ISRAEL
JAPAN
AUSTRIA
CANADA
CZECHOSLOVAKIA

SCOTT®

1995 Standard Postage Stamp Catalogue

ONE HUNDRED AND FIFTY-FIRST EDITION IN FIVE VOLUMES

VOLUME 3

EUROPEAN COUNTRIES and COLONIES,
INDEPENDENT NATIONS of
AFRICA, ASIA, LATIN AMERICA

D-I

VICE PRESIDENT/PUBLISHER	Stuart J. Morrissey
EDITOR	William W. Cummings
ASSISTANT EDITOR	James E. Kloetzel
VALUING EDITOR	Martin J. Frankevicz
NEW ISSUES EDITOR	David C. Akin
COMPUTER CONTROL COORDINATOR	Denise Oder
VALUING ANALYST	Jose R. Capote
EDITORIAL ASSISTANTS	Judith E. Bertrand, Beth Brown
CONTRIBUTING EDITOR	Joyce Nelson
ART/PRODUCTION DIRECTOR	Janine C. S. Apple
PRODUCTION COORDINATOR	Nancy S. Martin
SALES MANAGER	William Fay
ADVERTISING	David Lodge
CIRCULATION/PRODUCT PROMOTION MANAGER	Tim Wagner

Scott Publishing Co.

911 Vandemark Road, Sidney, OH 45365

A division of AMOS PRESS, INC., publishers of *Linn's Stamp News, Coin World, Cars & Parts* magazine and *The Sidney Daily News.*

Table of Contents

See Volumes 2, 4 and 5 for nations of Africa, Asia, Europe, Latin America A-C, J-Q and R-Z and their affiliated territories.

See Volume 1 for United States and its affiliated territories, United Nations and the British Commonwealth of Nations.

Copyright Notice

Trademark Notice

ISBN 0-89487-202-8

Library of Congress Card No. 2-3301

Scott Publishing Co.

911 VANDEMARK ROAD, SIDNEY, OHIO 45365 513-498-0802

SCOTT

Dear Catalogue User:

As stamp collectors, we tend to be a demanding group. We're fussy about condition, particular about how our collections look in our albums and absolute pests about items on our wantlists. At times we can even be difficult, according to some dealers and spouses (although I believe that many such reports are grossly exaggerated).

Each edition of the Scott Catalogue must deliver for catalogue users to be satisfied. The 1995 edition delivers on many levels. There are more new and wonderful additions, improvements and revisions than any year in recent memory. And, values are definitely headed north for many countries.

Where to begin? I'm almost not sure. To make it easier, and to keep everything on the square, I've engaged an imaginary TV talk show host to ask me a few questions. I made sure that our host was a "fess-up, tell all" type, committed to getting down to the juicy stuff for the benefit of the home audience.

Stuart, in the past you have claimed the new edition was exciting and the best ever and so on. What's truly important this year?

The return of increasing values in Western Europe. Both France and Germany post many strong increases in Volume 3. There are more than 2,000 value changes in France, 1,800 in Germany and more than 1,300 in German Democratic Republic.

Let's get down to specifics.

In France for example, Scott 49, the 10¢ on 10¢ of 1871, which was never placed in use, moves to $1,000 from $825, and the perforated 4¢ gray Ceres of 1870, Scott 52, jumps to $250 unused, from $175. The 1935 Cardinal Richelieu 1.50fr, Scott 304, zips to $30 unused, from $24, and the 1937 Rene Descartes issues, Scott 330-331, leap to $7.25 unused, from $4.60. Scott 374, the Photography centenary 2.25fr, climbs to $5.75 unused, from $4.75. The 1956 Technical Achievements set, Scott 807-809, moves to $14.90 unused, from $9.75, and the 1980 French Cuisine 90¢, Scott 1696, rises to 65¢ unused from 28¢.

In Germany, many of the changes are found in the semipostals and the Berlin listings. The 1925 Traffic Exhibition set, Scott 345-346, rises to $37.50 never-hinged, from $27.50. The June 30, 1930 Rhineland Evacuation overprints, Scott 385-386, jump to $10 never-hinged, from $6.25. The 1932 surcharged semi-postals, Scott B42-B43, rise to $42.50 never-hinged, from $30; and $15.25 hinged, from $10.

In the Berlin issues, the 1955 Furtwangler 40pf, Scott 9N115, increases to $20 unused and $13 used, from $15 unused and $12 used, and the 1974 90pf Airlift 25th anniversary, Scott 9N346, flies to $1.25 unused and 85¢ used, from 75¢ unused and 65¢ used.

What else is hot?

Many sharp increases are found in East Germany. The 1950 May Day issue, Scott 53, jumps to $14 unused, from $12. Scott 82-84, the 1951 Friendship with Communist China set, rockets to $465 unused, from $225, while the 1953 Leipzig Zoo 24pf, Scott 179, roars to $1.75 unused, from 90¢.

Seems like everything is hot. Let's not pretend this is a philatelic land of Oz. What's going down?

Can we talk?

Talk to me.

In Hungary, most changes are downward. The 1926-27 Madonna and Child set, Scott 415-417, drops to $35.75 unused, from $41, and the 1938 St. Stephen souvenir sheet, Scott 528, falls to $13 never-hinged, from last year's $14 level. Many items issued from 1985-91 also show decreases. For example, Scott 3069, the 1987 Esztergom Cathedral Treasures souvenir sheet, falls to $4 unused, from $5, and the 1989 Moon Landing Anniversary souvenir sheet, Scott 3186, decreases to $4.50 unused, from $6.

Anything else on your mind?

I suspect that many collectors will be caught by surprise by Dominican Republic. There are more than 400 changes, most of which are dramatic increases. Most of the changes are for unused stamps and sets valued less than $1.

Many complain that they cannot find certain stamps in the catalogue. When will you give us a break?

I was afraid you wouldn't ask. The index and identifier section has been expanded, with an 8-page illustrated section that shows inscriptions in languages that do not use Latin letters, stamps that use pictures as identifying features, or those that just show numerals. The illustrated section will assist both novice and experienced collectors in identifying stamps when they don't have a clue where to start. When trying to find a stamp in the catalogue, it is essential to first identify the country of issue. Most stamps show the name of the country, usually in the native language. These inscriptions, along with other stamp inscriptions that are less obvious identifying features, are included in the index and identifier section.

Any other editorial improvements?

The period for which Hungary is now valued in both hinged and never-hinged condition has been moved to 1937 in postage, and as early as 1934 in postage dues.

Renumberings affect the 1985-89 Egyptian Officials, the 1989-94 definitives of Finland's Aland Islands, France's 1990-92 Marianne definitives, Germany's 1987-93 Historic Sites definitives, the 1992-93 airmail surcharges of Honduras and Italy's 1988-91 Castle coils.

All of the Ivory Coast stamps mentioned in the 1994 catalogue that the editors wanted to see were sent in by collectors and listed as majors. The editors wish to thank all collectors who sent in these hard-to-find stamps, which apparently were used for postage in Ivory Coast.

Minors for se-tenants have been added in German Democratic Republic, Greece and Iran. More set totals have been added in Iraq.

Issue dates have been refined in Estonia, Haiti and Honduras.

And, finally, what are this year's topics for the cross reference section?

Mushrooms and Space.

You're kidding. These topics could draw a whole new audience. As a matter of fact, next week we have a segment devoted to new-age lifestyles, and . . .

Until next time, Happy Collecting!

Stuart Morrissey

Stuart Morrissey
Publisher

Acknowledgments

Our appreciation and gratitude go to the following individuals and organizations who have assisted us in preparing information included in the 1995 Scott Catalogues. Some helpers prefer anonymity. These individuals have generously shared their stamp knowledge with others through the medium of the Scott Catalogue.

Those who follow provided information that is in addition to the hundreds of dealer price lists and advertisements and scores of auction catalogues and realizations which were used in producing the Catalogue Values. It is from those noted here that we have been able to obtain information on items not normally seen in published lists and advertisements. Support from these people of course goes beyond data leading to Catalogue Values, for they also are key to editorial changes.

American Air Mail Society
Stephen Reinhard, PO Box 110,
Mineola, NY 11501

American Philatelic Society
PO Box 8000,
State College, PA 16803

American Revenue Association
Bruce Miller, Suite 332,
701 South First Ave.,
Arcadia, CA 91006

American Stamp Dealers' Association
3 School St.,
Glen Cove, NY 11542

American Topical Association
PO Box 630,
Johnstown, PA 15907

Booklet Collectors Club
James Natale, PO Box 2461,
Cinnaminson, NJ 08077-5461

Bureau Issues Association
George V.H. Godin, PO Box 23707,
Belleville, IL 62223

Confederate Stamp Alliance
Richard L. Calhoun, 1749 W. Golf Rd.,
Suite 366, Mt. Prospect, IL 60056

Errors, Freaks, and Oddities Collectors Association
Jim McDevitt, 1903 Village Road West,
Norwood, MA 02062-2516

Fine and Performing Arts Philatelists
Dorothy E. Weihrauch,
Nine Island Ave., Apt. 906,
Miami Beach, FL 33139

International Society of Worldwide Stamp Collectors
Carol Cervenka, Route 1 Box 69A,
Caddo Mills, TX 75135

Junior Philatelists of America
Sally Horn, PO Box 850,
Boalsburg, PA 16827-0850

Masonic Stamp Club of New York
Bernard Nathan, 22 East 35th Street,
New York, NY 10016

National Duck Stamp Collectors Society
Peter Pierce, PO Box 566,
Oxford, MA 01540-0760

Plate Number Coil Collectors Club
Joann Lenz, 37211 Alper Drive,
Sterling Heights, MI 48312

Precancel Stamp Society
1750 Skippack Pk. #1603,
Center Square, PA 19422

Royal Philatelic Society
Francis Kiddle, 41 Devonshire Place,
London, U.K. W1N 1PE

Royal Philatelic Society of Canada
PO Box 100, First Canadian Place,
Toronto ONT, CANADA M6A 1T6

Scouts on Stamps Society International
Kenneth A. Shuker, 20 Cedar Lane,
Cornwall, NY 12518

United Postal Stationery Society
Joann Thomas, PO Box 48,
Redlands, CA 92373

US Philatelic Classics Society
Patricia S. Walker, Briarwood,
Lisbon, MD 21765

US Possessions Philatelic Society
Kenneth M. Koller, 217 Tyler Ave.,
Cuyahoga Falls, OH 44221

Society for the New Republics of the Former USSR (Armenia, etc.)
Michael Padwee,
163 Joralemon St., PO Box 1520,
Brooklyn, NY 11201-1520

Austria Philatelic Soc. of New York
Dr. Ernst Theimer, 150 Rumson Rd.,
Rumson, NJ 07760

American Belgian Philatelic Society
Kenneth L. Costilow, 621 Virginius Dr.,
Virginia Beach, VA 23452

Belize Philatelic Study Circle
Charles R. Gambill,
730 Collingswood,
Corpus Christi, TX 78412

Bermuda Collectors Society
Thomas J. McMahon, 86 Nash Road,
Purdys, NY 10578

Brazil Philatelic Association
Kurt Ottenheimer,
462 West Walnut St.,
Long Beach, NY 11561

British Caribbean Philatelic Study Group
Gale J. Raymond, PO Box 35695,
Houston, TX 77235

British North America Philatelic Society
Jerome C. Jarnick, 108 Duncan Drive,
Troy, MI 48098

Canal Zone Study Group
Richard H. Salz, 60 27th Ave.,
San Francisco, CA 94121

China Stamp Society
Paul H. Gault, 140 West 18th Ave.,
Columbus, OH 43210

COPAPHIL (Colombia & Panama)
David Leeds, PO Box 2245,
El Cajon, CA 92021

Society of Costa Rica Collectors
Dr. Hector Mena, PO Box 14831,
Baton Rouge, LA 70808

Croatian Philatelic Society (Croatia and other Balkan areas)
Eck Spahich, 1512 Lancelot Rd.,
Borger, TX 79007

Cuban Philatelic Society of America
PO Box 450207,
Miami, FL 33245-0207

Society for Czechoslovak Philately
Robert T. Cossaboom,
PO Box 332,
Scott AFB, IL 62225

Estonian Philatelic Society
Rudolf Hamar, 31 Addison Terrace,
Old Tappan, NJ 07675

Ethiopian Philatelic Society
Huguette Gagnon, PO Box 8110-45,
Blaine, WA 98230

Falkland Islands Philatelic Study Group
James Driscoll, PO Box 172,
South Dennis, NJ 08245

France & Colonies Philatelic Society
Walter Parshall, 103 Spruce St.,
Bloomfield, NJ 07003

Germany Philatelic Society
PO Box 779,
Arnold, MD 21012-4779

GDR Study Group of German Philatelic Society
Ken Lawrence, PO Box 8040,
State College, PA 16803-8040

Great Britain Collectors Club
Frank J. Koch, PO Box 309,
Batavia, OH 45103-0309

Hellenic Philatelic Society of America (Greece and related areas)
Dr. Nicholas Asimakopulos,
541 Cedar Hill Ave.,
Wyckoff, NJ 07481

International Society of Guatemala Collectors
Mrs. Mae Vignola, 105 22nd Ave.,
San Francisco, CA 94116

Haiti Philatelic Society
Dwight Bishop, 16434 Shamhart Dr.,
Granada Hills, CA 91344

Hong Kong Stamp Society
Dr. An-Min Chung, 120 Deerfield Rd.,
Broomall, PA 19008

Hong Kong Collectors Club
Nikolai Lau, 6021 Yonge Street #888,
North York, ON, CANADA M2M 3W2

Hungary Philatelic Society
Thomas Phillips, PO Box 1162,
Samp Mortar Sta., Fairfield, CT 06432

India Study Circle
John Warren, PO Box 70775,
Washington, DC 20024

Society of Indochina Philatelists
Paul Blake, 1466 Hamilton Way,
San Jose, CA 95125

Iran Philatelic Circle
A. John Ultee, 816 Gwynne Ave.,
Waynesboro, VA 22980

Eire Philatelic Association (Ireland)
Michael J. Conway,
74 Woodside Circle,
Fairfield, CT 06430

Society of Israel Philatelists
Howard D. Chapman,
28650 Settlers Lane,
Pepper Pike, OH 44124

Italy and Colonies Study Circle
David F. Emery, PO Box 86,
Philipsburg, NJ 08865

International Society for Japanese Philately
Kenneth Kamholz, PO Box 1283,
Haddonfield, NJ 08033

Korea Stamp Society
Harold L. Klein, PO Box 750,
Lebanon, PA 17042

Latin American Philatelic Society
Piet Steen, PO Box 6420,
Hinton, AB, CANADA T7B 1X7

Liberian Philatelic Society
William Thomas Lockard, PO Box 267,
Wellston, OH 45692

Plebiscite-Memel-Saar Study Group
Clay Wallace, 158 Arapaho Circle,
San Ramon, CA 94583

Mexico-Elmhurst Philatelic Society International
William E. Shelton, PO Box 39838,
San Antonio, TX 78218

Nepal & Tibet Philatelic Study Group
Roger D. Skinner, 1020 Covington Road,
Los Altos, CA 94022

American Society of Netherlands Philately
Jan Enthoven, W6428 Riverview Drive,
Onalaska, WI 54650

Nicaragua Study Group
Clyde R. Maxwell, Airport Plaza, 2041
Business Center Drive, Suite 101,
Irvine, CA 92715

Society of Australasian Specialists/ Oceania
Henry Bateman, PO Box 4862,
Monroe, LA 71211

Orange Free State Study Circle
J. R. Stroud, 28 Oxford St.,
Burnham-on-sea,
Somerset, U.K. TA8 1LQ

International Philippine Philatelic Society
Eugene A. Garrett, 446 Stratford Ave.,
Elmhurst, IL 60126-4123

American Society of Polar Philatelists (Antarctic areas)
S.H. Jacobson, PO Box 945,
Skokie, IL 60077

Pitcairn Islands Study Group
Nelson A.L. Weller, 2940 Wesleyan
Lane, Winston-Salem, NC 27106

Polonus Philatelic Society (Poland)
864 N. Ashland Ave.,
Chicago, IL 60622

International Society for Portuguese Philately
Nancy M. Gaylord,
1116 Marineway West,
North Palm Beach, FL 33408

Rhodesian Study Circle
William R. Wallace, PO Box 16381,
San Francisco, CA 94116

Romanian Chapter of Croatian Philatelic Society
Dan Demetriade, PO Box 10182,
Detroit, MI 48210

Rossica Society of Russian Philately
Gary Combs, 8241 Chalet Ct.,
Millersville, MD 21108

Canadian Society of Russian Philately
Andrew Cronin, PO Box 5722, Station A,
Toronto, ON, CANADA M5W 1P2

Ryukyu Philatelic Specialist Society
Carmine J. DiVincenzo, PO Box 381,
Clayton, CA 94517-0381

St. Helena, Ascension & Tristan Society
Dr. Russell V. Skavaril,
222 East Torrance Road,
Columbus, OH 43214-3834

Associated Collectors of El Salvador
Jeff Brasor,
7365 NW 68th Way,
Pompano Beach, FL 33067-3918

Sarawak Specialists' Society
Art Bunce, PO Box 2516,
Escondido, CA 92033

Arabian Philatelic Society
ARAMCO Box 1929,
Dhahran, SAUDI ARABIA 31311

Scandinavia Collectors Club
Jared H. Richter, PO Box 302,
Lawrenceville, GA 30246-0302

Philatelic Society for Greater Southern Africa
William C. Brooks VI,
PO Box 2698,
San Bernardino, CA 92406-2698

Slovakia Stamp Society
Jack Benchik, PO Box 555,
Notre Dame, IN 46556

Spanish Philatelic Society
Bob Penn, PO Box 3804,
Gettysburg, PA 17325

American Helvetia Philatelic Society (Switzerland, Liechtenstein)
Richard T. Hall,
PO Box 666,
Manhattan Beach, CA 90266-0666

Society for Thai Philately
H.R. Blakeney, PO Box 25644,
Oklahoma City, OK 73125

Tonga/Tin Can Mail Study Circle
Paul Stanton, PO Box 700257,
Plymouth, MI 48170

Turkey and Ottoman Philatelic Society
Gary F. Paiste, 4249 Berritt St.,
Fairfax, VA 22030

Tuvalu & Kiribati Philatelic Society
Frank Caprio, PO Box 218071,
Nashville, TN 37221

Ukrainian Philatelic & Numismatic Society
Val Zabijaka, PO Box 3711,
Silver Spring, MD 20918

United Nations Philatelists
Helen Benedict,
408 S. Orange Grove Blvd.,
Pasadena, CA 91105

Vatican Philatelic Society
Louis Padavan, PO Box 127,
Remsenburg, NY 11960

Yugoslavia Study Group
Michael Lenard, 1514 North 3rd Ave.,
Wausau, WI 54401

George F. Ackerman
Michael E. Aldrich
A.R. Allison
B.J. Ammel
Mike Armus
Robert Ausubel
Don Bakos
Vladimir Barrio-Lemm
Jules K. Beck
John Birkinbine II
Torbjorn Bjork
Joan R. Bleakley
Brian M. Bleckwenn
Al Boerger
John R. Boker, Jr.
Jeff Brasor
George W. Brett
Roger Brody
William C. Brooks VI
Joseph Bush
Lawrence A. Bustillo
Peter Bylen
Nathan Carlin
E. J. Chamberlin
Albert F. Chang
Henry Chlanda
Andrew Cronin
Charles Cwiakala
Dan Demetriade
Rich Drews
P. J. Drossos
Bob Dumaine
Victor E. Engstrom
Leon Finik
Fabio Famiglietti
J. A. Farrington
Henry Fisher
Geoffrey Flack
William Fletcher
Joseph E. Foley
Marvin Frey
Huguette Gagnon
Earl H. Galitz
Peter Georgiadis
Brian M. Green
Fred F. Gregory
Henry Hahn
Rudolf Hamar
Erich E. Hamm
John Head
Robert R. Hegland
Dale Hendricks
Clifford O. Herrick
Lee H. Hill, Jr.
Dr. Eugene Holmok
Rollin C. Huggins, Jr.
Eric Jackson
Peter C. Jeannopoulos
Clyde Jennings
Jack Jonza
Henry Karen
Stanford M. Katz
Dr. James Kerr
Charles Kezbers
William V. Kriebel
William Langs
Ken Lawrence
Anshan Li
Pedro Llach
William Thomas Lockard
David MacDonnell
Walter J. Mader
Leo Malz
Robert L. Markovits
Clyde R. Maxwell
Menachim Mayo
P. J. McGowan
Timothy M. McRee
Dr. Hector Mena
Robert Meyersburg
Jack Molesworth
Gary M. Morris
Peter Mosiondz, Jr.
Bruce M. Moyer
Richard H. Muller
James Natale
Gregg Nelson
Victor Ostolaza
Michael Padwee
Souren Panirian
Sheldon Paris
Robert H. Penn
Donald J. Peterson
Vernon Pickering
Stanley Piller
S. Pinchot
Gilbert N. Plass
Louis Repeta
Peter A. Robertson
Jon Rose
Larry Rosenblum
Frans H. A. Rummens
Richard H. Salz
Byron Sandfield
Jacques C. Schiff, Jr.
Richard Schwartz
F. Burton Sellers
Martin Sellinger
Michael Shamilzadeh
Dr. Hubert Skinner
Sherwood Springer
Richard Stambaugh
Scott Trepel
Ming W. Tsang
A. John Ultee
James O. Vadoboncoeur
Xavier Verbeck
George P. Wagner
Jerome S. Wagshal
Richard A. Washburn
Irwin Weinberg
Larry S. Weiss
William R. Weiss, Jr.
Hans A. Westphal
Robert F. Yacano
Clarke Yarbrough
Val Zabijaka
Nathan Zankel

Catalogue Information

Catalogue Value

The Scott Catalogue value is a retail price, what you could expect to pay for the stamp in a grade of Fine-Very Fine. The value listed is a reference which reflects recent actual dealer selling prices.

Dealer retail price lists, public auction results, published prices in advertising, and individual solicitation of retail prices from dealers, collectors, and specialty organizations have been used in establishing the values found in this catalogue.

Use this catalogue as a guide in your own buying and selling. The actual price you pay for a stamp may be higher or lower than the catalogue value because of one or more of the following: the amount of personal service a dealer offers, increased interest in the country or topic represented by the stamp or set, whether an item is a "loss leader," part of a special sale, or otherwise is being sold for a short period of time at a lower price, or if at a public auction you are able to obtain an item inexpensively because of little interest in the item at that time.

For unused stamps, more recent issues are valued as never-hinged, with the beginning point determined on a country-by-country basis. Notes to show the beginning points are prominently noted in the text.

Grade

A stamp's grade and condition are crucial to its value. Values quoted in this catalogue are for stamps graded at Fine-Very Fine and with no faults. Exceptions are noted in the text. The accompanying illustrations show an example of a Fine-Very Fine grade between the grades immediately below and above it: Fine and Very Fine.

FINE stamps have the design noticeably off-center on two sides. Imperforate stamps may have small margins and earlier issues may show the design touching one edge of the stamp. Used stamps may have heavier than usual cancellations.

FINE-VERY FINE stamps may be somewhat off-center on one side, or only slightly off-center on two sides. Imperforate stamps will have two margins at least normal size and the design will not touch the edge. *Early issues of a country may be printed in such a way that the design naturally is very close to the edges.* Used stamps will not have a cancellation that detracts from the design. This is the grade used to establish Scott Catalogue values.

VERY FINE stamps may be slightly off-center on one side, with the design well clear of the edge. Imperforate stamps will have three margins at least normal size. Used stamps will have light or otherwise neat cancellations.

Condition

The above definitions describe *grade,* which is centering and (for used stamps) cancellation. *Condition* refers to the soundness of the stamp, i.e., faults, repairs, and other factors influencing price.

Copies of a stamp which are of a lesser grade and/or condition trade at lower prices. Those of exceptional quality often command higher prices.

Factors that can increase the value of a stamp include exceptionally wide margins, particularly fresh color, and the presence of selvage.

Factors other than faults that decrease the value of a stamp include loss of gum or regumming, hinge remnant, foreign object adhering to gum, natural inclusion, or a straight edge.

Faults include a missing piece, tear, clipped perforation, pin or other hole, surface scuff, thin spot, crease, toning, oxidation or other form of color changeling, short or pulled perforation, stains or such man-made changes as reperforation or the chemical removal or lightening of a cancellation.

Scott Publishing Co. recognizes that there is no formal, enforced grading scheme for postage stamps, and that the final price you pay for a stamp or obtain for a stamp you are selling will be determined by individual agreement at the time of the transaction.

Catalogue Listing Policy

It is the intent of Scott Publishing to list all postage stamps of the world in the *Scott Standard Postage Stamp Catalogue.* The only strict criteria for listing is that stamps be decreed legal for postage by the issuing country. Whether the primary intent of issuing a given stamp or set was for sale to postal patrons or to stamp collectors is not part of our listing criteria. Scott's role is to provide comprehensive stamp information. It is up to each stamp collector to choose which items to include in a collection.

It is Scott's objective to seek reasons why a stamp should be listed, rather than why it should not. Nevertheless, there are certain types of items which will not be listed:

1. Unissued items, even if they "accidentally" are distributed to the philatelic or even postal market. If such items later are officially issued by the country, they will be listed. Unissued items consist of those which have been printed and then held from sale for reasons such as change in government, error found on stamp, or even something objectionable about a stamp subject or design.
2. Stamps "issued" by non-existent entities or fantasy countries, such as Nagaland, Occusi-Ambeno, and others.
3. Semi-official or unofficial items not required for postage. Examples are items issued by private agencies for their own express services. When such items are required or valid as prepayment of postage, they will be listed.
4. Local stamps issued for local use only. Stamps issued by government specifically for "domestic" use, such as Haiti Scott 219-228 or the U.S. non-denominated stamps, are not considered to be locals.
5. Items not valid for postal use. For example, a few countries have issued souvenir sheets not valid for postage.
6. Intentional varieties, such as imperforate stamps issued in very small quantities with the same design as perforate stamps.
7. Items distributed by the issuing government only to a limited group, such as a stamp club or a single stamp dealer, and then brought to market at inflated prices. These items normally will be included in a footnote.

The fact that a stamp has been used successfully as postage, even on international mail, is not sufficient to prove that it was legitimately issued. Numerous examples of "stamps" from non-existent countries are known to have been used to post letters that have passed through the international mail.

Those items that will still not appear in the catalogue represent a very small percentage, perhaps as little as two percent, of the more than 400,000 stamps currently listed in the Scott catalogue system, or the 8,000 or so new issues that are listed each year.

There are certain items that are subject to interpretation. When a stamp falls outside our specifications, it will be listed and a cautionary footnote added.

A series of factors are considered in our approach to how a stamp is listed. Following is a list of various factors, presented here primarily to share with catalogue users the complexity of the listing process.

Additional printings – "additional printings" of a previously issued stamp may range from something that is totally different to cases where it is virtually impossible to differentiate it from the original. We will assign at least a minor number (a small-letter suffix) if there is a distinct change in stamp color, the design is noticeably redrawn, or the perforation measurement is different. A major number (numeral or numeral and capital-letter combination) will be assigned if we believe the "additional printing" is sufficiently different from the original that it constitutes a whole new issue.

Commemoratives – where practical, or where advance information is available, like commemoratives will be placed in a set, for example, the U.S. Credo issue of 1960-61 and the Constitution Bicentennial series of 1989-90. Japan and Korea issue such material on a regular basis, with an announced or, at least, predictable number of stamps known in advance.

Definitive sets – blocks of numbers are reserved for definitive sets, based on previous experience with that country. If more stamps are issued than expected, but it looks as if only a few more stamps will be issued for that series, they will be inserted into the original set with a capital-letter suffix, such as U.S. Scott 1059A. If it appears that many more stamps are yet to be issued in the set, a new block of numbers will be reserved, and the original grouping closed off, as in the case of the U.S. Transportation coil series and the Great Americans series.

New country – the important consideration is correct placement of the listings within the catalogue, either as a separate country listing or as a "state" following the "mother country" listing, for example, Aland Islands following Finland. Membership in the Univeral Postal Union is not a consideration for listing status or order of placement in the Catalogue.

"No release date" items – very complete information is readily available from certain countries for new issues before the stamps are issued; in some cases no information is available; while others fall somewhere in between. Often countries will provide denominations of upcoming stamps or souvenir sheets not released at the time of issue. Sometimes philatelic agencies, private firms employed by postal administrations, will add these later-issued items to sets months or years after the formal release date. If the items are officially issued by the country, the later material will be inserted into the proper set.

In order to understand how new issues come to market, it is important to know how philatelic agents operate. A philatelic agent is employed by a postal administration to perform duties ranging from complete development of all new issues including concept, design, printing and philatelic distribution to simply publicizing and selling new issues. Many countries do not have agents, or use them only for special projects.

Overprints – color of an overprint is always noted if it is other than black. Where more than one color ink is used on overprints of a set, the color used for a particular stamp is noted in the description line of that stamp.

Early overprint and surcharge illustrations were altered to prevent their use for counterfeiting.

Se-tenants – including pairs and blocks, will be listed in the format most commonly collected. If the stamps are collected as a unit, the major number will be assigned to the multiple and the minor numbers to the individual increments. When the items are usually collected as singles, then each individual stamp is given a major number and the entire se-tenant item is given a minor number of the last item in sequence. The manner in which an item is listed generally depends on the stamp's usage in the country of issue. Where stamps are used widely for postal purposes, even if se-tenant issues will be collected as a unit, each stamp will be given a major number, such as the stamps of the United States, Canada, Germany, and Great Britain.

Understanding the Listings

On the following page is an enlarged "typical" listing from this catalogue. Following are detailed explanations of each of the highlighted parts of the listing.

1 **Scott number** – Stamp collectors use Scott numbers to identify specific stamps when buying, selling, or trading stamps, and for ease in organizing their collections. Each stamp issued by a country has a unique number. Therefore, Germany Scott 99 can only refer to a single stamp. Although the Scott Catalogue usually lists stamps in chronological order by date of issue, when a country issues a set of stamps over a period of time the stamps within that set are kept together without regard of date of issue. This follows the normal collecting approach of keeping stamps in their natural sets.

When a country is known to be issuing a set of stamps over a period of time, a group of consecutive catalogue numbers is reserved for the stamps in that set, as issued. If that group of numbers proves to be too few, capital-letter suffixes are added to numbers to create enough catalogue numbers to cover all items in the set. Scott uses a suffix letter, e.g., "A," "b," etc., only once. If there is a Scott 16A in a set, there will not be a Scott 16a also. Suffix letters are not cumulative. A minor variety of Scott 16A would be Scott 16b, not Scott 16Ab. Any exceptions, such as Great Britain Scott 358cp, are clearly shown.

There are times when the block of numbers is too large for the set, leaving some numbers unused. Such gaps in the sequence also occur when the editors move an item elsewhere in the catalogue or removed from the listings entirely. Scott does not attempt to account for every possible number, but rather it does attempt to assure that each stamp is assigned its own number.

Scott numbers designating regular postage normally are only numerals. Scott numbers for other types of stamps, i.e., air post, semi-postal, and so on, will have a prefix of either a capital letter or a combination of numerals and capital letters.

2 **Illustration number** – used to identify each illustration. For most sets, the lowest face-value stamp is shown. It then serves as an example of the basic design approach for the set. Where more than one stamp in a set uses the same illustration number but has no different design, that number needs to be used with the design paragraph or description line (noted below) to be certain of the exact design on each stamp within the set. Where there are both vertical and horizontal designs in a set, a single illustration may be used, with the exceptions noted in the design paragraph or description line. When an illustration is followed by a lower-case letter in parentheses, such as "A2(b)," the trailing letter indicates which overprint illustration applies from those shown.

Illustrations normally are 75 percent of the original size of the stamp. An effort has been made to note all illustrations not at that percentage. Overprints are shown at 100 percent of the original, unless otherwise noted. In some cases, the illustration will be placed above the set, between listings, or omitted completely. Overprint and surcharge illustrations are not placed in this catalogue for purposes of expertizing stamps.

3 **Paper color** – The color of the paper is noted in italic type when the paper used is not white.

4 **Listing styles** – there are two principal types of catalogue listings: major and minor. *Majors* normally are in a larger type style than minor listings. They also may be distinguished by having as their catalogue number a numeral with or without a capital-letter suffix and with or without a prefix.

Minors are in a smaller type style and have a small-letter suffix (or, only have the small letter itself shown if the listing is immediately beneath its major listing). These listings show a variety of the "normal," or major item. Examples include color variation or a different watermark used for that stamp only.

Examples of major numbers are 16, 28A, B97, C13A, 10N5, and 10N6A. Examples of minor numbers are 16a and C13b.

5 **Basic information on stamp or set** – introducing each stamp issue, this section normally includes the date of issue, method of printing, perforation, watermark, and sometimes some additional information. *New information on method of printing, watermark or perforation measurement will appear when that information changes in the sequential order of the listings.* Stamps created by overprinting or surcharging previous stamps are assumed to have the same perforation, watermark and printing method as the original. Dates of issue are as precise as Scott is able to confirm.

6 **Denomination** – normally the face value of the stamp, i.e., the cost of the stamp at the post office at the time of issue. When the denomination is shown in parentheses, it does not appear on the stamp.

7 **Color or other description** – this line provides information to solidify identification of the stamp. Historically, when stamps normally were printed in a single color, only the color appeared here. With modern printing techniques, which include multicolor presses which mix inks on the paper, earlier methods of color identification are no longer applicable. In many cases, a description of the stamp design appears in this space.

8 **Year of issue** – in stamp sets issued over more than one year, the number in parentheses is the year that stamp appeared. Stamps without a date appeared during the first year of the span. Dates are not always given for minor varieties.

9 **Value unused** and **Value used** – the catalogue values are based on stamps which are in a grade of Fine-Very Fine. Unused values refer to items which have not seen postal or other duty for which they were intended. For pre-1900 issue, unused stamps must have at least most of their original gum; for later issues full original gum is expected. It is probably that they will show evidence of hinging if issued before the never-hinged breakpoint. Stamps issued without gum are noted. Modern issues with PVA gum may appear ungummed. Unused values are for never-hinged stamps beginning at the point immediately following a prominent notice in the actual listing. The same information also appears at the beginning of the country's information. See the section "Catalogue Values" for an explanation of the meaning of these values. Information about catalogue values shown in italics may be found in the section "Understanding Valuing Notations."

10 **Changes in basic set information** – bold type is used to show any change in the basic data on within a set of stamps, i.e., perforation from one stamp to the next or a different paper or printing method or watermark.

11 **Total value of set** – the total value of sets of five or more stamps, issued after 1900, are shown. The line also notes the range of Scott numbers and total number of stamps included in the total. *Set value* is the term used to indicate the value of a set when it is less than the total of the individual stamps.

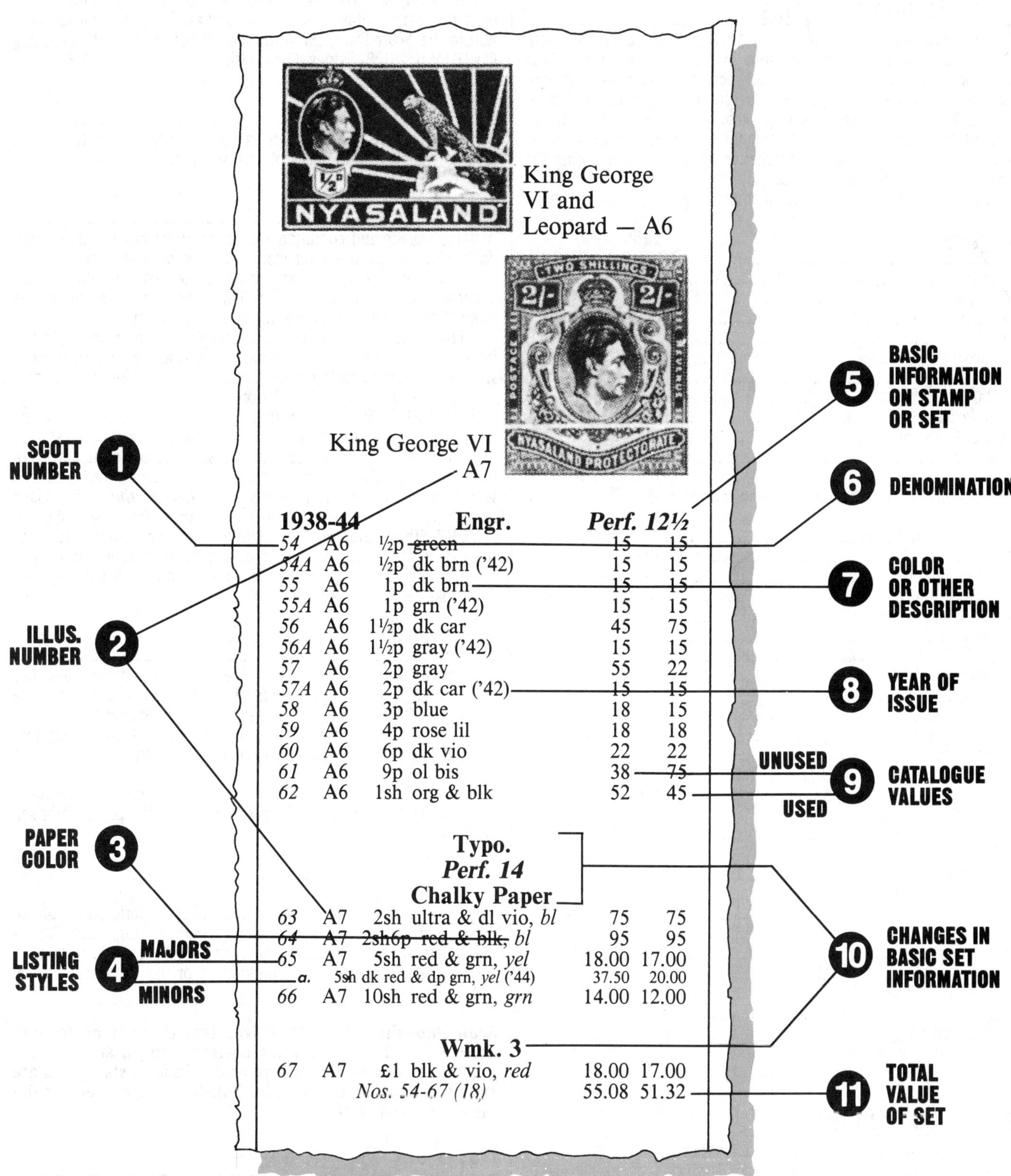

King George VI and Leopard — A6

King George VI A7

1938-44			**Engr.**	***Perf. 12½***	
54	A6	½p	green	15	15
54A	A6	½p	dk brn ('42)	15	15
55	A6	1p	dk brn	15	15
55A	A6	1p	grn ('42)	15	15
56	A6	1½p	dk car	45	75
56A	A6	1½p	gray ('42)	15	15
57	A6	2p	gray	55	22
57A	A6	2p	dk car ('42)	15	15
58	A6	3p	blue	18	15
59	A6	4p	rose lil	18	18
60	A6	6p	dk vio	22	22
61	A6	9p	ol bis	38	75
62	A6	1sh	org & blk	52	45

Typo.
Perf. 14
Chalky Paper

63	A7	2sh	ultra & dl vio, *bl*	75	75
64	A7	2sh6p	red & blk, *bl*	95	95
65	A7	5sh	red & grn, *yel*	18.00	17.00
a.		5sh	dk red & dp grn, *yel* ('44)	37.50	20.00
66	A7	10sh	red & grn, *grn*	14.00	12.00

Wmk. 3

67	A7	£1	blk & vio, *red*	18.00	17.00
			Nos. 54-67 (18)	55.08	51.32

Special Notices

Classification of stamps

The *Scott Standard Postage Stamp Catalogue* lists stamps by country of issue. The next level is a listing by section on the basis of the function of the stamps. The principal sections cover regular postage stamps; air post stamps; postage due stamps, registration stamps, special delivery and express stamps, semi-postal stamps, and, so on. Except for regular postage, Catalogue numbers for all sections include a prefix letter (or number-letter combination) denoting the class to which the stamp belongs.

Following is a listing of the most commonly used of the prefixes.

Category	**Prefix**
Air Post	C
Military	M
Newspaper	P
Occupation - Regular Issues	N
Official	O
Parcel Post	Q
Postage Due	J
Postal Tax	RA
Semi-Postal	B
Special Delivery	E
War Tax	MR

Other prefixes used by more than one country are:

Acknowledgment of Receipt	H
Air Post Official	CO
Air Post Parcel Post	CQ
Air Post Postal Tax	RAC
Air Post Registration	CF
Air Post Semi-Postal	CB
Air Post Semi-Postal Official	CBO
Air Post Special Delivery	CE
Authorized Delivery	EY
Franchise	S
Insured Letter	G
Marine Insurance	GY
Military Air Post	MC
Military Parcel Post	MQ
Occupation - Air Post	NC
Occupation - Official	NO
Occupation - Postage Due	NJ
Occupation - Postal Tax	NRA
Occupation - Semi-Postal	NB
Occupation - Special Delivery	NE
Parcel Post Authorized Delivery	QY
Postal-fiscal	AR
Postal Tax Due	RAJ
Postal Tax Semi-Postal	RAB
Registration	F
Semi-Postal Special Delivery	EB
Special Delivery Official	EO
Special Handling	QE

New issue listings

Updates to this catalogue appear each month in the *Scott Stamp Monthly.* Included in this update are additions to the listings of countries found in *Scott Standard Postage Stamp Catalogue* and the *Specialized Catalogue of United States Stamps,* new issues of countries not listed in the catalogues, and corrections and updates to current editions of this catalogue.

From time to time there will be changes in the listings from the *Scott Stamp Monthly* to the next edition of the catalogue, as additional information becomes available.

The catalogue update section of the *Scott Stamp Monthly* is the most timely presentation of this material available. Annual subscription to the *Scott Stamp Monthly* is available from Scott Publishing Co., P.O. Box 828, Sidney, OH 45365.

Number changes

A list of catalogue number changes from the previous edition of the catalogue appears at the back of each volume.

Grade

A stamp's grade and condition are crucial to its value. Values quoted in this catalogue are for stamps graded at Fine-Very Fine and with no faults. Exceptions are noted in the text. The illustrations show an example of a Fine-Very Fine grade between the grades immediately below and above it: Fine and Very Fine.

FINE stamps have the design noticeably off-center on two sides. Imperforate stamps may have small margins and earlier issues may show the design touching one edge of the stamp. Used stamps may have heavier than usual cancellations.

FINE-VERY FINE stamps may be somewhat off-center on one side, or only slightly off-center on two sides. Imperforate stamps will have two margins at least normal size and the design will not touch the edge. *Early issues of a country may be printed in such a way that the design naturally is very close to the edges.* Used stamps will not have a cancellation that detracts from the design.

VERY FINE stamps maybe slightly off-center on one side, with the design well clear of the edge. Imperforate stamps will have three margins at least normal size. Used stamps will have light or otherwise neat cancellations.

Condition

The above definitions describe *grade,* which is centering and (for used stamps) cancellation. *Condition* refers to the soundness of the stamp, i.e., faults, repairs, and other factors influencing price.

Copies of a stamp which are of a lesser grade and/or condition trade at lower prices. Those of exceptional quality often command higher prices.

Factors that can increase the value of a stamp include exceptionally wide margins, particularly fresh color, and the presence of selvage.

Factors other than faults that decrease the value of a stamp include no gum or regumming, hinge remnant, foreign object adhering to gum, natural inclusion, or a straight edge.

Faults include a missing piece, tear, clipped perforation, pin or other hole, surface scuff, thin spot, crease, toning, oxidation or other form of color changeling, short or pulled perforation, stains or such man-made changes as reperforation or the chemical removal or lightening of a cancellation.

Scott Publishing Co. recognizes that there is no formal, enforced grading scheme for postage stamps, and that the final price you pay for a stamp or obtain for a stamp you are selling will be determined by individual agreement at the time of the transaction.

Catalogue Value

The Scott Catalogue value is a retail price, what you could expect to pay for the stamp in a grade of Fine-Very Fine. The value listed is a reference which reflects recent actual dealer selling prices.

Dealer retail price lists, public auction results, published prices in advertising, and individual solicitation of retail prices from dealers, collectors, and specialty organizations have been used in establishing the values found in this catalogue.

Use this catalogue as a guide in your own buying and selling. The actual price you pay for a stamp may be higher or lower than the catalogue value because of one or more of the following: the amount of personal service a dealer offers, increased interest in the country or topic represented by the stamp or set, whether an item is a "loss leader," part of a special sale, or otherwise is being sold for a short period of time at a lower price, or if at a public auction you are able to obtain an item inexpensively because of little interest in the item at that time.

For unused stamps, more recent issues are valued as never-hinged, with the beginning point determined on a country-by-country basis. Notes in the text prominently show the beginning points of these designations.

As a point of philatelic-economic fact, the lower the value shown for an item in this catalogue, the greater the percentage of that value which is attributed to dealer mark-up and profit margin. Thus, a packet of 1,000 different items - each of which has a catalogue value of 15 cents - normally sells for considerably less than 150 dollars!

Persons wishing to establish the specific value of a stamp or other philatelic item may wish to consult with recognized stamp experts (collectors or dealers) and review current information or recent developments which would affect stamp prices.

Scott Publishing Co. assumes no obligation to revise the values during the distribution period of this catalogue or to advise users of other facts, such as stamp availability, political and economic conditions, or collecting preferences, any of which may have an immediate positive or negative impact on values.

Understanding valuing notations

The *absence of a value* does not necessarily suggest that a stamp is scarce or rare. In the U.S. listings, a dash in the value column means that the stamp is known in a stated form or variety, but information is lacking or insufficient for purposes of establishing a usable catalogue value.

Stamp values in *italics* generally refer to items which are difficult to value accurately. For expensive items, i.e., value at $1,000 or more, a value in italics represents an item which trades very seldom, such as a unique item. For inexpensive items, a value in italics represents a warning. One example is a "blocked" issue where the issuing postal administration controlled one stamp in a set in an attempt to make the whole set more valuable. Another example is a single item with a very low face value which sells in the marketplace, at the time of issue, at an extreme multiple of face value. Some countries have released back issues of stamps in a canceled-to-order form, sometimes covering at much as 10 years.

The Scott Catalogue values for used stamps reflect canceled-to-order material when such are found to predominate in the marketplace for the issue involved. Frequently notes appear in the stamp listings to specify items which are valued as canceled-to-order or if there is a premium for postally used examples.

Another example of a warning to collectors is a stamp that used has a value considerably higher than the unused version. Here, the collector is cautioned to be certain the used version has a readable, contemporary cancellation. The type of cancellation on a stamp can be an important factor in determining its sale price. Catalogue values do not apply to fiscal or telegraph cancels, unless otherwise noted.

The *minimum catalogue value* of a stamp is 15 cents, to cover a dealer's costs and then preparing it for resale. As noted, the sum of these values does not properly represent the "value" of sets with a number of minimum-value stamps, or packets of stamps.

Values in the "unused" column are for stamps that have been hinged, unless there is a specific note in a listing after which unused stamps are valued as never-hinged. A similar note will appear at the beginning of the country's listings, noting exactly where the dividing point between hinged and never-hinged is for each section of the listings. Where a value for a used stamp is considerably higher than for the unused stamp, the value applies to a stamp showing a distinct contemporary postmark of origin.

Many countries sell canceled-to-order stamps at a marked reduction of face value. Countries which sell or have sold canceled-to-order stamps at *full* face value include Australia, Netherlands, France, and Switzerland. It may be almost impossible to identify such stamps, if the gum has been removed, because official government canceling devices are used. Postally used copies on cover, of these items, are usually worth more than the canceled-to-order stamps with original gum.

Abbreviations

Scott Publishing Co. uses a consistent set of abbreviations throughout this catalogue to conserve space while still providing necessary information. The first block shown here refers to color names only:

COLOR ABBREVIATIONS

amb........................amber
anil........................aniline
ap..........................apple
aqua.......................aquamarine
az..........................azure
bis.........................bister
bl...........................blue
bld.........................blood
blk.........................black
bril.........................brilliant
brn.........................brown
brnsh.....................brownish
brnz.......................bronze
brt..........................bright
brnt........................burnt
car.........................carmine
cer.........................cerise
chlky......................chalky
cham......................chamois
chnt.......................chestnut
choc.......................chocolate
chr.........................chrome
cit...........................citron
cl............................claret
cob.........................cobalt
cop.........................copper
crim........................crimson
cr............................cream
dk...........................dark
dl............................dull
dp...........................deep
db...........................drab
emer.......................emerald
gldn........................golden
grysh......................grayish
grn..........................green
grnsh......................greenish
hel..........................heliotrope
hn...........................henna
ind..........................indigo
int...........................intense
lav..........................lavender
lem.........................lemon
lil............................lilac
lt.............................light
mag........................magenta
man........................manila
mar.........................maroon
mv..........................mauve
multi.......................multicolored
mlky.......................milky
myr.........................myrtle
ol............................olive
olvn........................olivine
org..........................orange
pck..........................peacock
pnksh......................pinkish
Prus........................Prussian
pur..........................purple
redsh.......................reddish
res...........................reseda
ros...........................rosine
ryl............................royal
sal...........................salmon
saph........................sapphire
scar.........................scarlet
sep..........................sepia
sien.........................sienna
sil............................silver
sl.............................slate
stl............................steel
turq.........................turquoise
ultra........................ultramarine
ven..........................Venetian
ver...........................vermilion
vio...........................violet
yel...........................yellow
yelsh........................yellowish

When no color is given for an overprint or surcharge, black is the color used. Abbreviations for colors used for overprints and surcharges are: "(B)" or "(Blk)," black; "(Bl)," blue; "(R)," red; "(G)," green; etc.

Additional abbreviations in this catalogue are shown below:

Adm. ....Administration
AFL ....American Federation of Labor
Anniv. ....Anniversary
APU ....Arab Postal Union
APS ....American Philatelic Society
ASEAN ....Association of South East Asian Nations
ASPCA ....American Society for the Prevention of Cruelty to Animals
Assoc. ....Association
ASSR. ....Autonomous Soviet Socialist Republic

b. ....Born
BEP ....Bureau of Engraving and Printing
Bicent. ....Bicentennial
Bklt. ....Booklet
Brit. ....British
btwn. ....Between
Bur. ....Bureau

c. or ca. ....Circa
CAR ....Central African Republic
Cat. ....Catalogue
CCTA. ....Commission for Technical Cooperation in Africa South of the Sahara
Cent. ....Centennial, century, centenary
CEPT ....Conference Europeenne des Administrations des Postes et des Telecommunications
CIO ....Congress of Industrial Organizations
Conf. ....Conference
Cong. ....Congress
Cpl. ....Corporal
CTO ....Canceled to order

d. ....Died
Dbl. ....Double
DDR ....German Democratic Republic (East Germany)

ECU ....European currency unit
EEC ....European Economic Community
EKU ....Earliest known use
Engr. ....Engraved
Exhib. ....Exhibition
Expo. ....Exposition

FAO ....Food and Agricultural Organization of the United Nations
Fed. ....Federation
FIP ....Federation International de Philatelie

GB. ....Great Britain
Gen. ....General
GPO ....General post office

Horiz. ....Horizontal

ICAO. ....International Civil Aviation Organization
ICY. ....International Cooperation Year
IEY. ....International Education Year
ILO. ....International Labor Organization
Imperf. ....Imperforate
Impt. ....Imprint
Intl. ....International
Invtd. ....Inverted
INTELSAT ......International Telecommunications Satellite Consortium
IQSY. ....International Quiet Sun Year
ITU. ....International Telecommunications Union
ITY. ....International Tourism Year
IWY. ....International Women's Year
IYC. ....International Year of the Child
IYD. ....International Year of the Disabled
IYP. ....International Year of Peace
IYSH. ....International Year of Shelter for the Homeless
IYY. ....International Youth Year

L. ....Left
Lieut., lt. ....Lieutenant
Litho. ....Lithographed
LL. ....Lower left
LR ....Lower right

mm ....Millimeter
Ms. ....Manuscript

NASA ....National Aeronautics and Space Administration
Natl. ....National
NATO ....North Atlantic Treaty Organization
No. ....Number
NY. ....New York
NYC ....New York City

OAU. ....Organization of African Unity
OPEC ....Organization of Petroleum Exporting Countries
Ovpt. ....Overprint
Ovptd. ....Overprinted

P ....Plate number
Perf. ....Perforated, perforation
Phil. ....Philatelic
Photo. ....Photogravure
PO. ....Post office
Pr. ....Pair
P.R. ....Puerto Rico
PRC. ....People's Republic of China (Mainland China)
Prec. ....Precancel, precanceled
Pres. ....President
PTT ....Post, Telephone and Telegraph
PUAS. ....Postal Union of the Americas and Spain
PUASP. ....Postal Union of the Americas, Spain and Portugal

QE2. ....Queen Elizabeth II (ship)

Rio ....Rio de Janeiro
ROC. ....Republic of China (Taiwan)

SEATO ....South East Asia Treaty Organization
Sgt. ....Sergeant
Soc. ....Society
Souv. ....Souvenir
SSR. ....Soviet Socialist Republic, see ASSR
St. ....Saint, street
Surch. ....Surcharge

Typo. ....Typographed

UAE ....United Arab Emirates
UAMPT ....Union of African and Malagasy Posts and Telecommunications

UAR. ....United Arab Republic
UL..................Upper left
UN ....United Nations
UNCTAD ....United Nations Conference on Trade and Development
UNESCO........United Nations Educational, Scientific and Cultural Organization
UNICEF..........United Nations Children's Fund
UAR ....United Arab Republic
UNPA.............United Nations Postal Administration
Unwmkd. ....Unwatermarked
UPAE ....Union Postal de las Americas y Espana
UPU ....Universal Postal Union
UR..................Upper Right
US ....United States
USPO ....United States Post Office Department
USPS ....United States Postal Service
USSR..............Union of Soviet Socialist Republics

Vert. ....Vertical
VP ....Vice president

WCY ....World Communications Year
WFUNA ....World Federation of United Nations Associations
WHO..............World Health Organization
Wmk. ....Watermark
Wmkd. ....Watermarked
WMO............World Meteorological Organization
WRY...............World Refugee Year
WWF.............World Wildlife Fund
WWI ....World War I
WWII ....World War II

YAR................Yemen Arab Republic
Yemen PDR....Yemen People's Democratic Republic

Examination

Scott Publishing Co. will not pass upon the genuineness, grade or condition of stamps, because of the time and responsibility involved. Rather, there are several expertizing groups which undertake this work for both collectors and dealers. Neither can Scott Publishing Co. appraise or identify philatelic material. The Company cannot take responsibility for unsolicited stamps or covers.

How to order from your dealer

It is not necessary to write the full description of a stamp as listed in this catalogue. All that you need is the name of the country, the Scott Catalogue number and whether the item is unused or used. For example, "Japan Scott 422 unused" is sufficient to identify the stamp of Japan listed as "422 A206 5y brown."

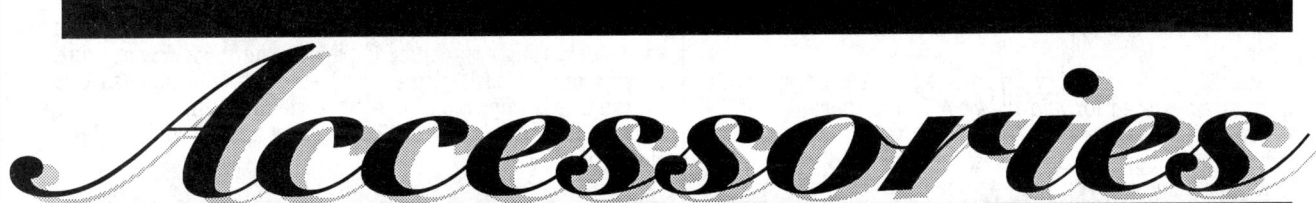

Basic Stamp Information

A stamp collector's knowledge of the combined elements that make a given issue of a stamp unique determines his or her ability to identify stamps. These elements include paper, watermark, method of separation, printing, design and gum. On the following pages each of these important areas is described.

PAPER

Paper is a material composed of a compacted web of cellulose fibers formed into sheets. Paper may be manufactured in sheets, or may have been part of a roll before being cut to size. The fibers most often used for the paper on which stamps are printed are bark, wood, straw and certain grasses with linen or cotton rags added for greater strength. Grinding and bleaching these fibers reduces them to a slushy pulp. Sizing and sometimes coloring matter are added to the pulp. Thin coatings of pulp are poured onto sieve-like frames, which allow the water to run off while retaining the matted pulp. Mechanical processes convert the pulp, when it is almost dry, by passing it through smooth or engraved rollers - dandy rolls - or placed between cloth in a press then flattens and dries the product under pressure.

Stamp paper falls broadly into two types: wove and laid. The nature of the surface of the frame onto which the pulp is first fed causes the differences in appearance between the two. If the surface is smooth and even the paper will be of uniform texture throughout, showing no light and dark areas when held to a light. This is known as *wove paper.* Early paper-making machines poured the pulp onto continuously circulating web of felt, but modern machines feed the pulp onto a cloth-like screen made of closely interwoven fine wires. This paper, when held to a light, will show little dots or points very close together. The proper name for this is "wire wove," but the type is still considered wove. Any U.S. or British stamp printed after 1880 will serve as an example of wire wove paper.

Closed spaced parallel wires, with cross wires at wider intervals, make up the frames used for *laid paper.* A greater thickness of the pulp will settle between the wires. The paper, when held to a light, will show alternate light and dark lines. The spacing and the thickness of the lines may vary, but on any one sheet of paper they are all alike. See Russia Scott 31-38 for an example of laid paper.

Batonne, from the French word meaning "a staff," is used if the lines are spaced quite far apart, like the ruling on a writing tablet. Batonne paper may be either wove or laid. If laid, fine laid lines can be seen between the batons. The laid lines, which are a form of watermark, may be geometrical figures such as squares, diamonds, rectangles, or wavy lines.

Quadrille is the term used when the lines form little squares. *Oblong quadrille* is the term used when rectangles rather than squares are formed. See Mexico-Guadalajara Scott 35-37.

Paper also is classified as thick or thin, hard or soft, and by color if dye is added during manufacture. Such colors may be yellowish, greenish, bluish and reddish. Following are brief explanations of other types of paper used for stamps:

Pelure – A very thin, hard and often brittle paper, it is sometimes bluish or grayish. See Serbia Scott 169-170.

Native – A term applied to handmade papers used to produce some of the early stamps of the Indian states. Japanese paper, originally made of mulberry fibers and rice flour, is part of this group. See Japan Scott 1-18.

Manila – Often used to make stamped envelopes and wrappers, it is a coarse textured stock, usually smooth on one side and rough on the other. A variety of colors are known.

Silk – Introduced by the British in 1847 as a safeguard against counterfeiting, bits of colored silk thread are scattered throughout it. Silk-thread paper has uninterrupted threads of colored silk arranged so that one or more threads run through the stamp or postal stationery. See Great Britain Scott 5-6.

Granite – Filled with minute fibers of various colors and lengths, this should not be confused with either type of silk paper. See Austria Scott 172-175.

Chalky – A chalk-like substance coats the surface to discourage the cleaning and reuse of canceled stamps. Because the design is imprinted on the water-soluble coating of the stamp, any attempt to remove a cancellation will destroy the stamp. *Do not soak these stamps in any fluid.* To remove a stamp printed on chalky paper from an envelope, wet the paper from underneath the stamp until the gum dissolves enough to release the stamp from the paper. See St. Kitts-Nevis Scott 89-90.

India – Another name for this paper, originally introduced from China about 1750, is "China Paper." It is a thin, opaque paper often used for plate and die proofs by many countries.

Double – In philately, this has two distinct meanings. The first, used experimentally as a means to discourage reuse, is two-ply paper, usually a combination of a thick and a thin sheet, joined during manufacture. The design is printed on the thin paper. Any attempt to remove a cancellation would destroy the design. The second occurs on the rotary press, when the end of one paper roll is glued to the next roll to save time feeding the paper through the press. Stamp designs are printed over the joined paper and, if overlooked by inspectors, may get into post office stocks.

Goldbeater's Skin – Used for the 1866 issue of Prussia, it was made of a tough translucent paper. The design was printed in reverse on the back of the stamp, and the gum applied over the printing. It is impossible to remove stamps printed on this type of paper from the paper to which they are affixed without destroying the design.

Ribbed – An uneven, corrugated surface made by passing the paper through ridged roller. This type exists on some copies of U.S. Scott 156-165.

Various other substances have been used for stamp manufacture, including wood, aluminum, copper, silver and gold foil; plastic; and silk and cotton fabrics. Stamp collectors and dealers consider most of these as novelties designed for sale to collectors.

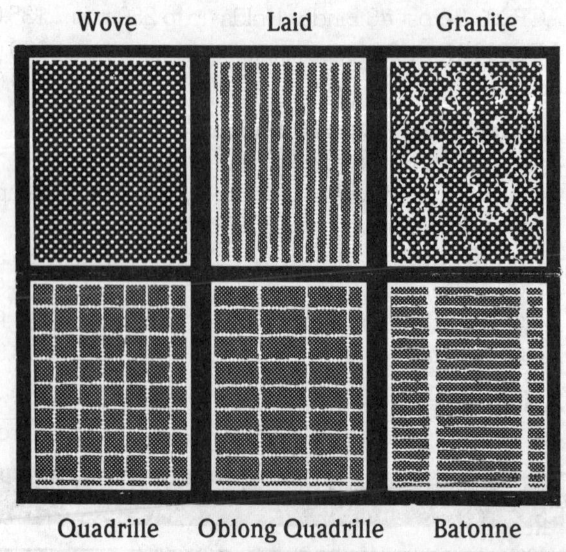

WATERMARKS

Watermarks are an integral part of the paper, for they are formed in the process of paper manufacture. They consist of small designs formed of wire or cut from metal and soldered to the surface of the dandy roll or mold. The designs may be in the form of crowns, stars, anchors, letters, etc. These pieces of metal - known in the paper-making industry as "bits" - impress a design into the paper. The design may be seen by holding the stamp to the light. Some are more easily seen with a watermark detector. This important tool is a small black tray into which the stamp is placed face down and dampened with a watermark detection fluid that brings up the watermark in the form of dark lines against a lighter background.

Multiple watermarks of Crown Agents and Burma

Watermarks of Uruguay, Vatican and Jamaica

WARNING: Some inks used in the photogravure process dissolve in watermark fluids. (See section below on Soluble Printing Inks.) Also, see "chalky paper." There also are electric watermark detectors, which come with plastic filter disks of various colors. The disks neutralize the color of the stamp, permitting the watermark to be seen more easily.

Watermarks may be found reversed, inverted, sideways or diagonal, as seen from the back of the stamp. The relationship of watermark to stamp design depends on the position of the printing plates or how paper is fed through the press. On machine-made paper, watermarks normally are read from right to left. The design is repeated closely throughout the sheet in a "multiple-watermark design." In a "sheet watermark," the design appears only once on the sheet, but extends over many stamps. Individual stamps may carry only a small fraction or none of the watermark.

"Marginal watermarks" occur in the margins of sheets or panes of stamps. They occur outside the border of paper (ostensibly outside the area where stamps are to be printed) a large row of letters may spell the name of the country or the manufacturer of the paper. Careless press feeding may cause parts of these letters to show on stamps of the outer row of a pane.

For easier reference, Scott Publishing Co. identifies and assigns a number to watermarks. See the numerical index of watermarks at the back of this volume.

Soluble Printing Inks

WARNING: Most stamp colors are permanent. That is, they are not seriously affected by light or water. Some colors may fade from excessive exposure to light. There are stamps printed with inks which dissolve easily in water or fluids used to detect watermarks. Use of these inks is intentional to prevent the removal of cancellations. Water affects all aniline prints, those on safety paper, and some photogravure printings - all known as *fugitive colors.*

Separation

"Separation" is the general term used to describe methods of separating stamps. The earliest issues, such as the 1840 Penny Black of Great Britain (Scott 1), did not have any means provided for separating. It was expected they would be cut apart with scissors. These are imperforate stamps. Many stamps first issued imperforate were later issued perforated. Care therefore must be observed in buying imperforate stamps to be certain they were issued imperforate and are not perforated copies that have been altered by having the perforations trimmed away. Imperforate stamps sometimes are valued as singles, as within this catalogue. But, imperforate varieties of normally perforated stamps should be collected in pairs or larger pieces as indisputable evidence of their imperforate character.

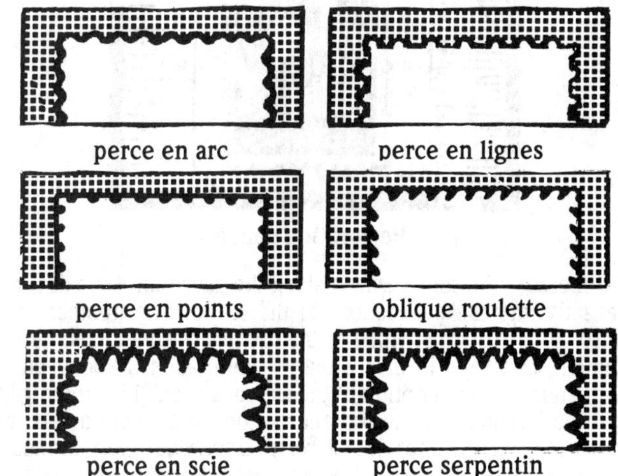

ROULETTING

Separation is brought about by two general methods during stamp production, rouletting and perforating. In rouletting, the paper is cut partly or wholly through, with no paper removed. In perforating, a part of the paper is removed. Rouletting derives its name from the French roulette, a spur-like wheel. As the wheel is rolled over the paper, each point makes a small cut. The number of cuts made in two centimeters determines the gauge of the roulette, just as the number of perforations in two centimeters determines the gauge of the perforation (see below).

The shape and arrangement of the teeth on the wheels varies. Various roulette types generally carry French names:

Perce en lignes – rouletted in lines. The paper receives short, straight cuts in lines. See Mexico Scott 500.

Perce en points – pin-perforated. This differs from a small perforation because no paper is removed, although round, equidistant holes are pricked through the paper. See Mexico Scott 242-256.

Perce en arc and perce en scie – pierced in an arc or sawtoothed designs, forming half circles or small triangles. See Hanover (German States) Scott 25-29.

Perce en serpentin – serpentine roulettes. The cuts form a serpentine or wavy line. See Brunswick (German States) Scott 13-18.

PERFORATION

The other chief style of separation of stamps, and the one which is in universal use today, is perforating. By this process, paper between the stamps is cut away in a line of holes, usually round, leaving little bridges of paper between the stamps to hold them together. These little bridges, which project from the stamp when it is torn from the pane are called the teeth of the perforation. As the size of the perforation is sometimes the only way to differentiate between two otherwise identical stamps, it is necessary to be able to measure and describe them. This is done with a perforation gauge, usually a ruler-like device that has dots to show how many perforations may be counted in the space of two centimeters. Two centimeters is the space universally adopted in which to measure perforations.

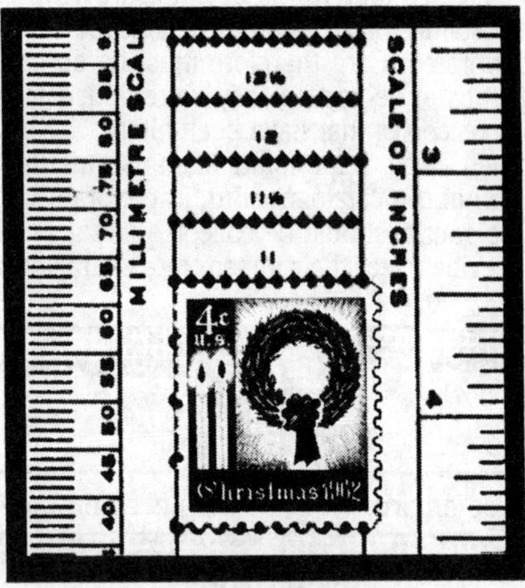

Perforation gauge

To measure the stamp, run it along the gauge until the dots on it fit exactly into the perforations of the stamp. The number to the side of the line of dots which fit the stamp's perforation is the measurement, i.e., an "11" means that 11 perforations fit between two centimeters. The description of the stamp is "perf. 11." If the gauge of the perforations on the top and bottom of a stamp differs from that on the sides, the result is a *compound perforation.* In measuring compound perforations, the gauge at top and bottom is always given first, then the sides. Thus, a stamp that measures 10 1/2 at top and bottom and 11 at the sides is "perf. 10 1/2 x 11." See U.S. Scott 1526.

There are stamps known with perforations different on three or all four sides. Descriptions of such items are in clockwise order, beginning with the top of the stamp.

A perforation with small holes and teeth close together is a "fine perforation." One with large holes and teeth far apart is a "coarse perforation." Holes jagged rather than clean cut, are "rough perforations." *Blind perforations* are the slight impressions left by the perforating pins if they fail to puncture the paper. Multiples of stamps showing blind perforations may command a slight premium over normally perforated stamps.

Printing Processes

ENGRAVING (Intaglio)

Master die – The initial operation in the engraving process is making of the master die. The die is a small flat block of soft steel on which the stamp design is recess engraved in reverse.

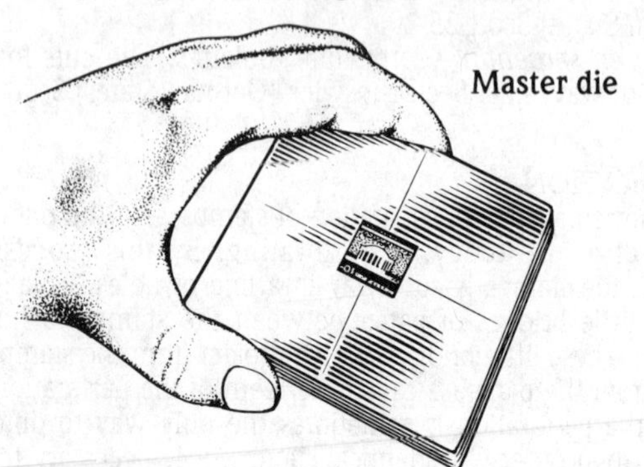
Master die

Photographic reduction of the original art is made to the appropriate size, and it serves as a tracing guide for the initial outline of the design. After completion of the engraving, the die is hardened to withstand the stress and pressures of later transfer operations.

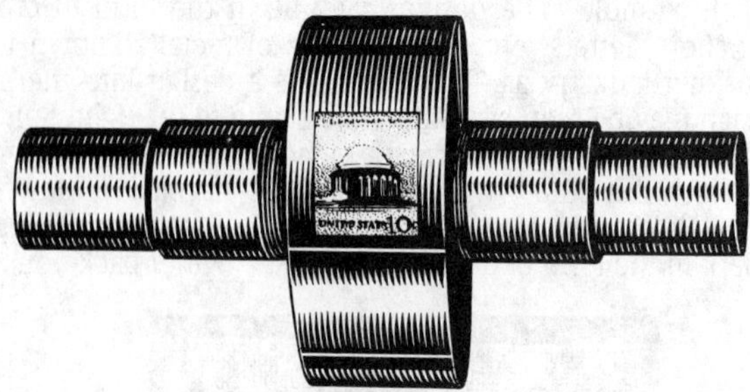
Transfer roll

Transfer roll – Next is production of the transfer roll which, as the name implies, is the medium used to transfer the subject from the die to the plate. A blank roll of soft steel, mounted on a mandrel, is placed under the bearers of the transfer press to allow it to roll freely on its axis. The hardened die is placed on the bed of the press and the face of the transfer roll is applied on the die, under pressure. The bed is then rocked back and forth under increasing pressure until the soft steel of the roll is forced into every engraved line of the die. The resulting impression on the roll is known as a "relief" or a "relief transfer." After the required number of reliefs are "rocked in," the soft steel transfer roll is also hardened.

A "relief" is the normal reproduction of the design on the die in reverse. A "defective relief" may occur during the "rocking in" process because of a minute piece of foreign material lodging on the die, or some other cause. Imperfections in the steel of the transfer roll may result in a breaking away of parts of the design. A damaged relief continued in use will transfer a repeating defect to the plate. Deliberate alterations of reliefs sometimes occur. "Broken reliefs" and "altered reliefs" designate these changed conditions.

Plate – The final step in the procedure is the making of the printing plate. A flat piece of soft steel replaces the die on the bed of the transfer press. One of the reliefs on the transfer roll is applied on this soft steel. "Position dots" determine the position on the plate. The dots have been lightly marked in advance. After the correct position of the relief is determined, pressure is applied. By following the same method used in making the transfer roll, a transfer is entered. This transfer reproduces the design of the relief in reverse and in detail. There are as many transfers entered on the plate as there are subjects printed on the sheet of stamps.

Transferring the design to the plate

Following the entering of the required transfers, the position dots, layout dots and lines, scratches, etc., generally are burnished out. Added at this time are any required *guide lines, plate numbers* or other *marginal markings.* A proof impression is then taken and, if approved, the plate machined for fitting to the press, hardened and sent to the plate vault ready for use.

On press, the plate is inked and the surface automatically wiped clean, leaving the ink in the depressed lines only. Paper under pressure is forced down into the engraved depressed lines, thereby receiving the ink. Thus, the ink lines on engraved stamps are slightly raised; and, conversely, slight depressions occur on the back of the stamp. Historically, paper had been dampened before inking. Newer processes do not require this procedure. Thus, there are both *wet* and *dry printings* of some stamps.

Rotary Press – Until 1915, only flat plates were used to print engraved stamps. Rotary press printing was introduced in 1915. After approval, *rotary press plates* require additional machining. They are curved to fit the press cylinder. "Gripper slots" are cut into the back of each plate to receive the "grippers," which hold the plate securely on the press. The plate is then hardened. Stamps printed from rotary press plates are usually longer or wider than the same stamps printed from flat press plates. The stretching of the plate during the curving process causes this enlargement.

Re-entry – In order to execute a re-entry, the transfer roll is reapplied to the plate, usually at some time after its first use on the press. Worn-out designs can be resharpened by carefully re-entering the transfer roll. If the transfer roll is not precisely in line with the impression of the plate, the registration will not be true and a double transfer will result. After a plate has been curved for the rotary press, it is impossible to make a re-entry.

Double Transfer – This is a description of the condition of a transfer on a plate that shows evidence of a duplication of all, or a portion of the design. It is usually the result of the changing of the registration between the transfer roll and the plate during the rocking-in of the original entry.

It is sometimes necessary to remove the original transfer from a plate and repeat the process a second time. If the finished re-transfer shows indications of the original impression attributable to incomplete erasure, the result is a double transfer.

Re-engraved – Either the die that has been used to make a plate or the plate itself may have it's "temper" drawn (softened) and be re-cut. The resulting impressions from such a re-engraved die or plate may differ slightly from the original issue, and are known as "re-engraved."

Short Transfer – Sometimes the transfer roll is not rocked its entire length in entering a transfer onto a plate, so that the finished transfer fails to show the complete design. This is known as a "short transfer." See U.S. Scott 8.

TYPOGRAPHY (Letterpress, Surface Printing)
As it relates to the printing of postage stamps, typography is the reverse of engraving. Typography includes all printing where the design is above the surface area, whether it is wood, metal, or in some instances hard rubber.

The master die and the engraved die are made in much the same manner. In this instance, however, the area not used as a printing surface is cut away, leaving the surface area raised. The original die is then reproduced by stereotyping or electrotyping. The resulting electrotypes are assembled in the required number and format of the desired sheet of stamps. The plate used in printing the stamps is an electroplate of these assembled electrotypes.

Ink is applied to the raised surface and the pressure of the press transfers the ink impression to the paper. In contrast with engraving, the fine lines of typography are impressed on the surface of the stamp. When viewed from the back (as on a typewritten page), the corresponding linework will be raised slightly above the surface.

PHOTOGRAVURE (Rotogravure, Heliogravure)
In this process, the basic principles of photography are applied to a sensitized metal plate, as opposed to photographic paper. The design is transferred photographically to the plate through a halftone screen, breaking the reproduction into tiny dots. The plate is treated chemically and the dots form depressions of varying depths, depending on the degrees of shade in the design. Ink is lifted out of the depressions in the plate when the paper is pressed against the plate in a manner similar to that of engraved printing.

LITHOGRAPHY
The principle that oil and water will not mix is the basis for lithography. The stamp design is drawn by hand or transferred from engraving to the surface of a lithographic stone or metal plate in a greasy (oily) ink. The stone (or plate) is wet with an acid fluid, causing it to repel the printing ink in all areas not covered by the greasy ink.

Transfer paper is used to transfer the design from the original stone of plate. A series of duplicate transfers are grouped and, in turn, transferred to the final printing plate.

Photolithography – The application of photographic processes to lithography. This process allows greater flexibility of design, related to use of halftone screens combined with linework.

Offset – A development of the lithographic process. A rubber-covered blanket cylinder takes up the impression from the inked lithographic plate. From the "blanket" the impression is *offset* or transferred to the paper. Greater flexibility and speed are the principal reasons offset printing has largely displaced lithography. The term "lithography" covers both processes, and results are almost identical.

Sometimes two or even three printing methods are combined in producing stamps.

EMBOSSED (Relief) Printing
Embossing is a method in which the design first is sunk into the metal of the die. Printing is done against a yielding platen, such as leather or linoleum. The platen is forced into the depression of the die, thus forming the design on the paper in relief.

Embossing may be done without color (see Sardinia Scott 4-6); with color printed around the embossed area (see Great Britain Scott 5 and most U.S. envelopes); and with color in exact registration with the embossed subject (see Canada Scott 656-657).

INK COLORS
Inks or colored papers used in stamp printing usually are of mineral origin. The tone of any given color may be affected by many aspects: heavier pressure will cause a more intense color, slight interruptions in the ink feed will cause a lighter tint.

Hand-mixed ink formulas produced under different conditions (humidity and temperature) at different times account for notable color variations in early printings, mostly 19th century, of the same stamp (see U.S. Scott 248-250, 279B, etc.).

Papers of different quality and consistency used for the same stamp printing may affect color shade. Most pelure papers, for example, show a richer color when compared with wove or laid papers. See Russia Scott 181a.

The very nature of the printing processes can cause a variety of differences in shades or hues of the same stamp. Some of these shades are scarcer than others and are of particular interest to the advanced collector.

Tagged Stamps

Tagging also is known as *luminescence, fluorescence,* and *phosphorescence.* Some tagged stamps have bars (Great Britain and Canada), frames (South Africa), or an overall coating of luminescent material applied after the stamps have been printed (United States). Another tagging method is to incorporate the luminescent material into some or all colors of the printing ink. See Australia Scott 366 and Netherlands Scott 478. A third is to mix the luminescent material with the pulp during the paper manufacturing process or apply it as a surface coating afterwards: "fluorescent" papers. See Switzerland Scott 510-514 and Germany Scott 848.

The treated stamps show up in specific colors when exposed to ultraviolet light. The wave length of light radiated by the luminescent material determines the colors and activates the triggering mechanism of the electronic machinery for sorting, facing or canceling letters.

Various fluorescent substances have been used as paper whiteners, but the resulting "hi-brite papers" show up differently under ultraviolet light and do not trigger the machines. The Scott Catalogue does not recognize these papers.

Many countries now use tagging in its various forms to expedite mail handling, following introduction by Great Britain, on an experimental basis, in 1959. Among these countries, and dates of their introduction, are Germany, 1961; Canada and Denmark, 1962; United States, Australia, Netherlands and Switzerland, 1963; Belgium and Japan, 1966; Sweden and Norway, 1967; Italy, 1968; and Russia, 1969.

Certain stamps were issued with and without the luminescent feature. In those instances, Scott lists the "tagged" variety in the United States, Canada, Great Britain and Switzerland listings and notes the situation in some of the other countries.

Gum

The gum on the back of a stamp may be smooth, rough, dark, white, colored or tinted. It may be either obvious or virtually invisible as on Canada Scott 453 or Rwanda Scott 287-294. Most stamp gumming adhesives use gum arabic or dextrine as a base. Certain polymers such as polyvinyl alcohol (PVA) have been used extensively since World War II. The PVA gum which the security printers Harrison & Sons of Great Britain introduced in 1968 is dull, slightly yellowish and almost invisible.

The *Scott Standard Postage Stamp Catalogue* does not list items by types of gum. The *Scott Specialized Catalogue of United States Stamps* does differentiate among some types of gum for certain issues.

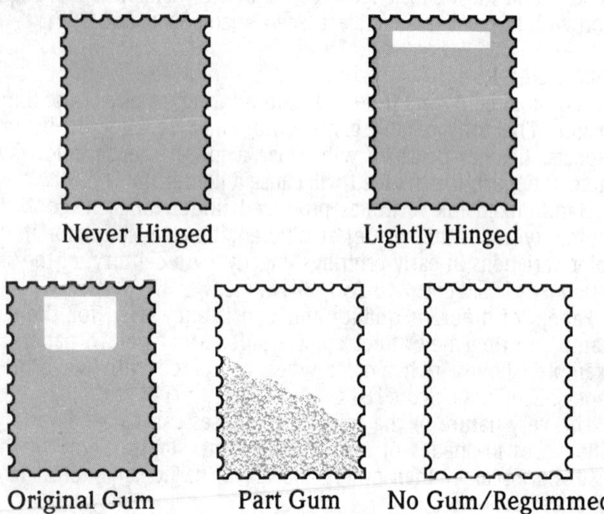

Never Hinged Lightly Hinged

Original Gum Part Gum No Gum/Regummed

For purposes of determining the grade of an unused stamp, Scott Publishing Co. presents the following (with accompanying illustrations) definitions: **Never Hinged (NH)** – Full original gum with no hinge mark or other blemish or disturbance. The presence of an expertizer's mark does not disqualify a stamp from this designation; **Lightly Hinged (LH)** – Full original gum with a light disturbance or the gum from the removal of a peelable hinge; **Original Gum (OG)** – Hinging and other disturbances should affect 20 percent or less of the original gum. **Part Gum (PG)** – Between 20 and 80 percent of the original gum remains. The stamp may have hinge remnants; **No Gum (NG) or Regummed (RE)** – A stamp with no gum or less than 20 percent of the original gum. A regummed stamp, considered the same as a stamp with none of its original gum, fits this category.

Stamps having full *original gum* sell for more than those from which the gum has been removed. Reprints of stamps may have gum differing from the original issues.

Many stamps have been issued without gum and the catalogue will note this fact. See China Scott 1438-1440. Sometimes, gum may have been removed to preserve the stamp. Germany Scott B68 is valued in the catalogue with gum removed.

Reprints and Reissues

These are impressions of stamps (usually obsolete) made from the original plates or stones. If valid for postage and from obsolete issues, they are *reissues.* If they are from current issues, they are *second, third,* etc., *printings.* If designated for a particular purpose, they are *special printings.*

Scott normally lists those reissues and reprints that are valid for postage.

When reprints are not valid for postage, but made from original dies and plates by authorized persons, they are *official reprints. Private reprints* are made from original plates and dies by private hands. *Official reproductions* or imitations are made from new dies and plates by government authorization.

For the United States' 1876 Centennial, the U.S. government made official imitations of its first postage stamps. Produced were copies of the first two stamps (listed as Scott 3-4), reprints of the demonetized pre-1861 issues and reissues of the 1861 stamps, the 1869 stamps and the then-current 1875 denominations. An example of the private reprint is that of the New Haven, Connecticut, postmaster's provisional.

Most reprints differ slightly from the original stamp in some characteristic, such as gum, paper, perforation, color or watermark. Sometimes the details are followed so meticulously that only a student of that specific stamp is able to distinguish the reprint from the original.

Remainders and Canceled to Order

Some countries sell their stock of old stamps when a new issue replaces them. To avoid postal use, the *remainders* usually are canceled with a punch hole, a heavy line or bar, or a more-or-less regular cancellation. The most famous merchant of remainders was Nicholas F. Seebeck. In the 1880's and 1890's, he arranged printing contracts between the Hamilton Bank Note Co., of which he was a director, and several Central and South American countries. The contracts provided that the plates and all remainders of the yearly issues became the property of Hamilton. Seebeck saw to it that ample stock remained. The "Seebecks," both remainders and reprints, were standard packet fillers for decades.

Some countries also issue stamps *canceled to order (CTO),* either in sheets with original gum or stuck onto pieces of paper or envelopes and canceled. Such CTO items generally are worth less than postally used stamps. Most can be detected by the presence of gum. However, as the CTO practice goes back at least to 1885, the gum inevitably has been washed off some stamps so they could pass for postally used. The normally applied postmarks usually differ slightly and specialists are able to tell the difference. When applied individually to envelopes by philatelically minded persons, CTO material is known as *favor canceled* and generally sells at large discounts.

Cinderellas and Facsimiles

Cinderella is a catchall term used by stamp collectors to describe phantoms, fantasies, bogus items, municipal issues, exhibition seals, local revenues, transportation stamps, labels, poster stamps, and so on. Some cinderella collectors include in their collections local postage issues, telegraph stamps, essays and proofs, forgeries and counterfeits.

A *fantasy* is an adhesive created for a nonexistent stamp issuing authority. Fantasy items range from imaginary countries (Kingdom of Sedang, Principality of Trinidad, or Occusi-Ambeno), to nonexistent locals (Winans City Post), or nonexistent transportation lines (McRobish & Co.'s Acapulco-San Francisco Line).

On the other hand, if the entity exists and might have issued stamps or did issue other stamps, the items are *bogus* stamps. These would include the Mormon postage stamps of Utah, S. Allan Taylor's Guatemala and Paraguay inventions, the propaganda issues for the South Moluccas and the adhesives of the Page & Keyes local post of Boston.

Phantoms is another term for both fantasy and bogus issues.

Facsimiles are copies or imitations made to represent original stamps, but which do not pretend to be originals. A catalogue illustration is such a facsimile. Illustrations from the Moens catalogue of the last century were occasionally colored and passed off as stamps. Since the beginning of stamp collecting, facsimiles have been made for collectors as space fillers or for reference. They often carry the word "facsimile," "falsch" (German), "sanko" or "mozo" (Japanese), or "faux" (French) overprinted on the face or stamped on the back.

Counterfeits or Forgeries

Unauthorized imitations of stamps, intended to deprive the post office of revenue, are *postal counterfeits* or *postal forgeries.* These items often command higher prices in the philatelic marketplace than the genuine stamps they imitate. Sales are illegal. Governments can, and do, prosecute those who trade in them.

The first postal forgery was of Spain's 4-cuarto carmine of 1854 (the real one is Scott 25). The forgers lithographed it, though the original was typographed. Apparently they were not satisfied and soon made an engraved forgery, which is common, unlike the scarce lithographed counterfeit. Postal forgeries quickly followed in Spain, Austria, Naples, Sardinia and the Roman States.

An infamous counterfeit to defraud is the 1-shilling Great Britain "Stock Exchange" forgery of 1872, used on telegraphs at the exchange that year. It escaped detection until a stamp dealer noticed it in 1898. Many postal counterfeits are known of U.S. stamps.

Wartime propaganda stamps of World War I and World War II may be classed as postal counterfeits. They were distributed by enemy governments or resistance groups.

Philatelic forgeries or *counterfeits* are unauthorized imitations of stamps designed to deceive and defraud stamp collectors. Such spurious items first appeared on the market around 1860 and most old-time collections contain one or more. Many are crude and easily spotted, but some can deceive the experts.

An important supplier of these early philatelic forgeries was the Hamburg printer Gebruder Spiro. Many others with reputations in this craft were S. Allan Taylor, George Hussey, James Chute, George Forune, Benjamin & Sarpy, Julius Goldner, E. Oneglia and L.H. Mercier. Among the noted 20th century forgers were Francois Fournier, Jean Sperati, and the prolific Raoul DeThuin.

Fraudulently produced copies are known of most classic rarities, many medium-priced stamps and, in this century, cheap stamps destined for beginners' packets. Few new philatelic forgeries have appeared in recent decades. Successful imitation of engraved work is virtually impossible.

It has proven far easier to produce a fake by altering a genuine stamp than to duplicate a stamp completely.

Repairs, Restoration and Fakes

Scott Publishing Co. bases its catalogue values on stamps which are free of defects and otherwise meet the standards set forth earlier in this introduction. Stamp collectors desire to have the finest copy of an item possible. Even within given grading categories there are variances. This leads to practice that is not universally defined, nor accepted, that of stamp *restoration.*

There are differences of opinion about what is "permissible" when it comes to restoration. Applying a soft eraser carefully to a stamp to remove dirt marks is one form of restoration, as is the washing of the stamp in mild soap and water. More severe forms of restoration are the pressing out of creases, or the removal of stains caused by tape. To what degree each of the above is "acceptable" is dependent on the individual situation. Further along the spectrum is the freshening of a stamp's color by removing oxide build-up or removing toning or the effects of wax paper left next to stamps shipped to the tropics.

At some point along this spectrum the concept of *repair* replaces that of "restoration." Repairs include filling in thin spots, mending tears by reweaving, adding a missing perforation tooth. Regumming stamps may have been acceptable as a restoration technique decades ago, but today it is considered a form of fakery.

Restored stamps may not sell at a discount, and it is possible that the value of individual restored items may be enhanced over that of their pre-restoration state. Specific situations will dictate the resultant value of such an item. Repaired stamps sell at substantial discounts.

When the purchaser of an item has any reason to suspect an item has been repaired, and the detection of such a repair is beyond his own ability, he should seek expert advice. There are services that specialize in such advice.

Fakes are genuine stamps altered in some way to make them more desirable. One student of this part of stamp collecting has estimated that by the 1950's more than 30,000 varieties of fakes were known. That number has grown. The widespread existence of fakes makes it important for stamp collectors to study their philatelic holdings and use relevant literature. Likewise, they should buy from reputable dealers who will guarantee their stamps and make full and prompt refund should a purchase be declared not genuine by some mutually agreed-upon authority. Because fakes always have some genuine characteristics, it is not always possible to obtain unanimous agreement among experts regarding specific items. These students may change their opinions as philatelic knowledge increases. More than 80 percent of all fakes on the philatelic market today are regummed, reperforated (or, perforated for the first time), or bear altered overprints, surcharges or cancellations.

Stamps can be chemically treated to alter or eliminate colors. For example, a pale rose stamp can be recolored into a blue of high market value, or a "missing color" variety can be created. Designs may be changed by "painting," or a stroke or a dot added or bleached out to turn an ordinary variety into a seemingly scarcer stamp. Part of a stamp can be bleached and reprinted in a different version, achieving an inverted center or frame. Margins can be added or repairs done so deceptively that the stamps move from the "repaired" into the "fake" category.

The fakers have not left the backs of the stamps untouched. They may create false watermarks, add fake grills or press out genuine grills. A thin India paper proof may be glued onto a thicker backing to "create" an issued stamp, or a proof printed on cardboard may be shaved down. Silk threads are impressed into paper and stamps have been split so that a rare paper variety is "added" to an otherwise inexpensive stamp. The most common treatment to the back of a stamp, however, is regumming.

Some in the business of faking stamps openly advertise "foolproof" application of "original gum" to stamps that lack it. This is faking, not counterfeiting. It is believed that few early stamps have survived without being hinged. The large number of never-hinged examples of such earlier material offered for sale thus suggests the widespread extent of regumming activity. Regumming also may be used to hide repairs or thin spots. Dipping the stamp into watermark fluid often will reveal these flaws.

Fakers also tamper with separations. Ingenious ways to add margins are known. Perforated wide-margin stamps may be falsely represented as imperforate when trimmed. Reperforating is commonly done to create scarce coil or perforation varieties and to eliminate the straight-edge stamps found in sheet margin positions of many earlier issues. Custom has made straight edges less desirable. Fakers have obliged by perforating straight-edged stamps so that many are now uncommon, if not rare.

Another fertile field of the faker is that of the overprint, surcharge and cancellation. The forging of rare surcharges or overprints began in the 1880's or 1890's. These forgeries are sometimes difficult to detect, but the experts have identified almost all. Only occasionally are overprints or cancellations removed to create unoverprinted stamps or seemingly unused items. "SPECIMEN" overprints may be removed - scraping and repainting is one way - to create unoverprinted varieties. Fakers use inexpensive revenues or pen-canceled stamps to generate "unused" stamps for further faking by adding other markings. The quartz lamp and a high-powered magnifying glass help in detecting cancellation removal.

The bigger problem, however, is the addition of overprints, surcharges or cancellations - many with such precision that they are very difficult to ascertain. Plating of the stamps or the overprint can be an important method of detection.

Fake postmarks may range from many spurious fancy cancellations, to the host of markings applied to transatlantic covers, to adding "normal" postmarks to World War II-vintage definitives of some countries whose stamps are valued at far more used than unused. With the advance of cover collecting and the widespread interest in postal history, a fertile new field for fakers has come about. Some have tried to create entire covers. Others specialize in adding stamps, tied by fake cancellations, to genuine stampless covers, or replacing less expensive or damaged stamps with more valuable ones. Detailed study of postal rates in effect at the time of the cover in question, including the analysis of each handstamp in the period, ink analysis and similar techniques, usually will unmask the fraud.

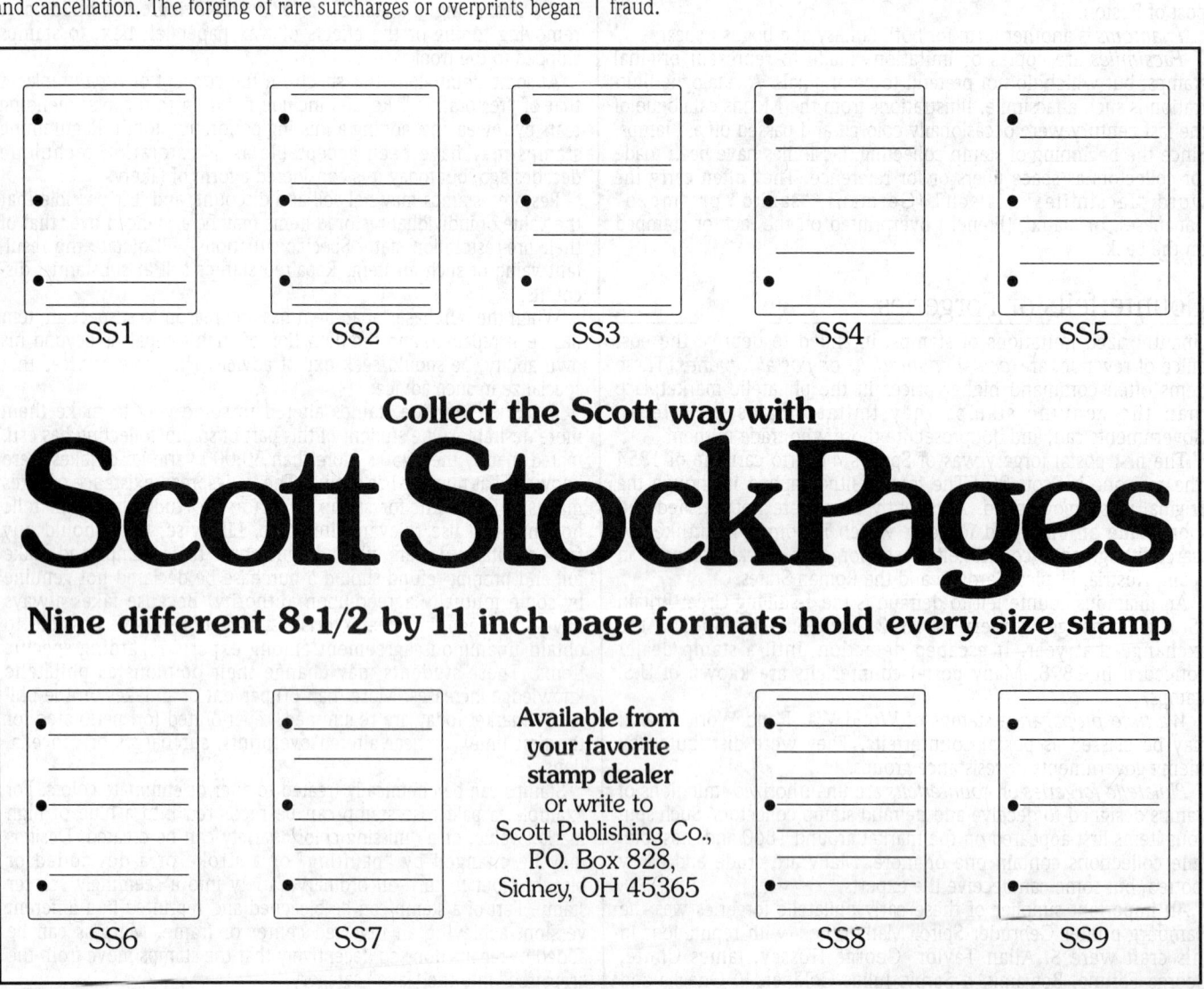

Terminology

Booklets – Many countries have issued stamps in small booklets for the convenience of users. This idea is becoming increasingly more popular today in many countries. Booklets have been issued in all sizes and forms, often with advertising on the covers, on the panes of stamps or on the interleaving.

The panes may be printed from special plates or made from regular sheets. All panes from booklets issued by the United States and many from those of other countries contain stamps that are straight edged on the bottom and both sides, but perforated between. Any stamp-like unit in the pane, either printed or blank, which is not a postage stamp, is considered a label in the catalogue listings.

Scott lists and values panes only. Complete booklets are listed only in a very few cases. See Grenada Scott 1055. Panes are listed only when they are not fashioned from existing sheet stamps and, therefore, are identifiable from their sheet-stamp counterparts.

Panes usually do not have a "used" value because there is little market activity in used panes, even though many exist used.

Cancellations – the marks or obliterations put on a stamp by the postal authorities to show that the stamp has done service and is no long valid for postage. If made with a pen, the marking is a "pen cancellation." When the location of the post office appears in the cancellation, it is a "town cancellation." When calling attention to a cause or celebration, it is a "slogan cancellation." Many other types and styles of cancellations exist, such as duplex, numerals, targets, etc.

Coil Stamps – stamps issued in rolls for use in dispensers, affixing and vending machines. Those of the United States, Canada, Sweden and some other countries are perforated horizontally or vertically only, with the outer edges imperforate. Coil stamps of some countries, such as Great Britain, are perforated on all four sides.

Covers – envelopes, with or without adhesive postage stamps, which have passed through the mail and bear postal or other markings of philatelic interest. Before the introduction of envelopes in about 1840, people folded letters and wrote the address on the outside. Many people covered their letters with an extra sheet of paper on the outside for the address, producing the term "cover." Used airletter sheets, stamped envelopes, and other items of postal stationery also are considered covers.

Errors – stamps having some unintentional deviation from the normal. Errors include, but are not limited to, mistakes in color, paper, or watermark; inverted centers or frames on multicolor printing, surcharges or overprints, and double impressions. Factually wrong or misspelled information, if it appears on all examples of a stamp, even if corrected later, is not classified as a philatelic error.

Overprinted and Surcharged Stamps – Overprinting is a wording or design placed on stamps to alter the place of use (i.e., "Canal Zone" on U.S. stamps), to adapt them for a special purpose ("Porto" on Denmark's 1913-20 regular issues for use as postage due stamps, Scott J1-J7), or for a special occasion (Guatemala Scott 374-378).

A *surcharge* is an overprint which changes or restates the face value of the item.

Surcharges and overprints may be handstamped, typeset or, occasionally, lithographed or engraved. A few hand-written overprints and surcharges are known.

Precancels – stamps canceled before they are placed in the mail. Precanceling is done to expedite the handling of large mailings.

In the United States, precancellations generally identified the point of origin. That is, the city and state names or initials appeared, usually centered between parallel lines. More recently, bureau precancels retained the parallel lines, but the city and state designation was dropped. Recent coils have a "service inscription" to show the mail service paid for by the stamp. Since these stamps do not receive any further cancellation when used as intended, they fall under the general precancel umbrella.

Such items may not have parallel lines as part of the precancellation.

In France, the abbreviation *Affranchts* in a semicircle together with the word *Postes* is the general form. Belgian precancellations are usually a box in which the name of the city appears. Netherlands' precancellations have the name of the city enclosed between concentric circles, sometimes called a "lifesaver."

Precancellations of other countries usually follow these patterns, but may be any arrangement of bars, boxes and city names.

Precancels are listed in the catalogue only if the precancel changes the denomination (Belgium Scott 477-478); the precanceled stamp is different from the non-precancel version (untagged U.S. stamps); or, if the stamp only exists precanceled (France Scott 1096-1099, U.S. Scott 2265).

Proofs and Essays – Proofs are impressions taken from an approved die, plate or stone in which the design and color are the same as the stamp issued to the public. Trial color proofs are impressions taken from approved dies, plates or stones in varying colors. An essay is the impression of a design that differs in some way from the stamp as issued.

Provisionals – stamps issued on short notice and intended for temporary use pending the arrival of regular issues. They usually are issued to meet such contingencies as changes in government or currency, shortage of necessary postage values, or military occupation.

In the 1840's, postmasters in certain American cities issued stamps that were valid only at specific post offices. In 1861, postmasters of the Confederate States also issued stamps with limited validity. Both of these examples are known as "postmaster's provisionals."

Se-tenant – joined, referring to an unsevered pair, strip or block of stamps differing in design, denomination or overprint. See U.S. Scott 2158a.

Unless the se-tenant item has a continuous design (see U.S. Scott 1451a, 1694a) the stamps do not have to be in the same order as shown in the catalogue (see U.S. Scott 2158a).

Specimens – One of the regulations of the Universal Postal Union requires member nations to send samples of all stamps they put into service to the International Bureau in Switzerland. Member nations of the UPU receive these specimens as samples of what stamps are valid for postage. Many are overprinted, handstamped or initial-perforated "Specimen," "Canceled" or "Muestra." Some are marked with bars across the denominations (China-Taiwan), punched holes (Czechoslovakia) or back inscriptions (Mongolia).

Stamps distributed to government officials or for publicity purposes, and stamps submitted by private security printers for official approval, also may receive such defacements.

These markings prevent postal use, and all such items generally are known as "specimens."

Tete Beche – A pair of stamps in which one is upside down in relation to the other. Some of these are the result of intentional sheet arrangements, e.g. Morocco Scott B10-B11. Others occurred when one or more electrotypes accidentally were placed upside down on the plate. See Colombia Scott 57a. Separation of the stamps, of course, destroys the tete beche variety.

Currency Conversion

	Dollar	Pound	Swiss Franc	Guilder	Yen	Lira	HK Dollar	D-Mark	French Franc	Canadian Dollar	Australian Dollar
Australia	1.4017	2.1163	0.9991	0.7552	0.0138	0.0009	0.1815	0.8475	0.2475	1.0142	....
Canada	1.3821	2.0867	0.9851	0.7446	0.0136	0.0009	0.1789	0.8356	0.2440	....	0.9860
France	5.6645	8.5523	4.0374	3.0518	0.0557	0.0036	0.7333	3.4247	....	4.0985	4.0412
Germany	1.654	2.4972	1.1789	0.8911	0.0163	0.0010	0.2141	....	0.2920	1.1967	1.18
Hong Kong	7.725	11.663	5.5061	4.1619	0.076	0.0049	....	4.6705	1.3636	5.5893	5.5112
Italy	1586	2394.5	1130.4	854.48	15.603	....	205.31	958.89	279.99	1147.53	1131.48
Japan	101.7	153.47	72.452	54.77	....	0.0641	13.159	61.457	17.945	73.548	72.519
Netherlands	1.8561	2.8023	1.323	....	0.0183	0.0012	0.2403	1.1222	0.3277	1.3430	1.3242
Switzerland	1.403	2.1182	....	0.7559	0.0138	0.0009	0.1816	0.8483	0.2477	1.0151	1.0009
U.K.	0.6623	....	0.4721	0.3568	0.0065	0.0004	0.0857	0.4005	0.1169	0.4792	0.4725
U.S	....	1.5098	0.7128	0.5388	0.0098	0.0006	0.1295	0.6046	0.1765	0.7235	0.7134

Country	Currency	U.S. $ Equiv.
Denmark	krone	.1530
Djibouti	franc	.0056
Dominican Republic	peso	.0766
Ecuador	sucre	.00049
Egypt	pound	.2955
Equatorial Guinea	CFA franc	.00175
Estonia	kroon	.0751
Ethiopia	burr	.20
Faroe Islands	krone	.1530
Finland	markka	.1852
France	franc	.1765
French Polynesia	Community of French Pacific (CFP) franc	.0096
French Southern & Antarctic Territory	franc	.1765
Gabon	Community of French Africa (CFA) franc	.00175
Germany	deutsche mark	.6046
Greece	drachma	.0041
Greenland	krone	.1530
Guatemala	quetzal	.1728
Guinea	CFA franc	.00175
Guinea-Bissau	peso	.00008
Haiti	gourde	.0833
Honduras	lempira	.1323
Hungary	forint	.00975
Iceland	krona	.0140
Indonesia	rupiah	.00046
Israel	new shekel	.3322
Italy	lira	.0006
Ivory Coast	CFA franc	.00175

*Source: **Wall Street Journal** May 2, 1994. Figures reflect values as of Apr. 29, 1994.*

Colonies, Former Colonies, Offices, Territories Controlled by Parent States

Belgium

Belgian Congo
Ruanda-Urundi

Denmark

Danish West Indies
Faroe Islands
Greenland
Iceland

Finland

Aland Islands

France

COLONIES PAST AND PRESENT, CONTROLLED TERRITORIES

Afars & Issas, Territory of
Alaouites
Alexandretta
Algeria
Alsace & Lorraine
Ajouan
Annam & Tonkin
Benin
Cambodia (Khmer)
Cameroun
Castellorizo
Chad
Cilicia
Cochin China
Comoro Islands
Dahomey
Diego Suarez
Djibouti (Somali Coast)
Fezzan
French Congo
French Equatorial Africa
French Guiana
French Guinea
French India
French Morocco
French Polynesia (Oceania)
French Southern & Antarctic Territories
French Sudan
French West Africa
Gabon
Germany
Ghadames
Grand Comoro
Guadeloupe
Indo-China
Inini
Ivory Coast
Laos
Latakia
Lebanon
Madagascar
Martinique
Mauritania
Mayotte
Memel
Middle Congo
Moheli
New Caledonia
New Hebrides
Niger Territory
Nossi-Be
Obock
Reunion
Rouad, Ile
Ste.-Marie de Madagascar
St. Pierre & Miquelon
Senegal
Senegambia & Niger
Somali Coast
Syria
Tahiti
Togo
Tunisia
Ubangi-Shari
Upper Senegal & Niger
Upper Volta
Viet Nam
Wallis & Futuna Islands

POST OFFICES IN FOREIGN COUNTRIES

China
Crete
Egypt
Turkish Empire
Zanzibar

Germany

EARLY STATES

Baden
Bavaria
Bergedorf
Bremen
Brunswick
Hamburg
Hanover
Lubeck
Mecklenburg-Schwerin
Mecklenburg-Strelitz
Oldenburg
Prussia
Saxony
Schleswig-Holstein
Wurttemberg

FORMER COLONIES

Cameroun (Kamerun)
Caroline Islands
German East Africa
German New Guinea
German South-West Africa
Kiauchau
Mariana Islands
Marshall Islands
Samoa
Togo

Italy

EARLY STATES

Modena
Parma
Romagna
Roman States
Sardinia
Tuscany
Two Sicilies
  Naples
  Neapolitan Provinces
  Sicily

FORMER COLONIES, CONTROLLED TERRITORIES, OCCUPATION AREAS

Aegean Islands
  Calimno (Calino)
  Caso
  Cos (Coo)
  Karki (Carchi)
  Leros (Lero)
  Lipso
  Nisiros (Nisiro)
  Patmos (Patmo)
  Piscopi
  Rodi (Rhodes)
  Scarpanto
  Simi
  Stampalia
Castellorizo
Corfu
Cyrenaica
Eritrea
Ethiopia (Abyssinia)
Fiume
Ionian Islands
  Cephalonia
  Ithaca
  Paxos
Italian East Africa
Libya
Oltre Giuba
Saseno
Somalia (Italian Somaliland)
Tripolitania

POST OFFICES IN FOREIGN COUNTRIES

"ESTERO"*
Austria
China
  Peking
  Tientsin
Crete
Tripoli
Turkish Empire
  Constantinople
  Durazzo
  Janina
Jerusalem
Salonika
Scutari
Smyrna
Valona

*Stamps overprinted "ESTERO" were used in various parts of the world.

Netherlands

Aruba
Netherlands Antilles (Curacao)
Netherlands Indies
Netherlands New Guinea
Surinam (Dutch Guiana)

Portugal

COLONIES PAST AND PRESENT, CONTROLLED TERRITORIES

Angola
Angra
Azores
Cape Verde
Funchal
Horta
Inhambane
Kionga
Lourenco Marques
Macao
Madeira
Mozambique
Mozambique Co.
Nyassa
Ponta Delgada
Portuguese Africa
Portuguese Congo
Portuguese Guinea
Portuguese India
Quelimane
St. Thomas & Prince Islands
Tete
Timor
Zambezia

Russia

ALLIED TERRITORIES AND REPUBLICS, OCCUPATION AREAS

Armenia
Aunus (Olonets)
Azerbaijan
Batum
Estonia
Far Eastern Republic
Georgia
Karelia
Latvia
Lithuania
North Ingermanland
Ostland
Russian Turkestan
Siberia
South Russia
Tannu Tuva
Transcaucasian Fed. Republics
Ukraine
Wenden (Livonia)
Western Ukraine

Spain

COLONIES PAST AND PRESENT, CONTROLLED TERRITORIES

Aguera, La
Cape Juby
Cuba
Elobey, Annobon & Corisco
Fernando Po
Ifni
Mariana Islands
Philippines
Puerto Rico
Rio de Oro
Rio Muni
Spanish Guinea
Spanish Morocco
Spanish Sahara
Spanish West Africa

POST OFFICES IN FOREIGN COUNTRIES

Morocco
Tangier
Tetuan

Common Design Types

Pictured in this section are issues where one illustration has been used for a number of countries in the Catalogue. Not included in this section are overprinted stamps or those issues which are illustrated in each country.

EUROPA

Europa Issue, 1956

The design symbolizing the cooperation among the six countries comprising the Coal and Steel Community is illustrated in each country.

Belgium 496-497
France 805-806
Germany 748-749
Italy 715-716
Luxembourg 318-320
Netherlands 368-369

Europa Issue, 1958

"E" and Dove – CD1

European Postal Union at the service of European integration.

1958, Sept. 13

Belgium 527-528
France 889-890
Germany 790-791
Italy 750-751
Luxembourg 341-343
Netherlands 375-376
Saar 317-318

Europa Issue, 1959

6-Link Endless Chain – CD2

1959, Sept. 19

Belgium 536-537
France 929-930
Germany 805-806
Italy 791-792
Luxembourg 354-355
Netherlands 379-380

Europa Issue, 1960

19-Spoke Wheel – CD3

First anniverary of the establishment of C.E.P.T. (Conference Europeenne des Administrations des Postes et des Telecommunications.)

The spokes symbolize the 19 founding members of the Conference.

1960, Sept.

Belgium 553-554
Denmark 379
Finland 376-377
France 970-971
Germany 818-820
Great Britain 377-378
Greece 688
Iceland 327-328
Ireland 175-176
Italy 809-810
Luxembourg 374-375
Netherlands 385-386
Norway 387
Portugal 866-867
Spain 941-942
Sweden 562-563
Switzerland 400-401
Turkey 1493-1494

Europa Issue, 1961

19 Doves Flying as One – CD4

The 19 doves represent the 19 members of the Conference of European Postal and Telecommunications Administrations C.E.P.T.

1961-62

Belgium 572-573
Cyprus 201-203
France 1005-1006
Germany 844-845
Great Britain 383-384
Greece 718-719
Iceland 340-341
Italy 845-846
Luxembourg 382-383
Netherlands 387-388
Spain 1010-1011
Switzerland 410-411
Turkey 1518-1520

Europa Issue, 1962

Young Tree with 19 Leaves – CD5

The 19 leaves represent the 19 original members of C.E.P.T.

1962-63

Belgium 582-583
Cyprus 219-221
France 1045-1046
Germany 852-853
Greece 739-740
Iceland 348-349
Ireland 184-185
Italy 860-861
Luxembourg 386-387
Netherlands 394-395
Norway 414-415
Switzerland 416-417
Turkey 1553-1555

Europa Issue, 1963

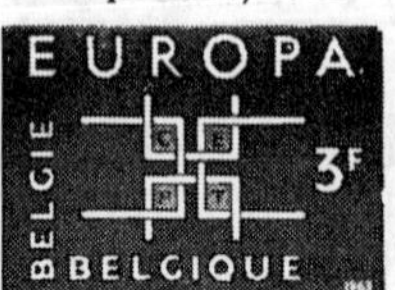

Stylized Links, Symbolizing Unity – CD6

1963, Sept.

Belgium 598-599
Cyprus 229-231
Finland 419
France 1074-1075
Germany 867-868
Greece 768-769
Iceland 357-358
Ireland 188-189
Italy 880-881
Luxembourg 403-404
Netherlands 416-417
Norway 441-442
Switzerland 429
Turkey 1602-1603

Europa Issue, 1964

Symbolic Daisy – CD7

5th anniversary of the establishment of C.E.P.T. The 22 petals of the flower symbolize the 22 members of the Conference.

1964, Sept.

Austria 738
Belgium 614-615
Cyprus 244-246
France 1109-1110
Germany 897-898
Greece 801-802
Iceland 367-368
Ireland 196-197
Italy 894-895
Luxembourg 411-412
Monaco 590-591
Netherlands 428-429
Norway 458
Portugal 931-933
Spain 1262-1263
Switzerland 438-439
Turkey 1628-1629

Europa Issue, 1965

Leaves and "Fruit" – CD8

1965

Belgium 636-637
Cyprus 262-264
Finland 437
France 1131-1132
Germany 934-935
Greece 833-834
Iceland 375-376
Ireland 204-205
Italy 915-916
Luxembourg 432-433
Monaco 616-617
Netherlands 438-439
Norway 475-476
Portugal 958-960
Switzerland 469
Turkey 1665-1666

Europa Issue, 1966

Symbolic Sailboat – CD9

1966, Sept.

Andorra, French 172
Belgium 675-676
Cyprus 275-277
France 1163-1164
Germany 963-964
Greece 862-863
Iceland 384-385
Ireland 216-217
Italy 942-943
Liechtenstein 415
Luxembourg 440-441
Monaco 639-640
Netherlands 441-442
Norway 496-497
Portugal 980-982
Switzerland 477-478
Turkey 1718-1719

Europa Issue, 1967

Cogwheels – CD10

1967

Andorra, French 174-175
Belgium 688-689
Cyprus 297-299
France 1178-1179
Greece 891-892
Germany 969-970
Iceland 389-390
Ireland 232-233
Italy 951-952
Liechtenstein 420
Luxembourg 449-450
Monaco 669-670
Netherlands 444-447
Norway 504-505
Portugal 994-996
Spain 1465-1466
Switzerland 482
Turkey B120-B121

Europa Issue, 1968

Golden Key with C.E.P.T. Emblem CD11

1968

Andorra, French 182-183
Belgium 705-706
Cyprus 314-316
France 1209-1210
Germany 983-984
Greece 916-917
Iceland 395-396
Ireland 242-243
Italy 979-980
Liechtenstein 442
Luxembourg 466-467
Monaco 689-691
Netherlands 452-453
Portugal 1019-1021
San Marino 687
Spain 1526
Turkey 1775-1776

Europa Issue, 1969

"EUROPA" and "CEPT" – CD12

Tenth anniversary of C.E.P.T.

1969

Andorra, French 188-189
Austria 837
Belgium 718-719
Cyprus 326-328
Denmark 458
Finland 483
France 1245-1246
Germany 996-997
Great Britain 585
Greece 947-948
Iceland 406-407
Ireland 270-271

Italy..1000-1001
Liechtenstein...453
Luxembourg....................................474-475
Monaco..722-724
Netherlands....................................475-476
Norway...533-534
Portugal.......................................1038-1040
San Marino.....................................701-702
Spain...1567
Sweden..814-816
Switzerland.....................................500-501
Turkey..1799-1800
Vatican..470-472
Yugoslavia...................................1003-1004

Europa Issue, 1970

Interwoven Threads CD13

1970
Andorra, French.................................196-197
Belgium...741-742
Cyprus...340-342
France...1271-1272
Germany..1018-1019
Greece...985, 987
Iceland..420-421
Ireland...279-281
Italy...1013-1014
Liechtenstein...470
Luxembourg....................................489-490
Monaco..768-770
Netherlands....................................483-484
Portugal.......................................1060-1062
San Marino.....................................729-730
Spain...1607
Switzerland.....................................515-516
Turkey..1848-1849
Yugoslavia...................................1024-1025

Europa Issue, 1971

"Fraternity, Cooperation, Common Effort" – CD14

1971
Andorra, French.................................205-206
Belgium...803-804
Cyprus...365-367
Finland...504
France...1304
Germany..1064-1065
Greece...1029-1030
Iceland..429-430
Ireland...305-306
Italy...1038-1039
Liechtenstein...485
Luxembourg....................................500-501
Malta...425-427
Monaco..797-799
Netherlands....................................488-489
Portugal.......................................1094-1096
San Marino.....................................749-750
Spain...1675-1676
Switzerland.....................................531-532
Turkey..1876-1877
Yugoslavia...................................1052-1053

Europa Issue, 1972

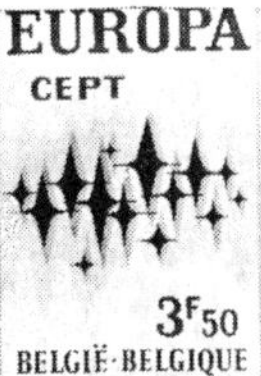

Sparkles, Symbolic of Communications CD15

1972
Andorra, French.................................210-211
Andorra, Spanish...................................62
Belgium...825-826
Cyprus...380-382
Finland...512-513
France...1341
Germany..1089-1090
Greece...1049-1050
Iceland..439-440
Ireland...316-317
Italy...1065-1066
Liechtenstein...504
Luxembourg....................................512-513
Malta...450-453
Monaco..831-832
Netherlands....................................494-495
Portugal.......................................1141-1143
San Marino.....................................771-772
Spain...1718
Switzerland.....................................544-545
Turkey..1907-1908
Yugoslavia...................................1100-1101

Europa Issue, 1973

Post Horn and Arrows CD16

1973
Andorra, French.................................319-320
Andorra, Spanish...................................76
Belgium...839-840
Cyprus...396-398
Finland...526
France...1367
Germany..1114-1115
Greece...1090-1092
Iceland..447-448
Ireland...329-330
Italy...1108-1109
Liechtenstein....................................528-529
Luxembourg....................................523-524
Malta...469-471
Monaco..866-867
Netherlands....................................504-505
Norway...604-605
Portugal.......................................1170-1172
San Marino.....................................802-803
Spain...1753
Switzerland.....................................580-581
Turkey..1935-1936
Yugoslavia...................................1138-1139

PORTUGAL & COLONIES

Vasco da Gama Issue

Fleet Departing – CD20

Fleet Arriving at Calicut – CD21

Embarking at Rastello – CD22

Muse of History – CD23

San Gabriel, da Gama and Camoens – CD24

Archangel Gabriel, the Patron Saint CD25

Flagship San Gabriel CD26

Vasco da Gama CD27

Fourth centenary of Vasco da Gama's discovery of the route to India.

1898
Azores...93-100
Macao...67-74
Madeira..37-44
Portugal..147-154
Port. Africa..1-8
Port. India.......................................189-196
Timor...45-52

Pombal Issue

POSTAL TAX

Marquis de Pombal CD28

Planning Reconstruction of Lisbon, 1755 CD29

Pombal Monument, Lisbon – CD30

Sebastiao Jose de Carvalho e Mello, Marquis de Pombal (1699-1782), statesman, rebuilt Lisbon after earthquake of 1755. Tax was for the erection of Pombal monument. Obligatory on all mail on certain days throughout the year.

1925
Angola...RA1-RA3
Azores...RA9-RA11
Cape Verde......................................RA1-RA3
Macao...RA1-RA3
Madeira..RA1-RA3
Mozambique....................................RA1-RA3
Portugal...RA11-RA13
Port. Guinea....................................RA1-RA3
Port. India......................................RA1-RA3
St. Thomas & Prince Islands..............RA1-RA3
Timor...RA1-RA3

Pombal Issue

POSTAL TAX DUES

CD31

CD32

CD33

1925
Angola..RAJ1-RAJ3
Azores..RAJ2-RAJ4
Cape Verde....................................RAJ1-RAJ3
Macao..RAJ1-RAJ3
Madeira..RAJ1-RAJ3
Mozambique..................................RAJ1-RAJ3
Portugal.......................................RAJ2-RAJ4
Port. Guinea..................................RAJ1-RAJ3
Port. India....................................RAJ1-RAJ3
St. Thomas & Prince Islands............RAJ1-RAJ3
Timor...RAJ1-RAJ3

Vasco da Gama CD34

Mousinho de Albuquerque CD35

Dam CD36

Prince Henry the Navigator – CD37

Affonso de Albuquerque CD38

Plane over Globe CD39

1938-39
Angola...274-291
Cape Verde......................................234-251
Macao..289-305
Mozambique....................................270-287
Port. Guinea....................................233-250
Port. India......................................439-453
St. Thomas & Prince Islands..............302-319, 323-340
Timor...223-239

1938-39
Angola...C1-C9
Cape Verde......................................C1-C9

Macao C7-C15
Mozambique C1-C9
Port. Guinea C1-C9
Port. India C1-C8
St. Thomas & Prince Islands C1-C18
Timor C1-C9

Lady of Fatima Issue

Our Lady of the Rosary, Fatima, Portugal CD40

1948-49

Angola 315-318
Cape Verde 266
Macao 336
Mozambique 325-328
Port. Guinea 271
Port. India 480
St. Thomas & Prince Islands 351
Timor 254

A souvenir sheet of 9 stamps was issued in 1951 to mark the extension of the 1950 Holy Year. The sheet contains: Angola No. 316, Cape Verde No. 266, Macao No. 336, Mozambique No. 325, Portuguese Guinea No. 271, Portugese India Nos. 480, 485, St. Thomas & Prince Islands No. 351, Timor No. 254.

The sheet also contains a portrait of Pope Pius XII and is inscribed "Encerramento do Ano Santo, Fatima 1951." It was sold for 11 escudos.

Holy Year Issue

Church Bells and Dove CD41

Angel Holding Candelabra CD42

Holy Year, 1950.

1950-51

Angola 331-332
Cape Verde 268-269
Macao 339-340
Mozambique 330-331
Port. Guinea 273-274
Port. India 490-491, 496-503
St. Thomas & Prince Islands 353-354
Timor 258-259

A souvenir sheet of 8 stamps was issued in 1951 to mark the extension of the Holy Year. The sheet contains: Angola No. 331, Cape Verde No. 269, Macao No. 340, Mozambique No. 331, Portuguese Guinea No. 275, Portuguese India No. 490, St. Thomas & Prince Islands No. 354, Timor No. 258, some with colors changed. The sheet contains doves and is inscribed "Encerramento do Ano Santo, Fatima 1951." It was sold for 17 escudos.

Holy Year Conclusion Issue

Our Lady of Fatima CD43

Conclusion of Holy Year. Sheets contain alternate vertical rows of stamps and labels bearing quotation from Pope Pius XII, different for each colony

1951

Angola 357
Cape Verde 270
Macao 352
Mozambique 356
Port. Guinea 275
Port. India 506
St. Thomas & Prince Islands 355
Timor 270

Medical Congress Issue

Medical Examination CD44

First National Congress of Tropical Medicine, Lisbon, 1952.

Each stamp has a different design.

1952

Angola 358
Cape Verde 287
Macao 364
Mozambique 359
Port. Guinea 276
Port. India 516
St. Thomas & Prince Islands 356
Timor 271

POSTAGE DUE STAMPS

CD45

1952

Angola J37-J42
Cape Verde J31-J36
Macao J53-J58
Mozambique J51-J56
Port. Guinea J40-J45
Port. India J47-J52
St. Thomas & Prince Islands J52-J57
Timor J31-J36

Sao Paulo Issue

Father Manuel de Nobrega and View of Sao Paulo – CD46

400th anniversary of the founding of Sao Paulo, Brazil.

1954

Angola 385
Cape Verde 297
Macao 382
Mozambique 395
Port. Guinea 291
Port. India 530
St. Thomas & Prince Islands 369
Timor 279

Tropical Medicine Congress Issue

Securidaca Longipedunculata – CD47

Sixth International Congress for Tropical Medicine and Malaria, Lisbon, Sept. 1958.

Each stamp shows a different plant.

1958

Angola 409
Cape Verde 303
Macao 392
Mozambique 404
Port. Guinea 295
Port. India 569
St. Thomas & Prince Islands 371
Timor 289

Sports Issue

Flying – CD48

Each stamp shows a different sport.

1962

Angola 433-438
Cape Verde 320-325
Macao 394-399
Mozambique 424-429
Port. Guinea 299-304
St. Thomas & Prince Islands 374-379
Timor 313-318

Anti-Malaria Issue

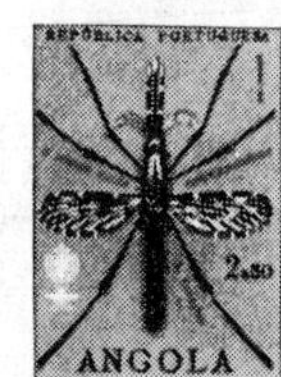

Anopheles Funestus and Malaria Eradication Symbol – CD49

World Health Organization drive to eradicate malaria.

1962

Angola 439
Cape Verde 326
Macao 400
Mozambique 430
Port. Guinea 305
St. Thomas & Prince Islands 380
Timor 319

Airline Anniversary Issue

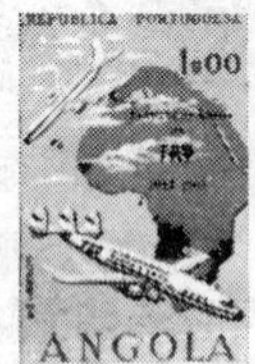

Map of Africa, Super Constellation and Jet Liner – CD50

Tenth anniversary of Transportes Aereos Portugueses (TAP).

1963

Angola 490
Cape Verde 327
Mozambique 434
Port. Guinea 318
St. Thomas & Prince Islands 381

National Overseas Bank Issue

Antonio Teixeira de Sousa – CD51

Centenary of the National Overseas Bank of Portugal.

1964, May 16

Angola 509
Cape Verde 328
Port. Guinea 319
St. Thomas & Prince Islands 382
Timor 320

ITU Issue

ITU Emblem and St. Gabriel CD52

Centenary of the International Communications Union.

1965, May 17

Angola 511
Cape Verde 329
Macao 402
Mozambique 464
Port. Guinea 320
St. Thomas & Prince Islands 383
Timor 321

National Revolution Issue

St. Paul's Hospital, and Commercial and Industrial School – CD53

40th anniversary of the National Revolution.

Different buildings on each stamp.

1966, May 28

Angola 525
Cape Verde 338
Macao 403
Mozambique 465
Port. Guinea 329
St. Thomas & Prince Islands 392
Timor 322

Navy Club Issue

Mendes Barata and Cruiser Dom Carlos I – CD54

Centenary of Portugal's Navy Club.

Each stamp has a different design.

1967, Jan. 31

Angola 527-528
Cape Verde 339-340
Macao 412-413
Mozambique 478-479
Port. Guinea 330-331
St. Thomas & Prince Islands 393-394
Timor 323-324

Admiral Coutinho Issue

Admiral Gago Coutinho and his First Ship – CD55

Centenary of the birth of Admiral Carlos Viegas Gago Coutinho (1869-1959), explorer and aviation pioneer.

Each stamp has a different design.

1969, Feb. 17

Angola....547
Cape Verde....355
Macao....417
Mozambique....484
Port. Guinea....335
St. Thomas & Prince Islands....397
Timor....335

Administration Reform Issue

Luiz Augusto Rebello da Silva – CD56

Centenary of the administration reforms of the overseas territories.

1969, Sept. 25

Angola....549
Cape Verde....357
Macao....419
Mozambique....491
Port. Guinea....337
St. Thomas & Prince Islands....399
Timor....338

Marshal Carmona Issue

Marshal A.O. Carmona CD57

Birth centenary of Marshal Antonio Oscar Carmona de Fragoso (1869-1951), President of Portugal.

Each stamp has a different design.

1970, Nov. 15

Angola....563
Cape Verde....359
Macao....422
Mozambique....493
Port. Guinea....340
St. Thomas & Prince Islands....403
Timor....341

Olympic Games Issue

Racing Yachts and Olympic Emblem CD59

20th Olympic Games, Munich, Aug. 26-Sept. 11.

Each stamp shows a different sport.

1972, June 20

Angola....569
Cape Verde....361
Macao....426
Mozambique....504
Port. Guinea....342
St. Thomas & Prince Islands....408
Timor....343

Lisbon-Rio de Janeiro Flight Issue

"Santa Cruz" over Fernando de Noronha – CD60

50th anniversary of the Lisbon to Rio de Janeiro flight by Arturo de Sacadura and Coutinho, March 30-June 5, 1922.

Each stamp shows a different stage of the flight.

1972, Sept. 20

Angola....570
Cape Verde....362
Macao....427
Mozambique....505
Port. Guinea....343
St. Thomas & Prince Islands....409
Timor....344

WMO Centenary Issue

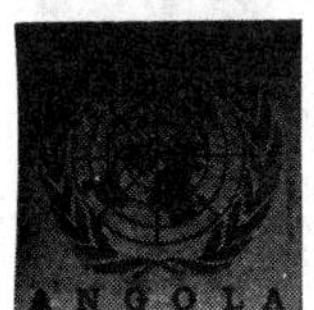

WMO Emblem – CD61

Centenary of international meterological cooperation.

1973, Dec. 15

Angola....571
Cape Verde....363
Macao....429
Mozambique....509
Port. Guinea....344
St. Thomas & Prince Islands....410
Timor....345

FRENCH COMMUNITY

Upper Volta can be found under Burkina Faso in Vol. 2

Colonial Exposition Issue

People of French Empire – CD70

Women's Heads – CD71

France Showing Way to Civilization CD72

"Colonial Commerce" – CD73

International Colonial Exposition, Paris 1931.

1931

Cameroun....213-216
Chad....60-63
Dahomey....97-100
Fr. Guiana....152-155
Fr. Guinea....116-119
Fr. India....100-103
Fr. Polynesia....76-79
Fr. Sudan....102-105
Gabon....120-123
Guadeloupe....138-141
Indo-China....140-142
Ivory Coast....92-95
Madagascar....169-172
Martinique....129-132
Mauritania....65-68
Middle Congo....61-64
New Caledonia....176-179
Niger....73-76
Reunion....122-125
St. Pierre & Miquelon....132-135
Senegal....138-141
Somali Coast....135-138
Togo....254-257
Ubangi-Shari....82-85
Upper Volta....66-69
Wallis & Futuna Isls....85-88

Paris International Exposition Issue
Colonial Arts Exposition Issue

"Colonial Resources" CD74 CD77

Overseas Commerce – CD75

Exposition Building and Women – CD76

"France and the Empire" – CD78

Cultural Treasures of the Colonies CD79

Souvenir sheets contain one imperf. stamp.

1937

Cameroun....217-222A
Dahomey....101-107
Fr. Equatorial Africa....27-32, 73
Fr. Guiana....162-168
Fr. Guinea....120-126
Fr. India....104-110
Fr. Polynesia....117-123
Fr. Sudan....106-112
Guadeloupe....148-154
Indo-China....193-199
Inini....41
Ivory Coast....152-158
Kwangchowan....132
Madagascar....191-197
Martinique....179-185
Mauritania....69-75
New Caledonia....208-214
Niger....72-83
Reunion....167-173
St. Pierre & Miquelon....165-171
Senegal....172-178
Somali Coast....139-145
Togo....258-264
Wallis & Futuna Isls....89

Curie Issue

Pierre and Marie Curie – CD80

40th anniversary of the discovery of radium. The surtax was for the benefit of the International Union for the Control of Cancer.

1938

Cameroun....B1
Dahomey....B2
France....B76
Fr. Equatorial Africa....B1
Fr. Guiana....B3
Fr. Guinea....B2
Fr. India....B6
Fr. Polynesia....B5
Fr. Sudan....B1
Guadeloupe....B3
Indo-China....B14
Ivory Coast....B2
Madagascar....B2
Martinique....B2
Mauritania....B3
New Caledonia....B4
Niger....B1
Reunion....B4
St. Pierre & Miquelon....B3
Senegal....B3
Somali Coast....B2
Togo....B1

Caillie Issue

Rene Caille and Map of Northwestern Africa – CD81

Death centenary of Rene Caillie (1799-1838), French explorer.

All three denominations exist with colony name omitted.

1939

Dahomey....108-110
Fr. Guinea....161-163
Fr. Sudan....113-115
Ivory Coast....160-162
Mauritania....109-111
Niger....84-86
Senegal....188-190
Togo....265-267

New York World's Fair Issue

Natives and New York Skyline – CD82

1939

Cameroun 223-224
Dahomey 111-112
Fr. Equatorial Africa 78-79
Fr. Guiana 169-170
Fr. Guinea 164-165
Fr. India 111-112
Fr. Polynesia 124-125
Fr. Sudan 116-117
Guadeloupe 155-156
Indo-China 203-204
Inini 42-43
Ivory Coast 163-164
Kwangchowan 121-122
Madagascar 209-210
Martinique 186-187
Mauritania 112-113
New Caledonia 215-216
Niger 87-88
Reunion 174-175
St. Pierre & Miquelon 205-206
Senegal 191-192
Somali Coast 179-180
Togo 268-269
Wallis & Futuna Isls. 90-91

French Revolution Issue

Storming of the Bastille – CD83

150th anniversary of the French Revolution. The surtax was for the defense of the colonies.

1939

Cameroun B2-B6
Dahomey B3-B7
Fr. Equatorial Africa B4-B8, CB1
Fr. Guiana B4-B8, CB1
Fr. Guinea B3-B7
Fr. India B7-B11
Fr. Polynesia B6-B10, CB1
Fr. Sudan B2-B6
Guadeloupe B4-B8
Indo-China B15-B19, CB1
Inini B1-B5
Ivory Coast B3-B7
Kwangchowan B1-B5
Madagascar B3-B7, CB1
Martinique B3-B7
Mauritania B4-B8
New Caledonia B5-B9, CB1
Niger B2-B6
Reunion B5-B9, CB1
St. Pierre & Miquelon B4-B8
Senegal B4-B8, CB1
Somali Coast B3-B7
Togo B2-B6
Wallis & Futuna Isls. B1-B5

Plane over Coastal Area – CD85

All five denominations exist with colony name omitted.

1940

Dahomey C1-C5
Fr. Guinea C1-C5
Fr. Sudan C1-C5
Ivory Coast C1-C5
Mauritania C1-C5
Niger C1-C5
Senegal C12-C16
Togo C1-C5

Colonial Infantryman CD86

1941

Cameroun B13B
Dahomey B13
Fr. Equatorial Africa B8B
Fr. Guiana B10
Fr. Guinea B13
Fr. India B13
Fr. Polynesia B12
Fr. Sudan B12
Guadeloupe B10
Indo-China B19B
Inini B7
Ivory Coast B13
Kwangchowan B7
Madagascar B9
Martinique B9
Mauritania B14
New Caledonia B11
Niger B12
Reunion B11
St. Pierre & Miquelon B8B
Senegal B14
Somali Coast B9
Togo B10B
Wallis & Futuna Isls. B7

Cross of Lorraine and Four-motor Plane – CD87

1941-5

Cameroun C1-C7
Fr. Equatorial Africa C17-C23
Fr. Guiana C9-C10
Fr. India C1-C6
Fr. Polynesia C3-C9
Fr. West Africa C1-C3
Guadeloupe C1-C2
Madagascar C37-C43
Martinique C1-C2
New Caledonia C7-C13
Reunion C18-C24
St. Pierre & Miquelon C1-C7
Somali Coast C1-C7

Transport Plane CD88

Caravan and Plane CD89

1942

Dahomey C6-C13
Fr. Guinea C6-C13
Fr. Sudan C6-C13
Ivory Coast C6-C13
Mauritania C6-C13
Niger C6-C13
Senegal C17-C25
Togo C6-C13

Red Cross Issue

Marianne CD90

The surtax was for the French Red Cross and national relief.

1944

Cameroun B28
Fr. Equatorial Africa B38
Fr. Guiana B12
Fr. India B14
Fr. Polynesia B13
Fr. West Africa B1
Guadeloupe B12
Madagascar B15
Martinique B11
New Caledonia B13
Reunion B15
St. Pierre & Miquelon B13
Somali Coast B13
Wallis & Futuna Isls. B9

Eboue Issue

Felix Eboue – CD91

Felix Eboue, first French colonial administrator to proclaim resistance to Germany after French surrender in World War II.

1945

Cameroun 296-297
Fr. Equatorial Africa 156-157
Fr. Guiana 171-172
Fr. India 210-211
Fr. Polynesia 150-151
Fr. West Africa 15-16
Guadeloupe 187-188
Madagascar 259-260
Martinique 196-197
New Caledonia 274-275
Reunion 238-239
St. Pierre & Miquelon 322-323
Somali Coast 238-239

Victory Issue

Victory – CD92

European victory of the Allied Nations in World War II.

1946, May 8

Cameroun C8
Fr. Equatorial Africa C24
Fr. Guiana C11
Fr. India C7
Fr. Polynesia C10
Fr. West Africa C4
Guadeloupe C3
Indo-China C19
Madagascar C44
Martinique C3
New Caledonia C14
Reunion C25
St. Pierre & Miquelon C8
Somali Coast C8
Wallis & Futuna Isls. C1

Chad to Rhine Issue

Leclerc's Departure from Chad – CD93

Battle at Cufra Oasis – CD94

Tanks in Action, Mareth – CD95

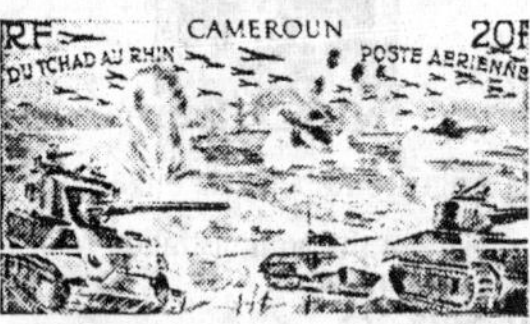

Normandy Invasion – CD96

Entering Paris – CD97

Liberation of Strasbourg – CD98

"Chad to the Rhine" march, 1942-44, by Gen. Jacques Leclerc's column, later French 2nd Armored Division.

1946, June 6

Cameroun C9-C14
Fr. Equatorial Africa C25-C30
Fr. Guiana C12-C17
Fr. India C8-C13
Fr. Polynesia C11-C16
Fr. West Africa C5-C10
Guadeloupe C4-C9
Indo-China C20-C25
Madagascar C45-C50
Martinique C4-C9
New Caledonia C15-C20
Reunion C26-C31
St. Pierre & Miquelon C9-C14
Somali Coast C9-C14
Wallis & Futuna Isls. C2-C7

UPU Issue

French Colonials, Globe and Plane CD99

75th anniversary of the Universal Postal Union.

1949, July 4

Cameroun C29
Fr. Equatorial Africa C34
Fr. India C17
Fr. Polynesia C20
Fr. West Africa C15
Indo-China C26

Madagascar.......................C55
New Caledonia.......................C24
St. Pierre & Miquelon.......................C18
Somali Coast.......................C18
Togo.......................C18
Wallis & Futuna Isls.......................C10

Tropical Medicine Issue

Doctor Treating Infant – CD100

The surtax was for charitable work.

1950
Cameroun.......................B29
Fr. Equatorial Africa.......................B39
Fr. India.......................B15
Fr. Polynesia.......................B14
Fr. West Africa.......................B3
Madagascar.......................B17
New Caledonia.......................B14
St. Pierre & Miquelon.......................B14
Somali Coast.......................B14
Togo.......................B11

Military Medal Issue

Medal, Early Marine and Colonial Soldier – CD101

Centenary of the creation of the French Military Medal.

1952
Cameroun.......................332
Comoro Isls.......................39
Fr. Equatorial Africa.......................186
Fr. India.......................233
Fr. Polynesia.......................179
Fr. West Africa.......................57
Madagascar.......................286
New Caledonia.......................295
St. Pierre & Miquelon.......................345
Somali Coast.......................267
Togo.......................327
Wallis & Futuna Isls.......................149

Liberation Issue

Allied Landing, Victory Sign and Cross of Lorraine – CD102

10th anniversary of the liberation of France.

1954, June 6
Cameroun.......................C32
Comoro Isls.......................C4
Fr. Equatorial Africa.......................C38
Fr. India.......................C18
Fr. Polynesia.......................C23
Fr. West Africa.......................C17
Madagascar.......................C57
New Caledonia.......................C25
St. Pierre & Miquelon.......................C19
Somali Coast.......................C19
Togo.......................C19
Wallis & Futuna Isls.......................C11

FIDES Issue

Plowmen CD103

Efforts of FIDES, the Economic and Social Development Fund for Overseas Possessions (Fonds d' Investissement pour le Developpement Economique et Social).

Each stamp has a different design.

1956
Cameroun.......................326-329
Comoro Isls.......................43
Fr. Polynesia.......................181
Madagascar.......................292-295
New Caledonia.......................303
Somali Coast.......................268
Togo.......................331

Flower Issue

Euadania CD104

Each stamp shows a different flower.

1958-9
Cameroun.......................333
Comoro Isls.......................45
Fr. Equatorial Africa.......................200-201
Fr. Polynesia.......................192
Fr. So. & Antarctic Terr.......................11
Fr. West Africa.......................79-83
Madagascar.......................301-302
New Caledonia.......................304-305
St. Pierre & Miquelon.......................357
Somali Coast.......................270
Togo.......................348-349
Wallis & Futuna Isls.......................152

Human Rights Issue

Sun, Dove and U.N. Emblem – CD105

10th anniversary of the signing of the Universal Declaration of Human Rights.

1958
Comoro Isls.......................44
Fr. Equatorial Africa.......................202
Fr. Polynesia.......................191
Fr. West Africa.......................85
Madagascar.......................300
New Caledonia.......................306
St. Pierre & Miquelon.......................356
Somali Coast.......................274
Wallis & Futuna Isls.......................153

C.C.T.A. Issue

Map of Africa & Cogwheels – CD106

10th anniversary of the Commission for Technical Cooperation in Africa south of the Sahara.

1960
Cameroun.......................335
Cent. African Rep.......................3
Chad.......................66
Congo, P.R.......................90
Dahomey.......................138
Gabon.......................150
Ivory Coast.......................180
Madagascar.......................317
Mali.......................9
Mauritania.......................117
Niger.......................104
Upper Volta.......................89

Air Afrique Issue, 1961

Modern and Ancient Africa, Map and Planes – CD107

Founding of Air Afrique (African Airlines).

1961-62
Cameroun.......................C37
Cent. African Rep.......................C5
Chad.......................C7
Congo, P.R.......................C5
Dahomey.......................C17
Gabon.......................C5
Ivory Coast.......................C18
Mauritania.......................C17
Niger.......................C22
Senegal.......................C31
Upper Volta.......................C4

Anti-Malaria Issue

Malaria Eradication Emblem – CD108

World Health Organization drive to eradicate malaria.

1962, Apr. 7
Cameroun.......................B36
Cent. African Rep.......................B1
Chad.......................B1
Comoro Isls.......................B1
Congo, P.R.......................B3
Dahomey.......................B15
Gabon.......................B4
Ivory Coast.......................B15
Madagascar.......................B19
Mali.......................B1
Mauritania.......................B16
Niger.......................B14
Senegal.......................B16
Somali Coast.......................B15
Upper Volta.......................B1

Abidjan Games Issue

Relay Race – CD109

Abidjan Games, Ivory Coast, Dec. 24-31, 1961.

Each stamp shows a different sport.

1962
Chad.......................83-84
Cent. African Rep.......................19-20
Congo, P.R.......................103-104
Gabon.......................163-164
Niger.......................109-111
Upper Volta.......................103-105

African and Malagasy Union Issue

Flag of Union – CD110

First anniversary of the Union.

1962, Sept. 8
Cameroun.......................373
Cent. African Rep.......................21
Chad.......................85
Congo, P.R.......................105
Dahomey.......................155
Gabon.......................165
Ivory Coast.......................198
Madagascar.......................332
Mauritania.......................170
Niger.......................112
Senegal.......................211
Upper Volta.......................106

Telstar Issue

Telstar and Globe Showing Andover and Pleumeur-Bodou – CD111

First television connection of the United States and Europe through the Telstar satellite, July 11-12, 1962.

1962-63
Andorra, French.......................154
Comoro Isls.......................C7
Fr. Polynesia.......................C29
Fr. So. & Antarctic Terr.......................C5
New Caledonia.......................C33
Somali Coast.......................C31
St. Pierre & Miquelon.......................C26
Wallis & Futuna Isls.......................C17

Freedom From Hunger Issue

World Map and Wheat Emblem – CD112

United Nations Food and Agriculture Organization's "Freedom from Hunger" campaign.

1963, Mar. 21
Cameroun.......................B37-B38
Cent. African Rep.......................B2
Chad.......................B2
Congo, P.R.......................B4
Dahomey.......................B16
Gabon.......................B5
Ivory Coast.......................B16
Madagascar.......................B21
Mauritania.......................B17
Niger.......................B15
Senegal.......................B17
Upper Volta.......................B2

Red Cross Centenary Issue

Centenary Emblem – CD113

Centenary of the International Red Cross.

1963, Sept. 2

Comoro Isls. 55
Fr. Polynesia 205
New Caledonia 328
St. Pierre & Miquelon 367
Somali Coast 297
Wallis & Futuna Isls. 165

African Postal Union Issue

UAMPT Emblem, Radio Masts, Plane and Mail – CD114

Establishment of the African and Malagasy Posts and Telecommunications Union, UAMPT.

1963, Sept. 8

Cameroun C47
Cent. African Rep. C10
Chad C9
Congo, P.R. C13
Dahomey C19
Gabon C13
Ivory Coast C25
Madagascar C75
Mauritania C22
Niger C27
Rwanda 36
Senegal C32
Upper Volta C9

Air Afrique Issue, 1963

Symbols of Flight – CD115

First anniversary of Air Afrique and inauguration of DC-8 service.

1963, Nov. 19

Cameroun C48
Chad C10
Congo, P.R. C14
Gabon C18
Ivory Coast C26
Mauritania C26
Niger C35
Senegal C33

Europafrica Issue

Europe and Africa Linked – CD116

Signing of an economic agreement between the European Economic Community and the African and Malagasy Union, Yaounde, Cameroun, July 20, 1963.

1963-64

Cameroun 402
Chad C11
Cent. African Rep. C12
Congo, P.R. C16
Gabon C19
Ivory Coast 217
Niger C43
Upper Volta C11

Human Rights Issue

Scales of Justice and Globe – CD117

15th anniversary of the Universal Declaration of Human Rights.

1963, Dec. 10

Comoro Isls. 58
Fr. Polynesia 206
New Caledonia 329
St. Pierre & Miquelon 368
Somali Coast 300
Wallis & Futuna Isls. 166

PHILATEC Issue

Stamp Album, Champs Elysees Palace and Horses of Marly – CD118

"PHILATEC," International Philatelic and Postal Techniques Exhibition, Paris, June 5-21, 1964.

1963-64

Comoro Isls. 60
France 1078
Fr. Polynesia 207
New Caledonia 341
St. Pierre & Miquelon 369
Somali Coast 301
Wallis & Futuna Isls. 167

Cooperation Issue

Maps of France and Africa and Clasped Hands – CD119

Cooperation between France and the French-speaking countries of Africa and Madagascar.

1964

Cameroun 409-410
Cent. African Rep. 39
Chad 103
Congo, P.R. 121
Dahomey 193
France 1111
Gabon 175
Ivory Coast 221
Madagascar 360
Mauritania 181
Niger 143
Senegal 236
Togo 495

ITU Issue

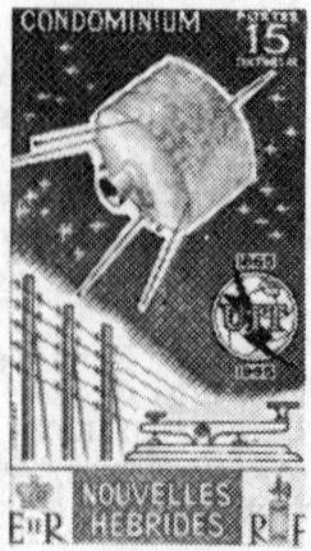

Telegraph, Syncom Satellite and ITU Emblem – CD120

Centenary of the International Telecommunication Union.

1965, May 17

Comoro Isls. C14
Fr. Polynesia C33
Fr. So. & Antarctic Terr. C8
New Caledonia C40
New Hebrides 124-125
St. Pierre & Miquelon C29
Somali Coast C36
Wallis & Futuna Isls. C20

French Satellite A-1 Issue

Diamant Rocket and Launching Installation – CD121

Launching of France's first satellite, Nov. 26, 1965.

1965-66

Comoro Isls. C15-C16
France 1137-1138
Fr. Polynesia C40-C41
Fr. So. & Antarctic Terr. C9-C10
New Caledonia C44-C45
St. Pierre & Miquelon C30-C31
Somali Coast C39-C40
Wallis & Futuna Isls. C22-C23

French Satellite D-1 Issue

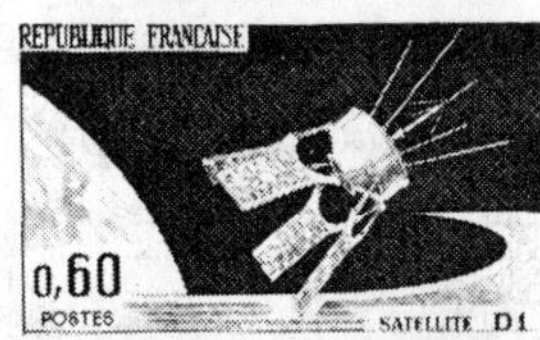

D-1 Satellite in Orbit – CD122

Launching of the D-1 satellite at Hammaguir, Algeria, Feb. 17, 1966.

1966

Comoro Isls. C17
France 1148
Fr. Polynesia C42
Fr. So. & Antarctic Terr. C11
New Caledonia C46
St. Pierre & Miquelon C32
Somali Coast C49
Wallis & Futuna Isls. C24

Air Afrique Issue, 1966

Planes and Air Afrique Emblem – CD123

Introduction of DC-8F planes by Air Afrique.

1966

Cameroun C79
Cent. African Rep. C35
Chad C26
Congo, P.R. C42
Dahomey C42
Gabon C47
Ivory Coast C32
Mauritania C57
Niger C63
Senegal C47
Togo C54
Upper Volta C31

African Postal Union, 1967

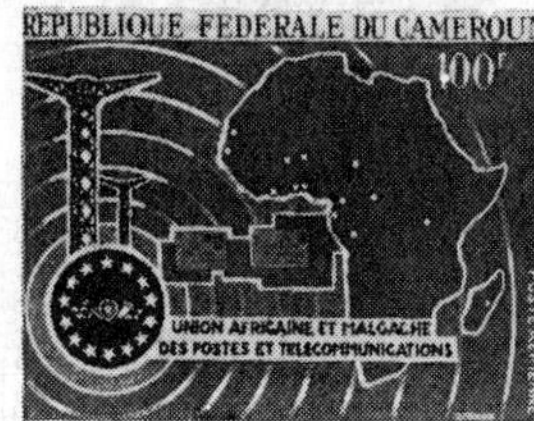

Telecommunications Symbols and Map of Africa – CD124

Fifth anniversary of the establishment of the African and Malagasy Union of Posts and Telecommunications, UAMPT.

1967

Cameroun C90
Cent. African Rep. C46
Chad C37
Congo, P.R. C57
Dahomey C61
Gabon C58
Ivory Coast C34
Madagascar C85
Mauritania C65
Niger C75
Rwanda C1-C3
Senegal C60
Togo C81
Upper Volta C50

Monetary Union Issue

Gold Token of the Ashantis, 17-18th Centuries – CD125

Fifth anniversary of the West African Monetary Union.

1967, Nov. 4

Dahomey 244
Ivory Coast 259
Mauritania 238
Niger 204
Senegal 294
Togo 623
Upper Volta 181

WHO Anniversary Issue

Sun, Flowers and WHO Emblem CD126

20th anniversary of the World Health Organization.

1968, May 4

Afars & Issas 317
Comoro Isls. 73
Fr. Polynesia 241-242

Fr. So. & Antarctic Terr.	31
New Caledonia	367
St. Pierre & Miquelon	377
Wallis & Futuna Isls.	169

Human Rights Year Issue

Human Rights Flame – CD127

International Human Rights Year.

1968, Aug. 10

Afars & Issas	322-323
Comoro Isls.	76
Fr. Polynesia	243-244
Fr. So. & Antarctic Terr.	32
New Caledonia	369
St. Pierre & Miquelon	382
Wallis & Futuna Isls.	170

2nd PHILEXAFRIQUE Issue

Gabon No. 131 and Industrial Plant CD128

Opening of PHILEXAFRIQUE, Abidjan, Feb. 14. Each stamp shows a local scene and stamp.

1969, Feb. 14

Cameroun	C118
Cent. African Rep.	C65
Chad	C48
Congo, P.R.	C77
Dahomey	C94
Gabon	C82
Ivory Coast	C38-C40
Madagascar	C92
Mali	C65
Mauritania	C80
Niger	C104
Senegal	C68
Togo	C104
Upper Volta	C62

Concorde Issue

Concorde in Flight – CD129

First flight of the prototype Concorde super-sonic plane at Toulouse, Mar. 1, 1969.

1969

Afars & Issas	C56
Comoro Isls.	C29
France	C42
Fr. Polynesia	C50
Fr. So. & Antarctic Terr.	C18
New Caledonia	C63
St. Pierre & Miquelon	C40
Wallis & Futuna Isls.	C30

Development Bank Issue

Bank Emblem CD130

Fifth anniversary of the African Development Bank.

1969

Cameroun	499
Chad	217
Congo, P.R.	181-182
Ivory Coast	281
Mali	127-128
Mauritania	267
Niger	220
Senegal	317-318
Upper Volta	201

ILO Issue

ILO Headquarters, Geneva, and Emblem – CD131

50th anniversary of the International Labor Organization.

1969-70

Afars & Issas	337
Comoro Isls.	83
Fr. Polynesia	251-252
Fr. So. & Antarctic Terr.	35
New Caledonia	379
St. Pierre & Miquelon	396
Wallis & Futuna Isls.	172

ASECNA Issue

Map of Africa, Plane and Airport – CD132

10th anniversary of the Agency for the Security of Aerial Navigation in Africa and Madagascar (ASECNA, Agence pour la Securite de la Navigation Aerienne en Afrique et a Madagascar).

1969-70

Cameroun	500
Cent. African Rep.	119
Chad	222
Congo, P.R.	197
Dahomey	269
Gabon	260
Ivory Coast	287
Mali	130
Niger	221
Senegal	321
Upper Volta	204

U.P.U. Headquarters Issue

U.P.U. Headquarters and Emblem CD133

New Universal Postal Union headquarters, Bern, Switzerland.

1970

Afars & Issas	342
Algeria	443
Cameroun	503-504
Cent. African Rep.	125
Chad	225
Comoro Isls.	84
Congo, P.R.	216
Fr. Polynesia	261-262
Fr. So. & Antarctic Terr.	36
Gabon	258
Ivory Coast	295
Madagascar	444
Mali	134-135
Mauritania	283
New Caledonia	382
Niger	231-232
St. Pierre & Miquelon	397-398
Senegal	328-329
Tunisia	535
Wallis & Futuna Isls.	173

De Gaulle Issue

General de Gaulle 1940 – CD134

First anniversay of the death of Charles de Gaulle, (1890-1970), President of France.

1971-72

Afars & Issas	356-357
Comoro Isls.	104-105
France	1322-1325
Fr. Polynesia	270-271
Fr. So. & Antarctic Terr.	52-53
New Caledonia	393-394
Reunion	377, 380
St. Pierre & Miquelon	417-418
Wallis & Futuna Isls.	177-178

African Postal Union Issue, 1971

Carved Stool, UAMPT Building, Brazzaville, Congo – CD135

10th anniversary of the establishment of the African and Malagasy Posts and Telecommunications Union, UAMPT.

Each stamp has a different native design.

1971, Nov. 13

Cameroun	C177
Cent. African Rep.	C89
Chad	C94
Congo, P.R.	C136
Dahomey	C146
Gabon	C120
Ivory Coast	C47
Mauritania	C113
Niger	C164
Rwanda	C8
Senegal	C105
Togo	C166
Upper Volta	C97

West African Monetary Union Issue

African Couple, City, Village and Commemorative Coin – CD136

10th anniversary of the West African Monetary Union.

1972, Nov. 2

Dahomey	300
Ivory Coast	331
Mauritania	299
Niger	258
Senegal	374
Togo	825
Upper Volta	280

African Postal Union Issue, 1973

Telecommunications Symbols and Map of Africa – CD137

11th anniversary of the African and Malagasy Posts and Telecommunications Union (UAMPT).

1973, Sept. 12

Cameroun	574
Cent. African Rep.	194
Chad	272
Congo, P.R.	289
Dahomey	311
Gabon	320
Ivory Coast	361
Madagascar	500
Mauritania	304
Niger	287
Rwanda	540
Senegal	393
Togo	849
Upper Volta	285

Philexafrique II — Essen Issue

Buffalo and Dahomey No. C33 – CD138

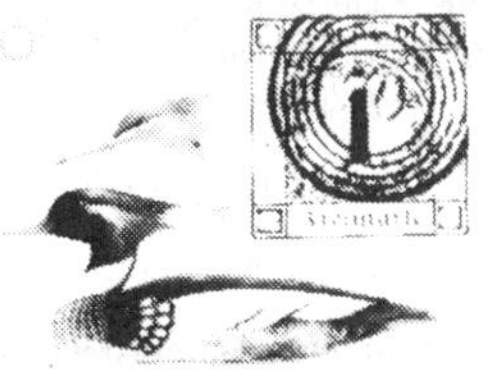

Wild Ducks and Baden No. 1 – CD139

Designs: Indigenous fauna, local and German stamps.

Types CD138-CD139 printed horizontally and vertically se-tenant in sheets of 10 (2x5). Label between horizontal pairs alternately commemoratives Philexafrique II, Libreville, Gabon, June 1978, and 2nd International Stamp Fair, Essen, Germany, Nov. 1-5.

1978-1979

Benin	C285-C286
Central Africa	C200-C201
Chad	C238-C239
Congo Republic	C245-C246
Djibouti	C121-C122
Gabon	C215-C216
Ivory Coast	C64-C65
Mali	C356-C357
Mauritania	C185-C186
Niger	C291-C292
Rwanda	C12-C13
Senegal	C146-C147
Togo	C363-C364
Upper Volta	C253-C254

The Topical Cross Reference

The topical cross reference is a listing of stamps relating to a specific topic or theme. Each year, two topics are selected for this treatment. The topics chosen for this edition are mushrooms and space. The listings are organized by country and sequentially by Scott number.

Topical collections are based on the design of the stamp. As is the case for any type of stamp collection, you may extend your collection as far as you like, including perforation differences, paper differences, related cancellations and so on. Or you may want to narrowly collect within a topic. For the space topic, as an example, you may choose to limit your collection to space ships, comets, planets, Copernicus, views of earth, etc.

The listings we present are based on individual handbooks published by the American Topical Association (ATA). Since it is our intent to present topical listings as current as the stamp listings in our catalogue, we have supplemented that which is found in the ATA-published listings with more current information.

Topical listings found in each volume of the 1995 edition will include items issued by countries found in that volume. Thus, the listings that follow will cover only Volume 3 (D-I) countries.

Following the topical listings is information on the ATA, including a list of its available handbooks and checklists. The ATA is a membership organization, offering a variety of services.

Mushrooms, from the ATA Checklist Service

This listing includes the Latin names of the mushrooms and fungi. Individuals listed include Carl von Linne (nomenclature of living things), Sir Alexander Fleming (penicillin) and Selman Abraham Waksman (streptomycin).

Space, by Leo Malz

This listing includes a broad overview of the areas collected under the space topic. Selected astromomy issues have been included, such as observatories, planetariums, Copernicus, Kepler, Galileo, and so forth. Jules Verne and John F. Kennedy are included only when the designs include space themes. International Quiet Sun Year, International Telecommunications Union, World Communications Year and World Meteorological Organization issues generally are included. In some cases entire sets are listed even though some of the stamps do not show space related subjects. Because so many of the stamps are normally described by ITU, WMO, etc., rather than the space subject shown on the stamps, only Scott numbers are being shown in this section.

Mushrooms

Denmark
624, Morchella esculenta; 625, Boletus satanas.

Djibouti
518, Fleming; 625, Macrolepiota imbricata; 626, Lentinus squarrosulus; 627, Terfezia boudieri.

Equatorial Guinea
173, Termitomyces globulus; 174, Termitomyces le testui; 175, Termitomyces robustus.

Faroe Islands
96, Fleming.

Finland
634, in design (lichen); B200, Gyromitra esculenta; B201, Cantharellus cibarius; B202, Boletus edulis; B215, Lactarius deterrimus; B216, Lepiota procera (macrolepiota); B217, Rozites caperata; B221, Lactarius torminosus; B222, Boletus versipellis (leccinum vers.); B223, Russula paludosa.

France
1630, Amanita caesuarea; 1631, Craterellus cornucopoides; 1632, Clitocybe olearia; 1633, Clavaria botrytes; 2050, Gyroporus cyanescens; 2051, Gomphus clavatus; 2052, Morchella conica; 2053, Russula virescens; B482, in design.

French Southern and Antarctic Territories
127, Neuropogon taylori (lichen).

Gabon
420, Fleming, penicillin formula; 693A, unidentified; 723, termite mushroom mound.

Germany
1340, Bracket fungi.

German Democratic Republic
389, Carl von Linne; 1299, mushrooms: Durer painting; 1413, Amanita muscaria; 1533, Rhodophyllus sinuatus; 1534, Boletus satanas; 1535, Amanita pantherina; 1536, Amanita muscaria; 1537, Gyromitra esculenta; 1538, Inocybe patouillrdii; 1539, Amanita phalloides; 1540, Clitocybe dealbata; 2137, Leccinum testaceo scabrum; 2138, Boletus erythropus; 2139, Agaricus campestris (psalliota); 2140, Boletus badius (xerocomus); 2141, Boletus edulis; 2142, Cantharellus cibarius; 2451, in design.

Guinea
724, 726a, Collybia fusipes; 725, Lycoperdon perlatum; 726, 726a, Boletus edulis; 726a, Agaricus heterocystis; 727, Lactarius deliciosus; 728, Agaricus campestris (psalliota); 918, 962, Rhodophyllus callidermus; 919, 963, Agaricus niger; 920, 964, Termitomyces globulus; 921, 965, Amanita robusta; 922, 966, Lepiota subradicans; 923, 967, Cantharellus rhodophyllus; 924, 968, Phlebopus sylvaticus, Agaricus h.; C131, Morchella esculenta; C132, Lepiota procera (macrolepiota); C133, Cantharellus cibarius.

Guinea Bissau
374c, Fleming; 635a, Clitocybe gibba; 635b, morchella elata; 635c, Lepista nuda; 635d, Lactarius deliciosus; 635e, Russula virescens; 635f, Chroogomphus rutilus; 765, Peziza aurantia; 766, Morchella; 767, Amanita caesarea; 768, Amanita muscaria; 769, Amanita phalloides; 770, Agaricus bisporus; 771, Cantharellus cibarius.

Hungary
1277, in design "Cricket & Ant"; 1341-1342, in design; 2699, Fleming; 2873, Boletus edulis; 2874, Marasmius oreades; 2875, Morchella esculenta; 2876, Agaricus campestris (psalliota); 2877, Lepiota procera (macrolepiota); 2878, Canthaarellus cibarius; 2879, Armillariella mellea; 3046, Amanita phalloides; 3047, Inocybe patouillardii; 3048, Amanita muscaria; 3049, Omphalotus olearius; 3050, Amanita pantherina; 3051, Gyromitra esculenta; 3391, Ramaria botrytis; 3392, Craterelius cornucopoides; 3393, Amanita caesarea; B79, in design.

Italy
1272, in design; 1590, in design.

Space

Dahomey
196-197; 202; 311; 349; C25; C57; C67-C68a; C102; C103-C104; C117; C118; C120; C142-C143; C185-C186; C188; C199; C208; C213; C221-C224; C224-C229; C203-C231; C232; C238-C242; C255-C258; J35; J43.

Danzig
B16.

Denmark
288, B14; 293; 300; 420; 489; 524; 732; 936-937.

Djibouti
454; 518; 524; 528; 547; 561; 610-611; 647; 702-703; C135-C136; C137; C140; C144-C146; C149-C150; C151-C152; C155-C157; C165; C188-C189; C207-C208; C213-C214; C215-C217; C227-C228; C233-C234; C243.

Dominican Republic
598-601, C135-C136a; 637, C178; 640, C156-C157; 673, C178; 694, C197; 711, C208; 741, C229; 742-743, C230; B21-B25, CB13-CB15; C144-C145; C269; C333; C383.

Dubai
118; 121-124; 126; 143; 146, C55-C56; 153; C28-C35a.

Ecuador
650; 718; 748-748E, 748f, 748g; 749-749E, 749f, 749g; 750B; 756-756B, 756c; 758-758E, 758f; 772, 772e; 869; [illegible]; 1138-1141; 1174-1175; 1217-1219; 1260; C422; C610.

Egypt
567; 651; 655-667; 711; 741; 831; 841; 867; 996-997; 1037; 1083; 1096; 1115; 1143; 1160; 1171; 1199; 1211; 1228; 1250; 1299; 1428; 1527; C96; C106; C140; C154; C157; N126-N128; N132; NC37.

Equatorial Guinea
65-66; 91-92; 114-115.

Estonia
108, 110.

Ethiopia
439-441; 541-543; 599-603; 661-663; 668-670; 941-945; 1069-1071.

Faroe Islands
173-174; 220-221.

Fernando Po
254-256.

Finland
325; 373-374; 435; 461; 531; 677-678; 696; 741; 767; 781; 810-811; 866-867.

France
390; 608-609; 626; 673; 770; 792; 857; 861; 869; 870; 871; 925; 987; 1047-1048; 1067; 1100; 1122; 1137-1138; 1148; 1184; 1259; 1270; 1281; 1347; 1416; 1485; 1522-1523; 1578; 1586; 1657; 1683; 1725; 1835; 1862; 1863-1864; 1903; 1934; 1936; 2001; 2016; 2087; 2088-2099; 2109-2110; 2146; 2154; 2231; 2254-2255; 2287-2288; B202; B241; B270; B298; B384; B548-B549; B575; C51; C53.

France - Reunion
294; 343-344; 358-359.

French Polynesia
291; 485; 577; 587-590; C29; C33; C40-C41; C42; C95; C160; C164; C185.

French Southern and Antarctic Territories
8-10; 23-24, C6; 29; 137; C5; C6; C8; C9-C10; C11; C12; C15-C16; C39-C40; C49-C53; C67; C73-C75; C92; C95; C98; C114; C122; C130-C131.

Gabon
167-168; 170; 179; 180; 257; 271; 276; 294; 318; 320; 350; 363; 376; 432; 465; 510; 514; 536-537; 538; 555; 564; 571; 586; 589; 597; 616; 644; 662; 706; 739; 772; 768; 773; C10, C10a; C43-C44; C56; C90; C92-C94a; C108-C108F, C108g, C108h; C119; C137, C137a; C144; C149; C152; C169; C197; C224; C232; C245-C247a; C273-C274; C277.

Germany
472; 725; 862; 920; 924; 927; 1072; 1102; 1104; 1170; 1174; 1175; 1183; 1192; 1246; 1269; 1299; 1404; B268; B584.

Germany - Berlin
9N92; 9N232; 9N313; 9N359; 9N363; 9N364; 9N372; 9N376; 9N569; 9N578; 9NB177.

German Democratic Republic
58, 63; 106; 293; 370-372; 353; 383-384; 426-427; 454; 549-551; 576-581; 630; 634; 655-656; 673-676; 694; 733; 745-747; 762-763; 771-772; 792-794; 819; 898; 982-984; 985-986; 1262-1269; 1275; 1285; 1305; 1336-1338; 1362-1364; 1383; 1402-1407; 1409-1410; 1422; 1456; 1461; 1467; 1494; 1501; 1566; 1604; 1642-1643; 1656; 1661-1664; 1683-1685; 1712-1713; 1718; 1742; 1771; 1772; 1811; 1813; 1856-1857; 1898-1901; 1904-1905; 1944; 1945-1949; 1963; 1990; 2086; 2097; 2292; 2319-2322; 2343-2348; 2471; 2528-2531; 2655; 2675-2677; 2698-2700, 2698a-2700a; 2752-2753; 2800-2803; 2820-2824; 2849-2852.

Greece
820; 827-829; 835; 983-984; 1046; 1350-1351; 1621-1622; 1715-1716b.

Greenland
114; 122.

Guatemala
225; 230; 233; C425-C430; C454; C516; C444-C446; C609a; C762; CB17, CB20.

Guinea
309-311, C50-C51; 380-381, C73-C74; 387a, 393a; 401-404, C78-C79; 529-530, C112-C112B; 541a-547; 560-563; 593-598; 604-607, C120-C121; 653-659; 677; 719-722a; 769-773, C146-C147; 807-814; 839-845, 844A, 845A; 869-875, 874A, 875A; 882; 904-910, 909A, 910A; 911-917; 925-931A; 932; 936; 946-952; 984-990; 1016; 1017-1021; 1028; 1033; 1034-1040; 1061; 1081-1087; 1099; 1108; 1134; 1135; 1141; 1142a; 1151; 1168; 1170-1171; 1182A, 1182O, 1182Q; 1183; 1187B; 1189; 1209; 1212; 1230, 1237; B38-B44; C35-C38; C62-C63; C69-C70; C115, C115A; C167-C169; C171; C172.

Guinea-Bissau
349; 368-368F; 374A; 375-375F; 382-382F; 385-386; 392-392F; 396-396F; 397A-397B; 412A, 412D; 413-413C, C23-C25; 464; 465-472; 537-544; 578; 688a-688l; 703; 889-890; C10-C10F; C11-C11A; C28; C46.

Haiti
417-420, C113-C114a; 424-427, C119-C121A; 484-485, C186-C187; 496-499, C200-C202; 503-504, C206-C207; 503a-504a, C206a-C207a; 521-523, C233-C235; 526-528, C242-C245; 537-539, C255-C256; 544-547, C263-C265; 558, C272; 584, C296-C298; 600, C314-C316, B41, CB61-CB62; 624-624I; 639-639O; 656-656O; 680-681, C415-C420; 695; 710-712, C466-C468; 742-751; 789-794; B2-B3, C89; B41, CB61-CB62; C344A-C344D; C444; C460-C463.

Honduras
C436-C442; C446-C448; C450-C453; C454-C458; C500; C501-C504; C555.

Hungary
1212-1218; 1262; 1381-1382; 1385-1388; 1389-1391; 1562-1569; 1592; 1618; 1659-1668; 1679; 1738-1739; 1803-1810; 1861; 2019; 2132-2133; 2218; 2220; 2228; 2273-2278, C347-C348; 2307; 2312; 2367; 2393; 2410; 2420; 2424, C365; 2441; 2456; 2485; 2492; 2498-2503, C375; 2530; 2540; 2665; 2696; 2733; 2743-2749; 2806-2812; 2813; 2971; 2972-2977; 3061; 3186; 3204; 3286-3287; 3312; 3353; 3390; B242a, B242b; B257a, B257b; B262a, B262b; B293; B300-B301; C209; C210-C218; C219-C220; C221-C227; C236-C247; C248; C251-C252; C253-C260; C275; C284; C285-C286; C287-C294; C295; C304; C305; C308; C310; C311; C312; C314; C315; C324; C326; C327; C328; C336; C346; C350; C351; C354-C361; C363; C366-C373; C388; C393-C399; C408; C409; C417; C425; C426; C434; CB30a, CB30b; CB36.

Iceland
370-371; 460; 547; 580; 738-739.

Ifni
149-151.

Indonesia
460-464; 740-741; 776-777; 802; 819-821; 840; 931; 976-977a; 1006; 1062; 1174-1175; 1191-1194; 1196-1198; 1199; 1215-1216; 1295; 1313-1314; 1366; 1390; 1519-1521.

Iran
947-948; 1048-1050; 1226-1227; 1285; 1324; 1516; 1521; 1534; 1549; 1721; 1728; 1824; 1835; 1862-1863; 1900; 1943; 1983; 1984; 1995; 2023; 2042; 2054; 2057; 2071; 2106; 2118; 2138; 2141; 2157; 2183; 2221; 2269; 2321; 2355-2358; 2362-2363; 2368; 2377-2378; 2379; 2440; 2455; 2489a-2489e; 2506; 2544; B1-B15, B17-B21, B31-B35; C90.

Iraq
377-378a; 425-426; 703-704; 768-770; 844-846; 945-947; 959-961; 997-999; 1006-1009; 1012; 1042; 1050-1052; 1113-1116; 1117; C63-C65.

Israel
74; 117; 132; 190-202; 215-217; 294; 496; 952; 1066; 1089-1091; 1112; 1114.

Italy
419-422; 717; 888-889; 909; 922; 997; 1189; 1324; 1356; 1377-1378; 1406b; 1550-1553; 1558-1559; 1573-1575; 1613; 1839-1840; D16; D18.

Ivory Coast
213; 228; 280; 294; 315; 317; 328; 361; 459; 465; 512; 520; 542-545; 583-584; 585-589; 630; 682A-682B; 715; C54; C97-C98; C99-C103.

ADDITIONAL VOLUME 2 LISTINGS

Albania
553-554; 604-606; 621-624; 654-657; 680-685; 740-744; 777-786; 814-815; 816-820; 941-944; 1208-1210; 1360-1363; 1481-1486; 2086-2087; 2243; 2311, 2313; C68-C72; C73-C74.

Burkina Faso
297; 868; C164; C169; C257; C309-C312.

Croatia
59-60.

American Topical Association

In addition to the specific American Topical Association (ATA) handbooks and checklists used in developing the previous listings, considerably more material is available for a wide variety of topics. Following are two sets of such information, one showing handbooks and their prices from ATA and the other showing checklists. Handbooks are large and normally more broad in scope. Checklists may deal with much tighter specialties.

Only ATA members may take advantage of the checklist service, and therefore cost information on checklists is not included here. Membership information is available for a SASE from the ATA Central Office, P.O. Box 630-C, Johnstown, PA 15907.

Handbooks may not be current, based on publication date of each.

ATA Handbooks

Adventures in Topical Stamp Collecting (HB96), $8.
Americana on Foreign Stamps, volume 1 (HB58), $6.
Americana on Foreign Stamps, volume 2 (HB85), $6.
Astronomy and Philately (HB90), $5.
Bicentennial of American Independence (HB97), $6.
Bicentennial of Postmarks 1972-1984 (HB110), $5.
Birds of the World in Philately (HB106), $14.
Birds of the World in Philately, supplement 1 (HB106-1), $6.
Birds of the World in Philately, supplement 2 (HB106-2), $10.
Christmas Stamps of the World (HB120), $17.
Christopher Columbus in Philately (HB121), $5.
Fairy Tales and Folk Tales on Stamps (HB73), $4.
Fishes, Amphibia, and Reptiles on Stamps of the World (HB91), $8.
Holy Family on Stamps (HB92), $8.
Horses & Horse Relatives (HB116), $16.
Insects on Stamps (HB123), $15.
Mammals of the World on Stamps (HB79), $5.
Map Stamps of the World (HB104), $7.
Medicine Stamps (HB66), $7.
Music World of Stamps (HB84), $6.
Old Glory Around the World (HB75), $3.
Orchids on Stamps (HB118), $9.
Pharmaceutical Philately (HB114), $9.
Plants on Stamps, volume 1 (HB94), $10.
Plants on Stamps, volume 2 (HB112), $12.
Railway Stamps (HB102), $11.
Railway Stamps, supplement 1 (HB102-1), $5.
Science Stamps (HB87), $7.
Space Stamps (HB99), $11.
Sports & Recreation Checklist (HB83), $4.
Stamps on Stamps (HB122), $17.
Statue of Liberty Stamps and Postmarks (HB111), $5.
Watercraft on Stamps (HB117), $17.
Women on Stamps, volume 1 (HB71), $4.
Women on Stamps, volume 2 (HB93), $7.
Women on Stamps, volume 3 (HB124), $17.

ATA Checklists

These listings are continually updated. The number of pages is approximate.

African & Asian Folktales, 1 page, Sept. 1987
African Postal Union, 2 pages, Oct. 1988
AIDS, 1 page+, Dec. 1993
Airlines, 7 pages, Mar. 1992
Airports, 5 pages, Mar. 1992
Airships (Zeppelins), 8 pages, Nov. 1992
Andersen, Hans Christian, 2 pages, July 1992
Anti-Alcohol, 1 page, Nov. 1993
Anti-Drug, 2 pages, Dec. 1993
Anti-Malaria (WHO), 4 pages, Jan. 1991
Anti-Polio, 2 pages, Nov. 1992
Anti-Smoking, 2 pages, Sept. 1993
Arabian Nights Folktales, 1 page, Aug. 1987
Arab Postal Union, 1 page, Dec. 1987
Archery, 7 pages, Jan. 1992
Audubon, 4 pages, June 1992
Automobiles, 31 pages, July 1991

Bach, Johann Sebastian, 1 page*, Nov. 1992
Badger, 1 page, Nov. 1992
Badminton, 2 pages, May 1993
Bagpipes, 2 pages, June 1992
Ballet, 3 pages, Jan. 1991
Balloons, 13 pages, Aug. 1991
  Toy, 2 pages, Aug. 1991
  Weather, 2 pages, Aug. 1991
Baltic Fairy Tales, 1 page, Aug. 1987
Bananas, 4 pages, Nov. 1993
Baseball, 8 pages, Mar. 1993
Basketball, 9 pages*, Mar. 1993
Bats, 2 pages, Nov. 1992
Bears, 8 pages, Jan. 1993
Beauty Queens, 2 pages, Jan. 1992
Bees, 8 pages, Nov. 1991
Beethoven, 2 pages, Nov. 1992
Bells, 19 pages, Dec. 1987
Biathlon, 2 pages*, Apr. 1993
Birds of Prey, 14 pages, Aug. 1990
Bison, 2 pages, May 1992
Black Americans, 5 pages, Nov. 1992
Blacksmiths, 3 pages, Mar. 1990
Blood Donation, 3 pages, Sept. 1993
Bobsled, Luge, Sled & Toboggan, 3 pages, Jan. 1991
Bonsai, 2 pages, Nov. 1992
Bowling, 1 page, July 1993
Boxing, 10 pages, Sept. 1993
Braille, Louis, 1 page, Mar. 1993
Brasses, 2 pages, Jan. 1991
Breast Feeding, 3 pages, Dec. 1991
Bridges, 15 pages, Oct. 1991
Bromeliads (Pineapple Plants), 2 pages, July 1993
Buffalo, 2 pages, May 1992
Butterflies, 11 pages*, Aug. 1989

Cameras & Photography, 6 pages, Sept. 1991
Cards, Gambling & Lottery, 3 pages+, Feb. 1994
Carnivals, 3 pages, Nov. 1993
Castles, 16 pages, Oct. 1989
Cattle, 9 pages, Aug. 1991
Cats, Domestic, 11 pages, Nov. 1992
Cats, Feral, 21 pages, Feb. 1991
Chess, 9 pages, Dec. 1993
Children, Caring for, 8 pages, June 1989
Children's Classics, 2 pages, Nov. 1987
Children's Drawings, 6 pages*, Jan. 1989
Children's Stories, 1 page, Nov. 1987
Chopin, 1 page, Nov. 1992
Churchill, Sir Winston, 4 pages, Nov. 1989
Circus, 5 pages, Nov. 1993
Civets & Genets, 1 page, Feb. 1991
Clocks (Timepieces), 11 pages, Nov. 1987
Clowns, 3 pages, Nov. 1993
Cockatoos, Lories, Parrots & Parakeets, 7 pages, Dec. 1988
Coffee, 5 pages, Dec. 1988
Coffee and Tea Service, 4 pages, Aug. 1990
Columbus, Christopher, 7 pages, Nov. 1991
Computers, 5 pages, Nov. 1992
Cook, Capt. James, 4 pages, Oct. 1990
Copernicus, 4 pages, Apr. 1993
Costumes, 7 pages, Apr. 1988
  Folk - full length, 2 pages, Sept. 1987
Cotton, 3 pages*, June 1989
Crabs, 6 pages, Dec. 1991
Cricket (Sport), 6 pages, Mar. 1992
Crocodile, 6 pages, Apr. 1993
Curie, Marie & Pierre, 2 pages, Oct. 1993
Dams and Hydroelectric Plants, 10 pages, Oct. 1992
Dance (no ballet), 11 pages, Feb. 1989
Darwin, Charles, 1 page, Apr. 1993
Dentistry, 3 pages, July 1993
Detectives, fictional, 1 page+, Feb. 1994
Diamonds, 2 pages, Apr. 1992
Dickens, Charles, 2 pages, Feb. 1992
Dinosaurs and Flying Reptiles, 6 pages, Apr. 1993
Discus, 5 pages, Oct. 1990
Disney, Walt, 7 pages, Apr. 1993
Diving Competition, 4 pages, Oct. 1993
Dog Sleds, 2 pages, Oct. 1992
Dogs, 11 pages, Feb. 1993
Dolls, 5 pages, July 1993
Dolphins, 4 pages, Nov. 1992
Don Quixote, 2 pages, Nov. 1992
Dragonflies, 3 pages, July 1991
Drums, 5 pages, Dec. 1989
Ducks, 6 pages, Nov. 1992

Early Man, 1 page, Apr. 1993
Eastern Art: Icons, Mosaics & Wall Paintings, 12 pages+, Feb. 1994
Einstein, Albert, 1 page, Dec. 1993
Elephants, 14 pages, July 1992
Elvis Presley, 1 page, Sept. 1993
Esperanto, 2 pages, Jan. 1991
Europa, 14 pages*, July 1988
European Fairy Tales, 1 page, Sept. 1987

Fables, 2 pages, July 1992
Fairy Tales & Folklore, 10 pages+, Feb. 1994
Fans (Hand-held), 4 pages, Aug. 1992
Fencing, 8 pages, Aug. 1993
Field Hockey, 3 pages, Mar. 1993
Firearms, 2 pages, Oct. 1993
Fire Fighting, 8 pages, Mar. 1993
Fireworks, 2 pages, Nov. 1993
Fleming, Alexander, 1 page, Apr. 1992
Flowers (minimal descriptions), 22 pages, Dec. 1990
Folktales, 2 pages, Sept. 1987
Fossils and Prehistoric Animals, 13 pages+, Feb. 1994
Foxes, 3 pages, Sept. 1993

Frogs and Toads, 5 pages, July 1993
Fruits and Berries, 21 pages, Apr. 1993

Galileo, 1 page, Apr. 1993
Gandhi Mahatma, 2 pages*, Jan. 1993
Geese, 3 pages, Nov. 1992
Gems and Minerals, 11 pages, Apr. 1992
Giraffes, 2 pages, Apr. 1993
Girl Guides and Girl Scouts, 4 pages, July 1993
Glass, 2 pages, June 1988
Goats, 3 pages, Nov. 1992
Golf, 2 pages, July 1993
Grimm Brothers, 2 pages, Sept. 992
Guitar, Mandolin and Zither, 2 pages, Jan. 1991
Gymnastics, Men, 6 pages, Mar. 1992
Gymnastics, Women, 8 pages, Mar. 1992

Halley's Comet, 6 pages, Oct. 1993
Hammarskjold, Dag, 1 page, Nov. 1991
Hammer Throw, 2 pages, Oct. 1990
Helicopters (Vertical Flight), 7 pages, Sept. 1992
Hercules: Life and Labors, 1 page, Sept. 1987
Hermes (Mercury), 6 pages, Feb. 1989
Hibiscus, 9 pages, Aug. 1989
High Jump, 4 pages, Oct. 1990
Hippopotamus, 2 pages, Nov. 1992
Horse Racing, 4 pages, Nov. 1992
Hugo, Victor, 1 page, Oct. 1989
Hummel Figurines, 2 pages, Sept. 1993
Hummingbirds, 4 pages, July 1993
Hunting Scenes, 5 pages, Sept. 1993
Hurdles, 6 pages, Oct. 1990

Ice Hockey, 7 pages, Mar. 1993
Int'l Education Year, 1 page*, Dec. 1988
Int'l Labor Organization (ILO) 50th Anniversary, 2 pages*, June 1989
Int'l Letter Writing Week, 2 pages, June 1988
Int'l Quiet Sun Year, 1 page*, Oct. 1988
Int'l Telecommunications Union (ITU) Centenary, 4 pages*, June 1989
Int'l Year of the Child, 6 pages*, Nov. 1987
Int'l Year of the Disabled, 3 pages*, Dec. 1987
Iris, 4 pages, Aug. 1989

Japanese Fairy Tales, 1 page, Aug. 1987
Javelin, 5 pages, Oct. 1990
Jaycees, 1 page, July 1993
Jazz Musicians, 2 pages, Sept. 1993
Jesuits, 7 pages, Oct. 1990
Jewelry, 2 pages, Dec. 1989
Joint Issues, 4 pages, Mar. 1990
Joint Issues with U.S., 2 pages, Mar. 1990
Judo, 4 pages, Nov. 1992

Kangaroos, 2 pages, July 1993
Karate, 2 pages, Sept. 1993
Kennedy, John F., 5 pages, Sept. 1992
Keyboard, 1 page, Jan. 1991
King, Martin Luther, Jr., 2 pages*, Mar. 1992
Kites, 2 pages, Jan. 1992
Koalas, 2 pages, Nov. 1992
Koch, Dr. Robert, 2 pages*, Dec. 1992

Legends, 3 pages, Nov. 1987
Leonardo da Vinci, 3 pages, Sept. 1993
Liberty Bell, 1 page, June 1989
Lifesaving, 1 page, Mar. 1990
Lindbergh, 2 pages, Oct. 1990
Lizards, 6 pages, June 1992
Lobsters and Crayfish, 3 pages, Oct. 1992
Long Jump, 3 pages, Oct. 1990
Loons, 1 page, Nov. 1992
Lute, 2 pages, Jan. 1991
Luther, Martin, 1 page, Apr. 1993

Magnifying Glasses, 2 pages, Jan. 1991
Maritime Disasters, 6 pages, Mar. 1990
Martial Arts, 6 pages, Aug. 1992
Masks, 14 pages+, Feb. 1994
Comedy/Tragedy, 2 pages, Dec. 1991
Mermaids, 3 pages, Apr. 1993
Methodist Religion, 2 pages, Mar. 1990
Mice and Rats, 2 pages, Feb. 1991
Microscopes, 7 pages, Nov. 1991
Mining, 5 pages, Apr. 1993
Mosaics, 6 pages, Aug. 1992
Motorcycles, 12 pages, Mar. 1993
Mountain Climbing, 3 pages*, Apr. 1992
Mozart, 3 pages, July 1993
Mushrooms, 25 pages, Dec. 1993

Nobel Chemistry Prize, 3 pages, Jan. 1992
Nobel Literature Prize, 8 pages, Jan. 1992
Nobel Medicine Prize, 5 pages, Jan. 1992
Nobel Peace Prize, 8 pages, Jan. 1992
Nobel Physics Prize, 6 pages, Jan. 1992
North American Indians, 5 pages, Sept. 1991
Nubian Monuments, 3 pages, Dec. 1992
Nursery Rhymes, 1 page, Nov. 1987
Nurses and Nursing, 18 pages, Mar. 1992

Octopus and Squid, 2 pages, Oct. 1992
Olympic Mascots, 1 page, Jan. 1993
Opera, 23 pages, Mar. 1990
Owls, 5 pages, Nov. 1992

Pandas, 1 page, Oct. 1992
Parachute, 3 pages, Nov. 1992
Pasteur, Louis, 1 page, Oct. 1993
Peace, 12 pages+, Feb. 1994
Pegasus and Winged Horses, 2 pages, June 1988
Penguins, 4 pages, Dec. 1993
Peonies, 2 pages, Aug. 1987
Perrault, Charles, 1 page, Aug. 1987
Phoenix, 2 pages, Mar. 1990
Phonographs and Records, 1 page, Nov. 1993
Picasso, 8 pages, Oct. 1993
Pigs, Hogs and Wild Boar, 5 pages, Oct. 1990
Pinocchio, 1 page, July 1992
Pipe Organs, 3 pages, Feb. 1993
Pirates, 3 pages, July 1989
Playing Cards, 2 pages, Nov. 1993
Poinsettias, 1 page, July 1993
Pole Vault, 3 pages, Oct. 1990
Polo, 1 page, June 1993
Popes, 7 pages, Apr. 1991
Pope John Paul II, 3 pages, Apr. 1991
Primates (Apes and Monkeys), 7 pages, May 1993
Puffins, 2 pages, Nov. 1992
Puppets, 2 pages, Jan. 1991

Rabbits, 5 pages, Apr. 1993
Rainbows, 4 pages*, Dec. 1991
Red Cross Societies, 30 pages*, Dec. 1987
Red Cross Supplement One, 4 pages* Dec. 1989
Relay Race, 2 pages, Oct. 1990
Rockwell, Norman, 3 pages, Sept. 1993
Roller Skating, 1 page, Apr. 1992
Roses, 11 pages*, May 1989
Rotary International, 4 pages, Dec. 1992
Rowing, 4 pages, Jan. 1992
Rugby, 2 pages, Aug. 1992
Running, 18 pages, Oct. 1990
Russian Folklore, 1 page, Sept. 1987

St. George and Dragon, 4 pages, 1991
Sailing, 8 pages, Nov. 1992
Salvation Army, 2 pages, Feb. 1991
Santa Claus, 4 pages, July 1993
Scales (Measuring and Weighing), 9 pages, Feb. 1990
Scandinavian Fairy Tales, 1 page, Sept. 1987
Schweitzer, Dr. Albert, 2 pages, Jan. 1994
Scuba, 5 pages, Mar. 1993
Seahorses, 2 pages, Apr. 1993
Seals and Walruses, 4 pages, Nov. 1992
Seaplanes and Flying Boats, 10 pages, Apr. 1993
Shakespeare, 3 pages, Nov. 1993
Sheep, 4 pages, Oct. 1990
Shells, 6 pages*, Sept. 1992
Shooting Competitions, 4 pages, Oct. 1993
Shot Put, 3 pages, Oct. 1990
Skating (no Ice Hockey), 9 pages, May 1993
Skiing (no Biathlon), 20 pages, Apr. 1993
Smoking and Tobacco, 7 pages, Dec. 1992
Snakes, 9 pages, June 1992
Cadaceus/WHO Emblem, 2 pages, June 1992
Soccer, 29 pages, July 1993
South and Central American Folktales, 1 page, Sept. 1987
Spiders, 1 page, Nov. 1992
Stained Glass, 6 pages, Nov. 1992
Streetcars, 4 pages, Mar. 1990
Submarines, 3 pages, Nov. 1993
Sugar, 7 pages, Sept. 1987
Surveying, 8 pages, Dec. 1993
Swans, 3 pages, Mar. 1993
Swimming, 9 pages, Oct. 1993

Table Tennis, 3 pages, Apr. 1992
Teddy Bears, 3 pages, Sept. 1993
Telephone Centenary, 2 pages*, Apr. 1987
Tennis, 11 pages+, Feb. 1994
3-D Stamps and Holograms, 2 pages, July 1993
Toys, 4 pages, Apr. 1988
Traffic Safety, 9 pages, Oct. 1991
Triple Jump, 1 page, Oct. 1990
Turtles, 9 pages, Mar. 1992
Twain, Mark, 1 page, Sept. 1992

Umbrellas, 7 pages, 1987
Unesco Building in Paris, 1 page*, Dec. 1987
Uniforms, 4 pages*, Aug. 1987
Universities, 11 pages, May 1991
U.P.U., 13 pages, Feb. 1989
U.S. Stage and Screen Stars, 8 pages, Sept. 1993

Vegetables, 5 pages, Nov. 1992
Verne, Jules, 2 pages, June 1993
Violin Family, 4 pages, Apr. 1992
Volleyball, 5 pages, Feb. 1993

Wagner, Richard, 2 pages, Nov. 1992
Walking Race, 1 page, Oct. 1990
Waterfalls, 9 pages, Jan. 1988
Water Polo, 2 pages, Oct. 1993
Water Skiing & Surfing, 2 pages*, Nov. 1992
Whales, 6 pages, Nov. 1992
Whaleboats, 2 pages, July 1990
Windmills, 6 pages, Feb. 1991
Windsurfing, 2 pages*, Nov. 1992
Wine, 9 pages, Dec. 1988
Wolves, 3 pages, Nov. 1992
Woodpeckers, 4 pages, Feb. 1989
Woodwinds, 2 pages, Jan. 1991
World Refugee Year, 2 pages*, Dec. 1992
World Wildlife Fund, 3 pages*, Dec. 1992
Wrestling, 7 pages, Jan. 1992

X-ray, 1 page, Oct. 1993
Xylophone, 1 page, Jan. 1991

Zebras, 3 pages, June 1991
Zodiac: Eastern & Western, 4 pages, Dec. 1988

* indicates checklist without descriptions.
\+ indicates checklists available on 3 1/2" or 5 1/4" IBM diskettes.

DAHOMEY

LOCATION — West coast of Africa
GOVT. — Republic
AREA — 43,483 sq. mi.
POP. — 3,030,000 (est. 1974)
CAPITAL — Porto-Novo

Formerly a native kingdom including Benin, Dahomey was annexed by France in 1894. It became part of the colonial administrative unit of French West Africa in 1895. Stamps of French West Africa superseded those of Dahomey in 1945. The Republic of Dahomey was proclaimed Dec. 4, 1958.

The republic changed its name to the People's Republic of Benin on Nov. 30, 1975. See Benin for stamps issued after that date.

100 Centimes = 1 Franc

Catalogue values for unused stamps in this country are for Never Hinged items, beginning with Scott 137 in the regular postage section, Scott B15 in the semi-postal section, Scott C14 in the airpost section, Scott CQ1 in the airpost parcel post section, Scott J29 in the postage due section, and Scott Q1 in the parcel post section.

See French West Africa No. 71 for stamp inscribed "Dahomey" and "Afrique Occidentale Francaise."

Navigation and Commerce — A1

Perf. 14x13½

1899-1905 Typo. Unwmk.

Name of Colony in Blue or Carmine

No.	Type	Description	Unused	Used
1	A1	1c black, *lil bl* ('01)	40	40
2	A1	2c brown, *buff* ('04)	55	55
3	A1	4c claret, *lav* ('04)	85	85
4	A1	5c yellow grn ('04)	1.65	1.65
5	A1	10c red ('01)	1.65	1.10
6	A1	15c gray ('01)	1.10	55
7	A1	20c red, *grn* ('04)	6.25	6.25
8	A1	25c black, *rose* ('99)	6.25	4.75
9	A1	25c blue ('01)	6.25	5.00
10	A1	30c brown, *bis* ('04)	8.50	6.75
11	A1	40c red, *straw* ('04)	8.50	6.75
12	A1	50c brn, *az* (name in red) ('01)	10.00	7.75
12A	A1	50c brn, *az* (name in bl) ('05)	15.00	11.00
13	A1	75c dp vio, *org* ('04)	37.50	27.50
14	A1	1fr brnz grn, *straw* ('04)	20.00	16.00
15	A1	2fr violet, *rose* ('04)	57.50	45.00
16	A1	5fr red lilac, *lav* ('04)	75.00	65.00
		Nos. 1-16 (17)	256.95	206.85

Perf. 13½x14 stamps are counterfeits.
For surcharges see Nos. 32-41.

Gen. Louis Faidherbe — A2

Oil Palm — A3

Dr. Noel Eugène Ballay — A4

1906-07 *Perf. 13½x14*

Name of Colony in Red or Blue

No.	Type	Description	Unused	Used
17	A2	1c slate	50	50
18	A2	2c chocolate	50	50
19	A2	4c choc, *gray bl*	90	75
20	A2	5c green	3.25	75
21	A2	10c carmine (B)	6.50	90
22	A3	20c black, *azure*	5.25	3.50
23	A3	25c blue, *pnksh*	6.50	3.25
24	A3	30c choc, *pnksh*	6.25	4.00
25	A3	35c black, *yellow*	40.00	3.75
26	A3	45c choc, *grnsh* ('07)	6.50	5.25
27	A3	50c deep violet	7.00	5.25
28	A3	75c blue, *orange*	8.00	6.50
29	A4	1fr black, *azure*	9.00	6.25
30	A4	2fr blue, *pink*	55.00	50.00
31	A4	5fr car, *straw* (B)	45.00	40.00
		Nos. 17-31 (15)	200.15	131.15

Stamps of 1901-05 Surcharged in Black or Carmine

05 **10**

1912 *Perf. 14x13½*

No.	Description	Unused	Used
32	5c on 2c brn, *buff*	35	35
33	5c on 4c claret, *lav* (C)	60	60
a.	Double surcharge	110.00	
34	5c on 15c gray (C)	60	60
35	5c on 20c red, *grn*	60	60
36	5c on 25c blue (C)	60	60
a.	Inverted surcharge	90.00	
37	5c on 30c brown, *bis* (C)	60	60
38	10c on 40c red, *straw*	60	60
a.	Inverted surcharge	140.00	
39	10c on 50c brn, *az*, name in bl (C)	65	65
40	10c on 50c brn, *az*, name in red (C)	600.00	650.00
41	10c on 75c violet, *org*	2.75	2.75
	Nos. 32-39,41 (9)	7.35	7.35

Two spacings between the surcharged numerals are found on Nos. 32 to 41.

Man Climbing Oil Palm — A5

1913-39 *Perf. 13½x14*

No.	Type	Description	Unused	Used
42	A5	1c violet & blk	15	15
43	A5	2c choc & rose	15	15
44	A5	4c black & brn	15	15
45	A5	5c yel grn & bl grn	15	15
46	A5	5c vio brn & vio ('22)	15	15
47	A5	10c org red & rose	40	28
48	A5	10c yel grn & bl grn ('22)	16	16
49	A5	10c red & ol ('25)	15	15
50	A5	15c brn org & dk vio ('17)	15	15
51	A5	20c gray & choc	15	15
52	A5	20c bluish grn & grn ('26)	15	15
53	A5	20c mag & blk ('27)	15	15
54	A5	25c ultra & dp blue	65	35
55	A5	25c vio brn & org ('22)	32	32
56	A5	30c choc & vio	90	70
57	A5	30c red org & rose ('22)	90	90
58	A5	30c yellow & vio ('25)	15	15
59	A5	30c dl grn & grn ('27)	15	15
60	A5	35c brown & blk	40	35
61	A5	35c bl grn & grn ('38)	15	15
62	A5	40c black & red org	16	15
63	A5	45c gray & ultra	16	16
64	A5	50c chocolate & brn	1.60	1.40
65	A5	50c ultra & bl ('22)	45	45
66	A5	50c brn red & bl ('26)	15	15
67	A5	55c gray grn & choc ('38)	15	15
68	A5	60c vio, *pnksh* ('25)	15	15
69	A5	65c yel brn & ol grn ('26)	35	35
70	A5	75c blue & violet	32	25
71	A5	80c henna brn & ultra ('38)	15	15
72	A5	85c dk bl & ver ('26)	55	55
73	A5	90c rose & brn red ('30)	32	28
74	A5	90c yel bis & red org ('39)	32	22
75	A5	1fr blue grn & blk	60	35
76	A5	1fr dk bl & ultra ('26)	60	60
77	A5	1fr yel brn & lt red ('28)	62	40
78	A5	1fr dk red & red org ('38)	40	25
79	A5	1.10fr vio & bis ('28)	1.00	1.00
80	A5	1.25fr dp bl & dk brn ('33)	8.00	3.25
81	A5	1.50fr dk bl & lt bl ('30)	40	28
82	A5	1.75fr dk brn & dp buff ('33)	1.50	80
83	A5	1.75fr ind & ultra ('38)	35	22
84	A5	2fr yel org & choc	60	45
85	A5	3fr red violet ('30)	1.00	70
86	A5	5fr violet & dp bl	1.00	80
		Nos. 42-86 (45)	26.58	18.52

The 1c gray and yellow green and 5c dull red and black are Togo Nos. 193a, 196a.

For surcharges see Nos. 87-96, B1, B8-B11.

Type of 1913 Surcharged **60** **60**

1922-25

No.	Type	Description	Unused	Used
87	A5	60c on 75c vio, *pnksh*	32	32
a.		Double surcharge	100.00	100.00
88	A5	65c on 15c brn org & dk vio ('25)	70	70
89	A5	85c on 15c brn org & dk vio ('25)	70	70

Stamps and Type of 1913-39 Surcharged with New Value and Bars

1924-27

No.	Type	Description	Unused	Used
90	A5	25c on 2fr org & choc	32	32
91	A5	90c on 75c cer & brn red ('27)	75	75
92	A5	1.25fr on 1fr dk bl & ultra (R) ('26)	32	32
93	A5	1.50fr on 1fr dk bl & grnsh bl ('27)	85	85
94	A5	3fr on 5fr olvn & dp org ('27)	4.00	4.00
95	A5	10fr on 5fr bl vio & red brn ('27)	3.50	3.50
96	A5	20fr on 5fr ver & dl grn ('27)	3.50	3.50
		Nos. 90-96 (7)	13.24	13.24

Common Design Types pictured in section at front of book.

Colonial Exposition Issue
Common Design Types

1931 Engr. *Perf. 12½*

Name of Country in Black

No.	Type	Description	Unused	Used
97	CD70	40c deep green	2.50	2.50
98	CD71	50c violet	2.50	2.50
99	CD72	90c red orange	2.50	2.50
100	CD73	1.50fr dull blue	2.50	2.50

Paris International Exposition Issue
Common Design Types

1937 Engr. *Perf. 13*

No.	Type	Description	Unused	Used
101	CD74	20c deep violet	45	45
102	CD75	30c dark green	55	55
103	CD76	40c carmine rose	55	55
104	CD77	50c dark brown	45	45
105	CD78	90c red	45	45
106	CD79	1.50fr ultra	55	55
		Nos. 101-106 (6)	3.00	3.00

Souvenir Sheet

Imperf

No.	Type	Description	Unused	Used
107	CD77	3fr dp blue & blk	2.50	2.50

Caillié Issue
Common Design Type

1939, Apr. 5 Engr. *Perf. 12½x12*

No.	Type	Description	Unused	Used
108	CD81	90c org brn & org	65	65
109	CD81	2fr brt violet	68	68
110	CD81	2.25fr ultra & dk blue	70	70

New York World's Fair Issue
Common Design Type

1939 Engr.

No.	Type	Description	Unused	Used
111	CD82	1.25fr carmine lake	40	40
112	CD82	2.25fr ultra	40	40

Man Poling a Canoe — A7

Pile House — A8

Sailboat on Lake Nokoué — A9

Dahomey Warrior — A10

1941 *Perf. 13*

No.	Type	Description	Unused	Used
113	A7	2c scarlet	15	15
114	A7	3c deep blue	15	15
115	A7	5c brown violet	20	20
116	A7	10c green	15	15
117	A7	15c black	15	15
118	A8	20c violet brown	15	15
119	A8	30c dk violet	15	15
120	A8	40c scarlet	32	32
121	A8	50c slate green	32	32
122	A8	60c black	15	15
123	A8	70c brt red violet	15	15
124	A9	80c brown black	25	25
125	A9	1fr violet	35	35
126	A9	1.30fr brown violet	40	40
127	A9	1.40fr green	50	50
128	A9	1.50fr brt rose	50	50
129	A9	2fr brown orange	62	62
130	A10	2.50fr dark blue	50	50
131	A10	3fr scarlet	55	55
132	A10	5fr slate green	42	42
133	A10	10fr violet brown	80	80
134	A10	20fr black	1.10	1.10
		Nos. 113-134 (22)	8.03	8.03

Stamps of type A8 without "RF" were issued in 1944 by the Vichy Government, but were not placed on sale in the colony.

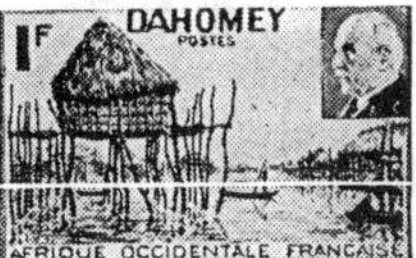

Pile House and Marshal Pétain A11

1941 *Perf. 12½x12*

No.	Type	Description	Unused
135	A11	1fr green	32
136	A11	2.50fr blue	32

Catalogue values for unused stamps in this section, from this point to the end of the section, are for Never Hinged items.

Republic

Village Ganvié — A12

Unwmk.

1960, Mar. 1 Engr. *Perf. 12*

No.	Type	Description	Unused	Used
137	A12	25fr dk blue, brn & red	25	15

For overprint see No. 152.

Imperforates
Most Dahomey stamps from 1960 onward exist imperforate in issued and trial colors, and also in small presentation sheets in issued colors.

C.C.T.A. Issue
Common Design Type

1960, May 16

No.	Type	Description	Unused	Used
138	CD106	5fr rose lilac & ultra	25	22

Emblem of the Entente A13

Prime Minister Hubert Maga A14

Council of the Entente Issue

1960, May 29 Photo. ***Perf. 13x13½***
139 A13 25fr multicolored 40 35

1st anniv. of the Council of the Entente (Dahomey, Ivory Coast, Niger and Upper Volta).

1960, Aug. Engr. ***Perf. 13***
140 A14 85fr deep claret & blk 80 22

Issued on the occasion of Dahomey's proclamation of independence, Aug. 1, 1960.
For surcharge see No. 149.

Weaver — A15

Doves, UN Building and Emblem — A16

Designs: 2fr, 10fr, Wood sculptor. 3fr, 15fr, Fisherman and net, horiz. 4fr, 20fr, Potter, horiz.

1961, Feb. 17 Engr. ***Perf. 13***
141 A15 1fr rose, org & red lilac 15 15
142 A15 2fr bister brn & choc 15 15
143 A15 3fr green & orange 15 15
144 A15 4fr olive bis & claret 15 15
145 A15 6fr rose, lt vio & ver 15 15
146 A15 10fr blue & green 16 15
147 A15 15fr red lilac & violet 18 15
148 A15 20fr bluish vio & Prus bl 25 16
Set value 90 65

For surcharges see Nos. Q1-Q7.

No. 140 Surcharged with New Value, Bars and: "Président de la République"

1961, Aug. 1
149 A14 100fr on 85fr dp cl & blk 1.10 1.00

First anniversary of Independence.

1961, Sept. 20 Unwmk. ***Perf. 13***
150 A16 5fr multicolored 15 15
151 A16 60fr multicolored 45 40

1st anniv. of Dahomey's admission to the UN. See #C16 and souvenir sheet #C16a.

No. 137 Overprinted: "JEUX SPORTIFS D'ABIDJAN 24 AU 31 DECEMBRE 1961"

1961, Dec. 24
152 A12 25fr dk blue, brn & red 30 18

Abidjan Games, Dec 24-31.

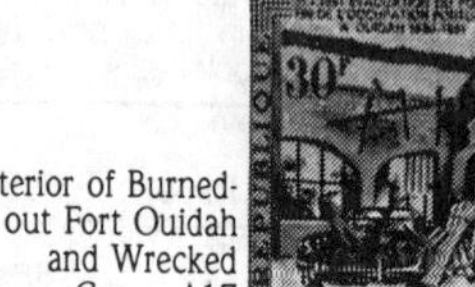

Interior of Burned-out Fort Ouidah and Wrecked Car — A17

1962, July 31 Photo. ***Perf. 12½***
153 A17 30fr multicolored 30 15
154 A17 60fr multicolored 60 35

First anniversary of the evacuation of Fort Ouidah by the Portuguese, and its occupation by Dahomey.

African and Malgache Union Issue

Common Design Type

1962, Sept. 8 ***Perf. 12½x12***
155 CD110 30fr red lil, bluish grn, red & gold 50 20

Red Cross Nurses and Map — A18

1962, Oct. 5 Engr. ***Perf. 13***
156 A18 5fr blue, choc & red 15 15
157 A18 20fr blue, dk grn & red 20 16
158 A18 25fr blue, brown & red 25 20
159 A18 30fr blue, black & red 35 20

Ganvié Woman in Canoe — A19

Peuhl Herdsman and Cattle — A20

Designs: 3fr, 65fr, Bariba chief of Nikki. 15fr, 50fr, Ouidah witch doctor, rock python. 20fr, 30fr, Nessoukoué women carrying vases on heads, Abomey. 25fr, 40fr, Dahomey girl. 60fr, Peuhl herdsman and cattle. 85fr, Ganvié woman in canoe.

1963, Feb. 18 Unwmk. ***Perf. 13***
160 A19 2fr grnsh bl & vio 15 15
161 A19 3fr blue & black 15 15
162 A20 5fr brown, blk & grn 15 15
163 A19 15fr brn, bl grn & red brn 15 15
164 A19 20fr green, blk & car 15 15
165 A20 25fr dk brn, bl & bl grn 18 15
166 A19 30fr brn org, choc & mag 22 15
167 A20 40fr choc, grn & brt bl 30 15
168 A19 50fr blk, grn, brn & red brn 38 18
169 A20 60fr choc, org red & ol 42 20
170 A19 65fr orange brn & choc 45 25
171 A19 85fr brt blue & choc 65 38
Nos. 160-171 (12) 3.35
Set value 1.65

For surcharges see Nos. 211, 232.

Boxers — A21

Designs: 1fr, 20fr, Soccer goalkeeper, horiz. 2fr, 5fr, Runners.

1963, Apr. 11 Engr.
172 A21 50c green & blue 15 15
173 A21 1fr olive, blk & brn 15 15
174 A21 2fr olive, blue & brn 15 15
175 A21 5fr brown, crim & blk 15 15
176 A21 15fr dk violet & brn 16 15
177 A21 20fr multicolored 25 20
Set value 63 54

Friendship Games, Dakar, Apr. 11-21.

President's Palace, Cotonou A22

1963, Aug. 1 Photo. ***Perf. 12½x12***
178 A22 25fr multicolored 25 16

Third anniversary of independence.

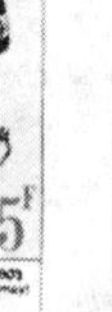

Gen. Toussaint L'Ouverture — A23

UN Emblem, Flame, "15" — A24

1963, Nov. 18 Unwmk. ***Perf. 12x13***
179 A23 25fr multicolored 20 15
180 A23 30fr multicolored 22 15
181 A23 100fr ultra, brn & red 75 50

Pierre Dominique Toussaint L'Ouverture (1743-1803), Haitian gen., statesman and descendant of the kings of Allada (Dahomey).

1963, Dec. 10 ***Perf. 12***
182 A24 4fr multicolored 15 15
183 A24 6fr multicolored 15 15
184 A24 25fr multicolored 25 20
Set value 37 30

15th anniversary of the Universal Declaration of Human Rights.

Somba Dance — A25

Regional Dances: 3fr, Nago dance, Pobe-Ketou, horiz. 10fr, Dance of the baton. 15fr, Nago dance, Ouidah, horiz. 25fr, Dance of the Sakpatassi. 30fr, Dance of the Nessouhouessi, horiz.

1964, Aug. 8 Engr. ***Perf. 13***
185 A25 2fr red, emerald & blk 15 15
186 A25 3fr dull red, blue & grn 15 15
187 A25 10fr purple, blk & red 15 15
188 A25 15fr magenta, blk & grn 16 15
189 A25 25fr Prus blue, brn & org 25 16
190 A25 30fr dk red, choc & org 30 22
Set value 00 65

Runner — A26

1964, Oct. 20 Photo. ***Perf. 11***
191 A26 60fr shown 50 38
192 A26 85fr Bicyclist 80 60

18th Olympic Games, Tokyo, Oct. 10-25.

Cooperation Issue

Common Design Type

1964, Nov. 7 Engr. ***Perf. 13***
193 CD119 25fr org, vio & dk brn 25 16

UNICEF Emblem, Mother and Child — A27

IQSY Emblem and Apollo — A28

Design: 25fr, Mother holding child in her arms.

1964, Dec. 11 Unwmk. ***Perf. 13***
194 A27 20fr yel grn, dk red & blk 20 16
195 A27 25fr blue, dk red & blk 25 16

18th anniv. of UNICEF.

1964, Dec. 22 Photo. ***Perf. 13x12½***

Design: 100fr, IQSY emblem and Nimbus weather satellite.

196 A28 25fr green & lt yellow 35 15
197 A28 100fr deep plum & yellow 1.00 60

International Quiet Sun Year, 1964-65.

Abomey Tapestry — A29

Designs (Abomey tapestries): 25fr, Warrior and fight scenes. 50fr, Birds and warriors, horiz. 85fr, Animals, ship and plants, horiz.

1965, Apr. 12 Photo. ***Perf. 12½***
198 A29 20fr multicolored 20 15
199 A29 25fr multicolored 25 20
200 A29 50fr multicolored 50 35
201 A29 85fr multicolored 80 60
a. Min. sheet of 4, #198-201 1.50 1.50

Issued to publicize the local rug weaving industry.

Baudot Telegraph Distributor and Ader Telephone A30

1965, May 17 Engr. ***Perf. 13***
202 A30 100fr lilac, org & blk 1.00 40

Cent. of the ITU.

Cotonou Harbor — A31

Design: 100fr, Cotonou Harbor, denomination at left.

1965, Aug. 1 Photo. *Perf. 12½*

203 A31 25fr multicolored 30 16
204 A31 100fr multicolored 1.10 65
a. Pair, #203-204 1.50

The opening of Cotonou Harbor. No. 204a has a continuous design.
For surcharges see Nos. 219-220.

REPUBLIQUE DU DAHOMEY 10f POSTES CYBIUM TRITOR

Cybium Tritor — A32

Fish: 25fr, Dentex filosus. 30fr, Atlantic sailfish. 50fr, Blackish tripletail.

1965, Sept. 20 Engr. *Perf. 13*

205 A32 10fr black & brt blue 15 15
206 A32 25fr brt blue, org & blk 25 20
207 A32 30fr violet bl & grnsh bl 30 20
208 A32 50fr black, gray bl & org 50 35

Independence Monument — A33

1965, Oct. 28 Photo. *Perf. 12x12½*

209 A33 25fr gray, black & red 25 15
210 A33 30fr lt ultra, black & red 30 16

October 28 Revolution, 2nd anniv.

No. 165 Surcharged

1 F

1965, Nov. Engr. *Perf. 13*

211 A20 1fr on 25fr 15 15

Porto Novo Cathedral A34

Designs: 50fr, Ouidah Pro-Cathedral, vert. 70fr, Cotonou Cathedral.

1966, Mar. 21 Engr. *Perf. 13*

212 A34 30fr Prus bl, vio brn & grn 30 20
213 A34 50fr vio brn, Prus bl & brn 50 30
214 A34 70fr grn, Prus bl & vio brn 70 42

Jewelry — A35

Designs: 30fr, Architecture. 50fr, Musician. 70fr, Crucifixion, sculpture.

1966, Apr. 4 Engr. *Perf. 13*

215 A35 15fr dull red brn & blk 16 15
216 A35 30fr dk brn, ultra & brn red 30 16
217 A35 50fr brt blue & dk brn 50 25
218 A35 70fr red brown & blk 70 42

International Negro Arts Festival, Dakar, Senegal, Apr. 1-24.

Nos. 203-204 Surcharged

ACCORD DE COOPERATION
FRANCE - DAHOMEY
5e Anniversaire - 24 Avril 1966

15 F

1966, Apr. 24 Photo. *Perf. 12½*

219 A31 15fr on 25fr multi 16 15
220 A31 15fr on 100fr multi 16 15
Set value 20

Fifth anniversary of the Cooperation Agreement between France and Dahomey.

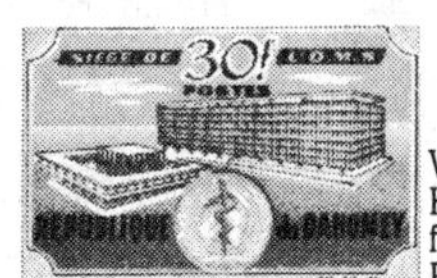

WHO Headquarters from the East — A36

1966, May 3 *Perf. 12½x13*
Size: 35x22½mm

221 A36 30fr multicolored 30 20

Inauguration of the WHO Headquarters, Geneva. See No. C32.

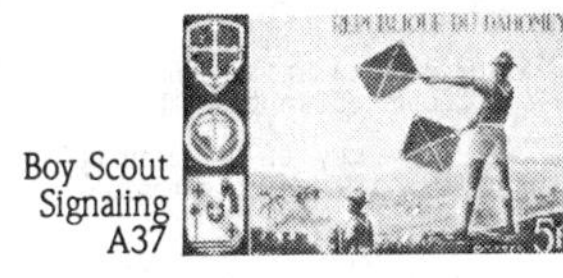

Boy Scout Signaling A37

Designs: 10fr, Patrol standard with pennant, vert. 30fr, Campfire and map of Dahomey, vert. 50fr, Scouts building foot bridge.

1966, Oct. 17 Engr. *Perf. 13*

222 A37 5fr dk brn, ocher & red 15 15
223 A37 10fr black, grn & rose cl 15 15
224 A37 30fr org, red brn & pur 25 16
225 A37 50fr vio bl, grn & dk brn 45 25
a. Min. sheet of 4, #222-225 1.10 1.10
Set value 50

Clappertonia Ficifolia — A38

Lions Emblem, Dancing Children, Bird — A39

Flowers: 3fr, Hewittia sublobata. 5fr, Butterfly pea. 10fr, Water lily. 15fr, Commelina forskalaei. 30fr, Eremomastax speciosa.

1967, Feb. 20 Photo. *Perf. 12x12½*

226 A38 1fr multicolored 15 15
227 A38 3fr multicolored 15 15
228 A38 5fr multicolored 15 15
229 A38 10fr multicolored 16 15
230 A38 15fr multicolored 20 15
231 A38 30fr multicolored 40 20
Set value 1.00 54

Nos. 170-171 Surcharged with New Value and Heavy Bar

1967, Mar. 1 Engr. *Perf. 13*

232 A19 30fr on 65fr 30 22
a. Double surcharge 15.00
233 A19 30fr on 85fr 30 25
a. Double surcharge 22.50
b. Inverted surcharge 22.50

1967, Mar. 20

234 A39 100fr dl vio, dp bl & grn 1.10 35

50th anniversary of Lions International.

EXPO '67 "Man in the City" Pavilion A40

Design: 70fr, "The New Africa" exhibit.

1967, June 12 Engr. *Perf. 13*

235 A40 30fr green & choc 22 15
236 A40 70fr green & brn red 50 32

EXPO '67, International Exhibition, Montreal, Apr. 28-Oct. 27, 1967. See No. C57 and miniature sheet No. C57a.

Europafrica Issue, 1967

Trade (Blood) Circulation, Map of Europe and Africa — A41

1967, July 20 Photo. *Perf. 12x12½*

237 A41 30fr multicolored 25 15
238 A41 45fr multicolored 42 16

Scouts Climbing Mountain, Jamboree Emblem A42

Design: 70fr, Jamboree emblem and Scouts launching canoe.

1967, Aug. 7 Engr. *Perf. 13*

239 A42 30fr brt bl, red brn & sl 30 15
240 A42 70fr brt bl, sl grn & dk brn 65 42

12th Boy Scout World Jamboree, Farragut State Park, Idaho, Aug. 1-9. For souvenir sheet see No. C59a.

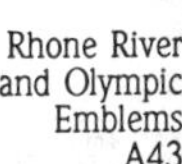

Rhone River and Olympic Emblems A43

Designs (Olympic Emblems and): 45fr, View of Grenoble, vert. 100fr, Rhone Bridge, Grenoble, and Pierre de Coubertin.

1967, Sept. 2 Engr. *Perf. 13*

241 A43 30fr bis, dp bl & grn 25 15
242 A43 45fr ultra, grn & brn 42 15
243 A43 100fr choc, grn & brt bl 85 45
a. Min. sheet of 3, #241-243 1.65 1.65

10th Winter Olympic Games, Grenoble, Feb. 6-18, 1968.

Monetary Union Issue
Common Design Type

1967, Nov. 4 Engr. *Perf. 13*

244 CD125 30fr grn, dk car & dk brn 30 16

Cape Buffalo — A45

Animals from the Pendjari Reservation: 30fr, Lion. 45fr, Buffon's kob. 70fr, African slender-snouted crocodile. 100fr, Hippopotamus.

1968, Mar. 18 Photo. *Perf. 12½x13*

245 A45 15fr multicolored 16 15
246 A45 30fr purple & multi 30 15
247 A45 45fr blue & multi 45 20
248 A45 70fr multicolored 65 30
249 A45 100fr multicolored 1.00 55
Nos. 245-249 (5) 2.56 1.35

For surcharge see No. 310.

WHO Emblem A46

1968, Apr. 22 Engr. *Perf. 13*

250 A46 30fr multicolored 30 15
251 A46 70fr multicolored 65 38

20th anniv. of WHO.

Leopard A47

Animals: 5fr, Warthog. 60fr, Spotted hyena. 75fr, Anubius baboon. 90fr, Hartebeest.

1969, Feb. 10 Photo. *Perf. 12½x12*

252 A47 5fr dark brown & multi 15 15
253 A47 30fr deep ultra & multi 30 15
254 A47 60fr dark green & multi 60 25
255 A47 75fr dark blue & multi 70 38
256 A47 90fr dark green & multi 90 45
Nos. 252-256 (5) 2.65 1.38

Heads, Symbols of Agriculture and Science, and Globe — A48

1969, Mar. 10 Engr. *Perf. 13*

257 A48 30fr orange & multi 30 15
258 A48 70fr maroon & multi 65 35

50th anniv. of the ILO.

Arms of Dahomey A49

1969, June 30 Litho. *Perf. 13½x13*

259 A49 5fr yellow & multi 15 15
260 A49 30fr orange red & multi 25 16
Set value 30 21

See No. C101.

Development Bank Issue

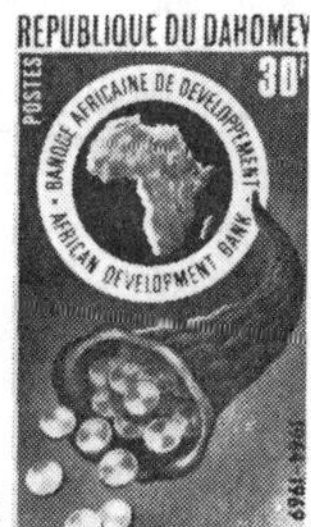

Cornucopia and Bank Emblem — A50

1969, Sept. 10 Photo. *Perf. 13*

261 A50 30fr black, grn & ocher 35 16

African Development Bank, 5th anniv.

Europafrica Issue

Ambary (Kenaf) Industry, Cotonou A51

Design: 45fr, Cotton industry, Parakou.

1969, Sept. 22 Litho. *Perf. 14*

262 A51 30fr multicolored 40 25
263 A51 45fr multicolored 60 30

See Nos. C105-C105a.

Sakpata Dance and Tourist Year Emblem — A52

Dances and Tourist Year Emblem: 30fr, Guelede dance. 45fr, Sato dance.

1969, Dec. 15 Litho. *Perf. 14*

264 A52 10fr multicolored 15 15
265 A52 30fr multicolored 30 15
266 A52 45fr multicolored 42 22

See No. C108.

UN Emblem, Garden and Wall — A53

1970, Apr. 6 Engr. *Perf. 13*

267 A53 30fr ultra, red org & slate 30 15
268 A53 40fr ultra, brn & sl grn 40 20

25th anniversary of the United Nations.
For surcharge see No. 294.

ASECNA Issue
Common Design Type

1970, June 1 Engr. *Perf. 13*

269 CD132 40fr red & purple 40 22

Mt. Fuji, EXPO '70 Emblem, Monorail Train — A54

1970, June 15 Litho. *Perf. 13½x14*

270 A54 5fr green, red & vio bl 15 15

EXPO '70 International Exhibition, Osaka, Japan, Mar. 15-Sept. 13, 1970. See Nos. C124-C125.

Alkemy, King of Ardres — A55

Designs: 40fr, Sailing ships "La Justice" and "La Concorde," Ardres, 1670. 50fr, Matheo Lopes, ambassador of the King of Ardres and his coat of arms. 200fr, Louis XIV and fleur de-lis.

1970, July 6 Engr. *Perf. 13*

271 A55 40fr brt grn, ultra & brn 32 15
272 A55 50fr dk car, choc & emer 38 15
273 A55 70fr gray, lemon & choc 50 20
274 A55 200fr Prus bl, dk car & choc 1.40 60

300th anniv. of the mission from the King of Ardres to the King of France, and of the audience with Louis XIV on Dec. 19, 1670.

Star of the Order of Independence A56

Bariba Warrior A57

1970, Aug. 1 Photo. *Perf. 12*

275 A56 30fr multicolored 22 15
276 A56 40fr multicolored 35 16

10th anniversary of independence.

1970, Aug. 24 *Perf. 12½x13*

Designs: 2fr, 50fr, Two horsemen. 10fr, 70fr, Horseman facing left.

277 A57 1fr yellow & multi 15 15
278 A57 2fr gray grn & multi 15 15
279 A57 10fr blue & multi 15 15
280 A57 40fr yellow grn & multi 38 20
281 A57 50fr gold & multi 42 20
282 A57 70fr lilac rose & multi 65 35
Set value 1.65 92

For surcharge see Benin Nos. 350-351.

Globe and Heart — A58

Design: 40fr, Hands holding heart, vert.

1971, June 7 Engr. *Perf. 13*

283 A58 40fr red, green & dk brn 35 20
284 A58 100fr green, red & blue 70 40

Intl. year against racial discrimination.

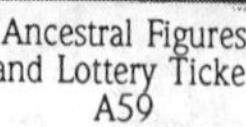

Ancestral Figures and Lottery Ticket A59

King Behanzin's Emblem (1889-1894) A60

1971, June 24 Litho. *Perf. 14*

285 A59 35fr multicolored 20 15
286 A59 40fr multicolored 35 16

4th anniv. of the National Lottery.

Photo.; Litho. (25fr, 135fr)
1971-72 *Perf. 12½*

Emblems of the Kings of Abomey: 25fr, Agoliagbo (1894-1900). 35fr, Ganyehoussou (1620-45), bird and cup, horiz. 100fr, Guezo (1818-58), bull, tree and birds. 135fr, Ouegbadja (1645-85), horiz. 140fr, Glèle (1858-89), lion and sword, horiz.

287 A60 25fr multicolored 20 15
288 A60 35fr green & multi 30 15
289 A60 40fr green & multi 35 16
290 A60 100fr red & multi 80 30
291 A60 135fr multicolored 90 45
292 A60 140fr brown & multi 1.10 60
Nos. 287-292 (6) 3.65 1.81

Issue dates: 25fr, 135fr, July 17, 1972. Others, Aug. 3, 1971.

Kabuki Actor, Long-distance Skiing — A61

Brahms and "Soir d'été" — A62

1972, Feb. Engr. *Perf. 13*

293 A61 35fr dk car, brn & bl grn 25 15

11th Winter Olympic Games, Sapporo, Japan, Feb. 3-13. See No. C153.

No. 268 Surcharged

1972

294 A53 35fr on 40fr multi 30 16

1972, June 29 Engr. *Perf. 13*

Design: 65fr, Brahms, woman at piano and music, horiz.

295 A62 30fr red brn, blk & lil 25 16
296 A62 65fr red brn, blk & lil 55 35

75th anniversary of the death of Johannes Brahms (1833-1897), German composer.

The Hare and The Tortoise, by La Fontaine — A63

Fables: 35fr, The Fox and The Stork, vert. 40fr, The Cat, The Weasel and Rabbit.

1972, Aug. 28 Engr. *Perf. 13*

297 A63 10fr multicolored 15 15
298 A63 35fr dark red & multi 30 16
299 A63 40fr ultra & multi 35 20

Jean de La Fontaine (1621-1695), French fabulist.

West African Monetary Union Issue
Common Design Type

1972, Nov. 2 Engr. *Perf. 13*

300 CD136 40fr choc, ocher & gray 30 16

Dr. Hansen, Microscope, Bacilli — A65

Design: 85fr, Portrait of Dr. Hansen.

1973, May 14 Engr. *Perf. 13*

301 A65 35fr ultra, vio brn & brn 20 15
302 A65 85fr yel grn, bis & ver 50 35

Centenary of the discovery by Dr. Armauer G. Hansen of the Hansen bacillus, the cause of leprosy.

Arms of Dahomey — A66

1973, June 25 Photo. *Perf. 13*

303 A66 5fr ultra & multi 15 15
304 A66 35fr ocher & multi 20 15
305 A66 40fr red orange & multi 22 15
Set value 47 27

INTERPOL Emblem and Spiderweb A67

Design: 50fr, INTERPOL emblem and communications symbols, vert.

1973, July Engr.

306 A67 35fr ver, grn & brn 22 15
307 A67 50fr green, brn & red 35 20

50th anniversary of International Criminal Police Organization (INTERPOL).

Education in Hygiene and Nutrition A68

WHO, 25th Anniv.: 100fr, Prenatal examination and care, WHO emblem.

1973, Aug. 2 Photo. *Perf. 12½x13*

308 A68 35fr multicolored 22 15
309 A68 100fr multicolored 55 35

No. 248 Surcharged with New Value, 2 Bars, and Overprinted in Red: "SECHERESSE SOLIDARITE AFRICAINE"

1973, Aug. 16

310 A45 100fr on 70fr multi 80 42

African solidarity in drought emergency.

African Postal Union Issue
Common Design Type

1973, Sept. 12 Engr. *Perf. 13*

311 CD137 100fr red, purple & blk 65 38

Epinephelus Aeneus — A69

Fish: 15fr, Drepane africana. 35fr, Pragus ehrenbergi.

1973, Sept. 18

312 A69 5fr slate blue & indigo 15 15
313 A69 15fr black & brt blue 15 15
314 A69 35fr emerald, ocher & sep 20 15
Set value 36 22

Chameleon A70

Design: 40fr, Emblem over map of Dahomey, vert.

1973, Nov. 30 Photo. *Perf. 13*

315 A70 35fr olive & multi 22 15
316 A70 40fr multicolored 25 20

1st anniv. of the Oct. 26 revolution.

The Chameleon in the Tree — A71

Designs: 5fr, The elephant, the hen and the dog, vert. 10fr, The sparrowhawk and the dog, vert. 25fr, The chameleon in the tree. 40fr, The eagle, the viper and the hen.

1974, Feb. 14 Photo. *Perf. 13*

317 A71 5fr emerald & multi 15 15
318 A71 10fr slate blue & multi 15 15
319 A71 25fr slate blue & multi 15 15
320 A71 40fr light blue & multi 22 15
Set value 48 32

Folktales of Dahomey.

German Shepherd — A72

1974, Apr. 25 Photo. *Perf. 13*

321 A72 40fr shown 22 15
322 A72 50fr Boxer 25 16
323 A72 100fr Saluki 55 40

Council Issue

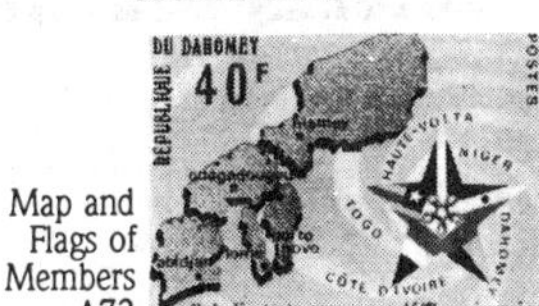

Map and Flags of Members A73

1974, May 29 Photo. *Perf. 13x12½*

324 A73 40fr blue & multi 22 15

15th anniversary of the Council of Accord.

Locomotive 232, 1911 — A74

Designs: Locomotives.

1974, Sept. 2 Photo. *Perf. 13x12½*

325 A74 35fr shown 20 15
326 A74 40fr Freight, 1877 22 15
327 A74 100fr Crampton, 1849 60 40
328 A74 200fr Stephenson, 1846 1.10 80

Globe, Money, People in Bank — A75

1974, Oct. 31 Engr. *Perf. 13*

329 A75 35fr multicolored 22 15

World Savings Day.

Dompago Dance, Hissi Tribe — A76

Flags of Dahomey and Nigeria over Africa — A77

Folk Dances: 25fr, Fetish Dance, Vaudou-Tchinan. 40fr, Bamboo Dance, Agbehoun. 100fr, Somba Dance, Sandoua, horiz.

1975, Aug. 4 Litho. *Perf. 12*

330 A76 10fr yellow & multi 15 15
331 A76 25fr dk green & multi 15 15
332 A76 40fr red & multi 22 15
333 A76 100fr multicolored 60 35
Set value 63

1975, Aug. 11 Photo. *Perf. 12½x13*

Design: 100fr, Arrows connecting maps of Dahomey and Nigeria, horiz.

334 A77 65fr multicolored 38 22
335 A77 100fr green & multi 60 38

Year of intensified cooperation between Dahomey and Nigeria.

Map, Pylons, Emblem — A78

Benin Electric Community Emblem and Pylon — A79

1975, Aug. 18

336 A78 40fr multicolored 22 16
337 A79 150fr multicolored 80 60

Benin Electric Community and Ghana-Togo-Dahomey cooperation.

Map of Dahomey, Rising Sun — A80

Albert Schweitzer, Nurse, Patient — A81

1975, Aug. 25 Photo. *Perf. 12½x13*

338 A80 35fr multicolored 15 15

Cooperation Year for the creation of a new Dahoman society.

1975, Sept. 22 Engr. *Perf. 13*

339 A81 200fr olive, grn & red brn 1.10 70

Birth centenary of Albert Schweitzer (1875-1965), medical missionary and musician.

Woman Speaking on Telephone, IWY Emblem — A82

Design: 150fr, International Women's Year emblem and linked rings.

1975, Oct. 20 Engr. *Perf. 12½x13*

340 A82 50fr Prus blue & lilac 25 16
341 A82 150fr emerald, brn & org 80 42

International Women's Year 1975.

Later issues are listed under Benin.

SEMI-POSTAL STAMPS

Regular Issue of 1913 Surcharged in Red

1915 Unwmk. *Perf. 14x13½*

B1 A5 10c + 5c orange red & rose 50 40

Curie Issue

Common Design Type

1938 *Perf. 13*

B2 CD80 1.75fr + 50c brt ultra 4.50 4.50

French Revolution Issue

Common Design Type

1939 Photo.

Name and Value Typo. in Black

B3 CD83 45c + 25c green 3.00 3.00
B4 CD83 70c + 30c brown 3.25 3.25
B5 CD83 90c + 35c red org 3.25 3.25
B6 CD83 1.25fr + 1fr rose pink 3.25 3.25
B7 CD83 2.25fr + 2fr blue 3.25 3.25
Nos. B3-B7 (5) 16.00 16.00

Postage Stamps of 1913-38 Surcharged in Black

SECOURS
+ 1 fr.
NATIONAL

1941 *Perf. 13½x14*

B8 A5 50c + 1fr brn red & bl 65 65
B9 A5 80c + 2fr hn brn & ultra 2.25 2.25
B10 A5 1.50fr + 2fr dk bl & lt bl 3.00 3.00
B11 A5 2fr + 3fr yel org & choc 3.00 3.00

Common Design Type and

Radio Operator — SP1

Senegalese Artillerymen SP2

1941 Photo. *Perf. 13½*

B12 SP1 1fr + 1fr red 65
B13 CD86 1.50fr + 3fr claret 65
B14 SP2 2.50fr + 1fr blue 65

Surtax for the defense of the colonies

Stamps of type A11 surcharged "OEUVRES COLONIALES" and new values were issued in 1944 by the Vichy Government, but were not placed on sale in the colony.

Catalogue values for unused stamps in this section, from this point to the end of the section, are for Never Hinged items.

Republic
Anti-Malaria Issue
Common Design Type

1962, Apr. 7 Engr. *Perf. 12½x12*

B15 CD108 25fr + 5fr orange brn 42 42

Freedom from Hunger Issue
Common Design Type

1963, Mar. 21 Unwmk. *Perf. 13*

B16 CD112 25fr + 5fr ol, brn red & brn 42 42

AIR POST STAMPS

Common Design Type

1940 Unwmk. Engr. *Perf. 12½*

C1 CD85 1.90fr ultra 15 15
C2 CD85 2.90fr dk red 20 20
C3 CD85 4.50fr dk gray grn 32 32
C4 CD85 4.90fr yel bister 42 42
C5 CD85 6.90fr deep org 65 65
Nos. C1-C5 (5) 1.74 1.74

Common Design Types

1942

C6 CD88 50c car & bl 15
C7 CD88 1fr brn & blk 15
C8 CD88 2fr dk grn & red brn 20
C9 CD88 3fr dk bl & scar 40
C10 CD88 5fr vio & brn red 40

Frame Engr., Center Typo.

C11 CD89 10fr ultra, ind & org 50
C12 CD89 20fr rose car, mag & gray blk 50
C13 CD89 50fr yel grn, dl grn & dp bl 1.25 1.60
Nos. C6-C13 (8) 3.55

There is doubt whether Nos. C6-C12 were officially placed in use.

Catalogue values for unused stamps in this section, from this point to the end of the section, are for Never Hinged items.

Republic

Somba House — AP4

Design: 500fr, Royal Court of Abomey.

Unwmk.

1960, Apr. 1 Engr. *Perf. 13*
C14 AP4 100fr multi 75 22
C15 AP4 500fr multi 3.50 65

Type of Regular Issue, 1961

1961, Sept. 20
C16 A16 200fr multi 1.40 1.00
a. Souv. sheet of 3, #150-151, C16 2.50 2.50

Air Afrique Issue
Common Design Type

1962, Feb. 17 *Perf. 13*
C17 CD107 25fr ultra, blk & org brn 35 16

Palace of the African and Malgache Union, Cotonou — AP5

1963, July 27 Photo. *Perf. 13x12*
C18 AP5 250fr multi 2.00 1.10

Assembly of chiefs of state of the African and Malgache Union held at Cotonou in July.

African Postal Union Issue
Common Design Type

1963, Sept. 8 Unwmk. *Perf. 12½*
C19 CD114 25fr brt bl, ocher & red 30 20

See note after Cameroun No. C47.

Boeing 707 — AP6

Designs (Boeing 707): 200fr, On the ground. 300fr, Over Cotonou airport. 500fr, In the air.

1963, Oct. 25 Engr. *Perf. 13*
C20 AP6 100fr multi 65 20
C21 AP6 200fr multi 1.25 65
C22 AP6 300fr multi 1.75 90
C23 AP6 500fr multi 3.00 1.25

For surcharges see Nos. CQ1-CQ5.

Priests Carrying Funerary Boat, Isis Temple, Philae — AP7

1964, Mar. 9 Unwmk. *Perf. 13*
C24 AP7 25fr vio bl & brn 45 35

UNESCO world campaign to save historic monuments in Nubia.

Weather Map and Symbols — AP8

1965, Mar. 23 Photo. *Perf. 12½*
C25 AP8 50fr multi 55 35

Fifth World Meteorological Day.

ICY Emblem and Men of Various Races — AP9

1965, June 26 Engr. *Perf. 13*
C26 AP9 25fr dl pur, mar & grn 25 15
C27 AP9 85fr dp bl, mar & sl grn 80 55

International Cooperation Year, 1965

Winston Churchill — AP10

1965, June 15 Photo. *Perf. 12½*
C28 AP10 100fr multi 1.10 80

Abraham Lincoln — AP11

1965, July 15 *Perf. 13*
C29 AP11 100fr multi 1.10 80

Centenary of death of Lincoln
For surcharge see No. C55.

John F. Kennedy and Arms of Dahomey — AP12

1965, Nov. 22 Photo. *Perf. 12½*
C30 AP12 100fr dp grn & blk 1.10 80

President John F. Kennedy (1917-63).
For surcharge see No. C56.

Dr. Albert Schweitzer and Patients — AP13

1966, Jan. 17 Photo. *Perf. 12½*
C31 AP13 100fr multi 1.10 80

Dr. Albert Schweitzer (1875-1965), medical missionary, theologian and musician.

WHO Type of Regular Issue

Design: 100fr, WHO Headquarters from the West.

1966, May 3 Unwmk. *Perf. 13*
Size: 47x28mm
C32 A36 100fr ultra, yel & blk 1.10 65

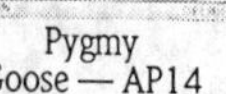
Pygmy Goose — AP14

Broad-billed Rollers — AP15

Birds: 100fr, Firey-breasted bush-shrike. 250fr, Emerald cuckoos. 500fr, Emerald starling.

1966-67 *Perf. 12½*
C33 AP14 50fr multi 50 20
C34 AP14 100fr multi 90 35
C35 AP15 200fr multi 1.75 70
C36 AP15 250fr multi 2.00 1.00
C37 AP14 500fr multi 3.50 1.75
Nos. C33-C37 (5) 8.65 4.00

Issue dates: 50fr, 100fr, 500fr, June 13, 1966. Others, Jan. 20, 1967.
For surcharge see No. C107.

Industrial Symbols — AP16

1966, July 21 Photo. *Perf. 12x13*
C38 AP16 100fr multi 1.00 60

3rd anniversary of agreement between European Economic Community and the African and Malagache Union.

Pope Paul VI and St. Peter's, Rome — AP17

Pope Paul VI and UN General Assembly AP18

Design: 70fr, Pope Paul VI and view of New York City.

1966, Aug. 22 Engr. *Perf. 13*
C39 AP17 50fr multi 45 20
C40 AP17 70fr multi 65 30
C41 AP18 100fr multi 1.00 50
a. Min. sheet of 3, #C39-C41 2.50 2.50

Pope Paul's appeal for peace before the UN General Assembly, Oct. 4, 1965.

Air Afrique Issue, 1966
Common Design Type

1966, Aug. 31 Photo. *Perf. 12½*
C42 CD123 30fr dk vio, blk & gray 35 16

"Science" — AP20

Designs: 45fr, "Art" (carved female statue, vert). 100fr, "Education" (book and letters).

1966, Nov. 4 Engr. *Perf. 13*
C43 AP20 30fr mag, ultra & vio brn 20 15
C44 AP20 45fr mar & grn 35 20
C45 AP20 100fr blk, mar & brt bl 75 45
a. Min. sheet of 3, #C43-C45 2.00 2.00

20th anniversary of UNESCO.

Madonna by Alessio Baldovinetti AP21

Christmas: 50fr, Nativity after 15th century Beaune tapestry. 100fr, Adoration of the Shepherds, by José Ribera.

1966, Dec. 25 Photo. *Perf. 12½x12*
C46 AP21 50fr multi 1.10 65
C47 AP21 100fr multi 2.00 1.40
C48 AP21 200fr multi 3.40 2.50

See Nos. C95-C96, C109-C115. For surcharge see No. C60.

1967, Apr. 10 *Perf. 12½x12*

Paintings by Ingres: No. C49, Self-portrait, 1804. No. C50, Oedipus and the Sphinx.

C49 AP21 100fr multi 1.00 75
C50 AP21 100fr multi 1.00 75

Jean Auguste Dominique Ingres (1780-1867), French painter.

Three-master Suzanne — AP22

Windjammers: 45fr, Three-master Esmeralda (vert). 80fr, Schooner Marie Alice (vert). 100fr, Four-master Antonin.

1967, May 8 *Perf. 13*

C51 AP22	30fr multi		35	16
C52 AP22	45fr multi		45	30
C53 AP22	80fr multi		80	40
C54 AP22	100fr multi		1.00	60

Nos. C29-C30 Surcharged

29 MAI 1967
50e Anniversaire
de la naissance
de
John F. Kennedy

125F

1967, May 29 Photo. *Perf. 13, 12½*

C55 AP11	125fr on 100fr	1.00	50
C56 AP12	125fr on 100fr	1.00	50

50th anniv. of the birth of Pres. John F. Kennedy.

EXPO '67 "Man In Space" Pavilion — AP23

1967, June 12 Engr. *Perf. 13*

C57 AP23	100fr dl red & Prus bl	75	42
a.	Min. sheet of 3, #235-236, C57	1.65	1.65

EXPO '67, International Exhibition, Montreal, Apr. 28-Oct. 27, 1967.

Europafrica Issue, 1967

Konrad Adenauer, by Oscar Kokoschká AP24

1967, July 19 Photo. *Perf. 12½x12*

C58 AP24	70fr multi	80	60
a.	Souv. sheet of 4	3.50	3.50

Konrad Adenauer (1876-1967), chancellor of West Germany (1949-1963).

Jamboree Emblem, Ropes and World Map — AP25

1967, Aug. 7 Engr. *Perf. 13*

C59 AP25	100fr lil, sl grn & dp bl	1.00	60
a.	Souv. sheet of 3, #239-240, C59	2.00	1.75

12th Boy Scout World Jamboree, Farragut State Park, Idaho, Aug. 1-9.

No. C48 Surcharged in Red

150F

RICCIONE
12-29
Août
1967

1967, Aug. 12 Photo. *Perf. 12½x12*

C60 AP21	150fr on 200fr	1.25	1.00
a.	"150F" omitted	80.00	80.00

Riccione, Italy Stamp Exhibition.

African Postal Union Issue, 1967
Common Design Type

1967, Sept. 9 Engr. *Perf. 13*

C61 CD124	100fr red, brt lil & emer	1.00	65

Charles de Gaulle AP26

1967, Nov. 21 Photo. *Perf. 12½x13*

C62 AP26	100fr multi	1.25	1.00
a.	Souv. sheet of 4	5.00	5.00

Pres. Charles de Gaulle of France on the occasion of Pres. Christophe Soglo's state visit to Paris, Nov. 1967.

Madonna, by Matthias Grunewald AP27

Paintings: 50fr, Holy Family by the Master of St. Sebastian, horiz. 100fr, Adoration of the Magi by Ulrich Apt the Elder. 200fr, Annunciation, by Matthias Grunewald.

1967, Dec. 11 Photo. *Perf. 12½*

C63 AP27	30fr multi	18	15
C64 AP27	50fr multi	35	20
C65 AP27	100fr multi	75	45
C66 AP27	200fr multi	1.50	70

Christmas 1967.

Venus de Milo and Mariner 5 — AP28

Gutenberg Monument, Strasbourg Cathedral — AP29

Design: No. C68, Venus de Milo and Venus 4 Rocket.

1968, Feb. 17 Photo. *Perf. 13*

C67 AP28	70fr grnsh bl & multi	65	30
C68 AP28	70fr dp bl & multi	65	30
a.	Souv. sheet of 2, #C67-C68	1.25	1.25

Explorations of the planet Venus, Oct. 18-19, 1967.
For surcharges see Nos. C103-C104.

1968, May 20 Litho. *Perf. 14x13½*

Design: 100fr, Gutenberg Monument, Mainz, and Gutenberg press.

C69 AP29	45fr grn & org	35	18
C70 AP29	100fr dk & lt bl	65	32
a.	Souv. sheet of 2, #C69-C70	1.25	1.25

500th anniv. of the death of Johann Gutenberg, inventor of printing from movable type.

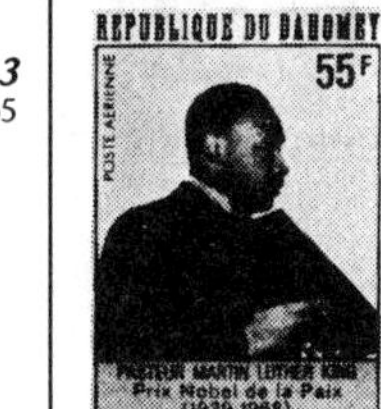
Martin Luther King, Jr. — AP30

Designs: 30fr, "We must meet hate with creative love" in French, English and German. 100fr, Full-face portrait.

Perf. 12½, 13½x13
1968, June 17 Photo.
Size: 26x46mm

C71 AP30	30fr red brn, yel & blk	20	15

Size: 26x37mm

C72 AP30	55fr multi	35	20
C73 AP30	100fr multi	65	32
a.	Min. sheet of 3, #C71-C73	1.40	1.40

Martin Luther King, Jr. (1929-68), American civil rights leader.

Robert Schuman — AP31

Designs: 45fr, Alcide de Gasperi. 70fr, Konrad Adenauer.

1968, July 20 Photo. *Perf. 13*

C74 AP31	30fr dp yel, blk & grn	20	15
C75 AP31	45fr org, dk brn & ol	30	15
C76 AP31	70fr multi	50	22

5th anniversary of the economic agreement between the European Economic Community and the African and Malgache Union.

Battle of Montebello, by Henri Philippoteaux — AP32

Paintings: 45fr, 2nd Zouave Regiment at Magenta, by Riballier. 70fr, Battle of Magenta, by Louis Eugène Charpentier. 100fr, Battle of Solferino, by Charpentier.

1968, Aug. 12 *Perf. 12½x12*

C77 AP32	30fr multi	22	15
C78 AP32	45fr multi	35	15
C79 AP32	70fr multi	50	25
C80 AP32	100fr multi	75	38

Issued for the Red Cross.

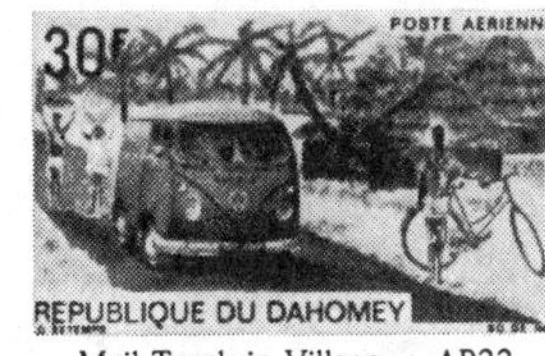
Mail Truck in Village — AP33

Designs: 45fr, Mail truck stopping at rural post office. 55fr, Mail truck at river bank. 70fr, Mail truck and train.

1968, Oct. 7 Photo. *Perf. 13x12½*

C81 AP33	30fr multi	20	15
C82 AP33	45fr multi	40	20
C83 AP33	55fr multi	45	25
C84 AP33	70fr multi	60	35

Aztec Stadium, Mexico City — AP34

Designs (Olympic Rings and); 45fr, Ball player, Mayan sculpture, vert. 70fr, Wrestler, sculpture from Uxpanapan, vert. 150fr, Olympic Stadium, Mexico City.

1968, Nov. 20 Engr. *Perf. 13*

C85 AP34	30fr dp cl & sl grn	30	15
C86 AP34	45fr ultra & dk rose brn	40	18
C87 AP34	70fr sl grn & dk brn	60	28
C88 AP34	150fr dk car & dk brn	1.40	70
a.	Min. sheet of 4, #C85-C88	3.00	3.00

19th Olympic Games, Mexico City, Oct. 12-27. No. C88a is folded down the vertical gutter separating Nos. C85-C86 se-tenant at left and Nos. C87-C88 se-tenant at right.

The Annunciation, by Foujita — AP35

Paintings by Foujita: 30fr, Nativity, horiz. 100fr, The Virgin and Child. 200fr, The Baptism of Christ.

Perf. 12x12½, 12½ x12

1968, Nov. 25 **Photo.**
C89 AP35 30fr multi 25 15
C90 AP35 70fr multi 45 22
C91 AP35 100fr multi 75 32
C92 AP35 200fr multi 1.50 65

Christmas 1968.

PHILEXAFRIQUE Issue

Painting: 100fr, Diderot, by Louis Michel Vanloo.

1968, Dec. 16 *Perf. 12½x12*
C93 AP35 100fr multi 1.00 65

PHILEXAFRIQUE, Philatelic Exhibition in Abidjan, Feb. 14-23. Printed with alternating bluish violet label.

2nd PHILEXAFRIQUE Issue
Common Design Type

Design: 50fr, Dahomey No. 119 and aerial view of Cotonou.

1969, Feb. 14 **Engr.** *Perf. 13*
C94 CD128 50fr bl, brn & pur 50 40

Christmas Painting Type

Paintings: No. C95, Virgin of the Rocks, by Leonardo da Vinci. No. C96, Virgin with the Scales, by Cesare da Sesto.

1969, Mar. 17 **Photo.** *Perf. 12½x12*
C95 AP21 100fr vio & multi 65 32
C96 AP21 100fr grn & multi 65 32

Leonardo da Vinci (1452-1519).

General Bonaparte, by Jacques Louis David AP36

Paintings: 60fr, Napoleon I in 1809, by Robert J. Lefevre. 75fr, Napoleon on the Battlefield of Eylau, by Antoine Jean Gros, horiz. 200fr, Gen. Bonaparte at Arcole, by Gros.

1969, Apr. 14 **Photo.** *Perf. 12½x12*
C97 AP36 30fr multi 60 42
C98 AP36 60fr multi 90 65
C99 AP36 75fr multi 1.25 85
C100 AP36 200fr multi 2.75 2.65

Bicentenary of the birth of Napoleon I.

Arms Type of Regular Issue, 1969

1969, June 30 **Litho.** *Perf. 13½x13*
C101 A49 50fr multi 40 20

Apollo 8 Trip Around the Moon AP37

Embossed on Gold Foil

1969, July *Die-cut Perf. 10½*
C102 AP37 1000fr gold 10.00 10.00

US Apollo 8 mission, which put the 1st men into orbit around the moon, Dec. 21-27, 1968.

ALUNISSAGE
APOLLO XI
JUILLET 1969

Nos. C67-C68 Surcharged

125F

1969, Aug. 1 **Photo.** *Perf. 13*
C103 AP28 125fr on 70fr grnsh bl & multi 1.40 65
C104 AP28 125fr on 70fr dp bl & multi 1.40 65

Man's 1st landing on the moon, July 20, 1969; US astronauts Neil A. Armstrong, Col. Edwin E. Aldrin, Jr., with Lieut. Col. Michael Collins piloting Apollo 11.

Europafrica Issue
Type of Regular Issue, 1969

Design: 100fr, Oil palm industry, Cotonou.

1969, Sept. 22 **Litho.** *Perf. 14*
C105 A51 100fr multi 1.25 65
a. Souv. sheet of 3, #262-263, C105 2.25 2.25

Dahomey Rotary Emblem — AP38

1969, Sept. 25 *Perf. 14x13½*
C106 AP38 50fr multi 60 32

No. C33 Surcharged **10F**

1969, Nov. 15 **Photo.** *Perf. 12½*
C107 AP14 10fr on 50fr multi 15 15

Dance Type of Regular Issue

Design: 70fr, Teke dance and Tourist Year emblem.

1969, Dec. 15 **Litho.** *Perf. 14*
C108 A52 70fr multi 60 25

Painting Type of 1966

Paintings: 30fr, Annunciation, by Vrancke van der Stockt. 45fr, Nativity, Swabian School, horiz. 110fr, Madonna and Child, by the Master of the Gold Brocade. 200fr, Adoration of the Kings, Antwerp School.

Perf. 12½x12, 12x12½

1969, Dec. 20
C109 AP21 30fr multi 35 22
C110 AP21 45fr red & multi 50 35
C111 AP21 110fr multi 1.40 80
C112 AP21 200fr multi 2.25 1.50

Christmas 1969.

1969, Dec. 27 *Perf. 12½x12*

Paintings: No. C113, The Artist's Studio (detail), by Gustave Courbet. No. C114, Self-portrait with Gold Chain, by Rembrandt. 150fr, Hendrickje Stoffels, by Rembrandt.

C113 AP21 100fr red & multi 65 40
C114 AP21 100fr grn & multi 65 40
C115 AP21 150fr multi 1.00 50

Franklin D. Roosevelt — AP39

Astronauts, Rocket, US Flag — AP40

1970, Feb. **Photo.** *Perf. 12½*
C116 AP39 100fr ultra, yel grn & blk 80 35

25th anniversary of the death of Pres. Franklin Delano Roosevelt (1882-1945).

1970, Mar. 9 **Photo.** *Perf. 12½*

Designs: 50fr, Astronauts riding rocket through space. 70fr, Astronauts in landing module approaching moon. 110fr, Astronauts planting US flag on moon.

C117 AP40 30fr multi 20 15

Souvenir Sheet

C118 Sheet of 4 1.75 1.75
a. AP40 50fr violet blue & multi 30 30
b. AP40 70fr violet blue & multi 42 42
c. AP40 110fr violet blue & multi 65 65

See note after No. C104. No. C118 contains Nos. C117, C118a, C118b and C118c.

For surcharge see No. C120.

Walt Whitman and Dahoman Huts — AP41

1970, Apr. 30 **Engr.** *Perf. 13*
C119 AP41 100fr Prus bl, brn & emer 65 25

Walt Whitman (1818-92), American poet.

No. C117 Surcharged in Silver with New Value, Heavy Bar and: "APOLLO XIII / SOLIDARITE / SPATIALE / INTERNATIONALE"

1970, May 15 **Photo.** *Perf. 12½*
C120 AP40 40fr on 30fr multi 65 65

The flight of Apollo 13.

Soccer Players and Globe AP42

Designs: 50fr, Goalkeeper catching ball. 200fr, Players kicking ball.

1970, May 19
C121 AP42 40fr multi 30 18
C122 AP42 50fr multi 50 20
C123 AP42 200fr multi 1.50 75

9th World Soccer Championships for the Jules Rimet Cup, Mexico City, May 30-June 21, 1970.

For surcharge see No. C126.

EXPO '70 Type of Regular Issue

Designs (EXPO '70 Emblems and): 70fr, Dahomey pavilion. 120fr, Mt. Fuji, temple and torii.

1970, June 15 **Litho.** *Perf. 13½x14*
C124 A54 70fr yel, red & dk vio 85 40
C125 A54 120fr yel, red & grn 1.50 75

No. C123 Surcharged with New Value and Overprinted: "Bresil-Italie / 4-1"

1970, July 13 **Photo.** *Perf. 12½*
C126 AP42 100fr on 200fr multi 1.00 42

Brazil's victory in the 9th World Soccer Championships, Mexico City.

Mercury, Map of Africa and Europe AP43

Ludwig van Beethoven AP44

Europafrica Issue, 1970

1970, July 20 **Photo.** *Perf. 12x13*
C127 AP43 40fr multi 35 20
C128 AP43 70fr multi 60 25

1970, Sept. 21 **Litho.** *Perf. 14x13½*
C129 AP44 90fr brt bl & vio blk 80 35
C130 AP44 110fr yel grn & dk brn 90 45

Bicentenary of the birth of Ludwig van Beethoven (1770-1827), composer.

Symbols of Learning — AP45

1970, Nov. 6 **Photo.** *Perf. 12½*
C131 AP45 100fr multi 80 35

Laying of the foundation stone for the University at Calavi.

Annunciation, Rhenish School, c.1340 — AP46

Paintings of Rhenish School, circa 1340: 70fr, Nativity. 110fr, Adoration of the Kings. 200fr, Presentation at the Temple.

1970, Nov. 9 *Perf. 12½x12*
C132 AP46 40fr gold & multi 25 15
C133 AP46 70fr gold & multi 45 18
C134 AP46 110fr gold & multi 65 30
C135 AP46 200fr gold & multi 1.40 55

Christmas 1970.

Charles de Gaulle, Arc de Triomphe and Flag — AP47

Design: 500fr, de Gaulle as old man and Notre Dame Cathedral, Paris.

1971, Mar. 15 Photo. *Perf. 12½*

C136 AP47 40fr multi 30 15
C137 AP47 500fr multi 3.00 1.50

Gen. Charles de Gaulle (1890-1970), President of France.

L'Indifférent, by Watteau AP48

Painting: No. C139, Woman playing stringed instrument, by Watteau.

1971, May 3 Photo. *Perf. 13*

C138 AP48 100fr red brn & multi 80 55
C139 AP48 100fr red brn & multi 80 55

For overprints see Nos. C151-C152.

1971, May 29 Photo. *Perf. 13*

Dürer Paintings: 100fr, Self-portrait, 1498. 200fr, Self-portrait, 1500.

C140 AP48 100fr bl grn & multi 60 40
C141 AP48 200fr dk grn & multi 1.40 80

Albrecht Dürer (1471-1528), German painter and engraver. See #C151-C152, C174-C175.

Johannes Kepler and Diagram — AP49

Designs: 200fr, Kepler, trajectories, satellite and rocket.

1971, July 12 Engr. *Perf. 13*

C142 AP49 40fr brt rose lil, blk & vio bl 35 16
C143 AP49 200fr red, blk & dk bl 2.00 80

Kepler (1571-1630), German astronomer

Europafrica Issue

Jet Plane, Maps of Europe and Africa — AP50

Designs: 100fr, Ocean liner, maps of Europe and Africa.

1971, July 19 Photo. *Perf. 12½x12*

C144 AP50 50fr blk, lt bl & org 40 20
C145 AP50 100fr multi 80 40

African Postal Union Issue, 1971

Common Design Type

Design: 100fr, Dahomey coat of arms and UAMPT building, Brazzaville, Congo.

1971, Nov. 13 *Perf. 13x13½*

C146 CD135 100fr bl & multi 80 40

Flight into Egypt, by Van Dyck — AP51

Paintings: 40fr, Adoration of the Shepherds, by the Master of the Hausbuch, c. 1500, vert. 70fr, Adoration of the Kings, by Holbein the Elder, vert. 200fr, The Birth of Christ, by Dürer.

1971, Nov. 22 *Perf. 13*

C147 AP51 40fr gold & multi 25 15
C148 AP51 70fr gold & multi 45 22
C149 AP51 100fr gold & multi 60 25
C150 AP51 200fr gold & multi 1.20 60

Christmas 1971

Painting Type of 1971 Inscribed: "25e ANNIVERSAIRE DE L'UNICEF"

Paintings: 40fr, Prince Balthazar, by Velasquez. 100fr, Infanta Margarita Maria, by Velázquez.

1971, Dec. 11

C151 AP48 40fr gold & multi 35 20
C152 AP48 100fr gold & multi 80 35

25th anniv. of UNICEF.

Olympic Games Type

Design: 150fr, Sapporo '72 emblem, ski jump and stork flying.

1972, Feb. Engr. *Perf. 13*

C153 A61 150fr brn, dp rose lil & bl 1.00 50

11th Winter Olympic Games, Sapporo, Japan, Feb. 3-13.

Boy Scout and Scout Flag — AP52

Designs: 40fr, Scout playing marimba. 100fr, Scouts doing farm work.

1972, Mar. 19 Photo. *Perf. 13*

Size: 26x35mm

C154 AP52 35fr multi 15 15
C155 AP52 40fr multi 25 15

Size: 26x46mm

C156 AP52 100fr yel & multi 60 30
a. Souvenir sheet of 3, #C154-C156, perf. 12½ 1.25 1.25

World Boy Scout Seminar, Cotonou, Mar. 1972.

Workers Training Institute and Friedrich Naumann — AP53

Design: 250fr, Workers Training Institute and Pres. Theodor Heuss of Germany.

1972, Mar. 29 Photo. *Perf. 13x12*

C157 AP53 100fr brt rose, blk & vio 70 38
C158 AP53 250fr bl, blk & vio 2.00 80

Laying of foundation stone for National Workers Training Institute.

Mosaic Floor, St. Mark's, Venice — AP54

12th Century Mosaics from St. Mark's Basilica: 40fr, Roosters carrying fox on a pole. 65fr, Noah sending out dove.

1972, Apr. 10 *Perf. 13*

C159 AP54 35fr gold & multi 35 20
C160 AP54 40fr gold & multi 40 25
C161 AP54 65fr gold & multi 60 40

UNESCO campaign to save Venice.

Neapolitan and Dahoman Dancers — AP55

1972, May 3 *Perf. 13½x13*

C162 AP55 100fr multi 80 45

12th Philatelic Exhibition, Naples.

Running, German Eagle, Olympic Rings — AP56

Designs (Olympic Rings and): 85fr, High jump and Glyptothek, Munich. 150fr, Shot put and Propylaeum, Munich.

1972, June 12 Engr. *Perf. 13*

C163 AP56 20fr ultra, grn & brn 15 15
C164 AP56 85fr brn, grn & ultra 55 25
C165 AP56 150fr grn, brn & ultra 1.10 55
a. Min. sheet of 3, #C163-C165 2.25 2.25

20th Olympic Games, Munich, Aug. 26-Sept. 10.
For overprints see Nos. C170-C172.

Louis Blériot and his Plane — AP57

1972, June 26

C166 AP57 100fr vio, cl & brt bl 60 32

Birth centenary of Louis Blériot (1872-1936), French aviation pioneer.

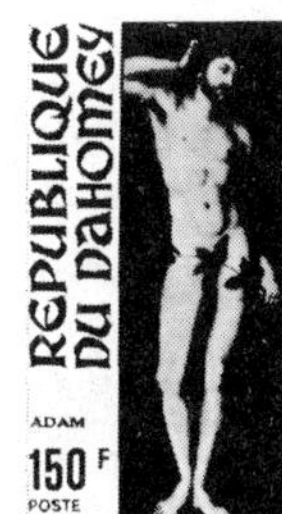

Adam, by Lucas Cranach — AP58

Design: 200fr, Eve, by Lucas Cranach.

1972, Oct. 24 Photo.

C167 AP58 150fr multi 1.40 65
C168 AP58 200fr multi 1.60 70

Lucas Cranach (1472-1553), German painter.

Pauline Borghese, by Canova — AP59

1972, Nov. 8

C169 AP59 250fr multi 2.00 1.00

Antonio Canova (1757-1822), Italian sculptor.

Nos. C163-C165 Overprinted:
a. 5.000m-10.000m. / VIREN / 2 MEDAILLES D'OR
b. HAUTEUR DAMES / MEYFARTH / MEDAILLE D'OR
c. POIDS / KOMAR / MEDAILLE D'OR

1972, Nov. 13 Engr. *Perf. 13*

C170 AP56(a) 20fr multi 15 15
C171 AP56(b) 85fr multi 50 25
C172 AP56(c) 150fr multi 1.00 60
a. Miniature sheet of 3 3.75 3.75

Gold medal winners in 20th Olympic Games: Lasse Viren, Finland, 5,000m. and 10,000m. races (20fr); Ulrike Meyfarth, Germany, women's high jump (85fr); Wladyslaw Komar, Poland, shot put (150fr).

Louis Pasteur — AP60

1972, Nov. 30

C173 AP60 100fr brt grn, lil & brn 80 42

Pasteur (1822-95), chemist and bacteriologist.

Painting Type of 1971

Paintings by Georges de La Tour (1593-1652), French painter: 35fr, Vielle player. 150fr, The Newborn, horiz.

1972, Dec. 11 Photo.

C174 AP48 35fr multi 28 15
C175 AP48 150fr multi 1.40 70

Values quoted in this catalogue are for stamps graded Fine-Very Fine and with no faults. An illustrated guide to grade is provided beginning on Page 8A.

Annunciation, School of Agnolo Gaddi — AP61

Paintings: 125fr, Nativity, by Simone dei Crocifissi. 140fr, Adoration of the Shepherds, by Giovanni di Pietro. 250fr, Adoration of the Kings, by Giotto.

1972, Dec. 15
C176 AP61 35fr gold & multi 20 15
C177 AP61 125fr gold & multi 60 30
C178 AP61 140fr gold & multi 80 40
C179 AP61 250fr gold & multi 1.40 75

Christmas 1972. See Nos. C195-C198, C234, C251, C253-C254.

Statue of St. Teresa, Basilica of Lisieux AP62

Design: 100fr, St. Teresa, roses, and globe, vert.

1973, May 14 Photo. *Perf. 13*
C180 AP62 40fr blk, gold & lt ultra 25 16
C181 AP62 100fr gold & multi 65 38

St. Teresa of Lisieux (Therese Martin, 1873-97), Carmelite nun.

Scouts, African Scout Emblem — AP63

Designs (African Scout Emblem and): 20fr, Lord Baden-Powell, vert. 40fr, Scouts building bridge.

1973, July 2 Engr. *Perf. 13*
C182 AP63 15fr bl, grn & choc 15 15
C183 AP63 20fr ol & Prus bl 15 15
C184 AP63 40fr grn, Prus bl & brn 25 15
a. Souvenir sheet of 3 55 55
Set value 31

24th Boy Scout World Conference, Nairobi, Kenya, July 16-21. No. C184a contains 3 stamps similar to Nos. C182-C184 in changed colors (15fr in ultramarine, slate green and chocolate; 20fr in chocolate, ultramarine and indigo; 40fr in slate green, indigo and chocolate).

For surcharges see Nos. C217-C218.

Copernicus, Venera and Mariner Satellites — AP64

Design: 125fr, Copernicus, sun, earth and moon, vert.

1973, Aug. 20 Engr. *Perf. 13*
C185 AP64 65fr blk, dk brn & org 55 30
C186 AP64 125fr bl, sl grn & pur 80 42

500th anniversary of the birth of Nicolaus Copernicus (1473-1543), Polish astronomer.

Head and City Hall, Brussels — AP64a

1973, Sept. 17 Engr. *Perf. 13*
C187 AP64a 100fr blk, Prus bl & dk grn 60 40

African Weeks, Brussels, Sept. 15-30, 1973.

WMO Emblem, World Weather Map — AP65

1973, Sept. 25
C188 AP65 100fr ol grn & lt brn 65 40

Cent. of intl. meteorological cooperation.
For surcharge see No. C199.

Europafrica Issue

AP66

Design: 40fr, similar to 35fr.

1973, Oct. 1 Engr. *Perf. 13*
C189 AP66 35fr multi 22 15
C190 AP66 40fr bl, sep & ultra 25 20

John F. Kennedy — AP67

1973, Oct. 18
C191 AP67 200fr bl grn, vio & sl grn 1.00 60
a. Souvenir sheet 1.25 1.25

Pres. John F. Kennedy (1917-63). No. C191a contains one stamp in changed colors (bright blue, magenta & brown).

Soccer — AP68

Designs: 40fr, Two soccer players. 100fr, Three soccer players.

1973, Nov. 19 Engr. *Perf. 13*
C192 AP68 35fr multi 20 15
C193 AP68 40fr multi 25 16
C194 AP68 100fr multi 60 42

World Soccer Cup, Munich 1974.
For surcharges see Nos. C219-C220.

Painting Type of 1972

Christmas: 35fr, Annunciation, by Dirk Bouts. 100fr, Nativity, by Giotto. 150fr, Adoration of the Kings, by Botticelli. 200fr, Adoration of the Shepherds, by Jacopo Bassano, horiz.

1973, Dec. 20 Photo. *Perf. 13*
C195 AP61 35fr gold & multi 18 15
C196 AP61 100fr gold & multi 50 30
C197 AP61 150fr gold & multi 75 50
C198 AP61 200fr gold & multi 1.00 65

No C188 Surcharged in Violet with New Value and: "OPERATION SKYLAB / 1973-1974"

1974, Feb. 4 Engr. *Perf. 13*
C199 AP65 200fr on 100fr multi 1.10 80

Skylab US space missions, 1973-74.

Skiers, Snowflake, Olympic Rings — AP69

1974, Feb. 25 Engr. *Perf. 13*
C200 AP69 100fr vio bl, brn & brt bl 60 42

50th anniversary of first Winter Olympic Games, Chamonix, France.

Marie Curie AP70

1974, June 7 Engr. *Perf. 13*
C201 AP70 50fr Lenin 30 20
C202 AP70 125fr shown 70 50
C203 AP70 150fr Churchill 90 60

50th anniv. of the death of Lenin; 40th anniv. of the death of Marie Sklodowska Curie; cent. of the birth of Winston Churchill.

Bishop, Persian, 18th Century — AP71

Frederic Chopin — AP72

Design: 200fr, Queen, Siamese chess piece, 19th century.

1974, June 14 Photo. *Perf. 12½x13*
C204 AP71 50fr org & multi 35 22
C205 AP71 200fr brt grn & multi 1.10 80

21st Chess Olympiad, Nice, June 6-30, 1974.
See Benin No. Q11 for overprint.

1974, June 24 Engr. *Perf. 13*

Design: No. C207, Ludwig van Beethoven.

C206 AP72 150fr blk & copper red 80 60
C207 AP72 150fr blk & copper red 80 60

Famous musicians: Frederic Chopin and Ludwig van Beethoven.

Astronaut on Moon, and Earth — AP73

1974, July 10 Engr. *Perf. 13*
C208 AP73 150fr multi 80 65

5th anniversary of the first moon walk.

Litho. & Embossed 'Gold Foil' Stamps
These stamps generally are of a different design format than the rest of the issue. Since there is a commemorative inscription tying them to the issue a separate illustration is not being shown.

There is some question as to the status of 4 sets, Nos. C209-C216, C225-C232, C238-C249.

World Cup Soccer Championships, Munich — AP74

World Cup trophy and players and flags of: 35fr, West Germany, Chile, Australia, DDR. 40fr, Zaire, Scotland, Brazil, Yugoslavia. 100fr, Sweden, Bulgaria, Uruguay, Netherlands. 200fr, Italy, Haiti, Poland, Argentina. 300fr, Stadium. 500fr, Trophy and flags.

Perf. 14x13, 13x14

1974, July 16 Litho.
C209 AP74 35fr multicolored
C210 AP74 40fr multicolored
C211 AP74 100fr multicolored
C212 AP74 200fr multicolored
C213 AP74 300fr multi, horiz.

Souvenir Sheet

C215 AP74 500fr multi, horiz.

It is uncertain if this issue was valid for postage or recognized by the Dahomey government.

Nos. C182-C183 Surcharged and Overprinted in Black or Red: "XIe JAMBOREE PANARAGE DE BATROUN-LIBAN"

1974, July 19
C217 AP63 100fr on 15fr multi 75 40
C218 AP63 140fr on 20fr multi (R) 1.25 70

11th Pan-Arab Jamboree, Batrun, Lebanon, Aug. 1974. Overprint includes 2 bars over old denomination; 2-line overprint on No. C217, 3 lines on No. C218.

Nos. C193-C194 Overprinted and Surcharged with New Value and Two Bars: "R F A 2 / HOLLANDE 1"

1974, July 26 Engr. *Perf. 13*

C219 AP68 100fr on 40fr 55 22
C220 AP68 150fr on 100fr 80 38

World Cup Soccer Championship, 1974, victory of German Federal Republic.

Earth and UPU Emblem — AP75

Designs (UPU Emblem and): 65fr, Concorde in flight. 125fr, French railroad car, c. 1860. 200fr, African drummer and Renault mail truck, pre-1939.

1974, Aug. 5 Engr. *Perf. 13*

C221 AP75 35fr rose cl & vio 20 15
C222 AP75 65fr Prus grn & cl 40 15
C223 AP75 125fr multi 70 28
C224 AP75 200fr multi 1.10 45

Centenary of Universal Postal Union.

UPU, Cent. — AP76

Communications and transportation: 50fr, Rocket, Indian shooting arrow. 100fr, Airplane, dog sled, vert. 125fr, Rocket launch, balloon. 150fr, Rocket re-entry into Earth's atmosphere, drum. 200fr, Locomotive, Pony Express rider. 500fr, UPU headquarters. No. C230, Train, 1829. No. C232, Astronaut canceling envelope on moon.

1974 Litho. *Perf. 13x14, 14x13*

C225 AP76 50fr multicolored
C226 AP76 100fr multicolored
C227 AP76 125fr multicolored
C228 AP76 150fr multicolored
C229 AP76 200fr multicolored

Litho. & Embossed

Perf. 13½

Size: 48x60mm

C230 AP76 1000fr gold & multi

Souvenir Sheets

Litho.

Perf. 13x14

C231 AP76 500fr multicolored

Litho. & Embossed

Perf. 13½

C232 AP76 1000fr gold & multi

Issue dates: Nos. C230, C232, Oct. 9, others, Aug. 5.

It is uncertain if this issue was valid for postage or recognized by the Dahomey government.

Painting Type of 1972 and

Lion of Belfort by Frederic A. Bartholdi — AP77

Painting: 250fr, Girl with Falcon, by Philippe de Champaigne.

1974, Aug. 20 Engr. *Perf. 13*

C233 AP77 100fr rose brn 65 22
C234 AP61 250fr multi 1.60 65

Prehistoric Animals — AP78

1974, Sept. 23 Photo.

C235 AP78 35fr Rhamphorhynchus 20 15
C236 AP78 150fr Stegosaurus 80 38
C237 AP78 200fr Tyrannosaurus 1.00 45

Conquest of Space — AP79

Various spacecraft and: 50fr, Mercury. 100fr, Venus. 150fr, Mars. 200fr, Jupiter. 400fr, Sun.

1974, Oct. 31 Litho. *Perf. 13x14*

C238 AP79 50fr multicolored
C239 AP79 100fr multicolored
C240 AP79 150fr multicolored
C241 AP79 200fr multicolored

Souvenir Sheet

C242 AP79 400fr multicolored

It is uncertain if this issue was valid for postage or recognized by the Dahomey government.

West Germany, World Cup Soccer Champions — AP80

Designs: 100fr, Team. 125fr, Paul Breitner. 150fr, Gerd Muller. 300fr, Presentation of trophy. 500fr, German team positioned on field.

1974, Nov. Litho. *Perf. 13x14*

C243 AP80 100fr multicolored
C244 AP80 125fr multicolored
C245 AP80 150fr multicolored
C246 AP80 300fr multicolored

Souvenir Sheet

C248 AP80 500fr multicolored

It is uncertain if this issue was valid for postage or recognized by the Dahomey government.

Europafrica Issue

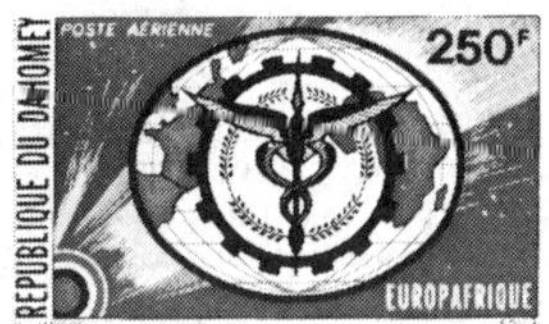

Globe, Cogwheel, Emblem — AP81

1974, Dec. 20 Typo. *Perf. 13*

C250 AP81 250fr red & multi 1.60 65

Printed tête bêche in sheets of 10.

Christmas Type of 1972 and

Nativity, by Martin Schongauer AP82

Paintings: 35fr, Annunciation, by Schongauer. 100fr, Virgin in Rose Arbor, by Schongauer. 250fr, Virgin and Child, with St. John the Baptist, by Botticelli.

1974, Dec. 23 Photo. *Perf. 13*

C251 AP61 35fr gold & multi 15 15
C252 AP82 40fr gold & multi 20 15
C253 AP61 100fr gold & multi 50 18
C254 AP61 250fr gold & multi 1.25 50

Apollo and Soyuz Spacecraft AP83

Designs: 200fr, American and Russian flags, rocket take-off. 500fr, Apollo-Soyuz link-up.

1975, July 16 Litho. *Perf. 12½*

C255 AP83 35fr multi 20 15
C256 AP83 200fr vio bl, red & bl 1.10 45
C257 AP83 500fr vio bl, ind & red 2.75 1.50

Apollo Soyuz space test project (Russo-American cooperation); launching July 15; link-up, July 17.

Nos. C255-C256 Surcharged in Silver or Black: "RENCONTRE / APOLLO-SOYOUZ / 17 Juil. 1975"

1975, July 17 Litho. *Perf. 12½*

C258 AP83 100fr on 35fr (S) 40 18
C259 AP83 300fr on 200fr 1.20 50

Apollo-Soyuz link-up in space, July 17, 1975.

ARPHILA Emblem, "Stamps" and Head of Ceres — AP84

1975, Aug. 22 Engr. *Perf. 13*

C260 AP84 100fr blk, bl & lilac 60 22

ARPHILA 75, International Philatelic Exhibition, Paris, June 6-16.

Holy Family, by Michelangelo AP85

Infantry and Stars AP86

Europafrica Issue

1975, Sept. 29 Litho. *Perf. 12*

C261 AP85 300fr gold & multi 1.75 65

1975, Nov. 18 Engr. *Perf. 13*

American bicentennial (Stars and): 135fr, Drummers and fifer. 300fr, Artillery with cannon. 500fr, Cavalry.

C262 AP86 75fr grn car & purple 30 15
C263 AP86 135fr bl, mag & sepia 55 22
C264 AP86 300fr vio bl, ver & choc 1.20 50
C265 AP86 500fr ver, dk grn & brn 2.00 90

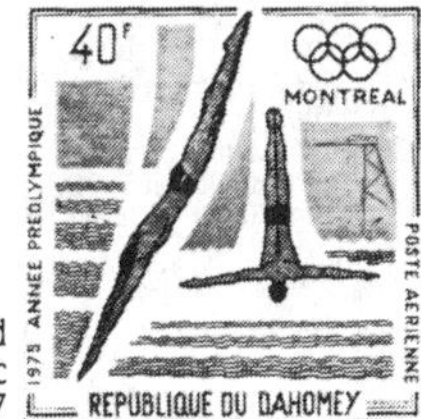

Diving and Olympic Rings — AP87

Design: 250fr, Soccer and Olympic rings.

1975, Nov. 24

C266 AP87 40fr vio, grnsh bl & ol brn 22 15
C267 AP87 250fr red, emer & brn 1.40 60

Pre-Olympic Year 1975.

AIR POST SEMI-POSTAL STAMPS

V1

V2

V4

Stamps of the preceding designs were issued in 1942 by the Vichy Government, but were not placed in use in the colony.

AIR POST PARCEL POST STAMPS

Catalogue values for unused stamps in this section are for Never Hinged items.

Nos. C20-C23, C14 Surcharged in Black or Red

300F

COLIS POSTAUX

1967-69 Engr. *Perf. 13*

CQ1	AP6	200fr on 200fr	2.75	2.00
CQ2	AP6	300fr on 100fr	3.25	2.75
CQ3	AP6	500fr on 300fr	6.00	4.25
CQ4	AP6	1000fr on 500fr	12.00	10.00
CQ5	AP4	5000fr on 100fr (R) ('69)	55.00	55.00
		Nos. CQ1-CQ5 (5)	79.00	74.00

On No. CQ5, "Colis Postaux" is at top, bar at right.

POSTAGE DUE STAMPS

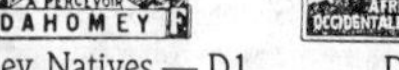
Dahomey Natives — D1

D2

1906 Unwmk. Typo. *Perf. 14x13½*

J1	D1	5c grn, *grnsh*	1.10	1.10
J2	D1	10c red brn	2.00	2.00
J3	D1	15c dark blue	4.00	4.00
J4	D1	20c blk, *yellow*	2.50	2.50
J5	D1	30c red, *straw*	3.25	3.25
J6	D1	50c violet	11.75	11.75
J7	D1	60c blk, *buff*	7.00	7.00
J8	D1	1fr blk, *pinkish*	17.50	17.50
		Nos. J1-J8 (8)	49.10	49.10

1914

J9	D2	5c green	15	15
J10	D2	10c rose	15	15
J11	D2	15c gray	25	25
J12	D2	20c brown	40	40
J13	D2	30c blue	40	40
J14	D2	50c black	62	62
J15	D2	60c orange	90	90
J16	D2	1fr violet	90	90
		Nos. J9-J16 (8)	3.77	3.77

Type of 1914 Issue Surcharged **2F.**

1927

J17	D2	2fr on 1fr lilac rose	2.25	2.25
J18	D2	3fr on 1fr org brn	2.00	2.00

Carved Mask — D3

1941 Engr. *Perf. 14x13*

J19	D3	5c black	15	15
J20	D3	10c lilac rose	15	15
J21	D3	15c dark blue	15	15
J22	D3	20c bright yel green	15	15
J23	D3	30c orange	20	20
J24	D3	50c violet brown	40	40
J25	D3	60c slate green	55	55
J26	D3	1fr rose red	65	65
J27	D3	2fr yellow	65	65
J28	D3	3fr dark purple	90	90
		Nos. J19-J28 (10)	3.95	3.95

Stamps of type D3 with value numerals replacing "RF" at upper left corner were issued in 1943-44 by the Vichy Government, but were not placed on sale in the colony.

Catalogue values for unused stamps in this section, from this point to the end of the section, are for Never Hinged items.

Republic

Panther and Man — D4

Perf. 14x13½

1963, July 22 Typo. Unwmk.

J29	D4	1fr green & rose	15	15
J30	D4	2fr brn & emerald	15	15
J31	D4	5fr org & vio bl	16	16
J32	D4	10fr magenta & blk	40	40
J33	D4	20fr vio bl & org	60	60
		Nos. J29-J33 (5)	1.46	1.46

Mail Boat D5

Designs: No. J35, Heliograph. No. J36, Morse receiver. No. J37, Mailman on bicycle. No. J38, Early telephone. No. J39, Autorail. No. J40, Mail truck. No. J41, Radio tower. No. J42, DC-8F jet plane. No. J43, Early Bird communications satellite.

1967, Oct. 24 Engr. *Perf. 11*

J34	D5	1fr brn, dl pur & bl	15	15
J35	D5	1fr dl pur, brn & bl	15	15
J36	D5	3fr dk brn, dk grn & org	15	15
J37	D5	3fr dk grn, dk brn & org	15	15
J38	D5	5fr ol bis, lil & bl	20	20
J39	D5	5fr lil, ol bis & bl	20	20
J40	D5	10fr brn org, vio & grn	35	35
J41	D5	10fr vio, brn org & grn	35	35
J42	D5	30fr Prus bl, mar & vio	55	55
J43	D5	30fr vio, Prus bl & mar	55	55
		Nos. J34-J43 (10)	2.80	2.80

The two designs of each value in Nos. J34-J43 were printed tete beche, se-tenant at the base.

PARCEL POST STAMPS

Catalogue values for unused stamps in this section are for Never Hinged items.

Nos. 141-146 and 148 Surcharged

COLIS POSTAUX

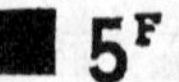

1967, Jan. Unwmk. Engr. *Perf. 13*

Q1	A15	5fr on 1fr multi	15	15
Q2	A15	10fr on 2fr multi	20	20
Q3	A15	20fr on 6fr multi	25	25
Q4	A15	25fr on 3fr multi	38	38
Q5	A15	30fr on 4fr multi	42	42
Q6	A15	50fr on 10fr multi	65	65
a.		"20" instead of "50"	55.00	
Q7	A15	100fr on 20fr multi	1.40	1.40
		Nos. Q1-Q7 (7)	3.45	3.45

The surcharge is arranged to fit the shape of the stamp.

No. Q6a occurred once on the sheet.

DALMATIA

LOCATION — A promontory in the northwestern part of the Balkan Peninsula, together with several small islands in the Adriatic Sea.

GOVT. — Part of the former Austro-Hungarian crownland of the same name.

AREA — 113 sq. mi.

POP. — 18,719 (1921)

CAPITAL — Zara.

Stamps were issued during Italian occupation. This territory was subsequently annexed by Italy.

100 Centesimi = 1 Corona = 1 Lira

Issued under Italian Occupation

Italy No. 87 Surcharged **una corona**

1919, May 1 Wmk. 140 *Perf. 14*

1	A46	1cor on 1 l brn & grn	40	*1.75*

Italian Stamps of 1906-08 Surcharged — a **5 centesimi di corona**

1921-22

2	A48	5c on 5c green	25	*50*
3	A48	10c on 10c claret	25	*50*
4	A49	25c on 25c blue('22)	32	*85*
5	A49	50c on 50c vio ('22)	80	*1.25*

Italian Stamps of 1901-10 Surcharged — b **1 corona**

6	A46	1cor on 1 l brn & grn ('22)	65	*2.00*
7	A46	5cor on 5 l bl & rose ('22)	3.00	*9.25*
8	A51	10cor on 10 l gray grn & red ('22)	4.50	*13.00*
		Nos. 1-8 (8)	10.17	*29.10*

Surcharges similar to these but differing in style or arrangement of type were used in Austria under Italian occupation.

SPECIAL DELIVERY STAMPS

Italian Special Delivery Stamp No. E1 Surcharged type "a"

1921 Wmk. 140 *Perf. 14*

E1	SD1	25c on 25c rose red	25	*1.50*
a.		Double surcharge	25.00	

Italian Special Delivery Stamp Surcharged **LIRE 1,20 DI CORONA**

1922

E2	SD2	1.20 l on 1.20 l	4.00	

No. E2 was not placed in use.

POSTAGE DUE STAMPS

Italian Postage Due Stamps Surcharged types "a" or "b"

1922 Wmk. 140 *Perf. 14*

J1	D3 (a)	50c on 50c buff & mag	65	*2.00*
J2	D3 (b)	1cor on 1 l bl & red	85	*2.50*
J3	D3 (b)	2cor on 2 l bl & red	3.00	*9.25*
J4	D3 (b)	5cor on 5 l bl & red	4.50	*13.00*

DANISH WEST INDIES

LOCATION — A group of islands in the West Indies, lying east of Puerto Rico

GOVT. — A former Danish colony

AREA — 132 sq. mi.

POP. — 27,086 (1911)

CAPITAL — Charlotte Amalie

The US bought these islands in 1917 and they became the US Virgin Islands, using US stamps and currency.

100 Cents = 1 Dollar
100 Bit = 1 Franc (1905)

Watermarks

Wmk. 111- Small Crown

Wmk. 112- Crown

Wmk. 113- Crown

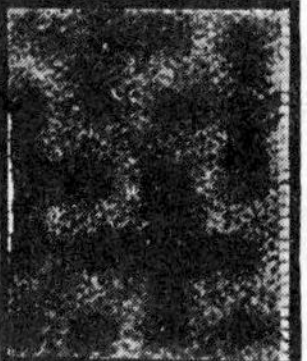
Wmk. 114- Multiple Crosses

Coat of Arms — A1

Yellowish Paper
Yellow Wavy-line Burelage, UL to LR

1856 Wmk. 111 Typo. *Imperf.*

1	A1	3c dk car, brown gum	125.00	160.00
a.		3c dark carmine, yellow gum	135.00	170.00
b.		3c carmine, white gum	*3,000.*	*3,000.*

Reprint: 1981, carmine, back-printed across two stamps ("Reprint by Dansk Post og Telegrafmuseum 1978"), value, pair, $10.

White Paper
Yellow Wavy-line Burelage, UR to LL

1866

2	A1	3c rose	40.00	35.00

No. 2 reprints unwatermarked: 1930 carmine, value $100. 1942 rose carmine, back-printed across each row ("Nytryk 1942 G. A. Hagemann Danmark og Dansk Vestindiens Friemaerker Bind 2"), value $50.

1872 *Perf. 12½*

3	A1	3c rose	75.00	125.00

1873

Without Burelage

4	A1	4c dull blue	100.00	250.00
a.		Imperf., pair	600.00	—
b.		Horiz. pair, imperf. vert.	500.00	—

#4 reprints, unwatermarked, imperf.: 1930, ultramarine, value $100. 1942, blue back-printed like 1942 reprint of #2, value $50.

A2

Normal Frame

Inverted Frame

The arabesques in the corners have a main stem and a branch. When the frame is in normal position, in the upper left corner the branch leaves the main stem half way between two little leaflets. In the lower right corner the branch starts at the foot of the second leaflet. When the frame is inverted the corner designs are, of course, transposed.

White Wove Paper, Varying from Thin to Thick

1874-79 Wmk. 112 *Perf. 14x13½*

5 A2 1c green & brn red 13.00 10.00
a. 1c grn & rose lilac, thin paper 75.00 75.00
b. 1c grn & red violet, medium paper 40.00 40.00
c. 1c green & violet, thick paper 13.00 10.00
e. Inverted frame 13.00 10.00
6 A2 3c blue & carmine 15.00 10.00
d. Imperf., pair 300.00
e. Inverted frame 15.00 10.00
7 A2 4c brn & dull blue 12.00 15.00
b. 4c brown & ultramarine 150.00 175.00
c. Diagonal half used as 2c on cover 100.00
d. Inverted frame *1,500.* *1,500.*
8 A2 5c green & gray ('76) 20.00 15.00
b. Inverted frame 20.00 15.00
9 A2 7c lilac & orange 20.00 *35.00*
a. 7c lilac & yellow 40.00 50.00
b. Inverted frame 30.00 60.00
10 A2 10c blue & brn ('76) 20.00 10.00
b. "cent.s" 25.00 15.00
c. Inverted frame 20.00 10.00
11 A2 12c red lilac & yel green ('77) 22.50 40.00
a. 12c lilac & deep green 75.00 75.00
12 A2 14c lilac & green 350.00 500.00
a. Inverted frame *2,000.* *2,500.*
13 A2 50c violet, thin paper ('79) 60.00 75.00
a. 50c gray violet, thick porous paper 100.00 150.00

The central element in the fan-shaped scrollwork at the outside of the lower left corner of Nos. 5a and 7b looks like an elongated diamond.

See Nos. 16-20. For surcharges see Nos. 14-15, 23-28, 40.

Nos. 9 and 13 Surcharged in Black

I CENT

10 CENTS 1895

1887-95

14 A2 1c on 7c lilac & org 50.00 90.00
a. 1c on 7c lilac & yellow 75.00 125.00
b. Double surcharge 200.00 300.00
c. Inverted frame 65.00 90.00
15 A2 10c on 50c violet ('95) 20.00 50.00

Type of 1873

1896-1901 *Perf. 13*

16 A2 1c green & red vio ('98) 8.00 8.00
a. Normal frame 200.00 300.00
17 A2 3c blue & lake ('98) 8.00 8.00
a. Normal frame 225.00 250.00
18 A2 4c bister & dull blue ('01) 9.00 9.00
a. Diagonal half used as 2c on cover 25.00
b. Inverted frame 35.00 30.00
19 A2 5c green & gray 35.00 20.00
a. Normal frame 500.00 650.00
20 A2 10c blue & brown ('01) 85.00 55.00
a. Inverted frame 800.00 1,100.
b. "cent.s" 60.00 95.00
Nos. 16-20 (5) 145.00 100.00

Arms — A5

1900

21 A5 1c light green 2.00 2.00
22 A5 5c light blue 8.00 12.00

See Nos. 29-30. For surcharges see Nos. 41-42.

Nos. 6, 17, 20 Surcharged:

2 CENTS 1902
c

8 Cents 1902
d

Surcharge "c" in Black

1902 *Perf. 14x13½*

23 A2 2c on 3c blue & car 500.00 400.00
a. "2" in date with straight tail 525.00 450.00
b. Normal frame *2,500.* —

Perf. 13

24 A2 2c on 3c blue & lake 8.00 12.50
a. "2" in date with straight tail 15.00 20.00
b. Dated "1901" 325.00 400.00
c. Normal frame 150.00 175.00
d. Dark green surcharge 1,250.
e. As "d" & "a" 1,500.
f. As "d" & "c" *6,000.*
25 A2 8c on 10c blue & brn 15.00 20.00
a. "2" with straight tail 15.00 22.50
b. On No. 20b 15.00 25.00
c. Inverted frame 250.00 300.00

Only one copy of No. 24f can exist.

Surcharge "d" in Black

27 A2 2c on 3c blue & lake 8.00 17.00
a. Normal frame 200.00 300.00
28 A2 8c on 10c blue & brn 7.00 7.00
a. On No. 20b 9.00 9.00
b. Inverted frame 200.00 250.00

1903 Wmk. 113

29 A5 2c carmine 8.00 10.00
30 A5 8c brown 16.00 20.00

King Christian IX — A8

St. Thomas Harbor — A9

1905 Typo. *Perf. 13*

31 A8 5b green 3.00 2.00
32 A8 10b red 4.00 2.00
33 A8 20b green & blue 8.00 8.00
34 A8 25b ultramarine 7.00 7.00
35 A8 40b red & gray 8.00 8.00
36 A8 50b yellow & gray 7.00 9.00

Frame Typo., Center Engr.
Wmk. Two Crowns (113)
Perf. 12

37 A9 1fr green & blue 13.00 *22.50*
38 A9 2fr org red & brown 30.00 *50.00*
39 A9 5fr yellow & brown 65.00 *150.00*
Nos. 31-39 (9) 145.00

Favor cancels exist on #37-39. Value 25% less.

Nos. 18, 22, 30 Surcharged in Black

5 BIT 1905

1905 Wmk. 112 *Perf. 13*

40 A2 5b on 4c bis & dull blue 9.00 *15.00*
a. Inverted frame 30.00 *45.00*
41 A5 5b on 5c light blue 8.00 *14.00*

Wmk. 113

42 A5 5b on 8c brown 8.00 *15.00*

Frederik VIII — A10

Christian X — A11

Frame Typo., Center Engr.

1907-08 Wmk. 113 *Perf. 13*

43 A10 5b green 1.50 1.00
44 A10 10b red 1.50 1.00
45 A10 15b violet & brown 3.50 3.50
46 A10 20b green & blue 30.00 14.00
47 A10 25b blue & dk blue 1.50 1.00
48 A10 30b claret & slate 40.00 35.00
49 A10 40b ver & gray 4.00 4.00
50 A10 50b yellow & brown 4.00 5.00
Nos. 43-50 (8) 86.00 64.50

1915 Wmk. 114 *Perf. 14x14½*

51 A11 5b yellow green 2.00 *5.00*
52 A11 10b red 2.00 *35.00*
53 A11 15b lilac & red brown 2.00 *35.00*
54 A11 20b green & blue 2.00 *35.00*
55 A11 25b blue & dark blue 2.00 *5.00*
56 A11 30b claret & black 2.00 *35.00*
57 A11 40b orange & black 2.00 *35.00*
58 A11 50b yellow & brown 2.00 *35.00*
Nos. 51-58 (8) 16.00

Forged and favor cancellations exist.

POSTAGE DUE STAMPS

Royal Cipher, "Christian 9 Rex" — D1

1902 Unwmk. Litho. *Perf. 11½*

J1 D1 1c dark blue 5.00 10.00
J2 D1 4c dark blue 6.00 15.00
J3 D1 6c dark blue 25.00 45.00
J4 D1 10c dark blue 15.00 20.00

There are five types of each value. On the 4c they may be distinguished by differences in the figures "4"; on the other values the differences are minute.

Used values of Nos. J1-J4 are for canceled copies. Uncanceled examples without gum have probably been used. Value 60% of unused.

Counterfeits of Nos. J1-J4 exist.

D2

1905-13 *Perf. 13*

J5 D2 5b red & gray 4.00 *5.00*
J6 D2 20b red & gray 8.00 *12.50*
J7 D2 30b red & gray 7.00 *12.50*
J8 D2 50b red & gray 9.00 *9.00*
a. Perf. 14x14½ ('13) 25.00 *100.00*
b. Perf. 11½ 500.00

All values of this issue are known imperforate, but were not regularly issued.

Used values of Nos. J5-J8 are for canceled copies. Uncanceled examples without gum have probably been used. Value 60% of unused.

Counterfeits of Nos. J5-J8 exist.

Danish West Indies stamps were replaced by those of the US in 1917, after the US bought the islands.

DANZIG

LOCATION — In northern Europe bordering on the Baltic Sea
GOVT. — Former free city and state
AREA — 754 sq. mi.
POP. — 407,000 (approx. 1939)
CAPITAL — Danzig

Established as a "Free City and State" under the protection of the League of Nations in 1920, Danzig was seized by Germany in 1939. It became a Polish province in 1945.

100 Pfennig = 1 Gulden (1923)
100 Pfennig = 1 Mark

Watermarks

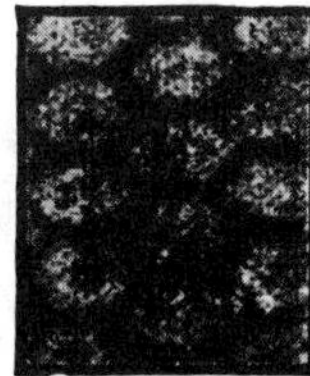

Wmk. 108- Honeycomb

Wmk. 109- Webbing

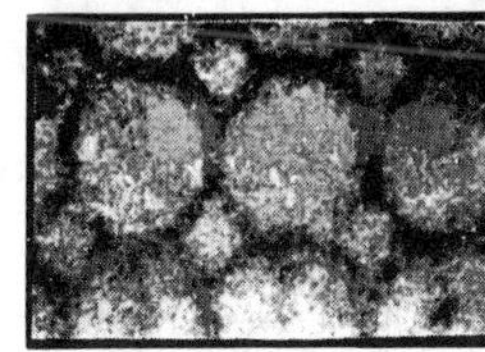

Wmk. 110- Octagons

Wmk. 125- Lozenges

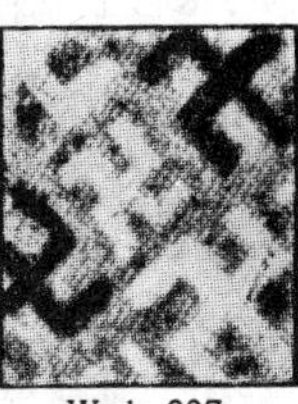

Wmk. 237- Swastikas

Used Values of 1920-23 are for favor-canceled stamps unless otherwise noted. Postally used copies bring higher prices.

German Stamps of 1906-20 Overprinted in Black

Danzig

Perf. 14, 14½, 15x14½

1920 Wmk. 125

1 A16 5pf green 18 15
2 A16 10pf carmine rose 18 15
3 A22 15pf violet brown 18 15
4 A16 20pf blue violet 18 15
5 A16 30pf org & blk, *buff* 24 18
6 A16 40pf carmine rose 20 15
7 A16 50pf pur & blk, *buff* 24 18
8 A17 1m red 45 35
9 A17 1.25m green 45 35
10 A17 1.50m yellow brn 55 65
11 A21 2m blue 90 90
a. Double overprint *625.00*
12 A21 2.50m lilac rose 1.10 1.75
13 A19 3m black violet 4.00 7.75
14 A16 4m black & rose 3.00 4.25
15 A20 5m slate & car 1.25 1.50
a. Center inverted *4,500.*
b. Inverted overprint *7,500.*
Nos. 1-15 (15) 13.10 18.61

The 5pf brown, 10pf orange and 40pf lake and black with this overprint were not regularly issued. Value for trio, $450.

For surcharges see Nos. 19-23, C1-C3.

Nos. 5, 4 Surcharged in Various Sizes — A1

1920

19 A16 5pf on 30pf (V) 15 15
20 A16 10pf on 20pf (R) 15 15
a. Double surcharge 115.00 165.00
21 A16 25pf on 30pf (G) 15 15
a. Inverted surcharge 115.00 165.00
22 A16 60pf on 30pf (Br) 42 50
a. Double surcharge 115.00 165.00
23 A16 80pf on 30pf (V) 42 50

German Stamps Surcharged in Various Styles

1 MARK 1 MARK **2 Mark 2**

Danzig **DANZIG**

10 Mark 10

Danzig

Gray Burelage with Points Up

25 A16 1m on 30pf org & blk, *buff* (Bk) 45 1.00
a. Pair, one without surcharge

26 A16 1¼m on 3pf brn (R) 45 1.00
27 A22 2m on 35pf red brn (Bl) 55 1.00
d. Surcharge omitted 55.00 75.00
28 A22 3m on 7½pf org (G) 55 1.00
29 A22 5m on 2pf gray (R) 55 1.00
30 A22 10m on 7½pf org (Bk) 1.75 5.25

Gray Burelage with Points Down

26a A16 1¼m on 3pf brown 12.50 20.00
27a A22 2m on 35pf red brown 150.00 135.00
28a A22 3m on 7½pf orange 5.50 6.25
29a A22 5m on 2pf gray 4.50 11.00
30a A22 10m on 7½pf orange 2.25 5.00

Violet Burelage with Points Up

25b A16 1m on 30pf org & blk, *buff* 17.50 25.00
26b A16 1¼m on 3pf brown 2.00 3.50
27b A22 2m on 35pf red brown 6.00 10.00
28b A22 3m on 7½pf org 70 1.25
29b A22 5m on 2pf gray 75 1.10
30b A22 10m on 7½pf org 75 1.00

Violet Burelage with Points Down

25c A16 1m on 30pf org & blk, *buff* 55 1.75
26c A16 1¼m on 3pf brown 2.00 7.50
27c A22 2m on 35pf red brown 6.50 27.50
28c A22 3m on 7½pf orange 17.50 50.00
29c A22 5m on 2pf gray 2.00 4.00
30c A22 10m on 7½pf orange 7.50 17.50

Excellent counterfeits of the surcharges are known.

German Stamps of 1906-20 Overprinted in Blue

1920

31 A22 2pf gray 60.00 110.00
32 A22 2½pf gray 75.00 150.00
33 A16 3pf brown 5.50 11.00
a. Double overprint 55.00 55.00
34 A16 5pf green 20 22
a. Double overprint 27.50
35 A22 7½pf orange 15.00 32.50
36 A16 10pf carmine 2.25 4.00
37 A22 15pf dk violet 30 40
b. Double overprint 27.50
38 A16 20pf blue violet 30 40

Overprinted in Carmine or Blue

39 A16 25pf org & blk, *yel* 30 40
40 A16 30pf org & blk, *buff* 24.00 55.00
42 A16 40pf lake & blk 1.25 2.50
a. Inverted overprint
b. Double overprint
43 A16 50pf pur & blk, *buff* 75.00 150.00
44 A16 60pf mag (Bl) 950.00 *2,000.*
45 A16 75pf green & blk 30 40
46 A16 80pf lake & blk, *rose* 3.00 2.75
47 A17 1m carmine 475.00 *800.00*
a. Double overprint *3,750.*

Overprinted in Carmine

48 A21 2m gray blue 700.00 *1,200.*

Counterfeit overprints of Nos. 31-48 exist.

Nos. 44, 47 and 48 were issued in small quantities and usually affixed directly to the mail by the postal clerk.

For surcharge see No. 62.

Hanseatic Trading Ship
A8 A9

Serrate Roulette 13½

1921, Jan. 31 **Typo.** **Wmk. 108**

49 A8 5pf brown & violet 25 18
50 A8 10pf orange & dk vio 25 18
51 A8 25pf green & car rose 38 55
52 A8 40pf carmine rose 2.25 2.25
53 A8 80pf ultra 28 42
54 A9 1m car rose & blk 1.10 1.40
55 A9 2m dk blue & dk grn 3.50 4.00
56 A9 3m black & grnsh blue 1.25 1.65
57 A9 5m indigo & rose red 1.25 1.65
58 A9 10m dk grn & brn org 1.90 3.50
Nos. 49-58 (10) 12.41 15.78

Issued in commemoration of the Constitution.

Nos. 49 and 50 with center in red instead of violet and Nos. 49, 50 and 54 with center inverted are probably proofs. All values of this issue exist imperforate but are not known to have been regularly issued in that condition.

1921, Mar. 11 ***Perf. 14***

59 A8 25pf green & car rose 48 55
60 A8 40pf carmine rose 60 60
61 A8 80pf ultra 3.00 6.50

No. 45 Surcharged in Black ≡60≡

1921, May 6 **Wmk. 125**

62 A16 60pf on 75pf 32 55
a. Double surcharge 60.00 60.00

Arms — A11

Coat of Arms — A12

Wmk. 108 (Vert. or Horiz.)

1921-22 ***Perf. 14***

63 A11 5(pf) orange 15 15
64 A11 10(pf) dark brown 15 15
65 A11 15(pf) green 15 15
66 A11 20(pf) slate 15 15
67 A11 25(pf) dark green 15 15
68 A11 30(pf) blue & car 20 15
a. Center inverted 19.00
69 A11 40pf green & car 15 15
a. Center inverted 19.00
70 A11 50pf dk green & car 15 15
71 A11 60pf carmine 25 28
72 A11 80pf black & car 25 35

Paper With Faint Gray Network

73 A11 1m orange & car 15 18
a. Center inverted 19.00
74 A11 1.20m blue violet 75 65
75 A11 2m gray & car 2.00 2.25
76 A11 3m violet & car 5.50 6.50

Serrate Roulette 13½

77 A12 5m grn, red & blk 95 1.40
78 A12 9m rose, red & org ('22) 1.90 3.75
79 A12 10m ultra, red & blk 95 1.40
80 A12 20m red & black 95 1.40
Nos. 63-80 (18) 14.90 19.36

In this and succeeding issues the mark values usually have the face of the paper covered with a gray network. This network is often very faint and occasionally is omitted.

Nos. 64, 66, 69-76 exist imperf. Value, each $20-$40.

See Nos. 81-93, 99-105. For surcharges and overprints see Nos. 96-98, O1-O33.

Type of 1921 and

Coat of Arms
A13 A13a

1922 **Wmk. 108** ***Perf. 14***

81 A11 75(pf) deep violet 15 15
82 A11 80(pf) green 15 15
83 A11 1.25m violet & car 15 15
84 A11 1.50m slate gray 15 18
85 A11 2m carmine rose 15 15
86 A11 2.40m dk brn & car 55 1.10
87 A11 3m carmine lake 15 18
88 A11 4m dark blue 55 85
89 A11 5m deep green 15 15
90 A11 6m carmine lake 15 18
a. 6m car rose, wmk. 109 horiz. *1,900.*
91 A11 8m light blue 18 50
92 A11 10m orange 15 18
93 A11 20m orange brn 15 18
94 A13 50m gold & car 85 1.80
a. 50m gold & red 5.50 8.00
95 A13a 100m metallic grn & red 1.80 3.00
Nos. 81-95 (15) 5.43 8.90

No. 95 has buff instead of gray network.

Nos. 81-83, 85-86, 88 exist imperf. Value, each $20.

Nos. 94-95 exist imperf. Value, each $50

Nos. 87, 88 and 91 Surcharged in Black or Carmine

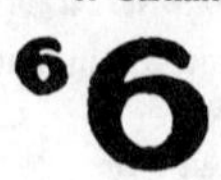

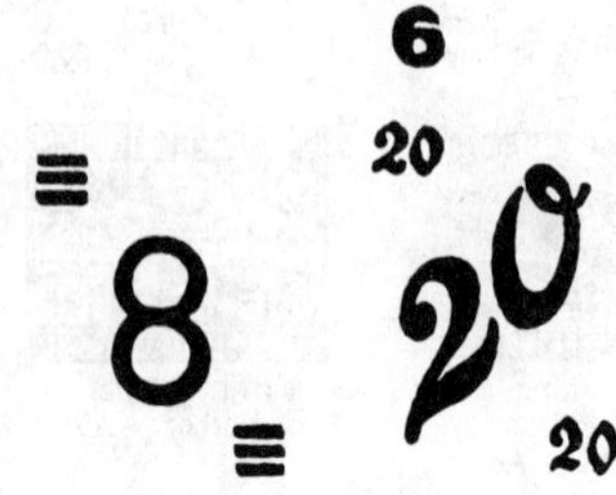

1922

96 A11 6m on 3m car lake 15 25
a. Double surcharge
97 A11 8m on 4m dk blue 15 40
a. Double surcharge 47.50 47.50
98 A11 20m on 8m lt bl (C) 18 32

Wmk. 109 (Vert. or Horiz.)

1922-23 ***Perf. 14***

99 A11 4m dark blue 15 18
100 A11 5m dark green 15 18
102 A11 10m orange 15 18
103 A11 20m orange brn 15 18

Paper Without Network

104 A11 40m pale blue 15 15
105 A11 80m red 15 15
Set value 54

Nos. 104-105 exist imperf. Value, each $15.

A15

A15a

Coat of Arms
A16

1923 ***Perf. 14***

Paper With Gray Network

106 A15 50m pale bl & red 15 22
107 A15a 100m dk green & red 15 22
108 A15a 150m violet & red 15 22
109 A16 250m violet & red 15 28
110 A16 500m gray blk & red 15 28
111 A16 1000m brown & red 15 28
112 A16 5000m silver & red 75 3.50

Paper Without Network

113 A15 50m pale blue 15 18
114 A15a 100m deep green 15 18
115 A15 200m orange 15 18
Set value 1.65

#109-112 exist imperf. Value, each $25.
#113-115 exist imperf. Value, each $17.50.

See Nos. 123-125. For surcharges and overprints see Nos. 126, 137-140, 143, 156-167, O35-O38.

A17

1923 ***Perf. 14***

Paper With Gray Network

117 A17 250m violet & red 15 20
118 A17 300m blue grn & red 15 22
119 A17 500m gray & red 15 20
120 A17 1000m brown & red 15 20
121 A17 3000m violet & red 15 20
123 A16 10,000m orange & red 25 40
124 A16 20,000m pale bl & red 32 70
125 A16 50,000m green & red 25 55
Set value 1.30

#117-125 exist imperf. Value, each $17.50.

See Nos. 127-135. For surcharges and overprints see Nos. 141-142, 144-155, O39-O41.

No. 124 Surcharged in Red **100 000**

1923, Aug. 14

126 A16 100,000m on 20,000m 75 *4.00*

1923 ***Perf. 14***

Paper Without Network

127 A17 1000m brown 15 20
129 A17 5000m rose 15 20
131 A17 20,000m pale blue 15 20
132 A17 50,000m green 15 20

Paper With Gray Network

133 A17 100,000m deep blue 15 20
134 A17 250,000m violet 15 20
135 A17 500,000m slate 15 20
Set value 63

Nos. 126-135 exist imperf.

Abbreviations: th=(tausend) thousand mil=million

Nos. 115, 114, 132, and Type of 1923 Surcharged **100 Tausend**

1923 ***Perf. 14***

Paper Without Network

137 A15 40th m on 200m 40 *95*
a. Double surcharge 60.00
138 A15 100th m on 200m 40 *95*
139 A15 250th m on 200m 4.00 *6.50*
140 A15a 400th m on 100m 25 30
141 A17 500th m on 50,000m 25 30
142 A17 1mil m on 10,000m org 1.90 *4.00*

The surcharges on Nos. 140 to 142 differ in details from those on Nos. 137 to 139.

Type of 1923 Surcharged **10 Millionen**

Paper With Gray Network

143 A16 10mil m on 1,000,000m org 25 20
Nos. 137-143 (7) 7.45 *13.20*

#142-143 exist imperf. Value, each $17.50.

Type of 1923 Surcharged **1 Million**

Paper Without Network

10,000m rose

144 A17 1mil m on 10,000m 15 22
145 A17 2mil m on 10,000m 15 22
146 A17 3mil m on 10,000m 15 22
147 A17 5mil m on 10,000m 15 22
b. Double surcharge 60.00

10,000m gray lilac

148 A17 10mil m on 10,000m 25 32
149 A17 20mil m on 10,000m 25 32
150 A17 25mil m on 10,000m 20 32
151 A17 40mil m on 10,000m 20 32
a. Double surcharge 50.00
152 A17 50mil m on 10,000m 20 32

Type of 1923 Surcharged in Red

300 Millionen

10,000m gray lilac

No.	Type	Description	Unused	Used
153	A17	100mil m on 10,000m	20	32
154	A17	300mil m on 10,000m	20	32
155	A17	500mil m on 10,000m	20	32
		Nos. 144-155 (12)	2.30	3.44

#144-147 exist imperf. Value, each $17.50. #153-155 exist imperf. Value, each $20.

Types of 1923 Surcharged

10 Pfennige

1923 Wmk. 110 *Perf. 14*

No.	Type	Description	Unused	Used
156	A15	5pf on 50m rose	40	32
157	A15	10pf on 50m rose	40	32
158	A15a	20pf on 100m rose	40	32
159	A15	25pf on 50m rose	3.50	6.25
160	A15	30pf on 50m rose	2.00	1.25
161	A15a	40pf on 100m rose	1.65	1.65
162	A15a	50pf on 100m rose	2.75	2.25
163	A15a	75pf on 100m rose	6.50	10.00

Type of 1923 Surcharged

2 Gulden

No.	Type	Description	Unused	Used
164	A16	1g on 1mil m rose	3.50	4.00
165	A16	2g on 1mil m rose	10.00	10.00
166	A16	3g on 1mil m rose	22.50	40.00
167	A16	5g on 1mil m rose	22.50	42.50
		Nos. 156-167 (12)	76.10	118.86

Coat of Arms — A19

1924-37 Wmk. 109 *Perf. 14*

No.	Type	Description	Unused	Used
168	A19	3pf brn, *yelsh* ('36)	90	65
a.		3pf dp brn, *white* ('27)	1.65	90
170	A19	5pf org, *yelsh* ('36)	2.75	24
a.		White paper	3.25	18
c.		Tête bêche pair	575.00	
d.		Syncopated perf., #170 ('37)	7.50	6.50
e.		Syncopated perf., #170a ('32)	12.50	6.50
171	A19	7pf yellow grn ('33)	1.10	1.40
172	A19	8pf yellow grn ('37)	1.65	3.00
173	A19	10pf grn, *yelsh* ('36)	4.25	18
a.		White paper	4.50	18
c.		10pf blue grn, *yellowish* ('37)	3.25	28
d.		Tête bêche pair	575.00	
e.		Syncopated perf., #173 ('37)	14.00	7.25
f.		Syncopated perf., #173a ('32)	16.00	11.00
g.		Syncopated perf., #173c ('37)	5.50	8.50
175	A19	15pf gray	2.50	42
176	A19	15pf red, *yelsh* ('36)	2.00	15
a.		White paper ('25)	2.00	15
177	A19	20pf carmine & red	6.00	28
178	A19	20pf gray ('35)	1.65	1.40
179	A19	25pf slate & red	10.00	1.40
180	A19	25pf carmine ('35)	10.50	60
181	A19	30pf green & red	5.25	45
182	A19	30pf dk violet ('35)	1.25	2.25
183	A19	35pf ultra ('25)	1.25	55
184	A19	40pf dk blue & blue	4.00	45
185	A19	40pf yel brn & red ('35)	6.50	12.00
186	A19	40pf dk blue ('35)	1.10	1.40
a.		Imperf.	30.00	
187	A19	50pf blue & red	7.50	2.75
a.		Yellowish paper ('36)	8.00	3.50
188	A19	55pf plum & scar ('37)	4.00	7.00
189	A19	60pf dk grn & red ('35)	6.00	11.00
190	A19	70pf yel grn & red ('35)	2.25	2.75
191	A19	75pf violet & red	6.00	3.25
a.		Yellowish paper ('36)	5.00	3.50
192	A19	80pf dk org brn & red ('35)	2.75	3.50
		Nos. 168-192 (23)	91.15	57.07

The 5pf and 10pf with syncopated perforations (Netherlands type C) are coils.

See Nos. 225-232. For overprints and surcharges see Nos. 200-209, 211-215, 241-252, B9-B11, O42-O52.

Oliva Castle and Cathedral — A20

St. Mary's Church — A23

Council Chamber on the Langenmarkt — A24

Designs: 2g, Mottlau River and Krantor. 3g, View of Zoppot.

1924-32 Engr. Wmk. 125

No.	Type	Description	Unused	Used
193	A20	1g yel grn & blk	22.50	20.00
		Parcel post cancel		10.50
194	A20	1g org & gray blk ('25)	10.50	1.25
a.		1g red orange & blk ('32)	15.00	6.00
		Parcel post cancel		90
195	A20	2g red vio & blk	40.00	60.00
		Parcel post cancel		35.00
196	A20	2g rose & blk ('25)	2.00	2.00
		Parcel post cancel		1.50
197	A20	3g dk blue & blk	3.00	3.75
		Parcel post cancel		1.90
198	A23	5g brn red & blk	4.00	4.75
		Parcel post cancel		1.65
199	A24	10g dk brn & blk	27.50	32.50
		Parcel post cancel		16.00
		Nos. 193-199 (7)	109.50	124.25

See No. 233. For overprints and surcharges see Nos. 210, 253-254, C31-C35.

Stamps of 1924-25 Overprinted in Black, Violet or Red

1920 15. November 1930

1930, Nov. 15 Typo. Wmk. 109

No.	Type	Description	Unused	Used
200	A19	5pf orange	1.90	1.50
201	A19	10pf yellow grn (V)	2.75	2.00
202	A19	15pf red	4.50	5.00
203	A19	20pf carmine & red	2.25	2.50
204	A19	25pf slate & red	3.75	5.00
205	A19	30pf green & red	7.75	12.50
206	A19	35pf ultra (R)	32.50	37.50
207	A19	40pf dk bl & bl (R)	9.50	14.00
208	A19	50pf dp blue & red	32.50	37.50
209	A19	75pf violet & red	32.50	37.50

Wmk. Lozenges. (125)
Engr.

No.	Type	Description	Unused	Used
210	A20	1g orange & blk (R)	32.50	37.50
		Nos. 200-210 (11)	162.40	192.50

10th anniversary of the Free State. Counterfeits exist.

Nos. 171 and 183 Surcharged in Red Blue or Green:

Nos. 211-214 No. 215

1934-36

No.	Type	Description	Unused	Used
211	A19	6pf on 7pf (R)	90	95
212	A19	8pf on 7pf (Bl) ('35)	2.25	2.25
213	A19	8pf on 7pf (R) ('36)	1.40	1.40
214	A19	8pf on 7pf (G) ('36)	90	95
215	A19	30pf on 35pf (Bl)	8.00	10.50
		Nos. 211-215 (5)	13.45	16.05

Bathing Beach, Brösen A25

View of Brösen Beach A26

War Memorial at Brösen A27

Skyline of Danzig A28

1936, June 23 Typo. Wmk. 109

No.	Type	Description	Unused	Used
216	A25	10pf deep green	45	80
217	A26	25pf rose red	80	1.50
218	A27	40pf bright blue	1.25	2.50

Village of Brösen, 125th anniversary. Exist imperf. Value of set, $150.

1937, Mar. 27

No.	Type	Description	Unused	Used
219	A28	10pf dark blue	50	80
220	A28	15pf violet brown	70	1.50

Air Defense League.

Danzig Philatelic Exhibition Issue
Souvenir Sheet

St. Mary's Church A29

1937, June 6 Wmk. 109 *Perf. 14*

No.	Type	Description	Unused	Used
221	A29	50pf dark green	1.50	2.75

Danzig Philatelic Exhib., June 6-8, 1937.

Arthur Schopenhauer
A30 A31

Design: 40pf, Full-face portrait, white hair.

Unwmk.
1938, Feb. 22 Photo. *Perf. 14*

No.	Type	Description	Unused	Used
222	A30	15pf dull blue	90	1.50
223	A31	25pf sepia	2.00	3.75
224	A31	40pf orange ver	1.00	2.50

150th anniv. of the birth of Schopenhauer.

Type of 1924-35

1938-39 Typo. Wmk. 237 *Perf. 14*

No.	Type	Description	Unused	Used
225	A19	3pf brown	48	*3.25*
226	A19	5pf orange	48	95
b.		Syncopated perf.	90	*3.75*
227	A19	8pf yellow grn	3.00	*8.25*
228	A19	10pf blue green	48	60
b.		Syncopated perf.	1.40	*4.00*
229	A19	15pf scarlet	1.40	*3.75*
230	A19	25pf carmine	1.40	*3.75*
231	A19	40pf dark blue	1.40	*5.00*
232	A19	50pf brt bl & red ('39)	1.75	*5.00*

Engr.

No.	Type	Description	Unused	Used
233	A20	1g red org & blk	3.00	*6.50*
		Nos. 225-233 (9)	13.39	*37.05*

Sizes: #233, 32½x21¼mm; #194, 31x21mm.

Nos. 226b and 228b are coils with Netherlands type C perforation.

Knights in Tournament, 1500 — A33

French Leaving Danzig, 1814 — A35

Stamp Day: 10pf, Signing of Danzig-Sweden neutrality treaty, 1630. 25pf, Battle of Weichselmünde, 1577.

Unwmk.
1939, Jan. 7 Photo. *Perf. 14*

No.	Type	Description	Unused	Used
234	A33	5pf dark green	70	*1.25*
235	A33	10pf copper brown	95	*1.40*
236	A35	15pf slate black	1.10	*1.65*
237	A35	25pf brown violet	1.25	*2.00*

Gregor Mendel — A37

Designs: 15pf, Dr. Robert Koch. 25pf, Wilhelm Roentgen.

1939, Apr. 29 Photo. *Perf. 13x14*

No.	Type	Description	Unused	Used
238	A37	10pf copper brown	30	55
239	A37	15pf indigo	50	70
240	A37	25pf dark olive green	70	1.10

Issued in honor of the achievements of Mendel, Koch and Roentgen.

Issued under German Administration
Stamps of Danzig, 1925-39, Surcharged in Black:

Rpf Deutsches Reich Rpf
a

4 Rpf 4 Deutsches Reich 4 Rpf 4
b

1 Reichsmark

c

Deutsches Reich

1939 Wmk. 109 *Perf. 14*

No.	Type	Description	Unused	Used
241	A19(b)	4rpf on 35pf ultra	65	1.10
242	A19(b)	12rpf on 7pf yel grn	70	1.25
243	A19(a)	20rpf gray	1.90	3.75

Wmk. 237

No.	Type	Description	Unused	Used
244	A19(a)	3rpf brown	65	1.10
245	A19(a)	5rpf orange	65	1.10
246	A19(a)	8rpf yellow grn	1.00	1.90
247	A19(a)	10rpf blue grn	1.25	2.00
248	A19(a)	15rpf scarlet	1.75	3.00
249	A19(a)	25rpf carmine	1.75	3.00
250	A19(a)	30rpf dk violet	1.10	2.00
251	A19(a)	40rpf dk blue	2.25	3.00
252	A19(a)	50rpf brt bl & red	2.25	4.00
253	A20(c)	1rm on 1g red org & blk	8.75	17.50

Wmk. 125

254 A20(c) 2rm on 2g rose & blk 12.50 21.00
Nos. 241-254 (14) 37.15 65.70

#241-254 were valid throughout Germany.

SEMI-POSTAL STAMPS

St. George and Dragon — SP1

Wmk. 108

1921, Oct. 16 Typo. *Perf. 14*

Size: 19x22mm

B1 SP1 30pf + 30pf grn & org 50 35
B2 SP1 60pf + 60pf rose & org 90 90

Size: 25x30mm

Serrate Roulette 13½

B3 SP1 1.20m + 1.20m dk bl & org 1.65 1.65

Aged Pensioner SP2

1923, Mar. Wmk. 109 *Perf. 14*

Paper With Gray Network

B4 SP2 50m + 20m lake 15 75
B5 SP2 100m + 30m red violet 15 75

Philatelic Exhibition Issue

Neptune Fountain — SP3

Various Frames.

1929, July 7 Engr. Unwmk.

B6 SP3 10pf yel grn & gray 2.00 2.25
B7 SP3 15pf car & gray 2.00 2.25
B8 SP3 25pf ultra & gray 6.50 6.00
a. 25pf violet blue & black 30.00 55.00

These stamps were sold exclusively at the Danzig Philatelic Exhibition, June 7-14, 1929, at double their face values, the excess being for the aid of the exhibition.

Regular Issue of 1924-25 Surcharged in Black

5
W. H. W.

1934, Jan. 15 Wmk. 109

B9 A19 5pf + 5pf orange 7.75 12.50
B10 A19 10pf + 5pf yellow grn 22.50 32.50
B11 A19 15pf + 5pf carmine 12.00 18.00

Surtax for winter welfare. Counterfeits exist.

Stock Tower — SP4

George Hall — SP6

City Gate, 16th Century SP5

1935, Dec. 16 Typo. *Perf. 14*

B12 SP4 5pf + 5pf orange 48 1.40
B13 SP5 10pf + 5pf green 75 1.40
B14 SP6 15pf + 10pf scarlet 1.25 2.25

Surtax for winter welfare.

Milk Can Tower SP7

Frauentor SP8

Krantor — SP9

Langgarter Gate SP10

High Gate SP11

1936, Nov. 25

B15 SP7 10pf + 5pf dk blue 1.00 2.00
a. Imperf. 50.00
B16 SP8 15pf + 5pf dull green 1.00 2.75
B17 SP9 25pf + 10pf red brown 1.40 2.75
B18 SP10 40pf + 20pf brn & red brn 2.00 3.50
B19 SP11 50pf + 20pf bl & dk bl 3.25 6.50
Nos. B15-B19 (5) 8.65 17.50

Surtax for winter welfare.

SP12

SP13

1937, Oct. 30

B20 SP12 25pf + 25pf dk carmine 1.65 3.50
B21 SP13 40pf + 40pf blue & red 1.65 3.50
a. Souvenir sheet of 2, #B20-B21 17.50 27.50

Founding of Danzig community at Magdeburg.

Madonna SP14

Mercury SP15

Weather Vane, Town Hall SP16

Neptune Fountain SP17

St. George and Dragon — SP18

1937, Dec. 13

B23 SP14 5pf + 5pf brt violet 1.65 2.50
B24 SP15 10pf + 10pf dk brown 1.65 3.00
B25 SP16 15pf + 5pf bl & yel brn 1.90 3.75
B26 SP17 25pf + 10pf bl grn & grn 2.00 4.25
B27 SP18 40pf + 25pf brt car & bl 3.75 6.75
Nos. B23-B27 (5) 10.95 20.25

Surtax for winter welfare. Designs are from frieze of the Artushof.

"Peter von Danzig" Yacht Race — SP19

Ships: 10pf+5pf, Dredger Fu Shing. 15pf+10pf, S. S. Columbus. 25pf+10pf, S. S. City of Danzig. 40pf+15pf, Peter von Danzig, 1472.

1938, Nov. 28 Photo. Unwmk.

B28 SP19 5pf + 5pf dk blue grn 95 1.50
B29 SP19 10pf + 5pf gldn brown 1.25 2.00
B30 SP19 15pf + 10pf olive grn 1.40 2.25
B31 SP19 25pf + 10pf indigo 1.90 3.00
B32 SP19 40pf + 15pf violet brn 2.50 3.75
Nos. B28-B32 (5) 8.00 12.50

Surtax for winter welfare.

AIR POST STAMPS

No. 6 Surcharged in Blue or Carmine

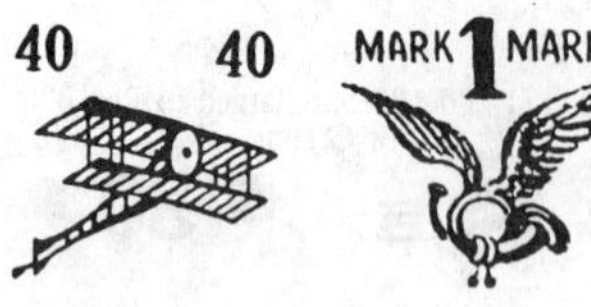

1920, Sept. 29 Wmk. 125 *Perf. 14*

C1 A16 40pf on 40pf 85 1.65
a. Double surcharge 350.00 350.00
C2 A16 60pf on 40pf (C) 85 1.65
a. Double surcharge 350.00 350.00
C3 A16 1m on 40pf 85 1.65

Plane faces left on No. C2.

Plane over Danzig
AP3 AP4

Wmk. Honeycomb (108)

1921-22 Typo. *Perf. 14*

C4 AP3 40(pf) blue green 24 38
C5 AP3 60(pf) dk violet 24 38
C6 AP3 1m carmine 24 38
C7 AP3 2m orange brown 24 38

Serrate Roulette 13½

Size: 34½x23mm

C8 AP4 5m violet blue 65 1.10
C9 AP4 10m dp green ('22) 1.50 2.50
Nos. C4-C9 (6) 3.11 5.12

Nos. C4-C9 exist imperf. Value, each $50.

1923 Wmk. Webbing (109) *Perf. 14*

C10 AP3 40(pf) blue green 22 1.10
C11 AP3 60(pf) dk violet 22 1.10
a. Double impression 50.00
C12 AP3 1m carmine 22 1.40
C13 AP3 2m org brown 22 1.40
C14 AP3 25m pale blue 22 35

Serrate Roulette 13½

Size: 34½x23mm

C15 AP4 5m violet blue 22 50
C16 AP4 10m deep green 22 50

Paper With Gray Network

C17 AP4 20m orange brown 22 50

Size: 40x23mm

C18 AP4 50m orange 22 40
C19 AP4 100m red 22 40
C20 AP4 250m dark brown 22 40
C21 AP4 500m carmine rose 22 40
Nos. C10-C21 (12) 2.64 8.45

Nos. C14, C18-C21 exist imperf. Value, each $35.

Post Horn and Airplanes — AP5

1923, Oct. 18 *Perf. 14*

Paper Without Network

C22 AP5 250,000m scarlet 18 80
C23 AP5 500,000m scarlet 18 80

Exist imperf. Value, each $37.50.

Surcharged

2
Millionen

C24 AP5 2mil m on 100,000m scar 18 80
C25 AP5 5mil m on 50,000m scar 18 80
b. Cliché of 10,000m in sheet of 50,000m 20.00 30.00

Exist imperf. Value, each $45.

Nos. C24 and C25 were not regularly issued without surcharge, although copies have been passed through the post. Value, uncanceled, each $7.50.

Plane over Danzig
AP6 AP7

1924

C26 AP6 10(pf) vermilion 11.00 2.50
C27 AP6 20(pf) carmine rose 1.25 1.10
C28 AP6 40(pf) olive brown 2.50 1.65
C29 AP6 1g deep green 2.50 1.65
C30 AP7 2½g violet brown 18.00 27.50
Nos. C26-C30 (5) 35.25 34.40

Exist imperf. Value No. C30, $150, others, each $62.50.

Danzig stamps can be mounted in the Scott Germany album part II.

Nos. 193, 195, 197-199 Surcharged in Various Colors

10 ▬ 10
Luftpost-Ausstellung
1932

1932 Wmk. 125

C31 A20 10pf on 1g (G) 8.25 9.50
C32 A20 15pf on 2g (V) 8.25 9.50
C33 A20 20pf on 3g (Bl) 8.25 9.50
C34 A23 25pf on 5g (R) 8.25 9.50
C35 A24 30pf on 10g (Br) 8.25 9.50
Nos. C31-C35 (5) 41.25 47.50

Intl. Air Post Exhib. of 1932. The surcharges were variously arranged to suit the shapes and designs of the stamps. The stamps were sold at double their surcharged values, the excess being donated to the exhibition funds.

Airplane
AP8 AP9

1935 Wmk. 109

C36 AP8 10pf scarlet 1.25 55
C37 AP8 15pf yellow 1.50 1.00
C38 AP8 25pf dark green 1.25 1.00
C39 AP8 50pf gray blue 5.00 6.25
C40 AP9 1g magenta 3.50 *7.00*
Nos. C36-C40 (5) 12.50 *15.80*

See Nos. C42-C45.

Souvenir Sheet

St. Mary's Church
AP10

1937, June 6 ***Perf. 14***

C41 AP10 50pf dark blue 1.50 2.50

Danzig Phil. Exhib., June 6-8, 1937.

Type of 1935

1938-39 Wmk. 237

C42 AP8 10pf scarlet 1.25 *4.50*
C43 AP8 15pf yellow ('39) 1.25 *4.75*
C44 AP8 25pf dark green 1.25 *4.75*
C45 AP8 50pf gray blue ('39) 4.50 *11.00*

POSTAGE DUE STAMPS

Danzig Coat of Arms
D1 D2

Wmk. Honeycomb (108)

1921-22 Typo. *Perf. 14*

Paper Without Network

J1 D1 10(pf) deep violet 18 24
J2 D1 20(pf) deep violet 18 24
J3 D1 40(pf) deep violet 18 24
J4 D1 60(pf) deep violet 18 24
J5 D1 75(pf) dp violet ('22) 18 24
J6 D1 80(pf) deep violet 18 24
J7 D1 120(pf) deep violet 18 24
J8 D1 200(pf) dp violet ('22) 65 95
J9 D1 240(pf) deep violet 18 24
J10 D1 300(pf) dp violet ('22) 65 95
J11 D1 400(pf) deep violet 65 95
J12 D1 500(pf) deep violet 65 95
J13 D1 800(pf) deep violet ('22) 65 95
J14 D1 20m dp violet ('22) 65 95
Nos. J1-J14 (14) 5.34 7.62

Nos. J1-J14 exist imperf. Value, each $15.

1923 Wmk. 109

J15 D1 100(pf) deep violet 35 40
J16 D1 200(pf) deep violet 2.00 2.25
J17 D1 300(pf) deep violet 35 35
J18 D1 400(pf) deep violet 35 35
J19 D1 500(pf) deep violet 35 35
J20 D1 800(pf) deep violet 60 60
J21 D1 10m deep violet 35 42
J22 D1 20m deep violet 35 42
J23 D1 50m deep violet 35 42

Paper With Gray Network

J24 D1 100m deep violet 35 42
J25 D1 500m deep violet 35 42
Nos. J15-J25 (11) 5.75 6.40

#J22-J25 exist imperf. Value, each $12.50.

Nos. J22-J23 and Type of 1923 Surcharged

10000

1923, Oct. 1

Paper without Network

J26 D1 5000m on 50m 18 30
J27 D1 10,000m on 20m 18 30
J28 D1 50,000m on 500m 18 30
J29 D1 100,000m on 20m 65 90

On No. J26 the numerals of the surcharge are all of the larger size.

A 1000(m) on 100m deep violet was prepared but not issued. Value, $110.

Nos. J26-J28 exist imperf. Value, each $25.

1923-28 Wmk. 110

J30 D2 5(pf) blue & black 60 60
J31 D2 10(pf) blue & black 45 45
J32 D2 15(pf) blue & black 90 90
J33 D2 20(pf) blue & black 1.10 1.50
J34 D2 30(pf) blue & black 5.00 1.50
J35 D2 40(pf) blue & black 1.40 1.90
J36 D2 50(pf) blue & black 1.40 1.75
J37 D2 60(pf) blue & black 9.00 12.00
J38 D2 100(pf) blue & black 9.00 5.00
J39 D2 3g blue & carmine 5.00 *30.00*
a. "Guldeu" instead of "Gulden" 165.00 *325.00*
Nos. J30-J39 (10) 33.85 *55.60*

Used values of Nos. J30-J39 are for postally used copies.

See Nos. J43-J47.

Postage Due Stamps of 1923 Issue Surcharged in Red

1932, Dec. 20

J40 D2 5pf on 40(pf) 1.40 *6.00*
J41 D2 10pf on 60(pf) 30.00 4.50
J42 D2 20pf on 100(pf) 1.50 *4.75*

Type of 1923

1938-39 Wmk. 237 *Perf. 14*

J43 D2 10(pf) blue & blk ('39) 85 *11.00*
J44 D2 30(pf) blue & black 1.25 *12.00*
J45 D2 40(pf) blue & blk ('39) 3.75 *25.00*
J46 D2 60(pf) blue & blk ('39) 4.75 *25.00*
J47 D2 100(pf) blue & black 5.75 *25.00*
Nos. J43-J47 (5) 16.35 *98.00*

OFFICIAL STAMPS

Regular Issues of 1921-22 Overprinted

a 

1921-22 Wmk. 108 *Perf. 14x14½*

O1 A11 5(pf) orange 20 25
O2 A11 10(pf) dark brown 15 20
a. Inverted overprint 50.00
O3 A11 15(pf) green 15 20
O4 A11 20(pf) slate 15 20
O5 A11 25(pf) dark green 15 20
O6 A11 30(pf) blue & car 38 48
O7 A11 40(pf) green & car 18 22
O8 A11 50(pf) dk grn & car 18 22
O9 A11 60(pf) carmine 18 22
O10 A11 75(pf) dp violet ('22) 15 25
O11 A11 80(pf) black & car 1.00 1.10
O12 A11 80(pf) green ('22) 15 25

Paper With Faint Gray Network

O14 A11 1m orange & car 15 22
O15 A11 1.20m blue violet 1.00 1.10
O16 A11 1.25m vio & car ('22) 15 25
O17 A11 1.50m slate gray ('22) 15 18
O18 A11 2m gray & car 11.00 8.25
a. Inverted overprint
O19 A11 2m car rose ('22) 15 25
O20 A11 2.40m dk brn & car ('22) 65 1.75
O21 A11 3m violet & car 7.50 7.75
O22 A11 3m car lake ('22) 15 18
O23 A11 4m dk blue ('22) 65 1.75
O24 A11 5m dp green ('22) 15 18
O25 A11 6m car lake ('22) 15 20
O26 A11 10m orange ('22) 15 20
O27 A11 20m orange brn ('22) 15 18
Nos. O1-O27 (26) 25.17 26.23

Double overprints exist on Nos. O1-O2, O5-O7, O10 and O12. Value, each $17.50.

Same Overprint on No. 96

O28 A11 6m on 3m 15 50
a. Inverted overprint 25.00

No. 77 Overprinted 

1922 *Serrate Roulette 13½*

O29 A12 5m grn, red & blk 2.00 4.25

Nos. 99-103, 106-107 Overprinted Type "a"

1923 Wmk. 109 *Perf. 14*

O30 A11 4m dark blue 15 22
O31 A11 5m dark green 18 30
O32 A11 10m orange 15 22
O33 A11 20m orange brn 15 22
O34 A15 50m pale blue & red 15 20
O35 A15a 100m dk green & red 15 20

Nos. 113-115, 118-120 Overprinted Type "a"

O36 A15 50m pale blue 15 20
a. Inverted overprint 20.00
O37 A15a 100m dark green 15 20
O38 A15 200m orange 15 20
a. Inverted overprint 20.00

Paper With Gray Network

O39 A17 300m bl grn & red 15 20
O40 A17 500m gray & red 15 20
O41 A17 1000m brown & red 15 20
Set value 1.50

Regular Issue of 1924-25 Overprinted *Dienst-marke*

1924-25 *Perf. 14x14½*

O42 A19 5pf orange 1.25 95
O43 A19 10pf yellow grn 1.25 95
O44 A19 15pf gray 1.25 95
O45 A19 15pf red ('25) 10.00 6.00
O46 A19 20pf carmine & red 1.50 95
O47 A19 25pf slate & red 10.00 11.00
O48 A19 30pf green & red 1.90 1.65
O49 A19 35pf ultra ('25) 27.50 35.00
O50 A19 40pf dk bl & dull bl 3.25 5.00
O51 A19 50pf dp blue & red 10.00 16.00
O52 A19 75pf violet & red 25.00 *55.00*
Nos. O42-O52 (11) 92.90 *133.45*

Double overprints exist on Nos. O42-O44, O47, O50-O52. Value, each $65.

DENMARK

LOCATION — Northern part of a peninsula which separates the North and Baltic Seas, and includes the surrounding islands
GOVT. — Kingdom
AREA — 16,631 sq. mi.
POP. — 5,112,130 (1984)
CAPITAL — Copenhagen

96 Skilling = 1 Rigsbank Daler
100 Ore = 1 Krone (1875)

Catalogue values for unused stamps in this country are for Never Hinged items, beginning with Scott 297 in the regular postage section, Scott B15 in the semi-postal section, and Scott Q28 in the parcel post section.

Watermarks

Wmk. 111- Small Crown

Wmk. 112- Crown

Wmk. 113- Crown

Wmk. 114- Multiple Crosses

Values of early Denmark stamps vary according to condition. Quotations for Nos. 1-15 are for fine copies. Very fine to superb specimens sell at much higher prices, and inferior or poor copies sell at reduced prices, depending on the condition of the individual specimen.

A1

Royal Emblems — A2

1851 Typo. Wmk. 111 *Imperf.*

With Yellow Brown Burelage

1 A1 2rs blue *2,500.* 700.00
a. First printing *5,750.* *2,250.*
2 A2 4rs brown 600.00 32.50
a. First printing 750.00 60.00
b. 4rs yellow brown 750.00 55.00

The first printing of Nos. 1 and 2 had the burelage printed from a copper plate, giving a clear impression with the lines in slight relief. The subsequent impressions had the burelage typographed, with the lines fainter and not rising above the surface of the paper.

Nos. 1-2 were reprinted in 1885 and 1901 on heavy yellowish paper, unwatermarked and imperforate, with a brown burelage. No. 1 was also reprinted without burelage, on both yellowish and white paper. Value for least costly reprint of No. 1, $40.

No. 2 was reprinted in 1951 in 10 shades with "Colour Specimen 1951" printed on the back. It was also reprinted in 1961 in 2 shades without burelage and with "Farve Nytryk 1961" printed on the back. Value for least costly reprint of No. 2, $8.50.

Dotting in Spandrels — A3

Wavy Lines in Spandrels — A4

1854-57

3 A3 2s blue ('55) 65.00 37.50
4 A3 4s brown 250.00 7.50
a. 4s yellow brown 250.00 7.50
5 A3 8s green ('57) 325.00 45.00
a. 8s yellow green 325.00 45.00
6 A3 16s gray lilac ('57) 500.00 110.00

See No. 10.

1858-62

7 A4 4s brown 47.50 4.75
a. 4s yellow brown 47.50 4.75
b. Wmk. 112 ('62) 47.50 5.50
8 A4 8s green 375.00 45.00

Nos. 2 to 8 inclusive are known with unofficial perforation 12 or 13, and Nos. 4, 5, 7 and 8 with unofficial roulette 9½.

Nos. 3, 6-8 were reprinted in 1885 on heavy yellowish paper, unwatermarked, imperforate and without burelage. Nos. 4-5 were reprinted in 1924 *on white paper, unwatermarked, imperforate, gummed and without burelage. Value for No. 3, $11; Nos. 4-5, each $100; No. 6, $15; Nos. 7-8, each $10.*

1863 Wmk. 112 *Rouletted 11*

9 A4 4s brown 65.00 12.50
  a. 4s deep brown 65.00 12.50
10 A3 16s violet 1,500. 675.00

Royal Emblems — A5

1864-68 *Perf. 13*

11 A5 2s blue ('65) 70.00 32.50
12 A5 3s red vio ('65) 70.00 45.00
13 A5 4s red 35.00 4.00
14 A5 8s bister ('68) 425.00 65.00
15 A5 16s olive green 475.00 75.00

Nos. 11-15 were reprinted in 1886 on heavy yellowish paper, unwatermarked, imperforate and without gum. The reprints of all values except the 4s were printed in two vertical rows of six, inverted with respect to each other, so that horizontal pairs are always tête bêche. Value $10 each.

Nos. 13 and 15 were reprinted in 1942 with printing on the back across each horizontal row: "Nytryk 1942. G. A. Hagemann: Danmarks og Vestindiens Frimaerker, Bind 2." Value, $65 each.

Imperf., Pairs

11a A5 2s blue 175.00 175.00
12a A5 3s red violet 300.00
13a A5 4s red 140.00 225.00
14a A5 8s bister 825.00
15a A5 16s olive green 1,050.

Perf. 12½

11b A5 2s blue 360.00 325.00
12b A5 3s red violet 375.00 265.00
14b A5 8s bister 425.00 265.00
15b A5 16s olive green 850.00 850.00

A6

The arabesques in the corners have a main stem and a branch. When the frame is in normal position, in the upper left corner the branch leaves the main stem half way between two little leaflets. In the lower right corner the branch starts at the foot of the second leaflet. When the frame is inverted the corner designs are, of course, transposed.

1870-71 Wmk. 112 *Perf. 14x13½*

Paper Varying from Thin to Thick

16 A6 2s gray & ultra ('71) 55.00 17.50
  a. 2s gray & blue 55.00 15.00
17 A6 3s gray & brt lil ('71) 125.00 55.00
18 A6 4s gray & car 60.00 8.00
19 A6 8s gray & brn ('71) 200.00 50.00
20 A6 16s gray & grn ('71) 350.00 100.00

Perf. 12½

21 A6 2s gray & bl ('71) 1,750. 2,500.
22 A6 4s gray & car 200.00 65.00
24 A6 48s brn & lilac 675.00 150.00

Nos. 16-20, 24 were reprinted in 1886 on thin white paper, unwatermarked, imperforate and without gum. These were printed in sheets of 10 in which 1 stamp has the normal frame (value $32.50 each) and 9 the inverted (value $11 each).

Imperf., Pairs

16b A6 2s 150.00
17a A6 3s 415.00
18a A6 4s 200.00
19a A6 8s 450.00
20a A6 16s 675.00
24a A6 48s 950.00

Inverted Frame

16c A6 2s 950.00 650.00
17b A6 3s 1,900. 1,300.
18b A6 4s 825.00 130.00
19b A6 8s 1,500. 825.00
20b A6 16s 1,300. 1,050.
24b A6 48s 2,750. 2,000.

1875-79 *Perf. 14x13½*

25 A6 3o gray blue & gray 12.00 5.75
  a. 1st "A" of "DANMARK" missing 52.50 110.00
  b. Imperf.
  c. Inverted frame 12.00 5.75
26 A6 4o slate & blue 10.00 20
  a. 4o gray & blue 10.00 20
  b. 4o slate & ultra 62.50 6.50
  c. 4o gray & ultra 62.50 6.50
  d. Imperf., pair 165.00
  e. Inverted frame 15.00 15
27 A6 5o rose & blue ('79) 30.00 35.00
  a. Ball of lower curve of large "5" missing 165.00 250.00
  b. Inverted frame 1,150. 1,450.
28 A6 8o slate & car 10.00 20
  a. 8o gray & carmine 35.00 2.00
  b. Imperf., pair 200.00
  c. Inverted frame 16.00 20
29 A6 12o sl & dull lake 7.50 2.00
  a. 12o gray & bright lilac 35.00 8.00
  b. 12o gray & dull magenta 7.50 3.50
  c. Inverted frame 10.00 2.00
30 A6 16o slate & brn 52.50 2.25
  a. 16o light gray & brown 55.00 7.50
  b. Inverted frame 25.00 2.00
31 A6 20o rose & gray 62.50 13.00
  a. 20o carmine & gray 62.50 13.00
  b. Inverted frame 62.50 15.00
32 A6 25o gray & green 55.00 14.00
  a. Inverted frame 80.00 45.00
33 A6 50o brown & vio 62.50 13.00
  a. 50o brown & blue violet 415.00 95.00
  b. Inverted frame 75.00 13.00
34 A6 100o gray & org ('77) 80.00 22.50
  a. Imperf., pair 350.00
  b. Inverted frame 130.00 52.50

The stamps of this issue on thin semi-transparent paper are far scarcer than those on thicker paper.

See Nos. 41-42, 44, 46-47, 50-52. For surcharges see Nos. 55, 79-80, 136.

Arms — A7

Two types of numerals in corners:

⑤ ⑤

1882

Small Corner Numerals

35 A7 5o green 185.00 90.00
37 A7 20o blue 165.00 30.00

1884-85

Larger Corner Numerals

38 A7 5o green 10.00 1.00
  a. Imperf.
39 A7 10o carmine ('85) 11.00 65
  a. Small numerals in corners 475.00 475.00
  b. Imperf., pair 175.00
  c. Pair, Nos. 39, 39a 500.00 625.00
40 A7 20o blue 17.50 65
  a. Pair, Nos. 37, 40 375.00 600.00
  b. Imperf., pair *1,900.*

Stamps with large corner numerals have white line around crown and lower oval touches frame.

The plate for No. 39, was damaged and 3 clichés in the bottom row were replaced by clichés for post cards, which had small numerals in the corners.

Two clichés with small numerals were inserted in the plate of No. 40.

See Nos. 43, 45, 48-49, 53-54. For surcharge see No. 56.

1895-1901 Wmk. 112 *Perf. 13*

41 A6 3o blue & gray 9.00 2.50
42 A6 4o slate & bl ('96) 5.00 15
43 A7 5o green 7.00 55
44 A6 8o slate & car 4.50 15
45 A7 10o rose car 8.00 65
46 A6 12o sl & dull lake 5.50 2.25
47 A6 16o slate & brown 18.00 3.00
48 A7 20o blue 9.50 1.25
49 A7 24o brown ('01) 10.50 3.75
50 A6 25o gray & grn ('98) 55.00 7.50
51 A6 50o brown & vio ('97) 55.00 12.00
52 A6 100o slate & org 60.00 16.00
  Nos. 41-52 (12) 247.00 49.75

Inverted Frame

41b A6 3o 10.50 2.75
42a A6 4o 5.00 15
44a A6 8o 4.50 15
46a A6 12o 12.50 2.25
47a A6 16o 22.50 3.00
50a A6 25o 47.50 12.00
51a A6 50o 65.00 21.00
52a A6 100o 52.50 15.00

1902-04 Wmk. 113

41c A6 3o blue & gray 3.75 3.50
42b A6 4o slate & blue 17.00 7.50
43a A7 5o green 2.75 25
44d A6 8o slate & carmine 450.00 275.00
45a A7 10o rose carmine 2.75 30
48a A7 20o blue 12.00 2.75
50b A6 25o gray & green 14.00 6.00
51b A6 50o brown & violet 45.00 18.00
52b A6 100o slate & orange 32.50 18.00

Inverted Frame

41d A6 3o 75.00 50.00
42c A6 4o 110.00 95.00
50c A6 25o 135.00 55.00
51c A6 50o 200.00 95.00
52c A6 100o 225.00 130.00

1902 Wmk. 113

53 A7 1o orange 75 32
  a. Imperf., pair 205.00
54 A7 15o lilac 11.00 60
  a. Imperf., pair

Nos. 44d, 44, 49 Surcharged:

a

15 15
ØRE

b

1904-12 Wmk. 113

55 A6(a) 4o on 8o sl & car 2.25 2.25
  a. Wmk. 112 ('12) 22.50 45.00
  b. As "a," inverted frame

Wmk. 112

56 A7(b) 15o on 24o brown 3.75 3.75
  a. Short "15" at right 32.50 45.00

A10

King Christian IX — A11

King Frederik VIII — A12

1905-17 Wmk. 113 *Perf. 13*

57 A10 1o orange ('06) 95 28
58 A10 2o carmine 1.10 15
  a. Perf. 14x14½ ('17) 2.75 2.25
59 A10 3o gray 2.75 25
60 A10 4o dull blue 2.75 15
  a. Perf. 14x14½ ('17) 7.25 4.50
61 A10 5o dp green ('12) 3.25 15
62 A10 10o dp rose ('12) 3.50 15
63 A10 15o lilac 10.00 32
64 A10 20o dk blue ('12) 22.50 55
  Nos. 57-64 (8) 46.80 2.00

The three wavy lines in design A10 are symbolical of the three waters which separate the principal Danish islands.

See Nos. 85-96. For surcharges and overprints see Nos. 163, 181, J1, J38, O1-O2.

1904-05 Engr.

65 A11 10o scarlet 3.00 15
66 A11 20o blue 11.00 50
67 A11 25o brown ('05) 11.00 1.40
68 A11 50o dull vio ('05) 32.50 26.00
69 A11 100o ocher ('05) 19.00 21.00
  Nos. 65-69 (5) 76.50 49.05

1905-06 Re-engraved

70 A11 5o green 3.25 15
71 A11 10o scarlet ('06) 10.00 15

The re-engraved stamps are much clearer than the originals, and the decoration on the king's left breast has been removed.

1907-12

72 A12 5o green 1.10 15
  a. Imperf.
73 A12 10o red 1.65 15
  a. Imperf.
74 A12 20o indigo 4.75 20
  a. 20o bright blue ('11) 7.25 65
75 A12 25o olive brn 9.00 38
76 A12 35o dp org ('12) 6.50 2.25
77 A12 50o claret 27.50 3.00
78 A12 100o bister brn 55.00 1.75
  Nos. 72-78 (7) 105.50 7.88

Nos. 47, 31 and O9 Surcharged:

35 ØRE
c

35 ØRE FRIMÆRKE
d

Dark Blue Surcharge

1912 Wmk. 112 Perf. 13

79 A6(c) 35o on 16o 11.00 *30.00*
a. Inverted frame 200.00 375.00

Perf. 14x13½

80 A6(c) 35o on 20o 9.00 *25.00*
a. Inverted frame 65.00 125.00

Black Surcharge

81 O1(d) 35o on 32o 18.00 37.50

General Post Office, Copenhagen
A15

1912 Engr. Wmk. 113 Perf. 13

82 A15 5k dark red 300.00 70.00

See Nos. 135, 843.

Perf. 14x14½

1913-30 Typo. Wmk. 114

85 A10 1o dp orange ('14) 38 15
a. Bklt. pane, 2 ea #85, 91 + 2 labels 18.00
86 A10 2o car ('13) 55 15
a. Imperf., pair 195.00 300.00
b. Booklet pane, 4 + 2 labels 24.00
87 A10 3o gray ('13) 1.10 15
88 A10 4o blue ('13) 3.25 15
a. Half used as 2o on cover 1,000.
89 A10 5o dk brown ('21) 55 15
a. Imperf., pair 275.00
b. Booklet pane, 4 + 2 labels 12.50
90 A10 5o lt green ('30) 80 15
a. Booklet pane, 4 + 2 labels 12.50
b. Booklet pane of 50
91 A10 7o apple grn ('26) 1.10 15
a. Booklet pane, 4 + 2 labels 15.00
92 A10 7o dk violet ('30) 4.50 1.25
93 A10 8o gray ('21) 2.75 38
94 A10 10o green ('21) 55 15
a. Imperf., pair 275.00
b. Booklet pane, 4 + 2 labels 32.50
95 A10 10o bister brn ('30) 95 15
a. Booklet pane, 4 + 2 labels 14.00
b. Booklet pane of 50
96 A10 12o violet ('26) 10.50 1.00
Nos. 85-96 (12) 26.98
Set value 3.40

No. 88a was used with No. 97 in Faroe Islands, Jan. 3-23, 1919.

See surcharge and overprint note following #64.

King Christian X
A16 A17

1913-28 Typo. Perf. 14x14½

97 A16 5o green 75 15
a. Booklet pane of 4 10.00
98 A16 7o orange ('18) 1.25 25
99 A16 8o dk gray ('20) 2.25 1.00
100 A16 10o red 95 15
a. Imperf., pair 275.00
b. Booklet pane of 4 10.00
101 A16 12o gray grn ('18) 5.00 4.50
102 A16 15o violet 1.10 15
103 A16 20o dp blue 4.00 15
104 A16 20o brown ('21) 50 15
105 A16 20o red ('26) 1.50 15
106 A16 25o dk brown 4.50 20
107 A16 25o brn & blk ('20) 26.00 1.75
108 A16 25o red ('22) 1.75 25
109 A16 25o yel grn ('25) 1.75 15
110 A16 27o ver & blk ('18) 22.50 30.00
111 A16 30o green & blk ('18) 6.25 75
112 A16 30o orange ('21) 1.50 35
113 A16 30o dk blue ('25) 1.50 30
114 A16 35o orange 7.25 1.50
115 A16 35o yel & blk ('19) 5.00 1.10
116 A16 40o vio & blk ('18) 6.00 85
117 A16 40o gray bl & blk ('20) 12.50 3.00
118 A16 40o dk blue ('22) 2.50 75
119 A16 40o orange ('25) 1.65 28
120 A16 50o claret 17.50 1.40
121 A16 50o claret & blk ('19) 32.50 75
122 A16 50o lt gray ('22) 3.75 15
a. 50o dark gray ('21) 20.00 1.00
123 A16 60o brn & bl ('19) 20.00 1.40
a. 60o brown & ultra ('19) 65.00 6.00
124 A16 60o grn bl ('21) 5.25 50
125 A16 70o brn & grn ('20) 10.50 1.00
126 A16 80o bl grn ('15) 30.00 10.00
127 A16 90o brn & red ('20) 10.00 1.00
128 A16 1k brn & bl ('22) 20.00 85
129 A16 2k gray & cl ('25) 32.50 7.50
130 A16 5k vio & brn ('27) 6.75 3.75
131 A16 10k ver & yel grn ('28) 225.00 30.00
Nos. 97-131 (35) 531.70 106.18

#97 surcharged "2 ORE" is Faroe Islands #1.

Nos. 87 and 98, 89 and 94, 89 and 104, 90 and 95, 97 and 103, 100 and 102 exist se-tenant in coils for use in vending machines.

For surcharges and overprints see Nos. 161-162, 176-177, 182-184, J2-J8, M1-M2, O3-O10.

1913-20 Engr.

132 A17 1k yellow brown 57.50 60
133 A17 2k gray 55.00 2.75
134 A17 5k purple ('20) 13.00 6.00

For overprint see No. O11.

G.P.O. Type of 1912

Perf. 14x14½

1915 Wmk. 114 Engr.

135 A15 5k dark red ('15) 350.00 75.00

Nos. 46 and O10 Surcharged in Black type "c" and:

DANMARK 80 ØRE POSTFRIM.
e

1915 Wmk. 112 Typo. Perf. 13

136 A6 (c) 80o on 12o 30.00 67.50
a. Inverted frame 415.00 500.00
137 O1 (e) 80o on 8o 35.00 75.00
a. "POSTERIM" 65.00 125.00

POSTFRIM.

Newspaper Stamps Surcharged ØRE 27 ØRE

DANMARK

On Issue of 1907

1918 Wmk. 113 Perf. 13

138 N1 27o on 1o olive 85.00 140.00
139 N1 27o on 5o blue 85.00 140.00
140 N1 27o on 7o car 85.00 140.00
141 N1 27o on 10o dp lil 85.00 140.00
142 N1 27o on 68o yel brn 5.25 14.00
143 N1 27o on 5k rose & yel grn 6.00 8.25
144 N1 27o on 10k bis & bl 5.25 12.50
Nos. 138-144 (7) 356.50 594.75

On Issue of 1914-15

Wmk. Multiple Crosses (114)

Perf. 14x14½

145 N1 27o on 1o ol gray 3.00 5.00
146 N1 27o on 5o blue 6.00 10.50
147 N1 27o on 7o rose 2.75 3.75
148 N1 27o on 8o green 3.00 6.25
149 N1 27o on 10o dp lil 2.75 4.00
150 N1 27o on 20o green 2.75 5.00
151 N1 27o on 29o org yel 2.75 4.00
152 N1 27o on 38o orange 30.00 37.50
153 N1 27o on 41o yel brn 6.50 *18.00*
154 N1 27o on 1k bl grn & mar 2.75 3.75
Nos. 145-154 (10) 62.25 97.75

Kronborg Castle — A20

Sonderborg Castle — A21

Roskilde Cathedral — A22

Perf. 14½x14, 14x14½

1920, Oct. 5 Typo.

156 A20 10o red 3.25 38
157 A21 20o slate 3.00 38
158 A22 40o dark brown 12.00 4.50

Reunion of Northern Schleswig with Denmark. See #159-160. For surcharges see #B1-B2.

1921

159 A20 10o green 6.50 32
160 A22 40o dark blue 32.50 5.00

Stamps of 1918 Surcharged in Blue  8

1921-22

161 A16 8o on 7o org ('22) 2.00 1.65
162 A16 8o on 12o gray grn 2.00 3.00

No. 87 Surcharged 8

1921

163 A10 8o on 3o gray 1.80 1.90

Christian X — A23

Christian IV — A24

A25

A26

1924, Dec. 1 Perf. 14x14½

164 A23 10o green 3.00 90
165 A24 10o green 3.00 90
166 A25 10o green 3.00 90
167 A26 10o green 3.00 90
168 A23 15o violet 3.00 90
169 A24 15o violet 3.00 90
170 A25 15o violet 3.00 90
171 A26 15o violet 3.00 90
172 A23 20o dark brown 3.00 90
173 A24 20o dark brown 3.00 90
174 A25 20o dark brown 3.00 90
175 A26 20o dark brown 3.00 90
a.-c. 3 Blocks of 4, #164-175 60.00 75.00
Nos. 164-175 (12) 36.00 10.80

300th anniv. of the Danish postal service.

The sheets of each value are composed of stamps of types A23, A24, A25 and A26, arranged in groups of four as illustrated.

Stamps of 1921-22 Surcharged:

20 20
k

20 ■ 20 ■
l

1926

176 A16 (k) 20o on 30o org 3.25 5.00
177 A16 (l) 20o on 40o dk blue 5.00 4.00

A27

A28

1926, Mar. 11 Perf. 14x14½

178 A27 10o dull green 1.00 15
179 A28 20o dark red 1.25 15
180 A28 30o dark blue 6.00 45
Set value 61

75th anniv. of the introduction of postage stamps in Denmark.

Stamps of 1913-26 Surcharged in Blue or Black

7 No. 181 — **7 7** Nos. 182-184

1926-27 *Perf. 14x14½*
181 A10 7o on 8o gray (Bl) 1.00 2.00
182 A16 7o on 27o ver & blk 3.50 7.50
183 A16 7o on 20o red ('27) 55 40
184 A16 12o on 15o violet 2.50 3.25

Surcharged on Official Stamps of 1914-23

185 O1 (e) 7o on 1o orange 2.75 4.50
186 O1 (e) 7o on 3o gray 6.50 12.50
187 O1 (e) 7o on 4o blue 2.75 7.00
188 O1 (e) 7o on 5o green 47.50 62.50
189 O1 (e) 7o on 10o green 2.75 5.50
190 O1 (e) 7o on 15o violet 3.00 5.50
191 O1 (e) 7o on 20o indigo 12.50 21.00
a. Double surcharge *475.00 475.00*
Nos. 181-191 (11) 85.30 131.65

Caravel A30

Christian X A31

1927 **Typo.** *Perf. 14x14½*
192 A30 15o red 2.25 15
193 A30 20o gray 3.50 25
194 A30 25o light blue 38 15
195 A30 30o ocher 38 15
196 A30 35o red brown 8.25 25
197 A30 40o yel green 8.25 15
Nos. 192-197 (6) 23.01
Set value 80

See #232-238J. For surcharges & overprints see #244-245, 269-272, Q12-Q14, Q19-Q25.

1930, Sept. 26
210 A31 5o apple grn 1.50 15
a. Booklet pane, 4 + 2 labels 17.50
211 A31 7o violet 5.50 1.75
212 A31 8o dk gray 22.50 6.50
213 A31 10o yel brn 4.00 18
a. Booklet pane, 4 + 2 labels 25.00
214 A31 15o red 8.25 15
215 A31 20o lt gray 20.00 1.75
216 A31 25o lt blue 7.75 24
217 A31 30o yel buff 8.25 1.40
218 A31 35o red brown 8.25 2.50
219 A31 40o dp green 8.25 75
Nos. 210-219 (10) 94.25 15.37

60th birthday of King Christian X.

Wavy Lines and Numeral of Value — A32

Type of 1905-12 Issue
Engraved, Redrawn

1933-40 **Unwmk.** *Perf. 13*
220 A32 1o gray blk 15 15
221 A32 2o scarlet 15 15
222 A32 4o blue 32 15
223 A32 5o yel grn 1.10 15
a. 5o gray green 20.00 20.00
b. Tête bêche pair 10.00 10.00
c. Booklet pane of 4 8.00
d. Bklt. pane, 1 #223a, 3 #B6 25.00
224 A32 5o rose lake ('38) 15 15
a. Booklet pane of 4 32
b. Booklet pane of 10 65
224C A32 6o orange ('40) 25 15
225 A32 7o violet 2.00 15
226 A32 7o yel grn ('38) 1.25 18
226A A32 7o lt brown ('40) 25 15
227 A32 8o gray 52 15
227A A32 8o yellow grn ('40) 30 15
228 A32 10o yellow org 11.50 15
a. Tête bêche pair 40.00 20.00
b. Booklet pane of 4 57.50
229 A32 10o lt brown ('37) 10.00 15
a. Booklet pane of 4 50.00
b. Booklet pane of 4, 1 #229, 3 #B7 22.50
230 A32 10o violet ('38) 52 15
a. Booklet pane of 4 2.50
b. Bklt. pane, 2 #230, 2 #B10 4.00
Nos. 220-230 (14) 28.46
Set value 1.15

The stamps of 1905-12 were typographed. They had a solid background with groups of small hearts below the heraldic lions in the upper corners and below "DA" and "RK" of "DANMARK." The numerals of value were enclosed in single-lined ovals.

The 1933-40 stamps are line-engraved and have a background of crossed lines. The hearts have been removed and the numerals of value are now in double-lined ovals. Two types exist of some values.

The 1ö, No. 220, was issued on fluorescent paper in 1969.

No. 230 with wide margins is from booklet pane No. 230b.

Of the tête bêche pairs, those with gutters are twice as plentiful. Values are for the less costly.

Surcharges of 20, 50 & 60öre on #220, 224 and 224C are listed as Faroe Islands #2-3, 5-6.

See Nos. 318, 333, 382, 416, 437-437A, 493-498, 629, 631, 688-695, 793-795, 883-890. For overprints and surcharges see Nos. 257, 263, 267-268, 355-356, Q15-Q17, Q31, Q43.

Certain Tête Bêche pairs of 1938-55 issues which reached the market in 1971, and were not regularly issued, are not listed. This group comprises 24 different major-number vertical pairs of types A32, A47, A61 and SP3 (13 with gutters, 11 without), and pairs of some minor numbers and shades. They were removed from booklet pane sheets.

Type of 1927 Issue
Type I

Type I- Two columns of squares between sail and left frame line.

1933-34 **Engr.** *Perf. 13*
232 A30 20o gray 8.50 15
233 A30 25o blue 42.50 6.00
234 A30 25o brown ('34) 27.50 15
235 A30 30o orange yel 1.25 80
236 A30 30o blue ('34) 1.25 15
237 A30 35o violet 65 15
238 A30 40o yellow grn 3.25 15
Nos. 232-238 (7) 84.90 7.55

Type II

Type II- One column of squares between sail and left frame line.

1933-40
238A A30 15o deep red 3.50 15
k. Booklet pane of 4 22.50
l. Bklt. pane, 1 #238A, 3 #B8 35.00
238B A30 15o yel grn ('40) 8.50 15
238C A30 20o gray blk ('39) 4.75 15
238D A30 20o red ('40) 90 15
238E A30 25o dp brown ('39) 90 15
238F A30 30o blue ('39) 3.50 25
238G A30 30o orange ('40) 75 15
238H A30 35o violet ('40) 1.10 30
238I A30 40o yel grn ('39) 10.00 18
238J A30 40o blue ('40) 1.25 15
Nos. 238A-238J (10) 35.15
Set value 1.30

Nos. 232-238J, engraved, have crosshatched background. Nos. 192-197, typographed, have solid background.

No. 238A surcharged 20 ore is listed as Faroe Islands No. 4.

See note on surcharges and overprints following No. 197.

King Christian X — A33

1934-41 *Perf. 13*
239 A33 50o gray 1.25 15
240 A33 60o blue grn 2.75 15
240A A33 75o dk blue ('41) 52 15
241 A33 1k lt brown 3.50 15
242 A33 2k dull red 7.50 40
243 A33 5k violet 11.00 1.75
Nos. 239-243 (6) 26.52 2.75
Set, never hinged 40.00

For overprints see Nos. Q26-Q27.

Nos. 233, 235 Surcharged in Black — **4**

1934, June 9
244 A30 4o on 25o blue 50 20
245 A30 10o on 30o org yel 3.25 1.25
Set, never hinged 4.75

"The Ugly Duckling" A34

Andersen A35

"The Little Mermaid" — A36

1935, Oct. 4 *Perf. 13*
246 A34 5o lt green 3.50 15
a. Tête bêche pair 15.00 9.00
b. Booklet pane of 4 17.50
247 A35 7o dull vio 3.00 50
248 A36 10o orange 5.50 15
a. Tête bêche pair 22.50 15.00
b. Booklet pane of 4 30.00
249 A35 15o red 13.00 15
a. Tête bêche pair 45.00 24.00
b. Booklet pane of 4 75.00
250 A35 20o gray 12.00 40
251 A35 30o dl bl 3.50 20
Nos. 246-251 (6) 40.50
Set value 1.25
Set, never hinged 67.50

Centenary of the publication of the earliest installment of Hans Christian Andersen's "Fairy Tales."

Note on tête bêche pair values after No. 230 applies to Nos. 246a, 248a and 249a.

Nikolai Church — A37

Hans Tausen — A38

Ribe Cathedral — A39

1936 *Perf. 13*
252 A37 5o green 1.65 15
a. Booklet pane of 4 17.50
253 A37 7o violet 1.65 50
254 A38 10o lt brown 2.25 15
a. Booklet pane of 4 18.00
255 A38 15o dull rose 3.25 15
256 A39 30o blue 14.00 28
Nos. 252-256 (5) 22.80
Set value 1.00
Set, never hinged 40.00

400th anniv. of the Church Reformation in Denmark.

No. 229 Overprinted in Blue — **K.P.K. 17.-26. SEPT. 19 37**

1937, Sept. 17
257 A32 10o lt brown 1.90 1.90
Never hinged 2.50

Jubilee Exhib. held by the Copenhagen Phil. Club on their 50th anniv. The stamps were on sale at the Exhib. only, each holder of a ticket of admission (1k) being entitled to purchase 20 stamps at face value; of a season ticket (5k), 100 stamps.

Yacht and Summer Palace, Marselisborg A40

Christian X in Streets of Copenhagen A41

Equestrian Statue of Frederik V and Amalienborg Palace — A42

1937, May 15 *Perf. 13*
258 A40 5o green 1.75 22
a. Booklet pane of 4 10.50
259 A41 10o brown 1.75 15
a. Booklet pane of 4 10.50
260 A42 15o scarlet 1.75 15
a. Booklet pane of 4 12.00
261 A41 30o blue 15.00 1.25
Set, never hinged 30.00

25th anniv. of the accession to the throne of King Christian X.

Emancipation Column, Copenhagen — A43

1938, June 20 *Perf. 13*
262 A43 15o scarlet 75 15
Never hinged 1.25

150th anniversary of the abolition of serfdom in Denmark.

No. 223 Overprinted in Red on Alternate Stamps — **D.F.U. FRIM-UDST. 19 38**

1938, Sept. 2
263 A32 5o yellow grn, pair 3.50 5.25
Never hinged 4.75

10th Danish Philatelic Exhibition.

Bertel Thorvaldsen A44

Statue of Jason A45

1938, Nov. 17 **Engr.** *Perf. 13*
264 A44 5o rose lake 55 15
265 A45 10o purple 55 15
266 A44 30o dark blue 1.90 28
Set value 42
Set, never hinged 5.00

The return to Denmark in 1838 of Bertel Thorvaldsen, Danish sculptor.

Stamps of 1933-39 Surcharged with New Values in Black:

6 (a) — **15** (b) — **20** (c)

1940
267 A32 (a) 6o on 7o yel grn 20 22
268 A32 (a) 6o on 8o gray 18 15
269 A30 (b) 15o on 40o #238 1.25 3.00
270 A30 (b) 15o on 40o #238I 1.25 65
271 A30 (c) 20o on 15o dp red 1.40 15
272 A30 (b) 40o on 30o #238F 1.25 22
Nos. 267-272 (6) 5.53 4.39
Set, never hinged 7.00

Bering's Ship — A46

1941, Nov. 27 Engr. *Perf. 13*

277 A46 10o dk violet 35 15
278 A46 20o red brown 75 25
279 A46 40o dk blue 45 32
Set, never hinged 1.85

200th anniv. of the death of Vitus Bering, explorer.

King Christian X — A47

1942-46 Unwmk. *Perf. 13*

280 A47 10o violet 15 15
281 A47 15o yel grn 35 15
282 A47 20o red 35 15
283 A47 25o brown ('43) 60 15
284 A47 30o orange ('43) 45 15
285 A47 35o brt red vio ('44) 45 15
286 A47 40o blue ('43) 45 15
286A A47 45o ol brn ('46) 60 15
286B A47 50o gray ('45) 90 15
287 A47 60o bluish grn ('44) 75 15
287A A47 75o dk blue ('46) 60 15
Nos. 280-287A (11) 5.65
Set value 82
Set, never hinged 6.75

For overprints see Nos. O28-O30.

Round Tower — A48

Condor Plane — A49

1942, Nov. 27

288 A48 10o violet 15 15
Never hinged 16

300th anniv. of the Round Tower, Copenhagen.
For surcharge see No. B14.

1943, Oct. 29

289 A49 20o red 18 15
Never hinged 20

25th anniv. of the Danish Aviation Company (Det Danske Luftfartsselskab).

Ejby Church — A50

Designs: 15ö, Oesterlars Church. 20ö, Hvidbjerg Church.

1944 Engr. *Perf. 13*

290 A50 10o violet 16 15
291 A50 15o yellow grn 22 35
292 A50 20o red 16 15
Never hinged 60

Ole Roemer A53

Christian X A54

1944, Sept. 25

293 A53 20o henna brown 18 15
Never hinged 20

300th anniv. of the birth of Ole Roemer, astronomer.

1945, Sept. 26

294 A54 10o lilac 15 15
295 A54 20o red 20 15
296 A54 40o deep blue 40 25
Set value 45
Never hinged 85

75th birthday of King Christian X.

Catalogue values for unused stamps in this section, from this point to the end of the section, are for Never Hinged items.

Small State Seal — A55

Tycho Brahe — A56

1946-47 Unwmk. *Perf. 13*

297 A55 1k brown 85 15
298 A55 2k red ('47) 70 15
299 A55 5k dull blue 1.25 15
Set value 16

Nos. 297-299 issued on ordinary and fluorescent paper.
See Nos. 395-400, 441A-444D, 499-506, 644-650, 716-720A, 804-815. For overprints see Nos. O35, O40, O46-O48.

1946, Dec. 14 Engr.

300 A56 20o dark red 18 15

400th anniv. of the birth of Tycho Brahe, astronomer.

First Danish Locomotive A57

Modern Steam Locomotive A58

Diesel Locomotive — A59

1947, June 27

301 A57 15o steel blue 25 25
302 A58 20o red 25 15
303 A59 40o deep blue 85 55

Cent. of the inauguration of the Danish State Railways.

Jacobsen — A60

Frederik IX — A61

1947, Nov. 10 *Perf. 13*

304 A60 20o dark red 28 15

60th anniv. of the death of Jacob Christian Jacobsen, founder of the Glyptothek Art Museum, Copenhagen.

1948-50 Unwmk. *Perf. 13*

Three types among 15ö, 20ö, 30ö:
I- Background of horizontal lines. No outline at left for cheek and ear. King's uniform textured in strong lines.
II- Background of vertical and horizontal lines. Contour of cheek and ear at left. Uniform same.
III- Background and facial contour lines as in II. Uniform lines double and thinner.

306 A61 15(o) green (II) 2.50 15
a. Type III ('49) 1.65 15
307 A61 20(o) dk red (I) 1.10 15
a. Type III ('49) 1.10 15
308 A61 25(o) lt brown 1.50 15
309 A61 30(o) org (II) 15.00 15
a. Type III ('50) 17.00 15
310 A61 40(o) dl blue ('49) 4.25 40
311 A61 45(o) olive ('50) 1.65 15
312 A61 50(o) gray ('49) 1.65 15
313 A61 60(o) grnsh bl ('50) 2.50 15
314 A61 75(o) lil rose ('50) 1.25 15
Nos. 306-314 (9) 31.40
Set value 1.00

See Nos. 319-326, 334-341, 354. For surcharges see Nos. 357-358, 370, B20, B61-B62, O32-O34, O36-O39.

Legislative Assembly, 1849 — A62

Symbol of UPU — A63

1949, June 5

315 A62 20o red brown 30 15

Centenary of the adoption of the Danish constitution.

1949, Oct. 9

316 A63 40o dull blue 65 50

75th anniv. of the UPU.

Kalundborg Radio Station and Masts — A64

1950, Apr. 1 Engr. *Perf. 13*

317 A64 20o brown red 40 15

25th anniv. of radio broadcasting in Denmark.

Types of 1933-50

1950-51 Unwmk. *Perf. 13*

318 A32 10o green 15 15
319 A61 15(o) lilac 70 15
b. 15(o) gray lilac 3.25 15
320 A61 20(o) lt brown 40 15
321 A61 25(o) dark red 3.50 15
322 A61 35(o) gray grn ('51) 1.00 15
323 A61 40(o) gray 1.00 15
324 A61 50(o) dark blue 3.25 15
325 A61 55(o) brown ('51) 18.00 1.65
326 A61 70(o) deep green 3.00 15
Nos. 318-326 (9) 31.00
Set value 2.15

Warship of 1701 A65

Oersted A66

1951, Feb. 26 Engr. *Perf. 13*

327 A65 25o dark red 48 15
328 A65 50o deep blue 2.75 75

250th anniv. of the foundation of the Naval Officers' College.

1951, Mar. 9 Unwmk.

329 A66 50o blue 1.40 45

Cent. of the death of Hans Christian Oersted, physicist.

Post Chaise ("Ball Post") A67

Marine Rescue A68

1951, Apr. 1 *Perf. 13*

330 A67 15o purple 75 15
331 A67 25o henna brown 75 15

Cent. of Denmark's 1st postage stamp.

1952, Mar. 26

332 A68 25o red brown 55 20

Cent. of the foundation of the Danish Lifesaving Service.

Types of 1933-50

1952-53 *Perf. 13*

333 A32 12o lt yel grn 32 15
334 A61 25(o) lt blue 1.10 15
335 A61 30(o) brown red 1.10 15
336 A61 50(o) aqua ('53) 52 15
337 A61 60(o) dp blue ('53) 65 15
338 A61 65(o) gray ('53) 65 15
339 A61 80(o) orange ('53) 65 15
340 A61 90(o) olive ('53) 2.75 15
341 A61 95(o) red org ('53) 1.10 22
Nos. 333-341 (9) 8.84
Set value 78

Jelling Runic Stone — A69

Designs: 15o, Vikings' camp, Trelleborg. 20o, Church of Kalundborg. 30o, Nyborg castle. 60o, Goose tower, Vordinborg.

1953-56 *Perf. 13*

342 A69 10o dp green 15 15
343 A69 15o lt rose vio 15 15
344 A69 20o brown 15 15
345 A69 30o red ('54) 15 15
346 A69 60o dp blue ('54) 40 16

Designs: 10o, Manor house, Spottrup. 15o, Hammershus castle ruins. 20o, Copenhagen stock exchange. 30o, Statue of Frederik V, Amalienborg. 60o, Soldier statue at Fredericia.

347 A69 10o green ('54) 15 15
348 A69 15o lilac ('55) 15 15
349 A69 20o brown ('55) 15 15
350 A69 30o red ('55) 15 15
351 A69 60o deep blue ('56) 70 16
Nos. 342-351 (10) 2.30
Set value 84

1000th anniv. of the Kingdom of Denmark. Each stamp represents a different century.

Telegraph Equipment of 1854 A70

Frederik V A71

1954, Feb. 2 *Perf. 13*

352 A70 30o red brown 48 15

Cent. of the telegraph in Denmark.

1954, Mar. 31

353 A71 30o dark red 65 15

200th anniv. of the founding of the Royal Academy of Fine Arts.

Type of 1948-50

1955, Apr. 27

354 A61 25o lilac 20 15

Nos. 224C and 226A Surcharged with New Value in Black. Nos. 307 and 321 Surcharged with New Value and 4 Bars

1955-56

355 A32 5o on 6o org 15 15
356 A32 5o on 7o lt brn 15 15
357 A61 30(o) on 20(o) dk red (I) 24 15
  a. Type III 42 15
  b. Double surcharge 400.00 400.00
358 A61 30(o) on 25(o) dk red ('56) 55 15
  a. Double surcharge
  Set value 36

Soren Kierkegaard — A72

1955, Nov. 11 **Unwmk.**
359 A72 30o dark red 35 15

100th anniv. of the death of Sören Kierkegaard, philosopher and theologian.

Ellehammer's Plane — A73

1956, Sept. 12 **Engr.**
360 A73 30o dull red 60 15

50th anniv. of the 1st flight made by Jacob Christian Hansen Ellehammer in a heavier-than-air craft.

Northern Countries Issue

Whooper Swans — A74

1956, Oct. 30 ***Perf. 13***
361 A74 30o rose red 3.00 22
362 A74 60o ultramarine 1.75 65

Issued to emphasize the close bonds among the northern countries: Denmark, Finland, Iceland, Norway and Sweden.

Prince's Palace A75

Harvester A76

Design: 60ö, Sun God's Chariot.

1957, May 15 **Unwmk.**
363 A75 30o dull red 1.10 15
364 A75 60o dark blue 1.10 32

150th anniv. of the National Museum.

1958, Sept. 4 **Engr.** ***Perf. 13***
365 A76 30o fawn 20 15

Centenary of the Royal Veterinary and Agricultural College.

Frederik IX — A77

Ballet Dancer — A78

1959, Mar. 11
366 A77 30o rose red 60 15
367 A77 35o rose lilac 35 35
368 A77 60o ultra 35 20

King Frederik's 60th birthday.

1959, May 16
369 A78 35o rose lilac 22 15

Danish Ballet and Music Festival, May 17-31. See Nos. 401, 422.

No. 319 Surcharged

1960, Apr. 7
370 A61 30o on 15o purple 22 15

Issued to publicize World Refugee Year, July 1, 1959-June 30, 1960.

Seeder and Farm — A79

Designs: 30ö, Harvester combine. 60ö, Plow.

1960, Apr. 28 **Engr.** ***Perf. 13***
371 A79 12o green 15 15
372 A79 30o dull red 24 15
373 A79 60o dk blue 50 22

King Frederik IX and Queen Ingrid — A80

1960, May 24 **Unwmk.**
374 A80 30o dull red 45 15
375 A80 60o blue 45 18

25th anniversary of the marriage of King Frederik IX and Queen Ingrid.

Bascule Light — A81

Finsen — A82

1960, June 8 **Engr.**
376 A81 30o dull red 28 15

400th anniv. of the Lighthouse Service.

1960, Aug. 1 ***Perf. 13***
377 A82 30o dark red 28 15

Centenary of the birth of Dr. Niels R. Finsen, physician and scientist.

Nursing Mother — A83

DC-8 Airliner — A84

1960, Aug. 16 **Unwmk.**
378 A83 60o ultra 65 20

10th meeting of the regional committee for Europe of WHO, Copenhagen, Aug. 16-20.

Europa Issue, 1960
Common Design Type

1960, Sept. 19 ***Perf. 13***
Size: 28x21mm
379 CD3 60o ultra 70 20

1961, Feb. 24
380 A84 60o ultra 65 20

10th anniv. of the Scandinavian Airlines System, SAS.

Landscape — A85

Frederik IX — A86

1961, Apr. 21 ***Perf. 13***
381 A85 30o copper brown 20 15

50th anniv. of Denmark's Society of Nature Lovers.

Fluorescent Paper
as well as ordinary paper, was used in printing many definitive and commemorative stamps, starting in 1962. These include No. 220, 224; the 15, 20, 25, 30, 35 (Nos. 386 and 387), 50 and 60ö, 1.20k, 1.50k and 25k definitives of following set, and Nos. 297-299, 318, 318a-318b, 333, 380, 401-427, 429-435, 438-439, 493, 543, 548, B30.
Only fluorescent paper was used for Nos. 436-437, 437A and 440 onward; in semipostals from B31 onward.

1961-63 **Engr.** ***Perf. 13***
382 A32 15o green ('63) 20 15
383 A86 20o brown 52 15
384 A86 25o brown ('63) 25 15
385 A86 30o rose red 65 15
386 A86 35o olive grn 65 50
387 A86 35o rose red ('63) 25 15
388 A86 40o gray 1.00 15
389 A86 50o aqua 65 15
390 A86 60o ultra 85 15
391 A86 70o green 1.65 20
392 A86 80o red orange 1.65 15
393 A86 90o olive bister 4.50 20
394 A86 95o claret ('63) 1.00 70
  Nos. 382-394 (13) 13.82
  Set value 2.15

See Nos. 417-419, 438-441. For overprints see Nos. O41-O42, O44-O45.

State Seal Type of 1946-47

1962-65
395 A55 1.10k lilac ('65) 3.50 60
396 A55 1.20k gray 3.00 15
397 A55 1.25k orange 3.00 15
398 A55 1.30k green ('65) 3.50 30
399 A55 1.50k red lilac 1.75 15
400 A55 25k yellow grn 4.75 15
  Nos. 395-400 (6) 19.50
  Set value 1.25

Dancer Type of 1959 Inscribed "15-31 MAJ"

1962, Apr. 26
401 A78 60o ultra 32 15

Issued to publicize the Danish Ballet and Music Festival, May 15-31.

Old Mill — A87

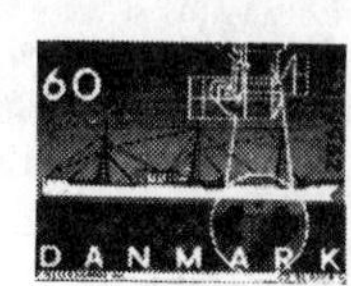

M.S. Selandia — A88

1962, May 10 **Unwmk.** ***Perf. 13***
402 A87 10o red brown 15 15

Cent. of the abolition of mill monopolies.

1962, June 14 **Engr.**
403 A88 60o dark blue 1.65 2.00

M.S. Selandia, the 1st Diesel ship, 50th anniv.

Violin Scroll, Leaves, Lights and Balloon A89

1962, Aug. 31
404 A89 35o rose violet 18 15

150th anniv. of the birth of Georg Carstensen, founder of Tivoli amusement park, Copenhagen.

Cliffs on Moen Island — A90

Germinating Wheat — A91

1962, Nov. 22
405 A90 20o pale brown 15 15

Issued to publicize preservation of natural treasures and landmarks.

1963, Mar. 21 **Engr.**
406 A91 35o fawn 22 15

FAO "Freedom from Hunger" campaign.

Railroad Wheel, Tire Tracks, Waves and Swallow — A92

Sailing Vessel, Coach, Postilions and Globe — A93

1963, May 14 **Unwmk.** ***Perf. 13***
407 A92 15o green 18 15

Inauguration of the "Bird Flight Line" railroad link between Denmark and Germany.

1963, May 27
408 A93 60o dark blue 45 18

Cent. of the 1st Intl. Postal Conf., Paris, 1863.

Niels Bohr and Atom Diagram — A94

Early Public School Drawn on Slate — A95

1963, Nov. 21 **Engr.**

409 A94 35o red brown 28 15
410 A94 60o dark blue 55 15
Set value 18

50th anniv. of Prof. Niels Bohr's (1885-1962) atom theory.

1964, June 19 **Unwmk.** ***Perf. 13***

411 A95 35o red brown 18 15

150th anniversary of the royal decrees for the public school system.

Fish and Chart — A96

Danish Watermarks and Perforations — A97

1964, Sept. 7 **Engr.**

412 A96 60o violet blue 35 18

Conference of the International Council for the Exploration of the Sea, Copenhagen.

1964, Oct. 10 ***Perf. 13***

413 A97 35o pink 25 15

25th anniv. of Stamp Day and to publicize the Odense Stamp Exhibition, Oct. 10-11.

Landscape — A98

Calculator, Ledger and Inkwell — A99

1964, Nov. 12 **Engr.**

414 A98 25o brown 15 15

Issued to publicize preservation of natural treasures and landmarks.

1965, Mar. 8 **Unwmk.**

415 A99 15o lt olive grn 15 15

Centenary of the first Business School in Denmark.

Types of 1933 and 1961

1965, May 15 **Engr.** ***Perf. 13***

416 A32 25o apple green 22 15
417 A86 40o brown 22 15
418 A86 50o rose red 30 15
419 A86 80o ultra 85 15
Set value 25

For overprints see Nos. Q41-Q42.

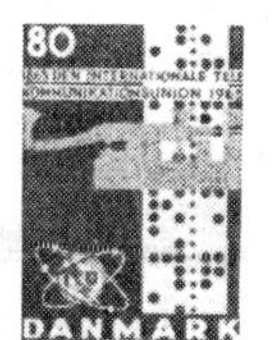
ITU Emblem, Telegraph Key, Teletype Paper A100

Carl Nielsen (1865-1931), Composer A101

1965, May 17

420 A100 80o dark blue 38 15

Cent. of the ITU.

1965, June 9 **Engr.**

421 A101 50o brown red 18 15

Dancer Type of 1959 Inscribed "15-31 MAJ"

1965, Sept. 23

422 A78 50o rose red 25 15

Issued to publicize the Danish Ballet and Music Festival, May 15-31.

Bogo Windmill A102

Mylius Dalgas Surveying Wasteland A103

1965, Nov. 10 **Engr.** ***Perf. 13***

423 A102 40o brown 22 15

Issued to publicize the preservation of natural treasures and landmarks.

1966, Feb. 24

424 A103 25o olive green 18 15

Cent. of the Danish Heath Soc. (reclamation of wastelands), founded by Enrico Mylius Dalgas.

Christen Kold (1816-70), Educator — A104

1966, Mar. 29 ***Perf. 13***

425 A104 50o dull red 22 15

Poorhouse, Copenhagen A105

Holte Allée, Bregentved A106

Dolmen (Grave) in Jutland — A107

1966 **Unwmk.**

426 A105 50o dull red 22 15
427 A106 80o dk blue 55 15
428 A107 1.50k dk slate grn 80 15
Set value 32

Nos. 426-428 issued to publicize preservation of national treasures and ancient monuments. Issue dates: 50o, May 12; 80o, June 16; 1.50k, Nov. 24.

George Jensen by Einar Nielsen — A108

Music Bar and Instruments — A109

1966, Aug. 31 **Engr.** ***Perf. 13***

429 A108 80o dark blue 60 15

Centenary of the birth of George Jensen, silversmith.

1967, Jan. 9

430 A109 50o dark red 22 15

Royal Danish Academy of Music, cent.

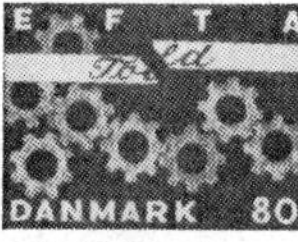
Cogwheels, and Broken Customs Duty Ribbon — A110

1967, Mar. 2

431 A110 80o dark blue 80 15

European Free Trade Association. Industrial tariffs were abolished Dec. 31, 1966, among EFTA members: Austria, Denmark, Finland, Great Britain, Norway, Portugal, Sweden and Switzerland.

Windmill and Medieval Fortress — A111

Designs: 40ö, Ship's rigging and baroque house front. 50ö, Old Town Hall. 80ö, New building construction.

1967 **Engr.** ***Perf. 13***

432 A111 25o green 30 15
433 A111 40o sepia 25 15
434 A111 50o red brown 25 15
435 A111 80o dk blue 75 24

The 800th anniversary of Copenhagen.
Issue dates: Nos. 432-433, Apr. 6; Nos. 434-435, May 11.

Princess Margrethe and Prince Henri — A112

1967, June 10

436 A112 50o red 32 15

Marriage of Crown Princess Margrethe and Prince Henri de Monpezat.

Types of 1933-1961

1967-71 **Engr.** ***Perf. 13***

437 A32 30o dk green 22 15
437A A32 40o orange ('71) 22 15
438 A86 50o brown 85 15
439 A86 60o rose red 85 15
440 A86 80o green 85 15
441 A86 90o ultra 90 15
441A A55 1.20k Prus grn ('71) 2.00 18
442 A55 2.20k orange 3.50 15
443 A55 2.80k gray 3.00 15
444 A55 2.90k rose vio 4.00 15
444A A55 3k dk sl grn ('69) 70 15
444B A55 3.10k plum ('70) 6.00 15
444C A55 4k gray ('69) 1.00 15
444D A55 4.10k olive ('70) 6.00 15
Nos. 437-444D (14) 30.09
Set value 1.15

Issue dates: Nos. 437-441, June 30, 1967; Nos. 442-443, July 8, 1967; No. 444, Apr. 29, 1968; Nos. 444A, 444C, Aug. 28, 1969; Nos. 444B, 444D, Aug. 27, 1970; Nos. 437A, 441A, June 24, 1971.
For overprints see Nos. Q44-Q45.

Sonne — A113

Cross-anchor and Porpoise — A114

1967, Sept. 21

445 A113 60o red 22 15

150th anniv. of the birth of Hans Christian Sonne, pioneer of the cooperative movement in Denmark.

1967, Nov. 9 **Engr.** ***Perf. 13***

446 A114 90o dk blue 45 22

Centenary of the Danish Seamen's Church in Foreign Ports.

Esbjerg Harbor — A115

Koldinghus — A116

1968, Apr. 24

447 A115 30o dk yellow grn 18 15

Centenary of Esbjerg Harbor.

1968, June 13

448 A116 60o copper red 22 15

700th anniversary of Koldinghus Castle.

Shipbuilding Industry A117

Sower A118

Designs: 50o, Chemical industry. 60o, Electric power. 90o, Engineering.

1968, Oct. 24 **Engr.** ***Perf. 13***

449 A117 30o green 22 15
450 A117 50o brown 22 15
451 A117 60o red brown 25 15
452 A117 90o dark blue 40 24
Set value 48

Issued to publicize Danish industries.

1969, Jan. 29

453 A118 30o gray green 18 15

200th anniv. of the Royal Agricultural Society of Denmark.

Five Ancient Ships — A119

Frederik IX — A120

Nordic Cooperation Issue

1969, Feb. 28 **Engr.** ***Perf. 13***

454 A119 60o brown red 1.10 16
455 A119 90o blue 1.65 70

50th anniv. of the Nordic Soc. and cent. of postal cooperation among the northern countries: Denmark, Finland, Iceland, Norway and Sweden. The design is taken from a coin found at the site of Birka, an ancient Swedish town.

1969, Mar. 11

456 A120 50o sepia 20 15
457 A120 60o dull red 20 15
Set value 16

70th birthday of King Frederik IX.

Europa Issue, 1969

Common Design Type

1969, Apr. 28

Size: 28x20mm

458 CD12 90o chalky blue 70 52

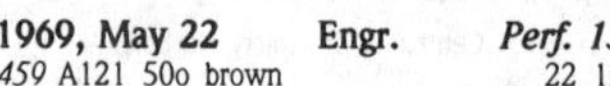
Kronborg Castle — A121 Danish Flag — A122

1969, May 22 **Engr.** ***Perf. 13***
459 A121 50o brown 22 15

50th anniversary of the association of Danes living abroad.

1969, June 12
460 A122 60o bluish blk, red & gray 30 15

750th anniversary of the fall of the Dannebrog (Danish flag) from heaven.

Nexo — A123 Stensen — A124

1969, Aug. 28
461 A123 80o deep green 38 15

Centenary of the birth of Martin Andersen Nexo (1869-1954), novelist.

1969, Sept. 25
462 A124 1k deep brown 42 15

300th anniv. of the publication of Niels Stensen's geological work "On Solid Bodies."

Abstract Design A125 Symbolic Design A126

1969, Nov. 10 **Engr.** ***Perf. 13***
463 A125 60o rose, red & ultra 22 15

1969, Nov. 20
464 A126 30o olive green 20 15

Valdemar Poulsen (1869-1942), electrical engineer and inventor.

Post Office Bank — A127 School Safety Patrol — A128

1970, Jan. 15 **Engr.** ***Perf. 13***
465 A127 60o dk red & org 22 15

50th anniv. of post office banking service.

1970, Feb. 19
466 A128 50o brown 22 15

Issued to publicize road safety.

Candle in Window A129 Deer A130

1970, May 4 **Engr.** ***Perf. 13***
467 A129 50o sl, dull bl & yel 22 15

25th anniv. of liberation from the Germans.

1970, May 28
468 A130 60o yel grn, red & brn 22 15

Tercentenary of Jaegersborg Deer Park.

Elephant Figurehead, 1741 — A131 "The Homecoming" by Povl Christensen — A132

1970, June 15 ***Perf. 11½***
469 A131 30o multicolored 22 20

Royal Naval Museum, tercentenary.

1970, June 15 ***Perf. 13***
470 A132 60o org, dl vio & ol grn 22 15

50th anniversary of the union of North Schleswig and Denmark.

Electromagnet A133

1970, Aug. 13 **Engr.**
471 A133 80o gray green 35 15

150th anniversary of Hans Christian Oersted's discovery of electromagnetism.

Bronze Age Ship — A134

Ships: 50o, Viking shipbuilding, from Bayeux tapestry. 60o, Thuroe schooner with topgallant. 90o, Tanker.

1970, Sept. 24
472 A134 30o ocher & brown 24 20
473 A134 50o brn red & rose brn 24 15
474 A134 60o gray ol & red brn 42 15
475 A134 90o blue grn & ultra 75 60

UN Emblem A135

1970, Oct. 22 **Engr.** ***Perf. 13***
476 A135 90o blue, grn & red 65 48

25th anniversary of the United Nations.

Bertel Thorvaldsen A136 Mathide Fibiger A137

1970, Nov. 19
477 A136 2k slate blue 70 15

Bicentenary of the birth of Bertel Thorvaldsen (1768-1844), sculptor.

1971, Feb. 25
478 A137 80o olive green 38 15

Danish Women's Association centenary.

Refugees A138 Hans Egede A139

1971, Mar. 26 **Engr.** ***Perf. 13***
479 A138 50o brown 24 15
480 A138 60o brown red 35 15
Set value 16

Joint northern campaign for the benefit of refugees.

1971, May 27
481 A139 1k brown 40 15

250th anniversary of arrival of Hans Egede in Greenland and beginning of its colonization.

A140 A141

1971, Oct. 14
482 A140 30o Swimming 24 20
483 A140 50o Gymnastics 24 15
484 A140 60o Soccer 35 15
485 A140 90o Sailing 60 35

1971, Nov. 11 **Engr.** ***Perf. 13***
486 A141 90o dark blue 42 15

Centenary of first lectures given by Georg Brandes (1842-1927), writer and literary critic.

A142 A143

1972, Jan. 27
487 A142 80o slate green 42 15

Centenary of Danish sugar production.

1972, Mar. 11 **Engr.** ***Perf. 13***
488 A143 60o red brown 28 15

Frederik IX (1899-1972).

Abstract Design A144

1972, Mar. 11
489 A144 1.20k brt rose lil, bl gray & brn 60 48

Centenary of the Danish Meteorological Institute.

Nikolai F. S. Grundtvig A145 Locomotive, 1847, Ferry, Travelers A146

1972, May 4 **Engr.** ***Perf. 13***
490 A145 1k sepia 38 20

Nikolai Frederik Severin Grundtvig (1783-1872), theologian and poet.

1972, June 26
491 A146 70o rose red 38 15

125th anniversary of Danish State Railways.

Rebild Hills — A147 "Tinker Turned Politician" — A148

1972, June 26
492 A147 1k bl, sl grn & mar 38 15

Types of 1933-46

1972-78 **Engr.** ***Perf. 13***
493 A32 20o slate bl ('74) 15 15
494 A32 50o sepia ('74) 15 15
a. Bklt. pane of 12 (4 #318, 4 #493, 4 #494) ('85) 2.00
495 A32 60o apple grn ('76) 1.75 15
496 A32 60o gray ('78) 65 35
497 A32 70o red 1.00 15
498 A32 70o apple grn ('77) 15 15
499 A55 2.50k orange 1.65 15
500 A55 2.80k olive ('75) 85 20
501 A55 3.50k lilac 2.00 15
502 A55 4.5k olive 4.50 15
503 A55 6k vio blk ('76) 1.10 15
504 A55 7k red lilac ('78) 1.25 15
505 A55 9k brown ol ('77) 1.75 15
506 A55 10k lemon ('76) 2.00 15
Nos. 493-506 (14) 18.95
Set value 1.50

1972, Sept. 14
507 A148 70o dark red 30 15

250th anniv. of the comedies of Ludvig Holberg (1684-1754) on the Danish stage.

WHO Building, Copenhagen A149

1972, Sept. 14
508 A149 2k bl, blk & lt red brn 75 28

Opening of WHO Building, Copenhagen.

Bridge Across Little Belt — A150 Aeroskobing House c. 1740 — A151

Highway engineering (Diagrams): 60o, Hanstholm Harbor. 70o, Lim Fjord Tunnel. 90o, Knudshoved Harbor.

1972, Oct. 19 Engr. *Perf. 13*

509 A150 40o dk green 20 18
510 A150 60o dk brown 35 15
511 A150 70o dk red 35 15
512 A150 90o dk blue grn 45 20
Set value 50

1972, Nov. 23

Danish Architecture: 60o, East Bornholm farmhouse, 17th century, horiz. 70o, House, Christianshavn, c. 1710. 1.20k, Hvide Sande Farmhouse, c. 1810, horiz.

Size: 20x28mm, 27x20mm

513 A151 40o red, brn & blk 35 24
514 A151 60o blk, vio bl & grn 35 24

Size: 18x37mm, 36x20mm

515 A151 70o red, dk red & blk 42 15
516 A151 1.20k dk brn, red & grn 60 55

Jensen A152

Guard Rails, Cogwheels A153

1973, Feb. 22 Engr. *Perf. 13*

517 A152 90o green 32 15

Centenary of the birth of Johannes Vilhelm Jensen (1873-1950), lyric poet and novelist.

1973, Mar. 22

518 A153 50o sepia 22 15

Centenary of first Danish Factory Act for labor protection.

Abildgaard A154

Rhododendron A155

1973, Mar. 22

519 A154 1k dull blue 38 38

Bicentenary of Royal Veterinary College, Christianshaven, founded by Prof. P. C. Abildgaard.

1973, Apr. 26

Design: 70o, Dronningen of Denmark rose.

520 A155 60o brn, grn & vio 40 15
521 A155 70o dk red, rose & grn 40 15

Centenary of the founding of the Horticultural Society of Denmark.

Nordic Cooperation Issue 1973

Nordic House, Reykjavik A156

1973, June 26 Engr. *Perf. 13*

522 A156 70o multicolored 48 18
523 A156 1k multicolored 1.75 30

A century of postal cooperation among Denmark, Finland, Iceland, Norway and Sweden, and in connection with the Nordic Postal Conference, Reykjavik.

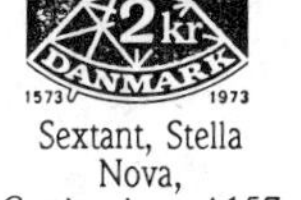

Sextant, Stella Nova, Cassiopeia — A157

St. Mark, from 11th Cent. Book of Dalby — A158

1973, Oct. 18 Engr. *Perf. 13*

524 A157 2k dark blue 70 18

400th anniversary of the publication of "De Nova Stella," by Tycho Brahe.

1973, Oct. 18 Photo. *Perf. 14x14½*

525 A158 120o buff & multi 70 55

300th anniversary of Royal Library.

Devil and Gossips, Fanefjord Church, 1480 — A159

Frescoes: No. 527, Queen Esther and King Ahasuerus, Tirsted Church, c.1400. No. 528, Miraculous Harvest, Jetsmark Church, c.1474. No. 529, Jesus carrying cross, and wearing crown of thorns, Biersted Church, c.1400. No. 530, Creation of Eve, Fanefjord Church, c.1480.

1973, Nov. 28 Engr. *Perf. 13*

Cream Paper

526 A159 70o dk red, yel & grn 1.25 32
527 A159 70o dk red, yel & grn 1.25 32
528 A159 70o dk red, yel & grn 1.25 32
529 A159 70o dk red, yel & grn 1.25 32
530 A159 70o dk red, yel & grn 1.25 32
a. Booklet pane, 2 each #526-530 35.00
b. Strip of 5, #526-530 6.25
Nos. 526-530 (5) 6.25 1.60

Nos. 526-530 printed se-tenant in sheets of 50.

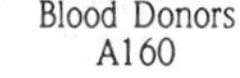

Blood Donors A160

Queen Margrethe A161

1974, Jan. 24

531 A160 90o purple & red 35 15

"Blood Saves Lives."

1974-81 Engr. *Perf. 13*

532 A161 60o brown 45 15
533 A161 60o orange 45 15
534 A161 70o red 45 15
535 A161 70o dk brown 45 15
536 A161 80o green 45 15
537 A161 80o dp brn ('76) 45 15
538 A161 90o red lilac 45 15
539 A161 90o dull red 45 15
540 A161 90o slate grn ('76) 45 15
541 A161 100o dp ultra 55 15
542 A161 100o gray ('75) 55 15
543 A161 100o red ('76) 45 15
544 A161 100o brown ('77) 45 15
a. Bklt. pane of 5 (#544, #494, 2 #493, #318) 1.50
545 A161 110o orange ('78) 45 15
546 A161 120o slate 55 15
547 A161 120o red ('77) 45 15
548 A161 130o ultra ('75) 1.75 60
549 A161 150o vio bl ('78) 70 42
550 A161 180o slate grn ('77) 55 30
551 A161 200o blue ('81) 90 30
Nos. 532-551 (20) 11.40
Set value 3.00

See #630, 632-643. For overprint see #O49.

Pantomime Theater — A162

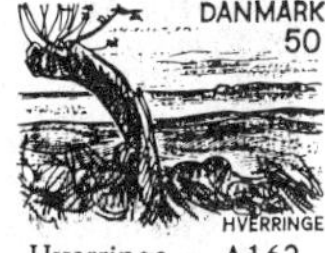

Hverringe — A163

1974, May 16

552 A162 100o indigo 42 20

Cent. of the Pantomime Theater, Tivoli.

1974, June 20 Engr. *Perf. 13*

Views: 60o, Norre Lyndelse, Carl Nielsen's childhood home. 70o, Odense, Hans Chr. Andersen's childhood home. 90o, Hesselagergaard, vert. 120o, Hindsholm.

553 A163 50o brown & multi 42 22
554 A163 60o sl grn & multi 35 25
555 A163 70o red brn & multi 35 25
556 A163 90o dk green & mar 48 15
557 A163 120o red org & dk grn 65 38
Nos. 553-557 (5) 2.25 1.25

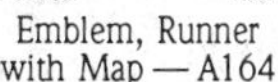

Emblem, Runner with Map — A164

Iris — A165

1974, Aug. 22 Engr. *Perf. 13*

558 A164 70o shown 35 24
559 A164 80o Compass 35 24

World Orienteering Championships 1974.

1974, Sept. 19

560 A165 90o shown 35 15
561 A165 120o Purple orchid 55 25

Copenhagen Botanical Garden centenary.

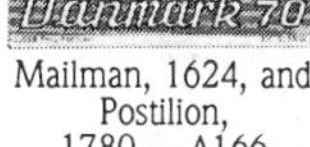

Mailman, 1624, and Postilion, 1780 — A166

Carrier Pigeon — A167

Design: 90o, Balloon and sailing ships.

1974, Oct. 9 Engr. *Perf. 13*

562 A166 70o lemon & dk brn 32 35
563 A166 90o dull grn & sep 40 16
564 A167 120o dark blue 55 30

350th anniv. of Danish PO (70o, 90o) and cent. of UPU (120o).

Souvenir Sheet

Ferslew's Essays, 1849 and 1852 A168

Engraved and Photogravure

1975, Feb. 27 *Perf. 13*

565 A168 Sheet of 4 5.25 6.00
a. 70o Coat of arms 1.25 1.40
b. 80o King Frederik VII 1.25 1.40
c. 90o King Frederik VII 1.25 1.40
d. 100o Mercury 1.25 1.40

HAFNIA 76 Intl. Stamp Exhib., Copenhagen, Aug. 20-29, 1976. Sold for 5k.
See No. 585.

Early Radio Equipment A169

Flora Danica Plate A170

1975, Mar. 20 Engr. *Perf. 13*

566 A169 90o dull red 42 15

Danish broadcasting, 50th anniversary.

1975, May 22

Danish China: 90o, Flora Danica tureen. 130o, Vase and tea caddy, blue fluted china.

567 A170 50o slate grn 30 15
568 A170 90o brown red 60 15
569 A170 130o violet bl 90 90

Church of Moravian Brethren, Christiansfeld A171

Designs: 120o, Kongsgaard farmhouse, Lejre. 150o, Anna Queenstraede, Helsingor, vert.

1975, June 19

570 A171 70o sepia 32 24
571 A171 120o olive grn 1.10 30
572 A171 150o violet blk 52 15

European Architectural Heritage Year 1975.

Andersen A172

Watchman's Square, Abenra A173

Designs: 70o, Numbskull Jack, drawing by Vilh. Pedersen. 130o, The Marshking's Daughter, drawing by L. Frohlich.

1975, Aug. 28 Engr. *Perf. 13*

573 A172 70o brown & blk 55 50
574 A172 90o brn red & dk brn 1.00 15
575 A172 130o blue blk & sep 1.25 1.25

Hans Christian Andersen (1805-75), writer.

1975, Sept. 25

Designs: 90o, Haderslev Cathedral, vert. 100o, Mögeltönder Polder. 120o, Mouth of Vidaaen at Höjer Floodgates.

576 A173 70o multicolored 35 24
577 A173 90o multicolored 42 15
578 A173 100o multicolored 42 15
579 A173 120o multicolored 60 30

European Kingfisher — A174

1975, Oct. 23 Engr. *Perf. 13*

580 A174 50o shown 45 24
581 A174 70o Hedgehog 45 24
582 A174 90o Cats 45 15
583 A174 130o Avocets 85 75
584 A174 200o Otter 70 16
Nos. 580-584 (5) 2.90 1.54

Protected animals, and for the centenary of the Danish Society for the Prevention of Cruelty to Animals (90ő).

HAFNIA Type of 1974
Souvenir Sheet

1975, Nov. 20 Engr. & Photo.

585 A168 Sheet of 4 2.75 3.50
a. 50o buff & brown, No. 2 65 85
b. 70o buff, brown & blue, No. 1 65 85
c. 90o buff, blue & brown, No. 11 65 85
d. 130o olive, brown & buff, No. 19 65 85

HAFNIA 76 Intl. Stamp Exhib., Copenhagen, Aug. 20-29, 1976. Sold for 5k.

Copenhagen, Center — A175

View from Round Tower — A176

Copenhagen, Views: 100o, Central Station, interior. 130o, Harbor.

1976, Mar. 25 Engr. *Perf. 12½*

586 A175 60o multicolored 52 20
587 A176 80o multicolored 52 15
588 A176 100o multicolored 32 15
589 A175 130o multicolored 1.50 1.50

Postilion, by Otto Bache A177

Emil Chr. Hansen, Physiologist, in Laboratory A178

1976, June 17 Engr. *Perf. 12½*

590 A177 130o multicolored 1.25 1.25

Souvenir Sheet

591 A177 130o multicolored 7.00 8.25

HAFNIA 76 Intl. Stamp Exhib., Copenhagen, Aug. 20-29. No. 591 contains one stamp similar to No. 590 with design continuous into sheet margin. Sheet shows painting "A String of Horses Outside an Inn" of which No. 590 shows a detail. Sheet sold for 15k including exhibition ticket.

1976, Sept. 23 Engr. *Perf. 13*

592 A178 100o orange red 38 15

Carlsberg Foundation (art and science), centenary.

Glass Blower Molding Glass — A179

Five Water Lilies — A180

Danish Glass Production: 80o, Finished glass removed from pipe. 130o, Glass cut off from foot. 150o, Glass blown up in mold.

1976, Nov. 18 Engr. *Perf. 13*

593 A179 60o slate 20 18
594 A179 80o dk brown 25 18
595 A179 130o dk blue 70 65
596 A179 150o red brown 52 15

Photogravure and Engraved

1977, Feb. 2 *Perf. 12½*

597 A180 100o brt green & multi 45 22
598 A180 130o ultra & multi 1.40 1.25

Nordic countries cooperation for protection of the environment and 25th Session of Nordic Council, Helsinki, Feb. 19.

Road Accident — A181

Allinge — A182

1977, Mar. 24 Engr. *Perf. 12½*

599 A181 100o brown red 35 15

Road Safety Traffic Act, May 1, 1977.

1977, May 2 Engr. *Perf. 12½*

Europa: 1.30k, View, Ringsted.

600 A182 1k dull red 50 25
601 A182 1.30k dk blue 2.50 3.00

Kongeaen — A183

Hammers and Horseshoes — A184

Landscapes, Southern Jutland: 90o, Skallingen. 150o, Torskind. 200o, Jelling.

1977, June 30 Engr. *Perf. 12½*

602 A183 60o multicolored 85 75
603 A183 90o multicolored 40 24
604 A183 150o multicolored 52 30
605 A183 200o multicolored 60 18

See Nos. 616-619, 655-658, 666-669.

1977, Sept. 22 Engr. *Perf. 12½*

Designs: 1k, Chisel, square and plane. 1.30k, Trowel, ceiling brush and folding ruler.

606 A184 80o dk brown 32 25
607 A184 1k red 40 15
608 A184 1.30k violet bl 70 32

Danish crafts.

Globe Flower — A185

Handball — A186

Endangered Flora: 1.50k, Cnidium dubium.

1977, Nov. 17 Engr. *Perf. 12½*

609 A185 1k multicolored 42 15
610 A185 1.50k multicolored 90 55

1978, Jan. 19 *Perf. 12½*

611 A186 1.20k red 32 15

Men's World Handball Championships.

Christian IV, Frederiksborg Castle A187

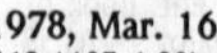

Frederiksborg Museum A188

1978, Mar. 16

612 A187 1.20k brown red 42 15
613 A188 1.80k black 70 28

Frederiksborg Museum, centenary.

Europa Issue

Jens Bang's House, Aalborg A189

Frederiksborg Castle, Ground Plan and Elevation A190

1978, May 11 Engr. *Perf. 12½*

614 A189 1.20k red 28 15
615 A190 1.50k dk bl & vio bl 85 60

Landscape Type of 1977

Landscapes, Central Jutland: 70o, Kongenshus Memorial Park. 120o, Post Office, Old Town in Aarhus. 150o, Lignite fields, Soby. 180o, Church wall, Stadil Church.

1978, June 15 Engr. *Perf. 12½*

616 A183 70o multicolored 25 18
617 A183 120o multicolored 45 15
618 A183 150o multicolored 55 42
619 A183 180o multicolored 60 35

Boats in Harbor — A191

Edible Morel — A192

Danish fishing industry: 1k, Eel traps. 1.80k, Boats in berth. 2.50k, Drying nets.

1978, Sept. 7 Engr. *Perf. 12½*

620 A191 70o olive gray 42 20
621 A191 1k redsh brown 42 15
622 A191 1.80k slate 42 20
623 A191 2.50k sepia 90 30

1978, Nov. 16 Engr. *Perf. 12½*

Design: 1.20k, Satan's mushroom.

624 A192 1k sepia 35 32
625 A192 1.20k dull red 48 32

Telephones — A193

1979, Jan. 25 Engr. *Perf. 12½*

626 A193 1.20k dull red 42 15

Centenary of Danish telephone.

University Seal A194

Pentagram: University Faculties A195

1979, Apr. 5 Engr. *Perf. 12½*

627 A194 1.30k vermilion 45 15
628 A195 1.60k dk vio blue 60 55

University of Copenhagen, 500th anniv.

Types of 1933-1974

1979-82 Engr. *Perf. 13*

629 A32 80o green 22 15
630 A161 90o slate 1.00 90
631 A32 100o dp green ('81) 28 15
632 A161 110o brown 30 15
a. Bklt. pane of 5 (#493-494, #632, 2 #318) ('79) 1.00
633 A161 130o red 45 15
a. Bklt. pane of 10, 2 each #494, 629, 632, 4 #633 ('79) 4.00
634 A161 130o brown ('81) 55 24
635 A161 140o red org ('80) 90 70
636 A161 150o red org ('81) 60 45
637 A161 160o ultra 70 55
638 A161 160o red ('81) 52 15
a. Bklt. pane of 14 (2 each #318, 634, 638, 8 #494) 8.00
639 A161 180o ultra ('80) 70 60
640 A161 210o gray ('80) 90 75
641 A161 230o ol grn ('81) 90 28
642 A161 250o blue grn ('81) 90 35
643 A55 2.80k dull grn 70 15
644 A55 3.30k brn red ('81) 70 20
645 A55 3.50k grnsh bl ('82) 75 45
646 A55 4.30k brn red ('80) 1.25 75
647 A55 4.70k rose lil ('81) 1.25 90
648 A55 8k orange 1.75 15
649 A55 12k red brn ('81) 2.50 45
650 A55 14k dk red brn ('82) 3.00 55
Nos. 629-650 (22) 20.82 9.17

A196

A197

Europa: 1.30k, Mail cart, 1785. 1.60k, Morse key and amplifier.

1979, May 10 *Perf. 12½*

651 A196 1.30k red 35 15
652 A196 1.60k dark blue 75 75

1979, June 14 Engr. *Perf. 13*

Viking Art: 1.10k, Gripping beast pendant. 2k, Key with gripping beast design.

653 A197 1.10k sepia 40 15
654 A197 2k grnsh gray 60 15

Landscape Type of 1977

Landscapes, Northern Jutland: 80o, Mols Bjerge. 90o, Orslev Kloster. 200o, Trans. 280o, Bovbjerg.

1979, Sept. 6 Engr. *Perf. 12½*

655 A183 80o multicolored 25 24
656 A183 90o multicolored 60 48
657 A183 200o multicolored 45 15
658 A183 280o multicolored 65 45

Adam Oehlenschläger (1799-1850), Poet and Dramatist — A198

1979, Oct, 4 Engr. *Perf. 13*

659 A198 1.30k dk carmine 40 15

Score, Violin, Dancing Couple — A199

Ballerina — A200

1979, Nov. 8 Engr. *Perf. 13x12½*
660 A199 1.10k brown 35 18
661 A200 1.60k ultra 65 30

Jacob Gade (b. 1879), composer; August Bournoville (1805-1879), ballet master.

Royal Mail Guards' Office, Copenhagen, 1779 — A201

1980, Feb. 14 Engr. *Perf. 13*
662 A201 1.30k brown red 40 15

National Postal Service, 200th anniversary.

Symbols of Occupation, Health and Education — A202

1980, May 5 Engr. *Perf. 13*
663 A202 1.60k dark blue 55 38

World Conference of the UN Decade for Women, Copenhagen, July 14-30.

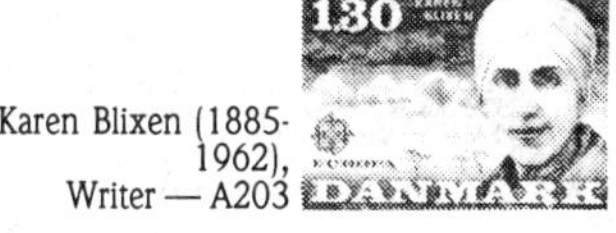

Karen Blixen (1885-1962), Writer — A203

Europa: 1.60k, August Krogh (1874-1949), physiologist.

1980, May 5
664 A203 1.30k red 35 15
665 A203 1.60k blue 65 45

Landscape Type of 1977

Landscapes, Northern Jutland: 80o, Viking ship burial grounds, Lindholm Hoje. 110o, Lighthouse, Skagen, vert. 200o, Boreglum Monastery. 280o, Fishing boats, Vorupor Beach.

1980, June 19 Engr. *Perf. 13*
666 A183 80o multicolored 35 25
667 A183 110o multicolored 35 25
668 A183 200o multicolored 55 15
669 A183 280o multicolored 90 52

Nordic Cooperation Issue

Silver Tankard, by Borchardt Rollufse, 1641 — A204

1980, Sept. 9 Engr. *Perf. 13*
670 A204 1.30k shown 35 16
671 A204 1.80k Bishop's bowl, Copenhagen faience, 18th cent. 75 85

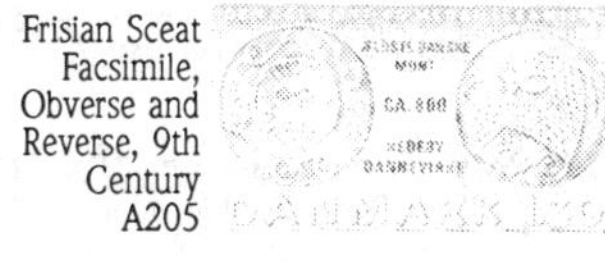
Frisian Sceat Facsimile, Obverse and Reverse, 9th Century A205

Coins: 1.40k Silver coin of Valdemar the Great and Absalom, 1157-1182, 1.80k, Gold 12-mark coin of Christian VII, 1781.

1980, Oct. 9 Engr. *Perf. 13*
672 A205 1.30k red & redsh brn 30 24
673 A205 1.40k ol gray & sl grn 55 85
674 A205 1.80k dk bl & sl bl 55 85

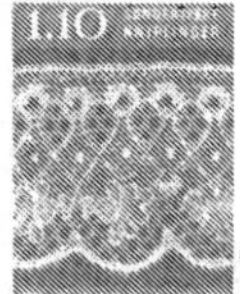

Tonder Lace Pattern, North Schleswig — A206

Designs: Tonder lace patterns.

1980, Nov. 13 Engr. *Perf. 13*
675 A206 1.10k brown 40 20
676 A206 1.30k brown red 48 15
677 A206 2k olive gray 70 18

Nyboder Development, Copenhagen, 350th Anniversary — A207

Design: 1.30k, View of Nyboder, diff.

1981, Mar. 19
678 A207 1.30k dp org & ocher 55 32
679 A207 1.60k dp org & ocher 55 15

Tilting at a Barrel on Shrovetide — A208

Design: 2k, Midsummer's Eve bonfire.

1981, May 4 Engr. *Perf. 13*
680 A208 1.60k brown red 50 16
681 A208 2k dk blue 70 30

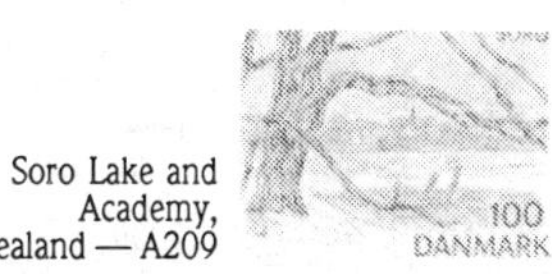

Soro Lake and Academy, Zealand — A209

Designs: Views of Zealand.

1981, June 18 Engr. *Perf. 13*
682 A209 100o shown 35 15
683 A209 150o Poet N.F.S. Grundtvig's home, Udby 55 20
684 A209 160o Kaj Munk's home, Opager 60 15
685 A209 200o Gronsund 60 24
686 A209 230o Bornholm Isld. 70 30
Nos. 682-686 (5) 2.80 1.04

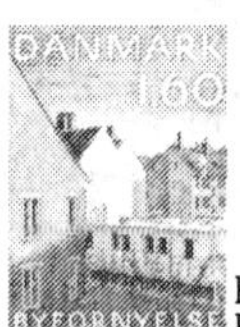

European Urban Renaissance Year — A210

1981, Sept. 10 Engr. *Perf. 12½x13*
687 A210 1.60k dull red 50 18

Type of 1933

1981-85 Engr. *Perf. 13*
688 A32 30o orange 15 15
a. Bklt. pane 10 (2 #318, 2 #688, 6 #494)('84) 1.75
689 A32 40o purple 15 15
a. Bklt. pane of 10 (4 #318, 2 #689, 4 #494) ('89) 1.25
690 A32 80o ol bis ('85) 15 15
691 A32 100o blue ('83) 40 15
b. Bklt. pane of 8 (2 #494, 4 #691, 2 #706) ('83) 6.00
692 A32 150o dk green ('82) 55 22
693 A32 200o green ('83) 60 35
694 A32 230o brt yel grn ('84) 40 20
695 A32 250o brt yel grn ('85) 60 20
Nos. 688-695 (8) 3.00
Set value 1.25

Ellehammer's 18-horsepower Biplane, 1906 — A211

1981, Oct. 8 Engr. *Perf. 13*
696 A211 1k shown 35 30
697 A211 1.30k R-1 Fokker CV reconnaissance plane, 1926 60 45
698 A211 1.60k Bellanca J-300, 1931 45 18
699 A211 2.30k DC-7C, 1957 70 38

Queen Margrethe II, 10th Anniv. of Accession — A212

1982-85 Engr. *Perf. 13*
700 A212 1.60k dull red 55 15
701 A212 1.60k dk ol grn 90 70
702 A212 1.80k sepia 70 40
703 A212 2k dull red 70 15
b. Bklt. pane of 10 (4 #494, 2 each #493, 702, 703) 10.00
704 A212 2.20k ol grn ('83) 55 40
705 A212 2.30k violet 75 15
706 A212 2.50k org red ('83) 60 30
707 A212 2.70k dk blue 1.00 35
708 A212 2.70k cop red ('84) 70 25
c. Booklet pane of 8 (3 #688, 2 #494, 3 #708) ('84) 5.00
709 A212 2.80k cop red ('85) 70 25
b. Booklet pane of 8 (3 #493, 2 #494, 3 #709) ('85) 4.00
710 A212 3k violet ('83) 75 35
711 A212 3.30k bluish blk ('84) 80 28
712 A212 3.50k blue ('83) 85 20
713 A212 3.50k dk vio ('85) 90 30
714 A212 3.70k dp blue ('84) 90 32
715 A212 3.80k dk blue ('85) 95 32

See Nos. 796-803, 891-899.

Arms Type of 1946

Engr. *Perf. 13*
716 A55 4.30k dk ol grn ('84) 1.10 38
717 A55 5.50k dk bl grn ('84) 1.40 50
718 A55 16k cop red ('83) 3.75 70
719 A55 17k cop red ('84) 4.00 75
720 A55 18k brn vio ('85) 4.75 75
720A A55 50k dk red ('85) 11.50 2.50
Nos. 700-720A (22) 38.80 10.45

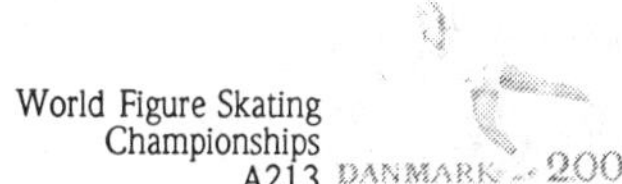

World Figure Skating Championships A213

1982, Feb. 25
721 A213 2k dark blue 60 15

A214

A215

1982, Feb. 25 Engr. *Perf. 12½*
722 A214 1.60k Revenue schooner Argus 52 15

Customs Service centenary

1982, May 3 Engr. *Perf. 12½*
723 A215 2k Abolition of adscription, 1788 55 15
724 A215 2.70k Women's voting right, 1915 90 35

Europa.

Butter Churn, Barn, Hjedding — A216

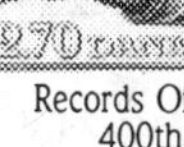

Records Office, 400th Anniv. — A217

1982, June 10 Engr. *Perf. 13*
725 A216 1.80k brown 60 20

Cooperative dairy farming centenary.

1982, June 10
726 A217 2.70k green 85 15

Steen Steensen Blicher (1782-1848), Poet, by J.V. Gertner — A218

1982, Aug. 26 Engr. *Perf. 13*
727 A218 2k brown red 65 15

Robert Storm Petersen (1882-1949), Cartoonist A219

Printing in Denmark, 500th Anniv. A220

Characters: 1.50k, Three little men and the number man. 2k, Peter and Ping the penguin, horiz.

1982, Sept. 23 Engr. *Perf. 12½*
728 A219 1.50k dk bl & red 60 25
729 A219 2k red & ol grn 65 20

1982, Sept. 23
730 A220 1.80k Press, text, ink balls 60 20

A221

A222

1982, Nov. 4
731 A221 2.70k Library seal 85 20

500th anniv. of University Library.

1983, Jan. 27 Engr. *Perf. 13*
732 A222 2k multicolored 55 20

World Communications Year.

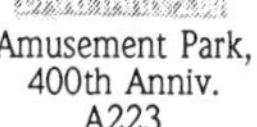
Amusement Park, 400th Anniv. A223

Badminton Championship A224

1983, Feb. 24
733 A223 2k multicolored 55 20

1983, Feb. 24
734 A224 2.70k multicolored 80 20

Nordic Cooperation Issue — A225

1983, Mar. 24

735 A225 2.50k Egeskov Castle	60	20
736 A225 3.50k Troll Church, North Jutland	1.00	50

50th Anniv. of Steel Plate Printed Stamps — A226

1983, Mar. 24 Engr. *Perf. 13*

737 A226 2.50k car rose 65 20

Europa 1983 — A227

Weights and Measures Ordinance, 300th Anniv. — A228

Designs: 2.50k, Kildekovshallen Recreation Center, Copenhagen. 3.50k, Salling Sound Bridge.

1983, May 5 Engr. *Perf. 13*

738 A227 2.50k multicolored 60 20
739 A227 3.50k multicolored 1.00 50

1983, June 16

740 A228 2.50k red 55 20

A229

A230

1983, Sept. 8 Engr.

741 A229 5k Codex titlepage 1.10 40

Christian V Danish law, 300th anniv.

1983, Oct. 6 Engr. *Perf. 13*

742 A230 1k Car crash, police 28 15
743 A230 2.50k Fire, ambulance service 55 20
744 A230 3.50k Sea rescue 90 50

Life saving and salvage services.

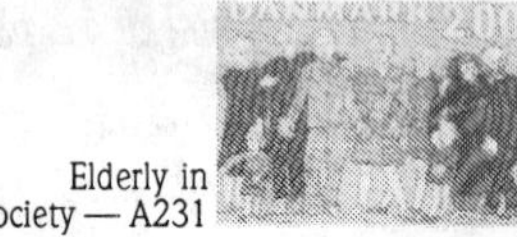
Elderly in Society — A231

1983, Oct. 6

745 A231 2k Stages of life 48 25
746 A231 2.50k Train passengers 60 15

N.F.S. Grundtvig (1783-1872), Poet — A232

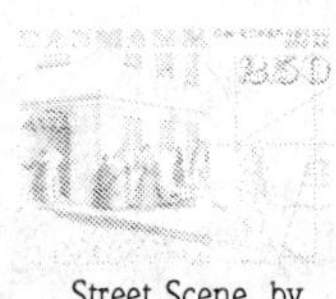
Street Scene, by C.W. Eckersberg (1783-1853) — A233

1983, Nov. 3 Engr.

747 A232 2.50k brown red 55 20
748 A233 2.50k brown red 55 20

A234

A235

1984, Jan. 26 Litho. & Engr.

749 A234 2.70k Shovel, sapling 55 15

Plant a tree campaign.

1984, Jan. 26 Engr.

750 A235 3.70k Game 85 25

1984 Billiards World Championships, Copenhagen, May 10-13.

Hydrographic Dept. Bicentenary — A236

Pilotage Service, 300th Anniv. — A237

1984, Mar. 22 Engr. *Perf. 13*

751 A236 2.30k Compass 52 32
752 A237 2.70k Boat 60 25

2nd European Parliament Elections — A238

Scouts Around Campfire, Emblems — A239

1984, Apr. 12 Litho. & Engr. *Perf. 13*

753 A238 2.70k org & dk bl 60 15
754 A239 2.70k multi 60 15

Europa (1959-84) — A240

1984, May 3 Engr. *Perf. 12½*

755 A240 2.70k red 60 15
756 A240 3.70k blue 90 50

Prince Henrik, 50th Birthday A241

D Day, 40th Anniv. A242

1984, June 6 Engr.

757 A241 2.70k brown red 60 15
758 A242 2.70k War Memorial, Copenhagen 60 15

See Greenland No. 160.

17th Cent. Inn — A243

1984, June 6

759 A243 3k multicolored 75 40

Fishing and Shipping — A244

1984, Sept. 6 Engr.

760 A244 2.30k Research (Herring) 55 60
761 A244 2.70k Sea transport 60 15
762 A244 3.30k Deep-sea fishing 75 70
763 A244 3.70k Deep-sea, diff. 90 50

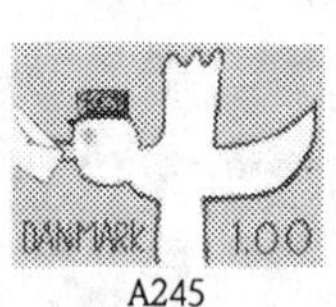
A245

A246

1984, Oct. 5 Litho. & Engr.

764 A245 1k Post bird 28 15

1984, Oct. 5

Holberg Meets with an Officer, by Wilhelm Marstrand (1810-73).

765 A246 2.70k multicolored 65 22

Ludvig Holberg (1684-1754), writer.

Jewish Community in Copenhagen, 300th Anniv. — A247

1984, Oct. 5

766 A247 3.70k Woman blessing Sabbath candles 85 60

Carnival in Rome, by Christoffer W. Eckersberg (1783-1853) — A248

Paintings: 10k, Ymer and Odhumble (Nordic mythology figures), by Nicolai A. Abildgaard (1743-1809), vert.

Perf. 12½x13, 13x12½

1984, Nov. 22 Litho. & Engr.

767 A248 5k multicolored 1.25 1.10
768 A248 10k multicolored 2.50 1.90

German and French Reform Church, 300th Anniv. — A249

1985, Jan. 24 Engr. *Perf. 13*

769 A249 2.80k magenta 80 20

Bonn-Copenhagen Declaration, 30th Anniv. — A250

1985, Feb. 21 Litho. *Perf. 14*

770 A250 2.80k Map, flags 80 20

A251

A252

1985, Mar. 14 *Perf. 13*

771 A251 3.80k multicolored 1.00 45

Intl. Youth Year.

Souvenir Sheet

Early postal ordinances.

1985, Mar. 14 Litho. & Engr.

772 Sheet of 4 4.75 5.00
a. A252 1k Christian IV's Ordinance on Postmen, 1624 1.10 1.25
b. A252 2.50k Plague Mandate, 1711 1.10 1.25
c. A252 2.80k Ordinance on Prohibition of Mail by Means other than the Post, 1775 1.10 1.25
d. A252 3.80k Act on Postal Articles, 1831 1.10 1.25

HAFNIA '87 phil. exhib. Sold for 15k.

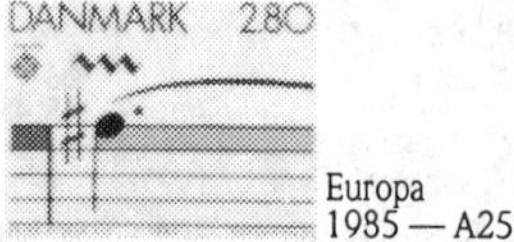
Europa 1985 — A253

1985, May 2

773 A253 2.80k Musical staff 70 25
774 A253 3.80k Musical staff, diff. 1.00 15

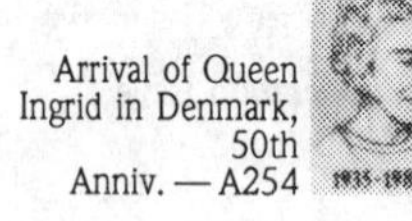

Arrival of Queen Ingrid in Denmark, 50th Anniv. — A254

1985, May 21

775 A254 2.80k Queen Mother, chrysanthemums 75 15

See Greenland No. 163.

Opening of the Faro Bridges — A255

1985, May 21 Litho. *Perf. 13*

776 A255 2.80k Faro-Falster Bridge 75 15

St. Cnut's Land Grant to Lund Cathedral, 900th Anniv. — A256

Seal of King Cnut and: 2.80k, Lund Cathedral. 3k, City of Helsingdorg, Sweden.

1985, May 21 **Engr.**

777	A256	2.80k multi	80	15
778	A256	3k multi	85	40

See Sweden Nos. 1538-1539.

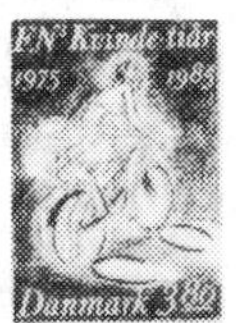

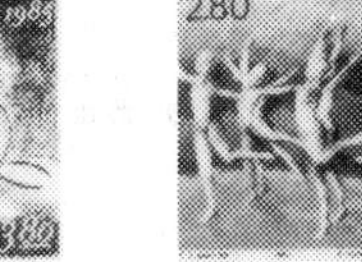

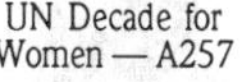

UN Decade for Women — A257

Sports — A258

1985, June 27 **Litho. & Engr.**

779	A257	3.80k Cyclist	1.00	40

1985, June 27

780	A258	2.80k Women's floor exercise	75	20
781	A258	3.80k Canoe & kayak	1.10	40
782	A258	6k Cycling	1.50	65

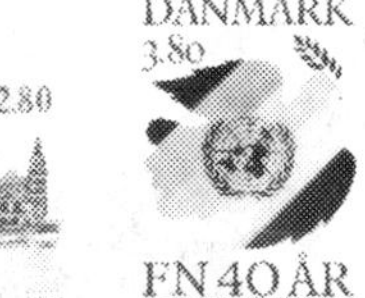

Kronborg Castle, Elsinore, 400th Anniv. A259

UN 40th Anniv. A260

1985, Sept. 5

783	A259	2.80k multi	75	22

1985, Sept. 5

784	A260	3.80k Dove, emblem	1.00	40

Niels Bohr (1885-1962), Physicist — A261

1985, Oct. 3 ***Perf. 13x12½***

785	A261	2.80k With wife Margrethe	80	40

Winner of 1922 Nobel Prize in Physics for theory of atomic structure.

Hand Signing "D" — A262

Boat, by Helge Refn — A263

1985, Nov. 7 **Engr.** ***Perf. 13***

786	A262	2.80k multicolored	75	32

Danish Assoc. for the Deaf, 50th anniv.

1985, Nov. 7 **Litho.**

787	A263	2.80k multicolored	75	32

Abstract Iron Sculpture by Robert Jacobsen A264

Lithographed and Engraved

1985, Nov. 7 ***Perf. 13x12½***

788	A264	3.80k multicolored	1.00	52

Abstract Painting by Bjorn Wiinblad A265

1986, Jan. 23 **Litho.** ***Perf. 13x12½***

789	A265	2.80k multicolored	75	20

Amnesty Intl., 25th Anniv. A266

Lithographed and Engraved

1986, Jan. 23 ***Perf. 13***

790	A266	2.80k multicolored	75	20

Miniature Sheet

HAFNIA '87 — A267

1986, Feb. 20

791		Sheet of 4	6.00	5.75
a.	A267	100o Holstein carriage, c. 1840	1.40	1.40
b.	A267	250o Iceboat, c. 1880	1.40	1.40
c.	A267	280o 1st mail van, 1908	1.40	1.40
d.	A267	380o Airmail service 1919	1.40	1.40

Sold for 15k.

Changing of the Guard — A268

1986, Mar. 20 ***Perf. 13***

792	A268	2.80k multicolored	80	28

Royal Danish Life Guards barracks and Rosenborg Drilling Ground, bicent.

Types of 1933-82

1986-90 **Engr.** ***Perf. 13***

793	A32	5o brn org ('89)	15	15
794	A32	270o brt yel grn	80	15
b.		Bklt. pane, 6 #318, 2 #691, 2 #794	3.00	
795	A32	300o brt yel grn	85	15
796	A212	3k cop red	85	15
797	A212	3.20k deep vio	90	15
798	A212	3.20k carmine	90	15
c.		Bklt. pane, 2 #693, 4 #798	5.00	
799	A212	3.40k dk grn	95	15
800	A212	3.80k dark vio	1.00	15
801	A212	4.10k dark blue	1.10	15
802	A212	4.20k dk pur	1.15	15
803	A212	4.40k dp bl	1.25	15
804	A55	4.60k gray	1.25	15
805	A55	6.50k dp grn	1.75	75
806	A55	6.60k green	1.75	30
807	A55	7.10k brn vio	2.00	35
808	A55	7.30k green	2.00	38
809	A55	7.70k dk brn vio	2.15	40
810	A55	11k brown	3.00	90
811	A55	20k dp ultra	5.25	2.25
812	A55	22k henna brn	5.75	3.00
813	A55	23k dark olive grn	7.10	1.75
814	A55	24k dark olive grn	6.50	2.00
815	A55	26k dark olive grn	7.25	2.25
		Nos. 793-815 (23)	55.65	16.13

Issue dates: 6.50k, 20k, Jan. 9. 22k, Jan. 3, 1987. 270o, 3k, No. 797, 3.80k, 4.10k, 4.60k, 6.60k, 7.10k, 24k, Jan. 7, 1988. No. 794b, Jan. 28, 1988. 300o, No. 798, 3.40k, 4.20k, 4.40k, 7.30k, 7.70k, 11k, 26k, Jan. 26, 1989. 5k, 1989. 23k, Jan. 11, 1990.

No. 793 issued for use in lieu of currency of the same face value.

Soro Academy, 400th Anniv. — A269

1986, Apr. 28 **Litho. & Engr.**

816	A269	2.80k multi	65	28

A270

A271

1986, Apr. 28

817	A270	3.80k multi	85	65

Intl. Peace Year

1986, May 26 **Litho.**

818	A271	2.80k multi	65	28

Crown Prince Frederik, 18th birthday.

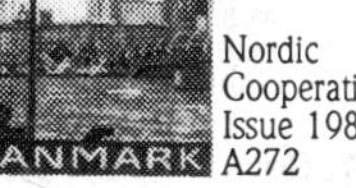

Nordic Cooperation Issue 1986 A272

Sister towns.

1986, May 27 **Engr.**

819	A272	2.80k Aalborg Harbor	65	28
820	A272	3.80k Thisted Church and Town Hall	85	42

Hoje Tastrup Train Station Opening, May 31 — A273

1986, May 27 **Litho.**

821	A273	2.80k multi	65	28

Mailbox, Telegraph Lines, Telephone A274

Natl. Bird Candidates A275

1986, June 19 **Litho.** ***Perf. 13***

822	A274	2.80k multi	65	28

19th European Intl. PTT Congress, Copenhagen, Aug. 12-16.

1986, June 19 **Litho. & Engr.**

Finalists: a, Corvus corax. b, Sturnus vulgaris. c, Cygnus olor (winner). d, Vanellus vanellus. e, Alauda arvensis.

823		Strip of 5	4.75	2.25
a.-e.	A275	2.80k any single	95	42

A276

HAFNIA '87 — A277

1986, June 19

824	A276	2.80k multi	65	28

Danish Rifle, Gymnastics and Sports Club, 125th anniv.

Souvenir Sheet

1986, Sept. 4

825		Sheet of 4	5.00	5.00
a.	A277	100o Mailcoach, c. 1841	1.10	1.10
b.	A277	250o Postmaster, c. 1840	1.10	1.10
c.	A277	280o Postman, c. 1851	1.10	1.10
d.	A277	380o Rural postman, c. 1893	1.25	1.25

Sold for 15k.

Europa 1986 — A278

Cupid — A279

1986, Sept. 4 **Engr.**

826	A278	2.80k Street sweeper	65	28
827	A278	3.80k Garbage truck	85	42

1986, Oct. 9 **Litho.**

828	A279	3.80k multi	85	42

Premiere of The Whims of Cupid and the Ballet Master, by Vincenzo Galeotti, bicent.

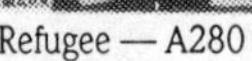

Refugee — A280

A281

1986, Oct. 9 **Litho. & Engr.**
829 A280 2.80k multi 65 28

Danish Refugee Council Relief Campaign.

1986, Oct. 9 **Litho.** *Perf. 13*

Protestant Reformation in Denmark, 450th Anniv.: Sermon, altarpiece detail, 1561, Thorslunde Church, Copenhagen.

830 A281 6.50k multi 1.60 75

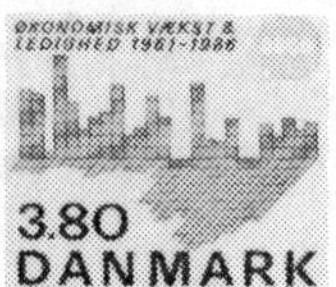

A282

Abstract by Lin Utzon — A283

1986, Nov. 6 **Litho. & Engr.**
831 A282 3.80k multi 85 42

Organization for Economic Cooperation and Development, 25th anniv.

1987, Jan. 22 **Litho.** *Perf. 13*
832 A283 2.80k multi 65 25

Art appreciation.

A284

RIBE DOMKIRKE
DANMARK 3.00

A285

1987, Feb. 26 **Engr.** *Perf. 13*
833 A284 2.80k lake & black 65 25

Danish Consumer Council, 40th anniv.

1987, Apr. 9 **Litho.** *Perf. 13*

Religious art (details) from Ribe Cathedral.

834 A285 3k Fresco 65 30
835 A285 3.80k Stained-glass window 85 40
836 A285 6.50k Mosaic 1.40 60

Ribe Cathedral redecoration, 1982-1987, by Carl-Henning Pedersen.

A286

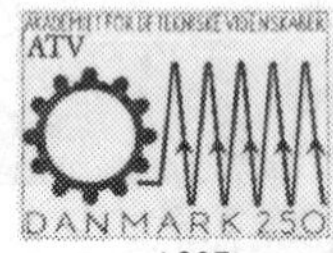

A287

Europa (Modern architecture): 2.80k, Central Library, Gentofte, 1985. 3.80k, Hoje Tastrup High School, 1985, horiz.

1987, May 4 **Engr.** *Perf. 13*
837 A286 2.80k rose claret 85 28
838 A286 3.80k bright ultra 1.15 40

1987, May 4
839 A287 2.50k dark red & blue blk 75 38

Danish Academy of Technical Sciences (ATV), 50th anniv.

DANMARK 2.80

8th Gymnaestrada, Herning, July 7-11 — A288

1987, June 18 **Litho. & Engr.**
840 A288 2.80k multi 80 30

A289

A290

1987, June 18
841 A289 3.80k multi 1.20 40

Danish Cooperative Bacon Factories, cent.

1987, Aug. 27 **Litho.**
842 A290 3.80k Single-sculler 1.10 35

World Rowing Championships, Aug. 23-30.

HAFNIA '87, Bella Center, Copenhagen, Oct. 16-25 — A291

Perf. 13x12½

1987, Aug. 27 **Litho. & Engr.**
843 A291 280o Type A15, mail train c. 1912 80 40

Souvenir Sheet

843A A291 280o like No. 843, green lawn and locomotive 15.00 15.00

Purchase of No. 843A included admission to the exhibition. Sold for 45k.

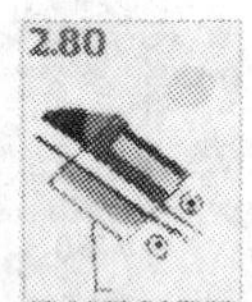

Abstact by Ejler Bille — A292

1987, Sept. 24 **Litho.** *Perf. 13*
844 A292 2.80k multi 82 25

Rasmus Rask (1787-1832), Linguist — A293

1987, Oct. 15 **Engr.** *Perf. 13x12½*
845 A293 2.80k dark henna brown 82 25

A294

A295

Emblem: Miraculous Catch (Luke 5:4-7), New Testament.

1987, Oct. 15 *Perf. 13*
846 A294 3k carmine lake 88 30

Clerical Assoc. for the Home Mission in Denmark, 125th anniv.

Photo. & Engr., Litho. (4.10k)

1988, Feb. 18 *Perf. 13*

Designs: 3k, Two lions from the gate of Rosenburg Castle around the monogram of Christian IV. 4.10k, Portrait of the monarch painted by P. Isaacsz, vert.

847 A295 3k blue gray & gold 95 32
848 A295 4.10k multi 1.30 42

Accession of Christian IV (1577-1648), King of Denmark and Norway (1588-1648), 400th anniv.

Ole Worm (1588-1654), Archaeologist, and Runic Artifacts — A296

1988, Feb. 18 **Engr.**
849 A296 7.10k chocolate 2.25 65

Odense, 1000th Anniv. — A297

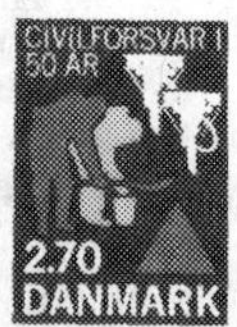

A298

Design: St. Cnut's Church and statue of Hans Christian Andersen, Odense.

1988, Mar. 10 **Engr.**
850 A297 3k multi 98 32

1988, Apr. 7 **Litho.**
851 A298 2.70k multi 88 30

Danish Civil Defense and Emergency Planning Agency, 50th Anniv.

WHO, 40th Anniv. — A299

Abolition of *Stavnsbaand*, 200th Anniv. — A300

1988, Apr. 7 **Litho. & Engr.**
852 A299 4.10k multi 1.35 45

1988, May 5 **Litho.**

Painting: King Christian VII riding past the Liberty Memorial, Copenhagen, by C.W. Eckersberg (1783-1853).

853 A300 3.20k multi 1.05 35

Stavnsbaand (adscription) provided that all Danish farmers' sons from age 4 to 40 would be bound as villeins to the estates on which they were born, thus providing landowners with free labor.

A301

A302

Europa: Transport and communication.

1988, May 5
854 A301 3k Postwoman on bicycle 95 32
855 A301 4.10k Mobile telephone 1.30 45

1988, June 16 **Litho.**
856 A302 4.10k multi 1.30 45

1988 Individual Speedway World Motorcycle Championships, Denmark, Sept. 3.

Federation of Danish Industries, 150th Anniv. — A303

Painting (detail): *The Industrialists*, by P.S. Kroyer.

1988, June 16 *Perf. 13½x13*
857 A303 3k multi 95 48

Danish Metalworkers' Union, Cent. — A304

1988, Aug. 18 **Litho.** *Perf. 13*
858 A304 3k Glass mosaic by Niels Winkel 88 45

Tonder Teachers' Training College, 200th Anniv. — A305

1988, Aug. 18 **Engr.** *Perf. 13x12½*
859 A305 3k lake 88 45

Homage to Leon Degand, Sculpture by Robert Jacobsen A306

1988, Sept. 22 *Perf. 11½x13*
860 A306 4.10k black, lake & gray 1.20 60

Danish-French cultural exchange program, 10th anniv. See France No. 2130.

Preservation of Historic Sites — A307

1988, Oct. 13 Engr. *Perf. 13x12½*
861 A307 3k Lumby Windmill, 1818 90 45
862 A307 7.10k Vejstrup Water Mill, 1837 2.15 1.10

Paintings in the State Museum of Art, Copenhagen — A308

Designs: 4.10k, *Bathing Boys,* 1902, by Peter Hansen (1868-1928). 10k, *The Hill at Overkaerby,* 1917, by Fritz Syberg (1862-1939).

1988, Nov. 3 Litho. & Engr. *Perf. 13*
863 A308 4.10k multi 1.25 62
864 A308 10k multi 3.00 1.50

See Nos. 881-882, 951-952, 972-973.

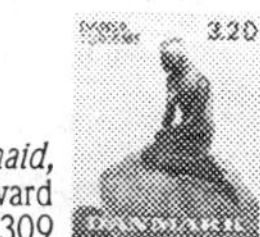
The Little Mermaid, Sculpture by Edvard Eriksen — A309

1989, Feb. 16 Engr.
865 A309 3.20k dark green 95 48

Tourism industry, cent.

Danish Soccer Assoc., Cent. — A310

NATO Membership, 40th Anniv. — A311

1989, Mar. 16 Litho.
866 A310 3.20k multi 90 45

1989, Mar. 16
867 A311 4.40k dk blue, gold & lt blue 1.25 62

Nordic Cooperation Issue — A312

Folk costumes.

1989, Apr. 20 Litho. & Engr.
868 A312 3.20k Woman from Valby 92 45
869 A312 4.40k Pork butcher 1.25 62

European Parliament 3rd Elections A313

1989, May 11 Litho.
870 A313 3k blue & yellow 85 42

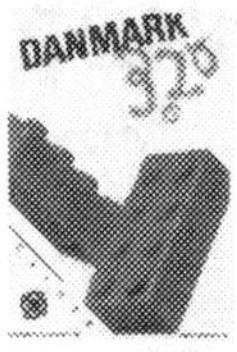
Europa 1989 — A314

Children's toys.

1989, May 11 Litho. & Engr. *Perf.*
871 A314 3.20k Lego blocks 90 45
872 A314 4.40k Wooden soldiers, by Kay Bojesen 1.25 62

Agricultural Museum, Cent. — A315

1989, June 15 Engr. *Perf. 13*
873 A315 3.20k Tractor, 1889 90 45

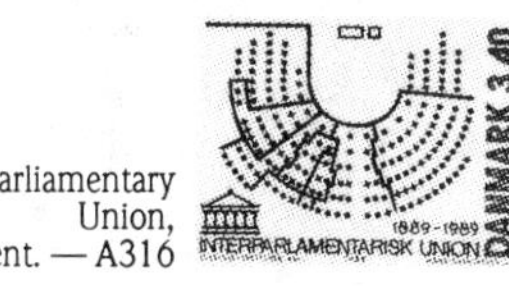
Interparliamentary Union, Cent. — A316

1989, June 15 Litho. & Engr.
874 A316 3.40k Folketing Chamber layout 98 50

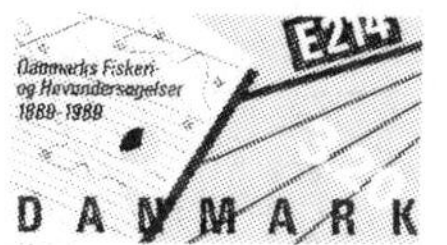
Danish Fishery and Marine Research Institute, Cent. A317

1989, Aug. 24 Litho. & Engr.
875 A317 3.20k multi 82 40

Bernhard Severin Ingemann (1789-1862), Poet and Novelist — A318

1989, Aug. 24 Engr.
876 A318 7.70k dark green 2.00 1.00

A319

A320

Danish Film Office, 50th Anniv.: 3k, Scene from the short feature film *They Reached the Ferry,* 1948. 3.20k, Bodil Ipsen (d. 1964), actress. 4.40k, Carl Th. Dreyer (1889-1968), screenwriter and director.

1989, Sept. 28 Litho.
877 A319 3k multi 80 40
878 A319 3.20k multi 85 42
879 A319 4.40k multi 1.15 58

1989, Nov. 10 Litho. & Engr.
880 A320 3.20k multi 88 45

Stamp Day, 50th anniv.

Art Type of 1988

Paintings: 4.40k, *Part of the Northern Gate of the Citadel Bridge,* c. 1837, by Christen Kobke (1810-1848). 10k, *A Little Girl, Elise Kobke, With a Cup in Front of Her,* c. 1850, by Constantin Hansen (1804-1880).

1989, Nov. 10 *Perf. 12½x13*
881 A308 4.40k multi 1.20 60
882 A308 10k multi 2.75 1.40

Types of 1933-82 and:

Queen Margrethe II — A321

1990-94 Engr. *Perf. 12½*
883 A32 25o bluish black 15 15
a. Bklt. pane, 4 #691, 2 #883 1.75
886 A32 125o carmine lake 40 15
890 A32 325o lt yellow green 1.00 15
890A A32 350o yellow green 1.30 15
891 A212 3.50k dark red 1.10 15
a. Bklt. pane, 2 each #691, 890, 891 5.00
892 A321 3.50k henna brown 1.10 15
b. Bklt. pane, 4 each #883, #886, #892 ('91) 7.35
893 A212 3.75k dark green 1.15 15
894 A321 3.75k green 1.30 15
895 A321 3.75k red 1.40 15
a. Bklt. pane, 4 each #886, #895 7.30
897 A212 4.50k brown violet 1.40 15
898 A321 4.50k violet 1.60 15
899 A212 4.75k dark blue 1.45 18
900 A321 4.75k blue 1.65 15
901 A321 4.75k violet 1.75 15
903 A321 5k blue 1.80 15
904 A321 5.50k green 1.65 15
Nos. 883-904 (16) 20.20
Set value 1.40

Queen Margrethe II's 50th birthday (No. 892).
Issued: No. 892, Apr. 5. Nos. 894, 898, 900, 1990. No. 892a, Feb. 14, 1991. Nos. 890A, 895, 895a-895b, 901, 903, June 10, 1992. 5.50k, Jan. 13, 1994. Others, Jan. 11.
This is an expanding set. Numbers will change if necessary.

A322

A323

Design: Silver coffee pot designed by Axel Johannes Kroyer, Copenhagen, 1726.

1990, Feb. 15 Engr. *Perf. 13*
911 A322 3.50k dark blue & black 1.10 55

Museum of Decorative Art, cent.

1990, Feb. 15

Steam engine, 200th anniv.: Steam engine built by Andrew Mitchell, 1790.

912 A323 8.25k dull red brown 2.50 1.25

Nyholm, 300th Anniv. A324

1990, Apr. 5 Engr.
913 A324 4.75k black 1.50 75

Europa 1990 — A325

1990, Apr. 5 Litho.
914 A325 3.50k Royal Monogram, Haderslev P.O. 1.10 55
915 A325 4.75k Odense P.O. 1.50 75

A326

A327

Pieces from the Flora Danica Banquet Service produced for King Christian VII.

1990, May 3 Litho.
916 A326 3.50k Bell-shaped lid, dish 1.10 55
917 A326 3.50k Gravy boat, dish 1.10 55
918 A326 3.50k Ice pot, casserole, lid 1.10 55
919 A326 3.50k Serving dish 1.10 55
a. Strip of 4, #916-919 4.50

Flora Danica porcelain, 200th anniv.

1990, June 14

Endangered plant species.

920 A327 3.25k Marshmallow 1.05 52
921 A327 3.50k Red helleborine 1.15 58
922 A327 3.75k Purple orchis 1.20 60
923 A327 4.75k Lady's slipper 1.50 75

Village Churches, Jutland — A328

Perf. 13x12½, 12½x13
1990, Aug. 30 Engr.
924 A328 3.50k Gjellerup 1.10 55
925 A328 4.75k Veng 1.40 75
926 A328 8.25k Bredsten, vert. 2.55 1.30

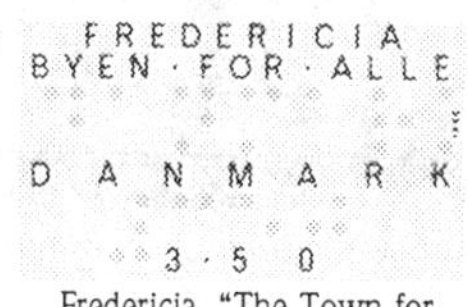

Fredericia, "The Town for Everybody" — A329

Engr. & Embossed
1990, Oct. 5 *Perf. 13*
927 A329 3.50k black & red 1.10 55

Tordenskiold (Peter Wessel, 1690-1720), Admiral — A330

1990, Oct. 5 Litho. ***Perf. 13½x13***
928 A330 3.50k multicolored 1.10 55

Prevent Bicycle Thefts — A331

Design: 3.50k, Stop drunk driving.

1990, Nov. 8 Litho. ***Perf. 13x12½***
930 A331 3.25k shown 1.05 52
931 A331 3.50k Automobile, wine glass 1.10 55

Locomotives — A332

1991, Mar. 14 Engr. ***Perf. 13***
932 A332 3.25k IC3 1990 1.05 55
933 A332 3.50k Class A 1882 1.15 55
934 A332 3.75k Class MY 1954 1.20 60
935 A332 4.75k Class P 1907 1.55 75

Europa — A333

Jutland Law, 750th Anniv. — A334

Satellite photographs showing temperatures of Danish: 3.50k, Waters. 4.75k, Land.

1991, May 2 Litho. ***Perf. 13***
936 A333 3.50k multicolored 1.10 55
937 A333 4.75k multicolored 1.45 75

1991, May 2
938 A334 8.25k multicolored 2.35 1.20

Danish Islands — A335

1991, June 6
939 A335 3.50k Fano 1.00 50
940 A335 4.75k Christianso 1.35 70

Decorative Art — A336

Keep Denmark Clean — A337

Designs: 3.25k, Earthenware bowl and jars by Christian Poulsen. 3.50k, Chair by Hans Wegner, vert. 4.75k, Silver cutlery by Kay Bojesen, vert. 8k, Lamp by Poul Henningsen.

1991, Aug. 22 Litho. ***Perf. 13***
941 A336 3.25k multicolored 95 42
942 A336 3.50k multicolored 1.00 50
943 A336 4.75k multicolored 1.40 70
944 A336 8.25k multicolored 2.50 1.25

1991, Sept. 19 Engr. ***Perf. 13***

Designs: 3.50k, Cleaning up after dog. 4.75k, Picking up litter.

945 A337 3.50k red 1.80 90
946 A337 4.75k blue 2.45 1.20

Posters from Danish Museum of Decorative Arts — A338

Posters for: 3.50k, Nordic Advertising Congress, by Arne Ungermann (1902-1981). 4.50k, Poster Exhibition at Copenhagen Zoo (baboon), by Valdemar Andersen (1875-1928). 4.75k, Danish Air Lines, by Ib Andersen (1907-1969). 12k, The Sinner, by Sven Brasch (1886-1970).

1991, Sept. 19 Litho.
947 A338 3.50k multicolored 1.10 55
948 A338 4.50k multicolored 1.40 70
949 A338 4.75k multicolored 1.45 72
950 A338 12k multicolored 3.75 1.80

Art Type of 1988

Designs: 4.75k, Lady at her Toilet by Harald Giersing (1881-1927), vert. 14k, Road through a Wood by Edvard Weie (1879-1943), vert.

Perf. 13x12½
1991, Nov. 7 Litho. & Engr.
951 A308 4.75k multicolored 1.50 75
952 A308 14k multicolored 4.45 2.25

A339

A340

Treasures of Natl. Museum: 3.50k, Earthenware bowl, Skarpsalling. 4.50k, Bronze dancer, Grevensvaenge. 4.75k, Bottom plate of silver cauldron, Gundestrup. 8.25k, Flint knife, Hindsgavl.

1992, Feb. 13 Engr. ***Perf. 13***
953 A339 3.50k dk vio & brown 1.15 58
954 A339 4.50k dk bl & dk ol green 1.45 75
955 A339 4.75k brown & black 1.55 80
956 A339 8.25k dk ol grn & vio brown 2.70 1.35

1992, Mar. 12 ***Perf. 13½x13***
957 A340 3.50k rose carmine 1.15 58

Danish Society of Chemical, Civil, Electrical, and Mechanical Engineers, cent.

Souvenir Sheet

Queen Margaret I (1353-1412) — A341

Litho. & Engr.
1992, Mar. 12 ***Perf. 12½***
958 A341 Sheet of 2 3.75 1.85
a. 3.50k Fresco 1.60 80
b. 4.75k Alabaster bust 2.15 1.05

Nordia '94, Scandinavian Philatelic Exhibition. No. 958 sold for 12k to benefit the exhibition.

Discovery of America, 500th Anniv. — A342

1992, May 7 Engr. ***Perf. 12½***
959 A342 3.50k Potato plant 1.15 58
960 A342 4.75k Ear of corn 1.50 75

Europa.

Protect the Environment A343

1992, June 10 Litho. & Engr. ***Perf. 13***
961 A343 3.75k Hare beside road 1.40 70
962 A343 5k Fish, water pollution 1.80 90
963 A343 8.75k Cut trees, vert. 3.20 1.60

Queen Margrethe II and Prince Henrik, 25th Wedding Anniv. — A344

1992, June 10 Litho. ***Perf. 12½x13***
964 A344 3.75k multicolored 1.40 70

A345

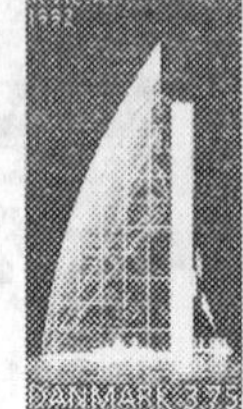

A346

1992, July 16 ***Perf. 13***
965 A345 3.75k multicolored 1.40 70

Denmark, European soccer champions.

1992, Aug. 27 Engr. ***Perf. 13***
966 A346 3.75k blue 1.40 70

Danish Pavilion, Expo '92, Seville.

A347

A348

1992, Oct. 8 Litho. & Engr. ***Perf. 13***
967 A347 3.75k blue & org 1.40 70

Single European market.

Litho. & Engr.
1992, Oct. 8 ***Perf. 12½***

Cartoon characters: 3.50k, A Hug, by Ivar Gjorup. 3.75k, Love Letter, by Phillip Stein Jonsson. 4.75k, Domestic Triangle, by Nikoline Werdelin. 5k, Poet and His Little Wife, by Jorgen Mogensen.

968 A348 3.50k multicolored 1.30 65

Engr.
969 A348 3.75k red & purple 1.40 70
970 A348 4.75k blk & red brn 1.80 90
971 A348 5k blue & red brn 1.85 92

Art Type of 1988

Designs: 5k, Landscape from Vejby, 1843, by John Thomas Lundbye. 10k, Motif from Halleby Brook, 1847, by Peter Christian Skovgaard.

Perf. 12½x13
1992, Nov. 12 Litho. & Engr.
972 A308 5k multicolored 1.65 82
973 A308 10k multicolored 3.30 1.65

A349

A350

1992, Nov. 12 *Perf. 13*

974 A349 3.75k Jacob's fight with angel 1.25 62

Publication of new Danish bible.

1993, Feb. 4 Litho. & Engr. *Perf. 13*

Archaeological Treasures. Anthropomorphic gold foil figures found in: 3.75k, Lundeborg, horiz. 5k, Bornholm.

975 A350 3.75k multicolored 1.25 62
976 A350 5k multicolored 1.65 80

A351

A352

Butterflies.

1993, Mar. 11 **Litho.**

977 A351 3.75k Small tortoiseshell 1.25 62
978 A351 5k Large blue 1.65 80
979 A351 8.75k Marsh fritillary 3.00 1.50
980 A351 12k Red admiral 4.00 2.00

1993, May 6 Litho. *Perf. 12½*

Posters: 3.75k, Pierrot, by Thor Bogelund, 1947, horiz. 5k, Balloons, by Wilhelm Freddie, 1987.

981 A352 3.75k multicolored 1.25 65
982 A352 5k multicolored 1.65 80

Tivoli Gardens, 150th anniv.

A353

A354

1993, May 6 *Perf. 13*

Europa (Contemporary paintings by): 3.75k, Troels Worsel, horiz. 5k, Stig Brogger.

983 A353 3.75k multicolored 1.25 62
984 A353 5k multicolored 1.65 80

1993, June 17 Engr. *Perf. 13*

985 A354 5k dark blue green 1.60 80

Danish-Russian relations, 500th anniv. See Russia No. 6154.

Training Ships
A355 A356

Perf. 13, 13½x13 (#987)

1993, June 17 Litho. & Engr.

986 A355 3.75k Danmark 1.20 60
987 A356 4.75k Jens Krogh 1.50 75
988 A355 5k Georg Stage, horiz. 1.55 78

Size: 39x28mm

Perf. 13x13½

989 A356 9.50k Marilyn Anne, horiz. 3.00 1.50

Child's Drawing of Viking Ships — A357

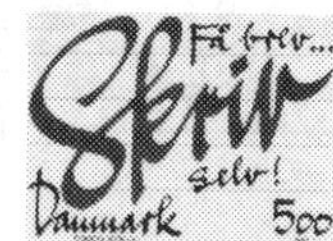

Letter Writing Campaign — A358

1993, Aug. 19 Litho. *Perf. 13*

990 A357 3.75k multicolored 1.10 58
991 A358 5k lt blue, dk blue & black 1.50 75

Ethnic Jewelry — A359

1993, Sept. 16 Litho. *Perf. 13*

992 A359 3.50k Falster 1.10 55
993 A359 3.75k Amager 1.25 60
994 A359 5k Laeso 1.65 80
995 A359 8.75k Romo 2.75 1.40

Cubist Paintings A360

Designs: 5k, Assemblage, by Vilhelm Lundstrom, 1929. 15k, Composition, by Franciska Clausen, 1929.

Litho. & Engr.

1993, Nov. 11 *Perf. 12½*

996 A360 5k multicolored 1.50 75
997 A360 15k multicolored 4.50 2.25

Conservation — A361

1994, Jan. 27 Litho. *Perf. 13*

998 A361 3.75k Save water 1.10 55
999 A361 5k CO2 1.50 75

SEMI-POSTAL STAMPS

Nos. 159, 157 Surcharged in Red ✚ 5 ✚

Wmk. Multiple Crosses (114)

1921, June 17 *Perf. 14½x14*

B1 A20 10o + 5o green 15.00 16.00
B2 A21 20o + 10o slate 19.00 20.00
Set, never hinged 50.00

Crown and Staff of Aesculapius — SP1

Dybbol Mill — SP2

1929, Aug. 1 **Engr.**

B3 SP1 10o yellow green 3.25 3.50
a. Booklet pane of 2 21.00
B4 SP1 15o brick red 4.25 3.50
a. Booklet pane of 2 25.00
B5 SP1 25o deep blue 17.50 20.00
a. Booklet pane of 2 100.00
Set, never hinged 38.00

These stamps were sold at a premium of 5 öre each for benefit of the Danish Cancer Committee.

1937, Jan. 20 Unwmk. *Perf. 13*

B6 SP2 5o + 5o green 90 90
B7 SP2 10o + 5o lt brown 3.00 3.00
B8 SP2 15o + 5o carmine 3.00 3.00
Set, never hinged 9.50

The surtax was for a fund in memory of H. P. Hanssen, statesman.

Nos. 223a and B6, Nos. 229 and B7, Nos. 238A and B8 are found se-tenant in booklets. For booklet panes, see Nos. 223d, 229b and 238e.

Queen Alexandrine SP3

Princesses Ingrid and Margrethe SP4

1939-40 *Perf. 13*

B9 SP3 5o + 3o rose lake & red ('40) 20 20
a. Booklet pane of 4 2.00 2.00
B10 SP3 10o + 5o dk violet & red 25 18
B11 SP3 15o + 5o scarlet & red 50 50
Set, never hinged 1.25

The surtax was for the Danish Red Cross.

Nos. 230 and B10 have been issued se-tenant in booklets. See No. 230b. In this pane No. 230 measures 23½x31mm from perf. to perf.

1941-43

B12 SP4 10o + 5o dk violet 16 22
a. Booklet pane of 10 19.00
B13 SP4 20o + 5o red ('43) 16 22
Set, never hinged 45

Surtax for the Children's Charity Fund.

No. 288 Surcharged in Red ✚ 5

1944, May 11

B14 A48 10o + 5o violet 16 20
a. Booklet pane of 10 27.50
Never hinged 20

The surtax was for the Danish Red Cross.

Catalogue values for unused stamps in this section, from this point to the end of the section, are for Never Hinged items.

Symbols of Freedom SP5

Explosions at Rail Junction SP6

Danish Flag — SP7

Princess Anne-Marie — SP8

1947, May 4 Engr. *Perf. 13*

B15 SP5 15o + 5o green 35 30
B16 SP6 20o + 5o dark red 35 30
B17 SP7 40o + 5o deep blue 90 75

Issued in memory of the Danish struggle for liberty and the liberation of Denmark. The surtax was for the Liberty Fund.

For surcharges see Nos. B22-B23.

1950, Oct. 19 **Unwmk.**

B18 SP8 25o + 5o rose brown 60 60

The surtax was for the National Children's Welfare Association.

S. S. Jutlandia — SP9

1951, Sept. 13 *Perf. 13*

B19 SP9 25o + 5o red 75 75

The surtax was for the Red Cross.

No. 335 Surcharged in Black **NL ✚ 10**

1953, Feb. 13

B20 A61 30o + 10o brown red 1.65 1.50

The surtax was for flood relief in the Netherlands.

Stone Memorial — SP10

1953, Mar. 26 *Perf. 13*

B21 SP10 30o + 5o dark red 1.50 1.40

The surtax was for cultural work of the Danish Border Union.

Nos. B15 and B16 Surcharged with New Value and Ornamental Screen in Black

1955, Feb. 17

B22 SP5 20o + 5o on No. B15 1.10 1.00
B23 SP6 30o + 5o on No. B16 1.10 1.00

The surtax was for the Liberty Fund.

No. 341 Surcharged **30 + 5 Ungarns-hjælpen**

1957, Mar. 25

B24 A61 30o + 5o on 95o red org 60 60

The surtax went to the Danish Red Cross for aid to Hungary.

#335 Surcharged: "Gronlandsfonden + 10"

1959, Feb. 23

B25 A61 30o + 10o brown red 1.00 1.00

The surtax was for the Greenland Fund.

Globe Encircled by Red Cross Flags — SP11

Queen Ingrid — SP12

1959, June 24 Engr. *Perf. 13*

B26 SP11 30o + 5o rose red 48 40
B27 SP11 60o + 5o lt ultra & car 80 75

Centenary of the Intl. Red Cross idea. The surtax was for the Red Cross. Crosses photogravure on No. B27.

1960, Oct. 25 Unwmk.

B28 SP12 30o + 10o dark red 75 85

Queen Ingrid's 25th anniv. as a Girl Scout. The surtax was for the Scouts' fund for needy and sick children.

African Mother, Child — SP13

Healthy and Crippled Hands — SP14

1962, May 24

B29 SP13 30o + 10o dark red 75 1.10

Issued to aid underdeveloped countries.

1963, June 24 *Perf. 13*

B30 SP14 35o + 10o dark red 1.25 1.25

The surtax was for the benefit of the Cripples' Foundation.

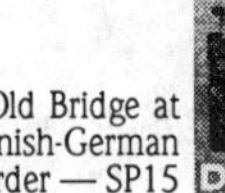

Old Bridge at Danish-German Border — SP15

1964, May 28 Engr.

B31 SP15 35o + 10o henna brown 1.00 1.00

Surtax for the Danish Border Union.

Princesses Margrethe, Benedikte, Anne-Marie — SP16

Happy Child — SP17

1964, Aug. 24

B32 SP16 35o + 10o dull red 85 85
B33 SP16 60o + 10o dk blue & red 1.10 1.10

The surtax was for the Red Cross.

1965, Oct. 21 Engr. *Perf. 13*

B34 SP17 50o + 10o brick red 48 48

The surtax was for the National Children's Welfare Association.

"Red Cross" in 32 Languages and Red Cross, Red Lion and Sun, and Red Crescent Emblems SP18

1966, Jan. 20 Engr. *Perf. 13*

B35 SP18 50o + 10o red 50 50

Engraved and Photogravure

B36 SP18 80o + 10o dk blue & red 1.00 1.00

The surtax was for the Red Cross.

"Refugees 66" — SP19

Symbolic Rose — SP20

1966, Oct. 24 Engr. *Perf. 13*

B37 SP19 40o + 10o sepia 90 90
B38 SP19 50o + 10o rose red 90 90
B39 SP19 80o + 10o blue 1.25 1.25

The surtax was for aid to refugees.

1967, Oct. 12

B40 SP20 60o + 10o brown red 45 45

The surcharge was for the Salvation Army.

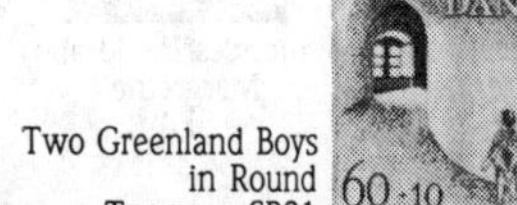

Two Greenland Boys in Round Tower — SP21

1968, Sept. 12 Engr. *Perf. 13*

B41 SP21 60o + 10o dark red 55 55

The surtax was for child welfare work in Greenland.

Princess Margrethe and Prince Henrik with Prince Frederik — SP22

1969, Dec. 11

B42 SP22 50o + 10o brown & red 60 60
B43 SP22 60o + 10o brn red & red 60 60

The surtax was for the Danish Red Cross.

Child Seeking Help — SP23

1970, Mar. 13

B44 SP23 60o + 10o brown red 48 48

Surtax for "Save the Children Fund."

Child — SP24

Marsh Marigold — SP25

1971, Apr. 29 Engr. *Perf. 13*

B45 SP24 60o + 10o copper red 52 52

Surtax was for the National Children's Welfare Association.

1972, Aug. 17

B46 SP25 70o + 10o green & yel 45 45

Cent. of the Soc. and Home for the Disabled.

Heimaey Town and Volcano — SP26

1973, Oct. 17 Engr. *Perf. 13*

B47 SP26 70o + 20o vio blue & red 65 65

The surtax was for the victims of the eruption of Heimaey Volcano, Jan. 23, 1973.

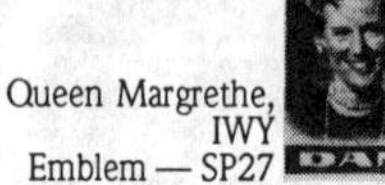

Queen Margrethe, IWY Emblem — SP27

1975, Mar. 20 Engr. *Perf. 13*

B48 SP27 90o + 20o red & buff 65 65

International Women's Year 1975. Surtax was for a foundation to benefit women primarily in Greenland and Faroe Islands.

Skuldelev I SP28

Ships: 90o+20o, Thingvalla, emigrant steamer. 100o+20o, Liner Frederick VIII, c. 1930. 130o+20o, Three-master Danmark.

1976, Jan. 22 Engr. *Perf. 13*

B49 SP28 70 + 20o olive brown 90 1.00
B50 SP28 90 + 20o brick red 90 1.00
B51 SP28 100 + 20o olive green 1.00 1.25
B52 SP28 130 + 20o violet blue 1.00 1.25

Bicentenary of American Declaration of Independence.

People and Red Cross SP29

Invalid in Wheelchair SP30

1976, Feb. 26 Engr. *Perf. 13*

B53 SP29 100o + 20o red & black 35 35
B54 SP29 130o + 20o blue, red & blk 55 55

Centenary of Danish Red Cross.

1976, May 6 Engr. *Perf. 13*

B55 SP30 100o + 20o vermilion & blk 45 45

The surtax was for the Foundation to Aid the Disabled.

Mother and Child — SP31

Anti-Cancer Campaign — SP32

1977, Mar. 24 Engr. *Perf. 12½*

B56 SP31 1k + 20o multicolored 45 45

Danish Society for the Mentally Handicapped, 25th anniversary. Surtax was for the Society.

1978, Oct. 12 Engr. *Perf. 13*

B57 SP32 120o + 20o red 48 48

Danish Anti-Cancer Campaign, 50th anniversary. Surtax was for campaign.

Child and IYC Emblem — SP33

1979, Jan. 25 Engr. *Perf. 12½*

B58 SP33 1.20k + 20o red & brown 48 48

International Year of the Child.

Foundation for the Disabled, 25th Anniversary — SP34

1980, Apr. 10 Engr. *Perf. 13*

B59 SP34 130o + 20o brown red 40 40

Children Playing Ball — SP35

Intl. Year of the Disabled — SP36

1981, Feb. 5 Engr. *Perf. 12½x13*

B60 SP35 1.60k + 20o brown red 60 60

Surtax was for child welfare.

1981, Sept. 10 Engr. *Perf. 12½x13*

B61 SP36 2k + 20o dark blue 65 65

Stem and Broken Line — SP37

1982, May 3 Engr. *Perf. 13*

B62 SP37 2k + 40o dull red 65 65

Surtax was for Danish Multiple Sclerosis Society.

Nurse with Patient — SP38

1984 Olympic Games — SP39

1983, Jan. 27 **Engr.**
B63 SP38 2k + 40o multicolored 65 65

1984, Feb. 23 **Litho. & Engr.**
B64 SP39 2.70k + 40o multicolored 1.00 1.00

Electrocardiogram Reading, Heart — SP40

1984, Sept. 6 **Engr.** ***Perf. 12½***
B65 SP40 2.70k + 40o red 1.00 1.00

Surtax was for Heart Foundation.

SP41

SP42

1985, May 2 **Litho.** ***Perf. 13***
B66 SP41 2.80k + 50o multicolored 1.00 1.00

Liberation from German Occupation, 40th Anniv. Surtax for benefit of World War II veterans.

1985, Oct. 3 **Litho. & Engr.**

Design: Tapestry detail, by Caroline Ebbeson (1852-1936), former patient, St. Hans Hospital, Roskilade.

B67 SP42 2.80k + 40o multicolored 85 65

Natl. Society for the Welfare of the Mentally Ill, 25th Anniv. Surtax benefited the mentally ill.

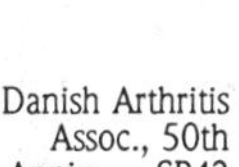

Danish Arthritis Assoc., 50th Anniv. — SP43

1986, Mar. 20 **Litho.** ***Perf. 13***
B68 SP43 2.80k + 50o multicolored 70 40

Surtax for the Arthritis Assoc.

Poul Reichhart (1913-1985), as Papageno in The Magic Flute — SP44

1986, Feb. 6 **Litho.** ***Perf. 13***
B69 SP44 2.80k + 50o multicolored 70 42

Surtax for the physically handicapped.

Danish Society for the Blind, 75th Anniv. — SP45

1986, Feb. 20 **Litho. & Engr.** ***Perf. 13***
B70 SP45 2.80k +50o blk, vio brn & dk red 70 45

Danish Assoc. of Epileptics, 25th Anniv. SP46

1987, Sept. 24 **Engr.** ***Perf. 13***
B71 SP46 2.80k +50o dk red, brt ultra & dk grn 95 48

Folkekirkens Nodhjaelp Relief Organization — SP47

1988, Mar. 10 **Engr.**
B72 SP47 3k +50o multicolored 1.15 58

Surtax for the relief organization.

Natl. Council for Unwed Mothers, 5th Anniv. — SP48

1988, Sept. 22 **Photo.**
B73 SP48 3k +50o dk rose brown 1.05 52

SP49

SP50

1989, Feb. 16 **Litho.** ***Perf.***
B74 SP49 3.20k +50o multi 1.10 55

Salvation Army.

1990, Aug. 30 **Litho.** ***Perf. 13***
B75 SP50 3.50k +50o Insulin crystal 1.25 65

Danish Diabetes Assoc., 50th anniv.

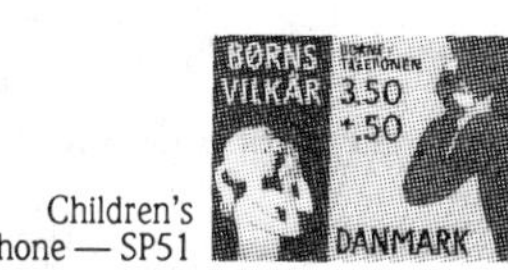

Children's Telephone — SP51

1991, June 6 **Engr.** ***Perf. 13***
B76 SP51 3.50k +50o dark blue 1.15 60

Surtax benefits Borns Vilkar, children's welfare organization.

Danish Dyslexia Assoc., 50th Anniv. SP52

Litho. & Engr.

1992, Aug. 27 ***Perf. 13***
B77 SP52 3.75k +50o multi 1.60 80

YMCA Social Work, 75th Anniv. — SP53

1993, Aug. 19 **Litho.** ***Perf. 13***
B78 SP53 3.75k +50o multi 1.25 65

AIR POST STAMPS

Airplane and Plowman AP1

Towers of Copenhagen AP2

Wmk. Multiple Crosses (114)

1925-29 **Typo.** ***Perf. 12x12½***
C1 AP1 10o yel grn 13.00 15.00
C2 AP1 15o violet ('26) 27.50 25.00
C3 AP1 25o scarlet 25.00 22.50
C4 AP1 50o lt gray ('29) 65.00 70.00
C5 AP1 1k choc ('29) 57.50 50.00
Nos. C1-C5 (5) 188.00 182.50
Set, never hinged 375.00

Unwmk.

1934, June 9 **Engr.** ***Perf. 13***
C6 AP2 10o orange 80 90
C7 AP2 15o red 2.75 3.50
C8 AP2 20o Prus blue 3.25 3.50
C9 AP2 50o olive blk 2.75 3.50
C10 AP2 1k brown 9.00 10.00
Nos. C6-C10 (5) 18.55 21.40
Set, never hinged 30.00

LATE FEE STAMPS

LF1

Coat of Arms — LF2

Perf. 14x14½

1923 **Typo.** **Wmk. 114**
I1 LF1 10o green 5.00 1.00
a. Double overprint

No. I1 was, at first, not a postage stamp but represented a tax for the services of the post office clerks in filling out postal forms and writing addresses. In 1923 it was put into use as a Late Fee stamp.

1926-31
I2 LF2 10o green 1.65 95
I3 LF2 10o brown ('31) 1.50 32

1934 **Unwmk.** **Engr.** ***Perf. 13***
I4 LF2 5o green 20 15
I5 LF2 10o orange 20 15
Set value 21

POSTAGE DUE STAMPS

Regular Issues of 1913-20 Overprinted **PORTO**

Perf. 14x14½

1921, May 1 **Wmk. 114**
J1 A10 1o deep orange 1.25 90
J2 A16 5o green 2.00 1.25
J3 A16 7o orange 1.90 1.10
J4 A16 10o red 11.00 5.50
J5 A16 20o deep blue 6.00 3.00
J6 A16 25o brown & blk 9.00 2.00
J7 A16 50o claret & blk 4.25 1.25
Nos. J1-J7 (7) 35.40 15.00

Same Overprint in Dark Blue On Military Stamp of 1917

1921, Nov. 23
J8 A16 10o red 4.25 3.00
a. "S" inverted 100.00 125.00

Numeral of Value — D1

Typographed (Solid Panel)

1921-30 ***Perf. 14x14½***
J9 D1 1o orange ('22) 35 40
J10 D1 4o blue ('25) 1.10 1.10
J11 D1 5o brown ('22) 90 65
J12 D1 5o lt green ('30) 60 52
J13 D1 7o apple grn ('27) 9.50 10.50
J14 D1 7o dk violet ('30) 14.00 16.00
J15 D1 10o yel grn ('22) 75 40
J16 D1 10o lt brown ('30) 65 32
J17 D1 20o grnsh bl ('21) 90 50
a. Double impression 1,500.
J18 D1 20o gray ('30) 1.25 85
J19 D1 25o scarlet ('23) 1.65 70
J20 D1 25o violet ('26) 1.65 90
J21 D1 25o lt blue ('30) 3.00 2.25
J22 D1 1k dk blue ('21) 27.50 4.50
J23 D1 1k brn & dk bl ('25) 9.00 2.75
J24 D1 5k purple ('25) 15.00 5.25
Nos. J9-J24 (16) 87.80 47.59

Engraved (Lined Panel)

1934-55 **Unwmk.** ***Perf. 13***
J25 D1 1o slate 15 15
J26 D1 2o carmine 15 15
J27 D1 5o yellow grn 15 15
J28 D1 6o dk olive ('41) 40 15
J29 D1 8o magenta ('50) 1.25 1.50
J30 D1 10o orange 15 15
J31 D1 12o dp ultra ('55) 30 25
J32 D1 15o violet ('37) 40 15
J33 D1 20o gray 35 15
J34 D1 25o blue 40 15
J35 D1 30o green ('53) 40 15
J36 D1 40o claret ('49) 50 15
J37 D1 1k brown 65 15
Nos. J25-J37 (13) 5.25
Set value 2.70

No. 96 Surcharged in Black **PORTO 15**

1934 **Wmk. 114** ***Perf. 14x14½***
J38 A10 15o on 12o violet 1.65 70

MILITARY STAMPS

Nos. 97 and 100 Overprinted in Blue **S F**

1917 **Wmk. 114** ***Perf. 14x14½***
M1 A16 5o green 12.50 16.00
a. "S" inverted 185.00 275.00
M2 A16 10o red 11.00 13.00
a. "S" inverted 150.00 200.00

The letters "S F" are the initials of "Soldater Frimaerke" (Soldier's Stamp).
For overprint see No. J8.

OFFICIAL STAMPS

Small State Seal — O1

Wmk. Crown (112)

1871 Typo. Perf. 14x13½

O1 O1 2s blue 82.50 45.00
a. 2s ultra 82.50 45.00
b. Imperf., pair 400.00
O2 O1 4s carmine 47.50 8.00
a. Imperf., pair 375.00
O3 O1 16s green 210.00 150.00
a. Imperf., pair 475.00

Perf. 12½

O4 O1 4s carmine 3,250. 250.00
O5 O1 16s green 225.00 190.00

Nos. O1-O3 were reprinted in 1886 upon white wove paper, unwatermarked and imperforate. Value $10 each.

1875 Perf. 14x13½

O6 O1 3o violet 2.25 6.50
O7 O1 4o grnsh bl 3.50 1.65
O8 O1 8o carmine 3.50 90
a. Imperf., pair
O9 O1 32o green 27.50 19.00

For surcharge see No. 81.

1899-02 Perf. 13

O9A O1 3o red lil ('02) 2.75 2.25
c. Imperf., pair 350.00
O9B O1 4o blue 1.25 95
O10 O1 8o carmine 13.00 7.25

For surcharge see No. 137.

1902-06 Wmk. 113

O11 O1 1o orange 1.65 1.40
O12 O1 3o red lil ('06) 65 55
O13 O1 4o blue ('03) 1.40 80
O14 O1 5o green 1.00 20
O15 O1 10o carmine 1.00 75
Nos. O11-O15 (5) 5.70 3.70

1914-23 Wmk. 114 Perf. 14x14½

O16 O1 1o orange 1.10 75
O17 O1 3o gray ('18) 3.00 2.25
O18 O1 4o blue ('16) 21.00 19.00
O19 O1 5o grn ('15) 65 18
O20 O1 5o choc ('23) 3.00 *10.00*
O21 O1 10o red ('17) 2.75 65
O22 O1 10o green ('21) 1.00 1.00
O23 O1 15o vio ('19) 21.00 19.00
O24 O1 20o indigo ('20) 7.25 3.50
Nos. O16-O24 (9) 60.75 56.33

For surcharges see Nos. 185-191.
Official stamps were discontinued Apr. 1, 1924.

NEWSPAPER STAMPS

Numeral of Value — N1

1907 Typo. Wmk. 113 Perf. 13

P1 N1 1o olive 3.25 1.10
P2 N1 5o blue 13.00 6.50
P3 N1 7o carmine 4.00 38
P4 N1 10o deep lilac 8.00 1.65
P5 N1 20o green 7.25 55
P6 N1 38o orange 10.50 55
P7 N1 68o yel brn 21.00 11.00
P8 N1 1k bl grn & cl 8.00 80
P9 N1 5k rose & yel grn 60.00 11.00
P10 N1 10k bis & bl 60.00 11.00
Nos. P1-P10 (10) 195.00 44.53

For surcharges see Nos. 138-144.

1914-15 Wmk. 114 Perf. 14x14½

P11 N1 1o ol gray 3.25 32
P12 N1 5o blue 9.25 3.75
P13 N1 7o rose 7.25 32
P14 N1 8o green ('15) 8.00 32
P15 N1 10o deep lilac 8.00 32
P16 N1 20o green 92.50 95
a. Imperf., pair *450.00*
P17 N1 29o org yel ('15) 12.00 75
P18 N1 38o orange 2,500. 90.00
P19 N1 41o yel brn ('15) 12.00 70
P20 N1 1k bl grn & mar 20.00 35
Nos. P11-P17,P19-P20 (9) 172.25 7.78

For surcharges see Nos. 145-154.

PARCEL POST STAMPS

These stamps were for use on postal packets sent by the Esbjerg-Fano Ferry Service.

Regular Issues of 1913-30 Overprinted **POSTFÆRGE**

1919-41 Wmk. 114 Perf. 14x14½

Q1 A10 10o green ('22) 11.00 6.00
Q2 A10 10o bis brn ('30) 10.00 3.75
Q3 A16 10o red 40.00 40.00
a. "POSFFAERGE" 165.00 250.00
Q4 A16 15o violet 14.00 13.00
a. "POSFFAERGE" 165.00 *350.00*
Q5 A16 30o orange ('22) 10.00 10.00
Q6 A16 30o dk blue ('26) 2.50 2.50
Q7 A16 50o cl & blk ('20) 175.00 165.00
Q8 A16 50o lt gray ('22) 15.00 5.25
a. 50o dark gray ('22) 100.00 125.00
Q9 A16 1k brn & bl ('24) 45.00 10.50
Q9A A16 5k vio & brn ('41) 2.80 1.75
Q10 A16 10k ver & grn ('30) 55.00 55.00

Engr.

Q11 A17 1k yel brn 110.00 90.00
a. "POSFFAERGE" 1,300. 2,000.
Nos. Q1-Q11 (12) 490.30 402.75

1927-30

Q12 A30 15o red ('27) 15.00 8.50
Q13 A30 30o ocher ('27) 15.00 9.00
Q14 A30 40o yel grn ('30) 14.00 5.00

Overprinted on Regular Issues of 1933-40

1936-42 Unwmk. Perf. 13

Q15 A32 5o rose lake ('42) 15 15
Q16 A32 10o yel org 26.00 22.50
Q17 A32 10o lt brown ('38) 1.25 1.40
Q18 A32 10o purple ('39) 22 24
Q19 A30 15o dp red 85 1.00
Q20 A30 30o blue, I 5.00 4.25
Q21 A30 30o blue, II ('40) 6.50 8.75
Q22 A30 30o org, II ('42) 65 60
Q23 A30 40o yel grn, I 5.00 4.25
Q24 A30 40o yel grn, II ('40) 6.50 7.75
Q25 A30 40o blue, II ('42) 85 90
Q26 A33 50o gray 1.50 1.50
Q27 A33 1k lt brown 1.10 1.00
Nos. Q15-Q27 (13) 55.57 54.29

Catalogue values for unused stamps in this section, from this point to the end of the section, are for Never Hinged items.

Overprinted on Nos. 284, 286, 286B

1945

Q28 A47 30o orange 1.50 1.25
Q29 A47 40o blue 1.25 1.25
Q30 A47 50o gray 1.50 1.25

Ovptd. on Nos. 318, 309, 310, 312, 297

1949-53

Q31 A32 10o green ('53) 28 28
Q32 A61 30o orange 2.00 1.50
Q33 A61 40o dull blue 2.00 1.50
Q34 A61 50o gray ('50) 12.00 2.75
Q35 A55 1k brown ('50) 1.50 1.40
Nos. Q31-Q35 (5) 17.78 7.43

Ovptd. on Nos. 335, 323, 336, 326, 397

1955-65

Q36 A61 30o brown red 75 65
Q37 A61 40o gray 60 60
Q38 A61 50o aqua 75 75
Q39 A61 70o deep green 75 75
Q40 A55 1.25k orange ('65) 4.25 4.75
Nos. Q36-Q40 (5) 7.10 7.50

Overprinted on Nos. 417 and 419

1967 Engr. Perf. 13

Q41 A86 40o brown 60 60
Q42 A86 80o ultra 60 60

Nos. 224, 438, 441, 297-299 Overprinted **POSTFÆRGE**

1967-74 Engr. Perf. 13

Q43 A32 5o rose lake 18 18
Q44 A86 50o brown ('74) 42 42
Q45 A86 90o ultra ('70) 85 85
Q46 A55 1k brown 1.10 90
Q47 A55 2k red ('72) 1.40 1.40
Q48 A55 5k dull bl ('72) 3.00 2.75
Nos. Q43-Q48 (6) 6.95 6.50

Nos. Q44-Q45, Q47-Q48 are on fluorescent paper.

Overprinted on No. 541

1975, Feb. 27

Q49 A161 100o deep ultra 50 50

DIEGO-SUAREZ

LOCATION — A town at the northern end of Madagascar
GOVT. — Former French colony
POP. — 12,237

From 1885 to 1896 Diego-Suarez, (Antsirane), a French naval base, was a separate colony and issued its own stamps. These were succeeded by stamps of Madagascar.

100 Centimes = 1 Franc

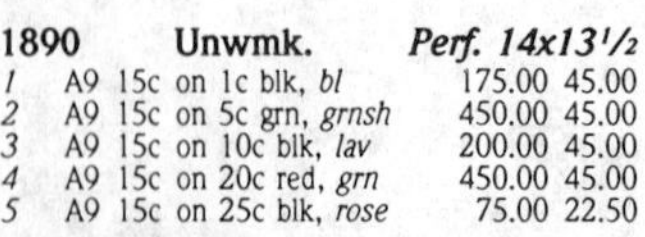

Stamps of French Colonies Handstamp Surcharged in Violet

1890 Unwmk. Perf. 14x13½

1 A9 15c on 1c blk, *bl* 175.00 45.00
2 A9 15c on 5c grn, *grnsh* 450.00 45.00
3 A9 15c on 10c blk, *lav* 200.00 45.00
4 A9 15c on 20c red, *grn* 450.00 45.00
5 A9 15c on 25c blk, *rose* 75.00 22.50

This surcharge is found inverted, double, etc. Counterfeits exist.

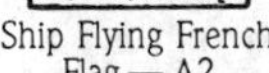
Ship Flying French Flag — A2

France — A5

Symbolical of Union of France and Madagascar
A3 A4

1890 Litho. Imperf.

6 A2 1c black 750.00 160.00
7 A3 5c black 725.00 125.00
8 A4 15c black 175.00 55.00
9 A5 25c black 200.00 65.00

Counterfeits exist of Nos. 6-9.

A6

1891

10 A6 5c black 140.00 57.50

Excellent counterfeits exist of No. 10.

Stamps of French Colonies Surcharged in Red or Black:

No. 11

No. 12

1892 Perf. 14x13½

11 A9 5c on 10c blk, *lav* (R) 110.00 50.00
a. Inverted surcharge 275.00 190.00
12 A9 5c on 20c red, *grn* 100.00 35.00
a. Inverted surcharge 275.00 190.00

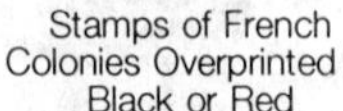
Stamps of French Colonies Overprinted in Black or Red

1892

13 A9 1c blue (R) 17.50 9.00
14 A9 2c brown, *buff* 17.50 9.00
15 A9 4c claret, *lav* 30.00 20.00
16 A9 5c green, *grnsh* 67.50 47.50
17 A9 10c black, *lavender* 20.00 15.00
18 A9 15c black, *blue* 17.50 11.00
19 A9 20c red, *grn* 20.00 14.00
20 A9 25c black, *rose* 15.00 9.00
21 A9 30c brown, *bis* (R) 800.00 550.00
22 A9 35c black, *yellow* 800.00 450.00
23 A9 75c carmine, *rose* 42.50 25.00
24 A9 1fr brnz grn, *straw* (R) 42.50 25.00
a. Double overprint 150.00 125.00

Inverted Overprint

13a A9 1c 125. 100.
14a A9 2c 125. 100.
16a A9 5c 125. 100.
17a A9 10c 125. 100.
20a A9 25c 125. 100.
21a A9 30c 1,000.
22a A9 35c 1,000.

Navigation and Commerce
A10 A11

1892 Typo. Perf. 14x13½
Name of Colony in Blue or Carmine

25 A10 1c black, *blue* 1.10 1.10
26 A10 2c brown, *buff* 1.25 1.10
27 A10 4c claret, *lav* 1.00 1.00
28 A10 5c green, *grnsh* 2.50 1.60
29 A10 10c black, *lavender* 3.75 2.00
30 A10 15c bl, quadrille paper 4.25 3.50
31 A10 20c red, *green* 8.00 6.25
32 A10 25c black, *rose* 7.00 5.00
33 A10 30c brown, *bister* 9.00 6.25
34 A10 40c red, *straw* 11.00 7.50
35 A10 50c carmine, *rose* 21.00 11.00
36 A10 75c violet, *org* 35.00 14.00
37 A10 1fr brnz grn, *straw* 35.00 20.00
Nos. 25-37 (13) 139.85 80.30

Perf. 13½x14 stamps are counterfeits.

1894 Perf. 14x13½

38 A11 1c black, *blue* 60 65
39 A11 2c brown, *buff* 1.25 1.00
40 A11 4c claret, *lav* 1.25 1.00
41 A11 5c green, *grnsh* 2.25 1.75
42 A11 10c black, *lavender* 3.50 2.25
43 A11 15c blue, quadrille paper 3.50 2.25
44 A11 20c red, *grn* 7.00 5.00
45 A11 25c black, *rose* 4.00 2.25
46 A11 30c brown, *bister* 4.50 3.00
47 A11 40c red, *straw* 5.00 3.00
48 A11 50c carmine, *rose* 7.00 6.00
49 A11 75c violet, *org* 5.00 3.00
50 A11 1fr brnz grn, *straw* 11.00 9.00
Nos. 38-50 (13) 55.85 40.15

Bisected stamps of type A11 are mentioned in note after Madagascar No. 62.
For surcharges see Madagascar #56-57, 61-62.
Perf. 13½x14 stamps are counterfeits.

POSTAGE DUE STAMPS

D1

D2

1891 Unwmk. Litho. Imperf.

J1 D1 5c violet 90.00 35.00
J2 D2 50c black 90.00 35.00

Excellent counterfeits exist of Nos. J1-J2.

Postage Due Stamps of French Colonies Overprinted Like Nos. 13-24

1892

J3	D1	1c black	62.50	25.00
J4	D1	2c black	62.50	25.50
a.		Inverted overprint	225.00	175.00
J5	D1	3c black	62.50	27.50
J6	D1	4c black	62.50	27.50
J7	D1	5c black	62.50	27.50
J8	D1	10c black	17.50	12.00
a.		Inverted overprint	225.00	160.00
J9	D1	15c black	17.50	12.00
a.		Double overprint	350.00	275.00
J10	D1	20c black	110.00	52.50
J11	D1	30c black	52.50	27.50
a.		Inverted overprint	225.00	160.00
J12	D1	60c black	750.00	350.00
J13	D1	1fr brown	1,400.	750.00

DJIBOUTI

LOCATION — East Africa
GOVT. — Republic
AREA — 8,880 sq. mi.
POP. — 340,000 (est. 1983)
CAPITAL — Djibouti

The French territory of Afars and Issas became the Republic of Djibouti June 27, 1977. For 1894-1902 issues with "Djibouti" or "DJ," see Somali Coast.

Catalogue values for all unused stamps in this country are for Never Hinged items.

Afars and Issas Issues of 1972-1977 Overprinted and Surcharged with Bars and "REPUBLIQUE DE DJIBOUTI" in Black, Dark Green, Blue or Brown

Printing and Perforations as Before

1977

439	A63	1fr on 4fr (#358;B)	15	15
440	A81	2fr on 5fr (#433;B)	15	15
441	A75	5fr on 20fr (#421;B)	15	15
442	A70	8fr (#380;B)	15	15
443	A71	20fr (#387;DG)	30	30
444	A81	30fr (#434;B)	40	40
445	A71	40fr (#388;DG)	50	50
446	A71	45fr (#389;Bl)	60	60
447	A78	45fr (#428;B)	60	60
448	A72	50fr (#394;B)	75	75
449	A71	60fr (#391;Br)	80	80
450	A79	70fr (#430;B)	1.00	1.00
451	A81	70fr (#435;B)	1.00	1.00
452	A74	100fr (#418;B)	1.40	1.40
453	A72	150fr (#399;B)	2.00	2.00
454	A76	200fr (#422;B)	2.75	2.75
455	A80	200fr (#432;B)	2.75	2.75
456	A74	300fr (#419;B)	4.25	4.25
		Nos. 439-456,C106-C108 (21)	28.05	27.30

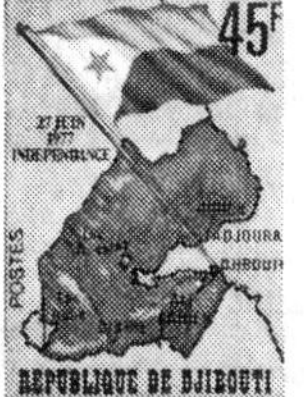
Map and Flag of Djibouti — A83

Water Pipe — A84

Design: 65fr, Map and flag of Djibouti, map of Africa, horiz.

1977, June 27 Litho. *Perf. 12½*

457	A83	45fr multicolored	65	40
458	A83	65fr multicolored	1.00	50

Independence, June 27.

1977, July 4

459	A84	10fr Headrest, horiz.	15	15
460	A84	20fr shown	30	15
461	A84	25fr Pitcher	40	18
		Set value		40

Ostrich — A85

1977, Aug. 11 Litho. *Perf. 12½*

462	A85	90fr shown	1.10	80
463	A85	100fr Weaver	1.50	1.00

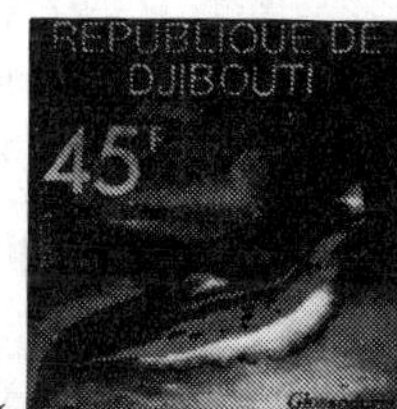
Snail — A86

Designs: 15fr, Fiddler crab. 50fr, Klipspringers. 70fr, Green turtle. 80fr, Priacanthus hamrur (fish). 150fr, Dolphinfish.

1977 Litho. *Perf. 12½*

464	A86	15fr multicolored	15	15
465	A86	45fr multicolored	30	25
466	A86	50fr multicolored	60	40
467	A86	70fr multicolored	60	35
468	A86	80fr multicolored	65	40
469	A86	150fr multicolored	2.00	1.10
		Nos. 464-469 (6)	4.30	2.65

Issue dates: 45fr, 70fr, 80fr, Sept. 14. Others, Dec. 5.

Pres. Hassan Gouled Aptidon and Djibouti Flag — A87

1978, Feb. 12 Litho. *Perf. 13*

470	A87	65fr multicolored	75	40

Charaxes Hansali — A88

Necklace — A89

Butterflies: 20fr, Colias electo. 25fr, Acraea chilo. 150fr, Junonia hierta.

1978, Mar. 13 Litho. *Perf. 12½x13*

471	A88	5fr multicolored	15	15
472	A88	20fr multicolored	15	15
473	A88	25fr multicolored	30	20
474	A88	150fr multicolored	1.40	60
		Set value		92

1978, May 29 Litho. *Perf. 12½x13*

Design: 55fr, Necklace, diff.

475	A89	45fr pink & multi	40	22
476	A89	55fr blue & multi	50	28

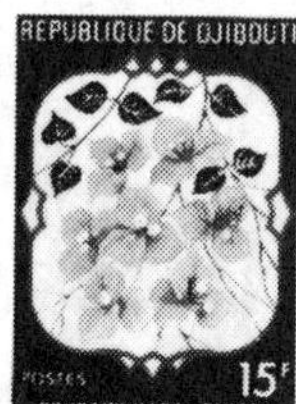
Bougainvillea — A90

Flowers: 35fr, Hibiscus schizopetalus. 250fr, Caesalpinia pulcherrima.

1978, July 10 Photo. *Perf. 12½x13*

477	A90	15fr multicolored	18	15
478	A90	35fr multicolored	42	24
479	A90	250fr multicolored	2.50	1.10

Charonia Nodifera — A91

Sea Shell: 80fr, Charonia variegata.

1978, Oct. 9 Litho. *Perf. 13*

480	A91	10fr multicolored	15	15
481	A91	80fr multicolored	75	30
		Set value		35

Chaetodon A92

Fish: 30fr, Yellow surgeonfish. 40fr, Harlequinfish.

1978, Nov. 20 Litho. *Perf. 13x12½*

482	A92	8fr multicolored	15	15
483	A92	30fr multicolored	28	15
484	A92	40fr multicolored	35	15
		Set value		30

Alsthom BB 1201 at Dock — A93

Locomotives: 55fr, Steam locomotive 231. 60fr, Steam locomotive 130 and map of route. 75fr, Diesel.

1979, Jan. 29 Litho. *Perf. 13*

485	A93	40fr multicolored	1.10	40
486	A93	55fr multicolored	1.40	50
487	A93	60fr multicolored	1.50	50
488	A93	75fr multicolored	2.25	60

Djibouti-Addis Ababa railroad.

Children and IYC Emblem — A94

Design: 200fr, Mother, child, IYC emblem.

1979, Feb. 26 Litho. *Perf. 13*

489	A94	20fr multicolored	20	15
490	A94	200fr multicolored	2.00	1.10

International Year of the Child.

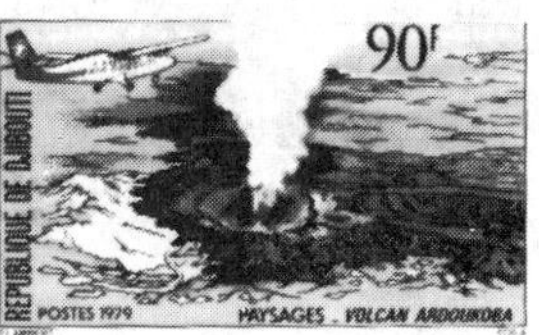
Plane over Ardoukoba Volcano — A95

Design: 30fr, Helicopter over Ardoukoba Volcano, vert.

1979, Mar. 19

491	A95	30fr multicolored	30	25
492	A95	90fr multicolored	90	50

Rowland Hill, Postal Clerks, No. C109 — A96

Designs: 100fr, Somali Coast No. 22, Djibouti No. 457, letters, Rowland Hill. 150fr, Letters hoisted onto ship, smoke signals, Rowland Hill.

1979, Apr. 17 Litho. *Perf. 13x12½*

493	A96	25fr multicolored	25	15
494	A96	100fr multicolored	1.00	40
495	A96	150fr multicolored	1.40	65

Sir Rowland Hill (1795-1879), originator of penny postage.

View of Djibouti, Bird and Local Woman — A97

Design: 80fr, Map and flag of Djibouti, UPU emblem, Concorde, train and mail runner.

1979, June 8 Litho. *Perf. 13x12½*

496 A97 55fr multicolored	80	60
497 A97 80fr multicolored	1.10	80

Philexafrique II, Libreville, Gabon, June 8-17. Nos. 496, 497 each printed in sheets of 10 with 5 labels showing exhibition emblem.

Solanacea A98

Flowers: 2fr, Opuntia, vert. 15fr, Trichodesma. 45fr, Acacia etbaica. 50fr, Thunbergia alata, vert.

Perf. 13x13½, 13½x13
1979, June 18

498 A98 2fr multicolored	15	15
499 A98 8fr multicolored	15	15
500 A98 15fr multicolored	15	15
501 A98 45fr multicolored	35	15
502 A98 50fr multicolored	42	15
Nos. 498-502 (5)	1.22	
Set value		40

Running — A99

Olympic Emblem and: 70fr, Basketball. 200fr, Soccer, horiz.

Perf. 12½x13, 13x12½
1979, Oct. 22 Litho.

503 A99 70fr multicolored	60	25
504 A99 120fr multicolored	1.10	50
505 A99 200fr multicolored	2.00	75

Pre-Olympic Year.

Cypraecassis Rufa — A100

Shells: 40fr, Lambis chiragra arthritica. 300fr, Harpa connaidalis.

1979, Dec. 22 Litho. *Perf. 13*

506 A100 10fr multicolored	15	15
507 A100 40fr multicolored	35	15
508 A100 300fr multicolored	2.50	1.10

Rotary International, 75th Anniversary — A101

1980, Feb. 19 Litho. *Perf. 13x12½*

509 A101 90fr multicolored	1.00	50

Lions Club of Djibouti — A102

1980, Feb. 19

510 A102 100fr multicolored	1.10	50

Colotis Danae — A103

1980, Mar. 17 *Perf. 13x13½*

511 A103 5fr *shown*	15	15
512 A103 55fr *Danaus chrysippus*	1.00	20
Set value		25

Chess Players, Knight — A104

Chess Federation Creation: 75fr, Chess Game, Florence, 1493.

1980, June 9 Litho. *Perf. 13*

513 A104 20fr multicolored	28	15
514 A104 75fr multicolored	80	28

Cribraria A105

1980, Aug. 12 Litho. *Perf. 13*

515 A105 15fr *shown*	15	15
516 A105 85fr *Nautilius pompilius*	75	30
Set value		36

Alexander Fleming, Discoverer of Penicillin — A106

Design: 130fr, Jules Verne, French science fiction writer; earth, moon and spacecraft.

1980, Sept. 1

517 A106 20fr multicolored	20	15
518 A106 130fr multicolored	1.10	50

Capt. Cook and Endeavor — A107

Capt. James Cook Death Bicentenary: 90fr, Ships and Maps of voyages.

1980, Nov. 20 Litho. *Perf. 13*

519 A107 55fr multicolored	40	20
520 A107 90fr multicolored	75	40

Souvenir sheets of 1 exist, perf. 12½x12.

Angel Fish — A108

1981, Apr. 13 Litho. *Perf. 12½*

521 A108 25fr shown	20	15
522 A108 55fr Moorish idol	40	20
523 A108 70fr Scad	50	30

13th World Telecommunications Day — A109

1981, May 17 Litho. *Perf. 13*

524 A109 140fr multicolored	1.10	50

Type 231 Steam Locomotive, Germany, 1958 and Amtrak, US, 1980 — A110

Locomotives: 55fr, Stephenson and his Rocket, Djibouti Railways 230 engine. 65fr, Type TGV, France, Type 962, Japan.

1981, June 9 Litho. *Perf. 13*

525 A110 40fr multicolored	30	20
526 A110 55fr multicolored	40	20
527 A110 65fr multicolored	50	22

Radio Amateurs Club — A111

1981, June 25

528 A111 250fr multicolored	1.50	75

Prince Charles and Lady Diana — A112

1981, June 29

529 A112 180fr shown	1.50	1.50
530 A112 200fr Couple, diff.	1.60	1.00

Royal Wedding.

Lord Nelson and Victory A113

1981, July 6 Litho. *Perf. 13x12½*

531 A113 100fr multicolored	65	40
532 A113 175fr multicolored	1.00	65

Lord Horatio Nelson (1758-1805).

Scout Tending Campfire — A114

1981, July 16 Litho. *Perf. 13*

533 A114 60fr shown	50	30
534 A114 105fr Scout giving sign	80	40

28th World Scouting Conference, Dakar, Aug. (60fr); 4th Pan-African Scouting Conference, Abidjan, Aug. (105fr).

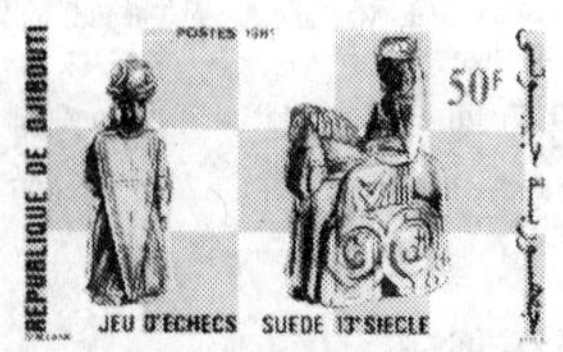

Pawn and Queen, Swedish Bone Chess Pieces, 13th Cent. — A115

1981, Oct. 15 Litho. *Perf. 13*

535 A115 50fr shown	40	25
536 A115 130fr Pawn, knight, Chinese, 19th cent., vert.	1.10	65

For overprints see Nos. 542-543.

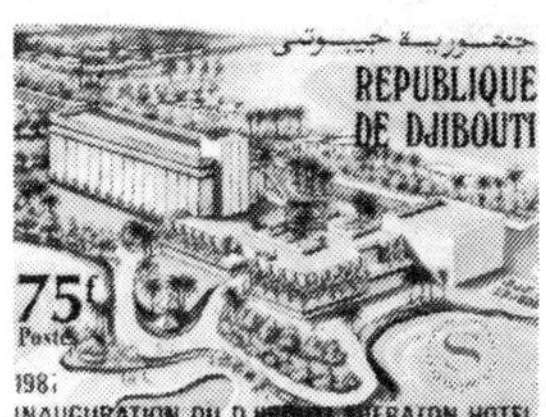

Sheraton Hotel Opening — A116

1981, Nov. 15 Litho. *Perf. 13x12½*

537 A116 75fr multicolored 60 40

For surcharge see No. 623.

Acacia Mellifera A117

1981, Dec. 21 *Perf. 13*

538 A117 10fr Clitoria ternatea, vert. 15 15
539 A117 30fr shown 25 15
540 A117 35fr Punica granatum 28 20
541 A117 45fr Malvaceous plant, vert. 35 20
Set value 58

See Nos. 558-560.

Nos. 535-536 Overprinted with Winners' Names

1981, Dec. Litho. *Perf. 13*

542 A115 50fr multicolored 40 30
543 A115 130fr multicolored 1.10 75

World Chess Championship.

TB Bacillus Centenary A117a

1982 Litho. *Perf. 13*

544 A117a 305fr Koch, slide, microscope 1.50 1.00

A117b A118

1982, Apr. 8 Litho. *Perf. 13*

545 A117b 125fr Ivory bishop 1.00 65
546 A117b 175fr Queen, pawn, 19th cent. 1.50 80

1982 World Chess Championship.

1982, May 17

547 A118 150fr multicolored 1.10 80

14th World Telecommunications Day.

Bus and Jeep — A119

1982, July 27 Litho. *Perf. 13*

548 A119 20fr shown 15 15
549 A119 25fr Dhow, ferry 20 15
550 A119 55fr Train, jet 42 30

Shells from the Red Sea — A120

1982, Nov. 20 Litho. *Perf. 12½*

551 A120 10fr Cypraea erythraeensis 15 15
552 A120 15fr Conus sumatrensis 15 15
553 A120 25fr Cypraea pulchra 20 15
554 A120 30fr Conus inscriptus 25 15
555 A120 70fr Casmaria ponderosa 60 38
556 A120 150fr Cypraea exusta 1.10 80
Nos. 551-556 (6) 2.45 1.78

See Nos. 563-567.

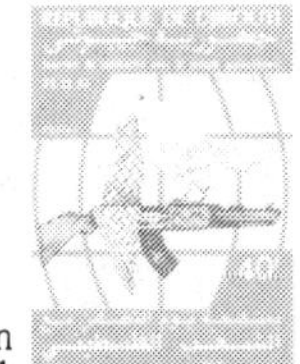

Intl. Palestinian Solidarity Day — A121

1982, Nov. 29 Litho. *Perf. 13*

557 A121 40fr multicolored 40 28

Local Flowers type of 1981

Various flowers. 5fr, 55fr, vert.

1983, Apr. 14 Litho. *Perf. 13*

558 A117 5fr multicolored 15 15
559 A117 50fr multicolored 55 40
560 A117 55fr multicolored 60 42

World Communications Year — A123

1983, June 20 Litho. *Perf. 13*

561 A123 500fr multicolored 4.50 3.00

Conference of Donors, Nov. 21-23 — A124

1983, Nov. 21 Litho. *Perf. 13x12½*

562 A124 75fr multicolored 75 55

Shell Type of 1982

1983, Dec. 20 Litho. *Perf. 12½*

563 A120 15fr Marginella obtusa 15 15
564 A120 30fr Conus jickelli 25 20
565 A120 55fr Cypraea macandrewi 50 40
566 A120 80fr Conus cuvieri 75 60
567 A120 100fr Turbo petholatus 1.00 75
Nos. 563-567 (5) 2.65 2.10

Local Butterflies A125

1984, Jan. 24 Litho. *Perf. 13½x13*

568 A125 5fr Colotis chrysonome 15 15
569 A125 20fr Colias erate 20 15
570 A125 30fr Junonia orithyia 28 22
571 A125 75fr Acraea doubledayi 75 55
572 A125 110fr Byblia ilithya 1.00 75
Nos. 568-572 (5) 2.38 1.82

Landscapes and Animals — A126

1984, Apr. 29 Litho. *Perf. 13*

573 A126 2fr Randa Klipspringer 15 15
574 A126 8fr Ali Sabieh, gazelles 15 15
575 A126 10fr Lake Assal, oryx 15 15
576 A126 15fr Tadjoura, gazelle 15 15
577 A126 40fr Alaila Dada, jackal, vert. 40 28
578 A126 45fr Lake Abbe, warthog 42 35
579 A126 55fr Obock, seagull 55 40
580 A126 125fr Presidential Palace, bird 1.10 80
Nos. 573-580 (8) 3.07 2.43

For surcharges see Nos. 657-658, 660.

Fire Prevention — A127

1984, Sept. 9 Litho. *Perf. 13*

581 A127 25fr Fire truck 22 20
582 A127 95fr Hook & ladder 1.00 65
583 A127 100fr Fire plane 1.00 75

International Olympic Committee Membership A128

1984, July 22 Litho. *Perf. 13*

584 A128 45fr Runners 45 35

Motor Carriage, 1886 A128a

1984, Nov. 11 Litho. *Perf. 12½*

585 A128a 35fr shown 35 25
586 A128a 65fr Cabriolet, 1896 60 45
587 A128a 90fr Phoenix, 1900 90 65

Gottlieb Daimler (1834-1900), pioneer automobile manufacturer.

Marie and Pierre Curie — A129

1984, Dec. 3 Litho. *Perf. 12½*

588 A129 150fr Pierre Curie 1.40 1.10
589 A129 150fr Marie Curie 1.40 1.10

Audubon Bicentenary — A130

1985, Jan. 27 Litho. *Perf. 13*

590 A130 5fr Merops albicollis 15 15
591 A130 15fr Pterocles exustus 15 15
592 A130 20fr Trachyphonus margaritatus somalicus 20 15
593 A130 25fr Coracias garrulus 22 20
Set value 50

Intl. Youth Year — A131

1985, Mar. 26 Litho. *Perf. 13*

594 A131 10fr multicolored 15 15
595 A131 30fr multicolored 28 22
596 A131 40fr multicolored 38 28

German Railways, 150th Anniv. — A132

Designs: 55fr, Engine No. 29, Addis Ababa-Djibouti Railways. 75fr, Adler, museum facsimile of the first German locomotive.

1985, Apr. 22 Litho. *Perf. 13*

597 A132 55fr multicolored 55 40
598 A132 75fr multicolored 75 55

A133 A134

1985, May 23

599 A133 35fr Planting saplings 35 25
600 A133 65fr Hygiene, family health care 60 45

Scouting.

1985, June 24 **Litho.**

Writers: 80fr, Victor Hugo (1802-1885), Novelist. 100fr, Arthur Rimbaud (1854-1891), poet.

601 A134 80fr brt blue & slate 75 60
602 A134 100fr multicolored 1.00 75

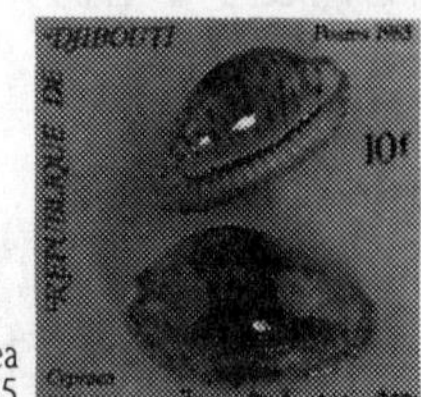

Sea Shells — A135

1985, July 15 **Litho.** ***Perf. 12½***

603 A135 10fr Cypraea nebrites 15 15
604 A135 15fr Cypraea turdus 15 15
605 A135 30fr Conus acuminatus 28 22
606 A135 40fr Cypraea camelopardalis 38 28
607 A135 55fr Conus terebra 50 40
Nos. 603-607 (5) 1.46 1.20

1st World Cup Marathon '85, Hiroshima A136

1985, Sept. 2 ***Perf. 12½x13***

608 A136 75fr Winners 70 55
609 A136 100fr Approaching finish 1.00 70

Halley's Comet — A137

Designs: 85fr, Bayeux Tapestry, Comet and Halley. 90fr, Vega I, Giotto space probes, map of planets, comet trajectory.

1986, Jan. 27 **Litho.** ***Perf. 13***

610 A137 85fr multicolored 80 60
611 A137 90fr multicolored 85 65

ISERST Solar Energy Installation — A138

Designs: 50fr, Runners on beach. 150fr, Windmill, headquarters, power control station.

1986, Mar. 20

612 A138 50fr multicolored 45 35
613 A138 150fr multicolored 1.50 1.10

Ships from Columbus's Fleet, 1492 — A139

1986, Apr. 14

614 A139 60fr Santa Maria 60 42
615 A139 90fr Nina, Pinta 80 65

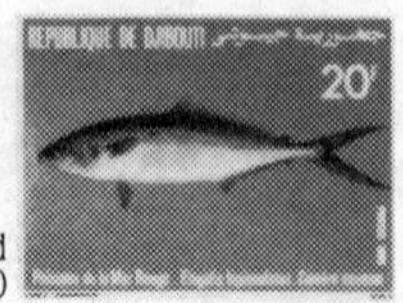

Fish, Red Sea — A140

1986, June 16 **Litho.** ***Perf. 13½x13***

616 A140 20fr Elagatis bipinnulatus 20 15
617 A140 25fr Valamugil seheli 22 20
618 A140 55fr Lutjanus rivulatus 50 40

Public Buildings — A141

Designs: 105fr, People's Palace. 115fr, Ministry of the Interior, Posts and Telecommunications.

1986, July 21 **Litho.** ***Perf. 13***

619 A141 105fr multicolored 1.00 75
620 A141 115fr multicolored 1.10 85

Sea-Me-We Building, Keyboard — A142

1986, Sept. 8 **Litho.** ***Perf. 13***

621 A142 100fr multicolored 1.00 70

Souvenir Sheet

Perf. 12½

622 A142 250fr multicolored 2.25 1.75

Southeast Asia, Middle East, Western Europe Submarine Cable System inauguration.

No. 537 Surcharged "5e ANNIVERSAIRE."

1986, Nov. 15 ***Perf. 13x12½***

623 A116 55fr on 75fr multi 50 40

Pasteur Institute, Cent. — A143

1987, Feb. 19 **Litho.** ***Perf. 13***

624 A143 220fr multicolored 2.25 1.50

Natl. Vaccination Campaign.

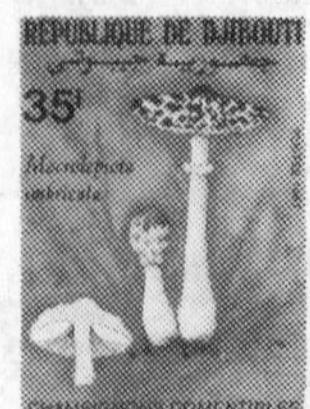

Edible Mushrooms — A144

1987, Apr. 16 **Litho.** ***Perf. 13x12½***

625 A144 35fr Macrolepiota imbricata 50 38
626 A144 50fr Lentinus squarrosulus 70 52
627 A144 95fr Terfezia boudieri 1.40 1.00

Wildlife A145

1987, May 14 ***Perf. 12½x13***

628 A145 5fr Hare 15 15
629 A145 30fr Dromedary 45 35
630 A145 140fr Cheetah 2.00 1.50

1988 Olympics, Seoul and Calgary — A146

Designs: 85fr, Pierre de Coubertin (1863-1937), founder of the modern Olympics, and lighting of the flame. 135fr, Ski jumping. 140fr, Running.

1987, July 16 ***Perf. 13***

631 A146 85fr multicolored 1.20 90
632 A146 135fr multicolored 1.90 1.40
633 A146 140fr multicolored 2.00 1.50

Traditional Art — A147

UN Universal Immunization by 1990 Campaign — A148

1988, Jan. 31 **Litho.** ***Perf. 13***

634 A147 30fr Nomad's comb 45 32
635 A147 70fr Wash jug 1.00 75

1988, Mar. 12 ***Perf. 12½***

636 A148 125fr multicolored 1.80 1.35

16th Africa Cup Soccer Championships, Morocco — A149

1988, Mar. 12 ***Perf. 13***

637 A149 55fr Athletes, view of Rabat 80 60

1988 Winter Olympics, Calgary — A150

1988, Mar. 27 **Litho.** ***Perf. 13***

638 A150 45fr Ski jump 65 50

Campaign Against Thirst A151

1988, Sept. 10 **Litho.** ***Perf. 12½x13***

639 A151 50fr multicolored 68 52

Intl. Fund for Agricultural Development, 10th Anniv. — A152

1988, Nov. 14 ***Perf. 13***

640 A152 135fr multicolored 1.80 1.35

Michel Lafoux Air Club, 40th Anniv. — A153

1988, Dec. 6

641 A153 145fr 1948 Tiger Moth, 1988 Tobago 10 1.95 1.50

Marine Life — A154

1989, Jan. 29 **Litho.** ***Perf. 12½***

642 A154 90fr *Lobophyllia costata* 1.10 82
643 A154 160fr *Lambis truncata* 1.90 1.45

Colotis protomedia A155

1989, Feb. 2
644 A155 70fr multicolored 95 72

Nos. 573 and 547 Surcharged

1989, Mar. 5 *Perf. 13*
646 A126 70fr on 2fr No. 573 95 72
647 A118 70fr on 150fr No. 547 95 72

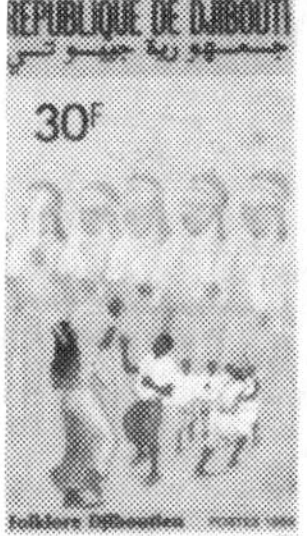
Folk Dances — A157

Francolin of Djibouti — A159

1989, Jan. 29
648 A157 30fr shown 40 30
649 A157 70fr multicolored, diff. 95 72

1989, Apr. 25 Litho. *Perf. 12½*
651 A159 35fr multicolored 48 35

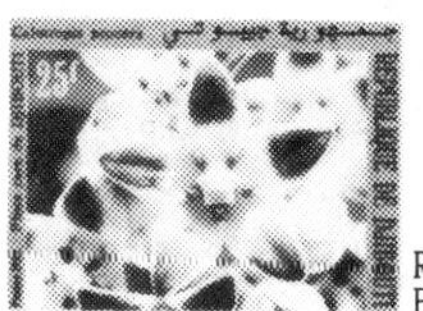
Rare Flora — A160

1989, June 12
652 A160 25fr *Calotropis procera* 35 25

A161 A162

1989, Aug. 9 Litho. *Perf. 13*
653 A161 70fr multicolored 90 68

Interparliamentary Union, cent.

1989, Oct. 1
654 A162 145fr multicolored 1.85 1.40

Intl. Literacy Year.

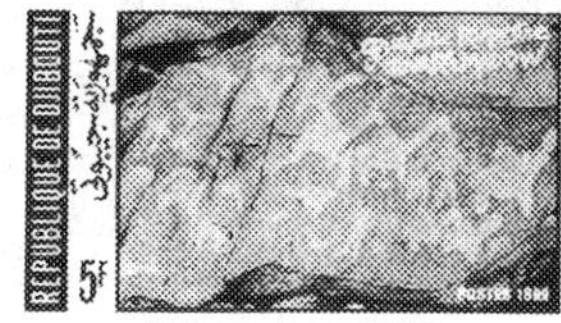
Petroglyph — A163

1989, Nov. 18 Litho. *Perf. 13*
655 A163 5fr multicolored 15 15

Girl — A164

1989, Dec. 6
656 A164 55fr multicolored 70 52

Nos. 574, 576-577 Surcharged

1990 Litho. *Perf. 13*
657 A126 30fr on 8fr multi 42 32
658 A126 50fr on 40fr multi 80 60
660 A126 120fr on 15fr multi 1.90 1.45

Issue dates: 50fr, July 3; 120fr, Mar. 17.

Water Conservation A165

1990, Mar. 17 Litho. *Perf. 11½*
665 A165 120fr multicolored 1.90 1.45

Traditional Jewelry A166

1990, Mar. 21
666 A166 70fr multicolored 1.15 85

Commiphora A167

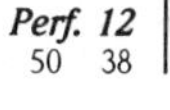

1990, Apr. 16 *Perf. 12*
667 A167 30fr multicolored 50 38

Baskets A168

1990, May 5
668 A168 30fr multicolored 50 38

A169

A170

1990, June 12 *Perf. 11½*
669 A169 100fr multicolored 1.45 1.10

World Cup Soccer Championships, Italy.

1990, July 3 *Perf. 11½*
670 A170 55fr shown 50 38

20 kilometer race of Djibouti.

Vaccination Campaign A171

1990, Aug. 22 Litho. *Perf. 11½*
Granite Paper
671 A171 300fr multicolored 5.25 4.00

Charles de Gaulle — A172

African Tourism Year — A173

1990, Sept. 16
Granite Paper
672 A172 200fr multicolored 3.50 2.65

1991, Jan. 23 Litho. *Perf. 13*
673 A173 115fr multicolored 2.00 1.50

Corals — A174

Aquatic Birds — A175

1991, Jan. 28 *Perf. 12½*
674 A174 40fr Acropora 70 55
675 A174 45fr Seriatopora hytrise 80 60

1991, Feb. 12
676 A175 10fr Pelecanus rufescens 18 15
677 A175 15fr Egretta gularis 28 20
678 A175 20fr Ardea goliath, horiz. 35 28
679 A175 25fr Platalea leucorodia, horiz. 45 35

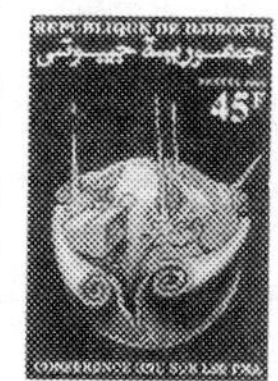
A176

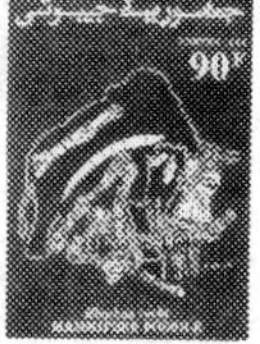
Fossils — A177

1990, Oct. 9 Litho. *Perf. 11½x12*
Granite Paper
680 A176 45fr multicolored 80 60

1990, Nov. 12
Granite Paper
681 A177 90fr pur, org & blk 1.60 1.20

Papio Hamadryas — A178

1990, Dec. 6
Granite Paper
682 A178 50fr multicolored 90 70

Pandion Haliaetus A179

1991, Mar. 27 Litho. *Perf. 12x11½*
683 A179 200fr multicolored 3.60 2.70

Traditional Game A180

1991, Apr. 4
684 A180 250fr multicolored 4.50 3.40

See No. 696.

Djibouti-Ethiopia Railroad — A181

1991, May 25 Litho. *Perf. 11½*
685 A181 85fr multicolored 1.25 95

World Environment Day — A182

1991, June 10
686 A182 110fr multicolored 1.65 1.25

Philexafrique A183

1991 Litho. *Perf. 11½*
687 A183 120fr Islands 2.10 1.60

A184

A185

1991
688 A184 175fr Handball 3.05 2.30

Pre-Olympic year.

1991 Litho. *Perf. 11½x12*
689 A185 105fr multicolored 1.85 1.40

World Food Day.

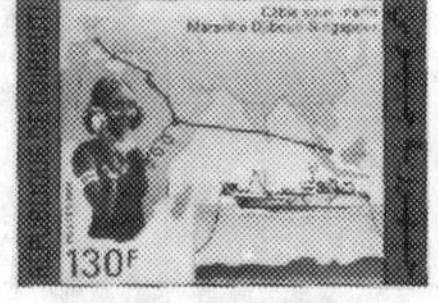

Underwater Cable Network A186

1991, Nov. 23 *Perf. 12x11½*
690 A186 130fr multicolored 2.25 1.70

Discovery of America, 500th Anniv. A187

1991, Dec. 19 Litho. *Perf. 11½*
691 A187 145fr multicolored 2.40 1.80

Arthur Rimbaud (1854-1891) Poet and Merchant A188

1991-92 *Perf. 11½*
692 A188 90fr Young man, ship 1.50 1.15
693 A188 150fr Old man, camels 2.50 1.90

Issue dates: 90fr, Feb. 5, 1992. 150fr, Dec. 23, 1991.

Djibouti-Ethiopia Railroad — A189

Design: 250fr, Locomotive, map.

1992 Litho. *Perf. 12x11½*
694 A189 70fr multicolored 1.15 90

Souvenir Sheet
Perf. 13x12½
695 A189 250fr multicolored 4.35 3.25

Issue dates: 70fr, Feb. 2; 250fr, Jan. 30.

Traditional Game Type of 1991

1992, Feb. 10 *Perf. 11½*
696 A180 100fr Boys playing Go 1.65 1.25

A190

A191

1992, Apr. 24 Litho. *Perf. 14*
697 A190 80fr multicolored 1.40 1.05

1992 Summer Olympics, Barcelona.

1992, June 9 Litho. *Perf. 14x13½*

Traditional food preparation.

698 A191 30fr Pounding grain 52 40
699 A191 70fr Winnowing grain 1.20 90

Discovery of America, 500th Anniv. A192

1992, May 16 Litho. *Perf. 11½*
700 A192 125fr multicolored 2.00 1.50

African Soccer Championships A193

Intl. Space Year A194

1992, July 22 *Perf. 14*
701 A193 15fr multicolored 25 18

Perf. 14x13½, 13½x14
1992, Sept. 28
702 A194 120fr Rocket, satellite 1.90 1.40
703 A194 135fr Astronaut, satellite, horiz. 2.15 1.60

Wildlife A195

1992, Nov. 11 *Perf. 14*
704 A195 5fr Dik-dik 15 15
705 A195 200fr Caretta caretta 3.25 2.50

Nomad Girls in Traditional Costumes — A196

1993, Feb. 10 Litho. *Perf. 13*
706 A196 70fr Girl beside hut 1.15 90
707 A196 120fr shown 1.90 1.40

White-eyed Seagull A197

1993, Mar. 10 Litho. *Perf. 12½*
708 A197 300fr multicolored 4.75 3.55

AIR POST STAMPS

Afars and Issas Nos. C104-C105, C103 Overprinted with Bars and "REPUBLIQUE DE DJIBOUTI" in Brown or Black

1977 Engr. *Perf. 13*
C106 AP37 55fr multi (Br) 1.00 1.00
C107 AP37 75fr multi 1.10 1.10

Litho. *Perf. 12*
C108 AP36 500fr multi 6.25 5.50

Map of Djibouti, Dove, UN Emblem — AP38

1977, Oct. 19 Photo. *Perf. 13*
C109 AP38 300fr multi 2.75 2.00

Djibouti's admission to the United Nations.

Marcel Brochet MB 101, 1955 — AP39

Djibouti Aero Club: 85fr, Tiger Moth, 1960. 200fr, Rallye-Commodore, 1973.

1978, Feb. 27 Litho. *Perf. 13*
C110 AP39 60fr multi 60 35
C111 AP39 85fr multi 80 50
C112 AP39 200fr multi 2.00 1.00

Old Man, by Rubens AP40

Design: 500fr, Hippopotamus Hunt, by Rubens, horiz.

1978, Apr. 24 Photo. *Perf. 13*
C113 AP40 50fr multi 50 30
C114 AP40 500fr multi 5.00 3.00

Peter Paul Rubens (1577-1640), 400th birth anniversary.

Player Holding Soccer Cup — AP41

Design: 300fr, Soccer player, map of South America with Argentina, Cup and emblem.

1978, June 20 Litho. *Perf. 13*
C115 AP41 100fr multi 75 30
C116 AP41 300fr multi 2.25 90

11th World Cup Soccer Championship, Argentina, June 1-25.
For overprints see Nos. C117-C118.

Nos. C115-C116 Overprinted:
a. ARGENTINE/CHAMPION 1978
b. ARGENTINE/HOLLANDE/3-1

1978, Aug. 20 Litho. *Perf. 13*
C117 AP41 (a) 100fr multi 85 38
C118 AP41 (b) 300fr multi 2.50 1.10

Argentina's victory in 1978 Soccer Championship.

Tahitian Women, by Gauguin — AP42

Young Hare, by Dürer — AP43

Perf. 13x12½, 12½x13

1978, Sept. 25 **Litho.**
C119 AP42 100fr multi 1.00 40
C120 AP43 250fr multi 2.50 1.50

Paul Gauguin (1848-1903) and Albrecht Dürer (1471-1528), painters.

Philexafrique II-Essen Issue
Common Design Types

Designs: No. C121, Lynx and Djibouti No. 456. No. C122, Jay and Brunswick No. 3.

1978, Dec. 13 **Litho.** ***Perf. 13x12½***
C121 CD138 90fr multi 1.10 1.00
C122 CD139 90fr multi 1.10 1.00

Nos. C121-C122 printed se-tenant.

UPU Emblem, Map of Djibouti, Dove — AP44

1978, Dec. 18 **Engr.** ***Perf. 13***
C123 AP44 200fr multi 2.00 1.10

Centenary of Congress of Paris.

Junkers JU-52 and Dewoitine D-338 — AP45

Powered Flight, 75th Anniversary: 250fr, Potez P63-11, 1941 and Supermarine Spitfire HF-VII, 1942. 500fr, Concorde, 1969 and Sikorsky S-40 "American Clipper," 1931.

1979, May 21 **Litho.** ***Perf. 13x12½***
C124 AP45 140fr multi 1.10 50
C125 AP45 250fr multi 2.25 1.00
C126 AP45 500fr multi 5.00 1.65

Common Design Types pictured in section at front of book.

The Laundress, by Honore Daumier AP46

1979, July 10 **Litho.** ***Perf. 12½x13***
C127 AP46 500fr multi 4.50 2.25

Olympic Emblem, Skis, Sleds — AP47

1980, Jan. 21 **Litho.** ***Perf. 13***
C128 AP47 150fr multi 1.50 60

13th Winter Olympic Games, Lake Placid, N.Y., Feb. 12-24.

For surcharges see Nos. C133-C134.

Cathedral of the Archangel, Basketball, Moscow '80 Emblem — AP48

Designs: 120fr, Lomonossov Univ., Moscow, Soccer. 250fr, Cathedral of the Annunciation, Running.

1980, Apr. 10 **Litho.** ***Perf. 13***
C129 AP48 60fr multi 50 20
C130 AP48 120fr multi 1.00 40
C131 AP48 250fr multi 2.00 1.00

22nd Summer Olympic Games, Moscow, July 18-Aug. 3.

Air Djibouti, 1st Anniversary — AP49

1980, Mar. 29 **Litho.** ***Perf. 13x12½***
C132 AP49 400fr multi 2.50 1.00

No. C128 Surcharged in Black and Blue or Purple:
80fr. A.M. MOSER-PROEL / AUTRICHE / DESCENTE DAMES / MEDAILLE D'OR
200fr. HEIDEN / USA / 5 MEDAILLES D'OR / PATINAGE DE VITESSE

1980, Apr. 5 **Litho.** ***Perf. 13***
C133 AP47 80fr on 150fr 65 40
C134 AP47 200fr on 150fr (P) 1.60 1.10

Apollo 11 Moon Landing, 10th Anniversary — AP50

Space Conquests: 300fr, Apollo-Soyuz space project, 5th anniversary.

1980, May 8
C135 AP50 200fr multi 1.75 60
C136 AP50 300fr multi 2.50 1.00

Satellite Earth Station Inauguration — AP51

1980, July 3 **Litho.** ***Perf. 13***
C137 AP51 500fr multi 3.00 1.75

Graf Zeppelin — AP52

1980, Oct. 2 **Litho.** ***Perf. 13***
C138 AP52 100fr shown 85 40
C139 AP52 150fr Ferdinand von Zeppelin, blimp 1.10 60

Zeppelin flight, 80th anniversary.

Voyager Passing Saturn — AP53

1980, Dec. 21 **Litho.** ***Perf. 13***
C140 AP53 250fr multi 1.50 75

AP54 AP55

World Cup Soccer Preliminary Games: 200fr, Players (diff.).

1981, Jan. 14
C141 AP54 80fr multi 50 25
C142 AP54 200fr multi 1.25 60

1981, Feb. 10 **Litho.** ***Perf. 13***
C143 AP55 100fr multi 80 40

European-African Economic Convention.

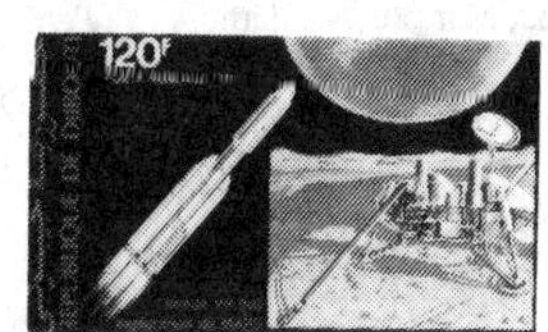

5th Anniversary of Viking I Take-off to Mars — AP56

20th Anniversary of Various Space Flights: 75fr, Vostok I, Yuri Gagarin, vert. 150fr, Freedom 7, Alan B. Shepard, vert.

1981, Mar. 9 **Litho.** ***Perf. 13***
C144 AP56 75fr multi 45 25
C145 AP56 120fr multi 75 35
C146 AP56 150fr multi 90 45

Football Players, by Picasso (1881-1973) — AP57

Design: 400fr Man Wearing a Turban, by Rembrandt (1606-1669), vert.

Perf. 13x12½, 12½x13

1981, Aug. 3 **Litho.**
C147 AP57 300fr multi 2.50 1.10
C148 AP57 400fr multi 3.25 1.75

Columbia Space Shuttle — AP58

1981, Sept. 24 **Litho.** ***Perf. 13***
C149 AP58 90fr Shuttle, diff., vert. 75 40
C150 AP58 120fr shown 1.00 60

Nos. C149-C150 Overprinted in Brown with Astronauts' Names and Dates

1981, Nov. 12 **Litho.** ***Perf. 13***
C151 AP58 90fr multi 75 50
C152 AP58 120fr multi 1.00 75

1982 World Cup Soccer — AP59

Designs: Various soccer players.

1982, Jan. 20
C153 AP59 110fr multi 65 40
C154 AP59 220fr multi 1.25 75

For overprints see Nos. C166-C167.

Space Anniversaries — AP60

Designs: 40fr, Luna 9 moon landing, 15th, vert. 60fr, John Glenn's flight, 20th, vert. 180fr, Viking I Mars landing, 5th.

1982, Feb. 15
C155 AP60 40fr multi 30 20
C156 AP60 60fr multi 50 30
C157 AP60 180fr multi 1.40 80

21st Birthday of Princess Diana of Wales
AP61

1982, Apr. 29 Litho. *Perf. 12½x13*

C158 AP61 120fr Portrait 1.00 75
C159 AP61 180fr Portrait, diff. 1.50 1.00

For overprints see Nos. C168-C169.

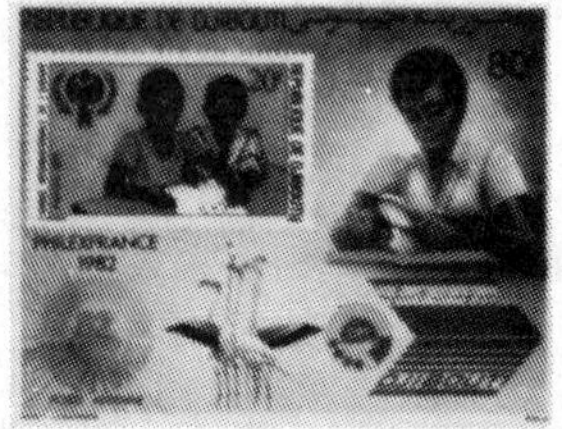

No. 489, Boy Examining Collection — AP62

1982, May 10 *Perf. 13x12½*

C160 AP62 80fr shown 65 50
C161 AP62 140fr No. 495 1.10 80

PHILEXFRANCE '82 Stamp Exhibition, Paris, June 11-21. Nos. C160-C161 se-tenant with label showing show emblem, dates.

1350th Anniv. of Mohammed's Death at Medina — AP63

1982, June 8 Litho. *Perf. 13*

C162 AP63 500fr Medina Mosque 4.00 2.00

Scouting Year — AP64

1982, June 28

C163 AP64 95fr Baden-Powell 80 50
C164 AP64 200fr Camp, scouts 1.60 1.00

2nd UN Conference on Peaceful Uses of Outer Space, Vienna, Aug. 9-21 — AP65

1982, Aug. 19

C165 AP65 350fr multi 3.00 1.40

Nos. C153-C154 Overprinted with Winner's Name and Scores

1982, July 21 Litho. *Perf. 13*

C166 AP59 110fr multi 80 60
C167 AP59 220fr multi 1.60 1.10

Italy's victory in 1982 World Cup.

Nos. C158-C159 Overprinted in Blue or Red with Date, Name and Title

1982, Aug. 9 *Perf. 12½x13*

C168 AP61 120fr multi 1.00 75
C169 AP61 180fr multi (R) 1.50 1.00

Birth of Prince William of Wales, June 21.

Franklin D. Roosevelt (1882-1945) — AP66

1982, Oct. 7 Litho. *Perf. 13*

C170 AP66 115fr shown 80 50
C171 AP66 250fr George Washington 2.00 1.00

Manned Flight Bicentenary
AP67

Pre-olympic Year
AP68

1983, Jan. 20 Litho.

C172 AP67 35fr Montgolfiere, 1783 32 22
C173 AP67 45fr Giffard, Paris Exposition, 1878 45 28
C174 AP67 120fr Double Eagle II, 1978 1.10 80

1983, Feb. 15

C175 AP68 75fr Volleyball 75 50
C176 AP68 125fr Wind surfing 1.25 80

50th Anniv. of Air France — AP69

1983, Mar. 20 Litho. *Perf. 13*

C177 AP69 25fr Bloch 220 25 16
C178 AP69 100fr DC-4 1.00 65
C179 AP69 175fr Boeing 747 1.90 1.10

AP70 AP71

Design: 180fr, Martin Luther King, Jr. (1929-68), civil rights leader. 250fr, Alfred Nobel (1833-96).

1983, May 18 Litho. *Perf. 13*

C180 AP70 180fr multi 2.00 1.25
C181 AP70 250fr multi 2.75 2.00

1983, July 18 Litho. *Perf. 13*

Service Clubs: 90fr, Rotary Club Intl., Sailing Show, Toronto, June 5-9. 150fr, Lions Club Intl., Honolulu Meeting, June 22-24, Djibouti lighthouse.

C182 AP71 90fr multi 90 60
C183 AP71 150fr multi 1.50 1.00

Printed se-tenant with label showing emblems.

Vintage Motor Cars — AP72

1983, July 18 Litho. *Perf. 13x12½*

C184 AP72 60fr Renault, 1904 60 40
C185 AP72 80fr Mercedes, 1910, vert. 80 55
C186 AP72 110fr Lorraine-Dietrich, 1912 1.10 75

Vostok VI
AP74

1983, Oct. 20 Litho. *Perf. 12*

C188 AP74 120fr shown 1.20 80
C189 AP74 200fr Explorer I 2.00 1.10

1984 Winter Olympics — AP75

1984, Feb. 14 Litho. *Perf. 13*

C190 AP75 70fr Speed skating 65 50
C191 AP75 130fr Figure skating 1.10 1.00

For overprints see Nos. C196-C197.

Souvenir Sheet

Ship
AP76

1984, Feb. 14 Litho. *Perf. 12½*

C192 AP76 250fr multi 2.25 1.75

Sea-Me-We (South-east Asia-Middle East-Western Europe) submarine cable construction agreement.

Motorized Hang Gliders — AP77

Various hang gliders.

1984, Mar. 12 *Perf. 13x12½*

C193 AP77 65fr multi 60 50
C194 AP77 85fr multi 80 60
C195 AP77 100fr multi 1.00 75

Nos. C190-C191 Overprinted with Winners' Names and Country

1984, Mar. 28 *Perf. 13*

C196 AP75 70fr multi 65 50
C197 AP75 130fr multi 1.25 1.00

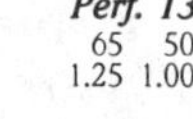

Portrait of Marguerite Matisse, 1910, by Henri Matisse
AP78

Design: 200fr, Portrait of Mario Varvogli, by Amedeo Modigliani.

1984, Apr. 15 Litho. *Perf. 12½x13*

C198 AP78 150fr multi 1.50 1.00
C199 AP78 200fr multi 2.00 1.40

1984 Summer Olympics — AP79

1984, May 24 *Perf. 13*

C200 AP79 50fr Running 50 38
C201 AP79 60fr High jump 60 42
C202 AP79 80fr Swimming 75 60

Battle Scene AP80

1984, June 16 Litho. *Perf. 13x12½*

C203 AP80 300fr multi 3.00 2.25

125th anniv. of Battle of Solferino and 120th anniv. of Red Cross.

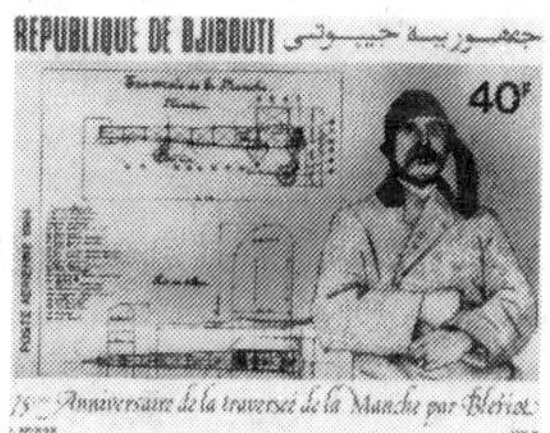

Bleriot's Flight over English Channel, 75th Anniv. — AP81

1984, July 8

C204 AP81 40fr 14-Bis plans 40 30
C205 AP81 75fr Britten-Norman Islander 75 55
C206 AP81 90fr Air Djibouti jet 80 65

375th Anniv., Galileo's Telescope — AP82

1984, Oct. 7 Litho. *Perf. 13*

C207 AP82 120fr Telescopes, spacecraft 1.10 80
C208 AP82 180fr Galileo, telescopes 1.75 1.10

1984 Soccer Events — AP83

1984, Oct. 20 Litho. *Perf. 13*

C209 AP83 80fr Euro Cup 75 60
C210 AP83 80fr Los Angeles Olympics 75 60

Issued se-tenant, separated by pictorial label.

Service Clubs — AP84

1985, Feb. 23 Litho. *Perf. 13*

C211 AP84 50fr Lions, World Leprosy Day 50 38
C212 AP84 60fr Rotary, chess board, pieces 60 45

Telecommunications Technology — AP85

Designs: No. C213, Technician, researchist, operator. No. C214, Offshore oil rig, transmission tower, government building.

1985, July 2 *Perf. 13x12½*

C213 AP85 80fr multi 75 55
C214 AP85 80fr multi 75 55

PHILEXAFRICA '85, Lome. Nos. C213-C214 printed se-tenant with center label picturing map of Africa or UAPT emblem.

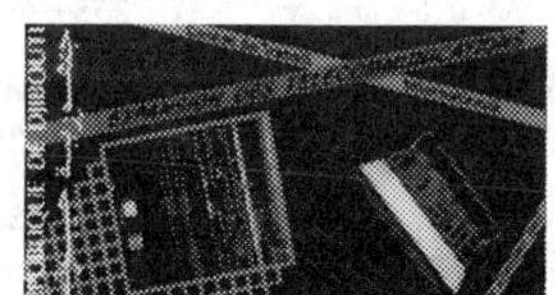
Telecommunications Development — AP86

1985, Oct. 2 *Perf. 13*

C215 AP86 50fr Intl. transmission center 50 35
C216 AP86 90fr Ariane rocket, vert. 90 65
C217 AP86 120fr ARABSAT satellite 1.10 90

Youths Windsurfing, Playing Tennis — AP87

Design: No. C219, Tadjoura Highway construction.

1985, Nov. 13 *Perf. 13x12½*

C218 AP87 100fr multi 1.00 70
C219 AP87 100fr multi 1.00 70

PHILEXAFRICA '85, Lome, Togo, Nov. 16-24. Nos. C218-C219 printed se-tenant with center label picturing map of Africa or UAPT emblem.

1986 World Cup Soccer Championships, Mexico — AP88

1986, Feb. 24 Litho. *Perf. 13*

C220 AP88 75fr shown 70 50
C221 AP88 100fr Players, stadium 1.00 70

For overprints see Nos. C223-C224.

Statue of Liberty, Cent. — AP89

1986, May 21

C222 AP89 250fr multi 2.25 1.75

Nos. C220-C221 Ovptd. with Winners

1986, Sept. 15 Litho. *Perf. 13*

C223 AP88 75fr "FRANCE - BELGIQUE / 4-2" 70 55
C224 AP88 100fr "3-2 ARGENTINE-RFA" 1.00 70

1986 World Chess Championships, May 1-19 — AP89a

Malayan animal chess pieces.

1986, Oct. 13 Litho. *Perf. 13*

C225 AP89a 80fr Knight, bishops 70 60
C226 AP89a 120fr Rook, king, pawn 1.10 90

Yuri Gagarin, Sputnik Spacecraft — AP90

1986, Nov. 27 Litho. *Perf. 13*

C227 AP90 150fr shown 1.40 1.10
C228 AP90 200fr Space rendezvous, 1966 1.50 1.25

First man in space, 25th anniv.; Gemini 8-Agena link-up, 20th anniv.

Historic Flights — AP91

1987, Jan. 22 Litho. *Perf. 13*

C229 AP91 55fr Amiot 370 55 40
C230 AP91 80fr Spirit of St. Louis 70 55
C231 AP91 120fr Voyager 1.10 90

First flight from Istria to Djibouti, 1942; Lindbergh's Transatlantic flight, 1927; nonstop world circumnavigation without refueling.

For surcharge see No. C240.

Pres. Aptidon, Natl. Crest and Flag — AP92

1987, June 27 Litho. *Perf. 12½x13*

C232 AP92 250fr multi 2.50 1.50

Natl. independence, 10th anniv.

Telstar, 25th Anniv. — AP93

1987, Oct. 1 *Perf. 13*

C233 AP93 190fr shown 2.00 1.25
C234 AP93 250fr Samuel Morse, telegraph key 2.50 1.50

Invention of the telegraph, 150th anniv. (250fr).

City of Djibouti, Cent. — AP94

Designs: 100fr, Djibouti Creek and quay, 1887. 150fr, Aerial view of city, 1987. 250fr, Somali Coast Nos. 6, 20, and postmarks of 1898 and 1903.

1987, Nov. 15 Litho. *Perf. 13x12½*

C235 AP94 100fr blk & buff 1.45 1.10
C236 AP94 150fr multi 2.15 1.60

Souvenir Sheet

C237 AP94 250fr multi 3.55 2.70

Nos. C235-C236 printed se-tenant with various center labels. No. C237 has decorative margin like design of 100fr.

Intl. Red Cross and Red Crescent Organizations, 125th Anniv. — AP95

1988, Feb. 17 Litho. *Perf. 13*

C238 AP95 300fr multi 4.25 3.25

1988 Summer Olympics, Seoul — AP96

1988, June 15 Litho. *Perf. 13*
C239 AP96 105fr multi 1.40 1.05

For overprint see No. C242.

No. C229 Surcharged in Black

PARIS - DJIBOUTI - ST DENIS DE LA REUNION
RALLYE ROLAND GARROS

70F

1988, June 28
C240 AP91 70fr on 55fr multi 95 72

Air race in memory of the Paris-Djibouti-St. Denis flight of French aviator Roland Garros (1888-1913).

World Post Day — AP97

1988, Oct. 9 Litho. *Perf. 13*
C241 AP97 1000fr multi 13.50 10.00

No. C239 Ovptd. "AHMED SALAH / 1re MEDAILLE OLYMPIQUE"

1988, Dec. 15 Litho. *Perf. 13*
C242 AP96 105fr multi

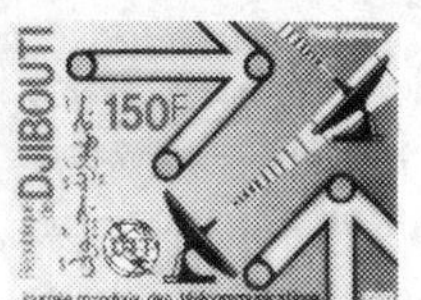

World Telecommunications Day — AP98

1989, May 17 Litho. *Perf. 12½*
C243 AP98 150fr multi 2.00 1.50

PHILEXFRANCE '89, Declaration of Human Rights and Citizenship Bicent. — AP99

1989, July 7 Litho. *Perf. 12½x13*
C244 AP99 120fr multi 1.60 1.20

Salt, Lake Assal — AP100

1989, Sept. 15 Litho. *Perf. 13*
C245 AP100 300fr multicolored 3.85 2.90

POSTAGE DUE STAMP

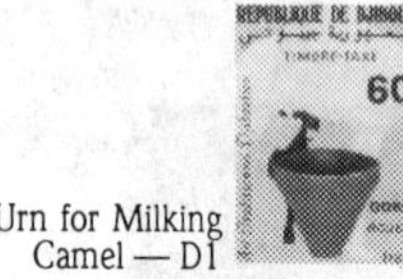

Urn for Milking Camel — D1

1988, Jan. 31 Litho. *Perf. 13*
J1 D1 60fr multi 88 65

DOMINICAN REPUBLIC

LOCATION — Comprises about two-thirds of the island of Hispaniola in the West Indies
GOVT. — Republic
AREA — 18,700 sq. mi.
POP. — 5,982,000 (est. 1983)
CAPITAL — Santo Domingo

8 Reales = 1 Peso
100 Centavos = 1 Peso (1880)
100 Centimos = 1 Franco (1883)
100 Centavos = 1 Peso (1885)

Catalogue values for unused stamps in this country are for Never Hinged items, beginning with Scott 437 in the regular postage section, Scott B1 in the semi-postal section, Scott C75 in the airpost section, Scott CB1 in the airpost semi-postal section, Scott E7 in the special delivery section, Scott G24 in the insured letter section, Scott J14 in the postage due section, Scott O26 in the officials section, and Scott RA20 in the postal tax section.

Watermarks

Wmk 115 Diamonds

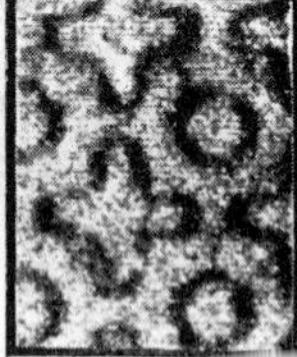
Wmk. 116 Crosses and Circles

Values of early Dominican Republic stamps vary according to condition. Quotations for Nos. 1-31 are for fine to very fine copies. Very fine to superb specimens sell at much higher prices, and inferior or poor copies sell at reduced prices, depending on the condition of the individual specimen.

Coat of Arms
A1 A2

1865 Unwmk. Typo. *Imperf.*

Wove Paper

1 A1 ½r blk, *rose* 475.00 475.00
2 A1 1r blk, *dp grn* 850.00 850.00

Twelve varieties of each.

Laid Paper

3 A2 ½r blk, *pale grn* 475.00 425.00
4 A2 1r blk, *straw* 800.00 800.00

Twelve varieties of the ½r, ten of the 1r.

A3 A4

1866 Laid Paper Unwmk.

5 A3 ½r blk, *straw* 175.00 150.00
6 A3 1r blk, *pale grn* 775.00 775.00
7 A4 1r blk, *pale grn* 150.00 125.00

Nos. 5-8 have 21 varieties (sheets of 21).

Wmk. 115

8 A3 1r blk, *pale grn* 2,750. 2,750.

1866-67 Wove Paper Unwmk.

9 A3 ½r blk, *rose* ('67) 47.50 47.50
10 A3 1r blk, *pale grn* 85.00 75.00
a. Inscription dbl., top & bottom *400.00 400.00*
11 A3 1r blk, *bl* ('67) 40.00 30.00
a. 1r blk, *light blue* ('67) 40.00 30.00
b. No space btwn. "Un" and "real" 225.00 200.00
c. Without inscription at top & bottom 400.00 200.00
d. Inscription invtd., top & bottom

1867-71

Pelure Paper

13 A3 ½r blk, *rose* 100.00 75.00
15 A3 ½r blk, *lav* ('68) 210.00 210.00
a. Without inscription at top and bottom 525.00
b. Dbl. inscriptions, one invtd. *425.00*
16 A3 ½r blk, *grnsh gray* ('68) 225.00 225.00
18 A3 ½r blk, *ol* ('69) 2,500. 2,500.
23 A3 1r blk, *lavender* 225.00 200.00
24 A4 1r blk, *rose* ('68) 225.00 225.00
25 A4 1r blk, *mag* ('69) 900.00 900.00
26 A4 1r blk, *sal* ('71) 225.00 225.00

1870-73

Ordinary Paper

27 A3 ½r blk, *magenta* 1,000. 1,000.
28 A3 ½r bl, *rose* (blk inscription) ('71) 50.00 42.50
a. Blue inscription 500.00 500.00
b. Without inscription at top and bottom
29 A3 ½r blk, *yel* ('73) 30.00 21.00
a. Without inscription at top and bottom 375.00 375.00
30 A4 1r blk, *vio* ('73) 30.00 21.00
a. Without inscription at top and bottom 700.00 700.00
31 A4 1r blk, *dk grn* 60.00 50.00

Nos. 9-31 have 21 varieties (sheets of 21). Nos. 29 and 30 are known pin-perforated, unofficially.

Bisects are known of several of the early 1r stamps.

A5 A6

1879 *Perf. 12½x13*

32 A5 ½r violet 2.50 1.50
a. Imperf., pair 9.00 9.00
b. Horiz. pair, imperf. vert. 17.00
33 A5 ½r vio, *bluish* 2.50 1.50
a. Imperf., pair 9.00 7.50
34 A5 1r carmine 3.50 1.50
a. Imperf., pair 11.50 9.00
b. Perf. 13 11.50 7.50
c. Perf. 13x12½ 11.50 7.50
35 A5 1r car, *sal* 2.50 1.50
a. Imperf., pair 8.25 8.25

In 1891 15 stamps of 1879-83 were surcharged "U P U," new values and crossed diagonal lines.

1880 Typo. *Rouletted in Color*

36 A6 1c green 1.25 90
b. Laid paper 50.00 50.00
37 A6 2c red 1.00 75
a. Pelure paper 40.00 40.00
b. Laid paper 40.00 40.00
38 A6 5c blue 1.25 60
39 A6 10c rose 3.25 90
40 A6 20c brown 2.00 75
41 A6 25c violet 2.25 1.10
42 A6 50c orange 2.50 1.50
43 A6 75c ultra 5.00 2.50
a. Laid paper 40.00 40.00
44 A6 1p gold 6.50 4.00
a. Laid paper 50.00 50.00
b. Double impression 42.50 42.50
Nos. 36-44 (9) 25.00 13.00

1881

Network Covering Stamp

45 A6 1c green 90 45
46 A6 2c red 90 45
47 A6 5c blue 1.25 45
48 A6 10c rose 1.50 60
49 A6 20c brown 1.50 80
50 A6 25c violet 1.75 90
51 A6 50c orange 2.00 1.25
52 A6 75c ultra 6.00 4.00
53 A6 1p gold 8.00 6.50
Nos. 45-53 (9) 23.80 15.40

Preceding Issues (Type A6) Surch. with Value in New Currency:

5 céntimos.
a

5 céntimos
b

5 céntimos.
c

1 franco.
d

1 Franco.
e

1 franco
f

1 franco, 25 céntimos.
g

5 francos.
h

5 francos
i

1883

Without Network

54 (a) 5c on 1c grn 1.35 1.50
b. Inverted surcharge 21.00 21.00
c. Surcharged "25 céntimos" 50.00 50.00
d. Surcharged "10 céntimos" 27.50 27.50
55 (b) 5c on 1c grn 25.00 9.00
b. Double surcharge 100.00
c. Inverted surcharge 65.00 65.00
56 (c) 5c on 1c grn 17.00 9.50
b. Surcharged "10 céntimos" 35.00 35.00
c. Surcharged "25 céntimos" 37.50 37.50
57 (a) 10c on 2c red 5.00 3.00
a. Inverted surcharge 27.50 27.50
d. Surcharged "5 céntimos" 52.50 52.50
e. Surcharged "25 céntimos" 75.00 75.00
58 (c) 10c on 2c red 4.50 3.50
a. "Céntimso"
b. Inverted surcharge 37.50 37.50
c. Surcharged "25 céntimos" 60.00 60.00
d. "10" omitted 60.00
59 (a) 25c on 5c blue 6.50 4.00
a. Surcharged "5 céntimos" 52.50
b. Surcharged "10 céntimos" 52.50 52.50
c. Surcharged "50 céntimos" 75.00 75.00
d. Inverted surcharge 50.00 50.00
60 (c) 25c on 5c bl 7.50 3.50
a. Inverted surcharge 45.00 37.50
b. Surcharged "10 céntimos" 45.00 37.50
e. "25" omitted 75.00
f. Surcharged on back 75.00
61 (a) 50c on 10c rose 25.00 11.50
a. Inverted surcharge 50.00 45.00
62 (c) 50c on 10c rose 35.00 17.50
a. Inverted surcharge 52.50 52.50
63 (d) 1fr on 20c brown 15.00 9.75
64 (e) 1fr on 20c brown 17.50 9.75
a. Comma after "Franco," 27.50 27.50

65	(f)	1fr on 20c brown	25.00	17.50
a.		Inverted surcharge		75.00
66	(g)	1fr25c on 25c violet	21.00	15.00
a.		Inverted surcharge	65.00	65.00
67	(g)	2fr50c on 50c orange	15.00	10.50
a.		Inverted surcharge	35.00	27.50
68	(g)	3fr75c on 75c ultra	27.50	25.00
b.		Inverted surcharge	60.00	60.00
c.		Laid paper	75.00	75.00
70	(i)	5fr on 1p gold	550.00	500.00
a.		"s" of "francos" inverted	700.00	700.00

With Network

71	(a)	5c on 1c green	3.00	2.50
b.		Inverted surcharge	22.50	22.50
c.		Double surcharge	22.50	22.50
d.		Surcharged "25 céntimos"	42.50	42.50
e.		"5" omitted	75.00	75.00
72	(b)	5c on 1c green	21.00	9.00
b.		Inverted surcharge	60.00	60.00
73	(c)	5c on 1c green	27.50	11.50
b.		Surcharged "10 céntimos"	50.00	42.50
c.		Surcharged "25 céntimos"	60.00	
74	(a)	10c on 2c red	3.75	2.25
a.		Surcharged "5 céntimos"	52.50	45.00
b.		Surcharged "25 céntimos"	67.50	67.50
c.		"10" omitted	57.50	
75	(c)	10c on 2c red	3.00	2.00
a.		Inverted surcharge	30.00	17.00
76	(a)	25c on 5c blue	7.50	3.50
a.		Surcharged "10 céntimos"	75.00	
b.		Surcharged "5 céntimos"	60.00	
c.		Surcharged "50 céntimos"	67.50	
77	(c)	25c on 5c blue	60.00	30.00
a.		Inverted surcharge		
b.		Surcharged on back		
78	(a)	50c on 10c rose	25.00	7.50
a.		Inverted surcharge	50.00	30.00
b.		Surcharged "25 céntimos"	60.00	
79	(c)	50c on 10c rose	30.00	9.50
a.		Inverted surcharge	60.00	
80	(d)	1fr on 20c brown	12.00	9.75
81	(e)	1fr on 20c brown	14.50	12.50
a.		Comma after "Franco"	35.00	35.00
b.		Inverted surcharge	75.00	
82	(f)	1fr on 20c brown	25.00	20.00
83	(g)	1fr25c on 25c violet	45.00	30.00
a.		Inverted surcharge	75.00	
84	(g)	2fr50c on 50c orange	19.00	12.50
a.		Inverted surcharge	35.00	27.50
85	(g)	3fr75c on 75c ultra	45.00	42.50
86	(h)	5fr on 1p gold	175.00	175.00
a.		Inverted surcharge		
87	(i)	5fr on 1p gold	190.00	190.00

Many minor varieties exist in Nos. 54-87: accent on "i" of "centimos"; "5" with straight top; "1" with straight serif.

A7

A7a

1885-91 **Engr.** *Perf. 12*

88	A7	1c	green	90	45
89	A7	2c	vermilion	90	45
90	A7	5c	blue	1.25	45
91	A7a	10c	orange	2.00	60
92	A7a	20c	dark brown	2.00	75
93	A7a	50c	violet ('91)	7.00	6.00
94	A7	1p	carmine ('91)	18.00	12.00
95	A7	2p	red brown ('91)	22.50	14.00
			Nos. 88-95 (8)	54.55	34.70

Nos. 93, 94, 95 were issued without gum.
Imperf. varieties are proofs.
For surcharges see Nos. 166-168.

Coat of Arms — A8

1895 *Perf. 12½x14*

96	A8	1c	green	1.10	45
97	A8	2c	orange red	1.10	45
98	A8	5c	blue	1.10	45
99	A8	10c	orange	2.25	1.40

Nos. 96 to 99 are known imperforate but were not issued in this condition.

1897 *Perf. 14*

96a	A8	1c	green	1.40	52
97a	A8	2c	orange red	8.00	75
98a	A8	5c	blue	1.40	75
99a	A8	10c	orange	2.75	1.50

Voyage of Diego Méndez from Jamaica — A9

Enriquillo's Revolt
A10

Sarcophagus of Columbus
A11

"Española" Guarding Remains of Columbus
A12

Toscanelli Replying to Columbus
A13

Bartolomé de las Casas Defending Indians — A14

Columbus at Salamanca
A15

Columbus' Mausoleum
A16

1899, Feb. 27 **Litho.** *Perf. 11½*

100	A9	1c	brown violet	5.00	4.00
102	A10	2c	rose red	1.75	70
103	A11	5c	blue	2.00	70
104	A12	10c	orange	4.25	1.25
a.			Tête bêche pair	42.50	42.50
105	A13	20c	brown	6.50	5.00
106	A14	50c	yellow green	8.00	6.00
a.			Tête bêche pair	57.50	57.50
107	A15	1p	black, *gray bl*	20.00	15.00
108	A16	2p	bister brown	37.50	37.50

1900, Jan.

109	A11	¼c	black	70	1.25
110	A15	½c	black	70	1.25
110A	A9	1c	gray green	70	52
			Nos. 100-110A (11)	87.10	73.17

Nos. 100-110A were issued to raise funds for a Columbus mausoleum.

Imperf., Pairs

100a	A9	1c	brown violet	15.00	
102a	A10	2c	rose red	5.00	
103a	A11	5c	blue	5.75	
104b	A12	10c	orange	8.75	
105a	A13	20c	brown	15.00	
106b	A14	50c	yellow green	17.50	
c.			As "b," tête bêche pair	125.00	
107a	A15	1p	black, *gray blue*	42.50	
108a	A16	2p	bister brown	70.00	
109a	A11	¼c	black	2.10	2.50
110b	A15	½c	black	2.10	2.50
110c	A9	1c	gray green	3.50	

Map of Hispaniola — A17

A18

1900, Oct. 21 **Unwmk.** *Perf. 14*

111	A17	¼c	dark blue	65	42
112	A17	½c	rose	65	42
113	A17	1c	olive green	65	42
114	A17	2c	deep green	65	42
115	A17	5c	red brown	65	42
a.			Vertical pair, imperf. between	17.50	

Perf. 12

116	A17	10c	orange	65	42
117	A17	20c	lilac	2.75	2.10
a.			20c rose (error)	5.75	5.75
118	A17	50c	black	2.50	2.25
119	A17	1p	brown	2.75	2.25
			Nos. 111-119 (9)	11.90	9.12

Several varieties in design are known in this issue. They were deliberately made. Counterfeits of Nos. 111-119 abound.

1901-06 **Typo.** *Perf. 14*

120	A18	½c	carmine & vio	65	35
121	A18	½c	blk & org ('05)	1.50	85
122	A18	½c	grn & blk ('06)	80	30
123	A18	1c	ol grn & vio	65	18
124	A18	1c	blk & ultra ('05)	1.50	70
125	A18	1c	car & blk ('06)	1.00	45
126	A18	2c	dp grn & vio	70	18
127	A18	2c	blk & vio ('05)	2.00	60
128	A18	2c	org brn & blk ('06)	1.00	15
129	A18	5c	org brn & vio	75	22
130	A18	5c	black & cl ('05)	2.25	1.00
131	A18	5c	blue & blk ('06)	1.25	28
132	A18	10c	orange & vio	1.25	35
133	A18	10c	blk & grn ('05)	3.75	2.00
134	A18	10c	red vio & blk ('06)	1.25	35
135	A18	20c	brn vio & vio	2.25	70
136	A18	20c	blk & ol ('05)	11.50	7.50
137	A18	20c	ol grn & blk ('06)	6.50	2.50
138	A18	50c	gray blk & vio	7.00	5.00
139	A18	50c	blk & red brn ('05)	40.00	30.00
140	A18	50c	brn & blk ('06)	7.50	7.00
141	A18	1p	brn & vio	16.00	9.50
142	A18	1p	blk & gray ('05)	175.00	200.00
143	A18	1p	violet & blk ('06)	17.50	12.00
			Nos. 120-143 (24)	303.55	282.16

Issue dates: Nov. 15, 1901, May 11, 1905, Aug. 17, 1906.
See #172-176. For surcharges see #151-156.

Francisco Sánchez — A19

Juan Pablo Duarte — A20

Ramón Mella — A21

Ft. Santo Domingo — A22

1902, Feb. 25 **Engr.** *Perf. 12*

144	A19	1c	dk green & blk	25	25
145	A20	2c	scarlet & blk	25	25
146	A20	5c	blue & blk	25	25
147	A19	10c	orange & blk	25	25
148	A21	12c	purple & blk	25	25
149	A21	20c	rose & blk	35	35
150	A22	50c	brown & blk	52	52
			Nos. 144-150 (7)	2.12	2.12

Center Inverted

144a	A19	1c	3.25
145a	A20	2c	3.25
146a	A20	5c	3.25
148a	A21	12c	3.25
149a	A21	20c	3.25
150a	A22	50c	3.25
		Nos. 144a-150a (6)	19.50

400th anniversary of Santo Domingo.
Imperforate varieties of Nos. 144 to 150 were never sold to the public.

Nos. 138, 141 Surcharged in Black

2
dos cts

1904, Aug.

151	A18	2c on 50c	7.00	6.00
152	A18	2c on 1p	10.50	7.00
b.		"2" omitted	50.00	50.00
153	A18	5c on 50c	3.75	2.10
154	A18	5c on 1p	4.00	3.50
155	A18	10c on 50c	7.00	6.50
156	A18	10c on 1p	7.00	6.50
		Nos. 151-156 (6)	39.25	31.60

Inverted Surcharge

151a	A18	2c on 50c	14.00	14.00
152a	A18	2c on 1p	14.00	14.00
c.		As "a," "2" omitted	80.00	80.00
153a	A18	5c on 50c	5.00	3.50
154a	A18	5c on 1p	7.00	6.50
155a	A18	10c on 50c	14.00	14.00
156a	A18	10c on 1p	10.00	10.00

16 de Agosto

Official Stamps of 1902 Overprinted

1904

Red Overprint

1904, Aug. 16

157	O1	5c dk blue & blk	5.00	2.75
a.		Inverted overprint	6.50	5.50

Black Overprint

158	O1	2c scarlet & blk	12.50	4.00
a.		Inverted overprint	15.00	5.00
159	O1	5c dk blue & blk	700.00	700.00
160	O1	10c yellow grn & blk	9.25	9.00
a.		Inverted overprint	12.50	12.50

Surcharged

16 de Agosto

1 1904 1

161	O1	1c on 20c yellow & blk	4.00	2.75
a.		Inverted surcharge	6.50	5.00

Nos. J1-J2 Surcharged or Overprinted

REPUBLICA
DOMINICANA
1
CENTAVOS
CORREOS

Surcharged "CENTAVOS"

1904-05

Black Surcharge

162	D1	1c on 2c olive gray	100.00	100.00
a.		"entavos"		
b.		"Dominican"	200.00	200.00
c.		"Centavo"	200.00	200.00

Carmine Surcharge or Overprint

163	D1	1c on 2c olive gray	2.25	1.00
a.		Inverted surcharge	3.50	2.50
b.		"Domihicana"	15.00	15.00
c.		As "b," inverted	40.00	40.00
d.		"Dominican"	10.50	10.50
e.		"Centavos" omitted	30.00	30.00
g.		"entavos"	30.00	
163F	D1	1c on 4c olive gray	35.00	7.00
164	D1	2c olive gray	80	50
a.		"Domihicana"	11.00	11.00
b.		Inverted overprint	1.90	1.90
c.		As "a," inverted	25.00	25.00
d.		"Dominican"	5.75	5.75
e.		"Centavo" omitted	12.50	10.00
f.		"entavos"	12.50	12.50
g.		As "f," inverted	40.00	40.00
h.		As "d," inverted	40.00	40.00

Surcharged "CENTAVO"

165	D1	1c on 4c olive gray	80	65
a.		"Domihicana"	10.00	10.00
c.		Inverted surcharge	1.75	1.75
d.		"1" omitted	3.50	3.50
e.		As "a," inverted	32.50	32.50
f.		As "d," inverted	40.00	40.00
g.		Double surcharge	30.00	30.00

No. 92 Surcharged in Red

DOS
1905
CENTAVOS

1905, Apr. 4

166 A7a 2c on 20c dk brown 7.00 5.00
a. Inverted surcharge 15.00 15.00
167 A7a 5c on 20c dk brown 4.00 1.75
a. Inverted surcharge 16.00 16.00
b. Double surcharge 25.00 25.00
168 A7a 10c on 20c dk brown 7.00 5.00

Nos. 166-168 exist with inverted "A" for "V" in "CENTAVOS" in surcharge.

Nos. J2, J4, J3 Surcharged:

REPUBLICA DOMINICANA. UN centavo. — REPUBLICA DOMINICANA. DOS centavos.

1906, Jan. 16 *Perf. 14*

Red Surcharge

169 D1 1c on 4c olive gray 85 50
a. Inverted surcharge 10.50 10.50
b. Double surcharge 25.00

1906, May 1

Black Surcharge

170 D1 1c on 10c olive gray 1.00 42
a. Inverted surcharge 10.50 10.50
b. Double surcharge 14.00 14.00
c. "OMINICANA" 20.00 20.00
d. As "c," inverted 150.00
171 D1 2c on 5c olive gray 1.00 42
a. Inverted surcharge 10.50 10.50
b. Double surcharge 35.00

The varieties small "C" or small "A" in "REPUBLICA" are found on #169, 170, 171.

Arms Type of 1901-06

1907-10 **Wmk. 116**

172 A18 ½c grn & blk ('08) 75 18
173 A18 1c carmine & blk 75 15
174 A18 2c orange brn & blk 75 15
175 A18 5c blue & blk 75 22
176 A18 10c red vio & blk ('10) 8.00 1.05
Nos. 172-176 (5) 11.00 1.75

No. O6 Overprinted in Red — HABILITADO 1911

Perf. 13½x14, 13½x13

1911, July 11

177 O2 2c scarlet & black 1.25 52
a. "HABILITAOO" 8.75 6.00
b. Inverted overprint 21.00
c. Double overprint 21.00

A23

Juan Pablo Duarte — A24

1911-13 *Perf. 14*

Center in Black

178 A23 ½c orange ('13) 25 15
179 A23 1c green 25 15
180 A23 2c carmine 25 15
181 A23 5c gray blue ('13) 75 15
182 A23 10c red violet 1.25 42
183 A23 20c olive green 8.00 7.00
184 A23 30c yellow brn ('12) 3.25 3.25
185 A23 1p violet ('12) 5.50 3.50
Nos. 178-185 (8) 19.50 14.77

See Nos. 230-232.

1914, Apr. 13 *Perf. 13x14*

Background Red, White and Blue

186 A24 ½c orange & blk 50 40
187 A24 1c green & blk 50 40
188 A24 2c rose & blk 50 40
189 A24 5c slate & blk 50 50
190 A24 10c magenta & blk 1.00 85
191 A24 20c olive grn & blk 2.25 2.50
192 A24 50c brown & blk 3.00 3.25
193 A24 1p dull lilac & blk 5.00 5.00
Nos. 186-193 (8) 13.25 13.30

Cent. of the birth of Juan Pablo Duarte (1813-1876), patriot and revolutionary.

Official Stamps of 1909-12 Surcharged in Violet or Overprinted in Red:

Habilitado 1915 MEDIO CENTAVO — a

Habilitado 1915 — b

1915, Feb. *Perf. 13½x13, 13½x14*

194 O2 (a) ½c on 20c orange & blk 52 35
a. Inverted surcharge 6.00 6.00
b. Double surcharge 8.75 8.75
c. "Habilitado" omitted 5.25 5.25
195 O2 (b) 1c blue grn & blk 80 25
a. Inverted overprint 6.00 6.00
b. Double overprint 7.00
c. Overprinted "1915" only 12.50
196 O2 (b) 2c scarlet & blk 80 25
a. Inverted overprint 5.25 5.25
b. Double overprint 7.75 7.75
c. Overprinted "1915" only 8.75
d. "1915" double
197 O2 (b) 5c dk blue & blk 1.00 25
a. Inverted overprint 7.00 7.00
b. Double overprint 8.75 8.75
c. Double ovpt., one invtd. 27.50
d. Overprinted "1915" only 8.50
198 O2 (b) 10c yellow grn & blk 2.75 2.50
a. Inverted overprint 15.00
199 O2 (b) 20c orange & blk 9.00 6.50
a. "Habilitado" omitted
Nos. 194-199 (6) 14.87 10.10

Nos. 194, 196-198 are known with both perforations. Nos. 195 and 199 are only perf. 13½x13.

The variety capital "I" for "1" in "Habilitado" occurs once in each sheet in all denominations.

A25

Type of 1911-13 Redrawn Overprinted "1915" in Red

TWO CENTAVOS:
Type I - "DOS" in small letters.
Type II - "DOS" in larger letters with white dot at each end of the word.

1915 **Unwmk.** **Litho.** *Perf. 11½*

200 A25 ½c violet & blk 75 18
a. Imperf., pair 5.75
201 A25 1c yellow brn & blk 75 15
a. Imperf., pair 6.50
b. Vert. pair, imperf. horiz. 10.50
c. Horiz. pair, imperf. vert. 10.50
202 A25 2c ol grn & blk (I) 3.75 25
a. Imperf., pair 10.00
203 A25 2c ol grn & blk (II) 6.00 18
a. Center omitted 87.50
b. Frame omitted 87.50
c. Imperf., pair 15.00
d. Horiz. pair, imperf. vert. 15.00
204 A25 5c magenta & blk 3.25 25
a. Pair, one without overprint 65.00
b. Imperf., pair 6.50
205 A25 10c gray blue & blk 3.75 50
a. Imperf., pair 7.75
b. Horiz. pair, imperf. vert. 35.00
206 A25 20c rose red & blk 6.50 1.50
a. Imperf., pair 12.50
207 A25 50c green & blk 8.50 4.00
a. Imperf., pair 25.00
208 A25 1p orange & blk 17.50 7.00
a. Imperf., pair 52.50
Nos. 200-208 (9) 50.75 14.01

Type of 1915 Overprinted "1916" in Red

1916

209 A25 ½c violet & blk 1.25 15
a. Imperf., pair 21.00
210 A25 1c green & blk 2.00 15
a. Imperf., pair 21.00

Type of 1915 Overprinted "1917" in Red

1917-19

213 A25 ½c red lilac & blk 2.25 28
a. Horiz. pair, imperf. btwn. 47.50 47.50
214 A25 1c yellow grn & blk 1.50 15
a. Vert. pair, imperf. btwn. 50.00
215 A25 2c olive grn & blk 1.40 15
a. Imperf., pair 35.00
216 A25 5c magenta & blk 16.00 70

Type of 1915 Overprinted "1919" in Red

1919

219 A25 2c olive grn & blk 10.00 15

Type of 1915 Overprinted "1920" in Red

1920-27

220 A25 ½c lilac rose & blk 50 22
a. Horiz. pair, imperf. btwn. 25.00 25.00
b. Inverted overprint
c. Double overprint
d. Double overprint, one invtd.
221 A25 1c yellow grn & blk 75 15
a. Overprint omitted 70.00
b. Horiz. pair, imperf. btwn. 40.00
222 A25 2c olive grn & blk 75 15
a. Vertical pair, imperf. between 27.50
223 A25 5c dp rose & blk 9.00 50
224 A25 10c blue & black 5.00 22
225 A25 20c rose red & blk ('27) 7.00 52
226 A25 50c green & blk ('27) 52.50 17.50
Nos. 220-226 (7) 75.50 19.26

Type of 1915 Overprinted "1921" in Red

1921

227 A25 1c yellow grn & blk 3.00 28
a. Horiz. pair, imperf. btwn. 45.00 45.00
b. Imperf., pair 45.00 45.00
228 A25 2c olive grn & blk 5.00 32
a. Vert. pair, imperf. btwn. 45.00

Redrawn Design of 1915 without Overprint

1922

230 A25 1c green 2.25 15
231 A25 2c carmine (II) 2.50 15
232 A25 5c blue 4.00 25
Set value 45

Exist imperf.

A26

A27

Second Redrawing

TEN CENTAVOS:
Type I - Numerals 2mm high. "DIEZ" in thick letters with large white dot at each end.
Type II - Numerals 3mm high. "DIEZ" in thin letters with white dot with colored center at each end.

1924-27

233 A26 1c green 90 15
a. Vert. pair, imperf. btwn. 35.00 35.00
234 A26 2c red 70 15
235 A26 5c blue 1.10 15
236 A26 10c pale bl & blk (I) ('26) 12.00 3.00
236A A26 10c pale bl & blk (II) 22.50 1.10
236B A26 50c gray grn & blk ('26) 45.00 27.50
237 A26 1p orange & blk ('27) 16.00 10.50
Nos. 233-237 (7) 98.20 42.55

In the second redrawing the shield has a flat top and the design differs in many details from the stamps of 1911-13 and 1915-22.

1927

238 A27 ½c lilac rose & blk 28 15

Exhibition Pavilion — A28

1927 **Unwmk.** *Perf. 12*

239 A28 2c carmine 80 50
240 A28 5c ultra 1.75 50

Natl. and West Indian Exhib. at Santiago de los Caballeros.

Ruins of Columbus' Fortress A29

1928

241 A29 ½c lilac rose 60 35
242 A29 1c deep green 50 15
a. Horiz. pair, imperf. btwn. 25.00
243 A29 2c red 50 15
244 A29 5c dark blue 1.50 35
245 A29 10c light blue 1.75 28
246 A29 20c rose 3.00 42
247 A29 50c yellow green 10.50 6.50
248 A29 1p orange yellow 27.50 20.00
Nos. 241-248 (8) 45.85 28.20

Reprints exist of 1c, 2c and 10c.
Issue dates: 1c, 2c, 10c, Oct. 1. Others, Dec.

Horacio Vasquez — A30

Convent of San Ignacio de Loyola — A31

1929, May-June

249 A30 ½c dull rose 50 30
250 A30 1c gray green 50 15
251 A30 2c red 60 15
252 A30 5c dark ultra 1.25 35
253 A30 10c pale blue 1.75 50
Nos. 249-253 (5) 4.60 1.45

Signing of the "Frontier" treaty with Haiti.
Issue dates: 2c, May, others, June.

Imperf., Pairs

249a A30 ½c 12.50
250a A30 1c 12.50
251a A30 2c 12.50
252a A30 5c 14.00

1930, May 1 *Perf. 11½*

254 A31 ½c red brown 65 45
a. Imperf., pair 55.00 55.00
255 A31 1c deep green 50 15
256 A31 2c vermilion 50 15
a. Imperf., pair 60.00
257 A31 5c deep blue 1.25 35
258 A31 10c light blue 3.00 1.05
Nos. 254-258 (5) 5.90 2.15

Cathedral of Santo Domingo, First Church in America — A32

1931 *Perf. 12*

260 A32 1c deep green 70 15
a. Imperf., pair 50.00
261 A32 2c scarlet 52 15
a. Imperf., pair 50.00
262 A32 3c violet 70 15
263 A32 7c dark blue 2.00 25
264 A32 8c bister 2.75 85
265 A32 10c light blue 4.50 1.05
a. Imperf., pair 35.00
Nos. 260-265 (6) 11.17 2.60

Issue dates: 3c-7c, Aug. 1. Others, July 11.
For overprint see No. RAC8.

A33

Overprinted or Surcharged in Black

1932, Dec. 20 *Perf. 12*

Cross in Red

265B A33 1c yellow green 52 42
265C A33 3c on 2c violet 70 50
265D A33 5c blue 4.00 4.25
265E A33 7c on 10c turq bl 5.50 5.75

Proceeds of sale given to Red Cross. Valid Dec. 20 to Jan. 5, 1933.

Inverted and pairs, one without surcharge or overprint, exist on Nos. 265B-265D, as well as missing letters.

Fernando Arturo de Merino (1833-1906) as President — A35

Cathedral of Santo Domingo — A36

Designs: ½c, 5c, 8c, Tomb of Merino. 1c, 3c, 10c, as Archbishop.

1933, Feb. 27 Engr. *Perf. 14*

266 A35 ½c lt violet 30 25
267 A35 1c yellow green 30 15
268 A35 2c lt red 1.00 80
269 A35 3c deep violet 40 15
270 A35 5c dark blue 75 28
271 A35 7c ultra 1.25 42
272 A35 8c dark green 1.40 1.25
273 A35 10c orange yel 1.25 28
274 A35 20c carmine rose 2.75 2.00
275 A36 50c lemon 10.50 7.00
276 A36 1p dark brown 27.50 17.50
Nos. 266-276 (11) 47.40 30.08

For surcharges see Nos. G1-G7.

Tower of Homage, Ozama Fortress — A37

1932 Litho. *Perf. 12*

278 A37 1c green 75 15
279 A37 3c violet 52 15
Set value 21

Issue dates: 1c, July 2; 3c, June 22.

"CORREOS" added at left

1933, May 28

283 A37 1c dark green 50 15

President Rafael L. Trujillo
A38 A39

1933, Aug. 16 Engr. *Perf. 14*

286 A38 1c yellow grn & blk 85 50
287 A39 3c dp violet & blk 85 22
288 A38 7c ultra & blk 2.00 1.00

42nd birthday of President Rafael Leonidas Trujillo Molina.

San Rafael Bridge — A40

1934 Litho. *Perf. 12*

289 A40 ½c dull violet 65 35
290 A40 1c dark green 90 18
291 A40 3c violet 1.40 15

Opening of San Rafael Bridge.
Issue dates: ½c, 3c, Mar. 3; 1c, Feb. 17.

Trujillo Bridge A41

1934

292 A41 ½c red brown 65 25
293 A41 1c green 90 15
294 A41 3c purple 1.25 15
Set value 43

Opening of the General Trujillo Bridge near Ciudad Trujillo.
Issue dates: 1c, Aug. 24. Others, Sept. 7.

Ramfis Bridge A42

1935, Apr. 6

295 A42 1c green 45 15
296 A42 3c yellow brown 50 15
297 A42 5c brown violet 1.65 1.05
298 A42 10c rose 3.25 1.40

Issued in commemoration of the opening of the Ramfis Bridge over the Higuamo River.

President Trujillo — A43

A44

A45

1935 *Perf. 11*

299 A43 3c yellow & brown 32 18
300 A44 5c org red, bl, red & bis 40 15
301 A45 7c ultra, bl, red & bis 60 15
302 A44 10c red vio, bl, red & bis 90 15
Set value 48

Ratification of a treaty setting the frontier between Dominican Republic and Haiti.
Issue dates: 3c, Oct. 29; 5c, 10c, Nov. 25; 7c, Nov. 8.

National Palace — A46

1935, Apr. 1 *Perf. 11½*

303 A46 25c yellow orange 2.25 18

Obligatory for all mail addressed to the president and cabinet ministers.

Post Office, Santiago A47

1936

304 A47 ½c bright violet 32 35
305 A47 1c green 32 15

Issue dates: ½c, Jan. 14; 1c, Jan. 4.

George Washington Ave., Ciudad Trujillo — A48

1936, Feb. 22

306 A48 ½c brn & vio brn 42 45
a. Imperf., pair 52.50
307 A48 2c carmine & brn 42 32
308 A48 3c yellow org & red brn 65 18
309 A48 7c ultra, blue & brn 1.25 1.25
a. Imperf., pair 52.50

Dedication of George Washington Avenue, Ciudad Trujillo.

José Nuñez de Cáceres — A49 Felix M. del Monte — A55

Proposed National Library — A56

Designs: 1c, Gen. Gregorio Luperon. 2c, Emiliano Tejera. 3c, President Trujillo. 5c, Jose Reyes. 7c, Gen. Antonio Duverge. 25c, Francisco J. Peynado. 30c, Salome Urena. 50c, Gen. Jose M. Cabral. 1p, Manuel de Jesus Galvan. 2p, Gaston F. Deligne.

1936 Unwmk. Engr. *Perf. 13½, 14*

310 A49 ½c dull violet 30 15
311 A49 1c dark green 24 15
312 A49 2c carmine 28 15
313 A49 3c violet 28 15
314 A49 5c deep ultra 55 30
315 A49 7c slate blue 1.00 55
316 A55 10c orange 1.00 30
317 A56 20c olive green 3.75 2.75
318 A55 25c gray violet 6.00 8.00
319 A55 30c scarlet 7.50 10.00
320 A55 50c black brown 8.00 5.50
321 A55 1p black 27.50 32.50
322 A55 2p yellow brown 65.00 80.00
Nos. 310-322 (13) 121.40 140.50

The funds derived from the sale of these stamps were returned to the National Treasury Fund for the erection of a building for the National Library and Archives.
Issue dates: 3c, 7c, Mar. 18; others, May 22.

President Trujillo and Obelisk — A62

1937, Jan. 11 Litho. *Perf. 11½*

323 A62 1c green 18 15
324 A62 3c violet 38 15
325 A62 7c blue & turq blue 1.05 1.00

1st anniv. of naming Ciudad Trujillo.

Discus Thrower and Flag — A63

1937, Aug. 14
Flag in Red and Blue

326 A63 1c dark green 3.00 75
327 A63 3c violet 3.75 45
328 A63 7c dark blue 6.00 2.75

1st Natl. Olympic Games, Aug. 16, 1937.

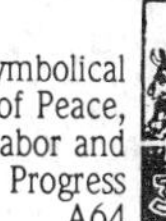

Symbolical of Peace, Labor and Progress A64

1937, Sept. 18 *Perf. 12*

329 A64 3c purple 30 15

"8th Year of the Benefactor."

Monument to Father Francisco Xavier Billini (1837-90) — A65

1937, Dec. 29

330 A65 ½c deep orange 15 15
331 A65 5c purple 42 15
Set value 22

Globe and Torch of Liberty — A66

1938, Feb. 22 *Perf. 11½*

332 A66 1c green 38 15
333 A66 3c purple 52 15
334 A66 10c orange 1.00 18
Set value 30

150th anniv. of the Constitution of the US.

Pledge of Trinitarians, City Gate and National Flag — A67

1938, July 16 *Perf. 12*

335 A67 1c green, red & dk bl 38 18
336 A67 3c purple, red & bl 45 15
337 A67 10c orange, red & bl 90 42

Trinitarians and patriots, Francisco Del Rosario Sanchez, Ramon Matias Mella and Juan Pablo Duarte, who helped free their country from foreign domination.

Seal of the University of Santo Domingo — A68

1938, Oct. 28
338 A68 ½c orange 28 25
339 A68 1c dp green & lt green 30 15
340 A68 3c purple & pale vio 38 15
341 A68 7c dp blue & lt blue 75 40

Founding of the University of Santo Domingo, on Oct. 28, 1538.

Trylon and Perisphere, Flag and Proposed Columbus Lighthouse — A69

1939, Apr. 30 Litho. *Perf. 12*
Flag in Blue and Red
342 A69 ½c red org & org 35 18
343 A69 1c green & lt green 38 15
344 A69 3c purple & pale vio 42 15
345 A69 10c orange & yellow 1.25 65
Nos. 342-345,C33 (5) 3.65 1.73

New York World's Fair.

A70 A71

1939, Sept. Typo.
346 A70 ½c black & pale gray 28 15
347 A70 1c black & yel grn 38 15
348 A70 3c black & yel brn 42 15
349 A70 7c black & dp ultra 1.00 90
350 A70 10c black & brt red vio 1.50 40
Nos. 346-350 (5) 3.58 1.75

José Trujillo Valdez (1863-1935), father of President Trujillo Molina.

1940, Apr. 14 Litho. *Perf. 11½*

Map of the Americas and flags of 21 American republics.

Flags in National Colors
351 A71 1c deep green 24 15
352 A71 2c carmine 35 25
353 A71 3c red violet 48 15
354 A71 10c orange 1.00 18
355 A71 1p chestnut 15.00 12.00
Nos. 351-355 (5) 17.07 12.73

Pan American Union, 50th anniv.

Sir Rowland Hill — A72

1940, May 6 *Perf. 12*
356 A72 3c brt red vio & rose lilac 3.00 38
357 A72 7c dk blue & lt blue 6.00 1.40

Centenary of first postage stamp.

Julia Molina Trujillo A73

1940, May 26
358 A73 1c grn, lt grn & dk grn 28 15
359 A73 2c brt red, buff & dp rose 38 24
360 A73 3c org, dl org & brn org 45 15
361 A73 7c bl, pale bl & dk bl 1.00 40
Set value 78

Issued in commemoration of Mother's Day.

Map of Caribbean A74

1940, June 6 *Perf. 11½*
362 A74 3c brt car & pale rose 38 15
363 A74 7c dk blue & lt blue 75 15
364 A74 1p yel grn & pale grn 7.50 6.50

2nd Inter-American Caribbean Conf. held at Ciudad Trujillo, May 31 to June 6.

Marion Military Hospital — A75

1940, Dec. 24
365 A75 ½c chestnut & fawn 24 18

Fortress, Ciudad Trujillo A76

Statue of Columbus, Ciudad Trujillo — A77

1941
366 A76 1c dk green & lt green 15 15
367 A77 2c brt red & rose 15 15
368 A77 10c orange brn & buff 52 15
Set value 21

Issue dates: 1c, Mar. 27; others, Apr. 7.

Sánchez, Duarte, Mella and Trujillo — A78

1941, May 16
369 A78 3c brt red lil & red vio 22 15
370 A78 4c brt red, crim & pale rose 30 20
371 A78 13c dk blue & lt blue 60 25
372 A78 15c orange brn & buff 2.00 1.50
373 A78 17c lt bl, bl & pale bl 2.00 1.50
374 A78 1p org, yel brn & pale org 7.75 7.00
375 A78 2p lt gray & pale gray 17.00 7.25
Nos. 369-375 (7) 29.87 17.85

Trujillo-Hull Treaty signed Sept. 24, 1940 and effective Apr. 1, 1941.

Bastion of February 27 — A79

1941, Oct. 20
376 A79 5c brt blue & lt blue 48 18

School, Torch of Knowledge, Pres. Trujillo — A80

1941
377 A80 ½c chestnut & fawn 18 15
378 A80 1c dk green & lt green 24 15
Set value 16

Education campaign.
Issue dates: ½c, Dec. 12, 1c, Dec. 2.

Reserve Bank of Dominican Republic — A81

1942 Unwmk.
379 A81 5c lt brown & buff 38 15
380 A81 17c dp blue & lt blue 70 45

Founding of the Reserve Bank, Oct. 24, 1941.

Representation of Transportation A82

Virgin of Altagracia A83

1942, Aug. 15
381 A82 3c dk brn, grn yel & lt bl 50 15
382 A82 15c pur, grn, yel & lt bl 1.25 45
Set value 51

Day of Posts and Telegraph, 8th anniv.

1942, Aug. 15
383 A83 ½c gray & pale gray 75 15
384 A83 1c dp green & lt green 1.50 15
385 A83 3c brt red lil & lil 9.50 15
386 A83 5c dk vio brn & vio brn 2.00 15
387 A83 10c rose pink & pink 6.75 24
388 A83 15c dp blue & lt blue 7.25 30
Nos. 383-388 (6) 27.75
Set value 84

20th anniv. of the coronation of Our Lady of Altagracia.

Bananas A84 Cows A85

1942-43
389 A84 3c dk brn & grn ('43) 45 15
390 A84 4c vermilion & blk ('43) 48 28
391 A85 5c dp blue & cop brn 48 15
392 A85 15c dk purple & blue grn 75 35

Issue date: 5c, 15c, Aug. 18.

Emblems of Dominican and Trujillista Parties — A86

1943, Jan. 15
393 A86 3c orange 38 15
394 A86 4c dark red 48 20
395 A86 13c brt red lilac 95 18
396 A86 1p lt blue 4.50 1.65

Re-election of President Rafael Trujillo Molina, May 16, 1942.

Model Market, Ciudad Trujillo — A87

1944
397 A87 2c dk brown & buff 15 15

Bastion of Feb. 27 and National Flag — A88

1944, Feb. 27 Unwmk.
Flag in Dark Blue and Carmine
398 A88 ½c ocher 15 15
399 A88 1c yellow green 15 15
400 A88 2c scarlet 15 15
401 A88 3c brt red vio 15 15
402 A88 5c yellow orange 18 15
403 A88 7c brt blue 24 22
404 A88 10c orange brown 38 30
405 A88 20c olive green 60 60
406 A88 50c lt blue 1.90 1.75
Nos. 398-406,C46-C48 (12) 6.70 5.42

Souvenir Sheet
Imperf
407 Sheet of 12 90.00 90.00
a.-l. Single stamp 3.00 3.00

Centenary of Independence.
No. 407 contains one each of Nos. 398-406, C46-C48 with simulated perforations. Size: 141x205mm.

Battlefield and Nurse with Child A90

1944, Aug. 1
408 A90 1c dk bl grn, buff & car 15 15
a. Vertical pair, imperf. btwn. 15.00
b. Horiz. pair, imperf. vert. 15.00
409 A90 2c dk brn, buff & car 30 15
410 A90 3c brt bl, buff & car 30 15
411 A90 10c rose car, buff & car 60 15
Set value 36

80th anniv. of the Intl. Red Cross.

Municipal Building, San Cristóbal A91

Emblem of Communications A92

Unwmk.

1945, Jan. 10 Litho. *Perf. 12*

412 A91	½c blue & lt blue	15	15
413 A91	1c dk green & green	15	15
414 A91	2c red org & org	15	15
415 A91	3c dk brown & brown	15	15
416 A91	10c ultra & gray blue	42	15
	Set value	78	36

Centenary of the constitution.

1945, Sept. 1

Center in Dark Blue and Carmine

417 A92	3c orange	15	15
418 A92	20c yellow green	75	18
419 A92	50c light blue	1.50	55
	Nos. 417-419,C53-C56 (7)	3.63	1.58

Palace of Justice, Ciudad Trujillo — A93

1946 *Perf. 11½*

420 A93	3c dk red brown & buff	18	15

Map of Hispaniola A94

1946, Aug. 4 *Perf. 12*

421 A94	10c rose brn, yel, lil, bl, red & grn	38	15

450th anniv. of the founding of Santo Domingo. See Nos. C62-C63.

Waterfall of Jimenoa — A95

1946-47

Center Multicolored

422 A95	1c yellow grn ('47)	15	15
423 A95	2c carmine ('47)	15	15
424 A95	3c deep blue	15	15
425 A95	13c red violet ('47)	42	24
426 A95	20c chocolate ('47)	90	24
427 A95	50c orange ('47)	1.65	90
	Nos. 422-427,C64-C67 (10)	5.22	3.33

Nos. 422-423, 425-427 issued Mar. 18.
For surcharge see No. 540.

Executive Palace — A96

1948, Feb. 27

428 A96	1c yellow green	15	15
429 A96	3c deep blue	15	15
	Set value	21	15

See Nos. C68-C69.

Church of San Francisco Ruins — A97

1949, Apr. 13 *Perf. 11½*

430 A97	1c dk grn & pale grn	15	15
431 A97	3c dp bl & pale bl	15	15
	Nos. 430-431,C70-C73 (6)	1.65	
	Set value		90

Gen. Pedro Santana — A98

Pigeon and Globe — A99

1949, Aug. 10

432 A98	3c deep blue & blue	15	15

Centenary of the Battle of Las Carreras. See No. C74.

1949, Sept. 15

Center and Inscriptions in Brown

433 A99	1c green & pale green	15	15
434 A99	2c yel grn & yel	15	15
435 A99	5c blue & pale blue	18	15
436 A99	7c dk vio bl & pale bl	40	15
	Set value		35

75th anniv. of the UPU.

Catalogue values for unused stamps in this section, from this point to the end of the section, are for Never Hinged items.

Hotel Jimani A100

Hotels: 1c, 2c, Hamaca. 5c, Montana. 15c, San Cristobal. 20c, Maguana.

1950-52

437 A100	½c org brn & buff	15	15
438 A100	1c dp grn & grn ('51)	15	15
439 A100	2c red org & sal ('52)	15	15
440 A100	5c blue & lt blue	25	15
441 A100	15c dp orange & yel	52	15
442 A100	20c lilac & rose lilac	1.00	16
443 A100	1p chocolate & yel	4.00	1.65
	Nos. 437-443,C75-C76 (9)	8.79	4.71

Issue dates: 1c, Dec. 1, 1951; 2c, Jan. 11, 1952. Others, Sept. 8, 1950.
The ½c, 15c and 20c exist imperf.

Ruins of Church and Hospital of San Nicolas de Bari — A101

School of Medicine — A102

Queen Isabella I — A103

1950, Oct. 2

444 A101	2c dk green & rose brn	24	15
445 A102	5c vio blue & org brn	32	15
	Set value		18

13th Pan-American Health Conference. Exist imperf. See No. C77.

1951, Oct. 12

446 A103	5c dk blue & red brn	28	15

500th anniversary of the birth of Queen Isabella I of Spain. Exists imperf.

Dr. Salvador B. Gautier Hospital A104

1952, Aug.

447 A104	1c dark green	15	15
448 A104	2c red	15	15
449 A104	5c violet blue	28	15
	Nos. 447-449,C78-C79 (5)	3.13	2.85

Columbus Lighthouse and Flags of 21 Republics A105

1953, Jan. 6 Engr. *Perf. 13*

450 A105	2c dark green	25	15
451 A105	5c deep blue	35	15
452 A105	10c deep carmine	60	24
	Nos. 450-452,C80-C86 (10)	5.33	3.52

Miniature sheet containing Nos. 450-452 and C80-C86 is listed as No. C86a.

Treasury Building, Ciudad Trujillo A106

Sugar Industry, "Central Rio Haina" A107

1953 Litho. *Perf. 11½*

453 A106	½c brown	15	15
454 A106	2c dark blue	15	15
455 A107	5c blue & vio brn	20	15
456 A106	15c orange	60	20
	Set value		37

For surcharge see No. 539.

José Marti — A108

Monument to the Peace of Trujillo — A109

1954 *Perf. 12½*

457 A108	10c dp blue & dk brown	45	15

Centenary of the birth of Jose Marti (1853-1895), Cuban patriot.

1954, May 25

458 A109	2c green	15	15
459 A109	7c blue	25	15
460 A109	20c orange	75	15
	Set value		23

See No. 493.

Rotary Emblem A110

1955, Feb. 23 *Perf. 12*

461 A110	7c deep blue	60	20

50th anniv., Rotary Intl. See No. C90.

Gen. Rafael L. Trujillo — A111

Designs: 4c, Trujillo in civilian clothes. 7c, Trujillo statue. 10c, Symbols of culture and prosperity.

1955, May 16 Engr. *Perf. 13½x13*

462 A111	2c red	15	15
463 A111	4c lt olive green	15	15
464 A111	7c indigo	25	15
465 A111	10c brown	50	16
	Nos. 462-465,C91-C93 (7)	2.75	
	Set value		1.25

25th anniversary of the Trujillo era.

General Rafael L. Trujillo — A112

Angelita Trujillo — A113

1955, Dec. 20 Unwmk. *Perf. 13*

466 A112	7c deep claret	35	15
467 A112	10c dark blue	50	15
	Set value		25

See No. C94.

1955, Dec. 20 Litho. *Perf. 12½*

468 A113	10c blue & ultra	45	15

Nos. 466-468 were issued to publicize the International Fair of Peace and Brotherhood in Ciudad Trujillo, Dec. 1955.

Airport A114 — Cedar A115

1956, Apr. 6 — *Perf. 12½*

469	A114	1c	brown	15 15
470	A114	2c	red orange	15 15
			Set value	25 15

3rd Caribbean conf. of the ICAO. See #95.

1956, Dec. 8 — *Perf. 11½x12*

471	A115	5c	car rose & grn	24 15
472	A115	6c	red vio & grn	28 15
			Set value	20

Issued to publicize the reforestation program. See No. C96.

Fair Emblem A116 — Fanny Blankers-Koen, Netherlands A117

1957, Jan. 10 — *Perf. 12½*

473	A116	7c	blue, lt brn & ver	35 15

2nd International Livestock Show, Ciudad Trujillo, Jan. 10-20, 1957. Exists imperf.

Engraved & Lithographed

1957, Jan. 24 — *Perf. 11½, Imperf.*

Olympic Winners and Flags: 2c, Jesse Owens, US. 3c, Kee Chung Sohn, Japan. 5c, Lord Burghley, England. 7c, Bob Mathias, US.

Flags in National Colors

474	A117	1c	brn, lt bl, vio & mar	15 15
475	A117	2c	dk brn, lt bl & vio	15 15
476	A117	3c	red lilac & red	15 15
477	A117	5c	red org & vio	15 15
478	A117	7c	green & violet	15 15
			Set value, #474-478, C97-C99	85 73

16th Olympic Games, Melbourne, Nov. 22-Dec. 8, 1956.

Miniature sheets of 5 exist, perf. and imperf., containing Nos. 474-478. Value, 2 sheets, perf. and imperf., $8.50.

For surcharges see Nos. B1-B5, B26-B30, CB1-CB3, CB16-CB18.

Lars Hall, Sweden, Pentathlon — A118

Olympic Winners and Flags: 2c, Betty Cuthbert, Australia, 100 & 200 meter dash. 3c, Egil Danielsen, Norway, javelin. 5c, Alain Mimoun, France, marathon. 7c, Norman Read, New Zealand, 50 km. walk.

Perf. 13½, Imperf.

1957, July 18 — **Photo.** — **Unwmk.**

Flags in National Colors

479	A118	1c	brn & brt bl	15 15
480	A118	2c	org ver & dk bl	15 15
481	A118	3c	dark blue	15 15
482	A118	5c	ol & dk bl	15 15
483	A118	7c	rose brn & dk bl	15 15
			Set value, #479-483, C100-C102	85 73

1956 Olympic winners.

Miniature sheets of 8 exist, perf. and imperf., containing Nos. 479-483 and C100-C102. The center label in these sheets is printed in two forms: Olympic gold medal or Olympic flag. Sheets measure 140x140mm. Value, 4 sheets, perf. and imperf., medal and flag, $18.

A third set of similar miniature sheets (perf. and imperf.) with center label showing an incorrect version of the Dominican Republic flag (colors transposed) was printed. These sheets are said to have been briefly sold on the first day, then withdrawn as the misprint was discovered. Value, 2 sheets, perf. & imperf., $150.

For surcharges see Nos. B6-B10, CB4-CB6.

Gerald Ouellette, Canada, Small Bore Rifle, Prone — A119

Ron Delaney, Ireland, 1,500 Meter Run — A120

Olympic Winners and Flags: 3c, Tenley Albright, US, figure skating. 5c, Joaquin Capilla, Mexico, platform diving. 7c, Ercole Baldini, Italy, individual road race (cycling).

Engraved and Lithographed

1957, Nov. 12 — *Perf. 13½, Imperf.*

Flags in National Colors

484	A119	1c	red brown	15 15
485	A120	2c	gray brown	15 15
486	A119	3c	violet	15 15
487	A120	5c	red orange	15 15
488	A119	7c	Prus green	15 15
			Set value, #484-488, C103-C105	85 73

1956 Olympic winners.

Miniature sheets of 5 exist, perf. and imperf., containing Nos. 484-488. Value, 2 sheets, perf. and imperf., $5.50.

For surcharges see Nos. B11-B20, CB7-CB12.

Mahogany Flower — A121 — Cervantes, Globe, Book — A122

1957-58 — **Litho.** — *Perf. 12½*

489	A121	2c	green & maroon	15 15

Perf. 12

490	A121	4c	lilac & rose ('58)	15 15
491	A121	7c	ultra & gray grn	35 15
492	A121	25c	brown & org ('58)	70 28
			Set value	54

Sizes: No. 489, 25x29¼mm; Nos. 490-492, 24x28¾mm. In 1959, the 2c was reissued in size 24¼x28½mm with slightly different tones of green and maroon.

Issue dates: 2c, Oct. 24; 7c, Nov. 6; 4c and 25c, Apr. 7, 1958.

For surcharges see Nos. 537-538.

Type of 1954, Redrawn

Perf. 12x11½

1957, June 12 — **Unwmk.**

493	A109	7c	bright blue	50 16

On No. 493 the cent symbol is smaller, the shading of the sky and steps stronger and the letters in "Correos" shorter and bolder.

1958, Apr. 23 — **Litho.** — *Perf. 12½*

494	A122	4c	yellow green	15 15
495	A122	7c	red lilac	20 15
496	A122	10c	lt olive brown	35 15
			Set value	28

4th Book Fair, Apr. 23-28. Exist imperf.

Gen. Rafael L. Trujillo — A123

1958, Aug. 16 — *Perf. 12*

497	A123	2c	red lilac & yel	15 15
498	A123	4c	green & yel	15 15
499	A123	7c	brown & yel	20 15
a.			Souv. sheet of 3, #497-499, imperf.	75 60
			Set value	37 21

25th anniv. of Gen. Trujillo's designation as "Benefactor of his country."

S. S. Rhadames A124

1958, Oct. 27 — *Perf. 12½*

500	A124	7c	bright blue	40 15

Day of the Dominican Merchant Marine. Exists imperf.

Shozo Sasahara, Japan, Featherweight Wrestling — A125

Olympic Winners and Flags: 1c, Gillian Sheen, England, fencing, vert. 2c, Milton Campbell, US, decathlon, vert. 5c, Madeleine Berthod, Switzerland, downhill skiing. 7c, Murray Rose, Australia, 400 & 1,500 meter freestyle.

Perf. 13½, Imperf.

1958, Oct. 30 — **Photo.**

Flags in National Colors

501	A125	1c	rose, ind & ultra	15 15
502	A125	2c	brown & blue	15 15
503	A125	3c	gray, vio, blk & buff	15 15
504	A125	5c	rose, dk bl, brn & red	15 15
505	A125	7c	lt brn, dk bl & red	15 15
			Set value, #501-505, C106-C108	85 73

1956 Olympic winners.

Miniature sheets of 5 exist, perf. and imperf. containing Nos. 501-505. Value, 2 sheets, perf. and imperf., $5.

For surcharges see Nos. B21-B25, CB13-CB15.

Globe and Symbolic Fire — A126

1958, Nov. 3 — **Litho.** — *Perf. 11½*

506	A126	7c	blue & dp carmine	24 15

Opening of UNESCO Headquarters in Paris, Nov. 3.

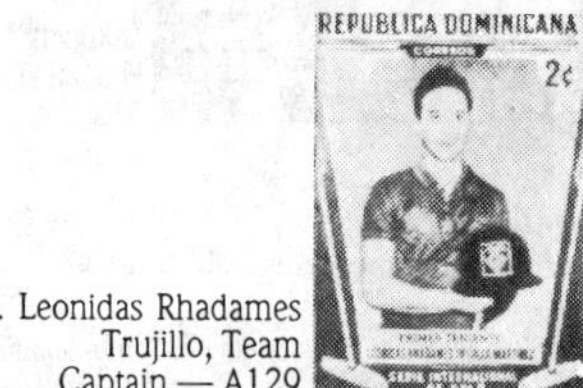

Dominican Republic Pavilion, Brussels Fair — A127

1958, Dec. 9 — **Unwmk.** — *Perf. 12½*

507	A127	7c	blue green	24 15

Universal and International Exposition at Brussels. See Nos. C109-C110a.

Gen. Trujillo Placing Wreath on Altar of the Nation — A128

1959, July 10 — *Perf. 12*

508	A128	9c	brn, grn, red & gold	24 15
a.			Souv. sheet of 1, imperf.	48 48

29th anniversary of the Trujillo regime.

Lt. Leonidas Rhadames Trujillo, Team Captain — A129

Jamaican Polo Team — A130

Design: 10c, Lt. Trujillo on polo pony.

1959, May 15

509	A129	2c	violet	15 15
510	A130	7c	yellow brown	40 25
511	A130	10c	green	45 28

Jamaica-Dominican Republic polo match at Ciudad Trujillo.

See No. C111.

Symbolical of Census A131

1959, Aug. 15 Litho. *Perf. 12½*
Flag in Ultramarine and Red

512 A131 1c blue & black 15 15
513 A131 9c green & black 30 20
514 A131 13c orange & black 50 28

Issued to publicize the 1960 census.

Trujillo Stadium A132

1959, Aug. 27

515 A132 9c green & gray 40 24

Issued to publicize the 3rd Pan American Games, Chicago, Aug. 27-Sept. 7.

Charles V — A133

Rhadames Bridge — A134

1959, Oct. 12 Unwmk. *Perf. 12*

516 A133 5c bright pink 16 15
517 A133 9c violet blue 24 15
Set value 20

400th anniv. of the death of Charles V (1500-1558), Holy Roman Emperor.

1959-60 Litho. *Perf. 12*

Designs: 1c and No. 520, Different view of bridge.

518 A134 1c green & gray ('60) 15 15
519 A134 2c ultra & gray 15 15
520 A134 2c red & gray ('60) 15 15
521 A134 5c brn & dull red brn 22 15
Set value 33

Issue dates: No. 519, Oct. 22; 5c, Nov. 30; 1c, No. 520, Feb. 6, 1960.
For surcharge see No. 536.

Sosua Refugee Settlement and WRY Emblem A135

1960, Apr. 7 *Perf. 12½*
Center in Gray

522 A135 5c red brn & yel grn 15 15
523 A135 9c carmine & lt blue 18 15
524 A135 13c orange & green 24 15
Nos. 522-524,C113-C114 (5) 1.29 1.05

Issued to publicize World Refugee Year, July 1, 1959-June 30, 1960.
For surcharges see Nos. B31-B33.

Sholam Takhti, Iran, Lightweight Wrestling — A136

Olympic Winners: 2c, Mauru Furukawa, Japan, 200 meter breast stroke. 3c, Mildred McDaniel, USA, high jump. 5c, Terence Spinks, England, featherweight boxing. 7c, Carlo Pavesi, Italy, fencing.

Perf. 13½, Imperf.
1960, Sept. 14 Photo.
Flags in National Colors

525 A136 1c red, yel grn & blk 15 15
526 A136 2c org, grnsh bl & brn 15 15
527 A136 3c henna brn & bl 15 15
528 A136 5c brown & ultra 15 15
529 A136 7c grn, bl & rose brn 15 15
Set value, #525-529, C115-C117 68 68

17th Olympic Games, Rome, Aug. 25-Sept. 11.
Miniature sheets of 5 exist, perf. and imperf., containing Nos. 525-529. Value, 2 sheets, perf. & imperf., $5.
For surcharges see Nos. B34-B38, CB21-CB23.

Post Office, Ciudad Trujillo A137

1960, Aug. 26 Litho. *Perf. 11½x12*

530 A137 2c ultra & gray 15 15

Exists imperf.

Cattle A138

1960, Aug. 30

531 A138 9c carmine & gray 25 15

Issued to publicize the Agricultural and Industrial Fair, San Juan de la Maguana.

Nos. 518, 490-491, 453, 427 Surcharged in Red, Black or Blue

HABILITADO PARA 2¢

1960-61 *Perf. 12*

536 A134 2c on 1c grn & gray (R) 15 15
537 A121 9c on 4c lilac & rose 50 15
a. Inverted surcharge 21.00
538 A121 9c on 7c ultra & gray grn (R) 50 15
539 A106 36c on ½c brown 1.40 1.25
a. Inverted surcharge 18.00
540 A95 1p on 50c multi (Bl) 3.00 2.50
Nos. 536-540 (5) 5.55 4.20

Issue dates: No. 536, Dec. 30, 1960; No. 537, Dec. 20, 1960. Others, Feb. 4, 1961.

Trujillo Memorial — A139

Coffee, Cacao — A140

1961 Unwmk. *Perf. 11½*

548 A139 1c brown 15 15
549 A139 2c green 15 15
550 A139 4c rose lilac 52 65
551 A139 5c light blue 22 15
552 A139 9c red orange 28 18
Nos. 548-552 (5) 1.32
Set value 87

Gen. Rafael L. Trujillo (1891-1961).
Issued: 2c, Aug. 7, 4c, Oct. 24, others Aug. 30.

1961, Dec. 30 Litho. *Perf. 12½*

553 A140 1c blue green 15 15
554 A140 2c orange brown 15 15
555 A140 4c violet 15 15
556 A140 5c blue 15 15
557 A140 9c gray 35 15
Nos. 553-557,C118-C119 (7) 1.71
Set value 1.00

Exist imperf.

Dagger Pointing at Mosquito — A141

1962, Apr. 29 Photo. *Perf. 12*

558 A141 10c brt pink & red lilac 15 15
559 A141 20c pale brown & brown 30 28
560 A141 25c pale grn & yel grn 40 30
Nos. 558-560,B39-B40,C120-C121,CB24-CB25 (9) 2.55 2.30

WHO drive to eradicate malaria.

Broken Fetters and Laurel A142

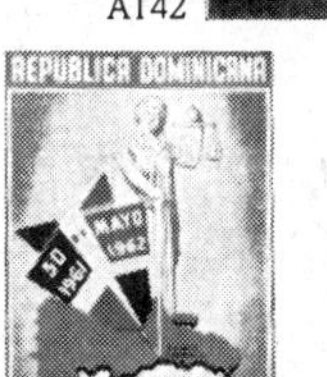

"Justice," Map of Dominican Republic — A143

Farm, Factory and Flag — A144

Design: 20c, Flag, torch and inscription.

1962, May 30 Litho. *Perf. 12½*

561 A142 1c grn, yel, ultra & red 15 15
562 A143 9c bister ultra & red 28 15
563 A142 20c lt blue, ultra & red 60 28
a. Souvenir sheet of 3, #561-563 90 90
564 A143 1p lilac, ultra & red 3.00 1.75
Nos. 561-564,C122-C123 (6) 5.36 3.30

1st anniv. of end of Trujillo era. Exist imperf.

1962, May 22

565 A144 1c ultra, red & green 15 15
566 A144 2c ultra & red 15 15
567 A144 3c ultra, red & brown 15 15
568 A144 5c ultra, red & blue 15 15
569 A144 15c ultra, red & orange 24 15
Set value 54 32

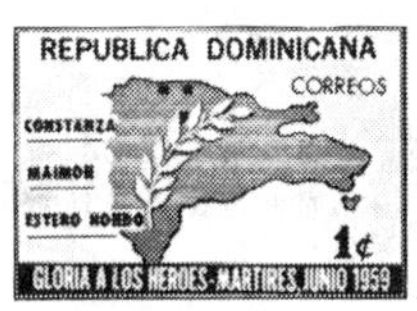

Map and Laurel A145

1962, June 14 Litho.

570 A145 1c black 22 15

Issued to honor the martyrs of June 1959 revolution.

Western Hemisphere and Carrier Pigeon — A146

Archbishop Adolfo Alejandro Nouel — A147

1962, Oct. 23 Unwmk. *Perf. 12½*

571 A146 2c rose red 15 15
572 A146 9c orange 22 15
573 A146 14c blue green 18 15
Nos. 571-573,C124-C125 (5) 1.15
Set value 1.00

50th anniv. of the founding of the Postal Union of the Americas and Spain, UPAE.

1962, Dec. 18

574 A147 2c bl grn & dull bl 15 15
575 A147 9c orange & red brn 22 15
576 A147 13c maroon & vio brn 28 18
Nos. 574-576,C126-C127 (5) 1.48 1.21

Cent. of the birth of Archbishop Adolfo Alejandro Nouel, President of Dominican Republic in 1911.

Globe, Banner and Emblems A148

1963, Apr. 15 Unwmk. *Perf. 11½*
Banner in Dark Blue & Red

577 A148 2c green 15 15
578 A148 5c brt rose lilac 15 15
579 A148 9c orange 24 15
Set value, #577-579, B41-B43 78 55

FAO "Freedom from Hunger" campaign.

Juan Pablo Duarte — A149

1963, July 7 Litho. *Perf. 12x11½*

580 A149 2c shown 15 15
581 A149 7c Francisco Sanchez 15 15
582 A149 9c Ramon Mella 15 15
Set value 32 29

120th anniversary of separation from Haiti. See No. C128.

Ulises F. Espaillat, Benigno F. de Rojas and Pedro F. Bono A150

Designs: 4c, Generals Santiago Rodriguez, Jose Cabrera and Benito Moncion. 5c, Capotillo monument. 9c, Generals Gaspar Polanco, Gregorio Luperon and Jose A. Salcedo.

1963, Aug. 16 Unwmk. *Perf. 11½*

583 A150 2c green 15 15
584 A150 4c red orange 15 15
585 A150 5c brown 15 15
586 A150 9c bright blue 15 15
a. Souvenir sheet of 4 50 50
Set value 36 30

Cent. of the Restoration. #586a contains 4 imperf. stamps similar to #583-586.

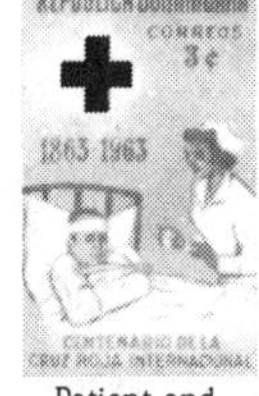

Patient and Nurse — A151

Scales, Globe, UNESCO Emblem — A152

1963, Oct. 25 Unwmk. *Perf. 12½*

587 A151 3c gray & carmine	15	15
588 A151 6c emerald & red	20	15
Set value	30	16

Centenary of International Red Cross. Exist imperf. See No. C129.

1963, Dec. 10 Litho.

589 A152 6c pink & deep pink	15	15
590 A152 50c lt green & green	65	65

Universal Declaration of Human Rights, 15th anniv. Exist imperf.

See Nos. C130-C131.

Ramses II Battling the Hittites (from Abu Simbel)
A153

Design: 6c, Two heads of Ramses II.

1964, Mar. 8 Unwmk. *Perf. 12½*

591 A153 3c pale pink & ver	15	15
592 A153 6c pale blue & ultra	15	15
593 A153 9c pale rose & red brn	18	15
Nos. 591-593,C132-C133 (5)	94	
Set value		63

UNESCO world campaign to save historic monuments in Nubia.

For surcharges see Nos. B44-B46.

Maximo Gomez — A154

Palm Chat — A155

1964, Apr. 30 Litho.

594 A154 2c lt blue & blue	15	15
595 A154 6c dull pink & dull claret	15	15
Set value	17	15

Bicent. of the founding of the town of Bani.

1964, June 8 Unwmk. *Perf. 12½*

Design: 6c, Hispaniolan parrot.

Size: 27x37½mm

596 A155 3c ultra, brn & yel	15	15
597 A155 6c gray & multi	20	15
Set value		21

See Nos. 602-604, C134.

Rocket Leaving Earth
A156

Designs: 1c, Launching of rocket, vert. 3c, Space capsule orbiting earth. 6c, As 2c.

1964, July 28 Litho.

598 A156 1c sky blue	15	15
599 A156 2c emerald	15	15
600 A156 3c blue	15	15
601 A156 6c sky blue	22	15
Nos. 598-601,C135-C136 (6)	1.21	
Set value		72

Issued to commemorate the conquest of space.

Bird Type of 1964

Designs: 1c, Narrow-billed tody. 2c, Hispaniolan emerald hummingbird. 6c, Hispaniolan trogon.

1964, Nov. 7 *Perf. 11½*

Size: 26x37mm

Birds in Natural Colors

602 A155 1c bright pink	15	15
603 A155 2c dark brown	15	15
604 A155 6c blue	25	15
Set value	50	24

Universal Postal Union and United Nations Emblems
A157

1964, Dec. 5 Litho. *Perf. 12½*

605 A157 1c red	15	15
606 A157 4c green	15	15
607 A157 5c orange	15	15
Set value	32	21

15th UPU Cong., Vienna, Austria, May-June 1964. See No. C138.

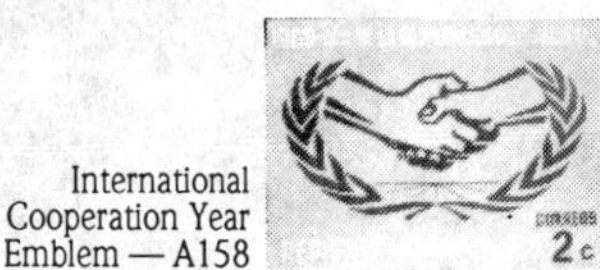

International Cooperation Year Emblem — A158

1965, Feb. 16 Unwmk. *Perf. 12½*

608 A158 2c lt blue & ultra	15	15
609 A158 3c emerald & dk grn	15	15
610 A158 6c salmon pink & red	15	15
Set value	22	16

UN Intl. Cooperation Year. See No. C139.

Virgin of Altagracia — A159

Flags of 21 American Nations — A160

Design: 2c, Hands holding lily.

1965, Mar. 18 Unwmk. *Perf. 12½*

611 A159 2c green, emer & dp rose	15	15
612 A159 6c multicolored	30	24
Set value		29

4th Mariological Cong. and 11th Intl. Marian Cong. #612 exists imperf. See #C140.

1965, Apr. 14 Litho. *Perf. 11½*

613 A160 2c brown, yel & multi	15	15
614 A160 6c red lilac & multi	15	15
Set value	17	15

Organization of American States.

Stamp of 1865 (No. 1) — A161

1965, Dec. 28 Litho. *Perf. 12½*

615 A161 1c pink, buff & blk	15	15
616 A161 2c blue, buff & blk	15	15
617 A161 6c emerald, buff & blk	15	15
a. Souvenir sheet of 2	70	70
Set value, #615-617, C142-C143	71	60

Cent. of 1st Dominican postage stamps. No. 617a shows replicas of Nos. 1-2. Sold for 50c.

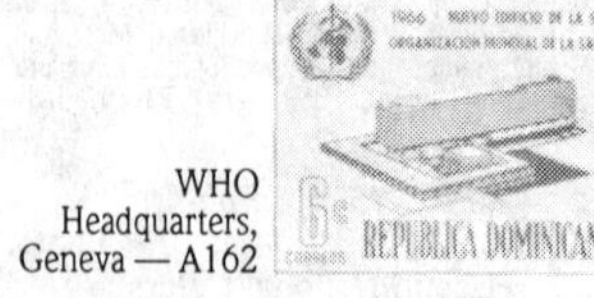

WHO Headquarters, Geneva — A162

1966, May 21 Litho. *Perf. 12½*

618 A162 6c blue	15	15
619 A162 10c red lilac	22	15
Set value		18

New WHO Headquarters, Geneva.

Man Holding Map of Republic — A163

1966, May 23

620 A163 2c black & brt green	15	15
621 A163 6c black & dp orange	15	15
Set value	17	15

General elections, June 1, 1966.

Ascia Monuste — A164

Natl. Altar — A165

1966 Litho. *Perf. 12½*

Various Butterflies in Natural Colors

Size: 31x21mm

622 A164 1c blue & vio bl	15	15
623 A164 2c lt grn & brt grn	15	15
624 A164 3c lt gray & gray	15	15
625 A164 6c pink & magenta	22	18
626 A164 8c buff & brown	35	35
Nos. 622-626,C146-C148 (8)	6.02	2.81

Issue dates: 1c, Sept. 7; 3c, Sept. 11; others, Nov. 8.

For surcharges see #B47-B51, CB28-CB30.

1967, Jan. 18 Litho. *Perf. 11½*

627 A165 1c bright blue	15	15
628 A165 2c carmine rose	15	15
629 A165 3c emerald	15	15
630 A165 4c gray	15	15
631 A165 5c orange yellow	15	15
632 A165 6c orange	15	15
Set value, #627-632, C149-C151	88	74

Map of Republic and Emblem
A166

1967, Mar. 30 Litho. *Perf. 12½*

633 A166 2c yellow, blue & blk	15	15
634 A166 6c orange, blue & blk	15	15
635 A166 10c emerald, blue & blk	22	15
Set value	39	23

Development Year, 1967.

Rook and Knight
A167

1967, June 23 Litho. *Perf. 12½*

636 A167 25c multicolored	70	38

5th Central American Chess Championships, Santo Domingo. See Nos. C152-C152a.

Alliance for Progress
A168

Institute Emblem
A169

1967, Sept. 16 Litho. *Perf. 12½*

637 A168 1c bright green	15	15

6th anniv. of the Alliance for Progress. See Nos. C153-C154.

1967, Oct. 7

638 A169 3c bright green	15	15
639 A169 6c salmon pink	15	15
Set value	18	15

25th anniversary of the Inter-American Agriculture Institute. See No. C155.

Globe and Satellite
A170

1968, June 15 Typo. *Perf. 12*

640 A170 6c black & multi	22	15

Issued to commemorate World Meteorological Day, Mar. 23. See Nos. C156-C157.

Boxers
A171

1968, June 29

641 A171 6c rose red & dp cl	15	15

Fight between Carlos Ortiz, Puerto Rico, and Teo Cruz, Dominican Republic, for the World Lightweight Boxing Championship. See Nos. C158-C159.

Lions Emblem — A172

1968, Aug. 9 Litho. *Perf. 11½*
642 A172 6c brown & multi 15 15

50th anniv. (in 1967) of Lions Intl. See No. C160.

Wrestling and Olympic Emblem A173

Designs (Olympic Emblem and): 6c, Running. 25c, Boxing.

1968, Nov. 12 Litho. *Perf. 11½*
643 A173 1c sky blue & multi 15 15
644 A173 6c pale green & multi 22 15
645 A173 25c pale lilac & multi 75 38
Nos. 643-645,C161-C162 (5) 2.12 1.50

19th Olympic Games, Mexico City, Oct. 12-27.

Map of Americas and House — A174

Stool in Human Form — A175

1969, Jan. 25 Litho. *Perf. 12½*
646 A174 6c brt bl, lt bl & grn 15 15

Issued to publicize the 7th Inter-American Conference for Savings and Loans, Santo Domingo, Jan. 25-31. See No. C163.

1969, Jan. 31 Litho. *Perf. 12½*

Taino Art: 2c, Wood carved mother figure, vert. 3c, Face carved on 3-cornered stone. 4c, Stone hatchet, vert. 5c, Clay pot.

647 A175 1c yellow, org & blk 15 15
648 A175 2c lt grn, grn & blk 15 15
649 A175 3c citron, ol & brt grn 15 15
650 A175 4c lt lil, lil & brt grn 15 15
651 A175 5c yellow, org & brn 15 15
Set value, #647-651, C164-C166 1.10 1.00

Taino art flourished in the West Indies at the time of Columbus.

Community Day Emblem A176

COTAL Emblem A177

Headquarters Building and COTAL Emblem — A178

1969, Mar. 25 Litho. *Perf. 12½*
652 A176 6c dull green & gold 15 15

Community Development Day, Mar. 22.

1969, May 25 Litho. *Perf. 12½*

Design: 2c, Boy and COTAL emblem.

653 A177 1c lt & dk blue & red 15 15
654 A177 2c emerald & dk grn 15 15
655 A178 6c vermilion & pink 15 15
Set value 23 16

12th Congress of the Confederation of Latin American Tourist Organizations (COTAL), Santo Domingo, May 25-29.

See No. C167.

ILO Emblem — A179

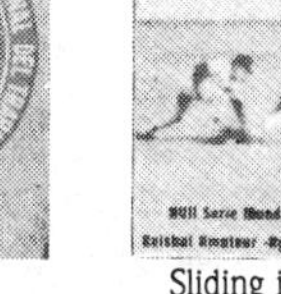

Sliding into Base — A180

1969, June 27 Litho. *Perf. 12½*
656 A179 6c lt grnsh bl, grnsh bl & blk 24 15

50th anniv. of the ILO. See No. C168.

1969, Aug. 15 Litho. *Perf. 12½*

Designs: 1c, Catching a fly ball. 2c, View of Cibao Stadium, horiz.

Size: 21x31mm (1c, 3c); 43x30mm (2c)

657 A180 1c green & gray 15 15
658 A180 2c green & lt green 18 15
659 A180 3c purple & red brown 18 15
Nos. 657-659,C169-C171 (6) 3.61 2.66

17th World Amateur Baseball Championships, Santo Domingo.

Las Damas Dam — A181

Tavera Dam A182

Designs: 2c, Las Damas hydroelectric station, vert. 6c, Arroyo Hondo substation.

1969 Litho. *Perf. 12*
660 A181 2c green & multi 15 15
661 A181 3c dk blue & multi 15 15
662 A181 6c brt rose lilac 15 15
663 A182 6c multicolored 25 15
Set value, #660-663, C172-C173 1.00 47

National electrification plan.

Issue dates: Nos. 660-662, Sept. 15. No. 663, Oct. 15.

Juan Pablo Duarte A183

Map of Republic, People, Census Emblem A184

1970, Jan. 26 Litho. *Perf. 12*
664 A183 1c emerald & dk grn 15 15
665 A183 2c sal pink & dp car 15 15
666 A183 3c brt pink & plum 15 15
667 A183 6c blue & violet blue 15 15
Set value, #664-667, C174 46 31

Issued for Duarte Day in memory of Juan Pablo Duarte (1813-1876), liberator.

1970, Feb. 6 *Perf. 11*

Design: 6c, Census emblem and inscription.

668 A184 5c emerald & blk 15 15
669 A184 6c ultra & blue 15 15
Set value 24 15

Census of 1970. See No. C175.

Abelardo Rodriguez Urdaneta — A185

"One of Many" A186

1970, Feb. 20 Litho. *Perf. 12½*
670 A185 3c ultramarine 15 15
671 A186 6c green & yel grn 15 15
Set value 24 15

Issued to honor Abelardo Rodriguez Urdaneta, sculptor. See No. C176.

Masonic Symbols — A187

1970, Mar. 2
672 A187 6c green 15 15

8th Inter-American Masonic Conference, Santo Domingo, Mar. 1-7. See No. C177.

Communications Satellite — A188

1970, May 25 Litho. *Perf. 12½*
673 A188 20c olive & gray 48 28

World Telecommunications Day. See #C178.

UPU Headquarters, Bern — A189

1970, June 5 *Perf. 11*
674 A189 6c gray & brown 15 15

Inauguration of the new UPU headquarters in Bern. See No. C179.

Education Year Emblem A190

Pedro Alejandrino Pina A191

1970, June 26 Litho. *Perf. 12½*
675 A190 4c rose lilac 15 15

Issued for International Education Year, 1970. See No. C180.

1970, Aug. 24 Litho. *Perf. 12½*
676 A191 6c lt red brn & blk 15 15

150th anniv. of the birth and the cent. of the death of Pedro Alejandrino Pina (1820-70), author.

Children Reading — A192

1970, Oct. 12 Litho. *Perf. 12½*
677 A192 5c dull green 15 15

1st World Exhibition of Books and Culture Festival, Santo Domingo, Oct. 11-Dec. 11. See Nos. C181-C182.

Virgin of Altagracia — A193

Rodriguez Objio — A194

1971, Jan. 20 Litho. *Perf. 12½*
678 A193 3c multicolored 15 15

Inauguration of the Basilica of Our Lady of Altagracia. See No. C184.

1971, June 18 Litho. *Perf. 11*
679 A194 6c light blue 15 15

Manuel Rodriguez Objio (1838-1871), poet.

Boxing and Canoeing — A195

1971, Sept. 10
680 A195 2c shown 15 15
681 A195 5c Basketball 18 15
Set value 25 15

2nd National Games. See No. C186.

Goat and Fruit A196

Designs: 2c, Cow and goose. 3c, Cacao and horse. 6c, Bananas, coffee and pig.

1971, Sept. 29 *Perf. 12½*
682 A196 1c brown & multi 15 15
683 A196 2c plum & multi 15 15
684 A196 3c green & multi 15 15
685 A196 6c blue & multi 22 15
Set value, #682-685, C187 1.00 54

6th Natl. agriculture and livestock census.

José Nuñez de Cáceres — A197

Shepherds and Star — A198

1971, Dec. 1 *Perf. 11*
686 A197 6c lt bl, lil & dk bl 15 15

Sesquicentennial of first national independence. See No. C188.

1971, Dec. 10 *Perf. 12½*
687 A198 6c blue, brown & yel 15 15

Christmas 1971. See No. C189.

UNICEF Emblem, Child on Beach — A199

1971, Dec. 14 **Litho.** *Perf. 11*
688 A199 6c gray blue & multi 15 15

UNICEF, 25th anniv. See No. C190.

Book Year Emblem — A200

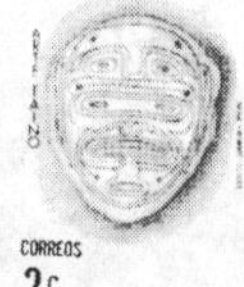

Taino Mask — A201

1972, Jan. 25 *Perf. 12½*
689 A200 1c green, ultra & red 15 15
690 A200 2c brown, ultra & red 15 15
Set value 15 15

Intl. Book Year 1972. See No. C191.

1972, May 10 **Litho.** *Perf. 11*

Taino Art: 4c, Ladle and amulet. 6c, Human figure.

691 A201 2c pink & multi 15 15
692 A201 4c black, bl & ocher 15 15
693 A201 6c gray & multi 18 15
Nos. 691-693,C194-C196 (6) 1.36
Set value 68

Taino art. See note after No. 651.

Globe A202

1972, May 17 *Perf. 12½*
694 A202 6c blue & multi 15 15

4th World Telecommunications Day. See No. C197.

"1972," Stamps and Map of Dominican Republic — A203

1972, June 3
695 A203 2c green & multi 15 15

First National Philatelic Exhibition, Santo Domingo, June 3-17. See No. C198.

Basketball — A204

1972, Aug. 25 **Litho.** *Perf. 12½*
696 A204 2c blue & multi 15 15

20th Olympic Games, Munich, Aug. 26-Sept. 11. See No. C199.

Club Emblem A205

1972, Sept. 29 **Litho.** *Perf. 10½*
697 A205 1c lt green & multi 15 15

50th anniversary of the Club Activo 20-30 International. See No. C200.

Emilio A. Morel A206

1972, Oct. 20 *Perf. 12½*
698 A206 6c brt pink & multi 15 15

Emilio A. Morel (1884-1958), poet and journalist. See No. C201.

Central Bank Building A207

1972, Oct. 23
699 A207 1c shown 15 15
700 A207 5c 1-peso note 15 15
Set value 17 15

25th anniv. of Central Bank. See No. C202.

Holy Family — A208

Poinsettia A209

1972, Nov. 21
701 A208 2c rose lil, pur & gold 15 15
702 A209 6c red & multi 18 15
Set value 25 15

Christmas 1972. See No. C203.

Mail Box and Student A210

1972, Dec. 15
703 A210 2c rose red 15 15
704 A210 6c blue 15 15
705 A210 10c emerald 18 15
Set value 35 20

Publicity for correspondence schools.

Tavera Dam — A211

1973, Feb. 26 **Litho.** *Perf. 12½*
706 A211 10c multicolored 18 15

Inauguration of the Tavera Dam.

Various Sports — A212

Designs: a, UL. b, UR. c, LL. d, LR.

1973, Mar. 30 *Perf. 13½x13*
707 A212 Block of 4 38 50
a.-d. 2c, any single 15 15
708 A212 Block of 4 1.90 2.00
a.-d. 25c, any single 45 24
Nos. 707-708,C204-C205 (4) 5.28 4.75

12th Central American and Caribbean Games, Santo Domingo, Summer 1974.

Christ Carrying the Cross — A213

Design: 6c, Belfry of Church of Our Lady of Carmen, vert.

1973, Apr. 18 **Litho.** *Perf. 10½*
709 A213 2c multicolored 15 15
710 A213 6c multicolored 18 15
Set value 25 15

Holy Week, 1973. See No. C206.

WMO Emblem, Weather Satellite, "Weather" — A214

Mask, Cibao — A215

1973, Aug. 10 **Litho.** *Perf. 13½x13*
711 A214 6c magenta & multi 15 15

Centenary of international meteorological cooperation. See No. C208.

1973, Oct. 12 **Litho.** *Perf. 10½*
712 A215 1c Maguey drum, horiz 15 15
713 A215 2c Carved amber, horiz 15 15
714 A215 4c shown 15 15
715 A215 6c Pottery 15 15
Set value, #712-715, C210-C211 60 43

Opening of Museum of Mankind in Santo Domingo.

Nativity A216

Design: 6c, Stained glass window, vert.

Perf. 13½x13, 13x13½
1973, Nov. 26
716 A216 2c black, bl & yel 15 15
717 A216 6c rose & multi 15 15
Set value 22 17

Christmas 1973. See No. C212.
No. 717 exists imperf.

Dominican Scout Emblem A217

Design: 5c, Scouts and flag.

1973, Dec. 7 Litho. *Perf. 12*

Size: 35x35mm

718 A217 1c ultra & multi 15 15

Size: 26x36mm

719 A217 5c black & multi 15 15
Set value 18 15

50th anniversary of Dominican Republic Boy Scouts. See No. C213.

Sports Palace, Basketball Players A218

Design: 6c, Bicyclist and race track.

1974, Feb. 25 Litho. *Perf. 13½*

720 A218 2c red brown & multi 15 15
721 A218 6c yellow & multi 15 15
Set value 22 15

12th Central American and Caribbean Games, Santo Domingo, 1974. See Nos. C214-C215.

Bell Tower, Cathedral of Santo Domingo — A219

Mater Dolorosa — A220

1974, June 27 Litho. *Perf. 13½*

722 A219 2c multicolored 15 15
723 A220 6c multicolored 22 15
Set value 17

Holy Week 1974. See No. C216.

Francisco del Rosario Sanchez Bridge A221

1974, July 12 *Perf. 12*

724 A221 6c multicolored 15 15

See No. C217.

Map, Emblem and Patient A222

Design: 5c, Map of Dominican Republic, diabetics' emblem and pancreas.

1974, Aug. 22 Litho. *Perf. 13*

725 A222 4c blue & multi 15 15
726 A222 5c yellow grn & multi 15 15
Set value 20 20

Fight against diabetes. See Nos. C218-C219.

Train and UPU Emblem A223

Design: 6c, Mail coach and UPU emblem.

1974, Oct. 9 Litho. *Perf. 13½*

727 A223 2c blue & multi 15 15
728 A223 6c brown & multi 15 15
Set value 18 15

Cent. of UPU. See Nos. C220-C221a.

Golfers — A224

Design: 2c, Championship emblem and badge of Dominican Golf Association, horiz.

Perf. 13x13½, 13½x13

1974, Oct. 24

729 A224 2c yellow & blk 15 15
730 A224 6c blue & multi 22 15

World Amateur Golf Championships. See Nos. C222-C223.

Christmas Decorations A225

Virgin and Child A226

1974, Dec. 3 Litho. *Perf. 12*

731 A225 2c multicolored 15 15
732 A226 6c multicolored 18 15
Set value 26 15

Christmas 1974. See No. C224.

Tomatoes, FAO Emblem — A227

1974, Dec. 5

733 A227 2c shown 15 15
734 A227 3c Avocados 15 15
735 A227 5c Coconuts 15 15
Set value 24 20

World Food Program, 10th anniv. See No. C225.

Fernando A. Defillo — A228

Tower, Our Lady of the Rosary Convent — A229

1975, Feb. 14 Litho. *Perf. 13½x13*

736 A228 1c dull brown 15 15
737 A228 6c dull green 15 15
Set value 15 15

Dr. Fernando A. Defillo (1874-1949), physician.

1975, Mar. 26 Litho. *Perf. 13½*

Design: 2c, Jesus saying "I am the Resurrection and the Life."

738 A229 2c brown & multi 15 15
739 A229 6c multicolored 15 15
Set value 25 20

Holy Week 1975. See No. C226.

Hands (Steel Beams) with Symbols of Agriculture, Industry A230

1975, May 19 Litho. *Perf. 10½x10*

740 A230 6c dull blue & multi 15 15

16th Assembly of the Governors of the International Development Bank, Santo Domingo, May 1975. See No. C228.

Satellite Tracking Station — A231

1975, June 21 Litho. *Perf. 13½*

741 A231 5c multicolored 15 15

Opening of first earth satellite tracking station in Dominican Republic. See No. C229.

Apollo — A232

1975, July 24

Size: 35x25mm

742 A232 1c shown 15 15
743 A232 4c Soyuz 15 15
Set value 21 21

Apollo Soyuz space test project (Russo-American cooperation), launching July 15; link-up, July 17. See No. C230.

Father Rafael C. Castellanos — A233

1975, Aug. 6 Litho. *Perf. 12*

744 A233 6c brown & buff 15 15

Castellanos (1875-1934), 1st Apostolic Administrator in Dominican Republic.

Women and Men Around IWY Emblem A234

1975, Aug. 6 *Perf. 13*

745 A234 3c orange & multi 15 15

International Women's Year 1975.

Guacanagarix A235

Basketball A236

Indian Chiefs: 2c, Guarionex. 3c, Caonabo. 4c, Bohechio. 5c, Cayacoa. 6c, Anacona (woman). 9c, Hatuey.

1975, Sept. 27 Litho. *Perf. 12*

746 A235 1c yellow & multi 15 15
747 A235 2c salmon & multi 15 15
748 A235 3c violet bl & multi 15 15
749 A235 4c green & multi 15 15
750 A235 5c blue & multi 15 15
751 A235 6c violet & multi 15 15
752 A235 9c rose & multi 25 20
Set value, #746-752, C231-C233 1.40 1.05

1975, Oct. 24 Litho. *Perf. 12*

Design: 6c, Baseball and Games' emblem.

753 A236 2c pink & multi 15 15
754 A236 6c orange & multi 18 15
Set value 27 15

7th Pan-American Games, Mexico City, Oct. 13-26. See Nos. C234-C235.

Carolers A237

Design: 6c, Dominican nativity with farmers and shepherds.

1975, Dec. 12 Litho. *Perf. 13x13½*

755 A237 2c yellow & multi 15 15
756 A237 6c blue & multi 15 15
Set value 25 20

Christmas 1975. See No. C236.

Abudefdul Marginatus — A238

1976, Jan. 23 **Litho.** ***Perf. 13***
757 A238 10c shown 35 24
758 A238 10c Doncella 35 24
759 A238 10c Carajuelo 35 24
760 A238 10c Reina de los Angeles 35 24
761 A238 10c Pargo Colorado 35 24
a. Strip of 5, #757-761 1.75 1.50
Nos. 757-761 (5) 1.75 1.20

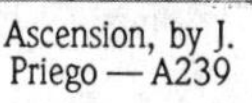

Ascension, by J. Priego — A239

"Separacion Dominicana" and Adm. Cambiaso — A240

Design: 2c, Mary Magdalene, by Enrique Godoy.

1976, Apr. 14 **Litho.** ***Perf. 13½***
762 A239 2c blue & multi 15 15
763 A239 6c yellow & multi 18 15
Set value 26 15

Holy Week 1976. See No. C238.

1976, Apr. 15 ***Perf. 13½x13***
764 A240 20c multicolored 30 25

Naval Battle off Tortuga, Apr. 15, 1844.

Maps of US and Dominican Republic — A241

Design: 9c, Maps within cogwheels.

1976, May 29 **Litho.** ***Perf. 13½***
765 A241 6c violet bl & multi 16 15
766 A241 9c violet bl & multi 15 15
Set value 26 15

American Bicentennial. See #C239-C240.

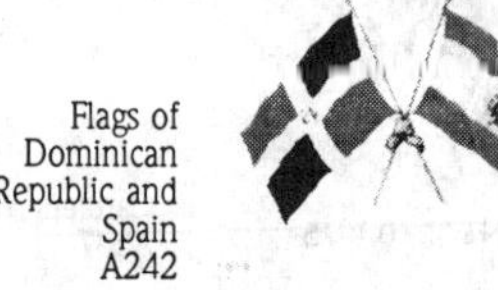

Flags of Dominican Republic and Spain
A242

1976, May 31
767 A242 6c multicolored 35 15

Visit of King Juan Carlos I and Queen Sofia of Spain. See No. C241.

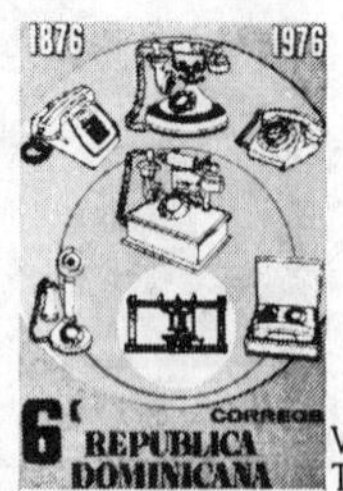

Various Telephones — A243

1976, July 15 ***Perf. 12x12½***
768 A243 6c multicolored 15 15

Cent. of 1st telephone call by Alexander Graham Bell, Mar. 10, 1876. See No. C242.

Vision of Duarte, by Luis Desangles
A244

Juan Pablo Duarte, by Rhadames Mejia — A245

1976, July 20 **Litho.** ***Perf. 13x13½***
769 A244 2c multicolored 15 15

Perf. 13½
770 A245 6c multicolored 15 15
Set value 21 15

Juan Pablo Duarte, liberation hero, death centenary. See Nos. C243-C244.

Fire Hydrant — A246

Design: 6c, Firemen's emblem.

1976, Sept. 13 **Litho.** ***Perf. 12***
771 A246 4c multicolored 15 15
772 A246 6c multicolored 15 15
Set value 18 15

Honoring firemen. Nos. 771-772 inscribed "Correos." See No. C245.

Radio and Atom Symbols — A247

1976, Oct. 8 **Litho.** ***Perf. 13½***
773 A247 6c red & black 15 15

Dominican Radio Club, 50th anniversary. See No. C246.

Spain, Central and South America, Galleon
A248

1976, Oct. 22 **Litho.** ***Perf. 13½***
774 A248 6c multicolored 18 15

Spanish heritage. See No. C247.

Boxing and Montreal Emblem
A249

Design: 3c, Weight lifting.

1976, Oct. 22 ***Perf. 12***
775 A249 2c blue & multi 15 15
776 A249 3c multicolored 15 15
Set value 16 15

21st Olympic Games, Montreal, Canada, July 17-Aug. 1. See Nos. C248-C249.

Virgin and Child — A250

Three Kings — A251

1976, Dec. 8 **Litho.** ***Perf. 13½***
777 A250 2c multicolored 15 15
778 A251 6c multicolored 18 15
Set value 27 15

Christmas 1976. See No. C250.

Cable Car and Beach Scenes
A252

1977, Jan. 7
779 A252 6c multicolored 15 15

Tourist publicity. See Nos. C251-C253.

Championship Emblem
A253

1977, Mar. 4 **Litho.** ***Perf. 13½***
780 A253 3c rose & multi 15 15
781 A253 5c yellow & multi 15 15
Set value 16 15

10th Central American and Caribbean Children's and Young People's Swimming Championships, Santo Domingo.
See Nos. C254-C255.

Christ Carrying Cross — A254

Design: 6c, Head with crown of thorns.

1977, Apr. 18 **Litho.** ***Perf. 13½x13***
782 A254 2c multicolored 15 15
783 A254 6c black & rose 22 15
Set value 15

Holy Week 1977. See No. C256.

Doves, Lions Emblem
A255

1977, May 6 ***Perf. 13½x13***
784 A255 2c lt blue & multi 15 15
785 A255 6c salmon & multi 15 15
Set value 18 15

12th annual Dominican Republic Lions Convention. See No. C257.

Battle Scene
A256

1977, June 15 **Litho.** ***Perf. 13x13½***
786 A256 20c multicolored 38 30

Dominican Navy.

Water Lily — A257

National Botanical Garden: 4c, "Flor de Mayo" (orchid). 6c, Sebesten.

1977, Aug. 19 **Litho.** ***Perf. 12***
787 A257 2c multicolored 15 15
788 A257 4c multicolored 15 15
789 A257 6c multicolored 15 15
Nos. 787-789,C259-C260 (5) 88
Set value 46

Chart and Computers — A258

1977, Nov. 30 **Litho.** ***Perf. 13***
790 A258 6c multicolored 15 15

7th Interamerican Statistics Conf. See #C261.

Solenodon Paradoxus — A259

Design: 20c, Iguana and Congress emblem.

1977, Dec. 29 Litho. *Perf. 13*
791 A259 6c multicolored 15 15
792 A259 20c multicolored 42 30
Set value 35

8th Pan-American Veterinary and Zoo-technical Congress. See Nos. C262-C263.

Main Gate, Casa del Cordon, 1503 — A260

Crown of Thorns, Tools at the Cross — A261

1978, Jan. 19 *Perf. 13x13½*
Size: 26x36mm
793 A260 6c multicolored 15 15

Spanish heritage. See No. C264.

1978, Mar. 21 Litho. *Perf. 12*

Design: 6c, Head of Jesus with crown of thorns.

Size: 22x33mm
794 A261 2c multicolored 15 15
795 A261 6c slate 18 15
Set value 28 15

Holy Week 1978. See Nos. C265-C266.

Cardinal Octavio A. Beras Rojas — A262

Pres. Manuel de Troncoso — A263

1978, May 5 Litho. *Perf. 13*
796 A262 6c multicolored 15 15

First Cardinal from Dominican Republic, consecrated May 24, 1976. See No. C268.

1978, June 12 Litho. *Perf. 13½*
797 A263 2c black, rose & brn 15 15
798 A263 6c black, gray & brn 15 15
Set value 15 15

Manuel de Jesus Troncoso de la Concha (1878-1955), pres. of Dominican Republic, 1940-42.

Father Juan N. Zegri y Moreno — A264

1978, July 11 Litho. *Perf. 13x13½*
799 A264 6c multicolored 15 15

Congregation of the Merciful Sisters of Charity, centenary. See No. C273.

Boxing and Games' Emblem A265

1978, July 21 *Perf. 12*
800 A265 2c shown 15 15
801 A265 6c Weight lifting 15 15
Set value 22 15

13th Central American & Caribbean Games, Medellin, Colombia. See Nos. C274-C275.

Sun over Landscape — A266

Ships of Columbus, Map of Dominican Republic — A267

Design: 6c, Sun over beach and boat.

1978, Sept. 12 Litho. *Perf. 12*
802 A266 2c multicolored 15 15
803 A266 6c multicolored 15 15
Set value 17 15

Tourist publicity. See Nos. C280-C281.

1978, Oct. 12 Litho. *Perf. 13½*
804 A267 2c multicolored 15 15

Spanish heritage. See No. C282.

Dove, Lamp, Poinsettia A268

Design: 6c, Dominican family and star, vert.

1978, Dec. 5 Litho. *Perf. 12*
805 A268 2c multicolored 15 15
806 A268 6c multicolored 22 15
Set value 15

Christmas 1978. See No. C284.

Starving Child, IYC Emblem — A269

Crucifixion — A270

1979, Feb. 26 Litho. *Perf. 12*
807 A269 2c orange & black 15 15

Intl. Year of the Child. See Nos. C287-C289.

1979, Apr. 9 Litho. *Perf. 13½*

Design: 3c, Jesus carrying cross, horiz.

808 A270 2c multicolored 20 15
809 A270 3c multicolored 26 15
Set value 15

Holy Week. See No. C290.

Stigmaphyllon Periplocifolium — A271

1979, May 17 Litho. *Perf. 12*
810 A271 50c multicolored 70 38

Dr. Rafael M. Moscoso National Botanical Garden. See Nos. C293-C295.

Heart, Diseased Blood Vessel A272

Design: 1p, Cardiology Institute and heart.

1979, June 2 Litho. *Perf. 13½*
811 A272 3c multicolored 15 15
812 A272 1p multicolored 1.40 75

Dominican Cardiology Institute. See No. C296.

Baseball, Games' Emblem A273

Design: 3c, Bicycling and Games' emblem, vert.

1979, June 20
813 A273 2c multicolored 15 15
814 A273 3c multicolored 15 15
Set value 17 15

8th Pan American Games, Puerto Rico, June 30-July 15. See No. C297.

Soccer — A274

Thomas A. Edison — A275

Design: 25c, Swimming, horiz.

1979, Aug. 9 Litho. *Perf. 12*
815 A274 2c multicolored 15 15
816 A274 25c multicolored 30 15
Set value 38 17

Third National Games. See No. C298.

1979, Aug. 27 *Perf. 13½*
817 A275 25c multicolored 50 40

Cent. of invention of electric light. See #C300.

Hand Holding Electric Plug — A276

Design: 6c, Filling automobile gas tank.

1979, Aug. 30
818 A276 2c multicolored 15 15
819 A276 6c multicolored 15 15
Set value 17 15

Energy conservation.

Parrot — A277

Birds: 6c, Temnotrogon roseigaster.

1979, Sept. 12 Litho. *Perf. 12*
820 A277 2c multicolored 15 15
821 A277 6c multicolored 16 15
Nos. 820-821,C301-C303 (5) 1.81
Set value 73

A278

A279

Design: Lions Emblem, Map of Dominican Republic.

1979, Nov. 13 Litho. *Perf. 12*
822 A278 20c multicolored 40 35

Lions International Club of Dominican Republic, 10th anniversary. See No. C304.

1979, Dec. 18 Litho. *Perf. 12*
823 A279 2c Holy Family 15 15

Christmas 1979. See No. C305.

A280

A281

Design: Jesus Carrying Cross.

1980, Mar. 27 Litho. *Perf. 12*
824 A280 3c multicolored 15 15

Holy Week. See Nos. C306-C307.

1980, May 15 **Litho.** ***Perf. 13½***

825 A281 1c shown 15 15
826 A281 2c Coffee 15 15
827 A281 3c Plantain 15 15
828 A281 4c Sugar cane 15 15
829 A281 5c Corn 15 15
Set value 32 31

Cacao Harvest (Agriculture Year)

Cotuf Gold Mine, Pueblo Viejo, Flag of Dominican Republic A282

1980, July 8 **Litho.** ***Perf. 13½***

830 A282 6c multicolored 20 20

Nationalization of gold mining. See Nos. C310-C311.

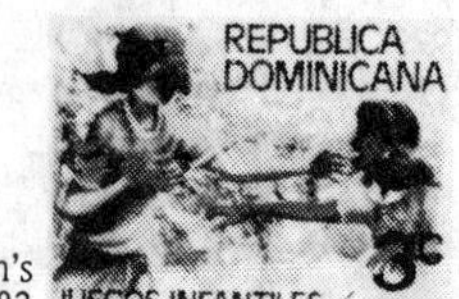

Blind Man's Buff — A283

1980, July 21 ***Perf. 12***

831 A283 3c shown 15 15
832 A283 4c Marbles 15 15
833 A283 5c Drawing in sand 15 15
834 A283 6c Hopscotch 15 15
Set value 36 25

Iguana A284

1980, Aug. 30 **Litho.** ***Perf. 12***

835 A284 20c multicolored 42 40
Nos. 835,C314-C317 (5) 2.05 1.98

Dance, by Jaime Colson A285

Perf. 13x13½, 13½x13

1980, Sept. 23 **Litho.**

836 A285 3c *shown* 15 15
837 A285 50c *Woman, by Gilberto Hernandez Ortega, vert.* 65 60

See Nos. C318-C319.

Three Kings — A286

Salcedo Province Cent. — A287

1980, Dec. 5 **Litho.** ***Perf. 13½***

838 A286 3c shown 15 15
839 A286 6c Carolers 18 15
Set value 26 16

Christmas 1980. See No. C327.

1981, Jan. 14 **Litho.** ***Perf. 13½***

840 A287 6c multicolored 15 15

See No. C328.

Juan Pablo Duarte, Liberation Hero, 105th Anniv. of Death — A288

1981, Feb. 6 **Litho.** ***Perf. 12***

841 A288 2c sepia & deep bister 15 15

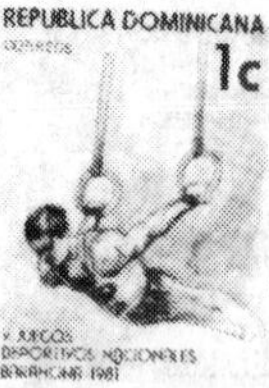

Gymnast — A289

Mother Mazzarello — A290

1981, Mar. 31 **Litho.** ***Perf. 13½***

842 A289 1c shown 15 15
843 A289 2c Running 15 15
844 A289 3c Pole vault 15 15
845 A289 6c Boxing 18 15
Set value, #842-845, C331 62 32

5th National Games.

1981, Apr. 14 ***Perf. 12***

846 A290 6c multicolored 15 15

Mother Maria Mazzarello (1837-1881), founder of Daughters of Mary.

A291

A292

1981, May 18 **Litho.** ***Perf. 13½***

847 A291 6c gray vio & lt gray 15 15

Pedro Henriquez Urena, Historian (1884-1946)

1981, June 30 **Litho.** ***Perf. 12***

848 A292 2c shown 15 15
849 A292 6c River, forest 15 15
Set value 18 15

Forest conservation.

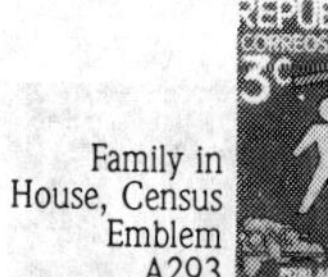

Family in House, Census Emblem A293

1981, Aug. 14 **Litho.** ***Perf. 12***

850 A293 3c shown 15 15
851 A293 6c Farmer 15 15
Set value 24 15

1981 natl. population and housing census.

A294 A295

1981, Dec. 23 **Litho.** ***Perf. 13½***

852 A294 2c Bells 15 15
853 A294 3c Poinsettia 15 15
Set value 16 15

Christmas. See No. C353

1982, Jan. 29 **Litho.** ***Perf. 13½***

854 A295 2c Juan Pablo Duarte 15 15

REPUBLICA DOMINICANA 2c ELECCIONES NACIONALES 1982 VOTAR ES UN DEBER CIUDADANO

National Elections A296

Designs: Voters casting votes. 3c, 6c vert.

1982, Mar. 30 **Litho.** ***Perf. 13½***

855 A296 2c multicolored 15 15
856 A296 3c multicolored 15 15
857 A296 6c multicolored 15 15
Set value 23 18

A297

A298

Energy Conservation: Various forms of energy.

1982, May 10 **Litho.** ***Perf. 12***

858 A297 1c multicolored 15 15
859 A297 2c multicolored 15 15
860 A297 3c multicolored 15 15
861 A297 4c multicolored 15 15
862 A297 5c multicolored 15 15
863 A297 6c multicolored 15 15
Set value 55 35

1982, Aug. 2 ***Perf. 12x12½***

864 A298 6c multicolored 15 15

Emilio Prud'Homme (1856-1932), composer.

Pres. Antonio Guzman Fernandez (1911-1982) A299

1982, Aug. 4 ***Perf. 13x13½***

865 A299 6c multicolored 15 15

14th Central American and Caribbean Games A300

1982, Aug. 13 ***Perf. 12, Imperf.***

866 A300 3c Baseball 15 15

See Nos. C368-C370.

San Pedro de Macoris Province Centenary — A301

1982, Aug. 26 ***Perf. 13***

867 A301 1c Wagon 15 15
868 A301 2c Stained-glass window 15 15
869 A301 5c Views 18 15
Set value 21

Size of 2c, 25x35mm. See No. C375.

St. Teresa of Jesus of Avila (1515-1582) — A302

1982, Nov. 17 **Litho.** ***Perf. 13½***

870 A302 6c multicolored 15 15

Christmas 1982 — A303

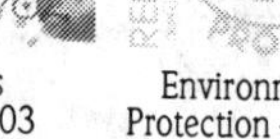

Environmental Protection — A304

Various Christmas balls.

1982, Dec. 8

871 A303 6c multicolored 15 15

See No. C380.

1982, Dec. 15 ***Perf. 12***

872 A304 2c Bird 15 15
873 A304 3c Water 15 15
874 A304 6c Forest 15 15
875 A304 20c Fish 24 18
Set value 44 34

Natl. Literacy Campaign A305

1983, Mar. 9 **Litho.** *Perf. 13½*

876 A305 2c Vowels on blackboard 15 15
877 A305 3c Writing, reading 15 15
878 A305 6c Children, pencil 15 15
Set value 26 15

A306

A307

1983, Apr. 4 *Perf. 12*

879 A306 1c multicolored 15 15
880 A306 5c multicolored 15 15
Set value 23 15

Mao City centenary.

1983, Apr. 25 **Litho.** *Perf. 12*

Famous Men: 2c, Antonio del Monte y Tejada (1780-1861). 3c, Manuel Ubaldo Gomez (1857-1941). 5c, Emiliano Tejera (1841-1923). 6c, Bernardo Pichardo (1877-1924). 7c, Americo Lugo (1870-1952). 10c, José Gabriel Garcia (1834-1910). 7c, 10c airmail.

881 A307 2c multicolored 15 15
882 A307 3c multicolored 15 15
883 A307 5c multicolored 15 15
884 A307 6c multicolored 15 15
885 A307 7c multicolored 15 15
886 A307 10c multicolored 22 15
Set value 75 36

National Anthem, 100th Anniv. A308

Design: Emilio Prud'Homme, and Jose Reyes, composer.

1983, Sept. 13 **Litho.** *Perf. 13½*

887 A308 6c cop red & blk 15 15

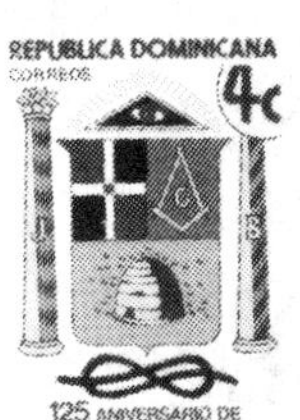

Free Masons, 125th Anniv. — A309

Church of Our Lady of Regla, 300th Anniv. — A310

1983, Oct. 24 **Litho.** *Perf. 12*

888 A309 4c Emblem 15 15

1983, Nov. 5 *Perf. 13½*

889 A310 3c Church 15 15
890 A310 6c Statue 15 15
Set value 15 15

450th Anniv. of Monte Cristi Province — A311

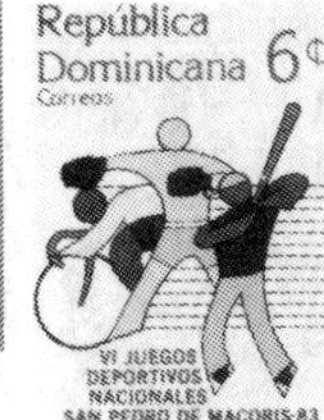

6th Natl. Games — A312

1983, Nov. 25 *Perf. 12*

891 A311 1c Tower 15 15
892 A311 2c Arms 15 15
893 A311 5c Cuban independence site, horiz. 15 15
894 A311 7c Workers, horiz. 15 15
Set value 46 27

1983, Dec. 9

895 A312 6c Bicycling, boxing, baseball 15 15
896 A312 10c Gymnast, weight lifting, swimming 18 15
Set value 15

10c airmail.

Restoration of the Republic, 120th Anniv. — A313

1983, Dec. 30 **Litho.** *Perf. 13½*

897 A313 1c Capotillo Heroes Monument 15 15

140th Anniv. of Independence A314

Designs: 6c, Matia Ramon Mella (Patriot), flag. 25c, Mella's Blunderbuss rifle, Gate of Deliverance (independence declaration site).

1984, Feb. 24 **Litho.** *Perf. 13½*

898 A314 6c multicolored 15 15
899 A314 25c multicolored 35 15
Set value 25

Heriberto Pieter (1884-1972), Physician, First Negro Graduate — A315

1984, Mar. 16

900 A315 3c multicolored 15 15

Battle of Barranquita, 67th Anniv. A316

1983, Dec. 30 *Perf. 12*

901 A316 5c multicolored 15 15

Battle of Santiago, 140th Anniv. A317

1984, Mar. 29 *Perf. 13½*

902 A317 7c multicolored 15 15

Coast Guard Ship DC-1, 1934 A318

1984, Apr. 13 **Litho.**

903 A318 10c multicolored 15 15

Navy Day and 140th anniv. of Battle of Tortuguero.

Birth Centenary of Pedro Henriquez Urena — A319

1984, June 29 **Litho.** *Perf. 12*

904 A319 7c Salome Urena 15 15
905 A319 10c Text 15 15
906 A319 22c Urena 25 15
Set value 27

Monument to Heroes of June 1959 A320

1984, June 20 *Perf. 13½*

907 A320 6c silver & blue 15 15

Gesta de Constanza Maimon and Estero Hondo, 25th anniv.

1984 Summer Olympics A321

1984, Aug. 1

908 A321 1p Hurdles 1.25 1.25
909 A321 1p Weightlifting 1.25 1.25
910 A321 1p Boxing 1.25 1.25
911 A321 1p Baseball 1.25 1.25
a. Block of 4, #908-911 5.00 5.00

Protection of Fauna — A322

1984, Oct. 3 **Litho.** *Perf. 12*

912 A322 10c Owl 15 15
913 A322 15c Flamingo 20 15
914 A322 25c Wild Pig 25 18
915 A322 35c Solenodon 35 35
Set value 70

500th Anniv. of Discovery of America A323

1984, Oct. 10 **Litho.** *Perf. 13½x13*

916 A323 10c Landing on Hispaniola 15 15
917 A323 35c Destruction of Ft. Navidad 38 30
918 A323 65c First Mass in America 65 60
919 A323 1p Battle of Santo Cerro 1.00 80

Visit of Pope John Paul II — A324

1984, Oct. 11 **Litho.** *Perf. 13x13½*

920 Block of 4 5.00 5.00
a. A324 75c shown 1.25 1.25
b. A324 75c Pope, map of Caribbean 1.25 1.25
c. A324 75c Pope, globe 1.25 1.25
d. A324 75c Bishop's crozier 1.25 1.25

150th Anniv. of Birth of Maximo Gomez (1986) A325

1984, Dec. 6 **Litho.** *Perf. 13½*

921 A325 10c Gomez on horseback 15 15
922 A325 20c Maximo Gomez 18 15
Set value 28 20

Christmas 1984 — A326

Perf. 13½x13, 13x13½

1984, Dec. 14 **Litho.**

923 A326 5c multicolored 15 15
924 A326 10c multicolored, vert. 15 15
Set value 16 15

Sacrifice of the Child, by Eligio Pichardo A327

Paintings and sculpture: 10c, The Pumpkin Sellers, by Gaspar Mario Cruz; 25c, The Market, by Celeste Woss y Gil; 50c, Horses in the Rain, by Dario Suro.

1984, Dec. 19 **Litho.** *Perf. 13½*

925 A327 5c multicolored 15 15
926 A327 10c multi, vert. 15 15
927 A327 25c multicolored 18 15
928 A327 50c multicolored 40 24
Set value 50

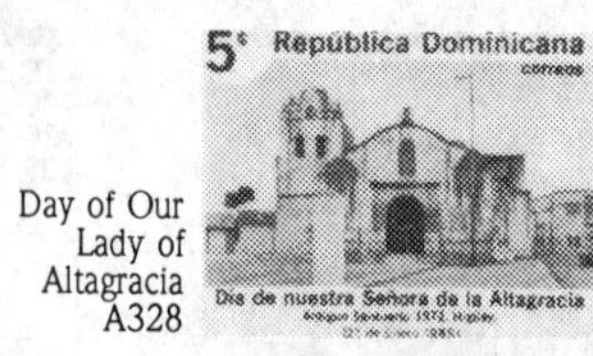

Day of Our Lady of Altagracia
A328

1985, Jan. 21

929 A328 5c Old church at Higuey, 1572 15 15
930 A328 10c Our Lady of Altagracia 1514, vert. 15 15
931 A328 25c Basilica of the Protector, Higuey 1971, vert. 30 15
Set value 48 17

Independence, 141st Anniv. — A329

Painting: The Fathers of Our Country (Duarte, Sanchez and Mella).

1985, Mar. 8 *Perf. 12½*

932 A329 5c multicolored 15 15
933 A329 10c multicolored 15 15
934 A329 25c multicolored 30 15
Set value 49 20

Battle of Azua, 141st Anniv. A330

1985, Apr. 8 Litho. *Perf. 13½*

935 A330 10c Gen. Antonio Duverge, Statue 15 15

A331 A332

1985, Apr. 15 **Litho.**

936 A331 25c Santo Domingo Lighthouse, 1853 25 15

Battle of Tortuguero, 141st anniv.

1985, Apr. 15 Litho. *Perf. 12*

937 A332 35c multicolored 42 28

American Airforces Cooperation System, 25th anniv.

A333 A334

1985, May 24 Litho. *Perf. 13½*

938 A333 10c Don Carlos M. Rojas, 1st gov. 15 15

Espaillat Province cent.

1985, July 5 Litho. *Perf. 12*

939 A334 5c Table tennis 15 15
940 A334 10c Walking race 15 15
Set value 22 15

MOCA '85, 7th Natl. Games.

Intl. Youth Year — A335

1985, July 29 *Perf. 13½*

941 A335 5c Youth 15 15
942 A335 25c The Haitises 35 25
943 A335 35c Mt. Duarte summit 42 30
944 A335 2p Mt. Duarte 2.50 2.00

Interamerican Development Bank, 25th Anniv. A336

Designs: 10c, Haina Harbor. 25c, Map of development sites. 1p, Tavera-Bao-Lopez Hydroelectric Complex.

1985, Aug. 23

945 A336 10c multicolored 15 15
946 A336 25c multicolored 30 22
947 A336 1p multicolored 1.25 80

Intl. Decade for Women — A337

15th Central American and Caribbean Games, Santiago — A338

Design: Evangelina Rodriguez (1879-1947), first Dominican woman doctor.

1985, Sept. 26

948 A337 10c multicolored 15 15

1985, Oct. 9 *Perf. 12*

949 A338 5c multicolored 15 15
950 A338 25c multicolored 35 22
Set value 27

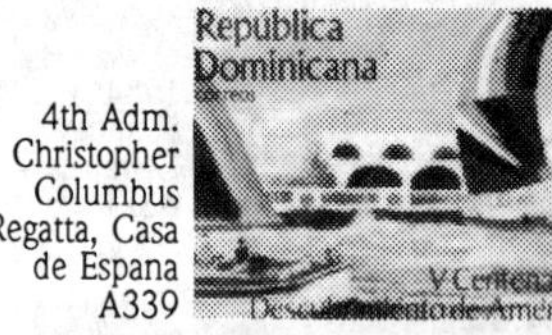

4th Adm. Christopher Columbus Regatta, Casa de Espana A339

Designs: 50c, Founding of Santo Domingo, 1496. 65c, Chapel of Our Lady of the Rosary, 1496, Santo Domingo. 1p, Columbus, American Indian and old Spanish coat of arms.

1985, Oct. 10 *Perf. 13½*

951 A339 35c multicolored 50 50
952 A339 50c multicolored 60 60
953 A339 65c multicolored 80 80
954 A339 1p multicolored 1.25 1.25

Discovery of America, 500th anniv. (in 1992).

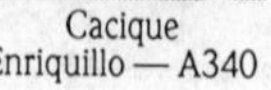

Cacique Enriquillo — A340

Archbishop Fernando Arturo de Merino — A341

Designs: 5c, Enriquillo in the Bahuroco Mountains, mural detail. 10c, Shown.

1985, Oct. 31

955 A340 5c multicolored 15 15
956 A340 10c multicolored 20 15
Set value 26 17

Enriquillo (d. 1536), leader of revolution against Spain. Size of No. 955: 47x33mm.

1985, Dec. 3 *Perf. 12*

957 A341 25c multicolored 30 22

Cent. of holy orders granted to Merino (1833-1906), pres. of the republic 1880-82.

Mirabal Sisters, Political Martyrs 1960 A342

1985, Dec. 18 *Perf. 13½*

958 A342 10c multicolored 15 15

Christmas A343

1985, Dec. 18

959 A343 10c multicolored 15 15
960 A343 25c multicolored 30 22

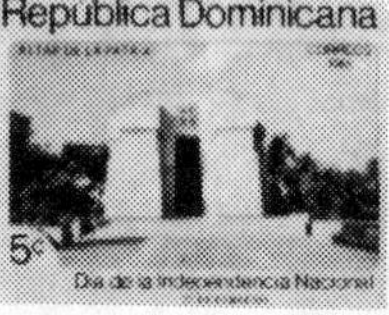

Day of Independence, Feb. 27 — A344

Design: Mausoleum of founding fathers Duarte, Sanchez and Mella.

1986, Feb. 26 Litho. *Perf. 13½*

961 A344 5c multicolored 15 15
962 A344 10c multicolored 15 15
Set value 18 15

Holy Week — A345

Colonial churches.

1986, Apr. 10

963 A345 5c San Miguel 15 15
964 A345 5c San Andres 15 15
965 A345 10c Santa Barbara 15 15
966 A345 10c San Lazaro 15 15
967 A345 10c San Carlos 15 15
Set value 52 34

Navy Day — A346

Design: Juan Bautista Cambiaso, Juan Bautista Maggiolo and Juan Alejandro Acosta, 1884 independence battle heroes.

1986, Apr. 15

968 A346 10c multicolored 15 15

Natl. Elections — A347

Natl. Postal Institute Inauguration — A348

1986, Apr. 29

969 A347 5c Voters, map 15 15
970 A347 10c Ballot box 15 15
Set value 20 15

1986, June 10

971 A348 10c gold, blue & red 15 15
972 A348 25c silver, blue & red 35 22
973 A348 50c black, blue & red 65 40

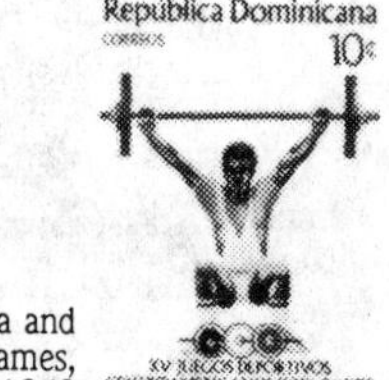

Central America and Caribbean Games, Santiago — A349

1986, July 17 Litho. *Perf. 13½*

974 A349 10c Weight lifting 15 15
975 A349 25c Gymnastics 30 22
976 A349 35c Diving 42 28
977 A349 50c Equestrian 60 40

Historians A350

Designs: 5c, Ercilia Pepin (b. 1886), vert. 10c, Ramon Emilio Jimenez (b. 1886) and Victor Garrido (1886-1972).

1986, Aug. 1 Litho. *Perf. 13½*

978 A350 5c silver & dull brn 15 15
979 A350 10c silver & dull brn 15 15
Set value 18 15

A351

A352

Discovery of America, 500th Anniv. (in 1992) — A353

Designs: 25c, Yachts racing, 5th Adm. Christopher Columbus Regatta, Casa de Espana. 50c, Columbus founding La Isabela City. 65c, Exploration of the hidalgos. 1p, Columbus returning to the Court of Ferdinand and Isabella. 1.50p, Emblems.

1986, Oct. 10 Litho. *Perf. 13½*

980	A351	25c multicolored	30	22
981	A352	50c multicolored	60	40
982	A352	65c multicolored	80	52
983	A352	1p multicolored	1.25	80

Textured Paper

Size: 86x58mm

Imperf

984	A353	1.50p multicolored	3.00	3.00
		Nos. 980-984 (5)	5.95	4.94

1986 World Cup Soccer Championships, Mexico — A354

Medicinal Plants — A355

Various soccer plays.

1986, Oct. 21 *Perf. 13½*

985	A354	50c multicolored	60	40
986	A354	75c multicolored	90	60

1986, Dec. 5

987	A355	5c Zea mays	15	15
988	A355	10c Bixa orellana	15	15
989	A355	25c Momordica charantia	30	22
990	A355	50c Annona muricata	60	40
		Set value		74

Second Caribbean Pharmacopeia Seminar.

Christmas A356

1986, Dec. 19

991	A356	5c Urban scene	15	15
992	A356	25c Rural scene	30	22
		Set value	36	27

A357

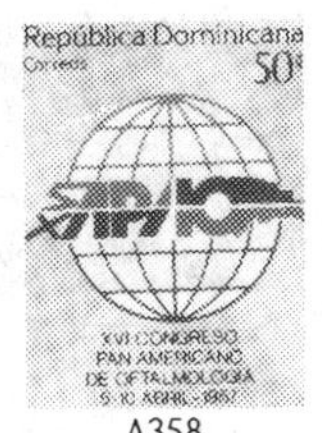

A358

1986, Dec. 31 Litho. *Perf. 13½*

993	A357	10c shown	15	15
994	A357	25c Portrait, c. 1900	30	22

Maximo Gomez (1836-1905), revolutionary, statesman.

1987, Mar. 30 Litho. *Perf. 13½*

995	A358	50c brt blue, blk & red	60	45

16th Pan American Ophthalmological Conf., Apr. 5-10.

A359

A360

Stained-glass window, San Juan Bosco church, Santo Domingo: Ascension of Christ to Heaven.

1987, May 28

996	A359	35c multicolored	42	32

1987, Aug. 21

Edible plants.

997	A360	5c Sorghum bicolor	15	15
998	A360	25c Martanta arundinacea	30	22
999	A360	65c Calathaea allouia	80	55
1000	A360	1p Voandzeia subterranea	1.25	90

Activo 20-30 Intl., 25th Anniv. A361

1987, Aug. 26

1001	A361	35c multicolored	42	32

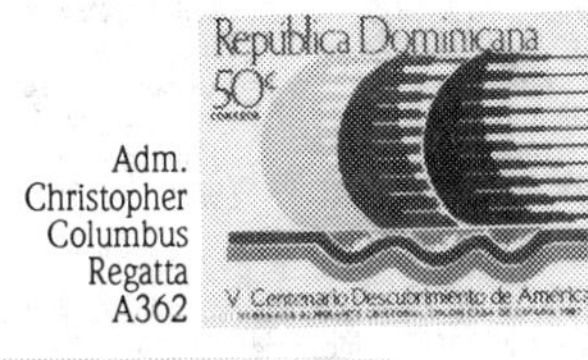

Adm. Christopher Columbus Regatta A362

A363

Columbus Memorial, Santo Domingo — A364

1987, Oct. 14

1002	A362	50c shown	60	45
1003	A363	75c shown	90	65
1004	A363	1p Building Ft. Santiago	1.25	90
1005	A363	1.50p Columbus imprisoned by Bombadilla	1.75	1.40

Size: 82x70mm

Imperf

1006	A364	2.50p shown	3.00	2.25
		Nos. 1002-1006 (5)	7.50	5.65

Discovery of America, 500th anniv. in 1992.

A365

A366

1987, Sept. 28

1007	A365	40c multicolored	48	35

Junior Olympics, La Vega, 50th anniv.

1987, Nov. 10 Litho. *Perf. 13½*

Historians and authors: 10c, Jose Antonio Hungria. 25c, Joaquin Sergio Inchaustegui.

1008	A366	10c buff & brown	15	15
1009	A366	25c pale grn & grn	30	22

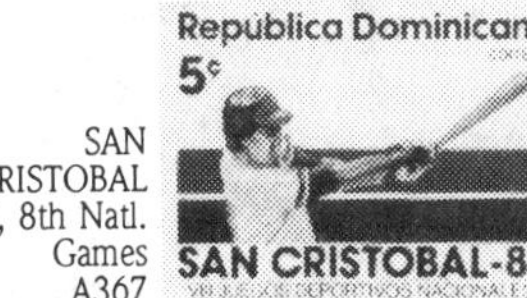

SAN CRISTOBAL '87, 8th Natl. Games A367

1987, Nov. 19

1010	A367	5c Baseball	15	15
1011	A367	10c Boxing	15	15
1012	A367	50c Judo	60	45
		Set value	78	59

Christmas 1987 — A368

1987, Dec. 9 Litho. *Perf. 13½*

1013	A368	10c Roasting pig	20	15
1014	A368	50c Arriving at airport	60	45

Fr. Xavier Billini (b. 1837) — A369

1987, Dec. 18 Litho. *Perf. 13½*

1015	A369	10c Statue	15	15
1016	A369	25c Portrait	30	22
1017	A369	75c Ana Hernandez de Billini, his mother	90	65

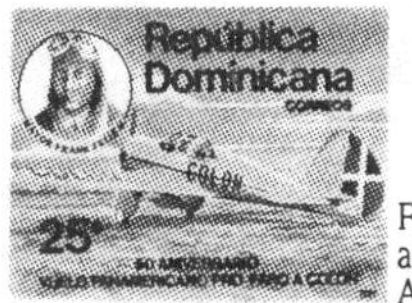

Frank Feliz, Sr., and Aircraft A370

1987, Dec. 22

1018	A370	25c shown	30	22

Size: 86x106mm

Imperf

1019	A370	2p No. C30, map	2.50	2.00

Pan-American goodwill flight to South American countries by the planes Colon, Pinta, Nina and Santa Maria, 50th anniv.

Flora — A371

1988, Feb. 3 Litho. *Perf. 13½*

1020	A371	50c Bromelia pinguin	60	45
1021	A371	50c Tillandsia fasciculata	60	45
1022	A371	50c Tillandsia hotteana, vert.	60	45
1023	A371	50c Tillandsia compacta, vert.	60	45

St. John Bosco (1815-1888) — A372

1988, Feb. 23 Litho. *Perf. 13½*

1024	A372	10c shown	15	15
1025	A372	70c Stained-glass window	85	65

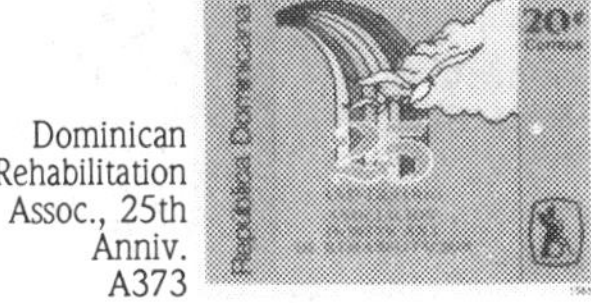

Dominican Rehabilitation Assoc., 25th Anniv. A373

1988, Mar. 1

1026	A373	20c multicolored	24	18

A374

A375

1988, Apr. 6 Litho. *Perf. 13½*

1027	A374	20c dk red brn & lt fawn	28	20

Dr. Manuel Emilio Perdomo (b.1886).

1988, Apr. 29 Litho. *Perf. 13½*

1028	A375	20c multicolored	28	20

Dominican College of Engineers, Architects and Surveyors (CODIA), 25th Anniv.

Independence Day, Mexico — A376

Flags and: No. 1029, Fr. Miguel Hidalgo y Costilla (1753-1811), Mexican revolutionary. No. 1030, Juan Pablo Duarte (1813-1876), father of Dominican independence.

1988, Sept. 12 Litho. *Perf. 13½*

1029 A376 50c multicolored	65	50
1030 A376 50c multicolored	65	50

1988 Summer Olympics, Seoul — A377

1988, Sept. 21 Litho. *Perf. 13½*

1031 A377 50c Running, vert.	65	45
1032 A377 70c Table tennis, vert.	90	65
1033 A377 1p Judo, vert.	1.40	90
1034 A377 1.50p Mural by Tete Marella	2.00	1.40

A378

Discovery of America, 500th Anniv. (in 1992) — A379

Designs: 50c, 7th Adm. Christopher Columbus Regatta, Casa de Espana, 1988. 70c, La Concepcion Fortress, La Vega Real, 1494. 1.50p, Ft. Bonao. 2p, Nicolas de Ovando (c. 1451-1511), governor of Spanish possessions in America from 1502 to 1509. 3p, Mausoleum of Christopher Columbus, Santo Domingo Cathedral.

1988, Oct. 14 *Perf. 13½*

1035 A378 50c multicolored	65	45
1036 A378 70c multicolored	90	65
1037 A378 1.50p multicolored	2.00	1.40
1038 A378 2p multicolored	2.75	1.75

Size: 78x109mm

Imperf

1039 A379 3p multicolored	3.00	2.00

Discovery of America, 500th anniv. (in 1992). No. 1038 inscribed "1501-1509."

Duverge Parish, Cent. — A380

1988, July 13 Litho. *Perf. 13½*

1040 A380 50c multicolored	60	40

A381

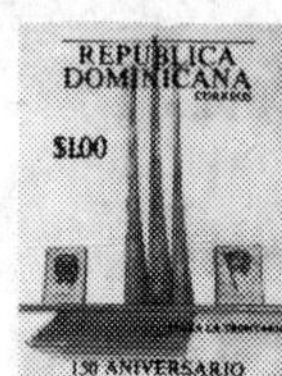
Trinitarians, 150th Anniv. — A382

1988, Nov. 11

1041 A381 10c shown	15	15
1042 A382 1p Trinitarian Plaza	1.25	80
1043 A382 5p Independence Plaza	6.00	4.00

See footnote after No. 337.

Pharmacology and Biochemistry A383

The Holy Family, 1504, by Miguel Angel A384

1988, Nov. 28 Litho. *Perf. 13½*

1044 A383 1p multicolored	2.00	1.35

13th Pan American and 16th Central American Congresses.

1988, Dec. 12

1045 A384 10c shown	20	15
1046 A384 20c Stained-glass window	40	28

Christmas.

Municipal Technical Advisory Organization (LIGA), 50th Anniv. — A385

Ana Teresa Paradas (1890-1960), 1st Female Lawyer of the Republic, 1913 — A386

1988, Dec. 23

1047 A385 20c multicolored	40	28

1988, Dec. 26

1048 A386 20c deep claret	40	28

French Revolution Bicent. A387

1989, Mar. 10 Litho. *Perf. 13½*

1049 A387 3p red & violet blue	1.50	1.40

Battle of Tortuga, Apr. 15, 1844 A388

1989, Apr. 14 Litho. *Perf. 13½*

1050 A388 40c multicolored	60	45

Natl. Anti-drug Campaign A389

1989, May 15

1051 A389 10c multicolored
1052 A389 20c multicolored
1053 A389 50c multicolored
1054 A389 70c multicolored
1055 A389 1p multicolored
1056 A389 1.50p multicolored
1057 A389 2p multicolored
1058 A389 5p multicolored
1059 A389 10p multicolored

Mother's Day — A390

1989, May 30 Litho. *Perf. 13½*

1060 A390 20c multicolored	22	16

Eugenio Maria de Hostos (b. 1839) — A391

Gen. Gregorio Luperon (b. 1839) — A392

1989, Aug. 22 Litho. *Perf. 13½*

1061 A391 20c multicolored	22	16

1989, Aug. 28

1062 A392 20c multicolored	22	16

Little League Baseball, 50th Anniv. A393

1989, Sept. 29

1063 A393 1p multicolored	1.10	82

Diabetes '89, 7th Latin American Congress A394

1989, Oct. 9 Litho. *Perf. 13½*

1064 A394 1p multicolored	1.10	82

America Issue — A395

UPAE emblem, pre-Columbian artifacts and customs: 20c, Cohoba silver statue and ritual dance. 1p, Taina mortar, pestle and family preparing cazabe.

1989, Oct. 12

1065 A395 20c multicolored	22	16
1066 A395 1p multicolored	1.10	82

8th Adm. Christopher Columbus Regatta, Casa de Espana — A396

European Colonization of the Americas A397

Designs: 70c, Fr. Pedro de Cordoba converting the Indians to Catholicism. 1p, Christopher Columbus trading with the Indians. 3p, Sermon of Pedro de Cordoba.

1989, Oct. 13

1067 A396 50c shown	32	24
1068 A397 70c shown	45	35
1069 A397 1p multicolored	65	48
1070 A397 3p multicolored	1.90	1.45

Discovery of America, 500th anniv. (in 1992).

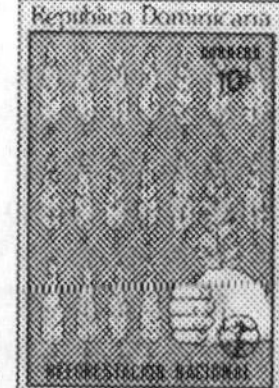
Natl. Afforestation — A398

1989, Oct. 30 Litho. *Perf. 13½*

1071 A398 10c shown 15 15
1072 A398 20c Tree 22 16
1073 A398 50c Forest 55 42
1074 A398 1p Sapling, mature trees 1.10 82

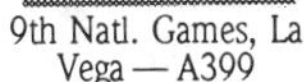

9th Natl. Games, La Vega — A399

Holy Week (Easter) — A400

1990, Mar. 20 Litho. *Perf. 13½*

1075 A399 10c Cycling 15 15
1076 A399 20c Running 30 22
1077 A399 50c Basketball 75 58

1990, Apr. 5

1078 A400 20c shown 30 22
1079 A400 50c Jesus carrying cross 75 58

Labor Day, Cent. — A401

1990 Litho. *Perf. 13½*

1080 A401 1p multicolored 1.50 1.15

Urban Renewal A402

1990

1081 A402 10c shown 15 15
1082 A402 20c Highway underpass 30 22
1083 A402 50c Library 75 58
1084 A402 1p City street 1.50 1.15

No. 1084 inscribed $100 instead of $1.00.

Penny Black, 150th Anniv. — A403

1990

1085 A403 1p multicolored 1.50 1.15

Size: 62x80mm

Imperf

1086 A403 3p Sir Rowland Hill, Penny Black 4.50 3.40

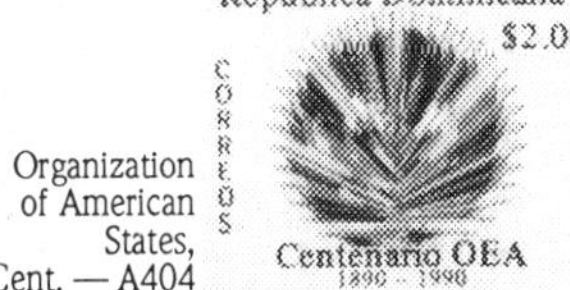

Organization of American States, Cent. — A404

1990 Litho. *Perf. 13½*

1087 A404 2p Flags 3.00 2.25

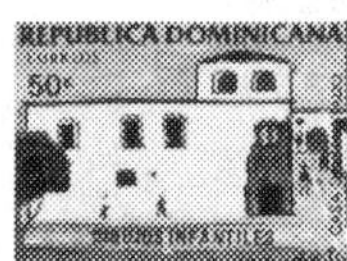

Children's Drawings A405

1990

1088 A405 50c House of Tostado 75 55
1089 A405 50c Ruins of St. Nicolas of Bari 75 55

Discovery of America, 500th Anniv. (in 1992) — A406

Designs: 1p, Fight at the Gulf of Arrows. 2p, Columbus talking with Guacanagari Indians. 5p, Columbus and Caonabo Indian prisoner.

1990

1090 A406 1p multicolored 1.50 1.10
1091 A406 2p multicolored 3.00 2.25
1092 A406 5p multicolored 7.50 5.65

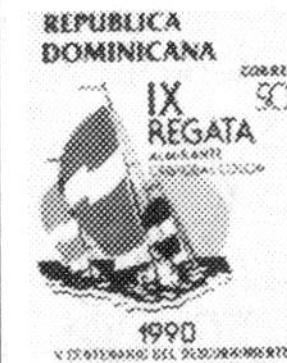

9th Adm. Christopher Columbus Regatta — A407

1990

1093 A407 50c multicolored 75 55

America Issue — A408

UPAE emblem and: 50c, Men in canoe. 3p, Man on hammock.

1990 Litho. *Perf. 13½*

1094 A408 50c multicolored 75 55
1095 A408 3p multicolored 4.50 3.40

A409

A410

Discovery of Hispaniola: 50c, 1st official mass in Americas. 1p, Arms of 1st religious order in Americas. 3p, Map of island, horiz. 4p, Christopher Columbus, 1st viceroy and governor in Americas.

1991 Litho. *Perf. 13½*

1096 A409 50c multicolored
1097 A409 1p multicolored
1098 A409 3p multicolored
1099 A409 4p multicolored

1991

1100 A410 30c Boxing
1101 A410 50c Cycling
1102 A410 1p Bowling

11th Pan American Games, Havana.

Dr. Tomas Eudoro Perez Rancier, Birth Cent. — A411

1991

1103 A411 2p yellow & black

10th Columbus Regatta, Casa de Espana — A412

Discovery of America, 500th Anniv. (in 1992) — A413

Designs: 50c, Encounter of three cultures. 3p, Columbus and Dr. Alvarez Chanca caring for sick. 4p, Rebellion of Enriquillo.

1991 Litho. *Perf. 13½*

1104 A412 30c multicolored
1105 A413 50c multicolored
1106 A413 3p multicolored
1107 A413 4p multicolored

See No. 1116.

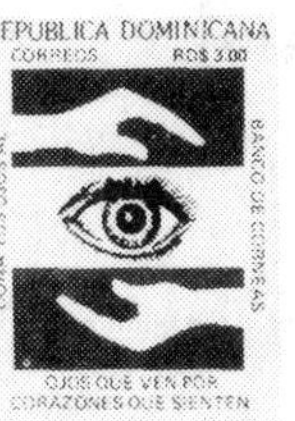

A414

A415

1991

1108 A414 3p black & red

Cornea Bank.

1991 Litho. *Perf. 13½*

1109 A415 1p Santa Maria
1110 A415 3p Christopher Columbus

America issue.

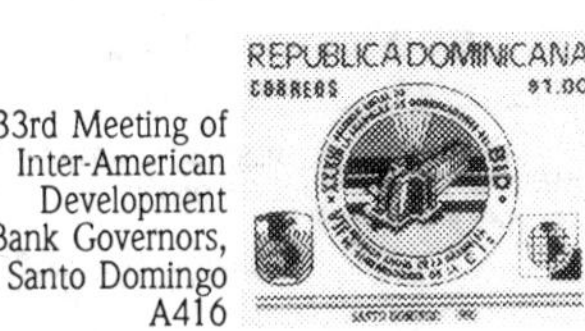

33rd Meeting of Inter-American Development Bank Governors, Santo Domingo A416

1992 Litho. *Perf. 13½*

1111 A416 1p multicolored

A417

A418

1992 Litho. *Perf. 13½*

1112 A417 3p multicolored

Espanola '92 Philatelic Exposition.

1992 Litho. *Perf. 13½*

Design: Valentin Salinero, Founder of Order of the Apostles.

1113 A418 1p blue & brown

Order of the Apostles, cent.

Ruins of Monastery of San Francisco A419

Designs: 3p, Ruins of San Nicolas hospital, first in the Americas.

1992

1114 A419 50c multicolored
1115 A419 3p multicolored

Type of 1991 and

A420

Designs: 50c, Racing yacht. 1p, Native women, Columbus. 2p, Natives offering Columbus tobacco. 3p, Native woman, Columbus, corn.

1992 Litho. *Perf. 13½*

1116 A412 50c multicolored
1117 A420 1p multicolored
1118 A420 2p multicolored
1119 A420 3p multicolored

11th Columbus Regatta (#1116), Discovery of America, 500th anniv. (#1117-1119).

23rd Convention of the Alliance of Panamerican Round Tables, Santo Domingo — A421

1992

1120 A421 1p multicolored

Visit by Pope John Paul II A422

Cathedrals: 50c, Vega. 3p, Santo Domingo.

1992 Photo.

1121 A422 50c multicolored
1122 A422 3p multicolored

Columbus Lighthouse A423

1992 **Litho.**

1123 A423 30c multicolored
1124 A423 1p multicolored

Size: 70x133mm

Imperf

1125 A423 3p Lighthouse at night

America Issue — A424

Designs: 50c, First royal residence in America, Santo Domingo. 3p, First viceregal residence in America, Royal Palace, Colon.

1992 **Litho.** ***Perf. 13½***

1126 A424 50c multicolored
1127 A424 3p multicolored

A425

Natl. Census — A426

1992 **Litho.** ***Perf. 13½***

1128 A425 30c Torch bearer
1129 A425 1p Emblems
1130 A425 4p Judo

1992 Natl. Sports Games, San Juan. Secretary of Sports, Education, Exercise and Recreation (#1129).

1993 **Litho.** ***Perf. 13½***

1131 A426 50c black, buff & blue
1132 A426 1p black, brown, & blue
1133 A426 3p black, gray & blue
1134 A426 4p black, yellow green & blue

A427

A428

1993

1135 A427 30c multicolored
1136 A427 50c multicolored
1137 A427 1p multicolored

Ema Balaguer, humanitarian.

1993 **Litho.** ***Perf. 13½***

1138 A428 30c shown
1139 A428 1p Emblem, flags

Rotary Club of Santo Domingo, 50th anniv.

17th Central American & Caribbean Games, Ponce — A429

1993 **Litho.** ***Perf. 13½***

1140 A429 50c Tennis
1141 A429 4p Swimming

Natl. Education Plan — A430

Spanish America — A431

1993

1142 A430 1.50p multicolored

1993

1143 A431 50c First university lecturn
1144 A431 3p First city coat of arms

America Issue — A432

1993

1145 A432 1p Aratinga chloroptera
1146 A432 3p Cyclura cornuta

REPUBLICA DOMINICANA

Opening of New Natl. Post Office — A433

1993

Color of Inscription

1147 A433 1p olive
1148 A433 3p red
1149 A433 4p blue
1150 A433 5p green
1151 A433 10p black

Size: 105x96mm

Imperf

1152 A433 5p black

SEMI-POSTAL STAMPS

Catalogue values for unused stamps in this section are for Never Hinged items.

Nos. 474-478 Surcharged in Red

Engraved and Lithographed

1957, Feb. 8 **Unwmk.** ***Perf. 11½***

Flags in National Colors

B1	A117	1c + 2c brn, lt bl, vio & mar	15	15
B2	A117	2c + 2c dk brn, lt bl & vio	15	15
B3	A117	3c + 2c red lilac & red	15	15
B4	A117	5c + 2c red orange & vio	20	20
B5	A117	7c + 2c green & violet	28	28
		Nos. B1-B5,CB1-CB3 (8)	2.01	2.01

The surtax was to aid Hungarian refugees. A similar 25c surcharge was applied to the miniature sheets described in the footnote following No. 478. Value, 2 sheets, perf. and imperf., $25.

Nos. 479-483 Surcharged in Red Orange

1957, Sept. 9 **Photo.** ***Perf. 13½***

Flags in National Colors

B6	A118	1c + 2c brown & brt bl	20	20
B7	A118	2c + 2c org ver & dk bl	28	28
B8	A118	3c + 2c dark blue	32	32
B9	A118	5c + 2c olive & dk bl	45	45
B10	A118	7c + 2c rose brn & dk bl	52	52
		Nos. B6-B10,CB4-CB6 (8)	3.52	3.47

Cent. of the birth of Lord Baden Powell and the 50th anniv. of the Scout Movement. The surtax was for the Dominican Republic Boy Scouts.

A similar 5c surcharge was applied to the miniature sheets described in the footnote following No. 483. Value 4 sheets, perf. and imperf., medal and flag, $40.

Types of Olympic Regular Issue, 1957, Surcharged in Carmine

+2¢ +2¢

REFUGIADOS REFUGIADOS

a b

1958, May 26 **Engr. & Litho.**

Flags in National Colors

Pink Paper

B11	A119(a)	1c + 2c red brown	20	20
B12	A119(b)	1c + 2c red brown	20	20
B13	A120(a)	2c + 2c gray brown	24	24
B14	A120(b)	2c + 2c gray brown	24	24
B15	A119(a)	3c + 2c violet	24	24
B16	A119(b)	3c + 2c violet	24	24
B17	A120(a)	5c + 2c red orange	32	32
B18	A120(b)	5c + 2c red orange	32	32
B19	A119(a)	7c + 2c Prus green	40	40
B20	A119(b)	7c + 2c Prus green	40	40
		Nos. B11-B20,CB7-CB12 (16)	4.90	4.90

Surtax for the UN Relief and Works Agency for Palestine Refugees.

A similar 5c surcharge, plus marginal United Nations emblem and "UNRWA," was applied to the miniature sheets described in the footnote following No. 488. Value, 4 sheets, perf. and imperf., $20.

Nos. 501-505 Surcharged

Perf. 13½

1959, Apr. 13 **Photo.** **Unwmk.**

Flags in National Colors

B21	A125	1c + 2c rose, indigo & ultra	28	28
B22	A125	1c + 2c brown & blue	35	35
B23	A125	3c + 2c gray, vio, blk & buff	40	40
B24	A125	5c + 2c rose, dk bl, brn & red	48	48
B25	A125	7c + 2c lt brn, dk bl & red	52	52
		Nos. B21-B25,CB13-CB15 (8)	4.30	4.30

International Geophysical Year, 1957-58.

A similar 5c surcharge was applied to the miniature sheets described in the footnote following No. 505. Value, 2 sheets, perf. and imperf., $40.

Type of 1957 Surcharged in Red

Engraved and Lithographed

1959, Sept. 10 **Unwmk.** ***Imperf.***

Flags in National Colors

B26	A117	1c + 2c brn, lt bl, vio & mar	30	30
B27	A117	2c + 2c dk brn, lt bl & vio	30	30
B28	A117	3c + 2c red lilac & red	32	32
B29	A117	5c + 2c red orange & vio	35	35
B30	A117	7c + 2c green & violet	45	45
		Nos. B26-B30,CB16-CB18 (8)	3.24	3.24

3rd Pan American Games, Chicago, Aug. 27-Sept. 7, 1959.

Nos. 522-524 Surcharged in Red

1960, Apr. 7 **Litho.** ***Perf. 12½***

Center in Gray

B31	A135	5c + 5c red brn & yel grn	15	15
B32	A135	9c + 5c carmine & lt bl	18	18
B33	A135	13c + 5c orange & green	35	35
		Nos. B31-B33,CB19-CB20 (5)	1.02	1.01

World Refugee Year, July 1, 1959-June 30, 1960. The surtax was for aid to refugees.

Souvenir sheets exist perf. and imperf., containing one each of Nos. B31-B33 and CB19-CB20. Value, 2 sheets, perf. and imperf., $10.

Nos. 525-529 Surcharged: "XV ANIVERSARIO DE LA UNESCO +2c"

1962, Jan. 8 **Photo.** ***Perf. 13½***

Flags in National Colors

B34	A136	1c + 2c red, yel grn & blk	15	15
B35	A136	2c + 2c org, grnsh bl & brn	15	15
B36	A136	3c + 2c henna brn & bl	15	15
B37	A136	5c + 2c brown & ultra	15	15
B38	A136	7c + 2c grn, bl & rose brn	15	15
		Set value, #B34-B38, CB21-CB23	1.25	1.25

15th anniv. (in 1961) of UNESCO.

A similar 5c surcharge was applied to the miniature sheets described in the footnote following No. 529. Value, 2 sheets, perf. and imperf., $12.50.

Anti-Malaria Type of 1962

1962, Apr. 29 **Litho.** ***Perf. 12***

B39	A141	10c + 2c brt pink & red lil	18	15
B40	A141	20c + 2c pale brn & brn	30	24

Freedom from Hunger Type of 1963

1963, Apr. 15 **Unwmk.** ***Perf. 11½***

Banner in Dark Blue & Red

B41	A148	2c + 1c green	15	15
B42	A148	5c + 2c brt rose lil	15	15
B43	A148	9c + 2c orange	18	18
		Set value	33	32

A souvenir sheet contains three imperf. stamps similar to #B41-B43. Value, $1.25.

Nos. 591-593 Surcharged

1964, Mar. 8 ***Perf. 12½***

B44	A153	3c + 2c pale pink & ver	15	15
B45	A153	6c + 2c pale blue & ultra	15	15
B46	A153	9c + 2c pale rose & red brn	24	24
		Set value, #B44-B46, CB26-CB27	69	69

UNESCO world campaign to save historic monuments in Nubia.

Nos. 622-626 Surcharged

PRO DAMNIFICADOS CICLON INES

1966, Dec. 9 **Litho.** ***Perf. 12½***

Size: 31x21mm

B47	A164	1c + 2c multi	25	25
B48	A164	2c + 2c multi	20	20
B49	A164	3c + 2c multi	20	20
B50	A164	6c + 4c multi	25	25
B51	A164	8c + 4c multi	35	35
		Nos. B47-B51,CB28-CB30 (8)	3.50	2.70

Surtax for victims of Hurricane Inez.

AIR POST STAMPS

Map of Hispaniola — AP1

Perf. 11½

1928, May 31 **Litho.** **Unwmk.**

C1 AP1 10c deep ultra 4.50 2.50

1930

C2 AP1 10c ocher 3.00 3.00
a. Vert. pair, imperf. btwn. *600.00*
C3 AP1 15c scarlet 6.00 4.00
C4 AP1 20c dull green 2.75 75
C5 AP1 30c violet 6.00 4.75

#C2-C5 have only "CENTAVOS" in lower panel. Issue dates: 10c, 20c, Jan. 24; 15c, 30c, Feb. 14.

1930

C6 AP1 10c light blue 1.50 60
C7 AP1 15c blue green 3.00 90
C8 AP1 20c yellow brown 3.25 45
a. Horiz. pair, imperf. vert. 400.00 400.00
C9 AP1 30c chocolate 5.50 1.50

Issue dates: 10c, 15c, 20c, Sept.; 30c, Oct.

Batwing Sundial Erected in 1753 — AP2

1931-33 *Perf. 12*

C10 AP2 10c carmine 3.25 50
C11 AP2 10c light blue 1.40 45
C12 AP2 10c dark green 5.50 2.50
C13 AP2 15c rose lilac 2.50 45
C14 AP2 20c dark blue 5.50 2.00
a. Numerals reading up at left and down at right 6.00 2.50
b. Imperf., pair 250.00
C15 AP2 30c green 2.25 30
C16 AP2 50c red brown 5.50 60
C17 AP2 1p deep orange 9.00 2.25
Nos. C10-C17 (8) 34.90 9.05

Issue dates: Aug. 16; July 2, 1932; May 28, 1933.

Airplane and Ozama Fortress AP3

1933, Nov. 20

C18 AP3 10c dark blue 3.25 50

Airplane and Trujillo Bridge AP4

1934, Sept. 20

C19 AP4 10c dark blue 2.75 50

Symbolic of Flight — AP5

1935, Apr. 29

C20 AP5 10c lt blue & dk blue 1.40 40

AP6

1936, Feb. 11 *Perf. 11½*

C21 AP6 10c dk bl & turq bl 2.25 40

Allegory of Flight — AP7

1936, Oct. 17

C22 AP7 10c dk bl, bl & turq bl 2.00 30

Macoris Airport AP8

1937, Oct. 22

C23 AP8 10c green 90 15

Fleet of Columbus AP9

Air Fleet AP10

Proposed Columbus Lighthouse AP11

1937, Nov. 9 *Perf. 12*

C24 AP9 10c rose red 1.50 1.25
C25 AP10 15c purple 1.25 90
C26 AP11 20c dk bl & lt bl 1.25 90
C27 AP10 25c red violet 1.75 1.00
C28 AP11 30c yellow green 1.65 1.00
C29 AP10 50c brown 3.25 1.25
C30 AP11 75c dk olive grn 9.00 9.00
C31 AP9 1p orange 5.50 1.75
Nos. C24-C31 (8) 25.15 17.05

Goodwill flight to all American countries by the planes "Colon," "Pinta," "Nina" and "Santa Maria."

#C30 was reproduced imperf. on #1019.

Pan American Clipper AP12

1938, July 30

C32 AP12 10c green 90 15

Trylon and Perisphere, Plane and Proposed Columbus Lighthouse — AP13

1939, Apr. 30

C33 AP13 10c green & lt green 1.25 60

New York World's Fair.

Airplane AP14

1939, Oct. 18

C34 AP14 10c green & dp green 1.40 18
a. Pair, imperf. btwn. *450.00*

Proposed Columbus Lighthouse, Plane and Caravels — AP15

Christopher Columbus and Proposed Lighthouse — AP16

Proposed Lighthouse — AP17

Christopher Columbus — AP18

Caravel — AP19

1940, Oct. 12

C35 AP15 10c sapphire & lt bl 45 45
C36 AP16 15c org brn & brn 70 70
C37 AP17 20c rose red & red 70 70
C38 AP18 25c brt red lil & red vio 70 40
C39 AP19 50c green & lt green 1.40 1.25
Nos. C35-C39 (5) 3.95 3.50

Discovery of America by Columbus and proposed Columbus memorial lighthouse in Dominican Republic.

Posts and Telegraph Building, San Cristobal — AP20

1941, Feb. 21

C40 AP20 10c brt red lil & pale lil rose 40 15

Globe, Wing and Letter AP21

1942, Feb. 13

C41 AP21 10c dark violet brn 48 15
C42 AP21 75c deep orange 3.00 2.00

Plane AP22

1943, Sept. 1

C43 AP22 10c brt red lilac 35 15
C44 AP22 20c dp blue & blue 42 15
C45 AP22 25c yellow olive 4.75 3.00

Plane, Flag, Coat of Arms and Torch of Liberty — AP23

1944, Feb. 27 *Perf. 11½*

Flag in Gray, Dark Blue, Carmine

C46 AP23 10c multicolored 35 15
C47 AP23 20c multicolored 45 15
C48 AP23 1p multicolored 2.00 1.50

Centenary of Independence. See No. 407 for souvenir sheet listing.

Communications Building, Ciudad Trujillo — AP24

1944, Nov. 12 **Litho.** *Perf. 12*

C49 AP24 9c yellow grn & blue 18 15
C50 AP24 13c dull brn & rose car 22 15
C51 AP24 25c orange & dull red 35 15
b. Vert. pair, imperf. btwn. 45.00
C52 AP24 30c black & ultra 75 65
Set value 88

Twenty booklets of 100 (25 panes of 4) of the 25c were issued. Single panes are unknown to experts.

Communications Type of Regular Issue

1945, Sept. 1

Center in Dark Blue and Carmine

C53 A92 7c deep yellow green 18 22
C54 A92 12c red orange 22 15
C55 A92 13c deep blue 28 15
C56 A92 25c orange brown 55 18

AP26

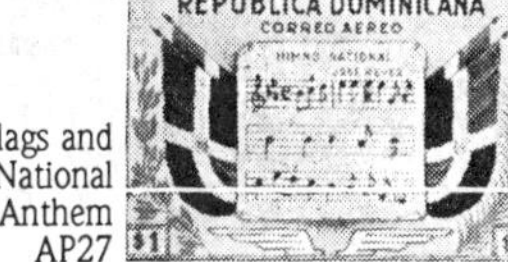

Flags and National Anthem AP27

Unwmk.

1946, Feb. 27 Litho. *Perf. 12*

Center in Dark Blue, Deep Carmine and Black

C57 AP26 10c carmine 42 35
C58 AP26 15c blue 1.00 90
C59 AP26 20c chocolate 1.25 90
C60 AP26 35c orange 1.25 1.00
C61 AP27 1p grn, yel grn & cit 12.00 10.50
Nos. C57-C61 (5) 15.92 13.65

Nos. C57-C61 exist imperf.

Map Type of Regular Issue

1946, Aug. 4

C62 A94 10c multicolored 30 15
C63 A94 13c multicolored 52 15

See note after No. 421.

Waterfall Type of Regular Issue

1947, Mar. 18 Litho.

Center Multicolored

C64 A95 18c light blue 35 35
C65 A95 23c carmine 35 35
C66 A95 50c red violet 35 35
C67 A95 75c chocolate 75 45

Palace Type of Regular Issue

1948, Feb. 27

C68 A96 37c orange brown 75 75
C69 A96 1p orange yellow 2.00 1.50

Ruins Type of Regular Issue

1949 Unwmk. *Perf. 11½*

C70 A97 7c ol grn & pale ol grn 15 15
C71 A97 10c orange brn & buff 15 15
C72 A97 15c brt rose & pale pink 45 22
C73 A97 20c green & pale green 60 42

Issue dates: 10c, Apr. 4; others, Apr. 13.

Las Carreras Monument — AP32

1949, Aug. 10

C74 AP32 10c red & pink 22 15

Cent. of the Battle of Las Carreras.

Catalogue values for unused stamps in this section, from this point to the end of the section, are for Never Hinged items.

Hotel Type of Regular Issue

Hotels: 12c, Montana. 37c, San Cristobal.

1950, Sept. 8

C75 A100 12c dk blue & blue 32 15
C76 A100 37c carmine & pink 2.25 2.00

Map, Plane and Caduceus — AP34

1950, Oct. 2

C77 AP34 12c orange brn & yel 48 15

13th Pan-American Health Conf. Exists imperf.

Hospital Type of Regular Issue

1952, Aug.

C78 A104 23c deep blue 80 1.00
C79 A104 29c carmine 1.75 1.40

Columbus Lighthouse and Plane AP36

Ano Mariano Initials in Monogram AP37

1953, Jan. 6 Engr. *Perf. 13*

C80 AP36 12c ocher 28 20
C81 AP36 14c dark blue 20 15
C82 AP36 20c black brown 60 48
C83 AP36 23c deep plum 35 30
C84 AP36 25c dark blue 70 55
C85 AP36 29c deep green 60 50
C86 AP36 1p red brown 1.40 80
a. Miniature sheet of 10 6.00 6.00
Nos. C80-C86 (7) 4.13 2.98

No. C86a is lithographed and contains Nos. 450-452 and C80-C86, in slightly different shades. Sheet measures 190x130mm and is imperf. with simulated perforations.

A miniature sheet similar to No. C86a, but measuring 200x163mm and in folder, exists. Value $100.

1954, Aug. 5 Litho. *Perf. 11½*

C87 AP37 8c claret 20 15
C88 AP37 11c blue 15 15
C89 AP37 33c brown orange 80 52
Set value 69

Marian Year. Nos. C87-C89 exist imperf.

Rotary Type of Regular Issue, 1955

1955, Feb. 23 *Perf. 12*

C90 A110 11c rose red 35 16

Flags — AP39

Portraits of General Hector B. Trujillo: 25c, In civilian clothes. 33c, In uniform.

1955, May 16 Engr. *Perf. 13½x13*

C91 AP39 11c blue, yel & car 35 15
C92 AP39 25c rose violet 55 32
C93 AP39 33c orange brown 80 48

The center of No. C91 is litho. 25th anniv. of the inauguration of the Trujillo era.

Fair Type of Regular Issue, 1955

1955, Dec. 20 Unwmk. *Perf. 13*

C94 A112 11c vermilion 32 15

ICAO Type of Regular Issue, 1956

1956, Apr. 6 Litho. *Perf. 12½*

C95 A114 11c ultra 28 15

Tree Type of Regular Issue, 1956

Design: 13c, Mahogany tree.

1956, Dec. 8 Litho. *Perf. 11½x12*

C96 A115 13c orange & green 35 15

Type of Regular Issue, 1957

Olympic Winners and Flags: 11c, Paavo Nurmi, Finland. 16c, Ugo Frigerio, Italy. 17c, Mildred Didrikson ("Didrickson" on stamp), US.

Engraved and Lithographed

Perf. 11½, Imperf.

1957, Jan. 24 Unwmk.

Flags in National Colors

C97 A117 11c ultra & red org 16 16
C98 A117 16c carmine & lt grn 20 20
C99 A117 17c black, vio & red 20 20

16th Olympic Games, Melbourne, Nov. 22-Dec. 8, 1956.

Souvenir sheets of 3 exist, perf. and imperf., containing Nos. C97-C99.

Value, 2 sheets, perf. & imperf., $7.

For surcharges see Nos. CB1-CB3, CB16-CB18..

Type of Regular Issue, 1957

Olympic Winners and Flags: 11c, Robert Morrow, US, 100 & 200 meter dash. 16c, Chris Brasher, England, steeplechase. 17c, A. Ferreira Da Silva, Brazil, hop, step and jump.

Perf. 13½, Imperf.

1957, July 18 Photo.

Flags in National Colors

C100 A118 11c yellow grn & dk bl 16 16
C101 A118 16c lilac & dk blue 20 20
C102 A118 17c brown & blue grn 20 20

1956 Olympic winners.

See note on miniature sheets following No. 483.

For surcharges see Nos. CB4-CB6.

Types of Regular Issue, 1957

Olympic Winners and Flags: 11c, Hans Winkler, Germany, individual jumping. 16c, Alfred Oerter, US, discus throw. 17c, Shirley Strickland, Australia, 800 meter hurdles.

Engraved and Lithographed

Perf. 13½, Imperf.

1957, Nov. 12 Unwmk.

Flags in National Colors

C103 A119 11c ultra 16 16
C104 A120 16c rose carmine 20 20
C105 A119 17c claret 20 20

1956 Olympic winners.

Miniature sheets of 3 exist, perf. and imperf., containing Nos. C103-C105. Value, 2 sheets, perf. and imperf., $5.50.

For surcharges see Nos. CB7-CB12.

Type of Regular Issue, 1958

Olympic Winners and Flags: 11c, Charles Jenkins, 400 & 800 meter run, and Thomas Courtney, 1,600 meter relay, US. 16c, Field hockey team, India. 17c, Yachting team, Sweden.

Perf. 13½, Imperf.

1958, Oct. 30 Unwmk. Photo.

Flags in National Colors

C106 A125 11c blue, olive & brn 16 16
C107 A125 16c lt grn, org & dk bl 20 20
C108 A125 17c ver, blue & yel 20 20

1956 Olympic winners.

Miniature sheets of 3 exist, perf. and imperf., containing Nos. C106-C108. Value, 2 sheets, perf. and imperf., $3.

For surcharges see Nos. CB13-CB15.

Fair Type of Regular Issue, 1958

1958, Dec. 9 Litho. *Perf. 12½*

C109 A127 9c gray 24 16
C110 A127 25c lt violet 60 35
a. Souv. sheet of 3, #C109-C110, 507, imperf. 1.75 1.40

Polo Type of Regular Issue, 1959

Design: 11c, Dominican polo team.

1959, May 15 *Perf. 12*

C111 A130 11c orange 35 32

"San Cristobal" Plane — AP42

Perf. 11½

1960, Feb. 25 Unwmk. Litho.

C112 AP42 13c org, bl, grn & gray 28 15

Dominican Civil Aviation.

Children and WRY Emblem AP43

1960, Apr. 7 *Perf. 12½*

C113 AP43 10c plum, gray & grn 32 28
C114 AP43 13c gray & green 40 32

Issued to publicize World Refugee Year, July 1, 1959-June 30, 1960.

For surcharges see Nos. CB19-CB20.

Olympic Type of Regular Issue

Olympic Winners: 11c, Pat McCormick, US, diving. 16c, Mithat Bayrack, Turkey, welterweight wrestling. 17c, Ursula Happe, Germany, 200 meter breast stroke.

Perf. 13½, Imperf.

1960, Sept. 14 Photo.

Flags in National Colors

C115 A136 11c blue, gray & brn 15 15
C116 A136 16c red, brown & ol 15 15
C117 A136 17c black, blue & ocher 15 15
Set value 24

17th Olympic Games, Rome, Aug. 25-Sept. 11.

Miniature sheets of 3 exist, perf. and imperf., containing Nos. C115-C117. Value, 2 sheets, perf. and imperf., $3.75.

For surcharges see Nos. CB21-CB23.

Coffee-Cacao Type of Regular Issue

1961, Dec. 30 Litho. *Perf. 12½*

C118 A140 13c orange ver 24 24
C119 A140 33c brt yellow 52 52

Exist imperf.

Anti-Malaria Type of Regular Issue

1962, Apr. 29 Unwmk. *Perf. 12*

C120 A141 13c pink & red 22 18
C121 A141 33c orange & dp orange 45 45

See Nos. CB24-CB25.

Type of Regular Issue, 1962

Designs: 13c, Broken fetters and laurel. 50c, Flag, torch and inscription.

1962, May 30 *Perf. 12½*

C122 A142 13c brn, yel, ol, ultra & red 28 22
C123 A142 50c rose lilac, ultra & red 1.05 75

No. C122 exists imperf.

UPAE Type of Regular Issue, 1962

1962, Oct. 23 *Perf. 12½*

C124 A146 13c bright blue 30 18
C125 A146 22c dull red brown 30 50

Exist imperf.

Nouel Type of Regular Issue, 1962

Design: Frame altered with rosary and cross surrounding portrait.

1962, Dec. 18

C126 A147 13c blue & pale blue 35 18
C127 A147 25c vio & pale vio 48 55
a. Souv. sheet of 2, #C126-C127, imperf. 75 75

Exist imperf.

Sanchez, Duarte, Mella — AP44

1963, July 7 Litho. *Perf. 11½x12*

C128 AP44 15c orange 24 18

120th anniv. of separation from Haiti.

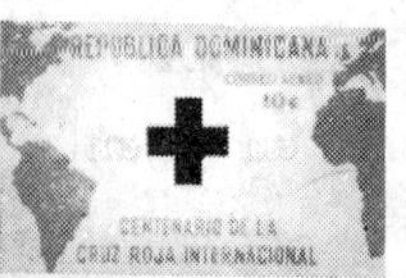

World Map — AP45

1963, Oct. 25 Unwmk. *Perf. 12½*

C129 AP45 10c gray & carmine 24 22

Cent. of Intl. Red Cross. Exists imperf.

Human Rights Type of Regular Issue

1963, Dec. 10 **Litho.**

C130 A152 7c fawn & red brn 18 15
C131 A152 10c lt blue & blue 22 15

Exist imperf.

Ramses II Battling the Hittites (from Abu Simbel) — AP46

1964, Mar. 8 ***Perf. 12½***

C132 AP46 10c brt violet 22 15
C133 AP46 13c yellow 24 22

UNESCO world campaign to save historic monuments in Nubia. Exist imperf.

For surcharges see Nos. CB26-CB27.

Striated Woodpecker — AP47

1964, June 8 **Litho.**

C134 AP47 10c multicolored 35 18

Type of Space Issue, 1964

Designs: 7c, Rocket leaving earth. 10c, Space capsule orbiting earth.

1964, July 28 **Unwmk.** ***Perf. 12½***

C135 A156 7c brt green 24 15
C136 A156 10c violet blue 30 24
a. Souvenir sheet 3.00 3.00

No. C136a contains 7c and 10c stamps similar to Nos. C135-C136 with simulated perforation.

Pres. John F. Kennedy — AP48

1964, Nov. 22 ***Perf. 11½***

C137 AP48 10c buff & dk brown 42 24

President John F. Kennedy (1917-63). Sheets of 10 (5x2) and sheets of 50.

UPU Type of Regular Issue

1964, Dec. 5 **Litho.** ***Perf. 12½***

C138 A157 7c blue 15 15

ICY Type of Regular Issue, 1965

1965, Feb. 16 **Unwmk.** ***Perf. 12½***

C139 A158 10c lilac & violet 22 18

Basilica of Our Lady of Altagracia AP49

1965, Mar. 18 **Unwmk.** ***Perf. 12½***

C140 AP49 10c multicolored 30 22

Fourth Mariological Congress and the Eleventh International Marian Congress.

Abraham Lincoln — AP50

1965, Apr. 15 **Litho.** ***Perf. 12½***

C141 AP50 17c bright blue 35 35

Cent. of the death of Abraham Lincoln.

Stamp Centenary Type of 1965

Design: Stamp of 1865, (No. 2).

1965, Dec. 28 **Litho.** ***Perf. 12½***

C142 A161 7c violet, lt grn & blk 22 18
C143 A161 10c yellow, lt grn & blk 24 22

ITU Emblem, Old and New Communication Equipment AP51

1966, Apr. 6 **Litho.** ***Perf. 12½***

C144 AP51 28c pink & carmine 60 60
C145 AP51 45c brt green & green 90 90

Cent. (in 1965) of the ITU.

Butterfly Type of Regular Issue

1966, Nov. 8 **Litho.** ***Perf. 12½***

Various Butterflies in Natural Colors

Size: 35x24mm

C146 A164 10c lt violet & violet 1.00 18
C147 A164 50c orange & dp orange 2.00 75
C148 A164 75c pink & rose red 2.00 90

For surcharges see Nos. CB28-CB30.

Altar Type of Regular Issue

1967, Jan. 18 **Litho.** ***Perf. 11½***

C149 A165 7c lt olive green 15 15
C150 A165 10c lilac 16 15
C151 A165 20c yellow brown 28 22
Set value 43

Chess Type of Regular Issue

Design: 10c, Pawn and Bishop.

1967, June 23 **Litho.** ***Perf. 12½***

C152 A167 10c olive, lt olive & blk 35 22
a. Souvenir sheet 1.00 1.00

No. C152a contains 2 imperf. stamps similar to Nos. 636 and C152.

Alliance for Progress Type

1967, Sept. 16 **Litho.** ***Perf. 12½***

C153 A168 8c gray 18 18
C154 A168 10c blue 18 15

Cornucopia and Emblem — AP52

Latin American Flags — AP53

1967, Oct. 7

C155 AP52 12c multicolored 22 15

25th anniversary of the Inter-American Agriculture Institute.

Satellite Type of Regular Issue

1968, June 15 **Typo.** ***Perf. 12***

C156 A170 10c dp blue & multi 24 18
C157 A170 15c purple & multi 35 28

Boxing Type of Regular Issue

Designs: Two views of boxing match.

1968, June 29

C158 A171 7c orange yel & grn 16 15
C159 A171 10c gray & blue 22 15

See note after No. 641.

Lions Type of Regular Issue

1968, Aug. 9 **Litho.** ***Perf. 11½***

C160 A172 10c ultra & multi 22 15

Olympic Type of Regular Issue

Designs (Olympic Emblem and): 10c, Weight lifting. 33c, Pistol shooting.

1968, Nov. 12 **Litho.** ***Perf. 11½***

C161 A173 10c buff & multi 25 22
C162 A173 33c pink & multi 75 60

1969, Jan. 25 **Litho.** ***Perf. 12½***

C163 AP53 10c pink & multi 22 15

7th Inter-American Savings and Loan Conference, Santo Domingo, Jan. 25-31.

Taino Art Type of Regular Issue

Taino Art: 7c, Various vomiting spoons with human heads, vert. 10c, Female torso forming drinking vessel. 20c, Vase with human head, vert.

1969, Jan. 31 **Litho.** ***Perf. 12½***

C164 A175 7c lt bl, bl & lem 18 18
C165 A175 10c pink, ver & brn 24 18
C166 A175 20c yellow, org & brn 32 30

COTAL Type of Regular Issue

Design: 10c, Airport of the Americas and COTAL emblem.

1969, May 25 **Litho.** ***Perf. 12½***

C167 A178 10c brown & pale fawn 22 15

See note after No. 655.

ILO Type of Regular Issue

1969, June 27 **Litho.** ***Perf. 12½***

C168 A179 10c rose, red & black 18 15

Baseball Type of Regular Issue

Designs: 7c, Bleachers, Tetelo Vargas Stadium, horiz. 10c, Batter, catcher and umpire. 1p, Quisqueya Stadium, horiz.

1969, Aug. 15 **Litho.** ***Perf. 12½***

Size: 43x30mm (7c, 1p); 21x31mm (10c)

C169 A180 7c magenta & org 40 22
C170 A180 10c maroon & rose red 45 24
C171 A180 1p violet blue & brn 2.25 1.75

Electrification Types of Regular Issue

Design: No. C172, Rio Haina steam plant. No. C173, Valdesa Dam.

1969 **Litho.** ***Perf. 12***

C172 A181 10c orange ver 18 15
C173 A182 10c multicolored 35 15
Set value 21

Issue dates: #C172, Sept. 15; #C173, Oct. 15.

Duarte Type of Regular Issue

1970, Jan. 26 **Litho.** ***Perf. 12***

C174 A183 10c brown & dk brown 18 15

Census Type of Regular Issue

Design: 10c, Buildings and census emblem.

1970, Feb. 6 ***Perf. 11***

C175 A184 10c lt blue & multi 22 15

Sculpture Type of Regular Issue

Design: 10c, The Prisoner, by Abelardo Rodriguez Urdaneta, vert.

1970, Feb. 20 **Litho.** ***Perf. 12½***

C176 A186 10c bluish gray 30 15

Masonic Type of Regular Issue

1970, Mar. 2

C177 A187 10c brown 15 15

Satellite Type of Regular Issue

1970, May 25 **Litho.** ***Perf. 12½***

C178 A188 7c blue & gray 18 15

UPU Type of Regular Issue

1970, June 5 ***Perf. 11***

C179 A189 10c yellow & brown 18 15

Education Year Type of Regular Issue

1970, June 26 **Litho.** ***Perf. 12½***

C180 A190 15c bright pink 22 15

Dancers — AP54

Album, Globe and Emblem — AP55

Design: 10c, UN emblem and wheel.

1970, Oct. 12 **Litho.** ***Perf. 12½***

C181 AP54 7c blue & multi 22 15
C182 AP54 10c pink & multi 24 15
Set value 22

1st World Exhib. of Books and Culture Festival, Santo Domingo, Oct. 11-Dec. 11.

1970, Oct. 26 **Litho.** ***Perf. 11***

C183 AP55 10c multicolored 24 15

Issued to publicize EXFILCA 70, 2nd Interamerican Philatelic Exhibition, Caracas, Venezuela, Nov. 27-Dec. 6.

Basilica of Our Lady of Altagracia — AP56

1971, Jan. 20 **Litho.** ***Perf. 12½***

C184 AP56 17c multicolored 40 22

Inauguration of the Basilica of Our Lady of Altagracia.

Map of Dominican Republic, CARE Package — AP57

1971, May 28 **Litho.** ***Perf. 12½***

C185 AP57 10c blue & green 15 15

25th anniversary of CARE, a US-Canadian Cooperative for American Relief Everywhere.

Sports Type of Regular Issue

1971, Sept. 10 ***Perf. 11***

C186 A195 7c Volleyball 20 20

Animal Type of Regular Issue

Design: 25c, Cock and grain.

1971, Sept. 29 ***Perf. 12½***

C187 A196 25c black & multi 50 30

Independence Type of Regular Issue

Design: 10c, Dominican-Colombian flag of 1821.

1971, Dec. 1 ***Perf. 11***

C188 A197 10c vio bl, yel & red 22 15

Christmas Type of Regular Issue

1971, Dec. 10 ***Perf. 12½***

C189 A198 10c Bell, 1493 20 15

UNICEF Type of Regular Issue

Design: 15c, UNICEF emblem and child on beach.

1971, Dec. 14 ***Perf. 11***

C190 A199 15c multicolored 30 30

Book Year Type of Regular Issue

1972, Jan. 25 Litho. *Perf. 12½*
C191 A200 12c lilac, dk bl & red 20 20

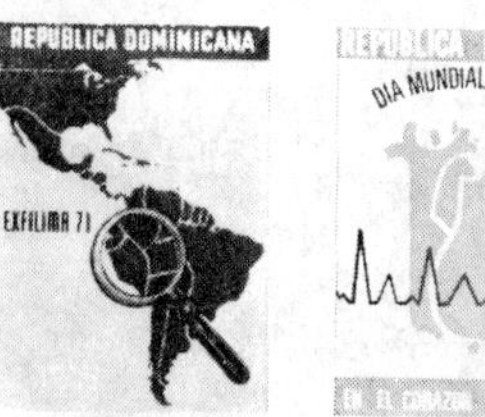

Magnifying Glass over Peru on Map of Americas — AP58

"Your Heart is your Health" — AP59

1972, Mar. 7 Litho. *Perf. 12*
C192 AP58 10c blue & multi 30 22

EXFILIMA '71, 3rd Inter-American Philatelic Exposition, Lima, Peru, Nov. 6-14, 1971.

1972, Apr. 27 Litho. *Perf. 11*
C193 AP59 7c red & multi 25 15

World Health Day.

Taino Art Type of 1972

Taino Art: 8c, Ritual vessel showing human figures. 10c, Trumpet (shell). 25c, Carved vomiting spoons. All horiz.

1972, May 10 Litho. *Perf. 11*
C194 A201 8c multicolored 15 15
C195 A201 10c lt blue & multi 28 15
C196 A201 25c multicolored 45 24
Set value 39

Telecommunications Type of Regular Issue

1972, May 17 *Perf. 12½*
C197 A202 21c yellow & multi 40 22

Exhibition Type of Regular Issue

1972, June 3
C198 A203 33c orange & multi 60 40

Olympic Type of Regular Issue

1972, Aug. 25 Litho. *Perf. 12½*
C199 A204 33c Running 65 50

Club Type of Regular Issue

1972, Sept. 29 Litho. *Perf. 10½*
C200 A205 20c blue & multi 40 25

Morel Type of Regular Issue

1972, Oct. 20 Litho. *Perf. 12½*
C201 A206 10c multicolored 20 15

Bank Type of Regular Issue

Design: 25c, Silver coin, 1947, and entrance to the Mint.

1972, Oct. 23
C202 A207 25c ocher & multi 45 22

"La Navidad" Fortress, 1492 AP60

1972, Nov. 21 Litho. *Perf. 12½*
C203 AP60 10c multicolored 18 15

Christmas 1972.

Sports Type of Regular Issue

Designs: Various sports; a, UL. b, UR. c, LL. d, LR.

1973, Mar. 30 Litho. *Perf. 13½x13*
C204 A212 Block of 4 1.00 1.00
a.-d. 8c, any single 24 24
C205 A212 Block of 4 2.00 1.25
a.-d. 10c, any single 50 30

Easter Type 1973

Design: 10c, Belfry of Church of Our Lady of Help.

1973, Apr. 18 Litho. *Perf. 10½*
C206 A213 10c multicolored 24 15

North and South America on Globe — AP61

1973, May 29 Litho. *Perf. 12*
C207 AP61 7c multicolored 25 15

Pan-American Health Organization, 70th anniversary (in 1972).

WMO Type of Regular Issue

1973, Aug. 10 Litho. *Perf. 13½x13*
C208 A214 7c green & multi 25 15

INTERPOL Emblem Police Scientist AP62

1973, Sept. 28 Litho. *Perf. 10½*
C209 AP62 10c vio bl, bl & emer 18 15

50th anniversary of International Criminal Police Organization.

Handicraft Type of Regular Issue

1973, Oct. 12
C210 A215 7c Sailing ship, mosaic 15 15
C211 A215 10c Maracas rattles, horiz. 25 15
Set value 21

Christmas Type of Regular Issue

Design: 10c, Angels adoring Christ Child.

1973, Nov. 26 Litho. *Perf. 13½x13*
C212 A216 10c multicolored 22 15

Scout Type of Regular Issue

Design: 21c, Scouts cooking and Lord Baden-Powell.

1973, Dec. 7 Litho. *Perf. 12*
C213 A217 21c red & multi 35 35

Sport Type of Regular Issue

Designs: 10c, Olympic swimming pool and diver. 25c, Olympic Stadium, soccer and discus.

1974, Feb. 25 Litho. *Perf. 13½*
C214 A218 10c blue & multi 15 15
C215 A218 25c multicolored 40 18
Set value 24

The Last Supper AP63

1974, June 27 Litho. *Perf. 13½*
C216 AP63 10c multicolored 24 15

Holy Week 1974.

Bridge Type of 1974

Design: 10c, Higuamo Bridge.

1974, July 12 *Perf. 12*
C217 A221 10c multicolored 22 15

Diabetes Type of 1974

Designs (Map of Dominican Republic, Diabetics' Emblem and): 7c, Kidney. 33c, Eye and heart.

1974, Aug. 22 Litho. *Perf. 13*
C218 A222 7c yellow & multi 25 25
C219 A222 33c lt blue & multi 1.00 75

UPU Type of 1974

1974, Oct. 9 Litho. *Perf. 13½*
C220 A223 7c Ships 15 15
C221 A223 33c Jet 50 24
a. Souvenir sheet of 4 85 45

No. C221a contains Nos. 727-728, C220-C221 forming continuous design.

Golfers and Championship Emblem — AP64

Design: 20c, Golfer and Golf Association emblem.

1974, Oct. 24 Litho. *Perf. 13x13½*
C222 AP64 10c green & multi 28 18
C223 AP64 20c green & multi 45 40

World Amateur Golf Championships.

Hand Holding Dove — AP65

1974, Dec. 3 Litho. *Perf. 12*
C224 AP65 10c multicolored 26 15

Christmas 1974.

FAO Type of 1974

Design: 10c, Bee, beehive and barrel of honey.

1974, Dec. 5
C225 A227 10c multicolored 24 15

Chrismon, Lamb, Candle and Palm — AP66

Spain No. 1, España 75 Emblem — AP67

1975, Mar. 26 Litho. *Perf. 13½*
C226 AP66 10c gold & multi 26 15

Holy Week 1975.

1975, Apr. 10
C227 AP67 12c red, yel & blk 25 15

Espana 75, International Philatelic Exhibition, Madrid, Apr. 4-13.

Development Bank Type of 1975

1975, May 19 Litho. *Perf. 10½x10*
C228 A230 10c rose car & multi 22 18

Three Satellites and Globe AP68

1975, June 21 Litho. *Perf. 13½*
C229 AP68 15c multicolored 35 35

Opening of first earth satellite tracking station in Dominican Republic.

Apollo Type of 1975

Design: 2p, Apollo-Soyuz link-up over earth.

1975, July 24 *Perf. 13*
Size: 42x28mm
C230 A232 2p multicolored 2.50 2.50

Indian Chief Type of 1975

Designs: 7c, Mayobanex. 8c, Cotubanama and Juan de Esquivel. 10c, Enriquillo and Mencia.

1975, Sept. 27 Litho. *Perf. 12*
C231 A235 7c lt green & multi 20 15
C232 A235 8c orange & multi 30 25
C233 A235 10c gray & multi 30 18

Volleyball AP69

Design: 10c, Weight lifting and Games' emblem.

1975, Oct. 24 Litho. *Perf. 12*
C234 AP69 7c blue & multi 18 15
C235 AP69 10c multicolored 26 18

7th Pan-American Games, Mexico City, Oct. 13-26.

Christmas Type of 1975

Design: 10c, Dove and peace message.

1975, Dec. 12 Litho. *Perf. 13x13½*
C236 A237 10c yellow & multi 24 15

Valdesia Dam AP70

1976, Jan. 26 Litho. *Perf. 13*
C237 AP70 10c multicolored 25 15

Holy Week Type 1976

Design: 10c, Crucifixion, by Eliezer Castillo.

1976, Apr. 14 Litho. *Perf. 13½*
C238 A239 10c multicolored 28 18

Bicentennial Type of 1976 and

George Washington, Independence Hall — AP71

Design: 10c, Hands holding maps of US and Dominican Republic.

1976, May 29 Litho. *Perf. 13½*

C239 A241 10c vio bl, grn & blk 25 15
C240 AP71 75c black & orange 75 75

American Bicentennial; No. C240 also for Interphil 76 International Philatelic Exhibition, Philadelphia, Pa., May 29-June 6.

King Juan Carlos I and Queen Sofia — AP72

1976, May 31

C241 AP72 21c multicolored 55 50

Visit of King Juan Carlos I and Queen Sofia of Spain.

Telephone Type of 1976

Design: 10c, Alexander Graham Bell and telephones, 1876 and 1976.

1976, July 15

C242 A243 10c multicolored 22 15

Duarte Types of 1976

Designs: 10c, Scroll with Duarte letter and Dominican flag. 33c, Duarte leaving for Exile, by E. Godoy.

1976, July 20 Litho. *Perf. 13½*

C243 A245 10c blue & multi 22 15

Perf. 13x13½

C244 A244 33c brown & multi 75 60

Fire Engine AP73

1976, Sept. 13 Litho. *Perf. 12*

C245 AP73 10c multicolored 20 15

Honoring firemen.

Radio Club Type of 1976

1976, Oct. 8 Litho. *Perf. 13½*

C246 A247 10c blue & black 24 15

Various People — AP74

1976, Oct. 22 Litho. *Perf. 13½*

C247 AP74 21c multicolored 35 35

Spanish heritage.

Olympic Games Type of 1976

Design (Montreal Olympic Games Emblem and): 10c, Running. 25c, Basketball.

1976, Oct. 22 *Perf. 12*

C248 A249 10c ocher & multi 18 15
C249 A249 25c green & multi 35 25

Christmas Type of 1976

Design: 10c, Angel with bells.

1976, Dec. 8 Litho. *Perf. 13½*

C250 A251 10c multicolored 25 18

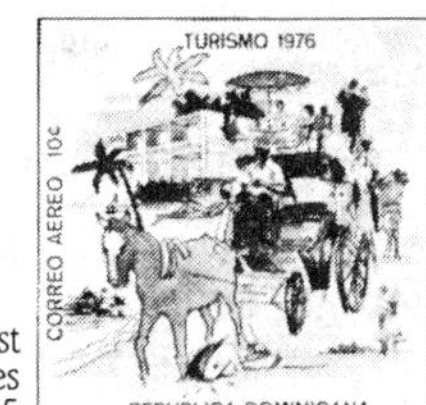

Tourist Activities AP75

Tourist publicity: 12c, Angling and hotel. 25c, Horseback riding and waterfall, vert.

1977, Jan. 7

Size: 36x36mm

C251 AP75 10c multicolored 20 15

Size: 34x25½mm, 25½x34mm

C252 AP75 12c multicolored 20 15
C253 AP75 25c multicolored 48 25

Championship Type of 1977

1977, Mar. 4 Litho. *Perf. 13½*

C254 A253 10c yel grn & multi 22 15
C255 A253 25c lt brown & multi 32 15

Holy Week Type 1977

Design: 10c, Belfry and open book.

1977, Apr. 18 Litho. *Perf. 13½x13*

C256 A254 10c multicolored 24 15

Lions Type of 1977

1977, May 6 *Perf. 13½x13*

C257 A255 7c lt green & multi 15 15

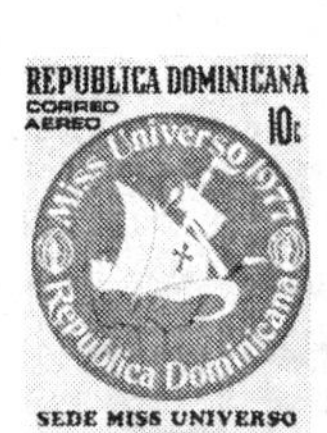

Caravel under Sail — AP76 Melon Cactus — AP77

1977, July 16 Litho. *Perf. 13*

C258 AP76 10c multicolored 22 15

Miss Universe Contest, held in Dominican Republic.

1977, Aug. 19 Litho. *Perf. 12*

Design: 33c, Coccothrinax (tree).

C259 AP77 7c multicolored 18 15
C260 AP77 33c multicolored 25 18

National Botanical Garden.

Chart and Factories — AP78

1977, Nov. 30 Litho. *Perf. 13x13½*

C261 AP78 28c multicolored 50 50

7th Interamerican Statistics Conference.

Animal Type of 1977

Designs (Congress Emblem and): 10c, "Dorado," red Roman stud bull. 25c, Flamingo, vert.

1977, Dec. 29 Litho. *Perf. 13*

C262 A259 10c multicolored 22 15
C263 A259 25c multicolored 45 30

Spanish Heritage Type of 1978

Design: 21c, Window, Casa del Tostado, 16th century.

1978, Jan. 19 *Perf. 13x13½*

Size: 28x41mm

C264 A260 21c multicolored 42 35

Holy Week Type, 1978

Designs: 7c, Facade, Santo Domingo Cathedral. 10c, Facade of Dominican Convent.

1978, Mar. 21 Litho. *Perf. 12*

Size: 27x36mm

C265 A261 7c multicolored 20 15
C266 A261 10c multicolored 30 18

Schooner Duarte AP79

1978, Apr. 15 Litho. *Perf. 13½*

C267 AP79 7c multicolored 15 15

Dominican naval forces training ship.

Cardinal Type of 1978

1978, May 5 Litho. *Perf. 13*

C268 A262 10c multicolored 25 15

Antenna AP80

1978, May 17 Litho. *Perf. 13½*

C269 AP80 25c silver & multi 45 30

10th World Telecommunications Day.

No. C1 and Map — AP81

1978, June 6

C270 AP81 10c multicolored 24 15

50th anniversary of first Dominican Republic airmail stamp.

Globe, Soccer Ball, Emblem — AP82 Crown, Cross and Rosary Emblem — AP83

Design: 33c, Soccer field, Argentina '78 emblem and globe.

1978, June 29

C271 AP82 12c multicolored 35 30
C272 AP82 33c multicolored 70 70

11th World Cup Soccer Championship, Argentina, June 1-25.

1978, July 11 *Perf. 13x13½*

C273 AP83 21c multicolored 35 35

Congregation of the Merciful Sisters of Charity, centenary.

Sports Type of 1978

Designs (Games' Emblem and): 7c, Baseball, vert. 10c, Soccer, vert.

1978, July 21 Litho. *Perf. 13½*

C274 A265 7c multicolored 15 15
C275 A265 10c multicolored 25 18

Wright Brothers and Glider, 1902 — AP84

Designs: 7c, Diagrams of Flyer I and jet, vert. 13c, Diagram of air flow over wing. 45c, Flyer I over world map.

1978, Aug. 8 *Perf. 12*

C276 AP84 7c multicolored 22 18
C277 AP84 10c multicolored 28 15
C278 AP84 13c multicolored 42 38
C279 AP84 45c multicolored 75 75

75th anniversary of first powered flight.

Tourist Type of 1978

Designs: 7c, Sun and musical instruments. 10c, Sun and plane over Santo Domingo.

1978, Sept. 12 Litho. *Perf. 12*

C280 A266 7c multicolored 15 15
C281 A266 10c multicolored 18 18
Set value 25

People and Globe AP85

1978, Oct. 12 Litho. *Perf. 13½*

C282 AP85 21c multicolored 40 40

Spanish heritage.

REPUBLICA DOMINICANA
1956-1978
22 años de apoyo al desarrollo dominicano
Programa de Naciones Unidas para el desarrollo
33c
33 ANIVERSARIO ONU

Dominican Republic and UN Flags — AP86

1978, Oct. 23 *Perf. 12*

C283 AP86 33c multicolored 60 60

33rd anniversary of the United Nations.

Statue of the Virgin — AP87 Pope John Paul II — AP88

1978, Dec. 5 Litho. *Perf. 12*

C284 AP87 10c multicolored 28 22

Christmas 1978.

1979, Jan. 25 Litho. *Perf. 13½*

C285 AP88 10c multicolored 3.00 3.00

Visit of Pope John Paul II to the Dominican Republic, Jan. 25-26.

Map of Beata Island — AP89

1979, Jan. 25 ***Perf. 12***
C286 AP89 10c multicolored 18 15

1st expedition of radio amateurs to Beata Is.

Year of the Child Type, 1979

Designs (ICY Emblem and): 7c, Children reading book. 10c, Symbolic head and protective hands. 33c, Hands and jars.

1979, Feb. 26
C287 A269 7c multicolored 18 15
C288 A269 10c multicolored 25 15
C289 A269 33c multicolored 60 60

Pope John Paul II Giving Benediction
AP90

Adm. Juan Bautista Cambiaso
AP91

1979, Apr. 9 **Litho.** ***Perf. 13½***
C290 AP90 10c multicolored 1.00 75

Holy Week.

1979, Apr. 14 ***Perf. 12***
C291 AP91 10c multicolored 18 15

135th anniv. of the Battle of Tortuguero.

Map of Dominican Rep., Album, Magnifier
AP92

1979, Apr. 18
C292 AP92 33c multicolored 60 60

EXFILNA, 3rd National Philatelic Exhibition, Apr. 18-22.

Flower Type of 1979

Designs: 7c, Passionflower. 10c, Isidorea pungens. 13c, Calotropis procera.

1979, May 17 **Litho.** ***Perf. 12***
C293 A271 7c multicolored 20 20
C294 A271 10c multicolored 30 18
C295 A271 13c multicolored 40 35

Cardiology Type, 1979

Design: 10c, Figure of man showing blood circulation, vert.

1979, June 2 **Litho.** ***Perf. 13½***
C296 A272 10c multicolored 24 15

Sports Type of 1979

Design: 7c, Runner and Games' emblem, vert.

1979, June 20
C297 A273 7c multicolored 20 18

Soccer Type of 1979

1979, Aug. 9 **Litho.** ***Perf. 12***
C298 A273 10c Tennis, vert. 30 20

Rowland Hill, Dominican Republic No. 1 — AP93

1979, Aug. 21 ***Perf. 13½***
C299 AP93 2p multicolored 3.00 2.50

Sir Rowland Hill (1795-1879), originator of penny postage.

Electric Light Type of 1979

Design: 10c, "100" and light bulb, horiz.

1979, Aug. 27 ***Perf. 13½***
C300 A275 10c multicolored 30 20

Bird Type of 1979

Birds: 7c, Phaenicophilus palmarum. 10c, Calyptophilus frugivorus tertius. 45c, Icterus dominicensis.

1979, Sept. 12 **Litho.** ***Perf. 12***
C301 A277 7c multicolored 25 22
C302 A277 10c multicolored 35 22
C303 A277 45c multicolored 90 60

Lions Type of 1979

Design: 10c, Melvin Jones, organization founder.

1979, Nov. 13 **Litho.** ***Perf. 12***
C304 A278 10c multicolored 25 15

Christmas Type of 1979

Christmas: 10c, Three Kings riding camels.

1979, Dec. 18 **Litho.** ***Perf. 12***
C305 A279 10c multicolored 24 18

Holy Week Type of 1980

1980, Mar. 27 **Litho.** ***Perf. 12***
C306 A280 7c Crucifixion 16 15
C307 A280 10c Resurrection 25 18

Navy Day — AP94

1980, Apr. 15 **Litho.** ***Perf. 13½***
C308 AP94 21c multicolored 40 30

Dominican Philatelic Society, 25th Anniversary
AP95

1980, Apr. 18
C309 AP95 10c multicolored 18 15

Gold Type of 1980

1980, July 8 **Litho.** ***Perf. 13½***
C310 A282 10c Drag line mining 35 35
C311 A282 33c Mine 60 55

Tourism Secretariat Emblem — AP96

1980, Aug. 26 **Litho.** ***Perf. 13½***
C312 AP96 10c shown 28 26
C313 AP96 33c Conf. emblem 90 75

World Tourism Conf., Manila, Sept. 27.

Iguana Type of 1980

1980, Aug. 30 ***Perf. 12***
C314 A284 7c American crocodile 25 25
C315 A284 10c Cuban rat 28 28
C316 A284 25c Manatee 45 40
C317 A284 45c Turtle 65 65

Painting Type of 1980

1980, Sept. 23 **Litho.** ***Perf. 13½x13***
C318 A285 10c Abstract, by Paul Guidicelli, vert. 28 22
C319 A285 17c Farmer, by Yoryi Morel, vert. 42 35

Visit of Radio Amateurs to Catalina Island
AP97

1980, Oct. 3
C320 AP97 7c multicolored 24 22

Rotary International, 75th Anniversary
AP98

1980, Oct. 23 **Litho.** ***Perf. 12***
C321 AP98 10c Globe, emblem, vert. 32 28
C322 AP98 33c shown 60 60

Carrier Pigeons, UPU Emblem
AP99

1980, Oct. 31 ***Perf. 13½***
C323 AP99 33c shown 30 22
C324 AP99 45c Pigeons, diff. 40 28
C325 AP99 50c Pigeon, stamp 65 40

Souvenir Sheet

Imperf

C326 AP99 1.10p UPU emblem 1.10 1.00

UPU cent. No. C326 contains one 48½x31mm stamp.

Christmas Type of 1980

1980, Dec. 5 **Litho.** ***Perf. 13½***
C327 A286 10c Holy Family 28 22

Christmas 1980.

Salcedo Type of 1981

Design: Map and arms of Salcedo.

1981, Jan. 14 **Litho.** ***Perf. 13½***
C328 A287 10c multicolored 24 20

AP100

AP101

Design: Industrial Symbols, Seminar Emblem.

1981, Feb. 18 **Litho.** ***Perf. 13½***
C329 AP100 10c shown 25 24
C330 AP100 33c Seminar emblem 42 24

CODIA Chemical Engineering Seminar.

National Games Type of 1981

1981, Mar. 31 **Litho.** ***Perf. 13½***
C331 A289 10c Baseball 20 15

1981, Apr. 15

Design: Admiral Juan Alejandro Acosta.

C332 AP101 10c multicolored 18 15

Battle of Tortuguero anniversary.

13th World Telecommunications Day — AP102

1981, May 16 **Litho.** ***Perf. 12***
C333 AP102 10c multicolored 22 15

Heinrich von Stephan
AP103

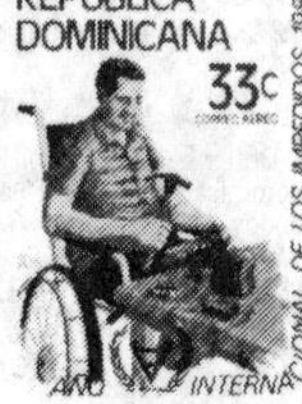

Worker in Wheelchair
AP104

1981, July 15 **Litho.** ***Perf. 13½***
C334 AP103 33c tan & lt red brn 60 60

Birth sesquicentennial of Universal Postal Union founder.

1981, July 24
C335 AP104 7c Stylized people 25 25
C336 AP104 33c shown 60 60

Intl. Year of the Disabled.

EXPURIDOM '81 Intl. Stamp Show, Santo Domingo, July 31-Aug. 2 — AP105

1981, July 31
C337 AP105 7c multicolored 15 15

Bullet Holes in Target, Competition Emblem
AP106

1981, Aug. 12
C338 AP106 10c shown 18 15
C339 AP106 15c Riflemen 28 24
C340 AP106 25c Pistol shooting 45 40

2nd World Sharpshooting Championship.

Exports — AP107

World Food Day — AP108

1981, Oct. 16 Litho. *Perf. 12*

C341 AP107 7c Jewelry 24 22
C342 AP107 10c Handicrafts 28 22
C343 AP107 11c Fruit 26 20
C344 AP107 17c Vegetables 42 30

1981, Oct. 16 Litho. *Perf. 13½*

C345 AP108 10c Fruits 35 18
C346 AP108 50c Vegetables 80 70

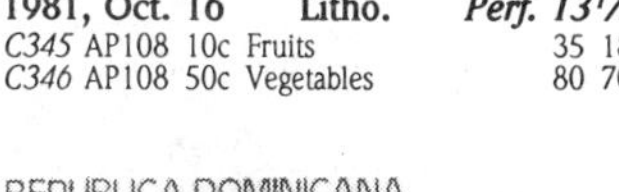

5th Natl. Games AP109

1981, Dec. 5 Litho. *Perf. 13½*

C347 AP109 10c Javelin, vert. 24 22
C348 AP109 50c Cycling 1.25 1.25

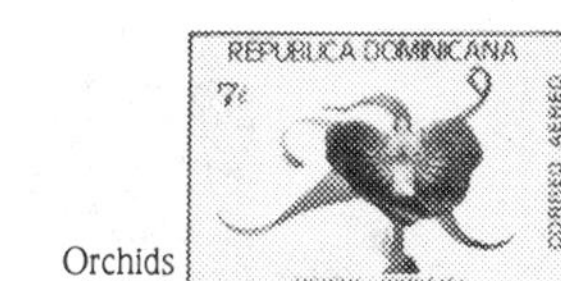
Orchids AP110

1981, Dec. 14

C349 AP110 7c Encyclia cochleata 15 15
C350 AP110 10c Broughtonia domingensis 22 18
C351 AP110 25c Encyclia truncata 30 20
C352 AP110 75c Elleanthus capitatus 75 75

Christmas Type of 1981

1981, Dec. 23

C353 A294 10c Dove, sun 28 22

Battle of Tortuguero Anniv. AP111

1982, Apr. 15 Litho. *Perf. 13½*

C354 AP111 10c Naval Academy, cadets 20 18

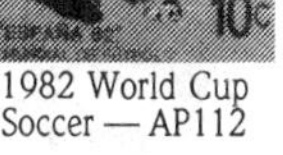
1982 World Cup Soccer — AP112

American Air Forces Cooperation System — AP113

Designs: Various soccer players.

1982, Apr. 19

C355 AP112 10c multicolored 30 25
C356 AP112 21c multicolored 30 20
C357 AP112 33c multicolored 60 60

1982, Apr. 12 *Perf. 12*

C358 AP113 10c multicolored 20 20

Scouting Year AP114

1982, Apr. 30 Litho. *Perf. 13½*

C359 AP114 10c Baden-Powell, vert. 15 15
C360 AP114 15c Globe 24 22
C361 AP114 25c Baden-Powell, scout, vert. 35 22

Dancers — AP115

Espamer '82 Emblem — AP116

1982, June 1 Litho. *Perf. 13½*

C362 AP115 7c Emblem 15 15
C363 AP115 10c Cathedral, Casa del Tostado, Santo Domingo 20 15
C364 AP115 33c shown 60 60

Tourist Org. of the Americas, 25th Congress (COTAL '82), Santo Domingo.

1982, July 5

Espamer '82 Intl. Stamp Exhibition, San Juan, Oct. 12-17: Symbolic stamps. 7c, 13c horiz.

C365 AP116 7c multicolored 15 15
C366 AP116 13c multicolored 22 18
C367 AP116 50c multicolored 1.00 80

Sports Type of 1982

1982, Aug. 13 *Perf. 12, Imperf.*

C368 A300 10c Basketball 18 15
C369 A300 13c Boxing 30 15
C370 A300 25c Gymnast 30 20
Set value 41

Harbor, by Alejandro Bonilla — AP117

Paintings: 10c, Portrait of a Woman, by Leopoldo Navarro. 45c, Amelia Francasci, by Luis Desangles. 2p, Portrait, by Abelardo Rodriguez Urdaneta. 10c, 45c, 2p vert.

1982, Aug. 20 *Perf. 13, Imperf.*

C371 AP117 7c multicolored 20 15
C372 AP117 10c multicolored 22 15
C373 AP117 45c multicolored 60 18
C374 AP117 2p multicolored 2.00 1.50

San Pedro de Macoris Type of 1982

1982, Aug. 26

Size: 42x29mm

C375 A301 7c Lake 25 22

35th Anniv. of Central Bank AP118

1982, Oct. 22 Litho. *Perf. 13½x13*

C376 AP118 10c multicolored 18 16

490th Anniv. of Discovery of America AP119

1982, Oct. 7 Litho. *Perf. 13½*

C377 AP119 7c Map *65* 15
C378 AP119 10c Santa Maria, vert. *85* 15
C379 AP119 21c Columbus, vert. *1.00* 15
Set value 36

Christmas Type of 1982

1982, Dec. 8

C380 A303 10c multicolored 20 18

French Alliance Centenary — AP120

1983, Mar. 31 Litho. *Perf. 13½*

C381 AP120 33c multicolored 40 35

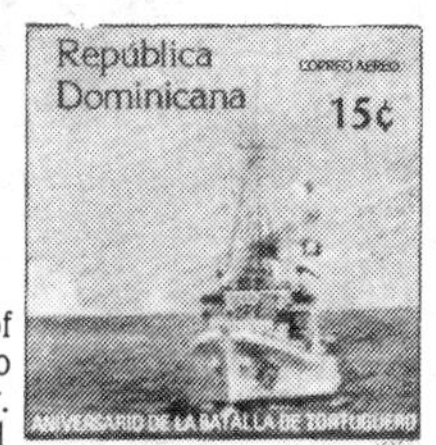
Battle of Tortuguero Anniv. AP121

1983, Apr. 15 Litho. *Perf. 13½*

C382 AP121 15c Frigate Mella-451 22 15

World Communications Year — AP122

1983, May 6 Litho. *Perf. 13½*

C383 AP122 10c dk blue & blue 22 22

AP123

AP124

1983, July 5 Litho. *Perf. 13½*

C384 AP123 9c multicolored 15 15

Simon Bolivar (1783-1830).

1983, Aug. 22 Litho. *Perf. 12*

C385 AP124 7c Gymnast, basketball 15 15
C386 AP124 10c Highjump, boxing 18 15
C387 AP124 15c Baseball, weight lifting, bicycling 22 15
Set value 31

9th Pan American Games, Caracas, Aug. 13-28.

491st Anniv. of Discovery of America AP125

1983, Oct. 11 Litho. *Perf. 13½*

C388 AP125 10c Columbus' ships, map *60* 15
C389 AP125 21c Santa Maria (trophy) *90* 15
C390 AP125 33c Yacht Sotavento, vert. *1.00* 15
Set value 27

Size: 103x103mm

Imperf

C391 AP125 50c Ship models

10th Anniv. of Latin American Civil Aviation Commission AP126

1983, Dec. 7

C392 AP126 10c dark blue 15 15

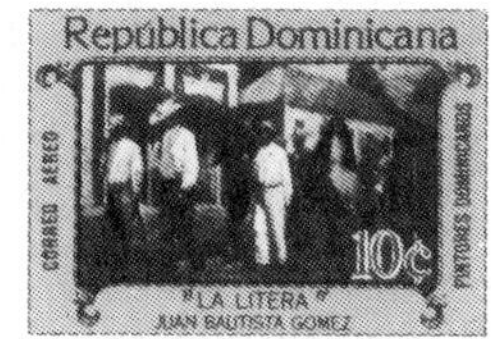
Funeral Procession, by Juan Bautista Gomez — AP127

Designs: 15c, Meeting of Maximo Gomez and Jose Marti in Guayubin, by Enrique Garcia Godoy. 21c, St. Francis, by Angel Perdomo, vert. 33c, Portrait of a Girl, by Adriana Billini, vert.

1983, Dec. 26 *Perf. 13½*

C393 AP127 10c multicolored 15 15
C394 AP127 15c multicolored 15 15
C395 AP127 21c multicolored 24 15
C396 AP127 33c multicolored 32 15
Set value 37

Christmas 1983 — AP128

1983, Dec. 13 Litho. *Perf. 13½*

C397 AP128 10c Bells, ornaments 18 15

AIR POST SEMI-POSTAL STAMPS

Catalogue values for unused stamps in this section are for Never Hinged items.

Nos. C97-C99 Surcharged in Red like Nos. B1-B5

Engraved and Lithographed

1957, Feb. 8 Unwmk. *Perf. 11½*

Flags in National Colors

CB1 A117 11c + 2c ultra & red org 28 28
CB2 A117 16c + 2c car & lt grn 38 38
CB3 A117 17c + 2c blk, vio & red 42 42

The surtax was to aid Hungarian refugees. A similar 25c surcharge was applied to the souvenir sheets described in the footnote following No. C99. Value, 2 sheets, perf. and imperf., $17.50.

Nos. C100-C102 Surcharged in Red Orange like Nos. B6-B10

1957, Sept. 9 Photo. *Perf. 13½*
Flags in National Colors

CB4 A118 11c + 2c yel grn & dk bl 50 45
CB5 A118 16c + 2c lilac & dk bl 60 60
CB6 A118 17c + 2c brn & bl grn 65 65

See note after No. B10.

A similar 5c surcharge was applied to the miniature sheets described in the footnote following No. 483. Value, 4 sheets, perf. & imperf., medal and flag, $40.

Types of Olympic Air Post Stamps, 1957, Surcharged in Carmine like Nos. B11-B20

1958, May 26 Engr. & Litho.
Flags in National Colors
Pink Paper

CB7 A119(a) 11c + 2c ultra 28 28
CB8 A119(b) 11c + 2c ultra 28 28
CB9 A120(a) 16c + 2c rose car 35 35
CB10 A120(b) 16c + 2c rose car 35 35
CB11 A119(a) 17c + 2c claret 42 42
CB12 A119(b) 17c + 2c claret 42 42
Nos. CB7-CB12 (6) 2.10 2.10

A similar 5c surcharge, plus marginal UN emblem and "UNRWA," was applied to the miniature sheets described in the footnote following No. C105. Value, 4 sheets, perf. and imperf., $20.

Nos. C106-C108 Surcharged like Nos. B21-B25

1959, Apr. 13 Photo. *Perf. 13½*
Flags in National Colors

CB13 A125 11c + 2c blue, ol & brn 52 52
CB14 A125 16c + 2c lt grn, org & dk bl 70 70
CB15 A125 17c + 2c ver bl & yel 1.05 1.05

A similar 5c surcharge was applied to the miniature sheets described in the footnote following No. C108. Value, 2 sheets, perf. and imperf., $25.

Type of Regular Issue 1957 Surcharged in Red like Nos. B26-B30

Engraved and Lithographed
1959, Sept. 10 *Imperf.*
Flags in National Colors

CB16 A117 11c + 2c ultra & red org 45 45
CB17 A117 16c + 2c carmine & lt grn 52 52
CB18 A117 17c + 2c black, vio & red 55 55

Nos. C113-C114 Surcharged in Red like Nos. B31-B33

1960, Apr. 7 Litho. *Perf. 12½*

CB19 AP43 10c + 5c plum, gray & grn 16 15
CB20 AP43 13c + 5c gray & green 18 18

World Refugee Year.
For souvenir sheets see note after No. B33.

Nos. C115-C117 Surcharged: "XV ANIVERSARIO DE LA UNESCO + 2c"

Perf. 13½
1962, Jan. 8 Unwmk. Photo.
Flags in National Colors

CB21 A136 11c + 2c blue, gray & brn 22 22
CB22 A136 16c + 2c red, brn & ol 30 30
CB23 A136 17c + 2c blk, bl & ocher 32 32

See note after No. B38.

A similar 5c surcharge was applied to the miniature sheets described in the footnote following No. C117. Value, 2 sheets, perf. and imperf., $7.50.

Anti-Malaria Type of 1962

1962, Apr. 29 Litho. *Perf. 12*

CB24 A141 13c + 2c pink & red 15 15
CB25 A141 33c + 2c org & dp org 40 40

Souvenir sheets exist, perf. and imperf. containing one each of Nos. B39-B40, CB24-CB25 and a 25c+2c pale green and yellow green.

Nos. C132-C133 Surcharged like Nos. B44-B46

1964, Mar. 8

CB26 AP46 10c + 2c brt violet 15 15
CB27 AP46 13c + 2c yellow 16 15

Nos. C146-C148 Surcharged like Nos. B47-B51

1966, Dec. 9 Litho. *Perf. 12½*
Size: 35x24mm

CB28 A164 10c + 5c multi 50 15
CB29 A164 50c + 10c multi 75 60
CB30 A164 75c + 10c multi 1.00 70

AIR POST OFFICIAL STAMPS

Nos. O13-O14 Overprinted in Blue

CORREO
AEREO

Unwmk.
1930, Dec. 3 Typo. *Perf. 12*

CO1 O3 10c light blue 10.50 11.00
a. Pair, one without ovpt. *900.00*
CO2 O3 20c orange 10.50 11.00

SPECIAL DELIVERY STAMPS

Biplane — SD1

Perf. 11½
1920, Apr. Unwmk. Litho.

E1 SD1 10c deep ultra 6.00 1.25
a. Imperf., pair

Special Delivery Messenger — SD2

1925

E2 SD2 10c dark blue 16.00 4.50

SD3

1927

E3 SD3 10c red brown 6.00 1.25
a. "E EXPRESO" at top 55.00 55.00

Type of 1927

1941 Redrawn

E4 SD3 10c yellow green 2.50 3.00
E5 SD3 10c dark blue green 2.00 60

The redrawn design differs slightly from SD3. Issue dates: #E4, Mar. 27; #E5, Aug. 7.

Emblem of Communications — SD4

1945, Sept. 1 *Perf. 12*

E6 SD4 10c rose car, car & dk bl 45 18

Catalogue values for unused stamps in this section, from this point to the end of the section, are for Never Hinged items.

SD5

1950 Litho. Unwmk.

E7 SD5 10c multicolored 52 18

Exists imperf.

Modern Communications System — SD6

1956, Aug. 18 *Perf. 11½*

E8 SD6 25c green 1.05 30

Carrier Pigeon SD7

1967 Litho. *Perf. 11½*

E9 SD7 25c light blue 55 24

Carrier Pigeon, Globe — SD8

Messenger, Plane — SD9

1978, Aug. 2 Litho. *Perf. 13½*

E10 SD8 25c multicolored 45 30

1979, Nov. 30 *Perf. 13½*

E11 SD9 25c multicolored 20 20

Motorcycling SD10

1989, May Litho. *Perf. 13½*

E12 SD10 1p multicolored 35 35

INSURED LETTER STAMPS

PRIMA
VALORES DECLARADOS

Merino Issue of 1933 Surcharged in Red or Black

SERVICIO INTERIOR
8
CENTAVOS

1935, Feb. 1 Unwmk. *Perf. 14*

G1 A35 8c on 7c ultra 60 15
a. Inverted surcharge 18.00
G2 A35 15c on 10c org yel 60 15
a. Inverted surcharge 18.00
G3 A35 30c on 8c dk green 1.75 90
G4 A35 45c on 20c car rose (Bk) 3.00 1.00
G5 A36 70c on 50c lemon 6.00 1.25
Nos. G1-G5 (5) 11.95 3.45

PRIMA
VALORES DECLARADOS

Merino Issue of 1933 Surcharged in Red

SERVICIO INTERIOR

CENTAVOS

1940

G6 A35 8c on ½c lt vio 2.00 2.00
G7 A35 8c on 7c ultra 2.25 2.25

Coat of Arms — IL1

1940-45 Litho. *Perf. 11½*
Arms in Black

G8 IL1 8c brown red 60 15
a. 8c dk red, no shading on inner frame 1.00 15
G9 IL1 15c dp orange ('45) 1.25 15
G10 IL1 30c dk green ('41) 1.50 15
a. 30c yellow green 1.50 15
G11 IL1 45c ultra ('44) 1.50 30
G12 IL1 70c olive brn ('44) 1.75 28
Nos. G8-G12 (5) 6.60 1.03

See Nos. G13-G16, G24-G27.

Redrawn Type of 1940-45

1952-53
Arms in Black

G13 IL1 8c car lake ('53) 1.00 50
G14 IL1 15c red orange ('53) 1.75 75
G15 IL1 70c dp brown car 4.25 1.50

Larger and bolder numerals on 8c and 15c. Smaller and bolder "70." There are many other minor differences in the design.

Type of 1940-45

1954
Arms in Black, 15x16mm

G16 IL1 10c carmine 75 25

Coat of Arms — IL2

1955-69 Unwmk. Litho. *Perf. 11½*
Arms in Black, 13½x11½mm

G17 IL2 10c carmine rose 35 15
G18 IL2 15c red orange ('56) 1.75 1.25
G19 IL2 20c red orange ('58) 75 30
a. 20c orange ('69) 90 28
b. 20c orange, retouched ('69) 3.50 1.25
G20 IL2 30c dark green ('55) 1.40 30
G21 IL2 40c dark green ('58) 1.65 90
a. 40c lt yellow grn ('62) 1.40 45
G22 IL2 45c ultra ('56) 4.00 3.75
G23 IL2 70c dp brn car ('56) 3.00 2.00
Nos. G17-G23 (7) 12.90 8.65

On No. G19b the horizontal shading lines of shield are omitted.
See Nos. G28-G37.

Catalogue values for unused stamps in this section, from this point to the end of the section, are for Never Hinged items.

Type of 1940-45
Second Redrawing

1963 *Perf. 12½*
Arms in Black, 17x16mm

G24 IL1 10c red orange 1.25 30
G25 IL1 20c orange 1.50 50

Third Redrawing

1966 Litho. *Perf. 12½*
Arms in Black, 14x14mm

G26 IL1 10c violet 40 18
G27 IL1 40c orange 1.50 1.05

Type of 1955-62

1968 Litho. *Perf. 11½*
Arms in Black, 13½x11½mm

G28 IL2 20c red 2.00 75
G29 IL2 60c yellow 1.50 1.50

1973-76 Litho. *Perf. 12½*
Arms in Black, 11x11mm

G30 IL2 10c car rose ('76) 40 35
G31 IL2 20c yellow 1.40 90
G32 IL2 20c orange ('76) 1.75 48
G33 IL2 40c yel grn 1.65 1.00
a. 40c green ('76) 3.00 3.00
G34 IL2 70c blue 1.75 1.90

1973 *Perf. 11½*
Arms in Black, 13½x11½mm
G35 IL2 10c dark violet 90 30

1978, Aug. 9 *Perf. 10½*
Arms in Black, 11x11mm
G36 IL2 10c rose magenta 35 15
G37 IL2 40c bright green 1.50 1.50

IL3

1982-83 Litho. *Perf. 10½*
Arms in Black
G38 IL3 10c deep magenta 18 15
G39 IL3 20c deep orange 35 22
G40 IL3 40c bluish green 75 50

IL4

1986 Litho. *Perf. 10½*
Arms in Black
G41 IL4 20c brt rose lilac 24 16
G42 IL4 60c orange 70 48
G43 IL4 1p light blue 1.25 80
G44 IL4 1.25p pink 1.50 1.00
G45 IL4 1.50p vermilion 1.75 1.25
G46 IL4 3p light green 3.75 2.50
G47 IL4 3.50p olive bister 4.25 2.75
G48 IL4 4p yellow 4.75 3.25
G49 IL4 4.50p lt blue grn 5.50 3.75
G50 IL4 5p brown olive 6.00 4.00
G51 IL4 6p gray 7.25 4.75
G52 IL4 6.50p lt ultra 7.75 5.25
Nos. G41-G52 (12) 44.69 29.94

Issue dates: #G42-G43, G45, July 16. #G46-G52, Sept. 2. #G41, G44, Nov. 6.

Coat of Arms — IL5

1989-90 Litho. *Perf. 13½*
Arms in Black
G53 IL5 20c brt lilac rose 15 15
G53A IL5 60c orange ('90) 25 18
G54 IL5 1p sky blue 45 28
G54A IL5 1.25p lt salmon pink 55 50
G55 IL5 1.50p dark red 60 40
Nos. G53-G55 (5) 2.00 1.51

"RD$" in lower left square on #G54-G55.
This is an expanding set. Numbers will change if necessary.

POSTAGE DUE STAMPS

D1

1901 Unwmk. Typo. *Perf. 14*
J1 D1 2c olive gray 70 15
J2 D1 4c olive gray 90 20
J3 D1 5c olive gray 1.50 30
J4 D1 10c olive gray 2.75 75

For surcharges and overprint see Nos. 162-165, 169-171.

1909 Wmk. 116
J5 D1 2c olive gray 1.50 50
J6 D1 4c olive gray 1.50 50
J7 D1 6c olive gray 2.00 75
J8 D1 10c olive gray 4.00 2.50

1913
J9 D1 2c olive green 45 15
J10 D1 4c olive green 50 20
J11 D1 6c olive green 80 35
J12 D1 10c olive green 90 40

1922 Unwmk. Litho. *Perf. 11½*
J13 D1 1c olive green 45 40

Catalogue values for unused stamps in this section, from this point to the end of the section, are for Never Hinged items.

D2

D3

1942
J14 D2 1c dk red & pale pink 15 15
J15 D2 2c dk bl & pale bl 15 15
J16 D2 4c dk grn & pale grn 15 15
J17 D2 6c green & buff 22 22
J18 D2 8c yel org & pale yel 22 22
J19 D2 10c mag & pale pink 28 28
Nos. J14-J19 (6) 1.17 1.17

1955
Size: 20½x25mm
J20 D2 2c dark blue 1.40 1.00

1959 Litho. *Perf. 11½*
Size: 21x25½mm
J21 D3 1c dark car rose 1.25 1.25
J22 D3 2c dark blue 1.25 1.25
J23 D3 4c green 3.00 3.00

OFFICIAL STAMPS

Bastion of February 27 — O1

Unwmk.
1902, Feb. 25 Litho. *Perf. 12*
O1 O1 2c scarlet & blk 50 30
O2 O1 5c dk blue & blk 65 25
O3 O1 10c yel grn & blk 75 45
O4 O1 20c yellow & blk 1.00 42
a. Imperf., pair 10.00

For overprints and surcharge see #157-161.

Bastion of Feb. 27 — O2

Columbus Lighthouse — O3

Perf. 13½x13, 13½x14
1909-12 Wmk. 116 Typo.
O5 O2 1c blue grn & blk 20 15
O6 O2 2c scarlet & blk 25 15
O7 O2 5c dk blue & blk 55 25
O8 O2 10c yel grn & blk ('12) 1.00 60
O9 O2 20c orange & blk ('12) 1.50 1.25
Nos. O5-O9 (5) 3.50 2.40

The 2c, 5c are found in both perforations; 1c, 20c perf. 13½x13; 10c perf. 13½x14.
For overprints and surcharge see #177, 194-199.

1928 Unwmk. *Perf. 12*
O10 O3 1c green 15 15
O11 O3 2c red 15 15
O12 O3 5c ultramarine 20 15
O13 O3 10c light blue 25 22
O14 O3 20c orange 30 30
Nos. O10-O14 (5) 1.05
Set value 80

For overprints see Nos. CO1-CO2.

Proposed Columbus Lighthouse O4

1937 Litho. *Perf. 11½*
O15 O4 3c dark purple 60 15
O16 O4 7c indigo & blue 60 25
O17 O4 10c orange yellow 70 36

Proposed Columbus Lighthouse O5

1939-41
O18 O5 1c dp grn & lt grn 15 15
O19 O5 2c crim & pale pink 15 15
O20 O5 3c purple & lt vio 15 15
O21 O5 5c dk bl & lt bl ('40) 30 15
O21A O5 5c lt blue ('41) 75 65
O22 O5 7c brt bl & lt bl ('41) 50 15
O23 O5 10c yel org & pale org ('41) 50 20
O24 O5 20c brn org & buff ('41) 1.50 30
O25 O5 50c brt red lil & pale lil ('41) 1.75 1.00
Nos. O18-O25 (9) 5.75
Set value 2.20

Catalogue values for unused stamps in this section, from this point to the end of the section, are for Never Hinged items.

Type of 1939
1950 Redrawn
O26 O5 50c dp car & rose 3.00 1.10

The numerals "50" measure 3mm, and are close to left and right frames; numerals measure 4mm on No. O25. There are other minor differences.

Denominations in "Centavos Oro"
1950
O27 O5 5c light blue 55 15
O28 O5 10c yel & pale yel 65 25
O29 O5 20c dl org brn & buff 70 50

Letters of top inscription are 1½mm high.

Type of 1939-41
Second Redrawing
Denominations in "Centavos Oro"
1956 Unwmk. *Perf. 11½*
O30 O5 7c blue & lt blue 55 55
O31 O5 20c yellow brn & buff 1.25 1.25
O32 O5 50c red lil & brt pink 3.25 3.25

The letters of top inscription are 2mm high, the trees at base of monument have been redrawn, etc. On No. O32 the numerals are similar to No. O26.

POSTAL TAX STAMPS

Santo Domingo after Hurricane PT1

Hurricane's Effect on Capital PT2

1930, Dec. Unwmk. Litho. *Perf. 12*
RA1 PT1 1c green & rose 15 15
RA2 PT1 2c red rose 18 15
RA3 PT2 5c ultra & rose 30 15
RA4 PT2 10c yellow & rose 35 30

Imperf
RA5 PT1 1c green & rose 42 30
RA6 PT1 2c red & rose 48 32
RA7 PT2 5c ultra & rose 60 48
RA8 PT2 10c yellow & rose 90 75
Nos. RA1-RA8 (8) 3.38 2.60

For surcharges see Nos. RAC1-RAC7.

Tête bêche Pairs
RA1a PT1 1c green & rose 1.75 1.75
RA2a PT1 2c red rose 1.75 1.50
RA3a PT1 5c ultra & rose 1.75 2.10
RA4a PT1 10c yellow & rose 2.10 2.10

Imperf
RA5a PT1 1c green & rose 1.75 1.75
RA6a PT1 2c red & rose 1.75 1.75
RA7a PT1 5c ultra & rose 2.10 2.10
RA8a PT1 10c yellow & rose 2.10 2.10

Dr. Martos Sanatorium — PT3

Nurse and Child — PT4

1944, Apr. 1 Litho. *Perf. 11½*
RA9 PT3 1c dp bl, sl bl & red 22 15

1947, Apr. 1 Unwmk.
RA10 PT4 1c dp bl, pale bl & car 22 15

Sanatorium of the Holy Help — PT5

1949, Apr. 1
RA11 PT5 1c dp bl, pale bl & car 18 15

Youth Holding Banner PT6

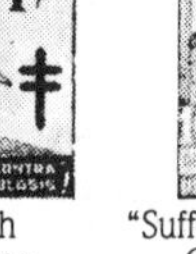
"Suffer Little Children to Come Unto Me" PT7

1950, Apr. 1 *Perf. 11½*
RA12 PT6 1c dp bl, pale bl & car 18 15

1950, Dec. 1 *Perf. 12*
Size: 22½x32mm
RA13 PT7 1c lt bl & pale bl 45 15
b. Perf. 12½ ('52) 3.00 20

Vertical line centering side borders merges into dots toward the bottom. See Nos. RA13A, RA17, RA19, RA26, RA32, RA35.
The tax was for child welfare.

1951, Dec. 1 Redrawn
RA13A PT7 1c lt blue & pale blue 2.25 20

In the redrawn stamp, the standing child, a blonde in No. RA13, is changed to a brunette; more foliage has been added above child's head and to branches showing in upper right corner. Vertical dashes in side borders.

Tuberculosis Sanatorium, Santiago — PT8

1952, Apr. 1 Litho. *Perf. 11½*
RA14 PT8 1c lt blue & car 18 15

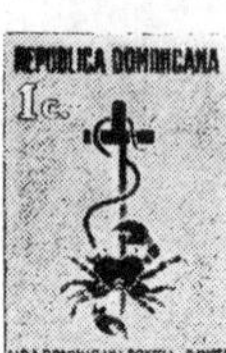

Sword, Serpent and Crab — PT9

1953, Feb. 1 Unwmk. *Perf. 12.*
RA15 PT9 1c carmine 28 15

The tax was for the Dominican League Against Cancer. See Nos. RA18, RA21, RA43, RA46, RA51, RA56, RA61, RA67, RA72, RA76, RA82, RA88, RA93, RA96.

Tuberculosis Dispensary for Children — PT10

1953, Apr. 1 Litho. *Perf. 12½*
RA16 PT10 1c dp bl, pale bl & red 18 15

See No. RA22.

Jesus Type of 1950
Second Redrawing

1953, Dec. 1 *Perf. 11½*
Size: 22x31mm
RA17 PT7 1c blue 35 15

Solid shading in sky reduced to a few scattered dots. Girl's left arm indicated. Rough white dots in side borders.

Cancer Type of 1952

1954, Oct. 1 Redrawn *Perf. 12½*
RA18 PT9 1c rose carmine 22 15
a. 1c red orange ('58) 30 15
b. 1c carmine ('70) 1.25 18

Upper right serif of numeral "1" eliminated; diagonal line added through "C" and period removed; sword extended, placing top on a line with top of "1." Dots of background screen arranged diagonally. Many other differences.

The tax was for the Dominican League Against Cancer. No. RA18a exists imperf.

On No. RA18b background screen eliminates white outline of crab.

Jesus Type of 1950

1954, Dec. 1 Third Redrawing
Size: 23x32¾mm
RA19 PT7 1c bright blue 24 15
a. 1c pale blue ('59) 15 15

Center completely screened. Tiny white horizontal rectangles in side borders.

Catalogue values for unused stamps in this section, from this point to the end of the section, are for Never Hinged items.

Lorraine Cross as Bell Clapper — PT11

1955, Apr. 1 Litho. *Perf. 11½x12*
RA20 PT11 1c black, yel & red 18 15

Cancer Type of 1952
Second Redrawing

1956, Oct. 1 *Perf. 12½*
RA21 PT9 1c carmine 35 15
a. 1c red orange ('64) 1.00 52

Similar to No. RA18, but dots of background screen arranged in vertical and horizontal rows. Outlines of central device, lettering and frame clearly delineated. "C" of cent-sign smaller. Upper claw in solid color.

TB Dispensary Type of 1953
Redrawn

1954, Apr. 1
RA22 PT10 1c blue & red 35 15
a. Red (cross) omitted 55.00

No. RA22 has third color omitted; clouds added; bolder letters and numerals.

Angelita Trujillo — PT12

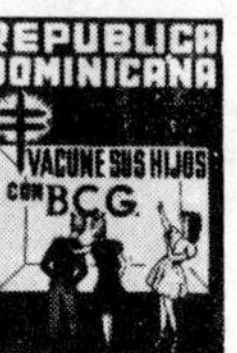

Lorraine Cross — PT13

1955, Dec. 1 Unwmk. *Perf. 12½*
RA23 PT12 1c violet 18 15

The tax was for child welfare.

1956, Apr. 1 Litho. *Perf. 11½*
RA24 PT13 1c blk, grn, lem & red 18 15

The tax was for the Anti-Tuberculosis League. Inscribed: B.C.G. (Bacillus Calmette-Guerin).

PT14

PT15

1957, Apr. 1
RA25 PT14 1c red, blk, yel, grn & bl 18 15

Jesus Type of 1950
Fourth Redrawing

1956, Dec. 1 Unwmk. *Perf. 12*
Size: 21¾x31¼mm
RA26 PT7 1c blue 30 15

Thin white lines around numeral boxes. Girl's bouquet touches Jesus' sleeve. Tiny white squares or rectangles in side borders. Foliage at either side of "Era de Trujillo" panel.

1958, Apr. 1 Litho. *Perf. 12½*
RA27 PT15 1c brown car & red 15 15

Inscribed "1959"

1959, Apr. 1
RA28 PT15 1c brown car & red 15 15

PT16

PT17

1960, Apr. 1 Litho. *Perf. 12*
RA29 PT16 1c bl, pale yel & red 18 15

1961, Apr. 1 Unwmk. *Perf. 11½*
RA30 PT17 1c blue & red 15 15

Nos. RA29-RA30: tax was for the Anti-Tuberculosis League.
See No. RA33.

Maria de los Angeles M. de Trujillo and Housing Project PT18

1961, Aug. 1 Litho. *Perf. 12*
RA31 PT18 1c carmine rose 18 15

The tax was for aid to the needy.
Nos. RA31-RA33 exist imperf.

Jesus Type of 1950
Fifth Redrawing

1961, Dec. 1 Unwmk. *Perf. 12½*
RA32 PT7 1c blue 18 15

No. RA32 is similar to No. RA19, but "Era de Trujillo" has been replaced by a solid color panel.

Type of 1961 Dated "1962"

1962, Apr. 2 *Perf. 12½*
RA33 PT17 1c blue & red 15 15

Tax for the Anti-Tuberculosis League.

Man's Chest PT19

Hibiscus PT20

1963, Apr. 1 *Perf. 12x11½*
RA34 PT19 1c ultra & red 15 15

Jesus Type of 1950
Sixth Redrawing

1963, Dec. 1 *Perf. 11½*
Size: 21¾x32mm
RA35 PT7 1c blue 15 15
a. 1c deep blue ('64) 15 15

No. RA35 is similar to No. RA26, but "Era de Trujillo" panel has been omitted.

1966, Apr. 1 Litho. *Perf. 11½*
RA36 PT20 1c emerald & car 15 15

Tax for the Anti-Tuberculosis League.

Domingoa Nodosa — PT21

Civil Defense Emblem — PT22

1967, Apr. 1 Litho. *Perf. 12½*
RA37 PT21 1c lilac & red 15 15

Tax for the Anti-Tuberculosis League.

1967, July 1 Litho. *Rouletted 13*
RA38 PT22 1c multicolored 18 15

Tax for the Civil Defense Organization.

Boy, School and Yule Bells — PT23

Hand Holding Invalid — PT24

1967, Dec. 1 Litho. *Perf. 12½*
RA39 PT23 1c rose red & pink 22 15

1968 *Perf. 11*
RA40 PT23 1c vermilion 28 15

No. RA40 has screened background; No. RA39, smooth background.
The tax was for child welfare.
See Nos. RA49A, RA52, RA57, RA62, RA68, RA73, RA77, RA81.

1968, Mar. 19 Litho. *Perf. 12½*
RA41 PT24 1c green & yellow 15 15
a. 1c olive green & deep yellow, perf. 11½x12 ('69) 15 15

The tax was for the rehabilitation of the handicapped. See Nos. RA47, RA50, RA54.

Dogbane PT25

Schoolyard, Torch PT26

1968, Apr. 25 Litho. *Perf. 12½*
RA42 PT25 1c emerald, yel & red 15 15

The tax was for the Anti-Tuberculosis League. See Nos. RA45, RA49.

Redrawn Cancer Type of 1955

1968, Oct. 1 Litho. *Perf. 12*
RA43 PT9 1c emerald 15 15

The tax was for the Dominican League against Cancer.

1969, Feb. 1 Litho. *Perf. 12½*
RA44 PT26 1c light blue 15 15

Issued for Education Year 1969.

Flower Type of 1968

Design: No. RA45, Violets.

1969, Apr. 25 Litho. *Perf. 12½*
RA45 PT25 1c emerald, lil & red 15 15

Tax for the Anti-Tuberculosis League.

Redrawn Cancer Type of 1955

1969, Oct. 1 Litho. *Perf. 11*
RA46 PT9 1c brt rose lilac 15 15

The tax was for the Dominican League against Cancer.

Invalid Type of 1968

1970, Mar. 2 *Perf. 12½*
RA47 PT24 1c blue 15 15

The tax was for the rehabilitation of the handicapped.

Book, Sun and Education Year Emblem — PT27

Communications Emblem — PT28

1970, Feb. 6 *Perf. 11*
RA48 PT27 1c bright pink 15 15

International Education Year.

Flower Type of 1968

Design: 1c, Eleanthus capitatus; cross in upper left corner, denomination in lower right.

1970, Apr. 30 *Perf. 11*
RA49 PT25 1c emerald, red & yel 15 15

Tax for Anti-Tuberculosis League.

Boy Type of 1967

1970, Dec. 1 *Perf. 12½*
RA49A PT23 1c orange 24 15

1971, Jan. 2 Litho. *Perf. 11*
Size: 17½x20½mm
RA49B PT28 1c vio bl & red (white frame) 22 15

Tax was for Postal and Telegraph Communications School.
See Nos. RA53, RA58, RA63, RA69, RA78, RA91.

Invalid Type of 1968

1971, Mar. 1 Litho. *Perf. 11*
RA50 PT24 1c brt rose lilac 15 15

Tax for rehabilitation of the handicapped.

Cancer Type of 1952
Third Redrawing

1971, Oct. 1 *Perf. 11½*
RA51 PT9 1c dp yellow green 15 15

Background of No. RA51 appears white and design stands out. No. RA43 has greenish background and design appears faint. Numeral "1" on No. RA51 is 3½mm high, on No. RA43 it is 3mm.

Boy Type of 1967

1971, Dec. 1 Litho. *Perf. 11*
RA52 PT23 1c green 22 15

Communications Type of 1971

1972, Jan. 3 Litho. *Perf. 12½*
Size: 19x22mm
RA53 PT28 1c dk bl & red (bl frame) 15 15

Tax was for the Postal and Telegraph Communications School.

Invalid Type of 1968

1972, Mar. 1 Litho. *Perf. 11½*
RA54 PT24 1c brown 15 15

Orchid — PT29

1972, Apr. 2 *Perf. 11*
RA55 PT29 1c lt grn, red & yel 16 15

Tax was for the Anti-Tuberculosis League.

Redrawn Cancer Type of 1954-58

1972, Oct. 2 *Perf. 12½*
RA56 PT9 1c orange 15 15

Tax for Dominican League against Cancer.

Boy Type of 1967

1972, Dec. 1 *Perf. 12*
RA57 PT23 1c violet 20 15

Tax was for child welfare.

Communications Type of 1971

1973, Jan. 2 *Perf. 10½*
Size: 19x22mm
RA58 PT28 1c dk bl & red (red frame) 15 15

Tax was for Postal and Telegraph Communications School.

Invalid PT30

Hibiscus PT31

1973, Mar. 1 Litho. *Perf. 12½*
Size: 21x25mm
RA59 PT30 1c olive 15 15

Tax was for the Dominican Rehabilitation Association. See Nos. RA66, RA70, RA74, RA79, RA86.

1973, Apr. 17 Litho. *Perf. 10½*
RA60 PT31 1c multicolored 15 15

Tax was for Anti-Tuberculosis League. Exists imperf.

Cancer Type of 1952 Redrawn and "1973" Added

1973, Oct. 1 *Perf. 13½*
RA61 PT9 1c olive green 15 15

Tax was for Dominican League Against Cancer.

Boy Type of 1967

1973, Dec. 1 Litho. *Perf. 13x13½*
RA62 PT23 1c blue 15 15

Communications Type of 1971

1973, Nov. 3 *Perf. 10½*
Size: 19x22mm
RA63 PT28 1c bl & red (lt grn frame) 15 15

Tax was for Postal and Telegraph Communications School. Exists imperf.

Invalid Type of 1973

1974, Mar. 1 Litho. *Perf. 10½*
Size: 22x27½mm
RA66 PT30 1c light ultra 15 15

See note after No. RA59.

Cancer Type of 1952 Redrawn and "1974" Added

1974, Oct. 1 *Perf. 12*
RA67 PT9 1c orange 15 15

Tax for Dominican League Against Cancer.

Boy Type of 1967

1974, Dec. 2 Litho. *Perf. 11½*
RA68 PT23 1c dk brown & buff 15 15

Communications Type of 1971

1974, Nov. 13 *Perf. 10½*
RA69 PT28 1c blue & red (yel frame) 15 15

Invalid Type of 1973 Dated "1975"

1975, Mar. 1 *Perf. 13½x13*
Size: 21x32mm
RA70 PT30 1c olive brown 15 15

See note after No. RA59.

Catteeyopsis Rosea PT32

Oncidium Colochilum PT33

1975, Apr. 1 *Perf. 12*
RA71 PT32 1c blue & multi 95 68

Tax was for Anti-Tuberculosis League.

Cancer Type of 1952 Redrawn and "1975" Added

1975, Oct. 1 Litho. *Perf. 12*
RA72 PT9 1c violet blue 15 15

Tax was for Dominican League Against Cancer. Exists imperf.

Boy Type of 1967

1975, Dec. 1 Litho. *Perf. 12*
RA73 PT23 1c red orange 15 15

Tax was for child welfare.

Invalid Type of 1973 Dated "1976"

1976, Mar. 1 Litho. *Perf. 12*
Size: 21x31mm
RA74 PT30 1c ultra 15 15

See note after No. RA59.

1976, Apr. 6 *Perf. 13x13½*
RA75 PT33 1c green & multi 15 15

Tax was for Anti-Tuberculosis League.
See No. RA80, RA84.

Cancer Type of 1952 Redrawn and "1976" Added

1976, Oct. 1 Litho. *Perf. 13½*
RA76 PT9 1c green 15 15

Tax was for Dominican League Against Cancer.

Boy Type of 1967

1976, Dec. 1 Litho. *Perf. 13½*
RA77 PT23 1c purple 15 15

Tax was for child welfare.

Communications Type of 1971

1977, Jan. 7 Litho. *Perf. 10½*
Size: 19x22mm
RA78 PT28 1c blue & red (lil frame) 15 15

Tax was for Postal and Telegraph Communications School.

Invalid Type of 1973 Dated "1977"

1977, Mar. 11 *Perf. 12*
Size: 21x31mm
RA79 PT30 1c ultra 15 15

See note after No. RA59.

Orchid Type of 1976 Dated "1977"

Orchid: Oncidium variegatum.

1977, Apr. 22 Litho. *Perf. 13½*
RA80 PT33 1c multicolored 15 15

Tax was for Anti-Tuberculosis League.

Boy Type of 1967

1977, Dec. 27 Litho. *Perf. 12*
RA81 PT23 1c emerald 15 15

Tax was for child welfare.

Cancer Type of 1952 Redrawn and "1977" Added

1978, Oct. 2 Litho. *Perf. 13½*
RA82 PT9 1c lilac rose 15 15

Tax for Dominican League Against Cancer.

Mother, Child, Holly — PT34

University Seal — PT35

1978, Dec. 1 Litho. *Perf. 13½*
RA83 PT34 1c green 15 15

Tax was for child welfare.
See Nos. RA89, RA92, RA97.

Orchid Type of 1973 Dated "1978"

Flower: Yellow alder.

1979, Apr. Litho. *Perf. 13½*
RA84 PT33 1c lt blue & multi 15 15

Tax was for Anti-Tuberculosis League.

1979, Feb. 10 Litho. *Perf. 13½*
RA85 PT35 2c ultra & gray 15 15

450th anniv. of University of Santo Domingo.

Invalid Type of 1973 Dated "1978"

1979, Mar. 1 Litho. *Perf. 12*
RA86 PT30 1c emerald 15 15

See note after No. RA59.

Invalid — PT36

Turnera Ulmifolia (Marilope) — PT37

1980, Mar. 28 Litho. *Perf. 13½*
RA87 PT36 1c olive & citron 15 15

Cancer Type of 1952 Redrawn and "1980" Added

1980, Oct. 1
RA88 PT9 1c violet & dk pur 15 15

Mother and Child Type of 1978

1980, Dec. 1 Litho. *Perf. 13½*
RA89 PT34 1c bright blue 15 15

1981, Apr. 27 Litho. *Perf. 12*
RA90 PT37 1c multicolored 15 15

Tax was for Anti-Tuberculosis League.
See Nos. RA98-RA99.

Communications Type of 1971

1981, Feb. Litho. *Perf. 10½*
RA91 PT28 1c blue & red (lt bl frame) 15 15

Mother and Child Type of 1978

1982, Dec. 1 Litho. *Perf. 12x12½*
RA92 PT34 1c lt bluish green 15 15

Inscribed 1981.

Cancer Type of 1952 Redrawn and "1981" Added

1982 **Litho.** *Perf. 13½*
RA93 PT9 1c blue & dp blue 15 15

PT38 Disabled — PT39

1983, Apr. 29 **Litho.** *Perf. 12*
RA94 PT38 1c multicolored 15 15

Tax was for Red Cross.

1984 **Litho.** *Perf. 13½*
RA95 PT39 1c sky blue 15 15

Cancer Type of 1952 Redrawn and "1983" Added

1983, Oct. 1 **Litho.** *Perf. 13½*
RA96 PT9 1c lt bluish grn & dk grn 15 15

Mother and Child Type of 1978

1983, Dec. 1 **Litho.** *Perf. 12*
RA97 PT34 1c light green 15 15

Inscribed 1983.

Flower Type of 1981 Dated "1983" or "1984"

1983-85 **Litho.** *Perf. 12x12½*
RA98 PT37 1c 1983 15 15
RA99 PT37 1c 1984 15 15
Set value 15 15

Issue dates: No. RA98, Apr. 19, 1983. No. RA99, Apr. 1, 1985.

POSTAL TAX AIR POST STAMPS

HABILITADO PARA
CORREO AEREO

Postal Tax Stamps Surcharged in Red or Gold

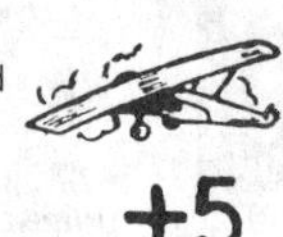

+5

1930, Dec. 3 **Unwmk.** *Perf. 12*
RAC1 PT2 5c + 5c blk & rose (R) 18.00 18.00
a. Tête bêche pair 125.00
b. "Habilitado Para" missing 52.50
RAC2 PT2 10c + 10c blk & rose (R) 18.00 18.00
a. Tête bêche pair 125.00
b. "Habilitado Para" missing 52.50
c. Gold surcharge 80.00 80.00
d. As "c," tête bêche pair 450.00
e. As "c" and "b" 250.00

Nos. RAC1-RAC2 were on sale one day.

RAC4 PT2 5c + 5c ultra & rose (R) 6.00 6.00
a. Tête bêche pair 45.00
b. Inverted surcharge 42.50
c. Tête bêche pair, inverted surcharge 600.00
d. Pair, one without surcharge 190.00
e. "Habilitado Para" missing 15.00
RAC5 PT2 10c + 10c yel & rose (G) 4.50 4.50
a. Tête bêche pair 42.50
b. "Habilitado Para" missing 18.00

Imperf

RAC6 PT2 5c + 5c ultra & rose (R) 6.00 6.00
a. Tête bêche pair 52.50
b. "Habilitado Para" missing 18.00
RAC7 PT2 10c + 10c yel & rose (G) 6.00 6.00
a. Tête bêche pair 52.50
b. "Habilitado Para" missing 18.00

It was obligatory to use Nos. RA1-RA8 and RAC1-RAC7 on all postal matter, in amounts equal to the ordinary postage.

This surtax was for the aid of sufferers from the hurricane of Sept. 3, 1930.

No. 261 Overprinted in Green **CORREO AEREO INTERNO**

1933, Oct. 11
RAC8 A32 2c scarlet 35 28
a. Double overprint 9.00
b. Pair, one without ovpt. 375.00

By official decree a copy of this stamp, in addition to the regular postage, had to be used on every letter, etc., sent by the internal air post service.

DUBAI

LOCATION — Oman Peninsula, Arabia, on Persian Gulf
GOVT. — Sheikdom under British protection
AREA — 1,500 sq. mi.
POP. — 60,000
CAPITAL — Dubai

Dubai is one of six Persian Gulf sheikdoms to join the United Arab Emirates which proclaimed its independence Dec. 2, 1971. See United Arab Emirates.

100 Naye Paise = 1 Rupee
100 Dirhams = 1 Riyal (1966)

Imperforate
Many issues were accompanied by smaller quantities of imperforate stamps.

Catalogue values for all unused stamps in this country are for Never Hinged items.

Hermit Crab — A1

Sheik Rashid bin Said al Maktum — A2

Designs: 2np, 20np, Cuttlefish. 3np, 25np, Snail. 4np, 30np, Crab. 5np, 35np, Sea urchin. 10np, 50np, Sea shell. 1r, Fortress wall. 2r, View of Dubai. 3r, Fortress wall. 5r, View of Dubai.

Perf. 12x11½

1963, June 15 **Litho.** **Unwmk.**
1 A1 1np dl bl & car rose 18 15
2 A1 2np lt bl & bis brn 18 15
3 A1 3np green & sepia 18 15
4 A1 4np pink & orange 18 15
5 A1 5np violet & blk 18 15
6 A1 10np brn org & blk 18 15
7 A1 15np gray ol & dp car 30 15
8 A1 20np rose red & org brn 32 15
9 A1 25np ap grn & red brn 38 15
10 A1 30np gray & red 45 20
11 A1 35np dl lil & dl vio 50 20
12 A1 50np org & sepia 80 30
13 A1 1r brt bl & red org 1.65 60
14 A1 2r dull yel & brn 3.50 1.25
15 A1 3r rose car & blk 5.25 1.75
16 A1 5r grn & dl red brn 8.25 3.00

Perf. 12

17 A2 10r rose lake, grnsh bl & blk 17.00 6.00
Nos. 1-17 (17) 39.48 14.65

Dhows — A3

Designs: 2np, First-aid tent. 3np, Camel caravan. 4np, Butterfly.

1963, Sept. 1 **Unwmk.** *Perf. 12*
18 A3 1np ultra, yel & red 15 15
19 A3 2np brn, yel & red 15 15
20 A3 3np red brn, org & red 15 15
21 A3 4np brn, brt grn & red 15 15
Nos. 18-21,C9-C12 (8) 2.57 2.57

Centenary of International Red Cross. Exist perf. 10½.

Four imperf. souvenir sheets exist in the denominations and designs of Nos. C9-C12, with "Air-Mail" omitted and colors changed. Size: 119x99mm.

For overprints see Nos. C52-C54.

A4

A5

Anopheles Mosquito: 2np, Mosquito and entwined snakes. 3np, Mosquitoes over swamp.

1963, Dec. 20 **Unwmk.** *Perf. 12*
22 A4 1np emer & red brn 15 15
23 A4 1np red & dark brn 15 15
24 A4 1np blue & carmine 15 15
25 A4 2np brn & orange 15 15
26 A4 2np carmine & blue 15 15
27 A4 3np org brn & blue 15 15
Nos. 22-27,C13-C15 (9) 2.23 2.23

WHO drive to eradicate malaria.

1964 **Unwmk.**

Designs: 1np, Scouts forming pyramid. 2np, Bugler. 3np, Cub Scouts. 4np, Scouts and bugler. 5np, Scouts presenting flag.

28 A5 1np dk brn & ocher 15 15
29 A5 2np car rose & sep 15 15
30 A5 3np blue & red org 15 15
31 A5 4np carmine & blue 15 15
32 A5 5np ind & bluish grn 15 15
Nos. 28-32,C20-C24 (10) 2.55 2.55

11th Boy Scout Jamboree, Marathon, Greece, Aug., 1963.

For overprints see Nos. C47-C51.

Unisphere, New York Skyline and Dubai Harbor — A6

Design: 2np, 4np, 10np, Views of New York and Dubai.

1964, Apr. 22 **Litho.** *Perf. 12*
33 A6 1np dk bl & rose red 15 15
34 A6 2np dl red, lil rose & bl 15 15
35 A6 3np brown & green 15 15
36 A6 4np emer, brt grn & red 15 15
37 A6 5np ol, sl grn & lil 15 15
38 A6 10np brn org, red org & blk 50 50
Nos. 33-38,C36-C38 (9) 3.70 3.70

New York World's Fair, 1964-65.

Gymnast A8

Designs: 2np, 5np, 20np, 40np, Various exercises on bar. 3np, 30np, Various exercises on vaulting horse. 4np, 10np, 1r, Various exercises on rings.

1964 **Photo.** *Perf. 14*
43 A8 1np org brn & yel grn 15 15
44 A8 2np dk brn & grnsh bl 15 15
45 A8 3np ultra & org brn 15 15
46 A8 4np dk pur & yel 15 15
47 A8 5np ocher & dk bl 15 15
48 A8 10np brt bl & ocher 25 25
49 A8 20np ol & lil rose 55 55
50 A8 30np dk bl & yel 65 65
51 A8 40np Prus grn & dl org 1.10 1.10
52 A8 1r rose vio & grnsh bl 2.50 2.50
Nos. 43-52 (10) 5.80 5.80

18th Olympic Games, Tokyo, Oct. 10-25, 1964. An imperf. miniature sheet contains a 67x67mm stamp similar to No. 52. Value $6.

Palace — A9

5 RUPEES POSTAGE
DUBAI

Sheik Rashid bin Said — A10

Designs: 20np, 25np, View of new Dubai. 35np, 40np, Bridge and dhow. 60np, 1r, Bridge. 1.25r, Minaret. 1.50r, 3r, Old Dubai.

1966, May 30 **Photo.** *Perf. 14x14½*

Size: 23x18mm

53 A9 5np brown & indigo 20 20
54 A9 10np black & orange 20 20
55 A9 15np ultra & brown 22 22

Perf. 13

Size: 27½x20½mm

56 A9 20np blue & red brn 30 30
57 A9 25np org ver & ultra 38 38
58 A9 35np violet & emer 52 52
59 A9 40np grnsh bl & bl 55 55

Perf. 14½

Size: 31½x24mm

60 A9 60np yel grn & org ver 90 90
61 A9 1r ultra & blue 1.50 1.50
62 A9 1.25r brn org & blk 1.90 1.90
63 A9 1.50r rose lil & yel grn 2.25 2.25
64 A9 3r dk ol bis & vio 4.50 4.50

Engr.

Perf. 14

65 A10 5r rose carmine 7.50 7.50
66 A10 10r dark blue 15.00 15.00
Nos. 53-66 (14) 35.92 35.92

Nos. 53-62, 64-66 Overprinted with New Currency Names and Bars

1967
67 A9 5d on 5np 25 25
68 A9 10d on 10np 25 25
69 A9 15d on 15np 35 35
70 A9 20d on 20np 40 40
71 A9 25d on 25np 50 50
72 A9 35d on 35np 60 60
73 A9 40d on 40np 65 65
74 A9 60d on 60np 75 75
75 A9 1r on 1r 1.00 1.00
76 A9 1.25r on 1.25r 1.75 1.75
77 A9 3r on 3r 4.00 4.00
78 A10 5r on 5r 6.50 6.50
79 A10 10r on 10r 12.00 12.00
Nos. 67-79 (13) 29.00 29.00

Sheik and Falcon — A11

Dhow — A12

Litho. & Engr.

1967, Aug. 21 *Perf. 13½*

80 A11	5d dp car & org	15	15
81 A11	10d sepia & green	15	15
82 A11	20d dp cl & bl gray	15	15
83 A11	35d slate & car	32	32
84 A11	60d vio bl & emer	65	65
85 A11	1r green & lilac	90	90
86 A12	1.25r lt bl & claret	1.25	1.25
87 A12	3r dull vio & cl	3.00	3.00
88 A12	5r brt grn & vio	5.00	5.00
89 A12	10r lil rose & grn	5.75	5.75
	Nos. 80-89 (10)	17.32	17.32

S. S. Bamora, 1914 — A13

Designs: 35d, De Havilland 66 plane, 1930. 60d, S. S. Sirdhana, 1947. 1r, Armstrong Whitworth 15 "Atlanta," 1938. 1.25r, S. S. Chandpara, 1949. 3r, BOAC Sunderland amphibian plane, 1943. No. 96, Freighter Bombala, 1961, and BOAC Super VC10, 1967.

1969, Feb. 12 Litho. *Perf. 14x13½*

90 A13	25d lt grn, bl & blk	15	*15*
91 A13	35d multicolored	16	*15*
92 A13	60d multicolored	32	*15*
93 A13	1r lil, blk & dl yel	52	*15*
94 A13	1.25r gray, blk & dp org	65	*15*
95 A13	3r pink, blk & bl grn	1.60	*32*
	Nos. 90-95 (6)	3.40	
	Set value		*69*

Miniature Sheet

Imperf

96 A13	1.25r pink, blk & bl grn	3.25	3.25

60 years of postal service.

Mother and Children, by Rubens — A14

Arab Mother's Day: 60d, Madonna and Child, by Murillo. 1r, Mother and Child, by Francesco Mazzuoli. 3r, Madonna and Child, by Correggio.

1969, Mar. 21 Litho. *Perf. 13½*

97 A14	60d silver & multi	50	*15*
98 A14	1r silver & multi	90	*15*
99 A14	1.25r silver & multi	1.10	*15*
100 A14	3r silver & multi	2.50	*38*
	Set value		*70*

Porkfish — A15

1969, May 26 Litho. *Perf. 11*

101 A15	60d shown	65	*32*
102 A15	60d Spotted grouper	65	*32*
103 A15	60d Moonfish	65	*32*
104 A15	60d Sweetlips	65	*32*
105 A15	60d Blue angel	65	*32*
106 A15	60d Texas skate	65	*32*
107 A15	60d Striped butterflyfish	65	*32*
108 A15	60d Imperial angelfish	65	*32*
	Nos. 101-108 (8)	5.20	*2.56*

Nos. 101-108 printed in same sheet of 16 (4x4).

Explorers and Map of Arabia A16

1969, July 21 Litho. *Perf. 13½x13*

109 A16	35d brown & green	50	*15*
110 A16	60d vio & sepia	90	*15*
111 A16	1r green & dl bl	1.50	*15*
112 A16	1.25r gray & rose car	2.00	*15*
	Set value		*37*

European explorers of Arabia: Sir Richard Francis Burton (1821-1890), Charles Montagu Doughty (1843-1926), Johann Ludwig Burckhardt (1784-1817) and Wilfred Patrick Thesiger (1910-).

Construction of World's First Underwater Oil Storage Tank — A17

Designs: 20d, Launching of oil storage tank. 35d, Oil storage tank in place on ocean ground. 60d, Sheik Rashid bin Said, offshore drilling platform and monument commemorating first oil export. 1r, Offshore production platform and helicopter port.

1969, Oct. 13 Litho. *Perf. 11*

113 A17	5d blue & multi	20	*15*
114 A17	20d blue & multi	32	*15*
115 A17	35d blue & multi	60	*15*
116 A17	60d blue & multi	1.00	*15*
117 A17	1r blue & multi	1.25	*15*
	Nos. 113-117 (5)	3.37	
	Set value		*30*

Astronauts Collecting Moon Rocks — A18

Designs: 1r, Astronaut at foot of ladder. 1.25r, Astronauts planting American flag.

1969, Dec. 15 Litho. *Perf. 14½*

118	Strip of 3	2.25	*30*
a.	A18 60d multicolored	30	*15*
b.	A18 1r multicolored	60	*15*
c.	A18 1.25r multicolored (airmail)	1.25	*15*

The 1.25r is inscribed "AIRMAIL."

Sizes: 60d and 1r, 28½x41mm; 1.25r, 60½x41mm.

See note after US No. C76.

Ocean Weather Ship Launching Radio Sonde, and Hastings Plane — A19

WMO Emblem and: 1r, Kew-type radio sonde, weather balloon and radar antenna. 1.25r, Tiros satellite and weather sounding rocket. 3r, Ariel satellite and rocket launching.

1970, Mar. 23 Litho. *Perf. 11*

121 A19	60d dl grn, brn & blk	32	*15*
122 A19	1r brown & multi	60	*15*
123 A19	1.25r dk blue & multi	70	*15*
124 A19	3r multicolored	1.65	*28*
	Set value		*54*

9th World Meteorological Day.

UPU Headquarters and Monument, Bern — A20

Design: 60d, UPU monument, Bern, telecommunications satellite and London PO tower.

1970, May 20 Litho. *Perf. 13½x14*

125 A20	5d lt grn & multi	35	*15*
126 A20	60d dp bl & multi	1.00	*15*
	Set value		*15*

UPU Headquarters opening, May 20.

Charles Dickens, London Skyline A21

Designs: 60d, Dickens' portrait, vert. 1.25r, Dickens and "Old Curiosity Shop." 3r, Bound volumes.

1970, July 23 Litho. *Perf. 13½*

127 A21	60d olive & multi	50	*15*
128 A21	1r multicolored	75	*15*
129 A21	1.25r buff & multi	1.00	*20*
130 A21	3r multicolored	2.50	*50*

Charles Dickens (1812-1870), English novelist.

The Graham Children, by William Hogarth — A22

Paintings: 60d, Caroline Murat and her Children, by Franois Pascal Gerard, vert. 1r, Napoleon with the Children on the Terrace in St. Cloud, by Louis Ducis.

1970, Oct. 1 Litho. *Perf. 13½*

131 A22	35d multicolored	40	*15*
132 A22	60d multicolored	70	*15*
133 A22	1r multicolored	1.10	*15*
	Set value		*18*

Issued for Children's Day.

National Bank of Dubai — A24

Sheik Rashid bin Said — A23

Television Station — A25

Designs: 10d, Boat building. 20d, Al Maktum Bascule Bridge. 35d, Great Mosque, Dubai, vert. 1r, Dubai International Airport, horiz. 1.25r, Port Rashid harbor project, horiz. 3r, Rashid Hospital, horiz. 5r, Dubai Trade School, horiz.

Perf. 14x14½, 14½x14

1970-71 Litho.

134 A23	5d multi ('71)	18	*15*
135 A24	10d multi ('71)	20	*15*
136 A24	20d multi ('71)	30	*15*
137 A24	35d multi ('71)	40	*15*
138 A24	60d multicolored	65	*15*

Perf. 14

139 A25	1r multicolored	90	*15*
140 A25	1.25r multicolored	1.00	*15*
141 A25	3r multicolored	2.00	*25*
142 A25	5r multicolored	3.25	*40*
143 A25	10r multi ('71)	5.75	*85*
	Nos. 134-143 (10)	14.63	
	Set value		*1.90*

Dubai Airport A26

Designs: 1.25r, Airport entrance.

1971, May 15 Litho. *Perf. 13½x14*

144 A26	1r multicolored	1.00	*15*
145 A26	1.25r multicolored	1.25	*20*

Opening of Dubai International Airport.

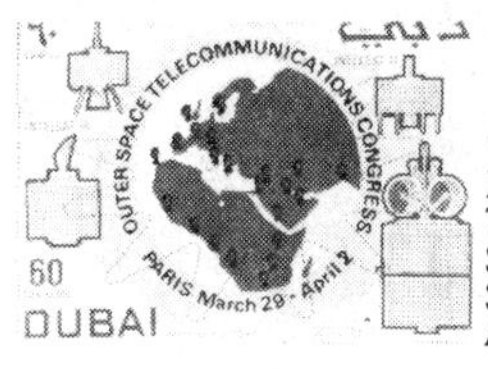

Map With Tracking Stations, Satellites A27

1971, June 21 Litho. *Perf. 14½*

146 A27	60d multicolored	45	*28*

Outer Space Telecommunications Cong., Paris, Mar. 29-Apr. 2. See Nos. C55-C56.

Fan, Scout Emblem, Map of Japan — A28

Designs: 1r, Boy Scouts in kayaks. 1.25r, Mountaineering. 3r, Campfire, horiz.

Perf. 14x13½, 13½x14

1971, Aug. 30 Litho.

147 A28	60d multicolored	42	*15*
148 A28	1r multicolored	75	*15*
149 A28	1.25r multicolored	90	*15*
150 A28	3r multicolored	2.00	*30*
	Set value		*57*

13th Boy Scout World Jamboree, Asagiri Plain, Japan, Aug. 2-10.

Albrecht Dürer, Self-portrait — A29

1971, Oct. 18 *Perf. 14x13½*

151 A29 60d gold & multi 50 *15*

See Nos. C57-C59.

Boy in Meadow — A30

Design: 5r, Boys playing and UNICEF emblem, horiz.

1971, Dec. 11 *Perf. 13½*

152 A30 60d gold & multi 42 *15*
153 A30 5r gold & multi 2.00 *25*
Set value *30*

25th anniv. of UNICEF. See No. C60.

Ludwig van Beethoven — A31

Portrait: 10d, Leonardo da Vinci.

1972, Feb. 7

154 A31 10d lt tan & multi 15 *15*
155 A31 35d lt tan & multi 25 *15*
Set value *15*

See Nos. C61-C62.

Olympic Emblems, Gymnast on Rings — A32

1972, July 31 **Litho.** *Perf. 13½*

156 A32 35d shown 30 *15*
157 A32 40d Fencing 38 *15*
158 A32 65d Hockey 45 *15*
Nos. 156-158,C65-C67 (6) 3.03
Set value *48*

20th Olympic Games, Munich, Aug. 26-Sept. 11.
Stamps of Dubai were replaced in 1972 by those of United Arab Emirates.

AIR POST STAMPS

Type of Regular Issue and

Peregrine Falcon — AP1

Wheat — AP2

Design: A1, Falcon over bridge.

Perf. 12x11½, 11½x12

1963, June 15 **Litho.** **Unwmk.**

C1 A1 20np dk red brn & lt blue 75 25
C2 AP1 25np ol & blk brn 80 30
C3 A1 30np red org & blk 90 35
C4 AP1 40np grayish brn & dk violet 1.00 40
C5 A1 50np emer & rose cl 1.25 52
C6 AP1 60np brn org & blk 1.50 55
C7 A1 75np vio & dp grn 1.75 60
C8 AP1 1r org & red brn 2.75 75
Nos. C1-C8 (8) 10.70 3.72

Red Cross Type of Regular Issue

Designs: 20np, Dhows. 30np, First-aid tent. 30np, Camel caravan. 4np, Butterfly.

1963, Sept. 1 **Unwmk.** *Perf. 12*

C9 A3 20np brown, yel & red 30 30
C10 A3 30np dk bl, buff & red 42 42
C11 A3 40np black, yel & red 55 55
C12 A3 50np vio, lt bl & red 70 70

Malaria Type of Regular Issue

Designs: 30np, Anopheles mosquito. 40np, Mosquito and coiled arrows. 70np, Mosquitoes over swamp.

1963, Dec. 20 **Unwmk.** *Perf. 12*

C13 A4 30np purple & emer 30 30
C14 A4 40np red & dull grn 38 38
C15 A4 70np slate & citron 65 65

Three imperf. souv. sheets exist containing 4 stamps each in changed colors similar to Nos. C13-C15.

1963, Dec. 30 **Litho.**

Designs: 40np, Wheat and palm tree. 70np, Hands holding wheat. 1r, Woman carrying basket.

C16 AP2 30np vio bl & ocher 30 30
C17 AP2 40np red & olive 45 45
C18 AP2 70np green & orange 65 65
C19 AP2 1r org brn & Prus bl 1.00 1.00

Boy Scout Type of Regular Issue

Designs: 20np, Human pyramid. 30np, Bugler. 40np, Cub Scouts. 70np, Scouts and bugler. 1r, Scouts presenting flag.

1964, Jan. 20

C20 A5 20np green & dk brn 15 15
C21 A5 30np lilac & ocher 22 22
C22 A5 40np vio bl & yel grn 28 28
C23 A5 70np dk grn & gray 45 45
C24 A5 1r vio bl & red org 70 70
Nos. C20-C24 (5) 1.80 1.80

Five imperf. souv. sheets exist containing 4 stamps each in changed colors similar to Nos. C20-C24.
For overprints, see Nos. C47-C51.

John F. Kennedy and US Seal — AP3

1964, Jan. 15 **Litho.**

C25 AP3 75np grn & blk, *lt grn* 52 52
C26 AP3 1r ocher & blk, *tan* 65 65
C27 AP3 1.25r mag & blk, *gray* 85 85

Pres. John F. Kennedy (1917-1963). A souvenir sheet contains one imperf. 1.25r in buff and black with simulated perforations.
For overprints, see Nos. C52-C54.

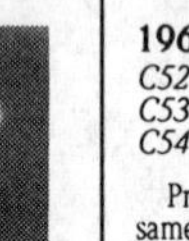
Spacecraft — AP4

Designs: 1np, 5np, Ascending rocket (vert.). 2np, 1r, Mercury capsule (vert.). 4np, 2r, Twin spacecraft.

1964, Jan. 25 **Unwmk.** *Perf. 12*

C28 AP4 1np emer & org 15 15
C29 AP4 2np multicolored 15 15
C30 AP4 3np multicolored 15 15
C31 AP4 4np multicolored 15 15
C32 AP4 5np bl & orange 15 15
C33 AP4 1r vio bl, dp car & buff 70 70
C34 AP4 1.50r vio bl, dp car & buff 1.20 1.20
C35 AP4 2r bl, yel & red 1.50 1.50
Nos. C28-C35 (8) 4.15 4.15

Issued to honor the astronauts. An imperf. souvenir sheet contains one stamp similar to No. C35.

New York World's Fair Type of Regular Issue

Design: Statue of Liberty and ships in Dubai harbor.

1964, Apr. 22 **Litho.**

C36 A6 75np gray bl, ultra & blk 50 50
C37 A6 2r gray grn, dk brn & bis 85 85
C38 A6 3r dl grn, gray ol & dp org 1.10 1.10

An imperf. souvenir sheet contains 2 stamps in Statue of Liberty design: 2r dark brown and rose carmine, and 3r ultramarine and gold.

Scales and Flame — AP5

1964, Apr. 30 **Litho.** *Perf. 12*

C39 AP5 35np bl, brn & scar 28 28
C40 AP5 50np lt bl, dk grn & scar 35 35
C41 AP5 1r grnsh bl, blk & scar 60 60
C42 AP5 3r lt ultra, ultra, & scar 2.00 2.00

15th anniv. of the Universal Declaration of Human Rights. An imperf. souvenir sheet contains one 3r light green, ultramarine and scarlet stamp.

Nos. C20-C24 Overprinted in Red and Black (Shield in Red)

1964, June 20

C47 A5 20np green & dk brn 75 38
C48 A5 30np lilac & ocher 1.00 50
C49 A5 40np vio bl & yel grn 1.50 75
C50 A5 70np dk grn & gray 2.50 1.25
C51 A5 1r vio bl & red org 3.75 1.75
Nos. C47-C51 (5) 9.50 4.63

9th Winter Olympic Games, Innsbruck, Austria, Jan. 29-Feb. 9, 1964.
A similar but unauthorized overprint, with shield in black, exists on Nos. 28-32, C20-C24, and the five souvenir sheets mentioned below No. C24. The Dubai G.P.O. calls this black-shield overprint "bogus."

Nos. C25-C27 Overprinted in Brown or Green

MAY
29

1964, Sept. 15

C52 AP3 75np (Br) 1.50 1.50
C53 AP3 1r (G) 1.75 1.75
C54 AP3 1.25r (G) 2.25 2.25

Pres. John F. Kennedy 48th birth anniv. The same overprint in black was applied to the souv. sheet noted after No. C27.

Communications Type of Regular Issue

Designs: 1r, Intelsat 4, tracking station on globe and rocket. 5r, Eiffel Tower, Syncom 3 and Goonhilly radar station.

1971, June 21 **Litho.** *Perf. 14½*

C55 A27 1r lt brn & multi 45 *15*
C56 A27 5r multicolored 2.25 *45*

Portrait Type of Regular Issue

Portraits: 1r, Sir Isaac Newton. 1.25r, Avicenna. 3r, Voltaire.

1971, Oct. 18 **Litho.** *Perf. 14x13½*

C57 A29 1r gold & multi 60 *15*
C58 A29 1.25r gold & multi 75 *15*
C59 A29 3r gold & multi 2.25 *45*

UNICEF Type of Regular Issue

Design: 1r, Mother, children and UNICEF emblem.

1971, Dec. 11 *Perf. 13½*

C60 A30 1r gold & multi 50 *15*

Portrait Type of Regular Issue

Portraits: 75d, Khalil Gibran. 5r, Charles de Gaulle.

1972, Feb. 7 **Litho.** *Perf. 13½*

C61 A31 75d lt tan & multi 25 *15*
C62 A31 5r lt tan & multi 1.75 *32*
Set value *37*

Infant Health Care AP6

Design: 75d, Nurse supervising children at meal, and WHO emblem (vert.).

1972, Apr. 7 **Litho.** *Perf. 14x13½*

C63 AP6 75d multicolored 1.00 *15*
C64 AP6 1.25r multicolored 1.50 *25*

World Health Day.

Olympic Type of Regular Issue

1972, July 31 **Litho.** *Perf. 13½*

C65 A32 75d Water polo 50 *15*
C66 A32 1r Steeplechase 65 *15*
C67 A32 1.25r Running 75 *15*
Set value *33*

POSTAGE DUE STAMPS

Type of Regular Issue, 1963.

Designs: 1np, 4np, 15np, Clam. 2np, 5np, 25np, Mussel. 3np, 10np, 35np, Oyster.

Perf. 12x11½

1963, June 15 **Litho.** **Unwmk.**

J1 A1 1np gray grn & ver 38 22
J2 A1 2np lemon & brt bl 45 30
J3 A1 3np dl rose & green 75 52
J4 A1 4np light grn & mag 1.10 75
J5 A1 5np vermilion & blk 1.25 90
J6 A1 10np citron & violet 1.65 1.25
J7 A1 15np brt ultra & ver 2.25 1.50
J8 A1 25np buff & olive grn 2.50 1.65
J9 A1 35np turq bl & dp org 3.00 1.90
Nos. J1-J9 (9) 13.33 8.99

Sheik Rashid bin Said — D1

1972, May 22 Litho. *Perf. 14x14½*

J10	D1	5d blk & gray grn	40	40
J11	D1	10d vio bl, blk & bis	40	40
J12	D1	20d sl grn, blk & brick red	60	60
J13	D1	30d grnsh gray, blk & lil	90	90
J14	D1	50d lilac, brn & bis	1.50	1.50
		Nos. J10-J14 (5)	3.80	3.80

EASTERN RUMELIA

(South Bulgaria)

LOCATION — In southern Bulgaria
GOVT. — A former autonomous unit of the Turkish Empire.
CAPITAL — Philippopolis (Plovdiv)

In 1885 the province of Eastern Rumelia revolted against Turkish rule and united with Bulgaria, adopting the new name of South Bulgaria. This union was assured by the Treaty of Bucharest in 1886, following the war between Serbia and Bulgaria.

40 Paras = 1 Piaster

Counterfeits of all overprints are plentiful.

No. 1 

A2

A3

Stamps of Turkey, 1876-84, Overprinted in Blue

1880 Unwmk. *Perf. 13½*

1	A1	½pi on 20pa yel grn	27.50	27.50
3	A2	10pa blk & rose	*30.00*	
4	A2	20pa vio & grn	28.00	28.00
6	A2	2pi blk & buff	57.50	57.50
7	A2	5pi red & bl	190.00	190.00
8	A3	10pa blk & red lil	18.00	

Nos. 3 & 8 were not placed in use.
Inverted and double overprints of all values exist.

Same, with Extra Overprint "R. O."

9	A3	10pa blk & red lil	30.00	30.00

Crescent and Turkish Inscriptions of Value — A4

1881 Typo. *Perf. 13½*

10	A4	5pa blk & olive	1.50	45
11	A4	10pa blk & green	5.50	45
12	A4	20pa blk & rose	22	45
13	A4	1pi blk & blue	2.25	1.90
14	A4	5pi rose & blue	18.00	27.50

Tête bêche pairs, imperforates and all perf. 11½ copies of Nos. 10-14 were not placed in use, and were found only in the remainder stock. This is true also of a 10pa cliché in the 20pa plate, and of a cliché of Turkey No. 63 in the 1pi plate.

1884 *Perf. 11½*

15	A4	5pa lil & pale lil	15	15
16	A4	10pa grn & pale grn	15	15
17	A4	20pa car & pale rose	15	
18	A4	1pi bl & pale bl	15	
19	A4	5pi brn & pale brn	*110.00*	

Nos. 17-19 were not placed in use.
Nos. 15-19 imperf. are from remainders.
For overprints see Turkey Nos. 542-545.

South Bulgaria

Counterfeits of all overprints are plentiful.

Nos. 10-14 Overprinted in Two Types:

a

b

Type a - Four toes on each foot.
Type b - Three toes on each foot.

1885 Unwmk. *Perf. 13½*

Blue Overprint

20	A4	5pa blk & olive	*75.00*	*75.00*
21	A4	10pa blk & grn	*275.00*	*275.00*
22	A4	20pa blk & rose	75.00	75.00
23	A4	1pi blk & blue	15.00	17.50
24	A4	5pi rose & bl, "b"	*225.00*	*240.00*
a.		Type "a"	*400.00*	*400.00*

Nos. 20-21 are type "a." Nos. 22-23 are types "a" and "b," same values.

Black Overprint

25	A4	1pi blk & bl	12.50	15.00
26	A4	5pi rose & bl	*300.00*	*300.00*

No. 25 is types "a" and "b," same values, No. 26 type "b."

Same Overprint on Nos. 15-17

Perf. 11½, 13½

Blue Overprint

27	A4	5pa lil & pale lil, perf. 11½	6.75	11.00
a.		Perf. 13½	17.50	20.00
28	A4	10pa grn & pale grn	6.75	11.00
29	A4	20pa car & pale rose	60.00	67.50

Black Overprint

30	A4	5pa lil & pale lil	12.00	15.00
31	A4	10pa grn & pale grn	12.00	15.00
32	A4	20pa car & pale rose	11.00	15.00

#27-32 are types "a" and "b," same values.

Nos. 10-17 Handstamped in Black in Two Types:

a

b

Type a - First letter at top circular.
Type b - First letter at top oval.

1885 *Perf. 13½*

33	A4	5pa blk & olive	*225.00*	
34	A4	10pa blk & grn	*225.00*	
35	A4	20pa blk & rose	30.00	40.00
36	A4	1pi blk & bl	30.00	35.00
37	A4	5pi rose & bl, "b"	*225.00*	*275.00*
a.		Type "a"	*400.00*	*400.00*

#33-36 are types "a" and "b," same values.

Perf. 11½

38	A4	5pa lil & pale lil, perf. 13½	8.50	8.50
a.		Perf. 11½, "a"	75.00	80.00
39	A4	10pa grn & pale grn	7.50	8.00
40	A4	20pa car & pale rose	7.50	11.00

Nos. 38-40 are types "a" and "b," same values.

Nos. 20-40 exist with inverted and double handstamps. Overprints in unlisted colors are proofs.

The stamps of South Bulgaria were superseded in 1886 by those of Bulgaria.

EASTERN SILESIA

LOCATION — In central Europe
GOVT. — Former Austrian crownland
AREA — 1,987 sq. mi.
POP. — 680,422 (estimated 1920)
CAPITAL — Troppau

After World War I, this territory was occupied by Czechoslovakia and eventually was divided between Poland and Czechoslovakia, the dividing line running through Teschen.

100 Heller = 1 Krone
100 Fennigi = 1 Marka

Plebiscite Issues

Stamps of Czechoslovakia 1918-20, Overprinted in Black, Blue, Violet or Red

SO
1920

1920 Unwmk. *Imperf.*

1	A2	1h dk brn	22	22
2	A1	3h red vio	15	15
3	A2	5h bl grn	25.00	20.00
4	A2	15h red	14.00	6.50
5	A1	20h bl grn	15	15
6	A2	25h dl vio	80	80
7	A1	30h bister (R)	16	16
8	A1	40h red org	16	16
9	A2	50h dl vio	35	35
10	A2	50h dk bl	1.10	1.10
11	A2	60h org (Bl)	50	50
12	A2	75h slate (R)	35	35
13	A2	80h ol grn (R)	35	35
14	A1	100h brown	45	45
15	A2	120h gray blk (R)	1.10	1.10
16	A1	200h ultra (R)	1.10	1.10
17	A2	300h grn (R)	1.60	1.60
18	A1	400h pur (R)	1.40	1.40
20	A2	500h red brn (Bl)	4.00	3.25
a.		Black overprint	8.00	6.50
21	A2	1000h vio (Bl)	11.00	6.50
a.		Black overprint	140.00	80.00
		Nos. 1-21 (20)	63.94	46.19

Perf. 11½, 14

22	A2	1h dk brn	15	15
23	A2	5h bl grn	16	16
24	A2	10h yel grn	15	15
a.		Imperf.	*250.00*	*250.00*
25	A2	15h red	15	15
26	A2	20h rose	22	22
a.		Imperf.	*200.00*	*200.00*
27	A2	25h dl vio	22	22
28	A2	30h red vio (Bl)	22	22
29	A2	60h org (Bl)	35	35
30	A1	200h ultra (R)	2.50	2.50
		Nos. 22-30 (9)	4.12	4.12

The letters "S. O." are the initials of "Silésie Orientale."

Forged cancellations are found on #1-30.

Overprinted in Carmine or Violet

SO
19 20

31	A4	500h sl, *grysh* (C)	80.00	
32	A4	1000h blk brn, *brnsh*	80.00	

Excellent counterfeits of this overprint exist.

Stamps of Poland, 1919, Overprinted

S. O.
1920.

1920 *Perf. 11½*

41	A10	5f green	15	15
42	A10	10f red brn	15	15
43	A10	15f light red	15	15
44	A11	25f olive green	15	15
45	A11	50f blue green	15	15

Overprinted **S. O. 1920.**

46	A12	1k deep green	15	15
47	A12	1.50k brown	15	15
48	A12	2k dark blue	15	15
49	A13	2.50k dull violet	15	15
50	A14	5k slate blue	15	15
		Set value	55	64

SPECIAL DELIVERY STAMPS

Czechoslovakia Special Delivery Stamps Overprinted in Blue

S O
19 20

1920 Unwmk. *Imperf.*

E1	SD1	2h red violet, *yel*	15	15
a.		Black overprint	1.00	80
E2	SD1	5h yellow green, *yel*	15	15
a.		Black overprint	6.00	5.00
		Set value	16	18

POSTAGE DUE STAMPS

SO

Czechoslovakia Postage Due Stamps Overprinted In Blue or Red

1920

1920 Unwmk. *Imperf.*

J1	D1	5h deep bis (Bl)	15	15
a.		Black overprint	37.50	30.00
J2	D1	10h deep bister	15	15
J3	D1	15h deep bister	15	15
J4	D1	20h deep bister	25	15
J5	D1	25h deep bister	25	15
J6	D1	30h deep bister	25	15
J7	D1	40h deep bister	40	35
J8	D1	50h deep bister	40	35
J9	D1	100h blk brn (R)	80	62
J10	D1	500h gray grn (R)	3.50	2.50
J11	D1	1000h purple (R)	6.25	5.75
		Nos. J1-J11 (11)	12.55	10.47

Forged cancellations exist.

NEWSPAPER STAMPS

Czeckoslovakia Newspaper Stamps Overprinted in Black like Nos. 1-30

1920 Unwmk. *Imperf.*

P1	N1	2h gray green	25	25
P2	N1	6h red	15	15
P3	N1	10h dull violet	20	20
P4	N1	20h blue	25	25
P5	N1	30h gray brown	25	25
		Nos. P1-P5 (5)	1.10	1.10

ECUADOR

LOCATION — Northwest coast of South America, bordering on the Pacific Ocean
GOVT. — Republic
AREA — 116,270 sq. mi.
POP. — 8,420,000 (est. 1984)
CAPITAL — Quito

The Republic of Ecuador was so constituted on May 11, 1830, after the Civil War which separated the original members of the Republic of Colombia, founded by Simon Bolivar by uniting the Presidency of Quito with the Viceroyalty of New Grenada and the Captaincy of Venezuela. The Presidency of Quito became the Republic of Ecuador.

8 Reales = 1 Peso
100 Centavos = 1 Sucre (1881)

Catalogue values for unused stamps in this country are for Never Hinged items, beginning with Scott 453 in the regular postage section, Scott C147 in the airpost section, Scott CO19 in the airpost officials section, Scott O201 in the officials section, Scott RA60 in the postal tax section, and all entries in the Galapagos section.

Watermarks

Wmk. 117-Liberty Cap

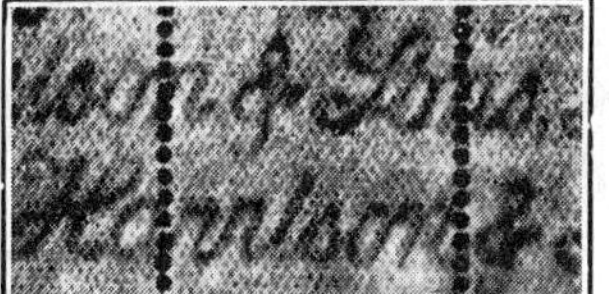
Wmk. 233- "Harrison & Sons, London" in Script Letters

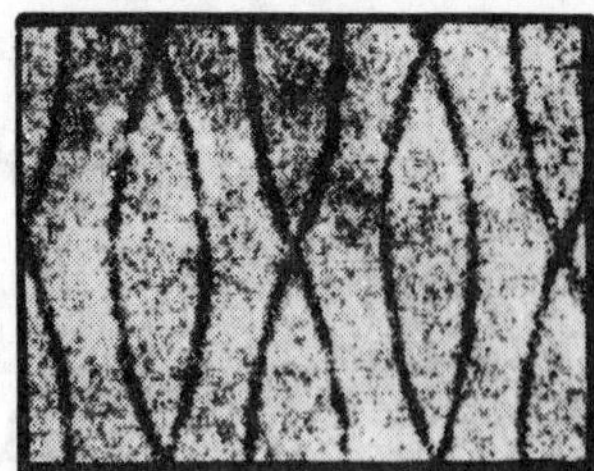

Wmk. 340- Alternating Interlaced Wavy Lines

Wmk. 367- Liberty Cap, Emblem, Inscription

Coat of Arms
A1 A2

1865-72 Unwmk. Typo. *Imperf.*

Quadrille Paper

1 A1 1r yellow ('72) 25.00 24.00

Wove Paper

2 A1 ½r ultra 15.00 8.00
a. ½r gray blue ('67) 15.00 8.00
b. Batonne paper ('70) 22.50 14.00
c. Blue paper ('72) 110.00 75.00
3 A1 1r buff 20.00 10.00
a. 1r orange buff 25.00 12.00
4 A1 1r yellow 12.00 8.50
a. 1r olive yellow ('66) 17.00 10.00
b. Laid paper 110.00 75.00
c. Half used as ½r on cover 200.00
d. Batonne paper 22.50 17.00
5 A1 1r green 170.00 20.00
a. Half used as ½r on cover 200.00
6 A2 4r red ('66) 185.00 90.00
a. 4r red brown ('66) 185.00 90.00
b. Arms in circle 185.00 90.00
c. Printed on both sides 300.00
d. Half used as 2r on cover 1,300.

Letter paper embossed with arms of Ecuador was used in printing a number of sheets of Nos. 2, 4-6.

Papermakers' watermarks are known on No. 2 ("Bath" and crown) and No. 4 ("Rolland Freres").

On the 4r the oval holding the coat of arms is usually 13½-14mm wide, but on about one-fifth of the stamps in the sheet it is 15-15½mm wide, almost a circle.

The 2r, 8r and 12r, type A1, are bogus.

Proofs of the ½r, type A1, are known in black and green.

An essay of type A2 shows the condor's head facing right.

1871-72

Blue-surface Paper

7 A1 ½r ultra 20.00 13.00
8 A1 1r yellow 110.00 40.00

Unofficial reprints of types A1-A2 differ in color, have a different sheet makeup and lack gum. Type A1 reprints usually have a double frameline at left. All stamps on blue paper with horiz. blue lines are reprints.

A3

A4

1872 White Paper Litho. *Perf. 11*

9 A3 ½r blue 12.00 2.75
10 A4 1r yellow 14.00 4.00
11 A3 1p rose 2.75 *9.00*

The 1r surcharged 4c is fraudulent.

A5

A6

A7

A8

A9

A10

1881, Nov. 1 Engr. *Perf. 12*

12 A5 1c yellow brn 15 15
13 A6 2c lake 15 15
14 A7 5c blue 2.50 35
15 A8 10c orange 15 15
16 A9 20c gray violet 15 15
17 A10 50c blue green 70 *2.00*
Nos. 12-17 (6) 3.80 *2.95*

The 1c surcharged 3c, and 20c surcharged 5c are fraudulent.

For overprints see Nos. O1-O6.

No. 17 Surcharged in Black

DIEZ
CENTAVOS

1883, Apr.

18 A10 10c on 50c blue grn 17.00 14.00
a. Double surcharge

Dangerous forgeries exist.

A12

A13

A14

A15

1887

19 A12 1c blue green 22 15
20 A13 2c vermilion 35 15
21 A14 5c blue 1.10 22
22 A15 80c olive green 2.00 *5.50*

For overprints see Nos. O7-O10.

President Juan Flores — A16

1892

23 A16 1c orange 15 15
24 A16 2c dk brown 15 15
25 A16 5c vermilion 15 15
26 A16 10c green 15 15
27 A16 20c red brown 15 15
28 A16 50c maroon 15 *28*
29 A16 1s blue 18 *70*
30 A16 5s purple 50 *1.00*
Set value 1.28 *2.30*

The issues of 1892, 1894, 1895 and 1896 were printed by the Hamilton Bank Note Co., New York, to the order of N. F. Seebeck, who held a contract for stamps with the government of Ecuador.

No. 30 in green is said to be an essay or color trial.

For surcharges and overprints see Nos. 31-37, O11-O17.

Nos. 29 and 30 Surcharged in Black

5 CENTAVOS

1893

Surcharge Measures 25½x2½mm

31 A16 5c on 1s blue 2.00 2.00
32 A16 5c on 5s purple 4.75 3.50
a. Double surcharge

Surcharge Measures 24x2¼mm

33 A16 5c on 1s blue 1.25 1.00
a. Double surcharge, one inverted
34 A16 5c on 5s purple 5.00 4.00
a. Double surcharge, one inverted

Nos. 28-30 Surcharged in Black

5 CENTAVOS

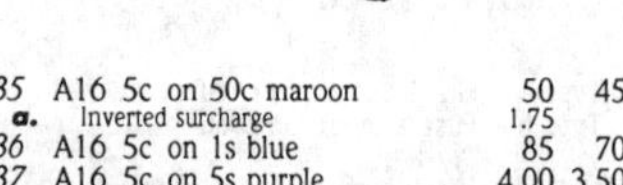

35 A16 5c on 50c maroon 50 45
a. Inverted surcharge 1.75
36 A16 5c on 1s blue 85 70
37 A16 5c on 5s purple 4.00 3.50

Pres. Juan Flores — A19

Pres. Vicente Rocafuerte — A20

38 A19 5c on 5s lake 1.00 1.00

It is stated that No. 38 was used exclusively as a postage stamp and not for telegrams.

1894 Dated 1894 *Perf. 12*

Various Frames

39 A20 1c blue 20 20
40 A20 2c yellow brn 20 20
41 A20 5c green 20 20
b. Perf. 14 2.75 1.00
42 A20 10c vermilion 35 28
43 A20 20c black 50 35
44 A20 50c orange 2.75 1.00
45 A20 1s carmine 4.50 2.00
46 A20 5s dark blue 5.50 3.00
Nos. 39-46 (8) 14.20 7.23

1895

Same, Dated "1895"

47 A20 1c blue 40 35
48 A20 2c yellow brn 40 35
49 A20 5c green 35 24
50 A20 10c vermilion 35 20
51 A20 20c black 50 45
52 A20 50c orange 1.75 1.00
53 A20 1s carmine 8.50 4.00
54 A20 5s dark blue 4.00 2.00
Nos. 47-54 (8) 16.25 8.59

Reprints of the 2c, 10c, 50c, 1s and 5s of the 1894-95 issues are generally on thick paper. Original issues are on thin to medium thick paper. To distinguish reprints from originals, a comparison of paper thickness, paper color, gum, printing clarity and direction of paper weave is necessary. Value 15 cents each.

For overprints see #77-112, O20-O33, O50-O91.

A21

A22

A23

A24

A25

A26

A27 A28

1896 Wmk. 117

55 A21 1c dk green 35 30
56 A22 2c red 35 15
57 A23 5c blue 35 15
58 A24 10c bister brn 25 *35*
59 A25 20c orange 60 *1.00*
60 A26 50c dark blue 1.00 *1.50*
61 A27 1s yellow brn 1.75 *1.75*
62 A27 5s violet *7.00* *2.75*
Nos. 55-62 (8) 11.65 *7.95*

Unwmk.

62A A21 1c dk green 50 15
62B A22 2c red 50 15
62C A23 5c blue 50 30
62D A24 10c bister brn 35 *70*
62E A25 20c orange 3.00 *2.75*
62F A26 50c dark blue 50 *1.40*
62G A27 1s yellow brn 3.00 *4.00*
62H A28 5s violet *7.00* *2.75*
Nos. 62A-62H (8) 15.35 *12.20*

Reprints of Nos. 55-62H are on very thick paper, with paper weave direction vertical. Value 15 cents each.

For surcharges and overprints see Nos. 74, 76, 113-114, O34-O49.

Vicente Roca, Diego Noboa and José Olmedo — A28a

General Juan Francisco Elizalde — A28b

Perf. 11½

1896, Oct. 9 Unwmk. Litho.

63 A28a 1c rose 32 40
64 A28b 2c blue 32 40
65 A28a 5c green 38 48
66 A28b 10c ocher 38 48
67 A28a 20c red 48 *1.00*
68 A28b 50c violet 65 *1.65*
69 A28a 1s orange 1.25 *2.00*
Nos. 63-69 (7) 3.78 *6.41*

Success of the Liberal Party in 1845 & 1895.

For overprints see Nos. 115-125.

A29

Black Surcharge

1896, Nov. *Perf. 12*

70 A29 1c on 1c ver, "1893-1894" 50 28
a. Inverted surcharge 1.25 1.00
b. Double surcharge 4.00 3.50
71 A29 2c on 2c bl, "1893-1894" 1.00 85
a. Inverted surcharge 2.00 1.75
72 A29 5c on 10c org, "1887-1888" 1.00 28
a. Inverted surcharge 2.00 85
b. Double surcharge 3.50 2.00
c. Surcharged "2cts" 50 40
d. "1893-1894" 2.75 2.50
73 A29 10c on 4c brn, "1887-1888" 1.00 52
a. Inverted surcharge 2.00 85
b. Double surcharge 3.00 1.75
c. Double surcharge, one inverted
d. Surcharged "1 cto" 1.00 1.40
e. "1891-1892" 8.50 6.75

Similar surcharges of type A29 include: Dated "1887-1888"- 1c on 1c blue green, 1c on 2c red, 1c on 4c brown, 1c on 10c yellow; 2c on 2c red, 2c on 10c yellow; 10c on 1c green.
Dated "1891-1892"- 1c on 1c blue green, 1c on 4c brown.
Dated "1893-1894"- 2c on 10c yellow; 10c on 1c vermilion, 10c on 10s black.
For overprints see Nos. O18-O19.

Nos. 59-60 Surcharged in Black or Red

1896, Oct. **Wmk. 117**

74 A25 5c on 20c orange 16.00 16.00
76 A26 10c on 50c dk bl (R) 16.00 16.00
a. Double surcharge

The surcharge is diagonal, horizontal or vertical.

Overprinted 1897 1898

On Issue of 1894

1897 **Unwmk.**

77 A20 1c blue 1.00 1.00
78 A20 2c yellow brn 85 60
79 A20 5c green 40 40
80 A20 10c vermilion 1.25 1.00
81 A20 20c black 1.40 1.25
82 A20 50c orange 3.00 1.50
83 A20 1s carmine 8.75 3.00
84 A20 5s dark blue 50.00 40.00
Nos. 77-84 (8) 66.65 48.75

On Issue of 1895

85 A20 1c blue 2.75 2.50
86 A20 2c yellow brn 1.00 1.00
87 A20 5c green 85 75
88 A20 10c vermilion 3.00 2.75
89 A20 20c black 85 85
90 A20 50c orange 15.00 6.00
91 A20 1s carmine 6.75 3.50
92 A20 5s dark blue 6.75 6.75
Nos. 85-92 (8) 36.95 24.10

Overprinted

On Issue of 1894

93 A20 1c blue 70 40
94 A20 2c yellow brn 52 35
95 A20 5c green 28 15
96 A20 10c vermilion 1.50 85
97 A20 20c black 1.75 1.25
98 A20 50c orange 3.00 1.25
99 A20 1s carmine 5.50 4.00
100 A20 5s dark blue 50.00 40.00
Nos. 93-100 (8) 63.25 48.25

On Issue of 1895

101 A20 1c blue 1.50 70
102 A20 2c yellow brn 70 70
103 A20 5c green 85 50
104 A20 10c vermilion 2.75 2.00
105 A20 20c black 2.50 55
106 A20 50c orange 90 90
107 A20 1s carmine 4.00 3.50
108 A20 5s dark blue 4.75 4.75
Nos. 101-108 (8) 17.95 13.60

Overprints on Nos. 77-108 are to be found reading upward from left to right and downward from left to right, as well as inverted.

Overprinted **1897 Y 1898**

On Issue of 1894

1897

109 A20 10c vermilion *60.00 50.00*

On Issue of 1895

110 A20 2c yellow brn *45.00 40.00*
111 A20 1s carmine *60.00 50.00*
112 A20 5s dark blue *60.00 45.00*

Nos. 56, 59 Overprinted like Nos. 93-108

1897, June **Wmk. 117**

113 A22 2c red 45.00 35.00
114 A25 20c orange 50.00 42.50

Many forged overprints on Nos. 77-114 exist, made on original stamps and reprints.

Stamps or Types of 1896 Overprinted like Nos. 93-108

1897 **Unwmk.** *Perf. 11½*

115 A28a 1c rose 1.25 1.25
116 A28b 2c blue 1.00 1.00
117 A28b 10c ocher 1.00 1.00
118 A28a 1s yellow 5.00 5.00

No. 63 Overprinted like Nos. 77-92

1897

119 A28a 1c rose 60 50

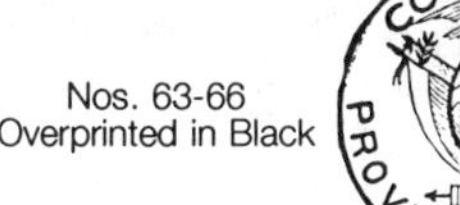
Nos. 63-66 Overprinted in Black

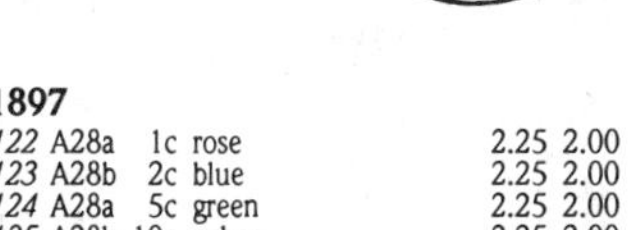

1897

122 A28a 1c rose 2.25 2.00
123 A28b 2c blue 2.25 2.00
124 A28a 5c green 2.25 2.00
125 A28b 10c ocher 2.25 2.00
a. Double overprint 5.25 4.75

The 20c, 50c and 1s with this overprint in black and all values of the issue overprinted in blue are reprints.

Overprint Inverted

122a A28a 1c 3.00 2.75
123a A28b 2c 3.00 2.75
124a A28a 5c 3.00 2.75
125b A28b 10c 2.75 2.75

Coat of Arms — A33

1897, June 23 **Engr.** *Perf. 14-16*

127 A33 1c dk yellow grn 15 15
128 A33 2c orange red 15 15
129 A33 5c lake 15 15
130 A33 10c dk brown 15 16
131 A33 20c yellow 20 40
132 A33 50c dull blue 26 65
133 A33 1s gray 50 80
134 A33 5s dark lilac 75 *1.10*
Nos. 127-134 (8) 2.37 *3.56*

No. 135

No. 136

1899, May

135 A33 1c on 2c orange red 1.50 75
136 A33 5c on 10c brown 1.25 50
a. Double surcharge

Luis Vargas Torres
A36

Abdón Calderón
A37

Juan Montalvo
A38

José Mejía
A39

Santa Cruz y Espejo — A40

Pedro Carbo — A41

José Joaquin Olmedo
A42

Pedro Moncayo
A43

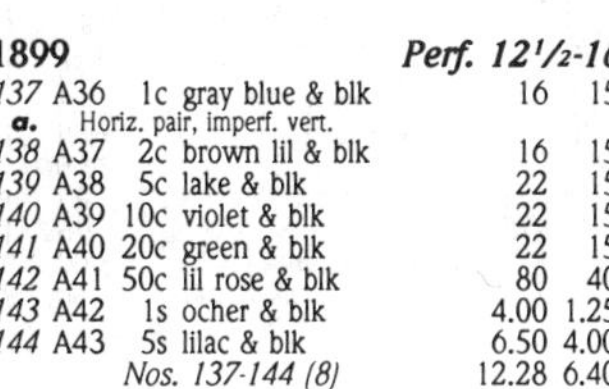

1899 *Perf. 12½-16*

137 A36 1c gray blue & blk 16 15
a. Horiz. pair, imperf. vert.
138 A37 2c brown lil & blk 16 15
139 A38 5c lake & blk 22 15
140 A39 10c violet & blk 22 15
141 A40 20c green & blk 22 15
142 A41 50c lil rose & blk 80 40
143 A42 1s ocher & blk 4.00 1.25
144 A43 5s lilac & blk 6.50 4.00
Nos. 137-144 (8) 12.28 6.40

1901

145 A36 1c scarlet & blk 15 15
146 A37 2c green & blk 15 15
147 A38 5c gray lil & blk 15 15
148 A39 10c dp blue & blk 15 15
149 A40 20c gray & blk 15 15
150 A41 50c lt blue & blk 65 40
151 A42 1s brown & blk 2.75 1.75
152 A43 5s gray blk & blk 4.00 3.00
Nos. 145-152 (8) 8.15 5.90

In July, 1902, following the theft of a quantity of stamps during a fire at Guayaquil, the Government authorized the governors of the provinces to handstamp their stocks. Many varieties of these handstamps exist.
Other control marks were used in 1907.
For overprints see Nos. O103-O106, O167.

A44

Surcharged on Revenue Stamp Dated 1901-1902

1903-06 *Perf. 14, 15*

153 A44 1c on 5c gray lil ('06) 25 16
154 A44 1c on 20c gray ('06) 3.00 3.00
155 A44 1c on 25c yel 50 16
a. Double surcharge
156 A44 1c on 1s bl ('06) 25.00 17.00
157 A44 3c on 5c gray lil ('06) 3.00 2.00
158 A44 3c on 20c gray ('06) 7.50 7.50
159 A44 3c on 25c yel ('06) 7.50 7.50
159A A44 3c on 1s blue ('06) 1.00 1.00
Nos. 153-159A (8) 47.75 38.32

Counterfeits are plentiful. See #191-197.

Capt. Abdón Calderón
A45 A46

1904, July 31 *Perf. 12*

160 A45 1c red & blk 30 22
161 A45 2c blue & blk 30 22
162 A46 5c yellow & blk 1.10 75
163 A45 10c red & blk 2.25 75
164 A45 20c blue & blk 6.00 1.90
165 A46 50c yellow & blk 50.00 30.00
Nos. 160-165 (6) 59.95 33.84

Centenary of the birth of Calderón.

Presidents

Vicente Roca — A47

Diego Noboa — A48

Francisco Robles — A49

José M. Urvina — A50

García Moreno — A51

Jerónimo Carrión — A52

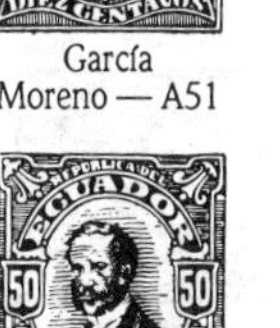
Javier Espinoza — A53

Antonio Borrero — A54

1907, July *Perf. 14, 15*

166 A47 1c red & blk 25 15
167 A48 2c pale blue & blk 50 15
168 A49 3c orange & blk 75 15
169 A50 5c lilac rose & blk 1.00 15
170 A51 10c dp blue & blk 2.00 18
171 A52 20c yellow grn & blk 3.00 22
172 A53 50c violet & blk 6.00 52
173 A54 1s green & blk 8.00 1.40
Nos. 166-173 (8) 21.50 2.92

The stamps of the 1907 issue frequently have control marks similar to those found on the 1899 and 1901 issues. These marks were applied to distinguish the stamps issued in the various provinces and to serve as a check on local officials.

Locomotive — A55

García Moreno
A56

Gen. Eloy Alfaro A57

Abelardo Moncayo — A58

Archer Harman A59

James Sivewright — A60

Mt. Chimborazo A61

1908, June 25

174	A55	1c red brown	65	65
175	A56	2c blue & blk	1.00	85
176	A57	5c claret & blk	2.00	1.75
177	A58	10c ocher & blk	1.25	1.00
178	A59	20c green & blk	1.25	1.25
179	A60	50c gray & blk	1.25	1.25
180	A61	1s black	2.75	2.75
		Nos. 174-180 (7)	10.15	9.50

Opening of the Guayaquil-Quito Railway.

José Mejía Vallejo — A62

Principal Exposition Building — A70

Designs: 2c, Francisco J. E. Santa Cruz y Espejo. 3c, Francisco Ascásubi. 5c, Juan Salinas. 10c, Juan Pio de Montúfar. 20c, Carlos de Montúfar. 40c, Juan de Dios Morales. 1s, Manuel R. de Quiroga.

1909, Aug. 10 *Perf. 12*

181	A62	1c green	22	44
182	A62	2c blue	22	44
183	A62	3c orange	22	48
184	A62	5c claret	22	48
185	A62	10c yellow brn	26	48
186	A62	20c gray	26	70
187	A62	50c vermilion	26	70
188	A62	1s olive grn	26	95
189	A70	5s violet	75	1.90
		Nos. 181-189 (9)	2.67	6.57

National Exposition of 1909.

Surcharged CINCO CENTAVOS

1909

190	A68	5c on 50c vermilion	55	50

Revenue Stamps Surcharged as in 1903

1910 *Perf. 14, 15*

Stamps Dated 1905-1906

191	A44	1c on 5c green	1.00	70
192	A44	5c on 20c blue	4.00	85
193	A44	5c on 25c violet	7.50	1.50

Stamps Dated 1907-1908

194	A44	1c on 5c green	20	15
195	A44	5c on 20c blue	6.00	4.00
196	A44	5c on 25c violet	50	16

Stamp Dated 1909-1910

197	A44	5c on 20c blue	*30.00*	*25.00*

Presidents

Roca — A71

Noboa — A72

Robles — A73

Urvina — A74

Moreno A75

Borrero A76

1911-28 *Perf. 12*

198	A71	1c scarlet & blk	30	15
199	A71	1c orange ('16)	30	15
200	A71	1c lt blue ('25)	15	15
201	A72	2c blue & blk	40	15
202	A72	2c green ('16)	40	15
203	A72	2c dk violet ('25)	40	15
204	A73	3c orange & blk ('13)	1.00	24
205	A73	3c black ('15)	50	15
206	A74	5c scarlet & blk	75	15
207	A74	5c violet ('15)	75	15
208	A74	5c rose ('25)	25	15
209	A74	5c dk brown ('28)	25	15
210	A75	10c dp blue & blk	1.00	15
211	A75	10c dp blue ('15)	1.00	15
212	A75	10c yellow grn ('25)	25	15
213	A75	10c black ('28)	75	15
214	A76	1s green & blk	5.00	1.00
215	A76	1s orange & blk ('27)	3.50	20
		Nos. 198-215 (18)	16.95	
		Set value		2.25

For overprints see Nos. 260-262, 264-265, O107-O122, O124-O134, O156-O157, O160-O162, O1654-O166, O168-O173, O175-O178, O183-O184, O189, RA1.

A77

1912 *Perf. 14, 15*

216	A77	1c on 1s green	40	40
217	A77	2c on 2s carmine	1.00	60
218	A77	2c on 5s dull blue	60	60
219	A77	2c on 10s yellow	2.00	2.00
a.		Inverted surcharge	7.50	6.00

No. 216 exists with narrow "V" and small "U" in "UN" and Nos. 217, 218 and 219 with "D" with serifs or small "O" in "DOS."

Enrique Váldez — A78

Jerónimo Carrión — A79

Javier Espinoza — A80

1915-17 *Perf. 12*

220	A78	4c red & blk	15	15
221	A79	20c green & blk ('17)	1.40	16
222	A80	50c dp violet & blk	2.25	32
		Set value		52

For overprints see #O123, O135, O163, O174.

Olmedo A86

Monument to "Fathers of the Country" A95

Laurel Wreath and Star — A104

Designs: 2c, Rafael Ximena. 3c, Roca. 4c, Luis F. Viviero. 5c, Luis Febres Cordero. 6c, Francisco Lavayen. 7c, Jorge Antonio de Elizalde. 8c, Baltazar Garcia. 9c, Jose de Antepara. 15c, Luis Urdaneta. 20c, Jose M. Villamil. 30c, Miguel Letamendi. 40c, Gregorio Escobedo. 50c, Gen. Antonio Jose de Sucre. 60c, Juan Illingworth. 70c, Roca. 80c, Rocafuerte. 1s, Simon Bolivar.

1920

223	A86	1c yellow grn	20	15
224	A86	2c carmine	16	15
225	A86	3c yellow brn	16	15
226	A86	4c myrtle green	28	15
227	A86	5c pale blue	28	15
228	A86	6c red orange	50	28
229	A86	7c brown	1.25	50
230	A86	8c apple green	70	32
231	A86	9c lake	2.25	1.00
232	A95	10c lt blue	1.00	15
233	A86	15c dk gray	1.25	32
234	A86	20c dk violet	1.25	16
235	A86	30c brt violet	2.25	85
236	A86	40c dk brown	4.00	1.40
237	A86	50c dk green	2.75	32
238	A86	60c dk blue	5.00	1.50
239	A86	70c gray	8.00	3.25
240	A86	80c orange yel	8.50	3.25
241	A104	90c green	9.00	3.25
242	A86	1s pale blue	12.50	5.50
		Nos. 223-242 (20)	61.28	22.80

Cent. of the independence of Guayaquil.
For overprints and surcharges see Nos. 263, 274-292, O136-O155, O179-O182, O185-O188.

Postal Tax Stamp of 1924 Overprinted POSTAL

1925

259	PT6	20c bister brown	1.25	50

Stamps of 1915-25 Overprinted in Black or Red Upright (1c, 3c, 5c) or Inverted (2c, 4c, 10c)

1926

260	A71	1c lt blue	3.00	2.00
261	A72	2c dk violet	3.00	2.00
262	A73	3c black (R)	2.25	2.00
263	A86	4c myrtle green	2.25	2.00
264	A74	5c rose	4.00	2.00
265	A75	10c yellow grn	4.00	2.00
		Nos. 260-265 (6)	18.50	12.00

Quito-Esmeraldas railway opening.

Upright overprints on 2c, 4c, 10c and inverted overprints on 1c, 3c, 5c sell for more.

Postal Tax Stamps of 1920-24 Overprinted **POSTAL**

1927

266	PT6	1c olive green	15	15
a.		"POSTAI"	1.40	85
b.		Double overprint	2.00	85
c.		Inverted overprint	2.00	85
267	PT6	2c deep green	15	15
a.		"POSTAI"	1.40	85
b.		Double overprint	2.00	85
268	PT6	20c bister brown	70	15
a.		"POSTAI"	8.50	5.00
		Set value		20

Quito Post Office — A109

1927, June

269	A109	5c orange	25	15
270	A109	10c dark green	35	15
271	A109	20c violet	40	16
		Set value		33

Opening of new Quito P.O.
For overprint see No. O190.

Postal Tax Stamp of 1924 Overprinted in Dark Blue **POSTAL**

1928

273	PT6	20c bister brown	25	15
a.		Double overprint, one inverted	2.00	70

See No. 339 for 10c with same overprint.

A110

Nos. 235, 239-240 Overprinted in Red Brown and Surcharged in Dark Blue

1928, July 8

274	A110	10c on 30c violet	4.00	4.00
275	A110	50c on 70c gray	5.00	5.00
276	A110	1s on 80c org yel	6.00	6.00

Quito-Cayambe railway opening.

Stamps of 1920 Surcharged ASAMBLEA NCNAL. 1928 5 CTVOS.

1928, Oct. 9

277	A86	1c on 1c yel grn	8.00	6.75
278	A86	1c on 2c car	20	20
279	A86	2c on 3c yel brn	1.25	1.25
a.		Dbl. surch., one reading up	7.25	7.25
280	A86	2c on 4c myr grn	60	60
381	A86	2c on 5c lt blue	30	30
a.		Dbl. surch., one reading up	5.00	5.00
282	A86	2c on 7c brown	10.50	8.25
283	A86	5c on 6c red org	20	15
a.		"5 ctvos." omitted	14.00	14.00
284	A86	10c on 7c brown	50	40
285	A86	20c on 8c apple grn	20	15
a.		Double surcharge		
286	A95	40c on 10c blue	2.25	2.00
287	A86	40c on 15c dk gray	50	50
288	A86	50c on 20c dk vio	7.50	6.00
289	A86	1s on 40c dk brown	2.00	2.00
290	A86	5s on 50c dk green	2.50	2.50
291	A86	10s on 60c dk blue	8.75	6.00

With Additional Surcharge in Red **0.10**

292 A86 10c on 2c on 7c brn		20	15
a. Red surcharge double		5.00	5.00
	Nos. 277-292 (16)	45.45	37.20

National Assembly of 1928.
Counterfeit overprints exist of #277-291.

A111

A112

Surcharged in Various Colors

1928, Oct. 31 *Perf. 14*

293 A111 5c on 20c gray lil (Bk)	80	70
294 A111 10c on 20c gray lil (R)	80	70
295 A111 20c on 1s grn (O)	80	70
296 A111 50c on 1s grn (Bl)	95	52
297 A111 1s on 1s grn (V)	1.25	70
298 A111 5s on 2s red (G)	3.75	3.50
299 A111 10s on 2s red (Br)	4.75	4.75
a. Black surcharge	5.00	5.00
Nos. 293-299 (7)	13.10	11.57

Quito-Otavalo railway opening.
See Nos. 586-587.

Postal Tax Stamp of 1924 Overprinted in Red **POSTAL**

1929 *Perf. 12*

302 PT6 2c deep green 15 15

There are two types of overprint on No. 302 differing slightly.

1929

Red Overprint

303 A112 1c dark blue	15	15
a. Overprint reading down	15	15

See Nos. 586-587.

Plowing — A113

Cultivating Cacao — A114

Cacao Pod — A115

Loading Sugar Cane — A119

Growing Tobacco — A116

Exportation of Fruits — A117

Landscape A118

Scene in Quito A120

Scene in Quito A121

Olmedo — A122

Monument to Simón Bolívar — A125

Designs: 2s, Sucre. 5s, Bolivar.

1930, Aug. 1 *Perf. 12½*

304 A113 1c yellow & car	15	15
305 A114 2c yellow & grn	15	15
306 A115 5c dp grn & vio brn	15	15
307 A116 6c yellow & red	15	16
308 A117 10c orange & ol grn	25	15
309 A118 16c red & yel grn	30	26
310 A119 20c ultra & yel	40	15
311 A120 40c orange & sepia	60	15
312 A121 50c orange & sepia	50	15
313 A122 1s dp green & blk	2.00	16
314 A122 2s dk blue & blk	3.25	32
315 A122 5s dk violet & blk	5.75	50
316 A125 10s car rose & blk	16.00	4.00
Nos. 304-316 (13)	29.65	6.45

Centenary of founding of republic.
For surcharges and overprints see Nos. 319-320, 331-338, RA25, RA33, RA43.

A126

A127

Red Overprint

1933 *Perf. 15*

317 A126 10c olive brown 50 15

Blue Overprint

318 A127 10c olive brown	30	15
a. Inverted overprint	5.00	5.00
Set value		17

For overprint see No. 339.

Nos. 307, 309 Surcharged in Black

1933 *Perf. 12½*

319 A116 5c on 6c yellow & red	20	15
320 A118 10c on 16c red & yel grn	40	15
a. Inverted overprint	4.00	4.00
Set value		20

Landscape A128

Mt. Chimborazo A129

1934-45 *Perf. 12*

321 A128 5c violet	15	15
322 A128 5c blue	20	15
323 A128 5c dk brown	20	15
323A A128 5c slate blk ('45)	20	15
324 A128 10c rose	20	15
325 A128 10c dk green	20	15
326 A128 10c brown	20	15
327 A128 10c orange	20	15
328 A128 10c olive grn	20	15
329 A128 10c gray blk ('35)	20	15
329A A128 10c red lilac ('44)	15	15

Perf. 14

330 A129 1s car rose	1.00	40
Nos. 321-330 (12)	3.10	
Set value		95

Stamps of 1930 Surcharged or Ovptd. in various colors similar to:

INAUGURACION MONUMENTO A BOLIVAR

QUITO, 24 DE JULIO DE 1935

1935 *Perf. 12½*

331 A116 5c on 6c (Bl)	20	15
332 A116 10c on 6c (G)	30	15
333 A119 20c (R)	40	15
334 A120 40c (G)	50	20
335 A121 50c (G)	60	32
336 A122 1s on 5s (Gold)	1.50	1.00
337 A122 2s on 5s (Gold)	2.00	1.50
338 A125 5s on 10s (Bl)	3.25	3.25
Nos. 331-338,C35-C38 (12)	25.75	23.72

Unveiling of a monument to Bolivar at Quito, July 24, 1935.

The 5-stamp Sociedad Colombista Panamericana series of 1935 and 5 air-mail stamps of a similar design are not recognized by this Catalogue as having been issued primarily for postal purposes.

Telegraph Stamp Overprinted Diagonally in Red like No. 273

1935 *Perf. 14½*

339 A126 10c olive brown 25 15

Map of Galápagos Islands A130

Galapagos Land Iguana A131

Galápagos Tortoise A132

Charles R. Darwin A133

Columbus A134

Island Scene A135

1936 *Perf. 14*

340 A130 2c black	15	15
341 A131 5c olive grn	25	15
342 A132 10c brown	50	15
343 A133 20c dk violet	50	15
344 A134 1s dk carmine	1.00	35
345 A135 2s dark blue	1.50	70
Nos. 340-345 (6)	3.90	1.65

Cent. of the visit of Charles Darwin to the Galápagos Islands, Sept. 17, 1835.
For overprints see Nos. O191-O195.

Tobacco Stamp Overprinted in Black

POSTAL

1936 ***Rouletted 7***

346 PT7 1c rose red 15 15
a. Horiz. pair, imperf. vert.
b. Double surcharge

No. 346 is similar to type PT7 but does not include "CASA CORREOS."

Louis Godin, Charles M. de la Condamine and Pierre Bouguer A136

Portraits: 5c, 20c, Antonio Ulloa, La Condamine and Jorge Juan.

1936 **Engr.** *Perf. 12½*

347 A136 2c dp blue	15	15
348 A136 5c dk green	15	15
349 A136 10c dp orange	15	15
350 A136 20c violet	30	15
351 A136 50c dk red	50	24
Nos. 347-351,C39-C42 (9)	2.39	
Set value		95

Bicentenary of Geodesical Mission to Quito.

Independence Monument — A137

1936 *Perf. 13½x14*

352 A137 2c green	1.10	50
353 A137 5c dk violet	1.10	50
354 A137 10c car rose	1.10	60
355 A137 20c black	1.10	75

356	A137	50c blue	2.00	1.50
357	A137	1s dk red	2.25	2.00
		Nos. 352-357,C43-C50 (14)	29.35	26.32

1st Intl. Philatelic Exhibition at Quito.

Coat of Arms — A138

Overprint in Black or Red

1937 *Perf. 12½*

359	A138	5c olive green	50	15
360	A138	10c dark blue (R)	50	15
		Set value		15

For overprint see No. 562.

Andean Landscape A139

Atahualpa, the Last Inca A140

Hat Weavers — A141

Coast Landscape — A142

Gold Washing — A143

1937, Aug. 19 *Perf. 11½*

361	A139	2c green	15	15
362	A140	5c deep rose	15	15
363	A141	10c blue	16	15
364	A142	20c deep rose	60	16
365	A143	1s olive green	75	24
		Nos. 361-365 (5)	1.81	
		Set value		55

For overprints see Nos. O196-O200.

"Liberty" Carrying Flag of Ecuador — A144

Engraved and Lithographed

1938, Feb. 22 *Perf. 12*

Center Multicolored

366	A144	2c blue	15	15
367	A144	5c violet	18	15
368	A144	10c black	22	15
369	A144	20c brown	30	15
370	A144	50c black	45	15
371	A144	1s olive blk	75	16
372	A144	2s dk brn	1.50	50
		Nos. 366-372,C57-C63 (14)	7.55	
		Set value		2.20

US Constitution, 150th anniversary.

For overprints and surcharges see Nos. 413-415, 444-446, RA46, RA52.

A145

A146

A147

A148

Designs: 10c, Winged figure holding globe. 50c, Cactus, winged wheel. 1s, "Communications." 2s, "Construction."

Perf. 13, 13x13½

1938, Oct. 30 **Engr.**

373	A145	10c brt ultra	15	15
374	A146	50c dp red vio	15	15
375	A147	1s copper red	30	15
376	A148	2s dk grn	45	15
		Set value		32

Progress of Ecuador Exhibition.

For overprints see Nos. C105-C113.

Parade of Athletes — A149

Runner — A150

Basketball — A151

Wrestlers A152

Diver A153

1939, Mar. *Perf. 12*

377	A149	5c car rose	1.65	35
378	A150	10c deep blue	2.00	42
379	A151	50c gray olive	2.25	52
380	A152	1s dull vio	4.25	52
381	A153	2s dull ol grn	6.00	70
		Nos. 377-381,C65-C69 (10)	31.65	4.07

First Bolivarian Games (1938), La Paz.

Dolores Mission A154

Trylon and Perisphere A155

1939, June 16 *Perf. 12½x13*

382	A154	2c blue green	15	15
383	A154	5c rose red	15	15
384	A154	10c ultra	15	15
385	A154	50c yellow brn	50	15
386	A154	1s black	75	15
387	A154	2s purple	1.00	15
		Nos. 382-387,C73-C79 (13)	4.75	
		Set value		1.00

Golden Gate International Exposition.

For surcharges see Nos. 429, 436.

1939, June 30

388	A155	2c lt olive grn	15	15
389	A155	5c red orange	15	15
390	A155	10c ultra	15	15
391	A155	50c slate gray	50	15
392	A155	1s rose car	75	18
393	A155	2s black brown	1.00	22
		Nos. 388-393,C80-C86 (13)	4.75	
		Set value		1.30

New York World's Fair.

For surcharge see No. 437.

Flags of the 21 American Republics — A156

1940 *Perf. 12*

394	A156	5c dp rose & blk	15	15
395	A156	10c dk blue & blk	15	15
396	A156	50c Prus grn & blk	30	15
397	A156	1s dp vio & blk	42	22
		Nos. 394-397,C87-C90 (8)	2.77	
		Set value		1.30

Pan American Union, 50th anniversary.

Francisco J. E. Santa Cruz y Espejo — A157

1941, Dec. 15

398	A157	30c blue	50	15
399	A157	1s red orange	1.50	15
		Set value		21

Exposition of Journalism held under the auspices of the Natl. Newspaper Men's Union. See Nos. C91-C92.

Francisco de Orellana A158

Gonzalo Pizarro A159

View of Guayaquil — A160

View of Quito — A161

1942, Jan. 30

400	A158	10c sepia	30	15
401	A159	40c deep rose	60	15
402	A160	1s violet	90	15
403	A161	2s dark blue	1.25	26
		Nos. 400-403,C93-C96 (8)	6.05	1.69
		Set value		1.40

400th anniv. of the discovery and exploration of the Amazon River by Orellana.

Remigio Crespo Toral — A162

Alfredo Baquerizo Moreno — A163

1942 *Perf. 13½*

404	A162	10c green	15	15
405	A162	50c brown	25	15
		Set value		20

See No. C97.

1942

406	A163	10c green	15	15

Mt. Chimborazo A164

1942-47 *Perf. 12*

407	A164	30c red brn	25	15
407A	A164	30c lt bl ('43)	25	15
407B	A164	30c red org ('44)	15	15
407C	A164	30c grn ('47)	25	15
		Set value		20

View of Guayaquil — A165

1942-44

408	A165	20c red	25	15
408A	A165	20c dp blue ('44)	25	15
		Set value		18

Gen. Eloy Alfaro — A166

Devil's Nose — A167

Designs: 30c, Military College. 1s, Montecristi, Alfaro's birthplace.

1942

409	A166	10c dk rose & blk	15	15
410	A167	20c ol blk & red brn	30	30
411	A167	30c ol gray & grn	60	60
412	A167	1s slate & sal	1.00	1.00
		Nos. 409-412,C98-C101 (8)	4.98	4.00

President Alfaro (1842-1912).

Nos. 370-372 Overprinted in Red Brown

BIENVENIDO — WALLACE

Abril 15 — 1943

1943, Apr. 15 *Perf. 11½*

413	A144	50c multicolored	32	32
414	A144	1s multicolored	65	65
415	A144	2s multicolored	1.00	1.00
		Nos. 413-415,C102-C104 (6)	5.37	4.52

Visit of US Vice-Pres. Henry A. Wallace.

"30 Centavos" — A170

Black Surcharge

1943 *Perf. 12½*
416 A170 30c on 50c red brn 35 15
a. Without bars 35 15

Map Showing US and Ecuador — A171

1943, Oct. 9 *Perf. 12*
417 A171 10c dull violet 16 16
418 A171 20c red brown 16 16
419 A171 30c orange 22 22
420 A171 50c olive green 26 26
421 A171 1s dp violet 32 32
422 A171 10s olive bis 3.25 3.25
Nos. 417-422,C114-C118 (11) 11.29 10.01

Good will tour of Pres. Arroyo del Rio in 1942.

1944, Feb. 7
423 A171 10c yellow grn 15 15
424 A171 20c rose pink 15 15
425 A171 30c dk gray brn 16 16
426 A171 50c dp red lil 26 26
427 A171 1s olive gray 32 32
428 A171 10s red orange 3.25 3.25
Nos. 423-428,C119-C123 (11) 7.89 7.08

For surcharges see Nos. B1-B6.

No. 385 Surcharged in Black

30
Centavos

1944 **Unwmk.** *Perf. 12½x13*
429 A154 30c on 50c yel brn 15 15

Archbishop Federico González Suárez, Birth Cent. — A172

1944 *Perf. 12*
430 A172 10c dp blue 15 15
431 A172 20c green 15 15
432 A172 30c dk vio brn 20 20
433 A172 1s dull violet 40 40
Nos. 430-433,C124-C127 (8) 3.50 2.48

Air Post Stamps Nos. C76 and C83 Surcharged in Black

POSTAL
30
Centavos

1944 *Perf. 12½x13*
434 AP15 30c on 50c rose vio 15 15
435 AP16 30c on 50c sl grn 15 15
Set value 24 15

Nos. 382 and 388 Surcharged in Black

CINCO
Centavos

1944-45
436 A154 5c on 2c bl grn 15 15
a. Double surcharge
437 A155 5c on 2c lt ol grn ('45) 15 15
Set value 20 16

Government Palace, Quito — A173

1944 **Engr.** *Perf. 11*
438 A173 10c dk green 15 15
439 A173 30c blue 15 15
Set value 20 16

For surcharges see Nos. 452, RAC1-RAC2.

Symbol of the Red Cross — A174

1945, Apr. 25 *Perf. 12*
Cross in Rose
440 A174 30c bister brn 40 16
441 A174 1s red brown 50 20
442 A174 5s turq green 1.00 65
443 A174 10s scarlet 2.75 1.65
Nos. 440-443,C131-C134 (8) 10.97 7.35

International Red Cross, 80th anniversary.

Nos. 370 to 372 Overprinted in Dark Blue and Gold

LOOR A CHILE
OCTUBRE 2 1945

1945, Oct. 2 *Perf. 11½*
Center Multicolored
444 A144 50c black 18 15
a. Double overprint
445 A144 1s olive blk 28 20
446 A144 2s dk brown 60 52
Nos. 444-446,C139-C141 (6) 2.47 2.28

Visit of Pres. Juan Antonio Rios of Chile.

General Antonio José de Sucre, 150th Birth Anniv. — A175

1945, Nov. 14 **Engr.** *Perf. 12*
447 A175 10c olive 25 25
448 A175 20c red brown 25 15
449 A175 40c olive gray 25 15
450 A175 1s dark green 50 25
451 A175 2s sepia 75 50
Nos. 447-451,C142-C146 (10) 4.63 3.00

No. 438 Surcharged in Blue

VEINTE
CENTAVOS

1945 *Perf. 11*
452 A173 20c on 10c dk green 15 15
a. Fancy bar omitted

Catalogue values for unused stamps in this section, from this point to the end of the section, are for Never Hinged items.

Map of Pan-American Highway and Arms of Loja — A176

1946, Apr. 22 **Engr.** *Perf. 12*
453 A176 20c red brown 15 15
454 A176 30c brt green 15 15
455 A176 1s brt ultra 16 16
456 A176 5s dp red lil 75 75
457 A176 10s scarlet 1.50 1.10
Nos. 453-457,C147-C151 (10) 5.84 3.81

Torch of Democracy A177

Popular Suffrage A178

Flag of Ecuador A179

Pres. José M. Velasco Ibarra A180

1946, Aug. 9 **Unwmk.** *Perf. 12½*
458 A177 5c dk blue 15 15
459 A178 10c Prus green 15 15
460 A179 20c carmine 16 15
461 A180 30c chocolate 26 15
Set value, #458-461, C152-C155 1.50 88

2nd anniv. of the Revolution of May 28, 1944.

"30 Ctvs." — A181

Black Surcharge

1946
462 A181 30c on 50c red brown 35 15

For overprint see No. 484.

Nos. CO13-CO14 With Additional Overprint in Black

POSTAL

1946 *Perf. 11½*
463 AP7 10c chestnut 15 15
464 AP7 20c olive black 15 15
Set value 15 15

Instructor and Student — A182

1946, Sept. 16 *Perf. 12½*
465 A182 10c dp blue 15 15
466 A182 20c chocolate 15 15
467 A182 30c dk green 15 15
468 A182 50c bluish blk 26 26
469 A182 1s dk red 40 40
470 A182 10s dk violet 2.50 65
Nos. 465-470,C156-C160 (11) 7.89 3.29

Campaign for adult education.

Mariana de Jesus Paredes y Flores — A183

Urn — A184

1946, Nov. 28
471 A183 10c black brown 15 15
472 A183 20c green 15 15
473 A183 30c purple 16 15
474 A184 1s rose brown 32 25
Nos. 471-474,C161-C164 (8) 3.00 2.31

300th anniv. of the death of the Blessed Mariana de Jesus Paredes y Flores.

Pres. Vicente Rocafuerte A185

Jesuits' Church Quito A186

Design: 45c, 50c, 80c, F.J.E. de Santa Cruz y Espejo.

1947, Nov. 27 *Perf. 12*
475 A185 5c redsh brown 15 15
476 A185 10c sepia 15 15
477 A185 15c gray black 15 15
478 A186 20c redsh brown 15 15
479 A186 30c red violet 15 15
480 A186 40c brt ultra 16 15
481 A185 45c dk slate grn 20 15
482 A185 50c olive blk 26 15
483 A185 80c orange red 32 15
Set value, #475-483, C165-C171 2.58 1.20

For overprints and surcharges see Nos. 489, 496, 525-527.

Type of 1946, Overprinted "POSTAL" in Black but Without Additional Surcharge

1948 **Engr.**
484 A181 10c orange 40 15

Andrés Bello A188

Flagship of Columbus A189

1948, Apr. 21 *Perf. 13*
485 A188 20c lt blue 15 15
486 A188 30c rose car 16 15
487 A188 40c blue green 20 15
488 A188 1s black brn 38 15
Nos. 485-488,C172-C174 (7) 1.68 1.15

83rd anniversary of the death of Andrés Bello (1781-1865), educator.

No. 480 Overprinted in Black

CONFERENCIA
ECONOMICA
GRANCOLOMBIANA
MAYO 24 DE 1.948

1948, May 24 *Perf. 12*
489 A186 40c brt ultra 25 25

See No. C175.

1948 *Perf. 14*
490 A189 10c dk blue grn 20 20
491 A189 20c brown 30 30
492 A189 30c dk purple 40 40
493 A189 50c dp claret 50 50
494 A189 1s ultra 1.10 1.10
495 A189 5s carmine 2.00 2.00
Nos. 490-495,C176-C180 (11) 7.18 5.66

Issued to publicize the proposed Columbus Memorial Lighthouse near Ciudad Trujillo, Dominican Republic.

No. 483 Overprinted in Blue

Feria Nacional
1 9 4 8
de hoy y del
ECUADOR
MAÑANA

1948 *Perf. 12*
"MANANA" Reading Down
496 A185 80c orange red 25 25

Issued to publicize the National Fair of Today and Tomorrow, 1948. See No. C181.

Telegrafo I in Flight — A190

Book and Pen — A191

1948 **Engr.** *Perf. 12½*
497 A190 30c red orange 15 15
498 A190 40c rose lilac 15 15
499 A190 60c violet blue 15 15
500 A190 1s brown red 18 15
501 A190 3s brown 65 30
502 A190 5s gray black 70 28
Nos. 497-502,C182-C187 (12) 4.03 2.86

25th anniversary (in 1945) of the first postal flight in Ecuador.

1948, Oct. 12 **Unwmk.** *Perf. 14*
503 A191 10c dp claret 15 15
504 A191 20c brown 25 25
505 A191 30c dk green 40 40
506 A191 50c red 50 25
507 A191 1s purple 70 50
508 A191 10s dull blue 2.00 75
Nos. 503-508,C188-C192 (11) 6.75 3.33

Campaign for adult education.

Franklin D. Roosevelt and Two of "Four Freedoms"
A192 A193

1948, Oct. 24 *Perf. 12½*
509 A192 10c rose brn & gray 18 15
510 A192 20c brn ol & bl 20 15
511 A193 30c ol bis & car rose 24 20
512 A193 40c red vio & sep 32 15
513 A193 1s org brn & car 38 30
Nos. 509-513,C193-C197 (10) 3.10 1.76

Maldonado and Map — A194

Riobamba Aqueduct A195

Maldonado on Bank of Riobamba A196

Pedro V. Maldonado A197

1948, Nov. 17 **Engr.** **Unwmk.**
514 A194 5c gray blk & ver 25 15
515 A195 10c car & gray blk 35 15
516 A196 30c bis brn & ultra 40 15
517 A195 40c sage grn & vio 75 15
518 A194 50c grn & car 75 15
519 A197 1s brn & slate bl 1.00 15
Nos. 514-519,C198-C201 (10) 4.58
Set value 95

Bicentenary of the death of Pedro Vicente Maldonado, geographer.
For overprints and surcharges see Nos. 537-540.

A198

Miguel de Cervantes Saavedra A199

1949, May 2 *Perf. 12½x12*
520 A198 30c dk car rose & dp ultra 40 15
521 A199 60c bis & brn vio 60 30
522 A198 1s grn & rose car 1.00 18
523 A199 2s gray blk & red brn 2.00 28
524 A198 5s choc & aqua 3.50 1.00
Nos. 520-524,C202-C206 (10) 13.75 4.65

400th anniv. of the birth of Miguel de Cervantes Saavedra, novelist, playwright and poet.

No. 480 Surcharged in Carmine

II CONGRESO
Junio 1949
0.10
Eucarístico Ncl.

1949, June 15 *Perf. 12*
525 A186 10c on 40c brt ultra 16 15
526 A186 20c on 40c brt ultra 22 15
a. Double surcharge
527 A186 30c on 40c brt ultra 26 20
Nos. 525-527,C207-C209 (6) 1.12
Set value 78

Second National Eucharistic Congress, Quito, June, 1949.
No. 526 exists se-tenant with No. 527.

Monument on Equator — A200

1949, June **Engr.** *Perf. 12½x12*
528 A200 10c deep plum 20 15

For overprint see No. 536.

No. 542 Surcharged in Black and Carmine

0.30
75 ANIVERSARIO
U. P. U.

1949 *Perf. 12x12½*
529 A203 10c on 50c green 15 15
530 A203 20c on 50c green 18 15
531 A203 30c on 50c green 26 15
Nos. 529-531,C210-C213 (7) 2.49 1.80

Universal Postal Union, 75th anniversary.

Consular Service Stamps Surcharged in Black

Arms of Ecuador — R1

POSTAL
20 ctvs.

1949 *Perf. 12*
532 R1 20c on 25c red brown 15 15
533 R1 30c on 50c gray 15 15
Set value 15

For other overprints and surcharges on type R1 see Nos. 544-549, 566-570, C245, C249-C252, RA60-RA62, RA72.

Nos. RA49A and RA55 Overprinted in Black

a **POSTAL**

1950 **Unwmk.** *Perf. 12*
534 PT18 5c green 15 15
535 PT21 5c blue 15 15
Set value 15

Overprint 15mm on No. 534.

Nos. 528 and 517 to 519 Overprinted or Surcharged in Black or Carmine

ALFABETIZACION

1950, Feb. 10 *Perf. 12½x12*
536 A200 10c dp plum 25 25
Perf. 12½
537 A195 20c on 40c sage grn & vio 40 40
538 A195 30c on 40c sage grn & vio 50 50
539 A194 50c grn & car 75 75
540 A197 1s brn & sl bl (C) 90 90

No. C220 Overprinted Type "a" in Carmine
Perf. 11
Overprint 15mm long
541 A173 10s violet 2.50 1.25
Nos. 536-541,C216-C220 (11) 8.25 6.00

Nos. 536-541 publicize adult education.

San Pablo Lake — A203

Perf. 12x12½
1950, May **Engr.** **Unwmk.**
542 A203 50c green 25 15

For surcharges see Nos. 529-531.

Consular Service Stamp Surcharged "CORREOS" and New Value Vertically in Black

1950 *Perf. 12*
544 R1 30c on 50c gray 15 15

Coat of Arms — R2

Consular Service Stamps Overprinted or Surcharged in Black

b: **POSTAL 20 Ctvs. 20**
c: **POSTAL**
d: **CORREOS**
e: **50 ctvs. POSTAL**

1951 **Unwmk.** *Perf. 12*
545 R1 (b) 5c on 10c car rose 15 15
546 R1 (c) 10c car rose 15 15
547 R1 (d) 10c car rose 15 15
548 R1 (b) 20c on 25c red brn 15 15
549 R1 (b) 30c on 50c gray 25 15
550 R2 (b) 40c on 25c blue 35 15
551 R2 (e) 50c on 25c blue 40 15
Nos. 545-551 (7) 1.60
Set value 38

Surcharge on No. 545 expressed: "5 ctvs." Small (lower case) "c" in "ctvs." on No. 550.
See Nos. 552-554, C233-C234, C246-C248, RA67.

Consular Service Stamps Surcharged in Black

CAMPAÑA
Alfabetización
20 Ctvs. 20

1951
552 R2 20c on 25c blue 35 15
553 R2 30c on 25c blue 35 15
Set value 15

Adult education. See Nos. C225-C226.

Consular Service Stamp Surcharged Type "e" in Black

1951

554 R2 $0.30 on 50c car rose 20 15

Reliquary of St. Mariana and Vatican — A204

Perf. 12½x12

1952, Feb. Engr. Unwmk.

555 A204 10c emer & red brn 25 15
556 A204 20c dp bl & pur 25 15
557 A204 30c car & bl grn 25 15
Nos. 555-557,C227-C230 (7) 2.19
Set value 72

Issued to publicize the canonization of Mariana de Jesus Paredes y Flores.

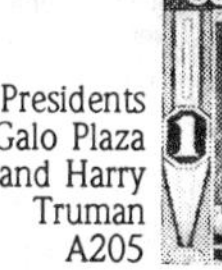

Presidents Galo Plaza and Harry Truman A205

Design: 2s, Pres. Plaza addressing US Congress.

1952, Mar. 26 *Perf. 12*

558 A205 1s rose car & gray blk 20 20
559 A205 2s dl bl & sepia 40 40

1951 visit of Pres. Galo Plaza y Lasso to the US. See Nos. C231-C232.

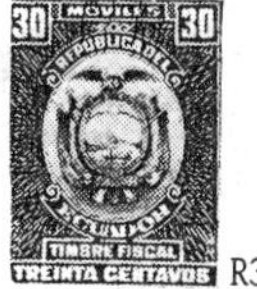

R3

Fiscal Stamps Surcharged or Overprinted Type "c" Horizontally in Carmine or Black

1952 Unwmk. Engr. Perf. 12

560 R3 20c on 30c dp bl (C) 25 15
561 R3 30c deep blue 25 15

Diagonal Overprint

562 A138 50c purple 25 15
Set value 25

For overprints and surcharge see Nos. RA68-RA69, RA71.

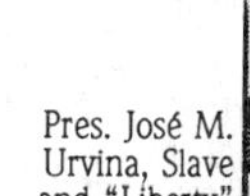

Pres. José M. Urvina, Slave and "Liberty" A206

1952 Litho. *Hyphen-hole Perf. 7x6½*

563 A206 20c red & green 15 15
564 A206 30c red & vio bl 15 15
565 A206 50c blue & car 25 25
Nos. 563-565,C236-C239 (7) 4.55 1.63

Centenary of abolition of slavery in Ecuador. Counterfeits exist.

Consular Service Stamps Surcharged in Black — f

POSTAL
10
Centavos

1952-53 Unwmk. *Perf. 12*

566 R1 10c on 20s blue ('53) 20 15
567 R1 20c on 10s gray ('53) 20 15
568 R1 20c on 20s blue 20 15
569 R1 30c on 10s gray ('53) 20 15
570 R1 30c on 20s blue 20 15
Nos. 566-570 (5) 1.00 75
Set value 25

Similar surcharges of 60c and 90c on the 20s blue are said to be bogus.

Teacher and Students — A207

New Citizens Voting — A208

Designs: 10c, Instructor with student. 30c, Teaching the alphabet.

1953, Apr. 13 Engr.

571 A207 5c lt bl 30 15
572 A207 10c dk car rose 30 15
573 A208 20c brt brn org 30 15
574 A208 30c dp red lil 30 15
Nos. 571-574,C240-C241 (6) 2.30
Set value 55

1952 adult education campaign.

A209

Cuicocha Lagoon — A210

Black Surcharge

1953

575 A209 40c on 50c purple 35 15

1953 Engr. *Perf. 13x12½*

Designs: 10c, Equatorial Line monument. 20c, Quininde countryside. 30c, Tomebamba river. 40c, La Chilintosa rock. 50c, Iliniza Mountains.

Frames in Black

576 A210 5c brt bl 15 15
577 A210 10c brt grn 15 15
578 A210 20c purple 15 15
579 A210 30c brown 15 15
580 A210 40c orange 15 15
581 A210 50c dp car 30 15
Set value 66 51

Carlos Maria Cardinal de la Torre and Arches — A211

1954, Jan. Photo. *Perf. 8½*

582 A211 30c blk & ver 25 15
583 A211 50c blk & rose lil 25 15
Nos. 582-583,C253-C255 (5) 1.60
Set value 51

1st anniv. of the elevation of Archbishop de la Torre to Cardinal.

Queen Isabella I (1451-1504) of Spain, 500th Birth Anniv. — A212

1954, Apr. 22

584 A212 30c blk & gray 35 35
585 A212 50c blk brn & yel 35 35
Nos. 584-585,C256-C260 (7) 2.11 1.90

Type of 1929; "POSTAL" Overprint Larger, No Letterspacing

1954-55 Unwmk. *Perf. 12*

586 A112 5c ol grn ('55) 25 15
587 A112 10c orange 25 15
Set value 15

The normal overprint on Nos. 586-587 reads up. It also exists reading down.

Indian Messenger A213

Products of Ecuador A214

1954, Aug. 2 Litho. *Perf. 11*

588 A213 30c dk brn 25 15

Issued to publicize the Day of the Postal Employee. See No. C263.

1954, Sept. 24 Photo.

589 A214 10c orange 15 15
590 A214 20c vermilion 15 15
591 A214 30c rose pink 15 15
592 A214 40c dk gray grn 20 15
593 A214 50c yel brn 20 15
Nos. 589-593 (5) 85
Set value 33

José Abel Castillo A215

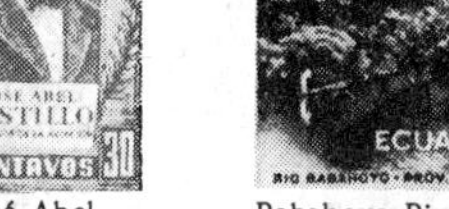

Babahoyo River Los Rios A216

Perf. 11½x11

1955, Oct. 19 Engr. Unwmk.

594 A215 30c olive bister 25 25
595 A215 50c dk gray 25 25
Nos. 594-595,C282-C286 (7) 1.95 1.55

30th anniv. of the 1st flight of the "Telegrafo I" and to honor Castillo, aviation pioneer.

1955-56 Photo. *Perf. 13*

Designs: 5c, Palms, Esmeraldas. 10c, Fishermen, Manabi. 30c, Guayaquil, Guayas. 50c, Pital River, El Oro. 70c, Cactus, Galapagos Isls. 80c, Orchids, Napo-Pastaza. 1s, Aguacate Mission, Zamora-Chinchipe. 2s, Jibaro Indian, Morona-Santiago.

596 A216 5c yel grn ('56) 15 15
597 A216 10c blue ('56) 15 15
598 A216 20c brown 15 15
599 A216 30c dk gray 15 15
600 A216 50c bl grn 15 15
601 A216 70c ol ('56) 20 15
602 A216 80c dp vio ('56) 50 15
603 A216 1s org ('56) 25 15
604 A216 2s rose red ('56) 50 15
Nos. 596-604 (9) 2.20
Set value 68

See #620-630, 670, C288-C297, C310-C311.

Brother Juan Adam Schwarz, S. J. — A217

1956, Aug. 27 Engr. *Perf. 13½*

605 A217 5c yel grn 15 15
606 A217 10c org red 15 15
607 A217 20c lt vio 15 15
608 A217 30c dk grn 15 15
609 A217 40c blue 15 15
610 A217 50c dp ultra 15 15
611 A217 70c orange 15 15
Set value, #605-611, C302-C305 1.35 86

Bicentennial of printing in Ecuador and honoring Brother Juan Adam Schwarz, S.J.

Andres Hurtado de Mendoza — A218

Gil Ramirez Davalos A219

Designs: 20c, Brother Vincent Solano.

1957, Apr. 7 Unwmk. *Perf. 12*

612 A218 5c dk bl, *pink* 15 15
613 A219 10c grn, *grnsh* 15 15
614 A218 20c choc, *buff* 15 15
a. Souvenir sheet of 4 40 40
Set value, #612-614, C312-C314 64 37

4th cent. of the founding of Cuenca.

No. 614a contains two 5c gray and two 20c brown red stamps in designs similar to Nos. 612 and 614. It was printed on white ungummed paper, imperf.

Francisco Marcos, Gen. Pedro Alcantara Herran and Santos Michelena A220

1957, Sept. 5 Engr. *Perf. 14½x14*

615 A220 40c yellow 15 15
616 A220 50c ultra 15 15
617 A220 2s dk red 35 16
Set value 55 26

7th Postal Congress of the Americas and Spain (in 1955).

Souvenir Sheets

Various Railroad Scenes — A221

1957 Litho. *Perf. 10½x11*

618 A221 20c Sheet of 5 1.00 1.00
619 A221 30c Sheet of 5 1.00 1.00

Issued to commemorate the opening of the Quito-Ibarra-San Lorenzo railroad.

Nos. 618-619 contain 2 orange yellow, 1 ultramarine and 2 carmine stamps, each in a different design.

Scenic Type of 1955-56.

Designs as before, except: 40c, Cactus, Galapagos Islands. No. 629, San Pablo, Imbabura.

1957-58 Photo. *Perf. 13*

620 A216 5c light blue 15 15
621 A216 10c brown 15 15
622 A216 20c crimson rose 15 15
623 A216 20c yel green 15 15
624 A216 30c rose red 15 15
625 A216 40c chalky blue 26 15
626 A216 50c lt vio 15 15
627 A216 90c brt ultra 26 25
628 A216 1s dark brown 15 15
629 A216 1s gray blk ('58) 15 15
630 A216 2s brown 32 20
Set value 1.60 95

Blue and Yellow Macaw — A222

Birds: 20c, Red-breasted toucan. 30c, Condor. 40c, Black-tailed and sword-tailed hummingbirds.

Perf. 13½x13
1958, Jan. 7 Litho. Unwmk.
Birds in Natural Colors

634 A222 10c red brn 16 15
635 A222 20c dk gray 16 15
636 A222 30c brt yel grn 38 15
637 A222 40c red org 38 15
Set value 39

Carlos Sanz de Santamaria — A223

Richard M. Nixon and Flags — A224

Design: No. 640, Dr. Ramon Villeda Morales and flags. 2.20s, José Carlos de Macedo Soares and horizontal flags.

1958 *Perf. 12*
Flags in Red, Blue, Yellow & Green

638 A223 1.80s dl vio 30 15
639 A224 2s dk grn 30 15
640 A224 2s dk brn 30 15
641 A223 2.20s blk brn 30 15

Visits: Colombia's Foreign Minister Dr. Carlos Sanz de Santamaria; US Vice Pres. Nixon, May 9-10; Pres. Ramon Villeda Morales of Honduras; Brazil's Foreign Minister José Carlos de Macedo Soares. See Nos. C419-C421. For overprints and surcharges see Nos. 775-775C, C419-C421, C460.

Locomotive of 1908 — A225

Garcia Moreno, Jose Caamano, L. Plaza and Eloy Alfaro — A226

Design: 50c, Diesel locomotive.

Perf. 13½x14, 14
1958, Aug. 9 Photo. Unwmk.

642 A225 30c brn blk 30 15
643 A225 50c dk car 30 15
644 A226 5s dk brn 60 35
Set value 46

Guayaquil-Quito railroad, 50th anniv.

Cardinal — A227

Birds: 30c, Andean cock-of-the-rock. 50c, Glossy cowbird. 60c, Red-fronted Amazon.

1958 Litho. *Perf. 13½x13*
Birds in Natural Colors

645 A227 20c bluish grn, blk & red 15 15
646 A227 30c buff, blk & brt bl 15 15
647 A227 50c org, blk & grn 15 15
648 A227 60c pale rose, blk & bluish grn 18 15
Set value 48 26

UNESCO Building and Eiffel Tower, Paris — A228

1958, Nov. 3 Engr. *Perf. 12½*

649 A228 80c brown 20 15

UNESCO Headquarters in Paris opening, Nov. 3.

Globe and Satellites — A229

Virgin of Quito — A230

1958, Dec. 20 Photo. *Perf. 14x13½*

650 A229 1.80s dark blue 80 35

International Geophysical Year, 1957-58.
For overprints see Nos. 718, C422.

1959, Sept. 8 Unwmk. *Perf. 13*

651 A230 5c ol grn 15 15
652 A230 10c yel brn 15 15
653 A230 20c purple 15 15
654 A230 30c ultra 15 15
655 A230 80c dk car rose 15 15
Set value 37 26

See No. C290. For surcharges and overprint see Nos. 695-699.

Uprooted Oak Emblem — A231

1960, Apr. 7 Litho. *Perf. 14x13*

656 A231 80c rose car & grn 15 15

Issued to publicize World Refugee Year, July 1, 1959-June 30, 1960.
For overprints see Nos. 709, 719, O205.

Great Anteater and Arms — A232

Animals: 40c, Tapir and map. 80c, Spectacled bear and arms. 1s, Puma and map.

1960, May 14 Photo. *Perf. 13*

657 A232 20c org, grn & blk 15 15
658 A232 40c yel grn, bl grn & brn 15 15
659 A232 80c bl, blk & red brn 25 15
660 A232 1s Prus bl, plum & ocher 50 20
Set value 46

Founding of the city of Baeza, 4th cent.
See Nos. 676-679.

Hotel Quito A233

Designs: No. 662, Dormitory, Catholic University. No. 663, Dormitory, Central University. No. 664, Airport, Quito. No. 665, Overpass on Highway to Quito. No. 666, Security Bank. No. 667, Ministry of Foreign Affairs. No. 668, Government Palace. No. 669, Legislative Palace.

Perf. 11x11½
1960, Aug. 8 Engr. Unwmk.

661 A233 1s dk pur & redsh brn 15 15
662 A233 1s dk bl & brn 15 15
663 A233 1s blk & red 15 15
664 A233 1s dk bl & ultra 15 15
665 A233 1s dk pur & dk car rose 15 15
666 A233 1s blk & ol bis 15 15
667 A233 1s dk pur & turq 15 15
668 A233 1s dk bl & grn 15 15
669 A233 1s blk & vio 15 15
Set value 1.08 90

11th Inter-American Conference, Quito.
For surcharges see Nos. 700-708

Type of Regular Issue, 1955-56
Souvenir Sheet

Design: Orchids, Napo-Pastaza.

1960 Photo. *Perf. 13*
Yellow Paper

670 Sheet of 2 35 35
a. A216 80c deep violet 15 15
b. A216 90c deep green 15 15

25th anniv. of Asociacion Filatelica Ecuatoriana. Marginal inscription in silver. Exists with silver inscription omitted.

"Freedom of Expression" A234

Manabi Bridge A235

Designs: 10c, "Freedom to vote." 20c, "Freedom to work." 30c, Coins, "Monetary stability."

1960, Aug. 29 Litho. *Perf. 13*

671 A234 5c dk bl 15 15
672 A234 10c lt vio 15 15
673 A234 20c orange 15 15
674 A234 30c bluish grn 15 15
675 A235 40c brn & bluish grn 18 18
Set value 48 48

Achievements of President Camilo Ponce Enriquez. See Nos. C370-C374.

Animal Type of 1960.

Animals: 10c, Collared peccary. 20c, Kinkajou. 80c, Jaguars. 1s, Mountain coati.

Unwmk.
1961, July 13 Photo. *Perf. 13*

676 A232 10c grn, rose red & blk 15 15
677 A232 20c vio, grnsh bl & brn 15 15
678 A232 80c red org, dl yel & blk 22 15
679 A232 1s brn, brt grn & org 26 15
Set value 65 38

Founding of the city of Tena, 400th anniv.

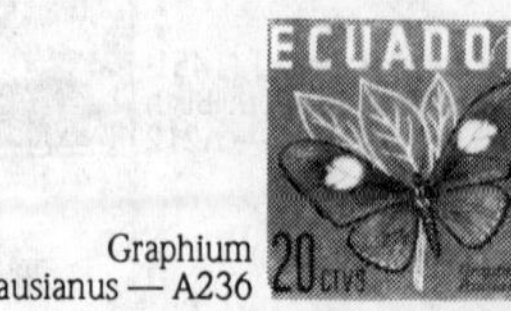

Graphium Pausianus — A236

Butterflies: 30c, Papilio torquatus leptalea. 50c, Graphium molops molops. 80c, Battus lycidas.

1961, July 13 Litho. *Perf. 13½*

680 A236 20c pink & multi 15 15
681 A236 30c lt ultra & multi 15 15
682 A236 50c org & multi 30 15
683 A236 80c bl grn & multi 40 15
Set value 38

See Nos. 711-713.

Galapagos Islands Nos. L1-L3 Overprinted in Black or Red

1961
Estación de Biología Marítima de Galápagos

XXXXXXXXXXXX

1961, Oct. 31 Photo. *Perf. 12*

684 A1 20c dk brn 20 20
685 A2 50c violet 20 20
686 A1 1s dk ol grn (R) 30 30
Nos. 684-686,C389-C391 (6) 1.72 1.44

Establishment of maritime biological stations on Galapagos Islands by UNESCO. Overprint arranged differently on 20c, 1s.
See Nos. C389-C391.

Daniel Enrique Proano School A237

Designs: 60c, Loja-Zamora highway, vert. 80c, Aguirre Abad College, Guayaquil. 1s, Army quarters, Quito.

Perf. 11x11½, 11½x11
1962, Jan. 10 Engr. Unwmk.

687 A237 50c dl bl & blk 15 15
688 A237 60c ol grn & blk 15 15
689 A237 80c org red & blk 15 15
690 A237 1s rose lake & blk 18 15
Set value 47 29

Pres. Arosemena, Flags of Ecuador, US — A238

Protection for The Family — A239

Designs (Arosemena and): 10c, Flags of Ecuador. 20c, Flags of Ecuador and Panama.

1963, July 1 Litho. *Perf. 14*

691 A238 10c buff & multi 15 15
692 A238 20c multi 15 15
693 A238 60c multi 15 15
Set value, #691-693, C409-C411 1.15 1.15

Issued to commemorate Pres. Carlos J. Arosemena's friendship trip, July 1962.

1963, July 9 Unwmk. *Perf. 14*

694 A239 10c ultra, red, gray & blk 15 15

Social Insurance, 25th anniv. See #C413.

No. 655 Overprinted or Surcharged in Black or Blue

1961
DIA DEL EMPLEADO POSTAL
10

1963 Photo. *Perf. 13*
695 A230 10c on 80c dk car rose 15 15
696 A230 20c on 80c dk car rose 15 15
697 A230 50c on 80c dk car rose 15 15
698 A230 60c on 80c dk car rose (Bl) 15 15
699 A230 80c dk car rose 18 15
Set value 47 35

Nos. 661-669 Surcharged 0,10 XXXXX

1964, Apr. 20 Engr. *Perf. 11x11½*
700 A233 10c on 1s dk pur & redsh brn 15 15
701 A233 10c on 1s dk pur & turq 15 15
702 A233 20c on 1s dk bl & brn 15 15
703 A233 20c on 1s dk bl & grn 15 15
704 A233 30c on 1s dk pur & dk car rose 15 15
705 A233 40c on 1s blk & ol bis 15 15
706 A233 60c on 1s blk & red 15 15
707 A233 80c on 1s dk bl & ultra 15 15
708 A233 80c on 1s blk & vio 15 15
Set value 72 54

No. 656 Overprinted in Black or Light Ultramarine

1964 Litho. *Perf. 14x13*
709 A231 80c rose car & grn 1.40 1.00

Butterfly Type of 1961

Butterflies: Same as on Nos. 680, 682-683.

1964, June Litho. *Perf. 13½*
711 A236 20c brt grn & multi 15 15
712 A236 50c sal pink & multi 35 15
713 A236 80c lt red brn & multi 50 15
Set value 20

Alliance for Progress Emblem, Agriculture and Industry A240

Designs: 50c, Emblem, gear wheels, mountain and seashore. 80c, Emblem, banana worker, fish, factory and ship.

1964, Aug. 26 Unwmk. *Perf. 12*
715 A240 40c bis brn & vio 15 15
716 A240 50c red org & blk 15 15
717 A240 80c bl & dk brn 18 15
Set value 20

Issued to publicize the Alliance for Progress which aims to stimulate economic growth and raise living standards in Latin America.

No. 650 Overprinted in Red

FARO DE COLON

1964 Photo. *Perf. 14x13½*
718 A229 1.80s dark blue 2.00 2.00

No. 656 Overprinted

(Reduced Size)
Overprint covers four stamps

1964, July Litho. *Perf. 14x13*
719 A231 80c block of 4 2.00 2.00

Organization of American States.

World Map and Banana Tree — A241

1964, Oct. 26 *Perf. 12½x12*
720 A241 50c dk brn, gray & gray ol 15 15
721 A241 80c blk, org & gray ol 15 15
Set value 15 15

Issued to publicize the Banana Conference, Oct.-Nov. 1964. See Nos. C427-C428a.

King Philip II of Spain and Map of Upper Amazon River A242

Designs (Map and): 20c, Juan de Salinas de Loyola. 30c, Hernando de Santillan.

1964, Dec. 6 Litho. *Perf. 13½*
722 A242 10c rose, blk & buff 15 15
723 A242 20c bl grn, blk & buff 15 15
724 A242 30c bl, blk & buff 15 15
Set value 25 17

4th centenary of the establishment of the Royal High Court in Quito.

Pole Vaulting A243

1964, Dec. 16 *Perf. 14x13½*
725 A243 80c vio bl, yel grn & brn 15 15

18th Olympic Games, Tokyo, Oct. 10-25. See Nos. C432-C434.

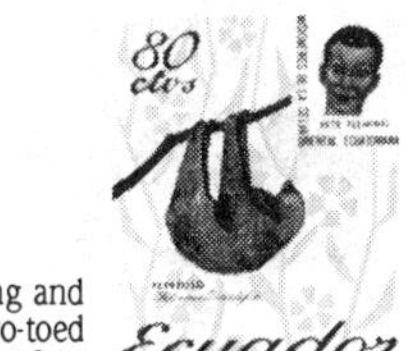

Peter Fleming and Two-toed Sloth — A244

Designs: 20c, James Elliot and armadillo. 30c, T. Edward McCully, Jr., and squirrel. 40c, Roger Youderian and deer. 60c, Nathaniel (Nate) Saint and plane over Napo River.

1965 Unwmk. *Perf. 13½*
726 A244 20c emerald & multi 15 15
727 A244 30c yellow & multi 15 15
728 A244 40c lilac & multi 15 15
729 A244 60c multi 15 15
730 A244 80c multi 15 15
Nos. 726-730 (5) 75
Set value 32

Issued in memory of five American Protestant missionaries, killed by the Auca Indians, Jan. 8, 1956.
Issue dates: 80c, May 11; others, July 8.

Juan B. Vázquez and Benigno Malo College A245

1965, June 6 Litho. *Perf. 14*
731 A245 20c blk, yel & vio bl 15 15
732 A245 60c blk, red, yel & vio bl 15 15
733 A245 80c blk, emer, yel & vio bl 15 15
Set value 25 21

Centenary (in 1964) of the founding of Benigno Malo National College.

National Anthem, Juan Leon Mera and Antonio Neumane A246

1965, Aug. 10 Litho. *Perf. 13½*
734 A246 50c pink & blk 15 15
735 A246 80c lt grn & blk 25 15
736 A246 5s bis & blk 60 35
737 A246 10s lt ultra & blk 1.00 75

Cent. of the national anthem. The name of the poet Juan Leon Mera is misspelled on the stamps.
For surcharges see Nos. 766C, 766H.

Torch and Athletes (Shot Put, Discus, Javelin and Hammer Throw) — A247

Torch and Athletes: 50c, 1s, Runners. 60c, 1.50s, Soccer.

1965, Nov. 20 *Perf. 12x12½*
738 A247 40c org, gold, & blk 20 15
739 A247 50c org ver, gold & blk 20 15
740 A247 60c bl, gold & blk 20 15
741 A247 80c brt yel grn, gold & blk 30 15
742 A247 1s lt vio, gold & blk 30 15
743 A247 1.50s brt pink, gold & blk 50 35
Nos. 738-743,C435-C440 (12) 4.10
Set value 1.90

Issued to publicize the 5th Bolivarian Games, held at Guayaquil and Quito.
For surcharges see Nos. 766B, 766D, C449.

Stamps of 1865 — A248

1965, Dec. 30 Litho. *Perf. 13½*
Stamps of 1865 in Yellow, Ultramarine & Green
744 A248 80c rose red 20 15
745 A248 1.30s rose lilac 30 15
746 A248 2s chocolate 50 15
747 A248 4s black 1.00 20
a. Souv. sheet of 4, #744-747, imperf. 2.50 2.50
Set value 51

Cent. of Ecuadorian postage stamps.

The postal validity of some of the following sets has been questioned.

ITU Centenary — A248a

1966, Jan. 27 Litho. *Perf. 12x12½*
748 A248a 10c Telstar
748A A248a 10c Syncom
748B A248a 80c Relay
748C A248a 1.50s Luna 3
748D A248a 3s Echo II
f. Souv. sheet of 3, #748, 748B, 748D, perf. 14x12½
748E A248a 4s E. Branly, Marconi, Bell, E. Belin
g. Souv. sheet of 3, #748A, 748C, 748E, perf. 14x12½

1.50s, 3s, 4s are airmail.
Nos. 748f-748g are printed on surface colored paper. Exist imperf.

Space Exploration — A248b

Designs: 10c, Edward White's space walk, June 8, 1965. 1s, Gemini 5, Aug. 21, 1965. 1.30s, Solar system. 2s, Charles Conrad, L. Gordon Cooper, Gemini 5, Aug. 21-29, 1965. 2.50s, Gemini 6. 3.50s, Alexei L. Leonov's space walk, Mar. 18, 1965.

1966, Jan. 27 *Perf. 12x12½*
749 A248b 10c multicolored
749A A248b 1s multicolored
749B A248b 1.30s multicolored
749C A248b 2s multicolored
749D A248b 2.50s multicolored
749E A248b 3.50s multicolored
f. Souv. sheet of 3, #749, 749B, 749E, perf. 14x12½

1.30s, 2s, 2.50s, 3.50s are airmail.
No. 749f is printed on surface colored paper. Exists imperf.

Dante's Dream by Rossetti — A248c

Designs: 80c, Dante and Beatrix by Holliday. 2s, Galileo Galilei, 400th birth cent., vert. 3s, Dante, 700th birth cent., vert.

1966, June *Perf. 13½x14, 14x13½*
750 A248c 10c multicolored
750A A248c 80c multicolored
750B A248c 2s multicolored
750C A248c 3s multicolored
d. Souv. sheet of 3, #750, 750A, 750C, perf. 12x12½

Nos. 750A-750B are airmail. No. 750d exists imperf.

Pavonine Quetzal — A249

Birds: 50c, Blue-crowned motmot. 60c, Paradise tanager. 80c, Wire-tailed manakin.

1966, June 17 Litho. *Perf. 13½*
Birds in Natural Colors
751 A249 40c dl rose & blk 20 15
751A A249 50c sal & blk 20 15
751B A249 60c lt ocher & blk 20 15
751C A249 80c lt bl & blk 20 15
Nos. 751-751C,C441-C448 (12) 4.80
Set value 1.50

For surcharges see Nos. 766E-766F, C450, C455-C457.

Pope Paul VI — A249a

Pope Paul VI and: 1.30s, Nativity. 3.50s, Virgin of Merced.

1966, June 24 *Perf. 12½x12*

752 A249a 10c multicolored
752A A249a 1.30s multicolored
752B A249a 3.50s multicolored
c. Souv. sheet of 3, #752, perf. 14x13½, 752A-752B, perf. 12½x12

Nos. 752A-752B are airmail.
No. 752c is printed on surface colored paper. Exists imperf.

Sir Winston Churchill, (1874-1965) — A249b

Famous Men: 10c, Dag Hammarskjold, vert. 1.50s, Albert Schweitzer, vert. 2.50s, John F. Kennedy, vert. 4s, Churchill, Kennedy.

Perf. 14x13½, 13½x14

1966, June 24

753 A249b 10c vio bl, brn & blk
753A A249b 1s ver, bl & blk
753B A249b 1.50s brn, lil rose & blk
753C A249b 2.50s ver, bl & blk
753D A249b 4s bl, blk & brn
e. Souv. sheet of 3, #753, 753B, 753D

Nos. 753C-753D are airmail.
No. 753e is printed on surface colored paper. 10c stamp is perf. 14x13½, 1.50s is perf. 14x13½x14x12, 4s is perf. 12x12½x13x12½. Exists imperf.

History of Summer Olympics — A249c

1966, June 27 *Perf. 12x12½*

754 A249c 10c Long jump
754A A249c 10c Wrestling
754B A249c 80c Discus, javelin
754C A249c 1.30s Chariot racing
754D A249c 3s High jump
f. Souv. sheet of 3, #754, 754B, 754D
754E A249c 3.50s Discus
g. Souv. sheet of 3, #754A, 754C, 754E

Nos. 754C-754D are airmail.
Nos. 754f-754g are printed on surface colored paper.

1968 Winter Olympics, Grenoble — A249d

1966, June 27 *Perf. 14*

755 A249d 10c Speedskating
755A A249d 1s Ice hockey
755B A249d 1.50s Ski jumping
755C A249d 2s Cross country skiing
755D A249d 2.50s Downhill skiing
755E A249d 4s Figure skating
f. Souv. sheet of 3, #755, 755B, 755E, perf. 14x13½

Nos. 755B-755E are airmail.
No. 755f is printed on surface colored paper. Exists imperf.

French-American Cooperation in Space — A249e

Designs: 1.50s, French satellite D-1, Mt. Gros observatory, vert. 4s, John F. Kennedy, satellites.

1966 *Perf. 13½x14, 14x13½*

756 A249e 10c multicolored
756A A249e 1.50s multicolored
756B A249e 4s multicolored
c. Sheet of 3, #756-756B

Nos. 756A-756B are airmail.

Moon Exploration A249f

1966 *Perf. 14*

758 A249f 10c Surveyor
758A A249f 80c Luna 10
758B A249f 1s Luna 9
758C A249f 2s Astronaut flight trainer
758D A249f 2.50s Ranger 7
758E A249f 3s Lunar Orbiter 1
f. Sheet of 3, #758, 758A, 758E

Nos. 758C-758E are airmail. Stamps in No. 758f have colored pattern in border. No. 758f exists imperf.

1968 Summer Olympics, Mexico City — A249g

Paintings by Mexican artists: 10c, Wanderer by Diego Rivera. 1s, Workers by Jose Orozco. 1.30s, Pres. Juarez by Orozco. 2s, Mother and Child by David Siqueiros. 2.50s, Two Women by Rivera. 3.50s, New Democracy by Siqueiros.

1967, Mar. 13 *Perf. 14*

759 A249g 10c multicolored
759A A249g 1s multicolored
759B A249g 1.30s multicolored
759C A249g 2s multicolored
759D A249g 2.50s multicolored
759E A249g 3.50s multicolored
f. Sheet of 3, #759, 759B, 759E

Nos. 759B-759E are airmail.
No. 759f is printed on surface colored paper that differs slightly from Nos. 759-759E. Exists imperf.

1968 Summer Olympics, Mexico City — A249h

1967, Mar. 13

760 A249h 10c Soccer
760A A249h 10c Hurdles
760B A249h 80c Track
760C A249h 1.50s Fencing
760D A249h 3s High jump
f. Souv. sheet of 3, #760A, 760B, 760D
760E A249h 4s Swimming
g. Souv. sheet of 3, #760, 760C, 760E

Nos. 760C-760E are airmail.
Nos. 760f-760g are printed on surface colored paper. Exist imperf.

4th Natl. Eucharistic Congress A249i

Paintings: 10c, Madonna and Child by unknown artist. 60c, Holy Family by Rodriguez. 80c, Madonna and Child by Samaniego. 1s, Good Shepherd by Samaniego. 1.50s, Assumption of the Virgin by Vargas. 2s, Man in Prayer by Santiago.

1967, May 10

761 A249i 10c multicolored
761A A249i 60c multicolored
761B A249i 80c multicolored
761C A249i 1s multicolored
761D A249i 1.50s multicolored
761E A249i 2s multicolored

Nos. 761D-761E are airmail. Frames and inscriptions vary greatly.

Madonna and Child Enthroned by Guido Reni A249j

Paintings of the Madonna and Child by: 40c, van Hemesen. 50c, Memling. 1.30s, Durer. 2.50s, Raphael. 3s, Murillo.

1967, May 25 *Perf. 14x13½*

762 A249j 10c multicolored
762A A249j 40c multicolored
762B A249j 50c multicolored
762C A249j 1.30s multicolored
762D A249j 2.50s multicolored
762E A249j 3s multicolored

Nos. 762C-762E are airmail.

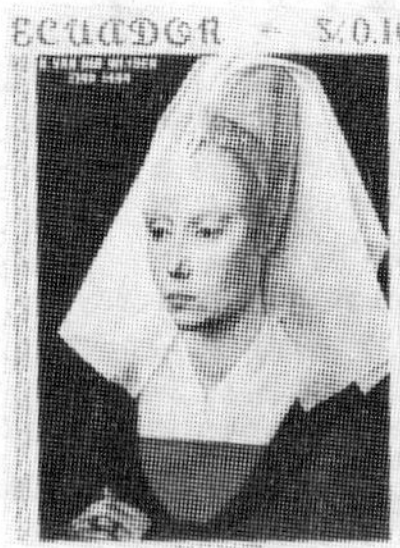

Portrait of a Young Woman by Rogier van der Weyden A249k

Designs: 1s, Helene Fourment by Rubens. 1.50s, Venetian Woman by Durer. 2s, Lady Sheffield by Gainsborough. 2.50s, Suzon by Manet. 4s, Lady with a Unicorn by Raphael.

1967, Sept. 9 *Perf. 14x13½*

763 A249k 10c multicolored
763A A249k 1s multicolored
763B A249k 1.50s multicolored
763C A249k 2s multicolored
763D A249k 2.50s multicolored
763E A249k 4s multicolored
f. Sheet of 3, #763, 763B, 763E, perf. 14

Nos. 763B-763E are airmail.
Stamps in No. 763f have colored pattern in border. Exists imperf.

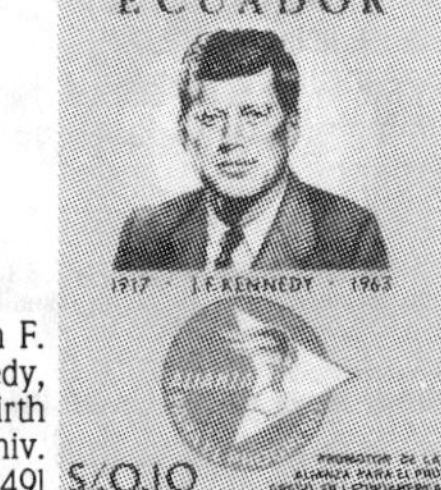

John F. Kennedy, 50th Birth Anniv. A249l

JFK and: No. 764A, Dag Hammarskjold. 80c, Pope Paul VI. 1.30s, Konrad Adenauer. 3s, Charles de Gaulle. 2.50s, Winston Churchill.

Perf. 14x13½, 13½x14

1967, Sept. 11

764 A249l 10c lil, brn & bl
764A A249l 10c yel, brn & sky bl
764B A249l 80c yel, brn & sal
764C A249l 1.30s yel, brn & pink
764D A249l 3s yel, brn & yel grn
764E A249l 3.50s yel, brn & bl

Souvenir Sheets

764F Sheet of 3
h. like #764, 35x27mm
i. like #764B, 35x27mm
j. like #764D, 35x27mm
764G Sheet of 3
k. like #764A, 35x27mm
l. like #764C, 35x27mm
m. like #764E, 35x27mm

Nos. 764C-764E are airmail. Nos. 764A-764E horiz. Stamps in Nos. 764F-764G have colored pattern in border.

Christmas — A249m

Designs: No. 765A, Children's procession. 40c, Candlelight procession. 50c, Children singing. 60c, Processional. 2.50s, Christmas celebration.

1967, Dec. 29 *Perf. 13x14*

765 A249m 10c multicolored
765A A249m 10c multicolored
765B A249m 40c multicolored
765C A249m 50c multicolored
765D A249m 60c multicolored
765E A249m 2.50s multicolored

No. 765E is airmail. See Nos. 768-768F.

Various Surcharges on Issues of 1956-66

1967-68

766	AP72	30c on 1.10s (C337)	20	20
766A	AP66	40c on 1.70s (C292)	20	20
766B	A247	40c on 3.50s (C438)	20	15
766C	A246	50c on 5s (736) ('68)	20	20
766D	A247	80c on 1.50s (743)	25	15
766E	A249	80c on 2.50s (C445)	25	15
766F	A249	1s on 4s (C447)	30	15
766G	AP66	1.30s on 1.90s (C293)	40	40
766H	A246	2s on 10s (737) ('68)	50	20
		Nos. 766-766H,C449-C450 (11)	3.00	2.20

The surcharge on Nos. 766B-766C, 766E and 766G-766H includes "Resello." The obliteration of old denomination and arrangement of surcharges differ on each stamp.

Bust of Peñaherrera, Central University, Quito — A250

Designs: 50c, Law books. 80c, Open book and laurel, horiz.

Perf. 12x12½, 12½x12

1967, Dec. 29 **Litho.**

767	A250	50c brt grn & blk	15	15
767A	A250	60c rose & blk	15	15
767B	A250	80c rose lil & blk	15	15
		Nos. 767-767B,C451-C452 (5)	75	
		Set value		37

Cent. (in 1964) of the birth of Dr. Victor Manuel Peñaherrera (1864-1932), author of the civil and criminal codes of Ecuador.

Christmas Type of 1967

Native Christian Art: 10c, Mourning of the Death of Christ, by Manuel Chili. 80c, Ascension of the Holy Virgin, vert. 1s, The Holy Virgin. 1.30s, Coronation of the Holy Virgin, by Bernardo Rodriguez, vert. 1.50s, Madonna and Child with the Heavenly Host, vert. 2s, Madonna and Child, by Manuel Samaniego, vert. 3s, Immaculate Conception, by Bernardo de Legranda, vert. 3.50s, Passion of Christ, by Chili, vert. 4s, The Holy Virgin of Quito, by de Legranda, vert.

1968 Jan. 19 *Perf. 13½x14, 14x13½*

768 A249m 10c multicolored
768A A249m 80c multicolored
768B A249m 1s multicolored
768C A249m 1.30s multicolored
768D A249m 1.50s multicolored
768E A249m 2s multicolored

Souvenir Sheet

Perf. 14

768F Sheet of 3
g. A249m 3s multicolored
h. A249m 3.50s multicolored
i. A249m 4s multicolored

Nos. 768C-768F are airmail. No. 768F exists imperf.

Tourism Year — A250a

Designs: 20c, Woman from Otavalo. 30c, Colorado Indian. 40c, Petroglyph of a cat. 50c, Petroglyph of a mythological predator. 60c, Woman in a bazaar. 80c, 1s, 1.30s, Petroglyphs, diff. 1.50s, Colonial street, Quito. 2s, Amulet.

1968, Apr. 1 *Perf. 13½x14*

769 A250a 20c multicolored
769A A250a 30c multicolored
769B A250a 40c multicolored
769C A250a 50c multicolored
769D A250a 60c multicolored
769E A250a 80c multicolored
769F A250a 1s multicolored
769G A250a 1.30s multicolored
769H A250a 1.50s multicolored
769I A250a 2s multicolored

Ninth Congress of the Confederation of Latin American Tourist Organizations (COTAL). Nos. 769G-769I are airmail.

Otto Arosemena Gomez — A251

Lions Emblem — A252

Design: 1s, Page from the Constitution.

1968, May 9 **Litho.** *Perf. 13½x14*

770	A251	80c lil & multi	15	15
770A	A251	1s multi	15	15
		Set value		15

First anniversary of the administration of Pres. Otto Arosemena Gomez. See Nos. C453-C454.

1968, May 24 **Litho.** *Perf. 13½x14*

771	A252	80c multi	20	20
771A	A252	1.30s multi	25	15
771B	A252	2s pink & multi	30	15
c.		Souv. sheet of 1	3.00	3.00
		Set value		40

50th anniv. (in 1967) of Lions Intl.

No. 771c contains one 5s 39x49mm stamp. Exists imperf.

Pope Paul VI, Visit to Latin America — A252a

39th Intl. Eucharistic Congress, Bogota, Colombia A252b

Designs: 60c, Pope Paul VI, vert. 1s, Madonna by Botticelli. 1.30s, Pope Paul VI with flags of South American nations. 2s, Madonna and Child by Durer.

1969 *Perf. 13½x14, 14x13½*

772 A252a 40c multicolored
772A A252a 60c multicolored
772B A252b 1s multicolored
772C A252a 1.30s multicolored
e. Souv. sheet of 3, #772, 772A, 772C, imperf.
772D A252b 2s multicolored
f. Souv. sheet of 2, #772B, 772D, imperf.

Nos. 772C-772D are airmail. Nos. 772-772f overprinted in silver with the national coat of arms.

Madonna with the Angel by Rogier van der Weyden A252c

Paintings by various artists showing the life of the Virgin Mary.

1969 *Perf. 14x13½, 13½x14*

773 A252c 40c shown
773A A252c 60c Van der Weyden, diff.
773B A252c 1s Raphael
773C A252c 1.30s Veronese
e. Souv. sheet of 2, #773B-773C, imperf.
773D A252c 2s Van der Weyden, horiz.
f. Souv. sheet of 3, #773-773A, 773D, imperf.

Nos. 773-773f overprinted in silver with the national coat of arms. Nos. 773C-773D are airmail.

Nos. C331 and C326 Surcharged in Violet and Dark Blue

RESELLO

$ 0,40

a

$ 0,50

RESELLO

b

1969, Jan. 10 *Perf. 11½, 14x13½*

774	AP79 (a)	40c on 1.30s (V)	25	25
774A	AP76 (b)	50c on 1.30s (DBl)	25	25

Type of 1958 Surcharged and Overprinted in Plum and Black

RESELLO

$ 0,50

Design: Ignacio Luis Arcaya, Foreign Minister of Venezuela.

1969, Mar. **Litho.** *Perf. 12*

Flags in Red, Blue and Yellow

775	A223	50c on 2s sepia	20	20
775A	A223	80c on 2s sepia	20	20
775B	A223	1s on 2s sepia	20	20
775C	A223	2s sepia	20	20
		Nos. 775-775C,C455-C457 (7)	1.55	1.28

Nos. 775-775C were not issued without overprint. The obliteration of old denomination on No. 775A is a small square around a star. Overprint is plum, except for the black small coat of arms on right flag.

Map of Ecuador and Oriental Region — A253

Surcharge typographed in Dark Blue, Red Brown, Black or Lilac

1969 **Litho.** *Perf. 14*

776	A253	20c on 30c (DBl)	15	15
776A	A253	40c on 30c (RBr)	15	15
777	A253	50c on 30c (DBl)	15	15
778	A253	60c on 30c (DBl)	15	15
779	A253	80c on 30c (Bk)	20	15
780	A253	1s on 30c (L)	20	15
781	A253	1.30s on 30c (Bk)	30	15
782	A253	1.50s on 30c (Bk)	30	30
783	A253	2s on 30c (DBl)	40	15
784	A253	3s on 30c (DBl)	45	18
785	A253	4s on 30c (Bk)	50	15
786	A253	5s on 30c (Bk)	60	25
		Nos. 776-786 (12)	3.55	
		Set value		1.50

Not issued without surcharge.

M. L. King, John and Robert Kennedy — A254

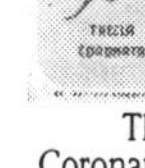

Thecla Coronata — A255

1969-70 **Typo.** *Perf. 12½*

787	A254	4s blk, bl, grn & buff	40	15

Perf. 13½

788	A254	4s blk, lt bl & grn ('70)	40	15

In memory of John F. Kennedy, Robert F. Kennedy and Martin Luther King, Jr.

1970 **Litho.** *Perf. 12½*

Butterflies: 20c, Papilio zabreus. 30c, Heliconius chestertoni. 40c, Papilio pausanias. 50c, Pereute leucodrosime. 60c, Metamorpha dido. 80c, Morpho cypris. 1s, Catagramma astarte.

789	A255	10c buff & multi	30	30
790	A255	20c lt grn & multi	30	30
791	A255	30c pink & multi	30	30
792	A255	40c lt bl & multi	30	15
793	A255	50c gold & multi	30	15
794	A255	60c salmon & multi	30	15
795	A255	80c silver & multi	30	15
796	A255	1s lt grn & multi	30	15

Same, White Background

Perf. 13½

797	A255	10c multi	30	30
798	A255	20c multi	30	30
799	A255	30c multi	30	30
800	A255	40c multi	30	15
801	A255	50c multi	30	15
802	A255	60c multi	30	15
803	A255	80c multi	30	15
804	A255	1s multi	30	15
		Nos. 789-804,C461-C464 (20)	6.80	
		Set value		2.65

Surcharged Revenue Stamps
A256 A257

1970, June 16 **Litho.** *Perf. 14*

Red Surcharge

805	A256	1s on 1s light blue	15	15
806	A256	1.30s on 1s light blue	20	15
807	A256	1.50s on 1s light blue	25	25
808	A256	2s on 1s light blue	30	20
809	A256	5s on 1s light blue	60	30
810	A256	10s on 1s light blue	1.00	50
		Nos. 805-810 (6)	2.50	1.55

1970 **Typo.** *Perf. 12*

Black Surcharge

811	A257	60c on 1s violet	15	15
812	A257	80c on 1s violet	15	15
813	A257	1s on 1s violet	15	15
814	A257	1.10s on 1s violet	20	15
815	A257	1.30s on 1s violet	20	15
816	A257	1.50s on 1s violet	25	15
817	A257	2s on 1s violet	30	15
818	A257	2.20s on 1s violet	35	15
819	A257	3s on 1s violet	45	15
		Nos. 811-819 (9)	2.20	
		Set value		1.00

1970

820 A257 1.10s on 2s green 20 20
821 A257 1.30s on 2s green 20 15
822 A257 1.50s on 2s green 25 15
823 A257 2s on 2s green 30 15
824 A257 3.40s on 2s green 45 15
825 A257 5s on 2s green 60 20
826 A257 10s on 2s green 1.00 15
827 A257 20s on 2s green 2.00 50
828 A257 50s on 2s green 4.00 2.00
Nos. 820-828 (9) 9.00 3.65

1970

829 A257 3s on 5s blue 45 15
830 A257 5s on 5s blue 55 25
831 A257 10s on 40s orange 1.00 50

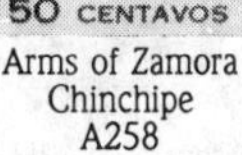

Arms of Zamora Chinchipe A258

Flags of Ecuador and Chile A259

Design: 1s, Arms and flag of Esmeraldas.

1971 Litho. *Perf. 10½*

832 A258 50c pale yel & multi 20 15
833 A258 1s sal & multi 20 15
Nos. 832-833,C465-C469 (7) 2.90
Set value 1.10

1971, Sept. *Perf. 12½*

840 A259 1.30s blk & multi 15 15

Visit of Pres. Salvador Allende of Chile, Aug. 24. See Nos. C481-C482.

Ismael Pérez Pazmiño — A260

1971, Sept. 16 *Perf. 12x11½*

841 A260 1s grn & multi 15 15

50th anniversary of "El Universo," newspaper founded by Ismael Pérez Pazmiño. See Nos. C485-C486.

CARE Package — A261

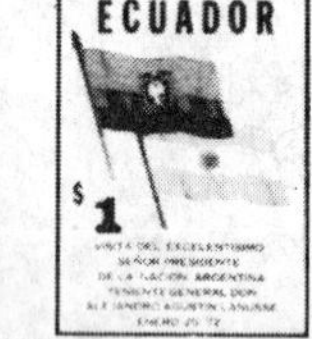

Flags of Ecuador and Argentina — A262

1971-72 *Perf. 12½*

842 A261 30c lilac ('72) 15 15
843 A261 40c emerald ('72) 15 15
844 A261 50c blue 15 15
845 A261 60c carmine 15 15
846 A261 80c lt brn ('72) 15 15
Nos. 842-846 (5) 75
Set value 35

25th anniversary of CARE, a US-Canadian Cooperative for American Relief Everywhere.

1972 *Perf. 11½*

847 A262 1s blk & multi 15 15

Visit of Lt. Gen. Alejandro Agustin Lanusse, president of Argentina, Jan. 25.
See Nos. C491-C492.

Jesus Giving Keys to St. Peter, by Miguel de Santiago — A263

Ecuadorian Paintings: 1.10s, Virgin of Mercy, Quito School. 2s, Virgin Mary, by Manuel Samaniego.

1972, Apr. 24 Litho. *Perf. 14x13½*

848 A263 50c blk & multi 15 15
849 A263 1.10s blk & multi 25 25
850 A263 2s blk & multi 40 40
a. Souv. sheet of 3 1.00 1.00
Nos. 848-850,C494-C495 (5) 1.80 1.55

No. 850a contains 3 imperf. stamps similar to Nos. 848-850.

1972, May 4

Ecuadorian Statues: 50c, Our Lady of Sorrow, by Caspicara. 1.10s, Nativity. Quito School, horiz. 2s, Virgin of Quito, anonymous.

851 A263 50c blk & multi 15 15
852 A263 1.10s blk & multi 25 25
853 A263 2s blk & multi 40 40
a. Souv. sheet of 3 1.00 1.00
Nos. 851-853,C496-C497 (5) 1.80 1.55

Letters of "Ecuador" 3mm high on Nos. 851-853, 7mm high on Nos. 848-850. No. 853a contains 3 imperf. stamps similar to Nos. 851-853.

A264

A265

Designs: 30c, Gen. Juan Ignacio Pareja. 40c, Juan José Flores. 50c, Leon de Febres Cordero. 60c, Ignacio Torres. 70c, Francisco de Paula Santander. 1s, José M. Cordova.

1972, May 24 *Perf. 12½*

854 A264 30c bl & multi 15 15
855 A264 40c bl & multi 15 15
856 A264 50c bl & multi 15 15
857 A264 60c bl & multi 15 15
858 A264 70c bl & multi 15 15
859 A264 1s bl & multi 15 15
Nos. 854-859,C498-C503 (12) 3.10
Set value 2.05

Sesquicentennial of the Battle of Pichincha and the liberation of Quito.

1972, July Photo. *Perf. 13*

Designs: 2s, Woman Wearing Poncho. 3s, Striped poncho. 5s, Embroidered poncho. 10s, Metal vase.

860 A265 2s multi 20 20
861 A265 3s multi 30 30
862 A265 5s multi 50 50
863 A265 10s dp bl & multi 1.00 1.00
a. Souvenir sheet of 4 1.40 1.40
Nos. 860-863,C504-C507 (8) 4.00 4.00

Handicraft of Ecuador. No. 863a contains 4 imperf. stamps similar to Nos. 860-863.

Sucre Statue, Santo Domingo — A266

Radar Station — A267

Designs: 1.80s, San Agustin Convent. 2.30s, Plaza de la Independencia. 2.50s, Bolivar statue, La Alameda. 4.75s, Chapel door.

1972, Dec. 6 Litho. *Perf. 11½*

864 A266 1.20s yel & multi 15 15
865 A266 1.80s yel & multi 20 15
866 A266 2.30s yel & multi 20 15
867 A266 2.50s yel & multi 25 15
868 A266 4.75s yel & multi 40 40
Nos. 864-868,C518-C524 (12) 4.95 2.95

Sesquicentennial of the Battle of Pichincha.

1973, Apr. 5 Wmk. 367

869 A267 1s multi 25 15

Inauguration of earth telecommunications station, Oct. 19, 1972.

Blue-footed Boobies A268

Wmk. 367, Unwmkd. (#872)

1973 Litho. *Perf. 11½x12*

870 A268 30c shown 15 15
871 A268 40c Blue-faced booby 15 15
872 A268 50c Oyster-catcher 15 15
873 A268 60c California sea lions 15 15
874 A268 70c Galapagos giant tortoise 20 20
875 A268 1s California sea lion 20 15
Nos. 870-875,C527-C528 (8) 2.00
Set value 88

Elevation of Galapagos Islands to a province of Ecuador.
Issue dates: 50c, Oct. 3; others Aug. 16.

Black-chinned Mountain Tanager — A269

Birds of Ecuador: 2s, Moriche oriole. 3s, Toucan barbet, vert. 5s, Masked crimson tanager, vert. 10s, Blue-necked tanager, vert.

Perf. 11x11½, 11½x11

1973, Dec. 6 Litho. Unwmk.

876 A269 1s brick red & multi 15 15
877 A269 2s lt bl & multi 18 18
878 A269 3s lt grn & multi 18 18
879 A269 5s pale lil & multi 40 40
880 A269 10s pale yel grn & multi 85 60
Nos. 876-880 (5) 1.76 1.51

Two souvenir sheets exist: one contains 2 imperf. stamps similar to Nos. 876-877 with yellow margin and black inscription; the other 3 stamps similar to Nos. 878-880; gray margin and black inscription including "Aereo." Both sheets dated "1972." Size: 143x84mm.

Marco T. Varea, Botanist — A270

Portraits: 60c, Pio Jaramillo Alvarado, writer. 70c, Prof. Luciano Andrade M. No. 883, Marco T. Varea, botanist. No. 884, Dr. Juan Modesto Carbo Noboa, medical researcher. No. 885, Alfredo J. Valenzuela. No. 886, Capt. Edmundo Chiriboga G. 1.20s, Francisco Campos R., scientist. 1.80s, Luis Vernaza Lazarte, philanthropist.

1974 Unwmk. *Perf. 12x11½*

881 A270 60c crim rose 15 15
882 A270 70c lilac 15 15
883 A270 1s ultra 15 15
884 A270 1s orange 15 15
885 A270 1s emerald 15 15
886 A270 1s brown 15 15
887 A270 1.20s apple grn 15 15
889 A270 1.80s lt blue 25 25
Nos. 881-889 (8) 1.30
Set value 85

Arcade — A271

Designs: 30c, Monastery, entrance. 40c, Church. 50c, View of Church through gate, vert. 60c, Chapel, vert. 70c, Church and cemetery, vert.

Perf. 11½x12, 12x11½

1975, Feb. 4 Litho.

896 A271 20c yellow & multi 15 15
897 A271 30c yellow & multi 15 15
898 A271 40c yellow & multi 15 15
899 A271 50c yellow & multi 15 15
900 A271 60c yellow & multi 15 15
901 A271 70c yellow & multi 15 15
Nos. 896-901 (6) 90
Set value 40

Colonial Monastery, Tilipulo, Cotopaxi Province.

Angel Polibio Chaves, Founder of Bolivar Province — A272

Portrait: No. 903, Emilio Estrada Ycaza (1916-1961), archeologist.

1975 Litho. *Perf. 12x11½*

902 A272 80c vio bl & lt bl 15 15
903 A272 80c ver & pink 15 15
Set value 20 20

Issue dates: #902, Feb. 21; #903, Mar. 25.

R. Rodriguez Palacios and A. Duran Quintero — A273

"Woman of Action" — A274

1975, Apr. 1 Litho. *Perf. 12x11½*

910 A273 1s multi 15 15

Meeting of the Ministers for Public Works of Ecuador and Colombia, July 27, 1973.
See Nos. C547-C548.

1975, June

Design: No. 912, "Woman of Peace."

911 A274 1s yel & multi 15 15
912 A274 1s bl & multi 15 15
Set value 16

International Women's Year 1975.

Planes, Soldier and Ship — A275

1975, July 9 *Perf. 11½x12*

913	A275	2s multi	16	15

3 years of Natl. Revolutionary Government.

Hurdling — A276

Designs: Modern sports drawn Inca style.

1975, Sept. 11 **Litho.** *Perf. 11½*

914	A276	20c shown	15	15
915	A276	20c Chess	15	15
916	A276	30c Basketball	15	15
917	A276	30c Boxing	15	15
918	A276	40c Bicycling	15	15
919	A276	40c Steeplechase	15	15
920	A276	50c Soccer	15	15
921	A276	50c Fencing	15	15
922	A276	60c Golf	15	15
923	A276	60c Vaulting	15	15
924	A276	70c Judo (standing)	15	15
925	A276	70c Wrestling	15	15
926	A276	80c Swimming	15	15
927	A276	80c Weight lifting	15	15
928	A276	1s Table Tennis	15	15
929	A276	1s Paddle ball	15	15
		Nos. 914-929,C554-C558 (21)	3.65	
		Set value		1.25

3rd Ecuadorian Games.

Genciana A277

Designs: Ecuadorian plants.

Perf. 12x11½, 11½x12

1975, Nov. 18 **Litho.**

930	A277	20c Orchid, vert	15	15
931	A277	30c shown	15	15
932	A277	40c Bromeliaceae cactaceae, vert	15	15
933	A277	50c Orchid	15	15
934	A277	60c Orchid	15	15
935	A277	80c Flowering cactus	15	15
936	A277	1s Orchid	15	15
		Nos. 930-936,C559-C563 (12)	2.40	
		Set value		1.00

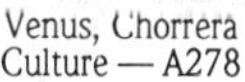

Venus, Chorrera Culture — A278

Female Mask, Tolita Culture — A279

Designs: 30c, Venus, Valdivia Culture. 40c, Seated man, Chorrera Culture. 50c, Man with poncho, Panzaleo Culture (late). 60c, Mythical head, Cashaloma Culture. 80c, Musician, Tolita Culture. No. 943, Chief Priest, Mantefia Culture. No. 945, Ornament, Tolita Culture. No. 946, Angry mask, Tolita Culture.

1976, Feb. 12 **Litho.** *Perf. 11½*

937	A278	20c multi	15	15
938	A278	30c multi	15	15
939	A278	40c multi	15	15
940	A278	50c multi	15	15
941	A278	60c multi	15	15
942	A278	80c multi	15	15
943	A278	1s multi	15	15
944	A279	1s multi	15	15
945	A279	1s multi	15	15
946	A279	1s multi	15	15
		Nos. 937-946,C568-C572 (15)	3.80	
		Set value		1.70

Archaeological artifacts.

Strawberries A280

Carlos Amable Ortiz (1859-1937) A281

1976, Mar. 30

947	A280	1s blue & multi	15	15

25th Flower and Fruit Festival, Ambato. See Nos. C573-C574.

1976, Mar. 15 **Litho.** *Perf. 11½*

Portraits: No. 949, Sixto Maria Duran (1875-1947). No. 950, Segundo Cueva Celi (1901-1969). No. 951, Cristobal Ojeda Davila (1910-1952). No. 952, Luis Alberto Valencia (1918-1970).

948	A281	1s ver & multi	15	15
949	A281	1s org & multi	15	15
950	A281	1s lt grn & multi	15	15
951	A281	1s bl & multi	15	15
952	A281	1s lt brn & multi	15	15
		Nos. 948-952 (5)	75	
		Set value		25

Ecuadorian composers and musicians.

Institute Emblem A282

1977, Aug. 15 **Litho.** *Perf. 11½x12*

953	A282	2s multi	16	15

11th General Assembly of Pan-American Institute of Geography and History, Quito, Aug. 15-30. See Nos. C597-C597a.

Hands Holding Rotary Emblem — A283

José Peralta — A284

1977, Aug. 31 **Litho.** *Perf. 13*

954	A283	1s multi	20	15
955	A283	2s multi	30	15

Souvenir Sheets

Imperf

956	A283	5s multi	50	24
957	A283	10s multi	1.00	48

Rotary Club of Guayaquil, 50th anniv.

1977 **Litho.** *Perf. 11½*

Design: 2.40s, Peralta statue.

958	A284	1.80s multi	15	15
959	A284	2.40s multi	20	20

José Peralta (1855-1937), writer, 40th death anniversary. See No. C609.

Blue-faced Booby — A285

Galapagos Birds: 1.80s, Red-footed booby. 2.40s, Blue-footed boobies. 3.40s, Gull. 4.40s, Galapagos hawk. 5.40s, Map of Galapagos Islands and boobies, vert.

Perf. 11½x12, 12x11½

1977, Nov. 29 **Litho.**

960	A285	1.20s multi	20	20
961	A285	1.80s multi	30	30
962	A285	2.40s multi	40	40
963	A285	3.40s multi	55	55
964	A285	4.40s multi	75	75
965	A285	5.40s multi	90	90
		Nos. 960-965 (6)	3.10	3.10

Dr. Corral Moscoso Hospital, Cuenca A286

1978, Apr. 12 **Litho.** *Perf. 11½x12*

966	A286	3s multi	25	15

Inauguration (in 1977) of Dr. Vicente Corral Moscoso Regional Hospital, Cuenca. See Nos. C613-C614.

Surveyor Plane over Ecuador — A287

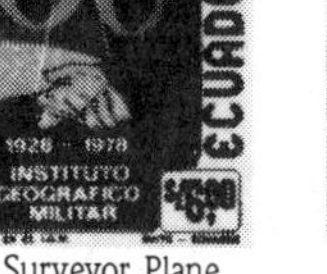

Latin-American Lions Emblem — A288

1978, Apr. 12 **Litho.** *Perf. 11½*

967	A287	6s multi	40	24

Military Geographical Institute, 50th anniversary. See Nos. C619-C620.

1978

968	A288	3s multi	25	15
969	A288	4.20s multi	40	16

7th meeting of Latin American Lions, Jan. 25-29. See Nos. C621-C623.

70th Anniversary Emblem — A289

1978, Sept. **Litho.** *Perf. 11½*

970	A289	4.20s gray & multi	32	16

70th anniversary of Filanbanco (Philanthropic Bank). See No. C626.

Goalmouth and Net — A290

Designs: 1.80s, "Gauchito" and Games emblem, vert. 4.40s, "Gauchito," vert.

1978, Nov. 1 **Litho.** *Perf. 12*

971	A290	1.20s multi	15	15
972	A290	1.80s multi	15	15
973	A290	4.40s multi	28	16
		Nos. 971-973,C627-C629 (6)	1.70	1.11

11th World Cup Soccer Championship, Argentina, June 1-25.

Symbols for Male and Female — A291

1979, Feb. 15 **Litho.** *Perf. 12x11½*

974	A291	3.40s multi	24	15

Inter-American Women's Commission, 50th anniversary.

Emblem A292

1979, June 21 **Litho.** *Perf. 11½x12*

975	A292	4.40s multi	32	16
976	A292	5.40s multi	40	25

Ecuadorian Mortgage Bank, 16th anniv.

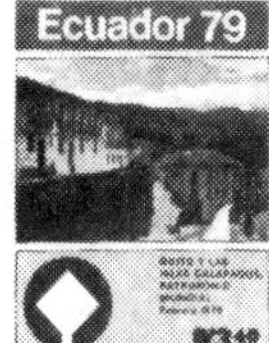

Street Scene, Quito — A293

Perf. 12x11½

1979, Aug. 3 **Litho.** **Unwmk.**

977	A293	3.40s multi	24	20

National heritage: Quito and Galapagos Islands. See Nos. C651-C653.

Jose Joaquin de Olmedo (1780-1847), Physician — A294

Chief Enriquillo, Dominican Republic — A295

1980, Apr. 29 Litho. *Perf. 12x11½*
978 A294 3s multi 20 15
979 A294 5s multi 32 25

First President of Free State of Guayaquil, 1820. See No. C662.

Wmk. 367, Unwmkd. (#981-983)
1980, May 12

Indo-American Tribal Chiefs: 3.40s, Guaycaypuro, Venezuela. No. 982, Abayuba, Uruguay. No. 983, Atlacatl, Salvador.

980 A295 3s multi 25 15
981 A295 3.40s multi 30 25
982 A295 5s multi 50 40
983 A295 5s multi 50 40
Nos. 980-983,C663-C678 (20) 13.80 7.29

King Juan Carlos and Queen Sofia, Visit to Ecuador — A296

Perf. 11½x12
1980, May 18 Unwmk.
984 A296 3.40s multi 24 15

See No. C679.

Cofan Indian, Napo Province — A297

1980, June 10 Litho. *Perf. 12x11½*
985 A297 3s shown 25 15
986 A297 3.40s Zuleta woman, Imbabura 30 20
987 A297 5s Chota woman, Imbabura 50 40
Nos. 985-987,C681-C684 (7) 3.70 2.21

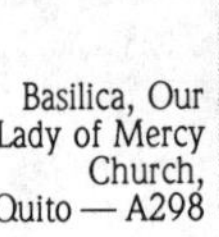

Basilica, Our Lady of Mercy Church, Quito — A298

1980, July 7 Litho. *Perf. 11½*
988 A298 3.40s shown 24 20
989 A298 3.40s Balcony 24 20
989A A298 3.40s Dome and cupolas 24 20

Sizes: 91x116mm, 116x91mm
Imperf
990 A298 5s multi 50 50
990A A298 5s multi, horiz. 50 50
990B A298 5s multi 50 50
Nos. 988-990B,C685-C691 (13) 7.22 4.63

Virgin of Mercy, patron saint of Ecuadorian armed forces. No. 990 contains designs of Nos. C686, C685, 989. No. 990A contains designs of Nos. C688, C691, C690. No. 990B contains designs of Nos. C689, C687, 989A, 988.

Olympic Torch and Rings — A299

Coronation of Virgin of Cisne, 50th Anniv. — A300

Perf. 12x11½
1980, July 19 Wmk. 395
991 A299 5s multi 32 20
992 A299 7.60s multi 48 30

Souvenir Sheet
Imperf
993 A299 30s multi 3.00 3.00

22nd Summer Olympic Games, Moscow, July 19-Aug. 3. See Nos. C695-C696.
No. 993 contains vignettes in designs of Nos. 991 and C695.

1980 Litho. *Perf. 11½*
994 A300 1.20s shown 15 15
995 A300 3.40s Different statue 30 20

J.J. Olmeda, Father de Velasco, Flags of Ecuador and Riobamba, Constitution A301

1980, Sept. 20 Litho. *Perf. 11½*
996 A301 3.40s multi 20 20
997 A301 5s multi 50 30

Souvenir Sheet
Imperf
998 A301 30s multi 2.50 2.50

Constitutional Assembly of Riobamba sesquicentennial. #998 contains vignettes in designs of #996-997. See #C700-C702.

First Lady Mrs. Aguilera — A302

Perf. 12x11½
1980, Oct. 9 Litho. Wmk. 395
999 A302 1.20s multi 15 15
1000 A302 3.40s multi 30 20

Democratic government, 1st anniversary. See Nos. C703-C705.

OPEC Emblem — A303

1980, Nov. 8 *Perf. 11½x12*
1001 A303 3.40s multi 30 20

20th anniversary of OPEC. See No. C706.

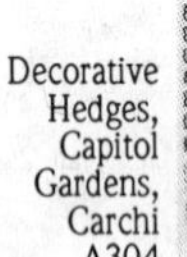

Decorative Hedges, Capitol Gardens, Carchi A304

1980, Nov. 21 *Perf. 13*
1002 A304 3s multi 20 15

Carchi province centennial. See #C707-C708.

Cattleya Maxima A305

Designs: Orchids.

1980, Nov. 22 *Perf. 11½x12*
1003 A305 1.20s *shown* 15 15
1004 A305 3s *Comparattia speciosa* 25 25
1005 A305 3.40s *Cattleya tricolor* 30 30
Nos. 1003-1005,C709-C712 (7) 5.80 4.52

Souvenir Sheet
Imperf
1006 A305 20s multi 2.50 2.50

No. 1006 contains vignettes in designs of Nos. 1003-1005.

Pope John Paul II and Children — A306

1980, Dec. 27 *Perf. 12*
1007 A306 3.40s multi 30 20

Christmas 1980 and visit of Pope John Paul II. See Nos. C715-C716.

Carlos and Jorge Mantilla Ortega, Editors of El Comercio — A307

El Comercio Newspaper, 75th Anniversary: 3.40s, Editors Cesar and Carlos Mantilla Jacome.

1981, Jan. 6
1008 A307 2s multi 15 15
1009 A307 3.40s multi 20 15
Set value 20

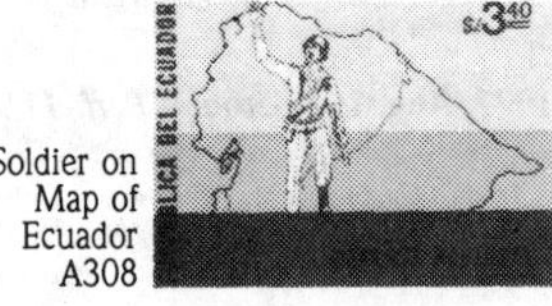

Soldier on Map of Ecuador A308

1981, Mar. 10 Litho. *Perf. 13*
1010 A308 3.40s shown 20 15
1011 A308 3.40s Pres. Roldos 20 15

National defense.

Theodore E. Gildred and Ecuador I A309

1981, Mar. 31 Litho. *Perf. 13*
1012 A309 2s lt bl & blk 15 15

Ecuador-US flight, 50th anniv.

A310

A311

1981, Apr. 10
1013 A310 2s multi 15 15

Octavio Cordero Palacios (1870-1930), humanist.

1981 Litho. *Perf. 13*
1014 A311 2s multi 15 15

Radio station HCJB, 50th anniv. See Nos. C721-C722.

Virgin of Dolorosa A312

1981, Apr. 30 Litho. *Perf. 12*
1015 A312 2s shown 15 15
1016 A312 2s San Gabriel College Church 15 15
Set value 24 16

Miracle of the painting of the Virgin of Dolorosa at San Gabriel College, 75th anniv.

Dr. Rafael Mendoza Aviles Bridge Inauguration A313

1981, July 25 *Perf. 13*
1017 A313 2s multi 15 15

Pablo Picasso (1881-1973), Painter — A313a

1981, Oct. 26 Litho. *Imperf.*
1017A A313a 20s multi 1.75 70

No. 1017A contains design of No. C728, additional portrait. See Nos. C728-C731.

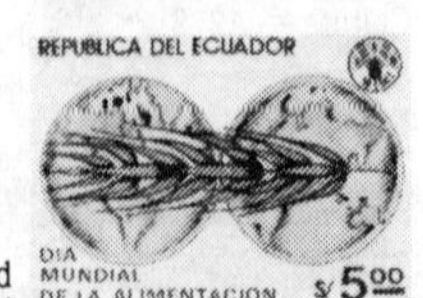

World Food Day — A314

1981, Dec. 31 Litho. *Perf. 13½x13*
1018 A314 5s multi 40 16

See No. C732

Transnave Shipping Co. 10th Anniv.
A315

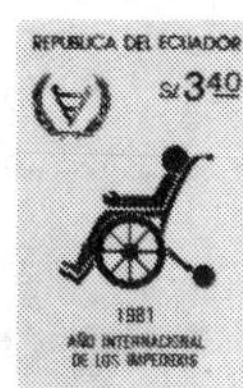

Intl. Year of the Disabled
A316

1982, Jan. 21 **Litho.** ***Perf. 13***
1019 A315 3.50s Freighter Isla Salango 28 15

1982, Feb. 25
1020 A316 3.40s Man in wheelchair 24 15

See Nos. C733-C734.

Arch — A317

Juan Montalvo Birth Sesqui. — A318

1982, May **Litho.** ***Perf. 13***
1021 A317 2s shown 15 15
1022 A317 3s Houses 20 15
Set value 16

Souvenir Sheet

1023 Sheet of 4, 18th cent. map of Quito 2.50 80
a.-d. A317 6s multi 60 20

QUITEX '82, 4th Natl. Stamp Exhibition, Quito, Apr. 16-22. No. 1023 contains 4 stamps (48x31mm, perf. 12½).

1982
1024 A318 2s Portrait 15 15
1025 A318 3s Mausoleum 20 15
Set value 16

See No. C735.

American Air Forces Cooperation System — A319

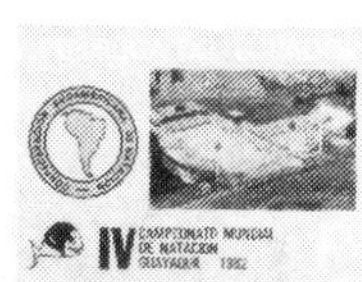

4th World Swimming Champ., Guayaquil — A320

1982
1026 A319 5s Emblem 32 16

1982, July 30
1027 A320 1.80s Stadium 15 15
1028 A320 3.40s Water polo 20 15
Set value 20

See Nos. C736-C737.

A321

A322

1982, Dec. **Litho.** ***Perf. 13***
1029 A321 5.40s shown 32 16
1030 A321 6s Statue 35 16

Juan L. Mera (1832-?), Writer, by Victor Mideros.

1983, Mar. 28 **Litho.** ***Perf. 13***
1031 A322 2s multi 15 15

St. Teresa of Jesus of Avila (1515-82).

Sea Lions
A323

Flamingoes
A324

1983, June 17 **Litho.** ***Perf. 13***
1032 A323 3s multi 15 15
1033 A324 5s multi 25 15
Set value 15

Sesquicentennial of Ecuadorian rule over Galapagos Islds. (3s); Charles Darwin (1809-1882).

Pres. Vicente Rocafuerte Birth Bicentenary
A325

Simon Bolivar
A326

Perf. 13x13½

1983, Aug. 26 **Litho.** **Wmk. 395**
1034 A325 5s Statue 16 15
1035 A325 20s Portrait 60 28
1036 A326 20s Portrait 60 28

Vicente Rocafuerte Bejarano, president, 1833-39 (Nos. 1034-1035).

A327

A328

1983, Sept. 3
1037 A327 5s River 15 15
1038 A327 10s Dam 24 16
Set value 24

Souvenir Sheet

Imperf

1039 A327 20s Dam, river 2.00 1.25

Paute hydroelectric plant opening. No. 1039 is airmail.

Wmk. 395

1983, Nov. 10 **Litho.** ***Perf. 13***
1040 A328 2s multi 15 15

World Communication Year.

A329

A330

1983, Sept. **Litho.** ***Perf. 13***
1041 A329 3s multi 15 15

Centenary of Bolivar and El Oro Provinces (1984).

1984, Mar. **Litho.** ***Perf. 13***
1042 A330 15s Engraving 24 15

Atahualpa (1497-1529), last Incan ruler.

Christmas 1983 — A331

Creche figures.

Perf. 13½x13, 13x13½

1984, July 7 **Litho.**
1043 A331 5s Jesus and lawyers 15 15
1044 A331 5s Three kings 15 15
1045 A331 5s Holy Family 15 15
1046 A331 6s Priest, vert. 15 15
Set value 42 20

Foreign Policy of Pres. Hurtado
A332

State visits.

1984, July 10 ***Perf. 13½x13***
1047 A332 8s Brazil 16 15
1048 A332 9s PRC 18 15
1049 A332 24s UN 48 20
1050 A332 28s US 55 22
1051 A332 29s Venezuela 60 24
1052 A332 37s Latin American Economic Conf., Quito 75 30
Nos. 1047-1052 (6) 2.72 1.26

Miguel Diaz Cueva (1884-1942), Lawyer
A333

1984, Aug. 8 **Litho.** ***Perf. 13½x13***
1053 A333 10s Cueva, arms 35 15

1984 Winter Olympics
A334

Manned Flight Bicentenary
A335

Perf. 13x13½, 12x11½ (6s)

1984, Aug. 15
1054 A334 2s Emblem 15 15
1055 A334 4s Ice skating 15 15
1056 A334 6s Skating, diff. 18 15
1057 A334 10s Skiing 28 15
Set value 64 35

1984, Aug. 15 ***Perf. 13x13½***
1058 A335 3s Montgolfier 15 15
1059 A335 6s Charlier's balloon, Paris, 1789 25 15
Set value 15

Souvenir Sheet

1060 A335 20s Graf Zeppelin, Montgolfier 75 75

No. 1060 is airmail and contains one imperf. stamp (50x37mm).

SAN MATEO '83, Esmeraldas
A336

1984 **Litho.** ***Perf. 13***
1061 A336 8s La Marimba folk dance 28 15

Size: 89x110mm

Imperf

1061A A336 15s La Marimba, diff. 45 45

No. 1061A is airmail.

Jose Maria de Jesus Yerovi (b. 1824), 4th Archbishop of Quito — A337

1984
1062 A337 5s multi 20 15

Canonization of Brother Miguel — A338

1984 **Litho.** ***Perf. 13***
1063 A338 9s Academy of Languages 28 16
1064 A338 24s Vatican City, vert. 60 35
1065 A338 28s Home of Brother Miguel 65 40

No. 1065, airmail, has black control number. Size: 110x90mm.

State Visit of Pope John Paul II — A339

Beatification of Mercedes de Jesus Molina — A340

1985, Jan. 23 **Litho.** ***Perf. 13x13½***
1066 A339 1.60s Papal arms 15 15
1067 A339 5s Blessing crowd 15 15
1068 A339 9s World map, itinerary 20 15
1069 A339 28s Pope waving 55 28
1070 A339 29s Portrait 60 30

Size: 90x109mm

Imperf

1071 A339 30s Pope holding crosier 3.50 1.75
Nos. 1066-1071 (6) 5.15 2.78

1985, Jan. 23

Paintings, sculpture.

1072 A340 1.60s Portrait 15 15
1073 A340 5s Czestochowa Madonna 15 15
1074 A340 9s Alborada Madonna 15 15

Size: 90x110mm

Imperf

1075 A340 20s Mercedes de Jesus, children 1.65 80
Set value 95

Visit of Pope John Paul II, birth bimillennium of the Virgin Mary.

Samuel Valarezo Delgado, Naturalist, Politician — A341

1985, Feb.

1076 A341 2s Bird 15 15
1077 A341 3s Swordfish, tuna 15 15
1078 A341 6s Portrait 20 15
Set value 30 20

ESPANA '84, Madrid A342

1985, Apr. 25 ***Perf. 13½x13***

1079 A342 6s Emblem 15 15
1080 A342 10s Spanish royal family 28 15

Size: 110x90mm

Imperf

1081 A342 15s Retiro Park, exhibition site 80 40

Dr. Pio Jaramillo Alvarado (1884-1968), Historian A343

1985, May 17

1082 A343 6s multi 20 15

Ingenio Valdez Sugar Refinery — A344

Designs: 50s, Sugar cane, emblem. 100s, Rafael Valdez Cervantes, founder.

1985, June **Litho.** ***Perf. 13***

1082A A344 50s multi 80 40
1082B A344 100s multi 1.65 80

Size: 110x90mm

Imperf

1083 A344 30s multi 48 24

Chamber of Commerce, 10th Anniv. A345

Design: 50s, Natl. and American Statues of Liberty.

1985, Aug. 15 ***Perf. 13½x13***

1084 A345 24s multi 52 26
1085 A345 28s multi 60 30

Size: 110x90mm

Imperf

1086 A345 50s multi 90 45

Natl. Philatelic Assoc., AFE, 50th Anniv. — A346

1985, Aug. 25 ***Perf. 12***

1087 A346 25s AFE emblem 52 25
1088 A346 30s No. 357, horiz. 65 32

Guayaquil Fire Dept., 150th Anniv. A347

1985, Oct. 10 ***Perf. 13½x13***

1089 A347 6s Steam fire pump, 1882 15 15
1090 A347 10s Fire Wagon, 1899 16 15
1091 A347 20s Anniv. emblem, natl. flag 30 16
Set value 29

Natl. Infant Survival Campaign — A348

1st Natl. Phil. Cong., Quito, Nov. 25-28 — A349

1985, Oct. ***Perf. 13x13½***

1092 A348 10s Boy, girl, tree 24 15

1985, Nov. ***Perf. 13x13½, 13½x13***

20th cent. illustrations, natl. cultural collection: 5s, Supreme Court, Quito, by J. M. Roura. 10s, Riobamba Cathedral, by O. Munaz. 15s, House of 100 Windows, by J. M. Roura, horiz. 20s, Rural cottage near Cuenca, by J. M. Roura.

No. 1097a, Stampless cover, 1779, Riobamba. b, Hand press, 1864, Quito. c, Postrider, 1880, Cuenca. d, Monoplane, 1st airmail flight, 1919, Guayaquil.

1093 A349 5s multi 15 15
1094 A349 10s multi 25 15
1095 A349 15s multi 30 15
1096 A349 20s multi 50 20

Souvenir Sheet

1097 Sheet of 4 60 30
a.-d. A349 5s, any single 15 15

AFE, 50th anniv. #1097 contains 53x42mm stamps, perf. 13x12½ on 2 sides.

10th Bolivarian Games, Cuenca — A350

1985, Nov. ***Perf. 13½x13***

1098 A350 10s Boxing 20 15
1099 A350 25s Women's gymnastics 52 26
1100 A350 30s Discus 60 30

BAE Calderon, Navy Cent. — A351

Military anniversaries: No. 1102, Fighter plane, Air Force 65th anniv. No. 1103, Army and paratroops emblems, Special Forces 30th anniv.

1985, Dec. ***Perf. 13x13½***

1101 A351 10s multi 20 15
1102 A351 10s multi 20 15
1103 A351 10s multi 20 15
Set value 30

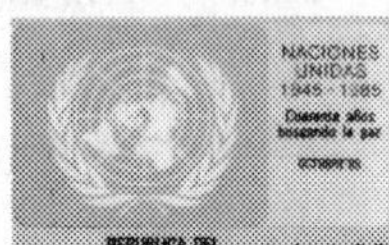

UN, 40th Anniv. A352

1985, Oct. **Litho.** ***Perf. 13***

1104 A352 10s UN flag 24 15
1105 A352 20s Natl. flag 35 18

Size: 110x90mm

Imperf

1106 A352 50s UN Building 80 40

Christmas — A353

Indigenous Flowers — A354

1985, Nov.

1107 A353 5s Child riding donkey 15 15
1108 A353 10s Baked goods 20 15
1109 A353 15s Riding donkey, diff. 28 15

Size: 90x110mm

Imperf

1110 A353 30s like 5s 48 24
Set value 54

1986, Feb.

1111 A354 24s Embotrium grandiforum 50 25
1112 A354 28s Topobea sp. 55 28
1113 A354 29s Befaria resinosa mutis 60 30

Size: 110x90mm

Imperf

1114 A354 15s multi 28 15

No. 1114 contains designs of Nos. 1111, 1113, 1112; black control number.

Discovery of the Galapagos Islds., 450th Anniv. A355

Map of the Islands — A356

1986, Feb. 12

1115 A355 10s Land iguana 20 15
1116 A355 20s Sea lion 38 20
1117 A355 30s Frigate birds 55 28
1118 A355 40s Penguins 75 38
1119 A355 50s Sea turtle 1.00 50
1120 A355 100s Charles Darwin 2.00 1.00
1121 A355 200s Bishop Tomas de Berlenga, discoverer 4.00 2.00

Perf. 12½ on 2 Sides

1122 A356 Sheet of 4 3.50 1.75
a.-d. 50s, any single 85 42
Nos. 1115-1122 (8) 12.38 6.26

No. 1122 contains 53x42mm stamps.

Inter-American Development Bank, 25th Anniv. — A357

Designs: 5s, Antonio Ortiz Mena, president 1971- . 10s, Felipe Herrera, president 1960-1971. 50s, Emblem.

1986, Mar. 6

1123 A357 5s multi 15 15
1124 A357 10s multi 22 15
1125 A357 50s multi 95 48

Guayaquil Tennis Club, 75th Anniv. — A358

1986, Mar. 7

1126 A358 10s Emblem 18 15
1127 A358 10s Francisco Segura Cano, vert. 18 15
1128 A358 10s Andres Gomez Santos, vert. 18 15
Set value 30

1986 World Cup Soccer Championships, Mexico — A359

1986, May 5

1129 A359 5s Shot 15 15
1130 A359 10s Block 18 15
Set value 18

An imperf. stamp exists picturing flags, player and emblem.

Meeting of Presidents Cordero and Betancourt of Colombia, Feb. 1985 — A360

1986 Litho. *Perf. 13½x13*
1131 A360 20s Presidents 35 18
1132 A360 20s Embracing 35 18

Exports
A361

Designs: 35s, 1137c, Shrimp. 40s, No. 1137b, Tuna. 45s, No. 1137a, Sardines. No. 1137d, MICIP emblem.

1986, Apr. 12
1133 A361 35s ultra & ver 60 30
1134 A361 40s red & yel grn 65 32
1135 A361 45s car & dk yel 75 38

Perf. 12½ on 2 Sides
1137 Sheet of 4 60 32
a.-d. A361 10s, any single 15 15

No. 1137 contains 4 53x42mm stamps.

A362

La Condamine's First Geodesic Mission, 250th Anniv. — A363

Designs: No. 1141a, Triangulation map for determining equatorial meridian, 1736. No. 1141b, Partial map of the Maranon and Amazon Rivers, by Samuel Fritz, 1743-1744. No. 1141c, Base of measurement, Yaruqui plains. No. 1141d, Caraburo and Dyambaru Pyramids near Quito. Nos. 1141c-1141d printed se-tenant in a continuous design.

1986, July 10 Litho. *Perf. 13½x13*
1138 A362 10s La Condamine 18 15
1139 A362 15s Maldonado 25 15
1140 A362 20s Middle of the World, Quito 30 15

Souvenir Sheet
Perf. 12½ on 2 Sides
1141 Sheet of 4 60 32
a.-d. A363 10s, any single 15 15

Chambers of Commerce
A364

1986 Litho. *Perf. 13½x13*
1142 A364 10s Pichincha 18 15
1143 A364 10s Cuenca 18 15
1144 A364 10s Guayaquil 18 15
Set value 30

Civil Service and Communications Ministry, 57th Anniv. — A365

Organization emblems.

1986, Dec. Litho. *Perf. 13x13½*
1145 A365 5s State railway 15 15
1146 A365 10s Post office 20 15
1147 A365 15s Communications 30 15
1148 A365 20s Ministry of Public Works 40 20
Set value 50

A366 A367

1987, Feb. 16 Litho. *Perf. 13x13½*
1149 A366 5s multi 15 15

Chamber of Agriculture of the 1st Zone, 50th anniv.

1988, Jan. 6 Litho. & Typo. *Perf. 13*

Col. Luis Vargas Torres (d. 1887): 50s, Portrait. No. 1151, Combat unit, c. 1885. No. 1152a, Torres and his mother, Delfina. No. 1152b, Letter to Delfina written by Torres during imprisonment, 1882. No. 1152c, Arms of Ecuador and combat unit.

1150 A367 50s yel grn, blk & gold 65 32
1151 A367 100s ver, gold & ultra 1.30 65

Size: 95x140mm
Perf. 12 on One or Two Sides
1152 Block of 3 3.90 1.95
a.-c. A367 100s any single 1.30 65

Sizes: Nos. 1152a, 1152c, 95x28mm. No. 1152b, 95x83mm.

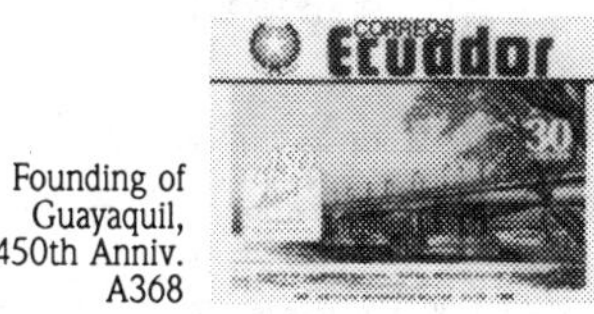

Founding of Guayaquil, 450th Anniv.
A368

Designs: 15s, Street in Las Penas, vert. 30s, Rafael Mendoza Aviles Bridge. 40s, Francisco de Orellana (c. 1490-1546), Spanish explorer, founder, and reenactment of landing, 1538.

1988, Feb. 19 Litho. *Perf. 13*
1153 A368 15s multi 15 15
1154 A368 30s multi 28 15
1155 A368 40s multi 38 20

Social Security Foundation (IESS), 60th Anniv.
A369

1988, Mar. 11
1156 A369 50s shown 45 22
1157 A369 100s multi, diff. 92 45

Dr. Pedro Moncayo y Esparza (1807-1888), Author, Politician
A370

1988, Apr. 28 Litho. *Perf. 14x13½*
1158 A370 10s Yaguarcocha Lake 15 15
1159 A370 15s shown 15 15
1160 A370 20s Residence 16 15

Size: 89x110mm
Imperf
1161 A370 100s Full-length portrait 85 42
Set value 60

A371

Avianca Airlines, 60th Anniv. — A372

1988, May 12 Litho. *Perf. 14x13½*
1162 A371 10s Junkers F-13 15 15
1163 A371 20s Dornier Wal seaplane 16 15
1164 A371 30s Ford 5AT trimotor 25 15
1165 A371 40s Boeing 247-D 35 18
1166 A371 50s Boeing 720-059B 42 22
1167 A371 100s Douglas DC-3 85 42
1168 A371 200s Boeing 727-200 1.70 85
1169 A371 300s Sikorsky S-38 2.55 1.30

Perf. 13½x14
1170 A372 500s shown 4.25 2.15
Nos. 1162-1170 (9) 10.68 5.57

San Gabriel College, 125th Anniv.
A373

1988, July 25 Litho. *Perf. 14x13½*
1171 A373 15s Contemporary facility 15 15
1172 A373 35s College entrance, 19th cent. 32 16
Set value 24

A374

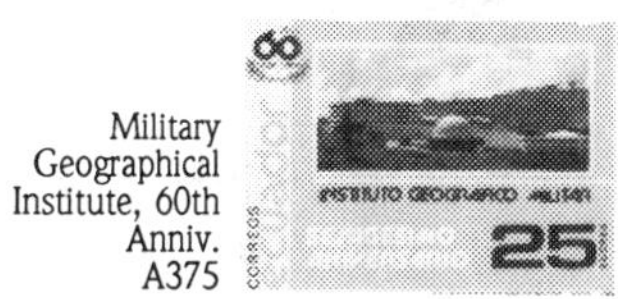

Military Geographical Institute, 60th Anniv.
A375

1988, July 25 *Perf. 12½ on 2 Sides*
Size of No. 1173: 110x90mm
1173 A374 Block of 4 32 20
a.-d. 5s any single 15 15

Perf. 13½
1174 A375 25s Planetarium 22 15
1175 A375 50s Zeiss projector 42 20
1176 A375 60s Anniv. emblem 52 25
1177 A375 500s Creation, mural by E. Kingman 4.25 2.10

Salesian Brothers in Ecuador, Cent. — A376

Designs: 10s, St. John Bosco (1815-88), vert. 50s, 1st Salesian Cong. in Ecuador. 100s, Bosco, Salesian Brothers monument and Andes Mountains.

1988, July 29 Litho. *Perf. 13½*
1178 A376 10s multi 15 15
1179 A376 50s multi 48 25

Size: 89x110mm
Imperf
1180 A376 100s multi 95 48

Eduardo Arosemena, 1st Director — A377

Social Services Council, Guayaquil, Cent. — A378

Flag: a, Emblem (upper left portion). b, Emblem (upper right portion). c, Emblem (lower left portion) and "100 AÑOS." d, Emblem (lower right portion) and "DE TRADICION DE FE, AMPARO Y ESPERANZA."

1988, Nov. 24 Litho. *Perf. 13½x14*
1181 A377 15s Francisco Coello, founder 15 15
1182 A377 20s shown 15 15
1183 A377 45s Emblem 32 16

Size: 110x90mm
Perf. 12½ on 2 Sides
1184 A378 Block of 4 32 20
a.-d. 10s any single 15 15
Set value 48

A379

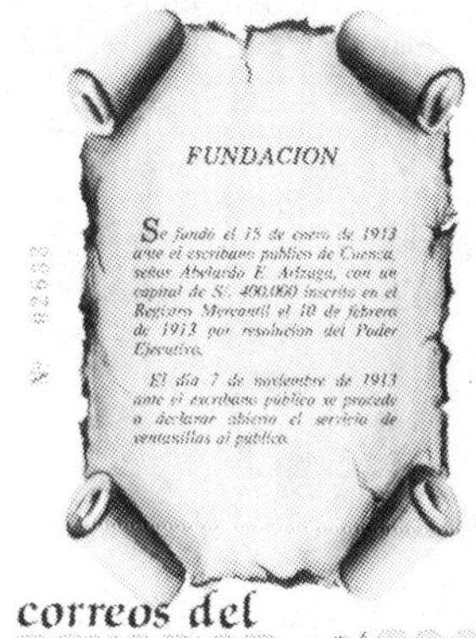

Azuay Bank, 75th Anniv. — A380

Perf. 14x13½, 13½x14
1989, Mar. 1 Litho.
1185 A379 20s shown 15 15
1186 A379 40s multi, vert. 25 15

Size: 90x110mm
Imperf
1187 A380 500s shown 2.85 1.45

1988 Summer Olympics, Seoul — A381

Character trademark demonstrating sports.

1989, Mar. 20 *Perf. 13½x14*

1188 A381 10s Running 15 15
1189 A381 20s Boxing 15 15
1190 A381 30s Cycling 15 15
1191 A381 40s Shooting 20 15
1192 A381 100s Diving 50 25
1193 A381 200s Weight lifting 1.00 50
1194 A381 300s Tae kwon do 1.50 75

Size: 90x110mm

Imperf

1195 A381 200s Emblems 1.05 52
Nos. 1188-1195 (8) 4.70 2.62

RUMINAHUI '88 — A382

Designs: 50s, *Bird,* by Joaquin Tinta, vert. 70s, Matriz Church, Sangolqui. 300s, Monument to Ruminahui in Sangolqui, Pichincha.

Perf. 14x13½, 13½x14

1989, May 2 Litho. Wmk. 395

1196 A382 50s multi 25 15
1197 A382 70s multi 35 18

Size: 90x111mm

Imperf

1198 A382 300s multi 1.50 75

Cantonization, 50th anniv.

Benjamin Carrion Mora, Educator A383

Perf. 13½x14, 14x13½

1989, May 10 Litho.

1199 A383 50s Portrait, vert. 25 15
1200 A383 70s Loja landscape 35 18
1201 A383 1000s University 5.00 2.50

Size: 110x90mm

Imperf

1202 A383 200s Portrait, diff. 1.00 50

2nd Intl. Art Biennial A384

Prize-winning art: 40s, *The Gilded Frame,* by Myrna Baez. 70s, *Paraguay III,* by Carlos Colorabino, vert. 100s, Ordinance establishing the art exhibition. 180s, *Modulation 892,* by Julio Le Parc, vert.

Perf. 14x13½, 13½x14, Imperf. (100s)

1989, June 2 Litho.

Size of No. 1205: 110x90mm

1203 A384 40s multi 20 15
1204 A384 70s multi 38 20
1205 A384 100s multi 52 25
1206 A384 180s multi 95 48

Guayaquil Chamber of Commerce, Cent. — A385

Perf. 13½x14, 14x13½, Imperf. (No. 1208)

1989, June 20 Litho.

Size of No. 1208: 110x91mm

1207 A385 50s Founder Ignacio Molestina, vert. 25 15
1208 A385 200s Flags 1.05 52
1209 A385 300s Headquarters 1.50 75
1210 A385 500s Flags, diff. 2.50 1.25

French Revolution, Bicent. A386

Designs: 20s, French natl. colors, anniv. emblem, vert. 50s, Cathedral fresco. 100s, Rooster, vert. 200s, Symbols of the revolution, vert. 600s, Story board showing events of the revolution, vert.

Perf. 13½x14, 14x13½

1989, July 11

1211 A386 20s multi 15 15
1212 A386 50s multi 25 15
1213 A386 100s multi 52 25

Size: 90x110mm

Imperf

1214 A386 200s multi 1.00 50
1215 A386 600s multi 3.00 1.50

A387

Ministry of Public Works and Communications A388

Designs: No. 1216a, MOP emblem, two-lane roadway. No. 1216b, State railway emblem, train. No. 1216c, Postal service emblem, airmail cover. No. 1216d, Telecommunications (IETEL) emblem, wall telephone. No. 1217, MOP, IETEL, postal service and state railway emblems. 100s, IETEL emblem. 200s, MOP emblem.

1989, July 7 *Perf. 12½ on 2 Sides*

1216 Block of 4 1.00 50
a.-d. A387 50s any single 25 15

Perf. 13½x14

1217 A388 50s shown 25 15
1218 A388 100s multi 50 25
1219 A388 200s multi 1.00 50

MOP, 60th anniv.; national communications, 105th anniv. (No. 1216d, 100s).

Natl. Red Cross, Intl. Red Cross and Red Crescent Societies, 125th Annivs. A389

1989, Sept. 14 Litho. *Perf. 13½*

1220 A389 10s Medical volunteer, vert. 15 15
1221 A389 30s shown 15 15
1222 A389 200s Two volunteers 95 48
Set value 60

Juan Montalvo (1832-1889), Writer A390

1989, Nov. 11 Litho. *Perf. 14x13½*

1223 A390 50s Mausoleum, Ambato 30 15
1224 A390 100s Portrait (detail) 58 30
1225 A390 200s Monument, Ambato 1.15 58

Size: 90x110mm

Imperf

1226 A390 200s Portrait 90 45

America Issue A391

UPAE emblem and pre-Columbian pottery.

1990, Mar. 6 Litho. *Perf. 13½*

1227 A391 200s La Tolita incensory, vert. 58 30
1228 A391 300s Warrior (plate) 85 42

Dated 1989.

Dr. Luis Carlos Jaramillo Leon, Founder A392

Designs: No. 1233a, Dr. Leon. Nos. 1230, 1233b, Federico Malo Andrade, honorary president. 130s, No. 1233c, Roberto Crespo Toral, first president. 200s, Alfonso Jaramillo Leon, founder.

1990, Jan. 17 Litho. *Perf. 13½*

1229 A392 100s shown 38 18
1230 A392 100s multicolored 38 18
1231 A392 130s multicolored 50 25
1232 A392 200s multicolored 75 35

Size: 91x38mm

Perf. 12½ Horiz. on 1 or 2 sides

1233 Block of 3 1.15 55
a.-c. A392 100s any single 38 18

Chamber of Commerce, 70th anniversary.

World Cup Soccer, Italy — A393

1990, July 12 Litho. *Perf. 13½*

1234 A393 100s shown 38 18
1235 A393 200s Soccer player 75 35
1236 A393 300s Map of Italy, trophy 1.15 58

Imperf

Size: 110x90mm

1237 A393 200s Player, flags 75 25

Size: 60x90mm

1238 A393 300s World Cup Trophy 1.15 58

Nos. 1235-1236, 1238 vert.

A394 A396

A395

1990, June 12 *Perf. 13½*

1239 A394 100s multi 38 18
1240 A394 200s Church tower, book 75 35

College of St. Mariana, cent.

1990, Sept. 7 Litho. *Perf. 13½*

Tourism: No. 100s, No. 1244c, Iguana. 200s, No. 1244b, La Compania Church, Quito. 300s, No. 1244a, Old man from Vilcabamba. No. 1244d, Locomotive.

1241 A395 100s multi 32 15
1242 A395 200s multi, vert. 65 30
1243 A395 300s multi 95 45

Size: 111x90mm

Perf. 12½ on 2 sides

1244 Block of 4 1.30 60
a.-d. A395 100s any single 32 15

1990, Sept. 1 *Perf. 13½*

National Census: 100s, No. 1248a, People and house. 200s, No. 1248b, Map. 300s, No. 1248c, Census breakdown, pencil.

1245 A396 100s multicolored 32 15
1246 A396 200s multicolored, horiz. 65 30
1247 A396 300s multicolored 95 45

Size: 109x88mm

Perf. 12½ on 2 sides

1248 Block of 3 95 45
a.-c. A396 100s any single 32 15

A397 A398

1990, Nov. 2 Litho. *Perf. 14*

1249 A397 200s Flags 65 32
1250 A397 300s shown 95 45

Organization of Petroleum Exporting Countries (OPEC), 30th anniv.

1990, Oct. 31 *Perf. 13½x14*

1251 A398 200s Emblem 65 32
1252 A398 300s Wooden parrots 95 45

Size: 92x110mm

Imperf

1253 A398 200s Wooden parrots, diff. 65 32

Artisans' Organization, 25th anniv.

Flowers — A399

Perf. 13½

1990, Nov. 12 Litho. Wmk. 395

1254 A399 100s Sobralia	32	16
1255 A399 100s Blakea, vert.	32	16
1256 A399 100s Cattleya, vert.	32	16
1257 A399 100s Loasa, vert.	32	16

Discovery of America, 500th Anniv. (in 1992) A400

1990, Dec. 31 Litho. *Perf. 13½*

1258 A400 100s Ancient dwelling	32	16
1259 A400 200s Mangrove swamp	65	32

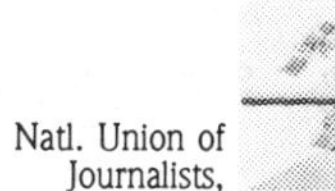

Natl. Union of Journalists, 50th Anniv. — A401

1991, Feb. 28

1260 A401 200s shown	65	32
1261 A401 300s Eugenio Espejo, writer	1.00	50
1262 A401 400s Union emblem	1.30	65

Radio Quito, 50th Anniv. A402

Designs: 200s, Man with microphone, vert. 500s, Family listening to radio.

1991, Apr. 10

1263 A402 200s multicolored	45	24
1264 A402 500s multicolored	1.15	55

Dr. Pablo A. Suarez, Birth Cent. — A403

1991, Sept. 16 Wmk. 395

1265 A403 70s multicolored	20	15

Dated 1990.

America Issue — A404

UPAEP emblem and: 200s, Columbus' ships. 500s, Columbus, landing in America.

1991, Oct. 18 Litho. *Perf. 13½x13*

1266 A404 200s multicolored	50	25
1267 A404 500s multicolored	1.20	60

A405

A406

Designs: Cultural artifacts.

Perf. 13½

1991, Nov. 14 Litho. Wmk. 395

1268 A405 100s Cat censer	25	15
1269 A405 200s Statue of old man's head	50	25
1270 A405 300s Zoomorphic statue	75	38

Dated 1990. See No. 1291.

1991 *Perf. 13*

Design: 500s, Woman in profile.

1271 A406 300s shown	75	38
1272 A406 500s multicolored	1.20	60

Day of Non-violence Toward Women.

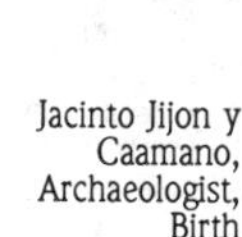

Jacinto Jijon y Caamano, Archaeologist, Birth Cent. — A407

1991, Dec. 11 *Perf. 13½*

1273 A407 200s Portrait, vert.	50	25
1274 A407 300s shown	75	38

Pres. Rodrigo Borja, Ecuador and Pres. Jaime Paz Zamora, Bolivia — A408

1991, Dec. 10 *Perf. 14x13½*

1275 A408 500s multicolored	1.20	60

Pres. Rodrigo Borja's Visit to the UN — A409

Wmk. 395

1992, Jan. 24 Litho. *Perf. 14*

1276 A409 100s multicolored	22	15
1277 A409 1000s Flags, world map	2.15	1.10

Battle of Jambeli, 50th Anniv. — A410

Designs: No. 1278, Gunboat Calderon and Capt. Raphael Moran Valverde. No. 1279, Dispatch boat Atahualpa and Ens. Victor Naranjo Fiallo. No. 1280, Valverde, Fiallo and ships.

1992, Apr. 7

1278 A410 300s multicolored	65	32
1279 A410 500s multicolored	1.10	52

Size: 110x90mm

Imperf

1280 A410 500s multicolored	1.10	52

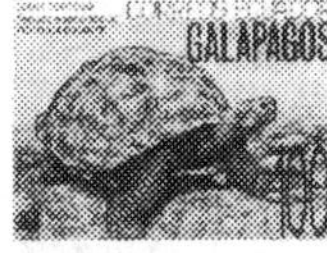

Galapagos Islands Wildlife — A411

Designs: No. 1281, Giant tortoise. No. 1282, Galapagos penguin, vert. No. 1283, Zalophus calfornianus, vert. No. 1284, Swallow-tailed gull. No. 1285, Fregata minor. No. 1286, Land iguana.

1992, Apr. 10 Litho. *Perf. 13½*

1281 A411 100s multicolored	22	15
1282 A411 100s multicolored	22	15
1283 A411 100s multicolored	22	15
1284 A411 100s multicolored	22	15
1285 A411 100s multicolored	22	15
1286 A411 100s multicolored	22	15
Nos. 1281-1286 (6)	1.32	
Set value		65

Vicente Rocafuerte National College, 150th Anniv. (in 1991) A412

Perf. 14x13½

1992, Apr. 29 Litho. Wmk. 395

1287 A412 200s shown	42	22
1288 A412 400s Vicente Rocafuerte	85	42

Eloy Alfaro (1842-1912), President — A413

Designs: 300s, Portrait, vert.

Perf. 13½x14, 14x13½

1992, Aug. 26 Litho. Wmk. 395

1289 A413 300s multicolored	55	28
1290 A413 700s multicolored	1.30	65

Cultural Artifacts Type of 1991

1992, Sept. 6 Litho. *Perf. 13½*

1291 A405 400s Ceremonial mask	75	38

Dated 1990.

Discovery of America, 500th Anniv. A414

Perf. 13½

1992, Oct. 15 Litho. Wmk. 395

1292 A414 200s Sailing ship	45	22
1293 A414 400s Columbus, map, vert.	90	45

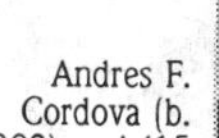

Andres F. Cordova (b. 1892) — A415

1992, Nov. 17 Litho. *Perf. 13½*

1294 A415 300s multicolored	65	32

Beatification of Narcisa of Jesus — A416

1992, Nov. 30 *Perf. 13½*

1295 A416 100s multicolored	22	15

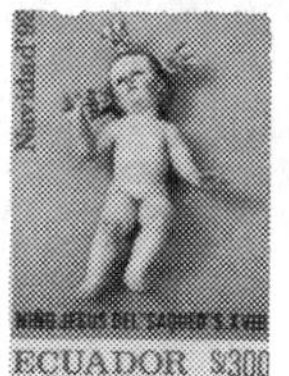

A417

A418

Christmas: 300s, Infant Jesus of Saqueo, 18th cent. 600s, Stable scene, Infant Jesus asleep on hay.

1992, Dec. 14 *Perf. 13½*

1296 A417 300s multicolored	65	32
1297 A417 600s multicolored	1.30	65

1992, Dec. 29

1298 A418 200s multicolored	45	22

Father Juan de Velasco, Death Bicent.

Frogs — A419

A420

Perf. 13½x14

1993, Jan. 28 Litho. Wmk. 395

1299 A419 300s Agalychnis spurelli	32	16
1300 A419 300s Atelopus bomolochos	32	16
1301 A419 600s Gastrotheca plumbea	65	32
1302 A419 600s Hyla picturata	65	32
1303 A419 900s Dendrobates sp.	95	48
1304 A419 900s Sphaenorhyncus lacteus	95	48
Nos. 1299-1304 (6)	3.84	1.92

1993, Feb. 16 Litho. *Perf. 13x13½*

1305 A420 300s blue	32	16

J. Roberto Paez, (1893-1983), co-founder of social security.

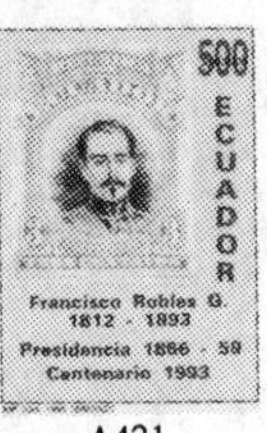

A421 A422

1993, Mar. 16 *Perf. 13½x14*

1306 A421 500s No. 168	55	28

Francisco Robles (1811-93).

Perf. 13½x14

1993, Mar. 25 Litho. Wmk. 395

1307 A422 300s Natl. police	55	28

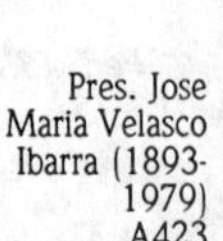

Pres. Jose Maria Velasco Ibarra (1893-1979) A423

Perf. 14x13½

1993, Mar. 31 Litho. Wmk. 395

1308 A423 500s multicolored	55	28

Insects — A424

Perf. 13½

1993, May 27 Litho. Wmk. 395

1309 A424 150s Fulgora laternaria	25	15
1310 A424 200s Semiotus ligneus	32	16
1311 A424 300s Taeniotes pulverulenta	48	25
1312 A424 400s Danaus plexippus	65	32
1313 A424 600s Erotylus onagga	1.00	50
1314 A424 700s Xylocopa darwini	1.10	55
Nos. 1309-1314 (6)	3.80	1.93

A425

Perf. 13½

1993, May 31 Litho. Wmk. 395

1315 A425 1000s multicolored	1.65	80

Pedro Fermin Cevallos Villacreces (1812-93), historian and founder of Academy of Language.

First Latin-American Children's Peace Assembly, Quito — A426

1993, June 7

1316 A426 300s multicolored	55	28

Juan Benigno Vela Hervas (1843-97), Jurist — A427

Perf. 13x13½

1993, July 8 Litho. Wmk. 395

1317 A427 2000s multicolored	3.25	1.65

Guillermo Bustamante, Birth Cent. — A428

1993 *Perf. 13½*

1318 A428 1500s multicolored	2.75	1.25

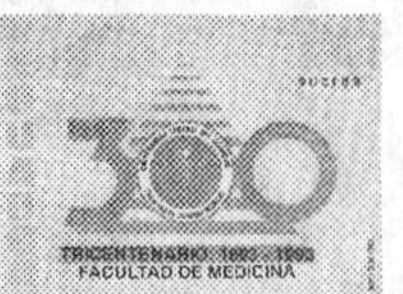

University of Ecuador School of Medicine, 300th Anniv. A429

Perf. 14x13½

1993, Sept. 7 Litho. Wmk. 395

1319 A429 300s multicolored	55	28

Maldonado-La Condamine Amazon Expedition, 250th Anniv. — A430

Designs: 150s, Cinchona cordifolia. 200s, Pedro V. Maldonado, 1500s, Charles La Condamine (1701-74), explorer.

1993, Aug. 20

1320 A430 150s multicolored	22	15
1321 A430 200s multicolored	30	15
1322 A430 1500s multicolored	2.25	1.10

A431 A432

1993 Litho. Wmk. 395 *Perf. 13*

1323 A431 500s multicolored	75	35

Dr. Carlos A. Arroyo del Rio, birth cent.

1993 *Perf. 13½x13, 13x13½*

Endangered species: 400s, Dinomys branickii, horiz. 800s, Ara severa.

1324 A432 400s multicolored	15	15
1325 A432 800s multicolored	30	15

America issue.

Christmas A433

Designs: 600s, Holy Family, 18th cent. Tagua miniatures. 900s, Mother and child, vert.

1993 Litho. Wmk. 395 *Perf. 13*

1326 A433 600s multicolored	95	48
1327 A433 900s multicolored	1.40	70

SEMI-POSTAL STAMPS

Nos. 423-428 Surcharged in Carmine or Blue:

Hospital

Méndez + $ 0.50

1944, May 9 Unwmk. *Perf. 12*

B1 A171 10c + 10c yel grn (C)	30	30
B2 A171 20c + 20c rose pink	30	30
B3 A171 30c + 20c dk gray brn	30	30
B4 A171 50c + 20c dp red lil	60	60
B5 A171 1s + 50c ol gray (C)	1.00	1.00
B6 A171 10s + 2s red orange	3.50	3.50
Nos. B1-B6 (6)	6.00	6.00

The surtax aided Mendez Hospital.

AIR POST STAMPS

In 1928-30, the internal airmail service of Ecuador was handled by the Sociedad Colombo-Alemana de Transportes Aereos ("SCADTA") under government sanction. During this period SCADTA issued stamps which were the only legal franking for airmail service except that handled under contract with Pan American-Grace Airways. SCADTA issues are Nos. C1-C6, C16-C25.

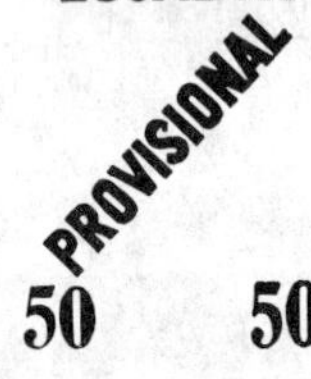

Colombia Air Post Stamps of 1923 Surcharged in Carmine

"Provisional" at 45 degree Angle

Perf. 14x14½

1928, Aug. 28 Wmk. 116

C1 AP6 50c on 10c grn	80.00	60.00
C2 AP6 75c on 15c car	165.00	110.00
C3 AP6 1s on 20c gray	55.00	35.00
C4 AP6 1½s on 30c blue	40.00	30.00
C5 AP6 3s on 60c brn	70.00	40.00
Nos. C1-C5 (5)	410.00	275.00

"Provisional" at 41 degree Angle

1929, Mar. 20

C1a AP6 50c on 10c grn	110.00	100.00
C2a AP6 75c on 15c car	140.00	125.00
C3a AP6 1s on 20c gray	110.00	125.00

Same with "Cts." Between Surcharged Numerals

C6 AP6 50c on 10c grn	*400.00*	*350.00*

A 75c on 15c carmine with "Cts." between the surcharged numerals exists. There is no evidence that it was regularly issued or used.

For overprints see Nos. CF3-CF3a.

Plane over River Guayas — AP1

Unwmk.

1929, May 5 Engr. *Perf. 12*

C8 AP1 2c black	15	15
C9 AP1 5c car rose	15	15
C10 AP1 10c dp brn	16	15
C11 AP1 20c dk vio	26	15
C12 AP1 50c dp grn	80	22
C13 AP1 1s dk bl	2.25	1.25
C14 AP1 5s org yel	6.50	5.00
C15 AP1 10s org red	32.50	26.00
Nos. C8-C15 (8)	42.77	33.07

Establishment of commercial air service in Ecuador. The stamps were available for all forms of postal service and were largely used for franking ordinary letters.

Nos. C13-C15 show numerals in color on white background. Counterfeits of No. C15 exist.

See #C26-C31. For overprints and surcharge see #C35-C38, C287, CO1-CO12.

Quito Cathedral AP2 Mount Chimborazo AP3

Wmk. 127

1929, Apr. 1 Litho. *Perf. 14*

C16 AP2 50c red brn	2.00	2.00
C17 AP2 75c green	2.00	2.00
C18 AP2 1s rose	3.00	2.00
C19 AP2 1½s gray bl	3.00	2.00
C20 AP2 2s violet	5.00	4.00
C21 AP2 3s brown	5.00	4.00
C22 AP3 5s lt bl	16.00	12.00
C23 AP3 10s lt red	35.00	26.00
C24 AP3 15s violet	60.00	50.00
C25 AP3 25s ol grn	80.00	60.00
Nos. C16-C25 (10)	211.00	164.00

For overprint see No. CF2.

Plane Type of 1929

1930-44 Unwmk. Engr. *Perf. 12*

C26 AP1 1s car lake	2.25	35
C27 AP1 1s grn ('44)	40	15
C28 AP1 5s ol grn	3.25	2.50
C29 AP1 5s pur ('44)	80	15
C30 AP1 10s black	10.00	3.50
C31 AP1 10s brt ultra ('44)	1.50	15
Nos. C26-C31 (6)	18.20	6.80

Nos. C26-C31 show numerals in color on white background.

For surcharge see No. C287.

Overprinted in Various Colors

AP4

1930, June 4

C32 AP4 1s car lake (Bk)	17.50	17.50
a. Double ovpt. (R Br + Bk)	70.00	
C33 AP4 5s ol grn (Bl)	17.50	17.50
C34 AP4 10s blk (R Br)	17.50	17.50

Flight of Capt. Benjamin Mendez from Bogota to Quito, bearing a crown of flowers for the tomb of Grand Marshal Sucre.

Air Post Official Stamps of 1929-30 Overprinted in Various Colors or Surcharged Similarly in Upper & Lower Case

INAUGURACION MONUMENTO A BOLIVAR QUITO, 24 DE JULIO DE 1935

1935, July 24

C35 AP1 50c dp grn (Bl)	4.25	4.25
C36 AP1 50c ol brn (R)	4.25	4.25
C37 AP1 1s on 5s ol grn (Bk)	4.25	4.25
a. Double surcharge	87.50	
C38 AP1 2s on 10s blk (R)	4.25	4.25

Unveiling of a monument to Bolívar at Quito, July 24th, 1935.

Geodesical Mission Issue

Nos. 349-351 Overprinted in Blue or Black and Type of Regular issue **AÉREO**

1936, July 3 *Perf. 12½*

C39 A136 10c dp org (Bl) 18 15
C40 A136 20c violet (Bk) 18 15
C41 A136 50c dk red (Bl) 28 15
C42 A136 70c black 50 24
Set value 46

For surcharge see No. RA42.

Philatelic Exhibition Issue

Type of Regular Issue Overprinted "AEREA"

1936, Oct. 20 *Perf. 13½x14*

C43 A137 2c rose 3.25 3.25
C44 A137 5c brn org 3.25 3.25
C45 A137 10c brown 3.25 3.25
C46 A137 20c ultra 3.25 3.25
C47 A137 50c red vio 3.25 3.25
C48 A137 1s green 3.25 3.25
Nos. C43-C48 (6) 19.50 19.50

Condor and Plane — AP6

C49 AP6 70c org brn 60 42
C50 AP6 1s dl vio 60 55

Nos. C43-C50 were issued for the 1st Intl. Phil. Exhib. at Quito.

Condor over "El Altar" — AP7

1937-46 *Perf. 11½, 12*

C51 AP7 10c chestnut 15 15
C52 AP7 20c olive blk 25 15
C53 AP7 40c rose car ('46) 25 15
C54 AP7 70c blk brn 35 15
C55 AP7 1s gray blk 50 16
C56 AP7 2s dark vio 1.00 22
Nos. C51-C56 (6) 2.50
Set value 62

Issue dates: 40c, Oct. 7; others, Aug. 19.
For overprints see #463-464, CO13-CO17.

Portrait of Washington, American Eagle and Flags — AP8

1938, Feb. 9 Engr. Litho. *Perf. 12*
Center Multicolored

C57 AP8 2c brown 15 15
C58 AP8 5c black 15 15
C59 AP8 10c brown 18 15
C60 AP8 20c dk bl 35 15
C61 AP8 50c violet 52 15
C62 AP8 1s black 90 18
C63 AP8 2s violet 1.75 52
Nos. C57-C63 (7) 4.00
Set value 1.10

150th anniv. of the US Constitution.
In 1947, Nos. C61-C63 were overprinted in dark blue: "Primero la Patria!" and plane. These revolutionary propaganda stamps were later renounced by decree.
For overprints see #C102-C104, C139-C141.

AEREO
SEDTA
0,65

No. RA35 Surcharged in Red

1938, Nov. 16 *Perf. 13½*

C64 PT12 65c on 3c ultra 15 15

A national airmail concession was given to the Sociedad Ecuatoriano de Transportes Aereos (SEDTA) in July, 1938. No. RA35 was surcharged for SEDTA postal requirements. SEDTA operated through 1940.

Army Horseman — AP9

Woman Runner — AP10

Tennis — AP11

Boxing — AP12

Olympic Fire — AP13

1939, Mar. Engr. *Perf. 12*

C65 AP9 5c lt grn 55 15
C66 AP10 10c salmon 70 18
C67 AP11 50c redsh brn 3.50 18
C68 AP12 1s blk brn 4.25 35
C69 AP13 2s rose car 6.50 70
Nos. C65-C69 (5) 15.50 1.56

First Bolivarian Games (1938), La Paz.

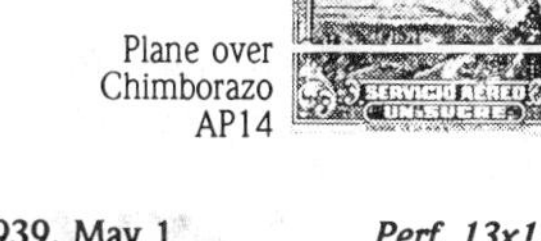

Plane over Chimborazo AP14

1939, May 1 *Perf. 13x12½*

C70 AP14 1s yel brn 16 15
C71 AP14 2s rose vio 32 15
C72 AP14 5s black 80 15
Set value 30

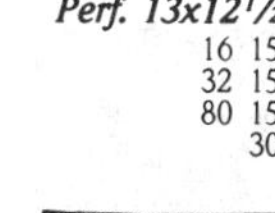

Golden Gate Bridge and Mountain Peak — AP15

Empire State Building and Mountain Peak — AP16

1939 *Perf. 12½x13*

C73 AP15 2c black 15 15
C74 AP15 5c rose red 15 15
C75 AP15 10c indigo 15 15
C76 AP15 50c rose vio 15 15
C77 AP15 1s chocolate 30 15
C78 AP15 2s yel brn 40 15
C79 AP15 5s emerald 75 15
Set value 1.75 50

Golden Gate International Exposition.
For surcharge & overprint see #434, CO18.

1939

C80 AP16 2c brn org 15 15
C81 AP16 5c dk car 15 15
C82 AP16 10c indigo 15 15
C83 AP16 50c slate grn 15 15
C84 AP16 1s dp org 30 15
C85 AP16 2s dk red vio 40 16
C86 AP16 5s dark gray 75 15
Set value 1.75 60

New York World's Fair.
For surcharge see No. 435.

Map of the Americas and Airplane — AP17

Francisco J. E. Santa Cruz y Espejo — AP18

1940, July 9

C87 AP17 10c red org & blue 15 15
C88 AP17 70c sepia & bl 20 15
C89 AP17 1s copper brn & bl 30 15
C90 AP17 10s blk & blue 1.10 55
Set value 79

Pan American Union, 50th anniversary.

1941, Dec. 15

C91 AP18 3s rose car 90 15
C92 AP18 10s yel org 1.75 22

See note after No. 399.

Old Map of South America Showing Amazon River — AP19

Panoramic View of Amazon River — AP20

Designs: 70c, Gonzalo de Pineda. 5s, Painting of the expedition.

1942, Jan. 30

C93 AP19 40c blk & buff 50 15
C94 AP19 70c olive 75 15
C95 AP20 2s dk grn 75 20
C96 AP19 5s rose 1.00 48

See note after No. 403.

Remigio Crespo Toral — AP21

1942, Sept. 1 *Perf. 13½*

C97 AP21 10c dull violet 22 15

Alfaro Types of Regular Issue

Designs: 70c, Gen. Eloy Alfaro. 1s, Devils's Nose. 3s, Military College. 5s, Montecristi, Alfaro's birthplace.

1943, Feb. 16 *Perf. 12*

C98 A166 70c dk rose & blk 38 20
C99 A167 1s ol blk & red brn 55 40
C100 A167 3s ol gray & grn 75 60
C101 A167 5s slate & sal 1.25 75

President Alfaro (1842-1912).

Nos. C61-C63 Overprinted in Red Brown

BIENVENIDO — WALLACE
Abril 15 — 1943

1943, Apr. 15 *Perf. 11½*
Center Multicolored

C102 AP8 50c violet 90 60
C103 AP8 1s black 1.10 70
C104 AP8 2s violet 1.40 1.25

Visit of US Vice-Pres. Henry A. Wallace.

Nos. 374-376 Overprinted "AEREO LOOR A BOLIVIA JUNIO 11-1943" (like Nos. C111-C113)

1943, June 11 *Perf. 13*

C105 A146 50c dp red vio 15 15
C106 A147 1s copper red 30 22
C107 A148 2s dark grn 42 25

Visit of Pres. Eurique Penaranda of Bolivia.
Vertical overprints on Nos. C105-C106.

Nos. 374-376 Overprinted "AEREO LOOR A PARAGUAY JULIO 5-1943" (like Nos. C111-C113)

1943, July 5

C108 A146 50c dp red vio 15 15
a. Double overprint 30.00
C109 A147 1s copper red 30 22
C110 A148 2s dark green 42 25

Visit of Pres. Higinio Morinigo of Paraguay.
Vertical overprints on Nos. C108-C109.

Nos. 374-376 Overprinted in Black

AEREO
LOOR A VENEZUELA
JULIO 23 — 1943

1943, July 23

C111 A146 50c dp red vio 15 15
C112 A147 1s copper red 30 22
C113 A148 2s dark green 42 25

Issued to commemorate the visit of President Isaias Medina Angarita of Venezuela.
Vertical overprint on Nos. C111-C112.
See Nos. C105-C110.

President Arroyo del Rio Addressing US Congress — AP26

1943, Oct. 9 *Perf. 12*

C114 AP26 50c dk brn 35 30
C115 AP26 70c brt rose 42 42
C116 AP26 3s dk bl 55 42
C117 AP26 5s dk grn 1.10 75
C118 AP26 10s olive blk 4.50 3.75
Nos. C114-C118 (5) 6.92 5.64

Good will tour of Pres. Arroyo del Rio in 1942.
For surcharges see Nos. CB1-CB5.

1944, Feb. 7

C119 AP26 50c dp red lil 35 28
C120 AP26 70c red brn 55 28
C121 AP26 3s turq grn 55 28
C122 AP26 5s brt ultra 90 70
C123 AP26 10s scarlet 1.25 1.25
Nos. C119-C123 (5) 3.60 2.79
Nos. C114-C123 (10) 10.52 8.43

Church of San Francisco, Quito — AP27

1944, Feb. 13

C124 AP27 70c turq grn 45 35
C125 AP27 1s olive 45 35
C126 AP27 3s red org 75 40
C127 AP27 5s car rose 95 48

See note after No. 433.

Palace Type of Regular Issue

1944 Engr. *Perf. 11*

C128 A173 3s orange 35 15
C129 A173 5s dark brown 55 15
C130 A173 10s dark red 1.10 15
Set value 31

See No. C221. For overprints and surcharges see Nos. 541, C136-C138, C210-C213, C218-C220, C223-C224, C277-C279.

Symbol of the Red Cross — A174

1945, Apr. 25 Unwmk. *Perf. 12*

Cross in Rose

No.	Type	Description	Unused	Used
C131	A174	2s deep blue	52	52
C132	A174	3s green	90	52
C133	A174	5s dk vio	1.40	90
C134	A174	10s car rose	3.50	2.75

80th anniversary of the founding of the International Red Cross.

No. RA55 Surcharged in Black

AEREO
40
Ctvs.

1945, June 8

No.	Type	Description	Unused	Used
C135	PT21	40c on 5c blue	15	15
a.		Double surcharge	7.00	

Counterfeits exist.

Nos. C128-C130 Overprinted in Green

SETIEMBRE 5
1945

1945, Sept. 6 *Perf. 11*

No.	Type	Description	Unused	Used
C136	A173	3s orange	42	42
a.		Inverted overprint	21.00	
b.		Double overprint	21.00	
C137	A173	5s dk brn	52	52
C138	A173	10s dk red	1.75	1.75

Nos. C61-C63 Overprinted in Dark Blue and Gold

LOOR A CHILE
OCTUBRE 2 1945

1945, Oct. 2 *Perf. 12*

Center Multicolored

No.	Type	Description	Unused	Used
C139	AP8	50c violet	45	45
C140	AP8	1s black	48	48
C141	AP8	2s violet	48	48

Visit of Pres. Juan Antonio Rios of Chile.

Monument to Liberty — AP30

1945, Nov. 14 Engr.

No.	Type	Description	Unused	Used
C142	AP30	30c blue	15	15
C143	AP30	40c rose car	18	15
C144	AP30	1s dl vio	45	18
C145	AP30	3s gray blk	75	52
C146	AP30	5s pur brn	1.10	70
		Nos. C142-C146 (5)	2.63	1.70

Gen. Antonio Jose de Sucre, 150th birth anniv.

Catalogue values for unused stamps in this section, from this point to the end of the section, are for Never Hinged items.

Highway Type of Regular Issue

1946, Apr. 22 Unwmk.

No.	Type	Description	Unused	Used
C147	A176	1s car rose	30	20
C148	A176	2s violet	38	26
C149	A176	3s turq grn	60	32
C150	A176	5s red org	75	40
C151	A176	10s dk bl	1.10	32
		Nos. C147-C151 (5)	3.13	1.50

Revolution Types of Regular Issue

1946, Aug. 9 *Perf. 12½*

No.	Type	Description	Unused	Used
C152	A177	40c deep claret	15	15
C153	A178	1s sepia	15	15
C154	A179	2s indigo	32	15
C155	A180	3s olive green	48	30
		Set value		60

National Union of Periodicals, Initials and Quill Pen — AP36

1946, Sept. 16

No.	Type	Description	Unused	Used
C156	AP36	50c dl pur	30	18
C157	AP36	70c dk grn	38	20
C158	AP36	3s red	60	28
C159	AP36	5s indigo	75	35
C160	AP36	10s chocolate	2.25	52
		Nos. C156-C160 (5)	4.28	1.53

Campaign for adult education.

The Blessed Mariana Teaching Children — AP37

"Lily of Quito" — AP38

1946, Nov. 28 Unwmk.

No.	Type	Description	Unused	Used
C161	AP37	40c chocolate	22	15
C162	AP37	60c dp bl	30	24
C163	AP38	3s org yel	60	52
C164	AP38	5s green	1.10	70

30th anniv. of the death of the Blessed Mariana de Jesus Paredes y Flores.

Juan de Velasco — AP39

Riobamba Irrigation Canal — AP40

1947, Nov. 27 *Perf. 12*

No.	Type	Description	Unused	Used
C165	AP39	60c dark green	15	15
C166	AP39	70c purple	15	15
C167	AP39	1s blk brown	15	15
C168	AP39	1.10s car rose	15	15
C169	AP40	1.30s deep blue	15	15
C170	AP40	1.90s olive bister	28	15
C171	AP40	2s olive green	28	15
		Nos. C165-C171 (7)	1.31	
		Set value		52

For overprints and surcharges see Nos. C175, C181, C207-C209, C215, C216-C217, C222, C235.

Bello Type of Regular Issue

1948, Apr. 21 *Perf. 13*

No.	Type	Description	Unused	Used
C172	A188	60c magenta	18	15
C173	A188	1.30s dk bl grn	35	15
C174	A188	1.90s dk rose car	26	25

No. C166 Overprinted in Black

CONFERENCIA
ECONOMICA
GRANCOLOMBIANA
MAYO 24 DE 1.948

1948, May 24 *Perf. 12*

No.	Type	Description	Unused	Used
C175	AP39	70c purple	38	25

Columbus — AP42

1948, May 26 *Perf. 14*

No.	Type	Description	Unused	Used
C176	AP42	50c ol grn	15	15
C177	AP42	70c rose car	15	15
C178	AP42	3c ultra	38	30
C179	AP42	5s brown	75	26
C180	AP42	10s dp vio	1.25	30
		Nos. C176-C180 (5)	2.68	1.16

See note after No. 495.

No. C169 Overprinted in Carmine

Feria Nacional
1948
de hoy y del
ECUADOR **MAÑANA**

1948, Aug. 26 Unwmk. *Perf. 12*

No.	Type	Description	Unused	Used
C181	AP40	1.30s dp bl	35	25

Issued to publicize the National Fair of Today and Tomorrow, 1948.

Elia Liut and Telegrafo I AP43

Teacher and Pupils AP44

1948, Sept. 10 *Perf. 12½*

No.	Type	Description	Unused	Used
C182	AP43	60c rose red	22	18
C183	AP43	1s green	22	22
C184	AP43	1.30s dp claret	22	22
C185	AP43	1.90s dp vio	26	26
C186	AP43	2s dk brn	38	30
C187	AP43	5s blue	75	50
		Nos. C182-C187 (6)	2.05	1.68

25th anniv. (in 1945) of the 1st postal flight in Ecuador.

1948, Oct. 12 *Perf. 14*

No.	Type	Description	Unused	Used
C188	AP44	50c violet	25	15
C189	AP44	70c dp bl	25	15
C190	AP44	3s dk grn	50	20
C191	AP44	5s red	50	18
C192	AP44	10s brown	1.25	35
		Nos. C188-C192 (5)	2.75	1.03

Campaign for adult education.

Franklin D. Roosevelt and Two of "Four Freedoms"
AP45 AP46

1948, Oct. 24 *Perf. 12½*

No.	Type	Description	Unused	Used
C193	AP45	60c emer & org brn	15	15
C194	AP45	1s car rose & sl	15	15
C195	AP46	1.50s grn & red brn	20	15
C196	AP46	2s red & blk	48	18
C197	AP46	5s ultra & blk	80	18
		Nos. C193-C197 (5)	1.78	81

Maldonado Types of Regular Issue

1948, Nov. 17

No.	Type	Description	Unused	Used
C198	A196	60c dp org & rose car	22	15
C199	A197	90c red & gray blk	22	15
C200	A196	1.30s pur & dp org	32	15
C201	A197	2s dp bl & dl grn	32	15
		Set value		46

See note after No. 519.

Juan Montalvo and Cervantes AP47

Don Quixote AP48

1949, May 2 Engr. *Perf. 12½x12*

No.	Type	Description	Unused	Used
C202	AP47	1.30s ol brn & ultra	2.00	2.00
C203	AP48	1.90s grn & rose car	50	22
C204	AP47	3s vio & org brn	50	22
C205	AP48	5s red & gray blk	1.25	15
C206	AP47	10s red lil & aqua	2.00	15
		Nos. C202-C206 (5)	6.25	2.74

400th anniv. of the birth of Miguel de Cervantes Saavedra, novelist, playwright and poet, and the 60th anniv. of the death of Juan Montalvo (1832-89), Ecuadorean writer.

For surcharges see Nos. C225-C226.

No. C168 Surcharged in Blue

II CONGRESO
Junio 1949
Eucarístico Ncl.
50 —— 50

1949, June 15 *Perf. 12*

No.	Type	Description	Unused	Used
C207	AP39	50c on 1.10s car rose	15	15
C208	AP39	60c on 1.10s car rose	15	15
C209	AP39	90c on 1.10s car rose	18	18

2nd Eucharistic Cong., Quito, June 1949.

No. C128 Surcharged in Black

75 Aniversario
* **U. P. U.** *
* *
* *
* *
* *
60 centavos 60

1949, Oct. 11 *Perf. 11*

No.	Type	Description	Unused	Used
C210	A173	60c on 3s orange	35	35
a.		Double surcharge	15.00	
C211	A173	90c on 3s orange	30	30
C212	A173	1s on 3s orange	35	35
C213	A173	2s on 3s orange	90	35

"SUCRE(S)" in capitals on Nos. C212-C213.
75th anniv. of the UPU.

AP49

Black Surcharge

1950 Unwmk. *Perf. 12*

C214 AP49 60c on 50c gray 25 15
a. Double surcharge 15.00

No. C170 Surcharged with New Value in Black

C215 AP40 90c on 1.90s ol bis 30 15
Set value 17

Nos. C168, C128-C129 and Type of 1944 Surcharged or Overprinted in Black or Carmine

ALFABETIZACION

1950, Feb. 10 *Perf. 12*

C216 AP39 50c on 1.10s car rose 30 30
C217 AP39 70c on 1.10s car rose 30 30

Perf. 11

C218 A173 3s orange 50 50
C219 A173 5s dk brn (C) 75 35
C220 A173 10s vio (C) 1.10 50
Nos. C216-C220 (5) 2.95 1.95

Issued to publicize adult education.
For overprint see No. 541.

Govt. Palace Type of 1944

1950, May 15 Engr. *Perf. 11*

C221 A173 10s violet 1.00 15

For surcharges see Nos. C277-C279.

No. C169 Surcharged with New Value in Black

1950 *Perf. 12*

C222 AP40 90c on 1.30s dp bl 25 15

See No. C235.

Nos. C128-C129 Overprinted in Black

20.000 Cruce
Línea Ecuatorial
PANAGRA
26-Julio-1951

1951, July 28 Unwmk. *Perf. 11*

C223 A173 3s orange 60 60
C224 A173 5s dk brn 1.00 1.00

20,000th crossing of the equator by Pan American-Grace Airways planes.

Nos. C202-C203 Surcharged in Black

CAMPANA
●
Alfabetización
60 Ctvs. 60

CAMPAÑA ● ALFABETIZACION
1,00 Sucre 1,00

1951 Unwmk. *Perf. 12½x12*

C225 AP47 60c on 1.30s 25 15
C226 AP48 1s on 1.90s 25 15
a. Inverted surcharge 12.00
Set value 20

Issued to publicize adult education.

St. Mariana de Jesus — AP50

1952, Feb. 15 Engr.

C227 AP50 60c plum & aqua 32 15
C228 AP50 90c dk grn & lt ultra 32 15
C229 AP50 1s car & dk grn 40 15
C230 AP50 2s indigo & rose lil 40 15
Set value 48

Issued to publicize the canonization of Mariana de Jesus Paredes y Flores.

Presidents Galo Plaza and Harry Truman AP51

1951 visit of Pres. Galo Plaza to the US: 5s, Plaza addressing US Congress.

1952, Mar. 26 *Perf. 12*

C231 AP51 3s lilac & bl grn 45 45
C232 AP51 5s red brn & ol gray 90 90
a. Souv. sheet of 2, #C231-C232 1.90 1.90

Consular Service Stamps Surcharged "AEREO" and New Value in Black

1952 Unwmk. *Perf. 12*

C233 R2 60c on 1s green 25 15
C234 R2 1s on 1s green 25 15

Type R2 illustrated above No. 545.

No. C169 Surcharged with New Value in Carmine

C235 AP40 90c on 1.30s dp bl 15 15
Set value 15

See No. C222.

Pres. José M. Urvina and Allegory of Freedom AP52

Torch of Knowledge AP53

Hyphen-hole Perf. 7x6½

1952, Nov. 18 Litho.

C236 AP52 60c rose red & bl 1.00 40
C237 AP52 90c lil & red 1.00 32
C238 AP52 1s org & grn 1.00 16
C239 AP52 2s red brn & bl 1.00 20

Centenary of abolition of slavery in Ecuador. Counterfeits exist.

Unwmk.

1953, Apr. 13 Engr. *Perf. 12*

Design: 2s, Aged couple studying alphabet.

C240 AP53 1s dark blue 45 15
C241 AP53 2s red orange 65 15
Set value 20

1952 adult education campaign.

Globe Showing Part of Western Hemisphere AP54

1953, June 5 *Perf. 12½x12*

C242 AP54 60c org yel 22 22
C243 AP54 90c dk bl 26 22
C244 AP54 3s carmine 55 38

Issued to publicize the crossing of the equator by the Pan-American highway.

Consular Service Stamps Surcharged in Black

AEREO
1
SUCRE
a

AEREO 1 SUCRE
b

1953-54 *Perf. 12*

C245 R1 (a) 60c on 2s brn 25 15
C246 R2 (a) 60c on 5s sep ('54) 25 15
C247 R2 (a) 70c on 5s sep ('54) 25 15
C248 R2 (a) 90c on 50c car rose ('54) 25 15
C249 R1 (b) 1s on 2s brn 25 15
C250 R1 (a) 1s on 2s brn ('54) 25 15
C251 R1 (a) 2s on 2s brn ('54) 40 15
C252 R1 (a) 3s on 5s vio ('54) 60 15
Nos. C245-C252 (8) 2.50
Set value 80

Surcharge reads up on Nos. C250-C252.

Carlos Maria Cardinal de la Torre — AP55

Queen Isabella I — AP56

1954, Jan. 13 Photo. *Perf. 8½*
Center in Black

C253 AP55 60c rose lilac 25 15
C254 AP55 90c green 35 15
C255 AP55 3s orange 50 20
Set value 36

1st anniv. of the elevation of Archbishop de la Torre to Cardinal.

1954, Apr. 22

C256 AP56 60c dk grn & grn 15 25
C257 AP56 90c lil rose 18 30
C258 AP56 1s blk & pale lil 18 25
C259 AP56 2s blk brn & pale bl 25 20
C260 AP56 5s blk brn & buff 65 20
Nos. C256-C260 (5) 1.41 1.20

See note with No. 585.

Post Office, Guayaquil AP57

1954, May 19 Engr. *Perf. 12½x12*
Black Surcharge

C261 AP57 80c on 20c red 15 15
C262 AP57 1s on 20c red 18 15
Set value 20

25th anniversary of Pan American-Grace Airways' operation in Ecuador.

Plane, Gateway and Wheel — AP58

Unwmk.

1954, Aug. 2 Litho. *Perf. 11*

C263 AP58 80c blue 15 15

Day of the Postal Employee.

San Pablo Lagoon — AP59

1954, Sept. 24 Photo.

C264 AP59 60c orange 15 15
C265 AP59 70c rose pink 15 15
C266 AP59 90c dp grn 15 15
C267 AP59 1s dk gray grn 20 15
C268 AP59 2s blue 30 15
C269 AP59 3s yel brn 40 15
Nos. C264-C269 (6) 1.35
Set value 43

Glorification of Abdon Calderon Garaicoa AP60

Capt. Calderon — AP61

1954, Oct. 1

C270 AP60 80c rose pink 30 15
C271 AP61 90c blue 30 15
Set value 20

150th anniversary of the birth of Capt. Abdon Calderon Garaicoa.

El Cebollar College — AP62

Brother Miguel Instructing Boys — AP63

Designs: 90c, Francisco Febres Cordero (Brother Miguel). 2.50s, Tomb of Brother Miguel. 3s, Monument to Brother Miguel.

1954, Dec. 3 Unwmk. *Perf. 11*

C272 AP62 70c dk grn 15 15
C273 AP63 80c dk brn 15 15
C274 AP63 90c dk gray bl 15 15
C275 AP63 2.50s indigo 25 15
C276 AP62 3s lil rose 50 25
Nos. C272-C276 (5) 1.20
Set value 60

Centenary of the birth of Francisco Febres Cordero (Brother Miguel).

No. C221 Surcharged in Various Colors

E. M. P. 1955
$ 1,00

1955, May 25

C277 A173 1s on 10s vio (Bk) 18 15
C278 A173 1.70s on 10s vio (C) 30 15
C279 A173 4.20s on 10s vio (Br) 55 35
Set value 52

Denomination in larger type on No. C279.
National Exhibition of Daily Periodicals.

"La Rotonda," Guayaquil, and Rotary Emblem AP64

Design: 90c, Eugenio Espejo hospital, Quito, and Rotary emblem.

1955, July 9 Engr. *Perf. 12½*

C280 AP64 80c dk brn 26 20
C281 AP64 90c dk grn 26 24

50th anniv. of the founding of Rotary Intl.

José Abel Castillo AP65

Design: 2s, 5s, José Abel Castillo and Map of Ecuador.

1955, Oct. 19 *Perf. 11x11½*

C282 AP65 60c chocolate 25 20
C283 AP65 90c lt ol grn 25 15
C284 AP65 1s lilac 25 15
C285 AP65 2s vermilion 25 20
C286 AP65 5s ultra 45 35
Nos. C282-C286 (5) 1.45 1.05

See note after No. 595.

No. C29 Surcharged in Black

1
X SUCRE X

1955, Oct. 24 *Perf. 12*

C287 AP1 1s on 5s purple 16 15

A similar surcharge on No. C29, set in two lines with letters 5mm high and no X's or black-out line of squares, was privately applied.

San Pablo, Imbabura — AP66

Designs: 50s, Rumichaca Caves. 1.30s, Virgin of Quito. 1.50s, Cotopaxi Volcano. 1.70s, Tungurahua Volcano, Tungurahua. 1.90s, Guanacos. 2.40s, Mat market. 2.50s, Ruins at Incapirca. 4.20s, El Carmen, Cuenca, Azuay. 4.80s, Santo Domingo Church.

1956, Jan. 2 Photo. *Perf. 13*

C288 AP66 50c slate bl 30 15
C289 AP66 1s ultra 30 15
C290 AP66 1.30s crimson 35 20
C291 AP66 1.50s dp grn 25 15
C292 AP66 1.70s yel brn 20 15
C293 AP66 1.90s olive 30 16
C294 AP66 2.40s red org 35 16
C295 AP66 2.50s violet 35 16
C296 AP66 4.20s black 40 20
C297 AP66 4.80s yel org 60 32
Nos. C288-C297 (10) 3.40
Set value 1.48

See Nos. C310-C311. For surcharges see Nos. 766A, 766G.

Honorato Vazquez — AP67

Title Page of First Book — AP68

1956, May 28 Engr.

Various Portraits

C298 AP67 1s yel grn 16 15
C299 AP67 1.50s red 20 15
C300 AP67 1.70s brt bl 16 15
C301 AP67 1.90s slate bl 20 15

Birth centenary (in 1955) of Honorato Vazquez, statesman.

1956, Aug. 27 Unwmk. *Perf. 13½*

C302 AP68 1s black 15 15
C303 AP68 1.70s slate bl 16 15
C304 AP68 2s blk brn 25 15
C305 AP68 3s redsh brn 30 20
Set value 51

Bicentenary of printing in Ecuador.

Hands Reaching for UN Emblem AP69

1956, Oct. 24 *Perf. 14*

C307 AP69 1.70s red org 38 15

10th anniv. of the UN (in 1955).
See No. C319. For overprint see No. C426.

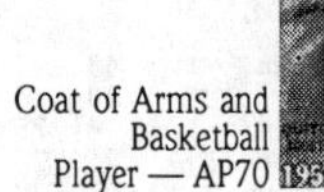

Coat of Arms and Basketball Player — AP70

Designs: 1.70s, Map of South America with flags and girl basketball players.

1956, Dec. 28 Photo. *Perf. 14½x14*

C308 AP70 1s red lilac 18 15
C309 AP70 1.70s deep green 30 15
Set value 21

6th South American Women's Basketball Championship, Aug. 1956.

Scenic Type of 1956

1957, Jan. 2 *Perf. 13*

C310 AP66 50c bl grn 25 15
C311 AP66 1s orange 25 15
Set value 17

Type of Regular Issue, 1957

Designs: 50c, Map of Cuenca, 16th century. 80c, Cathedral of Cuenca. 1s, Modern City Hall.

Unwmk.

1957, Apr. 7 Photo. *Perf. 12*

C312 A219 50c brn, *cr* 15 15
a. Souvenir sheet of 4 60 60
C313 A219 80c red, *bluish* 15 15
C314 A219 1s pur, *yel* 16 15
a. Souvenir sheet of 3 90 90
Set value 36 22

No. C312a contains 4 imperf. 50c stamps similar to No. 613, but inscribed "AEREO" and printed in green. The sheet is printed on white ungummed paper.

No. C314a contains 3 imperf. stamps in designs similar to Nos. C312-C314, but with colors changed to orange (50c), brown (80c), violet (1s). The sheet is printed on white ungummed paper.

Gabriela Mistral — AP71

Arms of Espejo, Carchi — AP72

Unwmk.

1957, Sept. 18 Litho. *Perf. 14*

C315 AP71 2s lt bl, blk & red 22 15

Issued to honor Gabriela Mistral (1889-1957), Chilean poet and educator.
See Nos. C406-C407.

1957, Nov. 16 *Perf. 14½x13½*

Arms of Cantons: 2s, Montufar. 4.20s, Tulcan.

Coat of Arms Multicolored

C316 AP72 1s carmine 15 15
C317 AP72 2s black 18 15
C318 AP72 4.20s ultra 45 28
Set value 45

Province of Carchi.
See Nos. C334-C337, C355-C364, C392-C395. For surcharge see No. 766.

Redrawn UN Type of 1956

1957, Dec. 10 Engr. *Perf. 14*

C319 AP69 2s greenish blue 35 24

Honoring the UN. Dates, as on No. C307, are omitted; inscribed: "Homenaje a las Naciones Unidas."

Mater Dolorosa, San Gabriel College — AP73

Rafael Maria Arizaga — AP74

Design: No. C321, 1s, Door of San Gabriel College, Quito.

1958, Apr. 27 Engr. *Perf. 14*

C320 AP73 30c rose cl, *dp rose* 15 15
C321 AP73 30c rose cl, *dp rose* 15 15
a. Pair, #C320-C321 30 20
C322 AP73 1s dk bl, *lt bl* 15 15
C323 AP73 1.70s dk bl, *lt bl* 17 18
a. Pair, #C322-C323 30 28
Set value 45

50th anniversary of the miracle of San Gabriel College, Quito.

1958, July 21 Litho.

C324 AP74 1s multi 15 15

Rafael Maria Arizaga (1858-1933), writer.
See Nos. C343, C350, C412.

Daule River Bridge AP75

1958, July 25 Engr. *Perf. 13½x14*

C325 AP75 1.30s green 18 15

Issued to commemorate the opening of the River Daule bridge in Guayas province.
See Nos. C367-C369.

Basketball Player — AP76

Symbolical of the Eucharist — AP77

1958, Sept. 1 Photo. *Perf. 14x13½*

C326 AP76 1.30s dk grn & lt brn 35 28

South American basketball championships.
For surcharge see No. 774A.

1958, Sept. 25 Litho. Unwmk.

Design: 60c, Cathedral of Guayaquil.

C327 AP77 10c vio & buff 15 15
C328 AP77 60c org & vio brn 15 15
C329 AP77 1s brn & lt bl 15 15
Set value 31 24

Souvenir Sheet

Symbolical of the Eucharist — AP78

Perf. 13½x14

C330 AP78 Sheet of 4 48 48
a.-d. 40c dark blue, any single 15 15

3rd National Eucharistic Congress.

Stamps of 1865 and 1920 AP79

Designs: 2s, Stamps of 1920 and 1948. 4.20s, Municipal museum and library.

1958, Oct. 8 Photo. *Perf. 11½*

Granite Paper

C331 AP79 1.30s grn & brn red 18 15
C332 AP79 2s bl & vio 35 24
C333 AP79 4.20s dk brn 60 45

National Philatelic Exposition (EXFIGUA), Guayaquil, Oct. 4-14.
For surcharge see No. 774.

Coat of Arms Type of 1957
Province of Imbabura

Arms of Cantons: 50c, Cotacachi. 60c, Antonio Ante. 80c, Otalvo. 1.10s, Ibarra.

1958, Nov. 9 Litho. *Perf. 14½x13½*

Coats of Arms Multicolored

C334 AP72 50c blk & red 15 15
C335 AP72 60c blk, bl & red 15 15
C336 AP72 80c blk & yel 15 15
C337 AP72 1.10s blk & red 25 15
Set value 36

Charles V — AP80

Paul Rivet — AP81

Engr. & Photo.

1958, Dec. 12 *Perf. 14x13½*

C338 AP80 2s brn red & dk brn 22 15
C339 AP80 4.20s dk gray & red brn 45 35

400th anniv. of the death of Charles V, Holy Roman Emperor.

1958, Dec. 29 Photo. *Perf. 11½*
Granite Paper

C340 AP81 1s brown 15 15

Issued in honor of Paul Rivet (1876-1958), French anthropologist.

1959, May 6

Portrait: 2s, Alexander von Humboldt.

C341 AP81 2s slate 16 15

Cent. of the death of Alexander von Humboldt, German naturalist and geographer.

Front Page of "El Telegrafo" AP82

1959, Feb. Litho. *Perf. 13½*

C342 AP82 1.30s bl grn & blk 16 15

75th anniv. of Ecuador's oldest newspaper.

Portrait Type of 1958

Portrait: José Luis Tamayo (1858-1947), lawyer.

1959, June 26 Unwmk. *Perf. 14*
Portrait Multicolored

C343 AP74 1.30s lt grn, bl & sal 16 15

El Sagrario & House of Manuela Canizares — AP83

Condor — AP84

Designs: 80c, Hall at San Agustin. 1s, First words of the constitutional act. 2s, Entrance to Cuartel Real. 4.20s, Allegory of Liberty.

Unwmk.

1959, Aug. 28 Photo. *Perf. 14*

C344 AP83 20c ultra & lt brn 15 15
C345 AP83 80c brt bl & dp org 15 15
C346 AP83 1s dk red & dk ol 15 15
C347 AP84 1.30s brt bl & org 18 15
C348 AP84 2s ultra & org brn 18 15
C349 AP84 4.20s scar & brt bl 45 30
Nos. C344-C349 (6) 1.26
Set value 68

Sesquicentennial of the revolution.

Portrait Type of 1958

Portrait: 1s, Alfredo Baquerizo Moreno (1859-1951), statesman.

1959, Sept. 26 Litho. *Perf. 14*

C350 AP74 1s gray, red & sal 15 15

Pope Pius XII — AP85

1959, Oct. 9 Unwmk. *Perf. 14½*

C351 AP85 1.30s multi 22 16

Issued in memory of Pope Plus XII.

Flags of Argentina, Bolivia, Brazil, Guatemala, Haiti, Mexico and Peru — AP86

Flags of: 80c, Chile, Costa Rica, Cuba, Dominican Republic, Panama, Paraguay, United States. 1.30s, Colombia, Ecuador, Honduras, Nicaragua, Salvador, Uruguay, Venezuela.

1959, Oct. 12 *Perf. 13½.*

C352 AP86 50c multi 15 15
C353 AP86 80c yel, red & bl 15 15
C354 AP86 1.30s multi 18 16
Set value 36

Organization of American States.
For overprints see #C423-C425, CO19-CO21.

Coat of Arms Type of 1957
Province of Pichincha

Arms of Cantons: 10c, Rumiñahui. 40c, Pedro Moncayo. 1s, Mejia. 1.30s, Cayambe. 4.20s, Quito.

Perf. 14½x13½

1959-60 Unwmk. Litho.
Coat of Arms Multicolored

C355 AP72 10c blk & dk red ('60) 15 15
C356 AP72 40c blk & yel 15 15
C357 AP72 1s blk & brn ('60) 15 15
C358 AP72 1.30s blk & grn ('60) 15 15
C359 AP72 4.20s blk & org 32 25
Nos. C355-C359 (5) 92 85
Set value 68 51

Province of Cotopaxi

Arms of Cantons: 40c, Pangua. 60c, Pujili. 70c, Saquisili. 1s, Salcedo. 1.30s, Latacunga.

1960
Coat of Arms Multicolored

C360 AP72 40c blk & car 15 15
C361 AP72 60c blk & bl 15 15
C362 AP72 70c blk & turq 16 15
C363 AP72 1s blk & red org 16 15
C364 AP72 1.30s blk & org 18 15
Nos. C360-C364 (5) 80 75
Set value 63 42

Flags of American Nations AP87

1960, Feb. 23 *Perf. 13x12½*

C365 AP87 1.30s multi 15 15
C366 AP87 2s multi 18 16
Set value 24

11th Inter-American Conference, Feb. 1960.

Bridge Type of 1958.

Bridges: No. C367, Juntas. No. C368, Saracay. 2s, Railroad bridge, Ambato.

1960 Litho. *Perf. 13½*

C367 AP75 1.30s chocolate 15 15

Photo. *Perf. 12½*

C368 AP75 1.30s emerald 15 15
C369 AP75 2s brown 20 15
Set value 21

Building of three new bridges.

Bahia-Chone Road — AP88

Pres. Camilo Ponce Enriquez AP89

Designs: 4.20s, Public Works Building, Cuenca. 5s, El Coca airport. 10s, New Harbor, Guayaquil.

1960, Aug. Litho. *Perf. 14*

C370 AP88 1.30s blk & dl yel 15 15
C371 AP88 4.20s rose car & lt grn 28 26
C372 AP88 5s dk brn & yel 42 32
C373 AP88 10s dk bl & bl 90 65

Perf. 11x11½

C374 AP89 2s org brn & blk 1.40 26
Nos. C370-C374 (5) 3.15 1.64

Nos. C370-C374 issued to publicize the achievements of Pres. Camilo Ponce Enriquez (1956-1960).

Issue dates: Nos. C370-C373, Aug. 24. No. C374, Aug. 31.

Red Cross Building, Quito and Henri Dunant — AP90

1960, Oct. 5 Unwmk. *Perf. 13x14*

C375 AP90 2s rose vio & car 28 15

Centenary (in 1959) of Red Cross idea.
For overprint see No. C408.

El Belen Church, Quito — AP91

1961, Jan. 14 *Perf. 12½*

C376 AP91 3s multi 38 18

Ecuador's participation in the 1960 Barcelona Philatelic Congress.

Map of Ecuador and Amazon River System AP92

1961, Feb. 27 Litho. *Perf. 10½*

C377 AP92 80c salmpn, claret & grn 16 15
C378 AP92 1.30s gray, slate & grn 20 18
C379 AP92 2s beige, red & grn 22 20

Amazon Week, and the 132nd anniversary of the Battle of Tarqui against Peru.

Juan Montalvo, Juan Leon Mera, Juan Benigno Vela — AP93

Hugo Ortiz G. — AP94

1961, Apr. 13 Unwmk. *Perf. 13*

C380 AP93 1.30s salmon & blk 20 15

Centenary of Tungurahua province.

1961, May 25 *Perf. 14x14½*

Design: No. C382, Ortiz monument.

C381 AP94 1.30s grnsh bl, blk & yel 15 15
C382 AP94 1.30s grnsh bl, pur, ol & brn 15 15
Set value 20

Issued in memory of Lieutenant Hugo Ortiz G., killed in battle Aug. 2, 1941.

Condor and Airplane Stamp of 1936 AP95

Designs: 1.30s, Map of South America and stamp of 1865. 2s, Bolivar monument stamp of 1930.

Perf. 10½

1961, May 25 Litho. Unwmk.
Size: 41x28mm

C383 AP95 80c org & vio 16 15

Size: 41x34mm

C384 AP95 1.30s bl, yel, ol & car 28 25

Size: 40½x37mm

C385 AP95 2s car rose & blk 35 20

Third National Philatelic Exhibition, Quito, May 25-June 3, 1961.

Arms of Los Rios and Egret — AP96

1961, May 27 *Perf. 14½x13½*
Coat of Arms Multicolored

C386 AP96 2s bl & blk 28 18

Centenary (in 1960) of Los Rios province.

Gabriel Garcia Moreno — AP97

Remigio Crespo Toral — AP98

1961, Sept. 24 Unwmk. *Perf. 12*

C387 AP97 1s bl, brn & buff 15 15

Centenary of the restoration of national integrity.

1961, Nov. 3 Unwmk. *Perf. 14*

C388 AP98 50c multi 15 15

Centenary of the birth of Remigio Crespo Toral, poet laureate of Ecuador.

Galapagos Islands Nos. LC1-LC3 Overprinted in Black or Red: "Estacion de Biologia Maritima de Galapagos" and "UNESCO 1961" (Similar to #684-686)

1961, Oct. 31 Photo. *Perf. 12*

C389 A1 1s dp bl 24 16
 a. "de Galapagos" on top line 2.00 2.00
C390 A1 1.80s rose vio 30 18
 a. UNESCO emblem omitted 1.25 1.25
C391 A1 4.20s blk (R) 48 40

Establishment of maritime biological stations on Galapagos Islands by UNESCO.

Coat of Arms Type of 1957
Province of Tungurahua

Arms of Cantons: 50c, Pillaro. 1s, Pelileo. 1.30s, Baños. 2s, Ambato.

Perf. 14½x13½

1962, Mar. 30 Litho. Unwmk.

Coats of Arms Multicolored

C392 AP72 50c black 15 15
C393 AP72 1s black 18 15
C394 AP72 1.30s black 25 15
C395 AP72 2s black 35 22
 Set value 47

Pres. Arosemena and Prince Philip, Arms of Ecuador and Great Britain and Equator Monument
AP99

Perf. 14x13½

1962, Feb. 17 Wmk. 340

C396 AP99 1.30s bl, sep, red & yel 16 16
C397 AP99 2s multi 20 15

Visit of Prince Philip, Duke of Edinburgh, to Ecuador, Feb. 17-20, 1962.

Mountain Farming — AP100

Perf. 12½

1963, Mar. 21 Unwmk. Litho.

C398 AP100 30c emer, yel & blk 15 15
C399 AP100 3s dl red, grn & org 32 20
C400 AP100 4.20s bl, blk & yel 48 35

FAO "Freedom from Hunger" campaign.

Mosquito and Malaria Eradication Emblem
AP101

1963, Apr. 17 Unwmk. *Perf. 12½*

C401 AP101 50c multi 15 15
C402 AP101 80c multi 15 15
C403 AP101 2s multi 20 16
 Set value 36 30

WHO drive to eradicate malaria.

Stagecoach and Jet Plane — AP102

1963, May 7 Litho.

C404 AP102 2s org & car rose 30 15
C405 AP102 4.20s claret & ultra 42 35

1st Intl. Postal Conference, Paris, 1863.

Type of 1957 Inscribed "Islas Galapagos," Surcharged with New Value and Overprinted "Ecuador" in Black or Red

1963, June 19 Unwmk. *Perf. 14*

C406 AP71 5s on 2s gray, dk bl & red 50 50
C407 AP71 10s on 2s gray, dk bl & red (R) 1.00 1.00

The basic 2s exists without surcharge and overprint. No. C407 exists with "ECUADOR" omitted, and with both "ECUADOR" and "10 SUCRES" double.

No. C375 Overprinted: "1863-1963/Centenario/de la Fundación/ de la Cruz Roja/Internacional"

1963, June 21 Photo. *Perf. 13x14*

C408 AP90 2s rose vio & car 22 15

Intl. Red Cross, centenary.

Type of Regular Issue, 1963

Designs (Arosemena and): 70c, Flags of Ecuador. 2s, Flags of Ecuador and Panama. 4s, Flags of Ecuador and US.

1963, July 1 Litho. *Perf. 14*

C409 A238 70c pale bl & multi 15 15
C410 A238 2s pink & multi 25 25
C411 A238 4s lt bl & multi 55 55

Portrait Type of 1958

Portrait: 2s, Dr. Mariano Cueva (1812-82).

Unwmk.

1963, July 4 Litho. *Perf. 14*

C412 AP74 2s lt grn & multi 35 15

Social Insurance Symbol — AP103

Mother and Child — AP104

1963, July 9 Litho.

C413 AP103 10s brn, bl, gray & ocher 60 50

25th anniversary of Social Insurance.

1963, July 28 *Perf. 12½*

C414 AP104 1.30s org, dk bl & blk 20 20
C415 AP104 5s gray, red & brn 40 40

7th Pan-American and South American Pediatrics Congresses, Quito.

Simon Bolivar Airport, Guayaquil
AP105

1963, July 25 *Perf. 14*

C416 AP105 60c gray 15 15
C417 AP105 70c dl grn 15 15
C418 AP105 5s brn vio 45 30
 Set value 45

Opening of Simon Bolivar Airport, Guayaquil, July 15, 1962.

Nos. 638, 640-641 Overprinted "AEREO"

1964 *Perf. 12*

Flags in National Colors

C419 A223 1.80s dl vio 35 35
C420 A224 2s dk brn 35 35
C421 A223 2.20s blk brn 35 35

On 1.80s and 2.20s, "AEREO" is vertical, reading down.

No. 650 Overprinted in Gold: "FARO DE COLON / AEREO"

1964 Photo. *Perf. 14x13½*

C422 A229 1.80s dk bl 2.50 1.75

Nos. C352-C354 Overprinted **1961**

1964 Litho. *Perf. 13½*

C423 AP86 50c bl & multi 60 40
C424 AP86 80c yel & multi 60 40
C425 AP86 1.30s pale grn & multi 60 40

No. C307 Overprinted: "DECLARACION / DERECHOS HUMANOS / 1964 / XV-ANIV"

Unwmk.

1964, Sept. 29 Engr. *Perf. 14*

C426 AP69 1.70s red org 28 15

15th anniversary (in 1963) of the Universal Declaration of Human Rights.

Banana Type of Regular Issue

1964, Oct. 26 Litho. *Perf. 12½x12*

C427 A241 4.20s blk, bis & gray ol 26 20
C428 A241 10s blk, scar & gray ol 50 40
 a. Souv. sheet of 4 90 90

No. C428a contains imperf. stamps similar to Nos. 720-721 and C427-C428.

John F. Kennedy, Flag-draped Coffin and John Jr. — AP106

1964, Nov. 22 Litho. *Perf. 14*

C429 AP106 4.20s multi 65 55
C430 AP106 5s multi 85 65
C431 AP106 10s multi 1.10 75
 a. Souv. sheet of 3 3.75 3.75

President John F. Kennedy (1917-63).

No. C431a contains stamps similar to Nos. C429-C431, imperf.

Olympic Type of Regular Issue

Designs: 1.30s, Gymnast, vert. 1.80s, Hurdler. 2s, Basketball.

Perf. 13½x14, 14x13½

1964, Dec. 16 Unwmk.

C432 A243 1.30s vio bl, ver & brn 20 20
C433 A243 1.80s vio bl & multi 20 15
C434 A243 2s red & multi 26 20
 a. Souv. sheet of 4 2.50 2.50

No. C434a contains stamps similar to Nos. 725 and C432-C434, imperf.

Sports Type of Regular Issue, 1965

Torch and Athletes: 2s, 3s, Diver, gymnast, wrestlers and weight lifter. 2.50s, 4s, Bicyclists. 3.50s, 5s, Jumpers.

1965, Nov. 20 Litho. *Perf. 12x12½*

C435 A247 2s bl, gold & blk 40 15
C436 A247 2.50s org, gold & blk 40 15
C437 A247 3s brt pink, gold & blk 40 15
C438 A247 3.50s lt vio, gold & bl 40 40
C439 A247 4s brt yel grn, gold & blk 40 20
C440 A247 5s red org, gold & blk 40 24
 a. Souv. sheet of 12 4.00 4.00
 Nos. C435-C440 (6) 2.40 1.29

No. C440a contains 12 imperf. stamps similar to Nos. 738-743 and C435-C440.

For surcharges see Nos. 766B, C449.

Bird Type of Regular Issue

Birds: 1s, Yellow grosbeak. 1.30s, Black-headed parrot. 1.50s, Scarlet tanager. 2s, Sapphire quail-dove. 2.50s, Violet-tailed sylph. 3s, Lemon-throated barbet. 4s, Yellow-tailed oriole. 10s, Collared puffbird.

1966, June 17 Litho. *Perf. 13½*

Birds in Natural Colors

C441 A249 1s lt red brn & blk 25 15
C442 A249 1.30s pink & blk 25 15
C443 A249 1.50s pale grn & blk 25 15
C444 A249 2s sal & blk 40 15
C445 A249 2.50s lt yel grn & blk 40 15
C446 A249 3s sal & blk 50 20
C447 A249 4s gray & blk 70 24
C448 A249 10s beige & blk 1.25 35
 Nos. C441-C448 (8) 4.00
 Set value 1.20

For surcharges see Nos. 766E-766F, C450, C455-C457.

Nos. C436 and C443 Surcharged

1967

C449 A247 80c on 2.50s multi 25 25
C450 A249 80c on 1.50s multi 25 15

Old denomination on No. C449 is obliterated with heavy bar; the surcharge on No. C450 includes "Resello" and an ornament over old denomination.

Peñaherrera Monument, Quito — AP107

Design: 2s, Peñaherrera statue.

1967, Dec. 29 Litho. *Perf. 12x12½*

C451 AP107 1.30s blk & org 15 15
C452 AP107 2s blk & lt ultra 15 15
 Set value 22

See note after No. 763.

Arosemena Type of Regular Issue

Designs: 1.30s, Inauguration of Pres. Arosemena. 2s, Pres. Arosemena speaking in Punta del Este.

1968, May 9 Litho. *Perf. 13½x14*

C453 A251 1.30s multi 15 15
C454 A251 2s multi 15 15
 Set value 21

No. C448 Surcharged in Plum, Dark Blue or Green

RESELLO

$ 0,80

1969, Jan. 9 Litho. *Perf. 13½*

Bird in Natural Colors

C455 A249 80c on 10s beige (P) 25 15
C456 A249 1s on 10s beige (DBl) 25 15
C457 A249 2s on 10s beige (G) 25 18

"Operation Friendship" AP108

1969-70 Typo. *Perf. 13½*

C458 AP108 2s yel, blk, red & lt bl 20 15
a. Perf. 12½ 20 15
C459 AP108 2s bl, blk, car & yel ('70) 20 15
Set value 20

Friendship campaign. Medallion background on Nos. C458 and C458a is blue; on No. C459, yellow.

No. 639 Surcharged in Gold "S/. 5 AEREO" and Bar

1969, Nov. 25 Litho. *Perf. 12*

C460 A224 5s on 2s multi 1.50 52

Butterfly Type of Regular Issue

Butterflies: 1.30s, Morpho peleides. 1.50s, Anartia amathea.

1970 Litho. *Perf. 12½*

C461 A255 1.30s multi 50 15
C462 A255 1.50s pink & multi 50 15
Set value 15

Same, White Background

1970 *Perf. 13½*

C463 A255 1.30s multi 50 15
C464 A255 1.50s multi 50 15
Set value 15

Arms Type of Regular Issue

Provincial Arms and Flags: 1.30s, El Oro. 2s, Loja. 3s, Manabi. 5s, Pichincha. 10s, Guayas.

1971 Litho. *Perf. 10½*

C465 A258 1.30s pink & multi 20 15
C466 A258 2s multi 30 15
C467 A258 3s multi 40 25
C468 A258 5s multi 60 25
C469 A258 10s multi 1.00 25
Nos. C465-C469 (5) 2.50 1.05

Presentation of the Virgin — AP109

Pres. Allende and Chilean Flag — AP110

Art of Quito: 1.50s, Blessed Anne at Prayer. 2s, St. Theresa de Jesus. 2.50s, Altar of Carmen, horiz. 3s, Descent from the Cross. 4s, Christ of St. Mariana de Jesus. 5s, Shrine of St. Anthony. 10s, Cross of San Diego.

1971 *Perf. 11½*

Inscriptions in Black

C473 AP109 1.30s multi 15 15
C474 AP109 1.50s multi 25 15
C475 AP109 2s multi 25 15
C476 AP109 2.50s multi 30 15
C477 AP109 3s multi 30 15
C478 AP109 4s multi 40 18
C479 AP109 5s multi 50 22
C480 AP109 10s multi 1.00 45
Nos. C473-C480 (8) 3.15
Set value 1.35

1971, Aug. 24 *Perf. 12½*

Design: 2.10s, Pres. José M. Velasco Ibarra of Ecuador, Pres. Salvador Allende of Chile and national flags.

C481 AP110 2s multi 15 15
C482 AP110 2.10s multi 15 15
Set value 16

Visit of Pres. Salvador Allende of Chile, Aug. 24.

Globe and Emblem AP111

1971

C483 AP111 5s black 45 15
C484 AP111 5.50s dl pur & blk 45 15

Opening of Postal Museum, Aug. 24, 1971.

Pazmiño Type of Regular Issue

1971, Sept. 16 *Perf. 12x11½*

C485 A260 1.50s grn & multi 15 15
C486 A260 2.50s grn & multi 15 15
Set value 20

AP112

AP113

Designs: 5s, Map of Americas. 10s, Converging roads and map. 20s, Map of Americas and Equator. 50s, Mountain road and monument on Equator.

1971 *Perf. 11½*

C487 AP112 5s org & multi 65 25
C488 AP112 10s org & blk 1.00 50
C489 AP112 20s blk, bl & brt rose 1.65 85
C490 AP112 50s bl, blk & gray 2.50 1.25

11th Pan-American Road Congress.
Issue dates: 5s, 10s, 50s, Nov. 15; 20s, Nov. 22.

1972

Design: 3s, Arms of Ecuador and Argentina. 5s, Presidents José M. Velasco Ibarra and Alejandro Agustin Lanusse.

C491 AP113 3s blk & multi 18 15
C492 AP113 5s blk & multi 28 20

Visit of Lt. Gen. Alejandro Agustin Lanusse, president of Argentina, Jan. 25.

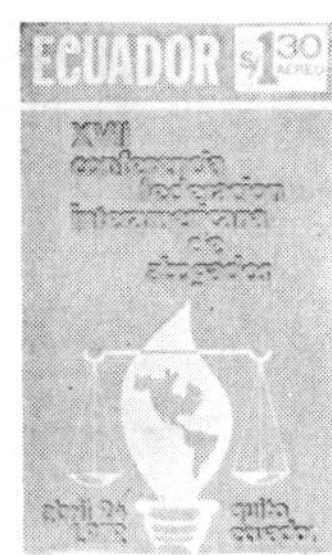

Flame, Scales, Map of Americas — AP114

1972, Apr. 24 Litho. *Perf. 12½*

C493 AP114 1.30s bl & red 15 15

17th Conference of the Interamerican Federation of Lawyers, Quito, Apr. 24.

Religious Paintings Type of Regular Issue

Ecuadorian Paintings: 3s, Virgin of the Flowers, by Miguel de Santiago. 10s, Virgin of the Rosary, by Quito School.

1972, Apr. 24 *Perf. 14x13½*

C494 A263 3s blk & multi 25 25
C495 A263 10s blk & multi 75 50
a. Souv. sheet of 2, #C494-C495 1.00 1.00

1972, May 4

Ecuadorian Statues: 3s, St. Dominic, Quito School. 10s, St. Rosa of Lima, by Bernardo de Legarda.

C496 A263 3s blk & multi 25 25
C497 A263 10s blk & multi 75 50
a. Souv. sheet of 2, #C496-C497 1.00 1.00

Letters of "Ecuador" 3mm high on #C496-C497, 7mm high on #C494-C495.

Portrait Type of Regular Issue

Designs (Generals, from Paintings): 1.30s, José Maria Saenz. 3s, Tomás Wright. 4s, Antonio Farfan. 5s, Antonio José de Sucre. 10s, Simon Bolivar. 20s, Arms of Ecuador.

1972, May 24

C498 A264 1.30s bl & multi 15 15
C499 A264 3s bl & multi 16 15
C500 A264 4s bl & multi 20 15
C501 A264 5s bl & multi 26 20
C502 A264 10s bl & multi 48 32
C503 A264 20s bl & multi 95 65
Nos. C498-C503 (6) 2.20 1.62

Artisan Type of Regular Issue

Handicraft of Ecuador: 2s, Woman wearing flowered poncho. 3s, Striped poncho. 5s, Poncho with roses. 10s, Gold sunburst sculpture.

1972, July Photo. *Perf. 13*

C504 A265 2s multi 20 20
C505 A265 3s multi 25 25
C506 A265 5s multi 55 55
C507 A265 10s org red & multi 1.00 1.00
a. Souv. sheet of 4, #C504-C507 2.00 2.00

Epidendrum Orchid — AP115

1972 Photo. *Perf. 12½*

C508 AP115 4s shown 40 40
C509 AP115 6s Canna 60 60
C510 AP115 10s Jimson weed 1.00 1.00
a. Souv. sheet of 3, #C508-C510 2.25 2.25

Exists imperf.

Oil Drilling Towers AP116

Coat of Arms AP117

1972, Oct. 17 Litho. *Perf. 11½*

C511 AP116 1.30s bl & multi 15 15

Ecuadorian oil industry.

1972, Nov. 18 Litho. *Perf. 11½*

Arms Multicolored

C512 AP117 2s black 15 15
C513 AP117 3s black 20 15
C514 AP117 4s black 26 16
C515 AP117 4.50s black 26 16
C516 AP117 6.30s black 50 26
C517 AP117 6.90s black 50 26
Nos. C512-C517 (6) 1.87 1.14

Pichincha Type of Regular Issue

Designs: 2.40s, Corridor, San Agustin. 4.50s, La Merced Convent. 5.50s, Column base. 6.30s, Chapter Hall, San Agustin. 6.90s, Interior, San Agustin. 7.40s, Crucifixion, Cantuña Chapel. 7.90s, Decorated ceiling, San Agustin.

1972, Dec. 6 Wmk. 367

C518 A266 2.40s yel & multi 25 15
C519 A266 4.50s yel & multi 40 18
C520 A266 5.50s yel & multi 50 22
C521 A266 6.30s yel & multi 55 35
C522 A266 6.90s yel & multi 60 35
C523 A266 7.40s yel & multi 70 35
C524 A266 7.90s yel & multi 75 35
Nos. C518-C524 (7) 3.75 1.95

UN Emblem AP118

OAS Emblem AP119

1973, Mar. 23 Litho. Unwmk.
Perf. 11½

C525 AP118 1.30s lt bl & blk 15 15

25th anniversary of the Economic Committee for Latin America (CEPAL).

Perf. 11½

1973, Apr. 14 Litho. Wmk. 367

C526 AP119 1.50s multi 15 15
a. Unwatermarked

Day of the Americas and "Philately for Peace."

Bird Type of Regular Issue

1973 Unwmk. *Perf. 11½x11*

C527 A268 1.30s Blue-footed booby 40 15
C528 A268 3s Brown pelican 60 15
Set value 23

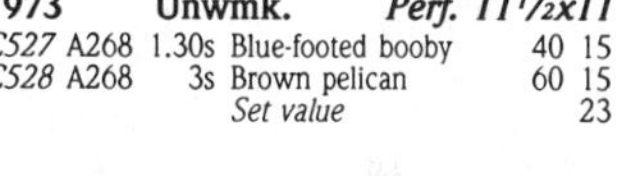

Presidents Lara and Caldera AP120

1973, June 15 Wmk. 367

C529 AP120 3s multi 30 15

Visit of Pres. Rafael Caldera of Venezuela, Feb. 5-7.

Silver Coin, 1934 — AP121

Globe, OPEC Emblem, Oil Derrick — AP122

Ecuadorian Coins: 10s, Silver coin, obverse. 50s, Gold coin, 1928.

Unwmk.

1973, Dec. 14 Photo. *Perf. 14*

C530 AP121 5s multi 40 20
C531 AP121 10s multi 75 35
C532 AP121 50s multi 3.75 2.00
a. Souvenir sheet of 3 5.25 5.25

No. C532a contains one each of Nos. C530-C532; Dated "1972." Exists imperf.

A gold marginal overprint was applied in 1974 to No. C532a (perf. and imperf.): "X Campeonato Mundial de Football / Munich -1974."

A carmine overprint was applied in 1974 to No. C532a (perf. and imperf.): "Seminario de Telecomunicaciones Rurales, / Septiembre-1974 / Quito-Ecuador" and ITU emblem.

1974, June 15 Litho. *Perf. 11½*

C533 AP122 2s multi 15 15

Meeting of Organization of Oil Exporting Countries, Quito, June 15-24.

Ecuadorian Flag, UPU Emblem — AP123

1974, July 15 Litho. *Perf. 11½*

C534 AP123 1.30s multi 15 15

Centenary of Universal Postal Union.

Teodoro Wolf AP124

Capt. Edmundo Chiriboga AP125

1974 Litho. *Perf. 12x11½*

C535 AP124 1.30s blk & ultra 15 15
C536 AP125 1.50s gray 15 15
Set value 15

Teodoro Wolf, geographer; Edmundo Chiriboga, national hero. Issue dates, No. C535, Nov. 29; No. C536, Dec. 4.

Congress Emblem AP126

1974, Dec. 8 Litho. *Perf. 11½x12*

C537 AP126 5s bl & multi 28 15

8th Inter-American Postmasters' Cong., Quito.

Map of Americas and Coat of Arms AP127

Manuel J. Calle, Journalist AP128

1975, Feb. 1 *Perf. 12x11½*

C538 AP127 3s bl & multi 18 15

EXFIGUA Stamp Exhibition and 5th General Assembly of Federation Inter-Americana de Filatelia, Guayaquil, Nov. 1973.

1975 *Perf. 12x11½*

Portraits: No. C540, Leopoldo Benites V., president of UN General Assembly, 1973-74; No. C541, Adofo H. Simmonds G. (1892-1969), journalists; No. C542, Juan de Dios Martinez Mera, President of Ecuador, birth centenary.

C539 AP128 5s lilac rose 40 15
C540 AP128 5s gray 40 15
C541 AP128 5s violet 40 25
C542 AP128 5s blk & rose red 40 15

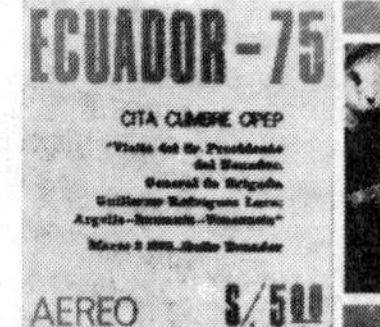

Pres. Guillermo Rodriguez Lara — AP129

1975 Unwmk. *Perf. 12*

C546 AP129 5s ver & blk 50 15

State visit of Pres. Guillermo Rodriguez Lara to Algeria, Romania and Venezuela.

Meeting Type of 1975

Designs: 1.50s, Rafael Rodriguez Palacio and Argelino Duran Quintero meeting at border in Ruichacha. 2s, Signing border agreement.

1975, Apr. 1 Litho. *Perf. 12x11½*

C547 A273 1.50s multi 15 15
C548 A273 2s multi 16 15
Set value 18

Sacred Heart (Painting) AP130

Quito Cathedral AP131

Design: 2s, Monstrance.

1975, Apr. 28 Litho. *Perf. 12x11½*

C549 AP130 1.30s yel & multi 15 15
C550 AP130 2s bl & multi 20 15
C551 AP131 3s multi 30 15
Set value 24

3rd Bolivarian Eucharistic Congress, Quito, June 9-16, 1974.

J. Delgado Panchana with Trophy — AP132

J. Delgado Panchana Swimming AP133

Perf. 12x11½, 11½x12

1975, June 12 Unwmk.

C552 AP132 1.30s bl & multi 15 15
C553 AP133 3s blk & multi 22 15
Set value 17

Jorge Delgado Panchana, South American swimming champion, 1971 and 1974.

Sports Type of 1975

1975, Sept. 11 Litho. *Perf. 11½*

C554 A276 1.30s Tennis 15 15
C555 A276 2s Target shooting 20 15
C556 A276 2.80s Volleyball 25 15
C557 A276 3s Raft with sails 25 15
C558 A276 5s Mask 40 15
Nos. C554-C558 (5) 1.25
Set value 36

Flower Type of 1975

1975, Nov. 18 Litho. *Perf. 11½x12*

C559 A227 1.30s Pitcairnia pungens 15 15
C560 A227 2s Scarlet sage 25 15
C561 A227 3s Amaryllis 25 15
C562 A227 4s Opuntia quitense 30 15
C563 A227 5s Amaryllis 40 15
Nos. C559-C563 (5) 1.35
Set value 55

Tail Assemblies and Emblem AP134

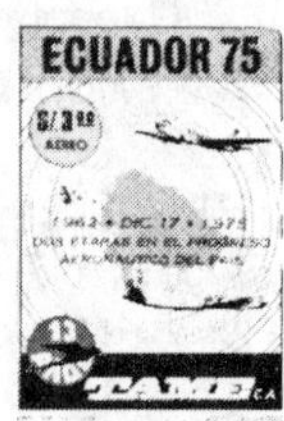

Planes over Map of Ecuador AP135

1975, Dec. 17 Litho. *Perf. 11½*

C564 AP134 1.30s bl & multi 15 15
C565 AP135 3s multi 18 15
Set value 17

TAME, Military Transport Airline, 13th anniversary.

Benalcázar Statue — AP136

1976, Feb. 6 Litho. *Perf. 11½*

C566 AP136 2s multi 15 15
C567 AP136 3s multi 22 15
Set value 15

Sebastián de Benalcázar (1495-1550), Spanish conquistador, founder of Quito.

Archaeology Type of 1975

Designs: 1.30s, Seated man, Carchi Culture. 2s, Funerary urn, Tuncahuan Culture. 3s, Priest, Bahia de Caraquez Culture. 4s, Snail's shell, Cuasmal Culture. 5s, Bowl supported by figurines, Guangala Culture.

1976, Feb. 12 Litho. *Perf. 11½*

C568 A278 1.30s multi 20 20
C569 A278 2s multi 30 15
C570 A278 3s multi 40 15
C571 A278 4s multi 60 15
C572 A278 5s multi 80 15
Nos. C568-C572 (5) 2.30
Set value 66

Fruit Type of 1976

1976, Mar. 30

C573 A280 2s Apples 15 15
C574 A280 5s Rose 28 15
Set value 21

Lufthansa Jet — AP137

1976, June 25 Litho. *Perf. 12*

C575 AP137 10s bl & multi 65 35

Lufthansa, 50th anniversary.

An imperf. 20s miniature sheet exists, similar to No. C575 enlarged, with overprinted black bar covering line below "Lufthansa." Size: 90x115mm.

Projected PO, Quito — AP138

Fruit Peddler — AP139

1976, Aug. 10 Litho. *Perf. 12*

C576 AP138 5s blk & multi 28 15

Design for new General Post Office, Quito.

1976, July 25

Designs: No. C578, Longshoreman. No. C579, Cerros del Carmen and Santa Ana, hills of Guayaquil, horiz. No. C580, Sebastián de Belalcázar. No. C581, Francisco de Orellana. No. C582, Chief Guayas and his wife Quila.

C577 AP139 1.30s red & multi 15 15
C578 AP139 1.30s red & multi 15 15
C579 AP139 1.30s red & multi 15 15
C580 AP139 2s red & multi 20 15
C581 AP139 2s red & multi 20 15
C582 AP139 2s red & multi 20 15
Nos. C577-C582 (6) 1.05
Set value 66

Founding of Guayaquil, 441st anniversary.

Emblem and Laurel AP140

1976, Aug. 9

C583 AP140 1.30s yel & multi 15 15

Bolivarian Soc. of Ecuador, 50th anniv.

Western Hemisphere and Equator Monument AP141

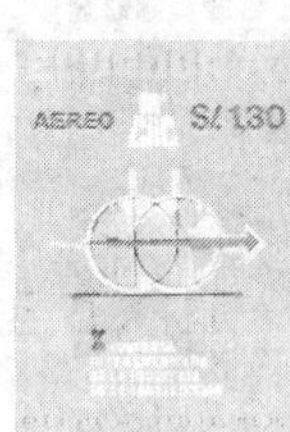
Congress Emblem AP142

1976, Sept. 6

C584 AP141 2s multi 15 15

Souvenir Sheet

Imperf

C585 AP141 5s multi 2.50 2.50

3rd Conference of Pan-American Transport Ministers, Quito, Sept. 6-11. No. C585 contains design similar to No. C584 with black denomination and red control number in margin.

1976, Sept. 27 Litho. *Perf. 11½*

C586 AP142 1.30s bl & multi 15 15
C587 AP142 3s bl & multi 30 30

Souvenir Sheet

Imperf

C588 AP142 10s bl & multi 1.00 1.00

10th Inter-American Congress of the Construction Industry, Quito, Sept. 27-30.

George Washington AP143

American Bicentennial: 5s, Naval battle, Sept. 23, 1779, in which the Bonhomme Richard, commanded by John Paul Jones, defeated and captured the Serapis, British man-of-war, off Yorkshire coast, horiz.

1976, Oct. 18 Litho. *Perf. 12*

C589 AP143 3s blk & multi 60 30
C590 AP143 5s red brn & yel 90 45

Dr. Hideyo Noguchi — AP144

Luis Cordero — AP145

1976 Litho. *Perf. 11½*

C591 AP144 3s yel & multi 25 25

Dr. Hideyo Noguchi (1876-1928), bacteriologist (at Rockefeller Institute). A 10s imperf. miniature sheet in same design exists without "Aereo." Size: 95x114mm.

1976, Dec. Litho. *Perf. 11½*

C592 AP145 2s multi 15 15

Luis Cordero (1833-1912), president of Ecuador.

Mariuxi Febres Cordero — AP146

1976, Dec. *Perf. 11½*

C593 AP146 3s multi 25 15

Mariuxi Febres Cordero, South American swimming champion.

Flags and Monument AP147

1976, Nov. 9 *Perf. 12*

C594 AP147 3s multi 25 15

Miniature Sheet

Imperf

C595 AP147 5s multi 50 50

2nd Meeting of the Agriculture Ministers of the Andean Countries, Quito, Nov. 8-10.

Sister Catalina AP148

Congress Hall, Quito AP149

1977, June 17 Litho. *Perf. 12x11½*

C596 AP148 1.30s blk & pale sal 15 15

Sister Catalina de Jesus Herrera (1717-1795), writer.

1977, Aug. 15 Litho. *Perf. 12x11½*

C597 AP149 5s multi 40 15
a. 10s souvenir sheet 1.00 1.00

11th General Assembly of Pan-American Institute of Geography and History, Quito, Aug. 15-30. No. C597a contains the designs of types A282 and AP149 without denominations and with simulated perforations.

Pres. Alfonso López Michelsen, Flag of Colombia — AP150

Designs: 5s, Pres. López M. of Colombia, Pres. Alfredo Povedo B. of Ecuador and aide. 7s, as 5s, vert. 9s, 10s, Presidents with aides.

1977 *Perf. 12*

C598 AP150 2.60s multi 30 15
C599 AP150 5s multi 60 15
C600 AP150 7s multi 60 15
C601 AP150 9s multi 75 50

Imperf

C602 AP150 10s multi 70 70

Meeting of the Presidents of Ecuador and Colombia and Declaration of Putumayo, Feb. 25, 1977. Nos. C598-C602 are overprinted in multiple fluorescent, colorless rows: INSTITUTO GEOGRAFICO MILITAR GOBIERNO DEL ECUADOR.

Ceramic Figure, Tolita Culture AP151

Designs: 9s, Divine Shepherdess, sculpture by Bernardo de Legarda. 11s, The Fruit Seller, sculpture by Legarda. 20s, Sun God, pre-Columbian gold mask.

1977, Aug. 24 *Perf. 12*

C603 AP151 7s gold & multi 60 30
C604 AP151 9s gold & multi 80 35
C605 AP151 11s gold & multi 1.00 75

Souvenir Sheet

Gold Embossed

Imperf

C606 AP151 20s vio, bl, blk & gold 2.50 2.50

Central Bank of Ecuador, 50th anniversary. Nos. C603-C605 overprinted like Nos. C598-C602.

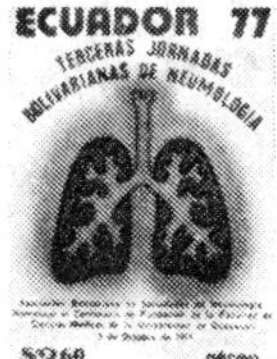

Lungs — AP152

Brother Miguel, St. Peter's, Rome — AP153

1977, Oct. 5 Litho. *Perf. 12x11½*

C607 AP152 2.60s multi 22 22

3rd Cong. of the Bolivarian Pneumonic Soc. and cent. of the founding of the medical faculty of the University of Guayaquil.

1977

C608 AP153 2.60s multi 22 15

Beatification of Brother Miguel.

Peralta Type of 1977

Design: 2.60s, Titles of works by Peralta and his bookmark.

1977 *Perf. 11½*

C609 A284 2.60s multi 22 22

Broadcast Tower — AP154

Remigio Romero y Cordero — AP155

1977, Dec. 2 Litho. *Perf. 12x11½*

C610 AP154 5s multi 40 40

9th World Telecommunications Day.

1978, Mar. 2 Litho. *Perf. 12½x11½*

C611 AP155 3s multi 15 15
C612 AP155 10.60s multi 55 25

Imperf

C612A AP155 10s multi 75 75

Remigio Romero y Cordero (1895-1967), poet. No. C612A contains a vignette similar to Nos. C611-C612.

Dr. Vicente Corral Moscoso — AP156

Faces — AP157

Design: 5s, Hospital emblem with Caduceus.

1978, Apr. 12 Litho. *Imperf.*

C613 AP156 5s multi 40 15

Perf. 12x11½

C614 AP156 7.60s multi 60 60

Inauguration (in 1977) of Dr. Vicente Corral Moscoso Regional Hospital, Cuenca.

1978, Mar. 17

Designs: 9s, Emblems and flags of Ecuador. 10s, 11s, Hands reaching for light.

C615 AP157 7s multi 42 20
C616 AP157 9s multi 55 20
C617 AP157 11s multi 65 20

Imperf

C618 AP157 10s multi 55 55

Ecuadorian Social Security Institute, 50th anniversary.

Geographical Institute Type of 1978

Design: 7.60s, Plane over map of Ecuador with mountains.

1978, Apr. 12 Litho. *Perf. 11½*

C619 A287 7.60s multi 60 40

Imperf

C620 A287 10s multi 90 90

No. C620 contains 2 vignettes with simulated perforations in designs of Nos. 967 and C619.

Lions Type of 1978

1978 *Perf. 11½*

C621 A288 5s multi 28 20
C622 A288 6.20s multi 35 25

Imperf

C623 A288 10s multi 55 55

No. C623 contains a vignette similar to Nos. C621-C622.

San Martin — AP158

1978, Apr. 13 Litho. *Perf. 12*

C624 AP158 10.60s multi 65 25

Imperf

C625 AP158 10s multi 55 55

Gen. José de San Martin (1778-1850), soldier and statesman. No. C625 contains a vignette similar to No. C624.

Bank Type of 1978

Design: 5s, Bank emblem.

1978, Sept. Litho. *Perf. 11½*

C626 A289 5s gray & multi 28 15

Soccer Type of 1978

Designs: 2.60s, "Gauchito" and Games' emblem. 5s, "Gauchito." 7s, Soccer ball. 9s, Games' emblem, vert. 10s, Games' emblem.

1978, Nov. 1 *Perf. 12*

C627 A290 2.60s multi 15 15
C628 A290 7s multi 42 25
C629 A290 9s multi 55 25

Imperf

C630 A290 5s blk & bl 50 50
C631 A290 10s blk & bl 1.00 1.00

Bernardo O'Higgins AP159

Old Men of Vilcabamba AP160

1978, Nov. 11 Litho. *Perf. 12x11½*

C632 AP159 10.60s multi 65 32

Imperf

C633 AP159 10s multi 55 55

Gen. Bernardo O'Higgins (1778-1842), Chilean soldier and statesman. No. C633 contains a vignette similar to No. C632.

1978, Nov. 11 *Perf. 12x11½*

C634 AP160 5s multi 40 25

Vilcabamba, valley of longevity.

Humphrey
AP161

Virgin and Child
AP162

1978, Nov. 27 Litho. *Perf. 12x11½*

C635 AP61 5s multi	40	25

Hubert H. Humphrey (1911-1978), Vice President of the US.

1978

Children's Drawings: 4.60s, Holy Family. 6.20s, Candle and children.

C636 AP162 2.20s multi	20	15
C637 AP162 4.60s multi	40	25
C638 AP162 6.20s multi	60	35

Christmas 1978.

Village, by Anibal Villacis — AP163

Ecuadorian Painters: No. C640, Mountain Village, by Gilberto Almeida. No. C641, Bay, by Roura Oxandaberro. No. C642, Abstract, by Luis Molinari. No. C643, Statue, by Oswaldo Viteri. No. C644, Tools, by Enrique Tabara.

1978, Dec. 9 *Perf. 12*

C639 AP163 5s multi	40	25
C640 AP163 5s multi	40	25
C641 AP163 5s multi	40	25
C642 AP163 5s multi	40	25
C643 AP163 5s multi	40	25
C644 AP163 5s multi	40	25
Nos. C639-C644 (6)	2.40	1.50

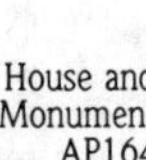

House and Monument AP164

Design: 3.40s, Monument, vert.

1979, Feb. 27 Litho. *Perf. 12*

C645 AP164 2.40s multi	15	15
C646 AP164 3.40s multi	18	18

Imperf

C647 AP164 10s multi	65	65

Sesquicentennial of Battle of Portete and Tarqui. #C647 contains vignettes similar to #C645-C646.

Fish and Ship — AP165

Flags of Ecuador and US — AP166

Designs: 7s, Map of Ecuador and Galapagos showing territorial waters, horiz. 9s, Map of South America with west-coast territorial waters.

Perf. 12x11½, 11½x12

1979, July 23 Litho. Wmk. 367

C648 AP165 5s multi	50	25
C649 AP165 7s multi	60	25
C650 AP165 9s multi	90	25

Declaration of 200-mile territorial limit, 25th anniversary.

1979, Aug. 3 *Perf. 12x11½*

Designs: 10.60s, Bells in Quito clock tower, horiz. 13.60s, Aerial view of Galapagos coast.

C651 A293 10.60s multi	65	25
C652 A293 13.60s multi	70	25

Size: 115x91mm

Imperf

Unwmk.

C653 A293 10s multi	65	65

National heritage: Quito and Galapagos Islands. No. C653 contains vignettes similar to Nos. 977, C651-C652.

1979, Aug. Wmk. 367 *Perf. 11½x12*

C654 AP166 7.60s multi	40	40
C655 AP166 10.60s multi	60	60

Size: 115x91mm

Imperf

Unwmk.

C656 AP166 10s multi	65	65

5th anniv. of Ecuador-US Chamber of Commerce. No. C656 contains vignettes similar to Nos. C654-C655.

Smiling Girl, IYC Emblem — AP167

Perf. 12x11½

1979, Sept. 7 Litho. Wmk. 367

C657 AP167 10s multi	65	32

International Year of the Child.

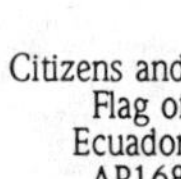
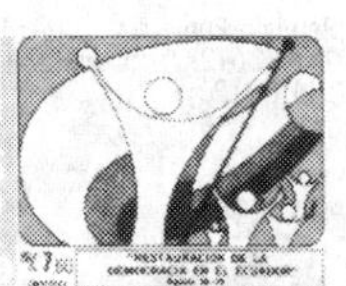

Citizens and Flag of Ecuador AP168

Design: 10.60s, Pres. Jaime Roldas Aguilera, flag of Ecuador, vert.

Perf. 11½

1979, Sept. 27 Litho. Unwmk.

C658 AP168 7.60s multi	75	30

Wmk. 367

C659 AP168 10.60s multi	90	25

Restoration of democracy to Ecuador.

Ecuador Coat of Arms, Olympic Rings and Eagle — AP169

Perf. 12x11½

1979, Nov. 23 Unwmk.

C660 AP169 28s multi	1.50	1.00

5th National Games, Cuenca.

CIESPAL Building, Quito AP170

Perf. 11½x12½

1979, Dec. 26 Wmk. 367

C661 AP170 10.60s multi	65	40

Opening of Ecuadorian Institute of Engineers building.

Olmedo Type of 1980

Perf. 12x11½

1980, Apr. 29 Litho. Unwmk.

C662 A294 10s multi	65	40

Tribal Chief Type of 1980

Wmk. 367 (#C663, C667), Unwmkd.

1980, May 12

Indo-American Tribal Chiefs: No. C663, Cuauhtemoc, Mexico. No. C664, Lempira, Honduras No. C665, Nicaragua. No. C666, Lambaré, Paraguay. No. C667, Urraca, Panama. No. C668, Anacaona, Haiti No. C669, Caupolican, Chile. No. C670, Tacun-Uman, Guatemala. No. C671, Calarca, Colombia. No. C672. Garabito, Costa Rica. No. C673, Hatuey, Cuba. No. C674, Cmarao, Brazil. No. C675, Tehuelche, Argentina. No. C676, Tupaj Katri, Bolivia. 17.80s, Sequoyah, US. 22.80s, Ruminahui, Ecuador.

C663 A295 7.60s multi	50	25
C664 A295 7.60s multi	50	25
C665 A295 7.60s multi	50	25
C666 A295 10s multi	65	32
C667 A295 10s multi	65	32
C668 A295 10.60s multi	65	32
C669 A295 10.60s multi	65	32
C670 A295 10.60s multi	65	32
C671 A295 12.80s multi	85	42
C672 A295 12.80s multi	85	42
C673 A295 12.80s multi	85	42
C674 A295 13.60s multi	85	42
C675 A295 13.60s multi	85	42
C676 A295 13.60s multi	85	42
C677 A295 17.80s multi	1.00	52
C678 A295 22.80s multi	1.40	70
Nos. C663-C678 (16)	12.25	6.09

Royal Visit Type of 1980

Perf. 11½x12

1980, May 18 Unwmk.

C679 A296 10.60s multi	65	32

Pichincha Provincial Development Council Building — AP171

1980, June 1 *Perf. 12x11½*

C680 AP171 10.60s multi	75	32

Progress in Pichincha Province.

Indian Type of 1980

1980, June 10 Litho. *Perf. 12x11½*

C681 A297 7.60s Salasaca boy, Tungurahua	50	40
C682 A297 10s Amula woman, Chimborazo	65	32
C683 A297 10.60s Canar woman, Canar	65	32
C684 A297 13.60s Colorado Indian, Pichincha	85	42

Virgin of Mercy Type of 1980

1980, July 7 Litho. *Perf. 11½*

C685 A298 7.60s Cupola, cloisters	50	35
C686 A298 7.60s Gold screen	50	35
C687 A298 7.60s Quito from basilica tower	50	35
C688 A298 10.60s Retable	75	32
C689 A298 10.60s Pulpit	75	32
C690 A298 13.60s Cupola	1.00	42
C691 A298 13.60s Statue of Virgin	1.00	42
Nos. C685-C691 (7)	5.00	2.53

UPU Monument AP172

Marshal Sucre, by Marco Sales AP173

Design: 17.80s, Mail box, 1880.

1980, July 7 *Perf. 12*

C692 AP172 10.60s multi	75	40
C693 AP172 17.80s multi	1.25	65

Souvenir Sheet

C694 AP172 25s multi	2.25	1.10

UPU membership cent. No. C694 contains designs of C692 and C693, horiz., perf. 11½.

Olympic Type of 1980.

Design: 10.60s, 13.60s, Moscow '80 emblem, Olympic rings.

Perf. 12x11½

1980, July 19 Wmk. 395

C695 A299 10.60s multi	65	45
C696 A299 13.60s multi	85	60

Souvenir Sheet

C697 A299 30s multi	3.00	3.00

No. C697 contains vignettes in designs of Nos. 991 and C695.

1980

C698 AP173 10.60s multi	65	45

Marshal Antonio Jose de Sucre, death sesquicentennial.

Rotary International, 75th Anniversary — AP174

1980, Aug. 4 *Perf. 11½*

C699 AP174 10s multi	1.00	50

Riobamba Type of 1980

Design: 7.60s, 10.60s, Monstrance, Riobamba Cathedral, vert.

1980, Sept. 20 Litho. *Perf. 11½*

C700 A301 7.60s multi	50	25
C701 A301 10.60s multi	65	32

Souvenir Sheet

Imperf

C702 A301 30s multi	1.75	85

No. C702 contains vignettes in designs of Nos. 996-997.

Democracy Type of 1980

Designs: 7.60s, 10.60s, Pres. Aguilera and voter.

Perf. 12x11½

1980, Oct. 9 Litho. Wmk. 395

C703 A302 7.60s multi	50	30
C704 A302 10.60s multi	65	30

Souvenir Sheet

Imperf

C705 A302 15s multi	90	45

No. C705 contains vignettes in designs of Nos. 999 and C703.

OPEC Type of 1980

20th Anniversary of OPEC: 7.60s, Men holding OPEC emblem, vert.

1980, Nov. 8 *Perf. 11½x12*

C706 A303 7.60s multi	50	35

Carchi Province Type of 1980

Designs: 10.60s, Governor's Palace, vert. 17.80s, Victory Museum, Central Square, vert.

1980, Nov. 21 *Perf. 13*
C707 A304 10.60c multi 75 40
C708 A304 17.80s multi 1.25 65

Orchid Type of 1980

Perf. 12x11½, 11½x12

1980, Nov. 22
C709 A305 7.60s *Anguloa uniflora* 70 50
C710 A305 10.60s *Scuticaria salesiana* 90 32
C711 A305 50s *Helcia sanguinolenta*, vert. 1.50 1.00
C712 A305 100s *Anguloa virginalis* 2.00 2.00

Souvenir Sheets

Imperf

C713 A305 20s multi 2.00 2.00
C714 A305 20s multi 2.00 2.00

Nos. C713-C714 contain vignettes in designs of Nos. C709-C710 and C711-C712 respectively.

Christmas Type of 1980

Designs: 7.60s, Pope blessing crowd, vert. 10.60s, Portrait, vert.

1980, Dec. 27 *Perf. 12*
C715 A306 7.60s multi 50 35
C716 A306 10.60s multi 65 32

Isidro Cueva — AP175

Simon Bolivar, by Marco Salas — AP176

1980, Nov. 20 *Perf. 13*
C717 AP175 18.20s multi 1.50 75

Dr. Isidro Ayora Cueva, former president, birth centenary.

1980, Dec. 17 *Perf. 11½*
C718 AP176 13.60s multi 1.25 50

Simon Bolivar death sesquicentennial.

Turtle, Galapagos Islands AP177

Design: 100s, Oldest Ecuadorian mail box, 1793, vert.

1981, Feb. 12 Litho. *Perf. 13*
C719 AP177 50s multi 4.00 3.00
C720 AP177 100s multi 5.75 3.75

HCJB Type of 1981

1981 Litho. *Perf. 13*
C721 A311 7.60s Emblem, horiz. 50 25
C722 A311 10.60s Emblem, diff. 65 25

Soccer Players — AP178

1981, July 8
C723 AP178 7.60s Emblem 70 35
C724 AP178 10.60s shown 90 32
C725 AP178 13.60s World Cup 1.25 50

Souvenir Sheets

C726 AP178 20s multi 2.00 2.00
C727 AP178 20s multi 2.00 2.00

1982 World Cup Soccer Championship. Nos. C726-C727 contain vignettes in designs of Nos. C723 and C724 respectively.

Picasso Type of 1981

1981, Oct. 26 Litho. *Perf. 13*
C728 A313a 7.60s Still-life 45 35
C729 A313a 10.60s First Communion, vert. 65 32
C730 A313a 13.60s Las Meninas, vert. 80 50

Size: 110x90mm

Imperf

C731 A313a 20s multi 1.25 1.25

No. C731 contains designs of Nos. C730, C729.

World Food Day Type of 1981

1981, Dec. 31 Litho. *Perf. 13x13½*
C732 A314 10s Farming, vert. 65 32

IYD Type of 1982

1982, Feb. 25 Litho. *Perf. 13*
C733 A316 7.60s Emblem 50 25
C734 A316 10.60s Man with crutch 65 32

Montalvo Type of 1982

1982 Litho. *Perf. 13*
C735 A318 5s Home, horiz. 70 35

Swimming Type of 1982

1982, July 30
C736 A320 10.20s Emblem, vert. 65 32
C737 A320 14.20s Diving, vert. 85 42

Pres. Jaime Roldos, (1940-81), Mrs. Martha Roldos, Independence Monument, Quito — AP179

1983, May 25 Litho. *Perf. 12*
C738 AP179 13.60s multi 45 35

Souvenir Sheet

Imperf

C739 AP179 20s multi 70 70

AIR POST SEMI-POSTAL STAMPS

Nos. C119-C123 Surcharged in Blue or Red:

Hospital
Méndez + $ 0,50

1944, May 9 Unwmk. *Perf. 12*
CB1 AP26 50c + 50c 3.00 3.00
CB2 AP26 70c + 30c 3.00 3.00
CB3 AP26 3s + 50c (R) 3.00 3.00
CB4 AP26 5s + 1s (R) 3.00 3.00
CB5 AP26 10s + 2s 3.00 3.00
Nos. CB1-CB5 (5) 15.00 15.00

The surtax aided Mendez Hospital.

AIR POST REGISTRATION STAMPS

Issued by Sociedad Colombo-Alemana de Transportes Aereos (SCADTA)

Nos. C3 and C3a Overprinted "R" in Carmine

1928-29 Wmk. 116 *Perf. 14x14½*
CF1 AP6 1s on 20c (#C3) 100.00 90.00
a. 1s on 20c (#C3a) ('29) 125.00 100.00

No. C18 Overprinted "R" in Black

1929, Apr. 1 Wmk. 127 *Perf. 14*
CF2 AP2 1s rose 60.00 50.00

AIR POST OFFICIAL STAMPS

Nos. C8-C15 Overprinted in Red or Black **OFICIAL**

1929, May Unwmk. *Perf. 12*
CO1 AP1 2c black (R) 40 40
CO2 AP1 5c car rose 40 40
CO3 AP1 10c deep brn 40 40
CO4 AP1 20c dark vio 40 40
CO5 AP1 50c deep grn 1.25 1.25
CO6 AP1 1s dark blue 1.25 1.25
a. Inverted overprint 225.00
CO7 AP1 5s org yel 6.00 5.00
CO8 AP1 10s org red 65.00 50.00
Nos. CO1-CO8 (8) 75.10 59.10

Establishment of commercial air service in Ecuador.
Counterfeits of No. CO8 exist.
See Nos. CO9-CO12. For overprints and surcharges see Nos. C35-C38.

1930, Jan. 9
CO9 AP1 50c olive brn 1.00 1.00
CO10 AP1 1s car lake 1.50 1.50
CO11 AP1 5s olive grn 3.00 3.00
CO12 AP1 10s black 7.50 7.50

For surcharges and overprint see Nos. C36-C38.

Air Post Stamps of 1937 Overprinted in Black **OFICIAL**

1937, Aug. 19
CO13 AP7 10c chestnut 16 15
CO14 AP7 20c olive blk 22 15
CO15 AP7 70c blk brn 22 15
CO16 AP7 1s gray black 32 15
CO17 AP7 2s dark vio 40 26
Nos. CO13-CO17 (5) 1.32 86

For overprints see Nos. 463-464.

No. C79 Overprinted in Black **OFICIAL**

1940, Aug. 1 *Perf. 12½x13*
CO18 AP15 5s emerald 80 60

Catalogue values for unused stamps in this section, from this point to the end of the section, are for Never Hinged items.

Nos. C352-C354 Overprinted: "1961 oficial"

1964 *Perf. 13½*
CO19 AP86 50c bl & multi 1.00 1.00
CO20 AP86 80c yel & multi 1.00 1.00
CO21 AP86 1.30s pale green & multi 1.00 1.00

SPECIAL DELIVERY STAMPS

SD1

1928 Unwmk. *Perf. 12*
E1 SD1 2c on 2c blue 4.00 *4.50*
E2 SD1 5c on 2c blue 3.50 *4.50*
E3 SD1 10c on 2c blue 3.50 *3.00*
a. "10 CTVOS" inverted 10.50 *13.00*
E4 SD1 20c on 2c blue 5.00 *4.50*
E5 SD1 50c on 2c blue 6.00 *4.50*
Nos. E1-E5 (5) 22.00 *21.00*

No. RA49A Surcharged in Red **EXPRESO 20 Ctvs.**

1945
E6 PT18 20c on 5c green 15 15

LATE FEE STAMP

No. RA49A Surcharged in Black **U. H. 10 Ctvs.**

1945 Unwmk. *Perf. 12*
I1 PT18 10c on 5c green 15 15

POSTAGE DUE STAMPS

Numeral D1

Coat of Arms D2

1896 Engr. Wmk. 117 *Perf. 12*
J1 D1 1c blue green 2.00 *2.00*
J2 D1 2c blue green 2.00 2.00
J3 D1 5c blue green 2.00 2.00
J4 D1 10c blue green 2.00 *5.00*
J5 D1 20c blue green 2.00 *5.00*
J6 D1 50c blue green 2.00 *5.00*
J7 D1 100c blue green 2.00 *3.75*
Nos. J1-J7 (7) 14.00 *24.75*

Reprints are on very thick paper with distinct watermark and vertical paper-weave direction. Value 15c each.

Unwmk.

J8 D1 1c blue green *2.50 3.00*
J9 D1 2c blue green *2.50 3.00*
J10 D1 5c blue green *2.50 3.00*
J11 D1 10c blue green *2.50 3.00*
J12 D1 20c blue green *2.50 3.75*
J13 D1 50c blue green *2.50 5.25*
J14 D1 100c blue green *2.50 7.50*
Nos. J8-J14 (7) 17.50 *28.50*

1929
J15 D2 5c deep blue 15 15
J16 D2 10c orange yellow 15 15
J17 D2 20c red 20 20

Numeral — D3

Perf. 13½

1958, Nov. Unwmk. Litho.
J18 D3 10c bright lilac 15 15
J19 D3 50c emerald 15 15
J20 D3 1s maroon 15 15
J21 D3 2s red 20 20
Set value 46 46

OFFICIAL STAMPS

Regular Issues of 1881 and 1887 Handstamped in Black **OFICIAL**

1886 Unwmk. *Perf. 12*

O1 A5 1c yel brn 75 75
O2 A6 2c lake 1.00 1.00
O3 A7 5c blue 2.00 2.50
O4 A8 10c orange 1.50 1.00
O5 A9 20c gray vio 1.50 1.50
O6 A10 50c bl grn 4.25 3.50
Nos. O1-O6 (6) 11.00 10.25

1887

O7 A12 1c green 1.00 75
O8 A13 2c vermilion 1.00 75
O9 A14 5c blue 1.50 75
O10 A15 80c ol grn 5.00 3.00

Nos. O1 to O10 are known with red handstamp but these are believed to be speculative.

The overprint on the 1886-87 issues is handstamped and is found in various positions.

Flores — O1

Arms — O1a

1892

Carmine Overprint

O11 O1 1c ultra 15 18
O12 O1 2c ultra 15 18
O13 O1 5c ultra 15 18
O14 O1 10c ultra 15 15
O15 O1 20c ultra 15 15
O16 O1 50c ultra 15 35
O17 O1 1s ultra 28 35
Set value 76

1894

O18 O1a 1c slate green (R) 8.00
O19 O1a 2c lake (Bk) 8.00

Nos. O18 and O19 were not placed in use.

Rocafuerte — O2

Dated 1894

1894

Carmine Overprint

O20 O2 1c gray black 18 35
O21 O2 2c gray black 18 18
O22 O2 5c gray black 18 18
O23 O2 10c gray black 15 15
O24 O2 20c gray black 22 18
O25 O2 50c gray black 1.00 1.00
O26 O2 1s gray black 1.40 1.40
Nos. O20-O26 (7) 3.31 3.44

Dated 1895

1895

Carmine Overprint

O27 O2 1c gray black 1.50 1.50
O28 O2 2c gray black 2.00 2.00
O29 O2 5c gray black 35 35
O30 O2 10c gray black 2.00 2.00
O31 O2 20c gray black 3.50 3.50
O32 O2 50c gray black *8.75 8.75*
O33 O2 1s gray black 1.00 1.00
Nos. O27-O33 (7) *19.10 19.10*

Reprints of 1894-95 issues are on very thick paper with paper weave found both horizontal and vertical for all denominations. Generally they are blacker than originals.

For overprints see Nos. O50-O91.

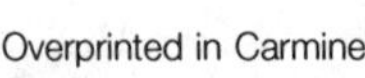
Overprinted in Carmine

1896 Wmk. 117

O34 A21 1c olive bister 25 25
O35 A22 2c olive bister 25 25
O36 A23 5c olive bister 25 25
O37 A24 10c olive bister 25 25
O38 A25 20c olive bister 25 25
O39 A26 50c olive bister 25 25
O40 A27 1s olive bister 70 52
O41 A28 5s olive bister 1.25 1.10
Nos. O34-O41 (8) 3.45 3.12

Reprints of Nos. O34-O41 are on thick paper with vertical paper weave direction.

Unwmk.

O42 A21 1c olive bister 70 70
O43 A22 2c olive bister 70 70
O44 A23 5c olive bister 70 50
O45 A24 10c olive bister 52 42
O46 A25 20c olive bister 70 70
O47 A26 50c olive bister 70 1.00
O48 A27 1s olive bister 1.40 90
O49 A28 5s olive bister 2.00 1.50
Nos. O42-O49 (8) 7.42 6.42

Reprints of Nos. O42-O49 all have overprint in black. Value 15 cents each.

Issue of 1894 Overprinted

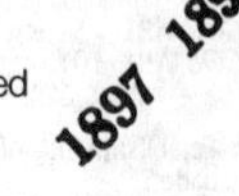

1897-98

O50 O2 1c gray black *3.50 3.50*
O51 O2 2c gray black *4.25 4.25*
O52 O2 5c gray black *45.00 45.00*
O53 O2 10c gray black *4.25 4.25*
O54 O2 20c gray black *1.90 1.25*
O55 O2 50c gray black *10.00 10.00*
O56 O2 1s gray black *15.00 15.00*
Nos. O50-O56 (7) *83.90 83.25*

Issue of 1894 Overprinted

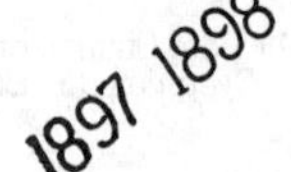

O57 O2 1c gray black *1.00 1.00*
O58 O2 2c gray black *2.50* 90
O59 O2 5c gray black *4.25 4.25*
O60 O2 10c gray black *45.00 45.00*
O61 O2 20c gray black *1.00 1.00*
O62 O2 50c gray black *4.25 3.50*
O63 O2 1s gray black *60.00 60.00*
Nos. O57-O63 (7) *118.00 115.65*

Issue of 1894 Overprinted **1897 Y 1898**

O64 O2 1c gray black *8.50 8.50*
O65 O2 2c gray black *8.50 8.50*
O66 O2 5c gray black *8.50 8.50*
O67 O2 10c gray black *8.50 8.50*
O68 O2 20c gray black *8.50 8.50*
O69 O2 50c gray black *8.50 8.50*
O70 O2 1s gray black *8.50 8.50*
Nos. O64-O70 (7) *59.50 59.50*

Issue of 1895 Overprinted in Black like Nos. O50-O56

O71 O2 1c gray black *2.00 2.00*
O72 O2 2c gray black *1.40 1.40*
O73 O2 5c gray black *2.00 2.00*
O74 O2 10c gray black *2.00 2.00*
O75 O2 20c gray black *3.50 3.50*
O76 O2 50c gray black *20.00*
O77 O2 1s gray black *40.00 40.00*
Nos. O71-O77 (7) *70.90*

Issue of 1895 Overprinted like Nos. O57-O63

O78 O2 1c gray black *90 90*
O79 O2 2c gray black *65 65*
O80 O2 5c gray black *1.75 1.75*
O81 O2 10c gray black *65 65*
O82 O2 20c gray black *70* 42
O83 O2 50c gray black *1.40* 52
O84 O2 1s gray black *5.25 5.25*
Nos. O78-O84 (7) *11.30 10.14*

Issue of 1895 Overprinted like Nos. O64-O70

O85 O2 1c gray black *40.00 40.00*
O86 O2 2c gray black *1.00 1.00*
O87 O2 5c gray black *80* 60
O88 O2 10c gray black *35.00 35.00*
O89 O2 20c gray black *60.00 60.00*
O90 O2 50c gray black *13.00 13.00*
O91 O2 1s gray black *80.00 80.00*
Nos. O85-O91 (7) *229.80 229.60*

Many forged overprints of Nos. O50-O91 exist, made on the original stamps and reprints.

O3

Black Surcharge

1898-99 *Perf. 15, 16*

O92 O3 5c on 50c lilac 22 22
a. Inverted surcharge 1.00 1.00
O93 O3 10c on 20s org 60 60
a. Double surcharge 1.50 1.50
O94 O3 10c on 50c lilac *65.00 65.00*
O95 O3 20c on 50c lilac 1.75 1.75
O96 O3 20c on 50s green 1.50 1.50
Nos. O92-O96 (5) *69.07 69.07*

Green Surcharge

O97 O3 5c on 50c lilac 90 90
a. Double surcharge 1.40
b. Double surcharge, blk and grn 4.50
c. Same as "b," blk surch. invtd. 1.40

Red Surcharge

1899

O98 O3 5c on 50c lilac 90 90
a. Double surcharge 1.40
b. Dbl. surch., blk and red 1.75
O99 O3 20c on 50s green 1.75 1.75
a. Inverted surcharge 3.50
b. Dbl. surch., red and blk 5.50

Similar Surcharge in Black

Value in Words in Two Lines

O100 O3 1c on 5c blue *80.00*

Red Surcharge

O101 O3 2c on 5c blue *125.00*
O102 O3 4c on 20c blue *100.00*

Types of Regular Issue of 1899 Overprinted in Black

OFICIAL

1899 *Perf. 14, 15*

O103 A37 2c org & blk 28 *70*
O104 A39 10c org & blk 28 *70*
O105 A40 20c org & blk 20 *1.10*
O106 A41 50c org & blk 20 *1.40*

For overprint see No. O167.

OFICIAL

The above overprint was applied to remainders of the postage stamps of 1904 with the idea of increasing their salability. They were never regularly in use as official stamps.

Regular Issue of 1911-13 Overprinted in Black

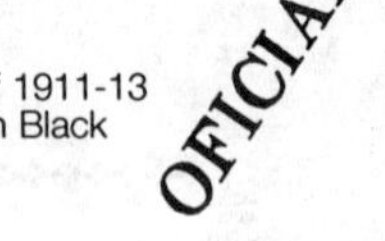

1913 *Perf. 12*

O107 A71 1c scar & blk 1.50 1.50
O108 A72 2c bl & blk 1.50 1.50
O109 A73 3c org & blk 1.00 1.00
O110 A74 5c scar & blk 2.00 2.00
O111 A75 10c bl & blk 2.00 2.00
Nos. O107-O111 (5) 8.00 8.00

Regular Issue of 1911-13 Overprinted

Overprint 22x3½mm

1916-17

O112 A72 2c bl & blk 10.00 7.50
O113 A74 5c scar & blk 10.00 7.50
O114 A75 10c bl & blk 6.00 5.00

Overprint 25x4mm

O115 A71 1c scar & blk 52 52
O116 A72 2c bl & blk 70 70
a. Inverted overprint 1.00 1.00
O117 A73 3c org & blk 42 42
O118 A74 5c scar & blk 70 70
O119 A75 10c bl & blk 70 70
Nos. O115-O119 (5) 3.04 3.04

Same Overprint On Regular Issue of 1915-17

O120 A71 1c orange 60 60
O121 A72 2c green 60 60
O122 A73 3c black 1.00 1.00
O123 A78 4c red & blk 1.00 1.00
a. Inverted overprint 5.00
O124 A74 5c violet 60 60
O125 A75 10c blue 1.25 1.25
O126 A79 20c grn & blk 7.50 7.50
Nos. O120-O126 (7) 12.55 12.55

Regular Issues of 1911-17 Overprinted in Black or Red

OFICIAL

O127 A71 1c orange 40 40
O128 A72 2c green 40 40
O129 A73 3c blk (Bk) 30 30
O130 A73 3c blk (R) 40 30
a. Inverted overprint
O131 A78 4c red & blk 40 40
O132 A74 5c violet 75 30
O133 A75 10c bl & blk 2.00 75
O134 A75 10c blue 40 40
O135 A79 20c grn & blk 2.00 75
Nos. O127-O135 (9) 7.05 4.00

Regular Issue of 1920 Overprinted **OFICIAL**

1920

O136 A86 1c green 50 50
a. Inverted overprint 4.25 4.25
O137 A86 2c carmine 40 40
O138 A86 3c yel brn 50 50
O139 A86 4c dk grn 75 75
a. Inverted overprint 6.00 10.00
O140 A86 5c blue 75 75
O141 A86 6c orange 50 50
O142 A86 7c brown 75 75
O143 A86 8c yel grn 1.00 1.00
O144 A86 9c red 1.25 1.25
O145 A95 10c blue 75 75
O146 A86 15c gray 4.00 4.00
O147 A86 20c dp vio 5.00 5.00
O148 A86 30c violet 6.00 6.00
O149 A86 40c dk brn 8.00 8.00
O150 A86 50c dk grn 5.00 5.00
O151 A86 60c dk bl 6.00 6.00
O152 A86 70c gray 6.00 6.00
O153 A86 80c yellow 7.50 7.50
O154 A104 90c green 8.00 8.00
O155 A86 1s blue 15.00 15.00
Nos. O136-O155 (20) 77.65 77.65

Cent. of the independence of Guayaquil.

Stamps of 1911 Overprinted

1922

O156 A71 1c scar & blk 3.25 3.25
O157 A72 2c blue & blk 1.75 1.75

Revenue Stamps of 1919-1920 Overprinted like Nos. O156 and O157

1924

O158 PT3 1c dark blue 75 75
O159 PT3 2c green 4.25 4.25

Regular Issues of 1911-17 Overprinted

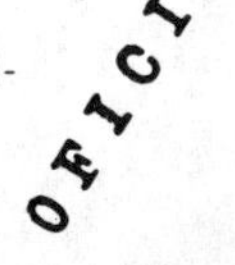

1924

O160 A71 1c orange 2.50 2.50
a. Inverted overprint 5.00

Overprinted in Black or Red **OFICIAL**

O161	A72	2c green	20	20
O162	A73	3c blk (R)	30	30
O163	A78	4c red & blk	50	50
O164	A74	5c violet	50	50
O165	A75	10c deep blue	50	50
O166	A76	1s grn & blk	2.50	2.50
		Nos. O160-O166 (7)	7.00	7.00

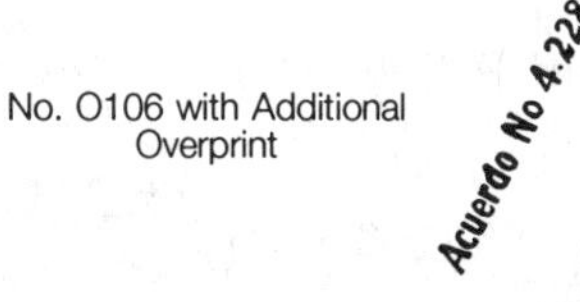

No. O106 with Additional Overprint **Acuerdo No 4.228**

1924 *Perf. 14, 15*

O167	A41	50c org & blk	1.00	1.00

Nos. O160-O167 exist with inverted overprint.

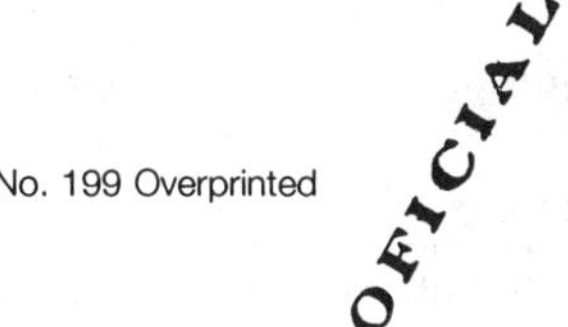

No. 199 Overprinted **OFICIAL**

1924 *Perf. 12*

O168	A71	1c orange	2.00	2.00

Regular Issues of 1911-25 Overprinted **OFICIAL**

1925

O169	A71	1c scar & blk	4.00	1.50
a.		Inverted overprint	5.00	
O170	A71	1c orange	20	20
a.		Inverted overprint	1.25	
O171	A72	2c green	20	20
a.		Inverted overprint	1.25	
O172	A73	3c blk (Bk)	25	18
O173	A73	3c blk (R)	40	40
O174	A78	4c red & blk	20	20
O175	A74	5c violet	30	30
O176	A74	5c rose	30	30
O177	A75	10c deep blue	20	20
		Nos. O169-O177 (9)	6.05	3.48

Regular Issues of 1916-25 Overprinted Vertically Up or Down **OFICIAL**

1927, Oct.

O178	A71	1c orange	75	75
O179	A86	2c carmine	75	75
O180	A86	3c yel brn	75	75
O181	A86	4c myr grn	75	75
O182	A86	5c pale bl	75	75
O183	A75	10c yel grn	75	75
		Nos. O178-O183 (6)	4.50	4.50

Regular Issues of 1920-27 Overprinted **OFICIAL**

1928

O184	A71	1c lt bl	40	40
O185	A86	2c carmine	40	40
O186	A86	3c yel brn	40	40
a.		Inverted overprint	2.00	
O187	A86	4c myr grn	40	40
O188	A86	5c lt bl	40	40
O189	A75	10c yel grn	40	40
O190	A109	20c violet	4.00	1.00
a.		Overprint reading up	1.50	1.00
		Nos. O184-O190 (7)	6.40	3.40

The overprint is placed vertically reading down on No. O190.

Regular Issue of 1936 Overprinted in Black **OFICIAL**

1936 *Perf. 14*

O191	A131	5c olive grn	20	15
O192	A132	10c brown	20	15
O193	A133	20c dark vio	30	30
O194	A134	1s dark car	50	50
O195	A135	2s dark blue	80	80
		Nos. O191-O195 (5)	2.00	1.90

Regular Postage Stamps of 1937 Overprinted in Black **OFICIAL**

1937 *Perf. 11½*

O196	A139	2c green	15	15
O197	A140	5c deep rose	15	15
O198	A141	10c blue	15	15
O199	A142	20c deep rose	15	15
O200	A143	1s olive green	16	15
		Set value	42	40

Catalogue values for unused stamps in this section, from this point to the end of the section, are for Never Hinged items.

Tobacco Stamp, Overprinted in Black
CORRESPONDENCIA OFICIAL

1946 **Unwmk.** *Rouletted*

O201	PT7	1c rose red	75	75

Communications Building, Quito — O4

1947 **Unwmk.** **Litho.** *Perf. 11*

O202	O4	30c brown	25	15
O203	O4	30c greenish blue	25	15
a.		Imperf., pair		
O204	O4	30c purple	25	15
		Set value		24

Nos. O202 to O204 overprinted "Primero la Patria!" and plane in dark blue are said to be essays.

No. 719 with Additional Diagonal Overprint *oficial*

1964 *Perf. 14x13*

O205	A231	80c block of 4	2.00	2.00

The "OEA" overprint covers four stamps, the "oficial" overprint is applied to every stamp.

A set of 20 imperforate items in the above Roosevelt design, some overprinted with the initials of various government ministries, was released in 1949. Later that year a set of 8 miniature sheets, bearing the same design plus a marginal inscription, "Presidencia (or Vicepresidencia) de la Republica," and a frame-line were released. In the editors' opinion, information justifying the listing of these issues has not been received.

POSTAL TAX STAMPS

Roca — PT1

1920 **Unwmk.** *Perf. 12*

RA1	PT1	1c orange	25	15

PT2

PT3

RA2	PT2	1c red & blue	50	15
a.		"de" inverted	4.00	4.00
b.		Double overprint	4.00	42
c.		Inverted overprint	4.00	42
RA3	PT3	1c deep blue	60	15
a.		Inverted overprint	2.50	70
b.		Double overprint	2.50	70

For overprints see Nos. O158-O159.

PT4

PT5

Red or Black Surcharge or Overprint

Stamp Dated 1911-1912

RA4	PT4	20c dp bl	27.50	15.00

Stamp Dated 1913-1914

RA5	PT4	20c dp bl (R)	1.00	35

Stamp Dated 1917-1918

RA6	PT4	20c ol grn (R)	3.00	50
a.		Dated 1919-20	*12.50*	
RA7	PT5	1c on 2c grn	40	15

Stamp Dated 1911-1912

RA8	PT5	1c on 5c grn	40	15
a.		Double surcharge		

Stamp Dated 1913-1914

RA9	PT5	1c on 5c grn	3.50	50
a.		Double surcharge	5.00	3.50

On Nos. RA7, RA8 and RA9 the surcharge is found reading upward or downward.
For surcharges see Nos. RA15-RA16.

Post Office — PT6

1920-24 **Engr.**

RA10	PT6	1c ol grn	15	15
RA11	PT6	2c dp grn	20	15
RA12	PT6	20c bis brn ('24)	65	15
RA13	PT6	2s violet	4.00	3.00
RA14	PT6	5s blue	7.00	5.00
		Nos. RA10-RA14 (5)	12.00	8.45

For overprints and surcharge see Nos. 259, 266-268, 273, 302, RA17.

Revenue Stamps of 1917-18 Surcharged Vertically in Red reading up or down

Casa de Correos VEINTE CTS. 1921—1922

1921-22

RA15	PT5	20c on 1c dk bl	25.00	3.00
RA16	PT5	20c on 2c grn	25.00	3.00

No. RA12 Surcharged in Green **DOS CENTAVOS — 2 —**

1924

RA17	PT6	2c on 20c bis brn	25	15
a.		Inverted surcharge	3.50	3.50
b.		Double surcharge	2.00	2.00

PT7

1924 *Rouletted 7*

RA18	PT7	1c rose red	40	15
a.		Inverted overprint	1.50	

Similar Design, Eagle at left

Perf. 12

RA19	PT7	2c blue	40	15
a.		Inverted overprint	1.50	1.50
		Set value		18

For overprints and surcharges see Nos. 346, O201, RA32, RA34, RA37, RA44-RA45, RA47.

PT8

Inscribed "Timbre Fiscal"

1924

RA20	PT8	1c yellow	2.00	75
RA21	PT8	2c dark blue	50	15

Inscribed "Region Oriental"

RA22	PT8	1c yellow	35	25
RA23	PT8	2c dark blue	65	35

Overprint on No. RA22 reads down or up.

Revenue Stamp Overprinted in Blue **CASA de Correos y Telegrafos de Guayaquil**

1934

RA24		2c green	15	15
a.		Blue overprint inverted	1.40	1.50
b.		Blue ovpt. dbl., one invtd.	1.75	1.00

Postage Stamp of 1930 Overprinted in Red

Perf. 12½

RA25	A119	20c ultra & yel	18	18
		Set value		25

Telegraph Stamp Overprinted in Red, like No. RA24, and Surcharged diagonally in Black

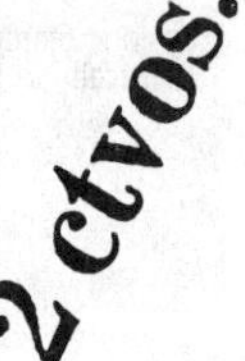

1934 *Perf. 14*
RA26 2c on 10c ol brn 30 15
a. Double surcharge 2.50

Overprint Blue, Surcharge Red

RA27 2c on 10c ol brn 30 15
Set value 20

PT9

PT10

Symbols of Post and Telegraph Service PT11

1934-36 *Perf. 12*
RA28 PT9 2c green 25 15
a. Both overprints in red ('36) 25 15

Postal Tax stamp of 1920-24, overprinted in red "POSTAL" has been again overprinted "CASA de Correos y Teleg. de Guayaquil" in black.

Perf. 14½x14
1934 **Photo.** **Wmk. 233**
RA29 PT10 2c yel grn 15 15

For the rebuilding of the GPO at Guayaquil. For surcharge see No. RA31.

1935
RA30 PT11 20c claret 15 15

For the rebuilding of the GPO at Guayaquil.

No. RA29 Surcharged in Red and Overprinted in Black

3 ctvs, Seguro Social del Campesino Quito, 16 de Otbre-1935

1935
RA31 PT10 3c on 2c yel grn 15 15
a. Double surcharge

Social and Rural Workers' Insurance Fund.

Tobacco Stamp Surcharged in Black

Seguro Social del Campesino 3 ctvs

1936 **Unwmk.** *Rouletted 7*
RA32 PT7 3c on 1c rose red 25 15
a. Lines of words reversed 1.00 15
b. Horiz. pair, imperf. vert.

Issued for the Social and Rural Workers' Insurance Fund.

No. 310 Overprinted in Black

Casa de Correos y Telégrafos de Guayaquil

1936 *Perf. 12½*
RA33 A119 20c ultra & yel 25 15
a. Double overprint

Tobacco Stamp Surcharged in Black

SEGURO SOCIAL DEL CAMPESINO 3 ctvs.

1936 *Rouletted 7*
RA34 PT7 3c on 1c rose red 25 15

Social and Rural Workers' Insurance Fund.

Worker — PT12

1936 **Engr.** *Perf. 13½*
RA35 PT12 3c ultra 15 15

Social and Rural Workers' Insurance Fund. For surcharges see Nos. C64, RA36, RA53-RA54.

Surcharged in Black

5 Centavos Dect. Junio 13 de 1936

1936
RA36 PT13 5c on 3c ultra 25 15

This combines the 2c for the rebuilding of the post office with the 3c for the Social and Rural Workers' Insurance Fund.

National Defense Issue

Tobacco Stamp, Surcharged in Black

TIMBRE PATRIOTICO DIEZ CENTAVOS

1936 *Rouletted 7*
RA37 PT7 10c on 1c rose 40 15
a. Double surcharge

Symbolical of Defense — PT14

1937-42 *Perf. 12½*
RA38 PT14 10c deep blue 40 15

A 1s violet and 2s green exist in type PT14. For surcharge see No. RA40.

PT15

Overprinted or Surcharged in Black

1937 **Engr. & Typo.** *Perf. 13½*
RA39 PT15 5c lt brn & red 1.00 25
d. Inverted overprint 10.00

1942 *Perf. 12, 11½*
RA39A PT15 20c on 5c rose pink & red 30.00
RA39B PT15 20c on 1s yel brn & red 30.00
RA39C PT15 20c on 2s grn & red 30.00

A 50c dark blue and red exists.

No. RA38 Surcharged in Red

5 5 POSTAL ADICIONAL

1937 **Engr.** *Perf. 12½*
RA40 PT14 5c on 10c dp bl 50 15

Map of Ecuador — PT16

1938 *Perf. 14x13½*
RA41 PT16 5c car rose 30 15

Social and Rural Workers' Insurance Fund.

No. C42 Surcharged in Red

20 20 CASA DE CORREOS Y TELEGRAFOS DE GUAYAQUIL 20 20

1938 *Perf. 12½*
RA42 AP5 20c on 70c blk 50 15

No. 307 Surcharged in Red

CAMPAÑA CONTRA EL CANCER 5 5

1938
RA43 A116 5c on 6c yel & red 15 15

This stamp was obligatory on all mail from Nov. 23rd to 30th, 1938. The tax was for the Intl. Union for the Control of Cancer.

Tobacco Stamp, Surcharged in Black

POSTAL ADICIONAL CINCO CENTAVOS

1939 *Rouletted*
RA44 PT7 5c on 1c rose 30 15
a. Double surcharge
b. Triple surcharge

Tobacco Stamp, Surcharged in Blue

CASAS DE CORREOS Y TELEGRAFOS CINCO CENTAVOS

1940
RA45 PT7 5c on 1c rose red 50 15
a. Double surcharge 3.50 3.50

No. 370 Surcharged in Carmine

CASA DE CORREOS y TELEGRAFOS DE GUAYAQUIL 20 20

1940 *Perf. 11½*
RA46 A144 20c on 50c blk & multi 25 15
a. Double surcharge, one inverted

Tobacco Stamp, Surcharged in Black

TIMBRE PATRIOTICO VEINTE CENTAVOS

1940 *Rouletted*
RA47 PT7 20c on 1c rose red 3.00 50

Farmer Plowing — PT17

Communication Symbols — PT18

1940 *Perf. 13x13½*
RA48 PT17 5c carmine rose 35 15

1940-43 *Perf. 12*
RA49 PT18 5c copper brown 30 15
RA49A PT18 5c green ('43) 30 15
Set value 15

For overprint and surcharges see #534, E6, I1.

Pursuit Planes — PT19

Warrior Shielding Women — PT20

1941 *Perf. 11½x13*
RA50 PT19 20c ultra 50 15

The tax was used for national defense.

1942-46 **Engr.** *Perf. 12*
RA51 PT20 20c dk bl 50 15
RA51A PT20 40c blk brn ('46) 50 15
Set value 15

The tax was used for national defense.

A 20c carmine, 20c brown and 30c gray exist lithographed in type PT20.

No. 370 Surcharged in Carmine

CASA DE CORREOS y TELEGRAFOS DE GUAYAQUIL VEINTE CENTAVOS

1942 *Perf. 11½*
RA52 A144 20c on 50c blk & multi 50 15
a. Double surcharge 5.00

No. RA35 Surcharged in Red

ADICIONAL CINCO CENTAVOS

1943 *Perf. 13½*
RA53 PT12 5c on 3c ultra 25 15

No. RA53 with Additional Surcharge in Black

5 Centavos
CASA DE CORREOS DE GQUIL. y

1943
RA54 PT12 5c on 5c on 3c ultra 25 15

Peons — PT21

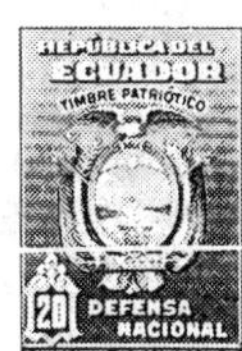

Coat of Arms — PT22

1943 *Perf. 12*
RA55 PT21 5c blue 40 15

The tax was for farm workers.
For overprint and surcharge see #535, C135.

Revenue Stamp (as No. RA64) Overprinted or Surcharged in Black

TIMBRE PATRIOTICO

TIMBRE PATRIOTICO
VEINTE CENTAVOS

1943 *Perf. 12½*
RA56 20c red org *30.00* 1.50

1943 *Perf. 12*
RA57 20c on 10c orange 1.00 25
a. Double surcharge

1943 *Perf. 12½*
RA58 PT22 20c orange red 25 15

The tax was for national defense.

No. RA58 Surcharged in Black

30 Centavos

1944
RA59 PT22 30c on 20c org red 30 15
a. Double surcharge

Catalogue values for unused stamps in this section, from this point to the end of the section, are for Never Hinged items.

Consular Service Stamps Surcharged in Black

TIMBRE ESCOLAR 20 ctvs. 20

1951 **Unwmk.** *Perf. 12*
RA60 R1 20c on 1s red 25 15
RA61 R1 20c on 2s brown 25 15
RA62 R1 20c on 5s violet 25 15
Set value 18

Teacher and Pupils in Schoolyard — PT23

PT24

1952 **Engr.** *Perf. 13*
RA63 PT23 20c blue green 25 15

Revenue Stamp Overprinted "PATRIOTICO / SANITARIO"

1952 *Perf. 12*
RA64 PT24 40(c) olive green 50 15

For overprints and surcharges see Nos. RA56-RA57

Woman Holding Flag — PT25

PT26

1953 *Perf. 12½*
RA65 PT25 40c ultra 60 15

Telegraph Stamp Surcharged "ESCOLAR 20 Centavos" in Black

1954 **Unwmk.** *Perf. 13*
RA66 PT26 20c on 30c red brn 60 15

Revenue Stamps Surcharged or Overprinted Horizontally in Black "PRO TURISMO 1954"

1954 **Unwmk.** *Perf. 12*
RA67 R2 10c on 25c blue 60 15
RA68 R3 10c on 50c org red 60 15
RA69 R3 10c carmine 60 15
Set value 29

PT27

Telegraph Stamp Surcharged "Pro-Turismo 1954 10 ctvs. 10"

1954 *Perf. 13*
RA70 PT27 10c on 30c red brn 75 15

Revenue Stamp Overprinted in Black

ESCOLAR

1954 *Perf. 12*
RA71 R3 20c olive black 75 15

Consular Service Stamp Surcharged in Black

0,20 0,20 ESCOLAR Veinte centavos

1954
RA72 R1 20c on 10s gray 75 15

Young Student at Desk — PT28

Globe, Ship, Plane — PT29

Imprint: "Heraclio Fournier.-Vitoria"

1954 **Photo.** *Perf. 11*
RA73 PT28 20c rose pink 50 15

See No. RA76.

1954 **Engr.** *Perf. 12*
RA74 PT29 10c dp magenta 50 15

Soldier Kissing Flag — PT30

1955 **Photo.** *Perf. 11*
RA75 PT30 40c blue 75 15

See No. RA77.

Types of 1954-55 Redrawn.
Imprint: "Thomas de la Rue & Co. Ltd."

1957 **Unwmk.** *Perf. 13*
RA76 PT28 20c rose pink 25 15

Perf. 14x14½

RA77 PT30 40c blue 75 20
Set value 26

No. RA77 is inscribed "Republica del Ecuador."

AIR POST POSTAL TAX STAMPS

No. 438 Surcharged in Black or Carmine

FOMENTO-AERO-COMUNICACIONES 20 Ctvs.

1945 **Unwmk.** *Perf. 11*
RAC1 A173 20c on 10c dk grn 25 15
a. Pair, one without surcharge 45.00
RAC2 A173 20c on 10c dk grn (C) 25 15
Set value 20

Obligatory on letters and parcel post carried on planes in the domestic service.

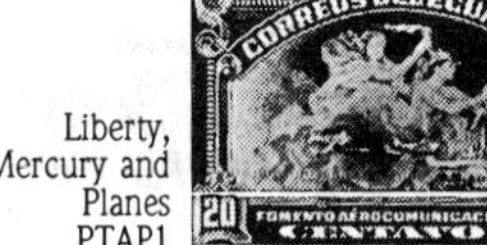

Liberty, Mercury and Planes PTAP1

1946 **Engr.** *Perf. 12*
RAC3 PTAP1 20c orange brown 20 15

GALAPAGOS ISLANDS

Issued for use in the Galapagos Islands (Columbus Archipelago), a province of Ecuador, but were commonly used throughout the country.

Catalogue values for unused stamps in this section are for Never Hinged items.

Sea Lions — A1

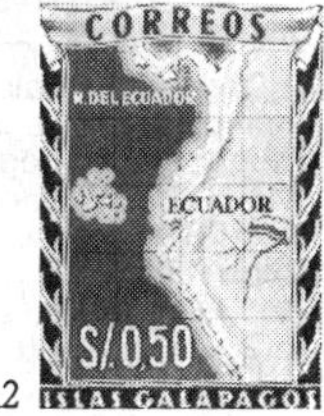

Map — A2

Design: 1s, Marine iguana.

Unwmk.

1957, July 15 **Photo.** *Perf. 12*
L1 A1 20c dark brown 30 15
L2 A2 50c violet 20 15
L3 A1 1s dull olive green 1.00 40

125th anniv. of Ecuador's possession of the Galapagos Islands, and publicizing the islands.
See Nos. LC1-LC3. For overprints see Nos. 684-686, C389-C391.

AIR POST STAMPS

Type of Regular Issue, 1957

Designs: 1s, Santa Cruz Island. 1.80s, Map of Galapagos archipelago. 4.20s, Galapagos giant tortoise.

Unwmk.

1957, July 19 **Photo.** *Perf. 12*
LC1 A1 1s deep blue 25 15
LC2 A1 1.80s rose violet 50 25
LC3 A1 4.20s black 1.50 60

For overprints see Nos. C389-C391.

Redrawn Type of Ecuador, 1956

1959, Jan. 3 **Engr.** *Perf. 14*
LC4 AP69 2s lt olive green 75 50

Issued to honor the United Nations.
See note after No. C407.

EGYPT

LOCATION — Northern Africa, bordering on the Mediterranean and the Red Sea
GOVT. — Republic
AREA — 386,900 sq. mi.
POP. — 46,000,000 (est. 1984)
CAPITAL — Cairo

Modern Egypt was a part of Turkey until 1914 when a British protectorate was declared over the country and the Khedive was deposed in favor of Hussein Kamil under the title of sultan. In 1922 the protectorate ended and the reigning sultan was declared king of the new monarchy. Egypt became a republic on June 18, 1953. Egypt merged with Syria in 1958 to form the United Arab Republic. Syria left this union in 1961. In 1971 Egypt took the name of Arab Republic of Egypt.

40 Paras = 1 Piaster
1000 Milliemes = 100 Piasters = 1 Pound (1888)
1000 Milliemes = 1 Pound (1953)
1000 Milliemes = 100 Piasters = 1 Pound (1982)

Catalogue values for unused stamps in this country are for Never Hinged items, beginning with Scott 241 in the regular postage section, Scott B1 in the semi-postal section, Scott C38 in the airpost section, Scott CB1 in the airpost semi-postal section, Scott E5 in the special delivery section, Scott J40 in the postage due section, Scott M5 in the military stamps section, Scott O60 in the officials section, Scott N1 in the occupation section, Scott NC1 in the occupation airpost section, Scott NE1 in the occupation special delivery section, and Scott NJ1 in the occupation postage due section.

Watermarks

Wmk. 118- Pyramid and Star

Wmk. 119- Crescent and Star

Wmk. 120- Triple Crescent and Star

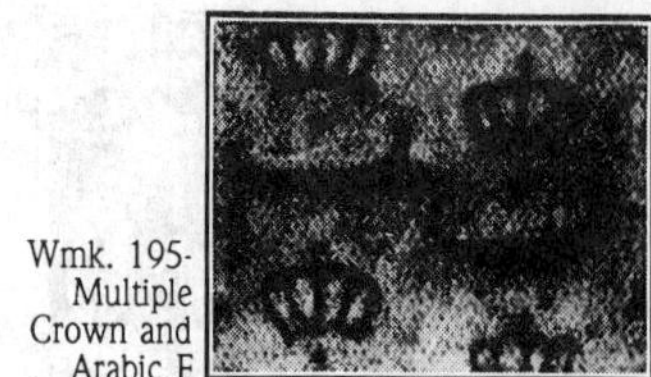
Wmk. 195- Multiple Crown and Arabic F

"F" in watermark stands for Fuad.

Wmk. 315- Multiple Eagle

Wmk. 318- Multiple Eagle and "Misr"

Wmk. 328- U A R

Wmk. 342- Coat of Arms, Multiple

Turkish Suzerainty

A1

A2

A3

A4

A5

A6

A7

Surcharged in Black

Perf. 12½

1866, Jan. 1 — Litho. — Wmk. 118

No.	Type	Description	Unused	Used
1	A1	5pa slate green	27.50	12.00
a.		Imperf., pair	225.00	
b.		Pair, imperf. between	275.00	
c.		Perf. 12½x13	35.00	35.00
d.		Perf. 13	275.00	325.00
2	A2	10pa brown	35.00	15.00
a.		Imperf., pair	160.00	
b.		Pair, imperf. between	160.00	
c.		Perf. 13	160.00	
d.		Perf. 12½x15	225.00	250.00
3	A3	20pa blue	35.00	21.00
a.		Imperf., pair	275.00	
b.		Pair, imperf. between	400.00	
c.		Perf. 12½x13	80.00	80.00
d.		Perf. 13	400.00	250.00
4	A4	2pi yellow	45.00	22.50
a.		Imperf.	80.00	37.50
b.		Imperf. vert. or horiz., pair	225.00	225.00
c.		Perf. 12½x15	100.00	
d.		Diagonal half used as 1pi on cover		1,000.
e.		Perf. 12½x13, 13x12½	80.00	25.00
5	A5	5pi rose	180.00	100.00
a.		Imperf.	200.00	150.00
b.		Imperf. vert. or horiz., pair	*650.00*	
d.		Inscription of 10pi, imperf.	350.00	
e.		Perf. 12½x13, 13x12½	200.00	150.00
f.		As "d," perf. 12½x15	400.00	300.00
6	A6	10pi slate bl	150.00	125.00
a.		Imperf.	150.00	140.00
b.		Pair, imperf. between	*1,400.*	
c.		Perf. 12½x13, 13x12½	350.00	250.00
d.		Perf. 13	*1,400.*	

Unwmk.

Typo.

No.	Type	Description	Unused	Used
7	A7	1pi rose lilac	35.00	2.50
a.		Imperf.	65.00	
b.		Horiz. pair, imperf. vert.	225.00	
c.		Perf. 12½x13, 13x12½	50.00	20.00
d.		Perf. 13	225.00	100.00

Single imperforates of types A1-A10 are sometimes simulated by trimming wide-margined copies of perforated stamps.

Proofs of #1-7 are on smooth white paper, unwatermarked and imperforate. Proofs of #7 are on thinner paper than No. 7a.

Sphinx and Pyramid — A8

Perf. 15x12½

1867 — Litho. — Wmk. 119

No.	Type	Description	Unused	Used
8	A8	5pa orange	9.00	5.00
a.		Imperf.	35.00	25.00
b.		Imperf. vert. or horiz., pair	140.00	
9	A8	10pa lilac	27.50	5.00
a.		10pa violet	27.50	5.00
b.		Half used as 5pa on newspaper piece		300.00
11	A8	20pa blue green	27.50	7.50
a.		20pa yellow green	30.00	7.50
13	A8	1pi rose red	3.25	75
a.		Imperf.	40.00	
b.		Pair, imperf. between	140.00	
c.		Half used as 20pa on cover		350.00
d.		Rouletted	35.00	
14	A8	2pi blue	50.00	6.00
a.		Imperf.	100.00	
b.		Horiz. pair, imperf. vert.	350.00	
c.		Diagonal half used as 1pi on cover		
d.		Perf. 12½		175.00
15	A8	5pi brown	175.00	75.00

There are 4 types of each value, so placed that any block of 4 contains all types.

A9

A10

Clear Impressions
Thick Opaque Paper

Typographed by the Government at Boulac

Perf. 12½x13½ Clean-cut

1872 — Wmk. 119

No.	Type	Description	Unused	Used
19	A9	5pa brown	6.00	2.50
20	A9	10pa lilac	5.00	2.00
21	A9	20pa blue	16.00	2.00
22	A9	1pi rose red	22.50	30
h.		Half used as 20pa on cover		150.00
23	A9	2pi dull yellow	35.00	3.00
24	A9	2½pi dull violet	30.00	3.00
25	A9	5pi green	165.00	20.00
i.		Tête bêche pair		

Perf. 13½ Clean-cut

No.	Type	Description	Unused	Used
19a	A9	5pa brown	12.50	6.00
20a	A9	10pa dull lilac	5.00	2.00
21a	A9	20pa blue	30.00	7.50
22a	A9	1pi rose red	35.00	2.00
23a	A9	2pi dull yellow	12.50	1.75
24a	A9	2½pi dull violet	675.00	
25a	A9	5pi green	250.00	40.00

Litho.

No.	Type	Description	Unused	Used
21m	A9	20pa blue, perf. 12½x13½	80.00	20.00
21n	A9	20pa blue, perf. 13½	140.00	40.00
21p	A9	20pa blue, imperf.	140.00	
22m	A9	1pi rose red, perf. 12½x13½	275.00	3.75
22n	A9	1pi rose red, perf. 13½		6.00

Typographed

Blurred Impressions
Thinner Paper

Perf. 12½ Rough

1874-75 — Wmk. 119

No.	Type	Description	Unused	Used
26	A10	5pa brown ('75)	4.00	1.50
e.		Imperf.		20.00
f.		Vert. pair, imperf. horiz.	100.00	75.00
g.		Tête bêche pair	35.00	25.00
20b	A9	10pa gray lilac	5.00	2.00
g.		Tête bêche pair	140.00	100.00
21b	A9	20pa gray blue	25.00	1.50
k.		Half used as 10pa on cover		200.00
22b	A9	1pi vermilion	2.50	45
f.		Imperf.	5.50	3.50
g.		Tête bêche pair	50.00	40.00
23b	A9	2pi yellow	20.00	2.00
i.		Tête bêche pair	350.00	250.00
24b	A9	2½pi deep violet	3.50	1.25
e.		Imperf.	15.00	11.25
f.		Tête bêche pair	250.00	200.00
25b	A9	5pi yellow green	22.50	5.00
e.		Imperf.	16.00	

No. 26f normally occurs tête-bêche.

Perf. 13½x12½ Rough

No.	Type	Description	Unused	Used
26c	A10	5pa brown	2.50	1.25
i.		Tête bêche pair	22.50	17.50
20c	A9	10pa gray lilac	4.00	1.50
i.		Tête bêche pair	140.00	100.00
21c	A9	20pa gray blue	3.00	2.00
h.		Pair, imperf. between	160.00	
22c	A9	1pi vermilion	7.00	50
i.		Tête bêche pair	200.00	150.00
23c	A9	2pi yellow	3.50	3.00
g.		Tête bêche pair	400.00	400.00
k.		Half used as 1pi on cover		*850.00*

Perf. 12½x13½ Rough

No.	Type	Description	Unused	Used
23d	A9	2pi yellow ('75)	12.50	3.00
h.		Tête bêche pair		
24d	A9	2½pi dp violet ('75)	10.00	6.00
i.		Tête bêche pair	450.00	400.00
25d	A9	5pi yel green ('75)	160.00	85.00

Stamp of 1872-75 Surcharged in Black

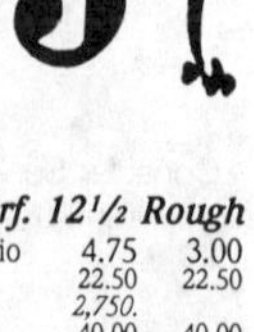

1879, Jan. 1 — *Perf. 12½ Rough*

No.	Type	Description	Unused	Used
27	A9	5pa on 2½pi dull vio	4.75	3.00
a.		Imperf.	22.50	22.50
b.		Tête bêche pair	*2,750.*	
c.		Inverted surcharge	40.00	40.00
d.		Perf. 12½x13½	4.00	4.00
e.		As "d," tête bêche pair		
f.		As "c," perf. 12½x13½	70.00	55.00
28	A9	10pa on 2½pi dull vio	3.25	3.00
a.		Imperf.		
b.		Tête bêche pair	1,000.	
c.		Inverted surcharge	45.00	35.00
d.		Perf. 12½x13½	7.00	6.00
e.		As "c," perf. 12½x13½	60.00	50.00

A11 A12

A13 A14

A15 A16

1879-93 Typo. *Perf. 14x13½*

No.	Type	Description	Unused	Used
29	A11	5pa brown	35	15
30	A12	10pa violet	21.00	1.50
31	A12	10pa lilac rose ('81)	37.50	2.00
32	A12	10pa gray ('82)	9.00	40
33	A12	10pa green ('84)	30	15
34	A13	20pa ultra	47.50	75
35	A13	20pa rose ('84)	9.00	25
36	A14	1pi rose	12.50	20
37	A14	1pi ultra ('84)	1.50	15
38	A15	2pi orange yel	14.00	25
39	A15	2pi orange brn	9.50	20
40	A16	5pi green	62.50	2.75
41	A16	5pi gray ('84)	9.50	25
		Nos. 29-41 (13)	234.15	9.00

Imperf. examples of #29-31, 35-41 are proofs.
Nos. 37, 39, 41, exist on both ordinary and chalky paper.
For overprints see Nos. 42, O6-O7.

A17

1884, Feb. 1

No.	Type	Description	Unused	Used
42	A17	20pa on 5pi green	7.00	60
a.		Inverted surcharge	27.50	22.50

A18 A19

A20 A21

A22

A23

1888-1906

No.	Type	Description	Unused	Used
43	A18	1m brown	15	15
44	A19	2m green	35	15
45	A20	3m maroon ('92)	1.90	40
46	A20	3m orange ('93)	95	15
47	A21	4m brown red ('06)	1.25	40
48	A22	5m carmine rose	65	15
49	A23	10p purple ('89)	18.00	30
		Nos. 43-49 (7)	23.25	
		Set value		95

Imperf. examples of #43-44, 47-48 are proofs.
Nos. 43-44, 46, 48-49 exist on both ordinary and chalky paper, No. 47 only on chalky-surfaced paper.
For overprints see Nos. O2-O3, O5, O8-O10, O14-O15.

Boats on Nile
A24

Cleopatra
A25

Ras-el-Tin Palace
A26

Giza Pyramids
A27

Sphinx
A28

Colossi of Thebes
A29

Pylon of Karnak and Temple of Khonsu — A30

Citadel at Cairo — A31

Rock Temple of Abu Simbel — A32

Aswan Dam — A33

Perf. 13½x14
1914, Jan. 8 Wmk. 119
Chalk-surfaced Paper

No.	Type	Description	Unused	Used
50	A24	1m olive brown	15	15
51	A25	2m dp green	25	15
52	A26	3m orange	42	15
53	A27	4m red	80	30
54	A28	5m lake	52	15
a.		Booklet pane of 6		
55	A29	10m dk blue	1.00	15

Perf. 14

No.	Type	Description	Unused	Used
56	A30	20m olive grn	2.50	15
57	A31	50m red violet	4.25	30
58	A32	100m black	8.25	30
59	A33	200m plum	20.00	52
		Nos. 50-59 (10)	38.14	
		Set value		1.80

All values of this issue exist imperforate on both watermarked and unwatermarked paper but are not known to have been issued in that condition.
See Nos. 61-69, 72-74. For overprints and surcharge see Nos. 60, 78-91, O11-O13, O16-O27, O29.

British Protectorate

No. 52 Surcharged

1915, Oct. 15

No.	Type	Description	Unused	Used
60	A26	2m on 3m orange	80	35
a.		Inverted surcharge	80.00	80.00

Scenic Types of 1914 and

Statue of Ramses II
A34 A35

1921-22 Wmk. 120 *Perf. 13½x14*
Chalk-surfaced Paper

No.	Type	Description	Unused	Used
61	A24	1m olive brown	15	15
62	A25	2m dp green	1.25	50
63	A25	2m red ('22)	30	15
64	A26	3m orange	1.40	16
65	A27	4m green ('22)	1.25	60
66	A28	5m lake	42	15
67	A28	5m pink	75	15
68	A29	10m dp blue	1.75	15
69	A29	10m lake ('22)	1.25	16
70	A34	15m indigo ('22)	1.00	15
71	A35	15m indigo ('22)	9.50	50

Perf. 14

No.	Type	Description	Unused	Used
72	A30	20m olive green	2.75	15
73	A31	50m maroon	5.50	16
74	A32	100m black	25.00	1.50
		Nos. 61-74 (14)	52.27	4.63

For overprints see Nos. O27-O28.

Independent Kingdom

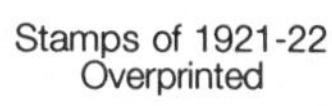
Stamps of 1921-22 Overprinted

1922, Oct. 10

No.	Type	Description	Unused	Used
78	A24	1m olive brown	25	15
a.		Inverted overprint	40.00	40.00
b.		Double overprint	50.00	50.00
79	A25	2m red	45	15
a.		Double overprint	40.00	40.00
80	A26	3m orange	80	28
81	A27	4m green	65	28
b.		Inverted overprint		
82	A28	5m pink	52	15
83	A29	10m lake	80	15
84	A34	15m indigo	2.00	15
85	A35	15m indigo	1.00	16

Perf. 14

No.	Type	Description	Unused	Used
86	A30	20m olive green	1.90	15
a.		Inverted overprint	140.00	140.00
b.		Double overprint	80.00	80.00
87	A31	50m maroon	2.50	15
a.		Inverted overprint	300.00	250.00
88	A32	100m black	8.25	32
a.		Inverted overprint	150.00	150.00
b.		Double overprint	150.00	150.00
		Nos. 78-88 (11)	19.12	
		Set value		1.50

Same Overprint on Nos. 58-59
Wmk. Crescent and Star (119)

No.	Type	Description	Unused	Used
90	A32	100m black	57.50	20.00
91	A33	200m plum	8.00	1.00

Proclamation of the Egyptian monarchy.
The overprint signifies "The Egyptian Kingdom, March 15, 1922". It exists in four types, one lithographed and three typographed on Nos 78-87, but lithographed only on Nos. 88-91.

King Fuad
A36 A37

Perf. 13½
1923-24 Photo. Wmk. 120
Size 18x22½mm

No.	Type	Description	Unused	Used
92	A36	1m orange	18	15
93	A36	2m black	28	15
94	A36	3m brown	55	15
a.		Imperf., pair	150.00	
95	A36	4m yellow grn	55	15
96	A36	5m orange brn	28	15
a.		Imperf., pair	20.00	
97	A36	10m rose	45	15
98	A36	15m ultra	55	15

Perf. 14
Size: 22x28mm

No.	Type	Description	Unused	Used
99	A36	20m dk green	1.10	15
100	A36	50m myrtle grn	3.75	15
101	A36	100m red violet	6.00	16
102	A36	200m violet ('24)	11.00	65
a.		Imperf., pair	250.00	
103	A37	£1 ultra & dk vio ('24)	72.50	6.50
a.		Imperf., pair	600.00	
		Nos. 92-103 (12)	97.19	8.66

For overprints & surcharge see #167, O31-O38.

Thoth Carving Name of King Fuad — A38

1925, Apr. Litho. *Perf. 11*

No.	Type	Description	Unused	Used
105	A38	5m brown	3.00	3.00
106	A38	10m rose	4.50	4.50
107	A38	15m ultra	6.50	6.50

International Geographical Congress, Cairo.
Nos. 106-107 exist with both white and yellowish gum.

Oxen Plowing
A39

1926 **Wmk. 195** ***Perf. 13x13½***

No.	Type	Description	Unused	Used
108	A39	5m lt brown	75	35
109	A39	10m brt rose	75	35
110	A39	15m dp blue	75	35
111	A39	50m Prus green	5.00	2.00
112	A39	100m brown vio	8.00	3.50
113	A39	200m brt violet	12.00	6.25
		Nos. 108-113 (6)	27.25	12.80

12th Agricultural and Industrial Exhibition at Gezira.
For surcharges see Nos. 115-117.

King Fuad — A40

Perf. 14x14½
1926, Apr. 2 **Photo.** **Wmk. 120**

No.	Type	Description	Unused	Used
114	A40	50p brn vio & red vio	52.50	5.50

58th birthday of King Fuad.
For overprint and surcharge see #124, 166.

Nos. 111-113 Surcharged **5 MILLIEMES**

Perf. 13x13½
1926, Aug. 24 **Wmk. 195**

No.	Type	Description	Unused	Used
115	A39	5m on 50m Prus green	1.25	70
116	A39	10m on 100m brown vio	1.25	70
117	A39	15m on 200m brt violet	1.25	70
a.		Double surcharge	160.00	

Ship of Hatshepsut A41

1926, Dec. 9 **Litho.** ***Perf. 13x13½***

No.	Type	Description	Unused	Used
118	A41	5m brown & blk	1.50	65
119	A41	10m dp red & blk	1.75	85
120	A41	15m dp blue & blk	1.75	85

International Navigation Congress, Cairo.
For overprints see Nos. 121-123.

Nos. 118-120, 114 Overprinted

PORT FOUAD *a* — PORT FOUAD *b*

1926, Dec. 21

No.	Type	Description	Unused	Used
121	A41 (a)	5m	90.00	60.00
122	A41 (a)	10m	90.00	60.00
123	A41 (a)	15m	90.00	60.00

Perf. 14x14½
Wmk. 120

No.	Type	Description	Unused	Used
124	A40 (b)	50p	1,100.	700.00

Inauguration of Port Fuad opposite Port Said.
Nos. 121-123 have a block over "Le Caire" at lower left.
Forgeries of Nos. 121-124 exist.

Branch of Cotton A42

Perf. 13x13½
1927, Jan. 25 **Wmk. 195**

No.	Type	Description	Unused	Used
125	A42	5m dk brown & sl grn	65	50
126	A42	10m dp red & sl grn	1.60	75
127	A42	15m dp blue & sl grn	1.60	75

International Cotton Congress, Cairo.

King Fuad
A43 A44

A45

A46

Perf. 13x13½
1927-37 **Wmk. 195** **Photo.**

No.	Type	Description	Unused	Used
128	A43	1m orange	15	15
129	A43	2m black	15	15
130	A43	3m olive brn	15	15
131	A43	3m dp green ('30)	16	15
132	A43	4m yellow grn	30	15
133	A43	4m brown ('30)	35	15
134	A43	4m dp green ('34)	65	16
135	A43	5m dk red brn ('29)	16	15
b.		5m chestnut	20	15
136	A43	10m dk red ('29)	40	15
a.		10m orange red	60	15
137	A43	10m purple ('34)	1.10	15
138	A43	13m car rose ('32)	35	15
139	A43	15m ultra	65	15
140	A43	15m dk violet ('34)	1.40	15
141	A43	20m ultra ('34)	2.25	15

Early printings of Nos. 128, 129, 130, 132, 135, 136 and 139 were from plates with screen of vertical dots in the vignette; later printings show screen of diagonal dots.

Perf. 13½x14

No.	Type	Description	Unused	Used
142	A44	20m olive grn	65	15
143	A44	20m ultra ('32)	1.50	15
144	A44	40m ol brn ('32)	80	15
145	A44	50m Prus green	65	15
a.		50m greenish blue	1.00	15
146	A44	100m brown vio	2.50	15
a.		100m claret	2.50	15
147	A44	200m dp violet	3.75	16

Printings of Nos. 142, 145 and 146, made in 1929 and later, were from new plates with stronger impressions and darker colors.

Lithographed; Center Photogravure
Perf. 13x13½

No.	Type	Description	Unused	Used
148	A45	500m choc & Prus bl ('32)	32.50	2.50
a.		Entirely photogravure	40.00	5.75
149	A46	£1 dk grn & org brn ('37)	42.50	2.00
a.		Entirely photogravure	42.50	3.50
		Nos. 128-149 (22)	93.07	
		Set value		5.50

Statue of Amenhotep, Son of Hapu — A47

1927, Dec. 29 **Photo.** ***Perf. 13½x13***

No.	Type	Description	Unused	Used
150	A47	5m orange brown	38	25
151	A47	10m copper red	70	35
152	A47	15m deep blue	1.50	40

Statistical Congress, Cairo.

Imhotep — A48

Mohammed Ali Pasha — A49

1928, Dec. 15

No.	Type	Description	Unused	Used
153	A48	5m orange brown	70	30
154	A49	10m copper red	70	30

Intl. Congress of Medicine at Cairo and the cent. of the Faculty of Medicine at Cairo.

Prince Farouk — A50

1929, Feb. 11 **Litho.**

No.	Type	Description	Unused	Used
155	A50	5m choc & gray	80	50
156	A50	10m dull red & gray	1.65	50
157	A50	15m ultra & gray	1.65	50
158	A50	20m Prus blue & gray	1.65	50

Ninth birthday of Prince Farouk.
Nos. 155-158 with black or brown centers are trial color proofs. They were sent to the UPU, but were never placed on sale to the public, although some are known used.

Tomb Fresco at El-Bersheh A51

1931, Feb. 15 ***Perf. 13x13½***

No.	Type	Description	Unused	Used
163	A51	5m brown	55	30
164	A51	10m copper red	1.25	30
165	A51	15m dark blue	1.65	38

14th Agricultural & Industrial Exhib., Cairo.

Nos. 114 and 103 Surcharged with Bars and

MILLS 50 — *a* — MILLS 100 — *b*

1932 **Wmk. 120** ***Perf. 14x14½***

No.	Type	Description	Unused	Used
166	A40	50m on 50p	6.00	80

Perf. 14

No.	Type	Description	Unused	Used
167	A37	100m on £1	100.00	65.00

Locomotive of 1852 — A52

Perf. 13x13½
1933, Jan. 19 **Litho.** **Wmk. 195**

No.	Type	Description	Unused	Used
168	A52	5m shown	1.90	75
169	A52	13m 1859	7.75	3.75
170	A52	15m 1862	7.75	3.75
171	A52	2m 1932	7.75	3.75

International Railroad Congress, Heliopolis.

Commercial Passenger Airplane — A56

Dornier Do-X A57

Graf Zeppelin A58

1933, Dec. 20 **Photo.**

No.	Type	Description	Unused	Used
172	A56	5m brown	2.50	1.25
173	A56	10m brt violet	8.00	4.75
174	A57	13m brown car	10.00	4.75
175	A57	15m violet	10.00	4.75
176	A58	20m blue	15.00	10.00
		Nos. 172-176 (5)	45.50	25.50

International Aviation Congress, Cairo.

Khedive Ismail Pasha
A59 A60

1934, Feb. 1 ***Perf. 13½***

No.	Type	Description	Unused	Used
177	A59	1m dp orange	15	15
178	A59	2m black	16	15
179	A59	3m brown	16	15
180	A59	4m blue green	24	22
181	A59	5m red brown	24	15
182	A59	10m violet	50	16
183	A59	13m copper red	70	45
184	A59	15m dull violet	55	16
185	A59	20m ultra	75	28
186	A59	50m Prus blue	2.50	28
187	A59	100m olive grn	5.25	45
188	A59	200m dp violet	12.00	2.25

Perf. 13½x13

No.	Type	Description	Unused	Used
189	A60	50p brown	60.00	32.50
190	A60	£1 Prus blue	110.00	50.00
		Nos. 177-190 (14)	193.20	87.35

10th Congress of UPU, Cairo.

King Fuad — A61

1936-37 ***Perf. 13½***

No.	Type	Description	Unused	Used
191	A61	1m dull orange	15	15
192	A61	2m black	16	15
193	A61	4m dk green	20	15
194	A61	5m chestnut	16	15
195	A61	10m purple ('37)	65	15
196	A61	15m brown violet	1.00	15
197	A61	20m sapphire	1.40	15
		Nos. 191-197 (7)	3.72	
		Set value		85

Entrance to Agricultural Building — A62

Agricultural Building A63

Design: 15m, 20m, Industrial Building.

1936, Feb. 15 *Perf. 13½x13*

No.	Type	Denomination & color	Unused	Used
198	A62	5m brown	42	35
		Perf. 13x13½		
199	A63	10m violet	60	50
200	A63	13m copper red	1.25	80
201	A63	15m dk violet	70	50
202	A63	20m blue	1.65	1.40
		Nos. 198-202 (5)	4.62	3.55

15th Agricultural & Industrial Exhib., Cairo.

Signing of Treaty — A65

1936, Dec. 22 *Perf. 11*

No.	Type	Denomination & color	Unused	Used
203	A65	5m brown	40	25
204	A65	15m dk violet	55	35
205	A65	20m sapphire	1.25	45

Signing of Anglo-Egyptian Treaty, Aug. 26, 1936.

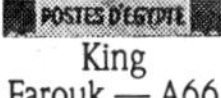

King Farouk — A66

Medal for Montreux Conf. — A67

1937-44 **Wmk. 195** *Perf. 13x13½*

No.	Type	Denomination & color	Unused	Used
206	A66	1m brown org	15	15
207	A66	2m vermilion	15	15
208	A66	3m brown	15	15
209	A66	4m green	15	15
210	A66	5m red brown	15	15
211	A66	6m lt yel grn ('40)	15	15
212	A66	10m purple	15	15
213	A66	13m rose car	15	15
214	A66	15m dk vio brn	16	15
215	A66	20m blue	20	15
216	A66	20m lil gray ('44)	22	15
		Set value	1.25	60

For overprints see Nos. 301, 303, 345, 348, 360E, N3, N6, N8, N22, N25, N27.

1937, Oct. 15 *Perf. 13½x13*

No.	Type	Denomination & color	Unused	Used
217	A67	5m red brown	35	16
218	A67	15m dk violet	60	28
219	A67 20m sapphire		65	32

Intl. Treaty signed at Montreux, Switzerland, under which foreign privileges in Egypt were to end in 1949.

Eye of Ré — A68

1937, Dec. 8 *Perf. 13x13½*

No.	Type	Denomination & color	Unused	Used
220	A68	5m brown	40	38
221	A68	15m dk violet	65	40
222	A68	20m sapphire	90	40

15th Ophthalmological Congress, Cairo, December, 1937.

King Farouk, Queen Farida — A69

1938, Jan. 20 *Perf. 11*

No.	Type	Denomination & color	Unused	Used
223	A69	5m red brown	6.50	1.25

Royal wedding of King Farouk and Farida Zulficar.

Inscribed: "11 Fevrier 1938"

1938, Feb. 11

No.	Type	Denomination & color	Unused	Used
224	A69	£1 green & sepia	100.00	65.00

King Farouk's 18th birthday.

Cotton Picker — A70

1938, Jan. 26 *Perf. 13½x13*

No.	Type	Denomination & color	Unused	Used
225	A70	5m red brown	42	35
226	A70	15m dk violet	1.40	70
227	A70	20m sapphire	1.00	60

18th International Cotton Congress at Cairo.

Pyramids of Giza and Colossus of Thebes A71

1938, Feb. 1 *Perf. 13x13½*

No.	Type	Denomination & color	Unused	Used
228	A71	5m red brown	55	50
229	A71	15m dk violet	1.00	65
230	A71	20m sapphire	1.40	65

Intl. Telecommunication Conf., Cairo.

Branch of Hydnocarpus — A72

1938, Mar. 21 *Perf. 13x13½*

No.	Type	Denomination & color	Unused	Used
231	A72	5m red brown	70	35
232	A72	15m dk violet	1.10	45
233	A72	20m sapphire	1.10	45

International Leprosy Congress, Cairo.

King Farouk and Pyramids — A73

King Farouk
A74 A75

Backgrounds: 40m, Hussan Mosque. 50m, Cairo Citadel. 100m, Aswan Dam. 200m, Cairo University.

1939-46 **Photo.** *Perf. 14x13½*

No.	Type	Denomination & color	Unused	Used
234	A73	30m gray	24	15
a.		30m slate gray	22	15
234B	A73	30m ol grn ('46)	24	15
235	A73	40m dk brown	38	15
236	A73	50m Prus green	40	15
237	A73	100m brown vio	60	15
238	A73	200m dk violet	1.75	15
		Perf. 13½x13		
239	A74	50p green & sep	4.00	28
240	A75	£1 dp bl & dk brn	7.25	35
		Nos. 234-240 (8)	14.86	
		Set value		90

For £1 with A77 portrait, see No. 269D. See Nos. 267-269D. For overprints see Nos. 310-314, 316, 355-358, 360, 363-364, N13-N19, N32-N38.

Catalogue values for unused stamps in this section, from this point to the end of the section, are for Never Hinged items.

King Fuad — A76

King Farouk — A77

1944, Apr. 28 *Perf. 13½x13*

No.	Type	Denomination & color	Unused	Used
241	A76	10m dk violet	20	15

8th anniv. of the death of King Fuad.

1944-50 **Wmk. 195** *Perf. 13x13½*

No.	Type	Denomination & color	Unused	Used
242	A77	1m yellow brn ('45)	15	15
243	A77	2m red org ('45)	15	15
244	A77	3m sepia ('46)	16	15
245	A77	4m dp green ('45)	16	15
246	A77	5m red brown ('46)	15	15
247	A77	10m dp violet	15	15
247A	A77	13m rose red ('50)	1.50	35
248	A77	15m dk violet ('45)	15	15
249	A77	17m olive grn	16	15
250	A77	20m dk gray ('45)	20	15
251	A77	22m dp blue ('45)	25	15
		Nos. 242-251 (11)	3.18	
		Set value		80

For overprints see Nos. 299-300, 302, 304-309, 343-344, 346-347, 349-354, 360B, 360D, 361, N1-N2, N4-N5, N7, N9-N12, N20-N21, N23-N24, N26, N28-N31.

King Farouk — A78

Khedive Ismail Pasha — A79

1945, Feb. 10 *Perf. 13½x13*

No.	Type	Denomination & color	Unused	Used
252	A78	10m dp violet	16	15

25th birthday of King Farouk.

1945, Mar. 2 **Photo.**

No.	Type	Denomination & color	Unused	Used
253	A79	10m dark olive	16	15

50th anniv. of death of Khedive Ismail Pasha.

Flags of Arab Nations — A80

1945, July 29

No.	Type	Denomination & color	Unused	Used
254	A80	10m violet	15	15
255	A80	22m dp yel grn	25	15
		Set value		16

League of Arab Nations Conference, Cairo, Mar. 22, 1945.

Flags of Egypt and Saudi Arabia A81

Perf. 13x13½

1946, Jan. 10 **Wmk. 195**

No.	Type	Denomination & color	Unused	Used
256	A81	10m dp yel grn	15	15

Visit of King Ibn Saud, Jan. 1946.

Citadel, Cairo A82

1946, Aug. 9

No.	Type	Denomination & color	Unused	Used
257	A82	10m yel brn & dp yel grn	16	16

Withdrawal of British troops from Cairo Citadel, Aug. 9, 1946.

King Farouk and Inchas Palace, Cairo — A83

Portraits: 2m, Prince Abdullah, Yemen. 3m, Pres. Bechara el-Khoury, Lebanon. 4m, King Abdul Aziz ibn Saud, Saudi Arabia. 5m, King Faisal II, Iraq. 10m, Amir Abdullah ibn Hussein, Jordan. 15m, Pres. Shukri el Kouatly, Syria.

1946, Nov. 9

No.	Type	Denomination & color	Unused	Used
258	A83	1m dp yel grn	15	15
259	A83	2m sepia	15	15
260	A83	3m dp blue	15	15
261	A83	4m brown org	15	15
262	A83	5m brown red	15	15

263 A83 10m dk gray 15 15
264 A83 15m dp violet 15 15
Set value 72 72

Arab League Cong. at Cairo, May 28, 1946.

Parliament Building, Cairo — A84

1947, Apr. 7 **Photo.**
265 A84 10m green 16 15

36th conf. of the Interparliamentary Union, Apr. 1947.

Raising Egyptian Flag over Kasr-el-Nil Barracks — A85

King Farouk — A85a

1947, May 6 ***Perf. 13½x13***
266 A85 10m dp plum & yel grn 18 15

Withdrawal of British troops from the Nile Delta.

Farouk Types 1939 Redrawn

1947-51 **Wmk. 195** ***Perf. 14x13½***
267 A73 30m olive green 22 15
268 A73 40m dk brown 28 15
269 A73 50m Prus grn ('48) 42 15
269A A73 100m dk brn vio ('49) 1.25 15
269B A73 200m dk violet ('49) 3.75 15

Perf. 13½x13

269C A85a 50p green & sep ('51) 12.00 1.75
269D A75 £1 dp bl & dk brn ('50) 24.00 1.00
Nos. 267-269D (7) 41.92 3.50

The king faces slightly to the left and clouds have been added in the sky on Nos. 267-269B. Backgrounds as in 1939-46 issue. Portrait on £1 as on type A77.

For overprints see Nos. 315, 359.

Field and Branch of Cotton — A86

Map and Infantry Column — A87

Perf. 13½x13

1948, Apr. 1 **Wmk. 195**
270 A86 10m olive green 20 15

Intl. Cotton Cong. held at Cairo in Apr. 1948.

1948, June 15 ***Perf. 11½x11***
271 A87 10m green 24 15

Arrival of Egyptian troops at Gaza, May 15, 1948.

Ibrahim Pasha (1789-1848) — A88

1948, Nov. 10 ***Perf. 13x13½***
272 A88 10m brn red & dp grn 20 15

Statue, "The Nile" — A89

Protection of Industry and Agriculture — A90

Perf. 13x13½

1949, Mar. 1 **Photo.** **Wmk. 195**
273 A89 1m dk green 15 15
274 A89 10m purple 16 16
275 A89 17m crimson 20 20
276 A89 22m deep blue 24 24

Perf. 11½x11

277 A90 30m dk brown 30 30
Nos. 273-277 (5) 1.05 1.05

Souvenir Sheets

Photo. & Litho.

Imperf

278 Sheet of 4 1.00 1.00
a. A89 1m red brown 20 20
b. A89 10m dark brown 20 20
c. A89 17m brown orange 20 20
d. A89 22m dark Prussian green 20 20
279 Sheet of 2 1.40 1.40
a. A90 10m violet gray 60 60
b. A90 30m red orange 60 60

16th Agricultural & Industrial Expo., Cairo.

Mohammed Ali and Map — A93

Globe — A94

Perf. 11½x11

1949, Aug. 2 **Photo.** **Wmk. 195**
280 A93 10m orange brn & grn 16 16

Centenary of death of Mohammed Ali.

1949, Oct. 9 ***Perf. 13½x13***
281 A94 10m rose brown 25 20
282 A94 22m violet 45 35
283 A94 30m dull blue 65 45

75th anniv. of the UPU.

Scales of Justice A95

1949, Oct. 14 ***Perf. 13x13½***
284 A95 10m dp olive green 16 15

Issued to commemorate the end of the Mixed Judiciary System, Oct. 14, 1949.

Desert Scene A96

1950, Dec. 27
285 A96 10m violet & red brn 20 16

Opening of the Fuad I Institute of the Desert.

Fuad I University A97

1950, Dec. 27
286 A97 22m dp green & claret 28 22

25th anniv. of the founding of Fuad I University.

Globe and Khedive Ismail Pasha A98

1950, Dec. 27
287 A98 30m claret & dp grn 32 25

75th anniv. of Royal Geographic Society of Egypt.

Picking Cotton — A99

1951, Feb. 24
290 A99 10m olive green 20 15

International Cotton Congress, 1951.

King Farouk and Queen Narriman — A100

1951, May 6 **Photo.** ***Perf. 11x11½***
291 A100 10m green & red brn 80 80
a. Souvenir sheet 1.40 1.25

Marriage of King Farouk and Narriman Sadek, May 6, 1951.

Stadium Entrance A101

Arms of Alexandria and Olympic Emblem — A102

King Farouk A103

1951, Oct. 5 ***Perf. 13x13½, 13½x13***
292 A101 10m brown 42 42
293 A102 22m dp green 70 70
294 A103 30m blue & dp grn 75 75
a. Souvenir sheet of 3, #292-294 4.00 4.00

Issued to publicize the first Mediterranean Games, Alexandria, Oct. 5-20, 1951.

Winged Figure and Map — A105

Designs: 22m, King Farouk and Map. 30m, King Farouk and Flag.

Dated "16 Oct. 1951"

1952, Feb. 11 ***Perf. 13½x13***
296 A105 10m dp green 42 42
297 A105 22m plum & dp grn 70 70
298 A105 30m green & brown 75 75
a. Souvenir sheet of 3, #296-298 4.00 4.00

Abrogation of the Anglo-Egyptian treaty.

Stamps of 1937-51 Overprinted in Various Colors

ملك مصر والسودان
١٦ اكتوبر سنة ١٩٥١

Perf. 13x13½

1952, Jan. 17 **Wmk. 195**
299 A77 1m yellow brown 15 15
300 A77 2m red org (Bl) 15 15
301 A66 3m brown (Bl) 15 15
302 A77 4m dp green (RV) 15 15
303 A66 6m lt yel grn (RV) 55 15
304 A77 10m dp vio (C) 18 15
305 A77 13m rose red (Bl) 65 15
306 A77 15m dk violet (C) 55 15
307 A77 17m olive grn (C) 75 15
308 A77 20m dk gray (RV) 80 15
309 A77 22m dp blue (C) 1.25 50

No. 244, the 3m sepia, exists with this overprint but was not regularly issued or used.

Same Overprint, 24½mm Wide, on Nos. 267 to 269B

Perf. 14x13½

310 A73 30m olive grn (DkBl) 30 15
a. Black overprint 50 15
311 A73 40m dk brown (G) 45 15
312 A73 50m Prus grn (C) 55 15
313 A73 100m dk brn vio (C) 80 16
314 A73 200m dk violet (C) 2.00 18

Same Overprint, 19mm Wide, on Nos. 269C-269D

Perf. 13½x13

315 A85a 50p green & sep (C) 11.00 2.00
316 A75 £1 dp bl & dk brn (Bl) 20.00 2.25
Nos. 299-316 (18) 40.43 7.04

The overprint translates: King of Egypt and the Sudan, Oct. 16, 1951.

Overprints in colors other than as listed are color trials.

Egyptian Flag — A106

Perf. 13½x13

1952, May 6 Photo. Wmk. 195

317 A106 10m org yel, dp bl & dp grn 16 16
a. Souvenir sheet of 1 1.00 1.00

Issued to commemorate the birth of Crown Prince Ahmed Fuad, Jan. 16, 1952.

"Dawn of New Era" A107

Symbolical of Egypt Freed — A108

Designs: 10m, "Egypt" with raised sword. 22m, Citizens marching with flag.

Perf. 13x13½, 13½x13

1952, Nov. 23

Dated: "23 Juillet 1952"

318 A107 4m dp green & org 15 15
319 A107 10m dp grn & cop brn 15 15
320 A108 17m brn org & dp grn 20 16
321 A108 22m choc & dp grn 28 22
Set value 68 55

Change of government, July 23, 1952.

Republic

Farmer A109

Soldier A110

Mosque of Sultan Hassan — A111

Queen Nefertiti — A112

1953-56 *Perf. 13x13½*

322 A109 1m red brown 15 15
323 A109 2m dk lilac 15 15
324 A109 3m brt blue 15 15
325 A109 4m dk green 15 15
326 A110 10m dk brown ("Defence") 15 15
327 A110 10m dk brown ("Defense") 15 15
328 A110 15m gray 15 15
329 A110 17m dk grnsh blue 15 15
330 A110 20m purple 15 15

Perf. 13½

331 A111 30m dull green 16 15
332 A111 32m brt blue 20 15
333 A111 35m violet ('55) 40 15
334 A111 37m gldn brn ('56) 1.25 15
335 A111 40m red brown 24 15
336 A111 50m violet brn 32 15
337 A112 100m henna brn 75 15
338 A112 200m dk grnsh blue 1.90 15
339 A112 500m purple 4.25 60
340 A112 £1 dk grn, blk & red 9.50 65
Nos. 322-340 (19) 20.32
Set value 2.15

Nos. 327-330 are inscribed "Defense."

See No. 490. For overprints and surcharges see Nos. 460, 500, N44-N56, N72.

Stamps of 1939-51 Overprinted in Black with Three Bars to Obliterate Portrait

1953 *Perf. 13x13½, 13½x13*

343 A77 1m yellow brn 15 15
344 A77 2m red orange 15 15
345 A66 3m brown 65 65
346 A77 3m sepia 15 15
347 A77 4m dp green 15 15
348 A66 6m lt yellow grn 16 16
349 A77 10m dp violet 15 15
350 A77 13m rose red 30 16
351 A77 15m dk violet 15 15
352 A77 17m olive grn 20 15
353 A77 20m dk gray 22 15
354 A77 22m deep blue 28 16
355 A73 30m ol grn (#267) 30 15
356 A73 50m Prus grn (#269) 48 15
357 A73 100m dk brn vio (#269A) 70 16
358 A73 200m dk violet (#269B) 2.75 65
359 A85a 50p green & sepia 5.75 1.40
360 A75 £1 dp bl & dk brn (#269D) 14.00 3.50
Nos. 343-360 (18) 26.69 8.34

No. 206 with this overprint is a forgery.

Same Overprint on Nos. 300, 303-305, 311 and 314

360B A77 2m red orange 22 16
360E A66 6m lt yel grn *2.25*
361 A77 10m dp violet 90 80
362 A77 13m rose red 45 25
363 A73 40m dk brown 55 25
364 A73 200m dk violet 2.75 40

Practically all values of Nos. 343-364 exist with double overprint. Other values of the 1952 overprinted issue are known with counterfeit bars.

Symbols of Electronic Progress A113

1953, Nov. 23 Photo. *Perf. 13x13½*

365 A113 10m brt blue 20 16

Electronics Exposition, Cairo, Nov. 23.

Crowd Acclaiming the Republic A114

Farmer A115

Design: 30m, Crowd, flag and eagle.

Perf. 13½x13

1954, June 18 Wmk. 195

366 A114 10m brown 15 15
367 A114 30m deep blue 25 22

Proclamation of the republic, 1st anniv.

1954-55 *Perf. 13x13½*

368 A115 1m red brown 15 15
369 A115 2m dark lilac 15 15
370 A115 3m brt blue 15 15
371 A115 4m dk green ('55) 15 15
372 A115 5m dp car ('55) 15 15
Set value 30 25

For overprints see Nos. N39-N43.

Egyptian Flag, Map — A116

Globe — A117

Design: 35m, Bugler, soldier and map.

1954, Nov. 4 *Perf. 13½x13*

373 A116 10m rose vio & grn 15 15
374 A116 35m ver, blk & bl grn 25 25

Agreement of Oct. 19, 1954, with Great Britain for the evacuation of the Suez Canal zone by British troops.

Arab Postal Union Issue

1955, Jan. 1

375 A117 5m yellow brn 15 15
376 A117 10m green 15 15
377 A117 37m violet 40 30
Set value 60 45

Founding of the Arab Postal Union, July 1, 1954.
For overprints see Nos. 381-383.

Paul P. Harris and Rotary Emblem — A118

Design: 35m, Globe, wings and Rotary emblem.

Perf. 13½x13

1955, Feb. 23 Wmk. 195

378 A118 10m claret 20 15
379 A118 35m blue 50 20
Set value 28

50th anniv. of the founding of Rotary Intl.

Nos. 375-377 Overprinted

مؤتمر البريد العربي
القاهرة-١٩٥٥/٣/١٥

1955, Nov. 1

381 A117 5m yellow brown 15 15
382 A117 10m green 16 16
383 A117 37m violet 45 45

Arab Postal Union Congress held at Cairo, Mar. 15, 1955.

Map of Africa and Asia, Olive Branch and Rings A119

Globe, Torch, Dove and Olive Branch — A120

Perf. 13x13½, 13½x13

1956, July 29

384 A119 10m chestnut & green 15 15
385 A120 35m org yel & dull pur 28 28
Set value 38

Afro-Asian Festival, Cairo, July, 1956.

Map of Suez Canal and Ship — A121

Queen Nefertiti — A122

Perf. 11½x11

1956, Sept. 26 Wmk. 195

386 A121 10m blue & buff 40 15

Nationalization of the Suez Canal, July 26, 1956.
See No. 393.

1956, Oct. 15 *Perf. 13½x13*

387 A122 10m dark green 1.50 75

Intl. Museum Week (UNESCO), Oct. 8-14.

Egyptians Defending Port Said — A123

1956, Dec. 20 Litho. *Perf. 11x11½*

388 A123 10m brown violet 35 16

Honoring the defenders of Port Said.

No. 388 Overprinted in Carmine Rose

الجلاء ٥٦/١٢/٢٣
EVACUATION 22·12·56

1957, Jan. 14

389 A123 10m brown violet 45 16

Evacuation of Port Said by British and French troops, Dec. 22, 1956.

Old and New Trains A124

1957, Jan. 30 Photo. *Perf. 13x13½*

390 A124 10m red violet & gray 15 15

100th anniv. of the Egyptian Railway System (in 1956).

Mother and Children A125

1957, Mar. 21

391 A125 10m crimson 15 15

Mother's Day, 1957.

Battle Scene
A126

Perf. 13x13½

1957, Mar. 28 **Wmk. 195**

392 A126 10m bright blue 15 15

150th anniv. of the victory over the British at Rosetta.

Type of 1956; New Inscriptions in English

1957, Apr. 15 *Perf. 11½x11*

393 A121 100m blue & yel grn 95 65

Reopening of the Suez Canal.
No. 393 is inscribed: "Nationalisation of Suez Canal Co. Guarantees Freedom of Navigation" and "Reopening 1957."

Map of Gaza Strip — A127

Perf. 13½x13

1957, May 4 **Photo.** **Wmk. 195**

394 A127 10m Prus blue 45 15

"Gaza Part of Arab Nation."
For overprint see No. N57.

Al Azhar University
A128

1957, Apr. 27 *Perf. 13x13½*

New Arabic Date in Red

395 A128 10m brt violet 20 15
396 A128 15m violet brown 25 16
397 A128 20m dark gray 35 25

Millenary of Al Azhar University, Cairo.

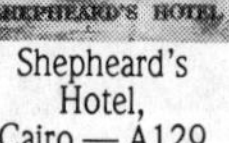

Shepheard's Hotel, Cairo — A129

Gate, Palace and Eagle — A130

Perf. 13½x13

1957, July 20 **Wmk. 195**

398 A129 10m brt violet 15 15

Reopening of Shepheard's Hotel, Cairo.

Perf. 11½x11

1957, July 22 **Wmk. 315**

399 A130 10m yellow & brown 15 15

First meeting of New National Assembly.

Amasis I in Battle of Avaris, 1580 B.C.
A131

Designs: No. 401, Sultan Saladin, Hitteen, 1187 A. D. No. 402, Louis IX of France in chains, Mansourah, 1250, vert. No. 403, Map of Middle East, Ein Galout, 1260. No. 404, Port Said, 1956.

Inscribed:
"Egypt Tomb of Aggressors 1957"

Perf. 13x13½, 13½x13

1957, July 26

400 A131 10m carmine rose 24 15
401 A131 10m dk olive grn 24 15
402 A131 10m brown violet 24 15
403 A131 10m grnsh blue 24 15
404 A131 10m yellow brown 24 15
Nos. 400-404 (5) 1.20
Set value 40

No. 400 exists with Wmk. 195.

Ahmed Arabi Speaking to the Khedive
A132

Perf. 13x13½

1957, Sept. 16 **Wmk. 315**

405 A132 10m deep violet 15 15

75th anniversary of Arabi Revolution.

Hafez Ibrahim — A133

Portrait: No. 407, Ahmed Shawky.

1957, Oct. 14 *Perf. 13½x13*

406 A133 10m dull red brn 15 15
407 A133 10m olive green 15 15
a. Pair, #406-407 20 18
Set value 16 15

25th anniv. of the deaths of Hafez Ibrahim and Ahmed Shawky, poets.

MiG and Ilyushin Planes
A134

Design: No. 409, Viscount plane.

1957, Dec. 19 *Perf. 13x13½*

408 A134 10m ultra 15 15
409 A134 10m green 15 15
a. Pair, #408-409 24 18
Set value 24 15

25th anniv. of the Egyptian Air Force and of Misrair, the Egyptian airline.

Pyramids, Dove and Globe
A135

1957, Dec. 26 **Photo.** **Wmk. 315**

410 A135 5m brown orange 15 15
411 A135 10m green 15 15
412 A135 15m brt violet 20 16
Set value 31

Issued to publicize the Afro-Asian Peoples Conference, Cairo, Dec. 26-Jan. 2.

Farmer's Wife
A136

Ramses II
A137

"Industry" — A138

1957-58 **Wmk. 315** *Perf. 13½*

413 A136 1m blue green ('58) 15 15
414 A137 10m violet 15 15
Set value 15 15

1958 **Wmk. 318**

415 A136 1m lt blue green 15 15
416 A138 5m brown 15 15
417 A137 10m violet 15 15
Set value 16 15

See #438-444, 474-488, 535. For overprints see #N58-N63, N66-N68, N75, N77-N78.

Cyclists — A139

Mustafa Kamel — A140

Perf. 13½x13

1958, Jan. 12 **Wmk. 315**

418 A139 10m lt red brown 15 15

5th Intl. Bicycle Race, Egypt, Jan. 12-26.

1958, Feb. 10 **Photo.** **Wmk. 318**

419 A140 10m blue gray 15 15

50th anniversary of the death of Mustafa Kamel, orator and politician.

United Arab Republic

Linked Maps of Egypt and Syria — A141

Cotton — A142

Perf. 11½x11

1958, Mar. 22 **Wmk. 318**

436 A141 10m yellow & green 15 15

Birth of United Arab Republic. See #C90.

1958, Apr. 5 *Perf. 13½x13*

437 A142 10m Prussian blue 15 15

Intl. Fair for Egyptian Cotton, Apr., 1958.

Types of 1957-58 Inscribed "U.A.R. EGYPT" and

Princess Nofret — A143

Designs: 1m, Farmer's wife. 2m, Ibn-Tulun's Mosque. 4m, 14th century glass lamp (design lacks "1963" of A217). 5m, "Industry" (factories and cogwheel). 10m, Ramses II. 35m, "Commerce" (eagle, ship and cargo).

1958 *Perf. 13½x14*

438 A136 1m crimson 15 15
439 A138 2m blue 15 15
440 A143 3m dk red brown 15 15
441 A217 4m green 15 15
442 A138 5m brown 15 15
443 A137 10m violet 15 15
444 A138 35m lt ultra 65 15
Set value 1.00 35

See Nos. 474-488, 532-533.

Qasim Amin — A144

Doves, Broken Chain and Globe — A145

1958, Apr. 23 *Perf. 13½x13*

445 A144 10m deep blue 15 15

50th anniversary of the death of Qasim Amin, author of "Emancipation of Women."

1958, June 18

446 A145 10m violet 15 15

Fifth anniversary of the republic to publicize the struggle of peoples and individuals for freedom.
For overprint see No. N69.

Cement Industry — A146

UAR Flag — A147

Industries: No. 448, Textile. No. 449, Iron & steel. No. 450, Petroleum (Oil). No. 451, Electricity and fertilizers.

Perf. 13½x13

1958, July 23 Photo. Wmk. 318

447 A146	10m	red brown	15	15
448 A146	10m	blue green	15	15
449 A146	10m	bright red	15	15
450 A146	10m	olive green	15	15
451 A146	10m	dark blue	15	15
a.		Strip of 5, #447-451	65	50
		Set value	60	40

Souvenir Sheet

Imperf

452 A147	50m	grn, dp car & blk	10.00	10.00

Revolution of July 23, 1952, 6th anniv.

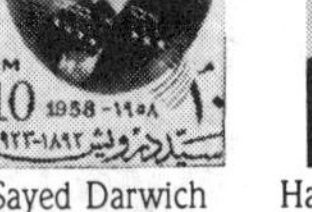

Sayed Darwich A148

Hand Holding Torch, Broken Chain and Flag A149

1958, Sept. 15 *Perf. 13½x13*

453 A148	10m	violet brown	15	15

35th anniv. of the death of Sayed Darwich, Arab composer.

1958, Oct. 14 Photo. Wmk. 318

454 A149	10m	carmine rose	15	15

Establishment of the Republic of Iraq.

Maps and Cogwheels A150

1958, Dec. 8 *Perf. 13x13½*

455 A150	10m	blue	15	15

Issued to publicize the Economic Conference of Afro-Asian Countries, Cairo, Dec. 8.

Overprinted in Red in English and Arabic in 3 Lines: "Industrial and Agricultural Production Fair"

1958, Dec. 9

456 A150	10m	lt red brown	15	15

Issued to publicize the Industrial and Agricultural Production Fair, Cairo, Dec. 9.

Dr. Mahmoud Azmy and UN Emblem A151

1958, Dec. 10

457 A151	10m	dull violet	15	15
458 A151	35m	green	35	22

10th anniv. of the signing of the Universal Declaration of Human Rights.

For overprints see Nos. N70-N71.

University Building, Sphinx, "Education" and God Thoth — A152

1958, Dec. 21 Photo. Wmk. 318

459 A152	10m	grnsh black	15	15

50th anniversary of Cairo University.

الجمهورية العربية المتحدة ══ ٥٥

No. 337 Surcharged

UAR ══ 55

1959, Jan. 20 Wmk. 195 *Perf. 13½*

460 A112	55m	on 100m henna brn	40	25

For overprint see No. N72.

Emblem A153

1959, Feb. 2 *Perf. 13x13½*

461 A153	10m	lt olive green	15	15

Afro-Asian Youth Conf., Cairo, Feb. 2.

See Syria UAR issues for stamps of designs A141, A149, A154, A156, A157, A162, A170, A172, A173, A179 with denominations in piasters (p).

Arms of UAR — A154

Perf. 13½x13

1959, Feb. 22 Photo. Wmk. 318

462 A154	10m	green, blk & red	15	15

First anniversary, United Arab Republic.

Nile Hilton Hotel A155

1959, Feb. 22 *Perf. 13x13½*

463 A155	10m	dark gray	15	15

Opening of the Nile Hilton Hotel, Cairo.

Globe, Radio and Telegraph A156

1959, Mar. 1

464 A156	10m	violet	15	15

Arab Union of Telecommunications.

United Arab States Issue

Flags of UAR and Yemen A157

1959, Mar. 8

465 A157	10m	sl grn, car & blk	15	15

First anniversary of United Arab States.

Oil Derrick and Pipe Line — A158

Perf. 13½x13

1959, Apr. 16 Litho. Wmk. 318

466 A158	10m	lt bl & dk bl	15	15

First Arab Petroleum Congress, Cairo.

Railroad A159

Designs: No. 468, Bus on highway. No. 469, River barge. No. 470, Ocean liner. No. 471, Telecommunications on map. No. 472, Stamp printing building, Heliopolis. No. 472A, Ship, train, plane and motorcycle mail carrier.

1959, July 23 Photo. *Perf. 13x13½*

Frame in Gray

467 A159	10m	maroon	15	15
468 A159	10m	green	15	15
469 A159	10m	violet	15	15
470 A159	10m	dark blue	15	15
471 A159	10m	dull purple	15	15
472 A159	10m	scarlet	15	15
		Set value	40	36

Souvenir Sheet

Imperf

472A A159	50m	green & red	*10.00*	*10.00*

No. 472A for the 7th anniv. of the Egyptian revolution of 1952 and was sold only with 5 sets of Nos. 467-472.

Globe, Swallows and Map — A160

1959, Aug. 8 *Perf. 13½x13*

473 A160	10m	maroon	15	15

Convention of the Assoc. of Arab Emigrants in the US.

Types of 1953-58 without "Egypt" and

St. Simon's Gate, Bosra, Syria — A161

Designs: 1m, Farmer's wife. 2m, Ibn-Tulun's Mosque. 3m, Princess Nofret. 4m, 14th century glass lamp (design lacks "1963" of A217). 5m, "Industry" (factories and cogwheel). 10m, Ramses II. 15m, Omayyad Mosque, Damascus. 20m, Lotus vase, Tutankhamen treasure. 35m, Eagle, ship and cargo. 40m, Scribe statue. 45m, Saladin's citadel, Aleppo. 55m, Eagle, cotton and wheat. 60m, Dam and factory. 100m, Eagle, hand, cotton and grain. 200m, Palmyra ruins, Syria. 500m, Queen Nefertiti, inscribed "UAR" (no ovpt.).

Perf. 13½x14, 14x13½

1959-60 Wmk. 328 Photo.

474 A136	1m	vermilion	15	15
475 A138	2m	dp blue ('60)	15	15
476 A143	3m	maroon	15	15
477 A217	4m	green ('60)	15	15
478 A138	5m	black ('60)	15	15
479 A137	10m	dk ol grn	15	15
480 A138	15m	deep claret	15	15
481 A138	20m	crimson ('60)	16	15
482 A161	30m	brown vio	28	15
483 A138	35m	lt vio bl ('60)	32	15
484 A143	40m	sepia	55	15
485 A161	45m	lil gray ('60)	90	15
486 A138	55m	brt blue grn	90	15
487 A138	60m	dp purple ('60)	55	15
488 A138	100m	org & sl grn ('60)	2.00	15
489 A161	200m	lt blue & mar	3.00	15
490 A112	500m	dk gray & red ('60)	5.75	20
		Nos. 474-490 (17)	15.46	
		Set value		1.00

Shield and Cogwheel — A162

Perf. 13½x13

1959, Oct. 20 Photo. Wmk. 328

491 A162	10m	brt car rose	15	15

Issued for Army Day, 1959.

Cairo Museum A163

1959, Nov. 18 *Perf. 13x13½*

492 A163	10m	olive gray	15	15

Centenary of Cairo museum.

Abu Simbel Temple of Ramses II — A164

1959, Dec. 22 *Perf. 11x11½*
493 A164 10m lt red brn, *pnksh* 20 15

Issued as propaganda to save historic monuments in Nubia threatened by the construction of Aswan High Dam.

Postrider, 12th Century A165

1960, Jan. 2 *Perf. 13x13½*
494 A165 10m dark blue 15 15

Issued for Post Day, Jan. 2.

Hydroelectric Power Station, Aswan Dam — A166

1960, Jan. 9
495 A166 10m violet blk 15 15

Inauguration of the Aswan Dam hydroelectric power station, Jan. 9.

Arabic and English Description of Aswan High Dam — A167

Architect's Drawing of Aswan High Dam — A168

1960, Jan. 9 *Perf. 11x11½*
496 A167 10m claret 16 15
497 A168 35m claret 32 15
a. Pair, #496-497 48 20
Set value 17

Start of work on the Aswan High Dam.

Symbols of Agriculture and Industry — A169

Arms and Flag — A170

1960, Jan. 16 *Perf. 13½x13*
498 A169 10m gray grn & sl grn 15 15

Industrial and Agricultural Fair, Cairo.

1960, Feb. 22 Photo. Wmk. 328
499 A170 10m green, blk & red 15 15

2nd anniversary of the proclamation of the United Arab Republic.

No. 340 Overprinted "UAR" in English and Arabic in Red

1960 Wmk. 195 *Perf. 13½*
500 A112 £1 dk grn, blk & red 10.00 1.00

"Art" — A171

Perf. 13½x13

1960, Mar. 1 Wmk. 328
501 A171 10m brown 15 15

Issued to publicize the 3rd Biennial Exhibition of Fine Arts in Alexandria.

Arab League Center, Cairo A172

1960, Mar. 22 Photo. *Perf. 13x13½*
502 A172 10m dull grn & blk 15 15

Opening of Arab League Center and Arab Postal Museum, Cairo.

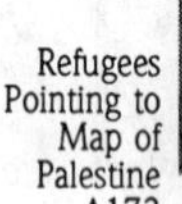

Refugees Pointing to Map of Palestine A173

1960, Apr. 7
503 A173 10m orange ver 22 15
504 A173 35m Prus blue 45 20
Set value 27

Issued to publicize World Refugee Year. July 1, 1959-June 30, 1960.
See Nos. N73-N74.

Weight Lifter — A174

Stadium, Cairo — A175

Sports: No. 506, Basketball. No. 507, Soccer. No. 508, Fencing. No. 509, Rowing. 30m, Steeplechase, horiz. 35m, Swimming, horiz.

Perf. 13½x13

1960, July 23 Photo. Wmk. 328
505 A174 5m gray 15 15
506 A174 5m brown 15 15
507 A174 5m dp claret 15 15
508 A174 10m brt carmine 15 15
509 A174 10m gray green 15 15
a. Vert. strip of 5, #505-509 50
510 A174 30m purple 30 15
511 A174 35m dark blue 38 16
Set value 1.15 53

Souvenir Sheet

Imperf

512 A175 100m car & brown 1.10 60

Nos. 505-511 for the 17th Olympic Games, Rome, Aug. 25-Sept. 11.

Dove and UN Emblem — A176

Design: 35m, Lights surrounding UN emblem, horiz.

Perf. 13½x13

1960, Oct. 24 Wmk. 328
513 A176 10m purple 15 15
514 A176 35m brt rose 24 15
Set value 32 17

15th anniversary of United Nations.

Abu Simbel Temple of Queen Nefertari — A177

Perf. 11x11½

1960, Nov. 14 Photo. Wmk. 328
515 A177 10m ocher, *buff* 30 15

Issued as propaganda to save historic monuments in Nubia and in connection with the UNESCO meeting, Paris, Nov. 14.

Model Post Office A178

1961, Jan. 2 *Perf. 13x13½*
516 A178 10m brt car rose 15 15

Issued for Post Day, Jan. 2.

Eagle, Fasces and Victory Wreath — A179

Wheat and Globe Surrounded by Flags — A180

1961, Feb. 22 *Perf. 13½x13*
517 A179 10m dull violet 15 15

3rd anniversary of United Arab Republic.

1961, Mar. 21 Wmk. 328
518 A180 10m vermilion 15 15

Intl. Agricultural Exhib., Cairo, Mar. 21-Apr. 20.

Patrice Lumumba and Map — A181

Reading Braille and WHO Emblem — A182

1961, Mar. 30 *Perf. 13½x13*
519 A181 10m black 15 15

Africa Day, Apr. 15 and 3rd Conf. of Independent African States, Cairo, Mar. 25-31.

1961, Apr. 6 Photo.
520 A182 10m red brown 15 15

WHO Day. See Nos. B21, N80.

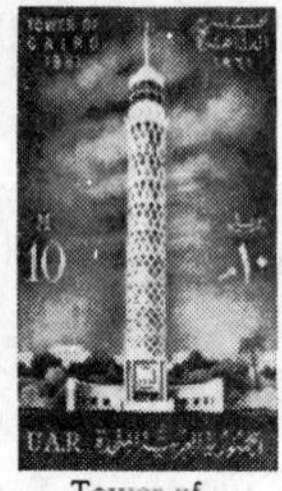

Tower of Cairo — A183

Arab Woman and Son, Palestine Map — A184

1961, Apr. 11 *Perf. 13½x13*
521 A183 10m grnsh blue 15 15

Opening of the 600-foot Tower of Cairo, on island of Gizireh. See No. C95.

1961, May 15 Wmk. 328
522 A184 10m brt green 45 15

Issued for Palestine Day.
See No. N79.

Set Values

A 15-cent minimum now applies to individual stamps and sets. Where the 15-cent minimum per stamp would increase the value of a set beyond retail, there is a "Set Value" notation giving the retail value of the set.

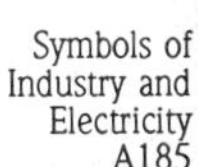

Symbols of Industry and Electricity
A185

Chart and Workers — A186

Designs: No. 524, New buildings and family. No. 525, Ship, train, bus and radio. No. 526, Dam, cotton and field. No. 527, Hand holding candle and family.

1961, July 23 Photo. *Perf. 13x13½*

523 A185	10m dp carmine		15	15
524 A185	10m brt blue		15	15
525 A185	10m dk vio brown		15	15
526 A185	35m dk green		20	15
527 A185	35m brt purple		20	15
	Set value		61	25

Souvenir Sheet

Imperf

528 A186 100m red brown 1.25 1.25

9th anniv. of the revolution.

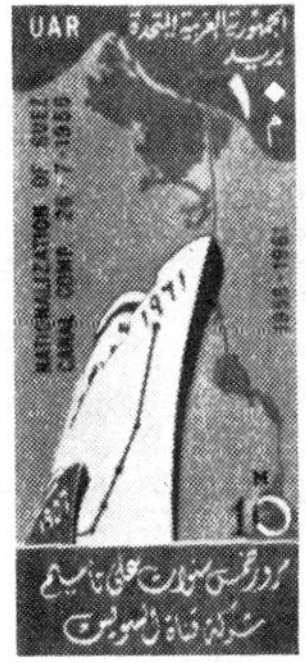

Map of Suez Canal and Ships — A187

Perf. 11½x11

1961, July 26 Unwmk.

529 A187 10m olive 15 15

Suez Canal Company nationalization, 5th anniv.

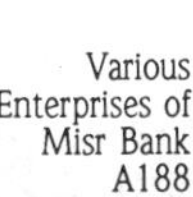

Various Enterprises of Misr Bank
A188

Perf. 13x13½

1961, Aug. 22 Wmk. 328

530 A188 10m red brn, *pnksh* 15 15

The 41st anniversary of Misr Bank.

Flag, Ship's Wheel and Battleship — A189

1961, Aug. 29 Photo. *Perf. 13½x13*

531 A189 10m deep blue 15 15

Issued for Navy Day.

Eagle of Saladin over Cairo — A190

UN Emblem, Book, Cogwheel, Corn — A191

Type A143 Redrawn, Type A138 and Type A190

Designs: 1m, Farmer's wife. 4m, 14th cent. glass lamp. 35m, "Commerce."

1961, Aug. 31 Unwmk. *Perf. 11½*

532 A143	1m blue	15	15
533 A143	4m olive	15	15
534 A190	10m purple	15	15
535 A138	35m slate blue	22	15
	Set value	40	20

Smaller of two Arabic inscriptions in new positions: 1m, at right above Egyptian numeral; 4m, upward to spot beside waist of lamp; 35m, upper left corner below "UAR." On 4m, "UAR" is 2mm deep instead of 1mm. "Egypt" omitted as in 1959-60.

Perf. 13½x13

1961, Oct. 24 Photo. Wmk. 328

Design: 35m, Globe and cogwheel, horiz.

536 A191	10m black & ocher	15	15
537 A191	35m blue grn & brn	15	15
	Set value	25	17

UN Technical Assistance Program and 16th anniv. of the UN.
See Nos. N81-N82.

Trajan's Kiosk, Philae — A192

1961, Nov. 4 Unwmk. *Perf. 11½*
Size: 60x27mm

538 A192 10m dp vio blue 32 16

15th anniv. of UNESCO, and to publicize UNESCO's help in safeguarding the monuments of Nubia.

The lack of a value for a listed item does not necessarily indicate rarity.

Palette, Brushes, Map of Mediterranean
A193

Atom and Educational Symbols
A194

1961, Dec. 14 Wmk. 328 *Perf. 13½*

539 A193 10m dk red brown 15 15

Issued to publicize the 4th Biennial Exhibition of Fine Arts in Alexandria.

1961, Dec. 18

540 A194 10m dull purple 15 15

Issued to publicize Education Day.
See No. N83.

Arms of UAR — A195

1961, Dec. 23 Unwmk. *Perf. 11½*

541 A195 10m brt pink, brt grn & blk 15 15

Victory Day. See No. N84.

Sphinx at Giza — A196

1961, Dec. 27 *Perf. 11x11½*

542 A196 10m black 15 15

Issued to publicize the "Sound and Light" Project, the installation of floodlights and sound equipment at the site of the Pyramids and Sphinx.

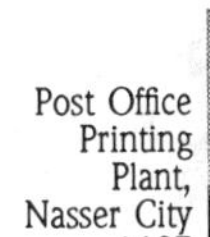

Post Office Printing Plant, Nasser City
A197

1962, Jan. 2 Photo. *Perf. 11½x11*

543 A197 10m dk brown 15 15

Issued for Post Day, Jan. 2.

Map of Africa, King Mohammed V of Morocco and Flags — A198

1962, Jan. 4 *Perf. 11x11½*

544 A198 10m indigo 15 15

African Charter, Casablanca, 1st anniv.

Girl Scout Saluting and Emblem
A199

Perf. 13x13½

1962, Feb. 22 Wmk. 328

545 A199 10m bright blue 22 15

Egyptian Girl Scouts' 25th anniversary.

Arab Refugees, Flag and Map — A200

Mother and Child — A201

1962, Mar. 7 *Perf. 13½x13*

546 A200 10m dark slate green 15 15

5th anniv. of the liberation of the Gaza Strip.
See No. N85.

1962, Mar. 21 Photo.

547 A201 10m dk violet brn 15 15

Issued for Arab Mother's Day, Mar. 21.

Map of Africa and Post Horn — A202

1962, Apr. 23 Wmk. 328

548 A202	10m crimson & ocher	15	15
549 A202	50m dp blue & ocher	32	15
	Set value		20

Establishment of African Postal Union.

Cadets on Parade and Academy Emblem
A203

1962, June 18 *Perf. 13x13½*

550 A203 10m green 15 15

150th anniv. of the Egyptian Military Academy.

Malaria Eradication Emblem A204

Theodor Bilharz A205

1962, June 20 *Perf. 13½x13*

551 A204 10m dk brown & red	15	15
552 A204 35m dk green & blue	15	15
Set value		19

WHO drive to eradicate malaria.
See Nos. N87-N88.

1962, June 24 *Perf. 11x11½*

553 A205 10m brown orange	15	15

Dr. Theodor Bilharz (1825-1862), German physician who first described bilharziasis, an endemic disease in Egypt.

Patrice Lumumba and Map of Africa — A206

Hand on Charter — A207

1962, July 1 **Photo.** **Wmk. 342**

554 A206 10m rose & red	15	15

Issued in memory of Patrice Lumumba (1925-61), Premier of Congo.

1962, July 10 *Perf. 11x11½*

555 A207 10m brt blue & dk brn	15	15

Proclamation of the National Charter.

"Birth of the Revolution" A208

Symbolic Designs: No. 557, Proclamation (Scroll and book). No. 558, Agricultural Reform (Farm and crescent). No. 559, Bandung Conference (Dove, globe and olive branch). No. 560, Birth of UAR (Eagle and flag). No. 561, Industrialization (cogwheel, factory, ship and bus). No. 562, Aswan High Dam. No. 563, Social Revolution (Modern buildings and emblem). 100m, Arms of UAR, emblems of Afro-Asian and African countries and UN.

1962, July 23 *Perf. 11½*

556 A208 10m brn, dk red brn & pink	15	15
557 A208 10m dk blue & sep	15	15
558 A208 10m sepia & brt bl	15	15
559 A208 10m olive & dk ultra	15	15
560 A208 10m grn, blk & red	15	15
561 A208 10m brn org & ind	15	15
562 A208 10m brn org & vio blk	15	15
563 A208 10m orange & blk	15	15
Set value	96	56

Souvenir Sheets

Perf. 11½, Imperf.

564 A208 100m grn, pink, red & blk	1.25	80

10th anniv. of the revolution.

Mahmoud Moukhtar, Museum and Sculpture A209

1962, July 24 *Perf. 11½x11*

565 A209 10m lt vio bl & olive	15	15

Opening of the Moukhtar Museum, Island of Gezireh. The sculpture is "La Vestale de Secrets" by Moukhtar.

Flag of Algeria and Map of Africa Showing Algeria — A210

1962, Aug. 15 *Perf. 11x11½*

566 A210 10m multicolored	15	15

Algeria's independence, July 1, 1962.

Rocket, Arms of UAR and Atom Symbol — A211

1962, Sept. 1 **Photo.** **Wmk. 342**

567 A211 10m brt grn, red & blk	15	15

Launching of UAR rockets.

Rifle and Target A212

Map of Africa, Table Tennis Paddle, Net and Ball — A213

1962, Sept. 18 *Perf. 11½*

568 A212 5m green, blk & red	15	15
569 A213 5m green, blk & red	15	15
a. Pair, #568-569	15	15
570 A212 10m bister, bl & dk grn	15	15
571 A213 10m bister, bl & dk grn	15	15
a. Pair, #570-571	25	25
572 A212 35m dp ultra, red & blk	30	30
573 A213 35m dp ultra, red & blk	30	30
a. Pair, #568-569	60	60
Set value	90	90

38th World Shooting Championships and the 1st African Table Tennis Tournament. Types A212 and A213 are printed se-tenant at the base.

Dag Hammarskjold and UN Emblem — A214

Perf. 11½x11

1962, Oct. 24 **Photo.** **Wmk. 342**

Portrait in Slate Blue

574 A214 5m deep lilac	15	15
575 A214 10m olive	15	15
576 A214 35m deep ultra	22	22
Set value	40	40

Dag Hammarskjold, Secretary General of the UN, 1953-61, and 17th anniv. of the UN.
See Nos. N89-N91.

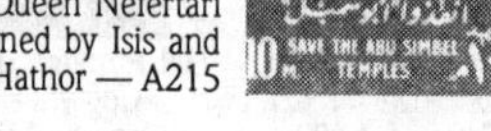

Queen Nefertari Crowned by Isis and Hathor — A215

1962, Oct. 31 *Perf. 11½*

577 A215 10m blue & ocher	22	15

Issued to publicize the UNESCO campaign to safeguard the monuments of Nubia.

Jet Trainer, Hawker Hart Biplane and College Emblem A216

1962, Nov. 2 *Perf. 11½x11*

578 A216 10m bl, dk bl & crim	15	15

25th anniversary of Air Force College.

14th Century Glass Lamp and "1963" — A217

Yemen Flag and Hand with Torch — A218

1963, Feb. 20 *Perf. 11x11½*

579 A217 4m dk brn, grn & car	15	15

Issued for use on greeting cards.
See Nos. 441, 477, N65, N76, N92. For overprint see No. N65.

1963, Mar. 14 **Photo.** **Wmk. 342**

580 A218 10m olive & brt car	15	15

Establishment of Yemen Arab Republic.

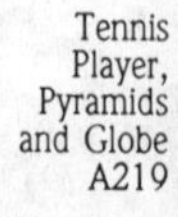

Tennis Player, Pyramids and Globe A219

Perf. 11½x11

1963, Mar. 20 **Unwmk.**

581 A219 10m gray, blk & brn	15	15

Issued to commemorate the International Lawn Tennis Championships, Cairo.

Cow, UN and FAO Emblems A220

Designs: 10m, Corn, wheat and emblems, vert. 35m, Wheat, corn and emblems.

Perf. 11½x11, 11x11½

1963, Mar. 21 **Wmk. 342**

582 A220 5m violet & dp org	15	15
583 A220 10m ultra & yel	15	15
584 A220 35m blue, yel & blk	26	15
Set value	45	25

FAO "Freedom from Hunger" campaign.
See Nos. N93-N95.

Centenary Emblem — A221

Design: 35m, Globe and emblem.

1963, May 8 **Unwmk.** *Perf. 11x11½*

585 A221 10m lt blue, red & mar	15	15
586 A221 35m lt blue & red	15	15
Set value	20	17

Centenary of the Red Cross.
See Nos. N96-N97.

Arab Socialist Union Emblem A222

Design: 50m, Tools, torch and symbol of National Charter.

Perf. 11½

1963, July 23 **Wmk. 342** **Photo.**

587 A222 10m slate & rose pink	15	15

Souvenir Sheets

Perf. 11½, Imperf.

588 A222 50m vio bl & org yel	1.00	1.00

11th anniv. of the revolution and to publicize the Arab Socialist Union.

Television Station, Cairo, and Screen A223

1963, Aug. 1 *Perf. 11½x11*

589 A223 10m dk blue & yel	15	15

Issued to publicize the 2nd International Television Festival, Alexandria, Sept. 1-10.

Queen Nefertari — A224

Swimmer and Map of Suez Canal — A225

Designs: 10m, Great Hypostyle Hall, Abu Simbel. 35m, Ramses in moonlight.

Wmk. 342

1963, Oct. 1 Photo. ***Perf. 11***
Size: 25x42mm (5m, 35m); 28x61mm (10m)

590 A224 5m brt vio blue & yel 15 15
591 A224 10m gray, blk & red org 15 15
592 A224 35m org yel & blk 28 20
Set value 42 32

UNESCO world campaign to save historic monuments in Nubia.
See Nos. N98-N100.

1963, Oct. 15
593 A225 10m blue & sal rose 15 15

Intl. Suez Canal Swimming Championship.

Ministry of Agriculture A226

Perf. 11½x11
1963, Nov. 20 Wmk. 342
594 A226 10m multicolored 15 15

50th anniv. of the Ministry of Agriculture.

Modern Building and Map of Africa and Asia A227

1963, Dec. 7
595 A227 10m multicolored 15 15

Afro-Asian Housing Congress, Dec. 7-12.

Scales, Globe, UN Emblem A228

1963, Dec. 10
596 A228 5m dk green & yel 15 15
597 A228 10m blue, gray & blk 15 15
598 A228 35m rose red, pink & red 22 15
Set value 35 24

15th anniv. of the Universal Declaration of Human Rights.
See Nos. N101-N103.

Sculpture, Arms of Alexandria and Palette with Flags — A229

1963, Dec. 12 ***Perf. 11x11½***
599 A229 10m pale bl, dk bl & brn 15 15

Issued to publicize the 5th Biennial Exhibition of Fine Arts in Alexandria.

Lion and Nile Hilton Hotel — A230

Vase, 13th Century — A231

Pharaoh Userkaf (5th Dynasty) A232

Designs: 1m, Vase, 14th century. 2m, Ivory headrest. 3m, Pharaonic calcite boat. 4m, Minaret and gate. 5m, Nile and Aswan High Dam. 10m, Eagle of Saladin over pyramids. 15m, Window, Ibn Tulun's mosque. No. 608, Mitwalli Gate, Cairo. 35m, Nefertari. 40m, Tower Hotel. 55m, Sultan Hassan's Mosque. 60m, Courtyard, Al Azhar University. 200m, Head of Ramses II. 500m, Funerary mask of Tutankhamen.

1964-67 Unwmk. Photo. ***Perf. 11***
Size: Nos. 608, 612, 19x24mm; others, 24x29mm

600 A231 1m citron & ultra 15 15
601 A230 2m magenta & bis 15 15
602 A230 3m salmon, org & bl 15 15
603 A235 4m ocher, blk & ultra 28 15
604 A230 5m brown & brt blue 15 15
a. 5m brown & dark blue 45 15
605 A231 10m green, dk brn & lt brn 15 15
606 A230 15m ultra & yel 15 15
607 A230 20m brown org & blk 22 15
608 A231 20m lt olive grn ('67) 22 15
609 A231 30m yellow & brown 30 15
610 A231 35m salmon, ocher & ultra 28 15
611 A231 40m ultra & yellow 38 15
612 A231 55m brt red lil ('67) 65 16
613 A231 60m grnsh bl & yel brn 55 16

Wmk. 342

614 A232 100m dk vio brn & sl 1.40 20
615 A232 200m bluish blk & yel brn 3.00 40
616 A232 500m ultra & dp org 5.25 80
Nos. 600-616 (17) 13.43
Set value 2.50

Nos. 603 & N107 lack the vertically arranged dates which appear at lower right on #619.
See Nos. N104-N116.

HSN Commission Emblem — A233

Perf. 11x11½
1964, Jan. 10 Wmk. 342
617 A233 10m dull bl, dk bl & yel 15 15

1st conf. of the Commission of Health, Sanitation and Nutrition.

Arab League Emblem — A234

1964, Jan. 13 ***Perf. 11***
618 A234 10m brt green & blk 15 15

1st meeting of the Heads of State of the Arab League, Cairo, January.
See No. N117.

Minaret at Night — A235

1964 Unwmk. ***Perf. 11***
619 A235 4m emerald, blk & red 15 15

Issued for use on greeting cards.
See Nos. 603, N107, N118.

Old and New Dwellings and Map of Nubia A236

Perf. 11½x11
1964, Feb. 27 Photo. Wmk. 342
620 A236 10m dull vio & yel 15 15

Resettlement of Nubian population.

Map of Africa and Asia and Train A237

1964, Mar. 21
621 A237 10m dull bl, dk bl & yel 15 15

Asian Railway Conference, Cairo, Mar. 21.

Ikhnaton and Nefertiti with Children — A238

1964, Mar. 21 ***Perf. 11x11½***
622 A238 10m dk brown & ultra 15 15

Issued for Arab Mother's Day, Mar. 21.

APU Emblem — A239

WHO Emblem — A240

1964, Apr. 1 Photo. Wmk. 342
623 A239 10m org brn & bl, *sal* 15 15

Permanent Office of the APU, 10th anniv.
See No. N119.

1964, Apr. 7
624 A240 10m dk blue & red 15 15

World Health Day (Anti-Tuberculosis).
See No. N120.

Statue of Liberty, World's Fair Pavilion and Pyramids
A241

1964, Apr. 22 ***Perf. 11½x11***
625 A241 10m brt green & ol, *grysh* 22 15

New York World's Fair, 1964-65.

Nile and Aswan High Dam A242

1964, May 15 Unwmk. ***Perf. 11½***
626 A242 10m black & blue 15 15

The diversion of the Nile.

"Land Reclamation" A243

Design: No. 628, "Electricity," Aswan High Dam hydroelectric station.

1964, July 23 ***Perf. 11½***
627 A243 10m yellow & emer 15 15
628 A243 10m green & blk 15 15
Set value 15

Land reclamation and hydroelectric power due to the Aswan High Dam.

An imperf. souvenir sheet, issued July 23, contains two 50m black and blue stamps showing Aswan High Dam before and after diversion of the Nile. Value $2.

Map of Africa and 34 Flags — A244

1964, July 17 **Photo.**
629 A244 10m brn, brt bl & blk 15 15

Assembly of Heads of State and Government of the Organization for African Unity at Cairo in July.

Jamboree Emblem — A245

Design: No. 631, Emblem of Air Scouts.

1964, Aug. 28 **Unwmk.** ***Perf. 11½***
630 A245 10m red, grn & blk 22 15
631 A245 10m green & red 22 15
a. Pair, #630-631 45 18
Set value 15

The 6th Pan Arab Jamboree, Alexandria.

Flag of Algeria A246

1964, Sept. 5 ***Perf. 11½x11***
Flags in Original Colors
632 A246 10m Algeria 24 15
633 A246 10m Iraq 24 15
634 A246 10m Jordan 24 15
635 A246 10m Kuwait 24 15
636 A246 10m Lebanon 24 15
637 A246 10m Libya 24 15
638 A246 10m Morocco 24 15
639 A246 10m Saudi Arabia 24 15
640 A246 10m Sudan 24 15
641 A246 10m Syria 24 15
642 A246 10m Tunisia 24 15
643 A246 10m UAR 24 15
644 A246 10m Yemen 24 15
Nos. 632-644 (13) 3.12
Set value 1.30

2nd meeting of the Heads of State of the Arab League, Alexandria, Sept. 1964.

World Map, Dove, Olive Branches and Pyramids — A247

1964, Oct. 5 ***Perf. 11½***
645 A247 10m slate blue & yel 15 15

Conference of Heads of State of Non-Aligned Countries, Cairo, Oct. 1964.

Pharaonic Athletes A248

Designs from ancient decorations: 10m, Four athletes, vert. 35m, Wrestlers, vert. 50m, Pharaoh in chariot hunting.

Perf. 11½x11, 11x11½
1964, Oct. 10 **Photo.** **Unwmk.**
Sizes: 39x22mm, 22x39mm
646 A248 5m lt green & org 15 15
647 A248 10m slate bl & lt brn 15 15
648 A248 35m dull vio & lt brn 35 18
Size: 58x24mm
649 A248 50m ultra & brn org 48 20
Set value 95 48

18th Olympic Games Tokyo, Oct. 10-25.

Emblem, Map of Africa and Asia — A249

Map of Africa, Communication Symbols — A250

1964, Oct. 10 ***Perf. 11x11½***
650 A249 10m violet & yellow 15 15

First Afro-Asian Medical Congress.

1964, Oct. 24
651 A250 10m green & blk 15 15

Pan-African and Malagasy Posts and Telecommunications Cong., Cairo, Oct. 24-Nov. 6.

Horus and Facade of Nefertari Temple, Abu Simbel A251

Ramses II — A252

Designs: 35m, A god holding rope of life, Abu Simbel. 50m, Isis of Kalabsha, horiz.

1964, Oct. 24 ***Perf. 11½, 11x11½***
652 A251 5m grnsh bl & yel brn 15 15
653 A252 10m sepia & brt yel 28 15
654 A251 35m brown org & ind 70 40

Souvenir Sheet
Imperf
655 A252 50m olive & vio blk 90 80

"Save the Monuments of Nubia" campaign. No. 655 contains one horiz. stamp.

Emblems of Cooperation, Rural Handicraft and Women's Work — A253

Perf. 11½x11
1964, Dec. 8 **Photo.** **Unwmk.**
656 A253 10m yellow & dk blue 15 15

25th anniv. of the Ministry of Social Affairs.

UN, UNESCO Emblems, Pyramids — A254

Minaret, Mardani Mosque — A255

1964, Dec. 24 ***Perf. 11x11½***
657 A254 10m ultra & yellow 15 15

Issued for UNESCO Day.

1965, Jan. 20 **Photo.** ***Perf. 11***
658 A255 4m blue & dk brown 15 15

Issued for use on greeting cards.
See No. N121.

Police Emblem over City — A256

Oil Derrick and Emblem — A257

Perf. 11x11½
1965, Jan. 25 **Wmk. 342**
659 A256 10m black & yellow 15 15

Issued for Police Day.

1965, Mar. 16 **Photo.**
660 A257 10m dk brown & yellow 15 15

5th Arab Petroleum Congress and the 2nd Arab Petroleum Exhibition.

Flags and Emblem of the Arab League — A258

Red Crescent and WHO Emblem — A259

Design: 20m, Arab League emblem, horiz.

1965, Mar. 22 **Wmk. 342**
661 A258 10m green, red & blk 15 15
662 A258 20m ultra & brown 15 15
Set value 24 16

20th anniversary of the Arab League.
See Nos. N122-N123.

1965, Apr. 7 **Photo.**
663 A259 10m blue & crimson 15 15

World Health Day (Smallpox: Constant Alert).
See No. N124.

Dagger in Map of Palestine — A260

1965, Apr. 9 ***Perf. 11x11½***
664 A260 10m black & red 45 22

Deir Yassin massacre, Apr. 9, 1948.
See No. N125.

ITU Emblem, Old and New Communication Equipment — A261

1965, May 17 ***Perf. 11½x11***
665 A261 5m violet blk & yel 15 15
666 A261 10m red & yellow 15 15
667 A261 35m dk blue, ultra & yel 15 15
Set value 32 22

Cent. of the ITU. See #N126-N128.

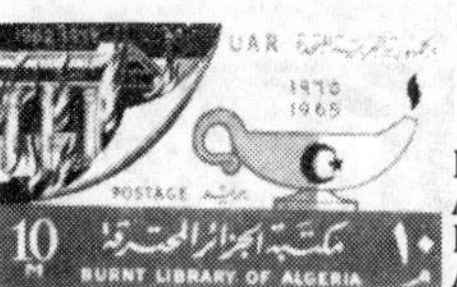

Library Aflame and Lamp A262

1965, June 7 **Photo.** **Wmk. 342**
668 A262 10m black, grn & red 15 15

Burning of the Library of Algiers, June 7, 1962.

Sheik Mohammed Abdo (1850-1905), Mufti of Egypt — A263

1965, July 11 ***Perf. 11x11½***
669 A263 10m Prus blue & bis brn 15 15

Pouring Ladle (Heavy Industry) A264

President Gamal Abdel Nasser and Emblems of Arab League, African Unity Organization, Afro-Asian Countries and UN — A265

Designs: No. 670, Search for off-shore oil. No. 672, Housing, construction in Nasser City (diamond shaped).

1965, July 23 *Perf. 11½*

670	A264	10m	indigo & lt blue	15	15
671	A264	10m	brown & yellow	15	15
672	A264	10m	yel brn & blk	15	15
673	A265	100m	lt green & blk	2.25	1.40

13th anniversary of the revolution.

The 100m was printed in sheets of six, consisting of two singles and two vertical pairs. Margins and gutters contain multiple UAR coat of arms in light green. Size: 240x330mm.

4th Pan Arab Games Emblem A266

Map and Emblems of Previous Games — A267

Designs: No. 675, Swimmers Zeitun and Abd el Gelil and arms of Alexandria. 35m, Race horse "Saadoon."

Perf. 11½x11; 11½ (#676)

1965, Sept. 2 **Photo.** **Wmk. 342**

674	A266	5m	blue & red	15	15
675	A266	10m	dp blue & dk brn	22	15
676	A267	10m	orange brn & dp blue	22	15
677	A266	35m	green & brown	40	20
			Set value		41

Issued to publicize the 4th Pan Arab Games, Cairo, Sept. 2-11. No. 675 commemorates the long-distance swimming competition at Alexandria, a part of the Games.

Map of Arab Countries, Emblem of Arab League and Broken Chain A268

1965, Sept. 13 **Photo.** *Perf. 11½*

678 A268 10m brown & yellow 15 15

3rd Arab Summit Conf., Casablanca, Sept. 13.

Land Forces Emblem and Sun — A269

Perf. 11x11½

1965, Oct. 20 **Wmk. 342**

679 A269 10m bister brn & blk 15 15

Issued for Land Forces Day.

Map of Africa, Torch and Olive Branches — A270

1965, Oct. 21 *Perf. 11½*

680 A270 10m dull pur & car rose 15 15

Assembly of Heads of State of the Organization for African Unity.

Ramses II, Abu Simbel, and ICY Emblem A271

Pillars, Philae, and UN Emblem — A272

Designs: 35m, Two Ramses II statues, Abu Simbel and UNESCO emblem. 50m, Cartouche of Ramses II and ICY emblem, horiz.

Perf. 11½

1965, Oct. 24 **Wmk. 342** **Photo.**

681	A271	5m	yellow & sl grn	15	15
682	A272	10m	blue & black	32	15
683	A271	35m	dk violet & yel	70	20
			Set value		40

Souvenir Sheet

Imperf

684 A272 50m brt ultra & dk brn 1.10 80

Intl. cooperation in saving the Nubian monuments. No. 684 also for the 20th anniv. of the UN. No. 684 contains one 42x25mm stamp.

Al-Maqrizi, Buildings and Books A273

Perf. 11½x11

1965, Nov. 20 **Photo.** **Wmk. 342**

685 A273 10m olive & dk sl grn 15 15

Ahmed Al-Maqrizi (1365-1442), historian.

Flag of UAR, Arms of Alexandria and Art Symbols — A274

1965, Dec. 16 *Perf. 11x11½*

686 A274 10m multicolored 15 15

6th Biennial Exhibition of Fine Arts in Alexandria, Dec. 16, 1965-Mar. 31, 1966.

Parchment Letter, Carrier Pigeon and Postrider A275

1966, Jan. 2 **Wmk. 342** *Perf. 11½*

687 A275 10m multicolored 15 15

Post Day, Jan. 2. See Nos. CB1-CB2.

Lamp and Arch — A276

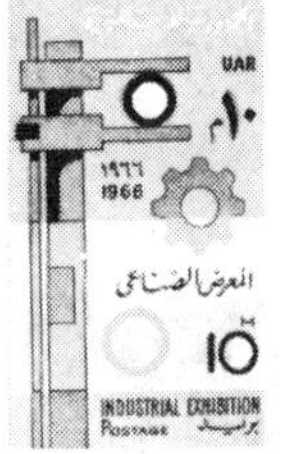
Exhibition Poster — A277

1966, Jan. 10 **Unwmk.** *Perf. 11*

688 A276 4m violet & dp org 15 15

Issued for use on greeting cards.

Perf. 11x11½

1966, Jan. 27 **Wmk. 342**

689 A277 10m lt blue & blk 15 15

Industrial Exhibition, Jan. 29-Feb.

Arab League Emblem A278

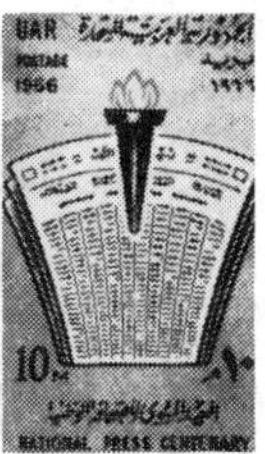
Printed Page and Torch A279

1966, Mar. 22 **Photo.** **Wmk. 342**

690 A278 10m brt yellow & pur 15 15

Arab Publicity Week, Mar. 22-28.

1966, Mar. 25 *Perf. 11x11½*

691 A279 10m dp orange & sl blue 15 15

Centenary of the national press.

Traffic Signal at Night — A280

Hands Holding Torch, Flags of UAR & Iraq — A281

1966, May 4 **Photo.** **Wmk. 342**

692 A280 10m green & red 15 15

Issued for Traffic Day.

1966, May 26 *Perf. 11x11½*

693 A281 10m dp cl, rose red & brt grn 15 15

Friendship between UAR and Iraq.

Workers and UN Emblem A282

Perf. 11½x11

1966, June 1 **Photo.** **Wmk. 342**

694	A282	5m	blue grn & blk	15	15
695	A282	10m	brt rose lil & grn	15	15
696	A282	35m	orange & black	25	15
			Set value	40	22

50th session of the ILO.

Mobilization Dept. Emblem, People and City — A283

1966, June 30 *Perf. 11x11½*

697 A283 10m dull pur & brn 15 15

Population sample, May 31-June 16.

"Salah el Din," Crane and Cogwheel
A284

Present-day Basket Dance and Pharaonic Dance — A285

Designs: No. 699, Transfer of first stones of Abu Simbel. No. 700, Development of Sinai (map of Red Sea area and Sinai Peninsula). No. 701, El Maadi Hospital and nurse with patient.

Perf. 11½

1966, July 23 Photo. Wmk. 342

698 A284	10m	orange & multi	15	15
699 A284	10m	brt green & multi	15	15
700 A284	10m	yellow & multi	15	15
701 A284	10m	lt blue & multi	15	15
		Set value	24	20

Souvenir Sheet

Imperf

702 A285 100m multicolored 2.00 2.00

14th anniv. of the revolution.

Suez Canal Headquarters, Ships and Map of Canal — A286

1966, July 26 ***Perf. 11½***

703 A286 10m blue & crimson 18 15

Nationalization of the Suez Canal, 10th anniv.

Cotton, Farmers with Plow and Tractor
A287

Perf. 11½x11

1966, Sept. 9 Photo. Wmk. 342

704 A287	5m	shown	15	15
705 A287	10m	Rice	15	15
706 A287	35m	Onions	15	15
		Set value	24	22

Issued for Farmer's Day.

WHO Headquarters, Geneva — A288

Designs: 10m, UN refugee emblem. 35m, UNICEF emblem.

Perf. 11½x11

1966, Oct. 24 Wmk. 342

707 A288	5m	olive & brt pur	15	15
708 A288	10m	orange & brt pur	16	15
709 A288	35m	lt blue & brt pur	45	15
		Set value		22

21st anniversary of the United Nations.

See Nos. N129-N131.

World Map and Festival Emblem
A289

1966, Nov. 8 Photo.

710 A289 10m brt purple & yellow 15 15

5th Intl. Television Festival, Nov. 1-10.

Arms of UAR, Rocket and Pylon
A290

1966, Dec. 23 Wmk. 342 ***Perf. 11½***

711 A290 10m brt grn & car rose 15 15

Issued for Victory Day.
See No. N132.

Jackal
A291

Design: 35m, Alabaster head from Tutankhamen treasure.

1967, Jan. 2 Photo.

712 A291	10m	slate, yel & brn	70	16
713 A291	35m	blue, dk vio & ocher	1.40	35

Issued for Post Day, Jan. 2.

Carnations
A292

Workers Planting Tree
A293

1967, Jan. 10 Unwmk. ***Perf. 11***

714 A292 4m citron & purple 15 15

Issued for use on greeting cards.

Perf. 11x11½

1967, Mar. 15 Wmk. 342

715 A293 10m brt green & blk vio 15 15

Issued to publicize the Tree Festival.

Gamal el-Dine el-Afghani and Arab League Emblem — A294

1967, Mar. 22 Photo. Wmk. 342

716 A294 10m dp green & dk brn 15 15

Arab Publicity Week, Mar. 22-28.
See No. N133.

Census Emblem, Man, Woman and Factory
A295

1967, Apr. 23 ***Perf. 11½x11***

717 A295 10m black & dp org 15 15

First industrial census.

Brickmaking Fresco, Tomb of Rekhmire, Thebes, 1504-1450 B.C.
A296

1967, May 1 Photo. Wmk. 342

718 A296 10m olive & orange 15 15

Issued for Labor Day, 1967.
See No. N134.

Ramses II and Queen Nefertari — A297

Design: 35m, Shooting geese, frieze from tomb of Atet at Meidum, c. 2724 B. C.

Perf. 11½x11

1967, June 7 Photo. Wmk. 342

719 A297	10m	multicolored	50	16
720 A297	35m	dk green & org	75	35
		Nos. 719-720,C113-C115 (5)	4.24	1.22

Issued for International Tourist Year, 1967.

President Nasser, Crowd and Map of Palestine
A298

1967, June 22 ***Perf. 11½***

721 A298 10m dp org, yel & ol 40 25

Issued to publicize Arab solidarity for "the defense of Palestine."

Souvenir Sheet

National Products — A299

1967, July 23 Wmk. 342 ***Imperf.***

722 A299 100m multicolored 2.00 75

15th anniv. of the revolution.

Salama Higazi — A300

Perf. 11x11½

1967, Oct. 14 Photo. Wmk. 342

723 A300 20m brown & dk blue 15 15

50th anniversary of the death of Salama Higazi, pioneer of Egyptian lyric stage.

Stag on Ceramic Disk — A301

Design: 55m, Apse showing Christ in Glory, Madonna and Saints, Coptic Museum, and UNESCO Emblem.

1967, Oct. 24 ***Perf. 11½***

724 A301	20m	dull rose & dk bl	15	15
725 A301	55m	dk slate grn & yel	45	25

22nd anniv. of the UN. See No. C117.

Savings Bank and Postal Authority Emblems
A302

1967, Oct. 31 ***Perf. 11½x11***

726 A302 20m sal pink & dk blue 15 15

International Savings Day.

Rose — A303

Unwmk.

1967, Dec. 15 Photo. ***Perf. 11***

727 A303 5m green & rose lil 15 15

Issued for use on greeting cards.

Pharaonic Dress — A304

Aswan High Dam and Power Lines — A305

Designs: Various pharaonic dresses from temple decorations.

Perf. 11x11½

1968, Jan. 2 **Wmk. 342**

728 A304 20m brown, grn & buff	45	15
729 A304 55m lt grn, yel & sep	1.00	28
730 A304 80m dk brn, bl & brt rose	1.40	60

Issued for Post Day, Jan. 2.

1968, Jan. 9

731 A305 20m yel, bl & dk brn	15	15

1st electricity generated by the Aswan Hydroelectric Station.

Alabaster Vessel, Tutankhamen Treasure — A306

Girl, Moon and Paint Brushes — A308

Capital of Coptic Limestone Pillar A307

Perf. 11x11½, 11½

1968, Jan. 20 **Photo.** **Wmk. 342**

732 A306 20m dk ultra, yel & brn	15	15
733 A307 80m lt grn, dk pur & ol grn	35	28

2nd International Festival of Museums.

1968, Feb. 15 *Perf. 11x11½*

734 A308 20m brt blue & black	15	15

7th Biennial Exhibition of Fine Arts, Alexandria, Feb. 15.

Cattle and Veterinarian — A309

Perf. 11½x11

1968, May 4 **Photo.** **Wmk. 342**

735 A309 20m brown, yel & grn	15	15

8th Arab Veterinary Congress, Cairo.

Human Rights Flame — A310

Perf. 11x11½

1968, July 1 **Photo.** **Wmk. 342**

736 A310 20m citron, crim & grn	15	15
737 A310 60m sky blue, crim & grn	20	15
Set value		20

International Human Rights Year, 1968.

Open Book with Symbols of Science, Victory Election Result A311

Workers, Cogwheel with Coat of Arms and Open Book — A312

1968, July 23 *Perf. 11½*

738 A311 20m rose red & sl grn	15	15

Souvenir Sheet

Imperf

739 A312 100m lt green, org & pur	90	80

16th anniversary of the revolution.

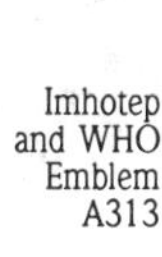

Imhotep and WHO Emblem A313

Design: No. 741, Avicenna and WHO emblem.

Perf. 11½x11

1968, Sept. 1 **Photo.** **Wmk. 342**

740 A313 20m blue, yel & brn	28	15
741 A313 20m yellow, bl & brn	28	15
a. Pair, #740-741	60	30
Set value		16

20th anniv. of the WHO. Nos. 740-741 printed in checkerboard sheets of 50 (5x10).

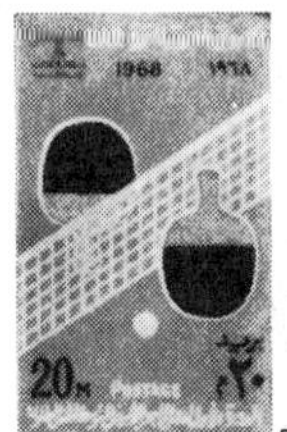

Table Tennis — A314

Perf. 11x11½

1968, Sept. 20 **Photo.** **Wmk. 342**

742 A314 20m lt green & dk brn	15	15

First Mediterranean Table Tennis Tournament, Alexandria, Sept. 20-27.

Factories and Fair Emblem A315

1968, Oct. 20 **Wmk. 342** *Perf. 11½*

743 A315 20m bl gray, red & sl bl	15	15

Cairo International Industrial Fair.

Temples of Philae — A316

Refugees, Map of Palestine, Refugee Year Emblem A317

Design: 55m, Temple at Philae and UNESCO emblem.

1968, Oct. 24 **Photo.**

744 A316 20m multicolored	15	15
745 A317 30m multicolored	90	16
746 A317 55m lt blue, yel & blk	45	20
Set value		42

Issued for United Nations Day, Oct. 24.

Egyptian Boy Scout Emblem — A318

1968, Nov. 1

747 A318 10m dull org & vio bl	22	15

50th anniversary of Egyptian Boy Scouts.

Pharaonic Sports A319

Design: 30m, Pharaonic sports (different).

1968, Nov. 1

748 A319 20m pale ol, pale sal & blk	20	15
749 A319 30m pale blue, buff & pur	30	15
Set value		15

19th Olympic Games, Mexico City, Oct. 12-27.

Aly Moubarak — A320

Lotus — A321

1968, Nov. 9 *Perf. 11½*

750 A320 20m green, brn & bis	22	15

Aly Moubarak (1823-93), founder of the modern educational system in Egypt.

1968, Dec. 11 **Photo.** **Wmk. 342**

751 A321 5m brt blue, grn & yel	28	15

Issued for use on greeting cards.

Son of Ramses III — A322

Hefni Nassef — A323

Pharaonic Dress: No. 753, Ramses III. No. 754, Girl carrying basket on her head. 55m, Queen of the New Empire in transparent dress.

1969, Jan. 2 **Photo.** *Perf. 11½*

752 A322 5m blue & multi	45	20
753 A322 20m blue & multi	70	40
754 A322 20m blue & multi	1.25	60
755 A322 55m blue & multi	55	28

Issued for Post Day, Jan. 2.

Perf. 11x11½

1969, Mar. 2 **Photo.** **Wmk. 342**

Portrait: No. 757, Mohammed Farid.

756 A323 20m purple & brown	28	15
757 A323 20m emerald & brown	28	15
a. Pair, #756-757	60	30
Set value		16

50th anniv. of the death of Hefni Nassef (1860-1919) writer and government worker, and Mohammed Farid (1867-1919), lawyer and Speaker of the Nationalist Party.

Teacher and Children A324

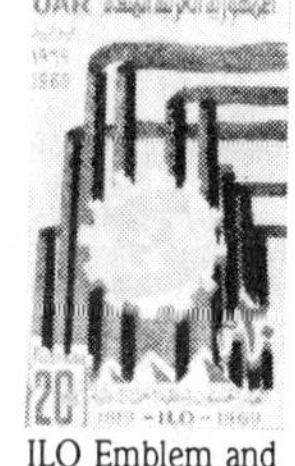

ILO Emblem and Factory Chimneys A325

1969, Mar. 2 *Perf. 11x11½*

758 A324 20m multicolored	15	15

Arab Teacher's Day.

1969, Apr. 11 **Photo.** **Wmk. 342**

759 A325 20m brown, ultra & car	15	15

50th anniv. of the ILO.

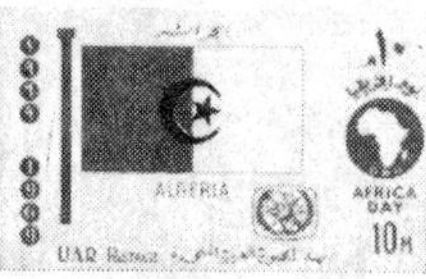

Flag of Algeria, Africa Day and Tourist Year Emblems
A326

Perf. 11½x11

1969, May 25 Litho. Wmk. 342

No.	Type	Value	Description	Unused	Used
760	A326	10m	Algeria	45	22
761	A326	10m	Botswana	45	22
762	A326	10m	Burundi	45	22
763	A326	10m	Cameroun	45	22
764	A326	10m	Cent. Afr. Rep.	45	22
765	A326	10m	Chad	45	22
766	A326	10m	Congo, ex-Belgian	45	22
767	A326	10m	Congo, ex-French	45	22
768	A326	10m	Dahomey	45	22
769	A326	10m	Equatorial Guinea	45	22
770	A326	10m	Ethiopia	45	22
771	A326	10m	Gabon	45	22
772	A326	10m	Gambia	45	22
773	A326	10m	Ghana	45	22
774	A326	10m	Guinea	45	22
775	A326	10m	Ivory Coast	45	22
776	A326	10m	Kenya	45	22
777	A326	10m	Lesotho	45	22
778	A326	10m	Liberia	45	22
779	A326	10m	Libya	45	22
780	A326	10m	Malagasy	45	22
781	A326	10m	Malawi	45	22
782	A326	10m	Mali	45	22
783	A326	10m	Mauritania	45	22
784	A326	10m	Mauritius	45	22
785	A326	10m	Morocco	45	22
786	A326	10m	Niger	45	22
787	A326	10m	Nigeria	45	22
788	A326	10m	Rwanda	45	22
789	A326	10m	Senegal	45	22
790	A326	10m	Sierra Leone	45	22
791	A326	10m	Somalia	45	22
792	A326	10m	Sudan	45	22
793	A326	10m	Swaziland	45	22
794	A326	10m	Tanzania	45	22
795	A326	10m	Togo	45	22
796	A326	10m	Tunisia	45	22
797	A326	10m	Uganda	45	22
798	A326	10m	UAR	45	22
799	A326	10m	Upper Volta	45	22
800	A326	10m	Zambia	45	22
			Nos. 760-800 (41)	18.45	9.02

El Fetouh Gate, Cairo
A327

Sculptures from the Egyptian Museum, Cairo — A328

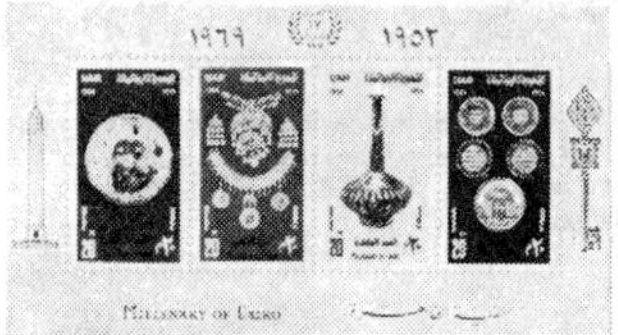

Millenary of Cairo — A329

Designs: No. 802, Al Azhar University. No. 803, The Citadel. No. 805, Sculptures, Coptic Museum. No. 806, Glass plate and vase, Fatimid dynasty, Islamic Museum. No. 807a, Islamic coin. No. 807b, Fatimist era jewelry. No. 807c, Copper vase. No. 807d, Coins and plaque.

Perf. 11½x11

1969, July 23 Photo. Wmk. 342

801 A327 10m dk brown & multi 45 20
802 A327 10m green & multi 45 20
803 A327 10m blue & multi 45 20

Perf. 11½

804 A328 20m yellow grn & multi 75 32
805 A328 20m dp ultra & multi 75 32
806 A328 20m brown & multi 75 32
Nos. 801-806 (6) 3.60 1.56

Souvenir Sheet

807 A329 Sheet of 4 5.00 5.00
a. 20m dark blue & multi 90 90
b. 20m lilac & multi 90 90
c. 20m yellow & multi 90 90
d. 20m dark green & multi 90 90

Millenium of the founding of Cairo.

African Development Bank Emblem — A330

Perf. 11x11½

1969, Sept. 10 Photo. Wmk. 342

808 A330 20m emerald, yel & vio 15 15

African Development Bank, 5th anniv.

Pharaonic Boat and UN Emblem
A331

Temple of Philae Inundated and UNESCO Emblem
A332

Design: 5m, King and Queen from Abu Simbel Temple and UNESCO Emblem (size: 21x38mm).

Perf. 11x11½, 11½x11

1969, Oct. 24 Photo. Wmk. 342

809 A332 5m brown & multi 15 15
810 A331 20m yellow & ultra 55 20

Perf. 11½

811 A332 55m yellow & multi 45 20
Set value 45

Issued for United Nations Day.

Ships of 1869 and 1967 and Maps of Africa and Suez Canal — A333

1969, Nov. 15 *Perf. 11½x11*

812 A333 20m lt blue & multi 15 15

Centenary of the Suez Canal.

Cairo Opera House and Performance of Aida — A334

1969, Nov. 15

813 A334 20m multicolored 25 15

Centenary of the Cairo Opera House.

Crowd with Egyptian and Revolutionary Flags — A335

1969, Nov. 15 *Perf. 11½x11*

814 A335 20m brt grn, dull lil & red 22 15

Revolution of 1919.

Ancient Arithmetic and Computer Cards
A336

Perf. 11½x11

1969, Dec. 17 Photo. Wmk. 342

815 A336 20m multicolored 15 15

Intl. Congress for Scientific Accounting, Cairo, Dec. 17-19.

Poinsettia
A337

Sakkara Step Pyramid
A338

El Fetouh Gate, Cairo — A339

Fountain, Sultan Hassan Mosque, Cairo — A340

King Khafre (Ruled c. 2850 B.C.)
A341

1969, Dec. 24 Unwmk. *Perf. 11*

816 A337 5m yellow, grn & car 15 15

Issued for use on greeting cards.

Wmk. 342 (20m, £1), Unwmkd.
Photo.; Engr. (20m, 55m)

1969-70 *Perf. 11*

Designs: 5m, Al Azhar Mosque. 10m, Luxor Temple. 50m, Qaitbay Fort, Alexandria.

817 A338 1m multicolored ('70) 15 15
818 A338 5m multicolored ('70) 15 15
819 A338 10m multicolored ('70) 22 15
820 A339 20m dark brown 45 15
821 A338 50m multicolored ('70) 70 16
822 A340 55m slate green 90 18

Perf. 11½

Photo. & Engr.

823 A341 £1 org & sl grn ('70) 7.75 3.25
Nos. 817-823 (7) 10.32 4.19

See #889-891, 893-897, 899, 901-902, 904.

Veiled Women, by Mahmoud Said — A342

Perf. 11x11½

1970, Jan. 2 Photo. Wmk. 342
Size: 45x89mm

824 A342 100m blue & multi 1.65 35

Post Day. Sheet of 8 with 2 panes of 4.

Parliament, Scales, Globe and Laurel — A343

1970, Feb. 2 *Perf. 11½x11*

825 A343 20m blue, vio bl & ocher 15 15

Intl. Conf. of Parliamentarians on the Middle East Crisis, Cairo, Feb. 2-5.

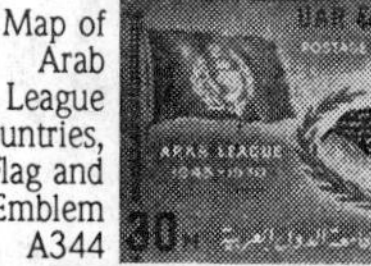

Map of Arab League Countries, Flag and Emblem
A344

Perf. 11½x11

1970, Mar. 22 Photo. Wmk. 342

826 A344 30m brn org, grn & dk pur 15 15

25th anniv. of the Arab League. See No. B42.

Mena House and Sheraton Hotel — A345

1970, Mar. 23

827 A345 20m olive, org & bl 25 15

Centenary of Mena House and the inauguration of the Cairo Sheraton Hotel.

Manufacture of Medicine — A346

1970, Apr. 20

828 A346 20m brown, yel & bl 25 15

Production of medicines in Egypt, 30th anniv.

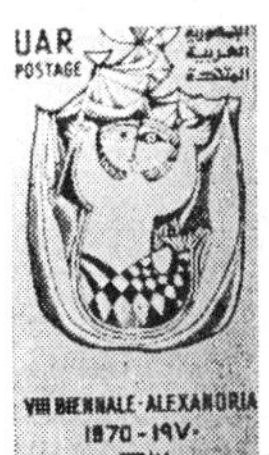
Mermaid — A347

1970, Apr. 20 *Perf. 11x11½*
829 A347 20m orange, blk & ultra 20 15

8th Biennial Exhibition of Fine Arts, Alexandria, March 12.

Misr Bank and Talaat Harb — A348

ITU Emblem — A349

1970, May 7 Photo. Wmk. 342
830 A348 20m multicolored 25 15

50th anniversary of Misr Bank.

1970, May 17 *Perf. 11x11½*
831 A349 20m dk brn, yel & dull bl 25 15

World Telecommunications Day.

UPU Headquarters, Bern — A350

1970, May 20 *Perf. 11½x11*
832 A350 20m multicolored 25 15

Inauguration of the UPU Headquarters in Bern. See No. C128.

Basketball Player and Map of Africa — A351

UPU, UN and U.P.A.F. Emblems A352

Designs: No. 834, Soccer player, map of Africa and cup, horiz.

Perf. 11x11½, 11½x11
1970, May 25 Photo. Wmk. 342
833 A351 20m lt blue, yel & brn 30 15
834 A351 20m yellow & multi 30 15
835 A352 20m ocher, grn & blk 30 15
Set value 18

Issued for Africa Day. No. 833 also commemorates the 5th African basketball championship for men; No. 834 the annual African Soccer championship and No. 835 publicizes the African Postal Union seminar.

Fist and Freed Bird — A353

1970, July 23 Photo. *Perf. 11*
836 A353 20m lt green, org & blk 25 15

Souvenir Sheet

Imperf

837 A353 100m lt blue, dp org & blk 90 35

18th anniv. of the revolution.

Al Aqsa Mosque on Fire — A354

1970, Aug. 21 Wmk. 342 *Perf. 11*
838 A354 20m multicolored 45 15
839 A354 60m brt blue & multi 90 20
Set value 26

1st anniv. of the burning of Al Aqsa Mosque, Jerusalem.

Standardization Emblems — A355

1970, Oct. 14 Wmk. 342 *Perf. 11*
840 A355 20m yellow, ultra & grn 20 15

World Standards Day and 25th anniv. of the Intl. Standardization Organization, ISO.

UN Emblem, Scales and Dove — A356

Temple at Philae A357

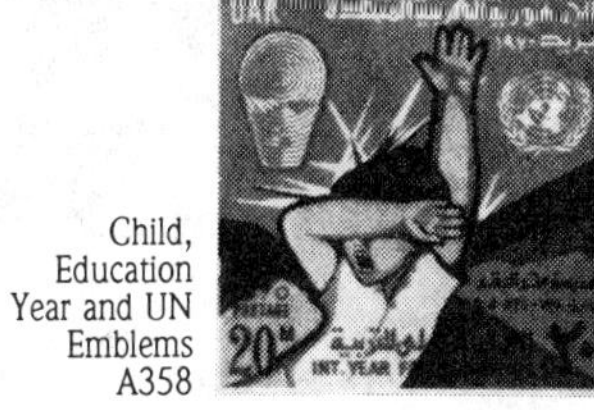
Child, Education Year and UN Emblems A358

Designs: 10m, UN emblem. No. 845, 2nd Temple at Philae (denomination at left).

Perf. 11 (5m), 11½ (others)
1970, Oct. 24 Photo. Wmk. 342
841 A356 5m lt bl, rose lil & sl 15 15
842 A357 10m yel, brn & lt bl 16 15
843 A358 20m slate & multi 28 16
844 A357 55m brn, bl & ocher 50 28
845 A357 55m brn, bl & ocher 50 25
a. Strip of 3, #842, 844-845 1.25 70
Nos. 841-845,B43 (6) 3.09 1.37

25th anniv. of the UN. No. 843 also commemorates Intl. Education Year; Nos. 842, 844-845, the work of UNESCO in saving the Temples of Philae. Nos. 842, 844-845 printed se-tenant in sheets of 35 (15 No. 842 and 10 each Nos. 844-845). Nos. 844-845 show continuous picture of the Temples at Philae.

Gamal Abdel Nasser — A359

1970, Nov. 6 Wmk. 342 *Perf. 11*
846 A359 5m sky blue & blk 15 15
847 A359 20m gray green & blk 25 15
Set value 32 15

Gamal Abdel Nasser (1918-1970), President of Egypt. See Nos. C129-C130.

Medical Association Building A360

Designs: No. 849, Old and new National Library. No. 850, Egyptian Credo (Nasser quotation). No. 851, Engineering Society, old and new buildings. No. 852, Government Printing Offices, old and new buildings.

1970, Dec. 20 Photo. *Perf. 11*
848 A360 20m yel, grn & brn 28 15
849 A360 20m green & multi 28 15
850 A360 20m lt blue & brn 28 15
851 A360 20m blue, yel & brn 28 15
852 A360 20m blue, yel & brn 28 15
a. Strip of 5, #848-852 1.50 50
Nos. 848-852 (5) 1.40
Set value 30

50th anniv. of Egyptian Medical Assoc. (#848); cent. of Natl. Library (#849); Egyptian Engineering Assoc. (#851); sesqui. of Government Printing Offices (#852).

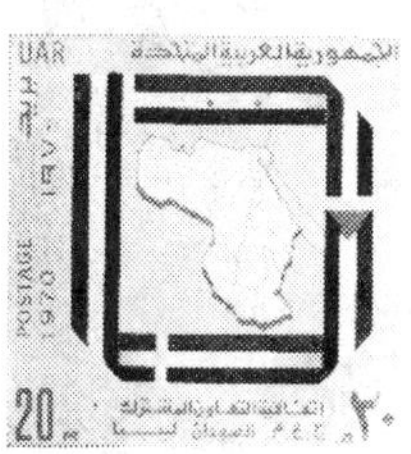
Map and Flags of UAR, Libya, Sudan A361

1970, Dec. 27 *Perf. 11½*
853 A361 20m lt grn, car & blk 20 15

Signing of the Charter of Tripoli affirming the unity of UAR, Libya and the Sudan, Dec. 27, 1970.

Qalawun Minaret — A362

Designs (Minarets): 10m, As Saleh. 20m, Isna. 55m, Al Hakim.

1971, Jan. 2 Wmk. 342 *Perf. 11*
854 A362 5m green & multi 35 20
855 A362 10m green & multi 1.00 40
856 A362 20m green & multi 2.00 80
857 A362 55m green & multi 3.50 1.60
a. Strip of 4, #854-857 + label 10.00 3.25

Post Day, 1971.
See Nos. 905-908, 932-935.

Gamal Abdel Nasser A363

Photogravure and Engraved
1971 Wmk. 342 *Perf. 11½*
858 A363 200m brn vio & dk bl 2.25 75
859 A363 500m blue & black 5.50 2.00

Souvenir Sheet

Design: Portrait facing right.

Imperf

860 Sheet of 2 5.50 2.75
a. A363 100m light green & black 2.25 75
b. A363 200m blue & black 1.75 1.25

No. 860 commemorates inauguration of the Aswan High Dam, which is shown in margin.
Issued: No. 860, Jan. 15; Nos. 858-859, Feb. 1.
See No. 903.

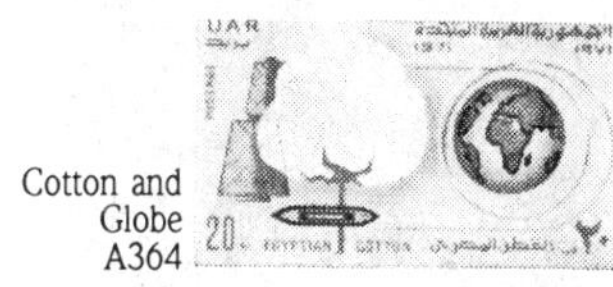
Cotton and Globe A364

1971, Mar. 6 Photo. *Perf. 11½x11*
861 A364 20m lt green, blue & brn 15 15

Egyptian cotton.

Arab Countries, and Arab Postal Union Emblem A365

1971, Mar. 6 Wmk. 342
862 A365 20m lt bl, org & sl grn 25 15

9th Arab Postal Congress, Cairo, March 6-25. See No. C131.

Cairo Fair Emblem — A366

1971, Mar. 6 *Perf. 11x11½*
863 A366 20m plum, blk & org 15 15

Cairo International Fair, March 2-23.

Nesy Ra, Apers Papyrus and WHO Emblem A367

Perf. 11½x11

1971, Apr. 30 Photo. Wmk. 342

864 A367 20m yellow bis & pur 25 15

World Health Organization Day.

Gamal Abdel Nasser — A368

1971, May 1 *Perf. 11*

865 A368 20m purple & bl gray 15 15
866 A368 55m blue & purple 40 16
Set value 22

Map of Africa, Telecommunications Symbols — A369

1971, May 17 *Perf. 11½x11*

867 A369 20m blue & multi 15 15

Pan-African telecommunications system.

Wheelwright A370

Hand Holding Wheat and Laurel A371

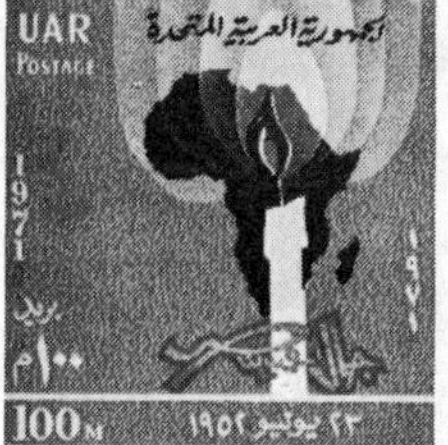

Candle Lighting Africa A372

Perf. 11x11½

1971, July 23 Photo. Wmk. 342

868 A370 20m yellow & multi 25 15
869 A371 20m tan, grn & ocher 25 15
Set value 15

Souvenir Sheet

Imperf

870 A372 100m blue & multi 1.00 50

19th anniv. of the July Revolution. No. 870 contains one stamp with simulated perforations in gold.

Arab Postal Union Emblem A373

1971, Aug. 3 *Perf. 11½*

871 A373 20m black, yel & grn 25 15

25th anniv. of the Conf. of Sofar, Lebanon, establishing the APU. See No. C135.

Arab Republic of Egypt

Three Links A374

Perf. 11½x11

1971, Sept. 28 Photo. Wmk. 342

872 A374 20m gray, org brn & blk 50 32

Confederation of Arab Republics (Egypt, Syria and Libya). See No. C136.

Gamal Abdel Nasser A375

Blood Donation A376

1971, Sept. 28 *Perf. 11x11½*

873 A375 5m slate grn & vio brn 15 15
874 A375 20m violet brn & ultra 18 15
875 A375 30m ultra & brown 28 15
876 A375 55m brown & emerald 45 20
Set value 46

Death of Pres. Gamal Abdel Nasser, 1st anniv.

1971, Oct. 24

877 A376 20m green & carmine 25 15

"Blood Saves Lives."

Princess Nursing Child, UNICEF Emblem — A377

Submerged Pillar, Philae, UNESCO Emblem — A379

Equality Year Emblem A378

Perf. 11x11½, 11½x11

1971, Oct. 24 Photo. Wmk. 342

878 A377 5m buff, blk & org brn 15 15
879 A378 20m red brn, grn, yel & blk 25 15
880 A379 55m black, lt bl, yel & brn 50 16
Set value 27

UN Day. No. 878 honors UN Intl. Children's Fund; No. 879 for Intl. Year Against Racial Discrimination; No. 880 honors UNESCO. See No. C137.

Postal Traffic Center, Alexandria A380

1971, Oct. 31 *Perf. 11½x11*

881 A380 20m blue & bister 15 15

Opening of Postal Traffic Center in Alexandria.

Sunflower A381

Abdalla El Nadim A382

1971, Nov. 13 *Perf. 11*

882 A381 5m lt blue & multi 15 15

For use on greeting cards.

1971, Nov. 14 *Perf. 11x11½*

883 A382 20m green & brown 25 15

Abdalla El Nadim (1845-1896), journalist, publisher, connected with Orabi Revolution.

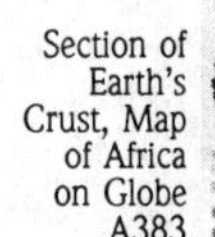

Section of Earth's Crust, Map of Africa on Globe A383

1971, Nov. 27 *Perf. 11½x11*

884 A383 20m ultra, yel & brn 15 15

75th anniv. of Egyptian Geological Survey and Intl. Conference, Nov. 27-Dec. 1.

Postal Union Emblem, Letter and Dove A384

Design: 55m, African Postal Union emblem and letter.

1971, Dec. 2

885 A384 5m multicolored 15 15
886 A384 20m olive, blk & org 15 15
887 A384 55m red, blk & blue 38 16
Set value 60 27

10th anniversary of African Postal Union. See No. C138.

Money and Safe Deposit Box — A385

1971, Dec. 23 *Perf. 11½*

888 A385 20m rose, brn & grn 25 15

70th anniversary of Postal Savings Bank.

Types of 1969-70, 1971 Inscribed "A. R. Egypt" and

Ramses II — A385a

Designs as before and: No. 894, King Citi I. No. 897, Queen Nefertari. No. 900, Sphinx and Middle Pyramid. 100m, Cairo Mosque. 200m, Head of Pharaoh Userkaf.

Wmk. 342 (#892A, 901-904)

1972-76 Photo. Unwmk. *Perf. 11*

889	A338	1m multicolored	15	15
890	A338	1m dk brown ('73)	15	15
891	A338	5m multicolored	15	15
892	A385a	5m olive ('73)	15	15
892A	A385a	5m bister ('76)	15	15
893	A338	10m multicolored	15	15
894	A338	10m lt brown ('73)	15	15
895	A339	20m olive	35	16
896	A339	20m purple ('73)	15	15
897	A338	50m multicolored	28	16
898	A385a	50m dull blue ('73)	22	15
899	A340	55m red lilac	30	20
900	A340	55m green ('74)	65	32
901	A339	100m lt blue, dp org & blk	45	28

Perf. 11½

Photo. & Engr.

902	A341	200m yel grn & brn	1.10	45
903	A363	500m blue & choc	6.50	4.00
904	A341	£1 orange & sl grn	8.75	6.00
		Nos. 889-904 (17)	19.80	12.92

Minaret Type of 1971

Designs: 5m, West Minaret, Nasser Mosque. 20m, East Minaret, Nasser Mosque. 30m, Minaret, Al Gawli Mosque. 55m, Minaret, Ibn Tulun Mosque.

Wmk. 342

1972, Jan. 2 Photo. *Perf. 11*

905 A362 5m dk green & multi 35 15
906 A362 20m dk green & multi 1.10 16
907 A362 30m dk green & multi 2.50 25
908 A362 55m dk green & multi 3.50 50
a. Strip of 4, #905-908 + label 11.00 1.40

Post Day, 1972.

Police Emblem and Activities — A386

1972, Jan. 25 *Perf. 11½*

909 A386 20m dull blue, brn & yel 25 15

Police Day 1972.

UNESCO, UN and Book Year Emblems — A387

1972, Jan. 25 *Perf. 11x11½*

910 A387 20m lt yel grn, vio bl & yel 15 15

International Book Year 1972.

Alexandria Biennale
A388

1972, Feb. 15 Wmk. 342 *Perf. 11½*
911 A388 20m black, brt rose & yel 15 15

9th Biennial Exhibition of Fine Arts, Alexandria, Mar., 1972.

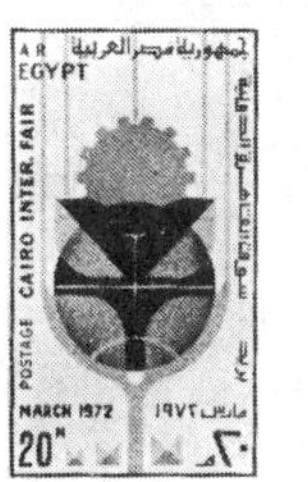
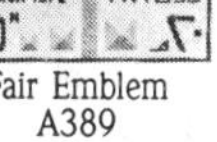

Fair Emblem
A389

Abdel Moniem Riad
A390

1972, Mar. 5 *Perf. 11x11½*
912 A389 20m blue, org & yel grn 25 15

International Cairo Fair.

1972, Mar. 21 Photo. Wmk. 342
913 A390 20m blue & brown 50 15

In memory of Brig. Gen. Abdel Moniem Riad (1919-1969), military hero.

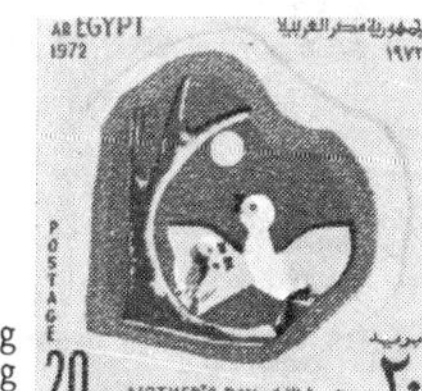

Bird Feeding Young
A391

1972, Mar. 21 *Perf. 11½*
914 A391 20m yellow & multi 25 15

Mother's Day.

Tutankhamen
A392

Design: 55m, Back of chair with king's name and symbols of eternity.

1972, May 22 Unwmk.
915 A392 20m gray, blk & ocher 75 20
916 A392 55m purple & yellow 1.50 35

50th anniversary of the discovery of the tomb of Tutankhamen by Howard Carter and Lord Carnarvon. See Nos. C142-C144.

Queen Nefertiti
A393

Perf. 11½
1972, May 22 Photo. Wmk. 342
917 A393 20m red, blk & gold 15 15

Soc. of the Friends of Art, 50th anniv.

Map of Africa — A394

1972, May 25 *Perf. 11x11½*
918 A394 20m purple, bl & brn 25 15

Africa Day.

Atom Symbol, "Faith and Science"
A395

Design: No. 920, Egyptian coat of arms.

1972, July 23 *Perf. 11½*
919 A395 20m blue, claret & blk 15 15
920 A395 20m ol grn, gold & blk 15 15
Set value 15

20th anniversary of the revolution.

Boxing, Olympic and Motion Emblems — A396

Designs (Olympic and Motion Emblems and): 10m, Wrestling. 20m, Basketball.

1972, Aug. 17 *Perf. 11½x11*
921 A396 5m blue & multi 15 15
922 A396 10m yellow & multi 20 15
923 A396 20m ver & multi 35 15
Nos. 921-923,C149-C152 (7) 1.90
Set value 45

20th Olympic Games, Munich, Aug. 26-Sept. 11.

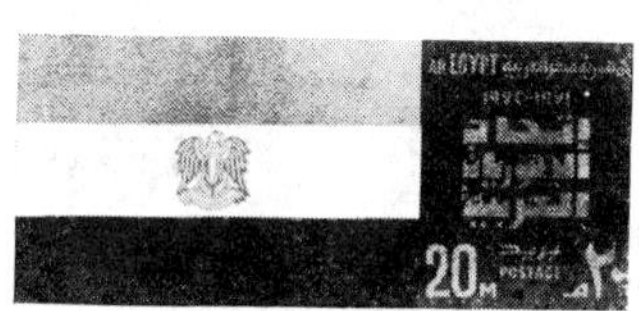

Flag of Confederation of Arab Republics — A397

1972, Sept. 1 Wmk. 342 *Perf. 11½*
924 A397 20m carmine, bis & blk 25 15

1st anniv. of Confederation of Arab Republics.

Red Crescent, TB and UN Emblems — A398

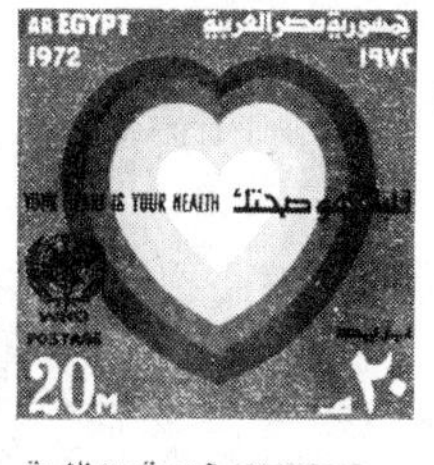

Heart and WHO Emblem
A399

Refugees, UNRWA Emblem, Map of Palestine — A400

Design: 55m, Inundated Temple of Philae, UNESCO emblem.

1972, Oct. 24 Photo. *Perf. 11x11½*
925 A398 10m brown org, red & bl 22 15

Perf. 11½
926 A399 20m green, yel & blk 45 15

Perf. 11
927 A400 30m lt blue, pur & lt brn 1.40 50

Perf. 11½
928 A399 55m brn, gold & bluish gray 1.50 55

UN Day. No. 925 is for the 14th Regional Tuberculosis Conf., Cairo, 1972; No. 926 is for World Health Month; No. 927 publicizes aid to refugees and No. 928 the UN campaign to save the Temples at Philae.

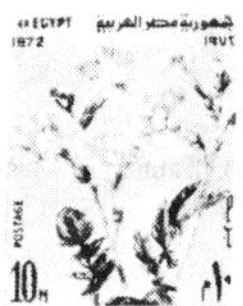

Morning Glory — A401

1972, Oct. 24 *Perf. 11*
929 A401 10m yel, lilac & grn 15 15

For use on greeting cards.

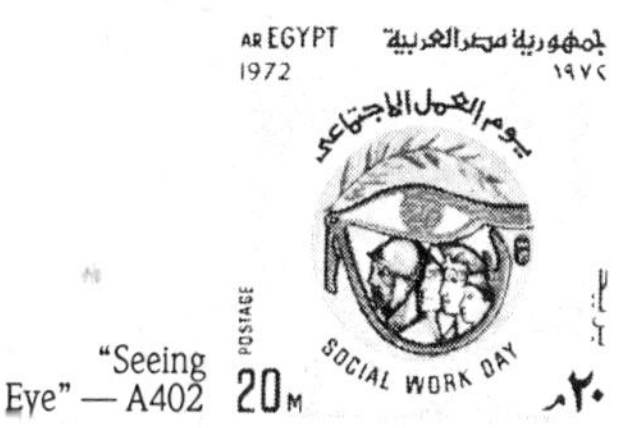

"Seeing Eye" — A402

1972, Nov. 30 *Perf. 11½*
930 A402 20m multicolored 15 15

Social Work Day.

Sculling Race, View of Luxor — A403

1972, Dec. 17 Wmk. 342 *Perf. 11*
931 A403 20m blue & brown 15 15

3rd Nile Intl. Rowing Festival, Dec. 1972.

Minaret Type of 1971

Minarets: 10m, Al Maridani, 1338. 20m, Bashtak, 1337. 30m, Qusun, 1330. 55m, Al Gashankir, 1306.

1973, Jan. 2
Frame in Bright Yellow Green
932 A362 10m multicolored 70 16
933 A362 20m multicolored 1.20 22
934 A362 30m multicolored 2.50 40
935 A362 55m multicolored 3.50 1.00
a. Strip of 4, #932-935 + Label 10.00 4.00

Post Day, 1973.

Cairo Fair Emblem
A404

Perf. 11½x11
1973, Mar. 21 Photo. Wmk. 342
936 A404 20m gray & multi 15 15

International Cairo Fair.

Family — A405

1973, Mar. 21 *Perf. 11x11½*
937 A405 20m multicolored 15 15

Family planning.

Sania Girls' School and Hoda Sharawi
A406

Perf. 11½x11
1973, July 15 Photo. Wmk. 342
938 A406 20m ultra & green 15 15

Centenary of education for girls and 50th anniversary of the Egyptian Women's Union, founded by Hoda Sharawi.

15-Cent Minimum Value
The minimum catalogue value is 15 cents. Separating se-tenant pieces into individual stamps does not increase the value of the stamps since demand for the separated stamps may be small.

Rifaa el Tahtawi — A407

1973, July 15 *Perf. 11x11½*

939 A407 20m brt green, ol & brn 25 15

Centenary of the death of Rifaa el Tahtawi, champion of democracy and principal of language school.

Omar Makram A408

Abdel Rahman al Gabarti, Historian A409

"Reconstruction and Battle" — A410

Design: No. 941, Mohamed Korayem, martyr.

1973, July 23

940 A408	20m	yel grn, bl & brn	15	15
941 A408	20m	lt grn, bl & brn	15	15
942 A409	20m	ocher & brown	15	15
		Set value	36	25

Souvenir Sheet

Imperf

943 A410 110m gold, bl & blk 1.00 1.00

Revolution establishing the republic, 21st anniv.

Grain, Cow, FAO Emblem A411

Perf. 11½x11

1973, Oct. 24 **Wmk. 342**

944 A411 10m brn, dk bl & yel grn 15 15

10th anniv. of the World Food Org.

Inundated Temples at Philae A412

1973, Oct. 24 *Perf. 11½*

945 A412 55m blue, pur & org 40 25

UNESCO campaign to save the temples at Philae.

Bank Building A413

1973, Oct. 24

946 A413 20m brn org, grn & blk 15 15

75th anniv. of the National Bank of Egypt.

Rose — A414

1973, Oct. 24 *Perf. 11*

947 A414 10m blue & multi 15 15

For use on greeting cards.

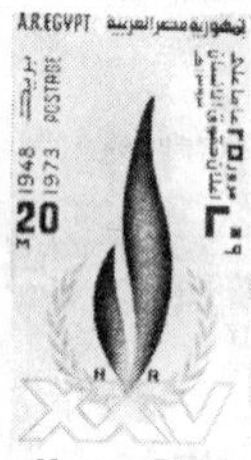

Human Rights Flame — A415

Taha Hussein — A416

Perf. 11x11½

1973, Dec. 8 **Photo.** **Wmk. 342**

948 A415 20m yel grn, dk bl & car 15 15

25th anniversary of the Universal Declaration of Human Rights.

1973, Dec. 10

949 A416 20m dk blue, brn & emer 15 15

Dr. Taha Hussein (1893-1973), "Father of Education" in Egypt, writer, philosopher.

Pres. Sadat, Flag and Battle of Oct. 6 — A417

1973, Dec. 23 *Perf. 11x11½*

950 A417 20m yellow, blk & red 2.25 1.00

October War against Israel (crossing of Suez Canal by Egyptian forces, Oct. 6, 1973). See No. 959.

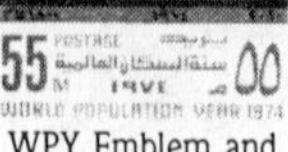

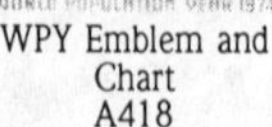

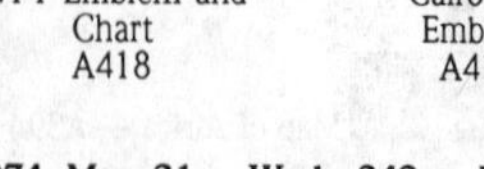

WPY Emblem and Chart A418

Cairo Fair Emblem A419

1974, Mar. 21 **Wmk. 342** *Perf. 11*

951 A418 55m org, grn & dk bl 30 20

World Population Year.

1974, Mar. 21 **Photo.**

952 A419 20m blue & multi 20 15

Cairo International Fair.

Nurse and Medal of Angels of Ramadan 10 — A420

1974, May 15 *Perf. 11½*

953 A420 55m multicolored 30 15

Nurses' and World Hospital Day.

Workers, Relief Carving from Queen Tee's Tomb, Sakhara — A421

1974, May 15 *Perf. 11*

954 A421 20m yellow, blue & brn 30 15

Workers' Day.

Pres. Sadat, Troops Crossing Suez Canal — A422

"Reconstruction," Map of Suez Canal and New Building — A423

Sheet of Aluminum A424

Design: 110m, Pres. Sadat's "October Working Paper," symbols of science and development.

1974, July 23 **Photo.** *Perf. 11x11½*

955 A422 20m multicolored 70 20

956 A423 20m blue, gold & blk 70 20

Perf. 11½

957 A424 20m plum & silver 40 15

Souvenir Sheet

Imperf

958 A424 110m green & multi 90 60

22nd anniversary of the revolution establishing the republic and for the end of the October War. No. 958 contains one stamp (52x59mm).

Pres. Sadat and Flag A425

Perf. 11x11½

1974, Oct. 6 **Wmk. 342**

959 A425 20m yellow, blk & red 1.50 75

1st anniv. of Battle. See No. 950.

Palette and Brushes A426

1974, Oct. 6 *Perf. 11½*

960 A426 30m purple, yel & blk 15 15

6th Exhibition of Plastic Art.

Teachers and Pupils — A427

1974, Oct. 6 *Perf. 11x11½*

961 A427 20m multicolored 15 15

Teachers' Day.

Souvenir Sheet

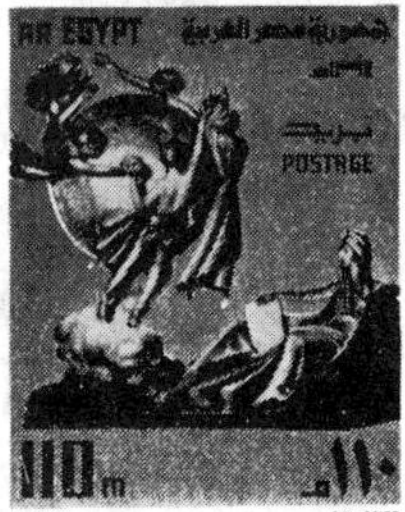

UPU Monument, Bern — A428

1974, Oct. 6 ***Imperf.***
962 A428 110m gold & multi 1.75 1.00

Cent. of the UPU.

Emblems, Cogwheel and Calipers — A429

Refugee Camp under Attack and UN Refugee Organization Emblem A430

Child and UNICEF Emblem A431

Temple of Philae — A432

1974, Oct. 24 ***Perf. 11½, 11x11½***
963 A429 10m black, bl & yel 22 15
964 A430 20m dp orange, bl & blk 70 40
965 A431 30m green, bl & brn 55 25
966 A432 55m black, bl & yel 80 35

United Nations Day. World Standards Day (10m); Palestinian refugee repatriation (20m); Family Planning (30m); Campaign to save Temple of Philae (55m).

Calla Lily — A433

1974, Nov. 7 ***Perf. 11***
967 A433 10m ultra & multi 15 15

For use on greeting cards.

10m-coins, Smokestacks and Grain A434

1974, Nov. 7 ***Perf. 11½x11***
968 A434 20m yel grn, dk bl & sil 15 15

International Savings Day.

Organization Emblem and Medical Services A435

1974, Nov. 7 ***Perf. 11½***
969 A435 30m vio, red & gold 15 15

Health Insurance Organization, 10th anniv.

Mustafa Lutfy El Manfalouty A436

Abbas Mahmoud El Akkad A437

Perf. 11x11½
1974, Dec. 8 Photo. Wmk. 342
970 A436 20m blue blk & brn 15 15
971 A437 20m brown & bl blk 15 15
a. Pair, #970-971 30 20
Set value 15

Arab writers; El Manfalouty (1876-1924) and El Akkad (1889-1964).

Goddess Maat Facing God Thoth — A438

Fish-shaped Vase — A439

Pharaonic Golden Vase — A440

Sign of Life, Mirror — A441

Perf. 11½
1975, Jan. 2 Photo. Wmk. 342
972 A438 20m silver & multi 22 15
973 A439 30m multicolored 28 20
974 A440 55m multicolored 35 25
975 A441 110m blue & multi 90 52

Post Day 1975. Egyptian art works from 12th-5th centuries B.C.

Om Kolthoum — A442

Perf. 11½
1975, Mar. 3 Photo. Unwmk.
976 A442 20m brown 20 15

In memory of Om Kolthoum, singer.

Crescent, Globe, Al Aqsa and Kaaba — A443

Cairo Fair Emblem — A444

1975, Mar. 25
977 A443 20m multicolored 45 25

Mohammed's Birthday.

Perf. 11x11½
1975, Mar. 25 Wmk. 342
978 A444 20m multicolored 15 15

International Cairo Fair.

Kasr El Ainy Hospital WHO Emblem A445

Perf. 11½x11
1975, May 7 Photo. Wmk. 342
979 A445 20m dk brown & blue 15 15

World Health Organization Day.

Children Reading Book — A446

Children and Line Graph — A447

1975, May 7 ***Perf. 11x11½***
980 A446 20m multicolored 15 15
981 A447 20m multicolored 15 15
Set value 25 15

Science Day.

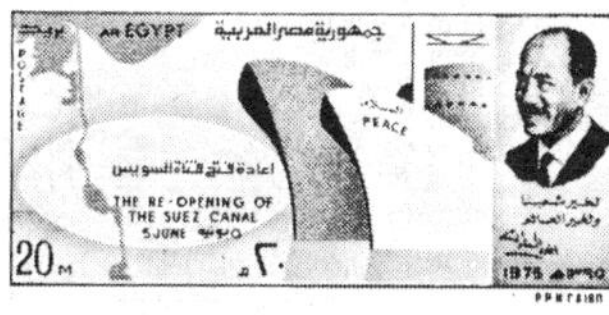

Suez Canal, Globe, Ships, Pres. Sadat — A448

1975, June 5 ***Perf. 11½***
982 A448 20m blue, brn & blk 70 30

Reopening of the Suez Canal, June 5. See Nos. C166-C167.

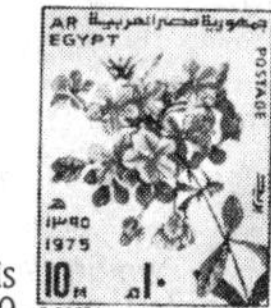

Belmabgoknis Flowers — A449

1975, July 30 Photo. Wmk. 342
983 A449 10m green & blue 15 15

For use on greeting cards.

Sphinx and Pyramids Illuminated A450

Rural Electrification A451

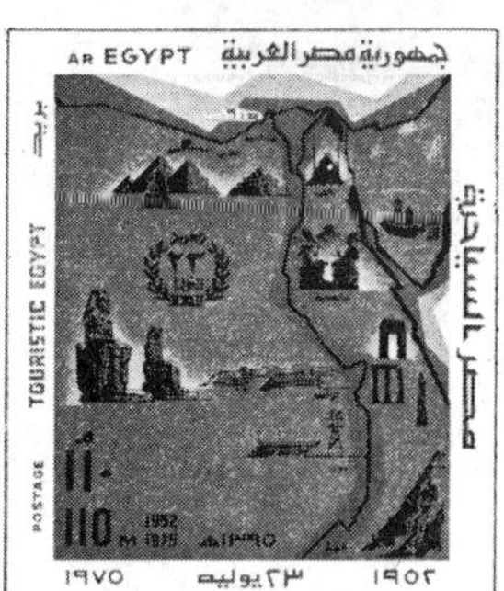

Map of Egypt with Tourist Sites — A452

1975, July 23
984 A450 20m black, org & grn 15 15

985 A451 20m dk blue & brown 15 15

Perf. 11

986 A452 110m multicolored 1.65 1.20

23rd anniversary of the revolution establishing the republic. No. 986 printed in sheets of 6 (2x3). Size: 71x80mm.

Volleyball — A453

1975, Aug. 2 Photo. *Perf. 11x11½*

987	A453	20m shown	18	15
988	A453	20m Running	18	15
989	A453	20m Torch and flag bearers	18	15
990	A453	20m Basketball	18	15
991	A453	20m Soccer	18	15
a.		Strip of 5, #987-991	1.00	50
		Nos. 987-991 (5)	90	
		Set value		40

6th Arab School Tournament.

Egyptian Flag and Tanks A454

1975 Photo. Unwmk. *Perf. 11½*

992 A454 20m multicolored 1.00 50

Two-line Arabic Inscription in Bottom Panel, "M" over "20"

992A A454 20m multicolored 1.00 50

No. 992 for 2nd anniv. of October War against Israel, "The Spark;" No. 992A, the Intl. Symposium on October War against Israel 1973, Cairo University, Oct. 27-31.

Issue dates: #992, Oct. 6. #992A, Oct. 24.

Arrows Pointing to Fluke, and Emblems A455

Submerged Wall and Sculpture, UNESCO Emblem A456

Perf. 11x11½

1975, Oct. 24 Wmk. 342

993 A455 20m multicolored 15 15

994 A456 55m multicolored 85 30

UN Day. 20m for Intl. Conf. on Schistosomiasis (Bilharziasis); 55m for UNESCO help in saving temples at Philae. See #C169-C170.

Pharaonic Gate, University Emblem — A457

Al Biruni — A458

1975, Nov. 15 Photo. Wmk. 342

995 A457 20m multicolored 15 15

Ain Shams University, 25th anniversary.

1975, Dec. 23 Photo. *Perf. 11x11½*

Arab Philosophers: No. 997, Al Farabi and lute. No. 998, Al Kanady, book and compass.

996	A458	20m blue, brn & grn	50	15
997	A458	20m blue, brn & grn	50	15
998	A458	20m blue, brn & grn	50	15
		Set value		18

Ibex (Prow) — A459

Post Day (from Tutankhamen's Tomb): 30m, Lioness. 55m, Cow's head (Goddess Hawthor). 110m, Hippopotamus' head (God Horus).

1976, Jan. 2 Unwmk. *Perf. 11½*

999 A459 20m multicolored 32 15

Wmk. 342

1000	A459	30m brown, gold & ultra	60	25
1001	A459	55m multicolored	80	30
1002	A459	110m multicolored	1.10	60

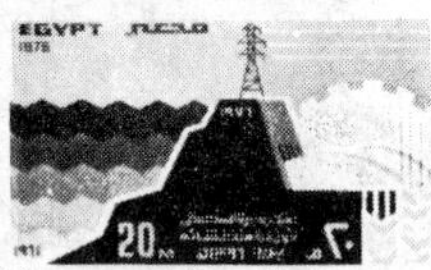

Lake, Aswan Dam, Industry and Agriculture A460

Perf. 11½x11

1976, Jan. 27 Photo. Wmk. 342

1003 A460 20m multicolored 15 15

Filling of lake formed by Aswan High Dam.

Fair Emblem — A461

Commemorative Medal — A462

1976, Mar. 15 *Perf. 11x11½*

1004 A461 20m orange & purple 15 15

9th International Cairo Fair, Mar. 8-27.

1976, Mar. 15 Wmk. 342

1005 A462 20m olive, yel & blk 15 15

11th Biennial Exhibition of Fine Arts, Alexandria.

Hands Shielding Invalid A463

1976, Apr. 7 Photo. *Perf. 11½*

1006 A463 20m dk grn, lt grn & yel 15 15

Founding of Faithfulness and Hope Society.

Eye and WHO Emblem A464

1976, Apr. 7

1007 A464 20m dk brown, yel & grn 15 15

World Health Day: "Foresight prevents blindness."

Pres. Sadat, Legal Department Emblem A465

Perf. 11½x11

1976, May 15 Photo. Wmk. 342

1008 A465 20m olive & multi 25 15

Centenary of State Legal Department.

Scales of Justice — A466

1976, May 15 *Perf. 11x11½*

1009 A466 20m carmine, blk & grn 15 15

5th anniversary of Rectification Movement.

Al-Ahram Front Page, First Issue A467

Perf. 11½x11

1976, June 25 Photo. Wmk. 342

1010 A467 20m bister & multi 15 15

Centenary of Al-Ahram newspaper.

World Map, Pres. Sadat and Emblems — A468

1976, July 23 *Perf. 11x11½*

1011 A468 20m blue, blk & yel 75 35

Souvenir Sheet

Imperf

1012 A468 110m blue, blk & yel 2.50 1.00

24th anniversary of the revolution. No. 1012 shows design of No. 1011 enlarged to fill entire area.

Scarborough Lily — A469

1976, Sept. 10 Photo. *Perf. 11*

1013 A469 10m multicolored 15 15

For use on greeting cards.

Reconstruction of Sinai by Irrigation — A470

Abu Redice Oil Wells and Refinery — A471

Unknown Soldier, Memorial Pyramid for October War — A472

1976, Oct. 6 *Perf. 11x11½*

1014 A470 20m multicolored 50 15

1015 A471 20m multicolored 50 15

Size: 65x77mm

1016 A472 110m green, blue & blk 2.00 80

October War against Israel, 3rd anniv.

Papyrus with Children's Animal Story — A473

Al Aqsa Mosque, Palestinian Refugees A474

Designs: 55m, Isis, from Philae Temple, UNESCO emblem, vert. 110m, UNESCO emblem and "30."

Perf. 11½, 11½x11

1976, Oct. 24 Photo. Wmk. 342

1017 A473 20m dk bl, bis & brn 15 15
1018 A474 30m brown, grn & blk 80 20
1019 A473 55m dk blue & bister 70 28
1020 A474 110m lt grn, vio bl & red 1.40 48

30th anniversary of UNESCO.

Census Chart A475

1976, Nov. 22 Photo. *Perf. 11½x11*

1021 A475 20m multicolored 15 15

10th General Population and Housing Census.

A476

A477

Design: Nile and commemorative medal.

1976, Nov. 22 *Perf. 11x11½*

1022 A476 20m green & brown 15 15

Geographical Soc. of Egypt, cent. (in 1975).

1977, Jan. 2 Photo. *Perf. 11x11½*

Post Day: 20m, Ikhnaton. 30m, Ikhnaton's daughter. 55m, Nefertiti, Ikhnaton's wife. 110m, Ikhnaton, front view.

1023 A477 20m multicolored 32 15
1024 A477 30m multicolored 28 16
1025 A477 55m multicolored 70 25
1026 A477 110m multicolored 1.40 60

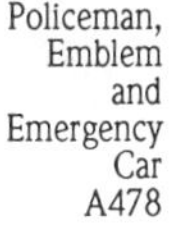

Policeman, Emblem and Emergency Car A478

Perf. 11½x11

1977, Feb. 25 Photo. Wmk. 342

1027 A478 20m multicolored 15 15

Police Day.

Map of Africa, Arab League Emblem — A479

1977, Mar 7 *Perf. 11x11½*

1028 A479 55m multicolored 25 15

First Afro-Arab Summit Conference, Cairo.

Fair Emblem, Pharaonic Ship A480

1977, Mar. 7 *Perf. 11½x11*

1029 A480 20m green, blk & red 18 15

10th International Cairo Fair.

King Faisal — A481

Healthy and Crippled Children — A482

1977, Mar. 22 Photo. *Perf. 11x11½*

1030 A481 20m indigo & brown 45 15

King Faisal Ben Abdel-Aziz Al Saud of Saudi Arabia (1906-1975).

1977, Apr. 12 Wmk. 342

1031 A482 20m multicolored 15 15

National campaign to fight poliomyelitis.

APU Emblem, Members' Flags — A483

1977, Apr. 12 *Perf. 11½*

1032 A483 20m blue & multi 15 15
1033 A483 30m gray & multi 16 15
Set value 15

25th anniv. of Arab Postal Union (APU).

Children's Village A484

Perf. 11½x11

1977, May 7 Photo. Wmk. 342

1034 A484 20m multicolored 15 15
1035 A484 55m multicolored 20 15
Set value 27 15

Inauguration of Children's Village, Cairo.

Loom, Spindle and Factory A485

1977, May 7

1036 A485 20m multicolored 15 15

Egyptian Spinning and Weaving Company, El Mehalla el Kobra, 50th anniv.

Satellite, Globe, ITU Emblem — A486

1977, May 17 *Perf. 11x11½*

1037 A486 110m dk blue & multi 1.00 40

World Telecommunications Day.

Flag and "25" A487

Egyptian Flag and Eagle — A488

Perf. 11½x11

1977, July 23 Photo. Wmk. 342

1038 A487 20m silver, car & blk 20 20

Perf. 11x11½

1039 A488 110m multicolored 1.25 50

25th anniversary of July 23rd Revolution. No. 1039 printed in sheets of six. Size: 75x83mm.

Saad Zaghloul A489

Archbishop Capucci, Map of Palestine A490

Perf. 11x11½

1977, Aug. 23 Photo. Wmk. 342

1040 A489 20m dk green & dk brn 15 15

Saad Zaghloul, leader of 1919 Revolution, 50th death anniversary.

1977, Sept. 1

1041 A490 45m emerald & blue 40 15

Palestinian Archbishop Hilarion Capucci, jailed by Israel in 1974.

Bird-of-Paradise Flower — A491

1977, Sept. 3

1042 A491 10m multicolored 15 15

For use on greeting cards.

Proclamation Greening the Land — A492

Perf. 11x11½

1977, Sept. 25 Photo. Wmk. 342

1043 A492 20m multicolored 15 15

Agraian Reform Law, 25th anniversary.

Soldier, Tanks, Medal of Oct. 6 — A493

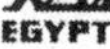

Anwar Sadat A494

1977, Oct. 6 *Perf. 11½x11*

1044 A493 20m multicolored 45 15

Unwmk.

Perf. 11

1045 A494 140m dk brn, gold & red 4.50 1.40

October War against Israel, 4th anniv. No. 1045 printed in sheets of 16.

Refugees Looking at Al Aqsa Mosque A495

Goddess Taueret and Spirit of Flight (Horus) A496

Mural Relief, Temple of Philae — A497

Wmk. 342

1977, Oct. 24 Photo. *Perf. 11*

1046 A495 45m green, red & blk 22 15
1047 A496 55m dp blue & yellow 28 15
1048 A497 140m olive bis & dk brn 65 25

United Nations Day.

Electric Trains, First Egyptian Locomotive A498

1977, Oct. 22
1049 A498 20m multicolored 15 15

125th anniversary of Egyptian railroads.

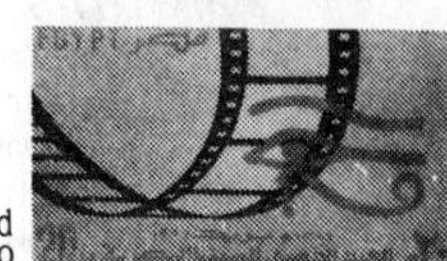

Film and Eye — A499

1977, Nov. 16 ***Perf. 11½x11***
1050 A499 20m gray, blk & gold 15 15

50th anniversary of Egyptian cinema.

Natural Gas Well and Refinery — A500

1977, Nov. 17 **Photo.**
1051 A500 20m multicolored 15 15

National Oil Festival, celebrating the acquisition of Sinai oil wells.

Pres. Sadat and Dome of the Rock A501

Perf. 11½x11

1977, Dec. 31 **Photo.** **Wmk. 342**
1052 A501 20m green, brn & blk 25 15
1053 A501 140m green, blk & brn 1.10 40

Pres. Sadat's peace mission to Israel.

Ramses II — A502

Post Day: 45m, Queen Nefertari, bas-relief.

1978, Jan. 2 ***Perf. 11½***
1054 A502 20m green, blk & gold 15 15
1055 A502 45m orange, blk & ol 22 15
Set value 15

Water Wheels, Fayum — A503

Flying Duck, from Floor in Ikhnaton's Palace A504

Designs: 5m, Birdhouse, 10m, Statue of Horus. 20m, Al Rifa'i Mosque, Cairo. 50m, Monastery, Wadi al-Natrun. 55m, Ruins of Edfu Temple. 70m, 80m, Bridge of Oct. 6. 85m, Medum pyramid. 100m, Facade, El Morsi Mosque, Alexandria. 200m, Column, Alexandria, and Sphinx. 500m, Arabian stallion.

Wmk. 342, Unwmkd. (30m, 70m, 80m)

1978-85 ***Perf. 11½***

1056 A503 1m slate blue 15 15
a. Unwmkd. ('79) 15 15
b. 1m gray ('83) 15 15
c. 1m gray, unwmkd. ('83) 15 15
1057 A503 5m bister brn 15 15
a. 5m dull brn, unwmkd. (79) 15 15
1058 A503 10m brt green 15 15
a. Unwmkd. ('79) 15 15
1059 A503 20m dk brown 15 15
b. Unwmkd. ('79) 15 15
1059A A503 30m sepia 15 15
1060 A503 50m Prus blue 22 15
a. Unwmkd. ('79) 22 15
b. Unwmkd., brt blure ('87) 22 15
1061 A503 55m olive 22 15
1062 A503 70m olive ('79) 30 15
1062A A503 80m olive ('82) 35 20
1063 A503 85m dp purple 38 15
a. Unwmkd. ('85) 38 15
1064 A503 100m brown 45 20
a. Unwmkd. ('85) 45 20
1065 A503 200m blue & indigo 90 40
1066 A504 500m multicolored 2.25 65
1067 A504 £1 multicolored 4.50 1.25
Nos. 1056-1067 (14) 10.32
Set value 3.30

Issue dates: 500m, £1, Feb. 27. Others, July 23, 70m, Aug. 22, 1979.

Fair Emblem and Wheat A505

1978, Mar. 15 ***Perf. 11½***
1072 A505 20m multicolored 15 15

11th Cairo International Fair, Mar. 11-25.

Emblem, Kasr El Ainy School A506

1978, Mar. 18 ***Perf. 11½x11***
1073 A506 20m lt blue, blk & gold 15 15

Kasr El Ainy School of Medicine, 150th anniversary.

Soldiers and Emblem — A507

Youssef El Sebai — A508

1978, Mar. 30 ***Perf. 11x11½***
1074 A507 20m multicolored 15 15
1075 A508 20m bister brown 15 15
a. Pair, #1074-1075 25 18
Set value 25 15

Youssef El Sebai, newspaper editor, assassinated on Cyprus and in memory of the commandos killed in raid on Cyprus.

Biennale Medal, Statue for Entrance to Port Said A509

1978, Apr. 1 ***Perf. 11½***
1076 A509 20m blue, grn & blk 15 15

12th Biennial Exhibition of Fine Arts, Alexandria.

Child with Smallpox, UN Emblem A510

1978, Apr. 7 **Photo.** ***Perf. 11½***
1077 A510 20m multicolored 15 15

Eradication of smallpox.

Heart & Arrow, UN Emblem — A511

Anwar Sadat — A512

1978, Apr. 7 **Wmk. 342**
1078 A511 20m multicolored 15 15

Fight against hypertension.

1978, May 15 **Photo.** ***Perf. 11½x11***
1079 A512 20m green, brn & gold 25 15

7th anniversary of Rectification Movement.

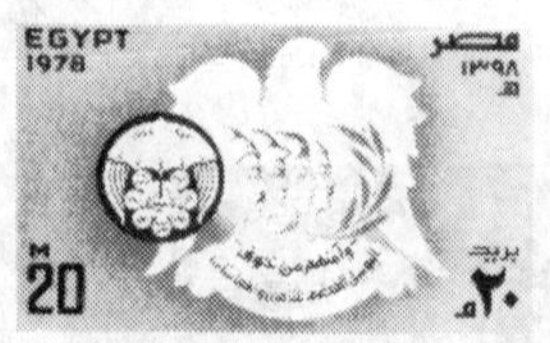

Social Security Emblem — A513

1978, May 16 ***Perf. 11***
1080 A513 20m lt green & dk brn 15 15

General Organization of Insurance and Pensions (Social Security), 25th anniversary.

New Cities on Map of Egypt — A514

Map of Egypt and Sudan, Wheat — A515

Perf. 11½

1978, July 23 **Photo.** **Wmk. 342**
1081 A514 20m multicolored 30 15
1082 A515 45m multicolored 50 15
Set value 15

26th anniversary of July 23rd revolution.

Symbols of Egyptian Ministries — A516

1978, Aug. 28 **Photo.** ***Perf. 11½x11***
1083 A516 20m multicolored 15 15

Centenary of Egyptian Ministerial System.

Pres. Sadat and "Spirit of Egypt" Showing Way — A517

1978, Oct. 6 **Photo.** ***Perf. 11x11½***
1084 A517 20m multicolored 25 15

October War against Israel, 5th anniv.

Human Rights Emblem — A518

Dove and Human Rights Emblem — A520

Kobet al Sakra Mosque, Refugee Camp A519

UN Day: 55m, Temple at Biga and UNESCO emblem, horiz.

Perf. 11, 11½ (45m)

1978, Oct. 24 Photo. Wmk. 342

1085 A518	20m	multicolored	15	15
1086 A519	45m	multicolored	75	25
1087 A518	55m	multicolored	28	15
1088 A520	140m	multicolored	65	25
		Set value		64

Pilgrims, Mt. Arafat and Holy Kaaba — A521

1978, Nov. 7 Photo. *Perf. 11*

1089 A521 45m multicolored 25 15

Pilgrimage to Mecca.

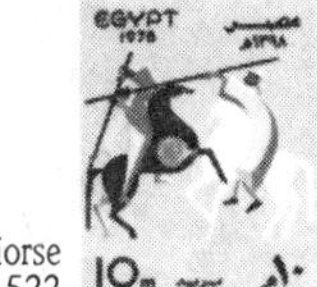

Tahtib Horse Dance — A522

1978, Nov. 7

1090 A522	10m	multicolored	15	15
1091 A522	20m	multicolored	15	15
		Set value	15	15

UN Emblem, Globe and Grain A523

1978, Nov. 11 Photo. *Perf. 11½*

1092 A523 20m green, dk bl & yel 15 15

Technical Cooperation Among Developing Countries Conf., Buenos Aires, Sept. 1978.

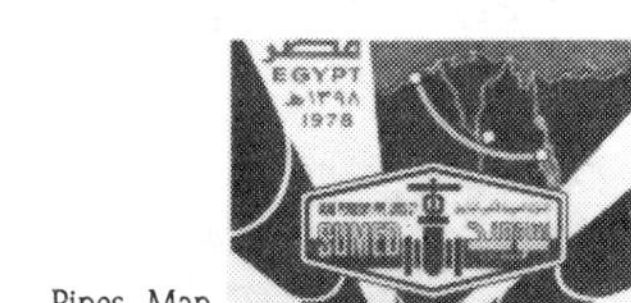

Pipes, Map and Emblem of Sumed Pipeline A524

1978, Nov. 11

1093 A524 20m brown, bl & yel 15 15

Inauguration of Sumed pipeline from Suez to Alexandria, 1st anniversary.

Mastheads A525

Abu el Walid A526

1978, Dec. 24 *Perf. 11x11½*

1094 A525 20m brown & black 15 15

150th anniversary of the newspaper El Wakea el Masriya.

1978, Dec. 24

1095 A526 45m brt green & indigo 18 15

800th death anniv. of Abu el Walid ibn Rashid.

Helwan Observatory and Sky — A527

1978, Dec. 30 Wmk. 342

1096 A527 20m multicolored 15 15

Helwan Observatory, 75th anniversary.

Second Daughter of Ramses II — A528

Ramses Statues, Abu Simbel, and Cartouches A529

1979, Jan. 2 Photo. *Perf. 11*

1097 A528 20m brown & yellow 15 15

Perf. 11½x11

1098 A529	140m	multicolored	80	25
		Set value		30

Post Day 1978.

Book, Reader and Globe A530

Perf. 11½x11

1979, Feb. 1 Photo. Wmk. 342

1099 A530 20m yellow grn & brown 15 15

Cairo 11th International Book Fair.

Wheat, Globe, Fair Emblem — A531

Perf. 11x11½

1979, Mar. 17 Photo. Unwmk.

1100 A531 20m blue, org & blk 15 15

12th Cairo International Fair, Mar.-Apr.

Skull, Poppy, Agency Emblem — A532

1979, Mar. 20 *Perf. 11*

1101 A532 70m multicolored 40 18

Anti-Narcotics General Administration, 50th anniversary.

Isis Holding Horus — A533

1979, Mar. 21

1102 A533 140m multicolored 80 35

Mother's Day.

World Map and Book A534

Perf. 11x11½

1979, Mar. 22 Wmk. 342

1103 A534 45m yellow, bl & brn 15 15

Cultural achievements of the Arabs.

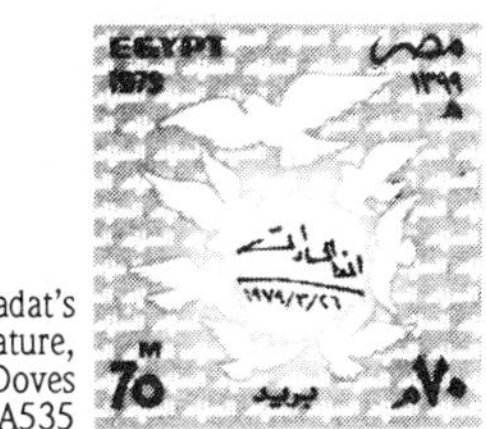

Pres. Sadat's Signature, Peace Doves A535

Perf. 11½

1979, Mar. 31 Photo. Wmk. 342

1104 A535	70m	brt green & red	50	18
1105 A535	140m	yellow grn & red	90	35

Signing of Peace Treaty between Egypt and Israel, Mar. 26.

1979, May 26 Photo. *Perf. 11½*

1106 A535 20m yellow & dk brn 32 15

Return of Al Arish to Egypt.

Honeycomb with Food Symbols A536

1979, May 15

1107 A536 20m multicolored 15 15

8th anniversary of movement to establish food security.

Coins, 1959, 1979 A537

Perf. 11½x11

1979, June 1 Wmk. 342 Photo.

1108 A537 20m yellow & gray 15 15

25th anniversary of the Egyptian Mint.

Egypt No. 1104 under Magnifying Glass — A538

1979, June 1 *Perf. 11*

1109 A538 20m green, blk & brn 25 15

Philatelic Society of Egypt, 50th anniversary.

Book, Atom Symbol, Rising Sun — A539

"23 July," "Revolution" and "Peace" — A540

Perf. 11½x11

1979, July 23 **Wmk. 342**
1110 A539 20m multicolored 15 15

Miniature Sheet

Imperf

1111 A540 140m multicolored 85 45

27th anniversary of July 23rd revolution.

Musicians — A541

1979, Aug. 22 *Perf. 11½*
1112 A541 10m multicolored 15 15

For use on greeting cards.

Dove over Map of Suez Canal A542

Perf. 11½

1979, Oct. 6 **Photo.** **Wmk. 342**
1113 A542 20m blue & brown 15 15

October War against Israel, 6th anniv.

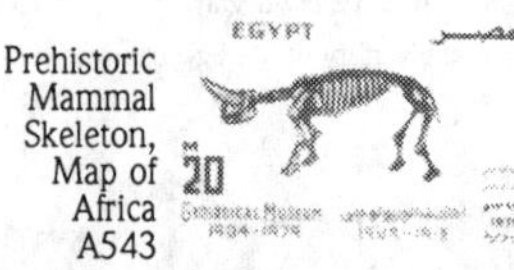

Prehistoric Mammal Skeleton, Map of Africa A543

Perf. 11½x11

1979, Oct. 9 **Photo.** **Wmk. 342**
1114 A543 20m multicolored 15 15

Egyptian Geological Museum, 75th anniv.

T Square on Drawing Board — A544

1979, Oct. 11 *Perf. 11*
1115 A544 20m multicolored 15 15

Engineers Day.

Human Rights Emblem Over Globe — A545

Boy Balancing IYC Emblem — A546

Perf. 11½

1979, Oct. 24 **Photo.** **Unwmk.**
1116 A545 45m multicolored 20 15
1117 A546 140m multicolored 75 35

UN Day and Intl. Year of the Child.

International Savings Day — A547

1979, Oct. 31
1118 A547 70m multicolored 25 18

A548 A549

Design: Shooting championship emblem.

1979, Nov. 16
1119 A548 20m multicolored 15 15

20th International Military Shooting Championship, Cairo.

1979, Nov. 29 *Perf. 11x11½*
1120 A549 45m multicolored 50 15

International Palestinian Solidarity Day.

Dove Holding Grain, Rotary Emblem, Globe A550

1979, Dec. 3 **Photo.** *Perf. 11½*
1121 A550 140m multicolored 30 35

Rotary International, 75th anniversary; Cairo Rotary Club, 50th anniversary.

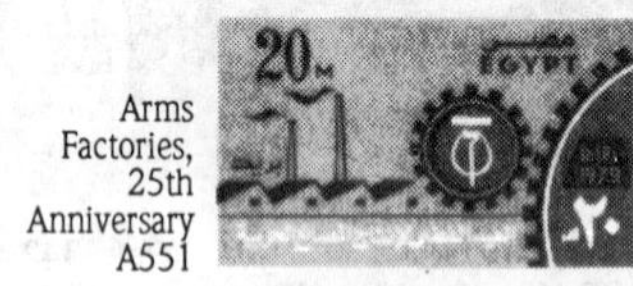

Arms Factories, 25th Anniversary A551

Perf. 11½x11

1979, Dec. 23 **Photo.** **Wmk. 342**
1122 A551 20m lt olive grn & brn 15 15

Aly El Garem (1881-1949) A552

Pharaonic Capital A553

Poets: No. 1124, Mahmoud Samy El Baroudy (1839-1904).

1979, Dec. 25 *Perf. 11x11½*
1123 A552 20m dk brown & yel brn 25 15
1124 A552 20m brown & dk brown 25 15
a. Pair, #1123-1124 50 22
Set value 15

1980, Jan. 2 **Unwmk.** *Perf. 11½*

Post Day: Various Pharaonic capitals.

1125 A553 20m multicolored 22 15
1126 A553 45m multicolored 35 15
1127 A553 70m multicolored 60 18
1128 A553 140m multicolored 95 35
a. Strip of 4, #1125-1128 2.25 1.00
Set value 68

Golden Goddess of Writing, Fair Emblem — A554

Exhibition Catalogue and Medal — A555

1980, Feb. 2 **Photo.** *Perf. 11½*
1129 A554 20m multicolored 25 15

12th Cairo Intl. Book Fair, Jan. 24-Feb. 4.

1980, Feb. 2
1130 A555 20m multicolored 15 15

13th Biennial Exhibition of Fine Arts, Alexandria.

13th Cairo International Fair — A556

1980, Mar. 8 **Photo.** *Perf. 11x11½*
1131 A556 20m multicolored 15 15

Kiosk of Trajan A557

1980, Mar. 10 *Perf. 11½*
1132 Strip of 4 + label 2.50 2.25
a. A557 70m, single stamp 35 22

UNESCO campaign to save Nubian monuments, 20th anniversary. Shown on stamps are Temples of Philae, Kalabsha, Korasy.

Physicians' Day — A558

1980, Mar. 18 *Perf. 11x11½*
1133 A558 20m multicolored 15 15

Rectification Movement, 9th Anniversary A559

Perf. 11½x11

1980, May 15 **Photo.** **Wmk. 342**
1134 A559 20m multicolored 25 15

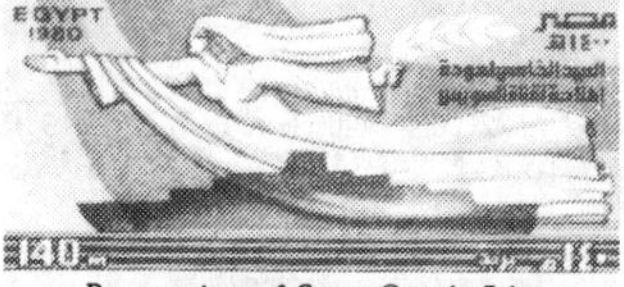

Re-opening of Suez Canal, 5th Anniversary — A560

1980, June 5 *Perf. 11½*
1135 A560 140m multicolored 70 35

Prevention of Cruelty to Animals Week A561

1980, June 5
1136 A561 20m lt yel grn & gray 40 15

Industry Day A562

Perf. 11½x11

1980, July 12 **Photo.** **Wmk. 342**
1137 A562 20m multicolored 15 15

Leaf with Text — A563

Family Protection Emblem A564

1980, July 23 *Perf. 11½*

1138 A563 20m multicolored 15 15

Souvenir Sheet

Imperf

1139 A564 140m multicolored 75 40

July 23rd Revolution, 28th anniv.; Social Security Year.

Erksous Seller and Nakrazan Player — A565

Perf. 11½

1980, Aug. 8 Unwmk. Photo.

1140 A565 10m multicolored 15 15

For use on greeting cards.

October War Against Israel, 7th Anniv. — A566

1980, Oct. 6 Litho.

1141 A566 20m multicolored 15 15

Islamic and Coptic Columns A567

International Telecommunications Union Emblem — A568

Perf. 11½

1980, Oct. 24 Photo. Wmk. 342

1142 A567 70m multicolored 35 18
1143 A568 140m multicolored 70 35

UN Day. Campaign to save Egyptian monuments (70m), Intl. Telecommunications Day (140m).

Hegira (Pilgrimage Year) — A569

1980, Nov. 9 Litho. *Perf. 11x11½*

1144 A569 45m multicolored 18 15

Opening of Suez Canal Third Branch A570

Perf. 11½x11

1980, Dec. 16 Photo. Wmk. 342

1145 A570 70m multicolored 35 18

Mustafa Sadek El-Rafai (1880-1927), Writer — A571

Famous Men: No. 1147, Ali Mustafa Mousharafa (1898-1950), mathematician. No. 1148, Ali Ibrahim (1880-1947), surgeon.

1980, Dec. 23 *Perf. 11x11½*

1146 A571 20m green & brown 22 15
1147 A571 20m green & brown 22 15
1148 A571 20m green & brown 22 15
a. Strip of 3, #1146-1148 70 50
Set value 24

See Nos. 1178-1179.

Ladybug Scarab Emblem — A572

von Stephan, UPU — A573

Perf. 11½

1981, Jan. 2 Photo. Unwmk.

1149 A572 70m shown 35 18
1150 A572 70m Scarab, reverse 35 18

Post Day.

Perf. 11x11½

1981, Jan. 7 Wmk. 342

1151 A573 140m grnsh bl & dk brn 45 35

Heinrich von Stephan (1831-97), founder of UPU.

13th Cairo International Book Fair — A574

1981, Feb. 1 *Perf. 11½x11*

1152 A574 20m multicolored 15 15

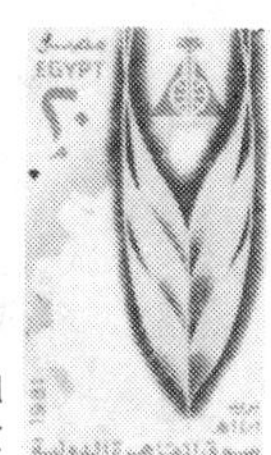

14th Cairo International Fair, Mar. 14-28 — A575

Perf. 11x11½

1981, Mar. 14 Photo. Wmk. 342

1153 A575 20m multicolored 15 15

Rural Electrification Authority, 10th Anniversary — A576

1981, Mar. 18

1154 A576 20m multicolored 15 15

Veterans' Day — A577

Intl. Dentistry Conf., Cairo — A578

1981, Mar. 26

1155 A577 20m multicolored 15 15

Perf. 11x11½

1981, Apr. 14 Photo. Wmk. 342

1156 A578 20m red & olive 15 15

Trade Union Emblem A579

Nurses' Day A580

Perf. 11x11½

1981, May 1 Photo. Wmk. 342

1157 A579 20m brt blue & dk brn 15 15

International Confederation of Arab Trade Unions, 25th anniv.

1981, May 12

1158 A580 20m multicolored 15 15

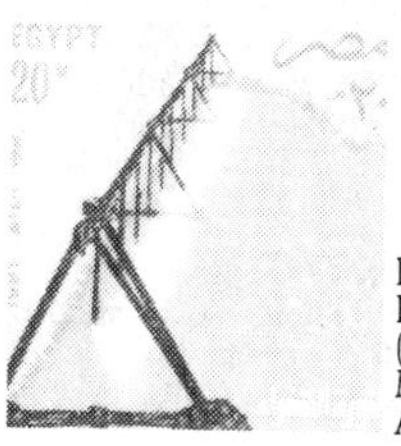

Irrigation Equipment (Electrification Movement) A581

1981, May 15 *Perf. 11½*

1159 A581 20m multicolored 15 15

Air Force Day — A582

Perf. 11x11½

1981, June 30 Photo. Wmk. 342

1160 A582 20m multicolored 15 15

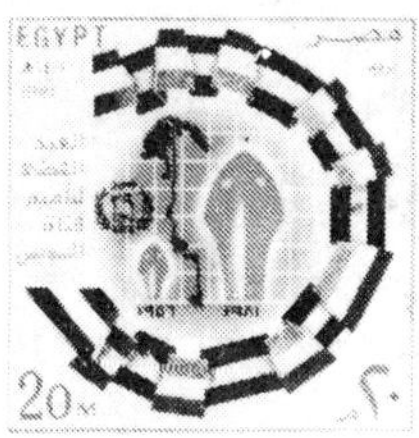

Flag Surrounding Map of Suez Canal A583

Perf. 11½

1981, July 23 Photo. Wmk. 342

1161 A583 20m multicolored 15 15
1162 A583 20m Emblems 15 15
Set value 15 15

July 23rd Revolution, 29th anniv.; Social Defense Year.

1981 Feasts — A584

Kemal Ataturk — A585

Wmk. 342

1981, July 29 Photo. *Perf. 11*

1163 A584 10m multicolored 15 15

1981, Aug. 10 *Perf. 11x11½*

1164 A585 140m dk green & brn 55 35

Arabi Pasha, Leader of Egyptian Force — A586

Athlete, Pyramids, Sphinx — A587

Perf. 11x11½

1981, Sept. 9 Photo. Wmk. 342

1165 A586 20m dk green & brn	15	15

Orabi Revolution centenary.

1981, Sept. 14

1166 A587 45m multicolored	18	15

World Muscular Athletics Championships, Cairo.

Ministry of Industry and Mineral Resources, 25th Anniv. — A588

Perf. 11x11½

1981, Sept. 26 Photo. Wmk. 342

1167 A588 45m multicolored	18	15

20th Intl. Occupational Health Congress, Cairo — A589

1981, Sept. 28 *Perf. 11½x11*

1168 A589 20m multicolored	18	15

October War Against Israel, 8th Anniv. A590

1981, Oct. 6

1169 A590 20m multicolored	22	15

World Food Day A591

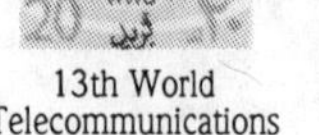

13th World Telecommunications Day — A592

Intl. Year of the Disabled — A593

Fight Against Apartheid A594

Perf. 11½x11, 11x11½

1981, Oct. 24 Photo. Wmk. 342

1170 A591 10m multicolored	15	15
1171 A592 20m multicolored	15	15
1172 A593 45m multicolored	22	15
1173 A594 230m multicolored	1.00	70
Set value		95

United Nations Day.

Pres. Anwar Sadat (1917-81) — A595

Perf. 11x11½

1981, Nov. 14 Unwmk.

1174 A595 30m multicolored	40	18
1175 A595 230m multicolored	1.65	75

Establishment of Shura Family Council — A596

Perf. 11½x11

1981, Dec. 12 Photo. Wmk. 342

1176 A596 45m purple & yellow	15	15

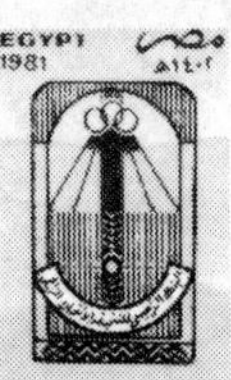

Agricultural Credit and Development Bank, 50th Anniv. — A597

1981, Dec. 15 *Perf. 11x11½*

1177 A597 20m multicolored	15	15

Famous Men Type of 1980

Designs: 30m, Ali el-Ghayati (1885-1956), journalist. 60m, Omar Ebn sl-Fared (1181-1234), Sufi poet.

Perf. 11x11½

1981, Dec. 21 Photo. Wmk. 342

1178 A571 30m green & brown	15	15
1179 A571 60m green & brown	20	15
a. Pair, #1178-1179	35	25
Set value		23

20th Anniv. of African Postal Union A598

1981, Dec. 21 *Perf. 11½x11*

1180 A598 60m multicolored	25	15

14th Cairo Intl. Book Fair — A599

Arab Trade Union of Egypt, 25th Anniv. — A600

1982, Jan. 28

1181 A599 3p brown & yellow	15	15

1982, Jan. 30

1182 A600 3p multicolored	15	15

Khartoum Branch of Cairo University, 25th Anniv. A601

Perf. 11½x11

1982, Mar. 4 Wmk. 342

1183 A601 6p blue & green	20	15

15th Cairo Intl. Fair — A602

1982, Mar. 13 *Perf. 11x11½*

1184 A602 3p multicolored	15	15

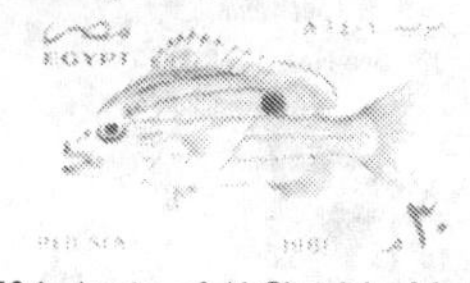

50th Anniv. of Al-Ghardaka Marine Biological Station A603

Fish of the Red Sea in continuous design.

1982, Apr. 24 Litho. *Perf. 11½x11*

1185 A603 10m Lined butterfly fish	15	15
1186 A603 30m Blue-banded sea perch	15	15
1187 A603 60m Batfish	30	15
1188 A603 230m Blue-spotted boxfish	1.10	60
a. Block of 4, #1185-1188	1.75	1.00

Liberation of the Sinai — A604

1982, Apr. 25 Photo. *Perf. 11x11½*

1189 A604 3p multicolored	15	15

50th Anniv. of Egypt Air A605

1982, May 7 Photo. *Perf. 11½x11*

1190 A605 23p multicolored	75	60

Minaret — A606

Al Azhar Mosque — A607

Perf. 11x11½

1982, June 28 Photo. Wmk. 342

1191 Strip of 4 + label	1.10	1.10
a. A606 6p any single, multi	25	25

Souvenir Sheet

Unwmk. *Imperf.*

1192 A607 23p multicolored	1.10	1.10

Al Azhar Mosque millennium.
No. 1192 airmail.

Dove — A608

Flower in Natl. Colors — A609

Perf. 11x11½

1982, July 23 Photo. Wmk. 342

1193 A608 3p multicolored	15	15

Souvenir Sheet

Imperf

1194 A609 23p multicolored	75	75

30th anniv. of July 23rd Revolution.

World Tourism Day A610

Design: Sphinx, pyramid of Cheops, St. Catherine's Tower.

Perf. 11½x11

1982, Sept. 27 Photo. Wmk. 342

1195 A610 23p multicolored	75	75

October War Against Israel, 9th Anniv. A611

1982, Oct. 6
1196 A611 3p Memorial, map 15 15

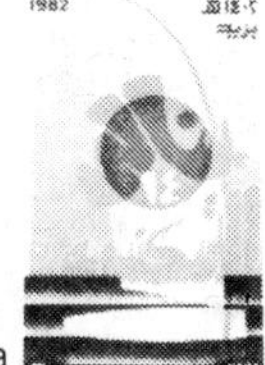
Biennale of Alexandria Art Exhibition — A612

1982, Oct. 17 ***Perf. 11x11½***
1197 A612 3p multicolored 15 15

10th Anniv. of UN Conference on Human Environment — A613

2nd UN Conference on Peaceful Uses of Outer Space, Vienna, Aug. 9-21 A614

Scouting Year — A615

TB Bacillus Centenary A616

Perf. 11½x11, 11½ (A615)
1982, Oct. 24
1198 A613 3p multicolored 15 15
1199 A614 6p multicolored 28 15
1200 A615 6p multicolored 28 15
1201 A616 8p multicolored 35 20

United Nations Day.

50th Anniv. of Air Force A617

1982, Nov. 2 ***Perf. 11½x11***
1202 A617 3p Jet, plane 15 15

Ahmed Chawki (1868-1932) and Hafez Ibrahim (1871-1932), Poets — A618

Perf. 11½x11
1982, Nov. 25 Photo. Wmk. 342
1203 A618 6p multicolored 20 15

Natl. Research Center, 25th Anniv. — A619

1982, Dec. 12 Photo. ***Perf. 11x11½***
1204 A619 3p red & blue 15 15

50th Anniv. of Arab Language Society A620

1982, Dec. 25 ***Perf. 11½x11***
1205 A620 6p multicolored 20 15

Year of the Aged — A621

Post Day — A622

1982, Dec. 25 ***Perf. 11x11½***
1206 A621 23p multicolored 75 60

1983, Jan. 2 ***Perf. 11½***
1207 A622 3p multicolored 15 15

15th Cairo Intl. Book Fair — A623

Perf. 11x11½
1983, Jan. 25 Photo. Wmk. 342
1208 A623 3p blue & red 15 15

Police Day A624

1983, Jan. 25 ***Perf. 11½x11***
1209 A624 3p multicolored 15 15

16th Cairo Intl. Fair — A625

5th UN African Map Conf., Cairo — A626

Perf. 11x11½
1983, Mar. 2 Photo. Wmk. 342
1210 A625 3p multicolored 15 15

1983, Mar. 2
1211 A626 3p lt green & blue 15 15

African Ministers of Transport, Communications and Planning, 3rd Conference — A627

1983, Mar. 8 ***Perf. 11½x11***
1212 A627 23p green & blue 75 60

A628

A629

1983, Mar. 20 ***Perf. 11x11½***
1213 A628 3p Heading 15 15
1214 A628 3p Kick 15 15
Set value 24 16

Victory in African Soccer Cup.

Perf. 11x11½
1983, Apr. 2 Photo. Wmk. 342
1215 A629 3p olive & red 15 15

World Health Day and Natl. Blood Donation Campaign.

Org. of African Trade Union Unity A630

Perf. 11½x11
1983, Apr. 21 Photo. Wmk. 342
1216 A630 3p multicolored 15 15

1st Anniv. of Sinai Liberation — A631

75th Anniv. of Entomology Society — A632

1983, Apr. 25 ***Perf. 11x11½***
1217 A631 3p multicolored 15 15

1983, May 23
1218 A632 3p Emblem (Holy Scarab) 15 15

Flowers — A633

1983, June 11 Photo. ***Perf. 11½x11***
1219 A633 20m green & org red 15 15

5th African Handball Championship, Cairo — A634

Perf. 11½x11
1983, July 22 Photo. Wmk. 342
1220 A634 6p brown & dk grn 20 15

31st Anniv. of Revolution A635

Simon Bolivar (1783-1830) A636

1983, July 23 ***Perf. 11½***
1221 A635 3p multicolored 15 15

1983, Aug. ***Perf. 11x11½***
1222 A636 23p brown & dull grn 75 60

Centenary of Arrival of Natl. Hero Orabi in Ceylon A637

Perf. 11½x11
1983, Aug. 25 Photo. Wmk. 342
1223 A637 3p Map, Orabi, El-Zahra School 15 15

Islamic Vase, Museum Building A638

1983, Sept. 14 Photo. ***Perf. 11½x11***
1224 A638 3p yel brn & dk brn 15 15

Reopening of Islamic Museum.

The Scott Catalogue value is a retail price; that is, what you could expect to pay for the stamp in a grade of Fine-Very Fine. The value listed reflects recent actual dealer selling prices.

October War Against Israel, 10th Anniv. — A639

2nd Pharaonic Race — A640

1983, Oct. 6 *Perf. 11½*
1225 A639 3p multicolored 15 15

1983, Oct. 17 *Perf. 11½*
1226 A640 23p multicolored 75 60

United Nations Day — A641

1983, Oct. 24 Photo. *Perf. 11*

1227	A641	3p	IMO, ships, horiz.	15	15
1228	A641	6p	ITU, UPU	15	15
1229	A641	6p	FAO, UN, grain	15	15
1230	A641	23p	UN, ocean	90	60

4th World Karate Championship, Cairo — A642

1983, Nov. Photo. *Perf. 13*
1231 A642 3p multicolored 15 15

Intl. Palestinian Cooperation Day — A643

1983, Nov. 29 Photo. *Perf. 13x13½*
1232 A643 6p Dome of the Rock 20 15

75th Anniv. of Faculty of Fine Arts, Cairo — A644

1983, Nov. 30 *Perf. 13*
1233 A644 3p multicolored 15 15

75th Anniv. of Cairo University — A645

1983, Nov. 30 *Perf. 11x11½*
1234 A645 3p multicolored 15 15

Intl. Egyptian Society of Mother and Child Care A646

1983, Nov. 30 *Perf. 11½x11*
1235 A646 3p multicolored 15 15

Org. of African Unity, 20th Anniv. — A647

World Heritage Convention, 10th Anniv. — A648

Perf. 11x11½
1983, Dec. 20 Photo. Wmk. 342
1236 A647 3p multicolored 15 15

1983, Dec. 24

1237	Strip of 3		30	22
a.	A648 3p Wood carving, Islamic		15	15
b.	A648 3p Coptic tapestry		15	15
c.	A648 3p Ramses II Thebes		15	15

Post Day — A649

Restored Forts: 6p, Quatbay. 23p, Mosque, Salah El-Din.

1984, Jan. 2 *Perf. 13*
1238 A649 6p multicolored 20 15
1239 A649 23p multicolored 80 60

Misr Insurance Co., 50 Anniv. A650

1984, Jan. 14 *Perf. 11½x11*
1240 A650 3p multicolored 15 15

16th Cairo Intl. Book Fair — A651

Perf. 13½x13
1984, Jan. 26 Photo. Wmk. 342
1241 A651 3p multicolored 15 15

17th Cairo Intl. Fair — A652

Perf. 11½x11
1984, Mar. 10 Photo. Wmk. 342
1242 A652 3p multicolored 15 15

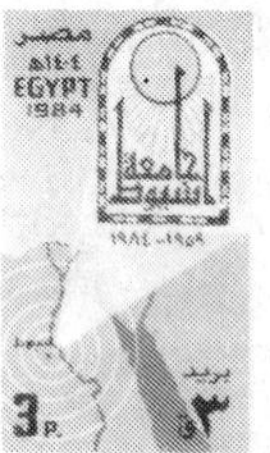

25th Anniv. of Assiout University — A653

75th Anniv. of Cooperative Unions — A654

1984, Mar. 10 *Perf. 11x11½*
1243 A653 3p multicolored 15 15

1984, Mar. 17
1244 A654 3p multicolored 15 15

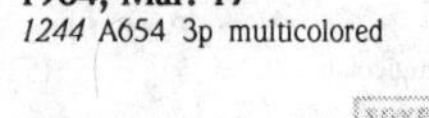

World Theater Day — A655

Mahmoud Mokhtar (1891-1934), Sculptor — A656

Perf. 11x11½, 11½x11
1984, Mar. 27 Photo. Unwmk.
1245 A655 3p Masks 15 15
1246 A656 3p Pride of the Nile 15 15
Set value 16

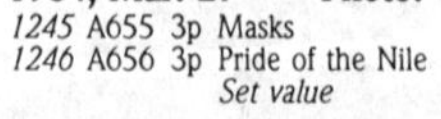

World Health Day and Fight Against Polio — A657

Perf. 11½x11
1984, Apr. 7 Photo. Wmk. 342
1247 A657 3p Polio vaccine 15 15

2nd Anniv. of Sinai Liberation — A658

1984, Apr. 25
1248 A658 3p Doves, map 15 15

Africa Day A659

Perf. 12½x13½
1984, May 25 Photo. Wmk. 342
1249 A659 3p Map, UN emblem 15 15

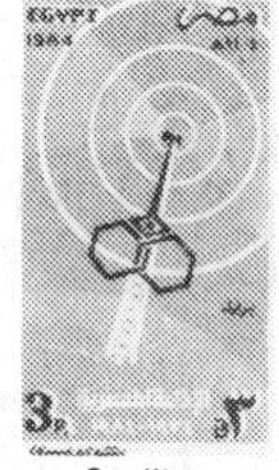

Satellite, Waves — A660

Flower — A661

1984, May 31 *Perf. 11x11½*
1250 A660 3p multicolored 15 15

Radio broadcasting in Egypt, 50th anniv.

1984, June 1
1251 A661 2p red & green 15 15

Intl. Cairo Arab Arts Biennale — A662

1984, June 1 *Perf. 13½x12½*
1252 A662 3p multicolored 15 15

July Revolution, 32nd Anniv. A663

Wmk. 342
1984, July 23 Photo. *Perf. 11*
1253 A663 3p Atomic energy, agriculture 15 15

A664

A665

1984 Summer Olympics: a, Boxing. b, Basketball. c, Volleyball. d, Soccer.

1984, July 28

1254 Strip of 4 + label 55 30
a.-d. A664 3p any single 15 15

Size: 130x80mm

Imperf

1255 A664 30p like #1254 1.00 65

Wmk. 342

1984, Aug. 13 Photo. *Perf. 11*

1256 A665 3p bl & multi 15 15
1257 A665 23p grn & multi 75 60

2nd Genl. Conference of Egyptians Abroad, Aug. 11-15, Cairo.

Youth Hostels, 30th Anniv. — A666

Egypt Tour Co., 50th Anniv. — A667

Perf. 11x11½

1984, Sept. 22 Photo. Wmk. 342

1258 A666 3p Youths, emblem 15 15

1984, Sept. 27

1259 A667 3p Emblem, sphinx 15 15

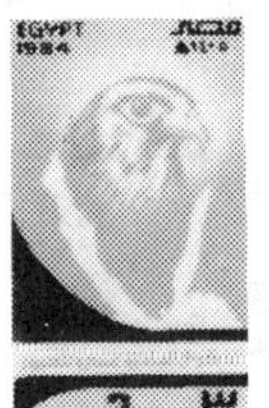

October War Against Israel, 11th Anniv. — A668

Egypt-Sudan Unity — A669

1984, Oct. 6

1260 A668 3p Map, eagle 15 15

1984, Oct. 12

1261 A669 3p Map of Nile, arms 15 15

UN Day — A670

Tanks, Emblem — A671

Perf. 13½x12½

1984, Oct. 24 Photo. Wmk. 342

1262 A670 3p UNICEF Emblem, child 15 15

UN campaign for infant survival.

1984, Nov. 10

1263 A671 3p multicolored 15 15

Military Equipment Exhibition, Cairo, Nov. 10-14.

Tolon Mosque, Egypt A672

1984, Dec. 23 Photo. *Perf. 11½x11*

1264 A672 3p multicolored 15 15

Ahmed Ebn Tolon (A.D. 835-884), Gov. of Egypt, founder of Kataea City.

A673

A674

1984, Dec. 23 *Perf. 11x11½*

1265 A673 3p multicolored 15 15

Kamel el-Kilany (1897-1959), author.

Perf. 11x11½

1984, Dec. 26 Photo. Wmk. 342

Globe and congress emblem.

1266 A674 3p lt blue, ver & blk 15 15

29th Intl. Congress on the History of Medicine, Dec. 27, 1984-Jan. 1, 1985, Cairo.

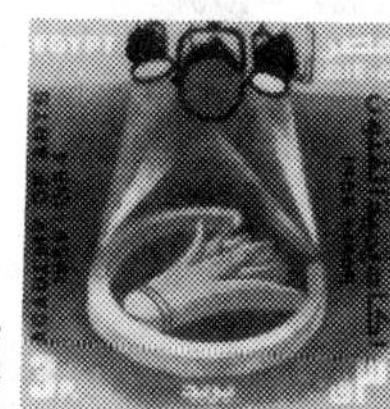

Academy of the Arts, 25th Anniv. — A675

1984, Dec. 31 *Perf. 13*

1267 A675 3p Emblem in spotlights 15 15

Pharaoh Receiving Message, Natl. Postal Museum, Cairo A676

1985, Jan. 2 *Perf. 11½x11*

1268 A676 3p brown, lt bl & ver 15 15

Postal Museum, 50th anniv.

Intl. Union of Architects, 15th Conference, Jan. 14-Feb. 15 — A677

1985, Jan. 20

1269 A677 3p multicolored 15 15

Seated Pharaonic Scribe A678

Wheat, Cogwheels, Fair Emblem A679

1985, Jan. 22 *Perf. 11x11½*

1270 A678 3p brt org & dk blue grn 15 15

17th Intl. Book Fair, Jan. 22-Feb. 3, Cairo.

1985, Mar. 9 *Perf. 13½x13*

1271 A679 3p multicolored 15 15

18th Intl. Fair, Mar. 9-22, Cairo.

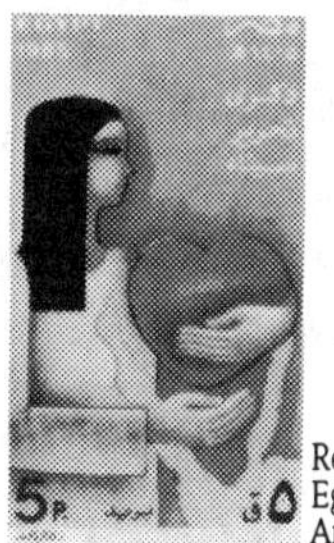

Return of Sinai to Egypt, 3rd Anniv. — A680

1985, Apr. 25 Wmk. 342 Litho.

1272 A680 5p multicolored 20 15

Ancient Artifacts — A681

A681a

Designs: 1p, God Mout, limestone sculpture, 360-340 B.C. 2p, No. 1281, Five wading birds, bas-relief. 3p, No. 1276, Seated statue, Ramses II, Temple of Luxor. No. 1276A, Vase. 8p, 15p, Slave bearing votive fruit offering, mural. 10p, Double-handled flask. 11p, Sculpted head of woman. No. 1282, Pitcher. 30p, 50p, Decanter. 35p, Temple of Karnak carved capitals. £1, Mosque.

1985-90 Photo. Unwmk. *Perf. 11½*

1273	A681	1p	brown olive	15	15
1274	A681	2p	brt grnsh bl	15	15
1275	A681	3p	yellow brown	15	15
1276	A681	5p	dk violet	15	15
1276A	A681	5p	lemon	15	15
1277	A681	8p	pale ol grn, sep & brn	25	20
1278	A681	10p	dk violet & blue	30	15
1279	A681	11p	dk violet	30	28
1280	A681	15p	pale yel, sep & brn	30	30
1281	A681	20p	yellow green	30	30
1282	A681	20p	dk green & yel	30	30
1283	A681	30p	olive bister & buff	35	35
1284	A681	35p	sepia & pale yel	40	40
1285	A681	50p	purple & buff	60	60
1285A	A681a	£1	brown & buff	1.50	1.50
1286	A681a	£2	sepia & yellow	2.50	2.50
			Nos. 1273-1286 (16)	7.85	7.63

Issue dates: 1p, 2p, 3p, #1276, 8p, 11p, 15p, May 1. 35p, July 7. No. 1281, Apr. 1, 1986. 10p, Oct. 1, 1989. £2, Dec. 1, 1989. #1282, Feb. 1, 1990; 30p, 50p, Feb. 5, 1990; £1, Feb. 8, 1990. #1276A, Dec. 15, 1990.

Nos. 1276A, 1278 are 18x23mm.

No. 1278 exists dated "1990."

See Nos. 1467, 1470, 1472.

Helwan University School of Music, 50th Anniv. A682

1985, May 15

1287 A682 5p multicolored 20 15

El-Moulid Bride, Folk Doll — A683

1985

1288 A683 2p orange & multi 15 15
1289 A683 5p red & multi 20 15
Set value 27 17

Festivals 1985. Issued: 2p, June 11. 5p, Aug. 10.

A684

A685

Designs and winning teams: a, b, Cairo Sports Stadium. c, El-Mokawiloon Club, white uniform, 1983. d, Natl. Club, red uniform, 1984. e, El-Zamalek Club, orange uniform, 1984.

1985, June 17 *Perf. 13½x13*

1290 Strip of 5 80 65
a.-e. A684 5p any single 15 15

1985 Africa Cup Soccer Championships. Cairo Sports Stadium, 25th anniv. Nos. 1290a-1290b have continuous design.

1985, July 23 *Perf. 11½x11*

1291 A685 5p blue, brn & yel 20 15

Egyptian Television, 25th anniv. Egyptian Revolution, 33rd anniv.

Suez Canal Reopening, 10th Anniv. — A686

Perf. 13x13½

1985, July 23 Litho. Wmk. 342

1292 A686 5p multicolored 20 15

Egyptian Revolution, 33rd anniv.

The only foreign revenue stamps listed in this catalogue are those also authorized for prepayment of postage.

Ahmed Hamdi Memorial Underwater Tunnel — A687

1985, July 23 *Perf. 13½x13*

1293 A687 5p blue, vio & org 20 15

Egyptian Revolution, 33rd anniv.

Souvenir Sheet

Aswan High Dam, 25th Anniv. — A688

Wmk. 342

1985, July 23 Photo. *Imperf.*

1294 A688 30p multicolored 1.00 75

Heart, Map, Olive Laurel, Conference Emblem — A689

1985, Aug. 10 Litho. *Perf. 13½x13*

1295 A689 15p multicolored 60 38

Egyptian Emigrants, 3rd general conference, Aug. 10-14, Cairo.

Natl. Tourism Ministry, 50th Anniv. — A690

1985, Sept. 10 *Perf. 13x13½*

1296 A690 5p multicolored 20 15

October War Against Israel, 12th Anniv. A691

1985, Oct. 6

1297 A691 5p multicolored 20 15

Air Scouts Assoc., 30th Anniv. A692

1985, Oct. 15 Photo. *Perf. 11½*

1298 A692 5p Emblem 20 15

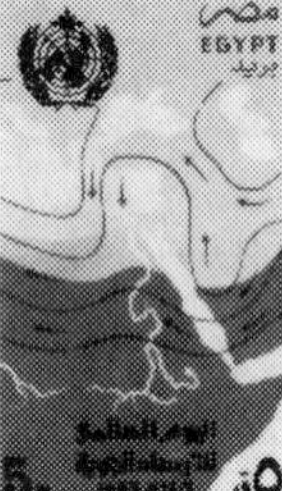

A693

UN, 40th Anniv. — A694

1985, Oct. 24

1299 A693 5p UN emblem, weather map 20 15

UN Day, Meteorology Day.

1985, Oct. 24

1300 A694 15p multicolored 60 38

Intl. Youth Year — A695

A696

1985, Oct. 24

1301 A695 5p multicolored 20 15

1985, Oct. 24

1302 A696 15p blue & int blue 60 38

Intl. Communications Development Program.

A697

A698

1985, Oct. 29 *Perf. 11x11½*

Emblem, hieroglyphics of Hassi Raa, 1st known dentist.

1303 A697 5p beige & pale bl vio 20 15

2nd Intl. Dentistry Conference.

1985, Nov. 18 Photo. *Perf. 11½*

1304 A698 5p Emblem, squash player 20 15

1985 World Squash Championships, Nov. 18-Dec. 4.

A699

A700

1985, Nov. 2 Litho. *Perf. 13½x13*

1305 A699 5p multicolored 20 15

4th Intl. Conference on the Biography and Sunna of Mohammed.

1985, Dec. 1 Photo. *Perf. 11x11½*

1306 A700 5p multicolored 20 15

1st Conference on the Development of Vocational Training.

Natl. Olympic Committee, 75th Anniv. — A701

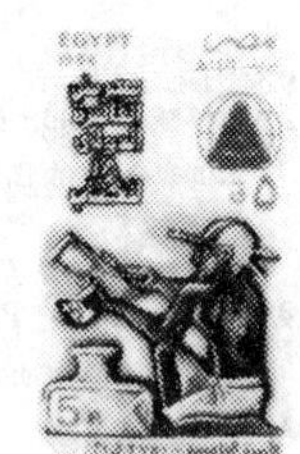

18th Intl. Book Fair, Cairo — A702

1985, Dec. 28 Photo. *Perf. 13x13½*

1307 A701 5p multicolored 20 15

1986, Jan. 21 *Perf. 11x11½*

1308 A702 5p Pharaonic scribe 20 20

CODATU III — A703

1986, Jan. 26 *Perf. 11½*

1309 A703 5p lt ol grn, ver & grnsh bl 20 20

3rd Intl. Conference on Urban Transportation in Developing Countries, Cairo.

Central Bank, 25th Anniv. — A704

1986, Jan. 30 *Perf. 13x13½*

1310 A704 5p multicolored 20 20

Cairo Postal Traffic Center Inauguration — A705

1986, Jan. 30 *Perf. 11½x11*

1311 A705 5p blue & dk brown 20 20

Pharaonic Mural, Btah Hotteb's Tomb at Saqqara A706

1986, Feb. 27 Photo. *Perf. 11½x11*

1312 A706 5p yel, gldn brn & brn 20 20

Faculty of Commerce, Cairo University, 75th anniv.

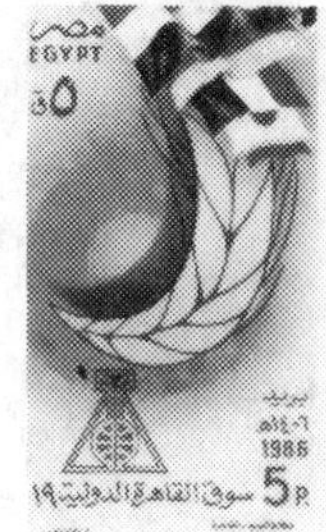

Cairo Intl. Fair, Mar. 8-21 — A707

1986, Mar. 8 Litho. *Perf. 13½x13*

1313 A707 5p multicolored 20 20

Queen Nefertiti, Sinai — A708

Perf. 13x13½

1986, Mar. 25 Litho. Wmk. 342

1314 A708 5p multicolored 20 20

Return of the Sinai to Egypt, 4th anniv.

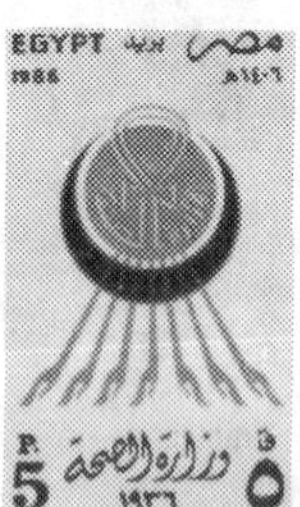

Ministry of Health, 50th Anniv. — A709

1986, Apr. 10 *Perf. 13½x13*

1315 A709 5p multicolored 20 20

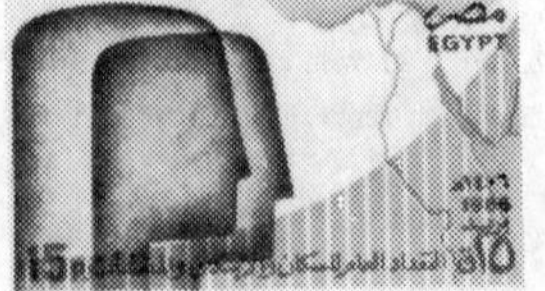

1986 Census — A710

1986, May 26 Photo. *Perf. 11½*

1316 A710 15p brn, grnsh bl & yel bis 60 60

Egypt, Winner of African Soccer Cup — A711

Festivals, Roses — A712

1986, May 31 *Perf. 13½x13*

1317 A711 5p English inscription below cup 20 20
1318 A711 5p Arabic 20 20
a. Pair, #1317-1318 40 40

1986, June 2 *Perf. 11½*

1319 A712 5p multicolored 20 20

World Environment Day — A713

1986, June 5 *Perf. 13½x13*

1320 A713 15p Emblem, smokestacks 60 60

July 23rd Revolution, 34th Anniv. A714

1986, July 23 **Litho.** *Perf. 13*

1321 A714 5p gray grn, scar & yel bister 20 20

6th African Roads Conference, Cairo, Sept. 22-26 — A715

Perf. 13½x13

1986, Sept. 21 **Litho.** **Wmk. 342**

1322 A715 15p multicolored 60 60

October War Against Israel, 13th Anniv. A716

1986, Oct. 6 **Litho.** *Perf. 13*

1323 A716 5p multicolored 20 20

Engineers' Syndicate, 40th Anniv. A717

1986, Oct. 11 **Photo.** *Perf. 11½*

1324 A717 5p lt blue, brn & pale grn 20 20

Workers' Cultural Education Assoc., 25th Anniv. — A718

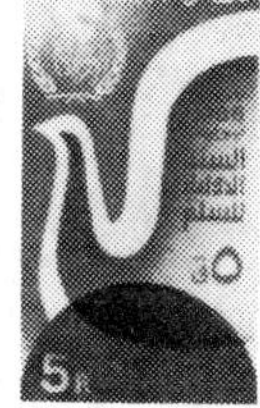

Intl. Peace Year — A719

1986, Oct. 11 *Perf. 11x11½*

1325 A718 5p orange & rose vio 20 20

1986, Oct. 24

1326 A719 5p blue, grn & pale sal 20 20

First Oil Well in Egypt, Cent. — A720

1986, Nov. 7 **Photo.** *Perf. 11½*

1327 A720 5p dull grn, blk & pale yel 20 20

UN Child Survival Campaign A721

1986, Nov. 20 **Litho.** *Perf. 13*

1328 A721 5p multicolored 20 20

Ahmed Amin, Philosopher — A722

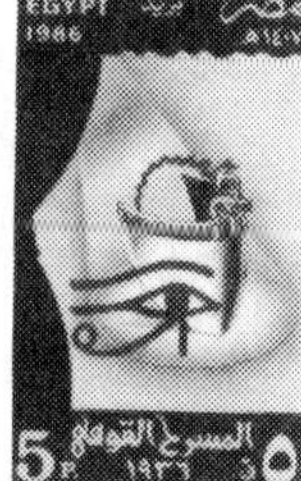

National Theater, 50th Anniv. — A723

1986, Dec. 20 *Perf. 11½*

1329 A722 5p pale grn, pale yel & brn 20 20

1986, Dec. 20 *Perf. 13½x13*

1330 A723 5p multicolored 20 20

Post Day A724

Design: Step Pyramid, Saqqara, King Zoser.

Perf. 13x13½

1987, Jan. 2 **Litho.** **Wmk. 342**

1331 A724 5p multicolored 20 20

19th Intl. Book Fair, Cairo — A725

1987, Jan. 25 **Litho.** *Perf. 13*

1332 A725 5p multicolored 20 20

5th World Conference on Islamic Education A726

Wmk. 342

1987, Mar. 8 **Litho.** *Perf. 13*

1333 A726 5p multicolored 20 20

20th Intl. Fair, Cairo — A727

1987, Mar. 21 **Photo.** *Perf. 11½*

1334 A727 5p Good workers medal 20 20

Veteran's Day — A728

1987, Mar. 26

1335 A728 5p multicolored 20 20

Intl. Gardens Inauguration, Nasser City — A729

1987, Mar. 30 **Litho.** *Perf. 13*

1336 A729 15p multicolored 60 60

World Health Day — A730

1987, Apr. 7 **Photo.** *Perf. 11½*

1337 A730 5p Mother feeding child 20 20

Litho.

Perf. 13

1338 A730 5p Oral rehydration therapy 20 20

A731

Natl. Team Victory at 1986 Intl. Soccer Championships — A732

Trophies: No. 1339a, Al Ahly Cup. No. 1339b, National Cup. No. 1339c, Al Zamalek Cup. No. 1340, Natl. flag, Cairo Stadium and trophies pictured on No. 1339.

1987, Apr. 19 **Litho.** *Perf. 13½x13*

1339 Strip of 3 60 60
a.-c. A731 5p any single 20 20

Size: 115x85mm

Imperf

1340 A732 30p multicolored 1.25 1.25

The Scott International album provides spaces for an extensive representative collection of the world's postage stamps.

Salah El Din Citadel, Pharoah's Is., Sinai — A733

1987, Apr. 25
1341 A733 5p sky blue & lt brown 20 20

Return of the Sinai to Egypt, 5th anniv.

Festivals — A734

1987, May 21 Photo. ***Perf. 11½***
1342 A734 5p Dahlia 20 20

Cultural Heritage Exhibition — A735

1987, June 17 Litho. ***Perf. 13x13½***
1343 A735 15p multicolored 60 60

Tourism Year — A736

Designs: a, Column and Sphinx, Alexandria. b, St. Catherine's Monastery, Mt. Sinai. c, Colossi of Thebes. d, Temple of Theban Triad, Luxor.

1987, June 18
1344 Block of 4 2.25 2.25
a.-d. A736 15p any single 55 55

See No. C187.

National Day — A737

1987, June 26 ***Perf. 13***
1345 A737 5p multicolored 20 20

Industry-Agriculture Exhibition — A738

1987, July 23 Photo. ***Perf. 11½***
1346 A738 5p grn, dull org & blk 20 20

Intl. Year of Shelter for the Homeless A739

1987, Sept. 2 Litho. ***Perf. 13***
1347 A739 5p multicolored 20 20

World Architects' Day.

Aida, Performed at Al Ahram Pyramid, Giza — A740

Design: Radamis and troops returning from Ethiopia.

1987, Sept. 21
1348 A740 15p multicolored 60 60

Size: 70x70mm

Imperf

1349 A740 30p multicolored 1.25 1.25

Greater Cairo Subway Inauguration — A741

1987, Sept. 27 ***Perf. 13x13½***
1350 A741 5p multicolored 20 20

Industry Day — A742

1987, Oct. 1 ***Perf. 13***
1351 A742 5p multicolored 20 20

Battle of Hettin, 700th Anniv. — A743

1987, Oct. 6 Photo. ***Perf. 11x11½***
1352 A743 5p multicolored 20 20

UPU Emblem A744

Perf. 11½

1987, Oct. 24 Unwmk. Photo.
1353 A744 5p multicolored 20 20

UN Executive Council, 40th anniv.; UPU Consultative Council, 30th anniv.

16th Art Biennial of Alexandria — A745

1987, Nov. 7 Litho. ***Perf. 13½x13***
1354 A745 5p multicolored 20 20

Second Intl. Defense Equipment Exhibition, Cairo, Nov. 9-13 — A746

Perf. 13x13½

1987, Nov. 9 Litho. Unwmk.
1355 A746 5p multicolored 20 20

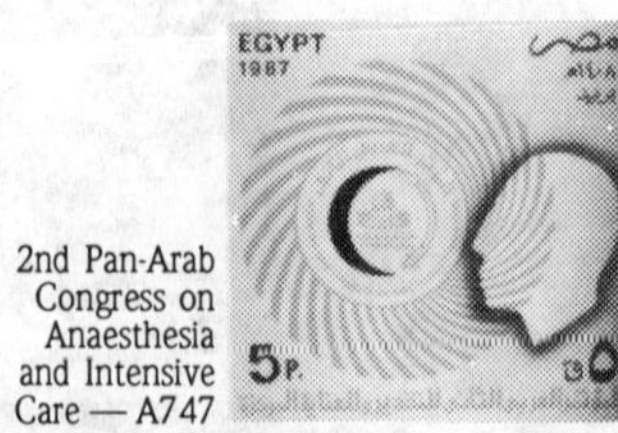

2nd Pan-Arab Congress on Anaesthesia and Intensive Care — A747

Unwmk.

1987, Dec. 1 Litho. ***Perf. 13***
1356 A747 5p multicolored 20 20

Intl. Orthopedic and Traumatology Conference — A748

1987, Dec. 1 ***Perf. 13½x13***
1357 A748 5p gray, red brn & bl 20 20

Selim Hassan (1887-1961), Egyptologist, and Hieroglyphs A749

Abdel Hamid Badawi (1887-1965), Jurist, and Scales of Justice A750

Perf. 13½x13

1987, Dec. 30 Litho. Unwmk.
1358 A749 5p multicolored 20 20
1359 A750 5p multicolored 20 20

Stamp Day 1988 — A751

Pyramids of the Pharaohs and: a, Cheops. b, Chefren. c, Mycerinus. No. 1360 has a continuous design.

1988, Jan. 2
1360 Strip of 3 1.50 1.50
a.-c. A751 15p any single 45 45

Afro-Asian Peoples Solidarity Organization, 30th Anniv. — A752

1988, Jan. 10 ***Perf. 13x13½***
1361 A752 15p multicolored 50 50

20th Intl. Book Fair, Cairo — A753

1988, Jan. 26 *Perf. 13½x13*
1362 A753 5p multicolored 20 20

Martrans (Natl. Shipping Line), 25th Anniv. A754

Unwmk.
1988, Mar. 3 Litho. *Perf. 13*
1363 A754 5p multicolored 20 20

Cairo Intl. Fair — A755

1988, Mar. 12 Photo. *Perf. 11½x11*
1364 A755 5p multicolored 20 20

World Health Day 1988: Diabetes A756

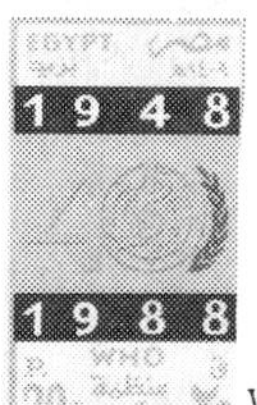

1988 Festivals A757

Perf. 11x11½
1988, Apr. 7 Photo. Unwmk.
1365 A756 5p multicolored 20 20

1988, Apr. 17 *Perf. 11½*
1366 A757 5p grn, brn org & brn 20 20

African Postal Union, 25th Anniv. — A758

1988, Apr. 23 Litho. *Perf. 13x13½*
1367 A758 15p brt blue 60 60

Oppose Racial Discrimination — A759

1988, May 25 Photo. *Perf. 11½*
1368 A759 5p multicolored 20 20

Taw Fek-Hakem (1902-1987), Playwright, Novelist — A760

1988, Aug. 5 Photo. *Perf. 11½*
1369 A760 5p brt grn blue & org brn 20 20

See #1479-1480, 1486, 1500-1502, 1543-1546.

Faculty of Art Education, 50th Anniv. A761

Perf. 11½
1988, Sept. 10 Photo. Unwmk.
1370 A761 5p multicolored 20 20

A762

1988 Summer Olympics, Seoul — A763

1988, Sept. 17 Litho. *Perf. 13*
1371 A762 15p multicolored 60 60

Size: 96x91mm
Imperf.
1372 A763 30p multicolored 1.00 1.00

No. 1371 is airmail.

October War Against Israel, 15th Anniv. — A764

Perf. 13x13½
1988, Oct. 6 Litho. Unwmk.
1373 A764 5p multicolored 20 20

A765

Opening of the Opera House — A766

1988, Oct. 10 *Perf. 11½*
1374 A765 5p multicolored 20 20

Size: 112x75mm
Imperf
1375 A766 50p multicolored 1.50 1.50

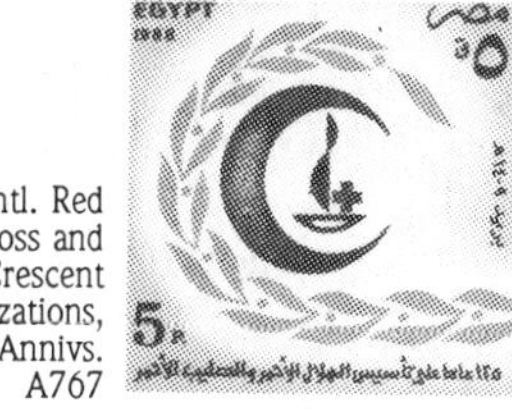

Intl. Red Cross and Red Crescent Organizations, 125th Annivs. A767

Perf. 11½
1988, Oct. 24 Photo. Unwmk.
1376 A767 5p green, blk & red 20 20

WHO, 40th Anniv. — A768

1988, Oct. 24 *Perf. 11x11½*
1377 A768 20p multicolored 80 80

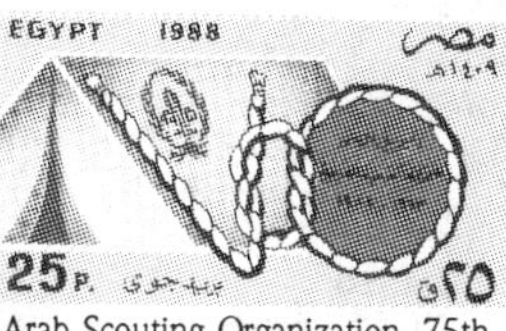

Naguib Mahfouz, 1988 Nobel Prize Winner for Literature — A769

1988, Nov. 7 Litho. *Perf. 13x13½*
1378 A769 5p multicolored 20 20

See No. C190.

Arab Scouting Organization, 75th Anniv. — A770

1988, Nov. 10
1379 A770 25p multicolored 80 80

Return of Taba to Egypt — A771

1988, Nov. 15
1380 A771 5p multicolored 20 20

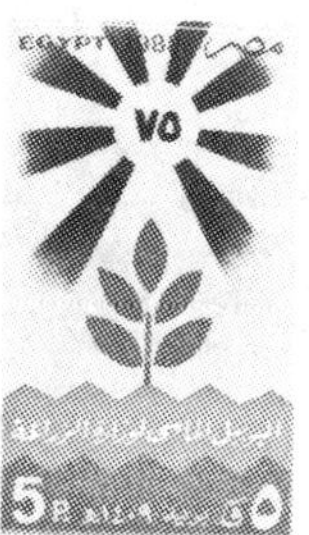

Intl. Conference on Orthopedic Surgery, Cairo, Nov. 15-18 A772

1988, Nov. 15 Photo. *Perf. 11½x11*
1381 A772 5p buff, brt yel grn & brn 20 20

A773

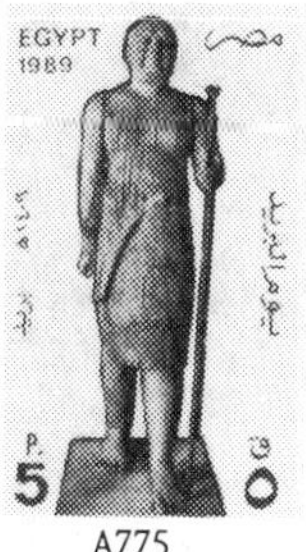

A774

1988, Dec. 3 *Perf. 11½*
1382 A773 5p multicolored 20 20

Ministry of Agriculture, 75th anniv.

Famous Men: No. 1383, Mohamed Hussein Hekal (1888-1956), author, politician. No. 1384, Ahmed Lotfi El Sayed (1872-1963), educator, politician.

Perf. 13½x13
1988, Dec. 29 Litho. Unwmk.
1383 A774 5p green & red brn 20 20
1384 A774 5p green & red brn 20 20
a. Pair, #1383-1384 40 40

A775

A776

Statues: 5p, Statue of K. Abr, a priest, 5th cent. No. 1386, Queen Nefert, 4th Dynasty. No. 1387, King Ra Hoteb, 4th Dynasty.

1989, Jan. 2

1385 A775 5p multicolored	20	20
1386 A775 25p multicolored	80	80
1387 A775 25p multicolored	80	80
a. Pair, #1386-1387	2.00	2.00

Stamp Day.

1989, Jan. 10

1388 A776 5p dull green 20 20

Jawaharlal Nehru (1889-1964), 1st Prime Minister of independent India.

Nile Hilton Hotel, 30th Anniv. — A777

1989, Feb. 22 Litho. *Perf. 13x13½*

1389 A777 5p multicolored 20 20

Return of Taba to Egypt A778

Unwmk.

1989, Mar. 15 Litho. *Perf. 13*

1390 A778 5p multicolored 20 20

2nd Stage of Cairo Subway A779

1989, Apr. 12 Litho. *Perf. 13*

1391 A779 5p multicolored 20 20

Festivals — A780

1989, May 4 Photo. *Perf. 11½*

1392 A780 5p multicolored 20 20

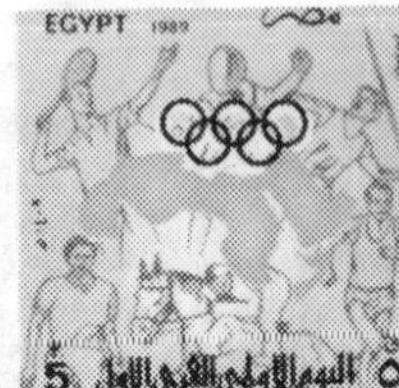

1st Arab Olympic Day — A781

1989, May 24

1393 A781 5p tan, blk & dull grn 20 20

Interparliamentary Union, Cent. — A782

Pyramids and the Parliament Building, Cairo.

1989, June 29 Litho. *Perf. 13x13½*

1394 A782 25p shown 1.00 1.00

Size: 87x76mm

Imperf

1395 A782 25p multi, diff. 1.00 1.00

French Revolution, Bicent. — A783

1989, July 14 Photo. *Perf. 11½*

1396 A783 25p multicolored 1.00 1.00

African Development Bank, 25th Anniv. — A784

Perf. 11½

1989, Oct. 1 Photo. Unwmk.

1397 A784 10p multicolored 15 15

A785

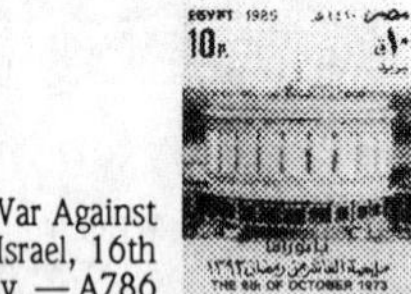

October War Against Israel, 16th Anniv. — A786

1989, Oct. 6 *Perf. 13*

1398 Strip of 3	45	45
a. A785 10p shown	15	15
b. A786 10p shown	15	15
c. A785 10p Battle scene	15	15

See No. 1424.

Aga Khan Award for Architecture A788

Perf. 11½

1989, Oct. 15 Photo. Unwmk.

1400 A788 35p multicolored 50 50

Natl. Health Insurance Plan, 25th Anniv. A789

1989, Oct. 24

1401 A789 10p blk, gray & ver 15 15

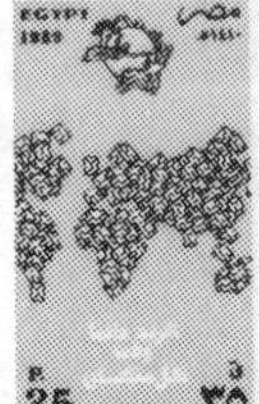

World Post Day — A790

1989, Oct. 24 *Perf. 11x11½*

1402 A790 35p blue, blk & brt yel 50 50

Statues of Memnon, Thebes — A791

Perf. 11½

1989, Nov. 12 Photo. Unwmk.

1403 A791 10p lt vio, blk & brt yel grn 15 15

Intl. Cong. & Convention Assoc. (ICCA) annual convention, Nov. 11-18, Cairo.

Cairo University School of Agriculture, Cent. — A792

1989, Nov. 15

1404 A792 10p pale grn, blk & brt yel 15 15

Cairo Intl. Conference Center A793

1989, Nov. 20 *Perf. 11½x11*

1405 A793 5p multicolored 15 15

Road Safety Soc., 20th Anniv. — A794

1989, Nov. 20 *Perf. 11½*

1406 A794 10p multicolored 15 15

Alexandria University, 50th Anniv. — A795

1989, Nov. 30 *Perf. 11x11½*

1407 A795 10p pale blue & tan 15 15

Portrait of Pasha, Monument in Opera Square, Cairo A796

Perf. 11½x11

1989, Dec. 31 Photo. Unwmk.

1408 A796 10p multicolored 15 15

Ibrahim Pasha (d. 1838), army commander from 1825 to 1828.

Famous Men

A797 A798

1989, Dec. 31 *Perf. 11x11½*

1409 A797 10p green & dk olive grn	15	15
1410 A798 10p golden brown	15	15

Abd El-Rahman El-Rafei (b. 1889), historian (No. 1409); Abdel Kader El Mazni (b. 1889), man of letters (No. 1410).

See Nos. 1431-1432.

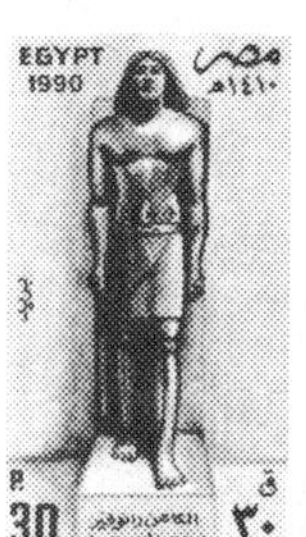
Statue of Priest Ranofr — A799

Relief Sculpture of Betah Hoteb — A800

1990, Jan. 2 *Perf. 13½x13*

1411 A799 30p multicolored 45 45
1412 A800 30p multicolored 45 45
a. Pair, #1411-1412 90 90

Stamp Day.

Arab Cooperation Council, 1st Anniv. — A801

Perf. 13x13½

1990, Feb. 16 Photo. Unwmk.

1413 A801 10p multicolored 15 15
1414 A801 35p multicolored 52 52

Emblem, Conference Center A802

Road Safety Emblems A803

Perf. 13½x13

1990, Mar. 10 Litho. Unwmk.

1415 A802 10p brt yel grn, red & blk 15 15

Size: 80x59mm

Imperf

1416 A802 30p multicolored 45 45

African Parliamentary Union 13th general conference, Mar. 10-15.

1990, Mar. 19 Photo. *Perf. 11x11½*

1417 A803 10p multicolored 15 15

Intl. Conference on Road Safety & Accidents in Developing Countries, Mar. 19-22.

Festivals 1990 — A804

1990, Apr. 24 *Perf. 11½*

1418 A804 10p multicolored 15 15

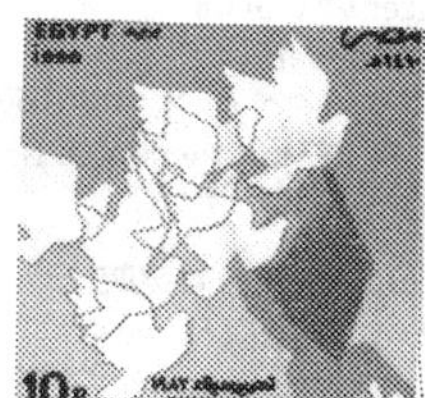
Sinai Liberation, 8th Anniv. A805

1990, Apr. 25

1419 A805 10p blue, blk & yel grn 15 15

World Cup Soccer Championships, Italy — A806

1990, May 26 Litho. *Perf. 13½x13*

1420 A806 10p multicolored 15 15

Souvenir Sheet

Imperf

1421 A806 50p Flags, trophy 75 75

World Basketball Championships, Argentina — A807

1990, Aug. 8 *Perf. 13x13½*

1422 A807 10p multicolored 15 15

Natl. Population Council, 5th Anniv. — A808

1990, Sept. 15 *Perf. 13½x13*

1423 A808 10p brown & yel grn 15 15

October War Against Israel Type of 1989

1990, Oct. 6 Litho. *Perf. 13x13½*

1424 Strip of 3 45 45
a. A785 10p Bunker, tank 15 15
b. A786 10p like #1398b 15 15
c. A785 10p Troops with flag, flame thrower 15 15

Egyptian Postal Service, 125th Anniv. — A809

1990, Oct. 9

1425 A809 10p lt blue, blk & red 15 15

Dar El Eloum Faculty, Cent. A810

1990, Oct. 13 Litho. *Perf. 13*

1426 A810 10p multicolored 15 15

UN Development Program, 40th Anniv. — A811

ITU, 125th Anniv. — A812

1990, Oct. 24 *Perf. 11½*

1427 A811 30p yel, bl grn & yel grn 45 45

Perf. 13

1428 A812 30p multicolored 45 45

UN Day.

Ras Mohammed Natl. Park A813

Various tropical fish and coral reefs.

1990, Dec. 22 Litho. *Perf. 13*

1429 Block of 4 90 90
a.-b. A813 10p any single 15 15
c.-d. A813 20p any single 30 30

No. 1429 has continuous design.

Day of the Disabled — A814

1990. Dec. 15 Photo. *Perf. 11*

1430 A814 10p multicolored 15 15

Mohamed Fahmy Abdel Meguid Bey, Medical Reformer A815

Nabaweya Moussa (1890-1951), Educator A816

Perf. 11x11½

1990, Dec. 30 Unwmk.

1431 A815 10p Prus bl, brn & org 15 15
1432 A816 10p grn, org brn & blk 15 15

Stamp Day — A817

1991, Jan. 1 Litho. *Perf. 13½x13*

1433 A817 5p No. 1 15 15
1434 A187 10p No. 2 15 15
1435 A817 20p No. 3 30 30
a. Strip of 3, #1433-1435 53 53

See Nos. 1443-1446, 1459-1460.

Veterinary Surgeon Syndicate, 50th Anniv. — A818

1991, Feb. 28 Photo. *Perf. 11½*

1436 A818 10p multicolored 15 15

Syndicate of Journalists, 50th Anniv. — A819

1991, Apr. Photo. *Perf. 11½*

1437 A819 10p multicolored 15 15

Festivals — A820

1991, Apr. 13

1438 A820 10p multicolored 15 15

Giza Zoo, Cent. — A821

1991, June 15 Litho. *Imperf.*
Size: 80x63mm

1439 A821 50p multicolored 75 75

Mahmoud Mokhtar (1891-1934), Sculptor — A822

Mohamed Nagi (1888-1956), Painter — A823

Perf. 13x13½, 13½x13
1991, June 11 Litho.

1440 A822 10p multicolored 15 15
1441 A823 10p multicolored 15 15

Faculty of Engineering A824

1991, June 30 *Perf. 13x13½*

1442 A824 10p multicolored 15 15

Stamp Day Type of 1991

Designs: No. 1443, #5. No. 1444, #4. No. 1445, #7. No. 1446, Sphinx, pyramid, #6.

1991, July 23 *Perf. 13*

1443 A817 10p orange & blk 15 15
1444 A817 10p yellow & blk 15 15
1445 A817 10p lilac & blk 15 15
a. Strip of 3, #1443-1445 45 45

Size: 80x60mm
Imperf

1446 A817 50p multicolored 75 75

Mohamed Abdel el Wahab, Musician A825

1991, Aug. 28 *Perf. 13*

1447 A825 10p multicolored 15 15

5th Africa Games, Cairo — A826

Designs: No. 1448, Karate, judo. No. 1449, Table tennis, field hockey, tennis. No. 1450, Running, gymnastics, swimming. No. 1451, Soccer, basketball, shooting. No. 1452, Boxing, wrestling, weightlifting. No. 1453, Handball, cycling, volleyball. No. 1454, Games mascot, vert. No. 1455, Mascot, emblem, torch.

Perf. 13x13½
1991, Sept. Litho. Unwmk.

1448 A826 10p multicolored 15 15
1449 A826 10p multicolored 15 15
a. Pair, #1448-1449 30 30
1450 A826 10p multicolored 15 15
1451 A826 10p multicolored 15 15
a. Pair, #1450-1451 30 30
1452 A826 10p multicolored 15 15
1453 A826 10p multicolored 15 15
a. Pair, #1452-1453 30 30

Perf. 13½x13

1454 A826 10p multicolored 15 15

Size: 80x60mm
Imperf

1455 A826 50p multicolored 75 75
Nos. 1448-1455 (8) 1.80 1.80

Intl. Statistics Institute, 48th Session A827

1991, Sept.

1456 A827 10p multicolored 15 15

Opening of Dar Al Eftaa Religious Center — A828

1991, Oct. 1 Litho. *Perf. 13*

1457 A828 10p multicolored 15 15

October War Against Israel, 18th Anniv. — A829

1991, Oct. 6 *Perf. 13x13½*

1458 A829 10p multicolored 15 15

Stamp Day Type of 1991

Designs: 10p, #6. £1, Stamp exhibition emblem, hieroglyphics, pyramids, sphinx.

1991, Oct. *Perf. 13*

1459 A817 10p blue & black 15 15

Size: 90x60mm
Imperf

1460 A817 £1 multicolored 1.50 1.50

Natl. Philatelic Exhibition, Cairo (#1460). No. 1460 sold two per person at exhibition.

Ancient Artifacts Type of 1985
Perf. 11½x11
1990-92 Unwmk. Photo.
Size: 18x23mm

1467 A681 10p like #1278 15 15
1470 A681 30p like #1283 45 45
1472 A681 50p like #1285 52 52

Issue dates: 10p, Nov. 20, 1990. 30p, Sept. 1, 1991. 50p, July 11, 1992.
This is an expanding set. Numbers will change if necessary.

United Nations Day — A830

Designs: No. 1477, Brick hands housing people. No. 1478, Woman learning to write, fingerprint, vert.

Perf. 13x13½, 13½x13
1991, Oct. 24 Litho.

1476 A830 10p shown 15 15
1477 A830 10p multicolored 15 15
1478 A830 10p multicolored 15 15
Set value 35 35

Famous Men Type of 1988
Inscribed "1991"

Designs: No. 1479, Dr. Zaki Mubarak (1891-1952), writer and poet. No. 1480, Abd El Kader Hamza (1879-1941), journalist.

1991, Dec. 23 Photo. *Perf. 13½x13*

1479 A760 10p olive brown 15 15
1480 A760 10p gray 15 15

A831

Post Day — A832

1992, Jan. 2 Litho. *Perf. 13*

1481 A831 10p shown 15 15
1482 A831 45p Bird mosaic 68 68

Perf. 14

1483 A832 70p shown 1.05 1.05

Nos. 1482-1483 are airmail.

Police Day — A833

1992, Jan. 25 *Perf. 14*

1484 A833 10p multicolored 15 15

25th Cairo Intl. Fair A834

1992, Mar. Litho. *Perf. 14*

1485 A834 10p multicolored 15 15

Famous Men Type of 1988
Inscribed "1992"

Design: 10p, Sayed Darwish (1882-1923), musician.

1992, Mar. Photo. *Perf. 14x13½*

1486 A760 10p dull orange & olive 15 15

Festivals — A835

1992, Mar. *Perf. 11½*

1487 A835 10p Egyptian hoopoe 15 15

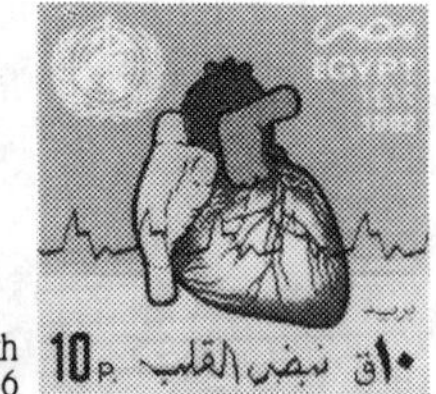

World Health Day — A836

1992, Apr. Litho. *Perf. 13*

1488 A836 10p multicolored 15 15

Aswan Dam, 90th Anniv. A837

1992, July Litho. *Perf. 13*

1489 A837 10p No. 487 15 15

20th Arab Scout Jamboree — A838

1992, July 10 ***Perf. 13x13½***
1490 A838 10p multicolored 15 15

A839

A840

1992, July 20 ***Perf. 13½x13***
1491 A839 10p multicolored 15 15

Size: 80x60mm

Imperf

1492 A839 70p Summer Games' emblem 75 75

1992 Summer Olympics, Barcelona.

1992, Sept. 14 Litho. ***Perf. 13½x13***
1493 A840 10p multicolored 15 15

El Helal Magazine, cent.

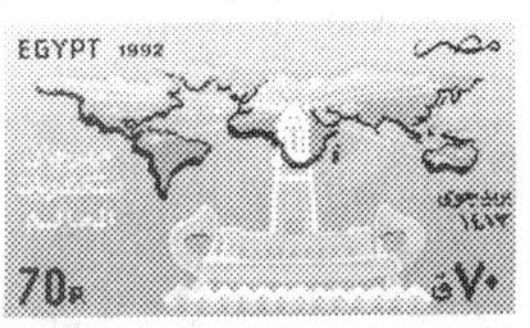

Alexandria World Festival — A841

1992, Sept. 27 ***Perf. 13x13½***
1494 A841 70p multicolored 75 75

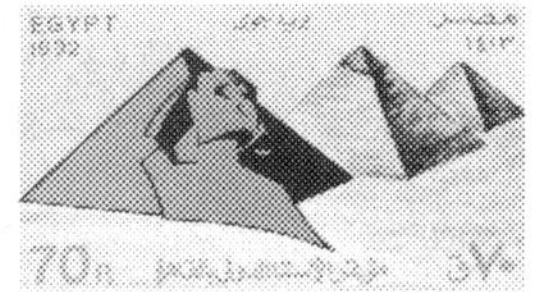

Congress of Federation of World and American Travel Companies, Cairo — A842

1992, Sept. 20
1495 A842 70p multicolored 75 75

World Post Day — A843

1992, Oct. 9 Litho. ***Perf. 13***
1496 A843 10p dk bl, lt bl & blk 15 15

Children's Day — A844

1992, Oct. 24 Litho. ***Perf. 13½x13***
1497 A844 10p multicolored 15 15

Intl. Conference on Food, Agriculture and World Health A845

1992, Oct. 24 ***Perf. 13***
1498 A845 70p multicolored 75 75

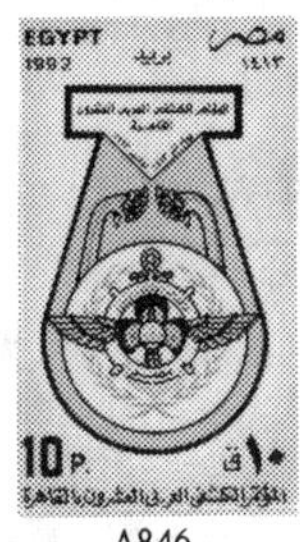

A846

A847

1992, Nov. 21 ***Perf. 13½x13***
1499 A846 10p multicolored 15 15

20th Arab Scout Conference, Cairo.

Famous Men Type of 1988 Inscribed 1992

Designs: No. 1500, Talaat Harb, economist. No. 1501, Mohamed Taymour, writer. No. 1502, Dr. Ahmed Zaki Abu Shadi (with glasses), physician & poet.

1992, Dec. 23 Photo. ***Perf. 13½x13***

1500	A760 10p	blue & brown	15	15
1501	A760 10p	citron & blue gray	15	15
1502	A760 10p	citron & blue gray	15	15
a.		Pair, #1501-1502	20	20
		Set value	30	30

1993, Jan. 2 Litho. ***Perf. 13½x13***

Pharaohs: 10p, Sesostris I. 45p, Amenemhet III. 70p, Hur I.

1503	A847 10p	brown & yellow	15	15
1504	A847 45p	brown & yellow	46	46
1505	A847 70p	brown & yellow	72	72
a.		Strip of 3, #1503-1505	1.30	1.30

Post Day.

A848

A849

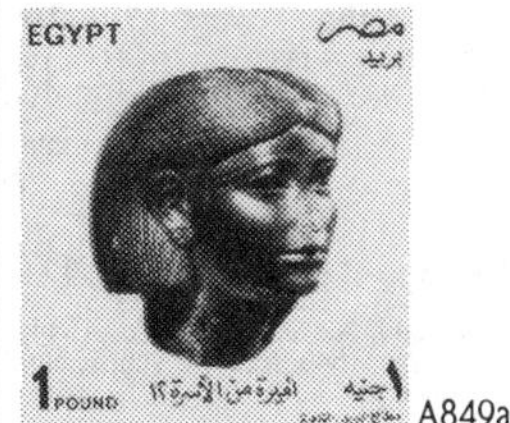

A849a

1993, Jan. 26 Litho. ***Perf. 13½x13***
1506 A848 15p multicolored 18 18

Intl. Book Fair, Cairo.

1993 Photo. Unwmk. ***Perf. 11½x11***

Artifacts: 5p, Ancient Egyptian. 15p, Sphinx. 25p, Statue of a princess. 55p, Ramses II. £1, Head of a woman. £2, Woman wearing headdress. £5, Pharaonic capital.

1510	A849	5p	multicolored	15	15
1515	A849	15p	brown & bister	18	18
1516	A849	15p	brown & bister	16	16
1517	A849	25p	brn & org brn	25	25
			Litho.		
1518	A849	55p	indigo & lt blue	60	60
			Perf. 11½		
1520	A849a	£1	slate & black	1.20	1.20
1521	A849a	£2	brown & green	2.40	2.40
1521A	A849a	£5	brown & gold	5.00	5.00
	Nos. 1510-1521A (8)			9.94	9.94

Body of Sphinx on No. 1516 stops above value, and extends through value on No. 1515.

Issued: 5p, No. 1515, Feb. 1. 25p, Mar. 10. £1, £2, Apr. 1. 55p, July 1. £5, Aug. 1.

This is an expanding set. Numbers may change.

Architects' Association, 75th Anniv. — A850

1993, Feb. 28 Litho. ***Perf. 13x13½***
1522 A850 15p multicolored 18 18

New Building for Ministry of Foreign Affairs A851

1993, Mar. 15 ***Perf. 13***
1523 A851 15p multicolored 18 18
1524 A851 80p multicolored 1.00 1.00

Diplomacy Day (#1523). No. 1524 is airmail.

Feasts — A852

1993, Mar. 20 Litho. ***Perf. 13x13½***
1525 A852 15p Opuntia 15 15

Newspaper, Le Progres Egyptien, Cent. — A853

1993, Apr. 15 Litho. ***Perf. 13x13½***
1526 A853 15p multicolored 18 18

A854

A855

1993, May 15 Litho. ***Perf. 13½x13***
1527 A854 15p multicolored 18 18

World Telecommunications Day.

1993, June 15 Litho. ***Perf. 13½x13***
1528 A855 15p multicolored 18 18

UN Conference on Human Rights, Vienna.

Organization of African Unity — A856

1993, June 26 ***Perf. 13***
1529 A856 15p yellow green & multi 18 18
1530 A856 80p red violet & multi 85 85

No. 1530 is airmail.

World PTT Conference, Cairo — A857

1993, Sept. Litho. ***Perf. 13***
1531 A857 15p multicolored 18 18

Salah El-Din El Ayubi (1137-1193), Dome of the Rock — A858

1993, Sept.
1532 A858 55p multicolored 60 60

A859 A860

1993, Oct. 6
1533 A859 15p multicolored 18 18

October War Against Israel, 20th Anniv.

1993, Oct. 12 ***Perf. 13½x13***
1534 A860 15p cream & multi 18 18
1535 A860 55p silver & multi 60 60
1536 A860 80p gold & multi 90 90

Imperf
Size: 90x70mm

1537 A860 80p multicolored 90 90

Pres. Mohamed Hosni Mubarak, Third Term.

Reduction of Natural Disasters A861

1993, Oct. 24 **Litho.** ***Perf. 13***
1538 A861 80p multicolored 90 90

Electricity in Egypt, Cent. — A862

1993, Oct. 24 ***Perf. 13½x13***
1539 A862 15p multicolored 18 18

Intl. Conference on Big Dams, Cairo — A863

1993, Nov. 19 **Litho.** ***Perf. 13***
1540 A863 15p multicolored 18 18

35th Military Intl. Soccer Championship — A864

1993, Dec. 1 **Litho.** ***Perf. 13x13½***
1541 A864 15p orange & multi 16 16
1542 A864 15p Trophy, emblem 16 16

9th Men's Junior World Handball Championship (#1542).

Famous Men Type of 1988 Inscribed 1993

Designs: No. 1543, A. Al. Bishry. No. 1544, M.F. Abu Hadeed. No. 1545, M.B. Al. Tunisy. No. 1546, Ali Moubarak.

1993, Dec. 25 ***Perf. 13½x13***
1543 A760 15p blue 16 16
1544 A760 15p blue black 16 16
1545 A760 15p light violet 16 16
1546 A760 15p green 16 16

Post Day — A865

1994, Jan. 2
1547 A865 15p Amenhotep III 16 16
1548 A865 55p Queen Hatshepsut 60 60
1549 A865 80p Thutmose III 90 90

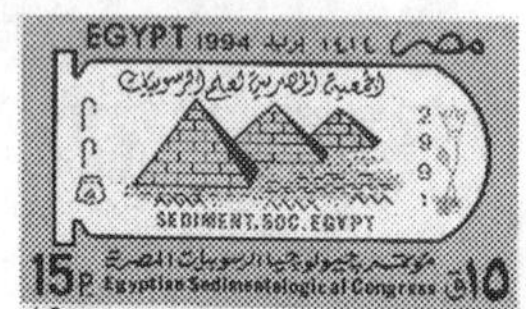

Congress of Egyptian Sedimentary Geology Society — A866

1994, Jan. 4 **Litho.** ***Perf. 13x13½***
1550 A866 15p multicolored 18 18

SEMI-POSTAL STAMPS

Catalogue values for unused stamps in this section are for Never Hinged items.

Princess Ferial — SP1

Perf. 13½x14

1940, May 17 **Photo.** **Wmk. 195**
B1 SP1 5m + 5m copper brown 50 40

No. B1 Overprinted in Green **1943** ١٩٤٣

1943, Nov. 17
B2 SP1 5m + 5m 4.50 3.75
a. Arabic date "1493" 175.00 150.00

The surtax on Nos. B1 and B2 was for the children's fund.

First Postage Stamp of Egypt SP2

Khedive Ismail Pasha SP3

Designs: 17m+17m, King Fuad. 22m+22m, King Farouk.

Perf. 13x13½

1946, Feb. 28 **Wmk. 195**
B3 SP2 1m + 1m gray 15 15
B4 SP3 10m + 10m violet 15 15
B5 SP3 17m + 17m brown 16 16
B6 SP3 22m + 22m yel grn 20 20
a. Souv. sheet, #B3-B6, perf. 8½ 32.50 17.50
b. As "a," imperf. 32.50 17.50
Set value 55 55

80th anniv. of Egypt's 1st postage stamp. Nos. B6a, B6b measure 129x171mm.

Goddess Hathor, King Men-kau-Re (Mycerinus) and Jackalheaded Goddess — SP7

Ramesseum, Thebes — SP8

Queen Nefertiti SP9

Funerary Mask of King Tutankhamen SP10

Perf. 13½x13

1947, Mar. 9 **Wmk. 195**
B9 SP7 5m + 5m slate 18 15
B10 SP8 15m + 15m dp blue 38 25
B11 SP9 30m + 30m henna brn 48 45
B12 SP10 50m + 50m brown 70 65

Intl. Exposition of Contemporary Art, Cairo.

Boy Scout Emblem — SP11

Scout Emblems: 20m+10m, Sea Scouts. 35m+15m, Air Explorers.

1956, July 25 **Photo.** ***Perf. 13½x13***
B13 SP11 10m + 10m green 32 15
B14 SP11 20m + 10m ultra 48 22
B15 SP11 35m + 15m blue 65 32

2nd Arab Scout Jamboree, Alexandria-Aboukir, 1956.

Souvenir sheets, perf. and imperf., contain one each of Nos. B13-B15. Size: 118x158mm. Value $500 each.

Ambulance — SP12

1957, May 13 ***Perf. 13x13½***
B16 SP12 10m + 5m rose red 18 15

50th anniv. of the Public Aid Society.

United Arab Republic

Eye and Map of Africa, Europe and Asia — SP13

Postal Emblem — SP14

Perf. 13½x13

1958, Mar. 1 **Photo.** **Wmk. 318**
B17 SP13 10m + 5m orange 40 30

First Afro-Asian Congress of Ophthalmology, Cairo.

The surtax was for centers to aid the blind.

1959, Jan. 2
B18 SP14 10m + 5m bl grn, red & blk 15 15

Post Day. The surtax went to the social fund for postal employees.

See Syria UAR issues No. B1 for similar stamp with denominations in piasters (p).

Children and UN Emblem — SP15

Arab League Building, Cairo, and Emblem — SP16

1959, Oct. 24 **Wmk. 328**
B19 SP15 10m + 5m brown lake 15 15
B20 SP15 35m + 10m dk blue 25 18
Set value 24

Issued for International Children's Day and to honor UNICEF.

Braille Type of Regular Issue, 1961

1961, Apr. 6 ***Perf. 13½x13***
B21 A182 35m + 15m yel & brn 50 25

1962, Mar. 22 **Photo.** **Wmk. 328**
B22 SP16 10m + 5m gray 25 15

Arab Publicity Week, Mar. 22-28.

See No. N86.

Postal Emblem — SP17

Stamp of 1866 — SP18

1963, Jan. 2 Wmk. 342 *Perf. 11½*

B23 SP17 20m +10m brt grn, red & blk 40 40
B24 SP18 40m +20m blk & brn org 60 60
B25 SP18 40m +20m brn org & blk 60 60
a. Pair, #B24-B25 1.25 1.25

Post Day, Jan. 2 and 1966 exhibition of the FIP.

Arms of UAR and Pyramids SP19

1964, Jan. 2 Wmk. 342 *Perf. 11*

B26 SP19 10m + 5m org yel & grn 65 40
B27 SP19 80m + 40m grnsh bl & blk 1.40 75
B28 SP19 115m + 55m org brn & blk 1.60 1.00

Issued for Post Day. Jan. 2.

Type of 1963 and

Postal Emblem — SP20

Designs: No. B30, Emblem of Postal Secondary School. 80m+40m, Postal emblem, gearwheel and laurel wreath.

Perf. 11½

1965, Jan. 2 Unwmk. Photo.

B29 SP20 10m + 5m lt green & car 15 15
B30 SP20 10m + 5m ultra, car & blk 15 15
B31 SP18 80m + 40m rose, brt grn & blk 65 50
Set value 62

Issued for Post Day, Jan. 2. No. B31 also publicizes the Stamp Centenary Exhibition.

Souvenir Sheet

Stamps of Egypt, 1866 — SP21

1966, Jan. 2 Wmk. 342 *Imperf.*

B32 SP21 140m + 60m blk, sl bl & rose 2.00 2.00

Post Day, 1966, and cent. of the 1st Egyptian postage stamps.

Pharaonic "Mediator" — SP22

Design: 115m+40m, Pharaonic guard.

1967, Jan. 2 Wmk. 342 *Perf. 11½*

B33 SP22 80m + 20m multi 1.50 65
B34 SP22 115m + 40m multi 2.75 90

Issued for Post Day, Jan. 2.

Grand Canal, Doges' Palace, Venice, and Santa Maria del Fiore, Florence — SP23

Design: 115m+30m, Piazetta and Campanile, Venice, and Palazzo Vecchio, Florence.

Perf. 11½x11

1967, Dec. 9 Photo. Wmk. 342

B35 SP23 80m + 20m grn, yel & brn 65 32
B36 SP23 115m + 30m ol, yel & sl bl 1.00 50

The surtax was to help save the cultural monuments of Venice and Florence, damaged in the 1966 floods.

Boy and Girl — SP24

Emblem and Flags of Arab League — SP25

Design: No. B38, Five children and arch.

Wmk. 342

1968, Dec. 11 Photo. *Perf. 11*

B37 SP24 20m + 10m car, bl & lt brn 25 15
B38 SP24 20m + 10m vio bl, sep & lt grn 25 15
Set value 20

Children's Day & 22nd anniv. of UNICEF.

1969, Mar. 22 *Perf. 11x11½*

B39 SP25 20m + 10m multi 22 15

Arab Publicity Week, Mar. 22-28.

Refugee Family SP26

1969, Oct. 24 Photo. *Perf. 11½*

B40 SP26 30m + 10m multi 65 25

Issued for United Nations Day.

Men of Three Races, Human Rights Emblem SP27

1970, Mar. 21 *Perf. 11½x11*

B41 SP27 20m + 10m multi 25 15

Issued to publicize the International Day for the Elimination of Racial Discrimination.

Arab League Type of Regular Issue

1970, Mar. 22 Wmk. 342

B42 A344 20m + 10m bl, grn & brn 65 25

Map of Palestine and Refugees SP28

Perf. 11½x11

1970, Oct. 24 Photo. Wmk. 342

B43 SP28 20m + 10m multi 1.50 38

25th anniv. of the UN and to draw attention to the plight of the Palestinian refugees.

Arab Republic of Egypt

Blind Girl, WHO and Society Emblems — SP29

1973, Oct. 24 Photo. *Perf. 11x11½*

B44 SP29 20m + 10m blue & gold 25 15

25th anniv. of WHO and for the Light and Hope Soc., which educates and helps blind girls.

Map of Africa, OAU Emblem SP30

Social Work Day Emblem SP31

Perf. 11x11½

1973, Dec. 8 Photo. Wmk. 342

B45 SP30 55m + 20m multi 1.40 75

Organization for African Unity, 10th anniv.

1973, Dec. 8

B46 SP31 20m + 10m multi 25 15

Social Work Day.

Jihan al Sadat Consoling Wounded Man — SP32

1974, Mar. 21 Wmk. 342 *Perf. 11*

B47 SP32 20m + 10m multi 50 15

Faithfulness and Hope Society.

Afghan Solidarity SP33

Perf. 11½

1981, July 15 Photo. Wmk. 342

B48 SP33 20m + 10m multi 15 15

Size: 30x25mm

1981 Photo. *Perf. 11½*

B49 SP33 20m + 10m multi 1.00 25

Map of Sudan, Dunes, Dead Tree — SP34

1986, Mar. 25 Photo. *Perf. 13x13½*

B50 SP34 15p + 5p multi 50 40

Fight against drought and desertification of the Sudan. Surtax for drought relief.

Organization of African Unity, 25th Anniv. SP35

1988, May 25 Litho. *Perf. 13*

B51 SP35 15p +10p multi 80 80

The first value column gives the catalogue value of an unused stamp, the second that of a used stamp.

AIR POST STAMPS

Mail Plane in Flight — AP1

Perf. 13x13½

1926, Mar. 10 Wmk. 195 Photo.
C1 AP1 27m deep violet 10.00 3.25

1929, July 17
C2 AP1 27m orange brown 4.00 2.00

Zeppelin Issue

No. C2 Surcharged in Blue or Violet

GRAF ZEPPELIN
AVRIL 1931
= 50 =

1931, Apr. 6
C3 AP1 50m on 27m (Bl) 20.00 15.00
a. "1951" instead of "1931" 25.00 25.00
C4 AP1 100m on 27m (V) 20.00 15.00

Airplane over Giza Pyramids AP2

1933-38 Litho. *Perf. 13x13½*
C5 AP2 1m orange & blk 15 15
C6 AP2 2m gray & blk 55 32
C7 AP2 2m org red & blk ('38) 52 45
C8 AP2 3m ol brn & blk 15 15
C9 AP2 4m green & blk 32 28
C10 AP2 5m dp brown & blk 20 15
C11 AP2 6m dk green & blk 45 40
C12 AP2 7m dk blue & blk 32 25
C13 AP2 8m violet & blk 15 15
C14 AP2 9m dp red & blk 52 48
C15 AP2 10m violet & brn 30 15
C16 AP2 20m dk green & brn 20 15
C17 AP2 30m dull blue & brn 30 15
C18 AP2 40m dp red & brn 5.75 15
C19 AP2 50m orange & brn 4.50 15
C20 AP2 60m gray & brn 1.50 15
C21 AP2 70m dk blue & bl grn 90 15
C22 AP2 80m ol brn & bl grn 90 15
C23 AP2 90m org & bl grn 1.40 15
C24 AP2 100m vio & bl grn 1.75 15
C25 AP2 200m dp red & bl grn 3.50 30
Nos. C5-C25 (21) 24.33 4.58

See Nos. C34-C37. For overprint see No. C38.

Type of 1933

1941-43 Photo.
C34 AP2 5m copper brn ('43) 15 15
C35 AP2 10m violet 25 15
C36 AP2 25m dk vio brn ('43) 25 15
C37 AP2 30m green 35 15

Catalogue values for unused stamps in this section, from this point to the end of the section, are for Never Hinged items.

No. C37 Overprinted in Black

مؤتمر الملاحة الجوية الدولى للشرق الأوسط

Le Caire 1946 - ١٩٤٦ القاهرة

1946, Oct. 1
C38 AP2 30m green 32 15
a. Double overprint 90.00 62.50
b. Inverted overprint 125.00 100.00

Middle East Intl. Air Navigation Congress, Cairo, Oct. 1946.

King Farouk, Delta Dam and DC-3 Plane AP3

Perf. 13x13½

1947, Feb. 19 Photo. Wmk. 195
C39 AP3 2m red orange 15 15
C40 AP3 3m dk brown 15 15
C41 AP3 5m red brown 15 15
C42 AP3 7m dp yel org 15 15
C43 AP3 8m green 15 15
C44 AP3 10m violet 15 15
C45 AP3 20m brt blue 18 15
C46 AP3 30m brown vio 28 15
C47 AP3 40m car rose 38 15
C48 AP3 50m Prus green 45 15
C49 AP3 100m olive grn 1.25 22
C50 AP3 200m dk gray 1.90 65
Nos. C39-C50 (12) 5.34
Set value 1.60

For overprints see Nos. C51-C64, C67-C89, NC1-NC30.

Nos. C49 and C50 Surcharged in Black

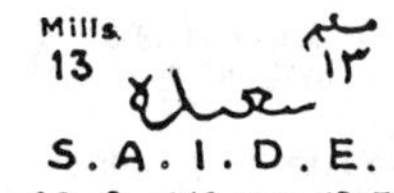

1948, Aug. 23
C51 AP3 13m on 100m 45 25
C52 AP3 22m on 200m 55 30
a. Date omitted

Inaugural flights of "Services Aeriens Internationaux d'Egypte" from Cairo to Athens and Rome, Aug. 23, 1948.

Nos. C39 to C50 Overprinted in Various Colors

Overprint 27mm Wide

1952, Jan. Wmk. 195 *Perf. 13x13½*
C53 AP3 2m red orange (Bl) 15 15
C54 AP3 3m dk brown (RV) 15 15
C55 AP3 5m red brown 15 15
C56 AP3 7m dp yel org (Bl) 18 15
C57 AP3 8m green (RV) 15 15
C58 AP3 10m violet (G) 35 24
C59 AP3 20m brt blue (RV) 90 50
C60 AP3 30m brown vio (G) 38 20
C61 AP3 40m car rose 1.90 40
C62 AP3 50m Prus green (RV) 1.10 75
C63 AP3 100m olive grn 2.25 1.25
C64 AP3 200m dk gray (RV) 3.25 2.00
Nos. C53-C64 (12) 10.91 6.09

See notes after No. 316.

Delta Dam and Douglas DC-3 AP4

1953 Photo.
C65 AP4 5m red brown 15 15
C66 AP4 15m olive green 45 15
Set value 15

For overprints see Nos. NC31-NC32.

Nos. C39-C49 Overprinted in Black with Three Bars to Obliterate Portrait

1953
C67 AP3 2m red orange 15 15
C68 AP3 3m dk brown 30 20
C69 AP3 5m red brown 15 15
C70 AP3 7m dp yel org 42 18
C71 AP3 8m green 15 15
C72 AP3 10m violet *7.75*
C73 AP3 20m brt blue 18 15
C74 AP3 30m brown vio 30 18
C75 AP3 40m car rose 35 22
C76 AP3 50m Prus grn 48 28
C77 AP3 100m olive grn 1.40 75
C77A AP3 200m gray *16.00*

Nos. C72 and C77A are in question. They are not known postally used.

Nos. C53-C64 Overprinted in Black with Three Bars to Obliterate Portrait

1953
C78 AP3 2m red orange 15 15
C79 AP3 3m dk brown 15 15
C80 AP3 5m red brown 15 15
C82 AP3 8m green 25 18
C83 AP3 10m violet 18 15
C85 AP3 30m brown vio 25 18
C87 AP3 50m Prus green 40 22
C88 AP3 100m ol green 55 38
C89 AP3 200m dk gray 5.75 1.75
Nos. C78-C89 (12) 7.83 1.56

Practically all values of Nos. C67-C89 exist with double overprint. The 7m, 20m and 40m with this overprint are forgeries.

United Arab Republic

Type of Regular Issue

Perf. 11½x11

1958, Mar. 22 Photo. Wmk. 318
C90 A141 15m ultra & red brn 30 15

Pyramids at Giza AP5

Al Azhar University AP6

Designs: 15m, Colossi of Memnon, Thebes. 90m, St. Catherine Monastery, Mt. Sinai.

1959-60 Wmk. 328 *Perf. 13x13½*
C91 AP5 5m bright red 15 15
C92 AP5 15m dk dull violet 15 15
C93 AP6 60m dk green 42 25
C94 AP5 90m brown car ('60) 80 20
Set value 58

Nos. C91-C93 exist imperf. See Nos. C101, C105, NC33.

Tower of Cairo Type of Regular Issue, Redrawn

1961, May 1 *Perf. 13½x13*
C95 A183 50m bright blue 40 18

Top inscription has been replaced by two airplanes.

Weather Vane, Anemometer and UN World Meteorological Organization Emblem — AP7

Perf. 11½x11

1962, Mar. 23 Photo. Unwmk.
C96 AP7 60m yellow & dp blue 45 25

2nd World Meteorological Day, Mar. 23.

Patrice Lumumba and Map of Africa — AP8

Perf. 13½x13

1962, July 1 Wmk. 328
C97 AP8 35m multicolored 30 15

Patrice Lumumba (1925-61), Premier of Congo.

Maritime Station, Alexandria AP9

Designs: 30m, International Airport, Cairo. 40m, Railroad Station, Luxor.

1963, Mar. 18 *Perf. 13x13½*
C98 AP9 20m dk brown 15 15
C99 AP9 30m carmine rose 20 15
C100 AP9 40m black 28 15
Set value 31

Type of 1959-60 and

Temple of Queen Nefertari, Abu Simbel AP10

Arch and Tower of Cairo — AP11

Designs: 80m, Al Azhar University seen through arch. 140m, Ramses II, Abu Simbel.

Perf. 11½x11, 11x11½

1963-65 Photo. Wmk. 342
C101 AP6 80m vio blk & brt bl 2.25 35
C102 AP10 115m brown & yel 70 45
C103 AP10 140m pale vio, blk & org red 85 60

Unwmk.
C104 AP11 50m yel brn & brt bl 38 20
C105 AP6 80m vio bl & lt bl 1.90 25
Nos. C101-C105 (5) 6.08 1.85

Issue dates: 50m, Nov. 2, 1964. No. C105, Feb. 13, 1965. Others, Oct. 24, 1963.
See Nos. NC34-NC36.

Weather Vane, Anemometer and WMO Emblem — AP12

Perf. 11½x11

1965, Mar. 23 Wmk. 342
C106 AP12 80m dk blue & rose lil 42 25

Fifth World Meteorological Day.
See No. NC37.

Game Board from Tomb of Tutankhamen — AP13

1965, July 1 Photo. Unwmk.
C107 AP13 10m yellow & dk blue 35 15

See No. NC38.

Temples at Abu Simbel — AP14

1966, Apr. 28 Wmk. 342 *Perf. 11½*

C108 AP14 20m multicolored 15 15
C109 AP14 80m multicolored 40 18
Set value 23

Issued to commemorate the transfer of the temples of Abu Simbel to a hilltop, 1963-66.

Scout Camp and Jamboree Emblem AP15

1966, Aug. 10 *Perf. 11½x11*

C110 AP15 20m olive & rose 25 15

7th Pan-Arab Boy Scout Jamboree, Good Daim, Libya, Aug. 12.

St. Catherine Monastery, Mt. Sinai — AP16

1966, Nov. 30 Photo. Wmk. 342

C111 AP16 80m multicolored 60 18

St. Catherine Monastery, Sinai, 1400th anniv.

Cairo Airport AP17

1967, Apr. 26 *Perf. 11½x11*

C112 AP17 20m sky bl, sl grn & lt brn 15 15

Hotel El Alamein and Map of Nile Delta AP18

Intl. Tourist Year: 80m, The Virgin's Tree, Virgin Mary and Child. 115m, Fishing in the Red Sea.

1967, June 7 Wmk. 342 *Perf. 11½*

C113 AP18 20m dull pur, sl grn & dl org 24 15
C114 AP18 80m blue & multi 1.00 18
C115 AP18 115m brown, org & bl 1.75 38

Oil Derricks, Map of Egypt AP19

1967, July 23 Photo.

C116 AP19 50m orange & bluish blk 40 15

15th anniversary of the revolution.

Type of Regular Issue, 1967

Design: 80m, Back of Tutankhamen's throne and UNESCO emblem.

1967, Oct. 24 Wmk. 342 *Perf. 11½*

C117 A301 80m blue & yellow 45 18

Koran — AP20

1968, Mar. 25 Wmk. 342 *Perf. 11½*

C118 AP20 30m lilac, bl & yel 75 25
C119 AP20 80m lilac, bl & yel 1.50 50

1400th anniv. of the Koran. Nos. C118-C119 are printed in miniature sheets of 4 containing 2 each of Nos. C118-C119.

St. Mark and St. Mark's Cathedral — AP21

1968, June 25 Wmk. 342 *Perf. 11½*

C120 AP21 80m brt grn, dk brn & dp car 60 18

Martyrdom of St. Mark, 1900th anniv. and the consecration of St. Mark's Cathedral, Cairo.

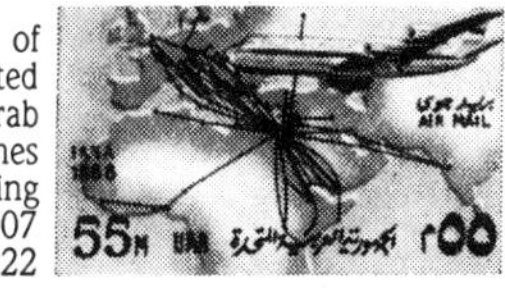

Map of United Arab Airlines and Boeing 707 AP22

Design: No. C122, Ilyushin 18 and routes of United Arab Airlines.

1968-69 Photo. *Perf. 11½x11*

C121 AP22 55m blue, ocher & car 35 15
C122 AP22 55m bl, yel & vio blk ('69) 35 15

1st flights of a Boeing 707 and an Ilyushin 18 for United Arab Airlines.

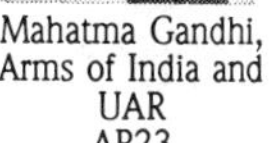

Mahatma Gandhi, Arms of India and UAR AP23

Imam El Boukhary AP24

1969, Sept. 10 *Perf. 11x11½*

C123 AP23 80m lt blue, ocher & brn 65 18

Mohandas K. Gandhi (1869-1948), leader in India's fight for independence.

1969, Dec. 27 Photo. Wmk. 342

C124 AP24 30m lt olive & dk brown 20 15

1100th anniv. of the death of the Imam El Boukhary (824-870), philosopher and writer.

Azzahir Beybars Mosque AP25

1969, Dec. 27 Engr. *Perf. 11½x11*

C125 AP25 30m red lilac 15 15

700th anniv. of the founding of the Azzahir Beybars Mosque, Cairo.

Lenin (1870-1924) — AP26

Perf. 11x11½

1970, Apr. 22 Photo. Wmk. 342

C126 AP26 80m lt green & brown 45 18

Phantom Fighters and Destroyed Factory AP27

1970, May 1 *Perf. 11½x11*

C127 AP27 80m yel, grn & dk vio brn 60 18

Issued to commemorate the destruction of the Abu-Zaabal factory by Israeli planes.

UPU Type of Regular Issue

1970, May 20 Photo. Wmk. 342

C128 A350 80m multicolored 40 18

Nasser and Burial Mosque — AP28

1970, Nov. 6 Wmk. 342 *Perf. 11*

C129 AP28 30m olive & blk 32 15
C130 AP28 80m brown & blk 70 18
Set value 26

Gamal Abdel Nasser (1918-70), Pres. of Egypt.

Postal Congress Type of Regular Issue

Perf. 11½x11

1971, Mar. 6 Photo. Wmk. 342

C131 A365 30m lt ol, org & sl grn 16 15

Nasser, El Rifaei and Sultan Hussein Mosques AP29

Designs: 85m, Nasser and Ramses Square, Cairo. 110m, Nasser, Sphinx and pyramids.

Perf. 11½x11

1971, July 1 Photo. Wmk. 342

C132 AP29 30m multicolored 45 15
C133 AP29 85m multicolored 1.10 25
C134 AP29 110m multicolored 1.65 35

APU Type of Regular Issue

1971, Aug. 3 Wmk. 342 *Perf. 11½*

C135 A373 30m brown, yel & bl 15 15

Arab Republic of Egypt

Confederation Type of Regular Issue

Perf. 11½x11

1971, Sept. 28 Photo. Wmk. 342

C136 A374 30m gray, sl grn & dk pur 15 15

Al Aqsa Mosque and Woman AP30

Perf. 11½

1971, Oct. 24 Photo. Wmk. 342

C137 AP30 30m bl, yel, brn & grn 75 25

25th anniv. of the UN (in 1970) and return of Palestinian refugees.

Postal Union Type of Regular Issue

Design: 30m, African Postal Union emblem and letter.

1971, Dec. 2 *Perf. 11½x11*

C138 A384 30m green, blk & bl 15 15

Aida, Triumphal March AP31

1971, Dec. 23 Wmk. 342 *Perf. 11½*

C139 AP31 110m dk brn, yel & sl grn 80 20

Centenary of the first performance of the opera Aida, by Giuseppe Verdi.

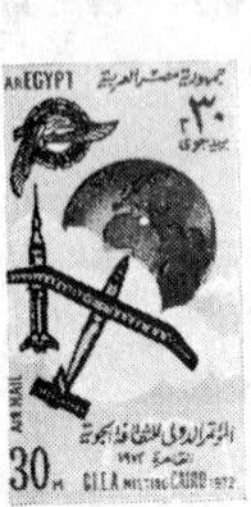

Globe, Glider, Rocket Club Emblem AP32

St. Catherine's Monastery on Fire AP33

1972, Feb. 11 ***Perf. 11x11½***
C140 AP32 30m blue, ocher & yel 18 15

International Aerospace Education Conference, Cairo, Jan. 11-13.

Perf. 11½x11
1972, Feb. 15 **Unwmk.**
C141 AP33 110m dp car, org & blk 60 20

The burning of St. Catherine's Monastery in Sinai Desert, Nov. 30, 1971.

Tutankhamen in Garden — AP34

Tutankhamen, from 2nd Sarcophagus — AP35

Design: No. C143, Ankhesenamun.

1972, May 22 **Photo.** ***Perf. 11½***
C142 AP34 110m brn org, bl & grn 2.25 60
C143 AP34 110m brn org, bl & grn 2.25 60
a. Pair, #C142-C143 5.00 1.50

Souvenir Sheet

Imperf

C144 AP35 200m gold & multi 6.50 6.50

50th anniv. of the discovery of the tomb of Tutankhamen. No. C143a has continuous design.

Souvenir Sheet

Flag of Confederation of Arab Republics — AP36

1972, July 23 **Photo.** ***Imperf.***
C145 AP36 110m gold, dp car & blk 1.75 75

20th anniversary of the revolution.

Temples at Abu Simbel AP37

Designs: 30m, Al Azhar Mosque and St. George's Church. 110m, Pyramids at Giza.

1972 **Wmk. 342** ***Perf. 11½x11***
C146 AP37 30m blue, brn & buff 22 15
C147 AP37 85m blue, brn & ocher 60 15
C148 AP37 110m multicolored 80 16
Set value 36

Issued: #C146, C148, Nov. 22; #C147, Aug. 1.

Olympic Type of Regular Issue

Designs (Olympic and Motion Emblems and): No. C149, Handball. No. C150, Weight lifting. 50m, Swimming. 55m, Gymnastics. All vertical.

1972, Aug. 17 ***Perf. 11x11½***
C149 A396 30m multicolored 20 15
C150 A396 30m yellow & multi 20 15
C151 A396 50m blue & multi 38 15
C152 A396 55m multicolored 42 15
Set value 30

Champollion, Rosetta Stone, Hieroglyphics — AP38

1972, Oct. 16
C153 AP38 110m gold, grn & blk 1.25 25

Sesquicentennial of the deciphering of Egyptian hieroglyphics by Jean-Francois Champollion.

World Map, Telephone, Radar, ITU Emblem — AP39

1973, Mar. 21 **Photo.** ***Perf. 11***
C154 AP39 30m lt bl, dk bl & blk 15 15

5th World Telecommunications Day.

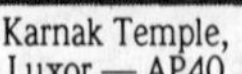

Karnak Temple, Luxor — AP40

Hand Dripping Blood and Falling Plane — AP41

1973, Mar. 21
C155 AP40 110m dp ultra, blk & rose 75 45

Sound and light at Karnak.

1973, May 1 ***Perf. 11x11½***
C156 AP41 110m multicolored 2.75 50

Israeli attack on Libyan civilian plane, Feb. 1973.

WMO Emblem, Weather Vane — AP42

1973, Oct. 24 ***Perf. 11x11½***
C157 AP42 110m blue, gold & pur 65 25

Cent. of intl. meteorological cooperation.

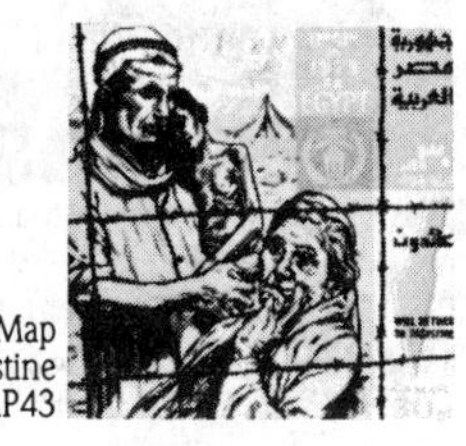

Refugees, Map of Palestine AP43

1973, Oct. 24 ***Perf. 11½***
C158 AP43 30m dk brn, yel & bl 1.00 18

Plight of Palestinian refugees.

INTERPOL Emblem AP44

Postal and UPU Emblems AP45

Perf. 11x11½
1973, Dec. 8 **Photo.** **Wmk. 342**
C159 AP44 110m black & multi 75 18

Intl. Criminal Police Organization, 50th anniv.

1974, Jan. 2 **Unwmk.** ***Perf. 11***

Post Day (UPU Emblems and): 30m, APU emblem. 55m, African Postal Union emblem. 110m, UPU emblem.

Size: 26x46½mm

C160 AP45 20m gray, red & blk 15 15
C161 AP45 30m salmon, blk & pur 15 15
C162 AP45 55m emerald, blk & brt mag 55 15

Size: 37x37½mm

Perf. 11½

C163 AP45 110m lt blue, blk & gold 80 25
Set value 47

Solar Bark of Khufu (Cheops) — AP46

Perf. 11½
1974, Mar. 21 **Wmk. 342** **Photo.**
C164 AP46 110m blue, gold & brn 1.00 25

Solar Bark Museum.

Hotel Meridien AP47

1974, Oct. 6 ***Perf. 11½x11***
C165 AP47 110m multicolored 75 25

Opening of Hotel Meridien, Cairo.

Suez Canal Type of 1975

1975, June 5 ***Perf. 11½***
C166 A448 30m bl, yel grn & ind 55 15
C167 A448 110m indigo & blue 1.40 25

Irrigation Commission Emblem — AP48

1975, July 20
C168 AP48 110m orange & dk grn 90 25

9th Intl. Congress on Irrigation and Drainage, Moscow, and 25th anniv. of the Intl. Commission on Irrigation and Drainage.

Refugees and UNWRA Emblem — AP49

Woman and IWY Emblem — AP50

Perf. 11x11½

1975, Oct. 24 Photo. Wmk. 342

C169 AP49 30m multicolored 75 25

Unwmk.

C170 AP50 110m olive, org & blk 1.10 32

UN Day. 30m publicizes UN help for refugees; 110m is for Intl. Women's Year 1975.

Step Pyramid, Sakhara, and Entrance Gate AP51

Designs: 45m, 60m, Plane over Giza Pyramids. 140m, Plane over boats on Nile.

Perf. 11½x11

1978-82 Photo. Wmk. 342

C171	AP51	45m yellow & brown	18	15
C171A	AP51	60m olive	24	15
C172	AP51	115m blue & brown	48	15
C173	AP51	140m blue & purple	55	25
C173A	AP51	185m bl, sep & gray brn	80	50
		Nos. C171-C173A (5)	2.25	1.20

Issue dates: 60m, Jan. 15, 1982. 185m, 1982. Others, Jan. 1, 1978.

Flyer and UN ICAO Emblem — AP52

Perf. 11x11½

1978, Dec. 30 Photo. Wmk. 342

C174 AP52 140m blue, blk & brn 60 28

75th anniversary of 1st powered flight.

Seeing Eye Medallion AP53

Perf. 11½x11

1981, Oct. 1 Photo. Wmk. 342

C175 AP53 230m multicolored 95 30

Hilton Ramses Hotel Opening — AP54

Perf. 11x11½

1982, Mar. 15 Photo. Wmk. 342

C176 AP54 18½p multi 75 25

Temple of Horus, Edfu AP55

Designs: 15p, like 6p. 18½p, 25p, Statue of Akhnaton, Thebes, hieroglyphics, vert. 23p, 30p, Giza pyramids.

1985 Photo. *Perf. 11½x11, 11x11½*

C177	AP55	6p lt blue & dk bl grn	18	15
C178	AP55	15p grnsh bl & brn	45	28
C179	AP55	18½p grn, sep & dp yel	50	35
C180	AP55	23p grnsh bl, sep & yel bis	65	40
C181	AP55	25p lt bl, sep & yel bis	70	40
a.		Unwmkd. ('87)	85	45
C182	AP55	30p grnsh bl, sep & org yel	1.00	55
a.		Unwmkd. ('87)	1.00	55
		Nos. C177-C182 (6)	3.48	2.13

Issue dates: 6p, 18½p, 23p, Mar. 1. 15p, 25p, 30p, May. 1.

Post Day — AP56

Narmer Board, oldest known hieroglyphic inscriptions: No. C183a, Tablet obverse. No. C183b, Reverse.

1986, Jan. 2 Photo. *Perf. 13½x13*

C183 AP56 Pair 1.25 1.25

a.-b. 15p any single 60 60

Map, Jet, AFRAA Emblem AP57

1986, Apr. 7 Photo. *Perf. 11½*

C184 AP57 15p blue, yel & blk 40 40

African Airlines Assoc., 18th General Assembly, Cairo, Apr. 7-10.

World Food Day AP58

UNESCO, 40th Anniv. — AP59

Perf. 13½x13, 13x13½

1986, Oct. 24 Litho.

C185 AP58 15p multicolored 70 70

C186 AP59 15p multicolored 70 70

UN Day.

Tourism Year — AP60

Design: Column and Sphinx in Alexandria, St. Catherine's Monastery in Mt. Sinai, Colossi of Thebes and Temple of Theban Triad in Luxor.

Unwmk.

1987, Sept. 30 Litho. *Imperf.*

Size: 140x90mm

C187 AP60 30p multicolored 1.40 1.40

Palestinian Uprising — AP61

1988, Sept. 28 Litho. *Perf. 12x13½*

C188 AP61 25p multicolored 80 80

UN Day AP62

1988, Oct. 20 Litho. *Perf. 13x13½*

C189 AP62 25p multicolored 80 80

Nobel Prize Type of 1988

1988, Nov. 7

C190 A769 25p multicolored 80 80

Arab Cooperation Council — AP63

Architecture and Art — AP64

1989, May 10 Litho. *Perf. 13½x13*

C191 AP63 25p Flags 80 80

Size: 89x80mm

Imperf

C192 AP63 50p Flags, seal 2.00 2.00

1989-91 Photo. *Perf. 11x11½*

C193	AP64	20p Balcony	30	30
C194	AP64	25p Brazier	38	38
C195	AP64	35p shown	52	52
C196	AP64	45p Tapestry	68	68
C196A	AP64	45p like #C195	68	68
C197	AP64	50p Stag (dish)	75	75
C198	AP64	55p 4 animals (plate)	82	82
C199	AP64	60p like #C197	90	90
C199A	AP64	65p like #C197	1.00	1.00
C200	AP64	70p like #C193	1.05	1.05
C201	AP64	85p like #C198	1.30	1.30
		Nos. C193-C201 (11)	8.38	8.38

Issue dates: 35p, 60p, Oct. 1, 1989. 55p, Jan. 1, 1990. Nos. C196A, C200, Jan. 25, 1991. 65p, 85p, July 20, 1991. Others, Apr. 1, 1989.

This is an expanding set. Numbers will change if necessary.

AP65

Funerary Mask of King Tutankhamen AP66

1993, Mar. 1 Litho. *Perf. 11½*

C205 AP65 55p multicolored 55 55

C206 AP66 80p multicolored 80 80

AIR POST SEMI-POSTAL STAMPS

Catalogue values for unused stamps in this section are for Never Hinged items.

United Arab Republic

Pharaonic Mail Carriers and Papyrus Plants SPAP1

Design: 115m+55m, Jet plane, world map and stamp of Egypt, 1926 (No. C1).

Perf. 11½

1966, Jan. 2 Wmk. 342 Photo.

CB1 SPAP1 80m + 40m multi 85 35

CB2 SPAP1 115m + 55m multi 1.25 42

a. Pair, #CB1-CB2 1.75 1.00

Post Day, Jan. 2.

SPECIAL DELIVERY STAMPS

Motorcycle Postman SD1

Perf. 13x13½

1926, Nov. 28 Photo. Wmk. 195

E1 SD1 20m dark green 4.25 1.00

1929, Sept.

E2 SD1 20m brown red & black 50 20

Inscribed "Postes Expres"

1943-44 Litho.

E3 SD1 26m brn red & gray blk 65 45

E4 SD1 40m dl brn & pale gray ('44) 50 15

For overprints see Nos. E5, NE1.

Catalogue values for unused stamps in this section, from this point to the end of the section, are for Never Hinged items.

No. E4 Overprinted in Black

ملك مصر والسودان
١٦ اكتوبر سنة ١٩٥١

Overprint 27mm Wide

1952, Jan.

E5 SD1 40m dl brn & pale gray 80 22

See notes after No. 316.

POSTAGE DUE STAMPS

D1

D2

Wmk. Crescent and Star (119)

1884, Jan. 1 Litho. *Perf. 10½*

J1 D1 10pa red 8.00 1.25
a. Horiz. pair, imperf. vert. 100.00
J2 D1 20pa red 12.00 1.65
J3 D1 1pi red 25.00 4.25
J4 D1 2pi red 40.00 2.25
J5 D1 5pi red 10.00 6.25

1886, Aug. 1 Unwmk.

J6 D1 10pa red 2.00 50
a. Horiz. pair, imperf. vert. 50.00 30.00
J7 D1 20pa red 50.00 5.00
J8 D1 1pi red 1.60 50
J9 D1 2pi red 1.60 25

1888, Jan. 1 *Perf. 11½*

J10 D2 2m green 1.00 38
a. Horiz. pair, imperf. between 50.00
J11 D2 5m rose red 1.60 38
J12 D2 1pi blue 16.00 4.25
J13 D2 2pi yellow 14.00 1.75
J14 D2 5pi gray 50.00 25.00
a. Period after "PIASTRES" 65.00 37.50
Nos. J10-J14 (5) 82.60 31.76

Excellent counterfeits of #J1-J14 are plentiful.
There are 4 types of each of Nos. J1-J14, so placed that any block of 4 contains all types.

D3

D4

Perf. 14x13½

1889 Wmk. 119 Typo.

J15 D3 2m green 60 15
a. Half used as 1m on cover 2.50
J16 D3 4m maroon 40 15
J17 D3 1pi ultra 1.00 15
J18 D3 2pi orange 1.20 15
Set value 27

Nos. J15-J18 exist on both ordinary and chalky paper. Imperf. examples of Nos. J15-J17 are proofs.

Black Surcharge

1898

J19 D4 3m on 2pi orange 20 16
a. Inverted surcharge 20.00 15.00
b. Double surcharge 65.00 50.00
c. Pair, one without surcharge 120.00

There are two types of this surcharge. In one type, the spacing between the last two Arabic characters at the right is 2mm. In the other type, this spacing is 3mm, and there is an added sign on top of the second character from the right.

D5

D6

1921 Wmk. 120 *Perf. 14x13½*

J20 D5 2m green 25 22
J21 D5 4m vermilion 1.00 38
J22 D6 10m deep blue 1.00 50

1921-22

J23 D5 2m vermilion 22 15
J24 D5 4m green 22 15
J25 D6 10m lake ('22) 35 15
Set value 21

Nos. J18, J23-J25 Overprinted

1922, Oct. 10 Wmk. 119

J26 D3 2pi orange 2.50 50
a. Overprint right side up 5.50 2.50

Wmk. 120

J27 D5 2m vermilion 35 15
J28 D5 4m green 50 25
J29 D6 10m lake 80 30

Overprint on Nos. J26-J29 is inverted.

Arabic Numeral — D7

Perf. 13x13½

1927-56 Litho. Wmk. 195

Size: 18x22½mm

J30 D7 2m slate 35 15
J31 D7 2m orange ('38) 16 15
J32 D7 4m green 25 15
J33 D7 4m ol brn ('32) 1.00 15
J34 D7 5m brown 65 15
J35 D7 6m gray grn ('41) 35 15
J36 D7 8m brn vio 35 15
J37 D7 10m brick red ('29) 42 15
a. 10m deep red 50 18
J38 D7 12m rose lake ('41) 60 15
J38A D7 20m dk red ('56) 1.00 38

Perf. 13½x14

Size: 22x28mm

J39 D7 30m purple 2.25 75
Nos. J30-J39 (11) 7.38
Set value 2.05

See Nos. J47-J59. For overprints see Nos. J40-J46, NJ1-NJ7.

Catalogue values for unused stamps in this section, from this point to the end of the section, are for Never Hinged items.

Postage Due Stamps and Type of 1927 Overprinted in Various Colors

ملك مصر والسودان
١٦ اكتوبر سنة ١٩٥١

1952, Jan. 16 *Perf. 13x13½*

J40 D7 2m orange (Bl) 15 15
J41 D7 4m green 20 15
J42 D7 6m gray grn (RV) 30 18
J43 D7 8m brn vio (Bl) 25 18
J44 D7 10m dl rose (Bl) 65 18
a. 10m brown red (Bk) 42 20
J45 D7 12m rose lake (Bl) 35 15

Perf. 14

J46 D7 30m purple (C) 1.00 28
Nos. J40-J46 (7) 2.90 1.27

See notes after No. 316.

United Arab Republic

1960 Wmk. 318 *Perf. 13x13½*

Size: 18x22½mm

J47 D7 2m orange 30 15
J48 D7 4m light green 38 15
J49 D7 6m green 50 15
J50 D7 8m brown vio 38 18
J51 D7 12m rose brown 65 25
J52 D7 20m dull rose brn 1.00 25

Perf. 14

Size: 22x28mm

J53 D7 30m violet 3.50 50
Nos. J47-J53 (7) 6.71 1.63

1962 Wmk. 328 *Perf. 13x13½*

Size: 18x22½mm

J54 D7 2m salmon 22 15
J55 D7 4m light green 45 18
J56 D7 10m red brown 65 25
J57 D7 12m rose brown 1.20 38
J58 D7 20m dull rose brn 1.60 75

Perf. 14

Size: 22x28mm

J59 D7 30m light violet 2.00 1.10
Nos. J54-J59 (6) 6.12 2.81

D8

1965 Unwmk. Photo. *Perf. 11*

J60 D8 2m org & vio blk 15 15
J61 D8 8m lt bl & dk bl 16 15
J62 D8 10m yel & emer 20 15
J63 D8 20m lt bl & vio blk 24 15
J64 D8 40m org & emer 48 15
Nos. J60-J64 (5) 1.23
Set value 38

MILITARY STAMPS

From Nov. 1, 1932 to Feb. 29, 1936 members of the British Forces in Egypt were permitted to send letters to Great Britain at reduced rates. Special seals were used in place of Egyptian stamps. These seals were replaced by special stamps Mar. 1, 1936.

Fuad Type of 1927
Inscribed "Army Post"

Perf. 13½x14

1936, Mar. 1 Photo. Wmk. 195

M1 A44 3m green 42 15
M2 A44 10m carmine 1.25 15
Set value 23

King Farouk — M1

1939, Dec. 16 *Perf. 13x13½*

M3 M1 3m green 42 *1.50*
M4 M1 10m carmine rose 1.25 15

Catalogue values for unused stamps in this section, from this point to the end of the section, are for Never Hinged items.

United Arab Republic

Arms of UAR and Military Emblems — M2

Perf. 11x11½

1971, Apr. 15 Photo. Wmk. 342

M5 M2 10m purple 15 15

OFFICIAL STAMPS

O1

Wmk. Crescent and Star (119)

1893, Jan. 1 Typo. *Perf. 14x13½*

O1 O1 orange brown 20 15

No. O1 exists on ordinary and chalky paper. Imperf. examples of No. O1 are proofs.

Regular Issues of 1884-93 Overprinted

O.H.H.S.
اميري

1907

O2 A18 1m brown 15 15
O3 A19 2m green 18 15
O4 A21 3m orange 18 15
O5 A20 5m car rose 28 15
O6 A14 1pi ultra 50 15
O7 A16 5pi gray 2.75 15
Nos. O2-O7 (6) 4.04
Set value 35

Nos. O2-O3, O5-O7 imperf.are proofs.

Overprinted **O.H.H.S.**

1913

O8 A20 5m carmine rose 20 15
a. Inverted overprint 25.00
b. No period after "S" 4.25 1.75

Regular Issues Overprinted

O.H.H.S.
اميرى

1914-15

On Issues of 1888-1906

O9 A19 2m green 24 15
a. Inverted overprint 14.00 10.00
b. Double overprint 160.00
c. No period after "S" 4.00 3.00
O10 A23 4m brown red 40 15
a. Inverted overprint 90.00 55.00

On Issue of 1914

O11 A24 1m olive brown 16 15
a. No period after "S" 1.60 1.25
O12 A26 3m orange 18 15
a. No period after "S" 3.50 2.50
O13 A28 5m lake 40 15
a. No period after "S" 2.50 2.00
b. Two periods after "S" 2.50 2.00
Nos. O9-O13 (5) 1.38
Set value 39

Regular Issues Overprinted

O.H.H.S.
أميرى

1915, Oct.

On Issues of 1888-1906

O14 A19 2m green 50 15
a. Inverted overprint 6.50 5.00
b. Double overprint 10.00
O15 A23 4m brown red 65 15

On Issue of 1914

O16 A28 5m lake 40 15
a. Pair, one without overprint 140.00
Set value 23

1922 Wmk. 120

On Issue of 1921-22

O17 A24 1m olive brown 3.50 1.00
O18 A25 2m red 3.50 1.00
O19 A26 3m orange 60.00 60.00
O20 A28 5m pink 3.50 1.50

Regular Issues of 1921-22 Overprinted

O.H.E.M.S.
الحكومة
الملكية المصرية

1922

O21 A24 1m olive brn 22 22
O22 A25 2m red 25 20
O23 A26 3m orange 1.10 80
O24 A27 4m green 1.60 1.10
a. Two periods after "H" none after "S" 65.00 65.00
O25 A28 5m pink 40 16
a. Two periods after "H" none after "S" 35.00 35.00
O26 A29 10m deep blue 1.10 65
O27 A29 10m lake ('23) 2.00 65
a. Two periods after "H" none after "S" 50.00 37.50
O28 A34 15m indigo 1.40 80
O29 A35 15m indigo 90.00 80.00
a. Two periods after "H" none after "S" 200.00 200.00
O30 A31 50m maroon 6.50 2.50
Nos. O21-O30 (10) 104.57 87.08

Regular Issue of 1923 Overprinted in Black or Red

أميرى

1924 *Perf. 13½x14*

O31 A36 1m orange 40 25
O32 A36 2m gray (R) 50 30
O33 A36 3m brown 1.40 55

O34 A36 4m yellow green 1.60 65
O35 A36 5m orange brown 50 15
O36 A36 10m rose 1.50 22
O37 A36 15m ultra 1.60 45

Perf. 14

O38 A36 50m myrtle green 4.00 1.25
Nos. O31-O38 (8) 11.50 3.82

O2 O3

Perf. 13x13½

1926-35 Litho. Wmk. 195

Size: 18½x22mm

O39 O2 1m lt orange 15 15
O40 O2 2m black 15 15
O41 O2 3m olive brn 15 15
O42 O2 4m lt green 15 15
O43 O2 5m brown 15 15
O44 O2 10m dull red 38 15
O45 O2 10m brt vio ('34) 20 15
O46 O2 15m dp blue 60 15
O47 O2 15m brown vio ('34) 22 15
O48 O2 20m dp blue ('35) 30 15

Perf. 13½

Size 22½x27½mm

O49 O2 20m olive green 1.50 15
O50 O2 50m myrtle green 1.10 15
Nos. O39-O50 (12) 5.05
Set value 65

1938, Dec.

Size 22½x19mm

O51 O3 1m orange 15 15
O52 O3 2m red 15 15
O53 O3 3m olive brown 15 15
O54 O3 4m yel green 15 15
O55 O3 5m brown 15 15
O56 O3 10m brt violet 15 15
O57 O3 15m rose violet 15 15
O58 O3 20m blue 20 15

Perf. 14x13½

Size 26½x22mm

O59 O3 50m myrtle green 42 15
Set value 1.20 48

Catalogue values for unused stamps in this section, from this point to the end of the section, are for Never Hinged items.

Nos. O51 to O59 Overprinted in Various Colors

ملك مصر والسودان
١٦ اكتوبر سنة ١٩٥١

Overprint 19mm Wide

1952, Jan. *Perf. 13x13½*

O60 O3 1m orange (Br) 15 15
O61 O3 2m red (Br) 15 15
O62 O3 3m olive brn (Bl) 15 15
O63 O3 4m yel green (Bl) 15 15
O64 O3 5m brown (Bl) 15 15
O65 O3 10m brt violet (Bl) 15 15
O66 O3 15m rose violet (Bl) 20 15
O67 O3 20m blue 26 18

Overprint 24½mm Wide

Perf. 14x13½

O68 O3 50m myrtle grn (RV) 75 38
Set value 1.75 95

See notes after No. 316.

United Arab Republic

O4 Arms of UAR — O5

Perf. 13x13½

1959 Litho. Wmk. 318

O69 O4 10m brown violet 42 15
O70 O4 35m chalky blue 80 15
Set value 15

1962-63 Wmk. 328

O71 O4 1m orange ('63) 15 15
O72 O4 4m yel grn ('63) 15 15
O73 O4 5m brown 15 15
O74 O4 10m dk brown 15 15
O75 O4 35m dark blue 25 25
O76 O4 50m green 40 40
O77 O4 100m violet ('63) 75 40
O78 O4 200m rose red ('63) 1.65 75
O79 O4 500m gray ('63) 4.00 2.25
Nos. O71-O79 (9) 7.65 4.65

Perf. 11½x11

1966-68 Unwmk. Photo.

O80 O5 1m ultra 15 15
O81 O5 4m brown 15 15
O82 O5 5m olive 15 15
O83 O5 10m brown blk 15 15
O84 O5 20m magenta 15 15
O85 O5 35m dk purple 25 15
O86 O5 50m orange 28 18
O87 O5 55m dk purple 30 20

Wmk. 342

O88 O5 100m brt grn & brick red 80 38
O89 O5 200m blue & brick red 1.50 50
O90 O5 500m olive & brick red 3.00 1.25
Nos. O80-O90 (11) 6.88
Set value 2.90

1969 Wmk. 342

O91 O5 10m magenta 15 15

Arab Republic of Egypt

Arms of Egypt
O6 O7

Wmk. 342

1972, June 30 Photo. *Perf. 11*

O92 O6 1m black & vio blue 15 15
a. 1m black & light blue ('75) 15 15
O93 O6 10m black & car 15 15
a. 10m black & rose red ('76) 15 15
O94 O6 20m black & olive 15 15
O95 O6 50m black & orange 25 15
O96 O6 55m black & purple 28 18
Set value 78 50

1973

O97 O6 20m lilac & sepia 15 15
a. 20m pur & light brn ('76) 15 15
O98 O6 70m black & grn ('79) 50 25

1982 Photo. Unwmk. *Perf. 11*

O99 O6 30m purple & brown 15 15
O100 O6 60m black & orange 25 15
O101 O6 80m black & green 30 20

Issue dates: 30m, Feb. 12; 60m, Feb. 24; 80m, Feb. 18.

1985-89 Photo. *Perf. 11½*

O102 O7 1p vermilion 15 15
O103 O7 2p brown 15 15
O104 O7 3p sepia 15 15
O105 O7 5p orange yel 16 15
O106 O7 8p green 25 20
O107 O7 10p brown olive 15 15
O108 O7 15p dull violet 50 38
O109 O7 20p blue 65 50
O110 O7 25p red 38 38
O111 O7 30p dull violet 45 45
O112 O7 50p green 1.60 1.25
O113 O7 60p myrtle green 90 90
Nos. O102-O113 (12) 5.49 4.81

Issue dates: 1p, 3p, 5p, 8p, 15p, May 1. 20p, 50p, Apr. 1988. 10p, 30p, 60p, Dec. 1, 1989. 2p, 25p, 1989.

1991 Wmk. 342

Size: 18x22mm

O114 O7 10p brown violet 15 15
O115 O7 30p dk violet 45 45
O116 O7 50p green 75 75

Issue dates: 10p, 30p, July 1. 50p, Dec. 1.

Perf. 11½x11

1993 Photo. Wmk. 342

Size: 18x22mm

O117 O7 5p orange yellow 15 15
O118 O7 15p brown 15 15
O119 O7 25p purple 25 25
O120 O7 55p red 58 58

Issued: 55p, Apr. 1, 1993.

This is an expanding set. Numbers will change when complete.

OCCUPATION STAMPS

Catalogue values for unused stamps in this section are for Never Hinged items.

For Use in Palestine

فلسطين

Stamps of 1939-46 Overprinted in Red, Green or Black — a

PALESTINE

Perf. 13x13½, 13½x13

1948, May 15 Wmk. 195

N1 A77 1m yellow brn (G) 15 15
N2 A77 2m red org (G) 15 15
N3 A66 3m brown (G) 15 15
N4 A77 4m dp green 15 15
N5 A77 5m red brown (Bk) 15 15
N6 A66 6m lt yel grn (Bk) 15 15
N7 A77 10m dp violet 15 15
N8 A66 13m rose car (G) 16 15
N9 A77 15m dk violet 15 15
N10 A77 17m olive green 18 15
N11 A77 20m dk gray 18 15
N12 A77 22m deep blue 25 18
N13 A74 50pi green & sep 4.75 3.00
N14 A75 £1 dp bl & dk brn 9.25 5.75

The two lines of the overprint are more widely separated on Nos. N13 and N14.

Nos. 267-269, 237 and 238 Overprinted in Red

فلسطين

b

PALESTINE

Perf. 14x13½

N15 A73 30m olive green 60 45
N16 A73 40m dark brown 75 45
N17 A73 50m Prus green 1.10 60
N18 A73 100m brown violet 1.40 85
N19 A73 200m dark violet 4.00 3.00
Nos. N1-N19 (19) 23.82 15.93

Overprint arranged to fit size of stamps.

Nos. N1-N19 Overprinted in Black with Three Bars to Obliterate Portrait

Perf. 13x13½, 13½x13, 14x13½

1953 Wmk. 195

N20 A77 1m yellow brown 15 15
N21 A77 2m red orange 15 15
N22 A66 3m brown 15 15
N23 A77 4m deep green 15 15
N24 A77 5m red brown 15 15
N25 A66 6m lt yel grn 20 15
N26 A77 10m deep violet 25 18
N27 A66 13m rose carmine 28 22
N28 A77 15m dark violet 28 22
N29 A77 17m olive green 32 25
N30 A77 20m dark gray 32 25
N31 A77 22m deep blue 50 38
N32 A73 30m olive green 55 42
N33 A73 40m dark brown 85 70
N34 A73 50m Prus green 1.25 95
N35 A73 100m brown violet 2.75 2.25
N36 A73 200m dark violet 6.25 4.75
N37 A74 50pi green & sepia 17.50 14.00
N38 A75 £1 dp bl & dk brn 27.50 21.00
Nos. N20-N38 (19) 59.55 46.47

Regular Issue of 1953-55 Overprinted Type "a" in Blue or Red

1954-56 *Perf. 13x13½*

N39 A115 1m red brown 15 15
N40 A115 2m dark lilac 15 15
N41 A115 3m brt blue (R) 15 15
N42 A115 4m dark green (R) 15 15
N43 A115 5m deep carmine 15 15
N44 A110 10m dark brown 15 15
N45 A110 15m gray (R) 15 15
N46 A110 17m dk grnsh bl (R) 16 15
N47 A110 20m purple (R) ('54) 16 15

فلسطين

Nos. 331-333 and 335-340 Overprinted in Blue or Red — c

PALESTINE

Perf. 13½

N48 A111 30m dull green (R) 26 22
N49 A111 32m brt blue (R) 30 25
N50 A111 35m violet (R) 35 26
N51 A111 40m red brown 55 42
N52 A111 50m violet brown 60 45
N53 A112 100m henna brown 1.50 1.10
N54 A112 200m dk grnsh bl (R) 2.75 2.25
N55 A112 500m purple (R) 12.00 9.00
N56 A112 £1 dk grn, blk & red (R) ('56) 20.00 15.00
Nos. N39-N56 (18) 39.68 30.30

Type of 1957 Overprinted in Red — d

فلسطين
PALESTINE

1957 Wmk. 195 *Perf. 13½x13*

N57 A127 10m blue green 1.10 65

Nos. 414-417 Overprinted Type "d" in Red

1957-58 Wmk. 315 *Perf. 13½*

N58 A137 10m violet 15 15

Wmk. 318

N59 A136 1m lt bl grn ('58) 15 15
N60 A138 5m brown ('58) 15 15
N61 A137 10m violet ('58) 15 15
Set value 36 28

United Arab Republic

Nos. 438-444 Overprinted Type "d" in Red or Green

Perf. 13½x14

1958 Wmk. 318 Photo.

N62 A136 1m crimson 15 15
N63 A138 2m blue 15 15
N64 A143 3m dk red brn (G) 15 15
N65 A217 4m green 15 15
N66 A138 5m brown 15 15
N67 A137 10m violet 15 15
N68 A138 35m lt ultra 25 20
Set value 58 50

Same Overprint in Red on Freedom Struggle Type of 1958

1958 *Perf. 13½x13*

N69 A145 10m dark brown 65 50

Same Overprint in Green on Declaration of Human Rights Type of 1958

1958 *Perf. 13x13½*

N70 A151 10m rose violet 65 50
N71 A151 35m red brown 1.00 75

No. 460 Overprinted Type "d" in Green

1959 Wmk. 195 *Perf. 13½*

N72 A112 55m on 100m henna brn 50 38

"PALESTINE" Added in English and Arabic to Stamps of Egypt

World Refugee Year Type

1960 Wmk. 328 *Perf. 13x13½*

N73 A173 10m orange brown 15 15
N74 A173 35m dk blue gray 32 18
Set value 23

Type of Regular Issue 1959-60

1960 *Perf. 13½x14*

N75 A136 1m brown orange 15 15
N76 A217 4m olive gray 15 15
N77 A138 5m dk dull pur 15 15
N78 A137 10m dk olive grn 15 15
Set value 27 23

Palestine Day Type

1961, May 15 *Perf. 13½x13*

N79 A184 10m purple 15 15

WHO Day Type

1961 Wmk. 328 *Perf. 13½x13*

N80 A182 10m blue 15 15

U.N.T.A.P. Type

1961, Oct. 24

N81 A191 10m dk blue & org 15 15
N82 A191 35m vermilion & blk 20 15
Set value 27 20

Education Day Type

1961, Dec. 18 Photo. *Perf. 13½*

N83 A194 10m red brown 15 15

Victory Day Type

1961, Dec. 23 Unwmk. *Perf. 11½*

N84 A195 10m brn org & brn 15 15

Gaza Strip Type

Perf. 13½x13

1962, Mar. 7 Wmk. 328

N85 A200 10m red brown 15 15

Arab Publicity Week Type

1962, Mar. 22 *Perf. 13½x13*

N86 SP16 10m dark purple 15 15

Anti-Malaria Type

1962, June 20 Photo.

N87 A204 10m brn & dk car rose 15 15
N88 A204 35m black & yellow 25 20

Hammarskjold Type

Perf. 11½x11

1962, Oct. 24 Wmk. 342

Portrait in Slate Blue

N89 A214 5m bright rose 15 15
N90 A214 10m brown 15 15
N91 A214 35m blue 25 20
Set value 46 35

Lamp Type of Regular Issue

Perf. 11x11½

1963, Feb. 20 Unwmk.

N92 A217 4m dk brn, org & ultra 15 15

"Freedom from Hunger" Type

Perf. 11½x11, 11x11½

1963, Mar. 21 Wmk. 342

N93 A220 5m lt grn & dp org 15 15
N94 A220 10m olive & yellow 15 15
N95 A220 35m dull pur, yel & blk 22 18
Set value 34 28

Red Cross Centenary Type

Designs: 10m, Centenary emblem, bottom panel added. 35m, Globe and emblem, top and bottom panels added.

1963, May 8 Unwmk. *Perf. 11x11½*

N96 A221 10m dk blue & crim 15 15
N97 A221 35m crim & dk blue 22 18
Set value 29 23

"Save Abu Simbel" Type, 1963

1963, Oct. 15 Wmk. 342 *Perf. 11*

N98 A224 5m black & yellow 15 15
N99 A224 10m gray, blk & yellow 15 15
N100 A224 35m org yel & violet 22 18
Set value 34 28

Human Rights Type, 1963

1963, Dec. 10 Photo. *Perf. 11½x11*

N101 A228 5m dk brown & yellow 15 15
N102 A228 10m dp claret, gray & blk 15 15
N103 A228 35m lt grn, pale grn & blk 22 18
Set value 34 28

Types of Regular Issue, 1964

1964 Unwmk. *Perf. 11*

N104 A231 1m citron & lt violet 15 15
N105 A230 2m orange & slate 15 15
N106 A230 3m blue & ocher 15 15
N107 A235 4m ol gray, ol, brn & rose 15 15
N108 A230 5m rose & brt blue 15 15
a. 5m rose & dark blue 1.00 75
N109 A231 10m olive, rose & brn 16 15
N110 A230 15m lilac & yellow 28 18
N111 A230 20m brown blk & ol 18 15
N112 A231 30m dp org & ind 28 18
N113 A231 35m buff, ocher & emer 42 25
N114 A231 40m ultra & emer 42 25
N115 A231 60m grnsh bl & brn org 80 50

Wmk. 342

N116 A232 100m bluish blk & yel brn 80 50
Nos. N104-N116 (13) 4.09
Set value 2.30

Arab League Council Type, 1964

1964, Jan. 13 Photo.

N117 A234 10m olive & black 15 15

Minaret Type, 1964

1964 Unwmk. *Perf. 11*

N118 A235 4m ol, red brn & red 15 15

Arab Postal Union Type, 1964

1964, Apr. 1 Wmk. 342 *Perf. 11*

N119 A239 10m emer & ultra, *lt grn* 15 15

WHO Type, 1964

1964, Apr. 7

N120 A240 10m violet blk & red 15 15

Minaret Type, 1965

1965, Jan. 20 Unwmk. *Perf. 11*

N121 A255 4m green & dk brn 15 15

Arab League Type, 1965

1965, Mar. 22 Wmk. 342 *Perf. 11*

N122 A258 10m green, red & blk 15 15
N123 A258 20m green & brown 15 15
Set value 21 15

World Health Day Type, 1965

1965, Apr. 7 Wmk. 342 *Perf. 11*

N124 A259 10m brt green & crim 15 15

Massacre Type, 1965

1965, Apr. 9 Photo.

N125 A260 10m slate blue & red 15 15

ITU Type, 1965

1965, May 17 Wmk. 342 *Perf. 11*

N126 A261 5m sl grn, sl bl & yel 15 15
N127 A261 10m car, rose red & gray 15 15
N128 A261 35m vio bl, ultra & yel 20 15
Set value 32 25

United Nations Type, 1966

Designs: 5m, WHO Headquarters Building, Geneva. 10m, UN Refugee emblem. 35m, UNICEF emblem.

1966, Oct. 24 Wmk. 342 *Perf. 11*

N129 A288 5m rose & brt pur 15 15
N130 A288 10m yel brn & brt pur 15 15
N131 A288 35m brt green & brt pur 20 15
Set value 30 25

Victory Day Type, 1966

Perf. 11½

1966, Dec. 23 Wmk. 342 Photo.

N132 A290 10m olive & car rose 15 15

Arab Publicity Week Type, 1967

Perf. 11x11½

1967, Mar. 22 Photo. Wmk. 342

N133 A294 10m vio blue & brn 15 15

Labor Day Type, 1967

Perf. 11½x11

1967, May 1 Photo. Wmk. 342

N134 A296 10m olive & sepia 15 15

OCCUPATION AIR POST STAMPS

Catalogue values for unused stamps in this section are for Never Hinged items.

Nos. C39-C50 Overprinted Type "b" in Black, Carmine or Red

Perf. 13x13½

1948, May 15 Wmk. 195

NC1 AP3 2m red org (Bk) 15 15
NC2 AP3 3m dk brn (C) 15 15
NC3 AP3 5m red brn (Bk) 15 15
NC4 AP3 7m dp yel org (Bk) 15 15
NC5 AP3 8m green (C) 15 15
NC6 AP3 10m violet 16 15
NC7 AP3 20m brt bl 26 18
NC8 AP3 30m brn vio (Bk) 42 25
NC9 AP3 40m car rose (Bk) 50 32
NC10 AP3 50m Prus grn 75 45
NC11 AP3 100m olive grn 1.25 75
NC12 AP3 200m dark gray 4.00 2.50
Nos. NC1-NC12 (12) 8.09 5.35

Nos. NC1-NC12 Overprinted in Black with Three Bars to Obliterate Portrait

1953

NC13 AP3 2m red org 70 45
NC14 AP3 3m dk brn 15 15
NC15 AP3 5m red brn 2.75 1.75
NC16 AP3 7m dp yel org 42 25
NC17 AP3 8m green 60 38
NC18 AP3 10m violet 20 15
NC19 AP3 20m brt bl 50 30
NC20 AP3 30m brn vio 60 38
NC21 AP3 40m car rose 60 38
NC22 AP3 50m Prus grn 3.00 2.00
NC23 AP3 100m olive grn 17.00 10.00
NC24 AP3 200m dk gray 8.00 5.00
Nos. NC13-NC24 (12) 34.52 21.19

Nos. NC1-NC3, NC6, NC10, NC11 with Additional Overprint in Various Colors

ملك مصر والسودان
١٦ اكتوبر سنة ١٩٥١

Overprinted in Black with Three Bars to Obliterate Portrait

1953

NC25 AP3 2m red org (Bk + Bl) 15 15
NC26 AP3 3m dk brn (Bk + RV) 2.00 1.25
NC27 AP3 5m red brn (Bk) 15 15
NC28 AP3 10m vio (R + G) 4.25 2.50
NC29 AP3 50m Prus grn (R + RV) 2.75 1.75
NC30 AP3 100m ol grn (R + Bk) 12.50 7.50
Nos. NC25-NC30 (6) 21.80 13.30

Nos. C65-C66 Overprinted Type "b" in Black or Red

1955 Wmk. 195 *Perf. 13x13½*

NC31 AP4 5m red brn 75 45
NC32 AP4 15m ol grn (R) 1.00 65

United Arab Republic

"PALESTINE" Added in Arabic and English to Air Post Stamps

Type of 1963

Perf. 11½x11

1963, Oct. 24 Photo. Wmk. 342

NC33 AP6 80m blk & brt bl 1.10 60
NC34 AP10 115m blk & yel 1.65 80
NC35 AP10 140m bl, ultra & org red 2.00 1.00

Cairo Tower Type, 1964

1964, Nov. 2 Unwmk. *Perf. 11x11½*

NC36 AP11 50m dl vio & lt bl 45 25

World Meteorological Day Type

1965, Mar. 23 Wmk. 342 *Perf. 11*

NC37 AP12 80m dk bl & org 80 50

Tutankhamen Type of 1965

1965, July 1 Photo. *Perf. 11*

NC38 AP13 10m brn org & brt grn 40 22

OCCUPATION SPECIAL DELIVERY STAMP

Catalogue values for unused stamps in this section are for Never Hinged items.

No. E4 Overprinted Type "b" in Carmine

1948 Wmk. 195 *Perf. 13x13½*

NE1 SD1 40m dl brn & pale gray 1.00 1.00

OCCUPATION POSTAGE DUE STAMPS

Catalogue values for unused stamps in this section are for Never Hinged items.

Postage Due Stamps of Egypt, 1927-41, Overprinted Type "a" in Black or Rose

1948 Wmk. 195 *Perf. 13x13½*

NJ1 D7 2m orange 15 15
NJ2 D7 4m green (R) 15 15
NJ3 D7 6m gray green 16 15
NJ4 D7 8m brown violet 25 15
NJ5 D7 10m brick red 25 15
NJ6 D7 12m rose lake 38 22

Overprinted Type "b" in Red

Perf. 14

Size: 22x28mm

NJ7 D7 30m purple 90 55
Nos. NJ1-NJ7 (7) 2.24 1.52

ELOBEY, ANNOBON AND CORISCO

LOCATION — A group of islands near the Guinea Coast of western Africa.

GOVT. — Spanish colonial possessions administered as part of the Continental Guinea District. A second district under the same governor-general included Fernando Po.

AREA — 13¾ sq. mi.

POP. — 2,950 (estimated 1910)

CAPITAL — Santa Isabel

100 Centimos = 1 Peseta

King Alfonso XIII — A1

1903 Unwmk. Typo. *Perf. 14*

Control Numbers on Back

1 A1 ¼c carmine 35 15
2 A1 ½c dk vio 35 15
3 A1 1c black 35 15
4 A1 2c red 35 15
5 A1 3c dk grn 35 15
6 A1 4c dk bl grn 35 15
7 A1 5c violet 35 15
8 A1 10c rose lake 70 45
9 A1 15c org buff 2.00 45
10 A1 25c dark blue 3.50 1.50
11 A1 50c red brn 5.00 2.25
12 A1 75c blk brn 5.00 3.00
13 A1 1p org red 7.50 4.00
14 A1 2p chocolate 20.00 11.50
15 A1 3p dp ol grn 30.00 14.00
16 A1 4p claret 60.00 21.00
17 A1 5p bl grn 70.00 21.00
18 A1 10p dull blue 125.00 32.50
Nos. 1-18 (18) 331.15 112.70

Dated "1905"

1905

Control Numbers on Back

19 A1 1c carmine 65 20
20 A1 2c dp vio 3.00 20
21 A1 3c black 65 20
22 A1 4c dull red 65 20
23 A1 5c dp grn 65 20
24 A1 10c bl grn 2.25 30
25 A1 15c violet 3.00 1.25
26 A1 25c rose lake 3.00 1.25
27 A1 50c org buff 5.25 1.75
28 A1 75c dark blue 5.25 1.75
29 A1 1p red brn 10.50 4.00
30 A1 2p blk brn 11.50 6.00
31 A1 3p org red 11.50 6.00
32 A1 4p dk brn 60.00 25.00
33 A1 5p bronze grn 60.00 25.00
34 A1 10p claret 215.00 70.00
Nos. 19-34 (16) 392.85 143.30

Nos. 19-22 Surcharged in Black or Red

1906

35 A1 10c on 1c rose (Bk) 6.00 4.50
a. Inverted surcharge 6.00 4.50
b. Value omitted 21.00 11.50
c. Frame omitted 11.00 5.25
d. Double surcharge 6.00 4.50
e. Surcharged "15 cents" 21.00 11.50
f. Surcharged "25 cents" 32.50 16.00
g. Surcharged "50 cents" 32.50 16.00
h. "1906" omitted 11.50 5.25
36 A1 15c on 2c dp vio (R) 6.00 4.50
a. Frame omitted 8.00 4.00
b. Surcharged "25 cents" 11.00 6.50
c. Inverted surcharge 6.00 4.50
d. Double surcharge 6.00 4.50
36E A1 15c on 2c dp vio (Bk) 11.00 6.50
37 A1 25c on 3c blk (R) 6.00 4.50
a. Inverted surcharge 6.00 4.50
b. Double surcharge 6.00 4.50
c. Surcharged "15 cents" 11.00 6.50
d. Surcharged "50 cents" 16.00 8.00
37E A1 25c on 3c blk (Bk) 11.00 6.50
f. Inverted surcharge 11.00 6.50
g. Surcharged "15 cents" 11.00 7.50
h. Surcharged "10 cents" 16.00 7.25
38 A1 50c on 4c red (Bk) 6.00 4.50
a. Inverted surcharge 6.00 4.50
b. Value omitted 26.00 13.00
c. Frame omitted 11.50 5.75
e. Double surcharge 6.00 4.50
f. "1906" omitted 11.50 5.75
g. Surcharged "10 cents" 22.50 11.50
h. Surcharged "25 cents" 22.50 11.50
Nos. 35-38 (6) 46.00 31.00

Eight other surcharges were prepared but not issued: 10c on 50c, 75c, 1p, 2p and 3p; 15c on 50c and 5p; 50c on 5c.

King Alfonso XIII — A2

1907

Control Numbers on Back

39	A2	1c dk vio	42	35
40	A2	2c black	42	35
41	A2	3c red org	42	35
42	A2	4c dk grn	42	35
43	A2	5c bl grn	42	35
44	A2	10c violet	3.75	1.90
45	A2	15c carmine	1.25	60
46	A2	25c orange	1.25	60
47	A2	50c blue	1.25	60
48	A2	75c brown	3.75	1.10
49	A2	1p blk brn	6.25	1.90
50	A2	2p org red	9.25	3.25
51	A2	3p dk brn	8.50	3.25
52	A2	4p bronze grn	9.25	2.75
53	A2	5p claret	12.50	3.25
54	A2	10p rose	30.00	9.25
		Nos. 39-54 (16)	89.10	30.20

Stamps of 1907 Surcharged

1908-09

Black Surcharge

55	A2	5c on 3c red org ('09)	2.75	1.25
56	A2	5c on 4c dk grn ('09)	2.75	1.25
57	A2	5c on 10c violet	5.75	5.00
58	A2	25c on 10c violet	30.00	15.00

1910

Red Surcharge

59	A2	5c on 1c dark violet	2.25	1.00
60	A2	5c on 2c black	2.25	1.00

Nos. 55-60 exist with surcharge inverted (value each $10 unused, $7.50 used); with double surcharge, one black, one red (value $15 each); with "PARA" omitted (value each $15 unused, $7.50 used).

The same 5c surcharge was also applied to Nos. 45-54, but these were not issued. Value $10 each.

In 1909, stamps of Spanish Guinea replaced those of Elobey, Annobon and Corisco.

1909 CORREOS
10 cen de peseta

Revenue stamps surcharged as above were unauthorized although some were postally used.

EPIRUS

LOCATION — Southeastern Europe comprising parts of Greece and Albania.

This territory formerly belonged to Turkey but is now divided between Greece and Albania. The northern part of the Greek section, now a part of Albania, set up a provisional government during 1912-13 and issued postage stamps but it collapsed in 1916, following Greek occupation. The name "Epirus" is taken from the Greek word meaning "Mainland."

100 Lepta = 1 Drachma

Epirus Greek Occupation stamps can be mounted in the Scott Greece album.

Chimarra Issue

Double-headed Eagle, Skull and Crossbones — A1

Handstamped

1914 (Feb.) Unwmk. *Imperf.*

Control Mark in Blue

Without Gum

1	A1	1 l black & blue		
2	A1	5 l blue & red		
3	A1	10 l red & blk		
4	A1	25 l blue & red		
		Nos. 1-4 (4)	800.00	600.00

All values exist without control mark. This mark is a solid blue oval, about 12x8mm, containing the colorless Greek letters "SP," the first two letters of Spiromilios, the Chimarra commander.

All four exist with value inverted and the 1, 5 and 10 l with value double.

Some experts question the official character of this issue. Counterfeits are plentiful.

Provisional Government Issues

Infantryman with Rifle
A2 A3

Serrate Roulette 13½

1914 (Mar.) Litho.

5	A2	1 l orange	30	30
6	A2	5 l green	30	30
7	A3	10 l carmine	30	30
8	A3	25 l deep blue	30	30
9	A2	50 l brown	80	80
10	A2	1d violet	1.90	1.90
11	A2	2d blue	14.00	14.00
12	A2	5d gray green	16.00	16.00
		Nos. 5-12 (8)	33.90	33.90

15 values, 5 l to 5d, of Turkish stamps surcharged "Epirus Autonomous" and new values in Greek were on sale for a few days in Argyrokastron (Gjirokaster).

Flag of Epirus — A5

1914 (Aug.)

15	A5	1 l brown & blue	75	75
16	A5	5 l green & blue	75	75
17	A5	10 l rose red & blue	75	75
18	A5	25 l dk blue & blue	75	75
19	A5	50 l violet & blue	75	75
20	A5	1d carmine & blue	3.25	3.25
21	A5	2d orange & blue	80	80
22	A5	5d dk green & blue	3.25	3.25
		Nos. 15-22 (8)	11.05	11.05

Koritsa Issue

A7

1914

26	A7	25 l dk blue & blue	2.50	2.50
27	A7	50 l violet & blue	3.75	3.75

Chimarra Issue

1911-23 Issues of Greece Overprinted

ΕΛΛΗΝΙΚΗ
1914
ΧΕΙΜΑΡΡΑ

1914 (Aug.)

34	A24	1 l green	*15.00*	*15.00*
35	A25	2 l carmine	*15.00*	*15.00*
36	A24	3 l vermilion	*20.00*	*20.00*
37	A26	5 l green	*20.00*	*20.00*
38	A24	10 l carmine	*15.00*	*15.00*
39	A25	20 l slate	*37.50*	*37.50*
40	A25	25 l blue	*65.00*	*65.00*
41	A26	50 l vio brn	*135.00*	*135.00*
		Nos. 34-41 (8)	*322.50*	*322.50*

The 2 l and 3 l are engraved stamps of the 1911-21 issue, the others are lithographed stamps of the 1912-23 issue.

Overprint reads: "Greek Chimarra 1914."

Stamps of this issue are with or without a black monogram (S.S., for S. Spiromilios) in manuscript. Counterfeits are plentiful.

Stamps of the following designs were not regularly issued for postal purposes in the opinion of the editors.

From 1914: 1st design, 3 varieties. 2nd design, 6 varieties. 3rd design, 7 varieties. 4th and 5th designs, 15 varieties.

From 1920: 6th design, 4 varieties.

OCCUPATION STAMPS

Issued under Greek Occupation.

Greek Occupation Stamps of 1913 Overprinted Horizontally

Β. ΗΠΕΙΡΟΣ

Serrate Roulette 13½

1914-15 Black Overprint Unwmk.

N1	O1	1 l brown	30	30
N2	O2	2 l red	30	30
b.		2 l rose	40	40
N4	O2	3 l orange	40	40
N5	O1	5 l green	75	30
N6	O1	10 l rose red	1.50	30
N7	O1	20 l violet	7.00	1.50
N8	O2	25 l pale blue	2.50	1.00
N9	O1	30 l gray green	9.25	6.00
N10	O2	40 l indigo	12.00	10.00
N11	O1	50 l dark blue	16.00	10.00
N12	O2	1d vio brown	50.00	50.00
		Nos. N1-N12 (11)	100.00	80.10

The overprint exists double on 6 denominations (1 l, 2 l both, 3 l, 5 l, 10 l and 1d); inverted on all but 25 l, 40 l; double, one inverted, 5 l. Values, $15 and up.

Red Overprint

N1a	O1	1 l brown	3.25
N2a	O2	2 l red	3.25
N4a	O2	3 l orange	3.25
N5a	O1	5 l green	3.25

Nos. N1a-N5a were not issued. Exist canceled.

Regular Issues of Greece, 1911-23, Overprinted

Β. ΗΠΕΙΡΟΣ

On Issue of 1911-21

1916 Engr.

N17	A24	3 l vermilion	45	45
N18	A26	30 l car rose	65.00	65.00
N19	A27	1d ultra	22.00	22.00
N20	A27	2d vermilion	45.00	45.00
N21	A27	3d car rose	50.00	50.00
N22	A27	5d ultra	325.00	325.00
a.		Double overprint	450.00	450.00
		Nos. N17-N22 (6)	507.45	507.45

On Issue of 1912-23

1916 Litho.

N23	A24	1 l green	40	40
N24	A25	2 l carmine	40	40
N25	A24	3 l vermilion	45	45
N26	A26	5 l green	45	45
N27	A24	10 l carmine	1.00	1.00
N28	A25	20 l slate	1.65	1.65
N29	A25	25 l blue	2.50	2.50
N30	A26	30 l rose	4.25	4.25
N31	A25	40 l indigo	6.00	6.00
N32	A26	50 l violet brown	9.00	9.00
		Nos. N23-N32 (10)	26.10	26.10

In each sheet there are two varieties in the overprint: the "I" in "Epirus" omitted and an inverted "L" in place of the first letter of the word.

Counterfeits exist of Nos. N1-N32.

Postage stamps issued in 1940-41, during Greek occupation, are listed under Greece.

EQUATORIAL GUINEA

LOCATION — Gulf of Guinea, West Africa
GOVT. — Republic
AREA — 10,832 sq. mi.
POP. — 310,000 (est. 1974)
CAPITAL — Malabo

The Spanish provinces Fernando Po and Rio Muni united and became independent as the Republic of Equatorial Guinea, Oct. 12, 1968.

100 Centimos = 1 Peseta

100 centimos = 1 ekuele, bipkwele is plural (1973)

100 centimes = 1 CFA franc (1985)

Catalogue values for all unused stamps in this country are for Never Hinged items.

Clasped Hands and Laurel — A1

Pres. Francisco Macias Nguema — A2

Unwmk.

1968, Oct. 12 Photo. *Perf. 13*

1	A1	1p	dp bl, gold & sep	15	15
2	A1	1.50p	dk grn, gold & brn	15	15
3	A1	6p	cop red, gold & brn	15	15
			Set value	24	17

Attainment of independence, Oct. 12, 1968.

1970, Jan. 27 *Perf. 13x12½*

4	A2	50c	dl org, brn & crim	15	15
5	A2	1p	pink, grn & lil	15	15
6	A2	1.50p	pale ol, brn & bl grn	15	15
7	A2	2p	buff, grn & ol	15	15
8	A2	2.50p	pale grn, dk grn & dk bl	15	15
9	A2	10p	bis, Prus bl & vio brn	65	15
10	A2	25p	gray, blk & brn	1.10	16
			Set value	2.00	52

Pres. Macias Nguema and Cock — A3

1971, Apr. Photo. *Perf. 13*

11	A3	3p	lt bl & multi	15	15
12	A3	5p	buff & multi	15	15
13	A3	10p	pale lilac & multi	25	15
14	A3	25p	pale grn & multi	40	20
			Set value		41

2nd anniv. of independence, Oct. 12, 1970.

REPUBLICA DE GUINEA ECUATORIAL
Torch, Bow and Arrows — A4

1972 Photo. *Perf. 11½*

15	A4	50p	ocher & multi	1.10	42

"3rd Triumphal Year."

Apollo 15, set of seven, 1p, 3p, 5p, 8p, 10p, airmail 15p, 25p, plus two airmail semi-postal gold foil perf. 200p+25p, imperf. 250p+50p, and two souv. sheets, perf. 25p+200p, imperf. 50p+250p, issued Jan. 28. Nos. 7201-7211.

1972 Winter Olympics, Sapporo, set of seven, 1p, 2p, 3p, 5p, 8p, airmail 15p, 50p, plus two airmail semi-postal gold foil perf., imperf., 200p+25p, 250p+50p, and two souv. sheets, perf. 200p+25p, imperf. 250p+50p, issued Feb. 3, 1972. Nos. 7212-7222.

Christmas, paintings, set of seven, 1p, 3p, 5p, 8p, 10p, airmail 15p, 25p, plus two airmail semi-postal gold foil perf. 200p+25p, imperf. 250p+50p, and two souv. sheets, perf. 25p+200p, imperf. 50p+250p (Virgin and Child by da Vinci, Murillo, Raphael, Mabuse, van der Weyden, Durer), issued Feb. 20. Nos. 7223-7233.

Easter, set of seven, 1p, 3p, 5p, 8p, 10p, airmail 15p, 25p, plus two airmail semi-postal gold foil perf., imperf., 200p+25p, 250p+50p (designs by Velazquez and El Greco), two souv. sheets, perf. (25p, 200p), and imperf. 250p+50p, issued Apr. 28. Nos. 7234-7244.

1976 Summer Olympics, Munich, set of seven, 1p, 2p, 3p, 5p, 8p, airmail 15p, 50p, plus two airmail semi-postal souv. sheets, perf. 200p+25p, imperf. 250p+50p, and presentation folder with two gold foil, perf. 200p+25p, imperf. 250p+50p, issued May 5, 1972. Nos. 7245-7255.

Gold Medal Winners, Sapporo, set of seven, 1p, 2p, 3p, 5p, 8p, airmail 15p, 50p, plus 12 airmail semi-postal gold foil perf. 200p+25p (6), imperf. 250p+50p (6), imperf. souv. sheet 250p+50p, and perf. souv. sheet of two (25p, 200p), issued May 25. Nos. 7256-7276.

Black Gold Medal Winners, Munich, set of seven, 1p, 2p, 3p, 5p, 8p, airmail 15p, 50p, plus 18 gold foil airmail semi-postal perf. 200p+25p (9), imperf. 250p+50p (9), and two souv. sheets, perf. 200p+25p, imperf. 250p+50p, issued June 26. Nos. 7277-72103.

Olympic Games, Regatta in Kiel and Oberschleissheim, set of seven, 1p, 2p, 3p, 5p, 8p, airmail 15p, 50p, plus four airmail semi-postal gold foil, perf. 200p+25p (2), imperf. 250p+50p (2), and two souv. sheets, perf. 200p+25p, imperf. 250p+50p, issued July 25. Nos. 72104-72116.

1972 Summer Olympics, Munich, set of seven, 1p, 2p, 3p, 5p, 8p, airmail 15p, 50p, plus two airmail semi-postal souv. sheets, perf. 200p+25p, imperf. 250p+50p, issued Aug. 10, 1972; and 20 gold foil, perf. 200p+25p (10), imperf. 250+50p (10), issued Aug. 17. Nos. 72117-72145.

Olympic Equestrian Events, set of seven, 1p, 2p, 3p, 5p, 8p, airmail 15p, 50p, plus two airmail semi-postal souv. sheets, perf. 200p+25p, imperf. 250p+50p, two gold foil, perf. 200p+25p, imperf. 250p+50p, four gold foil souv. sheets of two, 200p+25p (2 perf., 2 imperf.), and 16 souv. sheets, perf. 200p+25p (8), imperf. 250p+50p (8), issued Aug. 24. Nos. 72146-72176.

Japanese Railroad Cent. (locomotives), set of seven, 1p, 3p, 5p, 8p, 10p, airmail 15p, 25p, plus 2 airmail semi-postal souv. sheets, perf. 200p+25p, imperf. 250p+50p, 11 gold foil souv. sheets of 1, perf. 200p+25p (9), imperf. 200p+25p (2), and 2 souv. sheets of 2, perf., imperf., 200p+25p, issued Sept. 21. Nos. 72177-72198.

Gold Medal Winners, Munich, set of seven, 1p, 2p, 3p, 5p, 8p, airmail 15p, 50p, plus two airmail semi-postal souv. sheets, perf. 200p+25p, imperf. 250p+50p, and four gold foil souv. sheets, perf. 200p+25p (2), imperf. 250p+50p (2), issued Oct. 30. Nos. 72199-72211.

Christmas and 500th Birth Anniv. of Lucas Cranach, Madonnas and Christmas seals, set of seven, 1p, 3p, 5p, 8p, 10p, airmail 15p, 25p (Giotto, Schongauer, Fouquet, de Morales, Fini, David, Sassetta), plus two airmail semi-postal souv. sheets, perf. 200p+25p, imperf. 250p+50p, 12 gold foil souv. sheets, perf. 200p+25p (6), imperf. 250p+50p (6), two souv. sheets of two, perf., imperf., 200p+25p, and ovptd. 200p+25p stamp, issued Nov. 22. Nos. 772212-72234.

American and Russian Astronaut Memorial, set of seven, 1p, 3p, 5p, 8p, 10p, airmail 15p, 25p, plus two airmail semi-postal souv. sheets, perf. 200p+25p, imperf. 250p+50p, and four gold foil ovptd. "Apollo 16 and 17" perf. 200p+25p (2), imperf. 250p+50p (2), issued Dec. 14. Nos. 72235-72247.

United Natl. Workers' Party Emblem — A5

1973 Litho. *Perf. 13½x13*

16	A5	1p	multi	15	15
17	A5	1.50p	multi	15	15
18	A5	2p	multi	15	15
19	A5	4p	multi	15	15
20	A5	5p	multi	22	16
			Set value	66	46

Natl. Independence, 4th Anniv. — A6

Pres. Macias Nguema and: 1.50p, Agriculture. 2p, 4p, Education. 3p, 5p, Natl. defense.

1973 *Perf. 13½*

21	A6	1.50p	multi	15	15
22	A6	2p	multi	15	15
23	A6	3p	multi	15	15
24	A6	4p	multi	15	15
25	A6	5p	multi	25	20
			Nos. 21-25 (5)	85	
			Set value		55

1973

Transatlantic Yacht Race, set of seven, 1p, 2p, 3p, 5p, 8p, airmail 15p, 50p, and two airmail semi-postal souv. sheets, perf. 200p+25p, imperf. 250p+50p, issued Jan. 22. Nos. 7301-7309.

Renior paintings, set of seven, 1p, 2p, 3p, 5p, 8p, airmail 15p, 50p, plus two airmail semi-postal gold foil, perf. 200p+25p, imperf. 250p+50p, and two souv. sheets, perf. 200p+25p, imperf. 250p+50p, issued Feb. 22. Nos. 7310-7320.

Conquest of Venus (spacecraft), set of seven, 1p, 3p, 5p, 8p, 10p, airmail 5p, 25p, and two airmail semi-postal souv. sheets, perf. 200p+25p, imperf. 250p+50p, issued Mar. 22. Nos. 7321-7329.

Apollo 11-17 Flights, gold foil airmail semi-postal souv. sheets, perf. 200p+25p (7), 250p+50p (7), and four souv. sheets of two, perf. 200p+25p (2), imperf. 250p+50p (2), issued Mar. 22. Nos. 7330-7347.

Easter, paintings, set of seven, 1p, 3p, 5p, 8p, 10p, airmail 15p, 25p (Verrocchio, Perugino, Tintoretto, Witz, Pontormo), plus two airmail semi-postal souv. sheets, perf. 200p+25p, imperf. 250p+50p, and four gold foil issue of 1972 souv. sheets ovptd., perf. 200p+25p (2), imperf. 250p+50p (2), issued Apr. 25. Nos. 7348-7360.

Copernicus, 500th birth anniv. (US and USSR space explorations), four gold foil airmail semi-postal souv. sheets, perf. 200p+25p (2), imperf. 250p+50p (2), issued May 15. Nos. 7361-7364.

Tour de France bicycle race, set of seven, 1p, 2p, 3p, 5p, 8p, airmail 15p, 50p, and two airmail semi-postal souv. sheets, perf. 200p+25p, imperf. 250p+50p, issued May 22. Nos. 7365-7373.

Paintings, set of seven, 1p, 2p, 3p, 5p, 8p, airmail 15p, 50p, and two airmail semi-postal souv. sheets, 200p+25p, imperf. 250p+50p, issued June 29. Nos. 7374-7482.

1974 World Cup Soccer Championships, Munich, set of nine, 5c, 10c, 15c, 20c, 25c, 55c, 60c, airmail 5p, 70p, and two airmail souv. sheets, perf. 130p, imperf. 200p, issued Aug. 30. Nos. 7383-7393.

Rubens paintings, set of seven, 1p, 2p, 3p, 5p, 8p, airmail 15p, 50p, and two airmail semi-postal souv. sheets, perf. (25p, 200p), imperf. (50p, 250p), issued Sept. 23. Nos. 7394-73102.

1974 World Cup Soccer Championships, Munich, four gold foil airmail souv. sheets, perf. 130e (2), imperf. 200e (2), and two souv. sheets of two, perf. 130e, imperf. 200e, issued Oct. 24. Nos. 73103-73108.

Christmas, paintings, set of seven, 1p, 3p, 5p, 8p, 10p, airmail 15p, 25p, and two airmail semi-postal souv. sheets, perf. 200p+25p, imperf. 250p+50p (Nativity, by van der Weyden, Bosco, de Carvajal, Mabuse, Lucas Jordan, P. Goecke, Maino, Fabriano, Lochner), issued Oct. 30. Nos. 73109-73117.

Apollo Program and J.F. Kennedy, two gold foil airmail semi-postals, perf. 200p+25p, imperf. 250p+50p, and two souv. sheets, perf. 200p+25p, imperf. 250p+50p, issued Nov. 10. Nos. 73118-73121.

World Cup Soccer (famous players), set of nine, 30c, 35c, 40c, 45c, 50c, 65c, 70c, airmail 8p, 60p, and two airmail souv. sheets, perf. 130p, imperf. 200p, issued Nov. 20. Nos. 73122-73132.

Princess Anne's Wedding, six gold foil airmail souv. sheets, perf., imperf., two sheets of one, each 250e, one sheet of two 250e, issued Dec. 17. Nos. 73133-73141.

Pablo Picasso Memorial (Blue Period paintings), set of seven, 30c, 35c, 40c, 45c, 50c, airmail 8e, 60e, and two airmail souv. sheets, perf. 130e, imperf. 200e, issued Dec. 20. Nos. 73142-73150.

1974

Copernicus, 500th birth anniv., set of seven, 5c, 10c, 15c, 20c, 4e, airmail 10e, 70e, two airmail souv. sheets, perf. 130e, imperf. 200e, issued Feb. 8, 1974; eight gold foil airmail souv. sheets, perf. 130e (3), 250e, imperf. 200e (3), 300e, and four souv. sheets of two, perf. 250e (2), imperf. 250e (2), issued Apr. 10. Nos. 7401-7421.

World Cup Soccer Championships (final games), set of nine, 75c, 80c, 85c, 90c, 95c, 1e, 1.25e, airmail 10e, 50e, and two airmail souv. sheets, perf. 130e, imperf. 200e, issued Feb. 28. Nos. 7422-7432.

Easter, paintings, set of seven, 1p, 3p, 5p, 8p, 10p, airmail 15p, 25p (Fra Angelico, Castagno, Allori, Multscher, della Francesca, Pleydenwurff, Correggio), and two airmail semi-postal souv. sheets, perf. 200p+25p, imperf. 250p+50p, issued Mar. 27. Nos. 7433-7441.

Holy Year 1975 (famous churches), set of seven, 5c, 10c, 15c, 20c, 3.50e, airmail 10e, 70e, and two airmail souv. sheets, perf. 130e, imperf. 200e, issued Apr. 11. Nos. 7442-7450.

World Cup Soccer (contemporary players), set of nine, 1.50, 1.75, 2, 2.25, 2.50, 3, 3.50e, airmail 10, 60e, and 2 airmail souv. sheets of 2, perf. (2x65e), imperf. (2x100e), issued Apr. 30. Nos. 7451-7461.

UPU Cent. (transportation from messenger to rocket), set of seven, 60c, 70c, 80c, 1e, 1.50e, airmail 30e, 50e, and two airmail souv. sheets, perf. 225e, imperf. (150e, 150e), issued May 30; two airmail deluxe souv. sheets, 130e, and 2x130e, issued June 8. Nos. 7462-7472.

Picasso Memorial (Pink Period paintings), set of seven, 55c, 60c, 65c, 70c, 75c, airmail 10e, 50e, and two airmail souv. sheets, perf. 130e, imperf. 200e, issued June 28. Nos. 7473-7481.

World Cup Soccer Championships, gold foil airmail souv. sheets, four sheets of one, 130e (2), 250e (2), two sheets of two (2x130e; 2x250e), issued July 8. Nos. 7482-7487.

Aleksander Solzhenitsyn, two gold foil airmail souv. sheets, perf. 250e, imperf. 300e, issued July 25. Nos. 7488-7489.

Opening of American West, set of seven, 30c, 35c, 40c, 45c, 50c, airmail 8p, 60p, and two souv. sheets, perf. 130p, imperf. 200p, issued July 30. Nos. 7490-7498.

Flowers, set of 14, 5c, 10c, 15c, 20c, 25c, 1p, 3p, 5p, 8p, 10p, airmail 5p, 15p, 25p, 70p, and 4 airmail souv. sheets, perf. 130p, 25p+200p, imperf. 200p, 50p+250p, issued Aug. 20. Nos. 7499-74116.

Christmas, set of seven, 60c, 70c, 80c, 1e, 1.50e, airmail 30e, 50e, and two souv. sheets, perf. 225e, imperf. 300e, issued Sept. 16. Nos. 74117-74125.

Barcelona Soccer Team, 75th anniv., set of seven, 1e, 3e, 5e, 8e, 10e, airmail 15e, 60e, miniature sheet of seven plus label, two airmail souv. sheets, perf. 200e, imperf. 300e, and two gold foil airmail souv. sheets, perf., imperf., 200e each, issued Sept. 25. Nos. 74126-74137.

UPU Cent. and ESPANA 75, set of seven, 1.25e, 1.50e, 1.75e, 2e, 2.25e, airmail 35e, 60e, and 2 airmail souv. sheets, perf. 225e, imperf. 300e, issued Oct. 9; 6 gold foil sheets, perf. 250e, 250e, 2x250e, imperf. 300e, 300e, 2x300e, issued Oct. 14. Nos. 74138-74152.

Nature Protection

Australian Animals, set of seven, 80c, 85c, 90c, 95c, 1e, airmail 15e, 40e, and two airmail souv. sheets, perf. 130e, imperf. 200e, issued Oct. 25. Nos. 74153-74161.

African Animals, set of seven, 55c, 60c, 65c, 70c, 75c, airmail 10e, 70e, and two airmail souv. sheets, perf. 130e, imperf. 200e, issued Nov. 6. Nos. 74162-74170.

Australian and South American Birds, set of 14, 1.25p, 1.50p, 1.75p, 2p, 2.25p, 2.50p, 2.75p, 3p, 3.50p, 4p, airmail 20p, 25p, 30p, 35p, and four souv. sheets, perf. 130p (2), imperf. 200p (2), issued Nov. 26. Nos. 74171-74188.

Endangered Species, set of 15, 10c, 15c, 20c, 25c, 30c, 35c, 40c, 45c, 50c, 55c, 60c, 1e, 2e, airmail 10e, 70e, se-tenant in sheet of 15, issued Dec. 17. Nos. 74189-74203.

Monkeys, various species, set of 16, 5c, 10c, 15c, 20c, 25c, 30c, 35c, 40c, 45c, 50c, 55c, 60c, 1e, 2e, airmail 10e, 70e, se-tenant in sheet of 16, issued Dec. 27. Nos. 74204-74219.

Cats, various species, set of 16, 5c, 10c, 15c, 20c, 25c, 30c, 35c, 40c, 45c, 50c, 55c, 60c, 1e, 2e, airmail 10e, 70e, se-tenant in sheet of 16, issued Dec. 27. Nos. 74220-74235.

Fish, various species, set of 16, 5c, 10c, 15c, 20c, 25c, 30c, 35c, 40c, 45c, 50c, 55c, 60c, 1e, 2e, airmail 10e, 70e, se-tenant in sheet of 16, issued Dec. 27. Nos. 74236-74251.

Butterflies, various species, set of 16, 5c, 10c, 15c, 20c, 25c, 30c, 35c, 40c, 45c, 50c, 55c, 60c, 1e, 2e, airmail 10e, 70e, se-tenant in sheet of 16, issued Dec. 27. Nos. 74252-74267.

1975

Picasso Memorial (paintings from last period), set of seven, 5c, 10c, 15c, 20c, 25c, airmail 5e, 70e, and two souv. sheets, perf. 130e, imperf. 200e, issued Jan. 27. Nos. 7501-7509.

ARPHILA 75 Phil. Exhib., Paris, 8 gold foil airmail souv. sheets: perf. 3 sheets of 1 250e, 1 sheet of 2 250e, imperf. 3 sheets of 1 300e, 1 sheet of 2 300e, issued Jan. 27. Nos. 7510-7517.

Easter and Holy Year 1975, set of seven, 60c, 70c, 80c, 1e, 1.50e, airmail 30e, 50e, and two airmail souv. sheets, perf. 225e, imperf. 300e, issued Feb. 15. Nos. 7518-7526.

1976 Winter Olympics, Innsbruck, set of 11, 5c, 10c, 15c, 20c, 25c, 30c, 35c, 40c, 45c, 25e, 70e, two airmail souv. sheets, perf. 130e, imperf. 200e, and two gold foil airmail souv. sheets, 1 sheet of 1 250e, 1 sheet of 2 250e, issued Mar. 10. Nos. 7527-7541.

Don Quixote, set of seven, 30c, 35c, 40c, 45c, 50c, airmail 25e, 60e, and two airmail souv. sheets, perf. 130e, imperf. 200e, issued Apr. 4. Nos. 7542-7550.

American Bicent. (1st issue), set of nine, 5c, 20c, 40c, 75c, 2e, 5e, 8e, airmail 25e, 30e, and two airmail souv. sheets, perf. 130e, imperf. 200e, issued Apr. 30. Nos. 7551-7561.

American Bicent. (2nd issue), set of nine, 10c, 30c, 50c, 1e, 3e, 6e, 10e, airmail 12e, 40e, and two airmail souv. sheets, perf. 130e, imperf. 200e, issued Apr. 30. Nos. 7562-7572.

American Bicent. (Presidents), set of 18, 5c, 10c, 20c, 30c, 40c, 50c, 75c, 1e, 2e, 3e, 5e, 6e, 8e, 10e, airmail 12e, 25e, 30e, 40e, four airmail souv. sheets, perf. 225e (2), imperf. 300e (2), and six embossed gold foil airmail souv. sheets, perf. 200e, 200e, 2x200e, imperf. 300e, 300e, 2x300e, issued July 4. Nos. 7573-75100.

Bull Fight, set of seven, 80c, 85c, 90c, 95c, 8e, airmail 35e, 40e, and two airmail souv. sheets, perf. 130e, imperf. 200e, issued May 26. Nos. 75101-75109.

Apollo-Soyuz Space Project, set of 11, 1e, 2e, 3e, 5e, 5.50e, 7e, 7.50e, 9e, 15e, airmail 20e, 30e, and two airmail souv. sheets, perf. 225e, imperf. 300e, issued June 20, 1975; airmail souv. sheet, perf. 250e, issued July 17. Nos. 75110-75123.

Famous Painters, Nudes, set of 16, 5c, 10c, 15c, 20c, 25c, 30c, 35c, 40c, 45c, 50c, 55c, 60c, 1e, 2e, airmail 10e, 70e (Egyptian Greek, Roman, Indian art, Goes, Durer, Liss, Beniort, Renoir, Gauguin, Stenlen, Picasso, Modigliani, Matisse, Padua), se-tenant in sheet of 16, and 20 airmail embossed gold foil souv. sheetlets, perf. 200p+25p (10), imperf. 250p+50p (10), issued Aug. 10. Nos. 75124-75159.

Conquerors of the Sea, set of 14, 30c, 35c, 40c, 45c, 50c, 55c, 60c, 65c, 70c, 75c, airmail 8p, 10p, 50p, 60p, and four airmail souv. sheets, perf. 130p (2), imperf. 200p (2), issued Sept. 5. Nos. 75160-75177.

Christmas and Holy Year, 1975, set of seven, 60c, 70c, 80c, 1e, 1.50e, airmail 30e, 50e (Jordan, Barocci, Vereycke, Rubens, Mengs, Del Castillo, Cavedone), two airmail souv. sheets, perf. 225e, imperf. 300e, plus four embossed gold foil souv. sheets, perf. 200e (2), imperf. 300e (2), and two gold foil miniature sheets of two, perf. 200e+200e, imperf. 300e+300e, issued Oct. Nos. 75178-75192.

President Macias, IWY, set of eight, 1.50e, 3e, 3.50e, 5e, 7e, 10e, airmail 100e, 300e, and two imperf. airmail souv. sheets (world events), 100e (US 2c Yorktown), 300e, issued Dec. 25. Nos. 75193-75202.

1976

Cavalry Uniforms, set of seven, 5c, 10c, 15c, 20c, 25c, airmail 5p, 70p, and two airmail souv. sheets, perf. 130p, imperf. 200p, issued Feb. 2. Nos. 7601-7609.

1976 Winter Olympics, Innsbruck, set of 11, 50c, 55c, 60c, 65c, 70c, 75c, 80c, 85c, 90c, airmail 35e, 60e, and two airmail souv. sheets, perf. 130e, imperf. 200e, issued Feb. Nos. 7610-7622.

1976 Summer Olympics, Montreal, Ancient to Modern Games, set of seven, 50c, 60c, 70c, 80c, 90c, airmail 35e, 60e, and two airmail souv. sheets, perf. 225e, imperf. 300e, issued Feb. Nos. 7623-7631.

1976 Summer Olympics, Montreal, set of seven, 50c, 60c, 70c, 80c, 90c, airmail 30e, 60e, plus two airmail souv. sheets, perf. 225e, imperf. 300e, four embossed gold foil airmail souv. sheets, per. 250e (2), imperf. 300e (2), and two imperf. miniature sheets of two, perf. 2x250e, imperf. 2x300e, issued Mar. 5. Nos. 7632-7646.

El Greco, paintings, set of seven, 1e, 3e, 5e, 8e, 10e, airmail 15e, 25e, and two airmail semi-postal souv. sheets, perf. 200e+25e, imperf. 250e+50e, issued Apr. 5. Nos. 7647-7655.

1976 Summer Olympics, modern games, set of 11, 50c, 55c, 60c, 65c, 70c, 75c, 80c, 85c, 90c, airmail 35e, 60e, plus two airmail souv. sheets, perf. 225e, imperf. 300e, four embossed gold foil airmail souv. sheets, perf. 250e (2), imperf. 300e (2), and two miniature sheets of two, perf. 2x250e, imperf. 2x300e, issued May 7. Nos. 7656-7674.

UN 30th Anniv., airmail souv. sheet, 250e, issued June. No. 7675.

Contemporary Automobiles, set of seven, 1p, 3p, 5p, 8p, 10p, airmail 15p, 25p, and two airmail semi-postal souv. sheets, perf. 200p+24p, imperf. 250p+50p, issued June 10. Nos. 7675-7684.

Nature Protection

European Animals, set of seven, 5c, 10c, 15c, 20c, 25c, airmail 5p, 70p, and two airmail souv. sheets, perf. 130p, imperf. 200p, issued July 1. Nos. 7685-7693.

Asian Animals, set of seven, 30c, 35c, 40c, 45c, 8p, airmail 50c, 60p, and two airmail souv. sheets, perf. 130p, imperf. 200p, issued Sept. 20. Nos. 7694-74102.

Asian Birds, set of seven, 55c, 60c, 65c, 70c, 75c, airmail 10p, 50p, and two airmail souv. sheets, perf. 130p, imperf. 200p, issued Sept. 20. Nos. 76103-76111.

European Birds, set of seven, 5c, 10c, 15c, 20c, 25c, airmail 5p, 70p, and two airmail souv. sheets, perf. 130p, imperf. 200p, issued Sept. 20. Nos. 76112-76120.

North American Birds, set of seven, 80c, 85c, 90c, 95c, 1p, airmail 15p, 40p, and two airmail souv. sheets, perf. 130p, imperf. 200p, issued Sept. 20. Nos. 76121-76129.

Motorcycle Aces, set of 16, two each 1e, 2e, 3e, 4e, 5e, 10e, 30e, 40e, in se-tenant blocks of eight diff. values, issued July 22. Nos. 76130-76145.

1976 Summer Olympics, Montreal, set of five, 10e, 25e se-tenant strip of 3, airmail 200e, and imperf. airmail souv. sheet, 300e, issued Aug. 7. Nos. 76146-76151.

South American Flowers, set of seven, 30c, 35c, 40c, 45c, 50c, airmail 8p, 60p, and two airmail souv. sheets, perf. 130p, imperf. 200p, issued Aug. 16. Nos. 76152-76160.

Oceania, set of seven, 80c, 85c, 90c, 95c, 1p, airmail 15p, 40p, and two airmail souv. sheets, perf. 130p, imperf. 200p, issued 1976. Nos. 76161-76169.

1977

Butterflies, set of seven, 80c, 85c, 90c, 95c, 8e, airmail 35e, 40e, and two airmail souv. sheets, perf. 130e, imperf. 200e, issued Jan. Nos. 7701-7709.

Madrid Real, 75th Anniv., set of nine, 2e, 4e, 5e, 8e, 10e, 15e, airmail 20e, 35e, 150e, issued Jan. Nos. 7710-7718.

Ancient Carriages, set of 16, 5c, 10c, 15c, 20c, 25c, 30c, 35c, 40c, 45c, 50c, 55c, 60c, 1e, 2e, airmail 10e, 70e, issued Feb. Nos. 7719-7734.

Chinese Art, set of seven, 60c, 70c, 80c, 1e, 1.50e, airmail 30e, 50e, and two airmail souv. sheets, perf. 130e, imperf. 200e, issued Feb. Nos. 7735-7743.

African Masks, set of seven, 5c, 10c, 15c, 20c, 25c, airmail 5e, 70e, and two airmail souv. sheets, perf. 130e, imperf. 200e, issued Mar. Nos. 7744-7752.

North American Animals, set of seven, 1.25e, 1.50e, 1.75e, 2e, 2.25e, airmail 20e, 50e, and two airmail souv. sheets, perf. 130e, imperf. 200e, issued 1977. Nos. 7753-7761.

World Cup Soccer Championships, Argentina '78 (famous players), set of eight, 2e, 4e, 5e, 8e, 10e, 15e, airmail 20e, 35e, and two airmail souv. sheets, perf. 150e, imperf. 250e, issued July 25. Nos. 7762-7771.

World Cup Soccer (famous teams), se-tenant set of eight, 2e, 4e, 5e, 8e, 10e, 15e, airmail 20e, 35e, and two gold foil embossed souv. sheets, 500e (AMPHILEX '77, Cutty Sark, Concorde), airmail 500e (World Cup), issued Aug. 25. Nos. 7772-7781.

Napoleon, Life and Battle Scenes, se-tenant sheet of 16, 5c, 10c, 15c, 20c, 25c, 30c, 35c, 40c, 45c, 50c, 55c, 60c, 1e, 2e, airmail 10e, 70e, issued Aug. 20. Nos. 7782-7797.

Napoleon, Military Uniforms, se-tenant sheet of 16, 5c, 10c, 15c, 20c, 25c, 30c, 35c, 40c, 45c, 50c, 55c, 60c, 1e, 2e, airmail 10e, 70e, issued Aug. 20. Nos. 7798-77113.

South American Animals, set of seven, 2.50e, 2.75e, 3e, 3.50e, 4e, airmail 25e, 35e, and two airmail souv. sheets, perf. 130e, imperf. 200e, issued Aug. Nos. 77114-77122.

USSR Space Program, 20th Anniv., set of eight, 2e, 4e, 5e, 8e, 10e, 15e, airmail 20e, 35e, and two airmail souv. sheets, imperf. 150e, perf. 250e, issued Dec. 15. Nos. 77123-77132.

1978

Ancient Sailing Ships, set of 12, 5c, 10c, 15c, 20c, 25c, airmail 5e, 70e, also 5e, 10e, 20e, 25e, 70e, plus four airmail souv. sheets, perf. 150e, 225e, imperf. 250e, 300e, and two embossed gold foil airmail souv. sheets, perf., imperf., 500e, issued Jan. 6. Nos. 7801-7818.

1980 Winter Olympics, Lake Placid, set of five, 5e, 10e, 20e, 25e, airmail 70e, two airmail souv. sheets, perf. 150e, imperf. 250e, and two embossed gold foil airmail souv. sheets, perf., imperf., 500e, issued Jan. 17. Nos. 7819-7827.

1980 Summer Olympics, Moscow, set of eight, 2e, 3e, 5e, 8e, 10e, 15e, airmail 30e, 50e, two airmail souv. sheets, perf. 150e, imperf. 250e, and two embossed gold foil airmail souv. sheets, perf., imperf., 500e, issued Jan. 17. Nos. 7828-7839.

1980 Summer Olympic Water Games, Tallinn, set of five, 5e, 10e, 20e, 25e, airmail 70e, two airmail souv. sheets, perf. 150e, imperf. 250e, and two embossed gold foil airmail souv. sheets, perf., imperf., 500e, issued Jan. 17. Nos. 7840-7848.

Eliz. II Coronation, 25th Anniv., set of eight, 2e, 5e, 8e, 10e, 12e, 15e, airmail 30e, 50e, and two airmail souv. sheets, perf. 150e, imperf. 250e, issued Apr. 25. Nos. 7849-7858.

English Knights of 1200-1350 A.D., set of seven, 5e, 10e, 15e, 20e, 25e, airmail 15e, 70e, and two airmail souv. sheets, perf. 130e, imperf. 250e, issued Apr. 25. Nos. 7859-7867.

Old Locomotives, set of seven, 1e, 2e, 3e, 5e, 10e, airmail 25e, 70e, and two airmail souv. sheets, perf. 150e, imperf. 250e, issued Aug. Nos. 7868-7876.

Prehistoric Animals, set of seven, 30e, 35e, 40e, 45e, 50e, airmail 25e, 60e, and airmail souv. sheet, 130e, issued Aug. Nos. 7877-7884.

Francisco Goya, "Maja Vestida," airmail souv. sheet, 150e, issued Aug. No. 7885.

Peter Paul Rubens - UNICEF, airmail souv. sheet, 250e, issued Aug. No. 7886.

Europa - CEPT - Europhila '78, airmail souv. sheet, 250e, issued Aug. No. 7887.

30th Intl. Stamp Fair, Riccione, airmail souv. sheet, 150e, issued Aug. Nos. 7888.

Eliz. II Coronation, 25th anniv., airmail souv. sheet of three, 150e, issued Aug. Nos. 7889.

CEPT, airmail souv. sheet, 250e, issued Aug. Nos. 7890.

World Cup Soccer Championships, Argentina '78 and Spain '82, airmail souv. sheet, 150e, issued Aug. Nos. 7891.

Christmas, Titian painting, "The Virgin," airmail souv. sheet, 150e, issued Aug. Nos. 7892.

Natl. Independence, 5th Anniv. (in 1973) — A7

1979 *Perf. 13x13½*

26 A7 1e Ekuele coin 35 22

Natl. Independence, 5th Anniv. (in 1973) — A8

1979

27 A8 1e Port Bata 35 22
28 A8 1.50e State Palace 50 35
29 A8 2b Central Bank, Bata 65 45
30 A8 2.50b Nguema Biyogo Bridge 80 60
31 A8 3b Port, palace, bank, bridge 1.00 65
Nos. 27-31 (5) 3.30 2.27

Pres. Nguema — A9

Independence Martyrs — A10

1979 *Perf. 13½x13*

32 A9 1.50e multi 50 35

United Natl. Workers's Party (PUNT), 3rd Congress.

1979

33 A10 1e Enrique Nvo 35 22
34 A10 1.50e Salvador Ndongo Ekang 50 35
35 A10 2b Acacio Mane 65 45

Agricultural Experiment Year — A11

1979 *Perf. 13x13½*

36 A11 1e multi 35 22
37 A11 1.50e multi, diff. 50 35

Independence Martyrs — A12

Natl. Coat of Arms — A13

1981, Mar. Photo. *Perf. 13½x12½*

38 A12 5b Obiang Esono Nguema 15 15
39 A12 15b Fernando Nvara Engonga 20 15
40 A12 25b Ela Edjodjomo Mangue 35 22
41 A12 35b Obiang Nguema Moasogo, president 45 32
42 A12 50b Hipolito Micha Eworo 65 45
43 A13 100b multi 1.40 90
Nos. 38-43 (6) 3.20 2.19

Dated 1980.

Christmas 1980 A14

1981, Mar. 30 *Perf. 13½*

44 A14 8b Cathedral, infant 16 15
45 A14 25b Bells, youth 50 35

Dated 1980.

Souvenir Sheet

Pres. Obiang Nguema Mbasogo — A15

1981, Aug. 30 Litho. *Imperf.*

46 A15 400b multi 4.00 4.00

State Visit of King Juan Carlos of Spain — A16

Perf. 13x13½, 13½x13

1981, Nov. 30

47 A16 50b Government reception 45 30
48 A16 100b Arrival at airport 90 60
49 A16 150b King, Pres. Mbasogo, vert. 1.40 90

State Visit of Pope John Paul II — A17

1982, Feb. 18

50 A17 100b Papal and natl. arms
51 A17 200b Pres. Mbasogo greeting Pope
52 A17 300b Pope, vert.

Christmas 1981 A18

1982, Feb. 25 **Photo.**

53 A18 100b Carolers, vert. 1.10 80
54 A18 150b Magi, African youth 1.60 1.10

Dated 1981.

1982 World Cup Soccer Championships, Spain — A19

1982, June 13 *Perf. 13½*

55 A19 40b Emblem 35 22
56 A19 60b Naranjito character trademark 50 35
57 A19 100b World Cup trophy 80 60
58 A19 200b Players, palm tree, emblem 1.60 1.10

Fauna A20

1983, Feb. 4 **Litho.**

59 A20 40b Gorilla 30 20
60 A20 60b Hippopotamus 45 30
61 A20 80b Atherurus africanus 60 40
62 A20 120b Felis pardus 90 60

Dated 1982.

Christmas 1982 A21

1983, Feb. 25 **Photo.**

63 A21 100b Stars 80 60
64 A21 200b King offering frankincense 1.50 1.00

Dated 1982.

World Communications Year — A22

1983, July 18 **Litho.**

65 A22 150b Postal runner 65 45
66 A22 200b Microwave station, drimmer 1.50 1.00

Banana Trees A23

1983, Oct. 8

67 A23 300b shown 1.60 1.10
68 A23 400b Forest, vert. 2.25 1.60

Christmas 1983 A24

1984

69 A24 80b Folk dancer, musical instruments 65 45
70 A24 100b Holy Family 80 60

Dated 1983.

Constitution of State Powers A25

Scales of justice, fundamental lawbook and various maps.

1984, Feb. 15

71 A25 50b Annobon and Bioko 40 25
72 A25 100b Mainland regions 80 60

Turtle Hunting, Rio Muni — A26

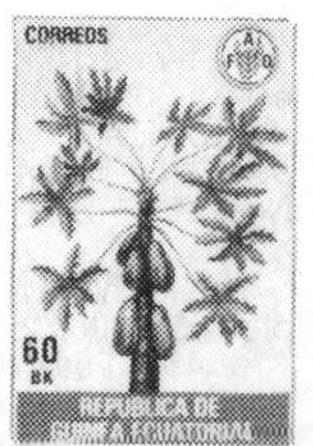

World Food Day — A27

1984, May 1

73 A26 125b Hunting Whales, horiz. 80 50
74 A26 150b shown 90 62

1984, Sept.

75 A27 60b Papaya 60 40
76 A27 80b Malanga 80 50

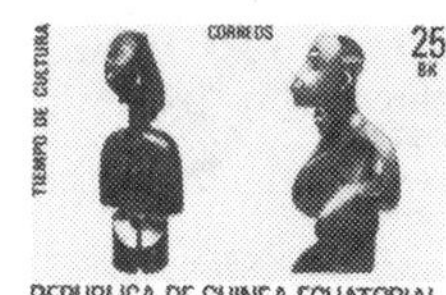

Abstract Wood-Carved Figurines and Art — A28

Designs: 25b, *Black Gazelle* and *Anxiety.* 30b, *Black Gazelle,* diff., and *Woman.* 60b, *Man and woman,* vert. 75b, *Poster,* vert. 100b, *Mother and Child,* vert. 150b, *Man and Woman,* diff., and *Bust of a Woman.*

1984, Nov. 15

77 A28 25b multi 16 15
78 A28 30b multi 20 15
79 A28 60b multi 40 25
80 A28 75b multi 50 35
81 A28 100b multi 65 45
82 A28 150b multi 1.00 65
Nos. 77-82 (6) 2.91 2.00

Christmas A29

1984, Dec. 24

83 A29 60b Mother and child, vert. 40 25
84 A29 100b Musical instruments 62 42

Immaculate Conception Missions, Cent. A30

Designs: 50fr, Emblem, vert. 60fr, Map, nun and youths, vert. 80fr, First Guinean nuns. 125fr, Missionaries landing at Bata Beach, 1885.

1985, Apr. *Perf. 14*

85 A30 50fr multi 20 15
86 A30 60fr multi 22 16
87 A30 80fr multi 30 20
88 A30 125fr multi 45 32

Jose Mavule Ndjong, First Postmaster A31

1985, July *Perf. 13½*

89 A31 50fr Postal emblem, vert. 32 20
90 A31 80fr shown 50 35

Equatorial Guinea Postal Service.

Christmas A32

1985, Dec.

91 A32 40fr Nativity 32 20
92 A32 70fr Folk band, dancers, mother and child 50 35

Nature Conservation — A33

1985

93 A33 15fr Crab, snail 15 15
94 A33 35fr Butterflies, bees, birds 15 15
95 A33 45fr Flowering plants 18 15
96 A33 65fr Spraying and harvesting cacao 25 18
Set value 45

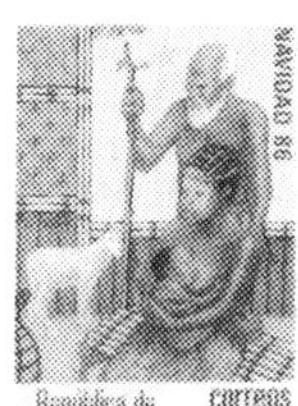

Folklore — A34

A35

1986, Apr. 15

97 A34 10fr Ndowe dance, Mekuyo, horiz. 15 15
98 A34 50fr Fang dance, Mokom 30 20
99 A34 65fr Cacha Bubi, Bisila 40 28
100 A34 80fr Fang dance, Ndong-Mba 50 35

1986, June 25

1986 World Cup Soccer Championships, Mexico: Various soccer plays.

101 A35 50fr multi, horiz. 30 20
102 A35 100fr multi, horiz. 60 40
103 A35 150fr multi 90 60
104 A35 200fr multi 1.20 90

Christmas — A36

Conf. of the Union of Central African States — A37

1986, Dec. 12

105 A36 100fr Musical instruments, horiz. 60 40
106 A36 150fr Holy Family, lamb 90 60

1986, Dec. 29

107 A37 80fr Flags, map 50 35
108 A37 100fr Emblem, map, horiz. 60 40

Campaign Against Hunger A38

1987, June 5

109 A38 60fr Chicken 35 24
110 A38 80fr Fish 50 35
111 A38 100fr Wheat 60 40

Intl. Peace Year — A39

1987, July 15 Litho. *Perf. 13½*

112 A39 100fr shown 75 50
113 A39 200fr Hands holding dove 1.50 1.00

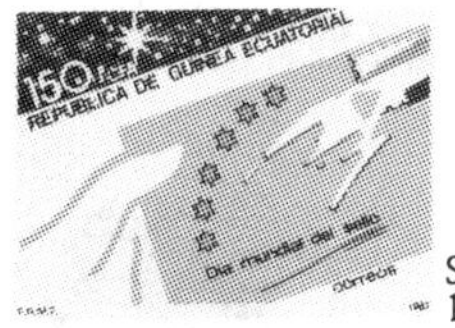

Stamp Day 1987 — A40

1987, Oct. 5 Litho. *Perf. 13½*

114 A40 150fr shown 1.05 70
115 A40 300fr Posting envelope 2.15 1.45

Christmas 1987 — A41

Mother and child (wood carvings).

1987, Dec. 22 Litho. *Perf. 13½*

116 A41 80fr multi 72 48
117 A41 100fr multi, diff. 90 60

Climbing Palm Tree — A42

Democratic Party — A43

1988, May 4 Litho. *Perf. 13½*

118 A42 50fr shown 50 32
119 A42 75fr Woman carrying fish 75 50
120 A42 150fr Chopping down trees 1.50 1.00

1988, Nov. 16

121 A43 40fr Crest 40 28
122 A43 75fr Torch, motto, horiz. 75 50
123 A43 100fr Torch, flag, weaving, horiz. 1.00 68

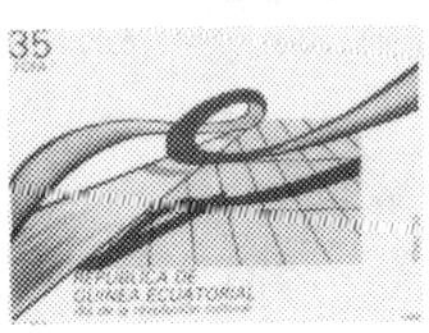

Cultural Revolution Day — A44

Geometric shapes.

1988, June 4

124 A44 35fr shown 35 24
125 A44 50fr Squares, sphere 50 32
126 A44 100fr Bird 1.00 68

Christmas — A45

1988, Dec. 22

127 A45 50fr shown 50 32
128 A45 100fr Mother and child 1.00 68

Natl. Independence, 20th Anniv. — A46

Designs: 10fr, Lumber on truck. 35fr, Folk dancers. 45fr, Officials on dais.

1989, Apr. 14 Litho. *Perf. 14*

129 A46 10fr multicolored 15 15
130 A46 35fr multicolored 38 25
131 A46 45fr multicolored 48 32

Youths Bathing, Ilachi Falls — A47

25fr, Waterfall in the jungle. 60fr, Boy drinking from fruit, boys swimming at Luba Beach.

1989, July 7 *Perf. 13½*

132 A47 15fr shown 15 15
133 A47 25fr multicolored 28 20
134 A47 60fr multicolored 62 40

1st Congress of the Democratic Party of Equatorial Guinea A48

1989, Oct. 23 Litho. *Perf. 13½*

135 A48 25fr shown 26 18
136 A48 35fr Torch, vert. 38 25
137 A48 40fr Pres. Nguema, vert. 42 28

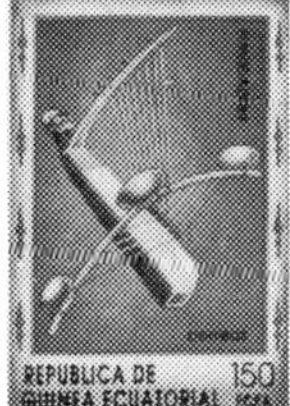

Christmas — A49

1989, Dec. 18 Litho. *Perf. 13½*

138 A49 150fr shown 1.60 1.05
139 A49 300fr Nativity, horiz. 3.20 2.10

Boy Scouts A50

1990, Mar. 23 Litho. *Perf. 13*

140 A50 100fr Lord Baden-Powell 1.10 75
141 A50 250fr Salute 2.70 1.75
142 A50 350fr Bugler 3.75 2.50

World Cup Soccer Championships, Italy — A51

1990, June 8 Litho. *Perf. 13*

143 A51 100fr Soccer player, map 1.25 80
144 A51 250fr Goalkeeper 3.00 2.00
145 A51 350fr Trophy 4.25 2.75

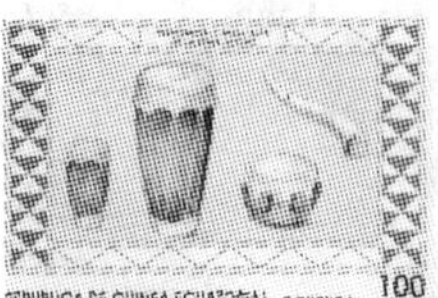
Musical Instruments of the Ndowe People A52

Instruments of the: 250fr, Fang. 350fr, Bubi.

1990, June 19

146 A52 100fr multicolored 1.25 80
147 A52 250fr multicolored 3.00 2.00
148 A52 350fr multicolored 4.25 2.75

Discovery of America, 500th Anniv. (in 1992) A53

1990, Oct. 10

149 A53 170fr Arrival in New World 2.00 1.30
150 A53 300fr Columbus' fleet 3.60 2.35

Christmas — A54

1990, Dec. 23 Litho. *Perf. 13½*

151 A54 170fr shown 2.00 1.30
152 A54 300fr Bubi tribesman 3.60 2.35

1992 Summer Olympics, Barcelona A55

1991 Litho. *Perf. 13½x14*

153 A55 150fr Tennis 1.80 1.20
154 A55 250fr Cycling 3.00 2.00

Souvenir Sheet

155 A55 500fr Equestrian 6.00 4.00

La Maja Desnuda by Goya — A56

Designs: 250fr, Eve by Durer, vert. 350fr, The Three Graces by Rubens, vert.

1991 Litho. *Perf. 14*

156 A56 100fr shown 1.20 80
157 A56 250fr multicolored 3.00 2.00
158 A56 350fr multicolored 4.20 2.80

Madrillus Sphinx — A57

1991 Litho. *Perf. 13½x14*

159 A57 25fr shown 30 20
160 A57 25fr Face 30 20
161 A57 25fr Seated 30 20
162 A57 25fr Walking, horiz. 30 20

World Wildlife Fund.

Discovery of America, 500th Anniv. A58

Captains, ships: 150fr, Vicente Yanez Pinzon, Nina. 260fr, Martin Alonso Pinzon, Pinta. 350fr, Christopher Columbus, Santa Maria.

1991 Litho. *Perf. 13½x14*

163 A58 150fr multicolored 1.80 1.20
164 A58 250fr multicolored 3.00 2.00
165 A58 350fr multicolored 4.20 2.80

Locomotives A59

Designs: 150fr, Electric, Japan, 1932. 250fr, Steam, US, 1873. 500fr, Steam, Germany, 1841.

1991

166 A59 150fr multicolored 1.80 1.20
167 A59 250fr multicolored 3.00 2.00

Souvenir Sheet

168 A59 500fr multicolored 6.00 4.00

1992 Summer Olympics, Barcelona A60

1992, Feb. Litho. *Perf. 13½x14*

169 A60 200fr Basketball 2.40 1.60
170 A60 300fr Swimming 3.60 2.40

Souvenir Sheet

171 A60 400fr Baseball 4.80 4.80

Souvenir Sheet

Discovery of America, 500th Anniv. — A61

Designs: a, 300fr, Columbus departing from Palos, Spain. b, 500fr, Columbus landing in New World.

1992, Apr.

172 A61 Sheet of 2, #a.-b. 9.60 9.60

Mushrooms — A62

Designs: 75fr, Termitomyces globulus. 125fr, Termitomyces le testui. 150fr, Termitomyces robustus.

1992, Nov. Litho. *Perf. 14x13½*

173 A62 75fr multicolored 90 60
174 A62 125fr multicolored 1.50 1.00
175 A62 150fr multicolored 1.80 1.20

Virgin and Child with Virtuous Saints, by Claudio Coello (c. 1635-1693) A63

Paintings, by Jacob Jordaens (1593-1678): 300fr, Apollo Conquering Marsias. 400fr, Meleager and Atalanta.

1993, Mar. Litho. *Perf. 13½x14*

176 A63 200fr multicolored 2.40 1.60
177 A63 300fr multicolored 3.60 2.40

Souvenir Sheet

178 A63 400fr multicolored 4.80 3.60

1992 Olympic Gold Medalists A64

Designs: 100fr, Quincy Watts, 400-meter dash, US. 250fr, Martin Lopez Zubero, swimming, Spain. 350fr, Petra Kronberger, women's slalom, Austria. 400fr, Flying Dutchman class yachting, Spain.

1993 Litho. *Perf. 13½x14*

179 A64 100fr multicolored 1.25 80
180 A64 250fr multicolored 3.00 2.00
181 A64 350fr multicolored 4.25 2.75
182 A64 400fr multicolored 4.75 3.25

Scene from Romeo and Juliet, by Tchaikovsky A65

Design: 200fr, Scene from Faust, by Charles-Francois Gounod (1818-1893).

1993, June Litho. *Perf. 13½x14*

183 A65 100fr multicolored 1.25 80
184 A65 200fr multicolored 2.50 1.65

First Ford Gasoline Engine, Cent. — A66

1993 *Perf. 13½x14, 14x13½*

185 A66 200fr First Ford vehicle 2.50 1.65
186 A66 300fr Ford Model T 3.50 2.50
187 A66 400fr Henry Ford, vert. 4.75 3.25

25th Anniv. of Independence A67

Designs: 150fr, Pres. Obiang Nguema Mbasogo, vert. 250fr, Cargo ship, map, communications . 300fr, Hydroelectric plant, Riaba. 350fr, Bridge.

1993 Litho. *Perf. 14x13½, 13½x14*

188 A67 150fr multicolored 1.90 1.25
189 A67 250fr multicolored 3.00 2.00
190 A67 300fr multicolored 3.75 2.50
191 A67 350fr multicolored 4.25 2.75

SPECIAL DELIVERY STAMPS

Archer with Crossbow — SD1

1971, Oct. 12 Photo. *Perf. 12½x13*

E1 SD1 4p blue & multi 15 15
E2 SD1 8p rose & multi 16 15
Set value 15

3rd anniversary of independence.

Buying Sets

It is often less expensive to purchase complete sets than individual stamps that make up the set. Set values are provided for many such sets.

ERITREA

LOCATION — In northeast Africa, bordering on the Red Sea
GOVT. — Former Italian Colony
AREA — 15,754 sq. mi. (1936)
POP. — 600,573 (1931)
CAPITAL — Asmara

Eritrea was incorporated as a State of Italian East Africa in 1936.

100 Centesimi = 1 Lira

Stamps of Italy Overprinted

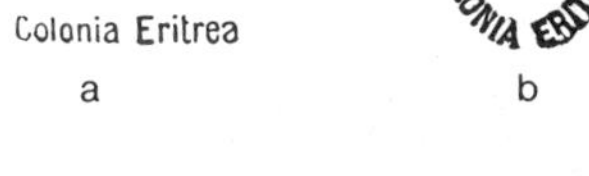

Colonia Eritrea COLONIA ERITREA

a b

1892 Wmk. 140 Perf. 14

Overprinted Type "a" in Black

1	A6	1c bronze grn	1.00	60
a.		Inverted overprint	130.00	100.00
b.		Double overprint	300.00	
2	A7	2c org brn	35	30
a.		Inverted overprint	225.00	130.00
b.		Double overprint	300.00	
3	A33	5c green	12.50	1.10
a.		Inverted overprint	2,000.	1,000.

Overprinted Type "b" in Black

4	A17	10c claret	5.00	85
5	A17	20c orange	32.50	85
6	A17	25c blue	110.00	4.50
7	A25	40c brown	2.00	2.00
8	A26	45c slate grn	2.00	3.00
9	A27	60c violet	2.00	3.50
10	A28	1 l brn & yel	3.25	5.00
11	A38	5 l bl & rose	95.00	40.00

1895-99

Overprinted type "a" in Black

12	A39	1c brown ('99)	2.00	3.00
13	A40	2c org brn ('99)	30	50
14	A41	5c green	30	40
a.		Inverted overprint	350.00	625.00

Overprinted type "b" in Black

15	A34	10c claret ('98)	35	50
16	A35	20c orange	50	52
17	A36	25c blue	62	85
18	A37	45c olive grn	2.00	4.00

1903-28

Overprinted type "a" in Black

19	A42	1c brown	15	30
a.		Inverted overprint	17.00	30.00
20	A43	2c org brn	15	24
21	A44	5c bl grn	8.00	30
22	A45	10c claret	10.50	30
23	A45	20c orange	24	30
24	A45	25c blue	55.00	3.00
a.		Double overprint	70.00	70.00
25	A45	40c brown	45.00	4.50
26	A45	45c ol grn	50	2.00
27	A45	50c violet	25.00	2.75
28	A46	75c dk red & rose ('28)	6.00	3.00
29	A46	1 l brn & grn	50	24
30	A46	1.25 l bl & ultra ('28)	5.00	2.00
31	A46	2 l dk grn & org ('25)	6.75	17.00
32	A46	2.50 l dk grn & org ('28)	17.00	10.50
33	A46	5 l bl & rose	6.00	5.50
		Nos. 19-33 (15)	185.79	51.93

Surcharged in Black

Colonia Eritrea
C. 15

1905

34	A45	15c on 20c orange	5.00	85

1908-28

Overprinted type "a" in Black

35	A48	5c green	20	15
36	A48	10c claret ('09)	20	15
37	A48	15c slate ('20)	1.65	1.00
38	A49	20c green ('25)	1.50	2.50
39	A49	20c lil brn ('28)	1.50	2.00
40	A49	25c blue ('09)	60	42
41	A49	30c gray ('25)	1.50	2.50
42	A49	40c brown ('16)	7.25	12.50
43	A49	50c vio ('16)	50	50
44	A49	60c brn car ('18)	3.50	4.50
45	A49	60c brn org ('28)	14.00	40.00
46	A51	10 l gray grn & red ('16)	60.00	175.00
		Nos. 35-46 (12)	92.40	241.22

See No. 53.

Government Building at Massaua

A1 A2

1910-29 Unwmk. Engr. Perf. 13½

47	A1	15c slate	45.00	2.75
a.		Perf. 11 ('29)	30.00	10.50
48	A2	25c dark blue	70	1.00
a.		Perf. 12		

For surcharges see Nos. 51-52.

Farmer Plowing

A3 A4

1914-28

49	A3	5c green	24	24
a.		Perf. 11 ('28)	65.00	13.00
50	A4	10c carmine	70	1.00
a.		Perf. 11 ('28)	12.50	10.50
b.		Perf. 13½x14	10.00	20.00

No. 47 Surcharged in Red or Black

Cent. 5

CENT. 20

1916

51	A1	5c on 15c slate (R)	1.50	4.50
52	A1	20c on 15c slate	50	50
a.		"CEN" for "CENT"	7.25	14.00
b.		"CENT" omitted	30.00	60.00
c.		"ENT"	10.00	20.00

Italy No. 113 Overprinted in Black — f

ERITREA

1921 Wmk. 140 Perf. 14

53	A50	20c brn org	85	3.00

Victory Issue

Italian Victory Stamps of 1921 Overprinted type "f" 13mm long

1922

54	A64	5c olive green	35	1.50
55	A64	10c red	35	1.50
56	A64	15c slate green	50	2.50
57	A64	25c ultra	50	2.00

Somalia Nos. 10-16 Overprinted In Black and Bars over Original Values

ERITREA

g

1922 Wmk. 140

58	A1	2c on 1b brn	2.50	3.50
59	A1	5c on 2b bl grn	2.50	2.50
60	A2	10c on 1a claret	2.50	50
61	A2	15c on 2a brn org	2.50	60
62	A2	25c on 2½a blue	2.50	60
63	A2	50c on 5a yellow	3.00	1.50
a.		"ERITREA" double		275.00
64	A2	1 l on 10a lilac	4.00	3.75
a.		"ERITREA" double	175.00	225.00
		Nos. 58-64 (7)	19.50	12.95

See Nos. 81-87.

Propagation of the Faith Issue

Italy Nos. 143-146 Overprinted

ERITREA

1923

65	A68	20c ol grn & brn org	1.25	5.50
66	A68	30c claret & brn org	1.25	5.50
67	A68	50c vio & brn org	1.00	4.50
68	A68	1 l bl & brn org	1.00	4.50

Fascisti Issue

Italy Nos. 159-164 Overprinted in Red or Black — j

ERITREA

1923 Unwmk. Perf. 14

69	A69	10c dk grn (R)	1.00	4.50
70	A69	30c dk vio (R)	1.00	4.50
71	A69	50c brn car	1.00	4.50

Wmk. 140

72	A70	1 l blue	1.00	4.50
73	A70	2 l brown	1.00	4.50
74	A71	5 l blk & bl (R)	1.00	7.50
		Nos. 69-74 (6)	6.00	30.00

Manzoni Issue

Italy Nos. 165-170 Overprinted in Red

ERITREA

1924 Perf. 14

75	A72	10c brn red & blk	55	5.00
76	A72	15c bl grn & blk	55	5.00
77	A72	30c blk & slate	55	5.00
78	A72	50c org brn & blk	55	5.00
79	A72	1 l bl & blk	8.75	55.00
80	A72	5 l vio & blk	200.00	900.00
		Nos. 75-79 (5)	10.95	75.00

On Nos. 79 and 80 the overprint is placed vertically at the left side.

Somalia Nos. 10-16 Overprinted type "g" in Blue or Red

1924

Bars over Original Values

81	A1	2c on 1b brn	5.25	10.00
82	A1	5c on 2b bl grn (R)	3.25	6.00
83	A2	10c on 1a rose red	2.00	3.00
84	A2	15c on 2a brn org	2.00	3.00
a.		Pair, one without "ERITREA"	400.00	
85	A2	25c on 2½a bl (R)	2.00	3.00
a.		Double surcharge	165.00	
86	A2	50c on 5a yellow	3.25	5.50
87	A2	1 l on 10a lil (R)	3.50	6.75
		Nos. 81-87 (7)	21.25	37.25

Stamps of Italy, 1901-08 Overprinted type "j" in Black

1924

88	A42	1c brown	1.00	2.50
a.		Inverted overprint	70.00	
89	A43	2c org brn	70	2.50
90	A48	5c green	1.25	2.50

Victor Emmanuel Issue

Italy Nos. 175-177 Overprinted — k

ERITREA

1925-26 Unwmk. Perf. 11

91	A78	60c brn car	15	1.50
a.		Perf. 13½	1.25	7.25
92	A78	1 l dark blue	20	1.50
a.		Perf. 13½	5,000.	1,050.

Perf. 13½

93	A78	1.25 l dk bl ('26)	50	6.50
a.		Perf. 11	85	6.50

Saint Francis of Assisi Issue

Italian Stamps of 1926 Overprinted

ERITREA

1926 Wmk. 140 Perf. 14

94	A79	20c gray grn	70	3.00
95	A80	40c dk vio	70	3.00
96	A81	60c red vio	70	3.00

Overprinted in Red

Eritrea

Unwmk. Perf. 11

97	A82	1.25 l dark blue	70	3.00

Perf. 14

98	A83	5 l + 2.50 l ol grn	1.75	5.25
		Nos. 94-98 (5)	4.55	17.25

Italian Stamps of 1926 Overprinted type "f" in Black

1926 Wmk. 140 Perf. 14

99	A46	75c dk red & rose	12.00	3.50
a.		Double overprint	95.00	
100	A46	1.25 l bl & ultra	8.25	1.50
101	A46	2.50 l dk grn & org	27.50	10.00

Volta Issue

Type of Italy, 1927, Overprinted — o

Eritrea

1927

102	A84	20c purple	2.50	7.25
103	A84	50c dp org	3.25	5.00
a.		Double overprint	12.50	
104	A84	1.25 l brt bl	3.75	7.25

Italian Stamps of 1925-28 Overprinted type "a" in Black

1928-29

105	A86	7½c lt brn ('29)	7.00	12.50
106	A86	50c brt vio	9.00	10.00

Italian Stamps of 1927-28 Overprinted type "f"

1928-29

107	A86	50c brt vio	15.00	14.00

Unwmk. Perf. 11

107A	A85	1.75 l dp brn	15.00	5.00

Italy No. 192 Overprinted type "o"

1928 Wmk. 140 Perf. 14

108	A85	50c brn & slate	4.50	1.00

Monte Cassino Issue

Types of 1929 Issue of Italy Overprinted in Red or Blue

ERITREA

1929 Perf. 14

109	A96	20c dk grn (R)	1.50	5.00
110	A96	25c red org (Bl)	1.50	5.00
111	A98	50c + 10c crim (Bl)	1.50	7.25
112	A98	75c + 15c ol brn (R)	1.50	7.25
113	A96	1.25 l + 25c dl vio (R)	2.75	7.25
114	A98	5 l + 1 l saph (R)	2.75	7.25

Overprinted in Red

Eritrea

Unwmk.

No.	Type	Description	Unused	Used
115	A100	10 l + 2 l gray brn	2.75	10.00
		Nos. 109-115 (7)	14.25	49.00

Royal Wedding Issue

Type of Italian Stamps of 1930 Overprinted ERITREA

1930 Wmk. 140

No.	Type	Description	Unused	Used
116	A101	20c yel grn	50	2.00
117	A101	50c + 10c dp org	35	2.50
118	A101	1.25 l + 25c rose red	35	3.00

Lancer — A5

Scene in Massaua A6

Designs: 2c, 35c, Lancer. 5c, 10c, Postman. 15c, Lineman. 25c, Askari (infantryman). 2 l, Railroad viaduct. 5 l, Asmara Deghe Selam. 10 l, Camels.

1930 Wmk. 140 Litho. Perf. 14

No.	Type	Description	Unused	Used
119	A5	2c brt bl & blk	55	1.00
120	A5	5c dk vio & blk	90	42
121	A5	10c yel brn & blk	90	24
122	A5	15c dk grn & blk	90	35
123	A5	25c gray grn & blk	90	24
124	A5	35c red brn & blk	2.75	3.00
125	A6	1 l dk bl & blk	1.10	15
126	A6	2 l choc & blk	2.00	3.00
127	A6	5 l ol grn & blk	3.75	5.00
128	A6	10 l dl bl & blk	3.75	6.50
		Nos. 119-128 (10)	17.50	19.90

Ferrucci Issue

Types of Italian Stamps of 1930 Overprinted type "f" in Red or Blue

1930

No.	Type	Description	Unused	Used
129	A102	20c vio (R)	35	1.50
130	A103	25c dk grn (R)	35	1.50
131	A103	50c blk (R)	35	1.50
132	A103	1.25 l dp bl (R)	35	1.50
133	A104	5 l + 2 l dp car (Bl)	1.50	3.00
		Nos. 129-133 (5)	2.90	9.00

Virgil Issue

Types of Italian Stamps of 1930 Overprinted in Red or Blue

ERITREA

1930 Photo.

No.	Type	Description	Unused	Used
134	A106	15c vio blk	28	1.50
135	A106	20c org brn	28	1.50
136	A106	25c dk grn	28	1.25
137	A106	30c lt brn	28	1.50
138	A106	50c dl vio	28	1.25
139	A106	75c rose red	28	1.50
140	A106	1.25 l gray bl	28	1.50

Unwmk. Engr.

No.	Type	Description	Unused	Used
141	A106	5 l + 1.50 l dk vio	1.40	6.00
142	A106	10 l + 2.50 l ol brn	1.40	6.00
		Nos. 134-142 (9)	4.76	22.00

Saint Anthony of Padua Issue

Types of Italian Stamps of 1931 Overprinted type "f" in Blue, Red or Black

1931 Photo. Wmk. 140

No.	Type	Description	Unused	Used
143	A116	20c brn (Bl)	50	2.00
144	A116	25c grn (R)	50	2.00
145	A118	30c gray brn (Bl)	50	2.00
146	A118	50c dl vio (Bl)	50	1.50
147	A120	1.25 l slate bl (R)	50	2.00

Unwmk. Engr.

No.	Type	Description	Unused	Used
148	A121	75c black (R)	50	2.00
149	A122	5 l + 2.50 l dk brn (Bk)	1.50	7.25
		Nos. 143-149 (7)	4.50	18.75

Victor Emmanuel III — A13

1931 Photo. Wmk. 140

No.	Type	Description	Unused	Used
150	A13	7½c olive brn	24	50
151	A13	20c slate bl & car	20	15
152	A13	30c ol grn & brn vio	24	15
153	A13	40c bl & yel grn	20	15
154	A13	50c bis brn & ol	15	15
155	A13	75c car rose	50	15
156	A13	1.25 l vio & indigo	60	15
157	A13	2.50 l dull green	85	60
		Nos. 150-157 (8)	2.98	
		Set value		1.62

Camel — A14

Temple Ruins — A18

Designs: 2c, 10c, Camel. 5c, 15c, Shark fishery. 25c, Baobab tree. 35c, Pastoral scene. 2 l, African elephant. 5 l, Eritrean man. 10 l, Eritrean woman.

1934 Photo. Wmk. 140

No.	Type	Description	Unused	Used
158	A14	2c deep blue	40	60
159	A14	5c black	45	35
160	A14	10c brown	65	24
161	A14	15c org brn	80	52
162	A14	25c gray grn	45	15
163	A14	35c purple	1.40	2.00
164	A18	1 l dk bl gray	15	15
165	A14	2 l olive blk	4.00	70
166	A18	5 l car rose	2.25	1.00
167	A18	10 l red org	2.50	1.25
		Nos. 158-167 (10)	13.05	6.96

Abruzzi Issue

Types of 1934 Issue Overprinted in Black or Red

ONORANZE AL DUCA DEGLI ABRUZZI

1934

No.	Type	Description	Unused	Used
168	A14	10c dl bl (R)	2.25	7.25
169	A14	15c blue	2.25	7.25
170	A14	35c grn (R)	1.50	7.25
171	A18	1 l copper red	1.50	7.25
172	A14	2 l rose red	3.50	7.25
173	A18	5 l purple (R)	1.75	7.25
174	A18	10 l ol grn (R)	1.75	7.25
		Nos. 168-174 (7)	14.50	50.75

Grant's Gazelle A22

1934 Photo.

No.	Type	Description	Unused	Used
175	A22	5c ol grn & brn	1.10	4.00
176	A22	10c yel brn & blk	1.10	4.00
177	A22	20c scar & indigo	1.10	4.00
178	A22	50c dk vio & brn	1.10	4.00
179	A22	60c org brn & ind	1.10	4.00
180	A22	1.25 l dk bl & grn	1.10	4.00
		Nos. 175-180 (6)	6.60	24.00

Second Colonial Arts Exhibition, Naples. See Nos. C1-C6.

Propaganda labels inscribed "Eritrea" appeared in 1978.

SEMI-POSTAL STAMPS

Many issues of Italy and Italian Colonies include one or more semipostal denominations. To avoid splitting sets, these issues are generally listed as regular postage, airmail, etc., unless all values carry a surtax.

Italy Nos. B1-B3 Overprinted type "f"

1915-16 Wmk. 140 Perf. 14

No.	Type	Description	Unused	Used
B1	SP1	10c + 5c rose	1.25	2.00
a.		"EPITREA"	6.00	8.50
b.		Inverted overprint	85.00	160.00
B2	SP2	15c + 5c slate	3.25	6.00
B3	SP2	20c + 5c org	1.90	3.00
a.		"EPITREA"	8.50	14.00
b.		Inverted overprint	50.00	70.00
c.		Pair, one without ovpt.		700.00

No. B2 Surcharged 20

1916

No.	Type	Description	Unused	Used
B4	SP2	20c on 15c+5c slate	3.25	6.00
a.		"EPITREA"	14.00	21.00
b.		Pair, one without overprint	125.00	

Counterfeits exist of the minor varieties of Nos. B1, B3-B4.

Holy Year Issue

Italy Nos. B20-B25 Overprinted in Black or Red

ERITREA

1925 Perf. 12

No.	Type	Description	Unused	Used
B5	SP4	20c + 10c dk grn & brn	75	3.00
B6	SP4	30c + 15c dk brn & brn	75	3.00
a.		Double overprint		
B7	SP4	50c + 25c vio & brn	75	3.00
B8	SP4	60c + 30c dp rose & brn	75	3.00
a.		Inverted overprint		
B9	SP8	1 l + 50c dp bl & vio (R)	75	3.00
B10	SP8	5 l + 2.50 l org brn & vio (R)	75	3.00
		Nos. B5-B10 (6)	4.50	18.00

Colonial Institute Issue

"Peace" Substituting Spade for Sword — SP1

1926 Typo. Perf. 14

No.	Type	Description	Unused	Used
B11	SP1	5c + 5c brown	15	1.65
B12	SP1	10c + 5c olive grn	15	1.65
B13	SP1	20c + 5c blue grn	15	1.65
B14	SP1	40c + 5c brown red	15	1.65
B15	SP1	60c + 5c orange	15	1.65
B16	SP1	1 l + 5c blue	15	1.65
		Nos. B11-B16 (6)	90	9.90

The surtax of 5c on each stamp was for the Italian Colonial Institute.

Types of Italian Semi-Postal Stamps of 1926 Overprinted type "k"

1927 Unwmk. Perf. 11½

No.	Type	Description	Unused	Used
B17	SP10	40c + 20c dk brn & blk	65	3.50
B18	SP10	60c + 30c brn red & ol brn	65	3.50
B19	SP10	1.25 l + 60c dp bl & blk	65	3.50
B20	SP10	5 l + 2.50 l dk grn & blk	1.00	4.50

The surtax on these stamps was for the charitable work of the Voluntary Militia for Italian National Defense.

Fascism and Victory — SP2

Agriculture — SP3

1928 Wmk. 140 Typo. Perf. 14

No.	Type	Description	Unused	Used
B21	SP2	20c + 5c bl grn	50	2.50
B22	SP2	30c + 5c red	50	2.50
B23	SP2	50c + 10c pur	50	2.50
B24	SP2	1.25 l + 20c dk bl	50	2.50

The surtax was for the Society Africana d'Italia, whose 46th anniversary was commemorated by the issue.

Types of Italian Semi-Postal Stamps of 1928 Overprinted type "f"

1929 Unwmk. Perf. 11

No.	Type	Description	Unused	Used
B25	SP10	30c + 10c red & blk	85	3.50
B26	SP10	50c + 20c vio & blk	85	3.50
B27	SP10	1.25 l + 50c brn & bl	1.00	5.00
B28	SP10	5 l + 2 l olive grn & blk	1.00	5.00

Surtax for the charitable work of the Voluntary Militia for Italian Natl. Defense.

Types of Italian Semi-Postal Stamps of 1929 Overprinted type "f" in Black or Red

1930 Perf. 14

No.	Type	Description	Unused	Used
B29	SP10	30c + 10c dk grn & bl grn (Bk)	3.25	10.00
B30	SP10	50c + 10c dk grn & vio	3.25	10.00
B31	SP10	1.25 l + 30c ol brn & red brn	3.25	10.00
B32	SP10	5 l + 1.50 l ind & grn	10.00	32.50

Surtax for the charitable work of the Voluntary Militia for Italian Natl. Defense.

1930 Photo. Wmk. 140

No.	Type	Description	Unused	Used
B33	SP3	50c + 20c ol brn	70	4.00
B34	SP3	1.25 l + 20c dp bl	70	4.00
B35	SP3	1.75 l + 20c green	70	4.00
B36	SP3	2.55 l + 50c purple	1.10	4.00
B37	SP3	5 l + 1 l dp car	1.10	4.00
		Nos. B33-37 (5)	4.30	20.00

Italian Colonial Agricultural Institute, 25th anniv. The surtax aided that institution.

AIR POST STAMPS

Desert Scene — AP1

Design: 80c, 1 l, 2 l, Plane and globe.

Wmk. Crowns (140)

1934 Photo. Perf. 14

No.	Type	Description	Unused	Used
C1	AP1	25c sl bl & org red	1.10	4.00
C2	AP1	50c grn & indigo	1.10	4.00
C3	AP1	75c brn & org red	1.10	4.00
C4	AP1	80c org brn & ol grn	1.10	4.00
C5	AP1	1 l scar & ol grn	1.10	4.00
C6	AP1	2 l dk bl & brn	1.10	4.00
		Nos. C1-C6 (6)	6.60	24.00

Second Colonial Arts Exhibition, Naples.

Plowing AP3

Plane and Cacti — AP6

Designs: 25c, 1.50 l, Plowing. 50c, 2 l, Plane over mountain pass. 60c, 5 l, Plane and trees. 75c, 10 l, Plane and cacti. 1 l, 3 l, Bridge.

1936 **Photo.**
C7 AP3 25c dp grn 50 1.00
C8 AP3 50c dk brn 30 20
C9 AP3 60c brn org 70 2.50
C10 AP6 75c org brn 60 50
C11 AP3 1 l deep blue 15 15
C12 AP3 1.50 l purple 42 25
C13 AP3 2 l gray blue 60 50
C14 AP3 3 l copper red 5.00 4.50
C15 AP3 5 l green 2.50 85
C16 AP6 10 l rose red 6.50 1.50
Nos. C7-C16 (10) 17.27 11.95

AIR POST SEMI-POSTAL STAMPS

King Victor Emmanuel III — SPAP1

1934 **Wmk. 140** **Photo.** ***Perf. 14***
CB1 SPAP1 25c + 10c 1.50 1.50
CB2 SPAP1 50c + 10c 1.50 1.50
CB3 SPAP1 75c + 15c 1.50 1.50
CB4 SPAP1 80c + 15c 1.50 1.50
CB5 SPAP1 1 l + 20c 1.50 1.50
CB6 SPAP1 2 l + 20c 1.50 1.50
CB7 SPAP1 3 l + 25c 14.00 14.00
CB8 SPAP1 5 l + 25c 14.00 14.00
CB9 SPAP1 10 l + 30c 14.00 14.00
CB10 SPAP1 25 l + 2 l 14.00 14.00
Nos. CB1-CB10 (10) 65.00 65.00

65th birthday of King Victor Emmanuel III and the nonstop flight from Rome to Mogadiscio. Used values are for stamps canceled to order.

AIR POST SEMI-POSTAL OFFICIAL STAMP

Type of Air Post Semi-Postal Stamps, 1934, Overprinted Crown and "SERVIZIO DI STATO" in Black

1934 **Wmk. 140** ***Perf. 14***
CBO1 SPAP1 25 l + 2 l cop red *900.00*

SPECIAL DELIVERY STAMPS

Special Delivery Stamps of Italy, Overprinted type "a"

1907 **Wmk. 140** ***Perf. 14***
E1 SD1 25c rose red 8.25 8.25
a. Double overprint

1909
E2 SD2 30c blue & rose 35.00 *42.50*

1920
E3 SD1 50c dull red 1.25 3.50

"Italia" SD1

1924 **Engr.** **Unwmk.**
E4 SD1 60c dk red & brn 2.00 *5.00*
a. Perf. 13½ 6.00 *12.50*
E5 SD1 2 l dk bl & red 4.50 *7.25*

For surcharges see Nos. E6-E8.

Nos. E4 and E5 Surcharged in Dark Blue or Red:

70 ٧٠
2,50 ٢,٥٠

1926
E6 SD1 70c on 60c (Bl) 2.00 *5.00*
E7 SD1 2.50 l on 2 l (R) 4.50 *7.25*

Type of 1924 Surcharged in Blue or Black:

LIRE 1,25 ١,٢٥

1927-35 ***Perf. 11***
E8 SD1 1.25 l on 60c dk red & brn (Bl) 2.00 50
a. Perf. 14 (Bl) ('35) 40.00 3.50
b. Perf. 11 (Bk) ('35) *2,250.* 125.00
c. Perf. 14 (Bk) ('35) 125.00 6.75

AUTHORIZED DELIVERY STAMP

Authorized Delivery Stamp of Italy, No. EY2, Overprinted Type "f" in Black

1939-41 **Wmk. 140** ***Perf. 14***
EY1 AD2 10c dk brn ('41) 15
a. 10c reddish brown 11.00 13.00

On No. EY1a, which was used in Eritrea, the overprint hits the figures "10." On No. EY1, which was sold in Rome, the overprint falls above the 10's.

POSTAGE DUE STAMPS

Postage Due Stamps of Italy Overprinted type "a" at Top

1903 **Wmk. 140** ***Perf. 14***
J1 D3 5c buff & mag 4.50 6.00
a. Double overprint 50.00
J2 D3 10c buff & mag 3.00 5.00
J3 D3 20c buff & mag 3.00 5.00
J4 D3 30c buff & mag 4.50 6.00
J5 D3 40c buff & mag 10.50 14.00
J6 D3 50c buff & mag 12.50 17.50
J7 D3 60c buff & mag 4.50 8.50
J8 D3 1 l bl & mag 3.00 1.50
J9 D3 2 l bl & mag 12.50 17.50
J10 D3 5 l bl & mag 42.50 65.00
J11 D3 10 l bl & mag 450.00 42.50

Same with Overprint at Bottom

1920-22
J1b D3 5c buff & magenta 24 1.25
c. Numeral and ovpt. inverted 50.00
J2a D3 10c buff & magenta 50 1.50
J3a D3 20c buff & magenta 55.00 60.00
J4a D3 30c buff & magenta 4.50 7.25
J5a D3 40c buff & magenta 3.00 7.25
J6a D3 50c buff & magenta 3.00 7.25
J7a D3 60c buff & magenta 4.50 10.00
J8a D3 1 l blue & magenta 6.75 7.25
J9a D3 2 l blue & magenta 385.00 280.00
J10a D3 5 l blue & magenta 50.00 85.00
J11a D3 10 l blue & magenta 2.50 12.50

1903 **Wmk. 140**
J12 D4 50 l yellow 125.00 55.00
J13 D4 100 l blue 75.00 14.00

1927
J14 D3 60c buff & brown 20.00 *30.00*

Postage Due Stamps of Italy, 1934, Overprinted type "j" in Black

1934
J15 D6 5c brown 20 *70*
J16 D6 10c blue 20 *70*
J17 D6 20c rose red 85 *1.00*
a. Inverted overprint 42.50
J18 D6 25c green 85 *1.00*
J19 D6 30c red orange 85 *1.50*
J20 D6 40c black brown 85 *2.00*
J21 D6 50c violet 85 35
J22 D6 60c black 1.25 *3.00*
J23 D7 1 l red orange 1.25 50
J24 D7 2 l green 10.50 14.00
J25 D7 5 l violet 14.00 17.50
J26 D7 10 l blue 14.00 17.50
J27 D7 20 l carmine rose 16.00 22.50
Nos. J15-J27 (13) 61.65 82.25

PARCEL POST STAMPS

These stamps were used by affixing them to the way bill so that one half remained on it following the parcel, the other half staying on the receipt given the sender. Most used halves are right halves. Complete stamps were obtainable canceled, probably to order. Both unused and used values are for complete stamps.

Parcel Post Stamps of Italy, 1914-17, Overprinted type "j" in Black on Each Half

1916 **Wmk. 140** ***Perf. 13½***
Q1 PP2 5c brown 21.00 *40.00*
Q2 PP2 10c deep blue *825.00* *1,150.*
Q3 PP2 25c red 30.00 *60.00*
Q4 PP2 50c orange 10.50 *20.00*
Q5 PP2 1 l violet 10.50 *20.00*
Q6 PP2 2 l green 8.50 *20.00*
Q7 PP2 3 l bister 60.00 *100.00*
Q8 PP2 4 l slate 60.00 *100.00*

Halves Used

Q1, Q7-Q8 1.25
Q2 20.00
Q3 65
Q4 15
Q5-Q6 20

Overprinted type "f" on Each Half

1917-24
Q9 PP2 5c brown 70 *2.00*
Q10 PP2 10c deep blue 70 *2.00*
Q11 PP2 20c black 70 *2.00*
Q12 PP2 25c red 70 *2.00*
Q13 PP2 50c orange 70 *2.00*
Q14 PP2 1 l violet 70 *2.00*
Q15 PP2 2 l green 70 *2.00*
Q16 PP2 3 l bister 1.00 *2.50*
Q17 PP2 4 l slate 1.50 *3.00*
Q18 PP2 10 l rose lil ('24) 17.50 *30.00*
Q19 PP2 12 l red brn ('24) 35.00 *65.00*
Q20 PP2 15 l olive grn ('24) 35.00 *65.00*
Q21 PP2 20 l brn vio ('24) 35.00 *65.00*
Nos. Q9-Q21 (13) 129.90 *244.50*

Halves Used

Q9-Q16 15
Q17 15
Q18 25
Q19 50
Q20 15
Q21 1.25

Parcel Post Stamps of Italy, 1927-39, Overprinted type "f" on Each Half

1927-37
Q21A PP3 10c dp bl ('37) *1,900.* 110.00
Q22 PP3 25c red ('37) 125.00 5.00
Q23 PP3 30c ultra ('29) 15 1.00
Q24 PP3 50c org ('36) 125.00 5.00
Q25 PP3 60c red ('29) 15 1.00
Q26 PP3 1 l brn vio ('36) 70.00 2.50
a. 1 l lilac 110.00 2.50
Q27 PP3 2 l grn ('36) 20.00 4.00
Q28 PP3 3 l bister 30 2.50
Q29 PP3 4 l gray 35 4.00
Q30 PP3 10 l rose lil ('36) 85.00 125.00
Q31 PP3 20 l lil brn ('36) 110.00 150.00
Nos. Q22-Q31 (10) 535.95
#Q21A-Q31 410.00

Halves Used

Q21A 5.25
Q22-Q25, Q27-Q28 15
Q26, Q26a, Q29 20
Q30 50
Q31 1.00

ESTONIA

LOCATION — Northern Europe, bordering on the Baltic Sea and the Gulf of Finland
GOVT. — Independent republic
AREA — 18,353 sq. mi.
POP. — 1,542,000 (1986)
CAPITAL — Tallinn

Formerly a part of Russia, Estonia declared its independence in 1918. In 1940 it was incorporated in the Union of Soviet Socialist Republics.

Estonia declared its independence on Aug. 20, 1991. Estonian independence was recognized by the Soviet Union on Sept. 6, 1991.

100 Kopecks = 1 Ruble (1918, 1991)
100 Penni = 1 Mark (1919)
100 Sents = 1 Kroon (1928, 1992)

Catalogue values for unused stamps in this country are for Never Hinged items, beginning with Scott 200 in the regular postage section, Scott B60 in the semi-postal section, and Scott F1 in the registration section.

Watermark

Wmk. 207- Arms of Finland in the Sheet

Illustration reduced. Watermark covers a large part of sheet.

A1

A2

1918-19 **Unwmk.** **Litho.** ***Imperf.***
1 A1 5k pale red 38 38
2 A1 15k bright blue 38 38
3 A2 35p brown ('19) 75 75
a. Printed on both sides 75.00
b. 35p olive 10.00 10.00
4 A2 70p olive grn ('19) 1.00 1.00

Nos. 1-4 exist privately perforated.

Russian Stamps of 1909-17 Handstamped in Violet or Black

1919 ***Perf. 14, 14½x15, 13½***
8 A14 1k orange *1,400.* *1,400.*
9 A14 2k green 19.00 19.00
10 A14 3k red 20.00 20.00
11 A14 5k claret 15.00 16.00
12 A15 10k dk bl (Bk) 22.50 22.50
13 A15 10k dk bl 55.00 57.50
14 A14 10k on 7k lt bl *200.00* *200.00*
15 A11 15k red brn & bl 20.00 20.00
16 A11 25k grn & vio 30.00 30.00
17 A11 35k red brn & grn *600.00* *600.00*
18 A8 50k vio & grn 65.00 65.00
19 A9 1r pale brn, brn & org 75.00 75.00
20 A13 10r scar, yel & gray *1,900.* *1,900.*

Imperf
21 A14 1k orange 20.00 22.50
22 A14 2k green *200.00* *225.00*
23 A14 3k red 37.50 37.50
24 A9 1r pale brn, brn & red org *150.00* *150.00*
25 A12 3½r mar & grn *200.00* *200.00*
26 A13 5r dk bl, grn & pale bl *300.00* *300.00*

Provisionally issued at Tallinn. This overprint has been extensively counterfeited.
No. 20 is always creased.

Gulls — A3

1919, May 13 *Imperf.*
27 A3 5p yellow 1.00 1.00

A4 A5 A6

A7

Viking Ship — A8

1919-20 *Perf. 11½*
28 A4 10p green 25 25

Imperf
29 A4 5p orange 15 15
30 A4 10p green 15 15
31 A5 15p rose 15 15
32 A6 35p blue 20 20
33 A7 70p dl vio ('20) 20 20
34 A8 1m bl & blk brn 50 25
a. Gray granite paper ('20) 35 18
35 A8 5m yel & blk 1.25 50
a. Gray granite paper ('20) 75 25
36 A8 15m yel grn & vio ('20) 2.50 50
37 A8 25m ultra & blk brn ('20) 3.50 1.50
Nos. 28-37 (10) 8.85 3.85

The 5m exists with inverted center. Not a postal item.
See #76-77. For surcharges see #55, 57.

Skyline of Tallinn — A9

1920-24 *Imperf.*

Pelure Paper
39 A9 25p green 20 15
40 A9 25p yellow ('24) 32 25
41 A9 35p rose 20 15
42 A9 50p green ('21) 20 15
43 A9 1m vermilion 38 15
44 A9 2m blue 50 15
45 A9 2m ultramarine 38 15
46 A9 2.50m blue 30 15
Nos. 39-46 (8) 2.48
Set value 90

Nos. 39 to 46 with sewing machine perforation are unofficial.
For surcharge see No. 56.

Stamps of 1919-20 Surcharged

1 Mk. 2 Mk.

1920 *Imperf.*
55 A5 1m on 15p rose 18 18
56 A9 1m on 35p rose 18 18
57 A7 2m on 70p dl vio 18 18

Weaver A10

Blacksmith A11

1922-23 **Typo.** *Imperf.*
58 A10 ½m org ('23) 1.25 1.65
59 A10 1m brn ('23) 1.50 1.50
60 A10 2m yel grn 1.50 1.50
61 A10 2½m claret 1.75 1.50
62 A11 5m rose 2.50 1.50
63 A11 9m red ('23) 4.50 3.00
64 A11 10m deep blue 2.75 1.75
Nos. 58-64 (7) 15.75 12.40

1922-25 *Perf. 14*
65 A10 ½m org ('23) 50 15
66 A10 1m brn ('23) 75 15
67 A10 2m yel grn 1.25 15
68 A10 2½m claret 1.25 15
69 A10 3m bl grn ('24) 1.40 15
70 A11 5m rose 2.00 15
71 A11 9m red ('23) 1.40 75
72 A11 10m deep blue 2.25 15
73 A11 12m red ('25) 2.50 90
74 A11 15m plum ('25) 2.00 25
75 A11 20m ultra ('25) 6.00 15
Nos. 65-75 (11) 21.30
Set value 2.50

See No. 89. For surcharges see Nos. 84-88.

Viking Ship Type of 1920

1922, June 8 *Perf. 14x13½*
76 A8 15m yel grn & vio 3.00 30
77 A8 25m ultra & blk brn 4.00 1.10

Map of Estonia — A13

1923-24

Paper with Lilac Network
78 A13 100m ol grn & bl 11.00 1.50

Paper with Buff Network
79 A13 300m brn & bl ('24) 24.00 4.50

For surcharges see Nos. 106-107.

National Theater, Tallinn — A14

1924, Dec. 9 *Perf. 14x13½*

Paper with Blue Network
81 A14 30m vio & blk 4.25 1.50

Paper with Rose Network
82 A14 70m car rose & blk 6.25 1.75

For surcharge see No. 105.

Vanemuine Theater, Tartu — A15

1927, Oct. 25

Paper with Lilac Network
83 A15 40m dp bl & ol brn 3.75 50

Stamps of 1922-25 Surcharged in New Currency in Red or Black

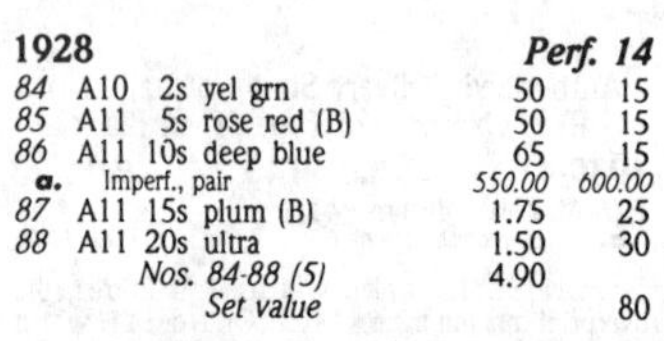

1918 24/II 1928

S. S.

1928 *Perf. 14*
84 A10 2s yel grn 50 15
85 A11 5s rose red (B) 50 15
86 A11 10s deep blue 65 15
a. Imperf., pair 550.00 600.00
87 A11 15s plum (B) 1.75 25
88 A11 20s ultra 1.50 30
Nos. 84-88 (5) 4.90
Set value 80

10th anniversary of independence.

3rd Philatelic Exhibition Issue

Blacksmith Type of 1922-23

1928, July 6
89 A11 10m gray 2.50 3.00
a. Imperf., pair

Sold only at Tallinn Philatelic Exhibition.

Arms — A16

Paper with Network in Parenthesis

1928-40 *Perf. 14, 14½x14*
90 A16 1s dk gray (bl) 30 15
a. Thick gray-toned laid paper ('40) 6.50 4.50
91 A16 2s yel grn (org) 40 15
92 A16 4s grn (brn) ('29) 50 15
93 A16 5s red (grn) 38 15
a. 5 feet on lowest lion 16.00 12.50
94 A16 8s vio (buff) ('29) 1.65 15
95 A16 10s lt bl (lilac) 1.00 15
96 A16 12s crimson (grn) 1.50 15
97 A16 15s yel (blue) 1.50 15
98 A16 15s car (gray) ('35) 5.00 45
99 A16 20s slate bl (red) 2.25 15
100 A16 25s red vio (grn) ('29) 5.50 15
101 A16 25s bl (brn) ('35) 5.00 38
102 A16 40s red org (bl) ('29) 3.75 30
103 A16 60s gray (brn) ('29) 4.00 50
104 A16 80s brn (bl) ('29) 7.50 1.00
Nos. 90-104 (15) 40.23
Set value 3.20

Types of 1924 Issues Surcharged:

KROON 1 KROON
a

2 KROONI 2
b

3 KROONI 3
c

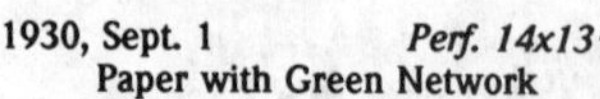

1930, Sept. 1 *Perf. 14x13½*

Paper with Green Network
105 A14 1k on 70m car & blk 4.25 2.50

Paper with Rose Network
106 A13 2k on 300m brn & bl 7.50 4.25

Paper with Blue Network
107 A13 3k on 300m brn & bl 19.00 11.00

University Observatory A17

University of Tartu A18

Paper with Network as in Parenthesis

1932, June 1 *Perf. 14*
108 A17 5s red (yellow) 3.25 30
109 A18 10s light bl (lilac) 1.00 15
110 A17 12s car (blue) 4.75 90
111 A18 20s dk bl (green) 4.00 20

University of Tartu tercentenary.

Narva Falls — A19

Ancient Bard Playing Harp — A20

1933, Apr. 1 **Photo.** *Perf. 14x13½*
112 A19 1k gray black 3.75 50

See No. 149.

Paper with Network as in Parenthesis

1933, May 29 **Typo.** *Perf. 14*
113 A20 2s green (orange) 1.50 20
114 A20 5s red (green) 2.00 20
115 A20 10s blue (lilac) 2.50 15

Tenth National Song Festival.

Woman Harvester A21

Pres. Konstantin Päts A22

1935, Mar. 1 **Engr.** *Perf. 13½*
116 A21 3k blk brn 45 75

1936-40 **Typo.** *Perf. 14*
117 A22 1s chocolate 38 15
118 A22 2s yel grn 38 15
119 A22 3s dp org ('40) 3.75 2.75
120 A22 4s rose vio 70 18
121 A22 5s lt bl grn 70 15
122 A22 6s rose lake 60 18
123 A22 6s dp grn ('40) 14.00 11.00
124 A22 10s greenish blue 75 15
125 A22 15s crim rose ('37) 1.25 15
126 A22 15s dp bl ('40) 4.00 25
127 A22 18s dp car ('39) 10.00 4.50
128 A22 20s brt vio 1.25 15
129 A22 25s dk bl ('38) 4.00 20
130 A22 30s bister ('38) 4.25 20
131 A22 30s ultra ('39) 7.50 1.25
132 A22 50s org brn 4.00 50
133 A22 60s brt pink 6.00 1.00
Nos. 117-133 (17) 63.51 22.91

Estonia stamps can be mounted in the annual Baltic States supplement.

St. Brigitta Convent Entrance A23

Ruins of Convent, Pirita River A24

Front View of Convent A25

Seal of Convent A26

Paper with Network as in Parenthesis

1936, June 10 *Perf. 13½*

134 A23	5s green (buff)	35	18
135 A24	10s blue (lil)	45	18
136 A25	15s red (org)	75	1.10
137 A26	25s ultra (brn)	1.00	1.40

St. Brigitta Convent, 500th anniversary.

Harbor at Tallinn — A27

1938, Apr. 11 **Engr.** *Perf. 14*

138 A27 2k blue 50 1.00

Friedrich R. Faehlmann A28

Friedrich R. Kreutzwald A29

1938 **Typo.** *Perf. 13½*

139 A28	5s dk grn	50	50
140 A29	10s dp brn	50	50
141 A29	15s dk car	65	90
142 A28	25s ultra	1.10	1.40
a.	Sheet of 4, #139-142	6.75	12.00

Society of Estonian Scholars centenary.

Hospital at Pärnu — A30

Beach Hotel — A31

1939, June 20 **Typo.**

144 A30	5s dk grn	70	40
145 A31	10s dp red vio	50	40
146 A30	18s dk car	1.50	1.50
147 A31	30s dp bl	1.75	1.75
a.	Sheet of 4, #144-147	10.00	20.00

Cent. of health resort and baths at Pärnu.

Narva Falls Type of 1933

1940, Apr. 15 **Engr.**

149 A19 1k slate green 50 1.25

The sky consists of heavy horizontal lines and the background consists of horizontal and vertical lines.

Carrier Pigeon and Plane — A32

1940, July 30 **Typo.**

150 A32	3s red orange	15	15
151 A32	10s purple	15	15
152 A32	15s rose brown	15	15
153 A32	30s dark blue	1.00	75
	Set value		1.00

Centenary of the first postage stamp.

Catalogue values for unused stamps in this section, from this point to the end of the section, are for Never Hinged items.

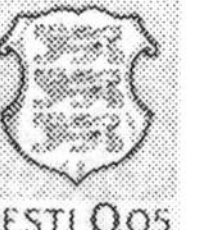

Natl. Arms — A40

A41

1991, Oct. 1 **Litho.** *Perf. 13x12½*

200 A40	5k salmon & red	25	25
201 A40	10k lt grn & dk bl grn	16	15
202 A40	15k lt bl & dk bl	25	15
203 A40	30k vio & gray	50	16
204 A40	50k org & brn	85	25
205 A40	70k pink & purple	1.25	35
206 A40	90k pur & rose lilac	1.50	55

Size: 20½x27mm

Engr.

Perf. 12½ Horiz.

207 A40	1r dark brown	1.50	50
208 A40	2r lt bl & dk bl	3.00	90
	Nos. 200-208 (9)	9.26	3.26

Perf. 13½x14, 14x13½

1991, Nov. 1 **Litho.**

209 A41	1.50r Flag, vert.	2.50	75
210 A41	2.50r shown	4.25	1.25

National Arms — A42

1992, Mar. 16 **Litho.** *Perf. 13x12½*

211 A42	E (1r) lemon	22	22
212 A42	I (20r) blue green	3.00	75
213 A42	A (40r) blue	6.00	1.50

No. 211 was valid for postage within Estonia. No. 212 was valid for postage within Europe. No. 213 was valid for overseas mail.

Arms Types of 1991-1992 and No. 202 Surcharged

0.60

And

Natl. Arms — A42a

Perf. 14, 13x12½ (#214, 217, 219-220)

1992-93

214 A42	E (10s) orange	25	25
215 A40	10s blue & gray	*15*	*15*
216 A40	50s gray & bright blue	*15*	*15*
217 A40	60s on 15k #202	*15*	*15*
218 A40	60s lilac & olive	*90*	*45*
219 A42	I (1k) emerald	2.50	75
220 A42	A (2k) violet blue	5.00	1.50
221 A42a	5k bister & red violet	*85*	*42*
222 A42a	10k blue & olive	*2.15*	*1.10*
223 A42a	20k pale lilac & slate grn	*3.25*	*1.65*

Coil Stamps

Engr.

Size: 20½x27mm

Perf. 12½ Horiz.

224 A42	X (10s) brown	25	25
225 A42	X (10s) olive	25	25
226 A42	X (10s) black	25	25
227 A42	Z (30s) red lilac	*18*	*15*
228 A42	Z (30s) red	*18*	*15*
229 A42	Z (30s) dark blue	*18*	*15*

Litho.

230 A42 60s lilac brown *18* *15*

Issue dates: Nos. 214, 219-220, June 22. No. 224, Aug. 29. No. 225, Sept. 25. No. 226, Oct. 31. No. 227, Nov. 16. No. 228, Dec. 1. No. 229, Dec. 22. No. 230, Jan. 8, 1993. No. 217, Mar. 5, 1993. 10s, 50s, Mar. 23 1993. 10k, May. 25, 1993. 5k, July 7, 1993. No. 218, Aug. 5, 1993. 20k, Sept. 8, 1993.

See note after No. 213. Nos. 224-229 were valid for postage within Estonia.

See No. F1.

A44

A45

Birds of the Baltic shores.

1992, Oct. 3 **Litho. & Engr.** *Perf. 13*

231 A44	1k Pandion haliaetus	22	15
232 A44	1k Limosa limosa	22	15
233 A44	1k Mergus merganser	22	15
234 A44	1k Tadorna todorna	22	15
a.	Booklet pane of 4, #231-234	1.00	

See Latvia Nos. 332-33a, Lithuania Nos. 427-430 and Sweden Nos. 1975-1978.

1992, Dec, 15 **Litho.** *Perf. 14*

235 A45	30s gray & multi	15	15
236 A45	2k light brown & multi	28	18

Christmas.

Friendship — A46

1993, Feb. 8 **Litho.** *Perf. 14*

237 A46	1k multicolored	*22*	*15*
a.	Booklet pane of 6	*1.30*	

See Finland No. 906.

A47

A48

1993, Feb. 16 *Perf. 13x13½*

238 A47	60s black & multi	*15*	*15*
239 A47	1k violet & multi	*25*	*15*
240 A47	2k blue & multi	*50*	*25*

First Republic, 75th anniv.

1993, June 9 **Litho.** *Perf. 13½x14*

241 A48	60s Wrestling	*15*	*15*
242 A48	1k +25s Viking ship, map	*30*	*15*
243 A48	2k Shot put with rock	*50*	*25*

First Baltic sea games.

Tallinn Castle — A49

Designs: 2.70k, Narva Fortress. 2.90k, Haapsalu Cathedral.

1993 **Litho.** *Perf. 14*

244 A49	2k tan & brown	*32*	*16*
246 A49	2.70k lt blue & dk blue	*65*	*32*
247 A49	2.90k lt green & dk green	*52*	*25*

Issue dates: 2k, Oct. 12. 2.70k, Dec. 10, 1993. 2.90k, Dec., 1993. While Nos. 246-247 were issued at about the same time, the dollar value of No. 247 was lower when it was released. This is an expanding set. Numbers may change.

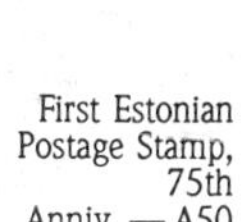

First Estonian Postage Stamp, 75th Anniv. — A50

1993, Nov. 13 **Litho.** *Perf. 14*

259 A50 1k multicolored *22* 15

Souvenir Sheet

Imperf

260 A50	4k multicolored	*1.00*	*1.00*
a.	Ovptd. in sheet margin	1.00	1.00

No. 260 sold for 5k. Overprint on No. 260a reads "FILATEELIANAITUS / MARE BALTICUM '93 / 24.-28. NOVEMBER 1993".

Christmas — A51

Designs: 80s, Haapsalu Cathedral. 2k, Tallinn Church, vert.

1993, Nov. Litho. *Perf. 14*

261 A51 80s red *15 15*
262 A51 2k blue *38 18*

Lydia Koidula — A52

1993, Dec. 14 Litho. *Perf. 14*

263 A52 1k multicolored *25 15*

1994 Winter Olympics, Lillehammer — A53

1994, Jan. 26

264 A53 1k +25s Ski jumping *20 15*
265 A53 2k Speed skating *32 16*

SEMI-POSTAL STAMPS

Assisting Wounded Soldier — SP1

Offering Aid to Wounded Hero — SP2

1920, June Unwmk. Litho. *Imperf.*

B1 SP1 35p + 10p red & ol grn 20 32
B2 SP2 70p + 15p dp bl & brn 20 32

Surcharged

2 MK

1920

B3 SP1 1m on No. B1 25 25
B4 SP2 2m on No. B2 25 25

Nurse and Wounded Soldier — SP3

1921, Aug. 1 *Imperf.*

B5 SP3 2½ (3½)m org, brn & car 50 70
B6 SP3 5 (7)m ultra, brn & car 50 70

1922, Apr. 26 *Perf. 13½x14*

B7 SP3 2½ (3½)m org, brn & car 75 1.00
a. Vert. pair, imperf. horiz. 7.50 10.00
B8 SP3 5 (7)m ultra, brn & car 75 1.00
a. Vert. pair, imperf. horiz. 7.50 10.00

Nos. B5-B8 Overprinted

Aita nädalist.

1923 *Imperf.*

B9 SP3 2½ (3½)m 13.00 19.00
B10 SP3 5 (7)m 16.00 22.50

Perf. 13½x14

B11 SP3 2½ (3½)m 19.00 27.50
a. Vert. pair, imperf. horiz. 75.00 95.00
B12 SP3 5 (7)m 22.50 30.00
a. Vert. pair, imperf. horiz. 75.00 95.00

Excellent forgeries are plentiful.

5 5

Nos. B7 and B8 Surcharged

6 6

1926, June 15

B13 SP3 5 (6)m on #B7 1.40 2.00
a. Vert. pair, imperf. horiz. 7.50 10.00
B14 SP3 10 (12)m on #B8 1.40 2.00
a. Vert. pair, imperf. horiz. 7.50 10.00

Nos. B5-B14 had the franking value of the lower figure. They were sold for the higher figure, the excess going to the Red Cross Society.

Kuressaare Castle — SP4

Tartu Cathedral — SP5

Tallinn Castle — SP6

Narva Fortress — SP7

View of Tallinn — SP8

Laid Paper

Perf. 14½x14

1927, Nov. 19 Typo. Wmk. 207

B15 SP4 5m + 5m bl grn & ol, *grysh* 32 50
B16 SP5 10m + 10m dp bl & brn, *cream* 32 50
B17 SP6 12m + 12m rose red & ol grn, *bluish* 32 75

Perf. 14x13½

B18 SP7 20m + 20m bl & choc, *gray* 62 1.10
B19 SP8 40m + 40m org brn & slate, *buff* 62 1.10
Nos. B15-B19 (5) 2.20 3.95

The money derived from the surtax was donated to the Committee for the commemoration of War for Liberation.

Red Cross Issue

Symbolical of Succor to Injured — SP9

Symbolical of "Light of Hope" — SP10

1931, Aug. 1 Unwmk. *Perf. 13½*

B20 SP9 2s + 3s grn & car 4.25 5.00
B21 SP10 5s + 3s red & car 4.25 5.00
B22 SP10 10s + 3s lt bl & car 4.25 5.00
B23 SP9 20s + 3s dk bl & car 6.50 7.50

Nurse and Child SP11

Taagepera Sanatorium SP12

Lorraine Cross and Flower — SP13

Paper with Network as in Parenthesis

1933, Oct. 1 *Perf. 14, 14½*

B24 SP11 5s + 3s ver (grn) 4.25 4.25
B25 SP12 10s + 3s lt bl & red (vio) 4.25 4.25
B26 SP13 12s + 3s rose & red (grn) 4.75 4.75
B27 SP12 20s + 3s dk bl & red (org) 7.50 7.50

The surtax was for a fund to combat tuberculosis.

Coats of Arms

Narva — SP14

Pärnu — SP15

Tartu — SP16

Tallinn — SP17

Paper with Network as in Parenthesis

1936, Feb. 1 *Perf. 13½*

B28 SP14 10s + 10s grn & ultra (gray) 3.50 3.75
B29 SP15 15s + 15s car & bl (gray) 3.50 3.75
B30 SP16 25s + 25s gray bl & red (brn) 4.50 5.00
B31 SP17 50s + 50s blk & dl org (ol) 10.00 14.00

Paide — SP18

Rakvere — SP19

Valga — SP20

Viljandi — SP21

Paper with Network as in Parenthesis

1937, Jan. 2

B32 SP18 10s + 10s grn (gray) 2.75 3.75
B33 SP19 15s + 15s red brn (gray) 2.75 3.75
B34 SP20 25s + 25s dk bl (lil) 4.00 5.00
B35 SP21 50s + 50s dk vio (gray) 7.50 10.00

Baltiski SP22

Võru SP23

Haapsalu SP24

Kuressaare SP25

Designs are the armorial bearings of various cities

1938, Jan. 21

Paper with Gray Network

B36 SP22 10s + 10s dk brn 2.50 3.25
B37 SP23 15s + 15s car & grn 3.00 3.50
B38 SP24 25s + 25s dk bl & car 4.00 5.00
B39 SP25 50s + 50s blk & org yel 6.00 8.75
a. Sheet of 4, #B36-B39 19.00 30.00

Annual charity ball, Tallinn, Jan. 2, 1938.

Viljandimaa — SP27

Pärnumaa — SP28

Tartumaa — SP29

Harjumaa — SP30

Designs are the armorial bearings of various districts

1939, Jan. 10

Paper with Gray Network

B41 SP27 10s + 10s dk bl grn 2.50 3.00
B42 SP28 15s + 15s carmine 3.00 3.50
B43 SP29 25s + 25s dk blue 4.00 4.75
B44 SP30 50s + 50s brn lake 6.25 10.00
a. Sheet of 4, #B41-B44 21.00 27.50

Võrumaa — SP32

Järvamaa — SP33

Läänemaa — SP34

Saaremaa — SP35

Designs are the armorial bearings of various districts

1940, Jan. 2 Typo. *Perf. 13½*

Paper with Gray Network

B46 SP32 10s + 10s dp grn & ultra 2.25 3.00
B47 SP33 15s + 15s dk car & ultra 2.25 3.00
B48 SP34 25s + 25s dk bl & scar 2.75 5.00
B49 SP35 50s + 50s ocher & ultra 3.75 8.00

Catalogue values for unused stamps in this section, from this point to the end of the section, are for Never Hinged items.

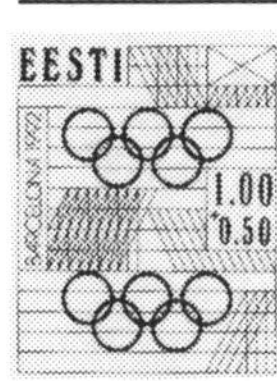

1992 Summer Olympics, Barcelona — SP40

1992, June 22 **Litho.** *Perf. 14*

B60	SP40	1r +50k red	18	18
B61	SP40	3r +1.50r green	50	50
B62	SP40	5r +2.50r blue & blk	85	85

While face values are shown in kopecks and rubles, the stamps were sold in the new currency at the rate of 1 ruble = 10 sents.

AIR POST STAMPS

Airplane AP1

Unwmk.

1920, Mar. 13 **Typo.** *Imperf.*

C1	AP1	5m yel, blk & lt grn	1.10	1.65

No. C1 Overprinted "1923" in Red

1923, Oct. 1

C2	AP1	5m multi	3.50	5.00

No. C1 Surcharged in Red

1923, Oct. 1

C3	AP1	15m on 5m multi	5.00	7.00

Pairs of No. C1 Surcharged in Black or Red

45 Marka

1923

1923, Oct.

C4	AP1	10m on 5m+5m (B)	6.00	*7.00*
C5	AP1	20m on 5m+5m	14.00	15.00
C6	AP1	45m on 5m+5m	45.00	47.50
		Rough Perf. 11½		
C7	AP1	10m on 5m+5m (B)	*125.00*	*150.00*
C8	AP1	20m on 5m+5m	*75.00*	*100.00*

The pairs comprising Nos. C7 and C8 are imperforate between. Forged surcharges and perforations abound.

Monoplane in Flight — AP2

Designs: Various views of planes in flight.

1924, Feb. 12 *Imperf.*

C9	AP2	5m yel & blk	1.40	2.25
C10	AP2	10m blue & blk	1.40	2.25
C11	AP2	15m red & blk	1.40	2.25
C12	AP2	20m grn & blk	1.40	2.25
C13	AP2	45m vio & blk	1.40	2.25
		Nos. C9-C13 (5)	7.00	11.25

The paper is covered with a faint network in pale shades of the frame colors. There are four varieties of the frames and five of the pictures.

1925, July 15 *Perf. 13½*

C14	AP2	5m yel & blk	1.00	1.50
C15	AP2	10m blue & blk	1.00	1.50
C16	AP2	15m red & blk	1.00	1.50
C17	AP2	20m grn & blk	1.00	1.50
C18	AP2	45m vio & blk	1.00	1.50
		Nos. C14-C18 (5)	5.00	7.50

Counterfeits of Nos. C1-C18 are plentiful.

REGISTRATION STAMPS

Catalogue values for unused stamps in this section are for Never Hinged items.

Arms Type of 1992

1992, Mar. 16 **Litho.** *Perf. 13x12½*

F1	A42	R (10r) pink & red	*2.25*	*2.25*

OCCUPATION STAMPS

Issued under German Occupation
For Use in Tartu (Dorpat)

Russian Stamps of 1909-12 Surcharged **20 Pfg.**

1918 **Unwmk.** *Perf. 14x14½*

N1	A15	20pf on 10k dk bl	20.00	*27.50*
N2	A8	40pf on 20k bl & car	20.00	*27.50*

Forged overprints exist.

Estonian Arms and Swastika — OS1

Perf. 11½

1941, Aug. **Typo.** **Unwmk.**

N3	OS1	15k brown	7.50	7.50
N4	OS1	20k green	5.50	5.50
N5	OS1	30k dark blue	5.50	5.50

Exist imperf. Value, set, $60.
Nos. N3-N5 were issued on both ordinary paper with colorless gum and thick chalky paper with yellow gum. Same values.

OCCUPATION SEMI-POSTAL STAMPS

Castle Tower, Tallinn — OSP1

Designs: 20k+20k, Stone Bridge, Tartu, horiz. 30k+30k, Narva Castle, horiz. 50k+50k, Tallinn view, horiz. 60k+60k, Tartu University. 100k+100k, Narva Castle, close view.

Paper with Gray Network

Perf. 11½

1941, Sept. 29 **Photo.** **Unwmk.**

NB1	OSP1	15k + 15k dk brn	45	*1.50*
NB2	OSP1	20k + 20k red lil	45	*1.50*
NB3	OSP1	30k + 30k dk bl	45	*1.50*
NB4	OSP1	50k + 50k bluish grn	60	*2.50*
NB5	OSP1	60k + 60k car	75	*2.50*
NB6	OSP1	100k + 100k gray	1.40	*3.00*
		Nos. NB1-NB6 (6)	4.10	*12.50*

Nos. NB1-NB6 exist imperf. Value, set unused $20, used $40.
A miniature sheet containing one each of Nos. NB1-NB6, imperf., exists in various colors. It was not postally valid. Reproductions are common.

ETHIOPIA

(Abyssinia)

LOCATION — Northeastern Africa
GOVT. — Republic (1988)
AREA — 471,800 sq. mi.
POP. — 40,000,000 (est. 1984)
CAPITAL — Addis Ababa

During the Italian occupation (1936-1941) Nos. N1-N7 were used, also stamps of Italian East Africa, Eritrea and Somalia.
During the British administration (1941-42) stamps of Great Britain and Kenya were used when available.

16 Guerche = 1 Menelik Dollar or 1 Maria Theresa Dollar
100 Centimes = 1 Franc (1905)
40 Paras = 1 Piaster (1908)
16 Mehalek = 1 Thaler or Talari (1928)
100 Centimes = 1 Thaler (1936)
100 Cents = 1 Ethiopian Dollar (1946)
100 Cents = 1 Birr (1978)

Catalogue values for unused stamps in this country are for Never Hinged items, beginning with Scott 268 in the regular postage section, Scott B6 in the semi-postal section, Scott C21 in the airpost section, Scott E1 in the special delivery section, and Scott J57 in the postage due section.

Watermark

Wmk. 282- Ethiopian Star and Amharic Characters, Multiple

Excellent forgeries of Nos. 1-86 exist.

On March 9, 1894 Menelik II awarded Alfred Ilg a concession to develop a railway, including postal service. Ilg's stamps were valid locally and to Djibouti. Mail to other countries had to bear stamps of Obock, Somali Coast, etc.
Ethiopia joined the UPU Nov. 1, 1908.

Menelik II — A1

Lion of Judah — A2

Perf. 14x13½

1894, Nov. 24 **Unwmk.** **Typo.**

1	A1	¼g green	1.75	1.75
2	A1	½g red	1.40	1.40
3	A1	1g blue	1.40	1.40
4	A1	2g dark brown	1.40	1.40
5	A2	4g lilac brown	1.40	1.40
6	A2	8g violet	1.40	1.40
7	A2	16g black	1.50	1.50
		Nos. 1-7 (7)	10.25	10.25

For 4g, 8g and 16g stamps of type A1, see Nos. J3a, J4a, and J7a.
Earliest reported use is Jan. 29, 1895.
Forged cancellations are plentiful.
For overprints see Nos. 8-86, J8-J28, J36-J42. For surcharges see Nos. 94-100, J29-J35.

Nos. 1-7 Handstamped in Violet or Blue **Ethiopie**

Overprint 9½x2¼mm, Serifs on "E"

1901, July 1

8	A1	¼g green	8.00	8.00
9	A1	½g red	8.00	8.00
10	A1	1g blue	8.00	8.00
11	A1	2g dark brown	8.00	8.00
12	A2	4g lilac brown	11.00	11.00
13	A2	8g violet	14.00	14.00
14	A2	16g black	15.00	15.00
		Nos. 8-14 (7)	72.00	72.00

Overprints 9¼mm and 8¼mm wide are official reproductions, value, set $25.

Nos. 1-7 Handstamped in Violet, Blue or Black **ቦስጣ።**

Overprint 11x3mm, Low Colons

1902, Apr. 1

15	A1	¼g green	3.75	3.75
16	A1	½g red	4.50	3.75
17	A1	1g blue	5.75	5.75
18	A1	2g dark brown	5.75	5.75
19	A2	4g lilac brown	9.50	9.50
20	A2	8g violet	13.00	13.00
21	A2	16g black	22.50	22.50
		Nos. 15-21 (7)	64.75	64.00

The handstamp reads "Bosta" (Post).
Overprints 10¾mm and 11mm wide with raised colons are official reproductions, value, set $25.

Nos. 1-7 Handstamped in Violet, Blue or Black **መልክት።**

Overprint 16x3¾mm

1903, Jan. 1

22	A1	¼g green	4.00	4.00
a.		On No. 15		
23	A1	½g red	4.00	4.00
24	A1	1g blue	5.75	5.75
a.		On No. 17		
25	A1	2g dark brown	7.75	7.75
26	A2	4g lilac brown	7.75	7.75
27	A2	8g violet	17.50	17.50
28	A2	16g black	24.00	24.00
		Nos. 22-28 (7)	70.75	70.75

The handstamp reads "Malekt." (Message).
Originals have blurred colons. Official reproductions have clean colons, value, set $25.

Nos. 1-7 Handstamped in Violet or Blue **ምልክት**

Overprint 18¼mm Wide

1903, Dec. 1

36	A1	¼g green	10.00
37	A1	½g red	10.00
38	A1	1g blue	12.00
39	A1	2g dark brown	15.00
40	A2	4g lilac brown	20.00
41	A2	8g violet	32.50
42	A2	16g black	47.50
		Nos. 36-42 (7)	147.00

The handstamp reads "Malekathe" (message). This set was never issued.

Preceding Issues Surcharged with New Values in French Currency in Blue, Violet, Rose or Black:

05 a **1,60** b

1905, Jan. 1

On Nos. 1-7

43	A1 (a)	5c on ¼g	5.00	5.00
44	A1 (a)	10c on ½g	5.00	5.00
45	A1 (a)	20c on 1g	5.00	5.00
46	A1 (a)	40c on 2g	6.50	6.50
47	A2 (a)	80c on 4g	11.00	11.00
48	A2 (b)	1.60fr on 8g	10.00	14.00
49	A2 (b)	3.20fr on 16g	20.00	20.00
		Nos. 43-49 (7)	62.50	66.50

Nos. 48-49 exist with period or comma.

On No. 8

50	A1 (a)	5c on ¼g	75.00	75.00

On Nos. 15-16

51	A1 (a)	5c on ¼g	15.00	15.00
51B	A1 (a)	10c on ½g	*180.00*	*180.00*

On No. 22

52	A1 (a)	5c on ¼g	32.50	32.50

On No. 36

53	A1 (a)	5c on ¼g	35.00	35.00

Official reproductions, value, Nos. 50, 51, 52, $10, No. 51B, $20. The 20c, 40c, 80c, and 1.60fr surcharges exist as official reproductions only. Value, each $15.

5%m
c

5
centimes.
d

1905

On No. 2

54	A1 (c)	5c on half of ½g	3.50	3.50

On Nos. 15 & 21

54B	A1 (c)	5c on ¼g grn	50.00	50.00
55	A2 (d)	5c on 16g blk	90.00	90.00

On No. 28

56	A2 (d)	5c on 16g blk	90.00	90.00

Nos. 55-56 issued Mar. 2.

The overprints and surcharges on Nos. 8 to 56 inclusive were handstamped, the work being very roughly done. Apparently any color of ink that was at hand was used.

As is usual with handstamped overprints and surcharges there are many inverted and double.

Surcharged with New Values in Various Colors

and in Violet:

1906, Jan. 1

57	A1	5c on ¼g grn	4.25	4.25
58	A1	10c on ½g red	5.75	5.75
59	A1	20c on 1g blue	5.75	5.75
60	A1	40c on 2g dk brn	5.75	5.75
61	A2	80c on 4g lil brn	7.25	7.25
62	A2	1.60fr on 8g vio	10.00	10.00
63	A2	3.20fr on 16g blk	27.50	27.50
		Nos. 57-63 (7)	66.25	66.25

Two types of the 4-character overprint ("Menelik"): 15x3½mm (Addis Ababa) and 16½x4½mm (Harar).

Surcharged with New Values

and in Violet: ምኒልክ።

1906, July 1

64	A1	5c on ¼g grn	4.75	4.75
a.		Surcharged "20"	40.00	40.00
65	A1	10c on ½g red	5.75	5.75
66	A1	20c on 1g blue	8.00	8.00
67	A1	40c on 2g dk brn	8.00	8.00
68	A2	80c on 4g lil brn	11.00	11.00
69	A2	1.60fr on 8g vio	11.00	11.00
70	A2	3.20fr on 16g blk	27.50	27.50
		Nos. 64-70 (7)	76.00	76.00

The control overprint reads "Menelik."

Surcharged in Violet:

ዳግማዊ። ዳግማዊ።

☆1/2☆ ✳ 1.✳
e f

1907, July 1

71	A1 (e)	¼ on ¼g grn	5.00	5.00
72	A1 (e)	½ on ½g red	5.00	5.00
73	A1 (f)	1 on 1g blue	6.00	6.00
74	A1 (f)	2 on 2g dk brn	7.25	7.25
a.		Surcharged "40"	45.00	
75	A2 (f)	4 on 4g lil brn	7.25	7.25
a.		Surcharged "80"	42.50	
76	A2 (f)	8 on 8g vio	15.00	15.00
77	A2 (f)	16 on 16g blk	20.00	20.00
		Nos. 71-77 (7)	65.50	65.50

Nos. 71-72 are also found with stars farther away from figures.

The control overprint reads "Dagmawi" ("Second"), meaning Emperor Menelik II.

Nos. 2, 23 Surcharged in Blue

1
PIASTRE

1908, Mar. 25

78	A1	1pi on ½g red (#2)	6.00	6.00
79	A1	1pi on ½g red (#23)		

Earliest known use is Aug. 1908.

Official reproductions exist. Value, set $25.

Forgeries exist.

The surcharges on Nos. 57-79 are handstamped and are found double, inverted, etc.

Surcharged in Black

1/4
piastre

1908, Nov. 1

80	A1	¼p on ¼g grn	1.00	1.00
81	A1	½p on ½g red	1.00	1.00
82	A1	1p on 1g blue	1.50	1.50
83	A1	2p on 2g dk brn	2.50	2.50
84	A2	4p on 4g lil brn	3.75	3.75
85	A2	8p on 8g vio	8.00	8.00
86	A2	16p on 16g blk	12.50	12.50
		Nos. 80-86 (7)	30.25	30.25

Surcharges on Nos. 80-85 are found double, inverted, etc.

These are the 1st stamps valid for international mail.

King Solomon's Throne — A3

Menelik in Native Costume — A4

Menelik in Royal Dress — A5

1909, Jan. *Perf. 11½*

87	A3	¼g blue green	48	40
88	A3	½g rose	48	40
89	A3	1g grn & org	2.75	1.00
90	A4	2g blue	2.00	1.25
91	A4	4g grn & car	3.00	2.50
92	A5	8g ver & dp grn	5.00	3.75
93	A5	16g ver & car	7.25	6.00
		Nos. 87-93 (7)	20.96	15.30

For overprints see Nos. 101-115, J43-J49, J55-J56. For surcharges see Nos. 116-119.

Nos. 1-7 Handstamped and Surcharged in ms.

AFF EXCEP
FAUTE TIMB
8 g.

1911, Oct. 1 *Perf. 14x13½*

94	A1	¼g on ¼g grn	90.00	37.50
95	A1	½g on ½g red	90.00	37.50
96	A1	1g on 1g blue	90.00	37.50
97	A1	2g on 2g dk brn	90.00	37.50
98	A2	4g on 4g lil brn	90.00	37.50
99	A2	8g on 8g vio	90.00	37.50
100	A2	16g on 16g blk	90.00	37.50
		Nos. 94-100 (7)	630.00	262.50

Nos. 94-100 are provisionals used at Dire-Dawa for 5 days. The overprint is abbreviated from "Affranchissement Exceptionnel Faute Timbres" (Special Franking Lacking Stamps). Nos. 94-100 exist without surcharge. Forgeries exist.

Stamps of 1909 Handstamped in Violet or Black:

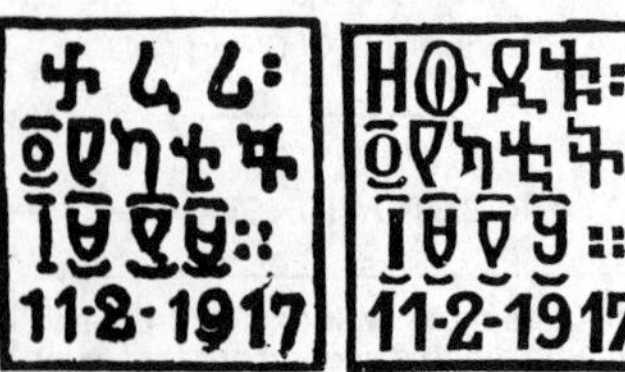

Nos. 101-102 Nos. 104-107

1917, Mar. 30 *Perf. 11½*

101	A3	¼g bl grn (V)	2.75	2.75
102	A3	½g rose (V)	2.75	2.75
104	A4	2g blue (Bk)	3.50	3.50
105	A4	4g grn & car (Bk)	6.25	6.25
106	A5	8g ver & dp grn (Bk)	10.50	10.50
107	A5	16g ver & car (Bk)	22.50	22.50
		Nos. 101-107 (6)	48.25	48.25

Coronation of Empress Zauditu and appointment of Prince Tafari as Regent and Heir to the throne.

Exist with overprint inverted and double.

Stamps of 1909 Overprinted in Blue, Black or Red:

11/2/1917 11/2/1917
Nos. 108-111 Nos. 112-115

1917, Apr. 5

108	A3	¼g bl grn (Bl)	22	22
109	A3	½g rose (Bl)	22	22
110	A3	1g grn & org (Bl)	1.50	1.50
111	A4	2g blue (R)	60.00	65.00
112	A4	2g blue (Bk)	26	22
113	A4	4g grn & car (Bl)	65	65
a.		Black overprint	8.75	8.75
114	A5	8g ver & dp grn (Bl)	52	52
115	A5	16g ver & car (Bl)	90	90
		Nos. 108-115 (8)	64.27	69.23

Coronation of Empress Zauditu.

Nos. 108-115 all exist with double overprint, inverted overprint, double overprint, one inverted, and various combinations.

Nos. 114-115 with Additional Surcharge

1/4 1/2 1 2
k l m n

1917, May 28

116	A5 (k)	¼g on 8g	2.00	2.00
117	A5 (l)	½g on 8g	2.00	2.00
118	A5 (m)	1g on 16g	5.25	5.25
119	A5 (n)	2g on 16g	5.25	5.25

Nos. 116-119 all exist with the numerals double and inverted and No. 116 with the Amharic surcharge missing.

Sommering's Gazelle — A6

Prince Tafari — A9

Cathedral of St. George — A12

Empress Waizeri Zauditu — A18

Designs: ¼g, Giraffes. ½g, Leopard. 2g, Prince Tafari (diff.). 4g, Prince Tafari (diff.). 8g, White rhinoceros. 12g, Somali ostriches. 1t, African elephant. 2t, Water buffalo. 3t, Lions. 5t, 10t, Empress Zauditu.

1919, July 16 **Typo.** *Perf. 11½*

120	A6	⅛g vio & brn	15	15
121	A6	¼g bl grn & db	15	15
122	A6	½g scar & ol grn	15	15
123	A9	1g rose lil & gray grn	15	15
124	A9	2g dp ultra & fawn	15	15
125	A9	4g turq bl & org	15	*1.50*
126	A12	6g lt bl & org	15	15
127	A12	8g ol grn & blk brn	20	15
128	A12	12g red vio & gray	30	16
129	A12	1t rose & gray blk	52	22
130	A12	2t blk & brn	1.40	
131	A12	3t grn & dp org	1.50	1.10
132	A18	4t brn & lil rose	1.75	1.50
133	A18	5t car & gray	2.25	2.25
134	A18	10t gray grn & bis	4.50	3.00
		Nos. 120-134 (15)	13.47	

No. 130 was not issued.

For overprints see Nos. J50-J54. For surcharges see Nos. 135-154.

Reprints have brownish gum that is cracked diagonally. Originals have smooth, white gum. Reprints exist imperf. and some values with inverted centers. Value for set, unused or canceled, $1.50.

No. 132 Surcharged in Blue

፬ ግርሽ ።
4guerches

1919, Oct.

135	A18	4g on 4t brn & lil rose	90	90

The Amharic surcharge indicates the new value and, therefore, varies on Nos. 135 to 154. There are numerous defective letters and figures, several types of the "2" of "½," the errors "guerhce," "gnerche," etc.

Stamps of 1919 Surcharged

አንድ ፡
ግርሽ ።
1 guerche

1921-22

136	A6	½g on ⅛g vio & brn ('22)	50	50
137	A6	1g on ¼g grn & db	50	50
138	A9	2g on 1g lil brn & gray grn ('22)	75	75
139	A18	2g on 4t brn & lil rose ('22)	27.50	27.50
140	A6	2½g on ½g scar & ol grn	75	75
141	A9	4g on 2g ultra & fawn ('22)	75	75
		Nos. 136-141 (6)	30.75	30.75

No. 139 has been forged.

Stamps and Type of 1919 Surcharged

፩ ግርሽ ፡
1 guerche

1925-28

142	A12	½g on 1t rose & gray blk ('26)	75	75
a.		Without colon ('28)	10.00	10.00
143	A18	½g on 5t car & gray ('26)	40	40
144	A12	1g on 6g bl & org	40	40
145	A12	1g on 12g lil & gray	80.00	80.00
146	A12	1g on 3t grn & org ('26)	17.50	17.50
147	A18	1g on 10t gray grn & bis ('26)	50	50
		Nos. 142-147 (6)	99.55	99.55

On No. 142 the surcharge is at the left side of the stamp, reading upward. On No. 142a it is at the right, reading downward. The two surcharges are from different, though similar, settings. On No. 146 the surcharge is at the right, reading upward. See note following No. 154.

There are many irregularly produced settings in imitation of Nos. 136-154 which differ slightly from the originals.

Type of 1919 Surcharged

፩ ገርሽ ፡

= 1 guerche =

1926

147A	A12	1g on 12g lil & gray	55.00	55.00

Forgeries exist.

Nos. 126-128 Surcharged

አንድ ፡ ግርሽ ፡

1 guerche 

1926

148	A12	½g on 8g	1.00	1.00
149	A12	1g on 6g	22.50	22.50
150	A12	1g on 12g	65.00	65.00

Nos. 126-128, 131 Surcharged

የግርሽ ፡ አላድ ፡

1/2 guerche 

1927

151	A12	½g on 8g	75	75
152	A12	1g on 6g	35.00	35.00
153	A12	1g on 12g	1.00	1.00
154	A12	1g on 3t	80.00	80.00

Many varieties of surcharge, such as double, inverted, lines transposed or omitted, and inverted "2" in "½," exist on Nos. 136-154.

Forgeries of No. 154 exist.

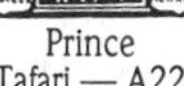

Prince Tafari — A22

Empress Zauditu — A23

1928, Sept. 5 Typo. *Perf. 13½x14*

155	A22	⅛m org & lt bl	40	32
156	A23	¼m ind & red org	24	24
157	A22	½m gray grn & blk	40	32
158	A23	1m dk car & blk	24	20
159	A22	2m dk bl & blk	24	20
160	A23	4m yel & olive	24	20
161	A22	8m vio & olive	65	48
162	A23	1t org brn & vio	80	65
163	A22	2t grn & bister	1.10	1.10
164	A23	3t choc & grn	1.65	1.25
		Nos. 155-164 (10)	5.96	4.96

For surcharges see Nos. 217-230. For overprints see Nos. 165-209, C1-C10.

Preceding Issue Overprinted in Black, Violet or Red

፲፱፻፳
ፖ፡ ቴ፡ ቴ፡
የተመረቀበት፡
ቀን፡ መታሰቢያ፡

1928, Sept. 1

165	A22	⅛m (Bk)	85	85
166	A23	¼m (V)	85	85
167	A22	½m (V)	85	85
168	A23	1m (V)	85	85
169	A22	2m (R)	85	85
170	A23	4m (Bk)	85	85
171	A22	8m (R)	85	85
172	A23	1t (Bk)	85	85
173	A22	2t (R)	1.25	1.25
174	A23	3t (R)	1.75	1.75
		Nos. 165-174 (10)	9.80	9.80

Opening of General Post Office, Addis Ababa.

Exist with overprint inverted, double, double, one inverted, etc.

Nos. 155, 157, 159, 161, 163 Handstamped in Violet, Red or Black

ንጉሥ፡ ተፈሪ፡
NEGOUS TEFERI

1928, Oct. 7

175	A22	⅛m (V)	90	90
176	A22	½m (R)	90	90
177	A22	2m (R)	90	90
178	A22	8m (Bk)	90	90
179	A22	2t (V)	90	90
		Nos. 175-179 (5)	4.50	4.50

Crowning of Prince Tafari as king (Negus) on Oct. 7, 1928.

Nos. 175-177 exist with overprint vertical, inverted, double, etc.

Forgeries exist.

Nos. 155-164 Overprinted in Red or Green

ቀዳማዊ
ኃይለ ሥላሴ
መንግሥተ ጽጌ ቀን
፲፱፻፳፪
HAYLE SELASSIE 1er
3 Avril 1930

1930, Apr. 3

180	A22	⅛m org & lt bl (R)	18	15
181	A23	¼m ind & red org (G)	22	18
182	A22	½m gray grn & blk (R)	18	15
183	A23	1m dk car & blk (G)	22	18
184	A22	2m dk bl & blk (R)	22	18
185	A23	4m yel & ol (R)	35	25
186	A22	8m vio & ol (R)	65	65
187	A23	1t org brn & vio (R)	1.50	1.50
188	A22	2t grn & bis (R)	2.00	2.00
189	A23	3t choc & grn (R)	2.50	2.50
		Nos. 180-189 (10)	8.02	7.74

Proclamation of King Tafari as King of Kings of Abyssinia under the name "Haile Selassie."

A similar overprint, set in four vertical lines, was printed on all denominations of the 1928 issue. It was not considered satisfactory and was rejected. The trial impressions were not placed on sale to the public, but some copies reached private hands and have been passed through the post.

Nos. 155-164 Overprinted in Red or Olive Brown

ቀዳማዊ ፡
ኃይለ ፡ ሥላሴ ፡
መንግሥት፡ጽጌ፡ቀን፡
፲፱፻፳፪
HAILE SELASSIE 1er
3 Avril 1930

1930, Apr. 3

190	A22	⅛m orange & lt bl	22	16
191	A23	¼m ind & red org (OB)	22	22
192	A22	½m gray grn & blk	22	16
193	A23	1m dk car & blk (OB)	22	22
194	A22	2m dk blue & blk	22	22
195	A23	4m yellow & ol	42	42
196	A22	8m violet & ol	65	65
197	A23	1t org brn & vio	1.50	1.50
198	A22	2t green & bister	2.00	2.00
199	A23	3t choc & grn	2.50	2.50
		Nos. 190-199 (10)	8.17	8.05

Proclamation of King Tafari as Emperor Haile Selassie.

All stamps of this series exist with "H" of "HAILE" omitted and with many other varieties.

Nos. 155-164 Handstamped in Violet or Red

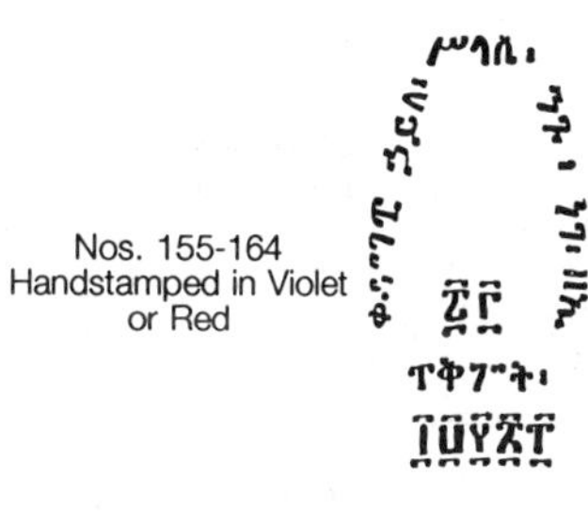

1930, Nov. 2

200	A22	⅛m (V)	25	20
201	A23	¼m (V)	25	20
202	A22	½m (R)	25	20
203	A23	1m (V)	25	20
204	A22	2m (R)	25	20
205	A23	4m (V)	25	20
206	A22	8m (V or R)	60	60
207	A23	1t (V)	85	85
208	A22	2t (V or R)	1.25	1.25
209	A23	3t (V or R)	1.90	1.90
		Nos. 200-209 (10)	6.10	5.80

Coronation of Emperor Haile Selassie, Nov. 2, 1930.

Haile Selassie Coronation Monument, Symbols of Empire — A24

1930, Nov. 23 Engr. *Perf. 12½*

210	A24	1g orange	18	18
211	A24	2g ultra	18	18
212	A24	4g violet	18	18
213	A24	8g dull green	32	28
214	A24	1t brown	45	45
215	A24	3t green	70	70
216	A24	5t red brown	70	70
		Nos. 210-216 (7)	2.71	2.67

Coronation of Emperor Haile Selassie.

Reprints of Nos. 210 to 216 exist. Colors are more yellow and the ink is thicker and slightly glossy. Ink on the originals is dull and granular. Value 15c each.

Nos. 158-160, 164 Surcharged in Green, Red or Blue

የመሐለቅ ፳ተኛ

1/8 Mehalek

የመሐለቅ ግማሽ — Type I

የመሐለቅ ፳ተኛ — Type II

1931, Mar. 20 *Perf. 13½x14*

217	A23	⅛m on 1m	25	25
218	A22	⅛m on 2m (R)	25	25
219	A23	⅛m on 4m	25	25
220	A23	¼m on 1m (Bl)	25	25
221	A22	¼m on 2m (R)	65	65
222	A23	¼m on 4m	65	65
225	A23	½m on 1m (Bl)	65	65
226	A22	½m on 2m (R)	65	65
227	A23	½m on 4m, type II	65	65
a.		½m on 4m, type I	6.25	6.25
228	A23	½m on 3t (R)	5.00	5.00
230	A22	1m on 2m (R)	85	85
		Nos. 217-230 (11)	10.10	10.10

The ½m on ⅛m orange & light blue and ½m on ¼m indigo & red orange were clandestinely printed and never sold at the post office.

No. 230 with double surcharge in red and blue is a color trial.

Many varieties exist.

Issued: 2g, Aug. 3; 4g, Sept. 24; others, June 27.

Prince Makonnen — A25

Empress Menen — A27

View of Hawash River and Railroad Bridge A26

Designs: 2g, 8g, Haile Selassie (profile). 4g, 1t, Statue of Menelik II. 3t, Empress Menen (full face). 5t, Haile Selassie (full face).

Perf. 12½, 12x12½, 12½x12

1931 Engr.

232	A25	⅛g red	15	15
233	A26	¼g olive green	15	15
234	A25	½g dark violet	20	15
235	A27	1g red orange	20	20
236	A27	2g ultra	25	25
237	A25	4g violet	35	35
238	A27	8g blue green	1.10	1.10
239	A25	1t chocolate	2.00	2.00
240	A27	3t yellow green	3.25	3.25
241	A27	5t red brown	6.00	5.00
		Nos. 232-241 (10)	13.65	12.60

For overprints see Nos. B1-B5. For surcharges see Nos. 242-246.

Reprints of Nos. 232-236, 238-240 are on thinner and whiter paper than the originals. On originals the ink is dull and granular. On reprints, heavy, caked and shiny. Value 15c each.

Nos. 232-236 Surcharged in Blue or Carmine similar to cut

2 c

፪ ሳንቲም

1936, Apr. 1 *Perf. 12x12½, 12½x12*

242	A25	1c on ⅛g red	1.10	75
243	A26	2c on ¼g ol grn (C)	1.10	75
244	A25	3c on ½g dk vio	1.10	85
245	A27	5c on 1g red org	2.00	1.25
246	A27	10c on 2g ultra (C)	2.50	1.50
		Nos. 242-246 (5)	7.80	5.10

Haile Selassie I

A32 A33

1942, Mar. 23 Litho. *Perf. 14x13½*

247	A32	4c lt bl grn, ind & blk	28	22
248	A32	10c rose, indigo & blk	90	45
249	A32	20c dp ultra, ind & blk	1.75	80

1942-43 Unwmk.

250	A33	4c lt bl grn & indigo	18	15
251	A33	8c yel org & indigo	22	15
252	A33	10c rose & indigo	35	18
253	A33	12c dull vio & indigo	38	22
254	A33	20c dp ultra & indigo	55	35
255	A33	25c dull grn & indigo	95	52
256	A33	50c dull brn & indigo	1.25	85
257	A33	60c lilac & indigo	2.25	1.10
		Nos. 250-257 (8)	6.13	3.52

Issued: 25c, 50c, 60c, Apr. 1, 1943; others, June 22, 1942.

For surcharges see #258-262, 284, C18-C20.

ኦበሊስክ :
OBELISK
3 Nov. 1943

Nos. 250-254 Surcharged in Black or Brown

፴
3

1943, Nov. 3

258	A33	5c on 4c	26.00	26.00
259	A33	10c on 8c	26.00	26.00
260	A33	15c on 10c	26.00	26.00
261	A33	20c on 12c (Br)	26.00	26.00
262	A33	30c on 20c (Br)	26.00	26.00
		Nos. 258-262 (5)	130.00	130.00

Restoration of the Obelisk in Myazzia Place, Addis Ababa, and the 14th anniv. of the coronation of Emperor Haile Selassie.

On No. 262, "3" is surcharged on "2" of "20" to make "30."

A small number of handstamped sets exist.

Palace of Menelik II A34

Menelik II — A35

Statue — A36

Designs: 50c, Mausoleum. 65c, Menelik II (with scepter).

1944, Dec. 31 Litho. *Perf. 10½*

263	A34	5c green	1.25	65
264	A35	10c red lilac	1.75	85
265	A36	20c deep blue	3.00	1.75
266	A34	50c dull purple	3.50	1.75
267	A35	65c bister brown	6.50	2.75
		Nos. 263-267 (5)	16.00	7.75

Cent. of the birth of Menelik II, Aug. 18, 1844.

Catalogue values for unused stamps in this section, from this point to the end of the section, are for Never Hinged items.

Unissued Semi-Postal Stamps Overprinted in Carmine:

Nurse & Baby — A39

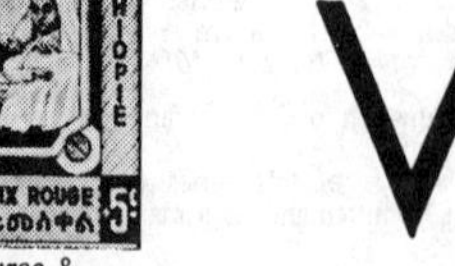

Various Designs Inscribed "Croix Rouge"

1945, Aug. 7 Photo. *Perf. 11½*

268	A39	5c brt green	40	40
269	A39	10c brt red	40	40
270	A39	25c brt blue	40	40
271	A39	50c dk yellow brn	2.25	1.75
272	A39	1t brt violet	3.50	2.50
		Nos. 268-272 (5)	6.95	5.45

Nos. 268-272 without overprint were ordered printed in Switzerland before Ethiopia fell to the invading Italians, so were not delivered to Addis Ababa. After that country's liberation, the set was overprinted "V" and issued for ordinary postage. These stamps exist without overprint, but were not so issued. Value $1.25.

Forged overprints exist.

For surcharges see Nos. B11-B15, B36-B40.

Lion of Judah A44

Menelik II A45

Mail Transport, Old and New A46

Designs: 50c, Old Post Office, Addis Ababa. 70c, Menelik II and Haile Selassie.

1947, Apr. 18 Engr. *Perf. 13*

273	A44	10c yellow org	1.75	60
274	A45	20c deep blue	2.25	75
275	A46	30c orange brn	3.50	1.25
276	A46	50c dk slate grn	8.00	2.50
277	A46	70c red violet	15.00	5.00
		Nos. 273-277 (5)	30.50	10.10

50th anniv. of Ethiopia's postal system.

Haile Selassie and Franklin D. Roosevelt — A49

Design: 65c, Roosevelt and US Flags.

Engraved and Photogravure

1947, May 23 Unwmk. *Perf. 12½*

278	A49	12c car lake & bl grn	35	20
279	A49	25c dk blue & rose	75	40
280	A49	65c blk, red & dp bl	1.50	1.00
		Nos. 278-280,C21-C22 (5)	12.60	10.10

King Sahle Selassie Reclining A50

King Sahle Selassie — A52

Design: 30c, View of Ankober.

1947, May 1 Engr. *Perf. 13*

281	A50	20c deep blue	1.50	75
282	A50	30c dark purple	2.50	1.00
283	A52	$1 deep green	6.00	3.00

150th anniversary of Selassie dynasty.

No. 255 Surcharged in Orange

12 centimes
፲፪ ሳንቲም

1947, July 14 *Perf. 14x13½*

284	A33	12c on 25c	40.00	40.00

Amba Alaguie A53

Designs: 2c, Trinity Church. 4c, Debra Sina. 5c, Mecan, near Achanguie. 8c, Lake Tana. 12c, 15c, Parliament Building, Addis Ababa. 20c, Aiba, near Mai Cheo. 30c, Bahr Bridge over Blue Nile. 60c, 70c, Canoe on Lake Tana. $1, Omo Falls. $3, Mt. Alamata. $5, Ras Dashan Mountains.

Perf. 13x13½

1947-53 Engr. Wmk. 282

285	A53	1c rose violet	15	15
286	A53	2c blue violet	15	15
a.		Unwatermarked ('51)		
287	A53	4c green	25	15
288	A53	5c dark green	25	15
289	A53	8c deep orange	40	20
290	A53	12c red	50	20
290A	A53	15c dk ol brn ('53)	45	20
291	A53	20c blue	75	30
292	A53	30c orange brown	1.25	40
292A	A53	60c red ('51)	1.50	70
293	A53	70c rose lilac	2.00	50
294	A53	$1 dk carmine rose	3.50	50
295	A53	$3 bright blue	9.00	2.00
296	A53	$5 olive	15.00	4.00
		Nos. 285-296 (14)	35.15	9.60

Issue dates: 15c, May 25, 1953; 60c, Feb. 10, 1951; others, Aug. 23, 1947.

For overprints see Nos. 355-356. For surcharges see Nos. B6-B10, B16-B20.

Empress Waizero Menen and Emperor Haile Selassie A54

1949, May 5 Wmk. 282 *Perf. 13*

297	A54	20c blue	1.00	50
298	A54	30c yellow org	1.00	65
299	A54	50c purple	2.50	1.25
300	A54	80c green	3.00	1.50
301	A54	$1 red	5.50	2.50
		Nos. 297-301 (5)	13.00	6.40

Central ornaments differ on each denomination.

8th anniv. of Ethiopia's liberation from Italian occupation.

Dejach Balcha Hospital A55

Abuna Petros — A56

Designs: 20c, Haile Selassie raising flag. 30c, Lion of Judah statue. 50c, Empress Waizero Menen, Haile Selassie and building.

Perf. 13x13½, 13½x13

1950, Nov. 2 Engr. Wmk. 282

302	A55	5c purple	60	30
303	A56	10c deep plum	1.50	60
304	A56	20c deep carmine	2.00	75
305	A56	30c green	3.50	1.50
306	A55	50c deep blue	6.00	3.00
		Nos. 302-306 (5)	13.60	6.15

20th anniv. of the coronation of Emperor Haile Selassie and Empress Menen.

Abbaye Bridge — A57

1951, Jan. 1 Unwmk. *Perf. 14*

308	A57	5c dk green & dk brn	3.50	30
309	A57	10c dp orange & blk	5.00	35
310	A57	15c dp blue & org brn	7.00	50
311	A57	30c olive & lil rose	12.50	65
312	A57	60c brown & dp bl	17.50	1.50
313	A57	80c purple & green	22.50	2.25
		Nos. 308-313 (6)	68.00	5.55

Issued to commemorate the opening of the Abbaye Bridge over the Blue Nile.

Tomb of Prince Makonnen A58

1951, Mar. 2

Center in Black

314	A58	5c dark green	1.75	25
315	A58	10c deep ultra	1.75	35
316	A58	15c blue	2.50	35
317	A58	30c claret	6.00	1.35
318	A58	80c rose carmine	8.00	2.00
319	A58	$1 orange brown	10.00	2.00
		Nos. 314-319 (6)	30.00	6.30

55th anniversary of the Battle of Adwa.

Emperor Haile Selassie — A59

1952, July 23 *Perf. 13½*

320 A59 5c dark green 35 20
321 A59 10c red orange 60 25
322 A59 15c black 85 35
323 A59 25c ultra 1.25 35
324 A59 30c violet 1.50 60
325 A59 50c rose red 2.25 85
326 A59 65c chocolate 3.75 1.50
Nos. 320-326 (7) 10.55 4.10

60th birthday of Haile Selassie.

Open Road to Sea — A60

Designs: 25c, 50c, Road and broken chain. 65c, Map. 80c, Allegory: Reunion. $1, Haile Selassie raising flag. $2, Ethiopian flag and seascape. $3, Haile Selassie addressing League of Nations.

Wmk. 282

1952, Sept. 11 **Engr.** *Perf. 13*

327 A60 15c brn car 75 30
328 A60 25c red brn 1.00 50
329 A60 30c yel brn 1.75 75
330 A60 50c purple 2.25 90
331 A60 65c gray 3.00 1.10
332 A60 80c bl grn 3.50 75
333 A60 $1 rose car 7.00 1.75
334 A60 $2 dp bl 13.00 3.00
335 A60 $3 magenta 27.50 5.00
Nos. 327-335 (9) 59.75 14.05

Issued to celebrate Ethiopia's federation with Eritrea, effected Sept. 11, 1952.

Haile Selassie and New Ethiopian Port — A61

Design: 15c, 30c, Haile Selassie on deck of ship.

1953, Oct. 4

337 A61 10c red & dk brn 1.25 75
338 A61 15c bl & dk grn 1.50 75
339 A61 25c org & dk brn 2.50 1.25
340 A61 30c red brn & dk grn 4.50 1.50
341 A61 50c pur & dk brn 8.50 3.25
Nos. 337-341 (5) 18.25 7.50

Federation of Ethiopia and Eritrea, 1st anniv.

Princess Tsahai at a Sickbed A62

Perf. 13x13½

1955, July 8 **Engr.** **Wmk. 282**

Cross Typo. in Red

342 A62 15c choc & ultra 1.00 50
343 A62 20c grn & org 1.50 60
344 A62 30c ultra & grn 2.50 75

Ethiopian Red Cross, 20th anniv.
For surcharges see Nos. B33-B35.

Promulgating the Constitution — A63

Bishops' Consecration by Archbishop — A64

Designs: 25c, Kagnew Battalion. 35c, Reunion with the Motherland. 50c, "Progress." 65c, Empress Waizero Menen and Emperor Haile Selassie.

Perf. 12½

1955, Nov. 3 **Unwmk.** **Engr.**

345 A63 5c grn & choc 50 25
346 A64 20c car & brn 1.10 35
347 A64 25c mag & gray 1.50 50
348 A63 35c brn & red org 2.00 65
349 A64 50c dk brn & ultra 3.00 1.00
350 A64 65c vio & car 4.25 1.50
Nos. 345-350 (6) 12.35 4.25

Silver jubilee of the coronation of Emperor Haile Selassie and Empress Waizero Menen.

Emperor Haile Selassie and Fair Emblem — A65

1955, Nov. 5 **Wmk. 282**

351 A65 5c grn & ol grn 60 15
352 A65 10c car & dp ultra 90 25
353 A65 15c vio blk & grn 1.25 35
354 A65 50c mag & red brn 1.75 90

Silver Jubilee Fair, Addis Ababa.

Nos. 291 and 292A Overprinted

የዓለም ስደተኞች ዓመት
World Refugee Year
1959-1960

1960, Apr. 7 *Perf. 13x13½*

355 A53 20c blue 35 25
356 A53 60c red 75 50

WRY, July 1, 1959-June 30, 1960.
The 60c without serifs is a trial printing.

Map of Africa, "Liberty" and Haile Selassie — A66

Emperor Haile Selassie — A67

Perf. 13½

1960, June 14 **Engr.** **Unwmk.**

357 A66 20c org & green 60 60
358 A66 80c org & violet 1.50 60
359 A66 $1 org & maroon 1.75 80

2nd Conf. of Independent African States at Tunis. Issued in sheets of 10.

1960, Nov. 2 **Wmk. 282** *Perf. 14*

360 A67 10c brown & blue 40 20
361 A67 25c vio & emerald 80 25
362 A67 50c dk bl & org yel 1.50 1.00
363 A67 65c sl grn & sal pink 2.00 1.00
364 A67 $1 ind & rose vio 3.00 1.50
Nos. 360-364 (5) 7.70 3.95

30th anniv. of the coronation of Emperor Haile Selassie.

Africa Hall, UN Economic Commission for Africa — A68

1961, Apr. 15 **Wmk. 282** *Perf. 14*

365 A68 80c ultra 1.00 50

Issued for Africa Freedom Day, Apr. 15, in sheets of 10.

Map of Ethiopia, Olive Branch A69

1961, May 5 *Perf. 13x13½*

366 A69 20c green 20 15
367 A69 30c violet blue 30 20
368 A69 $1 brown 1.25 60

20th anniv. of Ethiopia's liberation from Italian occupation.

African Wild Ass — A70

1961, June 16 **Wmk. 282** *Perf. 14*

369 A70 5c shown 15 15
370 A70 15c Eland 20 15
371 A70 25c Elephant 30 15
372 A70 35c Giraffe 40 20
373 A70 50c Beisa 50 35
374 A70 $1 Lion 1.50 85
Nos. 369-374 (6) 3.05 1.85

Issued in sheets of 10. Values are for CTO's.

Emperor Haile Selassie and Empress Waizero Menen — A71

1961, July 27 **Unwmk.** *Perf. 11*

375 A71 10c green 45 22
376 A71 50c vio bl 90 45
377 A71 $1 car rose 1.65 90

Golden wedding anniv. of the Emperor and Empress.

Warlike Horsemanship (Guks) — A72

Designs: 15c, Hockey. 20c, Bicycling. 30c, Soccer. 50c, 1960 Olympic marathon winner, Abebe Bikila.

Photogravure and Engraved

1962, Jan. 14 *Perf. 12x11½*

378 A72 10c yel grn & car 15 15
379 A72 15c pink & dk brn 20 15
380 A72 20c red & blk 25 15

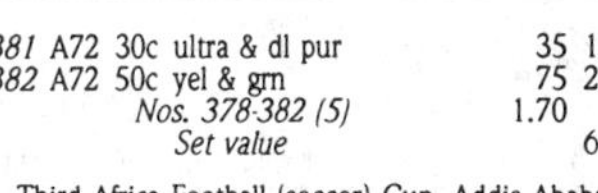

381 A72 30c ultra & dl pur 35 15
382 A72 50c yel & grn 75 25
Nos. 378-382 (5) 1.70
Set value 60

Third Africa Football (soccer) Cup, Addis Ababa, Jan. 14-22.

Malaria Eradication Emblem, World Map and Mosquito A73

Perf. 13½

1962, Apr. 7 **Wmk. 282** **Engr.**

383 A73 15c black 20 15
384 A73 30c purple 40 25
385 A73 60c red brown 1.00 60

WHO drive to eradicate malaria.

Abyssinian Ground Hornbill — A74

Birds: 15c, Abyssinian roller. 30c, Bataleur, vert. 50c, Double-toothed barbet, vert. $1, Didric cuckoo.

Perf. 11½

1962, May 5 **Unwmk.** **Photo.**

Granite Paper

386 A74 5c multi 20 15
387 A74 15c emer, brn & ultra 40 15
388 A74 30c lt brn, blk & red 75 25
389 A74 50c multi 1.50 60
390 A74 $1 multi 3.00 1.25
Nos. 386-390 (5) 5.85 2.40

See Nos. C77-C81, C97-C101, C107-C111.

Assab Hospital A75

Designs: 15c, School at Assab. 20c, Church at Massawa. 50c, Mosque at Massava. 60c, Assab port.

Perf. 13½

1962, Sept. 11 **Wmk. 282** **Engr.**

391 A75 3c purple 15 15
392 A75 15c dk bl 20 15
393 A75 20c green 25 15
394 A75 50c brown 50 25
395 A75 60c car rose 75 35
Nos. 391-395 (5) 1.85
Set value 85

Federation of Ethiopia and Eritrea, 10th anniv.

King Bazen, Madonna and Stars over Bethlehem A76

Designs: 15c, Ezana, obelisks and temple. 20c, Kaleb and sailing fleet. 50c, Lalibela, rock-church and frescoes, vert. 60c, King Yekuno Amlak and Abuna Tekle Haimanot preaching in Ankober. 75c, King Zara Yacob and Maskal celebration. $1, King Lebna Dengel and battle against Mohammed Gragn.

Perf. 14½

1962, Nov. 2 **Unwmk.** **Photo.**

396 A76 10c multi 15 15
397 A76 15c multi 25 15
398 A76 20c multi 30 15
399 A76 50c multi 50 20
400 A76 60c multi 55 30

401 A76 75c multi 90 50
402 A76 $1 multi 1.25 75
Nos. 396-402 (7) 3.90 2.20

32nd anniv. of the coronation of Emperor Haile Selassie and to commemorate ancient kings and saints.

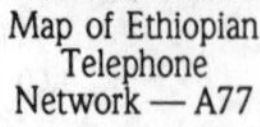

Map of Ethiopian Telephone Network — A77

Wheat Emblem — A78

Designs: 50c, Radio mast and waves. 60c, Telegraph pole and rising sun.

Perf. 13½x14

1963, Jan. 1 Engr. Wmk. 282

403 A77 10c dk red 40 15
404 A77 50c ultra 1.00 40
405 A77 60c brown 1.25 50

10th anniv. of the Imperial Board of Telecommunications.

1963, Mar. 21 Unwmk. *Perf. 13½*

406 A78 5c dp rose 15 15
407 A78 10c rose car 15 15
408 A78 15c vio bl 20 15
409 A78 30c emerald 30 20
Set value 45

FAO "Freedom from Hunger" campaign.

Abuna Salama — A79

Queen of Sheba — A80

Spiritual Leaders: 15c, Abuna Aregawi. 30c, Abuna Tekle Haimanot. 40c. Yared. 60c, Zara Yacob.

1964, Jan. 3 Unwmk. *Perf. 13½*

410 A79 10c blue 25 15
411 A79 15c dk grn 35 15
412 A79 30c brn red 60 35
413 A79 40c dk bl 1.00 60
414 A79 60c brown 1.50 1.10
Nos. 410-414 (5) 3.70 2.35

1964, Mar. 2 Photo. *Perf. 11½*

Ethiopian Empresses: 15c, Helen. 50c, Seble Wongel. 60c, Mentiwab. 80, Taitu, consort of Menelik II.

Granite Paper

415 A80 10c multi 50 15
416 A80 15c multi 60 20
417 A80 50c multi 1.25 55
418 A80 60c multi 2.00 85
419 A80 80c multi 2.50 1.25
Nos. 415-419 (5) 6.85 3.00

Priest Teaching Alphabet to Children A81

Eleanor Roosevelt (1884-1962) A82

Designs: 10c, Classroom. 15c, Woman learning to read, vert. 40c, Students in chemistry laboratory, vert. 60c, Graduation procession, vert.

1964, June 1 Unwmk. *Perf. 11½*
Granite Paper

420 A81 5c brown 15 15
421 A81 10c emerald 15 15
422 A81 15c rose vio 20 15
423 A81 40c vio bl 60 25
424 A81 60c dk pur 1.00 50
Nos. 420-424 (5) 2.10 1.20

Issued to publicize education.

1964, Oct. 11 Photo.
Granite Paper
Portrait in Slate Blue

425 A82 10c yel bis 15 15
426 A82 60c org brn 80 50
427 A82 80c grn & gold 1.00 70

King Serse Dengel and View of Gondar, 1563 A83

Ethiopian Leaders: 10c, King Fasiladas and Gondar in 1632. 20c, King Yassu the Great and Gondar in 1682. 25c, Emperor Theodore II and map of Ethiopia. 60c, Emperor John IV and Battle of Gura, 1876. 80c, Emperor Menelik II and Battle of Adwa, 1896.

1964, Dec. 12 Photo. *Perf. 14½x14*

428 A83 5c multi 15 15
429 A83 10c multi 15 15
430 A83 20c multi 28 15
431 A83 25c multi 45 18
432 A83 60c multi 90 50
433 A83 80c multi 1.10 70
Nos. 428-433 (6) 3.03 1.83

Ethiopian Rose — A84

Flowers: 10c, Kosso tree. 25c, St.-John's-wort. 35c, Parrot's-beak. 60c, Maskal daisy.

1965, Mar. 30 *Perf. 12x13½*

434 A84 5c multi 15 15
435 A84 10c multi 15 15
436 A84 25c multi 42 15
437 A84 35c multi 75 25
438 A84 60c grn, yel & org 1.00 42
Nos. 434-438 (5) 2.47
Set value 85

ITU Emblem, Old and New Communication Symbols — A85

Perf. 13½x14½

1965, May 17 Litho. Unwmk.

439 A85 5c bl, indigo & yel 15 15
440 A85 10c bl, indigo & org 25 15
441 A85 60c bl, indigo & lil rose 90 50
Set value 66

Cent. of the ITU.

Laboratory A86

Designs: 5c, Textile spinning mill. 10c, Sugar factory. 20c, Mountain road. 25c, Autobus. 30c, Diesel locomotive and bridge. 35c, Railroad station, Addis Ababa.

1965, July 19 Photo. *Perf. 11½*
Granite Paper
Portrait in Black

442 A86 3c sepia 15 15
443 A86 5c dl pur & buff 15 15
444 A86 10c blk & gray 15 15
445 A86 20c grn & pale yel 25 15
446 A86 25c dk brn & yel 35 15
447 A86 30c maroon & gray 55 25
448 A86 35c dk bl & gray 65 35
Nos. 442-448 (7) 2.25
Set value 1.00

For overprints see Nos. 609-612.

ICY Emblem — A87

1965, Oct. 24 Unwmk. *Perf. 11½*
Granite Paper

449 A87 10c bl & red brn 20 15
450 A87 50c dp bl & red brn 75 40
451 A87 80c vio bl & red brn 1.00 60

International Cooperation Year, 1965.

National Bank Emblem A88

Designs: 10c, Commercial Bank emblem. 60c, Natl. and Commercial Bank buildings.

1965, Nov. 2 Photo. *Perf. 13*

452 A88 10c dp car, blk & indigo 35 15
453 A88 30c ultra, blk & indigo 65 30
454 A88 60c blk, yel & indigo 95 50

Natl. and Commercial Banks of Ethiopia.

"Light and Peace" Press Building A89

1966, Apr. 5 Engr. *Perf. 13*

455 A89 5c pink & blk 15 15
456 A89 15c lt yel grn & blk 35 15
457 A89 30c org yel & blk 60 30
Set value 47

Opening of the "Light and Peace" Printing Press building.

Kabaro Drum — A90

Musical Instruments: 10c, Bagana harp. 35c, Messenko guitar. 50c, Krar lyre. 60c, Wachent flutes.

1966, Sept. 9 Photo. *Perf. 13½*

458 A90 5c brt grn & blk 15 15
459 A90 10c dl bl & blk 15 15
460 A90 35c org & blk 55 25
461 A90 50c yel & blk 80 35
462 A90 60c rose car & blk 1.00 60
Nos. 458-462 (5) 2.65 1.50

Emperor Haile Selassie — A91

1966, Nov. 1 Unwmk. *Perf. 12*

463 A91 10c blk, gold & grn 15 15
464 A91 15c blk, gold & dp car 30 15
465 A91 40c blk & gold 90 60
Set value 75

50 years of leadership of Emperor Haile Selassie.

UNESCO Emblem and Map of Africa A92

Perf. 13½

1966, Nov. 30 Wmk. 282 Litho.

466 A92 15c bl car & blk 35 15
467 A92 60c ol, brn & dk bl 90 45

20th anniv. of UNESCO.

WHO Headquarters, Geneva — A93

1966, Nov. 30

468 A93 5c ol, ultra & brn 20 15
469 A93 40c brn, pur & emer 65 35
Set value 40

Opening of WHO Headquarters, Geneva.

Expo '67 Ethiopian Pavilion and Columns of Axum (Replica) — A94

Perf. 12x13½

1967, May 2 Photo. Unwmk.

470 A94 30c brt bl & multi 52 22
471 A94 45c multi 65 30
472 A94 80c gray & multi 1.25 52

EXPO '67, Intl. Exhibition, Montreal, Apr. 28-Oct. 27, 1967.

Diesel Train and Map A95

1967, June 7 Photo. *Perf. 12*

473 A95 15c multi 35 15
474 A95 30c multi 75 30
475 A95 50c multi 1.25 35

Djibouti-Addis Ababa railroad, 50th anniv.

Papilionidae Aethiops A96

Various Butterflies.

Perf. 13½x13

1967, June 30 Photo. Unwmk.

476	A96	5c buff & multi	18	15
477	A96	10c lil & multi	35	15
478	A96	20c multi	65	15
479	A96	35c bl & multi	1.25	35
480	A96	40c multi	2.00	40
		Nos. 476-480 (5)	4.43	
		Set value		1.00

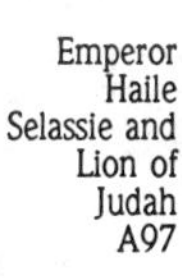

Emperor Haile Selassie and Lion of Judah A97

1967, July 21 *Perf. 11½*

Granite Paper

481	A97	10c dk brn, emer & gold	25	15
482	A97	15c dk brn, yel & gold	40	15
483	A97	$1 dk brn, red & gold	1.75	75

Souvenir Sheet

484	A97	$1 dk brn, pur & gold	4.00	3.75

75th birthday of Emperor Haile Selassie.

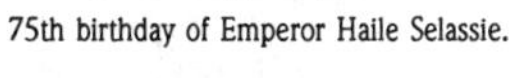

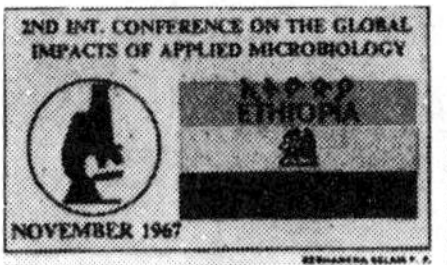

Microscope and Ethiopian Flag — A98

1967, Nov. 6 Litho. *Perf. 13*

Flag in Grn, Yel, Red & Blk

485	A98	5c blue	15	15
486	A98	30c ocher	50	25
487	A98	$1 violet	1.75	80

2nd Intl. Conf. on the Global Impact of Applied Microbiology, Addis Ababa, Nov. 6-12.

Wall Painting from Debre Berhan Selassie Church, Gondar, 17th Century — A99

Designs (ITY Emblem and): 25c, Votive throne from Atsbe Dera, 4th Cent. B.C., vert. 35c, Prehistoric cave painting, Harar Province. 50c, Prehistoric stone tools, Melke Kontoure, vert.

1967, Nov. 20 Photo. *Perf. 14½*

488	A99	15c multi	50	20
489	A99	25c yel grn, buff & blk	70	30
490	A99	35c grn, brn & blk	80	50
491	A99	50c yel & blk	1.00	75

International Tourist Year, 1967.

A100

A101

Crosses of Lalibela: 5c, Processional Bronze Cross, Biet-Maryam Church. 10c, Processional copper cross. 15c, Copper cross, Biet-Maryam church. 20c, Lalibela-style cross. 50c, Chiseled copper cross, Madhani Alem church.

1967, Dec. 7 Photo. *Perf. 14½*

Crosses in Silver

492	A100	5c yel & blk	15	15
493	A100	10c red org & blk	15	15
494	A100	15c vio & blk	25	15
495	A100	20c brt rose & blk	30	15
496	A100	50c org yel & blk	1.10	50
		Nos. 492-496 (5)	1.95	
		Set value		85

Perf. 14x13½

1968, Apr. 18 Litho. Unwmk.

Designs: 10c, Emperor Theodore (1818?-1868). 20c, Emperor Theodore and lions, horiz. 50c, Imperial crown.

497	A101	10c lt vio, ocher & brn	15	15
498	A101	20c lil, brn & dk vio	35	15
499	A101	50c dk grn, org & rose cl	1.00	40

Human Rights Flame A102

1968, May 31 Unwmk. *Perf. 14½*

500	A102	15c pink, red & blk	30	30
501	A102	$1 lt bl, brt bl & blk	1.50	1.50

International Human Rights Year, 1968.

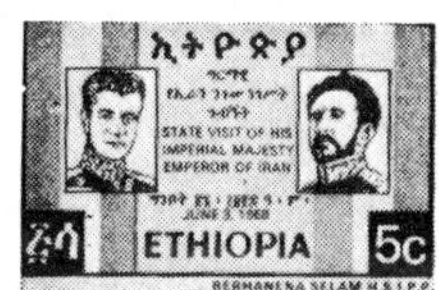

Shah Riza Pahlavi, Emperor and Flags A103

1968, June 3 Litho. *Perf. 13½*

502	A103	5c multi	15	15
503	A103	15c multi	25	25
504	A103	30c multi	85	85

Visit of Shah Mohammed Riza Pahlavi of Iran.

Emperor Haile Selassie Appealing to League of Nations, 1935 — A104

Designs: 35c, African Unity Building and map of Africa. $1, World map, symbolizing international relations.

1968, July 22 Photo. *Perf. 14x13½*

505	A104	15c bl, red, blk & gold	22	22
506	A104	35c blk, emer, red & gold	48	48
507	A104	$1 dk bl, lil, blk & gold	1.50	1.50

Ethiopia's struggle for peace.

WHO Emblem A105

Perf. 14x13½

1968, Aug. 30 Litho. Unwmk.

508	A105	15c brt grn & blk	25	25
509	A105	60c red lil & blk	90	90

20th anniv. of the WHO.

Abebe Bikila, Running A106

1968, Oct. 12 *Perf. 11½*

510	A106	10c shown	15	15
511	A106	15c Soccer	25	25
512	A106	20c Boxing	30	30
513	A106	40c Basketball	60	60
514	A106	50c Bicycling	90	90
		Nos. 510-514 (5)	2.20	2.20

Issued to commemorate the 19th Olympic Games, Mexico City, Oct. 12-27.

Arrussi Woman — A107

Regional Costumes: 15c, Man from Gemu Gefa. 20c, Gojam man. 30c, Kefa man. 35c, Harar woman. 50c, Ilubabor grass coat. 60c, Woman from Eritrea.

Perf. 13½x13

1968, Dec. 10 Photo. Unwmk.

515	A107	5c silver & multi	15	15
516	A107	15c silver & multi	15	15
517	A107	20c silver & multi	20	20
518	A107	30c silver & multi	30	30
519	A107	35c silver & multi	35	35
520	A107	50c silver & multi	60	60
521	A107	60c silver & multi	85	85
		Nos. 515-521 (7)	2.60	2.60

See Nos. 575-581.

Message Stick and Amharic Postal Emblem A108

1969, Mar. 10 Litho. *Perf. 14*

522	A108	10c emer, blk & brn	20	20
523	A108	15c yel, blk & brn	30	30
524	A108	35c multi	75	75

Ethiopian postal service, 75th anniv.

ILO Emblem A109

1969, Apr. 11 Litho. *Perf. 14½*

525	A109	15c org & blk	30	30
526	A109	60c emer & blk	1.25	1.25

50th anniv. of the ILO.

Dove, Red Cross, Crescent, Lion and Sun Emblems A110

1969, May 8 Wmk. 282 *Perf. 13*

527	A110	5c lt ultra, blk & red	15	15
528	A110	15c lt ultra, grn & red	30	30
529	A110	30c lt ultra, vio bl & red	60	60

League of Red Cross Societies, 50th anniv.

Endybis Silver Coin, 3rd Century — A111

Ancient Ethiopian Coins: 10c, Gold of Ezana, 4th cent. 15c, Gold of Kaleb, 6th cent. 30c, Bronze of Armah, 7th cent. 40c, Bronze of Wazena, 7th cent. 50c, Silver of Gersem, 8th cent.

1969, June 19 Photo. *Perf. 14½*

530	A111	5c ultra, blk & sil	15	15
531	A111	10c brt red, blk & gold	18	18
532	A111	15c brn, blk & gold	30	30
533	A111	30c dp car, blk & brnz	60	60
534	A111	40c dk grn, blk & brnz	70	70
535	A111	50c dp vio, blk & sil	90	90
		Nos. 530-535 (6)	2.83	2.83

Zebras and Tourist Year Emblem A112

Designs: 10c, Camping. 15c, Fishing. 20c, Water skiing. 25c, Mountaineering, vert.

Perf. 13x13½, 13½x13

1969, Aug. 29 Litho. Unwmk.

536	A112	5c multi	15	15
537	A112	10c multi	15	15
538	A112	15c multi	25	25
539	A112	20c multi	40	40
540	A112	25c multi	50	50
		Nos. 536-540 (5)	1.45	1.45

International Year of African Tourism.

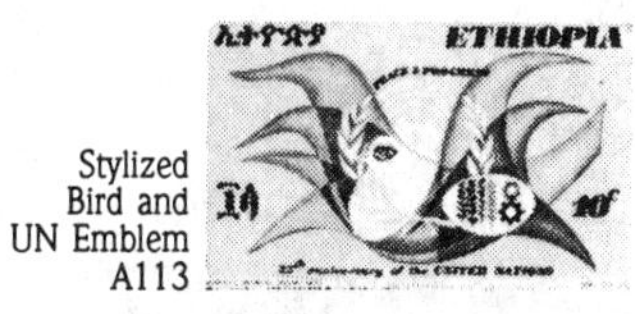

Stylized Bird and UN Emblem A113

UN 25th anniv.: 30c, Stylized flowers, UN and peace emblems, vert. 60c, Stylized bird, UN emblem and plane.

1969, Oct. 24 Unwmk. *Perf. 11½*

541	A113	10c lt bl & multi	15	15
542	A113	30c lt bl & multi	45	45
543	A113	60c lt bl & multi	1.00	1.00

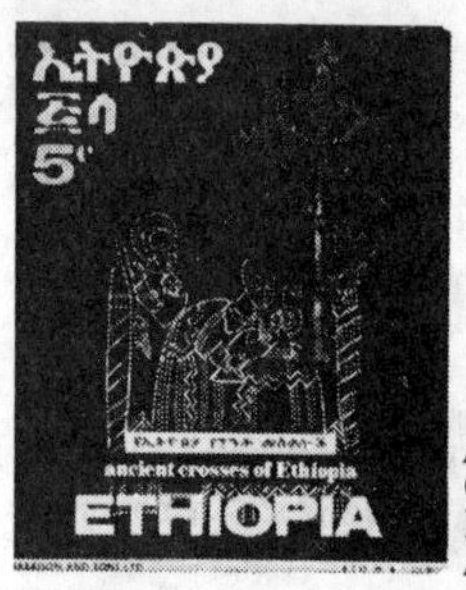

Ancient Cross and Holy Family
A114

Designs: Various ancient crosses.

Perf. 14½x13½

1969, Dec. 10 **Photo.**

544	A114	5c blk, yel & dk bl	15	15
545	A114	10c blk & yel	15	15
546	A114	25c blk, yel & grn	50	50
547	A114	60c blk & ocher	1.25	1.25

Ancient Figurines — A115

Ancient Ethiopian Pottery: 20c, Vases, Yeha period, 4th-3rd centuries B.C. 25c, Vases and jugs, Axum, 4th-6th centuries A.D. 35c, Bird-shaped jug and jugs, Matara, 4th-6th centuries A.D. 60c, Decorated pottery, Adulis, 6th-7th centuries A.D.

1970, Feb. 6 **Photo.** *Perf. 14½*

548	A115	10c blk & multi	15	15
549	A115	20c blk & multi	30	30
550	A115	25c blk & multi	35	35
551	A115	35c blk & multi	60	60
552	A115	60c blk & multi	1.10	1.10
		Nos. 548-552 (5)	2.50	2.50

Medhane Alem Church — A116

Rock Churches of Lalibela, 12th-13th Centuries: 10c, Bieta Emmanuel. 15c, The four Rock Churches of Lalibela. 20c, Bieta Mariam. 50c, Bieta Giorgis.

1970, Apr. 15 **Unwmk.** *Perf. 13*

553	A116	5c brn & multi	15	15
554	A116	10c brn & multi	15	15
555	A116	15c brn & multi	30	30
556	A116	20c brn & multi	50	50
557	A116	50c brn & multi	1.15	1.15
		Nos. 553-557 (5)	2.25	2.25

Sailfish Tang
A117

Tropical Fish: 10c, Undulate triggerfish. 15c, Orange butterflyfish. 25c, Butterflyfish. 50c, Imperial Angelfish.

1970, June 19 **Photo.** *Perf. 12½*

558	A117	5c multi	15	15
559	A117	10c multi	15	15
560	A117	15c multi	25	25
561	A117	25c multi	60	60
562	A117	50c multi	1.25	1.25
		Nos. 558-562 (5)	2.40	2.40

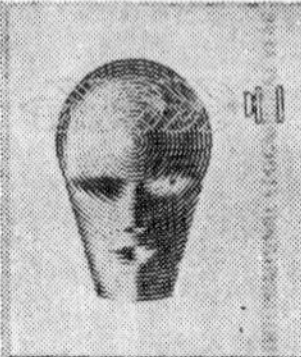

Education Year Emblem — A118

1970, Aug. 14 **Unwmk.** *Perf. 13½*

563	A118	10c multicolored	15	15
564	A118	20c gold, ultra & emer	35	35
565	A118	50c gold, emer & org	85	85

Issued for International Education Year.

Map of Africa
A119

Designs: 30c, Flag of Organization of African Unity. 40c, OAU Headquarters, Addis Ababa.

1970, Sept. 21 **Photo.** *Perf. 13½*

566	A119	20c multicolored	27	27
567	A119	30c multicolored	40	40
568	A119	40c green & multi	75	75

Africa Unity Day and Organization of African Unity.

Emperor Haile Selassie — A120

1970, Oct. 30 **Unwmk.** *Perf. 14½*

569	A120	15c Prus bl & multi	18	18
570	A120	50c multicolored	65	65
571	A120	60c multicolored	1.25	1.25

Coronation, 40th anniv.

Posts, Telecommunications and G.P.O. Buildings — A121

1970, Dec. 30 **Litho.** *Perf. 13½*

572	A121	10c ver & multi	18	18
573	A121	50c brown & multi	1.00	1.00
574	A121	80c multicolored	1.25	1.25

Opening of new Posts, Telecommunications and General Post Office buildings.

Costume Type of 1968

Regional Costumes: 5c, Warrior from Begemdir and Semien. 10c, Woman from Bale. 15c, Warrior from Welega. 20c, Woman from Shoa. 25c, Man from Sidamo. 40c, Woman from Tigre. 50c, Man from Welo.

1971, Feb. 17 **Photo.** *Perf. 11½*
Granite Paper

575	A107	5c gold & multi	15	15
576	A107	10c gold & multi	15	15
577	A107	15c gold & multi	25	25
578	A107	20c gold & multi	30	30
579	A107	25c gold & multi	40	40
580	A107	40c gold & multi	50	50
581	A107	50c gold & multi	1.00	1.00
		Nos. 575-581 (7)	2.75	2.75

Plane's Tail with Emblem — A122

Designs: 10c, Ethiopian scenes. 20c, Nose of Boeing 707. 60c, Pilots in cockpit, and engine. 80c, Globe with routes shown.

1971, Apr. 8 *Perf. 14½x14*

582	A122	5c multi	15	15
583	A122	10c multi	15	15
584	A122	20c multi	30	30
585	A122	60c multi	1.00	1.00
586	A122	80c multi	1.35	1.35
		Nos. 582-586 (5)	2.95	2.95

Ethiopian Airlines, 25th anniversary.

Fountain of Life, 15th Century Gospel Book — A123

Ethiopian Paintings: 10c, King David, 15th cent. manuscript. 25c, St. George, 17th cent. painting on canvas. 50c, King Lalibela, 18th cent. painting on wood. 60c, Yared singing before King Kaleb. Mural in Axum Cathedral.

1971, June 15 **Photo.** *Perf. 11½*
Granite Paper

587	A123	5c tan & multi	15	15
588	A123	10c pale sal & multi	15	15
589	A123	25c lemon & multi	30	30
590	A123	50c yellow & multi	80	80
591	A123	60c gray & multi	1.25	1.25
		Nos. 587-591 (5)	2.65	2.65

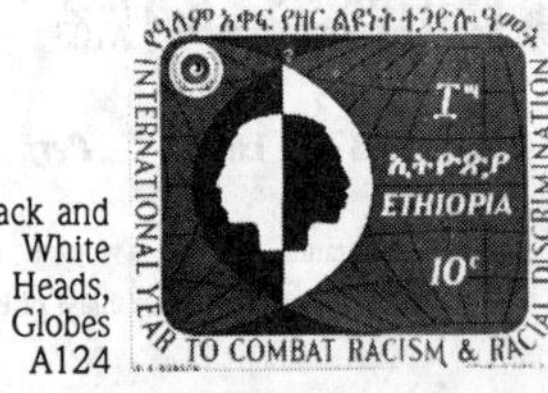

Black and White Heads, Globes
A124

Designs: 60c, Black and white hand holding globe. 80c, Four races, globes.

1971, Aug. 31 **Unwmk.**

592	A124	10c org, red brn & blk	20	20
593	A124	60c green, bl & blk	75	75
594	A124	80c bl, org, yel & blk	1.25	1.25

Intl. Year Against Racial Discrimination.

Emperor Menelik II and Reading of Treaty of Ucciali
A125

Contemporary Paintings: 30c, Menelik II on horseback gathering the tribes. 50c, Ethiopians and Italians in Battle of Adwa. 60c, Menelik II at head of his army.

1971, Oct. 20 **Litho.** *Perf. 13½*

595	A125	10c multi	20	20
596	A125	30c multi	50	50
597	A125	50c multi	75	75
598	A125	60c multi	1.25	1.25

75th anniversary of victory of Adwa over the Italians, March 1, 1896.

Haile Selassie Broadcasting and Map of Ethiopia — A126

Designs: 5c, Two telephones, 1897, Menelik II and Prince Makonnen. 30c, Ethiopians around television set. 40c, Telephone microwave circuits. 60c, Map of Africa on globe and telephone dial.

1971, Nov. 2

599	A126	5c brown & multi	15	15
600	A126	10c yellow & multi	15	15
601	A126	30c vio bl & multi	40	40
602	A126	40c black & multi	55	55
603	A126	60c vio bl & multi	1.10	1.10
		Nos. 599-603 (5)	2.35	2.35

Telecommunications in Ethiopia, 75th anniv.

UNICEF Emblem, Mother and Child — A127

UNICEF Emblem and: 10c, Children drinking milk. 15c, Man holding sick child. 30c, Kindergarten class. 50c, Father and son.

1971, Dec. 15 **Unwmk.**

604	A127	5c yellow & multi	15	15
605	A127	10c pale brn & multi	15	15
606	A127	15c rose & multi	22	22
607	A127	30c violet & multi	45	45
608	A127	50c green & multi	75	75
		Nos. 604-608 (5)	1.72	1.72

25th anniv. of UNICEF.

Nos. 445-448 Overprinted

U.N. SECURITY COUNCIL
FIRST MEETING
IN AFRICA 1972

1972, Jan. 28 **Photo.** *Perf. 11*
Portrait in Black

609	A86	20c grn & pale yel	30	30
610	A86	25c dk brn & yel	45	45
611	A86	30c maroon & gray	65	65
612	A86	35c dk blue & gray	80	80

1st meeting of UN Security Council in Africa.

River Boat on Lake Haik — A128

1972, Feb. 7 **Litho.** *Perf. 11½*
Granite Paper

613	A128	10c shown	15	15
614	A128	20c Boats on Lake Abaya	30	30
615	A128	30c on Lake Tana	60	60
616	A128	60c on Baro River	1.25	1.25

Proclamation of Cyrus the Great — A129

1972, Mar. 28 Photo. *Perf. 14x14½*

617	A129	10c red & multi	15	15
618	A129	60c emerald & multi	90	90
619	A129	80c gray & multi	1.25	1.25

2500th anniversary of the founding of the Persian empire by Cyrus the Great.

Houses, Sidamo Province A130

Ethiopian Architecture: 10c, Tigre Province. 20c, Eritrea Province. 40c, Addis Ababa. 80c, Shoa Province.

1972, Apr. 11 Litho. *Perf. 13½*

620	A130	5c black & multi	15	15
621	A130	10c black, gray & brn	15	15
622	A130	20c black & multi	30	30
623	A130	40c black, bl grn & brn	60	60
624	A130	80c black, brn & red brn	1.35	1.35
		Nos. 620-624 (5)	2.55	2.55

Hands Holding Map of Ethiopia — A131

Designs: 10c, Hands shielding Ethiopians. 25c, Map of Africa, hands reaching for African Unity emblem. 50c, Brown and white hands clasped, U.N. emblem. 60c, Hands protecting dove. Each denomination shows different portrait of the Emperor.

Perf. 14½x14

1972, July 21 Litho. Unwmk.

625	A131	5c scarlet & multi	15	15
626	A131	10c ultra & multi	15	15
627	A131	25c vio bl & multi	33	33
628	A131	50c lt blue & multi	65	65
629	A131	60c brown & multi	80	80
		Nos. 625-629 (5)	2.08	2.08

80th birthday of Emperor Haile Selassie.

Running, Flags of Mexico, Japan, Italy — A132

1972, Aug. 25 *Perf. 13½x13*

630	A132	10c shown	15	15
631	A132	30c Soccer	40	40
632	A132	50c Bicycling	80	80
633	A132	60c Boxing	1.10	1.10

20th Olympic Games, Munich, Germany, Aug. 26-Sept. 11.

Open Bible, Cross and Orbit A133

Designs: 50c, First and 1972 headquarters of the British and Foreign Bible Society, vert. 80c, First Amharic Bible.

1972, Sept. 25 Photo. *Perf. 13½*

634	A133	20c deep red & multi	27	27
635	A133	50c deep red & multi	65	65
636	A133	80c deep red & multi	1.25	1.25

United Bible Societies World Assembly, Addis Ababa, Sept. 1972.

Security Council Meeting A134

Designs: 60c, Building where Security Council met. 80c, Map of Africa with flags of participating members.

1972, Nov. 1 Litho. *Perf. 13½*

637	A134	10c lt bl & vio bl	15	15
638	A134	60c multicolored	75	75
639	A134	80c multicolored	1.50	1.50

First United Nations Security Council meeting, Addis Ababa, Jan. 28-Feb. 4, 1972.

Fish in Polluted Sea — A135

Designs: 30c, Fisherman, beacon, family. 80c, Polluted seashore.

1973, Feb. 23 Photo. *Perf. 13½*

640	A135	20c gold & multi	30	30
641	A135	30c gold & multi	45	45
642	A135	80c gold & multi	1.25	1.25

World message from the sea, Ethiopian anti-pollution campaign.

INTERPOL and Ethiopian Police Emblems A136

Designs: 50c, INTERPOL emblem and General Secretariat, Paris. 60c, INTERPOL emblem.

1973, Mar. 20 Photo. *Perf. 13½*

643	A136	40c dull orange & blk	65	65
644	A136	50c blue, blk & yel	85	85
645	A136	60c dk carmine & blk	1.00	1.00

50th anniversary of International Criminal Police Organization (INTERPOL).

Virgin of Emperor Zara Yaqob — A137

Ethiopian Art: 15c, Crucifixion, Zara Yaqob period. 30c, Virgin and Child, from Entoto Mariam Church. 40c, Christ, contemporary mosaic. 80c, The Evangelists, contemporary bas-relief.

1973, May 15 Photo. *Perf. 11½*

Granite Paper

646	A137	5c brown & multi	15	15
647	A137	15c dp blue & multi	20	20
648	A137	30c gray grn & multi	55	55
649	A137	40c multicolored	60	60
650	A137	80c slate & multi	1.50	1.50
		Nos. 646-650 (5)	3.00	3.00

Free African States in 1963 and 1973 — A138

Designs (Map of Africa and): 10c, Flags of OAU members. 20c, Symbols of progress. 40c, Dove and people. 80c, Emblems of various UN agencies.

1973 May 25 *Perf. 14½x14*

651	A138	5c red & multi	15	15
652	A138	10c ol gray & multi	17	17
653	A138	20c green & multi	33	33
654	A138	40c sepia & multi	65	65
655	A138	80c lt blue & multi	1.75	1.75
		Nos. 651-655 (5)	3.05	3.05

OAU, 10th anniv.

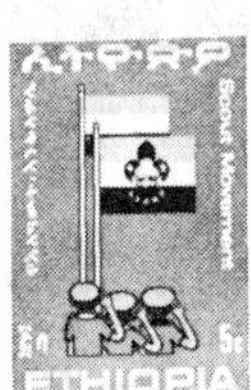

Scouts Saluting Ethiopian and Scout Flags — A139

Designs: 15c, Road and road sign. 30c, Girl Scout reading to old man. 40c, Scout and disabled people. 60c, Ethiopian Boy Scout.

1973, July 10 Photo. *Perf. 11½*

Granite Paper

656	A139	5c blue & multi	15	15
657	A139	15c lt green & multi	20	20
658	A139	30c yellow & multi	42	42
659	A139	40c crimson & multi	60	60
660	A139	60c violet & multi	1.10	1.10
		Nos. 656-660 (5)	2.47	2.47

24th Boy Scout World Conference, Nairobi, Kenya, July 16-21.

WMO Emblem A140

Designs: 50c, WMO emblem and anemometer. 60c, Weather satellite over earth, and WMO emblem.

1973, Sept. 4 Photo. *Perf. 13½*

661	A140	40c black, bl & dl bl	55	55
662	A140	50c dull blue & blk	65	65
663	A140	60c dull blue & multi	1.00	1.00

Cent. of intl. meteorological cooperation.

Prince Makonnen, Duke of Harar — A141

Human Rights Flame — A142

Designs: 5c, Old wall of Harar. 20c, Operating room. 40c, Boy Scouts learning first aid and hospital. 80c, Prince Makonnen and hospital.

1973, Nov. 1 Unwmk. *Perf. 14½*

664	A141	5c gray & multi	15	15
665	A141	10c red brn & multi	15	15
666	A141	20c green & multi	30	30
667	A141	40c brown red & multi	65	65
668	A141	80c ultra & multi	1.35	1.35
		Nos. 664-668 (5)	2.60	2.60

Opening of Prince Makonnen Memorial Hospital.

Perf. 11½

1973, Nov. 16 Photo. Unwmk.

Granite Paper

669	A142	40c yel, gold & dk grn	60	60
670	A142	50c lt grn, gold & dk grn	75	75
671	A142	60c org, gold & dk grn	1.00	1.00

25th anniversary of the Universal Declaration of Human Rights.

Emperor Haile Selassie — A143

1973, Nov. 5 Photo. *Perf. 11½*

672	A143	5c yellow & multi	15	15
673	A143	10c brt blue & multi	15	15
674	A143	15c green & multi	18	15
675	A143	20c dull yel & multi	25	15
676	A143	25c multi	30	15
677	A143	30c multi	35	15
678	A143	35c multi	42	17
679	A143	40c ultra & multi	48	20
680	A143	45c multi	55	22
681	A143	50c orange & multi	60	25
682	A143	55c magenta & multi	75	50
683	A143	60c multi	90	65
684	A143	70c red org & multi	1.00	70
685	A143	90c brt vio & multi	1.20	85
686	A143	$1 multi	1.60	1.10
687	A143	$2 orange & multi	3.00	2.00
688	A143	$3 multi	4.50	3.00
689	A143	$5 multi	7.50	5.00
		Nos. 672-689 (18)	23.88	15.54

Wicker Furniture A144

Designs: Various wicker baskets, wall hangings, dinnerware.

1974, Jan. 31 Photo. *Perf. 11½*

Granite Paper

690	A144	5c violet bl & multi	15	15
691	A144	10c violet bl & multi	15	15
692	A144	30c violet bl & multi	30	30
693	A144	50c violet bl & multi	60	60
694	A144	60c violet bl & multi	75	75
		Nos. 690-694 (5)	1.95	1.95

Cow, Calf, Syringe — A145

Designs: 15c, Inoculation of cattle. 20c, Bullock and syringe. 50c, Laboratory technician, cow's head, syringe. 60c, Map of Ethiopia, cattle, syringe.

1974, Feb. 20 Litho. ***Perf. 13½x13***

695	A145	5c	sepia & multi	15	15
696	A145	15c	ultra & multi	15	15
697	A145	20c	ultra & multi	20	20
698	A145	50c	orange & multi	75	75
699	A145	60c	gold & multi	1.00	1.00
			Nos. 695-699 (5)	2.25	2.25

Campaign against cattle plague.

Umbrella Makers A146

Designs: 30c, Weaving. 50c, Child care. 60c, Foundation headquarters.

1974, Apr. 17 Photo. ***Perf. 14½***

700	A146	10c	lt lilac & multi	15	15
701	A146	30c	multicolored	30	30
702	A146	50c	multicolored	60	60
703	A146	60c	blue & multi	75	75

20th anniv. of Haile Selassie Foundation.

Ceremonial Robe — A147

Designs: Ceremonial robes.

1974, June 26 Litho. ***Perf. 13***

704	A147	15c	multi	15	15
705	A147	25c	ocher & multi	25	25
706	A147	35c	green & multi	50	50
707	A147	40c	lt brown & multi	60	60
708	A147	60c	gray & multi	85	85
			Nos. 704-708 (5)	2.35	2.35

World Population Statistics A148

Designs: 50c, "Larger families-lower living standard." 60c, Rising population graph.

1974, Aug. 19 Photo. ***Perf. 14½***

709	A148	40c	yellow & multi	50	50
710	A148	50c	violet & multi	60	60
711	A148	60c	green & multi	75	75

World Population Year 1974.

UPU Emblem, Letter Carrier's Staff — A149

Celebration Around "Damara" Pillar — A150

Designs (UPU Emblem and): 50c, Letters and flags. 60c, Globe. 70c, Headquarters, Bern.

1974, Oct. 9 Photo. ***Perf. 11½***
Granite Paper

712	A149	15c	yellow & multi	15	15
713	A149	50c	multicolored	60	60
714	A149	60c	ultra & multi	75	75
715	A149	70c	multicolored	85	85

Centenary of Universal Postal Union.

1974, Dec. 17 Photo. ***Perf. 14x14½***

Designs: 5c, Site of Gishen Mariam Monastery. 20c, Cross and festivities. 80c, Torch (Chibos) Parade.

716	A150	5c	yellow & multi	15	15
717	A150	10c	yellow & multi	15	15
718	A150	20c	yellow & multi	25	25
719	A150	80c	yellow & multi	1.00	1.00

Meskel Festival, Sept. 26-27, commemorating the finding in the 4th century of the True Cross, of which a fragment is kept at Gishen Mariam Monastery in Welo Province.

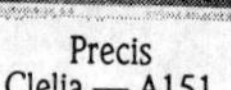

Precis Clelia — A151

Adoration of the Kings — A152

Butterflies: 25c, Charaxes achaemenes. 45c, Papilio dardanus. 50c, Charaxes druceanus. 60c, Papilio demodocus.

1975, Feb. 18 Photo. ***Perf. 12x12½***

720	A151	10c	silver & multi	15	15
721	A151	25c	gold & multi	25	25
722	A151	45c	purple & multi	65	65
723	A151	50c	green & multi	85	85
724	A151	60c	brt blue & multi	1.00	1.00
			Nos. 720-724 (5)	2.90	2.90

1975, Apr. 23 Photo. ***Perf. 11½***

Designs: 10c, Baptism of Jesus. 15c, Jesus teaching in the Temple. 30c, Jesus giving sight to the blind. 40c, Crucifixion. 80c, Resurrection.

Granite Paper

725	A152	5c	brown & multi	15	15
726	A152	10c	black & multi	15	15
727	A152	15c	dk brown & multi	15	15
728	A152	30c	dk brown & multi	30	30
729	A152	40c	black & multi	60	60
730	A152	80c	slate & multi	1.10	1.10
			Nos. 725-730 (6)	2.45	2.45

Murals from Ethiopian churches.

Wild Animals A153

1975, May 27 Photo. ***Perf. 11½***
Granite Paper

731	A153	5c	Warthog	15	15
732	A153	10c	Aardvark	15	15
733	A153	20c	Semien wolf	20	20
734	A153	40c	Gelada baboon	50	50
735	A153	80c	Civet	1.10	1.10
			Nos. 731-735 (5)	2.10	2.10

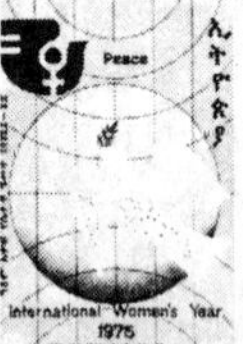

"Peace," Dove, Globe, IWY Emblem — A154

Designs (IWY Emblem and): 50c, Symbols of development. 90c, Equality between men and women.

1975, June 30 Litho. ***Perf. 14x14½***

736	A154	40c	blue & black	50	50
737	A154	50c	salmon & multi	60	60
738	A154	90c	multicolored	1.25	1.25

International Women's Year 1975.

Postal Museum A155

Designs: Various interior views of Postal Museum.

1975, Aug. 19 Photo. ***Perf. 13x12½***

739	A155	10c	ocher & multi	15	15
740	A155	30c	pink & multi	30	30
741	A155	60c	multicolored	75	75
742	A155	70c	lt green & multi	85	85

Ethiopian Natl. Postal Museum, opening.

Map of Ethiopia and Sun — A156

1975, Sept. 11 Photo. ***Perf. 11½***
Granite Paper

743	A156	5c	lilac & multi	15	15
744	A156	10c	ultra & multi	15	15
745	A156	25c	brown & multi	25	25
746	A156	50c	yellow & multi	60	60
747	A156	90c	brt green & multi	1.10	1.10
			Nos. 743-747 (5)	2.25	2.25

1st anniv. of Ethiopia Tikdem (Socialism).

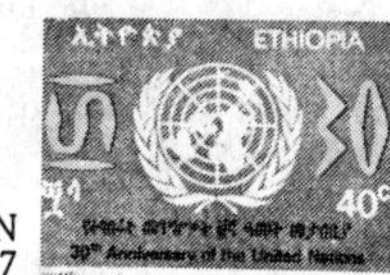

UN Emblem — A157

1975, Oct. 24 Photo. ***Perf. 11½***

748	A157	40c	lilac & multi	50	50
749	A157	50c	multicolored	60	60
750	A157	90c	blue & multi	1.10	1.10

United Nations, 30th anniversary.

Regional Hair Styles — A158

Delphinium Wellbyi — A159

1975, Dec. 15 Photo. ***Perf. 11½***

751	A158	5c	Ilubabor	15	15
752	A158	15c	Arusi	15	15
753	A158	20c	Eritrea	25	25
754	A158	30c	Bale	35	35
755	A158	35c	Kefa	50	50
756	A158	50c	Begemir	60	60
757	A158	60c	Shoa	75	75
			Nos. 751-757 (7)	2.75	2.75

See Nos. 832-838.

1976, Jan. 15 Photo. ***Perf. 11½***

Flowers: 10c, Plectocephalus varians. 20c, Brachystelma asmarensis, horiz. 40c, Ceropegia inflata. 80c, Erythrina brucei.

758	A159	5c	multi	15	15
759	A159	10c	multi	15	15
760	A159	20c	multi	25	25
761	A159	40c	multi	50	50
762	A159	80c	multi	1.00	1.00
			Nos. 758-762 (5)	2.05	2.05

Goalkeeper, Map of Africa, Games' Emblem A160

Designs: Various scenes from soccer, map of Africa and ball.

1976, Feb. 27 Photo. ***Perf. 14½***

763	A160	5c	orange & multi	15	15
764	A160	10c	yellow & multi	15	15
765	A160	25c	lilac & multi	30	30
766	A160	50c	green & multi	60	60
767	A160	90c	brt grn & multi	1.10	1.10
			Nos. 763-767 (5)	2.30	2.30

10th African Cup of Nations, Addis Ababa and Dire Dawa, Feb. 29-Mar. 14.

Telephones, 1876 and 1976 — A161

Ethiopian Jewelry — A162

Designs: 60c, Alexander Graham Bell. 90c, Transmission tower.

1976, Mar. 10 Litho. ***Perf. 12x13½***

768	A161	30c	lt ocher & multi	35	35
769	A161	60c	emerald & multi	75	75
770	A161	90c	ver, blk & buff	1.10	1.10

Centenary of first telephone call by Alexander Graham Bell, Mar. 10, 1876.

1976, May 14 Photo. ***Perf. 11½***

Designs: Women wearing various kinds of Ethiopian jewelry.

Granite Paper

771	A162	5c	blue & multi	15	15
772	A162	10c	plum & multi	15	15
773	A162	20c	gray & multi	30	30
774	A162	40c	green & multi	60	60
775	A162	80c	orange & multi	1.10	1.10
			Nos. 771-775 (5)	2.30	2.30

Boxing — A163

Hands Holding Map of Ethiopia — A164

Designs (Montreal Olympic Emblem and): 80c, Runner and maple leaf. 90c, Bicycling.

1976, July 15 Litho. ***Perf. 12½x12***

776	A163	10c	multicolored	15	15
777	A163	80c	brt red, blk & grn	1.00	1.00
778	A163	90c	brt red & multi	1.10	1.10

21st Olympic Games, Montreal, Canada, July 17-Aug. 1.

1976, Aug. 5 Photo. ***Perf. 14½***

779	A164	5c	rose & multi	15	15
780	A164	10c	olive & multi	15	15
781	A164	25c	orange & multi	25	25
782	A164	50c	multicolored	60	60
783	A164	90c	dk blue & multi	1.10	1.10
			Nos. 779-783 (5)	2.25	2.25

Development through cooperation.

Revolution Emblem: Eye and Map A165

1976, Sept. 9 Photo. *Perf. 13½*

No.	Type	Description	Unused	Used
784	A165	5c multi	15	15
785	A165	10c multi	15	15
786	A165	25c multi	25	25
787	A165	50c yellow & multi	60	60
788	A165	90c green & multi	1.10	1.10
		Nos. 784-788 (5)	2.25	2.25

2nd anniversary of the revolution (Tikdem).

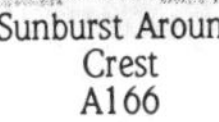

Sunburst Around Crest A166

Plane Over Man with Donkey A167

1976, Sept. 13 Photo. *Perf. 11½*

No.	Type	Description	Unused	Used
789	A166	5c green, gold & blk	15	15
790	A166	10c orange, gold & blk	15	15
791	A166	15c grnsh bl, gold & blk	15	15
792	A166	20c lilac, gold & blk	20	15
793	A166	25c brt grn, gold & blk	25	15
794	A166	30c car, gold & blk	30	15
795	A166	35c yel, gold & blk	35	18
796	A166	40c ol, gold & blk	40	20
797	A166	45c brt grn, gold & blk	45	22
798	A166	50c car rose, gold & blk	50	25
799	A166	55c ultra, gold & blk	55	28
800	A166	60c fawn, gold & blk	60	30
801	A166	70c rose, gold & blk	70	35
802	A166	90c blue, gold & blk	90	45
803	A166	$1 dull grn, gold & blk	1.00	50
804	A166	$2 gray, gold & blk	2.00	1.00
805	A166	$3 brn vio, gold & blk	3.00	1.50
806	A166	$5 slate bl, gold & blk	5.00	2.50
		Nos. 789-806 (18)	16.65	8.63

Denomination Expressed as "BIRR"

1983, June 16

No.	Type	Description
806A	A166	1b dull grn, gold & blk
806B	A166	2b
806C	A166	3b

1976, Oct. 28 Litho. *Perf. 12x12½*

Designs: 10c, Globe showing routes. 25c, Crew and passengers forming star. 50c, Propeller and jet engine. 90c, Airplanes surrounding map of Ethiopia.

No.	Type	Description	Unused	Used
807	A167	5c dull bl & multi	15	15
808	A167	10c lilac & multi	15	15
809	A167	25c multicolored	25	25
810	A167	50c orange & multi	50	50
811	A167	90c olive & multi	90	90
		Nos. 807-811 (5)	1.95	1.95

Ethiopian Airlines, 30th anniversary.

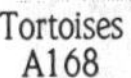

Tortoises A168

Hand Holding Makeshift Hammer A169

Reptiles: 20c, Chameleon. 30c, Python. 40c, Monitor lizard. 80c, Nile crocodiles.

1976, Dec. 15 Photo. *Perf. 14½*

No.	Type	Description	Unused	Used
812	A168	10c multi	15	15
813	A168	20c multi	20	20
814	A168	30c multi	30	30
815	A168	40c multi	40	40
816	A168	80c multi	80	80
		Nos. 812-816 (5)	1.85	1.85

1977, Jan. 20 Litho. *Perf. 12½*

Designs: 5c, Hands holding bowl and plane dropping food. 45c, Infant with empty bowl, and bank note. 60c, Map of affected area, footprints and tire tracks. 80c, Film strip, camera and Ethiopian sitting between eggshells.

No.	Type	Description	Unused	Used
817	A169	5c multi	15	15
818	A169	10c multi	15	15
819	A169	45c multi	45	45
820	A169	60c multi	60	60
821	A169	80c multi	80	80
		Nos. 817-821 (5)	2.15	2.15

Ethiopian Relief and Rehabilitation Commission for drought and disaster areas.

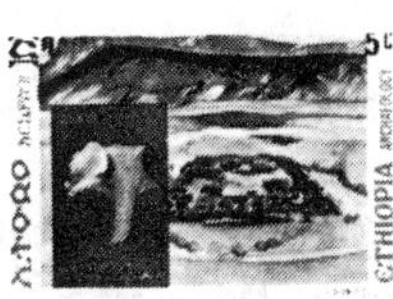

Elephant and Ruins, Axum, 7th Century A170

Designs: 10c, Ibex and temple, 5th century, B.C., Yeha. 25c, Megalithic dolmen and pottery, Sourre Kabanawa. 50c, Awash Valley, stone axe, Acheulean period. 80c, Omo Valley, hominid jawbone.

1977, Mar. 15 Photo. *Perf. 13½*

No.	Type	Description	Unused	Used
822	A170	5c gold & multi	15	15
823	A170	10c gold & multi	15	15
824	A170	25c gold & multi	25	25
825	A170	50c gold & multi	50	50
826	A170	80c gold & multi	80	80
		Nos. 822-826 (5)	1.85	1.85

Archaeological sites and finds in Ethiopia.

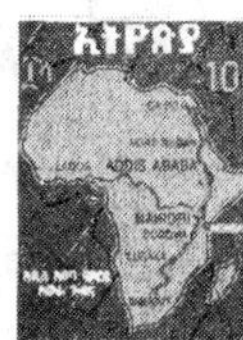

Map of Africa with Trans-East Highway — A171

1977, Mar. 30 *Perf. 14*

No.	Type	Description	Unused	Used
827	A171	10c gold & multi	15	15
828	A171	20c gold & multi	20	20
829	A171	40c gold & multi	40	40
830	A171	50c gold & multi	50	50
831	A171	60c gold & multi	60	60
		Nos. 827-831 (5)	1.85	1.85

Addis Ababa to Nairobi Highway and projected highways to Cairo, Egypt, and Gaborone, Botswana.

Hairstyle Type of 1975

1977, Apr. 28 Photo. *Perf. 11½*

No.	Type	Description	Unused	Used
832	A158	5c Welega	15	15
833	A158	10c Gojam	15	15
834	A158	15c Tigre	15	15
835	A158	20c Harar	20	20
836	A158	25c Gemu Gefa	25	25
837	A158	40c Sidamo	45	45
838	A158	50c Welo	60	60
		Nos. 832-838 (7)	1.95	1.95

Addis Ababa — A172

Towns of Ethiopia: 10c, Asmara. 25c, Harar. 50c, Jima. 90c, Dese.

1977, June 20 Photo. *Perf. 14½*

No.	Type	Description	Unused	Used
839	A172	5c silver & multi	15	15
840	A172	10c silver & multi	15	15
841	A172	25c silver & multi	25	25
842	A172	50c silver & multi	50	50
843	A172	90c silver & multi	90	90
		Nos. 839-843 (5)	1.95	1.95

Terebratula Abyssinica A173

Fractured Imperial Crown A174

Fossil Shells: 10c, Terebratula subalata. 25c, Cuculloea lefeburiaua. 50c, Ostrea plicatissima. 90c, Trigonia cousobrina.

1977, Aug. 15 Photo. *Perf. 14x13½*

No.	Type	Description	Unused	Used
844	A173	5c multi	15	15
845	A173	10c multi	15	15
846	A173	25c multi	25	25
847	A173	50c multi	50	50
848	A173	90c multi	90	90
		Nos. 844-848 (5)	1.95	1.95

1977, Sept. 9 Litho. *Perf. 15*

Designs: 10c, Symbol of the Revolution (spade, axe, torch). 25c, Warriors, hammer and sickle, map of Ethiopia. 60c, Soldier, farmer and map. 80c, Map and emblem of revolutionary government.

No.	Type	Description	Unused	Used
849	A174	5c multi	15	15
850	A174	10c multi	15	15
851	A174	25c multi	25	25
852	A174	60c multi	60	60
853	A174	80c multi	80	80
		Nos. 849-853 (5)	1.95	1.95

Third anniversary of the revolution.

Cicindela Petitii — A175

Lenin, Globe, Map of Ethiopia and Emblem — A176

Insects: 10c, Heliocopris dillonii. 25c, Poekilocerus vignaudii. 50c, Pepsis heros. 90c, Pepsis dedjaz.

1977, Sept. 30 Photo. *Perf. 14x13½*

No.	Type	Description	Unused	Used
854	A175	5c multi	15	15
855	A175	10c multi	15	15
856	A175	25c multi	25	25
857	A175	50c multi	50	50
858	A175	90c multi	90	90
		Nos. 854-858 (5)	1.95	1.95

1977, Nov. 15 Litho. *Perf. 12*

No.	Type	Description	Unused	Used
859	A176	5c org & multi	15	15
860	A176	10c multi	15	15
861	A176	25c sal & multi	25	25
862	A176	50c lt bl & multi	50	50
863	A176	90c yel & multi	90	90
		Nos. 859-863 (5)	1.95	1.95

60th anniv. of Russian October Revolution.

Chondrostoma Dilloni — A177

Salt-water Fish: 10c, Ostracion cubicus. 25c, Serranus summana. 50c, Serranus luti. 90c, Tetraodon maculatus.

1978, Jan. 20 Litho. *Perf. 15½*

No.	Type	Description	Unused	Used
864	A177	5c multi	15	15
865	A177	10c multi	15	15
866	A177	25c multi	25	25
867	A177	50c multi	50	50
868	A177	90c multi	90	90
		Nos. 864-868 (5)	1.95	1.95

Domestic Animals — A178

1978, Mar. 27 Litho. *Perf. 13½x14*

No.	Type	Description	Unused	Used
869	A178	5c Cattle	15	15
870	A178	10c Mules	15	15
871	A178	25c Goats	25	25
872	A178	50c Dromedaries	50	50
873	A178	90c Horses	90	90
		Nos. 869-873 (5)	1.95	1.95

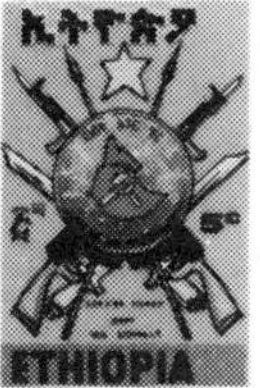

Weapons and Shield, Map of Ethiopia — A179

Bronze Ibex, 5th Century B.C. — A180

"Call of the Motherland." (Map of Ethiopia and): 10c, Civilian fighters. 25c, Map of Africa. 60c, Soldiers. 80c, Red Cross nurse and wounded man.

1978, May Litho. *Perf. 15½*

No.	Type	Description	Unused	Used
874	A179	5c multi	15	15
875	A179	10c multi	15	15
876	A179	25c multi	25	25
877	A179	60c multi	60	60
878	A179	80c multi	80	80
		Nos. 874-878 (5)	1.95	1.95

1978, June 21 Litho. *Perf. 15½*

Ancient Bronzes: 10c, Lion, Yeha, 5th cent. B.C., horiz. 25c, Lamp with ibex attacked by dog, Matara, 1st cent. B.C. 50c, Goat, Axum, 3rd cent. A.D., horiz. 90c, Ax, chisel and sickle, Yeha, 5th-4th centuries B.C.

No.	Type	Description	Unused	Used
879	A180	5c multi	15	15
880	A180	10c multi	15	15
881	A180	25c multi	25	25
882	A180	50c multi	50	50
883	A180	90c multi	90	90
		Nos. 879-883 (5)	1.95	1.95

See Nos. 1024-1027.

Globe and Argentina '78 Emblem A181

Designs (Argentina '78 Emblem and): 20c, Soccer player kicking ball. 30c, Two players embracing, net and ball. 55c, World map and ball. 70c, Soccer field, vert.

Perf. 14x13½, 13½x14

1978, July 19 Litho.

No.	Type	Description	Unused	Used
884	A181	5c multi	15	15
885	A181	20c multi	20	20
886	A181	30c multi	30	30
887	A181	55c multi	55	55
888	A181	70c multi	70	70
		Nos. 884-888 (5)	1.90	1.90

11th World Cup Soccer Championship, Argentina, June 1-25.

Map of Africa, Oppressed African — A182

Namibia Day: 10c, Policeman pointing gun. 25c, Sniper with gun. 60c, African caught in net. 80c, Head of free man.

1978, Aug. 25 *Perf. 12½x13½*

889 A182	5c multi		15	15
890 A182	10c multi		15	15
891 A182	25c multi		25	25
892 A182	60c multi		60	60
893 A182	80c multi		80	80
		Nos. 889-893 (5)	1.95	1.95

Soldiers, Guerrilla and Jets — A183

Design: 1b, People looking toward sun, crushing snake, flags.

1978, Sept. 8 **Photo.** *Perf. 14*

894 A183	80c multi	80	80
895 A183	1b multi	1.00	1.00

4th anniversary of revolution.

Hand and Globe with Tools — A184

Designs: 15c, Symbols of energy, communications, education, medicine, agriculture and industry. 25c, Cogwheels and world map. 60c, Globe and hands passing wrench. 70c, Flying geese and turtle over globe.

1978, Nov. 14 **Litho.** *Perf. 12x12½*

896 A184	10c multi		15	15
897 A184	15c multi		15	15
898 A184	25c multi		25	25
899 A184	60c multi		60	60
900 A184	70c multi		70	70
		Nos. 896-900 (5)	1.85	1.85

Technical Cooperation Among Developing Countries Conference, Buenos Aires, Argentina, Sept. 1978.

Human Rights Emblem — A185

Perf. 12½x13½

1978, Dec. 7 **Photo.**

901 A185	5c multi		15	15
902 A185	15c multi		15	15
903 A185	25c multi		25	25
904 A185	35c multi		35	35
905 A185	1b multi		1.00	1.00
		Nos. 901-905 (5)	1.90	1.90

Declaration of Human Rights, 30th anniv.

Broken Chain, Anti-Apartheid Emblem A186

Stele from Osole A187

1978, Dec. 28 **Litho.** *Perf. 12½x12*

906 A186	5c multi		15	15
907 A186	20c multi		20	20
908 A186	30c multi		30	30
909 A186	55c multi		55	55
910 A186	70c multi		70	70
		Nos. 906-910 (5)	1.90	1.90

Anti-Apartheid Year.

1979, Jan. 25 *Perf. 14*

Ancient Carved Stones, Soddo Region: 10c, Anthropomorphous stele, Gorashino. 25c, Leaning stone, Wado. 60c, Round stones, Ambeut. 80c, Bas-relief, Tiya.

911 A187	5c multi		15	15
912 A187	10c multi		15	15
913 A187	25c multi		25	25
914 A187	60c multi		60	60
915 A187	80c multi		80	80
		Nos. 911-915 (5)	1.95	1.95

Cotton Plantation A188

Shemma Industry: 10c, Women spinning cotton yarn. 20c, Man reeling cotton. 65c, Weaver. 80c, Shemma (Natl. dress).

1979, Mar. 15 **Litho.** *Perf. 15½x12*

916 A188	5c multi		15	15
917 A188	10c multi		15	15
918 A188	20c multi		20	20
919 A188	65c multi		65	65
920 A188	80c multi		80	80
		Nos. 916-920 (5)	1.95	1.95

"Grar" Tree — A189

Designs: Ethiopian trees.

1979, Apr. 26 **Photo.** *Perf. 13½x14*

921 A189	5c multi		15	15
922 A189	10c multi		15	15
923 A189	25c multi		25	25
924 A189	50c multi		50	50
925 A189	90c multi		90	90
		Nos. 921-925 (5)	1.95	1.95

Agricultural Development A190

Revolutionary Development Campaign: 15c, Industry. 25c, Transportation and communication. 60c, Education and health. 70c, Commerce.

1979, July 3 **Litho.** *Perf. 12x12½*

926 A190	10c multi		15	15
927 A190	15c multi		15	15
928 A190	25c multi		25	25
929 A190	60c multi		60	60
930 A190	70c multi		70	70
		Nos. 926-930 (5)	1.85	1.85

IYC Emblem — A191

Intl. Year of the Child: 15c, Adults leading children. 25c, Adult helping child. 60c, IYC emblem surrounded by children. 70c, Adult and children embracing.

1979, Aug. 16 **Litho.** *Perf. 12x12½*

931 A191	10c multi		15	15
932 A191	15c multi		15	15
933 A191	25c multi		25	25
934 A191	60c multi		60	60
935 A191	70c multi		70	70
		Nos. 931-935 (5)	1.85	1.85

Guerrilla Fighters — A192

Designs: 15c, Soldiers. 25c, Map of Africa within cogwheel and star. 60c, Students with book and torch. 70c, Family, hammer and sickle emblem.

1979, Sept. 11 **Photo.** *Perf. 14*

936 A192	10c multi		15	15
937 A192	15c multi		15	15
938 A192	25c multi		25	25
939 A192	60c multi		60	60
940 A192	70c multi		70	70
		Nos. 936-940 (5)	1.85	1.85

Fifth anniversary of revolution.

Telephone Receiver — A193

Incense Container — A194

Telecom Emblem and: 5c, Symbolic waves. 35c, Satellite beaming to earth. 45c, Dish antenna. 65c, Television cameraman.

1979, Sept. **Photo.** *Perf. 11½*

941 A193	5c multi		15	15
942 A193	30c multi		30	30
943 A193	35c multi		35	35
944 A193	45c multi		45	45
945 A193	65c multi		65	65
		Nos. 941-945 (5)	1.90	1.90

3rd World Telecommunications Exhibition, Geneva, Sept. 20-26.

1979, Nov. 15 **Litho.** *Perf. 15*

946 A194	5c shown		15	15
947 A194	10c Vase		15	15
948 A194	25c Earthenware cover		25	25
949 A194	60c Milk container		60	60
950 A194	80c Storage container		80	80
		Nos. 946-950 (5)	1.95	1.95

Wooden Grain Bowl — A195

Lappet-faced Vulture — A196

1980, Jan. **Litho.** *Perf. 13½x13*

951 A195	5c shown		15	15
952 A195	30c Chair, stool		30	30
953 A195	35c Mortar, pestle		35	35
954 A195	45c Buckets		45	45
955 A195	65c Storage jars		65	65
		Nos. 951-955 (5)	1.90	1.90

1980, Feb. 12 *Perf. 13½x14*

Birds of Prey: 15c, Long-crested hawk eagle. 25c, Secretary bird. 60c, Abyssinian long-eared owl. 70c, Lanner falcon.

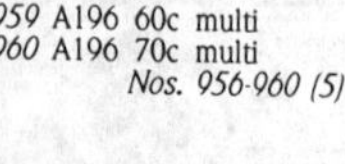

956 A196	10c multi		15	15
957 A196	15c multi		22	22
958 A196	25c multi		35	35
959 A196	60c multi		90	90
960 A196	70c multi		1.00	1.00
		Nos. 956-960 (5)	2.62	2.62

Fight Against Cigarette Smoking — A197

1980, Apr. 7 **Photo.** *Perf. 13x13½*

961 A197	20c shown	20	20
962 A197	60c Cigarette	60	60
963 A197	1b Respiratory system	1.00	1.00

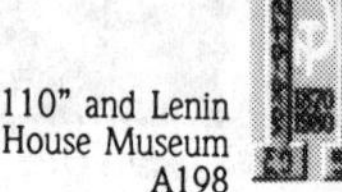

"110" and Lenin House Museum A198

Lenin, 110th "Birthday" (Paintings): 15c, In hiding. 20c, As a young man. 40c, Returning to Russia. 1b, Speaking on the Goelro Plan.

1980, Apr. 22 **Litho.** *Perf. 12x12½*

964 A198	5c multi		15	15
965 A198	15c multi		15	15
966 A198	20c multi		20	20
967 A198	40c multi		40	40
968 A198	1b multi		1.00	1.00
		Nos. 964-968 (5)	1.90	1.90

Grévy's Zebras — A199

1980, June 10 **Litho.** *Perf. 12½x12*

969 A199	10c shown		15	15
970 A199	15c Gazelles		22	22
971 A199	25c Wild hunting dogs		35	35
972 A199	60c Swayne's hartebeests		90	90
973 A199	70c Cheetahs		1.00	1.00
		Nos. 969-973 (5)	2.62	2.62

Runner, Moscow '80 Emblem — A200

1980, July 19 **Photo.** *Perf. 11½x12*

974 A200	30c shown	30	30
975 A200	70c Gymnast	70	70
976 A200	80c Boxing	80	80

22nd Summer Olympic Games, Moscow, July 19-Aug. 3.

Removing Blindfold A201

Bamboo Food Basket A202

1980, Sept. 11 Photo. *Perf. 14x13½*

977 A201 30c shown 30 30
978 A201 40c Revolutionary 40 40
979 A201 50c Woman breaking chain 50 50
980 A201 70c Russian & Ethiopian flags 70 70

6th anniversary of revolution.

1980, Oct. 23 Litho. *Perf. 14*

981 A202 5c shown 15 15
982 A202 15c Hand basket 15 15
983 A202 25c Stool 25 25
984 A202 35c Fruit basket 35 35
985 A202 1b Lamp shade 1.00 1.00
Nos. 981-985 (5) 1.90 1.90

Mekotkocha (Used in Weeding) A203

Traditional Harvesting Tools: 15c, Layda (grain separator). 40c, Mensh (fork). 45c, Mededekia (soil turner). 70c, Mofer & Kenber (plow and yoke).

1980, Dec. 18 Litho. *Perf. 12½x12*

986 A203 10c multi 15 15
987 A203 15c multi 15 15
988 A203 40c multi 40 40
989 A203 45c multi 45 45
990 A203 70c multi 70 70
Nos. 986-990 (5) 1.85 1.85

Baro River Bridge Opening A204

1981, Feb. 28 Photo. *Perf. 13½x13*

991 A204 15c Canoes and ferry 15 15
992 A204 65c Bridge construction 65 65
993 A204 1b shown 1.00 1.00

Semien National Park — A205

World Heritage Year: 5c, Wawel Castle, Poland. 15c, Quito Cathedral, Ecuador. 20c, Old Slave Quarters, Goree Island, Senegal. 30c, Mesa Verde Indian Village, US. 1b, L'Anse aux Meadows excavation, Canada.

Perf. 11x11½, 11½x11

1981, Mar. 10 Photo.

994 A205 5c multi 15 15
995 A205 15c multi 15 15
996 A205 20c multi 20 20
997 A205 30c multi 30 30
998 A205 80c multi 80 80
999 A205 1b multi 1.00 1.00

1981, June 16 Photo.

Designs: 10c, Biet Medhanialem Church, Ethiopia. 15c, Nahanni Natl. Park, Canada. 20c, Yellowstone River Lower Falls, US. 30c, Aachen Cathedral, Germany. 80c, Kicker Rock, San Cristobal Island, Ecuador. 1b, The Lizak corridor, Holy Cross Chapel, Cracow, Poland, vert.

1000 A205 10c multi 15 15
1001 A205 15c multi 15 15
1002 A205 20c multi 20 20
1003 A205 30c multi 30 30
1004 A205 80c multi 80 80
1005 A205 1b multi 1.00 1.00
Nos. 994-1005 (12) 5.20 5.20

Ancient Drinking Vessel — A206

1981, May 5 Litho. *Perf. 12½x12*

1006 A206 20c shown 20 20
1007 A206 25c Spice container 25 25
1008 A206 35c Jug 35 35
1009 A206 40c Cooking pot holder 40 40
1010 A206 60c Animal figurine 60 60
Nos. 1006-1010 (5) 1.80 1.80

Intl. Year of the Disabled A207

7th Anniv. of Revolution A208

1981, July 16 Photo. *Perf. 11½x12*

1011 A207 5c Prostheses 15 15
1012 A207 15c Boys writing 15 15
1013 A207 20c Activities 20 20
1014 A207 40c Knitting 40 40
1015 A207 1b Weaving 1.00 1.00
Nos. 1011-1015 (5) 1.90 1.90

1981, Sept. 10 *Perf. 14*

1016 A208 20c Children's Center 20 20
1017 A208 60c Heroes' Center 60 60
1018 A208 1b Serto Ader (state newspaper) 1.00 1.00

World Food Day — A209

Perf. 13½x12½

1981, Oct. 15 Litho.

1019 A209 5c Wheat airlift 15 15
1020 A209 15c Plowing 15 15
1021 A209 20c Malnutrition 20 20
1022 A209 40c Agriculture education 40 40
1023 A209 1b Cattle, corn 1.00 1.00
Nos. 1019-1023 (5) 1.90 1.90

Ancient Bronze Type of 1978

1981, Dec. 15 Litho. *Perf. 14x13½*

1024 A180 15c Pitcher 15 15
1025 A180 45c Tsenatsil (musical instrument) 45 45
1026 A180 50c Pitcher, diff. 50 50
1027 A180 70c Pot 70 70

Horn Artifacts — A210

1982, Feb. 18 Photo. *Perf. 12x12½*

1028 A210 10c Tobacco containers 15 15
1029 A210 15c Cup 15 15
1030 A210 40c Container, diff. 40 40
1031 A210 45c Goblet 45 45
1032 A210 70c Spoons 70 70
Nos. 1028-1032 (5) 1.85 1.85

Coffee Cultivation A211

1982, May, 6 Photo. *Perf. 13½*

1033 A211 5c Plants 15 15
1034 A211 15c Bushes 15 15
1035 A211 25c Mature bushes 25 25
1036 A211 35c Picking beans 35 35
1037 A211 1b Drinking coffee 1.00 1.00
Nos. 1033-1037 (5) 1.90 1.90

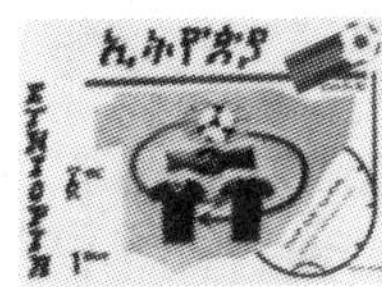

1982 World Cup — A212

Perf. 13½x12½

1982, June 10 Litho.

1038 A212 5c multi 15 15
1039 A212 15c multi 15 15
1040 A212 20c multi 20 20
1041 A212 40c multi 40 40
1042 A212 1b multi 1.00 1.00
Nos. 1038-1042 (5) 1.90 1.90

TB Bacillus Centenary A213

8th Anniv. of Revolution A214

Perf. 13½x12½

1982, July 12 Litho.

1043 A213 15c Cow 15 15
1044 A213 20c Magnifying glass 30 30
1045 A213 30c Koch, microscope 45 45
1046 A213 35c Koch 50 50
1047 A213 80c Man coughing 1.25 1.25
Nos. 1043-1047 (5) 2.65 2.65

1982, Sept. 10 *Perf. 12½x13½*

Designs: Symbols of justice.

1048 A214 80c multi 80 80
1049 A214 1b multi 1.00 1.00

World Standards Day — A215

Perf. 13½x12½

1982, Oct. 14 Litho.

1050 A215 5c Hand, foot, square 15 15
1051 A215 15c Scales 15 15
1052 A215 20c Rulers 20 20
1053 A215 40c Weights 40 40
1054 A215 1b Emblem 1.00 1.00
Nos. 1050-1054 (5) 1.90 1.90

10th Anniv. of UN Conference on Human Environment A216

1982, Dec. 13 Litho. *Perf. 12*

1055 A216 5c Wildlife conservation 15 15
1056 A216 15c Environmental health and settlement 15 15
1057 A216 20c Forest protection 20 20
1058 A216 40c Natl. literacy campaign 40 40
1059 A216 1b Soil and water conservation 1.00 1.00
Nos. 1055-1059 (5) 1.90 1.90

Cave of Sof Omar A217

Various views.

1983, Feb. 10 Photo. *Perf. 13½*

1060 A217 5c multi 15 15
1061 A217 10c multi 15 15
1062 A217 15c multi 15 15
1063 A217 70c multi 70 70
1064 A217 80c multi 80 80
Nos. 1060-1064 (5) 1.95 1.95

A218

A219

1983, Apr. 29 Photo. *Perf. 14*

1065 A218 80c multi 80 80
1066 A218 1b multi 1.00 1.00

25th Anniv. of Economic Commission for Africa.

Perf. 12½x11½

1983, June 3 Photo.

1067 A219 85c Emblem 85 85
1068 A219 1b Lighthouse, ship 1.00 1.00

25th Anniv. of Intl. Maritime Org.

WCY — A220

9th Anniv. of Revolution — A221

1983, July 22 Litho.

1069 A220 25c UPU emblem 25 25
1070 A220 55c Dish antenna, emblems 55 55
1071 A220 1b Bridge, tunnel 1.00 1.00

1983, Sept. 10 Litho. *Perf. 14½*

1072 A221 25c Dove 25 25
1073 A221 55c Star 55 55
1074 A221 1b Emblems 1.00 1.00

Musical Instruments A222

Charaxes Galawadiwosi A223

Perf. 12½x13½

1983, Oct. 17 Litho.

1075 A222 5c Hura 15 15
1076 A222 15c Dinke 15 15
1077 A222 20c Meleket 20 20
1078 A222 40c Embilta 40 40
1079 A222 1b Tom 1.00 1.00
Nos. 1075-1079 (5) 1.90 1.90

1983, Dec. 13 Photo. *Perf. 14*

1080 A223 10c shown 15 15
1081 A223 15c Epiphora elianae 20 20
1082 A223 55c Batuana rougeoti 70 70
1083 A223 1b Achaea saboeareginae 1.25 1.25

Intl. Anti-Apartheid Year (1983) — A224

Perf. 13½x12½

1984, Feb. 10 Litho.

1084 A224 5c multi 15 15
1085 A224 15c multi 15 15
1086 A224 20c multi 20 20

1087 A224 40c multi 40 40
1088 A224 1b multi 1.00 1.00
Nos. 1084-1088 (5) 1.90 1.90

Local Flowers — A225

Traditional Houses — A226

1984, Apr. 13 Litho. ***Perf. 13½***
1089 A225 5c Protea gaguedi 15 15
1090 A225 25c Sedum epidendrum 25 25
1091 A225 50c Echinops amplexicaulis 50 50
1092 A225 1b Canarina eminii 1.00 1.00

1984, Aug. 3 Photo.
1093 A226 15c Konso 15 15
1094 A226 65c Dorze 65 65
1095 A226 1b Harer 1.00 1.00

10th Anniv. of the Revolution A227

1984, Sept. 10 Photo. ***Perf. 11½***
1096 A227 5c Sept. 12, 1974 15 15
1097 A227 10c Mar. 4, 1975 15 15
1098 A227 15c Apr. 20, 1976 15 15
1099 A227 20c Feb. 11, 1977 20 20
1100 A227 25c Mar. 1978 25 25
1101 A227 40c July 8, 1980 40 40
1102 A227 45c Dec. 17, 1980 45 45
1103 A227 50c Sept. 15, 1980 50 50
1104 A227 70c Sept. 18, 1981 70 70
1105 A227 1b June 6, 1983 1.00 1.00
Nos. 1096-1105 (10) 3.95 3.95

Traditional Sports — A228

1984, Dec. 7 Photo. ***Perf. 14***
1106 A228 5c Gugs 15 15
1107 A228 25c Tigil 25 25
1108 A228 50c Genna 50 50
1109 A228 1b Gebeta 1.00 1.00

Birds — A229

1985, Jan. 4 Photo. ***Perf. 14½***
1110 A229 5c Francolinus harwoodi 15 15
1111 A229 15c Rallus rougetti 15 15
1112 A229 80c Merops pusillus 80 80
1113 A229 85c Malimbus rubriceps 85 85

Indigenous Fauna — A230

1985, Feb. 4 Litho. ***Perf. 12½x12***
1114 A230 20c Hippopotamus amphibius 20 20
1115 A230 25c Litocranius walleri 25 25
1116 A230 40c Sylivicapra grimmia 40 40
1117 A230 1b Rhynchotragus guentheri 1.00 1.00

Freshwater Fish A231

1985, Apr. 3 ***Perf. 13½***
1118 A231 10c Barbus degeni 15 15
1119 A231 20c Labeo cylindricus 20 20
1120 A231 55c Protopterus annectens 55 55
1121 A231 1b Alestes dentex 1.00 1.00

Medicinal Plants — A232

1985, May 23 ***Perf. 11½x12½***
1122 A232 10c Securidaca longependunculata 15 15
1123 A232 20c Plumbago zeylanicum 20 20
1124 A232 55c Brucea antidysenteric 55 55
1125 A232 1b Dorstenia barminiana 1.00 1.00

Ethiopian Red Cross Soc., 50th Anniv. — A233

1985, Aug. 6 Litho. ***Perf. 13½x13***
1126 A233 35c multi 35 35
1127 A233 55c multi 55 55
1128 A233 1b multi 1.00 1.00

Ethiopian Revolution, 11th Anniv. A234

Designs: 10c, Kombolcha Mills, Welo Region. 80c, Muger Cement Factory, Mokoda, Shoa. 1b, Relocating famine and drought victims.

1985, Sept. 10 Litho. ***Perf. 13½***
1129 A234 10c multicolored 15 15
1130 A234 80c multicolored 80 80
1131 A234 1b multicolored 1.00 1.00

UN 40th Anniv. — A235

1985, Nov. 22 Litho. ***Perf. 13½x14***
1132 A235 25c multicolored 25 25
1133 A235 55c multicolored 55 55
1134 A235 1b multicolored 1.00 1.00

Anti-Polio Campaign A236

Perf. 11½x12½
1986, Jan. 10 Litho.
1135 A236 5c Boy, prosthesis 15 15
1136 A236 10c Boy on crutches 15 15
1137 A236 20c Nurse, boy 20 20
1138 A236 55c Man, sewing machine 55 55
1139 A236 1b Nurse, mother, child 1.00 1.00
Nos. 1135-1139 (5) 2.05 2.05

Indigenous Trees — A237

1986, Feb. 10 ***Perf. 13½x14½***
1140 A237 10c Millettia ferruginea 15 15
1141 A237 30c Syzyigum guineense 30 30
1142 A237 50c Cordia africana 50 50
1143 A237 1b Hagenia abyssinica 1.00 1.00

Spices — A238

1986, Mar. 10 ***Perf. 13½***
1144 A238 10c Zingiber officinale rosc 15 15
1145 A238 15c Ocimum bacilicum 15 15
1146 A238 55c Sinapsis alba 55 55
1147 A238 1b Cuminum cyminum 1.00 1.00

Current Coins, Obverse and Reverse A239

1986, May 9 Litho. ***Perf. 13½x14***
1148 A239 5c 1-cent 15 15
1149 A239 10c 25-cent 15 15
1150 A239 35c 5-cent 35 35
1151 A239 50c 50-cent 50 50
1152 A239 1b 10-cent 1.00 1.00
Nos. 1148-1152 (5) 2.15 2.15

Discovery of 3.5 Million Year-old Hominid Skeleton, Dinkinesh — A240

1986, July 4 ***Perf. 13½***
1153 A240 2b multicolored 2.00 2.00

Ethiopian Revolution, 12th Anniv. A241

Designs: 20c, Military service. 30c, Tiglachin monument. 55c, Delachin Exhibition emblem. 85c, Food processing plant, Merti.

1986, Sept. 10 Litho. ***Perf. 14***
1154 A241 20c multicolored 20 20
1155 A241 30c multicolored 30 30
1156 A241 55c multicolored 52 52
1157 A241 85c multicolored 82 82

Ethiopian Airlines, 40th Anniv. — A242

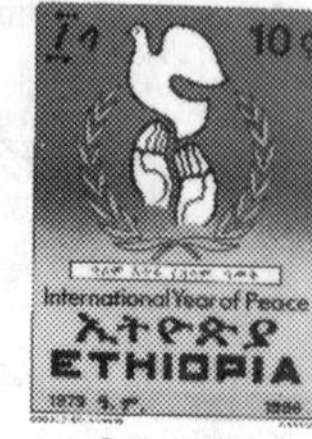

Intl. Peace Year — A243

1986, Oct. 14
1158 A242 10c DC-7 15 15
1159 A242 20c DC-3 20 20
1160 A242 30c Personnel, jet tail 30 30
1161 A242 40c Engine 38 38
1162 A242 1b DC-7, map 95 95
Nos. 1158-1162 (5) 1.98 1.98

1986, Nov. 13 ***Perf. 13½***
1163 A243 10c multicolored 15 15
1164 A243 80c multicolored 78 78
1165 A243 1b multicolored 95 95

UN Child Survival Campaign — A244

1986, Dec. 11 ***Perf. 12½***
1166 A244 10c Breast feeding 15 15
1167 A244 35c Immunization 35 35
1168 A244 50c Hygiene 48 48
1169 A244 1b Growth monitoring 95 95

Umbrellas — A245

1987, Feb. 10 ***Perf. 13½***
1170 A245 35c Axum 35 35
1171 A245 55c Negele-Borena 52 52
1172 A245 1b Jimma 95 95

Artwork by Afewerk Tekle (b. 1932) A246

Designs: 50c, Defender of His Country - Afar, stained glass window. 2b, Defender of His Country - Adwa, painting.

1987, Mar. 19 Litho. ***Perf. 13½***
1173 A246 50c multicolored 48 48
1174 A246 2b multicolored 1.90 1.90

Stained Glass Windows by Afewerk Tekle — A247

1987, June 16 Photo. ***Perf. 11½x12***
Granite Paper
1175 A247 50c multicolored

Size: 26x38mm

1176 A247 80c multicolored
1177 A247 1b multicolored

Struggle of the African People.
Sold out in Addis Ababa on date of issue.

Simien Fox — A248

1987, June 29 Litho. *Perf. 13½*

1178 A248 5c multicolored 15 15
1179 A248 10c multicolored 15 15
1180 A248 15c multicolored 15 15
1181 A248 20c multicolored 20 20
1182 A248 25c multicolored 25 25
1183 A248 45c multicolored 45 45
1184 A248 55c multicolored 52 52
Nos. 1178-1184 (7) 1.87 1.87

For overprints see Nos. 1234-1237.

Ethiopian Revolution, 13th Anniv. — A249

1987, Sept. 10 *Perf. 12½*

1185 A249 5c Constitution, freedom of press 15 15
1186 A249 10c Popular elections 15 15
1187 A249 80c Referendum 75 75
1188 A249 1b Bahir Dar Airport, map 95 95

Addis Ababa, Cent. — A251

"100" and views: 5c, Emperor Menelik II, Empress Taitu and city. 10c, Traditional buildings. 80c, Central Addis Ababa. 1b, Aerial view of city.

1987, Sept. 7 *Perf. 13½*

1193 A251 5c multi 15 15
1194 A251 10c multi 15 15
1195 A251 80c multi 75 75
1196 A251 1b multi 95 95

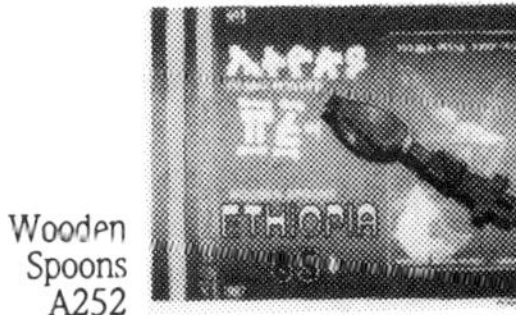
Wooden Spoons A252

1987, Nov. 30

1197 A252 85c Hurso, Harerge 80 80
1198 A252 1b Borena, Sidamo 95 95

Intl. Year of Shelter for the Homeless A253

1988, Jan. Litho. *Perf. 13*

1199 A253 10c Village revitalization program 15 15
1200 A253 35c Resettlement program 35 35
1201 A253 50c Urban improvement 50 50
1202 A253 1b Cooperative and government housing 1.00 1.00

October Revolution, Russia, 70th Anniv. (in 1987) A254

Painting: 1b, Lenin receiving Workers' Council delegates in the Smolny Institute.

1988, Feb. 17 *Perf. 12½x12*

1203 A254 1b multi 98 98

Traditional Hunting Methods and Prey — A255

1988, Mar. 30 Litho. *Perf. 13½*

1204 A255 85c Bow and arrow 85 85
1205 A255 1b Double-pronged spear 1.00 1.00

A256 A257

1988, May 6

1206 A256 85c multi 85 85
1207 A256 1b multi 1.00 1.00

Intl. Red Cross and Red Crescent Organizations, 125th annivs.

1988, June 7 Photo. *Perf. 11½x12*

1208 A257 2b multi 1.95 1.95

Organizaton of African Unity, 25th anniv.

Ethiopian Revolution, 14th Anniv. A258

Design: Various details of *The Victory of Ethiopia*, six-panel mural by Afewerk Tekle (b. 1932) in the museum of the Heroes Center, Debre Zeit.

1988, June 28 Litho. *Perf. 13½x13*

1209 A258 10c Jet over farm, vert. 15 15
1210 A258 20c Farm workers on road, vert. 20 20
1211 A258 35c Allegory of unity, vert. 35 35
1212 A258 55c Jet over industry 55 55
1213 A258 80c Steel works 80 80
1214 A258 1b Weaving 1.00 1.00
Nos. 1209-1214 (6) 3.05 3.05

Nos. 1209-1211 vert.

Women, Bracelets and Maps A259

1988, July 27 Litho. *Perf. 13x13½*

1215 A259 15c Sidamo 15 15
1216 A259 85c Arsi 85 85
1217 A259 1b Harerge 1.00 1.00

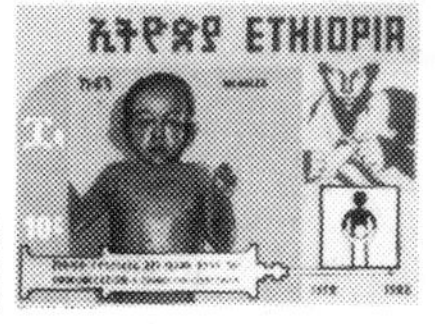
Immunize Every Child A260

1988, June 14 Litho. *Perf. 13x13½*

1218 A260 10c Measles 15 15
1219 A260 35c Tetanus 35 35
1220 A260 50c Whooping cough 50 50
1221 A260 1b Diphtheria 1.00 1.00

Intl. Fund for Agricultural Development (IFAD), 10th Anniv. A261

1988, Aug. 16 *Perf. 13½*

1222 A261 15c Monetary aid 15 15
1223 A261 85c Farming activities 85 85
1224 A261 1b Harvest 1.00 1.00

People's Democratic Republic of Ethiopia, 1st Anniv. A262

Designs: 5c, 1st Session of the natl. Shengo (congress). 10c, Mengistu Haile-Mariam, 1st president of the republic. 80c, Natl. crest, flag and crowd. 1b, State assembly building.

1988, Sept. 9 *Perf. 14*

1225 A262 5c multi 15 15
1226 A262 10c multi 15 15
1227 A262 80c multi 80 80
1228 A262 1b multi 1.00 1.00

Bank Notes A263

1988, Nov. 10 Photo. *Perf. 13*

1229 A263 5c 1-Birr 15 15
1230 A263 10c 5-Birr 15 15
1231 A263 20c 10-Birr 20 20
1232 A263 75c 50-Birr 75 75
1233 A263 85c 100-Birr 85 85
Nos. 1229-1233 (5) 2.10 2.10

Nos. 1181-1184 Overprinted "WORLD AIDS DAY" in Two Languages

1988, Dec. 1 Litho. *Perf. 13½*

1234 A248 20c multi 22 22
1235 A248 25c multi 28 28
1236 A248 45c multi 48 48
1237 A248 55c multi 58 58

Intl. Day for the Fight Against AIDS.

WHO, 40th Anniv. A264

1988, Dec. 30 Litho. *Perf. 14*

1238 A264 50c multi 50 50
1239 A264 65c multi 65 65
1240 A264 85c multi 85 85

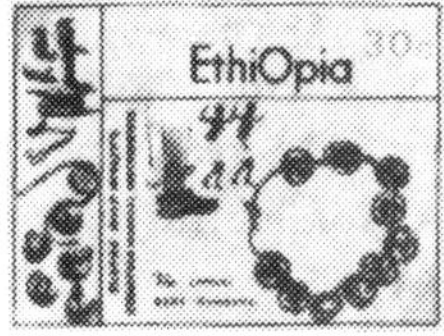
Traditional Musical Instruments A265

1989, Feb. 9 *Perf. 13x13½*

1241 A265 30c Gere 32 32
1242 A265 40c Fanfa 42 42
1243 A265 50c Chancha 52 52
1244 A265 85c Negareet 88 88

Ethiopian Shipping Lines, 25th Anniv. A266

1989, Mar. 27 Litho. *Perf. 14*

1245 A266 15c *Abyot* 16 16
1246 A266 30c *Wolwol* 32 32
1247 A266 55c *Queen of Sheba* 58 58
1248 A266 1b *Abbay Wonz* 1.05 1.05

Birds — A267

1989, May 18 Litho. *Perf. 13½x13*

1249 A267 10c Yellow-fronted parrot 15 15
1250 A267 35c White-winged cliff chat 35 35
1251 A267 50c Yellow-throated seed eater 50 50
1252 A267 1b Black-headed forest oriole 1.00 1.00

Production of Early Manuscripts A268

1989, June 16 Litho. *Perf. 13½*

1253 A268 5c Preparing vellum 15 15
1254 A268 10c Ink horns, pens 15 15
1255 A268 20c Scribe 20 20
1256 A268 75c Book binding 75 75
1257 A268 85c Illuminated manuscript 85 85
Nos. 1253-1257 (5) 2.10 2.10

Indigenous Wildlife — A269

1989, July 18

1258 A269 30c Greater kudu 30 30
1259 A269 40c Lesser kudu 40 40
1260 A269 50c Roan antelope 50 50
1261 A269 85c Nile lechwe 85 85

People's Democratic Republic of Ethiopia, 2nd Anniv. A270

Designs: 15c, Melka Wakana Hydroelectric Power Station. 75c, Adea Berga Dairy Farm. 1b, Pawe Hospital.

1989, Sept. 8

1262 A270 15c multi 15 15
1263 A270 75c multi 75 75
1264 A270 1b multi 1.00 1.00

African Development Bank, 25th Anniv. — A271

1989, Nov. 10 Litho. *Perf. 13¹/₂x13*

1265 A271 20c multicolored 20 20
1266 A271 80c multicolored 80 80
1267 A271 1b multicolored 1.00 1.00

Pan-African Postal Union, 10th Anniv. — A272

1990, Jan. 18 Litho. *Perf. 13¹/₂*

1268 A272 50c multicolored 50 50
1269 A272 70c multicolored 70 70
1270 A272 80c multicolored 80 80

UNESCO World Literacy Year — A273

Designs: 15c, Illiterate man holding newspaper upside down. 85c, Adults learning alphabet in school. 1b, Literate man holding newspaper upright.

1990, Mar. 13

1271 A273 15c multicolored 15 15
1272 A273 85c multicolored 85 85
1273 A273 1b multicolored 1.00 1.00

Abebe Bikila, Marathon Runner A274

1990, Apr. 17

1274 A274 5c Race 15 15
1275 A274 10c Flag bearer, Olympic team 15 15
1276 A274 20c Race, diff. 20 20
1277 A274 75c Race, diff. 75 75
1278 A274 85c Bikila, trophies, vert. 85 85
Nos. 1274-1278 (5) 2.10 2.10

Flag — A275

1990, Apr. 30 Litho. *Perf. 13¹/₂x13*

1279 A275 5c multicolored 15 15
1280 A275 10c multicolored 15 15
1281 A275 15c multicolored 15 15
1282 A275 20c multicolored 20 20
1283 A275 25c multicolored 25 25
1284 A275 30c multicolored 30 30
1285 A275 35c multicolored 35 35
1286 A275 40c multicolored 40 40
1287 A275 45c multicolored 45 45
1288 A275 50c multicolored 50 50
1289 A275 55c multicolored 55 55
1290 A275 60c multicolored 60 60
1291 A275 70c multicolored 70 70
1292 A275 80c multicolored 80 80
1293 A275 85c multicolored 85 85
1294 A275 90c multicolored 90 90
1295 A275 1b multicolored 1.00 1.00
1296 A275 2b multicolored 2.00 2.00
1297 A275 3b multicolored 3.00 3.00
Nos. 1279-1297 (19) 13.30 13.30

Dated 1989.

Sowing of Teff — A276

1990, May 18 Litho. *Perf. 13¹/₂*

1298 A276 5c shown 15 15
1299 A276 10c Harvesting 15 15
1300 A276 20c Threshing 20 20
1301 A276 75c Storage, preparation 75 75
1302 A276 85c Consumption 85 85
Nos. 1298-1302 (5) 2.10 2.10

Walia Ibex — A277

1990, June 18 *Perf. 14x13¹/₂*

1303 A277 5c multicolored 15 15
1304 A277 15c multicolored 15 15
1305 A277 20c multicolored 20 20
1306 A277 1b multi, horiz. 1.00 1.00

World AIDS Day — A278

1991, Jan. 31 Litho. *Perf. 14*

1307 A278 15c Stages of disease 15 15
1308 A278 85c Education 85 85
1309 A278 1b Causes, preventatives 1.00 1.00

Intl. Decade for Natural Disaster Reduction A279

Map of disaster-prone African areas and: 5c, Volcano. 10c, Earthquake. 15c, Drought. 30c, Flood. 50c, Red Cross health education. 1b, Red Cross assisting fire victims.

1991, Apr. 9 Litho. *Perf. 14*

1310 A279 5c multicolored 15 15
1311 A279 10c multicolored 15 15
1312 A279 15c multicolored 15 15
1313 A279 30c multicolored 30 30
1314 A279 50c multicolored 50 50
1315 A279 1b multicolored 1.00 1.00
Nos. 1310-1315 (6) 2.25 2.25

The Cannon of Tewodros A280

Designs: 15c, Villagers receiving cannon 85c, Warriors leaving with cannon. 1b, Hauling cannon up mountainside.

1991, June 18 Litho. *Perf. 13¹/₂*

1316 A280 15c multicolored 15 15
1317 A280 85c multicolored 85 85
1318 A280 1b multicolored 1.00 1.00

Fish — A281

1991, Sept. 6 Litho. *Perf. 13¹/₂*

1319 A281 5c Lacepede 15 15
1320 A281 15c Black-finned butterflyfish 15 15
1321 A281 80c Regal angelfish 80 80
1322 A281 1b Bleeker 1.00 1.00

A282

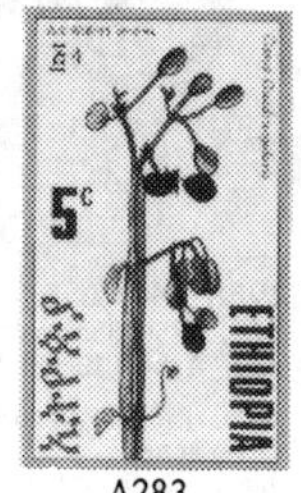

A283

Traditional Ceremonial Robes: Various robes.

1992, Jan. 1 Litho. *Perf. 13¹/₂x14*

1323 A282 5c yellow & multi 15 15
1324 A282 15c orange & multi 15 15
1325 A282 80c yel green & multi 80 80
1326 A282 1b blue & multi 1.00 1.00

1992, Mar. 5 Litho. *Perf. 13¹/₂x14*

Flowers: 5c, Cissus quadrangularis. 15c, Delphinium dasycaulon. 80c, Epilobium hirsutum. 1b, Kniphofia foliosa.

1327 A283 5c multicolored 15 15
1328 A283 15c multicolored 15 15
1329 A283 80c multicolored 80 80
1330 A283 1b multicolored 1.00 1.00

Traditional Homes — A284

1992, May 14 Litho. *Perf. 12¹/₂x12*

1331 A284 15c Afar 15 15
1332 A284 35c Anuak 35 35
1333 A284 50c Gimira 50 50
1334 A284 1b Oromo 1.00 1.00

A285

A286

Pottery.

1992, May Litho. *Perf. 13x13¹/₂*

1335 A285 15c Cover 15 15
1336 A285 85c Jug 85 85
1337 A285 1b Tall jar 1.00 1.00

1992, Sept. 29 *Perf. 14x13¹/₂*

1338 A286 20c multicolored 20 20
1339 A286 80c multicolored 80 80
1340 A286 1b multicolored 1.00 1.00

Pan-African Rinderpest campaign.

A287

Birds — A288

Musical instruments.

1993, Feb. 16 Litho. *Perf. 14x13¹/₂*

1341 A287 15c Catchel 15 15
1342 A287 35c Huldudwa 35 35
1343 A287 50c Dita 50 50
1344 A287 1b Atamo 1.00 1.00

1993, Apr. 22 Litho. *Perf. 14x13¹/₂*

1345 A288 15c Banded barbet 15 15
1346 A288 35c Ruppell's chat 18 18
1347 A288 50c Abyssinian catbird 25 25
1348 A288 1b White-billed starling 50 50

Animals A289

1993, May 14 *Perf. 13¹/₂x14*

1349 A289 15c Honey badger 15 15
1350 A289 35c Spotted necked otter 18 18
1351 A289 50c Rock hyrax 25 25
1352 A289 1b White-tailed mongoose 50 50

Herbs — A290

1993, June 10 *Perf. 14x13¹/₂*

1353 A290 5c Caraway seed 15 15
1354 A290 15c Garlic 15 15
1355 A290 80c Turmeric 40 40
1356 A290 1b Capsicum peppers 50 50
Set value 1.00 1.00

Butterflies — A291

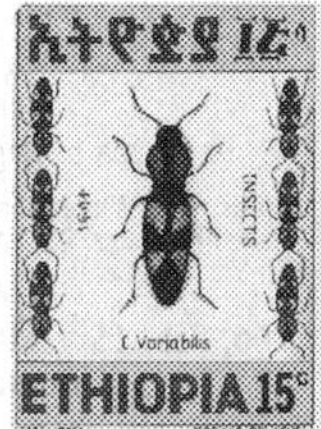

Insects — A292

1993, July 9 Litho. *Perf. 14x13½*

No.	Type	Description	Unused	Used
1357	A291	20c Papilio echeriodes	15	15
1358	A291	30c Papilio rex	15	15
1359	A291	50c Graphium policenes	25	25
1360	A291	1b Graphium leonidas	50	50

1993, Aug. 10

No.	Type	Description	Unused	Used
1361	A292	15c C. Variabilis	15	15
1362	A292	35c Lycus trabeatus	18	18
1363	A292	50c Malachius bifasciatus	25	25
1364	A292	1b Homoeogryllus xanthographus	50	50

Trees A293

1993, Oct. 12 Litho. *Perf. 13½x14*

No.	Type	Description	Unused	Used
1365	A293	15c Euphorbia ampliphylla	15	15
1366	A293	35c Erythrina brucei	18	18
1367	A293	50c Draceana steudneri	25	25
1368	A293	1b Allophylus abyssinicus	50	50

Lakes A294

1993, Dec. 14

No.	Type	Description	Unused	Used
1369	A294	15c Wonchi	15	15
1370	A294	35c Zuquala	15	15
1371	A294	50c Ashengi	22	22
1372	A294	1b Tana	42	42

SEMI-POSTAL STAMPS

Types of 1931, Overprinted in Red at Upper Left

Perf. 12x12½, 12½x12

1936, Feb. 25 Unwmk.

No.	Type	Description	Unused	Used
B1	A27	1g light green	35	30
B2	A27	2g rose	35	30
B3	A25	4g blue	35	30
B4	A27	8g brown	50	50
B5	A25	1t purple	50	50
		Nos. B1-B5 (5)	2.05	1.90

Nos. B1-B5 were sold at twice face value, the surtax going to the Red Cross.

Catalogue values for unused stamps in this section, from this point to the end of the section, are for Never Hinged items.

Nos. 289, 290 and 292 to 294 Surcharged in Blue

EXPOSITION
1949
+8c

Perf. 13x13½

1949, June 13 Wmk. 282

No.	Type	Description	Unused	Used
B6	A53	8c + 8c deep org	1.25	1.25
B7	A53	12c + 5c red	1.25	1.25
B8	A53	30c + 15c org brn	2.50	2.50
B9	A53	70c + 70c rose lilac	16.50	16.50
B10	A53	$1 + 80c dk car rose	20.00	20.00
		Nos. B6-B10 (5)	41.50	41.50

See Nos. B16-B20.

Type A39 Surcharged in Red or Carmine

+ 10 ct.

Perf. 11½

1950, May 8 Unwmk. Photo.

Various Designs

Inscribed "Croix Rouge"

No.	Type	Description	Unused	Used
B11	A39	5c + 10c brt grn	85	85
B12	A39	10c + 10c brt red	1.25	1.25
B13	A39	25c + 10c brt bl	2.00	2.00
B14	A39	50c + 10c dk yel brn	5.75	5.75
B15	A39	1t + 10c brt vio	9.00	9.00
		Nos. B11-B15 (5)	18.85	18.85

The surtax was for the Red Cross.

The surcharge includes two dots which invalidate the original surtax. The original surcharge was red, a 1951 printing was carmine. Forgeries exist.

Nos. B6-B10 Overprinted in Black

1951

Perf. 13x13½

1951, Nov. 17 Wmk. 282

No.	Type	Description	Unused	Used
B16	A53	8c + 8c dp org	65	65
B17	A53	12c + 5c red	65	65
B18	A53	30c + 15c org brn	1.00	1.00
B19	A53	70c + 70c rose lilac	8.75	8.75
B20	A53	$1 + 80c dk car rose	13.00	13.00
		Nos. B16-B20 (5)	24.05	24.05

Tree, Staff and Snake — SP1

Wmk. 282

1951, Nov. 25 Engr. *Perf. 13*

Lower Panel in Red

No.	Type	Description	Unused	Used
B21	SP1	5c + 2c dp bl grn	30	15
B22	SP1	10c + 3c orange	50	25
B23	SP1	15c + 3c dp bl	60	40
B24	SP1	30c + 5c red	1.35	1.00
B25	SP1	50c + 7c red brn	3.00	2.00
B26	SP1	$1 + 10c purple	5.25	3.00
		Nos. B21-B26 (6)	11.00	6.80

The surtax was for anti-tuberculosis work.

1958, Dec. 1

Lower Panel in Red

No.	Type	Description	Unused	Used
B27	SP1	20c + 3c dl pur	40	30
B28	SP1	25c + 4c emerald	50	35
B29	SP1	35c + 5c rose vio	75	40
B30	SP1	60c + 7c vio bl	1.50	80
B31	SP1	65c + 7c violet	3.00	1.75
B32	SP1	80c + 9c car rose	5.00	3.00
		Nos. B27-B32 (6)	11.15	6.60
		Nos. B21-B32 (12)	22.15	13.40

The surtax was for anti-tuberculosis work.

Nos. B21-B32 were the only stamps on sale from Dec. 1-25, 1958.

Type of Regular Issue, 1955, Overprinted and Surcharged

RED CROSS CENTENARY 1859 1959 +2c

Engr.; Cross Typo. in Red

1959, May 30 Wmk. 282

No.	Type	Description	Unused	Used
B33	A62	15c + 2c olive bister & rose red	60	60
B34	A62	20c + 3c vio & emer	75	75
B35	A62	30c + 5c rose car & grnsh bl	1.25	1.25

Cent. of the Intl. Red Cross idea. Surtax for the Red Cross.

The overprint includes the cross, "RED CROSS CENTENARY" and date in two languages. The surcharge includes the date in Amharic and the new surtax. The surcharge was applied locally.

Type A39 Surcharged

Silver Jubilee
1960
+ 5 ct.

Perf. 11½

1960, May 7 Photo. Unwmk.

No.	Type	Description	Unused	Used
B36	A39	5c + 1c brt green	35	25
B37	A39	10c + 2c brt red	50	30
B38	A39	25c + 3c brt blue	1.10	75
B39	A39	50c + 4c dk yel brn	1.75	1.50
B40	A39	1t + 5c brt vio	3.00	2.75
		Nos. B36-B40 (5)	6.70	5.55

25th anniversary of Ethiopian Red Cross.

Crippled Boy on Crutches — SP2

Perf. 13½

1963, July 23 Wmk. 282 Engr.

No.	Type	Description	Unused	Used
B41	SP2	10c + 2c ultra	25	25
B42	SP2	15c + 3c red	35	30
B43	SP2	50c + 5c brt green	1.10	1.00
B44	SP2	60c + 5c red lilac	1.75	1.25

The surtax was to aid the disabled.

AIR POST STAMPS

Regular Issue of 1928 Handstamped in Violet, Red, Black or Green

Perf. 13½x14

1929, Aug. 17 Unwmk.

No.	Type	Description	Unused	Used
C1	A22	⅛m org & lt bl	60	70
C2	A23	¼m ind & red org	60	70
C3	A22	½m gray grn & blk	60	70
C4	A23	1m dk car & blk	60	70
C5	A22	2m dk bl & blk	70	85
C6	A23	4m yel & olive	70	85
C7	A22	8m vio & olive	70	85
C8	A23	1t org brn & vio	85	85
C9	A22	2t grn & bister	1.10	1.40
C10	A23	3t choc & grn	1.10	1.40
		Nos. C1-C10 (10)	7.55	9.00

The overprint signifies "17 August 1929-Airplane of the Ethiopian Government." The stamps commemorate the arrival at Addis Ababa of the 1st airplane of the Ethiopian Government. There are 3 types of the overprint: (I) 19½mm high; "colon" at right of bottom word. (II) 20mm high; same "colon." (III) 19½mm high; no "colon." Many errors exist.

Symbols of Empire, Airplane and Map — AP1

1931, June 17 Engr. *Perf. 12½*

No.	Type	Description	Unused	Used
C11	AP1	1g orange red	15	20
C12	AP1	2g ultra	15	22
C13	AP1	4g violet	16	32
C14	AP1	8g blue green	40	65
C15	AP1	1t olive brn	95	80
C16	AP1	2t carmine	1.75	3.00
C17	AP1	3t yel green	2.50	4.00
		Nos. C11-C17 (7)	6.06	9.19

Nos. C11 to C17 exist imperforate.

Reprints of C11 to C17 exist. Paper is thinner and gum whiter than the originals and the ink is heavy and shiny. Originals have ink that is dull and granular. Reprints usually sell at about one-tenth of above values.

Nos. 250, 255 and 257 Surcharged in Black

a: 20 - 4 - 39 / II 12

b: AERIENNE / REPRISE POSTE / ETHIOPIENNE / 29/12/46 / Eth. Doll. 0,50

Perf. 14x13½

1947, Mar. 20 Unwmk.

No.	Type	Description	Unused	Used
C18	A33 (a)	12c on 4c	24.00	24.00
C19	A33 (b)	50c on 25c	24.00	24.00
a.		"26-12-46"	100.00	
C20	A33 (b)	$2 on 60c	40.00	40.00
a.		"26-12-46"	170.00	

Resumption of airmail service, Dec. 29, 1946.

Catalogue values for unused stamps in this section, from this point to the end of the section, are for Never Hinged items.

Franklin D. Roosevelt AP2

Design: $2, Haile Selassie.

Engraved and Photogravure

1947, May 23 *Perf. 12½*

No.	Type	Description	Unused	Used
C21	AP2	$1 dk pur & sepia	4.00	3.50
C22	AP2	$2 car & dp bl	6.00	5.00

Farmer Plowing AP3

Designs: 10c, 25c, Zoquala, extinct volcano. 30c, 35c, Tesissat Falls, Abai River. 65c, 70c, Amba Alaguie. $1, Sacala, source of Nile. $3, Gorgora and Dembia, Lake Tana. $5, Magdala, former capital. $10, Ras Dashan, mountain peak.

Perf. 13x13½

1947-55 Wmk. 282 Engr.

No.	Type	Description	Unused	Used
C23	AP3	8c pur brn	20	15
C24	AP3	10c brt grn	20	15
C25	AP3	25c dl pur ('52)	35	20
C26	AP3	30c org yel	50	15
C27	AP3	35c blue ('55)	50	25
C28	AP3	65c purple ('51)	60	40
C29	AP3	70c red	90	40
C30	AP3	$1 deep blue	1.00	50
C31	AP3	$3 rose lilac	4.00	2.50

C32 AP3 $5 red brown 7.50 3.50
C33 AP3 $10 rose violet 15.00 9.00
Nos. C23-C33 (11) 30.75 17.20

For overprints see Nos. C64-C70.

UPU Monument, Bern — AP4

1950, Apr. 3 Unwmk. *Perf. 12½*

C34 AP4 5c grn & red 20 15
C35 AP4 15c dk sl grn & car 25 25
C36 AP4 25c org yel & grn 30 25
C37 AP4 50c car & ultra 75 60

75th anniv. of the UPU.

Convair Plane over Mountains AP5

Engraved and Lithographed
1955, Dec. 30 Unwmk. *Perf. 12½*
Center Multicolored

C38 AP5 10c gray green 40 20
C39 AP5 15c carmine 50 25
C40 AP5 20c violet 75 40

10th anniversary of Ethiopian Airlines.

Promulgating the Constitution — AP6

Perf. 14x13½
1956, July 16 Engr. Wmk. 282

C41 AP6 10c redsh brn & ultra 30 20
C42 AP6 15c dk car rose & ol grn 40 25
C43 AP6 20c bl & org red 60 40
C44 AP6 25c pur & grn 75 50
C45 AP6 30c dk grn & red brn 1.00 75
Nos. C41-C45 (5) 3.05 2.10

25th anniversary of the constitution.

Aksum AP7

Ancient Capitals: 10c, Lalibela. 15c, Gondar. 20c, Mekele. 25c, Ankober.

1957, Feb. 7 *Perf. 14*
Centers in Green

C46 AP7 5c red brown 50 25
C47 AP7 10c rose carmine 50 25
C48 AP7 15c red orange 60 30
C49 AP7 20c ultramarine 85 45
C50 AP7 25c claret 1.25 65
Nos. C46-C50 (5) 3.70 1.90

Amharic "A" — AP8

Designs: Various Amharic characters and views of Addis Ababa. The characters, arranged by values, spell Addis Ababa.

1957, Feb. 14 Engr.
Amharic Letters in Scarlet

C51 AP8 5c ultra, *sal pink* 15 15
C52 AP8 10c ol grn, *pink* 25 15
C53 AP8 15c dl pur, *yel* 35 15
C54 AP8 20c grn, *buff* 50 25
C55 AP8 25c plum, *pale bl* 75 30
C56 AP8 30c red, *pale grn* 90 35
Nos. C51-C56 (6) 2.90 1.35

70th anniversary of Addis Ababa.

Map, Rock Church at Lalibela and Obelisk AP9

1958, Apr. 15 Wmk. 282 *Perf. 13½*

C57 AP9 10c green 20 15
C58 AP9 20c rose red 30 20
C59 AP9 30c bright blue 50 25

Conf. of Independent African States, Accra, Apr. 15-22.

Map of Africa and UN Emblem AP10

1958, Dec. 29 *Perf. 13*

C60 AP10 5c emerald 15 15
C61 AP10 20c carmine rose 25 20
C62 AP10 25c ultramarine 30 25
C63 AP10 50c pale purple 60 40

1st session of the UN Economic Conf. for Africa, opened in Addis Ababa Dec. 29.

Nos. C23-29 Overprinted
የአየር ፖስት ፴ኛ ዓመት
30th Airmail Ann.
1929 - 1959

Perf. 13x13½
1959, Aug. 16 Engr. Wmk. 282

C64 AP3 8c pur brn 30 25
C65 AP3 10c brt grn 40 30
C66 AP3 25c dl pur 60 35
C67 AP3 30c org yel 65 50
C68 AP3 35c blue 85 55
C69 AP3 65c purple 1.25 85
C70 AP3 70c red 1.60 1.10
Nos. C64-C70 (7) 5.65 3.90

30th anniv. of Ethiopian airmail service.

Ethiopian Soldier and Map of Congo — AP11

Globe with Map of Africa — AP12

Perf. 11½
1962, July 23 Unwmk. Photo.
Granite Paper

C71 AP11 15c org, bl, brn & grn 20 15
C72 AP11 50c pur, bl, brn & grn 40 30
C73 AP11 60c red, bl, brn & grn 70 35

2nd anniv. of the Ethiopian contingent of the UN forces in the Congo and in honor of the 70th birthday of Emperor Haile Selassie.

1963, May 22
Granite Paper

C74 AP12 10c mag & blk 20 15
C75 AP12 40c emer & blk 40 25
C76 AP12 60c bl & blk 70 35

Conf. of African heads of state for African Unity, Addis Ababa.

Bird Type of Regular Issue, 1962

Birds: 10c, Black-headed forest oriole. 15c, Broad-tailed paradise whydah, vert. 20c, Lammergeier, vert. 50c, White-checked touraco. 80c, Purple indigo bird.

1963, Sept. 12 *Perf. 11½*
Granite Paper

C77 A74 10c multi 20 15
C78 A74 15c multi 25 18
C79 A74 20c bl, blk & ocher 45 25
C80 A74 50c lem & multi 75 45
C81 A74 80c ultra, blk & brn 1.50 75
Nos. C77-C81 (5) 3.15 1.78

Swimming AP13

Sport: 10c, Basketball, vert. 15c, Javelin. 80c, Soccer game in stadium.

Perf. 14x13½
1964, Sept. 15 Litho. Unwmk.

C82 AP13 5c multi 15 15
C83 AP13 10c multi 15 15
C84 AP13 15c multi 30 30
C85 AP13 80c multi 1.25 60

18th Olympic Games, Tokyo, Oct. 10-25.

Queen Elizabeth II and Emperor Haile Selassie — AP14

1965, Feb. 1 Photo. *Perf. 11½*
Granite Paper

C86 AP14 5c multi 15 15
C87 AP14 35c multi 50 30
C88 AP14 60c multi 85 50

Issued to commemorate the visit of Queen Elizabeth II of Great Britain, Feb. 1-8.

Koka Dam and Power Plant — AP15

Designs: 15c, Sugar cane field. 50c, Blue Nile bridge. 60c, Gondar castles. 80c, Coffee tree. $1, Cattle at water hole. $3, Camels at well. $5, Ethiopian Air Lines jet plane.

1965, July 19 Unwmk. *Perf. 11½*
Granite Paper
Portrait in Black

C89 AP15 15c vio brn & buff 20 15
C90 AP15 40c vio bl & lt bl 50 30
C91 AP15 50c grn & lt bl 60 35
C92 AP15 60c claret & yel 75 45
C93 AP15 80c grn, yel & red 90 50
C94 AP15 $1 brn & lt bl 1.10 60
C95 AP15 $3 claret & pink 3.50 1.65
C96 AP15 $5 ultra & lt bl 7.50 3.00
Nos. C89-C96 (8) 15.05 7.00

Bird Type of Regular Issue, 1962

Birds: 10c, White-collared kingfisher. 15c, Blue-breasted bee-eater. 25c, African paradise flycatcher. 40c, Village weaver. 60c, White-collared pigeon.

1966, Feb. 15 Photo. *Perf. 11½*
Granite Paper

C97 A74 10c dl yel & multi 20 15
C98 A74 15c lt bl & multi 30 15
C99 A74 25c gray & multi 65 35
C100 A74 40c pink & multi 1.25 50
C101 A74 60c multi 1.50 75
Nos. C97-C101 (5) 3.90 1.90

Black Rhinoceros AP16

Animals: 10c, Leopard. 20c, Black-and-white colobus (monkey). 30c, Mountain nyala. 60c, Nubian ibex.

1966, June 20 Litho. *Perf. 13*

C102 AP16 5c dp grn, blk & gray 15 15
C103 AP16 10c grn, blk & ocher 20 15
C104 AP16 20c cit, blk & grn 40 15
C105 AP16 30c yel grn, blk & ocher 60 18
C106 AP16 60c yel grn, blk & dk brn 1.25 30
Nos. C102-C106 (5) 2.60 93

Bird Type of Regular Issue, 1962

Birds: 10c, Blue-winged goose, vert. 15c, Yellow-billed duck. 20c, Wattled ibis. 25c, Striped swallow. 40c, Black-winged lovebird, vert.

1967, Sept. 29 Photo. *Perf. 11½*
Granite Paper

C107 A74 10c lt ultra & multi 24 15
C108 A74 15c grn & multi 30 15
C109 A74 20c yel & multi 35 15
C110 A74 25c sal & multi 60 15
C111 A74 40c pink & multi 1.25 48
Nos. C107-C111 (5) 2.74 1.08

SPECIAL DELIVERY STAMPS

Catalogue values for unused stamps in this section are for Never Hinged items.

Motorcycle Messenger SD1

Addis Ababa Post Office SD2

Unwmk.
1947, Apr. 24 Engr. *Perf. 13*

E1 SD1 30c orange brown 60 50
E2 SD2 50c blue 2.00 1.50

1954-62 Wmk. 282

E3 SD1 30c org brown ('62) 1.00 75
E4 SD2 50c blue 90 50

POSTAGE DUE STAMPS

Menelik II — D1

Perf. 14x13½

1896, June 10 Unwmk.

Black Overprint

J1 D1 ¼g green 1.00
J2 D1 ½g red 1.00
J3 D1 4g lilac brown 75
a. Without overprint 75
J4 D1 8g violet 75
a. Without overprint 75

Red Overprint

J5 D1 1g blue 1.00
J6 D1 2g dark brown 1.00
J7 D1 16g black 75
a. Without overprint 75
Nos. J1-J7 (7) 6.25

No. 1-7 Handstamped in Various Colors:

a

b

1905, Jan. 1

J8 A1 (a) ¼g green 14.00 14.00
J9 A1 (a) ½g red 14.00 14.00
J10 A1 (a) 1g blue 14.00 14.00
J11 A1 (a) 2g dk brn 14.00 14.00
J12 A2 (a) 4g lil brn 14.00 14.00
J13 A2 (a) 8g violet 20.00 20.00
J14 A2 (a) 16g black 40.00 40.00

1905, June 1

J15 A1 (b) ¼g green 14.00 14.00
J16 A1 (b) ½g red 14.00 14.00
J17 A1 (b) 1g blue 14.00 14.00
J18 A1 (b) 2g dk brn 14.00 14.00
J19 A2 (b) 4g lil brn 14.00 14.00
J20 A2 (b) 8g violet 20.00 20.00
J21 A2 (b) 16g black 40.00 40.00
Nos. J8-J21 (14) 260.00 260.00

Excellent forgeries of Nos. J8-J42 exist.

Nos. 1-7 Handstamped in Blue or Violet

TAXE A PERCEVOIR T

1906, July 1

J22 A1 ¼g green 8.00 8.00
J23 A1 ½g red 8.00 8.00
J24 A1 1g blue 8.00 8.00
J25 A1 2g dark brown 8.00 8.00
J26 A2 4g lilac brown 8.00 8.00
J27 A2 8g violet 12.50 12.50
J28 A2 16g black 18.00 18.00
Nos. J22-J28 (7) 70.50 70.50

Nos. J22-J27 exist with inverted overprint, also No. J22 with double overprint.
Forgeries exist.

With Additional Surcharge of Value Handstamped as on Nos. 71-77

1907, July 1

J29 A1 (e) ¼ on ¼g grn 12.00 12.00
J30 A1 (e) ½ on ½g red 12.00 12.00
J31 A1 (f) 1 on 1g blue 12.00 12.00
J32 A1 (f) 2 on 2g dk brn 12.00 12.00
J33 A2 (f) 4 on 4g lil brn 12.00 12.00
J34 A2 (f) 8 on 8g vio 12.00 12.00
J35 A2 (f) 16 on 16g blk 19.00 19.00
Nos. J29-J35 (7) 91.00 91.00

Nos. J30-J35 exist with inverted surcharge. Nos. J30, J33-J35 exist with double surcharge.

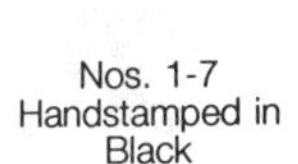
Nos. 1-7 Handstamped in Black

1908, Dec. 1

J36 A1 ¼g green 85 65
J37 A1 ½g red 85 65
J38 A1 1g blue 85 65
J39 A1 2g dark brown 1.10 85
J40 A2 4g lilac brown 1.50 1.25
J41 A2 8g violet 3.50 3.50
J42 A2 16g black 10.50 10.50
Nos. J36-J42 (7) 19.15 18.05

Nos. J36 to J42 exist with inverted overprint and Nos. J36, J37, J38 and J40 with double overprint.
Forgeries of Nos. J36-J56 exist.

Same Handstamp on Nos. 87-93

1912, Dec. 1 *Perf. 11½*

J43 A3 ¼g blue green 1.10 75
J44 A3 ½g rose 1.10 1.00

1913, July 1

J45 A3 1g green & org 3.50 2.50
J46 A4 2g blue 4.00 3.50
J47 A4 4g green & car 6.00 4.00
J48 A5 8g ver & dp grn 8.00 6.50
J49 A5 16g ver & car 20.00 15.00
Nos. J43-J49 (7) 43.70 33.25

Nos. J43 to J49, all exist with inverted, double and double, one inverted overprint.

Same Handstamp on Nos. 120-124 in Blue Black

1925-27 *Perf. 11½*

J50 A6 ⅛g vio & brn *18.00 18.00*
J51 A6 ¼g bl grn & db *18.00 18.00*
J52 A6 ½g scar & ol grn *20.00 20.00*
J53 A9 1g rose lil & gray grn 2.50 2.50
J54 A9 2g dp ultra & fawn *20.00 20.00*

Same Handstamp on Nos. 110, 112

1930 (?)

J55 A3 (i) 1g green & org *21.00 21.00*
J56 A4 (j) 2g blue *21.00 21.00*

The status of Nos. J55-J56 is questioned.

Catalogue values for unused stamps in this section, from this point to the end of the section, are for Never Hinged items.

D2

Perf. 11½

1951, Apr. 2 Unwmk. Litho.

J57 D2 1c emerald 30 15
J58 D2 5c rose red 42 15
J59 D2 10c violet 60 25
J60 D2 20c ocher 90 65
J61 D2 50c bright ultra 1.75 1.40
J62 D2 $1 rose lilac 3.50 2.00
Nos. J57-J62 (6) 7.47 4.60

OCCUPATION STAMPS

Issued under Italian Occupation

100 Centesimi = 1 Lira

Emperor Victor Emmanuel III
OS1 OS2

1936 Wmk. 140 *Perf. 14*

N1 OS1 10c orange brown 35 35
N2 OS1 20c purple 65 65
N3 OS2 25c dark green 45 45
N4 OS2 30c dark brown 45 45
N5 OS2 50c rose carmine 45 45
N6 OS1 75c deep orange 65 65
N7 OS1 1.25 l deep blue 1.40 1.40
Nos. N1-N7 (7) 4.40 4.40

Issue dates: #N3-N5, May 22. Others Dec. 5.
For later issues see Italian East Africa.

FAR EASTERN REPUBLIC

LOCATION — In Siberia east of Lake Baikal
GOVT. — Republic
AREA — 900,745 sq. mi.
POP. — 1,560,000 (approx. 1920)
CAPITAL — Chita

A short-lived independent government was established here in 1920.

100 Kopecks = 1 Ruble

Watermark

Wmk. 171- Diamonds

Vladivostok Issue

Russian Stamps Surcharged or Overprinted:

a

K.7 K.
b

DBP
K.10 K.
c

On Stamps of 1909-17

Perf. 14, 14½x15, 13½

1920 Unwmk.

2 A14(a) 2k green 6.50 8.00
3 A14(a) 3k red 7.50 10.00
4 A11(b) 3k on 35k red brn & grn 7.00 10.00
5 A15(a) 4k carmine 5.50 7.00
6 A11(b) 4k on 70k brn & org 6.00 7.00
8 A11(b) 7k on 15k red brn & bl 1.50 2.75
a. Inverted surcharge 25.00
b. Pair, one ovptd. "DBP" only
9 A15(a) 10k dark blue 50.00 55.00
a. Overprint on back 75.00
10 A12(c) 10k on 3½r mar & lt grn 15.00 17.50
11 A11(a) 14k blue & rose 16.00 19.00
12 A11(a) 15k red brn & bl 7.00 8.00
13 A8(a) 20k blue & car 42.50 55.00
14 A11(b) 20k on 14k bl & rose 6.00 6.00
a. Surcharge on back 30.00
15 A11(a) 25k green & vio 12.50 12.00
16 A11(a) 35k red brn & grn 30.00 30.00
17 A8(a) 50k brn vio & grn 10.00 11.50
18 A9(a) 1r pale brn, dk brn & org 200.00 250.00

On Stamps of 1917

Imperf

21 A14(a) 1k orange 7.50 8.50
22 A14(a) 2k gray grn 2.50 2.50
23 A14(a) 3k red 8.00 10.00
25 A11(b) 7k on 15k red brn & dp bl 1.00 1.00
a. Pair, one without surcharge
b. Pair, one ovptd. "DBP" only
26 A12(c) 10k on 3½r mar & lt grn 10.00 12.50
27 A9(a) 1r pale brn, brn & red org 10.00 11.00

On Stamps of Siberia 1919

Perf. 14, 14½x15

30 A14(a) 35k on 2k green 3.00 3.75
a. "DBP" on back 20.00 40.00

Imperf

31 A14(a) 35k on 2k green 7.00 7.50
32 A14(a) 70k on 1k orange 3.75 4.50

Counterfeit surcharges and overprints abound.

Postal Savings Stamps Surcharged for Postal Use

A1

Perf. 14½x15

Wmk. 171

35 A1(b) 1k on 5k green, *buff* 7.50 10.00
36 A1(b) 2k on 10k brown, *buff* 10.00 12.50

The letters on these stamps resembling "DBP," are the Russian initials of "Dalni Vostochini Respoublika" (Far Eastern Republic).

Chita Issue

A2

A2a

1921 Unwmk. Typo. *Imperf.*

38 A2 2k gray green 1.00 1.00
39 A2a 4k rose 1.10 1.10
40 A2 5k claret 2.00 2.00
41 A2a 10k blue 1.50 1.75

For overprints see Nos. 62-65.

Blagoveshchensk Issue

A3

1921 Litho. *Imperf.*

42 A3 2r red 2.50 2.00
43 A3 3r dark green 2.50 2.00
44 A3 5r dark blue 2.50 2.00
a. Tête bêche pair 25.00 25.00
45 A3 15r dark brown 2.50 2.00
46 A3 30r dark violet 2.50 2.00
a. Tête bêche pair 20.00 25.00
Nos. 42-46 (5) 12.50 10.00

Remainders of Nos. 42-46 were canceled in colored crayon or by typographed bars. These sell for half of foregoing values.

Chita Issue

A4

A5

1922 Litho. *Imperf.*

49 A4 1k orange 45 75
50 A4 3k dull red 25 45
51 A5 4k dp rose & buff 25 45
52 A4 5k orange brown 65 45
53 A4 7k light blue 65 1.25
a. Perf. 11½ 1.00 1.25
b. Rouletted 9 2.00 2.00
c. Perf. 11½x rouletted 4.00 3.00
54 A5 10k dk blue & red 30 65
55 A4 15k dull rose 45 75
56 A5 20k blue & red 45 75
57 A5 30k green & red org 50 1.00
58 A5 50k black & red org 85 1.50
Nos. 49-58 (10) 4.80 8.00

The 4k exists with "4" omitted.

Vladivostok Issue

Stamps of 1921 Overprinted in Red

1917
7-XI
1922

1922 *Imperf.*

62 A2 2k gray green 9.00 11.00
a. Inverted overprint 21.00
63 A2a 4k rose 9.00 11.00
a. Inverted overprint 32.50
b. Double overprint 30.00
64 A2 5k claret 12.00 15.00
a. Inverted overprint 32.50
b. Double overprint 30.00
65 A2a 10k blue 12.00 15.00
a. Inverted overprint 75.00

Russian revolution of Nov. 1917, 5th anniv.

Once in the setting the figures "22" of 1922 have the bottom stroke curved instead of straight. Value, each $15.

Vladivostok Issue

Russian Stamps of 1922-23 Surcharged in Black or Red

Д. В.
коп. 1 коп.
ЗОЛОТОМ

1923			*Imperf.*
66 A50 1k on 100r red	35	75
a. Inverted surcharge	27.50	
67 A50 2k on 70r violet	35	75
68 A49 5k on 10r blue (R)	35	75
69 A50 10k on 50r brown	60	1.25
a. Inverted surcharge	19.00	

Perf. 14½x15

70 A50 1k on 100r red	60	1.25
Nos. 66-70 (5)	2.25	4.75

OCCUPATION STAMPS

Issued under Occupation of General Semenov
Chita Issue

Russian Stamps of 1909-12 Surcharged:

p. 1 p. a

2p.50к. b

P. 5 P. c

1920 **Unwmk.**	*Perf. 14, 14x15½*	
N1 A15 (a) 1r on 4k carmine	20.00	22.50
N2 A8 (b) 2r50k on 20k bl & car	20.00	22.50
N3 A14 (c) 5r on 5k claret	10.00	15.00
a. Double surcharge	25.00	
N4 A11 (a) 10r on 70k brn & org	20.00	22.50

FAROE ISLANDS

(The Faroes)

LOCATION — North Atlantic Ocean
GOVT. — Self-governing part of Kingdom of Denmark
AREA — 540 sq. mi.
POP. — 52,347 (1984)
CAPITAL — Thorshavn

100 Ore = 1 Krone

Catalogue values for unused stamps in this country are for Never Hinged items, beginning with Scott 7.

Denmark No. 97 Handstamp Surcharged

2
ØRE

1919, Jan. **Typo.**	*Perf. 14x14½*	
1 A16 2o on 5o green	900.00	400.00

Counterfeits of surcharge exist.
Denmark No. 88a, the bisect, was used with Denmark No. 97 in Faroe Islands Jan. 3-23, 1919.

Denmark Nos. 220, 224, 238A, 224C Surcharged in Blue or Black

50 ≡ 50
Nos. 2, 5-6

20 |||| 20
No. 3

20
No. 4

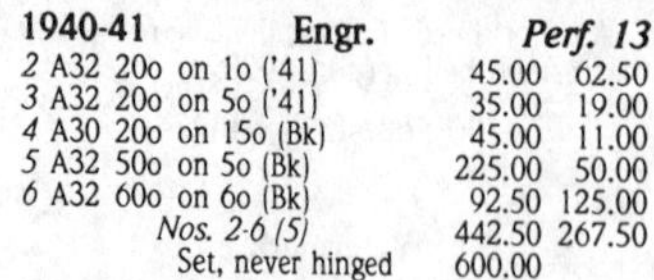

1940-41 **Engr.**	*Perf. 13*	
2 A32 20o on 1o ('41)	45.00	62.50
3 A32 20o on 5o ('41)	35.00	19.00
4 A30 20o on 15o (Bk)	45.00	11.00
5 A32 50o on 5o (Bk)	225.00	50.00
6 A32 60o on 6o (Bk)	92.50	125.00
Nos. 2-6 (5)	442.50	267.50
Set, never hinged	600.00	

Issued during British administration.

Catalogue values for unused stamps in this section, from this point to the end of the section, are for Never Hinged items.

Map of Islands, 1673 — A1

Map of North Atlantic, 1573 — A2

West Coast, Sandoy — A3

Vidoy and Svinoy, by Eyvindur Mohr — A4

Designs: 50o, 90o, like 5o. 60o, 80o, 120o, like 10o. 200o, like 70o. 250o, 300o, View of Streymoy and Vagar. 450o, Houses, Nes, by Ruth Smith. 500o, View of Hvitanes and Skalafjordur, by S. Joensen-Mikines.

Unwmk.

1975, Jan. 30 **Engr.**	*Perf. 13*	
7 A1 5o sepia	15	15
8 A2 10o emer & dark blue	15	15
9 A1 50o graysh green	15	15
10 A2 60o brown & dark blue	1.00	1.00
11 A3 70o vio blue & slate green	1.00	1.00
12 A2 80o ocher & dark blue	50	50
13 A1 90o red brown	1.00	1.00
14 A2 120o brt blue & dark blue	50	35
15 A3 200o vio blue & slate green	50	50
16 A3 250o multicolored	45	45
17 A3 300o multicolored	5.00	2.50

Photo.	*Perf. 12½x13*	
18 A4 350o multicolored	65	65
19 A4 450o multicolored	75	75
20 A4 500o multicolored	75	75
Nos. 7-20 (14)	12.55	9.90

Faroe Boat — A5

Faroe Flag — A6

Faroe Mailman — A7

Perf. 12½x13, 12 (A6)

1976, Apr. 1 **Engr.; Litho. (A6)**		
21 A5 125o copper red	2.25	1.10
22 A6 160o multicolored	35	32
23 A7 800o olive	1.10	80

Faroe Islands independent postal service, Apr. 1, 1976.

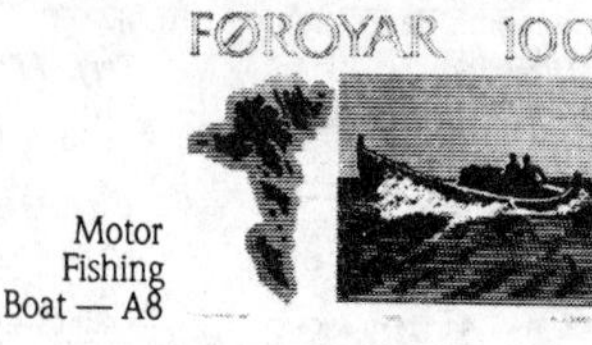
Motor Fishing Boat — A8

Faroese Fishing Vessels and Map of Islands: 125o, Inland fishing cutter. 160o, Modern seine fishing vessel. 600o, Deep-sea fishing trawler.

1977, Apr. 28 **Photo.**	*Perf. 14½x14*	
24 A8 100o green & black	6.50	4.75
25 A8 125o carmine & black	1.75	1.75
26 A8 160o blue & black	60	60
27 A8 600o brown & black	90	75

Common Snipe — A9

Photogravure & Engraved

1977, Sept. 29	*Perf. 14½x14*	
28 A9 70o shown	18	18
29 A9 180o Oystercatcher	35	35
30 A9 250o Whimbrel	55	55

North Coast, Puffins — A10

Mykines Village — A11

Mykines Island: 140o, Tilled fields and coast. 150o, Aerial view. 180o, Map.

Perf. 13x13½, 13½x13

1978, Jan. 26 **Photo.**

Size: 21x28mm, 28x21mm

31 A10 100o multicolored	22	22
32 A11 130o multicolored	28	28
33 A11 140o multicolored	55	55
34 A10 150o multicolored	38	38

Size: 37x26mm

Perf. 14½x14

35 A11 180o multicolored	38	38
Nos. 31-35 (5)	1.81	1.81

Sea Birds — A12

Old Library — A13

Lithographed and Engraved

1978, Apr. 13	*Perf. 12x12½*	
36 A12 140o Gannets	65	65
37 A12 180o Puffins	80	80
38 A12 400o Guillemots	65	65

1978, Dec. 7 *Perf. 13*

Design: 180o, New Library.

39 A13 140o gray green & lt green	50	50
40 A13 180o brown & buff	50	85

Completion of New Library Building.

Girl Guide, Tent and Fire — A14

Ram — A15

1978, Dec. 7 **Photo.**	*Perf. 13½*	
41 A14 140o multicolored	85	85

Faroese Girl Guides, 50th anniversary.

Lithographed and Engraved

1979, Mar. 19	*Perf. 12*	
42 A15 25k multicolored	5.00	4.00

Denmark No. 88a — A16

Europa: 180o, Faroe Islands No. 1.

1979, May 7	*Perf. 12½*	
43 A16 140o yellow & blue	65	65
44 A16 180o rose, green & black	65	65

Girl Wearing Festive Costume — A17

Children's Drawings and IYC Emblem: 150o, Fisherman. 200o, Two friends.

1979, Oct. 1	*Perf. 12*	
45 A17 110o multicolored	20	20
46 A17 150o multicolored	28	28
47 A17 200o multicolored	35	35

International Year of the Child.

Sea Plantain — A18

1980, Mar. 17 **Photo.**	*Perf. 12x11½*	
48 A18 90o *shown*	18	18
49 A18 110o *Glacier buttercup*	20	20
50 A18 150o *Purple saxifrage*	28	28
51 A18 200o *Starry saxifrage*	38	38
52 A18 400o *Lady's mantle*	70	70
Nos. 48-52 (5)	1.74	1.74

Jakob Jakobsen (1864-1918), Linguist — A19

Coat of Arms, Virgin and Child, Gothic Pew Gable — A20

Europa: 200o, Vensel Ulrich Hammershaimb (1819-1909), theologian, linguist and folklorist.

1980, Oct. 6 Engr. *Perf. 11½*

53	A19	150o dull green	30	30
54	A19	200o dull red brown	42	42

Photo. & Engr.

1980, Oct. 6 *Perf. 13½*

Kirkjubour Pew Gables, 15th Century: 140o, Norwegian coat of arms, John the Baptist. 150o, Christ's head, St. Peter. 200o, Hand in halo, Apostle Paul.

55	A20	110o multicolored	18	18
56	A20	140o multicolored	30	30
57	A20	150o multicolored	30	30
58	A20	200o multicolored	40	40

See Nos. 102-105.

Fishing Boats, Old Torshavn A21

Designs: Sketches of Old Torshavn by Ingalzur Reyni.

1981, Mar. 2 Engr.

59	A21	110o dark green	15	15
60	A21	140o black	28	28
61	A21	150o dark brown	28	28
62	A21	200o dark blue	38	38

The Ring Dance — A22

Europa: 200o, The garter dance.

1981, June 1 Engr. *Perf. 13x14*

63	A22	150o pale rose & grn	32	32
64	A22	200o pale yel grn & dk brn	38	38

Rune Stones, 800-1000 AD — A23

Historic Writings: 1k, Folksong, 1846. 3k, Sheep Letter excerpt, 1298. 6k, Seal and text, 1533. 10k, Titlepage from Faeroae et Faeroa, by Lucas Jacobson Debes, library.

Photo. & Engr.

1981, Oct. 19 *Perf. 11½*

65	A23	10o multicolored	15	15
66	A23	1k multicolored	22	22
67	A23	3k multicolored	58	58
68	A23	6k multicolored	1.10	1.10
69	A23	10k multicolored	2.00	2.00
		Nos. 65-69 (5)	4.05	4.05

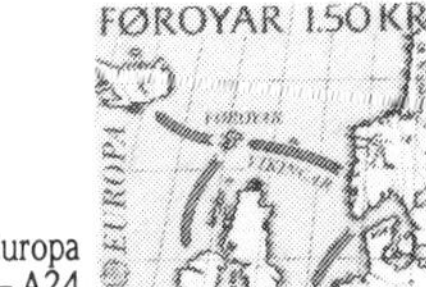

Europa 1982 — A24

1982, Mar. 15 Engr. *Perf. 13½*

81	A24	1.50k Viking North Atlantic routes	35	35
82	A24	2k Viking house foundation	40	40

View of Gjogv, by Ingalvur av Reyni A25

1982, June 7 Litho. *Perf. 12½x13*

83	A25	180o shown	38	38
84	A25	220o Hvalvik	1.90	70
85	A25	250o Kvivik	55	55

Ballad of Harra Paetur and Elinborg — A26

Designs: Scenes from the medieval ballad of chivalry.

1982, Sept. 27 Litho.

86	A26	220o multicolored	50	50
87	A26	250o multicolored	50	50
88	A26	350o multicolored	75	75
89	A26	450o multicolored	1.00	1.00

Cargo Ships — A27

1983, Feb. 21 Litho. *Perf. 14x14½*

90	A27	220o Arcturus, 1856	50	50
91	A27	250o Laura, 1882	50	50
92	A27	700o Thyra, 1866	1.40	1.40

Chessmen, by Pol i Buo (1791-1857) — A28

1983, May 2 Engr. *Perf. 13 Vert.*
Booklet Stamps

93	A28	250o King	70	70
94	A28	250o Queen	70	70
a.		Bklt. pane of 6 (3 each #93-94)	5.00	
b.		Pair, #93-94	1.50	

Europa 1983 — A29

Nobel Prizewinners in Medicine: 250o, Niels R. Finsen (1860-1903), ultraviolet radiation pioneer. 400o, Alexander Fleming (1881-1955), discoverer of penicillin.

1983, June 6 Engr. *Perf. 12x11½*

95	A29	250o dark blue	45	45
96	A29	400o red brown	85	85

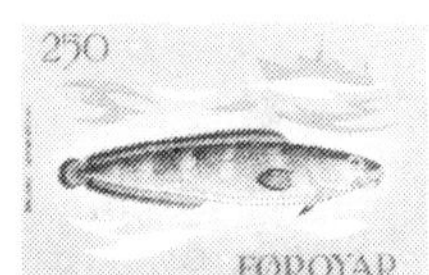

A30

1983, Sept. 19 Litho. *Perf. 12½x13*

97	A30	250o Tusk	60	60
98	A30	280o Haddock	75	75
99	A30	500o Halibut	1.10	1.10
100	A30	900o Catfish	2.00	2.00

Souvenir Sheet

Traditional Costumes — A31

Various national costumes.

1983, Nov. 4 Litho. *Perf. 12*

101		Sheet of 3	5.00	5.00
a.-c.	A31	250o multicolored	1.50	1.65

Nordic House Cultural Center opening. Margin shows Scandinavian flags.

Pew Gables Type of 1980

Designs: 250o, John, shield with three crowns. 300o, St. Jacob, shield with crossed keys. 350o, Thomas, shield with crossbeam. 400o, Judas Taddeus, Toulouse cross halo.

Photo. & Engr.

1984, Jan. 30 *Perf. 14x13½*

102	A20	250o lil, pur & dk brn	55	55
103	A20	300o red brn, dk buff & dk brn	70	70
104	A20	350o blk, lt gray & dk brn	80	80
105	A20	400o ol grn, pale yel & dk brn	95	95

Europa (1959-84) A33

1984, Apr. 2 Engr. *Perf. 13½*

106	A33	250o red	45	45
107	A33	500o dark blue	1.25	1.25

Sverri Patursson (1871-1960), Writer — A34

Poets: 2.50k, Joannes Patursson (1866-1946). 3k, J. H. O. Djurhuus (1881-1948). 4.50k, H.A. Djurhuus (1883-1951).

1984, May 28 Engr. *Perf. 13½*

108	A34	2k olive green	45	45
109	A34	2.50k red	55	55
110	A34	3k dark blue	65	65
111	A34	4.50k violet	1.00	1.00

Faroese Smack (Fishing Boat) — A35

Perf. 12½x13, 13x12½

1984, Sept. 10 Engr.

112	A35	280o shown	70	70
113	A35	300o Fishermen, vert.	70	70
114	A35	12k Helmsman, vert.	2.75	2.75

Fairytale Illustrations by Elinborg Lutzen — A36

1984, Oct. 29 Litho. *Perf. 13 Vert.*

Booklet Stamps

No.	Type	Denom.	Description	Unused	Used
115	A36	140o	Beauty of the Veils	90	90
116	A36	280o	Veils, diff.	90	90
117	A36	280o	Girl Shy Prince	90	90
118	A36	280o	The Glass Sword	90	90
119	A36	280o	Little Elin	90	90
120	A36	280o	The Boy and the Ox	90	90
a.			Bklt. pane of 6 (#115-120)	5.50	
			Nos. 115-120 (6)	5.40	5.40

View of Torshavn and the Forts, by Edward Dayes A37

Dayes' Landscapes, 1789: 280o, Skaeling. 550o, View Towards the North Seen from the Hills Near Torshavn in Stremoy, Faroes. 800o, The Moving Stones in Eysturoy, Faroes. Nos. 121-124 se-tenant.

1985, Feb. 4 Litho. & Engr. *Perf. 13*

No.	Type	Denom.	Description	Unused	Used
121	A37	250o	multicolored	40	40
122	A37	280o	multicolored	95	95
123	A37	550o	multicolored	90	90
124	A37	800o	multicolored	1.40	1.40

Europa 1985 — A38

Children taking music lessons.

1985, Apr. 1 Litho. *Perf. 13½x14½*

No.	Type	Denom.	Description	Unused	Used
125	A38	280o	multicolored	70	70
126	A38	550o	multicolored	1.25	1.25

Paintings, Faroese Museum of Art — A39

Designs: 550o, Winter's Day in Nolsoy, 1959, by Steffan Danielsen (1922-76). 450o, Self-Portrait, 1952, by Ruth Smith (1913-58), vert. 280o, The Garden, Hoyvik, 1973, by Thomas Arge (1942-78).

Litho. & Engr.

1985, June 3 *Perf. 12½*

No.	Type	Denom.	Description	Unused	Used
127	A39	280o	multicolored	70	70
128	A39	450o	multicolored	1.10	1.10
129	A39	550o	multicolored	1.25	1.25

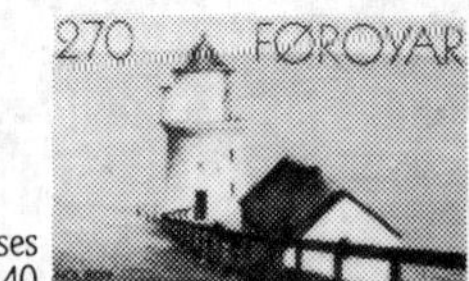

Lighthouses A40

1985, Sept. 23 Litho. *Perf. 13½x14*

No.	Type	Denom.	Description	Unused	Used
130	A40	270o	Nolsoy, 1893	70	70
131	A40	320o	Thorshavn, 1909	80	80
132	A40	350o	Mykines, 1909	95	95
133	A40	470o	Map of locations	1.25	1.25

Passenger Aviation in the Faroes, 22nd Anniv. A41

Perf. 13½ Horiz.

1985, Oct. 28 Photo.

Booklet Stamps

No.	Type	Denom.	Description	Unused	Used
134	A41	300o	Douglas DC-3	75	75
135	A41	300o	Fokker Friendship	75	75
136	A41	300o	Boeing 737	75	75
137	A41	300o	Interisland LM-IKB	75	75
138	A41	300o	Helicopter Snipan	75	75
a.			Booklet pane of 5, #134-138	4.00	4.00

Skrimsla, Ancient Folk Ballad — A42

1986, Feb. 3 Litho. *Perf. 12½x13*

No.	Type	Denom.	Description	Unused	Used
139	A42	300o	Peasant in woods	80	80
140	A42	420o	Meets Giant	1.10	1.10
141	A42	550o	Giant loses game	1.50	1.50
142	A42	650o	Giant grants Peasant's wish	1.75	1.75

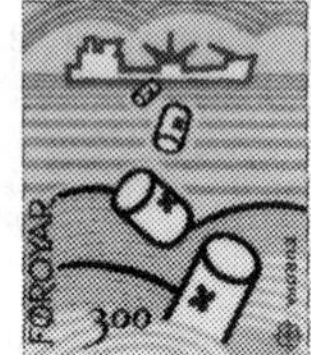

Europa 1986 — A43

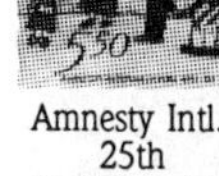

Amnesty Intl., 25th Anniv. — A44

1986, Apr. 7 Litho. *Perf. 13½*

No.	Type	Denom.	Description	Unused	Used
143	A43	3k	shown	75	75
144	A43	5.50k	Sea pollution	1.40	1.40

1986, June 2 *Perf. 14x13½*

Winning design competition artwork.

No.	Type	Denom.	Description	Unused	Used
145	A44	3k	Olivur vid Neyst	75	75
146	A44	4.70k	Eli Smith	1.10	1.10
147	A44	5.50k	Ranna Kunoy	1.40	1.40

Nos. 145-146 horiz.

Souvenir Sheet

HAFNIA '87, Copenhagen — A45

Design: East Bay of Torshavn, watercolor, 1782, by Christian Rosenmeyer (1728-1802).

1986, Aug. 29 Litho. *Perf. 13x13½*

No.	Type	Denom.	Description	Unused	Used
148			Sheet of 3	6.00	6.00
a.			A45 3k multicolored	2.00	2.00
b.			A45 4.70k multicolored	2.00	2.00
c.			A45 6.50k multicolored	2.00	2.00

Sold for 20k.

Old Stone Bridges A46

Designs: 2.70k, Glyvrar on Eysturoy. 3k, Leypanagjogv on Vagar, vert. 13k, Skaelinger on Streymoy.

Perf. 13½x14½, 14½x13½

1986, Oct. 13 Engr.

No.	Type	Denom.	Description	Unused	Used
149	A46	2.70k	dp brown vio	70	70
150	A46	3k	bluish blk	75	75
151	A46	13k	gray green	3.50	3.50

Farmhouses A47

Traditional architecture: 300o, Depil on Borooy, 1814. 420o, Depil, diff. 470o, Frammi vio Gjonna on Streymoy, c. 1814. 650o, Frammi, diff.

1987, Feb. 9 Engr. *Perf. 13x14½*

No.	Type	Denom.	Description	Unused	Used
152	A47	300o	pale blue & blue	75	75
153	A47	420o	buff & brown	1.00	1.00
154	A47	470o	pale grn & dp grn	1.10	1.10
155	A47	650o	pale gray & black	1.50	1.50

Europa 1987 — A48

Nordic House.

1987, Apr. 6 *Perf. 13x14*

No.	Type	Denom.	Description	Unused	Used
156	A48	300o	Exterior	80	80
157	A48	550o	Interior	1.50	1.50

Fishing Trawlers A49

1987, June 1 Litho. *Perf. 14x13½*

No.	Type	Denom.	Description	Unused	Used
158	A49	3k	Joannes Patursson	80	80
159	A49	5.50k	Magnus Heinason	1.40	1.40
160	A49	8k	Sjurdarberg	2.00	2.00

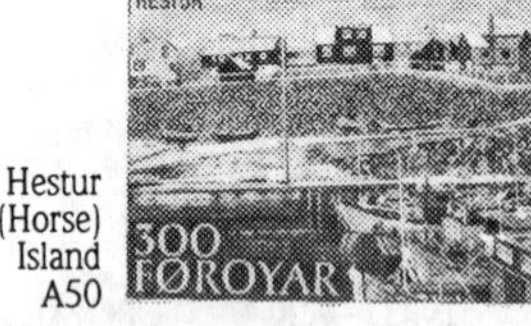

Hestur (Horse) Island A50

1987, Sept. 7 Litho. & Engr. *Perf. 13*

No.	Type	Denom.	Description	Unused	Used
161	A50	270o	Map	65	65
162	A50	300o	Seaport	75	75
163	A50	420o	Bird cliff	1.10	1.10
164	A50	470o	Pasture, sheep	1.25	1.25
165	A50	550o	Seashore	1.40	1.40
			Nos. 161-165 (5)	5.15	5.15

Nos. 161, 163 and 165 vert.

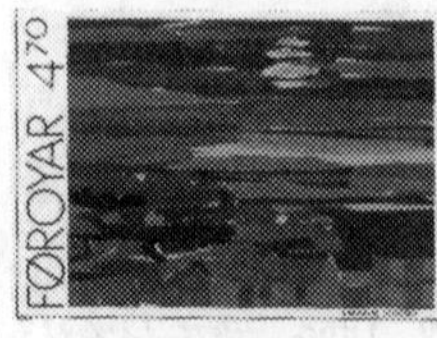

Abstract Collages by Zacharias Heinesen A51

West Bay of Torshavn, Watercolor by Rosenmeyer — A52

1987, Oct. 16 Litho. *Perf. 13½x14*

No.	Type	Denom.	Description	Unused	Used
166	A51	4.70k	Eystaravag	1.25	1.25
167	A51	6.50k	Vestarvag	1.50	1.50

Souvenir Sheet

Perf. 13½x13

No.	Type	Denom.	Description	Unused	Used
168	A52	3k	multicolored	1.40	1.40

HAFNIA '87. Sold for 4k.

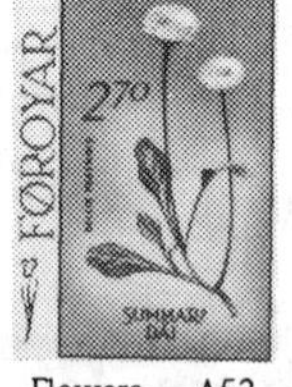

Flowers — A53

Europa — A54

1988, Feb. 8 Litho. *Perf. 11½*

Granite Paper

No.	Type	Denom.	Description	Unused	Used
169	A53	2.70k	Bellis perennis	80	80
170	A53	3k	Dactylorchis maculata	90	90
171	A53	4.70k	Potentilla erecta	1.40	1.40
172	A53	9k	Pinguicula vulgaris	1.90	1.90

1988, Apr. 11 Photo. *Perf. 11½*

Communication and transport.

No.	Type	Denom.	Description	Unused	Used
173	A54	3k	Satellite dish, satellite	85	85
174	A54	5.50k	Fork lift, crane, ship	1.50	1.50

A55

A56

Writers: 270o, Jorgen-Frantz Jacobsen (1900-38). 300o, Christian Matras (b. 1900). 470o, William Heinesen (b. 1900). 650o, Hedin Bru (1901-87).

1988, June 6 Engr. *Perf. 13½*

No.	Type	Denom.	Description	Unused	Used
175	A55	270o	myrtle green	65	65
176	A55	300o	rose lake	70	70
177	A55	470o	dark blue	1.10	1.10
178	A55	650o	brown black	1.50	1.50

1988, Sept. 5 Photo. *Perf. 12*

Text, illustrations and cameo portraits of organizers: 3k, Announcement and Djoni Geil, Enok Baerentsen and H.H. Jacobsen. 3.20k, Meeting, Rasmus Effersoe, C.L. Johannesen and Samal Krakusteini. 12k, Oystercatcher and lyrics of *Now the Hour Has Come,* by poet Sverri Patursson (1871-1960), Just A. Husum, Joannes Patursson and Jens Olsen.

Granite Paper

No.	Type	Denom.	Description	Unused	Used
179	A56	3k	multicolored	75	75
180	A56	3.20k	multicolored	80	80
181	A56	12k	multicolored	3.00	3.00

1888 Christmas meeting to preserve cultural traditions and the natl. language, cent.

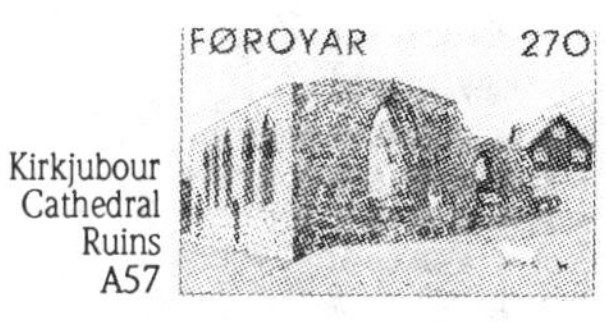
Kirkjubour Cathedral Ruins A57

Designs: 270o, Exterior. 300o, Arch, vert. 470o, Crucifixion, bas-relief, vert. 550o, Interior.

1988, Oct. 17 Engr. *Perf. 13*

182 A57 270o dark green 70 70
183 A57 300o dark blue 75 75
184 A57 470o dark brown 1.10 1.10
185 A57 550o dark violet 1.40 1.40

Havnar Church, Torshavn, 200th Anniv. A58

Designs: 350o, Church exterior. 500o, Crypt, vert. 15k, Bell, vert.

1989, Feb. 6 Engr. *Perf. 13*

186 A58 350o dark green 90 90
187 A58 500o dark brown 1.25 1.25
188 A58 15k deep blue 4.00 4.00

Folk Costumes — A59

Photo. & Engr.

1989, Apr. 10 *Perf. 13½*

189 A59 350o Man 90 90
190 A59 600o Woman 1.65 1.65

Europa 1989 — A60

Wooden children's toys.

Perf. 12x11½

1989, Apr. 10 Photo. Granite Paper

191 A60 3.50k Boat 90 90
192 A60 6k Horse 1.65 1.65

Island Games, July 5-13 — A61

1989, June 5 Photo. *Perf. 12½*

Granite Paper

193 A61 200o Rowing 50 50
194 A61 350o Handball 90 90
195 A61 600o Soccer 1.50 1.50
196 A61 700o Swimming 1.75 1.75

Faroe Islands stamps can be mounted in the Scott annually supplemented Scandinavia and Finland album.

A62

A63

Bird cliffs of Suduroy.

1989, Oct. 2 Engr. *Perf. 14x13½*

197 A62 320o Tvoran 85 85
198 A62 350o Skuvanes 90 90
199 A62 500o Beinisvord 1.30 1.30
200 A62 600o Asmundarstakkur 1.60 1.60

1990, Feb. 5 Litho. *Perf. 14x13½*

Modern fish factory (filleting station).

201 A63 3.50k Unloading fish 1.10 1.10
202 A63 3.70k Cleaning and sorting 1.15 1.15
203 A63 5k Filleting 1.55 1.55
204 A63 7k Packaged frozen fish 2.15 2.15

Europa 1990 — A64

Post offices.

1990, Apr. 9 Litho. *Perf. 13½x14*

205 A64 3.50k Gjogv 1.10 1.10
206 A64 6k Klaksvik 1.85 1.85

Souvenir Sheet

Recognition of the Merkid, Flag of the Faroes, by the British, 50th Anniv. — A65

Designs: a, Flag. b, Fishing trawler *Nyggjaberg*, disappeared, 1942. c, Sloop *Saana*, sunk by the Germans, 1942.

1990, Apr. 9 Photo. *Perf. 12*

Granite Paper

207 A65 Sheet of 3 3.25 3.25
a.-c. 3.50k any single 1.05 1.05

Whales A66

1990, June 6 Photo. *Perf. 11½*

Granite Paper

208 A66 320o *Mesoplodon bidens* 1.05 1.05
209 A66 350o *Balaena mysticetus* 1.15 1.15
210 A66 600o *Eubalaena glacialis* 1.90 1.90
211 A66 700o *Hyperoodon ampullatus* 2.25 2.25

Nolsoy Island by Steffan Danielsen A67

1990, Oct. 8 Photo. *Perf. 11½*

Granite Paper

212 A67 50o shown 16 16
213 A67 350o Coastline 1.15 1.15
214 A67 500o Town 1.60 1.60
215 A67 1000o Coastline, cliffs 2.30 2.30

Flora and Fauna — A68

Europa — A69

1991, Feb. 4 Litho. *Perf. 13*

216 A68 3.70k Plantago lanceolata 1.30 1.30
217 A68 4k Rumex longifolius 1.40 1.40
218 A68 4.50k Amara aulica 1.55 1.55
219 A68 6.50k Lumbricus terrestris 2.25 2.25

1991, Apr. 4 Litho. *Perf. 13*

Designs: 3.70k, Weather satellite. 6.50k, Celestial navigation.

220 A69 3.70k multicolored 1.30 1.30
221 A69 6.50k multicolored 2.25 2.25

Town of Torshavn, 125th Anniv. A70

1991, Apr. 4 *Perf. 14x13½*

222 A70 3.70k Town Hall 1.30 1.30
223 A70 3.70k View of town 1.30 1.30

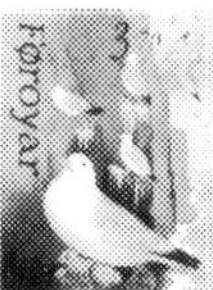
Birds — A71

1991, June 3 Litho. *Perf. 13½*

224 A71 3.70k Rissa tridactyla 1.30 1.30
225 A71 3.70k Sterna paradisaea 1.30 1.30
a. Bklt. pane, 3 each #224-225 7.80

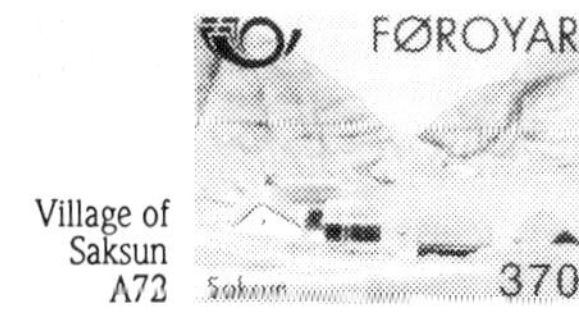
Village of Saksun A72

1991, June 3

226 A72 370o shown 1.30 1.30
227 A72 650o Cliffs of Vestmanna 2.25 2.25

Samal Joensen-Mikines (1906-1979), Painter — A73

1991, Oct. 7 Litho. *Perf. 13½*

228 A73 340o Funeral Procession 1.00 1.00
229 A73 370o The Farewell 1.10 1.10
230 A73 550o Handanagarthur 1.65 1.65
231 A73 1300o Winter morning 3.90 3.90

Mail Boats — A74

1992, Feb. 10 Litho. *Perf. 13½x14*

232 A74 200o Ruth 58 58
233 A74 370o Ritan 1.10 1.10
234 A74 550o Sigmundur 1.65 1.65
235 A74 800o Masin 2.35 2.35

Europa A75

Designs: 3.70k, Map of North Atlantic, Viking ship. 6.50k, Map of Central Atlantic region, one of Columbus' ships.

1992, Apr. 6 Litho. *Perf. 13½x14*

236 A75 3.70k multicolored 1.10 1.10
237 A75 6.50k multicolored 1.95 1.95

Souvenir Sheet

238 A75 Sheet of 2, #236-237 3.05 3.05

First landing in the Americas by Leif Erikson (#236). Discovery of America by Christopher Columbus, 500th anniv. (#237).

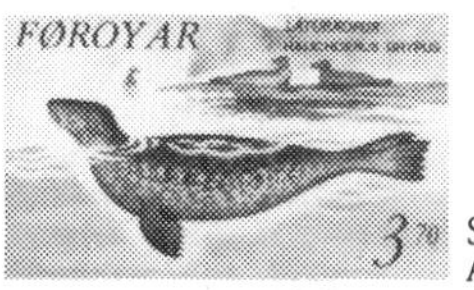
Seals A76

1992, June 9 Litho. *Perf. 14x13½*

239 A76 3.70k Halichoerus grypus 1.10 1.10
240 A76 3.70k Phoca vitulina 1.10 1.10
a. Bklt. pane of 3 #239, 3 #240 6.60

No. 240a contains 3 se-tenant pairs of Nos. 239-240.

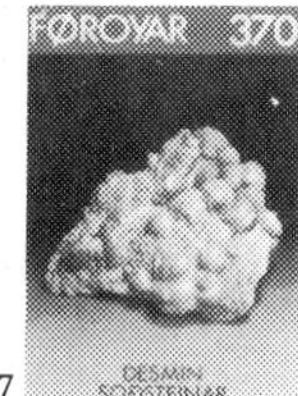
Minerals — A77

1992, June 9 Photo. *Perf. 12*

Granite Paper

241 A77 370o Desmine 1.10 1.10
242 A77 650o Mesolite 1.95 1.95

Traditional Houses A78

1992, Oct. 5 Litho. *Perf. 13½*

243 A78 3.40k Hja Glyvra Hanusi 1.20 1.20
244 A78 3.70k I Nordragotu 1.30 1.30
245 A78 6.50k Blasastova 2.25 2.25
246 A78 8k Jakupsstova 2.75 2.75

Nordic House Entertainers A79

No.	Type	Description	Unused	Used
1993, Feb. 8		**Litho.**		***Perf. 13½***
247	A79	400o Dancers	1.35	1.35
248	A79	400o Pianist	1.35	1.35
249	A79	400o Trio	1.35	1.35
a.		Souvenir sheet of 3, #247-249, perf. 12½	4.05	4.05

Village of Gjogv — A80

1993, Apr. 5

No.	Type	Description	Unused	Used
250	A80	4k View toward sea	1.35	1.35
251	A80	4k Ravine, village	1.35	1.35
a.		Booklet pane, 3 each #250-251	8.10	

A81 A82

Europa (Sculptures by Hans Pauli Olsen): 4k, Movement. 7k, Reflection.

1993, Apr. 5

No.	Type	Description	Unused	Used
252	A81	4k multicolored	1.35	1.35
253	A81	7k multicolored	1.35	1.35

Perf. 13½x13, 13x13½

1993, June 7 **Engr.**

Horses.

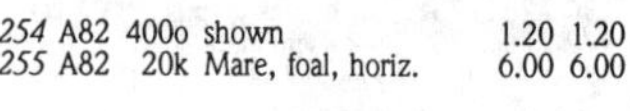

No.	Type	Description	Unused	Used
254	A82	400o shown	1.20	1.20
255	A82	20k Mare, foal, horiz.	6.00	6.00

Butterflies A83

No.	Type	Description	Unused	Used
1993, Oct. 4		**Litho.**		***Perf. 14½***
256	A83	350o Apamea zeta	1.00	1.00
257	A83	400o Hepialus humuli	1.25	1.25
258	A83	700o Vanessa atalanta	2.00	2.00
259	A83	900o Perizoma albulata	2.75	2.75

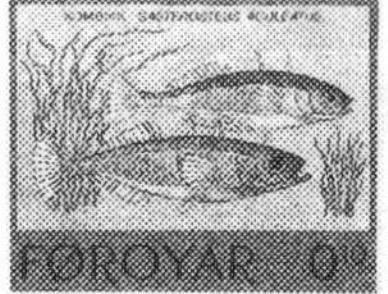

Fish — A84

No.	Type	Description	Unused	Used
1994, Feb. 7		**Litho.**		***Perf. 14½***
260	A84	10o Gasterosteus aculeatus	15	15
261	A84	4k Neocyttus helgae	1.10	1.10
262	A84	7k Salmo trutta fario	2.00	2.00
263	A84	10k Hoplostethus atlanticus	2.75	2.75

FERNANDO PO

LOCATION — An island in the Gulf of Guinea off west Africa.

GOVT. — Province of Spain

AREA — 800 sq. mi.

POP. — 62,612 (1960)

CAPITAL — Santa Isabel

Together with the islands of Elobey, Annobon and Corisco, Fernando Po came under the administration of Spanish Guinea. Postage stamps of Spanish Guinea were used until 1960.

The provinces of Fernando Po and Rio Muni united Oct. 12, 1968, to form the Republic of Equatorial Guinea.

100 Centimos = 1 Escudo = 2.50 Pesetas

100 Centimos = 1 Peseta

1000 Milesimas = 100 Centavos = 1 Peso (1882)

Catalogue values for unused stamps in this country are for Never Hinged items, beginning with Scott 181 in the regular postage section and Scott B1 in the semi-postal section.

Isabella II — A1

Alfonso XII — A2

No.	Type	Description	Unused	Used
1868		**Unwmk. Typo.**		***Perf. 14***
1	A1	20c brown	275.00	85.00

Forgeries exist.

1879

Centimos de Peseta

No.	Type	Description	Unused	Used
2	A2	5c green	22.50	5.00
3	A2	10c rose	22.50	5.00
4	A2	50c blue	26.00	5.00

1882-89

Centavos de Peso

No.	Type	Description	Unused	Used
5	A2	1c green	6.00	2.00
6	A2	2c rose	9.00	3.25
7	A2	5c gray blue	19.00	3.00
8	A2	10c dk brown ('89)	32.50	3.00

Nos. 5-7 Handstamp Surcharged in Blue, Black or Violet — a

1884-95

No.	Type	Description	Unused	Used
9	A2	50c on 1c green ('95)	42.00	8.50
11	A2	50c on 2c rose	15.00	3.50
12	A2	50c on 5c blue ('87)	62.50	14.00

Inverted and double surcharges exist. No. 12 exists overprinted in carmine.

King Alfonso XIII — A4

No.	Type	Description	Unused	Used
1894-97				***Perf. 14***
13	A4	⅛c slate ('96)	12.00	1.75
14	A4	2c rose ('96)	9.00	1.50
15	A4	5c blue grn ('97)	9.00	1.50
16	A4	6c dk vio ('96)	7.50	1.65
17	A4	10c brn vio ('94)	77.50	14.00
18	A4	10c lake ('95)	19.00	4.00
19	A4	10c org brn ('96)	7.50	1.50
20	A4	12½c dk brn ('96)	7.50	1.65
21	A4	20c slate bl ('96)	7.50	1.65
22	A4	25c claret ('96)	12.00	1.65
		Nos. 13-22 (10)	168.50	30.85

Stamps of 1894-97 Handstamped in Blue, Black or Red

b

c

Type "b" Surcharge

1896-98

No.	Type	Description	Unused	Used
23	A4	5c on 2c rose (Bl)	15.00	2.75
24	A4	5c on 10c brn vio (Bl)	52.50	7.00
25	A4	5c on 12½c brn (Bl)	12.00	2.75
a.		Black surcharge	12.00	2.75

Type "c" Surcharge

No.	Type	Description	Unused	Used
26	A4	5c on ⅛c slate (Bk)	10.00	2.75
27	A4	5c on 2c rose (Bl)	10.00	2.75
a.		Black surcharge	10.00	2.75
28	A4	5c on 5c green (R)	57.50	10.00
29	A4	5c on 6c dk vio (R)	7.25	5.00
a.		Violet surcharge	8.00	7.50
30	A4	5c on 10c org brn (Bk)	57.50	13.00
31	A4	5c on 12½c brn (R)	20.00	4.00
32	A4	5c on 20c sl bl (R)	13.00	4.00
33	A4	5c on 25c claret (Bk)	13.00	4.00
a.		Blue surcharge	15.00	4.50

Exist surcharged in other colors.

Type "a" Surch. in Blue or Black

1898-99

No.	Type	Description	Unused	Used
34	A4	50c on 2c rose	27.50	4.50
35	A4	50c on 10c brn vio	75.00	13.00
36	A4	50c on 10c lake	85.00	13.00
37	A4	50c on 10c org brn	75.00	13.00
38	A4	50c on 12½c brn (Bk)	57.50	10.00

The "a" surch. also exists on ⅛c, 5c & 25c.

A5

Arms

A6

Revenue Stamps Handstamped in Blue

No.	Type	Description	Unused	Used
1897-98				***Imperf.***
39	A5	5c on 10c rose	27.50	14.00
40	A6	10c rose	27.50	12.00

A7

Arms — A8

A9

A9a

Revenue Stamps Handstamped in Black or Red

No.	Type	Description	Unused	Used
1899				***Imperf.***
41	A7	15c on 10c green	35.00	19.00
a.		Blue surcharge, vertical	30.00	17.50
42	A8	10c on 25c green	92.50	57.50
43	A9	15c on 25c green	150.00	95.00
43A	A9a	15c on 25c green (R)	*3,000.*	*1,750.*
b.		Black surcharge	*3,000.*	*1,750.*

Surcharge on No. 41 is either horizontal, inverted or vertical.

On No. 42 "CORREOS" is ovptd. in red.

King Alfonso XIII — A10

No.	Type	Description	Unused	Used
1899				***Perf. 14***
44	A10	1m orange brn	1.50	35
45	A10	2m orange brn	1.50	35
46	A10	3m orange brn	1.50	35
47	A10	4m orange brn	1.50	35
48	A10	5m orange brn	1.50	35
49	A10	1c black vio	1.50	35
50	A10	2c dk blue grn	1.50	35
51	A10	3c dk brown	1.50	35
52	A10	4c orange	8.00	70
53	A10	5c car rose	1.50	35
54	A10	6c dark blue	1.50	35
55	A10	8c gray brn	4.25	35
56	A10	10c vermilion	2.50	35
57	A10	15c slate grn	2.50	35
58	A10	20c maroon	8.50	70
59	A10	40c violet	50.00	9.50
60	A10	60c black	50.00	9.50
61	A10	80c red brown	50.00	9.50
62	A10	1p yellow grn	190.00	50.00
63	A10	2p slate blue	200.00	50.00
		Nos. 44-63 (20)	580.75	134.45

Nos. 44-63 exist imperf. Value for set, $1,400.

See Nos. 66-85. For surcharges see Nos. 64-65, 88-88B.

1900

Surcharged type "a"

No.	Type	Description	Unused	Used
64	A10	50c on 20c maroon	12.00	2.25
a.		Blue surcharge	25.00	4.50

Surcharged type "b"

No.	Type	Description	Unused	Used
64B	A10	5c on 20c maroon	125.00	7.00

Surcharged type "c"

No.	Type	Description	Unused	Used
65	A10	5c on 20c maroon	7.00	2.25

Dated "1900"

1900

No.	Type	Description	Unused	Used
66	A10	1m black	1.75	38
67	A10	2m black	1.75	38
68	A10	3m black	1.75	38
69	A10	4m black	1.75	38
70	A10	5m black	1.75	38
71	A10	1c green	1.75	38
72	A10	2c violet	1.75	38
73	A10	3c rose	1.75	38
74	A10	4c black brn	1.75	38
75	A10	5c blue	1.75	38
76	A10	6c orange	1.75	1.25
77	A10	8c bronze grn	1.75	1.25
78	A10	10c claret	1.75	38
79	A10	15c dk violet	1.75	38

80	A10	20c olive brn	1.75	38
81	A10	40c brown	5.50	2.00
82	A10	60c green	12.50	2.00
83	A10	80c dark blue	12.50	2.25
84	A10	1p red brown	70.00	15.00
85	A10	2p orange	110.00	35.00
		Nos. 66-85 (20)	236.75	63.69

Nos. 66-85 exist imperf.

A11

A12

Revenue Stamps Overprinted or Surcharged with Handstamp in Red or Black

1900 *Imperf.*

86	A11	10c blue (R)	32.50	16.00
87	A12	5c on 10c blue	82.50	37.50

Nos. 52 and 80 Surcharged type "a" in Violet or Black

1900

88	A10	50c on 4c orange (V)	13.00	4.00
a.		Green surcharge	22.50	12.00
88B	A10	50c on 20c ol brn	13.00	3.50

A13

A14

1901 *Perf. 14*

89	A13	1c black	1.40	38
90	A13	2c orange brn	1.40	38
91	A13	3c dk violet	1.40	38
92	A13	4c lt violet	1.40	38
93	A13	5c orange red	95	38
94	A13	10c violet brn	95	38
95	A13	25c dp blue	95	38
96	A13	50c claret	1.40	38
97	A13	75c dk brown	1.25	38
98	A13	1p blue grn	30.00	2.75
99	A13	2p red brown	18.00	4.25
100	A13	3p olive grn	18.00	5.75
101	A13	4p dull red	18.00	5.75
102	A13	5p dk green	25.00	5.75
103	A13	10p buff	50.00	14.00
		Nos. 89-103 (15)	170.10	41.67

Dated "1902"

1902

Control Numbers on Back

104	A13	5c dk green	1.40	22
105	A13	10c slate	1.40	22
106	A13	25c claret	3.50	55
107	A13	50c violet brn	8.75	1.65
108	A13	75c lt violet	8.75	1.65
109	A13	1p car rose	11.00	2.25
110	A13	2p olive grn	22.50	5.75
111	A13	5p orange red	32.50	13.00
		Nos. 104-111 (8)	89.80	25.29

Exist imperf. Value for set, $425.

1903 *Perf. 14*

Control Numbers on Back

112	A14	¼c dk violet	25	15
113	A14	½c black	25	15
114	A14	1c scarlet	25	15
115	A14	2c dk green	25	15
116	A14	3c blue grn	25	15
117	A14	4c violet	25	15
118	A14	5c rose lake	30	15
119	A14	10c orange buff	38	15
120	A14	15c blue green	1.50	55
121	A14	25c red brn	1.75	70
122	A14	50c black brn	3.00	1.25
123	A14	75c carmine	10.00	2.25
124	A14	1p dk brn	15.00	3.75
125	A14	2p dk olive grn	19.00	4.75
126	A14	3p claret	19.00	4.75
127	A14	4p dark blue	25.00	7.50
128	A14	5p dp dull blue	37.50	9.50
129	A14	10p dull red	72.50	14.50
		Nos. 112-129 (18)	206.43	50.70

Dated "1905"

1905

Control Numbers on Back

136	A14	1c dp violet	22	15
137	A14	2c black	22	15
138	A14	3c vermilion	22	15
139	A14	4c dp green	22	15
140	A14	5c blue grn	30	15
141	A14	10c violet	95	28
142	A14	15c car lake	95	28
143	A14	25c orange buff	7.00	75
144	A14	50c green	5.25	1.25
145	A14	75c red brown	6.00	4.00
146	A14	1p dp gray brn	7.00	4.00
147	A14	2p carmine	13.00	6.00
148	A14	3p deep brown	20.00	7.00
149	A14	4p bronze grn	24.00	7.50
150	A14	5p claret	35.00	12.50
151	A14	10p deep blue	60.00	16.00
		Nos. 136-151 (16)	180.33	60.31

King Alfonso XIII — A15

1907

Control Numbers on Back

152	A15	1c blue black	15	15
153	A15	2c car rose	15	15
154	A15	3c dp violet	15	15
155	A15	4c black	15	15
156	A15	5c orange buff	15	15
157	A15	10c maroon	85	25
158	A15	15c bronze grn	28	15
159	A15	25c dk brown	14.00	5.00
160	A15	50c blue green	15	15
161	A15	75c vermilion	22	15
162	A15	1p dull blue	1.25	25
163	A15	2p brown	5.50	2.00
164	A15	3p lake	5.50	2.00
165	A15	4p violet	5.50	2.00
166	A15	5p black brn	5.50	2.00
167	A15	10p orange brn	5.50	2.00
		Nos. 152-167 (16)	45.00	16.70

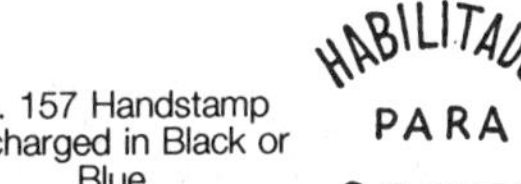

No. 157 Handstamp Surcharged in Black or Blue

1908

168	A15	5c on 10c mar (Bk)	2.50	1.75
169	A15	5c on 10c mar (Bl)	8.50	5.00

The surcharge on Nos. 168-169 exist inverted, double, etc. The surcharge also exists on other stamps. A 25c on 10c also exists.

Seville-Barcelona Issue of Spain, 1929, Overprinted in Blue or Red

FERNANDO POO

1929 *Perf. 11*

170	A52	5c rose lake	15	15
171	A53	10c green (R)	15	15
a.		Perf. 14	42	35
172	A50	15c Prus bl (R)	15	15
173	A51	20c purple (R)	15	15
174	A50	25c brt rose	15	15
175	A52	30c black brn	15	15
176	A53	40c dk blue (R)	24	22
177	A51	50c dp orange	36	35
178	A52	1p blue blk (R)	1.25	75
179	A53	4p deep rose	6.50	4.75
180	A53	10p brown	7.00	6.00
		Nos. 170-180 (11)	16.25	12.97

Catalogue values for unused stamps in this section, from this point to the end of the section, are for Never Hinged items.

Virgin Mary — A16

1960 Unwmk. Photo. *Perf. 13x12½*

181	A16	25c dull gray vio	15	15
182	A16	50c brown olive	15	15
183	A16	75c violet brn	15	15
184	A16	1p orange ver	15	15
185	A16	1.50p lt blue grn	15	15
186	A16	2p red lilac	15	15
187	A16	3p dark blue	2.50	65
188	A16	5p lt red brn	22	15
189	A16	10p lt olive grn	42	15
		Nos. 181-189 (9)	4.04	
		Set value		1.20

Tricorn and Windmill from "The Three-Cornered Hat" by Falla — A17

Manuel de Falla — A18

1960 *Perf. 13x12½, 12½x13*

190	A17	35c slate green	15	15
191	A18	80c Prus green	15	15
		Set value	22	15

Issued to honor Manuel de Falla (1876-1946), Spanish composer.

See Nos. B1-B2.

Map of Fernando Po — A19

General Franco A20

Designs: 70c, Santa Isabel Cathedral.

Perf. 13x12½, 12½x13

1961, Oct. 1 Photo. Unwmk.

192	A19	25c gray violet	15	15
193	A20	50c olive brown	15	15
194	A19	70c brt green	15	15
195	A20	1p red orange	15	15
		Set value	48	23

25th anniv. of the nomination of Gen. Francisco Franco as Chief of State.

Ocean Liner — A21

Design: 50c, S.S. San Francisco.

1962, July 10 *Perf. 12½x13*

196	A21	25c dull violet	18	15
197	A21	50c gray olive	18	15
198	A21	1p orange brn	18	15
		Set value		20

Mailman — A22

Mail Transport Symbols A23

Perf. 13x12½, 12½x13

1962, Nov. 23 **Unwmk.**

199	A22	15c dark green	18	15
200	A23	35c lilac rose	18	15
201	A22	1p brown	18	15
		Set value		20

Issued for Stamp Day.

Fetish — A24

1963, Jan. 29 *Perf. 13x12½*

202	A24	50c olive gray	15	15
203	A24	1p deep magenta	15	15
		Set value	20	15

Issued to help victims of the Seville flood.

Nuns — A25

Design: 50c, Nun and child, vert.

Perf. 12½x13, 13x12½

1963, July 6 Photo. Unwmk.

204	A25	25c bright lilac	15	15
205	A25	50c dull green	15	15
206	A25	1p red orange	15	15
		Set value	30	16

Issued for child welfare.

Child and Arms — A26

1963, July 12 *Perf. 12½x13*

207	A26	50c brown olive	15	15
208	A26	1p carmine rose	15	15
		Set value	15	15

Issued for Barcelona flood relief.

Governor Chacon A27

Orange Blossoms — A28

Men in Dugout Canoe — A29

1964, Mar. 6 *Perf. 12½x13, 13x12½*

No.	Type	Value	Color	Unused	Used
209	A27	25c	violet black	15	15
210	A28	50c	dark olive	15	15
211	A27	1p	brown red	15	15
			Set value	36	16

Issued for Stamp Day 1963.

1964, June 1 **Photo.** *Perf. 13x12½*

Design: 50c, Pineapple.

No.	Type	Value	Color	Unused	Used
212	A29	25c	purple	15	15
213	A28	50c	dull olive	15	15
214	A29	1p	deep claret	15	15
			Set value	36	17

Issued for child welfare.

Ring-necked Francolin — A30

Designs: 15c, 70c, 3p, Ring-necked francolin. 25c, 1p, 5p, Two mallards. 50c, 1.50p, 10p, Head of great blue touraco.

1964, July 1

No.	Type	Value	Color	Unused	Used
215	A30	15c	chestnut	15	15
216	A30	25c	dull violet	15	15
217	A30	50c	dk olive grn	15	15
218	A30	70c	green	15	15
219	A30	1p	brown org	15	15
220	A30	1.50p	grnsh blue	15	15
221	A30	3p	violet blue	60	15
222	A30	5p	dull purple	1.40	15
223	A30	10p	brt green	1.75	60
			Nos. 215-223 (9)	4.65	
			Set value		1.10

The Three Kings A31

Designs: 50c, 1.50p, Caspar, vert.

Perf. 13x12½, 12½x13

1964, Nov. 23 **Unwmk.**

No.	Type	Value	Color	Unused	Used
224	A31	50c	green	15	15
225	A31	1p	orange ver	15	15
226	A31	1.50p	deep green	15	15
227	A31	3p	ultra	1.40	65
			Set value		80

Issued for Stamp Day, 1964.

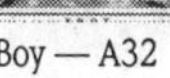

Boy — A32

Woman Fruit Picker — A33

Design: 1.50p, Girl learning to write, and church.

1964, Mar. 1 **Photo.** *Perf. 13x12½*

No.	Type	Value	Color	Unused	Used
228	A32	50c	indigo	15	15
229	A33	1p	dark red	15	15
230	A33	1.50p	grnsh blue	15	15
			Set value	26	17

Issued to commemorate 25 years of peace.

Plectrocnemia Cruciata — A34

Design: 1p, Metopodontus savagei, horiz.

Perf. 13x12½, 12½x13

1965, June 1 **Photo.** **Unwmk.**

No.	Type	Value	Color	Unused	Used
231	A34	50c	slate green	15	15
232	A34	1p	rose red	15	15
233	A34	1.50p	Prus blue	15	15
			Set value	26	17

Issued for child welfare.

Pole Vault — A35

Arms of Fernando Po — A36

Perf. 12½x13, 13x12½

1965, Nov. 23 **Photo.** **Unwmk.**

No.	Type	Value	Color	Unused	Used
234	A35	50c	yellow green	15	15
235	A36	1p	brt org brn	15	15
236	A35	1.50p	brt blue	15	15
			Set value	26	17

Issued for Stamp Day, 1965.

Children Reading A37

Design: 1.50p, St. Elizabeth of Hungary, vert.

Perf. 12½x13, 13x12½

1966, June 1 **Photo.** **Unwmk.**

No.	Type	Value	Color	Unused	Used
237	A37	50c	dark green	15	15
238	A37	1p	brown red	15	15
239	A37	1.50p	dark blue	15	15
			Set value	26	17

Issued for child welfare.

White-nosed Monkey — A38

Stamp Day: 40c, 4p, Head of moustached monkey, vert.

1966, Nov. 23 **Photo.** *Perf. 13*

No.	Type	Value	Color	Unused	Used
240	A38	10c	dk blue & yel	15	15
241	A38	40c	lt brn, bl & blk	15	15
242	A38	1.50p	ol bis, brn org & blk	15	15
243	A38	4p	sl grn, brn org & blk	20	15
			Set value	40	31

Flowers — A39

Designs: 40c, 4p, Six flowers.

1967, June 1 **Photo.** *Perf. 13*

No.	Type	Value	Color	Unused	Used
244	A39	10c	brt car & pale grn	15	15
245	A39	40c	red brn & org	15	15
246	A39	1.50p	red lil & lt red brn	15	15
247	A39	4p	dk blue & lt grn	20	15
			Set value	40	31

Issued for child welfare.

Linsang — A40

Stamp Day: 1.50p, Needle-clawed galago, vert. 3.50p, Fraser's scaly-tailed flying squirrel.

1967, Nov. 23 **Photo.** *Perf. 13*

No.	Type	Value	Color	Unused	Used
248	A40	1p	black & bister	15	15
249	A40	1.50p	brown & olive	15	15
250	A40	3.50p	rose lake & dl grn	25	20
			Set value		36

Stamp of 1868, No. 1, and Arms of San Carlos A41

Fernando Po No. 1 and: 1.50p, Arms of Santa Isabel. 2.50p, Arms of Fernando Po.

1968, Feb. 4 **Photo.** *Perf. 13*

No.	Type	Value	Color	Unused	Used
251	A41	1p	brt plum & brn org	15	15
252	A41	1.50p	dp blue & brn org	15	15
253	A41	2.50p	brn & brn org	20	15
			Set value		35

Centenary of the first postage stamp.

Signs of the Zodiac — A42

1968, Apr. 25 **Photo.** *Perf. 13*

No.	Type	Value	Color	Unused	Used
254	A42	1p	Libra	15	15
255	A42	1.50p	Leo	15	15
256	A42	2.50p	Aquarius	20	15
			Set value		35

Issued for child welfare.

SEMI-POSTAL STAMPS

Catalogue values for unused stamps in this section are for Never Hinged items.

Types of Regular Issue, 1960

Designs: 10c+5c, Manuel de Falla. 15c+5c, Dancers from "Love, the Magician."

Perf. 12½x13, 13x12½

1960 **Photo.** **Unwmk.**

No.	Type	Value	Color	Unused	Used
B1	A18	10c + 5c	maroon	15	15
B2	A17	15c + 5c	dk brn & bister	15	15
			Set value	25	15

The surtax was for child welfare.

Whale SP1

Design: Nos. B4, B6, Harpooning whale.

1961 *Perf. 12½x13*

No.	Type	Value	Color	Unused	Used
B3	SP1	10c + 5c	rose brown	15	15
B4	SP1	20c + 5c	dk slate grn	15	15
B5	SP1	30c + 10c	olive brn	15	15
B6	SP1	50c + 20c	dark brn	20	15
			Set value	38	21

Issued for Stamp Day, 1960.

Hand Blessing Woman — SP2

Design: 25c+10c, Boy making sign of the cross, and crucifix.

1961, June 21 *Perf. 13x12½*

No.	Type	Value	Color	Unused	Used
B7	SP2	10c + 5c	rose brn	15	15
B8	SP2	25c + 10c	gray vio	15	15
B9	SP2	80c + 20c	dk grn	15	15
			Set value	30	15

The surtax was for child welfare.

Ethiopian Tortoise SP3

Stamp Day: 25c+10c, 1p+10c, Native carriers, palms and shore.

1961, Nov. 23 *Perf. 12½x13*

No.	Type	Value	Color	Unused	Used
B10	SP3	10c + 5c	rose red	15	15
B11	SP3	25c + 10c	dk pur	15	15
B12	SP3	30c + 10c	vio brn	15	15
B13	SP3	1p + 10c	red org	15	15
			Set value	40	21

FINLAND

(Suomi)

LOCATION — Northern Europe bordering on the Gulfs of Bothnia and Finland
GOVT. — Republic
AREA — 130,119 sq. mi.
POP. — 4,869,858 (1984)
CAPITAL — Helsinki

Finland was a Grand Duchy of the Russian Empire from 1809 until December 1917, when it declared its independence.

100 Kopecks = 1 Ruble
100 Pennia = 1 Markka (1866)

Catalogue values for unused stamps in this country are for Never Hinged items, beginning with Scott 250 in the regular postage section, Scott B39 in the semi-postal section, Scott C2 in the airpost section, Scott M1 in the military stamp section, and Scott Q6 in the parcel post section.

Values of early Finland stamps vary according to condition. Quotations for Nos. 1-3B are for fine copies. Used values are for pen-canceled copies. Very fine to superb specimens sell at much higher prices, and inferior or poor copies sell at reduced prices, depending on the condition of the individual specimen.

Watermarks

Wmk. 121- Multiple Swastika

Wmk. 208- Post Horn

Wmk. 168- Wavy Lines and Letters

Wmk. 273- Roses

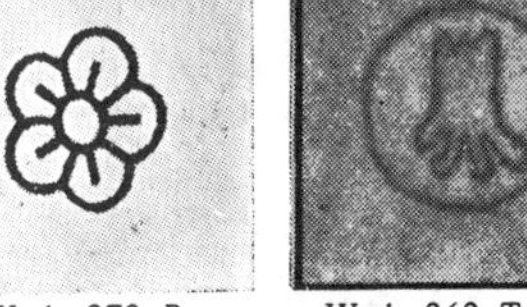

Wmk. 363- Tree Stump

Issues under Russian Empire

Coat of Arms — A1

1856 Unwmk. Typo. ***Imperf.***

Small Pearls in Post Horns

Wove Paper

No.	Type	Description	Unused	Used
1	A1	5k blue	*6,000.*	1,200.
		Pen and town cancellation		1,650.
		Town cancellation		2,500.
a.		Tête bêche pair		*30,000.*
		Pen and town cancellation		*37,500.*
2	A1	10k rose	7,250.	225.
		Pen and town cancellation		475.
		Town cancellation		800.
a.		Tête bêche pair		*17,500.*
		Pen and town cancellation		*22,500.*

1858

Wide Vertically Laid Paper

No.	Type	Description	Unused	Used
2C	A1	10k rose		1,050.
		Pen and town cancellation		1,500.
		Town cancellation		1,900.
d.		Tête bêche pair		

The wide vertically laid paper has 13-14 distinct lines per 2cm. The 10k rose also exists on a narrow laid paper with lines sometimes indistinct. Value, 60 per cent of that for a wide laid paper example.

A 5k blue with small pearls exists on narrow vertically laid paper.

Stamps on diagonally laid paper are envelope cut squares.

Large Pearls in Post Horns

Wove Paper

No.	Type	Description	Unused	Used
3	A1	5k blue	*6,000.*	1,050.
		Pen and town cancellation		1,350.
		Town cancellation		2,250.
a.		Tête bêche pair		*30,000.*
		Pen and town cancellation		*37,500.*

1859 Wide Vertically Laid Paper

No.	Type	Description	Unused	Used
3B	A1	5k blue		*10,500.*
		Pen and town cancellation		*15,000.*

Reprints of Nos. 2 and 3, made in 1862, are on brownish paper, on vertically laid paper, and in tête bêche pairs on normal and vertically laid paper. Reprints of 1871, 1881 and 1893 are on yellowish or white paper. Value for least costly of each, $85.

In 1956, Nos. 2 and 3 were reprinted for the Centenary with post horn watermark and gum. Value, $85 each.

Coat of Arms — A2

1860 ***Serpentine Roulette 7½, 8***

Nos. 4-13, with serpentine roulette, are seldom in perfect condition. Values are for specimens with "teeth" touching design and one or two missing. Copies with all teeth intact sell for many times more.

Four types of indentation are noted:

I- Depth 1-1¼mm

II- Depth 1½-1¾mm

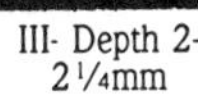

III- Depth 2-2¼mm

IV- Shovel-shaped teeth. Depth 1¼-1½mm

Wove Paper

No.	Type	Description	Unused	Used
4	A2	5k blue, *bluish*, I	275.00	75.00
a.		Roulette II	350.00	85.00
b.		Perf. vert.		
5	A2	10k rose, *pale rose*, I	225.00	30.00
a.		Roulette II	475.00	45.00

A3

A4

1866-74 ***Serpentine Roulette***

No.	Type	Description	Unused	Used
6	A3	5p pur brn, *lil*, I ('73)	110.00	40.00
a.		Roulette II		1,050.
b.		5p red brn, *lil*, III ('71)	110.00	40.00
7	A3	8p blk, *grn*, III ('67)	110.00	55.00
a.		Ribbed paper, III ('72)	450.00	175.00
b.		Roulette II ('74)	110.00	55.00
c.		As "b," ribbed paper ('74)	150.00	62.50
d.		Roulette I ('73)	165.00	75.00
e.		As "d," ribbed paper	450.00	175.00
f.		Serp. roulette 10½ ('67)		*7,000.*
8	A3	10p blk, *yel*, III ('70)	160.00	50.00
a.		10p blk, *buff*, II	275.00	85.00
b.		10p blk, *buff*, I ('73)	200.00	85.00
9	A3	20p bl, *bl*, III	150.00	24.00
a.		Roulette II	165.00	14.00
b.		Roulette I ('73)	225.00	30.00
c.		Roulette IV ('74)	*850.00*	*425.00*
d.		Perf. horiz.		*200.00*
e.		Printed on both sides (40p blue on back)		*5,000.*
10	A3	40p rose, *lil rose*, III	165.00	24.00
a.		Ribbed paper, III ('73)	225.00	27.50
b.		Roulette II	165.00	20.00
c.		As "b," ribbed paper ('73)	225.00	30.00
d.		Roulette I	350.00	32.50
e.		As "d," ribbed paper	250.00	32.50
f.		Roulette IV		*900.00*
g.		As "f," ribbed paper		*1,150.*
h.		Serp. roulette 10½		*3,500.*
11	A4	1m yel brn, III ('67)	750.00	275.00
a.		Roulette II	1,350.	475.00

Nos. 7f and 10h are private roulettes and are also known in compound serpentine roulette 10½ and 7½.

Nos. 4 to 11 were reprinted in 1893 on thick wove paper. Colors differ from originals. Roulette type IV. Value for Nos. 4-5, each $40, Nos. 6-10, each $50. Value for No. 11, $55.

Thin or Thick Laid Paper

No.	Type	Description	Unused	Used
12	A3	5p red brn, *lil*, III	110.00	40.00
a.		Roulette II	125.00	42.50
b.		Roulette I	125.00	47.50
d.		5p blk, *buff*, roul. III (error)		*6,250.*
e.		Tête bêche pair		*8,500.*
13	A3	10p black, *buff*, III	175.00	60.00
a.		10p black, *yel*, II	215.00	60.00
b.		10p black, *yel*, I	750.00	100.00
c.		10p red brown, *lil*, III (error)	*4,500.*	*2,750.*

Forgeries of No. 13c exist.

A5

A6

1875 ***Perf. 14x13½***

No.	Type	Description	Unused	Used
16	A5	32p lake	1,700.	450.

1875-81 ***Perf. 11***

No.	Type	Description	Unused	Used
17	A5	2p gray	40.00	40.00
18	A5	5p orange	100.00	10.00
a.		5p yellow	100.00	10.00
19	A5	8p blue green	165.00	62.50
a.		8p yellow green	165.00	52.50
20	A5	10p brown ('81)	275.00	52.50
21	A5	20p ultra	100.00	2.25
a.		20p blue	115.00	2.25
b.		20p Prussian blue	150.00	12.50
c.		Tête bêche pair		1,900.
22	A5	25p car ('79)	130.00	12.00
a.		25p rose	130.00	18.00

No.	Description	Unused	Used
23	A5 32p carmine	250.00	27.50
a.	32p rose	250.00	30.00
24	A5 1m violet ('77)	400.00	125.00

A souvenir card issued in 1974 for NORDIA 1975 reproduced a block of four of the unissued "1 MARKKAA" design.

Nos. 19, 23 were reprinted in 1893, perf. 12½. Value $17.50 each.

1881-83 *Perf. 12½*

No.	Description	Unused	Used
25	A5 2p gray	12.50	12.50
a.	Imperf., pair	100.00	
26	A5 5p orange	35.00	4.75
a.	Tête bêche pair	2,750.	2,250.
b.	Imperf. vert., pair	100.00	100.00
c.	Imperf. horiz., pair		115.00
27	A5 10p brown	75.00	13.00
28	A5 20p ultra	40.00	1.50
a.	20p blue	40.00	1.50
b.	Tête bêche pair	1,350.	1,700.
c.	Imperf., pair	65.00	
29	A5 25p rose	40.00	7.00
a.	25p carmine	40.00	7.00
b.	Tête bêche pair	3,000.	3,400.
30	A5 1m violet ('82)	275.00	30.00

Nos. 27-29 were reprinted in 1893 in deeper shades, perf. 12½. Value $35 each.

1881 *Perf. 11x12½*

No.	Description	Unused	Used
26d	A5 5p orange	250.00	52.50
27a	A5 10p brown	900.00	200.00
28d	A5 20p ultra	365.00	32.50
28e	A5 20p blue	365.00	32.50
29c	A5 25p rose	350.00	92.50
29d	A5 25p carmine	350.00	92.50
30a	A5 1m violet		1,000.

1881 *Perf. 12½x11*

No.	Description	Unused	Used
26e	A5 5p orange	250.00	52.50
27b	A5 10p brown	900.00	200.00
28f	A5 20p ultra	365.00	32.50
28g	A5 20p blue	365.00	32.50
29e	A5 25p rose	350.00	92.50
29f	A5 25p carmine	350.00	92.50

1885 *Perf. 12½*

No.	Description	Unused	Used
31	A5 5p emerald	16.00	28
a.	5p yellow green	16.00	28
b.	Tête bêche pair	4,300.	3,500.
32	A5 10p carmine	22.50	1.90
a.	10p rose	22.50	1.90
33	A5 20p orange	22.50	28
a.	20p yellow	27.50	1.75
b.	Tête bêche pair	2,500.	2,100.
34	A5 25p ultra	42.50	1.75
a.	25p blue	42.50	1.75
35	A5 1m gray & rose	25.00	11.00
36	A5 5m green & rose	350.00	275.00
37	A5 10m brown & rose	450.00	350.00

1889-92 *Perf. 12½*

No.	Description	Unused	Used
38	A6 2p slate ('90)	70	70
39	A6 5p green ('90)	22.50	22
40	A6 10p carmine ('90)	35.00	42
a.	10p rose ('90)	35.00	42
41	A6 20p orange ('92)	32.50	20
a.	20p yellow ('90)	35.00	1.00
42	A6 25p ultra ('91)	35.00	42
a.	25p blue	35.00	45
43	A6 1m slate & rose ('92)	5.25	2.75
a.	1m brnsh gray & rose ('90)	40.00	2.75
44	A6 5m green & rose ('90)	27.50	45.00
45	A6 10m brown & rose ('90)	55.00	75.00

The 2p slate, perf. 14x13, is believed to be an essay.

See Nos. 60-63.

See Russia for types similar to A7-A18.
Finnish stamps have "dot in circle" devices or are inscribed "Markka," "Markkaa," "Pen." or "Pennia."

Imperial Arms of Russia
A7 A8 A9

A10 A11

Laid Paper

1891-92 **Wmk. 168** *Perf. 14½x15*

No.	Description	Unused	Used
46	A7 1k orange yel	4.00	5.00
47	A7 2k green	4.75	5.25
48	A7 3k carmine	6.25	8.50
49	A8 4k rose	8.00	8.50
50	A7 7k dark blue	4.75	2.00
51	A8 10k dark blue	12.00	9.25
52	A9 14k blue & rose	18.00	14.00
53	A8 20k blue & car	12.00	10.00
54	A9 35k violet & grn	20.00	26.00
55	A8 50k violet & grn	26.00	20.00

Perf. 13½

No.	Description	Unused	Used
56	A10 1r brown & org	80.00	52.50
57	A11 3½r black & gray	275.00	300.00
a.	3½r black & yellow (error)	*7,000.*	*6,000.*
58	A11 7r black & yellow	165.00	135.00
	Nos. 46-58 (13)	635.75	596.00

Forgeries of Nos. 57, 57a, 58 exist.

Type of 1889-90
Wove Paper

1895-96 **Unwmk.** *Perf. 14x13*

No.	Description	Unused	Used
60	A6 5p green	50	15
61	A6 10p rose	65	15
a.	Imperf.	95.00	95.00
62	A6 20p orange	65	15
a.	Imperf.	82.50	95.00
63	A6 25p ultra	1.25	32
a.	25p blue	1.25	32
b.	Imperf.	95.00	95.00

A12 A13

A14 A15

1901 **Litho.** *Perf. 14½x15*
Chalky Paper

No.	Description	Unused	Used
64	A12 2p yellow	3.50	2.50
65	A12 5p green	10.00	45
66	A13 10p carmine	16.00	1.00
67	A12 20p dark blue	32.50	45
68	A14 1m violet & grn	150.00	4.75

Perf. 13½

No.	Description	Unused	Used
69	A15 10m black & gray	225.00	200.00
	Nos. 64-69 (6)	437.00	209.15

Imperf sheets of 10p and 20p, stolen during production, were privately perforated 11½ to defraud the P.O. Uncanceled imperfs. of Nos. 65-68 are believed to be proofs.

See Nos. 70-75, 82.

Types of 1901 Redrawn

No. 64 No. 70

2p. On No. 64, the "2" below "II" is shifted slightly leftward. On No. 70, the "2" is centered below "II."

No. 65 No. 71

5p. On No. 65, the frame lines are very close. On No. 71, a clear white space separates them.

Nos. 66, 67 Nos. 72, 73

10p, 20p. On Nos. 66-67, the horizontal central background lines are faint and broken. On Nos. 72-73, they are clear and solid, though still thin.

20p. On No. 67, "H" close to "2" with period midway. On No. 73 they are slightly separated with period close to "H."

No. 68 Nos. 74, 74a

1m. On No. 68, the "1" following "MARKKA" lacks serif at base. On Nos. 74-74a, this "1" has serif.

No. 69 No. 75

10m. On No. 69, the serifs of "M" and "A" in top and bottom panels do not touch. On No. 75, the serifs join.

1901-14 **Typo.** *Perf. 14, 14½x15*
Ordinary Paper

No.	Description	Unused	Used
70	A12 2p orange	60	60
71	A12 5p green	1.50	15
72	A13 10p carmine	45	15
b.	Background inverted	14.00	1.65
73	A12 20p dark blue	40	15
74	A14 1m lil & grn, perf. 14 ('14)	1.00	32
a.	1m violet & blue green, perf. 14½x15 ('02)	7.25	32
	Nos. 70-74 (5)	3.95	1.37

Perf. 13½

No.	Description	Unused	Used
75	A15 10m blk & drab ('03)	100.00	45.00

Imperf.

No.	Description	Unused	Used
70a	A12 2p	185.00	*200.00*
71b	A12 5p	75.00	105.00
72a	A13 10p	75.00	82.50
73a	A12 20p	75.00	82.50
74b	A14 1m	95.00	110.00

A16 A17 A18

1911-16 *Perf. 14, 14½x15*

No.	Description	Unused	Used
77	A16 2p orange	15	15
78	A16 5p green	24	15
a.	Imperf.	75.00	75.00
b.	Perf. 14½x15	200.00	57.50
79	A17 10p rose	18	15
a.	Imperf.	45.00	60.00
b.	Perf. 14½x15	1.00	65
80	A16 20p deep blue	18	15
a.	Imperf.	45.00	45.00
81	A18 40p violet & blue	15	15
a.	Perf. 14½x15	1,500.	1,500.
	Nos. 77-81 (5)	90	75

There are three minor types of No. 79.

Perf. 14½

No.	Description	Unused	Used
82	A15 10m blk & grnsh gray ('16)	125.00	165.00
a.	Horiz. pair, imperf. vert.	925.00	

Republic
Helsinki Issue

Arms of the Republic
A19 A20

Two types of the 40p.
Type I- Thin figures of value.

Type II- Thick figures of value.

1917-29 Unwmk. *Perf. 14, 14½x15*

83 A19 5p green 15 15
84 A19 5p gray ('19) 15 15
85 A19 10p rose 15 15
a. Imperf., pair 200.00 250.00
86 A19 10p green ('19) 1.10 15
a. Perf. 14½x15 1,200.
87 A19 10p lt blue ('21) 15 15
88 A19 20p buff 15 15
89 A19 20p rose ('20) 32 15
90 A19 20p brown ('24) 32 22
91 A19 25p blue 20 15
92 A19 25p lt brown ('19) 15 15
93 A19 30p green ('23) 25 15
94 A19 40p violet (I) 15 15
a. Perf. 14½x15 135.00 11.00
95 A19 40p bl grn (II) ('29) 15 32
a. Type I ('24) 6.50 3.00
96 A19 50p orange brn 15 15
97 A19 50p dp blue ('19) 2.75 15
a. Perf. 14½x15 415.00
98 A19 50p green ('21) 20 15
99 A19 60p red vio ('21) 32 15
a. Imperf., pair 75.00 100.00
100 A19 75p yellow ('21) 15 20
101 A19 1m dull rose & blk 9.25 15
102 A19 1m red org ('25) 25 *9.25*
103 A19 1½m bl grn & red vio ('29) 16 15
104 A19 2m green & blk ('21) 2.00 40
105 A19 2m dk blue & ind ('22) 65 15
106 A19 3m blue & blk ('21) 72.50 20
107 A19 5m red vio & blk 15.00 15
108 A19 10m brn & gray blk, perf. 14 55 55
a. 10m light brown & black, perf. 14½x15 ('29) 5.25 *350.00*
110 A19 25m dull red & yel ('21) 65 *13.00*
Nos. 83-108,110 (27) 107.97 *26.99*

Copies of a 2½p gray of this type exist. They are proofs from the original die which were distributed through the UPU. No plate was made for this denomination.

See Nos. 127-140, 143-152. For surcharge and overprints see Nos. 119-126, 153-154.

Vasa Issue

1918 Litho. *Perf. 11½*

111 A20 5p green 25 40
112 A20 10p red 22 35
113 A20 30p slate 65 1.25
114 A20 40p brown vio 20 40
115 A20 50p orange brn 32 90
116 A20 70p gray brown 1.50 8.50
117 A20 1m red & gray 32 65
118 A20 5m red violet & gray 65.00 95.00
Nos. 111-118 (8) 68.46 107.45

Nos. 111-118 exist imperforate but were not regularly issued in that condition.

Sheet margin copies, perf. on 3 sides, imperf. on margin side, were sold by post office.

Stamps and Type of 1917-29 Surcharged 50 50 50

1919 *Perf. 14*

119 A19 10p on 5p green 30 28
120 A19 20p on 10p rose 30 28
121 A19 50p on 25p blue 65 28
122 A19 75p on 20p orange 30 28

Stamps and Type of 1917-29 Surcharged:

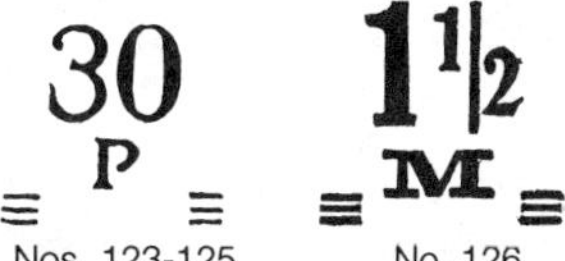

Nos. 123-125 No. 126

1921

123 A19 30p on 10p green 52 24
124 A19 60p on 40p red violet 2.75 35
125 A19 90p on 20p rose 15 15
126 A19 1½m on 50p blue 1.10 15
a. Thin "2" in "½" 5.25 2.75
b. Imperf., pair 150.00 300.00

Arms Type of 1917-29

Perf. 14, 14½x15

1925-29 Wmk. 121

127 A19 10p ultra ('27) 40 65
128 A19 20p brown 40 52
129 A19 25p brn org ('29) 60 *27.50*
130 A19 30p yel green 15 15
131 A19 40p blue grn (I) 2.00 15
a. Type II 2.00 15
132 A19 50p gray grn ('27) 32 15
133 A19 60p red violet 15 15
134 A19 1m dp orange 3.25 15
135 A19 1½m blue grn & red vio 5.50 15
136 A19 2m dk blue & indigo 25 32
137 A19 3m chlky blue & blk 85 15
138 A19 5m red violet & blk 22 15
139 A19 10m lt brn & blk ('27) 3.25 7.25
140 A19 25m dp org & yel ('27) 20.00 *200.00*
Nos. 127-140 (14) 37.34

A21

Wmk. 208

1927, Dec. 6 Typo. *Perf. 14*

141 A21 1½m deep violet 18 32
142 A21 2m deep blue 30 1.00

10th anniv. of Finnish independence.

Arms Type of 1917-29

1927-29 Wmk. 208 *Perf. 14½x15*

143 A19 20p lt brown ('29) 1.10 *4.50*
144 A19 40p bl grn (II) ('28) 15 15
145 A19 50p gray grn ('28) 15 15
146 A19 1m dp orange 15 15
a. Imperf., pair 125.00 140.00
b. Perf. 14 1.00 15
147 A19 1½m bl grn & red vio ('28) 2.00 15
a. Perf. 14 500.00 11.00
148 A19 2m dk bl & ind ('28) 32 32
149 A19 3m chlky bl & blk 32 32
a. Perf. 14 1.75 1.75
150 A19 5m red vio & blk ('28) 32 32
151 A19 10m lt brown & blk 1.00 *27.50*
152 A19 25m brown org & yel 1.10 *105.00*
Nos. 143-152 (10) 6.61

Nos. 146-147 Overprinted 1928 Postim. näytt. Frim. utställn.

1928, Nov. 10 Litho. Wmk. 208

153 A19 1m dp orange 6.50 12.00
154 A19 1½m bl grn & red vio 6.50 12.00

Nos. 153 and 154 were sold exclusively at the Helsinki Philatelic Exhibition, Nov. 10-18, 1928, and were valid only during that period.

S. S. "Bore" Leaving Turku A23

Turku Cathedral A24

Turku Castle — A25

Wmk. 208

1929, May 22 Typo. *Perf. 14*

155 A23 1m olive green 1.10 2.75
156 A24 1½m chocolate 2.00 2.25
157 A25 2m dark gray 65 2.75

Founding of the city of Turku (Abo), 700th anniv.

A26

1930-46 Unwmk. *Perf. 14*

158 A26 5p chocolate 15 15
159 A26 10p dull violet 15 15
160 A26 20p yellow grn 28 35
161 A26 25p yellow brn 15 15
162 A26 40p blue grn 2.50 16
163 A26 50p yellow 45 35
164 A26 50p bl grn ('32) 15 15
b. Imperf., pair 125.00 130.00
165 A26 60p dk gray 35 45
165A A26 75p dp org ('42) 15 15
166 A26 1m red orange 45 15
a. Booklet pane of 4 1.90
166B A26 1m yel grn ('42) 16 15
167 A26 1.20m crimson 35 52
168 A26 1.25m yellow ('32) 20 15
169 A26 1½m red vio 2.50 15
170 A26 1½m car ('32) 15 15
170A A26 1½m slate ('40) 15 15
170B A26 1.75m org yel ('40) 52 15
171 A26 2m indigo 28 15
172 A26 2m dp vio ('32) 7.00 15
173 A26 2m car ('36) 16 15
173B A26 2m yel org ('42) 28 15
173C A26 2m bl grn ('45) 16 15
174 A26 2½m brt bl ('32) 2.00 15
174A A26 2½m car ('42) 15 15
174B A26 2.75m rose vio ('40) 15 15
175 A26 3m olive blk 27.50 15
175B A26 3m car ('45) 20 15
175C A26 3m yellow ('45) 35 45
176 A26 3½m brt bl ('36) 5.50 15
176A A26 3½m olive ('42) 15 15
176B A26 4m olive ('45) 35 15
176C A26 4½m saph ('42) 15 15
176D A26 5m saph ('45) 35 15
176E A26 5m purple ('45) 35 15
j. Imperf., pair 125.00 130.00
176F A26 5m yellow ('46) 70 15
k. Imperf., pair 105.00 125.00
176G A26 6m car ('45) 35 15
m. Imperf., pair 125.00 130.00
176H A26 8m purple ('46) 15 15
176I A26 10m saph ('45) 70 15
Nos. 158-176I (38) 55.79
Set value 4.75

See Nos. 257-262, 270-274, 291-296, 302-304. For surcharges and overprints see Nos. 195-196, 212, 221-222, 243, 275, M2-M3.

Stamps of types A26-A29 overprinted "ITA KARJALA" are listed under Karelia, Nos. N1-N15.

Castle in Savonlinna — A27

Lake Saima — A28

Woodchopper A29

1930 Engr.

177 A27 5m blue 18 15
178 A28 10m gray lilac 72.50 2.50
179 A29 25m black brown 75 15

See #205, 305. For overprint see #NC1.

Elias Lönnrot — A30

Seal of Finnish Literary Society — A31

1931, Jan. 1 Typo.

180 A30 1m olive brown 3.00 2.50
181 A31 1½m dull blue 10.00 2.50

Centenary of Finnish Literary Society.

A32

1931, Feb. 28

182 A32 1½m red 2.50 3.00
183 A32 2m blue 2.50 3.50

1st use of postage stamps in Finland, 75th anniv.

Nos. 162-163 Surcharged 50 PEN.

1931, Dec.

195 A26 50p on 40p blue grn 1.00 20
196 A26 1.25m on 50p yellow 2.75 45

Svinhufvud A33

Alexis Kivi A34

1931, Dec. 15

197 A33 2m gray blue & blk 1.10 1.65

Pres. Pehr Eyvind Svinhufvud, 70th birthday.

Lake Saima Type of 1930

1932-43 Re-engraved

205 A28 10m red violet ('43) 35 15
a. 10m dark violet 16.00 50

On Nos. 205 and 205a the lines of the islands, the clouds and the foliage are much deeper and stronger than on No. 178.

1934, Oct. 10 Typo.

206 A34 2m red violet 1.75 1.90
Never hinged 4.00

Alexis Kivi, Finnish poet (1834-1872).

Bards Reciting the "Kalevala" A35

Goddess Louhi, As Eagle Seizing Magic Mill — A36

Kullervo — A37

1935, Feb. 28 Engr.

207 A35 1¼m brown lake 1.00 00
208 A36 2m black 3.00 70
209 A37 2½m blue 3.00 1.40
Set, never hinged 14.00

Cent. of the publication of the "Kalevala" (Finnish National Epic).

No. 170 Surcharged in Black 2 MARKKAA

1937, Feb.
212 A26 2m on 1½m car 3.50 45
Never hinged 9.50

Gustaf Mannerheim A38

Swede-Finn Co-operation in Colonization A39

1937, June 4 **Photo.** ***Perf. 14***
213 A38 2m ultra 45 85
Never hinged 85

70th birthday of Field Marshal Baron Carl Gustaf Mannerheim, June 4th, 1937.

1938, June 1
214 A39 3½m dark brown 1.25 1.75
Never hinged 2.50

Tercentenary of the colonization of Delaware by Swedes and Finns.

Early Post Office — A40

Designs: 1¼m, Mail delivery in 1700. 2m, Modern mail plane. 3½m, Helsinki post office.

1938, Sept. 6 **Photo.** ***Perf. 14***
215 A40 50p green 30 45
216 A40 1¼m dk blue 1.10 1.75
217 A40 2m scarlet 1.25 50
218 A40 3½m slate black 4.50 4.50
Set, never hinged 14.00

300th anniv. of the Finnish Postal System.

Post Office, Helsinki — A44

1939-42 **Photo.**
219 A44 4m brown black 15 15
Engr.
219A A44 7m black brn ('42) 45 15
219B A44 9m rose lake ('42) 45 15
Set value 30
Set, never hinged 2.10

See No. 248.

University of Helsinki — A45

1940, May 1 **Photo.**
220 A45 2m dp blue & blue 50 70
Never hinged 60

300th anniv. of the founding of the University of Helsinki.

Nos. 168 and 173 Surcharged in Black

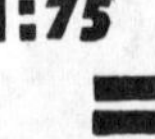

1940, June 16 **Typo.**
221 A26 1.75m on 1.25m yel 75 70
222 A26 2.75m on 2m carmine 2.25 20
Set, never hinged 8.25

President Kallio Reviewing Military Band — A46

1941, May 24 **Engr.**
223 A46 2.75m black 50 70
Never hinged 60

Pres. Kyösti Kallio (1873-1940).

Castle at Viborg — A47

1941, Aug. 30 **Typo.**
224 A47 1.75m yellow orange 32 65
225 A47 2.75m rose violet 32 65
226 A47 3.50m blue 65 1.25
Set, never hinged 2.10

Field Marshal Mannerheim — A48

Pres. Risto Ryti — A49

1941, Dec. 31 **Engr.** **Wmk. 273**
227 A48 50p dull green 55 85
228 A48 1.75m deep brown 55 85
229 A48 2m dark red 55 85
230 A48 2.75m dull vio brn 55 85
231 A48 3.50m deep blue 55 85
232 A48 5m slate blue 55 85
Nos. 227-232 (6) 3.30 5.10
Set, never hinged 5.25

233 A49 50p dull green 55 85
234 A49 1.75m deep brown 55 85
235 A49 2m dark red 55 85
236 A49 2.75m dull vio brn 55 85
237 A49 3.50m deep blue 55 85
238 A49 5m slate blue 55 85
Nos. 233-238 (6) 3.30 5.10
Set, never hinged 5.25

Types A48-A49 overprinted "ITA KARJALA" are listed under Karelia, Nos. N16-N27.

Häme Bridge, Tampere — A50

South Harbor, Helsinki — A51

1942 **Unwmk.**
239 A50 50m dull brown vio 1.00 15
240 A51 100m indigo 1.25 20
Set, never hinged 5.00

See No. 350.

Altar and Open Bible — A52

17th Century Printer — A53

1942, Oct. 10
241 A52 2.75m dk brown 28 65
242 A53 3.50m violet blue 55 1.10
Set, never hinged 1.30

300th anniv. of the printing of the 1st Bible in Finnish.

No. 174B Surcharged in Black

3½mk

1943, Feb. 1
243 A26 3.50m on 2.75m rose vio 16 16
Never hinged 30

Minna Canth (1844-96), Author and Playwright — A54

1944, Mar. 20
244 A54 3.50m dk olive grn 25 60
Never hinged 40

Pres. P. E. Svinhufvud A55

K. J. Stahlberg A56

1944, Aug. 1
245 A55 3.50m black 25 60
Never hinged 40

Death of President Svinhufvud (1861-1944).

1945, May 16 **Engr.** ***Perf. 14***
246 A56 3.50m brown vio 20 45
Never hinged 22

80th birthday of Dr. K. J. Stahlberg.

Castle in Savonlinna — A57

Jean Sibelius — A58

1945, Sept. 4
247 A57 15m lilac rose 70 15
248 A44 20m sepia 80 15
Set value 23
Set, never hinged 2.25

For a 35m of type A57, see No. 280.

1945, Dec. 8
249 A58 5m dk slate green 15 28
Never hinged 16

Jean Sibelius (1865-1957), composer.

Catalogue values for unused stamps in this section, from this point to the end of the section, are for Never Hinged items.

No. 176E Surcharged with New Value and Bars in Black

1946, Mar. 16
250 A26 8(m) on 5m purple 18 18

Victorious Athletes A59

Lighthouse at Uto A60

1946, June 1 **Engr.** ***Perf. 13½***
251 A59 8m brown violet 25 40

3rd Sports Festival, Helsinki, June 27-30, 1946.

1946, Sept. 19
252 A60 8m deep violet 25 40

250th anniv. of the Finnish Department of Pilots and Lighthouses.

Post Bus — A61

1946-47 **Unwmk.** ***Perf. 14***
253 A61 16m gray blk 50 50
253A A61 30m gray blk ('47) 1.75 15

Issue dates: 16m, Oct. 16, 30m, Feb. 10.

Old Town Hall, Porvoo — A62

Cathedral, Porvoo — A63

1946, Dec. 3
254 A62 5m gray black 18 30
255 A63 8m deep claret 28 42

600th anniv. of the founding of the city of Porvoo (Borga).

Waterfront, Tammisaari A64

1946, Dec. 14
256 A64 8m grnsh black 28 38

400th anniv. of the founding of the town of Tammisaari (Ekenas).

Lion Type of 1930

1947 **Typo.** ***Perf. 14***
257 A26 2½m dark green 60 15
258 A26 3m slate gray 30 15
259 A26 6m deep orange 1.50 15
260 A26 7m carmine 60 15
261 A26 10m purple 3.75 15
262 A26 12m deep blue 1.90 15
Nos. 257-262 (6) 8.65
Set value 50

Issue dates: 3m, June 9, 7m, 12m, Feb. 10, others, Jan. 20.

Pres. Juho K. Paasikivi A65

Postal Savings Emblem A66

1947, Mar. 15 **Engr.**
263 A65 10m gray black 32 38

1947, Apr. 1
264 A66 10m brown violet 28 38

60th anniv. of the foundation of the Finnish Postal Savings Bank.

Ilmarinen, the Plowman A67

Girl and Boy Athletes A68

1947, June 2
265 A67 10m gray black 28 38

2nd year of peace following WW II.

1947, June 2
266 A68 10m bright blue 28 38

Finnish Athletic Festival, Helsinki, June 29-July 3, 1947.

Wheat and Savings Bank Assoc. Emblem — A69

Sower — A70

1947, Aug. 21
267 A69 10m red brown 28 38

Finnish Savings Bank Assoc., 125th anniv.

1947, Nov. 1
268 A70 10m gray black 28 38

150th anniv. of Finnish Agricultural Societies.

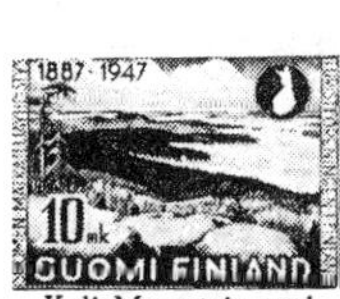

Koli Mountain and Lake Pielisjärvi A71

Statue of Michael Agricola A72

1947, Nov. 1
269 A71 10m indigo 28 38

60th anniv. of the Finnish Touring Assoc.

Lion Type of 1930

1948 **Typo.** ***Perf. 14***
270 A26 3m dk green 2.50 15
271 A26 6m yellow green 75 35
272 A26 9m carmine 55 15
273 A26 15m dk blue 4.75 15
274 A26 24m brown lake 1.50 22
Nos. 270-274 (5) 10.05
Set value 83

Issue dates: 3m, Feb. 9, 24m, Apr. 26, others, Sept. 13.

No. 261 Surcharged with New Value and Bars in Black

1948, Feb. 9
275 A26 12(m) on 10m purple 1.00 15

1948, Oct. 2 **Engr.** ***Perf. 14***

Design: 12m, Agricola translating New Testament.

276 A72 7m rose violet 85 1.10
277 A72 12m gray blue 85 1.10

400th anniv. of publication of the Finnish translation of the New Testament, by Michael Agricola.

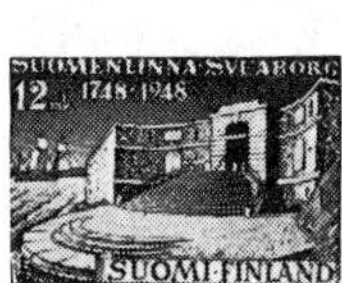

Sveaborg Fortress — A73

Post Rider — A74

1948, Oct. 15
278 A73 12m deep green 1.10 1.10

200th anniv. of the construction of Sveaborg Fortress on the Gulf of Finland.

1948, Oct. 27
279 A74 12m green 14.00 20.00

Helsinki Philatelic Exhibition. Sold only at exhibition for 62m, of which 50m was entrance fee.

Castle Type of 1945

1949
280 A57 35m violet 7.00 15

Sawmill and Cellulose Plant — A75

Pine Tree and Globe — A76

Woman with Torch — A77

1949, June 15
281 A75 9m brown 2.50 1.50
282 A76 15m dull green 2.50 1.50

Issued to publicize the Third World Forestry Congress, Helsinki, July 10-20, 1949.

1949, July 16 **Engr.** ***Perf. 14***
283 A77 5m dull green 4.50 *8.00*
284 A77 15m red *(Worker)* 4.50 *8.00*

50th anniv. of the Finnish labor movement.

Harbor of Lappeenranta (Willmanstrand) A78

Raahe (Brahestad) A79

1949
285 A78 5m dk blue grn 65 60
286 A79 9m brown car 85 85
287 A78 15m brt blue *(Kristiinan-kaupunki)* 1.25 1.25

300th anniv. of the founding of Willmanstrand, Brahestad and Kristinestad (Kristiinan-kaupunki). Issued: 5m, Aug. 6; 9m, Aug. 13; 15m, July 30.

Technical High School Badge — A80

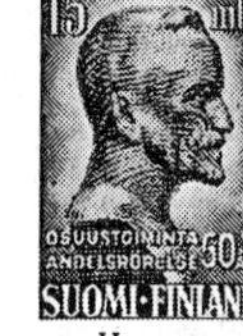

Hannes Gebhard — A81

1949, Sept. 13
288 A80 15m ultra 75 70

Founding of the technical school, cent.

1949, Oct. 2
289 A81 15m dull green 75 70

Establishment of Finnish cooperatives, 50th anniv.

Finnish Lake Country — A82

1949, Oct. 8
290 A82 15m blue 1.25 85

75th anniv. of the UPU.

Lion Type of 1930

1950, Jan. 9 **Typo.** ***Perf. 14***
291 A26 8m brt grn 80 65
292 A26 9m red org 1.25 32
293 A26 10m vio brn 5.50 15
294 A26 12m scarlet 80 15
295 A26 15m plum 14.00 15
296 A26 20m deep blue 5.50 15
Nos. 291-296 (6) 27.85
Set value 1.28

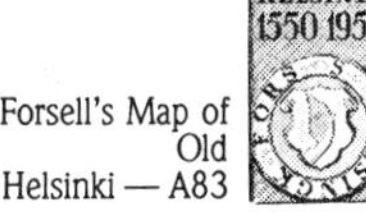

Forsell's Map of Old Helsinki — A83

J. A. Ehrenstrom and C. L. Engel — A84

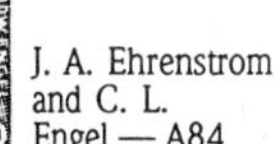

City Hall — A85

1950, June 11 **Engr.**
297 A83 5m emerald 50 50
298 A84 9m brown 80 80
299 A85 15m deep blue 55 55

400th anniv. of the founding of Helsinki.

J. K. Paasikivi A86

View of Kajaani A87

1950, Nov. 27
300 A86 20m deep ultra 55 38

80th birthday of Pres. J. K. Paasikivi.

1951, July 7 **Unwmk.** ***Perf. 14***
301 A87 20m red brn 60 50

Tercentenary of Kajaani.

Lion and Chopper Types of 1930

1952, Jan. 18 **Typo.**
302 A26 10m emerald 2.75 15
303 A26 15m red 4.00 15
304 A26 25m blue 5.00 15

Engr.

305 A29 40m blk brn 3.75 15
Set value 37

Arms of Pietarsaari A88

Rooftops of Vaasa A89

1952, June 19 **Unwmk.** ***Perf. 14***
306 A88 25m blue 80 60

300th anniv. of the founding of Pietarsaari (Jacobstad).

1952, Aug. 3
307 A89 25m brown 80 60

Centenary of the burning of Vaasa.

Chess Symbols — A90

Torch Bearers — A91

1952, Aug. 10
308 A90 25m gray 1.65 1.75

Issued to publicize the 10th Chess Olympics, Helsinki, Aug. 10-31, 1952.

1953, Jan. 27
309 A91 25m blue 1.00 65

Temperance movement in Finland, cent.

Air View of Hamina (Fredrikshamn) A92

Ivar Wilskman A93

1953, June 20

310 A92 25m dk gray grn	85	50

Tercentenary of Hamina.

1954, Feb. 26

311 A93 25m blue	75	45

Centenary of the birth of Prof. Ivar Wilskman, "father of gymnastics in Finland."

Arms of Finland A94

"In the Outer Archipelago" A95

1954-59 *Perf. 11½*

312	A94	1m red brn ('55)	45	15
313	A94	2m green ('55)	45	15
314	A94	3m dp org	45	15
314A	A94	4m gray ('58)	38	15
315	A94	5m vio bl	75	15
316	A94	10m bl grn	1.10	15
a.		Bklt. pane of 5 (vert. strip)	22.50	
317	A94	15m rose red	3.50	15
318	A94	15m yel org ('57)	7.50	15
319	A94	20m rose lilac	9.00	15
320	A94	20m rose red ('56)	3.00	15
321	A94	25m deep blue	3.75	15
322	A94	25m rose lil ('59)	13.00	15
323	A94	30m lt ultra ('56)	3.00	15
		Nos. 312-323 (13)	46.33	
		Set value		90

See Nos. 398, 400-405A, 457-459, 461A-462, 464-464B.

1954, July 21 *Perf. 14*

324 A95 25m black	65	48

Cent. of the birth of Albert Edelfelt, painter.

J. J. Nervander — A96

1955, Feb. 23

325 A96 25m blue	80	60

150th anniv. of the birth of J. J. Nervander, astronomer and poet.

Composite of Finnish Public Buildings — A97

Bishop Henrik with Foot on Lalli, his Murderer — A98

1955, Mar. 30 **Engr.** *Perf. 14*

326 A97 25m gray	15.00	17.50

Sold for 125m, which included the price of admission to the Natl. Postage Stamp Exhibition, Helsinki, Mar. 30-Apr. 3, 1955.

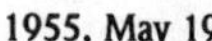

1955, May 19

Design: 25m, Arrival of Bishop Henrik and monks.

327 A98 15m rose brn	80	65
328 A98 25m green	80	65

Adoption of Christianity in Finland, 800th anniv.

Conference Hall, Helsinki — A99

1955, Aug. 25

329 A99 25m bluish green	1.10	90

44th conf. of the Interparliamentarian Union, Helsinki, Aug. 25-31, 1955.

Sailing Vessel and Merchant A100

1955, Sept. 2

330 A100 25m sepia	1.00	90

350th anniv. of founding of Oulu.

Town Hall, Lahti — A101

Radio Sender, Map of Finland — A102

1955, Nov. 1 *Perf. 14x13½*

331 A101 25m violet blue	1.10	75

50th anniversary of founding of Lahti.

1955, Dec. 10 *Perf. 14*

Designs: 15m, Otto Nyberg. 25m, Telegraph wires and pines under snow.

Inscribed: Lennatin 1855-1955 Telegrafen

332 A102 10m green	1.10	1.10
333 A102 15m dl vio	1.10	52
334 A102 25m lt ultra	1.10	52

Cent. of the telegraph in Finland.

Lighthouse and Porkkala Peninsula — A103

1956, Jan. 26 **Unwmk.** *Perf. 14*

335 A103 25m grnsh bl	70	48

Return of the Porkkala Region to Finland by Russia, Jan. 1956.

Church at Lammi — A104

Designs: 40m, House of Parliament. 60m, Fortress of Olavinlinna (Olofsborg).

1956-57 *Perf. 11½*

336	A104	30m gray olive	80	15
337	A104	40m dl pur	3.50	15
338	A104	50m gray ol ('57)	5.75	15
338A	A104	60m pale pur ('57)	13.00	15
		Set value		45

Issue dates: 30m, Mar. 4, 40m, Mar. 11, 50m, Mar. 3, 60m, Apr. 7. See Nos. 406-408A.

Johan V. Snellman A105

Gymnast and Athletes A106

1956, May 12 **Engr.** *Perf. 14*

339 A105 25m dk vio brn	65	48

Johan V. Snellman (1806-81), statesman.

1956, June 28

340 A106 30m vio bl	90	60

Finnish Gymnastic and Sports Games, Helsinki, June 28-July 1, 1956.

A107

Wmk. 208

1956, July 7 **Typo.** ***Rouletted***

341 A107 30m dp ultra	3.50	5.00
a. Tête bêche pair	7.25	10.50
b. Pane of 10	37.50	55.00

Issued to publicize the FINLANDIA Philatelic Exhibition, Helsinki, July 7-15, 1956.

Printed in sheets containing four 2x5 panes, with white margins around each group. The stamps in each double row are printed tete-beche, making the position of the watermark differ in the vertical row of each pane of ten.

Sold for 155m, price including entrance ticket to exhibition.

Town Hall at Vasa — A108

1956, Oct. 2 **Unwmk.** **Engr.** *Perf. 14*

342 A108 30m brt bl	75	48

350th anniversary of Vasa.

Northern Countries Issue

Whooper Swans — A108a

1956, Oct. 30 *Perf. 12½*

343 A108a 20m rose red	3.50	1.25
344 A108a 30m ultra	11.50	1.10

See footnote after Denmark No. 362.

University Clinic, Helsinki — A109

Scout Sign, Emblem and Globe — A110

1956, Dec. 17 *Perf. 11½*

345 A109 30m dl grn	1.25	40

Public health service in Finland, bicent.

1957, Feb. 22 *Perf. 14*

346 A110 30m ultra	1.50	70

50th anniversary of Boy Scouts.

Arms Holding Hammers and Laurel A111

"Lex" from Seal of Parliament A112

Design: 20m, Factories and cogwheel.

1957 **Engr.** *Perf. 13½*

347 A111 20m dark blue	75	45
348 A111 30m carmine	75	60

50th anniv.: Central Fed. of Finnish Employers (20m, issued 9/27); Finnish Trade Union Movement (30m, issued 4/15).

1957, May 23 *Perf. 14*

349 A112 30m olive gray	1.00	60

50th anniv. of the Finnish parliament.

Harbor Type of 1942

1957 **Unwmk.** *Perf. 14*

350 A51 100m grnsh bl	7.00	15

Ida Aalberg A114

Arms of Finland A115

1957, Dec. 4 *Perf. 14*

351 A114 30m vio gray & mar	70	55

Birth cent. of Ida Aalberg, Finnish actress.

1957, Dec. 6 *Perf. 11½*

352 A115 30m blue	75	55

40th anniv. of Finland's independence.

Jean Sibelius A116

Ski Jump A117

1957, Dec. 8 *Perf. 14*

353 A116 30m black	75	55

Jean Sibelius (1865-1957), composer.

1958, Feb. 1 Engr. *Perf. 11½*

Design: 30m, Skier, vert.

354 A117 20m slate grn 65 85
355 A117 30m blue 75 45

Nordic championships of the Intl. Ski Federation, Lahti.

"March of the Bjorneborgienses," by Edelfelt — A118

1958, Mar. 8

356 A118 30m vio gray 1.25 65

400th anniv. of the founding of Pori (Bjorneborg).

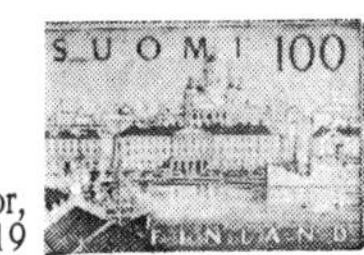

South Harbor, Helsinki — A119

1958, June 2 Unwmk. *Perf. 11½*

357 A119 100m bluish grn 22.50 15

See No. 410.

Seal of Jyväskylä Lyceum — A120

1958, Oct. 1 *Perf. 11½*

358 A120 30m rose car 1.25 70

Cent. of the founding of the 1st Finnish secondary school.

Chrismon and Globe — A121

Diet at Porvoo, 1809 — A122

1959, Jan. 19

359 A121 30m dl vio 85 38

Finnish Missionary Society, cent.

1959, Mar. 22 *Perf. 11½*

360 A122 30m dk bl gray 80 38

150th anniv. of the inauguration of the Diet at Porvoo.

Saw Cutting Log — A123

Pyhakoski Power Station — A124

1959, May 13 Engr.

361 A123 10m shown 45 45
362 A123 30m Forest 55 70

No. 361 for the cent. of the establishment of the 1st steam saw-mill in Finland; No. 362, the cent. of the Dept. of Forestry.

1959, May 24

363 A124 75m gray 4.00 15

See No. 409.

Oil Lamp — A125

Woman Gymnast — A126

1959, Dec. 19

364 A125 30m blue 75 38

Cent. of the liberation of the country trade.

1959, Nov. 14 Unwmk.

365 A126 30m rose lilac 75 38

Finnish women's gymnastics and the cent. of the birth of Elin Oihonna Kallio, pioneer of Finnish women's physical education.

Arms of Six New Towns — A127

1960, Jan. 2 *Perf. 14*

366 A127 30m lt vio 75 38

Issued to commemorate the founding of new towns in Finland: Hyvinkaa, Kouvola, Riihimaki, Rovaniemi, Salo and Seinajoki.

Type of 1860 Issue A128

1960, Mar. 25 Typo. *Rouletted 4½*

367 A128 30m bl & gray 8.50 8.50

Cent. of Finland's serpentine roulette stamps, and in connection with HELSINKI 1960, 40th anniv. exhib. of the Federation of Philatelic Societies of Finland, Mar. 25-31. Sold only at the exhibition for 150m including entrance ticket.

Mother and Child, Waiting Crowd and Uprooted Oak Emblem — A129

1960, Apr. 7 Engr. *Perf. 11½*

368 A129 30m rose claret 55 30
369 A129 40m dark blue 55 30

Issued to publicize World Refugee Year, July 1, 1959-June 30, 1960.

Johan Gadolin A130

Hj. Nortamo A131

1960, June 4 *Perf. 11½*

370 A130 30m dk brn 75 45

Bicent. of the birth of Gadolin, chemist.

1960, June 13 Unwmk.

371 A131 30m gray green 70 42

Cent. of the birth of Hj. Nortamo (Hjalmar Nordberg), writer.

Symbolic Tree and Cuckoo — A132

1960, June 18

372 A132 30m vermilion 75 42

Karelian Natl. Festival, Helsinki, June 18-19.

Geodetic Instrument A133

Urho Kekkonen A134

Design: 30m, Aurora borealis and globe.

1960, July 26 Unwmk. *Perf. 13½*

373 A133 10m bl & pale brn 40 32
374 A133 30m ver & rose car 75 40

12th General Assembly of the Intl. Union of Geodesy and Geophysics, Helsinki.

1960, Sept. 3 Engr. *Perf. 11½*

375 A134 30m vio bl 80 42

Issued to honor President Urho Kekkonen on his 60th birthday.

Common Design Types pictured in section at front of book.

Europa Issue, 1960

Common Design Type

1960, Sept. 19 *Perf. 13½*

Size: 30½x21mm.

376 CD3 30m dk bl & Prus bl 45 30
377 CD3 40m dk brn & plum 60 38

A 30m gray similar to No. 376 was printed with simulated perforations in a non-valid souvenir sheet privately released in London for STAMPEX 1961.

Values quoted in this catalogue are for stamps graded Fine-Very Fine and with no faults. An illustrated guide to grade is provided beginning on Page 8A.

Uno Cygnaeus A135

"Pommern" and Arms of Mariehamn A136

1960, Oct. 13 *Perf. 11½*

378 A135 30m dl vio 1.00 42

150th anniv. of the birth of Pastor Uno Cygnaeus, founder of elementary schools.

1961, Feb. 21 *Perf. 11½*

379 A136 30m grnsh bl 3.00 1.25

Centenary of the founding of Mariehamn.

Lake and Rowboat — A137

Turku Castle — A138

1961 Engr. Unwmk.

380 A137 5m green 32 15
381 A138 125m slate green 20.00 40

See Nos. 399, 411.

Postal Savings Bank Emblem A139

Symbol of Standardization A140

1961, May 24

382 A139 30m Prus grn 75 42

75th anniv. of Finland's Postal Savings Bank.

1961, June 5 Litho. *Perf. 14x13½*

383 A140 30m dk sl grn & org 75 42

Meeting of the Intl. Organization for Standardization (ISO), Helsinki, June 5.

Juhani Aho — A141

Various Buildings — A142

Perf. 11½

1961, Sept. 11 Unwmk. Engr.

384 A141 30m red brn 75 42

Juhani Aho (1861-1921), writer.

1961, Oct. 16 *Perf. 11½*

385 A142 30m slate 75 42

150 years of the Central Board of Buildings.

Arvid Jarnefelt — A143

1961, Nov. 16
386 A143 30m deep claret 75 42

Cent. of the birth of Arvid Jarnefelt, writer.

Bank of Finland A144 — First Finnish Locomotive A145

1961, Dec. 12 Engr. *Perf. 11½*
387 A144 30m brn vio 75 42

150th anniversary of Bank of Finland.

1962, Jan. 31 Unwmk. *Perf. 11½*

Designs: 30m, Steam locomotive and timber car. 40m, Diesel locomotive and passenger train.

388 A145 10m gray grn 90 45
389 A145 30m vio bl 1.10 45
390 A145 40m dl red brn 2.75 60

Centenary of the Finnish State Railways.

Mora Stone — A146

1962, Feb. 15
391 A146 30m gray brown 75 42

Issued to commemorate 600 years of political rights of the Finnish people.

Senate Place, Helsinki — A147

1962, Apr. 8 Unwmk. *Perf. 11½*
392 A147 30m vio brn 75 42

Sesquicentennial of the proclamation of Helsinki as capital of Finland.

Customs Emblem A148 — Staff of Mercury A149

1962, Apr. 11
393 A148 30m red 75 42

Finnish Board of Customs, sesquicentennial.

1962, May 21 Engr.
394 A149 30m bluish green 75 42

Cent. of the 1st commercial bank in Finland.

Santeri Alkio — A150

Finnish Labor Emblem and Conveyor Belt — A151

1962, June 17 Unwmk. *Perf. 11½*
395 A150 30m brown carmine 75 42

Cent. of the birth of Santeri Alkio, writer and pioneer of the young people's societies in Finland.

1962, Oct. 19
396 A151 30m chocolate 75 42

National production progress.

Survey Plane and Compass — A152

1962, Nov. 14
397 A152 30m yellow green 75 42

150th anniv. of the Finnish Land Survey Board.

Types of 1954-61 and

Log Floating — A153

1,75
SUOMI-FINLAND
Parainen Bridge — A154

Farm on Lake Shore — A155

Ristikallio in Kuusamo — A156

Designs: 40p, House of Parliament. 50p, Church at Lammi. 60p, 65p, Fortress of Olavinlinna. 2.50m, Aerial view of Punkaharju.

1963-67 Engr. *Perf. 11½*

398	A94	5p	violet blue	30	15
a.			Booklet pane of 2 (vert. pair)	20.00	
b.			Booklet pane of 2 (horiz. pair)	27.50	
399	A137	5p	green	22	15
400	A94	10p	blue green	38	15
a.			Booklet pane of 2 (vert. pair)	20.00	
401	A94	15p	yellow org	1.10	15
402	A94	20p	rose red	65	15
a.			Booklet pane of 1	20.00	
b.			Bklt. pane, 2 #400, 1 #402 + label; horiz. strip	37.50	
c.			Bklt. pane, 2 #398, 2 #400, 1 #402; horiz. strip	5.50	
403	A94	25p	rose lilac	45	15
404	A94	30p	lt ultra	6.00	15
404A	A94	30p	blue gray ('65)	55	15
405	A94	35p	blue	1.10	15
405A	A94	40p	ultra ('67)	1.50	15
406	A104	40p	dull purple	1.50	15
407	A104	50p	gray olive	1.50	15
408	A104	60p	pale purple	4.50	15
408A	A104	65p	pale purple ('67)	1.10	15
409	A124	75p	gray	1.50	15
410	A119	1m	bluish grn	40	15
411	A138	1.25m	slate grn	1.65	15
412	A153	1.50m	dk grnsh gray	80	15
413	A154	1.75m	blue	1.25	15
414	A155	2m	green ('64)	1.65	15
414A	A155	2.50m	ultra & yel ('67)	2.25	15
415	A156	5m	dk slate grn ('64)	6.00	35
			Nos. 398-415 (22)	36.35	
			Set value		1.80

Pennia denominations expressed: "0.05," "0.10," etc.

Four stamps of type A94 (5p, 10p, 20p, 25p) come in two types: I. Four vertical lines in "O" of SUOMI. II. Three lines in "O."

See Nos. 457-464B.

Mother and Child — A157

1963, Mar. 21 Unwmk. *Perf. 11½*
416 A157 40p red brown 60 38

FAO "Freedom from Hunger" campaign.

"Christ Today" — A158

Design: 10p, Crown of thorns and medieval cross of consecration.

1963, July 30 Engr. *Perf. 11½*
417 A158 10p maroon 32 45
418 A158 30p dark green 55 45

4th assembly of the Lutheran World Federation, Helsinki, July 30-Aug. 8.

Europa Issue, 1963
Common Design Type

1963, Sept. 16
Size: 30x20mm
419 CD6 40p red lilac 1.00 42

Assembly Building, Helsinki — A159

1963, Sept. 18
420 A159 30p violet blue 70 38

Representative Assembly of Finland, cent.

Convair Metropolitan A160

M. A. Castrén A161

Design: 40p, Caravelle jetliner.

1963, Nov. 1
421 A160 35p slate green 85 35
422 A160 40p brt ultra 85 35

40th anniversary of Finnish air traffic.

1963, Dec. 2 Unwmk.
423 A161 35p violet blue 90 40

Matthias Alexander Castrén (1813-52), ethnologist and philologist.

Stone Elk's Head, 2000 B.C. — A162

Emil Nestor Setälä — A163

1964, Feb. 5 Litho. *Perf. 11½*
424 A162 35p ocher & slate grn 90 40

Cent. of the Finnish Artists' Association. The soapstone sculpture was found at Huittinen.

1964, Feb. 27 Engr.
425 A163 35p dk red brown 90 40

Emil Nestor Setälä (1864-1946), philologist, minister of education and foreign affairs and chancellor of Abo University.

Staff of Aesculapius A164

1964, June 13 Unwmk. *Perf. 11½*
426 A164 40p slate green 1.10 40

18th General Assembly of the World Medical Association, Helsinki, June 13-19, 1964.

Ice Hockey — A165

1965, Jan. 4 Engr.
427 A165 35p dark blue 80 40

World Ice Hockey Championships, Finland, March 3-14, 1965.

Design from Centenary Medal — A166

1965, Feb. 6 Unwmk. *Perf. 11½*
428 A166 35p olive gray 80 40

Centenary of communal self-government in Finland.

K. J. Stahlberg and "Lex" by W. Runeberg — A167

1965, Mar. 22 Engr.
429 A167 35p brown 80 40

Kaarlo Juho Stahlberg (1865-1952), 1st Pres. of Finland.

International Cooperation Year Emblem — A168

1965, Apr. 2 Litho. *Perf. 14*
430 A168 40p bis, dull red, blk & grn 80 40

UN International Cooperation Year.

"Fratricide" by Gallen-Kallela
A169

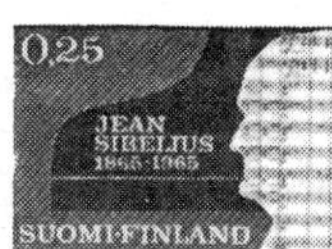

Sibelius, Piano and Score
A170

Design: 35p, Girl's Head by Akseli Gallen-Kallela.

1965, Apr. 26 *Perf. 13½x14*
431 A169 25p multicolored 1.25 45
432 A169 35p multicolored 1.25 45

Centenary of the birth of the painter Aksell Gallen-Kallela.

1965, May 15 Engr. *Perf. 11½*

Design: 35p, Musical score and bird.

433 A170 25p violet 70 38
434 A170 35p dull green 70 38

Jean Sibelius (1865-1957), composer.

Antenna for Satellite Telecommunication
A171

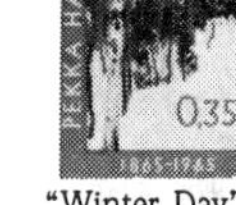

"Winter Day" by Pekka Halonen
A172

1965, May 17
435 A171 35p blue 80 40

Cent. of the ITU.

Perf. 14x13½
1965, Sept. 23 Litho. Unwmk.
436 A172 35p gold & multi 70 40

Centenary of the birth of the painter Pekka Halonen.

Europa Issue, 1965
Common Design Type
Engraved and Lithographed
1965, Sept. 27 *Perf. 13½x14*
437 CD8 40p bister, red brn, dk bl & grn 75 40

"Growth"
A173

Old Post Office
A174

1966, May 11 Litho. *Perf. 14*
438 A173 35p vio blue & blue 70 32

Centenary of the promulgation of the Elementary School Decree.

1966, June 11 Litho. *Perf. 14*
439 A174 35p ocher, yel, dk bl & blk 8.50 9.25

Cent. of the 1st postage stamps in Finnish currency, and in connection with the NORDIA Stamp Exhibition, Helsinki, June 11-15. The stamp was sold only to buyers of a 1.25m exhibition entrance ticket.

UNESCO Emblem and World Map
A175

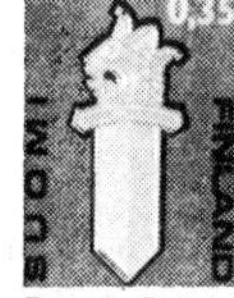

Finnish Police Emblem
A176

Lithographed and Engraved
1966, Oct. 9 *Perf. 14*
440 A175 40p grn, yel, blk & brn org 70 30

20th anniv. of UNESCO.

1966, Oct. 15
441 A176 35p dp ultra, blk & sil 70 30

Issued to honor the Finnish police.

Insurance Sesquicentennial Medal — A177

1966, Oct. 28 Engr. & Photo.
442 A177 35p maroon, ol & blk 70 30

150th anniv. of the Finnish insurance system.

UNICEF Emblem — A178

1966, Nov. 14
443 A178 15p lt ultra, pur & grn 42 30

Activities of UNICEF.

"FINEFTA," Finnish Flag and Circle — A179

1967, Feb. 15 Engr. *Perf. 14*
444 A179 40p ultra 1.00 30

European Free Trade Association, EFTA. See note after Denmark No. 431.

Windmill and Arms of Uusikaupunki
A180

Mannerheim Monument by Aimo Tukiainen
A181

Lithographed and Engraved
1967, Apr. 19 *Perf. 14*
445 A180 40p multicolored 70 30

350th anniv. of Uusikaupunki (Nystad).

1967, June 4 *Perf. 14*
446 A181 40p violet & multi 65 30

Cent. of the birth of Field Marshal Carl Gustav Emil Mannerheim.

Double Mortise Corner — A182

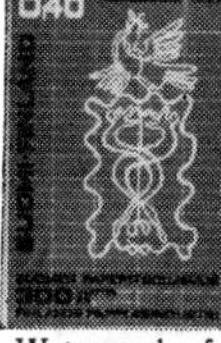

Watermark of Thomasböle Paper Mill — A183

1967, June 16 Litho. & Photo.
447 A182 40p multicolored 65 30

Issued to honor Finnish settlers in Sweden.

1967, Sept. 6 *Perf. 14*
448 A183 40p olive & black 65 30

300th anniv. of the Finnish paper industry.

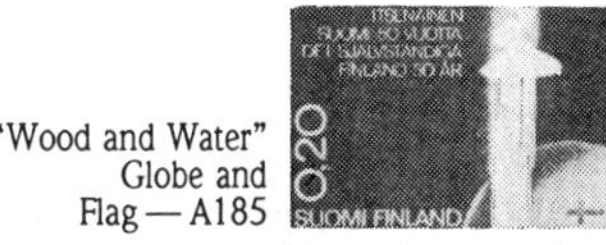

Martin Luther, by Lucas Cranach — A184

Photogravure and Engraved
1967, Nov. 4 *Perf. 14*
449 A184 40p bister & brown 65 30

450th anniversary of the Reformation.

"Wood and Water" Globe and Flag — A185

Designs (Globe, Flag and): 25p, Flying swan. 40p, Ear of wheat.

1967, Dec. 5 *Perf. 11½*
450 A185 20p green & blue 70 30
451 A185 25p ultra & blue 70 30
452 A185 40p magenta & bl 70 30

50th anniv. of Finland's independence.

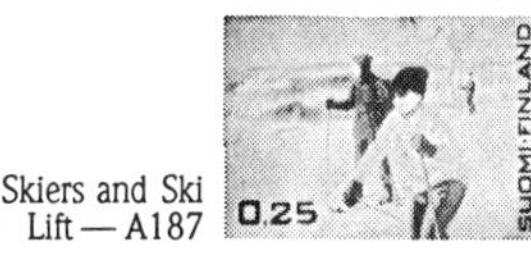

Zachris Topelius and Blue Bird — A186

1968, Jan. 14 Litho. *Perf. 14*
453 A186 25p blue & multi 65 30

Zachris Topelius (1818-98), writer and educator.

Skiers and Ski Lift — A187

1968, Feb. 19 Photo. *Perf. 14*
454 A187 25p multicolored 65 30

Winter Tourism in Finland.

Footnotes near stamp listings often refer to other stamps of the same design.

Paper Making, by Hannes Autere — A188

1968, Mar. 12 Litho. Wmk. 363
455 A188 45p dk red, brn & org 65 30

Finnish paper industry and 150th anniv. of the oldest Finnish paper mill, Tervakoski, whose own watermark was used for this stamp.

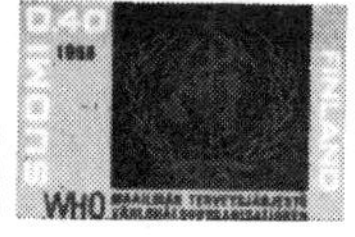

World Health Organization Emblem — A189

Lithographed and Photogravure
1968, Apr. 6 Unwmk. *Perf. 14*
456 A189 40p red org, dk blue & gold 65 30

To honor World Health Organization.

Lion Type of 1954-58 and

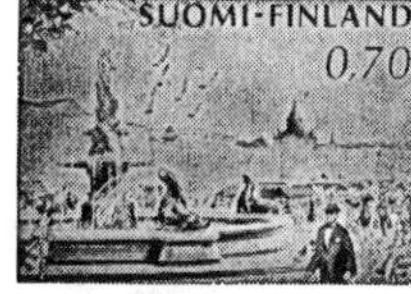

Market Place and Mermaid Fountain, Helsinki
A190

Keuru Wooden Church, 1758 — A191

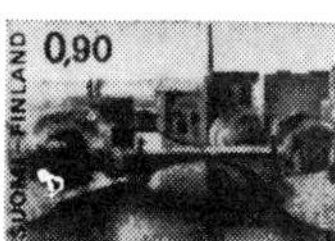

Häme Bridge, Tampere — A192

Finnish Arms from Grave of King Gustav Vasa, 1581 — A194

Designs: 25p, Post bus. 30p, Aquarium-Planetarium, Tampere. No. 463, P.O., Tampere. No. 465, National Museum, Helsinki, vert. No. 467A, like 70p. 1.30m, Helsinki railroad station.

Engr. (type A94); Litho. (#465 & type A190); Engr. & Litho. (others)
Perf. 11½; 12½ (type A190); 14 (#465, 470A); 13½ (#470)
1968-78
457 A94 1p lt red brn 40 15
458 A94 2p gray green 40 15
459 A94 4p gray 40 15
460 A192 25p multi ('71) 40 15
461 A191 30p multi ('71) 1.00 15
461A A94 35p dull org ('74) 40 15
b. Bklt. pane of 4 (#398, #401A, #400, #464A) + label 3.25
462 A94 40p orange ('73) 60 15
a. Bklt. pane of 3 (2 #404A, #462) + 2 labels 8.00
463 A192 40p multi ('73) 1.00 15
464 A94 50p lt ultra ('70) 1.00 15
c. Bklt. pane of 5 (#401, #403, #464, 2 #398) + 5 labels 9.50
464A A94 50p rose lake ('74) 80 15
d. Bklt. pane of 4 (#400, 2 #402, #464A) + label 2.50
464B A94 60p blue ('73) 60 15
465 A191 60p multi ('73) 48 15
466 A190 70p multi ('73) 80 15
467 A191 80p multi ('70) 2.50 15
467A A190 80p multi ('76) 48 15
468 A192 90p multicolored 2.00 15
469 A191 1.30m multi ('71) 1.00 15

470	A194	10m multi ('74)	3.25	40
470A	A194	20m multi ('78)	6.50	1.00
		Nos. 457-470A (19)	24.01	
		Set value		2.95

Infantry Monument, Vaasa — A195

Camping Ground — A196

Designs: 25p, War Memorial (cross), Hietaniemi Cemetery. 40p, Soldier, 1968.

1968, June 4 Photo. *Perf. 14*

471	A195	20p lt violet & multi	80	35
472	A195	25p lt blue & multi	80	35
473	A195	40p orange & multi	80	35

To honor Finnish national defense.

1968, June 10 Litho.

474 A196 25p multicolored 65 28

Issued to publicize Finland for summer vacations.

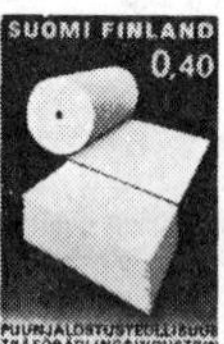

Paper, Pulp and Pine — A197

Mustola Lock, Saima Canal — A198

Lithographed and Embossed

1968, July 2 Unwmk. *Perf. 14*

475 A197 40p multicolored 65 28

Finnish wood industry.

1968, Aug. 5 Litho. *Perf. 14*

476 A198 40p multicolored 65 28

Opening of the Saima Canal.

Oskar Merikanto and Pipe Organ — A199

1968, Aug. 5 Unwmk.

477 A199 40p vio, silver & lt brn 65 28

Centenary of the birth of Oskar Merikanto, composer.

Ships in Harbor and Emblem of Central Chamber of Commerce A200

Welder A201

1968, Sept. 13 Litho. *Perf. 14*

478 A200 40p lt bl, brt bl & blk 65 28

Publicizing economic development and for the 50th anniv. of the Central Chamber of Commerce of Finland.

1968, Oct. 11 Litho. *Perf. 14*

479 A201 40p blue & multi 65 28

Finnish metal industry.

Lyre, Students' Emblem A202

Five Ancient Ships A203

Lithographed and Engraved

1968, Nov. 24 *Perf. 14*

480 A202 40p ultra, vio bl & gold 65 28

Issued to publicize the work of the student unions in Finnish social life.

Nordic Cooperation Issue

1968, Feb. 28 Engr. *Perf. 11½*

481 A203 40p lt ultra 1.75 28

See footnote after Denmark No. 455.

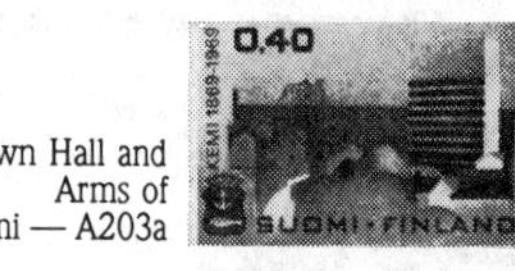

Town Hall and Arms of Kemi — A203a

1969, Mar. 5 Photo. *Perf. 14*

482 A203a 40p multicolored 65 28

Centenary of the town of Kemi.

Europa Issue, 1969

Common Design Type

1969, Apr. 28 Photo. *Perf. 14*

Size: 30x20mm

483 CD12 40p dl rose, vio bl & dk bl 2.75 50

ILO Emblem A204

Armas Järnefelt A205

Lithographed and Engraved

1969, June 2 *Perf. 11½*

484 A204 40p dp rose & vio blue 65 28

50th anniv. of the ILO.

1969, Aug. 14 Photo. *Perf. 14*

485 A205 40p multicolored 65 28

Järnefelt (1869-1958), composer and conductor. Portrait on stamp by Vilho Sjöström.

Emblems and Flag A206

Johannes Linnankoski A207

1969, Sept. 19 Photo. *Perf. 14*

486 A206 40p lt bl, blk, grn & lil 65 28

Issued to publicize the importance of National and International Fairs in Finnish economy.

1969, Oct. 18 Litho.

487 A207 40p dk brown red & multi 65 28

Linnankoski (1869-1913), writer.

Educational Symbols — A208

Lithographed and Engraved

1969, Nov. 24 *Perf. 11½*

488 A208 40p gray, vio & grn 65 28

Centenary of the Central School Board.

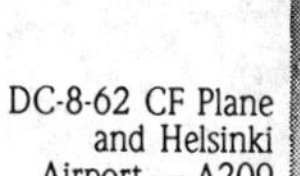

DC-8-62 CF Plane and Helsinki Airport — A209

1969, Dec. 22 Photo. *Perf. 14*

489 A209 25p sky blue & multi 85 28

Golden Eagle — A210

1970, Feb. 10 Litho. *Perf. 14*

490 A210 30p multicolored 2.75 65

Year of Nature Conservation, 1970.

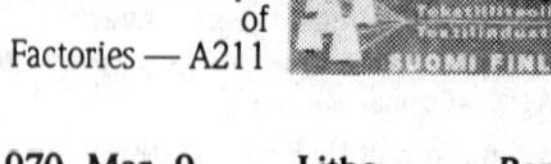
Swatches in Shape of Factories — A211

1970, Mar. 9 Litho. *Perf. 14*

491 A211 50p multicolored 70 28

Finnish textile industry.

Molecule Diagram and Factories — A212

UNESCO Emblem and Lenin — A213

Atom Diagram and Laurel — A214

UN Emblem and Globe — A215

1970, Mar. 26 Photo. *Perf. 14*

492 A212 50p multicolored 70 28

Finnish chemical industry.

1970 Litho. and Engr.

493	A213	30p gold & multi	70	25
494	A214	30p red & multi	70	25

Photogravure and Gold Embossed

495 A215 50p bl, vio bl & gold 70 25

25th anniv. of the UN. No. 493 also publicizes the UNESCO-sponsored Lenin Symposium, Tampere, Apr. 6-10. No. 494 also publicizes the Nuclear Data Conf. of the Atomic Energy Commission, Otaniemi (Helsinki), June 15-19.

Issue dates: No. 493, Apr. 6; No. 494, June 15; No. 495, Oct. 24.

Handicapped Volleyball Player A216

Meeting of Auroraseura Society A217

1970, June 27 Litho. *Perf. 14*

496 A216 50p orange, red & blk 75 28

Issued to publicize the position of handicapped civilians and war veterans in society and their potential contributions to it.

1970, Aug. 15 Photo. *Perf. 14*

497 A217 50p multicolored 65 28

200th anniv. of the Auroraseura Soc., dedicated to the study of Finnish history, geography, economy and language. The design of the stamp is after a painting by Eero Jarnefelt.

Uusikaarlepyy Arms, Church and 17th Cent. Building — A218

Design: No. 499, Arms of Kokkola, harbor, Sports Palace and 17th century building.

1970 *Perf. 14*

498	A218	50p multicolored	70	28
499	A218	50p multicolored	70	28

350th anniversaries of the towns of Uusikaarlepyy and Kokkola. Issue dates: No. 498, Aug. 21; No. 499, Sept. 17.

Set Values

A 15-cent minimum now applies to individual stamps and sets. Where the 15-cent minimum per stamp would increase the value of a set beyond retail, there is a "Set Value" notation giving the retail value of the set.

Urho Kekkonen, Medal by Aimo Tukiainen — A219

1970, Sept. 3 **Litho. & Engr.**
500 A219 50p ultra, sil & blk 75 28

70th birthday of Pres. Urho Kekkonen.

Globe, Maps of US, Finland, USSR A220

Pres. Paasikivi by Essi Renavall A221

Lithographed and Gold Embossed

1970, Nov. 2
501 A220 50p blk, bl, pink & gold 70 28

Issued to publicize the Strategic Arms Limitation Talks (SALT) between the US and USSR, Helsinki, Nov. 2-Dec. 18.

1970, Nov. 27 **Photo.** ***Perf. 14***
502 A221 50p gold, brt bl & sl 85 28

Centenary of the birth of Juho Kusti Paasikivi (1870-1956), President of Finland.

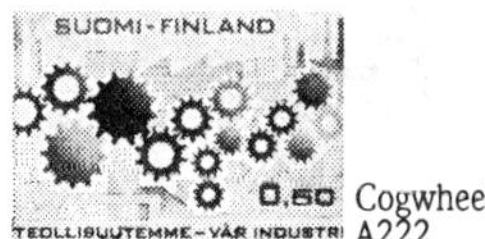

Cogwheels A222

1971, Jan. 28 **Litho.** ***Perf. 14***
503 A222 50p multicolored 70 28

Finnish industry.

Europa Issue, 1971
Common Design Type

1971, May 3 **Litho.** ***Perf. 14***
Size: 30x20mm
504 CD14 50p dp rose, yel & blk 1.65 38

Tornio Church A223

Front Page, January 15, 1771 A224

1971, May 12 **Litho.** ***Perf. 14***
505 A223 50p multicolored 85 28

350th anniversary of the town of Tornio.

1971, June 1 **Litho.** ***Perf. 14***
506 A224 50p multicolored 65 28

Bicentenary of the Finnish press.

Athletes in Helsinki Stadium — A225

Design: 50p, Running and javelin in Helsinki Stadium.

1971, July 5 **Litho.** ***Perf. 14***
507 A225 30p multicolored 90 40
508 A225 50p multicolored 1.90 40

European Athletic Championships.

Sailboats — A226

1971, July 14
509 A226 50p multicolored 1.00 32

International Lightning Class Championships, Helsinki, July 14-Aug. 1.

Silver Tea Pot, Guild's Emblem, Tools — A227

1971, Aug. 6
510 A227 50p lilac & multi 70 28

600th anniv. of Finnish goldsmiths' art.

"Plastic Buttons and Houses" — A228

Photogravure and Embossed

1971, Oct. 20 ***Perf. 14***
511 A228 50p multicolored 75 28

Finnish plastics industry.

Europa Issue 1972
Common Design Type

1972, May 2 **Litho.** ***Perf. 14***
Size: 20x30mm
512 CD15 30p dk red & multi 1.25 40
513 CD15 50p lt brn & multi 1.75 40

Finnish National Theater — A229

1972, May 22. **Litho.** ***Perf. 14***
514 A229 50p lt violet & multi 75 28

Centenary of the Finnish National Theater, founded by Kaarlo and Emilie Bergbom.

Globe, US and USSR Flags — A230

1972, June 2
515 A230 50p multicolored 1.40 35

Strategic Arms Limitation Talks (SALT), final meeting, Helsinki, Mar. 28-May 26; treaty signed, Moscow, May 26.

Map and Arms of Aland A231

Training Ship Suomen Joutsen A232

1972, June 9
516 A231 50p multicolored 4.00 75

50th anniv. of 1st Provincial Meeting of Aland.

1972, June 19
517 A232 50p orange & multi 1.10 35

Tall Ships' Race 1972, Helsinki, Aug. 20.

Costume from Perni, 12th Cent. — A233

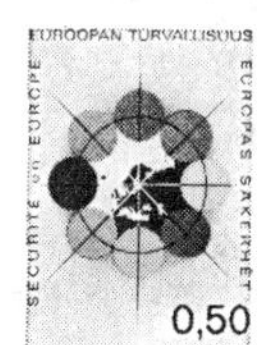

Circle Surrounding Map of Europe — A234

1972, Nov. 19 **Litho.** ***Perf. 13***
518 A233 50p shown 1.10 25
519 A233 50p Couple, Tenhola, 18th cent. 1.10 25
520 A233 50p Girl, Nastola, 19th cent. 1.10 25
521 A233 50p Man, Voyni, 19th cent. 1.10 25
522 A233 50p Lapps, Inari, 19th cent. 1.10 25
a. Booklet pane, 2 each #518-522 12.00
b. Strip of 5, #518-522 6.00
Nos. 518-522 (5) 5.50 1.25

Regional costumes.
See Nos. 533-537.

1972, Dec. 11 ***Perf. 14x13½***
523 A234 50p multicolored 2.50 42

Preparatory Conference on European Security and Cooperation.

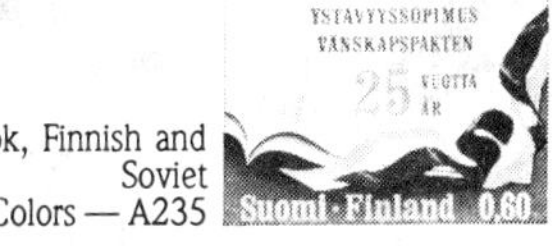

Book, Finnish and Soviet Colors — A235

Litho.; Gold Embossed

1973, Apr. 6 ***Perf. 14***
524 A235 60p gold & multi 70 28

Soviet-Finnish Treaty of Friendship, 25th anniv.

Kyösti Kallio (1873-1940), Pres. of Finland — A236

1973, Apr. 10 **Litho.** ***Perf. 13***
525 A236 60p multicolored 70 28

Europa Issue 1973
Common Design Type

1973, Apr. 30 **Photo.** ***Perf. 14***
Size: 31x21mm
526 CD16 60p bl, brt bl & emer 90 30

Nordic Cooperation Issue

Nordic House, Reykjavik A236a

1973, June 26 **Engr.** ***Perf. 12½***
527 A236a 60p multicolored 1.00 32
528 A236a 70p multicolored 1.00 32

A century of postal cooperation among Denmark, Finland, Iceland, Norway and Sweden, and in connection with the Nordic Postal Conference, Reykjavik.

Map of Europe, "EUROPA" as a Maze — A237

Litho. & Embossed

1973, July 3 ***Perf. 13***
529 A237 70p multicolored 80 28

Conference for European Security and Cooperation, Helsinki, July 1973.

Paddling A238

Radiosonde, WMO Emblem A239

1973, July 18 **Litho.** ***Perf. 14***
530 A238 60p multicolored 65 28

Canoeing World Championships, Tampere, July 26-29.

1973, Aug. 6 **Litho.** ***Perf. 14***
531 A239 60p multicolored 70 28

Cent. of intl. meteorological cooperation.

Eliel Saarinen and Design for Parliament, Helsinki A240

1973, Aug. 20 ***Perf. 12½x13***
532 A240 60p multicolored 70 28

Eliel Saarinen (1873-1950), architect.

Costume Type of 1972

1973, Oct. 10 **Litho.** ***Perf. 13***
533 A233 60p Woman, Kaukola 3.00 25
534 A233 60p Woman, Jaaski 3.00 25
535 A233 60p Married couple, Koivisto 3.00 25
536 A233 60p Mother and son, Sakyla 3.00 25
537 A233 60p Girl, Hainavesi 3.00 25
a. Strip of 5, #533-537 15.00
Nos. 533-537 (5) 15.00 1.25

Regional costumes.

DC10-30 Jet — A241

1973, Nov. 1 Litho. *Perf. 14*
538 A241 60p multicolored 70 28

50th anniv. of regular air service, Finnair.

Santa Claus in Reindeer Sleigh — A242

1973, Nov. 15 Litho. *Perf. 14*
539 A242 30p multicolored 65 18

Christmas 1973.

"The Barber of Seville" — A243

1973, Nov. 21
540 A243 60p multicolored 70 28

Centenary of opera in Finland.

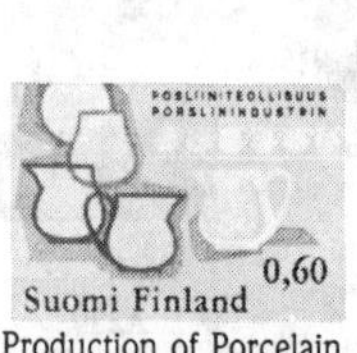

Production of Porcelain Jug A244

Nurmi, by Waino Aaltonen A245

1973, Nov. 23
541 A244 60p blue & multi 70 28

Finnish porcelain.

1973, Dec. 11
542 A245 60p multicolored 70 28

Paavo Nurmi (1897-1973), runner, Olympic winner, 1920-1924-1928.

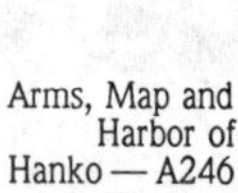

Arms, Map and Harbor of Hanko — A246

1974, Jan. 10 Litho. *Perf. 14*
543 A246 60p blue & multi 70 28

Centenary of the town of Hanko.

Ice Hockey — A247

1974, Mar. 5 Litho. *Perf. 14*
544 A247 60p multicolored 70 28

European and World Ice Hockey Championships, held in Finland.

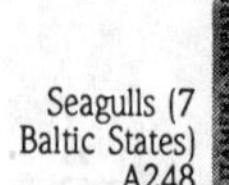

Seagulls (7 Baltic States) A248

1974, Mar. 18 *Perf. 12½*
545 A248 60p multicolored 70 28

Protection of marine environment of the Baltic Sea.

Goddess of Freedom, by Waino Aaltonen — A249

Ilmari Kianto and Old Pine — A250

1974, Apr. 29 Litho. *Perf. 13x12½*
546 A249 70p multicolored 1.10 28

Europa.

1974, May 7 *Perf. 13*
547 A250 60p multicolored 65 28

Ilmari Kianto (1874-1970), writer.

Society Emblem, Symbol — A251

Lithographed and Embossed

1974, June 12 *Perf. 13½x14*
548 A251 60p gold & multi 65 28

Centenary of Adult Education.

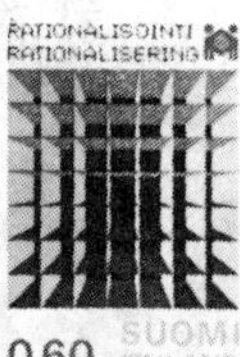

Grid — A252

UPU Emblem — A253

1974, June 14 Litho. *Perf. 14x13½*
549 A252 60p multicolored 65 28

Rationalization Year in Finland, dedicated to economic and business improvements.

1974, Oct. 10 Litho. *Perf. 13½x14*
550 A253 60p multicolored 65 28
551 A253 70p multicolored 65 28

Centenary of Universal Postal Union.

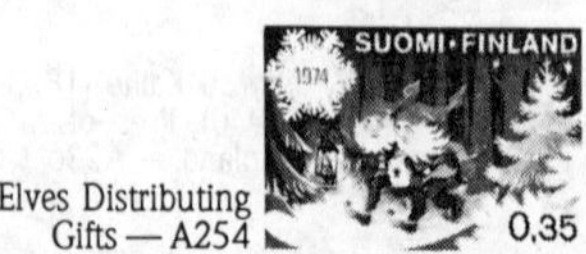

Elves Distributing Gifts — A254

1974, Nov. 16 Litho. *Perf. 14x13½*
552 A254 35p multicolored 1.10 28

Christmas 1974.

Concrete Bridge and Granite Bridge, Aunessilta — A255

Litho. & Engr.

1974, Dec. 17 *Perf. 14*
553 A255 60p multicolored 65 28

Royal Finnish Directorate of Roads and Waterways, 175th anniversary.

Coat of Arms, 1581 A256

Chimneyless Log Sauna A256a

Carved Wooden Distaffs — A258

Kirvu Weather Vane — A258a

Cheese Frames — A257

Design: 1.50m, Wood-carved high drinking bowl, 1542.

1975-90 Engr. *Perf. 11½; 14 (2m)*

No.	Type	Value	Description	Unused	Used
555	A256	10p	red lilac ('78)	15	15
a.			Bklt. pane of 4 (#555, 2 #556, #559) + label	2.50	
b.			Bklt. pane of 5 (2 #555, #557, #563, #564)	1.90	
c.			As #555a, no label	50	
d.			Perf. 13x12½	15	15
556	A256	20p	olive ('77)	15	15
a.			20p yellow bister ('87)	15	15
557	A256	30p	carmine ('77)	15	15
557A	A256	30p	car, litho.	15	15
558	A256	40p	orange	16	15
559	A256	50p	green ('76)	20	15
560	A256	60p	blue	25	15
a.			Perf. 13x12½	32	15
561	A256	70p	sepia	35	15
562	A256	80p	dl red & bl grn ('76)	38	15
a.			Perf. 13x12½	40	40
563	A256	90p	violet ('77)	42	15
564	A256	1.10m	yellow ('79)	45	15
565	A256	1.20m	dk blue ('79)	50	15
566	A258	1.50m	multi ('76)	60	15
567	A256a	2m	multi, litho. ('77)	75	18

Lithographed and Engraved

No.	Type	Value	Description	Unused	Used
568	A257	2.50m	multi ('76)	95	18
569	A258	4.50m	multi ('76)	1.65	18
570	A258a	5m	multi ('77)	1.90	18
			Nos. 555-570 (17)	9.16	
			Set value		1.40

Issue dates: #557A, June 3, 1980. #560a, July 25, 1988. #555d, July 25, 1989. #562a, Mar. 1, 1990.

See Nos. 629, 631-633, 711-715.

Finland No. 16 — A259

Girl Combing Hair, by Magnus Enckell — A260

Lithographed and Typographed

1975, Apr. 26 *Perf. 13*
571 A259 70p multicolored 3.75 4.00

Nordia 75 Philatelic Exhibition, Helsinki, Apr. 26-May 1. Sold only at exhibition for 3m including entrance ticket.

1975, Apr. 28 Litho. *Perf. 13x12½*

Europa: 90p, Washerwoman, by Tyko Sallinen (1879-1955).

572 A260 70p gray & multi 1.25 25
573 A260 90p tan & multi 1.25 25

Balance of Justice, Sword of Legality A261

Rescue Boat and Sinking Ship A262

1975, May 7 *Perf. 14*
574 A261 70p vio blue & multi 60 28

Sesquicentennial of State Economy Comptroller's Office.

1975, June 2 Litho. *Perf. 14*
575 A262 70p multicolored 65 28

12th Intl. Salvage Conf., Finland, stressing importance of coordinating sea, air and communications resources in salvage operations.

Safe and Unsafe Levels of Drugs — A263

1975, July 21 Litho. *Perf. 14*
576 A263 70p multicolored 60 28

Importance of pharmacological studies and for the 6th International Pharmacology Congress, Helsinki.

Olavinlinna Castle — A264

1975, July 29 *Perf. 13*
577 A264 70p multicolored 65 28

500th anniversary of Olavinlinna Castle.

Swallows over Finlandia Hall — A265

"Men and Women Working for Peace" — A266

1975, July 30
578 A265 90p multicolored 90 28

European Security and Cooperation Conference, Helsinki, July 30-Aug. 1. (The swallows of the design represent freedom, mobility and continuity.) See No. 709.

1975, Oct. 24 Litho. ***Perf. 13x12½***
579 A266 70p multicolored 60 28

International Women's Year 1975.

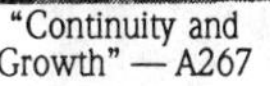
"Continuity and Growth" — A267

Boys as Three Kings and Herod — A268

1975, Oct. 29 ***Perf. 13***
580 A267 70p brown & multi 60 28

Industrial Art and for the centenary of the Finnish Society of Industrial Art.

1975, Nov. 8 ***Perf. 14***
581 A268 40p blue & multi 65 18

Christmas 1975.

Top Border of State Debenture — A269

Lithographed and Engraved

1976, Jan. 9 ***Perf. 11½***
582 A269 80p multicolored 60 28

Centenary of State Treasury.

Glider over Lake Region — A270

1976, Jan. 13 Litho. ***Perf. 14***
583 A270 80p multicolored 90 28

15th World Glider Championships, Rayskala, June 13-27.

Prof. Heikki Klemetti (1876-1953), Musician & Writer — A271

1976, Feb. 14 Litho. ***Perf. 13***
584 A271 80p green & multi 65 28

Map with Areas of Different Dialects — A272

Aino Ackté, by Albert Edelfelt — A273

1976, Mar. 10 Litho. ***Perf. 13***
585 A272 80p multicolored 65 28

Finnish Language Society, centenary.

1976, Apr. 23
586 A273 70p yellow & multi 80 28

Aino Ackté (1876-1944), opera singer.

Europa Issue 1976

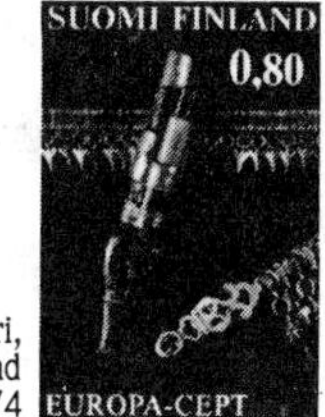

Knife from Voyri, Sheath and Belt — A274

1976, May 3 Litho. ***Perf. 13***
587 A274 80p violet bl & multi 1.90 35

Radio and Television A275

1976, Sept. 9 Litho. ***Perf. 13***
588 A275 80p multicolored 60 28

Radio broadcasting in Finland, 50th anniv.

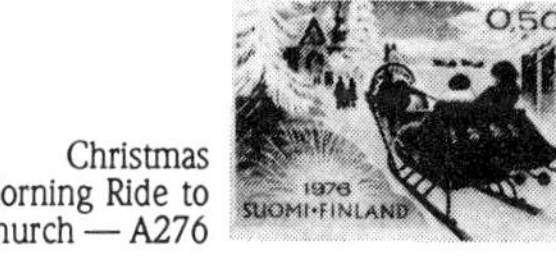

Christmas Morning Ride to Church — A276

1976, Oct. 23 Litho. ***Perf. 14***
589 A276 50p multicolored 60 20

Christmas 1976.

Turku Chapter Seal (Virgin and Child) A277

1976, Nov. 1 Litho. ***Perf. 12½***
590 A277 80p buff, brn & red 60 28

700th anniv. of the Cathedral Chapter of Turku.

Alvar Aalto, Finlandia Hall, Helsinki A278

1976, Nov. 4
591 A278 80p multicolored 60 28

Hugo Alvar Henrik Aalto (1898-1976), architect.

Ice Dancers — A280

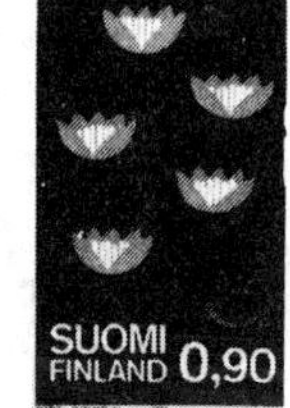

Five Water Lilies — A281

1977, Jan. 25 Litho. ***Perf. 13***
592 A280 90p multicolored 60 28

European Figure Skating Championships, Finland, Jan. 25-29.

Photogravure and Engraved

1977, Feb. 2 ***Perf. 12½***
593 A281 90p brt green & multi 80 30
594 A281 1m ultra & multi 80 30

Nordic countries cooperation for protection of the environment and 25th Session of Nordic Council, Helsinki, Feb. 19.

Icebreaker Rescuing Merchantman A282

1977, Mar. 2 Litho. ***Perf. 13***
595 A282 90p multicolored 55 28

Winter navigation between Finland and Sweden, centenary.

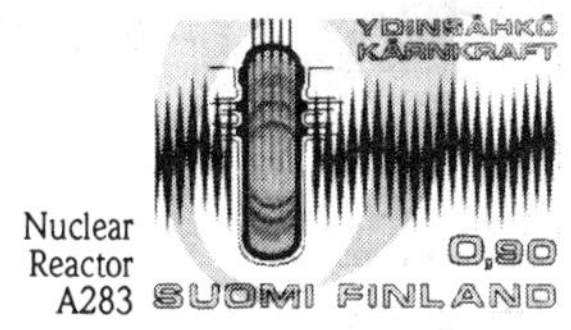

Nuclear Reactor A283

1977, Mar. 3 ***Perf. 12½x13***
596 A283 90p multicolored 55 28

Opening of nuclear power station on Hästholmen Island.

Europa Issue 1977

Autumn Landscape, Northern Finland A284

1977, May 2 Litho. ***Perf. 12½x13***
597 A284 90p multicolored 90 28

Tree, Birds and Nest — A285

Orthodox Church, Valamo Cloister — A286

1977, May 4 ***Perf. 13x12½***
598 A285 90p multicolored 55 28

75th anniversary of cooperative banks.

1977, May 31 Litho. ***Perf. 14***
599 A286 90p multicolored 55 28

Consecration festival of new Orthodox Church at Valamo Cloister, Heinävesi; 800th anniversary of introduction of orthodoxy in Karelia and of founding of Valamo Cloister.

Paavo Ruotsalainen (1777-1852), Lay Leader of Pietists in Finland — A287

1977, July 8 Litho. ***Perf. 13***
600 A287 90p multicolored 55 28

People Fleeing Fire and Water A288

Volleyball A289

1977, Sept. 14 Litho. ***Perf. 14***
601 A288 90p multicolored 55 28

Civil defense for security.

1977, Sept. 15
602 A289 90p multicolored 60 28

European Women's Volleyball Championships, Finland, Sept. 29-Oct. 2.

Children Bringing Water for Sauna — A290

1977, Oct. 25
603 A290 50p multicolored 50 18

Christmas 1977.

Finnish Flag A291

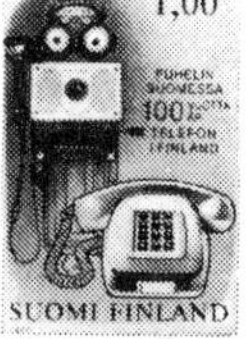

Wall Telephone, 1880, New Telephone A292

1977, Dec. 5 Litho. *Perf. 14*

Size: 31x21mm

604 A291 80p multicolored 60 25

Size: 37x25mm

Perf. 13

605 A291 1m multicolored 85 25

Finland's declaration of independence, 60th anniv.

1977, Dec. 9 *Perf. 14*

606 A292 1m multicolored 60 28

Centenary of first telephone in Finland.

Harbor, Sunila Factory, Kotka Arms — A293

1978, Jan. 2 Litho. *Perf. 14*

607 A293 1m multicolored 60 28

Centenary of founding of Kotka.

Paimio Sanitarium by Alvar Aalto — A294

Europa: 1.20m, Hvittrask studio house, 1902, horiz.

1978, May 2 Litho. *Perf. 13*

608 A294 1m multicolored 2.00 55

609 A294 1.20m multicolored 4.00 3.00

Rural Bus Service — A295

1978, June 8 Litho. *Perf. 14*

610 A295 1m multicolored 60 28

Eino Leino and Eagle — A296

1978, July 6 Litho. *Perf. 13*

611 A296 1m multicolored 60 28

Eino Leino (1878-1926), poet.

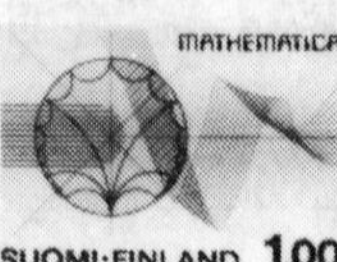

Function Theory and Rhythmical Lines — A297

1978, Aug. 15 Litho. *Perf. 14*

612 A297 1m multicolored 60 28

ICM 78, International Congress of Mathematicians, Helsinki, Aug. 15-23.

Child Feeding Birds — A298

1978, Oct. 23 Litho. *Perf. 14*

613 A298 50p multicolored 50 18

Christmas 1978.

A299 A300

1979, Jan. 2 Litho. *Perf. 13*

614 A299 1.10m multicolored 2.75 28

International Year of the Child.

1979, Feb. 7 Litho. *Perf. 14*

615 A300 1.10m Runner 90 28

8th Orienteering World Championships, Finland, Sept. 1-4.

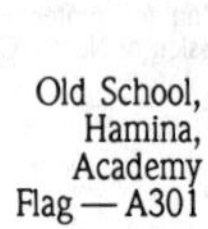

Old School, Hamina, Academy Flag — A301

1979, Mar. 20 Litho. *Perf. 14*

616 A301 1.10m multicolored 60 28

200th anniv. of Finnish Military Academy.

A302 A303

Design: Turku Cathedral and Castle, Prinkkala house, Brahe statue.

1979, Mar. 31

617 A302 1.10m multicolored 60 28

1979, May 2 Litho. *Perf. 14*

618 A303 1.10m Streetcar, Helsinki 60 28

Non-polluting urban transportation.

View of Tampere, 1779 — A304

View of Tampere, 1979 — A305

1979, May 2

619 A304 90p multicolored 60 28

1979, Oct. 1 *Perf. 13*

620 A305 1.10m multicolored 60 28

Bicentenary of founding of Tampere.

Optical Telegraph, 1796, Map of Islands — A306

Europa: 1.10m, Letter of Queen Christina to Per Brahe, 1638, establishing postal service, vert.

1979, May 2 *Perf. 13*

621 A306 1.10m multicolored 75 28

622 A306 1.30m multicolored 1.25 70

Shops and Merchants' Signs — A307

1979, Sept. 26 *Perf. 14*

623 A307 1.10m multicolored 60 28

Business and industry regulation centenary.

Old and New Cars, Street Crossing — A308

1979, Oct. 1

624 A308 1.10m multicolored 60 28

Road safety.

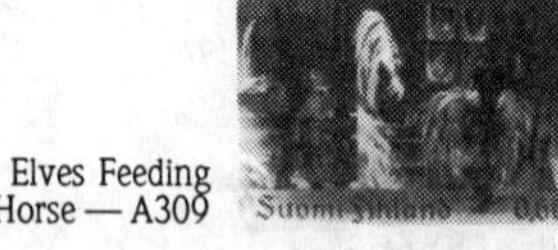

Elves Feeding Horse — A309

1979, Oct. 24

625 A309 60p multicolored 48 18

Christmas 1979.

Korppi House, Lapinjarvi A310

Farm houses, First Row: Syrjala House, Tammela, 2 stamps in continuous design; Murtovaara House, Valtimo; Antila House, Lapua. Second row: Lofts, Pohjanmaa; Courtyard gate, Kanajarvi House, Kalvola; Main door, Havuselka House, Kauhajoki; Maki-Rasinpera House and dinner bell tower; Gable and eaves, Rasula Kuortane granary.

1979, Oct. 27 Litho. *Perf. 13*

626 Booklet pane of 10 7.25

a.-j. A310 1.10m single stamp 70 35

See Nos. 672, 737.

Type of 1975 and

Kauhaneva Swamp A315

Hame Castle, Hameenlinna A316

Windmill, Harrstrom A318

Multiharju Forest, Seitseminen Natl. Park A319

Shuttle, Raanu Designs — A322

Kaspaikka Towel Design — A323

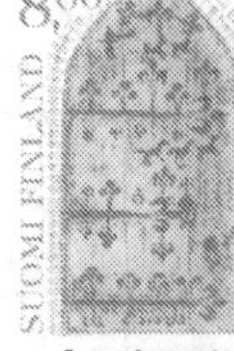

Bridal Rug, Teisko, 1815 A324

Iron-forged Door, Hollola Church A325

Iron Fish Spear c. 1100 — A326

Design: 1.80m, Eastern Gulf natl. park.

Litho. & Engr., Litho., Engr.

1979-85 *Perf. 11½, 14*

627 A315 70p multi ('81) 32 15

628 A316 90p brown red ('82) 35 25

629 A256 1m red brown ('81) 40 16

630 A318 1m bl & red brn ('83) 40 16

631 A256 1.30m dk green ('83) 48 16

a. Bklt. pane of 5, #555, #556, #557A, #560, #631 1.05

632 A256 1.40m purple ('84) 52 16

633 A256 1.50m grnsh blue ('85) 55 16

634 A319 1.60m multicolored 60 24

635 A315 1.80m multi ('83) 65 24

636 A322 3m multicolored 1.10 20

637 A323 6m multi ('80) 2.25 32

638 A324 7m multi ('82) 2.75 40

639 A325 8m multi ('83) 2.75 48

640 A326 9m blk & dk bl ('84) 3.25 48

Nos. 627-640 (14) 16.37 3.56

Issue date: #631a, Nov. 1, 1985.

Coil Stamps

Perf. 11½ Vert.

641 A316 90p brown red ('82) 40 22

Perf. 12½ Horiz.

642 A318 1m blue & red brn ('83) 50 24

Maria Jotuni (1880-1943), Writer — A327

1980, Apr. 9 **Litho.**
643 A327 1.10m multicolored 60 22

Frans Eemil Sillanpaa (1888-1964), Writer A328

Europa: 1.30m, Artturi Ilmari Virtanen (1895-1973), chemist, vert.

1980, Apr. 28 ***Perf. 13***
644 A328 1.10m multicolored 95 30
645 A328 1.30m multicolored 95 38

Pres. Urho Kekkonen, 80th Birthday — A329

1980, Sept. 3 **Litho.** ***Perf. 13***
646 A329 1.10m multicolored 65 24

Nordic Cooperation Issue

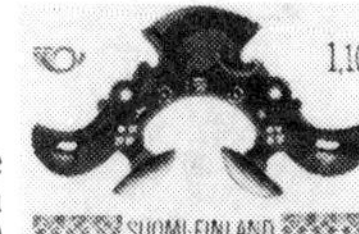

Back-piece Harness, 19th century — A330

1980, Sept. 9 ***Perf. 14***
647 A330 1.10m shown 60 30
648 A330 1.30m Collar harness, vert. 60 38

Biathlon — A331

1980, Oct. 17 **Litho.** ***Perf. 14***
649 A331 1.10m multicolored 60 24

World Biathlon Championship, Lahti, Feb. 10-15, 1981.

Pull the Roller, Weighing out the Salt — A332

Christmas 1980 (Traditional Games): 1.10m, Putting out the shoemaker's eye.

1980, Oct. 27
650 A332 60p multicolored 24 15
651 A332 1.10m multicolored 70 18

Boxing Match — A333

Glass Blowing — A334

1981, Feb. 28 **Litho.** ***Perf. 14***
652 A333 1.10m multicolored 60 22

European Boxing Championships, Tampere, May 2-10.

1981, Mar. 12
653 A334 1.10m multicolored 60 22

Glass industry, 300th anniversary.

Mail Boat Furst Menschikoff, 1836 — A335

1981, May 6 **Litho & Engr.** ***Perf. 13***
654 A335 1.10m brown & tan 3.50 3.25

Nordia '81 Stamp Exhibition, Helsinki, May 6-10. Sold only at exhibition for 3m including entrance ticket.

Europa Issue 1981

Rowing to Church A336

1981, May 18 **Litho.** ***Perf. 13***
655 A336 1.10m shown 70 22
656 A336 1.50m Midsummer's Eve dance 70 32

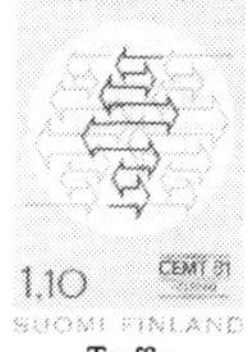

Traffic Conference Emblem A337

Boy and Girl Riding Pegasus A338

1981, May 26 **Litho.** ***Perf. 14***
657 A337 1.10m multicolored 45 22

European Conference of Ministers of Transport, May 25-28.

1981, June 11
658 A338 1m multicolored 45 22

Youth associations centenary.

Intl. Year of the Disabled — A339

1981, Sept. 2 **Litho.** ***Perf. 13***
659 A339 1.10m multicolored 60 22

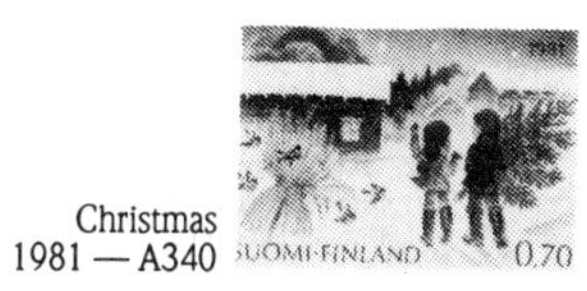

Christmas 1981 — A340

1981, Oct. 27 **Litho.** ***Perf. 14***
660 A340 70p Children, Christmas tree 32 16
661 A340 1.10m Decorating tree, vert. 50 30

"Om Konsten att Ratt Behaga" First Issue (Periodicals Bicentenary) A341

1982, Jan. 15
662 A341 1.20m multicolored 60 22

Kuopio Bicentenary A343

Score, String Instrument Neck A344

1982, Mar. 4 **Litho.** ***Perf. 14***
664 A343 1.20m multicolored 60 22

1982, Mar. 11 ***Perf. 13***
665 A344 1.20m multicolored 60 22

Centenaries of Sibelius Academy of Music and Helsinki Orchestra.

Electric Power Plant Centenary A345

1982, Mar. 15 ***Perf. 14***
666 A345 1.20m multicolored 60 22

Gardening A346

1982, Apr. 16 **Litho.** ***Perf. 14***
667 A346 1.10m multicolored 48 22

Europa — A347

Designs: 1.20m, Publication of Abckiria (first Finnish book), 1543. (Sculpture of Mikael Agricola, translator, by Oskari Jauhiainen, 1951). 1.50m, Turku Academy, first Finnish university (Turku Academy Inaugural Procession, 1640, after Albert Edelfelt).

1982, Apr. 29 **Litho.** ***Perf. 13x12½***
668 A347 1.20m multicolored 65 25

Size: 47x31mm
Perf. 12½
669 A347 1.50m multicolored 70 45

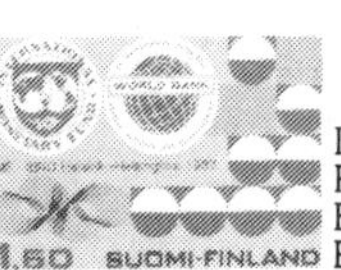

Intl. Monetary Fund and World Bank Emblems — A348

1982, May 12 ***Perf. 14***
670 A348 1.60m multicolored 72 22

IMF Interim Committee and IMF-WB Joint Development Committee Meeting, Helsinki, May 12-14.

75th Anniv. of Unicameral Parliament A349

1982, May 25
671 A349 2.40m Future, by Waino Aaltonen, Parliament 1.00 38

House Type of 1979

Manor Houses, First Row: a, Kuitia, Parainen, 1490. b, Louhisaari, Askainen, 1655. c, Frugard, Joroinen, 1780. d, Jokioinen, 1798. e, Moisio, Elimaki, 1820.

Second Row: f, Sjundby, Siuntio, 1560. g, Fagervik, Inkoo, 1773. h, Mustio, Karjaa, 1792. i, Fiskars, Pohja, 1818. j, Kotkaniemi, Vihti, 1836.

1982, June 14 **Litho.** ***Perf. 13x13½***
672 Booklet pane of 10 5.25
a.-j. A310 1.20m single stamp 50 25

Christmas 1982 — A350

1982, Oct. 25
673 A350 90p Feeding forest animals 52 22
674 A350 1.20m Children eating porridge 52 22

Nordic Cooperation A351

1983, Mar. 24 **Litho.** ***Perf. 14***
675 A351 1.20m Panning for gold 52 22
676 A351 1.30m Kitkajoki River rapids 52 22

World Communications Year — A352

1983, Apr. 9 **Litho.** ***Perf. 13***
677 A352 1.30m Postal services 55 22
678 A352 1.70m Sound waves, optical cables 65 38

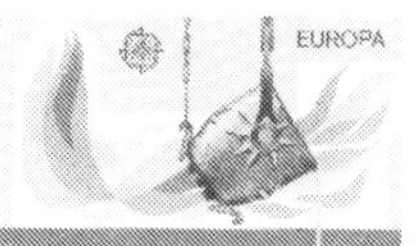

Europa 1983 A353

1983, May 2 Litho. *Perf. 12½x13*

679 A353 1.30m Flash smelting method 65 30
680 A353 1.70m Temppeliaukio Church 85 50

Pres. Lauri Kristian Relander (1883-1942) A354

Running A355

1983, May 31 Litho. *Perf. 14*

681 A354 1.30m multicolored 65 30

1983, June 6

682 A355 1.20m Javelin, horiz. 60 40
683 A355 1.30m shown 65 30

First World Athletic Championships, Helsinki, Aug. 7-14.

Toivo Kuula (1883-1918), Composer — A356

1983, July 7 *Perf. 14*

684 A356 1.30m multicolored 65 30

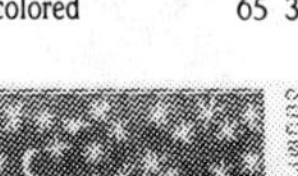

Christmas 1983 — A357

Childrens drawings: 1m, Santa, reindeer, sled and gifts by Eija Myllyviita. 1.30m, Two candles by Camilla Lindberg.

Engr., Litho.

1983, Nov. 4 *Perf. 12, 14*

685 A357 1m dark blue 50 30
686 A357 1.30m multi, vert. 65 30

President Mauno Henrik Koivisto, 60th Birthday — A358

1983, Nov. 25 Litho. *Perf. 14*

687 A358 1.30m brt blue & blk 65 30

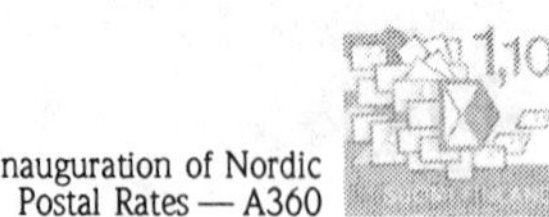

Inauguration of Nordic Postal Rates — A360

1984, Mar. 1 Engr. *Perf. 12*

689 A360 1.10m Letters (2nd class rate) 50 20

Photo. & Engr.

690 A360 1.40m Automated sorting (1st class rate), vert. 65 20

Museum Pieces — A361

Work and Skill — A362

Designs: No. 691, Pottery, 3200 B.C.; Silver chalice, 1416; Crossbow, 16th cent. No. 692, Kaplan hydraulic turbine.

1984, Apr. 30 Litho. *Perf. 13½*

691 A361 1.40m multicolored 65 32
692 A362 1.40m multicolored 65 32

Europa (1959-84) A363

1984, May 7 *Perf. 12½x13*

693 A363 1.40m multicolored 60 24
694 A363 2m multicolored 80 38

Dentistry — A364

1984, Aug. 27 Litho. *Perf. 14*

695 A364 1.40m Dentist, teeth 65 32

Astronomy A365

1984, Sept. 12

696 A365 1.10m Observatory, planets, sun 50 25

Aleksis Kivi (1934-72), Writer — A366

1984, Oct. 10 Litho. *Perf. 14*

697 A366 1.40m Song of my Heart 65 32

Christmas 1984 — A367

Litho. & Engr.

1984, Nov. 30 *Perf. 12*

698 A367 1.10m Father Christmas, brownie 50 25

Common Law of 1734 — A368

1984, Dec. 6 *Perf. 14*

699 A368 2m Statute Book 90 40

25th Anniv. of EFTA — A369

1985, Feb. 2 Litho.

700 A369 1.20m multicolored 55 25

100th Anniv. of Society of Swedish Literature in Finland — A370

1985, Feb. 5 Litho.

701 A370 1.50m Johan Ludvig Runeberg 70 30

100th Anniv. of Order of St. Sergei and St. Herman — A371

1985, Feb. 18 Litho. *Perf. 11½x12*

702 A371 1.50m Icon 70 30

150th Anniv. of Kalevala — A372

NORDIA 1985 — A373

Perf. 13x12½

1985, Feb. 28 Litho. & Engr.

703 A372 1.50m Pedri Semeikka 70 30
704 A372 2.10m Larin Paraske 95 45

Litho. & Engr.

1985, May 15 *Perf. 13*

705 A373 1.50m Mermaid and sea lions 5.00 6.25

NORDIA 1985 philatelic exhibition, May 15-19. Sold for 10m, which included admission ticket.

Finnish Banknote Cent. — A374

Europa 1985 — A375

Designs: Finnish banknotes of 1886, 1909, 1922, 1945 and 1955.

Photo. & Engr.

1985, May 18 *Perf. 11½*

706 Booklet pane of 8 5.50 5.50
a.-h. A374 1.50m any single 60 30

1985, June 17 Litho. *Perf. 13*

Designs: 1.50m, Children playing the recorder. 2.10m, Excerpt "Ramus Virens Olivarum" from the "Piae Cantiones," 1582.

707 A375 1.50m multicolored 70 30
708 A375 2.10m multicolored 95 45

Security Conference Type of 1975

1985, June 19 Litho.

709 A265 2.10m multicolored 95 45

European Security and Cooperation Conference, 10th Anniv.

Provincial Administration Established by Count Per Brahe, 350th Anniv. — A376

1985, Sept. 5 Litho. *Perf. 14*

710 A376 1.50m Provincial arms, Count's seal 70 30

Arms Type of 1975 and

Kerimaki Church — A376a

Urho Kekkonen Natl. Park — A376b

Tulip Damask Table Cloth, 18th Cent. A377

Postal Service A377a

Brown Bear — A377b

Perf. 11½, 13x12½ (2m)

1985-90 Engr., Litho. (2m)

711 A256 1.60m vermilion 75 20
712 A256 1.70m black 75 20
a. Bklt. pane, #558, 560, 2 each #555, 556a, 712 + 2 labels 2.50
713 A256 1.80m olive green 90 25
a. Bklt. pane of 6 (2 each Nos. 555d, 560a, 713b) 2.75
b. Perf. 13x12½ 98 32
714 A256 1.90m brt orange 95 25
715 A256 2m blue grn, bklt. stamp 1.00 30
a. Bklt. pane of 5 (2 each #715, 555d, 1 #562a) 2.10

Litho. *Perf. 14*

716 A376a 2.20m multicolored 1.10 35
717 A376b 2.40m multicolored 1.20 35
718 A377 12m multicolored 5.00 1.10

Perf. 13x12½

Litho. & Engr.

719 A377b 50m blk, grn & lt red brn 22.50 22.50
Nos. 711-719 (9) 34.15 25.50

No. 712a contains two labels inscribed to publicize FINLANDIA '88.

Issue dates: 12m, Sept. 13. 1.60m, Jan. 2, 1986. 1.70m, Jan. 2, 1987. No. 712a, Aug. 10, 1987. 1.80m, Jan. 4, 1988. 2.20m, 2.40m, Jan. 20, 1988. No. 713b, July 25, 1988. 1.90m, Jan. 2, 1989. 2m, Jan. 19, 1990. 50m, Aug. 30, 1989.

Booklet Stamps

Designs: No. 720, Telephone, mailbox. No. 721, Postal truck, transport plane. No. 722, Transport plane, fork lift. No. 723, Postman delivering letter. No. 724, Woman accepting letter.

Perf. 12½ on 3 Sides

1988, Feb. 1 **Litho.**

720 A377a 1.80m multicolored 90 90
721 A377a 1.80m multicolored 90 90
722 A377a 1.80m multicolored 90 90
723 A377a 1.80m multicolored 90 90
724 A377a 1.80m multicolored 90 90
a. Bklt. pane, 2 each #720-724 9.00
Nos. 720-724 (5) 4.50 4.50

Nos. 721-722 and 723-724 printed se-tenant in continuous designs. No. 724c sold for 14m to households on mainland Finland. Each household entitled to buy 2 booklets at discount price from Feb. 1 to May 31, with coupon.

Miniature Sheet

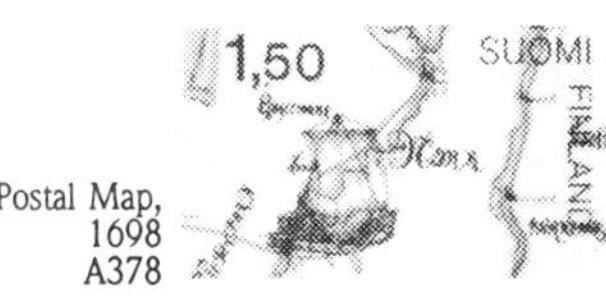

Postal Map, 1698
A378

Designs: a, Postman on foot. c, Sailing vessel, diff. d, Postrider, vert.

Litho. & Engr.

1985, Oct. 16 *Perf. 14*

728 Sheet of 4 3.50 3.50
a.-d. A378 1.50m any single 85 85

FINLANDIA '88, 350th anniv. of Finnish Postal Service, founded in 1638 by Gov.-Gen. Per Brahe. Sheet sold for 8m.

Intl. Youth Year — A379

Christmas 1985 — A380

1985, Nov. 1 **Litho.** *Perf. 13*

729 A379 1.50m multicolored 70 30

1985, Nov. 29 *Perf. 14*

730 A380 1.20m Bird, tulips 55 30
731 A380 1.20m Cross of St. Thomas, hyacinths 55 30

Natl. Geological Society, Cent.
A390

1986, Feb. 8 **Litho.** *Perf. 14*

732 A390 1.30m Orbicular granite 60 30
733 A390 1.60m Rapaviki 75 50
734 A390 2.10m Veined gneiss 95 50

Europa 1986
A391

1986, Apr. 10 *Perf. 12½x13*

735 A391 1.60m Saimaa ringed seal 75 50
736 A391 2.20m Environmental conservation 1.00 50

Conference Palace, Baghdad, 1982 — A392

Natl. Construction Year. b, Lahti Theater, 1983. c, Kuusamo Municipal Offices, 1978. d, Hamina Court Building, 1983. e, Finnish Embassy, New Delhi, 1986. f, Western Sakyla Daycare Center, 1980.

1986, Apr. 19 *Perf. 14*

737 Booklet pane of 6 4.50
a.-f. A392 1.60m, any single 75 30

Nordic Cooperation Issue
1986 — A393

Sister towns.

1986, May 27 **Litho.** *Perf. 14*

738 A393 1.60m Joensuu 75 40
739 A393 2.20m Jyvaskyla 1.00 50

Souvenir Sheet

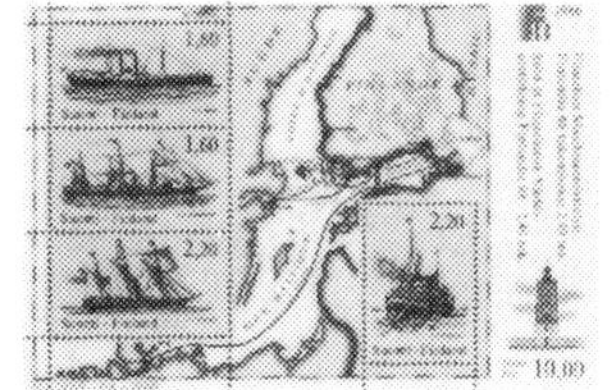

FINLANDIA '88 — A394

Postal ships: a, Iron paddle steamer Aura, Stockholm-St. Petersburg, 1858. b, Screw vessel Alexander, Helsinki-Tallinn-Lubeck, 1859. c, Steamship Nicolai, Helsinki-Tallinn-St. Petersburg, 1858. d, 1st Ice steamship Express II, Helsinki-Stockholm, 1877-98, vert.

Litho. & Engr.

1986, Aug. 29 *Perf. 13*

740 A394 Sheet of 4 4.25 4.75
a.-b. 1.60m, any single 1.00 1.10
c.-d. 2.20m, any single 1.00 1.10

Sold for 10k.

Pierre-Louis Moreau de Maupertuis (1698-1759) — A395

1986, Sept. 5 **Litho.** *Perf. 12½x13*

741 A395 1.60m multicolored 75 30

Lapland Expedition, 250th anniv., proved Earth's poles are flattened.
See France No. 2016.

Urho Kaleva Kekkonen (1900-86), Pres. — A396

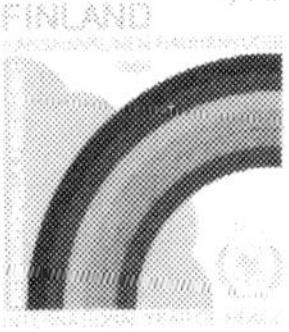

Intl. Peace Year — A397

1986, Sept. 30 **Engr.** *Perf. 14*

742 A396 5m black 2.00 2.00

1986, Oct. 13 **Litho.** *Perf. 13*

743 A397 1.60m multicolored 75 30

A398

Christmas
A399

Photo. & Engr.

1986, Oct. 31 *Perf. 12*

744 A398 1.30m shown 60 30
745 A398 1.30m Denomination at right 60 30
a. Pair, #744-745 1.25 75
746 A399 1.60m Elves 75 40

No. 744a has a continuous design.

Postal Savings Bank, Cent. — A400

1987, Jan. 2 **Litho.** *Perf. 14*

747 A400 1.70m multicolored 75 38

Natl. Tourism, Cent. — A401

1987, Feb. 4 **Litho.** *Perf. 14*

748 A401 1.70m Winter 75 38
749 A401 2.30m Summer 1.05 52

Metric System in Finland, Cent. — A402

1987, Feb. 4 *Perf. 14*

750 A402 1.40m multicolored 65 32

Leevi Madetoja (1887-1947), Composer
A403

1987, Feb. 17 **Litho.** *Perf. 14*

751 A403 2.10m multicolored 90 45

European Wrestling Championships
A404

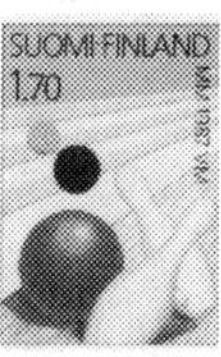

1987 World Bowling Championships
A405

1987, Feb. 17

752 A404 1.70m multicolored 75 38

1987, Apr. 13

753 A405 1.70m multicolored 75 38

Mental Health — A406

1987, Apr. 13

754 A406 1.70m multicolored 75 38

Souvenir Sheet

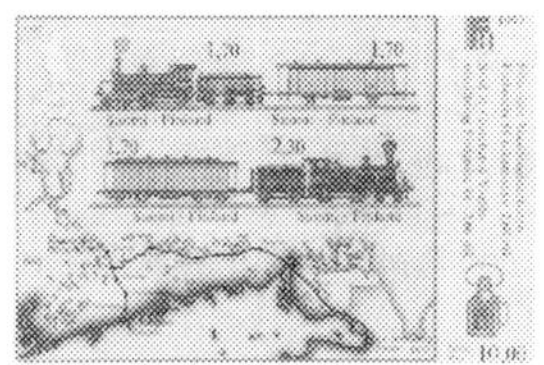

FINLANDIA '88 — A407

Locomotives and mail cars: a, Steam locomotive, 6-wheeled tender. b, 4-window mail car. c, 7-window mail car.

Perf. 12½x13

1987, May 8 **Litho. & Engr.**

755 A407 Sheet of 4 7.50 7.50
a.-c. 1.70m any single 1.50 1.50
d. 2.30m multicolored 1.50 1.50

Sold for 10m.

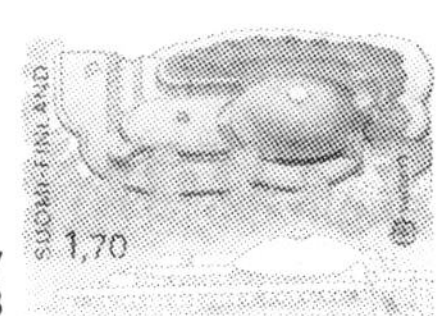

Europa 1987
A408

Modern architecture: 1.70m, Tampere Main Library, 1986, designed by Raili and Reima Pietila. 2.30m, Stoa Monument, Helsinki, c. 1981, by sculptor Hannu Siren.

1987, May 15 **Litho.** *Perf. 13*

756 A408 1.70m multicolored 80 40
757 A408 2.30m multicolored 1.10 55

Natl. Art Museum, Ateneum, Cent. — A409

Paintings: a, Strawberry Girl, by Nils Schillmark (1745-1804). b, Still-life on a Lady's Work Table, by Ferdinand von Wright (1822-1906). c, Old Woman with Basket, by Albert Edelfelt (1854-1906). d, Boy and Crow, by Akseli Gallen-Kallela (1865-1931). e, Late Winter, by Tyko Sallinen (1879-1955).

1987, May 15

758 Booklet pane of 5 4.00
a.-e. A409 1.70m any single 80 40

European Physics Soc. 7th Gen. Conf., Helsinki, Aug. 10-14 — A410

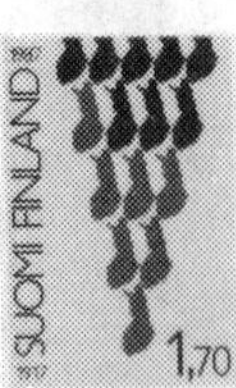

Natl. Independence, 70th Anniv. — A411

1987, Aug. 12 ***Perf. 14***

759 A410 1.70m multicolored 78 78

1987, Oct. 12

760 A411 1.70m ultra, sil & pale lt gray 75 75

Size: 30x41mm

761 A411 10m dark ultra, lt blue & sil 4.50 4.50

Ylppo, Child and Lastenlinna Children's Hospital — A412

1987, Oct. 27

762 A412 1.70m multicolored 75 75

Arvo Ylppo (b. 1887), pediatrics pioneer.

Christmas A413

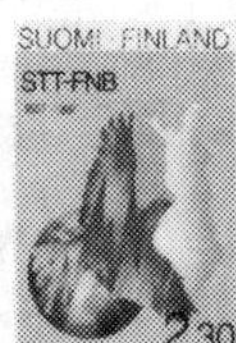

Finnish News Agency (STT), Cent. A414

1987, Oct. 30

763 A413 1.40m Santa Claus, youths, horiz. 65 65
764 A413 1.70m shown 75 75

1987, Nov. 1

765 A414 2.30m multicolored 1.05 1.05

Lauri "Tahko" Pihkala (1888-1981), Promulgator of Sports and Physical Education A415

1988, Jan. 5 **Litho.** ***Perf. 14***

766 A415 1.80m blk, chalky blue & brt blue 90 90

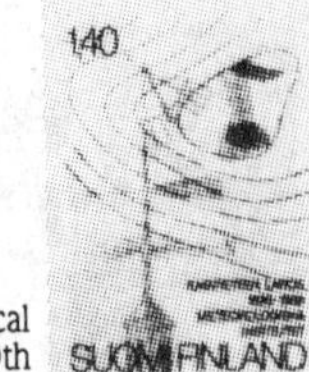

Meteorological Institute, 150th Anniv. — A416

1988, Mar. 14 **Litho.**

767 A416 1.40m multicolored 70 70

Settlement of New Sweden in America, 350th Anniv. — A417

Design: 17th Century European settlers negotiating with 3 American Indians, map of New Sweden, the Swedish ships Kalmar Nyckel and Fogel Grip, based on an 18th cent. illustration from a Swedish book about the American Colonies.

Litho. & Engr.

1988, Mar. 29 ***Perf. 13***

768 A417 3m multicolored 1.50 1.50

See US No. C117 and Sweden No. 1672.

FINLANDIA '88, June 1-12, Helsinki Fair Center — A418

Design: Agathon Faberge (1876-1951), famed philatelist, and rarities from his collection.

Booklet Stamp

1988, May 2 **Litho.** ***Perf. 13***

769 A418 5m Pane of 1+2 labels 15.00 15.00

350th Anniv. of the Finnish Postal Service. No. 769 sold for 30m to include the price of adult admission to the exhibition.

Achievements of Finnish Athletes at the 1988 Winter Olympics, Calgary A419

Design: Matti Nykanen, gold medalist in all 3 ski jumping events at the '88 Games.

1988, Apr. 6 ***Perf. 14***

770 A419 1.80m multicolored 90 90

Europa 1988 A420

Communication and transport.

1988, May 23 **Litho.** ***Perf. 13***

771 A420 1.80m shown 90 90
772 A420 2.40m Horse-drawn tram, 1890 1.20 1.20

Souvenir Sheet

FINLANDIA '88 — A421

1st airmail flights: a, Finnish air force Breguet 14 biplane transporting mail from Helsinki to Tallinn, Feb. 12, 1920. b, AERO Junkers F-13 making 1st airmail night flight from Helsinki to Copenhagen, May 15, 1930. c, AERO Douglas DC-3, 1st intl. route, Helsinki-Norrkoping-Copenhagen-Amsterdam, 1947. d, Douglas DC 10-30, 1975-88, inauguration of Helsinki-Beijing route, June 2, 1988.

Litho. & Engr.

1988, June 2 ***Perf. 13½***

773 Sheet of 4 5.50 5.50
a.-c. A421 1.80m any single 2.35 2.35
d. A421 2.40m multicolored 3.15 3.15

Sold for 11m.

Turku Fire Brigade, 150th Anniv. — A422

Design: 1902 Horse-drawn, steam-driven fire pump, preserved at the brigade.

1988, Aug. 15 **Litho.** ***Perf. 14***

774 A422 2.20m multicolored 1.05 1.05

A423

A424

Missale Aboense, the 1st printed book in Finland, 500th anniv.

1988, Aug. 17

775 A423 1.80m multicolored 85 85

Booklet Stamps

1988, Sept. 6 **Litho.** ***Perf. 13***

Finnish Postal Service, 350th Anniv.: #776, Postal tariff issued by Queen Christina of Sweden, Sept. 6, 1638. #777, Postal cart, c. 1880. #778, Leyland Sherpa 185 mail van, 1976. #779, Malmi P.O. interior. #780, Skier using mobile telephone, c. 1970. #781, Telecommunications satellite in orbit.

776 A424 1.80m multicolored 85 85
777 A424 1.80m multicolored 85 85
778 A424 1.80m multicolored 85 85
779 A424 1.80m multicolored 85 85
780 A424 1.80m multicolored 85 85
781 A424 1.80m multicolored 85 85
a. Booklet pane of 6, #776-781 5.10
Nos. 776-781 (6) 5.10 5.10

Children's Playgroups (Preschool) A425

1988, Oct. 10 ***Perf. 14***

782 A425 1.80m multicolored 85 85

Christmas A426

1988, Nov. 4 **Litho.**

783 A426 1.40m multicolored 65 65
784 A426 1.80m multicolored 82 82

Hameenlinna Township, 350th Anniv. — A427

Design: Market square, coat of arms and 17th century plan of the town.

1989, Jan. 19 **Litho.**

785 A427 1.90m multicolored 95 95

1989 Nordic Ski Championships, Lahti, Feb. 17-26 — A428

1989, Jan. 25

786 A428 1.90m multicolored 95 95

Salvation Army in Finland, Cent. — A429

Photography, 150th Anniv. — A430

1989, Feb. 6 **Litho.**

787 A429 1.90m multicolored 92 92

1989, Feb. 6

788 A430 1.50m Photographer, box camera, c.1900 75 75

31st Intl. Physiology Congress, Basel, July 9-14 — A431

Design: Congress emblem, silhouettes of Robert Tigerstedt and Ragnar Granit, eye, flowmeter measuring flow of blood through heart, color-sensitive retinal cells and microelectrode.

1989, Mar. 2

789 A431 1.90m multicolored 92 92

Sports — A432

1989, Mar. 10 **Booklet Stamps**

790 A432 1.90m Skiing 92 92
791 A432 1.90m Jogging 92 92
792 A432 1.90m Cycling 92 92
793 A432 1.90m Canoeing 92 92
a. Booklet pane of 4, #790-793 3.70 3.70

Souvenir Sheet

Finnish Kennel Club, Cent. — A433

Dogs: a, Lapponian herder. b, Finnish spitz. c, Karelian bear dog. d, Finnish hound.

1989, Mar. 17 Litho. *Perf. 14*

794 A433 Sheet of 4	3.60	3.60
a.-d. 1.90m any single	90	90

Europa — A434

A435

1989, Mar. 31 *Perf. 13*

795 A434 1.90m Hopscotch	90	90
796 A434 2.50m Sledding	1.20	1.20

1989, Apr. 20 *Perf. 14*

Nordic Cooperation Year: Folk Costumes.

797 A435 1.90m Sakyla (man)	90	90
798 A435 2.50m Veteli (woman)	1.20	1.20

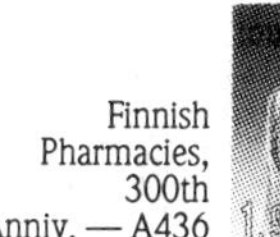

Finnish Pharmacies, 300th Anniv. — A436

Design: Foxglove, distilling apparatus, mortar, flask.

1989, June 2 Litho.

799 A436 1.90m multicolored	90	90

Savonlinna Municipal Charter, 350th Anniv. — A437

1989, June 2

800 A437 1.90m multicolored	90	90

Helsinki Zoo, Cent. — A438

1989, June 12

801 A438 1.90m *Panthera uncia*	90	90
802 A438 2.50m *Capra falconeri*	1.20	1.20

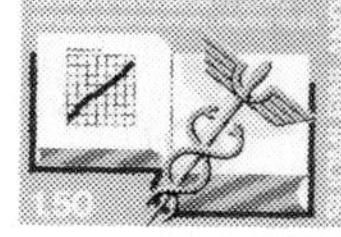

Vocational Training, 150th Anniv. — A439

Interparliamentary Union, Cent. — A440

Council of Europe, 40th Anniv. — A441

1989, Sept. 4 Litho. *Perf. 14*

803 A439 1.50m multicolored	68	68
804 A440 1.90m multicolored	85	85
805 A441 2.50m multicolored	1.15	1.15

Admission of Finland to the Council of Europe (2.50m).

Hannes Kolehmainen (1889-1966) Winning the 5000-meter Race at the Stockholm Olympics, 1912 — A442

1989, Oct. 9 Litho.

806 A442 1.90m multicolored	85	85

Continuing Education in Finland, Cent. — A443

1989, Oct. 20

807 A443 1.90m multicolored	85	85

A444

A445

Christmas: 1.90m, Sodankyla Church, Siberian jays in snow.

1989, Nov. 3

808 A444 1.50m shown	68	68
809 A444 1.90m multicolored	85	85

1990, Jan. 19 Litho. *Perf. 13x13½*

810 A445 1.90m multicolored	90	90
811 A445 2.50m multicolored	1.20	1.20

Incorporation of the State Posts and Telecommunications Services.

Emblem of the corporation was produced by holography. Soaking may affect the design.

Musical Soc. of Turku and Finnish Orchestras, 200th Annivs. — A446

1990, Jan. 26 *Perf. 14*

812 A446 1.90m multicolored	90	90

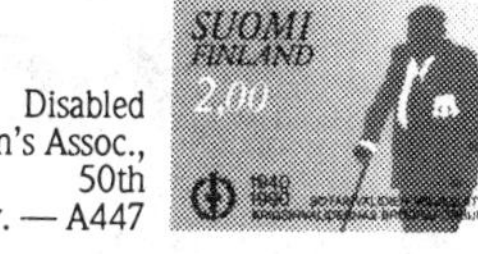

Disabled Veteran's Assoc., 50th Anniv. — A447

1990, Mar. 13 Litho.

813 A447 2m multicolored	1.00	1.00

End of the Winter (Russo-Finnish) War, 50th Anniv. — A448

1990, Mar. 13

814 A448 2m blue	1.00	1.00

University of Helsinki, 350th Anniv. — A449

University crest and: 2m, Queen Christina on horseback. 3.20m, Degree ceremony procession in front of the main university building.

1990, Mar. 26 Litho. *Perf. 13*

815 A449 2m multicolored	1.00	1.00
816 A449 3.20m multicolored	1.60	1.60

Europa 1990 A450

Post Offices: 2m, Lapp man, P.O. at Nuvvus, Mt. Nuvvus Ailigas. 2.70m, Turku main P.O.

1990, Mar. 26 *Perf. 12½x13*

817 A450 2m multicolored	1.00	1.00
818 A450 2.70m multicolored	1.40	1.40

Rural Postal Service and Address Reform, Cent. — A451

1990, Apr. 19 Litho. *Perf. 13*

819 A451 2m multicolored	1.00	1.00

"Ali Baba and the Forty Thieves" — A452

"Story of the Great Musician" — A453

"Story of the Giants, the Witches and the Daughter of the Sun" — A454

"The Golden Bird, the Golden Horse and the Princess" — A455

"Lamb Brother" — A456

"The Snow Queen" — A457

Fairy tale illustrations by Rudolf Koivu.

Booklet Stamps

Perf. 14 on 3 sides

1990, Aug. 29 Litho.

820 A452 2m multicolored	1.00	1.00
821 A453 2m multicolored	1.00	1.00
822 A454 2m multicolored	1.00	1.00
823 A455 2m multicolored	1.00	1.00
824 A456 2m multicolored	1.00	1.00
825 A457 2m multicolored	1.00	1.00
a. Booklet pane of 6, #820-825	6.00	6.00

Souvenir Sheet

Horse Care — A458

Designs: a, Feeding. b, Riding. c, Watering. d, Currying.

1990, Oct. 10 Litho. *Perf. 14*

826 Sheet of 4	4.00	4.00
a.-d. A458 2m any single	1.00	1.00

Christmas A459

1990, Nov. 2

827 A459 1.70m Santa's elves	85	85
828 A459 2m Santa, reindeer	1.00	1.00

Provincial Flowers A460

Labrador Tea A460a

1990-93 *Perf. 13x12½*

834 A460 2m Wood anemone	95	22
835 A460 2.10m Rowan	1.15	25
838 A460 2.70m Heather	1.30	38
839 A460 2.90m Sea buckthorn	1.60	52
841 A460 3.50m Oak	1.95	65
Nos. 834-841 (5)	6.95	2.02
842 A460 (2) Globeflower	85	85
843 A460 (1) Hepatica	1.10	1.10

No. 842 sold for 1.60m and No. 843 for 2.10m at time of release.

Self-Adhesive

Die Cut

843A A460 (2) Iris 65 65
b. Booklet pane of 20 13.00
844 A460 2.10m Rowan 1.15 50
845 A460 (1) Rosebay willowherb 80 80
845A A460a (1) multicolored 85 85
b. Booklet pane of 10 8.50

Issued: 2m, 2.70m, Jan. 19. No. 835, 2.90m, 3.50m, Feb. 5. 2.10m, 1991. Nos. 842-843, Mar. 2, 1992. No. 845, Oct. 9, 1992. No. 843A, Mar. 1, 1993. No. 845A, June 14, 1993.

No. 843A sold for 1.90m, No. 845 for 2.10m and No. 845A for 2.30m at time of release. Nos. 844-845 issued in sheets of 10.

The numbers on the stamps represent the class of mail for which each was intended at time of release.

This is an expanding set. Numbers will change if necessary.

World Hockey Championships, Turku — A461

1991, Mar. 1 ***Perf. 14***
846 A461 2.10m multicolored 1.15 1.15

Home Economics Teacher Education, Cent. — A462

1991, Mar. 1
847 A462 2.10m Cooking class 1.15 1.15

SUOMI 0.10 Birds — A463

1991-93 Litho. ***Perf. 13x12½***

Booklet Stamps

848 A463 10p Great tit 15 15
849 A463 10p Wagtail 15 15
850 A463 10p Aegolius funereus 15 15
850A A463 20p Phoenicurus phoenicurus 15 15
851 A463 60p Chaffinches 35 15
852 A463 60p Robin 28 28
856 A463 2.10m Bullfinch 1.15 38
a. Bklt. pane, #851, 2 each #848, 856 2.85
857 A463 2.10m Waxwing 95 95
a. Bklt. pane, #852, 2 each #849, 857 2.25
859 A463 2.30m Dendrocopos leucotos 78 78
a. Booklet pane of #850A, 2 each #850, #859 + 1 label 1.70
Nos. 848-857 (8) 3.33 2.36

Issued: Nos. 848, 851, 856, Mar. 20. Nos. 849, 852, 857, Apr. 22, 1992. Nos. 850, 850A, 859, June 4, 1993.

"SUOMI" is in upper left on Nos. 849, 852 and 857.

This is an expanding set. Numbers may change.

Fishing — A464

Tourism — A465

Designs: a, Fly fisherman, trout. b, Perch, bobber. c, Crayfish, trap. d, Trawling for herring. e, Stocking powan.

1991, Mar. 20 ***Perf. 14***
863 Booklet pane of 5 5.75 5.75
a.-e. A464 2.10m any single 1.15 1.15

1991, June 4 Litho. ***Perf. 14***
864 A465 2.10m Seurasaari Island 1.00 1.00
865 A465 2.90m Steamship, Lake Saimaa 1.35 1.35

Europa A466

European map and: 2.10m, Human figures. 2.90m, Satellites, dish antennae.

1991, June 7 Litho. ***Perf. 12½x13***
866 A466 2.10m multicolored 1.00 1.00
867 A466 2.90m multicolored 1.35 1.35

Alfred W. Finch (1854-1930) — A467

Designs: 2.10m, Iris, ceramic vase. 2.90m, Painting, The English Coast at Dover.

1991, Sept. 7 Litho. ***Perf. 13***
868 A467 2.10m multicolored 1.00 1.00
869 A467 2.90m multicolored 1.35 1.35

See Belgium No. 1410.

Finnish Candy Industry, Cent. — A468

1991, Sept. 17 Photo. ***Perf. 11½***
870 A468 2.10m multicolored 1.00 1.00

Souvenir Sheet

Children's Stamp Designs — A469

Skiing — A470

Designs: a, Sun. b, Rainbow. c, Cows grazing.

1991, Sept. 17 Litho. ***Perf. 13½***
871 Sheet of 3 3.00 3.00
a.-c. A469 2.10m any single 1.00 1.00

1991, Oct. 4 ***Perf. 14***

Color of skisuit: a, red. b, green. c, yellow. d, blue.

872 Sheet of 4 4.00 4.00
a.-d. A470 2.10m any single 1.00 1.00

Town Status for Iisalmi, Cent. — A471

1991, Oct. 18 Litho. ***Perf. 14***
873 A471 2.10m multicolored 1.00 1.00

Christmas A472

Designs: 1.80m, Santa, animals carrying candles. 2.10m, Reindeer pulling Santa's sleigh, vert.

1991, Nov. 1 Litho. ***Perf. 14***
874 A472 1.80m multicolored 90 90
875 A472 2.10m multicolored 1.10 1.10

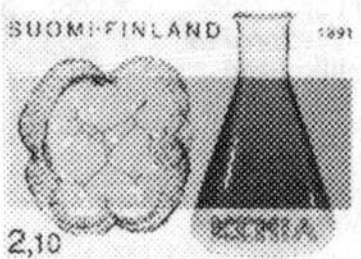

Chemists' Club, Finnish Chemists' Society, Cent. — A473

1991, Nov. 1
876 A473 2.10m multi 1.10 1.10
877 A473 2.10m multi, diff. 1.10 1.10
a. Pair, #876-877 + label 2.20 2.20

Second and third vertical branches merge while second and third branches below almost touch in the upper left part of camphor molecular structure on No. 877. Nos. 876-877 are designed to produce a three dimensional effect when viewed together.

1992 Olympic Games — A474

Designs: No. 878, Skier, Albertville. No. 879, Swimmer, Barcelona.

1992, Feb. 4 Litho. ***Perf. 14***
878 A474 2.10m multicolored 1.20 1.20
879 A474 2.90m multicolored 1.75 1.75

Expo '92, Seville — A475

1992, Mar. 20 Litho. ***Perf. 14***
880 A475 3.40m multicolored 1.60 1.60

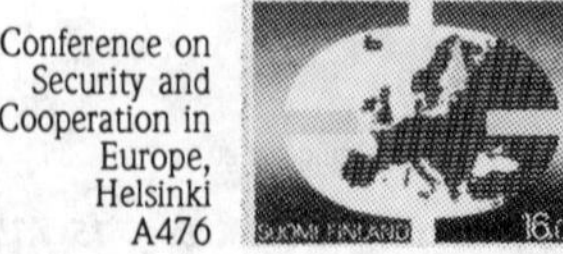

Conference on Security and Cooperation in Europe, Helsinki A476

1992, Mar. 20 ***Perf. 14½x15***
881 A476 16m multicolored 7.35 7.35

Town of Rauma, 550th Anniv. — A477

1992, Mar. 27 ***Perf. 14***
882 A477 2.10m multicolored 1.00 1.00

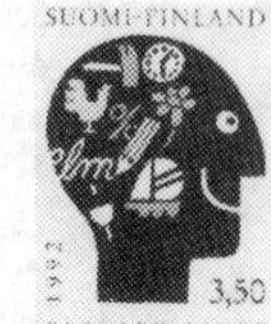

Healthy Brains — A478

1992, Mar. 27
883 A478 3.50m multicolored 1.60 1.60

Discovery of America, 500th Anniv. A479

1992, May 8 Litho. ***Perf. 12½x13***
884 A479 2.10m Santa Maria, map 1.00 1.00
885 A479 2.10m Map, Columbus 1.00 1.00
a. Pair, #884-885 2.00 2.00

Europa.

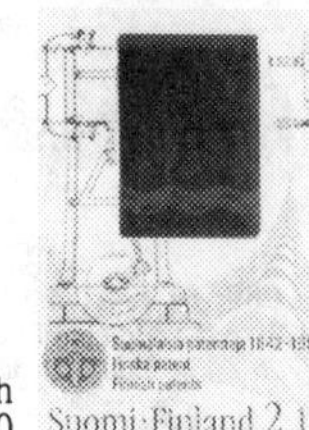

Finnish Technology — A480

Hologram of trees and: 2.10m, Drawing of blowing machine. 2.90m, Schematic of electronic circuits. 3.40m, Triangles and grid.

1992, May 8 ***Perf. 13x12½***
886 A480 2.10m multicolored 1.00 1.00
887 A480 2.90m multicolored 1.40 1.40
888 A480 3.40m multicolored 1.60 1.60

First Finnish patent granted, sesqui. (#886), Finnish chairmanship of Eureka (#887), Government Technology Research Center, 50th anniv. (#888).

Nos. 886-888 have holographic images. Soaking in water may affect the hologram.

Natl. Board of Agriculture, Cent. — A481

1992, June 4 Litho. ***Perf. 14***
889 A481 2.10m Currant harvesting 1.00 1.00

Finnish Women — A482

Designs: No. 890, Aurora Karamzin (1808-1902), founder of Deaconesses' Institution of Helsinki. No. 891, Baroness Sophie Mannerheim (1863-1928), reformer of nursing education. No. 892, Laimi Leidenius (1877-1938), physician and educator. No. 893, Miina Sillanpaa (1866-1952), Minister for social affairs. No. 894, Edith Sodergran (1892-1923), poet. No. 895, Kreeta Haapasalo (1813-1893), folk singer.

1992, June 8 Litho. & Engr. ***Perf. 14***

Booklet Stamps

890 A482 2.10m multicolored 1.10 1.10
891 A482 2.10m multicolored 1.10 1.10
892 A482 2.10m multicolored 1.10 1.10
893 A482 2.10m multicolored 1.10 1.10
894 A482 2.10m multicolored 1.10 1.10
895 A482 2.10m multicolored 1.10 1.10
a. Booklet pane of 6, #890-895 6.60
Nos. 890-895 (6) 6.60 6.60

Child's Painting — A483

Independence, 75th Anniv. — A484

1992, Oct. 5 Litho. *Perf. 13*
896 A483 2.10m multicolored 85 85

Souvenir Sheet
Perf. 13¹/₂
897 A484 2.10m multicolored 85 85

Nordia '93 — A485

A486

Illustrations depicting "Moomin" characters, by Tove Jansson: No. 898, Winter scene, ice covered bridges. No. 899, Winter scene in forest. No. 900, Boats in water. No. 901, Characters on beach.

Perf. 13 on 3 Sides
1992, Oct. 9 Litho.
Booklet Stamps
898 A485 2.10m multicolored 85 85
899 A485 2.10m multicolored 85 85
900 A485 2.10m multicolored 85 85
901 A485 2.10m multicolored 85 85
a. Booklet pane of 4, #898-901 3.40

1992, Oct. 20 Litho. *Perf. 13*
902 A486 2.10m multicolored 1.10 1.10

Printing in Finland, 350th anniv.

Christmas A487

Designs: 1.80m, Church of St. Lawrence, Vantaa. 2.10m, Stained glass window of nativity scene, Karkkila Church, vert.

1992, Oct. 30 Litho. *Perf. 14*
903 A487 1.80m multicolored 95 95
904 A487 2.10m multicolored 1.10 1.10

Central Chamber of Commerce, 75th Anniv. — A488

1993, Feb. 8 Litho. *Perf. 14*
905 A488 1.60m multicolored 65 65

Friendship A489

1993, Feb. 8 Litho. *Perf. 14*
906 A489 (1) multicolored 80 80
a. Booklet pane of 5 + label 4.00

No. 906 sold for 2m at time of release. See note following No. 845.
See Estonia No. 237.

Alopex Lagopus A490

Designs: a, Adult with winter white coat. b, Face, full view, winter white coat. c, Mother, kits, summer coat. d, Two on rock, summer coat.

1993, Mar. 19 Litho. *Perf. 12¹/₂x13*
907 A490 2.30m Block of 4, #a.-d. 3.15 3.15

World Wildlife Fund.

Sculptures A491

Europa: 2m, Rumba, by Martti Aiha. 2.90m, Complete Works, by Kari Caven.

1993, Apr. 26 *Perf. 13*
908 A491 2m multicolored 68 68
909 A491 2.90m multicolored 1.00 1.00

Organized Philately in Finland, Cent. — A492

1993, May 6 *Perf. 13x12¹/₂*
910 A492 2.30m Rosa pimpinellifolia 78 78

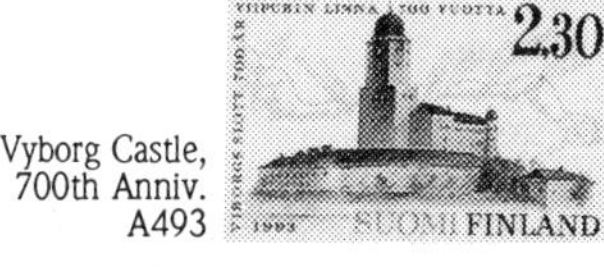

Vyborg Castle, 700th Anniv. A493

1993, May 6 *Perf. 13¹/₂*
911 A493 2.30m multicolored 78 78

Tourism A494

1993, May 7 *Perf. 13x12¹/₂*
912 A494 2.30m Naantali 78 78
913 A494 2.90m Imatra 1.00 1.00

550th anniv. of Naantali (#912).

A495

A496

Independent Finland Defense Forces, 75th Anniv.: 2.30m, Finnish landscape in form of soldier's silhouette. 3.40m, UN checkpoint of Finnish battalion, Middle East.

1993, June 4 Litho. *Perf. 14*
914 A495 2.30m multicolored 78 78
915 A495 3.40m multicolored 1.15 1.15

1993, June 14 Litho. *Perf. 12¹/₂x13*

Art by Martta Wendelin (1893-1986): No. 916, Boy on skis, 1936. No. 917, Mother, daughter knitting, 1931. No. 918, Children building snowman, 1931. No. 919, Mother, children at fence, 1935. No. 920, Girl with lamb, 1936.

Booklet Stamps
916 A496 2.30m multicolored 78 78
917 A496 2.30m multicolored 78 78
918 A496 2.30m multicolored 78 78
919 A496 2.30m multicolored 78 78
920 A496 2.30m multicolored 78 78
a. Booklet pane of 5, #916-920 4.00

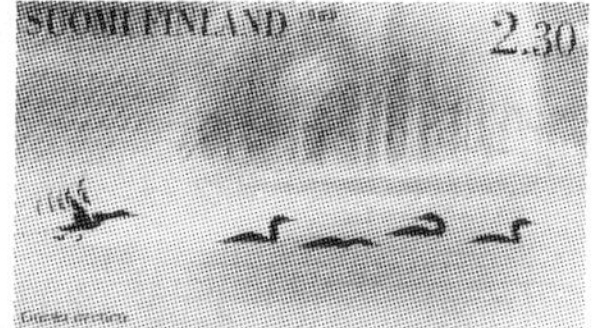

Water Birds — A497

Designs: No. 921, Flock of gavia arctica. No. 922, Pair of gavia arctica. No. 923, Mergus merganser. No. 924, Anas platyrhynchos. No. 925, Mergus serrator.

Perf. 12¹/₂x13 on 3 or 4 Sides
1993, Sept. 20 Litho.
Booklet Stamps
921 A497 2.30m multicolored 78 78
922 A497 2.30m multicolored 78 78

Size: 26x40mm
923 A497 2.30m multicolored 78 78
924 A497 2.30m multicolored 78 78
925 A497 2.30m multicolored 78 78
a. Booklet pane of 5, #921-925 4.00

Physical Education in Finnish Schools, 150th Anniv. — A498

1993, Oct. 8 *Perf. 14*
926 A498 2.30m multicolored 78 78

Souvenir Sheet

New Opera House, Helsinki — A499

Operas and ballet: a, 2.30m, Ostrobothnians, by Leevi Madetoja. b, 2.30m, The Faun (four dancers), by Claude Debussy. c, 2.90m, Giselle, by Adolphe Adam. d, 3.40m, The Magic Flute, by Wolfgang Amadeus Mozart.

1993, Oct. 8 *Perf. 13*
927 A499 Sheet of 4, #a.-d. 3.75 3.75

Christmas A500

Pres. Mauno Koivisto, 70th Birthday A501

Design: 1.80m, Christmas tree, elves. 2.30m, Three angels.

1993, Nov. 5 Litho. *Perf. 14*
928 A500 1.80m multicolored 60 60
a. Booklet pane of 10 6.00
929 A500 2.30m multicolored 80 80

1993, Nov. 25
930 A501 2.30m multicolored 80 80

Friendship — A502

Moomin characters: No. 931, Two standing. No. 932, Seven running.

1994, Jan. 27 Litho. *Perf. 12¹/₂x13*
Booklet Stamps
931 A502 (1) multicolored 80 80
932 A502 (1) multicolored 80 80
a. Booklet pane of 4 each, #931-932 6.50

Nos. 931-932 each sold for 2.30m at time of release. See note following No. 845.

Souvenir Sheet

Intl. Olympic Committee, Cent. — A503

Winter Olympics medalists from Finland: a, Marja-Liisa Kirvesniemi, Marjo Matikainen, cross-country skiing. b, Clas Thunberg, speed skating. c, Veikko Kankkonen, ski jumping. d, Veikko Hakulinen, cross-country skiing.

1994, Jan. 27 *Perf. 13*
933 A503 4.20m Sheet of 4, #a.-d. 5.75 5.75

Waino Aaltonen (1894-1966), Sculptor
A504 A505

1994, Mar. 8
934 A504 2m "Peace" 70 70
935 A505 2m "Muse" 70 70
a. Pair, #934-935 1.40 1.40

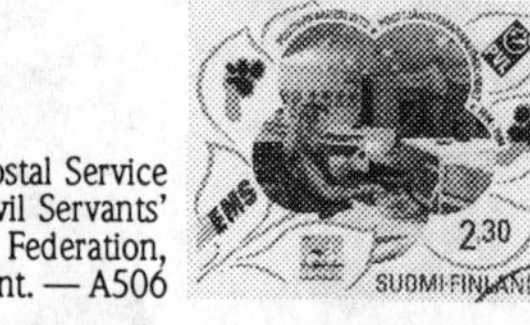

Postal Service Civil Servants' Federation, Cent. — A506

1994, Mar. 11

936 A506 2.30m multicolored 80 80

Finnish Technology A507

Europa: 2.30m, Paper roll, nitrogen fixation, safety lock, ice breaker MS Fennica. 4.20m, Radiosonde, fishing lure, mobile phone, wind power plant.

1994, Mar. 18

937 A507 2.30m multicolored 80 80
938 A507 4.20m multicolored 1.40 1.40

SEMI-POSTAL STAMPS

Arms — SP1

Unwmk.

1922, May 15 Typo. *Perf. 14*

B1 SP1 1m + 50p gray & red 50 *5.75*
Never hinged 1.10
a. Perf. 13x13½ 7.00
Never hinged 10.00

Red Cross Standard SP2

Symbolic SP3

Ship of Mercy — SP4

1930, Feb. 6

B2 SP2 1m + 10p red org & red 2.00 *6.00*
B3 SP3 1½m + 15p grysh grn & red 1.25 *6.00*
B4 SP4 2m + 20p dk bl & red 3.50 *24.00*
Set, never hinged 8.50

The surtax on this and subsequent similar issues was for the benefit of the Red Cross Society of Finland.

Church in Hattula — SP5

SP8

Designs: 1½m+15p, Castle of Hameenlinna. 2m+20p, Fortress of Viipuri.

1931, Jan. 1 Engr.

Cross in Red

B5 SP5 1m + 10p gray grn 1.10 *4.75*
B6 SP5 1½m + 15p lilac brn 6.00 6.50
B7 SP5 2m + 20p dull blue 95 *9.00*
Set, never hinged 19.00

1931, Oct. 15 Typo. *Rouletted 4, 5*

B8 SP8 1m + 4m black 20.00 *32.50*
Never hinged 35.00

The surtax was to assist the Postal Museum of Finland in purchasing the Richard Granberg collection of entire envelopes.

Helsinki University Library SP9

Nikolai Church at Helsinki SP10

Design: 2½m+25p, Parliament Building, Helsinki.

1932, Jan. 1 *Perf. 14*

B9 SP9 1¼m + 10p ol bis & red 1.40 *9.25*
B10 SP10 2m + 20p dp vio & red 70 *4.50*
B11 SP9 2½m + 25p lt blue & red 1.00 *15.00*
Set, never hinged 5.00

Bishop Magnus Tawast SP12

Michael Agricola SP13

Design: 2½m+25p, Isacus Rothovius.

1933, Jan. 20 Engr.

B12 SP12 1¼m + 10p blk brn & red 1.75 3.25
B13 SP13 2m + 20p brn vio & red 52 1.00
B14 SP13 2½m + 25p indigo & red 70 1.50
Set, never hinged 6.00

Evert Horn — SP15

Designs: 2m+20p, Torsten Stalhandske. 2½m+25p, Jakob (Lazy Jake) de la Gardie.

1934, Jan.

Cross in Red

B15 SP15 1¼m + 10p brown 75 1.25
B16 SP15 2m + 20p gray lilac 1.25 2.25
B17 SP15 2½m + 25p gray 75 1.65
Set, never hinged 4.75

Mathias Calonius SP18

Robert Henrik Rehbinder SP21

Designs: 2m+20p, Henrik C. Porthan. 2½m+25p, Anders Chydenius.

1935, Jan. 1

Cross in Red

B18 SP18 1¼m + 15p brown 70 1.25
B19 SP18 2m + 20p gray lilac 1.00 1.75
B20 SP18 2½m + 25p gray blue 52 1.50
Set, never hinged 4.50

1936, Jan. 1

Designs: 2m+20p, Count Gustaf Mauritz Armfelt. 2½m+25p, Count Arvid Bernard Horn.

Cross in Red

B21 SP21 1¼m + 15p dk brown 50 1.40
B22 SP21 2m + 20p vio brn 2.75 3.75
B23 SP21 2½m + 25p blue 50 2.00
Set, never hinged 7.50

Type "Uusimaa" SP24

Type "Turunmaa" SP25

Design: 3½m+35p, Type "Hameenmaa."

1937, Jan. 1

Cross in Red

B24 SP24 1¼m + 15p brown 60 1.65
B25 SP25 2m + 20p brn lake 11.00 4.50
B26 SP24 3½m + 35p indigo 60 2.00
Set, never hinged 30.00

Aukuste Makipeska SP27

Skiing SP31

Designs: 1¼m+15p, Robert Isidor Orn. 2m+20p, Edward Bergenheim. 3½m+35p, Johan Mauritz Nordenstam.

1938, Jan. 5 Engr.

Cross in Red

B27 SP27 50p + 5p dk green 45 65
B28 SP27 1¼m + 15p dk brown 65 1.25
B29 SP27 2m + 20p rose lake 6.00 4.50
B30 SP27 3½m + 35p dk blue 60 2.25
Set, never hinged 12.00

1938, Jan. 18

Designs: #B32, Skijumper. #B33, Skier.

B31 SP31 1.25m + 75p slate grn 3.50 6.00
B32 SP31 2m + 1m dk carmine 3.50 6.00
B33 SP31 3.50m + 1.50m dk blue 3.50 6.00
Set, never hinged 17.00

Ski championships held at Lahti.

Soldier — SP34

Battlefield at Solferino — SP35

1938, May 16

B34 SP34 2m + ½m blue 1.25 3.00
Never hinged 3.50

Victory of the White Army over the Red Guards. The surtax was for the benefit of the members of the Union of the Finnish Front.

1939, Jan. 2

Cross in Scarlet

B35 SP35 50p + 5p dk green 60 90
B36 SP35 1¼m + 15p dk brown 60 1.50
B37 SP35 2m + 20p lake 11.00 6.00
B38 SP35 3½m + 35p dk blue 48 2.00
Set, never hinged 25.00

Intl. Red Cross Soc., 75th anniv.

Catalogue values for unused stamps in this section, from this point to the end of the section, are for Never Hinged items.

Soldiers with Crossbows SP36

Arms of Finland SP40

Designs: 1¼m+15p, Cavalryman. 2m+20p, Soldier of Charles XII of Sweden. 3½m+35p, Officer and soldier of War with Russia, 1808-1809.

1940, Jan. 3

Cross in Red

B39 SP36 50p + 5p dk grn 70 1.00
B40 SP36 1¼m + 15p dk brn 1.50 1.65
B41 SP36 2m + 20p lake 2.00 1.65
B42 SP36 3½m + 35p dp ultra 2.00 2.00

The surtax aided the Finnish Red Cross.

1940, Feb. 15 Litho.

B43 SP40 2m + 2m indigo 42 80

The surtax was given to a fund for the preservation of neutrality.

Mason SP41

Soldier's Emblem SP45

Designs: 1.75m+15p, Farmer plowing. 2.75m+25p, Mother and child. 3.50m+35p, Finnish flag.

1941, Jan. 2 Engr.

Cross in Red

B44 SP41 50p + 5p grn 55 70
B45 SP41 1.75m + 15p brn 1.40 1.25
B46 SP41 2.75m + 25p brn car 7.25 6.50
B47 SP41 3.50m + 35p dp ultra 1.40 1.75

See Nos. B65-B68.

1941, May 24 Unwmk.

B48 SP45 2.75m + 25p brt ultra 65 75

The surtax was for the aid of the soldiers who fought in the Russo-Finnish War.

Aland Arms — SP46

Lapland Arms — SP51

Coats of Arms: 1.75m+15p, Nyland. 2.75m+25p, Finland's first arms. 3.50m+35p, Karelia. 4.75m+45p, Satakunta.

1942, Jan. 2 *Perf. 14*

Cross in Red

B49 SP46 50p + 5p grn 80 1.00
B50 SP46 1.75m + 15p brn 1.00 1.50
B51 SP46 2.75m + 25p dk red 1.00 1.50
B52 SP46 3.50m + 35p dp ultra 1.00 1.50
B53 SP46 4.75m + 45p dk sl grn 80 1.50
Nos. B49-B53 (5) 4.60 7.00

The surtax aided the Finnish Red Cross.

1943, Jan. 6 **Inscribed "1943"**

Coats of Arms: 2m+20p, Hame. 3.50m+35p, Eastern Bothnia. 4.50m+45p, Savo.

Cross in Red

B54 SP51 50p + 5p grn 40 85
B55 SP51 2m + 20p brn 80 1.25
B56 SP51 3.50m + 35p dk red 80 1.25
B57 SP51 4.50m + 45p brt ultra 1.25 3.25

The surtax aided the Finnish Red Cross.

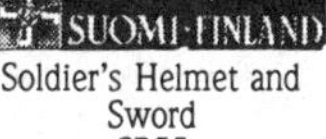

Soldier's Helmet and Sword SP55

Mother and Children SP56

1943, Feb. 1 *Perf. 13*

B58 SP55 2m + 50p dk brown 38 70
B59 SP56 3.50m + 1m brown red 38 70

The surtax was for national welfare.

Red Cross Train — SP57

Designs: 2m+50p, Ambulance. 3.50m+75p, Red Cross Hospital, Helsinki. 4.50m+1m, Hospital plane.

1944, Jan. 2 *Perf. 14*

Cross in Red

B60 SP57 50p + 25p green 24 24
B61 SP57 2m + 50p sepia 35 45
B62 SP57 3.50m + 75p ver 35 45
B63 SP57 4.50m + 1m brt ultra 70 1.10

The surtax aided the Finnish Red Cross.

Symbols of Peace SP61

Wrestling SP62

1944, Dec. 1

B64 SP61 3.50m + 1.50m dk red brn 38 65

The surtax was for national welfare.

Type of 1941 Inscribed "1945"

1945, May 2 **Photo. & Engr.**

Cross in Red

B65 SP41 1m + 25p green 15 28
B66 SP41 2m + 50p brown 20 45
B67 SP41 3.50m + 75p brn car 20 45
B68 SP41 4.50m + 1m dp ultra 40 80

The surtax was for the Finnish Red Cross.

1945, Apr. 16 **Engr.** *Perf. 13½*

Designs: 2m+1m, Gymnast. 3.50m+1.75m, Runner. 4.50m+2.25m, Skier. 7m+3.50m, Javelin thrower.

B69 SP62 1m + 50p bluish grn 18 55
B70 SP62 2m + 1m dp red 18 55
B71 SP62 3.50m + 1.75m dull vio 18 55
B72 SP62 4.50m + 2.25m ultra 32 70
B73 SP62 7m + 3.50m dull brn 50 1.10
Nos. B69-B73 (5) 1.36 3.45

Fishing SP67

Nurse and Children SP71

Designs: 3m+75p, Churning. 5m+1.25m, Reaping. 10m+2.50m, Logging.

Engraved; Cross Typo. in Red

1946, Jan. 7

B74 SP67 1m + 25p dull grn 32 45
B75 SP67 3m + 75p lilac brn 25 30
B76 SP67 5m + 1.25m rose red 32 45
a. Red cross omitted 450.00
B77 SP67 10m + 2.50m ultra 40 60

The surtax was for the Finnish Red Cross.

1946, Sept. 2 **Engr.**

Design: 8m+2m, Doctor examining infant.

B78 SP71 5m + 1m green 28 45
B79 SP71 8m + 2m brown vio 28 45

The surtax was for the prevention of tuberculosis.

Nos. B78 and B79 Surcharged with New Values in Black

1947, Apr. 1

B80 SP71 6m + 1m on 5m + 1m 28 55
B81 SP71 10m + 2m on 8m + 2m 28 55

The surtax was for the prevention of tuberculosis.

Medical Examination of Infants
SP73 SP74

Designs: 10m+2.50m, Infant held by the feet. 12m+3m, Mme. Alli Paasikivi and a child. 20m+5m, Infant standing.

1947, Sept. 15 **Engr.**

B82 SP73 2.50m + 1m green 35 55
B83 SP74 6m + 1.50m dk red 45 55
B84 SP74 10m + 2.50m red brn 55 55
B85 SP73 12m + 3m dp blue 70 80
B86 SP74 20m + 5m dk red vio 85 1.10
Nos. B82-B86 (5) 2.90 3.55

The surtax was for the prevention of tuberculosis.
For surcharges see Nos. B91-B93.

Zachris Topelius — SP78

Designs: 7m+2m, Fredrik Pacius. 12m+3m, Johan L. Runeberg. 20m+5m, Fredrik Cygnaeus.

Engraved; Cross Typo. in Red

1948, May 10 **Unwmk.** *Perf. 14*

B87 SP78 3m + 1m green 40 60
B88 SP78 7m + 2m rose red 50 65
B89 SP78 12m + 3m brt blue 55 75
B90 SP78 20m + 5m dk vio 65 90

The surtax was for the Finnish Red Cross.

Nos. B83, B84 and B86 Surcharged with New Values and Bars in Black

1948, Sept. 13 **Engr.** *Perf. 13½*

B91 SP74 7m + 2m on #B83 1.25 1.50
B92 SP74 15m + 3m on #B84 1.25 1.50
B93 SP74 24m + 6m on #B86 1.50 1.50

The surtax was for the prevention of tuberculosis.

Tying Birch Boughs — SP79

Wood Anemone — SP83

Designs: 9m+3m, Bathers in Sauna house. 15m+5m, Rural bath house. 30m+10m, Cold plunge in lake.

Engraved; Cross Typo. in Red

1949, May 5 *Perf. 13½x14*

B94 SP79 5m + 2m dull grn 35 50
B95 SP79 9m + 3m dk car 60 75
B96 SP79 15m + 5m dp blue 60 75
B97 SP79 30m + 10m dk vio brn 1.10 1.75

The surtax was for the Finnish Red Cross.

1949, June 2 **Engr.**

Inscribed: "1949"

B98 SP83 5m + 2m shown 38 75
B99 SP83 9m + 3m Wild rose 45 75
B100 SP83 15m + 5m Coltsfoot 55 1.10

The surtax was for the prevention of tuberculosis.

Similar to Type of 1949

Designs: 5m+2m, Water lily. 9m+3m, Pasqueflower. 15m+5m, Bell flower cluster.

1950, Apr. 1

Inscribed: "1950"

B101 SP83 5m + 2m emer 1.50 1.50
B102 SP83 9m + 3m rose car 1.40 1.40
B103 SP83 15m + 5m blue 1.40 1.40

The surtax was for the prevention of tuberculosis.

Hospital Entrance, Helsinki — SP84

Blood Donor's Medal — SP86

Design: 12m+3m, Giving blood.

Engraved; Cross Typo. in Red

1951, Mar. 17 **Unwmk.** *Perf. 14*

B104 SP84 7m + 2m chocolate 80 1.10
B105 SP84 12m + 3m bl vio 80 1.10
B106 SP86 20m + 5m car 1.50 2.00

The surtax was for the Finnish Red Cross.

Capercaillie — SP87

Designs: 12m+3m, European cranes. 20m+5m, Caspian terns.

1951, Oct. 26 **Engr.**

B107 SP87 7m + 2m dk grn 1.90 1.90
B108 SP87 12m + 3m rose brn 1.90 1.90
B109 SP87 20m + 5m bl 1.90 1.90

The surtax was for the prevention of tuberculosis.

Diver — SP88

Soccer Players — SP89

Designs: 20m+3m, Stadum, Helsinki. 25m+4m, Runners.

1951-52

B110 SP88 12m + 2m rose car 55 90
B111 SP89 15m + 2m grn ('52) 55 90
B112 SP88 20m + 3m dp bl 55 90
B113 SP89 25m + 4m brn ('52) 55 90

XV Olympic Games, Helsinki, 1952. The surtax was to help finance the games.

Margin blocks of four of each denomination were cut from regular or perf.-through-margin sheets and pasted by the selvage, overlapping, in a printed folder to create a kind of souvenir booklet. Value $35.

Field Marshal Mannerheim SP90

Great Titmouse SP91

Engraved; Cross Typo. in Red

1952, Mar. 4

B114 SP90 10m + 2m gray 1.50 1.50
B115 SP90 15m + 3m rose vio 1.50 1.50
B116 SP90 25m + 5m blue 1.50 1.50

The surtax was for the Red Cross.

1952, Dec. 4 **Engr.**

Designs: 15m+3m, Spotted flycatchers and nest. 25m+5m, Swift.

B117 SP91 10m + 2m grn 1.90 1.90
B118 SP91 15m + 3m plum 1.90 1.90
B119 SP91 25m + 5m dp bl 1.90 1.90

The surtax was for the prevention of tuberculosis.

European Red Squirrel — SP92

Designs: 15m+3m, Brown bear. 25m+5m, European elk.

Unwmk.

1953, Nov. 16 **Engr.** *Perf. 14*

B120 SP92 10m + 2m red brn 1.90 1.90
B121 SP92 15m + 3m vio 1.90 1.90
B122 SP92 25m + 5m dk grn 1.90 1.90

Surtax for the prevention of tuberculosis.

Children Receiving Parcel from Welfare Worker — SP93

Designs: 15m+3m, Aged woman knitting. 25m+5m, Blind basket-maker and dog.

Engraved; Cross Typo. in Red

1954, Mar. 8 *Perf. 11½*

B123 SP93 10m + 2m dk ol grn 1.25 1.25
B124 SP93 15m + 3m dk bl 1.25 1.25
B125 SP93 25m + 5m dk brn 1.25 1.25

The surtax was for the Finnish Red Cross.

Bumblebees, Dandelions SP94

European Perch SP95

Designs: 15m+3m, Butterfly. 25m+5m, Dragonfly.

Engraved; Cross Typo. in Red

1954, Dec. 7 ***Perf. 14***

B126	SP94	10m + 2m brown	1.50	1.50
B127	SP94	15m + 3m carmine	1.50	1.50
B128	SP94	25m + 5m blue	1.50	1.50

The surtax was for the prevention of tuberculosis.

Engraved; Cross Typo. in Red

1955, Sept. 26 ***Perf. 14***

Designs: 15m+3m, Northern pike. 25m+5m, Atlantic salmon.

B129	SP95	10m + 2m dl grn	1.50	1.50
B130	SP95	15m + 3m vio brn	1.50	1.50
B131	SP95	25m + 5m dk bl	1.50	1.50

The surtax was for the Anti-Tuberculosis Society.

Gen. von Dobeln in Battle of Juthas, 1808 SP96

Waxwing SP97

Illustrations by Albert Edelfelter from J. L. Runeberg's "Tales of Ensign Stal": 15m+3m, Col. J. Z. Duncker holding flag. 25m+5m, Son of fallen Soldier.

Engraved; Cross Typo. in Red

1955, Nov. 24

B132	SP96	10m + 2m dp ultra	1.25	1.25
B133	SP96	15m + 3m dk red brn	1.25	1.25
B134	SP96	25m + 5m green	1.25	1.25

The surtax was for the Red Cross.

Engraved; Cross Typo. in Red

1956, Sept. 25 ***Perf. 11½***

Birds: 20m+3m, Eagle owl. 30m+5m, Mute swan.

B135	SP97	10m + 2m dl red brn	1.25	1.25
B136	SP97	20m + 3m bl grn	1.40	1.40
B137	SP97	30m + 5m blue	1.40	1.40

The surtax was for the Anti-Tuberculosis Society.

Pekka Aulin SP98

Wolverine (Glutton) SP99

Portraits: 10m+2m, Leonard von Pfaler. 20m+3m, Gustaf Johansson. 30m+5m, Viktor Magnus von Born.

Engraved; Cross Typo. in Red

1956, Nov. 26 **Unwmk.**

B138	SP98	5m + 1m grysh grn	85	75
B139	SP98	10m + 2m brown	1.00	90
B140	SP98	20m + 3m magenta	1.10	1.10
B141	SP98	30m + 5m lt ultra	1.10	1.10

The surtax was for the Red Cross.

Engraved; Cross Typo. in Red

1957, Sept. 5 ***Perf. 11½***

Designs: 20m+3m, Lynx. 30m+5m, Reindeer.

B142	SP99	10m + 2m dl pur	1.10	1.00
B143	SP99	20m + 3m sepia	1.25	1.10
B144	SP99	30m + 5m dk bl	1.25	1.10

The surtax was for the Anti-Tuberculosis Society. See Nos. B160-B165.

Red Cross Flag SP100

Raspberry SP101

1957, Nov. 25 **Engr.** ***Perf. 14***

Cross in Red

B145	SP100	10m + 2m ol grn	1.65	1.40
B146	SP100	20m + 3m maroon	1.65	1.40
B147	SP100	30m + 5m dl bl	1.65	1.40

80th anniv. of the Finnish Red Cross.

Type of 1952

Flowers: 10m+2m, Lily of the Valley. 20m+3m, Red clover. 30m+5m, Hepatica.

Engraved; Cross Typo. in Red

1958, May 5 **Unwmk.** ***Perf. 14***

B148	SP91	10m + 2m green	1.10	90
B149	SP91	20m + 3m lil rose	1.25	1.10
B150	SP91	30m + 5m ultra	1.25	1.10

The surtax was for the Anti-Tuberculosis Society.

Engraved; Cross Typo. in Red

1958, Nov. 20 ***Perf. 11½***

Designs: 20m+3m, Cowberry. 30m+5m, Blueberry.

B151	SP101	10m + 2m orange	1.00	75
B152	SP101	20m + 3m red	1.40	1.10
B153	SP101	30m + 5m dk bl	1.40	1.10

The surtax was for the Red Cross.

Daisy — SP102

Reindeer — SP103

Designs: 20m+5m, Primrose. 30m+5m, Cornflower.

Engraved; Cross Typo. in Red

1959, Sept. 7 **Unwmk.**

B154	SP102	10m + 2m grn	1.90	1.10
B155	SP102	20m + 3m lt brn	2.50	1.40
B156	SP102	30m + 5m blue	2.50	1.40

The surtax was for the Anti-Tuberculosis Society.

Engraved; Cross Typo. in Red

1960, Nov. 24 ***Perf. 11½***

Designs: 20m+3m, Lapp and lasso. 30m+5m, Mountains.

B157	SP103	10m + 2m dk gray	1.10	90
B158	SP103	20m + 3m gray vio	1.65	1.40
B159	SP103	30m + 5m rose vio	1.65	1.40

The surtax was for the Red Cross.

Animal Type of 1957

Designs: 10m+2m, Muskrat. 20m+3m, Otter. 30m+5m, Seal.

Engr.; Cross at right, Typo. in Red

1961, Sept. 4

B160	SP99	10m + 2m brn car	1.10	90
B161	SP99	20m + 3m slate bl	1.65	1.40
B162	SP99	30m + 5m bl grn	1.65	1.40

The surtax was for the Anti-Tuberculosis Society.

Animal Type of 1957.

Designs: 10m+2m, Hare. 20m+3m, Pine marten. 30m+5m, Ermine.

Engraved; Cross Typo. in Red

1962, Oct. 1

B163	SP99	10m + 2m gray	1.25	90
B164	SP99	20m + 3m dl red brn	1.50	1.25
B165	SP99	30m + 5m vio bl	1.50	1.25

The surtax was for the Anti-Tuberculosis Society.

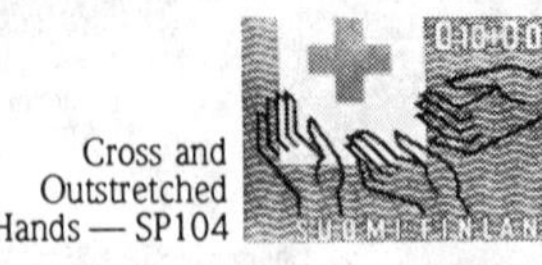

Cross and Outstretched Hands — SP104

Engraved; Cross Typo. in Red

1963, May 8 **Unwmk.** ***Perf. 11½***

B166	SP104	10p + 2p red brn	75	75
B167	SP104	20p + 3p violet	90	90
B168	SP104	30p + 5p green	90	90

The surtax was for the Red Cross.

Attending the Wounded SP105

Red Cross Activities: 25p+4p, Hospital ship. 35p+5p, Prisoner-of-war health examination. 40p+7p, Gift parcel distribution.

Engraved; Cross Typo. in Red

1964, May 26 ***Perf. 11½***

B169	SP105	15p + 3p vio bl	65	65
B170	SP105	25p + 4p green	90	75
B171	SP105	35p + 5p vio brn	90	75
B172	SP105	40p + 7p dk ol grn	90	75

The surtax was for the Red Cross.

Finnish Spitz SP106

Artificial Respiration SP107

Designs: 25p+4p, Karelian bear dog. 35p+5p, Finnish hunting dog.

Engraved; Cross Typo. in Red

1965, May 10 ***Perf. 11½***

B173	AP106	15p + 3p org brn	1.25	90
B174	AP106	25p + 4p black	1.40	1.10
B175	AP106	35p + 5p gray brn	1.40	1.10

Surtax for Anti-Tuberculosis Society.

1966, May 7 **Litho.** ***Perf. 14***

First Aid: 25p+4p, Skin diver rescuing occupants of submerged car. 35p+5p, Helicopter rescue in winter.

B176	SP107	15p + 3p multi	90	80
B177	SP107	25p + 4p multi	90	80
B178	SP107	35p + 5p multi	90	80

The surtax was for the Red Cross.

Birch — SP108

Horse-drawn Ambulance — SP109

Trees: 25p+4p, Pine. 40p+7p, Spruce.

1967, May 12 **Litho.** ***Perf. 14***

B179	SP108	20p + 3p multi	75	75
B180	SP108	25p + 4p multi	75	75
B181	SP108	40p + 7p multi	75	75

Surtax for Anti-Tuberculosis Society. See Nos. B185-B187.

1967, Nov. 24 **Litho.** ***Perf. 14***

Designs: 25p+4p, Ambulance, 1967. 40p+7p, Red Cross.

Cross in Red

B182	SP109	20p + 3p dl yel, grn & blk	75	75
B183	SP109	25p + 4p vio & blk	75	75
B184	SP109	40p + 7p dk grn, blk & dk ol	75	75

The surtax was for the Red Cross.

Tree Type of 1967

Trees: 20p+3p, Juniper. 25+4p, Aspen. 40p+7p, Chokecherry.

1969, May 12 **Litho.** ***Perf. 14***

B185	SP108	20p + 3p multi	75	75
B186	SP108	25p + 4p multi	75	75
B187	SP108	40p + 7p multi	75	75

Surtax for Anti-Tuberculosis Society.

"On the Lapp's Magic Rock" — SP110

Designs: 30p+6p, Juhani blowing horn on Impivaara Rock, vert. 50p+10p, The Pale Maiden. The designs are from illustrations by Askeli Gallen-Kallelas for "The Seven Brothers" by Aleksis Kivi.

1970, May 8 **Litho.** ***Perf. 14***

B188	SP110	25p + 5p multi	70	60
B189	SP110	30p + 6p multi	70	60
B190	SP110	50p + 10p multi	70	60

The surtax was for the Red Cross.

Cutting and Loading Timber — SP111

Designs: 30p+6p, Floating logs downstream. 50p+10p, Sorting logs at sawmill.

1971, Apr. 25 **Litho.** ***Perf. 14***

B191	SP111	25p + 5p multi	70	60
B192	SP111	30p + 6p multi	70	60
B193	SP111	50p + 10p multi	70	60

Surtax for Anti-Tuberculosis Society.

Blood Donor and Nurse — SP112

Designs: 30p+6p, Blood research (microscope, slides) vert. 50p+10p, Blood transfusion.

1972, Oct. 23

B194	AP112	25p + 5p multi	65	65
B195	AP112	30p + 6p multi	65	65
B196	AP112	50p + 10p multi	65	65

Surtax was for the Red Cross.

Girl with Lamb, by Hugo Simberg — SP113

Paintings: 40p+10p, Summer Evening, by Vilho Sjöström. 60p+15p, Woman at Mountain Foun ain, by Juho Rissanen.

1973, Sept. 12 Litho. *Perf. 13x12½*

B197 SP113 30p + 5p multi 60 60
B198 SP113 40p + 10p multi 90 90
B199 SP113 60p + 15p multi 90 90

Surtax for the Finnish Anti-Tuberculosis Assoc. Birth centenaries of featured artists.

Morel — SP114

Mushrooms: 50p+10p, Chanterelle. 60p+15p, Boletus edulis.

1974, Sept. 24 Litho. *Perf. 12½x13*

B200 SP114 35p + 5p multi 1.10 85
B201 SP114 50p + 10p multi 1.10 85
B202 SP114 60p + 15p multi 1.10 85

Finnish Red Cross.

Echo, by Ellen Thesleff (1869-1954) SP115

Paintings: 60p+15p, Hilda Wiik, by Maria Wiik (1853-1928). 70p+20p, At Home (old woman in chair), by Helene Schjerfbeck (1862-1946).

1975, Sept. 30 Litho. *Perf. 13x12½*

B203 SP115 40p + 10p multi 70 55
B204 SP115 60p + 15p multi 90 70
B205 SP115 70p + 20p multi 90 70

Finnish Red Cross. In honor of International Women's Year paintings by women artists were chosen.

Disabled Veterans' Emblem — SP116

Lithographed and Photogravure

1976, Jan. 15 *Perf. 14*

B206 SP116 70p + 30p multi 1.00 95

The surtax was for hospitals for disabled war veterans.

Wedding Procession SP117

Designs: 70p+15p, Wedding dance, vert. 80p+20p, Bride, groom, matron and pastor at wedding dinner.

1976, Sept. 15 Litho. *Perf. 13*

B207 SP117 50p + 10p multi 45 45
B208 SP117 70p + 15p multi 60 60
B209 SP117 80p + 20p multi 65 65

Surtax for Anti-Tuberculosis Society.

Disaster Relief — SP118

Designs: 80p+15p, Community work. 90p+20p, Blood transfusion service.

1977, Jan. 19 Litho. *Perf. 14*

B210 SP118 50p + 10p multi 50 50
B211 SP118 80p + 15p multi 70 70
B212 SP118 90p + 20p multi 70 70

Finnish Red Cross centenary.

Long-distance Skiing — SP119

Design: 1m+50p, Ski jump.

1977, Oct. 5 Litho. *Perf. 13*

B213 SP119 80p + 40p multi 2.75 2.75
B214 SP119 1m + 50p multi 1.75 1.75

Surtax was for World Ski Championships, Lahti, Feb. 17-26, 1978.

Saffron Milkcap SP120

Edible Mushrooms: 80p+15p, Parasol, vert. 1m+20p, Gypsy.

1978, Sept. 13 Litho. *Perf. 13*

B215 SP120 50p + 10p multi 75 75
B216 SP120 80p + 15p multi 1.10 1.10
B217 SP120 1m + 20p multi 1.10 1.10

Surtax was for Red Cross. See Nos. B221-B223.

Pehr Kalm, 1716-1779 SP121

Finnish Scientists: 90p+15p, Title page of Pehr Adrian Gadd's (1727-97) book, vert. 1.10m+20p, Petter Forsskal (1732-63).

Perf. 12½x13, 13x12½

1979, Sept. 26 Litho.

B218 SP121 60p + 10p multi 42 42
B219 SP121 90p + 15p multi 65 65
B220 SP121 1.10m + 20p multi 65 65

Surtax was for the Finnish Anti-Tuberculosis Association.

Mushroom Type of 1978

Edible Mushrooms: 60p+10p, Woolly milkcap. 90p+15p, Orange-cap boletus, vert. 1.10m+20p, Russula paludosa.

1980, Apr. 19 Litho. *Perf. 13*

B221 SP120 60p + 10p multi 45 45
B222 SP120 90p + 15p multi 65 60
B223 SP120 1.10m + 20p multi 65 60

Surtax was for Red Cross.

Fuchsia — SP122

1981, Aug. 24 Litho. *Perf. 13*

B224 SP122 70p + 10p shown 45 45
B225 SP122 1m + 15p African violet 60 60
B226 SP122 1.10m + 20p Geranium 75 75

Surtax was for Red Cross.

Garden Dormouse SP123

1982, Aug. 16 Litho. *Perf. 13*

B227 SP123 90p + 10p shown 42 35
B228 SP123 1.10m + 15p Flying squirrels 55 45
B229 SP123 1.20m + 20p European minks 60 50

Surtax was for Red Cross. No. B228 vert.

Forest and Wetland Plants — SP124

Designs: 1m+20p, Chickweed wintergreen. 1.20m+25p, Marsh violet. 1.30m+30p, Marsh marigold. Surtax was for Finnish Anti-Tuberculosis Assoc.

1983, July 7 Litho. *Perf. 13*

B230 SP124 1m + 20p multi 48 35
B231 SP124 1.20m + 25p multi 65 48
B232 SP124 1.30m + 30p multi 65 48

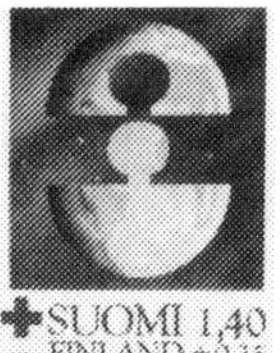

Globe Puzzle — SP125

Butterflies — SP126

Design: 2m+40p, Symbolic world communication. Surtax was for Red Cross.

1984, May 28 Litho. *Perf. 13*

B233 SP125 1.40m + 35p multi 55 55
B234 SP125 2m + 40p multi 75 75

1986, May 22 Litho. *Perf. 13*

B235 SP126 1.60m + 40p Anthocharis cardamines 90 85
B236 SP126 2.10m + 45p Nymphalis antiopa 1.25 1.25
B237 SP126 5m + 50p Parnassius apollo 2.25 2.00

Surtax for Red Cross.

Festivals — SP127

1988, Mar. 14 Litho. *Perf. 13*

B238 SP127 1.40m +40p Christmas 80 80
B239 SP127 1.80m +45p Easter 1.00 1.00
B240 SP127 2.40m +50p Midsummer 1.25 1.25

Surtax for the Red Cross.

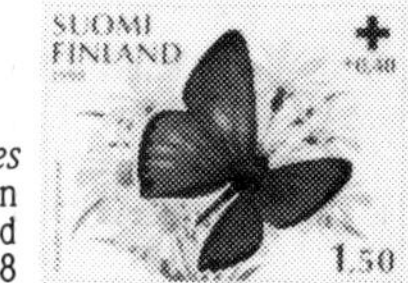

Heodes virgaureae on Goldrod Plant — SP128

Butterflies and plants: No. B242, *Agrodiaetus amandus* on meadow vetchling. No. B243, *Inachis io* on tufted vetch.

1990, Apr. 6 Photo. *Perf. 12x11½*

B241 SP128 1.50m +40p multi 95 95
B242 SP128 2m +50p multi 1.25 1.25
B243 SP128 2.70m +60p multi 1.70 1.70

Surtax for the natl. Red Cross Soc.

The Little Convalescent SP129

Paintings by Helene Schjerfbeck: B244b, Green Still-Life.

1991, Mar. 8 Litho. *Perf. 13*

B244 Pair 2.90 2.90
a.-b. SP129 2.10m +50p any single 1.45 1.45

Surtax for philately.

Butterflies SP130

Designs: 1.60m+40p, Xestia brunneopicta. 2.10m+50p, Acerbia alpina. 5m+60p, Baptria tibiale.

Litho. & Embossed

1992, Apr. 22 *Perf. 13*

B245 SP130 1.60m +40p multi 95 95
B246 SP130 2.10m +50p multi 1.25 1.25
B247 SP130 5m +60p multi 2.65 2.65

Surtax for Finnish Red Cross. Embossed "Arla 100" in braille for Arla Institute, training center for the blind, cent.

Autumn Landscape of Lake Pielisjarvi, by Eero Jarnefelt SP131

Designs: a, Tree-covered hill. b, Lake shoreline.

1993, Mar. 19 Litho. *Perf. 13*

B248 SP131 2.30m + 70p Pair, #a.-b. 1.60 1.60

Surtax for philately.

Finnhorses SP132

1994, Mar. 11 Litho. *Perf. 13*

B249 SP132 2m +40p Draft horses 85 85
B250 SP132 2.30m +50p Trotter 95 95
B251 SP132 4.20m +60p War horses, vert. 1.65 1.65

Surtax for Finnish Red Cross.

AIR POST STAMPS

No. 178 Overprinted in Red **ZEPPELIN 1930**

1930, Sept. 24 Unwmk. *Perf. 14*

C1 A28 10m gray lilac 110.00 190.00
Never hinged 190.00
a. 1830 for 1930 2,000. 3,250.

Overprinted expressly for use on mail carried in "Graf Zeppelin" on return flight from Finland to Germany on Sept. 24, 1930, after which trip the stamps ceased to be valid for postage. Forgeries are almost always on No. 205, rather than No. 178.

Catalogue values for unused stamps in this section, from this point to the end of the section, are for Never Hinged items.

Douglas DC-2 — AP1

1944 Engr.

C2 AP1 3.50m dark brown 35 65

20th anniv. of Air Transport Service, 1923-43.

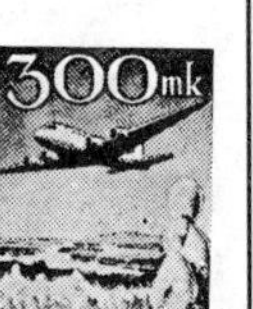

Douglas DC-6 Over Winter Landscape — AP2

1950, Feb. 13

C3 AP2 300m blue 20.00 6.25

Available also for ordinary postage.

Redrawn

1958, Jan. 20 *Perf. 11½*

C4 AP2 300(m) blue 35.00 1.00

On No. C4 "mk" is omitted.
See Nos. C9-C9a.

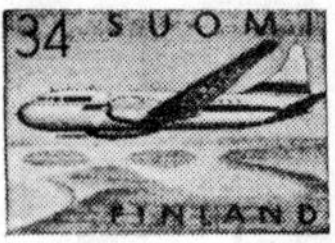

Convair 440 over Lakes — AP3

1958, Oct. 31 Unwmk. *Perf. 11½*

C5 AP3 34m blue 1.00 95

No. C5 Surcharged with New Value and Bars

1959, Apr. 5

C6 AP3 45m on 34m blue 2.00 2.00

1959, Nov. 2

C7 AP3 45m blue 2.00 52

1963, Feb. 15

C8 AP3 45p blue 1.40 55

On No. C7 the denomination is "45." On No. C8 it is "0.45."

DC-6 Type, Comma After "3"

Type I- 16 lines in "O"
Type II- 13 lines in "O"

1963, Oct. 10

C9 AP2 3m blue, Type II ('73) 1.75 18
a. Type I

Convair Type of 1958

1970, July 15

C10 AP3 57p ultra 1.40 45

MILITARY STAMPS

Catalogue values for unused stamps in this section are for Never Hinged items.

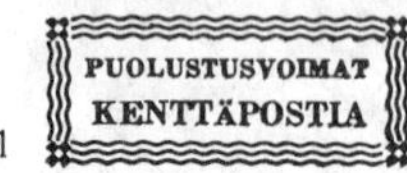

M1

1941, Nov. 1 Unwmk. Typo. *Imperf.*

M1 M1 (4m) blk, *dk org* 25 45

#M1 has simulated roulette printed in black.

Type of 1930-46 Overprinted in Black **KENTTÄ-POSTI FÄLTPOST**

1943, Oct. 16 *Perf. 14*

M2 A26 2m deep orange 28 35
M3 A26 3½m greenish blue 28 35

Post Horn and Sword — M2

1943 Size: 29½x19½mm

M4 M2 (2m) green 20 35
M5 M2 (3m) rose violet 20 35

1944 Size: 20x16mm

M6 M2 (2m) green 18 20
M7 M2 (3m) rose violet 18 20

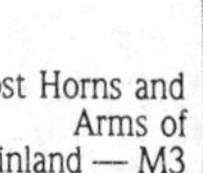
Post Horns and Arms of Finland — M3

1963, Sept. 26 Litho. *Perf. 14*

M8 M3 violet blue 190.00 150.00

Used during maneuvers Sept. 30-Oct. 5, 1963. Valid from Sept. 26.

No. M8 with overprint "1983" was issued in that year.

PARCEL POST STAMPS

PP1

Wmk. Rose & Triangles Multiple
Rouletted 6 on 2 or 3 Sides

1949-50 Typo.

Q1 PP1 1m brt grn & blk 1.25 4.50
Q2 PP1 5m red & blk 10.50 14.00
Q3 PP1 20m org & blk 20.00 22.50
Q4 PP1 50m bl & blk ('50) 7.25 11.00
Q5 PP1 100m brn & blk ('50) 8.25 11.00
Nos. Q1-Q5 (5) 47.25 63.00
Set, never hinged 67.50

Catalogue values for unused stamps in this section, from this point to the end of the section, are for Never Hinged items.

Mail Bus — PP2

1952-58 Unwmk. Engr. *Perf. 14*

Q6 PP2 5m car rose 4.00 5.00
Q7 PP2 20m orange 10.00 7.00
Q8 PP2 50m blue ('54) 25.00 10.00
Q9 PP2 100m brn ('58) 30.00 15.00

Mail Bus — PP3

1963 *Perf. 12*

Q10 PP3 5p red & blk 2.25 2.25
Q11 PP3 20p org & blk 2.00 1.10
Q12 PP3 50p blue & blk 3.75 1.40
Q13 PP3 1m brn & blk 95 1.10

Nos. Q1-Q13 were issued only in booklets: panes of 6 for Nos. Q1-Q5, 10 for Nos. Q6-Q9 and 5 for Nos. Q10-Q13.

Used values are for regular postal or mail-bus cancels. Pen strokes, cutting or other cancels sell for half as much.

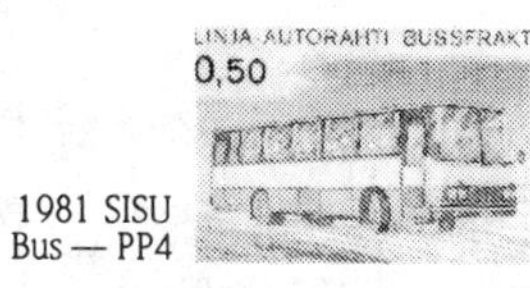

1981 SISU Bus — PP4

Perf. 12 Horiz.

1981, Dec. 7 Photo. & Engr.

Q14 PP4 50p dk bl & blk 50 2.50
Q15 PP4 1m dk brn & blk 75 2.50
Q16 PP4 5m grn & blk 3.00 5.25
Q17 PP4 10m red & blk 6.00 10.50

Parcel post stamps invalid after Jan. 9, 1985.

ALAND ISLANDS

Gaff-rigged Sloop — A1

Aland Flag — A2

Midsummer Pole — A3

Landscapes — A4

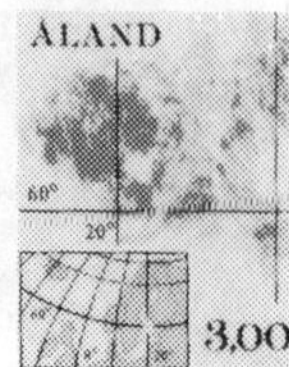

Map of Scandinavia — A5

Seal of St. Olaf and Aland Province, 1326 — A6

Artifacts — A7

Sea Birds — A8

Gothic Tower, Jomala Church, 12th Cent. — A9

Mariehamn Town Hall, Designed by Architect Lars Sonck — A9a

Designs: 1.50m, Statue of Frans Petter von Knorring, vicar from 1834 to 1875, and St. Michael's Church, Finstrom, 12th cent. 1.60m, Burial site, clay hands. 1.70m, Somateria mollissima. 2.20m, Bronze Staff of Finby, apostolic decoration. 2.30m, Aythya fuligula. 5m, Outer Aland Archipelago. 8m, Farm and windmill. 12m, Melantha fusca. 20m, Ancient court site, contemporary monument.

1984-90 Engr. Unwmk. *Perf. 12*

1 A1 10p magenta 15 15
2 A1 20p brown olive 15 15
3 A1 50p bright green 22 22
4 A1 1.10m deep blue 45 45
5 A1 1.20m black 50 50
6 A1 1.30m dark green 55 55

Litho.
Perf. 14, 13x14 (#8)

7 A2 1.40m multi 60 60
8 A9 1.40m multi 80 80
9 A3 1.50m multi, I 60 60
9A A3 1.50m multi, II 75 75
10 A9 1.50m multi 68 68

Perf. 13, 14 (#13)

11 A7 1.60m multi, vert. 75 75
12 A8 1.70m multi 85 85
13 A9a 1.90m multi 1.10 1.10
14 A4 2m multi 85 85
15 A7 2.20m multi, vert. 1.00 1.00
16 A8 2.30m multi 1.10 1.10
17 A5 3m multi 1.25 1.25
18 A4 5m multi, horiz. 2.00 2.00
19 A4 8m multi, horiz. 3.25 3.25

Litho. & Engr.

20 A6 10m multi 4.25 4.25

Litho.

21 A8 12m multi 6.00 6.00
22 A7 20m multi 9.25 9.25
Nos. 1-22 (23) 37.10 37.10

On No. 9A (type II) "Aland" is 10½mm long, figure support is 2mm wide, pole supports are thinner, diagonal black highlighting lines in pole greenery and horizontal black line on support under the man removed.

Issue dates: Nos. 2-4, 7, 17, 20, Mar. 1. Nos. 1, 5, 6, 9, 13, Jan. 2, 1985. Nos. 14, 18-19, Sept. 16, 1985. Nos. 11, 15, 22, Apr. 4, 1986. Nos. 12, 16, 21, Jan. 2, 1987. No. 8, Aug. 26, 1988. No. 10, Sept. 4, 1989. No. 9A, May 21, 1990.

See Nos. 39-42.

Bark Pommern and Car Ferries, Mariehamn West Harbor — A10

1984, Mar. 1 **Litho.** ***Perf. 14***
23 A10 2m multicolored 3.50 3.50

1986 Nordic Orienteering Championships, Aug. 30-31 — A11

1986, Jan. 2 **Litho.** ***Perf. 14***
24 A11 1.60m multicolored 75 75

Onningeby Artists' Colony, Cent. — A12

Design: Pallette, pen and ink drawing of Onningeby landscape, 1891, by Victor Westerholm (1860-1919), founder.

1986, Sept. 1 **Litho.**
25 A12 3.70m multicolored 1.75 1.75

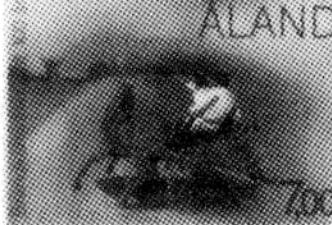

Mariehamn Volunteer Fire Brigade, Cent. — A13

1987, Apr. 27 **Litho.** ***Perf. 14***
26 A13 7m multicolored 3.25 3.25

Farjsund Bridge, 50th Anniv., Rebuilt in 1980 — A14

1987, Apr. 27 **Engr.** ***Perf. 13x13½***
27 A14 1m greenish black 45 45

Municipal Meeting, Finstrom, 1917 — A15

1987, Aug. 20 **Litho.** ***Perf. 14***
28 A15 1.70m multicolored 78 78

Movement for reunification with Sweden, 70th anniv.

Loading of Mail Barrels on Sailboat, Post Office, Eckero — A16

1988, Jan. 4 **Litho.** ***Perf. 14***
29 A16 1.80m multicolored 90 90

Postal Service, 350th anniv. From Feb. 1 to May 31, Alanders were entitled to buy 20 stamps for 28m with a discount coupon.

New Aland Farm School, Horse-Drawn Plow — A17

1988, Mar. 29 **Litho.** ***Perf. 14***
30 A17 2.20m multicolored 1.10 1.10

Haga Farm School, cent.; Aland Farm School, 75th anniv.; 50th anniv. of experimental farming on Aland.

Sailing Ships — A18

1988, June 4 **Litho.** ***Perf. 13***
31 A18 1.80m Albanus, 1904, vert. 90 90
32 A18 2.40m Ingrid, c. 1900 1.20 1.20
33 A18 11m Pamir, c. 1900 5.50 5.50

Type of 1988 and

Orchids — A19

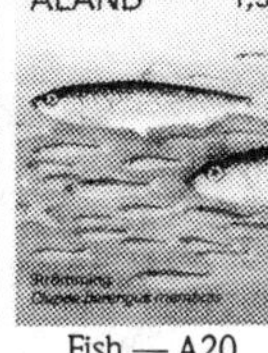

Fish — A20

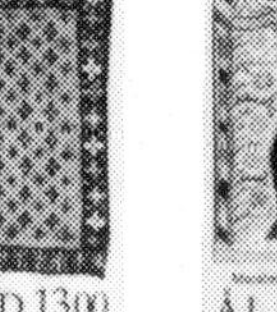

Handicrafts — A21

Fresco, St. Anna's Church of Kumlinge — A22

Mammals — A23

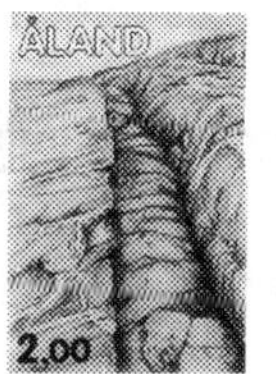

Geological Formations
A24 A25

Designs: 10p, Boulder field, Geta. #35, *Dactylorhiza sambucina.* #36, *Clupea harengus membras.* #37, *Erinaceus europauus.* #38, Drumlin, Finstrom. 1.70m, St. Andrew Church, Lumparland. #40, Vardo Church. #41, Hammarland Church. #42, Sottunga Church. #43, *Esox lucius.* #45, Diabase dike, Sottunga, Basskar. 2.10m, *Sciurus vulgaris.* 2.50m, *Cephalanthera longifolia.* #48, *Platichthys flesus.* #49, Pillow lava, Kumlinge, western Varpskar. #50, *Capreolus capreolus.* #51, Rouche Moutonne, Roda Kon, Lumparn. 6m, Folded gneiss, Sottunga, Gloskar. 13m, Tapestry, 1793. 14m, *Cypripedium calceolus.*

Perf. 13, 14 (#39-42, 44, 53), 15x14½ (10p, #38, 45, 49, 51-52)

1989-94 **Litho.**

No.	Type	Value	Color	Unused	Used
34	A26	10p	multicolored	15	15
35	A19	1.50m	multicolored	70	70
36	A20	1.50m	multicolored	75	75
37	A23	1.60m	multicolored	90	90
38	A25	1.60m	multicolored	55	55
39	A9	1.70m	multicolored	85	85
40	A9	1.80m	multicolored	85	85
41	A9	1.80m	multicolored	70	70
42	A9	1.80m	multicolored	60	60
43	A20	2m	multicolored	1.00	1.00
44	A22	2m	multicolored	1.00	1.00
45	A24	2m	multicolored	68	68
46	A23	2.10m	multicolored	1.15	1.15
47	A19	2.50m	multicolored	1.20	1.20
48	A20	2.70m	multicolored	1.35	1.35
49	A24	2.70m	multicolored	95	95
50	A23	2.90m	multicolored	1.60	1.60
51	A25	2.90m	multicolored	1.00	1.00
52	A24	6m	multicolored	2.05	2.05
53	A21	13m	multicolored	6.50	6.50
54	A19	14m	multicolored	6.50	6.50
			Nos. 34-54 (21)	31.03	31.03

Issued: 2.50m, 14m, #35, Apr. 10, 1989. 2.70m, #36, 43, Mar. 1, 1990. 13m, Apr. 19, 1990. 1.70m, #44, Sept. 10, 1990. 1.60m, 2.10m, #50, Mar. 3, 1991. #40, Oct. 9, 1991. #41 Oct. 5, 1992. #45, 49, 52, Sept. 3, 1993. #42, Oct. 8, 1993. 10p, #38, 51, Feb. 1, 1994.

Educational System of the Province, 350th Anniv. — A33

1989, May 31 **Litho.** ***Perf. 14***
57 A33 1.90m multicolored 90 90

Souvenir Sheet

1991 Aland Island Games — A34

Designs: a, Volleyball. b, Shooting. c, Soccer. d, Running.

1991, Apr. 5 **Litho.** ***Perf. 13x12½***
58 A34 2.10m Sheet of 4, #a.-d. 4.50 4.50

Autonomy of Aland, 70th Anniv. — A35

1991, June 4 ***Perf. 13***
59 A35 16m multicolored 7.75 7.75

Kayaking — A36

1991, June 4 ***Perf. 14***
60 A36 2.10m shown 1.00 1.00
61 A36 2.90m Cycling 1.40 1.40

Rev. Frans Peter Von Knorring (1792-1875), Educator — A37

Cape Horn Congress, Mariehamn, June 8-11 — A38

1992, Mar. 2 **Litho.** ***Perf. 13***
62 A37 (2) multicolored 85 85

Litho. & Engr.
Perf. 13½x14

63 A38 (1) multicolored 1.10 1.10

No. 62 sold for 1.60m, No. 63 for 2.10m. The numbers on the stamps represent the class of mail for which each was intended at time of release.

Lighthouses — A39

1992, May 8 **Litho.** ***Perf. 13***
Booklet Stamps

64 A39 2.10m Ranno 1.10 1.10
65 A39 2.10m Salskar 1.10 1.10
66 A39 2.10m Lagskar 1.10 1.10
67 A39 2.10m Market 1.10 1.10
a. Booklet pane of 4, #64-67 4.40

First Aland Provincial Parliament, 70th Anniv. — A40

1992, June 8 **Litho.** ***Perf. 13***
68 A40 3.40m multicolored 1.60 1.60

Joel Pettersson (1892-1937), Painter — A41

1992, June 8
69 A41 2.90m Landscape from Lemland 1.40 1.40
70 A41 16m Self-Portrait 7.55 7.55

Arms of Aland — A42

1993, Mar. 1 **Litho.** ***Perf. 14***
71 A42 1.60m gray, sepia & blue 58 58

Autonomy Act, Jan. 1.

Souvenir Sheet

Autonomous Postal Administration — A43

Designs: a, Inscriptions from old letter canceled in Kastelholm, vert. b, Mariehamn post office. c, Ferry, mail truck. d, New post office emblem, vert.

Perf. 12½x13, 14 (#b.-c.)
1993, Mar. 1 Litho., Engr. (#b.-c.)
72 A43 1.90m Sheet of 4, #a.-d. 2.70 2.70

Fiddler, Jan Karlsgarden Museum — A44

Folk Dresses — A45

Design: 2.30m, Boat Shed, Jan Karlsgarden Museum.

Perf. 13x12½, 12½x13
1993, May 7 Litho.
73 A44 2m multicolored 68 68
74 A44 2.30m multicolored 78 78

1993, June 1 *Perf. 12½*

Clothing from: 1.90m, Saltvik. 3.50m, Brando, Eckero, Mariehamn. 17m, Finstrom.

75 A45 1.90m multicolored 65 65
76 A45 3.50m multicolored 1.20 1.20
77 A45 17m multicolored 5.80 5.80

Butterflies — A46

Perf. 14 on 3 Sides
1994, Mar. 1 Litho.
Booklet Stamps
78 A46 2.30m Melitaea cinxia 80 80
79 A46 2.30m Quercusia querqus 80 80
80 A46 2.30m Parnassius mnemosyne 80 80
81 A46 2.30m Hesperia comma 80 80
a. Booklet pane, 2 each #78-81 3.25

FIUME

LOCATION — A city and surrounding territory on the Adriatic Sea
GOVT. — Formerly a part of Italy
AREA — 8 sq. mi.
POP. — 44,956 (estimated 1924)

Formerly a port of Hungary, Fiume was claimed by Yugoslavia and Italy following World War I. During the discussion, the poet, Gabriele d'Annunzio, organized his legionnaires and seized Fiume, together with the islands of Arbe, Carnaro and Veglia, in the name of Italy. Yugoslavia recognized Italy's claim and the city was annexed in January, 1924.

100 Filler = 1 Korona
100 Centesimi = 1 Corona (1919)
100 Centesimi = 1 Lira

Hungarian Stamps of 1916-18 Overprinted FIUME

1918, Dec. 2 Wmk. 137 *Perf. 15*
On Stamps of 1916
White Numerals
1 A8 10f rose 15.00 5.00
2 A8 15f violet 8.00 3.25

Nos. 1-2 overprints are handstamped.

On Stamps of 1916-18
Colored Numerals
3 A9 2f brown orange 22 15
4 A9 3f red violet 30 15
5 A9 5f green 30 15
6 A9 6f grnsh blue 30 15
7 A9 10f rose red 14.00 5.00
8 A9 15f violet 30 15
9 A9 20f gray brown 30 15
10 A9 25f deep blue 32 25
11 A9 35f brown 40 40
12 A9 40f olive green 6.00 1.25
White Numerals
13 A10 50f red vio & lil 32 25
14 A10 75f brt bl & pale bl 1.10 40
15 A10 80f grn & pale grn 85 25
16 A10 1k red brn & cl 4.50 1.10
17 A10 2k ol brn & bis 40 25
18 A10 3k dk vio & ind 3.50 1.10
19 A10 5k dk brn & lt brn 5.75 2.25
20 A10 10k vio brn & vio 40.00 22.50

Inverted or double overprints exist on most of Nos. 4-15.

On Stamps of 1918
21 A11 10f scarlet 32 15
22 A11 20f dark brown 32 15
23 A12 40f olive green 1.25 65

The overprint on Nos. 3-23 was applied both by press and handstamp. Values are for the less costly. Values of Nos. 7, 12, 20 and 23 are for handstamps.
Forgeries of Nos. 1-23 abound.

Postage Due Stamps of Hungary, 1915-20 Ovptd. & Surcharged in Black

FRANCO
FIUME
45

1919, Jan.
24 D1 45f on 6f green & red 1.10 50
25 D1 45f on 20f green & red 1.10 50

Hungarian Savings Bank Stamp Surcharged in Black — A2

1919, Jan. 29
26 A2 15f on 10f dk violet 1.10 50

"Italy" — A3

Italian Flag on Clock-Tower in Fiume — A4

"Revolution" A5

Sailor Raising Italian Flag at Fiume (1918) A6

1919 Unwmk. Litho. *Perf. 11½*
27 A3 2c dull blue 15 22
28 A3 3c gray brown 15 22
29 A3 5c yellow green 15 22
30 A4 10c rose 15 22
31 A4 15c violet 15 22
32 A4 20c green 15 22
33 A5 25c dark blue 15 22
34 A6 30c deep violet 15 22
35 A5 40c brown 18 30
36 A5 45c orange 15 22
37 A6 50c yellow green 15 22
38 A6 60c claret 15 22
39 A6 1cor brown orange 18 30
40 A6 2cor brt blue 22 35
41 A6 3cor orange red 22 35
42 A6 5cor deep brown 22 35
43 A6 10cor olive green 80 1.25
Nos. 27-43 (17) 3.47 5.32

The earlier printings of Jan. and Feb. are on thin grayish paper, the Mar. printing is on semi-transparent white paper, all in sheets of 70. An Apr. printing is on white paper of medium thickness in sheets of 100. Part-perf. examples of most of this series are known.
For surcharges see Nos. 58, 60, 64, 66-69.

A7

A8

A9

A10

1919, July 28 *Perf. 11½*
46 A7 5c yellow green 15 15
47 A8 10c rose 15 15
48 A9 30c violet 15 15
49 A10 40c yellow brown 42 42
50 A10 45c orange 15 15
51 A9 50c yellow green 15 15
52 A9 60c claret 15 15
a. Perf. 13x12½ 20.00 20.00
53 A9 10cor olive green 50 50
a. Perf. 13x12½ 20.00 20.00
b. Perf. 10½ 20.00 20.00
Set value 1.52 1.50

Five other denominations (25c, 1cor, 2cor, 3cor and 5cor) were not officially issued. Some copies of the 25c are known canceled.
For surcharges see Nos. 59, 61-63, 65, 70.

Stamps of 1919 Handstamp Surcharged FRANCO 5

1919-20
58 A4 5c on 20c green ('20) 15 15
59 A10 5c on 25c blue 15 15
60 A5 10c on 45c orange 15 15
61 A9 15c on 30c vio ('20) 15 15
62 A10 15c on 45c orange 15 15
63 A9 15c on 60c cl ('20) 15 18
64 A6 25c on 50c yel grn ('20) 60 65
65 A9 25c on 50c yel grn ('20) 15 18
66 A6 55c on 1cor brn org 60 65
67 A6 55c on 2cor brt bl 60 65
68 A6 55c on 3cor org red 60 65
69 A6 55c on 5cor dp brn 60 65
70 A9 55c on 10cor ol grn 80 75
Nos. 58-70 (13) 4.85 5.11

Semi-Postal Stamps of 1919 Surcharged:

Valore globale Cent. 5
a

Valore globale Cent. 45
b

1919-20
73 SP6(a) 5c on 5c green 15 15
74 SP6(a) 10c on 10c rose 15 15
75 SP6(a) 15c on 15c gray 15 15
76 SP6(a) 20c on 20c orange 15 15
77 SP9(a) 25c on 25c bl ('20) 15 15
78 SP7(b) 45c on 45c ol grn 15 15
79 SP7(b) 60c on 60c rose 15 15
80 SP7(b) 80c on 80c violet 18 18
81 SP7(b) 1cor on 1cor slate 18 18
82 SP8(a) 2cor on 2cor red brn 24 24
83 SP8(a) 3cor on 3cor blk brn 50 50
84 SP8(a) 5cor on 5cor yel brn 60 60
85 SP8(a) 10cor on 10cor dk vio ('20) 30 30
Nos. 73-85 (13) 3.05 3.05

Double or inverted surcharges, or imperf. varieties, exist on most of Nos. 73-85.
There were three settings of the surcharges on Nos. 73-85 except No. 77 which is known only with one setting.

Gabriele d'Annunzio — A11

Severing the Gordian Knot — A12

1920, Sept. 12 Typo. *Perf. 11½*
Pale Buff Background
86 A11 5c green 15 15
87 A11 10c carmine 15 15
88 A11 15c dark gray 20 20
89 A11 20c orange 20 20
90 A11 25c dark blue 32 32
91 A11 30c red brown 32 32
92 A11 45c olive gray 50 50
93 A11 50c lilac 50 50
94 A11 55c bister 50 50
95 A11 1 l black 80 80
96 A11 2 l red violet 1.65 1.65
97 A11 3 l dark green 1.65 1.65
98 A11 5 l brown 1.65 1.65
99 A11 10 l gray violet 2.00 2.00
Nos. 86-99 (14) 10.59 10.59

Counterfeits of Nos. 86 to 99 are plentiful.
For overprints see Nos. 134-148.

1920, Sept. 12

Designs: 10c, Ancient emblem of Fiume. 20c, Head of "Fiume." 25c, Hands holding daggers.

100 A12 5c green 5.00 5.00
101 A12 10c deep rose 1.00 1.00
102 A12 20c brown orange 1.25 1.00
103 A12 25c dark blue 10.00 7.25

Anniv. of the occupation of Fiume by d'Annunzio. They were available for franking the correspondence of the legionnaires on the day of issue only, Sept. 12, 1920.
Counterfeits of Nos. 100-103 are plentiful.
For overprints and surcharges see Nos. 104-133, E4-E9.

Nos. 100-103 Overprinted or Surcharged in Black or Red and New Values

Reggenza
Italiana
del
Carnaro

1920, Nov. 20

104	A12	1c on 5c green	15	15
105	A12	2c on 25c blue (R)	15	15
106	A12	5c green	15	15
107	A12	10c rose	20	20
108	A12	15c on 10c rose	20	20
109	A12	15c on 20c brn org	20	20
110	A12	15c on 25c blue (R)	25	25
111	A12	20c brown orange	25	25
112	A12	25c blue (R)	25	25
113	A12	25c blue (Bk)	25.00	21.00
114	A12	25c on 10c rose	85	85
115	A12	50c on 20c brn org	32	32
116	A12	55c on 5c green	32	32
117	A12	1 l on 10c rose	1.25	1.25
118	A12	1 l on 25c blue (R)	100.00	60.00
119	A12	2 l on 5c green	2.75	2.75
120	A12	5 l on 10c rose	15.00	8.50
121	A12	10 l on 20c brn org	60.00	21.00
		Nos. 104-121 (18)	207.29	117.79

The Fiume Legionnaires of d'Annunzio occupied the islands of Arbe and Veglia in the Gulf of Carnaro Nov. 13, 1920-Jan. 5, 1921.

Varieties of overprint or surcharge exist for most of Nos. 104-121.

Nos. 100-103 Overprinted or Surcharged at top **ARBE**

1920, Nov. 18

122	A12	5c green	85	65
123	A12	10c rose	1.00	85
124	A12	20c brown org	1.25	1.00
125	A12	25c deep blue	5.25	3.25
126	A12	50c on 20c brn org	1.75	1.10
127	A12	55c on 5c green	1.75	1.10
		Nos. 122-127 (6)	11.85	7.95

The overprint on Nos. 122-125 comes in two widths: 11mm and 14mm. Values are for the 11mm width.

Nos. 100-103 Overprinted or Surcharged at top **VEGLIA**

1920, Nov. 18

128	A12	5c green	50	40
129	A12	10c rose	60	50
130	A12	20c brown orange	80	60
131	A12	25c deep blue	3.25	2.00
132	A12	50c on 20c brn org	1.10	70
133	A12	55c on 5c green	1.10	70
		Nos. 128-133 (6)	7.35	4.90

The overprint on Nos. 128-131 comes in two widths: 17mm and 19mm. Values are for the 17mm width.

Nos. 122-133 exist with double and inverted overprints.

Counterfeits of these overprints exist.

Nos. 86-99 Overprinted

Governo
Provvisorio

1921, Feb. 2

Pale Buff Background

134	A11	5c green	15	15
135	A11	10c carmine	15	15
136	A11	15c dark gray	20	20
137	A11	20c orange	20	20
138	A11	25c dark blue	25	25
139	A11	30c red brown	25	25
140	A11	45c olive gray	32	32
141	A11	50c lilac	32	32
142	A11	55c bister	32	32
143	A11	1 l black	13.00	14.00
144	A11	2 l red violet	65	50
145	A11	3 l dark green	1.00	1.00
146	A11	5 l brown	1.25	50
147	A11	10 l gray violet	1.50	1.25

With Additional Surcharge LIRE UNA

148	A11	1 l on 30c red brown	32	20
		Nos. 134-148 (15)	19.88	19.61

Most of Nos. 134-143, 148 and E10-E11 exist with inverted or double overprint.

See Nos. E10-E11.

First Constituent Assembly

Nos. B4-B15 Overprinted

1921, Apr. 24

149	SP6	5c blue green	25	15
150	SP6	10c rose	20	15
151	SP6	15c gray	20	15
152	SP6	20c orange	20	15
153	SP7	45c olive green	32	22
154	SP7	60c car rose	40	32
155	SP7	80c brt violet	50	40

With Additional Overprint "L"

156	SP7	1 l on 1cor dk slate	65	55
157	SP8	2 l on 2cor red brn	2.00	32
158	SP8	3 l on 3cor black brn	3.25	4.00
159	SP8	5 l on 5cor yel brn	6.00	32
160	SP8	10 l on 10cor dk vio	6.00	6.50
		Nos. 149-160 (12)	19.97	13.23

The overprint exists inverted on several denominations.

Second Constituent Assembly

"Constitution" Issue of 1921 With Additional Overprint "1922"

1922

161	SP6	5c blue green	1.00	25
162	SP6	10c rose	15	15
163	SP6	15c gray	2.00	40
164	SP6	20c orange	15	15
165	SP7	45c olive grn	15	15
166	SP7	60c car rose	15	15
167	SP7	80c brt violet	15	15
168	SP7	1 l on 1cor dk slate	15	15
169	SP8	2 l on 2cor red brn	15	22
170	SP8	3 l on 3cor blk brn	15	32
171	SP8	5 l on 5cor yel brn	20	50
		Nos. 161-171 (11)	4.40	2.59

Nos. 161-171 have the overprint in heavier type than Nos. 149-160 and "IV" in Roman instead of sans-serif numerals.

The overprint exists inverted or double on almost all values.

Venetian Ship — A16

Roman Arch — A17

St. Vitus — A18

Rostral Column — A19

1923, Mar. 23 *Perf. 11½*

Pale Buff Background

172	A16	5c blue green	15	15
173	A16	10c violet	15	15
174	A16	15c brown	15	15
175	A17	20c orange red	15	15
176	A17	25c dark gray	15	15
177	A17	30c dark green	15	15
178	A18	50c dull blue	15	15
179	A18	60c rose	20	20
180	A18	1 l dark blue	20	20
181	A19	2 l violet brown	1.00	65
182	A19	3 l olive bister	5.25	4.00
183	A19	5 l yellow brown	2.25	2.00
		Nos. 172-183 (12)	9.95	8.10

Nos. 172-183 Overprinted

1924, Feb. 22

Pale Buff Background

184	A16	5c blue green	15	20
185	A16	10c violet	15	20
186	A16	15c brown	15	20
187	A17	20c orange red	15	20
188	A17	25c dk gray	15	20
189	A17	30c dk green	15	20
190	A18	50c dull blue	15	20
191	A18	60c red	15	20
192	A18	1 l dark blue	15	20
193	A19	2 l violet brown	32	65
194	A19	3 l olive	1.10	2.25
195	A19	5 l yellow brown	1.10	2.25
		Nos. 184-195 (12)	3.87	6.95

The overprint exists inverted on almost all values.

Nos. 172-183 Overprinted

22 Febb. 1924

1924, Mar. 1

Pale Buff Background

196	A16	5c blue green	15	20
197	A16	10c violet	15	20
198	A16	15c brown	15	20
199	A17	20c orange red	15	20
200	A17	25c dark gray	15	20
201	A17	30c dark green	15	20
202	A18	50c dull blue	15	20
203	A18	60c red	15	20
204	A18	1 l dark blue	15	20
205	A19	2 l violet brown	50	1.00
206	A19	3 l olive	50	1.00
207	A19	5 l yellow brown	50	1.00
		Set value	2.40	

Postage stamps of Fiume were superseded by stamps of Italy.

SEMI-POSTAL STAMPS

Semi-Postal Stamps of Hungary, 1916-17 Overprinted FIUME

1918, Dec. 2 **Wmk. 137** ***Perf. 15***

B1	SP3	10f + 2f rose	55	20
a.		Inverted overprint	18.00	5.75
B2	SP4	15f + 2f dl vio	60	20
a.		Inverted overprint	18.00	4.50
B3	SP5	40f + 2f brn car	85	60
a.		Inverted overprint	18.00	4.50

Examples of Nos. B1-B3 with overprint handstamped sell for higher prices.

Statue of Romulus and Remus Being Suckled by Wolf — SP6

Venetian Galley — SP7

Church of St. Mark's, Venice — SP8

Perf. 11½

1919, May 18 **Unwmk.** **Typo.**

B4	SP6	5c +5 l bl grn	90	95
B5	SP6	10c +5 l rose	90	95
B6	SP6	15c +5 l dk gray	90	95
B7	SP6	20c +5 l orange	90	95
B8	SP7	45c +5 l ol grn	90	95
B9	SP7	60c +5 l car rose	90	95
B10	SP7	80c +5 l brt vio	90	95
B11	SP7	1cor +5 l dk slate	90	95
B12	SP8	2cor +5 l red brn	90	95
B13	SP8	3cor +5 l blk brn	90	95
B14	SP8	5cor +5 l yel brn	90	95
B15	SP8	10cor +5 l dk vio	90	95
		Nos. B4-B15 (12)	10.80	11.40

200th day of peace. The surtax aided Fiume students in Italy. "Posta di Fiume" is printed on the back of Nos. B4-B16.

The surtax is shown on the stamps as "LIRE 5" but actually was 5cor.

For surcharges and overprints see Nos. 73-85, 149-171, J15-J26.

Dr. Antonio Grossich — SP9

1919, Sept. 20

B16	SP9	25c + 2 l blue	15	15

Surtax for the Dr. Grossich Foundation.

SPECIAL DELIVERY STAMPS

Special Delivery Stamp of Hungary, 1916, Overprinted like Nos. 1-23

1918, Dec. 2 **Wmk. 137** ***Perf. 15***

E1	SD1	2f gray green & red	25	15

Handstamped overprints sell for more.

SD3

Perf. 11½

1920, Sept. 12 **Unwmk.** **Typo.**

E2	SD3	30c slate blue	50	50
E3	SD3	50c rose	50	50

For overprints see Nos. E10-E11.

Nos. 102 and 100 Surcharged

Reggenza
Italiana
del
Carnaro
50 50
ESPRESSO

1920, Nov.

E4	A12	30c on 20c brn org	12.00	8.00
E5	A12	50c on 5c green	4.00	2.00

Same Surcharge as on Nos. 124, 122

E6	A12	30c on 20c brn org	19.00	9.75
E7	A12	50c on 5c green	5.50	6.25

Overprint on Nos. E6-E7 is 11mm wide.

Same Surcharge as on Nos. 130, 128

E8	A12	30c on 20c brn org	19.00	9.75
E9	A12	50c on 5c green	5.50	6.25

Overprint on Nos. E8-E9 is 17mm wide.

Nos. E2 and E3 Overprinted

Governo Provvisorio

1921, Feb. 2

E10	SD3	30c slate blue	50	50
E11	SD3	50c rose	50	50

Fiume in 16th Century
SD4

1923, Mar. 23 *Perf. 11, 11½*

E12	SD4	60c rose & buff	32	32
E13	SD4	2 l dk bl & buff	32	32

Nos. E12-E13 Overprinted

1924, Feb. 22

E14	SD4	60c car & buff	32	65
E15	SD4	2 l dk bl & buff	32	65

Nos. E12-E13 Overprinted

1924, Mar. 1

E16	SD4	60c car & buff	32	65
E17	SD4	2 l dk bl & buff	32	70

POSTAGE DUE STAMPS

Postage Due Stamps of Hungary, 1915-1916, Overprinted FIUME

1918, Dec. **Wmk. 137** *Perf. 15*

J1	D1	6f green & black	47.50	14.00
J2	D1	12f green & black	35.00	14.00
J3	D1	50f green & black	20.00	7.50
J4	D1	1f green & red	6.00	3.50
J5	D1	2f green & red	20	15
J6	D1	5f green & red	2.75	1.00
J7	D1	6f green & red	20	15
J8	D1	10f green & red	3.25	1.25
J9	D1	12f green & red	20	15
J10	D1	15f green & red	5.00	3.25
J11	D1	20f green & red	20	15
J12	D1	30f green & red	4.00	2.75
		Nos. J4-J12 (9)	21.80	12.35

The overprint on Nos. J1-J12 was applied both by press and handstamp. Values are for the less costly. Inverted and double overprints exist. Excellent forgeries exist.

Eagle — D2

Perf. 11½

1919, July 28 **Unwmk.** **Typo.**

J13	D2	2c brown	15	15
J14	D2	5c brown	15	15
		Set value	20	20

Semi-Postal Stamps of 1919 with Overprint "Valore Globale" Surcharged:

1921, Mar. 21

J15	SP6	2c on 15c gray	15	20
J16	SP6	4c on 10c rose	15	15
J17	SP9	5c on 25c blue	15	15
J18	SP6	6c on 20c orange	15	15
J19	SP6	10c on 20c orange	25	32

Surcharged:

J20	SP7	20c on 45c olive grn	20	25
J21	SP7	30c on 1cor dk slate	20	30
J22	SP7	40c on 80c violet	15	20
J23	SP7	50c on 60c carmine	15	25
J24	SP7	60c on 45c olive grn	20	25
J25	SP7	80c on 45c olive grn	20	30

Surcharged like Nos. J15-J19

J26	SP8	1 l on 2cor red brown	32	50
		Nos. J15-J26 (12)	2.27	3.02

See note below No. 85 regarding settings of "Valore Globale" overprint.

NEWSPAPER STAMPS

Newspaper Stamp of Hungary, 1914, Overprinted like Nos. 1-23

1918, Dec. 2 **Wmk. 137** *Imperf.*

P1	N5	(2f) orange	35	24

Handstamped overprints sell for more.

Eagle — N1

1919 **Unwmk.** *Perf. 11½*

P2	N1	2c deep buff	35	60

Re-engraved

P3	N1	2c deep buff	60	1.10

In the re-engraved stamp the top of the "2" is rounder and broader, the feet of the eagle show clearly and the diamond at bottom has six lines instead of five.

Steamer
N2

1920, Sept. 12

P4	N2	1c gray green	22	38

No. P4 exists imperf.

See note on FIUME-KUPA Zone, Italian Occupation, after Yugoslavia No. NJ22.

FRANCE

LOCATION — Western Europe
GOVT. — Republic
AREA — 210,033 sq. mi.
POP. — 54,539,000 (est. 1984)
CAPITAL — Paris

100 Centimes = 1 Franc

Catalogue values for unused stamps in this country are for Never Hinged items, beginning with Scott 299 in the regular postage section, Scott B42 in the semi-postal section, Scott C18 in the airpost section, Scott CB1 in the airpost semi-postal section, Scott J69 in the postage due section, Scott M10 in the military stamps section, Scott 1O1 in the section for official stamps for the Council of Europe, Scott 2O1 for the section for UNESCO, Scott S1 for franchise stamps, Scott N27 for occupation stamps, and Scott 2N1 for AMG stamps.

Values of early French stamps vary according to condition. Quotations for Nos. 1-48 are for fine to very fine copies. Very fine to superb specimens sell at much higher prices, and inferior or poor copies sell at reduced prices, depending on the condition of the individual specimen.

Ceres — A1

FORTY CENTIMES

Type I — Type II

1849-50 Typo. Unwmk. *Imperf.*

No.		Description	Unused	Used
1	A1	10c bis, *yelsh* ('50)	*1,000.*	225.00
a.		10c dark bister, *yelsh*	1,150.	275.00
b.		10c greenish bister	1,900.	375.00
c.		Tête beche pair	*40,000.*	*8,500.*
2	A1	15c yel grn, *grnsh* ('50)	*8,500.*	875.00
a.		15c green, *grnsh*	*8,750.*	900.00
b.		Tête bêche pair		*95,000.*
3	A1	20c blk, *yelsh*	200.00	37.50
a.		20c black	250.00	42.50
b.		20c black, *buff*	1,150.	260.00
c.		Tête bêche pair	*4,000.*	*4,000.*
4	A1	20c dark blue	*1,050.*	
a.		20c blue, *bluish*	*1,150.*	
b.		20c blue, *yelsh*	*1,400.*	
c.		Tête bêche pair	*21,000.*	
6	A1	25c lt bl, *bluish*	*2,600.*	27.50
a.		25c blue, *bluish* ('50)	*3,200.*	35.00
b.		25c blue, *yelsh*	*2,600.*	37.50
c.		Tête bêche pair	*60,000.*	*6,250.*
7	A1	40c org, *yelsh* (I) ('50)	*1,500.*	375.00
a.		40c org ver, *yelsh* (I)	*1,900.*	475.00
b.		40c orange, *yelsh* (II)	*10,500.*	*2,600.*
c.		Pair, types I and II	*16,000.*	*5,600.*
8	A1	1fr dull org red	*21,000.*	*9,500.*
a.		1fr ver, *yelsh*	*38,500.*	*14,000.*
b.		Tête bêche pair	*160,000.*	*115,000.*
c.		1fr pale ver ("Vervelle")	*12,500.*	
9	A1	1fr dk car, *yelsh*	*4,500.*	625.00
a.		Tête bêche pair	*70,000.*	*15,000.*
b.		1fr brown carmine	*6,250.*	950.00
c.		1fr light carmine	*5,000.*	700.00

No. 4, which lacks gum, was not issued due to a rate change to 25c after the stamps were prepared.

An ungummed sheet of No. 8c was found in 1895 among the effects of Anatole A. Hulot, the printer. It was sold to Ernest Vervelle, a Parisian dealer, by whose name the stamps are known.

See Nos. 329-329e, 612-613, 624.

Nos. 1, 4a, 6a, 7 and 13 are of similar designs and colors to French Colonies Nos. 9, 11, 12, 14, and 8. There are numerous shades of each. They can seldom be correctly allocated except by the cancellations. Because of the date of issue the Colonies stamps are similar in shades and papers to the perforated French stamps, Nos. 23a, 54, 57-59, and are not as clearly printed. Except for No. 13, unused, the French Colonies stamps sell for much less than the values shown here for identifiable French versions.

1862 Re-issue

No.		Description	Unused
1d	A1	10c bister	175.00
2d	A1	15c yellow green	250.00
3d	A1	20c black, *yellowish*	160.00
4d	A1	20c blue	160.00
6d	A1	25c blue	160.00
7d	A1	40c orange (I)	250.00
7e	A1	40c orange (II)	*7,000.*
9d	A1	1fr pale lake	260.00

The re-issues are in lighter colors and on whiter paper than the originals. An official imitation of the essay, 25c on 20c blue, was made at the same time as the re-issues.

President Louis Napoleon — A2

Emperor Napoleon III — A3

1852

No.		Description	Unused	Used
10	A2	10c pale bister, *yelsh*	*12,500.*	325.
a.		10c dark bister, *yelsh*	*17,500.*	450.
11	A2	25c blue, *bluish*	*1,750.*	35.

1862 Re-issue

No.		Description	Unused
10b	A2	10c bister	200.00
11a	A2	25c blue	165.00

The re-issues are in lighter colors and on whiter paper than the originals.

1853-60 *Imperf.*

Die I. The curl above the forehead directly below "R" of "EMPIRE" is made up of two lines very close together, often appearing to form a single thick line. There is no shading across the neck.

Die II. The curl is made of two distinct, more widely separated lines. There are lines of shading across the upper neck.

No.		Description	Unused	Used
12	A3	1c ol grn, *pale bl* '60	110.00	50.00
a.		1c brnz grn, *pale bluish*	125.00	55.00
13	A3	5c grn, *grnsh* (I) ('54)	450.00	50.00
14	A3	10c bis, *yelsh* (I)	210.00	5.75
a.		10c yellow, *yelsh* (I)	1,250.	57.50
b.		10c bister brn, *yelsh* (I)	325.00	21.00
c.		10c bister, *yelsh* (II) ('60)	325.00	22.50
15	A3	20c bl, *bluish* (I) ('54)	110.00	70
a.		20c dark bl, *bluish* (I)	175.00	1.10
b.		20c milky blue (I)	190.00	10.50
c.		20c blue, *lilac* (I)	2,500.	62.50
d.		20c blue, *bluish* (II) ('60)	260.00	3.75
16	A3	20c bl, *grnsh* (I)	*2,750.*	125.00
a.		20c blue, *greenish* (II)	*2,750.*	160.00
17	A3	25c bl, *bluish* (I)	1,350.	190.00
18	A3	40c org, *yelsh* (I)	1,000.	9.50
a.		40c org ver, *yellowish*	*1,400.*	16.00
19	A3	80c lake, *yelsh* (I) ('54)	1,750.	35.00
a.		Tête bêche pair	*115,000.*	*11,000.*
20	A3	80c rose, *pnksh* (I) ('60)	675.00	35.00
a.		Tete bêche pair	*21,000.*	*5,600.*
21	A3	1fr lake, *yelsh* (I)	*3,250.*	*1,900.*
a.		Tête bêche pair	*125,000.*	*60,000.*

Most values of the 1853-60 issue are known unofficially rouletted, pin-perf., perf. 7 and percé en scie.

1862 Re-issue

No.		Description	Unused
17c	A3	25c blue (I)	175.
20c	A3	80c rose (I)	950.
21c	A3	1fr lake (I)	775.
d.		Tête bêche pair	*9,500.*

The re-issues are in lighter colors and on whiter paper than the originals.

1862-71 *Perf. 14x13½*

No.		Description	Unused	Used
22	A3	1c ol grn, *pale bl* (II)	70.00	27.50
a.		1c bronze grn, *pale bl* (II)	70.00	30.00
23	A3	5c yel grn, *grnsh* (I)	105.00	6.25
a.		5c deep green, *grnsh* (I)	130.00	8.75
24	A3	5c grn, *pale bl* ('71) (I)	700.00	52.50
25	A3	10c bis, *yelsh* (II)	600.00	2.75
a.		10c yel brn, *yelsh* (II)	700.00	3.50
26	A3	20c bl, *bluish* (II)	165.00	50
a.		Tête bêche pair (II)	3,000.	700.00
27	A3	40c org, *yelsh* (I)	700.00	4.50
28	A3	80c rose, *pnksh* (I)	700.00	30.00
a.		80c brt rose, *pinkish* (I)	700.00	45.00
b.		Tête bêche pair (I)	*7,750.*	*3,000.*

No. 26a imperf is from a trial printing.

Napoleon III
A4 A5

Napoleon
A6

1863-70 *Perf. 14x13½*

No.		Description	Unused	Used
29	A4	1c brnz grn, *pale bl* ('70)	15.00	8.75
a.		1c olive green, *pale blue*	17.00	10.50
b.		Imperf.	700.00	
30	A4	2c red brn, *yelsh*	40.00	19.00
a.		Imperf.	130.00	
31	A4	4c gray	95.00	37.50
a.		Tete beche pair	*7,000.*	*5,250.*
b.		Imperf.	105.00	
32	A5	10c bis, *yelsh* ('67)	190.00	3.50
a.		Imperf.	105.00	
33	A5	20c bl, *bluish* ('67)	115.00	90
a.		Imperf.	160.00	
34	A5	30c brn, *yelsh* ('67)	400.00	12.50
a.		30c dk brn, *yellowish*	575.00	26.00
c.		Imperf.	105.00	
35	A5	40c org, *yelsh* ('68)	450.00	7.75
a.		40c pale org, *yellowish*	475.00	9.00
b.		Imperf.	140.00	
36	A5	80c rose, *pnksh* ('68)	475.00	14.00
a.		80c carmine, *yellowish*	550.00	22.50
b.		Imperf.	250.00	
37	A6	5fr gray lil, *lav* ('69)	*3,500.*	600.00
a.		"5" and "F" omitted		*32,500.*
b.		Imperf.	*5,250.*	

No. 33 exists in two types, differing in the size of the dots at either side of POSTES.

On No. 37, the "5" and "F" vary in height from 3¾mm to 4½mm. All known copies of No. 37a are more or less damaged.

The imperforate varieties of Nos. 29-36 constitute the "Rothschild Issue," said to have been authorized exclusively for the banker to use on his correspondence. Used copies exist.

No. 29 was reprinted in 1887 by authority of Granet, Minister of Posts. The reprints show a yellowish shade under the ultraviolet lamp. Value $850.

For surcharge see No. 49.

Ceres
A7 A8

A9

A10

A11

Bordeaux Issue

On the lithographed stamps, except for type I of the 20c, the shading on the cheek and neck is in lines or dashes, not in dots. On the typographed stamps the shading is in dots. The 2c, 10c and 20c (types II and III) occur in two or more types. The most easily distinguishable are:

2c- Type A. To the left of and within the top of the left "2" are lines of shading composed of dots.

2c- Type B. These lines of dots are replaced by solid lines.

10c- Type A. The inner frame lines are of the same thickness as all other frame lines.

10c- Type B. The inner frame lines are much thicker than the others.

Three Types of the 20c.

A9- The inscriptions in the upper and lower labels are small and there is quite a space between the upper label and the circle containing the head. There is also very little shading under the eye and in the neck.

A10- The inscriptions in the labels are similar to those of the first type, the shading under the eye and in the neck is heavier and the upper label and circle almost touch.

A11- The inscriptions in the labels are much larger than those of the two preceding types, and are similar to those of the other values of the same type in the set.

1870-71 Litho. *Imperf.*

38	A7	1c ol grn, *pale bl*	35.00	60.00
a.		1c bronze green, *pale blue*	85.00	87.50
39	A7	2c red brn, *yelsh* (B)	125.00	150.00
a.		2c brick red, *yelsh* (B)	675.00	600.00
b.		2c chestnut, *yelsh* (B)	950.00	625.00
c.		2c chocolate, *yelsh* (A)	625.00	600.00
40	A7	4c gray	165.00	150.00
41	A8	5c grn, *grnsh*	175.00	100.00
a.		5c yel green, *greenish*	160.00	120.00
b.		5c emerald, *greenish*	1,750.	700.00
42	A8	10c bis, *yelsh* (A)	500.00	45.00
a.		10c bister, *yellowish* (B)	575.00	62.50
43	A9	20c bl, *bluish*	*9,250.*	475.00
a.		20c dark blue, *bluish*	*7,750.*	600.00
44	A10	20c bl, *bluish*	550.00	40.00
a.		20c dark blue, *bluish*	800.00	60.00
b.		20c ultra, *bluish*	*11,500.*	*2,100.*
45	A11	20c bl, *bluish* ('71)	600.00	12.50
a.		20c ultra, *bluish*	1,600.	475.00
46	A8	30c brn, *yelsh*	225.00	140.00
a.		30c blk brn, *yelsh*	1,050.	575.00
47	A8	40c org, *yelsh*	300.00	77.50
a.		40c yel orange, *yelsh*	275.00	77.50
b.		40c red orange, *yelsh*	425.00	125.00
c.		40c scarlet, *yelsh*	*3,750.*	*1,350.*
48	A8	80c rose, *pinkish*	325.00	165.00
a.		80c dull rose, *pinkish*	450.00	165.00

All values of the 1870 issue are known rouletted, pin-perf. and perf. 14, unofficially.

See Nos. 50-53.

A12

Blue Surcharge

1871 Typo. *Perf. 14x13½*

49 A12 10c on 10c bister 1,000.

#49 was never placed in use. Counterfeits exist.

A13

A14

Two types of the 40c as in the 1849-50 issue.

1870-73 Typo. *Perf. 14x13½*

50	A7	1c ol grn, *pale bl*	18.00	8.50
a.		1c bronze grn, *pale bl* ('72)	27.50	8.75
51	A7	2c red brn, *yelsh* ('70)	35.00	8.50
52	A7	4c gray ('70)	250.00	27.50
53	A7	5c yel grn, *pale bl* ('72)	85.00	5.25
a.		5c green	87.50	6.25
54	A13	10c bis, *yelsh*	250.00	35.00
a.		Tête beche pair	*2,750.*	*1,400.*
55	A13	10c bis, *rose* ('73)	210.00	6.00
a.		Tête bêche pair	2,100.	1,050.
56	A13	15c bis, *yelsh* ('71)	210.00	2.75
a.		Tête bêche pair	*19,000.*	*5,000.*
57	A13	20c dl bl, *bluish*	160.00	4.25
a.		20c bright blue, *bluish*	170.00	6.25
b.		Tête bêche pair	1,900.	950.00
58	A13	25c bl, *bluish* ('71)	65.00	65
a.		25c dk bl, *bluish*	70.00	70
b.		Tête bêche pair	*3,500.*	*1,750.*
59	A13	40c org, *yelsh* (I)	300.00	3.25
a.		40c orange yel, *yelsh* (I)	400.00	4.25
b.		40c orange, *yelsh* (II)	1,600.	105.00
c.		40c orange yel, *yelsh* (II)	1,600.	105.00
d.		Pair, types I and II	*2,750.*	350.00

No. 58 exists in three main plate varieties, differing in one or another of the flower-like corner ornaments.

Margins on this issue are extremely small.

Nos. 54, 57 and 58 were reprinted imperf. in 1887. See note after No. 37.

1872-75

Larger Numerals

60	A14	10c bis, *rose* ('75)	190.00	6.00
a.		Cliché of 15c in plate of 10c	*2,250.*	*2,600.*
b.		Pair, #60, 60a	*3,750.*	*3,750.*
61	A14	15c bister ('73)	175.00	3.25
62	A14	30c brn, *yelsh*	350.00	4.25
63	A14	80c rose, *pnksh*	375.00	8.75

Peace and Commerce ("Type Sage") — A15

Type I. The "N" of "INV" is under the "B" of "REPUBLIQUE."

Type II. The "N" of "INV" is under the "U" of "REPUBLIQUE."

1876-78

Type I

64	A15	1c grn, *grnsh*	80.00	37.50
65	A15	2c grn, *grnsh*	875.00	190.00
66	A15	4c grn, *grnsh*	75.00	32.50
67	A15	5c grn, *grnsh*	325.00	32.50
68	A15	10c grn, *grnsh*	475.00	17.50
69	A15	15c gray lil, *grysh*	475.00	12.50
70	A15	20c red brn, *straw*	350.00	12.00
71	A15	20c bl, *bluish*	*17,500.*	
72	A15	25c ultra, *bluish*	*5,500.*	37.50
73	A15	30c brn, *yelsh*	210.00	5.75
74	A15	40c red, *straw* ('78)	210.00	21.00
75	A15	75c car, *rose*	425.00	7.75
76	A15	1fr brnz grn, *straw*	375.00	7.00

No. 71 was never put into use.

The reprints of No. 71 are type II. They are imperforate or with forged perforation.

For overprints and surcharges see Offices in China Nos. 1-17, J7-J10, J20-J22, Offices in Egypt, Alexandria 1-15, Port Said 1-17, Offices in Turkish Empire 1-7, Cavalle 1-8, Dedeagh 1-8, Port Lagos 1-5, Vathy 1-9, Offices in Zanzibar 1-33, 50-54, Offices in Morocco 1-8, and Madagascar 14-27.

Imperf.

64a	A15	1c	110.00
65a	A15	2c	950.00
66a	A15	4c	110.00
67a	A15	5c	375.00
68a	A15	10c	425.00
69a	A15	15c	500.00
70a	A15	20c	300.00
73a	A15	30c	190.00
74a	A15	40c	190.00
75a	A15	75c	375.00
76a	A15	1fr	325.00

1876-77

Type II

77	A15	2c grn, *grnsh*	57.50	13.00
78	A15	5c grn, *grnsh*	13.00	20
a.		Imperf.	130.00	
79	A15	10c grn, *grnsh*	600.00	150.00
80	A15	15c gray lil, *grysh*	325.00	90
81	A15	25c ultra, *bluish*	250.00	20
a.		25c blue, *bluish*	250.00	35
b.		Pair, types I & II	*22,500.*	*7,000.*
c.		Imperf.	250.00	
82	A15	30c yel brn, *yelsh*	22.50	55
a.		30c brown, *yellowish*	25.00	55
b.		Imperf.	375.00	
83	A15	75c car, *rose* ('77)	1,100.	60.00
84	A15	1fr brnz grn, *straw* ('77)	50.00	3.75
a.		Imperf.	375.00	

1877-80

86	A15	1c blk, *lil bl*	1.60	42
a.		1c black, *gray blue*	1.75	45
b.		Imperf.	47.50	
87	A15	1c blk, *Prus bl* ('80)	*5,250.*	*2,750.*

Values for No. 87 are for copies with the perfs touching the design on at least one side.

88	A15	2c brn, *straw*	2.25	52
a.		2c brown, *yellow*	3.25	1.00
b.		Imperf.	47.50	
89	A15	3c yel, *straw* ('78)	150.00	32.50
a.		Imperf.	85.00	
90	A15	4c claret, *lav*	2.25	1.10
a.		4c vio brown, *lavender*	3.75	2.00
b.		Imperf.	47.50	
91	A15	10c blk, *lavender*	21.00	60
a.		10c black, *rose lilac*	22.50	90
b.		10c black, *lilac*	22.50	90
c.		Imperf.	52.50	
92	A15	15c blue ('78)	12.50	20
a.		Imperf.	67.50	
b.		15c blue, *bluish*	190.00	2.50
93	A15	25c blk, *red* ('78)	550.00	16.00
a.		Imperf.	500.00	
94	A15	35c blk, *yel* ('78)	225.00	25.00
a.		35c blk, *yel org*	325.00	25.00
b.		Imperf.	275.00	
95	A15	40c red, *straw* ('80)	37.50	90
a.		Imperf.	175.00	
96	A15	5fr vio, *lav*	400.00	60.00
a.		5fr red lilac, *lavender*	400.00	62.50
b.		Imperf.	550.00	

1879-90

97	A15	3c gray, *grysh* ('80)	1.60	70
a.		Imperf.	47.50	
98	A15	20c red, *yel grn*	21.00	1.60
a.		20c red, *deep green* ('84)	27.50	3.25
b.		Imperf.	57.50	
99	A15	25c yel, *straw*	175.00	2.75
a.		Imperf.	200.00	
100	A15	25c blk, *pale rose* ('86)	22.50	32
a.		Imperf.	85.00	
101	A15	50c rose, *rose* ('90)	110.00	70
a.		50c carmine, *rose*	87.50	70
102	A15	75c dp vio, *org* ('90)	125.00	21.00
a.		75c deep violet, *yellow*	135.00	25.00

1892

Quadrille Paper

103	A15	15c blue	7.50	20
a.		Imperf.	95.00	

1898-1900

Ordinary Paper

104	A15	5c yel grn	8.50	20
a.		Imperf.	62.50	

Type I

105	A15	5c yel grn	6.25	45
a.		Imperf.	225.00	
106	A15	10c blk, *lavender*	10.50	1.40
a.		Imperf.	125.00	
107	A15	50c car, *rose*	87.50	21.00
108	A15	2fr brn, *azure* ('00)	77.50	25.00
b.		Imperf.	*1,450.*	

See No. 226.

Reprints of A15, type II, were made in 1887 and left imperf. See note after No. 37. Value for set of 27, $2,750.

Liberty, Equality, Fraternity — A16

"The Rights of Man" — A17

Liberty and Peace — A18

1900-29 *Perf. 14x13½*

109	A16	1c gray	35	15
110	A16	2c vio brn	50	15
111	A16	3c orange	55	15
a.		3c red	12.50	3.25
112	A16	4c yel brn	2.50	48
113	A16	5c green	1.90	15
b.		Booklet pane of 10	25.00	
114	A16	7½c lilac ('26)	48	20
115	A16	10c lilac ('29)	3.25	15
116	A17	10c carmine	16.00	48
a.		Numerals printed separately	19.00	6.25
117	A17	15c orange	5.75	18
118	A17	20c brn vio	47.50	3.50
119	A17	25c blue	70.00	58
a.		Numerals printed separately	85.00	4.50
120	A17	30c violet	47.50	3.50
121	A18	40c red & pale bl	11.00	32
122	A18	45c grn & bl ('06)	14.00	58
123	A18	50c bis brn & lav	77.50	65
124	A18	60c vio & ultra ('20)	90	28
125	A18	1fr cl & ol grn	22.50	18
126	A18	2fr gray vio & yel	475.00	35.00
127	A18	2fr org & pale bl ('20)	32.50	20
128	A18	3fr vio & bl ('25)	16.00	3.25
129	A18	3fr brt vio & rose ('27)	40.00	70
130	A18	5fr dk bl & buff	65.00	1.75
131	A18	10fr grn & red ('26)	75.00	7.50
132	A18	20fr mag & grn ('26)	110.00	16.00
		Nos. 109-132 (24)	1,135.	76.08

In the 10c and 25c values, the first printings show the numerals to have been impressed by a second operation, whereas, in later printings, the numerals were inserted in the plates. Two operations were used for all 20c and 30c, and one operation for the 15c.

No. 114 was issued precanceled only. Values for precanceled stamps in first column are for those which have not been through the post and have original gum. Values in the second column are for postally used, gumless stamps.

See Offices in China Nos. 34, 40-44, Offices in Crete 1-5, 10-15, Offices in Egypt, Alexandria 16-20, 26-30, 77, 84-86, Port Said 18-22, 28-32, 83, 90-92, Offices in Turkish Empire 21-26, 31-33, Cavalle 9, Dedeagh 9.

For overprints and surcharge see Nos. 197, 246, C1-C2, M1, P7. Offices in China 57, 62-65, 71, 73, 75, 83-85, J14, J27, Offices in Crete 17-20, Offices in Egypt, Alexandria 31-32, 34-35, 40-48, 57-64, 66, 71-73, Port Said 33, 35 40, 43, 46-57, 59, 65-71, 73, 78-80, Offices in Turkish Empire 35-38, 47-49, Cavalle 13-15, Dedeagh 16-18, Offices in Zanzibar 39, 45-49, 55, Offices in Morocco 11-15, 20-22, 26-29, 35-41, 49-54, 72-76, 84-85, 87-89, B6.

Imperf.

109a A16 1c 26.00
110a A16 2c 55.00
111b A16 3c 40.00
112a A16 4c 110.00
113a A16 5c 47.50
116b A17 10c #116 or 116a 190.00 *125.00*
117a A17 15c 140.00 *100.00*
119b A17 25c #119 or 119a 475.00 *250.00*
121a A18 40c 140.00 95.00
122a A18 45c 140.00 100.00
123a A18 50c 225.00 175.00
124a A18 60c 325.00 240.00
125a A18 1fr 140.00 100.00
126a A18 2fr *1,600.* *950.00*
127a A18 2fr 375.00 275.00
129a A18 3fr 275.00
130a A18 5fr 700.00 375.00

Flat Plate & Rotary Press

The following stamps were printed by both flat plate and rotary press: Nos. 109-113, 144-146, 163, 166, 168, 170, 177-178, 185, 192 and P7.

"Rights of Man" — A19

Sower — A20

1902

133 A19 10c rose red 17.50 28
134 A19 15c pale red 7.00 20
135 A19 20c brn vio 72.50 10.00
136 A19 25c blue 80.00 1.10
137 A19 30c lilac 200.00 7.00
Nos. 133-137 (5) 377.00 18.58

Imperf., Without Gum

133a A19 10c rose red 150.00
134a A19 15c pale red 200.00
135a A19 20c brown violet 300.00
137a A19 30c lilac 475.00

See Offices in China Nos. 35-39, Offices in Crete 6-10, Offices in Egypt, Alexandria 21-25, 81-82, Port Said 23-27, 87-88, Offices in Turkish Empire 26-30, Cavalle 10-11, Dedeagh 10-11. For overprints and surcharges see Nos. M2, Offices in China 45, 58-61, 66-70, 76-82, J15-J16, J28-J30, Offices in Crete 16, Offices in Egypt, Alexandria 33, 36-39, 49-50, 52-56, 65, 67-70, B1-B4, Port Said 34, 41-42, 44-45, 57, 60-64, 77, 74-77, B1-B4, Offices in Turkish Empire 34, 39, Cavalle 12, Dedeagh 15, Offices in Zanzibar 40-44, 56-59, Offices in Morocco 16-19, 30-34, 42-48, 77-83, 86, B1-B5, B7, B9.

1903-38

138 A20 10c rose 6.25 15
139 A20 15c slate grn 2.50 15
b. Booklet pane of 10 37.50
140 A20 20c vio brn 62.50 1.20
141 A20 25c dull blue 67.50 85
142 A20 30c violet 160.00 3.75
143 A20 45c lt vio ('26) 4.25 48
144 A20 50c dull bl ('21) 17.00 35
145 A20 50c gray grn ('26) 6.75 30
146 A20 50c ver ('26) 45 15
a. Booklet pane of 10 9.00
147 A20 50c grnsh bl ('38) 1.50 15
148 A20 60c lt vio ('24) 6.75 80
149 A20 65c rose ('24) 3.25 60
150 A20 65c gray grn ('27) 9.00 90
151 A20 75c rose lil ('26) 5.25 30
152 A20 80c ver ('26) 40.00 5.25
153 A20 85c ver ('24) 16.00 60
154 A20 1fr dull blue ('26) 6.25 22
Nos. 138-154 (17) 415.20 16.20

See Nos. 941, 942A. For surcharges and overprints see Nos. 229-230, 232-233, 236, 256, B25, B29, B32, B36, B40, M3-M4, M6, Offices in Turkish Empire 46, 54.

Imperf.

138a A20 10c 75.00 47.50
139a A20 15c 75.00 47.50
140a A20 20c 175.00 95.00
141a A20 25c 150.00 75.00
142a A20 30c 525.00 260.00
144a A20 50c 67.50
145a A20 50c 135.00
146b A20 50c 90.00
147a A20 50c 60.00
149a A20 65c 185.00
151a A20 75c 475.00

Ground — A21

No Ground — A22

1906

With Ground Under Feet of Figure

155 A21 10c red 4.00 60
a. Imperf., pair, without gum 225.00

1906-37

TEN AND THIRTY-FIVE CENTIMES

Type I- Numerals and letters of the inscriptions thin.

Type II- Numerals and letters thicker.

No Ground Under the Feet

156 A22 1c olive bis ('33) 15 15
157 A22 2c dk green ('33) 15 15
158 A22 3c ver ('33) 15 15
159 A22 5c green 1.90 15
a. Imperf., pair 18.00
b. Booklet pane of 10 32.50
160 A22 5c orange ('21) 1.50 15
a. Booklet pane of 10 30.00
161 A22 5c cerise ('34) 15 15
162 A22 10c red (II) 1.90 15
a. Imperf., pair 18.00
b. 10c red (I) ('06) 7.50 20
c. Booklet pane of 10 (I) 105.00
d. Booklet pane of 10 (II) 62.50
e. Booklet pane of 6 (II) 210.00
163 A22 10c grn (II) ('21) 55 15
a. 10c green (I) ('27) 22.50 20.00
b. Booklet pane of 10 (II) 12.50
c. Booklet pane of 10 (I) 350.00
164 A22 10c ultra ('32) 95 15
165 A22 15c red brn ('26) 22 15
a. Booklet pane of 10 20.00
166 A22 20c brown 3.00 20
a. Imperf., pair 30.00
167 A22 20c red vio ('26) 22 15
a. Booklet pane of 10 5.50
168 A22 25c blue 1.90 15
a. Booklet pane of 10 26.00
b. Imperf., pair 30.00
169 A22 25c brn ('27) 15 15
170 A22 30c orange 12.00 60
a. Imperf., pair 92.50
171 A22 30c red ('21) 8.00 1.10
172 A22 30c cerise ('25) 95 20
a. Booklet pane of 10 10.50
173 A22 30c lt bl ('25) 2.10 15
a. Booklet pane of 10 30.00
174 A22 30c cop red ('37) 30 15
a. Booklet pane of 10 6.75
175 A22 35c vio (II) ('26) 8.50 35
a. Imperf., pair 95.00
b. 35c violet (I) ('06) 150.00 3.50
176 A22 35c grn ('37) 58 15
177 A22 40c olive ('25) 1.00 20
b. Booklet pane of 10 27.50
178 A22 40c ver ('26) 1.60 15
a. Booklet pane of 10 22.50
179 A22 40c vio ('27) 1.90 15
180 A22 40c lt ultra ('28) 1.25 15
181 A22 1.05fr ver ('25) 7.50 2.25
182 A22 1.10fr cerise ('27) 8.50 1.00
183 A22 1.40fr cerise ('26) 15.00 10.50
184 A22 2fr Prus grn ('31) 10.00 30
Nos. 156-184 (29) 92.07 19.55

The 10c and 35c, type I, were slightly retouched by adding thin white outlines to the sack of grain, the underside of the right arm and the back of the skirt. It is difficult to distinguish the retouches except on clearly-printed copies. The white outlines were made stronger on the stamps of type II.

Stamps of types A16, A18, A20 and A22 were printed in 1916-20 on paper of poor quality, usually grayish and containing bits of fiber. This is called G. C. (Grande Consommation) paper.

Nos. 160, 162b, 163, 175b and 176 also exist imperf.

See Nos. 241-241b. For surcharges and overprint see Nos. 227-228, 234, 238, 240, 400, B1, B24, B28, B31, B35, B37, B39, B41, M5, P8, Offices in Turkish Empire 40-45, 52, 55.

Louis Pasteur — A23

1923-26

185 A23 10c green 52 15
a. Booklet pane of 10 8.25
186 A23 15c green ('24) 1.50 15
187 A23 20c green ('26) 2.25 30
188 A23 30c red 32 22
189 A23 30c green ('26) 60 15
190 A23 45c red ('24) 1.50 65
191 A23 50c blue 3.00 15
192 A23 75c blue ('24) 2.75 20
a. Imperf., pair 175.00
193 A23 90c red ('26) 7.00 1.40
194 A23 1fr blue ('25) 15.00 15
195 A23 1.25fr blue ('26) 15.00 3.75
196 A23 1.50fr blue ('26) 3.75 15
Nos. 185-196 (12) 53.19 7.42
Set, never hinged 110.00

Nos. 185, 188 and 191 were issued to commemorate the cent. of the birth of Pasteur.

For surcharges and overprint see Nos. 231, 235, 257, B26, B30, B33, C4.

No. 125 Overprinted in Blue

CONGRES PHILATELIQUE
DE
BORDEAUX
1923

1923, June 15

197 A18 1fr claret & ol grn 275.00 275.00
Never hinged 500.00

Allegory of Olympic Games at Paris — A24

The Trophy — A25

Milo of Crotona — A26

Victorious Athlete — A27

1924, Apr. 1 ***Perf. 14x13½, 13½x14***

198 A24 10c gray grn & yel grn 1.10 35
199 A25 25c rose & dk rose 1.60 20
200 A26 30c brn red & blk 5.75 4.25
201 A27 50c ultra & dk bl 13.00 2.25
Set, never hinged 47.50

8th Olympic Games, Paris. Exist imperf.

Pierre de Ronsard (1524-85), Poet — A28

1924, Oct. 6 ***Perf. 14x13½***

219 A28 75c blue, *bluish* 85 50
Never hinged 2.00

"Light and Liberty" Allegory A29

Majolica Vase — A30

Potter Decorating Vase — A31

Terrace of Château A32

1924-25 ***Perf. 14x13½, 13½x14***

220 A29 10c dk grn & yel ('25) 45 26
221 A30 15c ind & grn ('25) 45 26
a. Imperf. 135.00
222 A31 25c vio brn & garnet 55 15
223 A32 25c gray bl & vio ('25) 85 30
a. Imperf. 250.00
224 A31 75c indigo & ultra 2.25 85
225 A29 75c dk bl & lt bl ('25) 9.00 3.50
a. Imperf. 175.00
Nos. 220-225 (6) 13.55 5.32
Set, never hinged 25.00

Intl. Exhibition of Decorative Modern Arts at Paris, 1925.

Philatelic Exhibition Issue
Souvenir Sheet

A32a

1925, May 2 ***Perf. 14x13½***

226 A32a Sheet of 4, A15 II 500.00 500.00
Never hinged 1,200.
a. Imperf. sheet *2,750.*
b. 5fr carmine, perf. 72.50 65.00
c. 5fr carmine, imperf. 475.00

These were on sale only at the Intl. Phil. Exhib., Paris, May, 1925. Size: 140x220mm.

Nos. 148-149, 152-153, 173, 175, 181, 183, 192, 195 Surcharged **=25c**

1926-27

227 A22 25c on 30c lt bl 25 15
228 A22 25c on 35c vio 25 20
a. Double surcharge 200.00
229 A20 50c on 60c lt vio 1.00 40
230 A20 50c on 65c rose 80 20
231 A23 50c on 75c blue 2.10 20
232 A20 50c on 80c ver 1.00 40
233 A20 50c on 85c ver 1.65 20
234 A22 50c on 1.05fr ver 1.25 30
235 A23 50c on 1.25fr bl 1.25 30
236 A20 55c on 60c lt vio 82.50 35.00
238 A22 90c on 1.05fr ver 2.50 1.75
240 A22 1.10fr on 1.40fr cer 90 30
Nos. 227-240 (12) 95.45 39.40
Set, never hinged 250.00

Issue dates: Nos. 229-230, 232-234, 1927.
No. 236 is known only precanceled. See second note after No. 132.
Nos. 229, 230, 234, 238 and 240 have three bars instead of two. The 55c surcharge has thinner, larger numerals and a rounded "c." Width, including bars, is 17mm, instead of 13mm.

Strasbourg Exhibition Issue
Souvenir Sheet

A32b

1927, June 4

241 A32b Sheet of 2 550.00 550.00
a. 5fr light ultra (A22) 125.00 125.00
b. 10fr carmine rose (A22) 125.00 125.00

Sold at the Strasbourg Philatelic Exhibition as souvenirs. Size: 111x140mm.

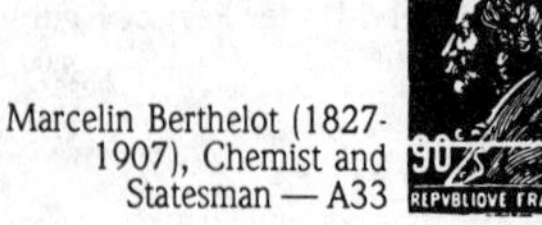

Marcelin Berthelot (1827-1907), Chemist and Statesman — A33

1927, Sept. 7

242 A33 90c dull rose 1.00 18
Never hinged 2.00

For surcharge see No. C3.

Lafayette, Washington, S. S. Paris and Airplane "Spirit of St. Louis" — A34

1927, Sept. 15

243 A34 90c dull red 90 65
a. Value omitted 1,100.
244 A34 1.50fr deep blue 2.50 90
a. Value omitted 1,000.
Set, never hinged 5.50

Visit of American Legionnaires to France, September, 1927. Exist imperf.

Joan of Arc — A35

1929, Mar.

245 A35 50c dull blue 1.50 18
Never hinged 2.25
a. Booklet pane of 10 120.00
b. Imperf. 135.00

500th anniv. of the relief of Orleans by the French forces led by Joan of Arc.

No. 127 Overprinted in Blue

EXPOSITION
LE HAVRE
1929
PHILATELIQUE

1929, May 18

246 A18 2fr org & pale bl *375.00 375.00*
Never hinged 550.00

Sold exclusively at the Intl. Phil. Exhib., Le Havre, May, 1929, for 7fr, which included a 5fr admission ticket.
Excellent counterfeits of No. 246 exist.

Reims Cathedral — A37

Dies I, II & III

Die IV

Die I Die II Die III

Die I - The window of the 1st turret on the left is made of 2 lines. The horizontal line of the frame surrounding 3F is not continuous.
Die II - Same as Die I but the line under 3F is continuous.
Die III - Same as Die II but there is a deeply cut line separating 3 and F.
Die IV - Same as Die III but the window of the first turret on the left is made of three lines.

Mont-Saint-Michel — A38

Die I Die II

Die I - The line at the top of the spire is broken.
Die II - The line is unbroken.

Port of La Rochelle A39

Dies I & II

Die III

Die I - The top of the "E" of "POSTES" has a serif. The oval of shading inside the "0" of "10 fr" and the outer oval are broken at their bases.
Die II - The same top has no serif. Interior and exterior of "0" broken as in Die I.
Die III - Top of "E" has no serif. Interior and exterior of "0" complete.

Pont du Gard, Nimes — A40

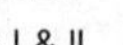

Dies I & II

Die III

Die I - Shading of the first complete arch in the left middle tier is made of horizontal lines. Size 36x20¾mm. Perf. 13½.
Die II - Same, size 35½x21mm. Perf. 11.
Die III - Shading of same arch is made of three diagonal lines. Thin paper. Perf. 13.

1929-33 **Engr.** ***Perf. 11, 13, 13½***

247 A37 3fr dk gray ('30) (I) 50.00 1.90
Never hinged 100.00
247A A37 3fr dk gray ('30) (II) 110.00 3.00
Never hinged 190.00
247B A37 3fr dk gray ('30) (III) 350.00 16.00
Never hinged 550.00
248 A37 3fr bluish sl ('31) (IV) 72.50 1.90
Never hinged 140.00
249 A38 5fr brn ('30) (I) 19.00 1.40
Never hinged 30.00
250 A38 5fr brn ('31) (II) 17.50 28
Never hinged 30.00
251 A39 10fr lt ultra (I) 92.50 9.75
Never hinged 165.00
251A A39 10fr ultra (II) 110.00 17.00
Never hinged 190.00
252 A39 10fr dk ultra ('31) (III) 75.00 5.00
Never hinged 140.00
253 A40 20fr red brown (I) 225.00 24.00
Never hinged 375.00
254 A40 20fr brt red brn ('33) (II) 575.00 175.00
Never hinged 1,100.

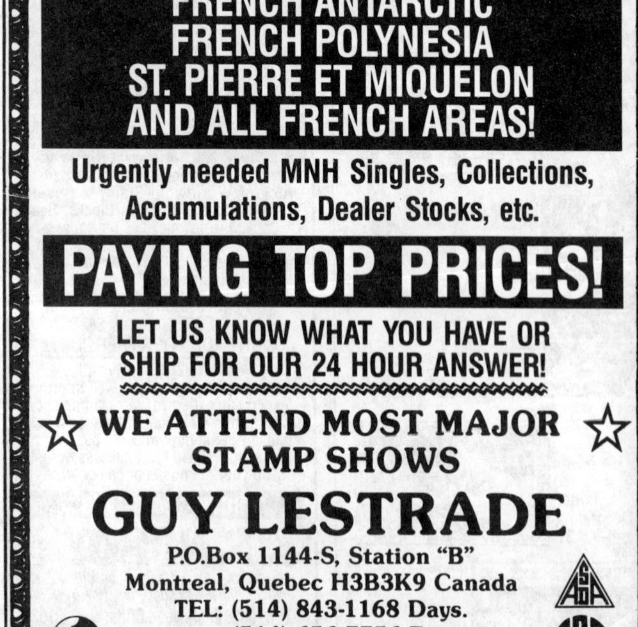

254A A40 20fr org brn ('31) (III) 165.00 16.50
Never hinged 325.00

View of Algiers — A41

1929, Jan. 1 **Typo.**
255 A41 50c blue & rose red 1.50 22
Never hinged 3.00

Cent. of the 1st French settlement in Algeria.

Nos. 146 and 196 Overprinted

CONGRÈS DU B. I. T. 1930

1930, Apr. 23 ***Perf. 14x13½***
256 A20 50c vermilion 2.10 1.25
257 A23 1.50fr blue 14.00 10.00
Set, never hinged 30.00

Intl. Labor Bureau, 48th Congress, Paris.

Colonial Exposition Issue

Fachi Woman A42

French Colonials A43

1930-31 **Typo.** ***Perf. 14x13½***
258 A42 15c gray black 55 20
259 A42 40c dark brown 1.40 20
260 A42 50c dark red 52 15
a. Booklet pane of 10 10.50
261 A42 1.50fr deep blue 8.00 25

Perf. 13½
Photo.
262 A43 1.50fr dp blue ('31) 32.50 1.00
Nos. 258-262 (5) 42.97 1.80
Set, never hinged 75.00

Arc de Triomphe A44

1931 **Engr.** ***Perf. 13***
263 A44 2fr red brown 17.50 32
Never hinged 40.00

Peace with Olive Branch — A45

1932-39 **Typo.** ***Perf. 14x13½***
264 A45 30c dp green 60 22
265 A45 40c brt violet 22 15
266 A45 45c yellow brown 1.65 35
267 A45 50c rose red 15 15
a. Imperf., pair 65.00
b. Booklet pane of 10 4.50
268 A45 55c dull vio ('37) 60 16
269 A45 60c ocher ('37) 18 16
270 A45 65c violet brown 30 15
271 A45 65c brt ultra ('37) 28 15
a. Booklet pane of 10 6.00
272 A45 75c olive green 15 15
273 A45 80c orange ('38) 15 15
274 A45 90c dk red 22.50 1.05
275 A45 90c brt green ('38) 15 15
276 A45 90c ultra ('38) 48 15
a. Booklet pane of 10 7.50
277 A45 1fr orange 1.25 15
278 A45 1fr rose pink ('38) 1.35 15
279 A45 1.25fr brown ol 52.50 1.65
280 A45 1.25fr rose car ('39) 1.25 55
281 A45 1.40fr brt red vio ('39) 5.00 2.50
282 A45 1.50fr deep blue 18 15
283 A45 1.75fr magenta 3.75 15
Nos. 264-283 (20) 92.69 8.44
Set, never hinged 190.00

The 50c is found in 4 types, differing in the lines below belt and size of "c."

For surcharges and overprints see Nos. 298, 333, 401-403, 405-409, M7-M9, S1.

Le Puy-en-Velay A46

1933 **Engr.** ***Perf. 13***
290 A46 90c rose 2.25 30
Never hinged 3.50

Aristide Briand — A47

Paul Doumer — A48

Victor Hugo — A49

1933, Dec. 11 **Typo.** ***Perf. 14x13½***
291 A47 30c blue green 11.50 4.50
292 A48 75c red violet 12.50 45
293 A49 1.25fr claret 3.25 45
Set, never hinged 60.00

Dove and Olive Branch — A50

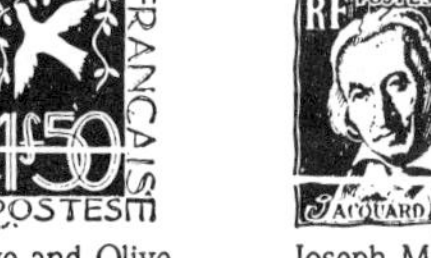
Joseph Marie Jacquard — A51

1934, Feb. 20
294 A50 1.50fr ultra 50.00 9.00
Never hinged 90.00

1934, Mar. 14 **Engr.** ***Perf. 14x13***
295 A51 40c blue 1.90 48
Never hinged 3.00

Jacquard (1752-1834), inventor of an improved loom for figured weaving.

Jacques Cartier A52

1934, July 18 ***Perf. 13***
296 A52 75c rose lilac 13.00 1.00
297 A52 1.50fr blue 30.00 1.90
Set, never hinged 90.00

Cartier's discovery of Canada, 400th anniv.

No. 279 Surcharged

50c

1934, Nov. ***Perf. 14x13½***
298 A45 50c on 1.25fr brn ol 2.75 18
Never hinged 5.00

Catalogue values for unused stamps in this section, from this point to the end of the section, are for Never Hinged items.

Breton River Scene — A53

1935, Feb. **Engr.** ***Perf. 13***
299 A53 2fr blue green 47.50 35

S. S. Normandie A54

1935, Apr.
300 A54 1.50fr dark blue 17.50 75
a. 1.50fr blue ('36) 80.00 10.50
b. 1.50fr blue green ('36) *3,500.*

Maiden voyage of the transatlantic steamship, the "Normandie".

Benjamin Delessert A55

1935, May 20
301 A55 75c blue green 25.00 52

Opening of the International Savings Bank Congress, May 20, 1935.

View of St. Trophime at Arles — A56

Victor Hugo (1802-85) — A57

1935, May 3
302 A56 3.50fr dark brown 40.00 1.40

1935, May 30 ***Perf. 14x13***
303 A57 1.25fr magenta 5.25 90

France stamps can be mounted in the Scott annually supplemented France album.

Cardinal Richelieu — A58

Jacques Callot — A59

1935, June 12 ***Perf. 13***
304 A58 1.50fr deep rose 30.00 90

Tercentenary of the founding of the French Academy by Cardinal Richelieu.

1935, Nov. ***Perf. 14x13***
305 A59 75c red 13.00 28

300th anniv. of the death of Jacques Callot, engraver.

André Marie Ampère (1775-1836), Scientist, by Louis Boilly — A60

1936, Feb. 27 ***Perf. 13***
306 A60 75c brown 25.00 65

Windmill at Fontvielle, Immortalized by Daudet A61

1936, Apr. 27
307 A61 2fr ultra 2.50 15

70th anniversary of the publication, in 1866, of Alphonse Daudet's "Lettres de mon Moulin".

Pilâtre de Rozier and his Balloon — A62

1936, June 4
308 A62 75c Prus blue 27.50 1.25

150th anniversary of the death of Jean Joseph Pilâtre de Rozier, balloonist.

Rouget de Lisle — A63

"La Marseillaise" A64

1936, June 27
309 A63 20c Prus green 3.25 50
310 A64 40c dark brown 6.75 1.40

Cent. of the death of Claude Joseph Rouget de Lisle, composer of "La Marseillaise."

Canadian War Memorial at Vimy Ridge — A65

1936, July 26

311 A65 75c henna brown 10.50 1.05
312 A65 1.50fr dull blue 19.00 5.00

Unveiling of the Canadian War Memorial at Vimy Ridge, July 26, 1936.

A66

Jean Léon Jaurès — A67

1936, July 30

313 A66 40c red brown 3.00 34
314 A67 1.50fr ultra 12.00 1.25

Assassination of Jean Léon Jaurès (1859-1914), socialist and politician.

Herald A68

Allegory of Exposition A69

1936, Sept. 15 Typo. *Perf. 14x13½*

315 A68 20c brt violet 60 20
316 A68 30c Prus green 3.25 65
317 A68 40c ultra 1.50 20
318 A68 50c red orange 1.25 15
319 A69 90c carmine 17.00 5.00
320 A69 1.50fr ultra 35.00 1.40
Nos. 315-320 (6) 58.60 7.60

Publicity for the 1937 Paris Exposition.

"Peace" A70

1936, Oct. 1 Engr. *Perf. 13*

321 A70 1.50fr blue 17.00 1.60

Skiing — A71

1937, Jan. 18

322 A71 1.50fr dark blue 8.50 70

Intl. Ski Meet at Chamonix-Mont Blanc.

Pierre Corneille, Portrait by Charles Le Brun — A72

1937, Feb. 15

323 A72 75c brown carmine 2.00 65

300th anniv. of the publication of "Le Cid."

Paris Exposition Issue

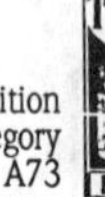

Exposition Allegory A73

1937, Mar. 15

324 A73 1.50fr turq blue 2.00 50

Jean Mermoz (1901-36), Aviator A74

Memorial to Mermoz — A75

1937, Apr. 27

325 A74 30c dk slate green 70 28
326 A75 3fr dark violet 6.75 2.00
a. 3fr violet 7.25 2.50

Electric Train — A76

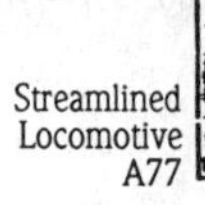
Streamlined Locomotive A77

1937, May 31

327 A76 30c dk green 1.65 75
328 A77 1.50fr dk ultra 9.50 5.00

13th International Railroad Congress.

Intl. Philatelic Exhibition Issue

Souvenir Sheet

Ceres Type A1 of 1849-50 A77a

1937, June 18 Typo. *Perf. 14x13½*

329 A77a Sheet of 4 200.00 150.00
a. 5c ultra & dark brown 27.50 27.50
b. 15c red & rose red 27.50 27.50
c. 30c ultra & rose red 27.50 27.50
d. 50c red & dark brown 27.50 27.50
e. Sheet of 4, imperf 1,300.

Issued in sheets measuring 150x220mm.

The sheets were sold only at the exhibition in Paris, a ticket of admission being required for each sheet purchased.

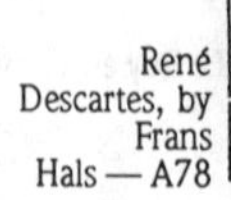

René Descartes, by Frans Hals — A78

1937, June Engr. *Perf. 13*

Inscribed "Discours sur la Méthode"

330 A78 90c copper red 1.75 65

Inscribed "Discours de la Méthode"

331 A78 90c copper red 5.50 65

3rd centenary of the publication of "Discours de la Méthode" by René Descartes.

France Congratulating USA — A79

1937, Sept. 17

332 A79 1.75fr ultra 2.25 70

150th anniv. of the US Constitution.

=

80c

No. 277 Surcharged in Red

1937, Oct. *Perf. 14x13½*

333 A45 80c on 1fr orange 45 20
a. Inverted surcharge 475.00

Mountain Road at Iseran — A80

1937, Oct. 4 Engr. *Perf. 13*

334 A80 90c dark green 1.50 15

Issued in commemoration of the opening of the mountain road at Iseran, Savoy.

Ceres — A81

1938-40 Typo. *Perf. 14x13½*

335 A81 1.75fr dk ultra 1.25 15
336 A81 2fr car rose ('39) 28 15
337 A81 2.25fr ultra ('39) 10.00 28
338 A81 2.50fr green ('39) 2.50 15
339 A81 2.50fr vio blue ('40) 95 32
340 A81 3fr rose lilac ('39) 95 15
Nos. 335-340 (6) 15.93 1.20

For surcharges see Nos. 397-399.

Léon Gambetta (1838-82), Lawyer and Statesman — A82

1938, Apr. 2 Engr. *Perf. 13*

341 A82 55c dark violet 40 28

Arc de Triomphe of Orange A82a

Miners — A83

Keep and Gate of Vincennes — A86

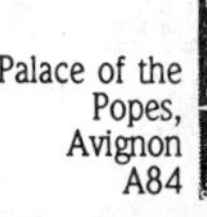

Palace of the Popes, Avignon A84

Medieval Walls of Carcassonne A85

Port of St. Malo — A87

1938

342 A82a 2fr brown black 1.50 65
343 A83 2.15fr violet brn 3.00 32
344 A84 3fr carmine brown 14.00 1.75
345 A85 5fr deep ultra 80 28
346 A86 10fr brown, *blue* 2.25 90
347 A87 20fr dk blue green 52.50 9.00
Nos. 342-347 (6) 74.05 12.90

For surcharges see Nos. 410-414.

Clément Ader, Air Pioneer A88

1938, June 16

348 A88 50fr ultra (thin paper) 110.00 42.50
a. 50fr dk ultra (thick paper) 125.00 55.00

Soccer Players A89

1938, June 1

349 A89 1.75fr dark ultra 12.50 4.25

World Cup Soccer Championship.

15-Cent Minimum Value

The minimum value for a single stamp is 15 cents. This value reflects the costs of handling inexpensive stamps.

Costume of Champagne Region — A90

Jean de La Fontaine — A91

1938, June 13

350 A90 1.75fr dark ultra 4.00 1.75

Tercentenary of the birth of Dom Pierre Pérignon, discoverer of the champagne process.

1938, July 8

351 A91 55c dk blue green 60 28

Issued to honor Jean de La Fontaine (1621-1695) the fabulist.

Seal of Friendship and Peace, Victoria Tower and Arc de Triomphe A92

1938, July 19

352 A92 1.75fr ultra 90 42

Visit of King George VI and Queen Elizabeth of Great Britain to France.

Mercury A93

Paul Cézanne, Self-portrait A95

1938-42 Typo. *Perf. 14x13½*

353 A93 1c dark brown ('39) 15 15
354 A93 2c slate grn ('39) 15 15
355 A93 5c rose 15 15
356 A93 10c ultra 15 15
357 A93 15c red orange 15 15
358 A93 15c orange brn ('39) 65 20
359 A93 20c red violet 15 15
360 A93 25c blue green 15 15
361 A93 30c rose red ('39) 15 15
362 A93 40c dk violet ('39) 15 15
363 A93 45c lt green ('39) 60 20
364 A93 50c deep blue ('39) 2.75 15
365 A93 50c dk green ('41) 60 15
366 A93 50c grnsh blue ('42) 15 15
367 A93 60c red orange ('39) 18 15
368 A93 70c magenta ('39) 20 15
369 A93 75c dk org brn ('39) 5.00 1.10
Nos. 353-369 (17) 11.48
Set value 2.25

No. 366 exists imperforate. See Nos. 455-458. For overprints and surcharge see #404, 499-502.

1939, Mar. 15 Engr. *Perf. 13*

370 A95 2.25fr Prussian blue 4.25 1.40

Paul Cézanne (1839-1906), painter.

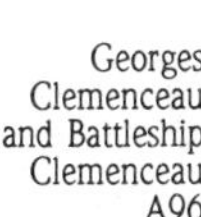

Georges Clemenceau and Battleship Clemenceau A96

1939, Apr. 18

371 A96 90c ultra 40 30

Laying of the keel of the warship "Clemenceau," Jan. 17, 1939.

Statue of Liberty, French Pavilion, Trylon and Perisphere A97

1939-40

372 A97 2.25fr ultra 6.75 1.75
373 A97 2.50fr ultra ('40) 4.00 1.40

New York World's Fair.

Joseph Nicéphore Niepce and Louis Jacques Mandé Daguerre A98

1939, Apr. 24

374 A98 2.25fr dark blue 5.75 2.50

Centenary of photography.

Iris — A99

Pumping Station at Marly — A100

1939-44 Typo. *Perf. 14x13½*

375 A99 80c red brown ('40) 32 15
376 A99 80c yellow grn ('44) 15 15
377 A99 1fr green 80 15
378 A99 1fr crimson ('40) 24 15
a. Booklet pane of 10 6.00
379 A99 1fr grnsh blue ('44) 15 15
380 A99 1.20fr violet ('44) 15 15
381 A99 1.30fr ultra ('40) 24 15
382 A99 1.50fr red org ('41) 32 20
383 A99 1.50fr henna brn ('44) 15 15
384 A99 2fr violet brn ('44) 16 15
385 A99 2.40fr car rose ('44) 16 15
386 A99 3fr orange ('44) 24 15
387 A99 4fr ultra ('44) 32 15
Nos. 375-387 (13) 3.40
Set value 1.15

1939 Engr. *Perf. 13*

388 A100 2.25fr brt ultra 7.75 1.40

France's participation in the International Water Exposition at Liège.

St. Gregory of Tours — A101

1939, June 10

389 A101 90c red 60 42

14th centenary of the birth of St. Gregory of Tours, historian and bishop.

"The Oath of the Tennis Court" by Jacques David A102

1939, June 20

390 A102 90c deep slate green 2.50 52

150th anniversary of French Revolution.

Cathedral of Strasbourg — A103

1939, June 23

391 A103 70c brown carmine 1.00 45

500th anniv. of the completion of Strasbourg Cathedral.

Porte Chaussée, Verdun A104

1939, June 23

392 A104 90c black brown 1.00 65

23rd anniv. of the Battle of Verdun.

View of Pau — A105

1939, Aug. 25

393 A105 90c brt rose, *gray bl* 1.10 35

Maid of Languedoc A106

Bridge at Lyons A107

1939

394 A106 70c black, *blue* 40 32
395 A107 90c dull brown vio 60 32

Imperforates

Nearly all French stamps issued from 1940 onward exist imperforate. Officially 20 sheets, ranging from 25 to 100 subjects, were left imperforate.

Georges Guynemer (1894-1917), World War I Ace — A108

1940, Nov. 7

396 A108 50fr ultra 10.00 6.00

Stamps of 1938-39 Surcharged in Carmine **1F**

1940-41 *Perf. 14x13½*

397 A81 1fr on 1.75fr dk ultra 18 15
398 A81 1fr on 2.25fr ultra ('41) 18 15
399 A81 1fr on 2.50fr grn ('41) 55 38

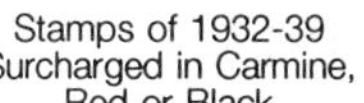

Stamps of 1932-39 Surcharged in Carmine, Red or Black

1940-41 *Perf. 13, 14x13½*

400 A22 30c on 35c grn (C) ('41) 15 15
401 A45 50c on 55c dl vio (C) ('41) 15 15
a. Inverted surcharge 375.00
402 A45 50c on 65c brt ultra (C) ('41) 15 15
403 A45 50c on 75c ol grn (C) ('41) 22 15
404 A93 50c on 75c dk org brn (C) ('41) 22 15
405 A45 50c on 80c org (C) ('41) 22 15
406 A45 50c on 90c ultra (C) ('41) 15 15
a. Inverted surcharge 200.00
b. "05" instead of "50" *3,000.*
407 A45 1fr on 1.25fr rose car (Bk) ('41) 22 15
408 A45 1fr on 1.40fr brt red vio (R) ('41) 22 15
a. Double surcharge 600.00
409 A45 1fr on 1.50fr dk bl (C) ('41) 55 38
410 A83 1fr on 2.15fr vio brn (C) 22 15
411 A85 2.50fr on 5fr dp ultra (C) ('41) 25 18
a. Double surcharge 140.00 57.50
412 A86 5fr on 10fr brn, *bl* (C) ('41) 1.75 1.25
413 A87 10fr on 20fr dk bl grn (C) ('41) 1.25 85
414 A88 20fr on 50fr dk ultra (#348a) (C) ('41) 42.50 30.00
a. 20fr on 50fr ultra, thin paper (#348) 47.50 32.50
Nos. 400-414 (15) 48.22 34.16

Marshal Pétain — A109

Frédéric Mistral — A110

1941 *Perf. 13*

415 A109 40c red brown 35 28
416 A109 80c turq blue 55 35
417 A109 1fr red 18 15
418 A109 2.50fr deep ultra 1.10 65

1941, Feb. 20 *Perf. 14x13*

419 A110 1fr brown lake 15 15

Issued in honor of Frédéric Mistral, poet and Nobel prize winner for literature in 1904.

Beaune Hospital A111

View of Angers A112

Ramparts of St. Louis, Aiguesmortes A113

1941

420 A111 5fr brown black 24 15
421 A112 10fr dark violet 35 20
422 A113 20fr brown black 48 35

Inscribed "Postes Francaises"

1942

Imprint: "FELTESSE" at right

423 A111 15fr brown lake 50 20

Marshal Pétain
A114 A115 A116

A117

A118

1941-42 Typo. *Perf.* 14x13½

No.	Type	Description	Unused	Used
427	A114	20c lilac ('42)	15	15
428	A114	30c rose red	15	15
429	A114	40c ultra	15	15
431	A115	50c dp green	15	15
432	A115	60c violet ('42)	15	15
433	A115	70c saph ('42)	15	15
434	A115	70c orange ('42)	15	15
435	A115	80c brown	15	15
436	A115	80c emerald ('42)	15	15
437	A115	1fr rose red	15	15
438	A115	1.20fr red brn ('42)	15	15
439	A116	1.50fr rose	15	15
440	A116	1.50fr dl red brn ('42)	15	15
a.		Booklet pane of 10	2.75	
441	A116	2fr blue grn ('42)	15	15
443	A116	2.40fr rose red ('42)	15	15
444	A116	2.50fr ultra	75	32
445	A116	3fr orange	15	15
446	A115	4fr ultra ('42)	15	15
447	A115	4.50fr dk green ('42)	75	18
		Set value	2.75	1.50

Nos. 431 to 438 measure 16½x20½mm.

No. 440 was forged by the French Underground ("Defense de la France") and used to frank clandestine journals, etc., from Feb. to June, 1944. The forgeries were ungummed, both perf. 11½ and imperf., with a back handstamp covering six stamps and including the words: "Atelier des Faux."

For surcharge see No. B134.

1942 Engr. *Perf.* 14x13

No.	Type	Description	Unused	Used
448	A115	4fr brt ultra	20	15
449	A115	4.50fr dark green	20	15
450	A117	5fr Prus green	15	15

***Perf.* 13**

No.	Type	Description	Unused	Used
451	A118	50fr black	3.00	1.75

Nos. 448 and 449 measure 18x21½mm.

Jules Massenet A119

Stendhal (Marie Henri Beyle) A120

1942, June 22 *Perf.* 14x13

No.	Type	Description	Unused	Used
452	A119	4fr Prus green	15	15

Jules Massenet (1842-1912), composer.

1942, Sept. 14 *Perf.* 13

No.	Type	Description	Unused	Used
453	A120	4fr blk brn & org red	22	22

Stendhal (1783-1842), writer.

André Blondel — A121

Town-Hall Belfry, Arras — A122

1942, Sept. 14

No.	Type	Description	Unused	Used
454	A121	4fr dull blue	22	22

André Eugène Blondel (1863-1938), physicist.

Mercury Type of 1938-42
Inscribed "Postes Franaises"

1942 *Perf.* 14x13½

No.	Type	Description	Unused	Used
455	A93	10c ultra	15	15
456	A93	30c rose red	15	15
457	A93	40c dark violet	15	15
458	A93	50c turq blue	15	15
		Set value	24	20

1942, Dec. 8 Engr. *Perf.* 13

No.	Type	Description	Unused	Used
459	A122	10fr green	15	15

Coats of Arms

Lyon — A123

1943 Typo. *Perf.* 14x13½

No.	Type	Description	Unused	Used
460	A123	5fr shown	30	15
461	A123	10fr Brittany	38	20
462	A123	15fr Provence	1.65	85
463	A123	20fr Ile de France	1.25	50

Antoine Lavoisier (1743-94), French Scientist — A127

1943, July 5 Engr. *Perf.* 14x13

No.	Type	Description	Unused	Used
464	A127	4fr ultra	15	15

Lake Lerie and Meije Dauphiné Alps — A128

1943, July 5 *Perf.* 13

No.	Type	Description	Unused	Used
465	A128	20fr dull gray grn	42	32

Nicolas Rolin, Guigone de Salins and Hospital of Beaune A129

1943, July 21

No.	Type	Description	Unused	Used
466	A129	4fr blue	20	18

500th anniv. of the founding of the Hospital of Beaune.

Arms of Flanders — A130

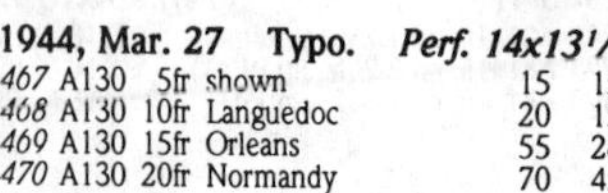

1944, Mar. 27 Typo. *Perf.* 14x13½

No.	Type	Description	Unused	Used
467	A130	5fr shown	15	15
468	A130	10fr Languedoc	20	15
469	A130	15fr Orleans	55	28
470	A130	20fr Normandy	70	45

Edouard Branly A134

Early Postal Car A135

1944, Feb. 21 Engr. *Perf.* 14x13

No.	Type	Description	Unused	Used
471	A134	4fr ultra	15	15

Cent. of the birth of Edouard Branly, electrical inventor.

1944, June 10 *Perf.* 13

No.	Type	Description	Unused	Used
472	A135	1.50fr dark blue green	30	20

Cent. of France's traveling postal service.

Chateau de Chenonceaux A136

Claude Chappe A137

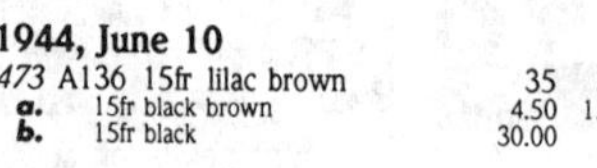

1944, June 10

No.	Type	Description	Unused	Used
473	A136	15fr lilac brown	35	30
a.		15fr black brown	4.50	1.00
b.		15fr black	30.00	

See No. 496.

1944, Aug. 14 *Perf.* 14x13

No.	Type	Description	Unused	Used
474	A137	4fr dark ultra	15	15

150th anniv. of the invention of an optical telegraph by Claude Chappe (1763-1805).

Gallic Cock A138

Marianne A139

1944 Litho. *Perf.* 12

No.	Type	Description	Unused	Used
477	A138	10c yellow grn	15	15
478	A138	30c dk rose vio	16	15
479	A138	40c blue	15	15
480	A138	50c dark red	15	15
481	A139	60c olive brown	15	15
482	A139	70c rose lilac	15	15
483	A139	80c yellow grn	50	45
484	A139	1fr violet	15	15
485	A139	1.20fr dp carmine	15	15
486	A139	1.50fr deep blue	15	15
487	A138	2fr indigo	15	15
488	A139	2.40fr red orange	95	90
489	A139	3fr dp blue grn	16	15
490	A139	4fr grnsh blue	16	15
491	A139	4.50fr black	15	15
492	A139	5fr violet blue	3.00	2.75
493	A138	10fr violet	3.50	3.25
494	A138	15fr olive brown	3.50	3.25
495	A138	20fr dk slate grn	3.50	3.25
		Nos. 477-495 (19)	16.93	15.80

Nos. 477-495 were issued first in Corsica after the Allied landing, and released in Paris Nov. 15, 1944.

Chateau Type Inscribed "RF"

1944, Oct. 30 Engr. *Perf.* 13

No.	Type	Description	Unused	Used
496	A136	25fr black	40	35

Thomas Robert Bugeaud — A141

1944, Nov. 20

No.	Type	Description	Unused	Used
497	A141	4fr myrtle green	15	15

Battle of Isly, Aug. 14th, 1844.

Church of St. Denis A142

1944, Nov. 20

No.	Type	Description	Unused	Used
498	A142	2.40fr brown carmine	15	15

800th anniv. of the Church of St. Denis.

Type of 1938-42, Overprinted in Black **RF**

Inscribed "Postes Francaises"

1944 *Perf.* 14x13½

No.	Type	Description	Unused	Used
499	A93	10c ultra	15	15
500	A93	30c rose red	15	15
501	A93	40c dark violet	15	15
502	A93	50c grnsh blue	15	15
		Set value	32	29

The overprint "RF" in various forms, with or without Lorraine Cross, was also applied to stamps of the French State at Lyon and fourteen other cities.

French Forces of the Interior and Symbol of Liberation — A143

1945, Jan.

No.	Type	Description	Unused	Used
503	A143	4fr dark ultra	18	15

Issued to commemorate the Liberation.

Stamps of the above design, and of one incorporating "FRANCE" in the top panel, were printed by photo. in England during WW II upon order of the Free French Government. They were not issued. There are 3 values in each design; 25c green, 1fr red, 2.50fr blue. Value: set, above design, $135; set inscribed "FRANCE," $525.

Marianne — A144

***Perf.* 11½x12½**

1944-45 Engr. Unwmk.

No.	Type	Description	Unused	Used
505	A144	10c ultra	15	15
506	A144	30c bister	15	15
507	A144	40c indigo	15	15

No.	Type	Value	Color	Unused	Used
508	A144	50c	red orange	15	15
509	A144	60c	chalky blue	15	15
510	A144	70c	sepia	15	15
511	A144	80c	deep green	15	15
512	A144	1fr	lilac	15	15
513	A144	1.20fr	dk ol grn	15	15
514	A144	1.50fr	rose ('44)	15	15
515	A144	2fr	dk brown	15	15
516	A144	2.40fr	red	15	15
517	A144	3fr	brt ol grn	15	15
518	A144	4fr	brt ultra	15	15
519	A144	4.50fr	slate gray	15	15
520	A144	5fr	brt orange	25	22
521	A144	10fr	yellow grn	35	30
522	A144	15fr	lake	35	30
523	A144	20fr	brown org	1.10	95
523A	A144	50fr	deep purple	2.25	2.00
			Set value	5.25	4.50

The 2.40fr exists imperf. in a miniature sheet of 4 which was not issued.

Coat of Arms A145

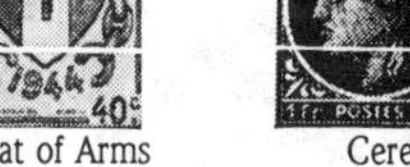

Ceres A146

Marianne — A147

1945-47 Typo. Perf. 14x13½

No.	Type	Value	Color	Unused	Used
524	A145	10c	brown black	15	15
525	A145	30c	dk blue green	15	15
526	A145	40c	lilac rose	15	15
527	A145	50c	violet blue	15	15
528	A146	60c	brt ultra	15	15
530	A146	80c	brt green	15	15
531	A146	90c	dull grn ('46)	75	30
532	A146	1fr	rose red	15	15
533	A146	1.20fr	brown black	15	15
534	A146	1.50fr	rose lilac	15	15
535	A147	1.50fr	rose pink	15	15
536	A147	2fr	myrtle green	15	15
536A	A146	2fr	lt bl grn ('46)	15	15
537	A147	2.40fr	scarlet	35	24
538	A146	2.50fr	brown ('46)	15	15
539	A147	3fr	sepia	15	15
540	A147	3fr	deep rose ('46)	15	15
541	A147	4fr	ultra	15	15
541A	A147	4fr	violet ('46)	15	15
541B	A147	4.50fr	ultra ('47)	15	15
542	A147	5fr	lt green	15	15
542A	A147	5fr	rose pink ('47)	15	15
543	A147	6fr	brt ultra	35	24
544	A147	6fr	crim rose ('46)	25	15
545	A147	10fr	red orange	35	15
546	A147	10fr	ultra ('46)	1.10	32
547	A147	15fr	brt red vio	1.75	65
			Set value	7.00	3.25

No. 531 is known only precanceled. See second note after No. 132.

Due to a reduction of the domestic postage rate, No. 542A was sold for 4.50fr.

See Nos. 576-580, 594-602, 614, 615, 650-654. For surcharges see Nos. 610, 706, Reunion 270-276, 278, 285, 290-291, 293, 295.

1945-46 Engr. Perf. 14x13

No.	Type	Value	Color	Unused	Used
548	A147	4fr	dark blue	20	15
549	A147	10fr	dp blue ('46)	50	20
550	A147	15fr	brt red vio ('46)	4.75	90
551	A147	20fr	blue grn ('46)	1.00	20
552	A147	25fr	red ('46)	4.00	70
			Nos. 548-552 (5)	10.45	2.15

Marianne — A148

1945 Engr. Perf. 13

No.	Type	Value	Color	Unused	Used
553	A148	20fr	dark green	1.50	42
554	A148	25fr	violet	1.65	65
555	A148	50fr	red brown	1.75	60
556	A148	100fr	brt rose car	8.50	3.50

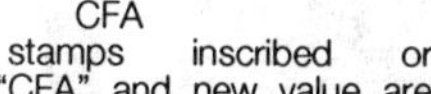

CFA

French stamps inscribed or surcharged "CFA" and new value are listed under Réunion at the end of the French listings.

Arms of Metz A149

Arms of Strasbourg A150

1945, Mar. 3 Perf. 14x13

No.	Type	Value	Color	Unused	Used
557	A149	2.40fr	dull blue	15	15
558	A150	4fr	black brown	15	15

Liberation of Metz and Strasbourg.

Costumes of Alsace and Lorraine and Cathedrals of Strasbourg and Metz — A151

1945, May 16 Perf. 13

No.	Type	Value	Color	Unused	Used
559	A151	4fr	henna brown	15	15

Liberation of Alsace and Lorraine.

World Map Showing French Possessions A152

1945, Sept. 17

No.	Type	Value	Color	Unused	Used
560	A152	2fr	Prussian blue	15	15

No. B193 Surcharged with New Value in Black

1946 Perf. 14x13½

No.	Type	Value	Color	Unused	Used
561	SP147	3fr on 2fr+1fr	red org	15	15

Arms of Corsica — A153

1946 Unwmk. Typo. Perf. 14x13½

No.	Type	Value	Color	Unused	Used
562	A153	10c	shown	15	15
563	A153	30c	Alsace	15	15
564	A153	50c	Lorraine	15	15
565	A153	60c	County of Nice	15	15
			Set value	24	20

For surcharges see Reunion Nos. 268-269.

Reaching for "Peace" — A157

Holding the Dove of Peace — A158

1946, July 29 Engr. Perf. 13

No.	Type	Value	Color	Unused	Used
566	A157	3fr	Prussian green	15	15
567	A158	10fr	dark blue	15	15

Peace Conference of Paris, 1946.

Vézelay A159

Luxembourg Palace A160

Rocamadour — A161

Pointe du Raz, Finistère A162

1946 Unwmk. Perf. 13

No.	Type	Value	Color	Unused	Used
568	A159	5fr	rose violet	40	16
569	A160	10fr	dark blue	40	15
570	A161	15fr	dk violet brn	1.50	25
571	A162	20fr	slate gray	50	15
			Set value		62

See Nos. 591-592. For surcharges see Reunion Nos. 277, 279.

Globe and Wreath — A163

1946, Nov.

No.	Type	Value	Color	Unused	Used
572	A163	10fr	dark blue	20	20

Gen. conf. of UNESCO, Paris, 1946.

Cannes A164

Stanislas Square, Nancy A165

1946-48 Engr. Perf. 13

No.	Type	Value	Color	Unused	Used
573	A164	6fr	rose red	55	40
574	A165	25fr	black brown	2.00	20
575	A165	25fr	dark blue ('48)	5.50	90

For surcharges see Reunion Nos. 280-281.

Ceres & Marianne Types of 1945

1947 Unwmk. Typo. Perf. 14x13½

No.	Type	Value	Color	Unused	Used
576	A146	1.30fr	dull blue	25	18
577	A147	3fr	green	65	15
578	A147	3.50fr	brown red	45	16
579	A147	5fr	blue	20	15
580	A147	6fr	carmine	35	25
			Nos. 576-580 (5)	1.90	
			Set value		74

Colonnade of the Louvre A166

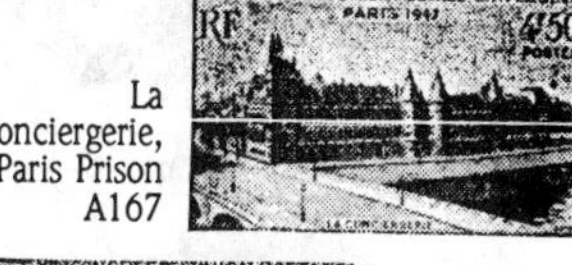

La Conciergerie, Paris Prison A167

La Cité, Oldest Section of Paris — A168

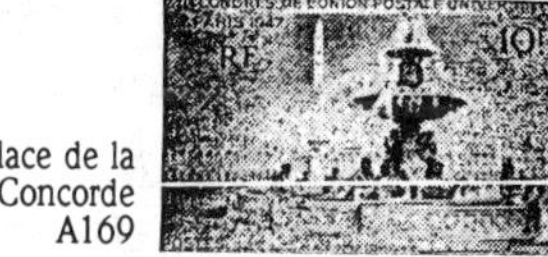

Place de la Concorde A169

1947, May 7 Engr. Perf. 13

No.	Type	Value	Color	Unused	Used
581	A166	3.50fr	chocolate	28	28
582	A167	4.50fr	dk slate gray	28	28
583	A168	6fr	red	55	55
584	A169	10fr	bright ultra	55	55

12th UPU Cong., Paris, May 7-July 7.

Auguste Pavie — A170

Francois Fénelon — A171

1947, May 30

No.	Type	Value	Color	Unused	Used
585	A170	4.50fr	sepia	15	15

Cent. of the birth of Auguste Pavie, French pioneer in Laos.

1947, July 12

No.	Type	Value	Color	Unused	Used
586	A171	4.50fr	chocolate	15	15

Issued to honor Francois de Salignac de la Mothe-Fénelon, prelate and writer.

Fleur-de-Lis and Double Carrick Bend — A172

1947, Aug. 2 Unwmk.

No.	Type	Value	Color	Unused	Used
587	A172	5fr	brown	16	16

6th World Boy Scout Jamboree held at Moisson, Aug. 9th-18th, 1947.

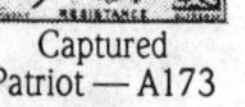

Captured Patriot — A173

View of Conques — A174

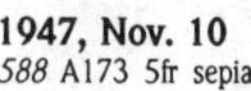

1947, Nov. 10 Engr. *Perf. 13*

588 A173 5fr sepia 40 35

No. 576 Surcharged in Carmine

1947, Nov. Typo. *Perf. 14x13½*

589 A146 1fr on 1.30fr dull blue 15 15

1947, Dec. 18 Engr. *Perf. 13*

590 A174 15fr henna brown 1.90 50

For surcharge see Reunion No. 282.

Types of 1946-47

1948 Re-engraved

591 A160 12fr rose carmine 95 50
592 A160 15fr bright red 42 35
593 A174 18fr dark blue 1.00 35

"FRANCE" substituted for inscriptions "RF" and "REPUBLIQUE FRANCAISE."

Marianne Type of 1945

1948-49 Typo. *Perf. 14x13½*

594 A147 2.50fr brown 2.75 1.25
595 A147 3fr lilac rose 25 15
596 A147 4fr lt blue grn 30 15
597 A147 4fr brown org 1.25 32
598 A147 5fr lt blue grn 65 15
599 A147 8fr blue 35 15
600 A147 10fr brt violet 22 15
601 A147 12fr ultra ('49) 1.25 15
602 A147 15fr crim rose ('49) 55 15
a. Booklet pane of 10 60.00
Nos. 594-602 (9) 7.57
Set value 2.00

No. 594 known only precanceled. See second note after No. 132.

Franois René de Chateaubriand A175

1948, July 3 Engr. *Perf. 13*

603 A175 18fr dark blue 22 18

Vicomte de Chateaubriand (1768-1848).

Philippe Franois M. de Hautecloque (Gen. Jacques Leclerc) A176

1948, July 3

604 A176 6fr gray black 25 20

See Nos. 692-692A.

Chaillot Palace A177

A178

1948, Sept. 21

605 A177 12fr carmine rose 25 24
606 A178 18fr indigo 30 28

Meeting of the UN General Assembly, Paris, 1948.

Genissiat Dam A179

Paul Langevin A180

1948, Sept. 21

607 A179 12fr carmine rose 30 28

1948, Nov. 17 *Perf. 14x13*

608 A180 5fr shown 15 15
609 A180 8fr Jean Perrin 15 15

Placing of the ashes of physicists Langevin (1872-1946) and Perrin (1870-1942) in the Pantheon.

No. 580 Surcharged with New Value and Bars in Black

1949, Jan. *Perf. 14x13½*

610 A147 5fr on 6fr carmine 15 15

Arctic Scene — A181

1949, May 2 *Perf. 13*

611 A181 15fr indigo 25 22

French polar explorations.

Types of 1849 and 1945

1949, May 9 Engr. *Imperf.*

612 A1 15fr red 3.75 3.75
a. Strip of 4, #612-615 + label 15.00 15.00
613 A1 25fr deep blue 3.75 3.75

Perf. 14x13

614 A147 15fr red 3.75 3.75
615 A147 25fr deep blue 3.75 3.75

Cent. of the 1st French postage stamps.

Arms of Burgundy — A182

Arms: 50c, Guyenne (Aquitania). 1fr, Savoy. 2fr, Auvergne. 4fr, Anjou.

1949, May 11 Typo. *Perf. 14x13½*

616 A182 10c blue, red & yel 15 15
617 A182 50c blue, red & yel 15 15
618 A182 1fr brown & red 22 15
619 A182 2fr green, yel & red 35 15
620 A182 4fr blue, red & yel 65 28
Nos. 616-620 (5) 1.52
Set value 65

See Nos. 659-663, 694-699, 733-739, 782-785. For surcharges see Reunion Nos. 283-284, 288-289, 297, 301, 305, 311.

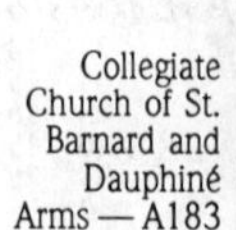

Collegiate Church of St. Barnard and Dauphiné Arms — A183

1949, May 14 Engr. *Perf. 13*

621 A183 12fr red brown 22 15

600th anniv. of France's acquisition of the Dauphiné region.

US and French Flags, Plane and Steamship A184

1949, May 14

622 A184 25fr blue & carmine 50 35

Issued to publicize Franco-American friendship.

Cloister of St. Wandrille Abbey A185

1949, May 18

623 A185 25fr deep ultra 22 15

See No. 649. For surcharge see Reunion No. 287.

Type of 1849 Inscribed "1849-1949" in Lower Margin

1949, June 1

624 A1 10fr brown orange 45.00 35.00
a. Sheet of 10 450.00 400.00

Cent. of the 1st French postage stamp.

No. 624 has wide margins, 40x52mm from perforation to perforation. Sold for 110fr, which included cost of admission to the Centenary Intl. Exhib., Paris, June 1949.

Claude Chappe — A186

Jean Racine — A187

Designs: 15fr, Franois Arago and André M. Ampère. 25fr, Emile Baudot. 50fr, Gen. Gustave A. Ferrié.

Inscribed: "C.I.T.T. PARIS 1949"

1949, June 13 Unwmk. *Perf. 13*

625 A186 10fr vermilion 55 45
626 A186 15fr sepia 85 55
627 A186 25fr deep claret 2.75 1.65
628 A186 50fr deep claret 4.00 1.65

International Telegraph and Telephone Conference, Paris, May-July 1949.

1949

629 A187 12fr sepia 28 28

250th anniv. of the death of Jean Racine, dramatist.

Abbey of St. Bertrand de Comminges A188

Meuse Valley, Ardennes A189

Mt. Gerbier de Jonc, Vivarais A190

1949 Engr.

630 A188 20fr dark red 26 15
631 A189 40fr Prus green 10.50 22
632 A190 50fr sepia 2.00 15

For surcharge see Reunion No. 286.

A191

1949, Oct. 18

633 A191 15fr deep carmine 22 22

50th anniv. of the Assembly of Presidents of Chambers of Commerce of the French Union.

UPU Allegory A192

1949, Nov. 7

634 A192 5fr dark green 24 24
635 A192 15fr deep carmine 32 24
636 A192 25fr deep blue 1.00 80

UPU, 75th anniversary.

Raymond Poincaré — A193

Franois Rabelais — A195

Charles Péguy and Cathedral at Chartres A194

1950, May 27 Unwmk. *Perf. 13*

637 A193 15fr indigo 25 18

1950, June

638 A194 12fr dk brown 20 20
639 A195 12fr red brown 25 25

Chateau of Chateaudun A196

1950, Nov. 25

640 A196 8fr choc & bis brn 32 25

Madame Récamier A197

Marie de Sévigné A198

1950

641 A197 12fr dark green 30 30
642 A198 15fr ultra 24 24

Palace of Fontainbleau A199

1951, Jan. 20
643 A199 12fr dark brown 35 28

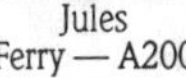

Jules Ferry — A200

Jean-Baptiste de la Salle — A202

Hands Holding Shuttle A201

1951, Mar. 17
644 A200 15fr bright red 38 30

1951, Apr. 9
645 A201 25fr deep ultra 80 65

Issued to publicize the International Textile Exposition at Lille, April-May, 1951.

1951, Apr. 28
646 A202 15fr chocolate 32 28

300th anniv. of the birth of Jean-Baptiste de la Salle, educator and saint.

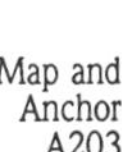

Map and Anchor A203

1951, May 12
647 A203 15fr deep ultra 45 40

50th anniv. of the creation of the French colonial troops.

Vincent d'Indy A204

1951, May 15
648 A204 25fr deep green 1.65 1.10

Centenary of the birth of Vincent d'Indy, composer.

Abbey Type of 1949

1951
649 A185 30fr bright blue 4.00 2.75

Marianne Type of 1945-47

1951 Typo. *Perf. 14x13½*

650	A147 5fr dull violet	60	15
651	A147 6fr green	5.50	40
652	A147 12fr red orange	1.10	15
653	A147 15fr ultra	25	15
a.	Booklet pane of 10	20.00	
654	A147 18fr cerise	14.00	90
	Nos. 650-654 (5)	21.45	
	Set value		1.50

Professors Nocard, Bouley and Chauveau; Gate at Lyons School A205

1951, June 8 Engr. *Perf. 13*
655 A205 12fr red violet 50 40

Issued to honor Veterinary Medicine.

Gen. Picqué, Cols. Roussin and Villemin; Val de Grace Dome — A206

1951, June 17 Unwmk.
656 A206 15fr red brown 50 40

Issued to honor Military Medicine.

St. Nicholas, by Jean Didier — A207

1951, June 23
657 A207 15fr indigo, dp cl & org 55 48

Chateau Bontemps, Arbois A208

1951, June 23
658 A208 30fr indigo 55 15

For surcharge see Reunion No. 296.

Arms Type of 1949

Arms of: 10c, Artois. 50c, Limousin. 1fr, Béarn. 2fr, Touraine. 3fr, Franche-Comté.

1951, June Typo. *Perf. 14x13½*

659	A182 10c red, vio bl & yel	15	15
660	A182 50c green, red & blk	15	15
661	A182 1fr blue, red & yel	20	15
662	A182 2fr vio bl, red & yel	60	15
663	A182 3fr red, vio bl & yel	75	20
	Nos. 659-663 (5)	1.85	
	Set value		58

Seal of Paris — A209

Maurice Noguès and Globe — A210

1951, July 7 Unwmk. Engr. *Perf. 13*
664 A209 15fr dp blue, dk brn & red 40 30

2,000th anniv. of the founding of Paris.

1951, Oct. 13
665 A210 12fr indigo & blue 55 30

Issued to honor Maurice Nogues, aviation pioneer.

Charles Baudelaire A211

Poets: 12fr, Paul Verlaine. 15fr, Arthur Rimbaud.

1951, Oct. 27

666	A211 8fr purple	40	40
667	A211 12fr gray	55	55
668	A211 15fr dp green	65	65

Georges Clemenceau, Birth Cent. — A212

1951, Nov. 11
669 A212 15fr black brown 28 28

Chateau du Clos, Vougeot A213

1951, Nov. 17
670 A213 30fr blk brn & brn 4.00 1.90

Chaillot Palace and Eiffel Tower A214

1951, Nov. 6

671	A214 18fr red	85	60
672	A214 30fr dp ultra	1.40	75

Opening of the Geneva Assembly of the United Nations, Paris, Nov. 6, 1951.

Observatory, Pic du Midi — A215

Abbaye aux Hommes, Caen — A216

1951, Dec. 22

673	A215 40fr violet	4.50	18
674	A216 50fr black brown	3.50	18

For surcharge see Reunion No. 294.

Marshal Jean de Lattre de Tassigny, 1890-1952 A217

1952, May 8 Unwmk. *Perf. 13*
675 A217 15fr violet brown 70 30

See No. 717.

Gate of France, Vaucouleurs — A218

1952, May 11
676 A218 12fr brown black 1.50 80

Flags and Monument at Narvik, Norway A219

1952, May 28
677 A219 30fr violet blue 2.25 1.25

Battle of Narvik, May 27, 1940.

Chateau de Chambord A220

1952, May 30
678 A220 20fr dark purple 38 15

For surcharge see Reunion No. 292.

Assembly Hall, Strasbourg A221

1952, May 31
679 A221 30fr dark green 8.00 4.50

Issued to honor the Council of Europe.

Monument, Bir-Hacheim Cemetery A222

1952, June 14
680 A222 30fr rose lake 2.75 1.00

10th anniv. of the defense of Bir-Hacheim.

Abbey of the Holy Cross, Poitiers — A223

1952, June 21
681 A223 15fr bright red 30 28

14th cent. of the foundation of the Abbey of the Holy Cross at Poitiers.

Leonardo da Vinci, Amboise Chateau and La Signoria, Florence A224

1952, July 9

682	A224	30fr deep ultra	7.00	3.00

500th anniv. of the birth of Leonardo da Vinci.

Garabit Viaduct A225

1952, July 5

683	A225	15fr dark blue	60	25

Sword and Military Medals, 1852-1952 A226

Dr. René Laennec A227

1952, July 5

684	A226	15fr choc, grn & yel	40	32

Cent. of the creation of the Military Medal.

1952, Nov. 7

685	A227	12fr dark green	38	32

Versailles Gate, Painted by Utrillo A228

1952, Dec. 20

686	A228	18fr violet brown	1.50	1.00

Publicity for the restoration of Versailles Palace. See No. 728.

Mannequin — A229

1953, Apr. 24 Unwmk. *Perf. 13*

687	A229	30fr blue blk & rose vio	70	28

Issued to publicize the dressmaking industry of France.

Gargantua of Franois Rabelais A230

Célimène from The Misanthrope A231

Figaro, from the Barber of Seville — A232

Hernani of Victor Hugo — A233

1953

688	A230	6fr dp plum & car	25	25
689	A231	8fr indigo & ultra	20	16
690	A232	12fr vio brn & dk grn	20	15
691	A233	18fr vio brn & blk brn	55	40

For surcharge see Reunion No. 298.

Type of 1948

Inscribed "Général Leclerc Maréchal de France"

1953-54

692	A176	8fr red brown	55	35
692A	A176	12fr dk grn & gray grn ('54)	2.00	1.10

Issued to honor the memory of General Jacques Leclerc.

Map and Cyclists, 1903-1953 A234

1953, July 26

693	A234	12fr red brn, ultra & blk	1.50	60

50th anniv. of the Bicycle Tour de France.

Arms Type of 1949

Coats of Arms: 50c, Picardy. 70c, Gascony. 80c, Berri. 1fr, Poitou. 2fr, Champagne. 3fr, Dauphiné.

1953 Typo. *Perf. 14x13½*

694	A182	50c blue, yel & red	24	22
695	A182	70c red, blue & yel	22	20
696	A182	80c blue, red & yel	22	20
697	A182	1fr black, red & yel	24	18
698	A182	2fr brown, bl & yel	24	18
699	A182	3fr red, blue & yel	45	20
		Nos. 694-699 (6)	1.61	1.18

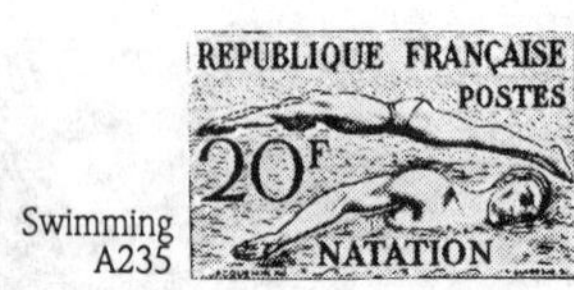

Swimming A235

1953, Nov. 28 Engr. *Perf. 13*

700	A235	20fr shown	2.25	24
701	A235	25fr Track	8.50	55
702	A235	30fr Fencing	2.25	32
703	A235	40fr Canoe racing	8.00	32
704	A235	50fr Rowing	4.75	24
705	A235	75fr Equestrian	30.00	13.00
		Nos. 700-705 (6)	55.75	14.67

For surcharges see Reunion Nos. 299-300.

No. 654 Surcharged with New Value and Bars in Black

1954 *Perf. 14x13½*

706	A147	15fr on 18fr cerise	52	15

Farm Woman — A236

Gallic Cock — A237

1954 Typo.

707	A236	4fr blue	30	15
708	A236	8fr brown red	4.50	70
709	A237	12fr cerise	3.25	32
710	A237	24fr blue green	13.00	3.50

Nos. 707-710 are known only precanceled. See second note after No. 132.

See Nos. 833-834, 840-844, 910-913, 939, 952-955. For surcharges see Reunion Nos. 324, 326-327.

Tapestry and Gobelin Workshop A238

Entrance to Exhibition Park A239

Designs: 30fr, Book manufacture. 40fr, Porcelain and glassware. 50fr, Jewelry and metalsmith's work. 75fr, Flowers and perfumes.

1954, May 6 Engr. *Perf. 13*

711	A238	25fr red brn car & blk brn	8.25	30
712	A238	30fr dk grn & lil gray	1.50	15
713	A238	40fr dk brn, vio brn & org brn	2.50	15
714	A238	50fr brt ultra, dl grn & org brn	1.75	15
715	A238	75fr dp car & magenta	10.00	45
		Nos. 711-715 (5)	24.00	
		Set value		1.00

For surcharges see Reunion Nos. 303-304.

1954, May 22

716	A239	15fr blue & dk car	35	30

Founding of the Fair of Paris, 50th anniv.

De Lattre Type of 1952

1954, June 5

717	A217	12fr vio bl & indigo	1.75	1.10

Allied Landings A240

1954, June 5

718	A240	15fr scarlet & ultra	1.25	50

The 10th anniversary of the liberation.

View of Lourdes A241

Street Corner, Quimper — A242

Views: 8fr, Seine valley, Les Andelys. 10fr, Beach at Royan. 18fr, Cheverny Chateau. 20fr, Beach, Gulf of Ajaccio.

1954

719	A241	6fr ultra, ind & dk grn	38	30
720	A241	8fr brt blue & dk grn	38	15
721	A241	10fr aqua & org brn	38	15
722	A242	12fr rose vio & dk vio	38	15
723	A241	18fr bl, dk grn & ind	2.50	60
724	A241	20fr blk brn, bl grn & red brn	2.00	15
		Nos. 719-724 (6)	6.02	1.50

See No. 873. For surcharges see Reunion Nos. 302, 306-310.

Abbey Ruins, Jumièges A243

St. Philibert Abbey, Tournus A244

1954, June 13

725	A243	12fr vio bl, ind & dk grn	1.40	80

13th centenary of Abbey of Jumièges.

1954, June 18

726	A244	30fr indigo & blue	6.00	3.75

1st conf. of the Intl. Center of Romance Studies.

View of Stenay A245

1954, June 26

727	A245	15fr dk brn & org brn	75	55

300th anniv. of the acquisition of Stenay by France.

Versailles Type of 1952

1954, July 10

728	A228	18fr dp bl, ind & vio brn	8.50	3.50

Villandry Chateau A246

1954, July 17

729	A246	18fr dk bl & dk bl grn	4.25	2.75

Napoleon Awarding Legion of Honor Decoration A247

1954, Aug. 14

730	A247	12fr scarlet	1.25	65

150th anniv. of the 1st Legion of Honor awards at Camp de Boulogne.

Cadets Marching Through Gateway A248

1954, Aug. 1

731	A248	15fr vio gray, dk bl & car	1.25	65

150th anniversary of the founding of the Military School of Saint-Cyr.

Allegory
A249

Duke de Saint-Simon
A250

1954, Oct. 4
732 A249 30fr indigo & choc 6.25 5.00

Issued to publicize the fact that the metric system was first introduced in France.

Arms Type of 1949

Arms: 50c, Maine. 70c, Navarre. 80c, Nivernais. 1fr, Bourbonnais. 2fr, Angoumois. 3fr, Aunis. 5fr, Saintonge.

1954 Typo. *Perf. 14x13½*

733	A182	50c	multicolored	16	15
734	A182	70c	green, red & yel	28	22
735	A182	80c	blue, red & yel	28	22
736	A182	1fr	red, blue & yel	18	15
737	A182	2fr	black, red & yel	15	15
738	A182	3fr	brown, red & yel	15	15
739	A182	5fr	blue & yellow	15	15
			Set value	1.10	80

1955, Feb. 5 Engr. *Perf. 13*
740 A250 12fr dk brn & vio brn 60 40

Louis de Rouvroy, Duke de Saint-Simon (1675-1755).

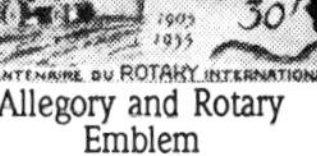
Allegory and Rotary Emblem
A251

Marianne
A252

1955, Feb. 23
741 A251 30fr vio bl, bl & org 1.40 1.00

50th anniv. of Rotary International.

1955-59 Typo. *Perf. 14x13½*

751	A252	6fr	fawn	2.75	1.75
752	A252	12fr	green	2.50	1.10
a.			Bklt. pane of 10 + 2 labels	30.00	
753	A252	15fr	carmine	30	15
a.			Booklet pane of 10	7.50	
754	A252	18fr	green ('58)	30	15
755	A252	20fr	ultra ('57)	45	15
756	A252	25fr	rose red ('59)	1.00	15
a.			Booklet pane of 8	10.00	
b.			Booklet pane of 10	11.00	
			Nos. 751-756 (6)	7.30	3.45

No. 751 was issued in coils of 1,000.

No. 752 was issued in panes of 10 stamps and two labels with marginal instructions for folding to form a booklet.

Nos. 754-755 are found in two types, distinguished by the numerals. On the 18fr there is no serif at base of "1" on the earlier type.

For surcharges see Reunion Nos. 330-331.

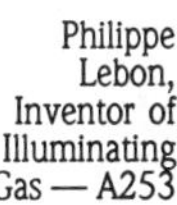

Philippe Lebon, Inventor of Illuminating Gas — A253

Inventors: 10fr, Barthélemy Thimonnier, sewing machine. 12fr, Nicolas Appert, canned foods. 18fr, Dr. E. H. St. Claire Deville, aluminum. 25fr, Pierre Martin, steel making. 30fr, Bernigaud de Chardonnet, rayon.

1955, Mar. 5 Engr.

757	A253	5fr	dk vio bl & bl	80	45
758	A253	10fr	dk brn & org brn	80	55
759	A253	12fr	dk green	1.10	65
760	A253	18fr	dk vio bl & ind	2.50	2.10
761	A253	25fr	dk brnsh pur & vio	2.50	1.90
762	A253	30fr	rose car & scar	2.50	1.90
			Nos. 757-762 (6)	10.20	7.55

St. Stephen Bridge, Limoges
A254

1955, Mar. 26 Unwmk. *Perf. 13*
763 A254 12fr yel brn & dk vio brn 1.25 70

Gloved Model in Place de la Concorde — A255

1955, Mar. 26
764 A255 25fr blk brn, vio bl & blk 75 16

French glove manufacturing.

Jean Pierre Claris de Florian
A256

1955, Apr. 2
765 A256 12fr blue green 60 35

200th anniv. of the birth of Jean Pierre Claris de Florian, fabulist.

Eiffel Tower and Television Antennas
A257

1955, Apr. 16
766 A257 15fr indigo & ultra 85 25

Issued to publicize French advancement in television.

Wire Fence and Guard Tower
A258

1955, Apr. 23
767 A258 12fr dk gray bl & brn blk 75 30

10th anniv. of the liberation of concentration camps.

Electric Train — A259

1955, May 11
768 A259 12fr blk brn & slate bl 2.00 60

Issued to publicize the electrification of the Valenciennes-Thionville railroad line.

Jacquemart of Moulins — A260

1955, May 28
769 A260 12fr black brown 1.40 65

Jules Verne and Nautilus
A261

1955, June 3
770 A261 30fr indigo 7.00 5.00

50th anniv. of the death of Jules Verne.

Auguste and Louis Lumière and Motion Picture Projector
A262

1955, June 12
771 A262 30fr rose brown 4.75 3.00

60th anniv. of the invention of motion pictures.

Jacques Coeur and His Mansion at Bourges
A263

1955, June 18
772 A263 12fr violet 2.00 1.20

5th centenary of the death of Jacques Coeur (1395?-1456), French merchant.

Corvette "La Capricieuse"
A264

1955, July 9
773 A264 30fr aqua & dk blue 5.50 3.25

Centenary of the voyage of La Capricieuse to Canada.

Bordeaux
A265

Designs: 8fr, Marseilles. 10fr, Nice. 12fr, Valentre bridge, Cahors. 18fr, Uzerche. 25fr, Fortifications, Brouage.

1955, Oct. 15

774	A265	6fr	carmine lake	32	22
775	A265	8fr	indigo	45	15
776	A265	10fr	dp ultra	40	15
777	A265	12fr	violet & brn	40	15
778	A265	18fr	bluish grn & ind	1.10	18
779	A265	25fr	org brn & red brn	1.25	15
			Nos. 774-779 (6)	3.92	
			Set value		78

See Nos. 838-839. For surcharges see Reunion Nos. 312-317, 323.

Mount Pelée, Martinique
A266

1955, Nov. 1
780 A266 20fr dk & lt purple 3.25 15

Gérard de Nerval — A267

1955, Nov. 11
781 A267 12fr lake & sepia 35 18

Centenary of the death of Gérard de Nerval (Labrunie), author.

Arms Type of 1949

Arms of: 50c, County of Foix. 70c, Marche. 80c, Roussillon. 1fr, Comtat Venaissin.

Perf. 14x13½
1955, Nov. 19 Typo. Unwmk.

782	A182	50c	multicolored	15	15
783	A182	70c	red, blue & yel	15	15
784	A182	80c	brown, yel & red	15	15
785	A182	1fr	blue, red & yel	15	15
			Set value	35	30

Concentration Camp Victim and Monument — A268

Belfry at Douai — A269

1956, Jan. 14 Engr. *Perf. 13*
786 A268 15fr brn blk & red brn 42 35

Natl. memorial for Nazi deportation victims erected at the Natzwiller Struthof concentration camp in Alsace.

1956, Feb. 11
787 A269 15fr ultra & indigo 35 30

Col. Emil Driant
A270

1956, Feb. 21
788 A270 15fr dark blue 30 25

40th anniv. of the death of Col. Emil Driant during the battle of Verdun.

The values of never-hinged stamps in superb condition are greater than catalogue value.

Trench Fighting — A271

1956, Mar. 3

789 A271 30fr indigo & dk olive 1.75 80

40th anniversary of Battle of Verdun.

Jean Henri Fabre, Entomology A272

Scientists: 15fr, Charles Tellier, Refrigeration. 18fr, Camille Flammarion, Popular Astronomy. 30fr, Paul Sabatier, Catalytic Chemistry.

1956, Apr. 7

790 A272 12fr vio brn & org brn 60 38
791 A272 15fr vio bl & int blk 90 55
792 A272 18fr brt ultra 2.25 1.25
793 A272 30fr Prus grn & dk grn 3.00 2.00

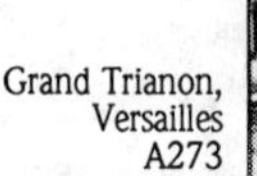

Grand Trianon, Versailles A273

1956, Apr. 14

794 A273 12fr vio brn & gray grn 1.25 85

Symbols of Latin American and French Culture A274

1956, Apr. 21

795 A274 30fr brown & red brn 1.75 1.10

Issued in recognition of the friendship between France and Latin America.

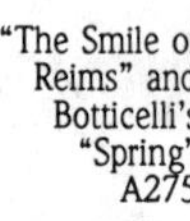

"The Smile of Reims" and Botticelli's "Spring" A275

1956, May 5

796 A275 12fr black & green 65 40

Issued to emphasize the cultural and artistic kinship of Reims and Florence.

Leprosarium and Maltese Cross — A276

1956, May 12

797 A276 12fr sepia, red brn & red 40 30

Issued in honor of the Knights of Malta.

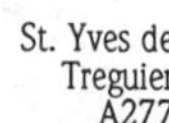

St. Yves de Treguier A277

1956, May 19

798 A277 15fr bluish gray & blk 30 20

St. Yves, patron saint of lawyers.

Marshal Franchet d'Esperey A278

Miners Monument A279

1956, May 26

799 A278 30fr deep claret 2.25 1.10

Centenary of the birth of Marshal Louis Franchet d'Esperey.

1956, June 2

800 A279 12fr violet brown 40 35

100th anniv. of the town Montceau-les-Mines.

Basketball A280

"Rebuilding Europe" A281

Sports: 40fr, Pelota (Jai alai). 50fr, Rugby. 75fr, Mountain climbing.

1956, July 7

801 A280 30fr gray vio & blk 1.00 18
802 A280 40fr brown & vio brn 3.25 28
803 A280 50fr rose vio & vio 2.00 15
804 A280 75fr indigo, grn & bl 6.50 1.50

For surcharges see Reunion Nos. 318-321.

Europa Issue

Perf. 13½x14

1956, Sept. 15 Typo. Unwmk.

805 A281 15fr rose & rose lake 1.00 22

Perf. 13

Engr.

806 A281 30fr lt blue & vio bl 5.25 85

Issued to symbolize the cooperation among the six countries comprising the Coal and Steel Community.

No. 805 measures 21x35½mm, No. 806 measures 22x35½mm.

Dam at Donzère-Mondragon — A282

Cable Railway to Pic du Midi — A283

Rhine Port of Strasbourg A284

1956, Oct. 6 Engr. *Perf. 13*

807 A282 12fr gray vio & vio brn 1.90 85
808 A283 18fr indigo 3.00 1.25
809 A284 30fr indigo & dk blue 10.00 2.50

French technical achievements.

Antoine-Augustin Parmentier — A285

1956, Oct. 27

810 A285 12fr brown red & brown 35 28

Parmentier, nutrition chemist, who popularized the potato in France.

Petrarch — A286

Portraits: 12fr, J. B. Lully. 15fr, J. J. Rousseau. 18fr, Benjamin Franklin. 20fr, Frederic Chopin. 30fr, Vincent van Gogh.

1956, Nov. 10

811 A286 8fr green 55 40
812 A286 12fr claret 55 40
813 A286 15fr dark red 80 60
814 A286 18fr ultra 2.50 1.40
815 A286 20fr brt violet 3.00 1.10
816 A286 30fr brt grnsh blue 3.50 2.25
Nos. 811-816 (6) 10.90 6.15

Issued in honor of famous men who lived in France.

Pierre de Coubertin and Olympic Stadium A287

1956, Nov. 24

817 A287 30fr dk blue gray & pur 1.25 70

Issued in honor of Baron Pierre de Coubertin, founder of the modern Olympic Games.

Homing Pigeon A288

1957, Jan. 12

818 A288 15fr dp ultra, ind & red brn 30 22

Victor Schoelcher — A289

1957, Feb. 16 Engr.

819 A289 18fr lilac rose 35 25

Issued in honor of Victor Schoelcher, who freed the slaves in the French Colonies.

Sèvres Porcelain A290

1957, Mar. 23 Unwmk. *Perf. 13*

820 A290 30fr ultra & vio blue 60 35

Bicentenary of the porcelain works at Sèvres (in 1956).

Gaston Planté and Storage Battery A291

Designs: 12fr, Antoine Béclère and X-ray apparatus. 18fr, Octave Terrillon, autoclave, microscope and surgical instruments. 30fr, Etienne Oemichen and early helicopter.

1957, Apr. 13

821 A291 8fr gray blk & dp cl 32 32
822 A291 12fr dk blue, blk & emer 40 38
823 A291 18fr rose red & magenta 1.25 1.25
824 A291 30fr green & slate grn 1.75 1.65

Uzès Chateau A292

1957, Apr. 27

825 A292 12fr slate bl & bis brn 30 25

Jean Moulin A293

Le Quesnoy A294

Portraits: 10fr, Honoré d'Estienne d'Orves. 12fr, Robert Keller. 18fr, Pierre Brossolette. 20fr, Jean-Baptiste Lebas.

1957, May 18

826 A293 8fr violet brown 52 35
827 A293 10fr black & vio bl 48 35
828 A293 12fr brown & sl grn 52 30
829 A293 18fr purple & blk 1.65 80
830 A293 20fr Prus bl & dk bl 90 45
Nos. 826-830 (5) 4.07 2.25

Issued in honor of the heroes of the French Underground of World War II.

See #879-882, 915-919, 959-963, 990-993.

1957, June 1

831 A294 8fr dk slate green 20 18

See No. 837. For surcharge see Reunion No. 322.

Symbols of Justice
A295

1957, June 1
832 A295 12fr sepia & ultra 30 30

150th anniv. of the French Cour des Comptes.

Farm Woman Type of 1954

1957-59 ***Perf. 14x13½***
833 A236 6fr orange 15 15
833A A236 10fr brt green ('59) 60 15
834 A236 12fr red lilac 18 15
Set value 31

Nos. 833-834 issued without precancellation.

Symbols of Public Works A296

1957, June 20 Engr. ***Perf. 13***
835 A296 30fr sl grn, brn & ocher 1.25 52

Brest — A297

1957, July 6
836 A297 12fr gray grn & brn ol 55 28

Scenic Types of 1955, 1957

Designs: 15fr, Le Quesnoy. 35fr, Bordeaux. 70fr, Valentre bridge, Cahors.

1957, July 19 Unwmk.
837 A294 15fr dk blue grn & sep 30 15
838 A265 35fr dk blue grn & sl grn 2.00 60
839 A265 70fr black & dull grn 9.50 1.75

Gallic Cock Type of 1954

1957 Typo. ***Perf. 14x13½***
840 A237 5fr olive bister 35 22
841 A237 10fr bright blue 75 28
842 A237 15fr plum 1.65 45
843 A237 30fr bright red 4.50 90
844 A237 45fr green 26.00 11.00
Nos. 840-844 (5) 33.25 12.85

Nos. 840-844 are known only precanceled. See second note after No. 132.

Leo Lagrange and Stadium A298

1957, Aug. 31 Engr. ***Perf. 13***
845 A298 18fr lilac gray & blk 40 20

Intl. University Games, Paris, Aug. 31-Sept. 8.

"United Europe" A299

Auguste Comte A300

1957, Sept. 16
846 A299 20fr red brown & green 30 18
847 A299 35fr dk brown & blue 95 38

Issued to publicize a united Europe for peace and prosperity.

1957, Sept. 14
848 A300 35fr brown red & sepia 40 35

Centenary of the death of Auguste Comte, mathematician and philosopher.

Roman Amphitheater, Lyon — A301

1957, Oct. 5 ***Perf. 13***
849 A301 20fr brn org & brn vio 38 22

2,000th anniv. of the founding of Lyon.

Sens River, Guadeloupe A302

Beynac-Cazenac, Dordogne A303

Nicolaus Copernicus A304

Designs: 10fr, Elysee Palace. 25fr, Chateau de Valencay, Indre. 35fr, Rouen Cathedral. 50fr, Roman Ruins, Saint-Remy. 65fr, Evian-les-Bains.

1957, Oct. 19
850 A302 8fr green & lt brn 15 15
851 A302 10fr dk ol bis & vio brn 15 15
852 A303 18fr indigo & dk brn 20 15
853 A302 25fr bl gray & vio brn 28 15
854 A303 35fr car rose & lake 28 15
855 A302 50fr ol grn & ol bis 38 15
856 A302 65fr dk blue & indigo 60 15
Nos. 850-856 (7) 2.04
Set value 56

See Nos. 907-909. For overprint see No. 101. For surcharges see Reunion Nos. 325, 328-329, 332-334

1957, Nov. 9 Engr. ***Perf. 13***

Portraits: 10fr, Michelangelo. 12fr, Miguel de Cervantes. 15fr, Rembrandt. 18fr, Isaac Newton. 25fr, Mozart. 35fr, Johann Wolfgang von Goethe.

857 A304 8fr dark brown 60 45
858 A304 10fr dark green 65 45
859 A304 12fr dark purple 75 45
860 A304 15fr brown & org brn 95 40
861 A304 18fr deep blue 1.25 90
862 A304 25fr lilac & claret 1.25 45
863 A304 35fr blue 1.50 1.10
Nos. 857-863 (7) 6.95 4.20

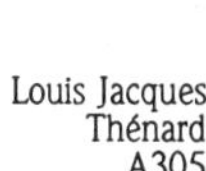

Louis Jacques Thénard A305

1957, Nov. 30 Unwmk.
864 A305 15fr ol bis & grnsh blk 30 30

Centenary of the death of L. J. Thenard, chemist, and the founding of the Charitable Society of the Friends of Science.

Dr. Philippe Pinel A306

Joseph Louis Lagrange A307

French Physicians: 12fr, Fernand Widal. 15fr, Charles Nicolle. 35fr, René Leriche.

1958, Jan. 25
865 A306 8fr brown olive 75 50
866 A306 12fr brt vio blue 75 50
867 A306 15fr deep blue 1.10 60
868 A306 35fr black 1.65 1.00

1958, Feb. 15 ***Perf. 13***

French Scientists: 12fr, Urbain Jean Joseph Leverrier. 15fr, Jean Bernard Leon Foucault. 35fr, Claude Louis Berthollet.

869 A307 8fr blue grn & vio bl 80 55
870 A307 12fr sepia & gray 95 70
871 A307 15fr slate grn & grn 1.90 95
872 A307 35fr maroon & cop red 2.00 1.10

Lourdes Type of 1954

1958
873 A241 20fr grnsh bl & ol 25 15

Le Havre — A308

Maubeuge — A309

Designs: 18fr, Saint-Die. 25fr, Sete.

1958, Mar. 29 Engr. ***Perf. 13***
874 A308 12fr ol grn & car rose 55 45
875 A309 15fr brt purple & brn 60 40
876 A309 18fr ultra & indigo 95 75
877 A308 25fr dk bl, bl grn & brn 1.25 75

Reconstruction of war-damaged cities.

French Pavilion, Brussels A310

1958, Apr. 12
878 A310 35fr brn, dk grn & bl 28 24

Issued for the Universal and International Exposition at Brussels.

Heroes Type of 1957

Portraits: 8fr, Jean Cavaillès. 12fr, Fred Scamaroni. 15fr, Simone Michel-Levy. 20fr, Jacques Bingen.

1958, Apr. 19
879 A293 8fr violet & black 40 30
880 A293 12fr ultra & green 40 30
881 A293 15fr brown & gray 1.10 90
882 A293 20fr olive & ultra 1.00 65

Issued in honor of the heroes of the French Underground in World War II.

Bowling A311

Sports: 15fr, Naval joust. 18fr, Archery, vert. 25fr, Breton wrestling, vert.

1958, Apr. 26
883 A311 12fr rose & brown 80 38
884 A311 15fr blue, ol gray & grn 1.10 55
885 A311 18fr green & brown 1.90 95
886 A311 25fr brown & indigo 2.50 1.25

Senlis Cathedral — A312

1958, May 17
887 A312 15fr ultra & indigo 30 30

Bayeux Tapestry Horsemen A313

1958, June 21
888 A313 15fr blue & carmine 35 25

Europa Issue, 1958

Common Design Type

1958, Sept. 13 Engr. ***Perf. 13***
Size: 22x36mm
889 CD1 20fr rose red 28 15
890 CD1 35fr ultra 52 28

Foix Chateau A314

1958, Oct. 11
891 A314 15fr ultra, grn & ol brn 20 15

City Halls, Paris and Rome — A315

1958, Oct. 11
892 A315 35fr gray, grnsh bl & rose red 30 24

Issued to publicize the cultural ties between Rome and Paris and the need for European unity.

Common Design Types pictured in section at front of book.

UNESCO Building, Paris — A316

Design: 35fr, Different view of building.

1958, Nov. 1 *Perf. 13*

893 A316 20fr grnsh blue & ol bis 15 15
894 A316 35fr dk sl grn & red org 20 18

Opening of UNESCO Headquarters in Paris, Nov. 3.

Soldier's Grave in Wheat Field A317

Arms of Marseilles A318

1958, Nov. 11

895 A317 15fr dk green & ultra 16 15

40th anniv. of the World War I armistice.

1958-59 **Typo.** *Perf. 14x13½*

Arms (Cities): 70c, Lyon. 80c, Toulouse. 1fr, Bordeaux. 2fr, Nice. 3fr, Nantes. 5fr, Lille. 15fr, Algiers.

896 A318 50c dk blue & ultra 15 15
897 A318 70c multicolored 15 15
898 A318 80c red, blue & yel 15 15
899 A318 1fr dk bl, yel & red 15 15
900 A318 2fr dk bl, red & grn 15 15
901 A318 3fr multicolored 15 15
902 A318 5fr dk brown & red 15 15
903 A318 15fr multi ('59) 18 15
Set value 75 45

See Nos. 938, 940, 973, 1040-1042, 1091-1095, 1142-1144. For surcharges see Reunion Nos. 336, 345-346, 350-351, 353.

Arc de Triomphe and Flowers — A319

1959, Jan. 17 **Engr.** *Perf. 13*

904 A319 15fr brn, bl, grn, cl & red 30 18

Paris Flower Festival.

Symbols of Learning and Medal A320

1959, Jan. 24 *Perf. 13*

905 A320 20fr lake, blk & vio 18 18

Sesquicentennial of the Palm Leaf Medal of the French Academy.

Charles de Foucauld A321

1959, Jan. 31

906 A321 50fr dp brn, bl & mar 45 35

Issued to honor Father Charles de Foucauld, explorer and missionary of the Sahara.

Type of 1957

Designs: 30fr, Elysee Palace. 85fr, Evian-les Bains. 100fr, Sens River, Guadeloupe.

1959, Feb. 10

907 A302 30fr dk slate green 1.40 22
908 A302 85fr deep claret 2.75 25
909 A302 100fr deep violet 16.00 42

Gallic Cock Type of 1954

1959 **Typo.** *Perf. 14x13½*

910 A237 8fr violet 60 22
911 A237 20fr yellow grn 1.75 65
912 A237 40fr henna brn 4.00 2.25
913 A237 55fr emerald 17.50 10.00

Nos. 910-913 were issued with precancellation. See second note after No. 132.

Miners' Tools and School A322

1959, Apr. 11 **Engr.** *Perf. 13*

914 A322 20fr red, blk & blue 15 15

175th anniv. of the National Mining School.

Heroes Type of 1957

Portraits: No. 915, The five martyrs of the Buffon school. No. 916, Yvonne Le Roux. No. 917, Médéric-Védy. No. 918, Louis Martin-Bret. 30fr, Gaston Moutardier.

1959, Apr. 25 **Engr.** *Perf. 13*

915 A293 15fr black & vio 30 20
916 A293 15fr mag & rose vio 38 28
917 A293 20fr green & grnsh bl 38 28
918 A293 20fr org brn & brn 55 38
919 A293 30fr magenta & vio 65 38
Nos. 915-919 (5) 2.26 1.52

Dam at Foum el Gherza A323

Marcoule Atomic Center — A324

Designs: 30fr, Oil field at Hassi Messaoud, Sahara. 50fr, C. N. I. T. Building (Centre National des Industries et des Techniques).

1959, May 23

920 A323 15fr olive & grnsh bl 24 18
921 A324 20fr brt car & red brn 32 22
922 A324 30fr dk blue, brn & grn 50 22
923 A323 50fr ol grn & sl blue 95 35

Issued to publicize French technical achievements.

Marceline Desbordes-Valmore — A325

1959, June 20

924 A325 30fr blue, brn & grn 25 22

Centenary of the death of Marceline Desbordes-Valmore, poet.

Pilots Goujon and Rozanoff A326

1959, June 13

925 A326 20fr lt blue & org brn 25 22

Issued in honor of Charles Goujon and Col. Constantin Rozanoff, test pilots.

Tancarville Bridge A327

1959, Aug. 1 **Engr.** *Perf. 13*

926 A327 30fr dk blue, brn & ol 25 18

Marianne and Ship of State — A328

Jean Jaures — A329

1959, July **Typo.** *Perf. 14x13½*

927 A328 25fr black & red 28 15

See No. 942. For surcharge see No. B336.

1959, Sept. 12 **Engr.** *Perf. 13*

928 A329 50fr chocolate 35 22

Centenary of the birth of Jean Jaures, socialist leader.

Europa Issue, 1959

Common Design Type

1959, Sept. 19

Size: 22x36mm

929 CD2 25fr bright green 30 18
930 CD2 50fr bright violet 60 25

Blood Donors A330

1959, Oct. 17 **Engr.**

931 A330 20fr magenta & gray 25 16

French-Spanish Handshake — A331

1959, Oct. 24 *Perf. 13*

932 A331 50fr blue, rose car & org 38 25

300th anniv. of the signing of the Treaty of the Pyrenees.

Polio Victim Holding Crutches A332

Henri Bergson A333

1959, Oct. 31

933 A332 20fr dark blue 16 15

Vaccination against poliomyelitis.

1959, Nov. 7

934 A333 50fr lt red brown 30 22

Centenary of the birth of Henri Bergson, philosopher.

Avesnes-sur-Helpe — A334

Design: 30fr, Perpignan.

1959, Nov. 14

935 A334 20fr sepia & blue 20 15
936 A334 30fr brn, dp cl & bl 28 16

New NATO Headquarters, Paris — A335

1959, Dec. 12

937 A335 50fr green, brn & ultra 60 40

10th anniv. of the NATO.

Types of 1958-59 and

Farm Woman A336

Sower A337

Designs: 5c, Arms of Lille. 15c, Arms of Algiers. 25c, Marianne and Ship of State.

Perf. 14x13½

1960-61 **Unwmk.** **Typo.**

938 A318 5c dk brown & red 7.25 15
939 A336 10c brt green 26 15
940 A318 15c red, ultra, yel & grn 60 15
941 A337 20c grnsh bl & car rose 18 15
942 A328 25c ver & ultra 2.25 15
b. Booklet pane of 8 27.50
c. Booklet pane of 10 32.50
942A A337 30c gray & ultra ('61) 2.00 28
Nos. 938-942A (6) 12.54
Set value 70

See Nos. 707-708, 833-834 for the Farm Woman type (A336), but with no decimals in denominations.

For surcharges see Reunion Nos. 337-338, 341. For overprint see Algeria No. 286.

Laon Cathedral A338

Kerrata Gorge — A339

Designs: 30c, Fougères Chateau. 50c, Mosque, Tlemcen. 65c, Sioule Valley. 85c, Chaumont Viaduct. 1fr, Cilaos Church, Reunion.

1960, Jan. 16 Engr. *Perf. 13*

943	A338	15c	blue & indigo	25	15
944	A338	30c	blue, sepia & grn	2.75	15
945	A339	45c	brt vio & ol gray	85	15
946	A339	50c	sl grn & lt cl	85	15
947	A338	65c	sl grn, bl & blk brn	1.00	15
948	A338	85c	blue, sep & grn	2.75	15
949	A339	1fr	vio bl, bl & grn	1.65	15
			Nos. 943-949 (7)	10.10	
			Set value		80

For surcharges see Reunion Nos. 335, 340, 342. For overprint see Algeria Nos. 288-289.

Pierre de Nolhac A340

1960, Feb. 13

950	A340	20c	black & gray	52	30

Centenary of the birth of Pierre de Nolhac, curator of Versailles and historian.

Museum of Art and Industry, Saint-Etienne A341

1960, Feb. 20

951	A341	30c	brn, car & slate	60	30

Gallic Cock Type of 1954

1960 Typo. *Perf. 14x13½*

952	A237	8c	violet	95	15
953	A237	20c	yellow grn	3.25	32
954	A237	40c	henna brn	7.75	2.00
955	A237	55c	emerald	27.50	12.00

Nos. 952-955 were issued only precanceled. See second note after No. 132.

View of Cannes A342

1960, Mar. 5 Engr. *Perf. 13*

956	A342	50c	red brn & lt grn	60	48

Meeting of European municipal administrators, Cannes, Mar., 1960.

Woman of Savoy and Alps — A343

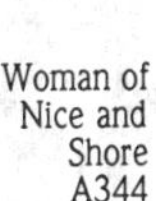

Woman of Nice and Shore A344

1960 Unwmk. *Perf. 13*

957	A343	30c	slate green	48	32
958	A344	50c	brown, yel & rose	52	28

Cent. of the annexation of Nice and Savoy.

Heroes Type of 1957

Portraits: No. 959, Edmund Debeaumarché. No. 960, Pierre Massé. No. 961, Maurice Ripoche. No. 962, Leonce Vieljeux. 50c, Abbé René Bonpain.

1960, Mar. 26

959	A293	20c	bister & blk	1.90	1.00
960	A293	20c	pink & rose cl	1.90	1.00
961	A293	30c	vio & brt vio	1.90	1.00
962	A293	30c	sl blue & brt bl	2.25	1.50
963	A293	50c	sl grn & red brn	2.75	1.90
			Nos. 959-963 (5)	10.70	6.40

Issued in honor of the heroes of the French Underground of World War II.

"Education" and Children A345

1960, May 21 Engr. *Perf. 13*

964	A345	20c	rose lilac, pur & blk	25	20

150th anniversary of the first secondary school in Strasbourg.

Blois Chateau A346

View of La Bourboule A347

1960, May

965	A346	30c	dk blue, sep & grn	55	28
966	A347	50c	ol brown, car & grn	70	35

Lorraine Cross A348

Marianne A349

1960, June 18

967	A348	20c	red brn, dk brn & yel grn	35	15

20th anniv. of the French Resistance Movement in World War II.

1960, June 18 Typo. *Perf. 14x13½*

968	A349	25c	lake & gray	15	15
a.			Booklet pane of 0	4.50	
b.			Booklet pane of 10	3.50	

For surcharge see Reunion No. 339. For overprint see Algeria No. 287.

Jean Bouin and Stadium A350

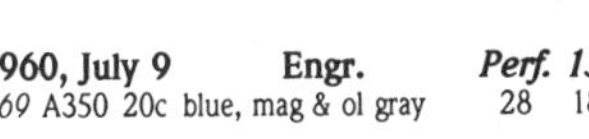

1960, July 9 Engr. *Perf. 13*

969	A350	20c	blue, mag & ol gray	28	18

17th Olympic Games, Rome, Aug. 25-Sept. 11.

Europa Issue, 1960

Common Design Type

1960, Sept. 17 *Perf. 13*

Size: 36x22mm

970	CD3	25c	green & bluish grn	15	15
971	CD3	50c	maroon & red lilac	28	18

Lisieux Basilica A351

1960, Sept. 24 *Perf. 13*

972	A351	15c	blue, gray & blk	22	18

Arms Type of 1958-59

Design: Arms of Oran.

1960, Oct. 15 Typo. *Perf. 14x13½*

973	A318	5c	red, bl, yel & emer	18	15

Madame de Stael by Franois Gerard — A352

1960, Oct. 22 Engr. *Perf. 13*

974	A352	30c	dull claret & brn	22	18

Madame de Stael (1766-1817), writer.

Gen. J. B. E. Estienne A353

1960, Nov. 5

975	A353	15c	lt lilac & black	20	15

Centenary of the birth of Gen. Jean Baptiste Eugene Estienne.

Marc Sangnier and Youth Hostel at Bierville A354

1960, Nov. 5

976	A354	20c	blue, blk & lilac	15	15

Issued to honor Marc Sangnier, founder of the French League for Youth Hostels.

Badge of Order of Liberation — A355

1960, Nov. 14 Engr. *Perf. 13*

977	A355	20c	black & brt green	32	18

Order of Liberation, 20th anniversary.

Lapwings A356

Birds: 30c, Puffin. 45c, European teal. 50c, European bee-eaters.

1960, Nov. 12

978	A356	20c	multicolored	28	20
979	A356	30c	multicolored	28	25
980	A356	45c	multicolored	95	50
981	A356	50c	multicolored	60	25

Issued to publicize wildlife protection.

André Honnorat A357

1960, Nov. 19

982	A357	30c	blue, blk & green	30	24

Honnorat, statesman, fighter against tuberculosis and founder of the University City of Paris, an intl. students' community.

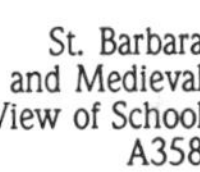

St. Barbara and Medieval View of School A358

1960, Dec. 3 Engr.

983	A358	30c	red, bl & ol brn	30	30

St. Barbara School, Paris, 500th anniv.

"Mediterranean" by Aristide Maillol — A359

1961, Feb. 18 Unwmk. *Perf. 13*

984	A359	20c	carmine & indigo	20	16

Aristide Maillol, sculptor, birth cent.

Marianne by Cocteau — A360

1961, Feb. 23

985	A360	20c	blue & carmine	15	15

A second type has an extra inverted V-shaped mark (a blue flag top) at right of hair tip. Value unused $1.75, used 35 cents.

For surcharge see Reunion No. 357.

Paris Airport, Orly — A361

1961, Feb. 25

986	A361	50c	blk, dk bl, & bluish grn	38	22

Inauguration of new facilities at Orly airport.

George Méliès and Motion Picture Screen A362

1961, Mar. 11

987 A362 50c pur, ind & ol bis 60 30

Cent. of the birth of George Méliès, motion picture pioneer.

Jean Baptiste Henri Lacordaire — A363

1961, Mar. 25 *Perf. 13*

988 A363 30c lt brown & black 25 25

Cent. of the death of the Dominican monk Lacordaire, orator and liberal Catholic leader.

A364

1961, Mar. 25

989 A364 30c grn, red brn & red 28 25

Introduction of tobacco use into France, fourth centenary. By error stamp portrays Jan Nicquet instead of Jean Nicot.

Heroes Type of 1957

Portraits: No. 990, Jacques Renouvin. No. 991, Lionel Dubray. No. 992, Paul Gateaud. No. 993, Mère Elisabeth.

1961, Apr. 22

990 A293 20c blue & lilac 70 40
991 A293 20c gray grn & blue 70 42
992 A293 30c brown org & blk 95 52
993 A293 30c violet & blk 1.25 60

Bagnoles-de-l'Orne — A365

1961, May 6

994 A365 20c ol, ocher, bl & grn 22 15

Dove, Olive Branch and Federation Emblem — A366

1961, May 6

995 A366 50c brt bl, grn & mar 28 22

World Federation of Ex-Service Men.

Deauville in 19th Century A367

1961, May 13 **Engr.**

996 A367 50c rose claret 1.50 75

Centenary of Deauville.

La Champmeslé A368

Mont-Dore, Snowflake and Cable Car A369

French actors: No. 998, Talma. No. 999, Rachel. No. 1000, Gérard Philipe. No. 1001, Raimu.

1961, June 10 **Unwmk.** *Perf. 13*

Dark Carmine Frame

997 A368 20c choc & yel grn 42 20
998 A368 30c brown & crimson 45 25
999 A368 30c yel grn & sl grn 45 25
1000 A368 50c olive & choc 85 40
1001 A368 50c bl grn & red brn 85 30
Nos. 997-1001 (5) 3.02 1.40

Issued to honor great French actors and in connection with the Fifth World Congress of the International Federation of Actors.

1961, July 1

1002 A369 20c orange & rose lil 25 20

Pierre Fauchard A370

St. Theobald's Church, Thann A371

1961, July 1

1003 A370 50c dk green & blk 45 30

Bicentenary of the death of Pierre Fauchard, 1st surgeon dentist.

1961, July 1

1004 A371 20c sl grn, vio & brn 45 30

800th anniversary of Thann.

Europa Issue, 1961

Common Design Type

1961, Sept. 16 *Perf. 13*

Size: 35x22mm

1005 CD4 25c vermilion 15 15
1006 CD4 50c ultramarine 28 18
Set value 26

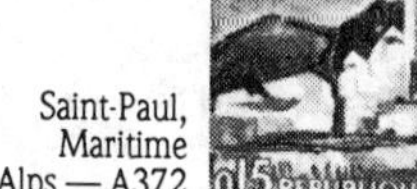

Saint-Paul, Maritime Alps — A372

Designs: 30c, Beach and sailboats, Arcachon. 45c, Sully-sur-Loire Chateau. 50c, View of Cognac. 65c, Rance Valley and Dinan. 85c, City hall and Rodin's Burghers, Calais. 1fr, Roman gates of Lodi, Medea, Algeria.

1961, Oct. 9 **Engr.** *Perf. 13*

1007 A372 15c blue & purple 15 15
1008 A372 30c ultra, sl grn & lt brn 25 15
1009 A372 45c vio bl, red brn & grn 30 15
1010 A372 50c grn, Prus bl & sl 48 15
1011 A372 65c red brn, sl grn & bl 48 15
1012 A372 85c sl grn, sl & red brn 75 15
1013 A372 1fr dk bl, sl & bis 2.50 15
Nos. 1007-1013 (7) 4.91
Set value 75

For surcharges see Reunion Nos. 347-348. For overprint see Algeria No. 290.

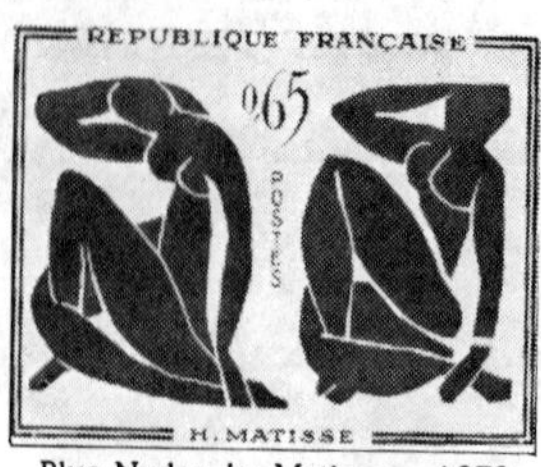

Blue Nudes, by Matisse — A373

Paintings: 50c, "The Messenger," by Braque. 85c, "The Cardplayers," by Cézanne. 1fr, "The 14th July," by Roger de La Fresnaye.

1961, Nov. 10 *Perf. 13x12*

1014 A373 50c dk brn, bl, blk & gray 2.75 1.50
1015 A373 65c grn, vio, & ultra 3.25 2.00
1016 A373 85c blk, brn, red & ol 2.50 1.65
1017 A373 1fr multicolored 3.75 2.50

Liner France A374

1962, Jan. 11 **Engr.** *Perf. 13*

1018 A374 30c dk blue, blk & car 45 25

New French liner France.

Skier Going Downhill A375

Maurice Bourdet A376

1962, Jan. 27 *Perf. 13*

1019 A375 30c shown 18 16
1020 A375 50c Slalom 32 22

Issued to publicize the World Ski Championships, Chamonix, Feb. 1962.

1962, Feb. 17

1021 A376 30c slate 20 15

60th anniv. of the birth of Maurice Bourdet, radio commentator and resistance hero.

Pierre-Fidele Bretonneau A377

1962, Feb. 17

1022 A377 50c brt lilac & blue 28 18

Centenary of the death of Pierre-Fidele Bretonneau, physician.

Chateau and Bridge, Laval, Mayenne A378

Gallic Cock A379

1962, Feb. 24

1023 A378 20c bis brn & sl grn 25 20

1962-65 *Perf. 13*

1024 A379 25c ultra, car & brn 25 15
a. Bklt. pane of 4 (horiz. strip) 2.50
1024B A379 30c gray grn, red & brn ('65) 85 15
c. Booklet pane of 5 5.00
d. Booklet pane of 10 10.00
Set value 15

No. 1024 was also issued on experimental luminescent paper in 1963.

Ramparts of Vannes A380

Dunkirk — A381

Paris Beach, Le Touquet A381a

1962 **Engr.** *Perf. 13*

1025 A380 30c dark blue 48 38
1026 A381 95c grn, bis & red lil 1.25 15
1027 A381a 1fr grn, red brn & bl 45 15

No. 1026 for the 300th anniv. of Dunkirk.

Stage Setting and Globe A382

1962, Mar. 24 **Unwmk.**

1028 A382 50c sl grn, ocher & mag 35 25

International Day of the Theater, Mar. 27.

Memorial to Fighting France, Mont Valerien A383

Resistance Heroes' Monument, Vercors — A384

Design: 50c, Ile de Sein monument.

1962, Apr. 7

1029 A383	20c olive & sl grn		65	22
1030 A384	30c bluish black		50	28
1031 A384	50c blue & indigo		85	35

Issued to publicize memorials for the French Underground in World War II.

Malaria Eradication Emblem and Swamp A385

Nurses with Child and Hospital A386

1962, Apr. 14 **Engr.**

1032 A385	50c dk blue & dk red	32	24

WHO drive to eradicate malaria.

1962, May 5 **Unwmk.** ***Perf. 13***

1033 A386	30c bl grn, gray & red brn	16	16

National Hospital Week, May 5-12.

Glider — A387

Design: 20c, Planes showing development of aviation.

1962, May 12

1034 A387	15c orange red & brn	30	22
1035 A387	20c lil rose & rose cl	35	25

Issued to publicize sports aviation.

School Emblem — A388

1962, May 19 **Engr.**

1036 A388	50c mar, ocher & dk vio	35	30

Watchmaker's School at Besanon, cent.

Louis XIV and Workers Showing Modern Gobelin A389

1962, May 26 **Unwmk.** ***Perf. 13***

1037 A389	50c olive, sl grn & car	35	25

300th anniv. of the Gobelin tapestry works, Paris.

Blaise Pascal A390

1962, May 26

1038 A390	50c sl grn & dp org	40	25

Blaise Pascal (1623-1662), mathematician, scientist and philosopher.

Palace of Justice, Rennes A391

1962, June 12

1039 A391	30c blk, grysh bl & grn	1.50	60

Arms Type of 1958-59

Arms: 5c, Amiens. 10c, Troyes. 15c, Nevers.

1962-63 **Typo.** ***Perf. 14x13½***

1040 A318	5c ver, ultra & yel	15	15
1041 A318	10c red, ultra & yel ('63)	15	15
1042 A318	15c ver, ultra & yel	15	15
	Set value	25	15

Phosphor Tagging

In 1970 France began to experiment with luminescence. Phosphor bands have been added to Nos. 1041, 1143, 1231, 1231C, 1292A-1294B, 1494-1498, 1560-1579B, etc.

Rose — A392

Design: 30c, Old-fashioned rose.

1962, Sept. 8 **Engr.** ***Perf. 13***

1043 A392	20c ol, grn & brt car	38	18
1044 A392	30c dk sl grn, ol & car	52	28

Europa Issue, 1962

Common Design Type

1962, Sept. 15

Size: 36x22mm

1045 CD5	25c violet	15	15
1046 CD5	50c henna brown	28	18

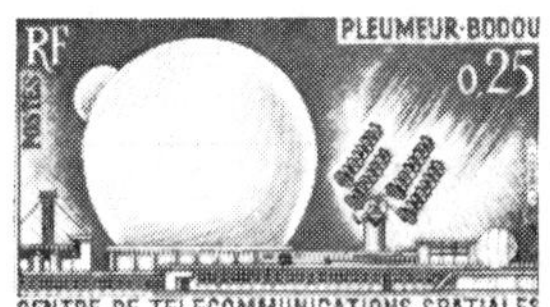

Space Communications Center, Pleumeur-Bodou, France — A394

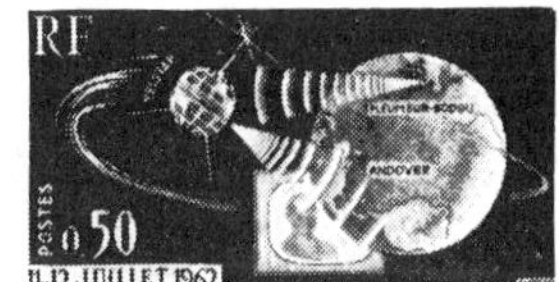

Telstar, Earth and Television Set — A395

1962, Sept. 29 **Engr.** ***Perf. 13***

1047 A394	25c gray, yel & grn	18	15
1048 A395	50c dk bl, grn & ultra	32	24

1st television connection of the US and Europe through Telstar satellite, July 11-12.

For surcharges see Reunion Nos. 343-344.

"Bonjour Monsieur Courbet" by Gustave Courbet — A396

Paintings: 65c, "Madame Manet on Blue Sofa," by Edouard Manet. 1fr, "Guards officer on horseback," by Theodore Géricault, vert.

1962, Nov. 9 ***Perf. 13x12, 12x13***

1049 A396	50c multicolored	3.25	1.65
1050 A396	65c multicolored	2.50	1.65
1051 A396	1fr multicolored	4.75	2.50

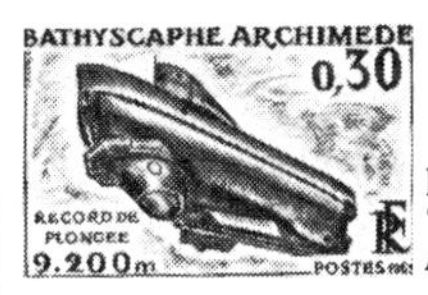

Bathyscaph "Archimede" A397

1963, Jan. 26 **Unwmk.** ***Perf. 13***

1052 A397	30c dk blue & blk	22	18

French deep-sea explorations.

Flowers and Nantes Chateau A398

1963, Feb. 11

1053 A398	30c vio bl, car & sl grn	22	18

Nantes flower festival.

St. Peter, Window at St. Foy de Conches A399

Design: 50c, Jacob Wrestling with the Angel, by Delacroix.

1963, Mar. 2 ***Perf. 12x13***

1054 A399	50c multicolored	3.25	1.75
1055 A399	1fr multicolored	4.75	3.00

See Nos. 1076-1077.

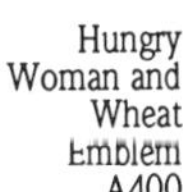

Hungry Woman and Wheat Emblem A400

1963, Mar. 21 **Engr.** ***Perf. 13***

1056 A400	50c slate grn & brn	30	18

FAO "Freedom from Hunger" campaign.

Cemetery and Memorial, Glières — A401

Design: 50c, Memorial, Ile de la Cité, Paris.

1963, Mar. 23 **Unwmk.** ***Perf. 13***

1057 A401	30c dk brown & ol	25	25
1058 A401	50c indigo	32	32

Heroes of the resistance against the Nazis.

Beethoven, Birthplace at Bonn and Rhine — A402

Designs: No. 1060, Emile Verhaeren, memorial at Roisin and residence. No. 1061, Giuseppe Mazzini, Marcus Aurelius statue and Via Appia, Rome. No. 1062, Emile Mayrisch, Colpach Chateau and blast furnace, Esch. No. 1063, Hugo de Groot, Palace of Peace, The Hague and St. Agatha Church, Delft.

1963, Apr. 27 **Unwmk.** ***Perf. 13***

1059 A402	20c ocher, sl & brt grn	28	24
1060 A402	20c purple, blk & mar	28	24
1061 A402	20c maroon, sl & ol	28	24
1062 A402	20c mar, dk brn & ocher	28	24
1063 A402	30c dk brn, vio & ocher	28	24
	Nos. 1059-1063 (5)	1.40	1.20

Issued to honor famous men of the European Common Market countries.

Hotel des Postes and Stagecoach, 1863 — A403

1963, May 4

1064 A403	50c grayish black	35	28

1st Intl. Postal Conference, Paris, 1863.

Lycée Louis-le-Grand, Belvédère, Panthéon and St. Etienne du Mont Church — A404

1963, May 18

1065 A404	30c slate green	32	30

400th anniversary of the Jesuit Clermont secondary school, named after Louis XIV.

St. Peter's Church and Ramparts, Caen — A405

1963, June 1 **Unwmk.** ***Perf. 13***

1066 A405	30c gray blue & brn	32	32

Radio Telescope, Nanay — A406

1963, June 8 **Engr.**

1067 A406 50c dk bl & dk brn 32 28

Amboise Chateau A407

Saint-Flour — A408

Designs: 50c, Côte d'Azur Varoise. 85c, Vittel. 95c, Moissac.

1963, June 15

1068 A407 30c slate, grn & bis 25 15
1069 A407 50c dk grn, dk bl & hn brn 38 15
1070 A408 60c ultra, dk grn & hn brn 42 18
1071 A407 85c dk grn, yel grn & brn 1.25 15
1072 A408 95c dk brown & black 75 18
Nos. 1068-1072 (5) 3.05
Set value 60

For surcharge see Reunion No. 355.

Water Skiing Slalom A409

1963, Aug. 31 **Unwmk.** ***Perf. 13***

1073 A409 30c sl grn, blk & car 22 18

World Water Skiing Championships, Vichy.

Europa Issue, 1963

Common Design Type

1963, Sept. 14

Size: 36x22mm

1074 CD6 25c red brown 16 15
1075 CD6 50c green 24 18

Type of 1963

Designs: 85c, "The Married Couple of the Eiffel Tower," by Marc Chagall. 95c, "The Fur Merchants," window, Chartres Cathedral.

1963, Nov. 9 **Engr.** ***Perf. 12x13***

1076 A399 85c multicolored 1.50 90
1077 A399 95c multicolored 80 48

Philatec Issue

Common Design Type

1963, Dec. 14 **Unwmk.** ***Perf. 13***

1078 CD118 25c dk gray, sl grn & dk car 15 15

For surcharge see Reunion No. 349.

Radio and Television Center, Paris — A411

1963, Dec. 15 **Engr.**

1079 A411 20c org brn, sl & ol 15 15

Fire Brigade Insignia, Symbols of Fire, Water and Civilian Defense A412

1964, Feb. 8 **Engr.** ***Perf. 13***

1082 A412 30c blue, org & red 28 20

Issued to honor the fire brigades and civilian defense corps.

Handicapped Laboratory Technician — A413

1964, Feb. 22 **Unwmk.** ***Perf. 13***

1083 A413 30c green, red brn & brn 25 20

Rehabilitation of the handicapped.

John II the Good (1319-64) by Girard d'Orleans A414

1964, Apr. 25 ***Perf. 12x13***

1084 A414 1fr multicolored 1.90 1.20

Stamp of 1900 — A415

Mechanized Mail Handling — A416

Designs: No. 1086, Stamp of 1900, Type A17. No. 1088, Telecommunications.

1964, May 9 ***Perf. 13***

1085 A415 25c bister & dk car 30 30
1086 A415 25c bister & blue 30 30
1087 A416 30c blk, bl & org brn 30 30
1088 A416 30c blk, car rose & bluish grn 30 30
a. Strip of 4, #1085-1088 + label 1.25 1.25

Printed in sheets of 20 stamps, containing five No. 1088a. The label shows the Philatec emblem in green.

Type of Semi-Postal Issue, 1959 with "25e ANNIVERSAIRE" added

1964, May 9

1089 SP208 25c multicolored 18 15

25th anniversary, night airmail service.

Madonna and Child from Rose Window of Notre Dame A417

1964, May 23 ***Perf. 12x13***

1090 A417 60c multicolored 48 35

Notre Dame Cathedral, Paris, 800th anniv.

Arms Type of 1958-59

Arms: 1c, Niort. 2c, Guéret. 12c, Agen. 18c, Saint-Denis, Réunion. 30c, Paris.

1964-65 **Typo.** ***Perf. 14x13½***

1091 A318 1c vio blue & yel 15 15
1092 A318 2c emer, vio bl & yel 15 15
1093 A318 12c black, red & yel 15 15
1094 A318 18c multicolored 15 15
1095 A318 30c vio bl & red ('65) 30 15
a. Booklet pane of 10 6.50
Set value 60 34

Gallic Coin — A418

Perf. 13½x14

1964-66 **Typo.** **Unwmk.**

1096 A418 10c emer & bister 85 15
1097 A418 15c org & bis ('66) 28 15
1098 A418 25c lilac & brn 45 20
1099 A418 50c brt blue & brn 95 40

Nos. 1096-1099 are known only precanceled. See second note after No. 132. See Nos. 1240-1242, 1315-1318, 1421-1424.

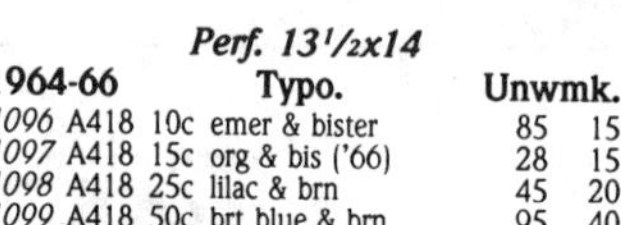

Postrider, Rocket and Radar Equipment — A419

1964, June 5 **Engr.** ***Perf. 13***

1100 A419 1fr brn, dk red & dk bl 20.00 17.00

Sold for 4fr, including 3fr admission to PHILATEC. Issued in sheets of 8 stamps and 8 labels (2x8 subjects with labels in horizontal rows 1, 4, 5, 8; stamps in rows 2, 3, 6, 7). Commemorative inscriptions on side margins.

Caesar's Tower, Provins — A420

Chapel of Notre Dame du Haut, Ronchamp A421

1964-65

1101 A421 40c sl grn, dk brn & brn ('65) 20 15
1102 A420 70c sl, grn & car 30 15
1103 A421 1.25fr brt bl, sl grn & ol 55 25
Set value 36

The 40c was issued in vertical coils in 1971. Every 10th coil stamp has a red control number printed twice on the back.

For surcharges see Reunion Nos. 352, 361.

Mandel — A422

Judo — A423

1964, July 4 **Unwmk.** ***Perf. 13***

1104 A422 30c violet brown 16 16

Georges Mandel (1885-1944), Cabinet minister, executed by the Nazis.

1964, July 4

1105 A423 50c dk blue & vio brn 25 18

Issued to publicize the 18th Olympic Games, Tokyo, Oct. 10-25, 1964.

Champlevé Enamel from Limoges, 12th Century A424

Design: No. 1107, The Lady (Claude Le Viste?) with the Unicorn, 15th cent. tapestry.

1964 ***Perf. 12x13***

1106 A424 1fr multicolored 1.40 80
1107 A424 1fr multicolored 48 35

No. 1106 shows part of an enamel sepulchral plate portraying Geoffrey IV, Count of Anjou and Le Maine (1113-1151), who was called Geoffrey Plantagenet.

Issue dates: #1106, July 4. #1107, Oct. 31.

Paris Taxis Carrying Soldiers to Front, 1914 — A425

1964, Sept. 5 **Unwmk.** ***Perf. 13***

1108 A425 30c black, blue & red 18 18

50th anniversary of Battle of the Marne.

Europa Issue, 1964

Common Design Type

1964, Sept. 12 **Engr.**

Size: 22x36mm

1109 CD7 25c dk car, dp ocher & grn 15 15
1110 CD7 50c vio, yel grn & dk car 20 18

Cooperation Issue

Common Design Type

1964, Nov. 6 **Unwmk.** ***Perf. 13***

1111 CD119 25c red brn, dk brn & dk bl 15 15

Joux Chateau — A427

1965, Feb. 6 **Engr.**
1112 A427 1.30fr redsh brn, brn red & dk brn 65 15

"The English Girl from the Star" by Toulouse-Lautrec — A428

St. Paul on the Damascus Road, Window, Cathedral of Sens — A429

Leaving for the Hunt — A430

Apocalypse Tapestry, 14th Century A431

"The Red Violin" by Raoul Dufy — A432

Designs: No. 1115, "August" miniature of Book of Hours of Jean de France, Duc de Berry ("Les Très Riches Heures du Duc de Berry"), painted by Flemish brothers, Pol, Hermant and Jannequin Limbourg, 1411-16. No. 1116, Scene from oldest existing set of French tapestries, showing the Wine-press of the Wrath of God (Revelations 14: 19-20).

1965 ***Perf. 12x13, 13x12***

1113 A428	1fr multicolored	40	40
1114 A429	1fr multicolored	38	38
1115 A430	1fr multicolored	38	38
1116 A431	1fr multicolored	38	38
1117 A432	1fr blk, pink & car	38	38
	Nos. 1113-1117 (5)	1.92	1.92

No. 1114 issued to commemorate the 800th anniversary of the Cathedral of Sens.

Dates of issue: No. 1113, Mar. 12. No. 1114, June 5. No. 1115, Sept. 25. No. 1116, Oct. 30. No. 1117, Nov. 6.

Paris Parade of Returning Deportees, 1945 — A433

1965, Apr. 1 **Unwmk.** ***Perf. 13***
1118 A433 40c Prussian green 40 30

20th anniv. of the return of people deported during World War II.

House of Youth and Culture, Troyes A434

1965, Apr. 10 **Engr.**
1119 A434 25c ind, brn & dk grn 25 15

20th anniv. of the establishment of recreational cultural centers for young people.

Woman Carrying Flowers — A435

Flags of France, US, USSR and Great Britain Crushing Swastika — A436

1965, Apr. 24 **Unwmk.** ***Perf. 13***
1120 A435 60c dk grn, dp org & ver 30 22

Issued to publicize the tourist Campaign of Welcome and Amiability.

1965, May 8
1121 A436 40c black, car & ultra 30 18

20th anniv. of victory in World War II.

Telegraph Key, Syncom Satellite and Pleumeur-Bodou Station — A437

1965, May 17
1122 A437 60c dk blue, brn & blk 35 22

Centenary of the ITU.

Croix de Guerre — A438

1965, May 22 **Engr.**
1123 A438 40c red, brn & brt grn 40 22

50th anniv. of the Croix de Guerre medal.

Cathedral of Bourges — A439

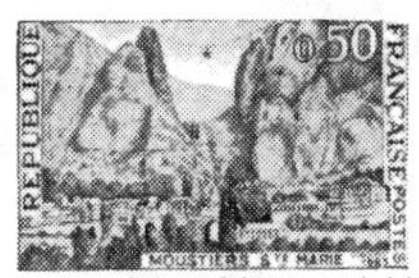
Moustiers-Sainte-Marie — A440

Views: 30c, Road and tunnel, Mont Blanc. 60c, Aix-les-Bains, sailboat. 75c, Tarn Gorge, Lozère mountains. 95c, Vendée River, man poling boat, and windmill. 1fr, Prehistoric stone monuments, Carnac.

1965

1124 A439	30c bl, vio bl & brn vio	20	15
1125 A439	40c gray bl & redsh brn	25	15
1126 A440	50c grn, bl gray & bis	28	15
1127 A439	60c blue & red brn	35	15
1128 A439	75c brown, bl & grn	85	32
1129 A440	95c brown, grn & bl	1.75	15
1130 A440	1fr gray grn & brn	80	15
	Nos. 1124-1130 (7)	4.48	
	Set value		1.00

No. 1124 for the opening of the Mont Blanc Tunnel. No. 1125 (Bourges Cathedral) was issued in connection with the French Philatelic Societies Federation Congress, held at Bourges.

Issue dates: 40c, June 5, 50c, June 19, 30c, 60c, July 17, others, July 10.

For surcharges see Reunion #354, 362, 365.

Europa Issue, 1965
Common Design Type

1965, Sept. 25 ***Perf. 13***
Size: 36x22mm

1131 CD8	30c red	16	15
1132 CD8	60c gray	26	20

Planting Seedling A441

Etienne Régnault, "Le Taureau" and Coast of Reunion A442

1965, Oct. 2
1133 A441 25c sl grn, yel grn & red brn 15 15

National reforestation campaign.

1965, Oct. 2
1134 A442 30c indigo & dk car 15 15

Tercentenary of settlement of Reunion.

Atomic Reactor and Diagram, Symbols of Industry, Agriculture and Medicine — A443

1965, Oct. 9
1135 A443 60c brt blue & blk 50 35

20th anniv. of the Atomic Energy Commission.

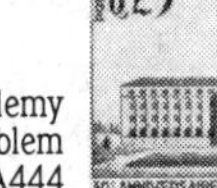

Air Academy and Emblem A444

1965, Nov. 6 ***Perf. 13***
1136 A444 25c dk blue & green 15 15

50th anniv. of the Air Academy, Salon-de-Provence.

French Satellite A-1 Issue
Common Design Type

Design: 60c, A-1 satellite.

1965, Nov. 30 **Engr.** ***Perf. 13***

1137 CD121	30c Prus bl, brt bl & blk	18	15
1138 CD121	60c blk, Prus bl & brt bl	26	18
a.	Strip of 2, #1137-1138 + label	45	42

Launching of France's 1st satellite, Nov. 26, 1965.

For surcharges see Reunion Nos. 358-359.

Arms of Auch — A446

Arms (Cities): 20c, Saint-Lô. 25c, Mont-de-Marsan.

Typographed, Photogravure (20c)
1966 ***Perf. 14x13; 14 (20c)***

1142 A446	5c blue & red	15	15
1143 A446	20c vio bl, sil, gold & red	15	15
1144 A446	25c red brown & ultra	45	15
	Set value		19

The 5c and 20c were issued in sheets and in vertical coils. In the coils, every 10th stamp has a red control number on the back.

360-360A.

French Satellite D-1 Issue
Common Design Type

1966, Feb. 18 **Engr.** ***Perf. 13***
1148 CD122 60c blue blk, grn & cl 22 18

Horses from Bronze Vessel of Vix — A448

Values quoted in this catalogue are for stamps graded Fine-Very Fine and with no faults. An illustrated guide to grade is provided beginning on Page 8A.

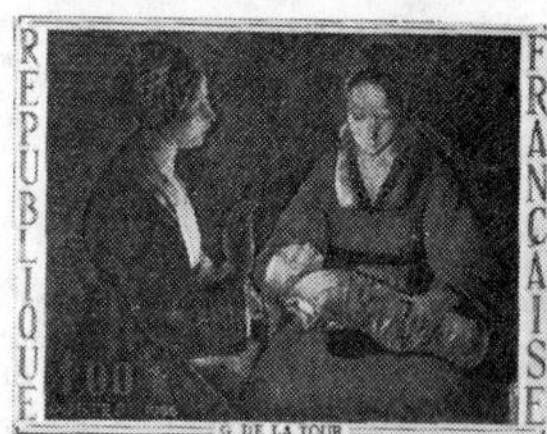

"The Newborn" by Georges de La Tour — A449

The Baptism of Judas (4th Century Bishop of Jerusalem) — A450

"The Moon and the Bull" Tapestry by Jean Lurat — A451

"Crispin and Scapin" by Honoré Daumier — A452

1966 ***Perf. 13x12, 12x13***

1149 A448 1fr multicolored 32 32
1150 A449 1fr multicolored 32 32
1151 A450 1fr multicolored 35 35
1152 A451 1fr multicolored 35 35
1153 A452 1fr multicolored 35 35
Nos. 1149-1153 (5) 1.69 1.69

The design of No. 1149 is a detail from a 6th century B.C. vessel, found in 1953 in a grave near Vix, Cote d'Or.

The design of No. 1151 is from a stained glass window in the 13th century Sainte-Chapelle, Paris.

No. 1150 exists in an imperf, ungummed souv. sheet with 2 progressive die proofs, issued for benefit of the Postal Museum, and not postally valid.

Issue dates: No. 1149, Mar. 26. No. 1150, June 25. No. 1151, Oct. 22. No. 1152, Nov. 19. No. 1153, Dec. 10.

Chessboard, Knight, Emblems for King and Queen — A453

St. Michael Slaying the Dragon — A455

Rhone Bridge, Pont-Saint-Esprit — A454

1966, Apr. 2 **Engr.** ***Perf. 13***
1154 A453 60c sep, gray & dk vio bl 40 30

Issued to publicize the Chess Festival.

1966, Apr. 23 **Unwmk.** ***Perf. 13***
1155 A454 25c black & dull blue 15 15

1966, Apr. 30 **Litho. & Engr.**
1156 A455 25c multicolored 15 15

Millenium of Mont-Saint-Michel.

Stanislas Leszczynski, Lunéville Chateau A456

1966, May 6 **Engr.**
1157 A456 25c slate, grn & brn 15 15

200th anniv. of the reunion of Lorraine and Bar (Barrois) with France.

St. Andrew's and Sèvre River, Niort — A457

1966, May 28 **Engr.** ***Perf. 13***
1158 A457 40c brt bl, ind & grn 20 15

Bernard Le Bovier de Fontenelle and 1666 Meeting Room A458

1966, June 4
1159 A458 60c dk car rose & brn 25 22

300th anniversary, Académie des Sciences.

William the Conqueror, Castle and Norman Ships — A459

1966, June 4
1160 A459 60c brown red & dp bl 30 28

900th anniversary of Battle of Hastings.

Tracks, Globe and Eiffel Tower A460

1966, June 11
1161 A460 60c dk brn, car & dull bl 90 30

19th International Railroad Congress.

Oléron Bridge A461

1966, June 20
1162 A461 25c Prus bl, brn & bl 15 15

Issued to commemorate the opening of Oléron Bridge, connecting Oléron Island in the Bay of Biscay with the French mainland.

Europa Issue, 1966
Common Design Type

1966, Sept. 24 **Engr.** ***Perf. 13***
Size: 22x36mm
1163 CD9 30c Prussian blue 15 15
1164 CD9 60c red 28 22

Vercingetorix at Gergovie, 52 B.C. — A462

Bishop Remi Baptizing King Clovis, 496 A.D. — A463

Design: 60c, Charlemagne attending school (page holding book for crowned king).

1966, Nov. 5 ***Perf. 13***
1165 A462 40c choc, grn & gray bl 22 15
1166 A463 40c dk red brn & blk 22 15
1167 A463 60c pur, rose car & brn 32 18

Map of Pneumatic Post and Tube A464

1966, Nov. 11
1168 A464 1.60fr maroon & indigo 60 28

Centenary of Paris pneumatic post system.

Val Chateau — A465

1966, Nov. 19 **Engr.** ***Perf. 13***
1169 A465 2.30fr dk bl, sl grn & brn 1.50 15

Rance Power Station A466

1966, Dec. 3
1170 A466 60c dk bl, sl grn & brn 38 16

Issued to publicize the tidal power station in the estuary of the Rance River on the English Channel.

European Broadcasting Union Emblem A467

1967, Mar. 4 **Engr.** ***Perf. 13***
1171 A467 40c dk blue & rose brn 18 16

3rd Intl. Congress of the European Broadcasting Union, Paris, Mar. 8-22.

Father Juniet's Gig by Henri Rousseau — A468

Francois I by Jean Clouet A469

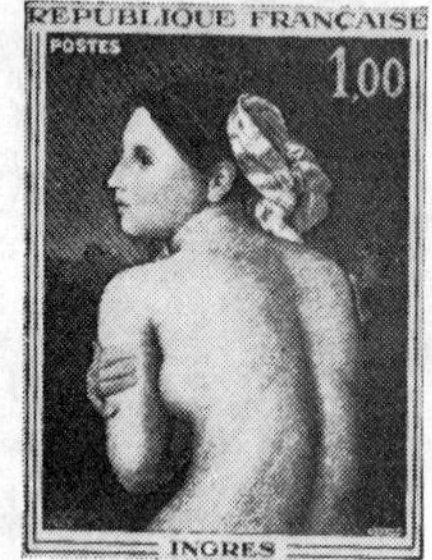

The Bather by Jean-Dominique Ingres — A470

St. Eloi, the Goldsmith, at Work — A471

1967 **Engr.** ***Perf. 13x12, 12x13***
1172 A468 1fr multicolored 45 42
1173 A469 1fr multicolored 45 42
1174 A470 1fr multicolored 40 38
1175 A471 1fr multicolored 40 38

The design of No. 1175 is from a 16th century stained glass window in the Church of Sainte Madeleine, Troyes.

Issue dates: No. 1172, Apr. 15. No. 1173, July 1. No. 1174, Sept. 9. No. 1175, Oct. 7.

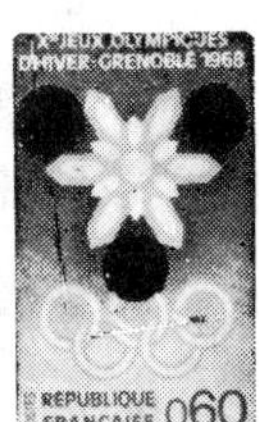

Snow Crystal and Olympic Rings — A472

1967, Apr. 22 Photo. *Perf. 13*
1176 A472 60c brt & lt blue & red 30 16

Issued to publicize the 10th Winter Olympic Games, Grenoble, Feb. 6-18, 1968.

French Pavilion, EXPO '67 — A473

1967, Apr. 22 Engr.
1177 A473 60c dull bl & bl grn 28 16

Intl. Exhibition EXPO '67, Montreal, Apr. 28-Oct. 27, 1967.
For surcharge see Reunion No. 363.

Europa Issue, 1967
Common Design Type

1967, Apr. 29
Size: 22x36mm
1178 CD10 30c blue & gray 15 15
1179 CD10 60c brown & lt blue 25 16
Set value 24

Great Bridge, Bordeaux A474

1967, May 8
1180 A474 25c olive, blk & brn 18 15

Nungesser, Coli and "L'Oiseau Blanc" A475

1967, May 8
1181 A475 40c slate, dk & lt brn 40 16

40th anniv. of the attempted transatlantic flight of Charles Nungesser and Franois Coil, French aviators.

Goüin House, Tours — A476

1967, May 13 Engr. *Perf. 13*
1182 A476 40c vio bl, red brn & red 30 16

Congress of the Federation of French Philatelic Societies in Tours.

Ramon and Alfort Veterinary School A477

1967, May 27
1183 A477 25c brn, dp bl & yel grn 15 15

200th anniv. of the Alfort Veterinary School and to honor Professor Gaston Ramon (1886-1963).

Robert Esnault-Pelterie, Diamant Rocket and A-1 Satellite — A478

1967, May 27
1184 A478 60c slate & vio blue 40 20

Issued to honor Robert Esnault-Pelterie (1881-1957), aviation and space expert.

City Hall, Saint-Quentin — A479

Saint-Germain-en-Laye — A480

Views: 60c, Clock Tower, Vire. 75c, Beach, La Baule, Brittany. 95c, Harbor, Boulogne-sur-Mer. 1fr, Rodez Cathedral. 1.50fr, Morlaix; old houses, grotesque carving, viaduct.

1967
1185 A479 50c blue, sl bl & brn 32 15
1186 A479 60c dp bl, sl bl & dk red brn 40 16
1187 A480 70c rose car, red brn & bl 40 15
1188 A480 75c multicolored 55 25
1189 A480 95c sky bl, lil & sl grn 70 25
1190 A479 1fr indigo & bl gray 52 15
1191 A479 1.50fr brt bl, brt grn & red brn 1.10 18
Nos. 1185-1191 (7) 3.99
Set value 1.00

Issue Dates: 1fr, 1.50fr, June 10; 70c, June 17; 50c, 60c, 95c, July 8; 75c, July 24.

Orchids — A481

Cross of Lorraine, Soldiers and Sailors — A483

Scales of Justice, City and Harbor A482

1967, July 29 Engr. *Perf. 13*
1192 A481 40c dp car, brt pink & pur 50 16

Orleans flower festival.

1967, Sept. 4
1193 A482 60c dk plum, dl bl & ocher 38 16

Issued to publicize the 9th International Accountancy Congress, Paris, Sept. 6-12.

1967, Oct. 7 Engr. *Perf. 13*
1194 A483 25c brn, dp ultra & bl 15 15

25th anniv. of the Battle of Bir Hacheim.

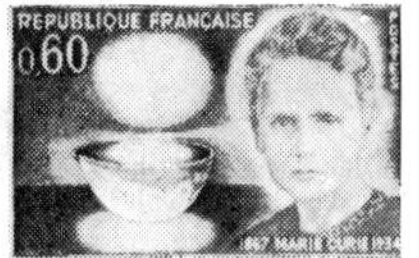

Marie Curie, Bowl Glowing with Radium A484

1967, Oct. 23 Engr. *Perf. 13*
1195 A484 60c dk blue & ultra 30 20

Marie Curie (1867-1934), scientist who discovered radium and polonium, Nobel prize winner for physics and chemistry.

Lions Emblem A485

Marianne (by Cheffer) A486

1967, Oct. 28
1196 A485 40c dk car & vio bl 75 30

50th anniversary of Lions International.
For surcharge see Reunion No. 364.

1967, Nov. 4 Engr.
1197 A486 25c dark blue 40 18
1198 A486 30c bright lilac 45 15
a. Booklet pane of 5 3.00
b. Booklet pane of 10 6.50
Set value 23

Coils (vertical) of Nos. 1197 and 1231 show a red number on the back of every 10th stamp.
See Nos. 1230-1231C. For surcharges see Reunion Nos. 367-368, 389.

King Philip II (Philip Augustus) at Battle of Bouvines — A487

Designs: No. 1200, Election of Hugh Capet as King, horiz. 60c, King Louis IX (St. Louis) holding audience for the poor.

1967, Nov. 13 Engr. *Perf. 13*
1199 A487 40c gray & black 26 18
1200 A487 40c steel bl & ultra 26 18
1201 A487 60c green & dk red brn 38 18

Commemorative Medal — A488

1968, Jan. 6 Engr. *Perf. 13*
1202 A488 40c dk slate grn & bis 20 18

50th anniversary of postal checking service.

Various Road Signs — A489

1968, Feb. 24
1203 A489 25c lil, red & dk bl grn 15 15

Issued to publicize road safety.

Prehistoric Paintings, Lascaux Cave — A490

Arearea (Merriment) by Paul Gauguin — A491

The Dance by Emile Antoine Bourdelle A492

Portrait of the Model by Auguste Renoir A493

1968 Engr. *Perf. 13x12, 12x13*

1204 A490 1fr multicolored 45 28
1205 A491 1fr multicolored 52 30
1206 A492 1fr car & gray olive 52 30
1207 A493 1fr multicolored 52 30

Issue dates: #1204, Apr. 13. #1205, Sept. 21. #1206, Oct. 26. #1207, Nov. 9.

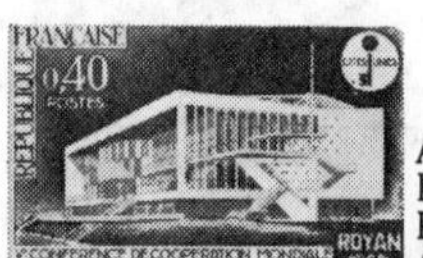

Audio-visual Institute, Royan A494

1968, Apr. 13 *Perf. 13*

1208 A494 40c sl grn, brn & Prus bl 20 18

5th Conference for World Cooperation with the theme of teaching living languages by audio-visual means.

Europa Issue, 1968

Common Design Type

1968, Apr. 27

Size: 36x22mm

1209 CD11 30c brt red lil & ocher 20 15
1210 CD11 60c brown & lake 30 18

Alain René Le Sage — A495

1968, May 4

1211 A495 40c blue & rose vio 20 15

Alain René Le Sage (1668-1747), novelist and playwright.

Chateau de Langeais A496

1968, May 4

1212 A496 60c sl bl, grn & red brn 30 22

Pierre Larousse A497

1968, May 11 Engr. *Perf. 13*

1213 A497 40c rose vio & brown 20 15

Pierre Larousse (1817-75), grammarian, lexicographer and encyclopedist.

Gnarled Trunk and Fir Tree — A498

1968, May 18 Engr. *Perf. 13*

1214 A498 25c grnsh bl, brn & grn 18 15

Twinning of Rambouillet Forest in France and the Black Forest in Germany.

Map of Papal Enclave, Valréas, and John XXII Receiving Homage A499

1968, May 25

1215 A499 60c brn, bis brn & pur 38 22

650th anniversary of the papal enclave at Valréas.

Louis XIV, Arms of France and Flanders A500

1968, June 29

1216 A500 40c rose car, gray & lem 20 15

300th anniv. of the Treaty of Aachen which reunited Flanders with France.

Martrou Bridge, Rochefort A501

1968, July 20

1217 A501 25c sky bl, blk & dk red brn 15 15

Letord Lorraine Bimotor Plane over Map of France A502

1968, Aug. 17 Engr. *Perf. 13*

1218 A502 25c brt blue, ind & red 40 18

50th anniv. of the 1st regularly scheduled air mail route in France from Paris to St. Nazaire.

Tower de Constance, Aigues-Mortes — A503

1968, Aug. 31

1219 A503 25c red brn, sky bl & olive bister 20 15

Bicentenary of the release of Huguenot prisoners from the Tower de Constance, Aigues-Mortes.

Cathedral and Pont Vieux, Beziers A504

1968, Sept. 7 Engr. *Perf. 13*

1220 A504 40c indigo, bis & grn 30 15

"Victory" over White Tower of Salonika — A505

1968, Sept. 28

1221 A505 40c red lilac & plum 25 20

50th anniv. of the armistice on the eastern front in World War I, Sept. 29, 1918.

Louis XV, Arms of France and Corsica A506

1968, Oct. 5 *Perf. 13*

1222 A506 25c ultra, grn & blk 15 15

200th anniv. of the return of Corsica to France.

Relay Race — A507

1968, Oct. 12

1223 A507 40c ultra, brt grn & ol brn 35 20

19th Olympic Games, Mexico City, Oct. 12-27.

Polar Camp with Helicopter, Plane and Snocat Tractor — A508

1968, Oct. 19

1224 A508 40c Prus bl, lt grnsh bl & brn red 30 20

20 years of French Polar expeditions.
For surcharge see Reunion No. 366.

Leon Bailby, Paris Opera Staircase and Hospital Beds — A509

"Victory" over Arc de Triomphe and Eternal Flame — A510

1968, Oct. 26

1225 A509 40c ocher & maroon 25 16

50th anniv. of the "Little White Beds" children's hospital fund.

1968, Nov. 9 Engr. *Perf. 13*

1226 A510 25c dk car rose & dp blue 15 15

50th anniv. of the armistice which ended World War I.

Death of Bertrand Du Guesclin at Chateauneuf-de-Randon, 1380 — A511

Designs: No. 1228, King Philip IV (the Fair) and first States-General assembly, 1302, horiz. 60c, Joan of Arc leaving Vaucouleurs, 1429.

1968, Nov. 16

1227 A511 40c cop red, grn & gray 30 26
1228 A511 40c green, ultra & brn 30 26
1229 A511 60c vio bl, sl bl & bis 40 26

See No. 1260.

Marianne Type of 1967

1969-70 Engr. *Perf. 13*

1230 A486 30c green 20 15
a. Booklet pane of 10 2.75
1231 A486 40c deep carmine 35 15
a. Booklet pane of 5 (horiz. strip) 2.50
b. Booklet pane of 10 4.00
d. With label ('70) 40 25

Typo. *Perf. 14x13*

1231C A486 30c blue green 18 15
Set value 20

No. 1231d was issued in sheets of 50 with alternating labels showing coat of arms of Perigueux, arranged checkerwise, to commemorate the inauguration of the Perigueux stamp printing plant.

The 40c coil is noted after No. 1198.

Church of Brou, Bourg-en-Bresse — A512

Views: 80c, Vouglans Dam, Jura. 85c, Chateau de Chantilly. 1.15fr, Sailboats in La Trinité-sur-Mer harbor.

1969 Engr. *Perf. 13*

1232 A512 45c olive, bl & red brn 25 15
1233 A512 80c ol bis, brn red & dk brn 45 15
1234 A512 85c sl grn, dl bl & gray 50 45
1235 A512 1.15fr brt bl, gray grn & brn 55 35

"February" Bas-relief from Amiens Cathedral A513

Philip the Good, by Roger van der Weyden A514

Sts. Savin and Cyprian before Ladicius, Mural, St. Savin, Vienne — A515

The Circus, by Georges Seurat A515a

1969 ***Perf. 12x13***

1236 A513 1fr dk green & brown 55 35
1237 A514 1fr multicolored 55 35
1238 A515 1fr multicolored 55 35
1239 A515a 1fr multicolored 55 35

Issue dates: No. 1236, Feb. 22; No. 1237, May 3; No. 1238, June 28; No. 1239, Nov. 8.

Gallic Coin Type of 1964-66

1969 **Typo.** ***Perf. 13½x14***

1240 A418 22c brt green & vio 80 15
1241 A418 35c red & ultra 1.65 40
1242 A418 70c ultra & red brn 6.00 2.00

Nos. 1240-1242 are known only precanceled. See note after No. 132.

Hautefort Chateau A516

1969, Apr. 5 **Engr.** ***Perf. 13***

1243 A516 70c blue, slate & bis 40 30

Irises — A517

1969, Apr. 12 **Photo.**

1244 A517 45c multicolored 35 28

Issued to publicize the 3rd International Flower Show, Paris, Apr. 23-Oct. 5.

Europa Issue, 1969

Common Design Type

1969, Apr. 26 **Engr.** ***Perf. 13***

Size: 36x22mm

1245 CD12 40c carmine rose 20 15
1246 CD12 70c Prussian blue 30 25

Albert Thomas and Thomas Memorial, Geneva A518

1969, May 10 **Engr.** ***Perf. 13***

1247 A518 70c brn, ol bis & ind 35 30

50th anniv. of the ILO and to honor Albert Thomas (1878-1932), director of the ILO (1920-32).

Garigliano Battle Scene, 1944 — A519

1969, May 10

1248 A519 45c black & violet 30 20

25th anniv. of the Battle of the Garigliano against the Germans.

Chateau du Marché, Chalons-sur-Marne A520

Parachutists over Normandy Beach A521

1969, May 24

1249 A520 45c bis, dull bl & grn 40 30

Federation of French Philatelic Societies, 42nd congress.

1969, May 31

1250 A521 45c dk blue & vio bl 50 30

25th anniv. of the landing of Special Air Service and Free French commandos in Normandy, June 6, 1944.

Monument of the French Resistance, Mt. Mouchet — A522

1969, June 7

1251 A522 45c dk grn, sl & ind 50 30

25th anniv. of the battle of Mt. Mouchet between French resistance fighters and the Germans, June 2 and 10, 1944.

French Troops Landing in Provence — A523

1969, Aug. 23 **Engr.** ***Perf. 13***

1252 A523 45c slate & blk brn 60 30

25th anniv. of the landing of French and American forces in Provence, Aug. 15, 1944.

Russian and French Aviators — A524

1969, Oct. 18 **Engr.** ***Perf. 13***

1253 A524 45c slate, dp bl & car 55 30

Issued to honor the French aviators of the Normandy-Neman Squadron who fought on the Russian Front, 1942-45.

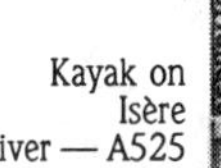
Kayak on Isère River — A525

1969, Aug. 2 **Engr.** ***Perf. 13***

1254 A525 70c org brn, ol & dk bl 40 30

Intl. Canoe and Kayak Championships, Bourg-Saint-Maurice, Savoy, July 31-Aug. 6.

Napoleon as Young Officer and his Birthplace, Ajaccio — A526

1969, Aug. 16

1255 A526 70c brt grnsh bl, ol & rose vio 45 30

Napoleon Bonaparte (1769-1821).
For surcharge see Reunion No. 370.

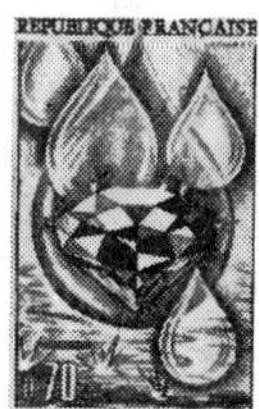

Drops of Water and Diamond A527

Mediterranean Mouflon A528

1969, Sept. 27

1256 A527 70c blk, dp bl & brt grn 50 30

European Water Charter.

1969, Oct. 11

1257 A528 45c ol, blk & org brn 35 30

Issued to publicize wildlife protection.

Central School of Arts and Crafts A529

1969, Oct. 18

1258 A529 70c dk grn, yel grn & org 30 25

Inauguration of the Central School of Arts and Crafts at Chatenay-Malabry.

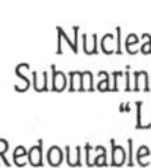
Nuclear Submarine "Le Redoutable" A530

1969, Oct. 25

1259 A530 70c dp bl, grn & sl grn 38 30

Type of 1968 and

Henri IV and Edict of Nantes — A531

Designs: No. 1260, Pierre Terrail de Bayard wounded at Battle of Brescia (after a painting in Versailles). No. 1262, Louis XI, Charles the Bold and map of France.

1969, Nov. 8 **Engr.** ***Perf. 13***

1260 A511 80c brn, bis & blk 40 25
1261 A531 80c blk & vio bl 50 25
1262 A531 80c ol, dp grn & dk red brn 40 25

"Firecrest" and Alain Gerbault — A532

1970, Jan. 10 **Engr.** ***Perf. 13***

1263 A532 70c indigo, brt bl & gray 55 30

Completion of Alain Gerbault's trip around the world aboard the "Firecrest," 1923-29, 40th anniv.

Gendarmery Emblem, Mountain Climber, Helicopter, Motorcyclists and Motorboat — A533

1970, Jan. 31

1264 A533 45c sl grn, dk bl & brn 1.25 50

National Gendarmery, founded 1791.

Field Ball Player — A534

1970, Feb. 21 **Engr.** ***Perf. 13***

1265 A534 80c slate green 40 20

7th Intl. Field Ball Games, Feb. 26-Mar. 8.

Alphonse Juin and Church of the Invalides — A535

1970, Feb. 28
1266 A535 45c gray bl & dk brn 28 20

Issued to honor Marshal Alphonse Pierre Juin (1888-1967), military leader.

Aerotrain A536

1970, Mar. 7
1267 A536 80c purple & gray 55 20

Introduction of the aerotrain, which reaches a speed of 320 miles per hour.

Pierre Joseph Pelletier, Joseph Bienaimé Caventou, Quinine Formula and Cell — A537

1970, Mar. 21 **Engr.** ***Perf. 13***
1268 A537 50c slate grn, sky bl & dp car 30 20

Discovery of quinine, 150th anniversary.

Pink Flamingos A538 — Diamant B Rocket and Radar A539

1970, Mar. 21
1269 A538 45c ol, gray & pink 30 18

European Nature Conservation Year, 1970.

1970, Mar. 28
1270 A539 45c bright green 45 18

Space center in Guyana and the launching of the Diamant B rocket, Mar. 10, 1970.

Europa Issue, 1970
Common Design Type
1970, May 2 **Engr.** ***Perf. 13***
Size: 36x22mm
1271 CD13 40c deep carmine 18 15
1272 CD13 80c sky blue 35 22

Annunication, by Primitive Painter of Savoy, 1480 — A540

The Triumph of Flora, by Jean Baptiste Carpeaux — A541

Diana Returning from the Hunt, by Franois Boucher — A542

Dancer with Bouquet, by Edgar Degas A543

1970 ***Perf. 12x13, 13x12***
1273 A540 1fr multicolored 85 32
1274 A541 1fr red brown 85 32
1275 A542 1fr multicolored 85 40
1276 A543 1fr multicolored 85 40

Issue dates: #1273, May 9. #1274, July 4. #1275, Oct. 10. #1276, Nov. 14.

Arms of Lens, Miner's Lamp and Pit Head A544

1970, May 16 **Engr.** ***Perf. 13***
1277 A544 40c scarlet 18 15

43rd Natl. Congress of the Federation of French Philatelic Societies, Lens, May 14-21.

Diamond Rock, Martinique A545

Haute Provence Observatory and Spiral Nebula — A546

Designs: 95c, Chancelade Abbey, Dordogne. 1fr, Gosier Islet, Guadeloupe.

1970, June 20 **Engr.** ***Perf. 13***
1278 A545 50c sl grn, brt bl & plum 35 15
1279 A545 95c lt ol, car & brn 1.10 40
1280 A545 1fr sl grn, brt bl & dk car rose 60 15
1281 A546 1.30fr dk bl, vio bl & dk grn 1.90 60

Hand Reaching for Freedom A547

Handicapped Javelin Thrower A548

1970, June 27
1282 A547 45c vio bl, bl & bis 38 18

Liberation of concentration camps, 25th anniversary.

1970, June 27
1283 A548 45c rose car, ultra & emer 40 22

Issued to publicize the International Games of the Handicapped, St. Etienne, June 1970.

Pole Vault — A549

1970, Sept. 11 **Engr.** ***Perf. 13***
1284 A549 45c car, bl & ind 38 22

First European Junior Athletic Championships, Colombes, Sept. 11-13.

Royal Salt Works, Arc-et-Senans A550

1970, Sept. 26
1285 A550 80c bl, brn & dk grn 1.00 45

Restoration of the 18th cent. Royal Salt Works buildings, by Claude Nicolas Ledoux (1736-1806) at Arc-et-Senans, for use as a center for studies of all aspects of future human life.

Armand Jean du Plessis, Duc de Richelieu — A551

Designs: No. 1287, Battle of Fontenoy, 1745. No. 1288, Louis XIV and Versailles.

1970, Oct. 17 **Engr.** ***Perf. 13***
1286 A551 45c blk, sl & car rose 50 18
1287 A551 45c org, brn & indigo 50 18
1288 A551 45c sl grn, lem & org brn 50 18

UN Headquarters in New York and Geneva A552

1970, Oct. 24 **Engr.** ***Perf. 13***
1289 A552 80c ol, dp ultra & dk pur 35 28

25th anniversary of the United Nations.

View of Bordeaux and France No. 43 — A553

1970, Nov. 7
1290 A553 80c vio bl & gray bl 35 28

Centerary of the Bordeaux issue.

Col. Denfert-Rochereau and Lion of Belfort, by Frederic A. Bartholdi — A554

1970, Nov. 14
1291 A554 45c dk bl, ol & red brn 30 18

Centenary of the siege of Belfort during Franco-Prussian War.

Marianne (by Bequet) — A555

1971-74 **Typo.** ***Perf. 14x13***
1292 A555 45c sky blue 30 15
1292A A555 60c green ('74) 90 15
Set value 15

For surcharges see Reunion #371, 397-398.

Engr. ***Perf. 13***
1293 A555 50c rose carmine 32 15
a. Bklt. pane of 5 (horiz. strip) 2.25
b. Booklet pane of 10 3.50
1294 A555 60c green ('74) 4.25 15
a. Booklet pane of 10 45.00
1294B A555 80c car rose ('74) 48 15
c. Booklet pane of 5 3.50
d. Booklet pane of 10 7.25
Set value 18

Nos. 1294 and 1294B issued also in vertical coils with control number on back of every 10th stamp.

No. 1293 issued only in booklets and in vertical coils with red control number on back of every 10th stamp.

See Nos. 1494-1498.

St. Matthew, Sculpture from Strasbourg Cathedral A556

Winnower, by Franois Millet A557

The Dreamer, by Georges Rouault A558

1971 Engr. *Perf. 12x13*

1295 A556 1fr dark red brown	85	48
1296 A557 1fr multicolored	85	42
1297 A558 1fr multicolored	85	42

Issue dates: No. 1295, Jan. 23; No. 1296, Apr. 3; No. 1297, June 5.

Figure Skating Pair — A560

1971, Feb. 20 Engr. *Perf. 13*

1299 A560 80c vio bl, sl & aqua 50 25

World Figure Skating Championships, Lyons, Feb. 23-28.

Underwater Exploration — A561

1971, Mar. 6

1300 A561 80c blue blk & bl grn 40 25

International Exhibition of Ocean Exploration, Bordeaux, Mar. 9-14.

Cape Horn Clipper "Antoinette" and Solidor Castle, Saint-Malo — A562

1971, Apr. 10 Engr. *Perf. 13*

1301 A562 80c blue, pur & slate 70 32

For surcharge see Reunion No. 372.

Pyrenean Chamois — A563

1971, Apr. 24 Engr. *Perf. 13*

1302 A563 65c bl, dk brn & brn ol 50 20

National Park of Western Pyrenees.

Europa Issue, 1971

Common Design Type and

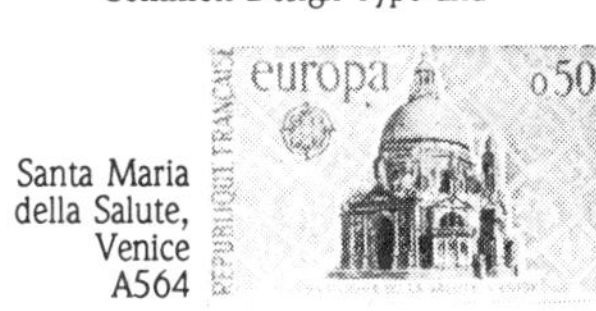
Santa Maria della Salute, Venice A564

1971, May 8 Engr. *Perf. 13*

1303 A564 50c blue gray & ol bis 30 15

Size: 36x22mm

1304 CD14 80c rose lilac 40 30

Cardinal, Nobleman and Lawyer — A565

Storming of the Bastille — A566

Design: No. 1306, Battle of Valmy.

1971

1305 A565 45c bl, rose red & pur	55	20
1306 A565 45c bl, ol bis & brn red	55	25
1307 A566 65c dk brn, gray bl & mag	85	30

No. 1305 commemorates the opening of the Estates General, May 5, 1789; No. 1306, Battle of Valmy (Sept. 20, 1792) between French and Prussian armies; 65c, Storming of the Bastille, Paris, July 14, 1789.

Issue dates: No. 1305, May 8; No. 1306, Sept. 18; 65c, July 10.

Grenoble A568

1971, May 29 Engr. *Perf. 13*

1308 A568 50c ocher, lil & rose red 28 15

44th Natl. Cong. of the Federation of French Philatelic Societies, Grenoble, May 30-31.

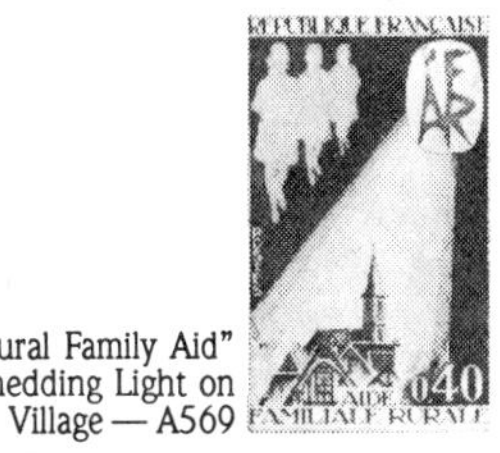
"Rural Family Aid" Shedding Light on Village — A569

1971, June 5

1309 A569 40c vio, bl & grn 20 15

Aid for rural families.

For surcharge see Reunion No. 373.

Chateau and Fort de Sedan A570

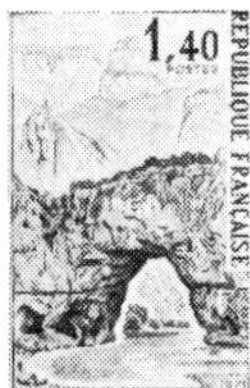
Pont d'Arc, Ardèche Gorge — A571

Views: 60c, Sainte Chapelle, Riom. 65c, Fountain and tower, Dole. 90c, Tower and street, Riquewihr.

1971 Engr. *Perf. 13*

1310 A571 60c black, grn & bl	24	15
1311 A571 65c lilac, ocher & blk	35	15
1312 A571 90c grn, vio brn & red brn	48	15
1313 A570 1.10fr sl grn, Prus bl & brn	60	20
1314 A571 1.40fr sl grn, bl & dk brn	75	15
Nos. 1310-1314 (5)	2.42	
Set value		68

Issue dates: 60c, June 19; 65c, 90c, July 3; 1.10fr, 1.40fr, June 12.

For surcharges see Reunion Nos. 374, 381.

Gallic Coin Type of 1964-66

1971, July 1 Typo. *Perf. 13½x14*

1315 A418 26c lilac & brn	52	15
1316 A418 30c lt brown & brn	90	20
1317 A418 45c dull green & brn	1.75	30
1318 A418 90c red & brown	2.25	48

Nos. 1315-1318 are known only precanceled. See second paragraph after No. 132.

Bourbon Palace A572

1971, Aug. 28 Engr. *Perf. 13*

1319 A572 90c violet blue 75 25

59th Conf. of the Interparliamentary Union.

Embroidery and Tool Making A573

1971, Oct. 16

1320 A573 90c brn red, brt lil & cl 50 30

40th anniv. of the first assembly of presidents of artisans' guilds.

For surcharge see Reunion No. 375.

Reunion Chameleon A574

1971, Nov. 6 Photo. *Perf. 13*

1321 A574 60c brn, yel, grn & blk 1.10 32

Nature protection.

De Gaulle Issue

Common Design Type and

De Gaulle in Brazzaville, 1944 — A576

Designs: No. 1324, De Gaulle entering Paris, 1944. No. 1325, Pres. de Gaulle, 1970.

1971, Nov. 9 Engr.

1322 CD134 50c black	1.10	35
1323 A576 50c ultra	1.10	35
1324 A576 50c rose red	1.10	35
1325 CD134 50c black	1.10	35
a. Strip of 4, #1322-1325 + label	4.50	2.50

First anniversary of the death of Charles de Gaulle (1890-1970).

See Reunion Nos. 377, 380.

Antoine Portal and first Session of Academy — A577

1971, Nov. 13

1326 A577 45c dk purple & magenta 25 20

Sesquicentennial of the founding of the National Academy of Medicine; Baron Antoine Portal was first president.

L'Etude, by Jean Honoré Fragonard A578

Women in Garden, by Claude Monet A579

St. Peter Presenting Pierre de Bourbon, by Maitre de Moulins A580

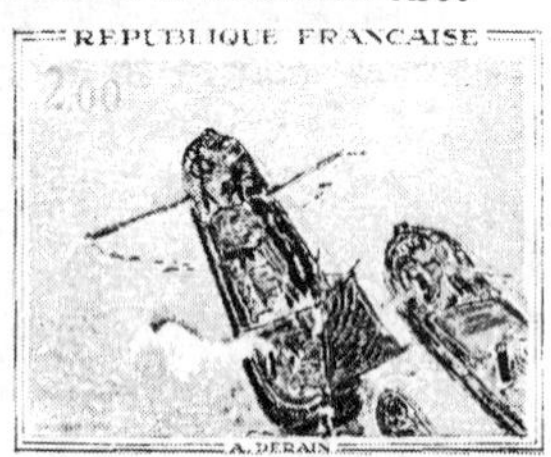

Boats, by André Derain — A581

1972 Engr. *Perf. 12x13, 13x12*

1327 A578	1fr black & multi		65	32
1328 A579	1fr slate grn & multi		95	32
1329 A580	2fr dk brown & multi		2.50	80
1330 A581	2fr yellow & multi		3.50	90

Issue dates: #1327, Jan. 22; #1328, June 17; #1329, Oct. 14; #1330, Dec. 16.

Map of South Indian Ocean, Penguin and Ships — A582

1972, Jan. 29 *Perf. 13*

1331 A582 90c black, bl & ocher 65 40

Bicentenary of discovery of the Crozet and Kerguelen Islands.

Slalom and Olympic Emblems A583

1972, Feb. 7

1332 A583 90c dk olive & dp car 50 30

11th Winter Olympic Games, Sapporo, Japan, Feb. 3-13.

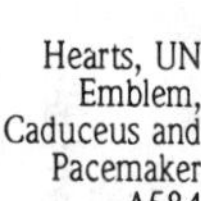

Hearts, UN Emblem, Caduceus and Pacemaker A584

1972, Apr. 8 Engr. *Perf. 13*

1333 A584 45c dk car, org & gray 30 20

"Your heart is your health," world health month.

Red Deer, Sologne Plateau — A585

Charlieu Abbey A585a

Bazoches-du-Morvand Chateau — A586

Saint-Just Cathedral, Narbonne A587

1972 *Perf. 13*

1334 A585	1fr ocher & red brn	55	15
1335 A585a	1.20fr sl & dull brn	48	15
1336 A586	2fr sl grn, blk & red brn	1.00	15
1337 A587	3.50fr bl, gray ol & car rose	1.40	20
	Set value		52

Issue dates: 1fr, Sept. 10; 1.20fr, Apr. 29; 2fr, Sept. 9; 3.5fr, Apr. 8.

For surcharge see Reunion No. 388.

Eagle Owl — A588

Nature protection: 60c, Salmon, horiz.

1972

1338 A588	60c grn, ind & brt bl	2.00	58
1339 A588	65c sl, ol brn & sep	1.25	32

Issue dates: 60c, May 27; 65c, Apr. 15.

Europa Issue 1972

Common Design Type and

Aix-la-Chapelle Cathedral — A589

1972, Apr. 22 Engr. *Perf. 13*

1340 A589 50c yel, vio brn & dk olive 24 15

Photo.

Size: 22x36mm

1341 CD15 90c red org & multi 48 30

Bouquet Made of Hearts and Blood Donors' Emblem A590

Newfoundlander "Côte d'Emeraude" A591

1972, May 5 Engr.

1342 A590 40c red 28 20

20th anniv. of the Blood Donors Association of Post and Telecommunications Employees.

For surcharge see Reunion No. 383.

1972, May 6

1343 A591 90c org, vio bl & sl grn 70 32

Cathedral, Saint-Brieuc A592

1972, May 20

1344 A592 50c lilac rose 28 15

45th Congress of the Federation of French Philatelic Societies, Saint-Brieuc, May 21-22.

Hand Holding Symbol of Postal Code A593

1972, June 3 Typo. *Perf. 14x13*

1345 A593	30c green, blk & car	16	15
1346 A593	50c car, blk & yel	28	15
	Set value		15

Introduction of postal code system.

For surcharges see Reunion Nos. 384-385.

Old and New Communications A594

1972, July 1 Engr. *Perf. 13*

1347 A594 45c slate & vio blue 30 20

21st Intl. Congress of P.T.T. (Post, Telegraph and Telephone) Employees, Paris, July 1-7.

Hurdler and Olympic Rings — A595

1972, July 8

1348 A595 1fr deep olive 50 20

20th Olympic Games, Munich, Aug. 26-Sept. 11.

Hikers and Mt. Aigoual A596

Bicyclist A597

1972, July 15 Photo. *Perf. 13*

1349 A596 40c brt rose & multi 1.50 60

Intl. Year of Tourism and 25th anniv. of the Natl. Hikers Association.

1972, July 22 Engr.

1350 A597 1fr gray, brn & lil 1.90 60

World Bicycling Championships, Marseille, July 29-Aug. 2.

"Incroyables and Merveilleuses," 1794 — A598

Designs: 60c, Bonaparte at the Arcole Bridge. 65c, Egyptian expedition (soldiers and scientists finding antiquities; pyramids in background).

1972 Engr. *Perf. 13*

1351 A598	45c ol, dk grn & car rose	52	20
1352 A598	60c red, blk & ind	55	25
1353 A598	65c ocher, ultra & choc	55	30

French history. Issue dates: 45c, Oct. 7; 60c, 65c, Nov. 11.

Champollion, Rosetta Stone with Key Inscription — A599

1972, Oct. 14

1354 A599 90c vio bl, brn red & blk 50 32

Sesquicentennial of the deciphering of hieroglyphs by Jean-Franois Champollion.

St. Teresa, Portal of Notre Dame of Alenon A600

1973, Jan. 6 Engr. *Perf. 13*
1355 A600 1fr Prus blue & indigo 60 30

Centenary of the birth of St. Teresa of Lisieux, the Little Flower (Thérèse Martin, 1873-1897), Carmelite nun.

Anthurium (Martinique) — A601

1973, Jan. 20 Photo.
1356 A601 50c gray & multi 35 20

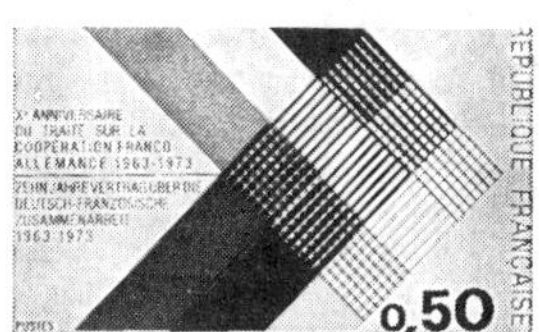
Colors of France and Germany Interlaced — A602

1973, Jan. 22
1357 A602 50c multicolored 38 20

10th anniv. of the Franco-German Cooperation Treaty. See Germany No. 1101.

Polish Immigrants — A603

1973, Feb. 3 Engr. *Perf. 13*
1358 A603 40c sl grn, dp car & brn 25 20

50th anniversary of Polish immigration into France, 1921-1923.

Last Supper, St. Austremoine Church, Issoire A604

Kneeling Woman, by Charles Le Brun — A605

Angel, Wood, Moutier-D'Ahun — A606

Lady Playing Archlute, by Antoine Watteau A607

1973 Engr. *Perf. 12x13*

1359	A604 2fr brown & multi	1.75	80
1360	A605 2fr dk red & yel	1.75	80
1361	A606 2fr ol brn & vio brn	1.75	80
1362	A607 2fr black & multi	1.75	80

Issue dates: #1359, Feb. 10; #1360, Apr. 28; #1361, May 26; #1362, Sept. 22.

Tuileries Palace, Telephone Relays A608

Oil Tanker, Francis I Lock — A609

Airbus A300-B A610

1973

1363	A608 45c ultra, sl grn & bis	32	15
1364	A609 90c plum, blk & bl	55	15
1365	A610 3fr dk brn, bl & blk	1.90	80

French technical achievements.
Issued: 45c, May 15; 90c, Oct. 27; 3fr, Apr. 7.

Europa Issue 1973

Common Design Type and

City Hall, Brussels, CEPT Emblem — A611

1973, Apr. 14 Engr. *Perf. 13*
1366 A611 50c brt pink & choc 45 15

Photo.

Size: 36x22mm

1367 CD16 90c sl grn & multi 95 30

Masonic Lodge Emblem A612

1973, May 12 Engr. *Perf. 13*
1368 A612 90c magenta & vio bl 55 30

Bicentenary of the Free Masons of France.

Guadeloupe Raccoon A613

White Storks A614

1973

1369	A613 40c lilac, sep & ol	35	20
1370	A614 60c blk, aqua & org red	52	25

Nature protection.
Issue dates: 40c, June 23; 60c, May 12.

Tourist Issue

Doubs Waterfall — A615

Clos-Lucé, Amboise — A617

Palace of Dukes of Burgundy, Dijon — A616

Design: 90c, Gien Chateau.

1973 Engr. *Perf. 13*

1371	A615 60c multicolored	22	15
1372	A616 65c red & purple	32	15
1373	A616 90c Prus bl, ind & brn	35	15
1374	A617 1fr ocher, bl & sl grn	35	15

Issue dates: 60c, Sept. 8; 65c, May 19; 90c, Aug. 18; 1fr, June 23.
For surcharge see Reunion No. 387.

Academy Emblem — A618

1973, May 26
1375 A618 1fr lilac, sl grn & red 40 25

Academy of Overseas Sciences, 50th anniv.

Racing Car and Clocks A619

1973, June 2
1376 A619 60c dk brown & blue 52 40

50th anniv. of the 24-hour automobile race at Le Mans.

Five-master France II — A620

1973, June 9
1377 A620 90c ultra, Prus bl & ind 60 25

For surcharge see Reunion No. 386.

Tower and Square, Toulouse — A621

1973, June 9
1378 A621 50c purple & red brn 25 15

46th Congress of the Federation of French Philatelic Societies, Toulouse, June 9-12.

Dr. Armauer G. Hansen — A622

Ducretet and his Transmission Diagram — A623

1973, Sept. 29 Engr. *Perf. 13*
1379 A622 45c grn, dk ol & ocher 25 20

Centenary of the discovery of the Hansen bacillus, the cause of leprosy.

1973, Oct. 6
1380 A623 1fr yel grn & magenta 40 18

75th anniversary of the first transmission of radio signals from the Eiffel Tower to the Pantheon by Eugene Ducretet (1844-1915).

Molière as Sganarelle — A624

1973, Oct. 20
1381 A624 1fr dk red & ol brn 42 20

Moliere (Jean-Baptiste Poquelin; 1622-1673), playwright and actor.

Pierre Bourgoin and Philippe Kieffer A625

1973, Oct. 27
1382 A625 1fr red, rose cl & vio bl 50 22

Pierre Bourgoin (1907-70), and Philippe Kieffer (1899-1963), heroes of the Free French forces in World War II.

Napoleon, Jean Portalis and Palace of Justice, Paris — A626

Exhibition Halls — A627

The Coronation of Napoleon, by Jean Louis David — A628

1973 **Engr.** ***Perf. 13***
1383 A626 45c blue, choc & gray 28 18
1384 A627 60c ol, sl grn & brn 40 18
1385 A628 1fr sl grn, ol & cl 60 20

History of France. 45c, for the preparation of the Code Napoleon; 60c, Napoleon's encouragement of industry; 1fr, his coronation.
Issued: 45c, Nov. 3; 60c, Nov. 24; 1fr, Nov. 12.

Eternal Flame, Arc de Triomphe — A629

Weather Vane — A630

1973, Nov. 10
1386 A629 40c pur, vio bl & red 28 18

50th anniv. of the Eternal Flame at the Arc de Triomphe, Paris.

1973, Dec. 1
1387 A630 65c ultra, blk & grn 28 18

50th anniv. of the Dept. of Agriculture.

Human Rights Flame and Man A631

Postal Museum A632

1973, Dec. 8 **Engr.** ***Perf. 13***
1388 A631 45c car, org & blk 22 15

25th anniversary of the Universal Declaration of Human Rights.

1973, Dec. 19
1389 A632 50c maroon & bister 20 15

Opening of new post and philately museum, Paris.

ARPHILA 75 Emblem A633

1974, Jan. 19 **Engr.** ***Perf. 13***
1390 A633 50c brn, bl & brt lil 25 15

ARPHILA 75 Philatelic Exhibition, Paris, June 1975.
For surcharge see Reunion No. 390.

Concorde over Charles de Gaulle Airport A634

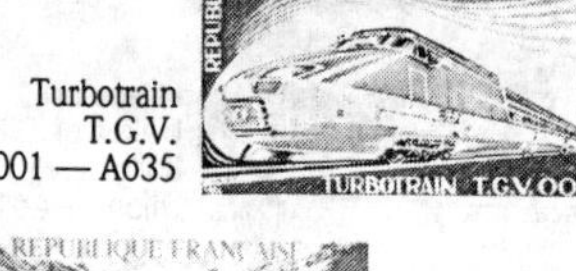

Turbotrain T.G.V. 001 — A635

Phenix Nuclear Power Station A636

1974 **Engr.** ***Perf. 13***
1391 A634 60c pur & ol gray 42 22
1392 A635 60c multicolored 1.10 35
1393 A636 65c multicolored 32 18

French technical achievements.
Issue dates: No. 1391, Mar. 18; No. 1392, Aug. 31; 65c, Sept. 21.

Cardinal Richelieu, by Philippe de Champaigne — A637

Painting by Joan Miró — A638

Canal du Loing, by Alfred Sisley — A639

"In Honor of Nicolas Fouquet," Tapestry by Georges Mathieu — A640

Engr., Photo. (#1395, 1397)

1974 ***Perf. 12x13, 13x12***
1394 A637 2fr multicolored 1.25 65
1395 A638 2fr multicolored 1.25 65
1396 A639 2fr multicolored 1.75 65
1397 A640 2fr multicolored 1.75 65

Nos. 1394-1397 are printed in sheets of 25 with alternating labels publicizing "ARPHILA 75," Paris, June 6-16, 1975.
Issue dates: #1394, Mar. 23; #1395, Sept. 14; #1396, Nov. 9; #1397, Nov. 16.
For surcharges see Reunion Nos. 391-394.

French Alps and Gentian A641

1974, Mar. 30 **Engr.** ***Perf. 13***
1398 A641 65c vio blue & gray 35 22

Centenary of the French Alpine Club.

Europa Issue 1974

"Age of Bronze," by Auguste Rodin — A642

"Air," by Aristide Maillol A643

1974, Apr. 20 ***Perf. 13***
1399 A642 50c brt rose lil & blk 32 15
1400 A643 90c olive & brown 65 22

Sea Rescue — A644

1974, Apr. 27
1401 A644 90c multicolored 40 22

Reorganized sea rescue organization.
For surcharge see Reunion No. 395.

Council Building, View of Strasbourg and Emblem — A645

1974, May 4 **Engr.** ***Perf. 13***
1402 A645 45c ind, bis & bl 28 15

25th anniversary of the Council of Europe.

Tourist Issue

View of Salers A646

Basilica of St. Nicolas de Porte — A647

Seashell over Corsica — A648

Design: 1.10fr, View of Lot Valley.

1974 **Engr.** ***Perf. 13***
1403 A646 65c yel grn & choc 24 18
1404 A646 1.10fr choc & sl grn 45 22
1405 A647 2fr gray & lilac 80 15
1406 A648 3fr multicolored 1.00 28

Issue dates: 65c, June 22; 1.10fr, Sept. 7; 2fr, Oct. 12; 3fr, May 11.

Bison — A649

Giant Armadillo of Guyana A650

1974
1407 A649 40c bis, choc & bl 32 15
1408 A650 65c sl, ol & grn 32 18

Nature protection.
Issue dates: #1407, May 25; #1408, Oct. 19.

Americans Landing in Normandy and Arms of Normandy — A651

General Marie-Pierre Koenig — A652

Order of the French Resistance — A653

1974

1409	A651	45c grn, rose & indigo	40	18
1410	A652	1fr multicolored	60	18
1411	A653	1fr multicolored	48	18

30th anniversary of the liberation of France from the Nazis. Design of No. 1410 includes diagram of battle of Bir-Hakeim and Free French and Bir-Hakeim memorials.

Issue dates: 45c, June 8. No. 1410, May 25. No. 1411, Nov. 23. See No. B478.

Pfister House, 16th Century, Colmar — A654

1974, June 1

1412	A654	50c multicolored	20	15

47th Congress of the Federation of French Philatelic Societies, Colmar, May 30-June 4.

Chess A655

1974, June 8

1413	A655	1fr dk brown & multi	55	30

21st Chess Olympiad, Nice, June 6-30.

Facade with Statue of Louis XIV, and 1675 Medal — A656

1974, June 15

1414	A656	40c indigo, bl & brn	18	15

300th anniversary of the founding of the Hotel des Invalides (Home for poor and sick officers and soldiers).

Peacocks Holding Letter, and Globe — A657

1974, Oct. 5 Engr. *Perf. 13*

1415	A657	1.20fr ultra, dp grn & dk car	48	28

Centenary of Universal Postal Union.
For surcharge see Reunion No. 396.

Copernicus and Heliocentric System — A658

1974, Oct. 12

1416	A658	1.20fr multicolored	42	28

500th anniversary of the birth of Nicolaus Copernicus (1473-1543), Polish astronomer.

Tourist Issue

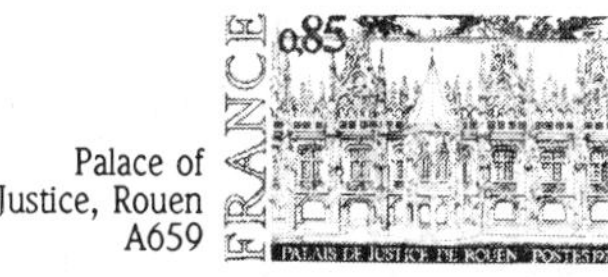

Palace of Justice, Rouen A659

Saint-Pol-de-Leon A660

Chateau de Rochechouart A661

1975 Engr. *Perf. 13*

1417	A659	85c multicolored	35	15
1418	A660	1.20fr bl, bis & choc	40	15
1419	A661	1.40fr brn, ind & grn	50	15

Issue dates: 85c, Jan. 25; 1.20fr, Jan. 18; 1.40fr, Jan. 11.

Snowy Egret — A662

Gallic Coin — A663

1975, Feb. 15 Engr. *Perf. 13*

1420	A662	70c brt blue & bister	40	22

Nature protection.

1975, Feb. 16 Typo. *Perf. 13½x14*

1421	A663	42c orange & mag	1.40	22
1422	A663	48c lt bl & red brn	1.65	22
1423	A663	70c brt pink & red	2.75	45
1424	A663	1.35fr lt green & brn	3.00	65

Nos. 1421-1424 are known only precanceled. See second note after No. 132. See Nos. 1460-1463, 1487-1490.

The Eye — A664

Ionic Capital — A665

Graphic Art — A666

Ceres A667

1975 Engr. *Perf. 13*

1425	A664	1fr red, pur & org	45	18
1426	A665	2fr grn, sl grn & mag	65	28
1427	A666	3fr dk car & ol grn	1.00	40
1428	A667	4fr red, sl grn & bis	1.40	55

Souvenir Sheet

1429	Sheet of 4	7.50	7.50
a.	A664 2fr dp car & slate blue	1.00	1.00
b.	A665 3fr brt bl, slate blue & dp car	1.40	1.40
c.	A666 4fr slate blue, brt bl & plum	2.00	2.00
d.	A667 6fr brt blue, slate blue & plum	2.50	2.50

ARPHILA 75, Intl. Philatelic Exhibition, Paris, June 6-16. Issued: 1fr, Mar. 1; 2fr, Mar. 22; 3fr, Apr. 19; 4fr, May 17; No. 1429, Apr. 2.

Pres. Georges Pompidou A668

Paul as Harlequin, by Picasso A669

1975, Apr. 3 Engr. *Perf. 13*

1430	A668	80c black & gray	30	15

Georges Pompidou (1911-74), President of France, 1969-74.

Europa Issue 1975

1975, Apr. 26 Photo. *Perf. 13*

Design: 1.20fr, Woman on Balcony, by Kees van Dongen, horiz.

1431	A669	80c multicolored	45	15
1432	A669	1.20fr multicolored	75	22

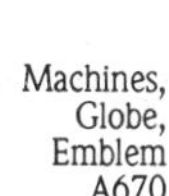

Machines, Globe, Emblem A670

1975, May 3 Engr.

1433	A670	1.20fr blue, blk & red	40	28

World Machine Tool Exhib., Paris, June 17-26.

Senate Assembly Hall — A671

1975, May 24 Engr. *Perf. 13*

1434	A671	1.20fr olive & dk car	42	28

Centenary of the Senate of the Republic.

Meter Convention Document, Atom Diagram and Waves — A672

1975, May 31

1435	A672	1fr multicolored	35	20

Cent. of Intl. Meter Convention, Paris, 1875.

Metro Regional Train — A673

"Gazelle" Helicopter A674

1975

1436 A673 1fr indigo & brt bl 90 22
1437 A674 1.30fr vio bl & grn 65 35

French technical achievements.
Issue dates: 1fr, June 21; 1.30fr, May 31.

Youth and Flasks, Symbols of Study and Growth — A675

1975, June 21

1438 A675 70c red pur & blk 25 20

Student Health Foundation.

People's Theater, Bussang, and Maurice Pottecher A676

1975, Aug. 9 Engr. ***Perf. 13***

1439 A676 85c multicolored 30 20

80th anniversary of the People's Theater at Bussang, founded by Maurice Pottecher.

Regions of France

Central France A677

Aquitaine A678

Limousin — A679

Picardy — A680

Burgundy A681

Loire A682

Guyana A683

Auvergne A684

Poitou-Charentes A685

Southern Pyrenees A686

Pas-de-Calais A687

1975-76 Engr. ***Perf. 13***

1440 A677 25c blue & yel grn 22 15
1441 A678 60c multicolored 22 16
1442 A679 70c multicolored 48 16
1443 A680 85c blue, grn & org 70 20
1444 A681 1fr red, yel & mar 70 20
1445 A682 1.15fr blue, bis & grn 70 25
1446 A683 1.25fr multicolored 55 30
1447 A684 1.30fr dk bl & red 55 20
1448 A685 1.90fr sl, ol & Prus bl 90 20
1449 A686 2.20fr multicolored 1.00 48
1450 A687 2.80fr car, bl & blk 1.40 52
Nos. 1440-1450 (11) 7.42 2.82

Issue dates- 1975: 85c, Nov. 15; 1fr, Oct. 25; 1.15fr, Sept. 6; 1.30fr, Oct. 4; 1.90fr, Dec. 6; 2.80fr, Dec. 13.

1976: 25c, Jan. 31; 2.20fr, Jan. 10; 60c, May 22; 70c, May 29; 125fr, Oct. 16.

French Flag, F.-H. Manhes, Jean Verneau, Pierre Kaan — A690

1975, Sept. 27

1453 A690 1fr multicolored 35 25

Liberation of concentration camps, 30th anniversary. F.-H. Manhes (1889-1959), Jean Verneau (1890-1944) and Pierre Kaan (1903-1945) were French resistance leaders, imprisoned in concentration camps.

Monument, by Joseph Riviere — A691

1975, Oct. 11

1454 A691 70c multicolored 25 20

Land Mine Demolition Service, 30th anniversary. Monument was erected in Alsace to honor land mine victims.

Symbols of Suburban Living A692

1975, Oct. 18

1455 A692 1.70fr brown, bl & grn 75 48

Creation of new towns.

Women and Rainbow — A693

1975, Nov. 8 **Photo.**

1456 A693 1.20fr silver & multi 45 30

International Women's Year 1975.

Saint-Nazaire Bridge A694

1975, Nov. 8 **Engr.**

1457 A694 1.40fr blue, ind & grn 60 20

French and Russian Flags A695

Frigate Melpomene A696

1975, Nov. 22

1458 A695 1.20fr blue, red & ocher 50 30

Franco-Soviet diplomatic relations, 50th anniversary.

1975, Dec. 6

1459 A696 90c multicolored 80 35

Gallic Coin Type of 1975

1976, Jan. 1 Typo. ***Perf. 13½x14***

1460 A663 50c lt green & brn 1.10 30
1461 A663 60c lilac & brn 1.75 30
1462 A663 90c orange & brn 2.25 65
1463 A663 1.60fr violet & brn 4.00 2.00

Nos. 1460-1463 are known only precanceled. See second note after No. 132.

Lintel, St. Genis des Fontaines Church A697

Venus of Brassempouy (Paleolithic) A698

"The Joy of Life," by Robert Delaunay A699

Ramses II, from Abu Simbel Temple, Egypt — A700

Still Life, by Maurice de Vlaminck — A701

1976 Engr. ***Perf. 13***

1464 A697 2fr blue & slate bl 1.25 60
1465 A698 2fr dk brn & yel 1.25 60

Photo. ***Perf. 12½x13***

1466 A699 2fr multicolored 1.25 60

Engr. ***Perf. 13x12½***

1467 A700 2fr multicolored 95 50

Perf. 13

1468 A701 2fr multicolored 95 50
Nos. 1464-1468 (5) 5.65 2.80

Issue dates: #1464, Jan. 24; #1465, Mar. 6; #1466, July 24; #1467, Sept. 4; #1468, Dec. 18.

Tourist Issue

Chateau Fort de Bonaguil A702

Lodève Cathedral A703

Biarritz A704

Thiers — A705

Ussel — A706

Chateau de Malmaison A707

1976	Engr.	*Perf. 13*		
1469 A702	1fr	multicolored	32	15
1470 A703	1.10fr	violet blue	38	20
1471 A704	1.40fr	multicolored	42	15
1472 A705	1.70fr	multicolored	55	15
1473 A706	2fr	multicolored	85	15
1474 A707	3fr	multicolored	95	20
		Nos. 1469-1474 (6)	3.47	1.00

Issue dates: 1fr, 2fr, July 10; 1.10fr, Nov. 13; 1.40fr, Sept. 25; 1.70fr, Oct. 9; 3fr, Apr. 10.

Destroyers, Association Emblem A708

1976, Apr. 24
1475 A708 1fr vio bl, mag & lem 52 20

Naval Reserve Officers Assoc., 50th anniv.

Gate, Rouen — A709

Young Person — A710

1976, Apr. 24
1476 A709 80c ol gray & salmon 35 15

49th Congress of the Federation of French Philatelic Societies, Rouen, Apr. 23-May 2.

1976, Apr. 27
1477 A710 60c bl grn, ind & car 35 15

JUVAROUEN 76, International Youth Philatelic Exhibition, Rouen, Apr. 25-May 2.

Europa Issue 1976

Ceramic Pitcher, Strasbourg, 18th Century A711

Design: 1.20fr, Sevres porcelain plate and CEPT emblem.

1976, May 8	Photo.	*Perf. 13*		
1478 A711	80c	multicolored	35	15
1479 A711	1.20fr	multicolored	60	20

Count de Vergennes and Benjamin Franklin — A712

1976, May 15 Engr. *Perf. 13*
1480 A712 1.20fr multicolored 42 28

American Bicentennial.

Battle of Verdun Memorial A713

Communication A714

1976, June 12 Engr.
1481 A713 1fr multicolored 45 20

Battle of Verdun, 60th anniversary.

1976, June 12 Photo.
1482 A714 1.20fr multicolored 40 22

Troncais Forest — A715

Cross of Lorraine — A716

1976, June 19 Engr.
1483 A715 70c green & multi 30 18

Protection of the environment.

1976, June 19
1484 A716 1fr multicolored 48 18

Association of Free French, 30th anniv.

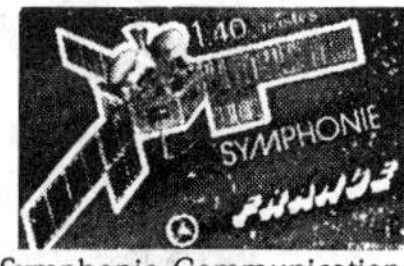

Symphonie Communications Satellite — A717

1976, June 26 Photo.
1485 A717 1.40fr multicolored 65 22

French technical achievements.

Gallic Coin Type of 1975

1976, July 1	Typo.	*Perf. 13½x14*		
1487 A663	52c	ver & dk brn	65	18
1488 A663	62c	vio & dk brn	1.25	35
1489 A663	95c	tan & dk brn	1.65	55
1490 A663	1.70fr	dk bl & dk brn	3.00	1.40

Nos. 1487-1490 are known only precanceled. See second note after No. 132.

Paris Summer Festival — A719

1976, July 10 Engr.
1491 A719 1fr multicolored 65 20

Summer festival in Tuileries Gardens, Paris.

Emblem and Soldiers A720

1976, July 8
1492 A720 1fr blk, dp bl & mag 38 18

Officers Reserve Corps, centenary.

Sailing — A721

1976, July 17
1493 A721 1.20fr blue, blk & vio 42 28

21st Olympic Games, Montreal, Canada, July 17-Aug. 1.

Marianne Type of 1971-74

1976	Typo.	*Perf. 14x13*		
1494 A555	80c	green	38	15
	Engr.	*Perf. 13*		
1495 A555	80c	green	42	15
a.		Booklet pane of 10	4.25	
1496 A555	1fr	carmine rose	42	15
a.		Booklet pane of 5	3.00	
b.		Booklet pane of 10	5.50	
		Set value		19

No. 1495 issued in booklets only. "POSTES" 6mm long on Nos. 1292A and 1494; 4mm on others.

#1494, 1496 were issued untagged in 1977.

Coil Stamps

1976, Aug. 1	Engr.	*Perf. 13 Horiz.*		
1497 A555	80c	green	42	22
1498 A555	1fr	carmine rose	42	18

Red control number on back of every 10th stamp.

Woman's Head, by Jean Carzou — A722

1976, Sept. 18 Engr. *Perf. 13x12½*
1499 A722 2fr multicolored 90 40

Old and New Telephones A723

1976, Sept. 25 Engr. *Perf. 13*
1500 A723 1fr multicolored 40 15

Centenary of first telephone call by Alexander Graham Bell, Mar. 10, 1876.

Festival Emblem and Trophy, Pyrenees, Hercules and Pyrène A724

Police Emblem A725

1976, Oct. 2
1501 A724 1.40fr multicolored 50 28

10th International Tourist Film Festival, Tarbes, Oct. 4-10.

1976, Oct. 9 Engr. *Perf. 13*
1502 A725 1.10fr ultra, red & ol 48 18

National Police, help and protection.

Atomic Particle Accelerator, Diagram A726

1976, Oct. 22 Photo.
1503 A726 1.40fr multicolored 65 22

European Center for Nuclear Research (CERN).

"Exhibitions" — A727

1976, Nov. 20 Engr. *Perf. 13*
1504 A727 1.50fr multicolored 75 28

Trade Fairs and Exhibitions.

Abstract Design A728

1976, Nov. 27 Photo.
1505 A728 1.10fr multicolored 45 20

Customs Service.

Atlantic Museum, Port Louis — A729

1976, Dec. 4 **Engr.**

1506 A729 1.45fr grnsh bl & ol	50	28

Regions of France

Réunion A730

Martinique A731

Franche-Comté A732

Brittany A733

Languedoc-Roussillon A734

Rhône-Alps A735

Champagne-Ardennes A736

Alsace A737

Photo. (1.45fr, 1.50fr, 2.50fr); Engr.
1977 ***Perf. 13***

1507 A730 1.45fr grn & lil rose	50	18
1508 A731 1.50fr multicolored	55	22
1509 A732 2.10fr multicolored	75	30
1510 A733 2.40fr multicolored	1.00	20
1511 A734 2.50fr multicolored	1.00	30
1512 A735 2.75fr Prus blue	1.25	28
1513 A736 3.20fr multicolored	1.25	48
1514 A737 3.90fr multicolored	1.65	55
Nos. 1507-1514 (8)	7.95	2.51

Issue dates: 1.45fr, Feb. 5; 1.50fr, Jan. 29; 2.10fr, Jan. 8; 2.40fr, Feb. 19; 2.50fr, Jan. 15; 2.75fr, Jan. 22; 3.20fr, Apr. 16; 3.90fr, Feb. 26.

Pompidou Cultural Center — A738

1977, Feb. 5 **Engr.** ***Perf. 13***

1515 A738 1fr multicolored	35	15

Inauguration of the Georges Pompidou National Center for Art and Culture, Paris.

Dunkirk Harbor A739

1977, Feb. 12

1516 A739 50c multicolored	25	15

Expansion of Dunkirk harbor facilities.

Bridge at Mantes, by Corot — A740

Virgin and Child, by Rubens A741

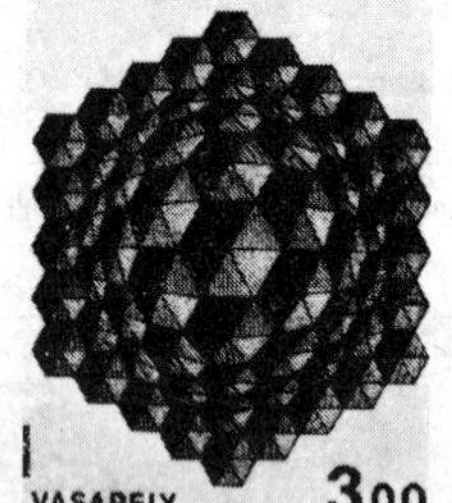
Tridimensional Design, by Victor Vasarely — A742

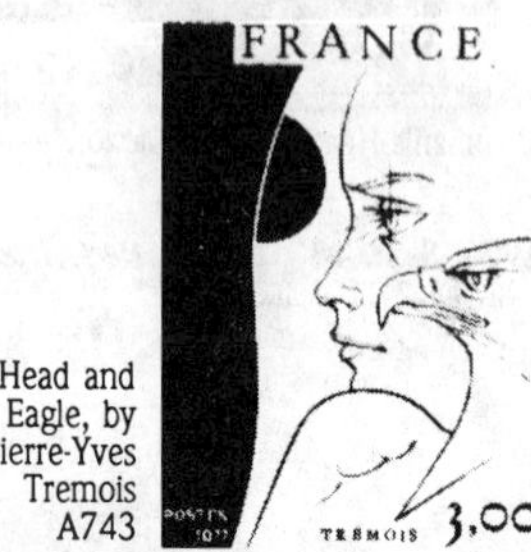
Head and Eagle, by Pierre-Yves Tremois A743

1977 **Engr.** ***Perf. 13x12½***

1517 A740 2fr multicolored	1.10	45

Perf. 12x13

1518 A741 2fr multicolored	1.10	45

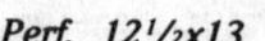
Perf. 12½x13

1519 A742 3fr ultra & sl grn	1.50	45

Photo.

1520 A743 3fr dark red & blk	1.90	55

Issue dates: No. 1517, Feb. 12; No. 1518, Nov. 5; No. 1519, Apr. 7; No. 1520, Sept. 17.

Hand Holding Torch and Sword — A744

Pisces — A745

1977, Mar. 5 **Engr.** ***Perf. 13***

1521 A744 80c ultra & multi	50	15

"France remembers its dead."

1977-78 **Engr.** ***Perf. 13***

Zodiac Signs: 58c, Cancer. 61c, Sagittarius. 68c, Taurus. 73c, Aries. 78c, Libra. 1.05fr, Scorpio. 1.15fr, Capricorn. 1.25fr, Leo. 1.85fr, Aquarius. 2fr, Virgo. 2.10fr, Gemini.

1522 A745 54c violet blue	65	28
1523 A745 58c emerald	1.00	30
1524 A745 61c brt blue	52	28
1525 A745 68c deep brown	85	35
1526 A745 73c rose carmine	1.50	55
1527 A745 78c vermilion	65	35
1528 A745 1.05fr brt lilac	1.50	75
1529 A745 1.15fr orange	2.25	1.10
1530 A745 1.25fr lt olive grn	1.25	60
1531 A745 1.85fr slate grn	2.75	90
1532 A745 2fr blue green	3.00	1.75
1533 A745 2.10fr lilac rose	1.65	1.00
Nos. 1522-1533 (12)	17.57	8.21

Issue dates: 54c, 68c, 1.05fr, 1.85fr, Apr. 1, 1977. Others, 1978.

Nos. 1522-1533 are known only precanceled. See second note after No. 132.

Village in Provence A746

Europa: 1.40fr, Brittany port.

1977, Apr. 23

1534 A746 1fr multicolored	45	15
1535 A746 1.40fr multicolored	65	18

Flowers and Gardening A747

1977, Apr. 23 **Engr.** ***Perf. 13***

1536 A747 1.70fr multicolored	70	28

National Horticulture Society, centenary.

Symbolic Flower — A748

1977, May 7

1537 A748 1.40fr multicolored	50	36

Intl. Flower Show, Nantes, May 12-23.

Battle of Cambray A749

1977, May 14

1538 A749 80c multicolored	35	20

300th anniversary of the capture of Cambray and the incorporation of Cambresis District into France.

Carmes Church, School, Map of France A750

Modern Constructions A751

1977, May 14

1539 A750 1.10fr multicolored	50	20

Catholic Institutes in France.

1977, May 21

1540 A751 1.10fr multicolored	55	25

European Federation of the Construction Industry.

Annecy Castle — A752

1977, May 28

1541 A752 1fr multicolored	60	15

Congress of the Federation of French Philatelic Societies, Annecy, May 28-30.

Tourist Issue

Abbey, Pont-à-Mousson A753

Abbey Tower, Saint-Amand-les-Eaux A754

Collegiate Church of Dorat A755

Fontenay Abbey A756

Bayeux Cathedral A757

Chateau de Vitré A758

1977 Engr. *Perf. 13*

1542 A753	1.25fr multicolored	40	15
1543 A754	1.40fr multicolored	42	15
1544 A755	1.45fr multicolored	42	16
1545 A756	1.50fr multicolored	48	20
1546 A757	1.90fr black & yel	58	25
1547 A758	2.40fr black & yel	70	20
Nos. 1542-1547 (6)		3.00	1.11

Issue dates: 1.25fr, Oct. 1; 1.40fr, Sept. 17; 1.45fr, July 16; 1.50fr, June 4; 1.90fr, July 9; 2.40fr, Sept. 24.

Polytechnic School and "X" — A759

1977, June 4 Engr. *Perf. 13*

1548 A759	1.70fr multicolored	55	20

Relocation at Palaiseau of Polytechnic School, founded 1794.

Soccer and Cup — A760

1977, June 11

1549 A760	80c multicolored	80	20

Soccer Cup of France, 60th anniversary.

De Gaulle Memorial — A761

Stylized Map of France — A762

1977, June 18 Photo. & Embossed

1550 A761	1fr gold & multi	75	15

5th anniversary of dedication of De Gaulle memorial at Colombey-les-Deux-Eglises.

1977, June 18 Engr. *Perf. 13*

1551 A762	1.10fr ultra & red	55	20

French Junior Chamber of Commerce.

Battle of Nancy A763

Arms of Burgundy A764

1977, June 25

1552 A763	1.10fr blue & slate	1.10	40

Battle of Nancy between the Dukes of Burgundy and Lorraine, 500th anniversary.

1977, July 2

1553 A764	1.25fr ol brn & sl grn	50	20

Annexation of Burgundy by the French Crown, 500th anniversary.

Association Emblem A765

1977, July 8

1554 A765	1.40fr ultra, ol & red	50	25

French-speaking Parliamentary Association.

Red Cicada — A766

1977, Sept. 10 Photo. *Perf. 13*

1555 A766	80c multicolored	50	16

Nature protection.

French Handicrafts A767

1977, Oct. 1 Engr. *Perf. 13*

1556 A767	1.40fr multicolored	50	20

French craftsmen.

Industry and Agriculture — A768

1977, Oct. 22

1557 A768	80c brown & olive	30	20

Economic & Social Council, 30th anniv.

Table Tennis — A769

1977, Dec. 17 Engr. *Perf. 13*

1558 A769	1.10fr multicolored	3.00	75

French Table Tennis Federation, 50th anniv., and French team, gold medal winner, Birmingham.

Abstract, by Roger Excoffon — A770

1977, Dec. 17 *Perf. 13x12½*

1559 A770	3fr multicolored	2.00	48

Sabine, after David — A771

1977-78 Engr. *Perf. 13*

1560 A771	1c	slate	15	15
1561 A771	2c	brt violet	15	15
1562 A771	5c	slate green	15	15
1563 A771	10c	red brown	15	15
1564 A771	15c	Prus blue	15	15
1565 A771	20c	brt green	15	15
1566 A771	30c	orange	15	15
1567 A771	50c	red lilac	15	15
1568 A771	80c	green ('77)	1.10	18
a.		Booklet pane of 10	11.00	
1569 A771	80c	olive	28	15
1570 A771	1fr	red ('77)	1.25	15
a.		Booklet pane of 5	8.50	
b.		Booklet pane of 10	15.00	
1571 A771	1fr	green	55	15
a.		Booklet pane of 10	5.50	
1572 A771	1.20fr	red	55	15
a.		Booklet pane of 5	4.25	
b.		Booklet pane of 10	7.75	
1573 A771	1.40fr	brt blue	2.00	18
1574 A771	1.70fr	grnsh blue	70	20
1575 A771	2fr	emerald	70	15
1576 A771	2.10fr	lilac rose	75	15
1577 A771	3fr	dark brown	1.00	28
Nos. 1560-1577 (18)			10.08	
Set value				1.60

Coil Stamps

1978 *Perf. 13 Horiz.*

1578 A771	80c	bright green	1.25	42
1579 A771	1fr	bright green	1.00	32
1579A A771	1fr	bright red	1.25	42
1579B A771	1.20fr	bright red	1.00	32

See Nos. 1658-1677.

For similar design inscribed "REPUBLIQUE FRANCAISE" see type A900.

Percheron, by Jacques Birr — A772

Osprey — A773

1978 Photo. *Perf. 13*

1580 A772	1.70fr multicolored	90	42

Engr.

1581 A773	1.80fr multicolored	75	22

Nature protection.
Issue dates: 1.70fr, Jan. 7; 1.80fr, Oct. 14.

Tournament, 1662, Etching A774

Institut de France and Pont des Arts, Paris, by Bernard Buffet — A776

Horses, by Yves Brayer — A777

1978 Engr. *Perf. 12x13*

1582 A774	2fr black	2.50	60

Perf. 13x12

1584 A776	3fr multicolored	2.75	42
1585 A777	3fr multicolored	2.00	42

Issue dates: 2fr, Jan. 14; No. 1584, Feb. 4; No. 1585, Dec. 9.

Communications School and Tower — A778

1978, Jan. 19 Engr. *Perf. 13*

1586 A778	80c Prussian blue	30	15

Natl. Telecommunications School, cent.

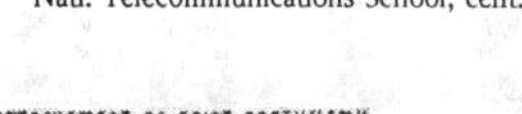

Swedish and French Flags, Map of Saint Barthelemy A779

1978, Jan. 19

1587 A779	1.10fr multicolored	45	18

Centenary of the reunion with France of Saint Barthelemy Island, West Indies.

Regions of France

Ile de France — A780

Tanker, Refinery, Flower, Upper Normandy A781

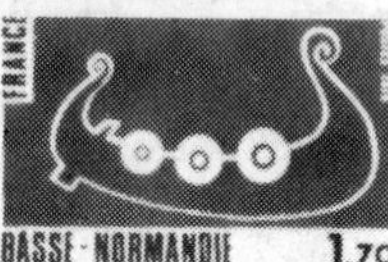

Lower Normandy A782

1978 **Photo.** ***Perf. 13***

1588	A780	1fr red, blue & blk	52	20

Engr.

1589	A781	1.40fr multicolored	55	20

Photo.

1590	A782	1.70fr multicolored	90	32

Issued: 1fr, Mar. 4; 1.40fr, Jan. 21; 1.70fr, Mar. 31.

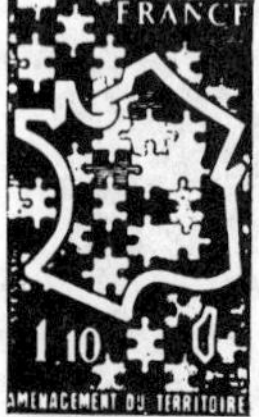

Stylized Map of France A788

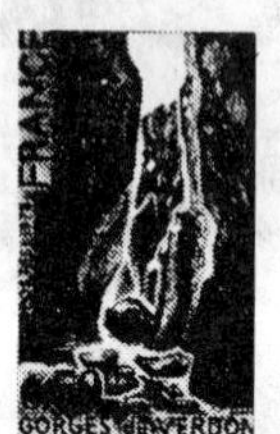

Young Stamp Collector A789

1978, Feb. 11 **Engr.** ***Perf. 13***

1596	A788	1.10fr violet & green	45	18

Program of administrative changes, 15th anniv.

1978, Feb. 25

1597	A789	80c multicolored	32	15

JUVEXNIORT, Youth Philatelic Exhibition, Niort, Feb. 25-March 5.

Tourist Issue

Verdon Gorge — A790

Saint-Saturnin Church — A792

Pont Neuf, Paris — A791

Our Lady of Bec-Hellouin Abbey A793

Chateau D'Esquelbecq A794

Aubazine Abbey A795

Fontevraud Abbey A796

1978 **Engr.** ***Perf. 13***

1598	A790	50c multicolored	18	15
1599	A791	80c multicolored	35	15
1600	A792	1fr black	38	15
1601	A793	1.10fr multicolored	50	15
1602	A794	1.10fr multicolored	38	22
1603	A795	1.25fr carmine & brn	50	20
1604	A796	1.70fr multicolored	70	22
		Nos. 1598-1604 (7)	2.99	1.24

Issue dates: 1.25fr, Feb. 18; 50c, Mar. 6; No. 1601, Mar. 26; 80c, May 27; 1fr, June 10; 1.70fr, June 3; No. 1602, June 17.

Fish and Underwater Flora — A797

1978, Apr. 15 **Photo.** ***Perf. 13***

1605	A797	1.25fr multicolored	95	42

Port Cros National Park, 15th anniversary.

Flowers, Butterflies and Houses — A798

1978, Apr. 22 **Engr.** ***Perf. 13***

1606	A798	1.70fr multicolored	2.75	32

50th anniversary of the beautification of France campaign.

Hands Shielding Source of Heat and Light — A799

1978, Apr. 22

1607	A799	1fr multicolored	60	15

Energy conservation.

World War I Memorial near Lens — A800

Fountain of the Innocents, Paris — A801

1978, May 6

1608	A800	2fr lemon & magenta	85	30

Colline Notre Dame de Lorette memorial of World War I.

1978, May 6

Europa: 1.40fr, Flower Park Fountain, Paris.

1609	A801	1fr multicolored	40	15
1610	A801	1.40fr multicolored	50	20

Maurois Palace, Troyes — A802

1978, May 13

1611	A802	1fr multicolored	40	15

51st Congress of the Federation of French Philatelic Societies, Troyes, May 13-15.

Roland Garros Tennis Court and Player — A803

1978, May 27

1612	A803	1fr multicolored	2.50	25

Roland Garros Tennis Court, 50th anniv.

Hand and Plant — A804

Printing Office Emblem — A805

1978, Sept. 9 **Engr.** ***Perf. 13***

1613	A804	1.30fr brown, red & grn	50	20

Encouragement of handicrafts.

1978, Sept. 23

1614	A805	1fr multicolored	35	15

National Printing Office, established 1538.

Fortress, Besanon, and Collegiate Church, Dole — A806

Valenciennes and Maubeuge A807

1978

1615	A806	1.20fr multicolored	50	15
1616	A807	1.20fr multicolored	50	15

Reunion of Franche-Comté and Valenciennes and Maubeuge with France, 300th anniversary.

Issue dates: #1615, Sept. 23; #1616, Sept. 30.

Sower Type of 1906-1937 and Academy Emblem — A808

Gymnasts, Strasbourg Cathedral, Storks — A809

1978, Oct. 7

1617	A808	1fr multicolored	40	16

Academy of Philately, 50th anniversary.

1978, Oct. 21

1618	A809	1fr multicolored	70	16

19th World Gymnastics Championships, Strasbourg, Oct. 23-26.

Various Sports A810

Polish Veterans' Monument A811

1978, Oct. 21

1619	A810	1fr multicolored	1.10	30

Sports for all.

1978, Nov. 11

1620	A811	1.70fr multicolored	60	25

Polish veterans of World War II.

Foreign postal stationery (stamped envelopes, postal cards and air letter sheets) is beyond the scope of this catalogue.

Railroad Car and Monument, Compiègne Forest, Rethondes
A812

1978, Nov. 11 Engr. *Perf. 13*

1621 A812 1.20fr indigo 75 15

60th anniversary of World War I armistice.

Handicapped People
A813

1978, Nov. 18

1622 A813 1fr multicolored 40 15

Rehabilitation of the handicapped.

Human Rights Emblem
A814

1978, Dec. 9 Engr. *Perf. 13*

1623 A814 1.70fr dk brown & blue 70 30

30th anniversary of Universal Declaration of Human Rights.

Child and IYC Emblem
A815

1979, Jan. 6 Engr. *Perf. 13*

1624 A815 1.70fr multicolored 4.00 1.50

International Year of the Child.

"Music," 15th Century Miniature — A816

1979, Jan. 13 *Perf. 13x12½*

1625 A816 2fr multicolored 1.40 48

Diana Taking a Bath, d'Ecouen Castle
A817

Church at Auvers-on-Oise, by Vincent Van Gogh — A818

Head of Marianne, by Salvador Dali — A819

Fire Dancer from The Magic Flute, by Chaplain Midy
A820

1979 Photo. *Perf. 12½x13*

1626 A817 2fr multicolored 90 40
1627 A818 2fr multicolored 6.75 65
1628 A819 3fr multicolored 1.25 40
1629 A820 3fr multicolored 1.25 48

Issue dates: #1626, Sept. 22; #1627, Oct. 27; #1628, Nov. 19; #1629, Nov. 26.

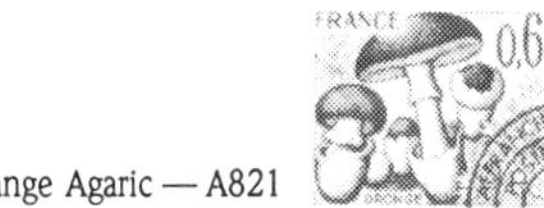

Orange Agaric — A821

Mushrooms: 83c, Death trumpet. 1.30fr, Olive wood pleurotus. 2.25fr, Cauliflower claveria.

1979, Jan. 15 Engr. *Perf. 13*

1630 A821 64c orange 32 25
1631 A821 83c brown 52 30
1632 A821 1.30fr yellow bister 80 42
1633 A821 2.25fr brown purple 1.25 70

Nos. 1630-1633 are known only precanceled. See second note after No. 132.

Victor Segalen
A822

1979, Jan. 20

1634 A822 1.50fr multicolored 50 20

Victor Segalen (1878-1919), physician, explorer and writer.

Hibiscus and Palms — A823

1979, Feb. 3

1635 A823 35c multicolored 15 15

International Flower Festival, Martinique.

Buddha, Stupas, Temple of Borobudur
A824

1979, Feb. 24

1636 A824 1.80fr ol & slate grn 60 30

Save the Temple of Borobudur, Java, campaign.

Boy, by Francisque Poulbot (1879-1946) — A825

1979, Mar. 24 Photo.

1637 A825 1.30fr multicolored 45 15

Tourist Issue

Chateau de Maisons, Laffitte
A826

Bernay and St. Pierre sur Dives Abbeys — A827

View of Auray — A827a

Steenvorde Windmill — A828

Wall Painting, Niaux Cave — A829

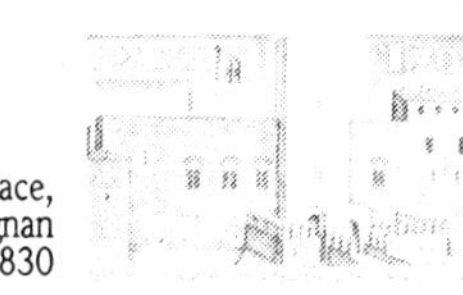

Royal Palace, Perpignan
A830

1979 Engr. *Perf. 13*

1638 A826 45c multicolored 16 15
1639 A827 1fr multicolored 32 15
1640 A827a 1fr multicolored 32 15
1641 A828 1.20fr multicolored 42 15
1642 A829 1.50fr multicolored 45 20
1643 A830 1.70fr multicolored 52 20
Nos. 1638-1643 (6) 2.19 1.00

Issue dates: 45c, Oct. 6; No. 1639, June 16; No. 1640, June 30; 1.20fr, May 12; 1.50fr, July 9; 1.70fr, Apr. 21.

Honey Bee — A831

1979, Mar. 31 Engr. *Perf. 13*

1644 A831 1fr multicolored 50 15

Nature protection.

St. Germain des Prés Abbey
A832

1979, Apr. 21

1645 A832 1.40fr multicolored 48 20

Simoun Mail Monoplanes, 1935, and Map of Mail Routes — A833

Europa: 1.70fr, Floating spheres used on Seine during siege of Paris, 1870.

1979, Apr. 28

1646 A833 1.20fr multicolored 45 15
1647 A833 1.70fr multicolored 55 25

Ship and View of Nantes
A834

1979, May 5 Engr. *Perf. 13*

1648 A834 1.20fr multicolored 42 15

52nd National Congress of French Philatelic Societies, Nantes, May 5-7.

Royal Palace, 1789 — A835

1979, May 19

1649 A835 1fr car rose & pur 40 20

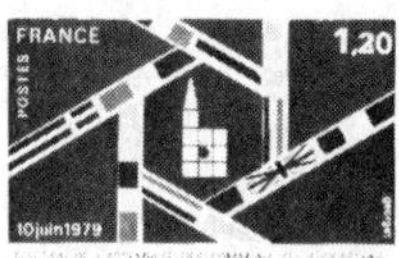

European Elections A836

1979, May 19 **Photo.** ***Perf. 13***

1650 A836 1.20fr multicolored 42 15

European Parliament, 1st direct elections, June 10.

Joan of Arc Monument A837

1979, May 24 **Engr.**

1651 A837 1.70fr brt lilac rose 70 30

Joan of Arc, the Maid of Orleans (1412-1431).

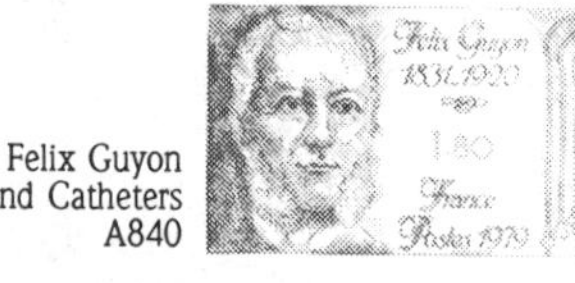

Felix Guyon and Catheters A840

1979, June 23

1652 A840 1.80fr sepia & blue 60 20

Felix Guyon (1831-1920), urologist.

Lantern Tower, La Rochelle — A841

Telecom '79 — A842

Towers: 88c, Chartres Cathedral. 1.40fr, Bourges Cathedral. 2.35fr, Amiens Cathedral.

1979, Aug. 13 **Engr.** ***Perf. 13***

1653 A841	68c	vio brn & blk	32	30
1654 A841	88c	ultra & blk	42	30
1655 A841	1.40fr	gray grn & blk	65	52
1656 A841	2.35fr	dull brn & blk	1.00	60

Nos. 1653-1656 are known only precanceled. See second note after No. 132. See Nos. 1684-1687, 1719-1722, 1814-1817.

1979, Sept. 22

1657 A842 1.10fr multicolored 38 15

3rd World Telecommunications Exhibition.

Sabine Type of 1977-78

1979-81 **Engr.** ***Perf. 13***

1658 A771	40c	brown ('81)	15	15
1659 A771	60c	red brown ('81)	16	15
1660 A771	70c	violet blue	20	15
1661 A771	90c	brt lilac ('81)	25	15
1662 A771	1fr	gray olive	25	15
1663 A771	1.10fr	green	70	15
1664 A771	1.20fr	green ('80)	45	15
1665 A771	1.30fr	rose red	70	15
1666 A771	1.40fr	rose red ('80)	52	15
1667 A771	1.60fr	purple	1.00	15
1668 A771	1.80fr	ocher	70	15
1669 A771	3.50fr	lt ol grn ('81)	1.00	15
1670 A771	4fr	brt car ('81)	1.10	20
1671 A771	5fr	brt grnsh bl ('81)	1.50	15
		Nos. 1658-1671 (14)	8.68	
		Set value		1.35

Coil Stamps

1979-80 ***Perf. 13 Horiz.***

1674 A771	1.10fr	green	1.10	20
1675 A771	1.20fr	green ('80)	50	20
1676 A771	1.30fr	rose red	1.10	20
1677 A771	1.40fr	rose red ('80)	55	20

Lorraine Region — A845

1979, Nov. 10

1678 A845 2.30fr multicolored 80 22

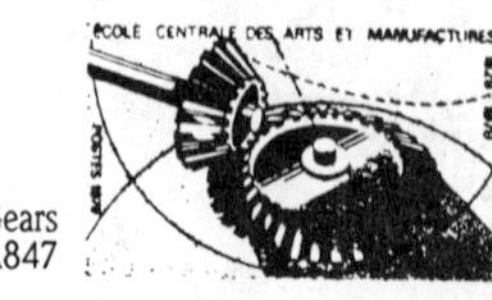

Gears A847

1979, Nov. 17 ***Perf. 13***

1680 A847 1.80fr multicolored 70 32

Central Technical School of Paris, 150th anniv.

Judo Throw A848

1979, Nov. 24 **Engr.**

1681 A848 1.60fr multicolored 52 28

World Judo Championships, Paris, Dec.

Violins — A849

1979, Dec. 10

1682 A849 1.30fr multicolored 52 15

Eurovision A850

1980, Jan. 12 **Engr.** ***Perf. 13x13½***

1683 A850 1.80fr multicolored 1.00 42

Tower Type of 1979

Designs: 76c, Chateau d'Angers. 99c, Chateau de Kerjean. 1.60fr, Chateau de Pierrefonds. 2.65fr, Chateau de Tarascon.

1980, Jan. 21 **Engr.**

1684 A841	76c	grnsh bl & blk	28	28
1685 A841	99c	slate grn & blk	38	32
1686 A841	1.60fr	red & blk	70	55
1687 A841	2.65fr	brn org & blk	1.10	65

Nos. 1684-1687 are known only precanceled. See second note after No. 132.

Self-portrait, by Albrecht Dürer, Philexfrance '82 Emblem A851

Woman Holding Fan, by Ossip Zadkine A852

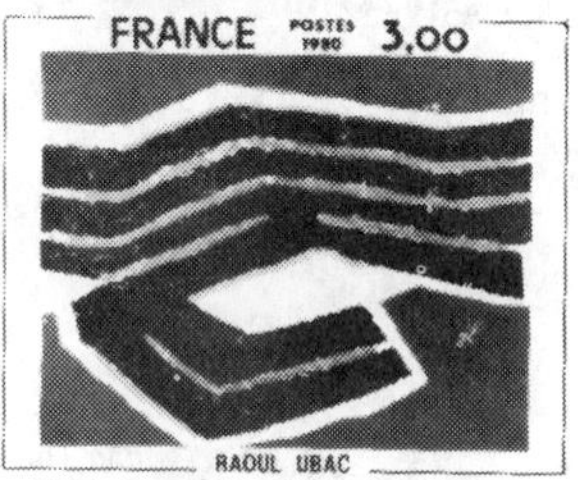

Abstract, by Raoul Ubak — A853

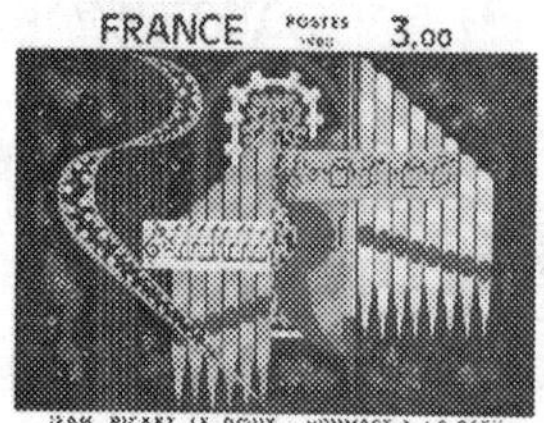

Hommage to J.S. Bach, by Jean Picart Le Doux — A854

Peasant, by Louis Le Nain A855

Woman with Blue Eyes, by Modigliani A856

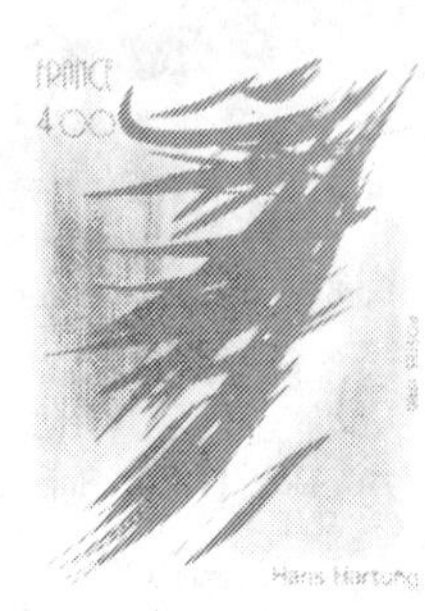

Abstract, by Hans Hartung A857

Engraved, Photogravure (#1691, 1694)

1980 ***Perf. 12½x13, 13x12½***

1688 A851	2fr	multicolored	85	42
1689 A852	3fr	multicolored	1.50	42
1690 A853	3fr	multicolored	1.50	42
1691 A854	3fr	multicolored	1.50	45
1692 A855	3fr	multicolored	1.50	35
1693 A856	4fr	multicolored	3.00	50
1694 A857	4fr	ultra & black	2.00	35
		Nos. 1688-1694 (7)	11.85	2.91

Issue dates: #1688, June 7; #1689, Jan. 19; #1690, Feb. 2; #1691, Sept. 20; #1693, Oct. 26; #1692, Nov. 10; #1694, Dec. 20.

Giants of the North Festival — A858

French Cuisine — A859

1980, Feb. 16 ***Perf. 13***

1695 A858 1.60fr multicolored 60 32

1980, Feb. 23

1696 A859 90c red & lt brown 65 15

Woman Embroidering A860

Fight Against Cigarette Smoking A861

Photogravure and Engraved

1980, Mar. 29 ***Perf. 13***

1697 A860 1.10fr multicolored 42 15

1980, Apr. 5 **Photo.** ***Perf. 13***

1698 A861 1.30fr multicolored 45 15

Europa Issue

Aristide Briand — A862

Design: 1.80fr, St. Benedict.

1980, Apr. 26 **Engr.** ***Perf. 13***

1699 A862 1.30fr multicolored 40 15

1700 A862 1.80fr red & red brown 60 18

Aristide Briand (1862-1932), prime minister, 1909-1911, 1921-1922; St. Benedict, patron saint of Europe.

Liancourt, College, Map of Northwestern France A863

1980, May 19 Engr. *Perf. 13*

1701 A863 2fr dk green & pur	65	20

National College of Arts and Handicrafts (founded by Larochefoucauld Liancourt) bicentenary.

Cranes, Town Hall Tower, Dunkirk — A864

1980, May 24

1702 A864 1.30fr multicolored	42	15

53rd Natl. Congress of French Federation of Philatelic Societies, Dunkirk, May 24-26.

Tourist Issue

Chateau de Maintenon A866

Cordes A865

Montauban A867

St. Peter's Abbey, Solesmes A868

Puy Cathedral A869

1980 Engr. *Perf. 13*

1703 A865 1.50fr multicolored	50	15
1704 A866 2fr multicolored	60	15
1705 A867 2.30fr multicolored	70	20
1706 A868 2.50fr multicolored	75	15
1707 A869 3.20fr multicolored	1.00	28
Nos. 1703-1707 (5)	3.55	93

Issue dates: No. 1703, Apr. 5; No. 1704, June 7; No. 1705, May 7; No. 1706, Sept. 20; No. 1707, May 12.

Graellsia Isabellae A870

1980, May 31 Photo.

1708 A870 1.10fr multicolored	60	20

Association Emblem — A871

1980, June 10 Photo.

1709 A871 1.30fr red & blue	45	16

Intl. Public Relations Assoc., 25th anniv.

Marianne, French Architecture A872

1980, June 21 Engr.

1710 A872 1.50fr bluish & gray blk	60	24

Heritage Year.

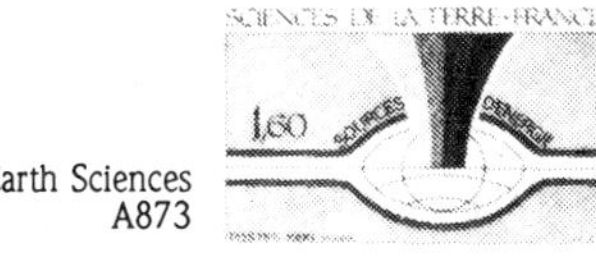

Earth Sciences A873

1980, July 5

1711 A873 1.60fr dk brown & red	55	28

International Geological Congress.

Rochambeau's Landing — A874

1980, July 15

1712 A874 2.50fr multicolored	1.00	35

Rochambeau's landing at Newport, R.I. (American Revolution), bicentenary.

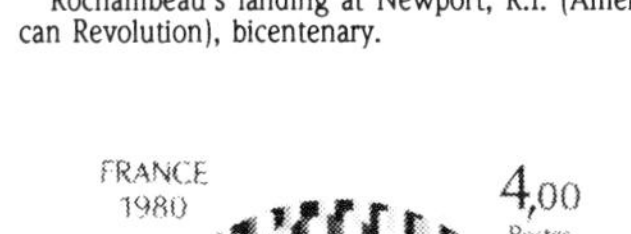

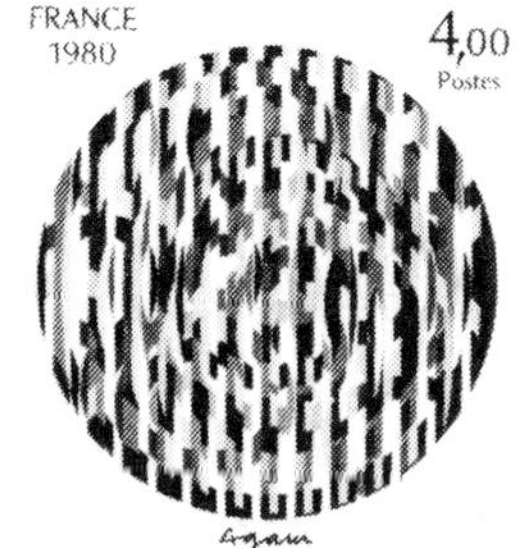

Message of Peace, by Yaacov Agam — A875

1980, Oct. 4 Photo. *Perf. 11½x13*

1713 A875 4fr multicolored	3.50	65

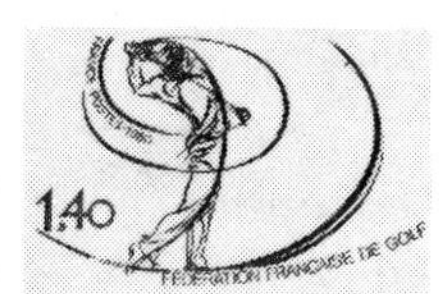

French Golf Federation A876

1980, Oct. 18 Engr.

1714 A876 1.40fr multicolored	55	16

Comedie Francaise, 300th Anniversary A877

1980, Oct. 18

1715 A877 2fr multicolored	65	22

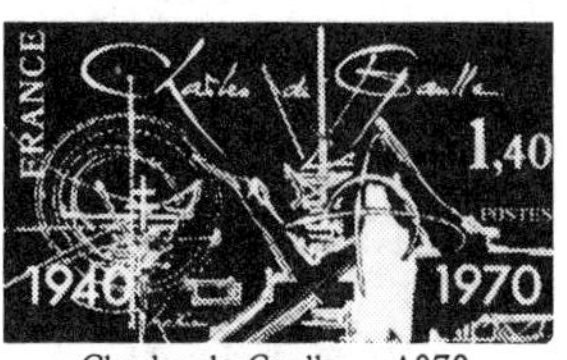

Charles de Gaulle — A878

1980, Nov. 10 Photo. *Perf. 13*

1716 A878 1.40fr multicolored	75	15

40th anniversary of De Gaulle's appeal of June 18, and 10th anniversary of his death.

Guardsman — A879

1980, Nov. 24 Engr. *Perf. 13*

1717 A879 1.70fr multicolored	65	35

Rambouillet Chateau A880

1980, Dec. 6 Engr. *Perf. 13*

1718 A880 2.20fr multicolored	90	16

Tower Type of 1979

Designs: 88c, Imperial Chapel, Ajaccio. 1.14fr, Astronomical Clock, Besancon. 1.84fr, Coucy Castle ruins. 3.05fr, Font-de-Gaume cave drawing, Les Eyzies de Tayac.

1981, Jan. 11 Engr. *Perf. 13*

1719 A841 88c dp magenta & blk	35	22
1720 A841 1.14fr ultra & blk	45	28
1721 A841 1.84fr dk green & blk	65	45
1722 A841 3.05fr brown red & blk	1.10	70

Nos. 1719-1722 are known only precanceled. See second note after No. 132.

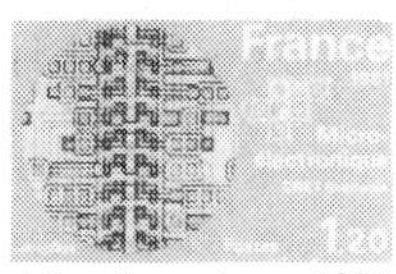

Microelectronics — A881

1981 Photo.

1723 A881 1.20fr shown	75	15
1724 A881 1.20fr Biology	42	18
1725 A881 1.40fr Energy	52	24
1726 A881 1.80fr Marine exploration	65	35
1727 A881 2fr Telemetry	80	18
Nos. 1723-1727 (5)	3.14	1.10

Issue dates: #1723, Feb. 5; others, Mar. 28.

Abstract, by Albert Gleizes A882

1981, Feb. 28 *Perf. 12½x13*

1728 A882 4fr multicolored	1.65	48

The Footpath by Camille Pissaro — A883

1981, Apr. 18 Engr. *Perf. 13x12½*

1729 A883 2fr multicolored	1.10	35

Child Watering Smiling Map of France — A884

1981, Mar. 14 Engr. *Perf. 13*

1730 A884 1.40fr multicolored	45	15

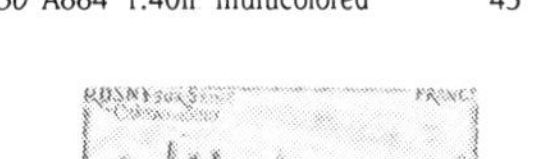

Sully Chateau, Rosny-sur-Seine — A885

1981, Mar. 21

1731 A885 2.50fr multicolored	95	15

Tourist Issue

Roman Temple, Nimes — A886

Church of St. Jean, Lyon — A887

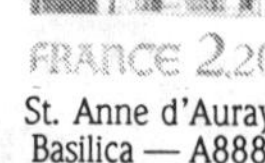

St. Anne d'Auray Basilica — A888

Vaucelles Abbey A889

Notre Dame of Louviers A890

1981, Apr. 11 **Engr.** ***Perf. 13***
1732 A886 1.70fr multicolored 60 22

1981
1733 A887 1.40fr dk red & dk brn 45 15
1734 A888 2.20fr blue & black 75 22

Issue dates: 1.40fr, May 30; 2.20fr, July 4.

1981
1735 A889 2fr red & black 60 16
1736 A890 2.20fr red brn & dk brn 75 28
Nos. 1732-1736 (5) 3.15 1.03

Issue dates: 2fr, Sept. 19; 2.20fr, Sept. 26.

Europa Issue 1981

Folkdances A891

1981, May 4 ***Perf. 13***
1737 A891 1.40fr Bouree 48 15
1738 A891 2fr Sardane 75 22

Bookbinding A892

Cadets A893

1981, Apr. 4 ***Perf. 13***
1739 A892 1.50fr ol & car rose 50 22

1981, May 16
1740 A893 2.50fr multicolored 85 16

Military College at St. Maixent centenary.

Man Drawing Geometric Diagram — A894

1981, May 23 **Photo.**
1741 A894 2fr shown 1.75 45
1742 A894 2fr Faces 1.75 45
a. Pair, #1741-1742 + label 3.50

PHILEXFRANCE '82 Stamp Exhibition, Paris, June 11-21, 1982.

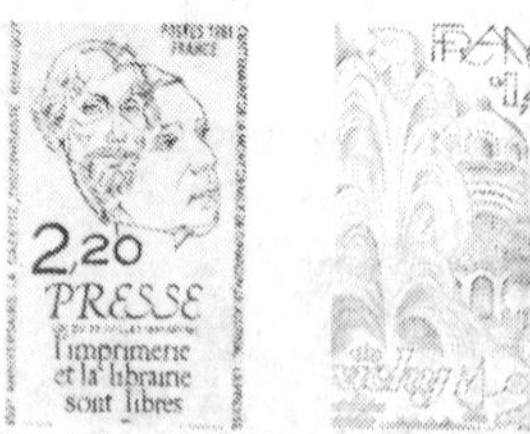

Theophraste Renaudot and Emile de Girardin — A895

Public Gardens, Vichy — A896

1981, May 30 **Engr.**
1743 A895 2.20fr black & red 75 38

350th anniversary of La Gazette (founded by Renaudot), and death centenary of founder of Le Journal (de Girardin).

1981, June 6
1744 A896 1.40fr multicolored 45 16

54th National Congress of French Federation of Philatelic Societies, Vichy.

Higher National College for Commercial Studies Centenary A897

1981, June 20 ***Perf. 13***
1745 A897 1.40fr multicolored 48 16

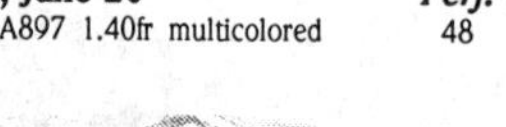

Sea Shore Conservation A898

1981, June 20
1746 A898 1.60fr multicolored 60 18

World Fencing Championship, Clermont-Ferrand, July 2-13 — A899

1981, June 27
1747 A899 1.80fr multicolored 60 24

Sabine, after David — A900

1981, Sept. 1 **Engr.**
1755 A900 1.40fr green 85 15
1756 A900 1.60fr red 1.00 25
1757 A900 2.30fr blue 1.40 40

Coil Stamps

1981 **Engr.** ***Perf. 13 Horiz.***
1758 A900 1.40fr green 55 22
1759 A900 1.60fr red 60 16

Highway Safety ("Drink or Drive") A901

1981, Sept. 5 ***Perf. 13***
1768 A901 1.60fr multicolored 60 15

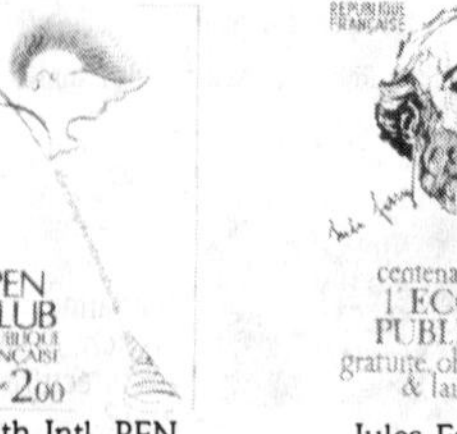

45th Intl. PEN Club Congress A902

Jules Ferry, Statesman A903

1981, Sept. 19 ***Perf. 13***
1769 A902 2fr multicolored 75 24

1981, Sept. 26 ***Perf. 12½x13***
1770 A903 1.60fr multicolored 60 16

Free compulsory public school centenary.

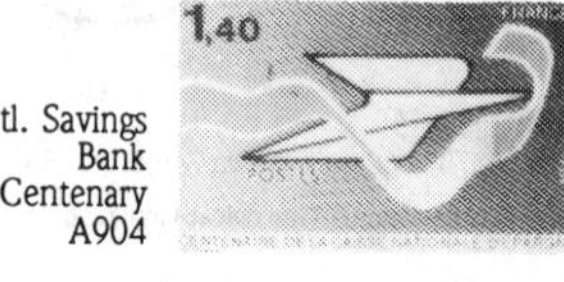

Natl. Savings Bank Centenary A904

1981, Sept. 21 **Photo.** ***Perf. 13***
1771 A904 1.40fr multicolored 48 16
1772 A904 1.60fr multicolored 52 16

The Divers, by Edouard Pignon — A905

1981, Oct. 3 ***Perf. 13x12½***
1773 A905 4fr multicolored 1.65 30

Alleluia, by Alfred Manessier A906

1981, Dec. 19 **Photo.** ***Perf. 12x13***
1774 A906 4fr multicolored 1.65 30

Tourist Issue

Saint-Emilion A907

Crest — A908

1981 **Engr.** ***Perf. 13x12½***
1775 A907 2.60fr dk red & lt ol grn 85 15
Perf. 13
1776 A908 2.90fr dk green 1.25 15
Set value 19

Issued: No. 1775, Oct. 10; No. 1776, Nov. 28.

150th Anniv. of Naval Academy A909

1981, Oct. 17 ***Perf. 13***
1777 A909 1.40fr multicolored 55 15

St. Hubert Kneeling Before the Stag, 15th Cent. Sculpture — A910

1981, Oct. 24
1778 A910 1.60fr multicolored 50 15

Museum of hunting and nature.

V. Schoelcher, J. Jaures, J. Moulin and the Pantheon — A911

1981, Nov. 2
1779 A911 1.60fr blue & dull pur 50 15

Intl. Year of the Disabled A912

1981, Nov. 7
1780 A912 1.60fr multicolored 50 15

Buying Sets
It is often less expensive to purchase complete sets than individual stamps that make up the set. Set values are provided for many such sets.

Men Leading Cattle, 2nd Cent. Roman Mosaic — A913

1981, Nov. 14 *Perf. 13x12*

1781 A913 2fr multicolored 1.10 32

Virgil's birth bimillennium.

Martyrs of Chateaubriant — A914

1981, Dec. 12 **Engr.** *Perf. 13*

1782 A914 1.40fr multicolored 50 15

Liberty, after Delacroix — A915

1982 **Engr.** *Perf. 13*

1783	A915	5c dk green	15	15
1784	A915	10c dull red	15	15
1785	A915	15c brt rose lilac	15	15
1786	A915	20c brt green	15	15
1787	A915	30c orange	15	15
1788	A915	40c brown	15	15
a.		Bklt. pane of 5, 4 No. 1784, No. 1788 ('87)	27	
1789	A915	50c lilac	15	15
1790	A915	60c lt red brn	15	15
1791	A915	70c ultra	15	15
1792	A915	80c lt olive grn	18	15
1793	A915	90c brt lilac	20	15
1794	A915	1fr olive green	22	15
1795	A915	1.40fr green	55	15
1796	A915	1.60fr green	40	15
1797	A915	1.60fr red	65	15
1798	A915	1.80fr red	52	15
1799	A915	2fr brt yellow grn	52	15
1800	A915	2.30fr blue	55	25
1801	A915	2.60fr blue	65	25
1802	A915	3fr chocolate	65	15
1803	A915	4fr brt carmine	90	15
1804	A915	5fr gray blue	1.10	15
		Nos. 1783-1804 (22)	8.44	
		Set value		1.80

Coil Stamps

Perf. 13 Horiz.

1805	A915	1.40fr green	1.00	28
1806	A915	1.60fr red	1.25	28
1807	A915	1.60fr green	48	16
1807A	A915	1.80fr red	60	15

Issued: 5c-50c, 1fr-1.40fr, 2fr, 2.30fr, 5fr, No. 1797, Jan. 2; 1.80fr, 2.60fr, No. 1796, June 1; 60c-90c, 3fr, 4fr, Nov. 3.

See Nos. 1878-1897A, 2077-2080. For surcharge see No. 2115.

Tourist Issue

St. Pierre and Miquelon A916

Corsica A917

Renaissance Fountain, Aix-en Provence A918

Collonges-la-Rouge — A919

Castle of Henry IV, Pau — A920

Lille — A921

Chateau Ripaille, Haute-Savoie A921a

1982 **Engr.** *Perf. 12½*

1808	A916	1.60fr dk blue & blk	48	15
1809	A917	1.90fr blue & red	60	20

Perf. 13

1810	A918	2fr multicolored	65	15
1811	A919	3fr multicolored	90	15
1812	A920	3fr ultra & dk bl	90	15

Issued: 1.60fr, 1.90fr, Jan. 9; 2fr, June 21, No. 1811, July 5, No. 1812, May 15.

1982 *Perf. 13x12½*

1813	A921	1.80fr dull red & ol	55	15
1813A	A921a	2.90fr multicolored	95	15
		Nos. 1808-1813A (7)	5.03	
		Set value		85

Issue dates: 1.80fr, Oct. 16; 2.90fr, Sept. 4.

Tower Type of 1979

Designs: 97c, Tanlay Castle, Yonne. 1.25fr, Salses Fort, Pyrenees-Orientales. 2.03fr, Montlhery Tower, Essonne. 3.36fr, Chateau d'If Bouches-du-Rhone.

1982, Jan. 11 **Engr.** *Perf. 13*

1814	A841	97c olive grn & blk	35	20
1815	A841	1.25fr red & blk	42	24
1816	A841	2.03fr sepia & blk	65	38
1817	A841	3.36fr ultra & blk	1.10	60

Nos. 1814-1817 are known only precanceled. See second note after No. 132.

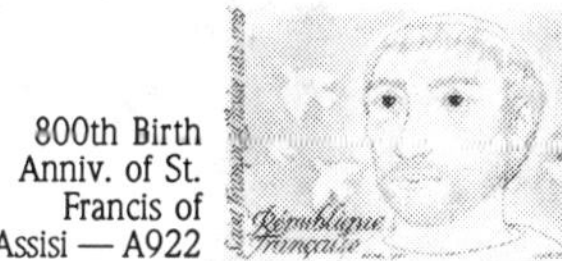
800th Birth Anniv. of St. Francis of Assisi — A922

1982, Feb. 6 **Photo. & Engr.**

1818 A922 2fr black & blue 70 18

Posts and Mankind A923

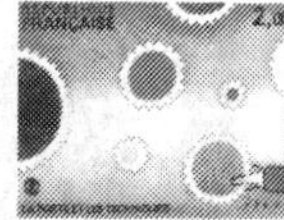
Posts and Technology A924

Illustration reduced.

1982, Feb. 13 **Photo.**

1819	A923	2fr multicolored	5.00	1.00
1820	A924	2fr multicolored	5.00	1.00
a.		Pair, #1819-1820 + label	10.00	

PHILEXFRANCE '82 Stamp Exhibition, Paris, June 11-21.

Souvenir Sheet

Marianne, by Jean Cocteau — A925

1982, June 11

1821	Sheet of 2	21.00	21.00
a.	A925 4fr red & blue	*9.00*	*9.00*
b.	A925 6fr blue & red	*10.00*	*10.00*

Sold only with 20fr show admission ticket.

Scouting Year — A926

1982, Feb. 20 **Engr.**

1822 A926 2.30fr yellow grn & blk 75 30

31st Natl. Census — A927

1982, Feb. 27 **Photo.**

1823 A927 1.60fr multicolored 50 15

Bale-Mulhouse Airport Opening — A928

1982, Mar. 15 **Engr.** *Perf. 13*

1824 A928 1.90fr multicolored 75 15

Fight Against Racism A929

1982, Mar. 20

1825 A929 2.30fr brn & red org 85 30

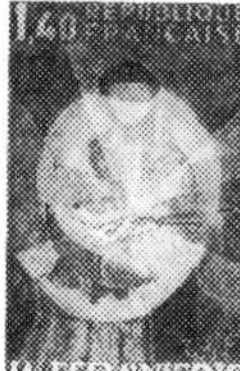
Blacksmith — A930

1982, Apr. 17

1826 A930 1.40fr multicolored 50 20

Europa 1982 A931

1982, Apr. 24

1827	A931	1.60fr Treaty of Rome, 1957	52	15
1828	A931	2.30fr Treaty of Verdun, 843	75	20

1982 World Cup A932

1982, Apr. 28

1829 A932 1.80fr multicolored 1.00 15

Young Greek Soldier, Hellenic Sculpture, Agude A933

1982, May 15 *Perf. 12½x13*

1830 A933 4fr multicolored 1.75 38

Embarkation for Ostia, by Claude Gellee — A934

The Lacemaker, by Vermeer A935

Turkish Chamber, by Balthus — A936

1982 Photo. *Perf. 13x12½, 12½x13*

1831	A934	4fr multicolored	1.65	35
1832	A935	4fr multicolored	1.65	35
1833	A936	4fr multicolored	1.65	30

Issue dates: No. 1831, June 19; No. 1832, Sept. 4; No. 1833, Nov. 6.

35th Intl. Film Festival, Cannes — A937

Natl. Space Studies Center, 20th Anniv. — A938

1982, May 15 Photo. *Perf. 13*

1834	A937	2.30fr multicolored	75	35

1982, May 15 Engr.

1835	A938	2.60fr multicolored	95	35

A939

A940

1982, June 4 Photo.

1836	A939	2.60fr multicolored	85	30

Industrialized Countries' Summit Meeting, Versailles, June 4-6.

1982, June 4 Engr. *Perf. 13*

1837	A940	1.60fr ol grn & dk grn	50	15

Jules Valles (1832-1885), writer.

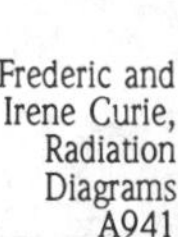

Frederic and Irene Curie, Radiation Diagrams A941

1982, June 26

1838	A941	1.80fr multicolored	70	15

Electric Street Lighting Centenary A942

1982, July 10

1839	A942	1.80fr dk blue & vio	70	15

The Family, by Marc Boyan A943

Photogravure and Engraved

1982, Sept. 18 *Perf. 12½x13*

1840	A943	4fr multicolored	1.90	32

Natl. Fed. of Firemen, Cent. A944

Marionettes A945

1982, Sept. 18 Engr. *Perf. 13*

1841	A944	3.30fr red & sepia	1.50	15

1982, Sept. 25

1842	A945	1.80fr multicolored	60	15

Rugby A946

1982, Oct. 9

1843	A946	1.60fr multicolored	1.00	15

Higher Education A947

1982, Oct. 16

1844	A947	1.80fr red & black	60	15

TB Bacillus Centenary A948

1982, Nov. 13

1845	A948	2.60fr red & black	80	30

St. Teresa of Avila (1515-82) A949

Leon Blum (1872-1950), Politician A950

1982, Nov. 20

1846	A949	2.10fr multicolored	65	20

1982, Dec. 18 Engr. *Perf. 13*

1847	A950	1.80fr dk brn & brn	65	15

Cavelier de la Salle (1643-1687), Explorer A951

1982, Dec. 18 *Perf. 13x12½*

1848	A951	3.25fr multicolored	1.00	20

Spring — A952

1983, Jan. 17 Engr. *Perf. 13*

1849	A952	1.05fr shown	32	16
1850	A952	1.35fr Summer	40	20
1851	A952	2.19fr Autumn	55	32
1852	A952	3.63fr Winter	1.00	55

Nos. 1849-1852 known only precanceled. See second note after No. 132.

Provence-Alpes-Cote d'Azur — A953

Brantome (Perigord) A954

Concarneau A955

Noirlac Abbey A956

Jarnac A957

Charleville-Mezieres — A958

Illustration A958 reduced.

1983 Photo. *Perf. 13*

1853	A953	1fr multicolored	40	15

Engr.

Perf. 13x12½

1854	A954	1.80fr multicolored	60	15

Perf. 13

1855	A955	3fr multicolored	1.00	20

Perf. 13x12½

1856	A956	3.60fr multicolored	1.25	28

Issued: 1fr, Jan. 8; 1.80fr, Feb. 5. 3fr, June 11; 3.60fr, July 2.

1983 *Perf. 13x12½*

1857	A957	2fr multicolored	70	15
1858	A958	3.10fr multicolored	1.10	60
		Nos. 1853-1858 (6)	5.05	1.53

Issued: 2fr, Oct. 8; 3.10fr, Sept. 17.

Martin Luther (1483-1546) — A959

1983, Feb. 12 Engr. *Perf. 13*

1859	A959	3.30fr dk brn & tan	1.25	25

Alliance Francaise Centenary A960

1983, Feb. 19

1860	A960	1.80fr multicolored	70	15

Danielle Casanova (d. 1942), Resistance Leader A961

1983, Mar. 8

1861	A961	3fr blk & red brn	95	24

World Communications Year — A962

1983, Mar. 12 Photo.

1862	A962	2.60fr multicolored	95	20

Manned Flight Bicentenary — A963

1983, Mar. 19 Photo. *Perf. 13*

1863	A963	2fr Hot air balloon	80	35
1864	A963	3fr Hydrogen balloon	1.10	48

Se-tenant with label.

Female Nude, by Raphael
A964

Aurora-Set, by Dewasne — A965

1983 Engr. *Perf. 13*
1865 A964 4fr multicolored 1.25 52

Photo.
1866 A965 4fr multicolored 1.25 52

Issue dates: #1866, Mar. 19; #1865, Apr. 9.

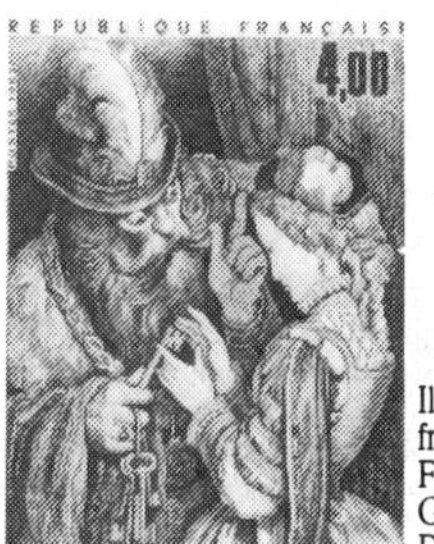

Illustration from Perrault's Folk Tales, by Gustave Dore — A966

1983, June 18 Engr. *Perf. 13*
1867 A966 4fr red & black 1.25 52

Homage to Jean Effel — A967

1983, Oct. 15
1868 A967 4fr multicolored 1.50 40

Le Lapin Agile, by Utrillo — A968

1983, Dec. 3 *Perf. 13x12½*
1869 A968 4fr multicolored 1.50 52

Thistle — A969

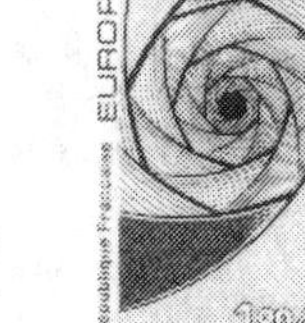

Europa 1983 — A970

1983, Apr. 23 Engr. *Perf. 12½x12*
1870 A969 1fr shown 28 15
1871 A969 2fr Martagon lily 80 15
1872 A969 3fr Aster 90 18
1873 A969 4fr Aconite 1.25 35

1983, Apr. 29 *Perf. 13*
1874 A970 1.80fr Symbolic shutter 3.25 22
1875 A970 2.60fr Lens-to-screen diagram 3.75 38

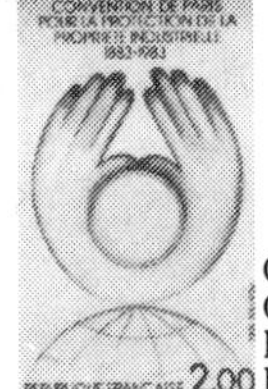

Centenary of Paris Convention for the Protection of Industrial Property — A971

1983, May 14 Photo. *Perf. 13*
1876 A971 2fr multicolored 70 16

French Philatelic Societies Congress, Marseilles
A972

1983, May 21 Engr. *Perf. 13*
1877 A972 1.80fr multicolored 70 15

Liberty Type of 1982

1983-87 Engr. *Perf. 13*

No.	Type	Value	Color	Unused	Used
1878	A915	1.70fr	green	42	15
1879	A915	1.80fr	green	40	15
1880	A915	1.90fr	green	50	15
1881	A915	2fr	red	55	15
1882	A915	2fr	green	55	15
1883	A915	2.10fr	red	55	15
1884	A915	2.20fr	red	55	15
a.		Booklet pane of 10		4.50	
b.		Bklt. pane, 5 #1788, 4 #1884		2.10	
c.		With label ('87)		55	15
1885	A915	2.80fr	blue	70	25
1886	A915	3fr	blue	85	18
1887	A915	3.20fr	blue	75	15
1888	A915	3.40fr	blue	95	16
1889	A915	3.60fr	blue	1.00	15
1890	A915	10fr	purple	2.25	15
1891	A915	(1.90fr)	green	50	15
1892	A915	(2fr)	green	60	15
	Nos. 1878-1892 (15)			11.12	
	Set value				1.45

Coil Stamps

Engr. *Perf. 13 Horiz.*

No.	Type	Value	Color	Unused	Used
1893	A915	1.70fr	green	55	15
1894	A915	1.80fr	green	60	15
1895	A915	1.90fr	green	65	15
1896	A915	2fr	red	85	15
1897	A915	2.10fr	red	1.00	35
1897A	A915	2.20fr	red	75	15
	Nos. 1893-1897A (6)			4.40	
	Set value				92

#1891 is inscribed "A," #1892 "B."

No. 1884c was issued in sheets of 50 plus 50 alternating labels picturing the PHILEXFRANCE '89 emblem to publicize the international philatelic exhibition.

Issued: 2.80fr, 10fr, #1881, June 1; 1.70fr, 2.10fr, 3fr, July 1, 1984; 1.80fr, 2.20fr, 3.20fr, Aug. 1, 1985; 3.40fr, #1891, Aug. 1, 1986; 1.90fr, Sept. 13, 1986; #1882, Oct. 15, 1987; 3.60fr, #1892, Aug. 1, 1987.

For surcharge see No. 2115.

50th Anniv. of Air France
A973

1983, June 18
1898 A973 3.45fr multicolored 1.10 32

Treaties of Versailles and Paris Bicentenary — A974

1983, Sept. 2 *Perf. 13x12½*
1899 A974 2.80fr multicolored 1.00 32

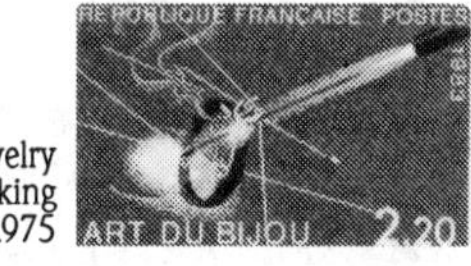

Jewelry Making
A975

1983, Sept. 10 Photo. *Perf. 13*
1900 A975 2.20fr multicolored 70 24

30th Anniv. of Customs Cooperation Council
A976

1983, Sept. 22 Engr. *Perf. 13x12½*
1901 A976 2.30fr multicolored 70 24

Michaux's Bicycle
A977

1983, Oct. 1 Engr. *Perf. 13*
1902 A977 1.60fr multicolored 60 15

Natl. Weather Forecasting — A978

1983, Oct. 22 Engr. *Perf. 12½x13*
1903 A978 1.50fr multicolored 60 15

Berthie Albrecht (1893-1943)
A979

1983, Nov. 5
1904 A979 1.60fr dk brown & olive 60 15
1905 A979 1.60fr Rene Levy (1906-1943) 60 15

Resistance heroines.

A980 A981

1983, Dec. 16
1906 A980 2fr dk gray & red 60 15

Pierre Mendes France (1907-1982), Premier.

1984, Mar. 22 *Perf. 13*
1907 A981 3.60fr Union leader Waldeck-Rousseau 1.25 30

Trade Union centenary.

Homage to the Cinema, by Cesar
A982

1984, Feb. 4 Engr. *Perf. 12½x13*
1908 A982 4fr multicolored 2.00 60

Four Corners of the Sky, by Jean Messagier — A983

1984, Mar. 31 Photo. *Perf. 13x12½*
1909 A983 4fr multicolored 1.75 60

Dining Room Corner, at Cannet, by Pierre Bonnard — A984

Photogravure and Engraved

1984, Apr. 14 *Perf. 12½x12*
1910 A984 4fr multicolored 1.75 60

Pythia, by Andre Masson
A985

Painter at the Feet of His Model, by Helion — A986

1984 Photo. *Perf. 12x13*
1911 A985 5fr multicolored 1.75 35
1912 A986 5fr multicolored 1.75 35

Issue dates: #1911, Oct. 13; #1912, Dec. 1.

Guadeloupe A987

1984, Feb. 25 *Perf. 13*
1913 A987 2.30fr Map, West Indian dancers 70 15

Vauban Citadel, Belle Ile-en-Mer A988

Cordouan Lighthouse — A989

La Grande Chartreuse Monastery, 900th Anniv. A990

Palais Ideal, Hauterives-Drome — A991

Montsegur Chateau A992

1984 Engr. *Perf. 13*
1914 A988 2.50fr multicolored 85 18
1915 A989 3.50fr multicolored 1.10 18

Issue dates: #1914, May 26; #1915, June 23.

1984
1916 A990 1.70fr multicolored 52 15
1917 A991 2.10fr multicolored 85 15
1917A A992 3.70fr multicolored 1.25 15
Nos. 1914-1917A (5) 4.57 81

Issue dates: 1.70fr, July 7; 2.10fr, June 30; 3.70fr, Sept. 15.

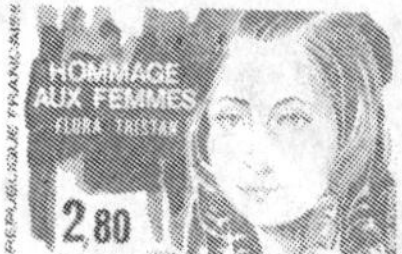
Flora Tristan (1803-44), Feminist A992a

1984, Mar. 8
1918 A992a 2.80fr multicolored 85 28

Playing Card Suits — A993

1984, Apr. 11 Engr.
1919 A993 1.14fr Hearts 40 20
1920 A993 1.47fr Spades 48 25
1921 A993 2.38fr Diamonds 70 48
1922 A993 3.95fr Clubs 1.40 80

Nos. 1919-1922 known only precanceled. See second note after No. 132.

450th Anniv. of Cartier's Landing in Quebec A994

1984, Apr. 20 Photo. & Engr.
1923 A994 2fr multicolored 75 15

See Canada No. 1011.

Philex '84, Dunkirk A995

1984, Apr. 21 *Perf. 13x12½*
1924 A995 1.60fr multicolored 50 18

Europa (1959-84) A996

1984, Apr. 28 Engr. *Perf. 13*
1925 A996 2fr red brown 60 15
1926 A996 2.80fr blue 90 30

2nd European Parliament Election A997

1984, Mar. 24 Photo. *Perf. 13*
1927 A997 2fr multicolored 65 15

Foreign Legion A998

1984, Apr. 30 Engr. *Perf. 13x12½*
1928 A998 3.10fr multicolored 95 30

40th Anniv. of Liberation A999

Photogravure and Engraved
1984, May 8 *Perf. 12½x13*
1929 A999 2fr Resistance 75 24
1930 A999 3fr Landing 1.10 35
a. Pair, #1929-1930 + label 1.90

Olympic Events — A1000

Illustration reduced.

1984, June 1 *Perf. 13*
1931 A1000 4fr multicolored 1.25 55

Intl. Olympic Committee, 90th anniv. and 1984 Summer Olympics.

Engraving — A1001

1984, June 8 Engr.
1932 A1001 2fr multicolored 60 15

Bordeaux A1002

1984, June 9 *Perf. 13x12½*
1933 A1002 2fr red 60 15

French Philatelic Societies Congress, Bordeaux.

Natl. Telecommunications College, 40th Anniv. — A1003

1984, June 16 Photo. *Perf. 13*
1934 A1003 3fr Satellite, phone, keyboard 90 24

25th Intl. Geography Congress, Paris — A1004

Illustration reduced.

1984, Aug. 25 Engr. *Perf. 13x12½*
1935 A1004 3fr Alps 90 24

Telecom I Satellite A1005

1984, Sept. 1 Photo. *Perf. 13*
1936 A1005 3.20fr multicolored 1.00 24

High-speed Train Mail Transport A1006

1984, Sept. 8
1937 A1006 2.10fr Electric train, Paris-Lyon 1.00 18

Local Birds A1007

Marx Dormoy (1888-1941) A1008

Photogravure and Engraved
1984, Sept. 22 *Perf. 12½x12*
1938 A1007 1fr Gypaetus barbatus 32 18
1939 A1007 2fr Circaetus gallicus 80 18
1940 A1007 3fr Accipiter nisus 90 24
1941 A1007 5fr Peregrine falcon 1.40 35

1984, Sept. 22 Engr. *Perf. 13*
1942 A1008 2.40fr multicolored 75 15

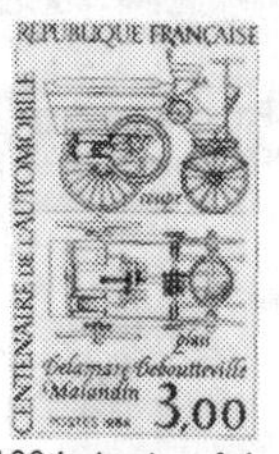
100th Anniv. of the Automobile A1009

Pres. Vincent Auriol (1884-1966) A1010

1984, Oct. 6 Engr. *Perf. 12½x13*
1943 A1009 3fr Automobile plans 1.10 15

1984, Nov. 3
1944 A1010 2.10fr multicolored 65 15

9th 5-Year Plan — A1011

1984, Dec. 8 Photo. *Perf. 13*
1945 A1011 2.10fr dk blue & scar 65 15

French Language Promotion — A1012

1985, Jan. 15 Engr. *Perf. 12½x13*

1946 A1012	3fr multicolored		90	15

Tourism Issue

View of Vienne A1013

Cathedral at Montpelier A1014

St. Michel de Cuxa (Codalet) Abbey — A1015

Talmont Church, Saintonge Romane A1016

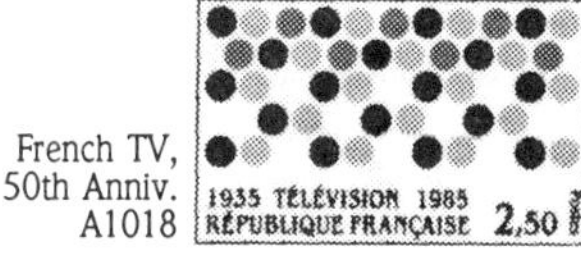

Solutre A1017

1985 *Perf. 13x12½*

1947 A1013	1.70fr	ol blk & dk grn	45	15
1948 A1014	2.10fr	sepia & orange	55	15
1949 A1015	2.20fr	multicolored	55	15
1950 A1016	3fr	multicolored	70	15
1951 A1017	3.90fr	multicolored	90	15
	Nos. 1947-1951 (5)		3.15	
	Set value			46

Issue dates: 1.70fr, Jan. 19; 2.10fr, Mar. 30; 2.20fr, July 6; 3fr, June 15; 3.90fr, Sept. 28.

French TV, 50th Anniv. A1018

1985, Jan. 26 Photo. *Perf. 13*

1952 A1018	2.50fr multicolored		75	15

Months of the Year — A1019

1985, Feb. 11 Engr.

1953 A1019	1.22fr	January	45	15
1954 A1019	1.57fr	February	50	15
1955 A1019	2.55fr	March	85	15
1956 A1019	4.23fr	April	1.50	15

1986, Feb. 10 Engr. *Perf. 13*

1957 A1019	1.28fr	May	42	15
1958 A1019	1.65fr	June	52	15
1959 A1019	2.67fr	July	90	15
1960 A1019	4.44fr	August	1.50	20

1987, Feb. 16 Engr.

1961 A1019	1.31fr	September	50	15
1962 A1019	1.69fr	October	65	15
1963 A1019	2.74fr	November	1.00	18
1964 A1019	4.56fr	December	1.75	32
	Nos. 1953-1964 (12)		10.54	
	Set value			1.50

Nos. 1953-1964 are known only precanceled. See second note after No. 132.

St. Valentine, by Raymond Peynet A1020

1985, Feb. 14 Photo. *Perf. 13x12½*

1965 A1020	2.10fr multicolored		75	15

Pauline Kergomard (1838-1925) A1021

1985, Mar. 8 Engr. *Perf. 13x12½*

1966 A1021	1.70fr int bl & cop red		50	15

Stained Glass Window, Strasbourg Cathedral A1022

Still-life with Candle, Nicolas de Stael — A1023

1985 Engraved *Perf. 12x13*

1967 A1022	5fr multicolored		3.75	22

Photo.

Perf. 13x12

1968 A1023	5fr multicolored		2.25	22

Issue dates: #1967, Apr. 13; #1968, June 1.

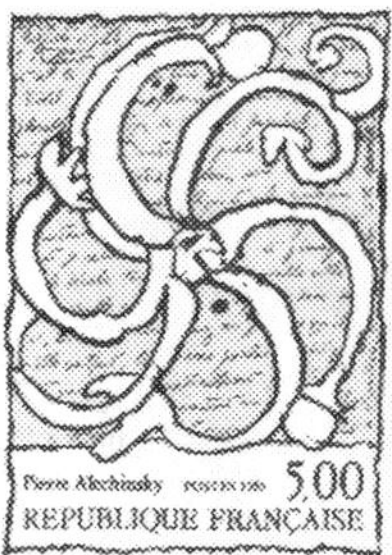

Untitled Abstract by Jean Dubuffet — A1024

Octopus Overlaid on Manuscript, by Pierre Alechinsky A1025

Photogravure; Engraved (#1970)

1985 *Perf. 13x12½*

1969 A1024	5fr multicolored		2.50	20
1970 A1025	5fr multicolored		2.50	20

Issue dates: #1969, Sept. 14; #1970, Oct. 12.

The Dog, Abstract by Alberto Giacometti (1901-1966) — A1026

1985, Dec. 7 Engr. *Perf. 13x12½*

1971 A1026	5fr grnsh blk & lt lem		2.50	25

Housing in Givors A1027

Contemporary architecture by Jean Renaude.

1985, Apr. 20 Engr. *Perf. 13*

1972 A1027	2.40fr blk, yel org & ol grn		80	15

Landevennec Abbey, 1500th Anniv. A1028

1985, Apr. 20 Engr. *Perf. 13x12½*

1973 A1028	1.70fr green & brn vio		60	15

A1029

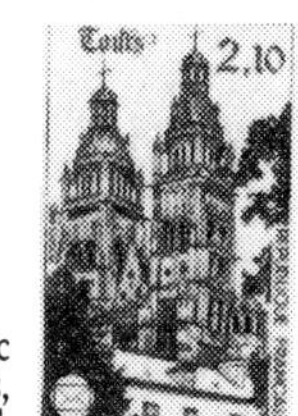

A1030

Europa: 2.10fr, Adam de la Halle (1240-1285), composer. 3fr, Darius Milhaud (1892-1974), composer.

1985, Apr. 27 *Perf. 12½x13*

1974 A1029	2.10fr dr bl, blk, & brt bl		75	15
1975 A1029	3fr dk bl, brt bl & blk		1.00	15

1985, May 8 *Perf. 13x12½*

1976 A1030	2fr Return of peace		75	15
1977 A1030	3fr Return of liberty		1.00	15
a.	Pair, #1976-1977 + label		1.75	

Liberation of France from German occupation forces, 40th anniv.

Natl. Philatelic Congress, Tours — A1031

1985, May 25 *Perf. 12½x13*

1978 A1031	2.10fr Tours Cathedral		65	15

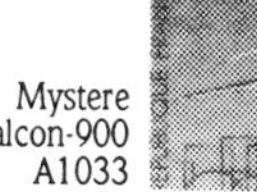

Rabies Vaccine Cent. A1032

1985, June 1 *Perf. 13x12½*

1979 A1032	1.50fr Pasteur inoculating patient		50	15

Mystere Falcon-900 A1033

1985, June 1 *Perf. 13*

1980 A1033	10fr blue		4.00	45

Lake Geneva Life-Saving Society Cent. A1034

1985, June 15

1981 A1034	2.50fr blk, red & brt ultra		75	15

UN, 40th Anniv. — A1035

Huguenot Cross — A1036

1985, June 26 *Perf. 13x12½*

1982 A1035	3fr multicolored		90	15

1985, Aug. 31 Engr. *Perf. 12½x13*

1983 A1036	2.50fr dp vio, dk red brn & dk red		75	15

King Louis XIV revoked the Edict of Nantes on Oct. 18, 1685, dispossessing French Protestants of religious and civil liberty.

A1037

A1038

Trees, leaves and fruit of the beech, elm, oak and spruce varieties.

1985, Sept. 21 Engr. *Perf. 12½*

1984 A1037 1fr shown 35 15
1985 A1037 2fr Ulmus montana 70 15
1986 A1037 3fr Quercus pedunculata 1.10 15
1987 A1037 5fr Picea abies 1.75 25
Set value 55

1985, Nov. 2 Engr. *Perf. 12½x13*

Design: La France Mourning the Dead, Eternal Flame.

1988 A1038 1.80fr brn, org & lake 70 15

Memorial Day.

A1039

A1040

1985, Nov. 9 Engr.

1989 A1039 3.20fr black & blue 1.00 16

Charles Dullin, 1885-1949, impresario, theater.

1985, Nov. 16 Engr. *Perf. 13x12½*

1990 A1040 2.20fr red & black 75 15

National information system.

Thai Ambassadors at the Court of King Louis XIV, Painting — A1041

1986, Jan. 25 Engr. *Perf. 13*

1991 A1041 3.20fr rose lake & blk 1.00 18

Normalization of diplomatic relations with Thailand, 300th anniv.

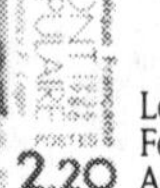

Leisure, by Fernand Leger A1042

1986, Feb. 1 Photo. *Perf. 13*

1992 A1042 2.20fr multicolored 75 15

1936 Popular Front, 50th anniv.

Venice Carnival, Paris — A1043

1986, Feb. 12 *Perf. 12½x13*

1993 A1043 2.20fr multicolored 80 15

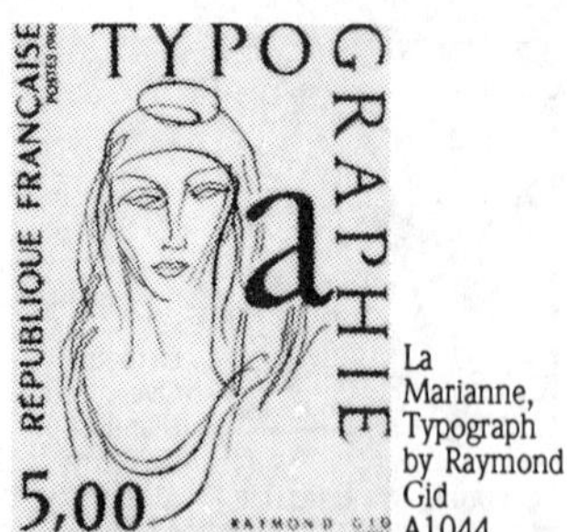

La Marianne, Typograph by Raymond Gid A1044

Photogravure & Engraved

1986, Mar. 3 *Perf. 12½x13½*

1994 A1044 5fr black & dk red 1.75 30

Tourism Issue

Filitosa, South Corsica A1045

Loches Chateau A1046

Norman Manor, St. Germain de Livet A1047

Notre-Dame-en-Vaux Monastery, Marne — A1048

Market Square, Bastide de Monpazier, Dordogne — A1049

Illustration A1049 reduced.

1986 Engr. *Perf. 13*

1995 A1045 1.80fr multicolored 55 15
1996 A1046 2fr int blue & blk 65 15
1997 A1047 2.20fr grnsh bl, brn & grn 70 15
1998 A1048 2.50fr henna brn & sepia 80 15

Perf. 13x12½

1999 A1049 3.90fr black & yel org 1.25 22
Nos. 1995-1999 (5) 3.95 82

Issue dates: 2.20fr, Mar. 3. 2fr, June 14; 2.50fr, June 9. 1.80fr, 3.90fr, July 5.

Louise Michel (1830-1905), Anarchist A1050

1986, Mar. 10 Engr.

2000 A1050 1.80fr dk red & gray blk 70 15

City of Science and Industry, La Villette — A1051

1986, Mar. 17

2001 A1051 3.90fr multicolored 1.25 18

Center for Modern Asia-Africa Studies A1052

1986, Apr. 12 Photo. *Perf. 13*

2002 A1052 3.20fr Map 1.00 18

Skibet, Abstract by Maurice Esteve — A1053

Virginia, Abstract by Alberto Magnelli — A1054

Abstract, by Pierre Soulages — A1055

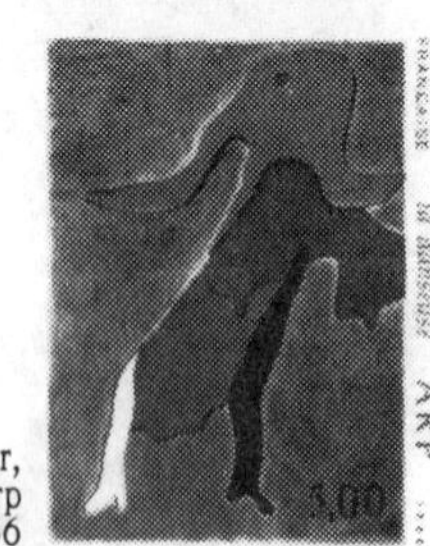

The Dancer, by Jean Arp A1056

Isabelle d'Este, by Leonardo da Vinci A1057

Perf. 12½x13, 13x12½ (#2005, 2006)

1986 Photo., Engr. (#2005, 2007)

2003 A1053 5fr multicolored 1.90 22
2004 A1054 5fr multicolored 1.90 28
2005 A1055 5fr brt vio, blk & brn gray 1.90 32
2006 A1056 5fr multicolored 1.90 30
2007 A1057 5fr blk, red brn & grnsh yel 1.90 32
Nos. 2003-2007 (5) 9.50 1.44

Issue dates: #2003, Apr. 14. #2004, June 25. #2005, Dec. 22. #2006, 2007, Nov. 10.

Victor Basch (1863-1944), IPY Emblem — A1058

1986, Apr. 28 Engr. *Perf. 13*

2008 A1058 2.50fr black & yel grn 75 15

International Peace Year.

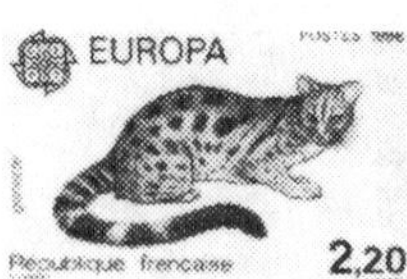

Europa 1986 A1059

1986, Apr. 28 *Perf. 13x12½*

2009 A1059 2.20fr Civet cat 70 15
2010 A1059 3.20fr Bat 1.00 15

St. Jean-Marie Vianney, Curé of Ars — A1060

1986, May 3 Engr. *Perf. 13x12½*

2011 A1060 1.80fr sepia, brn org & brn 55 15

Philatelic Societies Federation Congress, Nancy — A1061

1986, May 17 *Perf. 13*

2012 A1061 2.20fr Exposition Center 70 15

15-Cent Minimum Value

The minimum value for a single stamp is 15 cents. This value reflects the costs of handling inexpensive stamps.

Mens World Volleyball Championship A1062

Liberté 1886-1986

Statue of Liberty, Cent. A1063

1986, May 24 Engr. *Perf. 13*
2013 A1062 2.20fr dk vio, brn vio & scar 70 15

1986, July 4 *Perf. 13*
2014 A1063 2.20fr scar & dk blue 1.00 15

See US No. 2224.

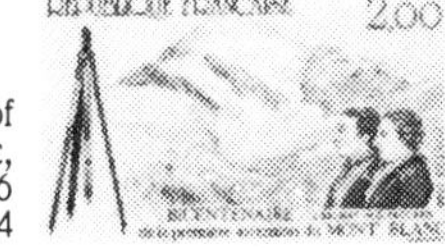

1st Ascent of Mt. Blanc, 1786 A1064

1986, Aug. 8 Engr. *Perf. 13x12½*
2015 A1064 2fr J. Balmat, M.G. Paccard 70 15

Pierre-Louis Moreau de Maupertuis (1698-1759), La Condamine and Sextant — A1065

1986, Sept. 5
2016 A1065 3fr lt bl, int bl & brt ultra 1.00 18

Lapland Expedition, 250th anniv., proved Earth's poles are flattened.
See Finland No. 741.

Marcassite — A1066

1986, Sept. 13 *Perf. 12½*

2017 A1066	2fr	shown	60	15
2018 A1066	3fr	Quartz	88	18
2019 A1066	4fr	Calcite	1.20	24
2020 A1066	5fr	Fluorite	1.50	30

Souvenir Sheet

Natl. Film Industry, 50th Anniv. — A1067

Personalities and film scenes: a, Louis Feuillade, The Vampires. b, Max Linder. c, Sacha Guitry, Romance of the Trickster. d, Jean Renoir, The Grand Illusion. e, Marcel Pagnol, The Baker's Woman. f, Jean Epstein, The Three-Sided Mirror. g, Rene Clair, Women of the Night. h, Jean Gremillon, Talk of Love. i, Jacques Becker, Helmet of Gold. j, Francois Truffaut, The Young Savage.

1986, Sept. 20 Photo. *Perf. 13x12½*
2021 Sheet of 10 8.00 8.00
a.-j. A1067 2.20fr any single 80 80

Scene from Le Grand Meaulnes, by Henry Alain-Fournier (b. 1886), Novelist — A1068

Professional Education, Cent. — A1069

1986, Oct. 4 Engr. *Perf. 12½x13*
2022 A1068 2.20fr black & dk red 75 15

1986, Oct. 4
2023 A1069 1.90fr brt vio & dp lil rose 65 15

World Energy Conf., Cannes — A1070

Mulhouse Technical Museum — A1071

1986, Oct. 5 Photo. *Perf. 13*
2024 A1070 3.40fr multicolored 1.10 22

1986, Dec. 1 Engr.
2025 A1071 2.20fr int blue, dk red & blk 90 15

Museum at Orsay, Opening — A1072

1986, Dec. 10 Photo.
2026 A1072 3.70fr bluish blk & pck bl 1.25 24

Fulgence Bienvenue (1852-1934), and the Metro A1073

1987, Jan. 17 Engr. *Perf. 13*
2027 A1073 2.50fr vio brn, brn & dk grn 85 16

A1074

A1075

1987, Jan. 24
2028 A1074 1.90fr green & grnsh blk 65 15

Raoul Follereau (1903-1977), care for lepers.

1987, Mar. 7 Engr. *Perf. 12½x13*
2029 A1075 1.90fr black & red 65 15

Cutlery industry, Thiers.

Tourist Issue

Redon, Ille et Vilaine A1076

Azay-le-Rideau Chateau A1077

Meuse District — A1078

De Gaulle's Home, Etretat A1079

Les Baux-de-Provence — A1080

Illustration A1078 reduced.

1987 Engr. *Perf. 13*

2030 A1076	2.20fr	dp rose lil, blk & brn ol	1.10	20
2031 A1077	2.50fr	Prus blue & olive grn	1.25	18
Perf. 12½				
2032 A1078	3.70fr	multicolored	1.75	25

Issue dates: 2.20fr, Mar. 7. 2.50fr, May 9. 3.70fr, May 30.

1987 Photo. *Perf. 13*

2033 A1079	2.20fr	multicolored	95	15
Engr.				
2034 A1080	3fr	dk ol bis & dp vio	1.40	18
		Nos. 2030-2034 (5)	6.45	96

Issue dates: 2.20fr, June 12. 3fr, June 27.

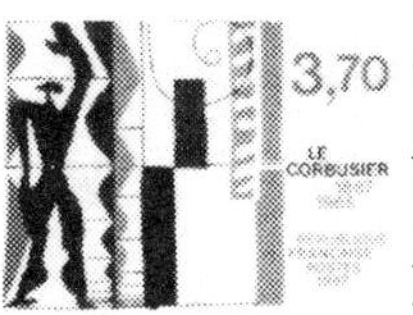

Charles Edouard Jenneret (Le Corbusier) (1887-1965), Architect A1081

1987, Apr. 11 Photo. *Perf. 13x12½*
2035 A1081 3.70fr Abstract 1.10 25

Europa 1987 A1082

Modern architecture: 2.20fr, Metal factory at Boulogne-Billancourt, by architect Claude Vasconi. 3.40fr, Rue Mallet-Stevens housing, by Robert Mallet-Stevens.

1987, Apr. 25 Engr. *Perf. 13x12½*
2036 A1082 2.20fr dk blue & grn 1.50 20
2037 A1082 3.40fr brown & dk grn 2.25 30

Abstract Painting, by Bram van Velde — A1083

Woman under Parasol, by Eugene Boudin (1824-1898) — A1084

Precambrien, by Camille Bryen A1085

World, Bronze Sculpture by Antoine Pevsner — A1086

Perf. 12½x13, 13x12½ (Nos. 2039, 2041)
Photo., Engr. (Nos. 2039, 2041)

1987

2038 A1083	5fr	multicolored	1.75	30
2039 A1084	5fr	multicolored	1.75	30
2040 A1085	5fr	multicolored	1.75	30
2041 A1086	5fr	bister & blk	1.75	24

Issue dates: #2038, Apr. 25. #2039, May 23. #2040, Sept. 12. #2041, Nov. 14.

Gaspard de Montagnes, from a Manuscript Illustration — A1087

1987, May 9 Engr. *Perf. 13*
2042 A1087 1.90fr dp green & sepia 55 15

Henri Pourrat (1887-1959), novelist.

Natl. Philatelic Societies Congress, Lens A1088

1987, June 6 *Perf. 13x13½*
2043 A1088 2.20fr chocolate & red 75 15

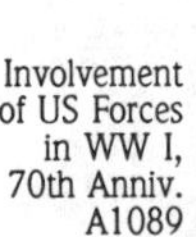

Involvement of US Forces in WW I, 70th Anniv. A1089

Design: Stars and Stripes, troops, Gen. John J. Pershing (1860-1948), American army commander.

1987, June 13 *Perf. 13*
2044 A1089 3.40fr olive grn, saph & ver 1.10 22

A1090 A1091

1987, June 17 Photo.
2045 A1090 2fr multicolored 65 15

6th Intl. Cable Car Transport Congress, Grenoble.

1987, June 20 Litho.
2046 A1091 1.90fr pale chalky blue & blk 65 15

Accession of Hugh Capet (c.938-996), 1st king of France, millenary.

A1092 A1093

1987, June 20 Engr. *Perf. 12½x13*
2047 A1092 2.20fr multicolored 75 15

La Fleche Natl. Military School.

1987, June 27 Photo. *Perf. 13*
2048 A1093 1.90fr multicolored 65 15

World Assembly of Expatriate Algerians, Nice.

World Wrestling Championships — A1094

1987, Aug. 21 Engr.
2049 A1094 3fr brt pur, vio gray & brt olive grn 95 18

Mushrooms A1095

William the Conqueror (c. 1027-1087) A1096

1987, Sept. 5 *Perf. 12½*
2050 A1095 2fr Gyroporus cyanescens 60 15
2051 A1095 3fr Gomphus clavatus 90 22
2052 A1095 4fr Morchella conica 1.25 28
2053 A1095 5fr Russula virescens 1.50 38

1987, Sept. 5 *Perf. 13*
2054 A1096 2fr Bayeux Tapestry detail 75 15

Montbenoit Le Saugeais A1097

Design: Abbey of Medieval Knights, cloisters, winter scene.

1987, Sept. 19
2055 A1097 2.50fr sapphire, blk & scar 85 16

Pasteur Institute, Cent. — A1098

1987, Oct. 3
2056 A1098 2.20fr dp blue & dk red 85 16

Blaise Cendrars (1887-1961), Poet and Novelist A1099

Treaty of Andelot, 1400th Anniv. A1100

Pen and ink portrait by Modigliani.

1987, Nov. 6 *Perf. 12½*
2057 A1099 2fr brt grn, buff & blk 75 15

1987, Nov. 28 *Perf. 12½x13*
2058 A1100 3.70fr multicolored 1.25 20

Gen. Leclerc (1902-1947), Marshal of France A1101

1987, Nov. 28 *Perf. 13x12½*
2059 A1101 2.20fr multicolored 85 15

Liberty Type of 1982

1987-90 *Perf. 13*
2077 A915 3.70fr brt lilac rose 1.10 15
2078 A915 (2.10fr) green ('90) 70 15
2079 A915 (2.30fr) red ('90) 75 15
Set value 27

Coil Stamp
Engr.
Perf. 13 Horiz.
2080 A915 2fr emerald green 70 15

Issue dates: 2fr, Aug. 1, 3.70fr, Nov. 16. Nos. 2078-2079, Jan. 2.
Nos. 2078-2079 are inscribed "C."

Franco-German Cooperation Treaty, 25th Anniv. — A1102

1988, Jan. 15 *Perf. 13*
2086 A1102 2.20fr Adenauer, De Gaulle 1.00 16

See Fed. Rep. of Germany No. 1546.

Marcel Dassault (1892-1986), Aircraft Designer — A1103

1988, Jan. 23 Photo.
2087 A1103 3.60fr brt ultra, gray blk & dk red 1.50 28

Communications A1104

Great Synagogue, Rue Victoire, Paris A1105

Angouleme Festival prize-winning cartoons.

1988, Jan. 29 Photo. *Perf. 13½x13*
2088 A1104 2.20fr Pellos 80 16
2089 A1104 2.20fr Reiser 80 16
2090 A1104 2.20fr Marijac 80 16
2091 A1104 2.20fr Fred 80 16
2092 A1104 2.20fr Moebius 80 16
2093 A1104 2.20fr Gillon 80 16
2094 A1104 2.20fr Bretecher 80 16
2095 A1104 2.20fr Forest 80 16
2096 A1104 2.20fr Mezieres 80 16
2097 A1104 2.20fr Tardi 80 16
2098 A1104 2.20fr Lob 80 16
2099 A1104 2.20fr Bilal 80 16
a. Bklt. pane of 12, #2088-2099 9.75
Nos. 2088-2099 (12) 9.60 1.92

Issued in booklets only.

1988, Feb. 7 Litho. *Perf. 13*
2100 A1105 2fr black & gold 75 15

The Four Elements — A1106

1988, Feb. 1 Engr. *Perf. 13*
2101 A1106 1.36fr Air 52 15
2102 A1106 1.75fr Water 65 15
2103 A1106 2.83fr Fire 1.00 15
2104 A1106 4.75fr Earth 1.75 22
Set value 48

Nos. 2101-2104 known only precanceled. See second note after No. 132.

PHILEXFRANCE '89 — A1107

1988, Mar. 4
2105 A1107 2.20fr #1885, emblem 80 16

Postal Training College, Cent. A1108

1988, Mar. 29
2106 A1108 3.60fr multicolored 1.40 25

Philex-Jeunes '88, Youth Stamp Show A1109

1988, Apr. 8 *Perf. 13x12½*
2107 A1109 2fr multicolored 75 15

Blood Donation — A1110

1988, Apr. 9 Photo. *Perf. 13½x13*
2108 A1110 2.50fr multicolored 90 18

Europa 1988 A1111

Communication and transportation.

1988, Apr. 30 Engr. *Perf. 13*
2109 A1111 2.20fr Cables, satellites 80 16
2110 A1111 3.60fr Rail cars 1.40 26

Jean Monnet (1888-1979), Economist — A1112

1988, May 10 *Perf. 12½x13*
2111 A1112 2.20fr black & brn ol 80 16

Philatelic Congress, Valence A1113

1988, May 21 *Perf. 13x12½*
2112 A1113 2.20fr multicolored 80 16

Intl. Medical Assistance A1114

1988, May 28 **Photo.** *Perf. 13*
2113 A1114 3.60fr multicolored 1.40 26

Aid to the Handicapped A1115

1988, May 28
2114 A1115 3.70fr multicolored 1.40 28

No. 1884 Surcharged in European Currency Units **ECU 0,31..**

1988, Apr. 16 **Engr.**
2115 A915 2.20fr red 70 15

Tourist Issue

Hermes Dicephalus (Roman Empire), Frejus — A1116

Ship Museum, Douarnenez A1117

Chateau Sedieres, Correze A1118

Cirque de Gavarnie A1119

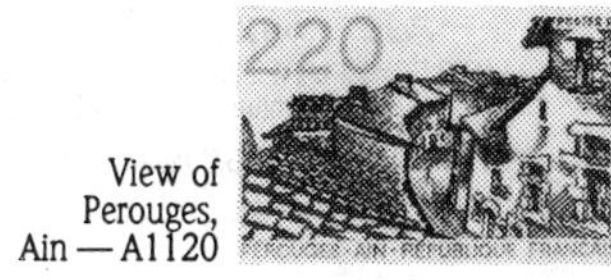

View of Perouges, Ain — A1120

1988, June 12 **Engr.** *Perf. 13x12½*
2116 A1116 3.70fr multicolored 1.40 28

1988 *Perf. 13, 12½x13 (#2118)*
2117 A1117 2fr multicolored 75 15
2118 A1118 2.20fr multicolored 80 15
2119 A1119 3fr multicolored 1.00 22

Issued: 2.20fr, July 2; 2fr, July 4; 3fr, July 23.

1988, Sept. 10 *Perf. 13x12½*
2120 A1120 2.20fr multicolored 75 15
Nos. 2116-2120 (5) 4.70 95

French Revolution, Bicent. — A1121

Designs: 3fr, Assembly of the Three Estates, Vizille. 4fr, Day of the Tiles (Barricades), Grenoble.

1988, June 18 **Engr.**
2121 A1121 3fr multicolored 1.10 22
2122 A1121 4fr multicolored 1.50 30

PHILEXFRANCE '89. Nos. 2121-2122 printed se-tenant with inscribed center label.

Buffon's Natural History — A1122

Alpine Troops, Cent. — A1123

1988, June 18 *Perf. 12½*
2123 A1122 2fr Otters 75 15
2124 A1122 3fr Stag 1.10 22
2125 A1122 4fr Fox 1.50 30
2126 A1122 5fr Badger 1.90 38

1988, June 25 *Perf. 13*
2127 A1123 2.50fr multicolored 95 18

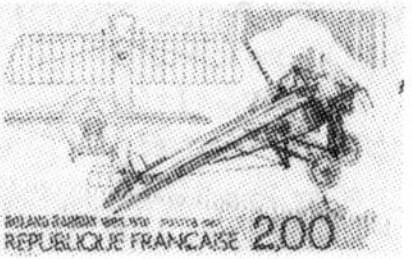

Roland Garros (1888-1918), 1st Pilot to Fly Across the Mediterranean, Sept. 23, 1913 A1124

1988, July 2 **Engr.** *Perf. 13x12½*
2128 A1124 2fr brt grn bl & olive 75 15

Nov. 11, 1918 Armistice Ending World War I, 70th Anniv. A1125

1988, Sept. 10 **Engr.** *Perf. 13*
2129 A1125 2.20fr brt blue, gray & blk 75 15

Homage to Leon Degand, Sculpture by Robert Jacobsen A1126

1988, Sept. 24 *Perf. 12½x13*
2130 A1126 5fr blk & dp claret 1.75 32

French-Danish cultural exchange program, 10th anniv. See Denmark No. 860.

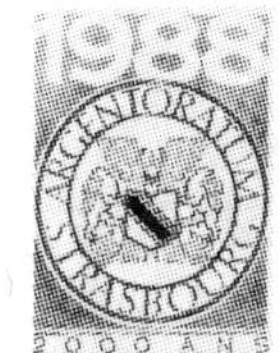

Strasbourg, 2000th Anniv. — A1127

1988, Sept. 24 *Perf. 13*
2131 A1127 2.20fr Municipal arms 80 15

St. Mihiel Sepulcher, by Ligier Richier (c. 1500-1567), Sculptor — A1128

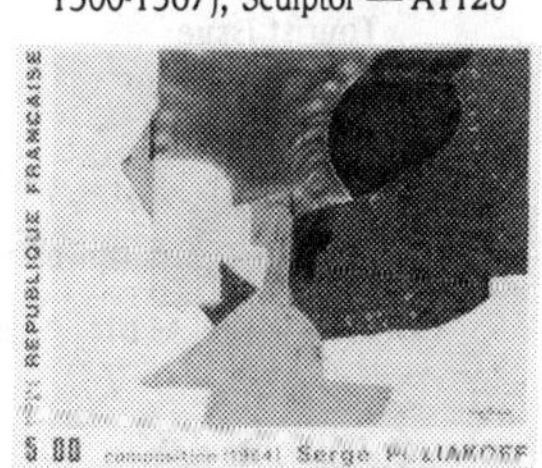

Composition, 1954, by Serge Poliakoff (1906-1969) — A1129

La Pieta de Villeneuve-les-Avignon, by Enguerrand Quarton (1444-1466) — A1130

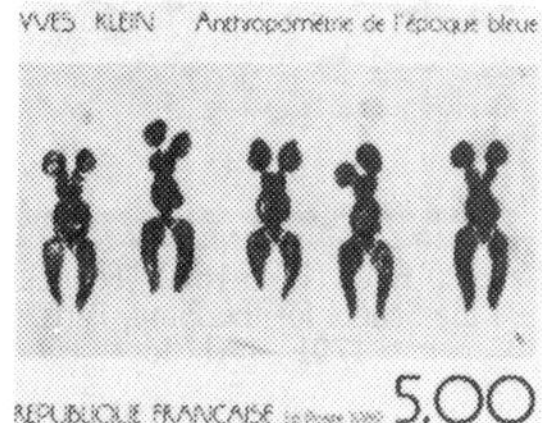

Anthropometry of the Blue Period, by Yves Klein — A1131

1988-89 **Engr.** *Perf. 13x12½*
2132 A1128 5fr black brown 1.65 32

Photo.

2133 A1129 5fr multicolored 1.65 32
2134 A1130 5fr multicolored 1.90 35
2135 A1131 5fr multi ('89) 1.90 35

Issue dates: #2132, Oct. 15. #2133, Oct. 22. #2134, Dec. 10. #2135, Jan. 21.

Thermal Springs A1132

1988, Nov. 21 **Engr.** *Perf. 13x12½*
2136 A1132 2.20fr multicolored 75 15

Metamecanique, by Jean Tinguely — A1133

1988, Nov. 26 **Photo.**
2137 A1133 5fr multicolored 1.75 35

See Switzerland No. 828.

UN Declaration of Human Rights, 40th Anniv. A1134

1988, Dec. 12 **Litho.** *Perf. 13*
2138 A1134 2.20fr dk bl & grnsh bl 1.00 15

French Revolution, Bicent. — A1135

1989, Jan. 1 Photo. *Perf. 13x12½*
2139 A1135 2.20fr red & vio blue 75 15

Valentin Hauy (1745-1822), Founder of the School for the Blind, Paris, 1791 — A1136

1989, Jan. 28 Photo. & Embossed
2140 A1136 2.20fr multicolored 75 15

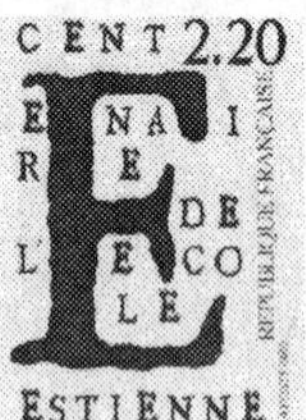

Estienne School, Cent. — A1137

1989, Feb. 4 Engr. *Perf. 12½*
2141 A1137 2.20fr gray, black & red 75 15

European Parliament Elections A1138

1989, Mar. 4 Litho. *Perf. 13*
2142 A1138 2.20fr multicolored 75 15

A1139

1989 Engr. *Perf. 12½x13*

2143	A1139 2.20fr Liberty	75	15
2144	A1139 2.20fr Equality	75	15
2145	A1139 2.20fr Fraternity	75	15
a.	Strip of 3, #2143-2145 + label	2.25	

Bicent. of the French revolution and the Declaration of Rights of Man and the Citizen. No. 2145a contains inscribed label picturing PHILEXFRANCE '89 emblem.

Issue dates: #2143, Mar. 18. #2144, Apr. 22. #2145, May 27. #2145a, July 14.

French-Soviet Joint Space Flight A1140

1989, Mar. 4 Litho. *Perf. 13*
2146 A1140 3.60fr multicolored 1.25 24

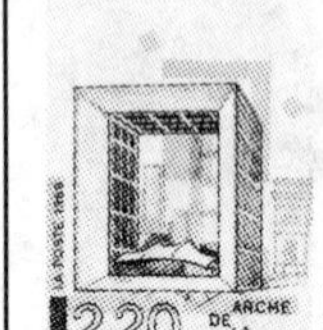

Historic Sights, Paris — A1141

Designs: No. 2147, Arche de la Defense. No. 2148, Eiffel Tower. No. 2149, Grand Louvre. No. 2150, Notre Dame Cathedral. No. 2151, Bastille Monument and Opera de la Bastille. Printed se-tenant in a continuous design.

1989, Apr. 21 Engr. *Perf. 13x12½*

2147 A1141 2.20fr multicolored	70	15
2148 A1141 2.20fr multicolored	70	15
2149 A1141 2.20fr multicolored	70	15
2150 A1141 2.20fr multicolored	70	15
2151 A1141 2.20fr multicolored	70	15
a. Strip of 5, #2147-2151	3.50	
Nos. 2147-2151 (5)	3.50	75

Europa 1989 A1142

Children's games.

1989, Apr. 29 *Perf. 13*
2152 A1142 2.20fr Hopscotch 75 15
2153 A1142 3.60fr Catch (ball) 1.10 22

ITU Plenipotentiaries Conference, Nice — A1143

1989, May 23 Litho.
2154 A1143 3.70fr dk bl, dl org & red 1.25 24

Tourist Issue

Fontainebleau Forest A1144

Vaux le Vicomte — A1145

La Brenne — A1146

Illustrations A1145-A1146 reduced.

1989, May 20 Engr. *Perf. 13*
2155 A1144 2.20fr multicolored 75 15

Perf. 13x12½
2156 A1145 3.70fr ol bis & blk 1.25 24
2157 A1146 4fr violet blue 1.25 24

Issue dates: 2.20fr, May 20. 3.70fr, July 14. 4fr, Aug. 25.

World Cycling Championships, Chambery — A1147

1989, June 3 Litho. *Perf. 13*
2158 A1147 2.20fr multi 75 15

Jehan de Malestroit, Dept. of Morbihan — A1148

1989, June 10 Engr. *Perf. 12½x13*
2159 A1148 3.70fr multicolored 1.25 24

Preliminary Sketch (Detail) for *Oath of the Tennis Court*, by David — A1149

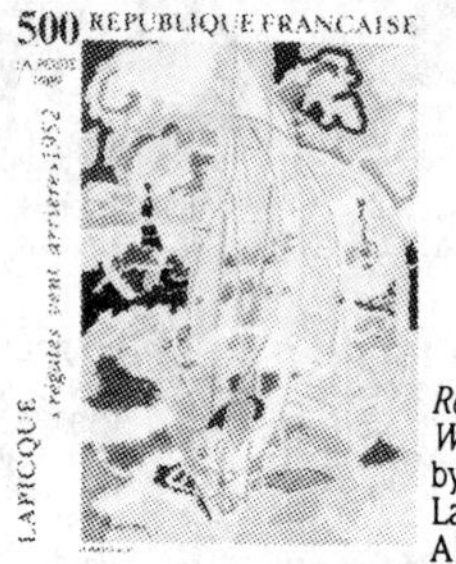

Regatta with Wind Astern, by Charles Lapicque A1150

1989, June 19 Photo. *Perf. 13x12½*
2160 A1149 5fr multicolored 1.65 32

Perf. 12½
2161 A1150 5fr multicolored 1.50 30

No. 2160 for French revolution bicent.
Issued: No. 2160, June 19. No. 2161, Sept. 23.

The lack of a value for a listed item does not necessarily indicate rarity.

Souvenir Sheet

Revolution Bicentennial — A1151

Revolutionaries: a, Madame Roland (1754-1793). b, Camille Desmoulins (1760-1794). c, Condorcet (1743-1794). d, Kellermann (1735-1820).

1989, June 26 Engr. *Perf. 13*
2162 A1151 Sheet of 4 3.00 3.00
a.-d. 2.20fr any single 75 75

15th Summit of the Arch Meeting of Leaders from Industrial Nations, July 14-16 A1152

1989, July 14 Photo.
2163 A1152 2.20fr multicolored 75 15

Declaration of the Rights of Man and the Citizen, Versailles, Aug. 26, 1789 — A1153

Details of an anonymous 18th-19th cent. painting in Carnavalet Museum: No. 2168a, Preamble, Article I. No. 2168b, Articles VII-XI. No. 2168c, Articles II-VI. No. 2168d, Articles XII-XVII.

Perf. 13x11½
1989, Aug. 26 Litho. & Engr.

2164 A1153 2.50fr Preamble, Article I	75	15
2165 A1153 2.50fr Articles II-VI	75	15
2166 A1153 2.50fr Articles VII-XI	75	15
2167 A1153 2.50fr Articles XII-XVII	75	15
a. Strip of 4, #2164-2167 + label	3.00	60

Souvenir Sheet

Perf. 13x12½

2168 Sheet of 4 *22.50 22.50*
a.-d. A1153 5fr any single *5.50 5.50*

No. 2168 contains 4 52x41mm stamps. Sold for 50fr, including admission fee to PHILEXFRANCE '89. Value of No. 2168 is for examples on plain paper. Examples on fluorescent paper seem to have been distributed in North America, and may not have been distributed widely or made available in Europe. At this time the fluorescent paper examples are selling for considerably more.

Musical Instruments — A1154

1989 Litho. *Perf. 12x12½*

2169 A1154	1.39fr Harp		42	15
2170 A1154	1.79fr Piano		52	15
2171 A1154	2.90fr Trumpet		90	15
2172 A1154	4.84fr Violin		1.50	18
	Set value			39

Nos. 2169-2172 are known only precanceled. See second note after No. 132.

See Nos. 2233-2239, 2273-2283, 2368-2371.

TGV Atlantic A1155

1989, Sept. 23 Photo. *Perf. 13*

2173 A1155 2.50fr dk blue, sil & red 75 15

Clermont-Ferrand Tramway, Cent. — A1156

1989, Oct. 28 Engr.

2174 A1156 3.70fr blk & dk ol bis 1.10 22

Villers-Cotterets Ordinance, 450th Anniv. — A1157

1989, Oct. 28 Engr.

2175 A1157 2.20fr blk, dp cl & red 70 15

Baron Augustin-Louis Cauchy (1789-1857), Mathematician — A1158

1989, Nov. 10 *Perf. 13x12½*

2176 A1158 3.60fr red, blk & bl grn 1.10 22

Marshal Jean de Lattre de Tassigny (1889-1952) A1159

1989, Nov. 18 *Perf. 13*

2177 A1159 2.20fr blue, blk & red 70 15

Harki Soldiers of France A1160

1989, Dec. 9 Photo.

2178 A1160 2.20fr multicolored 70 15

Marianne — A1161

1990-92 Engr. *Perf. 13*

2179	A1161	10c brown black	15	15
a.		Bklt. pane, 4 #2179, 1 #2180	32	
2180	A1161	20c lt green	15	15
2181	A1161	50c brt violet	18	15
2182	A1161	1fr orange	36	15
2183	A1161	2fr apple grn	72	15
2184	A1161	2.10fr dark green	75	15
2185	A1161	2.20fr dark green	75	16
2186	A1161	2.20fr emerald	78	15
2187	A1161	2.30fr red	75	15
a.		Bklt. pane, 4 #2187, 1 #2180	5.00	
2188	A1161	2.50fr red	85	15
2189	A1161	3.20fr blue	1.10	15
2190	A1161	3.40fr blue	1.15	15
2191	A1161	3.80fr lilac rose	2.75	15
2192	A1161	4fr lilac rose	1.35	15
2193	A1161	4.20fr lilac rose	1.65	15
2194	A1161	5fr dull blue	1.80	15
2195	A1161	10fr violet	3.60	15
2196	A1161	(2.20fr) dark green	75	16
2197	A1161	(2.50fr) red	85	18
		Nos. 2179-2197 (19)	20.44	
		Set value		1.75

Coil Stamps

Perf. 13 Horiz.

2198	A1161	2.10fr dark green	75	15
2199	A1161	2.20fr dark green	88	15
2200	A1161	2.30fr red	82	15
2201	A1161	2.50fr red	1.00	15
		Set value		30

Die Cut

Self-Adhesive

2202	A1161	2.30fr red	80	15
a.		Booklet pane of 10	8.00	
2203	A1161	2.50fr red	85	15
a.		Booklet pane of 10	8.50	
b.		Booklet pane of 5	4.50	
2204	A1161	(2.50fr) red	85	15
a.		Booklet pane of 10	8.50	

Issue dates: No. 2187, Jan. 2. No. 2198, Jan. 1. 10c, 20c, 50c, 3.20fr, 3.80fr, Mar. 26. No. 2202, Jan. 29. Nos. 2182-2183, 2194-2195, May 21. Nos. 2196-2197, Aug. 19, 1991. 2.20fr, 2.50fr, 3.40fr, 4fr, Sept. 30, 1991. Nos. 2179a, 2187a, 2199, 2201, 1991. 4.20fr, Sept. 24, 1992. Nos. 2203-2204, 1992. 2.10fr, 1993.

Peelable paper backing serves as booklet cover for Nos. 2202, 2203. No. 2203b has separate backing with no printing.

Nos. 2196-2197, 2204 inscribed "D."

See Nos. 2333-2351.

Lace Work A1162

1990, Feb. 3 Engr. *Perf. 13x12½*

2205 A1162 2.50fr red 82 16

1992 Winter Olympics, Albertville — A1163

1990, Feb. 9 Photo. *Perf. 13*

2206 A1163 2.50fr multicolored 82 16

Charles de Gaulle (1890-1970) A1164

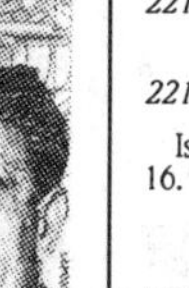

Max Hymans (1900-1961), Planes and ACC Emblem A1165

1990, Feb. 24 Engr. *Perf. 12½x13*

2207 A1164 2.30fr brt vio, vio bl & blk 82 16

1990, Mar. 3 *Perf. 13*

2208 A1165 2.30fr brt vio, brt bl & dk ol grn 82 16

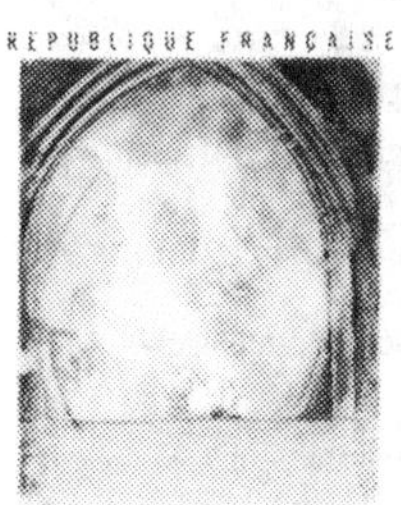

Profile of a Woman, by Odilon Redon A1166

Head of Christ, Wissembourg A1167

Cambodian Dancer by Auguste Rodin A1168

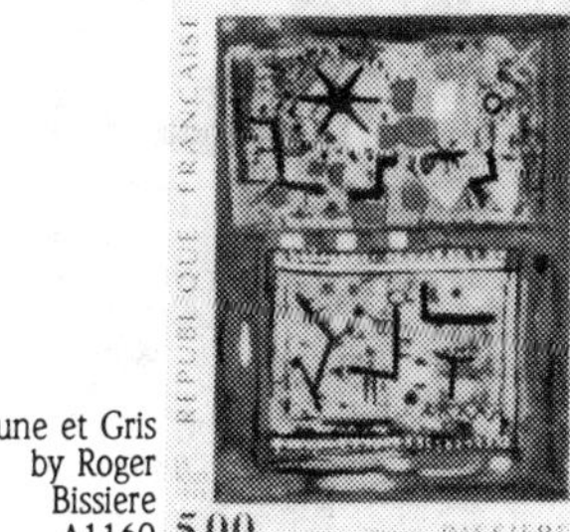

Jaune et Gris by Roger Bissiere A1169

1990 Litho. *Perf. 13½x14*

2209 A1166 5fr multicolored 1.75 35

Perf. 12½x13

Engr.

2210 A1167 5fr multicolored 1.75 35

2211 A1168 5fr multicolored 1.80 35

Photo.

2212 A1169 5fr multicolored 1.90 38

Issue dates: No. 2209, Mar. 3. No. 2210, June 16. No. 2211, June 9. No. 2212, Dec. 8.

Jean Guehenno (1890-1978) — A1170

Litho. & Engr.

1990, Mar. 24 *Perf. 13*

2213 A1170 3.20fr buff & red brown 1.10 22

Tourism Series

Flaran Abbey, Gers A1171

Cluny A1172

Pont Canal de Briare A1173

Cap Canaille, Cassis A1174

1990, Apr. 21 Engr. *Perf. 13*

2214 A1171 3.80fr sepia & blk 1.35 28

1990

2215 A1172	2.30fr multicolored	82	16
2216 A1173	2.30fr multicolored	82	16
2217 A1174	3.80fr multicolored	1.35	28

Issue dates: No. 2215, June 23. No. 2216, July 7. No. 2217, July 14.

Europa 1990 A1175

Post offices.

1990, Apr. 28 Engr. *Perf. 13*

2218 A1175	2.30fr Macon	80	16
2219 A1175	3.20fr Cerizay	1.10	22

Arab World Institute — A1176

1990, May 5 *Perf. 12½x13*
2220 A1176 3.80fr brt bl, dk red & dp bl 1.35 28

Labor Day, Cent. A1177

1990, May 1 **Photo.** *Perf. 13*
2221 A1177 2.30fr multicolored 80 16

Villefranche-sur-Saone — A1178

1990, June 2 **Engr.** *Perf. 13x12½*
2222 A1178 2.30fr multicolored 82 16

National philatelic congress.

A1179 A1181

1990, June 6 *Perf. 13x12½*
2223 A1179 2.30fr La Poste 82 16

Whitbread trans-global yacht race.

1990, June 17 *Perf. 12½x13*
2225 A1181 2.30fr multicolored 82 16

De Gaulle's Call for French Resistance, 50th anniv.

Franco-Brazilian House, Rio de Janeiro — A1182

1990, July 14 *Perf. 13*
2226 A1182 3.20fr multicolored 1.15 22

See Brazil No. 2255.

A1183 A1184

Designs: Fish.

1990, Oct. 6 **Engr.** *Perf. 12½*
2227 A1183 2fr Rutilus rutilus 70 16
2228 A1183 3fr Perca fluviatilis 1.00 20
2229 A1183 4fr Salmo salar 1.40 30
2230 A1183 5fr Esox lucius 1.80 35

1990, Sept. 29 **Photo.** *Perf. 12½x13*
2231 A1184 2.30fr multicolored 85 16

Natl. Institute of Geography, 50th anniv.

Souvenir Sheet

French Revolution, Bicentennial — A1185

Designs: a, Gaspard Monge. b, Abbe Gregoire. c, Creation of the Tricolor. d, Creation of the French departments.

1990, Oct. 15 **Engr.** *Perf. 13*
2232 A1185 Sheet of 4 3.60 3.60
a.-d. 2.50fr any single 90 90

Musical Instrument Type of 1989

1990, Sept. 1 **Litho.** *Perf. 13*
2233 A1154 1.46fr Accordion 52 15
2234 A1154 1.89fr Breton bagpipe 65 15
2235 A1154 3.06fr Tambourin 1.10 15
2236 A1154 5.10fr Hurdy-gurdy 1.80 20
Set value 42

1990, Nov. **Litho.** *Perf. 13*
2237 A1154 1.93fr like #2169 75 15
2238 A1154 2.39fr like #2170 90 15
2239 A1154 2.74fr like #2172 1.05 15
Set value 27

Nos. 2233-2239 are known only precanceled. See second note after No. 132.

Maurice Genevoix (1890-1980), Novelist — A1186

1990, Nov. 12 **Engr.** *Perf. 13*
2240 A1186 2.30fr lt green & blk 88 16

Organization for Economic Cooperation and Development, 30th Anniv. A1187

1990, Dec. 15 **Litho.**
2241 A1187 3.20fr dk & lt blue 1.20 25

"The Swing" by Auguste Renoir (1841-1919) A1188

1991, Feb. 23 **Engr.** *Perf. 12½x13*
2242 A1188 5fr multicolored 1.95 40

Youth Philatelic Exhibition, Cholet A1189

1991, Mar. 30 **Litho.** *Perf. 13*
2243 A1189 2.50fr multicolored 1.00 20

Art Series

Le Noeud Noir by Georges Seurat (1859-1891) A1190

Apres Nous La Maternite, by Max Ernst (1891-1976) A1191

Volte Faccia by Francois Rouan A1192

O Tableau Noir by Roberto Matta (b. 1911) — A1193

1991, Apr. 13 **Engr.** *Perf. 12½x13*
2244 A1190 5fr pale yellow & blk 1.95 40

1991, Oct. 10 **Photo.** *Perf. 13*
2245 A1191 2.50fr multicolored 85 18

1991, Nov. 9 **Engr.** *Perf. 12½x13*
2246 A1192 5fr black 1.85 38

1991, Nov. 30 **Photo.** *Perf. 13x12½*
2247 A1193 5fr multicolored 2.00 40

Wolfgang Amadeus Mozart (1756-1791), Composer A1194

1991, Apr. 9 **Photo.** *Perf. 13*
2248 A1194 2.50fr blue, blk & red 90 18

National Printing Office, 350th Anniv. — A1195

1991, Apr. 13
2249 A1195 4fr multicolored 1.40 28

Tourism Series

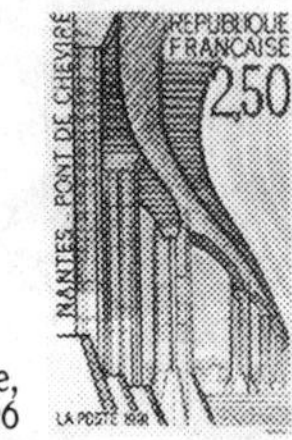

Chevire Bridge, Nantes — A1196

Carennac Castle A1197

Pipe Organ, Wasquehal A1198

Valley of Munster
A1199

1991 **Engr.** ***Perf. 13***
2250 A1196 2.50fr multicolored 90 18

Perf. 12x13
2251 A1197 2.50fr multicolored 90 18

Perf. 12
2252 A1198 4fr black & buff 1.40 28

Perf. 13x12½
2253 A1199 4fr violet 1.40 28

Issue dates: No. 2250, Apr. 27. Nos. 2251, 2253, July 6. No. 2252, June 22.

Europa
A1200

Concours Lepine, 90th Anniv.
A1201

1991, Apr. 27 ***Perf. 12½x13***
2254 A1200 2.50fr Ariane launch site, French Guiana 90 18
2255 A1200 3.50fr Television satellite 1.25 25

1991, Apr. 27 ***Perf. 13***
2256 A1201 4fr multicolored 1.40 28

French Assoc. of Small Manufacturers and Inventors.

Philatelic Society Congress, Perpignan
A1202

1991, May 18
2257 A1202 2.50fr multicolored 90 18

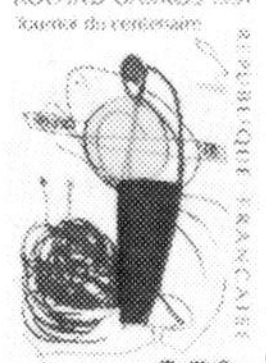

French Open Tennis Championships, Cent. — A1203

1991, May 24 **Engr.** ***Perf. 13***
2258 A1203 3.50fr multicolored 1.20 24

Souvenir Sheet

French Revolution, Bicent.
A1204

Designs: a, Theophile Malo Corret, La Tour d'Auvergne (1743-1800). b, Liberty Tree. c, National police, bicent. d, Louis Antoine-Leon de St. Just (1767-1794).

1991, June 1 **Engr.** ***Perf. 13***
2259 Sheet of 4 3.20 64
a.-d. A1204 2.50fr any single 80 16

A1205 A1206

1991, June 13 **Photo.** ***Perf. 13***
2260 A1205 2.50fr multicolored 90 18

Gaston III de Foix (Febus) (1331-1391), general.

1991, Sept. 14 **Engr.** ***Perf. 12½***

Designs: Wildlife.

2261 A1206 2fr Ursus arctos 68 15
2262 A1206 3fr Testudo hermanni 1.05 20
2263 A1206 4fr Castor fiber 1.35 28
2264 A1206 5fr Alcedo atthis 1.70 35

10th World Forestry Congress
A1207

1991, Sept. 22 **Engr.** ***Perf. 13x12½***
2265 A1207 2.50fr multicolored 85 18

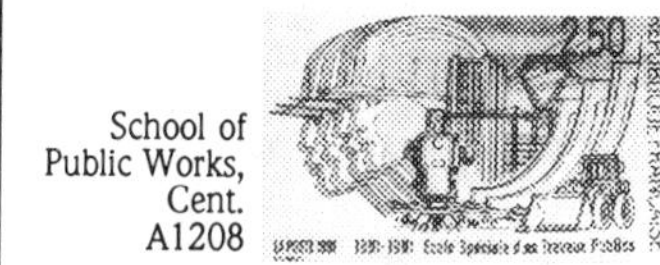

School of Public Works, Cent.
A1208

1991, Oct. 5 **Litho. & Engr.** ***Perf. 13***
2266 A1208 2.50fr multicolored 85 18

Marcel Cerdan (1916-1949), Middleweight Boxing Champion
A1209

1991, Oct. 19 **Photo.** ***Perf. 13***
2267 A1209 2.50fr black & red 85 18

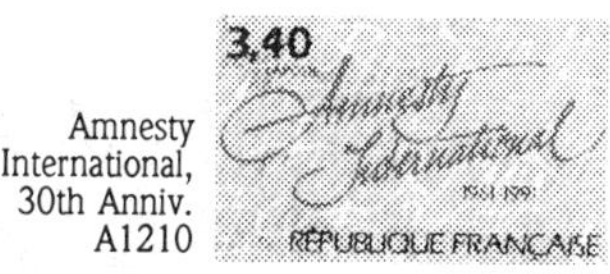

Amnesty International, 30th Anniv.
A1210

1991, Oct. 19
2268 A1210 3.40fr multicolored 1.15 25

Olympic Flame — A1211

1991, Nov. 14 **Engr.** ***Perf. 13***
2269 A1211 2.50fr blue, red & blk 90 18

1992 Winter Olympics, Albertville.

Fifth Handicapped Olympics — A1212

1991, Dec. 7 ***Perf. 13***
2270 A1212 2.50fr dk & lt blue 1.00 20

Voluntary Attachment of Mayotte to France, Sesquicentennial — A1213

1991, Dec. 21 **Engr.**
2271 A1213 2.50fr multicolored 1.00 20

French Pavilion, Expo '92, Seville
A1214

1992, Jan. 18 **Litho. & Engr.** ***Perf. 13***
2272 A1214 2.50fr multicolored 95 20

Musical Instruments Type of 1989

Perf. 13, 12½ (1.60fr, 3.19fr)

1992, Jan. 31 **Litho.**
2273 A1154 1.60fr Guitar 58 15
2274 A1154 1.98fr like #2233 72 15
2275 A1154 2.08fr Saxophone 75 15
2276 A1154 2.46fr like #2234 90 18
2277 A1154 2.98fr Banjo 1.05 20
2278 A1154 3.08fr like #2235 1.10 22
2279 A1154 3.14fr like #2236 1.10 22
2280 A1154 3.19fr like #2169 1.15 22
2281 A1154 5.28fr Xylophone 1.90 38
2282 A1154 5.30fr like #2170 1.95 38
2283 A1154 5.32fr like #2172 1.95 38
Nos. 2273-2283 (11) 13.15 2.63

Nos. 2273-2283 are known only precanceled. See second note after No. 132. See Nos. 2303-2306.

1992 Summer Olympics, Barcelona
A1215

1992, Apr. 3 **Photo.** ***Perf. 13***
2284 A1215 2.50fr multicolored 90 18

See Greece No. 1730.

Marguerite d'Angouleme (1492-1549) — A1216

1992, Apr. 11 **Litho.** ***Perf. 13***
2285 A1216 3.40fr multicolored 1.20 25

Founding of Ajaccio, 500th Anniv.
A1217

Design: 4fr, Virgin and Child Beneath a Garland by Botticelli.

1992, Apr. 30 **Photo.** ***Perf. 13***
2286 A1217 4fr multicolored 1.40 28

A1218

A1219

Discovery of America, 500th Anniv.: 2.50fr, Map, navigation instruments. 3.40fr, Sailing ship, map.

1992, May 9 **Engr.** ***Perf. 13x12½***
2287 A1218 2.50fr multicolored 90 18
2288 A1218 3.40fr multicolored 1.20 25

Europa.

1992, May 30 **Litho.** ***Perf. 13***
2289 A1219 3.40fr multicolored 1.25 25

Intl. Bread and Cereal Congress.

Tourism Series

Ourcq Canal
A1220

Mt. Aiguille
A1221

Biron Castle
A1223

Lorient
A1222

1992, May 30 **Engr.** ***Perf. 13***
2290 A1220 4fr black, blue & grn 1.45 28

1992, June 27 **Engr.** ***Perf. 13***
2291 A1221 3.40fr multicolored 1.35 28

First ascension of Mt. Aiguille, 500th anniv.

1992, July 4 **Engr.** ***Perf. 13***
2292 A1222 4fr multicolored 1.60 32

1992, July 4 ***Perf. 12½x13***
2293 A1223 2.50fr multicolored 1.00 20

Natl. Philatelic Societies Congress, Niort A1224

1992, June 6 Photo. *Perf. 13*

2294 A1224 2.50fr multicolored	90	18

Natl. Art Festival.

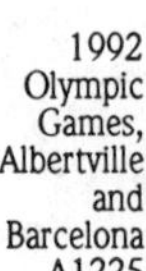

1992 Olympic Games, Albertville and Barcelona A1225

1992, June 19 *Perf. 12½x13½*

2295 A1225 2.50fr multicolored	90	18

Tautavel Man A1226

1992, June 20 Photo. *Perf. 13*

2296 A1226 3.40fr multicolored	1.35	28

Portrait of Jacques Callot (1592-1635), by Claude Deruet A1227

1992, June 27 Engr. *Perf. 12x13*

2297 A1227 5fr buff & brown	1.80	35

Flowers — A1228

Designs: 2fr, Pancratium maritimum. 3fr, Drosera rotundifolia. 4fr, Orchis palustris. 5fr, Nuphar luteum.

1992, Sept. 12 Engr. *Perf. 12½*

2298 A1228 2fr multicolored	78	15
2299 A1228 3fr multicolored	1.18	24
2300 A1228 4fr multicolored	1.55	30
2301 A1228 5fr multicolored	1.95	40

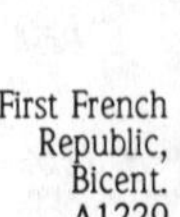

First French Republic, Bicent. A1229

1992, Sept. 26 *Perf. 13*

2302 A1229 2.50fr multicolored	1.00	20

Musical Instruments Type of 1989

1992, Oct. Litho. *Perf. 13*

2303 A1154 1.73fr like #2273	68	15
2304 A1154 2.25fr like #2275	88	18
2305 A1154 3.51fr like #2277	1.35	28
2306 A1154 5.40fr like #2281	2.10	42

Nos. 2303-2306 are known only precancelled. See second note after No. 132.

Proclamation of First French Republic, Bicent. — A1230

Paintings or drawings by contemporary artists: No. 2307, Tree of Freedom, by Pierre Alechinsky. No. 2308, Portrait of a Young Man, by Martial Raysse. No. 2309, Marianne with Body and Head of Rooster, by Gerard Garouste. No. 2310, "Republique Francaise," by Jean-Charles Blais.

1992, Sept. 26 Engr. *Perf. 13*

2307 A1230 2.50fr red	92	20
2308 A1230 2.50fr red	92	20
2309 A1230 2.50fr red	92	20
2310 A1230 2.50fr red	92	20

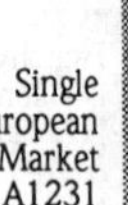

Single European Market A1231

Perf. 12½x13½

1992, Nov. 6 Photo.

2311 A1231 2.50fr multicolored	92	20

First Mail Flight from Nancy to Luneville, 80th Anniv. A1232

1992, Nov. 12 *Perf. 13*

2312 A1232 2.50fr multicolored	92	20

Marcel Paul (1900-1982), Minister of Industrial Production — A1233

1992, Nov. 13 Engr.

2313 A1233 4.20fr claret & blue	1.60	30

Contemporary Art — A1234

Designs: No. 2314, Le Rendezvous d'Ephese, by Paul Delvaux, Belgium. No. 2315, Abstract painting, by Alberto Burri, Italy. No. 2316, Abstract painting, by Antoni Tapies, Spain. No. 2317, Portrait of John Edwards, by Francis Bacon, Great Britain.

1992 Photo. *Perf. 13x12½*

2314 A1234 5fr multicolored	1.85	38
2315 A1234 5fr multicolored	1.85	38
2316 A1234 5fr multicolored	1.85	38
2317 A1234 5fr multicolored	1.85	38

Issue dates: No. 2314, Nov. 20. Nos. 2315-2317, Nov. 21.

See Nos. 2379-2390.

Gypsy Culture — A1235

1992, Dec. 5 Photo. *Perf. 13*

2318 A1235 2.50fr multicolored	95	20

Yacht "La Poste," Entrant in Whitbread Trans-Global Race A1236

1993, Feb. 6 Engr. *Perf. 12*

2319 A1236 2.50fr multicolored	95	20

See No. 2375.

Water Birds — A1237

1993, Feb. 6 *Perf. 12½x12*

2320 A1237 2fr Harle piette	75	15
2321 A1237 3fr Fuligule nyroca	1.15	22
2322 A1237 4fr Tadorne de belon	1.45	30
2323 A1237 5fr Harle huppe	1.80	35

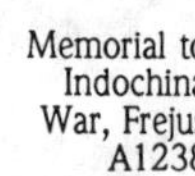

Memorial to Indochina War, Frejus A1238

Perf. 13x13½

1993, Feb. 16 Litho. & Engr.

2324 A1238 4fr multicolored	1.45	30

Stamp Day — A1239

1993, Mar. 6 Photo. *Perf. 13*

2325 A1239 2.50fr red & multi	1.00	20
2326 A1239 2.50fr +60c red & multi	1.25	25
a. Bklt. pane of 4 #2325, 3 #2326 + label	7.75	

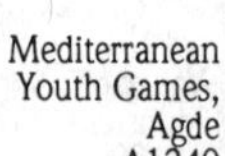

Mediterranean Youth Games, Agde A1240

1993, Mar. 13 Photo. *Perf. 13*

2327 A1240 2.50fr multicolored	90	20

Human Rights, Intl. Mixed Masonic Order, Cent. — A1241

1993, Apr. 3 Engr. *Perf. 13*

2328 A1241 3.40fr blue & black	1.25	26

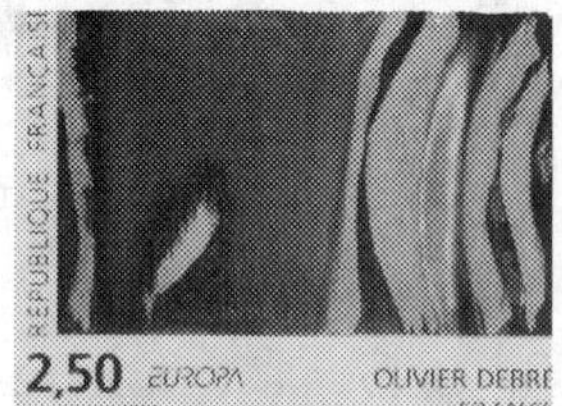

Contemporary Art — A1242

Europa: 2.50fr, Painting, Rouge Rythme Bleu, by Olivier Debre. 3.40fr, Sculpture, Le Griffu, by Germaine Richier, vert.

Perf. 13x12½, 12½x13

1993, Apr. 17 Litho.

2329 A1242 2.50fr multicolored	95	18
2330 A1242 3.40fr multicolored	1.25	25

Marianne Type of 1989

1993 Engr. *Perf. 13*

2333 A1161 2.40fr emerald	80	16
2336 A1161 3.50fr apple green	1.10	25
2338 A1161 4.40fr blue	1.50	30
2342 A1161 (2.50fr) red	95	18

Die Cut

Self-Adhesive

2350 A1161 70c brown	25	15
2351 A1161 (2.50fr) red	95	18
a. Booklet pane of 10	9.50	
b. Booklet pane of 4 + label	3.75	
c. Booklet pane, #2350, 3 #2351, + label	3.25	

Nos. 2342, 2351 pay postage for the first class letter rate and sold for 2.50fr when first released. They have no denomination or letter inscription.

Backing paper of Nos. 2351b and 2351c may have cuts along fold and were sold in a booklet for 20fr.

Issued: Nos. 2342, 2351, Apr. 19. 70c, July.

This is an expanding set. Numbers may change.

Tourism Series

Chinon — A1243

Illustration reduced.

Village of Minerve — A1244

Chaise-Dieu Abbey A1245

Montbeliard A1246

1993, Apr. 24 Engr. *Perf. 13x12½*
2355 A1243 4.20fr dk grn, ol grn & brn 1.60 32

1993, July 17 *Perf. 13*
2356 A1244 4.20fr red brown & yel grn 1.40 28

1993
2357 A1245 2.80fr multicolored 95 20
2358 A1246 4.40fr multicolored 1.50 30

Issued: No. 2357, Sept. 4. No. 2358, Sept. 11.

Ninth European Conference on Protection of Human Rights A1247

1993, May 8 Engr. *Perf. 12½x13*
2359 A1247 2.50fr multicolored 95 18

Django Reinhardt (1910-1953), Musician A1248

1993, May 14 Litho. *Perf. 13*
2360 A1248 4.20fr multicolored 1.60 32

Louise Weiss (1893-1983), Suffragist — A1249

1993, May 15 Engr. *Perf. 13x12½*
2361 A1249 2.50fr black, buff & red 95 18

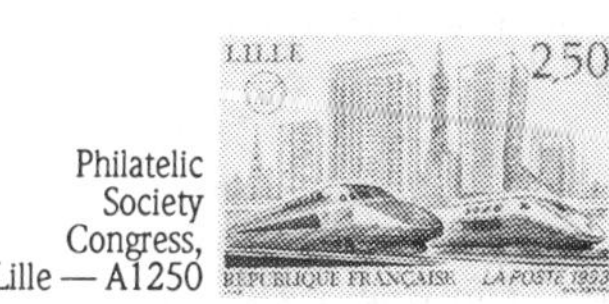

Philatelic Society Congress, Lille — A1250

1993, May 29 Engr. *Perf. 13x12½*
2362 A1250 2.50fr blue, dk blue & lilac 95 18

Natural History Museum, Bicent. A1251

1993, June 5 Litho. & Engr. *Perf. 13*
2363 A1251 2.50fr multicolored 95 18

Martyrs and Heroes of the Resistance
A1252 A1253

1993, June 18 Photo. *Perf. 13*
2364 A1252 2.50fr red, black & gray 95 18
2365 A1253 4.20fr red, black & gray 1.60 32
a. Pair, #2364-2365 2.55 50

A1254

A1255

1993, July 10 Engr. *Perf. 13x12½*
2366 A1254 2.50fr multicolored 95 18

Claude Chappe's Semaphore Telegraph, bicent.

1993, July 10 Engr. *Perf. 12½x13*
2367 A1255 3.40fr blue, green & red 1.15 24

Train to Lake Artouste, Laruns, highest train ride in Europe.

Musical Instruments Type of 1989

1993, July 1 Litho. *Perf. 13*
2368 A1154 1.82fr like #2171 60 15
2369 A1154 2.34fr like #2235 80 16
2370 A1154 3.86fr like #2236 1.25 25
2371 A1154 5.93fr like #2281 2.00 40

Nos. 2368-2371 are known only precanceled. See note after No. 132.

Liberation of Corsica, 50th Anniv. — A1256

1993, Sept. 9 Engr. *Perf. 13*
2372 A1256 2.80fr lake, blue & black 95 20

Saint Thomas, by Georges de la Tour (1593-1652) — A1257

1993, Sept. 9 Photo. *Perf. 12½x13*
2373 A1257 5fr multicolored 1.75 35

Service as Military Hospital of Val de Grace Monastery, Bicent. — A1258

1993, Sept. 25 Engr. *Perf. 13*
2374 A1258 3.70fr multicolored 1.25 25

Whitbread Trans-Global Race Type of 1993

1993, Sept. 27 Engr. *Perf. 12*
2375 A1236 2.80fr multicolored 95 20

The Muses, by Maurice Denis (1870-1943) A1259

1993, Oct. 2 Photo. *Perf. 12½x13*
2376 A1259 5fr multicolored 1.75 35

The Clowns, by Albert Gleizes (1881-1953) A1260

1993, Oct. 2 Photo. *Perf. 13½x12½*
2377 A1260 2.80fr multicolored 1.00 20

Natl. Circus Center, Chalons-sur-Marne.

Clock Tower Bellringer Statues of Lambesc — A1261

1993, Oct. 9 Engr. *Perf. 13x12½*
2378 A1261 4.40fr multicolored 1.50 30

European Contemporary Art Type of 1992

Designs: No. 2379, Abstract, by Takis. No. 2380, Abstract, by Maria Helena Vieira da Silva.

1993 Photo. *Perf. 13x12½*
2379 A1234 5fr black & vermilion 1.75 35
2380 A1234 5fr multicolored 1.65 32

Issued: No. 2379, Oct., 9. No. 2380, Dec. 11.

Greetings — A1266

Greeting, artist: No. 2383, Happy Birthday, Claire Wendling. No. 2384, Happy Birthday, Bernard Olivie. No. 2385, Happy Anniversary, Stephane Colman. No. 2386, Happy Anniversary, Guillaune Sorel. No. 2387, With Love, Jean-Michel Thiriet. No. 2388, Please Write, Etienne Davodeau. No. 2389, Congratulations, Johan de Moor. No. 2390, Good luck, "Mezzo." No. 2391, Best Wishes, Nicolas de Crecy. No. 2392, Best Wishes, Florence Magnin. No. 2393, Merry Christmas, Thierry Robin. No. 2394, Merry Christmas, Patrick Prugne.

1993, Oct. 21 Photo. *Perf. 13½x13*
2383 A1266 2.80fr multicolored 95 18
2384 A1266 2.80fr multicolored 95 18
2385 A1266 2.80fr multicolored 95 18
2386 A1266 2.80fr multicolored 95 18
2387 A1266 2.80fr multicolored 95 18
2388 A1266 2.80fr multicolored 95 18
2389 A1266 2.80fr multicolored 95 18
2390 A1266 2.80fr multicolored 95 18
2391 A1266 2.80fr multicolored 95 18
2392 A1266 2.80fr multicolored 95 18
2393 A1266 2.80fr multicolored 95 18
2394 A1266 2.80fr multicolored 95 18
a. Booklet pane of 12, #2383-2394 11.50
Nos. 2383-2394 (12) 11.40 2.16

Issued in booklets only.

Perf. 12½

2383a	A1266	2.80fr	95	18
2384a	A1266	2.80fr	95	18
2385a	A1266	2.80fr	95	18
2386a	A1266	2.80fr	95	18
2387a	A1266	2.80fr	95	18
2388a	A1266	2.80fr	95	18
2389a	A1266	2.80fr	95	18
2390a	A1266	2.80fr	95	18
2391a	A1266	2.80fr	95	18
2392a	A1266	2.80fr	95	18
2393a	A1266	2.80fr	95	18

2394b	A1266	2.80fr	95	18
c.	Booklet pane of 12, #2383a-2393a, 2394b		11.50	
	Nos. 2383a-2394b (12)		11.40	2.16

Souvenir Sheet

European Stamp Exhibition A1267

Designs: a, Rhododendrons. b, Flowers in park, Paris.

1993, Nov. 10 ***Perf. 13***

2395	A1267	2.40fr #a.-b.+ 2 labels	5.00	1.00

Louvre Museum, Bicent. A1268

1993, Nov. 20

2396	A1268	2.80fr Louvre, 1793	1.00	18
2397	A1268	4.40fr Louvre, 1993	1.50	30
a.		Pair, #2396-2397	2.50	50

Year Sets

Year set values are determined from price lists offering complete sets for each year. Not all dealers offer these sets. Values may be lower or higher than the total value of the individual stamps. Contents of the sets being offered may differ (complete booklets by some, singles from the booklets by others, etc.).

1969	#1230-1262, B423-B433, C42	26.00
1970	#1263-1291, B434-B444, C43	29.00
1971	#1292-1326, B445-B453, C44-C45	37.50
1972	#1327-1354, B454-B462, C46	36.00
1973	#1355-1389, B463-B472, C47	34.00
1974	#1390-1416, B473-B480	30.00
1975	#1417-1459, B481-B488	50.00
1976	#1460-1506, B489-B497, C48	46.00
1977	#1507-1577, B498-B504, C49	65.00
1978	#1578-1623, B505-B513, C50	52.50
1979	#1624-1682, B514-B522, C51	55.00
1980	#1683-1718, B523-B531, C52	45.00
1981	#1719-1782, B532-B540, C53-C54	55.00
1982	#1783-1848, B541-B549, C55	87.50
1983	#1849-1906, B550-B558	70.00
1984	#1907-1945, B559-B566, C56	60.00
1985	#1946-1956, 1965-1990, B567-B574, C57	90.00
1986	#1957-1960, 1991-2026, B575-B583, C58	85.00
1987	#1961-1964, 2027-2070, B584-B592, C59	80.00
1988	#2086-2138, B593-B601	67.50

Subject Index of French Commemorative Issues

SEMI-POSTAL STAMPS

SP1

SP2

Red Surcharge on No. B1

1914 Unwmk. Typo. *Perf. 14x13½*

B1 SP1 10c + 5c red 3.75 3.25
B2 SP2 10c + 5c red 22.50 2.25
a. Booklet pane of 10 425.00

Issue dates: #B1, Aug. 11; #B2, Sept. 10.
For overprint see Offices in Morocco #B8.

Widow at Grave — SP3

War Orphans — SP4

Woman Plowing — SP5

"Trench of Bayonets" SP6

Lion of Belfort — SP7

"La Marseillaise" SP8

1917-19

B3 SP3 2c + 3c vio brn 2.50 2.50
B4 SP4 5c + 5c green ('19) 5.50 4.00
B5 SP5 15c + 10c gray green 12.50 12.50
B6 SP5 25c + 15c deep blue 45.00 27.50
B7 SP6 35c + 25c slate & vio 77.50 65.00
B8 SP7 50c + 50c pale brn & dk brn 125.00 100.00
B9 SP8 1fr + 1fr claret & mar 225.00 200.00
B10 SP8 5fr + 5fr dp bl & blk 825.00 750.00
Nos. B3-B10 (8) 1,318. 1,161.

See #B20-B23. For surcharges see #B12-B19.

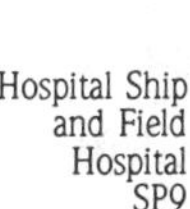

Hospital Ship and Field Hospital SP9

1918, Aug.

B11 SP9 15c + 5c slate & red 100.00 42.50

Semi-Postal Stamps of 1917-19 Surcharged

1922, Sept. 1

B12 SP3 2c + 1c violet brn 28 28
B13 SP4 5c + 2½c green 45 45
B14 SP5 15c + 5c gray grn 75 75
B15 SP5 25c + 5c deep blue 1.50 1.50
B16 SP6 35c + 5c slate & vio 6.50 6.50
B17 SP7 50c + 10c pale brn & dk brn 10.00 10.00
a. Pair, one without surcharge
B18 SP8 1fr + 25c claret & mar 15.00 15.00
B19 SP8 5fr + 1fr blue & blk 85.00 85.00
Nos. B12-B19 (8) 119.48 119.48

Style and arrangement of surcharge differs for each denomination.

Types of 1917-19

1926-27

B20 SP3 2c + 1c violet brn 70 70
B21 SP7 50c + 10c ol brn & dk brn 22.50 8.25
B22 SP8 1fr + 25c dp rose & red brn 35.00 22.00
B23 SP8 5fr + 1fr sl bl & blk 82.50 60.00
Set, never hinged 290.00

Sinking Fund Issues

Types of Regular Issues of 1903-07 Surcharged in Red or Blue

Caisse
d'Amortissement
+10c

1927, Sept. 26

B24 A22 40c + 10c lt blue (R) 3.50 3.50
B25 A20 50c + 25c green (Bl) 4.75 4.75

Surcharge on #B25 differs from illustration.

Type of Regular Issue of 1923 Surcharged in Black

+50c

B26 A23 1.50fr + 50c orange 8.00 8.00
Set, never hinged 32.50

See Nos. B28-B33, B35-B37, B39-B41.

Industry and Agriculture SP10

1928, May Engr. *Perf. 13½*

B27 SP10 1.50fr + 8.50fr dull blue 90.00 90.00
Never hinged 160.00
a. Blue green 300.00 300.00

Types of 1903-23 Issues Surcharged like Nos. B24-B26

1928, Oct. 1 *Perf. 14x13½*

B28 A22 40c + 10c gray lilac (R) 7.50 7.50
B29 A20 50c + 25c orange brn (Bl) 19.00 15.00
B30 A23 1.50fr + 50c rose lilac (Bk) 26.00 21.00
Set, never hinged 100.00

Types of 1903-23 Issues Surcharged like Nos. B24-B26

1929, Oct. 1

B31 A22 40c + 10c green 12.50 10.50
B32 A20 50c + 25c lilac rose 19.00 13.00
B33 A23 1.50fr + 50c chestnut 32.50 30.00
Set, never hinged 125.00

"The Smile of Reims" SP11

1930, Mar. 15 Engr. *Perf. 13*

B34 SP11 1.50fr + 3.50fr red violet 50.00 50.00
Never hinged 95.00
a. Booklet pane of 4 325.00 325.00

Types of 1903-07 Issues Surcharged like Nos. B24-B25

1930 Oct. 1 *Perf. 14x13½*

B35 A22 40c + 10c cerise 12.50 10.00
B36 A20 50c + 25c gray brown 27.50 16.00
B37 A22 1.50fr + 50c violet 47.50 40.00
Set, never hinged 160.00

Allegory, French Provinces SP12

1931, Mar. 1 *Perf. 13*

B38 SP12 1.50fr + 3.50fr green 105.00 105.00
Never hinged 165.00

Types of 1903-07 Issues Surcharged like Nos. B24-B25

1931, Oct. 1 *Perf. 14x13½*

B39 A22 40c + 10c olive green 30.00 30.00
B40 A20 50c + 25c gray violet 62.00 60.00
B41 A22 1.50fr + 50c deep red 70.00 67.50
Set, never hinged 335.00

Catalogue values for unused stamps in this section, from this point to the end of the section, are for Never Hinged items.

"France" Giving Aid to an Intellectual SP13

Symbolic of Music SP14

1935, Dec. 9 Engr. *Perf. 13*

B42 SP13 50c + 10c ultra 4.25 1.75
B43 SP14 50c + 2fr dull red 70.00 35.00

The surtax was for the aid of distressed and exiled intellectuals.
For surcharge see No. B47.

Statue of Liberty — SP15

Children of the Unemployed — SP16

1936-37

B44 SP15 50c + 25c dk blue ('37) 4.50 2.50
B45 SP15 75c + 50c violet 11.00 6.00

Surtax for the aid of political refugees.
For surcharge see No. B47.

1936, May

B46 SP16 50c + 10c copper red 5.75 4.50

The surtax was for the aid of children of the unemployed.

Type of 1935 Semi-Postal Surcharged in Black

+20c

1936, Nov.

B47 SP14 20c on 50c + 2fr dull red 3.50 3.00

Jacques Callot SP17

Anatole France (Jacques Anatole Thibault) — SP18

Hector Berlioz SP19

Victor Hugo — SP20

Auguste Rodin — SP21

Louis Pasteur SP22

1936-37 Engr.

B48 SP17 20c + 10c brown car 2.50 2.25
B49 SP18 30c + 10c emer ('37) 2.75 1.65
B50 SP19 40c + 10c emerald 3.00 2.50
B51 SP20 50c + 10c copper red 4.50 2.50
B52 SP21 90c + 10c rose red ('37) 6.00 4.00
B53 SP22 1.50fr + 50c deep ultra 24.00 15.00
Nos. B48-B53 (6) 42.75 27.90

The surtax was used for relief of unemployed intellectuals.

1938

B54 SP18 30c + 10c brown car 2.00 1.50
B55 SP17 35c + 10c dull green 3.50 2.00
B56 SP19 55c + 10c dull vio 6.25 2.50
B57 SP20 65c + 10c ultra 6.25 2.75
B58 SP21 1fr + 10c car lake 6.25 2.75
B59 SP22 1.75fr + 25c dp blue 17.50 7.00
Nos. B54-B59 (6) 41.75 18.50

Tug of War — SP23

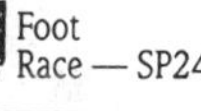
Foot Race — SP24

Hiking — SP25

1937, June 16

B60 SP23 20c + 10c brown 2.25 1.75
B61 SP24 40c + 10c red brown 2.25 1.75
B62 SP25 50c + 10c black brn 2.25 1.75

The surtax was for the Recreation Fund of the employees of the Post, Telephone and Telegraph.

Pierre Loti (Louis Marie Julien Viaud) — SP26

1937, Aug.

B63 SP26 50c + 20c rose carmine 3.75 2.75

The surtax was for the Pierre Loti Monument Fund.

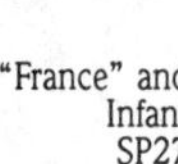

"France" and Infant SP27

1937-39

B64 SP27 65c + 25c brown vio 3.25 2.00
B65 SP27 90c + 30c pck bl ('39) 2.25 1.25

The surtax was used for public health work.

Winged Victory of Samothrace SP28

Jean Baptiste Charcot SP29

1937, Aug.

B66 SP28 30c blue green 110.00 32.50
B67 SP28 55c red 110.00 32.50

On sale at the Louvre for 2.50fr. The surtax of 1.65fr was for the benefit of the Louvre Museum.

1938-39

B68 SP29 65c + 35c dk bl grn 1.90 1.75
B69 SP29 90c + 35c brt red vio ('39) 10.50 8.50

Surtax for the benefit of French seamen.

Palace of Versailles SP30

1938, May 9

B70 SP30 1.75fr + 75c deep blue 25.00 14.00

Natl. Exposition of Painting and Sculpture at Versailles.

The surtax was for the benefit of the Versailles Concert Society.

French Soldier SP31

Monument SP32

1938, May 16

B71 SP31 55c + 70c brown vio 4.00 2.75
B72 SP31 65c + 1.10fr pck bl 4.00 2.75

The surtax was for a fund to erect a monument to the glory of the French Infantrymen.

1938, May 25

B73 SP32 55c + 45c vermilion 11.00 7.50

The surtax was for a fund to erect a monument in honor of the Army Medical Corps.

Reims Cathedral SP33

"France" Welcoming Her Sons SP34

1938, July 10

B74 SP33 65c + 35c ultra 9.25 8.50

Completion of the reconstruction of Reims Cathedral, July 10, 1938.

1938, Aug. 8

B75 SP34 65c + 60c rose car 5.00 4.00

The surtax was for the benefit of French volunteers repatriated from Spain.

Curie Issue

Common Design Type

1938, Sept. 1

B76 CD80 1.75fr + 50c deep ultra 8.25 8.00

Victory Parade Passing Arc de Triomphe SP36

1938, Oct. 8

B77 SP36 65c + 35c brown car 5.00 4.00

20th anniversary of the Armistice.

Student and Nurse — SP37

1938, Dec. 1

B78 SP37 65c + 60c pck blue 6.00 4.00

The surtax was for Student Relief.

Blind Man and Radio SP38

1938, Dec.

B79 SP38 90c + 25c brown vio 6.50 4.50

The surtax was used to help provide radios for the blind.

Civilian Facing Firing Squad — SP39

Red Cross Nurse — SP40

1939, Feb. 1

B80 SP39 90c + 35c black brn 7.50 4.75

The surtax was used to erect a monument to civilian victims of World War I.

1939, Mar. 24

B81 SP40 90c + 35c dk sl grn, turq bl & red 6.00 4.50

75th anniv. of the Intl. Red Cross Soc.

Army Engineer SP41

1939, Apr. 3

B82 SP41 70c + 50c vermilion 6.00 4.50

Army Engineering Corps. The surtax was used to erect a monument to those members who died in World War I.

Ministry of Post, Telegraph and Telephone SP42

1939, Apr. 8

B83 SP42 90c + 35c turq blue 16.00 8.50

The surtax was used to aid orphans of employees of the postal system. Opening of the new building for the Ministry of Post, Telegraph and Telephones.

Mother and Child — SP43

Eiffel Tower — SP44

1939, Apr. 24

B84 SP43 90c + 35c red 3.00 2.00

The surtax was used to aid children of the unemployed.

1939, May 5

B85 SP44 90c + 50c red violet 10.00 5.00

50th anniv. of the Eiffel Tower. The surtax was used for celebration festivities.

Puvis de Chavannes — SP45

Claude Debussy SP46

Honoré de Balzac SP47

Claude Bernard SP48

1939-40

B86 SP45 40c + 10c vermil-ion 1.65 85
B87 SP46 70c + 10c brn vio 1.90 1.10
B87A SP46 80c + 10c brn vio ('40) 3.00 2.00
B88 SP47 90c + 10c brt red vio 3.00 1.65
B88A SP47 1fr + 10c brt red vio ('40) 3.00 2.00
B89 SP48 2.25fr + 25c brt ultra 9.50 3.25
B89A SP48 2.50fr + 25c brt ultra ('40) 3.00 2.00
Nos. B86-B89A (7) 25.05 12.85

The surtax was used to aid unemployed intellectuals.

Mothers and Children SP49 SP50

1939, June 15

B90 SP49 70c + 80c bl, grn & vio 3.25 2.50
B91 SP50 90c + 60c dk brn, dl vio & brn 4.25 3.00

The surtax was used to aid France's repopulation campaign.

"The Letter" by Jean Honoré Fragonard — SP51

Statue of Widow and Children — SP52

1939, July 6

B92 SP51 40c + 60c brn, sep & pur 4.00 2.75

The surtax was used for the Postal Museum.

1939, July 20

B93 SP52 70c + 30c brown vio 8.00 4.50

Surtax for the benefit of French seamen.

French Soldier SP53

Colonial Trooper
SP54

1940, Feb. 15

B94 SP53	40c + 60c sepia	1.90	80
B95 SP54	1fr + 50c turq blue	1.90	80

The surtax was used to assist the families of mobilized men.

World Map Showing French Possessions
SP55

1940, Apr. 15

B96 SP55	1fr + 25c scarlet	2.50	1.75

Marshal Joseph J. C. Joffre — SP56

Marshal Ferdinand Foch — SP57

Gen. Joseph S. Gallieni
SP58

Woman Plowing
SP59

1940, May 1

B97	SP56	80c + 45c chocolate	3.00	2.00
B98	SP57	1fr + 50c dk violet	3.25	2.25
B99	SP58	1.50fr + 50c brown red	3.25	2.25
B100	SP59	2.50fr + 50c indigo & dl bl	4.00	2.75

The surtax was used for war charities.

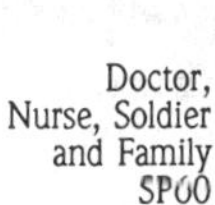

Doctor, Nurse, Soldier and Family
SP60

Nurse and Wounded Soldier
SP61

1940, May 12

B101 SP60	80c + 1fr dk green & red	5.00	3.25
B102 SP61	1fr + 2fr sepia & red	5.00	3.25

The surtax was used for the Red Cross.

Nurse with Injured Children — SP62

1940, Nov. 12

B103 SP62	1fr + 2fr sepia	75	65

The surtax was used for victims of the war.

Wheat Harvest
SP63

Sowing
SP64

Picking Grapes
SP65

Grazing Cattle
SP66

1940, Dec. 2

B104	SP63	80c + 2fr brown blk	1.65	1.25
B105	SP64	1fr + 2fr chestnut	1.65	1.25
B106	SP65	1.50fr + 2fr brt violet	1.65	1.25
B107	SP66	2.50fr + 2fr dp green	2.00	1.25

The surtax was for national relief.

Prisoners of War
SP67 SP68

1941, Jan. 1

B108 SP67	80c + 5fr dark green	1.00	90
B109 SP68	1fr + 5fr rose brown	1.00	90

The surtax was for prisoners of war.

Science Fighting Cancer
SP69

1941, Feb. 20

B110 SP69	2.50fr + 50c slate blk & brn	1.40	1.10

Surtax used for the control of cancer.

Type of 1941 Surcharged "+10c" in Blue

1941, Mar. 4

B111 A109	1fr + 10c crimson	15	15

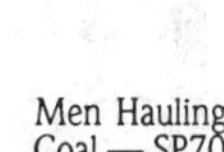

Men Hauling Coal — SP70

"France" Aiding Needy Man — SP71

1941

B112	SP70	1fr + 2fr sepia	1.25	60
B113	SP71	2.50fr + 7.50fr dk blue	4.25	2.00

The surtax was for Marshal Pétain's National Relief Fund.

Liner Pasteur
SP72

Red Surcharge

1941, July 17

B114 SP72	1fr + 1fr on 70c dk bl grn	15	15

World Map, Mercator Projection
SP73

1941

B115 SP73	1fr + 1fr multi	45	40

Fisherman — SP74

1941, Oct. 23

B116 SP74	1fr + 9fr dk blue grn	85	85

Surtax for benefit of French seamen.

Arms of Various Cities

Nancy
SP75

Lille
SP76

Rouen
SP77

Bordeaux
SP78

Toulouse
SP79

Clermont-Ferrand
SP80

Marseilles
SP81

Lyon
SP82

Rennes
SP83

Reims
SP84

Montpellier
SP85

Paris
SP86

1941 *Perf. 14x13*

B117	SP75	20c + 30c brown blk	1.90	1.90
B118	SP76	40c + 60c org brn	2.25	2.25
B119	SP77	50c + 70c grnsh blue	2.25	2.25
B120	SP78	70c + 80c rose vio	2.25	2.25
B121	SP79	80c + 1fr dp rose	2.25	2.25
B122	SP80	1fr + 1fr black	2.25	2.25
B123	SP81	1.50fr + 2fr dk blue	2.25	2.25
B124	SP82	2fr + 2fr dk vio	2.25	2.25
B125	SP83	2.50fr + 3fr brt grn	2.25	2.25
B126	SP84	3fr + 5fr org brn	2.25	2.25
B127	SP85	5fr + 6fr brt ultra	2.25	2.25
B128	SP86	10fr + 10fr dk red	2.50	2.50
		Nos. B117-B128 (12)	26.90	26.90

Count de La Pérouse
SP87

1942, Mar. 23 *Perf. 13*

B129 SP87	2.50fr + 7.50fr ultra	1.10	1.10

Jean Francois de Galaup de La Pérouse, (1741-88), French navigator and explorer. The surtax was for National Relief.

Planes over Fields — SP88

1942, Apr. 4

B130 SP88	1.50fr + 3.50fr lt violet	1.10	1.10

The surtax was for the benefit of French airmen and their familes.

Alexis Chabrier
SP89

1942, May 18

B131 SP89	2fr + 3fr sepia	75	75

Emmanuel Chabrier (1841-1894), composer, birth centenary. The surtax was for works of charity among musicians.

Symbolical of French Colonial Empire
SP90

1942, May 18

B132 SP90	1.50fr + 8.50fr black	55	55

The surtax was for National Relief.

Jean de Vienne
SP91

1942, June 16

B133 SP91	1.50fr + 8.50fr sepia	70	70

600th anniv. of the birth of Jean de Vienne, 1st admiral of France. The surtax was for the benefit of French seamen.

+ 50

Type of Regular Issue, 1941 Surcharged in Carmine

S N

1942, Sept. 10 *Perf. 14x13½*

B134 A116	1.50fr + 50c brt ultra	15	15

The surtax was for national relief ("Secours National").

Arms of Various Cities

Chambéry
SP92

La Rochelle
SP93

Poitiers
SP94

Orléans
SP95

Grenoble
SP96

Angers
SP97

Dijon
SP98

Limoges
SP99

Le Havre
SP100

Nantes
SP101

Nice
SP102

St. Etienne
SP103

Perf. 14x13

1942, Oct. Unwmk. Engr.

B135 SP92	50c + 60c black	2.25	2.25
B136 SP93	60c + 70c grnsh blue	2.25	2.25
B137 SP94	80c + 1fr rose	2.25	2.25
B138 SP95	1fr + 1.30fr dk green	2.50	2.50
B139 SP96	1.20fr + 1.50fr rose vio	2.50	2.50
B140 SP97	1.50fr + 1.80fr slate bl	2.50	2.50
B141 SP98	2fr + 2.30fr deep rose	2.50	2.50
B142 SP99	2.40fr + 2.80fr slate grn	2.50	2.50
B143 SP100	3fr + 3.50fr dp violet	2.50	2.50
B144 SP101	4fr + 5fr lt ultra	2.50	2.50
B145 SP102	4.50fr + 6fr red	2.50	2.50
B146 SP103	5fr + 7fr brt red vio	2.50	2.50
	Nos. B135-B146 (12)	29.25	29.25

The surtax was for national relief.

Tricolor Legion
SP104

1942, Oct. 12 *Perf. 13*

B147 SP104	1.20 + 8.80fr dk blue	7.50	7.50
a.	Vert. pair, #B147, B148 + albino impression	15.00	15.00
B148 SP104	1.20 + 8.80fr crimson	7.50	7.50

These stamps were printed in sheets of 20 stamps and 5 albino impressions arranged: 2 horizontal rows of 5 dark blue stamps, 1 row of 5 albino impressions, and 2 rows of 5 crimson stamps.

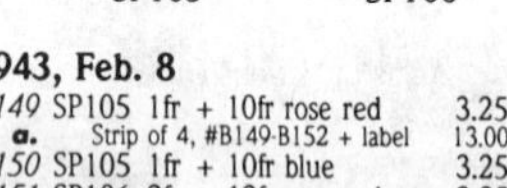
Marshal Henri Philippe Pétain
SP105 SP106

1943, Feb. 8

B149 SP105	1fr + 10fr rose red	3.25	3.25
a.	Strip of 4, #B149-B152 + label	13.00	13.00
B150 SP105	1fr + 10fr blue	3.25	3.25
B151 SP106	2fr + 12fr rose red	3.25	3.25
B152 SP106	2fr + 12fr blue	3.25	3.25

The surtax was for national relief. Printed in sheets of 20, the 10 blue stamps at left, the 10 rose red at right, separated by a vert. row of 5 white labels bearing a tri-colored battle-ax.

Marshal Pétain
SP107

"Work"
SP108

"Family"
SP109

"State"
SP110

Marshal Pétain — SP111

1943, June 7

B153 SP107	1.20fr + 1.40fr dull vio	11.00	11.00
a.	Strip of 5, #B153-B157	60.00	60.00
B154 SP108	1.50fr + 2.50fr red	11.00	11.00
B155 SP109	2.40fr + 7fr brown	11.00	11.00
B156 SP110	4fr + 10fr dk violet	11.00	11.00
B157 SP111	5fr + 15fr red brown	11.00	11.00
	Nos. B153-B157 (5)	55.00	55.00

Pétain's 87th birthday.
The surtax was for national relief.

Civilians Under Air Attack — SP112

Civilians Doing Farm Work — SP113

Prisoner's Family Doing Farm Work
SP114

1943, Aug. 23

B158 SP112	1.50fr + 3.50fr black	40	40

Surtax was for bomb victims at Billancourt, Dunkirk, Lorient, Saint-Nazaire.

1943, Sept. 27

B159 SP113	1.50fr + 8.50fr sepia	75	75
B160 SP114	2.40fr + 7.60fr dk green	75	75

The surtax was for families of war prisoners.

Michel de Montaigne
SP115

Picardy Costume
SP121

Designs: 1.20fr+1.50fr, Francois Clouet. 1.50fr+3fr, Ambrose Paré. 2.40fr+4fr, Chevalier Pierre de Bayard. 4fr+6fr, Duke of Sully. 5fr+10fr, Henri IV.

1943, Oct. 2

B161 SP115	60c + 80c Prus green	1.50	1.50
B162 SP115	1.20fr + 1.50fr black	1.50	1.50
B163 SP115	1.50fr + 3fr deep ultra	1.50	1.50
B164 SP115	2.40fr + 4fr red	1.50	1.50
B165 SP115	4fr + 6fr dull brn red	1.90	1.90
B166 SP115	5fr + 10fr dull green	1.90	1.90
	Nos. B161-B166 (6)	9.80	9.80

The surtax was for national relief. Issued to honor famous 16th century Frenchmen.

1943, Dec. 27

Designs: 18th Century Costumes: 1.20fr+2fr, Brittany. 1.50fr+4fr, Ile de France. 2.40+5fr, Burgundy. 4fr+6fr, Auvergne. 5fr+7fr, Provence.

B167 SP121	60c + 1.30fr sepia	1.65	1.65
B168 SP121	1.20fr + 2fr lt violet	1.65	1.65
B169 SP121	1.50fr + 4fr turq blue	1.65	1.65
B170 SP121	2.40fr + 5fr rose car	1.65	1.65
B171 SP121	4fr + 6fr chlky blue	2.25	2.25
B172 SP121	5fr + 7fr red	2.25	2.25
	Nos. B167-B172 (6)	11.10	11.10

The surtax was for national relief.

Admiral Tourville
SP127

Charles Gounod
SP128

1944, Feb. 21

B173 SP127	4fr + 6fr dull red brn	50	50

300th anniv. of the birth of Admiral Anne-Hilarion de Cotentin Tourville (1642-1701).

1944, Mar. 27 *Perf. 14x13*

B174 SP128	1.50fr + 3.50fr sepia	35	35

50th anniv. of the death of Charles Gounod, composer (1818-1893).

Marshal Pétain
SP129

Farming
SP130

Industry
SP131

1944, Apr. 24 *Perf. 13*

B175 SP129	1.50fr + 3.50fr sepia	2.25	2.25
B176 SP130	2fr + 3fr dp ultra	45	45
B177 SP131	4fr + 6fr rose red	45	45

Marshal Henri Pétain's 88th birthday.

Modern Streamliner, 19th Cent. Train SP132

Molière (Jean-Baptiste Poquelin) SP133

1944, Aug. 14

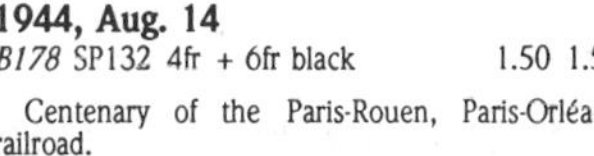

B178 SP132 4fr + 6fr black		1.50	1.50

Centenary of the Paris-Rouen, Paris-Orléans railroad.

1944, July 31

Designs: 80c+2.20fr, Jules Hardouin Mansart. 1.20fr+2.80fr, Blaise Pascal. 1.50fr+3.50fr, Louis II of Bourbon. 2fr+4fr, Jean-Baptiste Colbert. 4fr+6fr, Louis XIV.

B179	SP133	50c + 1.50fr rose car	1.00	1.00
B180	SP133	80c + 2.20fr dk green	1.00	1.00
B181	SP133	1.20fr + 2.80fr black	1.00	1.00
B182	SP133	1.50fr + 3.50fr brt ultra	1.00	1.00
B183	SP133	2fr + 4fr dull brn red	1.00	1.00
B184	SP133	4fr + 6fr red	1.00	1.00
		Nos. B179-B184 (6)	6.00	6.00

Noted 17th century Frenchmen.

Angoulême SP139

Chartres SP140

Amiens SP141

Beauvais SP142

Albi — SP143

1944, Nov. 20

B185	SP139	50c + 1.50fr black	25	25
B186	SP140	80c + 2.20fr rose vio	40	40
B187	SP141	1.20fr + 2.80fr brn car	52	52
B188	SP142	1.50fr + 3.50fr dp blue	52	52
B189	SP143	4fr + 6fr orange red	52	52
		Nos. B185-B189 (5)	2.21	2.21

French Cathedrals.

Coat of Arms of Renouard de Villayer SP144

Sarah Bernhardt SP145

1944, Dec. 9 **Engr.**

B190 SP144 1.50fr + 3.50fr dp brown		18	15

Stamp Day.

1945, May 16 **Unwmk.** ***Perf. 13***

B191 SP145 4fr + 1fr dk violet brn		20	20

100th anniv. of the birth of Sarah Bernhardt, actress.

War Victims SP146

1945, May 16

B192 SP146 4fr + 6fr dk violet brn		15	15

The surtax was for war victims of the P.T.T.

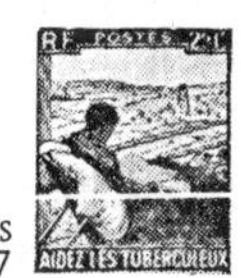

Tuberculosis Patient — SP147

1945, May 16 **Typo.** ***Perf. 14x13½***

B193 SP147 2fr + 1fr red orange		15	15

Surtax for the aid of tuberculosis victims.
For surcharge see No. 561.

Boy and Girl — SP148

Burning of Oradour Church — SP149

1945, July 9 **Engr.** ***Perf. 13***

B194 SP148 4fr + 2fr Prus green		18	18

The surtax was used for child welfare.

1945, Oct. 13

B195 SP149 4fr + 2fr sepia		18	18

Destruction of Oradour, June, 1944.

Louis XI and Post Rider — SP150

1945, Oct. 13

B196 SP150 2fr + 3fr deep ultra		20	20

Stamp Day.
For overprint see French West Africa #B2.

Ruins of Dunkirk SP151

Ruins of Rouen SP152

Ruins of Caen SP153

Ruins of Saint-Malo SP154

1945, Nov. 5

B197	SP151	1.50fr + 1.50fr red brown	20	15
B198	SP152	2fr + 2fr violet	20	15
B199	SP153	2.40fr + 2.60fr blue	20	15
B200	SP154	4fr + 4fr black	20	15

The surtax was to aid the suffering residents of Dunkirk, Rouen, Caen and Saint Malo.

Alfred Fournier SP155

Henri Becquerel SP156

1946, Feb. 4 **Engr.** ***Perf. 13***

B201	SP155	2fr + 3fr red brown	18	18
B202	SP156	2fr + 3fr violet	18	18

Issued to raise funds for the fight against venereal disease (#B201) and for the struggle against cancer (#B202).

No. B202 for the 50th anniv. of the discovery of radioactivity by Henri Becquerel.

See No. B221.

Church of the Invalides, Paris — SP157

1946, Mar. 11

B203 SP157 4fr + 6fr red brown		16	16

The surtax was to aid disabled war veterans.

French Warships SP158

1946, Apr. 8

B204 SP158 2fr + 3fr gray black		15	15

The surtax was for naval charities.

"The Letter" by Jean Siméon Chardin SP159

Fouquet de la Varane SP160

1946, May 25

B205 SP159 2fr + 3fr brown red		38	38

The surtax was used for the Postal Museum.

1946, June 29

B206 SP160 3fr + 2fr sepia		30	30

Stamp Day.

Franois Villon — SP161

Designs: 3fr+1fr, Jean Fouquet. 4fr+3fr, Philippe de Commynes. 5fr+4fr, Joan of Arc. 6fr+5fr, Jean de Gerson. 10fr+6fr, Charles VII.

1946, Oct. 28

B207	SP161	2fr + 1fr dk Prus grn	1.00	1.00
B208	SP161	3fr + 1fr dk blue vio	1.00	1.00
B209	SP161	4fr + 3fr henna brn	1.00	1.00
B210	SP161	5fr + 4fr ultra	1.00	1.00
B211	SP161	6fr + 5fr sepia	1.00	1.00
B212	SP161	10fr + 6fr red	1.25	1.25
		Nos. B207-B212 (6)	6.25	6.25

Church of St. Sernin, Toulouse SP167

Notre Dame du Port, Clermont-Ferrand SP168

Cathedral of St. Front, Perigueux SP169

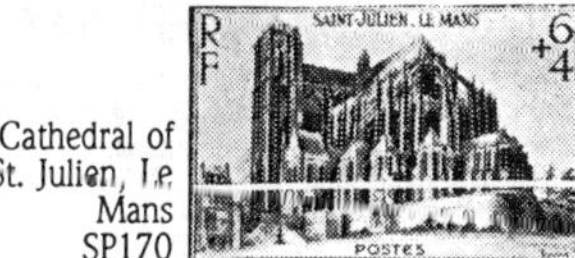

Cathedral of St. Julien, Le Mans SP170

Cathedral of Notre Dame, Paris — SP171

Franois Michel le Tellier de Louvois — SP172

1947 **Engr.**

B213 SP167 1fr + 1fr car rose 48 48
B214 SP168 3fr + 2fr dk blue vio 65 65
B215 SP169 4fr + 3fr henna brn 95 95
B216 SP170 6fr + 4fr deep blue 1.25 1.25
B217 SP171 10fr + 6fr dk gray grn 2.75 2.75
Nos. B213-B217 (5) 6.08 6.08

1947, Mar. 15

B218 SP172 4.50fr + 5.50fr car rose 1.00 1.00

Stamp Day, Mar. 15, 1947.

Submarine Pens, Shipyard and Monument SP173

1947, Aug. 2

B219 SP173 6fr + 4fr bluish black 35 35

British commando raid on the Nazi U-boat base at St. Nazaire, 1942.

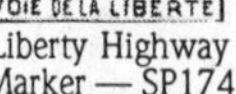

Liberty Highway Marker — SP174

Louis Braille — SP175

1947, Sept. 5

B220 SP174 6fr + 4fr dk green 50 50

The surtax was to help defray maintenance costs of the Liberty Highway.

Fournier Type of 1946

1947, Oct. 20

B221 SP155 2fr + 3fr indigo 16 16

1948, Jan. 19

B222 SP175 6fr + 4fr purple 30 30

Etienne Arago SP176

Alphonse de Lamartine SP177

1948, Mar. 6

B223 SP176 6fr + 4fr black brn 45 45

Stamp Day, March 6-7, 1948.

1948, Apr. 5 **Engr.** ***Perf. 13***

Designs: 3fr+2fr, Alexandre A. Ledru-Rollin. 4fr+3fr, Louis Blanc. 5fr+4fr, Albert (Alexandre Martin). 6fr+5fr, Pierre J. Proudhon. 10fr+6fr, Louis Auguste Blanqui. 15fr+7fr, Armand Barbés. 20fr+8fr, Dennis A. Affre.

B224 SP177 1fr + 1fr dk green 90 90
B225 SP177 3fr + 2fr henna brn 1.05 1.05
B226 SP177 4fr + 3fr violet brn 1.05 1.05
B227 SP177 5fr + 4fr lt blue grn 1.25 1.25
B228 SP177 6fr + 5fr indigo 1.25 1.25
B229 SP177 10fr + 6fr carmine rose 1.25 1.25
B230 SP177 15fr + 7fr slate blk 2.10 2.10
B231 SP177 20fr + 8fr purple 2.25 2.25
Nos. B224-B231 (8) 11.10 11.10

Centenary of the Revolution of 1848.

Dr. Léon Charles Albert Calmette SP178

1948, June 18

B232 SP178 6fr + 4fr dk grnsh blue 20 20

1st Intl. Congress on the Calmette-Guerin bacillus vaccine.

Farmer — SP179

Designs: 5fr+3fr, Fisherman. 8fr+4fr, Miner. 10fr+6fr, Metal worker.

1949, Feb. 14

B233 SP179 3fr + 1fr claret 60 35
B234 SP179 5fr + 3fr dk blue 65 52
B235 SP179 8fr + 4fr indigo 70 45
B236 SP179 10fr + 6fr dk red 1.10 65

Étienne Franois de Choiseul and Post Cart SP180

Baron de la Brède et de Montesquieu SP181

1949, Mar. 26

B237 SP180 15fr + 5fr dk green 1.00 1.00

Stamp Day, Mar. 26-27, 1949.

1949, Nov. 14

Designs: 8fr+2fr, Voltaire. 10fr+3fr, Antoine Watteau. 12fr+4fr, Georges de Buffon. 15fr+5fr, Joseph F. Dupleix. 25fr+10fr, A. R. J. Turgot.

B238 SP181 5fr + 1fr dk green 3.25 3.25
B239 SP181 8fr + 2fr indigo 3.25 3.25
B240 SP181 10fr + 3fr brown red 3.25 3.25
B241 SP181 12fr + 4fr purple 3.25 3.25
B242 SP181 15fr + 5fr rose car 4.00 4.00
B243 SP181 25fr + 10fr ultra 4.00 4.00
Nos. B238-B243 (6) 21.00 21.00

"Spring" SP182

Designs: 8fr+2fr, Summer. 12fr+3fr, Autumn. 15fr+4fr, Winter.

1949, Dec. 19

B244 SP182 5fr + 1fr green 1.65 1.65
B245 SP182 8fr + 2fr yellow org 1.65 1.65
B246 SP182 12fr + 3fr purple 2.00 2.00
B247 SP182 15fr + 4fr dp blue 2.25 2.25

Postman — SP183

1950, Mar. 11

B248 SP183 12fr + 3fr dp blue 2.50 1.65

Stamp Day, Mar. 11-12, 1950.

André de Chénier SP184

Alexandre Brongniart, Bust by Houdon SP185

Portraits: 8fr+3fr, J. L. David. 10fr+4fr, Lazare Carnot. 12fr+5fr, G. J. Danton. 15fr+6fr, Maximilian Robespierre. 20fr+10fr, Louis Hoche.

1950, July 10 **Engr.** ***Perf. 13***

Frames in Indigo

B249 SP184 5fr + 2fr brown vio 7.75 7.75
B250 SP184 8fr + 3fr black brn 7.75 7.75
B251 SP184 10fr + 4fr lake 7.75 7.75
B252 SP184 12fr + 5fr red brown 8.00 8.00
B253 SP184 15fr + 6fr dk green 9.50 9.50
B254 SP184 20fr + 10fr dk vio bl 9.50 9.50
Nos. B249-B254 (6) 50.25 50.25

1950, Dec. 22

Design: 15fr+3fr, "L'Amour" by Etienne M. Falconet.

B255 SP185 8fr + 2fr indigo & car 2.25 2.25
B256 SP185 15fr + 3fr red brn & car 2.25 2.25

The surtax was for the Red Cross.

Mail Car Interior SP186

Alfred de Musset SP187

1951, Mar. 10 **Unwmk.** ***Perf. 13***

B257 SP186 12fr + 3fr lilac gray 2.75 2.75

Stamp Day, Mar. 10-11, 1951.

1951, June 2

Designs: 8fr+2fr, Eugène Delacroix. 10fr+3fr, J.-L. Gay-Lussac. 12fr+4fr, Robert Surcouf. 15fr+5fr, C. M. Talleyrand. 30fr+10fr, Napoleon I.

Frames in Dark Brown

B258 SP187 5fr + 1fr dk green 6.75 6.75
B259 SP187 8fr + 2fr violet brn 7.25 7.25
B260 SP187 10fr + 3fr grnsh black 7.25 7.25
B261 SP187 12fr + 4fr dk vio brn 7.25 7.25
B262 SP187 15fr + 5fr brown car 7.50 7.50
B263 SP187 30fr + 10fr indigo 11.00 11.00
Nos. B258-B263 (6) 47.00 47.00

Child at Prayer by Le Maître de Moulins SP188

18th Century Child by Quentin de la Tour SP189

1951, Dec. 15

Cross in Red

B264 SP188 12fr + 3fr dk brown 3.25 3.25
B265 SP189 15fr + 5fr dp ultra 3.25 3.25

The surtax was for the Red Cross.

Stagecoach of 1844 SP190

1952, Mar. 8 ***Perf. 13***

B266 SP190 12fr + 3fr dp green 4.00 4.00

Stamp Day, Mar. 8, 1952.

Gustave Flaubert — SP191

Portraits: 12fr+3fr, Edouard Manet. 15fr+4fr, Camille Saint-Saens. 18fr+5fr, Henri Poincaré. 20fr+6fr, Georges-Eugene Haussmann. 30fr+7fr, Adolphe Thiers.

1952, Oct. 18

Frames in Dark Brown

B267 SP191 8fr + 2fr indigo 5.25 5.25
B268 SP191 12fr + 3fr vio blue 5.25 5.25
B269 SP191 15fr + 4fr dk green 5.25 5.25
B270 SP191 18fr + 5fr dk brown 5.25 5.25
B271 SP191 20fr + 6fr carmine 7.00 7.00
B272 SP191 30fr + 7fr purple 7.00 7.00
Nos. B267-B272 (6) 35.00 35.00

Cupid from Diana Fountain Versailles SP192

Design: 15fr+5fr, Similar detail, cupid facing left.

1952, Dec. 13

Cross in Red

B273 SP192 12fr + 3fr dark green 4.00 4.00
B274 SP192 15fr + 5fr indigo 4.00 4.00
a. Booklet pane of 10 65.00

The surtax was for the Red Cross.

Count d'Argenson SP193

St. Bernard SP194

1953, Mar. 14

B275 SP193 12fr + 3fr dp blue 2.00 2.00

Issued to commemorate the Day of the Stamp. The surtax was for the Red Cross.

1953, July 9

Portraits: 12fr+3fr, Olivier de Serres. 15fr+4fr, Jean Philippe Rameau. 18fr+5fr, Gaspard Monge. 20fr+6fr, Jules Michelet. 30fr+7fr, Marshal Hubert Lyautey.

B276 SP194 8fr + 2fr ultra 5.75 5.75
B277 SP194 12fr + 3fr dk green 5.75 5.75
B278 SP194 15fr + 4fr brown car 7.50 7.50
B279 SP194 18fr + 5fr dk blue 7.50 7.50
B280 SP194 20fr + 6fr dk purple 7.50 7.50
B281 SP194 30fr + 7fr brown 9.00 9.00
Nos. B276-B281 (6) 43.00 43.00

The surtax was for the Red Cross.

Madame Vigée-Lebrun and her Daughter — SP195

Count Antoine de La Vallette — SP196

Design: 15fr+5fr, "The Return from Baptism," by Louis Le Nain.

1953, Dec. 12

Cross in Red

B282 SP195 12fr + 3fr red brown 5.75 5.75
a. Bklt. pane, 4 each, gutter btwn. 65.00
B283 SP195 15fr + 5fr indigo 7.00 7.00

The surtax was for the Red Cross.

1954, Mar. 20 Engr. *Perf. 13*

B284 SP196 12fr + 3fr dp grn & choc 3.50 3.50

Stamp Day, Mar. 20, 1954.

Louis IX SP197

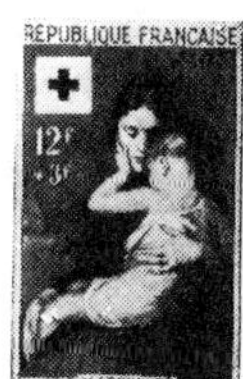
"The Sick Child," by Eugene Carrière SP198

Portraits: 15fr+5fr, Jacques Benigne Bossuet. 18fr+6fr, Sadi Carnot. 20fr+7fr, Antoine Bourdelle. 25fr+8fr, Dr. Emile Roux. 30fr+10fr, Paul Valéry.

1954, July 10

B285 SP197 12fr + 4fr dp blue 17.00 17.00
B286 SP197 15fr + 5fr purple 18.00 18.00
B287 SP197 18fr + 6fr dk brown 18.00 18.00
B288 SP197 20fr + 7fr crimson 22.50 22.50
B289 SP197 25fr + 8fr indigo 22.50 22.50
B290 SP197 30fr + 10fr dp claret 22.50 22.50
Nos. B285-B290 (6) 120.50 120.50

See Nos. B303-B308, B312-B317.

1954, Dec. 18

Design: 15fr+5fr, "Young Girl with Doves," by Jean Baptiste Greuze.

Cross in Red

B291 SP198 12fr + 3fr vio gray & indigo 7.50 7.50
a. Bklt. pane, 4 each, gutter btwn. 70.00
B292 SP198 15fr + 5fr dk brn & org brn 7.00 7.00

No. B291a for 90th anniv. of the Red Cross. The surtax was for the Red Cross.

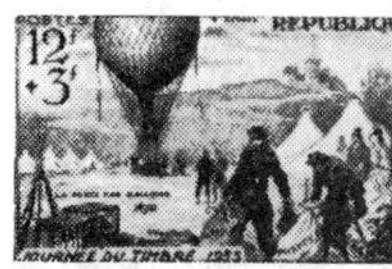
Balloon Post, 1870 SP199

1955, Mar. 19 Unwmk. *Perf. 13*

B293 SP199 12fr + 3fr multi 4.25 3.25

Stamp Day, Mar. 19-20, 1955.

King Philip II — SP200

Child with Cage by Pigalle — SP201

Portraits: 15fr+6fr, Francois de Malherbé. 18fr+7fr, Sebastien de Vauban. 25fr+8fr, Charles G. de Vergennes. 30fr+9fr, Pierre S. de Laplace. 50fr+15fr, Pierre Auguste Renoir.

1955, June 11

B294 SP200 12fr + 5fr brt pur 12.50 12.50
B295 SP200 15fr + 6fr dp blue 12.50 12.50
B296 SP200 18fr + 7fr dp green 14.00 14.00
B297 SP200 25fr + 8fr gray 19.00 19.00
B298 SP200 30fr + 9fr rose brn 20.00 20.00
B299 SP200 50fr + 15fr blue grn 22.50 22.50
Nos. B294-B299 (6) 100.50 100.50

See Nos. B321-B326.

1955, Dec. 17

Design: 15fr+5fr, Child with Goose, by Boethus of Chalcedon.

Cross in Red

B300 SP201 12fr + 3fr claret 5.00 5.00
B301 SP201 15fr + 5fr dk blue 5.00 5.00
a. Booklet pane of 10 60.00

The surtax was for the Red Cross.

Francois of Taxis — SP202

1956, Mar. 17 Engr. *Perf. 13*

B302 SP202 12fr + 3fr ultra, grn & dk brn 2.00 2.00

Stamp Day, Mar. 17-18, 1956.

Portrait Type of 1954

Portraits: No. 303, Guillaume Budé. No. B304, Jean Goujon. No. B305, Samuel de Champlain. No. B306, Jean Simeon Chardin. No. B307, Maurice Barrès. No. B308, Maurice Ravel.

1956, June 9 *Perf. 13*

B303 SP197 12fr + 3fr sapphire 4.50 4.50
B304 SP197 12fr + 3fr lilac gray 4.50 4.50
B305 SP197 12fr + 3fr brt red 5.75 5.75
B306 SP197 15fr + 5fr green 5.75 5.75
B307 SP197 15fr + 5fr violet brn 6.25 6.25
B308 SP197 15fr + 5fr dp violet 6.50 6.50
Nos. B303-B308 (6) 33.25 33.25

Peasant Boy by Le Nain — SP203

Design: 15fr+5fr, Gilles by Watteau.

1956, Dec. 8 Unwmk.

Cross in Red

B309 SP203 12fr + 3fr olive gray 2.50 2.50
a. Bklt. pane, 4 each, gutter btwn. 22.50
B310 SP203 15fr + 5fr rose lake 2.50 2.50

The surtax was for the Red Cross.

Genoese Felucca, 1750 SP204

1957, Mar. 16 *Perf. 13*

B311 SP204 12fr +3fr bluish gray & brn blk 1.50 1.40

Day of the Stamp, Mar. 16, 1957, and honoring the Maritime Postal Service.

Portrait Type of 1954

1957, June 15

Portraits: No. B312, Jean de Joinville. No. B313, Bernard Palissy. No. B314, Quentin de la Tour. No. B315, Hugues Félicité Robert de Lamennais. No. B316, George Sand. No. B317, Jules Guesde.

B312 SP197 12fr + 3fr ol gray & ol grn 1.90 1.90
B313 SP197 12fr + 3fr grnsh blk & grnsh bl 2.25 2.25
B314 SP197 15fr + 5fr cl & brt red 2.50 2.50
B315 SP197 15fr + 5fr ultra & ind 2.75 2.75
B316 SP197 18fr + 7fr grnsh blk & dk grn 3.00 3.00
B317 SP197 18fr + 7fr dk vio brn & red brn 3.25 3.25
Nos. B312-B317 (6) 15.65 15.65

Blind Man and Beggar, Engraving by Jacques Callot — SP205

Design: 20fr+8fr, Women beggars.

1957, Dec. 7 Engr. *Perf. 13*

B318 SP205 15fr + 7fr ultra & red 2.50 2.50
a. Bklt. pane, 4 each, gutter btwn. 22.50
B319 SP205 20fr + 8fr dk vio brn & red 2.50 2.50

The surtax was for the Red Cross.

Motorized Mail Distribution SP206

1958, Mar. 15

B320 SP206 15fr + 5fr multi 1.40 1.10

Stamp Day, Mar. 15.

Portrait Type of 1955

Portraits: No. B321, Joachim du Bellay. No. B322, Jean Bart. No. B323, Denis Diderot. No. B324, Gustave Courbet. 20fr+8fr, J. B. Carpeaux. 35fr+15fr, Toulouse-Lautrec.

1958, June 7 Engr. *Perf. 13*

B321 SP200 12fr + 4fr yellow grn 1.65 1.65
B322 SP200 12fr + 4fr dk blue 1.65 1.65
B323 SP200 15fr + 5fr dull claret 1.75 1.75
B324 SP200 15fr + 5fr ultra 1.75 1.75
B325 SP200 20fr + 8fr brt red 2.10 2.10
B326 SP200 35fr + 15fr green 2.10 2.10
Nos. B321-B326 (6) 11.00 11.00

St. Vincent de Paul — SP207

Portrait: 20fr+8fr, J. H. Dunant.

1958, Dec. 6 Unwmk.

Cross in Carmine

B327 SP207 15fr + 7fr grayish grn 1.00 1.00
a. Bklt. pane, 4 each, gutter btwn. 9.50
B328 SP207 20fr + 8fr violet 1.00 1.00

The surtax was for the Red Cross.

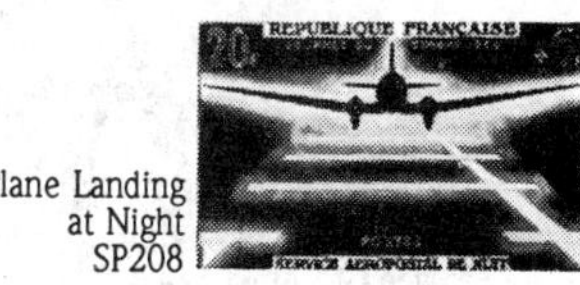
Plane Landing at Night SP208

1959, Mar. 21

B329 SP208 20fr + 5fr sl grn, blk & rose 45 45

Issued for Stamp Day, Mar. 21, and to publicize night air mail service.
The surtax was for the Red Cross.
See No. 1089.

Geoffroi de Villehardouin and Ships SP209

Designs: No. B331, André Le Nôtre and formal garden. No. B332, Jean Le Rond d'Alembert, books and wheel. No. B333, David d'Angers, statue and building. No. B334, M. F. X. Bichat and torch. No. B335, Frédéric Auguste Bartholdi, Statue of Liberty and Lion of Belfort.

1959, June 13 Engr. *Perf. 13*

B330 SP209 15fr + 5fr vio blue 1.05 1.05
B331 SP209 15fr + 5fr dk sl grn 1.05 1.05
B332 SP209 20fr + 10fr olive bis 1.20 1.20
B333 SP209 20fr + 10fr dk gray 1.20 1.20
B334 SP209 30fr + 10fr dk car rose 1.65 1.65
B335 SP209 30fr + 10fr orange brn 1.65 1.65
Nos. B330-B335 (6) 7.80 7.80

The surtax was for the Red Cross.

No. 927 Surcharged **FREJUS +5f**

1959, Dec. Typo. *Perf. 14x13½*

B336 A328 25fr + 5fr black & red 30 30

Surtax for the flood victims at Frejus.

Charles Michel de l'Épée — SP210

Design: 25fr+10fr, Valentin Hauy.

1959, Dec. 5 **Engr.** ***Perf. 13***

Cross in Carmine

B337 SP210 20fr + 10fr black & claret 1.00 1.00
a. Bklt. pane, 4 each, gutter btwn. 9.50
B338 SP210 25fr + 10fr dk blue & blk 1.00 1.00

The surtax was for the Red Cross.

Ship Laying Underwater Cable SP211

1960, Mar. 12

B339 SP211 20c + 5c grnsh bl & dk bl 90 90

Issued for the Day of the Stamp. The surtax went to the Red Cross.

Refugee Girl Amid Ruins — SP212

1960, Apr. 7

B340 SP212 25c + 10c grn, brn & indigo 24 20

World Refugee Year, July 1, 1959-June 30, 1960. The surtax was for aid to refugees.

Michel de L'Hospital SP213

Designs: No. B342, Henri de la Tour D'Auvergne, Viscount of Turenne. No. B343, Nicolas Boileau (Despreaux). No. B344, Jean-Martin Charcot, M.D. No. B345, Georges Bizet. 50c+15c, Edgar Degás.

1960, June 11 **Engr.** ***Perf. 13***

B341 SP213 10c + 5c pur & rose car 1.65 1.65
B342 SP213 20c + 10c ol & vio brn 1.75 1.75
B343 SP213 20c + 10c Prus grn & dp yel grn 2.10 2.10
B344 SP213 30c + 10c rose car & rose red 2.10 2.10
B345 SP213 30c + 10c dk bl & vio bl 2.50 2.50
B346 SP213 50c + 15c sl bl & gray 3.00 3.00
Nos. B341-B346 (6) 13.10 13.10

The surtax was for the Red Cross.
See Nos. B350-B355.

Staff of the Brotherhood of St. Martin — SP214

Letter Carrier, Paris 1760 — SP215

Design: 25c+10c, St. Martin, 16th century wood sculpture.

1960, Dec. 3 **Unwmk.** ***Perf. 13***

B347 SP214 20c + 10c rose cl & red 2.00 2.00
a. Bklt. pane, 4 each, gutter btwn. 20.00
B348 SP214 25c + 10c lt ultra & red 2.00 2.00

The surtax was for the Red Cross.

1961, Mar. 18 ***Perf. 13***

B349 SP215 20c + 5c sl grn, brn & red 75 75

Stamp Day. Surtax for Red Cross.

Famous Men Type of 1960

Designs: 15c+5c, Bertrand Du Guesclin. B351, Pierre Puget. #B352, Charles Coulomb. 30c+10c, Antoine Drouot. 45c+10c, Honoré Daumier. 50c+15c, Guillaume Apollinaire.

1961, May 20 **Engr.**

B350 SP213 15c + 5c red brn & blk 1.40 1.40
B351 SP213 20c + 10c dk grn & lt bl 1.40 1.40
B352 SP213 20c + 10c ver & rose car 1.40 1.40
B353 SP213 30c + 10c blk & brn org 1.40 1.40
B354 SP213 45c + 10c choc & dk grn 2.25 2.25
B355 SP213 50c + 15c dk car rose & vio 2.25 2.25
Nos. B350-B355 (6) 10.10 10.10

"Love" by Rouault SP216

Medieval Royal Messenger SP217

Designs from "Miserere" by Georges Rouault: 25c+10c, "The Blind Consoles the Seeing."

1961, Dec. 2 ***Perf. 13***

B356 SP216 20c + 10c brn, blk & red 2.00 2.00
a. Bklt. pane, 4 each, gutter btwn. 17.50
B357 SP216 25c + 10c brn, blk & red 2.00 2.00

The surtax was for the Red Cross.

1962, Mar. 17

B358 SP217 20c + 5c rose red, bl & sepia 70 42

Stamp Day. Surtax for Red Cross.

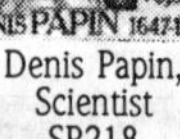

Denis Papin, Scientist SP218

Rosalie Fragonard by Fragonard SP219

Portraits: No. B360, Edme Bouchardon, sculptor. No. B361, Joseph Lakanal, educator. 30c+10c, Gustave Charpentier, composer. 45c+15c, Edouard Estaunlè, writer. 50c+20c, Hyacinthe Vincent, physician and bacteriologist.

1962, June 2 **Engr.**

B359 SP218 15c + 5c bluish grn & dk gray 2.00 2.00
B360 SP218 20c + 10c cl brn 2.00 2.00
B361 SP218 20c + 10c gray & sl 2.00 2.00
B362 SP218 30c + 10c brt bl & ind 2.50 2.50
B363 SP218 45c + 15c org brn & choc 2.50 2.50
B364 SP218 50c + 20c grnsh bl & blk 2.50 2.50
Nos. B359-B364 (6) 13.50 13.50

The surtax was for the Red Cross.

1962, Dec. 8

Design: 25c+10c, Child dressed as Pierrot.

Cross in Red

B365 SP219 20c + 10c redsh brown 1.10 1.10
a. Bklt. pane, 4 each, gutter btwn. 11.00
B366 SP219 25c + 10c dull green 1.10 1.10

The surtax was for the Red Cross.
For surcharges see Reunion Nos. B16-B17.

Jacques Amyot, Classical Scholar SP220

Portraits: 30c+10c, Pierre de Marivaux, playwright. 50c+20c, Jacques Daviel, surgeon.

1963, Feb. 23 **Unwmk.** ***Perf. 13***

B367 SP220 20c + 10c mar, gray & pur 1.00 1.00
B368 SP220 30c + 10c Prus grn & mar 95 95
B369 SP220 50c + 20c ultra, ocher & ol 1.00 1.00

The surtax was for the Red Cross.

Roman Chariot SP221

1963, Mar. 16 **Engr.**

B370 SP221 20c + 5c brn org & vio brn 22 22

Stamp Day. Surtax for Red Cross.

Étienne Méhul, Composer SP222

Designs: 30c+10c, Nicolas-Louis Vauquelin, chemist. 50c+20c, Alfred de Vigny, poet.

1963, May 25 **Unwmk.** ***Perf. 13***

B371 SP222 20c + 10c dp bl, dk brn & dp org 1.10 1.10
B372 SP222 30c + 10c mag, gray ol & blk 95 95
B373 SP222 50c + 20c sl, blk & brn 1.50 1.50

The surtax was for the Red Cross.

"Child with Grapes" by David d'Angers and Centenary Emblem — SP223

Design: 25c+10c, "The Fifer," by Edouard Manet.

1963, Dec. 9 **Unwmk.** ***Perf. 13***

B374 SP223 20c + 10c black & red 60 60
a. Bklt. pane, 4 each, gutter btwn. 5.00
B375 SP223 25c + 10c sl grn & red 60 60

Cent. of the Intl. and French Red Cross. Surtax for the Red Cross.
For surcharges see Reunion Nos. B18-B19.

Post Rider, 18th Century SP224

1964, Mar. 14 **Engr.**

B376 SP224 20c + 5c Prus green 20 15

Issued for Stamp Day.

Resistance Memorial by Watkin, Luxembourg Gardens — SP225

De Gaulle's 1940 Poster "A Tous les Francais" SP226

Allied Troops Landing in Normandy and Provence SP227

Designs: 20c+5c, "Deportation," concentration camp with watchtower and barbed wire. No. B380, Street fighting in Paris and Strasbourg.

1964 **Engr.** ***Perf. 13***

B377 SP225 20c + 5c slate blk 52 52

Perf. 12x13

B378 SP226 25c + 5c dk red, bl, red & blk 65 65

Perf. 13

B379 SP227 30c + 5c blk, bl & org brn 52 52
B380 SP227 30c + 5c org brn, cl & blk 60 60
B381 SP225 50c + 5c dark green 65 65
Nos. B377-B381 (5) 2.94 2.94

20th anniv. of liberation from the Nazis.
Issue dates: #B377, B381, Mar. 21; #B378, June 18; #B379, June 6; #B380, Aug. 22.

President René Coty SP229

Jean Nicolas Corvisart SP230

Portraits: No. B383, John Calvin. No. B384, Pope Sylvester II (Gerbert).

1964 **Unwmk.** ***Perf. 13***

B382 SP229 30c + 10c dp cl & blk 25 25
B383 SP229 30c + 10c dk grn, blk & brn 25 25
B384 SP229 30c + 10c slate & cl 25 25

The surtax was for the Red Cross.
Issue dates: No. B382, Apr. 25; No. B383, May 25; No. B384, June 1.

1964, Dec. 12 Engr.

Portrait: 25c+10c, Dominique Larrey.

Cross in Carmine

B385 SP230 20c + 10c black 25 25
a. Bklt. pane, 4 each, gutter btwn. 3.00
B386 SP230 25c + 10c black 25 25

Issued to honor Jean Nicolas Corvisart (1755-1821), physician of Napoleon I, and Dominique Larrey (1766-1842), Chief Surgeon of the Imperial Armies. The surtax was for the Red Cross.
For surcharges see Reunion Nos. B20-B21.

Paul Dukas, Composer — SP231

Portraits: No. B387, Duke Franois de La Rochefoucauld, writer. No. B388, Nicolas Poussin, painter. No. B389, Duke Charles of Orléans, poet.

1965, Feb. Engr. *Perf. 13*

B387 SP231 30c + 10c org brn & dk bl 42 42
B388 SP231 30c + 10c car & dk red brn 42 42
B389 SP231 40c + 10c dk red brn, dk red & Prus bl 48 48
B390 SP231 40c + 10c dk brn & sl bl 48 48

The surtax was for the Red Cross.
Nos. B387 and B390 were issued Feb. 13; Nos. B388-B389 were issued Feb. 20.

Packet "La Guienne" SP232

1965, Mar. 29 Unwmk. *Perf. 13*

B391 SP232 25c + 10c multi 50 50

Issued for Stamp Day, 1965. "La Guienne" was used for transatlantic mail service. Surtax was for the Red Cross.

Infant with Spoon by Auguste Renoir — SP233

Design: 30c+10c, Coco Writing (Renoir's daughter Claude).

1965, Dec. 11 Engr. *Perf. 13*

Cross in Carmine

B392 SP233 25c + 10c slate 20 20
a. Bklt. pane, 4 each, gutter btwn. 2.25
B393 SP233 30c + 10c dull red brn 25 25

The surtax was for the Red Cross.
For surcharges see Reunion Nos. B22-B23.

Francois Mansart and Carnavalet Palace, Paris SP234

Designs: No. B395, St. Pierre Fourier and Basilica of St. Pierre Fourier, Mirecourt. No. B396, Marcel Proust and St. Hilaire Bridge, Illiers. No. B397, Gabriel Fauré, monument and score of "Penelope." No. B398, Elie Metchnikoff, microscope and Pasteur Institute. No. B399, Hippolyte Taine and birthplace.

1966 Engr. *Perf. 13*

B394 SP234 30c + 10c dk red brn & grn 30 30
B395 SP234 30c + 10c blk & gray grn 30 30
B396 SP234 30c + 10c ind, sep & grn 30 30
B397 SP234 30c + 10c bis brn & ind 30 30
B398 SP234 30c + 10c blk & dl brn 30 30
B399 SP234 30c + 10c grn & ol brn 30 30
Nos. B394-B399 (6) 1.80 1.80

The surtax was for the Red Cross.
Issue dates: Nos. B394-B396, Feb. 12. Others, June 25.

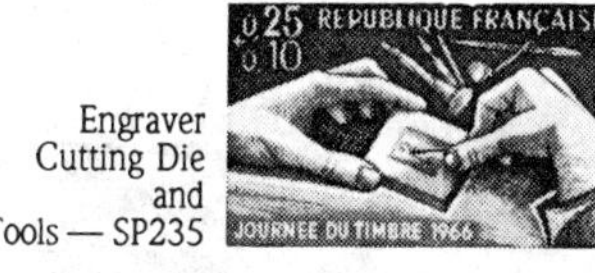

Engraver Cutting Die and Tools — SP235

1966, Mar. 19 Engr. *Perf. 13*

B400 SP235 25c + 10c sl, dk brn & dp org 30 30

Stamp Day. Surtax for Red Cross.

Angel of Victory, Verdun Fortress, Marching Troops — SP236

First Aid on Battlefield, 1859 — SP237

1966, May 28 *Perf. 13*

B401 SP236 30c + 5c Prus bl, ultra & dk bl 20 20

Victory of Verdun, 50th anniversary.

1966, Dec. 10 Engr. *Perf. 13*

Design: 30c+10c, Nurse giving first aid to child, 1966.

Cross in Carmine

B402 SP237 25c + 10c green 30 30
a. Bklt. pane, 4 each, gutter btwn. 3.00
B403 SP237 30c + 10c slate 30 30

The surtax was for the Red Cross.
For surcharges see Reunion Nos. B24-B25.

Emile Zola — SP238

Letter Carrier, 1865 — SP239

Portraits: No. B405, Beaumarchais (pen name of Pierre Augustin Caron). No. B406, St. Francois de Sales (1567-1622). No. B407, Albert Camus (1913-1960).

1967 Engr. *Perf. 13*

B404 SP238 30c + 10c sl bl & bl 30 30
B405 SP238 30c + 10c rose brn & lil 30 30
B406 SP238 30c + 10c dl vio & pur 30 30
B407 SP238 30c + 10c brn & dl cl 30 30

The surtax was for the Red Cross.
Issue dates: Nos. B404-B405, Feb. 4. Others, June 24.

1967, Apr. 8

B408 SP239 25c + 10c indigo, grn & red 20 20

Issued for Stamp Day.

Ivory Flute Player — SP240

Ski Jump and Long Distance Skiing — SP241

Design: 30c+10c, Violin player, ivory carving.

1967, Dec. 16 Engr. *Perf. 13*

Cross in Carmine

B409 SP240 25c + 10c dl vio & lt brn 30 30
a. Bklt. pane, 4 each, gutter btwn. 2.75
B410 SP240 30c + 10c grn & lt brn 30 30

The surtax was for the Red Cross.
For surcharges see Reunion Nos. B26-B27.

1968, Jan. 27

Designs: 40c+10c, Ice hockey. 60c+20c, Olympic flame and snowflakes. 75c+25c, Woman figure skater. 95c+35c, Slalom.

B411 SP241 30c + 10c ver, gray & brn 22 22
B412 SP241 40c + 10c lil, lem & brt mag 26 26
B413 SP241 60c + 20c dk grn, org & brt vio 35 35
B414 SP241 75c + 25c brt pink, yel grn & blk 45 45
B415 SP241 95c + 35c bl, brt pink & red brn 60 60
Nos. B411-B415 (5) 1.88 1.88

Issued for the 10th Winter Olympic Games, Grenoble, Feb. 6-18.

Rural Mailman, 1830 — SP242

1968, Mar. 16 Engr. *Perf. 13*

B416 SP242 25c + 10c multi 18 18

Issued for Stamp Day.

Franois Couperin, Composer, and Instruments SP243

Portraits: No. B418, Gen. Louis Desaix de Veygoux (1768-1800) and scene showing his death at the Battle of Marengo, Italy. No. B419, Saint-Pol-Roux (pen name of Paul-Pierre Roux, 1861-1940), Christ on the Cross and ruins of Camaret-sur-Mer. No. B420, Paul Claudel (poet and diplomat, 1868-1955) and Joan of Arc at the stake.

1968 Engr. *Perf. 13*

B417 SP243 30c + 10c pur & rose lil 22 22
B418 SP243 30c + 10c dk grn & brn 22 22
B419 SP243 30c + 10c cop red & ol bis 22 22
B420 SP243 30c + 10c dk brn & lil 22 22

Issue dates: Nos. B417-B418, Mar. 23; Nos. B419-B420, July 6.

Spring, by Nicolas Mignard — SP244

Designs (Paintings by Nicolas Mignard): 30c+10c, Fall. No. B423, Summer. No. B424, Winter.

1968-69 Engr. *Perf. 13*

Cross in Carmine

B421 SP244 25c + 10c pur & sl bl 22 22
a. Bklt. pane (4 #B421, 4 #B422 with gutter btwn.) 1.75
B422 SP244 30c + 10c brn & rose car 22 22
B423 SP244 40c + 15c dk brn & brn ('69) 28 28
a. Bklt. pane (4 #B423, 4 #B424 with gutter btwn.) 3.50
B424 SP244 40c + 15c pur & Prus bl ('69) 28 28

The surtax was for the Red Cross.
For surcharges see Reunion Nos. B28-B31.

Mailmen's Omnibus, 1881 SP245

1969, Mar. 15 Engr. *Perf. 13*

B425 SP245 30c + 10c brn, grn & blk 18 18

Issued for Stamp Day.
For surcharge see Reunion No. B32.

Gen. Francois Marceau — SP246

Portraits: No. B427, Charles Augustin Sainte-Beuve (1804-1869), writer. No. B428, Albert Roussel (1869-1937), musician. No. B429, Marshal Jean Lannes (1769-1809). No. B430, Georges Cuvier (1769-1832), naturalist. No. B431, André Gide, (1869-1951), writer.

1969

B426 SP246 50c + 10c brown red 42 42
B427 SP246 50c + 10c slate bl 42 42
B428 SP246 50c + 10c dp vio bl 42 42
B429 SP246 50c + 10c choc 42 42
B430 SP246 50c + 10c dp plum 42 42
B431 SP246 50c + 10c blue grn 42 42
Nos. B426-B431 (6) 2.52 2.52

The surtax was for the Red Cross.
Issue dates: Nos. B426-B428, Mar. 24. No. B429, May 10, Nos. B430-B431, May 17.

Gen. Jacques Leclerc, La Madeleine and Battle — SP247

1969, Aug. 23 Engr. *Perf. 13*

B432 SP247 45c + 10c slate & ol 60 60

25th anniversary of the liberation of Paris, Aug. 25, 1944.

Same Inscribed "Liberation de Strasbourg"

1969, Nov. 22 Engr. *Perf. 13*

B433 SP247 70c + 10c brn, choc & olive		1.40	1.40

25th anniv. of the liberation of Strasbourg.

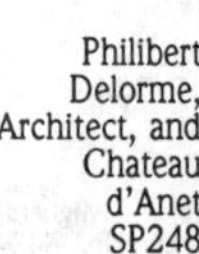

Philibert Delorme, Architect, and Chateau d'Anet SP248

Designs: No. B435, Louis Le Vau (1612-1670), architect, and Vaux-le-Vicomte Chateau, Paris. No. B436, Prosper Merimée (1803-1870), writer, and Carmen. No. B437, Alexandre Dumas (1820-1870), writer, and Three Musketeers. No. B438, Edouard Branly (1844-1940), physicist, electric circuit and convent of the Carmes, Paris. No. B439, Maurice de Broglie (1875-1960), physicist, and X-ray spectrograph.

1970 Engr. *Perf. 13*

B434 SP248 40c + 10c slate grn	42	42
B435 SP248 40c + 10c dk carmine	42	42
B436 SP248 40c + 10c Prus blue	42	42
B437 SP248 40c + 10c violet bl	42	42
B438 SP248 40c + 10c dp brown	42	42
B439 SP248 40c + 10c dk gray	42	42
Nos. B434-B439 (6)	2.52	2.52

The surtax was for the Red Cross.
Issue dates: No. B434-B436, Feb. 14; Nos. B437-B439, Apr. 11.

City Mailman, 1830 — SP249

"Life and Death" — SP250

1970, Mar. 14

B440 SP249 40c + 10c blk, ultra & dk car rose	30	30

Issued for Stamp Day.
For surcharge see Reunion No. B33.

1970, Apr. 4

B441 SP250 40c + 10c brt bl, ol & car rose	25	25

Issued to publicize the fight against cancer in connection with Health Day, Apr. 7.

Marshal de Lattre de Tassigny — SP251

1970, May 8 Engr. *Perf. 13*

B442 SP251 40c + 10c sl & vio bl	50	28

25th anniv. of the entry into Berlin of French troops under Marshal Jean de Lattre de Tassigny, May 8, 1945.

Lord and Lady, Dissay Chapel Fresco — SP252

Design: No. B444, Angel holding whips, from fresco in Dissay Castle Chapel, Vienne, c. 1500.

1970, Dec. 12 Engr. *Perf. 13*

Cross in Carmine

B443 SP252 40c + 15c green	55	45
a. Bklt. pane, 4 each, gutter btwn.	5.00	
B444 SP252 40c + 15c copper red	55	45

The surtax was for the Red Cross.
For surcharges see Reunion Nos. B34-B35.

Daniel-Francois Auber and "Fra Diavolo" Music — SP253

Designs: No. B446, Gen. Charles Diego Brosset (1898-1944), and Basilica of Fourvière. No. B447, Victor Grignard (1871-1935), chemist, and Nobel Prize medal. No. B448, Henri Farman (1874-1958) and plane. No. B449, Gen. Charles Georges Delestraint (1879-1945) and scroll. No. B450, Jean Eugène Robert-Houdin (1805-1871) and magician's act.

1971 Engr. *Perf. 13*

B445 SP253 50c + 10c brn vio & brn	75	60
B446 SP253 50c + 10c dk sl grn & ol gray	75	60
B447 SP253 50c + 10c brn red & olive	75	60
B448 SP253 50c + 10c vio bl & vio	75	60
B449 SP253 50c + 10c pur & cl	85	75
B450 SP253 50c + 10c sl grn & bl grn	85	75
Nos. B445-B450 (6)	4.70	3.90

The surtax was for the Red Cross.
Issue dates: Nos. B445-B446, Mar. 6. No. B447, May 8. No. B448, May 29. Nos. B449-B450, Oct. 16.

Army Post Office, 1914-1918 SP254

1971, Mar. 27 Engr. *Perf. 13*

B451 SP254 50c + 10c ol, brn & bl	35	28

Stamp Day, 1971.
For surcharge see Reunion No. B36.

Girl with Dog, by Greuze SP255

Aristide Bergès (1833-1904) SP256

Design: 50c+10c, "The Dead Bird," by Jean-Baptiste Greuze (1725-1805).

1971, Dec. 11

Cross in Carmine

B452 SP255 30c + 10c violet bl	55	55
a. Bklt. pane, 4 each, gutter btwn.	5.25	
B453 SP255 50c + 10c dp carmine	55	55

The surtax was for the Red Cross.
For surcharges see Reunion Nos. B37-B38.

1972 Engr. *Perf. 13*

Portraits: No. B455, Paul de Chomedey (1612-1676), founder of Montreal, and arms of Neuville-sur-Vanne. No. B456, Edouard Belin (1876-1963), inventor. No. B457, Louis Blériot (1872-1936), aviation pioneer. No. B458, Adm. Franois Joseph, Count de Grasse (1722-1788), hero of the American Revolution. No. B459, Théophile Gautier (1811-1872), writer.

B454 SP256 50c + 10c black & green	75	75
B455 SP256 50c + 10c black & blue	75	75
B456 SP256 50c + 10c blk & lil rose	75	75
B457 SP256 50c + 10c red & black	75	75
B458 SP256 50c + 10c orange & black	1.00	1.00
B459 SP256 50c + 10c black & brown	1.00	1.00
Nos. B454-B459 (6)	5.00	5.00

The surtax was for the Red Cross.
Issue dates: Nos. B454-B455, Feb. 19; No. B456, June 24; No. B457, July 1; Nos. B458-B459, Sept. 9.

Rural Mailman, 1894 SP257

Nicolas Desgenettes SP258

1972, Mar. 18 Engr. *Perf. 13*

B460 SP257 50c + 10c bl, yel & ol gray	75	35

Stamp Day 1972.
For surcharge see Reunion No. B39.

1972, Dec. 16 Engr. *Perf. 13*

Designs: 30c+10c, René Nicolas Dufriche, Baron Desgenettes, M.D. (1762-1837). 50c+10c, Franois Joseph Broussais, M.D. (1772-1838).

B461 SP258 30c + 10c sl grn & red	65	48
a. Bkit. pane, 4 each, gutter btwn.	5.50	
B462 SP258 50c + 10c red	65	48

The surtax was for the Red Cross.
For surcharges see Reunion Nos. B40-B41.

Gaspard de Coligny — SP259

Portraits: No. B463, Gaspard de Coligny (1519-1572), admiral and Huguenot leader. No. B464, Ernest Renan (1823-1892), philologist and historian. No. B465, Alberto Santos Dumont (1873-1932), Brazilian aviator. No. B466, Gabrielle-Sidonie Colette (1873-1954), writer. No. B467, René Duguay-Trouin (1673-1736), naval commander. No. B468, Louis Pasteur (1822-1895), chemist, bacteriologist. No. B469, Tony Garnier (1869-1948), architect.

1973 Engr. *Perf. 13*

B463 SP259 50c + 10c multi	85	60
B464 SP259 50c + 10c multi	85	60
B465 SP259 50c + 10c multi	85	60
B466 SP259 50c + 10c multi	85	60
B467 SP259 50c + 10c multi	85	60
B468 SP259 50c + 10c multi	85	65
B469 SP259 50c + 10c multi	85	65
Nos. B463-B469 (7)	5.95	4.30

Issue dates: No. B463, Feb. 17; No. B464, Apr. 28; No. B465, May 26; No. B466, June 2; No. B467, June 9; No. B468, Oct. 6; No. B469, Nov. 17.

Mail Coach, 1835 SP260

1973, Mar. 24 Engr. *Perf. 13*

B470 SP260 50c + 10c grnsh blue	35	30

Stamp Day, 1973.
For surcharge see Reunion No. B42.

Mary Magdalene SP261

St. Louis-Marie de Montfort SP262

Design: 50c+10c, Mourning woman. Designs are from 15th century Tomb of Tonnerre.

1973, Dec. 1

B471 SP261 30c + 10c sl grn & red	35	35
a. Bklt. pane, 4 each, gutter btwn.	3.50	
B472 SP261 50c + 10c dk gray & red	45	45

Surtax was for the Red Cross.
For surcharges see Reunion Nos. B43-B44.

1974, Feb. 23 Engr. *Perf. 13*

Portraits: No. B474, Francis Poulenc (1899-1963), composer. No. B475, Jules Barbey d'Aurevilly (1808-1889), writer. No. B476, Jean Giraudoux (1882-1944), writer.

B473 SP262 50c + 10c multi	1.10	1.10
B474 SP262 50c + 10c multi	70	70
B475 SP262 80c + 15c multi	80	80
B476 SP262 80c + 15c multi	80	80

Issue dates: No. B473, Mar. 9; No. B474, July 20; Nos. B475-B476, Nov. 16.

Automatically Sorted Letters — SP263

1974, Mar. 9 Engr. *Perf. 13*

B477 SP263 50c + 10c multi	25	20

Stamp Day 1974. Automatic letter sorting center, Orleans-la-Source, opened Jan. 30, 1973.
For surcharge see Reunion No. B45.

Order of Liberation and 5 Honored Cities — SP264

1974, June 15 Engr. *Perf. 13*

B478 SP264 1fr + 10c multi	55	30

30th anniv. of liberation from the Nazis.

"Summer"
SP265

"Winter"
SP266

Designs: B481, "Spring" (girl on swing). B482, "Fall" (umbrella and rabbits).

1974, Nov. 30 Engr. *Perf. 13*

B479	SP265	60c + 15c multi	48	35
a.		Bklt. pane, 4 each, gutter btwn.	3.75	
B480	SP266	80c + 15c multi	52	45

For surcharges see Reunion Nos. B46-B46.

1975, Nov. 29

B481	SP265	60c + 15c multi	40	28
a.		Bklt. pane, 4 each, gutter btwn.	4.25	
B482	SP266	80c + 20c multi	60	45

Surtax was for the Red Cross.

Dr. Albert Schweitzer
SP267

Edmond Michelet
SP268

André Siegfried and Map — SP269

Portraits: No. B483, Albert Schweitzer (1875-1965), medical missionary, birth centenary. No. B484, Edmond Michelet (1899-1970), Resistance hero, statesman. No. B485, Robert Schuman (1886-1963), promoter of United Europe. No. B486, Eugene Thomas (1903-1969), minister of PTT. No. B487, André Siegfried (1875-1959), political science professor, writer, birth centenary.

1975 Engr. *Perf. 13*

B483	SP267	80c + 20c multi	38	38
B484	SP268	80c + 20c blue & ind	38	38
B485	SP268	80c + 20c black & ind	38	38
B486	SP268	80c + 20c black & sl	38	38
B487	SP269	80c + 20c black & bl	45	45
		Nos. B483-B487 (5)	1.97	1.97

Issue dates: No. B483, Jan. 11; No. B484, Feb. 22; No. B485, May 10; No. B486, June 28; No. B487, Nov. 15.

Second Republic Mailman's Badge — SP270

1975, Mar. 8 Photo.

B488	SP270	80c + 20c multi	35	32

Stamp Day.

"Sage" Type of 1876
SP271

Marshal A. J. de Moncey
SP272

1976, Mar. 13 Engr. *Perf. 13*

B489	SP271	80c + 20c black & lilac	35	30

Stamp Day 1976.

1976 Engr. *Perf. 13*

Designs: No. B491, Max Jacob (1876-1944), Dadaist writer, by Picasso. No. B492, Jean Mounet-Sully (1841-1916), actor. No. B493, Gen. Pierre Daumesnil (1776-1832). No. B494, Eugène Fromentin (1820-1876), painter.

B490	SP272	80c + 20c multi	42	42
B491	SP272	80c + 20c red brn & ol	42	42
B492	SP272	80c + 20c multi	42	42
B493	SP272	1fr + 20c multi	48	48
B494	SP272	1fr + 20c multi	48	48
		Nos. B490-B494 (5)	2.22	2.22

Issue dates: No. B490, May 22; No. B491, July 22. No. B492, Aug. 28; No. B493, Sept. 4; No. B494, Sept. 25.

Anna de Noailles — SP273

St. Barbara — SP274

1976, Nov. 6 Engr. *Perf. 13*

B495	SP273	1fr + 20c multi	50	50

Anna de Noailles (1876-1933), writer & poet.

1976, Nov. 20

Design: 1fr+25c, Cimmerian Sibyl. Sculptures from Brou Cathedral.

Cross in Carmine

B496	SP274	80c + 20c violet	50	40
a.		Bklt. pane, 4 each, gutter btwn.	5.00	
B497	SP274	1fr + 25c dk brown	60	48

Surtax was for the Red Cross.

Marckolsheim Relay Station Sign — SP275

1977, Mar. 26 Engr. *Perf. 13*

B498	SP275	1fr + 20c multi	40	40

Stamp Day.

Edouard Herriot, Statesman and Writer
SP276

Christmas Figurine, Provence
SP277

Designs: No. B500, Abbé Breuil (1877-1961), archaeologist. No. B501, Guillaume de Machault (1305-1377), poet and composer. No. B502, Charles Cross (1842-1888).

1977 Engr. *Perf. 13*

B499	SP276	1fr + 20c multi	50	50
B500	SP276	1fr + 20c multi	50	50
B501	SP276	1fr + 20c multi	50	50
B502	SP276	1fr + 20c multi	50	50

Issue dates: #B499, Oct. 8; #B500, Oct. 15; #B501, Nov. 12; #B502, Dec. 3.

1977, Nov. 26

Design: 1fr+25c, Christmas figurine (woman), Provence.

B503	SP277	80c + 20c red & ind	45	45
a.		Bklt. pane, 4 each, gutter between	4.50	
B504	SP277	1fr + 25c red & sl grn	55	55

Surtax was for the Red Cross.

Marie Noel, Writer — SP278

Mail Collection, 1900 — SP279

Designs: No. B506, Georges Bernanos (1888-1948), writer. No. B507, Leo Tolstoi (1828-1910), Russian writer. No. B508, Charles Marie Leconte de Lisle (1818-1894), poet. No. B509, Voltaire (1694-1778) and Jean Jacques Rousseau (1712-1778). No. B510, Claude Bernard (1813-1878), physiologist.

1978 Engr. *Perf. 13*

B505	SP278	1fr + 20c multi	55	55
B506	SP278	1fr + 20c multi	55	55
B507	SP278	1fr + 20c multi	55	55
B508	SP278	1fr + 20c multi	55	55
B509	SP278	1fr + 20c multi	55	55
B510	SP278	1fr + 20c multi	55	55
		Nos. B505-B510 (6)	3.30	3.30

Issue dates: No. B505, Feb. 11; No. B506, Feb. 18; No. B507, Apr. 15; No. B508, Mar. 26; No. B509, July 1; No. B510, Sept. 16.

1978, Apr. 8 Engr. *Perf. 13*

B511	SP279	1fr + 20c multi	40	35

Stamp Day 1978.

SP280

SP281

Designs: 1fr+25c, The Hare and the Tortoise. 1.20fr+30c, The City Mouse and the Country Mouse.

1978, Dec. 2 Engr. *Perf. 13*

B512	SP280	1fr + 25c multi	55	35
a.		Bklt. pane, 4 each, gutter btwn.	4.50	
B513	SP280	1.20fr + 30c multi	70	45

Surtax was for the Red Cross.

1979 Engr. *Perf. 13*

Designs: No. B514, Ladislas Marshal de Berchény (1689-1778). No. B515, Leon Jouhaux (1879-1954), labor leader. No. B516, Peter Abelard (1079-1142), theologian and writer. No. B517, Georges Courteline (1860-1929), humorist. No. B518, Simone Weil (1909-1943), social philosopher. No. B519, André Malraux (1901-1976), novelist.

B514	SP281	1.20fr + 30c multi	55	55
B515	SP281	1.20fr + 30c multi	60	60
B516	SP281	1.20fr + 30c multi	55	55
B517	SP281	1.20fr + 30c multi	55	55
B518	SP281	1.30fr + 30c multi	60	60
B519	SP281	1.30fr + 30c multi	60	60
		Nos. B514-B519 (6)	3.45	3.45

Issue dates: Nos. B514, Jan. 13; B515, May 12; B516, June 9; B517, June 25; B518, Nov. 12; B519, Nov. 26.

General Post Office, from 1908 Post Card
SP282

1979, Mar. 10 Engr. *Perf. 13*

B520	SP282	1.20fr + 30c multi	48	34

Stamp Day 1979.

Woman, Stained-Glass Window — SP283

Stained-glass windows, Church of St. Joan of Arc, Rouen: 1.30fr+30c, Simon the Magician.

1979, Dec. 1

B521	SP283	1.10fr + 30c multi	50	40
a.		Bklt. pane, 4 each, gutter btwn.	4.75	
B522	SP283	1.30fr + 30c multi	60	42

Surtax was for the Red Cross.

Eugene Viollet le Duc (1814-1879), Architect
SP284

Jean-Marie de Le Mennais (1780-1860), Priest and Educator — SP285

Designs No. B524, Jean Monnet (1888-1979), economist and diplomat. No. B526, Frederic Mistral (1830-1914), poet. No. B527, Saint-John Perse (Alexis Leger, 1887-1975), poet and diplomat. No. B528, Pierre Paul de Riquet (1604-1680), canal builder.

1980 Engr. *Perf. 13*

B523	SP284	1.30fr + 30c multi	60	60
B524	SP285	1.30fr + 30c multi	70	70
B525	SP285	1.40fr + 30c blue	70	70
B526	SP285	1.40fr + 30c black	70	70
B527	SP285	1.40fr + 30c multi	70	70
B528	SP284	1.40fr + 30c multi	70	70
		Nos. B523-B528 (6)	4.10	4.10

Issue dates: No. B523, Feb. 16; No. B524, Nos. B525-B526, Sept. 6; Nos. B527-B528, Oct. 11.

The Letter to Melie, by Avati, Stamp Day, 1980 — SP286

1980, Mar. 8 **Photo.**

B529 SP286 1.30fr + 30c multi 60 42

Filling the Granaries, Choir Stall Detail, Amiens Cathedral — SP287

Design: 1.40fr+30c, Grapes from the Promised Land.

1980, Dec. 6 **Engr.** ***Perf. 13***

B530 SP287 1.20fr + 30c red & dk red brn 65 35
B531 SP287 1.40fr + 30c red & dk red brn 60 42
a. Bklt. pane, 4 each, gutter btwn. 5.00

Sister Anne-Marie Javouhey (1779-1851), Founded Congregation of St. Joseph of Cluny SP288

Designs: No. B532, Louis Armand (1905-1971), railway engineer. B533, Louis Jouvet (1887-1951), theater director. B534, Marc Boegner (1881-1970), peace worker. No. B536, Jacques Offenbach (1819-1880), composer. No. B537, Pierre Teilhard de Chardin (1881-1955), philosopher.
Nos. B532-B533, B537 vert.

1981 **Engr.** ***Perf. 13***

B532 SP288 1.20 + 30c multi 55 55
B533 SP288 1.20 + 30c multi 55 55
B534 SP288 1.40 + 30c multi 85 60
B535 SP288 1.40 + 30c multi 65 60
B536 SP288 1.40 + 30c multi 65 60
B537 SP288 1.40 + 30c multi 65 60
Nos. B532-B537 (6) 3.90 3.50

Issue dates: #B532, May 23; #B533, June 13; #B534, Nov. 14; #B535, Feb. 7; #B536, Feb. 14; #B537, May 23.

The Love Letter, by Goya — SP289

1981, Mar. 7 ***Perf. 13x12½***

B538 SP289 1.40 + 30c multi 1.00 32

Stamp Day 1981.

Scourges of the Passion SP290

Guillaume Postel (1510-1581), Theologian SP291

Stained-glass Windows, Church of the Sacred Heart, Audincourt: 1.60fr+30c, "Peace."

1981, Dec. 5 **Photo.** ***Perf. 13***

B539 SP290 1.40 + 30c multi 65 42
B540 SP290 1.60 + 30c multi 70 45
a. Bklt. pane, 4 each, gutter between 5.50

1982 **Engr.** ***Perf. 13***

Designs: No. B542, Henri Mondor (1885-1962), physician. No. B543, Andre Chantemesse (1851-1919), Scientist. No. B544, Louis Pergaud (1882-1915), writer. No. B545, Robert Debre (1882-1978), writer. No. B546, Gustave Eiffel (1832-1923), engineer.

B541 SP291 1.40 + 30c multi 60 48
B542 SP291 1.40 + 30c dk brn & dk bl 48 40
B543 SP291 1.60 + 30c multi 55 52
B544 SP291 1.60 + 40c multi 70 48
B545 SP291 1.60 + 40c dk blue 60 48
B546 SP291 1.80 + 40c sepia 60 60
Nos. B541-B546 (6) 3.53 2.96

Woman Reading, by Picasso — SP292

1982, Mar. 27 ***Perf. 13x12½***

B547 SP292 1.60 + 40c multi 80 42

Stamp Day.

SP293

SP294

Jules Verne books: 1.60fr+30c, Five Weeks in a Balloon. 1.80fr+40c, 20,000 Leagues under the Sea.

1982, Nov. 20 ***Perf. 13***

B548 SP293 1.60 + 30c multi 60 52
B549 SP293 1.80 + 40c multi 60 52
a. Bklt. pane, 4 each, gutter btwn. 4.25

Surtax was for Red Cross.

1983 **Engr.** ***Perf. 12½x13***

Designs: No. B550, Andre Messager (1853-1929). No. B551, J.A. Gabriel (1698-1782), architect. No. B552, Hector Berlioz (1803-1869), composer. No. B553, Max Fouchet (1913-1980). No. B554, Rene Cassin (1887-1976). No. B555, Stendhal (Marie Henri Beyle, 1783-1842).

B550 SP294 1.60 + 30c multi 65 65
B551 SP294 1.60 + 30c multi 65 65
B552 SP294 1.80 + 40c dp lil & blk 75 75
B553 SP294 1.80 + 40c multi 75 75
B554 SP294 2fr + 40c multi 80 80
B555 SP294 2fr + 40c multi 80 80
Nos. B550-B555 (6) 4.40 4.40

Issue dates: No. B550, Jan. 15; No. B551, Apr. 16; No. B552, Jan. 22; No. B553, Apr. 30; No. B554, June 25; No. B555, Nov. 12.

Man Dictating a Letter, by Rembrandt — SP295

Perf. 13X12½

1983, Feb. 26 **Photo. & Engr.**

B556 SP295 1.80 + 40c multi 65 35

Stamp Day.

Virgin with Child, Baillon, 14th Cent. — SP296

Design: No. B558, Virgin with Child, Genainville, 16th Cent.

1983, Nov. 26 **Engr.** ***Perf. 13***

B557 SP296 1.60 + 40c shown 65 45
B558 SP296 2fr + 40c multi 85 55
a. Bklt. pane, 4 each, gutter btwn. 6.50

Emile Littre (1801-1881), Physician SP297

Designs: No. B560, Jean Zay (1904-44). No. B561, Pierre Corneille (1606-1684). No. B562, Gaston Bachelard (1884-1962). No. B563, Jean Paulhan (1884-1968). No. B564, Evariste Galois (1811-1832).

1984 **Engr.** ***Perf. 13***

B559 SP297 1.60fr + 40c plum & blk 85 85
B560 SP297 1.60fr + 40c dk grn & blk 85 85
B561 SP297 1.70fr + 40c dp vio & blk 65 65
B562 SP297 2fr + 40c gray & blk 70 70
B563 SP297 2.10fr + 40c dk brn & blk 70 70
B564 SP297 2.10fr + 40c ultra & blk 70 70
Nos. B559-B564 (6) 4.45 4.45

SP298 SP299

Diderot Holding a Letter, by L.M. Van Loo.

1984, Mar. 17 **Engr.** ***Perf. 12½x13***

B565 SP298 2fr + 40c multi 75 35

1984, Nov. 24 **Photo.** ***Perf. 12½x13***

The Rose Basket, by Caly.

B566 SP299 2.10fr + 50c pnksh (basket) & multi 38 38
a. Salmon (basket) & multi, perf. 13½x13 38 38
b. As "a," bklt. pane of 10 + 2 labels 4.00

Surtax was for the Red Cross.

Jules Romains (1885-1972) SP300

Authors: No. B568, Jean-Paul Sartre (1905-1980). No. B569, Romain Rolland (1866-1944). No. B570, Roland Dorgeles (1885-1973). No. B571, Victor Hugo (1802-1885). No. B572, Francois Mauriac (1885-1970).

1985, Feb. 23 **Engr.** ***Perf. 13***

B567 SP300 1.70fr + 40c *2.50 2.50*
B568 SP300 1.70fr + 40c *2.50 2.50*
B569 SP300 1.70fr + 40c *2.50 2.50*
B570 SP300 2.10fr + 50c *3.00 3.00*
B571 SP300 2.10fr + 50c *3.00 3.00*
B572 SP300 2.10fr + 50c *3.00 3.00*
a. Bklt. pane, 1 each + 2 labels, perf. 15x14½
Nos. B567-B572 (6) *16.50 16.50*

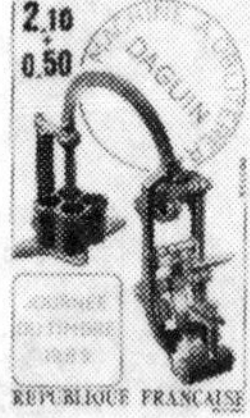

SP301

SP302

Stamp Day: Canceling apparatus invented by Eugene Daguin (1849-1888).

1985, Mar. 16 **Engr.** ***Perf. 12½x13***

B573 SP301 2.10fr + 50c brn blk & bluish gray 85 85

1985, Nov. 23 **Photo.**

Issenheim Altarpiece retable.

B574 SP302 2.20fr + 50c multi 85 85
a. As "b," bklt. pane of 10 8.50
b. Perf. 13½x13 85 85

Surtax for the Red Cross.

SP303

SP304

Famous men: No. B575, Francois Arago (1786-1853), physician, politician. No. B576, Henri Moissan (1852-1907), chemist. No. B577, Henri Fabre (1882-1984), engineer. No. B578, Marc Seguin (1786-1875), engineer. No. B579, Paul Heroult (1863-1914), chemist.

1986, Feb. 22 **Engr.** ***Perf. 13***

B575 SP303 1.80fr + 40c multi 95 95
B576 SP303 1.80fr + 40c multi 95 95
B577 SP303 1.80fr + 40c multi 95 95
B578 SP303 2.20fr + 50c multi 1.10 1.10
B579 SP303 2.20fr + 50c multi 1.10 1.10
a. Bklt. pane of 5, #B575-B579, + 3 labels 6.00
Nos. B575-B579 (5) 5.05 5.05

1986, Mar. 1 **Engr.** ***Perf. 13x12½***

B580 SP304 2.20fr + 50c brn blk *6.00 6.00*

Pierre Cot (1895-1977).

Mail Britzska SP305

1986, Apr. 5 *Perf. 13*
B581 SP305 2.20fr + 60c pale tan & dk vio brn 85 85

Booklet Stamp

B582 SP305 2.20fr + 60c buff & blk 85 85
a. Bklt. pane of 6 + label 6.00

Stamp Day. See Nos. B590-B591, B599-B600, B608-B609.

Stained Glass Window (detail), by Vieira da Silva, St. Jacques of Reims Church, Marne — SP306

1986, Nov. 24 Photo. *Perf. 12½x13*
B583 SP306 2.20fr + 60c multi 95 95
a. As "b," bklt. pane of 10 9.50
b. Perf. 13½x13 95 95

Surtaxed to benefit the natl. Red Cross.

Physicians and Biologists SP307

Designs: No. B584, Charles Richet (1850-1935). No. B585, Eugene Jamot (1879-1937). No. B586, Bernard Halpern (1904-1978). No. B587, Alexandre Yersin (1863-1943). No. B588, Jean Rostand (1894-1977). No. B589, Jacques Monod (1910-1976).

1987, Feb. 21 Engr. *Perf. 13*
B584 SP307 1.90fr + 50c deep ultra 95 95
B585 SP307 1.90fr + 50c dull lilac 95 95
B586 SP307 1.90fr + 50c grnish gray 95 95
B587 SP307 2.20fr + 50c grnish gray 1.10 1.10
B588 SP307 2.20fr + 50c deep ultra 1.10 1.10
B589 SP307 2.20fr + 50c dull lilac 1.10 1.10
a. Bklt. pane of 6, #B584-B589
Nos. B584-B589 (6) 6.15 6.15

Stamp Day Type of 1986

Stamp Day 1987: Berline carriage.

1987, Mar. 14 **Engr.**
B590 SP305 2.20fr + 60c buff & sepia 95 95

Booklet Stamp

B591 SP305 2.20fr + 60c pale & dk bl 95 95
a. Bklt. pane of 6 + 2 labels 5.75

Flight Into Egypt, Retable by Melchior Bruederlam, Charterhouse at Champmol — SP308

1987, Nov. 21 Photo. *Perf. 12½x13*
B592 SP306 2.20fr +60c multi 95 95
a. As "b," bklt. pane of 10 + 2 labels 9.50
b. Perf. 13½x13 95 95

Surtaxed to benefit the Red Cross.

Explorers SP309

Profiles and maps: No. B593, Marquis Abraham Duquesne (1610-1688), naval commander. No. B594, Pierre Andre de Suffren (1729-1788). No. B595, Jean-Francois de La Perouse (1741-1788). No. B596, Mahe de La Bourdonnais (1699-1753). No. B597, Louis-Antoine de Bougainville (1729-1811). No. B598, Jules Dumont d'Urville (1790-1842).

1988, Feb. 20 Engr. *Perf. 13*
B593 SP309 2fr + 50c multi 80 80
B594 SP309 2fr + 50c multi 80 80
B595 SP309 2fr + 50c multi 80 80
B596 SP309 2.20fr + 50c multi 85 85
B597 SP309 2.20fr + 50c multi 85 85
B598 SP309 2.20fr + 50c multi 85 85
a. Bklt. pane of 6, #B593-B598 5.00
Nos. B593-B598 (6) 4.95 4.95

Stamp Day Type of 1986

Stamp Day 1988: Postal coach.

1988, Mar. 29 **Engr.**
B599 SP305 2.20fr +60c dk lilac 1.00 1.00

Booklet Stamp

B600 SP305 2.20fr +60c sepia 1.00 1.00
a. Bklt. pane of 6 + 2 labels 6.00

Intl. Red Cross, 125th Anniv. — SP310

1988, Nov. 19 Engr. *Perf. 12½x13*
B601 SP310 2.20fr +60c multi 1.00 1.00
a. As "b," bklt. pane of 10+2 labels 10.00
b. Perf. 13½x13 1.00 1.00

Revolution Leaders and Heroes SP311

Designs: No. B602, Emmanuel Joseph Sieyes (1748-1836). No. B603, Honore Gabriel Riqueti, Comte de Mirabeau (1749-91). No. B604, Louis Marie de Noailles (1756-1804). No. B605, Lafayette. No. B606, Antoine Pierre Joseph Marie Barnave (1761-93). No. B607, Jean Baptiste Drouet (1763-1824).

1989, Feb. 25 Engr. *Perf. 13*
B602 SP311 2.20fr +50c multi 90 90
B603 SP311 2.20fr +50c multi 90 90
B604 SP311 2.20fr +50c multi 90 90
B605 SP311 2.20fr +50c multi 90 90
B606 SP311 2.20fr +50c multi 90 90
B607 SP311 2.20fr +50c multi 90 90
a. Bklt. pane, 1 each + 2 labels 5.75
Nos. B602-B607 (6) 5.40 5.40

French Revolution, bicent.

Stamp Day Type of 1986

Design: Paris-Lyon stagecoach.

1989, Apr. 15 Engr. *Perf. 13*
B608 SP305 2.20fr +60c pale bl & dk bl 95 95

Booklet Stamp

B609 SP305 2.20fr +60c pale lil & pur 95 95
a. Bklt. pane of 6 + 2 labels 5.75

Stamp Day 1989.

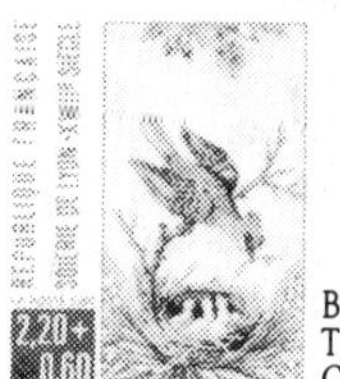

Bird From a Silk Tapestry, Lyon, 18th Cent. — SP312

1989, Nov. 18 Photo. *Perf. 12½x13*
B610 SP312 2.20fr +60c multi 90 90
a. As "b," bklt. pane of 10 9.00
b. Perf. 13½x13 90 90

Surtax for the natl. Red Cross.

1992 Winter Olympics, Albertville SP313

1990, Feb. 9 Engr. *Perf. 13*
B611 SP313 2.30fr +20c red, bl & blk 85 85

See Nos. B621-B627, B636-B637, B639.

Stamp Day — SP314

1990, Mar. 17 **Photo.**
B612 SP314 2.30fr +60c ultra, bl & brt yel 1.00 1.00

Booklet Stamp

B613 SP314 2.30fr +60c ultra, grn, yel & brt grn 1.00 1.00
a. Bklt. pane of 6 + 2 labels 6.25

SP315 SP316

Quimper or Brittany Ware Faience plate.

1990, May 5 Photo. *Perf. 12½x13*
B614 SP315 2.30fr +60c multi 1.00 1.00
a. As "b," bklt. pane of 10+2 labels 10.00
b. Perf. 13½x13 1.00 1.00

Surcharge benefited the Red Cross.

1990, June 16 Photo. *Perf. 13*

Designs: No. B615, Aristide Bruant. No. B616, Maurice Chevalier. No. B617, Tino Rossi. No. B618, Edith Piaf. No. B619, Jacques Brel. No. B620, Georges Brassens.

B615 SP316 2.30fr +50c multi 1.00 1.00
B616 SP316 2.30fr +50c multi 1.00 1.00
B617 SP316 2.30fr +50c multi 1.00 1.00
B618 SP316 2.30fr +50c multi 1.00 1.00
B619 SP316 2.30fr +50c multi 1.00 1.00
B620 SP316 2.30fr +50c multi 1.00 1.00
a. Bklt. pane, 1 each +2 labels 6.00
Nos. B615-B620 (6) 6.00 6.00

Albertville Olympic Type

Designs: No. B621, Ski jumping. No. B622, Speed skating. No. B623, Slalom skiing. No. B624, Cross-country skiing. No. B625, Ice hockey. No. B626, Luge. No. B627, Curling.

1990-91 Engr. *Perf. 13*
B621 SP313 2.30fr +20c multi 95 95
B622 SP313 2.30fr +20c multi 95 95
B623 SP313 2.30fr +20c multi 95 95
B624 SP313 2.30fr +20c multi 95 95
B625 SP313 2.30fr +20c multi 95 95
B626 SP313 2.50fr +20c multi 1.05 1.05
B627 SP313 2.50fr +20c multi 1.05 1.05
Nos. B621-B627 (7) 6.85 6.85

Issue dates: No. B621, Dec. 22. No. B622, Dec. 29. No. B623, Jan. 19, 1991. No. B624, Feb. 2, 1991. No. B625, Feb. 9, 1991. No. B626, Mar. 2, 1991. No. B627, Apr. 20, 1991.
No. B624 inscribed "La Poste 1992."

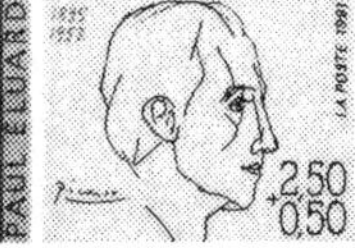

Paul Eluard (1895-1952) SP317

Poets: No. B629, Andre Breton (1896-1966). No. B630, Louis Aragon (1897-1982). No. B631, Francis Ponge (1899-1988). No. B632, Jacques Prevert (1900-1977). No. B633, Rene Char (1907-1988).

1991, Feb. 23 Engr. *Perf. 12½x13*
B628 SP317 2.50fr +50c multi 1.15 1.15
B629 SP317 2.50fr +50c multi 1.15 1.15
B630 SP317 2.50fr +50c multi 1.15 1.15
B631 SP317 2.50fr +50c multi 1.15 1.15
B632 SP317 2.50fr +50c multi 1.15 1.15
B633 SP317 2.50fr +50c multi 1.15 1.15
a. Bklt. pane, 1 each +2 labels, perf. 13 6.90 6.90
Nos. B628-B633 (6) 6.90 6.90

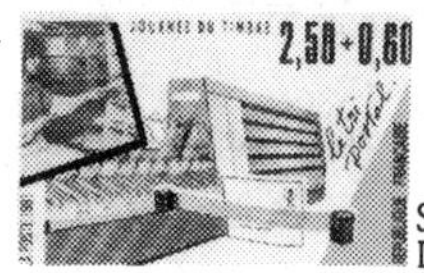

Stamp Day — SP318

1991, Mar. 16 Photo. *Perf. 13*
B634 SP318 2.50fr +60c blue machine 1.25 1.25
B635 SP318 2.50fr +60c purple machine 1.25 1.25
a. Bklt. pane of 6 + 2 labels 7.50

Winter Olympics Type of 1990

Designs: No. B636, Acrobatic skiing. No. B637, Alpine skiing.

1991 Engr. *Perf. 13*
B636 SP313 2.50fr +20c multi 95 95
B637 SP313 2.50fr +20c multi 95 95

Issue dates: #B636, Aug. 3. #B637, Aug. 17. Nos. B636-B637 inscribed "La Poste 1992."

The Harbor of Toulon by Francois Nardi — SP319

1991, Dec. 2 Photo. *Perf. 13x12½*
B638 SP319 2.50fr +60c multi 1.15 1.15
a. Perf. 13x13½ 1.15 1.15
b. As "a," bklt. pane of 10 + 2 labels 11.50

Surtax for the Red Cross.

Winter Olympics Type of 1990
Miniature Sheet

Designs: a, like #B611. b, like #B621. c, like #B622. d, like #B623. e, like #B624. f, like #B625.

1992, Feb. 8 Engr. *Perf. 13*
B639 Sheet of 10 + label 10.00 10.00
a.-f. SP313 2.50fr +20fr multi 1.00 1.00

No. B639 contains one each B626-B627, B636-B637, B639a-B639f. Central label is litho.

Stamp Day — SP320

1992, Mar. 7 Litho. *Perf. 13*
B640 SP320 2.50fr +60c gray people 1.10 1.10

Booklet Stamp

Photo.

B641 SP320 2.50fr +60c red people 1.10 1.10
a. Bklt. pane of 6 + 2 labels 6.60

SP321 SP322

Composers: No. B642, Cesar Franck (1822-1890). No. B643, Erik Satie (1866-1925). No. B644, Florent Schmitt (1870-1958). No. B645, Arthur Honegger (1892-1955). No. B646, Georges Auric (1899-1983). No. B647, Germaine Tailleferre (1892-1983).

1992, Apr. 11 Photo. *Perf. 13*

B642 SP321 2.50fr +50c multi	1.05	1.05
B643 SP321 2.50fr +50c multi	1.05	1.05
B644 SP321 2.50fr +50c multi	1.05	1.05
B645 SP321 2.50fr +50c multi	1.05	1.05
B646 SP321 2.50fr +50c multi	1.05	1.05
B647 SP321 2.50fr +50c multi	1.05	1.05
a. Bklt. pane of 6, #B642-B647	6.30	
Nos. B642-B647 (6)	6.30	6.30

1992, Nov. 28 Photo. *Perf. 13½x13*

B648 SP322 2.50fr +60c multi	1.15	1.15
a. Bklt. pane of 10 + 2 labels	11.50	

Mutual Aid, Strasbourg. Surtax for the Red Cross.

Writers SP323

Designs: No. B649, Guy de Maupassant (1850-1893). No. B650, Alain (Emile Chartier) (1868-1951). No. B651, Jean Cocteau (1889-1963). No. B652, Marcel Pagnol (1895-1974). No. B653, Andre Chamson (1900-1983). No. B654, Marguerite Yourcenar (1903-1987).

1993, Apr. 24 Engr. *Perf. 13*

B649 SP323 2.50fr +50fr multi	1.05	1.05
B650 SP323 2.50fr +50fr multi	1.05	1.05
B651 SP323 2.50fr +50fr multi	1.05	1.05
B652 SP323 2.50fr +50fr multi	1.05	1.05
B653 SP323 2.50fr +50fr multi	1.05	1.05
B654 SP323 2.50fr +50fr multi	1.05	1.05
a. Bklt. pane of 6, #B649-B654 + 2 labels	6.30	6.30
Nos. B649-B654 (6)	6.30	6.30

When Nos. B650-B654 are normally centered, inscriptions at base of the lower panel are not parallel to the perforations at bottom. On all six stamps the lower panel is not centered between the side perforations.

St. Nicolas, Image of Metz — SP324

1993, Nov. 27 Engr. *Perf. 12½x13*

B655 SP324 2.80fr +60c multi	1.10	1.10
a. Perf. 13½x13	1.10	1.10
b. as "a," Bklt. pane of 10 +2 labels	11.50	

Surtax for Red Cross.

AIR POST STAMPS

Nos. 127, 130 Overprinted in Dark Blue or Black

Perf. 14x13½

1927, June 25 Unwmk.

C1 A18 2fr org & bl (DB)	100.00	85.00
C2 A18 5fr dk bl & buff	100.00	85.00
Set, never hinged	450.00	

On sale only at the Intl. Aviation Exhib. at Marseilles, June, 1927. One set could be purchased by each holder of an admission ticket. Excellent counterfeits exist.

Nos. 242, 196 Surcharged

10 FR.

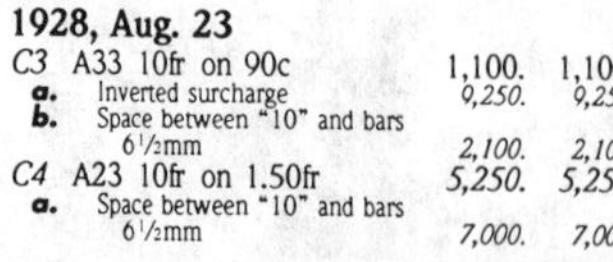

1928, Aug. 23

C3 A33 10fr on 90c	1,100.	1,100.
a. Inverted surcharge	*9,250.*	*9,250.*
b. Space between "10" and bars 6½mm	*2,100.*	*2,100.*
C4 A23 10fr on 1.50fr	*5,250.*	*5,250.*
a. Space between "10" and bars 6½mm	*7,000.*	*7,000.*

Nos. C3-C4 received their surcharge in New York by order of the French consul general. They were for use in paying the 10fr fee for letters leaving the liner Ile de France on a catapulted hydroplane when the ship was one day off the coast of France on its eastward voyage.

The normal space between "10" and bars is 4½mm, but on 10 stamps in each pane of 50 the space is 6½mm. Counterfeits exist.

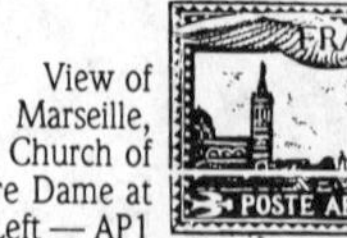

View of Marseille, Church of Notre Dame at Left — AP1

1930-31 Engr. *Perf. 13*

C5 AP1 1.50fr dp car	11.00	1.25
C6 AP1 1.50fr dk bl ('31)	10.50	1.10
a. 1.50fr ultramarine	25.00	7.50
b. With perf. initials "E.I.P.A.30"	250.00	225.00
Set, never hinged	50.00	

No. C6a was sold at the Intl. Air Post Exhib., Paris, Nov. 6-20, 1930, at face value plus 5fr, the price of admission. Most of the stamps of the first printing were perforated "E.I.P.A.30."

Blériot's Monoplane AP2

1934, Sept. 1 *Perf. 13*

C7 AP2 2.25fr violet	11.00	4.00
Never hinged	25.00	

Issued in commemoration of the first flight across the English Channel, by Louis Blériot.

Plane over Paris — AP3

1936

C8 AP3 85c dp green	1.65	65
C9 AP3 1.50fr blue	5.50	2.00
C10 AP3 2.25fr violet	12.50	3.75
C11 AP3 2.50fr rose	20.00	4.50
C12 AP3 3fr ultra	12.50	50
C13 AP3 3.50fr orange brn	45.00	11.50
C14 AP3 50fr emerald	450.00	175.00
a. 50fr deep green	825.00	375.00
Set, never hinged	840.00	
Nos. C8-C14 (7)	547.15	197.90

Monoplane over Paris — AP4

Paper with Red Network Overprint

1936, July 10 *Perf. 12½*

C15 AP4 50fr ultra	375.00	165.00
Never hinged	550.00	

Airplane and Galleon — AP5

Airplane and Globe — AP6

1936, Aug. 17 *Perf. 13*

C16 AP5 1.50fr dk ultra	10.00	1.50
C17 AP6 10fr Prus green	190.00	65.00
Set, never hinged	425.00	

Issued in commemoration of the 100th air mail flight across the South Atlantic.

Catalogue values for unused stamps in this section, from this point to the end of the section, are for Never Hinged items.

Centaur and Plane — AP7

Iris — AP8

Zeus Carrying Hebe — AP9

Chariot of the Sun — AP10

1946-47 Engr. Unwmk.

C18 AP7 40fr dk green	55	20
C19 AP8 50fr rose pink	55	20
C20 AP9 100fr dk blue ('47)	4.75	48
C21 AP10 200fr red	4.00	70

Issue dates: 50fr, 200fr, May 27. 40fr, July 1. 100fr, Jan.

For surcharges see Reunion Nos. C35-C38.

Ile de la Cité, Paris, and Gull AP11

1947, May 7

C22 AP11 500fr dk Prus green	40.00	25.00

UPU 12th Cong., Paris, May 7-July 7.

View of Lille — AP12

Air View of Paris — AP13

Designs: 200fr, Bordeaux. 300fr, Lyon. 500fr, Marseille.

1949-50 Unwmk. *Perf. 13*

C23 AP12 100fr sepia	80	18
C24 AP12 200fr dk blue grn	7.25	50
C25 AP12 300fr purple	16.00	8.25
C26 AP12 500fr brt red	37.50	3.25
C27 AP13 1000fr sep & blk, *bl* ('50)	75.00	16.00
Nos. C23-C27 (5)	136.55	28.18

For surcharges see Reunion Nos. C39-C41.

Alexander III Bridge and Petit Palais, Paris — AP14

1949, June 13

C28 AP14 100fr brown car	6.75	4.75

International Telegraph and Telephone Conference, Paris, May-July 1949.

Jet Plane, Mystère IV — AP15

Planes: 200fr, Noratlas. 500fr, Miles Magister. 1000fr, Provence.

1954, Jan. 16

C29 AP15 100fr red brn & bl	2.25	20
C30 AP15 200fr blk brn & vio bl	8.50	30
C31 AP15 500fr car & org	100.00	1.25
C32 AP15 1000fr vio brn, bl grn & ind	110.00	15.00

See No. C37. For surcharges see Reunion Nos. C42-C45, C48.

Maryse Bastié and Plane — AP16

1955, June 4 Unwmk. *Perf. 13*

C33 AP16 50fr dp plum & rose pink	5.25	3.75

Issued to honor Maryse Bastié, 1898-1952.

Caravelle AP17

Designs: 300fr, Morane Saulnier 760 "Paris." 1000fr, Alouette helicopter.

1957-59 Engr. *Perf. 13*

C34 AP17	300fr sl grn, grnsh bl & sep ('59)	4.25	2.00
C35 AP17	500fr dp ultra & blk	32.50	1.75
C36 AP17	1000fr lil, ol blk & blk ('58)	52.50	20.00

See Nos. C38-C41. For surcharges see Reunion Nos. C46-C47, C49-C51.

Types of 1954-59

Planes: 2fr, Noratlas. 3fr, MS760, Paris. 5fr, Caravelle. 10fr, Alouette helicopter.

1960, Jan. 11

C37 AP15	2fr vio bl & ultra	1.50	15
a.	2fr ultramarine	2.75	15
C38 AP17	3fr sl grn, grnsh bl & sep	1.40	15
C39 AP17	5fr dp ultra & blk	2.25	18
C40 AP17	10fr lil, ol blk & blk	12.50	95

Type of 1957-59

Design: 2fr, Jet plane, Mystère 20.

1965, June 12 Engr. *Perf. 13*

C41 AP17 2fr slate bl & indigo 85 15

Concorde Issue

Common Design Type

1969, Mar. 2 Engr. *Perf. 13*

C42 CD129 1fr indigo & brt bl 1.25 22

Jean Mermoz, Antoine de Saint-Exupéry and Concorde — AP19

1970, Sept. 19 Engr. *Perf. 13*

C43 AP19 20fr blue & indigo 7.50 32

Jean Mermoz (1901-36) and writer Antoine de Saint-Exupéry (1900-44), aviators and air mail pioneers.

Balloon, Gare d'Austerlitz, Paris — AP20

1971, Jan. 16 Engr. *Perf. 13*

C44 AP20 95c bl, vio bl, org & sl grn 1.00 55

Centenary of the balloon post from besieged Paris, 1870-71.

Didier Daurat, Raymond Vanier and Plane Landing at Night — AP21

1971, Apr. 17 Engr. *Perf. 13*

C45 AP21 5fr Prus bl, blk & lt grn 1.40 15

Didier Daurat (1891-1969) and Raymond Vanier (1895-1965), aviation pioneers.
For surcharge see Reunion No. C52.

Hélène Boucher, Maryse Hilsz and Caudron-Renault and Moth-Morane Planes — AP22

Design: 15fr, Henri Guillaumet, Paul Codos, Latécoère 521, Guillaumet's crashed plane in Andes, skyscrapers.

1972-73 Engr. *Perf. 13*

C46 AP22	10fr plum, red & sl	3.00	15
C47 AP22	15fr dp car, gray & brn ('73)	4.50	28

Hélène Boucher (1908-34), Maryse Hilsz (1901-46), Henri Guillaumet (1902-40) and Paul Codos (1896-1960), aviation pioneers.
Issue dates: 10fr, June 10; 15fr, Feb. 24.

Concorde AP23

1976, Jan. 10 Engr. *Perf. 13*

C48 AP23 1.70fr brt bl, red & blk 80 32

First flight of supersonic jet Concorde from Paris to Rio de Janeiro, Jan. 21.

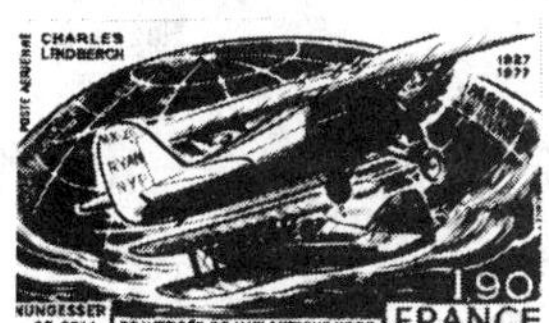

Planes over the Atlantic, New York-Paris — AP24

1977, June 4 Engr. *Perf. 13*

C49 AP24 1.90fr multicolored 80 32

1st transatlantic flight by Lindbergh from NY to Paris, 50th anniv., and 1st attempted westbound flight by French aviators Charles Nungesser and Francois Coli.

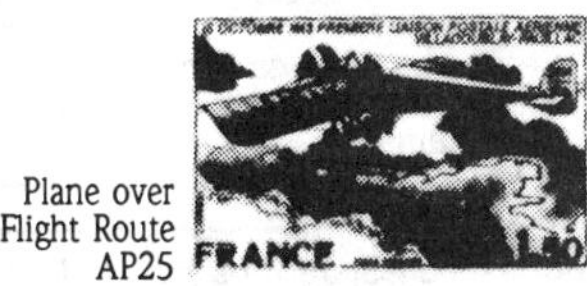

Plane over Flight Route AP25

1978, Oct. 14 Engr. *Perf. 13*

C50 AP25 1.50fr multicolored 1.00 28

75th anniversary of first airmail route from Villacoublay to Pauillac, Gironde.

Rocket, Concorde, Exhibition Hall — AP26

1979, June 9 Engr. *Perf. 13*

C51 AP26 1.70fr ultra, org & brn 90 35

33rd International Aerospace and Space Show, Le Bourget, June 11-15.

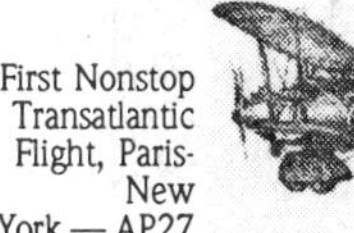

First Nonstop Transatlantic Flight, Paris-New York — AP27

1980, Aug. 30 Engr. *Perf. 13*

C52 AP27 2.50fr vio brn & ultra 75 28

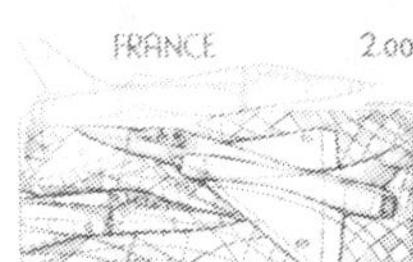

34th Intl. Space and Aeronautics Exhibition, June 5-14 — AP28

1981, June 6 Engr. *Perf. 13*

C53 AP28 2fr multicolored 2.00 35

Dieudonné Costes and Joseph Le Brix and their Breguet Bi-plane — AP29

1981, Sept. 12 Engr.

C54 AP29 10fr dk brown & red 3.00 15

1st So. Atlantic crossing, Oct. 14-15, 1927.

Seaplane Late-300 — AP30

1982, Dec. 4 Engr.

C55 AP30 1.60fr multicolored 75 35

Farman F-60 Goliath — AP31

Planes: 15fr, Farman F-60 Goliath. 20fr, CAMS-53 seaplane. 30fr, Wibault 283 Monoplane. 50fr, Dewoitine 338.

1984-87 Engr.

C56 AP31	15fr dark blue	3.75	34
C57 AP31	20fr dp orange ('85)	5.00	45
C58 AP31	30fr brt violet ('86)	7.50	1.40
C59 AP31	50fr green ('87)	12.50	2.25
	Nos. C55-C59 (5)	29.50	4.79

Issue dates: 15fr, Mar. 3; 20fr, Mar. 2; 30fr, Oct. 11; 50fr, Apr. 11.

AIR POST SEMI-POSTAL STAMPS

Catalogue values for unused stamps in this section are for Never Hinged items.

Antoine de Saint-Exupéry SPAP1

Col. Jean Dagnaux SPAP2

1948 Unwmk. Engr. *Perf. 13*

CB1 SPAP1	50fr + 30fr vio brn	1.75	1.75
CB2 SPAP2	100fr + 70fr dk blue	2.75	2.75

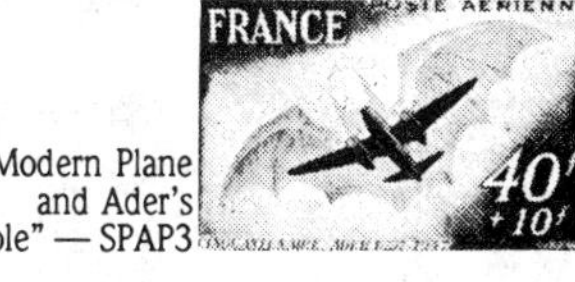

Modern Plane and Ader's "Eole" — SPAP3

1948, Feb.

CB3 SPAP3 40fr + 10fr dk blue 75 60

50th anniv. of the flight of Clément Ader's plane, the Eole, in 1897.

POSTAGE DUE STAMPS

D1

D2

1859-70 Unwmk. Litho. *Imperf.*

J1 D1	10c black	*9,000.*	165.00
J2 D1	15c black ('70)	100.00	180.00

In the lithographed stamps the central bar of the "E" of "CENTIMES" is very short, and the accent on "a" slants at an angle of 30 degree, for the 10c and 17 degree for the 15c, while on the typographed the central bar of the "E" is almost as wide as the top and bottom bars and the accent on the "a" slants at an angle of 47 degree.
No. J2 is known rouletted unofficially.

1859-78 Typo.

J3 D1	10c black	14.00	9.00
J4 D1	15c black ('63)	20.00	11.00
J5 D1	20c black ('77)	*1,800.*	
J6 D1	25c black ('71)	90.00	25.00
J7 D1	30c black ('78)	150.00	75.00
J8 D1	40c blue ('71)	225.00	250.00
a.	40c ultramarine	*4,250.*	*4,750.*
b.	40c Prussian blue	*2,000.*	
J9 D1	60c yellow ('71)	325.00	*950.00*
J10 D1	60c blue ('78)	40.00	65.00
a.	60c dark blue	450.00	525.00
J10B D1	60c black	*2,100.*	

The 20c & 60c black were not put into use.
Nos. J3, J4, J6, J8 and J9 are known rouletted unofficially and Nos. J4, J6, J7 and J10 pin-perf. unofficially.

1882-92 *Perf. 14x13½*

J11 D2	1c black	52	52
J12 D2	2c black	7.75	6.25
J13 D2	3c black	8.50	7.75
J14 D2	4c black	14.00	9.75
J15 D2	5c black	30.00	7.75
J16 D2	10c black	27.50	1.00
J17 D2	15c black	16.00	2.75
J18 D2	20c black	87.50	40.00
J19 D2	30c black	55.00	1.00
J20 D2	40c black	35.00	30.00
J21 D2	50c blk ('92)	200.00	22.50
J22 D2	60c blk ('84)	225.00	25.00
J23 D2	1fr black	300.00	180.00
J24 D2	2fr blk ('84)	475.00	340.00
J25 D2	5fr blk ('84)	1,200.	775.00

Excellent counterfeits exist of Nos. J23-J25.
See Nos. J26-J45A. For overprints and surcharges see Offices in China Nos. J1-J6, J33-J40, Offices in Egypt, Alexandria J1-J5, Port Said J1-J8, Offices in Zanzibar 60-62, J1-J5, Offices in Morocco 9-10, 24-25, J1-J5, J10-J12, J17-J22, J35-J41.

1884

J26 D2	1fr brown	175.00	45.00
J27 D2	2fr brown	110.00	72.50
J28 D2	5fr brown	200.00	140.00

1893-1941

J29 D2	5c blue ('94)	32	15
J30 D2	10c brown	32	15
J31 D2	15c lt grn ('94)	12.50	95
J32 D2	20c ol grn ('06)	2.10	15

J33	D2	25c rose ('23)	2.75	1.90
J34	D2	30c red ('94)	32	15
J35	D2	30c org red ('94)	325.00	37.50
J36	D2	40c rose ('25)	4.75	1.90
J37	D2	45c grn ('24)	3.50	2.50
J38	D2	50c brn vio ('95)	32	15
a.		50c lilac	32	15
J39	D2	60c bl grn ('25)	38	15
J40	D2	1fr rose, *straw* ('96)	350.00	300.00
J41	D2	1fr red brn, *straw* ('20)	2.75	15
J42	D2	1fr red brn ('35)	60	15
J43	D2	2fr red org ('10)	120.00	32.50
J44	D2	2fr brt vio ('26)	38	20
J45	D2	3fr magenta ('26)	38	20
J45A	D2	5fr red org ('41)	1.00	1.00

D3

D4

1908-25

J46	D3	1c olive grn	65	32
J47	D3	10c violet	70	20
a.		Imperf., pair	140.00	
J48	D3	20c bister ('19)	12.50	35
J49	D3	30c bister ('09)	6.75	20
J50	D3	50c red ('09)	165.00	35.00
J51	D3	60c red ('25)	1.50	75
		Nos. J46-J51 (6)	187.10	36.82

"Recouvrements" stamps were used to recover charges due on undelivered or refused mail which was returned to the sender.

For surcharges see Offices in Morocco Nos. J6-J9, J13-J16, J23-J26, J42-J45.

Nos. J49-J50 Surcharged **20c.**

1917

J52	D3	20c on 30c bister	6.25	1.65
J53	D3	40c on 50c red	6.25	1.50
a.		Double surcharge	130.00	

In Jan. 1917 several values of the current issue of postage stamps were handstamped "T" in a triangle and used as postage due stamps.

Recouvrements Stamps of 1908-25 Surcharged

1926

J54	D3	50c on 10c lilac	2.75	1.25
J55	D3	60c on 1c ol grn	4.25	2.00
J56	D3	1fr on 60c red	10.75	4.75
J57	D3	2fr on 60c red	10.75	5.50

1927-31

J58	D4	1c ol grn ('28)	80	28
J59	D4	10c rose ('31)	12.50	28
J60	D4	30c bister	2.75	16
J61	D4	60c red	2.50	22
J62	D4	1fr violet	9.00	1.75
J63	D4	1fr Prus grn ('31)	10.00	35
J64	D4	2fr blue	30.00	25.00
J65	D4	2fr ol brn ('31)	95.00	14.00
		Nos. J58-J65 (8)	162.55	42.04

Nos. J62 to J65 have the numerals of value double-lined.

Nos. J64, J62 Surcharged in Red or Black

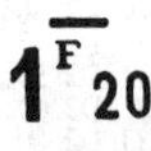

1929

J66	D4	1.20fr on 2fr blue	22.50	3.50
J67	D4	5fr on 1fr vio (Bk)	27.50	4.50

No. J61 Surcharged **UN FRANC**

1931

J68	D4	1fr on 60c red	19.00	1.10

Catalogue values for unused stamps in this section, from this point to the end of the section, are for Never Hinged items.

Sheaves of Wheat
D5 D6

Perf. 14x13½

1943-46 Unwmk. Typo.

J69	D5	10c sepia	20	18
J70	D5	30c brt red vio	20	18
J71	D5	50c blue grn	20	18
J72	D5	1fr brt ultra	20	18
J73	D5	1.50fr rose red	42	38
J74	D5	2fr turq blue	45	38
J75	D5	3fr brn org	45	38
J76	D5	4fr dp vio ('45)	4.00	3.00
J77	D5	5fr brt pink	60	38
J78	D5	10fr red org ('45)	3.50	38
J79	D5	20fr ol bis ('46)	6.50	2.50
		Nos. J69-J79 (11)	16.72	8.12

Type of 1943
Inscribed "Timbre Taxe"

1946-53

J80	D5	10c sepia ('47)	1.90	1.25
J81	D5	30c brt red vio ('47)	1.40	1.10
J82	D5	50c blue grn ('47)	11.00	5.50
J83	D5	1fr brt ultra ('47)	32	28
J85	D5	2fr turq blue	32	28
J86	D5	3fr brown org	32	28
J87	D5	4fr deep violet	42	28
J88	D5	5fr brt pink ('47)	42	18
J89	D5	10fr red org ('47)	42	18
J90	D5	20fr olive bis ('47)	2.00	38
J91	D5	50fr dk green ('50)	13.00	38
J92	D5	100fr dp green ('53)	57.50	5.75
		Nos. J80-J92 (12)	89.02	15.84

For surcharges see Reunion Nos. J36-J44.

1960 Typo. *Perf. 14x13½*

J93	D6	5c bright pink	1.65	30
J94	D6	10c red orange	2.00	30
J95	D6	20c olive bister	3.50	30
J96	D6	50c dark green	11.00	1.20
J97	D6	1fr deep green	42.50	1.65
		Nos. 93-97 (5)	60.65	3.75

For surcharges see Reunion Nos. J46-J48. For overprints see Algeria Nos. J49-J53.

Corn Poppy — D7

Ampedus Cinnabarinus — D8

Flowers: 5c, Centaury. 10c, Gentian. 20c, Violets. 30c, Forget-me-not. 40c, Columbine. 50c, Clover. 1fr, Soldanel.

1964-71 Typo. *Perf. 14x13½*

J98	D7	5c car rose, red & grn ('65)	15	15
J99	D7	10c car rose, brt bl & grn ('65)	15	15
J100	D7	15c brn, grn & red	15	15
J101	D7	20c dk grn, grn & vio ('71)	15	15
J102	D7	30c brn, ultra & grn	15	15
J103	D7	40c dk grn, scar & yel ('71)	24	15
J104	D7	50c vio bl, car & grn ('65)	24	15
J105	D7	1fr vio bl, lil & grn ('65)	38	15
		Nos. J98-J105 (8)	1.61	
		Set value		74

For surcharges see Reunion Nos. J49-J55.

1982-83 Engr. *Perf. 13*

J106	D8	10c shown	15	15
J107	D8	20c Dorcadion fuliginator	15	15
J108	D8	30c Leptura cordigera	15	15
J109	D8	40c Paederus littoralis	15	15
J110	D8	50c Pyrochroa coccinea	15	15
J111	D8	1fr Scarites laevigatus	30	15
J112	D8	2fr Trichius gallicus	55	15
J113	D8	3fr Adalia alpina	90	15
J114	D8	4fr Apoderus coryli	1.20	15
J115	D8	5fr Trichodes alvearius	1.50	15
		Nos. J106-J115 (10)	5.20	
		Set value		55

Issue dates: 30c, 40c, 3fr, 5fr, Jan. 3, 1983. Others, Jan. 4, 1982.

MILITARY STAMPS

Regular Issue Overprinted in Black or Red **F. M.**

1901-39 Unwmk. *Perf. 14x13½*

M1	A17	15c orange ('01)	55.00	7.50
a.		Inverted overprint	140.00	60.00
b.		Imperf., pair	325.00	
M2	A19	15c pale red ('03)	50.00	5.25
M3	A20	15c slate grn ('04)	40.00	6.00
a.		No period after "M"	100.00	40.00
b.		Imperf., pair	210.00	
M4	A20	10c rose ('06)	25.00	6.00
a.		No period after "M"	85.00	40.00
b.		Imperf., pair	200.00	
M5	A22	10c red ('07)	60	30
a.		Inverted overprint	65.00	37.50
b.		Imperf., pair	175.00	
M6	A20	50c vermilion ('29)	3.00	90
a.		No period after "M"	40.00	15.00
b.		Period in front of F	40.00	15.00
M7	A45	50c rose red ('34)	1.50	30
a.		No period after "M"	*20.00*	*12.50*
b.		Inverted overprint	95.00	45.00
M8	A45	65c brt ultra (R) ('38)	38	22
a.		No period after "M"	27.50	22.50
M9	A45	90c ultra (R) ('39)	45	38

"F. M." are initials of Franchise Militaire (Military Frank). See No. S1.

Catalogue values for unused stamps in this section, from this point to the end of the section, are for Never Hinged items.

M1

Flag — M2

1946-47 Typo.

M10	M1	dark green	1.50	65
M11	M1	rose red ('47)	25	15

Nos. M10-M11 were valid also in the French colonies.

1964, July 20 *Perf. 13x14*

M12	M2	multicolored	30	22

OFFICIAL STAMPS

FOR THE COUNCIL OF EUROPE

For use only on mail posted in the post office in the Council of Europe Building, Strasbourg.

Catalogue values for unused stamps in this section are for Never Hinged items.

For French stamp inscribed "Conseil de l'Europe" see No. 679.

France No. 854 Overprinted: "CONSEIL DE L'EUROPE"

Unwmk.

1958, Jan. 14 Engr. *Perf. 13*

1O1	A303	35fr car rose & lake	1.10	*2.25*

Council of Europe Flag — O1

1958-59

Flag in Ultramarine

1O2	O1	8fr red org & brn vio	15	15
1O3	O1	20fr yel & lt brn	30	25
1O4	O1	25fr lil rose & sl grn ('59)	60	35
1O5	O1	35fr red	45	45
1O6	O1	50fr lilac rose ('59)	1.10	1.00
		Nos. 1O2-1O6 (5)	2.60	2.20

1963, Jan. 3

Flag in Ultramarine

1O7	O1	20c yel & lt brn	1.25	50
1O8	O1	25c lil rose & sl grn	2.00	1.10
1O9	O1	50c lilac rose	2.00	1.65

Centime value stamps shown the denomination as "0,20," etc.

1965-71

Flag in Ultramarine & Yellow

1O10	O1	25c ver, yel & sl grn	85	65
1O11	O1	30c ver & yel	85	65
1O12	O1	40c ver, yel & gray	1.25	65
1O13	O1	50c red, yel & grn	2.50	1.25
1O14	O1	60c ver, yel & vio	1.00	65
1O15	O1	70c ver, yel & dk brn	3.75	2.50
		Nos. 1O10-1O15 (6)	10.20	6.35

Issue dates: 25c, 30c, 60c, Jan. 16, 1965. 50c, Feb. 20, 1971. Others, Mar. 24, 1969.

Type of 1958 Inscribed "FRANCE"

1975-76 Engr. *Perf. 13*

Flag in Ultramarine & Yellow

1O16	O1	60c org, yel & emer	1.25	65
1O17	O1	80c yel & mag	1.90	1.10
1O18	O1	1fr car, yel & gray ol ('76)	4.00	3.00
1O19	O1	1.20fr org, yel & bl	5.25	2.50

Issue dates: 1fr, Oct. 16; others, Nov. 22.

New Council Headquarters, Strasbourg
O2

1977, Jan. 22 Engr. *Perf. 13*

1O20	O2	80c car & multi	1.00	50
1O21	O2	1fr brown & multi	1.00	50
1O22	O2	1.40fr gray & multi	2.00	1.00

Human Rights Emblem in Upper Left Corner

1978, Oct. 14

1O23	O2	1.20fr red lilac & multi	45	40
1O24	O2	1.70fr blue & multi	75	55

30th anniversary of the Universal Declaration of Human Rights.

Council Headquarters Type of 1977

1980, Nov. 24 Engr. *Perf. 13*

1O25	O2	1.40fr olive	50	45
1O26	O2	2fr blue gray	60	55

New Council Headquarters, Strasbourg
O3

1981-84 Engr.

1O27	O3	1.40fr multicolored	48	40
1O28	O3	1.60fr multicolored	48	40
1O29	O3	1.70fr emerald	32	28
1O30	O3	1.80fr multicolored	70	55
1O31	O3	2fr multicolored	90	60
1O32	O3	2.10fr red	35	30
1O33	O3	2.30fr multicolored	75	65
1O34	O3	2.60fr multicolored	90	65
1O35	O3	2.80fr multicolored	1.00	75
1O36	O3	3fr brt blue	52	45
		Nos. 1O27-1O36 (10)	6.40	5.03

Issue dates: 1.40, 1.60, 2.30fr, Nov. 21. 1.80, 2.60fr, Nov. 13, 1982. 2, 2.80fr, No. 21, 1983. 1.70, 2.10, 3fr, Nov. 5, 1984.

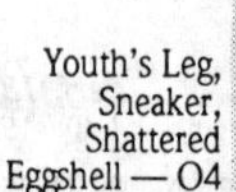

Youth's Leg, Sneaker, Shattered Eggshell — O4

1985, Aug. 31 Engr. *Perf. 13*

1O37	O4	1.80fr brt green	52	15
1O38	O4	2.20fr vermilion	65	15
1O39	O4	3.20fr brt blue	90	15
		Set value		22

New Council Headquarters, Strasbourg
O5

1986-87 Engr. *Perf. 13*

No.	Description	Unused	Used
1040 O5	1.90fr green	55	15
1041 O5	2fr brt yel grn	55	15
1042 O5	2.20fr red	65	15
1043 O5	3.40fr blue	1.00	15
1044 O5	3.60fr brt blue	95	16
Nos. 1040-1044 (5)		3.70	
Set value			57

Issue dates: 1.90fr, 2.20fr, 3.40fr, Dec. 13. 2fr, 3.60fr, Oct. 10, 1987.

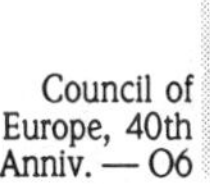

Council of Europe, 40th Anniv. — O6

1989, Feb. 4 Litho. & Engr.

No.	Description	Unused	Used
1045 O6	2.20fr multicolored	70	15
1046 O6	3.60fr multicolored	1.15	24

Denominations also inscribed in European Currency Units (ECUs).

Map of Europe — O7

1990, May 26 Litho. *Perf. 13*

No.	Description	Unused	Used
1047 O7	2.30fr multicolored	82	16
1048 O7	3.20fr multicolored	1.15	24

1991, Nov. 23

No.	Description	Unused	Used
1049 O7	2.50fr multicolored	1.00	20
1050 O7	3.40fr multicolored	1.30	28

FOR THE UNITED NATIONS EDUCATIONAL, SCIENTIFIC AND CULTURAL ORGANIZATION

For use only on mail posted in the post office in the UNESCO Building, Paris.

Catalogue values for unused stamps in this section are for Never Hinged items.

For French stamps inscribed "UNESCO" see Nos. 572, 893-894.

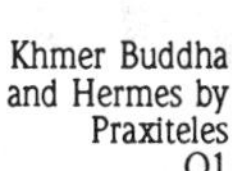

Khmer Buddha and Hermes by Praxiteles
O1

1961-65 Unwmk. Engr. *Perf. 13*

No.	Description	Unused	Used
201 O1	20c dk gray, ol bis & bl	25	25
202 O1	25c blk, lake & grn	38	30
203 O1	30c choc & bis brn ('65)	60	60
204 O1	50c blk, red & vio bl	1.50	1.25
205 O1	60c grnsh bl, red brn & rose lil ('65)	1.40	1.25
Nos. 201-205 (5)		4.13	3.65

Book and Globe — O2

1966, Dec. 17

No.	Description	Unused	Used
206 O2	25c gray	50	50
207 O2	30c dark red	65	65
208 O2	60c green	1.10	1.10

20th anniversary of UNESCO.

Human Rights Flame — O3

1969-71 Engr. *Perf. 13*

No.	Description	Unused	Used
209 O3	30c sl grn, red & dp brn	60	40
2010 O3	40c dk car rose, red & dp brn	95	60
2011 O3	50c ultra, car & brn ('71)	2.00	1.50
2012 O3	70c pur, red & sl	3.00	2.50

Universal Declaration of Human Rights.

Type of 1969 Inscribed "FRANCE"

1975, Nov. 15 Engr. *Perf. 13*

No.	Description	Unused	Used
2013 O3	60c grn, red & dk brn	1.10	65
2014 O3	80c ocher, red & red brn	1.65	1.10
2015 O3	1.20fr ind, red & brn	4.25	3.00

O4

1976-78 Engr. *Perf. 13*

No.	Description	Unused	Used
2016 O4	80c multi	85	65
2017 O4	1fr multi	85	65
2018 O4	1.20fr multi	48	45
2019 O4	1.40fr multi	2.25	1.40
2020 O4	1.70fr multi	75	60
Nos. 2016-2020 (5)		5.18	3.75

Issue dates: 1.20fr, 1.70fr, Oct. 14, 1978. Others, Oct. 23, 1976.

Slave Quarters, Senegal — O5

Designs: 1.40fr, Mohenjo-Daro excavations, Pakistan. 2fr, Sans-Souci Palace, Haiti.

1980, Nov. 17 Engr. *Perf. 13*

No.	Description	Unused	Used
2021 O5	1.20fr multi	45	36
2022 O5	1.40fr multi	50	40
2023 O5	2fr multi	65	55

Hue, Vietnam — O7

Designs: 1.40fr, Building, Fez, Morocco. 1.60fr, Seated deity, Sukhotai, Thailand. 2.20fr, Fort St. Elmo, Malta, horiz. 2.60fr, St. Michael Church ruins, Brazil.

1981-82

No.	Description	Unused	Used
2024 O7	1.40fr multi	48	40
2025 O7	1.60fr multi	48	40
2026 O7	1.80fr shown	60	55
2027 O7	2.30fr multi	70	60
2028 O7	2.60fr	70	65
Nos. 2024-2028 (5)		2.96	2.60

Issue dates: 1.80fr, 2.60fr, Oct. 23, 1982; others, Dec. 12, 1981.

Mosque, Chinguetti, Mauritania
O8

Architecture: 1.70fr, Church, Lalibela, Ethiopia. 1.80fr, Roman Theater and female standing sculpture, Carthage, Tunisia. 2.10fr, San'a, Yemen. 2.20fr, Old Town Square and wrought iron latticework, Havana. 2.80fr, Enclosure wall interior, Istanbul. 3fr, Church, Kotor, Yugoslavia. 3.20fr, Temple of Anuradhapura and bas-relief of two women, Sri Lanka.

1983-85 Engr.

No.	Description	Unused	Used
2029 O8	1.70fr multi	48	28
2030 O8	1.80fr multi	48	15
2031 O8	2fr multi	1.10	65
2032 O8	2.10fr multi	52	30
2033 O8	2.20fr multi	60	15
2034 O8	2.80fr multi	1.50	85
2035 O8	3fr multi	80	45
2036 O8	3.20fr multi	90	15
Nos. 2029-2036 (8)		6.38	2.98

Issue dates: 2fr, 2.80fr, Oct. 10, 1983. 1.70fr, 2.10fr, 3fr, Oct. 22, 1984. 1.80fr, 2.20fr, 3.20fr, Oct. 26, 1985.

Tikal Temple, Guatemala — O9

1986, Dec. 6 Engr. *Perf. 13*

No.	Description	Unused	Used
2037 O9	1.90fr shown	60	15
2038 O9	3.40fr Bagerhat Mosque, Bangladesh	1.00	15
Set value			23

The Parthenon, Athens — O10

1987, Dec. 5 Engr. *Perf. 13x12½*

No.	Description	Unused	Used
2039 O10	2fr shown	65	15
2040 O10	3.60fr Temple of Philae, Egypt	1.10	16

Shibam, Yemen People's Democratic Republic
O11

Perf. 13x12½, 12½x13

1990, Apr. 7 Engr.

No.	Description	Unused	Used
2041 O11	2.30fr San Francisco de Lima, Peru, vert.	82	16
2042 O11	3.20fr shown	1.15	24

Bagdaon Temple, Nepal — O12

Design: 3.40fr, Citadel of Harat, Afghanistan, horiz.

1991, Nov. 23

No.	Description	Unused	Used
2043 O12	2.50fr choc & dk red	90	18
2044 O12	3.40fr grn, brn & ol	1.20	18

Tassili N'Ajjer Natl. Park, Algeria
O13

Design: 2.80fr, Angkor Wat Archaeological Park, Cambodia, vert.

1993, Oct. 23 Litho. *Perf. 13*

No.	Description	Unused	Used
2045 O13	2.80fr multicolored	95	18
2046 O13	3.70fr multicolored	1.25	25

NEWSPAPER STAMPS

Coat of Arms — N1

1868 Unwmk. Typo. *Imperf.*

No.	Description	Unused	Used
P1 N1	2c lilac	200.00	32.50
P2 N1	2c (+ 2c) blue	425.00	200.00

Perf. 12½

No.	Description	Unused	Used
P3 N1	2c lilac	30.00	16.00
P4 N1	2c (+ 4c) rose	110.00	72.50
P5 N1	2c (+ 2c) blue	50.00	24.00
P6 N1	5c lilac	800.00	525.00

Nos. P2, P4, and P5 were sold for face plus an added fiscal charge indicated in parenthesis. Nos. P1, P3 and P6 were used simply as fiscals.

The 2c rose and 5c lilac imperforate and the 5c rose and 5c blue, both imperforate and perforated, were never put into use.

Nos. P1-P6 were reprinted for the 1913 Ghent Exhibition and the 1937 Paris Exhibition (PEXIP).

No. 109 Surcharged in Red

½ centime

1919 *Perf. 14x13½*

No.	Description	Unused	Used
P7 A16	½c on 1c gray	24	18
a.	Inverted surcharge	800.00	350.00

No. 156 Surcharged

1933

No.	Description	Unused	Used
P8 A22	½c on 1c olive bister	35	30

FRANCHISE STAMP

Catalogue values for unused stamps in this section are for Never Hinged items.

No. 276 Overprinted "F"

1939 Unwmk. *Perf. 14x13½*

No.	Description	Unused	Used
S1 A45	90c ultramarine	1.75	1.75
a.	Period after "F"	22.50	18.00

No. S1 was for the use of Spanish refugee soldiers in France. "F" stands for "Fugitives."

OCCUPATION STAMPS

Issued under German Occupation (Alsace and Lorraine)

OS1

1870 Typo. Unwmk. *Perf. 13½x14*

Network with Points Up

No.	Type	Description	Unused	Used
N1	OS1	1c olive grn	40.00	*75.00*
N2	OS1	2c red brown	75.00	95.00
a.		2c dark brown	90.00	120.00
N3	OS1	4c gray	70.00	45.00
N4	OS1	5c yel grn	45.00	7.50
N5	OS1	10c yel brn	22.50	2.75
a.		10c bister brown	42.50	3.50
b.		Network lemon yellow	55.00	6.00
N6	OS1	20c ultra	50.00	7.50
N7	OS1	25c brown	90.00	50.00
a.		25c black brown	120.00	72.50

There are three varieties of the 4c and two of the 10c, differing in the position of the figures of value, and several other setting varieties.

Network with Points Down

No.	Type	Description	Unused	Used
N8	OS1	1c olive grn	250.00	*575.00*
N9	OS1	2c red brn	110.00	*500.00*
N10	OS1	4c gray	120.00	80.00
N11	OS1	5c yel grn	1,800.	250.00
N12	OS1	10c bister	60.00	7.25
a.		Network lemon yellow	200.00	55.00
N13	OS1	20c ultra	165.00	75.00
N14	OS1	25c brown	350.00	200.00

Official imitations have the network with points downward. The "P" of "Postes" is 2½mm from the border in the imitations and 3mm in the originals. The word "Postes" measures 12¾ to 13mm on the imitations, and from 11 to 12½mm on the originals.

The imitations are perf. 13½x14½; originals, perf. 13½x14¼.

The stamps for Alsace and Lorraine were replaced by stamps of the German Empire on Jan. 1, 1872.

German Stamps of 1905-16 Surcharged:

3 Cent. 1 F

1916 Wmk. 125 *Perf. 14, 14½*

No.	Type	Description	Unused	Used
N15	A16	3c on 3pf brown	30	30
N16	A16	5c on 5pf green	30	45
N17	A22	8c on 7½pf org	60	*60*
N18	A16	10c on 10pf car	30	30
N19	A22	15c on 15pf yel brn	30	30
N20	A16	25c on 20pf blue	45	45
a.		25c on 20pf ultramarine	75	1.50
N21	A16	40c on 30pf org & blk, *buff*	60	1.20
N22	A16	50c on 40pf lake & blk	60	1.20
N23	A16	75c on 60pf mag	3.00	3.50
N24	A16	1fr on 80pf lake & blk, *rose*	3.00	5.50

✱ 1F.25Cent. ✱

No.	Type	Description	Unused	Used
N25	A17	1fr25c on 1m car	14.00	15.00
a.		Double surcharge	60.00	
N26	A21	2fr50c on 2m gray bl	14.50	12.00
a.		Double surcharge	60.00	
		Nos. N15-N26 (12)	37.95	40.80

These stamps were also used in parts of Belgium occupied by the German forces.

Catalogue values for unused stamps in this section, from this point to the end of the section, are for Never Hinged items.

Alsace

Issued under German Occupation

Stamps of Germany 1933-36 Overprinted in Black Elsaß

1940 Wmk. 237 *Perf. 14*

No.	Type	Description	Unused	Used
N27	A64	3pf olive bister	35	50
N28	A64	4pf dull blue	55	1.00
N29	A64	5pf brt green	35	50
N30	A64	6pf dark green	35	50
N31	A64	8pf vermilion	35	50
N32	A64	10pf chocolate	35	90
N33	A64	12pf dp carmine	38	60
N34	A64	15pt maroon	55	1.00
N35	A64	20pf brt blue	55	1.00
N36	A64	25pf ultra	75	1.35
N37	A64	30pf olive grn	1.40	1.60
N38	A64	40pf red violet	1.40	1.60
N39	A64	50pf dk grn & blk	2.00	2.50
N40	A64	60pf claret & blk	2.50	3.50
N41	A64	80pf dk blue & blk	2.75	5.00
N42	A64	100pf orange & blk	4.00	3.00
		Nos. N27-N42 (16)	18.58	25.05

Lorraine

Issued under German Occupation

Stamps of Germany 1933-36 Overprinted in Black Lothringen

1940 Wmk. 237 *Perf. 14*

No.	Type	Description	Unused	Used
N43	A64	3pf olive bister	95	*1.25*
N44	A64	4pf dull blue	95	*1.25*
N45	A64	5pf brt green	95	*1.25*
N46	A64	6pf dark green	95	65
N47	A64	8pf vermilion	95	*1.25*
N48	A64	10pf chocolate	95	95
N49	A64	12pf deep carmine	95	95
N50	A64	15pf maroon	95	*1.50*
a.		Inverted surcharge	125.00	
N51	A64	20pf brt blue	95	*1.75*
N52	A64	25pf ultra	1.10	*1.75*
N53	A64	30pf olive grn	1.25	*1.90*
N54	A64	40pf red violet	1.25	*1.90*
N55	A64	50pf dk grn & blk	1.90	*3.25*
N56	A64	60pf claret & blk	1.90	*3.75*
N57	A64	80pf dk blue & blk	2.25	*4.75*
N58	A64	100pf orange & blk	2.75	*7.50*
		Nos. N43-N58 (16)	20.95	*35.60*

Besetztes Gebiet Nordfrankreich

These three words, in a rectangular frame covering two stamps, were handstamped in black on Nos. 267, 367 and 369 and used in the Dunkerque region in July-August, 1940. The German commander of Dunkerque authorized the overprint.

ISSUED JOINTLY BY THE ALLIED MILITARY GOVERNMENT OF THE UNITED STATES AND GREAT BRITAIN, FOR CIVILIAN USE

Catalogue values for unused stamps in this section are for Never Hinged items.

Arc de Triomphe — OS2

1944 Unwmk. Litho. *Perf. 11*

No.	Type	Description	Unused	Used
2N1	OS2	5c brt red vio	15	15
2N2	OS2	10c lt gray	15	15
2N3	OS2	25c brown	15	15
2N4	OS2	50c olive bis	15	15
2N5	OS2	1fr pck green	15	15
2N6	OS2	1.50fr rose pink	15	15
2N7	OS2	2.50fr purple	15	15
2N8	OS2	4fr ultra	15	15
2N9	OS2	5fr black	15	15
2N10	OS2	10fr yellow org	17.50	14.00
		Set value	18.00	15.00

1945

Denominations in Black

No.	Type	Description	Unused	Used
2N11	OS2	30c orange	15	15
2N12	OS2	40c pale gray	15	15
2N13	OS2	50c olive bis	15	15
2N14	OS2	60c violet	15	15
2N15	OS2	80c emerald	15	15
2N16	OS2	1.20fr brown	15	15
2N17	OS2	1.50fr vermilion	15	15
2N18	OS2	2fr yellow	15	15
2N19	OS2	2.40fr dark rose	15	15
2N20	OS2	3fr brt red violet	15	15
		Set value	1.00	75

OFFICES IN CHINA

Prior to 1923 several of the world powers maintained their own post offices in China for the purpose of sending and receiving overseas mail. French offices were maintained in Canton, Hoi Hao (Hoihow), Kwang-chowan (Kouang-tchéou-wan), Mongtseu (Mong-tseu), Packhoi (Paknoi), Tong King (Tchongking), Yunnan Fou (Yunnanfu).

100 Centimes = 1 Franc
100 Cents = 1 Piaster
100 Cents = 1 Dollar

Peace and Commerce — A1

Stamps of France Overprinted in Red or Black

1894-1900 Unwmk. *Perf. 14x13½*

No.	Type	Description	Unused	Used
1	A1	5c grn, *grnsh* (R)	1.10	90
2	A1	5c yel grn, I (R) ('00)	1.25	65
a.		Type II	22.50	11.00
3	A1	10c blk, *lav*, I (R)	2.50	80
a.		Type II	9.00	6.00
4	A1	15c bl (R)	3.00	90
5	A1	20c red, *grn*	2.50	1.10
6	A1	25c blk, *rose* (R)	2.50	80
7	A1	30c brn, *bis*	2.50	1.60
8	A1	40c red, *straw*	3.00	1.75
9	A1	50c car, *rose*, I	6.50	4.25
a.		Red overprint	27.50	
b.		Type II (Bk)	7.00	3.50
10	A1	75c dp vio, *org* (R)	40.00	27.50
11	A1	1fr brnz grn, *straw*	4.75	1.75
a.		Double overprint	200.00	
12	A1	2fr brn, *az* ('00)	15.00	9.00
12A	A1	5fr red lil, *lav*	35.00	22.50
b.		Red overprint	240.00	

For surcharges and overprints see Nos. 13-17, J7-J10, J20-J23.

Surcharged in Black Chine 25

No.	Type	Description	Unused	Used
13	A1	25c on 1fr brnz, grn, *straw*	30.00	12.50

Surcharged in Red Chine 2 Cents

1901

No.	Type	Description	Unused	Used
14	A1	2c on 25c blk, *rose*	700.00	175.00
15	A1	4c on 25c blk, *rose*	575.00	175.00
16	A1	6c on 25c blk, *rose*	675.00	300.00
17	A1	16c on 25c blk, *rose*	190.00	140.00
a.		Black surcharge		*5,250.*

Stamps of Indo-China Surcharged in Black CHINE 二之五仙

1902-04

No.	Type	Description	Unused	Used
18	A3	1c blk, *lil bl*	1.10	80
19	A3	2c brn, *buff*	1.75	1.50
20	A3	4c claret, *lav*	1.25	1.00
21	A3	5c yel grn	1.40	1.10
22	A3	10c red	1.75	1.50
23	A3	15c gray	2.75	2.25
24	A3	20c red, *grn*	3.00	2.50
25	A3	25c blk, *rose*	4.00	3.50
26	A3	25c blue ('04)	3.50	3.00
27	A3	30c brn, *bis*	1.90	1.90
28	A3	40c red, *straw*	8.25	6.50
29	A3	50c car, *rose*	25.00	20.00
30	A3	50c brn, *az* ('04)	3.00	2.50
31	A3	75c vio, *org*	14.00	10.00
32	A3	1fr brnz grn, *straw*	17.00	13.00
33	A3	5fr red lil, *lavender*	42.50	35.00
		Nos. 18-33 (16)	132.15	106.05

The Chinese characters surcharged on Nos. 18-33 are the Chinese equivalents of the French values and therefore differ on each denomination. Another printing of these stamps was made in 1904 which differs from the first one principally in the size and shape of the letters in "CHINE," particularly the "H" which is much thinner in the second printing. Values are for the less expensive variety. Many varieties of surcharge exist.

Liberty, Equality and Fraternity — A3

"Rights of Man" — A4

A5

1902-03 Typo.

No.	Type	Description	Unused	Used
34	A3	5c green	75	65
35	A4	10c rose red ('03)	75	65
36	A4	15c pale red	1.10	70
37	A4	20c brn vio ('03)	1.90	1.90
38	A4	25c blue ('03)	1.90	1.00
39	A4	30c lilac ('03)	2.00	2.00
40	A5	40c red & pale bl	4.00	3.50
41	A5	50c bis brn & lav	4.75	3.75
42	A5	1fr claret & ol grn	7.25	4.25
43	A5	2fr gray vio & yel	24.00	16.00
44	A5	5fr dk bl & buff	35.00	21.00
		Nos. 34-44 (11)	83.40	55.40

For surcharges and overprints see Nos. 45, 57-85, J14-J16, J27-J30.

Surcharged in Black 5

1903

No.	Type	Description	Unused	Used
45	A4	5c on 15c pale red	6.25	3.50
a.		Inverted surcharge	40.00	40.00

Stamps of Indo-China, 1904-06, Surcharged as Nos. 18-33 in Black

1904-05

No.	Type	Description	Unused	Used
46	A4	1c olive grn	42	42
47	A4	2c vio brn, *buff*	42	42
47A	A4	4c cl, *bluish*	475.00	350.00
48	A4	5c deep grn	60	60
49	A4	10c carmine	60	60
50	A4	15c org brn, *bl*	60	60
51	A4	20c red, *grn*	3.25	3.25
52	A4	25c deep blue	1.40	75
53	A4	40c blk, *bluish*	2.00	1.50
54	A4	1fr pale grn	175.00	125.00
55	A4	2fr brn, *org*	9.00	7.00
56	A4	10fr org brn, *grn*	65.00	57.50
		Nos. 46-56 (12)	733.29	547.64

Many varieties of the surcharge exist.

Stamps of 1902-03 Surcharged in Black 2 CENTS 仙二

1907

No.	Type	Description	Unused	Used
57	A3	2c on 5c green	45	40
58	A4	4c on 10c rose red	45	40
a.		Pair, one without surcharge	*27.50*	
59	A4	6c on 15c pale red	55	42
60	A4	8c on 20c brn vio	1.75	1.40
a.		"8" inverted	27.50	27.50
61	A4	10c on 25c blue	24	24
62	A5	20c on 50c bis brn & lav	1.10	75
a.		Double surcharge		
b.		Triple surcharge	175.00	175.00
63	A5	40c on 1fr claret & ol grn	7.75	4.25
64	A5	2pi on 5fr dk bl & buff	7.75	4.50
a.		Double surcharge	*775.00*	*775.00*
		Nos. 57-64 (8)	20.04	12.36

Stamps of 1902-03 Surcharged in Black 2 CENTS 分二

1911-22

No.	Type	Description	Unused	Used
65	A3	2c on 5c green	28	20
66	A4	4c on 10c rose red	38	20
67	A4	6c on 15c org	70	28
68	A4	8c on 20c brn vio	55	28
69	A4	10c on 25c bl ('21)	55	28
70	A4	20c on 50c bl ('22)	21.00	14.00
71	A5	40c on 1fr cl & ol grn	1.10	75

No. 44 Surcharged

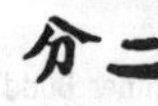

No.	Type	Description	Unused	Used
73	A5	$2 on 5fr bl & buff ('22)	67.50	52.50
		Nos. 65-73 (8)	92.06	68.49

Types of 1902-03 Surcharged like Nos. 65-71

1922

No.	Type	Description	Unused	Used
75	A3	1c on 5c org	1.25	65
76	A4	2c on 10c grn	2.10	1.75
77	A4	3c on 15c org	3.00	2.50
78	A4	4c on 20c red brn	4.25	3.00

No.	Type	Description	Unused	Used
79	A4	5c on 25c dk vio	2.25	1.10
80	A4	6c on 30c red	3.00	2.10
82	A4	10c on 50c blue	3.00	2.10
83	A5	20c on 1fr claret & ol grn	15.00	11.50
84	A5	40c on 2fr org & pale bl	15.00	11.50
85	A5	$1 on 5fr dk bl & buff	67.50	67.50
		Nos. 75-85 (10)	116.35	103.70

POSTAGE DUE STAMPS

Postage Due Stamps of France Handstamped in Red or Black — Chine

1901-07 Unwmk. Perf. 14x13½

No.	Type	Description	Unused	Used
J1	D2	5c lt bl (R)	1.75	1.05
J2	D2	10c choc (R)	3.00	2.10
J3	D2	15c lt grn (R)	3.00	2.10
J4	D2	20c ol grn (R) ('07)	3.50	2.50
J5	D2	30c carmine	5.25	3.50
J6	D2	50c lilac	5.50	3.50
		Nos. J1-J6 (6)	22.00	14.75

Stamps of 1894-1900 Handstamped in Carmine — A PERCEVOIR

1903

No.	Type	Description	Unused	Used
J7	A1	5c yel grn	1,700.	550.00
a.		Purple handstamp	1,700.	550.00
b.		5c green, greenish	3,750.	
J8	A1	10c blk, lavender	4,250.	3,500.
a.		Purple handstamp	4,250.	3,500.
J9	A1	15c blue	1,700.	525.00
a.		Purple handstamp	1,700.	550.00
J10	A1	30c brn, bister	950.00	60.00
a.		Purple handstamp	950.00	60.00

Same Handstamp on Stamps of 1902-03 in Carmine

1903

No.	Type	Description	Unused	Used
J14	A3	5c green	950.00	550.00
a.		Purple handstamp	950.00	550.00
J15	A4	10c rose red	450.00	70.00
a.		Purple handstamp	450.00	70.00
J16	A4	15c pale red	475.00	70.00
a.		Purple handstamp	475.00	70.00

Stamps of 1894-1900 Handstamped in Carmine

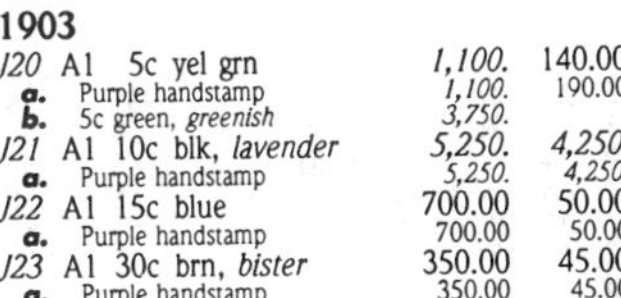

1903

No.	Type	Description	Unused	Used
J20	A1	5c yel grn	1,100.	140.00
a.		Purple handstamp	1,100.	190.00
b.		5c green, greenish	3,750.	
J21	A1	10c blk, lavender	5,250.	4,250.
a.		Purple handstamp	5,250.	4,250.
J22	A1	15c blue	700.00	50.00
a.		Purple handstamp	700.00	50.00
J23	A1	30c brn, bister	350.00	45.00
a.		Purple handstamp	350.00	45.00

Same Handstamp on Stamps of 1902-03 in Carmine or Purple

1903

No.	Type	Description	Unused	Used
J27	A3	5c green (C)	750.00	275.00
a.		Purple handstamp	750.00	275.00
J28	A4	10c rose red (C)	210.00	25.00
a.		Purple handstamp	210.00	25.00
J29	A4	15c pale red (C)	450.00	30.00
a.		Purple handstamp	450.00	30.00
J30	A4	30c lilac (P)	5,250.	4,250.

The handstamps on Nos. J7-J30 are found inverted, double, etc.

The cancellations on these stamps should have dates between Sept. 1, and Nov. 30, 1903, to be genuine.

Postage Due Stamps of France, 1893-1910 Surcharged like Nos. 65-71

1911

No.	Type	Description	Unused	Used
J33	D2	2c on 5c blue	55	42
a.		Double surcharge	52.50	52.50
J34	D2	4c on 10c choc	55	42
a.		Double surcharged	52.50	52.50
J35	D2	8c on 20c ol grn	60	60
a.		Double surcharge	52.50	52.50
J36	D2	20c on 50c lilac	75	60

1922

No.	Type	Description	Unused	Used
J37	D2	1c on 5c blue	32.50	27.50
J38	D2	2c on 10c brn	42.50	40.00
J39	D2	4c on 20c ol grn	42.50	40.00
J40	D2	10c on 50c brn vio	42.50	40.00

CANTON

Stamps of Indo-China, 1892-1900, Overprinted in Red — CANTON 州廣

1901 Unwmk. Perf. 14x13½

No.	Type	Description	Unused	Used
1	A3	1c blk, lil bl	70	70
1A	A3	2c brn, buff	70	70
2	A3	4c claret, lav	90	90
2A	A3	5c grn, grnsh	300.00	300.00
3	A3	5c yel grn	80	80
4	A3	10c blk, lavender	1.65	1.65
5	A3	15c blue, quadrille paper	1.00	1.00
6	A3	15c gray	1.65	1.65
a.		Double overprint	14.00	
7	A3	20c red, grn	2.75	2.75
8	A3	25c blk, rose	2.75	2.75
9	A3	30c brn, bister	6.25	6.25
10	A3	40c red, straw	7.00	7.00
11	A3	50c car, rose	12.50	12.50
12	A3	75c dp vio, org	19.00	19.00
13	A3	1fr brnz grn, straw	14.00	14.00
14	A3	5fr red lil, lav	105.00	105.00
		Nos. 1-14 (16)	476.65	476.65

The Chinese characters in the overprint on Nos. 1-14 read "Canton." On Nos. 15-64, they restate the denomination of the basic stamp.

Surcharged in Black — CANTON 仙六

1903-04

No.	Type	Description	Unused	Used
15	A3	1c blk, lil bl	1.10	1.10
16	A3	2c brn, buff	1.10	90
17	A3	4c claret, lav	1.10	90
18	A3	5c yel grn	1.10	90
19	A3	10c rose red	1.00	80
20	A3	15c gray	1.65	1.25
21	A3	20c red, grn	6.00	5.50
22	A3	25c blue	3.00	2.00
23	A3	25c blk, rose ('04)	3.00	2.00
24	A3	30c brn, bister	7.75	6.75
25	A3	40c red, straw	19.00	15.00
26	A3	50c car, rose	175.00	140.00
27	A3	50c brn, az ('04)	32.50	27.50
28	A3	75c dp vio, org	32.50	27.50
a.		"INDO-CHINE" inverted	16,000.	
29	A3	1fr brnz grn, straw	27.50	22.50
30	A3	5fr red lil, lav	35.00	25.00
		Nos. 15-30 (16)	348.30	279.60

Many varieties of the surcharge exist on Nos. 15-30.

Stamps of Indo-China, 1892-1906, Surcharged in Red or Black — CANTON 花銀八厘

A second printing of the 1906 surcharges of Canton, Hoi Hao, Kwangchowan, Mongtseu, Packhoi, Tong King and Yunnan Fou was made in 1908. The inks are grayish instead of full black and vermilion instead of carmine. Values are for the cheaper variety which usually is the second printing.

The 4c and 50c of the 1892 issue of Indo-China are known with this surcharge and similarly surcharged for other cities in China. The surcharges on these two stamps are always inverted. It is stated that they were irregularly produced and never issued.

1906

No.	Type	Description	Unused	Used
31	A4	1c ol grn (R)	70	70
32	A4	2c vio brn, buff	70	70
33	A4	4c cl, bluish (R)	70	70
34	A4	5c dp grn (R)	90	90
35	A4	10c carmine	1.05	1.00
36	A4	15c org brn, bl	2.50	2.50
37	A4	20c red, grn	1.05	1.05
38	A4	25c deep blue	1.05	1.05
39	A4	30c pale brn	1.90	1.75
40	A4	35c blk, yel (R)	1.05	1.00
41	A4	40c blk, bluish (R)	2.25	2.10
42	A4	50c bister brn	2.75	2.25
43	A3	75c dp vio, org (R)	21.00	19.00
44	A4	1fr pale grn	5.75	5.50
45	A4	2fr brn, org (R)	17.00	16.00
46	A3	5fr red lil, lav	35.00	27.50
47	A4	10fr org brn, grn	32.50	32.50
		Nos. 31-47 (17)	127.85	116.20

Surcharge exists inverted on 1c, 25c & 1fr.

Stamps of Indo-China, 1907, Surcharged "CANTON", and Chinese Characters, in Red or Blue

1908

No.	Type	Description	Unused	Used
48	A5	1c ol brn & blk	45	45
49	A5	2c brn & blk	45	45
50	A5	4c bl & blk	70	70
51	A5	5c grn & blk	70	70
52	A5	10c red & blk (Bl)	70	70
53	A5	15c vio & blk	1.05	1.05
54	A6	20c vio & blk	1.05	1.05
55	A6	25c bl & blk	1.05	1.05
56	A6	30c brn & blk	2.10	1.90
57	A6	35c ol grn & blk	2.10	1.90
58	A6	40c brn & blk	3.25	2.10
59	A6	50c car & blk (Bl)	3.50	2.50
60	A7	75c ver & blk (Bl)	3.50	2.75
61	A8	1fr car & blk (Bl)	5.25	4.25
62	A9	2fr grn & blk	17.00	16.00
63	A10	5fr bl & blk	22.50	17.50
64	A11	10fr pur & blk	37.50	32.50
		Nos. 48-64 (17)	102.85	87.55

Nos. 48-64 Surcharged with New Values in Cents or Piasters in Black, Red or Blue

1919

No.	Type	Description	Unused	Used
65	A5	2/5c on 1c	48	48
66	A5	4/5c on 2c	48	48
67	A5	1 3/5c on 4c (R)	65	55
68	A5	2c on 5c	65	55
69	A5	4c on 10c (Bl)	65	52
a.		Chinese "2" instead of "4"	15.50	15.50
70	A5	6c on 15c	1.00	70
71	A6	8c on 20c	1.00	80
72	A6	10c on 25c	1.10	70
73	A6	12c on 30c	1.10	70
a.		Double surcharge	62.50	62.50
74	A6	14c on 35c	1.10	70
a.		Closed "4"	5.00	5.00
75	A6	16c on 40c	1.10	80
76	A6	20c on 50c (Bl)	1.10	80
77	A7	30c on 75c (Bl)	1.10	70
78	A8	40c on 1fr (Bl)	4.25	2.75
79	A9	80c on 2fr (R)	5.25	3.50
80	A10	2pi on 5fr (R)	6.00	5.00
81	A11	4pi on 10fr (R)	6.75	6.25
		Nos. 65-81 (17)	33.76	25.98

HOI HAO

Stamps of Indo-China Overprinted in Red — HOI HAO 州瓊

1901 Unwmk. Perf. 14x13½

No.	Type	Description	Unused	Used
1	A3	1c blk, lil bl	1.65	1.65
2	A3	2c brn, buff	1.65	1.65
3	A3	4c claret, lav	1.65	1.65
4	A3	5c yel grn	1.65	1.65
5	A3	10c blk, lavender	2.00	2.00
6	A3	15c blue	1,150.	425.00
7	A3	15c gray	1.40	1.40
8	A3	20c red, grn	8.00	8.00
9	A3	25c blk, rose	3.75	2.25
10	A3	30c brn, bister	12.50	11.00
11	A3	40c red, straw	12.50	11.00
12	A3	50c car, rose	20.00	17.00
13	A3	75c dp vio, org	100.00	90.00
14	A3	1fr brnz grn, straw	500.00	450.00
15	A3	5fr red lil, lav	400.00	375.00
		Nos. 1-15 (15)	2,216.	1,399.

The Chinese characters in the overprint on Nos. 1-15 read "Hoi Hao." On Nos. 16-66, they restate the denomination of the basic stamp.

Surcharged in Black — HOI HAO 仙六

1903-04

No.	Type	Description	Unused	Used
16	A3	1c blk, lil bl	50	50
17	A3	2c brn, buff	50	50
18	A3	4c claret, lav	1.25	1.25
19	A3	5c yel grn	1.25	1.25
20	A3	10c red	1.25	1.25
21	A3	15c gray	1.25	1.25
22	A3	20c red, grn	3.00	3.00
23	A3	25c blue	1.40	1.40
24	A3	25c blk, rose ('04)	1.40	1.40
25	A3	30c brn, bister	1.40	1.40
26	A3	40c red, straw	15.00	15.00
27	A3	50c car, rose	15.00	15.00
28	A3	50c brn, az ('04)	47.50	47.50
29	A3	75c dp vio, org	19.00	19.00
a.		"INDO-CHINE" inverted	17,500.	
30	A3	1fr brnz grn, straw	21.00	21.00
31	A3	5fr red lil, lav	87.50	87.50
		Nos. 16-31 (16)	218.20	218.20

Many varieties of the surcharge exist on #1-31.

Stamps of Indo-China, 1892-1906, Surcharged in Red or Black — HOI HAO 花銀八厘

1906

No.	Type	Description	Unused	Used
32	A4	1c ol grn (R)	80	80
33	A4	2c vio brn, buff	80	80
34	A4	4c cl, bluish (R)	1.25	1.25
35	A4	5c dp grn (R)	1.40	1.40
36	A4	10c carmine	1.40	1.40
37	A4	15c org brn, bl	1.40	1.40
38	A4	20c red, grn	2.50	2.50
39	A4	25c deep blue	3.25	3.25
40	A4	30c pale brn	3.25	3.25
41	A4	35c blk, yel (R)	5.50	5.50
42	A4	40c blk, bluish (R)	5.75	5.75
43	A4	50c gray brn	6.00	6.00
44	A3	75c dp vio, org (R)	15.00	15.00
45	A4	1fr pale grn	15.00	15.00
46	A4	2fr brn, org (R)	15.00	15.00
47	A3	5fr red lil, lav	55.00	55.00
48	A4	10fr org brn, grn	67.50	67.50
		Nos. 32-48 (17)	200.80	200.80

Stamps of Indo-China, 1907, Surcharged "HOI HAO" and Chinese Characters, in Red or Blue

1908

No.	Type	Description	Unused	Used
49	A5	1c ol brn & blk	55	55
50	A5	2c brn & blk	55	55
51	A5	4c bl & blk	80	80
52	A5	5c grn & blk	1.05	1.05
53	A5	10c red & blk (Bl)	1.50	1.50
54	A5	15c vio & blk	2.10	2.10
55	A6	20c vio & blk	2.75	2.75
56	A6	25c bl & blk	2.75	2.75
57	A6	30c brn & blk	2.75	2.75
58	A6	35c ol grn & blk	2.75	2.75
59	A6	40c brn & blk	2.50	2.50
61	A6	50c car & blk (Bl)	3.25	3.25
62	A7	75c ver & blk (Bl)	3.50	3.50
63	A8	1fr car & blk (Bl)	8.00	8.00
64	A9	2fr grn & blk	17.00	17.00
65	A10	5fr bl & blk	35.00	35.00
66	A11	10fr pur & blk	50.00	50.00
		Nos. 49-66 (17)	136.80	136.80

Nos. 49-66 Surcharged with New Values in Cents or Piasters in Black, Red or Blue

1919

No.	Type	Description	Unused	Used
67	A5	2/5c on 1c	35	35
68	A5	4/5c on 2c	35	35
69	A5	1 3/5c on 4c (R)	55	55
70	A5	2c on 5c	35	35
71	A5	4c on 10c (Bl)	55	55
a.		Chinese "2" instead of "4"	3.00	3.00
72	A5	6c on 15c	55	55
73	A6	8c on 20c	95	95
a.		"S" of "CENTS" omitted	45.00	45.00
74	A6	10c on 25c	2.00	2.00
75	A6	12c on 30c	75	75
76	A6	14c on 35c	75	75
a.		Closed "4"	6.75	6.75
77	A6	16c on 40c	75	75
79	A6	20c on 50c (Bl)	90	90
80	A7	30c on 75c (Bl)	1.50	1.50
81	A8	40c on 1fr (Bl)	3.25	3.25
82	A9	80c on 2fr (R)	8.75	8.75
83	A10	2pi on 5fr (R)	27.50	27.50
a.		Triple surch. of new value	250.00	
84	A11	4pi on 10fr (R)	77.50	77.50
		Nos. 67-84 (17)	127.30	127.30

KWANGCHOWAN

A Chinese Territory leased to France, 1898 to 1945.

Stamps of Indo-China, 1892-1906, Surcharged in Red or Black — Kouang Tchéou-Wan 花銀八厘

1906 Unwmk. Perf. 14x13½

No.	Type	Description	Unused	Used
1	A4	1c ol grn (R)	1.00	1.00
2	A4	2c vio brn, buff	1.00	1.00
3	A4	4c cl, bluish (R)	1.40	1.40
4	A4	5c dp grn (R)	1.40	1.40
5	A4	10c carmine	1.40	1.40
6	A4	15c org brn, bl	3.00	3.00
7	A4	20c red, grn	1.40	1.40
8	A4	25c deep blue	1.40	1.40
9	A4	30c pale brn	1.75	1.75
10	A4	35c blk, yel (R)	2.50	2.50
11	A4	40c blk, bluish (R)	1.75	1.75
12	A4	50c bister brn	6.75	6.75
13	A3	75c dp vio, org (R)	9.25	9.25
14	A4	1fr pale grn	11.50	11.50
15	A4	2fr brn, org (R)	11.50	11.50

16 A3 5fr red lil, *lav* 80.00 80.00
17 A4 10fr org brn, *grn* 110.00 110.00
Nos. 1-17 (17) 247.00 247.00

Various varieties of the surcharge exist on Nos. 2-10.

Stamps of Indo-China, 1907, Surcharged "KOUANG-TCHEOU" and Value in Chinese in Red or Blue

1908

18 A5 1c ol brn & blk 20 20
19 A5 2c brn & blk 20 20
20 A5 4c bl & blk 20 20
21 A5 5c grn & blk 20 20
22 A5 10c red & blk (Bl) 20 20
23 A5 15c vio & blk 65 65
24 A6 20c vio & blk 1.10 1.10
25 A6 25c bl & blk 2.00 2.00
26 A6 30c brn & blk 3.50 3.50
27 A6 35c ol grn & blk 4.50 4.50
28 A6 40c brn & blk 4.50 4.50
30 A6 50c car & blk (Bl) 5.00 5.00
31 A7 75c ver & blk (Bl) 5.00 5.00
32 A8 1fr car & blk (Bl) 6.25 6.25
33 A9 2fr grn & blk 14.50 14.50
34 A10 5fr bl & blk 30.00 30.00
35 A11 10fr pur & blk 45.00 45.00
a. Double surcharge 450.00 450.00
b. Triple surcharge 450.00 450.00
Nos. 18-35 (17) 123.00 123.00

The Chinese characters overprinted on Nos. 1 to 35 repeat the denomination of the basic stamp.

Nos. 18-35 Surcharged with New Values in Cents or Piasters in Black, Red or Blue

1919

36 A5 2/5c on 1c 20 20
37 A5 4/5c on 2c 20 20
38 A5 1 3/5c on 4c (R) 30 30
39 A5 2c on 5c 30 30
a. "2 CENTS" inverted 35.00
40 A5 4c on 10c (Bl) 90 55
41 A5 6c on 15c 30 18
42 A6 8c on 20c 1.50 1.25
43 A6 10c on 25c 3.75 3.75
44 A6 12c on 30c 50 35
45 A6 14c on 35c 80 70
a. Closed "4" 16.00 13.00
46 A6 16c on 40c 65 50
48 A6 20c on 50c (Bl) 65 50
49 A7 30c on 75c (Bl) 2.50 2.10
50 A8 40c on 1fr (Bl) 3.00 3.00
a. "40 CENTS" inverted
51 A9 80c on 2fr (R) 3.25 2.75
52 A10 2pi on 5fr (R) 70.00 60.00
53 A11 4pi on 10fr (R) 8.75 7.50
Nos. 36-53 (17) 97.55 84.13

Stamps of Indo-China, 1922-23, Overprinted in Black, Red or Blue — **KOUANG-TCHEOU**

1923

54 A12 1/10c blk & sal (Bl) 15 15
55 A12 1/5c dp bl & blk (R) 15 15
a. Black overprint 65.00
56 A12 2/5c ol brn & blk (R) 18 18
57 A12 4/5c brt rose & blk 22 22
58 A12 1c yel brn & blk (Bl) 22 22
59 A12 2c gray grn & blk (R) 35 35
60 A12 3c vio & blk (R) 35 35
61 A12 4c org & blk 35 35
62 A12 5c car & blk 35 35
63 A13 6c dl red & blk 45 45
64 A13 7c ol grn & blk 35 35
65 A13 8c black (R) 60 60
66 A13 9c yel & blk 60 60
67 A13 10c bl & blk 60 60
68 A13 11c vio & blk 60 60
69 A13 12c brn & blk 60 60
70 A13 15c org & blk 80 80
71 A13 20c bl & blk, *straw* (R) 60 60
72 A13 40c ver & blk, *bluish* (Bl) 1.25 1.25
73 A13 1pi bl grn & blk, *grnsh* 3.50 3.50
74 A13 2pi vio brn & blk, *pnksh* (Bl) 6.00 6.00
Nos. 54-74 (21) 18.27 18.27

Indo-China Stamps of 1927 Overprinted in Black or Red — **KOUANG-TCHÉOU**

1927

75 A14 1/10c lt ol grn (R) 15 15
76 A14 1/5c yellow 18 18
77 A14 2/5c lt bl (R) 22 22
78 A14 4/5c dp brn 22 22
79 A14 1c orange 25 25
80 A14 2c bl grn (R) 35 35
81 A14 3c indigo (R) 35 35
82 A14 4c lilac rose 35 35
83 A14 5c dp vio 35 35
84 A15 6c dp red 35 35
85 A15 7c lt brn 35 35
86 A15 8c gray grn (R) 35 35
87 A15 9c red vio 45 45
88 A15 10c lt bl (R) 45 45
89 A15 11c orange 45 45
90 A15 12c myr grn (R) 45 45
91 A16 15c dl rose & ol brn 90 90
92 A16 20c vio & sl (R) 95 95
93 A17 25c org brn & lil rose 95 95
94 A17 30c dp bl & ol gray (R) 90 90
95 A18 40c ver & lt bl 90 90
96 A18 50c lt grn & sl (R) 90 90
97 A19 1pi dk bl, blk & yel (R) 2.00 2.00
98 A19 2pi red, dp bl & org (R) 2.00 2.00
a. Double overprint 75.00
Nos. 75-98 (24) 14.77 14.77

Stamps of Indo-China, 1931-41, Overprinted in Black or Red — **KOUANG-TCHÉOU**

1937-41 ***Perf. 13, 13½***

99 A20 1/10c Prus blue 15 15
100 A20 1/5c lake 15 15
101 A20 2/5c org red 15 15
102 A20 1/2c red brn 15 15
103 A20 4/5c dk vio 18 18
104 A20 1c blk brn 18 18
105 A20 2c dk grn 18 18
a. Inverted overprint 75.00
106 A21 3c dk grn 52 52
107 A21 3c yel brn ('41) 15 15
108 A21 4c dk bl (R) 35 35
109 A21 4c dk grn ('41) 18 18
110 A21 4c yel org ('41) 1.10 1.10
111 A21 5c dp vio 35 35
112 A21 5c dp grn ('41) 20 20
113 A21 6c org red 25 25
114 A21 7c blk (R) ('41) 25 25
115 A21 8c rose lake ('41) 25 25
116 A21 9c blk, *yel* (R) ('41) 25 25
d. Black overprint 4.50 4.50
117 A22 10c dk bl (R) 85 85
118 A22 10c ultra, *pink* (R) ('41) 35 35
119 A22 15c dk bl (R) 25 25
120 A22 18c bl (R) ('41) 15 15
121 A22 20c rose 25 25
122 A22 21c olive grn 25 25
123 A22 22c grn ('41) 20 20
124 A22 25c dp vio 1.65 1.65
125 A22 25c dk bl (R) ('41) 25 25
126 A22 30c org brn 25 25
127 A23 50c dk brn 70 70
128 A23 60c dl vio 70 70
129 A23 70c lt bl (R) ('41) 25 25
130 A23 1pi yel green 95 95
131 A23 2pi red 1.00 1.00
Nos. 99-131 (33) 13.04 13.04

Colonial Arts Exhibition Issue
Common Design Type
Souvenir Sheet

1937 **Engr.** ***Imperf.***

132 CD79 30c grn & sepia 2.75 2.75

New York World's Fair Issue
Common Design Type

1939 **Unwmk.** ***Perf. 12½x12***

133 CD82 13c car lake 65 65
134 CD82 23c ultra 65 65

Petain Issue

Indo-China Nos. 209-209A Overprinted "KOUANG TCHEOU" in Blue or Red

1941 **Engr.** ***Perf. 12½x12***

135 A27a 10c car lake (B) 35
136 A27a 25c blue (R) 35

Nos. 135-136 were issued by the Vichy government, and were not placed on sale in Kwangchowan. This is also true of 16 stamps of Indo-China types A20-A23 without "RF" and overprinted "KOUANG-TCHEOU."

SEMI-POSTAL STAMPS

French Revolution Issue
Common Design Type

1939 **Unwmk.** **Photo.** ***Perf. 13***
Name and Value typo. in Black

B1 CD83 6c + 2c green 3.00 3.00
B2 CD83 7c + 3c brown 3.00 3.00
B3 CD83 9c + 4c red org 3.00 3.00
B4 CD83 13c + 10c rose pink 3.00 3.00
B5 CD83 23c + 20c blue 3.00 3.00
Nos. B1-B5 (5) 15.00 15.00

Indo-China Nos. B19A and B19C Overprinted "KOUANG-TCHEOU" in Blue or Red, and Common Design Type

1941 **Photo.** ***Perf. 13½***

B6 SP1 10c + 10c red (B) 35
B7 CD86 15c + 30c mar & car 35
B8 SP2 25c + 10c blue (R) 45

Nos. B6-B8 were issued by the Vichy government, and were not placed on sale in Kwangchowan.

Nos. 135-136 were surcharged "OEUVRES COLONIALES" and surtax (including change of denomination of the 25c to 5c). These were issued in 1944 by the Vichy government, and not placed on sale in Kwangchowan.

AIR POST SEMI-POSTAL STAMPS.

Stamps of Indo-China types V4, V5 and V6 overprinted "KOUANG-TCHEOU" and type of Cameroons V10 inscribed "KOUANG-TCHEOU" were issued in 1942 by the Vichy Government, but were not placed on sale in the territory.

MONGTSEU (MENGTSZ)

Stamps of Indo-China Surcharged in Black — **MONGTZE** 仙 六

1903-04 **Unwmk.** ***Perf. 14x13½***

1 A3 1c blk, *lil bl* 3.00 3.00
2 A3 2c brn, *buff* 1.65 1.65
3 A3 4c claret, *lav* 3.00 3.00
4 A3 5c yel grn 2.25 2.25
5 A3 10c red 3.00 3.00
6 A3 15c gray 3.75 3.75
7 A3 20c red, *grn* 4.00 4.00
7C A3 25c blk, *rose* 300.00 300.00
8 A3 25c blue 4.25 4.25
9 A3 30c brn, *bister* 3.75 3.75
10 A3 40c red, *straw* 26.00 26.00
11 A3 50c car, *rose* 150.00 150.00
12 A3 50c brn, *az* ('04) 45.00 45.00
13 A3 75c dp vio, *org* 45.00 45.00
a. "INDO-CHINE" inverted 25,000.
14 A3 1fr brnz grn, *straw* 45.00 45.00
15 A3 5fr red lil, *lav* 45.00 45.00
Nos. 1-15 (16) 684.65 684.65

Many Surcharge varieties exist on #1-15.

Common Design Types pictured in section at front of book.

Stamps of Indo-China, 1892-1906, Surcharged in Red or Black — **Mong-Tseu** 花銀八厘

1906

16 A4 1c ol grn (R) 60 60
17 A4 2c vio brn, *buff* 60 60
18 A4 4c cl, *bluish* (R) 60 60
19 A4 5c dp grn (R) 60 60
20 A4 10c carmine 75 75
21 A4 15c org brn, *bl* 75 75
22 A4 20c red, *grn* 1.50 1.50
23 A4 25c deep blue 1.50 1.50
24 A4 30c pale brn 2.75 2.75
25 A4 35c blk, *yel* (R) 1.90 1.90
26 A4 40c blk, *bluish* (R) 2.25 2.25
27 A4 50c bister brn 6.25 6.25
28 A3 75c dp vio, *org* (R) 15.00 15.00
a. "INDO-CHINE" inverted 25,000.
29 A4 1fr pale grn 7.25 7.25
30 A4 2fr brn, *org* (R) 19.00 19.00
31 A3 5fr red lil, *lav* 42.50 42.50
32 A4 10fr org brn, *grn* 57.50 57.50
a. Chinese characters inverted 1,100. 1,400.
Nos. 16-32 (17) 161.30 161.30

Inverted varieties of the surcharge exist on Nos. 19, 22 and 32.

Stamps of Indo-China, 1907, Surcharged "MONGTSEU" and Value in Chinese in Red or Blue

1908

33 A5 1c ol brn & blk 22 22
34 A5 2c brn & blk 22 22
35 A5 4c bl & blk 35 35
36 A5 5c grn & blk 45 45
37 A5 10c red & blk (Bl) 60 60
38 A5 15c vio & blk 60 60
39 A6 20c vio & blk 1.90 1.90
40 A6 25c bl & blk 2.50 2.50
41 A6 30c brn & blk 1.50 1.50
42 A6 35c ol grn & blk 1.50 1.50
43 A6 40c brn & blk 1.50 1.50
45 A6 50c car & blk (Bl) 1.50 1.50
46 A7 75c ver & blk (Bl) 4.00 4.00
47 A8 1fr car & blk (Bl) 4.75 4.75
48 A9 2fr grn & blk 6.25 6.25
49 A10 5fr bl & blk 42.50 42.50
50 A11 10fr pur & blk 52.50 52.50
Nos. 33-50 (17) 122.84 122.84

The Chinese characters overprinted on Nos. 1 to 50 repeat the denomination of the basic stamp.

Nos. 33-50 Surcharged with New Values in Cents or Piasters in Black, Red or Blue

1919

51 A5 2/5c on 1c 25 25
52 A5 4/5c on 2c 25 25
53 A5 1 3/5c on 4c 65 65
54 A5 2c on 5c 40 40
55 A5 4c on 10c (Bl) 75 75
56 A5 6c on 15c 75 75
57 A6 8c on 20c 1.40 1.40
58 A6 10c on 25c 1.25 1.25
59 A6 12c on 30c 1.25 1.25
60 A6 14c on 35c 1.25 1.25
61 A6 16c on 40c 1.50 1.50
a. Closed "4" 4.75 4.75
63 A6 20c on 50c (Bl) 1.50 1.50
64 A7 30c on 75c (Bl) 1.40 1.40
65 A8 40c on 1fr (Bl) 3.50 3.50
66 A9 80c on 2fr (R) 2.00 2.00
a. Triple surch., one inverted 165.00 165.00
67 A10 2pi on 5fr (R) 55.00 55.00
a. Triple surch., one inverted 165.00 165.00
b. Double surcharge 165.00 165.00
68 A11 4pi on 10fr (R) 9.00 9.00
Nos. 51-68 (17) 82.10 82.10

PAKHOI

Stamps of Indo-China Surcharged in Black — **PACKHOI** 仙 六

1903-04 **Unwmk.** ***Perf. 14x13½***

1 A3 1c blk, *lil bl* 2.50 2.50
2 A3 2c brn, *buff* 1.75 1.75
3 A3 4c claret, *lav* 1.50 1.50
4 A3 5c yel grn 1.50 1.50
5 A3 10c red 1.25 1.25
6 A3 15c gray 1.25 1.25
7 A3 20c red, *grn* 2.50 2.50
8 A3 25c blue 2.50 2.50
9 A3 25c blk, *rose*('04) 1.75 1.75
10 A3 30c brn, *bister* 2.50 2.50
11 A3 40c red, *straw* 19.00 19.00
12 A3 50c car, *rose* 175.00 175.00
13 A3 50c brn, *az* ('04) 21.00 21.00
14 A3 75c dp vio, *org* 21.00 21.00
a. "INDO-CHINE" inverted 17,500.
15 A3 1fr brnz grn, *straw* 22.50 22.50
16 A3 5fr red lil, *lav* 40.00 40.00
Nos. 1-16 (16) 317.50 317.50

Many varieties of the surcharge exist.

Stamps of Indo-China 1892-1906, Surcharged in Red or Black — **PAK-HOI** 花銀八厘

1906

17 A4 1c ol grn (R) 55 55
18 A4 2c vio brn, *buff* 55 55
19 A4 4c cl, *bluish* (R) 55 55
20 A4 5c dp grn (R) 55 55
21 A4 10c carmine 55 55
22 A4 15c org brn, *bl* 1.90 1.90
23 A4 20c red, *grn* 1.25 1.25
24 A4 25c deep blue 1.25 1.25
25 A4 30c pale brn 1.25 1.25
26 A4 35c blk, *yel* (R) 1.25 1.25
27 A4 40c blk, *bluish*(R) 1.25 1.25
28 A4 50c bister brn 2.50 2.50
29 A3 75c dp vio, *org* (R) 17.00 17.00
30 A4 1fr pale grn 10.50 10.50
31 A4 2fr brn, *org*(R) 17.00 17.00
32 A3 5fr red lil, *lav* 42.50 42.50
33 A4 10fr org brn, *grn* 52.50 52.50
Nos. 17-33 (17) 152.90 152.90

Various surcharge varieties exist on #17-24.

Stamps of Indo-China, 1907, Surcharged "PAKHOI" and Value in Chinese in Red or Blue

1908

34 A5 1c ol brn & blk 20 20
35 A5 2c brn & blk 28 28
36 A5 4c bl & blk 28 28
37 A5 5c grn & blk 45 45
38 A5 10c red & blk (Bl) 45 45
39 A5 15c vio & blk 60 60
40 A6 20c vio & blk 60 60
41 A6 25c bl & blk 65 65
42 A6 30c brn & blk 1.00 1.00
43 A6 35c ol grn & blk 1.00 1.00
44 A6 40c brn & blk 1.00 1.00
46 A6 50c car & blk (Bl) 1.00 1.00
47 A7 75c ver & blk (Bl) 2.10 2.10
48 A8 1fr car & blk (Bl) 2.50 2.50
49 A9 2fr grn & blk 5.75 5.75

50	A10	5fr bl & blk	35.00	35.00
51	A11	10fr pur & blk	52.50	52.50
		Nos. 34-51 (17)	105.36	105.36

The Chinese characters overprinted on Nos. 1 to 51 repeat the denomination of the basic stamps.

Nos. 34-51 Surcharged with New Values in Cents or Piasters in Black, Red or Blue

1919

52	A5	2/5c on 1c	30	30
a.		"PAK-HOI" and Chinese dbl.	80.00	80.00
53	A5	4/5c on 2c	30	30
54	A5	1 3/5c on 4c (R)	30	30
55	A5	2c on 5c	45	45
56	A5	4c on 10c (Bl)	1.10	1.10
57	A5	6c on 15c	45	45
58	A6	8c on 20ck	1.10	1.10
59	A6	10c on 25c	1.40	1.40
60	A6	12c on 30ck	55	55
a.		"12 CENTS" double	65.00	65.00
61	A6	14c on 35c	30	30
a.		Closed "4"	3.50	3.50
62	A6	16c on 40c	85	85
64	A6	20c on 50c (Bl)	55	55
65	A7	30c on 75c (Bl)	85	85
66	A8	40c on 1fr (Bl)	3.75	3.75
67	A9	80c on 2fr (R)	1.75	1.75
68	A10	2pi on 5fr (R)	4.00	4.00
69	A11	4pi on 10fr (R)	7.50	7.50
		Nos. 52-69 (17)	25.50	25.50

TCHONGKING (CHUNGKING)

Stamps of Indo-China Surcharged in Black

TCHONGKING
仙 六

1903-04 Unwmk. *Perf. 14x13½*

1	A3	1c blk, *lil bl*	1.10	1.10
2	A3	2c brn, *buff*	1.10	1.10
3	A3	4c claret, *lav*	1.10	1.10
4	A3	5c yel grn	1.10	1.10
5	A3	10c red	1.10	1.10
6	A3	15c gray	1.10	1.10
7	A3	20c red, *grn*	1.10	1.10
8	A3	25c blue	16.00	16.00
9	A3	25c blk, *rose* ('04)	2.75	2.75
10	A3	30c brn, *bister*	4.00	4.00
11	A3	40c red, *straw*	16.00	16.00
12	A3	50c car, *rose*	95.00	95.00
13	A3	50c brn, *az* ('04)	52.50	52.50
14	A3	75c vio, *org*	16.00	16.00
15	A3	1fr brnz grn, *straw*	21.00	21.00
16	A3	5fr red lil, *lav*	37.50	37.50
		Nos. 1-16 (16)	268.45	268.45

Many surcharge varieties exist on #1-14.
Stamps of Indo-China and French China, issued in 1902 with similar overprint, but without Chinese characters, were not officially authorized.

Stamps of Indo-China, 1892-1906, Surcharged in Red or Black

Tch'ong
K'ing
花銀八厘

1906

17	A4	1c ol grn (R)	70	70
18	A4	2c vio brn, *buff*	70	70
19	A4	4c cl, *bluish* (R)	70	70
20	A4	5c dp grn (R)	70	70
21	A4	10c carmine	70	70
22	A4	15c org brn, *bl*	2.50	2.50
23	A4	20c red, *grn*	70	70
24	A4	25c deep blue	1.65	1.65
25	A4	30c pale brn	1.40	1.40
26	A4	35c blk, *yellow* (R)	1.40	1.40
27	A4	40c blk, *bluish* (R)	2.50	2.50
28	A4	50c bis brn	2.50	2.50
29	A3	75c dp vio, *org* (R)	12.00	12.00
30	A4	1fr pale grn	10.00	10.00
31	A4	2fr brn, *org* (R)	10.00	10.00
32	A3	5fr red lil, *lav*	50.00	50.00
33	A4	10fr org brn, *grn*	52.50	52.50
		Nos. 17-33 (17)	150.65	150.65

Variety "T" omitted in surcharge occurs once in each sheet of Nos. 17-33. Other surcharge varieties exist, such as inverted surcharge on 1c and 2c.

Stamps of Indo-China, 1907, Surcharged "TCHONGKING" and Value in Chinese in Red or Blue

1908

34	A5	1c ol brn & blk	15	15
35	A5	2c brn & blk	20	20
36	A5	4c bl & blk	24	24
37	A5	5c grn & blk	45	45
38	A5	10c red & blk (Bl)	55	55
39	A5	15c vio & blk	70	70
40	A6	20c vio & blk	1.40	1.40
41	A6	25c bl & blk	1.40	1.40
42	A6	30c brn & blk	1.50	1.50
43	A6	35c ol grn & blk	2.50	2.50
44	A6	40c brn & blk	5.00	5.00
45	A6	50c car & blk (Bl)	3.50	3.50
46	A7	75c ver & blk (Bl)	3.50	3.50
47	A8	1fr car & blk (Bl)	4.75	4.75
48	A9	2fr grn & blk	40.00	40.00
49	A10	5fr bl & blk	13.00	13.00
50	A11	10fr pur & blk	105.00	105.00
		Nos. 34-50 (17)	183.84	183.84

The Chinese characters overprinted on Nos. 1 to 50 repeat the denomination of the basic stamp.

Nos. 34-50 Surcharged with New Values in Cents or Piasters in Black, Red or Blue

1919

51	A5	2/5c on 1c	38	38
52	A5	4/5c on 2c	42	42
53	A5	1 3/5c on 4c (R)	55	55
54	A5	2c on 5c	50	38
55	A5	4c on 10c (Bl)	38	38
56	A5	6c on 15c	38	38
57	A6	8c on 20c	38	38
58	A6	10c on 25c	55	50
59	A6	12c on 30c	70	50
60	A6	14c on 35c	70	42
a.		Closed "4"	5.75	5.75
61	A6	16c on 40c	90	70
a.		"16 CENTS" double	67.50	67.50
62	A6	20c on 50c (Bl)	3.50	3.50
63	A7	30c on 75c (Bl)	90	90
64	A8	40c on 1fr (Bl)	1.40	90
65	A9	80c on 2fr (R)	2.00	1.50
66	A10	2pi on 5fr (R)	2.50	2.25
67	A11	4pi on 10fr (R)	4.00	3.25
		Nos. 51-67 (17)	20.14	17.29

YUNNAN FOU

(Formerly Yunnan Sen, later known as Kunming)

Stamps of Indo-China Surcharged in Black

YUNNANSEN
仙 六

1903-04 Unwmk. *Perf. 14x13½*

1	A3	1c blk, *lil bl*	2.10	1.75
2	A3	2c brn, *buff*	1.75	1.75
3	A3	4c claret, *lav*	1.75	1.75
4	A3	5c yel green	1.75	1.75
5	A3	10c red	1.75	1.75
6	A3	15c gray	2.75	1.75
7	A3	20c red, *grn*	3.00	2.25
8	A3	25c blue	1.75	2.25
9	A3	30c brn, *bister*	3.50	2.25
10	A3	40c red, *straw*	32.50	21.00
11	A3	50c car, *rose*	175.00	150.00
12	A3	50c brn, *az* ('04)	75.00	75.00
13	A3	75c dp vio, *org*	21.00	19.00
a.		"INDO-CHINE" inverted	17,500.	
14	A3	1fr brnz grn, *straw*	22.50	21.00
15	A3	5fr red lil, *lav*	47.50	45.00
		Nos. 1-15 (15)	393.60	348.25

The Chinese characters overprinted on Nos. 1 to 15 repeat the denomination of the basic stamp.
Many varieties of the surcharge exist.

Stamps of Indo-China, 1892-1906, Surcharged in Red or Black

Yunnan-Fou
花銀八厘

1906 Unwmk. *Perf. 14x13½*

17	A4	1c ol grn (R)	90	90
18	A4	2c vio brn, *buff*	1.10	1.10
19	A4	4c cl, *bluish* (R)	1.25	1.25
20	A4	5c dp grn (R)	1.25	1.25
21	A4	10c carmine	1.25	1.25
22	A4	15c org brn, *bl*	2.50	2.50
23	A4	20c red, *grn*	1.65	1.65
24	A4	25c deep blue	2.25	2.25
25	A4	30c pale brn	1.65	1.65
26	A4	35c blk, *yel* (R)	3.00	3.00
27	A4	40c blk, *bluish* (R)	2.25	2.25
28	A4	50c bister brn	3.00	3.00
29	A3	75c dp vio, *org* (R)	22.50	22.50
30	A4	1fr pale grn	7.75	7.75
31	A4	2fr brn, *org* (R)	7.75	7.75
32	A3	5fr red lil, *lav*	32.50	32.50
33	A4	10fr org brn, *grn*	35.00	35.00
		Nos. 17-33 (17)	127.55	127.55

Various varieties of the surcharge exist on Nos. 18, 20, 21 and 27.

Stamps of Indo-China, 1907, Surcharged "YUNNANFOU", and Value in Chinese in Red or Blue

1908

34	A5	1c ol brn & blk	50	50
35	A5	2c brn & blk	50	50
36	A5	4c bl & blk	50	50
37	A5	5c grn & blk	75	75
38	A5	10c red & blk (Bl)	50	50
39	A5	15c vio & blk	1.90	1.50
40	A6	20c vio & blk	2.25	1.75
41	A6	25c bl & blk	2.25	1.75
42	A6	30c brn & blk	3.00	2.50
43	A6	35c ol grn & blk	3.00	2.50
44	A6	40c brn & blk	3.25	3.25
45	A6	50c car & blk (Bl)	3.25	3.25
46	A7	75c ver & blk (Bl)	3.75	3.25
47	A8	1fr car & blk (Bl)	6.50	4.75
48	A9	2fr grn & blk	10.50	8.25
a.		"YUNANNFOU"	1,300.	1,300.
49	A10	5fr bl & blk	25.00	21.00
a.		"YUNANNFOU"	1,300.	1,300.
50	A11	10fr pur & blk	35.00	35.00
a.		"YUNANNFOU"	1,300.	1,300.
		Nos. 34-50 (17)	102.40	91.50

The Chinese characters overprinted on Nos. 17 to 50 repeat the denomination of the basic stamp.

Nos. 34-50 Surcharged with New Values in Cents or Piasters in Black, Red or Blue

1919

51	A5	2/5c on 1c	36	36
a.		New value double	45.00	
52	A5	4/5c on 2c	55	50
53	A5	1 3/5c on 4c (R)	65	55
54	A5	2c on 5c	55	50
a.		Triple surcharge	77.50	
55	A5	4c on 10c (Bl)	55	50
56	A5	6c on 15c	55	50
57	A6	8c on 20c	70	65
58	A6	10c on 25c	1.00	90
59	A6	12c on 30c	90	70
60	A6	14c on 35c	1.65	1.40
a.		Closed "4"	42.50	42.50
61	A6	16c on 40c	1.75	1.40
62	A6	20c on 50c (Bl)	1.00	1.00
63	A7	30c on 75c (Bl)	1.75	1.75
64	A8	40c on 1fr (Bl)	2.25	2.10
65	A9	80c on 2fr (R)	2.50	2.50
a.		Triple surch., one inverted	125.00	
66	A10	2pi on 5fr (R)	16.00	16.00
67	A11	4pi on 10fr (R)	5.25	5.25
		Nos. 51-67 (17)	37.96	36.56

OFFICES IN CRETE

Austria, France, Italy and Great Britain maintained their own post offices in Crete during the period when that country was an autonomous state.

100 Centimes = 1 Franc

Liberty, Equality and Fraternity — A1

"Rights of Man" — A2

Liberty and Peace (Symbolized by Olive Branch) — A3

Perf. 14x13½

1902-03 Unwmk. Typo.

1	A1	1c gray	70	70
2	A1	2c vio brn	75	75
3	A1	3c red org	75	75
4	A1	4c yel brn	75	75
5	A1	5c green	65	45
6	A2	10c rose red	90	90
7	A2	15c pale red ('03)	1.25	95
8	A2	20c brn vio ('03)	1.75	1.40
9	A2	25c blue ('03)	2.25	1.75
10	A2	30c lilac ('03)	3.25	3.00
11	A3	40c red & pale bl	5.00	4.00
12	A3	50c bis brn & lav	8.00	7.50
13	A3	1fr cl & ol grn	10.00	8.00
14	A3	2fr gray vio & yel	17.50	16.00
15	A3	5fr dk bl & buff	27.50	24.00
		Nos. 1-15 (15)	81.00	70.90

A4

A5

Black Surcharge

1903

16	A4	1pi on 25c blue	20.00	18.00
17	A5	2pi on 50c bis brn & lav	37.50	27.50
18	A5	4pi on 1fr claret & ol grn	55.00	47.50
19	A5	8pi on 2fr gray vio & yel	62.50	62.50
20	A5	20pi on 5fr dk bl & buff	100.00	90.00
		Nos. 16-20 (5)	275.00	245.50

OFFICES IN EGYPT

French post offices formerly maintained in Alexandria and Port Said.

100 Centimes = 1 Franc

ALEXANDRIA

A1

French Stamps Overprinted in Red, Blue or Black

1899-1900 Unwmk. *Perf. 14x13½*

1	A1	1c blk, *lil bl* (R)	45	45
a.		Double overprint	45.00	
b.		Triple overprint	45.00	
2	A1	2c brn, *buff* (Bl)	70	70
3	A1	3c gray, *grysh* (Bl)	90	70
4	A1	4c cl, *lav* (Bl)	80	65
5	A1	5c yel grn, (I) (R)	1.40	90
a.		Type II (R)	62.50	45.00
6	A1	10c blk, *lav*, (I) (R)	3.25	2.75
a.		Type II (R)	25.00	12.00
7	A1	15c blue (R)	2.75	1.75
8	A1	20c red, *grn*	5.25	2.75
a.		Double overprint		
9	A1	25c blk, *rose* (R)	2.25	1.40
a.		Inverted overprint	32.50	
b.		Double ovpt., one invtd.	55.00	
10	A1	30c brn, *bis*	5.75	4.25
11	A1	40c red, *straw*	4.75	4.75
12	A1	50c car, *rose* (II)	8.75	6.00
a.		Type I	72.50	6.25

13 A1 1fr brnz grn, *straw* 8.75 5.75
14 A1 2fr brn, *az* ('00) 42.50 30.00
15 A1 5fr red lil, *lav* 52.50 47.50
Nos. 1-15 (15) 140.75 110.30

A2

A3

A4

1902-03
16 A2 1c gray 25 15
17 A2 2c vio brn 25 15
18 A2 3c red org 25 15
19 A2 4c yel brn 35 20
20 A2 5c green 45 25
21 A3 10c rose red 55 25
22 A3 15c orange 45 30
a. 15c pale red ('03) 65 35
23 A3 20c brn vio ('03) 75 40
24 A3 25c blue ('03) 35 15
25 A3 30c violet ('03) 1.75 85
26 A4 40c red & pale bl 1.50 52
27 A4 50c bis brn & lav 2.25 75
28 A4 1fr cl & ol grn 3.00 90
29 A4 2fr gray vio & yel 5.50 3.25
30 A4 5fr dk bl & buff 7.25 5.00
Nos. 16-30 (15) 24.90 13.27

The 2c, 5c, 10c, 20c and 25c exist imperf. Value, each $15.

See Nos. 77-86. For surcharges see Nos. 31-73, B1-B4.

Stamps of 1902-03 Surcharged Locally in Black **4 Mill.**

1921
31 A2 2m on 5c grn 1.75 1.40
32 A2 3m on 3c red org 2.00 1.40
a. Larger numeral 27.50 24.00
33 A3 4m on 10c rose 1.50 1.40
34 A2 5m on 1c dk gray 2.25 1.75
35 A2 5m on 4c yel brn 2.25 1.75
36 A3 6m on 15c org 1.05 1.05
a. Larger numeral 27.50 27.50
37 A3 8m on 20c brn vio 1.75 1.40
a. Larger numeral 12.50 11.50
38 A3 10m on 25c blue 65 65
a. Inverted surcharge 14.00 14.00
b. Double surcharge 14.00 14.00
39 A3 12m on 30c vio 5.00 5.00
40 A2 15m on 2c vio brn 2.00 2.00

Nos. 26-30 Surcharged **15 Mill.**

41 A4 15m on 40c 5.50 5.00
42 A4 15m on 50c 2.25 2.25
43 A4 30m on 1fr 67.50 62.50
44 A4 60m on 2fr 95.00 95.00
a. Larger numeral 250.00 250.00
45 A4 150m on 5fr 140.00 140.00

Port Said Nos. 20 and 19 Surcharged like Nos. 32 and 40

45A A2 3m on 3c red org 42.50 42.50
46 A2 15m on 2c vio brn 42.50 42.50

Alexandria No. 28 Surcharged with Two New Values

1921
46A A4 30m on 15m on 1fr 500.00 500.00

The surcharge "15 Mill." was made in error and is canceled by a bar.

The surcharges were lithographed on Nos. 31, 33, 38, 39 and 42 and typographed on the other stamps of the 1921 issue. Nos. 34, 36 and 37 were surcharged by both methods.

Alexandria Stamps of 1902-03 Surcharged in Paris **2 MILLIEMES**

1921-23
47 A2 1m on 1c gray 60 60
48 A2 2m on 5c green 55 55
49 A3 4m on 10c rose 1.00 90
50 A3 4m on 10c grn ('23) 65 55
51 A2 5m on 3c red org ('23) 2.10 2.00
52 A3 6m on 15c org 60 52
53 A3 8m on 20c brn vio 45 35
54 A3 10m on 25c blue 45 32
55 A3 10m on 30c vio 1.25 1.10
56 A3 15m on 50c bl ('23) 80 55

Nos. 27-30 and Type of 1902 Surcharged **15 MILLIÈMES**

57 A4 15m on 50c 1.25 1.10
58 A4 30m on 1fr 80 70
59 A4 60m on 2fr *850.00 850.00*
60 A4 60m on 2fr org & pale bl ('23) 3.25 2.00
61 A4 150m on 5fr 4.00 2.00
Nos. 47-58,60-61 (14) 17.75 13.24

Stamps and Types of 1902-03 Surcharged with New Values and Bars in Black

1925
62 A2 1m on 1c gray 28 28
63 A2 2m on 5c orange 24 24
64 A2 2m on 5c green 52 52
65 A3 4m on 10c green 38 28
66 A2 5m on 3c red org 28 28
67 A3 6m on 15c orange 38 28
68 A3 8m on 20c brn vio 38 32
69 A3 10m on 25c blue 24 24
70 A3 15m on 50c blue 52 45
71 A4 30m on 1fr cl & ol grn 60 50
72 A4 60m on 2fr org & pale bl 1.25 1.00
73 A4 150m on 5fr dk bl & buff 1.50 1.25
Nos. 62-73 (12) 6.57 5.64

Types of 1902-03 Issue

1927-28
77 A2 3m orange ('28) 50 45
81 A3 15m slate blue 50 45
82 A3 20m rose lil ('28) 1.40 1.00
84 A4 50m org & blue 3.50 2.75
85 A4 100m sl bl & buff 4.25 3.50
86 A4 250m gray grn & red 8.00 5.75
Nos. 77-86 (6) 18.15 13.90

SEMI-POSTAL STAMPS

Regular Issue of 1902-03 Surcharged in Carmine ✚5c

1915 Unwmk. *Perf. 14x13½*
B1 A3 10c + 5c rose 28 28

Sinking Fund Issue

Type of 1902-03 Issue Surcharged in Blue or Black **+5 Mm** Caisse d'Amortissement

1927-30
B2 A3 15m + 5m deep org 95 95
B3 A3 15m + 5m red vio ('28) 1.40 1.40
a. 15m + 5m violet ('30) 3.25 3.25

Type of 1902-03 Issue Surcharged as in 1927-28

1929
B4 A3 15m + 5m fawn 2.25 2.25

POSTAGE DUE STAMPS

Postage Due Stamps of France, 1893-1920, Surcharged in Paris in Black **2 MILLIEMES**

1922 Unwmk. *Perf. 14x13½*
J1 D2 2m on 5c blue 80 80
J2 D2 4m on 10c brown 80 80
J3 D2 10m on 30c rose red 1.00 1.00
J4 D2 15m on 50c brn vio 1.10 1.10
J5 D2 30m on 1fr red brn, *straw* 1.75 1.75
Nos. J1-J5 (5) 5.45 5.45

D3

1928 Typo.
J6 D3 1m slate 75 75
J7 D3 2m light blue 60 60
J8 D3 4m lilac rose 80 80
J9 D3 5m gray green 55 55
J10 D3 10m light red 75 75
J11 D3 20m vio brn 60 60
J12 D3 30m green 2.00 2.00
J13 D3 40m light vio 1.90 1.90
Nos. J6-J13 (8) 7.95 7.95

Nos. J6 to J13 were also available for use in Port Said.

PORT SAID

A1

Stamps of France Overprinted in Red, Blue or Black

1899-1900 Unwmk. *Perf. 14x13½*
1 A1 1c blk, *lil bl* (R) 55 35
2 A1 2c brn, *buff* (bl) 65 48
3 A1 3c gray, *grysh* (Bl) 70 55
4 A1 4c claret, *lav* (Bl) 70 55
5 A1 5c yel grn (I) (R) 3.50 1.65
a. Type II (R) 18.50 5.00
6 A1 10c blk, *lav* (I) (R) 4.75 4.75
a. Type II (R) 20.00 13.50
7 A1 15c blue (R) 4.75 2.75
8 A1 20c red, *grn* 5.25 2.75
9 A1 25c blk, *rose* (R) 5.00 1.00
a. Double overprint 75.00
10 A1 30c brn, *bister* 5.25 2.75
a. Inverted overprint 75.00
11 A1 40c red, *straw* 5.75 3.00
12 A1 50c car, *rose* (II) 7.75 3.75
a. Type I 140.00 37.50
b. Double overprint (II) 100.00
13 A1 1fr brnz grn, *straw* 10.50 5.00
14 A1 2fr brn, *az* ('00) 30.00 20.00
15 A1 5fr red lil, *lav* 45.00 30.00
Nos. 1-15 (15) 130.10 79.33

Regular Issue Surcharged in Red PORT SAID **VINGT CINQ**

1899
16 A1 25c on 10c blk, *lav* 55.00 12.50

With Additional Surcharge "25"
17 A1 25c on 10c blk, *lav* 200.00 75.00

A2

A3

A4

1902-03 Typo.
18 A2 1c gray 25 20
19 A2 2c vio brn 25 20
20 A2 3c red org 30 20
21 A2 4c yel brn 35 25
22 A2 5c blue green 35 30
a. 5c yellow green 1.20 1.00
23 A3 10c rose red 60 35
24 A3 15c pale red ('03) 60 60
a. 15c orange 70 60
25 A3 20c brn vio ('03) 60 40
26 A3 25c blue ('03) 70 50
27 A3 30c violet ('03) 1.65 1.25
28 A4 40c red & pale bl 1.65 1.25
29 A4 50c bis brn & lav 2.25 1.65
30 A4 1fr claret & ol grn 2.75 2.00
31 A4 2fr gray vio & yel 4.50 4.00
32 A4 5fr dk bl & buff 10.50 8.75
Nos. 18-32 (15) 27.30 21.90

See Nos. 83-92. For surcharges see Nos. 33-80, B1-B4.

Stamps of 1902-03 Surcharged Locally **2 Milliemes**

1921
33 A2 2m on 5c grn 2.75 2.75
a. Inverted surcharge 18.00 18.00
34 A3 4m on 10c rose 2.75 2.75
a. Inverted surcharge 18.00 18.00
35 A2 5m on 1c .00 4.00
a. Inverted surcharge 35.00 35.00
c. Surcharged "2 Milliemes" 22.50 22.50
36 A2 5m on 2c 5.00 5.00
a. Surcharged "2 Milliemes" 27.50 27.50
b. As "a," inverted 47.50 47.50
37 A2 5m on 3c 4.00 4.00
a. Inverted surcharge 20.00 20.00
b. On Alexandria #18 140.00 140.00
38 A2 5m on 4c 4.00 4.00
a. Inverted surcharge 32.50 32.50
39 A2 10m on 2c 5.00 5.00
40 A2 10m on 4c 8.00 8.00
a. Inverted surcharge 32.50 32.50
41 A3 10m on 25c 2.50 2.50
a. Inverted surcharge 32.50 32.50
42 A3 12m on 30c 4.00 14.00
43 A2 15m on 4c 3.00 3.00
a. Inverted surcharge 32.50 32.50
44 A3 15m on 15c pale red 22.50 22.50
a. Inverted surcharge 45.00 45.00
45 A3 15m on 20c 22.50 22.50
a. Inverted surcharge 45.00 45.00
46 A4 30m on 50c 150.00 150.00
47 A4 60m on 50c 165.00 165.00
48 A4 150m on 50c 210.00 210.00

Nos. 46, 47 and 48 have a bar between the numerals and "Milliemes", which is in capital letters.

Same Surcharge on Stamps of French Offices in Turkey, 1902-03
49 A2 2m on 2c vio brn 35.00 35.00
50 A2 5m on 1c gray 35.00 35.00
a. "5" inverted 350.00 350.00

Nos. 28-32 Surcharged **15 MILLIEMES**

51 A4 15m on 40c 21.00 21.00
52 A4 15m on 50c 27.50 27.50
b. Bar below 15 22.50 22.50
53 A4 30m on 1fr 110.00 110.00
54 A4 60m on 2fr 40.00 40.00
55 A4 150m on 5fr 140.00 140.00

Overprinted "MILLtEMES"
51a A4 15m on 40c 52.50 50.00
52a A4 15m on 50c 135.00 135.00
53a A4 30m on 1fr 350.00 325.00
54a A4 60m on 2fr 140.00 110.00
55a A4 150m on 5fr 400.00 350.00

Stamps of 1902-03 Surcharged in Paris **2 MILLIEMES**

1921-23
56 A2 1m on 1c gray 35 35
57 A2 2m on 5c green 35 35
58 A3 4m on 10c rose 65 65
59 A2 5m on 3c red org 2.75 2.75
60 A3 6m on 15c org 85 85
a. 6m on 15c pale red 3.75 3.75
61 A3 8m on 20c brn vio 65 65
62 A3 10m on 25c blue 1.10 1.10
63 A3 10m on 30c vio 2.25 2.25
64 A3 15m on 50c blue 1.90 1.90

Nos. 29-32 and Type of 1902 Surcharged **15 MILLIEMES**

65 A4 15m on 50c 1.90 1.90
66 A4 30m on 1fr 2.25 2.25
67 A4 60m on 2fr 45.00 45.00
68 A4 60m on 2fr org & pale blue 3.25 3.25
69 A4 150m on 5fr 2.75 2.75
Nos. 56-69 (14) 66.00 66.00

Stamps and Types of 1902-03 Surcharged with New Values and Bars

1925
70 A2 1m on 1c gray 25 25
71 A2 2m on 5c green 30 30
72 A3 4m on 10c rose red 30 30
73 A2 5m on 3c red org 30 30
74 A3 6m on 15c org 48 48
75 A3 8m on 20c brn vio 30 30
76 A3 10m on 25c blue 50 50
77 A3 15m on 50c blue 50 50
78 A4 30m on 1fr cl & ol grn 55 55
79 A4 60m on 2fr org & pale blue 65 65
80 A4 150m on 5fr dk bl & buff 85 85
Nos. 70-80 (11) 4.98 4.98

Types of 1902-03 Issue

1927-28

83	A2	3m org ('28)	50	50
87	A3	15m slate bl	55	55
88	A3	20m rose lil ('28)	65	65
90	A4	50m org & blue	1.10	1.10
91	A4	100m slate bl & buff	1.50	1.50
92	A4	250m gray grn & red	2.75	2.75
		Nos. 83-92 (6)	7.05	7.05

SEMI-POSTAL STAMPS

Regular Issue of 1902-03 Surcharged in Carmine

+5c

1915 Unwmk. *Perf. 14x13½*

B1	A3	10c + 5c rose	52	52

Sinking Fund Issue

Type of 1902-03 Issue Surcharged like Alexandria Nos. B2-B3 in Blue or Black

1927-30

B2	A3	15m + 5m dp org (Bl)	95	95
B3	A3	15m + 5m red vio ('28)	95	95
a.		15m + 5m violet ('30)	1.65	1.65
B4	A3	15m + 5m fawn ('29)	1.00	1.00

POSTAGE DUE STAMPS

Postage Due Stamps of France, 1893-1906, Surcharged Locally in Black

15 Millièmes

1921 Unwmk. *Perf. 14x13½*

J1	D2	12m on 10c brn	18.00	18.00
J2	D2	15m on 5c blue	20.00	20.00
J3	D2	30m on 20c ol grn	22.50	22.50
a.		Inverted surcharge	275.00	275.00
J4	D2	30m on 50c red vio	*1,700.*	*1,700.*

Same Surcharged in Red or Blue

4 MILLIEMES

1921

J5	D2	2m on 5c bl (R)	18.00	18.00
a.		Blue surcharge	110.00	110.00
J6	D2	4m on 10c brn (Bl)	20.00	20.00
a.		Surcharged "15 Milliemes"	275.00	275.00
J7	D2	10m on 30c red (Bl)	18.00	18.00
a.		Inverted surcharge	45.00	45.00
J8	D2	15m on 50c brn vio (Bl)	24.00	24.00
a.		Inverted surcharge	47.50	47.50

Nos. J5-J8 exist with second "M" in "Milliemes" inverted, also with final "S" omitted.

Alexandria Nos. J6-J13 were also available for use in Port Said.

OFFICES IN TURKISH EMPIRE (LEVANT)

Various powers maintained post offices in the Turkish Empire before World War I by authority of treaties which ended with the signing of the Treaty of Lausanne in 1923. The foreign post offices were closed Oct. 27, 1923.

100 Centimes = 1 Franc
25 Centimes = 40 Paras = 1 Piaster

A1

Stamps of France Surcharged in Black or Red

1885-1901 Unwmk. *Perf. 14x13½*

1	A1	1pi on 25c yel, *straw*	200.00	3.75
a.		Inverted surcharge	*950.00*	*950.00*
2	A1	1pi on 25c blk, *rose* (R) ('86)	75	35
a.		Inverted surcharge	110.00	100.00
3	A1	2pi on 50c car, *rose* (II) ('90)	6.00	85
a.		Type I ('01)	125.00	15.00
4	A1	3pi on 75c car, *rose*	7.50	3.75
5	A1	4pi on 1fr brnz grn, *straw*	5.75	2.25
6	A1	8pi on 2fr brn, *az* ('00)	15.00	8.50
7	A1	20pi on 5fr red lil, *lav* ('90)	37.50	16.00

A2

A3

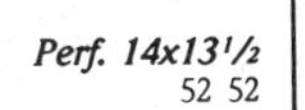
A4

A5

A6

1902-07 Typo. *Perf. 14x13½*

21	A2	1c gray	15	15
22	A2	2c vio brn	22	15
23	A2	3c red org	22	15
24	A2	4c yel brn	45	25
a.		Imperf., pair	24.00	
25	A2	5c grn ('06)	22	15
26	A3	10c rose red	28	15
27	A3	15c pale red ('03)	50	35
28	A3	20c brn vio ('03)	50	35
29	A3	25c blue ('07)	15.00	12.50
a.		Imperf., pair	140.00	
30	A3	30c lilac ('03)	1.25	70
31	A4	40c red & pale bl	1.25	70
32	A4	50c bis brn & lav ('07)	55.00	47.50
a.		Imperf., pair	350.00	
33	A4	1fr claret & ol grn ('07)	140.00	140.00
a.		Imperf., pair	350.00	

Black Surcharge

34	A5	1pi on 25c bl ('03)	28	15
a.		Second "1" omitted	6.00	5.00
b.		Double surcharge	19.00	14.00
35	A6	2pi on 50c bis brn & lavender	65	22
36	A6	4pi on 1fr cl & ol grn	85	30
a.		Imperf., pair	250.00	
37	A6	8pi on 2fr gray vio & yel	5.25	2.75
38	A6	20pi on 5fr dk bl & buff	1.90	80
		Nos. 21-38 (18)	223.97	207.32

Nos. 29, 32-33 were used during the early part of 1907 in the French Offices at Harar and Diredawa, Ethiopia. Djibouti and Port Said stamps were also used.

No. 27 Surcharged in Green

1 Piastre
Beyrouth

1905

39	A3	1pi on 15c pale red	900.00	125.00
a.		"Piastte"	*2,800.*	500.00

Stamps of France 1900-21 Surcharged:

30 PARAS	1 PIASTRE 20 PARAS	15 PIASTRES
On A22	On A20	On A18

1921-22

40	A22	30pa on 5c grn	28	18
41	A22	30pa on 5c org	28	18
42	A22	1pi20pa on 10c red	28	18
43	A22	1pi20pa on 10c grn	28	18
44	A22	3pi30pa on 25c bl	28	18
45	A22	4pi20pa on 30c org	28	18
a.		"4" omitted	350.00	
46	A20	7pi20pa on 50c bl	28	18
47	A18	15pi on 1fr car & ol grn	45	32
48	A18	30pi on 2fr org & pale bl	4.25	2.50
49	A18	75pi on 5fr dk bl & buff	2.50	1.50
		Nos. 40-49 (10)	9.16	5.58

Stamps of France, 1903-07, Handstamped

3 PIASTRES
30 PARAS

1923

52	A22	1pi20pa on 10c red	20.00	20.00
54	A20	3pi30pa on 15c gray grn	6.50	6.50
55	A22	7pi20pa on 35c vio	8.00	8.00
a.		1pi20pa on 35c violet	300.00	300.00

CAVALLE (CAVALLA)

A1

A2

Stamps of France Overprinted or Surcharged in Red, Blue or Black

1893-1900 Unwmk. *Perf. 14x13½*

1	A1	5c grn, *grnsh* (R)	5.75	5.00
2	A1	5c yel grn (I) ('00) (R)	6.25	4.00
3	A1	10c blk, *lav* (II)	6.50	4.75
a.		10c black, *lavender* (I)	67.50	60.00
4	A1	15c blue (R)	10.00	7.25
5	A2	1pi on 25c blk, *rose*	11.00	8.00
6	A2	2pi on 50c car, *rose*	30.00	22.00
7	A2	4pi on 1fr brnz grn, *straw* (R)	30.00	25.00
8	A2	8pi on 2fr brn, *az* ('00) (Bk)	42.50	40.00
		Nos. 1-8 (8)	142.00	116.00

A3

A4

A5

A6

1902-03

9	A3	5c green	45	45
10	A4	10c rose red ('03)	55	55
11	A4	15c orange	60	60
a.		15c pale red ('03)	2.75	2.75

Surcharged in Black

12	A5	1pi on 25c bl	1.00	90
13	A6	2pi on 50c bis brn & lav	2.50	2.00
14	A6	4pi on 1fr cl & ol grn	3.50	3.00
15	A6	8pi on 2fr gray vio & yel	5.00	4.75
		Nos. 9-15 (7)	13.60	12.25

DEDEAGH (DEDEAGATCH)

A1

A2

Stamps of France Overprinted or Surcharged in Red, Blue or Black

1893-1900 Unwmk. *Perf. 14x13½*

1	A1	5c grn, *grnsh* (II) (R)	4.75	4.25
2	A1	5c yel grn (I) ('00) (R)	4.75	4.25
3	A1	10c blk, *lav* (II)	7.00	6.25
a.		Type I	17.00	8.75
4	A1	15c blue (R)	9.75	8.50
5	A2	1pi on 25c blk, *rose*	9.75	8.50
6	A2	2pi on 50c car, *rose*	21.00	16.00
7	A2	4pi on 1fr brnz grn, *straw* (R)	25.00	19.00
8	A2	8pi on 2fr brn, *az* ('00) (Bk)	37.50	30.00
		Nos. 1-8 (8)	119.50	96.75

A3

A4

A5

A6

1902-03

9	A3	5c green	60	60
10	A4	10c rose red ('03)	85	60
11	A4	15c orange	1.25	90

Black Surcharge

15	A5	1pi on 25c bl ('03)	1.50	90
16	A6	2pi on 50c bis brn & lav	4.00	3.25
a.		Double surcharge	95.00	
17	A6	4pi on 1fr cl & ol grn	7.50	6.00
18	A6	8pi on 2fr gray vio & yel	11.00	10.00
		Nos. 9-18 (7)	26.70	22.25

PORT LAGOS

A1

A2

Stamps of France Overprinted or Surcharged in Red or Blue

1893 Unwmk. *Perf. 14x13½*

1	A1	5c grn, *grnsh* (R)	8.75	4.50
2	A1	10c blk, *lav*	18.00	8.75
3	A1	15c blue (R)	32.50	18.00
4	A2	1pi on 25c blk, *rose*	22.50	15.00
5	A2	2pi on 50c car, *rose*	75.00	30.00
6	A2	4pi on 1fr brnz grn, *straw* (R)	40.00	22.50

VATHY (SAMOS)

A1

A2

Stamps of France Overprinted or Surcharged in Red, Blue or Black

1894-1900 Unwmk. *Perf. 14x13½*

1	A1	5c grn, *grnsh* (R)	3.00	2.50
2	A1	5c yel grn (I) ('00) (R)	3.00	2.50
a.		Type II	37.50	35.00
3	A1	10c blk, *lav* (I)	4.50	3.75
a.		Type II	22.50	13.00
4	A1	15c blue (R)	4.00	4.00
5	A2	1pi on 25c blk, *rose*	4.50	3.50
6	A2	2pi on 50c car, *rose*	10.00	10.00
7	A2	4pi on 1fr brnz grn, *straw* (R)	11.50	11.00
8	A2	8pi on 2fr brn, *az* ('00) (Bk)	37.50	27.50
9	A2	20pi on 5fr lil, *lav* ('00) (Bk)	47.50	45.00
		Nos. 1-9 (9)	125.50	109.75

OFFICES IN ZANZIBAR

Until 1906 France maintained post offices in the Sultanate of Zanzibar, but in that year Great Britain assumed direct control over this protectorate and the French withdrew their postal system.

16 Annas = 1 Rupee

A1

A2

Stamps of France Surcharged in Red, Blue or Black

1894-96 Unwmk. *Perf. 14x13½*

1 A1 ½a on 5c grn, *grnsh* 2.75 2.25
2 A1 1a on 10c blk, *lav* (Bl) 5.25 4.00
3 A1 1½a on 15c bl ('96) 8.25 8.00
a. "ANNAS" 42.50 42.50
4 A1 2a on 20c red, *grn* ('96) (Bk) 5.25 4.00
5 A1 2½a on 25c blk, *rose* (Bl) 4.25 2.75
a. Double surcharge 75.00
6 A1 3a on 30c brn, *bis* ('96) (Bk) 8.25 7.25
7 A1 4a on 40c red, *straw* ('96) (Bk) 8.25 7.25
8 A1 5a on 50c car, *rose* (Bl) 14.00 11.50
9 A1 7½a on 75c vio, *org* ('96) 250.00 190.00
10 A1 10a on 1fr brnz grn, *straw* 22.50 18.00
11 A1 50a on 5fr red lil, *lav* ('96) (Bk) 175.00 125.00

1894

12 A2 ½a & 5c on 1c blk, *lil bl* (R) 75.00 75.00
13 A2 1a & 10c on 3c gray, *grysh* (R) 72.50 72.50
14 A2 2½a & 25c on 4c cl, *lav* (Bk) 100.00 100.00
15 A2 5a & 50c on 20c red, *grn* (Bk) 100.00 100.00
16 A2 10a & 1fr on 40c red, *straw* (Bk) 200.00 200.00

There are two distinct types of the figures 5c, four of the 25c and three of each of the others of this series.

A3

Surcharged in Red, Blue or Black

1896-1900

17 A3 ½a on 5c grn, *grnsh* (R) 2.50 1.75
18 A3 ½a on 5c yel grn (I) (R) 2.50 1.75
a. Type II 2.50 2.00
19 A3 1a on 10c blk, *lav* (II) (Bl) 2.75 2.00
a. Type I 5.00 4.50
20 A3 1½a on 15c bl (R) 2.50 1.75
21 A3 2a on 20c red, *grn* 2.50 2.25
a. "ZANZIBAR" double 37.50
b. "ZANZIBAR" triple 42.50
22 A3 2½a on 25c blk, *rose* (Bl) 3.25 2.75
23 A3 3a on 30c brn, *bis* 5.00 4.50
24 A3 4a on 40c red, *straw* 3.00 2.75
25 A3 5a on 50c rose, *rose* (II) (Bl) 12.50 9.50
a. Type I 24.00 21.00
26 A3 10a on 1fr brnz grn, *straw* (R) 6.50 5.00
27 A3 20a on 2fr brn, *az* 9.00 5.75
a. "ZANZIBAS" 250.00 250.00
28 A3 50a on 5fr lil, *lav* 24.00 16.00
a. "ZANZIBAS" *1,350.*
Nos. 17-28 (12) 76.00 55.75

For surcharges see Nos. 50-54.

A4

A5

1897

29 A4 2½a & 25c on ½a on 5c grn, *grnsh* 525.00 75.00
30 A4 2½a & 25c on 1a on 10c *lav* *2,100.* 475.00
31 A4 2½a & 25c on 1½a on 15c blue *2,100.* 400.00
32 A5 5a & 50c on 3a on 30c brn, *bis* *2,100.* 350.00
33 A5 5a & 50c on 4a on 40c red, *straw* *2,100.* 425.00

PosteFrance 2½ Annas 25c ZANZIBAR
A6

PosteFrance 5 Annas 50c ZANZIBAR
A7

Printed on the Margins of Sheets of French Stamps

1897

34 A6 2½a & 25c grn, *grnsh* 500.00
35 A6 2½a & 25c blk, *lav* *1,400.*
36 A6 2½a & 25c blue *1,400.*
37 A7 5a & 50c brn, *bis* *1,150.*
38 A7 5a & 50c red, *straw* *1,400.*

There are several varieties of figures in the above surcharges.

A8

A9

A10

Surcharged in Red or Black

1902-03

39 A8 ½a on 5c grn (R) 1.90 1.40
40 A9 1a on 10c rose red ('03) 2.25 2.10
41 A9 1½a on 15c pale red ('03) 4.50 4.00
42 A9 2a on 20c brn vio ('03) 5.75 4.75
43 A9 2½a on 25c bl ('03) 5.75 4.75
44 A9 3a on 30c lil ('03) 4.50 3.50
a. 5a on 30c (error) 150.00 150.00
45 A10 4a on 40c red & pale bl 7.50 6.75
46 A10 5a on 50c bis brn & lav 6.00 5.00
47 A10 10a on 1fr cl & ol grn 9.75 9.00
48 A10 20a on 2fr gray vio & yel 22.50 21.00
49 A10 50a on 5fr dk bl & buff 37.50 37.50
Nos. 39-49 (11) 107.90 99.75

For see Reunion Nos. 55-59.

Nos. 23-24 Surcharged in Black:

25 2½ — a
50 5 — b
1 fr 10 — c

1904

50 A3 25c & 2½a on 4a on 40c 450.00
51 A3 50c & 5a on 3a on 30c 575.00
52 A3 50c & 5a on 4a on 40c 575.00
53 A3 1fr & 10a on 3a on 30c 950.00
54 A3 1fr & 10a on 4a on 40c 950.00

Nos. 39-40, 44 Surcharged in Red or Black:

2 25
25c 2½

50c cinq
1 fr dix

55 A8 25c & 2a on ½a on 5c (R) *1,250.* 50.00
56 A9 25c & 2½a on 1a on 10c *2,500.* 57.50
a. Inverted surcharge 575.00
57 A9 25c & 2½a on 3a on 30c *1,500.*
a. Inverted surcharge *1,500.*
b. Double surch., both invtd. *1,900.*
58 A9 50c & 5a on 3a on 30c 500.00
59 A9 1fr & 10a on 3a on 30c 675.00

No. J1-J3 With Various Surcharges Overprinted:

"Timbre" in Red

60 D1 ½a on 5c blue 190.00

Overprinted "Affrancht" in Black

61 D1 1a on 10c brown 190.00

With Red Bars Across "CHIFFRE" and "TAXE"

62 D1 1½a on 15c green 425.00

The illustrations are not exact reproductions of the new surcharges but are merely intended to show their relative positions and general styles.

POSTAGE DUE STAMPS

D1

Stamps of France Surcharged in Red, Blue or Black

1897 Unwmk. *Perf. 14x13½*

J1 D1 ½a on 5c blue (R) 6.00 3.50
J2 D1 1a on 10c brn (Bl) 6.00 3.50
a. Inverted surcharge 57.50 57.50
J3 D1 1½a on 15c grn (R) 8.25 5.00
J4 D1 3a on 30c car (Bk) 9.75 7.25
J5 D1 5a on 50c lil (Bl) 9.75 7.25
a. 2½a on 50c lilac (Bl) 450.00 425.00
Nos. J1-J5 (5) 39.75 26.50

For overprints see Nos. 60-62.

REUNION

LOCATION — An island in the Indian Ocean about 400 miles east of Madagascar
GOVT. — Former French colony
AREA — 970 sq. mi.
POP. — 490,000 (est. 1974)
CAPITAL — St. Denis

The colony of Réunion became an integral part of the Republic, acquiring the same status as the departments in metropolitan France, under a law effective Jan. 1, 1947.

On Jan. 1, 1975, stamps of France replaced those inscribed or overprinted "CFA."

100 Centimes = 1 Franc

Catalogue values for unused stamps in this country are for Never Hinged items, beginning with Scott 224 in the regular postage section, Scott B15 in the semi-postal section, Scott C18 in the airpost section, and Scott J26 in the postage due section.

For French stamps inscribed "Reunion" see Nos. 949, 1507.

Values of early Reunion stamps vary according to condition. Quotations for Nos. 1-2 are for fine copies. Very fine to superb specimens sell at much higher prices, and inferior or poor copies sell at reduced prices, depending on the condition of the individual specimen.

A1

A2

1852 Unwmk. Typo. *Imperf.*

1 A1 15c black, *blue* *17,500.* *10,000.*
2 A2 30c black, *blue* *17,500.* *10,000.*

Four varieties of each value.

The reprints are printed on a more bluish paper than the originals. They have a frame of a thick and a thin line, instead of one thick and two thin lines. Value, $24 each.

Stamps of French Colonies Surcharged or Overprinted in Black:

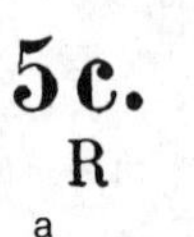

a

b

1885

3 A1(a) 5c on 40c org, *yelsh* 150.00 150.00
a. Inverted surcharge 500.00 500.00
4 A1(a) 25c on 40c org, *yelsh* 20.00 18.00
a. Inverted surcharge 180.00 180.00
b. Double surcharge 180.00 180.00
5 A5(a) 5c on 30c brn, *yelsh* 20.00 18.00
a. "5" inverted 650.00 650.00
b. Double surcharge 180.00 180.00
6 A4(a) 5c on 40c org, *yelsh* (I) 16.00 15.00
a. 5c on 40c org, *yelsh* (II) 700.00 700.00
b. Inverted surcharge (I)
c. Double surcharge (I)
7 A8(a) 5c on 30c brn, *yelsh* 3.00 3.00
8 A8(a) 5c on 40c ver, *straw* 40.00 30.00
a. Inverted surcharge
b. Double surcharge
9 A8(a) 10c on 40c ver, *straw* 4.00 3.50
10 A8(a) 20c on 30c brn, *yelsh* 25.00 20.00

Overprint Type "b"
With or Without Accent on "E"

1891

11 A4 40c org, *yelsh* (I) 225.00 175.00
a. 40c orange, *yelsh* (II) *1,600.* *1,600.*
12 A7 80c car, *pnksh* 25.00 20.00
13 A8 30c brn, *yelsh* 14.00 14.00
14 A8 40c ver, *straw* 10.00 10.00
15 A8 75c car, *rose* 140.00 140.00
16 A8 1fr brnz grn, *straw* 18.00 16.00

Perf. 14x13½

17 A9 1c blk, *lil bl* 1.40 1.20
a. Inverted overprint 8.00 8.00
b. Double overprint 12.50 12.50
18 A9 2c brn, *buff* 1.80 1.50
a. Inverted overprint 8.00 8.00
19 A9 4c claret, *lav* 3.25 2.50
a. Inverted overprint 25.00 25.00
20 A9 5c grn, *grnsh* 3.25 2.00
a. Inverted overprint 12.00 12.00
b. Double overprint 15.00 15.00
21 A9 10c blk, *lav* 12.00 2.00
a. Inverted overprint 20.00 20.00
b. Double overprint 20.00 17.50
22 A9 15c blue 16.00 2.00
a. Inverted overprint 35.00 35.00
23 A9 20c red, *grn* 12.00 9.00
a. Inverted overprint 42.50 42.50
b. Double overprint 35.00 32.50
24 A9 25c blk, *rose* 12.00 2.50
a. Inverted overprint 42.50 42.50
25 A9 35c dp vio, *yel* 9.00 9.00
b. Inverted overprint 50.00 50.00
26 A9 40c red, *straw* 25.00 21.00
a. Inverted overprint 65.00 65.00
27 A9 75c car, *rose* 250.00 200.00
a. Inverted overprint 450.00 450.00
28 A9 1fr brnz grn, *straw* 225.00 180.00
a. Inverted overprint 450.00 450.00

The varieties "RUNION", "RUENION", "REUNIONR", "REUNIOU" and "REUNOIN" are found on most stamps of this group. There are also many broken letters.

For surcharges see Nos. 29-33, 53-55.

No. 23 with Additional Surcharge in Black:

02c — c
2 — d
2 — e
2 — f

1891

29 A9(c) 02c on 20c red, *grn* 3.50 3.50
30 A9(c) 15c on 20c red, *grn* 5.00 5.00
31 A9(d) 2c on 20c red, *grn* 1.10 1.10
32 A9(e) 2c on 20c red, *grn* 90 90
33 A9(f) 2c on 20c red, *grn* 1.60 1.60

Navigation and Commerce — A14

1892-1905 Typo. *Perf. 14x13½*

Name of Colony in Blue or Carmine

34 A14 1c blk, *lil bl* 42 35
35 A14 2c brn, *buff* 42 35
36 A14 4c claret, *lav* 70 60
37 A14 5c grn, *grnsh* 2.00 80
38 A14 5c yel grn ('00) 42 42
39 A14 10c blk, *lav* 2.50 80
40 A14 10c red ('00) 55 55
41 A14 15c bl, quadrille paper 7.00 90
42 A14 15c gray ('00) 1.60 42
43 A14 20c red, *grn* 5.50 3.50
44 A14 25c blk, *rose* 5.25 80
a. "Reunion" double 110.00 110.00
45 A14 25c blue ('00) 6.25 6.25
46 A14 30c brn, *bis* 5.75 3.50
47 A14 40c red, *straw* 7.00 6.00
48 A14 50c car, *rose* 22.50 12.50
a. "Reunion" in red and blue 110.00 110.00
49 A14 50c brn, *az* ("Reunion" in car) ('00) 15.00 14.00
50 A14 50c brn, *az* ("Reunion" in bl) ('05) 18.00 15.00
51 A14 75c dp vio, *org* 20.00 15.00
a. "Reunion" double 110.00 110.00
52 A14 1fr brnz grn, *straw* 15.00 9.00
a. "Reunion" double 110.00 110.00
Nos. 34-52 (19) 135.86 90.74

Perf. 13½x14 stamps are counterfeits.

For surcharges and overprint see Nos. 56-59, 99-106, Q1.

French Colonies No. 52 Surcharged in Black:

2 c. 2 c. 2 c.
g h j

1893

53 A9(g) 2c on 20c red, *grn* 65 65
54 A9(h) 2c on 20c red, *grn* 1.40 1.40
55 A9(j) 2c on 20c red, *grn* 6.25 6.25

Reunion Nos. 47-48, 51-52 Surcharged in Black **5 c.**

1901

56 A14 5c on 40c red, *straw* 1.50 1.50
a. Inverted surcharge 11.00 11.00
b. No bar 55.00 55.00
c. Thin "5"
d. "5" inverted 375.00 375.00
57 A14 5c on 50c car, *rose* 1.60 1.60
a. Inverted surcharge 11.00 11.00
b. No bar 55.00 55.00
c. Thin "5"
58 A14 15c on 75c vio, *org* 5.50 5.50
a. Inverted surcharge 11.00 11.00
b. No bar 55.00 55.00
c. Thin "5" and small "1" 11.00 10.00
d. As "c," inverted
59 A14 15c on 1fr brnz grn, *straw* 5.50 5.50
a. Inverted surcharge 11.00 11.00
b. No bar 55.00 55.00
c. Thin "5" and small "1" 11.00 10.00
d. As "c," inverted

Map of Réunion A19

Coat of Arms and View of St. Denis — A20

View of St. Pierre — A21

1907-30 Typo.

60 A19 1c vio & car rose 15 15
61 A19 2c brn & ultra 15 15
62 A19 4c ol grn & red 15 15
63 A19 5c grn & red 15 15
64 A19 5c org & vio ('22) 15 15
65 A19 10c car & grn 60 15
66 A19 10c grn ('22) 15 15
67 A19 10c brn red & org red, *bluish* ('26) 15 15
68 A19 15c blk & ultra 15 15
69 A19 15c gray grn & bl grn ('26) 15 15
70 A19 15c bl & lt red ('28) 15 15
71 A20 20c gray grn & bl grn 15 15
72 A20 25c dp bl & vio brn 90 65
73 A20 25c lt brn & bl ('22) 15 15
74 A20 30c yel brn & grn 16 16
75 A20 30c rose & pale rose ('22) 15 15
76 A20 30c gray & car rose ('26) 15 15
77 A20 30c dp grn & yel grn ('28) 35 35
78 A20 35c ol grn & bl 40 16
79 A20 40c gray grn & brn ('25) 15 15
80 A20 45c vio & car rose 40 16
81 A20 45c red brn & ver ('26) 16 16
82 A20 45c vio & red org ('28) 80 80
83 A20 50c red brn & ultra 90 30
84 A20 50c bl & ultra ('22) 15 15
85 A20 50c yel & vio ('26) 15 15
86 A20 60c dk bl & yel brn ('26) 15 15
87 A20 65c vio & lt bl ('28) 35 30
88 A20 75c red & car rose 16 15
89 A20 75c ol brn & red vio ('28) 70 60
90 A20 90c brn red & brt red ('30) 2.50 2.25
91 A21 1fr ol grn & bl 30 20
92 A21 1fr blue ('26) 20 20
93 A21 1fr yel brn & lav ('28) 30 16
94 A21 1.10fr org brn & rose lil ('28) 40 30
95 A21 1.50fr dk bl & ultra ('30) 4.00 3.00
96 A21 2fr red & grn 1.50 1.00
97 A21 3fr red vio ('30) 4.25 3.00
98 A21 5fr car & vio brn 3.00 1.60
Nos. 60-98 (39) 25.03 18.35

For surcharges see #107-121, 178-180, B1-B3.

Stamps of 1892-1900 Surcharged in Black or Carmine

05 **10**

1912

99 A14 5c on 2c brn, *buff* 35 35
100 A14 5c on 15c gray (C) 35 35
a. Inverted surcharge 60.00 60.00
101 A14 5c on 20c red, *grn* 50 50
102 A14 5c on 25c blk, *rose* (C) 35 35
103 A14 5c on 30c brn, *bis* (C) 35 35
104 A14 10c on 40c red, *straw* 35 35
105 A14 10c on 50c brn, *az* (C) 1.25 1.25
106 A14 10c on 75c dp vio, *org* 3.50 3.50
Nos. 99-106 (8) 7.00 7.00

Two spacings between the surcharged numerals are found on Nos. 99 to 106.

No. 62 Surcharged **0,01**

1917

107 A19 1c on 4c ol grn & red 50 50
a. Inverted surcharge 15.00 15.00
b. Double surcharge 25.00 25.00

Stamps and Types of 1907-30 Surcharged in Black or Red **40**

1922-33

108 A20 40c on 20c grn & yel 25 25
109 A20 50c on 45c red brn & ver ('33) 35 28
109A A20 50c on 45c vio & red org ('33) 110.00 100.00
b. Double surcharge 550.00
110 A20 50c on 65c vio & lt bl ('33) 35 28
111 A20 60c on 75c red & rose 16 16
112 A19 65c on 15c blk & ultra (R) ('25) 45 45
113 A19 85c on 15c blk & ultra (R) ('25) 45 45
114 A20 85c on 75c red & cer ('25) 45 45
115 A20 90c on 75 brn red & rose red ('27) 60 60
Nos. 108-109 (2) 60 53

Stamps and Type of 1907-30 Surcharged with New Value and Bars in Black or Red

1924-27

116 A21 25c on 5fr car & brn 25 25
a. Double surcharge 27.50
117 A21 1.25fr on 1fr bl (R) ('26) 15 15
a. Double surcharge 32.50 32.50
118 A21 1.50fr on 1fr ind & ultra, *bluish* ('27) 25 25
a. Double surcharge 40.00 40.00
119 A21 3fr on 5fr dl red & lt bl ('27) 80 80
120 A21 10fr on 5fr bl grn & brn red ('27) 5.50 5.00
121 A21 20fr on 5fr blk brn & rose ('27) 7.00 6.00
Nos. 116-121 (6) 13.95 12.45

Colonial Exposition Issue

Common Design Types

1931 Engr. *Perf. 12½*

Name of Country Typo. in Black

122 CD70 40c dp grn 1.10 1.10
123 CD71 50c violet 1.25 1.25
124 CD72 90c red org 1.25 1.25
125 CD73 1.50fr dull blue 1.25 1.25

Cascade of Salazie — A22

Waterfowl Lake and Anchain Peak — A23

Léon Dierx Museum, St. Denis — A24

Perf. 12, 12½ and Compound

1933-40 Engr.

126 A22 1c violet 15 15
127 A22 2c dark brown 15 15
128 A22 3c rose vio ('40) 15 15
129 A22 4c olive green 15 15
130 A22 5c red orange 15 15
131 A22 10c ultramarine 15 15
132 A22 15c black 15 15
133 A22 20c indigo 15 15
134 A22 25c red brown 15 15
135 A22 30c dark green 15 15
136 A23 35c green ('38) 16 16
137 A23 40c ultramarine 15 15
138 A23 40c brn blk ('40) 15 15
139 A23 45c red violet 30 20
140 A23 45c green ('40) 15 15
141 A23 50c red 15 15
142 A23 55c brn org ('38) 16 15
143 A23 60c dull bl ('40) 15 15
144 A23 65c olive green 45 30
145 A23 70c ol grn ('40) 15 15
146 A23 75c dark brown 1.50 1.25
147 A23 80c black ('38) 16 16
148 A23 90c carmine 70 60
149 A23 90c dl rose vio ('39) 16 16
150 A23 1fr green 65 15
151 A23 1fr dk car ('38) 40 16
152 A23 1fr black ('40) 15 15
153 A24 1.25fr orange brown 16 15
154 A24 1.25fr brt car rose ('39) 32 32
155 A22 1.40fr pck bl ('40) 16 16
156 A24 1.50fr ultramarine 15 15
157 A22 1.60fr dk car rose ('40) 32 32
158 A24 1.75fr olive green 20 16
159 A22 1.75fr dk bl ('38) 20 16
160 A24 2fr vermilion 15 15
161 A22 2.25fr brt ultra ('39) 55 55
162 A22 2.50fr chnt ('40) 32 32
163 A24 3fr purple 15 15
164 A24 5fr magenta 35 16
165 A24 10fr dark blue 30 20
166 A24 20fr red brown 50 45
Set value 9.50 7.65

For overprints and surcharges see Nos. 177A, 181-220, 223, C1.

Paris International Exposition Issue

Common Design Types

1937 *Perf. 13*

167 CD74 20c dp vio 60 50
168 CD75 30c dk grn 65 65
169 CD76 40c car rose 65 65
170 CD77 50c dk brn & blk 70 70
171 CD78 90c red 70 70
172 CD79 1.50fr ultra 70 70
Nos. 167-172 (6) 4.00 3.90

Colonial Arts Exhibition Issue

Souvenir Sheet

Common Design Type

1937 *Imperf.*

173 CD74 3fr ultra 2.00 2.00

New York World's Fair Issue

Common Design Type

1939 Engr. *Perf. 12½x12*

174 CD82 1.25fr car lake 35 35
175 CD82 2.25fr ultra 35 35

For overprints see Nos. 221-222.

St. Denis Roadstead and Marshal Pétain A25

1941 Unwmk. *Perf. 11½x12*

176 A25 1fr brown 20
177 A25 2.50fr blue 20

Nos. 176-177 were issued by the Vichy government, and were not placed on sale in Réunion.

No. 144 Surcharged in Carmine

1943

177A A23 1fr on 65c olive grn 35 15

V1

Stamps of the above design and stamps of type A26, without "RF," were issued in 1943 and 1944 by the Vichy Government, but were not placed on sale in Réunion.

Stamps of 1907 Overprinted in Blue Violet

France Libre
q

1943 Unwmk. *Perf. 14x13½*

178 A19(q) 4c ol gray & pale red 1.20 1.20
179 A20(q) 75c red & lil rose 35 35
180 A21(q) 5fr car & vio brn 18.00 18.00

Stamps of 1933-40 Overprinted in Carmine, Black or Blue Violet

France

Libre
r

181 A22(r) 1c rose vio (C) 25 25
182 A22(r) 2c blk brn (C) 25 25
183 A22(r) 3c rose vio (C) 25 25
184 A22(r) 4c ol yel (C) 25 25
185 A22(r) 5c red org 25 25
186 A22(r) 10c ultra (C) 25 25
187 A22(r) 15c blk (C) 25 25
188 A22(r) 20c ind (C) 25 25
189 A22(r) 25c red brn (BlV) 25 25
190 A22(r) 30c dk grn (C) 25 25
191 A23(q) 35c green 25 25
192 A23(q) 40c dl ultra (C) 25 25

193 A23(q) 40c brn blk (C) 25 25
194 A23(q) 45c red vio 25 25
195 A23(q) 45c green 25 25
196 A23(q) 50c org red 25 25
197 A23(q) 55c brn org 25 25
198 A23(q) 60c dl bl (C) 90 90
199 A23(q) 65c ol grn 25 25
200 A23(q) 70c ol grn (C) 55 55
201 A23(q) 75c dk brn (C) 1.00 1.00
202 A23(q) 80c blk (C) 25 25
203 A23(q) 90c dl rose vio 25 25
204 A23(q) 1fr green 25 25
205 A23(q) 1fr dk car 25 25
206 A23(q) 1fr blk (C) 60 60
207 A24(q) 1.25fr org brn (BlV) 25 25
208 A24(q) 1.25fr brt car rose 55 55
209 A22(r) 1.40fr pck bl (C) 55 55
210 A24(q) 1.50fr ultra (C) 25 25
211 A22(r) 1.60fr dk car rose 60 60
212 A24(q) 1.75fr ol grn (C) 30 30
213 A22(r) 1.75fr dk bl (C) 1.20 1.20
214 A24(q) 2fr vermilion 25 25
215 A22(r) 2.25fr brt ultra (C) 55 55
216 A22(r) 2.50fr chnt (BlV) 1.90 1.90
217 A24(q) 3fr pur (C) 25 25
218 A24(q) 5fr brn lake (BlV) 55 55
219 A24(q) 10fr dk bl (C) 2.00 2.00
220 A24(q) 20fr red brn (BlV) 3.75 3.75

New York World's Fair Issue
Overprinted in Black or Carmine

221 CD82(q) 1.25fr car lake 65 65
222 CD82(q) 2.25fr ultra (C) 65 65
Nos. 178-222 (45) 42.35 42.35

No. 177A Overprinted Type "q"

1943 Unwmk. *Perf. 12½*
223 A23 1fr on 65c ol grn 25 25

Catalogue values for unused stamps in this section, from this point to the end of the section, are for Never Hinged items.

Produce of Réunion
A26

1943 Photo. *Perf. 14½x14*
224 A26 5c dull brn 15 15
225 A26 10c dark bl 15 15
226 A26 25c emerald 15 15
227 A26 30c deep org 15 15
228 A26 40c dk slate grn 15 15
229 A26 80c rose vio 16 16
230 A26 1fr red brn 15 15
231 A26 1.50fr crimson 16 16
232 A26 2fr black 16 16
233 A26 2.50fr ultra 16 16
234 A26 4fr dark vio 20 20
235 A26 5fr bister 25 25
236 A26 10fr dark brn 50 50
237 A26 20fr dark green 60 60
Set value 2.65 2.65

For surcharges see Nos. 240-247.

Eboue Issue
Common Design Type

1945 Engr. *Perf. 13*
238 CD91 2fr black 25 25
239 CD91 25fr Prussian green 35 35

Nos. 224, 226 and 233 Surcharged with New Values and Bars in Carmine or Black

1945 *Perf. 14½x14*
240 A26 50c on 5c dl brn (C) 15 15
241 A26 60c on 5c dl brn (C) 15 15
242 A26 70c on 5c dl brn (C) 15 15
243 A26 1.20fr on 5c dl brn (C) 15 15
244 A26 2.40fr on 25c emer 15 15
245 A26 3fr on 25c emer 20 20
246 A26 4.50fr on 25c emer 25 25
247 A26 15fr on 2.50fr ultra (C) 32 32
Set value 1.15 1.15

Cliff — A27

Cutting Sugar Cane — A28

Cascade
A29

Banana Tree
A30

Mountain Scene — A31

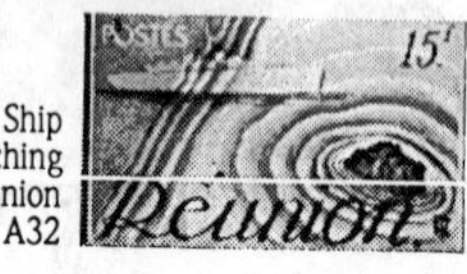

Ship Approaching Réunion
A32

1947 Unwmk. Photo. *Perf. 13½*
249 A27 10c org & grnsh blk 15 15
250 A27 30c org & brt bl 15 15
251 A27 40c org & brn 15 15
252 A28 50c bl grn & brn 15 15
253 A28 60c dk bl & brn 15 15
254 A28 80c brn & ol brn 16 15
255 A29 1fr dl bl & vio brn 15 15
256 A29 1.20fr bl grn & gray 16 16
257 A29 1.50fr org & vio brn 16 16
258 A30 2fr gray bl & bl grn 16 16
259 A30 3fr vio brn & bl grn 16 16
260 A30 3.60fr dl red & rose red 20 20
261 A30 4fr gray bl & buff 20 16
262 A31 5fr rose lil & brn 20 20
263 A31 6fr bl & brn 35 30
264 A31 10fr org & ultra 55 38
265 A32 15fr gray bl & vio brn 1.40 1.00
266 A32 20fr bl & org 1.60 1.40
267 A32 25fr rose lil & brn 2.00 1.50
Nos. 249-267 (19) 8.20 6.84

Stamps of France, 1945-49, Surcharged in Black or Carmine

2F-CFA
On A147 — b

10c
CFA
Others — a

1949 Unwmk. *Perf. 14x13½, 13*
268 A153 10c on 30c 16 15
269 A153 30c on 50c 15 15
270 A146 50c on 1fr 20 20
271 A146 60c on 2fr 3.25 60
272 A147 1fr on 3fr 38 30
273 A147 2fr on 4fr 1.90 50
274 A147 2.50fr on 5fr 9.00 6.00
275 A147 3fr on 6fr 80 30
276 A147 4fr on 10fr 80 40
277 A162 5fr on 20fr (C) 1.50 50
278 A147 6fr on 12fr 3.25 60
279 A160 7fr on 12fr 2.25 80
280 A165 8fr on 25fr (C) 11.00 2.00
281 A165 10fr on 25fr (C) 60 50
282 A174 11fr on 18fr (C) 3.75 1.00
Nos. 268-282 (15) 38.99 14.00

The letters "C. F. A." are the initials of "Colonies Francaises d'Afrique," referring to the currency which is expressed in French Africa francs.

The surcharge on Nos. 277, 279, 282 includes two bars.

1950 *Perf. 14x13½*
283 A182 10c on 50c bl, red & yel 15 15
284 A182 1fr on 2fr grn, yel & red (#619) 3.75 2.00
285 A147 2fr on 5fr lt grn 5.00 2.00

Surcharged Type "a" and Bars

1950-51 *Perf. 13*
286 A188 5fr on 20fr dk red 3.50 45
287 A185 8fr on 25fr dp ultra ('51) 1.60 50

Stamps of France, 1951-52, Surcharged in Black or Red

1951-52 *Perf. 14x13½, 13*
288 A182 50c on 1fr bl, red & yel 20 20
289 A182 1fr on 2fr vio bl, red & yel (#662) 35 30
290 A147 2fr on 5fr dl vio 55 40
291 A147 3fr on 6fr grn 2.00 1.00
292 A220 5fr on 20fr dk pur ('52) 55 50
293 A147 6fr on 12fr red org ('52) 3.25 60
294 A215 8fr on 40fr vio (R) ('52) 2.00 35
295 A147 9fr on 18fr cerise 3.50 1.90
296 A208 15fr on 30fr ind (R) 1.40 60
Nos. 288-296 (9) 13.80 5.85

The surcharge on Nos. 292, 294 and 296 include two bars.

France No. 697 Surcharged Type "a" in Black

1953 *Perf. 14x13½*
297 A182 50c on 1fr blk, red & yel 20 20

France No. 688 Surcharged in Black

c

3F CFA

Perf. 13
298 A230 3fr on 6fr dp plum & car 40 30

France Nos. 703 and 705 Surcharged Type "a" in Red or Blue

1954
299 A235 8fr on 40fr (R) 12.00 3.50
300 A235 20fr on 75fr 45.00 21.00

France Nos. 698, 721, 713, and 715 Surcharged Type "a" in Black

Perf. 14x13½, 13
301 A182 1fr on 2fr 60 30
302 A241 4fr on 10fr 80 38
303 A238 8fr on 40fr 3.00 20
304 A238 20fr on 75fr 3.50 50

The surcharge on Nos. 303 and 304 includes two bars.

France Nos. 737, 719 and 722-724 Surcharged in Black or Red

305 A182(a) 1fr on 2fr 30 30
306 A241(a) 2fr on 6fr (R) 30 25
307 A242(a) 6fr on 12fr 1.40 38
308 A241(b) 9fr on 18fr 3.50 2.50
309 A241(a) 10fr on 20fr 1.50 50
Nos. 299-309 (11) 71.90 29.81

The surcharge on Nos. 306-308 includes two bars; on No. 309 three bars.

France No. 720 Surcharged Type "c" in Red, Bars at Lower Left

1955 *Perf. 13*
310 A241 3fr on 8fr brt bl & dk grn 50 30

France Nos. 785, 774-779 Surcharged Type "a" in Black or Red

Perf. 14x13½, 13

1955-56 Typo., Engr.
311 A182 50c on 1fr 15 15
312 A265 2fr on 6fr ('56) 50 40
313 A265 3fr on 8fr 35 30
314 A265 4fr on 10fr 35 30
315 A265 5fr on 12fr (R) 60 30
316 A265 6fr on 18fr (R) 40 30
317 A265 10fr on 25fr 65 20
Nos. 311-317 (7) 3.00 1.95

The surcharge on Nos. 312-317 includes two bars.

France Nos. 801-804 Surcharged Type "a" or "b" in Black or Red

1956 Engr. *Perf. 13*
318 A280(a) 8fr on 30fr (R) 2.00 20
319 A280(b) 9fr on 40fr 2.50 80
320 A280(a) 15fr on 50fr 2.50 65
321 A280(a) 20fr on 75fr (R) 3.50 90

The surcharge on Nos. 318, 319 and 321 includes two bars.

France Nos. 837 and 839 Surcharged Type "a" in Red

1957 *Perf. 13*
322 A294 7fr on 15fr 60 40
323 A265 17fr on 70fr 3.00 1.20

The surcharge on Nos. 322-323 includes two bars.

No. 322 has three types of "7" in the sheet of 50. There are 34 of the "normal" 7; 10 of a slightly thinner 7, and 6 of a slightly thicker 7.

France Nos. 755-756, 833-834, 851-855, 908, 949 Surcharged in Black or Red Type "a", "b" or

d

50F CFA

Typographed, Engraved

1957-60 *Perf. 14x13½, 13*
324 A236(b) 2fr on 6fr 20 15
325 A302(b) 3fr on 10fr ('58) 20 20
326 A236(b) 4fr on 12fr 1.60 40
327 A236(b) 5fr on 10fr 90 25
328 A303(b) 6fr on 18fr 35 30
329 A302(a) 9fr on 25fr (R) ('58) 50 32
330 A252(a) 10fr on 20fr (R) 55 15
331 A252(a) 12fr on 25fr 2.50 20
332 A303(a) 17fr on 35fr 1.60 80
333 A302(a) 20fr on 50fr 80 42
334 A302(a) 25fr on 85fr 2.00 62
335 A339(d) 50fr on 1fr ('60) 1.50 45
Nos. 324-335 (12) 12.70 4.26

The surcharge includes two bars on Nos. 324, 326-327, 329-331, 333 and 335.

France Nos. 973, 939 and 968 Surcharged

2f CFA
e

12fCFA
f

1961-63 Typo. *Perf. 14x13½*
336 A318(e) 2fr on 5c multi 15 15
337 A336(e) 5fr on 10c brt grn 20 20
338 A336(b) 5fr on 10c brt grn ('63) 62 30
339 A349(f) 12fr on 25c lake & gray 16 15

The surcharge on No. 337 includes three bars. No. 338 has "b" surcharge and two bars.

France Nos. 943, 941 and 946 Surcharged "CFA" and New Value in Two Lines in Black or Red

Engraved, Typographed

1961 Unwmk. *Perf. 13, 14x13½*
340 A338 7fr on 15c 45 28
341 A337 10fr on 20c 15 15
342 A339 20fr on 50c (R) 7.50 2.25

Surcharge on No. 342 includes 3 bars.

France Nos. 1047-1048 Surcharged with New Value, "CFA" and Two Bars

1963, Jan. 2 Engr. *Perf. 13*
343 A394 12fr on 25c 50 50
344 A395 25fr on 50c 50 50

1st television connection of the US and Europe through the Telstar satellite, July 11-12, 1962.

France Nos. 1040-1041, 1007 and 1009 Surcharged Similarly to Type "e"

Typographed, Engraved

1963 *Perf. 14x13½, 13*
345 A318 2fr on 5c 15 15
346 A318 5fr on 10c 15 15
347 A372 7fr on 15c 20 20
348 A372 20fr on 45c 50 20

Two-line surcharge on No. 345; No. 347 has currency expressed in capital "F" and two heavy bars through old value; two thin bars on No. 348.

France No. 1078 Surcharged Type "e" in Two Lines in Dark Blue

1964, Feb. 8 Engr. *Perf. 13*
349 CD118 12fr on 25c 50 40

"PHILATEC," Intl. Philatelic and Postal Techniques Exhib., Paris, June 5-21, 1964.

France Nos. 1092, 1094 and 1102 Surcharged with New Value and "CFA"

Typographed, Engraved

1964 *Perf. 14x13½, 13*
350 A318 1fr on 2c 15 15
351 A318 6fr on 18c 20 20
352 A420 35fr on 70c 60 50

Surcharge on No. 352 includes two bars.

France Nos. 1095, 1126, 1070 Surcharged with New Value and "CFA"

1965
353 A318 15fr on 30c 20 15
354 A440 25fr on 50c 45 38
355 A408 30fr on 60c 60 50

Two bars obliterate old denomination on Nos. 354-355.

Etienne Regnault, "Le Taureau" and Coast of Reunion — A33

1965, Oct. 3 **Engr.** ***Perf. 13***
356 A33 15fr bluish blk & dk car 30 20

Tercentenary of settlement of Reunion.

France No. 985 Surcharged with New Value, Two Bars and "CFA"

1966, Feb. 13 **Engr.** ***Perf. 13***
357 A360 10fr on 20c bl & car 80 30

French Satellite A-1 Issue

France Nos. 1137-1138 Surcharged with New Value, Two Bars and "CFA" and Red

1966, Mar. 27 **Engr.** ***Perf. 13***
358 CD121 15fr on 30c 45 40
359 CD121 30fr on 60c 55 50
a. Strip of 2 + label 1.10 1.10

France Nos. 1142, 1143, 1101 and 1127 Surcharged with New Value, "CFA" and Two Bars

1967-69 **Typo.** ***Perf. 14x13***
360 A446 2fr on 5c bl & red 15 15

Photo. ***Perf. 13***
360A A446 10fr on 20c multi ('69) 15 15

Engr.
361 A421 20fr on 40c multi 28 25
362 A439 30fr on 60c bl & red brn 40 30

EXPO '67 Issue

France No. 1177 Surcharged with New Value, "CFA" and Two Bars

1967, June 12 **Engr.** ***Perf. 13***
363 A473 30fr on 60c dl bl & bl grn 50 45

EXPO '67, Montreal, Apr. 28-Oct. 27.

Lions Issue

France No. 1196 Surcharged in Violet Blue with New Value, "CFA" and Two Bars

1967, Oct. 29 **Engr.** ***Perf. 13***
364 A485 20fr on 40c 42 32

50th anniversary of Lions International.

France No. 1130 Surcharged in Violet Blue with New Value, "CFA" and Two Bars

1968, Feb. 26 **Engr.** ***Perf. 13***
365 A440 50fr on 1fr 65 50

France No. 1224 Surcharged with New Value, "CFA" and Two Bars

1968, Oct. 21 **Engr.** ***Perf. 13***
366 A508 20fr on 40c multi 40 35

20 years of French Polar expeditions.

France Nos. 1230-1231 Surcharged with New Value, "CFA" and Two Bars

1969, Apr. 13 **Engr.** ***Perf. 13***
367 A486 15fr on 30c green 25 20
368 A486 20fr on 40c dp car 30 15

France No. 1255 Surcharged with New Value, "CFA" and Two Bars

1969, Aug. 18 **Engr.** ***Perf. 13***
370 A520 35fr on 70c multi 70 50

Napoleon Bonaparte (1769-1821).

France No. 1293 Surcharged with New Value and "CFA"

1971, Jan. 16 **Engr.** ***Perf. 13***
371 A555 25fr on 50c rose car 35 15

France No. 1301 Surcharged with New Value and "CFA"

1971, Apr. 13 **Engr.** ***Perf. 13***
372 A562 40fr on 80c multi 55 50

France No. 1309 Surcharged with New Value, "CFA" and 2 Bars

1971, June 5 **Engr.** ***Perf. 13***
373 A569 15fr on 40c multi 30 30

Aid for rural families.

France No. 1312 Surcharged with New Value and "CFA"

1971, Aug. 30 **Engr.** ***Perf. 13***
374 A571 45fr on 90c multi 45 40

France No. 1320 Surcharged with New Value and "CFA"

1971, Oct. 18
375 A573 45fr on 90c multi 60 50

40th anniversary of the first assembly of presidents of artisans' guilds.

Réunion Chameleon A34

1971, Nov. 8 **Photo.** ***Perf. 13***
376 A34 25fr multi 50 30

Nature protection.

Common Design Type and

De Gaulle in Brazzaville, 1944 — A35

Designs: No. 377, Gen. de Gaulle, 1940. No. 379, de Gaulle entering Paris, 1944. No. 380, Pres. de Gaulle, 1970.

1971, Nov. 9 **Engr.**
377 CD134 25fr black 45 40
378 A35 25fr ultra 45 40
379 A35 25fr rose red 45 40
380 CD134 25fr black 45 40
a. Strip of 4 + label 2.00 1.60

Charles de Gaulle (1890-1970), president of France. Nos. 377-380 printed se-tenant in sheets of 20 containing 5 strips of 4 plus labels with Cross of Lorraine and inscription.

France No. 1313 Surcharged with New Value and "CFA"

1972, Jan. 17 **Engr.** ***Perf. 13***
381 A570 50fr on 1.10fr multi 60 50

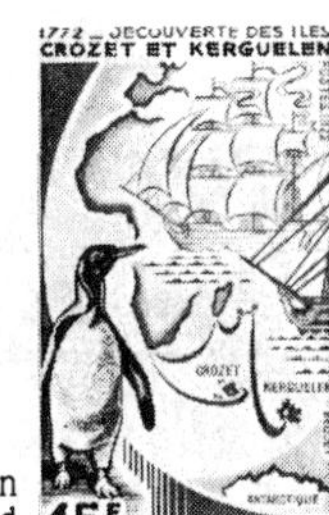

Map of South Indian Ocean, Penguin and Ships — A36

1972, Jan. 31 **Engr.** ***Perf. 13***
382 A36 45fr blk, bl & ocher 60 60

Bicentenary of the discovery of the Crozet and Kerguelen Islands.

France No. 1342 Surcharged with New Value, "CFA" and 2 Bars in Red

1972, May. 8 **Engr.** ***Perf. 13***
383 A590 15fr on 40c red 30 30

20th anniv. of Blood Donors' Assoc. of Post and Telecommunications Employees.

France Nos. 1345-1346 Surcharged with New Value, "CFA" and 2 Bars

1972, June 5 **Typo.** ***Perf. 14x13***
384 A593 15fr on 30c multi 20 20
385 A593 25fr on 50c multi 25 20

Introduction of postal code system.

France No. 1377 Surcharged with New Value, "CFA" and 2 Bars in Ultramarine

1973, June 12 **Engr.** ***Perf. 13***
386 A620 45fr on 90c multi 50 40

France Nos. 1374, 1336 Surcharged with New Value and "CFA" in Ultramarine or Red

1973 **Engr.** ***Perf. 13***
387 A617 50fr on 1fr multi (U) 45 38
388 A586 100fr on 2fr multi (R) 1.10 55

On No. 388, two bars cover "2.00". Issue dates: 50fr, June 24; 100fr, Oct. 13.

France No. 1231C Surcharged with New Value, "CFA" and 2 Bars

1973, Nov. **Typo.** ***Perf. 14x13***
389 A486 15fr on 30c bl grn 28 20

France No. 1390 Surcharged with New Value, "CFA" and 2 Bars in Red

1974, Jan. 20 **Engr.** ***Perf. 13***
390 A633 25fr on 50c multi 30 20

ARPHILA 75 Phil. Exhib., Paris, June 1975.

France Nos. 1394-1397 Surcharged "100 FCFA" in Black, Ultramarine or Brown

Engr. (#391, 393), Photo. (#392, 394)

1974 ***Perf. 12x13, 13x12***
391 A637 100fr on 2fr (Bk) 90 75
392 A638 100fr on 2fr (U) 90 75
393 A639 100fr on 2fr (Br) 1.00 75
394 A640 100fr on 2fr (U) 90 75

Nos. 391-394 printed in sheets of 25 with alternating labels publicizing "ARPHILA 75," Paris June 6-16, 1975.
Two bars obliterate original denomination on Nos. 391-393.

France No. 1401 Surcharged "45 FCFA" and 2 Bars in Red

1974, Apr. 29 **Engr.** ***Perf. 13***
395 A644 45fr on 90c multi 55 45

Reorganized sea rescue organization.

France No. 1415 Surcharged with New Value, 2 Bars and "FCFA" in Ultramarine

1974, Oct. 6 **Engr.** ***Perf. 13***
396 A657 60fr on 1.20fr multi 65 60

Centenary of Universal Postal Union.

France Nos. 1292A and 1294B Surcharged with New Value and "FCFA" in Ultramarine

1974, Oct. 19 **Typo.** ***Perf. 14x13***
397 A555 30fr on 60c grn 1.00 1.00

Engr.
Perf. 13
398 A555 40fr on 80c car rose 1.20 1.00

SEMI-POSTAL STAMPS

No. 65 Surcharged in Black or Red 5c

1915 **Unwmk.** ***Perf. 14x13½***
B1 A19 10c + 5c (Bk) 42.50 40.00
a. Inverted surcharge 100.00 80.00
B2 A19 10c + 5c (R) 50 50
a. Inverted surcharge 22.50 22.50

No. 65 Surcharged in Red

1916
B3 A19 10c + 5c 40 40

Curie Issue

Common Design Type

1938 ***Perf. 13***
B4 CD80 1.75fr + 50c brt ultra 5.00 5.00

French Revolution Issue

Common Design Type

1939 **Photo.** **Unwmk.**

Name and Value Typo. in Black
B5 CD83 45c + 25c grn 3.00 3.00
B6 CD83 70c + 30c brn 3.00 3.00
B7 CD83 90c + 35c red org 3.00 3.00
B8 CD83 1.25fr + 1fr rose pink 3.00 3.00
B9 CD83 2.25fr + 2fr blue 3.00 3.00
Nos. B5-B9 (5) 15.00 15.00

Common Design Type and

Artillery Colonel SP1

Colonial Infantry SP2

1941 **Unwmk.** ***Perf. 13½***
B10 SP1 1fr + 1fr red 40
B11 CD86 1.50fr + 3fr claret 40
B12 SP2 2.50fr + 1fr blue 40

Nos. B10-B12 were issued by the Vichy government and were not placed on sale in Reunion.
In 1944 the Vichy government surcharged Nos. 176-177 with "OEUVRES COLONIALES" and surtax, changing the denomination of the 2.50fr to 50c. These were not placed on sale in Reunion.

Catalogue values for unused stamps in this section, from this point to the end of the section, are for Never Hinged items.

Red Cross Issue

Common Design Type

1944 ***Perf. 14½x14***
B15 CD90 5fr + 20fr black 35 35

The surtax was for the French Red Cross and national relief.

France Nos. B365-B366 Surcharged with New Value, "CFA" and Two Bars

1962, Dec. 10 **Engr.** ***Perf. 13***
B16 SP219 10 + 5fr on 20 + 10c 1.20 1.20
B17 SP219 12 + 5fr on 25 + 10c 1.20 1.20

The surtax was for the Red Cross.

France Nos. B374-B375 Surcharged with New Value, "CFA" and Two Bars in Red

1963, Dec. 9
B18 SP223 10 + 5fr on 20 + 10c 1.50 1.50
B19 SP223 12 + 5fr on 25 + 10c 1.50 1.50

Centenary of the Intl. Red Cross. The surtax was for the Red Cross.

France Nos. B385-B386 Surcharged with New Value, "CFA" and Two Bars in Dark Blue

1964, Dec. 13 **Unwmk.** ***Perf. 13***
B20 SP230 10 + 5fr on 20 + 10c 80 80
B21 SP230 12 + 5fr on 25 + 10c 80 80

Jean Nicolas Corvisart (1755-1821) and Dominique Larrey (1766-1842), physicians. The surtax was for the Red Cross.

France Nos. B392-B393 Surcharged with New Value, "CFA" and Two Bars

1965, Dec. 12 **Engr.** ***Perf. 13***
B22 SP233 12 + 5fr on 25 + 10c 80 80
B23 SP233 15 + 5fr on 30 + 10c 80 80

The surtax was for the Red Cross.

France Nos. B402-B403 Surcharged with New Value, "CFA" and Two Bars

1966, Dec. 11 **Engr.** ***Perf. 13***
B24 SP237 12 + 5fr on 25 + 10c 65 60
B25 SP237 15 + 5fr on 30 + 10c 65 60

The surtax was for the Red Cross.

France Nos. B409-B410 Surcharged with New Value, "CFA" and Two Bars

1967, Dec. 17 Engr. *Perf. 13*
B26 SP240 12 + 5fr on 25 + 10c 1.25 1.25
B27 SP240 15 + 5fr on 30 + 10c 1.25 1.25

Surtax for the Red Cross.

France Nos. B421-B424 Surcharged with New Value, "CFA" and Two Bars

1968-69 Engr. *Perf. 13*
B28 SP244 12 + 5fr on 25 + 10c 1.00 80
B29 SP244 15 + 5fr on 30 + 10c 1.00 80
B30 SP244 20 + 7fr on 40 + 15c ('69) 70 70
B31 SP244 20 + 7fr on 40 + 15c ('69) 70 70

The surtax was for the Red Cross.

France No. B425 Surcharged with New Value, "CFA" and Two Bars

1969, Mar. 17 Engr. *Perf. 13*
B32 SP245 15fr + 5fr on 30c + 10c 50 50

Stamp Day.

France No. B440 Surcharged with New Value, "CFA" and Two Bars

1970, Mar. 16 Engr. *Perf. 13*
B33 SP249 20fr + 5fr on 40c + 10c 50 40

Stamp day.

France Nos. B443-B444 Surcharged with New Value "CFA" and Two Bars

1970, Dec. 14 Engr. *Perf. 13*
B34 SP252 20 + 7fr on 40 + 15c 1.25 1.10
B35 SP252 20 + 7fr on 40 + 15c 1.25 1.10

The surtax was for the Red Cross.

France No. B451 Surcharged with New Value, "CFA" and Two Bars

1971, Mar. 29 Engr. *Perf. 13*
B36 SP254 25fr + 5fr on 50c + 10c 40 35

Stamp Day.

France Nos. B452-B453 Surcharged with New Value, "CFA" and Two Bars

1971, Dec. 13
B37 SP255 15fr + 5fr on 30c + 10c 65 65
B38 SP255 25fr + 5fr on 50c + 10c 65 65

The surtax was for the Red Cross.

France No. B460 Surcharged with New Value and "CFA"

1972, Mar. 20 Engr. *Perf. 13*
B39 SP257 25fr + 5fr on 50c + 10c 42 42

Stamp Day.

France Nos. B461-B462 Surcharged with New Value, "CFA" and Two Bars in Red or Green

1972, Dec. 16 Engr. *Perf. 13*
B40 SP258 15 + 5fr on 30 + 10c 60 60
B41 SP258 25 + 5fr on 50 + 10c (G) 65 65

Surtax was for the Red Cross.

France No. B470 Surcharged with New Value, "CFA" and Two Bars in Red

1973, Mar. 26 Engr. *Perf. 13*
B42 SP260 25fr + 5fr on 50c + 10c 65 60

Stamp Day.

France Nos. B471-B472 Surcharged with New Value, "CFA" and Two Bars in Red

1973, Dec. 3 Engr. *Perf. 13*
B43 SP261 15 + 5fr on 30c + 10c 65 65
B44 SP261 25 + 5fr on 50c + 10c 80 80

Surtax was for the Red Cross.

France No. B477 Surcharged "25 + 5 FCFA"

1974, Mar. 11 Engr. *Perf. 13*
B45 SP263 25fr + 5fr on 50c + 10c 30 30

Stamp Day.

France Nos. B479-B480 Surcharged with New Value, "FCFA" and Two Bars in Green or Red

1974, Nov. 30 Engr. *Perf. 13*
B46 SP265 30 + 7fr on 60 + 15c (G) 65 65
B47 SP266 40 + 7fr on 80 + 15c (R) 80 80

Surtax was for the Red Cross.

AIR POST STAMPS

No. 141 Overprinted in Blue

RÉUNION - FRANCE
par avion
« *ROLAND GARROS* »

1937, Jan. 23 Unwmk. *Perf. 12½*
C1 A23 50c red 110. 100.
a. Vert. pair, one without overprint 600. 600.
b. Inverted overprint 1,500.

Flight of the "Roland Garros" from Reunion to France by aviators Laurent, Lenier and Touge in Jan.-Feb., 1937.

Airplane and Landscape — AP2

1938, Mar. 1 Engr. *Perf. 12½*
C2 AP2 3.65fr slate blue & car 30 30
C3 AP2 6.65fr brown & org red 30 30
C4 AP2 9.65fr car & ultra 30 30
C5 AP2 12.65fr brown & green 65 65

For overprints see Nos. C14-C17.

Plane and Bridge over East River AP3

Plane and Landscape AP4

1942, Oct. 19 *Perf. 12x12½*
C6 AP3 50c olive & pur 15
C7 AP3 1fr dk bl & scar 15
C8 AP3 2fr brn & blk 20
C9 AP3 3fr rose lil & grn 28
C10 AP3 5fr red org & red brn 28

Frame Engr., Center Photo.
C11 AP4 10fr dk grn, red org & vio 25
C12 AP4 20fr dk bl, brn vio & red 38
C13 AP4 50fr brn car, Prus grn & bl 42
Nos. C6-C13 (8) 2.11

There is doubt whether Nos. C6-C13 were officially placed in use.

V2

Stamps of the above design were issued in 1943 by the Vichy Government, but were not placed on sale in Réunion.

Nos. C2-C5 Overprinted in Black or Carmine **France Libre**

1943 Unwmk. *Perf. 12½*
C14 AP2 3.65fr sl bl & car 1.00 1.00
C15 AP2 6.65fr brn & org red 1.00 1.00
C16 AP2 9.65fr car & ultra (C) 1.00 1.00
C17 AP2 12.65fr brn & grn 1.00 1.00

Catalogue values for unused stamps in this section, from this point to the end of the section, are for Never Hinged items.

Common Design Type

1944 Photo. *Perf. 14½x14*
C18 CD87 1fr dk org 15 15
C19 CD87 1.50fr brt red 15 15
C20 CD87 5fr brn red 16 16
C21 CD87 10fr black 25 25
C22 CD87 25fr ultra 25 25
C23 CD87 50fr dk grn 25 25
C24 CD87 100fr plum 45 45
Nos. C18-C24 (7) 1.66 1.66

Victory Issue
Common Design Type

1946, May 8 Engr. *Perf. 12½*
C25 CD92 8fr olive gray 35 35

European victory of the Allied Nations in WWII.

Chad to Rhine Issue
Common Design Types

1946, June 6
C26 CD93 5fr orange 45 45
C27 CD94 10fr sepia 45 45
C28 CD95 15fr grnsh blk 45 45
C29 CD96 20fr lilac rose 55 55
C30 CD97 25fr greenish blue 60 60
C31 CD98 50fr green 60 60
Nos. C26-C31 (6) 3.10 3.10

Shadow of Plane — AP5

Plane over Réunion — AP6

Air View of Réunion and Shadow of Plane — AP7

Perf. 13x12½
1947, Mar. 24 Photo. Unwmk.
C32 AP5 50fr ol grn & bl gray 3.25 2.50
C33 AP6 100fr dk brn & org 4.50 4.00
C34 AP7 200fr dk bl & org 5.75 5.50

France, Nos. C18 to C21 Surcharged and Bars, in Carmine or Black

20F
CFA
c

1949 Unwmk. *Perf. 13*
C35 AP7 20fr on 40fr (C) 1.00 55
C36 AP8 25fr on 50fr 1.20 55
C37 AP9 50fr on 100fr (C) 3.25 1.90
C38 AP10 100fr on 200fr 15.00 11.00

France Nos. C24, C26 and C27 Surcharged Type "c" and Bars in Black

1949-51
C39 AP12 100fr on 200fr dk bl grn ('51) 45.00 13.50
C40 AP12 200fr on 500fr brt red 22.50 12.00
C41 AP13 500fr on 1000fr sep, *bl* ('51) 100.00 90.00

France Nos. C29-C32 Surcharged "CFA," New Value and Bars in Blue or Red

1954, Feb. 10
C42 AP15(c) 50fr on 100fr 1.40 65
C43 AP15 100fr on 200fr (R) 3.00 55
C44 AP15(c) 200fr on 500fr 14.00 9.00
C45 AP15 500fr on 1000fr 16.00 8.25

France Nos. C35-C36 Surcharged "CFA," New Values and Bars in Red or Black

1957-58 Engr. *Perf. 13*
C46 AP17 200fr on 500fr (R) 9.00 4.00
C47 AP17 500fr on 1000fr ('58) 14.00 8.00

France Nos. C37, C39-C40 Surcharged "CFA," New Value and Bars in Red or Black

1961-64
C48 AP15 100fr on 2fr 1.75 60
C49 AP17 200fr on 5fr 2.75 1.10
C50 AP17 500fr on 10fr (B;'64) 7.50 3.00

France No. C41 Surcharged "CFA," New Value and Two Bars in Red

1967, Jan. 27 Engr. *Perf. 13*
C51 AP17 100fr on 2fr sl bl & ind 1.00 40

France No. C45 Surcharged in Red with "CFA," New Value and Two Bars in Red

1972, May 14 Engr. *Perf. 13*
C52 AP21 200fr on 5fr multi 2.50 1.10

AIR POST SEMI-POSTAL STAMP

French Revolution Issue
Common Design Type

1939 Unwmk. *Perf. 13*
Name and Value Typo. in Orange
CB1 CD83 3.65fr + 4fr brn blk 7.00 7.00

V3

Stamps of the above design and type of Cameroun V10 inscribed "Réunion" were issued in 1942 by the Vichy Government, but were not placed on sale in Réunion.

POSTAGE DUE STAMPS

D1

D2

1889-92 Unwmk. Type-set *Imperf.*
J1 D1 5c black 6.25 3.75
J2 D1 10c black 8.50 3.75
J3 D1 15c black ('92) 18.00 9.00
J4 D1 20c black 15.00 8.25
J5 D1 30c black 12.50 7.00

Ten varieties of each value.
Nos. J1-J2, J4-J5 issued on yellowish paper in 1889; Nos. J1-J3, J5 on bluish white paper in 1892.
Nos. J1-J5 exist with double impression. Values $12.50-$25.

1907 Typo. *Perf. 14x13½*

J6	D2	5c carmine, *yel*	22	22
J7	D2	10c blue, *bl*	22	22
J8	D2	15c black, *bluish*	30	30
J9	D2	20c carmine	30	30
J10	D2	30c green, *grnsh*	45	45
J11	D2	50c red, *green*	55	55
J12	D2	60c carmine, *bl*	55	55
J13	D2	1fr violet	90	90
		Nos. J6-J13 (8)	3.49	3.49

Type of 1907 Issue Surcharged **=2F.=**

1927

J14	D2	2fr on 1fr org red	3.50	3.50
J15	D2	3fr on 1fr org brn	3.50	3.50

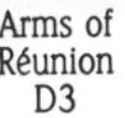
Arms of Réunion D3

Numeral D4

1933 Engr. *Perf. 13x13½*

J16	D3	5c deep violet	15	15
J17	D3	10c dark green	15	15
J18	D3	15c orange brown	15	15
J19	D3	20c light red	15	15
J20	D3	30c olive green	15	15
J21	D3	50c ultramarine	20	20
J22	D3	60c black brown	20	20
J23	D3	1fr light violet	20	20
J24	D3	2fr deep blue	20	20
J25	D3	3fr carmine	20	20
		Set value	1.25	1.25

Catalogue values for unused stamps in this section, from this point to the end of the section, are for Never Hinged items.

1947 Unwmk. Photo. *Perf. 13*

J26	D4	10c dark violet	15	15
J27	D4	30c brown	15	15
J28	D4	50c blue green	15	15
J29	D4	1fr orange	15	15
J30	D4	2fr red violet	15	15
J31	D4	3fr red brown	15	15
J32	D4	4fr blue	42	42
J33	D4	5fr henna brown	42	42
J34	D4	10fr slate green	42	42
J35	D4	20fr violet blue	55	55
		Nos. J26-J35 (10)	2.71	2.71

France, Nos. J83 to J92 Surcharged in Black

1949-53

J36	D5	10c on 1fr brt ultra	15	15
J37	D5	50c on 2fr turq bl	15	15
J38	D5	1fr on 3fr brn org	20	20
J39	D5	2fr on 4fr dp vio	30	30
J40	D5	3fr on 5fr brt pink	1.90	1.50
J41	D5	5fr on 10fr red org	55	50
J42	D5	10fr on 20fr ol bis	1.40	1.25
J43	D5	20fr on 50fr dk grn ('50)	4.25	2.50
J44	D5	50fr on 100fr dp grn ('53)	12.50	8.25
		Nos. J36-J44 (9)	21.40	14.80

Same Surcharge on France Nos. J93, J95-J96

1962-63 Typo. *Perf. 14x13½*

J46	D6	1fr on 5c brt pink ('63)	60	60
J47	D6	10fr on 20c ol bis ('63)	1.10	1.10
J48	D6	20fr on 50c dk grn	10.00	7.25

France Nos. J98-J102, J104-J105 Surcharged with New Value and "CFA"

1964-71 Unwmk. *Perf. 14x13½*

J49	D7	1fr on 5c	15	15
J50	D7	5fr on 10c	15	15
J51	D7	7fr on 15c	20	20
J52	D7	10fr on 20c ('71)	70	50
J53	D7	15fr on 30c	20	20
J54	D7	20fr on 50c	30	30
J55	D7	50fr on 1fr	90	60
		Nos. J49-J55 (7)	2.60	2.10

PARCEL POST STAMP

No. 40 Overprinted **Colis Postaux**

1906 Unwmk. *Perf. 14x13½*

Q1	A14	10c red	4.00	4.00

FRENCH COLONIES

From 1859 to 1906 and in 1944 and 1945 special stamps were issued for use in all French Colonies which did not have stamps of their own.

100 Centimes = 1 Franc

Catalogue values for unused stamps in this country are for Never Hinged items, beginning with Scott B1 in the semi-postal section and Scott J23 in the postage due section.

Perforations: Nos. 1-45 are known variously perforated unofficially.

Gum: Many of Nos. 1-45 were issued without gum. Some were gummed locally.

Reprints: Nos. 1-7, 9-12, 24, 26-42, 44 and 45 were reprinted officially in 1887. These reprints are ungummed and the colors of both design and paper are deeper or brighter than the originals. Value for Nos. 1-6, $20 each.

Values of early French Colonies stamps vary according to condition. Quotations for Nos. 1-23 are for fine copies. Very fine to superb specimens sell at much higher prices, and inferior or poor copies sell at reduced prices, depending on the condition of the individual specimen.

Eagle and Crown — A1

1859-65 Unwmk. Typo. *Imperf.*

1	A1	1c ol grn, *pale bl* ('62)	7.00	7.50
2	A1	5c yel grn, *grnsh* ('62)	8.00	5.50
3	A1	10c bister, *yel*	12.00	3.50
a.		Pair, one sideways	500.00	225.00
4	A1	20c bl, *bluish* ('65)	15.00	6.50
5	A1	40c org, *yelsh*	10.00	4.50
6	A1	80c car rose, *pnksh* ('65)	40.00	25.00

Napoleon III
A2 A3

Ceres — A4

Napoleon III — A5

1871-72 *Imperf.*

7	A2	1c ol grn, *pale bl* ('72)	33.00	33.00
8	A3	5c yel grn, *grnsh* ('72)	425.00	300.00
9	A4	10c bis, *yelsh*	190.00	80.00
a.		Tête bêche pair	*18,000.*	*14,000.*
10	A4	15c bis, *yelsh* ('72)	140.00	6.50
11	A4	20c blue, *bluish*	300.00	50.00
a.		Tête bêche pair		*9,500.*
12	A4	25c bl, *bluish* ('72)	80.00	5.50
13	A5	30c brn, *yelsh*	60.00	20.00
14	A4	40c org, *yelsh* (I)	140.00	8.00
a.		Type II	*2,000.*	*400.00*
b.		Pair, types I & II	*4,500.*	*1,100.*
15	A5	80c rose, *pnksh*	500.00	62.50

For types I and II of 40c see illustrations over No. 1 of France.

See note after France No. 9 for additional information on Nos. 8-9, 11-12, 14.

Ceres
A6 A7

1872-77 *Imperf.*

16	A6	1c ol grn, *pale bl* ('73)	7.50	8.00
17	A6	2c red brn, *yelsh* ('76)	275.00	500.00
18	A6	4c gray ('76)	*7,500.*	400.00
19	A6	5c grn, *pale bl*	8.00	5.00
20	A7	10c bis, *rose* ('76)	110.00	8.00
21	A7	15c bister ('77)	325.00	57.50
22	A7	30c brn, *yelsh*	55.00	10.00
23	A7	80c rose, *pnksh* ('73)	250.00	70.00

No. 17 was used only in Cochin China, 1876-77. Excellent forgeries of Nos. 17 and 18 exist.

With reference to the stamps of France and French Colonies in the same designs and colors see the note after France No. 9.

Peace and Commerce A8

Commerce A9

1877-78 Type I *Imperf.*

24	A8	1c grn, *grnsh*	15.00	20.00
25	A8	4c grn, *grnsh*	9.00	7.50
26	A8	30c brn, *yelsh* ('78)	17.50	17.50
27	A8	40c ver, *straw*	14.00	12.50
28	A8	75c car, *rose* ('78)	37.50	35.00
29	A8	1fr brnz grn, *straw*	17.50	11.00

Type II

30	A8	2c grn, *grnsh*	7.50	6.00
31	A8	5c grn, *grnsh*	9.00	3.00
32	A8	10c grn, *grnsh*	55.00	6.00
33	A8	15c gray, *grnsh*	150.00	45.00
34	A8	20c red brn, *straw*	32.50	4.00
35	A8	25c ultra *bluish*	20.00	5.50
a.		25c blue, *bluish* ('78)	*3,250.*	110.00
36	A8	35c vio blk, *org* ('78)	27.50	16.00

1878-80

Type II

38	A8	1c blk, *lil bl*	11.00	11.00
39	A8	2c brn, *buff*	10.00	7.50
40	A8	4c claret, *lav*	14.00	14.00
41	A8	10c blk, *lav* ('79)	60.00	12.00
42	A8	15c blue ('79)	16.00	7.50
43	A8	20c red, *grn* ('79)	50.00	7.50
44	A8	25c blk, *red* ('79)	300.00	200.00
45	A8	25c yel, *straw* ('80)	325.00	16.00

No. 44 was used only in Mayotte, Nossi-Be and New Caledonia. Forgeries exist.

The 3c yellow, 3c gray, 15c yellow, 20c blue, 25c rose and 5fr lilac were printed together with the reprints, and were never issued.

1881-86 *Perf. 14x13½*

46	A9	1c blk, *lil bl*	1.60	1.10
47	A9	2c brn, *buff*	2.00	1.60
48	A9	4c claret, *lav*	2.00	1.60
49	A9	5c grn, *grnsh*	2.00	80
50	A9	10c blk, *lavender*	4.00	2.25
51	A9	15c blue	6.00	80
52	A9	20c red, *yel grn*	15.00	7.50
53	A9	25c yel, *straw*	4.00	1.10
54	A9	25c blk, *rose* ('86)	4.00	1.00
55	A9	30c brn, *bis*	11.00	7.00
56	A9	35c vio blk, *yel org*	14.00	9.00
a.		35c violet black, *yellow*	25.00	12.50
57	A9	40c ver, *straw*	15.00	9.00
58	A9	75c car, *rose*	40.00	18.00
59	A9	1fr brnz grn, *straw*	25.00	12.50

Nos. 46-59 exist imperforate. They are proofs and were not used for postage, except the 10c.

For stamps of type A9 surcharged with numerals see: Cochin China, Diego Suarez, Gabon, Madagascar, Nossi-Be, New Caledonia, Reunion, Senegal, Tahiti.

SEMI-POSTAL STAMPS

Catalogue values for unused stamps in this section are for Never Hinged items.

Resistance Fighters — SP1

1943 Unwmk. Litho. *Rouletted*

B1	SP1	1.50fr + 98.50fr ind & gray	12.00	12.50

The surtax was for the benefit of patriots and the French Committee of Liberation.

No. B1 was printed in sheets of 10 (5x2) with adjoining labels showing the Lorraine cross.

Colonies Offering Aid to France — SP2

1943 *Perf. 12*

B2	SP2	9fr + 41fr red violet	70	80

Surtax for the benefit of French patriots.

Patriots and Map of France — SP3

1943

B3	SP3	50c + 4.50fr yel grn	40	60
B4	SP3	1.50fr + 8.50fr cerise	40	60
B5	SP3	3fr + 12fr grnsh bl	40	60
B6	SP3	5fr + 15fr ol gray	40	60

Surtax for the aid of combatants and patriots.

Refugee Family — SP4

1943

B7	SP4	10fr + 40fr dull blue	2.50	2.75

The surtax was for refugee relief work.

Woman and Child with Wing — SP5

1944

B8	SP5	10fr + 40fr grnsh blk	2.50	2.75

Surtax for the benefit of aviation.

Nos. B1-B8 were prepared for use in the French Colonies, but after the landing of Free French troops in Corsica they were used there and later also in Southern France. They became valid throughout France in Nov. 1944.

POSTAGE DUE STAMPS

D1

D2

1884-85 Unwmk. Typo. *Imperf.*

J1	D1	1c black	1.10	1.10
J2	D1	2c black	1.10	1.10
J3	D1	3c black	1.10	1.10
J4	D1	4c black	1.75	1.40
J5	D1	5c black	2.00	1.75
J6	D1	10c black	3.00	2.25
J7	D1	15c black	5.00	3.75
J8	D1	20c black	5.00	4.50
J9	D1	30c black	6.25	3.25
J10	D1	40c black	8.50	3.00
J11	D1	60c black	13.50	7.50
J12	D1	1fr brown	11.00	7.50
a.		1fr black	140.00	
J13	D1	2fr brown	9.00	6.25
a.		2fr black	140.00	
J14	D1	5fr brown	42.50	22.50
a.		5fr black	185.00	

Nos. J12a, J13a and J14a were not regularly issued.

1894-1906

J15	D1	5c pale blue	35	35
J16	D1	10c gray brown	35	35
J17	D1	15c pale green	35	35
J18	D1	20c olive grn ('06)	35	35
J19	D1	30c carmine	60	50
J20	D1	50c lilac	60	50
J21	D1	60c brown, *buff*	1.40	1.00
a.		60c dark violet, *buff*	1.60	1.00
J22	D1	1fr red, *buff*	2.00	1.60
a.		1fr rose, *buff*	10.00	9.00
		Nos. J15-J22 (8)	6.00	5.00

For overprints see New Caledonia Nos. J1-J8.

Catalogue values for unused stamps in this section, from this point to the end of the section, are for Never Hinged items.

1945 Litho. *Perf. 12*

J23	D2	10c slate blue	15	15
J24	D2	15c yel green	15	15
J25	D2	25c deep orange	15	15
J26	D2	50c greenish blk	25	25
J27	D2	60c copper brn	25	25
J28	D2	1fr deep red lil	15	15
J29	D2	2fr red	25	25
J30	D2	4fr slate gray	1.00	1.00
J31	D2	5fr brt ultra	1.00	1.00
J32	D2	10fr purple	5.50	4.00
J33	D2	20fr dull brown	1.10	1.10
J34	D2	50fr deep green	2.00	2.00
		Nos. J23-J34 (12)	11.95	10.45

FRENCH CONGO

LOCATION — Central Africa
GOVT. — French possession

French Congo was originally a separate colony, but was joined in 1888 to Gabon and placed under one commissioner-general with a lieutenant-governor presiding in Gabon and another in French Congo. In 1894 the military holdings in Ubangi were attached to French Congo, and in 1900 the Chad military protectorate was added. Postal service was not established in Ubangi or Chad, however, at that time. In 1906 Gabon and Middle Congo were separated and French Congo ceased to exist as such. Chad and Ubangi remained attached to Middle Congo as the joint dependency of "Ubangi-Chari-Chad," and Middle Congo stamps were used there.

Issues of the Republic of the Congo are listed under Congo People's Republic (ex-French).

100 Centimes = 1 Franc

Watermarks

Wmk. 122- Thistle Branch

Wmk. 123- Rose Branch

Wmk. 124- Olive Branch

Stamps of French Colonies Surcharged Horizontally in Red or Black

Congo français
5c.

1891 Unwmk. *Perf. 14x13½*

1	A9	5c on 1c blk, *lil bl* (R)	*4,500.*	*2,250.*
2	A9	5c on 1c blk, *lil bl*	75.00	42.50
a.		Double surcharge	350.00	160.00
3	A9	5c on 15c blue	160.00	65.00
a.		Double surcharge	350.00	160.00
5	A9	5c on 25c blk, *rose*	60.00	17.50
a.		Inverted surcharge		

First "O" of "Congo" is a Capital, "Francais" with Capital "F"

1891-92

6	A9	5c on 20c red, *grn*	650.00	225.00
7	A9	5c on 25c blk, *rose*	90.00	40.00
a.		Surcharge vertical	125.00	40.00
8	A9	10c on 25c blk, *rose*	90.00	25.00
a.		Inverted surcharge	175.00	60.00
b.		Surcharge vertical	100.00	42.50
c.		First "o" of "Congo" small		
d.		Double surcharge	200.00	62.50
9	A9	10c on 40c red, *straw*	1,350.	210.00
10	A9	15c on 25c blk, *rose*	90.00	17.50
a.		Surcharge vertical	125.00	27.50
b.		Inverted surcharge		
c.		Double surcharge	175.00	55.00

First "O" of Congo small
Surcharge Vert., Down or Up
No period

11	A9	5c on 25c blk, *rose*		
12	A9	10c on 25c blk, *rose*		
13	A9	15c on 25c blk, *rose*		

Postage Due Stamps of French Colonies Surcharged in Red or Black Reading Down or Up

Congo français
Timbres poste
10 c

1892 *Imperf.*

14	D1	5c on 5c blk (R)	70.00	62.50
15	D1	5c on 20c blk (R)	80.00	60.00
16	D1	5c on 30c blk (R)	110.00	70.00
17	D1	10c on 1fr brown	90.00	60.00
a.		Double surcharge		
b.		Surcharge horiz.		*1,000.*

Excellent counterfeits of Nos. 1-17 exist.

Navigation and Commerce — A3

1892-1900 Typo. *Perf. 14x13½*
Colony Name in Blue or Carmine

18	A3	1c blk, *lil bl*	80	65
19	A3	2c brn, *buff*	1.00	80
a.		Name double	65.00	60.00
20	A3	4c claret, *lav*	1.10	90
a.		Name in blk and in blue	65.00	60.00
21	A3	5c grn, *grnsh*	2.25	2.00
22	A3	10c blk, *lavender*	7.50	6.25
a.		Name double	310.00	225.00
23	A3	10c red ('00)	1.00	65
24	A3	15c blue, quadrille paper	25.00	6.00
25	A3	15c gray ('00)	3.25	2.25
26	A3	20c red, *grn*	10.00	6.25
27	A3	25c blk, *rose*	7.00	5.75
28	A3	25c blue ('00)	4.00	3.25
29	A3	30c brn, *bis*	12.50	6.50
30	A3	40c red, *straw*	17.50	10.00
31	A3	50c car, *rose*	17.50	10.00
32	A3	50c brn, *az* ('00)	4.00	3.25
a.		Name double	325.00	325.00
33	A3	75c dp vio, *org*	13.50	10.00
34	A3	1fr brnz grn, *straw*	25.00	12.50
		Nos. 18-34 (17)	152.90	87.00

Perf. 13½x14 stamps are counterfeits.
For surcharges see Nos. 50-51.

Leopard — A4

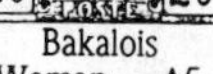
Bakalois Woman — A5

Coconut Grove — A6

1900 Wmk. 122 *Perf. 11*

35	A4	1c brn vio & gray lilac	28	28
a.		Background inverted	27.50	27.50
36	A4	2c brn & org	28	28
a.		2c dark red & red	65.00	
b.		Imperf., pair	27.50	27.50
37	A4	4c scar & gray bl	40	28
a.		4c dark red & red	400.00	
b.		Background inverted	32.50	32.50
38	A4	5c grn & gray grn	65	28
a.		Imperf., pair	60.00	60.00
39	A4	10c dk red & red	2.25	1.00
a.		Imperf., pair	60.00	60.00
40	A4	15c dl vio & ol grn	80	35
a.		Imperf. pair	35.00	35.00

Wmk. 123

41	A5	20c yel grn & org	80	55
42	A5	25c bl & pale bl	1.10	62
43	A5	30c car rose & org	1.40	65
44	A5	40c org brn & brt grn	2.00	90
a.		Imperf., pair	40.00	40.00
b.		Center inverted	62.50	62.50
45	A5	50c gray vio & lil	2.25	1.75
46	A5	75c red vio & org	3.75	3.00
a.		Imperf., pair	40.00	40.00

Wmk. 124

47	A6	1fr gray lil & ol	7.00	5.50
a.		Center inverted	140.00	140.00
b.		Imperf., pair	90.00	90.00
48	A6	2fr car & brn	13.50	7.00
a.		Imperf., pair	110.00	110.00
49	A6	5fr brn org & gray	37.50	22.50
a.		5fr ocher & gray	400.00	400.00
b.		Center inverted	200.00	200.00
c.		Wmk. 123	125.00	
d.		Imperf., pair	275.00	275.00
		Nos. 35-49 (15)	73.96	44.94

For surcharges see Nos. 52-53.

Nos. 26 and 29 Surcharged in Black

Valeur
15

1900 Unwmk. *Perf. 14x13½*

50	A3	5c on 20c red, *grn*	*14,000.*	*4,250.*
a.		Double surcharge		*8,500.*
51	A3	15c on 30c brn, *bis*	*7,000.*	*1,750.*
a.		Double surcharge		*3,750.*

Nos. 43 and 48 Surcharged in Black:

5c
— —
a

0,10
———
b

1903 Wmk. 123 *Perf. 11*

52	A5	5c on 30c	140.00	70.00
a.		Inverted surcharge	*1,250.*	

Wmk. 124

53	A6	10c on 2fr	200.00	65.00
a.		Inverted surcharge	*1,250.*	
b.		Double surcharge	*1,400.*	

Counterfeits of the preceding surcharges are known.

FRENCH EQUATORIAL AFRICA

LOCATION — North of Belgian Congo and south of Libya.
GOVT. — Former French Colony
AREA — 959,256 square miles
POP. — 4,491,785
CAPITAL — Brazzaville

In 1910 Gabon and Middle Congo, with its military dependencies, were politically united as French Equatorial Africa. The component colonies were granted administrative autonomy. In 1915 Ubangi-Chari-Chad was made an autonomous civilian colony and in 1920 Chad was made a civil colony. In 1934 the four colonies were administratively united as one colony, but this federation was not completed until 1936. Each colony had its own postal administration until 1936 when they were united. The postal issues of the former colonial subdivisions are listed under the names of those colonies.

In 1958, French Equatorial Africa was divided into four republics: Chad, Congo, Gabon and Central African Republic (formerly Ubangi-Chari).

Stamps other than Nos. 189-192 are inscribed with "Afrique Equatoriale Francaise" or "AEF" and the name of one of the component colonies. See listings in these colonies for such stamps.

100 Centimes = 1 Franc

Catalogue values for unused stamps in this country are for Never Hinged items, beginning with Scott 142 in the regular postage section, Scott B8A in the semi-postal section, Scott C17 in the airpost section, and Scott J12 in the postage due section.

Stamps of Gabon, 1932, Overprinted "Afrique Equatoriale Francaise" and Bars Similar to "a" and "b" in Black

Perf. 13x13½, 13½x13

1936 Unwmk.

1	A16	1c brown violet	15	15
2	A16	2c black, *rose*	15	15
3	A16	4c green	35	25
4	A16	5c grnsh blue	32	25
5	A16	10c red, *yel*	32	28
6	A17	40c brown violet	80	65
7	A17	50c red brown	80	48
8	A17	1fr yel grn, *bl*	12.50	4.50
9	A18	1.50fr dull blue	1.40	70
10	A18	2fr brown red	7.50	4.00
		Nos. 1-10 (10)	24.29	11.41

Stamps of Middle Congo, 1933 Overprinted in Black:

AFRIQUE
ÉQUATORIALE
FRANÇAISE

a

AFRIQUE ÉQUATORIALE
FRANÇAISE

b

AFRIQUE EQUATORIALE
FRANÇAISE

c

1936

No.	Type	Description	Unused	Used
11	A4 (b)	1c lt brown	15	15
12	A4 (b)	2c dull blue	15	15
13	A4 (b)	4c olive green	22	15
14	A4 (b)	5c red violet	25	20
15	A4 (b)	10c slate	55	35
16	A4 (b)	15c dk violet	60	35
17	A4 (b)	20c red, *pink*	45	25
18	A4 (b)	25c orange	1.25	90
19	A5 (a)	40c orange brn	1.40	1.00
20	A5 (c)	50c black violet	1.10	80
21	A5 (c)	75c black, *pink*	2.00	1.40
22	A5 (a)	90c carmine	1.10	90
23	A5 (c)	1.50fr dark blue	65	42
24	A6 (a)	5fr slate blue	25.00	15.00
25	A6 (a)	10fr black	14.00	11.00
26	A6 (a)	20fr dark brown	14.00	11.50
		Nos. 11-26 (16)	62.87	44.52

Paris International Exposition Issue

Common Design Types

1937, Apr. 15 Engr. *Perf. 13*

No.	Type	Description	Unused	Used
27	CD74	20c dark violet	1.00	1.00
28	CD75	30c dark green	1.00	1.00
29	CD76	40c carmine rose	1.10	1.10
30	CD77	50c dk brn & bl	90	90
31	CD78	90c red	1.10	1.10
32	CD79	1.50fr ultra	1.10	1.10
		Nos. 27-32 (6)	6.20	6.20

Logging on Loéme River — A1

People of Chad — A2

Pierre Savorgnan de Brazza — A3

Emile Gentil — A4

Paul Crampel A5

Governor Victor Liotard — A6

Two types of 25c:
I - Wide numerals (4mm).
II - Narrow numerals (3½mm).

1937-40 Photo. *Perf. 13½x13*

No.	Type	Description	Unused	Used
33	A1	1c brown & yel	15	15
34	A1	2c violet & grn	15	15
35	A1	3c blue & yel ('40)	15	15
36	A1	4c magenta & bl	15	15
37	A1	5c dk & lt green	15	15
38	A2	10c magenta & blue	15	15
39	A2	15c blue & buff	15	15
40	A2	20c brown & yellow	15	15
41	A2	25c cop red & bl (I)	22	15
a.		Type II	60	38
42	A3	30c gray grn & grn	16	16
43	A3	30c chlky bl, ind & buff ('40)	15	15
44	A2	35c dp grn & yel ('38)	45	32
45	A3	40c cop red & bl	15	15
46	A3	45c dk bl & lt grn	2.25	1.50
47	A3	45c dp grn & yel grn ('40)	16	16
48	A3	50c brown & yellow	15	15
49	A3	55c pur & bl ('38)	28	16
50	A3	60c mar & gray bl ('40)	16	16
51	A4	65c dk bl & lt grn	16	15
52	A4	70c dp vio & buff ('40)	16	16
53	A4	75c ol blk & dl yel	2.75	2.00
54	A4	80c brn & yel ('38)	16	15
55	A4	90c cop red & buff	16	15
56	A4	1fr dk vio & lt grn	60	25
57	A3	1fr cer & dl org ('38)	1.10	25
58	A4	1fr bl grn & sl grn ('40)	16	16
59	A5	1.25fr cop red & buff	45	40
60	A5	1.40fr dk brn & pale grn ('40)	25	25
61	A5	1.50fr dk & lt blue	70	28
62	A5	1.60fr dp vio & buff ('40)	25	25
63	A5	1.75fr brn & yel	70	35
64	A4	1.75fr bl & lt bl ('38)	16	15
65	A5	2fr dk & lt green	60	28
66	A6	2.15fr brn, vio & yel ('38)	28	20
67	A6	2.25fr bl & lt bl ('39)	60	60
68	A6	2.50fr rose lake & buff ('40)	28	28
69	A6	3fr dk blue & buff	35	16
70	A6	5fr dk & lt green	65	38
71	A6	10fr dk violet & bl	1.60	80
72	A6	20fr ol blk & dl yel	2.25	1.25
		Nos. 33-72 (40)	19.70	13.16

For overprints and surcharges see Nos. 80-127, 129-141, B2-B3, B10-B13, B22-B23.

Colonial Arts Exhibition Issue

Souvenir Sheet

Common Design Type

1937 *Imperf.*

No.	Type	Description	Unused	Used
73	CD79	3fr red brown	3.25	3.25

Count Louis Edouard Bouet-Willaumez and His Ship "La Malouine" — A7

1938, Dec. 5 *Perf. 13½*

No.	Type	Description	Unused	Used
74	A7	65c gray brown	45	45
75	A7	1fr deep rose	45	45
76	A7	1.75fr blue	75	75
77	A7	2fr dull violet	90	90

Centenary of Gabon.

New York World's Fair Issue

Common Design Type

1939, May 10 Engr. *Perf. 12½x12*

No.	Type	Description	Unused	Used
78	CD82	1.25fr carmine lake	60	60
79	CD82	2.25fr ultra	60	60

Common Design Types pictured in section at front of book.

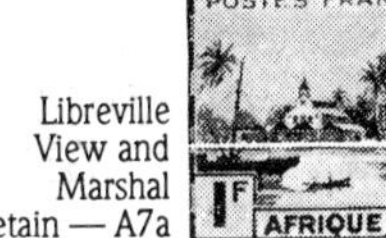

Libreville View and Marshal Petain — A7a

1941 Engr. *Perf. 12½x12*

No.	Type	Description	Unused	Used
79A	A7a	1fr bluish green	75	
79B	A7a	2.50fr blue	75	

Nos. 79A-79B were issued by the Vichy government, and were not placed on sale in the colony. This is also true of four stamps of types A2, A3 and A5 without "RF" monogram released in 1943-44.

Stamps of 1936-40, Overprinted in Carmine or Black:

AFRIQUE FRANÇAISE
LIBRE

Nos. 80-82, 84-88, 93

LIBRE

Nos. 83, 89-92, 94-125

1940-41 *Perf. 13½x13*

No.	Type	Description	Unused	Used
80	A1	1c brn & yel (C)	45	45
81	A1	2c vio & grn (C)	50	50
82	A1	3c blue & yel (C)	50	50
83	A4	4c ol grn (No. 13)	4.25	4.25
84	A1	5c dk grn & lt grn (C)	60	60
85	A2	10c magenta & bl	70	70
86	A2	15c blue & buff (C)	70	70
87	A2	20c brn & yel (C)	90	90
88	A2	25c cop red & bl	3.25	3.25
89	A3	30c gray grn & grn (C)	5.25	4.50
90	A3	30c gray grn & grn ('41)	90	70
91	A3	30c chlky bl, ind & buff (C) ('41)	5.00	4.25
92	A3	30c chlky bl, ind & buff ('41)	2.75	2.75
93	A2	35c dp grn & yel (C)	75	75
94	A3	40c cop red & bl	32	32
95	A3	45c dp grn & yel grn (C)	60	38
96	A3	45c dp grn & yel grn ('41)	32	32
97	A3	50c brn & yel (C)	3.00	2.00
98	A3	50c brn & yel ('41)	1.60	1.60
99	A3	55c pur & bl (C)	60	40
100	A3	55c pur & bl ('41)	32	32
101	A3	60c mar & gray bl	32	30
102	A4	65c dk bl & lt grn	32	30
103	A4	70c dp vio & buff	32	30
104	A4	75c ol blk & dl yel	18.00	18.00
105	A4	80c brown & yellow	30	30
106	A4	90c cop red & buff	50	50
107	A4	1fr bl grn & sl grn	2.25	2.00
108	A4	1fr bl grn & sl grn (C) ('41)	3.00	2.25
109	A3	1fr cer & dl org	70	65
110	A5	1.40fr dk brn & pale grn	30	30
111	A5	1.50fr dk bl & lt bl	30	30
112	A5	1.60fr dp vio & buff	30	30
113	A5	1.75fr brown & yel	65	45
114	A6	2.15fr brn, vio & yel	45	42
115	A6	2.25fr bl & lt bl (C)	60	50
116	A6	2.25fr bl & lt bl ('41)	90	80
117	A6	2.50fr rose lake & buff	45	45
118	A6	3fr dk bl & buff (C)	60	50
119	A6	3fr dk bl & buff ('41)	1.00	90
120	A6	5fr dk grn & lt grn (C)	1.90	1.75
121	A6	5fr dk grn & lt grn ('41)	57.50	30.00
122	A6	10fr dk vio & bl (C)	90	85
123	A6	10fr dk vio & bl ('41)	37.50	30.00
124	A6	20fr ol blk & dl yel (C)	90	85
125	A6	20fr ol blk & dl yel ('41)	5.50	5.50
		Nos. 80-125 (46)	168.72	128.61

For overprints and surcharges see Nos. 129-132, B12-B13, B22-B23.

Double Overprint

No.	Type	Description	Unused	Used
94a	A3	40c	16.00	
96a	A3	45c	4.25	4.25
98a	A3	50c	30.00	
100a	A3	55c	5.25	5.25
b.		one inverted	16.00	
102a	A4	65c	16.00	
103a	A4	70c	4.25	4.25
105a	A4	80c	16.00	
106a	A4	90c	16.00	
b.		one inverted	16.00	
110a	A5	1.40fr	3.50	3.50
111a	A5	1.50fr	5.25	5.25
114a	A6	2.15fr	3.50	3.50
115a	A6	2.25fr	5.25	5.25
116a	A6	2.25fr	16.00	
117a	A6	2.50fr	16.00	
119a	A6	3fr	4.75	4.75
123a	A6	10fr		

Nos. 48, 51 Surcharged in Black or Carmine

LIBRE
75c
═══

1940

No.	Type	Description	Unused	Used
126	A3	75c on 50c	25	25
a.		Double surcharge		
127	A4	1fr on 65c (C)	25	25
a.		Double surcharge	4.50	

Middle Congo No. 67 Overprinted in Carmine like No. 80

Perf. 13½

No.	Type	Description	Unused	Used
128	A4	4c olive green	21.00	18.00

Stamps of 1940 With Additional Overprint in Black

24-10-40

1940 *Perf. 13½x13*

No.	Type	Description	Unused	Used
129	A4	80c brown & yel	7.00	5.50
a.		Overprint without "2"	18.00	
130	A4	1fr bl grn & sl grn	6.75	5.50
131	A3	1fr cer & dull org	7.00	5.50
132	A5	1.50fr dk bl & lt bl	7.00	5.50

Arrival of General de Gaulle in Brazzaville, capital of Free France, Oct. 24, 1940.

These stamps were sold affixed to post cards and at a slight increase over face value to cover the cost of the cards.

For surcharges see Nos. B12-B13, B22-B23.

Stamps of 1937-40 Overprinted in Black

Afrique Française
Libre

1941

No.	Type	Description	Unused	Used
133	A1	1c brown & yel	55	55
134	A1	2c violet & grn	55	55
135	A1	3c blue & yel	55	55
136	A1	5c dk & lt green	55	55
137	A2	10c magenta & bl	55	55
138	A2	15c blue & buff	55	55
139	A2	20c brown & yel	55	55
140	A2	25c copper red & bl	1.90	1.90
141	A2	35c dp grn & yel	1.40	1.40
a.		Double overprint	10.00	
		Nos. 133-141 (9)	7.15	7.15

There are 2 settings of the overprint on Nos. 133-141 & C10. The 1st has 1mm between lines of the overprint, the 2nd has 2mm.

Catalogue values for unused stamps in this section, from this point to the end of the section, are for Never Hinged items.

Phoenix — A8

1941 Photo. *Perf. 14x14½*

No.	Type	Description	Unused	Used
142	A8	5c brown	15	15
143	A8	10c dark blue	15	15
144	A8	25c emerald	15	15
145	A8	30c deep orange	15	15
146	A8	40c dk slate grn	15	15
147	A8	80c red brown	15	15
148	A8	1fr deep red lilac	15	15
149	A8	1.50fr brt red	15	15
150	A8	2fr gray	15	15
151	A8	2.50fr brt ultra	26	20
152	A8	4fr dull violet	28	20
153	A8	5fr yellow bister	28	20
154	A8	10fr deep brown	32	26
155	A8	20fr deep green	55	26
		Set value	2.30	1.60

For surcharges see #158-165, B14-B21, B24-B35.

Eboue Issue

Common Design Type

1945 Unwmk. Engr. *Perf. 13*

No.	Type	Description	Unused	Used
156	CD91	2fr black	16	16
157	CD91	25fr Prussian green	80	80

Nos. 156 and 157 exist imperforate.

Nos. 142, 144 and 151 Surcharged with New Values and Bars in Red, Carmine or Black

1946 *Perf. 14x14½*

No.	Type	Description	Unused	Used
158	A8	50c on 5c (R)	32	32
159	A8	60c on 5c (R)	32	32
160	A8	70c on 5c (R)	26	26
161	A8	1.20fr on 5c (C)	26	26
162	A8	2.40fr on 25c	45	45
163	A8	3fr on 25c	65	65
164	A8	4.50fr on 25c	65	65
165	A8	15fr on 2.50fr (C)	65	65
		Nos. 158-165 (8)	3.56	3.56

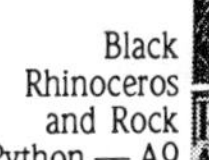

Black Rhinoceros and Rock Python — A9

Jungle Scene — A10

Mountainous Shore Line — A11

Gabon Forest — A12

Niger Boatman — A13

Young Bacongo Woman — A14

1946 Unwmk. Engr. *Perf.* 12½

166 A9	10c deep blue		15	15
167 A9	30c violet blk		15	15
168 A9	40c dp orange		15	15
169 A10	50c violet bl		15	15
170 A10	60c dk carmine		22	16
171 A10	80c dk ol grn		25	16
172 A11	1fr dp orange		25	16
173 A11	1.20fr dp claret		35	25
174 A11	1.50fr dk green		55	42
175 A12	2fr dk vio brn		15	15
176 A12	3fr rose carmine		15	15
177 A12	3.60fr red brown		90	75
178 A12	4fr deep blue		16	15
179 A13	5fr dk brown		25	15
180 A13	6fr deep blue		25	15
181 A13	10fr black		32	15
182 A14	15fr brown		60	15
183 A14	20fr dp claret		60	15
184 A14	25fr black		75	16
	Nos. 166-184 (19)		6.35	
	Set value			3.00

Imperforates

Most French Equatorial Africa stamps from 1951 onward exist imperforate in issued and trial colors, and also in small presentation sheets in issued colors.

Pierre Savorgnan de Brazza — A15

1951, Nov. 5 *Perf.* 13

185 A15 10fr indigo & dk grn 55 16

Cent. of the birth of Pierre Savorgnan de Brazza, explorer.

Military Medal Issue

Common Design Type

Engraved and Typographed

1952, Dec. 1 *Perf.* 13

186 CD101 15fr multicolored 2.25 2.00

Lt. Gov. Adolphe L. Cureau A16

1954, Sept. 20 Engr.

187 A16 15fr ol grn & red brn 65 32

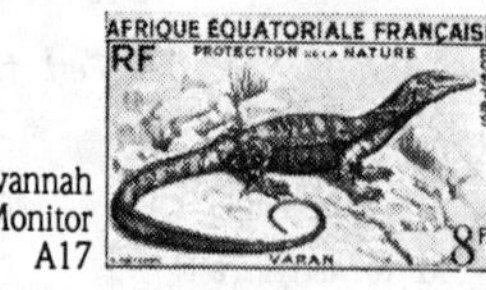
Savannah Monitor A17

1955, May 2 Unwmk.

188 A17 8fr dk grn & claret 1.25 60

International Exhibition for Wildlife Protection, Paris, May 1955.

FIDES Issue

Boali Waterfall and Power Plant, Ubangi-Chari A18

Designs: 10fr, Cotton, Chad. 15fr, Brazzaville Hospital, Middle Congo. 20fr, Libreville Harbor, Gabon.

1956, Apr. 25 *Perf.* 13x12½

189 A18	5fr dk brn & cl	25	18
190 A18	10fr blk & bluish grn	35	25
191 A18	15fr ind & gray vio	40	15
192 A18	20fr dk red & red org	48	25

See note after Common Design Type CD103.

Coffee Issue

Coffee — A19

1956, Oct. Engr. *Perf.* 13

193 A19 10fr brn vio & vio bl 40 15

Leprosarium at Mayumba and Maltese Cross — A20

1957, Mar. 11

194 A20 15fr grn, bl grn & red 40 15

Issued in honor of the Knights of Malta.

Giant Eland — A21

Animals: 2fr, Lions. 3fr, Elephant, vert. 4fr, Greater kudu, vert.

1957, Nov. 4

195 A21	1fr green & brown	15	15
196 A21	2fr Prus grn & ol grn	15	15
197 A21	3fr green, gray & bl	16	15
198 A21	4fr maroon & gray	16	16

WHO Building, Brazzaville A22

1958, May 19 Engr. *Perf.* 13

199 A22 20fr dk green & org brn 45 35

10th anniv. of WHO.

Flower Issue

Common Design Type

Design: 10fr, Euadania. 25fr, Spathodea.

1958, July 7 Photo. *Perf.* 12x12½

200 CD104	10fr dk vio, yel & grn	28	22
201 CD104	25fr green, yel & red	55	28

Human Rights Issue

Common Design Type

1958, Dec. 10 Engr. *Perf.* 13

202 CD105 20fr Prus grn & dk bl 60 55

SEMI-POSTAL STAMPS

Common Design Type

1938, Oct. 24 Engr.

B1 CD80 1.75fr + 50c brt ultra 9.00 9.00

Nos. 51, 64 Surcharged in Black or Red **+35c**

1938, Nov. 7 *Perf.* 13x13½

B2 A4	65c + 35c dk bl & lt grn (R)	1.10	1.05
B3 A4	1.75fr + 50c bl & lt bl	1.10	1.00

The surtax was for welfare.

French Revolution Issue

Common Design Type

Name and Value Typo. in Black

1939, July 5 Photo.

B4 CD83	45c + 25c green	6.00	6.00
B5 CD83	70c + 30c brown	6.00	6.00
B6 CD83	90c + 35c red org	6.00	6.00
B7 CD83	1.25fr + 1fr rose pink	6.00	6.00
B8 CD83	2.25fr + 2fr blue	6.00	6.00
	Nos. B4-B8 (5)	30.00	30.00

Surtax used for the defense of the colonies.

Catalogue values for unused stamps in this section, from this point to the end of the section, are for Never Hinged items.

Common Design Type and

Native Artilleryman SP1

Gabon Infantryman SP2

1941 Photo. *Perf.* 13½

B8A SP1	1fr + 1fr red	1.25
B8B CD86	1.50fr + 3fr maroon	1.25
B8C SP2	2.50fr + 1fr blue	1.25

Nos. B8A-B8C were issued by the Vichy government and not placed on sale in the colony.

Nos. 79A-79B were surcharged "OEUVRES COLONIALES" and surtax (including change of denomination of the 2.50fr to 50c). These were issued in 1944 by the Vichy government and not placed on sale in the colony.

Brazza and Stanley Pool — SP3

1941 Photo. *Perf.* 14½x14

B9 SP3 1fr + 2fr dk brn & red 40 40

The surtax was for a monument to Pierre Savorgnan de Brazza.

Nos. 67, 71 Surcharged in Red

Afrique Française Combattante + 50 fr.

1943, June 28 *Perf.* 13½x13

B10 A6	2.25fr + 50fr	5.50	5.50
B11 A6	10fr + 100fr	17.00	17.00

Nos. 129 and 132 with additional Surcharge in Carmine

LIBÉRATION

+ 10 fr.

1944

B12 A4	80c + 10fr	10.00	10.00
B13 A5	1.50fr + 15fr	10.00	10.00

Same surcharge printed Vertically on Nos. 142-146, 149, 150-151

***Perf.* 14x14½**

B14 A8	5c + 10fr brown	4.00	4.00
B15 A8	10c + 10fr dk bl	4.00	4.00
B16 A8	25c + 10fr emer	4.00	4.00
B17 A8	30c + 10fr dp org	4.00	4.00
B18 A8	40c + 10fr dk sl grn	4.00	4.00
B19 A8	1fr + 10fr dp red lil	4.00	4.00
B20 A8	2fr + 20fr gray	4.50	4.50
B21 A8	2.50fr + 25fr brt ultra	4.50	4.50
	Nos. B12-B21 (10)	53.00	53.00

Nos. 129 and 132 with additional Surcharge in Carmine

RÉSISTANCE

+ 10 fr.

1944 *Perf.* 13½x13

B22 A4	80c + 10fr	9.50	9.50
B23 A5	1.50fr + 15fr	9.50	9.50

Same Surcharge printed Vertically on Nos. 142-155

***Perf.* 14x14½**

B24 A8	5c + 10fr brn	2.75	2.75
B25 A8	10c + 10fr dk bl	2.75	2.75
B26 A8	25c + 10fr emer	2.75	2.75
B27 A8	30c + 10fr dp org	2.75	2.75
B28 A8	40c + 10fr dk sl grn	2.75	2.75
B29 A8	1fr + 10fr dp red lil	2.75	2.75
B30 A8	2fr + 20fr gray	2.75	2.75
B31 A8	2.50fr + 25fr brt ultra	2.75	2.75
B32 A8	4fr + 40fr dl vio	2.75	2.75
B33 A8	5fr + 50fr yel bis	2.75	2.75
B34 A8	10fr + 100fr dp brn	5.00	5.00
B35 A8	20fr + 200fr dp grn	5.00	5.00
	Nos. B22-B35 (14)	56.50	56.50

Nos. B12 to B35 were issued to raise funds for the Committee to Aid the Fighting Men and Patriots of France.

Red Cross Issue

Common Design Type

1944 Photo. *Perf.* 14½x14

B38 CD90 5fr + 20fr royal blue 60 60

The surtax was for the French Red Cross and national relief.

Tropical Medicine Issue
Common Design Type

1950, May 15 Engr. *Perf. 13*

B39	CD100 10fr + 2fr dk bl grn & vio brn	2.50	2.25

The surtax was for charitable work.

AIR POST STAMPS

Hydroplane over Pointe-Noire AP1

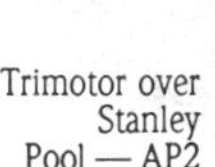

Trimotor over Stanley Pool — AP2

1937 Unwmk. Photo. *Perf. 13½*

C1	AP1	1.50fr ol blk & yel	15	15
C2	AP1	2fr mag & blue	16	16
C3	AP1	2.50fr grn & buff	16	16
C4	AP1	3.75fr brn & lt grn	35	35
C5	AP2	4.50fr cop red & bl	35	35
C6	AP2	6.50fr bl & lt grn	55	55
C7	AP2	8.50fr red brn & yel	55	55
C8	AP2	10.75fr vio & lt grn	55	55
		Nos. C1-C8 (8)	2.82	2.82

For overprints and surcharges see #C9-C16, CB2.

V4

Stamps of types AP1 and AP2 without "R F" and stamp of the design shown above were issued in 1943 and 1944 by the Vichy Government, but were not placed on sale in the colony.

Nos. C1, C3-C7 Overprinted in Black like Nos. 133-141

1940-41

C9	AP1	1.50fr ('41)	100.00	100.00
C10	AP1	2.50fr	70	70
C11	AP1	3.75fr ('41)	100.00	100.00
C12	AP2	4.50fr	70	70
C13	AP2	6.50fr	90	90
C14	AP2	8.50fr	70	70

Afrique Française Libre

50 fr.

No. C8 Surcharged in Carmine

C15	AP2	50fr on 10.75fr	4.25	4.25

Afrique Française Libre

No. C3 Surcharged in Black

C16	AP1	10fr on 2.50fr ('41)	47.50	47.50
		Nos. C9-C16 (8)	254.75	254.75

Counterfeits of Nos. C9 and C11 exist.
See note following No. 141.

Catalogue values for unused stamps in this section, from this point to the end of the section, are for Never Hinged items.

Common Design Type

1941 Photo. *Perf. 14½x14*

C17	CD87	1fr dk org	28	28
C18	CD87	1.50fr brt red	28	20
C19	CD87	5fr brn red	60	28
C20	CD87	10fr black	60	40
C21	CD87	25fr ultra	55	35
C22	CD87	50fr dk grn	35	35
C23	CD87	100fr plum	55	42
		Nos. C17-C23 (7)	3.21	2.28

Victory Issue
Common Design Type
Perf. 12½

1946, May 8 Unwmk. Engr.

C24	CD92	8fr lilac rose	55	42

Chad to Rhine Issue
Common Design Types

1946, June 6

C25	CD93	5fr dk vio	40	40
C26	CD94	10fr slate grn	40	40
C27	CD95	15fr deep blue	55	55
C28	CD96	20fr red org	65	65
C29	CD97	25fr sepia	70	70
C30	CD98	50fr brn car	70	70
		Nos. C25-C30 (6)	3.40	3.40

Palms and Village — AP3

Village and Waterfront — AP4

Bearers in Jungle — AP5

1946 Engr. *Perf. 13*

C31	AP3	50fr red brn	1.25	50
C32	AP4	100fr grnsh blk	2.00	75
C33	AP5	200fr deep blue	4.00	1.25

UPU Issue
Common Design Type

1949, July 4

C34	CD99	25fr green	5.50	5.50

Brazza Holding Map — AP6

1951, Nov. 5

C35	AP6	15fr brn, indigo & red	65	35

Cent. of the birth of Pierre Savorgnan de Brazza, explorer.

Archbishop Augouard and St. Anne Cathedral, Brazzaville — AP7

1952, Dec. 1

C36	AP7	15fr ol grn, dk brn & vio brn	2.00	1.40

Cent. of the birth of Archbishop Philippe-Prosper Augouard.

Anhingas — AP8

1953, Feb. 16

C37	AP8	500fr grnsh blk, blk & slate	20.00	4.00

Liberation Issue
Common Design Type

1954, June 6

C38	CD102	15fr vio & vio brn	2.00	2.00

Log Rafts AP9

Designs: 100fr, Fishing boats and nets, Lake Chad. 200fr, Age of mechanization.

1955, Jan. 24 Engr.

C39	AP9	50fr ind, brn & dk grn	80	45
C40	AP9	100fr aqua, dk grn & blk brn	2.75	45
C41	AP9	200fr red & dp plum	3.75	1.25

Gov. Gen. Félix Eboué, View of Brazzaville and the Pantheon — AP10

1955, Apr. 30 Unwmk. *Perf. 13*

C42	AP10	15fr sep, brn & sl bl	1.75	1.00

Gen. Louis Faidherbé and African Sharpshooter AP11

1957, July 20

C43	AP11	15fr sepia & org ver	1.15	90

Centenary of French African Troops.

AIR POST SEMI-POSTAL STAMPS

French Revolution Issue
Common Design Type

1939 Unwmk. Photo. *Perf. 13*
Name and Value Typo. in Orange

CB1	CD83	4.50fr + 4fr brn blk	12.50	12.50

V5

V6

V7

Stamps of the designs shown above and stamp of Cameroun type V10 inscribed "Afrique Equatoriale Frcaise" were issued in 1942 by the Vichy Government, but were not placed on sale in the colony.

#C8 Surcharged in Red like #B10-B11

1943, June 28 *Perf. 13½*

CB2	AP2	10.75fr + 200fr	85.00	85.00

Counterfeits exist.

POSTAGE DUE STAMPS

Numeral of Value on Equatorial Butterfly
D1 D2

1937 Unwmk. Photo. *Perf. 13*

J1	D1	5c redsh pur & lt bl	15	15
J2	D1	10c cop red & buff	15	15
J3	D1	20c dk grn & grn	15	15
J4	D1	25c red brn & buff	15	15
J5	D1	30c cop red & lt bl	15	15
J6	D1	45c mag & yel grn	30	30
J7	D1	50c dk ol grn & buff	28	28
J8	D1	60c redsh pur & yel	38	38
J9	D1	1fr brown & yel	45	45
J10	D1	2fr dk bl & buff	65	65
J11	D1	3fr red brn & lt grn	65	65
		Set value	3.00	3.00

Catalogue values for unused stamps in this section, from this point to the end of the section, are for Never Hinged items.

1947 Engr.

J12	D2	10c red	15	15
J13	D2	30c dp org	15	15
J14	D2	50c greenish bl	15	15
J15	D2	1fr carmine	15	15
J16	D2	2fr emerald	18	18
J17	D2	3fr dp red lil	26	26
J18	D2	4fr dp ultra	30	30
J19	D2	5fr red brown	45	45
J20	D2	10fr peacock blue	60	60
J21	D2	20fr sepia	65	65
		Set value	2.75	2.75

FRENCH GUIANA

LOCATION — On the northeast coast of South America bordering on the Atlantic Ocean.
GOVT. — Former French colony
AREA — 34,740 sq. mi.
POP. — 28,537 (1946)
CAPITAL — Cayenne

Formerly a colony, French Guiana became an overseas department of France in 1946.

100 Centimes = 1 Franc

Catalogue values for unused stamps in this country are for Never Hinged items, beginning with Scott 171 in the regular postage section, Scott B12 in the semi-postal section, Scott C9 in the airpost section, and Scott J22 in the postage due section.

See France No. 1446 for French stamp inscribed "Guyane."

Stamps of French Colonies Surcharged in Black

Déc. 1886.
GUY. FRANÇ.
0f 05

1886, Dec. Unwmk. *Imperf.*
1 A8 5c on 2c grn, *grnsh* 225.00 225.00
b. No "f" after "O" 250.00 250.00

Perf. 14x13½
2 A9 5c on 2c brn, *buff* 225.00 225.00
b. No "f" after "O" 160.00 150.00

Two types of No. 1: Surcharge 12mm high, and surcharge 10½mm high.

Avril 1887.
—
GUY FRANÇ
0f 20

Avril 1887.
—
GUY FRANÇ.
0f 25

"Av" of Date Line Inverted-Reversed
1887, Apr. *Imperf.*
4 A8 20c on 35c blk, *org* 20.00 18.00

Date Line Reads "Avril 1887"
5 A8 5c on 2c grn, *grnsh* 55.00 50.00
6 A8 20c on 35c blk, *org* 150.00 110.00
7 A7 25c on 30c brn, *yelsh* 14.00 12.00

Variety "small f omitted" occurs on #5-7.

French Colonies Nos. 22 and 26 Surcharged

DÉC. 1887.
GUY. FRANÇ.
5c

8 A7 5c on 30c brn, *yelsh* 60.00 50.00
a. Double surcharge 325.00 325.00
b. Inverted surcharge 400.00 400.00
c. Pair, one without surcharge 525.00 525.00
9 A8 5c on 30c brn, *yelsh* 750.00 750.00

French Colonies Nos. 22 and 28 Surcharged:

Février 1888
—
GUY. FRANÇ
5

Février 1888
—
GUY. FRANÇ
10

1888
10 A7 5c on 30c brn, *yelsh* 60.00 50.00
b. Double surcharge 225.00 225.00
c. Inverted surcharge 225.00 225.00
11 A8 10c on 75c car, *rose* 100.00 100.00

Stamps of French Colonies Overprinted in Black

1892, Feb. 20 *Imperf.*
12 A8 2c grn, *grnsh* 350.00 350.00
13 A7 30c brn, *yelsh* 60.00 60.00
14 A8 35c blk, *orange* 1,400. 1,100.
15 A8 40c red, *straw* 45.00 42.50
16 A8 75c car, *rose* 47.50 42.50
a. Inverted overprint 190.00 190.00
17 A8 1fr brnz grn, *straw* 60.00 60.00
a. Inverted overprint 250.00 250.00

1892 *Perf. 14x13½*
18 A9 1c blk, *lil bl* 18.00 12.50
19 A9 2c brn, *buff* 15.00 12.50
20 A9 4c claret, *lav* 15.00 12.50
21 A9 5c grn, *grnsh* 15.00 12.50
a. Inverted overprint 45.00 45.00
b. Double overprint 45.00
22 A9 10c blk, *lavender* 22.50 14.00
a. Inverted overprint 22.50 14.00
23 A9 15c blue 20.00 12.50
24 A9 20c red, *grn* 18.00 12.50
25 A9 25c blk, *rose* 25.00 12.50
26 A9 30c brn, *bis* 15.00 11.00
27 A9 35c blk, *orange* 90.00 90.00
28 A9 40c red, *straw* 55.00 50.00
a. Inverted overprint 80.00 70.00
29 A9 75c car, *rose* 50.00 42.50
30 A9 1fr brnz grn, *straw* 100.00 90.00

French Colonies No. 51 Surcharged

GUYANE.
DÉC. 92.
0f05

1892, Dec.
31 A9 5c on 15c blue 15.00 12.50

Navigation and Commerce — A12

1892-1904 Typo. *Perf. 14x13½*
Name of Colony in Blue or Carmine
32 A12 1c blk, *lil bl* 1.00 95
33 A12 2c brn, *buff* 70 75
34 A12 4c claret, *lav* 95 75
a. "GUYANE" double 125.00 125.00
35 A12 5c grn, *grnsh* 6.00 4.75
36 A12 5c yel grn ('04) 80 42
37 A12 10c blk, *lavender* 5.50 2.75
38 A12 10c red ('00) 2.00 80
39 A12 15c blue, quadrille paper 13.00 1.50
40 A12 15c gray, *lt gray* ('00) 50.00 37.50
41 A12 20c red, *grn* 8.00 5.50
42 A12 25c blk, *rose* 6.75 2.00
43 A12 25c blue ('00) 6.25 6.00
44 A12 30c brn, *bis* 7.25 5.50
45 A12 40c red, *straw* 8.25 5.50
46 A12 50c car, *rose* 13.00 5.50
47 A12 50c brn, *az* ('00) 9.00 7.50
48 A12 75c dp vio, *org* 15.00 8.00
49 A12 1fr brn grn, *straw* 6.00 5.50
50 A12 2fr vio, *rose* ('02) 90.00 6.00
Nos. 32-50 (19) 249.45 107.17

Perf. 13½x14 stamps are counterfeits.
For surcharges see Nos. 87-93.

Great Anteater — A13

Washing Gold — A14

Palm Grove at Cayenne A15

1905-28
51 A13 1c black 15 15
52 A13 2c blue 15 15
53 A13 4c red brn 15 15
54 A13 5c green 40 32
55 A13 5c org ('22) 15 15
56 A13 10c rose 15 15
57 A13 10c grn ('22) 15 15
58 A13 10c red, *bluish* ('25) 15 15
59 A13 15c violet 60 40
60 A14 20c red brn 15 15
61 A14 25c blue 75 28
62 A14 25c vio ('22) 35 15
63 A14 30c black 55 28
64 A14 30c rose ('22) 15 15
65 A14 30c red org ('25) 15 15
66 A14 30c dk grn, *grnsh* ('28) 42 42
67 A14 35c blk, *yel* ('06) 15 15
68 A14 40c rose 15 15
69 A14 40c black ('22) 20 15
70 A14 45c olive ('07) 35 15
71 A14 50c violet 80 60
72 A14 50c blue ('22) 15 15
73 A14 50c gray ('25) 35 15
74 A14 60c lil, *rose* ('25) 15 15
75 A14 65c myr grn ('26) 15 15
76 A14 75c green 45 28
77 A14 85c magenta ('26) 28 15
78 A15 1fr rose 32 15
79 A15 1fr bl, *bluish* ('25) 35 15
80 A15 1fr bl, *yel grn* ('28) 80 80
81 A15 1.10fr lt red ('28) 55 55
82 A15 2fr blue 40 28
83 A15 2fr org red, *yel* ('26) 70 60
84 A15 5fr black 3.00 1.50
85 A15 10fr grn, *yel* ('24) 6.00 4.75
a. Printed on both sides 20.00 20.00
86 A15 20fr brn lake ('24) 8.50 5.50
Nos. 51-86 (36) 28.37 19.86

For surcharges see Nos. 94-108, B1-B2.

Issue of 1892 Surcharged in Black or Carmine

05 10

1912
87 A12 5c on 2c brn, *buff* 40 40
88 A12 5c on 4c cl, *lav* (C) 35 35
89 A12 5c on 20c red, *grn* 40 40
90 A12 5c on 25c blk, *rose* (C) 1.40 1.40
91 A12 5c on 30c brn, *bis* (C) 60 60
92 A12 10c on 40c red, *straw* 35 35
93 A12 10c on 50c car, *rose* 75 75
a. Double surcharge 250.00
Nos. 87-93 (7) 4.25 4.25

Two spacings between the surcharged numerals are found on Nos. 87 to 93.

No. 59 Surcharged in Various Colors

0,01 =

1922
94 A13 1c on 15c vio (Bk) 18 18
95 A13 2c on 15c vio (Bl) 18 18
a. Inverted surcharge 40.00
96 A13 4c on 15c vio (G) 18 18
a. Double surcharge 40.00
97 A13 5c on 15c vio (R) 18 18

Type of 1905-28 Surcharged in Blue

VINGT
FRANCS

VINGT
FRANCS

1923
98 A15 10fr on 1fr grn, *yel* 6.00 6.00
99 A15 20fr on 5fr lilac, *rose* 6.00 6.00

Stamps and Types of 1905-28 Surcharged with New Value and Bars in Black or Red

1924-27
100 A13 25c on 15c vio ('25) 18 18
101 A15 25c on 2fr bl ('24) 18 18
a. Double surcharge 60.00
b. Triple surcharge 70.00
102 A14 65c on 45c ol (R) ('25) 48 48
103 A14 85c on 45c ol (R) ('25) 48 48
104 A14 90c on 75c red ('27) 48 48
105 A15 1.05fr on 2fr lt yel brn ('27) 48 48
106 A15 1.25fr on 1fr ultra (R) ('26) 48 48
107 A15 1.50fr on 1fr lt bl ('27) 60 60
108 A15 3fr on 5fr vio ('27) 60 60
a. No period after "F" 4.75 4.75
Nos. 100-108 (9) 3.96 3.96

Carib Archer — A16

Shooting Rapids, Maroni River — A17

Government Building, Cayenne A18

1929-40 *Perf. 13½x14*
109 A16 1c gray lil & grnsh bl 15 15
110 A16 2c dk red & bl grn 15 15
111 A16 3c gray lil & grnsh bl ('40) 15 15
112 A16 4c ol brn & red vio 15 15
113 A16 5c Prus bl & red org 15 15
114 A16 10c mag & brn 15 15
115 A16 15c yel brn & red org 15 15
116 A16 20c dk bl & ol grn 15 15
117 A16 25c dk red & dk brn 15 15

Perf. 14x13½
118 A17 30c dl & lt grn 22 15
119 A17 30c grn & brn ('40) 15 15
120 A17 35c Prus grn & ol grn ('38) 32 32
121 A17 40c org brn & ol gray 15 15
122 A17 45c grn & dk brn 32 32
123 A17 45c ol grn & lt grn ('40) 15 15
124 A17 50c dk bl & ol gray 15 15
125 A17 55c vio bl & car ('38) 40 40
126 A17 60c sal & grn ('40) 15 15
127 A17 65c sal & grn 35 35
128 A17 70c ind & sl bl ('40) 38 38
129 A17 75c ind & sl bl 50 50
130 A17 80c blk & vio bl ('38) 25 22
131 A17 90c dk red & ver 35 35
132 A17 90c red vio & brn ('39) 38 38
133 A17 1fr lt vio & brn 35 35
134 A17 1fr car & lt red ('38) 70 65
135 A17 1fr blk & vio bl ('40) 15 15
136 A18 1.05fr ver & olivine 2.50 1.60
137 A18 1.10fr ol brn & red vio 2.50 1.60
138 A18 1.25fr blk brn & bl grn ('33) 35 35
139 A18 1.25fr rose & lt red ('39) 20 20
140 A18 1.40fr ol brn & red vio ('40) 38 38
141 A18 1.50fr dk bl & lt bl 15 15
142 A18 1.60fr ol brn & bl grn ('40) 20 20
143 A18 1.75fr brn red & blk brn ('33) 70 65
144 A18 1.75fr vio bl ('38) 35 35
145 A18 2fr dk grn & rose red 15 15
146 A18 2.25fr vio bl ('39) 38 38
147 A18 2.50fr cop red & brn ('40) 38 38
148 A18 3fr brn red & red vio 32 32
149 A18 5fr dl vio & yel grn 32 32
150 A18 10fr ol gray & dp ultra 45 45
151 A18 20fr indigo & ver 65 60
Nos. 109-151 (43) 16.75 14.70

Colonial Exposition Issue
Common Design Types
1931 Engr. *Perf. 12½*
Name of Country in Black
152 CD70 40c dp grn 1.50 1.50
153 CD71 50c violet 1.50 1.50
154 CD72 90c red org 1.65 1.65
155 CD73 1.50fr dull blue 1.65 1.65

Recapture of Cayenne by d'Estrées, 1676 — A19

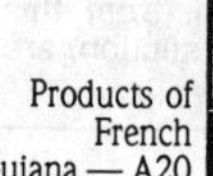

Products of French Guiana — A20

1935, Oct. 21 *Perf. 13*

156	A19	40c gray brn	1.90	1.75
157	A19	50c dull red	4.50	2.25
158	A19	1.50fr ultra	1.90	1.75
159	A20	1.75fr lilac rose	5.75	4.75
160	A20	5fr brown	4.50	3.00
161	A20	10fr bl grn	4.50	3.00
		Nos. 156-161 (6)	23.05	16.50

Tercentenary of the founding of French possessions in the West Indies.

Paris International Exposition Issue
Common Design Types

1937, Apr. 15

162	CD74	20c dp vio	45	45
163	CD75	30c dk grn	45	45
164	CD76	40c car rose	45	45
165	CD77	50c dk brn	45	45
166	CD78	90c red	50	50
167	CD79	1.50fr ultra	50	50
		Nos. 162-167 (6)	2.80	2.80

Colonial Arts Exhibition Issue
Souvenir Sheet
Common Design Type

1937 *Imperf.*

168 CD75 3fr violet 2.25 2.25

New York World's Fair Issue
Common Design Type

1939, May 10 Engr. *Perf. 12½x12*

169	CD82	1.25fr car lake	35	35
170	CD82	2.25fr ultra	35	35

View of Cayenne and Marshal Petain A21a

1941 Engr. *Perf. 12½x12*

170A	A21a	1fr deep lilac	35
170B	A21a	2.50fr blue	35

Nos. 170A-170B were issued by the Vichy government and were not placed on sale in the colony. This is also true of three stamps of types A16-A18 without "RF" released in 1944.

Common Design Types pictured in section at front of book.

Catalogue values for unused stamps in this section, from this point to the end of the section, are for Never Hinged items.

Eboue Issue
Common Design Type

1945 Engr. *Perf. 13*

171	CD91	2fr black	35	35
172	CD91	25fr Prussian green	55	55

This issue exists imperforate.

Arms of Cayenne A22

1945 Litho. *Perf. 12*

173	A22	10c deep gray vio	15	15
174	A22	30c brn org	15	15
175	A22	40c lt bl	15	15
176	A22	50c vio brn	15	15
177	A22	60c org yel	15	15
178	A22	70c pale brn	15	15
179	A22	80c lt grn	15	15
180	A22	1fr blue	15	15
181	A22	1.20fr brt vio	15	15
182	A22	1.50fr dp org	30	30
183	A22	2fr black	30	30
184	A22	2.40fr red	35	35
185	A22	3fr pink	35	35
186	A22	4fr dp ultra	35	35
187	A22	4.50fr dp yel grn	35	35
188	A22	5fr org brn	35	35
189	A22	10fr dk vio	35	35
190	A22	15fr rose car	50	50
191	A22	20fr olive grn	55	55
		Nos. 173-191 (19)	5.10	5.10

Hammock — A23

Guiana Girl — A26

Maroni River Bank — A24

Inini Scene — A25

Toucans A27

Parrots — A28

Unwmk.

1947, June 2 Engr. *Perf. 13.*

192	A23	10c dk bl grn	15	15
193	A23	30c brt red	15	15
194	A23	50c dk vio brn	15	15
195	A24	60c grnsh blk	15	15
196	A24	1fr red brn	18	18
197	A24	1.50fr blk brn	18	18
198	A25	2fr dp yel grn	35	18
199	A25	2.50fr dp ultra	35	30
200	A25	3fr red brn	48	42
201	A26	4fr blk brn	1.00	60
202	A26	5fr deep blue	85	60
203	A26	6fr red brn	90	60
204	A27	10fr dp ultra	2.50	1.75
205	A27	15fr blk brn	2.50	2.50
206	A27	20fr red brn	3.00	2.75
207	A28	25fr brt bl grn	4.00	3.00
208	A28	40fr blk brn	4.00	3.00
		Nos. 192-208 (17)	20.89	16.66

SEMI-POSTAL STAMPS

Regular Issue of 1905-28 Surcharged in Red

1915 Unwmk. *Perf. 13½x14*

B1	A13	10c + 5c rose	6.00	6.00
a.		Inverted surcharge	80.00	80.00
b.		Double surcharge	70.00	70.00

Regular Issue of 1905-28 Surcharged in Rose

B2 A13 10c + 5c rose 40 40

Curie Issue
Common Design Type

1938 *Perf. 13*

B3 CD80 1.75fr + 50c brt ultra 4.25 4.25

French Revolution Issue
Common Design Type

1939 Photo.

Name and Value in Black

B4	CD83	45c + 25c green	3.00	3.00
B5	CD83	70c + 30c brown	3.00	3.00
B6	CD83	90c + 35c red org	3.00	3.00
B7	CD83	1.25fr + 1fr rose pink	3.00	3.00
B8	CD83	2.25fr + 2fr blue	4.00	4.00
		Nos. B4-B8 (5)	16.00	16.00

Common Design Type and

Colonial Infantryman — SP1

Colonial Policeman SP2

1941 Photo. *Perf. 13½*

B9	SP1	1fr + 1fr red	55
B10	CD86	1.50fr + 3fr maroon	75
B11	SP2	2.50fr + 1fr blue	55

Nos. B9-B11 were issued by the Vichy government, and were not placed on sale in the colony.

Nos. 170A-170B were surcharged "OEUVRES COLONIALES" and surtax (including change of denomination of the 2.50fr to 50c). These were issued in 1944 by the Vichy government, and not placed on sale in the colony.

Catalogue values for unused stamps in this section, from this point to the end of the section, are for Never Hinged items.

Red Cross Issue
Common Design Type

1944 *Perf. 14½x14*

B12 CD90 5fr + 20fr dk cop brn 50 50

The surtax was for the French Red Cross and national relief.

AIR POST STAMPS

Cayenne AP1

Perf. 13½

1933, Nov. 20 Unwmk. Photo.

C1	AP1	50c org brn	15	15
C2	AP1	1fr yel grn	15	15
C3	AP1	1.50fr dk bl	15	15
C4	AP1	2fr orange	15	15
C5	AP1	3fr black	42	42
C6	AP1	5fr violet	20	20
C7	AP1	10fr olive grn	40	40
C8	AP1	20fr scarlet	42	42
		Nos. C1-C8 (8)	2.04	2.04

Catalogue values for unused stamps in this section, from this point to the end of the section, are for Never Hinged items.

V4

V5

Stamp of type AP1 without "RF" and stamps of the designs shown above were issued in 1942 and 1944 by the Vichy Government, but were not placed on sale in the colony.

Common Design Type

1945 Photo. *Perf. 14½x14*

C9	CD87	50fr dark green	40	40
C10	CD87	100fr plum	65	65

Victory Issue
Common Design Type

1946, May 8 Engr. *Perf. 12½*

C11 CD92 8fr black 50 50

Chad to Rhine Issue
Common Design Types

1946, June 6

C12	CD93	5fr dk slate bl	42	42
C13	CD94	10fr lilac rose	50	50
C14	CD95	15fr dk vio brn	50	50
C15	CD96	20fr dk slate grn	60	60
C16	CD97	25fr vio brown	65	65
C17	CD98	50fr bright lilac	80	80
		Nos. C12-C17 (6)	3.47	3.47

Eagles AP2

Tapir — AP3

Toucans — AP4

1947, June 2 Engr. *Perf. 13*

C18	AP2	50fr deep green	6.00	6.00
C19	AP3	100fr red brown	6.00	6.00
C20	AP4	200fr dk gray bl	13.00	13.00

AIR POST SEMI-POSTAL STAMP

French Revolution Issue
Common Design Type

Unwmk.

1939, July 5 Photo. *Perf. 13*

Name & Value Typo. in Orange

CB1 CD83 5fr + 4fr brn blk 7.00 7.00

V6

Stamps of the design shown above and stamp of Cameroun type V10 inscribed "Guyane Francaise" were issued in 1942 by the Vichy Government, but were not placed on sale in the colony.

POSTAGE DUE STAMPS

Postage Due Stamps of France, 1893-1926, Overprinted **GUYANE FRANÇAISE**

1925-27 Unwmk. *Perf. 14x13½*

J1 D2 5c light blue 15 15
J2 D2 10c brown 18 18
J3 D2 20c olive green 18 18
J4 D2 50c violet brown 42 30
J5 D2 3fr magenta ('27) 3.50 3.00

Surcharged in Black **GUYANE FRANÇAISE 25 centimes à percevoir**

J6 D2 15c on 20c ol grn 18 18
a. Blue surcharge 22.50
J7 D2 25c on 5c lt bl 40 25
J8 D2 30c on 20c ol grn 52 30
J9 D2 45c on 10c brn 30 22
J10 D2 60c on 5c lt bl 45 32
J11 D2 1fr on 20c ol grn 60 50
J12 D2 2fr on 50c vio brn 75 60
Nos. J1-J12 (12) 7.63 6.18

Royal Palms — D3

Guiana Girl — D4

1929, Oct. 14 Typo. *Perf. 13½x14*

J13 D3 5c indigo & Prus bl 15 15
J14 D3 10c bis brn & Prus grn 15 15
J15 D3 20c grn & rose red 15 15
J16 D3 30c ol brn & rose red 15 15
J17 D3 50c vio & ol brn 28 28
J18 D3 60c brn red & ol brn 42 42
J19 D4 1fr dp bl & org brn 60 60
J20 D4 2fr brn red & bluish grn 70 70
J21 D4 3fr vio & blk 1.40 1.40
Nos. J13-J21 (9) 4.00 4.00

Catalogue values for unused stamps in this section, from this point to the end of the section, are for Never Hinged items.

D5

1947, June 2 Engr. *Perf. 14x13*

J22 D5 10c dark car rose 15 15
J23 D5 30c dull green 15 15
J24 D5 50c black 15 15
J25 D5 1fr brt ultra 16 16
J26 D5 2fr dk brn red 16 16
J27 D5 3fr deep vio 25 25
J28 D5 4fr red 35 35
J29 D5 5fr brn vio 45 45
J30 D5 10fr bl grn 75 75
J31 D5 20fr lilac rose 90 90
Nos. J22-J31 (10) 3.47 3.47

FRENCH GUINEA

LOCATION — On the coast of West Africa, between Portuguese Guinea and Sierra Leone.
GOVT. — Former French colony
AREA — 89,436 sq. mi.
POP. — 2,058,442 (est. 1941)
CAPITAL — Conakry

French Guinea stamps were replaced by those of French West Africa around 1944-45. French Guinea became the Republic of Guinea Oct. 2, 1958. See "Guinea" for issues of the republic.

100 Centimes = 1 Franc

Navigation and Commerce A1

Fulah Shepherd A2

Perf. 14x13½

1892-1900 Typo. Unwmk.

Name of Colony in Blue or Carmine

1 A1 1c black, *lilac bl* 70 70
2 A1 2c brown, *buff* 80 80
3 A1 4c claret, *lav* 1.00 1.00
4 A1 5c green, *grnsh* 2.75 1.75
5 A1 10c blk, *lavender* 2.75 1.75
6 A1 10c red ('00) 16.00 12.50
7 A1 15c blue, quadrille paper 2.75 1.75
8 A1 15c gray, *lt gray* ('00) 52.50 42.50
9 A1 20c red, *grn* 7.00 5.00
10 A1 25c black, *rose* 4.00 3.00
11 A1 25c blue ('00) 9.50 6.50
12 A1 30c brown, *bis* 15.00 9.00
13 A1 40c red, *straw* 15.00 9.00
a. "GUINEE FRANCAISE" double 300.00 300.00
14 A1 50c car, *rose* 18.00 9.00
15 A1 50c brown, *az* ('00) 12.00 9.00
16 A1 75c dp vio, *org* 24.00 17.50
17 A1 1fr brnz grn, *straw* 17.50 12.00
Nos. 1-17 (17) 201.25 142.75

Perf. 13½x14 stamps are counterfeits.
For surcharges see Nos. 48-54.

1904

18 A2 1c black, *yel grn* 45 32
19 A2 2c vio brn, *buff* 45 45
20 A2 4c carmine, *bl* 70 50
21 A2 5c green, *grnsh* 70 50
22 A2 10c carmine 1.40 75
23 A2 15c violet, *rose* 2.75 1.50
24 A2 20c carmine, *grn* 4.50 3.75
25 A2 25c blue 5.25 3.75
26 A2 30c brown 8.50 7.00
27 A2 40c red, *straw* 10.00 9.00
28 A2 50c brown, *az* 10.00 9.00
29 A2 75c green, *org* 14.00 13.00
30 A2 1fr brnz grn, *straw* 18.00 16.00
31 A2 2fr red, *org* 40.00 34.00
32 A2 5fr green, *yel grn* 55.00 45.00
Nos. 18-32 (15) 171.70 144.52

For surcharges see Nos. 55-62.

Gen. Louis Faidherbé — A3

Oil Palm — A4

Dr. Noel Eugène Ballay — A5

1906-07

Name of Colony in Red or Blue

33 A3 1c gray 40 40
34 A3 2c brown 50 40
35 A3 4c brown, *bl* 65 50
36 A3 5c green 1.50 90
37 A3 10c carmine (B) 6.25 1.00
38 A4 20c black, *blue* 2.00 1.50
39 A4 25c blue, *pnksh* 2.50 1.75
40 A4 30c brown, *pnksh* 2.25 1.50
41 A4 35c black, *yellow* 1.40 90
42 A4 45c choc, *grnsh gray* 1.90 1.50
43 A4 50c dp violet 4.50 3.75
44 A4 75c blue, *org* 2.00 1.50
45 A5 1fr black, *az* 8.00 7.00
46 A5 2fr blue, *pink* 17.50 15.00
47 A5 5fr car, *straw* (B) 27.50 22.50
Nos. 33-47 (15) 78.85 60.10

Regular Issues Surcharged in Black or Carmine **05 10**

1912

On Issue of 1892-1900

48 A1 5c on 2c brown, *buff* 55 55
49 A1 5c on 4c claret, *lav* (C) 42 42
50 A1 5c on 15c blue (C) 42 42
51 A1 5c on 20c red, *grn* 1.40 1.40
52 A1 5c on 30c brn, *bis* (C) 1.40 1.40
53 A1 10c on 40c red, *straw* 80 80
54 A1 10c on 75c dp vio, *org* 2.50 2.50
a. Double surcharge, inverted 125.00

On Issue of 1904

55 A2 5c on 2c vio brn, *buff* 48 48
a. Pair, one without surcharge 350.00
56 A2 5c on 4c car, *blue* 48 48
57 A2 5c on 15c violet, *rose* 48 48
58 A2 5c on 20c car, *grn* 48 48
59 A2 5c on 25c blue (C) 48 48
60 A2 5c on 30c brown (C) 68 68
61 A2 10c on 40c red, *straw* 70 70
62 A2 10c on 50c brn, *az* (C) 1.40 1.40
Nos. 48-62 (15) 12.67 12.67

Two spacings between the surcharged numerals are found on Nos. 48 to 62.

Ford at Kitim — A6

1913-33 *Perf. 13½x14*

63 A6 1c violet & bl 15 15
64 A6 2c brn & vio brn 15 15
65 A6 4c gray & black 15 15
66 A6 5c yel grn & bl grn 15 15
67 A6 5c brn vio & grn ('22) 15 15
68 A6 10c red org & rose 15 15
69 A6 10c yel grn & bl grn ('22) 15 15
70 A6 10c vio & ver ('25) 15 15
71 A6 15c vio brn & rose ('16) 15 15
72 A6 15c gray grn & yel grn ('25) 15 15
73 A6 15c red brn & rose lil ('27) 15 15
74 A6 20c brown & violet 15 15
75 A6 20c grn & bl grn ('26) 52 32
76 A6 20c brn red & brn ('27) 15 15
77 A6 25c ultra & blue 70 55
78 A6 25c black & vio ('22) 45 28
79 A6 30c vio brn & grn 38 32
80 A6 30c red org & rose ('22) 15 15
81 A6 30c rose red & grn ('25) 15 15
82 A6 30c dl grn & bl grn ('28) 85 65
83 A6 35c blue & rose 15 15
84 A6 40c green & gray 55 42
85 A6 45c brown & red 75 52
86 A6 50c ultra & black 2.25 1.40
87 A6 50c ultra & bl ('22) 45 16
88 A6 50c yel brn & ol ('25) 15 15
89 A6 60c vio, *pnksh* ('25) 15 15
90 A6 65c yel brn & sl bl ('26) 80 65
91 A6 75c red & ultra 70 48
92 A6 75c ind & dl bl ('25) 45 28
93 A6 75c mag & yel grn ('27) 85 55
94 A6 85c ol grn & red brn ('26) 50 35
95 A6 90c brn red & rose ('30) 2.25 1.75
96 A6 1fr violet & black 75 40
97 A6 1.10fr vio & ol brn ('28) 2.00 1.60
98 A6 1.25fr vio & yel brn ('33) 70 50
99 A6 1.50fr dk bl & lt bl ('30) 1.90 1.10
100 A6 1.75fr ol brn & vio ('33) 75 60
101 A6 2fr orange & vio brn 1.10 60
102 A6 3fr red violet ('30) 3.50 2.75
103 A6 5fr black & vio 5.25 4.00
104 A6 5fr dl bl & blk ('22) 75 68
Nos. 63-104 (42) 31.85 23.61

Nos. 66 and 68 exist on both ordinary and chalky paper, No. 71 on chalky paper only.
For surcharges see Nos. 105-115, B1.

Type of 1913-33 Surcharged **60 = 60**

1922

105 A6 60c on 75c violet, *pnksh* 42 42

Stamps and Type of 1913-33 Surcharged with New Value and Bars

1924-27

106 A6 25c on 2fr org & brn (R) 15 15
107 A6 25c on 5fr dull bl & blk 15 15
108 A6 65c on 75c rose & ultra ('25) 90 90
109 A6 85c on 75c rose & ultra ('25) 90 90
110 A6 90c on 75c brn red & cer ('27) 95 95
111 A6 1.25fr on 1fr dk bl & ultra ('26) 42 42
112 A6 1.50fr on 1fr dp bl & lt bl ('27) 95 95
113 A6 3fr on 5fr mag & sl ('27) 1.75 1.75
114 A6 10fr on 5fr bl & bl grn, *bluish* ('27) 3.50 3.50
115 A6 20fr on 5fr rose lil & brn ol, *pnksh* ('27) 9.00 9.00
Nos. 106-115 (10) 18.67 18.67

Colonial Exposition Issue

Common Design Types

1931 Engr. *Perf. 12½*

Name of Country in Black

116 CD70 40c deep green 1.75 1.75
117 CD71 50c violet 1.75 1.75
118 CD72 90c red orange 1.75 1.75
119 CD73 1.50fr dull blue 1.40 1.40

Paris International Exposition Issue

Common Design Types

1937 *Perf. 13*

120 CD74 20c deep violet 75 75
121 CD75 30c dark green 75 75
122 CD76 40c carmine rose 85 85
123 CD77 50c dark brown 85 85
124 CD78 90c red 90 90
125 CD79 1.50fr ultra 90 90
Nos. 120-125 (6) 5.00 5.00

Colonial Arts Exhibition Issue

Souvenir Sheet

Common Design Type

1937 *Imperf.*

126 CD76 3fr Prussian green 2.00 2.00

Guinea Village — A7

Hausa Basket Workers A8

Forest Waterfall A9

Guinea Women — A10

1938-40 *Perf. 13*

No.	Type	Description	Unused	Used
128	A7	2c vermilion	15	15
129	A7	3c ultra	15	15
130	A7	4c green	15	15
131	A7	5c rose car	15	15
132	A7	10c peacock blue	15	15
133	A7	15c violet brown	15	15
134	A8	20c dk carmine	15	15
135	A8	25c pck blue	15	15
136	A8	30c ultra	15	15
137	A8	35c green	22	22
138	A8	40c blk brn ('40)	15	15
139	A8	45c dk green ('40)	15	15
140	A8	50c red brown	15	15
141	A9	55c dk ultra	35	25
142	A9	60c dk ultra ('40)	42	42
143	A9	65c green	38	22
144	A9	70c green ('40)	42	42
145	A9	80c rose violet	22	22
146	A9	90c rose vio ('39)	42	42
147	A9	1fr orange red	70	60
148	A9	1fr brn blk ('40)	28	28
149	A9	1.25fr org red ('39)	55	55
150	A9	1.40fr brown ('40)	55	55
151	A9	1.50fr brown	70	60
152	A10	1.60fr org red ('40)	55	55
153	A10	1.75fr ultra	30	28
154	A10	2fr magenta	50	28
155	A10	2.25fr brt ultra ('39)	65	65
156	A10	2.50fr brn blk ('40)	55	55
157	A10	3fr peacock blue	28	15
158	A10	5fr rose violet	35	28
159	A10	10fr slate green	60	42
160	A10	20fr chocolate	70	60
		Nos. 128-160 (33)	11.49	10.31

For surcharges see Nos. B8-B11.

Caillié Issue
Common Design Type

1939 **Engr.** *Perf. 12½x12*

No.	Type	Description	Unused	Used
161	CD81	90c org brn & org	35	35
162	CD81	2fr brt violet	35	35
163	CD81	2.25fr ultra & dk bl	35	35

René Caillié, French explorer, death cent.

New York World's Fair Issue
Common Design Type

1939

No.	Type	Description	Unused	Used
164	CD82	1.25fr carmine lake	35	35
165	CD82	2.25fr ultra	35	35

Ford at Kitim and Marshal Petain — A11

1941 *Perf. 12x12½*

No.	Type	Description	Unused	Used
166	A11	1fr green	28	
167	A11	2.50fr deep blue	28	

Nos. 166-167 were issued by the Vichy government. Seven stamps of types A7-A10 without "RF" are also Vichy issues (1943-44), but are believed not to have been placed on sale in the colony.

Stamps of French Guinea were followed by those of French West Africa.

Common Design Types pictured in section at front of book.

SEMI-POSTAL STAMPS

Regular Issue of 1913 Surcharged in Red

1915 **Unwmk.** *Perf. 13½x14*

No.	Type	Description	Unused	Used
B1	A6	10c + 5c org & rose	60	35

Exists on both ordinary and chalky paper.

Curie Issue
Common Design Type

1938 **Engr.** *Perf. 13*

No.	Type	Description	Unused	Used
B2	CD80	1.75fr + 50c brt ultra	4.00	4.00

French Revolution Issue
Common Design Type

1939 **Photo.**

Name and Value Typo. in Black

No.	Type	Description	Unused	Used
B3	CD83	45c + 25c green	2.75	2.75
B4	CD83	70c + 30c brown	2.75	2.75
B5	CD83	90c + 35c red org	2.75	2.75
B6	CD83	1.25fr + 1fr rose pink	2.75	2.75
B7	CD83	2.25fr + 2fr blue	2.75	2.75
		Nos. B3-B7 (5)	13.75	13.75

Stamps of 1938, Surcharged in Black

SECOURS
+ 1 fr.
NATIONAL

1941 **Unwmk.** *Perf. 13*

No.	Type	Description	Unused	Used
B8	A8	50c + 1fr red brn	60	60
B9	A9	80c + 2fr rose vio	1.60	1.50
B10	A9	1.50fr + 2fr brn	1.60	1.50
B11	A10	2fr + 3fr magenta	1.60	1.50

Common Design Type and

Senegalese Soldier
SP1

Colonial Infantryman
SP2

1941 **Unwmk.** *Perf. 13*

No.	Type	Description	Unused	Used
B12	SP1	1fr + 1fr red	45	
B13	CD86	1.50fr + 3fr maroon	45	
B14	SP2	2.50fr + 1fr blue	45	

Nos. B12-B14 were issued by the Vichy government, and were not placed on sale in the colony.

Nos. 166-167 were surcharged "OEUVRES COLONIALES" and surtax (including change of denomination of the 2.50fr to 50c). These were issued in 1944 by the Vichy government and not placed on sale in the colony.

AIR POST STAMPS

Common Design Type

1940 **Unwmk.** **Engr.** *Perf. 12½x12*

No.	Type	Description	Unused	Used
C1	CD85	1.90fr ultra	15	15
C2	CD85	2.90fr dk red	16	16
C3	CD85	4.50fr dk gray grn	20	20
C4	CD85	4.90fr yel bis	30	30
C5	CD85	6.90fr deep org	40	40
		Nos. C1-C5 (5)	1.21	1.21

Common Design Types

1942 **Engr.**

No.	Type	Description	Unused	Used
C6	CD88	50c car & bl	15	
C7	CD88	1fr brn & blk	15	
C8	CD88	2fr dk grn & red brn	15	
C9	CD88	3fr dk bl & scar	16	
C10	CD88	5fr vio & brn red	16	

Frame Engraved, Center Typographed

No.	Type	Description	Unused	Used
C11	CD89	10fr ultra, ind & vio	20	
C12	CD89	20fr rose car, mag & gray bl	20	
C13	CD89	50fr yel grn, dl grn & gray blk	35	1.00
		Nos. C6-C13 (8)	1.52	

There is doubt whether Nos. C6-C12 were officially placed in use.

AIR POST SEMI-POSTAL STAMPS

Stamps of types of Dahomey V1, V2 and V3, and of Cameroun V10, inscribed "Guinée", "Guinée Frcaise" or "Guinée Francaise," were issued in 1942 by the Vichy Government, but were not placed on sale in the colony.

POSTAGE DUE STAMPS

Fulah Woman
D1

Heads and Coast
D2

1905 **Unwmk.** **Typo.** *Perf. 14x13½*

No.	Type	Description	Unused	Used
J1	D1	5c blue	52	55
J2	D1	10c brown	52	55
J3	D1	15c green	2.00	1.40
J4	D1	30c rose	2.00	1.40
J5	D1	50c black	4.50	3.25
J6	D1	60c dull orange	5.75	3.75
J7	D1	1fr violet	17.50	14.00
		Nos. J1-J7 (7)	32.79	24.90

1906-08

No.	Type	Description	Unused	Used
J8	D2	5c grn, *grnsh* ('08)	8.25	5.50
J9	D2	10c vio brn ('08)	3.00	2.50
J10	D2	15c dk bl ('08)	2.00	2.50
J11	D2	20c blk, *yellow*	2.25	1.75
J12	D2	30c red, *straw* ('08)	13.00	8.00
J13	D2	50c violet ('08)	10.50	7.00
J14	D2	60c blk, *buff* ('08)	9.25	6.50
J15	D2	1fr blk, *pnksh* ('08)	6.50	4.00
		Nos. J8-J15 (8)	54.75	37.75

D3

D4

1914

No.	Type	Description	Unused	Used
J16	D3	5c green	15	15
J17	D3	10c rose	15	15
J18	D3	15c gray	20	20
J19	D3	20c brown	20	20
J20	D3	30c blue	20	20
J21	D3	50c black	40	40
J22	D3	60c orange	60	60
J23	D3	1fr violet	65	65
		Nos. J16-J23 (8)	2.55	2.55

Type of 1914 Issue Surcharged **2F.**

1927

No.	Type	Description	Unused	Used
J24	D3	2fr on 1fr lil rose	3.00	3.00
J25	D3	3fr on 1fr org brn	3.25	3.25

1938 **Engr.**

No.	Type	Description	Unused	Used
J26	D4	5c dk vio	15	15
J27	D4	10c carmine	15	15
J28	D4	15c green	15	15
J29	D4	20c red brn	15	15
J30	D4	30c rose vio	20	20
J31	D4	50c chocolate	30	30
J32	D4	60c peacock bl	50	50
J33	D4	1fr vermilion	50	50
J34	D4	2fr ultra	55	55
J35	D4	3fr black	60	60
		Set value	2.80	2.80

A 10c of type D4 without "RF" was issued in 1944 by the Vichy Government, but was not placed on sale in the colony.

FRENCH INDIA

LOCATION — East coast of India bordering on Bay of Bengal.
GOVT. — Former French Territory
AREA — 196 sq. mi.
POP. — 323,295 (1941)
CAPITAL — Pondichéry

French India was an administrative unit comprising the five settlements of Chandernagor, Karikal, Mahé, Pondichéry and Yanaon. These united with India in 1949 and 1954.

100 Centimes = 1 Franc
24 Caches = 1 Fanon (1923)
8 Fanons = 1 Rupie

Catalogue values for unused stamps in this country are for Never Hinged items, beginning with Scott 210 in the regular postage section, Scott B14 in the semi-postal section, and Scott C7 in the airpost section.

Navigation and Commerce — A1

A2

Perf. 14x13½

1892-1907 **Typo.** **Unwmk.**

Colony Name in Blue or Carmine

No.	Type	Description	Unused	Used
1	A1	1c blk, *lil bl*	70	50
2	A1	2c brn, *buff*	75	70
3	A1	4c claret, *lav*	80	75
4	A1	5c grn, *grnsh*	2.25	1.50
5	A1	10c blk, *lavender*	3.00	1.50
6	A1	10c red ('00)	1.50	1.10
7	A1	15c blue, quadrille paper	3.00	2.25
8	A1	15c gray, *lt gray* ('00)	11.00	10.00
9	A1	20c red, *grn*	3.50	2.50
10	A1	25c blk, *rose*	1.50	1.10
11	A1	25c blue ('00)	5.00	3.50
12	A1	30c brn, *bis*	22.50	20.00
13	A1	35c blk, *yel* ('06)	5.00	3.50
14	A1	40c red, *straw*	2.75	2.25
15	A1	45c blk, *gray grn* ('07)	2.50	1.75
16	A1	50c car, *rose*	2.75	2.25
17	A1	50c brn, *az* ('00)	4.00	3.00
18	A1	75c dp vio, *org*	3.25	3.25
19	A1	1fr brnz grn, *straw*	4.00	4.00
		Nos. 1-19 (19)	79.75	65.40

Perf. 13½x14 stamps are counterfeits.

Nos. 10 and 16 Surcharged in Carmine or Black **0,05**

1903

No.	Type	Description	Unused	Used
20	A1	5c on 25c blk, *rose*	150.00	100.00
21	A1	10c on 25c blk, *rose*	150.00	100.00
22	A1	15c on 25c blk, *rose*	50.00	50.00
23	A1	40c on 50c car, *rose* (Bk)	250.00	225.00

Counterfeits of Nos. 20-23 abound.

1903

No.	Type	Description	Unused	Used
24	A2	5c gray bl & blk	10.00	10.00

Brahma — A5

Kali Temple near Pondichéry — A6

1914-22 *Perf. 13½x14, 14x13½*

No.	Type	Description	Unused	Used
25	A5	1c gray & blk	15	15
26	A5	2c brn vio & blk	15	15
27	A5	2c grn & brn vio ('22)	15	15
28	A5	3c brn & blk	15	15
29	A5	4c org & blk	15	15
30	A5	5c bl grn & blk	25	25
31	A5	5c vio brn & blk ('22)	15	15
32	A5	10c dp rose & blk	32	32
33	A5	10c grn & blk ('22)	22	22
34	A5	15c vio & blk	35	35
35	A5	20c org red & blk	50	50
36	A5	25c blue & blk	50	50
37	A5	25c ultra & fawn ('22)	32	32
38	A5	30c ultra & blk	55	55
39	A5	30c rose & blk ('22)	40	40
40	A6	35c choc & blk	55	55
41	A6	40c org red & blk	55	55
42	A6	45c bl grn & blk	55	55

43 A6 50c dp rose & blk 50 50
44 A6 50c ultra & bl ('22) 50 50
45 A6 75c blue & blk 75 75
46 A6 1fr yel & blk 75 75
47 A6 2fr vio & blk 1.75 1.75
48 A6 5fr ultra & blk 70 70
49 A6 5fr rose & blk ('22) 1.10 1.10
Nos. 25-49 (25) 12.01 12.01

For surcharges see Nos. 50-79, 113-116, 156A, B1-B5.

No. 34 Surcharged in Various Colors

0,01 ≡

1922

50 A5 1c on 15c (Bk) 30 30
51 A5 2c on 15c (Bl) 30 30
53 A5 5c on 15c (R) 30 30

Stamps and Types of 1914-22 Surcharged with New Values in Caches, Fanons and Rupies in Black, Red or Blue:

1 FANON

2 CACHES

12 CACHES

3

ROUPIES

1923-28

54 A5 1ca on 1c gray & blk (R) 15 15
55 A5 2ca on 5c vio brn & blk 15 15
a. Horizontal pair, imperf. between
56 A5 3ca on 3c brn & blk 24 24
57 A5 4ca on 4c org & blk 38 38
58 A5 6ca on 10c grn & blk 48 48
59 A6 6ca on 45c bl grn & blk (R) 35 35
60 A5 10ca on 20c dp red & bl grn ('28) 80 80
61 A5 12ca on 15c vio & blk 48 48
62 A5 15ca on 20c org & blk 70 70
63 A6 16ca on 35c lt bl & yel brn ('28) 80 80
64 A5 18ca on 30c rose & blk 70 70
65 A6 20ca on 45c grn & dl red ('28) 80 60
66 A5 1fa on 25c dp grn & rose red ('28) 1.25 1.25
67 A6 1fa3ca on 35c choc & blk (Bl) 70 70
68 A6 1fa6ca on 40c org & blk (R) 80 52
69 A6 1fa12ca on 50c ultra & bl (Bl) 70 70
70 A6 1fa12ca on 75c bl & blk (Bl) 70 70
a. Double surcharge 70.00
71 A6 1fa16ca on 75c brn red & grn ('28) 1.25 95
72 A5 2fa9ca on 25c ultra & fawn (Bl) 80 60
73 A6 2fa12ca on 1fr vio & dk brn ('28) 95 95
74 A6 3fa3ca on 1fr yel & blk (R) 90 80
a. Double surcharge 70.00
75 A6 6fa6ca on 2fr vio & blk (Bl) 2.25 1.65
76 A6 1r on 1fr grn & dp bl (R) ('26) 2.50 2.25
77 A6 2r on 5fr rose & blk (R) 2.50 2.25
a. Double surcharge 70.00
78 A6 3r on 2fr gray & bl vio (R) ('26) 5.75 4.75
79 A6 5r on 5fr rose & blk, *grnsh* ('26) 7.50 6.75
Nos. 54-79 (26) 34.58 30.65

Nos. 60, 63, 66 and 73 have the original value obliterated by bars.

A7

A8

1929

80 A7 1ca dk gray & blk 15 15
81 A7 2ca vio brn & blk 15 15
82 A7 3ca brn & blk 15 15
83 A7 4ca org & blk 15 15
84 A7 6ca gray grn & grn 15 15
85 A7 10ca brn, red & grn 15 15
86 A8 12ca grn & lt grn 28 22
87 A7 16ca brt bl & blk 40 35
88 A7 18ca brn red & ver 40 35
89 A7 20ca dk bl & grn, *bluish* 32 28
90 A8 1fa gray grn & rose red 28 22
91 A8 1fa6ca red org & blk 28 22
92 A8 1fa12ca dp bl & ultra 28 22
93 A8 1fa16ca rose red & grn 42 40
94 A8 2fa12ca brt vio & brn 50 40
95 A8 6fa6ca dl vio & blk 50 40
96 A8 1r gray grn & dp bl 35 28
97 A8 2r rose & blk 65 35
98 A8 3r lt gray & gray lil 1.00 70
99 A8 5r rose & blk, *grnsh* 1.50 1.25
Nos. 80-99 (20) 8.06 6.54

For overprints and surcharges see Nos. 117-134, 157-176, 184-209G.

Colonial Exposition Issue
Common Design Types

1931 Engr. *Perf. 12½*

100 CD70 10ca dp grn 1.00 1.00
101 CD71 12ca violet 1.00 1.00
102 CD72 18ca red org 1.00 1.00
103 CD73 1fa12ca dull blue 1.00 1.00

Paris International Exposition Issue
Common Design Types

1937 *Perf. 13*

104 CD74 8ca dp vio 55 55
105 CD75 12ca dk grn 55 55
106 CD76 16ca car rose 55 55
107 CD77 20ca dk brn 55 55
108 CD78 1fa12ca red 55 55
109 CD79 2fa12ca ultra 55 55
Nos. 104-109 (6) 3.30 3.30

For overprints see Nos. 135-139, 177-181.

Colonial Arts Exhibition Issue
Souvenir Sheet
Common Design Type

1937 *Imperf.*

110 CD79 5fa red violet 2.00 2.00

For overprint see No. 140.

New York World's Fair Issue
Common Design Type

1939 Engr. *Perf. 12½x12*

111 CD82 1fa12ca car lake 75 75
112 CD82 2fa12ca ultra 80 80

For overprints see Nos. 141-142, 182-183.

Common Design Types pictured in section at front of book.

Temple near Pondichéry and Marshal Petain — A9

1941 Engr. *Perf. 12½x12*

112A A9 1fa16ca car & red 30
112B A9 4fa4ca blue 30

Nos. 112A-112B were issued by the Vichy government, and were not placed on sale in French India.

Nos. 62, 64, 67, 72 Overprinted in Carmine or Blue (#116):

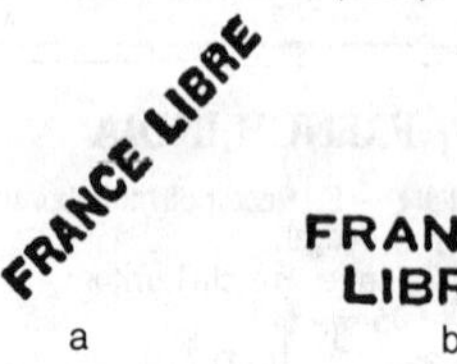

a b

1941 Unwmk. *Perf. 13½x14*

113 A5 (a) 15ca on 20c 30.00 30.00
114 A5 (a) 18ca on 30c 90 90
115 A6 (a) 1fa3ca on 35c 35.00 35.00
a. Horiz. overprint 40.00 40.00
116 A5 (b) 2fa9ca on 25c 450.00 400.00
a. Overprint "a" (Bl) 450.00 400.00
b. Overprint "b" (C) 900.00

Nos. 81-99 Overprinted Type "a" in Carmine or Blue

1941

117 A7 2ca (C) 3.50 3.50
118 A7 3ca (C) 90 90
119 A7 4ca (C) 2.25 2.00
120 A7 6ca (C) 60 60
121 A7 10ca (Bl) 75 65
122 A8 12ca (C) 75 65
123 A7 16ca (C) 1.00 75
123A A7 18ca (Bl) 475.00 425.00
124 A7 20ca (C) 75 65
125 A8 1fa (Bl) 65 65
126 A8 1fa6ca (C) 80 75
127 A8 1fa12ca (C) 1.75 1.60
128 A8 1fa16ca (C) 75 65
129 A8 2fa12ca (C) 75 65
130 A8 6fa6ca (C) 75 75
131 A8 1r (C) 75 75
132 A8 2r (C) 75 75
133 A8 3r (C) 90 90
134 A8 5r (C) 3.50 4.25
Nos. 117-123,124-134 (18) 21.85 21.40

Same Overprints on Paris Exposition Issue of 1937

1941 *Perf. 13*

135 CD74 (b) 8ca (C) 2.75 2.75
135A CD74 (b) 8ca (Bl) 110.00 110.00
135B CD74 (a) 8ca (C) 70.00 70.00
135C CD74 (a) 8ca (Bl) 100.00 100.00
136 CD75 (a) 12ca (C) 1.50 1.50
137 CD76 (a) 16ca (Bl) 1.50 1.50
138 CD78 (a) 1fa12ca (Bl) 1.50 1.50
139 CD79 (a) 2fa12ca (C) 1.50 1.50
Nos. 135-139 (8) 288.75 288.75

Inverted overprints exist.

Souvenir Sheet
No. 110 Overprinted "FRANCE LIBRE" Diagonally in Blue Violet

Two types of overprint:
I - Overprint 37mm. With serifs.
II - Overprint 24mm, as type "a" shown above No. 113. No serifs.

1941 Unwmk. *Imperf.*

140 CD79 5fa red vio (I) 250.00 225.00
a. Type II 300.00 300.00

Overprinted on New York World's Fair Issue, 1939
Perf. 12½x12

141 CD82 (a) 1fa12ca (Bl) 1.50 1.50
142 CD82 (a) 2fa12ca (C) 1.50 1.50

Lotus Flowers — A10

1942 Unwmk. Photo. *Perf. 14x14½*

143 A10 2ca brown 15 15
144 A10 3ca dk bl 15 15
145 A10 4ca emerald 15 15
146 A10 6ca dk org 15 15
147 A10 12ca grnsh blk 15 15
148 A10 16ca rose vio 15 15
149 A10 20ca dk red brn 35 35
150 A10 1fa brt red 35 28
151 A10 1fa18ca slate blk 55 35
152 A10 6fa6ca brt ultra 60 50
153 A10 1r dull vio 55 50
154 A10 2r bister 60 60
155 A10 3r chocolate 80 65
156 A10 5r dk grn 1.10 80
Nos. 143-156 (14) 5.80 4.93

Stamps of 1923-39 Overprinted in Blue or Carmine

c

FRANCE LIBRE

d

FRANCE LIBRE

1942-43 *Perf. 13½x14, 14x13½*
Overprinted on No. 64

156A A5 (c) 18ca on 30c (B) 140.00 100.00

Overprinted on Nos. 81-82, 84, 86-99

157 A7 (c) 2ca (C) 52 52
a. Black overprint 15.00 15.00
158 A7 (c) 3ca (C) 60 60
159 A7 (c) 6ca (Bl) 70 70
160 A8 (d) 12ca (Bl) 1.40 1.40
161 A7 (c) 16ca (C) 70 70
162 A7 (c) 18ca (Bl) 70 70
163 A7 (c) 20ca (Bl) ('43) 2.50 2.00
164 A7 (c) 20ca (C) 70 70
165 A8 (d) 1fa (Bl) 70 70
166 A8 (d) 1fa6ca (C) 90 90
167 A8 (d) 1fa12ca (C) 80 80
168 A8 (d) 1fa16ca (Bl) 70 70
169 A8 (d) 2fa12ca (Bl) 22.50 22.50
170 A8 (d) 2fa12ca (C) 80 80
171 A8 (d) 6fa6ca (C) 1.40 1.40
172 A8 (d) 1r (C) 3.25 3.25
173 A8 (d) 2r (C) 2.50 2.50
174 A8 (d) 3r (C) 3.25 3.25
175 A8 (d) 3r (Bl) ('43) 65.00 60.00
176 A8 (d) 5r (C) 3.50 3.50
Nos. 156A-176 (21) 253.12 207.62

Same Overprints on Paris International Exposition Issue of 1937
Perf. 13

177 CD74 (c) 8ca (Bl) 3.75 3.25
178 CD75 (d) 12ca (Bl) 3.25 3.25
179 CD76 (d) 16ca (Bl) 500.00 375.00
180 CD78 (d) 1fa12ca (Bl) 75 75
181 CD79 (d) 2fa12ca (C) 1.75 1.75

Same Overprint on New York World's Fair Issue, 1939
Perf. 12½x12

182 CD82 (d) 1fa12ca (Bl) 1.10 1.10
183 CD82 (d) 2fa12ca (C) 1.75 1.75

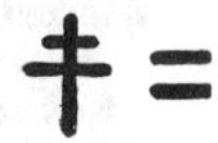

No. 87 Surcharged in Carmine

FRANCE LIBRE

2 fa 9 ca

1942-43 *Perf. 13½x14*

184 A7 1ca on 16ca 32.50 17.50
185 A7 4ca on 16ca ('43) 32.50 17.50
186 A7 10ca on 16ca 21.00 7.00
187 A7 15ca on 16ca 19.00 7.00
188 A7 1fa3ca on 16ca ('43) 32.50 15.00
189 A7 2fa9ca on 16ca ('43) 30.00 22.50
190 A7 3fa3ca on 16ca ('43) 22.50 10.00
Nos. 184-190 (7) 190.00 96.50

Nos. 95-99 Surcharged in Carmine

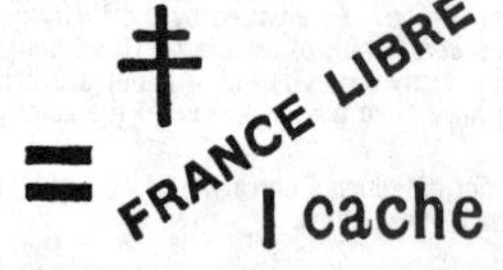

1943 *Perf. 14x13½*

191 A8 1ca on 6fa6ca 4.25 3.50
192 A8 4ca on 6fa6ca 5.00 4.50
193 A8 10ca on 6fa6ca 1.00 90
194 A8 15ca on 6fa6ca 2.00 1.00
195 A8 1fa3ca on 6fa6ca 3.00 1.40
196 A8 2fa9ca on 6fa6ca 2.50 2.00
197 A8 3fa3ca on 6fa6ca 3.50 2.25
198 A8 1ca on 1r 2.00 1.75
199 A8 2ca on 1r 75 75
200 A8 4ca on 1r 75 70
201 A8 6ca on 2r 70 60
202 A8 10ca on 2r 90 90
203 A8 12ca on 2r 70 60
204 A8 15ca on 3r 65 65
205 A8 16ca on 3r 65 65
206 A8 1fa3ca on 3r 70 70
207 A8 1fa6ca on 5r 90 90
208 A8 1fa12ca on 5r 90 80
209 A8 1fa16ca on 5r 90 80
Nos. 191-209 (19) 31.75 25.35

In 1943, 200 each of 27 stamps were overprinted in red or dark blue, "FRANCE TOUJOURS" and a Lorraine Cross within a circle measuring 17½mm in diameter. Overprinted were Nos. 81-99, 104-109, 111-112.

No. 95 Surcharged in Carmine with New Value and Bars

1943 Unwmk. *Perf. 14x13½*

209A	A8	1ca on 6fa6ca	12.00	7.50
209B	A8	4ca on 6fa6ca	12.00	7.50
209C	A8	10ca on 6fa6ca	3.75	2.75
209D	A8	15ca on 6fa6ca	3.75	2.75
209E	A8	1fa3ca on 6fa6ca	10.00	9.00
209F	A8	2fa9ca on 6fa6ca	10.00	9.00
209G	A8	3fa3ca on 6fa6ca	12.00	9.50
		Nos. 209A-209G (7)	63.50	48.00

Catalogue values for unused stamps in this section, from this point to the end of the section, are for Never Hinged items.

Eboue Issue

Common Design Type

1945 Engr. *Perf. 13*

210 CD91	3fa8ca black	28	28
211 CD91	5r1fa16ca Prus grn	60	60

Nos. 210 and 211 exist imperforate.

Apsaras — A11

Brahman Ascetic — A12

Designs: 6ca, 8ca, 10ca, Dvarabalagar. 12ca, 15ca, 1fa, Vishnu. 1fa6ca, 2fa, 2fa2ca, Dvarabalagar (foot raised). 2fa12ca, 3fa, 5fa, Temple Guardian. 7fa12ca, 1r2fa, 1r4fa12ca, Tigoupalagar.

1948 Photo. *Perf. 13x13½*

212 A11	1ca dk ol grn	15	15
213 A11	2ca org brn	15	15
214 A11	4ca vio, *cr*	15	15
215 A11	6ca yel org	40	20
216 A11	8ca gray blk	45	40
217 A11	10ca dl yel grn, *pale grn*	45	40
218 A11	12ca vio brn	20	15
219 A11	15ca Prus grn	20	15
220 A11	1fa vio, *pale rose*	60	28
221 A11	1fa6ca brn red	40	40
222 A11	2fa dk grn	40	28
223 A11	2fa2ca blue, *cr*	65	45
224 A11	2fa12ca brown	65	55
225 A11	3fa dp org	80	60
226 A11	5fa red vio, *rose*	70	60
227 A11	7fa12ca dk brn	60	60
228 A11	1r2fa brn blk	1.60	1.40
229 A11	1r4fa12ca ol grn	1.75	1.60
	Nos. 212-229 (18)	10.30	8.51

1952

230 A12	18ca rose red	60	60
231 A12	1fa15ca vio blue	80	80
232 A12	4fa olive grn	1.25	1.25

Military Medal Issue

Common Design Type

1952 Engr. and Typo. *Perf. 13*

233 CD101	1fa multi	1.60	1.60

SEMI-POSTAL STAMPS

Regular Issue of 1914 Surcharged in Red ✚ 5c

1915 Unwmk. *Perf. 14x13½*

B1	A5 10c + 5c rose & blk	45	45
a.	Inverted surcharge	35.00	35.00

There were two printings of this surcharge; in the first it was placed at the bottom of the stamp, in the second it was near the top.

Regular Issue of 1914 Surcharged in Red 5 ✠

1916

B2	A5 10c + 5c rose & blk	7.50	7.50
a.	Inverted surcharge	40.00	40.00
b.	Double surcharge	47.50	47.50

Surcharged ✠ 5 C

B3	A5 10c + 5c rose & blk	1.40	1.40

Surcharged ✚ 5 C

B4	A5 10c + 5c rose & blk	75	75

Surcharged ✚ 5c

B5	A5 10c + 5c rose & blk	75	75

Curie Issue

Common Design Type

1938 Engr. *Perf. 13*

B6	CD80 2fa12ca + 20ca brt ultra	5.00	5.00

French Revolution Issue

Common Design Type

1939 Photo.

Name and Value Typo. in Black

B7 CD83	18ca + 10ca grn	2.50	2.50
B8 CD83	1fa6ca + 12ca brn	2.50	2.50
B9 CD83	1fa12ca + 16ca red org	2.50	2.50
B10 CD83	1fa16ca + 1fa16ca rose pink	2.50	2.50
B11 CD83	2fa12ca + 3fa blue	2.50	2.50
	Nos. B7-B11 (5)	12.50	12.50

Common Design Type and

Non-Commissioned Officer, Native Guard — SP1

Sepoy — SP2

1941 Photo. *Perf. 13½*

B12 SP1	1fa16ca + 1fa16ca red	55
B13 CD86	2fa12ca + 5fa maroon	55
B13A SP2	4fa4ca + 1fa16ca bl	55

Nos. B12-B13A were issued by the Vichy government, and were not placed on sale in French India.

Nos. 112A-112B were surcharged "OEUVRES COLONIALES" and surtax (including change of denomination of the 4fa 4ca to 20ca). These were issued in 1944 by the Vichy government and were not placed on sale in French India.

Catalogue values for unused stamps in this section, from this point to the end of the section, are for Never Hinged items.

Red Cross Issue

Common Design Type

1944 Photo. *Perf. 14½x14*

B14 CD90	3fa + 1r4fa dk ol brn	60	60

The surtax was for the French Red Cross and national relief.

Tropical Medicine Issue

Common Design Type

1950 Engr. *Perf. 13*

B15 CD100	1fa + 10ca ind & dp bl	90	90

The surtax was for charitable work.

AIR POST STAMPS

Common Design Type

1942 Unwmk. Photo. *Perf. 14½x14*

C1 CD87	4fa dk org	25	25
C2 CD87	1r brt red	25	25
C3 CD87	2r brn red	45	45
C4 CD87	5r black	60	60
C5 CD87	8r ultra	70	70
C6 CD87	10r dk grn	75	75
	Nos. C1-C6 (6)	3.00	3.00

Catalogue values for unused stamps in this section, from this point to the end of the section, are for Never Hinged items.

Victory Issue

Common Design Type

1946 Engr. *Perf. 12½*

C7 CD92	4fa dk bl grn	50	50

Chad to Rhine Issue

Common Design Types

1946, June 6

C8 CD93	2fa12ca ol bis	35	35
C9 CD94	5fa dk bl	35	35
C10 CD95	7fa12ca dk pur	45	45
C11 CD96	1r2fa green	45	45
C12 CD97	1r4fa12ca dk car	50	50
C13 CD98	3r1fa vio brn	50	50
	Nos. C8-C13 (6)	2.60	2.60

A 3r ultramarine and red, picturing the Temple of Chindambaram, was sold at Paris June 7 to July 8, 1948, but not placed on sale in the colony.

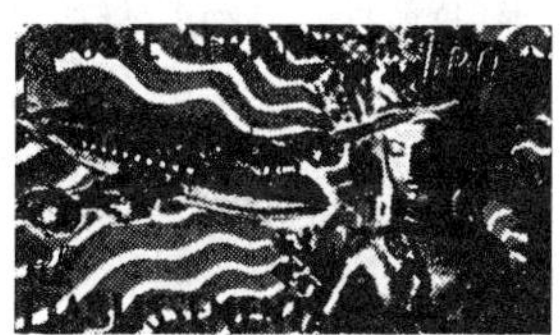

Bas-relief Figure of Goddess — AP1

Wing and Temple — AP2

Bird over Palms — AP3

Perf. 12x13, 13x12

1949 Photo. Unwmk.

C14 AP1	1r yel & plum	1.90	1.10
C15 AP2	2r grn & dk grn	2.50	2.25
C16 AP3	5r lt bl & vio brn	8.50	6.00

UPU Issue

Common Design Type

1949 Engr. *Perf. 13*

C17 CD99	6fa lilac rose	2.75	2.75

Universal Postal Union, 75th anniv.

Liberation Issue

Common Design Type

1954, June 6

C18 CD102	1fa sep & vio brn	2.25	2.25

AIR POST SEMI-POSTAL STAMPS

V4

Stamps of the above design and of Cameroun type V10 inscribed "Etabts Frcais dans l'Inde" were issued in 1942 by the Vichy Government, but were not placed on sale in French India.

POSTAGE DUE STAMPS

Postage Due Stamps of France (Type D2) Surcharged like Nos. 54-75 in Black, Blue or Red

1923 Unwmk. *Perf. 14x13½*

J1	D2	6ca on 10c brn	45	45
J2	D2	12ca on 25c rose (Bk)	45	45
J3	D2	15ca on 20c ol grn (R)	55	55
J4	D2	1fa6ca on 30c red	55	55
J5	D2	1fa12a on 50c brn vio	75	75
J6	D2	1fa15ca on 5c bl (Bk)	80	80
J7	D2	3fa3ca on 1fr red brn, *straw*	1.00	1.00
		Nos. J1-J7 (7)	4.55	4.55

Types of Postage Due Stamps of French Colonies, 1884-85, Surcharged with New Values as in 1923 in Red or Black Bars over Original Values

1928

J8	D1	4ca on 20c gray lil	50	50
J9	D1	1fa on 30c orange	70	70
J10	D1	1fa16ca on 5c bl blk (R)	75	75
J11	D1	3fa on 1fr lt grn	1.10	1.10

D3

D4

1929 Typo.

J12 D3	4ca deep red	28	28
J13 D3	6ca blue	35	35
J14 D3	12ca green	35	35
J15 D3	1fa brown	60	60
J16 D3	1fa12ca lilac gray	60	60
J17 D3	1fa16ca buff	62	62
J18 D3	3fa lilac	70	70
	Nos. J12-J18 (7)	3.50	3.50

1948 Unwmk. Photo. *Perf. 13x13½*

J19 D4	1ca dk vio	15	15
J20 D4	2ca dk brn	15	15
J21 D4	6ca bl grn	15	15
J22 D4	12ca dp org	22	22
J23 D4	1fa dk car rose	25	25
J24 D4	1fa12ca brown	40	40
J25 D4	2fa dk slate bl	55	55
J26 D4	2fa12ca henna brn	60	60
J27 D4	5fa dk olive grn	90	90
J28 D4	1r dk bl vio	1.10	1.10
	Nos. J19-J28 (10)	4.47	4.47

The Scott editorial staff regrettably cannot accept requests to identify, authenticate, or appraise stamps and postal markings.

FRENCH MOROCCO

LOCATION — Northwest coast of Africa
GOVT. — Former French Protectorate
AREA — 153,870 sq. mi.
POP. — 8,340,000 (estimated 1954)
CAPITAL — Rabat

French Morocco was a French Protectorate from 1912 until 1956 when it, along with the Spanish and Tangier zones of Morocco, became the independent country, Morocco.

Stamps inscribed "Tanger" were for use in the international zone of Tangier in northern Morocco.

100 Centimos = 1 Peseta
100 Centimes = 1 franc (1917)

Catalogue values for unused stamps in this country are for Never Hinged items, beginning with Scott 177 in the regular postage section, Scott B26 in the semi-postal section, Scott C27 in the airpost section, Scott CB23A in the airpost semi-postal section, and Scott J46 in the postage due section.

French Offices in Morocco

A1

A2

Stamps of France Surcharged in Red or Black

1891-1900 Unwmk. *Perf. 14x13½*

1 A1 5c on 5c grn, *grnsh* (R) 4.00 1.50
a. Imperf., pair 87.50
2 A1 5c on 5c yel grn (I) (R) ('99) 15.00 12.00
a. Type II 15.00 15.00
3 A1 10c on 10c blk, *lav* (II) (R) 12.00 1.65
a. Type I 22.50 5.50
b. 10c on 25c blk, *rose* 450.00
4 A1 20c on 20c red, *grn* 17.50 12.00
5 A1 25c on 25c blk, *rose* (R) 12.00 80
a. Double surcharge 140.00
b. Imperf., pair 95.00
6 A1 50c on 50c car, *rose* (II) 45.00 14.00
a. Type I 250.00 240.00
7 A1 1p on 1fr brnz grn, *straw* 45.00 40.00
8 A1 2p on 2fr brn, *az* (Bk) ('00) 175.00 145.00
Nos. 1-8 (8) 325.50 226.95

No. 3b was never sent to Morocco.

France Nos. J15-J16 Overprinted in Carmine

1893

9 A2 5c black 1,200. 400.00
10 A2 10c black 1,100. 250.00

Counterfeits exist.

A3

A4

A5

Surcharged in Red or Black

1902-10

11 A3 1c on 1c gray (R) ('08) 40 25
a. Surcharge omitted
12 A3 2c on 2c vio brn ('08) 48 50
13 A3 3c on 3c red org ('08) 55 50
14 A3 4c on 4c yel brn ('08) 4.00 3.00
15 A3 5c on 5c grn (R) 2.25 60
a. Double surcharge 140.00
16 A4 10c on 10c rose red ('03) 1.50 60
a. Surcharge omitted
17 A4 20c on 20c brn vio ('03) 9.50 7.00
18 A4 25c on 25c bl ('03) 9.50 1.00
19 A4 35c on 35c vio ('10) 14.00 10.00
20 A5 50c on 50c bis brn & lav ('03) 18.00 5.50
21 A5 1p on 1fr cl & ol grn ('03) 47.50 25.00
22 A5 2p on 2fr gray vio & yel ('03) 60.00 25.00
Nos. 11-22 (12) 167.68 78.95

Nos. 11-14 exist spelled CFNTIMOS or GENTIMOS.

The 25c on 25c with surcharge omitted is listed as No. 81a.

For overprints and surcharges see Nos. 26-37, 72-79, B1, B3.

Postage Due Stamps Nos. J1-J2 Handstamped

1903

24 D2 5c on 5c light blue 750.00 500.00
25 D2 10c on 10c chocolate 1,500. 1,200.

Nos. 24 and 25 were used only on Oct. 10, 1903. Used copies were not canceled, the overprint serving as a cancellation.

Counterfeits exist.

Types of 1902-10 Issue Surcharged in Red or Blue

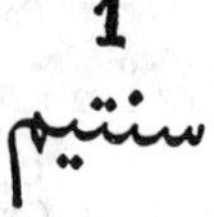

1911-17

26 A3 1c on 1c gray (R) 25 15
27 A3 2c on 2c vio brn 40 25
28 A3 3c on 3c orange 40 25
29 A3 5c on 5c green (R) 45 15
30 A4 10c on 10c rose 15 15
a. Imperf., pair 150.00
31 A4 15c on 15c org ('17) 80 65
32 A4 20c on 20c brn vio 1.75 1.25
33 A4 25c on 25c blue (R) 1.00 50
34 A4 35c on 35c violet (R) 3.00 1.25
35 A5 40c on 40c red & pale bl ('17) 3.00 2.50
36 A5 50c on 50c bis brn & lav (R) 12.50 6.00
37 A5 1p on 1fr cl & ol grn 8.00 2.50
Nos. 26-37 (12) 31.70 15.60

For surcharges see Nos. B1, B3.

Stamps of this design were issued by the Cherifien posts in 1912-13. The Administration Cherifinne des Postes, Telegraphes et Telephones was formed in 1911 under French guidance.

French Protectorate

A6

A7

A8

Issue of 1911-17 Overprinted "Protectorat Francais"

1914-21

38 A6 1c on 1c gray 30 30
39 A6 2c on 2c vio brn 30 22
40 A6 3c on 3c orange 60 42
41 A6 5c on 5c green 15 15
a. New value omitted 190.00 190.00
42 A7 10c on 10c rose 15 15
a. New value omitted 350.00 350.00
43 A7 15c on 15c org ('17) 18 15
a. New value omitted 70.00 70.00
44 A7 20c on 20c brn vio 2.00 1.10
a. "Protectorat Francais" double 225.00 225.00
45 A7 25c on 25c blue 75 15
a. New value omitted 225.00 225.00
46 A7 25c on 25c violet ('21) 60 15
a. "Protectorat Francais" omitted 42.50 42.50
b. "Protectorat Francais" double 110.00 110.00
c. "Protectorat Francais" dbl. (R + Bk) 100.00 100.00
47 A7 30c on 30c vio ('21) 6.00 5.25
48 A7 35c on 35c violet 2.00 75
49 A8 40c on 40c red & pale bl 7.00 3.75
a. New value omitted 225.00 225.00
50 A8 45c on 45c grn & bl ('21) 20.00 17.00
51 A8 50c on 50c bis brn & lav 52 18
a. "Protectorat Francais" invtd. 110.00 110.00
b. "Protectorat Francais" double
52 A8 1p on 1fr cl & ol grn 1.00 18
a. "Protectorat Francais" invtd. 250.00 250.00
b. New value double 110.00 110.00
c. New value dbl., one invtd. 110.00 100.00
53 A8 2p on 2fr gray vio & yel 1.75 75
a. New value omitted 125.00 125.00
b. "Protectorat Francais" omitted 75.00 75.00
c. New value double
d. New value dbl., one invtd.
54 A8 5p on 5fr dk bl & buff 6.75 2.25
Nos. 38-54 (17) 50.05 32.90

For surcharges see Nos. B2, B4-B5.

Tower of Hassan, Rabat — A9

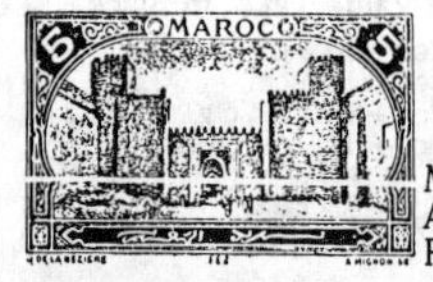
Mosque of the Andalusians, Fez — A10

City Gate Chella A11

Koutoubiah, Marrakesh A12

Bab Mansour, Meknes A13

Roman Ruins, Volubilis A14

1917 Engr. *Perf. 13½x14, 14x13½*

55 A9 1c grnsh gray 15 15
56 A9 2c brown lilac 28 25
57 A9 3c orange brn 25 18
a. Imperf., pair 35.00 35.00
58 A10 5c yellow grn 18 15
59 A10 10c rose red 18 15
60 A10 15c dark gray 18 15
a. Imperf., pair 27.50 27.50
61 A11 20c red brown 1.40 1.40
62 A11 25c dull blue 1.25 40
63 A11 30c gray violet 1.60 1.40
64 A12 35c orange 1.40 1.25
65 A12 40c ultra 80 45
66 A12 45c gray green 9.00 5.00
67 A13 50c dk brown 3.00 1.50
a. Imperf., pair 30.00 30.00
68 A13 1fr slate 3.50 1.90
a. Imperf., pair 25.00 25.00
69 A14 2fr black brown 82.50 37.50
70 A14 5fr dk gray grn 20.00 15.00
71 A14 10fr black 20.00 16.00
Nos. 55-71 (17) 145.67 82.83

See note following #115. See #93-105. For surcharges see #120-121.

Types of the 1902-10 Issue Overprinted **TANGER**

1918-24 *Perf. 14x13½*

72 A3 1c gray 15 15
73 A3 2c violet brn 18 18
74 A3 3c red orange 30 30
75 A3 5c green 42 35
76 A3 5c orange ('23) 85 80
77 A4 10c rose 42 42
78 A4 10c green ('24) 42 35
79 A4 15c orange 95 70
80 A4 20c violet brn 1.25 1.25
81 A4 25c blue 1.40 1.00
a. "TANGER" omitted 300.00 225.00
82 A4 30c red org ('24) 1.40 1.40
83 A4 35c violet 1.40 1.25
84 A5 40c red & pale bl 1.50 1.25
85 A5 50c bis brn & lav 9.00 5.00
86 A4 50c blue 7.00 3.75
87 A5 1fr cl & ol grn 4.50 2.50
88 A5 2fr org & pale bl ('24) 45.00 37.50
89 A5 5fr dk bl & buff ('24) 37.50 35.00
Nos. 72-89 (18) 113.64 93.15

Types of 1917 and

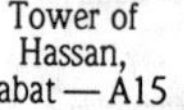
Tower of Hassan, Rabat — A15

Bab Mansour, Meknes — A16

Roman Ruins, Volubilis A17

1923-27 Photo. *Perf. 13½*

90 A15 1c olive green 15 15
91 A15 2c brown vio 15 15
92 A15 3c yellow brn 15 15
93 A10 5c orange 15 15
94 A10 10c yellow brn 15 15
95 A10 15c dk gray 15 15
96 A11 20c red brown 15 15
97 A11 20c red vio ('27) 28 25
98 A11 25c ultra 15 15
99 A11 30c deep red 15 15
100 A11 30c turq bl ('27) 45 25
101 A12 35c violet 45 40
102 A12 40c orange red 15 15
103 A12 45c deep green 15 15
104 A16 50c dull turq 15 15
105 A12 50c olive grn ('27) 32 15
106 A16 60c lilac 22 15
107 A16 75c red vio ('27) 42 22
108 A16 1fr deep brown 32 20
109 A16 1.05fr red brn ('27) 65 50
110 A16 1.40fr dull rose ('27) 35 25
111 A16 1.50fr turq bl ('27) 50 15
112 A17 2fr olive brn 60 40
113 A17 3fr dp red ('27) 60 45
114 A17 5fr dk gray grn 1.60 1.10
115 A17 10fr black 5.00 3.25
Nos. 90-115 (26) 13.56
Set value 8.15

Nos. 90-110, 112-115 exist imperf. The stamps of 1917 were line engraved. Those of 1923-27 were printed by photogravure and have in the margin at lower right the imprint "Helio Vaugirard."

See #B36. For surcharges see #122-123.

No. 102 Surcharged in Black

1930

120 A12	15c on 40c orange red		65	65

Nos. 100, 106 and 110 Surcharged in Blue Similarly to No. 176

1931

121 A11	25c on 30c turq blue	1.00	1.00
a.	Inverted surcharge	42.50	35.50
122 A16	50c on 60c lilac	35	15
a.	Inverted surcharge	50.00	45.00
123 A16	1fr on 1.40fr rose	1.25	65
a.	Inverted surcharge	50.00	45.00

Old Treasure House and Tribunal, Tangier — A18

Roadstead at Agadir — A19

Post Office at Casablanca A20

Moulay Idriss of the Zehroun A21

Kasbah of the Oudayas, Rabat — A22

Court of the Medersa el Attarine at Fez — A23

Saadiens' Tombs at Marrakesh — A25

Kasbah of Si Madani el Glaoui at Ouarzazat A24

1933-34 Engr. *Perf. 13*

124 A18	1c	olive blk	15	15
125 A18	2c	red violet	15	15
126 A19	3c	dark brown	15	15
127 A19	5c	brown red	15	15
128 A20	10c	blue green	15	15
129 A20	15c	black	15	15
130 A20	20c	red brown	15	15
131 A21	25c	dark blue	15	15
132 A21	30c	emerald	22	15
133 A21	40c	black brn	22	15
134 A22	45c	brown vio	25	25
135 A22	50c	dk blue grn	22	15
a.		Booklet pane of 10	10.00	
136 A22	65c	brown red	15	15
a.		Booklet pane of 10		
137 A23	75c	red violet	22	15
138 A23	90c	orange red	22	15
139 A23	1fr	deep brown	45	15
140 A23	1.25fr	black ('34)	62	30
141 A24	1.50fr	ultra	25	15
142 A24	1.75fr	myr grn ('34)	22	15
143 A24	2fr	yellow brn	1.40	15
144 A24	3fr	car rose	28.00	3.00
145 A25	5fr	red brown	2.75	60
146 A25	10fr	black	4.00	2.75
147 A25	20fr	bluish gray	5.00	2.75
		Nos. 124-147 (24)	45.39	
		Set value		10.50

Booklets containing No. 135a, and probably No. 135a, have two panes of 10 connected by a gutter. The panes are stapled into the booklet through the gutter.

For surcharges see Nos. 148, 176, B13-B20.

No. 135 Surcharged in Red

40c

1939

148 A22	40c on 50c dk bl grn	30	15

Mosque of Salé — A26

Sefrou — A27

Cedars — A28

Goatherd A29

Ramparts of Salé — A30

Scimitar-horned Oryxes — A31

Fez — A33

Valley of Draa — A32

1939-42

149 A26	1c	rose violet	15	15
150 A27	2c	emerald	15	15
151 A27	3c	ultra	15	15
152 A26	5c	dk bl grn	15	15
153 A27	10c	brt red vio	15	15
154 A28	15c	dk green	15	15
155 A28	20c	black grn	15	15
156 A29	30c	deep blue	15	15
157 A29	40c	chocolate	15	15
158 A29	45c	Prus green	28	20
159 A30	50c	rose red	80	40
159A A30	50c	Prus grn ('40)	15	15
160 A30	60c	turq blue	80	40
160A A30	60c	choc ('40)	15	15
161 A31	70c	dk violet	15	15
162 A32	75c	grnsh blk	20	20
163 A32	80c	pck bl ('40)	15	15
163A A32	80c	dk grn ('42)	15	15
164 A30	90c	ultra	15	15
165 A28	1fr	chocolate	15	15
165A A32	1.20fr	rose vio ('42)	20	15
166 A32	1.25fr	henna brn	55	28
167 A32	1.40fr	rose violet	20	15
168 A30	1.50fr	cop red ('40)	15	15
168A A30	1.50fr	rose ('42)	15	15
169 A33	2fr	Prus green	15	15
170 A33	2.25fr	dark blue	16	16
170A A26	2.40fr	red ('42)	15	15
171 A26	2.50fr	scarlet	55	28
171A A26	2.50fr	dp blue ('40)	50	28
172 A33	3fr	black brown	15	15
172A A26	4fr	dp ultra ('42)	15	15
172B A32	4.50fr	grnsh blk ('42)	28	15
173 A31	5fr	dark blue	28	15
174 A31	10fr	red	45	32
174A A31	15fr	Prus grn ('42)	2.25	2.00
175 A31	20fr	dk vio brn	80	80
		Set value	9.75	6.75

See Nos. 197-219. For surcharges see Nos. 244, 261-262, B21-B24, B26, B28, B32.

No. 136 Surcharged in Black

35c

1940

176 A22	35c on 65c brown red	80	50
a.	Pair, one without surcharge	1.50	1.00

The surcharge was applied on alternate rows in the sheet, making No. 176a. This was done to make a pair equal 1fr, the new rate.

Catalogue values for unused stamps in this section, from this point to the end of the section, are for Never Hinged items.

One Aim Alone-Victory A34

Tower of Hassan, Rabat A35

1943 Litho. *Perf. 12*

177 A34	1.50fr deep blue	15	15

1943

178 A35	10c	rose lilac	15	15
179 A35	30c	blue	15	15
180 A35	40c	lake	15	15
181 A35	50c	blue green	15	15
182 A35	60c	dk vio brn	15	15
183 A35	70c	rose violet	15	15
184 A35	80c	gray green	15	15
185 A35	1fr	car lake	15	15
186 A35	1.20fr	violet	15	15
187 A35	1.50fr	red	15	15
188 A35	2fr	lt bl grn	15	15
189 A35	2.40fr	car rose	15	15
190 A35	3fr	ol brn	15	15
191 A35	4fr	dk ultra	15	15
192 A35	4.50fr	slate blk	15	15
193 A35	5fr	dull blue	25	15
194 A35	10fr	orange brn	15	15
195 A35	15fr	slate grn	50	15
196 A35	20fr	deep plum	70	18
		Set value	2.40	1.10

Types of 1939-42

Perf. $13^1/_2$x14, 14x$13^1/_2$

1945-47 Typo. Unwmk.

197 A27	10c	red violet	15	15
199 A29	40c	chocolate	15	15
200 A30	50c	Prus grn	15	15
203 A28	1fr	choc ('46)	15	15
204 A32	1.20fr	vio brn ('46)	15	15
205 A27	1.30fr	blue ('47)	22	15
206 A30	1.50fr	deep red	20	16
207 A33	2fr	Prus grn	15	15
209 A33	3fr	black brn	15	15
210 A29	3.50fr	dk red ('47)	35	28
212 A31	4.50fr	magenta ('47)	16	15
214 A31	5fr	indigo	38	20
215 A32	6fr	chlky bl ('46)	16	15
216 A31	10fr	red	60	42
217 A31	15fr	Prus grn	65	38
218 A31	20fr	dk vio brn	1.00	65
219 A31	25fr	blk brn	1.40	1.00
		Nos. 197-219 (17)	6.17	
		Set value		3.65

For surcharges see #261-263, B26, B28, B32.

The Terraces — A37

Mountain District — A39

Fortress A38

Marrakesh A40

Gardens of Fez — A41

Ouarzazat District — A42

1947-48 Engr. Unwmk. *Perf. 13*

221 A37	10c	blk brn	15	15
222 A37	30c	brt red	15	15
223 A37	50c	brt grnsh bl	15	15
224 A37	60c	brt red vio	15	15
225 A38	1fr	black	15	15
226 A38	1.50fr	blue	15	15
227 A39	2fr	brt grn	15	15
228 A39	3fr	brn red	15	15
229 A40	4fr	dk bl vio	15	15
230 A41	5fr	dk grn	28	15
231 A40	6fr	crimson	15	15
232 A41	10fr	dp bl ('47)	15	15
233 A42	15fr	dk grn ('47)	60	42
234 A42	20fr	hn brn ('47)	40	15
235 A42	25fr	pur ('47)	1.00	42
		Set value	3.00	1.60

1948-49

236 A37	30c	purple	15	15
237 A38	2fr	vio brn ('49)	15	15
238 A40	4fr	green	15	15
239 A41	8fr	org ('49)	25	15
240 A41	10fr	blue	25	15
241 A42	10fr	car rose	25	16
242 A38	12fr	red	38	15
243 A42	18fr	deep blue	75	55
		Nos. 236-243 (8)	2.33	
		Set value		1.20

For surcharges see Nos. 293-294.

No. 175 Surcharged with New Value and Wavy Lines in Carmine

1948

244 A31	8fr on 20fr dk vio brn	40	28

Fortified Oasis — A43

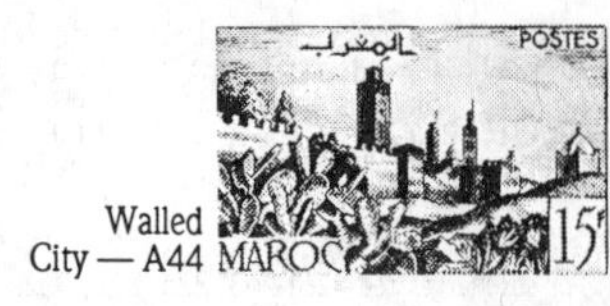

Walled City — A44

1949

245 A43 5fr blue green 15 15
246 A44 15fr red 75 15
247 A44 25fr ultra 75 15
Set value 18

See No. 300.

Detail, Gate of Oudayas, Rabat — A45

Nejjarine Fountain, Fez A46

Garden, Meknes A47

1949 *Perf. 14x13*

248 A45 10c black 15 15
249 A45 50c rose brn 15 15
250 A45 1fr bl vio 15 15
251 A46 2fr dk car rose 15 15
252 A46 3fr dark blue 15 15
253 A46 5fr brt grn 15 15
254 A47 8fr dk bl grn 40 15
255 A47 10fr brt red 55 15
Set value 1.30 45

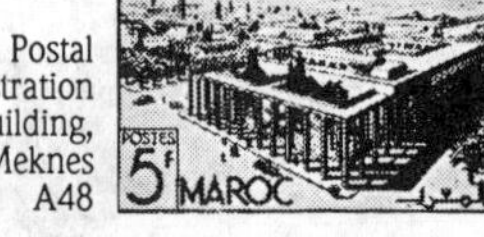

Postal Administration Building, Meknes A48

1949, Oct. *Perf. 13*

256 A48 5fr dark grn 65 65
257 A48 15fr deep car 70 70
258 A48 25fr deep blue 90 90

75th anniv. of the UPU.

Todra Valley — A49

1950

259 A49 35fr red brown 65 15
260 A49 50fr indigo 65 15
Set value 17

See No. 270.

Nos. 204 and 205 Surcharged in Black or Blue

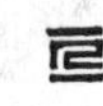

1fr

1950 *Perf. 14x13½, 13½x14*

261 A32 1fr on 1.20fr vio brn (Bk) 15 15
262 A27 1fr on 1.30fr blue (Bl) 15 15
Set value 20 20

The surcharge is transposed and spaced to fit the design on No. 262.

No. 231 Surcharged with New Value and Wavy Lines in Black

1951 *Perf. 13*

263 A40 5fr on 6fr crimson 15 15

Statue of Gen. Jacques Leclerc — A50

1951, Apr. 28 **Engr.**

264 A50 10fr blue green 80 80
265 A50 15fr deep carmine 1.00 1.00
266 A50 25fr indigo 1.00 1.00

Unveiling of a monument to Gen. Leclerc at Casablanca, Apr. 28, 1951. See No. C39.

Loustau Hospital, Oujda — A51

Designs: 15fr, New Hospital, Meknes. 25fr, New Hospital, Rabat.

1951

267 A51 10fr indigo & pur 75 75
268 A51 15fr Prus grn & red brn 75 75
269 A51 25fr dk brn & ind 1.00 1.00

Todra Valley Type of 1950

1951

270 A49 30fr ultramarine 60 28

Pigeons at Fountain — A52

Karaouine Mosque, Fez — A53

Patio, Oudayas — A54

Oudayas Point, Rabat — A55

Patio of Old House — A56

Type I (No. 275) Type II (No. 276)

Perf. 14x13, 13

1951-53 **Engr.** **Unwmk.**

271 A52 5fr magenta ('52) 15 15
272 A53 6fr bl grn ('52) 15 15
273 A52 8fr brown ('52) 15 15
273A A53 10fr rose red ('53) 15 15
274 A53 12fr dp ultra ('52) 28 15
275 A54 15fr red brn (I) 1.40 15
276 A54 15fr red brn (II) 32 15
277 A55 15fr pur ('52) 40 15
278 A55 18fr red ('52) 65 35
279 A56 20fr dp grnsh bl ('52) 45 32
Nos. 271-279 (10) 4.10
Set value 1.20

See Nos. 297-299.

8th-10th Cent. Capital A57

Casablanca Monument A58

Capitals: 20fr, 12th Cent. 25fr, 13th-14th Cent. 50fr, 17th Cent.

1952, Apr. 5 *Perf. 13*

280 A57 15fr deep blue 1.50 1.60
281 A57 20fr red 1.50 1.60
282 A57 25fr purple 1.50 1.60
283 A57 50fr deep green 1.60 1.75

1952 Sept. 22 **Engr. & Typo.**

284 A58 15fr multi 1.25 75

Creation of the French Military Medal, cent.

Daggers of South Morocco A59

Post Rider and Public Letter-writer A60

Designs: 20fr and 25fr, Antique brooches.

1953, Mar. 27 **Engr.**

285 A59 15fr dk car rose 1.50 1.50
286 A59 20fr vio brn 1.50 1.50
287 A59 25fr dark blue 1.50 1.50

See No. C46.

1953, May 16

288 A60 15fr vio brn 80 80

Stamp Day, May 16, 1953.

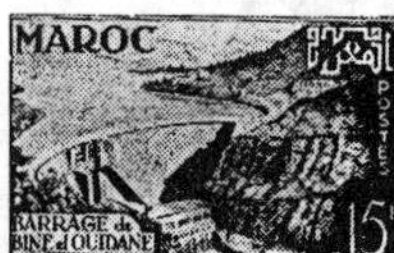

Bine el Ouidane Dam — A61

1953, Nov. 3 *Perf. 13*

290 A61 15fr indigo 80 80

See No. 295.

Mogador Fortress — A62

Design: 30fr, Moorish knights.

1953, Dec. 4

291 A62 15fr green 80 80
292 A62 30fr red brown 80 80

Issued to aid Army Welfare Work.

Nos. 226 and 243 Surcharged with New Value and Wavy Lines in Black

1954

293 A38 1fr on 1.50fr blue 15 15
294 A42 15fr on 18fr dp bl 35 35

Dam Type of 1953

1954, Mar. 8

295 A61 15fr red brn & indigo 50 20

Station of Rural Automobile Post — A63

1954, Apr. 10

296 A63 15fr dk bl grn 45 45

Stamp Day, April 10, 1954.

Types of 1951-53

1954 **Engr.** *Perf. 14x13*

297 A52 15fr dk bl grn 30 15

Typo.

298 A52 5fr magenta 20 15
299 A55 15fr rose violet 40 22
Set value 42

Walled City Type of 1949

1954 **Engr.** *Perf. 13*

300 A44 25fr purple 40 22

Marshal Lyautey at Rabat — A64

Lyautey, Builder of Cities — A65

Designs: 15fr, Marshal Lyautey at Khenifra. 50fr, Hubert Lyautey, Marshal of France.

1954, Nov. 17

301 A64 5fr indigo 1.25 1.25
302 A64 15fr dark green 1.25 1.25
303 A65 30fr rose brown 1.50 1.50
304 A65 50fr dk red brn 1.50 1.50

Marshal Hubert Lyautey, birth cent.

Franco-Moslem Education — A66

Moslem Student at Blackboard — A67

Designs: 30fr, Moslem school at Camp Boulhaut. 50fr, Moulay Idriss College at Fez.

1955, Apr. 16 **Unwmk.** *Perf. 13*

305 A66 5fr indigo 60 60
306 A67 15fr rose lake 70 70
307 A66 30fr chocolate 90 90
308 A67 50fr dk bl grn 1.00 1.00

Franco-Moslem solidarity.

Map and Rotary Emblem A68

1955, June 11

309	A68	15fr bl & org brn	80	65

Rotary Intl., 59th anniv.

Post Office, Mazagan A69

1955, May 24

310	A69	15fr red	42	42

Stamp Day.

Bab el Chorfa, Fez — A70

Mahakma (Courthouse), Casablanca — A71

Fortress, Safi — A72

Designs: 50c, 1fr, 2fr, Mrissa Gate, Salé. 10fr, 12fr, 15fr, Minaret at Rabat. 30fr, Menara Garden Marrakesh. 40fr, Tafraout Village. 50fr, Portuguese cistern, Mazagan. 75fr, Garden of Oudaya, Rabat.

1955 ***Perf. 13½x13, 13x13½, 13***

311	A70	50c brn vio	15	15
312	A70	1fr blue	15	15
313	A70	2fr red lilac	15	15
314	A70	3fr bluish blk	15	15
315	A70	5fr vermilion	48	15
316	A70	6fr green	15	15
317	A70	8fr org brn	38	20
318	A70	10fr vio brn	65	15
319	A70	12fr greenish bl	18	15
320	A70	15fr magenta	60	15
321	A71	18fr dk grn	75	35
322	A71	20fr brown lake	30	15
323	A72	25fr brt ultra	1.00	15
324	A72	30fr green	1.00	20
325	A72	40fr org red	52	15
326	A72	50fr blk brn	3.00	15
327	A71	75fr greenish bl	75	40
		Nos. 311-327 (17)	10.36	
		Set value		2.10

Succeeding issues, released under the Kingdom, are listed under Morocco in Vol. 4.

SEMI-POSTAL STAMPS

French Protectorate

No. 30 Surcharged in Red 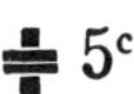

1914 **Unwmk.** ***Perf. 14x13½***

B1	A4	10c + 5c on 10c	*17,500.*	*17,500.*

Known only with inverted red surcharge.

Same Surcharge on No. 42 with "Protectorat Francais"

B2	A7	10c + 5c on 10c rose	1.50	1.50
a.		Double surcharge	65.00	65.00
b.		Inverted surcharge	85.00	85.00
c.		"c" omitted	40.00	40.00

On Nos. B1 and B2 the cross is set up from pieces of metal (quads), the horizontal bar being made from two long pieces, the vertical bar from two short pieces. Each cross in the setting of twenty-five differs from the others.

No. 30 Handstamp Surcharged in Red ✚ 5c

B3	A4	10c + 5c on 10c rose	*700.00*	*900.00*

No. B3 was issued at Oujda. The surcharge ink is water-soluble.

No. 42 Surcharged in Vermilion or Carmine 

B4	A7	10c + 5c on 10c (V)	9.00	9.00
a.		Double surcharge	75.00	75.00
b.		Inverted surcharge	90.00	90.00
c.		Double surch., one invtd.	90.00	90.00
B5	A7	10c +5c on 10c (C)	200.00	225.00

On Nos. B4-B5 the horizontal bar of the cross is single and not as thick as on Nos. B1-B2.
No. B5 was sold largely at Casablanca.

SP1

SP2

Carmine Surcharge

1915

B6	SP1	5c + 5c green	1.10	90
a.		Inverted surcharge	140.00	140.00

No. B6 was not issued without the Red Cross surcharge.

B7	SP2	10c + 5c rose	1.40	1.40

No. B7 was used in Tangier.

SP3

SP4

France No. B2 Overprinted in Black

B8	SP3	10c + 5c red	2.50	2.50

Carmine Surcharge

1917

B9	SP4	10c + 5c on 10c rose	90	90

On No. B9 the horizontal bar of the cross is made from a single, thick piece of metal.

Marshal Hubert Lyautey — SP5

1935, May 15 **Photo.** ***Perf. 13x13½***

B10	SP5	50c + 50c red	4.50	4.50
B11	SP5	1fr + 1fr dk grn	4.50	4.50
B12	SP5	5fr + 1fr blk brn	22.50	22.50

Stamps of 1933-34 Surcharged in Blue or Red **O.S.E. +3 c**

1938 ***Perf. 13***

B13	A18	2c + 2c red vio	2.50	2.50
B14	A19	3c + 3c dk brn	2.50	2.50
B15	A20	20c + 20c red brn	2.50	2.50
B16	A21	40c + 40c blk brn (R)	2.50	2.50
B17	A22	65c + 65c brn red	2.50	2.50
B18	A23	1.25fr + 1.25fr blk (R)	2.50	2.50
B19	A24	2fr + 2fr yel brn	2.50	2.50
B20	A25	5fr + 5fr red brn	2.50	2.50
		Nos. B13-B20 (8)	20.00	20.00

Stamps of 1939 Surcharged in Black

+2f
Enfants de France au Maroc

1942

B21	A29	45c + 2fr Prus grn	2.00	2.00
B22	A30	90c + 4fr ultra	2.00	2.00
B23	A32	1.25fr + 6fr henna brn	2.00	2.00
B24	A26	2.50fr + 8fr scarlet	2.00	2.00

The arrangement of the surcharge differs slightly on each denomination.

Catalogue values for unused stamps in this section, from this point to the end of the section, are for Never Hinged items.

No. 207 Surcharged in Black

AIDEZ LES TUBERCULEUX +1f

1945 **Unwmk.** ***Perf. 13½x14***

B26	A33	2fr + 1fr Prus green	16	16

For surcharge see No. B28.

Mausoleum of Marshal Lyautey — SP7

Statue of Marshal Lyautey — SP8

1945 **Litho.** ***Perf. 11½***

B27	SP7	2fr + 3fr dark blue	15	15

The surtax was for French works of solidarity.

No. B26 Surcharged in Red **3f**

1946 ***Perf. 13½x14***

B28	A33	3fr (+ 1fr) on 2fr + 1fr	15	15

Perf. 13½x14, 13

1946, Dec. 16 **Engr.**

B29	SP8	2fr + 10fr black	75	75
B30	SP8	3fr + 15fr cop red	90	90
B31	SP8	10fr + 20fr brt bl	1.50	1.50

The surtax was for works of solidarity.

No. 212 Surcharged in Rose Violet

JOURNÉE DU TIMBRE 1947
+5f50

1947, Mar. 15 ***Perf. 13½x14***

B32	A31	4.50fr + 5.50fr magenta	75	75

Stamp Day, 1947.

Map and Symbols of Prosperity from Phosphates SP9

1947 ***Perf. 13***

B33	SP9	4.50fr + 5.50fr green	50	50

25th anniv. of the exploitations of the Cherifien Office of Phosphates.

Power — SP10

Health — SP11

1948, Feb. 9

B34	SP10	6fr + 9fr red brn	1.00	1.00
B35	SP11	10fr + 20fr dp ultra	1.00	1.00

The surtax was for combined works of Franco-Moroccan solidarity.

Type of Regular Issue of 1923, Inscribed: "Journee du Timbre 1948"

1948, Mar. 6

B36	A16	6fr + 4fr red brown	45	45

Stamp Day, Mar. 6, 1948.

Battleship off Moroccan Coast — SP12

1948, Aug.

B37	SP12	6fr + 9fr purple	90	90

The surtax was for naval charities.

Wheat Field near Meknes SP13

Designs: 2fr+5fr, Olive grove, Taroudant. 3fr+7fr, Net and coastal view. 5fr+10fr, Aguedal Gardens, Marrakesh.

1949, Apr. 12 **Engr.** **Unwmk.**
Inscribed: "SOLIDARITÉ 1948"

B38	SP13	1fr + 2fr orange	75	75
B39	SP13	2fr + 5fr car	75	75
B40	SP13	3fr + 7fr pck bl	75	75
B41	SP13	5fr + 10fr dk brn vio	75	75
a.		Sheet of 4, #B38-B41	7.50	7.50
		Nos. B38-B41,CB31-CB34 (8)	6.20	6.20

Gazelle Hunter, from 1899 Local Stamp — SP14

1949, May 1

B42	SP14	10fr + 5fr choc & car rose	65	65

Stamp Day and 50th anniversary of Mazagan-Marrakesh local postage stamp.

Moroccan Soldiers, Flag — SP15

Rug Weaving — SP16

1949

B43	SP15	10fr + 10fr bright red	55	55

The surtax was for Army Welfare Work.

1950, Apr. 11

Designs: 2fr+5fr, Pottery making, 3fr+7fr, Bookbinding. 5fr+10fr, Copper work.

Inscribed: "SOLIDARITE 1949"

B44	SP16	1fr + 2fr dp car	1.10	1.10
B45	SP16	2fr + 5fr dk brnsh bl	1.10	1.10
B46	SP16	3fr + 7fr dk pur	1.10	1.10
B47	SP16	5fr + 10fr red brn	1.10	1.10
a.		Sheet of 4, #B44-B47	8.50	8.50
		Nos. B44-B47,CB36-CB39 (8)	7.60	7.60

Ruins of Sala Colonia at Chella SP17

1950, Sept. 25 Engr. *Perf. 13*

B48	SP17	10fr + 10fr dp magenta	65	65
B49	SP17	15fr + 15fr indigo	65	65

The surtax was for Army Welfare Work.

AIR POST STAMPS

French Protectorate

Biplane over Casablanca AP1

1922-27 Photo. Unwmk. *Perf. 13½*

C1	AP1	5c dp org ('27)	15	15
C2	AP1	25c dp ultra	42	15
C3	AP1	50c grnsh bl	15	15
C4	AP1	75c dp bl	35.00	4.00
C5	AP1	75c dp grn	15	15
C6	AP1	80c vio brn ('27)	80	20
C7	AP1	1fr vermilion	15	15
C8	AP1	1.40fr brn lake ('27)	65	50
C9	AP1	1.90fr dp bl ('27)	80	80
C10	AP1	2fr blk vio	60	45
a.		2fr deep violet	80	60
C11	AP1	3fr gray blk	65	50
		Nos. C1-C11 (11)	39.52	7.20

The 25c, 50c, 75c deep green and 1fr each were printed in two or three types, differing in frameline thickness, or hyphen in "Helio-Vaugirard" imprint.

Imperf., Pairs

C1a	AP1	5c	32.50
C2a	AP1	25c	40.00
C3a	AP1	50c	32.50
C4a	AP1	75c	350.00
C5a	AP1	75c	42.50
C6a	AP1	80c	35.00
C7a	AP1	1fr	40.00
C10b	AP1	2fr	125.00

Nos. C8-C9 Surcharged in Blue or Black

1931, Apr. 10

C12	AP1	1fr on 1.40fr (B)	80	80
a.		Inverted surcharge	160.00	160.00
C13	AP1	1.50fr on 1.90fr (Bk)	80	80

Rabat and Tower of Hassan — AP2

Casablanca AP3

1933, Jan. Engr.

C14	AP2	50c dark blue	42	22
C15	AP2	80c org brn	28	20
C16	AP2	1.50fr brn red	35	15
C17	AP3	2.50fr car rose	2.25	28
C18	AP3	5fr violet	1.00	65
C19	AP3	10fr bl grn	50	50
		Nos. C14-C19 (6)	4.80	2.00

For surcharges see Nos. CB22-CB23.

Storks and Minaret, Chella — AP4

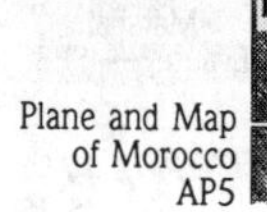
Plane and Map of Morocco AP5

1939-40 *Perf. 13*

C20	AP4	80c Prus green	15	15
C21	AP4	1fr dk red	15	15
C22	AP5	1.90fr ultra	15	15
C23	AP5	2fr red vio ('40)	15	15
C24	AP5	3fr chocolate	15	15
C25	AP4	5fr violet	50	35
C26	AP5	10fr turq blue	40	22
		Set value	1.10	80

Catalogue values for unused stamps in this section, from this point to the end of the section, are for Never Hinged items.

Plane over Oasis — AP6

1944 Litho. *Perf. 11½*

C27	AP6	50c Prus grn	15	15
C28	AP6	2fr ultra	15	15
C29	AP6	5fr scarlet	15	15
C30	AP6	10fr violet	35	35
C31	AP6	50fr black	55	55
C32	AP6	100fr dp bl & red	1.60	1.60
		Nos. C27-C32 (6)	2.95	2.95

For surcharge see No. CB24.

Plane — AP7

1945 Engr. *Perf. 13*

C33	AP7	50fr sepia	40	35

Moulay Idriss — AP8

La Medina AP9

1947-48

C34	AP8	9fr dk rose car	15	15
C35	AP8	40fr dark blue	45	22
C36	AP8	50fr dp claret ('47)	45	15
C37	AP9	100fr dp grnsh bl	1.10	45
C38	AP9	200fr henna brn	2.00	1.00
		Nos. C34-C38 (5)	4.15	1.97

Leclerc Type of Regular Issue

1951, Apr. 28

C39	A50	50fr purple	1.10	1.10

Unveiling of a monument to Gen. Leclerc at Casablanca, Apr. 28, 1951.

Kasbah of the Oudayas, Rabat — AP11

1951, May 22

C40	AP11	300fr purple	12.00	9.00

Ben Smine Sanatorium AP12

1951, June 4

C41	AP12	50fr pur & Prus grn	2.00	2.00

Fortifications, Chella AP13

Plane Near Marrakesh AP14

Fort, Anti-Atlas Mountains — AP15

View of Fez — AP16

1952, Apr. 19 Unwmk. *Perf. 13*

C42	AP13	10fr blue green	35	15
C43	AP14	40fr red	45	28
C44	AP15	100fr brown	1.25	28
C45	AP16	200fr purple	4.00	2.00

Antique Brooches — AP17

1953, Mar. 27

C46	AP17	50fr dark green	1.50	1.50

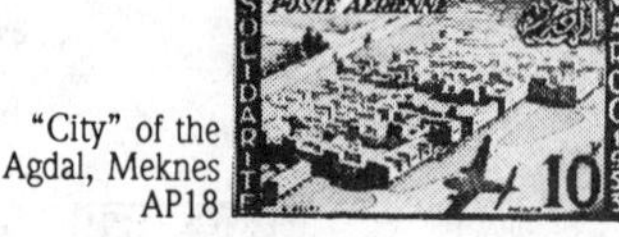
"City" of the Agdal, Meknes AP18

Designs: 20fr, Yakoub el Mansour, Rabat. 40fr, Ainchock, Casablanca. 50fr, El Aliya, Fedala.

1954, Mar. 8

C47	AP18	10fr olive brown	1.50	1.75
C48	AP18	20fr purple	1.50	1.75
C49	AP18	40fr red brown	1.50	1.75
C50	AP18	50fr deep green	1.50	1.75

Franco-Moroccan solidarity.

Naval Vessel and Sailboat AP19

Village in the Anti-Atlas AP20

"Ksar es Souk," Rabat and Plane — AP21

1954, Oct. 18

C51	AP19	15fr dk bl grn	80	80
C52	AP19	30fr vio bl	1.00	1.00

1955, July 25 Engr. *Perf. 13*

Designs: 200fr, Estuary of Bou Regreg, Rabat and Plane.

C53	AP20	100fr brt vio	1.50	30
C54	AP20	200fr brt car	2.25	70
C55	AP21	500fr grnsh bl	6.50	3.25

AIR POST SEMI-POSTAL STAMPS

French Protectorate

Moorish Tribesmen SPAP1

Designs: 25c, Moor plowing with camel and burro. 50c, Caravan nearing Saffi. 75c, Walls, Marrakesh. 80c, Sheep grazing at Azrou. 1fr, Gate at Fez. 1.50fr, Aerial view of Tangier. 2fr, Aerial view of Casablanca. 3fr, Storks on old wall, Rabat. 5fr, Moorish fete.

Perf. 13½

1928, July 26 Photo. Unwmk.

No.	Type	Description	Unused	Used
CB1	SPAP1	5c dp bl	2.00	2.00
CB2	SPAP1	25c brn org	2.00	2.00
CB3	SPAP1	50c red	2.00	2.00
CB4	SPAP1	75c org brn	2.00	2.00
CB5	SPAP1	80c ol grn	2.00	2.00
CB6	SPAP1	1fr orange	2.00	2.00
CB7	SPAP1	1.50fr Prus bl	2.00	2.00
CB8	SPAP1	2fr dp brn	2.00	2.00
CB9	SPAP1	3fr dp vio	2.00	2.00
CB10	SPAP1	5fr brn blk	2.00	2.00
		Nos. CB1-CB10 (10)	20.00	20.00

These stamps were sold in sets only and at double their face value. The money received for the surtax was divided among charitable and social organizations. The stamps were not sold at post offices but solely by subscription to the Moroccan Postal Administration.

Overprinted in Red or Blue (25c, 50c, 75c, 1fr) **Tanger**

1929, Feb. 1

No.	Type	Description	Unused	Used
CB11	SPAP1	5c dp bl	2.00	2.00
CB12	SPAP1	25c brn org	2.00	2.00
CB13	SPAP1	50c red	2.00	2.00
CB14	SPAP1	75c org brn	2.00	2.00
CB15	SPAP1	80c ol grn	2.00	2.00
CB16	SPAP1	1fr orange	2.00	2.00
CB17	SPAP1	1.50fr Prus bl	2.00	2.00
CB18	SPAP1	2fr dp brn	2.00	2.00
CB19	SPAP1	3fr dp vio	2.00	2.00
CB20	SPAP1	5fr brn blk	2.00	2.00
		Nos. CB11-CB20 (10)	20.00	20.00

These stamps were sold at double their face values and only in Tangier. The surtax benefited various charities.

Marshal Hubert Lyautey SPAP10

1935, May 15 *Perf. 13½*

No.	Type	Description	Unused	Used
CB21	SPAP10	1.50fr + 1.50fr blue	12.50	11.00

Nos. C14, C19 Surcharged in Red **O.S.E. +50 c**

1938 *Perf. 13*

No.	Type	Description	Unused	Used
CB22	AP2	50c + 50c dk bl	3.25	3.25
CB23	AP3	10fr + 10fr bl grn	3.25	3.25

Catalogue values for unused stamps in this section, from this point to the end of the section, are for Never Hinged items.

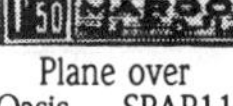

Plane over Oasis — SPAP11

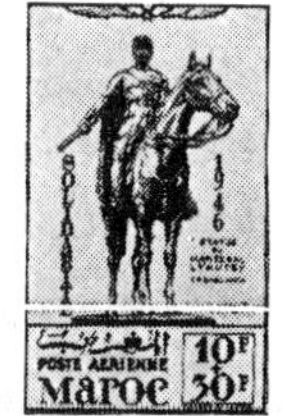

Statue of Marshal Lyautey — SPAP12

1944 Litho. *Perf. 11½*

No.	Type	Description	Unused	Used
CB23A	SPAP11	1.50fr + 98.50fr	80	80

The surtax was for charity among the liberated French.

No. C29 Surcharged in Black **+ 5F 18 Juin 1946 ‡ 18 Juin 1946**

1946, June 18 *Perf. 11*

No.	Type	Description	Unused	Used
CB24	AP6	5fr + 5fr scarlet	40	40

6th anniv. of the appeal made by Gen. Charles de Gaulle, June 18, 1940. The surtax was for the Free French Association of Morocco.

1946, Dec. Engr. *Perf. 13*

No.	Type	Description	Unused	Used
CB25	SPAP12	10fr +30fr dk grn	1.00	1.00

The surtax was for works of solidarity.

Replenishing Stocks of Food SPAP13

Agriculture SPAP14

1948, Feb. 9 Unwmk.

No.	Type	Description	Unused	Used
CB26	SPAP13	9fr +26fr dp grn	80	80
CB27	SPAP14	20fr +35fr brown	80	80

The surtax was for combined works of Franco-Moroccan solidarity.

Tomb of Marshal Hubert Lyautey — SPAP15

1948, May 18 *Perf. 13*

No.	Type	Description	Unused	Used
CB28	SPAP15	10fr +25fr dk grn	65	65

Lyautey Exposition, Paris, June, 1948.

P.T.T. Clubhouse SPAP16

1948, June 7 Engr.

No.	Type	Description	Unused	Used
CB29	SPAP16	6fr + 34fr dk grn	1.00	1.00
CB30	SPAP16	9fr + 51fr red brn	1.10	1.10

The surtax was used for the Moroccan P.T.T. employees vacation colony at Ifrane.

View of Agadir SPAP17

Plane over Globe SPAP18

Designs: 6fr+9fr, Fez. 9fr+16fr, Atlas Mountains. 15fr+25fr, Valley of Draa.

1949, Apr. 12 *Perf. 13*

Inscribed: "SOLIDARITÉ 1948"

No.	Type	Description	Unused	Used
CB31	SPAP17	5fr +5fr dk grn	80	80
CB32	SPAP17	6fr +9fr org red	80	80
CB33	SPAP17	9fr +16fr blk brn	80	80
CB34	SPAP17	15fr +25fr ind	80	80
a.		Sheet of 4, #CB31-CB34	5.00	5.00

1950, Mar. 11 Engr. & Typo.

No.	Type	Description	Unused	Used
CB35	SPAP18	15fr + 10fr bl grn & car	35	35

Day of the Stamp, Mar. 11-12, 1950, and 25th anniv. of the 1st post link between Casablanca and Dakar.

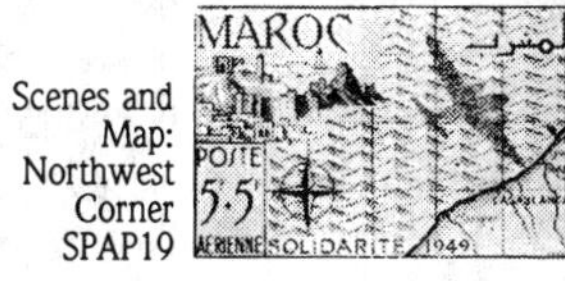

Scenes and Map: Northwest Corner SPAP19

Designs (quarters of map): 6fr+9fr, NE, 9fr+16fr, SW. 15fr+25fr, SE.

1950, Apr. 11 Engr.

Inscribed: "SOLIDARITE 1949"

No.	Type	Description	Unused	Used
CB36	SPAP19	5fr +5fr dp ultra	80	80
CB37	SPAP19	6fr +9fr Prus grn	80	80
CB38	SPAP19	9fr +16fr dk brn	80	80
CB39	SPAP19	15fr +25fr brn red	80	80
a.		Sheet of 4, #CB36-CB39	5.00	5.00

Arch of Triumph of Caracalla at Volubilis SPAP20

1950, Sept. 25 Unwmk.

No.	Type	Description	Unused	Used
CB40	SPAP20	10fr + 10fr sepia	65	65
CB41	SPAP20	15fr + 15fr bl grn	65	65

The surtax was for Army Welfare Work.

Casablanca Post Office and First Air Post Stamp SPAP21

1952, Mar. 8 *Perf. 13*

No.	Type	Description	Unused	Used
CB42	SPAP21	15fr + 5fr red brn & dp grn	2.50	2.50

Day of the Stamp, Mar. 8, 1952, and 30th anniv. of French Morocco's 1st air post stamp.

POSTAGE DUE STAMPS

French Offices in Morocco

Postage Due Stamps and Types of France Surcharged in Red or Black **5 CENTIMOS**

1896 Unwmk. *Perf. 14x13½*

On Stamps of 1891-93

No.	Type	Description	Unused	Used
J1	D2	5c on 5c lt bl (R)	2.00	1.25
J2	D2	10c on 10c choc (R)	3.25	1.25
J3	D2	30c on 30c car	7.25	5.00
a.		Pair, one without surcharge		
J4	D2	50c on 50c lilac	7.25	5.00
a.		"S" of "CENTIMOS" omitted		10.00
J5	D2	1p on 1fr lil brn	175.00	145.00

1909-10 On Stamps of 1908-10

No.	Type	Description	Unused	Used
J6	D3	1c on 1c ol grn (R)	55	55
J7	D3	10c on 10c violet	12.00	10.00
J8	D3	30c on 30c bister	15.00	14.00
J9	D3	50c on 50c red	22.50	22.50

Postage Due Stamps of France Surcharged in Red or Blue **5** (surcharge in Arabic)

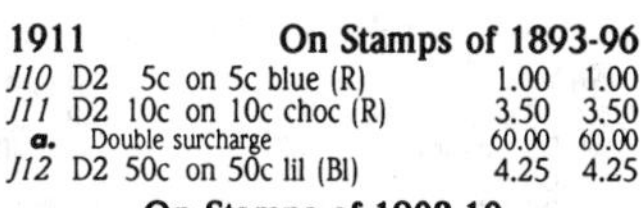

1911 On Stamps of 1893-96

No.	Type	Description	Unused	Used
J10	D2	5c on 5c blue (R)	1.00	1.00
J11	D2	10c on 10c choc (R)	3.50	3.50
a.		Double surcharge	60.00	60.00
J12	D2	50c on 50c lil (Bl)	4.25	4.25

On Stamps of 1908-10

No.	Type	Description	Unused	Used
J13	D3	1c on 1c ol grn (R)	45	45
J14	D3	10c on 10c vio (R)	1.40	1.40
J15	D3	30c on 30c bis (R)	2.00	2.00
J16	D3	50c on 50c red (Bl)	3.75	3.75
		Nos. J10-J16 (7)	16.35	16.35

For surcharges see Nos. JN23-J26.

French Protectorate

D4

D5

Type of 1911 Issue Overprinted "Protectorat Francais"

1915-17

No.	Type	Description	Unused	Used
J17	D4	1c on 1c black	15	15
a.		New value double	65.00	
J18	D4	5c on 5c blue	60	50
J19	D4	10c on 10c choc	80	65
J20	D4	20c on 20c ol grn	70	65
J21	D4	30c on 30c rose red	2.50	2.75
J22	D4	50c on 50c vio brn	4.50	2.25
		Nos. J17-J22 (6)	9.25	6.95

Nos. J13 to J16 With Additional Overprint "Protectorat Francais"

1915

No.	Type	Description	Unused	Used
J23	D3	1c on 1c ol grn	40	40
J24	D3	10c on 10c violet	80	65
J25	D3	30c on 30c bister	1.10	80
J26	D3	50c on 50c red	1.10	90

1917-26 Typo.

No.	Type	Description	Unused	Used
J27	D5	1c black	15	15
J28	D5	5c deep blue	15	15
J29	D5	10c brown	15	15
J30	D5	20c olive green	80	50
J31	D5	30c rose	15	15
J32	D5	50c lilac brown	15	15
J33	D5	1fr red brn, *straw* ('26)	60	18
J34	D5	2fr violet ('26)	70	42
		Nos. J27-J34 (8)	2.85	
		Set value		1.35

See #J49-J56. For surcharges see #J46-J48.

Postage Due Stamps of France, 1882-1906 Overprinted **TANGER**

1918

No.	Type	Description	Unused	Used
J35	D2	1c black	30	30
J36	D2	5c blue	52	52
J37	D2	10c chocolate	85	85
J38	D2	15c green	1.65	1.65
J39	D2	20c olive green	2.50	2.50
J40	D2	30c rose red	5.75	5.75
J41	D2	50c violet brown	9.50	9.50
		Nos. J35-J41 (7)	21.07	21.07

Postage Due Stamps of France, 1908-19 Overprinted **TANGER**

1918

No.	Type	Description	Unused	Used
J42	D3	1c olive green	32	32
J43	D3	10c violet	50	50
J44	D3	20c bister	2.75	2.75
J45	D3	40c red	6.00	6.00

Catalogue values for unused stamps in this section, from this point to the end of the section, are for Never Hinged items.

Nos. J31 and J29 Surcharged **50c**

1944 Unwmk. *Perf. 14x13½*

No.	Type	Description	Unused	Used
J46	D5	50c on 30c rose	1.25	1.25
J47	D5	1fr on 10c brown	1.90	1.60
J48	D5	3fr on 10c brown	5.00	4.00

Type of 1917-1926

1945-52 **Typo.**
J49 D5 1fr brn lake ('47) 40 38
J50 D5 2fr rose lake ('47) 55 40
J51 D5 3fr ultra 20 15
J52 D5 4fr red orange 20 15
J53 D5 5fr green 42 15
J54 D5 10fr yel brn 42 15
J55 D5 20fr carmine ('50) 65 50
J56 D5 30fr dull brn ('52) 1.10 80
Nos. J49-J56 (8) 3.94 2.68

PARCEL POST STAMPS

French Protectorate

PP1

1917 **Unwmk.** ***Perf. 13½x14***
Q1 PP1 5c green 32 15
Q2 PP1 10c carmine 35 20
Q3 PP1 20c lilac brown 38 22
Q4 PP1 25c blue 60 32
Q5 PP1 40c dark brown 1.10 50
Q6 PP1 50c red orange 1.25 40
Q7 PP1 75c pale slate 1.60 1.10
Q8 PP1 1f ultra 2.25 28
Q9 PP1 2f gray 3.50 40
Q10 PP1 5f violet 4.25 40
Q11 PP1 10f black 7.00 40
Nos. Q1-Q11 (11) 22.60 4.37

FRENCH POLYNESIA

(French Oceania)

LOCATION — South Pacific Ocean
GOVT. — French Overseas Territory
AREA — 1,522 sq. mi.
POP. — 172,000 (est. 1984)
CAPITAL — Papeete

In 1903 various French Establishments in the South Pacific were united to form a single colony. Most important of the island groups are the Society Islands, Marquesas Islands, the Tuamotu group and the Gambier, Austral, and Rapa Islands. Tahiti, largest of the Society group, ranks first in importance.

100 Centimes = 1 Franc

Catalogue values for unused stamps in this country are for Never Hinged items, beginning with Scott 124 in the regular postage section, Scott B6 in the semi-postal section, Scott C2 in the airpost section, Scott CB1 in the airpost semi-postal section, Scott J18 in the postage due section, and Scott O1 in the officials section.

Navigation and Commerce — A1

Perf. 14x13½

1892-1907 **Typo.** **Unwmk.**

Name of Colony in Blue or Carmine

1 A1 1c black, *lil bl* 75 65
2 A1 2c brown, *buff* 95 85
3 A1 4c claret, *lav* 1.65 1.25
4 A1 5c green, *grnsh* 3.75 4.00
5 A1 5c yellow grn ('06) 85 55
6 A1 10c blk, *lavender* 8.50 5.00
7 A1 10c red ('00) 70 55
8 A1 15c blue, quadrille paper 7.00 4.50
9 A1 15c gray, *lt gray* ('00) 1.10 1.25
10 A1 20c red, *grn* 6.00 4.00
11 A1 25c black, *rose* 15.00 9.25
12 A1 25c blue ('00) 5.00 3.50
13 A1 30c brown, *bis* 5.00 4.50
14 A1 35c black, *yel* ('06) 2.50 1.75
15 A1 40c red, *straw* 60.00 32.50
16 A1 45c blk, *gray grn* ('07) 1.90 1.40
17 A1 50c car, *rose* 3.75 2.75
18 A1 50c brown, *az* ('00) 92.50 70.00
19 A1 75c dp vio, *org* 5.00 3.50
20 A1 1fr brnz grn, *straw* 5.00 4.50
Nos. 1-20 (20) 226.90 156.25

Perf. 13½x14 stamps are counterfeits.
For overprint and surcharge see #55, B1.

Tahitian Girl — A2

Kanakas — A3

Fautaua Valley — A4

1913-30
21 A2 1c violet & brn 15 15
22 A2 2c brown & blk 15 15
23 A2 4c orange & bl 15 15
24 A2 5c grn & yel grn 15 15
25 A2 5c bl & blk ('22) 15 15
26 A2 10c rose & org 35 22
27 A2 10c bl grn & yel grn ('22) 20 20
28 A2 10c org red & brn red, *bluish* ('26) 40 40
29 A2 15c org & blk ('15) 15 15
a. Imperf., pair 18.00
30 A2 20c black & vio 15 15
a. Imperf., pair 22.50
31 A2 20c grn & bl grn ('26) 16 16
32 A2 20c brn red & dk brn ('27) 40 40
33 A3 25c ultra & blue 25 15
34 A3 25c vio & rose ('22) 15 15
35 A3 30c gray & brown 1.00 80
a. Imperf., pair 62.50
36 A3 30c rose & red org ('22) 35 35
37 A3 30c blk & red org ('26) 15 15
38 A3 30c slate bl & bl grn ('27) 40 40
39 A3 35c green & rose 25 15
40 A3 40c black & green 25 20
41 A3 45c orange & red 25 22
42 A3 50c dk brown & blk 4.50 4.00
43 A3 50c ultra & bl ('22) 25 25
44 A3 50c gray & bl vio ('26) 25 25
45 A3 60c green & blk ('26) 25 25
46 A3 65c ol brn & red vio ('27) 65 65
47 A3 75c vio brn & vio 60 40
48 A3 90c brn red & rose ('30) 5.50 5.50
49 A4 1fr rose & black 70 55
50 A4 1.10fr vio & dk brn ('28) 60 60
51 A4 1.40fr bis brn & vio ('29) 1.50 1.50
52 A4 1.50fr ind & bl ('30) 5.50 5.50
53 A4 2fr dk brown & grn 1.50 80
54 A4 5fr violet & bl 4.00 3.25
Nos. 21-54 (34) 31.41 28.50

For surcharges see Nos. 56-71, B2-B4.

No. 7 Overprinted **E F O 1915**

1915
55 A1 10c red 1.10 1.10
a. Inverted overprint 35.00 35.00

For surcharge see No. B1.

No. 29 Surcharged **10**

1916
56 A2 10c on 15c org & blk 45 45

Nos. 22, 41 and 29 Surcharged **05 1921**

1921
57 A2 5c on 2c brn & blk 12.50 12.50
58 A3 10c on 45c org & red 12.50 12.50
59 A2 25c on 15c org & blk 3.00 3.00

On No. 58 the new value and date are set wide apart and without bar.

Types of 1913-30 Issue Surcharged in Black or Red **60**

1923-27
60 A3 60c on 75c bl & brn 15 15
61 A4 65c on 1fr dk bl & ol (R) ('25) 40 40
62 A4 85c on 1fr dk bl & ol (R) ('25) 42 42
63 A3 90c on 75c brn red & cer ('27) 42 42

No. 26 Surcharged **45 c. 1924**

1924
64 A2 45c on 10c rose & org 65 65
a. Inverted surcharge 400.00 400.00

Stamps and Type of 1913-30 Surcharged with New Value and Bars in Black or Red

1924-27
65 A4 25c on 2fr dk brn & grn 52 52
66 A4 25c on 5fr vio & bl 60 60
67 A4 1.25fr on 1fr dk bl & ultra (R) ('26) 60 60
68 A4 1.50fr on 1fr dk bl & lt bl ('27) 1.00 1.00
69 A4 20fr on 5fr org & brt vio ('27) 10.00 7.75
Nos. 65-69 (5) 12.72 10.47

Surcharged in Black or Red **TROIS FRANCS**

1926
70 A4 3fr on 5fr gray & blue 75 60
71 A4 10fr on 5fr grn & blk (R) 1.90 1.50

Papetoai Bay, Moorea — A5

1929, Mar. 25
72 A5 3fr green & dk brn 2.00 2.00
73 A5 5fr lt blue & dk brn 3.50 3.50
74 A5 10fr lt red & dk brn 14.00 14.00
75 A5 20fr lilac & dk brn 16.00 16.00

For overprints see Nos. 128, 130, 132, 134.

Colonial Exposition Issue

Common Design Types

1931, Apr. 13 **Engr.** ***Perf. 12½***

Name of Country Printed in Black

76 CD70 40c deep green 1.90 1.90
77 CD71 50c violet 1.90 1.90
78 CD72 90c red orange 1.90 1.90
79 CD73 1.50fr dull blue 2.00 2.00

Spear Fishing — A12

Tahitian Girl — A13

Idols — A14

1934-39 **Photo.** ***Perf. 13½, 13½x13***
80 A12 1c gray black 15 15
81 A12 2c claret 15 15
82 A12 3c lt blue ('39) 15 15
83 A12 4c orange 15 15
84 A12 5c violet 28 28
85 A12 10c dark brown 15 15
86 A12 15c green 15 15
87 A12 20c red 15 15
88 A13 25c gray blue 15 15
89 A13 30c yellow green 40 40
90 A13 30c orange brn ('39) 15 15
91 A14 35c dp green ('38) 1.10 1.10
92 A13 40c red violet 15 15
93 A13 45c brown orange 3.25 3.25
94 A13 45c dk green ('39) 32 32
95 A13 50c violet 15 15
96 A13 55c blue ('38) 1.40 1.40
97 A13 60c black ('39) 15 15
98 A13 65c brown 1.00 1.00
99 A13 70c brt pink ('39) 25 25
100 A13 75c olive green 2.00 2.00
101 A13 80c violet brn ('38) 40 40
102 A13 90c rose red 25 25
103 A14 1fr red brown 15 15
104 A14 1.25fr brown violet 2.75 2.75
105 A14 1.25fr rose red ('39) 25 25
106 A14 1.40fr orange yel ('39) 25 25
107 A14 1.50fr blue 25 25
108 A14 1.60fr dull vio ('39) 25 25
109 A14 1.75fr olive 2.00 2.00
110 A14 2fr red 25 25
111 A14 2.25fr deep blue ('39) 22 22
112 A14 2.50fr black ('39) 32 32
113 A14 3fr brown org ('39) 32 32
114 A14 5fr red violet ('39) 32 32
115 A14 10fr dark green ('39) 1.00 1.00
116 A14 20fr dark brown ('39) 1.10 1.10
Nos. 80-116 (37) 21.88 21.88

For overprints see Nos. 126-127, 129, 131, 133, 135.

Paris International Exposition Issue

Common Design Types

1937 **Engr.** ***Perf. 13***
117 CD74 20c deep violet 65 65
118 CD75 30c dark green 65 65
119 CD76 40c carmine rose 65 65
120 CD77 50c dk brown & blue 80 80
121 CD78 90c red 1.00 1.00
122 CD79 1.50fr ultra 1.10 1.10
Nos. 117-122 (6) 4.85 4.85

Common Design Types pictured in section at front of book.

Colonial Arts Exhibition Issue

Souvenir Sheet
Common Design Type

1937 ***Imperf.***
123 CD78 3fr emerald 2.50 2.50

Catalogue values for unused stamps in this section, from this point to the end of the section, are for Never Hinged items.

New York World's Fair Issue

Common Design Type

1939, May 10 **Engr.** ***Perf. 12½x12***
124 CD82 1.25fr carmine lake 75 75
125 CD82 2.25fr ultra 75 75

Fautaua Valley and Marshal Petain — A15

1941 **Engr.** ***Perf. 12½x12***
125A A15 1fr bluish green 30
125B A15 2.50fr deep blue 30

Nos. 125A-125B were issued by the Vichy government, and were not placed on sale in the colony. This is also true of five stamps of types A12-A14 without "RF" released in 1942-44.

Stamps of 1929-39 Overprinted in Black or Red **FRANCE LIBRE**

1941 ***Perf. 14x13½, 13½x13***
126 A14 1fr red brown (Bk) 1.75 1.75
127 A14 2.50fr black 2.50 2.50
128 A5 3fr grn & dk brn 2.50 2.50
129 A14 3fr brn org (Bk) 2.50 2.50
130 A5 5fr lt bl & dk brn 2.50 2.50
131 A14 5fr red violet (Bk) 2.50 2.50
132 A5 10fr lt red & dk brn 6.25 6.25

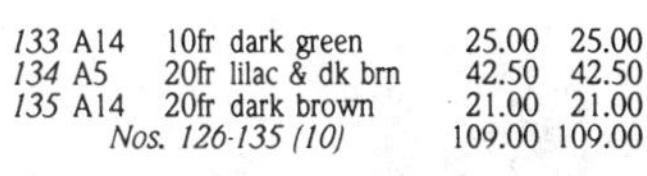
133 A14 10fr dark green 25.00 25.00
134 A5 20fr lilac & dk brn 42.50 42.50
135 A14 20fr dark brown 21.00 21.00
Nos. 126-135 (10) 109.00 109.00

Ancient Double Canoe A16

1942 Photo. Perf. 14½x14
136 A16 5c dark brown 15 15
137 A16 10c dk gray bl 15 15
138 A16 25c emerald 15 15
139 A16 30c red orange 15 15
140 A16 40c dk slate grn 15 15
141 A16 80c red brown 15 15
142 A16 1fr rose violet 15 15
143 A16 1.50fr brt red 16 15
144 A16 2fr gray black 16 16
145 A16 2.50fr brt ultra 65 65
146 A16 4fr dull violet 28 25
147 A16 5fr bister 40 38
148 A16 10fr deep brown 40 38
149 A16 20fr deep green 65 60
Set value 3.10 3.00

For surcharges see Nos. 152-159.

Eboue Issue
Common Design Type

1945 Engr. Perf. 13
150 CD91 2fr black 20 20
151 CD91 25fr Prus green 75 75

Nos. 150 and 151 exist imperforate.

Nos. 136, 138 and 145 Surcharged with New Values and Bars in Carmine or Black

1946 Perf. 14½x14
152 A16 50c on 5c (C) 15 15
153 A16 60c on 5c (C) 15 15
154 A16 70c on 5c (C) 15 15
155 A16 1.20fr on 5c (C) 15 15
156 A16 2.40fr on 25c (Bk) 45 45
157 A16 3fr on 25c (Bk) 28 28
158 A16 4.50fr on 25c (Bk) 65 65
159 A16 15fr on 2.50fr (C) 80 80
Nos. 152-159 (8) 2.78 2.78

Coast of Mooréa — A17

Fisherman and Catch — A18

Tahitian Girl — A20

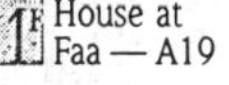
House at Faa — A19

Island of Borabora A21

Island Women — A22

1948 Unwmk. Engr. Perf. 13
160 A17 10c brown 15 15
161 A17 30c blue green 15 15
162 A17 40c deep blue 15 15
163 A18 50c red brown 15 15
164 A18 60c dk brown ol 15 15
165 A18 80c brt blue 15 15
166 A19 1fr red brown 15 15
167 A19 1.20fr slate 16 15
168 A19 1.50fr deep ultra 22 16
169 A20 2fr sepia 40 32
170 A20 2.40fr red brown 55 55
171 A20 3fr purple 4.50 1.10
172 A20 4fr blue black 45 45
173 A21 5fr sepia 55 45
174 A21 6fr steel blue 60 45
175 A21 10fr dk brown ol 1.00 40
176 A22 15fr vermilion 1.75 1.00
177 A22 20fr slate 1.90 1.00
178 A22 25fr sepia 2.25 1.25
Nos. 160-178 (19) 15.38 8.33

Imperforates
Most French Polynesia stamps from 1948 onward exist imperforate in issued and trial colors, and also in small presentation sheets in issued colors.

Military Medal Issue
Common Design Type

1952, Dec. 1 Engr. & Typo.
179 CD101 3fr multicolored 3.00 3.00

Girl of Borabora — A23

Girl Playing Guitar — A24

1955, Sept. 26 Engr.
180 A23 9fr dk brn, blk & red 7.00 5.00

FIDES Issue
Common Design Type

Design: 3fr, Dry dock at Papeete.

1956, Oct. 22 Engr. Perf. 13x12½
181 CD103 3fr grnsh blue 1.00 75

1958, Nov. 3 Unwmk. Perf. 13

Design: 4fr, 7fr, 9fr, Man with headdress. 10fr, 20fr, Girl with shells on beach.

182 A24 10c green & redsh brn 38 38
183 A24 25c slate grn, cl & car 38 38
184 A24 1fr brt bl, brn & red org 52 52
185 A24 2fr brn, vio brn & vio 52 52
186 A24 4fr sl grn & org yel 70 70
187 A24 7fr red brn, grn & org 1.10 90
188 A24 9fr vio brn, grn & org 2.00 1.65
189 A24 10fr dk blue, brn & car 2.25 1.75
190 A24 20fr pur, rose red & brn 4.50 3.00
Nos. 182-190 (9) 12.35 9.80

See Nos. 304-306.

Human Rights Issue
Common Design Type

1958, Dec. 10
191 CD105 7fr dk gray & dk bl 5.50 5.00

Flower Issue
Common Design Type

1959, Jan. Photo. Perf. 12½x12
192 CD104 4fr Breadfruit 3.00 2.25

Spear Fishing — A25

Tahitian Dancers A26

1960, May 16 Engr. Perf. 13
193 A25 5fr green, brn & lil 55 55
194 A26 17fr ultra, brt grn & red brn 2.75 1.10

Post Office, Papeete A27

1960, Dec. 15 Unwmk. Perf. 13
195 A27 16fr green, bl & claret 3.00 1.50

Saraca Indica — A28

1962, July 12 Photo. Perf. 13
196 A28 15fr shown 7.00 5.75
197 A28 25fr Hibiscus 9.00 8.00

Map of Australia and South Pacific — A29

1962, July 18 Perf. 13x12
198 A29 20fr multicolored 6.50 5.00

5th South Pacific Conf., Pago Pago, July 1962.

Spined Squirrelfish A30

Fish: 10fr, One-spot butterflyfish. 30fr, Radiate lionfish. 40fr, Horned boxfish.

1962, Dec. 15 Engr. Perf. 13
199 A30 5fr black, mag & bis 1.65 68
200 A30 10fr multicolored 2.25 1.25
201 A30 30fr multicolored 5.75 3.50
202 A30 40fr multicolored 8.50 5.75

Soccer — A30a

Design: 50fr, Throwing the javelin.

1963, Aug. 29 Photo. Perf. 12½
203 A30a 20fr brt ultra & brown 4.50 3.50
204 A30a 50fr brt car rose & ultra 7.00 5.00

Issued to publicize the South Pacific Games, Suva, Aug. 29-Sept. 7.

Red Cross Centenary Issue
Common Design Type

1963, Sept. 2 Engr. Perf. 13
205 CD113 15fr vio brn, gray & car 9.00 6.50

Human Rights Issue
Common Design Type

1963, Dec. 10 Unwmk. Perf. 13
206 CD117 7fr green & vio bl 7.00 6.00

Philatec Issue
Common Design Type

1964, Apr. 9 Unwmk. Perf. 13
207 CD118 25fr grn, dk sl grn & red 7.50 5.75

Tahitian Dancer A31

1964, May 14 Engr. Perf. 13
208 A31 1fr multicolored 25 25
209 A31 3fr dp claret, blk & org 50 50

Soldiers, Truck and Battle Flag — A32

1964, July 10 Photo. Perf. 12½
210 A32 5fr multicolored 4.50 2.25

Issued to honor the Tahitian Volunteers of the Pacific Battalion. See No. C31.

Tuamotu Scene — A33

Views: 4fr, Borabora. 7fr, Papeete Harbor. 8fr, Paul Gauguin's tomb, Marquesas. 20fr, Mangareva, Gambier Islands.

1964, Dec. 1 Litho. *Perf. 12½x13*

211 A33 2fr multicolored 30 25
212 A33 4fr multicolored 60 25
213 A33 7fr multicolored 90 55
214 A33 8fr multicolored 1.10 55
215 A33 20fr multicolored 3.00 1.40
Nos. 211-215,C32 (6) 10.40 5.00

Painting from a School Dining Room — A34

1965, Nov. 29 Engr. *Perf. 13*

216 A34 20fr dk brn, sl grn & dk car 9.00 6.75

Issued to publicize the School Canteen Program. See No. C38.

Outrigger Canoe on Lagoon A35

Ships: 11fr, Large cruising yacht, vert. 12fr, Motorboat for sport fishing. 14fr, Outrigger canoes with sails. 19fr, Schooner, vert. 22fr, Modern coaster "Oiseau des Isles II."

1966, Aug. 30 Engr. *Perf. 13*

217 A35 10fr brt ultra, emer & mar 1.00 60
218 A35 11fr mar, dk bl & sl grn 1.25 1.10
219 A35 12fr emer, dk bl & red lil 1.75 1.40
220 A35 14fr brn, bl & sl grn 2.25 1.50
221 A35 19fr scar, sl grn & dp bl 3.00 1.50
222 A35 22fr multicolored 4.00 3.00
Nos. 217-222 (6) 13.25 9.10

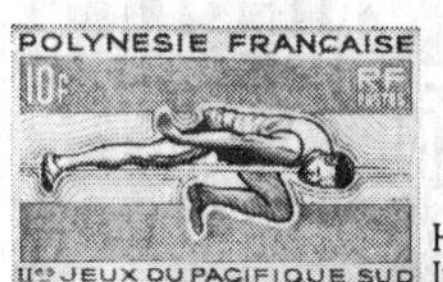

High Jump — A36

Designs: 20fr, Pole vault, vert. 40fr, Women's basketball, vert. 60fr, Hurdling.

1966, Dec. 15 Engr. *Perf. 13*

223 A36 10fr dk red, lem & blk 1.10 80
224 A36 20fr blue, emer & blk 2.50 1.20
225 A36 40fr emer, brt pink & blk 5.25 3.50
226 A36 60fr dull yel, bl & blk 9.00 6.00

2nd South Pacific Games, Nouméa, New Caledonia, Dec. 8-18.

15-Cent Minimum Value
The minimum catalogue value is 15 cents. Separating se-tenant pieces into individual stamps does not increase the value of the stamps since demand for the separated stamps may be small.

Poi Pounder A37

Javelin Throwing A38

1967, June 15 Engr. *Perf. 13*

227 A37 50fr orange & blk 8.50 5.00

Society for Oceanic Studies, 50th anniv.

1967, July 11

Designs: 5fr, Spring dance, horiz. 15fr, Horse race, horiz. 16fr, Fruit carriers' race. 21fr, Canoe race, horiz.

228 A38 5fr multicolored 80 70
229 A38 13fr multicolored 1.50 1.10
230 A38 15fr multicolored 1.65 1.40
231 A38 16fr multicolored 2.75 2.25
232 A38 21fr multicolored 5.00 3.50
Nos. 228-232 (5) 11.70 8.95

Issued to publicize the July Festival.

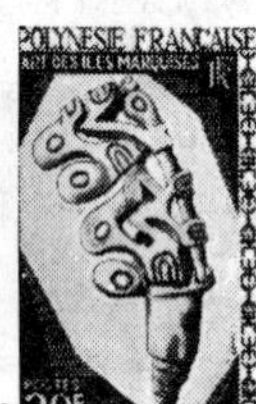

Earring — A39

Art of the Marquesas Islands: 10fr, Carved mother-of-pearl. 15fr, Decorated canoe paddle. 23fr, Oil vessel. 25fr, Carved stilt stirrups. 30fr, Fan handles. 35fr, Tattooed man. 50fr, Tikis.

1967-68 Engr. *Perf. 13*

233 A39 10fr dp cl, dl red & ultra 1.00 70
234 A39 15fr black & emerald 1.65 95
235 A39 20fr ol gray, dk car & lt bl 2.00 1.50
236 A39 23fr dk brn, ocher & bl 3.00 2.50
237 A39 25fr dk brn, dk bl & lil 3.75 2.50
238 A39 30fr brown & red lilac 5.00 2.75
239 A39 35fr ultra & dk brn 6.75 4.50
240 A39 50fr brn, sl grn & lt bl 7.25 5.00
Nos. 233-240 (8) 30.40 20.40

Issue dates: 20fr, 25fr, 30fr, 50fr, Dec. 19, 1967; others Feb. 28, 1968.

WHO Anniversary Issue
Common Design Type

1968, May 4 Engr. *Perf. 13*

241 CD126 15fr bl grn, mar & dp vio 4.00 1.90
242 CD126 16fr orange, lil & bl grn 4.75 2.50

Human Rights Year Issue
Common Design Type

1968, Aug. 10 Engr. *Perf. 13*

243 CD127 15fr blue, red & brn 4.25 3.25
244 CD127 16fr brn, brt pink & ultra 5.00 4.50

Tiare Apetahi — A40

Flower: 17fr, Tiare Tahiti.

1969, Mar. 27 Photo. *Perf. 12½x13*

245 A40 9fr multicolored 1.75 95
246 A40 17fr multicolored 2.50 1.40

Runner — A41

Designs: 9fr, Boxer, horiz. 17fr, High jump. 22fr, Long jump.

1969, Aug. 13 Engr. *Perf. 13*

247 A41 9fr blue, vio & sep 1.40 65
248 A41 17fr red, sep & cl 2.25 1.40
249 A41 18fr blue, brn ol & cl 3.50 2.25
250 A41 22fr brt green & choc 5.00 3.50

3rd South Pacific Games, Port Moresby, Papua and New Guinea, Aug. 13-23.

ILO Issue
Common Design Type

1969, Nov. 24 Engr. *Perf. 13*

251 CD131 17fr orange, emer & ol 4.25 2.75
252 CD131 18fr org, dk brn & vio bl 5.50 3.75

Territorial Assembly A42

Buildings: 14fr, Governor's Residence. 17fr, House of Tourism. 18fr, Maeva Hotel. 24fr, Taharaa Hotel.

1969, Dec. 22 Photo. *Perf. 12½x12*

253 A42 13fr black & multi 1.10 60
254 A42 14fr black & multi 1.50 1.00
255 A42 17fr black & multi 2.25 1.50
256 A42 18fr black & multi 3.25 1.50
257 A42 24fr black & multi 5.00 3.00
Nos. 253-257 (5) 13.10 7.60

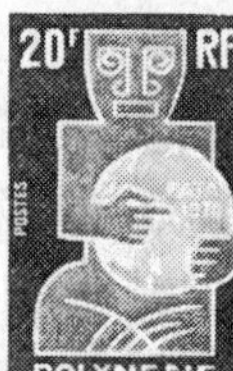

Stone Figure with Globe — A43

Designs: 40fr, Globe, plane, map of Polynesia and men holding "PATA" sign, horiz. 60fr, Polynesian carrying globe.

1970, Apr. 7 Engr. *Perf. 13*

258 A43 20fr deep plum, gray & bl 2.25 1.90
259 A43 40fr emer, rose lil & ultra 5.25 3.75
260 A43 60fr red brn, bl & dk brn 8.75 8.25

Issued to publicize the 1970 Pacific Area Travel Association Congress (PATA).

UPU Headquarters Issue
Common Design Type

1970, May 20 Engr. *Perf. 13*

261 CD133 18fr maroon, pur & brn 5.00 3.75
262 CD133 20fr lilac rose, ol & ind 6.50 4.50

Night Fishing — A44

1971, May 11 Photo. *Perf. 13*

263 A44 10fr multicolored 6.00 3.00

See Nos. C71-C73.

Flowers — A45

Designs: Various flowers. 12fr is horiz.

Perf. 12½x13, 13x12½

1971, Aug. 27

264 A45 8fr multicolored 90 75
265 A45 12fr multicolored 1.75 1.10
266 A45 22fr multicolored 3.25 2.25

Day of a Thousand Flowers.

Water-skiing Slalom — A46

Designs: 20fr, Water-skiing, jump, vert. 40fr, Figure water-skiing.

1971, Oct. 11 Engr. *Perf. 13*

267 A46 10fr grnsh bl, dk red & brn 1.75 1.50
268 A46 20fr carmine, emer & brn 4.50 2.75
269 A46 40fr brown, green & lilac 8.75 7.25

World water-skiing championships, Oct. 1971.

De Gaulle Issue
Common Design Type

Designs: 30fr, Gen. de Gaulle, 1940. 50fr, Pres. de Gaulle, 1970.

1971, Nov. 9 Engr. *Perf. 13*

270 CD134 30fr red lilac & blk 5.25 4.25
271 CD134 50fr red lilac & blk 7.75 6.75

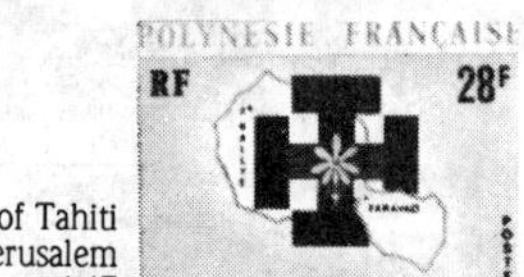

Map of Tahiti and Jerusalem Cross — A47

1971, Dec. 18 Photo. *Perf. 13x12½*

272 A47 28fr lt blue & multi 7.50 5.75

2nd rally of French Boy Scouts and Guides, Taravao, French Polynesia.

"Alcoholism" A48

Mother and Child A49

1972, Mar. 24 Photo. *Perf. 13*

273 A48 20fr brown & multi 4.00 2.75

Fight against alcoholism.

1973, Sept. 26 Photo. *Perf. 12½x13*

274 A49 28fr pale yellow & multi 4.50 2.25

Day nursery.

Polynesian Golfer — A50

Design: 24fr, Atimaono Golf Course.

1974, Feb. 27 Photo. *Perf. 13*
275 A50 16fr multicolored 3.00 1.10
276 A50 24fr multicolored 3.50 1.75

Atimaono Golf Course.

Hand Throwing Life Preserver to Puppy — A51

1974, May 9 Photo. *Perf. 13*
277 A51 21fr brt blue & multi 6.00 3.00

Society for the Protection of Animals.

Around a Fire, on the Beach — A52

Polynesian Views: 2fr, Lagoons and mountains. 6fr, Pebble divers. 10fr, Lonely Mountain and flowers, vert. 15fr, Sailing ship at sunset. 20fr, Lagoon and mountain.

1974, May 22
278 A52 2fr multicolored 25 25
279 A52 5fr multicolored 50 45
280 A52 6fr multicolored 65 42
281 A52 10fr multicolored 75 55
282 A52 15fr multicolored 1.65 75
283 A52 20fr multicolored 2.50 1.25
Nos. 278-283 (6) 6.30 3.67

Polynesian Woman and UPU Emblem — A53

Lion, Sun and Emblem — A54

1974, Oct. 9 Engr. *Perf. 13*
284 A53 65fr multicolored 6.50 4.00

Centenary of Universal Postal Union.

1975, June 17 Photo.
285 A54 26fr multicolored 5.50 2.00

15th anniv. of Lions Intl. in Tahiti.

Fish and Leaf A55

1975, July 9 Litho. *Perf. 12*
286 A55 19fr dp ultra & green 4.00 2.50

Polynesian Association for the Protection of Nature.

Georges Pompidou, Pres. of France — A55a

1976, Feb. 16 Engr. *Perf. 13*
287 A55a 49fr dk violet & black 5.00 3.75

See France No. 1430.

Alain Gerbault and Sailboat — A56

1976, May 25 Photo. *Perf. 13*
288 A56 90fr multicolored 7.50 6.50

50th anniversary of Alain Gerbault's arrival in Bora Bora.

Turtle — A57

Design: 42fr, Hand protecting bird.

1976, June 24 Litho. *Perf. 12½*
289 A57 18fr multicolored 3.75 1.50
290 A57 42fr multicolored 6.25 4.25

World Ecology Day.

A. G. Bell, Telephone, Radar and Satellite — A58

1976, Sept. 15 Engr. *Perf. 13*
291 A58 37fr multicolored 5.25 2.50

Centenary of first telephone call by Alexander Graham Bell, Mar. 10, 1876.

Dugout Canoes — A59

1976, Dec. 16 Litho. *Perf. 13x12½*
292 A59 25fr Marquesas 1.25 85
293 A59 30fr Raiatea 1.90 1.25
294 A59 75fr Tahiti 4.50 2.50
295 A59 100fr Tuamotu 6.50 4.50

Sailing Ship A60

Designs: Various sailing vessels.

1977, Dec. 22 Litho. *Perf. 13*
296 A60 20fr multicolored 1.25 90
297 A60 50fr multicolored 2.50 1.25
298 A60 85fr multicolored 3.50 2.25
299 A60 120fr multicolored 4.75 3.50

Hibiscus — A61

Girl with Shells on Beach — A62

Designs: 10fr, Vanda orchids. 16fr, Pua (fagraea berteriana). 22fr, Gardenia.

1978-79 Photo. *Perf. 12½x13*
300 A61 10fr multicolored 35 24
301 A61 13fr multicolored 90 55
302 A61 16fr multicolored 1.25 55
303 A61 22fr multicolored 60 42

Issue dates: Nos. 301-302, Aug. 23, 1978; Nos. 300, 303, Jan. 25, 1979.

1978, Nov. 3 Engr. *Perf. 13*

Designs (as type A24 with "1958 1978" added): 28fr, Man with headdress. 36fr, Girl playing guitar.

304 A62 20fr multicolored 1.10 32
305 A62 28fr multicolored 1.75 65
306 A62 36fr multicolored 2.25 1.00
a. Souvenir sheet of 3 9.50 9.50

20th anniv. of stamps inscribed: Polynesie Française. #306a contains #304-306 in changed colors.

Ships A63

1978, Dec. 29 Litho. *Perf. 13x12½*
307 A63 15fr Tahiti 90 75
308 A63 30fr Monowai 1.25 1.00
309 A63 75fr Tahitien 3.00 2.50
310 A63 100fr Mariposa 4.50 2.50

Porites Coral — A64

Design: 37fr, Montipora coral.

1979, Feb. 15 *Perf. 13x12½*
311 A64 32fr multicolored 1.50 70
312 A64 37fr multicolored 2.00 90

Raiatea — A65

Landscapes: 1fr, Moon over Bora Bora. 2fr, Mountain peaks, Ua Pou. 3fr, Sunset over Motu Tapu. 6fr, Palm and hut, Tuamotu.

1979, Mar. 8 Photo. *Perf. 13x13½*
313 A65 1fr multicolored 15 15
314 A65 2fr multicolored 15 15
315 A65 3fr multicolored 15 15
316 A65 4fr multicolored 22 15
317 A65 5fr multicolored 38 15
318 A65 6fr multicolored 45 38
Nos. 313-318 (6) 1.50
Set value 75

See Nos. 438-443 for redrawn designs.

Dance Costumes A66

1979, July 14 Litho. *Perf. 12½*
319 A66 45fr Fetia 1.25 80
320 A66 51fr Teanuanua 1.75 90
321 A66 74fr Temaeva 2.50 1.65

Hill, Great Britain No. 53, Tahiti No. 28 A67

1979, Aug. 1 Engr. *Perf. 13*
322 A67 100fr multicolored 3.50 2.75

Sir Rowland Hill (1795-1879), originator of penny postage.

Hastula Strigilata — A68

Statue Holding Rotary Emblem — A69

Shells: 28fr, Scabricola variegata. 35fr, Fusinus undatus.

1979, Aug. 21 **Litho.** ***Perf. 12½***

323	A68	20fr	multicolored	65	50
324	A68	28fr	multicolored	80	50
325	A68	35fr	multicolored	1.50	1.10

1979, Nov. 30 **Litho.** ***Perf. 13***

326	A69	47fr	multicolored	1.75	1.10

Rotary International, 75th anniversary; Papeete Rotary Club, 20th anniversary.

For overprint see No. 330.

Myripristis Murdjan A70

Fish: 8fr, Napoleon. 12fr, Emperor.

1980, Jan. 21 **Litho.** ***Perf. 12½***

327	A70	7fr	multicolored	40	24
328	A70	8fr	multicolored	40	24
329	A70	12fr	multicolored	70	40

No. 326 Overprinted and Surcharged in Gold: "75eme / ANNIVERSAIRE / 1905-1980"

1980, Feb. 23 **Litho.** ***Perf. 13***

330	A69	77fr	on 47fr multi	2.50	1.75

Rotary International, 75th anniversary.

CNEXO Fish Hatchery A71

1980, Mar. 17 **Photo.** ***Perf. 13x13½***

331	A71	15fr	shown	65	45
332	A71	22fr	Crayfish	75	50

Papeete Post Office Building Opening A72

1980, May 5 **Photo.** ***Perf. 13x12½***

333	A72	50fr	multicolored	1.50	1.10

Tiki and Festival Emblem — A73

1980, June 30 **Photo.** ***Perf. 13½***

334	A73	34fr	shown	65	50
335	A73	39fr	Drum (pahu)	90	70
336	A73	49fr	Ax (to'i)	1.75	1.25
a.			Souvenir sheet of 3, #334-336	5.00	5.00

South Pacific Arts Festival, Port Moresby, Papua New Guinea.

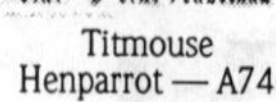

Titmouse Henparrot — A74

Charles de Gaulle — A75

Perf. 13x12½, 12½x13

1980, Oct. 20 **Photo.**

337	A74	25fr	White sea-swallow, horiz.	70	45
338	A74	35fr	shown	80	65
339	A74	45fr	Minor frigate bird, horiz.	1.10	85

1980, Nov. 9 **Engr.** ***Perf. 12½x13***

340	A75	100fr	multicolored	3.00	2.25

Naso Vlamingi (Karaua) A76

1981, Feb. 5 **Litho.** ***Perf. 12½***

341	A76	13fr	shown	55	42
342	A76	16fr	Lutjanus vaigensis (toau)	70	42
343	A76	24fr	Plectropomus leopardus (tonu)	1.00	55

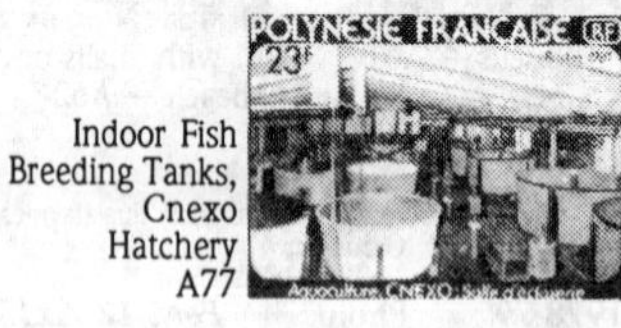

Indoor Fish Breeding Tanks, Cnexo Hatchery A77

1981, May 14 **Photo.** ***Perf. 13x13½***

344	A77	23fr	shown	55	45
345	A77	41fr	Mussels	90	60

Folk Dancers A78

Perf. 13x13½, 13½x13

1981, July 10 **Litho.**

346	A78	26fr	shown	55	35
347	A78	28fr	Dancer	60	48
348	A78	44fr	Dancers, vert.	1.10	70

Sterna Bergii — A79

1981, Sept. 24 **Litho.** ***Perf. 13***

349	A79	47fr	shown	90	60
350	A79	53fr	Ptilinopus purpuratus, vert.	1.10	70
351	A79	65fr	Estrilda astrild, vert.	1.25	1.10

See Nos. 370-372.

Huahine Island — A80

1981, Oct. 22 **Litho.** ***Perf. 12½***

352	A80	34fr	shown	65	45
353	A80	134fr	Maupiti	2.00	1.25
354	A80	136fr	Bora-Bora	2.00	1.25

A81

1982, Feb. 4 **Photo.** ***Perf. 13x13½***

355	A81	30fr	Parrotfish	60	52
356	A81	31fr	Regal angel	60	52
357	A81	45fr	Spotted bass	90	75

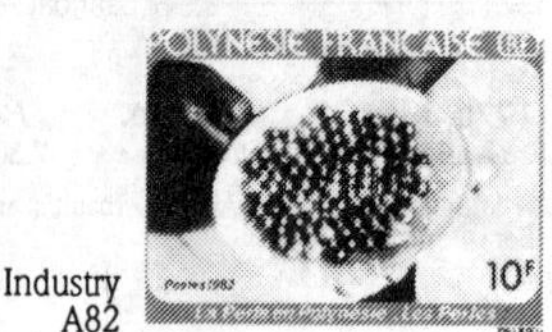

Pearl Industry A82

1982, Apr. 22 **Photo.** ***Perf. 13x13½***

358	A82	7fr	Pearl beds	15	15
359	A82	8fr	Extracting pearls	18	15
360	A82	10fr	Pearls	22	18

Tahiti "No. 1A," Emblem — A83

1982, May 12 **Engr.** ***Perf. 13***

361	A83	150fr	multicolored	3.75	3.25
a.			Souvenir sheet	9.00	9.00

PHILEXFRANCE Stamp Exhibition, Paris, June 11-21. No. 361a contains No. 361 in changed colors.

King Holding Carved Scepter — A84

Designs: Coronation ceremony.

1982, July 14 **Photo.** ***Perf. 13½x13***

362	A84	12fr	shown	25	15
363	A84	13fr	King, priest	25	15
364	A84	17fr	Procession	32	25

Championship Emblem — A85

1982, Aug. 13 ***Perf. 13***

365	A85	90fr	multicolored	1.65	1.40

4th Hobie-Cat 16 World Catamaran Sailing Championship, Tahiti, Aug. 15-21.

First Colloquium on New Energy Sources — A86

1982, Sept. 29 **Litho.**

366	A86	46fr	multicolored	80	65

Motu, Tuamotu Islet — A87

1982, Oct. 12 **Litho.** ***Perf. 13***

367	A87	20fr	shown	45	25
368	A87	33fr	Tupai Atoll	55	35
369	A87	35fr	Gambier Islds.	65	55

Bird Type of 1981

1982, Nov. 17 **Litho.** ***Perf. 13***

370	A79	37fr	Sacred egret	55	35
371	A79	39fr	Pluvialis dominica, vert.	65	45
372	A79	42fr	Lonchura castaneothorax	70	45

Fish — A88

1983, Feb. 9 **Litho.** ***Perf. 13x13½***

373	A88	8fr	Acanthurus lineatus	15	15
374	A88	10fr	Caranx melampygus	22	15
375	A88	12fr	Carcharhinus melanopterus	30	18

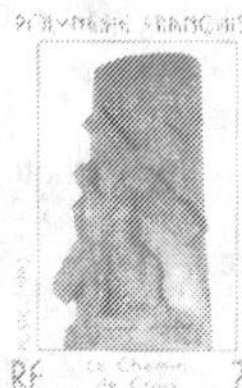

The Way of the Cross, Sculpture by Damien Haturau — A89

1983, Mar. 9 Litho. *Perf. 13*

376 A89 7fr shown 15 15
377 A89 21fr Virgin and Child 32 15
378 A89 23fr Christ 38 24
Set value 45

Traditional Hats — A90

1983, May 24 Litho. *Perf. 13x12½*

379 A90 11fr Acacia 18 18
380 A90 13fr Niau 25 18
381 A90 25fr Ofe 45 28
382 A90 35fr Ofe, diff. 65 42

See Nos. 393-396.

Chieftain in Traditional Costume, Sainte-Christine Isld. — A91

Traditional Costumes, Marquesas Islds.

1983, July 12 Photo. *Perf. 13*

383 A91 15fr shown 24 18
384 A91 17fr Man 30 24
385 A91 28fr Woman 42 30

See Nos. 397-399, 419-421.

Polynesian Crowns — A92

Various flower garlands.

1983, Oct. 19 Litho. *Perf. 13*

386 A92 41fr multicolored 65 55
387 A92 44fr multicolored 75 55
388 A92 45fr multicolored 75 55

See Nos. 400-402.

Martin Luther (1483-1546) — A93

Tiki Carvings — A94

1983, Nov. 19 Engr. *Perf. 13*

389 A93 90fr black, brn & lil gray 1.50 1.10

1984, Feb. 8 Litho. *Perf. 12½x13*

Various carvings.

390 A94 14fr multicolored 20 15
391 A94 16fr multicolored 25 16
392 A94 19fr multicolored 30 16

Hat Type of 1983

1984, June 20 Litho. *Perf. 13x12½*

393 A90 20fr Aeho ope 28 22
394 A90 24fr Paeore 35 22
395 A90 26fr Ofe fei 38 28
396 A90 33fr Hua 52 35

Costume Type of 1983

1984, Aug. 21 Litho. *Perf. 13*

397 A91 34fr Tahitian playing nose flute 50 30
398 A91 35fr Priest, Oei-eitia 50 30
399 A91 39fr Tahitian adult and child 52 35

Garland Type of 1983

1984, Oct. 24 Litho. *Perf. 13x12½*

400 A92 46fr Moto'i Lei 60 38
401 A92 47fr Pitate Lei 65 45
402 A92 53fr Bougainvillea Lei 75 55

4th Pacific Arts Festival, Noumea, New Caledonia, Dec. 8-22 — A95

1984, Nov. 20 Litho. *Perf. 13*

403 A95 150fr Statue, headdress 2.50 1.75

See No. C213.

Paysage D'Anaa, by Jean Masson — A96

Paintings: 50fr, Sortie Du Culte, by Jacques Boulaire. 75fr, La Fete, by Robert Tatin. 85fr, Tahitiennes Sur La Plage, by Pierre Heyman.

Perf. 12½x13, 13x12½

1984, Dec. 12 Litho.

404 A96 50fr multi, vert. 65 50
405 A96 65fr multicolored 80 50
406 A96 75fr multicolored 1.10 70
407 A96 85fr multicolored 1.25 90

Tiki Carvings — A97

Polynesian Faces — A98

1985, Jan. 23 Litho. *Perf. 13½*

408 A97 30fr multicolored 42 30
409 A97 36fr multicolored 50 40
410 A97 40fr multicolored 65 42

1985, Feb. 20 Photo. *Perf. 12½x13*

411 A98 22fr multicolored 28 20
412 A98 39fr multicolored 52 30
413 A98 44fr multicolored 55 45

Early Tahiti A99

Perf. 13x12½, 12½x13

1985, Apr. 24 Litho.

414 A99 42fr Entrance to Papeete 50 30
415 A99 45fr Girls, vert. 52 35
416 A99 48fr Papeete market 55 35

5th Intl. Congress on Coral Reefs, Tahiti A100

1985, May 28 Litho. *Perf. 13½*

417 A100 140fr Local reef formation 1.50 1.40

Printed se-tenant with label picturing congress emblem.

National Flag — A101

1985, June 28

418 A101 9fr Flag, natl. arms 20 15

Costume Type of 1983

18th-19th Cent. Prints, Beslu Collection.

1985, July 17 *Perf. 13*

419 A91 38fr Tahitian dancer 55 35
420 A91 55fr Man and woman from Otahiti, 1806 70 55
421 A91 70fr Traditional chief 1.00 70

Local Foods — A103

1985-86 Litho. *Perf. 13*

422 A103 25fr Roasted pig 38 25
423 A103 35fr Pit fire 50 38
423A A103 80fr Fish in coconut milk 1.25 75
423B A103 110fr Fafaru 1.65 1.25

Issue dates: 25fr, 35fr, Nov. 14. 80fr, 110fr, May 20, 1986.

See Nos. 458-459, 474-475.

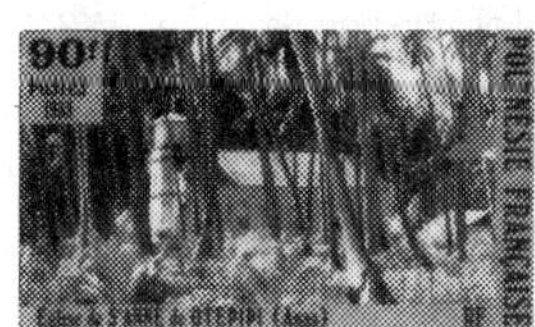

Catholic Churches — A104

1985, Dec. 11 Litho. *Perf. 13*

424 A104 90fr St. Anne's, Otepipi 1.50 1.10
425 A104 100fr St. Michael's Cathedral, Rikitea 1.65 1.25
426 A104 120fr Cathedral, exterior 2.00 1.50

Nos. 424-426 printed se-tenant with labels picturing local religious art.

Crabs A105

1986, Jan. 22 *Perf. 13½*

427 A105 18fr Fiddler 35 22
428 A105 29fr Hermit 55 35
429 A105 31fr Coconut 60 38

Faces of Polynesia A106

Perf. 12½x13, 13x12½

1986, Feb. 19

430 A106 43fr Boy, fish 75 50
431 A106 49fr Boy, coral 85 55
432 A106 51fr Boy, turtle, vert. 90 58

Old Tahiti A107

1986, Mar. 18 *Perf. 13x12½*

433 A107 52fr Papeete 90 60
434 A107 56fr Harpoon fishing 95 65
435 A107 57fr Royal Palace, Papeete 95 68

Tiki Rock Carvings — A108

1986, Apr. 16

436 A108 58fr Atuona, Hiva Oa 1.10 68
437 A108 59fr Ua Huka Hill, Hane Valley 1.10 70

Landscapes Type of 1979 Redrawn

1986-87 Litho. *Perf. 13½*

438 A65 1fr multicolored ('87) 15 15
439 A65 2fr multicolored 15 15
440 A65 3fr multicolored 15 15
441 A65 4fr multicolored ('87) 15 15
442 A65 5fr multicolored 15 15
443 A65 6fr multicolored 15 15
Set value 60 50

Nos. 439-440, 442-443 printed in sharper detail, box containing island name is taller and margin inscribed "CARTOR" instead of "DELRIEU."

Nos. 438, 441 printed in sharper detail, box containing island name is taller and margin is without "CARTOR" or "DELRIEU" inscription.

Traditional Crafts A109

Perf. 13x12½, 12½x13

1986, July 17 Litho.

444 A109 8fr Quilting, vert. 15 15
445 A109 10fr Baskets, hats 18 15
446 A109 12fr Grass skirts 22 16

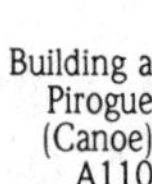

Building a Pirogue (Canoe) A110

1986, Oct. 21 **Litho.** *Perf. 13½*

447 A110 46fr Boat-builders 60 42
448 A110 50fr Close-up 60 48

Medicinal Plants — A111 Polynesians — A112

1986, Nov. 19 *Perf. 13*

449 A111 40fr Phymatosorus 60 45
450 A111 41fr Barringtonia asiatica 62 45
451 A111 60fr Ocimum bacilicum 90 68

See Nos. 495-497.

1987, Jan. 21 **Litho.** *Perf. 13½*

452 A112 28fr Old man 42 32
453 A112 30fr Mother and child 45 35
454 A112 37fr Old woman 55 42

Crustaceans A113

1987, Feb. 18 *Perf. 12½x13*

455 A113 34fr Carpilius maculatus 42 32
456 A113 35fr Parribacus antarticus 45 32
457 A113 39fr Justitia longimana 45 24

Local Foods Type of 1985

1987, Mar. 19 **Litho.** *Perf. 13*

458 A103 33fr Papaya poe 50 38
459 A103 65fr Chicken fafa 1.00 75

Polynesian Petroglyphs — A114

1987, May 13 *Perf. 12½*

460 A114 13fr Tipaerui, Tahiti 20 15
461 A114 21fr Turtle, Raiatea Is. 32 24

Calling Devices and Musical Instruments, Museum of Tahiti and the Isles — A115

1987, July 1 *Perf. 13½*

462 A115 20fr Wood horn 30 24
463 A115 26fr Triton's conch 40 30
464 A115 33fr Nose flutes 50 38

Medicinal Plants — A116

1987, Sept. 16 *Perf. 12½x13*

465 A116 46fr Thespesia populnea 70 52
466 A116 53fr Ophioglossum reticulatum 80 60
467 A116 54fr Dicrocephala latifolia 82 62

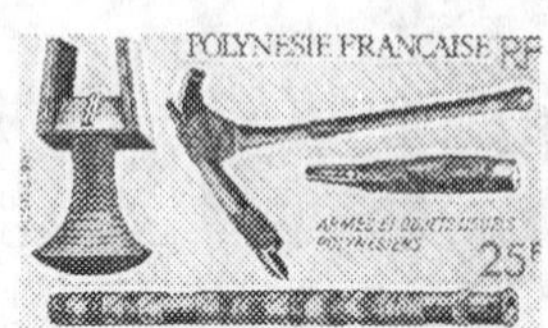

Ancient Weapons and Tools — A117

Designs: 25fr, Adze, war club, chisel, flute. 27fr, War clubs, tatooing comb, mallet. 32fr, Headdress, necklaces, nose flute.

1987, Oct. 14 **Engr.** *Perf. 13*

468 A117 25fr lt olive grn & blk 55 42
469 A117 27fr Prus grn & int blue 58 45
470 A117 32fr brt olive bis & brn blk 70 52

Catholic Missionaries — A118

Monsignors: 95fr, Rene Ildefonse Dordillon (1808-1888), bishop of the Marquesas Isls. 105fr, Tepano Jaussen (1815-1891), first bishop of Polynesia. 115fr, Paul Laurent Maze (1885-1976), archbishop of Papeete.

1987, Nov. 9 **Litho.**

471 A118 95fr multicolored 2.00 1.50
472 A118 105fr multicolored 2.25 1.70
473 A118 115fr multicolored 2.50 1.90

Local Foods Type of 1985

1988, Jan. 12 **Litho.** *Perf. 13*

474 A103 40fr Crayfish (varo) 78 58
475 A103 75fr Bananas in coconut milk 1.50 1.15

Nos. 474-475 are vert.

Authors — A119

Designs: 62fr, James Norman Hall (1887-1951). 85fr, Charles Bernard Nordhoff (1887-1947).

1988, Feb. 10

476 A119 62fr multicolored 1.20 90
477 A119 85fr multicolored 1.70 2.25

Traditional Housing — A120

Designs: 11fr, Taranpoo Opoa Is., Raiatea. 15fr, Tahaa Village. 17fr, Community meeting house, Tahiti.

1988, Mar. 16 **Litho.** *Perf. 13x12½*

478 A120 11fr multicolored 25 18
479 A120 15fr multicolored 32 25
480 A120 17fr multicolored 38 28

Point Venus Lighthouse, 120th Anniv. — A121

1988, Apr. 21 **Litho.** *Perf. 13*

481 A121 400fr multicolored 8.00 6.00

Tapa-cloth Paintings by Paul Engdahl A122

1988, May 20

482 A122 52fr multicolored 1.00 75
483 A122 54fr multicolored 1.05 78
484 A122 64fr multicolored 1.25 95

POLYSAT (Domestic Communications Network) — A123

1988, June 15 **Litho.** *Perf. 12½x12*

485 A123 300fr multicolored 6.00 4.75

Tahitian Dolls — A124

Designs: 42fr, Wearing grass skirt and headdress. 45fr, Wearing print dress and straw hat, holding guitar. 48fr, Wearing print dress and straw hat, holding straw bag.

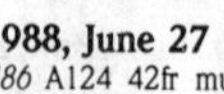

1988, June 27 *Perf. 13x12½*

486 A124 42fr multicolored 80 60
487 A124 45fr multicolored 85 65
488 A124 48fr multicolored 92 70

Visiting a Marae at Nuku Hiva, Engraving by J. & E. Verreaux A125

1988, Aug. 1 **Engr.** *Perf. 13*

489 A125 68fr black brown 1.25 95

Size: 143x101mm

490 A125 145fr violet brn & grn 2.65 2.65

SYDPEX '88, July 30-Aug. 7, Australia. No. 490 pictures a Russian navy officer (probably Krusenstern) visiting the Marquesas Islanders; denomination LR.

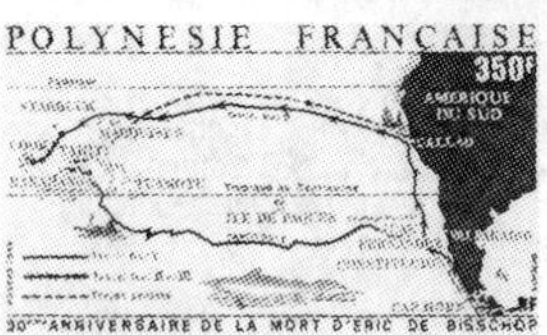

Map Linking South America and South Pacific Islands — A126

1988, Aug. 30 **Engr.**

491 A126 350fr multicolored 6.50 4.75

Eric de Bisschop (1890-1958), explorer who tried to prove that there was an exchange of peoples between the South Pacific islands and So. America, rather than that the island populations originated from So. America.

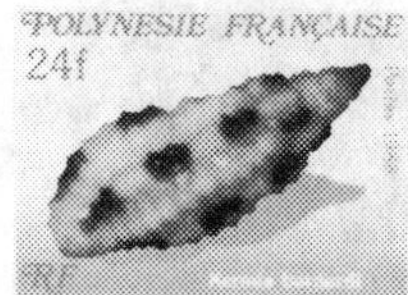

Seashells A127

1988, Sept. 21 **Litho.** *Perf. 13½*

492 A127 24fr Kermia barnardi 42 32
493 A127 35fr Vexillum suavis 62 48
494 A127 44fr Berthelinia 78 58

Medicinal Plants Type of 1986

1988, Oct. 18 **Engr.** *Perf. 13*

495 A111 23fr Davallia solida 40 30
496 A111 36fr Rorippa sarmentosa 65 48
497 A111 49fr Lindernia crustacea 88 65

Protestant Missionaries — A128

1988, Dec. 7 **Litho.**

498 A128 80fr Henry Nott (1774-1844) 1.40 1.05
499 A128 90fr Papeiha (1800-40) 1.60 1.20
500 A128 100fr Samuel Raapoto (1921-76) 1.75 1.30

Tahiti Post Office A129

1989, Jan. 12 **Engr.**
501 A129 30fr P.O., 1875 55 40
502 A129 40fr P.O., 1915 75 55

Center for Arts and Crafts A130

1989, Feb. 15 **Litho.** *Perf. 12½*
503 A130 29fr Marquesas Is. lidded bowl 52 38
504 A130 31fr Mother-of-pearl pendant 58 42

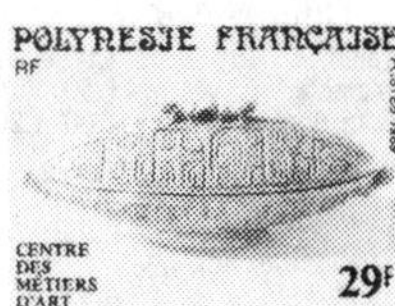
Copra Industry — A131

1989, Mar. 16 **Litho.** *Perf. 13*
505 A131 55fr Extracting copra from shell with a pa'aro, vert. *47.50 47.50*
506 A131 70fr shown *1.25* 95

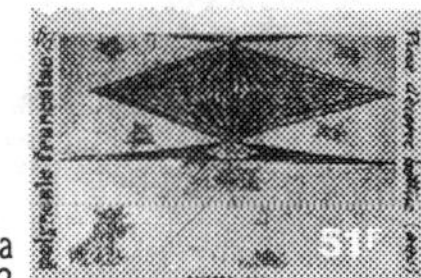
Tapa Art — A132

Designs: 43fr, Wood statue (pole), Marquesas Islands, vert. 51fr, Hand-painted bark tapestry, Society Is. 56fr, Concentric circles, Tubuai, Austral Islands.

1989, Apr. 18 **Litho.** *Perf. 13½*
507 A132 43fr multicolored 75 58
508 A132 51fr shown 88 65
509 A132 56fr multicolored 95 72

Polynesian Environment A133

1989, May 17 **Litho.** *Perf. 13x12½*
510 A133 120fr shown 2.15 1.00
511 A133 140fr Diving for seashells 2.50 1.90

Polynesian Folklore A134

Perf. 13x12½, 12½x13
1989, June 28 **Litho.**
512 A134 47fr Stone-lifting contest, vert. 80 60
513 A134 61fr Dancer, vert. 1.05 78
514 A134 67fr Folk singers 1.15 88

Bounty Castaways, from an Etching by Robert Dodd — A135

1989, July 7 **Engr.** *Perf. 13*
515 A135 100fr dp blue & bl grn 1.70 1.25

Souvenir Sheet
Imperf
516 A135 200fr dk ol grn & dk brn 3.75 3.75

PHILEXFRANCE '89 and 200th annivs. of the mutiny on the *Bounty* and the French revolution.
No. 515 printed se-tenant with label picturing exhibition emblem.

Reverend-Father Patrick O'Reilly (1900-1988) A136

1989, Aug. 7 **Engr.** *Perf. 13x13½*
517 A136 52fr yel brn & myrtle grn 88 65

Miniature Sheet

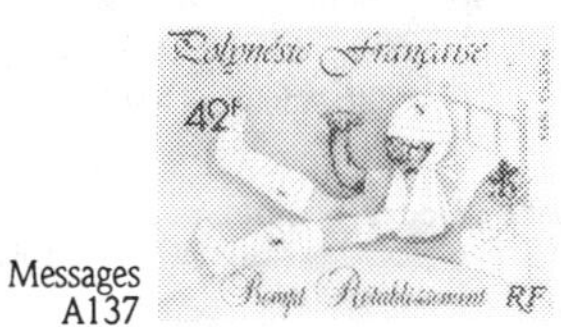
Messages A137

Messages: a, Get well soon. b, Good luck. c, Happy birthday. d, Keep in touch. e, Congratulations.

1989, Sept. 27 **Litho.** *Perf. 12½*
518 A137 42fr Sheet of 5, #a.-e. 3.50 3.50

Sea Shells A138

1989, Oct. 12 **Litho.** *Perf. 13½*
523 A138 60fr Triphoridae 1.05 80
524 A138 69fr Muricidae favartia 1.20 90
525 A138 73fr Muricidae morula 1.25 95

Te Faaturama, c. 1892, by Gauguin A139

1989, Nov. 19 **Litho.** *Perf. 12½x13*
526 A139 1000fr multicolored 17.25 13.00

Legends — A140

Designs: 66fr, Maui, birth of the islands, vert. 82fr, Mt. Rotui, the pierced mountain. 88fr, Princess Hina and the eel King of Lake Vaihiria.

1989, Dec. 6 **Litho.** *Perf. 13*
527 A140 66fr olive brn & blk 1.15 88
528 A140 82fr buff & blk 1.45 1.10
529 A140 88fr cream & blk 1.55 1.15

Vanilla Orchid — A141

1990, Jan. 11 **Litho.**
530 A141 34fr Flower 65 48
531 A141 35fr Bean pods 68 50

Marine Life — A142

1990, Feb. 9 **Litho.** *Perf. 13½*
532 A142 40fr *Kuhlia marginata* 78 58
533 A142 50fr *Macrobrachium* 98 75

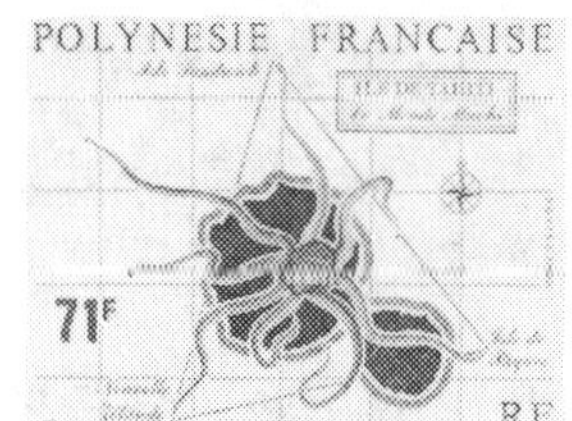
Tahiti, Center of Polynesian Triangle — A143

Maohi settlers and maps of island settlements: 58fr, Hawaiian Islands. 59fr, Easter Island. 63fr, New Zealand.

1990, Mar. 14 **Engr.** *Perf. 13*
534 A143 58fr black 1.25 82
535 A143 59fr bluish gray 1.25 85
536 A143 63fr olive green 1.35 90
537 A143 71fr Prussian blue 1.50 1.00

See Nos. 544-545.

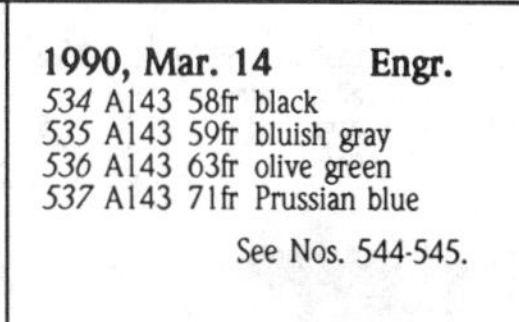
Papeete Village, Cent. — A144

1990, May 16 **Litho.**
538 A144 150fr New City Hall 3.25 2.25
539 A144 250fr Old Town Hall 5.25 3.65

A145

A146

Designs: Endangered birds.

1990, June 5 *Perf. 13½*
540 A145 13fr Porzana tabuensis 25 20
541 A145 20fr Vini ultramarina 40 30

1990, July 10 *Perf. 13*
542 A146 39fr multicolored 75 58

Lions Club in Papeete, 30th anniv.

Gen. Charles de Gaulle, Birth Cent. — A147

1990, Sept. 2 **Litho.**
543 A147 200fr multi 4.00 3.00

No. 536 with Different Colors and Inscriptions

1990, Aug. 24 **Engr.** *Perf. 13*
544 A143 125fr Man, map 2.60 2.00

Souvenir Sheet
Imperf
545 A143 230fr like No. 544 4.85 3.65

New Zealand 1990.

Intl. Tourism Day — A148

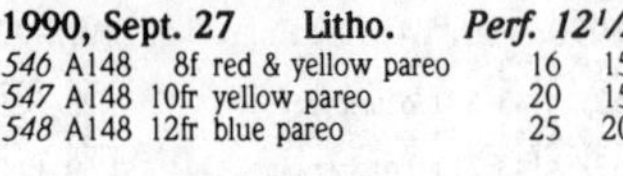

1990, Sept. 27 Litho. *Perf. 12½*

546 A148 8f red & yellow pareo 16 15
547 A148 10fr yellow pareo 20 15
548 A148 12fr blue pareo 25 20

Polynesian Legends — A149

Designs: 170fr, Legend of the Uru. 290fr, Pipirima, vert. 375fr, Hiro, God of Thieves, vert.

1990, Nov. 7 Litho. *Perf. 13*

549 A149 170fr multicolored 3.65 2.75
550 A149 290fr multicolored 6.25 4.70
551 A149 375fr multicolored 8.10 6.10

Tiare Flower — A150

Pineapple — A151

Designs: 28fr, Flower crown, lei. 30fr, Flowers in bloom. 37fr, Lei.

1990, Dec. 5 *Perf. 12½*

552 A150 28fr multicolored 60 45
553 A150 30fr multicolored 65 50
554 A150 37fr multicolored 80 60

1991, Jan. 9 *Die Cut*

Self-adhesive

555 A151 42fr shown 90 70
556 A151 44fr Pineapple field 95 75

#555-556 are on paper backing perf. 12½.

Marine Life — A152

1991, Feb. 7 *Perf. 12½*

557 A152 7fr Nudibranch 15 15
558 A152 9fr Galaxaura tenera 20 15
559 A152 11fr Adusta cumingii 25 20

Maohi Islands — A153

18th Century scenes of: 68fr, Woman of Easter Island, vert. 84fr, Twin-hulled canoe, Hawaii. 94fr, Maori village, New Zealand.

1991, Mar. 13 Engr. *Perf. 13*

560 A153 68fr olive 1.35 50
561 A153 84fr black 1.70 1.25
562 A153 94fr brown 1.90 1.40

Basketball, Cent. — A154

1991, May 15 Litho. *Perf. 13*

563 A154 80fr multicolored 1.60 1.25

Birds — A155

1991, June 5 *Perf. 13½*

564 A155 17fr Halcyon gambieri 35 26
565 A155 21fr Vini kuhlii 42 32

Still Life with Oranges in Tahiti by Paul Gauguin — A156

1991, June 9 Litho. *Perf. 13*

566 A156 700fr multicolored 15.00 11.25

Sculptures of the Marquesas Islands — A157

Designs: 56fr, White Tiki with Club, vert. 102fr, Warriors Carrying Tired Man, vert. 110fr, Native Canoe.

1991, July 17 Litho. *Perf. 13*

567 A157 56fr multicolored 1.10 82
568 A157 102fr multicolored 2.00 1.50
569 A157 110fr multicolored 2.25 1.75

Wolfgang Amadeus Mozart, Death Bicent. — A158

1991, Aug. 28 Engr. *Perf. 13x12½*

570 A158 100fr multicolored 2.00 1.50

Stone Fishing — A159

1991, Oct. 9 Litho. *Perf. 13*

571 A159 25fr Fishing boats, vert. 52 40
572 A159 57fr Man hurling stone, vert. 1.20 90
573 A159 62fr Trapped fish 1.30 1.00

Phila Nippon '91 — A160

Designs: 50fr, Drawings of marine life by Jules-Louis Lejeune, vert. 70fr, Sailing ship, La Coquille. 250fr, Contains designs from Nos. 574-575.

Perf. 12½x13, 13x12½

1991, Nov. 16 Engr.

574 A160 50fr multicolored 70 52
575 A160 70fr multicolored 1.00 75

Size: 100x75mm

Imperf

576 A160 250fr multicolored 3.45 3.45

Central Bank for Economic Co-operation, 50th Anniv. — A161

1991, Dec. 2 Litho. *Perf. 13x12½*

577 A161 307fr multicolored 6.50 4.90

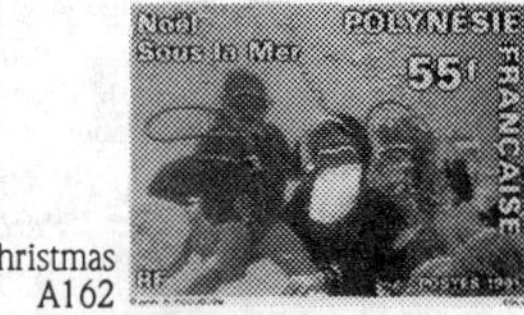

Christmas A162

Perf. 12½x13, 13x12½

1991, Dec. 11 Litho.

578 A162 55fr Scuba divers 1.00 75
579 A162 83fr Underwater scene 1.75 1.35
580 A162 86fr Nativity, vert. 2.00 1.50

Tourism — A163

1992, Feb. 12 *Perf. 13*

581 A163 1fr shown 15 15
582 A163 2fr Horses, beach 15 15
583 A163 3fr Girl holding fish 15 15
584 A163 4fr Waterfalls, vert. 15 15
585 A163 5fr Sailing 15 15
586 A163 6fr Waterfalls, helicopter, vert. 15 15
Set value 45 35

Views from Space — A164

1992, Mar. 18 Litho. *Perf. 13x12½*

587 A164 46fr Tahiti 1.00 75
588 A164 72fr Mataiva 1.50 1.15
589 A164 76fr Bora Bora 1.60 1.20

Size: 130x100mm

Imperf

590 A164 230fr Satellite imaging system 4.85 3.65

International Space Year.

World Health Day — A165

1992, Apr. 7 *Perf. 13½*

591 A165 136fr multicolored 3.00 2.25

Discovery of America, 500th Anniv. — A166

1992, May 22 *Perf. 13*

592 A166 130fr multicolored 2.85 2.15

Size: 140x100mm

Imperf

593 A166 250fr multicolored 5.50 4.10

World Columbian Stamp Expo '92, Chicago.

Traditional Dances — A167

Dance from: 95fr, Tahiti. 105fr, Hawaii. 115fr, Tonga.

1992, June 17 Engr. *Perf. 13*

594 A167 95fr brown black 2.25 1.65
595 A167 105fr olive brown 2.50 1.85
596 A167 115fr red brn & olive grn 2.75 2.00

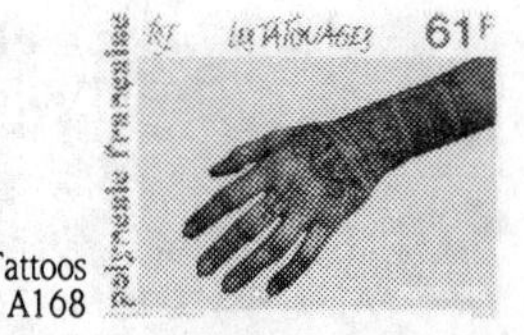

Tattoos A168

1992, July 8 Litho. *Perf. 12½*

597 A168 61fr Hand 1.30 95
598 A168 64fr Man, vert. 1.40 1.05

Children's Games A169

1992, Aug. 5 *Perf. 13½*

599 A169 22fr Outrigger canoe models	48	35
600 A169 31fr String game	65	45
601 A169 45fr Stilt game, vert.	98	70

Herman Melville, 150th Anniv. of Arrival in French Polynesia — A170

1992, Sept. 16 *Perf. 12½*

602 A170 78fr multicolored	1.70	1.25

6th Festival of Pacific Arts, Rarotonga — A171

Designs: 40fr, Men on raft. 65fr, Pirogues, Tahiti.

1992, Oct. 16 **Engr.** *Perf. 13*

603 A171 40fr lake	85	60
604 A171 65fr blue	1.40	1.00

First French Polynesian Postage Stamps, Cent. — A172

1992, Nov. 18 **Photo.** *Perf. 13*

605 A172 200fr multicolored	3.50	2.50

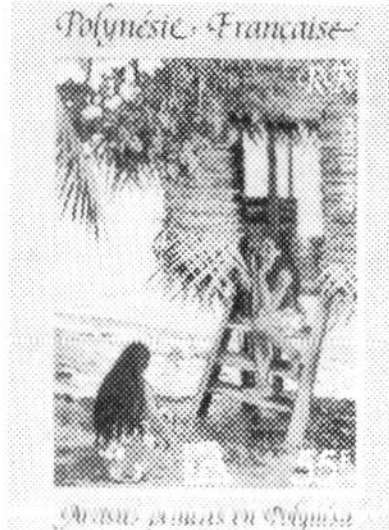

Paintings A173

Designs: 55fr, Two Women Talking, by Erhard Lux. 60fr, Bouquet of Flowers, by Uschi. 75fr, Spearfisherman, by Pierre Kienlen. 85fr, Mother Nursing Child, by Octave Morillot.

1992, Dec. 9 *Perf. 12½x13*

606 A173 55fr multicolored	1.20	85
607 A173 60fr multicolored	1.30	95
608 A173 75fr multicolored	1.60	1.15
609 A173 85fr multicolored	1.80	1.30

Net Thrower A174

Bonito Fishing A175

1993, Feb. 10 **Litho.** *Die Cut*

Self-Adhesive

Size: 17x23mm

610 A174 46fr blue & multi	90	70
611 A174 46fr green & multi	90	70
a. Booklet pane of 10	9.00	

1993, Mar. 10 *Perf. 13½*

612 A175 68fr Line & hook	1.30	1.00
613 A175 84fr Boat, horiz.	1.65	1.20
614 A175 86fr Drying catch	1.70	1.25

Allied Airfield on Bora Bora, 50th Anniv. — A176

1993, Apr. 5 *Perf. 13*

615 A176 120fr multicolored	2.35	1.75

Jacques Boullaire, Artist, Birth Cent. — A177

Various scenes depicting life on: 32fr, Moorea. 36fr, Tuamotu. 39fr, Rurutu. 51fr, Nuku Hiva.

1993, May 6 **Engr.**

616 A177 32fr brown black	65	48
617 A177 36fr brick red	70	52
618 A177 39fr violet	75	58
619 A177 51fr light brown	1.00	75

Sports Festival — A178

1993, May 15 **Litho.** *Perf. 12½*

620 A178 30fr multicolored	58	42

Australian Mathematics Competition, 15th Anniv. A179

1993, July 1 **Litho.** *Perf. 13½*

621 A179 70fr multicolored	1.35	1.00

Intl. Symposium on Inter-Plate Volcanism, French University of the Pacific, Punaauia — A180

1993, Aug. 2 **Litho.** *Perf. 13*

622 A180 140fr tan, black & brown	3.25	2.50

Taipei '93 — A181

Tourism — A182

1993, Aug. 14 **Litho.** *Perf. 13½*

623 A181 46fr multicolored	1.10	85

1993, Sept. 27

Designs: 14fr, Boat tour, horiz. 20fr, Groom preparing for traditional wedding. 29fr, Beachside brunch, horiz.

624 A182 14fr multicolored	48	35
625 A182 20fr multicolored	45	35
626 A182 29fr multicolored	65	45

Arrival of First French Gendarme in Tahiti, 150th Anniv. — A183

1993, Oct. 14 *Perf. 13*

627 A183 100fr multicolored	2.25	1.65

Alain Gerbault (1893-1941), Sailor — A184

1993, Nov. 17 **Engr.** *Perf. 13*

628 A184 150fr red, green & blue	3.50	2.75

Paintings — A185

Artists: 40fr, Vaea Sylvain. 70fr, A. Marere, vert. 80fr, J. Shelsher. 90fr, P.E. Victor, vert.

1993, Dec. 3 **Photo.** *Perf. 13*

629 A185 40fr multicolored	90	70
630 A185 70fr multicolored	1.65	1.25
631 A185 80fr multicolored	1.75	1.25
632 A185 90fr multicolored	2.00	1.50

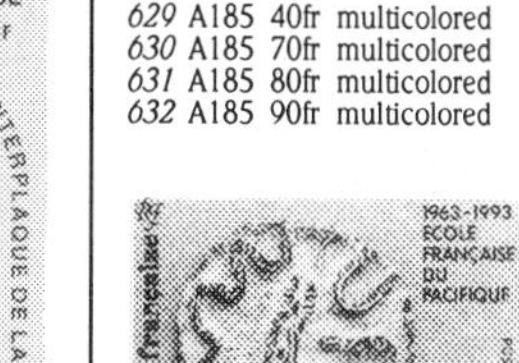

French School of the Pacific, 30th Anniv. A186

1993, Dec. 7 **Litho.** *Perf. 12½*

633 A186 200fr multicolored	4.75	3.50

Whales and Dolphins A187

1994, Jan. 12 **Litho.** *Perf. 13½*

634 A187 25fr Whale breeching	60	45
635 A187 68fr Dolphins	1.50	1.10
636 A187 72fr Humpback whales, vert.	1.65	1.25

SEMI-POSTAL STAMPS

Nos. 55 and 26 Surcharged in Red

1915 **Unwmk.** *Perf. 14x13½*

B1 A1 10c + 5c red	8.00	8.00
a. "e" instead of "c"	16.00	16.00
b. Inverted surcharge	42.50	37.50
B2 A2 10c + 5c rose & org	3.00	3.00
a. "e" instead of "c"	15.00	15.00
b. "c" inverted	15.00	15.00
c. Inverted surcharge	50.00	50.00

Surcharged in Carmine

B3 A2 10c + 5c rose & org	75	75
a. "e" instead of "c"	9.00	9.00
b. Inverted surcharge	50.00	50.00

Surcharged in Carmine +5c

1916

B4 A2 10c + 5c rose & org	75	75

Curie Issue

Common Design Type

1938 **Engr.** *Perf. 13*

B5 CD80 1.75fr + 50c brt ultra	5.50	5.50

Catalogue values for unused stamps in this section, from this point to the end of the section, are for Never Hinged items.

French Revolution Issue

Common Design Type

1939 **Photo.**

Name and Value Typo. in Black

B6 CD83 45c + 25c grn	5.00	5.00
B7 CD83 70c + 30c brn	5.00	5.00
B8 CD83 90c + 35c red org	5.00	5.00
B9 CD83 1.25fr + 1fr rose pink	5.00	5.00
B10 CD83 2.25fr + 2fr blue	5.00	5.00
Nos. B6-B10 (5)	25.00	25.00

Common Design Type and

Marine Officer — SP1

"L'Astrolabe" SP2

1941 Photo. *Perf. 13½*

B11	SP1	1fr + 1fr red	80
B12	CD86	1.50fr + 3fr maroon	80
B12A	SP2	2.50fr + 1fr blue	80

Nos. B11-B12A were issued by the Vichy government, and were not placed on sale in the colony.

Nos. 125A-125B were surcharged "OEUVRES COLONIALES" and surtax (including change of denomination of the 2.50fr to 50c). These were issued in 1944 by the Vichy government and not placed on sale in the colony.

Red Cross Issue
Common Design Type

1944 Photo. *Perf. 14½x14*

B13 CD90 5fr + 20fr peacock bl 45 45

The surtax was for the French Red Cross and national relief.

Tropical Medicine Issue
Common Design Type

1950 Engr. *Perf. 13*

B14 CD100 10fr + 2fr dk bl grn & dk grn 1.90 1.90

The surtax was for charitable work.

AIR POST STAMPS

Seaplane in Flight — AP1

Perf. 13½

1934, Nov. 5 Unwmk. Photo.

C1 AP1 5fr green 18 18

For overprint see No. C2.

Catalogue values for unused stamps in this section, from this point to the end of the section, are for Never Hinged items.

V4

Stamps of type AP1 without "RF" monogram and stamp of the above design were issued in 1944 by the Vichy Government, but were not placed on sale in the colony.

No. C1 Overprinted in Red **FRANCE LIBRE**

1941

C2 AP1 5fr green 1.75 1.75

Common Design Type

1942 *Perf. 14½x14*

C3 CD87	1fr dark orange	35	35
C4 CD87	1.50fr bright red	42	42
C5 CD87	5fr brown red	52	52
C6 CD87	10fr black	80	80
C7 CD87	25fr ultra	1.00	1.00
C8 CD87	50fr dark green	1.00	1.00
C9 CD87	100fr plum	1.00	1.00
	Nos. C3-C9 (7)	5.09	5.09

Victory Issue
Common Design Type

1946, May 8 Engr. *Perf. 12½*

C10 CD92 8fr dark green 1.00 1.00

Chad to Rhine Issue
Common Design Types

1946, June 6

C11 CD93	5fr red orange	90	90
C12 CD94	10fr dk olive bis	90	90
C13 CD95	15fr dk yellow grn	90	90
C14 CD96	20fr carmine	1.40	1.40
C15 CD97	25fr dk rose violet	1.40	1.40
C16 CD98	50fr black	2.25	2.25
	Nos. C11-C16 (6)	7.75	7.75

Shearwater and Moorea Landscape — AP2

Fishermen — AP3

Shearwater over Maupiti Shoreline — AP4

1948, Mar. 1 Unwmk. *Perf. 13*

C17 AP2	50fr red brown	11.00	7.50
C18 AP3	100fr purple	8.00	5.75
C19 AP4	200fr blue green	22.50	13.00

UPU Issue
Common Design Type

1949

C20 CD99 10fr deep blue 7.50 7.50

Bahia Peak, Borabora — AP6

Mother-of-Pearl Artist — AP7

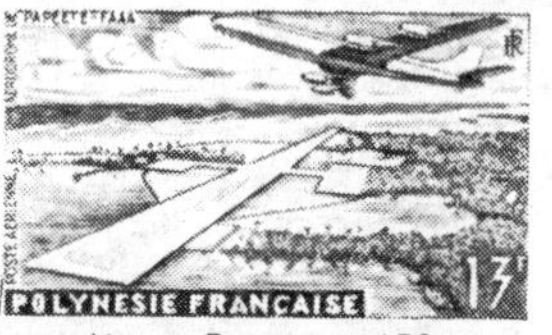

Airport, Papeete — AP8

Tahitian Dancer — AP10

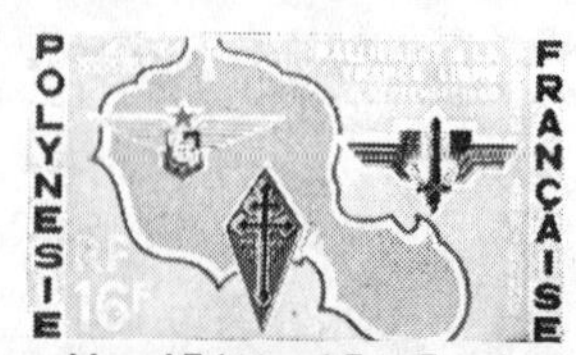

Map of Tahiti and Free French Emblems — AP11

Moorea Scene — AP12

Paul Gauguin — AP13

Skin Diver with Spear Gun AP14

Painting from a School Dining Room — AP15

Radio Tower, Globe and Palm — AP16

Gauguin's "Nafea faaipoipo" — AP5

1953, Sept. 24

C21 AP5 14fr dk brn, dk gray grn & red 45.00 40.00

50th anniv. of the death of Paul Gauguin.

Liberation Issue
Common Design Type

1954, June 6

C22 CD102 3fr dk grnsh bl & bl grn 2.00 2.00

1955, Sept. 26 Unwmk. *Perf. 13*

C23 AP6 13fr indigo & blue 5.50 3.75

Designs: 50fr, "Women of Tahiti," Gauguin, horiz. 100fr, "The White Horse," Gauguin. 200fr, Night fishing at Moorea, horiz.

1958, Nov. 3 Engr. *Perf. 13*

C24 AP7	13fr multicolored	3.25	2.50
C25 AP7	50fr multicolored	5.75	4.00
C26 AP7	100fr multicolored	9.50	6.75
C27 AP7	200fr lilac & slate	25.00	18.00

1960, Dec. 15

C28 AP8 13fr rose lil, vio, & yel grn 2.50 1.75

Telstar Issue
Common Design Type

1962, Dec. 5 *Perf. 13*

C29 CD111 50fr red lil, mar & vio bl 8.00 5.50

1964, May 14 Photo. *Perf. 13*

C30 AP10 15fr multicolored 2.50 1.75

1964, July 10 Unwmk.

C31 AP11 16fr multicolored 8.00 5.25

Issued to commemorate the rallying of French Polynesia to the Free French cause.

1964, Dec. 1 Litho. *Perf. 13*

C32 AP12 23fr multicolored 4.50 2.00

ITU Issue
Common Design Type

1965, May 17 Engr. *Perf. 13*

C33 CD120 50fr vio, red brn & blue 60.00 35.00

Design: 25fr, Gauguin Museum (stylized). 40fr, Primitive statues at Gauguin Museum.

1965 Engr. *Perf. 13*

C34 AP13	25fr olive green	6.00	3.75
C35 AP13	40fr blue green	11.00	6.00
C36 AP13	75fr brt red brown	17.50	12.50

Opening of Gauguin Museum, Papeete.

1965, Sept. 1 Engr. *Perf. 13*

C37 AP14 50fr red brn, dl bl & dk grn 50.00 40.00

World Championships in Underwater Fishing, Tuamotu Archipelago, Sept. 1965.

1965, Nov. 29

C38 AP15 80fr brn, bl, dl bl & red 16.00 12.00

School Canteen Program.

1965, Dec. 29 Engr. *Perf. 13*

C39 AP16 60fr orange, grn & dk brn 12.50 10.00

50th anniversary of the first radio link between Tahiti and France.

French Satellite A-1 Issue
Common Design Type

Designs: 7fr, Diamant Rocket and launching installations. 10fr, A-1 satellite.

1966, Feb. 7
C40 CD121 7fr choc, dp grn & lil 3.75 3.75
C41 CD121 10fr lil, dp grn & dk brn 5.00 5.00
a. Pair, #C40-C41 + label 10.00 10.00

French Satellite D-1 Issue
Common Design Type

1966, May 10 Engr. *Perf. 13*
C42 CD122 20fr brn, brt grn & claret 6.00 3.75

Papeete Harbor — AP17

1966, June 30 Photo. *Perf. 13*
C43 AP17 50fr multicolored 10.50 8.00

"Vive Tahiti" by A. Benichou — AP18

1966, Nov. 28 Photo. *Perf. 13*
C44 AP18 13fr multicolored 6.00 3.50

Explorer's Ship and Canoe — AP19

Designs: 60fr, Polynesian costume and ship. 80fr, Louis Antoine de Bougainville, vert.

1968 Engr. *Perf. 13*
C45 AP19 40fr green, bl & ocher 3.75 2.25
C46 AP19 60fr brt blue, org & blk 7.50 4.25
C47 AP19 80fr red lilac, sal & lake 7.75 5.25
a. Souvenir sheet of 3, #C45-C47 75.00 75.00

200th anniv. of the discovery of Tahiti by Louis Antoine de Bougainville.

The Meal, by Paul Gauguin — AP20

1968, July 30 Photo. *Perf. 12x12½*
C48 AP20 200fr multicolored 26.00 20.00

See Nos. C63-C67, C78-C82, C89-C93, C98.

Shot Put — AP21

PATA 1970 Poster — AP22

1968, Oct. 12 Engr. *Perf. 13*
C49 AP21 35fr dk car rose & brt grn 10.50 6.75

Issued to commemorate the 19th Olympic Games, Mexico City, Oct. 12-27.

Concorde Issue
Common Design Type

1969, Apr. 17
C50 CD129 40fr red brn & car rose 47.50 32.50

1969, July 9 Photo. *Perf. 12½x13*
C51 AP22 25fr blue & multi 6.00 4.00

Issued to publicize PATA 1970 (Pacific Area Travel Association Congress), Tahiti.

Underwater Fishing — AP23

Design: 52fr, Hand holding fish made up of flags, vert.

1969, Aug. 5 Photo. *Perf. 13*
C52 AP23 48fr blk, grnsh bl & red lil 9.50 6.50
C53 AP23 52fr blue, black & red 14.00 11.00

Issued to publicize the World Underwater Fishing Championships.

Gen. Bonaparte as Commander of the Army in Italy, by Jean Sebastien Rouillard AP24

1969, Oct. 15 Photo. *Perf. 12½x12*
C54 AP24 100fr carmine & multi 65.00 55.00

Bicentenary of the birth of Napoleon Bonaparte (1769-1821).

The index in each volume of the Scott Catalogue contains many listings that help identify stamps.

Eiffel Tower, Torii and EXPO Emblem — AP25

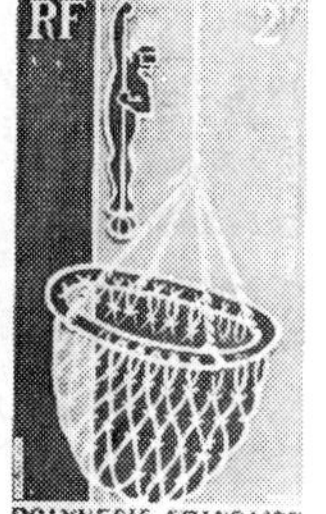

Pearl Diver Descending, and Basket — AP26

Design: 30fr, Mount Fuji, Tower of the Sun and EXPO emblem, horiz.

1970, Sept. 15 Photo. *Perf. 13*
C55 AP25 30fr multicolored 5.00 4.00
C56 AP25 50fr multicolored 7.25 5.50

EXPO '70 International Exposition, Osaka, Japan, Mar. 15-Sept. 13.

1970, Sept. 30 Engr. *Perf. 13*

Designs: 5fr, Diver collecting oysters. 18fr, Implantation into oyster, horiz. 27fr, Open oyster with pearl. 50fr, Woman with mother of pearl jewelry.

C57 AP26 2fr slate, grnsh bl & red brn 90 60
C58 AP26 5fr grnsh blue, ultra & org 1.65 85
C59 AP26 18fr slate, mag & org 2.75 1.75
C60 AP26 27fr brt pink, brn & dl lil 4.75 3.25
C61 AP26 50fr gray, red brn & org 8.50 5.50
Nos. C57-C61 (5) 18.55 11.95

Pearl industry of French Polynesia.

The Thinker, by Auguste Rodin and Education Year Emblem — AP27

1970, Oct. 15 Engr. *Perf. 13*
C62 AP27 50fr blue, ind & fawn 8.50 6.25

International Education Year.

Painting Type of 1968

Paintings by Artists Living in Polynesia: 20fr, Woman on the Beach, by Yves de Saint-Front. 40fr, Abstract, by Frank Fay. 60fr, Woman and Shells, by Jean Guillois. 80fr, Hut under Palms, by Jean Masson. 100fr, Polynesian Girl, by Jean-Charles Bouloc, vert.

Perf. 12x12½, 12½x12
1970, Dec. 14 Photo.
C63 AP20 20fr brown & multi 3.75 3.25
C64 AP20 40fr brown & multi 6.75 5.00
C65 AP20 60fr brown & multi 10.00 6.50
C66 AP20 80fr brown & multi 14.00 10.00
C67 AP20 100fr brown & multi 21.00 17.00
Nos. C63-C67 (5) 55.50 41.75

South Pacific Games Emblem — AP28

1971, Jan. 26 *Perf. 12½*
C68 AP28 20fr ultra & multi 4.00 3.25

Publicity for 4th South Pacific Games, held in Papeete, Sept. 8-19, 1971.

Memorial Flame — AP29

1971, Mar. 19 Photo. *Perf. 12½*
C69 AP29 5fr multicolored 3.00 2.00

In memory of Charles de Gaulle.

Soldier and Badge — AP30

1971, Apr. 21
C70 AP30 25fr multicolored 5.50 4.50

30th anniversary of departure of Tahitian volunteers to serve in World War II.

Water Sports Type of Regular Issue

Designs: 15fr, Surfing, vert. 16fr, Skin diving, vert. 20fr, Water-skiing with kite.

1971, May 11 Photo. *Perf. 13*
C71 A44 15fr multicolored 3.00 2.00
C72 A44 16fr multicolored 3.50 2.75
C73 A44 20fr multicolored 5.50 4.75

Sailing — AP31

1971, Sept. 8 *Perf. 12½*
C74 AP31 15fr shown 1.25 95
C75 AP31 18fr Golf 1.90 1.25
C76 AP31 27fr Archery 3.50 2.50
C77 AP31 53fr Tennis 6.00 4.00
a. Souv. sheet of 4, #C74-C77 55.00 55.00

4th So. Pacific Games, Papeete, Sept. 8-19.

Painting Type of 1968

Paintings by Artists Living in Polynesia: 20fr, Hut and Palms, by Isabelle Wolf. 40fr, Palms on Shore, by André Dobrowolski. 60fr, Polynesian Woman, by Franoise Séli, vert. 80fr, Holy Family, by Pierre Heymann, vert. 100fr, Crowd, by Nicolai Michoutouchkine.

1971, Dec. 15 Photo. *Perf. 13*
C78 AP20 20fr multicolored 3.75 3.50
C79 AP20 40fr multicolored 6.75 5.50
C80 AP20 60fr multicolored 10.00 8.00
C81 AP20 80fr multicolored 13.00 10.00
C82 AP20 100fr multicolored 22.50 20.00
Nos. C78-C82 (5) 56.00 47.00

Papeete Harbor — AP32

1972, Jan. 13
C83 AP32 28fr violet & multi 6.50 5.00

Free port of Papeete, 10th anniversary.

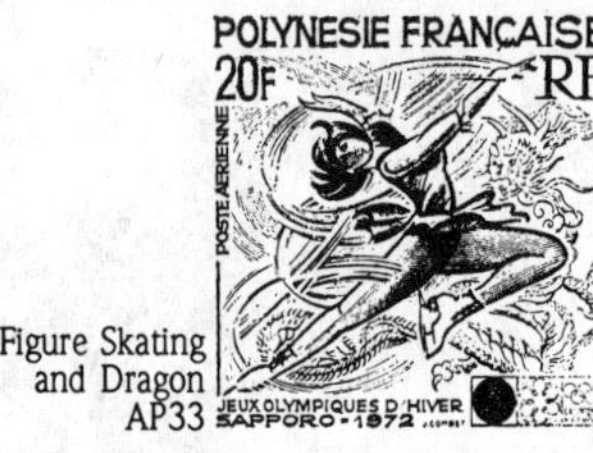

Figure Skating and Dragon AP33

1972, Jan. 25 Engr. *Perf. 13*

C84 AP33 20fr ultra, lake & brt grn 5.50 2.75

11th Winter Olympic Games, Sapporo, Japan, Feb. 3-13.

South Pacific Commission Headquarters, Noumea — AP34

1972, Feb. 5 Photo. *Perf. 13*

C85 AP34 21fr blue & multi 5.25 2.50

South Pacific Commission, 25th anniv.

Festival Emblem — AP35

1972, May 9 Engr. *Perf. 13*

C86 AP35 36fr orange, bl & grn 5.00 4.50

So. Pacific Festival of Arts, Fiji, May 6-20.

Kon Tiki and Route, Callao to Tahiti — AP36

1972, Aug. 18 Photo. *Perf. 13*

C87 AP36 16fr dk & lt bl, blk & org 4.25 2.00

25th anniversary of the arrival of the raft Kon Tiki in Tahiti.

Charles de Gaulle and Memorial — AP37

1972, Dec. 9 Engr. *Perf. 13*

C88 AP37 100fr slate 24.00 19.00

Painting Type of 1968

Paintings by Artists Living in Polynesia: 20fr, Horses, by Georges Bovy. 40fr, Sailboats, by Ruy Juventin, vert. 60fr, Harbor, by André Brooke. 80fr, Farmers, by Daniel Adam, vert. 100fr, Dancers, by Aloysius Pilioko, vert.

1972, Dec. 14 Photo.

C89 AP20 20fr gold & multi 4.25 3.00
C90 AP20 40fr gold & multi 7.25 4.25
C91 AP20 60fr gold & multi 12.00 7.25
C92 AP20 80fr dk grn, buff & dk brn 18.00 10.00
C93 AP20 100fr gold & multi 24.00 18.00
Nos. C89-C93 (5) 65.50 42.50

St. Teresa and Lisieux Basilica AP38

1973, Jan. 23 Engr. *Perf. 13*

C94 AP38 85fr multicolored 16.00 11.00

Centenary of the birth of St. Teresa of Lisieux (1873-1897), Carmelite nun.

Nicolaus Copernicus — AP39

1973, Mar. 7 Engr. *Perf. 13*

C95 AP39 100fr brn, vio bl & red lil 18.00 12.50

Copernicus (1473-1543), Polish astronomer.

Plane over Tahiti AP40

1973, Apr. 3 Photo. *Perf. 13*

C96 AP40 80fr ultra, gold & lt grn 15.00 12.00

Air France's World Tour via Tahiti.

DC-10 at Papeete Airport — AP41

1973, May 18 Engr. *Perf. 13*

C97 AP41 20fr bl, ultra & sl grn 7.00 3.25

Start of DC-10 service.

Painting Type of 1968

Design: 200fr, "Ta Matete" (seated women), by Paul Gauguin.

1973, June 7 Photo. *Perf. 13*

C98 AP20 200fr multicolored 18.00 12.00

70th anniversary of the death of Paul Gauguin (1848-1903), painter.

Pierre Loti and Characters from his Books — AP42

1973, July 4 Engr. *Perf. 13*

C99 AP42 60fr multicolored 16.00 11.00

Pierre Loti (1850-1923), French naval officer and writer.

"Sun," by Jean Francois Favre — AP43

Paintings by Artists Living in Polynesia: 40fr, Woman with Flowers, by Eliane de Gennes. 60fr, Seascape, by Alain Sidet. 80fr, Crowded Bus, by Francois Ravello. 100fr, Stylized Boats, by Jackie Bourdin, horiz.

1973, Dec. 13 Photo. *Perf. 13*

C100 AP43 20fr gold & multi 2.50 1.90
C101 AP43 40fr gold & multi 5.75 3.25
C102 AP43 60fr gold & multi 7.75 5.75
C103 AP43 80fr gold & multi 12.50 10.50
C104 AP43 100fr gold & multi 19.00 14.00
Nos. C100-C104 (5) 47.50 35.40

Bird, Fish, Flower and Water — AP44

Catamaran under Sail — AP45

1974, June 12 Photo. *Perf. 13*

C105 AP44 12fr blue & multi 4.50 1.75

Nature protection.

1974, July 22 Engr. *Perf. 13*

C106 AP45 100fr multicolored 14.00 10.00

2nd Catamaran World Championships.

Still-life, by Rosine Temarui-Masson — AP46

Paintings by Artists Living in Polynesia: 40fr, Palms and House on Beach, by Marcel Chardon. 60fr, Man, by Marie-Franoise Avril. 80fr, Polynesian Woman, by Henriette Robin. 100fr, Lagoon by Moon-light, by David Farsi, horiz.

1974, Dec. 12 Photo. *Perf. 13*

C107 AP46 20fr gold & multi 5.00 2.25
C108 AP46 40fr gold & multi 7.25 3.50
C109 AP46 60fr gold & multi 12.00 6.00
C110 AP46 80fr gold & multi 20.00 9.00
C111 AP46 100fr gold & multi 32.50 15.00
Nos. C107-C111 (5) 76.75 35.75

See Nos. C122-C126.

Polynesian Gods of Travel — AP47

Designs: 75fr, Tourville hydroplane, 1929. 100fr, Passengers leaving plane.

1975, Feb. 7 Engr. *Perf. 13*

C112 AP47 50fr sepia, pur & brn 4.25 3.50
C113 AP47 75fr green, bl & red 6.50 5.00
C114 AP47 100fr green, sep & car 10.00 8.50

Fifty years of Tahitian aviation.

French Ceres Stamp and Woman — AP48

1975, May 29 Engr. *Perf. 13*

C115 AP48 32fr ver, brn & blk 4.50 3.75

ARPHILA 75 International Philatelic Exhibition, Paris, June 6-16.

Shot Put and Games' Emblem AP50

1975, Aug. 1 Photo. *Perf. 13*

C117 AP50 25fr shown 3.00 2.25
C118 AP50 30fr Volleyball 3.75 2.25
C119 AP50 40fr Women's swim-ming 5.25 3.75

5th South Pacific Games, Guam, Aug. 1-10.

Flowers, Athlete, View of Montreal — AP51

1975, Oct. 15 **Engr.** ***Perf. 13***
C120 AP51 44fr brt bl, ver & blk 4.50 2.75

Pre-Olympic Year 1975.

UPU Emblem, Jet and Letters — AP52

1975, Nov. 5 **Engr.** ***Perf. 13***
C121 AP52 100fr brown, bl & ol 9.00 7.50

World Universal Postal Union Day.

Paintings Type of 1974

Paintings by Artists Living in Polynesia: 20fr, Beach Scene, by R. Marcel Marius, horiz. 40fr, Roofs with TV antennas, by M. Anglade, horiz. 60fr, Street scene with bus, by J. Day, horiz. 80fr, Tropical waters (fish), by J. Steimetz. 100fr, Women, by A. van der Heyde.

1975, Dec. 17 **Litho.** ***Perf. 13***
C122 AP46 20fr gold & multi 2.25 1.25
C123 AP46 40fr gold & multi 3.00 1.50
C124 AP46 60fr gold & multi 4.75 2.75
C125 AP46 80fr gold & multi 6.75 4.75
C126 AP46 100fr gold & multi 11.00 6.25
Nos. C122-C126 (5) 27.75 16.50

Concorde — AP53

1976, Jan. 21 **Engr.** ***Perf. 13***
C127 AP53 100fr carmine, bl & ind 11.50 8.00

First commercial flight of supersonic jet Concorde from Paris to Rio, Jan. 21.

Adm. Rodney, Count de la Perouse, "Barfleur" and "Triomphant" in Battle — AP54

Design: 31fr, Count de Grasse and Lord Graves, "Ville de Paris" and "Le Terible" in Chesapeake Bay Battle.

1976, Apr. 15 **Engr.** ***Perf. 13***
C128 AP54 24fr grnsh bl, lt brn & blk 2.25 1.50
C129 AP54 31fr magenta, red & lt brn 3.00 1.75

American Bicentennial.

King Pomaré I — AP55

Portraits: 21fr, King Pomaré II. 26fr, Queen Pomaré IV. 30fr, King Pomaré V.

1976, Apr. 28 **Litho.** ***Perf. 12½***
C130 AP55 18fr olive & multi 75 40
C131 AP55 21fr multicolored 1.10 60
C132 AP55 26fr gray & multi 1.40 75
C133 AP55 30fr plum & multi 1.65 1.10

Pomaré Dynasty. See Nos. C141-C144.

Running and Maple Leaf — AP56

Designs: 34fr, Long jump, vert. 50fr, Olympic flame and flowers.

1976, July 19 **Engr.** ***Perf. 13***
C134 AP56 26fr ultra & multi 2.00 1.65
C135 AP56 34fr ultra & multi 2.50 2.00
C136 AP56 50fr ultra & multi 5.00 3.75
a. Min. sheet of 3, #C134-C136 32.50 32.50

21st Olympic Games, Montreal, Canada, July 17-Aug. 1.

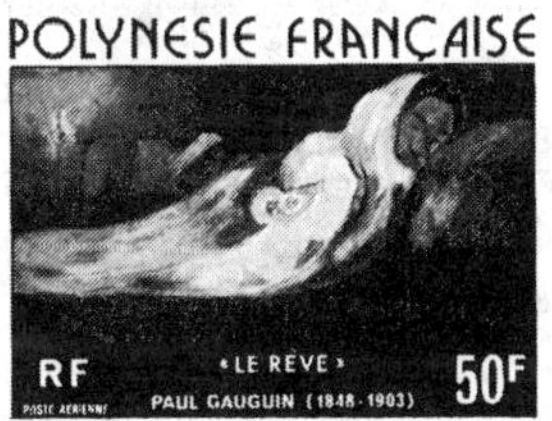

The Dream, by Paul Gauguin — AP57

1976, Oct. 17 **Photo.** ***Perf. 13***
C137 AP57 50fr multicolored 5.50 4.00

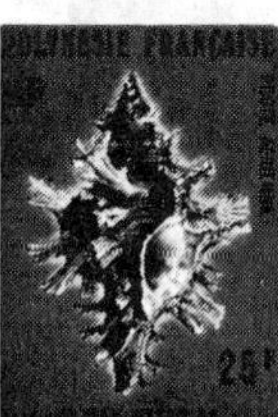

Murex Steeriae AP58

Pocillopora AP59

Sea Shells: 27fr, Conus Gauguini. 35fr, Conus marchionatus.

1977, Mar. 14 **Photo.** ***Perf. 12½x13***
C138 AP58 25fr violet bl & multi 1.50 85
C139 AP58 27fr ultra & multi 1.90 95
C140 AP58 35fr blue & multi 2.50 1.25

See Nos. C156-C158.

Royalty Type of 1976

Portraits: 19fr, King Maputeoa, Mangareva. 33fr, King Camatoa V, Raiatea. 39fr, Queen Vaekehu, Marquesas. 43fr, King Teurarii III, Rurutu.

1977, Apr. 19 **Litho.** ***Perf. 12½***
C141 AP55 19fr dull red & multi 80 50
C142 AP55 33fr dk blue & multi 95 80
C143 AP55 39fr ultra & multi 1.25 85
C144 AP55 43fr green & multi 1.65 1.10

Polynesian rulers.

Perf. 13x12½, 12½x13
1977, May 23 **Photo.**

Design: 25fr, Acropora, horiz.

C145 AP59 25fr multicolored 1.10 60
C146 AP59 33fr multicolored 1.50 75

3rd Symposium on Coral Reefs, Miami, Fla. See Nos. C162-C163.

De Gaulle Memorial — AP60

Tahitian Dancer — AP61

Photogravure and Embossed

1977, June 18 ***Perf. 13***
C147 AP60 40fr gold & multi 2.50 2.00

5th anniversary of dedication of De Gaulle memorial at Colombey-les-Deux-Eglises.

1977, July 14 **Litho.** ***Perf. 12½***
C148 AP61 27fr multicolored 1.90 95

Charles A. Lindbergh and Spirit of St. Louis — AP62

1977, Aug. 18 **Litho.** ***Perf. 12½***
C149 AP62 28fr multicolored 3.00 2.50

Lindbergh's solo transatlantic flight from New York to Paris, 50th anniv.

Mahoe — AP63

Palms on Shore — AP64

1977, Sept. 15 **Photo.** ***Perf. 12½x13***
C150 AP63 8fr shown 52 38
C151 AP63 12fr Frangipani 75 52

1977, Nov. 8 **Photo.** ***Perf. 12½x13***
C152 AP64 32fr multicolored 1.50 85

Ecology, protection of trees.

Rubens' Son Albert AP65

1977, Nov. 28 **Engr.** ***Perf. 13***
C153 AP65 100fr grnsh blk & rose cl 4.50 3.00

Peter Paul Rubens (1577-1640), painter, 400th birth anniversary.

Capt. Cook and "Discovery" — AP66

Design: 39fr, Capt. Cook and "Resolution."

1978, Jan. 20 **Engr.** ***Perf. 13***
C154 AP66 33fr multicolored 1.75 1.25
C155 AP66 39fr multicolored 2.25 1.50

Bicentenary of Capt. James Cook's arrival in Hawaii.

For overprints see Nos. C166-C167.

Shell Type of 1977

Sea Shells: 22fr, Erosaria obvelata. 24fr, Cypraea ventriculus. 31fr, Lambis robusta.

1978, Apr. 13 **Photo.** ***Perf. 13½x13***
C156 AP58 22fr brt blue & multi 90 50
C157 AP58 24fr brt blue & multi 1.00 50
C158 AP58 31fr brt blue & multi 1.25 70

Tahitian Woman and Boy, by Gauguin AP67

1978, May 7 ***Perf. 13***
C159 AP67 50fr multicolored 4.00 3.00

Paul Gauguin (1848-1903).

Antenna and ITU Emblem AP68

1978, May 17 **Litho.** ***Perf. 13***
C160 AP68 80fr gray & multi 4.25 3.00

10th World Telecommunications Day.

Soccer and Argentina '78 Emblem — AP69

1978, June 1
C161 AP69 28fr multicolored 1.75 1.25

11th World Cup Soccer Championship, Argentina, June 1-25.

Coral Type of 1977

Designs: 26fr, Fungia, horiz. 34fr, Millepora.

Perf. 13x12½, 12½x13
1978, July 13 **Photo.**
C162 AP59 26fr multicolored 70 55
C163 AP59 34fr multicolored 1.00 60

Radar Antenna, Polynesian Woman — AP70

1978, Sept. 5 **Engr.** ***Perf. 13***
C164 AP70 50fr blue & black 2.50 1.75

Papenoo earth station.

Bird and Rainbow over Island — AP71

1978, Oct. 5 **Photo.**
C165 AP71 23fr multicolored 1.25 80

Nature protection.

Nos. C154-C155 Overprinted in Black or Violet Blue: "1779-1979 / BICENTENAIRE / DE LA / MORT DE"

1979, Feb. 14 **Engr.** ***Perf. 13***
C166 AP66 33fr multicolored 1.65 90
C167 AP66 39fr multicolored (VBl) 2.00 1.50

Bicentenary of Capt. Cook's death. On No. C167 date is last line of overprint.

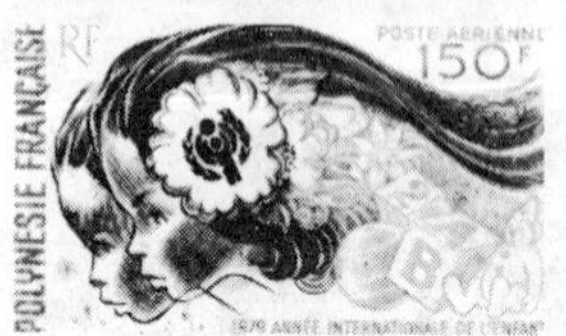

Children, Toys and IYC Emblem — AP72

1979, May 3 **Engr.** ***Perf. 13***
C168 AP72 150fr multicolored 6.00 5.00

International Year of the Child.

"Do you expect a letter?" by Paul Gauguin — AP73

1979, May 20 **Photo.** ***Perf. 13***
C169 AP73 200fr multicolored 6.50 4.50

Shell and Carved Head — AP74

1979, June 30 **Engr.** ***Perf. 13***
C170 AP74 44fr multicolored 1.75 1.40

Museum of Tahiti and the Islands.

Conference Emblem over Island AP75

1979, Oct. 6 **Photo.** ***Perf. 13***
C171 AP75 23fr multicolored 1.25 60

19th South Pacific Conf., Tahiti, Oct. 6-12.

Flying Boat "Bermuda" — AP76

Planes Used in Polynesia: 40fr, DC-4 over Papeete. 60fr, Britten-Norman "Islander." 80fr, Fairchild F-27A. 120fr, DC-8 over Tahiti.

1979, Dec. 19 **Litho.** ***Perf. 13***
C172 AP76 24fr multicolored 55 35
C173 AP76 40fr multicolored 90 65
C174 AP76 60fr multicolored 1.50 1.10
C175 AP76 80fr multicolored 2.00 1.25
C176 AP76 120fr multicolored 3.25 2.00
Nos. C172-C176 (5) 8.20 5.35

See Nos. C180-C183.

Window on Tahiti, by Henri Matisse AP77

1980, Feb. 18 **Photo.**
C177 AP77 150fr multicolored 5.50 3.50

Marshi Metua No Tehamana, by Gauguin AP78

1980, Aug. 18 **Photo.** ***Perf. 13***
C178 AP78 500fr multicolored 14.00 10.00

Sydpex '80, Philatelic Exhibition, Sydney Town Hall — AP79

1980, Sept. 29 **Photo.** ***Perf. 13***
C179 AP79 70fr multicolored 2.75 2.25

Aviation Type of 1979

1980, Dec. 15 **Litho.** ***Perf. 13***
C180 AP76 15fr Catalina 35 35
C181 AP76 26fr Twin Otter 60 50
C182 AP76 30fr CAMS 55 75 60
C183 AP76 50fr DC-6 1.10 90

And The Gold of their Bodies, by Gauguin — AP80

1981, Mar. 15 **Photo.** ***Perf. 13***
C184 AP80 100fr multicolored 2.75 1.90

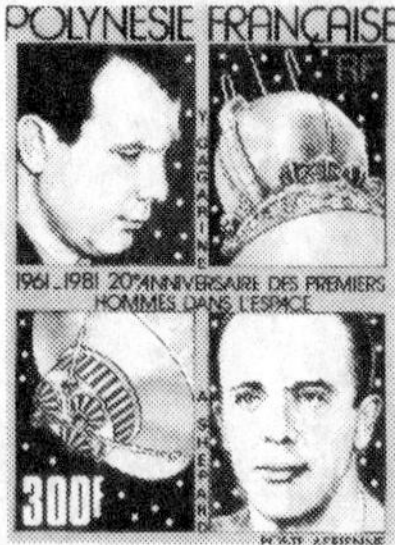

20th Anniv. of Manned Space Flight AP81

1981, June 13 **Litho.** ***Perf. 12½***
C185 AP81 300fr multicolored 6.00 4.50

First Intl. Pirogue (6-man Canoe) Championship — AP82

1981, July 25 **Litho.** ***Perf. 13x12½***
C186 AP82 200fr multicolored 4.50 3.75

Matavai Bay, by William Hodges — AP83

Paintings: 60fr, Poedea, by John Weber, vert. 80fr, Omai, by Joshua Reynolds, vert. 120fr, Point Venus, by George Tobin.

1981, Dec. 10 **Photo.** ***Perf. 13***
C187 AP83 40fr multicolored 75 60
C188 AP83 60fr multicolored 1.10 90
C189 AP83 80fr multicolored 1.60 1.25
C190 AP83 120fr multicolored 2.25 1.90

See Nos. C194-C197, C202-C205.

TB Bacillus Centenary — AP84

1982, Mar. 24 **Engr.** ***Perf. 13***
C191 AP84 200fr multicolored 3.50 2.50

1982 World Cup — AP85

1982, May 18 **Litho.** ***Perf. 13***
C192 AP85 250fr multicolored 5.00 3.75

French Overseas Possessions' Week, Sept. 18-25 — AP86

1982, Sept. 17 **Engr.**
C193 AP86 110fr multicolored 2.00 1.65

Painting Type of 1981

Designs: 50fr, The Tahitian, by M. Radiguet, vert. 70fr, Souvenir of Tahiti, by C. Giraud. 100fr, Beating Cloth Lengths, by Atlas JL the Younger. 160fr, Papeete Harbor, by C.F. Gordon Cumming.

1982, Dec. 15 **Photo.** ***Perf. 13***
C194 AP83 50fr multicolored 80 50
C195 AP83 70fr multicolored 1.00 70
C196 AP83 100fr multicolored 1.65 1.40
C197 AP83 160fr multicolored 2.75 1.65

Wood Cutter, by Gauguin AP87

Photo. & Engr.
1983, May 8 ***Perf. 12½x13***
C198 AP87 600fr multicolored 9.50 7.25

Voyage of Capt. Bligh — AP88

1983, June 9 **Litho.** ***Perf. 13***
C199 AP88 200fr Map, fruit 4.00 3.00

BRASILIANA '83 Intl. Stamp Exhibition, Rio de Janeiro, July 29-Aug. 7 — AP89

1983, July 29 **Litho.** ***Perf. 13x12½***
C200 AP89 100fr multicolored 2.00 1.65
a. Souvenir sheet 2.50 2.50

1983, Aug. 4 **Litho.** ***Perf. 13x12½***
C201 AP89 110fr Bangkok '83 2.25 1.75
a. Souvenir sheet 3.00 3.00

Painting Type of 1981

20th Century Paintings: 40fr, View of Moorea, by William Alister MacDonald (1861-1956). 60fr, The Fruit Carrier, by Adrian Herman Gouwe (1875-1965), vert. 80fr, Arrival of the Destroyer Escort, by Nicolas Mordvinoff (1911-1977), vert. 100fr, Women on a Veranda, by Charles Alfred Le Moine (1872-1918).

1983, Dec. 22 **Photo.** ***Perf. 13***
C202 AP83 40fr multicolored 75 60
C203 AP83 60fr multicolored 1.10 90
C204 AP83 80fr multicolored 1.50 1.10
C205 AP83 100fr multicolored 2.25 1.50

ESPANA '84 — AP90

Design: Maori canoers.

1984, Apr. 27 **Engr.** ***Perf. 13***
C206 AP90 80fr brn red & dk bl 1.40 1.10

Souvenir Sheet

C207 AP90 200fr dk blue & dk red 4.50 4.50

Woman with Mango, by Gauguin AP91

Photo. & Engr.
1984, May 27 ***Perf. 12½x13***
C208 AP91 400fr multicolored 7.00 6.00

Ausipex '84 — AP92

Details from Human Sacrifice of the Maori in Tahiti, 18th cent. engraving.

1984, Sept. 5 **Litho.** ***Perf. 13x12½***
C209 AP92 120fr Worshippers 3.25 2.25
C210 AP92 120fr Preparation 3.25 2.25
a. Pair, #C209-C210 + label 6.50 6.50

Souvenir Sheet

C211 AP92 200fr Entire 8.00 8.00

Painting by Gaugin (1848-1903) — AP93

Design: Where have we come from? What are we? Where are we going?
Illustration reduced.

1985, Mar. 17 **Litho.** ***Perf. 13½x13***
C212 AP93 550fr + label 7.75 6.25

4th Pacific Arts Festival Type of 1984

1985, July 3 **Litho.** ***Perf. 13***
C213 A95 200fr Islander, tiki, artifacts 3.00 2.00

Intl. Youth Year — AP95

1985, Sept. 18 **Litho.**
C214 AP95 250fr Island youths, frigate bird 3.50 2.50

ITALIA '85 — AP96

Designs: Ship sailing into Papeete Harbor, 19th century print.

1985, Oct. 22 **Engr.**
C215 AP96 130fr multicolored 2.00 1.50

Souvenir Sheet

C216 AP96 240fr multicolored 4.00 2.00

1st Intl. Marlin Fishing Contest, Feb. 27-Mar. 5 — AP97

1986, Feb. 27 **Litho.** ***Perf. 12½***
C217 AP97 300fr multicolored 5.25 3.25

Arrival of a Boat, c.1880 — AP98

1986, June 24 **Engr.** ***Perf. 13***
C218 AP98 400fr intense blue 6.75 4.50

STOCKHOLMIA '86 — AP99

Design: Dr. Karl Solander and Anders Sparrmann, Swedish scientists who accompanied Capt. Cook, and map of Tahiti.

1986, Aug. 28 **Engr.** ***Perf. 13***
C219 AP99 150fr multicolored 2.50 2.25

Souvenir Sheet

C220 AP99 210fr multicolored 4.50 4.50

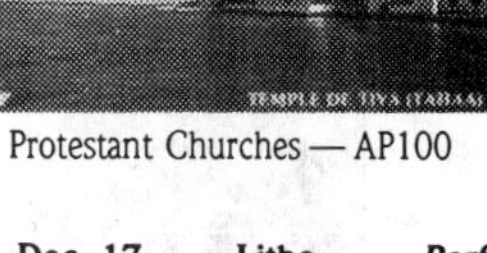

Protestant Churches — AP100

1986, Dec. 17 **Litho.** ***Perf. 13***
C221 AP100 80fr Tiva, 1955 1.20 90
C222 AP100 200fr Avera, 1880 3.00 2.25
C223 AP100 300fr Papetoai, 1822 4.50 3.40

Broche Barracks, 120th Anniv. — AP101

1987, Apr. 21 **Litho.** ***Perf. 12½x12***
C224 AP101 350fr multicolored 5.25 4.00

CAPEX '87 — AP102

Design: George Vancouver (1757-1798), English navigator and cartographer, chart and excerpt from ship's log.

1987, June 15 **Engr.** ***Perf. 13***
C225 AP102 130fr + label 2.00 1.50

Imperf

Size: 143x100mm

C226 AP102 260fr multicolored 4.00 3.00

Soyez Mysterieuses, from a 5-Panel Sculpture by Paul Gauguin, Gauguin Museum — AP103

Illustration reduced.

1987, Nov. 15 ***Perf. 13***
C227 AP103 600fr multicolored 12.50 9.50

AIR POST SEMI-POSTAL STAMP

Catalogue values for unused stamps in this section are for Never Hinged items.

French Revolution Issue
Common Design Type
Unwmk.

1939, July 5 **Photo.** ***Perf. 13***
Name and Value Typo. in Orange
CB1 CD83 5fr + 4fr brn blk 11.00 11.00

V5

Stamps of the above design and of Cameroun type V10 inscribed "Etabts Frcais de l'Océanie" were issued in 1942 by the Vichy Government, but were not placed on sale in the colony.

POSTAGE DUE STAMPS

Postage Due Stamps of French Colonies, 1894-1906, Overprinted

Établissements Français de l'Océanie

1926-27 Unwmk. *Perf. 14x13½*

J1	D1	5c	light blue	16	16
J2	D1	10c	brown	25	25
J3	D1	20c	olive green	40	40
J4	D1	30c	dull red	40	40
J5	D1	40c	rose	80	80
J6	D1	60c	blue green	60	60
J7	D1	1fr	red brown, *straw*	75	75
J8	D1	3fr	magenta ('27)	3.75	3.75

With Additional Surcharge of New Value

J9	D1	2fr on 1fr	orange red	1.10	1.10
			Nos. J1-J9 (9)	8.21	8.21

Fautaua Falls, Tahiti — D2

Tahitian Youth — D3

1929 Typo. *Perf. 13½x14*

J10	D2	5c	lt blue & dk brn	28	28
J11	D2	10c	vermilion & grn	28	28
J12	D2	30c	dk brn & dk red	60	60
J13	D2	50c	yel grn & dk brn	28	28
J14	D2	60c	dl vio & yel grn	1.40	1.40
J15	D3	1fr	Prus bl & red vio	60	60
J16	D3	2fr	brn red & dk brn	40	40
J17	D3	3fr	bl vio & bl grn	60	60
			Nos. J10-J17 (8)	4.44	4.44

Catalogue values for unused stamps in this section, from this point to the end of the section, are for Never Hinged items.

D4

Polynesian Club — D5

1948 Engr. *Perf. 14x13*

J18	D4	10c	brt blue grn	15	15
J19	D4	30c	black brown	15	15
J20	D4	50c	dk car rose	15	15
J21	D4	1fr	ultra	16	16
J22	D4	2fr	dk blue green	35	35
J23	D4	3fr	red	50	50
J24	D4	4fr	violet	60	60
J25	D4	5fr	lilac rose	65	65
J26	D4	10fr	slate	1.40	1.40
J27	D4	20fr	red brown	1.80	1.80
			Nos. J18-J27 (10)	5.91	5.91

1958 Unwmk. *Perf. 14x13*

J28	D5	1fr	dk brn & grn	30	30
J29	D5	3fr	bluish blk & hn brn	45	45
J30	D5	5fr	brown & ultra	75	75

Tahitian Bowl — D6

1984-87 Litho. *Perf. 13*

J31	D6	1fr	Mother-of-pearl fish hook, vert.	15	15
J32	D6	3fr	shown	15	15
J33	D6	5fr	Marquesan fan	15	15
J34	D6	10fr	Lamp stand, vert.	22	22
J35	D6	20fr	Wood headrest ('87)	30	22
J36	D6	50fr	Wood scoop ('87)	75	58
			Nos. J31-J36 (6)	1.72	1.47

Issue dates: Nos. J31-34, Mar. 16. Nos. J35-J36, Aug. 18.

OFFICIAL STAMPS

Catalogue values for unused stamps in this section are for Never Hinged items.

Breadfruit O1

Polynesian Fruits: 2fr, 3fr, 5fr, like 1fr. 7fr, 8fr, 10fr, 15fr, "Vi Tahiti." 19fr, 20fr, 25fr, 35fr, Avocados. 50fr, 100fr, 200fr, Mangos.

1977, June 9 Litho. *Perf. 12½*

O1	O1	1fr	ultra & multi	15	15
O2	O1	2fr	ultra & multi	15	15
O3	O1	3fr	ultra & multi	15	15
O4	O1	5fr	ultra & multi	15	15
O5	O1	7fr	red & multi	20	20
O6	O1	8fr	red & multi	20	20
O7	O1	10fr	red & multi	25	25
O8	O1	15fr	red & multi	35	35
O9	O1	19fr	black & multi	55	55
O10	O1	20fr	black & multi	55	55
O11	O1	25fr	black & multi	65	65
O12	O1	35fr	black & multi	85	85
O13	O1	50fr	black & multi	1.00	1.00
O14	O1	100fr	red & multi	3.25	3.25
O15	O1	200fr	ultra & multi	8.00	8.00
			Nos. O1-O15 (15)	16.45	16.45

Stamps and Postmarks — O2

Designs: 1fr, French Colonies #5. 2fr, French Colonies #27, #12. 3fr, French Colonies #29, 1884 Papeete postmark. 5fr, Newspaper franked with surcharge of Tahiti #2, 1884 Papeete postmark. 10fr, #4, 1894 octagonal postmark. 20fr, #6, #8. 46fr, #48. 70fr, Visit Tahiti postmark on postal card piece. 100fr, #181. 200fr, #C21, first day cancel.

1993, Jan. 13 Litho. *Perf. 13½*

O16	O2	1fr	multicolored	15	15
O17	O2	2fr	multicolored	15	15
O18	O2	3fr	multicolored	15	15
O19	O2	5fr	multicolored	15	15
O20	O2	10fr	multicolored	20	20
O21	O2	20fr	multicolored	38	38
O22	O2	46fr	multicolored	90	90
O23	O2	70fr	multicolored	1.40	1.40
O24	O2	100fr	multicolored	2.00	2.00
O25	O2	200fr	multicolored	4.00	4.00
			Nos. O16-O25 (10)	9.48	9.48

FRENCH SOUTHERN AND ANTARCTIC TERRITORIES

AREA — 9,000 sq. mi.
POP. — 168 (1983)

Formerly dependencies of Madagascar, these areas, comprising the Kerguelen Archipelago; St. Paul, Amsterdam and Crozet Islands and Adelle Land in Antarctica achieved territorial status on August 6, 1955.

100 Centimes = 1 Franc

Catalogue values for all unused stamps in this country are for Never Hinged items.

Madagascar No. 289 Overprinted in Red:

TERRES AUSTRALES ET ANTARCTIQUES FRANÇAISES

Unwmk.
1955, Oct. 28 Engr. *Perf. 13*

1	A25	15f	dk grn & dp ultra	12.00	15.00

Rockhopper Penguins, Crozet Archipelago — A1

New Amsterdam A2

Design: 10fr, 15fr, Elephant seal.

1956, Apr. 25 Engr. *Perf. 13*

2	A1	50c	dk blue, sep & yel	45	52
3	A1	1fr	ultra, org & gray	45	52
4	A2	5fr	blue & dp ultra	1.65	1.75
5	A2	8fr	gray vio & dk brn	12.50	13.00
6	A2	10fr	indigo	3.50	3.75
7	A2	15fr	indigo & brn vio	3.75	4.00
			Nos. 2-7 (6)	22.30	23.54

Polar Observation A3

1957, Oct. 11

8	A3	5fr	black & violet	3.00	3.00
9	A3	10fr	rose red	3.50	3.50
10	A3	15fr	dark blue	3.50	3.50

International Geophysical Year, 1957-58.

Imperforates

Most stamps of this French possession exist imperforate in issued and trial colors, and also in small presentation sheets in issued colors.

Flower Issue
Common Design Type

Design: Pringlea, horiz.

1959 Photo. *Perf. 12½x12*

11	CD104	10fr	sal, grn & yel	4.50	5.00

Common Design Types pictured in section at front of book.

Light-mantled Sooty Albatross — A4

Coat of Arms — A5

Designs: 40c, Skua, horiz. 12fr, King shag.

1959, Sept. 14 Engr. *Perf. 13*

12	A4	30c	blue, grn & red brn	40	40
13	A4	40c	blk, dl red brn & bl	40	40
14	A4	12fr	lt blue & blk	6.25	6.25

Typo. *Perf. 13x14*

15	A5	20fr	ultra, lt bl & yel	13.00	13.00

Sheathbills — A6

Designs: 4fr, Sea leopard, horiz. 25fr, Weddell seal at Kerguélen, horiz. 85fr, King penguin.

1960, Dec. 15 Engr. *Perf. 13*

16	A6	2fr	grnsh bl, gray & choc	1.50	1.50
17	A6	4fr	bl, dk brn & dk grn	5.75	5.75
18	A6	25fr	sl grn, bis brn & blk	52.50	52.50
19	A6	85fr	grnsh bl, org & blk	32.50	32.50

Yves-Joseph de Kerguélen-Trémarec — A7

1960, Nov. 22

20	A7	25fr	red org, dk bl & brn	20.00	20.00

Yves-Joseph de Kerguélen-Trémarec, discoverer of the Kerguélen Archipelago.

Charcot, Compass Rose and "Pourquoi-pas?" — A8

1961, Dec. 26 Unwmk. *Perf. 13*

21	A8	25fr	brn, grn & red	18.00	18.00

25th anniv. of the death of Commander Jean Charcot (1867-1936), Antarctic explorer.

Elephant Seals Fighting — A9

1963, Feb. 11 Engr. *Perf. 13*

22	A9	8fr	dk bl, blk & claret	8.50	8.50

See No. C4.

Penguins and Camp on Crozet Island — A10

Design: 20fr, Research station and IQSY emblem.

1963, Dec. 16 Unwmk. *Perf. 13*

23 A10 5fr blk, red brn & Prus bl 30.00 25.00
24 A10 20fr vio, sl & red brn 65.00 65.00

Issued to publicize the International Quiet Sun Year, 1964-65. See No. C6.

Great Blue Whale — A11

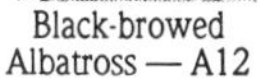
Black-browed Albatross — A12

Aurora Australis, Map of Antarctica and Rocket — A13

Designs: 10fr, Cape pigeons. 12fr, Phylica trees, Amsterdam Island. 15fr, Killer whale (orca).

1966-69 Engr. *Perf. 13*

25 A11 5fr brt bl & ind 10.00 10.00
26 A12 10fr sl, ind & ol brn 22.50 20.00
27 A11 12fr brt bl, sl grn & lemon 14.00 11.00
27A A11 15fr ol, dk bl & indigo 7.00 7.00
28 A12 20fr sl, ol & org 315.00 250.00
Nos. 25-28 (5) 368.50 298.00

Issue dates: 5fr, Dec. 12, 1966; 20fr, Jan. 31, 1968; 10fr, 12fr, Jan. 6, 1969; 15fr, Dec. 21, 1969.

1967, Mar. 4 Engr. *Perf. 13*

29 A13 20fr mag, bl & blk 21.00 18.00

Launching of the 1st space rocket from Adelie Land, Jan., 1967.

Dumont d'Urville A14

1968, Jan. 20

30 A14 30fr lt ultra, dk bl & dk brn 95.00 80.00

Jules Sébastien César Dumont D'Urville (1790-1842), French naval commander and South Seas explorer.

WHO Anniversary Issue

Common Design Type

1968, May 4 Engr. *Perf. 13*

31 CD126 30fr red, yel & bl 55.00 45.00

Human Rights Year Issue

Common Design Type

1968, Aug. 10 Engr. *Perf. 13*

32 CD127 30fr grnsh bl, red & brn 52.50 42.50

Polar Camp with Helicopter, Plane and Snocat Tractor — A15

1969, Mar. 17 Engr. *Perf. 13*

33 A15 25fr Prus bl, lt grnsh bl & brn red 16.00 12.00

20 years of French Polar expeditions.

ILO Issue

Common Design Type

1970, Jan. 1 Engr. *Perf. 13*

35 CD131 20fr org, dk bl & brn 12.50 9.00

UPU Headquarters Issue

Common Design Type

1970, May 20 Engr. *Perf. 13*

36 CD133 50fr bl, plum & ol bister 30.00 22.00

Ice Fish A16

Fish: Nos. 38-43, Antarctic cods, various species. 135fr, Zanchlorhynchus spinifer.

1971 Engr. *Perf. 13*

37 A16 5fr brt grn, ind & org 1.25 1.25
38 A16 10fr redsh brn & dp vio 1.40 1.40
39 A16 20fr dp cl, brt grn & org 2.25 2.25
40 A16 22fr pur, brn ol & mag 3.75 2.25
41 A16 25fr grn, ind & org 3.75 3.75
42 A16 30fr sep, gray & bl vio 5.50 5.50
43 A16 35fr sl grn, dk brn & ocher 4.50 3.75
44 A16 135fr Prus bl, dp org & ol grn 8.25 6.75
Nos. 37-44 (8) 30.65 26.90

Issue dates: Nos. 37-39, 41-42, Jan. 1; Nos. 40, 43-44, Dec. 22.

Map of Antarctica A17

Microzetia Mirabilis A18

1971, Dec. 22

45 A17 75fr red 20.00 20.00

10th anniversary of the Antarctic Treaty pledging peaceful uses of and scientific cooperation in Antarctica.

1972

Insects: 15fr, Christiansenia dreuxi. 22f, Phtirocoris antarcticus. 30fr, Antarctophytosus atriceps. 40fr, Paractora drenxi. 140fr, Pringleophaga Kerguelenensis.

46 A18 15fr cl, org & brn 5.75 4.00
47 A18 22fr vio bl, sl grn & yel 5.75 4.00
48 A18 25fr grn, rose lil & pur 5.75 4.00
49 A18 30fr blue & multi 7.00 5.75
50 A18 40fr dk brn, ocher & blk 5.75 4.75
51 A18 140fr bl, emer & brn 13.00 13.50
Nos. 46-51 (6) 43.00 36.00

Issue dates: Nos. 48, 50-51, Jan. 3; Nos. 46-47, 49, Dec. 16.

De Gaulle Issue

Common Design Type

Designs: 50fr, Gen. de Gaulle, 1940. 100fr, Pres. de Gaulle, 1970.

1972, Feb. 1 Engr. *Perf. 13*

52 CD134 50fr brt grn & blk 9.50 8.00
53 CD134 100fr brt grn & blk 16.00 15.00

Kerguelen Cabbage — A19

Designs: 61fr, Azorella selago, horiz. 87fr, Acaena ascendens, horiz.

1972-73

54 A19 45fr multicolored 3.75 3.50
55 A19 61fr multi ('73) 3.25 3.25
56 A19 87fr multi ('73) 3.50 3.50

Issue dates: 45fr, Dec. 18; others, Dec. 13.

Mailship Sapmer and Map of Amsterdam Island — A20

1974, Dec. 31 Engr. *Perf. 13*

57 A20 75fr bl, blk & dk brn 4.75 4.75

25th anniversary of postal service.

Antarctic Tern — A21

Designs: 50c, Antarctic petrel. 90c, Sea lioness. 1fr, Weddell seal. 1.20fr, Kerguelen cormorant, vert. 1.40fr, Gentoo penguin, vert.

1976, Jan. Engr. *Perf. 13*

58 A21 40c multicolored 1.90 1.25
59 A21 50c multicolored 2.50 1.90
60 A21 90c multicolored 3.75 3.25
61 A21 1fr multicolored 10.00 8.25
62 A21 1.20fr multicolored 10.00 10.00
63 A21 1.40fr multicolored 12.00 12.00
Nos. 58-63 (6) 40.15 36.65

James Clark Ross — A22

James Cook — A23

Design: 30c, Climbing Mount Ross.

1976, Dec. 16 Engr. *Perf. 13*

64 A22 30c multicolored 2.75 2.25
65 A22 3fr multicolored 3.25 3.25

First climbing of Mount Ross, Kerguelen Island, Jan. 5, 1975.

1976, Dec. 16

66 A23 70c multicolored 9.50 7.50

Bicentenary of Capt. Cook's voyage past Kerguelen Island. See No. C46.

Commerson's Dolphins A24

1977, Feb. 1 Engr. *Perf. 13*

67 A24	1.10fr Blue whale		2.75	2.00
68 A24	1.50fr shown		4.25	3.25

Macrocystis Algae — A25

Salmon Hatchery — A26

Magga Dan A27

Designs: 70c, Durvillea algae. 90c, Albatross. 1fr, Underwater sampling and scientists, vert. 1.40fr, Thala Dan and penguins.

1977, Dec. 20 Engr. *Perf. 13*

69 A25	40c ol brn & bis	38	32
70 A26	50c dk bl & pur	80	65
71 A25	70c blk, grn & brn	50	50
72 A26	90c grn, brt bl & brn	65	65
73 A27	1fr slate	75	75
74 A27	1.20fr multi	1.10	90
75 A27	1.40fr multi	1.40	1.00
	Nos. 69-75 (7)	5.58	4.77

See Nos. 77-79.

A28 A29

Explorer with French and Expedition Flags.

1977, Dec. 24

76 A28	1.90fr multicolored	5.00	4.00

French Polar expeditions, 1947-48, 30th anniversary.

Types of 1977

Designs: 40c, Forbin, destroyer. 50c Jeanne d'Arc, helicopter carrier. 1.40fr, Kerguelen cormorant.

1979, Jan. 1 Engr. *Perf. 13*

77 A27	40c black & blue	85	85
78 A27	50c black & blue	1.10	1.10
79 A26	1.40fr multicolored	1.10	1.10

1979, Jan. 1

80 A29	1.20fr citron & indigo	80	80

R. Rallier du Baty. See Nos. 97, 100, 111, 117, 129, 135, 188.

French Navigators Monument, Hobart — A30

1979, Jan. 1

81 A30	1fr multicolored	60	60

French navigators and explorers.

Petrel — A31

1979 Engr. *Perf. 13*

82 A31	70c Rockhopper penguins, vert.	85	65
83 A31	1fr shown	85	65

Commandant Bourdais — A32

1979

84 A32	1.10fr *Doudart de Lagree,* vert.	48	48
85 A32	1.50fr *shown*	75	75

Adm. Antoine d'Entrecasteaux A33

Sebastian de el Cano A34

1979

86 A33	1.20fr multicolored	90	65

1979

Discovery of Amsterdam Island, 1522: 4fr, Victoria, horiz.

87 A34	1.40fr multicolored	70	50
88 A34	4fr multicolored	1.65	1.65

Adelie Penguins — A35

Adelie Penguin — A36

Sea Leopard A37

1980, Dec. 15 Engr. *Perf. 13*

89 A35	50c rose violet	1.25	1.25
90 A36	60c multicolored	90	75
91 A35	1.20fr multicolored	1.25	1.00
92 A37	1.30fr multicolored	75	75
93 A37	1.80fr multicolored	90	75
	Nos. 89-93 (5)	5.05	4.50

20th Anniv. of Antarctic Treaty — A38

1981, June 23 Engr. *Perf. 13*

94 A38	1.80fr multicolored	4.75	4.75

Alouette II — A39

1981-82 Engr. *Perf. 13*

95 A39	55c brown & multi	45	30
96 A39	65c blue & multi	45	30

Explorer Type of 1979

1981

97 A29	1.40fr Jean Loranchet	60	55

Landing Ship Le Gros Ventre, Kerguelen — A41

1983, Jan. 3 Engr. *Perf. 13*

98 A41	55c multicolored	52	52

Our Lady of the Winds Statue and Church, Kerguelen — A42

1983, Jan. 3

99 A42	1.40fr multicolored	90	90

Explorer Type of 1979

Design: Martin de Vivies, Navigator.

1983, Jan. 3

100 A29	1.60fr multicolored	90	75

Eaton's Ducks A44

1983, Jan. 3

101 A44	1.50fr multicolored	60	60
102 A44	1.80fr multicolored	90	75

Trawler Austral — A45

1983, Jan. 3

103 A45	2.30fr multicolored	1.10	90

Freighter Lady Franklin — A46

1983, Aug. 4 Engr. *Perf. 13*

104 A46	5fr multicolored	3.50	2.00

Glaciology — A47

Design: Scientists examining glacier, base.

1984, Jan. 1 **Engr.** ***Perf. 13***
105 A47 15c multicolored 30 30
106 A47 1.70fr multicolored 55 55

Crab-eating Seal — A48

Penguins — A49

1984, Jan. 1
107 A48 60c multicolored 40 40
108 A49 70c multicolored 40 40
109 A49 2fr multicolored 90 90
110 A48 5.90fr multicolored 1.65 1.65

Explorer Type of 1979

1984, Jan. 1
111 A29 1.80fr Alfred Faure 75 60

Biomass — A51

1985, Jan. 1 **Engr.** ***Perf. 13***
112 A51 1.80fr multicolored 55 55
113 A51 5.20fr multicolored 1.75 1.75

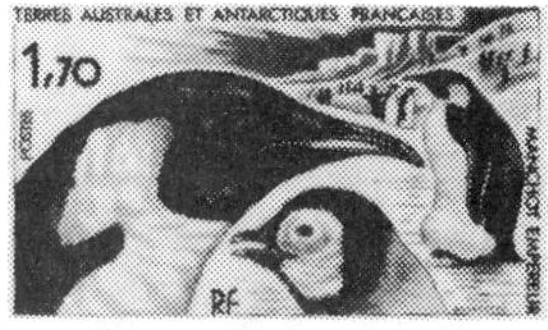

Emperor Penguins — A52

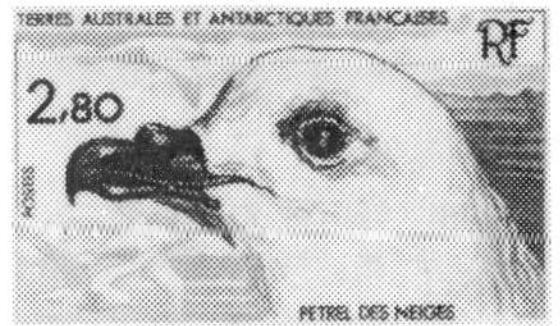

Snowy Petrel — A53

1985, Jan. 1 **Engr.** ***Perf. 13***
114 A52 1.70fr multicolored 60 48
115 A53 2.80fr multicolored 1.25 1.10

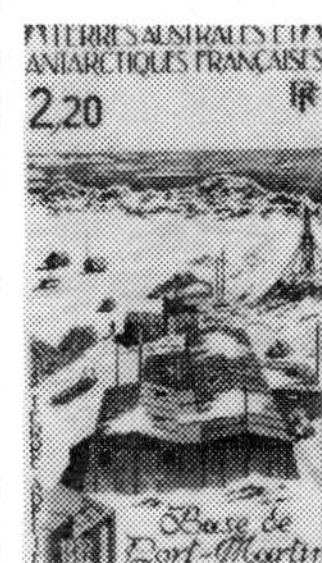

Port Martin — A54

1985, Jan. 1 **Engr.** ***Perf. 13***
116 A54 2.20fr multicolored 85 70

Explorer Type of 1979

1985, Jan. 1 **Engr.** ***Perf. 13***
117 A29 2fr Andre-Frank Liotard 75 60

Antarctic Fulmar — A56

1986, Jan. 1 **Engr.** ***Perf. 13***
118 A56 1fr shown 32 32
119 A56 1.70fr Giant petrels 60 60

See No. C91.

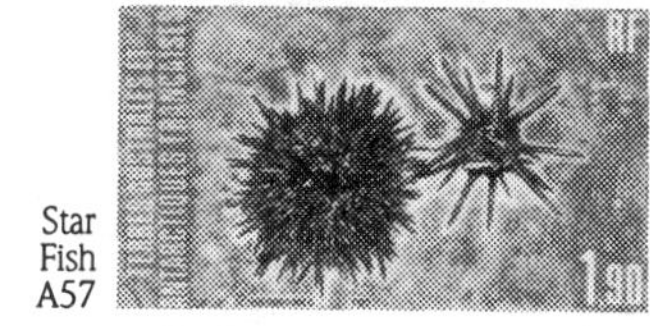

Star Fish A57

1986, Jan. 1
120 A57 1.90fr shown 60 60

Cotula Plumosa — A58

Shipping — A59

1986, Jan. 1
121 A58 2.30fr shown 75 75
122 A58 6.20fr Lycopodium. saururus 1.90 1.90

1986, Jan. 1
123 A59 2.10fr Var research ship 85 85
124 A59 3fr Polarbjorn support ship 1.25 1.25

Marine Life — A60

1987, Jan. 1 **Engr.** ***Perf. 13½x13***
125 A60 50c dk blue & org 25 25

Flora — A61

1987, Jan. 1
126 A61 1.80fr Poa cookii 50 50
127 A61 6.50fr Lichen, Neuropogon taylori 1.90 1.90

Marret Base, Adelie Land — A62

1987, Jan. 1
128 A62 2fr yel brn, dk ultra & lake 65 65

Explorer Type of 1979

1987, Jan. 1
129 A29 2.20fr Adm. Mouchez 70 70

Reindeer — A64

1987, Jan. 1
130 A64 2.50fr black 80 80

Transport Ship Eure — A65

1987, Jan. 1
131 A65 3.20fr dk ultra, Prus grn & dk grn 1.00 1.00

Macaroni Penguins — A66

1987, Jan. 1 ***Perf. 13x12½***
132 A66 4.80fr multicolored 1.65 1.65

Elephant Grass — A67

1988, Jan. 1 **Engr.** ***Perf. 13***
133 A67 1.70fr Prus grn, emer & olive 65 65

Rev.-Father Lejay, Explorer — A68

1988, Jan. 1
134 A68 2.20fr vio, ultra & blk 80 80

Explorer Type of 1979

Design: Robert Gessain (1907-86).

1988, Jan. 1
135 A29 3.40fr gray, dk red & blk 1.25 1.25

Le Gros Ventre, 18th Cent. — A70

1988, Jan. 1
136 A70 3.50fr dp ultra, bl grn & brn 1.25 1.25

Mermaid and B.A.P. Jules Verne, Research Vessel — A71

1988, Jan. 1
137 A71 4.90fr gray & dk blue 1.75 1.75

La Fortune, Early 19th Cent. — A72

1988, Jan. 1
138 A72 5fr blk & dull bl grn 1.75 1.75

Wilson's Petrel — A73

1988, Jan. 1
139 A73 6.80fr blk, sepia & dl bl grn 2.00 2.00

See Nos. 143-144.

Mt. Ross Campaign (in 1987) — A74

1988, Jan. 1 *Perf. 13x12½*

140 A74 2.20fr Volcanic rock cross-sections 70 70
141 A74 15.10fr Kerguelen Is. 5.00 5.00

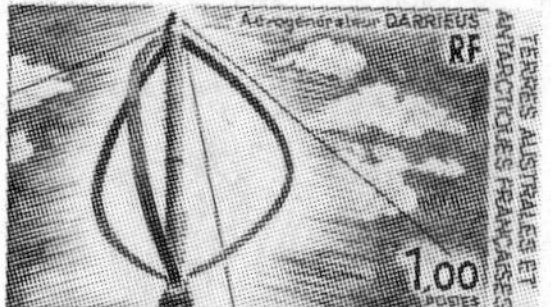

Darrieus System Wind Vane Electric Generator — A75

1988, Jan. 1 **Engr.** *Perf. 13*

142 A75 1fr dark blue & blue 35 35

Fauna Type of 1988

1989, Jan. 1 **Engr.**

143 A73 1.10fr Lithodes 35 35
144 A73 3.60fr Blue petrel 1.15 1.15

Seaweed — A76

1989, Jan. 1

145 A76 2.80fr blk, grn & dark red 90 90

Minerals A77

1989, Jan. 1

146 A77 5.10fr Mesotype 1.50 1.50
147 A77 7.30fr Analcime 2.00 2.00

Henri and Rene Bossiere, Pioneers of the Kerguelen Isls. — A78

1989, Jan. 1

148 A78 2.20fr multicolored 70 70

Kerguelen Is. Sheep — A79

1989, Jan. 1 *Perf. 13½x13*

149 A79 2fr multicolored 65 65

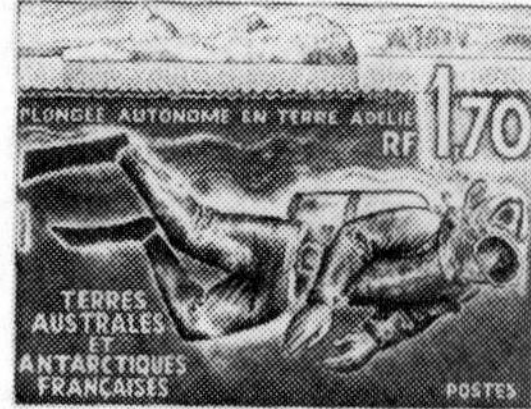

Scuba Diver, Adelie Coast — A80

1989, Jan. 1

150 A80 1.70fr dk olive bis, blue & dk grn 55 55

Map of Kerguelen Island, Protozoa and Copepod — A81

1990, Jan. 1 **Engr.** *Perf. 13*

151 A81 1.10fr blk, brt blue & red brn 40 40

Study of protista, Kerguelan Is.

Cattle on Farm, Sea Birds — A82

1990, Jan. 1

152 A82 1.70fr Prus blue, grn & brn blk 55 55

Rehabilitation of the environment, Amsterdam Is.

Quoy and *Copendium decollata* — A83

Dumont d'Urville (1790-1842), Explorer — A84

1990, Jan. 1 *Perf. 13½x13*

153 A83 2.20fr brt blue, blk & red brn 70 70

Jean Rene C. Quoy (1790-1869), naturalist, navigator.

1990, Jan. 1

154 A84 3.60fr ultra & blk 1.00 1.00

Yellow-billed Albatross — A85

1990, Jan. 1 *Perf. 13x12½*

155 A85 2.80fr multicolored 90 90

Aragonite A86

1990, Jan. 1

156 A86 5.10fr deep ultra & dark yel grn 1.65 1.65

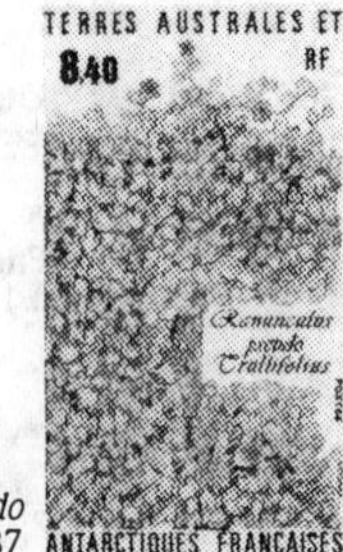

Ranunculus pseudo trullifolius — A87

1990, Jan. 1 *Perf. 13*

157 A87 8.40fr dp bl, org & emer grn 2.75 2.75

Penguin Type of Airpost 1974

1991, Jan. 1

158 AP18 50c blue grn, bl & blk 20 20

Postal Service at Crozet Island, 30th anniv.

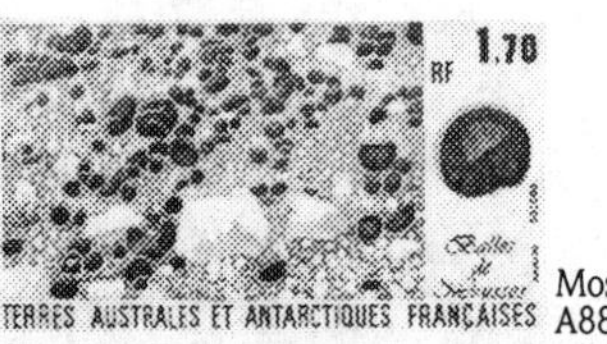

Moss A88

1991, Jan. 1 *Perf. 13x12½*

159 A88 1.70fr gray, brn & blk 65 65

Adm. Max Douguet (1903-1989) A89

1991, Jan. 1

160 A89 2.30fr org brn, blk & bl 90 90

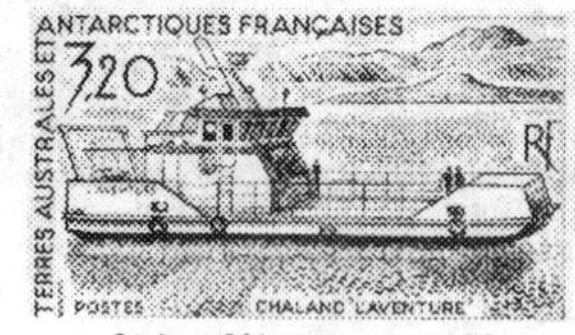

Lighter L'Aventure — A90

1991, Jan. 1 **Engr.** *Perf. 13*

161 A90 3.20fr brn, grn & bl 1.25 1.25

Sea Lions — A91

1991, Jan. 1 *Perf. 13*

162 A91 3.60fr blue & ol brn 1.40 1.40

Mordenite — A92

1991, Jan. 1

163 A92 5.20fr blk, grn bl & grn 2.00 2.00

Champsocephalus Gunnari — A93

1991, Jan. 1

164 A93 7.80fr blue & green 3.00 3.00

A94

A95

1991, Jan. 1

165 A94 9.30fr ol grn & rose red 3.50 3.50

Antarctic Treaty, 30th anniv.

1992, Jan. 1 **Engr.** *Perf. 13*

Design: Colobanthus Kerguelensis.

166 A95 1fr bl grn, grn & brn 40 40

Globe Challenge Yacht Race — A96

1992, Jan. 1 **Litho.**

167 A96 2.20fr multicolored 90 90

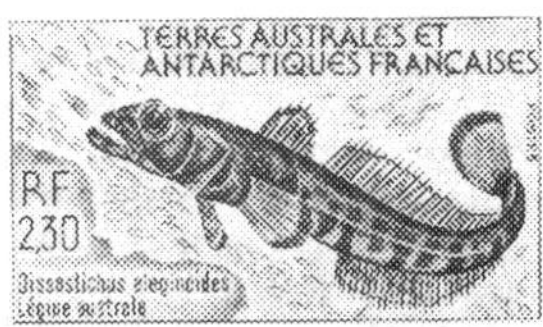

Dissostichus Eleginoides — A97

1992, Jan. 1 **Engr.**
168 A97 2.30fr blue, ol grn & red brn 95 95

Paul Tchernia A98

1992, Jan. 1 **Engr.** ***Perf. 13***
169 A98 2.50fr brown & green 1.00 1.00

Capt. Marion Dufresne (1724-1772) — A99

1992, Jan. 1 **Engr.** ***Perf. 13***
170 A99 3.70fr red, blk & bl 1.50 1.50

Supply Ship Tottan, 1951 — A100

1992, Jan. 1 **Engr.** ***Perf. 13***
171 A100 14fr blue grn, brn & bl 5.80 5.80

WOCE Program — A101

1992, Jan. 1
172 A101 25.40fr multi 10.50 10.50

Coat of Arms — A102

1992-93 **Engr.** ***Perf. 13***
173 A102 10c black 18 18
174 A102 20c greenish blue 15 15
175 A102 30c red 15 15
Set value 38 38

Issue dates: 10c, Jan. 1, 1992. 20c, 30c, Jan. 1, 1993.
This is an expanding set. Numbers may change.

Garnet A103

1993, Jan. 1 **Engr.** ***Perf. 13***
183 A103 1fr multicolored 38 28

Research Ship Marion Dufresne, 20th Anniv. A104

Lyallia Kerguelensis A105

1993, Jan. 1
184 A104 2.20fr multicolored 82 60

1993, Jan. 1
185 A105 2.30fr blue & green 85 62

A106

A107

1993, Jan. 1
186 A106 2.50fr Killer whale 95 68
187 A107 2.50fr Skua 95 68

Explorer Type of 1979 and

Weather station, Adelie Land — A108

Design: 2.50fr, Andre Prudhomme (1930-1959), Meteorologist.

1993, Jan. 1 ***Perf. 12½x13***
188 A29 2.50fr blue, blk & org 90 65
189 A108 22fr orange, blk & blue 8.10 5.80
a. Pair, #188-189 + label 9.00 6.45

Centriscops Obliquus — A109

1993, Jan. 1 ***Perf. 13***
190 A109 3.40fr multicolored 1.25 90

Freighter Italo Marsano — A110

1993, Jan. 1
191 A110 3.70fr multicolored 1.35 1.00

ECOPHY Program A111

1993, Jan. 1
192 A111 14fr black, blue & brn 5.15 3.75

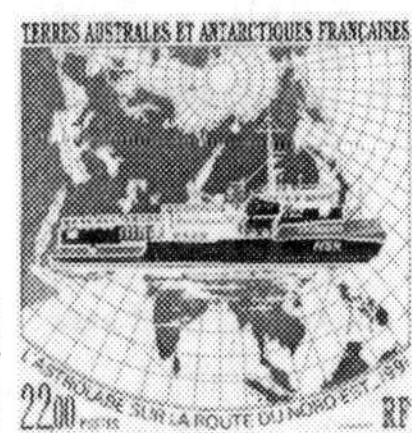

L'Astrolabe on Northeast Route, 1991 — A112

1993, Jan. 1
193 A112 22fr multicolored 8.00 5.75

A114

1994, Jan. 1 **Engr.** ***Perf. 13***
196 A114 2.40fr dk brown, blk & bl 90 65

A115

1994, Jan. 1
197 A115 2.80fr slate blue 1.00 70

Robert Pommier (1919-61) A116

1994, Jan. 1
198 A116 2.80fr multicolored 1.00 70

C.A. Vincendon Dumoulin (1811-58), Hydrographer — A117

Measuring Earth's Magnetic Field — A118

1994, Jan. 1 ***Perf. 12½x13***
199 A117 2.80fr black & blue 1.00 70
200 A118 23fr blue & black 8.00 5.75
a. Pair, #199-200 + label 9.00 6.50

Rascasse — A119

1994, Jan. 1 ***Perf. 13***
201 A119 3.70fr bl grn & red brn 1.40 95

TERRES AUSTRALES & ANTARCTIQUES FRANÇAISES 4,30 RF POSTES LE KERGUELEN DE TREMAREC

Kerguelen of Tremarec — A120

1994, Jan. 1
202 A120 4.30fr multicolored 1.50 1.10

Market value for a particular scarce stamp may remain relatively low if few collectors want it.

AIR POST STAMPS

Emperor Penguins and Map of Antarctica — AP1

Unwmk.

1956, Apr. 25 Engr. *Perf. 13*

C1	AP1 50fr lt ol grn & dk grn	30.00	25.00
C2	AP1 100fr dl bl & ind	30.00	25.00

Wandering Albatross — AP2

1959, Sept. 14

C3	AP2 200fr brn red, bl & blk	27.50	22.50

Adélie Penguins — AP3

1963, Feb. 11 Unwmk. *Perf. 13*

C4	AP3 50fr blk, dk bl & dp claret	37.50	35.00

Telstar Issue

Common Design Type

1963, Feb. 11

C5	CD111 50fr dp bl, ol & grn	22.50	17.50

Radio Towers, Adelie Penguins and IQSY Emblem — AP4

1963, Dec. 16 Engr.

C6	AP4 100fr bl, ver & blk	95.00	90.00

International Quiet Sun Year, 1964-65.

Discovery of Adelie Land — AP5

1965, Jan. 20 Engr. *Perf. 13*

C7	AP5 50fr blue & indigo	110.00	100.00

125th anniversary of the discovery of Adelie Land by Dumont d'Urville.

ITU Issue

Common Design Type

1965, May 17 Unwmk. *Perf. 13*

C8	CD120 30fr Prus bl, sep & dk car rose	225.00	190.00

French Satellite A-1 Issue

Common Design Type

Designs: 25fr, Diamant rocket and launching installations. 30fr, A-1 satellite.

1966, Mar. 2 Engr. *Perf. 13*

C9	CD121 25fr dk grn, choc & sl	12.50	10.00
C10	CD121 30fr choc, sl & dk grn	12.50	10.00
a.	Pair, #C9-C10 + label	25.00	20.00

French Satellite D-1 Issue

Common Design Type

1966, Mar. 27

C11	CD122 50fr dk pur, lil & org	42.50	32.50

Ionospheric Research Pylon, Adelie Land — AP6

1966, Dec. 12

C12	AP6 25fr plum, bl & dk brn	20.00	15.00

Port aux Franais, Emperor Penguin and Explorer — AP7

Design: 40fr, Aerial view of Saint Paul Island.

1968-69 Engr. *Perf. 13*

C13	AP7 40fr brt bl & dk gray	32.50	26.00
C14	AP7 50fr lt ultra, dk grn & blk	100.00	92.50

Issue dates: 50fr, Jan. 21; 40fr, Jan. 5, 1969.

Kerguelen Island and Rocket — AP8

Design: 30fr, Adelie Land.

1968, Apr. 22 Engr. *Perf. 13*

C15	AP8 25fr sl grn, dk brn & Prus bl	14.00	10.00
C16	AP8 30fr dk brn, sl grn & Prus bl	14.00	10.00
a.	Pair, #C15-C16 + label	30.00	22.50

Space explorations with Dragon rockets, 1967-68.

Eiffel Tower, Antarctic Research Station, Ship from Paris Arms and Albatross AP9

1969, Jan. 13

C17	AP9 50fr bright blue	35.00	27.50

5th Consultative Meeting of the Antarctic Treaty Powers, Paris, Nov. 18, 1968.

Concorde Issue

Common Design Type

1969, Apr. 17

C18	CD129 85fr indigo & blue	38.00	32.50

Map of Amsterdam Island AP10

Map of Kerguelen Island — AP11

Coat of Arms — AP12

Designs: 50fr, Possession Island. 200fr, Point Geology Archipelago.

1969-71 Engr. *Perf. 13*

C19	AP10 30fr brown	12.50	10.00
C20	AP11 50fr sl grn, bl & dk red	15.00	14.00
C21	AP11 100fr blue & blk	40.00	27.50
C22	AP10 200fr sl grn, brn & Prus bl	52.50	40.00
C23	AP12 500fr peacock blue	10.00	10.00
	Nos. C19-C23 (5)	130.00	101.50

30fr for the 20th anniv. of the Amsterdam Island Meteorological Station.

Issue dates: 100fr, 500fr, Dec. 21; 30fr, Mar. 27, 1970; 50fr, Dec. 22, 1970; 200fr, Jan. 1, 1971.

Port-aux-Franais, 1970 — AP13

Design: 40fr, Port-aux-Franais, 1950.

1971, Mar. 9 Engr. *Perf. 13*

C24	AP13 40fr bl, ocher & sl grn	12.00	10.00
C25	AP13 50fr bl, grn ol & sl grn	12.00	10.00
a.	Pair, #C24-C25 + label	27.50	22.50

20th anniversary of Port-aux-Franais on Kerguelen Island.

Marquis de Castries Taking Possession of Crozet Island, 1772 — AP14

Design: 250fr, Fleur-de-lis flag raising on Kerguelen Island.

1972 Engr. *Perf. 13*

C26	AP14 100fr black	35.00	27.50
C27	AP14 250fr black & dk brn	60.00	50.00

Bicentenary of the discovery of the Crozet and Kerguelen Islands.

Issue dates: 100fr, Jan. 24; 250fr, Feb. 23.

M. S. Galliéni — AP15

1973, Jan. 25 Engr. *Perf. 13*

C28	AP15 100fr black & blue	16.00	16.00

Exploration voyages of the Galliéni.

"Le Mascarin," 1772 — AP16

Designs: Sailing Ships: 145fr, "L'Astrolabe," 1840. 150fr, "Le Rolland," 1774. 185fr, "La Victoire," 1522.

1973, Dec. 13 Engr. *Perf. 13*

C29	AP16 120fr brown olive	3.25	2.50
C30	AP16 145fr brt ultra	3.25	3.00
C31	AP16 150fr slate	4.25	4.25
C32	AP16 185fr ocher	5.25	4.50

Ships used in exploring Antarctica.

See Nos. C37-C38.

Alfred Faure Base — AP17

Design: Nos. C33-C35 show panoramic view of Alfred Faure Base.

1974, Jan. 7 **Engr.** *Perf. 13*

C33	AP17 75fr Prus bl, ultra & brn	6.00	4.25
C34	AP17 110fr Prus bl, ultra & brn	8.50	5.75
C35	AP17 150fr Prus bl, ultra & brn	8.50	7.00
a.	Triptych, Nos. C33-C35	25.00	19.00
	Nos. C33-C35 (3)	23.00	17.00

Alfred Faure Antarctic Base, 10th anniv.

Penguin, Map of Antarctica, Letters — AP18

1974, Oct. 9 **Engr.** *Perf. 13*

C36	AP18 150fr multicolored	6.00	5.00

Centenary of Universal Postal Union.

Ship Type of 1973

Designs: 100fr, "Le Franais." 200fr, "Pourquoi-pas?"

1974, Dec. 16 **Engr.** *Perf. 13*

C37	AP16 100fr brt blue	3.00	2.00
C38	AP16 200fr dk car rose	4.50	3.00

Ships used in exploring Antarctica.

Rockets over Kerguelen Islands — AP19

Design: 90fr, Northern lights over map of northern coast of Russia.

1975, Jan. 26 **Engr.** *Perf. 13*

C39	AP19 45fr purple & multi	4.75	3.50
C40	AP19 90fr purple & multi	4.75	3.50
a.	Pair, #C39-C40 + label	13.00	13.00

Franco-Soviet magnetosphere research.

"La Curieuse" — AP20

Ships: 2.70fr, Commandant Charcot. 4fr, Marion-Dufresne.

1976, Jan. **Engr.** *Perf. 13*

C41	AP20 1.90fr multicolored	2.50	1.75
C42	AP20 2.70fr multicolored	4.25	3.50
C43	AP20 4fr red & multi	5.25	4.25

Dumont d'Urville Base, 1956 — AP21

Design: 4fr, Dumont d'Urville Base, 1976, Adelie Land.

1976, Jan.

C44	AP21 1.20fr multicolored	4.50	3.50
C45	AP21 4fr multicolored	9.00	6.75
a.	Pair, #C44-C45 + label	15.00	12.50

Dumont d'Urville Antarctic Base, 20th anniv.

Capt. Cook's Ships Passing Kerguelen Island — AP22

1976, Dec. 31 **Engr.** *Perf. 13*

C46	AP22 3.50fr slate & blue	7.00	6.00

Bicentenary of Capt. Cook's voyage past Kerguelen Island.

Sea Lion and Cub — AP23

1977-79 **Engr.** *Perf. 13*

C47	AP23 4fr dk blue grn ('79)	2.50	2.50
C48	AP23 10fr multicolored	9.50	9.50

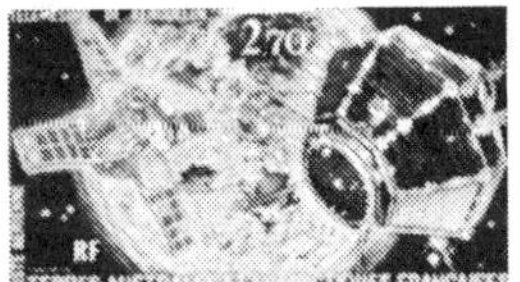

Satellite Survey, Kerguelen — AP24

Designs: 70c, Geophysical laboratory. 1.90fr, Satellite and Kerguelen tracking station. 3fr, Satellites, Adelie Land.

1977-79 **Engr.** *Perf. 13*

C49	AP24 50c multi ('79)	65	65
C50	AP24 70c multi ('79)	65	60
C51	AP24 1.90fr multi ('79)	1.40	1.25
C52	AP24 2.70fr multi ('78)	1.75	1.75
C53	AP24 3fr multicolored	3.00	3.00
	Nos. C49-C53 (5)	7.45	7.25

Elephant Seals — AP25

1979, Jan. 1

C54	AP25 10fr multicolored	4.00	4.00

Challenger — AP26

1979, Jan. 1

C55	AP26 2.70fr black & blue	1.65	1.65

Antarctic expeditions to Crozet and Kerguelen Islands, 1872-1876.

La Recherche and L'Esperance — AP27

1979

C56	AP27 1.90fr deep blue	95	75

Arrival of d'Entrecasteaux and Kermadec at Amsterdam Island, Mar. 28, 1792.

Lion Rock — AP28

1979

C57	AP28 90c multicolored	65	65

Natural Arch, Kerguelen Island, 1840 — AP29

1979

C58	AP29 2.70fr multicolored	95	85

Phylica Nitida, Amsterdam Island — AP30

1979

C59	AP30 10fr multicolored	3.25	3.25

Charles de Gaulle, 10th Anniversary of Death AP31

1980, Nov. 9 **Engr.** *Perf. 13*

C60	AP31 5.40fr multicolored	7.50	7.50

HB-40 Castor Truck and Trailer — AP32

1980, Dec. 15

C61	AP32 2.40fr multicolored	90	90

Supply Ship Saint Marcouf — AP33

1980, Dec. 15

C62	AP33 3.50fr shown	1.00	90
C63	AP33 7.30fr Icebreaker Norsel	2.00	1.75

Glacial Landscape, Dumont d'Urville Sea — AP34

Chionis — AP35

Adele Dumont d'Urville (1798-1842) AP36

The Scott Catalogue value is a retail price; that is, what you could expect to pay for the stamp in a grade of Fine-Very Fine. The value listed reflects recent actual dealer selling prices.

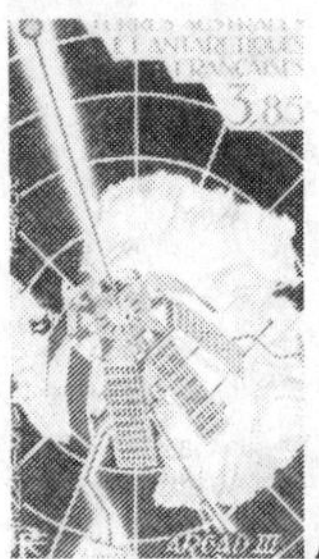
Arcad III — AP37

25th Anniv. of Charcot Station — AP38

Antares — AP39

1981 Engr. *Perf. 13, 12½x13 (2fr)*

C64 AP34 1.30fr multicolored 50 40
C65 AP35 1.50fr black 55 50
C66 AP36 2fr black & lt brn 85 85
C67 AP37 3.85fr multicolored 1.25 1.25
C68 AP38 5fr multicolored 1.75 1.50
C69 AP39 8.40fr multicolored 2.25 2.25
Nos. C64-C69 (6) 7.15 6.75

PHILEXFRANCE '82 Stamp Exhibition, Paris, June 11-21 — AP40

1982, June 11 Engr. *Perf. 13*

C70 AP40 8fr multicolored 5.25 5.25

French Overseas Possessions Week, Sept. 18-25 — AP41

1982, Sept. 17 Engr. *Perf. 13*

C71 AP41 5fr Commandant Charcot 1.75 1.75

Apostle Islands — AP42

1983, Jan. 3 Engr. *Perf. 13*

C72 AP42 65c multicolored 50 35

Sputnik I — AP43

Orange Bay Base, Cape Horn, 1883 — AP44

Intl. Polar Year Centenary and 24th Anniv. of Intl. Geophysical Year: 5.20fr, Scoresby Sound Base, Greenland, 1983.

1983, Jan. 3

C73 AP43 1.50fr multicolored 60 60
C74 AP44 3.30fr multicolored 1.65 1.65
C75 AP44 5.20fr multicolored 2.00 2.00
a. Strip of 3, #C73-C75 4.50 4.50

AP45

1983, Jan. 3

C76 AP45 4.55fr dark blue 3.50 2.75

Abstract, by G. Mathieu — AP46

Illustration reduced.

1983, Jan. 3 Photo. *Perf. 13x13½*

C77 AP46 25fr multicolored 9.00 9.00

Erebus off Antarctic Ice Cap, 1842 — AP47

Port of Joan of Arc, 1930 — AP48

1984, Jan. 1 Engr. *Perf. 13*

C78 AP47 2.60fr ultra & dk blue 1.25 1.10
C79 AP48 4.70fr multicolored 1.75 1.75

Aurora Polaris — AP49

1984, Jan. 1 Photo.

C80 AP49 3.50fr multicolored 1.75 1.25

Manned Flight Bicentenary (1983) — AP50

Various balloons and airships.

1984, Jan. 1 Engr.

C81 AP50 3.50fr multicolored 1.50 1.50
C82 AP50 7.80fr multicolored 2.50 2.50
a. Pair, #C81-C82 + label 4.00 4.00

Patrol Boat Albatros — AP51

1984, July 2 Engr. *Perf. 13*

C83 AP51 11.30fr multi 4.25 4.25

NORDPOSTA Exhibition — AP52

1984, Nov. 3 Engr. *Perf. 13*

C84 AP52 9fr Scientific Vessel Gauss 3.50 3.50

Issued se-tenant with label.

Corsican Sheep — AP53

Amsterdam Albatross — AP54

1985, Jan. 1 Engr. *Perf. 13*

C85 AP53 70c Mouflons 30 30
C86 AP54 3.90fr Diomedia amsterdamensis 1.50 1.25

La Novara, Frigate AP55

1985, Jan. 1 Engr. *Perf. 13*

C87 AP55 12.80fr La Novara at St. Paul 4.50 4.50

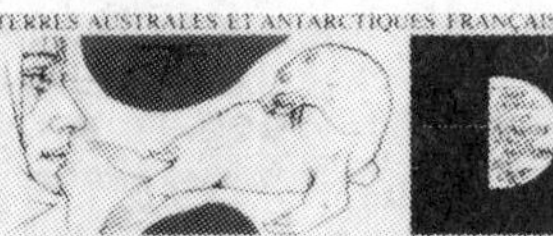

Explorer and Seal, by Tremois — AP56

Design: Explorer, seal, names of territories. Illustration reduced.

1985, Jan. 1 Photo. *Perf. 13x12½*

C88 AP56 30fr + label 8.00 8.00

Sailing Ships, Ropes, Flora & Fauna — AP57

1985, Aug. 6 Engr. *Perf. 13*

C89 AP57 2fr blk, brt bl & ol grn 52 52
C90 AP57 12.80fr blk, ol grn & brt bl 3.75 3.75
a. Pair, #C89-C90 + label 5.50 5.50

French Southern & Antarctic Territories, 30th anniv. No. C90a has continuous design with center label.

Bird Type of 1986

1986, Jan. 1 Engr. *Perf. 13½x13*

C91 A56 4.60fr Sea Gulls 1.50 1.50

Antarctic Atmospheric Research, 10th Anniv. — AP58

1986, Jan. 1

C92 AP58 14fr blk, dk red & brt org 4.00 4.00

Jean Charcot (1867-1936), Explorer — AP59

1986, Jan. 1

C93 AP59 2.10fr Ship Pourquoi Pas 60 60
C94 AP59 14fr Ship in storm 4.25 4.25
a. Pair, #C93-9C5 + label 5.00 5.00

SPOT Satellite over the Antarctic — AP60

1986, May 26 Engr. *Perf. 13*

C95 AP60 8fr dp ultra, sep & dk ol grn 2.50 2.50

J.B. Charcot — AP61

1987, Jan. 1 Engr. *Perf. 13x13½*

C96 AP61 14.60fr multi 4.50 4.50

Marine Oil Drilling Program — AP62

1987, Jan. 1 *Perf. 13½x13*

C97 AP62 16.80fr lem, dk ultra & bluish blk 4.50 4.50

INMARSAT — AP63

1987, Mar. 2 Engr. *Perf. 13*

C98 AP63 16.80fr multi 7.00 7.00

French Polar Expeditions, 40th Anniv. — AP64

1988, Jan. 1

C99 AP64 20fr lake, ol grn & plum 6.75 6.75

Views of Penguin Is. — AP65

1988, Jan. 1

C100 AP65 3.90fr dk blue & sepia 1.25 1.25
C101 AP65 15.10fr dp grn, choc brn & dk bl 5.00 5.00

Founding of Permanent Settlements in the Territories, 40th Anniv. — AP66

1989, Jan. 1 Engr. *Perf. 13½x13*

C102 AP66 15.50fr black 4.75 4.75

Apostle Islands — AP67

1989, Jan. 1

C103 AP67 8.40fr multi 2.50 2.50

La Curieuse — AP68

1989, Jan. 1 *Perf. 13x12½*

C104 AP68 2.20fr multicolored 70 70
C105 AP68 15.50fr multi, diff. 5.00 5.00
a. Pair, #C104-C105 + label 6.00 6.00

No. C105a label continues the design.

French Revolution, Bicent. — AP69

1989, July 14 Engr. *Perf. 13x12½*

C106 AP69 5fr pink, dark olive grn & dark blue 1.50 1.50

Souvenir Sheet

Perf. 13

C107 Sheet of 4 6.00 6.00
a. AP69 5fr Prussian green, bright ultra & dark red 1.50 1.50

No. C107 for PHILEXFRANCE '89.

15th Antarctic Treaty Summit Conference — AP70

1989, Oct. 9 Engr. *Perf. 13*

C108 AP70 17.70fr multicolored 5.75 5.75

Isle of Pigs, Crozet Isls. — AP71

1990, Jan. 1 Engr. *Perf. 13*

C109 AP71 7.30fr multicolored 2.40 2.40

L'Astrolabe, Expedition Team — AP72

1990, Jan. 1

C110 AP72 15.50fr dk red vio & blk 5.00 5.00

Discovery of Adelie Land by Dumont D'Urville, 150th anniv.

L'Astrolabe, Commanded by Dumont D'Urville, 1840 — AP73

1990, Jan. 1

C111 AP73 2.20fr *L'Astrolabe,* 1988 72 72
C112 AP73 15.50fr shown 5.00 5.00
a. Pair, #C111-C112 + label 6.00 6.00

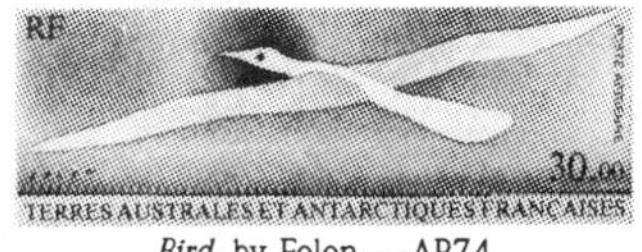

Bird, by Folon — AP74

Illustration reduced.

1990, Jan. 1 Litho. *Perf. 12½x13*

C113 AP74 30fr multicolored 10.50 10.50

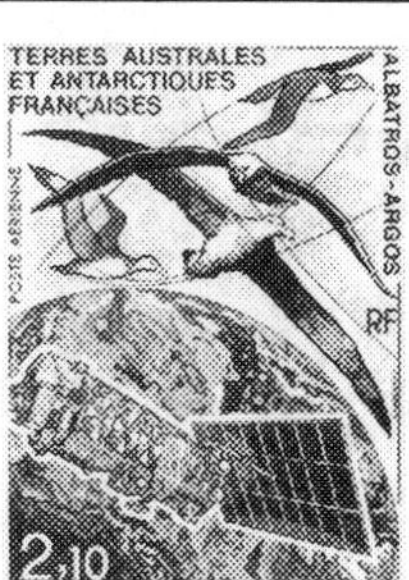

Albatross, Argos Satellite AP75

1991, Jan. 1

C114 AP75 2.10fr red brn, bl & brn 80 80

Climatological Research — AP76

1991, Jan. 1 Engr. *Perf. 13*

C115 AP76 3.60fr Weather balloons, instruments 1.40 1.40
C116 AP76 20fr Research ship 7.60 7.60
a. Pair, #C115-C116 + label 9.00 9.00

Charles de Gaulle (1890-1970) AP77

1991, Jan. 1

C117 AP77 18.80fr blk, red & bl 7.15 7.15

Cape Petrel — AP78

1992, Jan. 1 Engr. *Perf. 13*

C118 AP78 3.40fr multicolored 1.40 1.40

French Institute of Polar Research and Technology — AP79

Designs: No. C120, Polar bear with man offering flowers.

1991, Dec. 16 Engr. *Perf. 13x12*

C119 AP79 15fr multicolored 6.15 6.15
C120 AP79 15fr multicolored 6.15 6.15
a. Strip of 2, #C119-C120 + label 12.30 12.30

Christopher Columbus and Discovery of America — AP80

1992, Jan. 1 *Perf. 13*
C121 AP80 22fr multicolored 9.00 9.00

Mapping Satellite Poseidon — AP81

1992, Jan. 1 **Engr.** *Perf. 13*
C122 AP81 24.50fr multicolored 10.00 10.00

Dumont d'Urville Base, Adelie Land — AP82

Illustration reduced.

1992, Jan. 1 **Litho.** *Perf. 13x12½*
C123 AP82 25.70fr multi 10.50 10.50

Amateur Radio — AP83

1993, Jan. 1 **Engr.** *Perf. 13*
C124 AP83 2fr multicolored 75 55

New Animal Biology Laboratory, Adelie Land — AP84

1993, Jan. 1
C125 AP84 25.40fr multicolored 9.35 6.75

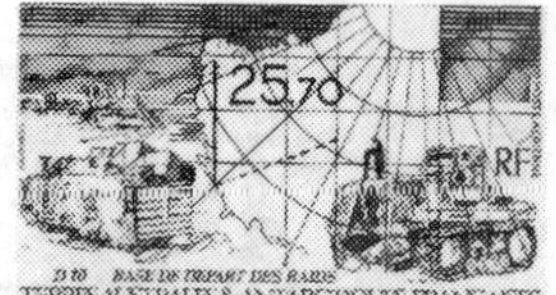

Support Base D10 — AP85

1993, Jan. 1
C126 AP85 25.70fr olive, red & blue 9.50 6.85

Opening of Adelie Land Airfield — AP86

1993, Jan. 1
C127 AP86 30fr multicolored 11.00 8.00

Krill — AP87

1994, Jan. 1 **Engr.** *Perf. 13*
C128 AP87 15fr black 5.25 4.00

Fishery Management — AP88

1994, Jan. 1
C129 AP88 23fr multicolored 8.00 5.75

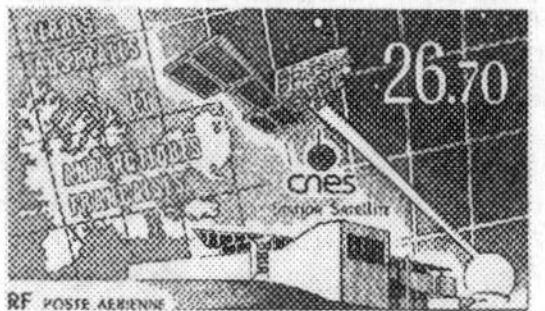

Satellite, Ground Station — AP89

Design: 27.30fr, Lidar Station.

1994, Jan. 1
C130 AP89 26.70fr multicolored 9.25 6.50
C131 AP89 27.30fr multicolored 9.50 6.75

Arrival of Emperor Penguins — AP90

Illustration reduced.

1994, Jan. 1 *Perf. 13x12½*
C132 AP90 28fr blue & black 9.75 7.25

FRENCH SUDAN

LOCATION — In northwest Africa, north of French Guinea and Ivory Coast
GOVT. — Former French Colony
AREA — 590,966 sq. mi.
POP. — 3,794,270 (1941)
CAPITAL — Bamako

In 1899 French Sudan was abolished as a separate colony and was divided among Dahomey, French Guinea, Ivory Coast, Senegal and Senegambia and Niger. Issues for French Sudan were resumed in 1921.

From 1906 to 1921 a part of this territory was known as Upper Senegal and Niger. A part of Upper Volta was added in 1933. See Mali.

100 Centimes = 1 Franc

Navigation and Commerce
A1 A2

Stamps of French Colonies, Surcharged in Black

Perf. 14x13½

1894, Apr. 12 **Unwmk.**

1	A1	15c	on 75c car, *rose*	*2,250.*	*1,250.*
2	A1	25c	on 1fr brnz grn, *straw*	*2,500.*	*1,000.*

The imperforate stamp like No. 1 was made privately in Paris from a fragment of the lithographic stone which had been used in the Colony for surcharging No. 1.

Counterfeit surcharges exist.

1894-1900 **Typo.** *Perf. 14x13½*

Name of colony in Blue or Carmine

3	A2	1c	blk, *lil bl*	80	80
4	A2	2c	brn, *buff*	90	90
5	A2	4c	claret, *lav*	2.25	2.00
6	A2	5c	grn, *grnsh*	3.00	2.50
7	A2	10c	blk, *lav*	6.50	6.50
8	A2	10c	red ('00)	1.50	1.60
9	A2	15c	blue, quadrille paper	2.00	1.75
10	A2	15c	gray, *lt gray* ('00)	3.00	3.00
11	A2	20c	red, *grn*	11.00	10.00
12	A2	25c	blk, *rose*	11.00	10.00
13	A2	25c	blue ('00)	2.50	2.50
14	A2	30c	brn, *bister*	21.00	16.00
15	A2	40c	red, *straw*	12.00	10.00
16	A2	50c	car, *rose*	22.50	22.50
17	A2	50c	brn, *az* ('00)	4.50	4.50
18	A2	75c	dp vio, *org*	16.00	16.00
19	A2	1fr	brnz grn, *straw*	4.00	4.00
			Nos. 3-19 (17)	124.45	114.55

Perf. 13½x14 stamps are counterfeits.

Nos. 8, 10, 13, 17 were issued in error. They were accepted for use in the other colonies.

Camel and Rider — A3

Stamps of Upper Senegal and Niger Overprinted in Black

1921-30 *Perf. 13½x14*

21	A3	1c	brn vio & vio	15	15
22	A3	2c	dk gray & dl vio	15	15
23	A3	4c	blk & blue	15	15
24	A3	5c	ol brn & dk brn	15	15
25	A3	10c	yel grn & bl grn	15	15
26	A3	10c	red vio & bl ('25)	15	15
27	A3	15c	red brn & org	15	15
28	A3	15c	yel grn & dp grn ('25)	15	15
29	A3	15c	org brn & vio ('27)	65	65
30	A3	20c	brn vio & blk	15	15
31	A3	25c	blk & bl grn	22	22
a.			Booklet pane of 4		
32	A3	30c	red org & rose	22	22
33	A3	30c	bl grn & blk ('26)	15	15
34	A3	30c	dl grn & bl grn ('28)	80	80
35	A3	35c	rose & vio	15	15
36	A3	40c	gray & rose	35	22
37	A3	45c	bl & ol brn	22	20
38	A3	50c	ultra & bl	32	25
39	A3	50c	red org & bl ('26)	38	22
40	A3	60c	vio, *pnksh* ('26)	22	15
41	A3	65c	bis & pale bl ('28)	60	60
42	A3	75c	org & ol brn	28	25
43	A3	90c	brn red & pink ('30)	2.50	2.50
44	A3	1fr	dk brn & dl vio	50	42
45	A3	1.10fr	gray lil & red vio ('28)	1.10	1.10
46	A3	1.50fr	dp bl & bl ('30)	2.50	2.50
47	A3	2fr	grn & bl	1.00	80
48	A3	3fr	red vio ('30)	4.25	4.25
a.			Double overprint	65.00	
49	A3	5fr	vio & blk	2.50	2.25
			Nos. 21-49 (29)	20.26	19.25

Type of 1921 Surcharged **60 = 60**

1922, Sept. 28
50 A3 60c on 75c vio, *pnksh* 22 22

Stamps and Type of 1921-30 Surcharged with New Values and Bars

1925-27

51	A3	25c	on 45c	22	22
52	A3	65c	on 75c	60	45
53	A3	85c	on 2fr	80	65
54	A3	85c	on 5fr	80	65
55	A3	90c	on 75c brn red & sal pink ('27)	90	80
56	A3	1.25fr	on 1fr dp bl & lt bl (R) ('26)	50	45
57	A3	1.50fr	on 1fr dp bl & ultra ('27)	50	45
58	A3	3fr	on 5fr dl red & brn org ('27)	1.60	1.10
59	A3	10fr	on 5fr brn red & bl grn ('27)	8.00	6.50
60	A3	20fr	on 5fr vio & ver ('27)	11.00	9.50
			Nos. 51-60 (10)	24.92	20.77

Sudanese Woman — A4

Entrance to the Residency at Djenné — A5

Sudanese Boatman — A6

1931-40 **Typo.** *Perf. 13x14*

61	A4	1c	dk red & blk	15	15
62	A4	2c	dp bl & org	15	15
63	A4	3c	dk red & blk ('40)	15	15
64	A4	4c	gray lil & rose	15	15
65	A4	5c	ind & grn	15	15
66	A4	10c	ol grn & rose	15	15
67	A4	15c	blk & brt vio	15	15
68	A4	20c	hn brn & lt bl	15	15
69	A4	25c	red vio & lt red	15	15
70	A5	30c	grn & lt grn	20	15
71	A5	30c	dk bl & red org ('40)	15	15
72	A5	35c	ol grn & grn ('38)	15	15
73	A5	40c	ol grn & pink	15	15
74	A5	45c	dk bl & red org	28	22
75	A5	45c	ol grn & grn ('40)	15	15
76	A5	50c	red & blk	15	15
77	A5	55c	ultra & car ('38)	20	20
78	A5	60c	brt bl & brn ('40)	38	38
79	A5	65c	brt vio & blk	15	15
80	A5	70c	vio bl & car rose ('40)	15	15
81	A5	75c	brt bl & ol brn	80	60
82	A5	80c	car & brn ('38)	15	15
83	A5	90c	dp red & red org	28	22
84	A5	90c	brt vio & sl blk ('39)	20	20
85	A5	1fr	ind & grn	3.25	55
86	A5	1fr	rose red ('38)	1.60	38
87	A5	1fr	car & brn ('40)	15	15
88	A6	1.25fr	vio & dl vio ('33)	28	22
89	A6	1.25fr	red ('39)	20	20
90	A6	1.40fr	brt vio & blk ('40)	20	20
91	A6	1.50fr	dk bl & ultra	15	15
92	A6	1.60fr	brn & dp bl ('40)	20	20
93	A6	1.75fr	dk brn & dp bl ('33)	20	20
94	A6	1.75fr	vio bl ('38)	20	20
95	A6	2fr	org brn & grn	28	15
96	A6	2.25fr	vio bl & ultra ('39)	32	32
97	A6	2.50fr	lt brn ('40)	40	40
98	A6	3fr	Prus grn & brn	28	15
99	A6	5fr	red & blk	65	38
100	A6	10fr	dl bl & grn	90	60
101	A6	20fr	red vio & brn	1.25	70
			Nos. 61-101 (41)	15.40	
			Set value		7.75

For surcharges see Nos. B7-B10.

Colonial Exposition Issue
Common Design Types

1931, Apr. 13 Engr. *Perf. 12½*
Name of Country Printed in Black

102 CD70 40c deep green 1.00 1.00
103 CD71 50c violet 1.00 1.00
104 CD72 90c red orange 1.00 1.00
105 CD73 1.50fr dull blue 1.00 1.00

Paris International Exposition Issue
Common Design Types

1937, Apr. 15 *Perf. 13*

106 CD74 20c dp vio 50 50
107 CD75 30c dk grn 50 50
108 CD76 40c car rose 50 50
109 CD77 50c dk brn 50 50
110 CD78 90c red 50 50
111 CD79 1.50fr ultra 50 50
Nos. 106-111 (6) 3.00 3.00

Colonial Arts Exhibition Issue
Souvenir Sheet
Common Design Type

1937 Engr. *Imperf.*

112 CD77 3fr magenta & blk 2.25 2.25

Caillie Issue
Common Design Type

1939, Apr. 5 *Perf. 12½x12*

113 CD81 90c org brn & org 35 35
114 CD81 2fr brt vio 35 35
115 CD81 2.25fr ultra & dk bl 35 35

New York World's Fair Issue
Common Design Type

1939, May 10

116 CD82 1.25fr car lake 42 42
117 CD82 2.25fr ultra 42 42

Entrance to the Residency at Djenné and Marshal Pétain — A7

1941 Engr. *Perf. 12x12½*

118 A7 1fr green 22 22
119 A7 2.50fr blue 22 22

Stamps of types A4 and A5 without "RF" were issued in 1943 and 1944 by the Vichy Government, but were not placed on sale in the colony.

Stamps of French Sudan were superseded by those of French West Africa.

See French West Africa No. 70 for stamp inscribed "Soudan Francais" and "Afrique Occidentale Francaise."

SEMI-POSTAL STAMPS

Curie Issue
Common Design Type
Unwmk.

1938, Oct. 24 Engr. *Perf. 13*

B1 CD80 1.75fr + 50c brt ultra 5.00 5.00

French Revolution Issue
Common Design Type

1939, July 5 Photo.
Name and Value Typo. in Black

B2 CD83 45c + 25c grn 3.25 3.25
B3 CD83 70c + 30c brn 3.25 3.25
B4 CD83 90c + 35c red org 3.25 3.25
B5 CD83 1.25fr + 1fr rose pink 3.25 3.25
B6 CD83 2.25fr + 2fr blue 3.25 3.25
Nos. B2-B6 (5) 16.25 16.25

Stamps of 1931-40, Surcharged in Black or Red

SECOURS
+ 1 fr.
NATIONAL

1941 *Perf. 13x14*

B7 A5 50c + 1fr red & blk (R) 65 65
B8 A5 80c + 2fr car & brn 3.50 3.50
B9 A6 1.50fr + 2fr dk bl & ultra 3.50 3.50
B10 A6 2fr + 3fr org brn & grn 3.50 3.50

Common Design Type and

Native Officer — SP1

Aviation Officer — SP2

1941 Photo. *Perf. 13½*

B11 SP1 1fr + 1fr red 42
B12 CD86 1.50fr + 3fr claret 42
B13 SP2 2.50fr + 1fr blue 42

Surtax for the defense of the colonies.
Issued by the Vichy government and not placed on sale in the colony.

Stamps of type A7, surcharged "OEUVRES COLONIALES" and new values, were issued in 1944 by the Vichy Government, but were not placed on sale in the colony.

AIR POST STAMPS

Common Design Type
Perf. 12½x12

1940, Feb. 8 Unwmk. Engr.

C1 CD85 1.90fr ultra 15 15
C2 CD85 2.90fr dark red 20 20
C3 CD85 4.50fr dk gray grn 40 40
C4 CD85 4.90fr yel bister 40 40
C5 CD85 6.90fr dp org 42 42
Nos. C1-C5 (5) 1.57 1.57

Common Design Types

1942, Oct. 19

C6 CD88 50c car & bl 15 25
C7 CD88 1fr brn & blk 15
C8 CD88 2fr dk grn & red brn 15
C9 CD88 3fr dk bl & scar 22
C10 CD88 5fr vio & brn red 22

Frame Engr., Center Typo.

C11 CD89 10fr ultra, ind & gray blk 22
C12 CD89 20fr rose car, mag & lt vio 28
C13 CD89 50fr yel grn, dl grn & dl bl 65 1.00
Nos. C6-C13 (8) 2.04

There is doubt whether Nos. C7-C12 were officially placed in use.

AIR POST SEMI-POSTAL STAMPS

Stamps of type of Dahomey V1, V2, V3 and V4 inscribed "Soudan Frcais", "Soudan" or "Soudan Francais" were issued in 1942 by the Vichy Government, but were not placed on sale in the colony.

POSTAGE DUE STAMPS

D1

D2

Postage Due Stamps of Upper Senegal and Niger Overprinted

Perf. 14x13½

1921, Dec. Unwmk. Typo.

J1 D1 5c green 20 20
J2 D1 10c rose 28 28
J3 D1 15c gray 28 28
J4 D1 20c brown 40 40
J5 D1 30c blue 40 40
J6 D1 50c black 60 60
J7 D1 60c orange 80 80
J8 D1 1fr violet 1.00 1.00
Nos. J1-J8 (8) 3.96 3.96

Type of 1921 Issue Surcharged **2F.**

1927, Oct. 10

J9 D1 2fr on 1fr lilac rose 2.50 2.50
J10 D1 3fr on 1fr org brown 2.50 2.50

1931, Mar. 9

J11 D2 5c green 15 15
J12 D2 10c rose 15 15
J13 D2 15c gray 15 15
J14 D2 20c dark brown 15 15
J15 D2 30c dark blue 15 15
J16 D2 50c black 15 15
J17 D2 60c deep orange 20 20
J18 D2 1fr violet 45 45
J19 D2 2fr lilac rose 60 60
J20 D2 3fr red brown 60 60
Set value 2.20 2.20

FRENCH WEST AFRICA

LOCATION — Northwestern Africa
GOVT. — Former French colonial administrative unit
AREA — 1,821,768 sq. mi.
POP. — 18,777,163 (est.)
CAPITAL — Dakar

French West Africa comprised the former colonies of Senegal, French Guinea, Ivory Coast, Dahomey, French Sudan, Mauritania, Niger and Upper Volta.

In 1958, these former colonies became republics, eventually issuing their own stamps. Until the republic issues appeared, stamps of French West Africa continued in use. The Senegal and Sudanese Republics issued stamps jointly as the Federation of Mali, starting in 1959.

Catalogue values for all unused stamps in this country are for Never Hinged items.

Many stamps other than Nos. 65-72 and 77 are inscribed "Afrique Occidentale Francaise" and the name of one of the former colonies. See listings in these colonies for such stamps.

Senegal No. 156 Surcharged in Red

50 fr.
=

1943 Unwmk. *Perf. 12½x12*

1 A30 1.50fr on 65c dk vio 32 32
2 A30 5.50fr on 65c dk vio 35 35
3 A30 50fr on 65c dk vio 1.10 1.10

Mauritania No. 91 Surcharged in Red

5 fr. =

1944 *Perf. 13*

4 A7 3.50fr on 65c dp grn 15 15
5 A7 4fr on 65c dp grn 25 15
6 A7 5fr on 65c dp grn 42 42
7 A7 10fr on 65c dp grn 45 35
Nos. 1-7 (7) 3.04 2.84

Senegal No. 143, 148 and 188 Surcharged with New Values in Black and Orange

1944 *Perf. 12½x12*

8 A29 1.50fr on 15c blk (O) 30 30
9 A29 4.50fr on 15c blk (O) 35 35
10 A29 5.50fr on 2c brn 70 70
11 A29 10fr on 15c blk (O) 70 70
12 CD81 20fr on 90c org brn & org 90 80
13 CD81 50fr on 90c org brn & org 1.50 1.40

Mauritania No. 109 Surcharged in Black

14 CD81 15fr on 90c org brn & org 55 45
Nos. 8-14 (7) 5.00 4.70

Eboue Issue
Common Design Type

1945 Engr. *Perf. 13*

15 CD91 2fr black 35 35
16 CD91 25fr Prussian green 80 80

Nos. 15 and 16 exist imperforate.

Colonial Soldier — A1

1945 Litho. *Perf. 12*

17 A1 10c indigo & buff 15 15
18 A1 30c olive & yel 15 15
19 A1 40c blue & buff 20 20
20 A1 50c red org & gray 15 15
21 A1 60c ol brn & bl 15 15
22 A1 70c mag & cit 22 22
23 A1 80c bl grn & pale lem 20 20
24 A1 1fr brn vio & cit 15 15
25 A1 1.20fr gray brn & cit 1.60 1.10
26 A1 1.50fr choc & pink 20 15
27 A1 2fr ocher and gray 35 20
28 A1 2.40fr red & gray 55 40
29 A1 3fr brn red & yelsh 15 15
30 A1 4fr ultra & pink 15 15
31 A1 4.50fr org brn & yelsh 15 15
32 A1 5fr dk pur & yelsh 15 15
33 A1 10fr ol grn & pink 60 15
34 A1 15fr org & yel 80 50
35 A1 20fr sl grn & grnsh 90 65
Nos. 17-35 (19) 6.97
Set value 4.15

Rifle Dance, Mauritania — A2

Shelling Coconuts, Togo — A6

Bamako Dike, French Sudan — A3

Trading Canoe, Niger River — A4

Oasis of Bilma, Niger — A5

Kouandé Weaving, Dahomey — A7

Donkey Caravan, Senegal — A8

Crocodile and Hippopotamus, Ivory Coast — A9

Gathering Coconuts, French Guinea — A10

Peul Woman of Dienné — A12

Bamako Fountain, French Sudan — A11

Bamako Market — A13

Dahomey Laborer — A14

Woman of Mauritania — A15

Fula Woman, French Guinea — A16

Djenné Mosque, French Sudan — A17

Monorail Train, Senegal A18

Agni Woman, Ivory Coast — A19

Azwa Women at Niger River — A20

1947 Engr. Unwmk. *Perf. 12½*

36	A2	10c blue	15	15
37	A3	30c red brn	15	15
38	A4	40c gray grn	15	15
39	A5	50c red brn	15	15
40	A6	60c gray blk	25	22
41	A7	80c brn vio	38	35
42	A8	1fr maroon	15	15
43	A9	1.20fr dk bl grn	65	45
44	A10	1.50fr ultra	65	45
45	A11	2fr red org	15	15
46	A12	3fr chocolate	25	15
47	A13	3.60fr brn red	75	55
48	A14	4fr deep blue	15	15
49	A15	5fr gray grn	15	15
50	A16	6fr dark blue	20	15
51	A17	10fr brn red	55	15
52	A18	15fr sepia	62	15
53	A19	20fr chocolate	55	15
54	A20	25fr grnsh blk	1.00	15
		Nos. 36-54 (19)	7.05	
		Set value		3.15

Types of 1947

1948 Re-engraved

55	A6	60c brown olive	35	22
56	A12	3fr chocolate	28	15

Nos. 40 and 46 are inscribed "TOGO" in lower margin. Inscription omitted on Nos. 55 and 56.

Imperforates

Most stamps of French West Africa from 1949 onward exist imperforate in issued and trial colors, and also in small presentation sheets in issued colors.

Military Medal Issue

Common Design Type

Engraved and Typographed

1952, Dec. 1 ***Perf. 13***

57 CD101 15fr blk, grn, yel & blk brn 2.50 2.50

Treich Laplène and Map — A21

1952, Dec. 1 Engr.

58 A21 40fr brown lake 80 15

Marcel Treich Laplène, a leading contributor to the development of Ivory Coast.

Medical Laboratory A22

1953, Nov. 18

59 A22 15fr brn, dk bl grn & blk brn 55 15

Couple Feeding Antelopes A23

1954, Sept. 20

60 A23 25fr multi 65 15

Gov. Noel Eugène Ballay — A24

1954, Nov. 29

61 A24 8fr indigo & brown 65 28

Chimpanzee A25

Giant Pangolin A26

1955, May 2 Unwmk. *Perf. 13*

62	A25	5fr gray & dk brn	65	35
63	A26	8fr brn & bl grn	65	35

International Exhibition for Wildlife Protection, Paris, May 1955.

Map, Symbols of Industry, Rotary Emblem — A27

1955, July 4

64 A27 15fr dark blue 65 40

50th anniv. of the founding of Rotary Intl.

FIDES Issue

Mossi Railroad Upper Volta — A28

Designs: 1fr, Date grove, Mauritania. 2fr, Milo Bridge, French Guinea. 4fr, Cattle raising, Niger. 15fr, Farm machinery and landscape, Senegal. 17fr, Woman and Niger River, French Sudan. 20fr, Palm oil production, Dahomey. 30fr, Road construction, Ivory Coast.

1956 Engr. *Perf. 13x12½*

65	A28	1fr dk grn & dk bl grn	30	22
66	A28	2fr dk bl grn & bl	30	22
67	A28	3fr dk brn & red brn	50	40
68	A28	4fr dk car rose	50	40
69	A28	15fr ind & ultra	60	22
70	A28	17fr dk bl & ind	65	28
71	A28	20fr rose lake	65	28
72	A28	30fr dk pur & claret	70	55
		Nos. 65-72 (8)	4.20	2.57

See note after Common Design Type CD103.

Coffee — A28a

1956, Oct. 22 ***Perf. 13***

73 A28a 15fr dk bl grn 28 15

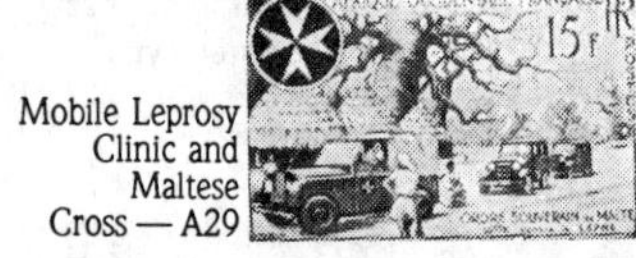

Mobile Leprosy Clinic and Maltese Cross — A29

1957, Mar. 11

74 A29 15fr dk red brn, pur & red 70 15

Issued in honor of the Knights of Malta.

Map of Africa — A30

1958, Feb. Unwmk. *Perf. 13*

75 A30 20fr grnsh bl, blk & dl red brn 65 40

Issued to publicize the sixth International Congress for African Tourism at Dakar.

"Africa" and Communications Symbols — A31

1958, Mar. 15 Engr.

76 A31 15fr org, ultra & choc 65 35

Stamp Day. See No. 86.

Abidjan Bridge — A32

1958, Mar. 15

77 A32 20fr dk sl grn & grnsh bl 65 35

Bananas — A33

1958, May 19 ***Perf. 13***

78 A33 20fr rose lil, dk grn & ol 45 16

Flower Issue

Common Design Type

Designs: 10fr, Gloriosa. 25fr, Adenopus. 30fr, Cyrtosperma. 40fr, Cistanche. 65fr, Crinum Moorei.

1958-59 Photo. *Perf. 12x12½*

79	CD104	10fr multi	35	15
80	CD104	25fr red, yel & grn	40	22
81	CD104	30fr multi	50	38
82	CD104	40fr blk brn, grn & yel	80	60
83	CD104	65fr multi	1.10	60
		Nos. 79-83 (5)	3.15	1.95

Issue dates: 25fr, 40fr, Jan. 5, 1959. Others, July 7, 1958.

Moro Naba Sagha and Map — A34

1958, Nov. 1 Engr. *Perf. 13*

84 A34 20fr ol brn, car & vio 60 35

10th anniv. of the reestablishment of the Upper Volta territory.

Human Rights Issue

Common Design Type

1958, Dec. 10

85 CD105 20fr mar & dk bl 90 90

Type of 1958 Redrawn

1959, Mar. 21 Engr. *Perf. 13*

86 A31 20fr red, grnsh bl & sl grn 1.10 80

Name of country omitted on No. 86; "RF" replaced by "CF," inscribed "Dakar-Abidjan." Stamp Day.

SEMI-POSTAL STAMPS

Red Cross Issue

Common Design Type

Perf. 14½x14

1944, Dec. Photo. Unwmk.

B1 CD90 5fr + 20fr plum 2.50 2.50

The surtax was for the French Red Cross and national relief.

Type of France, 1945, Overprinted in Black **A O F**

1945, Oct. 13 Engr. *Perf. 13*

B2 SP150 2fr + 3fr orange red		40	40

Tropical Medicine Issue
Common Design Type

1950, May 15 *Perf. 13*

B3 CD100 10fr +2fr red brn & sepia	3.00	3.00

The surtax was for charitable work.

AIR POST STAMPS

Common Design Type

1945 Photo. Unwmk. *Perf. 14½x14*

No.	Type	Description	Unused	Used
C1	CD87	5.50fr ultra	40	35
C2	CD87	50fr dk grn	1.65	35
C3	CD87	100fr plum	1.65	35

Victory Issue
Common Design Type

1946, May 8 Engr. *Perf. 12½*

No.	Type	Description	Unused	Used
C4	CD92	8fr violet	42	40

Chad to Rhine Issue
Common Design Types

1946, June 6

No.	Type	Description	Unused	Used
C5	CD93	5fr brn car	65	65
C6	CD94	10fr deep blue	65	65
C7	CD95	15fr brt vio	75	75
C8	CD96	20fr dk slate grn	95	95
C9	CD97	25fr olive brn	1.40	1.40
C10	CD98	50fr brown	1.90	1.90
		Nos. C5-C10 (6)	6.30	6.30

Antoine de Saint-Exupéry, Map and Natives — AP1

Plane over Dakar AP2

Great White Egrets in Flight AP3

Natives and Phantom Plane — AP4

1947, Mar. 24 Engr.

No.	Type	Description	Unused	Used
C11	AP1	8fr red brn	28	28
C12	AP2	50fr rose vio	1.10	28
C13	AP3	100fr ultra	4.25	2.00
C14	AP4	200fr slate gray	6.50	1.40

UPU Issue
Common Design Type

1949, July 4 *Perf. 13*

No.	Type	Description	Unused	Used
C15	CD99	25fr multi	4.00	4.00

Vridi Canal, Abidjan AP5

1951, Nov. 5 Unwmk. *Perf. 13*

No.	Type	Description	Unused	Used
C16	AP5	500fr red org, bl grn & dp ultra	12.00	3.00

Liberation Issue
Common Design Type

1954, June 6

No.	Type	Description	Unused	Used
C17	CD102	15fr indigo & ultra	2.00	1.50

Logging — AP6

Designs: 100fr, Radiotelephone exchange. 200fr, Baobab trees.

1954, Sept. 20

No.	Type	Description	Unused	Used
C18	AP6	50fr ol grn & org brn	1.50	40
C19	AP6	100fr ind, dk brn & dk grn	1.90	60
C20	AP6	200fr bl grn, grnsh blk & brn lake	5.75	1.75

Gen. Louis Faidherbé and African Sharpshooter — AP7

1957, July 20 Unwmk. *Perf. 13*

No.	Type	Description	Unused	Used
C21	AP7	15fr indigo & bl	80	80

Centenary of French African troops.

Gorée Island and Woman AP8

Designs: 20fr, Map with planes and ships. 25fr, Village and modern city. 40fr, Seat of Council of French West Africa. 50fr, Worker, ship and peanut plant. 100fr, Bay of N'Gor.

1958, Mar. 15 Engr.

No.	Type	Description	Unused	Used
C22	AP8	15fr blk brn, grn & vio	40	30
C23	AP8	20fr blk brn, dk bl & red brn	40	30
C24	AP8	25fr blk vio, bis & grn	40	30
C25	AP8	40fr dk bl, brn & grn	40	30
C26	AP8	50fr vio, brn & grn	60	45
C27	AP8	100fr brn, bl & grn	1.90	70
a.		Souv. sheet of 6, #C22-C27	6.00	6.00
		Nos. C22-C27 (6)	4.10	2.35

Centenary of Dakar.

Woman Playing Native Harp — AP9

1958, Dec. 1 Unwmk. *Perf. 13*

No.	Type	Description	Unused	Used
C28	AP9	20fr red brn, blk & gray	65	45

Inauguration of Nouakchott as capital of Mauritania.

POSTAGE DUE STAMPS

D1

1947 Engr. Unwmk. *Perf. 13*

No.	Type	Description	Unused	Used
J1	D1	10c red	15	15
J2	D1	30c deep orange	15	15
J3	D1	50c greenish blk	15	15
J4	D1	1fr carmine	15	15
J5	D1	2fr emerald	15	15
J6	D1	3fr red lilac	15	15
J7	D1	4fr deep ultra	25	25
J8	D1	5fr red brown	60	60
J9	D1	10fr peacock blue	90	90
J10	D1	20fr sepia	2.25	2.25
		Nos. J1-J10 (10)	4.90	4.90

OFFICIAL STAMPS

Mask — O1

Designs: Various masks.

Perf. 14x13

1958, June 2 Typo. Unwmk.

No.	Type	Description	Unused	Used
O1	O1	1fr dk brn red	20	20
O2	O1	3fr brt green	20	20
O3	O1	5fr crim rose	15	15
O4	O1	10fr light ultra	18	15
O5	O1	20fr bright red	30	15
O6	O1	25fr purple	30	15
O7	O1	30fr green	45	70
O8	O1	45fr gray black	50	45
O9	O1	50fr dark red	75	35
O10	O1	65fr brt ultra	1.10	45
O11	O1	100fr olive bister	2.00	35
O12	O1	200fr deep green	4.00	1.25
		Nos. O1-O12 (12)	10.13	4.55

FUJEIRA

LOCATION — Oman Peninsula, Arabia, on Persian Gulf

GOVT. — Sheikdom under British protection

Fujeira is one of six Persian Gulf sheikdoms to join the United Arab Emirates which proclaimed independence Dec. 2, 1971. See United Arab Emirates.

100 Naye Paise = 1 Rupee

Catalogue values for all unused stamps in this country are for Never Hinged items.

Sheik Hamad bin Mohammed al Sharqi and Grebe — A1

Sheik and: 2np, 50np, Arabian oryx. 3np, 70np, Hoopoe. 4np, 1r, Wild ass. 5np, 1.50r, Herons in flight. 10np, 2r, Arabian horses. 15np, 3r, Leopard. 20np, 5r, Camels. 30np, 10r, Hawks.

Photo. & Litho.

1964 Unwmk. *Perf. 14*

Size: 36x24mm

No.	Type	Description	Unused	Used
1	A1	1np gold & multi	15	15
2	A1	2np gold & multi	15	15
3	A1	3np gold & multi	15	15
4	A1	4np gold & multi	15	15
5	A1	5np gold & multi	15	15
6	A1	10np gold & multi	15	15
7	A1	15np gold & multi	15	15
8	A1	20np gold & multi	15	15
9	A1	30np gold & multi	15	15

Size: 43x28mm

No.	Type	Description	Unused	Used
10	A1	40np gold & multi	15	15
11	A1	50np gold & multi	15	15
12	A1	70np gold & multi	28	15
13	A1	1r gold & multi	22	15
14	A1	1.50r gold & multi	65	18
15	A1	2r gold & multi	45	22

Size: 53½x35mm

No.	Type	Description	Unused	Used
16	A1	3r gold & multi	65	32
17	A1	5r gold & multi	1.10	55
18	A1	10r gold & multi	3.50	1.10
		Nos. 1-18 (18)	8.50	
		Set value		3.00

Dates of issue: Nov. 14, for 20np, 30np, 70np, 1.50r, 3r and 10r; Sept. 22 for others.

Sheik Hamad and Shot Put A2

1964, Dec. 6 *Perf. 14*

Size: 43x28mm

No.	Type	Description	Unused	Used
19	A2	25np shown	15	15
20	A2	50np Discus	15	15
21	A2	75np Fencing	15	15
22	A2	1r Boxing	20	15
23	A2	1.50r Relay race	30	15
24	A2	2r Soccer	40	20

Size: 53½x35mm

No.	Type	Description	Unused	Used
25	A2	3r Pole vaulting	60	30
26	A2	5r Hurdling	1.00	50
27	A2	7.50r Equestrian	1.50	75
		Nos. 19-27 (9)	4.45	
		Set value		2.15

18th Olympic Games, Tokyo, Oct. 10-25, 1964.

John F. Kennedy — A3

John F. Kennedy: 10np, As sailor in the Pacific. 15np, As naval lieutenant. 20np, On speaker's rostrum. 25np, Sailing with family. 50np, With crowd of people. 1r, with Mrs. Kennedy and Lyndon B. Johnson. 2r, With Dwight D. Eisenhower on White House porch. 3r, With Mrs. Kennedy and Caroline. 5r, Portrait.

1965, Feb. 23 Photo. *Perf. 13½*

Size: 29x44mm

Black Design with Gold Inscriptions

No.	Type	Description	Unused	Used
28	A3	5np pale gray	15	15
29	A3	10np pale yellow	15	15
30	A3	15np pink	15	15
31	A3	20np pale greenish gray	15	15
32	A3	25np pale blue	15	15
33	A3	50np pale rose	15	15

Size: 33x51mm

No.	Type	Description	Unused	Used
34	A3	1r pale gray	22	15
35	A3	2r pale green	45	22
36	A3	3r pale gray	55	32
37	A3	5r pale yellow	80	55
		Set value	2.40	1.40

Pres. John F. Kennedy (1917-1963). A souvenir sheet contains 2 29x44mm stamps similar to Nos. 36-37 with pale blue (3r) and pale rose (5r) backgrounds.

Nos. 28-37 exist imperf.
Stamps of Fujeira were replaced in 1972 by those of United Arab Emirates.

AIR POST STAMPS

Arabian Oryx AP1

Photo. & Litho.
1965, Aug. 16 Unwmk. *Perf. 13½*
Size: 43x28mm

C1 AP1 15np Grebe 15 15
C2 AP1 25np shown 15 15
C3 AP1 35np Hoopoe 18 15
C4 AP1 50np Wild ass 15 15
C5 AP1 75np Herons in flight 35 15
C6 AP1 1r Arabian horses 22 15

Size: 53½x35mm

C7 AP1 2r Leopard 45 16
C8 AP1 3r Camels 60 28
C9 AP1 5r Hawks 1.50 50
Nos. C1-C9 (9) 3.75
Set value 1.30

AIR POST OFFICIAL STAMPS

Type of Air Post Issue, 1965
Photo. & Litho.
1965, Nov. 10 Unwmk. *Perf. 13½*
Size: 43x28mm

CO1 AP1 75np Arabian horses 20 15

Perf. 13
Size: 53½x35mm

CO2 AP1 2r Leopard 50 28
CO3 AP1 3r Camels 65 40
CO4 AP1 5r Hawks 1.75 65

OFFICIAL STAMPS

Type of Air Post Issue, 1965
Photo. & Litho.
1965, Oct. 14 Unwmk. *Perf. 13½*
Size: 43x28mm

O1 AP1 25np Grebe 15 15
O2 AP1 40np Arabian oryx 15 15
O3 AP1 50np Hoopoe 15 15
O4 AP1 75np Wild ass 20 15
O5 AP1 1r Herons in flight 28 16
Nos. O1-O5 (5) 93
Set value 47

FUNCHAL

LOCATION — A city and administrative district in the Madeira island group in the Atlantic Ocean northwest of Africa
GOVT. — A part of the Republic of Portugal
POP. — 150,574 (1900)

Postage stamps of Funchal were superseded by those of Madeira. These, in turn, were displaced by the stamps of Portugal.

1000 Reis = 1 Milreis

King Carlos
A1 A2

Perf. 11½, 12½, 13½
1892-93 Typo. Unwmk.

1 A1 5r yellow 1.00 65
a. Half used as 2½r on cover 16.00
b. Perf. 11½ 4.00 2.75
2 A1 10r red violet 1.10 80
3 A1 15r chocolate 1.75 1.25
4 A1 20r lavender 2.00 1.25
a. Perf. 13½ 4.00 3.00
5 A1 25r dark green 1.65 85
6 A1 50r ultra 2.75 65
a. Perf. 13½ 5.75 1.50
7 A1 75r carmine 5.50 4.00
8 A1 80r yel green 6.50 5.50
a. Perf. 13½ 9.50 8.00
9 A1 100r brn, *yel* ('93) 3.25 2.50
a. Diagonal half used as 50r on cover
10 A1 150r car, *rose* ('93) 15.00 10.00
11 A1 200r dk bl, *bl* ('93) 25.00 20.00
12 A1 300r dk bl, *sal* ('93) 30.00 22.50
Nos. 1-12 (12) 95.50 69.95

The reprints of this issue have shiny white gum and clean-cut perforation 13½. The shades differ from those of the originals and the uncolored paper is thin.

1897-1905 *Perf. 12*
Name and Value in Black except Nos. 25 and 34

13 A2 2½r gray 15 15
14 A2 5r orange 15 15
15 A2 10r light green 15 15
16 A2 15r brown 2.75 2.00
17 A2 15r gray grn ('99) 1.90 1.25
18 A2 20r gray vio 50 25
19 A2 25r sea green 1.25 32
20 A2 25r car rose ('99) 65 15
a. Booklet pane of 6
21 A2 50r dark blue 3.50 70
a. Perf. 12½ 10.50 2.00
22 A2 50r ultra ('05) 50 25
23 A2 65r slate blue ('98) 50 25
24 A2 75r rose 75 45
25 A2 75r brn & red, *yel* ('05) 80 1.00
26 A2 80r violet 65 40
27 A2 100r dark blue, *blue* 65 40
a. Diagonal half used as 50r on cover
28 A2 115r org brn, *pink* ('98) 1.50 1.50
29 A2 130r gray brown, *buff* ('98) 1.50 1.50
30 A2 150r lt brn, *buff* 1.90 1.50
31 A2 180r sl, *pnksh* ('98) 1.90 1.50
32 A2 200r red vio, *pale lil* 2.00 2.00
33 A2 300r blue, *rose* 2.00 1.75
34 A2 500r blk & red, *bl* 2.00 1.50
a. Perf. 12½ 6.00 4.25
Nos. 13-34 (22) 27.65 19.12

GABON

LOCATION — West coast of Africa, at the equator
GOVT. — Republic
AREA — 102,089 sq. mi.
POP. — 1,367,000 (est. 1984)
CAPITAL — Libreville

Gabon originally was under the control of French West Africa. In 1886, it was united with French Congo. In 1904, Gabon was granted a certain degree of colonial autonomy which prevailed until 1934, when it merged with French Equatorial Africa. Gabon Republic was proclaimed November 28, 1958.

100 Centimes = 1 Franc

Catalogue values for unused stamps in this country are for Never Hinged items, beginning with Scott 148 in the regular postage section, Scott B4 in the semi-postal section, Scott C1 in the airpost section, Scott CB1 in the airpost semi-postal section, Scott J34 in the postage due section, and Scott O1 in the officials section.

Stamps of French Colonies of 1881-86 Handstamp Surcharged in Black:

a

10
GAB
b

1886 Unwmk. *Perf. 14x13½*

1 A9 (a) 5c on 20c red, *grn* 225.00 225.00
2 A9 (b) 10c on 20c red, *grn* 225.00 225.00
3 A9 (b) 25c on 20c red, *grn* 20.00 15.00
e. 56 dots around "GAB" 2,250. 550.00
4 A9 (b) 50c on 15c blue 800.00 800.00
5 A9 (b) 75c on 15c blue 900.00 850.00

Nos. 1-3 exist with double surcharge of numeral; No. 3 with "GAB" double or inverted, or with "25" double.
On Nos. 3 and 5 the surcharge slants down; on No. 4 it slants up. The number of dots varies.
Counterfeits of Nos. 1-15 exist.

Handstamp Surcharged in Black **15**

1888-89

6 A9 15c on 10c blk, *lav* 2,250. 450.00
7 A9 15c on 1fr brnz grn, *straw* 1,200. 525.00
8 A9 25c on 5c grn, *grnsh* 550.00 110.00
9 A9 25c on 10c blk, *lav* 3,000. 725.00
10 A9 25c on 75c car, *rose* 1,600. 650.00

Official reprints exist.

Postage Due Stamps of French Colonies Handstamp Surcharged in Black

GABON
TIMBRE
15

1889 *Imperf.*

11 D1 15c on 5c black 100.00 70.00
12 D1 15c on 30c blk 3,000. 2,250.
13 D1 25c on 20c blk 50.00 40.00

Nos. 11 and 13 exist with "GABON," "TIMBRE" or "25" double; "TIMBRE" or "15" omitted, etc.

A8

1889 Typeset

14 A8 15c blk, *rose* 1,000. 525.00
15 A8 25c blk, *green* 550.00 375.00

Ten varieties of each. Nos. 14-15 exist with "GAB" inverted or omitted, and with small "f" in "Francaise."

Navigation and Commerce — A9

1904-07 Typo. *Perf. 14x13½*
Name of Colony in Blue or Carmine

16 A9 1c blk, *lil bl* 35 35
a. "GABON" double 175.00
17 A9 2c brn, *buff* 35 35
18 A9 4c claret, *lav* 60 60
19 A9 5c yel grn 90 90
20 A9 10c rose 2.75 2.75
21 A9 15c gray 2.75 2.75
22 A9 20c red, *grn* 4.25 4.25
23 A9 25c blue 2.75 2.75
24 A9 30c yel brn 6.00 6.00
25 A9 35c blk, *yel* ('06) 9.25 9.25
26 A9 40c red, *straw* 6.25 6.25
27 A9 45c blk, *gray grn* ('07) 13.00 13.00
28 A9 50c brn, *az* 4.75 4.75
29 A9 75c dp vio, *org* 8.50 8.50
30 A9 1fr brnz grn, *straw* 15.00 15.00
31 A9 2fr vio, *rose* 37.50 37.50
32 A9 5fr lil, *lav* 67.50 67.50
Nos. 16-32 (17) 182.45 182.45

Perf. 13½x14 stamps are counterfeits.
For surcharges see Nos. 72-84.

Fang Warrior — A10

Fang Woman — A12

Libreville A11

Inscribed: "Congo Francais"

1910 *Perf. 13½x14*

33 A10 1c choc & org 60 60
34 A10 2c blk & choc 90 90
35 A10 4c vio & dp bl 1.00 1.00
36 A10 5c ol gray & grn 1.20 1.20
37 A10 10c red & car 2.25 2.25
38 A10 20c choc & dk vio 2.25 2.25
39 A11 25c dp bl & choc 1.75 1.75
40 A11 30c gray blk & red 14.00 14.00
41 A11 35c dk vio & grn 7.25 7.25
42 A11 40c choc & ultra 10.00 10.00
43 A11 45c car & vio 16.00 16.00
44 A11 50c bl grn & gray 25.00 25.00
45 A11 75c org & choc 45.00 30.00
46 A12 1fr dk brn & bis 47.50 47.50
47 A12 2fr car & brn 130.00 130.00
48 A12 5fr bl & choc 120.00 120.00
Nos. 33-48 (16) 424.70 409.70

For surcharge see No. B1.

A13

A15

A14

Inscribed: "Afrique Equatoriale"

1910-22

49 A13 1c choc & org 15 15
50 A13 2c blk & choc 15 15
a. 2c gray blk & dp ol 15 15
51 A13 4c vio & dp bl 15 15
52 A13 5c ol gray & grn 26 15
53 A13 5c gray blk & ocher ('22) 26 26
54 A13 10c red & car 25 20
55 A13 10c yel grn & bl grn ('22) 26 26
56 A13 15c brn vio & rose ('18) 26 25
57 A13 20c ol brn & dk vio 3.00 2.50
58 A14 25c dp bl & choc 35 25
59 A14 25c Prus bl & blk ('22) 48 48
60 A14 30c gray blk & red 30 25
61 A14 30c rose & red ('22) 30 30
62 A14 35c dk vio & grn 52 32
63 A14 40c choc & ultra 35 25
64 A14 45c car & vio 30 25
65 A14 45c blk & red ('22) 48 48
66 A14 50c bl grn & gray 25 24
67 A14 50c dk bl & bl ('22) 30 30
68 A14 75c org & choc 2.50 2.00
69 A15 1fr dk brn & bis 1.20 1.00
70 A15 2fr car & brn 2.00 1.40
71 A15 5fr bl & choc 3.50 3.00
Nos. 49-71 (23) 17.57 14.59

For overprints and surcharges see Nos. 85-119, B2-B3.

Stamps of 1904-07 Surcharged in Black or Carmine

05 **10**

1912

72 A9 5c on 2c brn, *buff* 35 35
73 A9 5c on 4c cl, *lav* (C) 35 35
74 A9 5c on 15c gray (C) 25 25
75 A9 5c on 20c red, *grn* 25 25
76 A9 5c on 25c bl (C) 25 25
77 A9 5c on 30c pale brn (C) 25 25
78 A9 10c on 40c red, *straw* 25 25
79 A9 10c on 45c blk, *gray grn* (C) 35 35
80 A9 10c on 50c brn, *az* (C) 35 35
81 A9 10c on 75c dp vio, *org* 35 35
82 A9 10c on 1fr brnz grn, *straw* 35 35
83 A9 10c on 2fr vio, *rose* 40 40
a. inverted surch. 175.00 175.00
84 A9 10c on 5fr lil, *lav* 1.40 1.40
Nos. 72-84 (13) 5.15 5.15

Two spacings between the surcharged numerals are found on Nos. 72 to 84.

Stamps of 1910-22 Overprinted in Black, Blue or Carmine — **AFRIQUE EQUATORIALE FRANÇAISE**

1924-31

85 A13 1c brn & org 15 15
86 A13 2c blk & choc (Bl) 15 15
87 A13 4c vio & ind 15 15
88 A13 5c gray blk & ocher 15 15
89 A13 10c yel grn & bl grn 15 15
a. Double ovpt. (Bk & Bl) 70.00 70.00
90 A13 10c dk bl & brn ('26) (C) 15 15
91 A13 15c brn vio & rose (Bl) 25 25
92 A13 15c rose & brn vio ('31) (Bl) 50 50
93 A13 20c ol brn & dk vio (C) 25 25
a. Inverted ovpt. 75.00 75.00

Overprinted **AFRIQUE EQUATORIALE FRANÇAISE**

94 A14 25c Prus bl & blk (C) 25 25
95 A14 30c rose & red (Bl) 25 25
96 A14 30c blk & org ('26) 25 25
97 A14 30c dk grn & bl grn ('28) 50 50
98 A14 35c dk vio & grn (Bl) 22 22
99 A14 40c choc & ultra (C) 22 22
100 A14 45c blk & red (Bl) 40 40
101 A14 50c dk bl & bl (C) 22 22
102 A14 50c car & grn ('26) 16 16
103 A14 65c dp bl & red org ('28) 1.65 1.65
104 A14 75c org & brn (Bl) 60 60
105 A14 90c brn red & rose ('30) 1.10 1.10

Overprinted like Nos. 85 to 93

106 A15 1fr dk brn & bis 85 85
107 A15 1.10fr dl grn & rose red ('28) 2.75 2.25
108 A15 1.50fr pale bl & dk bl ('30) 60 60
109 A15 2fr rose & brn 85 85
110 A15 3fr red vio ('30) 3.00 2.75
111 A15 5fr dp bl & choc 2.50 2.50
Nos. 85-111 (27) 18.27 17.52

Types of 1924-31 Issues Surcharged with New Values in Black or Carmine

1925-28

112 A15 65c on 1fr ol grn & brn 50 50
113 A15 85c on 1fr ol grn & brn 50 50
114 A14 90c on 75c brn red & cer ('27) 75 75
115 A15 1.25fr on 1fr dk bl & ultra (C) 50 50
116 A15 1.50fr on 1fr lt bl & dk bl ('27) 65 65
117 A15 3fr on 5fr mag & ol brn 2.25 2.25
118 A15 10fr on 5fr org brn & grn ('27) 6.00 6.00
119 A15 20fr on 5fr red vio & org red ('27) 6.00 6.00
Nos. 112-119 (8) 17.15 17.15

Bars cover the old denominations on #114-119.

Colonial Exposition Issue
Common Design Types

1931 *Perf. 12½*

Name of Country in Black

120 CD70 40c dp grn 1.00 1.00
121 CD71 50c violet 1.00 1.00
122 CD72 90c red org 1.00 1.00
123 CD73 1.50fr dull blue 1.75 1.75

Timber Raft on Ogowe River — A16

Count Savorgnan de Brazza — A17

Village of Setta Kemma A18

1932-33 **Photo.** *Perf. 13x13½*

124 A16 1c brn vio 15 15
125 A16 2c blk, *rose* 15 15
126 A16 4c green 15 15
127 A16 5c grnsh bl 15 15
128 A16 10c red, *yel* 15 15
129 A16 15c red, *grn* 35 25
130 A16 20c dp red 48 35
131 A16 25c brn red 16 15
132 A17 30c yel grn 75 55
133 A17 40c brn vio 60 42
134 A17 45c blk, *dl grn* 80 75
135 A17 50c red brn 52 42
136 A17 65c Prus bl 2.50 1.75
137 A17 75c blk, *red org* 1.20 90
138 A17 90c rose red 1.40 80
139 A17 1fr yel grn, *bl* 10.00 8.00
140 A18 1.25fr dp vio ('33) 1.00 70
141 A18 1.50fr dull blue 1.40 70
142 A18 1.75fr dp grn ('33) 90 60
143 A18 2fr brn red 10.00 8.00
144 A18 3fr yel grn, *bl* 2.25 1.75
145 A18 5fr red brn 2.50 2.00
146 A18 10fr blk, *red org* 11.00 9.00
147 A18 20fr dk vio 20.00 16.00
Nos. 124-147 (24) 68.56 53.84

See French Equatorial Africa No. 192 for stamp inscribed "Gabon" and "Afrique Equatoriale Francaise."

Catalogue values for all unused stamps in this country are for Never Hinged items.

Republic

Prime Minister Leon Mba — A19

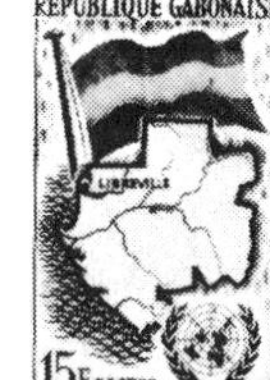

Flag & Map of Gabon & UN Emblem — A20

Design: 25fr, Leon Mba, profile.

Unwmk.

1959, Nov. 28 **Engr.** *Perf. 13*

148 A19 15fr chocolate 15 15
149 A19 25fr dk brn & grnsh blk 22 15
Set value 17

Proclamation of the Republic, 1st anniv.

Imperforates
Most Gabon stamps from 1959 onward exist imperforate in issued and trial colors, and also in small presentation sheets in issued colors.

C.C.T.A. Issue
Common Design Type

1960, May 21 **Engr.** *Perf. 13*

150 CD106 50fr vio brn & Prus bl 55 55

1961, Feb. 9

151 A20 15fr multi 20 15
152 A20 25fr multi 22 20
153 A20 85fr multi 80 60

Gabon's admission to United Nations.

Combretum A21

Designs: 1fr, 5fr, Tulip tree, vert. 2fr, 3fr, Yellow cassia.

1961, July 4 **Unwmk.** *Perf. 13*

154 A21 50c rose red & grn 15 15
155 A21 1fr sl grn, red & bis 15 15
156 A21 2fr dk grn & yel 15 15
157 A21 3fr ol grn & yel 15 15
158 A21 5fr multi 16 15
159 A21 10fr grn & rose red 22 16
Set value 66 60

President Leon Mba — A22

1962 **Engr.**

160 A22 15fr indigo, car & grn 16 15
161 A22 20fr brn blk, car & grn 20 15
162 A22 25fr brn, car & grn 22 15
Set value 31

Abidjan Games Issue
Common Design Type

1962, July 21 **Photo.** *Perf. 12½x12*

163 CD109 20fr Foot race, start 20 16
164 CD109 50fr Soccer 55 38

See No. C6.

African-Malgache Union Issue
Common Design Type

1962, Sept. 8 *Perf. 12½x12*

165 CD110 30fr emer, bluish grn, red & gold 65 50

Captain Ntchorere and Flags of France and Gabon A23

1962, Nov. 23 *Perf. 12*

166 A23 80fr multi 80 60

Issued to honor Capt. Ntchorere, who died for France, June 7, 1940.

Waves Around Globe — A23a

Design: 100fr, Orbit patterns around globe.

1963, Sept. 19 **Photo.** *Perf. 12½*

167 A23a 25fr ultra, grn & org 25 22
168 A23a 100fr grn, ultra & red brn 1.10 1.10

Issued to publicize space communications.

UNESCO Emblem, Scales and Tree A23b

1963, Dec. 10 **Engr.** *Perf. 13*

169 A23b 25fr grn, dk gray & red brn 22 20

15th anniv. of the Universal Declaration of Human Rights.

Common Design Types pictured in section at front of book.

Barograph and WMO Emblem A23c

1964, Mar. 23 **Unwmk.** *Perf. 13*

170 A23c 25fr ol bis, sl grn & ultra 30 25

UN's 4th World Meteorological Day, Mar. 23.

Arms of Gabon — A24

1964, June 15 **Photo.** *Perf. 13x12½*

171 A24 25fr ocher & multi 22 16

Tarpon A25

Designs: 60fr, Gorilla, vert. 80fr, Buffalo.

1964, July 15 **Engr.** *Perf. 13*

172 A25 30fr brn red, bl & blk 35 20
173 A25 60fr brn, grn & brn red 65 35
174 A25 80fr dk bl, grn & red brn 80 60

Cooperation Issue
Common Design Type

1964, Nov. 7

175 CD119 25fr gray, dk brn & lt bl 30 22

Dissotis Rotundifolia — A26

Flowers: 5fr, Gloriosa superba. 15fr, Eulophia horsfallii.

1964, Nov. 16 **Photo.** *Perf. 12x12½*

Flowers in Natural Colors

176 A26 3fr dp grn 15 15
177 A26 5fr green 15 15
178 A26 15fr dk brn 18 15
Set value 33 24

Sun and IQSY Emblem A27

1965, Feb. 25 *Perf. 12½x12*
179 A27 85fr multi 1.10 80

International Quiet Sun Year, 1964-65.

Morse Telegraph A28

1965, May 17 Engr. *Perf. 13*
180 A28 30fr multi 35 25

Cent. of the ITU.

Manganese Crusher, Moanda A29

Design: 60fr, Uranium mining, Mounana.

1965, June 15 Unwmk. *Perf. 13*
181 A29 15fr brt bl, pur & red 15 15
182 A29 60fr brn, brt bl & red 60 40

Issued to publicize Gabon's mineral wealth.

Field Ball — A30

Okoukoue Dance — A31

1965, July 15 Engr. *Perf. 13*
183 A30 25fr brt grn, blk & red 30 20

Issued to commemorate the First African Games, Brazzaville, July 18-25. See No. C35.

1965, Sept. 15 *Perf. 13*

Design: 60fr, Mukudji dance.

184 A31 25fr brn, grn & yel 25 16
185 A31 60fr blk, dk red & brn 60 42

Abraham Lincoln — A32

1965, Sept. 28 Photo. *Perf. 12½x13*
186 A32 50fr vio bl, blk, gold & buff 50 35

Centenary of death of Abraham Lincoln.

Old and New Post Offices and Mail Transport A33

1965, Dec. 18 Engr. *Perf. 13*
187 A33 30fr bl, brt grn & choc 30 20

Issued for Stamp Day, 1965.

Balumbu Mask — A34

Intl. Negro Arts Festival, Dakar, Senegal, Apr. 1-24: 10fr, Fang ancestral figure, Byeri. 25fr, Fang mask. 30fr, Okuyi mask, Myene. 85fr, Bakota leather mask.

1966, Apr. 18 Photo. *Perf. 12x12½*
188 A34 5fr red, brn, blk & buff 15 15
189 A34 10fr brt grnsh bl, dk brn & yel 15 15
190 A34 25fr multi 22 15
191 A34 30fr mar, yel & blk 28 18
192 A34 85fr multi 75 50
Nos. 188-192 (5) 1.55
Set value 94

WHO Headquarters, Geneva A35

1966, May 3 Photo. *Perf. 12½x13*
193 A35 50fr org yel, ultra & blk 50 30

Inauguration of the WHO Headquarters, Geneva.

Mother Learning to Write — A36

Soccer Player — A37

1966, June 22 Photo. *Perf. 12x12½*
194 A36 30fr multi 35 20

UNESCO literacy campaign.

1966, July 15 Engr. *Perf. 13*

Design: 90fr, Player facing left.

195 A37 25fr brn, grn & ultra 25 16
196 A37 90fr ultra & dk pur 1.00 60

8th World Cup Soccer Championship, Wembley, England, July 11-30. See No. C45.

Timber Industry — A38

Economic development: 85fr, Offshore oil rigs.

1966, Aug. 17 *Perf. 13*
197 A38 20fr red brn, lil & dk grn 22 15
198 A38 85fr dk brn, brt bl & brt grn 80 42

Woman with Children at Bank Window A39

1966, Sept. 23 Engr. *Perf. 13*
199 A39 25fr brt bl, vio brn & sl grn 22 15

Issued to publicize Savings Banks.

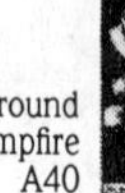

Scouts Around Campfire A40

Design: 50fr, Boy Scout pledging ceremony, vert.

1966, Oct. 17 Engr. *Perf. 13*
200 A40 30fr sl bl, car & dk brn 30 15
201 A40 50fr Prus bl, brn red & dk brn 55 30

Issued to honor Gabon's Boy Scouts.

Sikorsky S-43 Hydroplane and Map of West Africa — A41

1966, Dec. 17 Photo. *Perf. 12½x12*
202 A41 30fr multi 35 16

Issued for Stamp Day and to commemorate the 30th anniversary of the first air-mail service from Libreville to Port Gentil.

Hippopotami A42

Animals: 2fr, African crocodiles. 3fr, Water chevrotain. 5fr, Chimpanzees. 10fr, Elephants. 20fr, Leopards.

1967, Jan. 5 Photo. *Perf. 13x14*
203 A42 1fr multi 15 15
204 A42 2fr multi 15 15
205 A42 3fr multi 15 15
206 A42 5fr multi 15 15
207 A42 10fr multi 16 15
208 A42 20fr multi 25 15
Set value 65 42

Lions International Emblem A43

Design: 50fr, Lions emblem, map of Gabon and globe.

1967, Jan. 14 *Perf. 12½x13*
209 A43 30fr multi 30 15
210 A43 40fr bl & multi 50 25
a. Strip of 2, #209-210 + label 80 80

50th anniv. of Lions Intl.

Carnival Masks — A44

1967, Feb. 4 Photo. *Perf. 12x12½*
211 A44 30fr brn, yel bis & bl 35 20

Libreville Carnival, Feb. 4-7.

"Transportation" and Tourist Year Emblem — A45

1967, Feb. 15 *Perf. 12½x13*
212 A45 30fr multi 35 20

International Tourist Year, 1967.

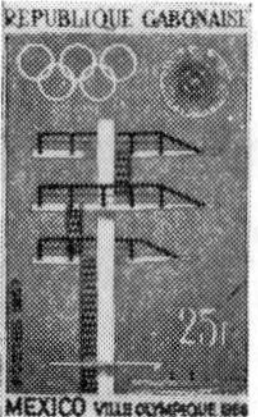

Olympic Diving Tower, Mexico City — A46

Symbolic of Atomic Energy Agency — A47

1968 Olympic Games: 30fr, Sun, snow crystals and Olympic rings. 50fr, Ice skating rink and view of Grenoble.

1967, Mar. 18 Engr. *Perf. 13*
213 A46 25fr dk vio, grnsh bl & ultra 25 15
214 A46 30fr grn, red lil & mar 30 16
215 A46 50fr ultra, grn & brn 55 35

1967, Apr. 15 Engr. *Perf. 13*
216 A47 30fr red brn, dk grn & ultra 35 16

International Atomic Energy Agency.

Pope Paul VI, Papal Arms and Libreville Cathedral A48

1967, June 1 Engr. *Perf. 13*
217 A48 30fr ultra, grn & blk 35 16

Issued to commemorate the "Populorum progressio" encyclical by Pope Paul VI concerning underdeveloped countries.

Flags, Tree, Logger, Map of Gabon and Mask — A49

1967, June 24 Engr. *Perf. 13*
218 A49 30fr multi 35 16

EXPO '67, International Exhibition, Montreal, Apr. 28-Oct. 27, 1967.

Europafrica Issue, 1967

Map of Europe and Africa and Products A50

1967, July 18 Photo. ***Perf. 12½x12***
219 A50 50fr multi 50 20

UN Emblem, Women and Child — A51

1967, Aug. 10 Engr. ***Perf. 13***
220 A51 75fr brt blue, dk brn & emer 75 40

United Nations Commission for Women.

19th Century Mail Ships — A52

Design: No. 222, Modern mail ships.

1967, Nov. 17 Photo. ***Perf. 12½***
221 A52 30fr multi 35 25
222 A52 30fr multi 35 25

Stamp Day. Nos. 221-222 printed se-tenant.

Draconea Fragrans — A53

Trees: 10fr, Pycnanthus angolensis. 20fr, Disthemonanthus benthamianus.

1967, Dec. 5 Engr. ***Perf. 13***
Size: 22x36mm
223 A53 5fr bl, emer & brn 15 15
224 A53 10fr grn, dk grn & bl 15 15
225 A53 20fr rose red, grn & ol 22 15
Nos. 223-225,C61-C62 (5) 2.17 1.28

For booklet pane see No. C62a.

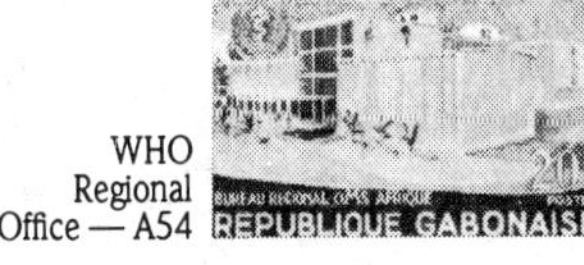
WHO Regional Office — A54

1968, Apr. 8 Engr. ***Perf. 13***
226 A54 20fr multi 22 15

20th anniv. of the WHO.

Dam, Power Station and UNESCO Emblem A55

1968, June 18 Engr. ***Perf. 13***
227 A55 15fr lake, org & Prus bl 15 15

Hydrological Decade (UNESCO), 1965-74.

Pres. Albert Bernard Bongo — A56

Design: 30fr, Pres. Bongo and arms of Gabon in background.

1968, June 24 Photo. ***Perf. 12x12½***
228 A56 25fr grn, buff & blk 20 15
229 A56 30fr rose lil, lt bl & blk 25 15
Set value 24

Tanker, Refinery, and Map of Area Served — A56a

1968, July 30 Photo. ***Perf. 12½***
230 A56a 30fr multi 30 16

Issued to commemorate the opening of the Port Gentil (Gabon) Refinery, June 12, 1968.

Open Book, Child and UNESCO Emblem A57

1968, Sept. 10 Engr. ***Perf. 13***
231 A57 25fr vio bl, dl red & brn 22 15

Issued for International Literacy Day.

A58

A60

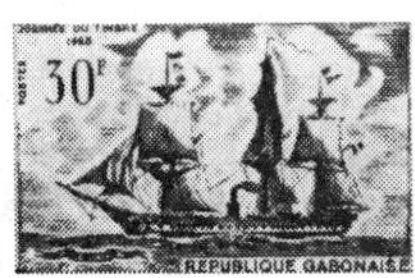
A59

1968, Oct. 15 Engr. ***Perf. 13***
232 A58 20fr Coffee 20 15
233 A58 40fr Cacao 38 16

1968, Nov. 23 Engr. ***Perf. 13***
234 A59 30fr "La Junon" 35 20

Issued for Stamp Day.

1968, Dec. 10

Design: Lawyer, globe and human rights flame.

235 A60 20fr blk, bl grn & car 20 15

International Human Rights Year.

Okanda Gap — A61

Designs: 15fr, Barracuda. 25fr, Kinguele Waterfall, vert. 30fr, Sitatunga trophies, vert.

1969, Mar. 28 Engr. ***Perf. 13***
236 A61 10fr brn, bl & sl grn 15 15
237 A61 15fr brn red, emer & ind 16 15
238 A61 25fr bl, pur & ol 22 15
239 A61 30fr multi 25 15
Set value 40

Year of African Tourism, 1969.

Mvet (Musical Instrument) A62

Musical Instruments: 30fr, Ngombi harp. 50fr, Ebele and Mbe drums. 100fr, Medzang xylophone.

1969, June 6 Engr. ***Perf. 13***
240 A62 25fr plum, ol & dp car 22 15
241 A62 30fr red brn, ol & dk brn 25 16
242 A62 50fr plum, ol & dp car 42 25
243 A62 100fr red brn, ol & dk brn 90 45
a. Min. sheet of 4, #240-243 2.50 2.50

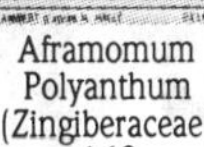
Aframomum Polyanthum (Zingiberaceae) A63

Tree of Life A64

African Plants: 2fr, Chlamydocola chlamydantha (Sterculiaceae). 5fr, Costus dinklagei (Zingiberaceae). 10fr, Cola rostrata (Sterculiaceae). 20fr, Dischistocalyx grandifolius (Acanthaceae).

1969, July 15 Photo. ***Perf. 12x12½***
244 A63 1fr multi 15 15
245 A63 2fr lt ol & multi 15 15
246 A63 5fr multi 15 15
247 A63 10fr slate & multi 16 15
248 A63 20fr yel & multi 22 16
Set value 56 40

1969, Aug. 17 Photo.
249 A64 25fr multi 22 15

National renovation.

Drilling for Oil on Land — A65

Workers and ILO Emblem — A66

Design: 50fr, Offshore drilling station.

1969, Sept. 13 ***Perf. 12x12½***
250 A65 25fr multi 20 15
251 A65 50fr multi 40 30
a. Strip of 2, #250-251 + label 70 70

20th anniv. of the ELF-SPAFE oil operations in Gabon.

1969, Oct. 29 Engr. ***Perf. 13***
252 A66 30fr bl, sl grn & dp car 25 16

50th anniv. of the ILO.

Arms of Port Gentil A67

Canoe Mail Transport A68

Coats of Arms: 20fr, Lambarene. 30fr, Libreville.

1969, Nov. 19 Photo. ***Perf. 12***
253 A67 20fr red, gold, sil & blk 16 15
254 A67 25fr bl, blk & gold 20 15
255 A67 30fr bl & multi 22 15
Set value 26

See Nos. 267-269, 291-293, 321-326, 340-348, 409-417, 492-501.

1969, Dec. 18 Engr. ***Perf. 13***
256 A68 30fr brt grn, grnsh bl & red brn 30 20

Issued for Stamp Day 1969.

Satellite, Globe, TV Screen and ITU Emblem A69

1970, May 17 Engr. ***Perf. 13***
257 A69 25fr dk bl, dk red brn & blk 25 16

International Telecommunications Day.

UPU Headquarters Issue
Common Design Type

1970, May 20 Engr. ***Perf. 13***
258 CD133 30fr brt grn, brt rose lil & brn 35 20

Geisha and African Drummer A70

1970, May 27 Photo. ***Perf. 12½x12***
259 A70 30fr ultra & multi 25 16

Issued to publicize EXPO '70 International Exhibition, Osaka, Japan, Mar. 15-Sept. 13.

ASECNA Issue
Common Design Type

1970, Aug. 26 Engr. ***Perf. 13***
260 CD132 100fr brt grn & bl grn 90 55

UN Emblem, Globe, Dove and Charts — A71

1970, Oct. 24 Photo. ***Perf. 12½x12***
261 A71 30fr Prus bl & multi 30 20

25th anniversary of the United Nations.

Bushbucks A72

Designs: 15fr, Pels scaly-tailed flying squirrel. 25fr, Gray-cheeked monkey, vert. 40fr, African golden cat. 60fr, Sevaline genet.

1970, Dec. 14 Photo. *Perf. 12½x13*

262 A72 5fr yel grn & multi	15	15
263 A72 15fr red org & blk	20	15
264 A72 25fr vio & multi	30	16
265 A72 40fr red & multi	40	22
266 A72 60fr bl & multi	60	25
Nos. 262-266 (5)	1.65	93

Arms Type of 1969

Coats of Arms: 20fr, Mouila. 25fr, Bitam. 30fr, Oyem.

1971, Feb. 16 Photo. *Perf. 12*

267 A67 20fr ver, blk, sil & gold	16	15
268 A67 25fr emer, gold & blk	20	15
269 A67 30fr emer, gold, blk & red	22	15
Set value		23

Men of Four Races and Emblem — A73

1971, Mar. 21 Engr. *Perf. 13*

270 A73 40fr multi 35 20

Intl. year against racial discrimination.

Map of Africa and Telecommunications System — A74

1971, Apr. 30 Photo. *Perf. 13*

271 A74 30fr org & multi 22 16

Pan-African telecommunications system.

Charaxes Smaragdalis — A75

Butterflies: 10fr, Euxanthe crossleyi. 15fr, Epiphora rectifascia. 25fr, Imbrasia bouvieri.

1971, May 26 Photo. *Perf. 13*

272 A75 5fr yel & multi	15	15
273 A75 10fr bl & multi	16	15
274 A75 15fr grn & multi	22	15
275 A75 25fr ol & multi	35	16
Set value		31

15-Cent Minimum Value
The minimum value for a single stamp is 15 cents. This value reflects the costs of handling inexpensive stamps.

Hertzian Center, Nkol Ogoum A76

1971, June 17 Engr. *Perf. 13*

276 A76 40fr grn, blk & dk car 38 22

3rd World Telecommunications Day.

Mother Nursing Child — A77

1971, Aug. 17 Engr. *Perf. 13*

277 A77 30fr lil rose, sep & ocher 25 20

15th anniversary of the Gabonese social security system.

UN Headquarters and Emblem — A78

1971, Sept. 30 Photo. *Perf. 13*

278 A78 30fr red & multi 22 15

10th anniv. of Gabon's admission to the UN.

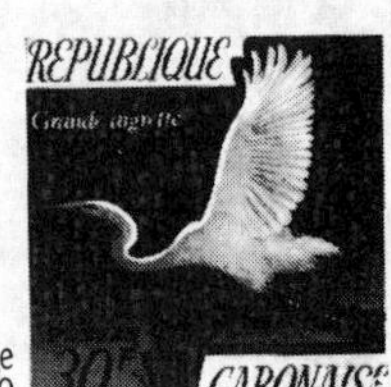
Large Egret — A79

Birds: 40fr, African gray parrot. 50fr, Woodland Kingfisher. 75fr, Cameroon bareheaded rock-fowl. 100fr, Gold Coast touraco.

1971, Oct. 12 Litho. *Perf. 13*

279 A79 30fr multi	25	16
280 A79 40fr multi	40	22
281 A79 50fr multi	50	25
282 A79 75fr multi	65	30
283 A79 100fr multi	80	38
Nos. 279-283 (5)	2.60	1.31

Asystasia Volgeliana A80

Designs: Flowers of Acanthus Family after paintings by Noel Hallé.

1972, Apr. 4 Photo. *Perf. 13*

284 A80 5fr pale cit & multi	15	15
285 A80 10fr multi	15	15
286 A80 20fr multi	22	16
287 A80 30fr lil rose & multi	35	20
288 A80 40fr dk grn & multi	42	35
289 A80 65fr red & multi	60	42
Nos. 284-289 (6)	1.89	1.43

Louis Pasteur — A81

1972, May 15 Engr. *Perf. 13*

290 A81 80fr dp org, pur & grn 55 20

Sesquicentennial of the birth of Louis Pasteur (1822-1895), scientist and bacteriologist.

Arms Type of 1969

Coats of Arms: 30fr, Franceville. 40fr, Makokou. 60fr, Tchibanga.

1972, June 2 Photo. *Perf. 12*

291 A67 30fr sil & multi	22	15
292 A67 40fr grn & multi	30	15
293 A67 60fr blk, grn & sil	50	16

Globe and Telecommunications Symbols — A81a

1972, July 25 *Perf. 13x12½*

294 A81a 40fr blk, yel & org 30 16

4th World Telecommunications Day.

Nat King Cole — A82

Black American Jazz Musicians: 60fr, Sidney Bechet. 100fr, Louis Armstrong.

1972, Sept. 1 Photo. *Perf. 13x13½*

295 A82 40fr bl & multi	35	20
296 A82 60fr org & multi	55	30
297 A82 100fr multi	80	50

Blanding's Rear-fanged Snake — A83

Designs: 2fr, Beauty snake. 3fr, Eggeating snake. 15fr, Striped ground snake. 25fr, Jameson's mamba. 50fr, Gabon viper.

1972, Oct. 2 Litho. *Perf. 13*

298 A83 1fr lem & multi	15	15
299 A83 2fr red brn & multi	15	15
300 A83 3fr brn org & multi	15	15
301 A83 15fr multi	20	15
302 A83 25fr grn & multi	25	15
303 A83 50fr multi	50	22
Set value	1.10	62

See Nos. 330-332, 354-357.

Dr. Armauer G. Hansen, Lambarene Leprosarium A84

1973, Jan. 28 Engr. *Perf. 13*

304 A84 30fr Prus grn, sl grn & brn 25 20

Centenary of the discovery of the Hansen bacilius, the cause of leprosy.

Charaxes Candiope — A85

Designs: Various butterflies.

1973, Feb. 23 Litho. *Perf. 13*

305 A85 10fr *shown*	15	15
306 A85 15fr *Eunica pechueli*	15	15
307 A85 20fr *Cyrestis camillus*	20	15
308 A85 30fr *Charaxes castor*	30	16
309 A85 40fr *Charaxes ameliae*	35	20
310 A85 50fr *Pseudacrea boisduvali*	50	22
Nos. 305-310 (6)	1.65	
Set value		75

Balloon of Santos-Dumont, 1901 — A86

History of Aviation: 1fr, Montgolfier's balloon, 1783, vert. 3fr, Octave Chanute's biplane, 1896. 4fr, Clement Ader's Plane III, 1897. 5fr, Louis Bleriot crossing the Channel, 1909. 10fr, Fabre's hydroplane, 1910.

1973, May 3 Engr. *Perf. 13*

311 A86 1fr grn, sl grn & dk red	15	15
312 A86 2fr sl grn & brt bl	15	15
313 A86 3fr bl, sl & org	15	15
314 A86 4fr lil & dk pur	15	15
315 A86 5fr slate grn & org	15	15
316 A86 10fr rose lil & Prus bl	15	15
Set value	44	30

1977 Coil Stamp

316A A86 10fr aqua 15 15

No. 316A has red control numbers on back of every 10th stamp.

INTERPOL Emblem — A87

1973, June 26 Engr. *Perf. 13*

317 A87 40fr magenta & ultra 25 15

50th anniversary of the International Criminal Police Organization (INTERPOL).

Earth Station "2 Decembre" A88

1973, July 2 Engr. *Perf. 13*

318 A88 40fr sl grn, bl & brn 25 15

Party Headquarters, Libreville — A89

1973, Aug. 17 **Photo.**
319 A89 30fr multi 20 15

African Postal Union Issue
Common Design Type

1973, Sept. 12 **Engr.** ***Perf. 13***
320 CD137 100fr red lil, pur & bl 60 40

Arms Type of 1969

Coats of Arms: 5fr, Gamba. 10fr, Ogowe-Lolo. 15fr, Fougamou. 30fr, Kango. 40fr, Booue. 60fr, Koula-Moutou.

1973-74 **Photo.** ***Perf. 12***
321 A67 5fr bl & multi ('74) 15 15
322 A67 10fr blk, red & gold ('74) 15 15
323 A67 15fr grn & multi ('74) 15 15
324 A67 30fr red & multi 22 15
325 A67 40fr red & multi 25 15
326 A67 60fr emer & multi 40 15
Set value 1.10 40

Issue dates: Nos. 321-323, Feb. 13, 1974; Nos. 324-326, Oct. 4, 1973.

St. Teresa of Lisieux — A90

Human Rights Flame — A91

Design: 40fr, St. Teresa and Jesus carrying cross.

1973, Dec. 4 **Photo.** ***Perf. 13***
327 A90 30fr blk & multi 22 16
328 A90 40fr blk & multi 30 22

St. Teresa of the Infant Jesus (Thérèse Martin, 1873-97), Carmelite nun.

1973, Dec. 10 **Engr.**
329 A91 20fr grn, red & ultra 15 15

25th anniversary of the Universal Declaration of Human Rights.

Wildlife Type of 1972

Monkeys: 40fr, Mangabey. 60fr, Cercopithecus cephus. 80fr, Mona monkey.

1974, Mar. 20 **Litho.** ***Perf. 14***
330 A83 40fr gray grn & multi 22 15
331 A83 60fr lt bl & multi 35 20
332 A83 80fr lil rose & multi 42 25

Ogowe River at Lambarene A93

Designs: 50fr, Cape Estérias. 75fr, Poubara rope bridge.

1974, July 30 **Photo.** ***Perf. 13x13½***
333 A93 30fr multi 16 15
334 A93 50fr multi 25 16
335 A93 75fr multi 40 25

Manioc A94

Design: 50fr, Palms and dates.

1974, Nov. 13 **Photo.** ***Perf. 13x12½***
336 A94 40fr org red & multi 22 15
337 A94 50fr bis & multi 25 15

UDEAC Issue

Presidents and Flags of Cameroun, CAR, Congo, Gabon and Meeting Center — A95

1974, Dec. 8 **Photo.** ***Perf. 13***
338 A95 40fr multi 22 15

See No. C156.

Hôtel du Dialogue — A96

1975, Jan. 20 **Photo.** ***Perf. 13***
339 A96 50fr multi 25 16

Opening of Hôtel du Dialogue.

Arms Type of 1969

Coats of Arms: 5fr, Ogowe-Ivindo. 10fr, Moabi. No. 342, Moanda. No. 343, Nyanga. 25fr, Mandji. No. 345, Mekambo. No. 346, Omboué. 60fr, Minvoul. 90fr, Mayumba.

1975-77 **Photo.** ***Perf. 12***
340 A67 5fr red & multi 15 15
341 A67 10fr gold & multi 15 15
342 A67 15fr red, sil & blk 15 15
343 A67 15fr bl & multi 15 15
344 A67 25fr grn & multi 15 15
345 A67 50fr blk, gold & red 25 15
346 A67 50fr multi 25 15
347 A67 60fr multi 35 15
348 A67 90fr multi 45 25
Set value 1.65 85

Issue dates: Nos. 340-342, Jan. 21, 1975. Nos. 343-345, Aug. 17, 1976. Nos. 346-348, July 12, 1977.

Map of Africa with Lion's Head, and Lions Emblem — A97

1975, May 2 **Typo.** ***Perf. 13***
349 A97 50fr grn & multi 25 20

Lions Club 17th congress, District 403, Libreville.

Hertzian Wave Transmitter Network, Map of Gabon — A98

1975, July 8 **Engr.** ***Perf. 13***
350 A98 40fr multi 25 16

City and Rural Women, Car, Train and Building — A99

1975, July 22 **Engr.** ***Perf. 13***
351 A99 50fr car, bl & brn 35 20

International Women's Year 1975.

Scoutmaster Ange Mba, Emblems and Rope — A100

Design: 50fr, Hand holding rope, Scout, camp, Boy Scout and Nordjamb 75 emblems.

1975, July 29
352 A100 40fr multi 25 16
353 A100 50fr grn, red & dk brn 35 20

Nordjamb 75, 14th Boy Scout Jamboree, Lillehammer, Norway, July 29-Aug. 7.

Wildlife Type of 1972

Fish: 30fr, Lutjanus goreensis. 40fr, Galeoides decadactylus. 50fr, Sardinella aurita. 120fr, Scarus hoefleri.

1975, Sept. 22 **Litho.** ***Perf. 14***
354 A83 30fr multi 16 15
355 A83 40fr multi 22 16
356 A83 50fr multi 25 20
357 A83 120fr multi 65 45

Agro-Industrial Complex — A102

1975, Dec. 15 **Litho.** ***Perf. 12½***
358 A102 60fr multi 35 22

Inauguration of Agro-Industrial Complex, Franceville.

Tchibanga Bridge — A103

Bridges of Gabon: 10fr, Mouila. 40fr, Kango. 50fr, Lambaréné, vert.

1976, Jan. 30 **Engr.** ***Perf. 13***
359 A103 5fr multi 15 15
360 A103 10fr multi 15 15
361 A103 40fr multi 20 16
362 A103 50fr multi 25 20
Set value 55 45

Telephones 1876 and 1976, Satellite, A. G. Bell — A104

1976, Mar. 10 **Engr.** ***Perf. 13***
363 A104 60fr dk bl, grn & sl grn 35 22

Centenary of first telephone call by Alexander Graham Bell, Mar. 10, 1876.

Msgr. Jean Remy Bessieux — A105

1976, Apr. 30 **Engr.** ***Perf. 13***
364 A105 50fr grn, bl & sep 25 20

Death centenary of Msgr. Bessieux.

Athletes, Torch, Map of Africa, Games Emblem — A106

1976, June 25 **Photo.** ***Perf. 13x12½***
365 A106 50fr multi 25 20
366 A106 60fr org & multi 35 22

First Central African Games (Zone 5), Libreville, June-July.

Motobécane, France A107

Motorcycles: 5fr, Bultaco, Spain. 10fr, Suzuki, Japan. 20fr, Kawasaki, Japan. 100fr, Harley-Davidson, US.

1976, July 20 **Litho.** ***Perf. 12½***
367 A107 3fr multi 15 15
368 A107 5fr org & multi 15 15
369 A107 10fr bl & multi 15 15
370 A107 20fr multi 15 15
371 A107 100fr car & multi 55 40
Set value 80 60

Rice — A108

1976, Oct. 15 **Litho.** ***Perf. 13x13½***
372 A108 50fr shown 25 15
373 A108 60fr Pepper plants 35 22

1977, Apr. 22 Litho. *Perf. 13x13½*

Designs: 50fr, Banana plantation. 60fr, Peanut market.

374 A108 50fr multi 25 20
375 A108 60fr multi 35 22

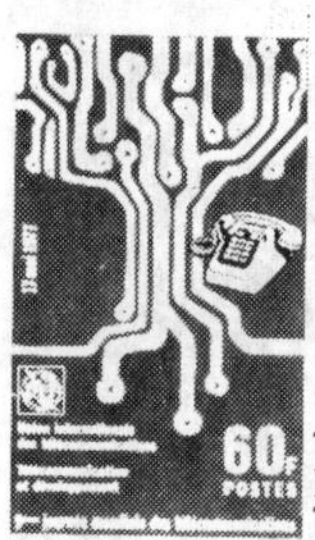

Telecommunications Emblem and Telephone — A109

1977, May 17 *Perf. 13*

376 A109 60fr multi 35 22

World Telecommunications Day.

View of Oyem — A110

Designs: 50fr, Cape Lopez. 70fr, Lebamba Cave.

1977, June 9 Litho. *Perf. 12½*

377 A110 50fr multi 25 20
378 A110 60fr multi 35 22
379 A110 70fr multi 38 25

Conference Hall — A111

1977, June 23 Photo. *Perf. 13x12½*

380 A111 100fr multi 55 38

Meeting of the OAU, Libreville.

Modern Buildings, Libreville — A113

Arms of Gabon — A112

1977 Engr. *Perf. 13*

Size: 23x36mm

381 A112 50fr blue 25 20

Size: 17x23mm

382 A112 60fr orange 35 15
a. Booklet pane of 5 1.90
383 A112 80fr red 42 35

#381 issued in coils, #382 in booklets only. Issue dates: #381-382, June 23. #383, Sept.

1977, Aug. 17 Litho. *Perf. 12*

387 A113 50fr multi 25 20

National Festival 1977.

Paris to Vienna, 1902 — A114

Renault Automobiles: 10fr, Coupé 1 2 CV, 1921. 30fr, Torpédo Scaphandrier, 1925. 40fr, Reinastella 40 CV, 1929. 100fr, Nerva Grand Sport, 1937. 150fr, Voiturette 1 CV, 1899. 200fr, Alpine Renault V6, 1977.

1977, Aug 30 Engr. *Perf. 13*

388 A114 5fr multi 15 15
389 A114 10fr multi 15 15
390 A114 30fr multi 15 15
391 A114 40fr multi 16 15
392 A114 100fr multi 42 28
Nos. 388-392 (5) 1.03
Set value 60

Miniature Sheet

393 Sheet of 2 + label 2.00 2.00
a. A114 150fr multi 75 75
b. A114 200fr multi 1.00 1.00

Louis Renault, French automobile pioneer, birth centenary. Nos. 383a-393b are perf. on 3 sides, without perforation between stamps and center label showing dark brown portrait of Renault.
See Nos. 395-400.

Globe A115

1978, Feb. 21 Engr. *Perf. 13x12½*

394 A115 80fr multi 42 35

World Leprosy Day.

Automobile Type of 1977

Citroen Cars: 10fr, Cabriolet, 1922. 50fr, Taxi, 1927. 60fr, Berline, 1932. 80fr, Berline, 1934. 150fr, Torpedo, 1919. 200fr, Berline, 1948. 250fr, Pallas, 1975.

1978, May 9 Engr. *Perf. 13*

395 A114 10fr multi 15 15
396 A114 50fr multi 35 22
397 A114 60fr multi 40 25
398 A114 80fr multi 55 35
399 A114 200fr multi 1.40 65
Nos. 395-399 (5) 2.85 1.62

Miniature Sheet

400 Sheet of 2 2.25 2.25
a. A114 150fr multi 75 75
b. A114 250fr multi 1.25 1.25

Andre Citroen (1878-1935), automobile designer and manufacturer.

Ndjole on Ogowe River — A116

Views: 40fr, Lambarene lake district. 50fr, Owendo Harbor.

1978, May 17 Litho. *Perf. 12½*

401 A116 30fr multi 20 15
402 A116 40fr multi 25 16
403 A116 50fr multi 35 20

Sternotomis Mirabilis — A117

Anti- Apartheid Emblem — A118

Various Coleopteras.

1978, June 21 Photo. *Perf. 12½x13*

404 A117 20fr multi 15 15
405 A117 60fr multi 40 25
406 A117 75fr multi 50 30
407 A117 80fr multi 55 35

1978, July 25 Engr. *Perf. 13*

408 A118 80fr multi 55 35

Arms Type of 1969

1978-80 Photo. *Perf. 12*

409 A67 5fr Oyem 15 15
410 A67 5fr Ogowe-Maritime ('79) 15 15
411 A67 10fr Lastoursville ('79) 15 15
412 A67 10fr Haut-Ogooue ('80) 15 15
413 A67 15fr M'Bigou ('79) 15 15
414 A67 20fr Estuaire ('80) 15 15
415 A67 30fr Bitam ('80) 20 15
416 A67 40fr Okondja 25 16
417 A67 60fr Mimongo 40 25
Set value 1.30 80

A119

1978, Oct. 24 Engr. *Perf. 13*

419 A119 80fr multi 55 35

UNESCO campaign to save the Acropolis.

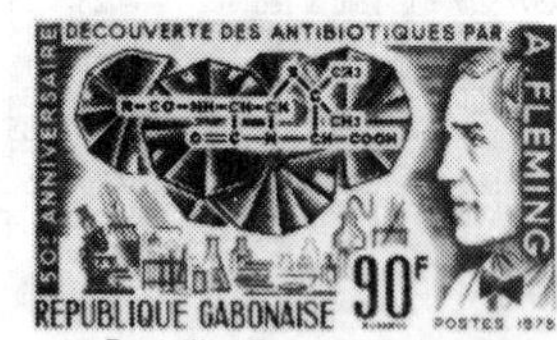

Penicillin Formula, — A120

1978, Nov. 21 Engr. *Perf. 13*

420 A120 90fr multi 60 38

Alexander Fleming's discovery of antibiotics, 50th anniversary.

The Visitation — A121

Designs: 80fr, Massacre of the Innocents. Woodcarvings from St. Michael's Church, Libreville.

1978, Dec. 15 Photo.

421 A121 60fr gold & multi 40 25
422 A121 80fr gold & multi 55 35

Christmas 1978. See Nos. 437-438.

Train and Map — A122

1978, Dec. 27 Litho. *Perf. 12½*

423 A122 60fr multi 40 25

Inauguration of Trans-Gabon Railroad, Libreville to Njolé.

A123

Pre-Olympic Year (Kremlin Towers, Olympic Emblem, Ancestral Figure and): 80fr, Long jump, vert. 100fr, Yachts.

1979, May 15 Engr. *Perf. 13*

424 A123 60fr multi 40 25
425 A123 80fr multi 55 35
426 A123 100fr multi 65 40
a. Miniature sheet of 3, #424-426 1.60 1.60

Rowland Hill, Messenger and Gabon No. O9 — A124

Allamanda Schottii A125

Designs: 80fr, Bakota mask and tulip tree flowers, vert. 150fr, Pigeon, UPU emblem, truck and canoe. No. 430b, Gloriosa superba. No. 430c, Phaeomeria magnifica, vert. No. 430d, Berlinia bracteosa, vert.

1979, June 8 Photo. *Perf. 13*

427 A124 50fr multi 35 20
428 A124 80fr multi 55 35

Engr.

429 A124 150fr multi 1.00 60

Souvenir Sheet

Photo. *Perf. 14*

430 Sheet of 4 3.00 3.00
a. A125 100fr multi 65
b. A125 100fr multi 65
c. A125 100fr multi 65
d. A125 100fr multi 65

Philexafrique II, Libreville, June 8-17. Nos. 427-429 each printed in sheets of 10 with 5 labels showing exhibition emblem. No. 427 also commemorates Sir Rowland Hill (1795-1879), originator of penny postage. No. 430 has label with exhibition emblem.

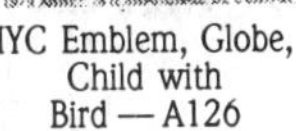

IYC Emblem, Globe, Child with Bird — A126

"TELECOM 79" — A127

1979, June 15 **Engr.** ***Perf. 13***
431 A126 100fr multi 65 40

International Year of the Child.

1979, Sept. 18 **Litho.** ***Perf. 13x12½***
432 A127 80fr multi 55 25

3rd World Telecommunications Exhibition, Geneva, Sept. 20-26.

Sugar Cane Harvest — A128

Judo Throw — A129

1979, Oct. 9 **Photo.** ***Perf. 12½x13***
433 A128 25fr shown 16 15
434 A128 30fr Yams 20 15
Set value 18

1979, Oct. 23 **Engr.** ***Perf. 13***
435 A129 40fr multi 25 15

World Judo Championships, Paris, Dec.

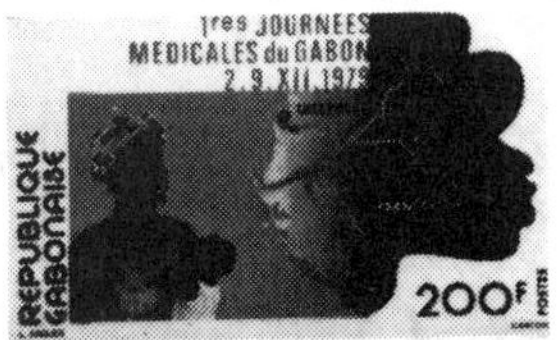

Mother and Child, Map of Congo River Basin — A130

1979, Dec. 2 **Litho.** ***Perf. 12***
436 A130 200fr multi 1.40 65

Medical Week, Dec. 2-9.

Christmas Type of 1978

Wood Carvings, St. Michael's Church, Libreville: 60fr, Flight into Egypt. 80fr, The Circumcision.

1979, Dec. 12 **Photo.** ***Perf. 13***
437 A121 60fr multi 40 20
438 A121 80fr multi 55 25

Pres. Omar Bongo, 44th Birthday — A131

OPEC, 20th Anniv. — A132

1979, Dec. 30 **Litho.** ***Perf. 12½***
439 A131 60fr multi 40 20

1980, Feb. 27 **Litho.** ***Perf. 12½***
440 A131 80fr multi 55 25

Pres. Hadj Omar Bongo, re-election and inauguration.

1980, Mar. 27 **Litho.** ***Perf. 13½x13***
441 A132 50fr multi 35 16

Donguila Church — A133

1980 Apr. 3 **Litho.** ***Perf. 12½***
442 A133 60fr shown 40 20
443 A133 80fr Bizengobibere Church 55 25

Easter 1980.

De Brazza (1852-1905), Map of Gabon with Franceville — A134

1980, June 30 **Litho.** ***Perf. 12½***
444 A134 165fr multi 1.10 55

Franceville Foundation centenary, founded by Savorgnan De Brazza.

20th Anniversary of Independence — A135

1980, Aug. 17 **Photo.** ***Perf. 13***
445 A135 60fr Leon Mba and Omar Bongo 40 20

World Tourism Conference, Manila, Sept. 27 — A136

1980, Sept. 10 **Engr.**
446 A136 80fr multi 55 25

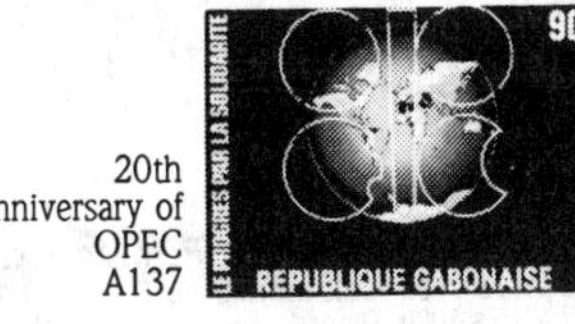

20th Anniversary of OPEC A137

1980, Sept. 15 **Litho.** ***Perf. 12½***
447 A137 90fr shown 60 30
448 A137 120fr Men Holding OPEC emblem, vert. 80 40

Pseudochelidon Eurystomina — A138

1980, Oct. 15 **Photo.** ***Perf. 14x14½***
449 A138 50fr *shown* 35 16
450 A138 60fr *Merops nubicus* 40 20
451 A138 80fr *Pitta angolensis* 55 25
452 A138 150fr *Scotopelia peli* 1.00 50

Statue of Bull, Bizangobibere Church — A139

Heinrich von Stephan — A140

1980, Dec. 10 **Photo.** ***Perf. 14x14½***
453 A139 60fr shown 40 20
454 A139 80fr Male statue 55 25

Christmas 1980.

1981, Jan. 7 **Engr.** ***Perf. 13***
455 A140 90fr brn & dk brn 60 30

Von Stephan (1831-97), UPU founder.

13th Anniversary of National Renovation Movement — A141

1981, Mar. 12 **Litho.** ***Perf. 13x12½***
456 A141 60fr multi 40 20

Lion Statue, Bizangobibere A142

Port Gentil Lions Club Banner A143

1981, Apr. 12 **Photo.** ***Perf. 14x14½***
457 A142 75fr multi 50 25
458 A142 100fr multi 65 35

Easter 1981.

1981, May 1 **Litho.** ***Perf. 12½***
459 A143 60fr shown 40 20
460 A143 75fr District 403 50 25
461 A143 80fr Libreville Cocotiers 55 25
462 A143 100fr Libreville Hibiscus 65 35
463 A143 165fr Ekwata 1.10 55
464 A143 200fr Haut-Ogooue 1.40 65
Nos. 459-464 (6) 4.60 2.25

Lions International, 23rd Congress of District 403, Libreville, May 1-3.

13th World Telecommunications Day — A144

1981, May 17 **Photo.** ***Perf. 13***
465 A144 125fr multi 80 42

Unity, Work and Justice A145

R.P. Klaine (Missionary), 70th Death Anniv. A146

1981-86 **Photo.** ***Perf. 13***
466 A145 5fr beige & blk 15 15
467 A145 10fr pale lil & blk 15 15
468 A145 15fr brt yel grn & blk 15 15
469 A145 20fr pink & blk 15 15
470 A145 25fr vio & blk 16 15
471 A145 40fr red org & blk 25 15
472 A145 50fr bluish grn & blk 35 16
473 A145 75fr bis brn & blk 50 25
473A A145 90fr lt bl & blk ('83) 25 15
474 A145 100fr yel & blk 65 35
474A A145 125fr grn & blk ('83) 35 16
474B A145 150fr brt pink & blk ('86) 40 20
Nos. 466-474B (12) 3.51
Set value 1.65

1981, July 2 **Litho.**

Design: 90fr, Archbishop Walker, 110th birth anniv.

475 A146 70fr multi 45 22
476 A146 90fr multi 60 30

Map of Gabon and Scout Sign — A147

Intl. Year of the Disabled — A148

1981, July 16 *Perf. 12½*
477 A147 75fr multi 50 25

4th Pan-African Scouting Congress, Abidjan, Aug.

No. 477 Overprinted: DAKAR / 28e CONFERENCE / MONDIALE DU / SCOUTISME

1981, July 23
478 A147 75fr multi 50 25

28th World Scouting Conf., Dakar, Aug.

1981, Aug. 6 **Engr.** *Perf. 13*
479 A148 100fr multi 65 35

Hypolimnas Salmacis A149

1981, Sept. 10 **Litho.** *Perf. 14½x14*
480 A149 75fr shown 50 25
481 A149 100fr Euphaedra themis 65 35
482 A149 150fr Amauris niavius 1.00 50
483 A149 250fr Cymothoe lucasi 1.60 80

Paul as Harlequin, by Pablo Picasso (1881-1973) A150

1981, Sept. 25 *Perf. 14½x13½*
484 A150 500fr multi 3.50 1.60

World Food Day A151

1981, Oct. 16 **Engr.** *Perf. 13*
485 A151 350fr multi 2.25 1.20

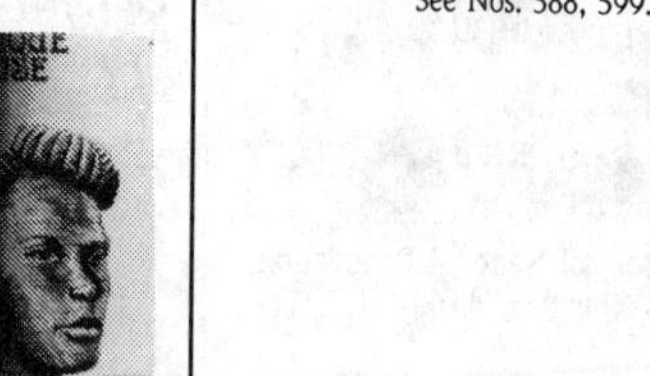

Traditional Hairstyle — A152

Designs: Various hairstyles.

1981, Nov. 12 **Litho.** *Perf. 14½x15*
486 A152 75fr multi 50 20
487 A152 100fr multi 65 35
488 A152 125fr multi 80 40
489 A152 200fr multi 1.40 65
a. Souvenir sheet of 4, #486-489 3.50 1.60

See Nos. 609A-609B, 676.

Christmas 1981 A153

Designs: Children's drawings.

1981, Dec. 10 *Perf. 14½x14*
490 A153 75fr Girls dancing 50 25
491 A153 100fr Dinner 65 35

Arms Type of 1969

Perf. 12, 13 (#495-497)

1982-92 **Photo.**
492 A67 75fr Moyen-Ogooue 50 25
493 A67 90fr Cocobeach ('84) 24 15
494 A67 100fr Woleu-N'tem 65 35
495 A67 100fr Lambarene ('86) 38 18
496 A67 100fr Port Gentil District ('91) 90 45
497 A67 100fr Medouneu 90 45
498 A67 125fr Mouila ('84) 35 16
499 A67 135fr N'Djole ('84) 38 15
500 A67 150fr N'Gounie 1.00 50
501 A67 160fr Leconi ('86) 55 30
Nos. 492-501 (10) 5.85 2.94

Issue dates: Nos. 492, 494, 500, Jan. 13. Nos. 493, 498, 499, Aug. 7. No. 496, Apr. 17. No. 497, Aug. 12.

A154

A155

1982, Feb. 16 **Litho.** *Perf. 13*
502 A154 100fr multi 65 35

Visit of Pope John Paul II, Feb. 17-19.

1982, Mar. 31 **Engr.** *Perf. 13*
503 A155 75fr black 50 25

Alfred de Musset (1810-1857), writer.

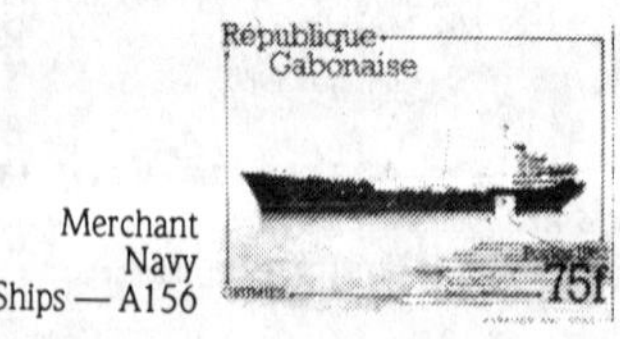

Merchant Navy Ships — A156

1982, Apr. 7 **Litho.** *Perf. 14½x14*
504 A156 75fr Timber carrier 50 25
505 A156 100fr Freighter 65 35
506 A156 200fr Oil tanker 1.40 65

See Nos. 588, 599.

TB Bacillus Centenary — A157

1982, Apr. 24 **Litho.** *Perf. 13*
507 A157 100fr multi 65 35

PHILEXFRANCE '82 Stamp Exhibition, Paris, June 11-21 — A158

1982, Apr. 28 *Perf. 12½*
508 A158 100fr Rope bridge 65 35
509 A158 200fr Sculptured head 1.40 65
a. Pair, #508-509 + label 2.10 1.50

14th World Telecommunications Day — A159

1982, May 17 *Perf. 13*
510 A159 75fr multi 50 25

1982 World Cup — A160

Designs: Various soccer players.

1982, May 19 *Perf. 14x14½*
511 A160 100fr multi 65 35
512 A160 125fr multi 80 40
513 A160 200fr multi 1.40 65
a. Souvenir sheet of 3, #511-513, perf. 14½ 2.75 1.50

For overprints see Nos. 516-518.

2nd UN Conf. on Peaceful Uses of Outer Space, Vienna, Aug. 9-21 — A161

1982, July 7 **Engr.** *Perf. 13*
514 A161 250fr Satellites 1.60 80

White Carnations A162

Designs: Various carnations.

1982, June 9 **Photo.** *Perf. 14½x14*
515 Strip of 3 2.25 1.10
a. A162 75fr multi 50 25
b. A162 100fr multi 65 35
c. A162 175fr multi 1.10 50

Nos. 511-513a Overprinted in Red with Semi-Finalists or Finalists

1982, Aug. 19 **Litho.** *Perf. 14x14½*
516 A160 100fr multi 65 35
517 A160 125fr multi 80 40
518 A160 200fr multi 1.40 65
a. Souvenir sheet of 3 3.00 1.50

Italy's victory in 1982 World Cup.

Phyllonotus Duplex A163

1982, Sept. 22 *Perf. 14½x14*
519 A163 75fr shown 50 25
520 A163 100fr Chama crenulata 65 35
521 A163 125fr Cardium hians 80 40

Okouyi Mask — A164

Christmas 1982 — A165

1982, Oct. 13 **Litho.** *Perf. 14x14½*
522 A164 75fr shown 50 25
523 A164 100fr Ondoumbo reliquary 65 35
524 A164 150fr Tsogho statuette 1.00 50
525 A164 250fr Fang bellows 1.60 80

1983, Dec. 15 **Litho.** *Perf. 14x14½*
526 A165 100fr St. Francis Xavier Church 65 35

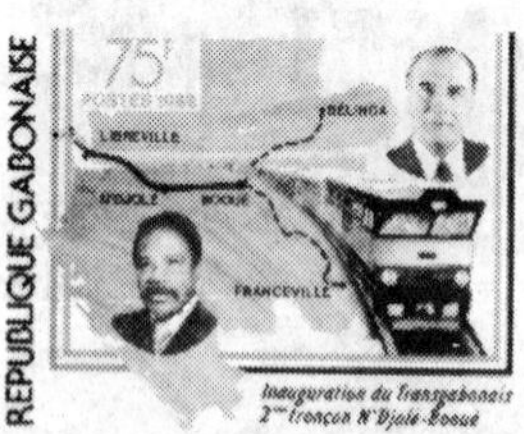

Trans-Gabon Railroad Inauguration — A166

1983, Jan. 18 *Perf. 12½*
527 A166 75fr multi 50 25

5th African Highway Conference, Libreville, Feb. 6-11 — A167

1983, Feb. 2 *Perf. 13*
528 A167 100fr multi 65 35

15th Anniv. of Natl. Renewal — A168

Provincial Symbols: a. Bakota mask, Ogowe Ivindo. b. Butterfly, Ogowe Lolo. c. Buffalo, Nyanga. d. Isogho hairdo, Ngounie. e. Tarpon, Ogowe Maritime. f. Manganese, Haut Ogowe. g. Crocodiles, Moyen Ogowe. h. Coffee plant. i. Epitorium trochiformis.

1983, Mar. 12 Litho. *Perf. 13x13½*
529 Strip of 9 + label 6.50 3.50
a. A168 75fr multi 50 25
b. A168 90fr multi 55 30
c. A168 90fr multi 60 30
d. A168 100fr multi 65 35
e. A168 125fr multi 80 40
f. A168 125fr multi 80 40
g. A168 125fr multi 80 40
h. A168 135fr multi 90 45
i. A168 135fr multi 90 45

25th Anniv. of Intl. Maritime Org. — A169

1983, Mar. 17 *Perf. 13*
530 A169 125fr multi 80 40

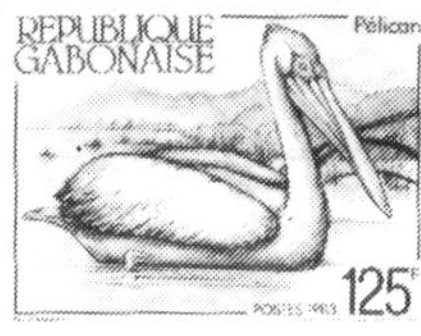

Pelican A170

1983, Apr. 20 Litho. *Perf. 15x14½*
531 A170 90fr Water musk deer 60 30
532 A170 125fr shown 80 40
533 A170 225fr Elephant 1.50 75
534 A170 400fr Iguana 2.50 1.25
a. Souv. sheet of 4, #531-534 5.75 2.75

25th Anniv. of UN Economic Commission for Africa — A171

1983, Apr. 29 Litho. *Perf. 12½*
535 A171 125fr multi 80 40

15th World Telecommunications Day — A172

1983, May 17 Litho. *Perf. 13*
536 A172 90fr multi 60 30
537 A172 90fr multi 60 30
a. Pair, #536-537 1.25 65

Denomination of No. 536 in lower right, No. 537, upper left.

Nkoltang Earth Satellite Station — A173

1983, July 2
538 A173 125fr multi 80 40

10th anniv. of station; World Communications Year.

Ivindo River Rapids — A174

1983, Sept. 7 Engr. *Perf. 13*
539 A174 90fr shown 60 30
540 A174 125fr Ogooue River 80 42
541 A174 185fr Wonga Wongue Preserve 1.20 60
542 A174 350fr Coastal view 2.25 1.20

Hand Drum, Mahongwe A175

Harmful Insects A176

1983, Oct. 12 Litho. *Perf. 14x14½*
543 A175 90fr shown 28 15
544 A175 125fr Okoukoue dancer 40 20
545 A175 135fr Four-stringed fiddle 42 22
546 A175 260fr Ndoumou dancer 80 40

1983, Nov. 9
547 A176 90fr Glossinidae 28 15
548 A176 125fr Belonogaster juncea 40 20
549 A176 300fr Aedes aegypti 1.00 45
550 A176 350fr Mylabris 1.20 60

Christmas 1983 A177

Wood Carvings, St. Michael's Church, Libreville.

Perf. 14½x13½
1983, Dec. 14 Litho.
551 A177 90fr Adultress 28 15
552 A177 125fr Good Samaritan 40 20

Boeing 737, No. 202 — A178

1984, Jan. 12 *Perf. 13x12½*
553 A178 125fr shown 40 20
554 A178 225fr Lufthansa jet, Germany No. C2 70 38

19th World UPU Congress, Hamburg, June 19-26. Se-tenant with label showing Congress emblem.

3rd Anniv. of Africa 1 Radio Transmitter — A179

1984, Feb. 7 Litho. *Perf. 12½*
555 A179 125fr multi 40 20

Local Flowers — A180

Various flowers.

1984, Apr. 18 Litho. *Perf. 14x15*
556 A180 90fr multi 28 15
557 A180 125fr multi 40 20
558 A180 135fr multi 42 22
559 A180 350fr multi 1.20 60

Fruit Trees — A181

1984, Mar. 1 Litho. *Perf. 14½x14*
560 A181 90fr Coconut 28 15
561 A181 100fr Papaya 33 16
562 A181 125fr Mango 40 20
563 A181 250fr Banana 80 40

World Telecommunications Day — A182

1984, May 17 *Perf. 13x13½*
564 A182 125fr multi 40 20

Black Jazz Musicians A183

1984, July 5 *Perf. 12½*
565 A183 90fr Lionel Hampton 28 15
566 A183 125fr Charlie Parker 40 20
567 A183 260fr Erroll Garner 80 40

View of Medouneu — A184

1984, Sept. 1 Litho. *Perf. 13*
568 A184 90fr shown 28 15
569 A184 125fr Canoes, Ogooue River 40 20
570 A184 165fr Railroad 55 25

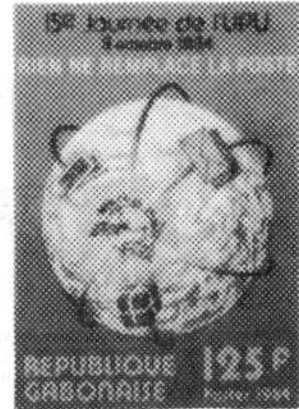

15th World UPU Day — A185

1984, Oct. 9 Litho. *Perf. 13½*
571 A185 125fr UPU emblem, globe, mail 40 20

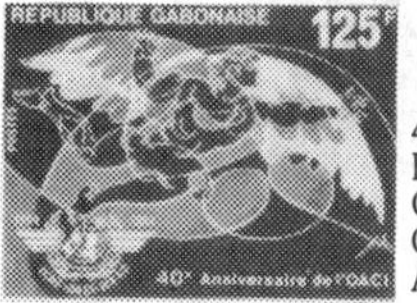

40th Anniv., International Civil Aviation Organization A186

1984, Dec. 1 Litho. *Perf. 13½*
572 A186 125fr Icarus 35 18

Christmas — A187

1984, Dec. 14 Litho. *Perf. 12½*
573 A187 90fr St. Michael's Church Libreville 25 15
574 A187 125fr St. Michael's, diff. 35 18
a. Pair, #573-574 60 35

World Leprosy Day — A188

1985, Jan. 27 Litho. *Perf. 12½*
575 A188 125fr Hospital, Libreville 35 18

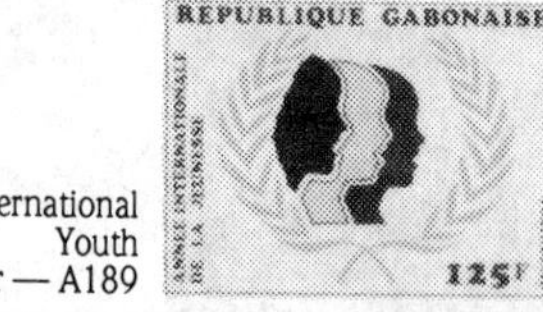
International Youth Year — A189

1985, Feb. 6 Litho. *Perf. 13x12½*
576 A189 125fr Silhouttes, wreath 35 18

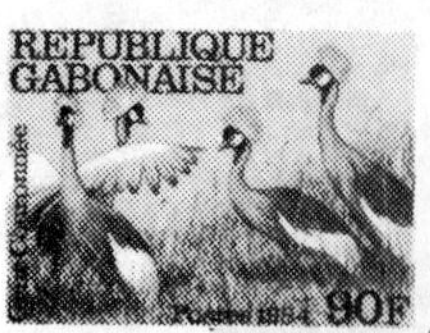
Birds A190

1984 Litho. *Perf. 15x14*
577 A190 90fr Crowned crane 22 15
578 A190 125fr Hummingbird 35 16
579 A190 150fr Toucan 40 20

Silhouettes, Emblem — A191

1985, Mar. 20 *Perf. 12½*
580 A191 125fr brt ultra, red & bl 35 16

Cultural and Technical Cooperation Agency, 15th anniv.

Wildlife A192

1985, Apr. 17 *Perf. 15x14*
581 A192 90fr Aulacode 22 15
582 A192 100fr Porcupine 25 15
583 A192 125fr Giant pangolin 35 16
584 A192 350fr Antelope 90 45
a. Souvenir sheet of 4, #581-584 1.90 90

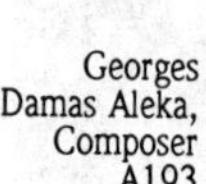

Georges Damas Aleka, Composer A193

1985, Apr. 30 *Perf. 13*
585 A193 90fr Portrait, La Concorde score 22 15

A194 A195

1985, May 17 *Perf. 13½*
586 A194 125fr multi 35 16

World Telecommunications Day. ITU, 120th anniv.

1985, June 9
587 A195 90fr Emblem 22 15

J.O.C., 30th anniv.

Merchant Navy Ships Type of 1982

1985, July 1 *Perf. 15x14*
588 A156 185fr Freighter Mpassa 55 25

Posts and Telecommunications Administration, 20th Anniv. — A196

1985, July 25 *Perf. 13*
589 A196 90fr Headquarters 25 15

President Bongo — A197

1985, Aug. 17 *Perf. 14*
590 A197 250fr multi 70 38
591 A197 500fr multi 1.50 80
a. Pair, #590-591 + 3 labels 2.25 1.50

Imperf

Size: 120x90mm

592 A197 1000fr View of Libreville 3.00 1.50

Natl. Independence, 25th anniv.
No. 592 has non-denominated vignettes of Nos. 590-591.

Org. of Petroleum Exporting Countries, 25th Anniv. — A198

1985, Sept. 25 *Perf. 13½*
593 A198 350fr multi 1.00 50

Intl. Center of the Bantu Civilizations A199

1985, Nov. 16 Litho. *Perf. 15x14*
594 A199 185fr multi 60 32

St. Andrew's Church, Libreville — A199a

1985 Litho. *Perf. 14x15*
594A A199a 90fr multicolored

Christmas.

UNESCO, 25th Anniv. — A200

1986, Jan. 5 Litho. *Perf. 12½*
595 A200 100fr multi 52 25

A201 A202

1986, May 1 Litho. *Perf. 13½*
596 A201 150fr multi 82 40

Rotary Intl. District 915, 4th conf.

1986, June 16 Litho. *Perf. 12½*
597 A202 150fr multi 82 40

Natl. Week of Cartography, Libreville, June 16-20.

Coffee Flowers, Berries, Beans — A203

1986, Aug. 27 Litho. *Perf. 12½*
598 A203 125fr multi 75 35

Organization of African and Madagascar Coffee Producers, 25th anniv.

Merchant Navy Ships Type of 1982

1986, June 24 Litho. *Perf. 15x14*
599 A156 250fr Merchantman L'Abanga 1.40 70

Natl. Postage Stamp, Cent. — A205

1986, July 10 *Perf. 13½x14½*
600 A205 500fr Boats, No. 4 3.00 1.50

Flowering Plants — A206

1986, July 23 *Perf. 14½x15*
601 A206 100fr Allamanda neriifolia 60 30
602 A206 150fr Musa cultivar 90 45
603 A206 160fr Dissotis decumbens 95 48
604 A206 350fr Campylospermum laeve 2.25 1.10

Butterflies A207

1986, Sept. 18 Litho. *Perf. 15x14*
605 A207 150fr Machaon 82 40
606 A207 290fr Urania 1.60 80

St. Pierre Church, Libreville A208

1986, Dec. 23 Litho. *Perf. 15x14½*
607 A208 500fr multi 2.75 1.40

Christmas.

Trans-Gabon Railway from Owendo to Franceville, Inauguration — A209

1986, Dec. 30 *Perf. 13*
608 A209 90fr multi 50 25

Souvenir Sheet

609 A209 250fr multi 1.40 70

Traditional Hairstyles Type of 1981

1986 Litho. *Perf. 14x15*
609A A152 100fr black, gray & yellow
609B A152 150fr tan, black & red brown 1.05 52

Fish — A210

1987, Jan. 15 *Perf. 15x14½*

610 A210 90fr Adioryx bastatus 50 25
611 A210 125fr Scarus boefleri 65 32
612 A210 225fr Cephalacanthus volitans 1.25 62
613 A210 350fr Dasyatis marmorata 2.00 95
a. Souv. sheet of 4, Nos. 610-613 5.75 2.90

No. 613a issued Oct. 1987.

Raoul Follereau (1903-1977) A211

1987, Jan. 23 *Perf. 12½*

614 A211 125fr multi 70 35

World Leprosy Day.

Pres. Bongo Accepting the 1986 Dag Hammarskjold Peace Prize — A212

1987, Mar. 31 **Litho.** *Perf. 13*

615 A212 125fr multi 70 35

World Telecommunications Day — A213

1987, May 17 **Litho.** *Perf. 13½*

616 A213 90fr multi 50 25

Lions Club of Gabon, 30th Anniv. — A214

Pierre de Coubertin, Father of the Modern Olympics — A215

1987, July 18 **Litho.** *Perf. 12x12½*

617 A214 90fr multi 50 25

1987, Aug. 29

618 A215 200fr multi 1.10 55

Lions Club Intl., 70th Anniv. — A216

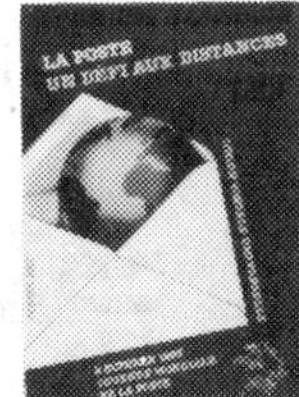

World Post Day — A217

1987, Oct. 1

619 A216 165fr multi 90 45

1987, Oct. 9 **Litho.** *Perf. 13½*

620 A217 125fr multi 85 42

Seashells A218

1987, Oct. *Perf. 15x14*

621 A218 90fr Natica fanel 60 30
622 A218 125fr Natica fulminea cruentata 85 42
a. Souv. sheet of 2, Nos. 621-622 1.50 75

Intl. Year of Shelter for the Homeless — A219

1987, Oct. 5 *Perf. 12½*

623 A219 90fr multi 65 32

Solidarity with the South West African Peoples' Organization (SWAPO) — A220

St. Anna of Odimba Mission — A221

1987, Sept. 15 **Litho.** *Perf. 14½x15*

624 A220 225fr Pres. Bongo, SWAPO leader 1.60 80

1987, Nov. 2 *Perf. 13½*

625 A221 90fr multi 65 32

Universal Child Immunization A222

1987, Nov. 16 *Perf. 15x14½*

626 A222 100fr multi 72 35

20th Anniv. of the Presidency of Omar Bongo — A223

1987, Dec. 2 *Perf. 14½x13½*

627 A223 1000fr multi 7.25 3.60

Christmas A224

1987, Dec. 15 *Perf. 15x14½*

628 A224 90fr St. Therese Church, Oyem 65 32

1988 Winter Olympics, Calgary — A225

1987, Dec. 30 *Perf. 13½x14½*

629 A225 125fr multi 90 45

Medicinal Plants — A226

1988, Jan. 26 **Litho.** *Perf. 14x15*

630 A226 90fr Cassia occidentalis 65 32
631 A226 125fr Tabernanthe iboga 90 45
632 A226 225fr Cassia alata 1.60 80
633 A226 350fr Anthocleista schweinfurthii 2.50 1.25
a. Miniature sheet of 4, #630-633 5.75 2.85

World Wildlife Fund — A227

African forest elephant, *Loxodonta africana cyclotis.*

1988, Feb. 29 **Litho.** *Perf. 13½*

634 A227 25fr multi 18 15
635 A227 40fr multi, diff. 30 15
636 A227 50fr multi, diff. 35 18
637 A227 100fr multi, diff. 72 35

Traditional Musical Instruments A228

1988, Feb. 17 *Perf. 14*

638 A228 90fr Obamba hochet 85 42
639 A228 100fr Fang sanza, vert. 95 48
640 A228 125fr Mitsogho harp, vert. 1.20 60
641 A228 165fr Fang xylophone 1.55 78
a. Souv. sheet of 4, Nos. 638-641 4.55 2.30

World Cup Rugby A229

1988, Mar. **Litho.** *Perf. 13½x14½*

642 A229 350fr multi 2.50 1.25

Delta Post Office Inauguration — A230

1988, Mar. 9

643 A230 90fr multi 60 30

World Telecommunications Day — A231

1988, May 17 *Perf. 13½*
644 A231 125fr multi 85 42

Storming of the Bastille, July 14, 1789 — A232

1988, May 30 Litho. *Perf. 13*
645 A232 125fr multi 85 42

PHILEXFRANCE '89.

Intl. Fund for Agricultural Development (IFAD), 10th Anniv. — A233

1988, June 20 *Perf. 13½*
646 A233 350fr multi 2.40 1.20

Intl. Red Cross and Red Crescent Organizations, 125th Annivs. — A234

1988, July 15 Litho. *Perf. 12½*
647 A234 125fr multi 80 40

1988 Summer Olympics, Seoul A235

1988, Sept. 17 Litho. *Perf. 15x14*

648	A235	90fr Tennis	62	30
649	A235	100fr Swimming	68	35
650	A235	350fr Running	2.35	1.15
651	A235	500fr Hurdles	3.35	1.65
a.		Souv. sheet of 4, Nos. 648-651	7.00	3.50

World Post Day A236

1988, Oct. 9 *Perf. 13½*
652 A236 125fr blk, brt yel & brt blue 85 42

Christmas A237

1988, Dec. 20 Litho. *Perf. 15x14*
653 A237 200fr Medouneu Church 1.30 65

A238

A239

1989, Feb. 21 *Perf. 13½*
654 A238 175fr multi 1.15 58

Chaine des Rotisseurs in Gabon, 10th anniv.

1989, Mar. 6 Litho. *Perf. 13½*
655 A239 125fr multi 75 38

Rabi Kounga oil field. See No. 707.

Traditional Games — A240

Perf. 13½x14½
1989, Mar. 20 Litho.
656 A240 90fr multicolored 58 30

Birds — A241

A242

1989, Apr. 17 Litho. *Perf. 14x15*

657	A241	100fr White-tufted bittern	60	30
658	A241	175fr Gabon gray parakeet	1.05	52
659	A241	200fr Pygmy hornbill	1.20	60
660	A241	500fr Pope's martin	3.00	1.50
a.		Souv. sheet of 4, Nos. 657-660	5.85	2.95

See Nos. 750-753.

1989, Apr. 27 *Perf. 13*
661 A242 125fr multi 75 38

8th Convention of Lions Intl. District 403, Libreville, Apr. 27-29.

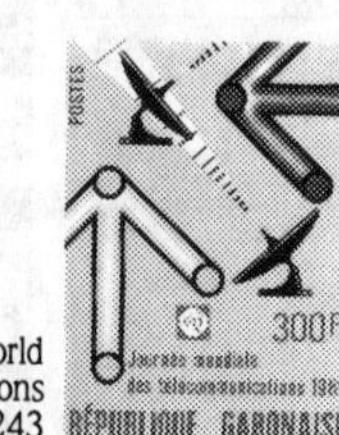

World Telecommunications Day — A243

1989, May 17 *Perf. 13½*
662 A243 300fr multi 1.80 90

PHILEXFRANCE '89 — A244

Symbols of the French revolution, 1789.

Wmk. 385
1989, July 7 Litho. *Perf. 13*
663 A244 175fr multi 1.15 58

French Revolution, Bicent. — A245

1989, July 14
664 A245 500fr multi 3.20 1.60

Fruit — A246

Perf. 14½x15
1989, May 30 Litho. Unwmk.

665	A246	90fr Coconuts	65	32
666	A246	125fr Cabosse	85	42
667	A246	175fr Pineapple	1.25	62
668	A246	250fr Breadfruit	1.75	88
a.		Souv. sheet of 4, #665-668	4.50	2.25

AIMF, 10th Anniv. — A247

1989, July 27 Litho. *Perf. 13*
669 A247 100fr multi 65 32

African Development Bank, 25th Anniv. — A248

1989, Aug. 2 Litho. *Perf. 13*
670 A248 100fr multi 60 30

Apples and Oranges, by Cezanne (1839-1906) — A249

Perf. 13½x14½
1989, June 22 Litho.
671 A249 500fr multicolored 3.20 1.60

1990 World Cup Soccer Championships, Italy — A250

Various athletes.

Perf. 15x14½
1989, Aug. 23 Litho. Unwmk.

672	A250	100fr shown	70	35
673	A250	175fr multi, diff.	1.25	60
674	A250	300fr multi, diff.	2.10	1.05
675	A250	500fr multi, diff.	3.50	1.75
a.		Souv. sheet of 4, #672-675	7.55	3.75

Traditional Hair Style Type of 1981

1989, Sept. 16 *Perf. 14½x15*
676 A152 175fr gray, black & vio 1.25 60

Post Day — A252

1989, Sept. 10 Litho. *Perf. 12*
Granite Paper
677 A252 175fr multicolored 1.40 70

Postal Service, 125th Anniv. (in 1987) — A255

Perf. 13½x14½

1989 Litho. Unwmk.

681 A255 90fr multicolored 65 32

Dated 1988.

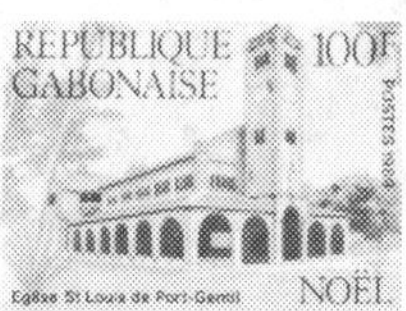

St. Louis Church, Port Gentil A256

1989, Dec. 15 Litho. ***Perf. 15x14***

682 A256 100fr multicolored 78 40

Christmas. See Nos. 725-726, 757.

L'Ogooue', N'Gomo A256a

1989 Litho. ***Perf. 15x14***

682A A256a 100fr multicolored

Libreville Coat of Arms — A257

World Health Day — A258

Perf. 13½

1990, Mar. 12 Litho. Wmk. 385

683 A257 100fr multicolored 82 40

1990, Apr. 7 Litho. ***Perf. 13***

684 A258 400fr multicolored 3.25 1.60

Souvenir Sheet

Prehistoric Tools A259

1990, Feb. 14 Litho. ***Perf. 15x14***

685 Sheet of 4 7.00 3.50
- **a.** A259 100fr Hand axe 72 40
- **b.** A259 175fr Knife blade 1.25 65
- **c.** A259 300fr Arrowhead 2.15 1.10
- **d.** A259 400fr Double bladed hand axe 2.85 1.45

See Nos. 727-730.

Souvenir Sheet

Fauna — A260

Illustration reduced.

1990, Apr. 13 ***Perf. 14***

686 A260 Sheet of 4 8.60 4.25
- **a.** 100fr Cercopitheque 90 45
- **b.** 175fr Potamocherus Porcus 1.55 75
- **c.** 200fr Antelope 1.75 85
- **d.** 500fr Mandrill 4.40 2.20

First Postage Stamps, 150th Anniv. — A261

1991, Jan. 9 Litho. ***Perf. 13½x14½***

687 A261 500fr multicolored 4.40 2.20

Independence, 30th Anniv. — A263

1990, Aug. 17 Litho. ***Perf. 13***

693 A263 100fr multicolored 90 45

Mushrooms A263a

1990 Litho. ***Perf. 15x14***

693A A263a 100fr multicolored

Numbers have been reserved for additional values in this set.

A264

A265

A264a

1990, Sept. 19 Litho. ***Perf. 13***

694 A264 200fr multicolored 1.75 90

Organization of Petroleum Exporting Countries (OPEC), 30th anniv.

1990 Litho. ***Perf. 15x14***

694A A264a 175fr multicolored

1990 World Cup Soccer Championships, Italy.

1990, Oct. 9 ***Perf. 13½***

695 A265 175fr blue, yel & blk 1.55 80

World Post Day.

Traditional Bwiti Dancer A265a

1990 Litho. ***Perf. 15x14***

695A A265a 175fr multicolored

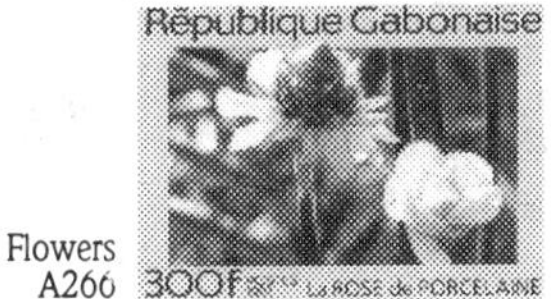

Flowers A266

1991, Jan. 9 Litho. ***Perf. 15x14***

696 A266 100fr Frangipanier 90 45
697 A266 175fr Boule de feu 1.55 75
698 A266 200fr Flamboyant 1.75 85
699 A266 300fr Rose de porcelaine 2.65 1.30
- **a.** Souvenir sheet of 4, #696-699 7.00 3.50

Petroglyphs A267

1991, Feb. 26 Litho. ***Perf. 15x14***

700 A267 100fr Lizard figure 90 45
701 A267 175fr Triangular figure 1.55 75
702 A267 300fr Incused lines 2.65 1.30
703 A267 500fr Concentric circles, circles in lines 4.40 2.20
- **a.** Souvenir sheet of 4, #700-703 9.50 4.75

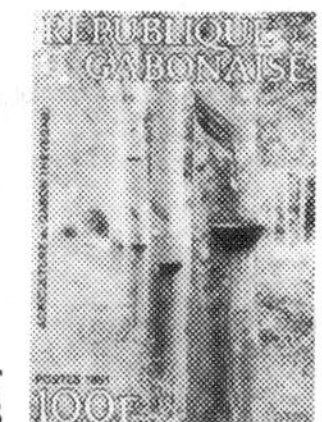

Rubber Trees — A268

1991, Mar. 20 Litho. ***Perf. 14x15***

705 A268 100fr multicolored 90 45

World Telecommunications Day — A269

1991, May 17 Litho. ***Perf. 13½***

706 A269 175fr multicolored 1.40 70

Rabi Kounga Oil Field Type of 1989

1991 Litho. ***Perf. 13½***

707 A239 175fr multicolored

Ngounie Women Washing Clothes A271

1991, July 17 Litho. ***Perf. 13½***

708 A271 100fr multicolored 90 45

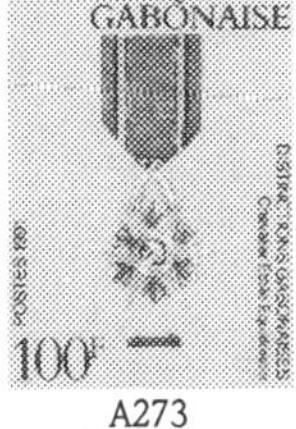

A272 A273

Designs: Craftsmen.

1991, June 19 ***Perf. 14x15***

709 A272 100fr Basket maker 90 45
710 A272 175fr Wood carver 1.55 75
711 A272 200fr Weaver 1.80 90
712 A272 500fr Thatch maker 4.50 2.25

1991, Aug. 18 Litho. ***Perf. 14x15***

Gabonese Medals: 100fr, Equatorial Knight's Star. 175fr, Equatorial Officer's Star. 200fr, Equatorial Commander's Star.

Gray Background

713 A273 100fr multicolored 80 40
714 A273 175fr multicolored 1.40 70
715 A273 200fr multicolored 1.60 80

See Nos. 735-737.

Fishing in Gabon A274

1991, Sept. 18 ***Perf. 15x14***

716 A274 100fr Bow-net fishing 80 40
717 A274 175fr Trammel fishing 1.40 70
718 A274 200fr Net fishing 1.60 80
719 A274 300fr Seine fishing 2.40 1.20
a. Souvenir sheet of 4, #716-719 6.20 3.10

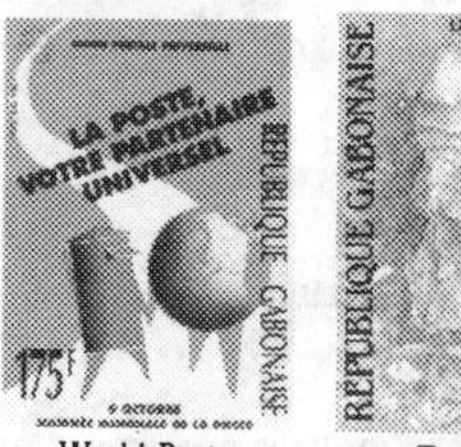

World Post Day — A275

Termite Mounds — A276

1991, Oct. 9 ***Perf. 13½***

720 A275 175fr blue & multi 1.40 70

See No. 749.

1991, Nov. 6 ***Perf. 14x15***

721 A276 100fr Phallic 80 40
722 A276 175fr Cathedral 1.40 70
723 A276 200fr Mushroom 1.60 80
724 A276 300fr Arboreal 2.40 1.20

Church Type of 1989

1991, Dec. 18 **Litho.** ***Perf. 15x14***

725 A256 100fr Church of Makokou 80 40
726 A256 100fr Church of Dibwangui 80 40

Christmas. No. 725 inscribed 1990.

Prehistoric Tools Type of 1990

Pottery: 100fr, Neolithic pot. 175fr, Bottle, 8th cent. 200fr, Vase, 8th cent. 300fr, Vase, 8th cent, diff.

1992, Jan. 9 **Litho.** ***Perf. 14x15***

727 A259 100fr multicolored 80 40
728 A259 175fr multicolored 1.40 70
729 A259 200fr multicolored 1.60 80
730 A259 300fr multicolored 2.40 1.20
a. Sheet of 4, #727-730 6.20 3.10

Nos. 727-730 are vert.

Occupations — A277

1992

731 A277 100fr Basket maker 80 40
732 A277 175fr Blacksmith 1.40 70
733 A277 200fr Boat builder 1.60 80
734 A277 300fr Hairdresser 2.40 1.20
a. Souvenir sheet of 4, #731-734 6.20 3.10

Issue dates: No. 734a, Feb. 9, others, Feb. 5.

Gabonese Medals Type of 1991

Designs: 100fr, Equatorial Grand Officer's Star. 175fr, Grand Cross of Dignity and Equatorial Star. 200fr, Order of Merit.

1992, Mar. 18 **Litho.** ***Perf. 14x15***

Aquamarine Background

735 A273 100fr multicolored 82 40
736 A273 175fr multicolored 1.45 72
737 A273 200fr multicolored 1.65 82

A278

A279

1992, Apr. 19 ***Perf. 13***

738 A278 500fr multicolored 4.15 2.10

Konrad Adenauer (1876-1967), German Statesman.

1992, May 17 ***Perf. 13½***

739 A279 175fr multicolored 1.50 75

World Telecommunications Day.

Butterflies A280

1992, June 10 **Litho.** ***Perf. 15x14***

740 A280 100fr Graphium policenes 90 45
741 A280 175fr Acraea egina 1.60 80

A281

A282

1992, July 25 ***Perf. 14x15***

742 A281 100fr Cycling 90 45
743 A281 175fr Boxing 1.60 80
744 A281 200fr Pole vault 1.80 90

1992 Summer Olympics, Barcelona.

1992, Sept. 16 **Litho.** ***Perf. 14x15***

Tribal masks.

745 A282 100fr Fang 90 45
746 A282 175fr Mpongwe 1.60 80
747 A282 200fr Kwele 1.80 90
748 A282 300fr Pounou 2.75 1.35
a. Souvenir sheet of 4, #745-748 7.05 3.50

World Post Day Type of 1991 Inscribed 1992

1992, Oct. 9 **Litho.** ***Perf. 13½***

749 A275 175fr bl grn & multi 1.45 75

Bird Type of 1989

1992, Nov. 4 **Litho.** ***Perf. 14x15***

750 A241 100fr African owl 85 42
751 A241 175fr Coliou strie 1.45 75
752 A241 200fr Vulture 1.65 85
753 A241 300fr Giant kingfisher 2.50 1.25
a. Souvenir sheet of 4, #750-753 6.45 3.25

Cattle A283

Various scenes of cattle in pasture.

1992, Dec. 10 ***Perf. 15x14***

754 A283 100fr multicolored 80 40
755 A283 175fr multicolored 1.40 70
756 A283 200fr multicolored 1.60 80

Church Type of 1989

1992, Dec. 16

757 A256 100fr Tchibanga Church 80 40

Christmas.

Intl. Conference on Nutrition, Rome — A284

1992, Dec. 20 ***Perf. 13½***

758 A284 100fr multicolored 80 40

Shells A285

1993, Jan. 6 **Litho.** ***Perf. 15x14***

759 A285 100fr Pugilina 80 40
760 A285 175fr Conus pulcher 1.40 70
761 A285 200fr Fusinus 1.60 80
762 A285 300fr Cymatium 2.40 1.20

World Leprosy Day — A286

1993, Jan. 28 ***Perf. 13½***

763 A286 175fr multicolored 1.40 70

Fernan-Vaz Mission A287

1993, Feb. 3 ***Perf. 15x14***

764 A287 175fr multicolored 1.40 70

Chappe's Semaphore Telegraph, Bicent. — A288

Designs: 100fr, Claude Chappe (1763-1805), engineer and inventor. 175fr, Chappe's signaling device and code. 200fr, Emile Baudot (1845-1903), devising telegraph code, early telegraph equipment. 300fr, Modern satellite, electronic chip and fiber optics.

1993, Mar. 10 **Litho.** ***Perf. 13½***

765 A288 100fr multicolored 85 42
766 A288 175fr multicolored 1.40 70
767 A288 200fr multicolored 1.65 85
768 A288 300fr multicolored 2.50 1.25
a. Souvenir sheet of 4, #765-768 6.50 3.25

Albert Schweitzer's Arrival in Lambarene, 80th Anniv. A289

1993, Apr. 6 **Litho.** ***Perf. 13***

769 A289 500fr multicolored 4.75 2.25
a. Booklet pane of 1 4.75

Booklet Stamps

Size: 26x37mm

Perf. 13½

770 A289 250fr Feeding chickens 2.25 1.10
a. Booklet pane of 4 9.00
771 A289 250fr Holding babies 2.25 1.10
a. Booklet pane of 4 9.00

Booklet containing one of each pane sold for 3000fr.

Nicolaus Copernicus, Heliocentric Solar System — A290

1993, May 5 **Litho.** ***Perf. 15x14***

772 A290 175fr multicolored 1.40 70

Polska '93.

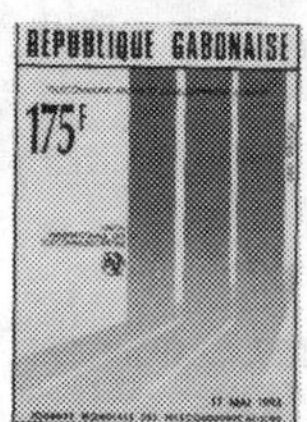

World Telecommunications Day — A291

1993, May 17 ***Perf. 13½***

773 A291 175fr multicolored 1.40 70

Traditional Wine Making — A292

Designs: 100fr, Still. 175fr, Extracting juice from palm roots. 200fr, Man in palm tree.

1993, June 9 **Litho.** ***Perf. 14***

774 A292 100fr multicolored 85 42
775 A292 175fr multicolored 1.40 70
776 A292 200fr multicolored 1.65 80
a. Souvenir sheet of 3, #774-776 4.00 2.00

Crustaceans A293

1993, July 21 Litho. *Perf. 15x14*

777 A293 100fr Spiny lobster 75 38
778 A293 175fr Violin crab 1.25 65
779 A293 200fr Crayfish 1.50 75
780 A293 300fr Spider crab 2.25 1.10

Paris '94 — A294

1993, Aug. 10 Litho. *Perf. 13*

781 A294 100fr multicolored 85 42

SEMI-POSTAL STAMPS

No. 37 Surcharged in Red

1916 Unwmk. *Perf. 13½x14*

B1 A10 10c + 5c red & car 7.25 7.25
a. Double surcharge 70.00 75.00

Same Surcharge on No. 54 in Red

B2 A13 10c + 5c red & car 10.50 10.00
a. Double surcharge 70.00 65.00

No. 54 Surcharged in Red

1917

B3 A13 10c + 5c car & red 40 40

> Catalogue values for unused stamps in this section, from this point to the end of the section, are for Never Hinged items.

Republic
Anti-Malaria Issue
Common Design Type

1962, Apr. 7 Engr. *Perf. 12½x12*

B4 CD108 25fr + 5fr yel grn 70 70

WHO drive to eradicate malaria.

Freedom from Hunger Issue
Common Design Type

1963, Mar. 21 Unwmk. *Perf. 13*

B5 CD112 25fr + 5fr dk red, grn & brn 60 60

AIR POST STAMPS

> Catalogue values for unused stamps in this section are for Never Hinged items.

Dr. Albert Schweitzer — AP1

Unwmk.

1960, July 23 Engr. *Perf. 13*

C1 AP1 200fr grn, dl red brn & ultra 2.25 1.25

Issued to honor Dr. Albert Schweitzer, medical missionary.
For surcharge see No. C11.

Workmen Felling Tree — AP2

1960, Oct. 8

C2 AP2 100fr red brn, grn & blk 1.40 70

5th World Forestry Cong., Seattle, WA, Aug. 29-Sept. 10.

Olympic Games Issue
French Equatorial Africa No. C37 Surcharged in Red Like Chad No. C1

1960, Dec. 15

C3 AP8 250fr on 500fr grnsh blk, blk & sl 4.00 4.00

Issued to commemorate the 17th Olympic Games, Rome, Aug. 25-Sept. 11.

Lyre-tailed Honey Guide — AP3

1961, May 30 *Perf. 13*

C4 AP3 50fr sl grn, red brn & ultra 60 40

See Nos. C14-C17.

Air Afrique Issue
Common Design Type

1962, Feb. 17 Engr. *Perf. 13*

C5 CD107 500fr sl grn, blk & bis 5.00 3.00

Long Jump — AP3a

1962, July 21 Photo. *Perf. 12x12½*

C6 AP3a 100fr dk & lt bl, brn & blk 1.40 70

Issued to publicize the Abidjan Games.

Breguet 14, 1928 — AP4

Development of air transport: 20fr, Dragon biplane transport. 60fr, Caravelle jet. 85fr, Rocket-propelled aircraft.

1962, Sept. 4 Engr. *Perf. 13*

C7 AP4 10fr dl red brn & sl 22 15
C8 AP4 20fr dk bl, sl & ocher 25 18
C9 AP4 60fr dk sl grn, blk & brn 65 50
C10 AP4 85fr dk bl, blk & org 1.10 1.00
a. Souv. sheet of 4, #C7-C10 2.50 2.50

Gabon's 1st phil. exhib., Libreville, Sept. 2-9.

No. C1 Surcharged in Red: "100F/JUBILE GABONAIS/1913-1963"

1963, Apr. 18

C11 AP1 100fr on 200fr 1.10 90

50th anniv. of Dr. Albert Schweitzer's arrival in Gabon.

Post Office, Libreville — AP5

1963, Apr. 28 Photo. *Perf. 13x12*

C12 AP5 100fr multi 90 65

African Postal Union Issue
Common Design Type

1963, Sept. 8 Unwmk. *Perf. 12½*

C13 CD114 85fr brt car, ocher & red 80 60

Bird Type of 1961

Birds: 100fr, Johanna's sunbird. 200fr, Blue-headed bee-eater, vert. 250fr, Crowned hawk-eagle, vert. 500fr, Narina trogon, vert.

1963-64 Engr. *Perf. 13*

C14 AP3 100fr dk grn, vio bl & car 1.20 55
C15 AP3 200fr ol, vio bl & red 2.25 1.20
C16 AP3 250fr grn, blk & dk brn ('64) 3.00 1.50
C17 AP3 500fr multi 5.75 2.75

1963 Air Afrique Issue
Common Design Type

1963, Nov. 19 Photo. *Perf. 13x12*

C18 CD115 50fr lt vio, gray, blk & grn 50 40

Europafrica Issue
Common Design Type

1963, Nov. 30 *Perf. 12x13*

C19 CD116 50fr vio, yel & dk brn 80 50

Chiefs of State Issue

Map and Presidents of Chad, Congo, Gabon and CAR — AP5a

1964, June 23 *Perf. 12½*

C20 AP5a 100fr multi 1.10 70

See note after Central African Republic No. C19.

Europafrica Issue, 1964

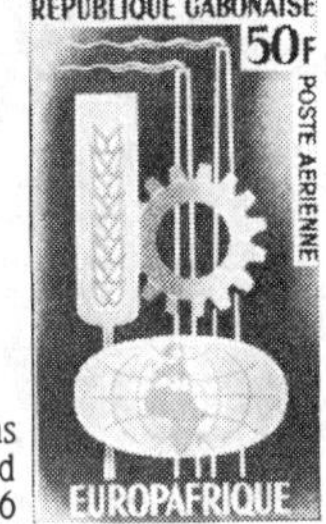

Globe and Emblems of Industry and Agriculture — AP6

1964, July 20 *Perf. 12x13*

C21 AP6 50fr red, ol & bl 55 40

See note after Cameroun No. 402.

Start of Race AP7

Athletes (Greek): 50fr, Massage at gymnasium, vert. 100fr, Anointing with oil before game, vert. 200fr, Four athletes.

1964, July 30 Engr. *Perf. 13*

C22 AP7 25fr sl grn, dk brn & org 22 18
C23 AP7 50fr dk brn, sl grn & org brn 50 35
C24 AP7 100fr vio bl, ol grn & dk brn 1.00 65
C25 AP7 200fr dk brn, mag & org red 2.00 1.40
a. Min. sheet of 4, #C22-C25 3.75 3.75

18th Olympic Games, Tokyo, Oct. 10-25.

Communications Symbols — AP7a

1964, Nov. 2 Litho. *Perf. 12½x13*

C26 AP7a 25fr lt grn, dk brn & lt red brn 22 20

See note after Chad No. C19.

John F. Kennedy (1917-63) — AP8

1964, Nov. 23 Photo. *Perf. 12½*

C27 AP8 100fr grn, org & blk 85 70
a. Souv. sheet of 4 3.50 3.50

Telephone Operator, Nurse and Police Woman — AP9

1964, Dec. 5 Engr. *Perf. 13*
C28 AP9 50fr car, bl & choc 55 35

Social evolution of Gabonese women.

World Map and ICY Emblem — AP10

1965, Mar. 25 Unwmk. *Perf. 13*
C29 AP10 50fr org, Prus bl & grnsh bl 55 38

International Cooperation Year.

Merchant Ship, 17th Century — AP11

Designs: 25fr, Galleon, 16th cent., vert. 85fr, Frigate, 18th cent., vert. 100fr, Brig, 19th cent.

1965, Apr. 22 Photo. *Perf. 13*

C30 AP11	25fr lil & multi	35	22
C31 AP11	50fr yel & multi	65	38
C32 AP11	85fr multi	1.00	65
C33 AP11	100fr multi	1.40	80

Red Cross Nurse Carrying Sick Child — AP12

1965, June 25 Engr. *Perf. 13*
C34 AP12 100fr brn, sl grn & red 1.00 65

Issued for the Gabonese Red Cross.

Women's Basketball — AP13

1965, July 15 Unwmk.
C35 AP13 100fr sep, red org & brt lil 1.00 65

African Games, Brazzaville, July 18-25.

Maps of Europe and Africa — AP14

1965, July 26 Photo. *Perf. 13x12*
C36 AP14 50fr multi 1.00 30

See note after Cameroun No. 421.

Pres. Leon Mba AP15

1965, Aug. 17 *Perf. 12½*
C37 AP15 25fr multi 25 20

Fifth anniversary of independence.

Sir Winston Churchill and Microphones — AP16

1965, Sept. 28 Photo. *Perf. 12½*
C38 AP16 100fr gold, blk & bl 1.10 70

Sir Winston Spencer Churchill (1874-1965), statesman and World War II leader.

Dr. Albert Schweitzer — AP17

Embossed on Gold Foil
Die-cut Perf. 14½, Approx.
1965, Dec. 4
C39 AP17 1000fr gold 16.00 16.00

Dr. Albert Schweitzer (1875-1965), medical missionary, theologian and musician.

Pope John XXIII and St. Peter's — AP18

1965, Dec. 10 Photo. *Perf. 13x12½*
C40 AP18 85fr multi 80 60

Issued in memory of Pope John XXIII.

Anti-Malaria Treatment — AP19

1966, Apr. 8 Photo. *Perf. 12½*

C41 AP19	50fr shown	40	25
a.	Min. sheet of 4	1.75	1.75
C42 AP19	100fr First aid	80	45
a.	Min. sheet of 4	3.50	3.50

Issued for the Red Cross.

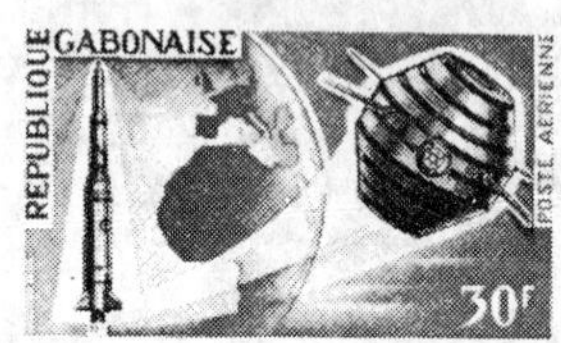
Diamant Rocket, A-1 Satellite and Map of Africa — AP20

Design: 90fr, FR-1 satellite, Diamant rocket and earth.

1966, May 18 Engr. *Perf. 13*

C43 AP20	30fr dk pur, brt bl & red brn	35	22
C44 AP20	90fr brt lil, red & pur	90	50

French achievements in space.

Soccer and World Map — AP21

1966, July 15 Engr. *Perf. 13*
C45 AP21 100fr sl & brn red 1.20 65

8th World Soccer Cup Championship, Wembley, England, July 11-30.

Symbols of Industry and Transportation AP22

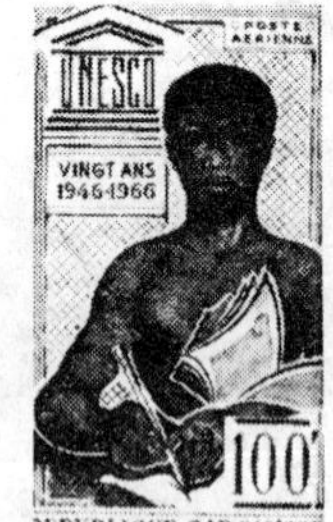
Student and UNESCO Emblem AP23

1966, July 26 Photo. *Perf. 12x13*
C46 AP22 50fr multi 55 25

3rd anniv. of the economic agreement between the European Economic Community and the African and Malgache Union.

Air Afrique Issue, 1966
Common Design Type
1966, Aug. 31 Photo. *Perf. 13*
C47 CD123 30fr org, blk & gray 25 15

1966, Nov. 4 Engr. *Perf. 13*
C48 AP23 100fr dl bl, ocher & blk 1.00 55

20th anniv. of UNESCO.

Libreville Airport — AP24

1966, Nov. 21 Engr. *Perf. 13*
C49 AP24 200fr dp bl & red brn 1.75 80

Inauguration of Libreville Airport.

Farman 190 — AP25

Planes: 300fr, De Havilland Heron. 500fr, Potez 56.

1967, Apr. 1 Engr. *Perf. 13*

C50 AP25	200fr ultra, lil & bl grn	1.75	55
C51 AP25	300fr brn, lil & brt bl	2.50	75
C52 AP25	500fr brn car, dk grn & ind	4.00	2.50

For surcharge see No. C128.

Planes, Runways and ICAO Emblem — AP26

1967, May 19 Engr. *Perf. 13*
C53 AP26 100fr plum, brt bl & yel grn 1.00 55

International Civil Aviation Organization.

Blood Donor and Bottles — AP27

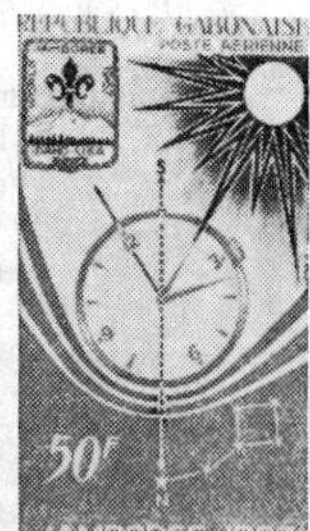
Jamboree Emblem and Symbols of Orientation — AP28

Design: 100fr, Human heart and transfusion apparatus.

1967, June 26 Photo. *Perf. 12½*

C54 AP27	50fr ocher, red & sl	50	25
a.	Souvenir sheet of 4	2.00	2.00
C55 AP27	100fr yel grn, red & gray	1.10	60
a.	Souvenir sheet of 4	4.50	4.50

Issued for the Red Cross. Nos. C54a, C55a each contain 2 vertical tête bêche pairs.

1967, Aug. 1 Engr. *Perf. 13*

Design: 100fr, Jamboree emblem, maps and Scouts of Africa and America.

C56 AP28	50fr multi	50	30
C57 AP28	100fr brt grn, dp car & bl	1.00	55

12th Boy Scout World Jamboree, Farragut State Park, Idaho, Aug. 1-9.

African Postal Union Issue, 1967
Common Design Type

1967, Sept. 9 Engr. *Perf. 13*
C58 CD124 100fr dl bl, ol & red brn 90 50

Mission Church — AP29

1967, Oct. 18 Engr. *Perf. 13*
C59 AP29 100fr brt bl, dk grn & blk 90 35

125th anniv. of the arrival of American Protestant missionaries in Baraka-Libreville.

UN Emblem, Sword, Book and People — AP30

Konrad Adenauer — AP31

1967, Nov. 7 Photo. *Perf. 13*
C60 AP30 60fr dk red, vio bl & bis 65 20

UN Commission on Human Rights.

Tree Type of Regular Issue

Designs: 50fr, Baillonella toxisperma. 100fr, Aucoumea klaineana.

1967, Dec. 5 Engr. *Perf. 13*
Size: 26½x47½mm
C61 A53 50fr grn, brt bl & brn 55 25
C62 A53 100fr multi 1.10 58
a. Bklt. pane (1 each #223-225 & C61-C62 with gutter btwn.) 2.25 2.25

1968, Feb. 20 Photo. *Perf. 12½*
C63 AP31 100fr blk, dl org & red 85 45
a. Souvenir sheet of 4 3.50 3.50

Issued in memory of Konrad Adenauer (1876-1967), chancellor of West Germany (1949-63). No. C63a includes 1967 CEPT (Europa) emblem.

Madonna of the Rosary by Murillo AP32

Paintings: 90fr, Christ in Bonds, by Luis de Morales. 100fr, St. John on Patmos, by Juan Mates, horiz.

1968, July 9 Photo. *Perf. 12½x12*
C64 AP32 60fr multi 50 25
C65 AP32 90fr multi 70 40
C66 AP32 100fr multi 85 50

See Nos. C77, C102-C104, C132-C133, C146-C148.

Europafrica Issue

Stylized Knot — AP32a

1968, July 23 Photo. *Perf. 13*
C67 AP32a 50fr yel brn, emer & lt ultra 55 25

See note after Congo Republic No. C69.

Support for Red Cross — AP33

Design: 50fr, Distribution of Red Cross gifts.

1968, Aug. 13
C68 AP33 50fr multi 45 22
C69 AP33 100fr multi 1.00 50
a. Bklt. pane of 2 (Nos. C68, C69 with gutter between) 1.50 1.50

Issued for the Red Cross.

High Jump AP34

Designs: 30fr, Bicycling, vert. 100fr, Judo, vert. 200fr, Boxing.

1968, Sept. 3 Engr.
C70 AP34 25fr dk brn, mag & gray 16 15
C71 AP34 30fr brick red, Prus bl & dk brn 22 15
C72 AP34 100fr brt bl, dk brn & dl yel 80 40
C73 AP34 200fr emer, gray & dk brn 1.50 75
a. Bklt. pane (1 each #C70-C71 & C72-C73 with gutter btwn.) 3.50 3.50

Issued to publicize the 19th Summer Olympic Games, Mexico City, Oct. 12-27.

Pres. Mba, Flag and Arms of Gabon AP35

Embossed on Gold Foil

1968, Nov. 28 *Perf. 14½*
C74 AP35 1000fr gold, grn, yel & dk bl 7.00 7.00

1st anniv. of the death of Pres. Léon Mba (1902-67).

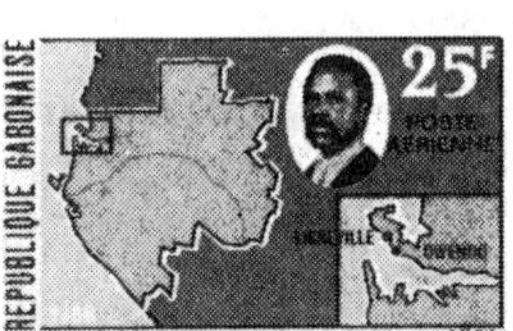

Pres. Bongo, Maps of Gabon and Owendo Harbor — AP36

Design: 30fr, Owendo Harbor.

1968, Dec. 16 Photo. *Perf. 12½*
C75 AP36 25fr multi 25 15
C76 AP36 30fr multi 35 16
a. Strip of 2, #C75-C76 + label 65 60

Laying of the foundation stone for Owendo Harbor, June 24, 1968.

PHILEXAFRIQUE Issue
Painting Type of 1968

Design: 100fr, The Convent of St. Mary of the Angels, by Francois Marius Granet.

1969, Jan. 8 Photo. *Perf. 12½x12*
C77 AP32 100fr multi 1.10 1.10

Issued to publicize PHILEXAFRIQUE Philatelic Exhibition in Abidjan, Feb. 14-23. Printed with alternating brown label.

Mahatma Gandhi — AP37

Portraits: 30fr, John F. Kennedy. 50fr, Robert F. Kennedy. 100fr, Martin Luther King, Jr.

1969, Jan. 15 *Perf. 12½*
C78 AP37 25fr pink & blk 20 15
C79 AP37 30fr lt yel grn & blk 22 15
C80 AP37 50fr lt bl & blk 38 18
C81 AP37 100fr brt rose lil & blk 75 32
a. Souv. sheet of 4, #C78-C81 2.00 2.00
Set value 69

Issued to honor exponents of non-violence.

2nd PHILEXAFRIQUE Issue
Common Design Type

1969, Feb. 14 Engr. *Perf. 13*
C82 CD128 50fr grn, ind & red brn 60 35

Battle of Rivoli, by Henri Philippoteaux — AP39

Paintings: 100fr, The Oath of the Army, by Jacques Louis David. 250fr, Napoleon with the Children on the Terrace in St. Cloud, by Louis Ducis.

1969, Apr. 23 Photo. *Perf. 12½x12*
C83 AP39 50fr brn & multi 80 50
C84 AP39 100fr grn & multi 1.50 1.00
C85 AP39 250fr lil & multi 4.00 2.50

Birth bicentenary of Napoleon I.

Red Cross Plane, Nurse and Biafran Children — AP40

Design: 20fr, Dispensary, ambulance and supplies. 25fr, Physician and nurse in children's ward. 30fr, Dispensary and playing children.

1969, June 20 Photo. *Perf. 14x13½*
C86 AP40 15fr lt ultra, dk brn & red 15 15
C87 AP40 20fr emer, blk, brn & red 22 15
C88 AP40 25fr grnsh bl, dk brn & red 25 16
C89 AP40 30fr org yel, dk brn & red 30 16

Red Cross help for Biafra.

A souvenir sheet contains four stamps similar to Nos. C86-C89, but lithographed and rouletted 13x13½. Gray margin with red inscription and Red Cross. Size: 118x75mm. Sold in cardboard folder. Value $1.20.

Astronauts and Lunar Landing Module, Apollo 11 — AP41

Embossed on Gold Foil

1969, July 25 *Die-cut Perf. 10½x10*
C90 AP41 1000fr gold 9.00 9.00

See note after Algeria No. 427.

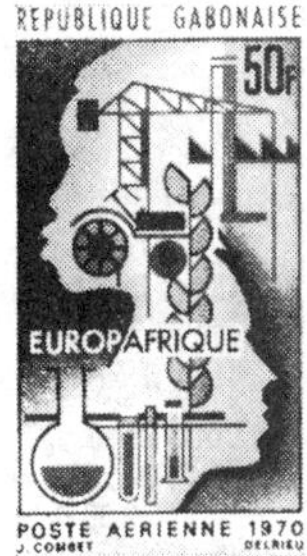

African and European Heads and Symbols — AP42

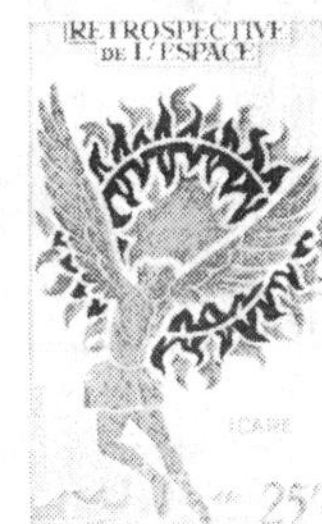

Icarus and Sun — AP43

Europafrica Issue, 1970

1970, June 5 Photo. *Perf. 12x13*
C91 AP42 50fr multi 50 22

1970, June 10 Engr. *Perf. 13*

Designs: 100fr, Leonardo da Vinci's flying man, 1519. 200fr, Jules Verne's space shell approaching moon, 1865.

C92 AP43 25fr ultra, red & org 20 15
C93 AP43 100fr ocher, plum & sl grn 70 45
C94 AP43 200fr gray, ultra & dk car 2.00 90
a. Min. sheet of 3, #C92-C94 3.25 3.25

UAMPT Emblem AP44

Embossed on Gold Foil

1970, June 18 *Die-cut Perf. 12½*
C95 AP44 200fr gold, yel grn & bl 1.90 1.10

Meeting of the Afro-Malagasy Union of Posts and Telecommuncations (UAMPT), Libreville, June 17-23.

Throwing Knives AP45

Gabonese Weapons: 30fr, Assegai and crossbow, vert. 50fr, War knives, vert. 90fr, Dagger and sheath.

1970, July 10 Engr. *Perf. 13*

C96 AP45 25fr multi 18 15
C97 AP45 30fr multi 22 15
C98 AP45 50fr multi 32 20
C99 AP45 90fr multi 70 35
a. Min. sheet of 4, #C96-C99 1.50 1.50
Set value 72

Japanese Masks, Mt. Fuji and Torii at Miyajima AP46

Embossed on Gold Foil

1970, July 31 *Die-cut Perf. 10*

C100 AP46 1000fr multi 10.00 10.00

Issued to publicize EXPO '70 International Exhibition, Osaka, Japan, Mar. 15-Sept. 13.

Pres. Albert Bernard Bongo — AP47

Lithographed; Gold Embossed

1970, Aug. 17 *Perf. 12½*

C101 AP47 200fr multi 2.00 1.10

10th anniversary of independence.

Painting Type of 1968

Paintings: 50fr, Portrait of a Young Man, School of Raphael. 100fr, Portrait of Jeanne d'Aragon, by Raphael. 200fr, Madonna with Blue Diadem, by Raphael.

1970, Oct. 16 Photo. *Perf. 12½x12*

C102 AP32 50fr multi 40 20
C102A AP32 100fr bl & multi 80 40
C102B AP32 200fr brn & multi 1.65 90

Raphael (1483-1520).

Miniature Sheets

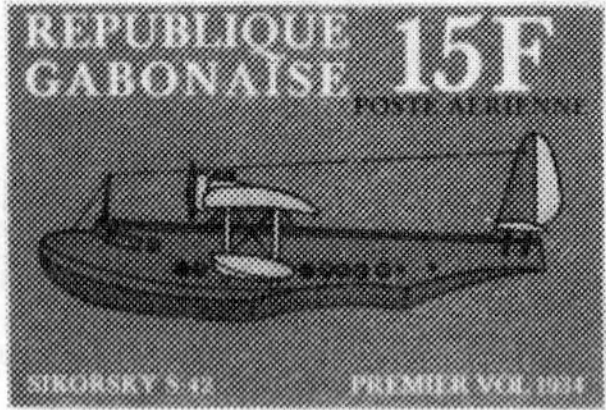

Sikorsky S-32 — AP47a

Hugo Junkers — AP47b

1970, Dec. 5 Litho. *Perf. 12*

C103 Sheet of 8
a. AP47a 15fr shown
b. AP47a 25fr Fokker "Southern Cross"
c. AP47a 40fr Dornier DO-18
d. AP47a 60fr Dornier DO-X
e. AP47a 80fr Breguet "Bizerte"
f. AP47a 125fr Douglas "Cloudster"
g. AP47a 150fr De Havilland DH-2
h. AP47a 200fr Vickers "Vini"

C104 Sheet of 4
a. AP47b 200fr shown
b. AP47b 300fr Claude Dornier
c. AP47b 400fr Anthony Fokker
d. AP47b 500fr Igor Sikorsky

Imperf

C105 Sheet of 8
a. AP47a 10fr Dornier "Spatz"
b. AP47a 20fr Douglas DC-3
c. AP47a 30fr Dornier DO-7 "Wal"
d. AP47a 50fr Sikorsky S-38
e. AP47a 75fr De Havilland "Moth"
f. AP47a 100fr Vickers "Spitfire"
g. AP47a 125fr Breguet XIX
h. AP47a 150fr Fokker "Universal"

Size: 80x90mm

C106 AP47b 1000fr Claude Dornier

Claude Dornier (1884-1969), aviation pioneer. No. C104 exists imperf.

Presidents Bongo and Pompidou — AP48

1971, Feb. 11 Photo. *Perf. 13*

C107 AP48 50fr multi 50 20

Visit of Georges Pompidou, Pres. of France.

Apollo 14 Liftoff — AP48a

1971, Feb. 19 *Perf. 14*

Yellow Inscriptions

C108 AP48a 15fr shown
C108A AP48a 25fr Achieving orbit
C108B AP48a 40fr Lunar module descent
C108C AP48a 55fr Lunar landing
C108D AP48a 75fr Lunar liftoff
C108E AP48a 120fr Earth re-entry

Souvenir Sheet

C108F Sheet of 2
g. AP48a 100fr Modules attached
h. AP48a 100fr like #C108E

Nos. C108-C108F exist imperf. with white inscriptions.

Flowers and Plane — AP49

Flowers and Planes: 25fr, Carnations. 40fr, Roses. 55fr, Daffodils. 75fr, Orchids. 120fr, Tulips.

1971, May 7 Litho. *Perf. 13½x14*

C109 AP49 15fr yel & multi 15 15
C109A AP49 25fr multi 20 15
C109B AP49 40fr pink & multi 30 15
C109C AP49 55fr bl & multi 40 20
C110 AP49 75fr multi 60 32
C111 AP49 120fr grn & multi 1.00 50
a. Souv. sheet of 2, #C110-C111 1.65 1.65
Nos. C109-C111 (6) 2.65 1.47

"Flowers by air."

Napoleon's Death Mask — AP50

Designs: 200fr, Longwood, St. Helena, by Jacques Marchand, horiz. 500fr, Sarcophagus in Les Invalides, Paris.

1971, May 12 Photo. *Perf. 13*

C112 AP50 100fr gold & multi 90 42
C113 AP50 200fr gold & multi 1.65 75
C114 AP50 500fr gold & multi 3.50 1.50

Napoleon Bonaparte (1769-1821).

Souvenir Sheet

Charles de Gaulle — AP51

Designs: 40fr, President de Gaulle. 80fr, General de Gaulle. 100fr, Quotation.

1971, June 18 Photo. *Perf. 12½*

C115 AP51 Sheet of 5 2.50 2.50
a. 40fr dark red & multi 25 25
b. 80fr dark green & multi 25 25
c. 100fr green, brown & yel 65 65

In memory of Gen. Charles de Gaulle (1890-1970), Pres. of France.
For surcharge see No. C126.

Red Crosses AP52

1971, June 29

C116 AP52 50fr multi 50 25

For the Red Cross of Gabon.
For surcharge see No. C143.

Uranium — AP53

1971, July 20 Photo. *Perf. 13x12½*

C117 AP53 85fr shown 70 40
C118 AP53 90fr Manganese 80 50

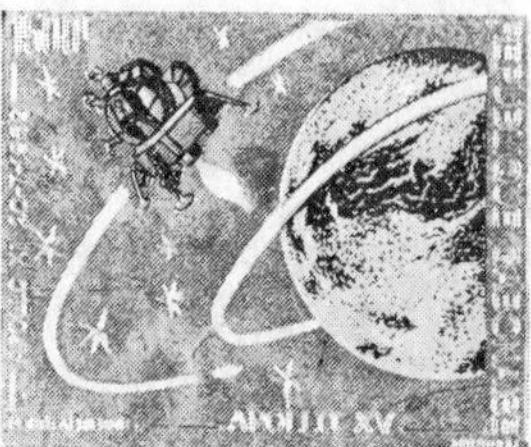

Landing Module over Moon — AP54

Embossed on Gold Foil

1971, July 30 *Die-cut Perf. 10*

C119 AP54 1500fr multi 14.00 14.00

Apollo 11 and 15 US moon missions.

African Postal Union Issue, 1971

Common Design Type

Design: 100fr, Bakota copper mask and UAMPT building, Brazzaville, Congo.

1971, Nov. 13 Photo. *Perf. 13x13½*

C120 CD135 100fr bl & multi 90 45

Ski Jump and Miyajima Torii — AP55

Design: 130fr, Speed skating and Japanese temple.

1972, Jan. 31 Engr. *Perf. 13*

C121 AP55 40fr hn brn, sl grn & vio bl 40 16
C122 AP55 130fr hn brn, sl grn & vio bl 1.20 42
a. Strip of 2, #C121-C122 + label 2.00 1.60

11th Winter Olympic Games, Sapporo, Japan, Feb. 3-13.

The Basin and Grand Canal, by Vanvitelli — AP56

Paintings: 70fr, Rialto Bridge, by Canaletto (erroneously inscribed Caffi), vert. 140fr, Santa Maria della Salute, by Vanvitelli, vert.

1972, Feb. 7 Photo. *Perf. 13*

C123 AP56 60fr gold & multi 40 15
C124 AP56 70fr gold & multi 60 15
C125 AP56 140fr gold & multi 1.20 35

UNESCO campaign to save Venice.

No. C115 Surcharged in Brown and Gold

Souvenir Sheet

1972, Feb. 11 *Perf. 12½*

C126 AP51 Sheet of 5 4.50 4.50
a. 60fr on 40fr multi 50 50
b. 120fr on 80fr multi 1.00 1.00
c. 180fr on 100fr multi 1.50 1.50

Publicity for the erection of a memorial for Charles de Gaulle. Nos. C126a-C126b have surcharge and Cross of Lorraine in gold, 2 bars obliterating old denomination in brown; No. C126c has surcharge, cross and bars in brown. Two Lorraine Crosses and inscription (MEMORIAL DU GENERAL DE GAULLE) in brown added in margin.

Hotel Inter-Continental, Libreville — AP57

1972, Feb. 26 **Engr.** ***Perf. 13***
C127 AP57 40fr bl, sl grn & org brn 35 15

No. C51 Surcharged

1972, Mar. 3
C128 AP25 50fr on 300fr multi 50 35

Official visit of the Grand Master of the Knights of Malta, March 3.

Discobolus, by Alcamenes — AP58

Designs: 100fr, Doryphoros, by Polycletus. 140fr, Borghese gladiator, by Agasias.

1972, May 10 **Engr.** ***Perf. 13***
C129 AP58 30fr rose cl & gray 20 15
C130 AP58 100fr rose cl & gray 65 18
C131 AP58 140fr rose cl & gray 90 25
a. Min. of sheet of 3, #C129-C131 2.00 2.00

20th Olympic Games, Munich, Aug. 26-Sept. 10.
For surcharges see Nos. C134-C136.

Painting Type of 1968

Paintings: 30fr, Adoration of the Magi, by Peter Brueghel, the Elder, horiz. 40fr, Madonna and Child, by Marco Basaiti.

1972, Oct. 30 **Photo.** ***Perf. 13***
C132 AP32 30fr gold & multi 25 16
C133 AP32 40fr gold & multi 35 16

Christmas 1972.

Nos. C129-C131 Surcharged with New Value, Two Bars and Names of Athletes.

1972, Dec. 5 **Engr.** ***Perf. 13***
C134 AP58 40fr on 30fr 35 20
C135 AP58 120fr on 100fr 1.00 50
C136 AP58 170fr on 140fr 1.50 80

Gold medal winners in 20th Olympic Games: Daniel Morelon, France, Bicycling (C134); Kipchoge Keino, Kenya, steeplechase (C135); Mark Spitz, US, swimming (C136).

Globe with Space Orbits, Simulated Stamps — AP59

1973, Feb. 20 **Photo.** ***Perf. 13***
C137 AP59 100fr multi 80 42
a. Souv. sheet of 4, perf. 12x12½ 3.75 3.75

PHILEXGABON 1973, Phil. Exhib., Libreville, Feb. 19-26. No. C137a exists imperf.

DC10-30 "Libreville" over Libreville Airport — AP60

1973, Mar. 19 **Typo.** ***Perf. 13***
C138 AP60 40fr blue & multi 35 18

Kinguélé Hydroelectric Station — AP61

Design: 40c, Kinguélé Dam.

1973, June 19 **Engr.** ***Perf. 13***
C139 AP61 30fr sl grn & dk ol 20 16
C140 AP61 40fr sl grn, dk ol & bl 25 20
a. Strip of 2, #C139-C140 + label 50 50

Hydroelectric installations at Kinguélé.

M'Bigou Stone Sculpture, Woman's Head — AP62

Design: 200fr, Sculpture, man's head.

1973, July 5
C141 AP62 100fr blk, bl & grn 80 55
C142 AP62 200fr grn, sep & sl grn 1.60 1.00

No. C116 Surcharged with New Value, 2 Bars, and Overprinted in Ultramarine: "SECHERESSE SOLIDARITE AFRICAINE"

1973, Aug. 16 **Photo.** ***Perf. 12½***
C143 AP52 100fr on 50fr multi 80 50

African solidarity in drought emergency.

Astronauts and Lunar Rover on Moon — AP63

1973, Sept. 6 **Engr.** ***Perf. 13***
C144 AP63 500fr multi 2.75 1.75

Apollo 17 US moon mission, Dec. 7-19, 1973.

Presidents Houphouet Boigny (Ivory Coast) and De Gaulle — AP64

1974, Apr. 30 **Engr.** ***Perf. 13***
C145 AP64 40fr rose lilac & indigo 22 15

30th anniv. of the Conf. of Brazzaville.

Painting Type of 1968

Impressionist Paintings: 40fr, Pleasure Boats, by Claude Monet, horiz. 50fr, Ballet Dancer, by Edgar Degas. 130fr, Young Girl with Flowers, by Auguste Renoir.

1974, June 11 **Photo.** ***Perf. 13***
C146 AP32 40fr gold & multi 22 15
C147 AP32 50fr gold & multi 25 16
C148 AP32 130fr gold & multi 70 40

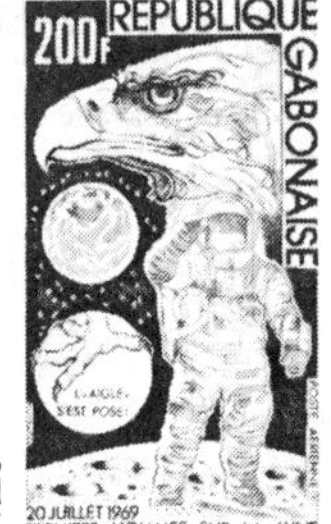

Astronaut on Moon, Eagle and Emblems — AP65

1974, July 20 **Engr.** ***Perf. 13***
C149 AP65 200fr multi 1.10 70

First men on the moon, 5th anniversary.

UPU Emblem, Letters, Pigeon AP66

UPU cent.: 300fr, UPU emblem, letters, pigeons (diff.).

1974, Oct. 9 **Engr.** ***Perf. 13***
C150 AP66 150fr lt bl & Prus bl 75 45
C151 AP66 300fr org & cl 1.50 80

Space Docking, US and USSR Crafts AP67

1974, Oct. 23 **Engr.** ***Perf. 13***
C152 AP67 1000fr grn, red & sl 5.50 3.50

Russo-American space cooperation.
For overprint see No. C169.

Soccer and Games Emblem — AP68

Designs: Soccer actions.

1974, Oct. 25
C153 AP68 40fr grn, red & brn 20 15
C154 AP68 65fr red, brn & grn 30 18
C155 AP68 100fr grn, red & brn 50 30
a. Souv. sheet of 3, #C153-C155 + 3 labels 1.10 1.10

World Cup Soccer Championship, Munich, June 13-July 7.

UDEAC Issue

Presidents and Flags of Cameroun, CAR, Gabon and Congo — AP68a

1974, Dec. 8 **Photo.** ***Perf. 13***
C156 AP68a 100fr gold & multi 60 38

Annunciation, Tapestry, 15th Century — AP69

Christmas: 40fr, Visitation from 15th century tapestry, Notre Dame de Beaune, vert.

1974, Dec. 11
C157 AP69 40fr gold & multi 25 16
C158 AP69 50fr gold & multi 35 20

Dr. Schweitzer and Lambarene Hospital — AP70

1975, Jan. 14 **Engr.** ***Perf. 13***
C159 AP70 500fr multi 2.50 1.75

Dr. Albert Schweitzer (1875-1965), medical missionary, birth centenary.

Crucifixion, by Bellini — AP71

Paintings: 150fr, Resurrection, Burgundian School, c. 1500.

1975, Apr. 8 **Photo.** ***Perf. 13½***
Size: 26x45mm
C160 AP71 140fr gold & multi 90 50
Size: 36x48mm
Perf. 13
C161 AP71 150fr gold & multi 1.00 50

Easter 1975.

Marc Seguin Locomotive, 1829 — AP72

Locomotives: 25fr, The Iron Duke, 1847. 40fr, Thomas Rogers, 1895. 50fr, The Soviet 272, 1934.

1975, Apr. 8 Engr. *Perf. 13*

C162 AP72 20fr multi 15 15
C163 AP72 25fr multi 15 15
C164 AP72 40fr multi 22 15
C165 AP72 50fr lil & multi 25 16
Set value 47

Swimming Pool, Montreal Olympic Games' Emblem — AP73

Designs: 150fr, Boxing ring and emblem. 300fr, Stadium, aerial view, and emblem.

1975, Sept. 30 Litho. *Perf. 13x12½*

C166 AP73 100fr multi 40 25
C167 AP73 150fr multi 60 40
C168 AP73 300fr multi 1.20 85
a. Min. sheet of 3, #C166-C168 2.25 2.25

Pre-Olympic Year 1975.

No. C152 Surcharged in Violet Blue: "JONCTION / 17 Juillet 1975"

1975, Oct. 20 Engr. *Perf. 13*

C169 AP67 1000fr multi 5.50 3.75

Apollo-Soyuz link-up in space, July 17, 1975.

Annunciation, by Maurice Denis — AP74

Painting: 50fr, Virgin and Child with Two Saints, by Fra Filippo Lippi.

1975, Dec. 9 Photo. *Perf. 13*

C170 AP74 40fr gold & multi 25 16
C171 AP74 50fr gold & multi 35 20

Christmas 1975.

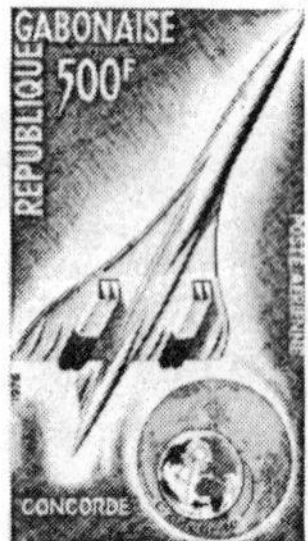

= 1000F
21 Janv. 1976
1er Vol
Commercial de
CONCORDE

Concorde and Globe — AP75

1975, Dec. 29 Engr. *Perf. 13*

C172 AP75 500fr bl, vio bl & red 2.50 1.90

For overprint see No. C198.

No. C172 Surcharged

1976, Jan. 21

C173 AP75 1000fr on 500fr 5.50 3.75

Nos. C172-C173 for the 1st commercial flight of supersonic jet Concorde from Paris to Rio, Jan. 21.

Slalom and Olympic Games Emblem — AP76

Design: 250fr, Speed skating and Winter Olympic Games emblem.

1976, Apr. 22 Engr. *Perf. 13*

C174 AP76 100fr blk, bl & red 40 30
C175 AP76 250fr blk, bl & red 1.00 70
a. Souvenir sheet 1.50 1.50

12th Winter Olympic Games, Innsbruck, Austria, Feb. 4-15. No. C175a contains 100fr and 250fr stamps in continuous design with additional inscription and skier between, but without perforations between the design elements.

Size of perforated area: 125x27mm.; size of sheet: 169x90mm.

Jesus Between the Thieves AP77

Design: 130fr, St. Thomas putting finger into wounds of Jesus. Both designs after wood carvings in Church of St. Michael, Libreville.

1976, Apr. 28 Litho. *Perf. 12½x13*

C176 AP77 120fr multi 65 42
C177 AP77 130fr multi 70 50

Easter 1976. See #C188-C189, C220-C221.

Boston Tea Party — AP78

Designs: 150fr, Battle of New York. 200fr, Demolition of statue of George III.

1976, May 3 Engr. *Perf. 13*

C178 AP78 100fr multi 55 40
C179 AP78 150fr multi 80 55
C180 AP78 200fr multi 1.10 65
a. Triptych, #C178-C180 + 2 labels 2.75 2.25

American Bicentennial.

Nos. C178-C180 Overprinted: "4 JUILLET 1976"

1976, July 4 Engr. *Perf. 13*

C181 AP78 100fr multi 55 40
C182 AP78 150fr multi 80 55
C183 AP78 200fr multi 1.10 65
a. Triptych, #C181-C183 + 2 labels 2.75 2.25

Independence Day.

Running — AP79

Designs (Olympic Rings and): 200fr, Soccer. 260fr, High jump.

1976, July 27 Litho. *Perf. 12½*

C184 AP79 100fr multi 40 30
C185 AP79 200fr multi 80 50
C186 AP79 260fr multi 1.00 70
a. Souv. sheet of 3, #C184-C186, perf. 13 2.25 2.25

21st Olympic Games, Montreal, Canada, July 17-Aug. 1.

Presidents Giscard d'Estaing and Bongo — AP80

1976, Aug. 5 Photo. *Perf. 13*

C187 AP80 60fr bl & multi 35 22

Visit of Pres. Valèrie Giscard d'Estaing of France.

Sculpture Type of 1976

Christmas: 50fr, Presentation at the Temple. 60fr, Nativity. Designs after wood Carvings in Church of St. Michael, Libreville.

1976, Dec. 6 Litho. *Perf. 12½x13*

C188 AP77 50fr multi 25 16
C189 AP77 60fr multi 35 22

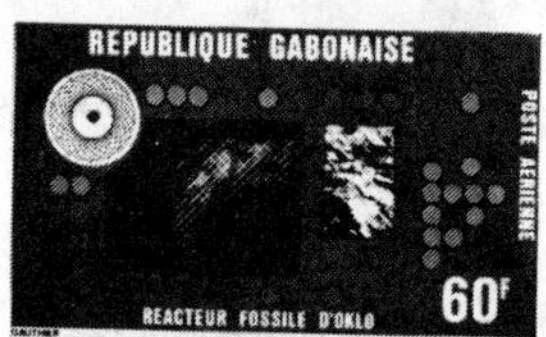

Oklo Fossil Reactor Station — AP81

1976, Dec. 15 Litho. *Perf. 13*

C190 AP81 60fr red & multi 35 22

The Last Supper, by Juste de Gand — AP82

Painting: 100fr, The Deposition, by Nicolas Poussin.

1977, Mar. 25 Litho. *Perf. 12½*

C191 AP82 50fr gold & multi 25 20
C192 AP82 100fr gold & multi 55 40

Easter 1977.

Air Gabon Plane and Insigne — AP83

1977, June 3 Litho. *Perf. 12½*

C193 AP83 60fr multi 35 22

Air Gabon's first intercontinental route.

Beethoven, Piano and Score — AP84

1977, June 15 Engr. *Perf. 13*

C194 AP84 260fr slate 1.40 90

Ludwig van Beethoven (1770-1827).

Lindbergh and Spirit of St. Louis — AP85

1977, Sept. 13 Engr. *Perf. 13*

C195 AP85 500fr multi 2.50 1.60

Charles A. Lindbergh's solo transatlantic flight from NY to Paris, 50th anniv.

Soccer — AP86

1977, Oct. 18 Photo. *Perf. 13x12½*

C196 AP86 250fr multi 1.40 90

Elimination games, World Soccer Cup, Buenos Aires, 1978.

Viking on Mars — AP87

1977, Nov. 17 Engr. *Perf. 13*

C197 AP87 1000fr multi 5.50 2.75

Viking, US space probe.

No. C172 Overprinted: "PARIS NEW-YORK / PREMIER VOL / 22.11.77"

1977, Nov. 22 Engr. *Perf. 13*

C198 AP75 500fr multi 2.75 2.00

Concorde, 1st commercial flight, Paris to NYC.

Lion Hunt, by Rubens — AP88

Rubens Paintings: 80fr, Hippopotamus Hunt. 200fr, Head of Black Man, vert.

1977, Nov. 24 Litho. *Perf. 13*

C199 AP88 60fr gold & multi	35	22
C200 AP88 80fr gold & multi	42	35
C201 AP88 200fr gold & multi	1.10	80
a. Souv. sheet of 3, #C199-C201	1.90	1.90

Peter Paul Rubens (1577-1640).

Adoration of the Kings, by Rubens — AP89

Design: 80fr, Flight into Egypt, by Rubens.

1977, Dec. 15 Litho. *Perf. 12½*

C202 AP89 60fr gold & multi	35	22
C203 AP89 80fr gold & multi	42	35

Christmas 1977; Peter Paul Rubens (1577-1640).

Paul Gauguin, Self-Portrait AP90

Design: 150fr, Flowers in vase and Maori statuette.

1978, Feb. 8 Litho. *Perf. 12½x12*

C204 AP90 150fr multi	80	40
C205 AP90 300fr multi	1.60	80

Paul Gauguin (1848-1903), French painter.

Pres. Bongo, Map of Gabon, Plane and Train AP91

Lithographed; Gold Embossed

1978, Mar. 12 *Perf. 12½*

C206 AP91 500fr multi	2.50	1.40

10th anniversary of national renewal.

Soccer and Argentina '78 Emblem — AP92

Designs (Argentina '78 Emblem and): 120fr, Three soccer players. 200fr, Jules Rimet Cup, vert.

1978, July 18 Engr. *Perf. 13*

C207 AP92 100fr red, grn & brn	40	20
C208 AP92 120fr grn, red & brn	50	30
C209 AP92 200fr brn & red	80	40
a. Min. sheet of 3, #C207-C209	1.75	1.75

11th World Cup Soccer Championship, Argentina, June 1-25.

Nos. C207-C209a Overprinted in Ultramarine or Black:
a. ARGENTINE / HOLLANDE / 3-1
b. BRESIL / ITALIE / 2-1
c. CHAMPION / DU MONDE 1978 / ARGENTINE

1978, July 21 Engr. *Perf. 13*

C210 AP92(a) 100fr multi	55	25
C211 AP92(b) 120fr multi	65	35
C212 AP92(c) 200fr multi	1.10	55
a. Min. sheet of 3 (Bk)	2.50	2.50

Argentina's World Cup victory.

Albrecht Dürer (age 13), Self-portrait AP93

Design: 250fr, Lucas de Leyde, by Dürer.

1978, Sept. 15 Engr. *Perf. 13*

C213 AP93 100fr red brn & sl	55	25
C214 AP93 250fr blk & red brn	1.40	65

Dürer (1474-1528), German painter.

Philexafrique II-Essen Issue

Common Design Types

Designs: No. C215, Gorilla and Gabon No. 280. No. C216, Stork and Saxony No. 1.

1978, Nov. 1 Litho. *Perf. 13x12½*

C215 CD138 100fr multi	55	25
C216 CD139 100fr multi	55	25

Nos. C215-C216 printed se-tenant.

Wright Brothers and Flyer AP94

1978, Dec. 19 Engr. *Perf. 13*

C217 AP94 380fr multi	2.00	1.00

75th anniversary of 1st powered flight.

Pope John Paul II AP95

Design: 200fr, Popes Paul VI and John Paul I, St. Peter's Basilica and Square, horiz.

1979, Jan. 24 Litho. *Perf. 12½*

C218 AP95 100fr multi	55	25
C219 AP95 200fr multi	1.10	55

Sculpture Type of 1976

Easter: 100fr, Disciples recognizing Jesus in the breaking of the bread. 150fr, Jesus appearing to Mary Magdalene. Designs after wood carvings in Church of St. Michael, Libreville.

1979, Apr. 10 Litho. *Perf. 12½x13*

C220 AP77 100fr multi	65	35
C221 AP77 150fr multi	1.00	50

Capt. Cook and Ships AP96

1979, July 10 Engr. *Perf. 13*

C222 AP96 500fr multi	3.50	1.60

Capt. James Cook (1728-1779), explorer, death bicentenary.

Flags and Map of England and France, Bleriot, Bleriot XI — AP97

Aviation Retrospect: 1000fr, Astronauts walking on moon (gold embossed inset).

Perf. 12½x12, 12

1979, Aug. 8 Litho.

C223 AP97 250fr multi	1.60	80
C224 AP97 1000fr multi	6.50	3.50

1st flight over English Channel, 70th anniv.; Apollo 11 moon landing, 10th anniv.

Demand, as well as supply, determine a stamp's market value.

Rotary Emblem, Map of Africa, Head — AP98

Eugene Jamot, Tsetse Fly — AP99

1979, Sept. 25 Photo. *Perf. 13*

C225 AP98 80fr multi	55	25

Rotary International, 75th anniversary.

1979, Nov. 23 Engr. *Perf. 13*

C226 AP99 300fr multi	2.00	1.00

Eugene Jamot (1879-1937), discoverer of sleeping sickness cure.

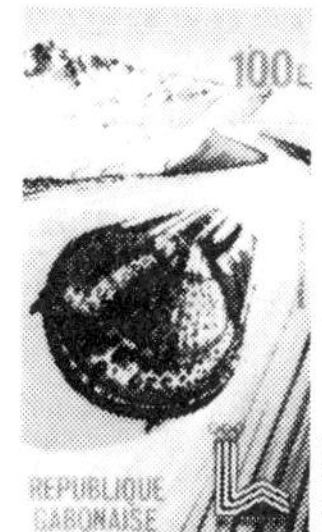

Bobsledding, Lake Placid '80 Emblem — AP100

1980, Feb. 25 Litho. *Perf. 12½*

C227 AP100 100fr shown	60	35
C228 AP100 200fr Ski jump	1.40	65
a. Souv. sheet of 2, #C227-C228	2.00	1.00

13th Winter Olympic Games, Lake Placid, NY, Feb. 12-24.

Jean Ingres AP101

1980, May 14 Engr. *Perf. 13*

C229 AP101 100fr shown	65	35
C230 AP101 200fr Jacques Offenbach	1.40	65
C231 AP101 360fr Gustave Flaubert	2.25	1.20

12th World Telecommunications Day — AP102

1980, May 17 Litho. *Perf. 12½*

C232 AP102 80fr multi	55	25

Costes, Bellonte and Plane — AP103

Design: 1000fr, Mermoz, sea plane.

1980, July 16 Engr. *Perf. 13*
C233 AP103 165fr multi 1.10 55
C234 AP103 1000fr multi 6.50 3.50

1st North Atlantic crossing, 50th anniv.; 1st South Atlantic air mail service, 50th anniv.

Running, Moscow '80 Emblem — AP104

1980, July 25 Litho.
C235 AP104 50fr shown 35 16
C236 AP104 100fr Pole vault 65 35
C237 AP104 250fr Boxing 1.50 80
a. Souv. sheet of 3, #C235-C237 2.50 1.40

22nd Summer Olympic Games, Moscow, July 19-Aug. 3.

Nos. C235-C237a Overprinted in Red, Brown, Ultramarine or Black

50fr: YIFTER (Eth.) / NYAMBUI (Tanz.) / MAANINKA (Finl.) / 5000 Metres
100fr: KOZIAKIEWICZ (Pol.) / (record du monde) / VOLKOV (Urss) et / SLUSARSKI (Pol.)
250fr: WELTERS / ALDAMA (Cuba) / MUGABI (Oug.) / KRUBER (Rda) / et SZCZERDA (Pol.)

1980, Sept. 25 Litho. *Perf. 13*
C238 AP104 50fr (R, vert. & horiz.) 35 16
C239 AP104 100fr (Br) 65 35
C240 AP104 250fr (U) 1.50 80
a. Souv. sheet of 3 (Blk) 2.50 1.40

Pres. Charles de Gaulle AP105

1980, Nov. 9 Photo. *Perf. 13*
C241 AP105 100fr shown 60 35
C242 AP105 200fr Pres. & Mrs. de Gaulle 1.40 65
a. Souv. sheet of 2, #C241-C242 2.00 1.00

Pres. Charles de Gaulle (1890-1970), 10th anniversary of death.

AP106 AP107

1981, Feb. 19 Litho. *Perf. 13*
C243 AP106 60fr Soccer Players 40 20
C244 AP106 190fr Soccer player 1.40 65

ESPANA '82 World Cup Soccer Championship.

1981, Mar. 26 Litho. *Perf. 13*

Spacecraft and Astronauts: 250fr, Yuri Gagarin. 500fr, Alan B. Shepard.

C245 AP107 150fr multi 1.00 50
C246 AP107 250fr multi 1.60 80
C247 AP107 500fr multi 3.50 1.60
a. Souv. sheet of 3, #C245-C247, perf. 12½ 6.25 3.25

200th anniv. of discovery of Uranus by William Herschel (1738-1822).

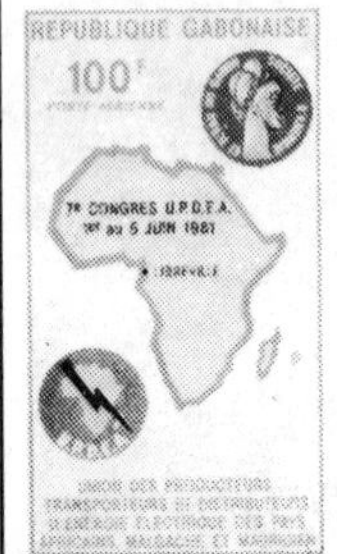
Map of Africa and Emblems — AP108

1981, June 1 Litho. *Perf. 12½*
C248 AP108 100fr multi 65 35

Electric Power Distribution Union, 7th Congress, Libreville, June 1-5.

D-51 Steam Locomotive, Japan, and SNCF Turbotrain TGV-001, France — AP109

200th Birth Anniv. of George Stephenson: 100fr, B&O Mallet 7100, US, Prussian T3 steam locomotive. 350fr, Stephenson and his Rocket, BB Alsthom electric locomotive, Central Africa.

1981, June 4 Engr. *Perf. 13*
C249 AP109 75fr multi 50 25
C250 AP109 100fr multi 65 35
C251 AP109 350fr multi 2.25 1.10
a. Souvenir sheet of 3 3.50 1.90

No. C251a contains Nos. C249-C251 in changed colors.

No. C251a Overprinted in 1 line across 3 stamps: 26 fevrier 1981-Record du monde de vitesse 380 km a l'heure
Souvenir Sheet

1981, June 13 Engr. *Perf. 13*
C252 AP109 Sheet of 3 3.50 1.90

New world railroad speed record, set Feb. 26.

Intl. Letter Writing Week, Oct. 9-16 — AP110

1981, Oct. 9 Photo. *Perf. 13*
C253 AP110 200fr multi 1.40 65

Still Life with a Mandolin, by George Braque (1882-1963) — AP111

Design: 350fr, Boy Blowing Bubbles, by Edouard Manet (1832-1883), vert.

Perf. 13x12½, 12½x13
1982, Oct. 5 Litho.
C254 AP111 300fr multi 2.00 1.00
C255 AP111 350fr multi 2.25 1.20

Pre-olympic Year AP112

Manned Flight Bicentenary AP113

1983, Feb. 16 Litho. *Perf. 13*
C256 AP112 90fr Gymnast 45 22
C257 AP112 350fr Wind surfing 1.75 90

1983, June 1 Engr. *Perf. 13*

Balloons.

C258 AP113 100fr Transatlantic flight, 5th anniv. 65 35
C259 AP113 125fr Montgolfiere, 1783 80 40
C260 AP113 350fr Rozier's balloon, 1783 2.25 1.20

Lady with Unicorn, by Raphael (1483-1520) AP114

1983, June 19 *Perf. 12½x13*
C261 AP114 1000fr multi 6.50 3.50

1984 Winter Olympics — AP115

1984, Feb. 8 Litho. *Perf. 12½*
C262 AP115 125fr Hockey 40 20
C263 AP115 350fr Figure skaters 1.10 55

See No. C268.

Paris-Libreville-Paris Air Race, Mar. 15-28 — AP116

1984, Mar. 15 Litho. *Perf. 13x12½*
C264 AP116 500fr Planes, emblem 1.60 80

The Racetrack, by Edgar Degas — AP117

1984, Mar. 21 *Perf. 13*
C265 AP117 500fr multi 1.60 80

1984 Summer Olympics AP118

Dr. Albert Schweitzer (1875-1965) AP119

1984, May 31 Litho. *Perf. 12½*
C266 AP118 90fr Basketball 28 15
C267 AP118 125fr Running 40 20

Souvenir Sheet
Nos. C262-C263, C266-C267 with Added Inscriptions

1984, Oct. 3 Litho. *Perf. 13*
C268 Sheet of 4 2.00 1.00
a. AP118 90fr MEDAILLE D'OR: U.S.A. 25 15
b. AP118 125fr MEDAILLE D'OR: KORIR 35 20
c. AP115 125fr Hockey sur glace: U.R.S.S. 35 20
d. AP115 350fr Danse couple: J. Torvill-C. Dean 1.00 50

1985, Sept. 5 Litho. *Perf. 12½*
C269 AP119 350fr multi 1.00 50

Flags of Gabon, UN — AP120

1985, Sept. 20
C270 AP120 225fr multi 65 35

Admission of Gabon to UN, 25th anniv.

Central Post Office, Libreville, UPU and Gabon Postal Emblems — AP121

1985, Oct. 9
C271 AP121 300fr multi 1.00 50

World Post Day.

UN, 40th Anniv. — AP122

1985, Oct. 24 Litho. *Perf. 12½*
C272 AP122 350fr multi 1.20 55

PHILEXAFRICA '85, Lome, Togo — AP123

1985, Oct. 30 *Perf. 13*
C273 AP123 100fr Scout campsite 35 16
C274 AP123 150fr Telecommunications, transportation 55 25

Nos. C273-C274 printed se-tenant with center labels picturing a map of Africa or UAPT emblem.

Gabon's Gift to the UN — AP124

Design: Mother and Child, carved wood statue, and UN emblem.

1986, Mar. 15 Litho. *Perf. 13½*
C275 AP124 350fr multi 1.75 85

Lastour Arriving in Gabon — AP125

1986, Mar. 25 Litho. *Perf. 12½*
C276 AP125 100fr multi 55 28

Lastoursville, cent.

World Telecommunications Day — AP126

1986, May 17 *Perf. 13½*
C277 AP126 300fr multi 1.65 82

1986 World Cup Soccer Championships, Mexico — AP127

1986, May 31 *Perf. 12½*
C278 AP127 100fr Goal 55 28
C279 AP127 150fr Dribbling, religious carving 82 40
C280 AP127 250fr Players, map, soccer cup 1.40 70
C281 AP127 350fr Stadium, flags 1.90 95
a. Souv. sheet of 4, #C278-C281 4.70 2.35

For overprints see Nos. C283-C286.

World Post Day — AP128

1986, Oct. 9 Litho. *Perf. 12½*
C282 AP128 500fr multi 2.75 1.40

Nos. C278-C281 Ovptd. "ARGENTINA 3 - R.F.A 2" in One or Two Lines in Red

1986, Oct. 23 Litho. *Perf. 12½*
C283 AP127 100fr multi 55 28
C284 AP127 150fr multi 82 40
C285 AP127 250fr multi 1.40 70
C286 AP127 350fr multi 1.90 95

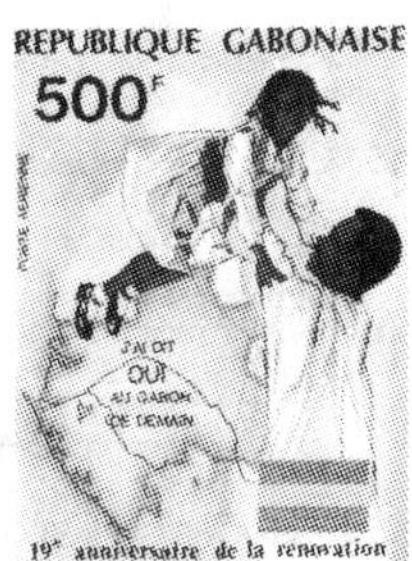

The Renewal, 19th Anniv. AP129

1987, Mar. 12 Litho. *Perf. 13*
C287 AP129 500fr multi 2.75 1.40

Konrad Adenauer (1876-1967), West German Chancellor — AP130

1987, Apr. 15 *Perf. 12x12½*
C288 AP130 300fr mar, chlky bl & blk 1.65 85

Schweitzer and Medical Settlement — AP131

1988, Apr. 17 Litho. *Perf. 12½x12*
C289 AP131 500fr multi 3.50 1.75

Dr. Albert Schweitzer (1875-1965), missionary physician and founder of the hospital and medical settlement, Lambarene, Gabon.

Port Gentil Refinery, 20th Anniv. — AP132

1988, Sept. 1 Litho. *Perf. 13½*
C290 AP132 350fr multi 2.35 1.20

De Gaulle's Call for French Resistance, 50th Anniv. — AP133

1990, June 18 Litho. *Perf. 13*
C291 AP133 500fr multicolored 3.50 1.75

Port of Marseilles by J. B. Jongkind (1819-1891) — AP134

1991, Feb. 9 Litho. *Perf. 13*
C292 AP134 500fr multicolored 4.40 2.20

Discovery of America, 500th Anniv. — AP135

1992, Oct. 12 Litho. *Perf. 13*
C293 AP135 500fr multicolored 4.25 2.10

AIR POST SEMI-POSTAL STAMPS

Catalogue values for unused stamps in this section are for Never Hinged items.

Ramses II Paying Homage to Four Gods, Wadi-es-Sabua — SPAP1

Unwmk.
1964, Mar. 9 Engr. *Perf. 13*
CB1 SPAP1 10fr + 5fr dk bl & bis brn 38 38
CB2 SPAP1 25fr + 5fr dk car rose & vio bl 50 50
CB3 SPAP1 50fr + 5fr sl grn & cl 65 65

UNESCO world campaign to save historic monuments in Nubia.

POSTAGE DUE STAMPS

GABON

Postage Due Stamps of France Overprinted

A. E. F.

1928 Unwmk. *Perf. 14x13½*
J1 D2 5c light blue 15 15
J2 D2 10c gray brown 15 15
J3 D2 20c olive green 32 32
J4 D2 25c bright rose 55 55
J5 D2 30c light red 60 60
J6 D2 45c blue green 65 65
J7 D2 50c brown violet 70 70
J8 D2 60c yellow brown 90 90
J9 D2 1fr red brown 90 90
J10 D2 2fr orange red 1.10 1.10
J11 D2 3fr bright violet 1.40 1.40
Nos. J1-J11 (11) 7.42 7.42

Chief Makoko, de Brazza's Aide — D3

Count Savorgnan de Brazza — D4

1930 Typo. Perf. 13½x14

No.	Type	Description	Unused	Used
J12	D3	5c dk bl & olive	55	55
J13	D3	10c dk red & brn	65	65
J14	D3	20c grn & brn	80	80
J15	D3	25c lt bl & brn	80	80
J16	D3	30c bis brn & Prus bl	1.00	1.00
J17	D3	45c Prus bl & ol	1.20	1.20
J18	D3	50c red vio & brn	1.65	1.65
J19	D3	60c gray lil & bl blk	2.75	2.75
J20	D4	1fr bis brn & bl blk	3.75	3.75
J21	D4	2fr vio & brn	5.50	5.50
J22	D4	3fr dp red & brn	6.50	6.50
		Nos. J12-J22 (11)	25.15	25.15

Fang Woman — D5

1932 Photo. Perf. 13x13½

No.	Type	Description	Unused	Used
J23	D5	5c dk bl, *bl*	45	45
J24	D5	10c red brn	70	70
J25	D5	20c chocolate	1.25	1.25
J26	D5	25c yel grn, *bl*	90	90
J27	D5	30c car rose	1.25	1.25
J28	D5	45c red org, *yel*	4.25	4.25
J29	D5	50c dk vio	1.25	1.25
J30	D5	60c dl bl	1.50	1.50
J31	D5	1fr blk, *red org*	4.25	4.25
J32	D5	2fr dk grn	6.00	6.00
J33	D5	3fr rose lake	5.25	5.25
		Nos. J23-J33 (11)	27.05	27.05

Catalogue values for unused stamps in this section, from this point to the end of the section, are for Never Hinged items.

Republic

Pineapple — D6

Unwmk.
1962, Dec. 10 Engr. Perf. 11

No.	Type	Description	Unused	Used
J34	D6	50c shown	15	15
J35	D6	50c Mangoes	15	15
J36	D6	1fr Avocados	15	15
J37	D6	1fr Tangerines	15	15
J38	D6	2fr Coconuts	15	15
J39	D6	2fr Grapefruit	15	15
J40	D6	5fr Oranges	30	30
J41	D6	5fr Papaya	30	30
J42	D6	10fr Breadfruit	65	65
J43	D6	10fr Guavas	65	65
J44	D6	25fr Lemons	75	75
J45	D6	25fr Bananas	75	75
		Nos. J34-J45 (12)	4.30	4.30

Stamps of the same denomination are printed together in the sheet, se-tenant at the base.

Charaxes Candiope — D7

Butterflies: 10fr, Charaxes ameliae. 25fr, Cyrestis camillus. 50fr, Charaxes castor. 100fr, Pseudacrea boisduvali.

1978, July 4 Litho. Perf. 13

No.	Type	Description	Unused	Used
J46	D7	5fr multi	15	15
J47	D7	10fr multi	15	15
J48	D7	25fr multi	15	15
J49	D7	50fr multi	30	18
J50	D7	100fr multi	60	35
		Nos. J46-J50 (5)	1.35	
		Set value		80

OFFICIAL STAMPS

Catalogue values for unused stamps in this section are for Never Hinged items.

Map of Gabon — O1

Flag of Gabon — O2

Designs: 25fr, 30fr, Flag of Gabon. 50fr, 85fr, 100fr, 200fr, Coat of Arms.

1968 Unwmk. Photo. Perf. 14

No.	Type	Description	Unused	Used
O1	O1	1fr olive & multi	15	15
O2	O1	2fr multi	15	15
O3	O1	5fr lilac & multi	15	15
O4	O1	10fr emer & multi	15	15
O5	O1	25fr brn & multi	28	15
O6	O1	30fr org & multi	30	15
O7	O1	50fr multi	50	18
O8	O1	85fr multi	90	32
O9	O1	100fr yel & multi	1.20	42
O10	O1	200fr gray & multi	2.25	1.00
		Nos. O1-O10 (10)	6.03	
		Set value		2.40

1971-84 Typo. Perf. 13x14

No.	Type	Description	Unused	Used
O11	O2	5fr multi ('81)	15	15
O12	O2	10fr multi	15	15
O13	O2	30fr multi ('78)	25	15
O14	O2	20fr multi ('81)	15	15
O15	O2	25fr multi ('84)	15	15
O16	O2	40fr multi ('72)	45	25
O17	O2	50fr multi ('76)	45	15
O18	O2	60fr multi ('77)	60	25
O19	O2	75fr multi ('81)	30	15
O20	O2	80fr multi ('77)	90	40
O21	O2	100fr multi ('78)	65	25
O22	O2	500fr multi ('78)	3.50	1.25
		Nos. O11-O22 (12)	7.70	
		Set value		3.00

GEORGIA

LOCATION — In the southern part of Russia, bordering on the Black Sea and occupying the entire western part of Trans-Caucasia
GOVT. — A Soviet Socialist Republic
AREA — 25,760 sq. mi. (1920)
POP. — 2,372,403 (1920)
CAPITAL — Tbilisi (Tiflis)

Georgia was formerly a province of the Russian Empire and later a part of the Transcaucasian Federation of Soviet Republics. Stamps of Georgia were replaced in 1923 by those of Transcaucasian Federated Republics.

On Mar. 1, 1994, Georgia joined the Commonwealth of Independent States.

100 Kopecks = 1 Ruble

Tiflis

A 6k local stamp, imperforate and embossed without color on white paper, was issued in November, 1857, at Tiflis by authority of the viceroy. The square design shows a coat of arms.

Georgia stamps can be mounted in the Scott Soviet Republics album part I.

National Republic

St. George
A1 A2

Perf. 11½, Imperf.

1919 Litho. Unwmk.

No.	Type	Description	Unused	Used
12	A1	10k blue	18	20
13	A1	40k red orange	18	20
a.		Tête bêche pair	7.50	7.50
14	A1	50k emerald	18	20
15	A1	60k red	18	22
16	A1	70k claret	18	24
17	A2	1r orange brown	18	24

Queen Thamar — A3

1920 Perf. 11½, Imperf.

No.	Type	Description	Unused	Used
18	A3	2r red brown	18	22
19	A3	3r gray blue	15	25
20	A3	5r orange	20	50

Nos. 12-20 with parts of design inverted, sideways or omitted are fraudulent varieties.

Overprints meaning "Day of the National Guard, 12, 12, 1920" (5 lines) and "Recognition of Independence, 27, 1, 1921" (4 lines) were applied, probably in Italy, to remainders taken by government officials who fled when Russian forces occupied Georgia.

"Constantinople" and new values were unofficially surcharged on stamps of 1919-20 by a consul in Turkey.

Soviet Socialist Republic

Soldier with Flag — A5

Peasant Sowing Grain — A6

Industry and Agriculture — A7

1922 Unwmk. Perf. 11½

No.	Type	Description	Unused	Used
26	A5	500r rose	2.25	1.90
27	A6	1000r bister brown	2.25	1.90
28	A7	2000r slate	4.00	3.25
29	A7	3000r brown	4.00	3.25
30	A7	5000r green	4.00	3.25
		Nos. 26-30 (5)	16.50	13.55

Nos. 26 to 30 exist imperforate but were not so issued. Value for set, $25.

Nos. 26-30 Handstamped with New Values in Violet

1923

No.	Type	Description	Unused	Used
36	A6	10,000r on 1000r	3.75	3.00
a.		Black surcharge	8.00	10.00
b.		20,000r on 1000r	200.00	
37	A7	15,000r on 2000r, blk surch.	4.75	5.50
a.		Violet surcharge	12.50	10.00
38	A5	20,000r on 500r	4.50	5.50
a.		Black surcharge	7.25	3.75
39	A7	40,000r on 5000r	3.25	3.00
a.		Black surcharge	7.00	7.50
40	A7	80,000r on 3000r	4.50	5.50
a.		Black surcharge	6.50	7.50
		Nos. 36-40 (5)	20.75	22.50

There were two types of the handstamped surcharges, with the numerals 5½mm and 6½mm high. The impressions are often too indistinct to measure or even to distinguish the numerals.

Double and inverted surcharges exist, as is usual with handstamps.

Printed Surcharge in Black

No.	Type	Description	Unused	Used
43	A6	10,000r on 1000r	5.25	6.00
44	A7	15,000r on 2000r	3.50	3.75
45	A5	20,000r on 500r	1.50	1.90
46	A7	40,000r on 5000r	2.75	3.50
47	A7	80,000r on 3000r	3.25	3.75
		Nos. 43-47 (5)	16.25	18.90

Nos. 43, 45, 46 and 47 exist imperforate but were not so issued. Value $4 each.

Russian Stamps of 1909-18 Handstamp Surcharged

Type I. Surcharge 20x5½mm.
Type II. Surcharge 22x7¼mm.

1923 Perf. 14½x15

No.	Type	Description	Unused	Used
48	A14	10,000r on 7k lt bl	40.00	40.00
49	A11	15,000r on 15k red brn & bl (I)	5.75	5.50
a.		Type II	5.75	5.50

Type I Surcharge Handstamped on Armenia No. 141

No.	Type	Description	Unused	Used
50	A11	15,000r on 5r on 15k red brn & bl	37.50	55.00
a.		Type II		

Russian Stamps and Types of 1909-18 Surcharged in Dark Blue or Black

1923 Perf. 11½, 14½x15

No.	Type	Description	Unused	Used
51	A14	75,000r on 1k org	3.00	4.25
a.		Imperf.	50.00	75.00
52	A14	200,000r on 5k cl	3.50	4.75
53	A8	300,000r on 20k bl & car (Bk)	3.50	4.75
a.		Dark blue surcharge	50.00	75.00
54	A14	350,000r on 3k red	5.50	7.25
a.		Imperf.	6.00	7.25

Imperf

No.	Type	Description	Unused	Used
55	A14	700,000r on 2k grn	6.50	7.75
a.		Perf. 14½x15	27.50	32.50
		Nos. 51-55 (5)	22.00	28.75

SEMI-POSTAL STAMPS

SP1

SP3

SP4

SP2

Surcharge in Red or Black

1922 Unwmk. Perf. 11½

No.	Type	Description	Unused	Used
B1	SP1	1000r on 50r vio (R)	30	50
B2	SP2	3000r on 100r brn red	30	50
B3	SP3	5000r on 250r gray grn	30	50
B4	SP4	10,000r on 25r blue (R)	30	50

Nos. B1-B4 exist imperf. but were not so issued. Value about twice that of perf.

GERMAN E. AFRICA

LOCATION — In East Africa, bordering on the Indian Ocean
GOVT. — Former German Colony
AREA — 384,180 sq. mi.
POP. — 7,680,132 (1913)
CAPITAL — Dar-es Salaam

Following World War I, the greater part of this German Colonial possession was mandated to Great Britain. The British ceded to the Belgians the provinces of Ruanda and Urundi. The Kionga triangle was awarded to the Portuguese and became part of the Mozambique Colony. The remaining area became the British Mandated Territory of Tanganyika.

64 Pesa = 1 Rupee
100 Heller = 1 Rupee (1905)
100 Centimes = 1 Franc (1916)

Stamps of Germany Surcharged in Black

10 PESA 10

Nos. 1-5

Nos. 6-10

1893 Unwmk. *Perf. 13½x14½*

1 A9 2pes on 3pf brown 40.00 60.00
2 A9 3pes on 5pf green 45.00 60.00
3 A10 5pes on 10pf car 30.00 24.00
4 A10 10pes on 20pf ultra 22.50 17.50
5 A10 25pes on 50pf red brn 40.00 37.50

The surcharge is 14¼, 15¼ or 16¼mm on #2-3; 15¼ or 16¾mm on #4; 16¾ or 17½mm on #5.

1896

6 A9 2pes on 3pf dk brn 2.00 *6.75*
a. 2pes on 3pf light brown 27.50 45.00
b. 2pes on 3pf grayish brown 11.00 5.75
7 A9 3pes on 5pf green 2.50 5.25
8 A10 5pes on 10pf car 2.50 4.25
9 A10 10pes on 20pf ultra 7.00 5.25
10 A10 25pes on 50pf red brn 25.00 27.50

Kaiser's Yacht "Hohenzollern"
A5 A6

1900 Typo. *Perf. 14*

11 A5 2p brown 3.50 1.65
12 A5 3p green 3.50 1.65
13 A5 5p carmine 3.75 1.90
14 A5 10p ultra 6.50 3.25
15 A5 15p org & blk, *sal* 6.50 4.50
16 A5 20p lake & blk 9.25 12.50
17 A5 25p pur & blk, *sal* 9.25 12.50
18 A5 40p lake & blk, *rose* 11.00 *22.50*

Engr.

Perf. 14½x14

19 A6 1r claret 22.50 *60.00*
20 A6 2r yel green 11.00 *92.50*
21 A6 3r car & slate 70.00 *165.00*
Nos. 11-21 (11) 156.75

Value in Heller

1905 Typo. *Perf. 14*

22 A5 2½h brown 2.50 2.00
23 A5 4h green 7.25 3.75
24 A5 7½h carmine 7.25 1.00
25 A5 15h ultra 13.00 5.50
26 A5 20h org & blk, *yel* 11.00 17.50
27 A5 30h lake & blk 9.00 8.00
28 A5 45h pur & blk 17.00 40.00
29 A5 60h lake & blk, *rose* 24.00 *125.00*
Nos. 22-29 (8) 91.00

1905-16 Wmk. Lozenges (125)

31 A5 2½h brn ('06) 85 75
32 A5 4h grn ('06) 85 75
b. Booklet pane of 4 + 2 labels 50.00
c. Booklet pane of 5 + label *375.00*
33 A5 7½h car ('06) 85 40
b. Booklet pane of 4 + 2 labels 50.00
c. Booklet pane of 5 + label *375.00*
34 A5 15h ultra ('06) 2.00 90
35 A5 20h org & blk, *yel* ('11) 2.50 *12.00*
36 A5 30h lake & blk ('09) 2.75 *7.75*
37 A5 45h pur & blk ('06) 5.00 *50.00*
38 A5 60h lake & blk, *rose* 35.00 *200.00*
Nos. 31-38 (8) 49.80

Engr.

Perf. 14½x14

39 A6 1r red ('16) 7.25 *21,500.*
40 A6 2r yel grn 45.00
41 A6 3r car & sl ('08) 22.50 *215.00*

No. 40 was never placed in use.
Forged cancellations are found on #35-39, 41.

OCCUPATION STAMPS

Issued under Belgian Occupation

Stamps of Belgian Congo, 1915, Handstamped "RUANDA" in Black or Blue

1916 Unwmk. *Perf. 13½ to 15*

N1 A29 5c grn & blk 13.00
N2 A30 10c car & blk 13.00
N3 A21 15c bl grn & blk 25.00
N4 A31 25c bl & blk 13.00
N5 A23 40c brn red & blk 13.00
N6 A24 50c brn lake & blk 14.00
N7 A25 1fr ol bis & blk 92.50
N8 A27 5fr ocher & blk *1,500.*
Nos. N1-N7 (7) 183.50

Stamps of Belgian Congo, 1915, Handstamped "URUNDI" in Black or Blue

N9 A29 5c grn & blk 13.00
N10 A30 10c car & blk 13.00
N11 A21 15c bl grn & blk 25.00
N12 A31 25c bl & blk 13.00
N13 A23 40c brn red & blk 13.00
N14 A24 50c brn lake & blk 14.00
N15 A25 1fr ol bis & blk 92.50
N16 A27 5fr ocher & blk *1,500.*
Nos. N9-N15 (7) 183.50

Stamps of Congo overprinted "Karema," "Kigoma" and "Tabora" were not officially authorized.
Nos. N1-N16 exist with forged overprint.

Stamps of Belgian Congo, 1915, Overprinted in Dark Blue

EST AFRICAIN ALLEMAND
OCCUPATION BELGE.

DUITSCH OOST AFRIKA
BELGISCHE BEZETTING.

1916 *Perf. 12½ to 15*

N17 A29 5c grn & blk 30 20
b. Inverted overprint 72.50 35.00
N18 A30 10c car & blk 40 32
N19 A21 15c bl grn & blk 30 20
N20 A31 25c bl & blk 1.75 1.10
N21 A23 40c brn red & blk 5.00 4.00
N22 A24 50c brn lake & blk 5.50 3.50
N23 A25 1fr ol bis & blk 60 42
N24 A27 5fr ocher & blk 90 70
Nos. N17-N24 (8) 14.75 10.44

Nos. N17-N18, N20-N22 Surcharged in Black or Red **·10c**

1922

N25 A24 5c on 50c brn lake & blk 22 22
N26 A29 10c on 5c grn & blk (R) 30 22
N27 A23 25c on 40c brn red & blk (R) 2.00 90
N28 A30 30c on 10c car & blk 20 20
N29 A31 50c on 25c bl & blk (R) 25 20
Nos. N25-N29 (5) 2.97 1.74

No. N25 has the surcharge at each side.

SEMI-POSTAL STAMPS

Issued under Belgian Occupation

Semi-Postal Stamps of Belgian Congo, 1918, Overprinted **A. O.**

1918 Unwmk. *Perf. 14, 15*

NB1 A29 5c + 10c grn & bl 20 20
NB2 A30 10c + 15c car & bl 20 20
NB3 A21 15c + 20c bl grn & bl 20 20
NB4 A31 25c + 25c dp bl & pale bl 20 20
NB5 A23 40c + 40c brn red & bl 30 30
NB6 A24 50c + 50c brn lake & bl 30 30
NB7 A25 1fr + 1fr ol bis & bl 1.10 1.10
NB8 A27 5fr + 5fr ocher & bl 6.25 4.00
NB9 A28 10fr + 10fr grn & bl 50.00 50.00
Nos. NB1-NB9 (9) 58.75 56.50

The letters "A.O." are the initials of "Afrique Orientale" (East Africa).

Stamps issued under British occupation are listed in Volume I.

GERMAN N. GUINEA

LOCATION — A group of islands in the west Pacific Ocean, including a part of New Guinea and adjacent islands of the Bismarck Archipelago.
GOVT. — A former German Protectorate
AREA — 93,000 sq. mi.
POP. — 601,427 (1913)
CAPITAL — Herbertshohe (later Kokopo)

The islands were occupied by Australian troops during World War I and renamed "New Britain." By covenant of the League of Nations they were made a mandated territory of Australia in 1920. The old name of "New Guinea" has since been restored. Postage stamps were issued under all regimes. For other listings see New Britain (1914-15), North West Pacific Islands (1915-22) and New Guinea in Vol. 1.

100 Pfennig = 1 Mark

Stamps of Germany Overprinted in Black

1897-99 Unwmk. *Perf. 13½x14½*

1 A9 3pf brown 8.50 11.50
a. 3pf reddish brown ('99) 35.00 65.00
b. 3pf yellow brown ('99) 25.00 50.00
2 A9 5pf green 4.25 6.25
3 A10 10pf carmine 7.25 9.50
4 A10 20pf ultra 11.00 14.00
5 A10 25pf orange ('98) 35.00 50.00
6 A10 50pf red brown 35.00 45.00

Kaiser's Yacht "Hohenzollern"
A3 A4

1901 Typo. *Perf. 14*

7 A3 3pf brown 85 90
8 A3 5pf green 9.25 1.10
9 A3 10pf carmine 32.50 1.75
10 A3 20pf ultra 1.10 *2.00*
11 A3 25pf org & blk, *yel* 1.25 *15.00*
12 A3 30pf org & blk, *sal* 1.25 *23.50*
13 A3 40pf lake & blk 1.25 *24.00*
14 A3 50pf pur & blk, *sal* 1.65 *22.50*
15 A3 80pf lake & blk, *rose* 3.75 *25.00*

Engr.

Perf. 14½x14

16 A4 1m carmine 4.00 *45.00*
17 A4 2m blue 6.00 *60.00*
18 A4 3m blk vio 8.00 *135.00*
19 A4 5m slate & car 150.00 *400.00*
Nos. 7-19 (13) 220.85

Fake cancellations exist on Nos. 10-19.

A5 A6

Wmk. Lozenges (125)

1914-19 Typo. *Perf. 14*

20 A3 3pf brown ('19) 65
21 A5 5pf green 1.75
22 A5 10pf carmine 1.75

Engr.

Perf. 14½x14

23 A6 5m slate & carmine 16.00

Nos. 20-23 were never placed in use.
Nos. 21-23 have "NEUGUINEA" as one word without a hyphen.

GERMAN S.W. AFRICA

LOCATION — In southwest Africa, bordering on the South Atlantic.
GOVT. — A former German Colony
AREA — 322,450 sq. mi. (1913)
POP. — 94,372 (1913)
CAPITAL — Windhoek

The Colony was occupied by South African troops during World War I and in 1920 was mandated to the Union of South Africa by the League of Nations. See South-West Africa in Vol. 1.

100 Pfennig = 1 Mark

Stamps of Germany Overprinted

1897 Unwmk. *Perf. 13½x14½*

1 A9 3pf dark brown 6.50 12.00
a. 3pf yellow brown 45.00
2 A9 5pf green 4.25 4.25
3 A10 10pf carmine 18.00 18.00
4 A10 20pf ultra 4.50 5.00
5 A10 25pf orange 225.00
6 A10 50pf red brown 225.00

Nos. 5 and 6 were prepared for issue but were not sent to the Colony.

Overprinted "Deutsch-Südwestafrika"

1899

7 A9 3pf dark brown 4.50 *30.00*
b. 3pf yellow brown 7.50 *9.00*
8 A9 5pf green 3.25 2.50
9 A10 10pf carmine 3.25 3.25
10 A10 20pf ultra 16.00 16.00
11 A10 25pf orange 375.00 350.00
12 A10 50pf red brown 13.00 13.00

Kaiser's Yacht "Hohenzollern"
A3 A4

1900 Typo. *Perf. 14*

13 A3 3pf brown 1.50 1.25
14 A3 5pf green 24.00 75
15 A3 10pf carmine 22.50 75
16 A3 20pf ultra 32.50 1.25
17 A3 25pf org & blk, *yel* 1.75 *5.00*
18 A3 30pf org & blk, *sal* 14.00 2.75
19 A3 40pf lake & blk 1.75 2.75
20 A3 50pf pur & blk, *sal* 1.75 2.25
21 A3 80pf lake & blk, *rose* 1.90 *6.50*

Engr.

Perf. 14½x14

No.	Design	Description	Unused	Used
22	A4	1m carmine	18.00	*27.50*
23	A4	2m blue	27.50	*35.00*
24	A4	3m blk vio	30.00	*40.00*
25	A4	5m slate & car	165.00	*135.00*
		Nos. 13-25 (13)	342.15	*260.75*

Wmk. Lozenges (125)

1906-19 Typo. *Perf. 14*

No.	Design	Description	Unused	Used
26	A3	3pf brown ('09)	85	80
27	A3	5pf green	85	65
b.		Bklt. pane of 6 (2 #27, 4 #28)	65.00	
c.		Booklet pane of 5 + label	300.00	
28	A3	10pf carmine	85	80
b.		Booklet pane of 5 + label	375.00	
29	A3	20pf ultra ('11)	85	*2.75*
30	A3	30pf org & blk, *buff* ('11)	4.75	*37.50*

Engr.

Perf. 14½x14

No.	Design	Description	Unused	Used
31	A4	1m carmine ('12)	5.25	*15.00*
32	A4	2m blue ('11)	5.25	*17.50*
33	A4	3m blk vio ('19)	10.00	
34	A4	5m slate & car	22.50	*150.00*
		Nos. 26-34 (9)	51.15	

No. 33 was never placed in use.
Forged cancellations are found on #30-32, 34.

GERMAN STATES

Watermarks

Wmk. 92- 17mm wide Wmk. 93- 14mm wide

Wmk. 94- Horiz. Wavy Lines Wide Apart

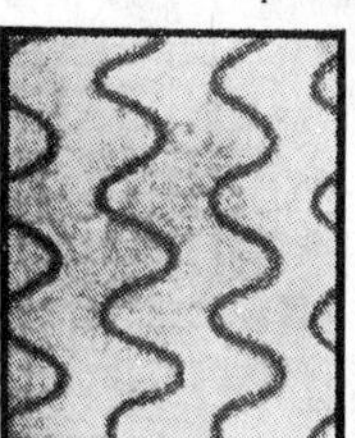

Wmk. 95v- Vert. Wavy Lines Close Together

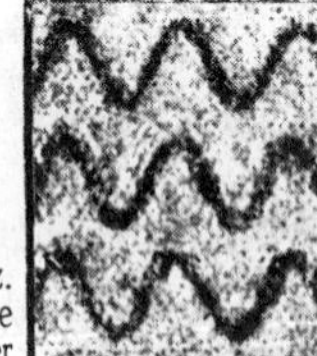

Wmk. 95h- Horiz. Wavy Lines Close Together

Wmk. 102- Post Horn Wmk. 116- Crosses and Circles

Baden stamps can be mounted in the Scott Germany albums part I and II.

Wmk. 128- Wavy Lines

Wmk. 130- Wreath of Oak Leaves Wmk. 148- Small Flowers

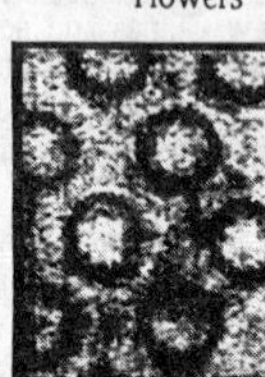

Wmk. 162- Laurel Wreath Wmk. 192- Circles

BADEN

LOCATION — In southwestern Germany
GOVT. — Former Grand Duchy
AREA — 5,817 sq. mi.
POP. — 1,432,000 (1864)
CAPITAL — (PRINCIPAL CITY) Karlsruhe

Baden was a member of the German Confederation. In 1870 it became part of the German Empire.

60 Kreuzer = 1 Gulden

Values for 1-9 unused are for copies without gum. Copies with gum sell for about twice as much. No. 10 and following numbers without gum sell for about half the prices.
Nos. 1-9 with margins all around and copies of Nos. 10-14 and 18 with all perforations intact sell considerably higher.

A1

1851-52 Unwmk. Typo. *Imperf.*

No.	Design	Description	Unused	Used
1	A1	1kr blk, *dk buff*	175.00	125.00
2	A1	3kr blk, *yellow*	90.00	13.00
3	A1	6kr blk, *yel grn*	400.00	27.50
4	A1	9kr blk, *lil rose*	60.00	14.00

Thin Paper (First Printing, 1851)

No.	Design	Description	Unused	Used
1a	A1	1kr black, *buff*	575.00	625.00
2a	A1	3kr black, *orange*	250.00	21.00
3a	A1	6kr black, *blue green*	1,400.	65.00
4a	A1	9kr black, *deep rose*	1,700.	110.00
4b	A1	9kr black, *bl grn* (error)		

1853-58

No.	Design	Description	Unused	Used
6	A1	1kr black	135.00	18.00
a.		Tête bêche gutter pair		*20,000.*
7	A1	3kr black, *green*	125.00	5.50
8	A1	3kr black, *bl* ('58)	200.00	22.50
a.		Printed on both sides		
9	A1	6kr black, *yellow*	190.00	16.00

Nos. 1-9 with margins all around sell considerably higher.
Reissues (1865) of Nos. 1, 2, 3, 6, 7 and 8 exist on thick paper and No. 9 on thin paper; the color of the last is brighter than that of the original.

Coat of Arms
A2 A3

1860-62 *Perf. 13½*

No.	Design	Description	Unused	Used
10	A2	1kr black	60.00	24.00
12	A2	3kr ultra ('61)	60.00	11.00
a.		3kr Prussian blue	225.00	11.00
13	A2	6kr red org ('61)	90.00	37.50
a.		6kr yellow orange ('62)	165.00	60.00
14	A2	9kr rose ('61)	190.00	110.00

Copies of Nos. 10-14 and 18 with all perforations intact sell considerably higher.

1862 *Perf. 10*

No.	Design	Description	Unused	Used
15	A2	1kr black	45.00	52.50
a.		1kr silver gray		*6,000.*
16	A2	6kr blue	87.50	47.50
17	A2	9kr brown	75.00	52.50
a.		9kr bister	95.00	100.00

Perf. 13½

No.	Design	Description	Unused	Used
18	A3	3kr rose	1,100.	300.00

1862-65 *Perf. 10*

No.	Design	Description	Unused	Used
19	A3	1kr black ('64)	35.00	11.00
a.		1kr silver gray		*1,250.*
20	A3	3kr rose	35.00	90
a.		Imperf.	*35,000.*	*12,000.*
22	A3	6kr ultra ('65)	6.75	15.00
a.		6kr Prussian blue ('64)	*275.00*	57.50
23	A3	9kr brn ('64)	12.00	15.00
a.		9kr bister	165.00	19.00
b.		Printed on both sides		*2,750.*
24	A3	18kr green	250.00	500.00
25	A3	30kr orange	21.00	*1,250.*

Forged cancellations are known on #25, 28a.

A4

1868

No.	Design	Description	Unused	Used
26	A4	1kr green	3.00	2.75
27	A4	3kr rose	1.50	90
28	A4	7kr dull blue	13.00	30.00
a.		7kr sky blue	30.00	85.00

The postage stamps of Baden were superseded by those of the German Empire on Jan. 1, 1872, but Official stamps were used during the year 1905.

Stamps of the Baden sector of the French Occupation Zone of Germany, issued in 1947-49, are listed under Germany, Occupation Issues.

RURAL POSTAGE DUE STAMPS

RU1

1862 Unwmk. *Perf. 10*

Thin Paper

No.	Design	Description	Unused	Used
LJ1	RU1	1kr blk, *yellow*	5.00	*225.00*
a.		Thick paper	125.00	*450.00*
LJ2	RU1	3kr blk, *yellow*	3.25	*100.00*
a.		Thick paper	75.00	*325.00*
LJ3	RU1	12kr blk, *yellow*	25.00	*15,000.*
a.		Half used as 6kr on cover		*18,000.*
b.		Quarter used as 3kr on cover		*6,500.*

On #LJ3, "LAND-POST" is a straight line.
Paper of #LJ1a, LJ2a is darker yellow.
Forged cancellations abound on #LJ1-LJ3.

OFFICIAL STAMPS

See Germany Nos. OL16-OL21.

BAVARIA

LOCATION — In southern Germany
GOVT. — Former Kingdom
AREA — 30,562 sq. mi. (1920)
POP. — 7,150,146 (1919)
CAPITAL — Munich

Bavaria was a member of the German Confederation and became part of the German Empire in 1870. After World War I, it declared itself a republic. It lost its postal autonomy on Mar. 31, 1920.

60 Kreuzer = 1 Gulden
100 Pfennig = 1 Mark (1874)

Values for unused stamps of 1849-78 issues are for copies with original gum. Copies without gum sell for about half the figures quoted.

A1

Broken Circle — A1a

1849 Unwmk. Typo. *Imperf.*

No.	Design	Description	Unused	Used
1	A1	1kr black	500.00	1,200.
a.		1kr deep black	1,750.	2,250.
b.		Tête bêche pair	*35,000.*	

With Silk Thread

No.	Design	Description	Unused	Used
2	A1a	3kr blue	35.00	1.10
a.		3kr greenish blue	42.50	1.40
b.		3kr deep blue	35.00	1.40
3	A1a	6kr brown	*5,500.*	135.00

No. 1 exists with silk thread but only as an essay.

Complete circle — A2

Coat of Arms — A3

1850-58 With Silk Thread

No.	Design	Description	Unused	Used
4	A2	1kr pink	100.00	14.00
5	A2	6kr brown	35.00	1.00
a.		Half used as 3kr on cover		*8,000.*
6	A2	9kr yel grn	60.00	7.25
a.		9kr blue green ('53)	*3,500.*	62.50
7	A2	12kr red ('58)	95.00	90.00
8	A2	18kr yel ('54)	100.00	125.00

1862

No.	Design	Description	Unused	Used
9	A2	1kr yellow	50.00	12.00
10	A1a	3kr rose	62.50	1.25
a.		3kr carmine	30.00	2.75
11	A2	6kr blue	50.00	6.25
a.		6kr ultra	*1,750.*	
b.		Half used as 3kr on cover		*6,000.*
12	A2	9kr bister	70.00	9.50
13	A2	12kr yel grn	75.00	52.50
a.		Half used as 6kr on cover		*18,000.*
14	A2	18kr ver red	525.00	90.00
a.		18kr pale red	125.00	225.00

No. 11a was not put in use.

1867-68 Embossed

No.	Design	Description	Unused	Used
15	A3	1kr yel grn	55.00	5.50
a.		1kr dark blue green	185.00	20.00
16	A3	3kr rose	45.00	32
a.		Printed on both sides		
17	A3	6kr ultra	30.00	15.00
a.		Half used as 3kr on cover		*16,000.*
18	A3	6kr bis ('68)	60.00	26.00
a.		Half used as 3kr on cover		*20,000.*
19	A3	7kr ultra ('68)	340.00	9.00
20	A3	9kr bister	25.00	27.50
21	A3	12kr lilac	325.00	62.50
22	A3	18kr red	100.00	130.00

The paper of the 1867-68 issues often shows ribbed or laid lines.

1870-72 Wmk. 92 *Perf. 11½*

Without Silk Thread

No.	Design	Description	Unused	Used
23	A3	1kr green	1.25	55
24	A3	3kr rose	4.00	25
25	A3	6kr bister	24.00	22.50
26	A3	7kr ultra	1.75	2.00
a.		7kr Prussian blue	6.00	5.00

27	A3	9kr pale brn ('72)	2.00	1.50
28	A3	10kr yellow	4.00	10.00
29	A3	12kr lilac, wmk. 93	200.00	*600.00*
30	A3	18kr red	6.50	7.00

The paper of the 1870-75 issues frequently appears to be laid with the lines either close or wide apart.

See Nos. 33-37.

Reprints exist.

Wmk. 93

23a	A3	1kr	50.00	5.75
24a	A3	3kr	40.00	1.25
25a	A3	6kr	125.00	40.00
26b	A3	7kr	75.00	22.50
27a	A3	9kr	200.00	*350.00*
28a	A3	10kr	200.00	225.00
29a	A3	12kr Wmk. 92	575.00	*1,500.*
30a	A3	18kr	200.00	150.00

A4

A5

1874-75 Wmk. 92 *Imperf.*

31	A4	1m violet	300.00	65.00

Perf. 11½

32	A4	1m violet ('75)	130.00	27.50

See Nos. 46-47, 54-57, 73-76.

1875 Wmk. 94

33	A3	1kr green	25	*9.00*
34	A3	3kr rose	25	*2.00*
35	A3	7kr ultra	2.75	*190.00*
36	A3	10kr yellow	27.50	*190.00*
37	A3	18kr red	25.00	*35.00*

False cancellations exist on #29, 29a, 33-37.

1876-78 Embossed *Perf. 11½*

38	A5	3pf lt grn	20.00	45
39	A5	5pf dk grn	40.00	5.50
40	A5	5pf lilac ('78)	65.00	9.00
41	A5	10pf rose	32.50	20
42	A5	20pf ultra	35.00	40
43	A5	25pf yel brn	90.00	3.00
44	A5	50pf scarlet	30.00	3.00
45	A5	50pf brn ('78)	225.00	17.00
46	A4	1m violet	1,400.	57.50
47	A4	2m orange	22.50	4.50

The paper of the 1876-78 issue often shows ribbed lines.

See Nos. 48-53, 58-72. For overprints and surcharge see Nos. 237, O1-O5.

1881-1906 Wmk. 95v *Perf. 11½*

48	A5	3pf green	12.00	20
a.		Imperf.	150.00	225.00
49	A5	5pf lilac	17.50	70
50	A5	10pf carmine	9.00	15
a.		Imperf.	150.00	200.00
51	A5	20pf ultra	12.00	55
52	A5	25pf yel brn	65.00	2.00
53	A5	50pf dp brn	67.50	2.00
54	A4	1m rose lil ('00)	1.75	22
a.		1m red lilac, toned paper	25.00	1.25
55	A4	2m org ('01)	2.75	2.75
a.		Toned paper ('90)	18.00	2.75
56	A4	3m ol gray ('00)	19.00	17.50
a.		White paper ('06)	40.00	150.00
57	A4	5m yel grn ('00)	19.00	17.50
a.		White paper ('06)	40.00	125.00

Nos. 56-57 are on toned paper. A 2m lilac was not regularly issued.

1888-1900 Wmk. 95h *Perf. 14½*

58	A5	2pf gray ('00)	1.25	20
59	A5	3pf green	3.50	40
60	A5	3pf brown ('00)	15	15
61	A5	5pf lilac	6.25	1.40
62	A5	5pf dk grn ('00)	15	15
63	A5	10pf carmine	15	60
64	A5	20pf ultra	15	15
65	A5	25pf yel brn	14.00	1.65
66	A5	25pf org ('00)	16	28
67	A5	30pf ol grn ('00)	16	28
68	A5	40pf yel ('00)	16	70
69	A5	50pf dp brn	22.50	1.65
70	A5	50pf mar ('00)	16	55
71	A5	80pf lilac ('00)	1.50	2.25

Nos. 59, 61, 65, 69 and 70 are on toned paper; Nos. 67-68 on white.

1888-99

Toned Paper

58a	A5	2pf ('99)	8.00	1.40
60a	A5	3pf ('90)	2.00	15
62a	A5	5pf ('90)	2.00	15
63a	A5	10pf	1.65	15
64a	A5	20pf	2.25	28
66a	A5	25pf ('90)	6.00	75
70a	A5	50pf ('90)	22.50	1.00
71a	A5	80pf ('99)	17.50	4.50

1911 Wmk. 95v

72	A5	5pf dark green	50	3.00

1911 Wmk. 95h *Perf. 11½*

73	A4	1m rose lilac	4.00	9.00
74	A4	2m orange	8.00	15.00
75	A4	3m olive gray	8.00	15.00
76	A4	5m pale yel grn	8.00	15.00

A6

A7

Prince Regent Luitpold A8

Perf. 14x14½

1911 Wmk. 95h Litho.

77	A6	3pf brn, *gray brn*	20	15
a.		"911" for "1911"	*275.00*	*275.00*
78	A6	5pf dk grn, *grn*	25	15
a.		Tête bêche pair	5.00	6.00
b.		Booklet pane of 4 + 2 labels		
c.		Bklt. pane of 5 + label		
d.		Bklt. pane of 6	27.50	
79	A6	10pf scar, *buff*	15	15
a.		Tête bèche pair	5.00	7.50
b.		"911" for "1911"	15.00	15.00
d.		Booklet pane of 5 + label		
80	A6	20pf dp bl, *bl*	1.25	15
81	A6	25pf vio brn, *buff*	1.75	75

Perf. 11½

Wmk. 95v

82	A7	30pf org buff, *buff*	1.00	55
83	A7	40pf ol grn, *buff*	1.50	50
84	A7	50pf cl, *gray brn*	1.75	1.10
84A	A7	60pf dk grn, *buff*	2.00	95
85	A7	80pf vio, *gray brn*	4.00	95
86	A8	1m brn, *gray brn*	1.65	1.25
87	A8	2m dk grn, *grn*	1.65	2.50
88	A8	3m lake, *buff*	10.00	13.00
89	A8	5m dk bl, *buff*	10.00	16.00
90	A8	10m org, *yel*	16.00	35.00
91	A8	20m blk brn, *yel*	14.00	20.00
		Nos. 77-91 (16)	67.15	93.15

90th birthday of Prince Regent Luitpold. All values exist in 2 types except #84A. Nos. 77-84, 85-91 exist imperf.

Prince Regent Luitpold — A9

1911, June 10 Unwmk.

92	A9	5pf grn, yel & blk	30	50
b.		Horiz. pair, imperf. btwn.	110.00	110.00
93	A9	10pf rose, yel & blk	45	1.00
b.		Pair, imperf. between	110.00	110.00

Silver Jubilee of Prince Regent Luitpold.

A10

A11

Bavaria stamps can be mounted in the Scott Germany album part II.

King Ludwig III
A12 A13

Perf. 14x14½

1914-20 Wmk. 95h Photo.

94	A10	2pf gray ('18)	15	15
95	A10	3pf brown	15	15
96	A10	5pf yel grn	15	15
a.		5pf dark green	1.60	30
b.		Tête bêche pair	6.00	9.00
c.		Booklet pane of 5 + 1 label	50.00	
97	A10	7½pf dp grn ('16)	15	15
a.		Tête bêche pair	3.50	5.25
b.		Booklet pane of 6	15.00	
98	A10	10pf vermilion	1.65	15
a.		Tête bêche pair	7.50	10.00
b.		Booklet pane of 5 + 1 label	50.00	
99	A10	10pf car rose ('16)	15	15
100	A10	15pf ver ('16)	15	15
a.		Tête bêche pair	4.00	5.25
b.		Booklet pane of 5 + 1 label	20.00	
101	A10	15pf car ('20)	1.65	*3.00*
102	A10	20pf blue	15	15
103	A10	25pf gray	15	15
104	A10	30pf orange	15	15
105	A10	40pf olive grn	15	15
106	A10	50pf red brn	15	15
107	A10	60pf bl grn	22	25
108	A10	80pf violet	25	38

Perf. 11½

Wmk. 95v

109	A11	1m brown	25	38
110	A11	2m violet	35	90
111	A11	3m scarlet	50	1.50

Wmk. 95h

112	A12	5m deep blue	1.10	2.25
113	A12	10m yel grn	1.50	*15.00*
114	A12	20m brown	3.50	*17.50*
		Nos. 94-114 (21)	12.62	

See #117-135. For overprints and surcharges see #115, 136-175, 193-236, B1-B3.

Used Values

of Nos. 94-275 are for postally used stamps. Canceled-to-order stamps, which abound, sell for same prices as unused.

No. 94 Surcharged

1916 Wmk. 95h *Perf. 14x14½*

115	A13	2½pf on 2pf gray	15	15
a.		Double surcharge		

Ludwig III Types of 1914-20

1916-20 *Imperf.*

117	A10	2pf gray	15	*1.65*
118	A10	3pf brown	15	*1.65*
119	A10	5pf pale yel grn	15	*1.65*
120	A10	7½pf dp grn	15	*1.65*
a.		Tête bêche pair	5.50	
121	A10	10pf car rose	15	*1.65*
122	A10	15pf vermilion	15	*1.65*
a.		Tête bêche pair	5.50	
123	A10	20pf blue	15	*1.65*
124	A10	25pf gray	15	*1.65*
125	A10	30pf orange	15	*1.65*
126	A10	40pf olive grn	15	*1.65*
127	A10	50pf red brn	15	*1.65*
128	A10	60pf dk grn	15	*1.65*
129	A10	80pf violet	15	*1.65*
130	A11	1m brown	25	*3.50*
131	A11	2m violet	35	*5.00*
132	A11	3m scarlet	50	*5.00*
133	A12	5m deep blue	1.00	*15.00*
134	A12	10m yel grn	1.75	*21.00*
135	A12	20m brown	2.25	*32.50*
		Nos. 117-135 (19)	8.05	

Stamps and Type of 1914-20 Overprinted:

Volksſtaat
Bayern
a

Volksſtaat
Bayern
b

Wmk. 95h or 95v

1919 *Perf. 14x14½*

Overprint "a"

136	A10	3pf brown	15	40
137	A10	5pf yel grn	15	16
138	A10	7½pf dp grn	15	40
139	A10	10pf car rose	15	16
140	A10	15pf vermilion	15	16
141	A10	20pf blue	15	40
142	A10	25pf gray	15	40
143	A10	30pf orange	15	40
144	A10	35pf orange	15	1.25
a.		Without overprint	135.00	
145	A10	40pf ol grn	15	32
146	A10	50pf red brn	15	32
147	A10	60pf dk grn	15	40
148	A10	75pf red brn	15	80
a.		Without overprint	35.00	*210.00*
149	A10	80pf violet	15	65

Perf. 11½

Overprint "a"

150	A11	1m brown	28	65
151	A11	2m violet	35	1.00
152	A11	3m scarlet	52	*2.75*

Overprint "b"

153	A12	5m deep blue	90	*4.75*
154	A12	10m yel grn	1.25	*10.00*
155	A12	20m dk brn	2.25	*20.00*
		Nos. 136-155 (20)	7.65	

Inverted overprints exist on Nos. 137-143, 145-147, 149. Value, each $10.

Double overprints exist on Nos. 137, 139, 143, 145, 150. Values, $20-$50.

Imperf

Overprint "a"

156	A10	3pf brown	15	60
157	A10	5pf pale yel grn	15	60
158	A10	7½pf dp grn	15	60
159	A10	10pf car rose	15	60
160	A10	15pf vermilion	15	60
161	A10	20pf blue	15	60
162	A10	25pf gray	15	60
163	A10	30pf orange	15	60
164	A10	35pf orange	15	60
a.		Without overprint	14.00	
165	A10	40pf ol grn	15	60
166	A10	50pf red brn	15	60
167	A10	60pf dk grn	15	60
168	A10	75pf red brn	15	60
a.		Without overprint	210.00	
169	A10	80pf violet	20	65
170	A11	1m brown	35	2.00
171	A11	2m violet	42	2.75
172	A11	3m scarlet	55	5.25

Overprint "b"

173	A12	5m deep blue	1.00	6.25
174	A12	10m yel grn	1.25	*20.00*
175	A12	20m brown	2.00	*20.00*
		Nos. 156-175 (20)	7.72	

Stamps of Germany 1906-19 Overprinted Freiſtaat Bayern

1919 Wmk. 125 *Perf. 14, 14½*

176	A22	2½pf gray	15	18
177	A16	3pf brown	15	15
178	A16	5pf green	15	15
179	A22	7½pf orange	15	15
180	A16	10pf carmine	15	15
181	A22	15pf dk vio	15	15
a.		Double overprint	130.00	*150.00*
182	A16	20pf ultra	15	15
183	A16	25pf org & blk, *yel*	15	48
184	A22	35pf red brn	15	55
185	A16	40pf lake & blk	22	55
186	A16	75pf grn & blk	38	90
187	A16	80pf lake & blk, *rose*	45	1.25
188	A17	1m car rose	95	1.75
189	A21	2m dl bl	1.10	3.50
190	A19	3m gray vio	1.50	4.75
191	A20	5m slate & car	1.90	4.75
a.		Inverted overprint	*2,100.*	
		Nos. 176-191 (16)	7.85	19.56

Bavarian Stamps of 1914-16 Overprinted:

Freiſtaat
Bayern
c

Freiſtaat
Bayern
d

Wmk. 95h or 95v

1919-20 *Perf. 14x14½*

Overprint "c"

193	A10	3pf brown	15	52
194	A10	5pf yel grn	15	15
195	A10	7½pf dp grn	15	*3.00*
196	A10	10pf car rose	15	15
197	A10	15pf vermilion	15	15
198	A10	20pf blue	15	20
199	A10	25pf gray	16	60
200	A10	30pf orange	16	60
201	A10	40pf olive grn	25	1.65
202	A10	50pf red brn	16	85
203	A10	60pf dk grn	35	*3.00*
204	A10	75pf olive bister	50	*4.00*
205	A10	80pf violet	35	1.65

Perf. 11½

Overprint "c"

206 A11 1m brown 35 1.65
207 A11 2m violet 35 2.25
208 A11 3m scarlet 50 4.00

Overprint "d"

209 A12 5m deep blue 1.10 *6.50*
210 A12 10m yel grn 1.90 *12.00*
211 A12 20m dk brn 2.25 *20.00*
Nos. 193-211 (19) 9.28

Imperf

Overprint "c"

212 A10 3pf brown 15 50
213 A10 5pf pale yel grn 15 50
214 A10 7½pf dp grn 15 *2.50*
215 A10 10pf car rose 15 50
216 A10 15pf vermilion 15 50
217 A10 20pf blue 15 50
a. Double overprint 47.50
218 A10 25pf gray 15 50
219 A10 30pf orange 15 50
220 A10 40pf ol grn 32 50
221 A10 50pf red brn 16 50
222 A10 60pf dk grn 32 50
223 A10 75pf ol bis 48 1.00
a. Without overprint 6.75
224 A10 80pf violet 20 52
225 A11 1m brown 32 1.65
226 A11 2m violet 32 2.25
227 A11 3m scarlet 60 4.00

Overprint "d"

228 A12 5m dp bl 90 6.50
229 A12 10m yel grn 2.25 *14.00*
230 A12 20m brown 2.25 *16.00*
Nos. 212-230 (19) 9.32

Ludwig Type of 1914, Printed in Various Colors and Surcharged

1,25 M Freistaat Bayern

1919 *Perf. 11½*

231 A11 1.25m on 1m yel grn 15 1.25
232 A11 1.50m on 1m org 15 2.00
233 A11 2.50m on 1m gray 18 4.00

1920 ***Imperf.***

234 A11 1.25m on 1m yel grn 20 *4.00*
a. Without surcharge 205.00
235 A11 1.50m on 1m org 20 *4.75*
a. Without surcharge 4.50
236 A11 2.50m on 1m gray 20 *6.50*
a. Without surcharge 4.50

No. 60 Surcharged in Dark Blue

20 20

20 20

1920 *Perf. 14½*

237 A5 20pf on 3pf brown 15 18
a. Inverted surcharge 9.75 18.00
b. Double surcharge 52.50 62.50

Plowman A14

"Electricity" Harnessing Light to a Water Wheel A15

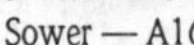

Sower — A16

Madonna and Child — A17

von Kaulbach's "Genius" — A18

TWENTY PFENNIG
Type I - Foot of "2" turns downward.
Type II - Foot of "2" turns upward.

Perf. 14x14½

1920 **Wmk. 95h** **Typo.**

238 A14 5pf yellow grn 15 15
239 A14 10pf orange 15 15
240 A14 15pf carmine 15 15
241 A15 20pf violet (I) 15 15
a. 20pf violet (II) 15.00 *250.00*
242 A15 30pf dp blue 15 45
243 A15 40pf brown 15 45
244 A16 50pf vermilion 18 75
245 A16 60pf blue green 18 75
246 A16 75pf lilac rose 18 1.25

Perf. 12x11½

Wmk. 95v

247 A17 1m car & gray 40 1.25
248 A17 1¼m ultra & ol bis 22 1.25
249 A17 1½m dk grn & gray 22 1.25
250 A17 2½m blk & gray 22 *4.00*

Perf. 11½x12

Wmk. 95h

251 A18 3m pale blue 35 6.50
252 A18 5m orange 70 6.75
253 A18 10m deep green 1.50 9.25
254 A18 20m black 2.00 13.00
Nos. 238-254 (17) 7.05

Imperf., Pair

238a A14 5pf yel grn 100.00
239a A14 10pf orange 225.00
241b A15 20pf vio (I) 100.00
243a A15 40pf brown 200.00
244a A16 50pf vermilion 25.00
245a A16 60pf blue green 55.00
246a A16 75pf lil rose 55.00

Wmk. 95v

247a A17 1m car & gray 10.00
248a A17 1¼m ultra & ol bis 10.00
249a A17 1½m dk grn & gray 10.00
250a A17 2½m blk & gray 16.00

Wmk. 95h

251a A18 3m pale blue 16.00
252a A18 5m orange 16.00
253a A18 10m deep green 16.00
254a A18 20m black 16.00

Perf. 12x11½

1920 **Litho.** **Wmk. 95v**

255 A17 2½m black & gray 1.00 *12.00*

On No. 255 the background dots are small, hazy and irregularly spaced. On No. 250 they are large, clear, round, white and regularly spaced in rows. The backs of the typo. stamps usually show a raised impression of parts of the design.

Stamps and Types of Preceding Issue Overprinted

Deutsches Reich

1920

256 A14 5pf yel grn 15 18
a. Inverted overprint 16.00
b. Imperf., pair 32.50
257 A14 10pf orange 15 18
a. Imperf., pair 32.50
258 A14 15pf carmine 15 18
259 A15 20pf violet 15 18
a. Inverted overprint 16.00
b. Double overprint 16.00
c. Imperf., pair 32.50
260 A15 30pf deep blue 15 18
a. Inverted overprint 16.00
b. Imperf., pair 45.00
261 A15 40pf brown 15 18
a. Inverted overprint 22.50
b. Imperf., pair 45.00
262 A16 50pf vermilion 15 18
263 A16 60pf blue green 15 18
264 A16 75pf lilac rose 30 95
265 A16 80pf dark blue 18 45
a. Without overprint *120.00*
b. Imperf., pair 32.50

Overprinted in Black or Red

Deutsches Reich

266 A17 1m car & gray 30 45
a. Imperf., pair 32.50
b. Inverted overprint 22.50
267 A17 1¼m ultra & ol bis 30 55
a. Imperf., pair 32.50
268 A17 1½m dk grn & gray 30 75
a. Imperf., pair 32.50
269 A17 2m vio & ol bis 60 1.10
a. Without overprint 50.00
b. Imperf., pair 32.50
270 A17 2½m (#250) (R) 15 48
c. Imperf., pair 32.50
270A A17 2½m (#255) (R) 55 *60.00*
b. Imperf., pair 32.50

Overprinted **Deutsches Reich**

271 A18 3m pale blue 2.25 3.00
272 A18 4m dull red 2.50 3.75
a. Without overprint 60.00
273 A18 5m orange 2.00 3.00
274 A18 10m dp grn 2.50 4.00
275 A18 20m black 3.75 5.00
Nos. 256-275 (21) 16.88

Nos. 256 to 275 were available for postage through all Germany, but were used almost exclusively in Bavaria.

SEMI-POSTAL STAMPS

Regular Issue of 1914-20 Surcharged in Black

5 Pf. für Kriegsbeschädigte Freistaat Bayern

1919 **Wmk. 95h** *Perf. 14x14½*

B1 A10 10pf + 5pf car rose 40 65
a. Inverted surcharge 12.00 30.00
b. Surcharge on back 24.00
c. Imperf., pair 325.00
B2 A10 15pf + 5pf ver 40 65
a. Inverted surcharge 12.00 30.00
b. Imperf., pair 160.00
B3 A10 20pf + 5pf blue 40 85
a. Inverted surcharge 12.00 30.00
b. Imperf., pair 200.00

Surtax was for wounded war veterans.

POSTAGE DUE STAMPS

D1

D2

With Silk Thread

1862 **Typeset** **Unwmk.** ***Imperf.***

J1 D1 3kr black 100.00 300.00
a. "Empfange" 325.00 *650.00*

Without Silk Thread

1870 **Typo.** **Wmk. 93** *Perf. 11½*

J2 D1 1kr black 11.00 *575.00*
a. Wmk. 92 25.00 *900.00*
J3 D1 3kr black 11.00 *325.00*
a. Wmk. 92 25.00 440.00

Type of 1876 Regular Issue Overprinted in Red "Vom Empfänger zahlbar"

1876 **Wmk. 94**

J4 D2 3pf gray 17.50 22.50
J5 D2 5pf gray 12.00 22.50
J6 D2 10pf gray 2.50 65

1883 **Wmk. 95v**

J7 D2 3pf gray 80.00 100.00
J8 D2 5pf gray 60.00 60.00
J9 D2 10pf gray 60 28
a. "Empfanper" 100.00 80.00
b. "zahlhar" 80.00 60.00
c. Imperf. 100.00

1895-1903 **Wmk. 95h** *Perf. 14½*

J10 D2 2pf gray 55 80
J11 D2 3pf gray ('03) 35 1.00
J12 D2 5pf gray ('03) 70 80
J13 D2 10pf gray ('03) 55 40

Nos. J10-J11 exist with inverted overprint.

1888

Rose-toned Paper

J10a D2 2pf gray 75 1.25
J11a D2 3pf gray 75 75
J12a D2 5pf gray 1.25 60
J13a D2 10pf gray 1.25 20
b. As "a," double overprint *1,750.*

No. J13b was used at Pirmasens.

Surcharged in Red in Each Corner

1895

J14 D2 2pf on 3pf gray

At least six copies exist, all used in Aichach.

OFFICIAL STAMPS

Nos. 77 to 81, 84, 95, 96, 98, 99 and 102, perforated with a large E were issued for official use in 1912-16.

Regular Issue of 1888-1900 Overprinted **E**

1908 **Wmk. 95h** *Perf. 14½*

O1 A5 3pf dk brn (R) 1.50 2.40
O2 A5 5pf dk grn (R) 15 15
O3 A5 10pf car (G) 15 15
O4 A5 20pf ultra (R) 50 35
O5 A5 50pf maroon 4.75 4.25
Nos. O1-O5 (5) 7.05 7.30

Nos. O1 to O5 were issued for the use of railway officials. "E" stands for "Eisenbahn."

Coat of Arms — O1

1916-17 **Typo.** *Perf. 11½*

O6 O1 3pf bis brn 15 25
O7 O1 5pf yel grn 15 25
O8 O1 7½pf grn, *grn* 15 25
O9 O1 7½pf grn ('17) 15 20
O10 O1 10pf dp rose 16 25
O11 O1 15pf red, *buff* 15 20
O12 O1 15pf red ('17) 16 40
O13 O1 20pf dp bl, *bl* 1.25 1.25
O14 O1 20pf dp bl ('17) 15 25
O15 O1 25pf gray 15 25
O16 O1 30pf orange 15 25
O17 O1 60pf dk grn 16 30
O18 O1 1m dl vio, *gray* 80 1.75
O19 O1 1m mar ('17) 3.25 *60.00*
Nos. O6-O19 (14) 6.98

Used Values of Nos. O6-O69 are for postally used stamps. Canceled-to-order stamps, which abound, sell for same prices as unused.

Official Stamps and Type of 1916-17 Overprinted

Volksstaat Bayern

1918

O20 O1 3pf bister brn 15 *3.50*
O21 O1 5pf yel green 15 25
O22 O1 7½pf gray green 15 30
O23 O1 10pf deep rose 15 20
O24 O1 15pf red 15 20
O25 O1 20pf blue 15 20
O26 O1 25pf gray 15 25
O27 O1 30pf orange 15 35
O28 O1 35pf orange 15 35
O29 O1 50pf olive gray 15 35
O30 O1 60pf dark grn 20 1.50
O31 O1 75pf red brown 25 1.50
O32 O1 1m dl vio, *gray* 75 2.50
O33 O1 1m maroon 4.00 *60.00*
Nos. O20-O33 (14) 6.70

O2 O3

O4

1920 Typo. *Perf. 14x14½*

No.	Design	Description	Unused	Used
O34	O2	5pf yel grn	15	*3.00*
O35	O2	10pf orange	15	*3.00*
O36	O2	15pf carmine	15	*3.00*
O37	O2	20pf violet	15	*3.00*
O38	O2	30pf dark blue	15	*4.50*
O39	O2	40pf bister	15	*5.00*

Perf. 14½x14

Wmk. 95v

No.	Design	Description	Unused	Used
O40	O3	50pf vermilion	15	*10.00*
O41	O3	60pf blue grn	15	*7.50*
O42	O3	70pf dk vio	15	*9.00*
a.		Imperf., pair	50.00	
O43	O3	75pf dp rose	15	12.50
O44	O3	80pf dl bl	15	20.00
O45	O3	90pf ol grn	15	25.00
O46	O3	1m dk brn	15	22.50
a.		Imperf., pair	80.00	
O47	O4	1¼m green	15	*27.50*
O48	O4	1½m vermilion	15	*30.00*
a.		Imperf. pair	40.00	
O49	O4	2½m deep blue	15	*32.50*
a.		Imperf. pair	80.00	
O50	O4	3m dark red	35	*35.00*
a.		Imperf. pair	32.00	
O51	O4	5m black	2.00	*45.00*
a.		Imperf., pair	80.00	
		Nos. O34-O51 (18)	4.75	

Stamps of Preceding Issue Overprinted **Deutsches Reich**

1920, Apr. 1

No.	Design	Description	Unused	Used
O52	O2	5pf yel grn	15	75
a.		Imperf., pair	45.00	
O53	O2	10pf orange	15	40
O54	O2	15pf carmine	15	40
O55	O2	20pf violet	15	40
O56	O2	30pf dark blue	15	20
O57	O2	40pf bister	15	20
O58	O3	50pf vermilion	15	20
a.		Imperf., pair	45.00	
O59	O3	60pf bl grn	15	20
O60	O3	70pf dk vio	1.25	1.40
O61	O3	75pf dp rose	32	60
O62	O3	80pf dull blue	15	40
O63	O3	90pf olive grn	80	1.00

Similar Ovpt., Words 8mm apart

No.	Design	Description	Unused	Used
O64	O4	1m dk brn	15	20
a.		Imperf., pair	45.00	
O65	O4	1¼m green	15	20
O66	O4	1½m vermilion	15	20
O67	O4	2½m deep blue	15	40
a.		Imperf., pair	60.00	
O68	O4	3m dark red	15	50
O69	O4	5m black	4.00	*15.00*
		Nos. O52-O69 (18)	8.47	

Nos. O52 to O69 could be used in all parts of Germany, but were almost exclusively used in Bavaria.

BERGEDORF

LOCATION — A town in northern Germany.
POP. — 2,989 (1861)

Originally Bergedorf belonged jointly to the Free City of Hamburg and the Free City of Lübeck. In 1867 it was purchased by Hamburg.

16 Schillings = 1 Mark

Values for unused stamps are for copies with gum. Copies without gum sell for about half the figures quoted.

Bergedorf stamps can be mounted in the Scott Germany album part II.

Combined Arms of Lübeck and Hamburg
A1 A2 A3

A4 A5

1861-67 Unwmk. Litho. *Imperf.*

No.	Design	Description	Unused	Used
1	A1	½s blk, *pale bl*	42.50	*375.00*
a.		½s black, *blue* ('67)	90.00	*2,500.*
2	A3	1s blk, *white*	42.50	*190.00*
a.		Tête bêche pair	200.00	
3	A4	1½s blk, *yellow*	22.50	*550.00*
a.		Tête bêche pair	*175.00*	
4	A2	3s blue, *pink*	27.50	*1,000.*
5	A5	4s blk, *brown*	27.50	*1,250.*

Counterfeit cancellations are plentiful.

The ½s on violet and 3s on rose, listed previously, as well as a 1s and 1½s on thick paper and 4s on light rose brown, come from proof sheets and were never placed in use. A 1½ "SCHILLUNG" (instead of SCHILLING) also exists only as a proof.

REPRINTS

½ SCHILLING

There is a dot in the upper part of the right branch of "N" of "EIN." The upper part of the shield is blank or almost blank. The horizontal bar of "H" in "HALBER" is generally defective.

1 SCHILLING

The "1" in the corners is generally with foot. The central horizontal bar of the "E" of "EIN" is separated from the vertical branch by a black line. The "A" of "POSTMARKE" has the horizontal bar incomplete or missing. The horizontal bar of the "H" of "SCHILLING" is separated from the vertical branches by a dark line at each side, sometimes the bar is missing.

1½ SCHILLINGE

There is a small triangle under the right side of the tower, exactly over the "R" of "POSTMARKE."

3 SCHILLINGE

The head of the eagle is not shaded. The horizontal bar of the second "E" of "BERGEDORF" is separated from the vertical branch by a thin line. There is generally a colored dot in the lower half of the "S" of "POSTMARKE."

4 SCHILLINGE

The upper part of the shield is blank or has two or three small dashes. In most of the reprints there is a diagonal dash across the wavy lines of the groundwork at the right of "I" and "E" of "VIER."

Reprints, value $1 each.

These stamps were superseded by those of the North German Confederation in 1868.

BREMEN

LOCATION — In northwestern Germany
AREA — 99 sq. mi.
POP. — 122,402 (1871)

Bremen was a Free City and member of the German Confederation. In 1870 it became part of the German Empire.

22 Grote = 10 Silbergroschen.

Values of Bremen stamps vary according to condition. Quotations are for fine copies. Very fine to superb specimens sell at much higher prices, and inferior or poor copies sell at reduced prices, depending on the condition of the individual specimen.

Values for unused stamps are for copies with gum. Copies without gum sell for about half the figures quoted.

Coat of Arms — A1

THREE GROTE
I II III

Type I. The central part of the scroll below the word Bremen is crossed by one vertical line.
Type II. The center of the scroll is crossed by two vertical lines.
Type III. The center of the scroll is crossed by three vertical lines.

1855 Unwmk. Litho. *Imperf.*

Horizontally Laid Paper

No.	Design	Description	Unused	Used
1	A1	3gr black, *blue*	175.00	250.00

Vertically Laid Paper

No.	Design	Description	Unused	Used
1A	A1	3gr black, *blue*	400.00	650.00

Nos. 1 and 1A can be found with parts of a papermaker's watermark, consisting of lilies. Value: unused $500; used $850.

See Nos. 9-10.

A2 A3

FIVE GROTE

Type I. The shading at the left of the ribbon containing "funf Grote" runs downward from the shield.
Type II. The shading at the left of the ribbon containing "funf Grote" runs upward.

1856-60 Wove Paper

No.	Design	Description	Unused	Used
2	A2	5gr blk, *rose*	125.00	175.00
a.		Printed on both sides		
b.		"Marken" (not issued)	10.00	
3	A2	7gr blk, *yel* ('60)	150.00	*475.00*
4	A3	5sgr green ('59)	125.00	225.00
a.		Chalky paper	50.00	*200.00*
b.		5sgr yellow green	100.00	150.00

See Nos. 6, 8, 12-13, 15.

A4 A5

1861-63 *Serpentine Roulette*

No.	Design	Description	Unused	Used
5	A4	2gr orange ('63)	150.00	*1,600.*
a.		2gr red orange	150.00	*1,600.*
b.		Chalky paper	180.00	*1,400.*
6	A2	5gr blk, *rose* ('62)	90.00	90.00
7	A5	10gr black	350.00	*775.00*
8	A3	5sgr green ('63)	400.00	125.00
a.		Chalky paper	425.00	250.00
b.		5sgr yellow green	175.00	115.00

See Nos. 11, 14.

1863

Horizontally (H) or Vertically (V) Laid Paper

No.	Design	Description	Unused	Used
9	A1	3gr blk, *blue* (V)	325.00	375.00
a.		3gr black, *blue* (H)	1,000.	*1,250.*

1866-67 *Perf. 13*

No.	Design	Description	Unused	Used
10	A1	3gr black, *blue*	80.00	150.00

Wove Paper

No.	Design	Description	Unused	Used
11	A4	2gr orange	70.00	*200.00*
a.		2gr red orange	125.00	*300.00*
b.		Horiz. pair, imperf. btwn.		*1,750.*
12	A2	5gr blk, *rose*	100.00	*110.00*
a.		Horiz. pair, imperf. btwn.		
13	A2	7gr blk, *yel* ('67)	90.00	*4,000.*
14	A5	10gr black ('67)	135.00	*700.00*
15	A3	5sgr green	110.00	*600.00*
a.		5sgr yellow green	110.00	100.00
b.		As "a," chalky paper	225.00	175.00

The stamps of Bremen were superseded by those of the North German Confederation on Jan. 1, 1868.

BRUNSWICK

LOCATION — In northern Germany
GOVT. — Former duchy
AREA — 1,417 sq. mi.
POP. — 349,367 (1880)
CAPITAL — Brunswick

Brunswick was a member of the German Confederation and, in 1870 became part of the German Empire.

12 Pfennigs = 1 Gutegroschen

30 Silbergroschen (Groschen) = 24 Gutegroschen = 1 Thaler

Values of Brunswick stamps vary according to condition. Quotations for Nos. 1-22 are for fine copies. Very fine to superb specimens sell at much higher prices, and inferior or poor copies sell at reduced prices, depending on the condition of the individual specimen.

Values for Nos. 1-3 unused are for copies without gum. Copies with gum sell for about three times the prices quoted. Nos. 4-26 without gum sell for about half the figures quoted.

The "Leaping Saxon Horse" — A1

The ½gr has white denomination and "Gr" in right oval.

1852 Unwmk. Typo. *Imperf.*

No.	Design	Description	Unused	Used
1	A1	1sgr rose	1,500.	200.00
2	A1	2sgr blue	900.00	125.00
a.		Half used as 1sgr on cover		
3	A1	3sgr vermilion	900.00	125.00

See Nos. 4-11, 13-22.

1853-63 Wmk. 102

No.	Design	Description	Unused	Used
4	A1	¼ggr blk, *brn* ('56)	200.00	165.00
5	A1	⅓sgr black ('56)	100.00	250.00
6	A1	½gr blk, *grn* ('63)	11.00	*150.00*
7	A1	1sgr blk, *orange*	90.00	32.50
a.		1sgr black, *orange buff*	90.00	32.50
8	A1	1sgr blk, *yel* ('61)	75.00	32.50
9	A1	2sgr blk, *blue*	65.00	40.00
a.		Half used as 1sgr on cover		*6,750.*
10	A1	3sgr blk, *rose*	175.00	40.00
11	A1	3sgr rose ('62)	200.00	165.00

A3 A4

1857

No.	Design	Description	Unused	Used
12	A3	Four ¼ggr blk, *brn* ('57)	25.00	60.00
a.		Four ¼ggr blk, *yel brown*	125.00	125.00

The bister on white paper was not issued. Value $12.

1864 *Serpentine Roulette 16*

No.	Design	Description	Unused	Used
13	A1	⅓sgr black	300.00	*1,900.*
14	A1	½gr blk, *green*	200.00	*1,500.*
15	A1	1sgr blk, *yellow*	*1,750.*	*1,000.*
16	A1	1sgr yellow	140.00	125.00
17	A1	2sgr blk, *blue*	250.00	300.00
a.		Half used as 1sgr on cover		*8,000.*
18	A1	3sgr rose	800.00	400.00

Rouletted 12

No.	Design	Description	Unused	Used
20	A1	1sgr blk, *yellow*		*9,000.*
21	A1	1sgr yellow	275.00	200.00
22	A1	3sgr rose	*2,650.*	*1,900.*

#13, 16, 18, 21-22 are on white paper.
Faked roulettes of Nos. 13-22 exist.

Serpentine Roulette

1865 Embossed Unwmk.

No.	Design	Description	Unused	Used
23	A4	⅓gr black	22.50	*250.00*
24	A4	1gr carmine	2.50	*30.00*
25	A4	2gr ultra	6.00	*150.00*
a.		2gr gray blue	6.00	*140.00*
c.		Half used as 1sgr on cover		*7,250.*
26	A4	3gr brown	5.50	*130.00*

Faked cancellations of Nos. 5-26 exist.

Imperf., Pair

23a A4 1/2gr 110.00
24a A4 1gr 32.50
25b A4 2gr 100.00
26a A4 3gr 125.00

Stamps of Brunswick were superseded by those of the North German Confederation on Jan. 1, 1868.

HAMBURG

LOCATION — Northern Germany
GOVT. — A former Free City
AREA — 160 sq. mi.
POP. — 453,869 (1880)
CAPITAL — Hamburg

Hamburg was a member of the German Confederation and became part of the German Empire in 1870.

16 Schillings = 1 Mark

Values of unused stamps are for copies without gum. Copies with gum sell for about twice the figures quoted.

Value Numeral on Arms — A1

1859 Typo. Wmk. 128 ***Imperf.***

1 A1 1/2s black 45.00 *500.00*
2 A1 1s brown 60.00 *55.00*
3 A1 2s red 55.00 *80.00*
4 A1 3s blue 45.00 *100.00*
5 A1 4s yellow green 50.00 *1,200.*
a. 4s green 75.00 *1,000.*
6 A1 7s orange 50.00 21.00
7 A1 9s yellow 70.00 *1,600.*

See Nos. 13-21.

A2 A3

1864 **Litho.**

9 A2 1 1/4s red lilac 50.00 60.00
a. 1 1/4s lilac 65.00 75.00
b. 1 1/4s gray 50.00 42.50
c. 1 1/4s blue 250.00 *500.00*
d. 1 1/4s greenish gray 50.00 *90.00*
12 A3 2 1/2s green 65.00 *110.00*

See Nos. 22-23.

The 1 1/4s and 2 1/2s have been reprinted on watermarked and unwatermarked paper.

1864-65 Typo. ***Perf. 13 1/2***

13 A1 1/2s black 3.50 9.00
a. Imperf. vert., pair 30.00
14 A1 1s brown 6.00 12.50
a. Half used as 1/2s on cover
15 A1 2s red 5.00 17.00
17 A1 3s ultra 15.00 22.50
a. Imperf., pair 40.00
b. Horiz. pair, imperf. vert.
c. 3s blue 20.00 30.00
18 A1 4s green 5.00 20.00
19 A1 7s orange 85.00 130.00
20 A1 7s vio ('65) 6.00 14.00
a. Imperf., pair 115.00
21 A1 9s yellow 10.00 *1,600.*
a. Vert. pair, imperf. btwn. 325.00

Litho.

22 A2 1 1/4s lilac 30.00 9.00
a. 1 1/4s red lilac 30.00 10.00
b. 1 1/4s violet 30.00 9.00
23 A3 2 1/2s yel grn 45.00 25.00
a. 2 1/2s blue green 45.00 25.00

The 1 1/4s has been reprinted on watermarked and unwatermarked paper; the 2 1/2s on unwatermarked paper.

Hamburg stamps can be mounted in the Scott Germany album part II.

A4 A5

Rouletted 10

1866 Unwmk. Embossed

24 A4 1 1/4s violet 15.00 22.50
a. 1 1/4s red violet 25.00 30.00
25 A5 1 1/2s rose 4.50 *60.00*

Reprints:

1 1/4s: The rosettes between the words of the inscription have a well-defined open circle in the center of the originals, while in the reprints this circle is filled up.

In the upper part of the top of the "g" of "Schilling", there is a thin vertical line which is missing in the reprints.

The two lower lines of the triangle in the upper left corner are of different thicknesses in the originals while in the reprints they are of equal thickness.

The labels at the right and left containing the inscriptions are 2 3/4mm in width in the originals while they are 2 1/2mm in reprints.

1 1/2s: The originals are printed on thinner paper than the reprints. This is easily seen by turning the stamps over, when on the originals the color and impression will clearly show through, which is not the case in the reprints.

The vertical stroke of the upper part of the "g" in Schilling is very short on the originals, scarcely crossing the top line, while in the reprints it almost touches the center of the "g".

The lower part of the "g" of Schilling in the originals, barely touches the inner line of the frame, in some stamps it does not touch it at all, while in the reprints the whole stroke runs into the inner line of the frame.

A6

1867 Typo. Wmk. 128 ***Perf. 13 1/2***

26 A6 2 1/2s dull green 4.00 *65.00*
a. 2 1/2s dark green 12.00 *50.00*
b. Imperf., pair 65.00

Forged cancellations exist on almost all stamps of Hamburg, especially on Nos. 4, 7, 21 and 25.

Nos. 1-23 and 26 exist without watermark, but they come from the same sheets as the watermarked stamps.

The stamps of Hamburg were superseded by those of the North German Confederation on Jan. 1, 1868.

HANOVER

LOCATION — Northern Germany
GOVT. — A former Kingdom
AREA — 14,893 sq. mi.
POP. — 3,191,000
CAPITAL — Hanover

Hanover was a member of the German Confederation and became in 1866 a province of Prussia.

10 Pfennigs = 1 Groschen
24 Gute Groschen = 1 Thaler
30 Silbergroschen = 1 Thaler (1858)

Values for unused stamps are for copies with gum. Copies without gum sell for about half the values quoted.

Coat of Arms
A1 A2

Wmk. Square Frame

1850 Rose Gum Typo. ***Imperf.***

1 A1 1g g blk, *gray bl* 3,000. 40.00

See Nos. 2, 11.

The reprints have white gum and no watermark.

1851-55 Wmk. 130

2 A1 1g g blk, *gray grn* 20.00 5.75
a. 1g g black, *yellow green* 165.00 17.50
3 A2 1/30th blk, *salmon* 52.00 32.50
a. 1/30th black, *crimson* ('55) 50.00 32.50
b. Bisect on cover
5 A2 1/15th blk, *gray bl* 75.00 37.50
a. Bisect on cover
6 A2 1/10th blk, *yellow* 75.00 37.50
a. 1/10th black, *orange* 75.00 37.50

Bisects Nos. 3b, 5a, 12a and 13a were used for 1/2g.

See Nos. 8, 12-13.

The 1/10th has been reprinted on unwatermarked paper, with white gum.

Crown and Numeral — A3

1853 Wmk. 130

7 A3 3pf rose 225.00 200.00

See Nos. 9, 16-17, 25.

The reprints of No. 7 have white gum.

Fine Network in Second Color

1855 Unwmk.

8 A2 1/10th blk & org 125.00 80.00
a. 1/10th black & yellow 140.00 110.00

No. 8 with olive yellow network and other values with fine network are essays.

Large Network in Second Color

1856-57

9 A3 3pf rose & blk 200.00 210.00
a. 3pf rose & gray 225.00 200.00
11 A1 1g g blk & grn 25.00 7.50
12 A2 1/30th blk & rose 65.00 22.50
a. Bisect on cover *3,500.*
13 A2 1/15th blk & bl 50.00 47.50
a. Bisect on cover *5,000.*
14 A2 1/10th blk & org ('57) 425.00 50.00

The reprints have white gum, and the network does not cover all the outer margin.

Without Network

1859-63

16 A3 3pf carmine rose 60.00 75.00
a. 3pf pink 50.00 70.00
17 A3 3pf grn (Drei Zehntel) ('63) 225.00 800.00

Copies of No. 25 with rouletting trimmed off sometimes pretend to be No. 17. Minimum size of No. 17 acknowledged as genuine: 21 1/2x24 1/2mm.

The reprints of No. 16 have pink gum instead of red; the extremities of the banderol point downward instead of outward.

Crown and Post Horn — A7

King George V — A8

1859-61 ***Imperf.***

18 A7 1/2g black ('60) 55.00 110.00
a. Rose gum 200.00 250.00
19 A8 1g rose 3.00 2.00
a. 1g vio rose 20.00 15.00
b. 1g carmine 8.00 12.50
c. Half used as 1/2g on cover *3,500.*
20 A8 2g ultra 8.00 22.50
a. Half used as 1g on cover *4,000.*
22 A8 3g yellow 125.00 57.50
a. 3g orange yellow 125.00 52.50
23 A8 3g brown ('61) 10.00 25.00
a. One third used as 1g on cover
24 A8 10g green ('61) 190.00 800.00

Reprints of 1/2g are on thick toned paper with yellowish gum. Originals are on white paper with rose or white gum. Reprints exist tête bêche.

Reprints of 3g yellow and 3g brown have white or pinkish gum. Originals have rose or orange gum.

1864 White Gum ***Perce en Arc 16***

25 A3 3pf grn (Drei Zehntel) 25.00 40.00
26 A7 1/2g black 125.00 200.00
27 A8 1g rose 4.00 2.50
28 A8 2g ultra 60.00 40.00
a. Half used as 1g on cover
29 A8 3g brown 60.00 35.00

Reprints of 3g are percé en arc 13 1/2.

Rose Gum

25a A3 3pf green 50.00 65.00
26a A7 1/2g black 200.00 300.00
27a A8 1g rose 20.00 20.00
29a A8 3g brown *1,250.* *1,250.*

The stamps of Prussia superseded those of Hanover on Oct. 1, 1866.

LUBECK

LOCATION — Situated on an arm of the Baltic Sea between the former German States of Holstein and Mecklenburg.
GOVT. — Former Free City and State
AREA — 115 sq. mi.
POP. — 136,413
CAPITAL — Lubeck

Lubeck was a member of the German Confederation and became part of the German Empire in 1870.

16 Schillings = 1 Mark

Values of Lubeck stamps vary according to condition. Quotations are for fine copies. Very fine to superb specimens sell at much higher prices, and inferior or poor copies sell at reduced prices, depending on the condition of the individual specimen.

Values for Nos. 1-7 unused are for copies without gum. Copies with gum sell for about twice the figures quoted. Nos. 8-14 without gum sell for about half the values quoted.

Coat of Arms — A1

1859 Litho. Wmk. 148 ***Imperf.***

1 A1 1/2g gray lilac 400.00 *1,250.*
2 A1 1s orange 400.00 *1,250.*
3 A1 2s brown 15.00 *200.00*
a. Value in words reads "ZWEI EIN HALB" 275.00 *6,250.*
4 A1 2 1/2s rose 30.00 *500.00*
5 A1 4s green 15.00 *225.00*

1862 Unwmk.

6 A1 1/2s lilac 20.00 *1,000.*
7 A1 1s yellow orange 30.00 *1,000.*

The reprints of the 1859-62 issues are unwatermarked and printed in bright colors.

A2

A3

1863 ***Rouletted 11 1/2***

Eagle embossed

8 A2 1/2s green 30.00 *65.00*
9 A2 1s orange 90.00 *130.00*
a. Rouletted 10 175.00 *425.00*
10 A2 2s rose 18.00 *60.00*
11 A2 2 1/2s ultra 40.00 *210.00*
12 A2 4s bister 30.00 *80.00*

The reprints are imperforate and without embossing.

1864 Litho. ***Imperf.***

13 A3 1 1/4s brown 18.00 *40.00*

A4

1865 *Rouletted 11½*

Eagle embossed

14 A4 1½s red lilac 18.00 *70.00*

The reprints are imperforate and without embossing.

Counterfeit cancellations are found on #1-14.

The stamps of Lübeck were superseded by those of the North German Confederation on Jan. 1, 1868.

MECKLENBURG-SCHWERIN

LOCATION — In northern Germany, bordering on the Baltic Sea.
GOVT. — A former Grand Duchy
AREA — 5,065 sq. mi. (approx.)
POP. — 674,000 (approx.)
CAPITAL — Schwerin

Mecklenburg-Schwerin was a member of the German Confederation and became part of the German Empire in 1870.

48 Schillings = 1 Thaler

Values of Mecklenburg-Schwerin stamps vary according to condition. Quotations are for fine copies. Very fine to superb specimens sell at much higher prices, and inferior or poor copies sell at reduced prices, depending on the condition of the individual specimen.
Values for unused stamps are for copies without gum.

Coat of Arms
A1 A2

1856 Unwmk. Typo. *Imperf.*

1 A1 Four ¼s red 100.00 100.00
a. ¼s red 15.00 12.50
2 A2 3s orange yellow 75.00 50.00
3 A2 5s blue 200.00 190.00

See Nos. 4, 6-8.

A3

1864-67 *Rouletted 11½*

4 A1 Four ¼s red *1,600.* *1,600.*
a. ¼s red 110.00 150.00
5 A3 Four ¼s red 50.00 45.00
a. ¼s red 8.00 8.00
6 A2 2s gray lil ('67) 150.00 *1,000.*
a. 2s red violet ('66) 200.00 225.00
7 A2 3s org yel, wide margin('67) 35.00 *200.00*
a. Narrow margin ('65) 150.00 75.00
8 A2 5s bister brn 150.00 *165.00*
a. Thick paper 200.00 *300.00*

The overall size of #7, including margin, is 24½x24½mm. That of #7a is 23½x23mm.

Counterfeit cancellations exist on those stamps valued higher used than unused.

These stamps were superseded by those of the North German Confederation on Jan. 1, 1868.

MECKLENBURG-STRELITZ

LOCATION — In northern Germany, divided by Mecklenburg-Schwerin
GOVT. — A former Grand Duchy
AREA — 1,131 sq. mi.
POP. — 106,347
CAPITAL — Neustrelitz

Mecklenburg-Strelitz was a member of the German Confederation and became part of the German Empire in 1870.

30 Silbergroschen = 48 Schillings = 1 Thaler

Values of Mecklenburg-Strelitz stamps vary according to condition. Quotations are for fine copies. Very fine to superb specimens sell at much higher prices, and inferior or poor copies sell at reduced prices, depending on the condition of the individual specimen.
Values for unused stamps are for copies without gum.

Coat of Arms
A1 A2

Rouletted 11½

1864 Unwmk. Embossed

1 A1 ¼sg orange 100. *2,200.*
a. ¼sg yellow orange 250. *4,000.*
2 A1 ⅓sg green 60. *1,200.*
a. ⅓sg dark green 100. *2,500.*
3 A1 1sch violet 175. *3,750.*
4 A2 1sg rose 75. 180.
5 A2 2sg ultra 25. *850.*
6 A2 3sg bister 35. *1,500.*

Counterfeit cancellations abound.

These stamps were superseded by those of the North German Confederation in 1868.

OLDENBURG

LOCATION — In northwestern Germany, bordering on the North Sea.
GOVT. — A former Grand Duchy
AREA — 2,482 sq. mi.
POP. — 483,042 (1910)
CAPITAL — Oldenburg

Oldenburg was a member of the German Confederation and became part of the German Empire in 1870.

30 Silbergroschen = 1 Thaler
30 Groschen = 1 Thaler

Values of Oldenburg stamps vary according to condition. Quotations for Nos. 1-15 are for fine copies. Very fine to superb specimens sell at much higher prices, and inferior or poor copies sell at reduced prices, depending on the condition of the individual specimen.
Values for Nos. 1-25 unused are for copies without gum.

A1 A2

1852-55 Unwmk. Litho. *Imperf.*

1 A1 ¹⁄₃₀th blk, *blue* 200.00 20.00
2 A1 ¹⁄₁₅th blk, *rose* 400.00 60.00
3 A1 ¹⁄₁₀th blk, *yellow* 450.00 70.00
4 A2 ⅓sgr blk, *grn* ('55) 700.00 400.00

There are three types of Nos. 1 and 2.

Oldenburg stamps can be mounted in the Scott Germany album part II.

A3 A4

1859

5 A3 ⅓g blk, *green* 1,500. *2,250.*
6 A3 1g blk, *blue* 425.00 20.00
7 A3 2g blk, *rose* 550.00 450.00
8 A3 3g blk, *yellow* 650.00 550.00
a. "OLBENBURG" 550.00 825.00

See Nos. 10, 13-15.

1861

9 A4 ¼g orange 150.00 *3,400.*
10 A3 ⅓g green 300.00 *750.00*
a. ⅓g bluish green 275.00 *650.00*
b. ⅓g moss green 1,000. *1,900.*
c. "OLDEIBURG" *350.00* *750.00*
d. "Dritto" *350.00* *750.00*
e. "Drittd" *350.00* *750.00*
f. Printed on both sides *3,750.*
12 A4 ½g redsh brn 200.00 325.00
a. ½g dark brown 300.00 400.00
13 A3 1g blue 150.00 140.00
a. 1g gray blue 250.00 140.00
b. Printed on both sides *5,000.*
14 A3 2g red 225.00 350.00
15 A3 3g yellow 325.00 325.00
a. "OLDEIBURG" *350.00* *350.00*
b. Printed on both sides *5,000.*

Forged cancellations are found on Nos. 9, 10, 12 and their minor varieties.

Coat of Arms — A5

1862 Embossed *Rouletted 11½*

16 A5 ⅓g green 140.00 200.00
17 A5 ½g orange 110.00 100.00
a. ½g orange red 140.00 140.00
18 A5 1g rose 65.00 11.00
19 A5 2g ultra 110.00 45.00
20 A5 3g bister 110.00 50.00

1867 *Rouletted 10*

21 A5 ⅓g green 10.00 *350.00*
22 A5 ½g orange 10.00 *275.00*
23 A5 1g rose 4.00 *35.00*
a. Half used as ½g on cover
24 A5 2g ultra 5.00 *175.00*
25 A5 3g bister 12.50 *275.00*

Forged cancellations are found on #21-25.

The stamps of Oldenburg were replaced by those of the North German Confederation on Jan. 1, 1868.

PRUSSIA

LOCATION — Formerly the greater part of northern Germany.
GOVT. — A former independent Kingdom
AREA — 134,650 sq. mi.
POP. — 40,165,219 (1910)
CAPITAL — Berlin

Prussia was a member of the German Confederation and became part of the German Empire in 1870.

12 Pfennigs = 1 Silbergroschen
60 Kreuzer = 1 Gulden (1867)

Values for unused stamps are for copies with gum. Copies without gum sell for about half the figures quoted.

King Frederick William IV
A1 A2

1850-56 Engr. Wmk. 162 *Imperf.*

Background of Crossed Lines

1 A1 4pf yel grn ('56) 67.50 47.50
a. 4pf dark green 67.50 55.00
2 A1 6pf (½sg) red org 55.00 22.50
3 A2 1sg black, *rose* 60.00 5.00
4 A2 2sg black, *blue* 60.00 7.00
a. Half used as 1sg on cover
5 A2 3sg black, *yellow* 70.00 7.75
a. 3sg black, *orange buff* 300.00 25.00

See Nos. 10-13.

Reprints exist on watermarked and unwatermarked paper.

A3 A4

Solid Background

1857 Typo. Unwmk.

6 A3 1sg rose 300.00 20.00
7 A3 2sg blue 1,050. 42.50
a. 2sg dark blue 1,500. 100.00
b. Half used as 1sg on cover
8 A3 3sg orange 105.00 25.00
a. 3sg yellow 215.00 60.00

The reprints of Nos. 6 to 8 inclusive have a period instead of a colon after "SILBERGR."

Background of Crossed Lines

1858-60 Typo.

9 A4 4pf green 52.50 20.00

Engr.

10 A1 6pf (½sg) org ('59) 90.00 80.00

Typo.

11 A2 1sg rose 35.00 1.90
12 A2 2sg blue 80.00 11.00
a. 2sg dark blue 125.00 21.00
b. Half used as 1sg on cover
13 A2 3sg orange 60.00 9.00
a. 3sg yellow 65.00 11.00

Coat of Arms
A6 A7

1861-65 Embossed *Rouletted 11½*

14 A6 3pf red lilac ('65) 16.00 17.50
a. 3pf red violet ('65) 40.00 45.00
15 A6 4pf yel grn 6.50 5.75
a. 4pf green 18.00 8.00
16 A6 6pf orange 6.50 7.25
a. 6pf vermilion 60.00 30.00
17 A7 1sg rose 2.50 32
18 A7 2sg ultra 7.00 90
a. 2sg blue 275.00 25.00
20 A7 3sg bister 7.00 1.25
a. 3sg gray brown ('65) 225.00 21.00

A8 A9

Typographed in Reverse on Paper Resembling Goldbeater's Skin

1866 *Rouletted 10*

21 A8 10sg rose 35.00 60.00
22 A9 30sg blue 50.00 125.00

Perfect copies of Nos. 21 and 22 are extremely rare.

A10

1867 Embossed *Rouletted 16*

23 A10 1kr green 21.00 14.00
24 A10 2kr orange 37.50 30.00
25 A10 3kr rose 18.00 20.00
26 A10 6kr ultra 18.00 14.00
27 A10 9kr bister brown 18.00 20.00

Imperforate stamps of the above sets are proofs.
The stamps of Prussia were superseded by those of the North German Confederation on Jan. 1, 1868.

OFFICIAL STAMPS

For stamps formerly listed as Nos. O1-O15, see Germany Nos. OL1-OL15.

SAXONY

LOCATION — In central Germany
GOVT. — A former kingdom
AREA — 5,787 sq. mi.
POP. — 2,500,000 (approx.)
CAPITAL — Dresden

Saxony was a member of the German Confederation and became a part of the German Empire in 1870.

10 Pfennings = 1 Neu-Groschen
30 Neu-Groschen = 1 Thaler

> Values of Saxony stamps vary according to condition. Quotations for Nos. 1-14 are for fine copies. Very fine to superb specimens sell at much higher prices, and inferior or poor copies sell at reduced prices, depending on the condition of the individual specimen.
> Values for unused stamps are for copies with gum. Copies without gum sell for about half the figures quoted.

A1

1850 Unwmk. Typo. *Imperf.*

1 A1 3pf red *5,500. 5,000.*
a. 3pf dark red *10,000. 10,000.*

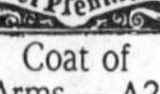
Coat of Arms — A2

Frederick Augustus II — A3

1851

2 A2 3pf green 70.00 37.50
a. 3pf yellow green 800.00 400.00

Nos. 2 and 2a with margins all around sell considerably higher.

1851-52 Engr.

3 A3 1/2ng black, *gray* 40.00 7.50
a. 1/2ng pale blue (error) *16,000.*
5 A3 1ng black, *rose* 40.00 6.00
6 A3 2ng black, *pale bl* 175.00 35.00
7 A3 2ng blk, *dk bl* ('52) 600.00 45.00
8 A3 3ng black, *yellow* 125.00 10.00

King John I — A4

1855-57

9 A4 1/2ng black, *gray* 8.00 1.75
a. "1/2" at left or right 375.00 200.00
10 A4 1ng black, *rose* 8.00 1.75
11 A4 2ng black, *blue* 10.00 14.00
a. 2ng black, *dark blue* 21.00 6.00
12 A4 3ng black, *yellow* 13.00 3.50
13 A4 5ng ver ('56) 70.00 22.50
a. 5ng orange brown ('56) 165.00 110.00
b. 5ng deep brown ('57) *750.00* 200.00
14 A4 10ng blue ('56) 250.00 165.00

The 1/2ng is found in 3 types, the 1ng in 2.
In 1861 the 5ng and 10ng were printed on hard, brittle, translucent paper.

A5

A6

Typo.; Arms Embossed

1863 *Perf. 13*

15 A5 3pf blue green 1.50 *9.00*
a. 3pf yellow green 8.00 *16.00*
16 A5 1/2ng orange 60 1.65
a. 1/2ng red orange 6.25 3.50
17 A6 1ng rose 75 90
a. Vert. pair, imperf. between *150.00*
b. Horiz. pair, imperf. between *275.00*
18 A6 2ng blue 1.65 3.50
a. 2ng dark blue 7.00 8.50
19 A6 3ng red brown 1.65 4.75
a. 3ng bister brown 5.00 2.75
20 A6 5ng dull violet 9.00 *22.50*
a. 5ng gray violet 9.00 *55.00*
b. 5ng gray blue 7.50 *20.00*
c. 5ng slate 40.00 *100.00*

The stamps of Saxony were superseded on Jan. 1, 1868, by those of the North German Confederation.

SCHLESWIG-HOLSTEIN

LOCATION — In northern Germany.
GOVT. — Former Duchies
AREA — 7,338 sq. mi.
POP. — 1,519,000 (approx.)
CAPITAL — Schleswig

Schleswig-Holstein was an autonomous territory from 1848 to 1851 when it came under Danish rule. In 1864, it was occupied by Prussia and Austria, and in 1866 it became a province of Prussia.

16 Schillings = 1 Mark

> Values of Schleswig-Holstein stamps vary according to condition. Quotations for Nos. 1-2, 15-17 are for fine copies. Very fine to superb specimens sell at much higher prices, and inferior or poor copies sell at reduced prices, depending on the condition of the individual specimen.
> Values for unused stamps are for copies with gum. Copies without gum sell for about half the figures quoted.

Coat of Arms — A1

Typographed; Arms Embossed

1850 Unwmk. *Imperf.*

With Silk Threads

1 A1 1s dl bl & grnsh bl 250.00 *3,500.*
a. 1s Prussian blue 425.00
2 A1 2s rose & pink 350.00 *4,250.*
a. 2s deep pink & rose 450.00
b. Double embossing 500.00

Forged cancellations are found on Nos. 1-2, 5-7, 9, 16 and 19.

A2

A3

1865 Typo. *Rouletted 11 1/2*

3 A2 1/2s rose 18.00 37.50
4 A2 1 1/4s green 8.00 9.50
5 A3 1 1/3s red lilac 40.00 *100.00*
6 A2 2s ultra 25.00 *165.00*
7 A3 4s bister 50.00 *1,000.*

Schleswig

A4

A5

1864 Typo. *Rouletted 11 1/2*

8 A4 1 1/4s green 25.00 9.00
9 A4 4s carmine 60.00 *325.00*

1865 *Rouletted 10, 11 1/2*

10 A4 1/2s green 25.00 50.00
11 A4 1 1/4s red lilac 30.00 10.00
a. 1 1/4s gray lilac ('67) 225.00 50.00
b. Half of #11a used as 1/2s on cover
12 A5 1 1/3s rose 25.00 50.00
13 A4 2s ultra 16.00 32.00
14 A4 4s bister 25.00 55.00

Holstein

A6

A7

Type I- Small lettering in frame. Wavy lines in spandrels close together.
Type II- Small lettering in frame. Wavy lines wider apart.
Type III- Larger lettering in frame and no periods after "H R Z G." Wavy lines as II.

1864 Litho. *Imperf.*

15 A6 1 1/4s bl & gray, I 45.00 32.50
a. Half used as 1/2s on cover *6,250.*
16 A6 1 1/4s bl & gray, II 400.00 *2,000.*
a. Half used as 1/2s on cover *22,500.*
17 A6 1 1/4s bl & gray, III 32.50 32.50
a. Half used as 1/2s on cover *7,000.*

1864 Typo. *Rouletted 8*

18 A7 1 1/4s blue & rose 30.00 12.00
a. Half used as 1/2s on cover *1,200.*

A8

1865 *Rouletted 8*

19 A8 1/2s green 50.00 85.00
20 A8 1 1/4s red lilac 35.00 13.00
21 A8 2s blue 42.50 35.00

A9

A10

1865-66 *Rouletted 7 and 8*

22 A9 1 1/4s red lilac ('66) 55.00 12.50
a. Half used as 1/2s on cover *3,000.*
23 A10 1 1/3s carmine 52.50 25.00
24 A9 2s blue ('66) 110.00 80.00
25 A10 4s bister 50.00 50.00

These stamps were superseded by those of North German Confederation on Jan. 1, 1868.

THURN AND TAXIS

30 Silbergroschen or Groschen = 1 Thaler

A princely house which, prior to the formation of the German Empire, enjoyed the privilege of a postal monopoly. These stamps were superseded on July 1, 1867, by those of Prussia, followed by those of the North German Postal District on Jan. 1, 1868, and later by stamps of the German Empire on Jan. 1, 1872.

> Values for unused stamps are for copies with gum. Copies without gum sell for about half the figures quoted.
> Values for the imperforate stamps are for fine to very copies with 3 margins. Stamps with 4 clear margins are scarce and command much higher prices.

Northern District

A1

A2

1852-58 Unwmk. Typo. *Imperf.*

1 A1 1/4sgr blk, *red brn* ('54) 125.00 55.00
2 A1 1/3sgr blk, *buff* ('58) 52.50 225.00
3 A1 1/2sgr blk, *green* 200.00 22.50
4 A1 1sgr blk, *dk bl* 325.00 50.00
5 A1 1sgr blk, *lt bl* ('53) 400.00 12.00
6 A1 2sgr blk, *rose* 300.00 14.00
7 A1 3sgr blk, *yellow* 250.00 12.00

Reprints of Nos. 1-12, 15-20, 23-24, were made in 1910. They have "ND" in script on the back. Value, $6 each.

1859-60

8 A1 1/4sgr red ('60) 30.00 35.00
9 A1 1/2sgr green 125.00 62.50
10 A1 1sgr blue 125.00 22.50
11 A1 2sgr rose ('60) 65.00 40.00
12 A1 3sgr red brn ('60) 65.00 52.50
13 A2 5sgr lilac 1.00 *250.00*
14 A2 10sgr orange 1.00 *575.00*

Excellent forged cancellations exist on Nos. 13 and 14. For reprints, see note after No. 7.

1862-63

15 A1 1/4sgr black ('63) 10.00 *35.00*
16 A1 1/3sgr green ('63) 12.00 *225.00*
17 A1 1/2sgr org yel 40.00 22.50
18 A1 1sgr rose ('63) 22.50 17.00
19 A1 2sgr blue ('63) 42.50 *45.00*
20 A1 3sgr bister ('63) 12.50 *21.00*

For reprints, see note after No. 7.

1865 *Rouletted*

21 A1 1/4sgr black 10.00 *525.00*
22 A1 1/3sgr green 12.50 *275.00*
23 A1 1/2sgr yellow 14.00 *30.00*
24 A1 1sgr rose 22.50 18.00
25 A1 2sgr blue 1.50 *50.00*
26 A1 3sgr bister 2.00 *17.50*

For reprints, see note after No. 7.

1866 *Rouletted in Colored Lines*

27 A1 1/4sgr black 1.25 *950.00*
28 A1 1/3sgr green 1.25 *700.00*
29 A1 1/2sgr yellow 1.25 *100.00*
30 A1 1sgr rose 1.25 *65.00*
a. Horizontal pair without rouletting between 85.00
b. Half used as 1/2sgr on cover *5,250.*
31 A1 2sgr blue 1.25 *750.00*
32 A1 3sgr bister 1.25 *125.00*

Forged cancellations on Nos. 2, 13-14, 15-16, 21-22, 25-32 are plentiful.

Southern District

60 Kreuzer = 1 Gulden

A1

A2

1852-53 Unwmk. *Imperf.*

42	A1	1kr blk, *lt grn*	90.00	12.00
43	A1	3kr blk, *dk bl*	350.00	22.50
44	A1	3kr blk, *bl* ('53)	400.00	9.50
45	A1	6kr blk, *rose*	300.00	13.00
46	A1	9kr blk, *yellow*	300.00	8.75

Reprints of Nos. 42-50, 53-56 were made in 1910. Each has "ND" in script on the back. Value, each $6.

1859

47	A1	1kr green	10.00	6.25
48	A1	3kr blue	250.00	16.00
49	A1	6kr rose	250.00	30.00
50	A1	9kr yellow	250.00	42.50
51	A2	15kr lilac	1.10	*105.00*
52	A2	30kr orange	1.10	*300.00*

Forged cancellations exist on Nos. 51 and 52. For reprints, see note after No. 46.

1862

53	A1	3kr rose	30.00	12.00
54	A1	6kr blue	7.25	13.00
55	A1	9kr bister	7.25	11.00

For reprints, see note after No. 46.

1865 *Rouletted*

56	A1	1kr green	11.00	11.00
57	A1	3kr rose	17.00	7.25
58	A1	6kr blue	1.50	*16.00*
59	A1	9kr bister	1.50	*17.50*

For reprint of No. 56, see note after No. 46.

1867 *Rouletted in Colored Lines*

60	A1	1kr green	1.40	*12.00*
61	A1	3kr rose	1.40	*20.00*
62	A1	6kr blue	1.40	*15.00*
63	A1	9kr bister	1.40	*22.50*

Forged cancellations exist on Nos. 51-52, 58-63.

The Thurn & Taxis Stamps, Northern and Southern Districts, were replaced on July 1, 1867, by those of Prussia.

WURTTEMBERG

LOCATION — In southern Germany
GOVT. — A former Kingdom
AREA — 7,530 sq. mi.
POP. — 2,580,000 (approx.)
CAPITAL — Stuttgart

Württemberg was a member of the German Confederation and became a part of the German Empire in 1870. It gave up its postal autonomy on March 31, 1902, but official stamps were issued until 1923.

16 Kreuzer = 1 Gulden
100 Pfennigs = 1 Mark (1875)

> Values of early Wurttemberg stamps vary according to condition. Quotations for Nos. 1-46 are for fine copies. Very fine to superb specimens sell at much higher prices, and inferior or poor copies sell at reduced prices, depending on the condition of the individual specimen.
>
> Values for Nos. 1-46 unused are for copies without gum. Copies with gum sell for about twice the figures quoted. Nos. 41-54 without gum sell for about half the prices.

A1

A1a

1851-52 Unwmk. Typo. *Imperf.*

1	A1	1kr blk, *buff*	265.00	40.00
a.		1kr black, *straw*	900.00	275.00
2	A1	3kr blk, *yellow*	150.00	2.75
a.		3kr black, *orange*	1,250.	150.00
4	A1	6kr blk, *yel grn*	600.00	17.50
a.		6kr black, *blue green*	1,300.	32.50
5	A1	9kr blk, *rose*	*3,750.*	17.50
6	A1a	18kr blk, *dl vio* ('52)	600.00	500.00

On the "reprints" the letters of "Württemberg" are smaller, especially the first "e"; the right branch of the "r's" of Württemberg runs upward in the reprints and downward in the originals.

Coat of Arms — A2

With Orange Silk Threads

1857 Typographed and Embossed

7	A2	1kr yel brn	180.00	60.00
a.		1kr dark brown	425.00	225.00
9	A2	3kr yel org	200.00	5.00
10	A2	6kr green	300.00	27.50
11	A2	9kr car rose	525.00	30.00
12	A2	18kr blue	750.00	475.00

Copies of Nos. 7-12 with margins all around sell considerably higher.

See Nos. 13-46, 53.

The reprints have red or yellow silk threads and are printed 2mm apart, while the originals are 3/4mm apart.

1859 Without Silk Threads

13	A2	1kr brown	250.00	50.00
a.		1kr dark brown	600.00	175.00
15	A2	3kr yel org	150.00	3.75
16	A2	6kr green	*3,750.*	57.50
17	A2	9kr car rose	675.00	37.50
18	A2	18kr dark blue	750.00	550.00

The colors of the reprints are brighter; they are also printed 2mm apart instead of 1 1/4mm.

1860 *Perf. 13 1/2*

19	A2	1kr brown	400.00	60.00
20	A2	3kr yel org	150.00	5.50
21	A2	6kr green	1,200.	40.00
22	A2	9kr carmine	600.00	90.00

1861 Thin Paper

23	A2	1kr brown	275.00	67.50
a.		1kr black brown	390.00	90.00
25	A2	3kr yel org	40.00	17.50
26	A2	6kr green	135.00	32.50
27	A2	9kr rose	350.00	100.00
a.		9kr claret	500.00	180.00
29	A2	18kr dark blue	550.00	550.00

Copies of Nos. 23-29 with all perforations intact sell considerably higher.

1862 *Perf. 10*

30	A2	1kr blk brn	200.00	200.00
31	A2	3kr yel org	200.00	27.50
32	A2	6kr green	195.00	70.00
33	A2	9kr claret	1,150.	550.00

1863

34	A2	1kr yel grn	22.50	6.00
a.		1kr green	150.00	47.50
36	A2	3kr rose	22.50	1.50
a.		3kr dark claret	550.00	225.00
37	A2	6kr blue	80.00	30.00
39	A2	9kr yel brn	225.00	60.00
a.		9kr red brown	125.00	30.00
b.		9kr black brown	300.00	75.00
40	A2	18kr orange	350.00	225.00

1866-68 *Rouletted 10*

41	A2	1kr yel grn	24.00	5.00
a.		1kr dark green	140.00	100.00
42	A2	3kr rose	13.00	1.50
a.		3kr claret	550.00	600.00
43	A2	6kr blue	125.00	30.00
44	A2	7kr slate bl ('68)	465.00	75.00
45	A2	9kr bis brn	425.00	40.00
a.		9kr red brown	365.00	40.00
46	A2	18kr orange	650.00	200.00

A3

1869-73 Typo. & Embossed

47	A3	1kr yel grn	8.00	1.25
48	A3	2kr orange	75.00	40.00
49	A3	3kr rose	8.00	75
50	A3	7kr blue	40.00	14.00
51	A3	9kr lt brn ('73)	50.00	20.00
52	A3	14kr orange	50.00	30.00
a.		14kr lemon yellow	1,000.	325.00

See No. 54.

1873 *Imperf.*

53	A2	70kr red violet	1,050.	1,100.
a.		70kr violet	1,650.	2,000.

Nos. 53 and 53a have single or double lines of fine black dots printed in the gutters between the stamps.

1874 *Perf. 11 1/2x11*

54	A3	1kr yellow green	40.00	32.50

A4

A5

1875-1900 Typo.

55	A4	2pf sl gray ('93)	1.65	48
56	A4	3pf green	6.50	1.00
57	A4	3pf brn ('90)	50	15
a.		Imperf. pair	90.00	
58	A4	5pf violet	8.00	35
59	A4	5pf grn ('90)	1.10	15
a.		5pf blue green	70.00	12.00
b.		Imperf., pair	90.00	
60	A4	10pf carmine	70	15
a.		10pf rose	40.00	40
b.		Imperf., pair	65.00	
61	A4	20pf ultra	70	15
a.		20pf dull blue	70	15
b.		Imperf., pair	85.00	
62	A4	25pf red brn	35.00	7.25
63	A4	25pf org ('90)	3.00	65
a.		Imperf., pair	80.00	
64	A5	30pf org & blk ('00)	3.50	2.00
65	A5	40pf dp rose & blk ('00)	3.50	3.50
66	A4	50pf gray	250.00	15.00
67	A4	50pf gray grn	25.00	2.00
68	A4	50pf pur brn ('90)	2.00	30
a.		50pf red brown	125.00	20.00
b.		Imperf., pair	100.00	
69	A4	2m yellow	450.00	200.00
70	A4	2m ver, *buff* ('79)	900.00	100.00
71	A5	2m org & blk ('86)	6.00	5.00
a.		2m yellow & black	175.00	15.00
b.		Imperf., pair	90.00	
		Telegraph cancel		1.75
72	A5	5m bl & blk ('81)	60.00	*100.00*
a.		Figure of value inverted		
		Telegraph cancel		45.00

No. 70 has "Unverkauflich" (not for sale) printed on its back to remind postal clerks that it, like No. 69, was for their use and not to be sold to the public.

The regular postage stamps of Württemberg were superseded by those of the German Empire in 1902. Official stamps were in use until 1923.

> Stamps for the Wurttemberg sector of the French Occupation Zone of Germany, issued 1947-1949, are listed under Germany, Occupation Issues.

OFFICIAL STAMPS

For the Communal Authorities

O1

Perf. 11 1/2x11

1875-1900 Typo. Unwmk.

O1	O1	2pf sl gray ('00)	1.00	45
O2	O1	3pf brn ('96)	1.00	16
O3	O1	5pf violet	20.00	1.00
a.		Imperf., pair		*1,750.*
O4	O1	5pf bl grn ('90)	1.50	16
a.		Imperf., pair	32.50	
O5	O1	10pf rose	4.75	16
a.		Imperf., pair	65.00	
O6	O1	25pf org ('00)	12.00	2.75
		Nos. O1-O6 (6)	40.25	4.68

See Nos. O12-O32. For overprints and surcharges see Nos. O7-O11, O40-O52, O59-O93.

> **Used Values**
>
> When italicized, used values for Nos. O7-O183 are for favor-canceled copies. Postally used copies command a premium.

Stamps of Previous Issues Overprinted in Black

1806 — 1906

1906, Jan. 30

O7	O1	2pf slate gray	40.00	65.00
O8	O1	3pf dk brn	14.00	7.50
O9	O1	5pf green	3.50	1.40
O10	O1	10pf deep rose	3.50	1.40
O11	O1	25pf orange	52.50	55.00
		Nos. O7-O11 (5)	113.50	130.30

Centenary of Kingdom of Württemberg.

Nos. O7-O11 also exist imperf. but it is doubtful if they were ever issued in that condition.

1906-21 Wmk. 116

O12	O1	2pf slate gray	30	15
O13	O1	2 1/2pf gray blk ('16)	30	15
O14	O1	3pf dk brn	30	15
O15	O1	5pf green	30	15
O16	O1	7 1/2pf org ('16)	30	15
O17	O1	10pf dp rose	30	15
O18	O1	10pf org ('21)	15	15
O19	O1	15pf yel brn ('16)	75	18
O20	O1	15pf purple ('17)	40	30
O21	O1	20pf dp ultra ('11)	30	15
O22	O1	20pf dp grn ('21)	15	15
O23	O1	25pf orange	30	15
O24	O1	25pf brn & blk ('17)	40	25
O25	O1	35pf brown ('19)	2.25	7.50
O26	O1	40pf rose red ('21)	15	15
O27	O1	50pf rose lake ('11)	8.00	5.00
O28	O1	50p vio brn ('21)	30	30
O29	O1	60pf olive grn ('21)	40	30
O30	O1	1.25m emerald ('21)	25	30
O31	O1	2m gray ('21)	25	30
O32	O1	3m brown ('21)	25	30
		Nos. O12-O32 (21)	16.10	16.38

No. O24 contains solid black numerals.

Nos. O12-O32 exist imperf. Value, each pair, $6-$16.

O3

Perf. 14 1/2x14

1916, Oct. 6 Typo. Unwmk.

O33	O3	2 1/2pf slate	2.75	*1.60*
O34	O3	7 1/2pf orange	1.90	*40*
O35	O3	10pf car rose	1.90	*40*
O36	O3	15pf yel brn	1.90	*40*
O37	O3	20pf blue	1.90	*40*
O38	O3	25pf gray blk	5.25	*1.25*
O39	O3	50pf red brn	9.25	*2.00*
		Nos. O33-O39 (7)	24.85	*6.45*

25th year of the reign of King Wilhelm II.

Stamps of 1900-06 Surcharged

25 Pf.

Perf. 11 1/2x11

1916, Sept. 10 Wmk. 116

O40	O1	25pf on 25pf org	2.25	2.25
a.		Without wmk.	25.00	

No. O13 Surcharged in Blue

2

1919 Wmk. 116

O42	O1	2pf on 2 1/2pf gray blk	75	1.25

Volksstaat

Official Stamps of 1906-19 Overprinted

Württemberg

1919

No.	Type	Description	Unused	Used
O43	O1	2½pf gray blk	15	20
O44	O1	3pf dk brn	6.25	2.25
O45	O1	5pf green	15	15
O46	O1	7½pf orange	30	20
O47	O1	10pf rose	15	15
O48	O1	15pf purple	15	15
O49	O1	20pf ultra	15	15
O50	O1	25pf brn & blk	15	15
O51	O1	35pf brown	2.75	35
O52	O1	50pf red brn	3.00	40
		Nos. O43-O52 (10)	13.20	4.15

Stag — O4

Perf. 14½

1920, Mar. 19 Litho. Wmk. 192

No.	Type	Description	Unused	Used
O53	O4	10pf maroon	70	75
O54	O4	15pf brown	70	75
O55	O4	20pf indigo	70	75
O56	O4	30pf deep green	70	75
O57	O4	50pf yellow	70	75
O58	O4	75pf bister	70	75
		Nos. O53-O58 (6)	4.20	4.50

Official Stamps of 1906-19 Overprinted **Deutsches Reich**

Perf. 11½x11

1920, Apr. 1 Wmk. 116

No.	Type	Description	Unused	Used
O59	O1	5pf green	3.50	3.00
O60	O1	10pf dp rose	2.25	1.75
O61	O1	15pf dp vio	1.90	1.75
O62	O1	20pf ultra	3.50	3.75
a.		Wmk. 192	5.00	5.00
O63	O1	50pf red brown	4.25	5.00
		Nos. O59-O63 (5)	15.40	15.25

Nos. O59 to O63 were available for official postage throughout all Germany but were used almost exclusively in Württemberg.

Stamps of 1917-21 Surcharged in Black, Red or Blue

1923

No.	Type	Description	Unused	Used
O64	O1	5m on 10pf org	15	15
O65	O1	10m on 15pf dp vio	15	15
O66	O1	12m on 40pf rose red	18	18
O67	O1	20m on 10pf org	15	18
O68	O1	25m on 20pf grn	15	15
O69	O1	40m on 20pf grn	18	25
O70	O1	50m on 60pf ol grn	15	15

Surcharged **60 Mark**

No.	Type	Description	Unused	Used
O71	O1	60m on 1.25m emer	15	15
O72	O1	100m on 40pf rose red	15	15
O73	O1	200m on 2m gray (R)	15	15
O74	O1	300m on 50pf red brn (Bl)	15	15
O75	O1	400m on 3m brn (Bl)	18	35
O76	O1	1000m on 60pf ol grn	18	30
O77	O1	2000m on 1.25m emer	18	15
		Nos. O64-O77 (14)	2.25	
		Set value		2.15

Abbreviations:
Th = (Tausend) Thousand
Mil = (Million) Million
Mlrd = (Milliarde) Billion

Surcharged **20 Tausend**

1923

No.	Type	Description	Unused	Used
O78	O1	5th m on 10pf org	18	22
O79	O1	20th m on 40pf rose red	18	15
O80	O1	50th m on 15pf vio	1.40	80
O81	O1	75th m on 2m gray	3.25	28
O82	O1	100th m on 20pf grn	15	28
O83	O1	250th m on 3m brn	15	15

Surcharged **2 Millionen**

No.	Type	Description	Unused	Used
O84	O1	1mil m on 60pf ol grn	1.10	80
O85	O1	2mil m on 50pf red brn	22	15
O86	O1	5mil m on 1.25m emer	32	32

Surcharged **10 Milliarden**

No.	Type	Description	Unused	Used
O87	O1	4 mlrd m on 50pf red brn	2.75	2.75
O88	O1	10 mlrd m on 3m brn	1.10	1.10
		Nos. O78-O88 (11)	10.80	7.00

No. O23 Surcharged with New Values in Rentenpfennig as **3**

1923, Dec.

No.	Type	Description	Unused	Used
O89	O1	3pf on 25pf orange	1.40	40
O90	O1	5pf on 25pf orange	22	15
O91	O1	10pf on 25pf orange	22	15
O92	O1	20pf on 25pf orange	45	45
O93	O1	50pf on 25pf orange	1.50	1.40
		Nos. O89-O93 (5)	3.79	2.55

For the State Authorities

O6

Perf. 11½x11

1881-1902 Typo. Unwmk.

No.	Type	Description	Unused	Used
O94	O6	2pf sl gray ('00)	38	22
O95	O6	3pf green	3.25	1.90
O96	O6	3pf dk brn ('90)	38	15
O97	O6	5pf violet	2.25	40
O98	O6	5pf grn ('90)	38	15
O99	O6	10pf rose	1.25	15
O100	O6	20pf ultra	38	15
O101	O6	25pf brown	8.75	2.00
O102	O6	25pf org ('90)	80	15
O103	O6	30pf org & blk ('02)	80	70
O104	O6	40pf dp rose & blk ('02)	80	70
O105	O6	50pf gray grn	16.00	3.50
O106	O6	50pf mar ('90)	80	40
a.		50pf red brown	145.00	625.00
O107	O6	1m yellow	90.00	150.00
O108	O6	1m vio ('90)	11.00	11.00

See Nos. O119-O135. For overprints and surcharges see Nos. O109-O118, O146-O164, O176-O183.

Overprinted in Black **1806 — 1906**

1906

No.	Type	Description	Unused	Used
O109	O6	2pf slate gray	32.50	42.50
O110	O6	3pf dk brn	6.00	3.50
O111	O6	5pf green	4.00	85
O112	O6	10pf dp rose	4.00	85
O113	O6	20pf ultra	4.00	2.00
O114	O6	25pf orange	12.00	8.50
O115	O6	30pf org & blk	12.00	8.50
O116	O6	40pf dp rose & blk	35.00	42.50
O117	O6	50pf red brown	35.00	42.50
O118	O6	1m purple	75.00	80.00
		Nos. O109-O118 (10)	219.50	231.70

Cent. of the kingdom of Wüttemberg.

Nos. O109 to O118 are also found imperforate, but it is doubtful if they were ever issued in that condition.

1906-19 Wmk. 116

No.	Type	Description	Unused	Used
O119	O6	2pf slate gray	28	15
O120	O6	2½pf gray blk ('16)	28	15
O121	O6	3pf dk brn	28	15
O122	O6	5pf green	28	15
O123	O6	7½pf orange ('16)	28	15
O124	O6	10pf deep rose	28	15
O125	O6	15pf yel brn ('16)	28	15
O126	O6	15pf purple ('17)	40	15
O127	O6	20pf ultra	28	15
O128	O6	25pf orange	28	15
O129	O6	25pf brn & blk ('17)	28	15
O130	O6	30pf org & blk	28	15
O131	O6	35pf brn ('19)	1.10	45
O132	O6	40pf dp rose & blk	28	15
O133	O6	50pf red brn	28	15
O134	O6	1m purple	1.90	2.50
O135	O6	1m sl & blk ('17)	1.90	1.10
		Nos. O119-O135 (17)	8.94	6.15

King Wilhelm II — O8

1916 Unwmk. Typo. *Perf. 14*

No.	Type	Description	Unused	Used
O136	O8	2½pf slate	2.75	70
O137	O8	7½pf orange	1.25	15
O138	O8	10pf carmine	1.25	32
O139	O8	15pf yel brn	1.25	15
O140	O8	20pf blue	1.25	25
O141	O8	25pf gray blk	2.75	32
O142	O8	30pf green	2.75	32
O143	O8	40pf claret	4.00	1.00
O144	O8	50pf red brn	6.25	1.50
O145	O8	1m violet	6.00	1.75
		Nos. O136-O145 (10)	29.50	6.46

25th year of the reign of King Wilhelm II.

Stamps of 1890-1906 Surcharged **25 Pf.**

1916-19 Wmk. 116 *Perf. 11½x11*

No.	Type	Description	Unused	Used
O146	O6	25pf on 25pf org	2.50	2.00
a.		Without watermark	35.00	20.00
O147	O6	50pf on 50pf red brn	2.50	1.10
a.		Inverted surcharge	30.00	

No. O120 Surcharged in Blue **2**

1919 Wmk. 116

No.	Type	Description	Unused	Used
O149	O6	2pf on 2½pf gray blk	90	70

Official Stamps of 1890-1919 Overprinted **Volksstaat Württemberg**

1919

No.	Type	Description	Unused	Used
O150	O6	2½pf gray blk	28	15
O151	O6	3pf dk brn	5.50	2.40
a.		Without watermark	62.50	
O152	O6	5pf green	18	15
O153	O6	7½pf orange	28	24
O154	O6	10pf rose	18	15
O155	O6	15pf purple	18	15
O156	O6	20pf ultra	20	15
O157	O6	25pf brn & blk	20	15
a.		Inverted overprint	70.00	100.00
O158	O6	30pf org & blk	45	15
a.		Inverted overprint	175.00	225.00
O159	O6	35pf brown	28	15
O160	O6	40pf rose & blk	32	18
O161	O6	50pf claret	32	24
O162	O6	1m sl & blk	70	48
		Nos. O150-O162 (13)	9.07	4.74

Nos. O151, O151a Surcharged in Carmine **75**

1920 Wmk. 116

No.	Type	Description	Unused	Used
O164	O6	75pf on 3pf dk brn	1.00	65
a.		Without watermark	27.50	

View of Stuttgart O9

Designs: 10pf, 50pf, 2.50m, 3m, View of Stuttgart. 15pf, 75pf, View of Ulm. 20pf, 1m, View of Tubingen. 30pf, 1.25m, View of Ellwangen.

Perf. 14½

1920, Mar. 25 Typo. Wmk. 192

No.	Type	Description	Unused	Used
O166	O9	10pf maroon	45	40
O167	O9	15pf brown	45	40
O168	O9	20pf indigo	45	40
O169	O9	30pf blue grn	45	40
O170	O9	50pf yellow	45	40
O171	O9	75pf bister	45	50
O172	O9	1m org red	45	50
O173	O9	1.25m dp vio	45	50
O174	O9	2.50m dk ultra	80	75
O175	O9	3m yel grn	80	75
		Nos. O166-O175 (10)	5.20	5.00

Official Stamps of 1906-19 Overprinted **Deutsches Reich**

1920 Wmk. 116 *Perf. 11½x11*

No.	Type	Description	Unused	Used
O176	O6	5pf green	20	38
O177	O6	10pf dp rose	15	15
O178	O6	15pf purple	15	15
O179	O6	20pf ultra	15	15
a.		Wmk. 192	65.00	85.00
O180	O6	30pf org & blk	15	20
O181	O6	40pf dp rose & blk	15	20

O182 O6 50pf red brn 15 *18*
O183 O6 1m slate & blk 15 *30*
Set value 75

The note after No. O63 will also apply to Nos. O176 to O183.

NORTH GERMAN CONFEDERATION

Northern District
30 Groschen = 1 Thaler
Southern District
60 Kreuzer = 1 Gulden
Hamburg
16 Schillings = 1 Mark

Unused values for Nos. 1-24 are for copies with original gum. Copies without gum sell for about half the figures quoted.

A1

A2

Rouletted 8 1/2 to 10, 11 to 12 1/2 and Compound

1868 Typo. Unwmk.

1	A1	1/4gr	red lilac	15.00	13.00
2	A1	1/3gr	green	7.50	2.00
3	A1	1/2gr	orange	15.00	90
4	A1	1gr	rose	9.00	30
b.		Half used as 1/2gr on cover			
5	A1	2gr	ultra	45.00	80
6	A1	5gr	bister	50.00	5.75
7	A2	1kr	green	16.00	6.75
8	A2	2kr	orange	32.50	27.50
9	A2	3kr	rose	32.50	1.50
10	A2	7kr	ultra	125.00	7.50
11	A1	18kr	bister	32.50	42.50

See Nos. 13-23.

Imperf

1a	A1	1/4gr	red lilac	105.00	*275.00*
2a	A1	1/3gr	green	47.50	*210.00*
3a	A1	1/2gr	orange	67.50	*300.00*
4a	A1	1gr	rose	35.00	*125.00*
5a	A1	2gr	ultra	140.00	*340.00*
6a	A1	5gr	bister	140.00	*300.00*
7a	A2	1kr	green	35.00	*60.00*
8a	A2	2kr	orange	105.00	42.50
9a	A2	3kr	rose	42.50	42.50
10a	A2	7kr	ultra	165.00	*340.00*
11a	A1	18kr	bister	165.00	*340.00*

A3

1868

12 A3 (1/2s) violet brown 60.00 25.00

See No. 24.

1869 ***Perf. 13 1/2x14***

13	A1	1/4gr	lilac	16.00	9.00
a.		1/4gr red violet		32.50	15.00
14	A1	1/3gr	green	3.00	65
15	A1	1/2gr	orange	3.00	45
16	A1	1gr	rose	2.50	40
17	A1	2gr	ultra	3.00	40
18	A1	5gr	bister	7.50	2.75
19	A2	1kr	green	12.00	6.00
20	A2	2kr	orange	35.00	*45.00*
21	A2	3kr	rose	6.00	80
22	A2	7kr	ultra	10.00	2.75
23	A2	18kr	bister	75.00	*775.00*

Counterfeit cancels exist on No. 23.

1869

24 A3 (1/2s) dull violet brown 2.00 2.50

A4

A5

25	A4	10gr	gray	300.00	400.00
		Pen cancellation			45.00
26	A5	30gr	blue	240.00	*900.00*
		Pen cancellation			*90.00*

Counterfeit cancels exist on No. 26.

See Germany designs A2, A3 and A8 for similar stamps.

OFFICIAL STAMPS

O1

1870 Unwmk. Typo. ***Perf. 14 1/2x14***

O1	O1	1/4gr	black & buff	24.00	45.00
O2	O1	1/3gr	black & buff	16.00	13.00
O3	O1	1/2gr	black & buff	2.25	2.25
O4	O1	1gr	black & buff	4.00	35
O5	O1	2gr	black & buff	6.00	2.50
O6	O1	1kr	black & gray	21.00	*250.00*
O7	O1	2kr	black & gray	60.00	*750.00*
O8	O1	3kr	black & gray	18.00	35.00
O9	O1	7kr	black & gray	35.00	*265.00*

Counterfeit cancels exist on Nos. O6-O9.

The stamps of the North German Confederation were replaced by those of the German Empire on Jan. 1, 1872.

GERMANY

LOCATION — In northern Europe bordering on the Baltic and North Seas
AREA — 182,104 sq. mi. (until 1945)
POP. — 67,032,242 (1946)
CAPITAL — Berlin

30 Silbergroschen or Groschen = 1 Thaler
60 Kreuzer = 1 Gulden
100 Pfennigs = 1 Mark (1875)
100 Pfennigs = 1 Deutsche Mark (1948)

Catalogue values for unused stamps in this country are for Never Hinged items, beginning with Scott 722 in the regular postage section, Scott B338 in the semi-postal section, Scott C61 in the airpost section, Scott 9N103 in the Berlin regular postage section and Scott 9NB12 in the Berlin semi-postal section.

Watermarks

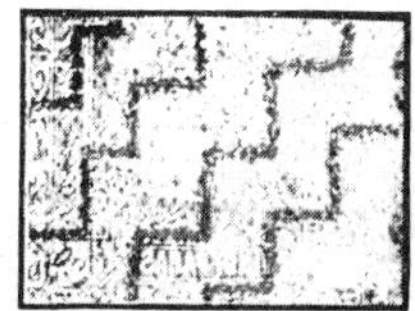
Wmk. 48- Diagonal Zigzag Lines

Wmk. 116- Crosses and Circles

Wmk. 125- Lozenges

Wmk. 126- Network

Wmk. 127- Quatrefoils

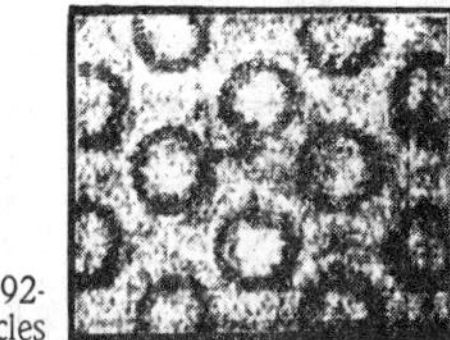
Wmk. 192- Circles

Wmk. 223- Eagle

Wmk. 237- Swastikas

Wmk. 241- Cross

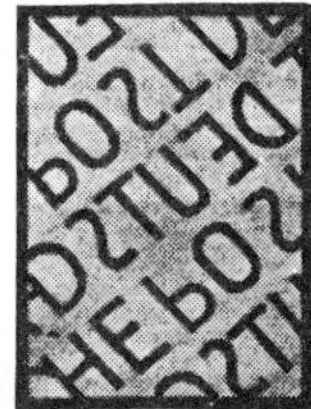
Wmk. 284- "DEUTSCHE POST" Multiple

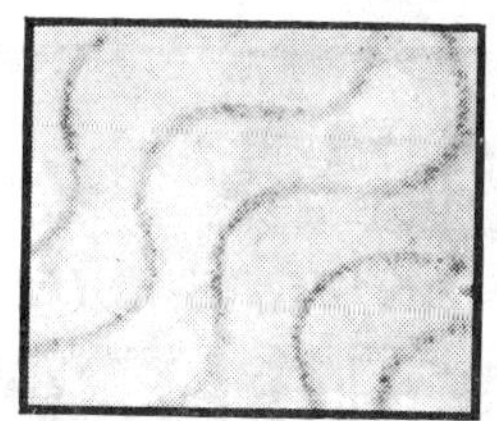
Wmk. 285- Marbleized Pattern

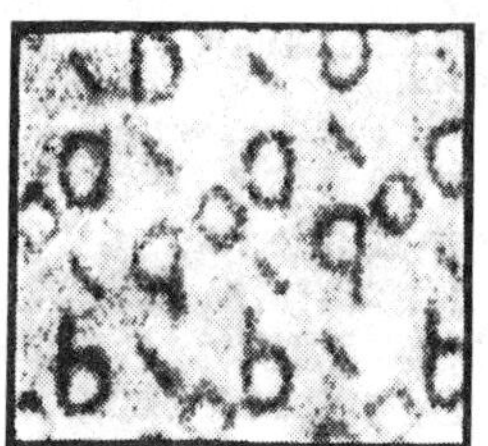
Wmk. 286- D P Multiple

Wmk. 292- Flowers, Multiple

Wmk. 295- B P and Zigzag Lines

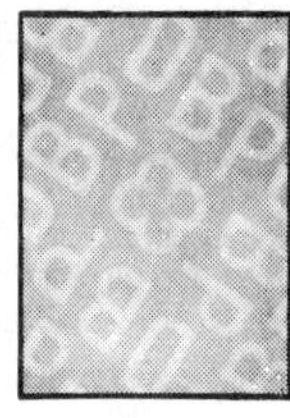
Wmk. 304- DBP and Rosettes Multiple

Empire

Values of early German Empire stamps vary according to condition. Quotations for Nos. 1-28 are for fine copies. Very fine to superb specimens sell at much higher prices, and inferior or poor copies sell at reduced prices, depending on the condition of the individual specimen.

Unused values for Nos. 1-13 are for stamps with original gum. Copies without gum sell at lower prices.

Imperial Eagle — A1

Typographed, Center Embossed

1872 Unwmk. ***Perf. 13 1/2x14 1/2***

Eagle with small shield

1	A1	1/4gr	violet	140.00	55.00
2	A1	1/3gr	green	300.00	25.00
a.		Imperf.			
3	A1	1/2gr	red orange	850.00	27.50
a.		1/2gr orange yellow		675.00	30.00
4	A1	1gr	rose	200.00	4.00
a.		Imperf.			
5	A1	2gr	ultra	650.00	7.50
a.		Imperf.			*8,500.*
6	A1	5gr	bister	425.00	57.50
a.		Imperf.			*8,500.*
7	A1	1kr	green	350.00	40.00
8	A1	2kr	orange	25.00	*100.00*
a.		2kr red orange		325.00	175.00
9	A1	3kr	rose	400.00	7.00
10	A1	7kr	ultra	1,250.	55.00
11	A1	18kr	bister	400.00	275.00

Values for imperforates are for copies postmarked at Leipzig (1/3gr), Coblenz (1gr), Huengen (2gr) and Leutersdorf (5gr).

A2

A3

1872 Typo. *Perf. 14½x13½*

12	A2	10gr gray	75.00	*1,000.*
		Pen cancellation		80.00
13	A3	30gr blue	110.00	*2,500.*
		Pen cancellation		*275.00*

For similar designs see A8, North German Confederation A4, A5.

A4

A5

1872
Center Embossed
Perf. 13½x14½
Eagle with large shield

14	A4	¼gr violet	42.50	57.50
15	A4	⅓gr yellow green	20.00	9.00
a.		½gr blue green	90.00	75.00
16	A4	½gr orange	27.50	3.25
a.		Imperf.		
17	A4	1gr rose	25.00	1.50
a.		Imperf.		*8,500.*
b.		Half used as ½gr on cover		*42,500.*
18	A4	2gr ultra	12.50	3.00
19	A4	2½gr orange brn	1,350.	37.50
a.		2½gr lilac brown	*5,250.*	250.00
20	A4	5gr bister	20.00	14.00
a.		Imperf.		*7,750.*
21	A4	1kr yellow green	22.50	20.00
a.		1kr blue green	125.00	150.00
22	A4	2kr orange	350.00	*1,750.*
23	A4	3kr rose	17.50	4.00
24	A4	7kr ultra	22.50	*50.00*
25	A4	9kr red brown	175.00	110.00
a.		9kr lilac brown	1,400.	300.00
26	A4	18kr bister	26.00	*1,500.*

Values for Nos. 17a and 20a are for copies postmarked at Potsdam (1gr), Damgarten or Anklam (5gr).

#14-26 with embossing inverted are fraudulent.

1874

Brown Surcharge

27	A5	2½gr on 2½gr brn	27.50	24.00
28	A5	9kr on 9kr brown	55.00	*170.00*

A6

A7

"Pfennige"

1875-77 Typo.

29	A6	3pf green	45.00	3.50
30	A6	5pf violet	80.00	1.00

Center Embossed

31	A7	10pf rose	30.00	20
32	A7	20pf ultra	175.00	75
33	A7	25pf red brown	325.00	12.00
34	A7	50pf gray	525.00	9.50
35	A7	50pf slate grn ('77)	2,000.	12.00

See Nos. 37-42. For surcharges see Offices in Turkey Nos. 1-6.

A8

1875-90 Typo. *Perf. 14½x13½*

36	A8	2m rose lilac ('90)	60.00	2.00
a.		2m purple	325.00	9.00
b.		2m dull violet	360.00	27.50

Types of 1875-77, "Pfennig" without final "e"

1880-83 *Perf. 13½x14½*

37	A6	3pf green	1.65	30
a.		Imperf.		
38	A6	5pf violet	1.25	38

Center Embossed

39	A7	10pf rose	8.00	15
a.		Imperf.	*350.00*	
40	A7	20pf ultra	5.50	15
41	A7	25pf orange brown	12.50	1.65
a.		25pf red brown ('83)	150.00	2.50
42	A7	50pf dp olive grn	6.50	50
a.		50pf gray green	6.50	50

Values for Nos. 37-42 are for stamps on thin paper. Those on thick paper sell for considerably more.

A9

A10

1889-1900 *Perf. 13½x14½*

45	A9	2pf gray ('00)	30	38
a.		"REIGHSPOST"	75.00	95.00
46	A9	3pf brown	1.90	15
a.		3pf yellow brown	8.00	35
b.		Imperf.	130.00	
c.		3pf reddish brown	50.00	10.00
47	A9	5pf green	90	15
48	A10	10pf carmine	1.50	15
a.		Imperf.	250.00	
49	A10	20pf ultra	7.50	15
a.		20pf Prus blue	350.00	45.00
50	A10	25pf orange ('90)	30.00	85
a.		Imperf.	165.00	
51	A10	50pf chocolate	24.00	15
a.		50pf copper brown	250.00	14.00
b.		Imperf.		
		Nos. 45-51 (7)	66.10	1.98

For surcharges and overprints see Offices in China Nos. 1-6, 16, Offices in Morocco 1-6, Offices in Turkey 8-12.

Germania — A11

1900, Jan. 1 *Perf. 14*

52	A11	2pf gray	35	15
a.		Imperf.	315.00	
53	A11	3pf brown	35	15
a.		Imperf.	250.00	
54	A11	5pf green	90	15
55	A11	10pf carmine	1.50	15
a.		Imperf.	62.50	
56	A11	20pf ultra	5.50	15
57	A11	25pf orange & blk, *yel*	10.50	1.50
58	A11	30pf orange & blk, *sal*	16.00	38
59	A11	40pf lake & black	20.00	75
60	A11	50pf pur & blk, *sal*	20.00	50
61	A11	80pf lake & blk, *rose*	27.50	1.40
		Nos. 52-61 (10)	102.60	5.28

Early printings of Nos. 57-61 had "REICHSPOST" in taller and thicker letters than on the ordinary stamps.

For surcharges see Nos. 65B, Offices in China 17-32, Offices in Morocco 7-15, 32A, Offices in Turkey 13-20, 25-27.

"REICHSPOST" Larger

57a	A11	25pf	*1,300.*	*2,500.*
58a	A11	30pf	*1,300.*	*2,500.*
59a	A11	40pf	*1,300.*	*2,500.*
60a	A11	50pf	*1,300.*	*2,500.*
61a	A11	80pf	*1,300.*	*2,500.*

General Post Office in Berlin — A12

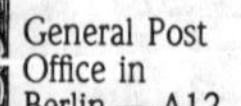

"Union of North and South Germany" A13

Unveiling Kaiser Wilhelm I Memorial, Berlin — A14

Wilhelm II Speaking at Empire's 25th Anniversary Celebration A15

Two types of 5m:
I - "5" is thick; "M" has slight serifs.
II - "5" thinner; "M" has distinct serifs.

Engr. *Perf. 14½x14*

62	A12	1m carmine rose	60.00	1.25
a.		Imperf.	*1,300.*	
63	A13	2m gray blue	60.00	2.75
64	A14	3m black violet	90.00	30.00
65	A15	5m slate & car, I	700.00	500.00
65A	A15	5m slate & car, II	275.00	225.00

Nos. 62-65 exist perf. 11½.

No. 65 exists with misaligned vignette. White paint was applied to the inner frame. Sometimes red was also used to retouch the vignette. Values, about ⅓ those of No. 65.

For surcharges see Offices in China Nos. 33-36A, Offices in Morocco 16-19A, Offices in Turkey 21-24B, 28-30.

Half of No. 54 Handstamp Surcharged in Violet **3PF**

1901 *Perf. 14*

65B	A11	3pf on half of 5pf	*6,500.*	*8,000.*

This provisional was produced at New Orleans when the German cruiser Vineta anchored there. The purser, with the ship commander's approval, surcharged and bisected 300 5pf stamps so the ship's post office could meet the need for a 3pf (printed matter rate). The crew wanted to send home newspapers reporting celebrations of the Kaiser's birthday.

A16

1902 Typo.

65C	A16	2pf gray	1.75	24
66	A16	3pf brown	1.00	15
a.		"DFUTSCHES"	8.00	*35.00*
67	A16	5pf green	2.75	15
68	A16	10pf carmine	6.75	15
69	A16	20pf ultra	26.00	18
70	A16	25pf org & blk, *yel*	42.50	1.40
71	A16	30pf org & blk, *sal*	47.50	55
72	A16	40pf lake & blk	65.00	85
73	A16	50pf pur & blk, *buff*	60.00	1.25
74	A16	80pf lake & blk, *rose*	100.00	2.25
		Nos. 65C-74 (10)	353.25	7.17

Nos. 65C-74 exist imperf. Value, set $2,000.

See Nos. 80-91, 118-119, 121-132, 169, 174, 210. For surcharges see Nos. 133-136, B1, Offices in China 37-42, 47-52, Offices in Morocco 20-28, 33-41, 45-53, Offices in Turkey 31-38, 43-50, 55-59.

A17

A18

A19

A20

Engr. *Perf. 14½*

75 A17 1m carmine rose	165.00	1.00
a. Imperf.	925.00	
76 A18 2m gray blue	85.00	70.00
77 A19 3m black violet	75.00	12.50
a. Imperf.	925.00	
78 A20 5m slate & car	125.00	15.00
a. Imperf.	925.00	

See Nos. 92, 94-95, 102, 111-113. For surcharges see Nos. 115-116, Offices in China 43, 45-46, 53, 55-56, Offices in Morocco 29, 31-32, 42, 44, 54, 56-57, Offices in Turkey 39, 41-42, 51, 53-54.

A21

79 A21 2m gray blue	75.00	2.00
a. Imperf.	925.00	

See Nos. 93, 114. For surcharges see Nos. 117, Offices in China 44, 54, Offices in Morocco 30, 43, 55, Offices in Turkey 40, 52.

1905-19 Typo. Wmk. 125 *Perf. 14*

80 A16 2pf gray	1.50	1.50
81 A16 3pf brown	25	15
82 A16 5pf green	15	15
b. Bklt. pane of 5 + label	400.00	
c. Bklt. pane of 4 + 2 labels	350.00	
d. Bklt. pane of 2 + 4 labels	350.00	
e. Bklt. pane, #82 + 5 #83	130.00	
f. Bklt. pane, 2 #82 + 4 #83	30.00	
g. Bklt. pane, 4 #82 + 2 #83	30.00	
83 A16 10pf carmine	75	15
b. Bklt. pane of 5 + label	775.00	
c. Bklt. pane of 4 + 2 labels	425.00	
84 A16 20pf blue vio ('18)	25	15
a. 20pf light blue	10.50	3.25
b. 20pf ultramarine	8.00	8.75
c. Imperf.	350.00	775.00
d. Half used as 10pf on cover		100.00
85 A16 25pf org & blk, *yel*	40	15
86 A16 30pf org & blk, *buff*	20	15
a. 30pf org & blk, *cr*	16.00	27.50
87 A16 40pf lake & black	85	15
88 A16 50pf pur & blk, *buff*	30	15
89 A16 60pf magenta ('11)	1.50	18
a. 60pf red violet	12.00	8.00
90 A16 75pf green & blk ('19)	15	15
91 A16 80pf lake & blk, *rose*	1.00	50

Engr.

92 A17 1m carmine rose	2.50	38
a. 1m carmine red	45.00	1.50
93 A21 2m brt blue	5.00	3.75
a. 2m gray blue	45.00	2.50
94 A19 3m violet gray	1.50	2.00
a. 3m black violet ('11)	47.50	22.50
95 A20 5m slate & car	1.50	1.75
a. Center inverted	*75,000.*	*100,000.*
Nos. 80-95 (16)	17.80	11.41

Pre-war printings of Nos. 80-95 have brighter colors and white instead of yellow gum. They sell for considerably more than the wartime printings which are valued here.

Labels in No. 82c contain an "X." The version with advertising is worth 3 times as much. No. 82f has three 10pf stamps in the top row. The version with 3 on the bottom row is worth 4 times as much.

Surcharged and overprinted stamps of designs A16-A22 are listed under Allenstein, Belgium, Danzig, France, Latvia, Lithuania, Marienwerder, Memel, Poland, Romania, Saar and Upper Silesia.

A22

1916-19 **Typo.**

96 A22 2pf lt gray ('18)	15	*2.00*
97 A22 2½pf lt gray	22	15
98 A22 7½pf red orange	18	15
b. Bklt. pane, 4 #98 + 2 #100	165.00	
c. Bklt. pane, 2 #98 + 4 #99	165.00	
d. Bklt. pane, 2 #98 + 4 #100	165.00	
e. Bklt. pane, 2 #82 + 4 #98	32.50	
f. 7½pf yel org	5.00	50
99 A22 15pf yellow brown	3.75	35
100 A22 15pf dk violet ('17)	15	15
b. Bklt. pane, 4 #82 + 2 #100	165.00	
c. Bklt. pane, 2 #83 + 4 #100	19.00	
101 A22 35pf red brown ('19)	15	35
Nos. 96-101 (6)	4.60	*3.15*

See No. 120. For surcharge see No. B2.

Nos. 98e and 100c have the 2 stamps first in the bottom row.

Type of 1902

1920 Engr. Wmk. 192 *Perf. 14½*

102 A19 3m black violet	1,500.	*1,900.*

Republic
National Assembly Issue

A23

A24

Rebuilding Germany — A25

Designs: A23, Live Stump of Tree Symbolizing that Germany will Survive her Difficulties. A24, New Shoots from Oak Stump Symbolical of New Government.

Perf. 13x13½

1919-20 Unwmk. Typo.

105 A23 10pf carmine rose	15	30
106 A24 15pf choc & blue	15	30
107 A25 25pf green & red	15	30
108 A25 30pf red vio & red ('20)	15	30
Set value	48	

Nos. 107-108 exist with date reading "1019" instead of "1919."

Types of 1902

Perf. 15x14½

1920 Wmk. 125 Offset

111 A17 1m red	1.50	35
112 A17 1.25m green	1.40	25
113 A17 1.50m yellow brown	16	22
114 A21 2.50m lilac rose	15	20
a. 2.50m magenta	1.10	35
b. 2.50m brown lilac	50	40

Nos. 111, 112 and 113 differ from the illustration in many minor respects. The numerals of Nos. 75 and 92 are outlined, with shaded background. Those of No. 111 are plain, with solid background and flags have been added to the top of the building, at right and left.

Types of 1902 Surcharged

* 1,25 m. *

1920 Engr. *Perf. 14½*

115 A17 1.25m on 1m green	35	*5.00*
116 A17 1.50m on 1m orange brn	35	*5.00*
117 A21 2.50m on 2m lilac rose	7.50	*150.00*

Germania Types of 1902-16

1920 Typo. *Perf. 14, 14½*

118 A16 5pf brown	15	15
119 A16 10pf orange	15	15
a. Tête bêche pair	65	*2.25*
d. Bklt. pane, 4 #119 + 2 #123	1.75	
120 A22 15pf violet brn	15	15
a. Imperf.	50.00	
c. Bklt. pane, 4 #84 + 2 #120	10.00	
121 A16 20pf green	15	15
a. Imperf.		125.00
123 A16 30pf dull blue	15	15
a. Tête bêche pair	65	*2.25*
d. Bklt. pane, 2 #123 + 4 #124	1.75	
124 A16 40pf carmine rose	15	15
a. Tête bêche pair	65	*2.25*
b. Imperf.	175.00	325.00
d. Bklt. pane, 2 #124 + 4 #126	2.25	
125 A16 50pf red lilac	65	50
126 A16 60pf olive green	15	15
a. Tête bêche pair	80	*4.00*
c. Imperf.	175.00	
127 A16 75pf red violet	15	20
128 A16 80pf blue violet	15	18
a. Imperf.	175.00	
129 A16 1m violet & grn	15	18
a. Imperf.	85.00	
130 A16 1¼m ver & mag	15	20
131 A16 2m carmine & bl	65	20
132 A16 4m black & rose	15	20
Set value	2.00	2.25

Stamps of 1920 Surcharged:

1,60 M No. 133 — 5 Mark No. 135

3 M 3 Nos. 134, 136

1921, Aug.

133 A16 1.60m on 5pf	15	28
134 A16 3m on 1¼m	15	28
135 A16 5m on 75pf (G)	15	28
136 A16 10m on 75pf	30	45
Set value	56	

In 1920 the current stamps of Bavaria were overprinted "Deutsches Reich". These stamps were available for postage throughout Germany, but because they were used almost exclusively in Bavaria, they are listed among the issues of that state.

A26

Iron Workers — A27

Miners A28

Farmers A29

Post Horn — A30

Numeral of Value — A31

Plowing — A32

Wmk. Lozenges (125)

1921 Typo. *Perf. 14*

137 A26 5pf claret	15	15
138 A26 10pf olive green	15	15
a. Tête bêche pair	70	*5.00*
b. Bklt. pane, 5 #138 + 1 #141	5.50	
139 A26 15pf grnsh blue	15	15
140 A26 25pf dark brown	15	15
141 A26 30pf blue green	15	15
a. Tête bêche pair	70	*5.00*
b. Bklt. pane, 2 #124 + 4 #141	3.00	
142 A26 40pf red orange	15	15
143 A26 50pf violet	40	50
144 A27 60pf red violet	15	15
145 A27 80pf carmine rose	15	*2.50*
146 A28 100pf yellow grn	38	*1.10*
147 A28 120pf ultra	15	18
148 A29 150pf orange	25	*75*
149 A29 160pf slate grn	15	*3.75*
150 A30 2m dp vio & rose	25	*1.25*
151 A30 3m red & yel	25	*5.00*
152 A30 4m dp grn & yel grn	15	*85*

Engr.

153 A31 5m brown orange	30	*38*
154 A31 10m carmine rose	50	*75*
155 A32 20m indigo & grn	1.10	*1.00*
a. Green background inverted	175.00	*500.00*
Set value	4.00	

See Nos. 156-209, 211, 222-223, 225, 227. For surcharges and overprints see Nos. 241-245, 247-248, 261-262, 273-276, B6-B7, O24.

1922 Litho. *Perf. 14½x14*

156 A31 100m brown vio, *buff* 24 25
157 A31 200m rose, *buff* 15 25
158 A31 300m green, *buff* 15 15
159 A31 400m bis brn, *buff* 40 *85*
160 A31 500m orange, *buff* 15 25
Nos. 156-160 (5) 1.09 *1.75*

Postally Used vs. CTO

Values quoted for canceled copies of the 1921-1923 issues are for postally used stamps. These bring higher prices than the plentiful canceled-to-order specimens made by applying genuine handstamps to remainders. C.T.O. examples sell for about the same price as unused stamps. Certification of postal usage by competent authorities is necessary.

Perf. 14, 14½

1921-22 Typo. Wmk. 126

161 A26 5pf claret 50 *140.00*
162 A26 10pf olive grn 2.00 *115.00*
163 A26 15pf grnsh blue 40 *130.00*
164 A26 25pf dark brown 15 *2.00*
165 A26 30pf blue green 65 *250.00*
166 A26 40pf red orange 15 *2.50*
167 A26 50pf violet ('21) 15 15
168 A27 60pf red violet 15 *16.00*
169 A16 75pf red violet 30 *1.65*
170 A26 75pf deep ultra 15 *1.65*
171 A27 80pf car rose 30 *47.50*
172 A28 100pf yellow green 15 15
a. Imperf. 45.00
173 A28 120pf ultra 65 *65.00*
174 A16 1¼m ver & mag 25 *50*
175 A29 150pf orange 15 15
a. Imperf. 3.50
176 A29 160pf slate green 75 *125.00*
177 A30 2m violet & rose 15 15
178 A30 3m red & yel ('21) 25 15
a. Imperf. 10.00
179 A30 4m dp grn & yel grn 15 22
180 A30 5m orange & yel 15 15
a. Imperf. 150.00
181 A30 10m car & pale rose 15 15
a. Pale rose (background) omitted 21.00
182 A30 20m violet & org 18 20
183 A30 30m brown & yel 15 15
184 A30 50m dk green & vio 15 15
Set value 7.15

1922-23

SIX MARKS:
Type I - Numerals upright.
Type II - Numerals leaning toward the right and slightly thinner.

EIGHT MARKS:
Type I - Numerals 2½mm wide with thick strokes.
Type II - Numerals 2mm wide with thinner strokes.

185 A30 2m deep violet 15 15
a. Imperf. 110.00
186 A30 3m red 15 15
187 A30 4m dark green 15 15
a. Imperf. 2.50
188 A30 5m orange 15 15
a. Imperf. 110.00
189 A30 6m dark blue (II) 15 15
a. 6m dark blue (I) 15 25
b. Imperf. 110.00
190 A30 8m olive green (I) 15 15
a. 8m olive green (II) 35 *17.50*
191 A30 20m dk violet ('23) 15 15
192 A30 30m dp brown ('23) 20 *3.75*
193 A30 40m lt green 15 15

Engr.

194 A31 5m brown orange 25 25
a. Imperf. 150.00
195 A31 10m carmine rose 65 75
196 A32 20m indigo & grn 15 1.25
a. Imperf. 150.00
b. Green background inverted 14.00 *140.00*
Set value 1.65

1922-23 Litho. *Perf. 14½x14*

198 A31 50m indigo 15 25
199 A31 100m brn vio, *buff* ('23) 28 38
200 A31 200m rose, *buff* ('23) 15 15
201 A31 300m grn, *buff* ('23) 15 15
202 A31 400m bis brn, *buff* ('23) 15 15
203 A31 500m org, *buff* ('23) 15 15
204 A31 1000m gray ('23) 15 15
205 A31 2000m blue ('23) 15 18
206 A31 3000m brown ('23) 15 18
207 A31 4000m violet ('23) 15 20
a. Imperf. 27.50
208 A31 5000m gray green ('23) 50 50
a. Imperf. 40.00
209 A31 100,000m vermilion ('23) 15 25
a. Imperf. 72.50
Set value 1.65

1920-22 Wmk. 127 Typo.

210 A16 1¼m ver & mag 325.00 350.00
211 A30 50m grn & vio ('22) 1.10 *350.00*

Wmk. 127 was intended for use only in printing revenue stamps.

Arms of Munich — A33

Wmk. Network (126)

1922, Apr. 22 Typo. *Perf. 13x13½*

212 A33 1¼m claret 15 25
213 A33 2m dark violet 15 25
214 A33 3m vermilion 22 32
215 A33 4m deep blue 18 32

Wmk. Lozenges (125)

216 A33 10m brown, *buff* 32 75
217 A33 20m deep rose, *pink* 2.50 6.00
Nos. 212-217 (6) 3.52 7.89

Munich Industrial Fair.

Type of 1921 and

Miners — A34

A35

1922-23 Wmk. 126 *Perf. 14*

221 A34 5m orange 15 *8.25*
222 A29 10m dull blue ('22) 15 15
223 A29 12m vermilion ('22) 15 15
224 A34 20m red lilac 15 15
225 A29 25m olive brown 15 15
226 A34 30m olive green 15 *32*
227 A29 40m green 15 15
228 A34 50m grnsh blue 35 *80.00*
229 A35 100m violet 15 15
230 A35 200m carmine rose 15 22
231 A35 300m green 15 22
232 A35 400m dark brown 15 *3.25*
233 A35 500m red orange 15 *3.25*
234 A35 1000m slate 15 25
Set value 1.15

The 50m was issued only in vertical coils.
Nos. 222-223 exist imperf.
For surcharges and overprints see Nos. 246, 249-260, 263-271, 277, 310, B5, O22-O23, O25-O28.

Wartburg Castle — A36

Cathedral of Cologne — A37

1923 Engr.

237 A36 5000m deep blue 25 *1.25*
a. Imperf. 325.00
238 A37 10,000m olive green 20 *1.65*

Abbreviations:
Th = (Tausend) Thousand
Mil = (Million) Million
Mlrd = (Milliarde) Billion

A38

1923 Typo.

238A A38 5th m grnsh blue 15 *10.00*
b. Imperf. 100.00
239 A38 50th m bister 15 25
a. Imperf. 18.00
240 A38 75th m dark violet 15 *6.50*
Set value 24
Set, never hinged 90

For surcharges see Nos. 272, 278.

Stamps and Types of 1922-23 Surcharged in Black, Blue or Green with Bars over Original Value

8 Tausend

1923 Wmk. Lozenges (125) *Perf. 14*

241 A26 8th m on 30pf 15 35
a. "8" inverted 22.50 *275.00*

Wmk. Network (126)

242 A26 5th m on 40pf 15 *75*
242A A26 8th m on 30pf 22.50 *3,750.*
243 A29 15th m on 40m 15 35
244 A29 20th m on 12m 15 35
a. Inverted surcharge
245 A29 20th m on 25m 15 *2.00*
246 A35 20th m on 200m 15 35
a. Inverted surcharge 85.00 165.00
247 A29 25th m on 25m 15 *12.50*
248 A29 30th m on 10m dp bl 15 35
a. Inverted surcharge 150.00
249 A35 30th m on 200m pale bl (Bl) 15 35
a. Without surcharge 165.00
250 A35 75th m on 300m yel grn 15 *12.50*
a. Imperf. 15.00 *42.50*
251 A35 75th m on 400m yel grn 15 35
252 A35 75th m on 1000m yel grn 15 35
a. Without surcharge 165.00
253 A35 100th m on 100m 15 *75*
a. Double surcharge 22.50
b. Inverted surcharge 15.00
254 A35 100th m on 400m bluish grn (G) 15 35
a. Imperf. 62.50
b. Without surcharge 165.00
255 A35 125th m on 1000m sal 15 35
256 A35 250th m on 200m 15 *3.50*
a. Inverted surcharge 27.50
b. Double surcharge 50.00
257 A35 250th m on 300m dp grn 15 *12.50*
a. Inverted surcharge 21.00
258 A35 250th m on 400m 15 *12.50*
a. Inverted surcharge 27.50
259 A35 250th m on 500m pink 15 35
a. Imperf. 62.50
260 A35 250th m on 500m red org 15 *10.50*
a. Double surcharge 21.00
b. Inverted surcharge 37.50
261 A26 800th m on 5pf lt grn (G) 15 *3.50*
a. Imperf. 8.50
262 A26 800th m on 10pf lt grn (G) 15 *4.25*
263 A35 800th m on 200m 15 *42.50*
a. Double surcharge 85.00
b. Inverted surcharge 50.00
264 A35 800th m on 300m lt grn (G) 15 *4.25*
a. Black surcharge 21.00
265 A35 800th m on 400m dk brn 15 *12.50*
a. Inverted surcharge 67.50
b. Double surcharge 70.00
266 A35 800th m on 400m lt grn (G) 15 *3.00*
267 A35 800th m on 500m lt grn (G) 15 *1,050.*
a. 800th m on 500m red org (Bk) 21.00
268 A35 800th m on 1000m lt grn (G) 15 35
269 A35 2mil m on 200m rose red 15 25
b. 2mil m on 200m car rose (#230) *500.00*
270 A35 2mil m on 300m dp grn 15 *85*
a. Inverted surcharge 67.50
b. Double surcharge 85.00
271 A35 2mil m on 500m dl rose 15 *4.25*
272 A38 2mil m on 5th m dl rose 15 35
b. Imperf. 42.50

Nos. 264a, 267a were not put in use.

Serrate Roulette 13½

273 A26 400th m on 15pf bis (Br) 15 *2.00*
a. Imperf. 77.50
274 A26 400th m on 25pf bis (Br) 15 *2.00*
a. Imperf. *425.00* *225.00*
275 A26 400th m on 30pf bis (Br) 15 *2.00*
a. Imperf. 50.00
276 A26 400th m on 40pf bis (Br) 15 *2.00*
a. Imperf. 50.00
277 A35 2mil m on 200m rose red 15 *125.00*
278 A38 2mil m on 5th m dull rose 15 *6.25*
Set, never hinged 60.00

Nos. 273-276 and 278 exist without surcharge. Value, $225-275 each.

A39

A39a

The stamps of types A39 and A39a usually have the value darker than the rest of the design.

1923 Wmk. 126 *Perf. 14*

280 A39 500th m brown 15 *2.00*
281 A39 1mil m grnsh blue 15 35
a. Imperf. 60.00
282 A39 2mil m dull vio 15 *22.50*
284 A39 4mil m yellow grn 15 75
a. Value double 100.00
b. Imperf. 50.00
285 A39 5mil m rose 15 35
286 A39 10mil m red 15 35
a. Value double 85.00 *300.00*
287 A39 20mil m ultra 15 50
288 A39 30mil m red brown 15 *10.50*
289 A39 50mil m dull green 15 35
a. Imperf. 62.50 *195.00*
b. Value inverted 35.00
290 A39 100mil m gray 15 35
291 A39 200mil m bister brn 15 35
a. Imperf. 6.25
293 A39 500mil m olive grn 15 35
294 A39a 1mlrd m choc 15 35
295 A39a 2mlrd m pale brn & grn 15 50
296 A39a 5mlrd m yellow & brn 15 50
297 A39a 10mlrd m ap grn & grn 15 50
a. Imperf. 30.00
298 A39a 20mlrd m bluish grn & brn 15 1.00
299 A39a 50mlrd m bl & dp bl 60 *22.50*
Set value 2.00
Set, never hinged 4.25

The variety "value omitted" exists on Nos. 280-281, 284-287, 290-291, 293-294, 296, 298-299 and 307. Values $90-$175.

See Nos. 301-309. For surcharges and overprints see Nos. 311-321, O40-O46.

Serrate Roulette 13½

301 A39 10mil m red 15 *42.50*
302 A39 20mil m ultra 15 *300.00*
303 A39 50mil m dull grn 15 *5.25*
304 A39 200mil m bis brn 15 *10.50*
305 A39a 1mlrd m choc 15 *5.00*
306 A39a 2mlrd m pale brn & grn 15 *2.25*
307 A39a 5mlrd m yel & brn 15 *1.65*
308 A39a 20mlrd m bluish grn & brn 40 *10.50*
309 A39a 50mlrd m bl & dp bl 1.25 *450.00*
Nos. 301-309 (9) 2.70
Set, never hinged 6.25

Stamps and Types of 1923 Surcharged with New Values

1923 ***Perf. 14***

310 A35 1mlrd m on 100m violet 15 *27.50*
a. Inverted surcharge 62.50
b. 1mlrd m on 100m deep reddish purple 77.50 *3,200.*
311 A39 5mlrd m on 2mil m dl vio 35 *100.00*
a. Inverted surcharge 30.00
b. Double surcharge 62.50
312 A39 5mlrd m on 4mil m yel grn 15 *27.50*
a. Inverted surcharge 42.50 *165.00*
b. Double surcharge 50.00
313 A39 5mlrd m on 10mil m red 15 *1.65*
a. Inverted surcharge 27.50 *165.00*
b. Double surcharge 30.00
314 A39 10mlrd m on 20mil m ultra 30 *1.65*
a. Double surcharge 72.50
b. Inverted surcharge 42.50
315 A39 10mlrd m on 50mil m dl grn 15 *1.65*
a. Inverted surcharge 30.00
b. Double surcharge 72.50
316 A39 10mlrd m on 100mil m gray 15 *5.00*
a. Inverted surcharge 37.50
b. Double surcharge 70.00
Set value 1.33
Set, never hinged 3.25

No. 310b was issued in Bavaria only and is known as the Hitler provisional. Excellent forgeries exist.

Serrate Roulette 13½

319 A39 5mlrd m on 10mil m red 1.00 *195.00*
a. Inverted surcharge 35.00
b. Double surcharge 30.00
320 A39 10mlrd m on 20mil m ultra 1.25 *90.00*
321 A39 10mlrd m on 50mil m dl grn 1.00 *42.50*
a. Inverted surcharge 35.00
Set, never hinged 5.75

A40

German Eagle — A41

1923 ***Perf. 14***

323 A40 3pf brown 40 15
324 A40 5pf dark green 40 15
325 A40 10pf carmine 40 15
326 A40 20pf deep ultra 1.00 15
327 A40 50pf orange 2.50 45
328 A40 100pf brown violet 8.25 55
Nos. 323-328 (6) 12.95
Set value 1.30
Set, never hinged 75.00

For overprints see Nos. O47-O52.

Imperf.

323a A40 3pf 165.00 *250.00*
324a A40 5pf 45.00 *250.00*
325a A40 10pf 130.00 130.00
326a A40 20pf 165.00 235.00
327a A40 50pf 180.00 300.00
328a A40 100pf 200.00

Value Omitted

323b A40 3pf 105.00 *250.00*
324b A40 5pf 140.00
325b A40 10pf 105.00
326b A40 20pf 100.00
327b A40 50pf 100.00
328b A40 100pf 140.00

1924 **Wmk. 126**

330 A41 3pf lt brown 24 15
331 A41 5pf lt green 32 15
332 A41 10pf vermilion 45 15
333 A41 20pf dull blue 1.25 15
334 A41 30pf rose lilac 1.90 20
335 A41 40pf olive green 13.00 45
336 A41 50pf orange 13.00 65
Nos. 330-336 (7) 30.16
Set value 1.50
Set, never hinged 275.00

The values above 5pf have "Pf" in the upper right corner.
For overprints see Nos. O53-O61.

Imperf.

330a A41 3pf 160.00 195.00
331a A41 5pf 210.00 *300.00*
332a A41 10pf 195.00
333a A41 20pf 195.00
334a A41 30pf 195.00
335a A41 40pf 200.00

Rheinstein Castle — A43

View of Cologne — A44

Marienburg Castle — A45

1924 **Engr.** **Wmk. 126**

337 A43 1m green 12.00 1.75
338 A44 2m blue 19.00 1.75
339 A45 3m claret 19.00 4.00
Set, never hinged 160.00

See No. 387.

Dr. Heinrich von Stephan
A46 A47

1924-28 **Typo.**

340 A46 10pf dark green 50 15
341 A46 20pf dark blue 70 35
342 A47 60pf red brown 4.25 15
a. Chalky paper ('28) 17.50 2.50
343 A47 80pf slate 6.50 85
Set, never hinged 67.50

Universal Postal Union, 50th anniversary.
No. 340 exists imperf. Value $300.

Traffic Wheel — A48

German Eagle Watching Rhine Valley — A49

1925, May 30 ***Perf. 13½x13***

345 A48 5pf deep green 3.00 3.50
346 A48 10pf vermilion 3.50 5.50
Set, never hinged 37.50

German Traffic Exhibition, Munich, May 30-Oct 11, 1925.

1925 ***Perf. 14***

347 A49 5pf green 42 15
348 A49 10pf vermilion 75 15
349 A49 20pf deep blue 4.25 70
Set, never hinged 27.50

Issued to commemorate 1000 years' union of the Rhineland with Germany.

Speyer Cathedral — A50

1925, Sept. 11 **Engr.**

350 A50 5m dull green 30.00 9.75
Never hinged 125.00

Johann Wolfgang von Goethe — A51

Designs: 3pf, 25pf, Goethe. 5pf, Friedrich von Schiller. 8pf, 20pf, Ludwig van Beethoven. 10pf, Frederick the Great. 15pf, Immanuel Kant. 30pf, Gotthold Ephraim Lessing. 40pf, Gottfried Wilhelm Leibnitz. 50pf, Johann Sebastian Bach. 80pf, Albrecht Durer.

1926-27 **Typo.** ***Perf. 14***

351 A51 3pf olive brown 45 15
352 A51 3pf bister ('27) 90 15
353 A51 5pf dark green 90 15
b. 5pf light green ('27) 1.10 15
354 A51 8pf blue grn ('27) 1.10 15
355 A51 10pf carmine 90 15
356 A51 15pf vermilion 2.25 15
a. Booklet pane of 8 + 2 labels 275.00
357 A51 20pf myrtle grn 11.00 60
358 A51 25pf blue 2.75 28
359 A51 30pf olive grn 6.25 16
360 A51 40pf dp violet 11.00 28
361 A51 50pf brown 12.00 4.75
362 A51 80pf chocolate 27.50 3.75
Nos. 351-362 (12) 77.00 10.72
Set, never hinged 800.00

Nos. 351-354, 356 and 357 exist imperf. Value each $175.

I.A.A.

Nos. 354, 356 and 358 Overprinted

10.-15.10.1927

1927, Oct. 10

363 A51 8pf blue green 17.00 35.00
364 A51 15pf vermilion 17.00 35.00
365 A51 25pf blue 17.00 35.00
Set, never hinged 130.00

"I.A.A." stands for "Internationales Arbeitsamt," (Intl. Labor Bureau), an agency of the League of Nations. Issued in connection with a meeting of the I.A.A. in Berlin, Oct. 10-15, 1927, they were on sale to the public.

Pres. Friedrich Ebert — A60

Pres. Paul von Hindenburg — A61

1928-32 **Typo.** ***Perf. 14***

366 A60 3pf bister 18 15
367 A61 4pf lt blue ('31) 30 15
a. Tête bêche pair 6.25 6.25
b. Bklt. pane of 9 + label 22.50
368 A61 5pf lt green 38 15
a. Tête bêche pair 6.75 6.75
b. Imperf. 250.00
c. Bklt. pane of 6 + 4 labels 19.00
d. Bklt. pane, 4 #368 + 6 #369 22.50
369 A60 6pf lt olive grn ('32) 38 15
a. Bklt. pane, 2 #369 + 8 #373 22.50
370 A60 8pf dark green 18 15
a. Tête bêche pair 7.75 7.75
371 A60 10pf vermilion 1.50 75
372 A60 10pf red violet ('30) 70 15
373 A61 12pf orange ('32) 65 15
a. Tête bêche pair 7.75 7.75
374 A61 15pf car rose 60 15
a. Tête bêche pair 10.50 10.50
b. Bklt. pane 6 + 4 labels 22.50
375 A60 20pf Prus green 3.00 1.40
a. Imperf. 500.00

376 A60 20pf gray ('30) 5.25 15
377 A61 25pf blue 8.00 30
378 A60 30pf olive green 4.75 20
379 A61 40pf violet 12.50 28
380 A60 45pf orange 7.00 1.10
381 A61 50pf brown 7.00 65
382 A60 60pf orange brn 8.00 1.10
383 A61 80pf chocolate 19.00 2.00
384 A61 80pf yel bis ('30) 6.00 48
Nos. 366-384 (19) 85.37 9.61
Set, never hinged 850.00

Stamps of 1928 Overprinted **30. JUNI 1930**

1930, June 30
385 A60 8pf dark green 75 15
386 A61 15pf carmine rose 75 20
Set, never hinged 10.00

Issued in commemoration of the final evacuation of the Rhineland by the Allied forces.

View of Cologne — A63

1930 Engr. Wmk. 126
Inscribed: "Reichsmark"
387 A63 2m dark blue 30.00 10.00
Never hinged 100.00

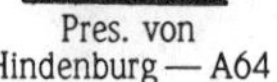

Pres. von Hindenburg — A64 Frederick the Great — A65

1932, Oct. 1 Typo. Wmk. 126
391 A64 4pf blue 60 15
392 A64 5pf brt green 60 15
393 A64 12pf dp orange 4.25 15
394 A64 15pf dk red 3.25 6.50
395 A64 25pf ultra 1.10 35
396 A64 40pf violet 7.75 1.00
397 A64 50pf dk brown 7.25 8.50
Nos. 391-397 (7) 24.80 16.80
Set, never hinged 130.00

85th birthday of von Hindenburg.

See Nos. 401-431, 436-441. For surcharges and overprints see France, Luxembourg and Poland.

1933, Apr. 12 Photo.
398 A65 6pf dk green 52 55
a. Tête bêche pair 12.50 14.00
399 A65 12pf carmine 52 55
a. Tête bêche pair 12.50 14.00
b. Bklt. pane of 5 + label 42.50
400 A65 25pf ultra 30.00 13.00
Set, never hinged 140.00

Celebration of Potsdam Day.

Hindenburg Type of 1932

1933 Typo.
401 A64 3pf olive bister 12.00 50
402 A64 4pf dull blue 3.25 50
403 A64 6pf dk green 1.40 15
404 A64 8pf dp orange 6.50 50
a. Bklt. pane, 3 #404 + 5 #406 130.00
b. Open "D" 27.50 3.00
405 A64 10pf chocolate 3.25 50
406 A64 12pf dp carmine 1.40 15
a. Bklt. pane, 4 #392 + 4 #406 60.00
407 A64 15pf maroon 4.50 *13.00*
408 A64 20pf brt blue 5.25 65
409 A64 30pf olive grn 6.50 40
410 A64 40pf red violet 24.00 1.25
411 A64 50pf dk grn & blk 15.00 1.65
412 A64 60pf claret & blk 24.00 52
413 A64 80pf dk blue & blk 9.00 90
414 A64 100pf orange & blk 18.00 6.50
Nos. 401-414 (14) 134.05 *27.17*
Set, never hinged 700.00

Hindenburg Type of 1932

1933-36 Wmk. 237 *Perf. 14*
415 A64 1pf black 15 15
a. Bklt. pane, 4 #415, 3 #417, label 5.00
b. Bklt. pane, 3 #415, 3 #416 + 2 #418 6.00
c. Bklt. pane, 2 #415, 5 #420, label 6.00
d. Bklt. pane, 4 #415 + 4 #422 3.50

416 A64 3pf olive bis ('34) 15 15
a. Bklt. pane, 4 #416 + 4 #418 1.75
b. Bklt. pane, 4 #416 + 4 #419 2.00
c. Bklt. pane, 6 #416, 1 #422, label 2.50
417 A64 4pf dull blue ('34) 15 15
a. Bklt. pane, 3 #417, 4 #422, label 6.00
418 A64 5pf brt green ('34) 15 15
a. Bklt. pane, 2 #418, 5 #419, label 5.00
b. Bklt. pane, 2 #418, 3 #419 + 3 #420 3.50
c. Bklt. pane, 4 #418 + 4 #420 4.00
419 A64 6pf dk green ('34) 15 15
b. Bklt. pane of 7 + label 1.75
c. Bklt. pane, 1 #419, 6 #422, label 17.00
420 A64 8pf dp orange ('34) 15 15
a. Bklt. pane, 3 #420, 4 #422, label 5.00
b. Open "D" 6.00 2.50
421 A64 10pf choc ('34) 15 15
422 A64 12pf dp car ('34) 15 15
a. Bklt. pane of 7 + label 6.00
423 A64 15pf maroon ('34) 25 15
424 A64 20pf brt blue ('34) 30 15
425 A64 25pf ultra ('34) 35 15
426 A64 30pf olive grn ('34) 55 15
427 A64 40pf red violet ('34) 55 15
428 A64 50pf dk grn & blk ('34) 85 15
429 A64 60pf claret & blk ('34) 70 15
430 A64 80pf dk bl & blk ('36) 2.25 50
431 A64 100pf orange & blk ('34) 4.00 32
Nos. 415-431 (17) 11.00
Set value 1.75
Set, never hinged 35.00

Franz Adolf E. Lüderitz — A66

Swastika, Sun and Nuremberg Castle — A70

Designs: 6pf, Dr. Gustav Nachtigal. 12pf, Karl Peters. 25pf, Hermann von Wissmann.

1934, June 30 *Perf. 13x13½*
432 A66 3pf brown & choc 2.00 2.75
433 A66 6pf dk green & choc 85 65
434 A66 12pf dk car & choc 1.00 38
435 A66 25pf brt blue & choc 6.50 9.00
Set, never hinged 80.00

Issued in remembrance of the lost colonies of Germany.

Hindenburg Memorial Issue
Type of 1932
With Black Border

1934, Sept. 4 *Perf. 14*
436 A64 3pf olive bister 65 20
437 A64 5pf brt green 65 32
438 A64 6pf dk green 1.10 15
439 A64 8pf vermilion 1.65 20
440 A64 12pf deep carmine 2.25 20
441 A64 25pf ultra 6.75 4.00
Nos. 436-441 (6) 13.05 5.07
Set, never hinged 57.50

1934, Sept. 1 Photo.
442 A70 6pf dark green 1.75 15
443 A70 12pf dark carmine 4.25 15
Set value 24
Set, never hinged 45.00

Nazi Congress at Nuremberg.
Imperfs exist. Value, each $400.

Allegory "Saar Belongs to Germany" — A71

German Eagle — A72

1934, Aug. 26 Typo. Wmk. 237
444 A71 6pf dark green 1.50 15
445 A72 12pf dark carmine 3.50 15
Set value 24
Set, never hinged 42.50

Issued to mark the Saar Plebiscite.

Friedrich von Schiller — A73

Germania Welcoming Home the Saar — A74

1934, Nov. 5
446 A73 6pf green 1.40 15
447 A73 12pf carmine 3.50 15
Set, never hinged 42.50

175th anniv. of the birth of von Schiller.

1935, Jan. 16 Photo.
448 A74 3pf brown 50 35
449 A74 6pf dark green 65 15
450 A74 12pf lake 2.50 15
451 A74 25pf dark blue 8.25 4.00
Set, never hinged 52.50

Return of the Saar to Germany.

German Soldier A75

Wreath and Swastika A76

1935, Mar. 15
452 A75 6pf dark green 90 85
453 A75 12pf copper red 90 85
Set, never hinged 8.00

Issued to commemorate War Heroes' Day.

1935, Apr. 26 Unwmk.
454 A76 6pf dark green 85 50
455 A76 12pf crimson 85 50
Set, never hinged 10.00

Issued in connection with the Young Workers' Professional Competitions.

Heinrich Schütz — A77

"The Eagle" — A80

Wmk. Swastikas (237)
1935, June 21 Engr. *Perf. 14*
456 A77 6pf shown 60 15
457 A77 12pf Bach 70 15
458 A77 25pf Handel 1.25 50
Set value 66
Set, never hinged 14.00

Schutz-Bach-Handel celebration.

1935, July 10 *Perf. 14*

Designs: 12pf, Modern express train. 25pf, "The Hamburg Flyer." 40pf, Streamlined locomotive.

459 A80 6pf dark green 80 22
460 A80 12pf copper red 80 22
461 A80 25pf ultra 6.50 85
462 A80 40pf red violet 8.00 85
Set, never hinged 57.50

Centenary of railroad in Germany.
Exist imperf. Value, $225 each.

Bugler of Hitler Youth Movement
A84

Eagle and Swastika over Nuremberg
A85

1935, July 25 **Photo.**

463 A84 6pf deep green 1.10 1.50
464 A84 15pf brown lake 1.10 1.50
Set, never hinged 9.00

Hitler Youth Meeting.

1935, Aug. 30 **Engr.**

465 A85 6pf gray green 65 15
466 A85 12pf dark carmine 1.00 15
Set value 18
Set, never hinged 6.25

1935 Nazi Congress at Nuremberg.

Nazi Flag Bearer and Feldherrnhalle at Munich — A86

Airplane — A87

1935, Nov. 5 **Photo.** ***Perf. 13½***

467 A86 3pf brown 25 15
468 A86 12pf dark carmine 40 15
Set, never hinged 4.50

12th anniv. of the 1st Hitler "Putsch" at Munich, Nov. 9, 1923.

1936, Jan. 6

469 A87 40pf sapphire 5.00 90
Never hinged 19.00

10th anniv. of the Lufthansa air service.

Gottlieb Daimler
A88

Carl Benz
A89

1936, Feb. 15 ***Perf. 14***

470 A88 6pf dark green 38 18
471 A89 12pf copper red 55 18
Set, never hinged 3.75

The 50th anniv. of the automobile; Intl. Automobile and Motorcycle Show, Berlin.

Otto von Guericke
A90

Symbolical of Municipalities
A91

1936, May 4

472 A90 6pf dark green 22 15
Never hinged 50

250th anniv. of the death of the German inventor, Otto von Guericke, May 11, 1686.

1936, June 3

473 A91 3pf dark brown 15 15
474 A91 5pf deep green 15 15
475 A91 12pf lake 25 15
476 A91 25pf dark ultra 65 65
Set value 90
Set, never hinged 4.25

6th Intl. Cong. of Municipalities, June 7-13.

Allegory of Recreation Congress
A92

Salute to Swastika
A93

1936, June 30

477 A92 6pf dark green 35 28
478 A92 15pf deep claret 50 38
Set, never hinged 4.00

World Congress for Vacation and Recreation held at Hamburg.

1936, Sept. 3 ***Perf. 14***

479 A93 6pf deep green 28 15
480 A93 12pf copper red 40 15
Set, never hinged 4.00

The 1936 Nazi Congress.

Shield Bearer — A94

German and Austrian Carrying Nazi Flag — A95

1937, Mar. 3 **Engr.** **Unwmk.**

481 A94 3pf brown 15 15
482 A94 6pf green 18 15
483 A94 12pf carmine 35 22
Set value 36
Set, never hinged 4.50

The Reich's Air Protection League.

Wmk. Swastikas (237)
1938, Apr. 8 **Photo.** ***Perf. 14x13½***
Size: 23x28mm

484 A95 6pf dark green 15 15
Never hinged 45

Unwmk. ***Perf. 12½***
Size: 21½x26mm

485 A95 6pf deep green 15 20
Never hinged 45

Union of Austria and Germany.

Cathedral Island — A96

Hermann Goering Stadium — A97

Town Hall, Breslau — A98

Centennial Hall, Breslau — A99

1938, June 21 **Engr.** ***Perf. 14***

486 A96 3pf dark brown 15 15
487 A97 6pf deep green 24 15
488 A98 12pf copper red 40 15
489 A99 15pf violet brown 65 50
Set value 74
Set, never hinged 6.00

16th German Gymnastic and Sports Festival held at Breslau, July 23-31, 1938.

Nazi Emblem — A100

1939, Apr. 4 **Photo.** **Wmk. 237**

490 A100 6pf dark green 1.75 2.50
491 A100 12pf deep carmine 1.75 2.50
Set, never hinged 10.00

Young Workers' Professional Competitions.

St. Mary's Church — A101

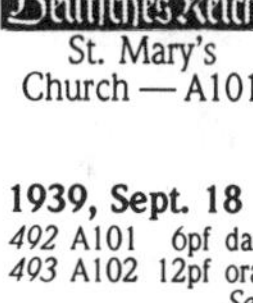
The Krantor, Danzig — A102

1939, Sept. 18

492 A101 6pf dark green 15 22
493 A102 12pf orange red 18 32
Set value 26
Set, never hinged 1.25

Unification of Danzig with the Reich.

Johannes Gutenberg and Library at Leipzig — A103

Designs: 6pf, "High House," Leipzig. 12pf, Old Town Hall, Leipzig. 25pf, View of Leipzig Fair.

Inscribed "Leipziger Messe"
Perf. 10½
1940, Mar. 3 **Photo.** **Unwmk.**

494 A103 3pf dark brown 15 22
495 A103 6pf dk gray green 15 22
496 A103 12pf henna brown 18 15
497 A103 25pf ultra 35 60
Set, never hinged 3.00

Leipzig Fair.

House of Nations, Leipzig — A107

Designs: 6pf, Concert Hall, Leipzig. 12pf, Leipzig Fair Office. 25pf, Railroad Terminal, Leipzig.

Inscribed: "Reichsmesse Leipzig, 1941"
1941, Mar. 1 ***Perf. 14x13½***

498 A107 3pf brown 16 28
499 A107 6pf green 16 28
500 A107 12pf dark red 22 30
501 A107 25pf bright blue 42 60
Set, never hinged 3.50

Leipzig Fair.

Fashion Allegory — A111

Vienna Fair Hall — A112

"Burgtheater"
A113

Monument to Prince Eugene
A114

1941, Mar. 8 ***Perf. 13½x14***

502 A111 3pf dark red brown 15 15
503 A112 6pf brt blue grn 15 15
504 A113 12pf scarlet 30 30
505 A114 25pf bright blue 52 52
Set, never hinged 4.50

Vienna Fair.

Adolf Hitler
A115 A116

1941-44 **Typo.** ***Perf. 14***
Size: 18½x22½mm

506 A115 1pf gray black 15 15
a. Bklt. pane, 4 #506 + 4 #509 2.00
507 A115 3pf lt brown 15 15
a. Bklt. pane, 6 #507 + 2 #510 2.00
508 A115 4pf slate 15 15
a. Bklt. pane, 4 #508, 2 #511 + 2 labels 2.25
509 A115 5pf dp yellow grn 15 15
510 A115 6pf purple 15 15
a. Bklt. pane of 7 + label 10.00
511 A115 8pf red 15 15
511A A115 10pf dk brown ('43) 15 15
511B A115 12pf carmine ('43) 15 15

Engr.

512 A115 10pf dark brown 30 15
513 A115 12pf brt carmine 30 15
a. Bklt. pane of 6 + 2 labels 6.00
514 A115 15pf brown lake 15 15
515 A115 16pf peacock green 15 55
516 A115 20pf blue 15 15
517 A115 24pf orange brown 15 35

Size: 21½x26mm

518 A115 25pf brt ultra 15 15
519 A115 30pf olive green 15 15
520 A115 40pf brt red vio 15 15
521 A115 50pf myrtle green 15 15
522 A115 60pf dk red brown 15 15
523 A115 80pf indigo 15 20
524 A116 1m dk slate grn ('44) 15 35
a. Perf. 12½ ('42) 1.40 15
525 A116 2m violet ('44) 38 75
a. Perf. 12½ ('42) 75 90

Perf. 12½

526 A116 3m copper red ('42) 75 1.25
a. Perf. 14 ('44) 1.25 1.75
527 A116 5m dark blue ('42) 1.90 4.50
a. Perf. 14 ('44) 2.50 3.50
Set value 4.90
Set, #506-527, never hinged 11.50
Set, #524a-527a, never hinged 7.00

Nos. 507, 510, 511, 511A, 511B, 520, 524-526 exist imperf.

For surcharge see No. MQ3. For overprints see Russia Nos. N9-N48.

Storm Trooper Emblem — A117

Adolf Hitler — A118

1942, Aug. 8 Photo. *Perf. 14*

528 A117 6pf purple 15 50
Never hinged 25

War Effort Day of the Storm Troopers.

1944 Engr.

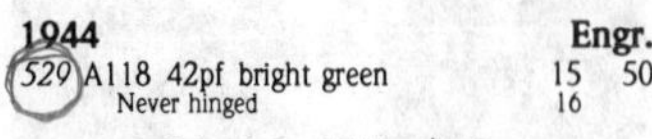

529 A118 42pf bright green 15 50
Never hinged 16

Exists imperf. Value $140.

A119

1946 Typo. Wmk. 284 *Perf. 14*

Size: 18x22mm

530 A119 1pf black 15 15
531 A119 2pf black 15 15
532 A119 3pf yellow brn 15 18
533 A119 4pf slate 15 22
534 A119 5pf yellow grn 15 15
535 A119 6pf purple 15 15
536 A119 8pf dp ver 15 15
537 A119 10pf chocolate 15 15
538 A119 12pf bright red 15 15
539 A119 12pf slate gray 15 15
a. Bklt. pane, 5 #539 + 3 #542 9.00 *45.00*
540 A119 15pf violet brn 15 18
541 A119 15pf lt yel grn 15 15
542 A119 16pf slate green 15 15
543 A119 20pf lt blue 15 15
544 A119 24pf orange brn 15 15
545 A119 25pf brt ultra 15 30
546 A119 25pf orange yel 15 15
547 A119 30pf olive 15 15
548 A119 40pf red violet 15 15
549 A119 42pf emerald 60 2.25
550 A119 45pf brt red 15 15
551 A119 50pf dk ol grn 15 15
552 A119 60pf brown red 15 15
553 A119 75pf deep ultra 15 15
554 A119 80pf dark blue 15 15
555 A119 84pf emerald 15 18

Size: 24½x29½mm

556 A119 1m olive green 15 18
Set value 1.25 4.90
Set, never hinged 1.90

Imperf. copies of Nos. 543, 544 and 548 are usually from the souvenir sheet No. B295. Most other denominations exist imperf.

For overprints see Nos. 585A-599, 9N64, 10N17-10N21.

Planting Olive A120

Sower A121

Laborer A122

Reaping Wheat A123

Germany Reaching for Peace — A124

Heinrich von Stephan — A125

1947-48 *Perf. 14*

557 A120 2pf brown blk 15 15
558 A120 6pf purple 15 15
559 A121 8pf red 15 15
560 A121 10pf yel grn ('48) 15 15
561 A122 12pf gray 15 15
562 A120 15pf choc ('48) 15 20
563 A123 16pf dk bl grn 15 15
564 A121 20pf blue 15 15
565 A123 24pf brown org 15 15
566 A120 25pf orange yel 15 15
567 A122 30pf red ('48) 15 24
568 A121 40pf red vio 15 15
569 A123 50pf ultra ('48) 15 40
571 A122 60pf red brn ('48) 15 15
a. 60pf brown red 15 15
572 A122 80pf dark blue 15 15
573 A123 84pf emerald 15 20

Engr.

574 A124 1m olive 15 15
575 A124 2m dk brown vio 15 15
576 A124 3m copper red 15 24
577 A124 5m dk blue ('48) 30 *1.00*
Set value 1.25 *3.00*
Set, never hinged 2.25

For overprints see Nos. 600-633, 9N1-9N34, 9N65-9N67, 10N1-10N16.

1947, May 15 Litho.

578 A125 24pf orange brown 15 15
579 A125 75pf dark blue 15 18
Set value 15 26
Set, never hinged 20

50th anniv. of the death of Heinrich von Stephan, 1st postmaster general of the German Empire.

Leipzig Fair Issues

Type of Semi-Postal Stamp of 1947

Designs: 12pf, Maximilian I granting charter, 1497. 75pf, Estimating and collecting taxes, 1365.

Perf. 13½x13

1947, Sept. 2 Litho. Wmk. 284

580 SP252 12pf carmine 15 15
581 SP252 75pf dk vio blue 15 15
Set value 15
Set, never hinged 20

Type of Semi-Postal Stamp of 1947, Dated 1948

Designs: 50pf, Merchants at customs barrier, 1388. 84pf, Arranging stocks of merchandise, 1433.

1948, Mar. 2 Engr.

582 SP252 50pf deep blue 15 15
583 SP252 84pf green 15 15
Set value 15
Set, never hinged 20

Exist imperf. Value, each, $400.

Hanover Fair Issue

Weighing Goods for Export — A126

1948, May 22 Typo. *Perf. 14*

584 A126 24pf deep carmine 15 15
585 A126 50pf ultra 15 22
c. Pair, #584-585 3.50 7.50
Pair, never hinged 4.00
Set value 15 30
Set, never hinged 20

For Use in the United States and British Zones

Stamps of Germany 1946-47 Overprinted in Black

a 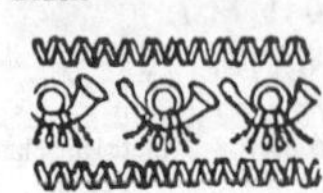

b 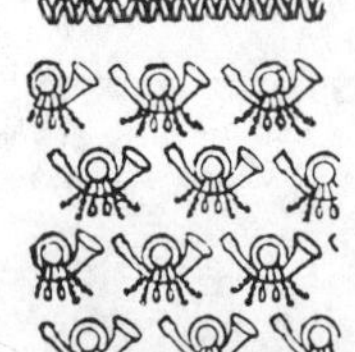

Overprint Type "a" on 1946 Numeral Issue

1948 Wmk. 284 *Perf. 14*

585A A119 2pf black 3.00 *16.00*
585B A119 8pf dp vermilion 6.00 *37.50*
586 A119 10pf chocolate 32 *3.00*
586A A119 12pf bright red 5.25 *27.50*
586B A119 12pf slate gray 87.50 *365.00*
586C A119 15pf violet brn 5.25 *27.50*
587 A119 15pf lt yel grn 5.00 *10.00*
587A A119 16pf slate green 26.00 *125.00*
587B A119 24pf orange brn 47.50 *137.50*
587C A119 25pf brt ultra 8.50 *32.50*
588 A119 25pf orange yel 65 *5.00*
589 A119 30pf olive 80 *5.00*
589A A119 40pf red violet 35.00 *130.00*
590 A119 45pf brt red 1.10 *5.00*
591 A119 50pf dk olive grn 1.10 *5.00*
592 A119 75pf dp ultra 3.25 *12.50*
593 A119 84pf emerald 3.25 *12.50*
Nos. 585A-593 (17) 239.47
Set, never hinged 475.00

Same, Overprinted Type "b"

593A A119 2pf black 8.25 *40.00*
593B A119 8pf dp vermilion 17.50 *75.00*
593C A119 10pf chocolate 15.00 *75.00*
593D A119 12pf bright red 5.25 *35.00*
593E A119 12pf slate gray 140.00 *700.00*
593F A119 15pf violet brown 5.75 *27.50*
594 A119 15pf lt yel grn 32 *4.50*
594A A119 16pf slate green 17.50 *95.00*
594B A119 24pf orange brown 22.50 *130.00*
594C A119 25pf brt ultra 6.75 *35.00*
594D A119 25pf orange yel 21.00 *105.00*
595 A119 30pf olive 70 *4.00*
595A A119 40pf red violet 27.50 *150.00*
596 A119 45pf bright red 1.10 *7.50*
597 A119 50pf dk olive grn 1.10 *7.50*
598 A119 75pf dp ultra 1.40 *8.50*
599 A119 84pf emerald 1.40 *8.00*
Nos. 593A-599 (17) 293.02
Set, never hinged 700.00

Nine other denominations of type A119 (1, 3, 4, 5, 6, 20, 42, 60 and 80pf) were also overprinted with types "a" and "b." These overprints were not authorized, but the stamps were sold at post offices and tolerated for postal use. Forgeries exist.

The overprints on Nos. 585A-599 have been extensively counterfeited.

Overprint Type "a" on Stamps and Types of 1947 Pictorial Issue

600 A120 2pf brown black 15 15
601 A120 6pf purple 15 15
602 A121 8pf dp vermilion 15 20
603 A121 10pf yellow green 15 15
604 A122 12pf slate gray 15 15
605 A120 15pf chocolate 4.75 8.75
606 A123 16pf dk blue green 90 1.65
607 A121 20pf blue 25 65
608 A123 24pf brown orange 15 15
609 A120 25pf orange yellow 25 42
610 A122 30pf red 1.25 2.50
611 A121 40pf red violet 60 90
612 A123 50pf ultra 60 90
614 A122 60pf red brown 60 90
a. 60pf brown red 32.50 *125.00*
615 A122 80pf dark blue 1.00 2.00
616 A123 84pf emerald 2.75 5.25
Nos. 600-616 (16) 13.85 24.87
Set, never hinged 20.00

Same, Overprinted Type "b"

617 A120 2pf brown black 50 75
618 A120 6pf purple 50 70
619 A121 8pf red 50 75
620 A121 10pf yellow green 15 15
621 A122 12pf gray 50 75
622 A120 15pf chocolate 15 18
623 A123 16pf dk blue green 15 15
624 A121 20pf blue 15 15
625 A123 24pf brown orange 40 65
626 A120 25pf orange yel 5.00 *7.50*
627 A122 30pf red 15 15
628 A121 40pf red violet 20 15
629 A123 50pf ultra 25 18
631 A122 60pf red brown 25 18
a. 60pf brown red 1.40 3.00
632 A122 80pf dark blue 25 15
633 A123 84pf emerald 50 75
Nos. 617-633 (16) 9.60
Set, never hinged 14.00

Most of Nos. 585A-633 exist with inverted and double overprints.

Frankfurt Town Hall — A127

Our Lady's Church, Munich — A128

Cologne Cathedral A129

Brandenburg Gate, Berlin A130

Holsten Gate, Lübeck — A131

Two types of mark values:
I- Four horiz. lines in stairs.
II- Seven horizontal lines.

Perf. 11½x11, 11

1948-51 Litho. Wmk. 286

634 A127 2pf black 15 15
a. Perf. 14 1.65 4.00
635 A128 4pf orange brown 15 15
a. Perf. 14 75 15
636 A129 5pf blue 15 15
a. Perf. 14 1.10 15
637 A128 6pf orange brown 15 25
638 A128 6pf orange 15 15
a. Perf. 14 9.75 6.00
639 A127 8pf orange yel 15 25
640 A128 8pf dk slate blue 15 15
641 A129 10pf green 14 15
a. Perf. 14 1.10 15
642 A128 15pf orange 90 2.00
643 A127 15pf violet 55 15
a. Perf. 14 6.75 15
644 A127 16pf bluish green 20 50
645 A127 20pf blue 42 1.10
646 A130 20pf carmine 30 15
a. Perf. 14 2.50 15
647 A130 24pf carmine 15 15
648 A129 25pf vermilion 42 15
a. Perf. 14 13.00 *25.00*
649 A130 30pf blue 50 15
a. Perf. 14 14.00 15
650 A128 30pf scarlet 1.25 *3.25*
651 A129 40pf rose lilac 70 15
a. Perf. 14 9.75 15
652 A130 50pf ultra 50 *1.10*
653 A128 50pf bluish green 70 15
a. Perf. 14 110.00 15
654 A129 60pf violet brn 25.00 15
a. Perf. 14 1.50 15
655 A130 80pf red violet 1.25 15
a. Perf. 14 62.50 15
656 A128 84pf rose violet 1.10 2.50
657 A129 90pf rose lilac 1.25 15
a. Perf. 14 85.00 15

Perf. 11, 11x11½

658 A131 1m yellow grn (I) 14.00 55
a. Perf. 14 (II) ('51) 65.00 15
b. Perf. 11 (II) 20.00 15
659 A131 2m violet (I) 14.00 55
a. Type II 30.00 32
660 A131 3m car rose (I) 15.00 2.50
a. Type II 100.00 85
661 A131 5m blue (I) 20.00 16.00
a. Type II 125.00 4.75
Set, never hinged 210.00
Set, 634a-658a, never hinged 700.00
Set, 658b-661a, never hinged 450.00

Imperforates of many values exist.

Specialists collect Nos. 634-661 with watermark in four positions: upright, D's facing left; upright, D's facing right; sideways, D's facing up; sideways, D's facing down.

Two types of perforation: line and comb. Nos. 634-657 are found both perf. 11 and 11½x11.

Herman Hildebrant Wedigh — A132

Wmk. 116

1949, Apr. 22 Engr. *Perf. 14*

662 A132 10pf green 1.25 85
663 A132 20pf carmine rose 1.25 85
664 A132 30pf blue 1.50 2.25
a. Sheet of 3, #662-664 50.00 *150.00*
Sheet, never hinged 95.00
Set, never hinged 9.00

Hanover Export Fair, 1949.
No. 664a sold for 1 mark.

Federal Republic

AREA—95,520 sq. mi.
POP.—62,040,000 (est. 1974)
CAPITAL—Bonn

"Reconstruction" A133

Bavaria Stamp A134

1949, Sept. 7 Litho. Wmk. 286

665 A133 10pf blue green 21.00 18.00
666 A133 20pf rose carmine 27.50 21.00
Set, never hinged 110.00

Opening of the first Federal Assembly.
Exist imperf. Value, each $425.

Wmk. 285
1949, Sept. 30 Litho. *Perf. 14*

Design: 30pf, Bavaria 6kr.

667 A134 20pf red & dull blue 22.50 24.00
668 A134 30pf dull blue & choc 27.50 47.50
Set, never hinged 100.00

Cent. of German postage stamps. See No. B309.

Heinrich von Stephan, General Post Office and Guild House, Bern
A135

1949, Oct. 9 Wmk. 286

669 A135 30pf ultra 27.50 32.50
Never hinged 72.50

75th anniv. of the UPU.

Numeral and Post Horn — A136

1951-52 Typo. Wmk. 295

670 A136 2pf yellow grn 18 65
671 A136 4pf yellow brn 18 15
a. Booklet pane, 3 #671 + 3 #673 + 4 #677 125.00
672 A136 5pf dp rose vio 2.00 15
673 A136 6pf orange 5.00 2.50
674 A136 8pf gray 6.00 6.75
675 A136 10pf dk green 55 15
a. Booklet pane, 4 #675 + 5 #677 + label 125.00
676 A136 15pf purple 9.50 90
677 A136 20pf carmine 55 15
678 A136 25pf dk rose lake 25.00 2.50

Engr.
Size: 20x24½mm

679 A136 30pf blue 15.00 20
680 A136 40pf rose lilac ('52) 40.00 20
681 A136 50pf blue gray ('52) 50.00 20
682 A136 60pf brown ('52) 40.00 20
683 A136 70pf dp yel ('52) 165.00 5.00
684 A136 80pf carmine ('52) 125.00 90
685 A136 90pf yel grn ('52) 175.00 1.10
Nos. 670-685 (16) 658.96 21.70
Set, never hinged 2,000.

Imperfs. exist of #671, 673, 675, 681 & 684.

W. K. Roentgen — A137

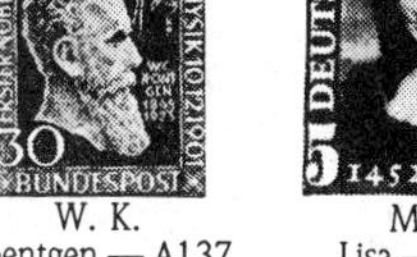
Mona Lisa — A138

1951, Dec. 10

686 A137 30pf blue 40.00 9.00
Never hinged 90.00

50th anniv. of the awarding of the Nobel prize in physics to Wilhelm K. Roentgen.

Perf. 13½
1952, Apr. 15 Wmk. 285 Litho.

687 A138 5pf multicolored 60 50
Never hinged 1.00

500th anniv. of the birth of Leonardo da Vinci.

N. A. Otto — A139

Martin Luther — A140

Wmk. 295
1952, July 25 Engr. *Perf. 14*

688 A139 30pf deep blue 16.00 9.00
Never hinged 37.50

75th anniv. of the four-cycle gas engine.

1952, July 25

689 A140 10pf green 6.75 3.50
Never hinged 16.00

Issued to publicize the Lutheran World Federation Assembly, Hanover, 1952.

Freighter Off Heligoland A141

Carl Schurz A142

1952, Sept. 6

690 A141 20pf red 7.00 5.50
Never hinged 19.00

Return of Heligoland, Mar. 1, 1952.

Perf. 13½
1952, Sept. 17 Litho. Wmk. 285

691 A142 20pf blue, blk & brn org 10.00 5.00
Never hinged 24.00

Centenary of Carl Schurz's arrival in America.

Thurn and Taxis Postilion — A143

Philipp Reis — A144

1952, Oct. 25

692 A143 10pf multicolored 2.75 1.25
Never hinged 6.50

1st Thurn and Taxis stamp, cent.

1952, Oct. 27 Photo. *Perf. 14*

693 A144 30pf blue 19.00 11.00
Never hinged 50.00

75 years of telephone service in Germany.

"Prevent Traffic Accidents" — A145

1953, Mar. 30 Litho. Wmk. 285

694 A145 20pf blk, red & bl grn 7.25 2.00
Never hinged 15.00

Justus von Liebig A146

Red Cross and Compass A147

1953, May 12 Engr. Wmk. 295

695 A146 30pf dark blue 20.00 12.50
Never hinged 45.00

150th anniv. of the birth of Justus von Liebig, chemist.

Perf. 14x13½
1953, May 8 Litho. Wmk. 285

696 A147 10pf dp ol grn & red 9.00 4.00
Never hinged 16.00

125th anniv. of the birth of Henri Dunant, founder of the Red Cross.

War Prisoner and Barbed Wire — A148

Train and Hand Signal — A149

Typographed and Embossed
1953, May 9 Unwmk. *Perf. 14*

697 A148 10pf gray & black 2.00 15
Never hinged 4.75

Issued in memory of the prisoners of war.

Wmk. 295
1953, June 20 Engr. *Perf. 14*

Designs: 10pf, Pigeon and planes. 20pf, Automobiles and traffic signal. 30pf, Ship, barges and buoy.

698 A149 4pf brown 3.25 3.25
699 A149 10pf deep green 7.75 6.00
700 A149 20pf red 10.00 7.00
701 A149 30pf deep ultra 24.00 13.00
Set, never hinged 80.00

Exhibition of Transport and Communications, Munich, 1953.

Pres. Theodor Heuss — A150

1954-60 Typo. *Perf. 14*
Size: 18½x22mm

702 A150 2pf citron 15 15
a. Booklet pane, 5 #702, 4 #704 + label ('55) 27.50
b. Booklet pane, 3 #702, 6 #704 + label ('56) 2.75
c. Booklet pane, 3 #702, 1 #707, 5 #708 + label ('56) 10.00
703 A150 4pf orange brn 15 15
704 A150 5pf rose lilac 15 15
a. Booklet pane, 2 #704, 7 #708 + label ('55) 27.50
705 A150 6pf lt brown 15 30
706 A150 7pf bluish green 15 15
707 A150 8pf gray 15 30
708 A150 10pf green 15 15
a. Booklet pane, 4 #708, 5 #710 + label ('55) 27.50
709 A150 15pf ultra 16 15
710 A150 20pf dk car rose 15 15
711 A150 25pf red brown 32 30

Engr.
Size: 19½x24mm

712 A150 30pf blue 7.25 1.65
713 A150 40pf red violet 3.25 15
714 A150 50pf gray 130.00 30
715 A150 60pf red brown 27.50 30
716 A150 70pf olive 7.25 65
717 A150 80pf deep rose 1.25 1.65
718 A150 90pf deep green 7.75 1.00

Size: 24½x29½mm

719 A150 1m olive green 70 15
720 A150 2m lt vio blue 1.10 65
721 A150 3m deep plum 2.00 75
Nos. 702-721 (20) 189.73 9.20
Set, never hinged 375.00

Coils and sheets of 100 were issued of the 5, 7, 10, 15, 20, 25, 40 and 70pf. Every fifth coil stamp has a control number on the back.
Printings of Nos. 704, 706, 708-711 and 708b were made on fluorescent paper beginning in 1960.
Nos. 702, 709, 714 exist imperf. Value about $375 each.
See Nos. 737b, 755-761.

Catalogue values for unused stamps in this section, from this point to the end of the section, are for Never Hinged items.

Paul Ehrlich and Emil von Behring — A151

15th Century Printer — A152

Perf. 13½
1954, Mar. 13 Wmk. 285 Litho.

722 A151 10pf dark green 14.00 2.25

Centenary of the births of Paul Ehrlich and Emil von Behring, medical researchers.
Exists imperf. Value $1,000.

1954, May 5 Typo. Wmk. 295

723 A152 4pf chocolate 90 20

500th anniversary of the publication of Gutenberg's 42-line Bible. Design from woodcut by Jost Amman.

Bishop's Miter and Sword — A153

Carl F. Gauss — A154

Engraved; Center Embossed
1954, June 5 Unwmk. *Perf. 13½x14*

724 A153 20pf gray & red 9.00 4.00

Martyrdom of Saint Boniface, 1200th anniv.

Wmk. 295
1955, Feb. 23 Engr. *Perf. 14*

725 A154 10pf deep green 3.50 28

Cent. of the death of Carl Friedrich Gauss, mathematician.

The only foreign revenue stamps listed in this catalogue are those also authorized for prepayment of postage.

A155

A156

Perf. 13½

1955, May 7 Litho. Wmk. 304
726 A155 10pf green 3.75 1.00

Cent. of the birth of Oskar von Miller, electrical engineer.

Engraved and Embossed

1955, May 9 Unwmk. *Perf. 13½x14*
727 A156 40pf blue 11.00 2.75

Friedrich von Schiller, poet, 150th death anniv.

1906 Automobile A157

Perf. 13½

1955, June 1 Typo. Wmk. 304
728 A157 20pf red & black 8.25 3.50

German postal motor-bus service, 50th anniv.

Arms of Baden-Württemberg A158

Globe and Atomic Symbol A159

Perf. 13x13½

1955, June 15 Litho. Wmk. 295
729 A158 7pf lemon, blk & brn red 2.75 2.25
730 A158 10pf lemon, blk & grn 4.00 2.25
a. Value omitted 325.00 475.00

Baden-Wurttemberg Exhibition, Stuttgart, 1955.

1955, June 24 Photo. *Perf. 13½x14*
731 A159 20pf rose brown 7.00 60

Issued to encourage scientific research.

Orb and Symbols of Battle — A160

Photogravure and Embossed

Perf. 14x13½

1955, Aug. 10 Unwmk.
732 A160 20pf red lilac 10.00 3.50

Issued in honor of Augsburg and the millenium of the Battle on the Lechfeld.

Set Values
A 15-cent minimum now applies to individual stamps and sets. Where the 15-cent minimum per stamp would increase the value of a set beyond retail, there is a "Set Value" notation giving the retail value of the set.

Family in Flight — A161

Railroad Signal, Tracks — A162

1955, Aug. 2 Engr. Wmk. 304
733 A161 20pf brown lake 2.75 25

Ten years of German expatriation. See No. 930.

Perf. 13½x14

1955, Oct. 5 Litho. Wmk. 304
734 A162 20pf red & black 7.25 1.10

European Timetable conf. at Wiesbaden, Oct. 5-15, 1955.

Stifter Monument and Stylized Trees — A163

1955, Oct. 22 Engr.
735 A163 10pf dark green 3.00 1.40

150th anniv, of the birth of Adalbert Stifter, poet.

United Nations Emblem — A164

Lithographed and Embossed

Perf. 14x13½

1955, Oct. 24 Unwmk.
736 A164 10pf lt green & red 4.00 4.25

United Nations Day, Oct. 24, 1955.

Numeral A165

Numeral and Signature A166

1955-58 Wmk. 304 Typo. *Perf. 14*
737 A165 1pf gray 20 15

Wmk. 295

737A A165 1pf gray ('58) 8.75 12.00
b. Bklt. pane of 10 (#707, 2 each #737A, #704, #708, 3 #710) 27.50

No. 737A was issued only in the booklet pane, No. 737b. No. 737 was issued on fluorescent paper in 1963.

1956, Jan. 7 Engr. Wmk. 304
738 A166 20pf dark red 5.25 1.65

125th anniv. of the birth of Heinrich von Stephan, co-founder of the UPU.

Clavichord A167

1956, Jan. 27 Litho.
739 A167 10pf dull lilac 40 18

200th anniv. of the birth of Wolfgang Amadeus Mozart, composer.

Heinrich Heine — A168

Perf. 13x13½

1956, Feb. 17 Wmk. 295
740 A168 10pf ol grn & blk 2.00 2.00

Centenary of death of Heinrich Heine, poet.

Old Buildings, Lüneburg — A169

Wmk. 304

1956, May 2 Engr. *Perf. 14*
741 A169 20pf dull red 6.50 2.50

Millenary of Lüneburg.

Olympic Rings A170

Robert Schumann A171

1956, June 9 *Perf. 13½x14*
742 A170 10pf slate green 48 32

Issued to publicize the Olympic year, 1956.

1956, July 28 Litho. Unwmk.
743 A171 10pf citron, blk & red 40 15

Schumann, composer, death cent.

Synod Emblem — A172

Thomas Mann — A173

Perf. 13½x13

1956, Aug. 8 Wmk. 304
744 A172 10pf green 2.25 2.00
745 A172 20pf brown carmine 2.75 2.25

Meeting of German Protestants (Evangelical Synod), Frankfurt-on-Main, Aug. 8-12.

1956, Aug. 11 Engr. *Perf. 13½x14*
746 A173 20pf pale rose vio 2.00 1.75

1st anniv. of the death of Thomas Mann, novelist.

Maria Laach Abbey A174

"Rebuilding Europe" A175

1956, Aug. 24 Photo. *Perf. 13x13½*
747 A174 20pf brn lake & gray 1.50 1.40

800th anniv. of the dedication of the Maria Laach Abbey.

Europa Issue, 1956

1956, Sept. 15 Engr. *Perf. 14*
748 A175 10pf green 75 15
749 A175 40pf blue 6.75 90

Issued to symbolize the cooperation among the six countries comprising the Coal and Steel Community.

Plan of Cologne Cathedral and Hand — A176

1956, Aug. 29 Litho. *Perf. 13x13½*
750 A176 10pf gray grn & red brn 1.50 1.50

Issued to commemorate the 77th meeting of German Catholics, Cologne, Aug. 29.

Map of the World and Policeman's Hand — A177

1956, Sept. 1 *Perf. 13½x13*
751 A177 20pf red org, grn & blk 2.00 1.50

Issued on the occasion of the International Police Show, Essen, Sept. 1-23.

Pigeon Holding Letter — A178

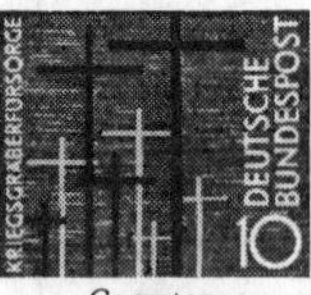
Cemetery Crosses — A179

1956, Oct. 27 Engr. *Perf. 14*
752 A178 10pf green 90 35

Issued to publicize the Day of the Stamp.

1956, Nov. 17 *Perf. 14x13½*
753 A179 10pf slate 90 35

Issued to commemorate the people of Germany who died during WWII and to promote the Society for the Care of Military Cemeteries.

Saar Coat of Arms — A180

1957, Jan. 2 Litho. *Perf. 13x13½*
754 A180 10pf bluish grn & brn 40 25

Issued to commemorate the return of the Saar to Germany. See Saar No. 262.

Heuss Type of 1954

1956-57 Wmk. 304 Engr. *Perf. 14*
Size: 18½x22mm

755 A150 30pf slate green		65	38
756 A150 40pf lt ultra		2.50	15
757 A150 50pf olive		1.65	15
758 A150 60pf lt brown		3.00	20
759 A150 70pf violet		12.00	15
760 A150 80pf red orange		6.25	1.10
761 A150 90pf bluish green		18.00	30
	Nos. 755-761 (7)	44.05	2.43

Nos. 755-756 were printed on both ordinary and fluorescent paper; Nos. 757-761 only on ordinary paper. Issue dates: 40pf, 1956. Others, 1957.

The 40pf and 70pf were also issued in coils. Every fifth coil stamp has control number on back.

Heinrich Hertz — A181

Paul Gerhardt — A182

1957, Feb. 22 Litho. *Perf. 14*
762 A181 10pf lt green & blk 1.00 32

Centenary of the birth of Heinrich Hertz, physicist.

1957, May 18 Engr.
763 A182 20pf carmine lake 40 28

350th anniv. of the birth of Paul Gerhardt, Lutheran clergyman and hymn writer.

Tulip and Post Horn — A183

1957, June 8
764 A183 20pf red orange 42 30

Flora & Philately Exhib., Cologne, June 8-10.

Arms of Aschaffenburg, 1332 — A184

Perf. 13x13½
1957, June 15 Wmk. 304
765 A184 20pf dp salmon & blk 42 30

1000th anniv. of the founding of the Abbey and town of Aschaffenburg.

Scholars (Sapiens Manuscript) A185

1957, June 24 *Perf. 13½x13*
766 A185 10pf blk, bl grn & red org 35 15

Founding of Freiburg University, 500th anniv.

Modern Passenger Freighter A186

1957, June 25 *Perf. 13½x14*
767 A186 15pf brt blue, blk & red 75 80

Merchant Marine Day, June 25.

Liebig Laboratory — A187

1957, July 3 Engr. *Perf. 14x13½*
768 A187 10pf dark green 30 20

350th anniv. of the Justus Liebig School at Ludwig University, Giessen.

Albert Ballin — A188

Television Screen — A189

Perf. 13½x14
1957, Aug. 15 Litho. Wmk. 304
769 A188 20pf dk car rose & blk 1.00 28

Centenary of the birth of Albert Ballin, founder of the Hamburg-America Steamship Line.

1957, Aug. 23 Engr. *Perf. 14x13½*
770 A189 10pf blue vio & grn 25 18

Issued to publicize the television industry.

Europa Issue, 1957

"United Europe" — A190

Lithographed; Tree Embossed
1957-58 Unwmk. *Perf. 14x13½*

771 A190 10pf yel grn & lt bl	24	15
a. Imperf.	*150.00*	*350.00*
772 A190 40pf dk bl & lt bl	4.00	25

Wmk. 304
772A A190 10pf yel grn & lt bl 8.00 7.25

A united Europe for peace and prosperity. Issued: #771-772, Sept. 16; #772A, Aug., 1958.

Water Lily — A191

European Robin — A192

Wmk. 304
1957, Oct. 4 Litho. *Perf. 14*
773 A191 10pf yel grn & org yel 28 18
774 A192 20pf multicolored 35 25

Protection of wild animals and plants.

Carrier Pigeons — A193

Baron vom Stein — A194

1957, Oct. 5
775 A193 20pf dp car & blk 60 28

Intl. Letter Writing Week, Oct. 6-12.

1957, Oct. 26 Engr. *Perf. 13½x14*
776 A194 20pf red 1.25 40

200th anniv. of the birth of Baron Heinrich Friedrich vom und zum Stein, Prussian statesman.

Leo Baeck — A195

Landschaft Building, Stuttgart — A196

1957, Nov. 2
777 A195 20pf dark red 1.25 40

1st anniv. of the death of Rabbi Leo Baeck of Berlin.

Perf. 13x13½
1957, Nov. 16 Litho. Wmk. 304
778 A196 10pf dk grn & yel grn 50 35

500th anniversary of the Wurttemberg Landtag (Assembly).

Coach — A197

"Max and Moritz" — A198

1957, Nov. 26 Engr. *Perf. 14*
779 A197 10pf olive green 50 32

Centenary of the death of Joseph V. Eichendorff, poet.

1958, Jan. 9 Litho. *Perf. 13½x13*

Design: 20pf, Wilhelm Busch.

780 A198 10pf lt ol grn & blk 20 20
781 A198 20pf red & black 40 28

50th anniv. of the death of Wilhelm Busch, humorist.

"Prevent Forest Fires" — A199

1958, Mar. 5 *Perf. 14*
782 A199 20pf brt red & blk 48 25

Rudolf Diesel A200

1958, Mar. 18 Engr. *Perf. 14*
783 A200 10pf dk blue grn 18 18

Centenary of the birth of Rudolf Diesel, inventor.

Giraffe and Lion — A201

View of Old Munich — A202

Perf. 13x13½
1958, May 7 Litho. Wmk. 304
784 A201 10pf brt yel grn & blk 30 28

Zoo at Frankfort on the Main, cent.
Exists imperf. Value $225.

1958, May 22 Engr. *Perf. 14x13½*
785 A202 20pf dark red 30 28

800th anniversary of Munich.

Market Cross, Trier — A203

Heraldic Eagle 5m Coin — A204

1958, June 3
786 A203 20pf dark red & black 30 28

Millennium of the market of Trier (Treves).

1958, June 20 Litho. *Perf. 13x13½*
787 A204 20pf red & black 35 28

10th anniv. of the German currency reform.
Exists imperf. Value $400.

Turner Emblem and Oak Leaf A205

Schulze-Delitzsch A206

Perf. 13½x14

1958, July 21 Wmk. 304
788 A205 10pf gray, blk & dl grn 16 18

150 years of German Turners and on the occasion of the 1958 Turner festival.

1958, Aug. 29 Engr. *Perf. 13½x14*
789 A206 10pf yellow green 16 18

150th anniv. of the birth of Hermann Schulze-Delitzsch, founder of German trade organizations.

Europa Issue, 1958
Common Design Type

1958, Sept. 13 Litho.
Size: 24½x30mm
790 CD1 10pf yel grn & blue 32 15
791 CD1 40pf lt blue & red 2.00 35
Set value 41

Nicolaus Cusanus (Nikolaus Krebs) — A207

Pres. Theodor Heuss — A208

1958, Dec. 3 Litho. *Perf. 14x13½*
792 A207 20pf dk car rose & blk 28 15

500th anniv. of the Cusanus Hospice at Kues, founded by Cardinal Nicolaus (1401-64).
Exists imperf. Value $250.

Common Design Types pictured in section at front of book.

1959 Wmk. 304 *Perf. 14*
793 A208 7pf blue green 24 15
794 A208 10pf green 38 15
795 A208 20pf dk car rose 50 15

Engr.
796 A208 40pf blue 12.00 95
797 A208 70pf deep purple 4.25 32
Nos. 793-797 (5) 17.37
Set value 1.45

Nos. 793-795 were issued in sheets of 100 and in coils. Every fifth coil stamp has a control number on the back.
An experimental booklet containing one pane of 10 of No. 794 was sold at Darmstadt in 1960. Value $650.

Jakob Fugger — A209

Adam Riese — A210

1959, Mar. 6 *Perf. 13x13½*
798 A209 20pf dk red & black 24 20

500th anniversary of the birth of Jakob Fugger the Rich, businessman and banker.

1959, Mar. 28 *Perf. 13½x13*
799 A210 10pf ol grn & blk 22 20

Adam Riese (c. 1492-1559), arithmetic teacher, 400th death anniversary.

The Scott International album provides spaces for an extensive representative collection of the world's postage stamps.

Alexander von Humboldt A211

Buildings, Buxtehude A212

1959, May 6 Engr. *Perf. 13½x14*
800 A211 40pf blue 80 80

Alexander von Humboldt (1769-1859), naturalist and geographer, death centenary.

1959, June 20 Litho. *Perf. 14*
801 A212 20pf lt blue, ver & blk 18 18

Millennium of town of Buxtehude.

Holy Coat of Trier — A213

Synod Emblem — A214

Lithographed; Coat Embossed
1959, July 18 Wmk. 304 *Perf. 14*
802 A213 20pf dull cl, buff & blk 18 18

Showing of the seamless robe of Christ at the Cathedral of Trier, July 19-Sept. 20.

1959, Aug. 12 Litho.
803 A214 10pf grn, brt vio & blk 20 15

Issued to honor the meeting of German Protestants (Evangelical Synod), Munich, Aug. 12-16.

Souvenir Sheet

A215

Portraits: 10pf, George Friedrich Handel. 15pf, Louis Spohr. 20pf, Ludwig van Beethoven. 25pf, Joseph Haydn. 40pf, Felix Mendelssohn-Bartholdy.

Perf. 14x13½

1959, Sept. 8 Engr. Wmk. 304
804 A215 Sheet of 5 27.00 *60.00*
a. 10pf deep green 3.75 5.25
b. 15pf blue 3.75 5.25
c. 20pf dark carmine 3.75 5.25
d. 25pf brown 3.75 5.25
e. 40pf dark blue 3.75 5.25

Opening of Beethoven Hall in Bonn and to honor various anniversaries of German composers.

Europa Issue, 1959
Common Design Type

1959, Sept. 19 Litho. *Perf. 13½x14*
Size: 24x29½mm
805 CD2 10pf olive green 15 15
806 CD2 40pf dark blue 90 32
Set value 38

Uprooted Oak Emblem — A216

1960, Apr. 7 *Perf. 13½x13*
807 A216 10pf grn, blk & lil 25 15
808 A216 40pf bl, blk & org 1.25 1.40

Issued to publicize World Refugee Year, July 1, 1959-June 30, 1960.

Philipp Melanchthon A217

Symbols of Christ's Sufferings A218

1960, Apr. 19 *Perf. 13½x14*
809 A217 20pf dk car rose & blk 1.00 70

400th anniversary of the death of Philipp Melanchthon, co-worker of Martin Luther in the German Reformation.

1960, May 17 *Perf. 14x13½*
810 A218 10pf Prus grn, gray & ocher 15 15

1960 Passion Play, Oberammergau, Bavaria.

Dove, Chalice and Crucifix — A219

1960, July 30 Engr. *Perf. 14x13½*
811 A219 10pf dull green 32 32
812 A219 20pf maroon 50 50

37th Eucharistic World Congress, Munich.

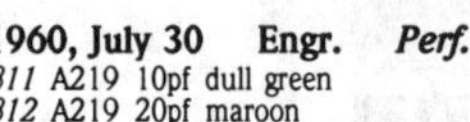

Wrestlers and Olympic Rings — A220

Hildesheim Cathedral, Miters, Cross and Crosier — A221

Sport scenes from Greek urns: 10pf, Sprinters. 20pf, Discus and Javelin throwers. 40pf, Chariot race.

1960, Aug. 8 Wmk. 304
813 A220 7pf red brn 15 15
814 A220 10pf olive green 18 15
815 A220 20pf vermilion 35 15
816 A220 40pf dark blue 60 95

17th Olympic Games, Rome, Aug. 25-Sept. 11.

1960, Sept. 6 Engr. *Perf. 13½x14*
817 A221 20pf claret 48 38

St. Bernward (960-1022) and St. Godehard (960-1038), bishops.

Europa Issue, 1960
Common Design Type

1960, Sept. 19 Wmk. 304
Size: 30x25mm
818 CD3 10pf ol grn & yel grn 15 15
819 CD3 20pf brt red & lt red 40 15
820 CD3 40pf bl & lt bl 60 75

George C. Marshall A222

Steam Locomotive A223

1960, Oct. 15 Litho. *Perf. 13x13½*
821 A222 40pf dp blue & blk 1.75 1.40

Issued to honor George C. Marshall, US general and statesman.

1960, Dec. 7 *Perf. 13½x14*
822 A223 10pf ol bis & blk 15 15

125th anniversary of German railroads.

St. George — A224

Wmk. 304
1961, Apr. 23 Engr. *Perf. 14*
823 A224 10pf green 15 15

Honoring Boy Scouts of the world on St. George's Day (patron saint of Boy Scouts).

Albrecht Dürer — A225

Portraits: 5pf, Albertus Magnus. 7pf, St. Elizabeth of Thuringia. 8pf, Johann Gutenberg. 15pf, Martin Luther. 20pf, Johann Sebastian Bach. 25pf, Balthasar Neumann. 30pf, Immanuel Kant. 40pf, Gotthold Ephraim Lessing. 50pf, Johann Wolfgang von Goethe. 60pf, Friedrich von Schiller. 70pf, Ludwig van Beethoven. 80pf, Heinrich von Kleist. 90pf, Prof. Franz Oppenheimer. 1m, Annette von Droste-Hülshoff. 2m, Gerhart Hauptmann.

1961-64 Typo. *Perf. 14*
Fluorescent or Ordinary Paper
824 A225 5pf olive 15 15
b. Tête bêche pair ('63) 50 60
825 A225 7pf dark bister 15 15
826 A225 8pf lilac 15 15
827 A225 10pf olive green 15 15
b. Tête bêche pair 50 1.00
828 A225 15pf blue 15 15
b. Tête bêche pair ('63) 75 1.00
829 A225 20pf dk red 15 15
b. Tête bêche pair ('63) 75 1.25
830 A225 25pf orange brn 15 15

Engr.
831 A225 30pf gray 15 15
832 A225 40pf blue 15 15
833 A225 50pf red brown 24 15
834 A225 60pf dk car rose ('62) 35 18
835 A225 70pf grnsh black 22 15
a. 70pf deep green 55 15
836 A225 80pf brown 55 30
837 A225 90pf yel ol ('64) 55 22
838 A225 1m violet blue 95 15
839 A225 2m yel grn ('62) 3.00 25
Nos. 824-839 (16) 7.21
Set value 1.95

Nos. 824-825, 827-830, 832, 834-835, 835a were issued in coils as well as in sheets. Every fifth coil stamp has a black control number on the back.
Nos. 824-839, including booklet panes and tête bêche pairs, were printed on fluorescent paper. Nos. 824-829 and 832 were also printed on ordinary paper.

Gottlieb Daimler's Car of 1886 and Signature — A226

Design: 20pf, Carl Benz's 3-wheel car of 1886 and signature.

1961, July 3 **Litho.**

840 A226 10pf green & blk 16 16
841 A226 20pf brick red & blk 22 22

75 years of motorized traffic.

Messenger, Nuremberg, 18th Century — A227

Cathedral, Speyer — A228

Photogravure and Engraved

1961, Aug. 31 **Wmk. 304** ***Perf. 14***

842 A227 7pf brown red & blk 15 15

Issued to publicize the exhibition "The Letter in Five Centuries," Nuremberg.

1961, Sept. 2 **Engr.**

843 A228 20pf vermilion 20 20

900th anniversary of Speyer Cathedral.

Europa Issue, 1961

Common Design Type

1961, Sept. 18 **Litho.**

Size: 28½x18½mm

844 CD4 10pf olive green 15 15
845 CD4 40pf violet blue 30 40
Set value 38 48

No. 844 was printed on both ordinary and fluorescent paper.

Reis Telephone — A229

Wmk. 304

1961, Oct. 26 **Engr.** ***Perf. 14***

846 A229 10pf green 15 15

Cent. of the demonstration of the 1st telephone by Philipp Reis.

Wilhelm Emanuel von Ketteler — A230

1961, Dec. 22 **Litho.**

847 A230 10pf olive grn & blk 15 15

Sesquicentennial of the birth of von Ketteler, Bishop of Mainz and pioneer in social development.

Fluorescent Paper was introduced for all stamps, starting with No. 848. Of the stamps before No. 848, those issued on both ordinary and fluorescent paper include Nos. 704, 706, 708-711, 737, 755-756, 824-829, 832, 844. Those issued only on fluorescent paper (up to No. 848) include Nos. 708b, 830-831, 833-839 and 842.

Drusus Stone and Old View of Mainz — A231

Notes and Tuning Fork — A232

1962, May 10 **Engr.** **Wmk. 304**

848 A231 20pf deep claret 15 15

The 2000th anniversary of Mainz.

1962, July 12 **Litho.** ***Perf. 14***

849 A232 20pf red & black 15 15

Issued to show appreciation of choral singing. The music is from the choral movement for three voices "In dulci jubilo" from "Musae Sioniae" by Michael Praetorius.

"Faith, Thanksgiving, Service" — A233

1962, Aug. 22 **Engr.** **Unwmk.**

850 A233 20pf magenta 15 15

Issued to commemorate the 79th meeting of German Catholics, Hanover, Aug. 22-29.

Open Bible, Chrismon and Chalice — A234

1962, Sept. 11 **Litho.** **Wmk. 304**

851 A234 20pf vermilion & blk 15 15

150th anniversary of the Württemberg Bible Society.

Europa Issue, 1962

Common Design Type

1962, Sept. 17 **Engr.**

Size: 28x23mm

852 CD5 10pf green 15 15
853 CD5 40pf blue 40 40
Set value 46 46

"Bread for the World" — A235

Lithographed and Embossed

1962, Nov. 23 ***Perf. 14***

854 A235 20pf brown red & blk 15 15

Issued in connection with the Advent Collection of the Protestant Church in Germany.

Mother and Child Receiving Gift Parcel — A236

1963, Feb. 9 **Engr.**

855 A236 20pf dark carmine 15 15

Issued to express gratitude to the American organizations, CRALOG (Council of Relief Agencies Licensed to Operate in Germany) and CARE (Cooperative for American Remittances to Everywhere), for help during 1946-1962.

Globe, Cross, Seeds and Stalks of Wheat — A237

Checkered Lily — A238

Lithographed and Engraved

1963, Feb. 27 **Wmk. 304** ***Perf. 14***

856 A237 20pf gray, blk & red 15 15

Issued to publicize the German Catholic "Miser-eor" (I have compassion) campaign against hunger and illness.

1963, Apr. 28 **Litho.** **Unwmk.**

Flowers: 15pf, Lady's slipper. 20pf, Columbine. 40pf, Beach thistle.

857 A238 10pf multi 15 15
858 A238 15pf multi 15 15
859 A238 20pf multi 15 15
860 A238 40pf multi 28 30
Set value 54 52

Flora and Philately Exhibition, Hamburg.

Heidelberg Catechism — A239

1963, May 2 **Litho. & Engr.**

861 A239 20pf dp org, brn org & blk 18 15

400th anniv. of the Heidelberg Catechism, containing the doctrine of the reformed church.

Cross of Golgotha, Darkened Sun and Moon — A240

1963, May 4 **Litho.** **Wmk. 304**

862 A240 10pf grn, dp car, blk & vio 15 15

Consecration of the Regina Martyrum Church, Berlin-Plötzensee, in memory of the victims of Nazism.

Arms of 18 Participating Countries, Paris Conference, 1863 — A241

Map Showing New Railroad Link, German and Danish Flags — A242

1963, May 7 **Engr.**

863 A241 40pf violet blue 25 22

Cent. of the 1st Intl. Postal Conf., Paris, 1863.

1963, May 14 **Litho.** **Unwmk.**

864 A242 20pf multi 15 15

Inauguration of the "Bird Flight Line" railroad link between Germany and Denmark.

Cross — A243

Synod Emblem and Crown of Barbed Wire — A244

Lithographed and Embossed

1963, May 24 **Unwmk.** ***Perf. 14***

865 A243 20pf mag, red & yel 15 15

Cent. of the founding of the Intl. Red Cross in connection with the German Red Cross cent. celebrations, Munster, May 24-26.

Perf. 13½x13

1963, July 24 **Litho.** **Wmk. 304**

866 A244 20pf dp orange & blk 22 22

Meeting of German Protestants (Evangelical Synod), Dortmund, July 24-28.

Europa Issue, 1963

Common Design Type

1963, Sept. 14 **Engr.** ***Perf. 14***

Size: 28x23½mm

867 CD6 15pf green 15 20
868 CD6 20pf red 15 15
Set value 22 26

Old Town Hall, Hanover — A245

State Capitals: No. 870, Hamburg harbor, 775th anniversary. No. 871, North Ferry pier, Kiel. No. 872, National Theater, Munich. No. 873, Fountain and building, Wiesbaden. No. 874, Reichstag Building, Berlin. No. 875, Gutenberg Museum, Mainz. No. 876, Jan Wellem (Johann Wilhelm II, 1658-1716) statue, Dusseldorf. No. 877, City Hall, Bonn. No. 878, City Hall, Bremen. No. 879, View of Stuttgart. No. 879A, Ludwig's Church, Saarbrucken.

1964-65 **Litho.** **Unwmk.** ***Perf. 14***

869 A245 20pf gray, blk & red 24 15
870 A245 20pf multi 24 15
871 A245 20pf multi 24 15
872 A245 20pf multi 24 15
873 A245 20pf multi 24 15
874 A245 20pf blue, blk, & grn 15 15
875 A245 20pf multi 15 15
876 A245 20pf multi 15 15
877 A245 20pf multi ('65) 15 15
878 A245 20pf multi ('65) 15 15
879 A245 20pf multi ('65) 15 15
879A A245 20pf multi ('65) 15 15
Set value 1.88 1.20

View of Ottobeuren Abbey — A246

Lithographed and Engraved

1964, May 29 ***Perf. 14***

880 A246 20pf pink, red & blk 15 15

Ottobeuren Benedictine Abbey, 1200th anniv.

Pres. Heinrich Lübke — A247

Sophie Scholl — A248

1964, July 1 Litho. *Perf. 14*

881	A247	20pf carmine	15	15
882	A247	40pf ultra	16	16
		Set value	22	22

Lübke's re-election. See Nos. 974-975.

1964, July 20 Litho. & Engr.

Designs: No. 884, Ludwig Beck. No. 885, Dietrich Bonhoeffer. No. 886, Alfred Delp. No. 887, Karl Friedrich Goerdeler. No. 888, Wilhelm Leuschner. No. 889, Count James von Moltke. No. 890, Count Claus Schenk von Stauffenberg.

883	A248	20pf blue gray & blk	1.10	2.25
884	A248	20pf blue gray & blk	1.10	2.25
885	A248	20pf blue gray & blk	1.10	2.25
886	A248	20pf blue gray & blk	1.10	2.25
887	A248	20pf blue gray & blk	1.10	2.25
888	A248	20pf blue gray & blk	1.10	2.25
889	A248	20pf blue gray & blk	1.10	2.25
890	A248	20pf blue gray & blk	1.10	2.25
		Nos. 883-890 (8)	8.80	18.00

Issued to honor the German resistance to the Nazis, 1943-45. Printed in sheet of eight, containing one each of Nos. 883-890, se-tenant. Size: 148x105mm. The stamps were valid; the sheet was not, though widely used.

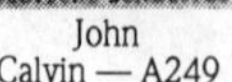

John Calvin — A249

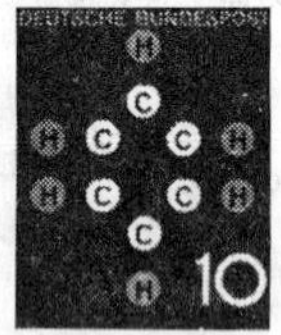

Benzene Ring, Kekulé's Formula — A250

1964, Aug. 3 Litho. *Perf. 14*

891	A249	20pf red & black	15	18

Issued to honor the meeting of the International Union of the Reformed Churches in Germany, Frankfort on the Main, Aug. 3-13.

1964, Aug. 14 Unwmk. *Perf. 14*

Designs: 15pf, Cerenkov radiation, reactor in operation. 20pf, German gas engine.

892	A250	10pf dk brn, brt grn & blk	15	15
893	A250	15pf brt grn, ultra & blk	15	15
894	A250	20pf red, grn & blk	15	15
		Set value	23	23

Progress in science and technology: 10pf, centenary of benzene formula by August Friedrich Kekulé; 15pf, 25 years of nuclear fission, Hahn and Strassmann; 20pf, centenary of German internal combustion engine, Nikolaus August Otto and Eugen Langen.

Ferdinand Lasalle — A251

Radiating Sun — A252

1964, Aug. 31 Litho.

895	A251	20pf slate bl & blk	15	15

Cent. of the death of Ferdinand Lasalle, a founder of the German Labor Movement.

1964, Sept. 2 Engr. Wmk. 304

896	A252	20pf gray & red	15	15

80th meeting of German Catholics, Stuttgart, Sept. 2-6. The inscription from Romans 12:2: ". . . be ye transformed through the renewing of your mind."

Europa Issue, 1964
Common Design Type
1964, Sept. 14 Litho. Unwmk.
Size: 23x29mm

897	CD7	15pf yellow grn & lil	16	15
898	CD7	20pf rose & lilac	16	15
		Set value		20

Judo — A253

Prussian Eagle — A254

1964, Oct. 10

899	A253	20pf multi	15	15

18th Olympic Games, Tokyo, Oct. 10-25.

Lithographed and Embossed
1964, Oct. 30 Unwmk. *Perf. 14*

900	A254	20pf brown org & blk	15	15

250 years of the Court of Accounts in Germany, founded as the Royal Prussian Upper Chamber of Accounts.

John F. Kennedy (1917-63) A255

Castle Gate, Ellwangen A256

1964, Nov. 21 Engr. Wmk. 304

901	A255	40pf dark blue	15	18

1964-66 Typo. Unwmk.

Designs: (German buildings through 12 centuries): 10pf, Wall pavilion, Zwinger, Dresden. 15pf, Tegel Castle, Berlin. 20pf, Portico, Lorsch. 40pf, Trifels Fortress, Palatinate. 60pf, Treptow Gate, Neubrandenburg. 70pf, Osthofen Gate, Soest. 80pf, Elling Gate, Weissenburg.

903	A256	10pf brown ('65)	15	15
904	A256	15pf dk green ('65)	15	15
b.		Tête bêche pair ('65)	1.00	1.00
905	A256	20pf brown red ('65)	15	15
b.		Tête bêche pair ('66)	1.00	1.00
		Engr.		
908	A256	40pf violet bl ('65)	32	15
909	A256	50pf olive bister	52	15
910	A256	60pf rose red	70	30
911	A256	70pf dark green ('65)	80	18
912	A256	80pf chocolate	90	28
		Nos. 903-912 (8)	3.69	
		Set value		1.10

Nos. 903-905, 908, 910-912 were issued in sheets of 100 and in coils. Every fifth coil stamp has a black control number on the back.

Illustrations from the Works of Matthias Claudius — A257

Otto von Bismarck by Franz von Lenbach — A258

1965, Jan. 21 Engr. *Perf. 14*

917	A257	20pf black & red	15	16

150th anniv. of the death of Matthias Claudius, poet and editor of the "Wandsbecker Bothe." Exists imperf. Value $350.

1965, Apr. 1 Litho. *Perf. 14*

918	A258	20pf black & dull red	15	16

Prince Otto von Bismarck (1815-1898), Prussian statesman and 1st chancellor of the German Empire.
Exists imperf. Value $250.

Jet Plane and Space Capsule — A259

Bouquet of Flowers — A260

Designs: 5pf, Traffic lights and signs. 10pf, Communications satellite and ground station. 15pf, Old and new post buses. 20pf, Semaphore telegraph and telecommunication tower. 40pf, Old and new railroad engines. 70pf, Sailing ship and ocean liner.

1965

919	A259	5pf gray & multi	15	15
920	A259	10pf multi	15	15
921	A259	15pf multi	15	15
922	A259	20pf maroon & multi	15	15
923	A259	40pf dk blue & multi	15	15
924	A259	60pf dull vio, yel & lt bl	20	30
925	A259	70pf multi	25	22
		Set value	85	85

Intl. Transport and Communications Exhib., Munich, June 25-Oct. 30. No. 924 also for the 10th anniv. of the reopening of air service by Lufthansa. Issue dates: 60pf, Apr. 1. Others, June 25.
No. 919 exists imperf.

1965, May 1 Litho.

926	A260	15pf multi	15	15

75th anniversary of May Day celebration in Germany.

ITU Emblem A261

Adolph Kolping A262

1965, May 17 Unwmk. *Perf. 14*

927	A261	40pf dp blue & blk	15	15

Cent. of the ITU.

1965, May 26 Typo.

928	A262	20pf black, gray & red	15	15

Kolping (1813-65), founder of the Catholic Unions of Journeymen, the Kolpingwork.

Rescue Ship — A263

Synod Emblem and Labyrinth — A264

1965, May 29 Litho. & Engr.

929	A263	20pf red & black	15	15

Cent. of the German Sea Rescue Service.

Type of 1955 dated "1945-1965"
Perf. 14x13½
1965, July 28 Engr. Wmk. 304

930	A161	20pf gray	15	15

20 years of German expatriation.

Lithographed and Engraved
Perf. 13½x14
1965, July 28 Unwmk.

931	A264	20pf dp bl, grnsh bl & blk	15	15

12th meeting of German Protestants (Evangelical Synod), Cologne, July 28-Aug. 1.

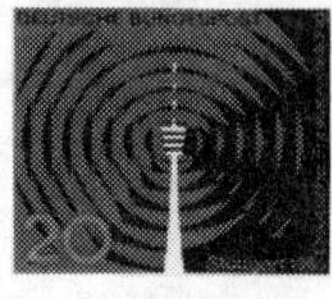

Waves and Stuttgart Television Tower — A265

1965, July 28 Litho. *Perf. 13½x13*

932	A265	20pf dp bl, blk & brt pink	15	15

Issued to publicize the German Radio Exhibition, Stuttgart, Aug. 27-Sept. 5.

Stamps of Thurn and Taxis, 1852-59 A266

1965, Aug. 28 *Perf. 14*

933	A266	20pf multi	15	15

125th anniv. of the introduction of postage stamps in Great Britain.

Europa Issue, 1965
Common Design Type
Perf. 14x13½
1965, Sept. 27 Engr. Wmk. 304
Size: 28x23mm

934	CD8	15pf green	15	16
935	CD8	20pf dull red	15	15
		Set value	24	22

Nordertor, Flensburg A267

Brandenburg Gate A268

Designs: 5pf, Berlin Gate, Stettin. 10pf, Wall Pavilion, Zwinger, Dresden. 20pf, Portico, Lorsch. 40pf, Trifels Fortress, Palatinate. 50pf, Castle Gate, Ellwangen. 60pf, Treptow Gate, Neubrandenburg. 70pf, Osthofen Gate, Soest. 80pf, Elling Gate, Weissenburg. 90pf, Zschocke Ladies' Home, Königsberg. 1m, Melanchthon House, Wittenberg. 1.10m, Trinity Hospital, Hildesheim. 1.30m, Tegel Castle, Berlin. 2m, Löwenberg, Town Hall, interior view.

1966-69 Unwmk. Engr. *Perf. 14*

936	A267	5pf olive	15	15
937	A267	10pf dk brown ('67)	15	15
939	A267	20pf dk green ('67)	16	15
940	A267	30pf yellow green	15	15
941	A267	30pf red ('67)	22	15
942	A267	40pf olive bis ('67)	30	15
943	A267	50pf blue ('67)	38	15
944	A267	60pf dp orange ('67)	1.75	80
945	A267	70pf slate grn ('67)	55	16
946	A267	80pf red brown ('67)	1.75	65
947	A267	90pf black	60	18
948	A267	1m dull blue	70	15
949	A267	1.10m red brown	90	22
950	A267	1.30m green ('69)	1.50	42
951	A267	2m purple	1.40	24
		Nos. 936-951 (15)	10.66	3.87

1966-68 Typo. *Perf. 14*

952	A268	10pf chocolate	15	15
a.		Bklt. pane, 4 #952, 2 #953, 4 #954 ('67)	3.50	
b.		Tête bêche pair	40	30
c.		Bklt. pane, 2 #952, 4 #953	2.00	
953	A268	20pf deep green	15	15
a.		Tête bêche pair ('68)	48	80
b.		Bklt. pane, 2 #953, 2 #954	1.50	
954	A268	30pf red	15	15
a.		Tête bêche pair ('68)	95	90
955	A268	50pf dark blue	65	30
956	A268	100pf dark blue ('67)	5.50	45
		Nos. 952-956 (5)	6.60	
		Set value		90

Nos. 952-956 were issued in sheets of 100 and in coils. Every fifth coil stamp has a black control number on the back.

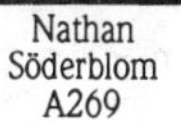

Nathan Söderblom A269

Cardinal von Galen A270

1966, Jan. 15 Litho. *Perf. 13x13½*

959 A269 20pf dull lilac & blk 15 15

Soderblom (1866-1931),Swedish Protestant theologian, who worked for the union of Christian churches and received 1930 Nobel Peace Prize.

1966, Mar. 22 Litho. *Perf. 14*

960 A270 20pf dp lil rose, sal pink & blk 15 15

Clemens August Cardinal Count von Galen (1878-1946), anti-Nazi Bishop of Munster.

"The Miraculous Draught" — A271

G. W. Leibniz — A272

1966, July 13 Litho. *Perf. 14*

961 A271 30pf dp orange & blk 15 15

Issued to commemorate the 81st meeting of German Catholics, Bamberg, July 13-17.

1966, Aug. 24 Unwmk. *Perf. 14*

962 A272 30pf rose car, pink & blk 15 15

Gottfried Wilhelm Leibniz (1646-1716), philosopher and mathematician.

Europa Issue, 1966

Common Design Type

1966, Sept. 24 *Perf. 14*

Size: 23x28½mm

963 CD9 20pf multi 15 18

964 CD9 30pf multi 15 15

Set value 24 24

Diagram of Three-Phase Transmission A273

UNICEF Emblem A274

1966, Sept. 28 Litho.

965 A273 20pf shown 15 15

966 A273 30pf Dynamo 15 15

Set value 20 24

Issued to publicize progress in science and technology: 20pf, 75th anniversary of three-phase power transmission; 30pf, centenary of discovery by Werner von Siemens of the dynamoelectric principle.

1966, Oct. 24 Litho. *Perf. 14*

967 A274 30pf red, blk & gray 15 15

Awarding of the 1965 Nobel Peace Prize to UNICEF.

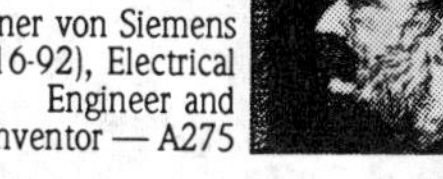
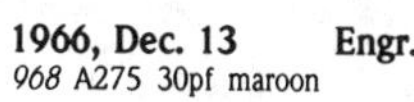

Werner von Siemens (1816-92), Electrical Engineer and Inventor — A275

1966, Dec. 13 Engr. *Perf. 14*

968 A275 30pf maroon 15 15

Europa Issue, 1967

Common Design Type

1967, May 2 Photo. *Perf. 14*

Size: 23x28mm

969 CD10 20pf multi 15 16

970 CD10 30pf multi 15 15

Set value 24 21

Franz von Taxis — A276

"Peace Is Among Us" — A277

Lithographed and Engraved

1967, June 3 *Perf. 14*

971 A276 30pf dp orange & blk 15 15

450th anniv. of the death of Franz von Taxis, founder of the Taxis (Thurn and Taxis) postal system.

1967, June 21

972 A277 30pf brt pink & blk 15 15

13th meeting of German Protestants (Evangelical Synod), Hanover, June 21-25.

Friedrich von Bodelschwingh A278

Perf. 13½x13

1967, July 1 Litho. Unwmk.

973 A278 30pf redsh brown & blk 15 15

Centenary of Bethel Institution (for the incurable). Friedrich von Bodelschwingh (1877-1946), manager of Bethel (1910-1946) and son of the founder.

Lübke Type of 1964

1967, Oct. 14 Litho. *Perf. 14*

974 A247 30pf carmine 15 15

975 A247 50pf ultra 28 20

Set value 28

Re-election of President Heinrich Lübke.

The Wartburg, Eisenach — A279

1967, Oct. 31 Engr. *Perf. 14*

976 A279 30pf red 15 15

450th anniversary of the Reformation.

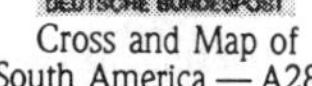
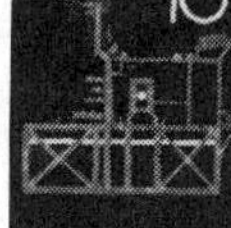
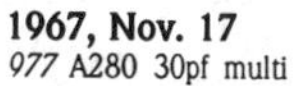

Cross and Map of South America — A280

Koenig Printing Press — A281

1967, Nov. 17 Photo. *Perf. 14*

977 A280 30pf multi 15 15

"Adveniat," aid movement of German Catholics for the Latin American church.

1968, Jan. 12 Litho. *Perf. 14*

Designs: 20pf, Zinc sulfide and lead sulfide crystals. 30pf, Schematic diagram of a microscope.

978 A281 10pf multi 15 15

979 A281 20pf multi 15 15

980 A281 30pf multi 18 20

Set value 32 34

Progress in science and technology: 10pf, 150th anniv. of the Koenig printing press; 20pf, 1000th anniv. of mining in the Harz Mountains; 30pf, cent. of scientific microscope construction.

Symbols of Various Crafts A282

1968, Mar. 8 Litho. *Perf. 14*

981 A282 30pf multi 15 15

Traditions and progress of the crafts. Exists imperf. Value $250.

Souvenir Sheet

Adenauer, Churchill, de Gasperi and Schuman — A283

Portraits: 10pf, Winston S. Churchill. 20pf, Alcide de Gasperi. 30pf, Robert Schuman. 50pf, Konrad Adenauer.

1968, Apr. 19 Litho. *Perf. 14*

Black Inscriptions

982 A283 Sheet of 4 1.90 2.75

a. 10pf dark red brown 40 55

b. 20pf green 40 55

c. 30pf dark red 40 55

d. 50pf bright blue 40 55

1st anniv. of the death of Konrad Adenauer (1876-1967), chancellor of West Germany (1949-63), and honoring leaders in building a united Europe.

Europa Issue, 1968

Common Design Type

1968, Apr. 29 Photo.

Size: 29x24½mm

983 CD11 20pf green, yel & brn 15 16

984 CD11 30pf car, yel & brn 18 15

Set value 22

Karl Marx (1818-83) A284

Pierre de Coubertin A285

Lithographed and Engraved

1968, Apr. 29 *Perf. 14*

985 A284 30pf red, black & gray 15 15

1968, June 6 Unwmk. *Perf. 14*

986 A285 30pf lilac & dk pur 18 15

Nos. 986,B434-B437 (5) 1.83 1.80

19th Olympic Games, Mexico City, Oct. 12-27.

Opening Bars, "Die Meistersinger von Nurnberg," by Wagner — A286

Lithographed and Photogravure

1968, June 21

987 A286 30pf gray, blk & fawn 15 15

Cent. of the 1st performance of Richard Wagner's "Die Meistersinger von Nurnberg."

Konrad Adenauer (1876-1967) — A287

1968, July 19 Litho. *Perf. 14*

988 A287 30pf dp orange & blk 15 15

Cross and Dove in Center of Universe A288

1968, July 19 Litho. & Engr.

989 A288 20pf brt grn, bl blk & yel 15 15

Issued to publicize the 82nd meeting of German Catholics, Essen, Sept. 4-8.

North German Confederation Nos. 4 and 10 — A289

1968, Sept. 5 Engr. *Perf. 14*

990 A289 30pf cop red, gray vio & blk 15 15

Cent. of the stamps of the North German Confederation.

Arrows Symbolizing Determination A290

Human Rights Flame A291

1968, Sept. 26 Photo. *Perf. 14*

991 A290 30pf multi	15	15

Centenary of the German trade unions.

1968, Dec. 10 Photo. *Perf. 14*

992 A291 30pf multi	15	15

International Human Rights Year.

Junkers 52 — A292

Design: 30pf, Boeing 707.

1969, Feb. 6 Litho. *Perf. 14*

993 A292 20pf green & multi	35	18
994 A292 30pf red & multi	50	18

50th anniv. of German airmail service.

Five-pointed Star — A293

1969, Apr. 28 Litho. *Perf. 13½x13*

995 A293 30pf red & multi	22	15

50th anniv. of the ILO.

Europa Issue, 1969
Common Design Type

1969, Apr. 28 Photo. *Perf. 14*
Size: 29x23mm

996 CD12 20pf green, blue & yel	28	16
997 CD12 30pf red brn, yel & blk	32	15
Set value		22

Heraldic Eagles of Federal and Weimar Republics A294

1969, May 23 Photo. *Perf. 14*

998 A294 30pf red, black & gold	38	18

20th anniversary of the German Basic Law, and the 50th anniversary of the proclamation of the Weimar Constitution.

Crosses — A295

1969, June 4 Litho. & Engr.

999 A295 30pf dk violet bl & cr	25	15

50th anniversary of the German War Graves Commission.

Seashore — A296

1969, June 4 *Perf. 14*

1000 A296 10pf shown	15	15
1001 A296 20pf Foothills	32	30
1002 A296 30pf Mountains	20	15
1003 A296 50pf Riverbed	40	40

Issued to publicize Nature Protection.

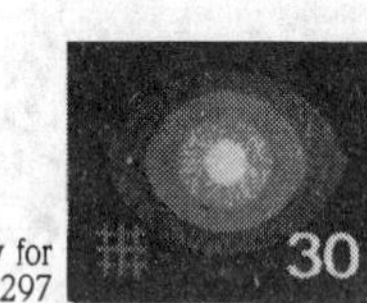
"Hungry for Justice" — A297

1969, July 7 Litho. *Perf. 14*

1004 A297 30pf multi	25	15

14th meeting of German Protestants (Evangelical Synod), Stuttgart, July 16-20.

Electromagnetic Field — A298

Maltese Cross — A299

1969, Aug. 11 Litho. *Perf. 14*

1005 A298 30pf red & multi	25	15

Issued to publicize the German Radio Exhibition, Stuttgart, Aug. 29-Sept. 7.

1969, Aug. 11 *Perf. 13x13½*

1006 A299 30pf red & black	25	15

Maltese Relief Service, founded 1955, worldwide activities in social services, first aid and disaster assistance.

Souvenir Sheet

Marie Juchacz, Marie-Elisabeth Lüders and Helene Weber — A300

1969, Aug. 11 Engr. *Perf. 14*

1007 A300 Sheet of 3	70	70
a. 10pf olive	15	15
b. 20pf dark green	22	15
c. 30pf lake	32	15

50th anniv. of universal women's suffrage, Marie Juchacz (1879-1956), Marie-Elisabeth Lüders (1878-1966) and Helene Weber (1881-1962) were members of the German Reichstag.

Bavaria No. 16 — A301

Brine Pipe Line — A302

1969, Sept. 4 Litho. & Embossed

1008 A301 30pf gray & rose	25	15

23rd meeting of the Federation of German Philatelists, Sept. 6, the 70th Philatelists' Day, Sept. 7, and the phil. exhib. "120 Years of Bavarian Stamps" in Garmish-Partenkirchen, Sept. 4-7.

1969, Sept. 4 Litho. *Perf. 13½x13*

1009 A302 20pf multi	25	15

350th anniversary of the Brine Pipe Line from Traunstein to Bad Reichenhall.

Rothenburg ob der Tauber — A303

Lithographed and Engraved

1969, Sept. 4 *Perf. 14*

1010 A303 30pf dark red & blk	25	15

See #1047-1049, 1067-1069A, 1106-1110.

Pope John XXIII (1881-1963) A304

Mahatma Gandhi (1869-1948) A305

1969, Oct. 2 Engr. *Perf. 13½x14*

1011 A304 30pf dark red	25	15

1969, Oct. 2 Litho.

1012 A305 20pf yellow grn & blk	25	15

Ernst Moritz Arndt A306

Ludwig van Beethoven A307

1969, Nov. 13 Litho. & Engr.

1013 A306 30pf gray & maroon	25	15

Arndt (1769-1860), historian, poet and member of German National Assembly.

1970, Mar. 20 *Perf. 13½x14*

Portraits: 20pf, Georg Wilhelm Hegel (1770-1831), philosopher. 30pf, Friedrich Hölderlin (1770-1843), poet.

1014 A307 10pf pale vio & blk	15	15
1015 A307 20pf olive & blk	16	15
1016 A307 30pf rose & blk	25	15
Set value		32

Bicentenary of births of Beethoven, Hegel and Hölderlin.

Saar No. 171 — A308

1970, Apr. 29 Photo. *Perf. 14x13½*

1017 A308 30pf blk, red & gray grn	25	15

Issued to publicize the SABRIA National Stamp Exhibition, Saarbrucken, Apr. 29-May 4. No. 1017 was issued Apr. 29 at the SABRIA post office in Saarbrucken, on May 4 throughout Germany.

Europa Issue, 1970
Common Design Type

1970, May 4 Engr. *Perf. 14x13½*
Size: 28x23mm

1018 CD13 20pf green	28	15
1019 CD13 30pf red	38	15
Set value		22

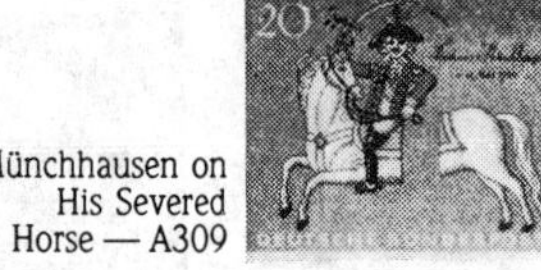
Münchhausen on His Severed Horse — A309

1970, May 11 Litho. *Perf. 13½x13*

1020 A309 20pf multi	22	15

Soldier and storyteller Count Hieronymus C. F. von Münchhausen (1720-97).

Seagoing Vessel and Underpass — A310

Nurse Assisting Elderly Woman — A311

1970, June 18 Litho. *Perf. 14*

1021 A310 20pf multi	22	15

North Sea-Baltic Sea Canal, 75th anniv.

1970 Photo.

Designs: 5pf, Welder (industrial protection). 10pf, Mountain climbers (rescuer bringing down casualty). 30pf, Fireman. 50pf, Stretcher bearer, casualty and ambulance. 70pf, Rescuer and drowning boy.

1022 A311 5pf dull blue & multi	15	15
1023 A311 10pf brown & multi	15	15
1024 A311 20pf green & multi	16	15
1025 A311 30pf red & multi	28	15
1026 A311 50pf blue & multi	45	35
1027 A311 70pf green & multi	52	48
Nos. 1022-1027 (6)	1.71	
Set value		1.20

Honoring various voluntary services.
Issued: 20pf, 30pf, June 18; others, Sept. 21.

Pres. Gustav Heinemann A312

Cross Seen through Glass A313

1970-73 Engr. *Perf. 14*

1028 A312 5pf dark gray	15	15
1029 A312 10pf brown	15	15
1030 A312 20pf green	16	15
1030A A312 25pf deep yel grn	22	15
1031 A312 30pf red brown	40	15
1032 A312 40pf brown org	45	15
1033 A312 50pf dark blue	1.50	15
1034 A312 60pf blue	1.00	15

1035 A312 70pf dark brown 80 28
1036 A312 80pf slate grn 80 20
1037 A312 90pf magenta 1.50 1.25
1038 A312 1m olive 80 35
1038A A312 110pf olive gray 1.00 35
1039 A312 120pf ocher 1.00 42
1040 A312 130pf ocher 1.10 35
1040A A312 140pf dk blue grn 1.25 48
1041 A312 150pf purple 1.25 32
1042 A312 160pf orange 1.40 60
1042A A312 170pf orange 1.50 32
1043 A312 190pf deep claret 2.25 55
1044 A312 2m deep violet 1.50 40
Nos. 1028-1044 (21) 20.18 7.07

Issue dates: 5pf, 1m, July 23. 10pf, 20pf, Oct. 23. 30pf, 90pf, 2m, Jan. 7, 1971. 40pf, 50pf, 70pf, 80pf, Apr. 8, 1971. 60pf, June 25, 1971. 25pf, Aug. 27, 1971. 120pf, 160pf, Mar. 8, 1972. 130pf, June 20, 1972. 150pf, July 5, 1972. 170pf, Sept. 11, 1972. 110pf, 140pf, 190pf, Jan. 16, 1973.

1970, Aug. 25 Litho.
1045 A313 20pf emerald & yellow 18 15

Issued to publicize the world mission of Catholic missionaries who bring the Gospel to all peoples.

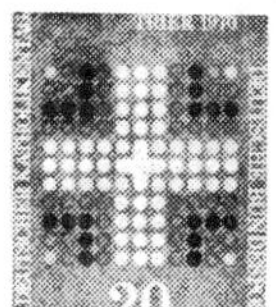

Cross
A314

Comenius
A315

1970, Sept. 4 *Perf. 13x13½*
1046 A314 20pf multi 18 15

Issued to publicize the 83rd meeting of German Catholics, Trier, Sept. 9-13.

Town Type of 1969

Designs: No. 1047, View of Cochem and Moselle River. No. 1048, Cathedral and view of Freiburg im Breisgau. No. 1049, View of Oberammergau.

1970 Litho. Engr. *Perf. 14*
1047 A303 20pf apple grn & blk 16 15
1048 A303 20pf green & dk brn 22 15
1049 A303 30pf dp orange & blk 25 15
Set value 38

Issue dates: No. 1047, Sept. 21; No. 1048, Nov. 4; No. 1049, May 11.

1970, Nov. 12 *Perf. 13½x14*
1050 A315 30pf dark red & blk 28 15

John Amos Comenius (1592-1670), theologian and educator.

Friedrich
Engels — A316

Imperial Eagle,
1872 — A317

1970, Nov. 27 Litho. *Perf. 14*
1051 A316 50pf red & vio blue 42 45

Engels (1820-95), socialist, collaborator with Marx.

1971, Jan. 18 Litho. *Perf. 13½x14*
1052 A317 30pf multi 25 15

Centenary of the German Empire.

Friedrich Ebert
(Germany No.
378) — A318

Molecule Diagram
Textile
Pattern — A319

1971, Jan. 18 *Perf. 13*
1053 A318 30pf red brn, ol & blk 25 15

Ebert (1871-1925), 1st Pres. of the German Republic.

1971, Feb. 18 Litho. *Perf. 13½x13*
1054 A319 20pf brt grn, red & blk 18 15

Synthetic textile fiber research, 125th anniversary.

School
Crossing — A320

Signal to
Pass — A321

Traffic Signs: 20pf, Proceed with caution. 30pf, Stop. 50pf, Pedestrian crossing.

1971, Feb. 18 *Perf. 14*
1055 A320 10pf black, ultra & red 15 15
1056 A320 20pf black, red & grn 20 15
1057 A320 30pf black, gray & red 30 15
1058 A320 50pf black, ultra & red 60 38
Set value 66

New traffic rules, effective Mar. 1, 1971.

1971, Apr. 16 Photo. *Perf. 14*

Traffic Signs: 10pf, Warning signal. 20pf, Drive at right. 30pf, "Observe pedestrian crossings."

1059 A321 5pf blue, blk & car 15 15
1060 A321 10pf multicolored 15 15
1061 A321 20pf brt grn, blk & car 15 15
1062 A321 30pf carmine & multi 30 18
Set value 59 50

New traffic rules, effective Mar. 1, 1971.

Luther Facing Charles
V, Woodcut by
Rabus — A322

Thomas à
Kempis — A323

1971, Mar. 18 *Perf. 14*
1063 A322 30pf red & black 28 15

450th anniversary of the Diet of Worms.

Europa Issue, 1971
Common Design Type

1971, May 3 Photo. *Perf. 14*
Size: 28½x23mm
1064 CD14 20pf green, gold & blk 20 15
1065 CD14 30pf dp car, gold & blk 40 15
Set value 15

1971, May 3 Engr.
1066 A323 30pf red & black 30 15

500th anniversary of the death of Thomas à Kempis (1379-1471), Augustinian monk, author of "The Imitation of Christ."

Town Type of 1969

Designs: 20pf, View of Goslar. No. 1068, View of Nuremberg. No. 1069, Heligoland. 40pf, Heidelberg.

1971-72 Litho. & Engr. *Perf. 14*
1067 A303 20pf brt green & blk 20 15
1068 A303 30pf vermilion & blk 35 15
1069 A303 30pf lt grn & blk ('72) 32 15
1069A A303 40pf orange & blk ('72) 40 16

Issue dates: 20pf, Sept. 15; No. 1068, May 21; Nos. 1069, 1069A, Oct. 20.

Dürer's
Signature — A324

1971, May 21 Engr.
1070 A324 30pf copper red & blk 30 15

500th anniversary of the birth of Albrecht Dürer (1471-1528), painter and engraver.

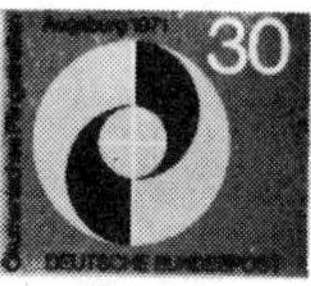

Congress
Emblem — A325

Illustration from
New
Astronomy, by
Kepler — A326

1971, May 28 Litho. *Perf. 13½x13*
1071 A325 30pf red, orange & blk 30 15

Ecumenical Meeting at Pentecost of the German Evangelical and Catholic Churches, Augsburg, June 2-5.

1971, June 25 Photo. *Perf. 14*
1072 A326 30pf brt car, gold & blk 30 15

Johannes Kepler (1571-1630), astronomer.

Dante
Alighieri — A327

"Matches Cause
Fires" — A328

1971, Sept. 3 Engr. *Perf. 14*
1073 A327 10pf black 15 15

650th anniversary of the death of Dante Alighieri (1265-1321), poet.

1971-74 Typo. *Perf. 14*

Designs: 10pf, Broken ladder. 20pf, Hand and circular saw. 25pf, "Alcohol and automobile." 30pf, Safety helmets prevent injury. 40pf, Defective plug. 50pf, Nail sticking from board. 60pf, 70pf, Traffic safety (ball rolling before car). 1m, Hoisted cargo. 1.50m, Fenced-in open manhole.

1074 A328 5pf orange 20 15
a. Bklt. pane, 2 each #1074, 1077 1079 ('74) 6.00
1075 A328 10pf dark brown 15 15
a. Bklt. pane, 4 #1075, 2 #1078 3.25
b. Bklt. pane, 2 each #1075-1076, 1078-1079 ('75) 6.00
c. Bklt. pane, 2 each #1079, 1075, 1078, 1076 19.00
1076 A328 20pf purple 20 15
1077 A328 25pf green 40 15
1078 A328 30pf dark red 22 15
1079 A328 40pf rose claret 28 15
1080 A328 50pf Prus blue 3.00 18
1081 A328 60pf violet blue 2.00 35
1082 A328 70pf green & vio bl 90 22
1083 A328 100pf olive 1.50 28
1085 A328 150pf red brown 6.00 70
Nos. 1074-1085 (11) 14.85
Set value 2.15

Accident prevention.

Issued in sheets of 100 and in coils. Every fifth coil stamp has a control number on the back.

Issue dates: 25pf, 60pf, Sept. 10. 5pf, Oct. 29. 10pf, 30pf, Mar. 8, 1972. 40pf, June 20, 1972. 20pf, 100pf, July 5, 1972. 150pf, Sept. 11, 1972. 50pf, Jan. 16, 1973. 70pf, June 5, 1973.

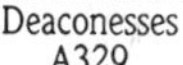

Deaconesses
A329

Senefelder's
Lithography Press
A330

1972, Jan. 20 Litho. *Perf. 13x13½*
1087 A329 25pf green, blk & gray 25 15

Wilhelm Löhe (1808-1872), founder of the Deaconesses Training Institute at Neuendettelsau.

1972, Apr. 14 Litho. *Perf. 13½x13*
1088 A330 25pf multi 25 15

175th anniversary of the invention of the lithographic printing process by Alois Senefelder in 1796.

Europa Issue 1972
Common Design Type

1972, May 2 Photo. *Perf. 13½x14*
Size: 23x29mm
1089 CD15 25pf yel grn, dk bl & yel 30 15
1090 CD15 30pf pale rose, dk & lt bl 40 15

Lucas Cranach, by
Dürer
A331

Archer in
Wheelchair
A332

Lithographed and Engraved

1972, May 18 *Perf. 14*
1091 A331 25pf green, buff & blk 25 15

Cranach (1472-1553), painter and engraver.

1972, July 18 Litho. *Perf. 14*
1092 A332 40pf yel, blk & red brn 38 20

21st Stoke-Mandeville Games for the Paralyzed, Heidelberg, Aug. 1-10.

Kurt
Schumacher — A333

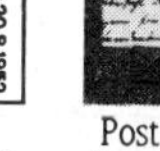

Post Horn and
Decree — A334

1972, Aug. 10 Litho. & Engr.
1093 A333 40pf red & black 38 15

Schumacher (1895-1952), 1st chairman of the German Social Democratic Party.

1972, Aug. 18 Photo.
1094 A334 40pf gold, car & blk 38 15

Centenary of the German Postal Museum, Berlin. Design shows page from Heinrich von Stephan's decree establishing the museum.

Open Book — A335

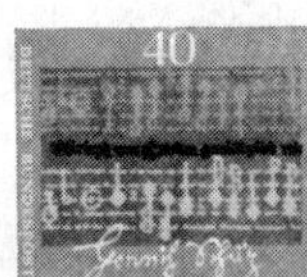

Music by Heinrich Schütz — A336

1972, Sept. 11 Photo. *Perf. 13x13½*
1095 A335 40pf red & multi 38 15

International Book Year 1972.

Lithographed and Engraved
1972, Sept. 29 *Perf. 14*
1096 A336 40pf multi 38 15

300th anniversary of the death of Heinrich Schütz (1585-1672), composer.

Carnival Dancers A337

1972, Nov. 10 Litho. *Perf. 14*
1097 A337 40pf red & multi 40 15

Cologne Carnival sesquicentennial.

Heinrich Heine (1797-1856), Poet A338

1972, Dec. 13 Litho. *Perf. 14*
1098 A338 40pf rose, blk & red 38 15

"Bread for the World" A339

1972, Dec. 13 Photo. *Perf. 14*
1099 A339 30pf grn & red 38 38

14th "Bread for the World-Developing Peace" campaign of the Protestant Church in Germany.

Würzburg Cathedral, 13th Century Seal — A340

1972, Dec. 13 Litho.
1100 A340 40pf dp car, lil rose & blk 38 15

Synod 72, meeting of Catholic bishoprics, Würzburg.

Colors of France and Germany Interlaced — A340a

1973, Jan. 22 Litho. *Perf. 14*
Size: 51x28mm
1101 A340a 40pf multi 38 18

10th anniversary of the Franco-German Cooperation Treaty.

Meteorological Map — A341

1973, Feb. 19 Litho. *Perf. 14*
1102 A341 30pf multi 30 15

Cent. of intl. meteorological cooperation.

Radio Tower and "Interpol" — A342

1973, Feb. 19 *Perf. 13½x13*
1103 A342 40pf blk & red 38 15

50th anniversary of International Criminal Police Organization (INTERPOL).

Copernicus and Solar System A343

1973, Feb. 19 *Perf. 14*
1104 A343 40pf blk & red 38 15

500th anniversary of the birth of Nicolaus Copernicus (1473-1543), astronomer.

Festival Poster — A344

Maximilian Kolbe — A345

1973, Mar. 15 Photo. *Perf. 14*
1105 A344 40pf multi 38 15

German Turner Festival, Stuttgart, June 12-17.

Town Type of 1969

Designs: 30pf, Saarbrücken. No. 1107, Ship in Hamburg Harbor. No. 1108, Rüdesheim. No. 1109, Aachen. No. 1110, Ships, Bremen Harbor.

1973 Lithographed and Engraved

1106 A303	30pf yel grn & blk	30	15
1107 A303	40pf red & blk	38	15
1108 A303	40pf org & blk	38	15
1109 A303	40pf brn red & blk	40	15
1110 A303	40pf red & blk	40	15
	Nos. 1106-1110 (5)	1.86	75

Issue dates: Nos. 1107-1108, Mar. 15; Nos. 1106, 1109-1110, Oct. 19.

Europa Issue 1973
Common Design Type
1973, Apr. 30 Photo. *Perf. 13½x14*
Size: 38½x21mm
1114 CD16 30pf grn, lt grn & yel 38 15
1115 CD16 40pf dp mag, lil & yel 55 15
Set value 24

1973, May 25 Litho. *Perf. 14*
1116 A345 40pf red, blk & brn 38 15

Maximilian Kolbe (1894-1941), Polish priest who died in Auschwitz and was beatified in 1971.

"R" for Roswitha A346

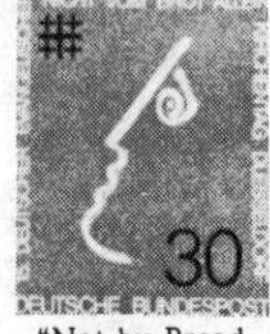

"Not by Bread Alone" A347

1973, May 25
1117 A346 40pf red, blk & yel 40 15

Millenary of the death of Roswitha of Gandersheim, Germany's first poetess.

1973, May 25 Photo.
1118 A347 30pf multi 35 15

15th meeting of German Protestants (Evangelical Synod), Dusseldorf, June 27-July 1.

Environment Emblem and "Waste" A348

Designs (Environment Emblem and): 30pf, "Water." 40pf, "Noise." 70pf, "Air."

1973, June 5 Litho.
1119 A348 25pf multi 24 15
1120 A348 30pf multi 30 15
1121 A348 40pf org & multi 42 20
1122 A348 70pf ultra & multi 75 65

International environment protection and Environment Day, June 5.

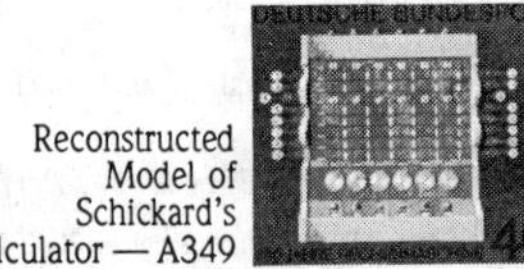

Reconstructed Model of Schickard's Calculator — A349

1973, June 12
1123 A349 40pf org & multi 45 45

350th anniv. of the calculator built by Prof. Wilhelm Shickard, University of Tubingen.

Otto Wels (1873-1939), Leader of German Social Democratic Party — A350

1973, Sept. 14 Litho. *Perf. 14*
1124 A350 40pf magenta & lilac 38 15

Lubeck Cathedral A351

1973, Sept. 14 Litho. & Engr.
1125 A351 40pf blk & multi 38 15

800th anniversary of Lubeck Cathedral.

Emblems from UN and German Flags A352

1973, Sept. 21 Litho.
1126 A352 40pf multi 52 15

Germany's admission to the UN.

Radio and Speaker, 1923 — A353

Luise Otto-Peters — A354

1973, Oct. 19 Photo. *Perf. 14*
1127 A353 30pf brt grn & multi 28 15

50 years of German broadcasting.

1974, Jan. 15 Litho. & Engr.
1128 A354 40pf shown 60 35
1129 A354 40pf Helene Lange 60 35
1130 A354 40pf Gertrud Bäumer 60 35
1131 A354 40pf Rosa Luxemburg 60 35

Honoring German women writers and leaders in political and women's movements.

Drop of Blood and Police Car Light A355

1974, Feb. 15 Photo. *Perf. 14*
1132 A355 40pf car & ultra 38 15

Blood donor service in conjunction with accident emergency service.

Handicapped People — A356

1974, Feb. 15 Litho. *Perf. 14*
1133 A356 40pf red & blk 38 15

Rehabilitation of the handicapped.

Thomas Aquinas Teaching — A357

1974, Feb. 15
1134 A357 40pf blk & red 38 15

St. Thomas Aquinas (1225-1274), scholastic philosopher.

Deer in Red, by Franz Marc — A358

Paintings: No. 1136, Girls under Trees, by August Macke, 40pf, Portrait in Blue, by Alexej von

Jawlensky, vert, 50pf, Pechstein (man) Asleep, by Erich Heckel, vert, 70pf, "Big Still-life," by Max Beckmann. 120pf, Old Farmer, by Ernst Ludwig Kirchner, vert.

1974 **Photo.**

1135	A358	30pf multi	28	15
1136	A358	30pf multi	25	15
1137	A358	40pf multi	40	15
1138	A358	50pf multi	52	20
1139	A358	70pf multi	65	45
1140	A358	120pf multi	1.40	95
		Nos. 1135-1140 (6)	3.50	2.05

German expressionist painters.
Issued: #1135, 1137, Feb. 15; #1136, 1138, Aug. 16; #1139-1140, Oct. 29.

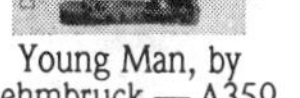

Young Man, by Lehmbruck — A359

Immanuel Kant — A360

Europa: 40pf, Kneeling Woman, by Wilhelm Lehmbruck.

1974, Apr. 17 **Litho.** ***Perf. 14***

1141	A359	30pf multi	35	15
1142	A359	40pf multi	45	15
		Set value		22

1974 **Litho. and Engr.** ***Perf. 14***

1143	A360	40pf Klopstock	35	16

Engr.

1144	A360	90pf shown	60	35

Friedrich Gottlieb Klopstock (1724-1803), poet, and Immanuel Kant (1724-1804), philosopher.
Issue dates: 40pf, May 15; 90pf, Apr. 17.

Souvenir Sheet

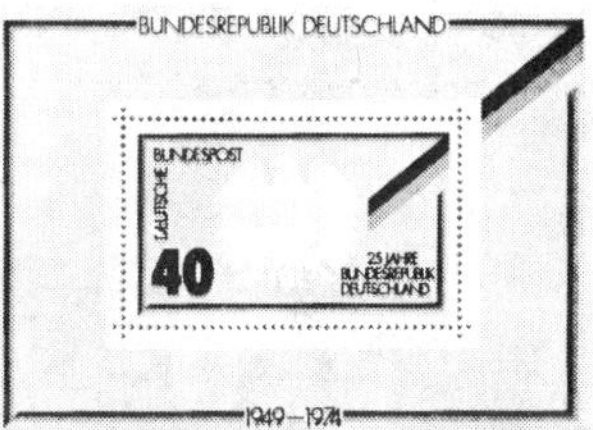

Federal Eagle and Flag — A361

1974, May 15 **Litho. & Embossed**

1145	A361	40pf gray & multi	95	95

Federal Republic of Germany, 25th anniv.

Soccer and Games Emblem A362

Design: 40pf, Three soccer players.

1974, May 15 **Litho.**

1146	A362	30pf grn & multi	55	15
1147	A362	40pf org & multi	75	18

World Cup Soccer Championship, Munich, June 13-July 7.

Crowned Cross Emblem of Diaconate A363

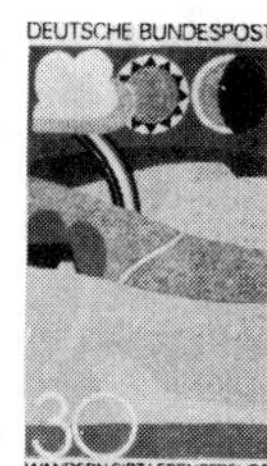

Landscape A364

1974, May 15

1148	A363	40pf multi	38	15

125th anniversary of the Diaconal Association of the German Protestant Church.

1974, May 15

1149	A364	30pf multi	30	15

To promote hiking and youth hostels.

Broken Bars of Prison Window — A365

1974, July 16 **Litho.** ***Perf. 14x13½***

1150	A365	70pf vio bl & blk	65	30

"Amnesty International," an organization for the protection of the rights of political, non-violent, prisoners.

Hans Holbein, Self-portrait — A366

Lithographed and Engraved

1974, July 16 ***Perf. 13½x14***

1151	A366	50pf multi	52	18

450th anniversary of the death of Hans Holbein the Elder (c. 1470-1524), painter.

Man and Woman Looking at Moon, by Friedrich — A367

1974, Aug. 16 **Photo.** ***Perf. 14***

1152	A367	50pf multi	48	22

Caspar David Friedrich (1774-1840), German Romantic painter.

Swiss and German 19th Century Mail Boxes — A368

Mothers and Foundation Emblem — A369

1974, Oct. 29 **Litho.** ***Perf. 14***

1153	A368	50pf red & multi	60	22

Centenary of Universal Postal Union.

1975, Jan. 15 **Litho.** ***Perf. 13***

1154	A369	50pf multi	48	15

Convalescent Mothers' Foundation, 25th anniversary.

Annette Kolb (1875-1967), Writer — A370

German women writers: 40pf, Ricarda Huch (1864-1947), writer. 50pf, Else Lasker-Schüler (1869-1945), poetess. 70pf, Gertrud von Le Fort (1876-1971), writer.

Lithographed and Engraved

1975, Jan. 15 ***Perf. 14***

1155	A370	30pf brown & multi	32	16
1156	A370	40pf multi	40	25
1157	A370	50pf claret & multi	60	28
1158	A370	70pf blue & multi	85	65

Dr. Albert Schweitzer A371

Design: 40pf, Hans Böckler.

1975 **Engr.**

1159	A371	40pf grn & blk	35	15
1160	A371	70pf bl & blk	70	30

Böckler (1875-1951), German Workers' Union leader, and of Dr. Albert Schweitzer (1875-1965), medical missionary. Issued: 40pf, Feb. 14; 70pf, Jan. 15.

Head, by Michelangelo A372

Plan of St. Peter's, Rome A373

1975, Feb. 14 **Photo.** ***Perf. 14***

1161	A372	70pf vio bl & blk	1.25	1.25

Michelangelo Buonarroti (1475-1564), Italian sculptor, painter and architect.

1975, Feb. 14

1162	A373	50pf red & multi	45	18

Holy Year 1975, the "Year of Reconciliation."

Ice Hockey A374

1975, Feb. 14 **Litho.** ***Perf. 14***

1163	A374	50pf bl & multi	48	18

Ice Hockey World Championship, Munich and Düsseldorf, Apr. 3-19.

Concentric Group, by Oskar Schlemmer — A375

Europa: 50pf, Bauhaus Staircase, painting by Oskar Schlemmer (1888-1943) and CEPT emblem.

1975, Apr. 15 **Litho. & Engr.**

1164	A375	40pf gray & multi	50	16
1165	A375	50pf gray & multi	65	16

Eduard Mörike, Weather Vane, Quill and Signature A376

1975, May 15

1166	A376	40pf multi	40	15

Eduard Mörike (1804-75), pastor and poet.

Joust, from Jousting Book of William IV — A377

1975, May 15 **Photo.** ***Perf. 14***

1167	A377	50pf multi	48	15

500th anniv. of the Wedding of Landshut, (last Duke of Landshut married the daughter of King of Poland, now a yearly local festival).

Cathedral of Mainz A378

1975, May 15 **Litho. & Engr.**

1168	A378	40pf multi	38	15

Millennium of the Cathedral of Mainz.

Buying Sets
It is often less expensive to purchase complete sets than individual stamps that make up the set. Set values are provided for many such sets.

View of Neuss, Woodcut A379

Space Laboratory A380

1975, May 15
1169 A379 50pf multi 48 15

500th anniv. of the unsuccessful siege of Neuss by Duke Charles the Bold of Burgundy.

1975-82 Engr. *Perf. 14*

1170	A380	5pf	Symphonie satellite	15	15
1171	A380	10pf	Electric train	15	15
1172	A380	20pf	Old Weser lighthouse	15	15
1173	A380	30pf	Rescue helicopter	25	15
1174	A380	40pf	Space	25	15
1175	A380	50pf	Radar station	35	15
1176	A380	60pf	X-ray machine	40	15
1177	A380	70pf	Shipbuilding	45	15
1178	A380	80pf	Tractor	52	20
1179	A380	100pf	Bituminous coal excavator	75	28
1180	A380	110pf	Color TV camera	80	30
1181	A380	120pf	Chemical plant	80	35
1182	A380	130pf	Brewery	95	38
1183	A380	140pf	Heating plant, Licterfelde	1.10	38
1184	A380	150pf	Power shovel	1.50	60
1185	A380	160pf	Blast furnace	1.65	45
1186	A380	180pf	Payloader	1.40	70
1187	A380	190pf	Shovel dredger	1.40	52
1188	A380	200pf	Oil drilling	1.65	45
1189	A380	230pf	Frankfurt Airport	1.90	70
1190	A380	250pf	Airport	1.90	70
1191	A380	300pf	Electro. RR	2.25	90
1192	A380	500pf	Effelsberg radio telescope	3.75	70
			Nos. 1170-1192 (23)	24.47	8.81

Issue dates: 40pf, 50pf, 100pf, May 15. 10pf, 30pf, 70pf, Aug. 14. 80pf, 120pf, 160pf, Oct. 15. 5pf, 140pf, 200pf, Nov. 14. 20pf, 500pf, Feb. 17, 1976. 60pf, Nov. 16, 1978. 230pf, May 17, 1979. 150pf, 180pf, July 12, 1979. 110pf, 130pf, 300pf, June 16, 1982. 190pf, 250pf, July 15, 1982.

Market and Town Hall, Alsfeld A381

Designs: No. 1197, Plönlein Corner, Siebers Tower and Kobolzeller Gate, Rothenburg. No. 1198, Town Hall (Steipe), Trier. No. 1199, View of Xanten.

1975, July 15 Litho. & Engr.
1196 A381 50pf multicolored 60 55
1197 A381 50pf multicolored 60 55
1198 A381 50pf multicolored 60 55
1199 A381 50pf multicolored 60 55

European Architectural Heritage Year.

Three Stages of Drug Addiction A382

1975, Aug. 14 Photo. *Perf. 14*
1200 A382 40pf multicolored 45 15

Fight against drug abuse.

Matthias Erzberger A383

1975, Aug. 14 Engr.
1201 A383 50pf red & black 48 15

Erzberger (1875-1921), statesman, signer of Compiègne Armistice (1918) at end of World War I.

Sign of Royal Prussian Post, 1776 — A384

1975, Aug. 14 Litho.
1202 A384 10pf blue & multi 25 15

Stamp Day, 1975, and 76th German Philatelists' Day, Sept. 21.

Souvenir Sheet

Gustav Stresemann, Ludwig Quidde, Carl von Ossietzky — A385

1975, Nov. 14 Engr. *Perf. 14*
1203 A385 Sheet of 3 1.50 1.50
a.-c. 50pf, single stamp 40 40

German winners of Nobel Peace Prize. No. 1203 has litho. marginal inscription.

Olympic Rings, Symbolic Mountains A386

Konrad Adenauer A387

1976, Jan. 5 Litho. & Engr.
1204 A386 50pf red & multi 48 15

12th Winter Olympic Games, Innsbruck, Austria, Feb. 4-15.

1976, Jan. 5 Engr.
1205 A387 50pf dark slate green 48 15

Konrad Adenauer (1876-1967), Chancellor (1949-63), birth centenary.

Books by Hans Sachs — A388

1976, Jan. 5 Litho.
1206 A388 40pf multicolored 40 15

Hans Sachs (1494-1576), poet (meister-singer), 400th death anniversary.

Junkers F 13, 1926 — A389

German Eagle — A390

1976, Jan. 5
1207 A389 50pf multicolored 55 15

Lufthansa, 50th anniversary.

1976, Feb. 17 Photo. *Perf. 14*
1208 A390 50pf red, blk & gold 55 15

Federal Constitutional Court, 25th anniv.

"EG" A391

1976, Apr. 6 Photo. *Perf. 14*
1209 A391 40pf red & multi 40 15

European Coal and Steel Community, 25th anniversary.

Wuppertal Suspension Train — A392

1976, Apr. 6 Litho.
1210 A392 50pf multicolored 48 15

Wuppertal suspension railroad, 75th anniv.

Girl Selling Trinkets and Prints — A393

Europa: 50pf, Boy selling copperplate prints, and CEPT emblem. Ludwigsburg china figurines, c. 1765.

1976, May 13 Photo.
1211 A393 40pf olive & multi 50 15
1212 A393 50pf scarlet & multi 65 15

Dr. Carl Sonnenschein A394

1976, May 13 Litho.
1213 A394 50pf carmine & multi 48 15

Sonnenschein (1876-1929), Roman Catholic clergyman and social reformer.

Weber Conducting "Freischutz" in Covent Garden — A395

1976, May 13
1214 A395 50pf red brown & blk 48 15

Carl Maria von Weber (1786-1826), composer, 150th death anniversary.

Hymn, by Paul Gerhardt A396

1976, May 13 Engr. & Litho.
1215 A396 40pf multicolored 38 15

Paul Gerhardt (1607-1676), Lutheran hymn writer, 300th death anniversary.

Carl Schurz, American Flag, Capitol A397

1976, May 13 Litho.
1216 A397 70pf multicolored 60 22

American Bicentennial.

Modern Stage A398

1976, July 14 Litho. *Perf. 14*
1217 A398 50pf multicolored 48 15

Bayreuth Festival, centenary.

Bronze Ritual Chariot c. 1000 B.C. A399

Archaeological Treasures: 40pf, Celtic gold vessel, 5th-4th centuries B.C. 50pf, Celtic silver torque, 2nd-1st centuries B.C. 120pf, Roman cup with masks, 1st century A.D.

1976, July 14

1218 A399	30pf multicolored		25	20
1219 A399	40pf multicolored		38	28
1220 A399	50pf multicolored		45	35
1221 A399	120pf multicolored		1.40	1.10

Golden Plover — A400

"Simplicissimus Teutsch" — A401

1976, Aug. 17

1222 A400 50pf multicolored 60 15

Protection of birds.

1976, Aug. 17

1223 A401 40pf multicolored 42 15

Johann Jacob Christoph von Grimmelshausen, 300th birth anniversary; author of the "Adventures of Simplicissimus Teutsch."

Imperial Post Emblem, Höchst am Main, 18th Cent. — A402

Caroline Neuber as Medea — A403

1976, Oct. 14 Litho. *Perf. 14*

1224 A402 10pf brown & multi 18 15

Stamp Day.

1976, Nov. 16 Photo.

German Actresses: 40pf, Sophie Schröder (1781-1868) as Sappho. 50pf, Louise Dumont (1862-1932) as Hedda Gabler. 70pf, Hermine Körner (1878-1960) as Lady Macbeth.

1225 A403	30pf multicolored	25	15
1226 A403	40pf multicolored	35	25
1227 A403	50pf multicolored	40	25
1228 A403	70pf multicolored	60	55

Palais de l'Europe, Strasbourg — A404

1977, Jan. 13 Engr. *Perf. 14*

1229 A404 140pf green & blk 1.25 45

Inauguration of the new Council of Europe Headquarters, Jan. 28.

Scenes from Till Eulenspiegel A405

Marksburg Castle A406

1977, Jan. 13 Litho.

1230 A405 50pf multicolored 60 15

Till Eulenspiegel (d. 1350), roguish fool and hero, his adventures reported in book of same name.

1977-79 Typo. *Perf. 14*

1231	A406	10pf Glucksburg	15	15
a.		Bklt. pane, 4 #1231, 2 each #1234, 1236	3.00	
b.		Bklt. pane, 4 #1231, 2 #1234, 2 #1310	2.50	
c.		Bklt. pane, 4 #1231, 2 #1310, 2 #1312	3.00	
d.		Bklt. pane, 2 each #1231, 1234, 1310-1311	3.00	
1232	A406	20pf Pfaueninsel	15	15
1233	A406	25pf Gemen	15	15
1234	A406	30pf Ludwigstein	24	15
1235	A406	40pf Eltz	38	15
1236	A406	50pf Neuschwanstein	75	15
1237	A406	60pf Marksburg	75	18
1238	A406	70pf Mespelbrunn	75	18
1239	A406	90pf Vischerenburg	95	28
1240	A406	190pf Pfaueninsel	1.65	45
1240A	A406	200pf Burresheim	1.90	45
1241	A406	210pf Schwanen-burg	2.00	60
1242	A406	230pf Lichtenberg	2.00	60
		Nos. 1231-1242 (13)	11.82	
		Set value		3.15

See Nos. 1308-1315.

Issued in sheets of 100 and in coils. Every fifth coil stamp has control number on the back.

Issue dates: 60pf, 200pf, Jan. 13. 40pf, 190pf, Feb. 16. 10pf, 30pf, Apr. 14. 50pf, 70pf, May 17. 230pf, Nov. 16, 1978. 25pf, 90pf, Jan. 11, 1979. 20pf, 210pf, Feb. 14, 1979.

Souvenir Sheet

German Art Nouveau — A407

Designs: 30pf, Floral ornament. 70pf, Athena, poster by Franz von Stuck. 90pf, Chair, c. 1902.

1977, Feb. 16 Litho. *Perf. 14*

1243 A407	Sheet of 3	1.75	1.25
a.	30pf multicolored	25	20
b.	70pf multicolored	48	32
c.	90pf multicolored	75	50

1st German Art Nouveau Exhib., 75th anniv.

Jean Monnet A408

1977, Feb. 16

1244 A408 50pf black & yellow 48 18

Jean Monnet (1888-1979), French proponent of unification of Europe, became first Honorary Citizen of Europe in Apr. 1976.

Flower Show Emblem A409

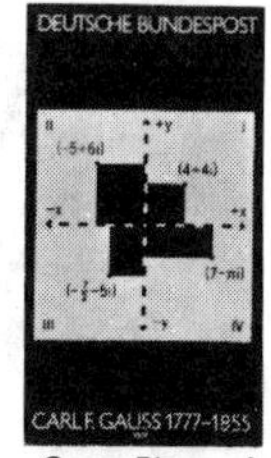

Gauss Plane of Complex Numbers A410

1977, Apr. 14

1245 A409 50pf green & multi 45 18

25th Federal Horticultural Show, Stuttgart, Apr. 29-Oct. 23.

1977, Apr. 14

1246 A410 40pf silver & multi 42 15

Carl Friedrich Gauss (1777-1855), mathematician, 200th birth anniversary.

Barbarossa Head, Cappenberg Reliquary — A411

1977, Apr. 14

1247 A411 40pf multicolored 45 15

Staufer Year 1977. "Time of the Hohenstaufen" Exhibition, Stuttgart, Mar. 25-June 5, in connection with the 25th anniversary of Baden-Wurttemberg.

Rhön Highway A412

Europa: 50pf, Rhine, Siebengebirge and train.

1977, May 7 Litho. & Engr.

1248 A412	40pf brt green & blk	50	15
1249 A412	50pf brt red & blk	65	15
	Set value		24

Rubens, Self-portrait A413

Ulm Cathedral A414

1977, May 17 Engr.

1250 A413 30pf brown black 28 15

Peter Paul Rubens (1577-1640), Flemish painter, 400th birth anniversary.

1977, May 17 Litho. & Engr.

1251 A414 40pf blue & sepia 42 15

600th anniversary of Ulm Cathedral.

Madonna, Oldest Rector's Seal — A415

Landgrave Philipp, Great Seal of University — A416

1977, May 17 Photo.

1252 A415	50pf indigo & org red	45	18
1253 A416	50pf indigo & org red	45	18

Mainz University, 500th anniv. (No. 1252); Marburg University, 450th anniv. (No. 1253).

Morning, by Runge — A417

1977, July 13 Litho. *Perf. 14*

1254 A417 60pf blue & multi 55 22

Philipp Otto Runge (1777-1810), painter.

Bishop Ketteler's Coat of Arms — A418

1977, July 13

1255 A418 50pf multicolored 52 15

Wilhelm Emmanuel von Ketteler (1811-1877), Bishop of Mainz, Reichstag member and social reformer, death centenary.

Fritz von Bodelschwingh A419

1977, July 13 Litho. & Engr.

1256 A419 50pf multicolored 48 15

Pastor Fritz von Bodelschwingh (1877-1946), manager of Bethel Institute (for the incurable sick), birth centenary.

Footnotes near stamp listings often refer to other stamps of the same design.

Jesus as Teacher, Great Seal of University — A420

Golden Hat, Schifferstadt, Bronze Age — A421

1977, Aug. 16 **Photo.**
1257 A420 50pf multicolored 48 15

Tübingen University, 500th anniversary.

1977, Aug. 16 **Litho.**

Archaeological heritage: 120pf, Gilt helmet, from Prince's Tomb, Krefeld-Gellep. 200pf, Bronze Centaur's head, Schwarzenacker.

1258 A421 30pf multicolored 32 22
1259 A421 120pf multicolored 1.25 1.25
1260 A421 200pf multicolored 1.75 1.40

Telephone Operator and Switchboard, 1881 — A422

1977, Oct. 13 **Litho.** ***Perf. 14***
1261 A422 50pf multicolored 48 15

German telephone centenary.

Arms of Hamburg, Post Emblem, c. 1861 — A423

Wilhelm Hauff — A424

1977, Oct. 13
1262 A423 10pf multicolored 15 15

Stamp Day.

1977, Nov. 10 **Photo.** ***Perf. 14***
1263 A424 40pf multicolored 38 15

Wilhelm Hauff (1802-1827), writer and fabulist, 150th death anniversary.

Traveling Surgeon — A425

Book Cover, by Alexander Schröder — A426

1977, Nov. 10 **Litho.**
1264 A425 50pf multicolored 48 15

Dr. Johann Andreas Eisenbarth (1663-1727), traveling surgeon and adventurer.

1978, Jan. 12 **Litho.** ***Perf. 14***
1265 A426 50pf multicolored 48 15

Rudolf Alexander Schröder (1878-1962), writer, designer, Lutheran minister.

"Refugees" A427

1978, Jan. 12 **Photo.**
1266 A427 50pf multicolored 48 15

Friedland Aid Society for displaced Germans, 20th anniversary.

Souvenir Sheet

Gerhart Hauptmann, Hermann Hesse, Thomas Mann — A428

1978, Feb. 16 **Litho.** ***Perf. 14***
1267 A428 Sheet of 3 1.40 1.40
a. 30pf multicolored 25 25
b. 50pf multicolored 40 40
c. 70pf multicolored 60 60

German winners of Nobel Literature Prize.

Martin Buber (1878-1965), Writer and Philosopher A429

1978, Feb. 16
1268 A429 50pf multicolored 48 15

Museum Tower and Observatory — A430

1978, Apr. 13 **Litho.** ***Perf. 14***
1269 A430 50pf multicolored 48 15

German Museum for Natural Sciences and Technology, Munich, 75th anniversary.

Old City Halls A431

Europa: 40pf, Bamberg. 50pf, Regensburg. 70pf, Esslingen on Neckar.

Lithographed and Engraved

1978, May 22 ***Perf. 14***
1270 A431 40pf multicolored 65 15
1271 A431 50pf multicolored 80 20
1272 A431 70pf multicolored 85 32

Pied Piper of Hamelin A432

1978, May 22 **Litho.**
1273 A432 50pf multicolored 50 15

The Pied Piper led 130 children of Hamelin away never to be seen again.

Janusz Korczak — A433

Fossil Bat — A434

1978, July 13 **Litho.** ***Perf. 14***
1274 A433 90pf multicolored 80 35

Dr. Janusz Korczak (1878-1942), physician, educator, proponent of children's rights.

1978, July 13

Design: 200pf, Eohippus (primitive horse), horiz.

1275 A434 80pf multicolored 2.50 2.00
1276 A434 200pf multicolored 2.50 2.00

Archaeological heritage from Messel opencast mine, c. 50 million years old.

Parliament, Bonn A435

1978, Aug. 17 **Litho.** ***Perf. 14***
1277 A435 70pf multicolored 60 24

65th Interparliamentary Conf., Bonn, Sept. 3-14.

Rose Window, Freiburg Cathedral — A436

1978, Aug. 17
1278 A436 40pf multicolored 38 15

85th Congress of German Catholics, Freiburg, Sept. 13-17.

Brentano as Butterfly, by Luise Duttenhofer A437

1978, Aug. 17
1279 A437 30pf multicolored 32 15

Clemens Brentano (1778-1842), poet.

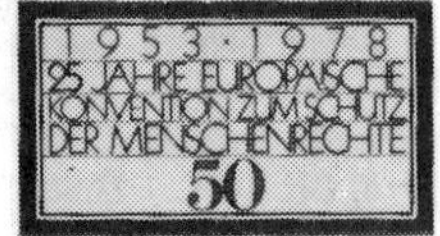

A438

1978, Aug. 17
1280 A438 50pf multicolored 45 15

European Human Rights Convention, 25th anniversary.

Bavarian Posthouse Sign, c. 1825 — A439

Saxony No. 1 with "World Philatelic Movement" Cancel — A440

1978, Oct. 12 **Litho.** ***Perf. 14***
1281 A439 40pf multicolored 40 15
1282 A440 50pf multicolored 50 15
a. Pair, #1281-1282 90 40

Stamp Day and German Philatelists' Meeting, Frankfurt am Main, Oct. 12-15.

Easter at Walchensee, by Lovis Corinth — A441

Impressionist Paintings: 70pf, Horseman on Shore, by Max Liebermann, vert. 120pf, Lady with Cat, by Max Slevogt, vert.

1978, Nov. 16 Photo. *Perf. 14*
1283 A441 50pf multicolored 48 15
1284 A441 70pf multicolored 65 40
1285 A441 120pf multicolored 1.10 70

Child and Building A442

1979, Jan. 11 Photo.
1286 A442 60pf black & rose 65 15

International Year of the Child and 20th anniv. of Declaration of Children's Rights.

Agnes Miegel — A443 Film — A444

1979, Feb. 14 Photo. *Perf. 14*
1287 A443 60pf multicolored 55 15

Agnes Miegel (1879-1964), poet.

1979, Feb. 14 Litho.
1288 A444 50pf black & green 45 15

25th German Short-Film Festival, Oberhausen, Apr. 23-28.

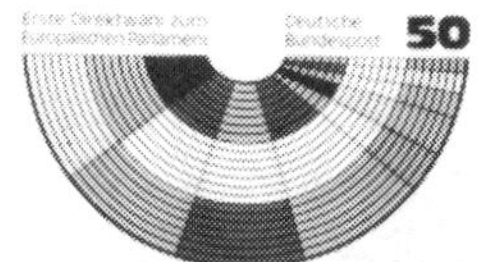

Parliament Benches in Flag Colors of Members — A445

1979, Feb. 14
1289 A445 50pf multicolored 48 15

European Parliament, first direct elections, June 7-10, 1979.

Emblems of Road Rescue Services A446

1979, Feb. 14
1290 A446 50pf multicolored 45 18

A447 A448

Europa: 50pf, Telegraph office, 1863. 60pf, Post Office window, 1854.

1979, May 17 Litho. *Perf. 14*
1291 A447 50pf multicolored 60 15
1292 A447 60pf multicolored 85 15

1979, May 17 Photo.
1293 A448 60pf red & black 52 18

Anne Frank (1929-45), author, Nazi victim.

First Electric Train, 1879 Berlin Exhibition A449

1979, May 17 Litho.
1294 A449 60pf multicolored 52 18

Intl. Transportation Exhib., Hamburg.

Hand Setting Radio Dial — A450

1979, July 12 Litho. *Perf. 14*
1295 A450 60pf multicolored 52 15

World Administrative Radio Conference, Geneva, Sept. 24-Dec. 1.

Moses Receiving Tablets of the Law, by Lucas Cranach — A451 Cross and Charlemagne's Emblem — A452

1979, July 12 Litho. & Engr.
1296 A451 50pf black & blue grn 45 18

450th anniv. of Martin Luther's Catechism.

1979, July 12 Litho. & Embossed
1297 A452 50pf multicolored 70 35

1979 pilgrimage to Aachen.

Hildegard von Bingen with Manuscript A453

1979, Aug. 9 Litho.
1298 A453 110pf multicolored 1.00 32

Hildegard von Bingen, Benedictine nun, mystic and writer, 800th death anniversary.

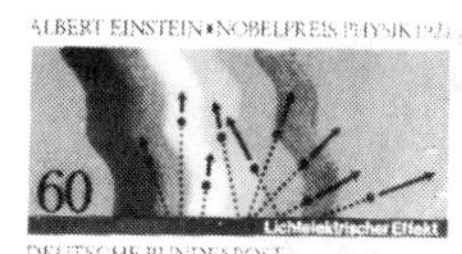

Diagram of Einstein's Photoelectric Effect — A454

Designs: No. 1300, Otto Hahn's diagram of the splitting of the uranium nucleus. No. 1301, Max von Laue's atom arrangement in crystals.

1979, Aug. 9 Photo.
1299 A454 60pf multicolored 55 25
1300 A454 60pf multicolored 55 25
1301 A454 60pf multicolored 55 25

Birth centenaries of German Nobel Prize winners: Albert Einstein, physics, 1921; Otto Hahn, chemistry, 1944; Max von Laue, physics, 1914.

Pilot on Board — A455

Lithographed and Engraved

1979, Oct. 11 *Perf. 14*
1302 A455 60pf multicolored 52 15

Three centuries of pilots' regulations.

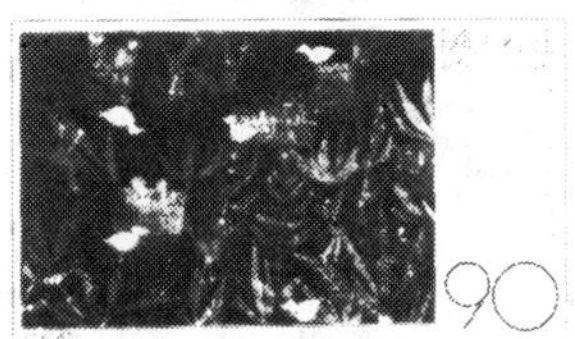

Birds in Garden, by Paul Klee — A456

1979, Nov. 14 Photo.
1303 A456 90pf multicolored 75 30

Paul Klee (1879-1940), Swiss artist.

Mephistopheles and Faust — A457

1979, Nov. 14 Litho.
1304 A457 60pf multicolored 52 20

Doctor Johannes Faust.

Energy Conservation — A458

1979, Nov. 14 *Perf. 13x13½*
1305 A458 40pf multicolored 38 15

Castle Type A406 of 1977-79

1979-82 Typo. *Perf. 14*

1308	35pf Lichtenstein	32	15
1309	40pf Wolfsburg	34	15
1310	50pf Inzlingen	40	15
1311	60pf Rheydt	55	15
1312	80pf Wilhelmsthal	65	24
1313	120pf Charlottenburg	1.00	35
1314	280pf Ahrensburg	2.50	85
1315	300pf Herrenhausen	2.50	90
	Nos. 1308-1315 (8)	8.26	2.94

Issue dates: 60pf, Nov. 14. 40pf, 50pf, Feb. 14, 1980. 35pf, 80pf, 300pf, June 16, 1982. 120pf, 280pf, July 15, 1982.

Iphigenia, by Anselm Feuerbach A459

1980, Jan. 10 Litho.
1321 A459 50pf multicolored 48 18

Anselm Feuerbach (1829-1880), historical and portrait painter.

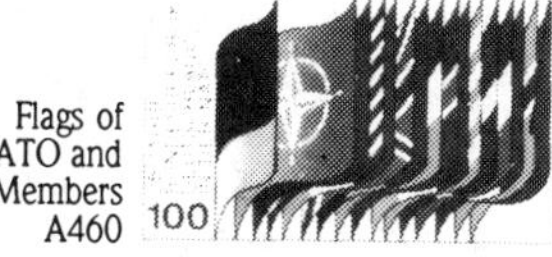

Flags of NATO and Members A460

1980, Jan. 10
1322 A460 100pf multicolored 1.00 52

Germany's membership in NATO, 25th anniversary.

Osnabruck, 1,200th Anniversary A461

1980, Jan. 10 Litho. & Engr.
1323 A461 60pf multicolored 52 20

Götz von Berlichingen, Painting on Glass — A462

1980, Jan. 10 Litho.
1324 A462 60pf multicolored 52 20

Götz von Berlichingen (1480-1562), knight.

Duden Dictionary, Old and New Editions — A463

1980, Jan. 14
1325 A463 60pf multicolored 52 20

Konrad Duden's German Language Dictionary, centenary of publication.

German Association for Public and Private Social Welfare Centenary — A464

1980, Apr. 10
1326 A464 60pf multicolored 52 20

A465

A466

Emperor Frederick I (Barbarossa) and Sons, Welf Chronicles, 12th century.

1980, Apr. 10
1327 A465 60pf multicolored 52 20

Imperial Diet of Geinhausen, 800th anniv.

1980, May 8 Litho. *Perf. 14*

Design: 50pf, Albertus Magnus (1193-1280), saint and doctor of the Church. 60pf, Gottfried Wilhelm Leibniz (1646-1716), philosopher.

1328 A466 50pf multicolored 60 16
1329 A466 60pf multicolored 80 22

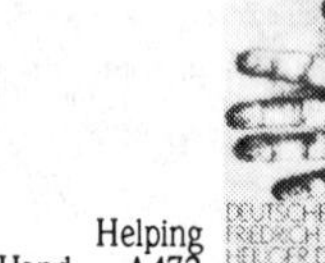
Confession of Augsburg, Engraving, 1630 — A467

1980, May 8
1330 A467 50pf multicolored 45 20

Reading of Confession of Augsburg to Charles V (first official creed of Lutheran Church), 400th anniversary.

Nature Preserves A468

1980, May 8 Photo.
1331 A468 40pf multicolored 38 15

Oscillogram Pulses and Ear — A469

Lithographed and Embossed

1980, July 10 *Perf. 14*
1332 A469 90pf multicolored 80 32

16th Intl. Cong. for the Training and Education of the Hard of Hearing, Hamburg, Aug. 4-8.

Book of Daily Bible Readings, Title Page, 1731 — A470

1980, July 10 Litho.
1333 A470 50pf multicolored 45 18

Moravian Brethren's Book of Daily Bible Readings, 250th edition.

St. Benedict of Nursia, 1500th Birth Anniv. — A471

1980, July 10 *Perf. 13x13½*
1334 A471 50pf multicolored 45 20

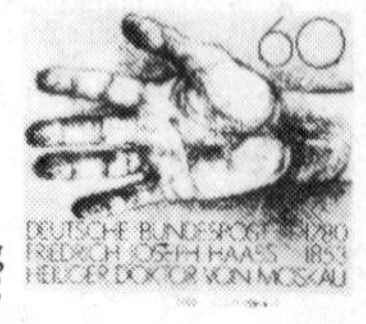
Helping Hand — A472

1980, Aug. 14 Litho. & Engr.
1335 A472 60pf multicolored 52 20

Dr. Friedrich Joseph Haass (1780-1853), physician and philanthropist.

Marie von Ebner-Eschenbach (1830-1916), Writer — A473

1980, Aug. 14 Photo.
1336 A473 60pf multicolored 52 20

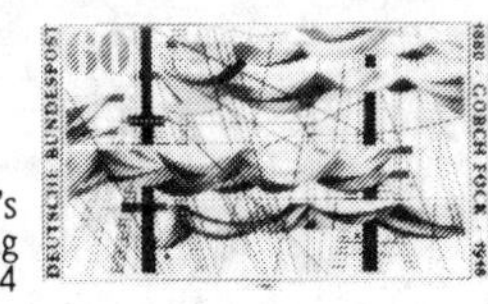
Ship's Rigging A474

1980, Aug. 14 Litho.
1337 A474 60pf multicolored 60 20

Gorch Fock (pen name of Johan Kinau) (1880-1916), poet and dramatist.

Hoeing, Pressing Grapes, Wine Cellar, 14th Century Woodcuts A475

1980, Oct. 9 Litho. *Perf. 14*
1338 A475 50pf multicolored 45 20

Wine production in Central Europe, 2000th anniversary.

Setting Final Stone in South Tower, Cologne Cathedral — A476

1980, Oct. 9
1339 A476 60pf multicolored 52 20

Completion of Cologne Cathedral, cent.

Landscape with Fir Trees, by Altdorfer A477

Lithographed and Engraved

1980, Nov. 13 *Perf. 14*
1340 A477 40pf multicolored 42 20

Albrecht Altdorfer (1480-1538), painter and engraver.

Elly Heuss-Knapp — A478

1981, Jan. 15 Photo.
1341 A478 60pf multicolored 52 20

Elly Heuss-Knapp (1881-1951), founded Elly Heuss-Knapp Foundation (Rest and Recuperation for Mothers).

International Year of the Disabled — A479

1981, Jan. 15 Litho.
1342 A479 60pf multicolored 52 20

European Urban Renaissance — A480

1981, Jan. 15 Litho. & Engr.
1343 A480 60pf multicolored 52 20

Georg Philipp Telemann, Title Page of "Singet dem Herrn" Cantata — A481

1981, Feb. 12 Photo.
1344 A481 60pf multicolored 52 20

Georg Telemann (1681-1767), composer.

Foreign Guest Worker Integration — A482

1981, Feb. 12 Litho.
1345 A482 50pf multicolored 48 20

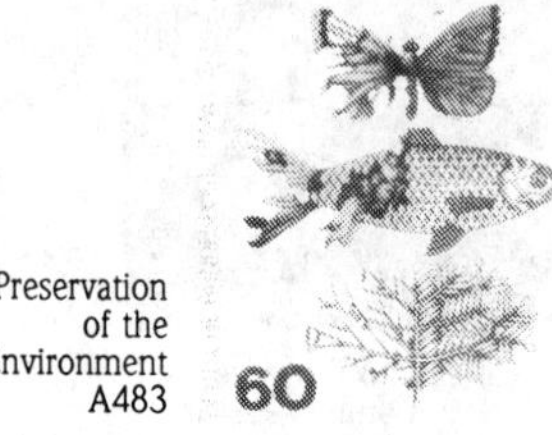
Preservation of the Environment A483

1981, Feb. 12
1346 A483 60pf multicolored 52 20

European Patent Office Centenary A484

1981, Feb. 12
1347 A484 60pf multicolored 52 20

A485 A486

1981, Feb. 12 *Perf. 13x13½*
1348 A485 40pf Chest scintigram 42 20

Early examination for the prevention of cancer.

1981, May 7 Litho. *Perf. 14*

South German couple dancing in regional costumes.

1349 A486 50pf shown 55 15
1350 A486 60pf Northern couple 75 15

Europa.

19th German Protestant Convention, Hamburg, June 17-21 A487

1981, May 7 Photo.
1351 A487 50pf multicolored 45 20

A488

A489

1981, May 7 Litho.
1352 A488 60pf Altar figures 52 20

Tilman Riemenschneider (1460-1531), sculptor, 450th death anniversary.

1981, July 16 Litho. *Perf. 14*
1353 A489 110pf multicolored 1.10 50

Georg von Neumayer polar research station.

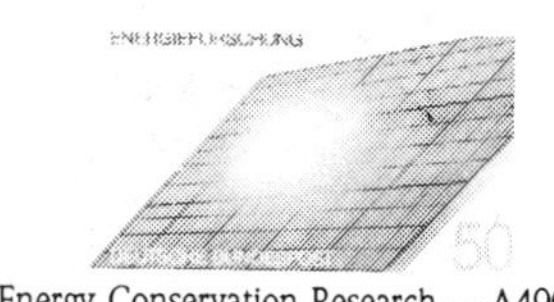
Energy Conservation Research — A490

1981, July 16
1354 A490 50pf Solar generator 45 18

Wildlife Protection — A491

1981, July 16
1355 A491 60pf Baby coot 52 20

Cooperation in Third World Development — A492

1981, July 16
1356 A492 90pf multicolored 80 45

Wilhelm Raabe (1831-1910), Poet — A493

1981, Aug. 13 **Litho. & Engr.**
1357 A493 50pf dk green & green 60 18

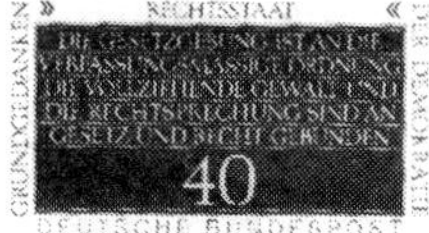
Statement of Constitutional Freedom (Fundamental Concept of Democracy) — A494

1981, Aug. 13 **Litho.** ***Perf. 14***
1358 A494 40pf shown 42 15
1359 A494 50pf Separation of powers 50 15
1360 A494 60pf Sovereignty of the people 65 16
Set value 36

A495

A496

People by Mailcoach, lithograph, 1855.

1981, Oct. 8 **Litho.**
1361 A495 60pf multicolored 85 25

Stamp Day, Oct. 25.

1981, Nov. 12 **Litho.** ***Perf. 14***
1362 A496 100pf multicolored 1.25 45

Antarctic Treaty, 20th anniv.

St. Elizabeth of Thuringia, 750th Anniv. of Death — A497

1981, Nov. 12
1363 A497 50pf multicolored 50 20

Karl von Clausewitz, by W. Wach — A498

1981, Nov. 12 **Photo.**
1364 A498 60pf multicolored 85 18

Prussian general and writer, (1780-1831).

Social Insurance Centenary A499

1981, Nov. 12
1365 A499 60pf multicolored 65 18

Pear-shaped Pot with Lid, 1715 — A500

1982, Jan. 13 **Litho.**
1366 A500 60pf multicolored 65 18

Johann Friedrich Bottger (1682-1719), originator of Dresden china, 300th birth anniv.

Energy Conservation — A501

1982, Jan. 13
1367 A501 60pf multicolored 65 18

A502

A503

Illustration from The Town Band of Bremen (folktale).

1982, Jan. 13
1368 A502 40pf red & black 45 18

1982, Feb. 18 **Photo.**
1369 A503 60pf multicolored 75 18

Johann Wolfgang von Goethe (1749-1832), by Georg Melchior Kraus, 1776.

Robert Koch (1843-1910), Discoverer of Tubercle Bacillus, (1882) A504

1982, Feb. 18
1370 A504 50pf multicolored 60 18

Die Fromme Helene, by Wilhelm Busch (1832-1908) — A505

1982, Apr. 15 **Litho.** ***Perf. 13½x14***
1371 A505 50pf multicolored 55 25

Europa 1982 A506

1982, May 5 **Litho.** ***Perf. 14***
1372 A506 50pf Hambach Meeting sesquicentennial 65 15
1373 A506 60pf Treaties of Rome, 1957-1982 80 20

Kiel Regatta Week Centenary A507

1982, May 5
1374 A507 60pf multicolored 60 18

Young Men's Christian Assoc. (YMCA) Centenary A508

1982, May 5
1375 A508 50pf multicolored 50 18

"Don't Drink and Drive" A509

1982, July 15 **Photo.**
1376 A509 80pf red & black 90 27

25th Anniv. of German Lepers' Org. — A510

1982, July 15 **Photo.**
1377 A510 80pf multicolored 90 27

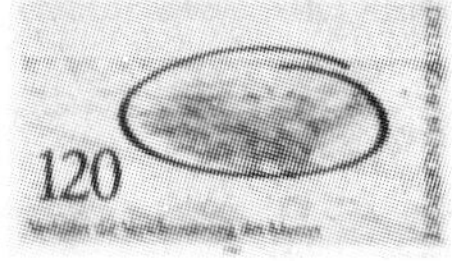
Prevent Water Pollution A511

1982, July 15
1378 A511 120pf multicolored 1.40 40

Urea Model and Synthesis Formula A512

1982, Aug. 12 **Photo.**
1379 A512 50pf multicolored 60 18

Friedrich Wohler (1800-1882), chemist, discoverer of organic chemistry.

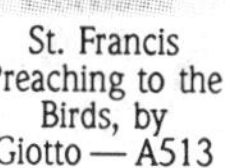
St. Francis Preaching to the Birds, by Giotto — A513

James Franck, Max Born — A514

1982, Aug. 12 **Litho.**
1380 A513 60pf multicolored 70 18

800th birth anniv. of St. Francis of Assisi and 87th German Catholics Cong., Dusseldorf, Sept. 1-5.

1982, Aug. 12 **Litho. & Engr.**
1381 A514 80pf multicolored 75 28

James Franck (1882-1964) and Max Born (1882-1970), Nobel Prize physicists, developed quantum theory.

Stamp Day, Oct. 24 A515

1982, Oct. 14 **Photo.** ***Perf. 14***
1382 A515 80pf Poster 1.25 28

400th Anniv. of the Gregorian Calendar — A516

Design: Calendar illumination, by Johannes Rasch, 1586.

1982, Oct. 14 **Litho.**
1383 A516 60pf multicolored 65 25

A517

A518

Presidents: a, Theodor Heuss, 1949-59. b, Heinrich Lubke, 1959-69. c, Gustav Heinemann, 1969-74. d, WalterScheel, 1974-79. e, Karl Carstens, 1979-84.

1982, Nov. 10

1384 Sheet of 5 4.25 6.00
a.-e. A517 80pf, single stamp 75 85

1983, Jan. 13 Litho. ***Perf. 14***

1385 A518 80pf gray & black 1.10 24

Edith Stein (d. 1942), philospher and Carmelite Nun.

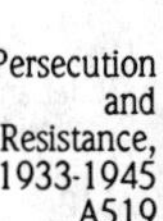

Persecution and Resistance, 1933-1945 A519

1983, Jan. 13

1386 A519 80pf multicolored 1.00 24

Light Space Modulator, 1930 — A520

Walter Gropius (1883-1969), Founder of Bauhaus Architecture: 60pf, Sanctuary, zinc lithograph, 1942. 80pf, Bauhaus Archives, Berlin, 1979.

1983, Feb. 8

1387 A520 50pf multicolored 55 16
1388 A520 60pf multicolored 70 20
1389 A520 80pf multicolored 85 24

Federahannes, Swabian-Alemannic Carnival — A521

1983, Feb. 8

1390 A521 60pf multicolored 70 20

4th Intl. Horticultural Show, Munich, Apr. 28-Oct. 9 — A522

1983, Apr. 12 Litho. ***Perf. 14***

1391 A522 60pf multicolored 70 24

Europa 1983 A523

Discoveries: 60pf, Printing press by Johannes Guttenburg. 80pf, Electromagnetic waves by Heinrich Hertz.

1983, May 5 Litho. ***Perf. 14***

1392 A523 60pf Movable type 90 28
1393 A523 80pf Resonant circuit, electric flux lines 1.00 28

Johannes Brahms (1833-1897), Composer — A524

1983, May 5 Photo.

1394 A524 80pf multicolored 1.00 24

Franz Kafka (1883-1924), Writer — A525

1983, May 5

1395 A525 80pf Signature, Tyn Church, Prague 90 24

Beer Pureness Law, 450th Anniv. A526

1983, May 5 Litho.

1396 A526 80pf Brewers, engraving, 1677 90 24

300th Anniv. of Immigration to US — A527

1983, May 5 Litho. & Engr.

1397 A527 80pf Concord 95 24

See US No. 2040.

Children and Road Safety A528

1983, July 14 Litho. ***Perf. 14***

1398 A528 80pf multicolored 90 20

50th Intl. Auto Show, Frankfurt, Sept. 15-25 A529

1983, July 14

1399 A529 60pf multicolored 65 20

Otto Warburg — A530 Christoph Martin Wieland (1733-1813), Poet — A531

1983, Aug. 11 Photo. ***Perf. 14***

1400 A530 50pf multicolored 50 18

Warburg (1883-1970), pioneer of modern biochemistry, 1931 Nobel prize winner in medicine.

1983, Aug. 11 Litho.

1401 A531 80pf multicolored 90 20

10th Anniv. of UN Membership A532

1983, Aug. 11 Photo.

1402 A532 80pf multicolored 1.00 20

Rauhe Haus Orphanage Sesquicentennial — A533

1983, Aug. 11 Litho.

1403 A533 80pf multicolored 90 20

Survey and Measuring Maps A534

1983, Aug. 11

1404 A534 120pf multicolored 1.25 30

Intl. Union of Geodesy and Geophysics Gen. Assembly, Hamburg, Aug. 15-26.

Stamp Day — A535

1983, Oct. 13 Litho. ***Perf. 13½***

1405 A535 80pf Postrider 1.25 24

Martin Luther (1483-1546) A536

1983, Oct. 13 ***Perf. 14***

1406 A536 80pf Engraving by G. Konig 85 24

Customs Union Sesquicentennial — A537

1983, Nov. 10

1407 A537 60pf multicolored 90 20

Territorial Authorities (Federation, Land, Communities) — A538

1983, Nov. 10 Litho.

1408 A538 80pf multicolored 75 24

Trier, 2000th Anniv. A539

1984, Jan. 12 Litho. & Engr.

1409 A539 80pf Black Gate, 175 A.D. 90 24

Philipp Reis (1834-1874) Physicist and Inventor — A540

1984, Jan. 12 Litho.

1410 A540 80pf multicolored 90 24

Gregor Mendel (1822-1884), Basic Laws of Heredity — A541

1984, Jan. 12 Litho.

1411 A541 50pf multicolored 70 16

500th Anniv. of Michelstadt Town Hall — A542

1984, Feb. 16 Litho.

1412 A542 60pf multicolored 70 20

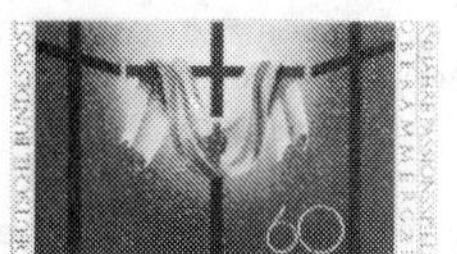

350th Anniv. of Oberammergau Passion Play — A543

1984, Feb. 16 Photo.

1413 A543 60pf multicolored 70 20

Second Election of Parliament, June 17 — A544

1984, Apr. 12 Litho. *Perf. 13½*
1414 A544 80pf multicolored 90 22

Europa (1959-1984) A545

1984, May 8 Photo. *Perf. 14*
1415 A545 60pf multicolored 85 18
1416 A545 80pf multicolored 1.00 24

A546 A547

1984, May 8 Engr.
1417 A546 60pf multicolored 90 22

Nursery Rhyme Illustration, by Ludwig Richter (1803-84).

1984, May 8
1418 A547 80pf Statue, 1693 90 22

St. Norbert von Xanten (1080-1134).

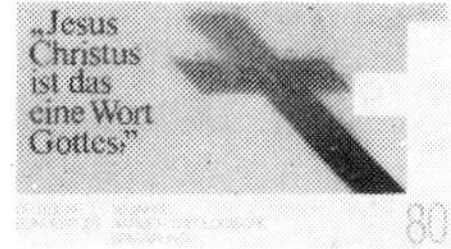

Barmer Theological Declaration, 50th Anniv. — A548

1984, May 8 Litho.
1419 A548 80pf Cross, text 90 22

Souvenir Sheet

1984 UPU Congress — A549

1984, June 19 Litho. *Perf. 14*
1420 Sheet of 3 3.25 3.25
a. A549 60pf Letter sorting, 19th cent. 70 70
b. A549 80pf Scanner 80 80
c. A549 120pf H. von Stephan, founder 1.40 1.40

City of Neuss Bimillenium A550

1984, June 19 Litho. & Engr.
1421 A550 80pf Tomb of Oclatius 90 22

Friedrich Wilhelm Bessel (1784-1846), Astronomer A551

1984, June 19
1422 A551 80pf Bessel function diagram 90 22

88th German Catholic Convention, Munich, July 4-8 — A552

1984, June 19 Photo.
1423 A552 60pf Pope Pius XII 65 18

Town Hall, Duderstadt A553

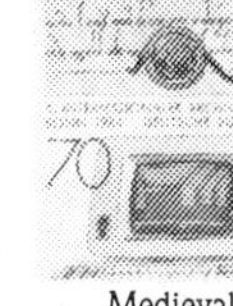

Medieval Document, Computer A554

1984, Aug. 21 Litho. *Perf. 14*
1424 A553 60pf multicolored 65 18

1984, Aug. 21
1425 A554 70pf multicolored 70 22

10th Intl. Archives Congress, Bonn.

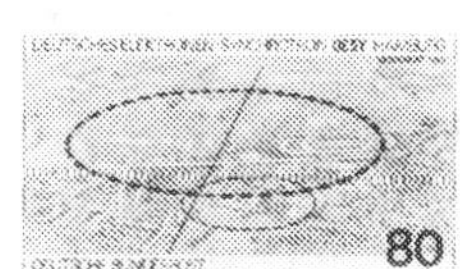

German Electron Synchrotron (DESY) Research Center, Hamburg — A555

1984, Aug. 21 Photo.
1426 A555 80pf multicolored 90 22

Schleswig-Holstein Canal Bicentenary — A556

1984, Aug. 21 Litho.
1427 A556 80pf Knoop lock 90 22

Stamp Day A557

1984, Oct. 18 Litho. *Perf. 14*
1428 A557 80pf Imperial Taxis Post-house, Augsburg 1.25 22

Anti-smoking Campaign — A558

1984, Nov. 8 Litho.
1429 A558 60pf Match, text 90 22

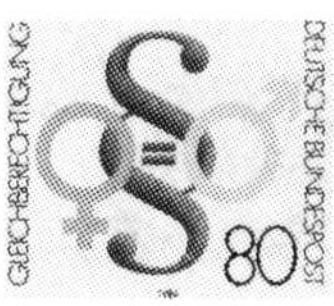

Equal Rights for Men and Women — A559

1984, Nov. 8
1430 A559 80pf Male & female symbols 90 22

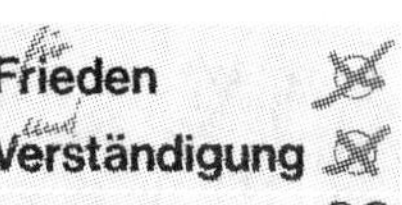

Peace and Understanding — A560

1984, Nov. 8
1431 A560 80pf Text 90 22

Augsburg, 2000th Anniv. A561

1985, Jan. 10 Litho.
1432 A561 80pf Roman Emperor Augustus, Augsburg buildings 90 22

Philipp Jakob Spener, Religious Leader (1635-1705) — A562

1985, Jan. 10 Litho.
1433 A562 80pf multicolored 90 22

Deutches Wortebuch A563

1985, Jan. 10 Litho.
1434 A563 80pf Bros. Grimm, text 90 22

Romano Guardini, Theologist (1885-1968) A564

1985, Jan. 10 Litho.
1435 A564 80pf multicolored 90 22

Market and Coinage Rights in Verden, 1000th Anniv. A565

1985, Feb. 21 Litho.
1436 A565 60pf multicolored 70 18

German-Danish Border Areas and Flags — A566

1985, Feb. 21
1437 A566 80pf multicolored 90 22

Bonn-Copenhagen declarations on mutual minorities, 30th anniv.

Johann Peter Hebel (1760-1826), Poet — A567

1985, Apr. 16 Litho.
1438 A567 80pf multicolored 1.00 22

Egon Erwin Kisch (1885-1948), Journalist — A568

1985, Apr. 16 Litho.
1439 A568 60pf Kisch using telephone 80 20

Europa 1985 — A569

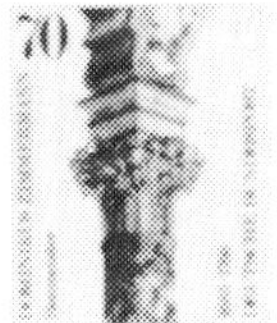

Dominikus Zimmermann (1685-1766), Architect — A570

European Music Year: 60pf, Georg Friedrich Handel. 80pf, Johann Sebastian Bach.

1985, May 7 Photo.
1440 A569 60pf Portrait of Handel 90 15
1441 A569 80pf Portrait of Bach 1.00 18

1985, May 7 Photo.
1442 A570 70pf Stucco column 70 20

St. George's Cathedral, 750th Anniv. — A571

1985, May 7 Litho. *Perf. 14*
1443 A571 60pf Cathedral, Limburg 75 20

Father Josef Kentenich (1885-1968) A572

1985, May 7 **Litho.**
1444 A572 80pf Portrait 90 22

Forest Conservation — A573

1985, July 16 **Litho.** ***Perf. 14***
1445 A573 80pf Clock, forest 90 22

Intl. Youth Year A574

1985, July 16 ***Perf. 14***
1446 A574 60pf Scouts, scouting and IYY emblems 65 18

30th World Scouting Conference, Munich, July 15-19.

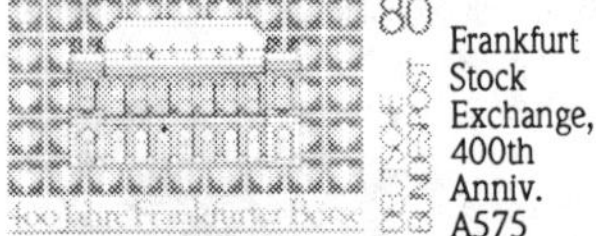

Frankfurt Stock Exchange, 400th Anniv. A575

Design: Bourse, est. 1879, and Frankfurt Eagle, the exchange emblem.

1985, Aug. 13 ***Perf. 14x14½***
1447 A575 80pf multicolored 90 22

The Sunday Walk, by Carl Spitzweg (1808-85) A576

1985, Aug. 13
1448 A576 60pf multicolored 70 22

Fritz Reuter (1810-1874), Dialect Author — A577

1985, Oct. 15 **Litho.** ***Perf. 14***
1449 A577 80pf Portrait, manuscript 1.00 22

Departure of the 1st Train from Nuremberg to Furth, 1835 A578

1985, Nov. 12 **Litho.** ***Perf. 14x14½***
1450 A578 80pf Adler locomotive 1.00 22

Founder Johannes Scharrer (1785-1844), German Railways 150th anniv.

Reintegration of German World War II Refugees, 40th Anniv. — A579

1985, Nov. 12 ***Perf. 14***
1451 A579 80pf multicolored 1.00 22

Natl. Armed Forces, 30th Anniv. A580

1985, Nov. 12 ***Perf. 14x14½***
1452 A580 80pf Iron Cross, natl. colors 1.00 22

Benz Tricycle, Saloon Car, 1912, and Modern Automobile — A581

1986, Jan. 16 **Litho.** ***Perf. 14***
1453 A581 80pf multicolored 1.00 22

Automobile cent.

Bad Hersfeld, 1250th Anniv. A582

1986, Feb. 13 **Litho.** ***Perf. 14***
1454 A582 60pf multicolored 80 20

Bach Contata, Detail, by Oskar Kokoschka (1886-1980) — A583

1986, Feb. 13
1455 A583 80pf Self portrait 90 22

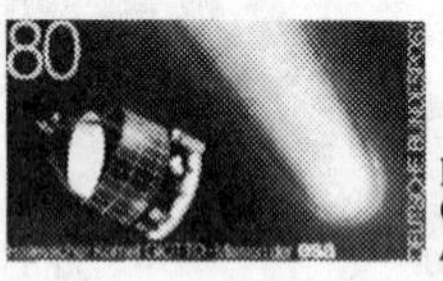

Halley's Comet A584

1986, Feb. 13
1456 A584 80pf multicolored 1.10 22

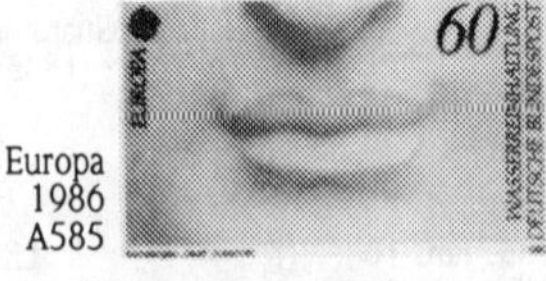

Europa 1986 A585

Details from Michelangelo's David: 60pf, Mouth (pure water). 80pf, Nose, (pure air).

1986, May 5 **Photo.** ***Perf. 14***
1457 A585 60pf multicolored 80 16
1458 A585 80pf multicolored 90 22

St. Johannis Monastery, Walsrode A586

1986, May 5 **Litho. & Engr.**
1459 A586 60pf multicolored 85 18

Monastery millennium and town of Walsrode, 603rd anniv.

King Ludwig II of Bavaria (1845-1886), Neuschwanstein Castle — A587

1986, May 5 **Litho.**
1460 A587 60pf multicolored 1.00 18

Karl Barth (1886-1968), Protestant Theologian — A588

1986, May 5 **Engr.**
1461 A588 80pf blk, dk red & red lil 1.00 22

Religion, Science, Friendship and Fatherland A589

1986, May 5 **Litho.**
1462 A589 80pf multicolored 1.00 22

Union of German Catholic Students, 100th assembly, Frankfurt, June 12-15.

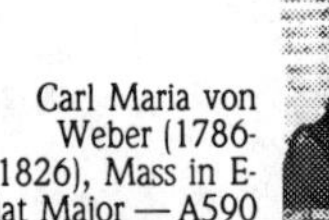

Carl Maria von Weber (1786-1826), Mass in E-flat Major — A590

1986, June 20 **Litho.** ***Perf. 14***
1463 A590 80pf multicolored 1.00 22

Franz Liszt and Signature A591

1986, June 20
1464 A591 80pf dk blue & dk org 1.00 22

Intl. Peace Year A592

1986, June 20
1465 A592 80pf multicolored 1.00 22

Souvenir Sheet

Reichstag, Berlin A593

Historic buildings: b, Koening Museum, Bonn. c, Parliament, Bonn.

1986, June 20
1466 Sheet of 3 3.25 3.25
a.-c. A593 80pf, any single 1.10 35

European Satellite Technology A594

Design: TV-SAT/TDF-1 over Europe.

1986, June 20
1467 A594 80pf multicolored 1.25 28

Augsburg Cathedral Stained Glass Window A595

1986, Aug. 14 ***Perf. 14***
1468 A595 80pf multicolored 1.25 28

Monuments protection.

King Frederick the Great (1712-1786) — A596

German Skat Congress, Cent. — A597

1986, Aug. 14
1469 A596 80pf multicolored 1.25 28

1986, Aug. 14
1470 A597 80pf Tournament card 1.25 28

Organization for Economic Cooperation and Development, 25th Anniv. — A598

1986, Aug. 14
1471 A598 80pf multicolored 1.25 28

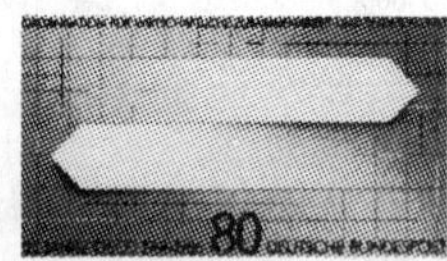

Heidelberg University, 600th Anniv. A599

1986, Oct. 16 **Litho.**
1472 A599 80pf multicolored 95 28

Stagecoach, Stamps from 1975-1984 — A600

1986, Oct. 16

1473 A600 80pf multicolored 1.25 28

Stamp Day, 50th Anniv.

A601 A602

1986, Nov. 13 Litho. *Perf. 14*

1474 A601 70pf multicolored 90 28

Mary Wigman (1886-1973), dancer.

1986-91 Engr. *Perf. 14*

Famous Women: 5pf, Emma Ihrer (1857-1911), politician, labor leader. 10pf, Paula Modersohn-Becker (1876-1907), painter. 20pf, Cilly Aussem (1909-63), tennis champion. 30pf, Kathe Kollwitz (1867-1945), painter, graphic artist. 40pf, Maria Sibylla Merian (1647-1717), naturalist, painter. 50pf, Christine Teusch (1888-1968), minister of education and cultural affairs. 60pf, Dorothea Erxleben (1715-62), physician. 70pf, Elisabet Boehm (1859-1943), social organizer. 80pf, Clara Schumann (1819-96), pianist, composer. 100pf, Therese Giehse (1898-1975), actress. 120pf, Elisabeth Selbert (1896-1986), politician. 130pf, Lise Meitner (1878-1968), physicist. 140pf, Cecile Vogt (1875-1962), neurologist. 150pf, Sophie Scholl (1921-43), member of anti-Nazi resistance. 170pf, Hannah Arendt (1906-75), American political scientist. 180pf, Lotte Lehmann (1888-1976), soprano. 200pf, Bertha von Suttner (1843-1914), 1905 Nobel Peace Prize winner. 240pf, Mathilde Franziska Anneke, (1817-84), American author. 250pf, Queen Louise of Prussia (1776-1810). 300pf, Fanny Hensel (1805-47), composer-conductor. 350pf, Hedwig Dransfeld (1871-1925), women's rights activist. 500pf, Alice Salomon (1872-1948), feminist and social activist.

1475	A602	5pf bluish gray & org brn	15	15
1476	A602	10pf vio & yel brn	15	15
1477	A602	20pf lake & Prus bl	25	15
1478	A602	30pf purple & olive	40	20
1479	A602	40pf dp bl & lil rose	45	22
1480	A602	50pf gray ol & Prus bl	50	25
1481	A602	60pf dk ol grn & dp vio	65	32
1482	A602	70pf lake & olive grn	95	48
1483	A602	80pf dk grn & lt red brn	80	40
1484	A602	100pf dk red & grnsh blk	1.10	55
1485	A602	120pf ol grn & dk red brn	1.40	70
1486	A602	130pf Prus bl & dk vio	1.60	80
1487	A602	140pf blk & dk ol bis	1.40	70
1488	A602	150pf choc & dk blue	1.85	95
1489	A602	170pf gray grn & dk brn	1.85	92
1490	A602	180pf blue & brn vio	1.80	90
1491	A602	200pf dp cl & lake	2.50	1.25
1492	A602	240pf Prus bl & yel brn	2.60	1.30
1493	A602	250pf dp lil rose & dp bl	2.50	1.25
1493A	A602	300pf dk vio & sage grn	3.00	1.50
1494	A602	350pf gray grn & lake	3.75	1.90
1494A	A602	500pf slate grn & brt ver	5.75	2.85
		Nos. 1475-1494A (22)	35.40	17.89

Issue dates: 50pf, 80pf, Nov. 18. 40pf, 60pf, Sept. 17, 1987. 120pf, Nov. 7, 1987. 10pf, Apr. 14, 1988. 20pf, 130pf, May 5, 1988. 100pf, 170pf, 240pf, 350pf, Nov. 10, 1988. 500pf, Jan. 12, 1989. 5pf, Feb. 9, 1989. 180pf, 250pf, July 13, 1989. 140pf, 300pf, Aug. 10, 1989. 30pf, 70pf, Jan. 8, 1991. 150pf, 200pf, Feb. 14, 1991.

See Nos. 1735, Berlin . 9N516-9N532.

Advent Collection for Church Projects in Latin America, 25th Anniv. A603

1986, Nov. 13 Litho. *Perf. 14*

1495 A603 80pf multicolored 90 25

Berlin, 750th Anniv. — A604

1987, Jan. 15 Litho.

1496 A604 80pf multicolored 1.00 25

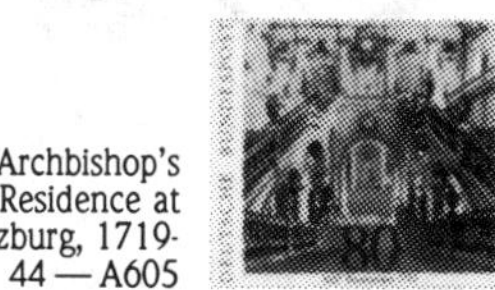
Archbishop's Residence at Wurzburg, 1719-44 — A605

1987, Jan. 15 Photo.

1497 A605 80pf multicolored 90 25

Balthasar Neumann (1687-1753), Baroque architect.

Ludwig Erhard (1897-1977), Economist, Chancellor 1963-66 — A606

1987, Jan. 15

1498 A606 80pf multicolored 90 25

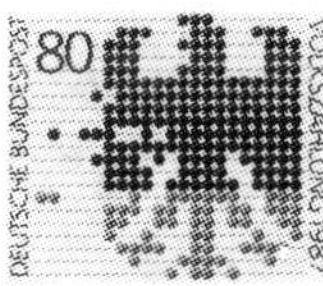

1987 Census — A607

1987, Jan. 15 Litho.

1499 A607 80pf Federal Eagle 90 25

Clemenswerth Hunting Castle, 250th Anniv. — A608

1987, Feb. 12 Litho.

1500 A608 60pf multicolored 90 20

Joseph von Fraunhofer (1787-1826), Optician, Physicist — A609

1987, Feb. 12 Litho. & Engr.

1501 A607 80pf Light spectrum diagram 90 25

Karl May (1842-1912), Novelist — A610

1987, Feb. 12 Photo.

1502 A610 80pf Apache Chief Winnetou 90 25

Papal Arms, Madonna and Child, Buildings in Kevelaer — A611

1987, Apr. 9 Litho.

1503 A611 80pf multicolored 88 25

State visit of Pope John Paul II, Apr. 30-May 4; 17th Marian and 10th Mariological World Congress, Kevelaer, Sept. 11-20.

German Choral Soc., 125th Anniv. A612

1987, Apr. 9

1504 A612 80pf multicolored 88 25

Europa 1987 A613

Modern architecture: 60pf, German Pavilion, designed by Ludwig Mies van der Rohe, 1928 World's Fair, Barcelona. 80pf, Kohlbrand Bridge, 1974, Hamburg, designed by Thyssen Engineering.

1987, May 5 Litho.

1505 A613 60pf multicolored 68 20

1506 A613 80pf multicolored 90 25

Organ Pipes, Signature A614

1987, May 5

1507 A614 80pf multicolored 90 25

Dietrich Buxtehude (c. 1637-1707), composer.

Wilhelm Kaisen (1887-1979), Bremen City Senate President — A615

1987, May 5

1508 A615 80pf multicolored 90 25

Johann Albrecht Bengel (1687-1752), Lutheran Theologian — A616

1987, May 5 Photo. *Perf. 14*

1509 A616 80pf multicolored 90 25

Kurt Schwitters (1887-1948), Artist — A617

1987, May 5 Litho.

1510 A617 80pf multicolored 90 25

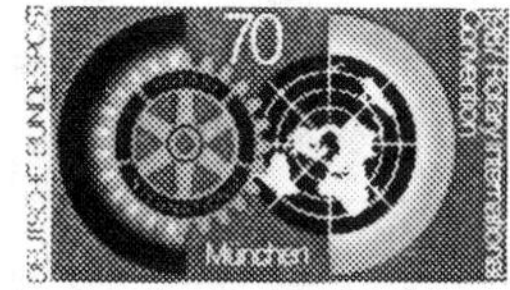
Rotary Intl. Convention, Munich, June 7-10 — A618

1987, May 5 Photo.

1511 A618 70pf multicolored 80 25

Dulmen's Wild Horses, Merfelder Bruch Nature Reserve — A619

1987, May 5

1512 A619 60pf multicolored 70 25

European Environmental Conservation Year.

Bishopric of Bremen, 1200th Anniv. — A620

Design: Charlemagne, Bremen Cathedral, city arms, Bishop Willehad.

1987, July 16 Litho. *Perf. 14*

1513 A620 80pf multicolored 90 25

7th European Rifleman's Festival, Lippstadt, Sept. 12-13 — A621

1987, Aug. 20 Litho. *Perf. 14*

1514 A621 80pf multicolored 90 25

Stamp Day — A622

1987, Oct. 15 **Litho.**
1515 A622 80pf Postmen, 1897 90 25

Historic Sites and Objects — A623

Designs: 5pf, Brunswick Lion. 10pf, Frankfurt Airport. 20pf, No. 1526, Queen Nefertiti of Egypt, bust, Egyptian Museum, Berlin. 30pf, Corner tower, Celle Castle, 14th cent. 33pf, 120pf, Schleswig Cathedral. 38pf, 280pf, Statue of Roland, Bremen. 40pf, Chile House, Hamburg. 41pf, 170pf, Russian church, Wiesbaden. 45pf, Rastatt Castle. 50pf, Filigree tracery on spires, Freiburg Cathedral. 60pf, Bavaria Munich, bronze statue above the Theresienwiese, Hall of Fame. No. 1527, Heligoland. 80pf, Entrance to Zollern II coal mine, Dortmund. 90pf, 140pf, Bronze flagon from Reinheim. 100pf, Altotting Chapel, Bavaria. 200pf, Magdeburg Cathedral. 300pf, Hambach Castle. 350pf, Externsteine Bridge near Horn-Bad Meinberg. 400pf, Opera House, Dresden. 450pf, New Gate, Neubrandenburg. 500pf, State Theatre, Cottbus. 700pf, German Theater, Berlin.

1987-93		**Typo.**		*Perf. 14*
1515A	5pf	Prus bl & gray	15	15
1516	10pf	chalky bl & slate bl	15	15
1517	20pf	dl bl & tan	22	15
1518	30pf	aqua & org brn	35	18
1519	33pf	tan & lt grn	40	20
1520	38pf	ol bis & brt grnsh bl	45	22
1521	40pf	ultra, dk red brn & org red	45	22
1522	41pf	ol bis & brt yel	52	26
1523	45pf	lt grnsh bl & dl org	55	28
1524	50pf	ultra & yel brn	58	30
1525	60pf	cob & pale gray	68	35
1526	70pf	dull bl & tan	85	42
1527	70pf	vio bl & henna brn	85	42
1528	80pf	cob & pale gray	90	45
	a.	Bklt. pane, 4 10pf, 2 50pf, 2 80pf ('89)	3.45	
	b.	Bklt. pane, 2 each 20pf, 80pf	2.50	
1529	90pf	dp bis & yel	98	50
1530	100pf	brt bluish grn & ol bis	1.10	55
	a.	Bklt. pane, 2 each 10, 60, 80, 100pf	5.60	
1531	120pf	brn org & lt grnsh bl	1.45	72
1532	140pf	dk ol bis & yel	1.60	80
1533	170pf	ol bis & brt yel	1.90	95
1534	200pf	light blue & buff	2.45	1.20
1535	280pf	sky bl & ol bis	3.00	1.50
1536	300pf	dk red brn & tan	3.75	1.80
1537	350pf	brt ultra & ol bis	3.75	1.90
1538	400pf	brn red & dl org	4.80	2.40
1539	450pf	gray bl & brn org	5.60	2.80
1540	500pf	claret & buff	6.00	3.00
1540A	700pf	gray grn & yel	8.25	4.25
		Nos. 1515A-1540A (27)	51.73	26.12

Issue dates: 30pf, 50pf, 60pf, 80pf, Nov. 6. 10pf, 300pf, Jan. 14, 1988. 120pf, No. 1526, July 14, 1988. 40pf, 90pf, 280pf, Aug. 11, 1988. 20pf, 33pf, 38pf, 140pf, Jan. 12, 1989. 100pf, 350pf, Feb. 9, 1989. 5pf, Feb. 15, 1990. 45p, No. 1527, June 21, 1990. 170pf, June 4, 1991. 400pf, Oct. 10, 1991. 450pf, Aug. 13, 1992. 200pf, Apr. 15, 1993. 500pf, June 17, 1993. 41pf, Aug. 12, 1993. 700pf, Sept. 16, 1993.

See #1655-1663, Berlin #9N543-9N557.

Christoph Willibald Gluck (1714-1787), Composer, and Score from the Opera Armide — A624

1987, Nov. 6 *Perf. 14*
1541 A624 60pf car lake & dk gray 70 25

Gerhart Hauptmann (1862-1946), Playwright — A625

1987, Nov. 6 **Litho.**
1542 A625 80pf black & brick red 90 25

German Agro Action Organization, 125th Anniv. — A626

1987, Nov. 6 **Photo.**
1543 A626 80pf Rice field 90 25

Mainz Carnival, 150th Anniv. — A627

1988, Jan. 14 **Litho.** *Perf. 14*
1544 A627 60pf Jester 75 20

Jacob Kaiser (1888-1961), Labor Leader — A628

1988, Jan. 14 **Litho. & Engr.**
1545 A628 80pf black 1.00 25

Franco-German Cooperation Treaty, 25th Anniv. — A629

1988, Jan. 14
1546 A629 80pf Adenauer, De Gaulle 1.00 25

See France No. 2086.

Beatification of Edith Stein and Rupert Mayer by Pope John Paul II in 1987 — A630

1988, Jan. 14 **Photo.**
1547 A630 80pf brown, blk & ver 1.00 25

A631 A632

Woodcut (detail) by Ludwig Richter.

1988, Feb. 18 **Litho.**
1548 A631 60pf multicolored 75 20

Woodcut inspired by poem Solitude of the Green Woods, by Baron Joseph von Eichendorff (1788-1857).

1988, Feb. 18 **Photo.**
1549 A632 80pf dk red & brn blk 1.00 25

Arthur Schopenhauer (1788-1860), philosopher.

Friedrich Wilhelm Raiffeisen (1818-1888), Economist — A633

1988, Feb. 18 **Litho.**
1550 A633 80pf black & brt yel grn 1.00 25

The German Raiffeisen Assoc., an agricultural cooperative credit soc., was founded by Raiffeisen.

Ulrich Reichsritter von Hutten (1488-1523), Humanist — A634

Design: Detail from an engraving published with Hutten's *Conquestiones.*

1988, Apr. 14 **Litho. & Engr.**
1551 A634 80pf multicolored 95 25

Europa 1988 A635

Transport and communication: 60pf, Airbus A320. 80pf, Integrated Services Digital Network (ISDN) system.

1988, May 5 **Litho.**
1552 A635 60pf multicolored 70 20
1553 A635 80pf multicolored 95 25

City of Dusseldorf, 700th Anniv. — A636

1988, May 5
1554 A636 60pf multicolored 70 20

Cologne University, 600th Anniv. A637

1988, May 5
1555 A637 80pf multicolored 95 25

Jean Monnet (1888-1979), French Statesman A638

1988, May 5
1556 A638 80pf multicolored 95 25

Theodor Storm (1817-1888), Poet, Novelist — A639

1988, May 5
1557 A639 80pf multicolored 95 25

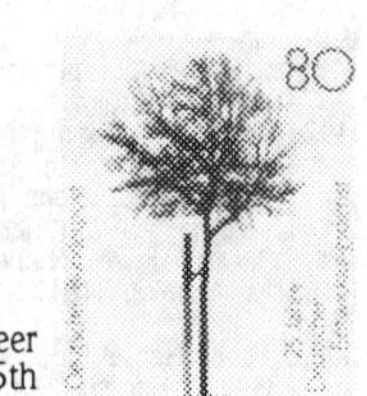

German Volunteer Service, 25th Anniv. — A640

1988, May 5
1558 A640 80pf multicolored 95 25

Town of Meersburg, Millennium — A641

1988, July 14 **Litho.** *Perf. 14*
1559 A641 60pf multicolored 72 20

Leopold Gmelin (1788-1853), Chemist — A642

1988, July 14 **Litho. & Engr.**
1560 A642 80pf multicolored 95 25

Vernier Scale as a Symbol of Precision and Quality — A643

1988, July 14 **Litho.**
1561 A643 140pf multicolored 1.65 75

Made in Germany.

August Bebel (1840-1913), Founder of the Social Democratic Party — A644

1988, Aug. 11 **Photo.**
1562 A644 80pf multicolored 85 25

Intl. Red Cross, 125th Anniv. — A645

Stamp Day — A646

1988, Oct. 13 **Litho. & Engr.**
1563 A645 80pf scarlet & black 85 25

1988, Oct. 13 **Litho.**
1564 A646 20pf Carrier pigeon 25 15

1st Nazi Pogrom, Nov. 9, 1938 A647

Design: Star, "Remembering is the secret of redemption," and burning synagogue in Baden-Baden.

1988, Oct. 13 **Photo.**
1565 A647 80pf dull pale pur & blk 85 25

Postage Stamps for Bethel, Cent. A648

1988, Nov. 10 **Litho.**
1566 A648 60pf multicolored 65 20

The Postage Stamps for Bethel program was founded by Pastor Friedrich V. Bodelschwingh to employ disabled residents of Bethel.

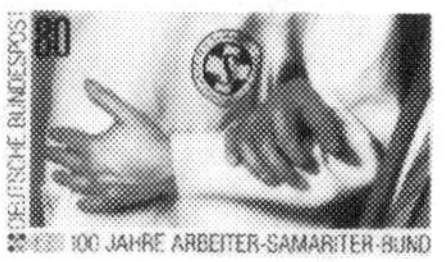

Samaritan Association of Workers (ASB) Rescue Service, Cent. A649

1988, Nov. 10
1567 A649 80pf multicolored 85 25

Bonn Bimillennium — A650

1989, Jan. 12 **Litho.**
1568 A650 80pf multicolored 90 30

Bonn as capital of the federal republic, 40th anniv.

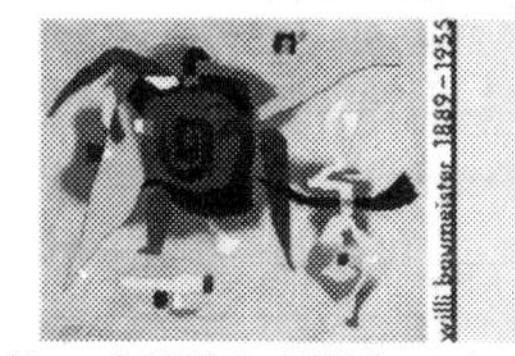

Bluxao I, 1955, by Willi Baumeister (1889-1955) — A651

1989, Jan. 12
1569 A651 60pf multicolored 75 25

Misereor and Brot fur die Welt, 30th Annivs. A652

1989, Jan. 12 **Photo.**
1570 A652 80pf Barren and verdant soil 90 30

Church organizations helping Third World nations to become self-sufficient in food production.

Cats in the Attic, Woodcut by Gerhard Marcks (1889-1981) — A653

1989, Feb. 9 **Litho.** *Perf. 14*
1571 A653 60pf multicolored 65 25

European Parliament 3rd Elections, June 18 A654

Flags of member nations.

1989, Apr. 20 **Litho.**
1572 A654 100pf multicolored 1.10 45

Europa 1989 A655

1989, May 5
1573 A655 60pf Kites 65 32
1574 A655 100pf Puppets 1.10 45

Hamburg Harbor, 800th Anniv. A656

1989, May 5
1575 A656 60pf multicolored 65 25

Cosmas Damian Asam (1686-1739), Painter, Architect — A657

1989, May 5 **Litho. & Engr.**
1576 A657 60pf Fresco 65 25

Federal Republic of Germany, 40th Anniv. — A658

1989, May 5 **Photo.**
1577 A658 100pf Natl. crest, flag, presidents' signatures 1.10 45

Council of Europe, 40th Anniv. — A659

1989, May 5 *Perf. 14*
1578 A659 100pf Parliamentary Assembly, stars 1.10 45

Franz Xaver Gabelsberger (1789-1849), Inventor of a German Shorthand — A660

1989, May 5 **Litho.**
1579 A660 100pf multicolored 1.10 45

Sts. Kilian, Colman and Totnan (d. 689), Martyred Missionaries, and Clover — A661

1989, June 15 **Litho.**
1580 A661 100pf multicolored 1.10 45

See Ireland No. 748.

Friedrich Silcher (1789-1860), Composer, and *Lorelai* Score — A662

1989, June 15
1581 A662 80pf multicolored 85 30

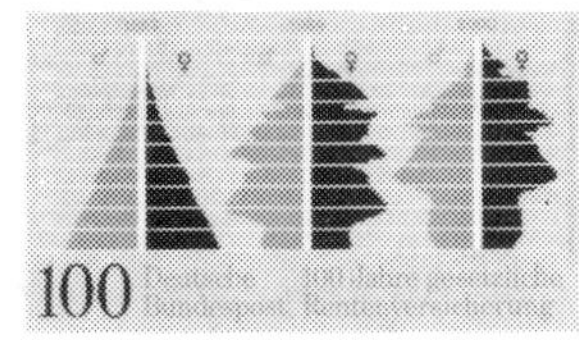

Social Security Pension Insurance, Cent. — A663

1989, June 15
1582 A663 100pf dull ultra, bl & ver 1.10 45

Friedrich List (1789-1846), Economist — A664

1989, July 13 **Engr.** *Perf. 14*
1583 A664 170pf black & dark red 1.75 75

Summer Evening, 1905, by Heinrich Vogler — A665

1989, July 13 **Litho.**
1584 A665 60pf multicolored 60 25

Worpswede Artists' Village, cent.

A666

A667

1989, July 13 **Photo.**
1585 A666 100pf slate grn, blk & gray 1.00 45

Reverend Paul Schneider (d. 1939), martyr of Buchenwald concentration camp.

1989, Aug. 10 **Litho.**
1586 A667 60pf multicolored 60 25

Frankfurt Cathedral, 750th anniv.

Child Welfare A668

1989, Aug. 10 ***Perf. 14***
1587 A668 100pf multicolored 1.00 45

Trade Union of the Mining and Power Industries, Cent. A669

1989, Aug. 10 ***Perf. 14***
1588 A669 100pf multicolored 1.00 45

Reinhold Maier (1889-1971), Politician — A670

1989, Oct. 12 **Litho.**
1589 A670 100pf multicolored 1.10 45

Restoration of St. James Church Organ, Constructed by Arp Schnitger, 1689 — A671

1989, Nov. 16
1590 A671 60pf multicolored 65 30

Speyer, 2000th Anniv. A672

1990, Jan. 12 **Litho.** ***Perf. 14x14½***
1591 A672 60pf multicolored 65 32

A673

A674

Design: *The Young Post Rider*, an Engraving by Albrecht Durer.

1990, Jan. 12 **Litho. & Engr.** ***Perf. 14***
1592 A673 100pf buff, vio brn & gray 1.10 45

Postal communications in Europe, 500th anniv. See Austria No. 1486, Belgium No. 1332 and DDR No. 2791.

1990, Jan. 12 **Litho.**
1593 A674 100pf multicolored 1.10 45

Riesling Vineyards, 500th anniv.

Addition of Lubeck to the UNESCO World Heritage List, 1987 A675

1990, Jan. 12 **Litho. & Engr.**
1594 A675 100pf multicolored 1.10 45

Seal of Col. Spittler, 1400, and Teutonic Order Heraldic Emblem — A676

1990, Feb. 15 **Litho.**
1595 A676 100pf multicolored 1.10 45

Teutonic Order, 800th anniv.

Seal of Frederick II and Galleria Reception Hall at the Frankfurt Fair A677

1990, Feb. 15
1596 A677 100pf multicolored 1.10 45

Granting of fair privileges to Frankfurt by Frederick II, 750th anniv.

Youth Science and Technology Competition, 25th Anniv. — A678

1990, Feb. 15
1597 A678 100pf multicolored 1.10 45

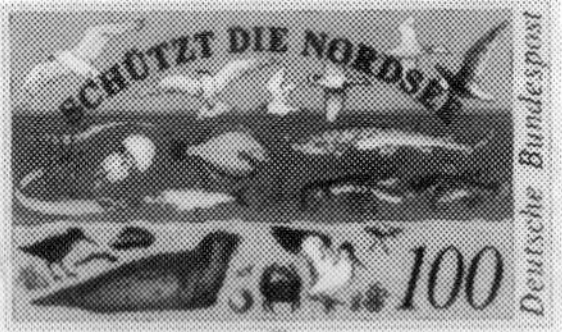

Nature and Environmental Protection — A679

1990, Feb. 15
1598 A679 100pf North Sea 1.10 45

Labor Day, Cent. A680

1990, Apr. 19 **Photo.** ***Perf. 14***
1599 A680 100pf dark red & blk 1.10 45

German Assoc. of Housewives, 75th Anniv. — A681

1990, Apr. 19 **Litho.**
1600 A681 100pf multicolored 1.10 45

Europa A682

Post offices in Frankfurt am Main: 60pf, Thurn and Taxis Palace. 100pf, Modern Giro office.

1990, May 3 **Litho.**
1601 A682 60pf multicolored 72 36
1602 A682 100pf multicolored 1.20 45

German Students' Fraternity, 175th Anniv. A683

1990, May 3 **Litho. & Engr.**
1603 A683 100pf multicolored 1.20 45

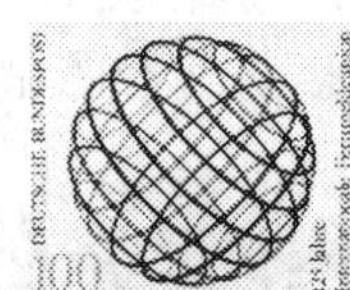

Intl. Telecommunication Union, 125th Anniv. — A684

1990, May 3 **Litho.**
1604 A684 100pf multicolored 1.20 45

German Life Boat Institution, 125th Anniv. A685

1990, May 3
1605 A685 60pf multicolored 65 36

Wilhelm Leuschner (1890-1944), Politician — A686

1990, May 3 **Litho. & Engr.**
1606 A686 100pf lt gray violet 1.20 45

Rummelsberg Diaconal Institution, Cent. — A687

1990, May 3 **Litho.**
1607 A687 100pf multicolored 1.20 45

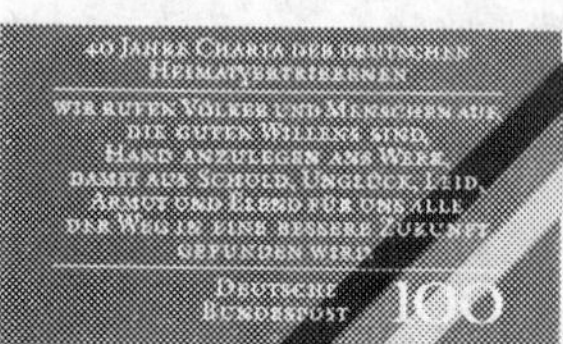

Charter of German Expellees, 40th Anniv. — A688

1990, June 21 **Photo.**
1608 A688 100pf multicolored 1.20 45

Intl. Chamber of Commerce, 30th Universal Congress A689

1990, June 21 **Litho.**
1609 A689 80pf multicolored 1.00 40

Matthias Claudius (1740-1815), Writer — A691

1990, Aug. 9 **Litho.**
1611 A691 100pf multicolored 1.20 45

German Reunification — A692

1990, Oct. 3 **Litho.** ***Perf. 14***
1612 A692 50pf black, red & yel 60 30
1613 A692 100pf black, red & yel 1.20 60

First Postage Stamps, 150th Anniv. — A693

1990, Oct. 11 **Litho.**
1614 A693 100pf multicolored 1.20 60

Heinrich Schliemann (1822-1890), Archaeologist — A694

1990, Oct. 11
1615 A694 60pf multicolored 70 35

See Greece No. 1705.

Kathe Dorsch (1912-1957), Actress — A695

Opening of Berlin Wall, 1st Anniv. — A696

1990, Nov. 6 **Photo.**

1616 A695 100pf red & violet 1.20 60

1990, Nov. 6 **Photo.** ***Perf. 14***

1617 A696 50pf shown 62 30
1618 A696 100pf Brandenburg Gate 1.25 62

Souvenir Sheet

1619 Sheet of 2 1.87 92
a. A696 50pf like No. 1617 62 30
b. A696 100pf like No. 1618 1.25 62

Rainbow continuous on stamps from #1619.

Pharmacy Profession, 750th Anniv. — A697

1991, Jan. 8 **Litho.**

1620 A697 100pf multicolored 1.25 68

Hanover, 750th Anniv. — A698

1991, Jan. 8

1621 A698 60pf multicolored 75 40

Brandenburg Gate, Bicentennial — A699

1991, Jan. 8 **Litho. & Engr.**

1622 A699 100pf gray, dk bl & red 1.25 68

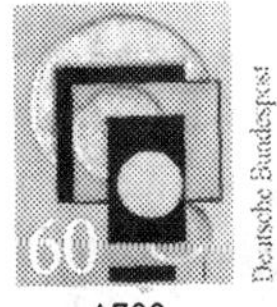

A700 A701

1991, Jan. 8 **Photo.**

1623 A700 60pf multicolored 75 40

Erich Buchholz (1891-1972), painter and architect.

1991, Jan. 8 **Litho.**

1624 A701 100pf multicolored 1.25 68

Walter Eucken (1891-1950), economist.

25th Intl. Tourism Exchange, Berlin — A702

1991, Jan. 8

1625 A702 100pf multicolored 1.25 68

Souvenir Sheet

World Bobsled Championships, Altenberg — A703

1991, Jan. 8 ***Perf. 12½x13***

1626 A703 100pf multicolored 1.25 68

Friedrich Spee von Langenfeld (1591-1635), Poet — A704

1991, Feb. 14 **Litho.** ***Perf. 14***

1627 A704 100pf multicolored 1.10 60

A705

1991, Feb. 14

1628 A705 100pf multicolored 1.10 60

Ludwig Windthorst (1812-1891), politician.

A706

1991, Mar. 12

1629 A706 60pf multicolored 70 35

Jan von Werth (1591-1652), general.

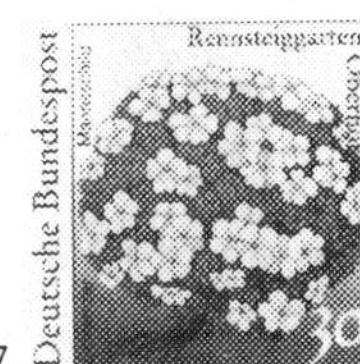

Flowers — A707

1991, Mar. 12 ***Perf. 13***

1630 A707 30pf Schweizer mannschild 35 18
1631 A707 50pf Wulfens primel (primula) 60 30
1632 A707 80pf Sommerenzian (gentian) 90 45
1633 A707 100pf Preiselbeere (cranberry) 1.15 60
1634 A707 350pf Alpenedelweiss 4.00 2.00
Nos. 1630-1634 (5) 7.00 3.53

Battle of Legnica, 750th Anniv. A708

1991, Apr. 9 **Litho. & Engr.** ***Perf. 14***

1635 A708 100pf multicolored 1.10 50

See Poland No. 3019.

Choral Singing Academy of Berlin, Bicent. A709

1991, Apr. 9

1636 A709 100pf multicolored 1.10 50

Lette Foundation, 125th Anniv. — A710

1991, Apr. 9 **Photo.**

1637 A710 100pf multicolored 1.10 50

Historic Aircraft A711

1991, Apr. 9

1638 A711 30pf Junkers F13, 1930 35 18
1639 A711 50pf Grade Eindecker, 1909 60 30
1640 A711 100pf Fokker FIII, 1922 1.15 60
1641 A711 165pf Graf Zeppelin LZ 127, 1928 1.90 95

Europa — A712

Satellites: 60pf, ERS-1. 100pf, Copernicus.

1991, May 2 **Litho.** ***Perf. 14***

1642 A712 60pf multicolored 70 35
1643 A712 100pf multicolored 1.15 60

Town Charters, 700th Anniv. — A713

Design: Arms of Bernkastel, Mayen, Montabaur, Saarburg, Welschbillig, and Wittlich.

1991, May 2

1644 A713 60pf multicolored 70 35

Max Reger (1873-1916), Composer — A714

1991, May 2

1645 A714 100pf multicolored 1.15 60

Inter-City Express Railway A715

1991, May 2

1646 A715 60pf multicolored 70 35

18th World Gas Congress, Berlin A716

Designs: 60pf, Wilhelm August Lampadius (1772-1842), chemist. 100pf, Gas street lamp.

1991, June 4 **Litho.** ***Perf. 13x12½***

1647 A716 60pf lt blue & black 65 32
1648 A716 100pf lt blue & black 1.00 50
a. Pair, #1647-1648 + label 1.65 82

Sea Birds — A717

Designs: 60pf, Kampflaufer, Philomachus pugnax. 80pf, Zwergseeschwalbe, Sterna albifrons. 100pf, Ringelgans, Branta bernicla. 140pf, Seeadler, Haliaeetus albicilla.

1991, June 4 **Litho.** ***Perf. 14***

1649 A717 60pf multicolored 65 32
1650 A717 80pf multicolored 90 45
1651 A717 100pf multicolored 1.10 55
1652 A717 140pf multicolored 1.55 78

Paul Wallot (1841-1912), Architect — A718

1991, June 4 **Litho. & Engr.** ***Perf. 14***

1653 A718 100pf multicolored 1.10 55

Historic Sites Type of 1987

1991 Litho. ***Die Cut, Imperf.***

Self-Adhesive

1655 A623	10pf like No. 1516	15	15
1659 A623	60pf like No. 1523	65	32
1661 A623	80pf like No. 1525	90	45
1663 A623	100pf like No. 1527	1.10	55
a.	Bklt. pane, 2 each #1655, 1659, 1661, 1663	5.75	2.75

Issued: #1655, 1659, 1661, 1663, June 4.

Nos. 1655, 1659, 1661, 1663 issued on peelable paper backing serving as booklet cover.

This is an expanding set. Numbers will change if necessary.

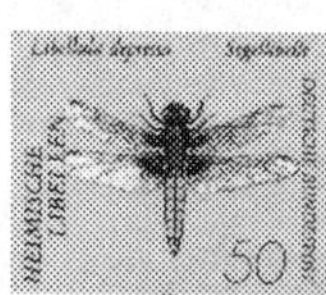

Dragonflies — A719

Designs: 50pf, No. 1671, Libellula depressa. No. 1672, 70pf, Sympetrum sanguineum. No. 1673, 80pf, Cordulegaster boltonii. No. 1674, 100pf, Aeshna viridis.

1991, July 9 Photo. ***Perf. 14***

1670 A719	50pf multicolored	55	28
1671 A719	60pf multicolored	65	32
1672 A719	60pf multicolored	65	32
1673 A719	60pf multicolored	65	32
1674 A719	60pf multicolored	65	32
a.	Block of 4, #1671-1674	2.70	1.35
1675 A719	70pf multicolored	78	40
1676 A719	80pf multicolored	90	45
1677 A719	100pf multicolored	1.10	55
	Nos. 1670-1677 (8)	5.93	2.96

Traffic Safety A720

1991, July 9 Litho.

1678 A720 100pf multicolored 1.10 55

Geneva Convention on Refugees, 40th Anniv. — A721

1991, July 9

1679 A721 100pf black, gray & pink 1.10 55

Intl. Radio Exhibition, Berlin A722

1991, July 9

1680 A722 100pf multicolored 1.10 55

Reinold von Thadden-Trieglaff (1891-1976), Founder of German Protestant Convention — A723

1991, Aug. 8 Litho. ***Perf. 14***

1681 A723 100pf multicolored 1.20 60

August Heinrich Hoffman von Fallersleben (1798-1874), Poet and Philologist — A724

1991, Aug. 8

1682 A724 100pf multicolored 1.20 60

German national anthem, 150th anniv.

3-Phase Energy Transmission, Cent. — A725

1991, Aug. 8

1683 A725 170pf multicolored 2.00 1.00

Rhine-Ruhr Harbor, Duisburg, 275th Anniv. A726

1991, Sept. 12 Litho. ***Perf. 14***

1684 A726 100pf multicolored 1.20 60

Souvenir Sheet

Theodor Korner (1791-1813), Poet — A727

1991, Sept. 12 ***Perf. 13x12½***

1685 A727	Sheet of 2	1.90	95
a.	60pf Sword and pen	70	35
b.	100pf Portrait	1.20	60

Hans Albers (1891-1960), Actor — A728

1991, Sept. 12 Photo. ***Perf. 14***

1686 A728 100pf multicolored 1.20 60

Postman, Spreewald Region — A729

1991, Oct. 10 Litho. ***Perf. 14***

1687 A729 100pf multicolored 1.20 60

Stamp Day.

Bird Monument by Max Ernst — A730

1991, Oct. 10

1688 A730 100pf multicolored 1.20 60

Sorbian Legends — A731

1991, Nov. 5 ***Perf. 13***

1689 A731	60pf Fiddler, water sprite	75	35
1690 A731	100pf Midday woman, woman from Nochten	1.20	60

Souvenir Sheet

Wolfgang Amadeus Mozart, Death Bicent. — A732

1991, Nov. 5 Litho. ***Perf. 14***

1691 A732 100pf multicolored 1.20 60

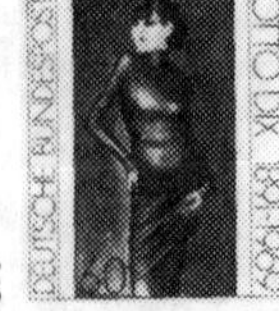

Otto Dix (1891-1969), Painter — A733

Designs: 60pf, Portrait of the Dancer Anita Berber. 100pf, Self-portrait.

1991, Nov. 5 Photo. ***Perf. 14***

1692 A733	60pf multicolored	72	35
1693 A733	100pf multicolored	1.20	60

Julius Leber (1891-1945), Politician A734

1991, Nov. 5 Litho.

1694 A734 100pf black & red 1.20 60

Nelly Sachs (1891-1970), Writer — A735

1991, Nov. 5

1695 A735 100pf violet 1.20 60

City of Koblenz, 2000th Anniv. A736

1992, Jan. 9 ***Perf. 13x12½***

1696 A736 60pf multicolored 72 36

Terre Des Hommes Child Welfare Organization, 25th Anniv. — A737

1992, Jan. 9 Litho. ***Perf. 14***

1697 A737 100pf multicolored 1.20 60

Martin Niemoller (1892-1984), Theologian — A738

1992, Jan. 9

1698 A738 100pf multicolored 1.20 60

Coats of Arms of States of the Federal Republic of Germany A739

1992-94 ***Perf. 13½***

1699 A739	100pf Baden-Wurttemberg	1.20	60
1700 A739	100pf Bavaria	1.20	60
1701 A739	100pf Berlin	1.25	65
1702 A739	100pf Brandenburg	1.30	65
1703 A739	100pf Bremen	1.30	65
1704 A739	100pf Hamburg	1.30	65
1705 A739	100pf Hesse	1.20	60
1706 A739	100pf Mecklenburg-Western Pomerania	1.20	60
1707 A739	100pf Lower Saxony	1.20	60
1708 A739	100pf North Rhine - Westphalia	1.25	65
1709 A739	100pf Rhineland-Palatinate	1.25	60
1710 A739	100pf Saar	1.10	55
1711 A739	100pf Saxony	1.10	55
	Nos. 1699-1711 (13)	15.85	7.95

Issued: #2699, Jan. 9; #1700, Mar. 12; #1701, June 11; #1702, July 16; #1703, Aug. 13; #1704,

Sept. 10; #1705. Mar. 11, 1993; #1706, June 17, 1993. #1707, July 15, 1993; #1708, Aug. 12, 1993; #1709, Sept. 16, 1993; #1710, Jan. 13, 1994. #1711, Mar. 10, 1994.
This is an expanding set. Numbers will change if necessary.

Famous Women Type of 1986

Design: 400pf, Charlotte von Stein (1742-1827), confidant of Goethe. 450pf, Hedwig Courths-Mahler (1867-1950), novelist.

1992 Engr. *Perf. 14*
1734 A602 400pf lake & blk 4.80 2.40
1735 A602 450pf brt blue & blue 5.65 2.80

Issue date: 400pf, Jan. 9, 1992; 450pf, June 11. This is an expanding set. Numbers will change if necessary.

Arthur Honegger (1892-1955), Composer — A740

1992, Feb. 6 Photo. *Perf. 14*
1736 A740 100pf sepia & black 1.20 60

Ferdinand von Zeppelin (1838-1917), Airship Builder — A741

1992, Feb. 6 Litho.
1737 A741 165pf multicolored 2.00 1.00

City of Kiel, 750th Anniv. A742

1992, Mar. 12
1738 A742 60pf multicolored 75 38

Konrad Adenauer — A743

1992, Mar. 12 Photo.
1739 A743 100pf black & dull org 1.20 60

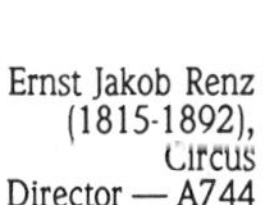

Ernst Jakob Renz (1815-1892), Circus Director — A744

1992, Mar. 12 Litho.
1740 A744 100pf multicolored 1.20 60

Berlin Sugar Institute, 125th Anniv. A745

1992, Mar. 12 *Perf. 13x12½*
1741 A745 100pf multicolored 1.20 60

Johann Adam Schall von Bell (1592-1666), Astronomer and Missionary — A746

1992, Apr. 9 Litho. *Perf. 13x12½*
1742 A746 140pf multicolored 1.60 80

Erfurt, Capital of Thuringia, 1250th Anniv. — A747

1992, May 7 Litho. *Perf. 14*
1743 A747 60pf multicolored 75 38

Discovery of America, 500th Anniv. — A748

Europa: 60pf, Woodcut illustrating letters from Columbus, 1493. 100pf, Rene de Laudonniere and Chief Athore by Jacques le Moyne de Morgues, 1564.

1992, May 7 *Perf. 13½*
1744 A748 60pf multicolored 75 38
1745 A748 100pf multicolored 1.20 60

A749 A750

1992, May 7 *Perf. 13*
1746 A749 100pf multicolored 1.20 60

Order of Merit, 150th anniv.

1992, May 7 Litho. *Perf. 14*
1747 A750 100pf multicolored 1.25 65

St. Ludgerus, 1250th birth anniv.

Adam Riese (1492-1559), Mathematician A751

1992, May 7
1748 A751 100pf multicolored 1.25 65

Georg Christoph Lichtenberg (1742-1799), Physicist — A752

1992, June 11 Litho. *Perf. 14*
1749 A752 100pf multicolored 1.20 60

20th Century Paintings — A753

Designs: 60pf, Landscape with a Horse, by Franz Marc (1880-1916). 100pf, Fashion Shop, by August Macke (1887-1914). 170pf, Murnau with a Rainbow, by Vassily Kandinsky (1866-1944).

1992, June 11 Litho. *Perf. 14*
1750 A753 60pf multicolored 75 38
1751 A753 100pf multicolored 1.25 65
1752 A753 170pf multicolored 2.10 1.05

Leipzig Botanical Garden A754

1992, July 16 Litho. *Perf. 13x12½*
1753 A754 60pf multicolored 78 40

Family Living — A755

1992, July 16 *Perf. 13½*
1754 A755 100pf multicolored 1.30 65

17th World Congress on Home Economics, Hanover A756

1992, July 16 Photo. *Perf. 14*
1755 A756 100pf multicolored 1.30 65

Egid Quirin Asam (1692-1750), Architect and Sculptor — A757

1992, Aug. 13 Litho. *Perf. 14*
1756 A757 60pf multicolored 75 38

German State Opera, Berlin, 250th Anniv. A758

1992, Aug. 13
1757 A758 80pf multicolored 1.05 58

Federation of German Amateur Theaters, Cent. — A759

1992, Aug. 13
1758 A759 100pf multicolored 1.30 65

Construction of First Globe by Martin Behaim, 500th Anniv. — A760

1992, Sept. 10 *Perf. 13½*
1759 A760 60pf multicolored 75 38

Opening of Main-Danube Canal — A761

1992, Sept. 10 *Perf. 14*
1760 A761 100pf multicolored 1.30 65

Werner Bergengruen (1892-1964), Writer — A762

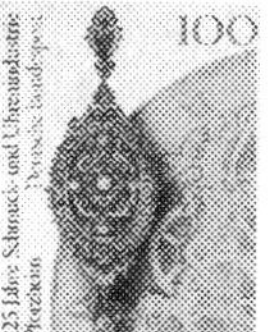

Jewelry & Watch Industries in Pforzheim, 225th Anniv. — A763

1992, Sept. 10
1761 A762 100pf blk, bl & gray 1.30 65

1992, Sept. 10
1762 A763 100pf multicolored 1.30 65

Balloon Post — A764

1992, Oct. 15 Litho. *Perf. 14*
1763 A764 100pf multicolored 1.25 60

Stamp Day.

Hugo Distler (1908-1942), Composer A765

1992, Oct. 15
1764 A765 100pf violet & black 1.25 60

Association of German Plant and Machine Builders, Cent. A766

1992, Oct. 15 **Litho. & Engr.**
1765 A766 170pf multicolored 2.10 1.05

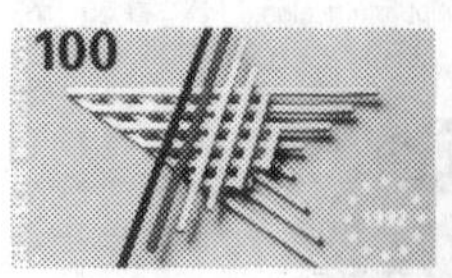

Single European Market A767

1992, Nov. 5 **Litho.** ***Perf. 14***
1766 A767 100pf multicolored 1.25 60

Jochen Klepper (1903-1942), Writer — A768

1992, Nov. 5 **Litho. & Engr.** ***Perf. 14***
1767 A768 100pf multicolored 1.25 60

A769 A770

1992, Nov. 5 **Photo.**
1768 A769 100pf sepia & black 1.25 60

Werner von Siemens (1816-1892), electrical engineer.

1992, Nov. 5 **Litho.**
1769 A770 100pf multicolored 1.25 60

Gebhard Leberecht von Blucher (1742-1819), Commander of Prussian Army.

City of Munster, 1200th Anniv. — A771

1993, Jan. 14 **Litho.** ***Perf. 14***
1770 A771 60pf multicolored 70 35

Sir Isaac Newton, Scientist A772

1993, Jan. 14 **Litho. & Engr.**
1771 A772 100pf multicolored 1.20 60

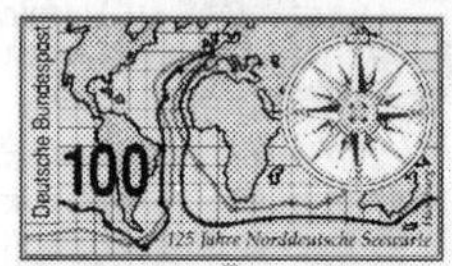

North German Naval Observatory, Hamburg, 125th Anniv. — A773

1993, Jan. 14 **Litho.** ***Perf. 13x12½***
1772 A773 100pf multicolored 1.20 60

A774 A775

1993, Jan. 14 **Photo.** ***Perf. 14***
1773 A774 100pf blk, yel & bl 1.20 60

Health and safety in workplace.

1993, Jan. 14
1774 A775 170pf multicolored 2.00 1.00

Association of German Electrical Engineers, cent.

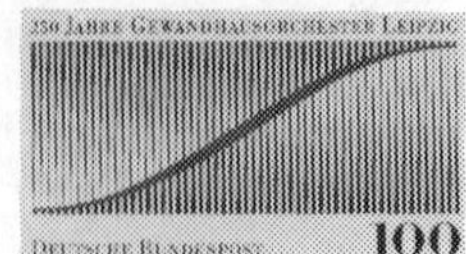

Leipzig Gewandhaus Orchestra, 250th Anniv. — A776

1993, Feb. 11 **Litho.** ***Perf. 13x12½***
1775 A776 100pf black & gold 1.20 60

St. John of Nepomuk, 600th Death Anniv. A777

1993, Mar. 11
1776 A777 100pf multicolored 1.20 60

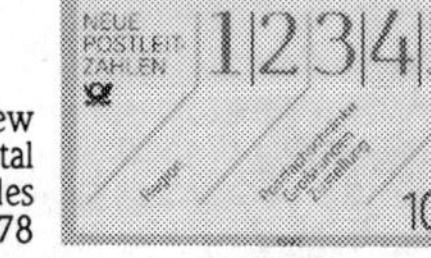

New Postal Codes A778

1993, Mar. 11 ***Perf. 14***
1777 A778 100pf multicolored 1.20 60

20th Century German Paintings — A779

Designs: No. 1778, Cafe, by George Grosz (1893-1959). No. 1779, Sea and Sun, by Otto Pankok (1893-1966). No. 1780, Audience, by A. Paul Weber (1893-1980).

1993, Mar. 11
1778 A779 100pf multicolored 1.20 60
1779 A779 100pf multicolored 1.20 60
1780 A779 100pf multicolored 1.20 60

Benedictine Abbeys of Maria Laach and Bursfelde, 900th Anniv. — A780

1993, Apr. 15 **Litho. & Engr.** ***Perf. 14***
1781 A780 80pf multicolored 1.00 50

5th Intl. Horticultural Show, Stuttgart — A781

1993, Apr. 15 **Litho.** ***Perf. 13x12½***
1782 A781 100pf multicolored 1.20 60

Contemporary Art — A782

Europa: 80pf, Storage Place, by Joseph Beuys (1921-1986). 100pf, Homage to the Square, by Joseph Albers (1888-1976).

1993, May 5 **Litho.** ***Perf. 13½x14***
1783 A782 80pf multicolored 95 48
1784 A782 100pf multicolored 1.20 60

Dahlwitz Hoppegarten (Hippodrome), Berlin, 125th Anniv. — A783

1993, May 5 **Litho.** ***Perf. 14***
1785 A783 80pf multicolored 95 48

Lake Constance Steamer Hohentwiel A784

1993, May 5 **Photo.**
1786 A784 100pf multicolored 1.20 60

See Austria No. 1618, Switzerland No. 931.

Schulpforta School for Boys, 450th Anniv. — A785

1993, May 5 **Litho.**
1787 A785 100pf multicolored 1.20 60

Coburger Convent, 125th Anniv. A786

1993, May 5 **Litho. & Engr.**
1788 A786 100pf black, green & red 1.20 60

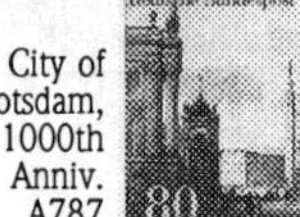

City of Potsdam, 1000th Anniv. A787

1993, June 17 **Litho.** ***Perf. 13x12½***
1789 A787 80pf multicolored 1.00 50

German UNICEF Committee, 40th Anniv. A788

1993, June 17 **Litho.**
1790 A788 100pf multicolored 1.20 60

A789

A790

1993, June 17 **Photo.** ***Perf. 14***
1791 A789 100pf multicolored 1.20 60

Friedrich Holderlin (1770-1843), writer.

1993, July 15
1792 A790 100pf multicolored 1.20 60

Hans Fallada (1893-1947), novelist.

Scenic Regions in Germany — A791

1993 **Litho.** ***Perf. 14***
1793 A791 100pf Rugen Island 1.20 60
1794 A791 100pf Harz Mountains 1.20 60
1795 A791 100pf Rhon Mountains 1.20 60

Issued: Nos. 1793-1795, July 15. Numbers have been reserved for additional values in this set.

Mathias Klotz (1653-1743), Violin Maker — A792

1993, Aug. 12 **Litho.** ***Perf. 13x12½***
1808 A792 80pf multicolored 1.00 50

Heinrich George (1893-1946), Actor — A793

1993, Aug. 12 ***Perf. 14***
1809 A793 100pf multicolored 1.25 65

Intl. Radio Exhibition, Berlin A794

1993, Aug. 12
1810 A794 100pf multicolored 1.25 65

Hans Leip (1893-1983), Poet and Painter — A795

1993, Sept. 16 **Litho.** ***Perf. 13***
1811 A795 100pf red, black & blue 1.25 60

Birger Forell (1893-1958), Swedish Priest — A796

1993, Sept. 16 ***Perf. 14***
1812 A796 100pf multicolored 1.25 60

Souvenir Sheet

For the Children — A797

1993, Sept. 16
1813 A797 100pf multicolored 1.25 1.25

Peter I. Tchaikovsky (1840-93), Composer — A798

1993, Oct. 14
1814 A798 80pf multicolored 1.00 50

Max Reinhardt (1873-1943), Theatrical Director — A799

1993, Oct. 14
1815 A799 100pf buff, black & red 1.25 60

St. Hedwig of Silesia, 750th Death Anniv. — A800

1993, Oct. 14
1816 A800 100pf multicolored 1.25 60

See Poland No. 3176.

Paracelsus (1493-1541), Physician, Teacher — A801

Litho. & Engr.

1993, Nov. 10 ***Perf. 14***
1817 A801 100pf multicolored 1.25 60

Claudio Monteverdi (1567-1643), Composer — A802

1993, Nov. 10 **Litho.** ***Perf. 13x12½***
1818 A802 100pf multicolored 1.25 60

Willy Brandt (1913-92), Statesman A803

1994, Nov. 10 ***Perf. 14***
1819 A803 100pf multicolored 1.25 60

Staade, 1000th Anniv. A804

1994, Jan. 13. **Litho. & Engr.** ***Perf. 14***
1820 A804 80pf multicolored 90 45

Intl. Year of the Family A805

1994, Jan. 13 **Litho.**
1821 A805 100pf multicolored 1.10 55

Heinrich Hertz (1857-94), Physicist A806

1994, Jan. 13 *Perf. 13x12½*

1822 A806 200pf multicolored 2.25 1.10

Frankfurt Am Main, 1200th Anniv. A807

1994, Feb. 10

1823 A807 80pf multicolored 90 45

Fulda, 1250th Anniv. A808

1994, Mar. 10 *Perf. 14*

1824 A808 80pf multicolored 90 45

German Women's Associations, German Women's Council, Cent. — A809

1994, Mar. 10 *Perf. 13x12½*

1825 A809 100pf black, red & yellow 1.10 55

Fourth European Parliamentary Elections — A810

1994, Mar. 10 *Perf. 14*

1826 A810 100pf multicolored 1.10 55

Foreigners in Germany: Living Together A811

1994, Mar. 10

1827 A811 100pf multicolored 1.10 55

SEMI-POSTAL STAMPS

Issues of the Republic

Regular Issue of 1906-17 Surcharged

1919, May 1 **Wmk. 125** *Perf. 14*

B1 A16 10pf + 5pf carmine 15 *4.00*
B2 A22 15pf + 5pf dk vio 20 *3.50*
Set, never hinged 70

4 Mark für Alters- und Kinderhilfe

"Planting Charity" — SP1

Feeding the Hungry — SP2

1922, Dec. 11 **Litho.** **Wmk. 126**

B3 SP1 6m + 4m ultra & brn 15 *15.00*
B4 SP1 12m + 8m red org & bl gray 15 *15.00*
Set, never hinged 1.10

Nos. 221, 225 and 196 Surcharged

500 M Rhein-Ruhr-Hilfe

1923, Feb. 19

B5 A34 5m + 100m 15 *5.00*
B6 A29 25m + 500m 15 *16.00*
a. Inverted surcharge 125.00
B7 A32 20m + 1000m 1.65 *90.00*
a. Inverted surcharge 400.00 *1,250.*
b. Green background inverted 125.00 275.00
Set, never hinged 6.00

Note following No. 160 applies to #B1-B7.

1924, Feb. 25 **Typo.** *Perf. 14½x15*

Designs: 10pf+30pf, Giving drink to the thirsty. 20pf+60pf, Clothing the naked. 50pf+1.50m, Healing the sick.

B8 SP2 5pf + 15pf dk green 95 1.90
B9 SP2 10pf + 30pf vermilion 95 1.50
B10 SP2 20pf + 60pf dk blue 5.00 5.25
B11 SP2 50pf + 1.50m red brn 24.00 40.00
Set, never hinged 110.00

The surtax was used for charity.
See No. B58.

Prussia — SP6

1925, Dec. 15 *Perf. 14*

Inscribed: "1925"

B12 SP6 5pf + 5pf shown 30 32
B13 SP6 10pf + 10pf Bavaria 95 50
B14 SP6 20pf + 20pf Saxony 6.50 8.25
a. Bklt. pane of 2 + 2 labels 225.00
Set, never hinged 35.00

1926, Dec. 1

Inscribed: "1926"

B15 SP6 5pf + 5pf Wurttemberg 75 80
B16 SP6 10pf + 10pf Baden 1.25 1.40
a. Bklt. pane of 6 + 2 labels 150.00
B17 SP6 25pf + 25pf Thuringia 7.75 12.50
B18 SP6 50pf + 50pf Hesse 35.00 47.50
Set, never hinged 165.00

See Nos. B23-B32.

Pres. Paul von Hindenburg — SP13

1927, Sept. 26 **Photo.**

B19 SP13 8pf dark green 40 55
a. Bklt. pane, 4 #B19, 3 #B20 + label 70.00
B20 SP13 15pf scarlet 65 90
B21 SP13 25pf deep blue 8.00 11.00
B22 SP13 50pf bister brown 11.00 15.00
Set, never hinged 80.00

80th birthday of Pres. Hindenburg. The stamps were sold at double face value. The surtax was given to a fund for War Invalids.

Arms Type of 1925

Design: 8pf+7pf, Mecklenberg-Schwerin.

1928, Nov. 15 **Typo.**

Inscribed: "1928"

B23 SP6 5pf + 5pf Hamburg 35 60
B24 SP6 8pf + 7pf multi 35 60
a. Bklt. pane, 4 #B24, 3 #B25 + label 125.00
B25 SP6 15pf + 15pf Oldenburg 70 1.00
B26 SP6 25pf + 25pf Brunswick 8.00 16.00
B27 SP6 50pf + 50pf Anhalt 37.50 57.50
Nos. B23-B27 (5) 46.90 75.70
Set, never hinged 165.00

1929, Nov. 4

Coats of Arms: 8pf+4pf, Lippe-Detmold. 25pf+10pf, ecklenburg-Strelitz. 50pf+40pf, Schaumburg-Lippe.

Inscribed: "1929"

B28 SP6 5pf + 2pf Bremen 40 75
a. Bklt. pane of 6 + 2 labels 30.00
B29 SP6 8pf + 4pf multi 40 75
a. Bklt. pane, 4 #B29, 3 #B30 + label 75.00
B30 SP6 15pf + 5pf Lubeck 55 1.10
B31 SP6 25pf + 10pf multi 8.25 20.00
B32 SP6 50pf + 40pf choc, ocher & red 37.50 50.00
a. "PE" for "PF" 200.00 275.00
Nos. B28-B32 (5) 47.10 72.60
Set, never hinged 140.00

Cathedral of Aachen — SP24

Brandenburg Gate, Berlin — SP25

Castle of Marienwerder SP26

Statue of St. Kilian and Marienburg Fortress at Würzburg SP27

Souvenir Sheet

Wmk. 223

1930, Sept. 12 **Engr.** *Perf. 14*

B33 Sheet of 4 350.00 *700.00*
a. SP24 8pf + 4pf dark green 30.00 50.00
b. SP25 15pf + 5pf carmine 30.00 50.00
c. SP26 25pf + 10p dark blue 30.00 50.00
d. SP27 50pf + 40pf dark brown 30.00 50.00
Sheet, never hinged 575.00

Intl. Phil. Exhib., Berlin, Sept. 12-21, 1930.

No. B33 is watermarked Eagle on each stamp and "IPOSTA"-"1930" in the margins. Size: 105x150. Each holder of an admission ticket was entitled to purchase one sheet. The ticket cost 1m and the sheet 1.70m (face value 98pf, charity 59pf, special paper 13pf).

The margin of the souvenir sheet is ungummed.

Types of International Philatelic Exhibition Issue

1930, Nov. 1 **Wmk. 126**

B34 SP24 8 + 4pf dp green 30 30
a. Bklt. pane of 7 + label 40.00
b. Bklt. pane, 3 #B34, 4 #B35 + label 50.00
B35 SP25 15 + 5pf car 45 40
B36 SP26 25 + 10pf dk blue 9.25 11.00
B37 SP27 50 + 40pf dp brown 24.00 35.00
Set, never hinged 92.50

The surtax was for charity.

The Zwinger at Dresden SP28

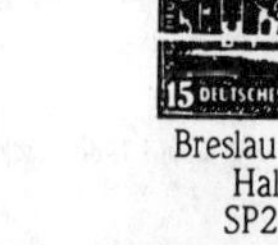

Breslau City Hall SP29

Heidelberg Castle — SP30

Holsten Gate, Lübeck — SP31

1931, Nov. 1

B38 SP28 8 + 4pf dk green 35 38
a. Bklt. pane of 7 + label 40.00
b. Bklt. pane, 3 #B38, 4 #B39 + label 50.00
B39 SP29 15 + 5pf carmine 55 60
B40 SP30 25 + 10pf dk blue 11.00 14.00
B41 SP31 50 + 40pf dp brown 45.00 45.00
Set, never hinged 150.00

The surtax was for charity.

Nos. B38-B39 Surcharged

12+3 Rpf 12 12

1932, Feb. 2

B42 SP28 6 + 4pf on 8 + 4pf 7.25 11.00
B43 SP29 12 + 3pf on 15 + 5pf 8.00 9.25
Set, never hinged 42.50

Wartburg Castle — SP32

Stolzenfels Castle — SP33

Nuremberg Castle — SP34

Lichtenstein Castle — SP35

Marburg Castle — SP36

1932, Nov. 1 **Engr.**

B44 SP32 4 + 2pf lt blue 30 28
a. Bklt. pane, 5 #B44, 5 #B45 30.00
B45 SP33 6 + 4pf olive grn 30 55
B46 SP34 12 + 3pf lt red 60 42
b. Bklt. pane of 8 + 2 labels 30.00
B47 SP35 25 + 10pf dp blue 9.50 11.00
B48 SP36 40 + 40pf brown vio 37.50 35.00
Nos. B44-B48 (5) 48.20 47.25
Set, never hinged 140.00

The surtax was for charity.

"Tannhäuser" SP37

Designs: 4pf+2pf, "Der Fliegende Hollander." 5pf+2pf, "Das Rheingold." 6pf+4pf, "Die Meistersinger." 8pf+4pf, "Die Walkure." 12pf+3pf, "Siegfried." 20pf+10pf, "Tristan und Isolde." 25pf+15pf, "Lohengrin." 40pf+35pf, "Parsifal."

Wmk. Swastikas (237)

1933, Nov. 1 *Perf. 13½x13*

B49 SP37 3 + 2pf bister brn 1.25 3.75
B50 SP37 4 + 2pf dk blue 95 1.25
b. Bklt. pane, 5 #B50, 5 #B52 37.50
B51 SP37 5 + 2pf brt green 2.50 4.25
B52 SP37 6 + 4pf gray grn 95 1.25
B53 SP37 8 + 4pf dp orange 1.25 1.75
b. Bklt. pane, 5 #B53, 4 #B53, 4 #B54 + label 82.50
B54 SP37 12 + 3pf brown red 1.50 1.75
B55 SP37 20 + 10pf blue 125.00 130.00
B56 SP37 25 + 15pf ultra 24.00 27.50
B57 SP37 40 + 35pf magenta 95.00 110.00
Nos. B49-B57 (9) 252.40 281.50
Set, never hinged 1,300.

Perf. 13½x14

B50a SP37 4 + 2pf dark blue 80 1.50
B52a SP37 6 + 4pf gray green 80 1.50
B53a SP37 8 + 4pf deep orange 1.00 2.75
B54a SP37 12 + 3pf brown red 1.40 2.75
B55a SP37 20 + 10pf blue 100.00 95.00
Nos. B50a-B55a (5) 104.00 103.50

Types of Semi-Postal Stamps of 1924 Issue Overprinted "1923-1933"

Souvenir Sheet

1933, Nov. 29 Typo. *Perf. 14½*

B58	Sheet of 4	950.00	*4,000.*
a.	SP2 5 + 15pf dark green	90.00	150.00
b.	SP2 10 + 30pf vermilion	90.00	150.00
c.	SP2 20 + 60pf dark blue	90.00	150.00
d.	SP2 50pf + 1.50m dk brown	90.00	150.00

The Swastika watermark covers the four stamps and above them appears a further watermark "10 Jahre Deutsche Nothilfe" and "1923-1933" below. Sheet size: 208x148mm.

The margin of the souvenir sheet is ungummed.

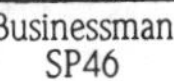

Businessman SP46 Judge SP54

Designs: 4pf+2pf, Blacksmith. 5pf+2pf, Mason. 6pf+4f, Miner. 8pf+4pf, Architect. 12pf+3pf, Farmer. 20pf+10pf, Agricultural Chemist. 25pf+15pf, Sculptor.

1934, Nov. 5 Engr. *Perf. 13x13½*

B59	SP46 3 + 2pf brown	90	90
B60	SP46 4 + 2pf black	60	70
a.	Bklt. pane, 5 #B60, 5 #B62	20.00	
B61	SP46 5 + 2pf green	5.00	5.50
B62	SP46 6 + 4pf dull green	45	42
B63	SP46 8 + 4pf orange brn	60	75
a.	Bklt. pane, 5 #B63, 4 #B64 + label	30.00	
B64	SP46 12 + 3pf henna brn	45	42
B65	SP46 20 + 10pf Prus blue	12.50	17.00
B66	SP46 25 + 15pf ultra	12.50	17.00
B67	SP54 40 + 35pf plum	37.50	52.50
	Nos. B59-B67 (9)	70.50	95.19
	Set, never hinged	275.00	

Souvenir Sheet

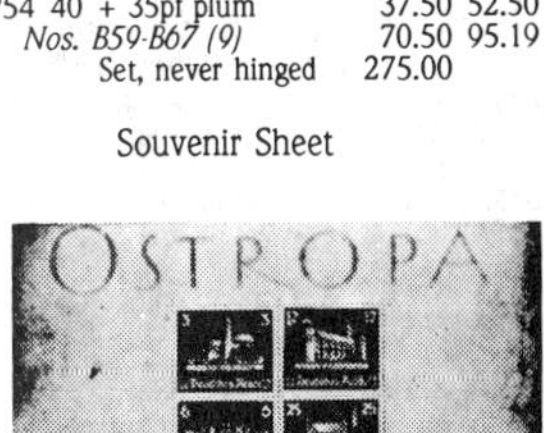

SP55

1935, June 23 Wmk. 241 *Perf. 14*

B68	SP55 Sheet of 4	425.00	475.00
a.	3pf red brown	24.00	35.00
b.	6pf dark green	24.00	35.00
c.	12pf dark carmine	24.00	35.00
d.	25pf dark blue	24.00	35.00

Watermarked cross on each stamp and "OSTROPA 1935" in the margins of the sheet. Size: 148x104mm. 1.70m was the price of a ticket of admission to the Intl. Exhib., Königsberg, June 23-July 3, 1935.

Because the gum on No. B68 contains sulphuric acid and tends to damage the sheet, some collectors prefer to remove it. **Catalogue unused values are for sheet and singles without gum.**

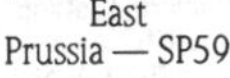

East Prussia — SP59 Skating — SP69

Designs (Costumes of Various Sections of Germany): 4pf+3pf, Silesia. 5pf+3pf, Rhineland. 6pf+4pf, Lower Saxony. 8pf+4pf, Brandenburg. 12pf+6pf, Black Forest. 15pf+10pf, Hesse. 25pf+15pf, Upper Bavaria. 30pf+20pf, Friesland. 40pf+35pf, Franconia.

Wmk. Swastikas (237)

1935, Oct. 4 *Perf. 14x13½*

B69	SP59 3 + 2pf dk brown	15	15
a.	Bklt. pane, 4 #B69, 5 #B74 + label	12.00	
B70	SP59 4 + 3pf gray	30	65
B71	SP59 5 + 3pf emerald	18	48
a.	Bklt. pane, 5 #B71, 5 #B72	3.50	
B72	SP59 6 + 4pf dk green	15	15
B73	SP59 8 + 4pf yellow brn	1.25	95
B74	SP59 12 + 6pf dk carmine	20	15
B75	SP59 15 + 10pf red brown	2.75	3.00
B76	SP59 25 + 15pf ultra	2.75	3.75
B77	SP59 30 + 20pf olive brn	12.00	13.00
B78	SP59 40 + 35p plum	8.75	7.50
	Nos. B69-B78 (10)	28.48	29.78
	Set, never hinged	110.00	

1935, Nov. 25 *Perf. 13½*

Designs: 12pf+6pf, Ski jump. 25pf+15pf, Bobsledding.

B79	SP69 6 + 4pf green	40	30
B80	SP69 12 + 6pf carmine	90	40
B81	SP69 25 + 15pf ultra	4.75	5.50
	Set, never hinged	30.00	

Winter Olympic Games held in Bavaria, Feb. 6-16, 1936.

1936, May 8

Designs: 3pf+2pf, Horizontal bar. 4pf+3pf, Diving. 6pf+4pf, Soccer. 8pf+4pf, Throwing javelin. 12pf+6pf, Torch runner. 15pf+10pf, Fencing. 25pf+15pf, Sculling. 40pf+35pf, Equestrian.

B82	SP69 3 + 2pf brown	15	15
a.	Bklt. pane, 5 #B82, 5 #B86	8.00	
B83	SP69 4 + 3pf indigo	18	50
a.	Bklt. pane, 5 #B83, 5 #B84	8.00	
B84	SP69 6 + 4pf green	15	15
B85	SP69 8 + 4pf red org	4.00	90
B86	SP69 12 + 6pf carmine	32	15
B87	SP69 15 + 10pf brn vio	5.75	2.75
B88	SP69 25 + 15pf ultra	3.25	2.75
B89	SP69 40 + 35pf violet	6.00	5.00
	Nos. B82-B89 (8)	19.80	12.35
	Set, never hinged	62.50	

Summer Olympic Games, Berlin, Aug. 1-16, 1936.

See Nos. B91-B92.

Souvenir Sheet

Horse Race — SP80

1936, June 22 Wmk. 237 *Perf. 14*

B90	SP80 42pf brown	7.50	12.50
	Never hinged	16.00	

A surtax of 1.08m was to provide a 100,000m sweepstakes prize. Wmk. 237 appears on the stamp, with "Munchen Riem 1936" watermarked on sheet margin.

For overprint see No. B105.

Type of 1935

Souvenir Sheets

1936, Aug. 1 *Perf. 14x13½*

B91	SP69 Sheet of 4	22.50	35.00
B92	SP69 Sheet of 4	22.50	35.00
	Set, never hinged	95.00	

11th Olympic Games, Berlin. No. B91 contains Nos. B82-B84, B89. No. B92 contains Nos. B85-B88.

Wmk. 237 appears on each stamp with "XI Olympische Spiele-Berlin 1936" watermarked on sheet margin. Sold for 1m each.

Frontier Highway, Munich — SP81

Designs: 4pf+3pf, Ministry of Aviation. 5pf+3pf, Nuremberg Memorial. 6pf+4pf, Bridge over the Saale, Saxony. 8pf+4pf, Germany Hall, Berlin. 12pf+6pf, German Alpine highway. 15pf+10pf, Fuhrer House, Munich. 25pf+15pf, Bridge over the Mangfall. 40pf+35pf, Museum of German Art, Munich.

Inscribed: "Winterhilfswerk"

Perf. 13½x14

1936, Sept. 21 Unwmk.

B93	SP81 3pf + 2pf black brn	15	15
a.	Bklt. pane, 4 #B93 + 5 #B98 + label	6.00	
B94	SP81 4pf + 3pf black	15	42
B95	SP81 5pf + 3pf brt green	15	15
a.	Bklt. pane, 5 #B95, 5 #B96)	2.25	
B96	SP81 6pf + 4pf dk green	15	15
B97	SP81 8pf + 4pf brown	45	85
B98	SP81 12pf + 6pf brn car	15	15
B99	SP81 15pf + 10pf vio brn	2.50	3.00
B100	SP81 25pf + 15pf indigo	1.40	2.25
B101	SP81 40pf + 35pf rose vio	2.75	3.75
	Nos. B93-B101 (9)	7.85	10.87
	Set, never hinged	37.50	

Souvenir Sheets

Adolf Hitler SP90

Wmk. 237

1937, Apr. 5 Photo. *Perf. 14*

B102	SP90 Sheet of 4	8.50	8.50
	Never hinged	32.50	
a.	6pf dark green	80	40

48th birthday of Adolf Hitler. Sold for 1m.

See Nos. B103-B104. For overprint see No. B106.

1937, Apr. 16 *Imperf.*

B103	SP90 Sheet of 4	26.00	21.00
	Never hinged	100.00	
a.	6pf dark green	2.50	3.00

German Natl. Phil. Exhib., Berlin, June 16-18, 1937 and the Phil. Exhib. of the Stamp Collectors Group of the Strength Through Joy Organization at Hamburg, Apr. 17-20, 1937.

Sold at the Exhib. post offices for 1.50m.

No. B102 with Marginal Inscriptions

Perf. 14 and Rouletted

1937, June 10 Wmk. 237

B104	SP90 Sheet of 4	35.00	55.00
	Never hinged	100.00	
a.	6pf dark green + 25pf label	5.50	5.50

No. B104 inscribed in the margin beside each stamp "25 Rpf. einschliesslich Kulturspende" in three lines.

The sheets were rouletted to allow for separation of each stamp with its component label. Sold at the post office as individual stamps with labels attached or in complete sheets.

Souvenir Sheet No. B90 Overprinted in Red

1937, Aug. 1 *Perf. 14*

B105	SP80 42pf brown	37.50	110.00
	Never hinged	100.00	

4th running of the "Brown Ribbon" horse race at the Munich-Riem Race Course, Aug. 1, 1937.

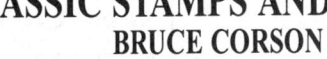

Souvenir Sheet No. B104 Overprinted in Black on Each Stamp

Reichsparteitag
Nürnberg 1937

Perf. 14 and Rouletted

1937, Sept. 3 Wmk. 237

B106 SP90 Sheet of 4 35.00 32.50
Never hinged 110.00
a. 6pf dark green + 25pf label 4.50 2.25

1937 Nazi Congress at Nuremburg.

Lifeboat — SP91

Designs: 4pf+3pf, Lightship "Elbe I." 5pf+3pf, Fishing smacks. 6pf+4pf, Steamer. 8pf+4pf, Sailing vessel. 12pf+6pf, The "Tannenberg." 15pf+10pf, Sea-Train "Schwerin." 25pf+15pf, S. S. Hamburg. 40pf+35pf, S. S. Bremen.

Perf. 13½

1937, Nov. 4 Engr. Unwmk.
Inscribed: "Winterhilfswerk"

B107 SP91 3pf + 2pf dk brown 15 25
a. Bklt. pane, 4 #B107 + 5 #B112 + label 6.75
B108 SP91 4pf + 3pf black 35 65
B109 SP91 5pf + 3pf yellow grn 15 25
a. Bklt. pane, 5 #B109, 5 #B110 2.75
B110 SP91 6pf + 4pf blue grn 15 25
B111 SP91 8pf + 4pf orange 70 1.00
B112 SP91 12pf + 6pf car lake 16 15
B113 SP91 15pf + 10pf vio brn 2.00 2.75
B114 SP91 25pf + 15pf ultra 3.75 2.75
B115 SP91 40pf + 35pf red vio 5.00 5.75
Nos. B107-B115 (9) 12.41 13.80
Set, never hinged 45.00

No. B115 actually pictures the S.S. Europa.

Youth Carrying Torch and Laurel — SP100

Adolf Hitler — SP101

Wmk. 237

1938, Jan. 28 Photo. *Perf. 14*

B116 SP100 6 + 4pf dk green 70 55
B117 SP100 12 + 8pf brt car 95 95
Set, never hinged 8.00

5th anniv. of the assumption of power by the Nazis.

1938, Apr. 13 Engr. Unwmk.

B118 SP101 12 + 38pf copper red 1.75 1.50
Never hinged 5.25

Hitler's 49th birthday.

Horsewoman SP102

1938, July 20

B119 SP102 42 + 108pf dp brown 22.50 32.50
Never hinged 77.50

5th "Brown Ribbon" at Munich.

Adolf Hitler SP103

Theater at Saarbrücken SP104

1938, Sept. 1

B120 SP103 6 + 19pf deep green 2.50 2.25
Never hinged 10.00

1938 Nazi Congress at Nuremberg. The surtax was for Hitler's National Culture Fund.

1938, Oct. 9 Photo. Wmk. 237

B121 SP104 6 + 4pf blue grn 75 75
B122 SP104 12 + 8pf dk car 1.75 1.65
Set, never hinged 6.50

Inauguration of the theater of the District of Saarpfalz at Saarbrücken. The surtax was for Hitler's National Culture Fund.

Castle of Forchtenstein SP105

Designs (scenes in Austria and various flowers): 4pf+3pf, Flexenstrasse in Vorarlberg. 5pf+3pf, Zell am See, Salzburg. 6pf+4pf, Grossglockner. 8pf+4pf, Ruins of Aggstein. 12pf+6pf, Prince Eugene Monument, Vienna. 15pf+10pf, Erzberg. 25pf+15pf, Hall, Tyrol. 40pf+35pf, Braunau.

Unwmk.

1938, Nov. 18 Engr. *Perf. 14*
Inscribed: "Winterhilfswerk"

B123 SP105 3 + 2pf olive brn 15 15
a. Bklt. pane, 4 #B123, 5 #B128 + label 12.00
B124 SP105 4 + 3pf indigo 1.25 80
B125 SP105 5 + 3pf emerald 15 20
a. Bklt. pane, 5 #B125, 5 #B126 3.00
B126 SP105 6 + 4pf dk green 15 15
B127 SP105 8 + 4pf red orange 1.25 80
B128 SP105 12 + 6pf dk carmine 18 15
B129 SP105 15 + 10pf dp claret 3.00 2.75
B130 SP105 25 + 15pf dk blue 3.00 2.75
B131 SP105 40 + 35pf plum 5.75 4.75
Nos. B123-B131 (9) 14.88 12.50
Set, never hinged 50.00

The surtax was for "Winter Help."

Sudeten Couple SP114

Early Types of Automobiles SP115

1938, Dec. 2 Photo. Wmk. 237

B132 SP114 6 + 4pf blue grn 70 1.00
B133 SP114 12 + 8pf dk car 2.25 2.00
Set, never hinged 12.00

Issued in commemoration of the annexation of the Sudeten Territory. The surtax was for Hitler's National Culture Fund.

1939

Designs: 12pf+8pf, Racing cars. 25pf+10pf, Modern automobile.

B134 SP115 6 + 4pf dk green 3.50 2.25
B135 SP115 12 + 8pf brt car 3.50 2.50
B136 SP115 25 + 10pf dp blue 5.25 5.25
Set, never hinged 30.00

Berlin Automobile and Motorcycle Exhibition. The surtax was for Hitler's National Culture Fund. For overprints see #B141-B143.

Adolf Hitler SP118

Exhibition Building SP119

Unwmk.

1939, Apr. 13 Engr. *Perf. 14*

B137 SP118 12 + 38pf carmine 2.25 3.00
Never hinged 5.75

Hitler's 50th birthday. The surtax was for Hitler's National Culture Fund.

1939, Apr. 22 Photo. *Perf. 12½*

B138 SP119 6 + 4pf dk green 1.10 1.50
B139 SP119 15 + 5pf dp plum 1.10 1.50
Set, never hinged 6.75

Horticultural Exhib. held at Stuttgart. Surtax for Hitler's National Culture Fund.

Adolf Hitler — SP120

Perf. 14x13½

1939, Apr. 28 Wmk. 237

B140 SP120 6 + 19pf black brn 2.00 3.50
Never hinged 7.25

Day of National Labor. The surtax was for Hitler's National Culture Fund.
See No. B147.

Nos. B134-B136 Overprinted in Black

Nürburgring-Rennen

1939, May 18 *Perf. 14*

B141 SP115 6 + 4pf dk green 24.00 22.50
B142 SP115 12 + 8pf brt car 24.00 22.50
B143 SP115 25 + 10pf dp blue 24.00 22.50
Set, never hinged 150.00

Nurburgring Auto Races held May 21 and July 23, 1939.

Racehorse "Investment" and Jockey — SP121

1939, June 18 Engr. Unwmk.

B144 SP121 25 + 50pf ultra 15.00 12.00
Never hinged 42.50

70th anniv. of the German Derby. The surtax was divided between Hitler's National Culture Fund and the race promoters.

Man Holding Rearing Horse — SP122

"Venetian Woman" by Albrecht Dürer — SP123

1939, July 12

B145 SP122 42 + 108pf dp brown 16.00 22.50
Never hinged 42.50

6th "Brown Ribbon" at Munich.

1939, July 12 Photo. Wmk. 237

B146 SP123 6 + 19pf dk green 4.50 4.50
Never hinged 17.00

Day of German Art. The surtax was used for Hitler's National Culture Fund.

Hitler Type of 1939
Inscribed "Reichsparteitag 1939"

1939, Aug. 25 *Perf. 14x13½*

B147 SP120 6 + 19pf black brn 2.75 4.75
Never hinged 8.50

1939 Nazi Congress at Nuremberg.

Meeting in German Hall, Berlin — SP124

Designs: 4pf+3pf, Meeting of postal and telegraph employees. 5pf+3pf, Professional competitions. 6pf+4pf, 6pf+9pf, Professional camp. 8pf+4pf, 8pf+12pf, Gold flag competitions. 10pf+5pf, Awarding prizes. 12&f+6pf, 12pf+18pf, Automobile race. 15pf+10pf, Sports. 16pf+10pf, 16pf+24pf, Postal police. 20pf+10pf, 20pf+30pf, Glider workshops. 24pf+10pf, 24pf+36pf, Mail coach. 25pf+15pf, Convalescent home, Konigstein.

Perf. 13½x14

1939-41 Unwmk. Photo.
Inscribed: "Kameradschaftsblock der Deutschen Reichpost"

B148 SP124 3 + 2pf bister brn 2.25 3.50
B149 SP124 4 + 3pf slate blue 1.90 3.00
B150 SP124 5 + 3pf brt bl grn 65 1.10
B151 SP124 6 + 4pf myrtle grn 65 1.10
B151A SP124 6 + 9pf dk grn ('41) 45 95
B152 SP124 8 + 4pf dp orange 60 95
B152A SP124 8 + 12pf hn brn ('41) 40 75
B153 SP124 10 + 5pf dk brown 60 95
B154 SP124 12 + 6pf rose brown 95 1.40
B154A SP124 12 + 18pf dk car rose ('41) 40 75
B155 SP124 15 + 10pf dp red lilac 95 1.40
B156 SP124 16 + 10pf slate grn 1.25 1.90
B156A SP124 16 + 24pf black ('41) 1.25 2.50
B157 SP124 20 + 10pf ultra 1.25 1.90
B157A SP124 20 + 30pf ultra ('41) 1.25 2.00
B158 SP124 24 + 10pf ol grn 1.90 2.50
B158A SP124 24 + 36pf pur ('41) 3.50 4.50
B159 SP124 25 + 15pf dk blue 1.90 3.00
Nos. B148-B159 (18) 22.10 34.15
Set, never hinged 52.50

The surtax was used for Hitler's National Culture Fund and the Postal Employees' Fund.
See Nos. B273, B275-B277.

Elbogen Castle — SP136

Buildings: 4pf+3pf, Drachenfels on the Rhine. 5pf+3pf, Kaiserpfalz at Goslar. 6pf+4pf, Clocktower at Graz. 8pf+4pf, Town Hall, Frankfurt. 12pf+6pf, Guild House, Klagenfurt. 15pf+10pf, Ruins of Schreckenstein Castle. 25pf+15pf, Fortress of Salzburg. 40pf+35pf, Castle of Hohentwiel.

1939 Unwmk. Engr. *Perf. 14*
Inscribed: "Winterhilfswerk"

B160 SP136 3 + 2pf dk brown 15 32
a. Bklt. pane, 4 #B160, 5 #B165 + label 9.75
B161 SP136 4 + 3pf gray blk 1.10 1.90
B162 SP136 5 + 3pf emerald 20 32
a. Bklt. pane, 5 #B162, 5 #B163 3.25
B163 SP136 6 + 4pf slate grn 20 32
B164 SP136 8 + 4pf red org 85 1.10
B165 SP136 12 + 6pf dk car 20 32
B166 SP136 15 + 10pf brown vio 2.75 4.50

B167	SP136	25 + 15pf ultra	1.65	4.50
B168	SP136	40 + 35pf rose vio	2.75	5.00
		Nos. B160-B168 (9)	9.85	18.28
		Set, never hinged	32.50	

Hall of Honor at Chancellery, Berlin — SP145

Child Greeting Hitler — SP146

1940, Mar. 28

B169	SP145	24 + 76pf dk green	5.50	9.50
		Never hinged	20.00	

2nd National Stamp Exposition, Berlin.

Perf. 14x13½

1940, Apr. 10 Photo. Wmk. 237

B170	SP146	12 + 38pf copper red	2.25	3.50
		Never hinged	7.50	

51st birthday of Adolf Hitler.

Armed Warrior SP147

Horseman SP148

1940, Apr. 30 Unwmk. *Perf. 14*

B171	SP147	6 + 4pf sl grn & lt grn	22	40
		Never hinged	45	

Issued to commemorate May Day.

Perf. 14x13½

1940, June 22 Wmk. 237

B172	SP148	25 + 100pf dp ultra	3.00	6.50
		Never hinged	10.00	

Blue Ribbon race, Hamburg, June 30, 1940. Surtax for Hitler's National Culture Fund.

Chariot — SP149

Unwmk.

1940, July 20 Engr. *Perf. 14*

B173	SP149	42 + 108pf brown	15.00	25.00
		Never hinged	45.00	

7th "Brown Ribbon" at Munich.
The surtax was for Hitler's National Culture Fund and the promoters of the race.

View of Malmedy — SP150

Design: 12pf+8pf, View of Eupen.

Perf. 14x13½

1940, July 25 Photo. Wmk. 237

B174	SP150	6 + 4pf dk green	55	1.00
B175	SP150	12 + 8pf org red	55	1.00
		Set, never hinged	3.50	

Issued on the occasion of the reunion of Eupen-Malmedy with the Reich.

Rocky Cliffs of Heligoland — SP152

Artushof in Danzig — SP153

1940, Aug. 9 Unwmk.

B176	SP152	6 + 94pf brt bl grn & red org	3.00	5.00
		Never hinged	12.00	

Heligoland's 50th year as part of Germany.

1940, Nov. 5 Engr. *Perf. 14*

Buildings: 4pf+3pf, Town Hall, Thorn. 5pf+3pf, Castle at Kaub. 6pf+4pf, City Theater, Poznan. 8pf+4pf, Castle at Heidelberg. 12pf+6pf, Porta Nigra Trier. 15pf+10pf, New German Theater, Prague. 25pf+15pf, Town Hall, Bremen. 40pf+35pf, Town Hall, Munster.

Inscribed: "Winterhilfswerk"

B177	SP153	3 + 2pf dk brown	15	15
a.		Bklt. pane, 4 #B177 + 5 #B182 + label	6.50	
B178	SP153	4 + 3pf bluish blk	75	55
B179	SP153	5 + 3pf yel grn	20	28
a.		Bklt. pane, 5 #B179, 5 #B180	3.00	
B180	SP153	6 + 4pf dk green	20	15
B181	SP153	8 + 4pf dp org	70	75
B182	SP153	12 + 6pf carmine	20	15
B183	SP153	15 + 10pf dk vio brn	70	1.40
B184	SP153	25 + 15pf dp ultra	1.00	2.25
B185	SP153	40 + 35pf red lilac	2.00	3.50
		Nos. B177-B185 (9)	5.90	9.18
		Set, never hinged	20.00	

von Behring SP162

Postilion SP163

1940, Nov. 26 Photo.

B186	SP162	6 + 4pf dp green	60	1.40
B187	SP162	25 + 10pf brt ultra	80	1.65
		Set, never hinged	3.75	

Dr. Emil von Behring (1854-1917), bacteriologist.

1941, Jan. 12 *Perf. 14x13½*

B188	SP163	6 + 24pf dp green	48	1.25
		Never hinged	1.25	

Postage Stamp Day. The surtax was for Hitler's National Culture Fund.

Benito Mussolini and Adolf Hitler SP164

Perf. 13½x14

1941, Jan. 30 Wmk. 237

B189	SP164	12 + 38pf rose brn	95	1.50
		Never hinged	2.75	

Issued as propaganda for the Rome-Berlin Axis. The surtax was for Hitler's National Culture Fund.

Adolf Hitler — SP165

Race Horse — SP166

1941, Apr. 17 *Perf. 14x13½*

B190	SP165	12 + 38pf dk red	1.00	1.75
		Never hinged	3.50	

52nd birthday of Adolf Hitler. The surtax was for Hitler's National Culture Fund.

Perf. 13½x14

1941, June 20 Engr. Unwmk.

B191	SP166	25 + 100pf sapphire	3.25	6.00
		Never hinged	6.50	

Issued in commemoration of the Blue Ribbon race held at Hamburg, June 29, 1941.

Amazons — SP167

1941, July 20 *Perf. 14*

B192	SP167	42 + 108pf brown	1.75	3.25
		Never hinged	4.50	

8th "Brown Ribbon" at Munich.

Brandenburg Gate, Berlin — SP168

1941, Sept. 9

B193	SP168	25 + 50pf dp ultra	2.00	3.50
		Never hinged	5.00	

Issued in honor of the Berlin races.

Marburg SP169

Veldes SP170

Pettau — SP171

Triglav — SP172

1941, Sept. 29 Photo.

B194	SP169	3 + 7pf brown	48	1.10
B195	SP170	6 + 9pf purple	50	1.25
B196	SP171	12 + 13pf rose brn	80	1.50
B197	SP172	25 + 15pf dk blue	1.40	2.75
		Set, never hinged	8.50	

Annexation of Styria and Carinthia.

View from Belvedere Palace, Vienna — SP173

Belvedere Gardens, Vienna — SP174

1941, Sept. 16 Engr.

B198	SP173	12 + 8pf dp red	75	1.00
B199	SP174	15 + 10pf violet	75	1.25
		Set, never hinged	4.25	

Issued to commemorate the Vienna Fair.

Mozart — SP175

Philatelist — SP176

1941, Nov. 28

B200	SP175	6 + 4pf dk rose vio	15	35
		Never hinged	35	

Wolfgang Amadeus Mozart (1756-91).

1942, Jan. 11 Photo.

B201	SP176	6 + 24pf dp purple	45	1.25
		Never hinged	1.50	

To commemorate Stamp Day.

Soldier's Head — SP177

Adolf Hitler — SP178

1942, Mar. 10 *Perf. 14x13½*

B202	SP177	12 + 38pf slate blk	30	65
		Never hinged	90	

To commemorate Hero Memorial Day.

1942, Apr. 13

B203	SP178	12 + 38pf lake	1.50	3.50
		Never hinged	6.50	

To commemorate Hitler's 53rd birthday.

Racing Three-year-old SP179

1942, June 16 Engr. *Perf. 14*

B204	SP179	25 + 100pf dk blue	4.75	8.50
		Never hinged	10.00	

73rd Hamburg Derby.

Race Horses — SP180

1942, July 14

B205	SP108	42 + 108pf brown	1.40	3.50
		Never hinged	3.75	

9th "Brown Ribbon" at Munich.

Lüneburg Lion and Nüremberg Betrothal Cup SP181

Henlein Monument, Nüremberg SP182

1942, Aug. 8 Photo. ***Perf. 14x13½***

B206	SP181	6 + 4pf copper red	20	45
B207	SP181	12 + 88pf green	30	75
		Set, never hinged	1.40	

10th anniv. of the German Goldsmiths' Society and the 1st Goldsmiths' Day in Germany.

1942, Aug. 29 ***Perf. 14***

B208	SP182	6 + 24pf rose vio	25	80
		Never hinged	85	

400th anniversary of the death of Peter Henlein, inventor of the pocket watch.

Postilion and Map of Europe SP183

Postilion and Globe — SP184

Postilion SP185

Perf. 13½x14, 14x13½

1942, Oct. 12 **Photo.**

B209	SP183	3 + 7pf dull blue	15	32
		Engr.		
B210	SP184	6 + 14pf ultra & dp brn	18	45
B211	SP185	12 + 38pf rose red & dp brn	38	85
		Set, never hinged	2.00	

European Postal Congress, Vienna.

Nos. B209 to B211 Overprinted in Black ***19.Okt.1942***

1942, Oct. 19

B212	SP183	3 + 7pf	50	1.25
B213	SP184	6 + 14pf	50	1.25
B214	SP185	12 + 38pf	65	1.50
		Set, never hinged	4.50	

To commemorate the signing of the European postal-telegraph agreement at Vienna.

Mail Coach — SP186

1943, Jan. 10 **Engr.**

B215	SP186	6 + 24pf gray, brn & yel	15	65
		Never hinged	35	

To commemorate Stamp Day. The surtax went to Hitler's National Culture Fund.

Brandenburg Gate SP187

Nazi Emblem SP188

1943, Jan. 26 **Photo.**

B216	SP187	54 + 96pf copper red	25	80
		Never hinged	55	

10th anniversary of the assumption of power by the Nazis.

1943, Jan. 26

B217	SP188	3 + 2pf olive bister	15	50
		Never hinged	50	

Used to secure special philatelic cancellations.

Submarine SP189

Designs: 4pf+3pf, Schutz-Staffel Troops. 5pf+4pf, Motorized marksmen. 6pf+9pf, Signal Corps. 8pf+7pf, Engineer Corps. 12pf+8pf, Grenade assault. 15pf+10pf, Heavy artillery. 20pf+14pf, Anti-aircraft units in action. 25pf+15pf, Dive bombers. 30pf+30pf, Paratroops. 40pf+40pf, Tank. 50pf+50pf, Speed boat.

1943, Mar. 21 **Engr.**

B218	SP189	3 + 2pf dk brown	20	50
B219	SP189	4 + 3pf brown	20	50
B220	SP189	5 + 4pf dk green	20	50
B221	SP189	6 + 9pf dp violet	20	50
B222	SP189	8 + 7pf brn org	20	50
B223	SP189	12 + 8pf car lake	20	50
B224	SP189	15 + 10pf vio brn	22	45
B225	SP189	20 + 14pf slate bl	30	60
B226	SP189	25 + 15pf indigo	30	95
B227	SP189	30 + 30pf green	45	1.00
B228	SP189	40 + 40pf red lilac	45	1.25
B229	SP189	50 50pf grnsh blk	85	2.25
		Nos. B218-B229 (12)	3.77	9.50
		Set, never hinged	10.00	

Army Day and Hero Memorial Day.
Nos. B220 and B224 exist imperf. Value, each $67.50.

Nazi Flag and Children — SP201

1943, Mar. 26 **Photo.**

B230	SP201	6 + 4pf dk green	15	40
		Never hinged	50	

To commemorate the Day of Youth Obligation when all German boys and girls had to take an oath of allegiance to Hitler.

Adolf Hitler — SP202

1943, Apr. 13

B231	SP202	3 + 7pf brown blk	35	80
B232	SP202	6 + 14pf dk green	35	80
B233	SP202	8 + 22pf dk chlky bl	35	80
B234	SP202	12 + 38pf copper red	35	80
B235	SP202	24 + 76pf vio brn	60	1.40
B236	SP202	40 + 160pf dk ol grn	65	1.75
		Nos. B231-B236 (6)	2.65	6.35
		Set, never hinged	7.00	

Hitler's 54th birthday. No. B231 exists imperf. Value $100.

Reich Labor Service Corpsmen SP203 SP204

Designs: 6pf+14pf, Corpsman chopping. 12pf+18pf, Corpsman with implements.

1943, June 26 **Engr.**

B237	SP203	3 + 7pf bis brn	15	18
B238	SP204	5 + 10pf pale ol grn	15	18
B239	SP204	6 + 14pf dp blue	15	18
B240	SP204	12 + 18pf dk red	18	38
		Set value	42	
		Set, never hinged	1.25	

Anniversary of Reich Labor Service.
Nos. B237-B238, B240 exist imperf.

Rosegger's Birthplace, Upper Styria SP207

Peter Rosegger SP208

Perf. 13½x14, 14x13½

1943, July 27 **Photo.**

B241	SP207	6 + 4pf green	15	32
B242	SP208	12 + 8pf copper red	15	32
		Set value	25	
		Set, never hinged	70	

Centenary of the birth of Peter Rosegger, Austrian writer.

Hunter — SP209

1943, July 27 **Engr.**

B243	SP209	42 + 108pf brown	15	75
		Never hinged	45	

10th "Brown Ribbon" at Munich.
No. B243 exists imperf. Value $300.

Race Horse SP210

Mother and Children SP211

1943, Aug. 14

B244	SP210	6 + 4pf vio blk	15	50
B245	SP210	12 + 88pf dk car	15	50
		Set value	24	
		Set, never hinged	55	

Grand Prize of the Freudenau, the Vienna race track, Aug. 15, 1943.

1943, Sept. 1

B246	SP211	12 + 38pf dark red	15	45
		Never hinged	35	

10th anniversary of Winter Relief.

St. George in Gold — SP212

Ancient Lübeck — SP213

1943, Oct. 1

B247	SP212	6 + 4pf dk ol grn	15	30
B248	SP212	12 + 88pf vio brn	15	35
		Set value	25	
		Set, never hinged	65	

German Goldsmiths' Society.

1943, Oct. 24 **Photo.**

B249	SP213	12 + 8pf copper red	15	50
		Never hinged	40	

800th anniv. of the Hanseatic town of Lubeck.
No. B249 exists imperf. Value, $75.

"And Despite All, You Were Victorious" — SP214

Dr. Robert Koch — SP215

1943, Nov. 5

B250	SP214	24 + 26pf henna	20	50
		Never hinged	55	

20th anniv. of the Nazis' Munich beer-hall putsch and to honor those who died for the Nazi movement. #B250 exists imperf.

1944, Jan. 25 **Engr.** **Unwmk.**

B251	SP215	12 + 38pf sepia	15	55
		Never hinged	40	

Centenary of the birth of the bacteriologist, Robert Koch (1843-1910).

Hitler and Nazi Emblems — SP216

1944, Jan. 29 **Photo.**

B252	SP216	54 + 96pf yel brn	15	60
		Never hinged	60	

Assumption of power by the Nazis, 11th anniv.

Airport Scene — SP217

Seaplane — SP218

Plane Seen from Above — SP219

Perf. 14x13½, 13½x14

1944, Feb. 11 **Photo.** **Unwmk.**

B252A	SP217	6 + 4pf dk grn	15	25
B252B	SP218	12 + 8pf maroon	15	32
B252C	SP219	42 + 108pf dp sl bl	15	42
		Set value	33	
		Set, never hinged	80	

25th anniv. of German air mail. The surtax was for the National Culture Fund.

Infant's Crib — SP220

Assault Boat — SP221

Designs: 6pf+4pf, Public nurse. 12pf+8pf, "Mother and Child" clinic. 15pf+10pf, Expectant mothers.

1944, Mar. 2

B253	SP220	3 + 2pf dk brn	15	18
B254	SP220	6 + 4pf dk grn	15	18
B255	SP220	12 + 8pf dp car	15	18
B256	SP220	15 + 10pf vio brn	15	38
		Set value	26	60
		Set, never hinged	70	

10th anniv. of "Mother and Child" aid.

1944, Mar. 11

Designs: 4pf+3pf, Chain-wheel vehicle. 5pf+3pf, Paratroops. 6pf+4pf, Submarine officer. 8pf+4pf, Schutz-Staffel grenade throwers. 10pf+5pf, Searchlight. 12pf+6pf, Infantry. 15pf+10pf, Self-propelled gun. 16pf+10pf, Speed boat. 20pf+10pf, Sea raider. 24pf+10pf, Railway artillery. 25pf+15pf, Rockets. 30pf+20pf, Mountain trooper.

Inscribed: "Grossdeutsches Reich"

B257	SP221	3 + 2pf yel brn	15	40
B258	SP221	4 + 3pf royal bl	15	40
B259	SP221	5 + 3pf dp yel grn	15	40
B260	SP221	6 + 4pf dp vio	15	40
B261	SP221	8 + 4pf org ver	15	40
B262	SP221	10 + 5pf chocolate	15	40
B263	SP221	12 + 6pf carmine	15	40
B264	SP221	15 + 10pf dp claret	15	40
B265	SP221	16 + 10pf dk bl grn	18	50
B266	SP221	20 + 10pf brt bl	20	60
B267	SP221	24 + 10pf dl org brn	25	70
B268	SP221	25 + 15pf vio bl	35	1.00
B269	SP221	30 + 20pf olive grn	32	95
		Nos. B257-B269 (13)	2.50	6.95
		Set, never hinged	6.00	

To commemorate Hero Memorial Day.

Flora Statue in Fulda's Schloss Garden — SP234

Adolf Hitler — SP235

1944, Mar. 11

B270	SP234	12 + 38pf dp brown	15	40
		Never hinged	35	

1,200th anniversary of town of Fulda.

1944, Apr. 14 Engr. Unwmk.

B271	SP235	54 + 96pf rose car	25	70
		Never hinged	80	

To commemorate Hitler's 55th birthday.

Type of 1939-41 and

Woman Mail Carrier — SP236

Field Post in the East — SP237

Designs: 8pf+12pf, Mail coach. 16pf+24pf, Automobile race. 20pf+30pf, Postal police. 24pf+36pf, Glider workshops.

1944, May 3 Photo.
Designs measure 29½x24½mm

B272	SP236	6 + 9pf vio bl	15	20
B273	SP124	8 + 12pf gray blk	15	20
B274	SP237	12 + 18pf dp plum	15	20
B275	SP124	16 + 24pf dk grn	15	20
B276	SP124	20 + 30pf blue	15	30
B277	SP124	24 + 36pf dk pur	15	30
		Set value	48	
		Set, never hinged	95	

Surtax for the Postal Employees' Fund.

Soldier and Tirolese Rifleman SP238

Albert I, Duke of Prussia SP239

1944, July

B278	SP238	6 + 4pf dp grn	15	30
B279	SP238	12 + 8pf brn lake	15	30
		Set value	20	
		Set, never hinged	65	

To commemorate the 7th National Shooting Matches at Innsbruck.

1944, July

B280	SP239	6 + 4pf dk bl grn	25	55
		Set, never hinged	65	

400th anniv. of Albert University, Königsberg.

Labor Corps Girl SP240

Labor Corpsman SP241

1944, June Engr.

B281	SP240	6 + 4pf green	15	24
B282	SP241	12 + 8pf carmine	15	35
		Set value	15	
		Set, never hinged	50	

Issued to honor an exhibit of the Reich Labor Service.

Race Horse and Foal — SP242

1944, July 23 ***Perf. 14x13½***

B283	SP242	42 + 108pf brown	15	70
		Never hinged	40	

11th "Brown Ribbon" at Munich.

Race Horse's Head in Oak Wreath — SP243

Nautilus Cup in Green Vault, Dresden — SP244

1944, Aug. Photo. ***Perf. 14***

B284	SP243	6 + 4pf Prus green	15	30
B285	SP243	12 + 88pf car lake	15	40
		Set value	15	
		Set, never hinged	70	

Vienna Grand Prize Race.

1944, Sept. 11

B286	SP244	6 + 4pf dk green	15	30
B287	SP244	12 + 88pf car brn	15	40
		Set value	15	
		Set, never hinged	45	

Issued in honor of the German Goldsmiths' Society.
No. B287 exists imperf. Value $175.

Post Horn and Letter — SP245

1944, Oct. 2

B288	SP245	6 + 24pf dk green	15	55
		Never hinged	40	

To commemorate Stamp Day.

Eagle and Serpent — SP246

Count Anton Günther — SP247

1944, Nov. 9

B289	SP246	12 + 8pf rose red	15	50
		Never hinged	40	

21st anniv. of the Munich putsch.

1945, Jan. 6 Typo. ***Perf. 13½x14***

B290	SP247	6 + 14pf brown vio	15	50
		Never hinged	45	

600th anniv. of municipal law in Oldenburg.

People's Army — SP248

1945, Feb. Photo. ***Perf. 14x13½***

B291	SP248	12 + 8pf rose car	18	75
		Never hinged	60	

Proclamation of the People's Army (Volkssturm) in East Prussia to fight the Russians.

Elite Storm Trooper (S. S.) — SP249

Storm Trooper (S. A.) — SP250

1945, Apr. 21 ***Perf. 13½x14***

B292	SP249	12 + 38pf brt car	7.50	*16.00*
B293	SP250	12 + 38pf brt car	7.50	*16.00*
		Set, never hinged	27.50	

12th anniv. of the assumption of power by the Nazis. Nos. B292-B293 were on sale in Berlin briefly before the collapse of that city.
Exist imperf. Value same as perf.

Souvenir Sheets

SP251

Wmk. 284

1946, Dec. 8 Typo. ***Perf. 14***

B294	SP251	Sheet of 3	22.50	*90.00*
		Never hinged	40.00	

Imperf

B295	SP251	Sheet of 3	37.50	*125.00*
		Never hinged	50.00	
a.	A119	20pf light blue	6.50	17.50
b.	A119	24pf orange brown	6.50	17.50
c.	A119	40pf red violet	6.50	17.50

No. B294 contains Nos. 543, 544 and 548.
Nos. B294-B295 sold for 5m each. Surtax for refugees and the aged.

Leipzig Proclaimed Market Place, 1160 SP252

Design: 60pf+40pf, Foreign merchants displaying their wares, 1268.

Wmk. 48

1947, Mar. 5 Engr. ***Perf. 13***

B296	SP252	24 +26pf chestnut brn	15	35
B297	SP252	60 + 40pf dp vio blue	15	45
		Set value	22	
		Set, never hinged	30	

1947 Leipzig Fairs.
No. B296 exists imperf. Value $150.
See Nos. 580-583, 10NB1-10NB2, 10NB4-10NB5, 10NB12-10NB13 and German Democratic Republic Nos. B15-B16.

Madonna SP254

Cathedral Towers SP255

Designs: 12pf+8pf, Three Kings. 24pf+16pf, Cologne Cathedral.

Wmk. 286

1948, Aug. 15 Typo. ***Perf. 11***

B298	SP254	6 + 4pf orange brn	15	48
a.		"1948-1248"	4.00	7.25
B299	SP254	12 + 8pf grnsh blue	50	1.25
a.		"1948-1948"	5.75	9.25
B300	SP254	24 + 16pf carmine	1.00	2.50
B301	SP255	50 + 50pf blue	2.00	5.75
		Set, never hinged	9.50	

700th anniv. of the laying of the cornerstone of Cologne Cathedral. The surtax was to aid in its reconstruction.
Specialists collect Nos. B298-B301 with watermark in four positions: upright, D's facing left; upright, D's facing right; sideways, D's facing up; sideways, D's facing down. Two types of perforation: line and comb.

The values of never-hinged stamps in superb condition are greater than catalogue value.

Brandenburg Gate, Berlin SP256

Bicycle Racers SP257

Perf. 10½x11½, 11

1948, Dec. **Litho.**

B302 SP256 10 + 5pf green 1.50 4.00
B303 SP256 20 + 10pf rose car 2.00 4.00
Set, never hinged 10.00

The surtax was for aid to Berlin.

Wmk. 116

1949, May 15 **Engr.** ***Perf. 14***

B304 SP257 10 + 5pf green 1.50 2.75
B305 SP257 20 + 10pf brn org 3.75 *12.00*
Set, never hinged 14.00

1949 Bicycle Tour of Germany.

Goethe at Rome — SP258

Goethe — SP259

Design: 30pf+15pf, Goethe portrait facing left.

1949, Aug. 15

B306 SP258 10 + 5pf green 1.00 3.25
B307 SP259 20 + 10pf red 1.00 3.50
B308 SP259 30 + 15pf blue 4.50 *13.00*
Set, never hinged 24.00

Bicentenary of the birth of Johann Wolfgang von Goethe.
The surtax was for the reconstruction of Goethe House, Frankfurt-on-Main.

Federal Republic

Bavaria Stamp of 1849 SP260

St. Elisabeth SP261

1949, Sept. 30 **Litho.** **Wmk. 285**

B309 SP260 10 + 2pf green & blk 5.50 14.00
Never hinged 13.00

Centenary of German postage stamps.

1949, Dec. 14 **Engr.** **Wmk. 286**

Designs: 10pf+5pf, Paracelsus. 20pf+10pf, F. W. A. Froebel. 30pf+15pf, J. H. Wichern.

B310 SP261 8 + 2pf brn vio 10.00 16.00
B311 SP261 10 + 5pf yel grn 7.00 8.00
B312 SP261 20 + 10pf red 7.75 8.00
B313 SP261 30 + 15pf vio bl 37.50 72.50
Set, never hinged 140.00

The surtax was for welfare organizations.

Seal of Johann Sebastian Bach — SP262

Frescoes from Marienkirche — SP263

1950, July 28 ***Perf. 14***

B314 SP262 10 + 2pf dk green 30.00 35.00
B315 SP262 20 + 3pf dk car 35.00 42.50
Set, never hinged 140.00

Bicentenary of the death of Bach.

1951, Aug. 30 **Photo.** **Wmk. 286**
Center in Gray

B316 SP263 10 + 5pf green 35.00 55.00
B317 SP263 20 + 5pf brn lake 40.00 70.00
Set, never hinged 200.00

Construction of Marienkirche, Lübeck, 700th anniv.
The surtax aided in its reconstruction.

Stamps Under Magnifying Glass — SP264

St. Vincent de Paul — SP265

Wmk. 295

1951, Sept. 14 **Typo.** ***Perf. 14***

B318 SP264 10 + 2pf yel grn, blk & yel 22.50 40.00
B319 SP264 20 + 3pf dp mag, blk & yel 22.50 40.00
Set, never hinged 100.00

Natl. Philatelic Exposition, Wuppertal, 1951.

1951, Oct. 23 **Engr.**

Portraits: 10pf+3pf, Friedrich von Bodelschwingh. 20pf+5pf, Elsa Brandstrom. 30pf+10pf, Johann Heinrich Pestalozzi.

B320 SP265 4 + 2pf brown 3.50 5.00
B321 SP265 10 + 3pf green 7.00 6.25
B322 SP265 20 + 5pf rose red 7.00 6.25
B323 SP265 30 + 10pf dp blue 60.00 95.00
Set, never hinged 155.00

The surtax was for charitable purposes.

Nuremberg Madonna SP266

Boy Hikers and Youth Hostel SP267

1952, Aug. 9

B324 SP266 10 + 5pf green 10.00 17.50
Never hinged 19.00

Centenary of the founding of the Germanic National Museum, Nuremberg. The surtax was for the museum.

1952, Sept. 17 ***Perf. 13½x14***

Design: 20pf+3pf, Girls and Hostel.

B325 SP267 10 + 2pf green 12.00 17.50
B326 SP267 20 + 3pf dp car 12.00 17.50
Set, never hinged 45.00

The surtax was to aid the youth program of the Federal Republic.

Elizabeth Fry SP268

Owl and Cogwheel SP269

Portraits: 10pf+5pf, Dr. Carl Sonnenschein. 20pf+10pf, Theodor Fliedner. 30pf+10pf, Henri Dunant.

1952, Oct. 1

B327 SP268 4 + 2pf org brn 3.75 5.00
B328 SP268 10 + 5pf green 3.75 4.00
B329 SP268 20 + 10pf brn car 9.00 9.25
B330 SP268 30 + 10pf dp blue 37.50 60.00
Set, never hinged 125.00

The surtax was for welfare organizations.

1953, May 7 **Wmk. 295** ***Perf. 14***

B331 SP269 10 + 5pf dp green 15.00 24.00
Never hinged 30.00

50th anniv. of the founding of the German Museum in Munich.

Thurn and Taxis Palace Gate — SP270

August Hermann Francke — SP271

Design: 20pf+3pf, Telecommunications Bldg., Frankfurt-on-Main.

Perf. 13½

1953, July 29 **Litho.** **Wmk. 285**

B332 SP270 10 + 2pf yel grn, bl & fawn 13.00 19.00
B333 SP270 20 + 3pf fawn, blk & gray 17.00 24.00
Set, never hinged 62.50

The surtax was for the International Stamp Exhibition, Frankfurt-on-Main, 1953.

Wmk. 295

1953, Nov. 2 **Engr.** ***Perf. 14***

Designs: 10pf+5pf, Sebastian Kneipp. 20pf+10pf, Dr. Johann Christian Senckenberg. 30pf+10pf, Fridtjof Nansen.

B334 SP271 4 + 2pf choc 2.75 3.25
B335 SP271 10 + 5pf bl grn 4.75 4.25
B336 SP271 20 + 10pf red 7.75 5.50
B337 SP271 30 + 10pf blue 30.00 37.50
Set, never hinged 80.00

The surtax was for welfare organizations.

Catalogue values for unused stamps in this section, from this point to the end of the section, are for Never Hinged items.

Käthe Kollwitz SP272

Carrier Pigeon and Magnifying Glass SP273

Portraits: 10pf+5pf, Lorenz Werthmann. 20pf+10pf, Johann Friedrich Oberlin. 40pf+10pf, Bertha Pappenheim.

1954, Dec. 28 ***Perf. 13½x14***

B338 SP272 7pf + 3pf brown 3.00 2.25
B339 SP272 10pf + 5pf green 2.25 1.25
B340 SP272 20pf + 10pf red 11.00 2.25
B341 SP272 40pf + 10pf blue 37.50 30.00

The surtax was for welfare organizations.

1955, Sept. 14 **Wmk. 304** ***Perf. 14***

Design: 20pf+3pf, Post horn and stamp tongs.

B342 SP273 10pf + 2pf green 6.50 5.75
B343 SP273 20pf + 3pf red 12.00 9.25

WESTROPA, 1955, philatelic exhibition at Dusseldorf. The surtax aided the Society of German Philatelists.

Amalie Sieveking — SP274

Portraits: 10pf+5pf, Adolph Kolping. 20pf+10pf, Dr. Samuel Hahnemann. 40pf+10pf, Florence Nightingale.

1955, Nov. 15 **Photo. & Litho.**

B344 SP274 7 + 3pf olive bis 2.25 1.50
B345 SP274 10 + 5pf dk green 1.75 65
B346 SP274 20 + 10pf red org 2.25 90
B347 SP274 40 + 10pf grnsh blue 32.50 27.50

The surtax was for independent welfare organizations.

Boy and Geometrical Designs — SP275

Design: 10pf+5pf, Girl playing flute.

Unwmk.

1956, July 21 **Litho.** ***Perf. 14***

B348 SP275 7pf + 3pf multi 3.00 2.50
B349 SP275 10pf + 5pf multi 7.00 9.25

The surtax was for the Youth Hostel Organization.

The Midwife — SP276

Designs: 10pf+5pf, Ignaz Philipp Semmelweis. 20pf+10pf, The mother. 40pf+10pf, The children's nurse.

1956, Oct. 1 **Photo.**
Design and Inscription in Black

B350 SP276 7pf + 3pf org brn 1.00 1.10
B351 SP276 10pf + 5pf green 60 42
B352 SP276 20pf + 10pf brt red 70 42
B353 SP276 40pf + 10pf brt blue 12.50 12.00

Issued to honor Ignaz Philipp Semmelweis, the discoverer of the cause of puerperal fever. The surtax was for independent welfare organizations.

Children Leaving — SP277

Design: 20pf+10pf, Child arriving.

1957, Feb. 1 Litho. *Perf. 13½x13*

B354 SP277 10pf + 5pf gray grn & red org 1.40 1.25
B355 SP277 20pf + 10pf red org & lt bl 1.90 1.75

The surtax was for vacations for the children of Berlin.

Young Miner — SP278

"The Fox who Stole the Goose" — SP279

Designs: 10pf+5pf, Miner with drill. 20pf+10pf, Miner and conveyor. 40pf+10pf, Miner and coal elevator.

1957, Oct. 1 Wmk. 304 *Perf. 14*

B356 SP278 7pf + 3pf bis brn & blk 1.10 1.10
B357 SP278 10pf + 5pf blk & yel grn 60 42
B358 SP278 20pf + 10pf black & red 85 42
B359 SP278 40pf + 10pf black & blue 13.00 13.00

The surtax was for independent welfare organizations.

1958, Apr. 1 Litho.

Design: 20pf+10pf, "A Hunter from the Palatinate."

B360 SP279 10pf + 5pf brn red, grn & blk 1.25 1.25
B361 SP279 20pf + 10pf multi 2.25 2.25

The surtax was to finance young peoples' study trips to Berlin.

Friedrich Wilhelm Raiffeisen SP280

Dairy Maid SP281

Designs: 20pf+10pf, Girl picking grapes. 40pf+10pf, Farmer with pitchfork.

1958, Oct. 1 Wmk. 304 *Perf. 14*

B362 SP280 7pf + 3pf gldn brn & dk brn 32 40
B363 SP281 10pf + 5pf grn, red & yel 28 20
B364 SP281 20pf + 10pf red, yel & bl 42 28
B365 SP281 40pf + 10pf blue & ocher 5.50 5.50

The surtax was for independent welfare organizations.

Stamp of Hamburg, 1859 — SP282

Design: 20pf+10pf, Stamp of Lübeck, 1859.

1959, May 22 Engr. Wmk. 304

B366 SP282 10pf + 5pf green & brn 85 1.10
  a. 10pf + 5pf yel green & brown 15 18
B367 SP282 20pf + 10pf mar & red brn 1.10 1.40
  a. 20pf + 10pf red org & red brn 15 35

"Interposta" Philatelic Exhibition, Hamburg, May 22-31, 1959 for the cent. of the 1st stamps of Hamburg and Lübeck.

The surtax on Nos. B366a and B367a was for vacations for the children of Berlin. Issued Aug. 22, 1959.

Girl Giving Bread to Beggar — SP283

Jacob and Wilhelm Grimm — SP284

Designs (from "Star Dollars" fairy tale): 10pf+5pf, Girl giving coat to boy, 20pf+10pf, Star-Money from Heaven.

1959, Oct. 1 Litho. *Perf. 14*

B368 SP283 7pf + 3pf brown & yel 15 24
B369 SP283 10pf + 5pf green & yel 20 18
B370 SP283 20pf + 10pf brick red & yel 32 18
B371 SP284 40pf + 10pf bl, blk, ocher & emer 2.50 3.00

The surtax was for independent welfare organizations.

Little Red Riding Hood and the Wolf — SP285

Various Scenes from Little Red Riding Hood.

1960, Oct. 1 Wmk. 304 *Perf. 14*

B372 SP285 7pf + 3pf brn ol, red & blk 20 28
B373 SP285 10pf + 5pf grn, red & blk 24 15
B374 SP285 20pf + 10pf brick red, emer & blk 30 18
B375 SP285 40pf + 20pf brt bl, red & blk 2.50 2.75

The surtax was for independent welfare organizations.

1961, Oct. 2

Various Scenes from Hansel and Gretel.

B376 SP285 7pf + 3pf multi 15 16
B377 SP285 10pf + 5pf multi 15 15
B378 SP285 20pf + 10pf multi 20 15
B379 SP285 40pf + 20pf multi 1.10 1.40

The surtax was for independent welfare organizations.
See B384-B387, B392-B395, B400-B403.

Fluorescent Paper was introduced for semipostal stamps, starting with No. B380.

Apollo — SP286

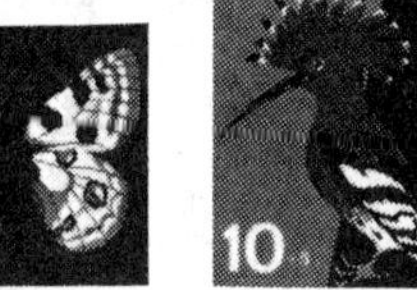
Hoopoe — SP287

Butterflies: 10pf+5pf, Camberwell beauty. 20pf+10pf, Tortoise-shell. 40pf+20pf, Tiger swallowtail.

Wmk. 304
1962, May 25 Litho. *Perf. 14*
Butterflies in Natural Colors, Black Inscriptions

B380 SP286 7pf + 3pf bister brn 24 22
B381 SP286 10pf + 5pf brt green 25 25
B382 SP286 20pf + 10pf dp crim 70 60
B383 SP286 40pf + 20pf brt blue 1.10 1.10

Issued for the benefit of young people.
Nos. B381-B383 exist without watermark. Value, each $900 unused, $750 used.

Fairy Tale Type of 1960

Various Scenes from Snow White (Schneewittchen).

1962, Oct. 10 *Perf. 14*

B384 SP285 7pf + 3pf multi 15 15
B385 SP285 10pf + 5pf multi 15 15
B386 SP285 20pf + 10pf multi 22 15
B387 SP285 40pf + 20pf multi 80 90

The surtax was for independent welfare organizations.

1963, June 12 Unwmk. *Perf. 14*

Birds: 15pf+5pf, European golden oriole. 20pf+10pf, Bullfinch. 40pf+20pf, European kingfisher.

B388 SP287 10pf + 5pf multi 32 24
B389 SP287 15pf + 5pf multi 32 30
B390 SP287 20pf + 10pf multi 40 30
B391 SP287 40pf + 20pf multi 1.40 1.10

Issued for the benefit of young people.

Fairy Tale Type of 1960

Various Scenes from the Grimm Brothers' "The Wolf and the Seven Kids."

1963, Sept. 23 Litho.

B392 SP285 10pf + 5pf multi 15 15
B393 SP285 15pf + 5pf multi 15 15
B394 SP285 20pf + 10pf multi 16 15
B395 SP285 40pf + 20pf multi 55 65
Set value 93

The surtax was for independent welfare organizations.

Herring — SP288

Woodcock — SP289

Fish: 15pf+5pf, Rosefish. 20pf+10pf, Carp. 40pf+20pf, Cod.

1964, Apr. 10 Unwmk. *Perf. 14*

B396 SP288 10pf + 5pf multi 22 28
B397 SP288 15pf + 5pf multi 22 25
B398 SP288 20pf + 10pf multi 35 25
B399 SP288 40pf + 20pf multi 1.00 1.25

Issued for the benefit of young people.

Fairy Tale Type of 1960

Various Scenes from Sleeping Beauty (Dornroschen).

1964, Oct. 6 Litho. *Perf. 14*

B400 SP285 10pf + 5pf multi 15 15
B401 SP285 15pf + 5pf multi 15 15
B402 SP285 20pf + 10pf multi 15 15
B403 SP285 40pf + 20pf multi 55 70

The surtax was for independent welfare organizations.

1965, Apr. 1 Unwmk. *Perf. 14*

Birds: 15pf+5pf, Ring-necked pheasant. 20pf+10pf, Black grouse. 40pf+20pf, Capercaillie.

B404 SP289 10pf + 5pf multi 15 15
B405 SP289 15pf + 5pf multi 15 15
B406 SP289 20pf + 10pf multi 18 15
B407 SP289 40pf + 20pf multi 38 55

Issued for the benefit of young people.

Cinderella Feeding Pigeons — SP290

Roe Deer — SP291

Various Scenes from Cinderella.

1965, Oct. 6 Litho. *Perf. 14*

B408 SP290 10pf + 5pf multi 15 15
B409 SP290 15pf + 5pf multi 15 15
B410 SP290 20pf + 10pf multi 15 15
B411 SP290 40pf + 20pf multi 48 55
Set value 78

The surtax was for independent welfare organizations.
See Nos. B418-B421, B426-B429.

1966, Apr. 22 Litho. *Perf. 14*

Designs: 20pf+10pf, Chamois. 30pf+15pf, Fallow deer. 50pf+25pf, Red deer.

B412 SP291 10pf + 5pf multi 16 15
B413 SP291 20pf + 10pf multi 20 15
B414 SP291 30pf + 15pf multi 28 20
B415 SP291 50pf + 25pf multi 65 65

Issued for the benefit of young people.
See Nos. B422-B425.

Prussian Letter Carrier — SP292

Design: 30pf+15pf, Bavarian mail coach.

1966 Litho. *Perf. 14*

B416 SP292 30pf + 15pf multi 42 60
B417 SP292 50pf + 25pf multi 32 52

Issued to publicize the meeting of the Federation Internationale de Philatélie (FIP), Munich, Sept. 26-29, and the stamp exhibition, Municipal Museum, Sept. 24-Oct. 1. The surcharge was for the Foundation for the Promotion of Philately and Postal History. Issue dates: No. B416, Sept. 24; No. B417, July 13.

Fairy Tale Type of 1965

Various Scenes from The Princess and the Frog.

1966, Oct. 5 Litho. *Perf. 14*

B418 SP290 10pf + 5pf multi 15 15
B419 SP290 20pf + 10pf multi 15 15
B420 SP290 30pf + 15pf multi 20 15
B421 SP290 50pf + 25pf multi 50 75

The surtax was for independent welfare organizations.

Animal Type of 1966

Designs: 10pf+5pf, Rabbit. 20pf+10pf, Ermine. 30pf+15pf, Hamster. 50pf+25pf, Red fox.

1967, Apr. 4 Litho. *Perf. 14*

B422 SP291 10pf + 5pf multi 20 18
B423 SP291 20pf + 10pf multi 20 22
B424 SP291 30pf + 15pf multi 32 30
B425 SP291 50pf + 25pf multi 1.00 1.10

Issued for the benefit of young people.

Fairy Tale Type of 1965

Various Scenes from Frau Holle.

1967, Oct. 3 Litho. *Perf. 14*

B426 SP290 10pf + 5pf multi 15 16
B427 SP290 20pf + 10pf multi 15 15
B428 SP290 30pf + 15pf multi 25 15
B429 SP290 50pf + 25pf multi 65 90

The surtax was for independent welfare organizations.

Wildcat — SP293

Animals: 20pf+10pf, Otter. 30pf+15pf, Badger. 50pf+25pf, Beaver.

1968, Feb. 2 Photo. Unwmk.

B430	SP293	10pf + 5pf multi	28	42
B431	SP293	20pf + 15pf multi	35	55
B432	SP293	30pf + 15pf multi	65	90
B433	SP293	50pf + 25pf multi	1.75	2.50

The surtax was for the benefit of young people.

Olympic Games Type of Regular Issue

Designs (Olympic Rings and): 10pf+5pf, Karl-Friedrich Freiherr von Langen, equestrian. 20pf+10pf, Rudolf Harbig, runner. 30pf+15pf, Helene Mayer, fencer. 50pf+25pf, Carl Diem, sports organizer.

Lithographed and Engraved

1968, June 6 Unwmk. *Perf. 14*

B434	A285	10pf + 5pf olive & dk brn	15	15
B435	A285	20pf + 10pf dp emer & dk grn	30	30
B436	A285	30pf + 15pf dp rose & dk red	45	45
B437	A285	50pf + 25pf brt bl & dk bl	75	75

The surtax was for the Foundation for the Promotion of the 1972 Olympic Games in Munich.

Doll, c. 1878 — SP294

Pony — SP295

Designs: Various 19th Century Dolls. Nos. B438-B440 are from Germanic National Museum, Nuremberg; No. B441 is from Altona Museum, Hamburg.

1968, Oct. 3 Litho. *Perf. 14*

B438	SP294	10pf + 5pf multi	15	18
B439	SP294	20pf + 10pf multi	16	15
B440	SP294	30pf + 15pf multi	20	18
B441	SP294	50pf + 25pf multi	60	95

The surtax was for independent welfare organizations.

1969, Feb. 6 Litho. *Perf. 14*

Horses: 20pf+10pf, Work horse. 30pf+15pf, Hotblood. 50pf+25pf, Thoroughbred.

B442	SP295	10pf + 5pf multi	28	28
B443	SP295	20pf + 10pf multi	35	35
B444	SP295	30pf + 15pf multi	75	80
B445	SP295	50pf + 25pf multi	1.75	1.75

Surtax for the benefit of young people.

Track and Olympic Rings — SP296

Toy Locomotive of Tin — SP297

Designs (Olympic Rings and): 20pf+10pf, Hockey. 30pf+15pf, Archery. 50pf+25pf, Sailing.

1969, June 4 Photo. *Perf. 14*

B446	SP296	10pf + 5pf dk brn & lem	15	18
B447	SP296	20pf + 10pf bl grn & emer	32	38
B448	SP296	30pf + 15pf mag & dp lil rose	45	55
B449	SP296	50pf + 25pf dp bl & brt bl	1.10	1.25

Issued to publicize the 1972 Olympic Games in Munich. The surtax was for the German Olympic Committee.

1969, Oct. 2 Litho. *Perf. 13½x14*

Tin Toys: 20pf+10pf, Gardener. 30pf+15pf, Bird seller. 50pf+25pf, Knight on horseback.

B450	SP297	10pf + 5pf multi	15	15
B451	SP297	20pf + 10pf multi	18	18
B452	SP297	30pf + 15pf multi	32	32
B453	SP297	50pf + 25pf multi	80	80

The surtax was for independent welfare organizations.

Tin Toy Type of 1969 Inscribed: "Weihnachtsmarke 1969"

Christmas: 10pf+5pf, Jesus in Manger.

1969, Nov. 13 *Perf. 13½x14*

B454	SP297	10pf + 5pf multi	25	25

Heinrich von Rugge — SP298

Minnesingers: 20pf+10pf, Wolfram von Eschenbach. 30pf+15pf, Walther von Metz. 50pf+25pf, Walther von der Vogelweide.

1970, Feb. 5 Photo. *Perf. 13½x14*

B455	SP298	10pf + 5pf multi	25	25
B456	SP298	20pf + 10pf multi	35	35
B457	SP298	30pf + 15pf multi	52	52
B458	SP298	50pf + 25pf multi	1.25	1.25

Surtax was for benefit of young people.

Residenz (Palace), Munich SP299

Munich Buildings: 20pf+10pf, Propylaea. 30pf+15pf, Glyptothek. 50pf+25pf, Bavaria Statue and Colonnade.

1970, June 5 Engr. *Perf. 14*

B459	SP299	10pf + 5pf olive bis	20	20
B460	SP299	20pf + 10pf dk bl grn	40	40
B461	SP299	30pf + 15pf carmine	50	50
B462	SP299	50pf + 25pf dk blue	1.00	1.00

The surtax was for the Foundation for the Promotion of the 1972 Olympic Games in Munich.

Jester — SP300

King Caspar — SP301

Puppets: 20pf+10pf, "Hanswurst." 30pf+15pf, Clown. 50pf+25pf, Harlequin.

1970, Oct. 6 Litho. *Perf. 13½x14*

B463	SP300	10pf + 5pf multi	15	15
B464	SP300	20pf + 10pf multi	16	16
B465	SP300	30pf + 15pf multi	30	30
B466	SP300	50pf + 25pf multi	75	75

The surtax was for independent welfare organizations.

1970, Nov. 12

Christmas: 10pf+5pf, Rococo Angel, from Ursuline Sisters' Convent, Innsbruck.

B467	SP300	10pf + 5pf multi	20	20

1971, Feb. 5 Litho. *Perf. 14*

Children's Drawings: 20pf+10pf, Flea. 30pf+15pf, Puss-in-Boots. 50pf+25pf, Snake.

B468	SP301	10pf + 5pf multi	16	16
B469	SP301	20pf + 10pf multi	35	35
B470	SP301	30pf + 15pf multi	55	55
B471	SP301	50pf + 25pf multi	1.10	1.10

Surtax for the benefit of young people.

Ski Jump — SP302

Women Churning Butter — SP303

Designs: 20pf+10pf, Figure skating. 30pf+15pf, Downhill skiing. 50pf+25pf, Ice hockey.

"1971" at Lower Right

1971, June 4 Litho. *Perf. 14*

B472	SP302	10pf + 5pf brn org & blk	28	32
B473	SP302	20pf + 10pf green & blk	55	65
B474	SP302	30pf + 15pf rose red & blk	70	80
B475	SP302	50pf + 25pf blue & blk	1.40	1.65
a.		Souvenir sheet of 4	3.50	3.50
b.		10pf + 5pf brown org & blk	75	75
c.		20pf + 10pf green & black	75	75
d.		30pf + 15pf rose red & black	75	75
e.		50pf + 25pf blue & black	75	75

Olympic Games 1972.

No. B475a contains Nos. B475b-B475e which lack the minute date ("1971") at lower right.

1971, Oct. 5 Litho. *Perf. 14*

Wooden Toys: 25pf+10pf, Horseback rider. 30pf+15pf, Nutcracker. 60pf+30pf, Dovecot.

B476	SP303	20pf + 10pf multi	15	15
B477	SP303	25pf + 10pf multi	18	18
B478	SP303	30pf + 15pf multi	24	24
B479	SP303	60pf + 30pf multi	85	85

Surtax for independent welfare organizations.

1971, Nov. 11

Christmas: 20pf+10pf, Christmas angel with lights.

B480	SP303	20pf + 10pf multi	28	28

Ducks Crossing Road — SP304

Olympic Rings and Wrestling — SP305

Designs: 25pf+10pf, Hunter chasing deer and rabbits. 30pf+15pf, Girl protecting birds from cat. 60pf+30pf, Boy annoying swans.

1972, Feb. 4 Litho. *Perf. 14*

B481	SP304	20pf + 10pf multi	60	60
B482	SP304	25pf + 10pf multi	70	70
B483	SP304	30pf + 15pf multi	90	90
B484	SP304	60pf + 30pf multi	1.75	1.75

Animal protection. Surtax for the benefit of young people.

1972, June 5 Photo. *Perf. 14*

Designs (Olympic Rings and): 25pf+10pf, Sailing. 30pf+15pf, Gymnastics. 60pf+30pf, Swimming.

B485	SP305	20pf + 10pf multi	42	42
B486	SP305	25pf + 10pf multi	52	52
B487	SP305	30pf + 15pf multi	65	65
B488	SP305	60pf + 30pf multi	1.75	1.75

20th Olympic Games, Munich, Aug. 26 Sept. 10. See No. B490.

Souvenir Sheet

Olympic Games Site, Munich — SP306

1972, July 5 Litho. *Perf. 14*

B489	SP306	Sheet of 4	7.50	7.50
a.		25pf + 10pf Gymnastics stadium	1.65	1.65
b.		30pf + 15pf Soccer stadium	1.65	1.65
c.		40pf + 20pf Tent and lake	1.65	1.65
d.		70pf + 35pf Television tower, vert.	1.65	1.65

20th Olympic Games, Munich. Surcharge was for the Foundation for the Promotion of the Munich Olympic Games.

Olympic Games Type of 1972
Souvenir Sheet

1972, Aug. 18 Litho. *Perf. 14*

B490		Sheet of 4	7.25	7.25
a.	SP305	25pf + 5pf Long jump, women's	1.65	1.65
b.	SP305	30pf + 10pf Basketball	1.65	1.65
c.	SP305	40pf + 10pf Discus, women's	1.65	1.65
d.	SP305	70pf + 10pf Canoeing	1.65	1.65
e.		Bklt. pane of 4, #B490a-b490d	20.00	

20th Olympic Games, Munich.

Knight — SP307

Adoration of the Kings — SP308

1972, Oct. 5

B491	SP307	25pf + 10pf shown	30	30
B492	SP307	30pf + 15pf Rook	35	35
B493	SP307	40pf + 20pf Queen	45	45
B494	SP307	70pf + 35pf King	1.50	1.50

19th century chess pieces made by Faience Works, Gien, France; now in Hamburg Museum. The surtax was for independent welfare organizations.

1972, Nov. 10 Litho.

B495	SP308	30pf + 15pf multi	52	52

Christmas 1972.

Osprey SP309

Hesse-Kassel SP310

Birds of Prey: 30pf+15pf, Buzzard. 40pf+20pf, Red kite. 70pf+35pf, Montagu's harrier.

1973, Feb. 6 Photo. *Perf. 14*

B496 SP309 25pf + 10pf multi 1.25 1.25
B497 SP309 30pf + 15pf multi 1.50 1.50
B498 SP309 40pf + 20pf multi 2.00 2.00
B499 SP309 70pf + 35pf multi 5.00 5.00

Surtax was for benefit of young people.

1973, Apr. 5 Litho. *Perf. 14*

Posthouse Signs: No. B501, Prussia. No. B502a, Württemberg. No. B502b, Bavaria.

B500 SP310 40pf + 20pf multi 1.00 1.00
B501 SP310 70pf + 35pf multi 1.50 1.50

Souvenir Sheet

B502 Sheet of 2 6.50 6.50
a. SP310 40pf + 20pf multi 3.00 3.00
b. SP310 70pf + 35pf multi 3.00 3.00

IBRA München 1973 International Philatelic Exhibition, Munich, May 11-20. No. B502 sold for 2.20 mark.

French Horn, 19th Century SP311

Christmas Star SP312

Musical Instruments: 30pf+15pf, Pedal piano, 18th century. 40pf+20pf, Violin, 18th century. 70pf+35pf, Pedal harp, 18th century.

1973, Oct. 5 Litho. *Perf. 14*

B503 SP311 25pf + 10pf multi 35 30
B504 SP311 30pf + 15pf multi 38 35
B505 SP311 40pf + 20pf multi 60 52
B506 SP311 70pf + 35pf multi 1.65 1.50

Surtax was for independent welfare organizations.

1973, Nov. 9 Litho. & Engr.

B507 SP312 30pf + 15pf multi 65 65

Christmas 1973.

Young Builder SP313

Campion SP314

Designs: 30pf+15pf, Girl in national costume. 40pf+20pf, Boy studying. 70pf+35pf, Girl with microscope.

1974, Apr. 17 Photo. *Perf. 14*

B508 SP313 25pf + 10pf multi 1.10 1.10
B509 SP313 30pf + 15pf multi 1.25 1.25
B510 SP313 40pf + 20pf multi 2.00 2.00
B511 SP313 70pf + 35pf multi 2.75 2.75

Surtax was for benefit of young people.

1974, Oct. 15 Litho. *Perf. 14*

Flowers: 40pf+20pf, Foxglove. 50pf+25pf, Mallow. 70pf+35pf, Bellflower.

B512 SP314 30pf + 15pf multi 32 32
B513 SP314 40pf + 20pf multi 42 42
B514 SP314 50pf + 25pf multi 55 55
B515 SP314 70pf + 35pf multi 1.50 1.50

Surtax was for independent welfare organizations.

1974, Oct. 29

Christmas: 40pf+20pf, Advent decoration.

B516 SP314 40pf + 20pf multi 65 60

Diesel Locomotive Class 218 SP315

Locomotives: 40pf+20pf, Electric engine Class 103. 50pf+25pf, Electric rail motor train Class 403. 70pf+35pf, Magnetic suspension train "Transrapid" (model).

1975, Apr. 15 Litho. *Perf. 14*

B517 SP315 30pf + 15pf multi 60 60
B518 SP315 40pf + 20pf multi 80 80
B519 SP315 50pf + 25pf multi 1.25 1.25
B520 SP315 70pf + 35pf multi 1.65 1.65

Surtax was for benefit of young people.

Edelweiss — SP316

Alpine Flowers: 40pf+20pf, Trollflower. 50pf+25pf, Alpine rose. 70pf+35pf, Pasqueflower.

1975, Oct. 15 Litho. *Perf. 14*

B521 SP316 30pf + 15pf multi 35 25
B522 SP316 40pf + 20pf multi 50 40
B523 SP316 50pf + 25pf multi 70 52
B524 SP316 70pf + 35pf multi 1.50 1.10

Surtax was for independent welfare organizations.

1975, Nov. 14

Christmas: Snow rose.

B525 SP316 40pf + 20pf multi 70 70

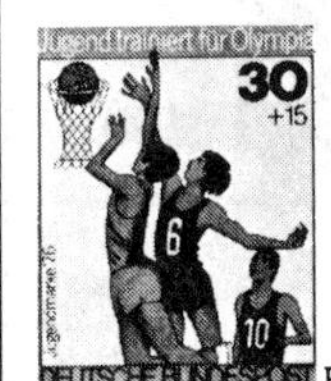

Basketball — SP317

Designs: 40pf+20pf, Rowing. 50pf+25pf, Gymnastics, women's. 70pf+35pf, Volleyball.

1976, Apr. 6 Litho. *Perf. 14*

B526 SP317 30pf + 15pf multi 65 65
B527 SP317 40pf + 20pf multi 90 90
B528 SP317 50pf + 25pf multi 1.10 1.10
B529 SP317 70pf + 35pf multi 1.50 1.50

Youth training for Olympic Games. Surtax was for benefit of young people.

Swimmer and Olympic Rings SP318

Designs (Olympic Rings and): 30pf+15pf, Hockey. 50pf+25pf, High jump. 70pf+35pf, Rowing, coxed four.

1976, Apr. 6

B530 SP318 40pf + 20pf multi 55 55
B531 SP318 50pf + 25pf multi 70 70

Souvenir Sheet

B532 Sheet of 2 1.75 1.75
a. SP318 30pf + 15pf multi 85 85
b. SP318 70pf + 35pf multi 85 85

21st Olympic Games, Montreal, Canada, July 17-Aug. 1. The surtax was for the German Sports Aid Foundation.

Phlox SP319

Flowers: 40pf+20pf, Marigolds. 50pf+25pf, Dahlias. 70pf+35pf, Pansies.

1976, Oct. 14 Litho. *Perf. 14*

B533 SP319 30pf + 15pf multi 40 40
B534 SP319 40pf + 20pf multi 52 52
B535 SP319 50pf + 25pf multi 65 65
B536 SP319 70pf + 35pf multi 1.10 1.10

Surtax was for independent welfare organizations.

Souvenir Sheet

Nativity, Window, Frauenkirche, Esslingen — SP320

1976, Nov. 16 Litho. & Engr.

B537 SP320 50pf + 25pf multi 75 75

Christmas 1976.

Wapen von Hamburg, c. 1730 SP321

Historic Ships: 40pf+20pf, Preussen, 5-master, 1902. 50pf+25pf, Bremen, 1929. 70pf+35pf, Freighter Sturmfels, 1972.

1977, Apr. 14 Litho. *Perf. 14*

B538 SP321 30pf + 15pf multi 60 60
B539 SP321 40pf + 20pf multi 95 95
B540 SP321 50pf + 25pf multi 1.10 1.10
B541 SP321 70pf + 35pf multi 1.50 1.50

Surtax was for benefit of young people.

Caraway — SP322

Meadow Flowers: 40pf+20pf, Dandelion. 50pf+25pf, Red clover. 70pf+35pf, Meadow sage.

1977, Oct. 13 Litho. *Perf. 14*

B542 SP322 30pf + 15pf multi 45 45
B543 SP322 40pf + 20pf multi 55 55
B544 SP322 50pf + 25pf multi 70 70
B545 SP322 70pf + 35pf multi 1.00 1.00

Surtax was for independent welfare organizations. See Nos. B553-B556.

Souvenir Sheet

King Caspar Offering Gold, Window, St. Gereon's, Cologne — SP323

1977, Nov. 10

B546 SP323 50pf + 25pf multi 75 75

Christmas 1977.

Giant Slalom SP324

Design: No. B548, Steeplechase.

1978 Litho. *Perf. 14*

B547 SP324 50pf + 25pf multi 1.75 1.75
B548 SP324 70pf + 35pf multi 4.50 4.50

Issued: #B547, Jan. 12, #B548, Apr. 13.
Surtax was for the German Sports Foundation.

Balloon Ascent, Oktoberfest, Munich, 1820 — SP325

Designs: 40pf+20pf, Airship LZ 1, 1900. 50pf+25pf, Bleriot monoplane, 1909. 70pf+35pf, Grade monoplane, 1909.

1978, Apr. 13 Litho. *Perf. 14*

B549 SP325 30pf + 15pf multi 55 55
B550 SP325 40pf + 20pf multi 70 70
B551 SP325 50pf + 25pf multi 95 95
B552 SP325 70pf + 35pf multi 1.25 1.25

Surtax was for benefit of young people.

Flower Type of 1977

Woodland Flowers: 30pf+15pf, Arum. 40pf+20pf, Weaselsnout. 50pf+25pf, Turk's-cap lily. 70pf+35pf, Liverwort.

1978, Oct. 12 Litho. *Perf. 14*

B553 SP322 30pf + 15pf multi 38 38
B554 SP322 40pf + 20pf multi 50 50
B555 SP322 50pf + 25pf multi 60 60
B556 SP322 70pf + 35pf multi 1.10 1.10

Surtax was for independent welfare organizations.

Souvenir Sheet

Christ Child, Window, Frauenkirche, Munich — SP326

1978, Nov. 16 **Litho.** ***Perf. 14***
B557 SP326 50pf + 25pf multi 75 75

Christmas 1978.

Dornier Wal, 1922
SP327

Airplanes: 50pf+25pf, Heinkel HE70, 1932. 60pf+30pf, Junkers W33 Bremen, 1928. 90pf+45pf, Focke-Wulf FW61, 1936.

1979, Apr. 5 **Litho.** ***Perf. 14***
B558 SP327 40pf + 20pf multi 60 60
B559 SP327 50pf + 25pf multi 85 85
B560 SP327 60pf + 30pf multi 1.00 1.00
B561 SP327 90pf + 45pf multi 1.50 1.50

Surtax was for benefit of young people. See Nos. B570-B573.

Handball
SP328

Design: 90pf+45pf, Canoeing.

1979, Apr. 5
B562 SP328 60pf + 30pf multi 1.00 1.00
B563 SP328 90pf + 45pf multi 1.40 1.40

Surtax was for German Sports Foundation.

Post House Sign, Altheim, Saar, 1754 — SP329

1979, Oct. 11 **Litho.** ***Perf. 14***
B564 SP329 60pf + 30pf multi 1.00 1.00

Stamp Day. Surtax was for Foundation of Promotion of Philately and Postal History. Issued in sheet of 10.

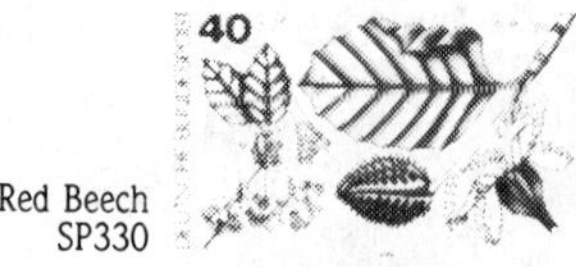

Red Beech
SP330

Woodland Plants: 50pf+25pf, English oak. 60pf+30pf, Hawthorn. 90pf+45pf, Mountain pine.

1979, Oct. 11 **Litho.** ***Perf. 14***
B565 SP330 40pf + 20pf multi 48 48
B566 SP330 50pf + 25pf multi 60 60
B567 SP330 60pf + 30pf multi 65 65
B568 SP330 90pf + 45pf multi 1.10 1.10

Surtax was for independent welfare organizations.

Nativity, Medieval Manuscript
SP331

1979, Nov. 14 **Litho.** ***Perf. 13½***
B569 SP331 60pf + 30pf multi 80 80

Christmas 1979.

Aviation Type of 1979

Designs: 40pf+20pf, FS 24 Phoenix, 1957. 50pf+25pf, Lockheed Super Constellation, 1950. 60pf+30pf, Airbus A300, 1972. 90pf+45pf, Boeing 747, 1969.

1980, Apr. 10 **Litho.** ***Perf. 14***
B570 SP327 40 + 20pf multi 55 55
B571 SP327 50 + 25pf multi 75 75
B572 SP327 60 + 30pf multi 95 95
B573 SP327 90 + 45pf multi 1.50 1.50

Surtax was for benefit of young people.

Soccer
SP332

Designs: 60pf+30pf, Equestrian. 90pf+45pf, Cross-country skiing.

1980, May 8 **Photo.** ***Perf. 14***
B574 SP332 50 + 25pf multi 70 70
B575 SP332 60 + 30pf multi 90 90
B576 SP332 90 + 45pf multi 1.40 1.40

Surtax was for German Sports Foundation.

Ceratocephalus
SP333

Wildflowers: 50pf+25pf, Climbing meadow pea. 60pf+30pf, Corn cockle. 90pf+45pf, Grape hyacinth.

1980, Oct. 9 **Litho.** ***Perf. 14***
B577 SP333 40 + 20pf multi 55 55
B578 SP333 50 + 25pf multi 70 70
B579 SP333 60 + 30pf multi 80 80
B580 SP333 90 + 45pf multi 1.25 1.25

Surtax was for independent welfare organizations.

Post House Sign, 1754, Altheim, Saar — SP334

1980, Nov. 13 **Litho.** ***Perf. 14***
B581 SP334 60 + 30pf multi 70 70

49th FIP Congress (Federation Internationale de Philatelie), Essen, Nov. 12-13.

Nativity, Altomunster Manuscript, 12th Century — SP335

1980, Nov. 13 ***Perf. 14x13½***
B582 SP335 60 + 30pf multi 75 75

Christmas 1980.

Borda Circle, 1800 — SP336

Historic Optical Instruments: 50pf+25pf, Reflecting telescope, 1770. 60pf+30pf, Binocular microscope, 1860. 90pf+45pf, Octant, 1775.

1981, Apr. 10 **Litho.** ***Perf. 13½***
B583 SP336 40 + 20pf multi 60 60
B584 SP336 50 + 25pf multi 75 75
B585 SP336 60 + 30pf multi 1.00 1.00
B586 SP336 90 + 45pf multi 1.50 1.50

Surtax was for benefit of young people.

Rowing
SP337

1981, Apr. 10 ***Perf. 14***
B587 SP337 60 + 30pf shown 90 90
B588 SP337 90 + 45pf Gliding 1.25 1.25

Surtax was for the German Sports Foundation.

Water Nut — SP338

Endangered Species: 50pf+25pf, Floating heart. 60pf+30pf, Water gillyflower. 90pf+45pf, Water lobelia.

1981, Oct. 8 **Litho.**
B589 SP338 40 + 20pf multi 60 60
B590 SP338 50 + 25pf multi 75 75
B591 SP338 60 + 30pf multi 90 90
B592 SP338 90 + 45pf multi 1.25 1.25

Surtax was for independent welfare organizations.

Nativity, 19th Cent. Painting
SP339

1981, Nov. 12 **Litho.**
B593 SP339 60 + 30pf multi 90 90

Christmas 1981.

Antique Cars
SP340

Designs: 40+20pf, Benz, 1886. 50+25pf, Mercedes, 1913. 60+30pf, Hanomag, 1925. 90+45pf, Opel Olympia, 1937.

1982, Apr. 15 **Litho.**
B594 SP340 40 + 20pf multi 65 65
B595 SP340 50 + 25pf multi 75 75
B596 SP340 60 + 30pf multi 95 95
B597 SP340 90 + 45pf multi 1.40 1.40

Surtax was for benefit of young people.

Jogging
SP341

1982, Apr. 15 **Litho.**
B598 SP341 60 + 30pf shown 85 85
B599 SP341 90 + 45pf Archery 1.40 1.40

Surtax was for the German Sports Foundation.

Tea-rose Hybrid — SP342

Christmas — SP343

Designs: 60pf+30pf, Floribunda. 80pf+40pf, Bourbon rose. 120pf+60pf, Polyantha hybrid.

1982, Oct. 14 **Litho.** ***Perf. 14***
B600 SP342 50 + 20pf multi 70 70
B601 SP342 60 + 30pf multi 90 90
B602 SP342 80 + 40pf multi 1.10 1.10
B603 SP342 120 + 60pf multi 1.75 1.75

Surtax was for independent welfare organizations.

1982, Nov. 10

Designs: Nativity, Oak altar, St. Peter's Church, Hamburg, 1380.

B604 SP343 80 + 40pf multi 1.25 1.25

Historic Motorcycles — SP344

Designs: 50pf+20pf, Daimler-Mayback, 1885. 60pf+30pf, NSU, 1901. 80pf+40pf, Megola-Sport, 1922. 120pf+60pf, BMW, 1936.

1983, Apr. 12 **Litho.** ***Perf. 14***
B605 SP344 50 + 20pf multi 75 75
B606 SP344 60 + 30pf multi 90 90
B607 SP344 80 + 40pf multi 1.10 1.10
B608 SP344 120 + 60pf multi 1.75 1.75

Surtax was for benefit of young people.

1983 Sports Championships — SP345

Designs: 80pf+40pf, Gymnastics Festival. 120pf+60pf, Modern Pentathlon World Championships.

1983, Apr. 12

B609 SP345	80 + 40pf multi	1.25	1.25
B610 SP345	120 + 60pf multi	1.75	1.75

Surtax was for German Sports Foundation.

Swiss Androsace — SP346

Designs: 60pf+30pf, Krain groundsel. 80pf+40pf, Fleischer's willow herb. 120pf+60pf, Alpine sow-thistle.

1983, Oct. 13 Litho. *Perf. 14*

B611 SP346	50 + 20pf multi	70	55
B612 SP346	60 + 30pf multi	90	70
B613 SP346	80 + 40pf multi	1.25	1.00
B614 SP346	120 + 60pf multi	1.75	1.40

Surtax was for welfare organizations.

Christmas — SP347

Insects — SP348

1983, Nov. 10 Litho.

B615 SP347	80 + 40pf Carolers	1.40	1.25

Surtax was for free welfare work.

1984, Apr. 12 Litho.

Designs: 50pf+20pf, Trichodes apoarius. 60pf+30pf, Vanessa atalanta. 80pf+40pf, Apis mellifera. 120pf+60pf, Chrysotoxum festivum.

B616 SP348	50 + 20pf multi	85	80
B617 SP348	60 + 30pf multi	1.10	1.00
B618 SP348	80 + 40pf multi	1.50	1.50
B619 SP348	120 + 60pf multi	2.25	2.00

Surtax was for German Youth Stamp Foundation.

Women's Discus SP349

Olympic Sports: 80pf+40pf, Rhythmic gymnastics. 120pf+60pf, Wind surfing.

1984, Apr. 12

B620 SP349	60 + 30pf multi	1.10	1.00
B621 SP349	80 + 40pf multi	1.50	1.40
B622 SP349	120 + 60pf multi	2.25	2.25

Surtax was for German Sports Foundation.

Orchids — SP350

Designs: 50pf+20pf, Aceras anthropophorum. 60pf+30pf, Orchis ustulata. 80pf+40pf, Limodorum abortivum. 120+60pf, Dactylorhiza sambucina.

1984, Oct. 18 Litho. *Perf. 14*

B623 SP350	50 + 20pf multi	85	75
B624 SP350	60 + 30pf multi	1.10	1.00
B625 SP350	80 + 40pf multi	1.50	1.40
B626 SP350	120 + 60pf multi	2.00	2.00

Surtax was for welfare organizations.

Christmas 1984 SP351

1984, Nov. 8 Litho.

B627 SP351	80pf + 40pf St. Martin	1.75	1.75

Surtax was for welfare organizations.

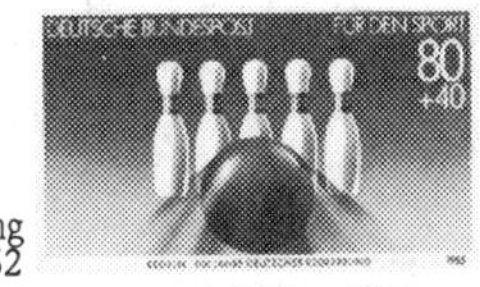

Bowling SP352

1985, Feb. 21 Photo.

B628 SP352	80pf + 40pf multi	1.75	1.50
B629 SP352	120pf + 60pf Kayaking	2.25	2.50

Surtax was for German Sports Foundation.

Antique Bicycles — SP353

Designs: 50pf+20pf, Draisienne, 1817. 60pf+30pf, NSU Germania, 1886. 80pf+40pf, Cross-frame, 1887. 120pf+60pf, Adler tricycle, 1888.

1985, Apr. 16 Litho.

B630 SP353	50pf + 20pf multi	1.10	1.00
B631 SP353	60pf + 30pf multi	1.50	1.40
B632 SP353	80pf + 40pf multi	2.00	1.90
B633 SP353	120pf + 60pf multi	2.75	2.75

Surtax was for benefit of young people. Each stamp also shows the International Youth Year emblem.

MOPHILA '85, Hamburg, Sept. 11-15 SP354

1985, Aug. 13 Litho. *Perf. 14x14½*

B634 SP354	60 + 20pf Coachman, horses	1.65	1.65
B635 SP354	80 + 20pf Stagecoach	2.00	2.00
a.	Pair, #B634-B635	3.75	3.75

Surtax for the benefit of the Philatelic & Postal History Foundation. No. B635a has continuous design.

SP355

Designs: Various ornamental borders, medieval prayer book, Prussian State Library, Berlin.

1985, Oct. 15 Litho. *Perf. 14*

B636 SP355	50pf + 20pf multi	80	70
B637 SP355	60pf + 30pf multi	1.00	90
B638 SP355	80pf + 40pf multi	1.40	1.25
B639 SP355	120pf + 60pf multi	2.00	2.00

Surtax for welfare organizations.

Christmas 1985 — SP356

Woodcut: The Birth of Christ, by Hans Baldung Grien (1485-1545), Freiburg Cathedral High Altar.

1985, Nov. 12 Litho. *Perf. 14*

B640 SP356	80pf + 40pf multi	1.25	1.25

Surtax for welfare organizations.

European World Sports Championships — SP357

1986, Feb. 13 Litho. *Perf. 14*

B641 SP357	80 + 40pf Running	1.25	1.25
B642 SP357	120 + 55pf Bobsledding	1.75	1.75

Surtax for the Natl. Sports Promotion Foundation.

Vocational Training SP358

1986, Apr. 10

B643 SP358	50 + 25pf Optician	1.10	1.10
B644 SP358	60 + 30pf Mason	1.40	1.40
B645 SP358	70 + 35pf Beautician	1.75	1.65
B646 SP358	80 + 40pf Baker	2.00	1.90

Surtax for German Youth Stamp Foundation.

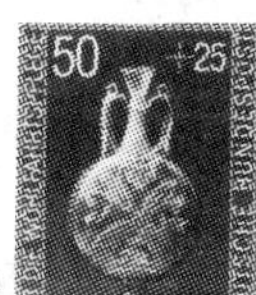

Glassware in German Museums — SP359

1986, Oct. 16 Litho.

B647 SP359	50 + 25pf Ornamental flask, c. 300	85	75
B648 SP359	60 + 30pf Goblet, c. 1650	1.00	90
B649 SP359	70 + 35pf Imperial eagle tankard, c. 1662	1.10	1.05
B650 SP359	80 + 40pf Engraved goblet, c. 1720	1.40	1.20

Surtax for public welfare organizations.

Christmas SP360

Adoration of the Infant Jesus, Ortenberg Altarpiece, c. 1430, Hesse Museum, Darmstadt.

1986, Nov. 13 Litho. *Perf. 14*

B651 SP360	80 + 40pf multi	1.50	1.20

Surtax for public welfare organizations.

World Championships — SP361

1987, Feb. 12 Litho.

B652 SP361	80 + 40pf Sailing	1.35	1.35
B653 SP361	120 + 55pf Cross-country skiing	1.95	1.95

Surtax for the benefit of the national Sports Promotion Foundation.

Youth in Industry SP362

1987, Apr. 9 Litho.

B654 SP362	50 + 25pf Plumber	82	82
B655 SP362	60 + 30pf Dental technician	1.00	1.00
B656 SP362	70 + 35pf Butcher	1.15	1.15
B657 SP362	80 + 40pf Bookbinder	1.30	1.30

Surtax for youth organizations.

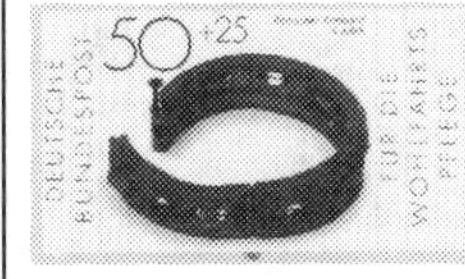

Gold and Silver Artifacts SP363

1987, Oct. 15

B658 SP363	50 + 25pf Roman bracelet, 4th cent.	85	85
B659 SP363	60 + 30pf Gothic buckle, 6th cent.	1.00	1.00
B660 SP363	70 + 35pf Merovingian disk fibula, 7th cent.	1.20	1.20
B661 SP363	80 + 40pf Purse-shaped reliquary, 8th cent.	1.35	1.35

Surtax for welfare organizations sonsoring free museum exhibitions.

Christmas SP364

Illustration from Book of Psalms, 13th cent., Bavarian Natl. Museum: Birth of Christ.

1987, Nov. 6

B662 SP364	80 + 40pf multi	1.25	1.00

Surtax for public welfare organizations.

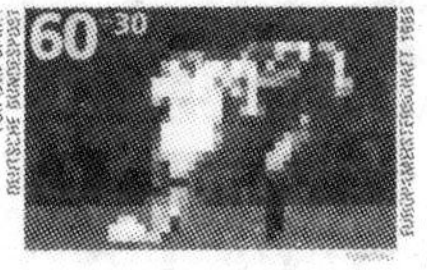

Sports SP365

1988, Feb. 18 Litho.

B663 SP365	60 + 30pf Soccer	1.00	1.00
B664 SP365	80 + 40pf Tennis	1.25	1.25
B665 SP365	120 + 55pf Diving	1.90	1.90

Surtax for Stiftung Deutsche Sporthilfe, a foundation for the promotion of sports in Germany.

Rock Stars
SP366

Designs: No. B666, Buddy Holly (1936-1959). No. B667, Elvis Presley (1935-1977). No. B668, Jim Morrison (1943-1971). No. B669, John Lennon (1940-1980).

1988, Apr. 14 **Litho.** ***Perf. 14***

B666 SP366 50 + 25pf multi 1.05 1.05
B667 SP366 60 + 30pf multi 1.10 1.10
B668 SP366 70 + 35pf multi 1.30 1.30
B669 SP366 80 + 40pf multi 1.50 1.50

Surtax for German Youth Stamp Foundation.

Gold and Rock Crystal Reliquary, c. 1200, Schnutgen Museum, Cologne
SP367

Gold and silver artifacts: No. B671, Bust of Charlemagne, 14th cent., Aachen cathedral. No. B672, Crown of Otto III, 10th cent., Essen cathedral. No. B673, Flower bouquet, c. 1620, Schmuck Museum, Pforzheim.

1988, Oct. 13 **Litho.**

B670 SP367 50 + 25pf multi 80 80
B671 SP367 60 + 30pf multi 90 90
B672 SP367 70 + 35pf multi 1.10 1.10
B673 SP367 80 + 40pf multi 1.25 1.25

Surtax for welfare organizations.

Christmas
SP368

Illumination from *The Gospel Book of Henry the Lion,* Helmarshausen, 1188, Prussian Cultural Museum, Bavaria: Adoration of the Magi.

1988, Nov. 10 **Litho.**

B674 SP368 80 + 40pf multi 1.25 1.00

Surtax for public welfare organizations.

World Championship Sporting Events Hosted by Germany — SP369

1989, Feb. 9 **Litho.**

B675 SP369 100pf + 50pf Table tennis 1.65 1.65
B676 SP369 140pf + 60pf Gymnastics 2.15 2.15

Surtax for the Natl. Sports Promotion Foundation.

IPHLA Philatelic Literature Exhibition, Frankfurt, Apr. 19-23
SP370

1989, Apr. 20 **Litho.**

B677 SP370 100 + 50pf multi 1.65 1.65

Surtax benefited the Foundation for the Promotion of Philately and Postal History.

Circus
SP371

1989, Apr. 20

B678 SP371 60 +30pf Elephants 1.00 1.00
B679 SP371 70 + 30pf Bareback rider 1.10 1.10
B680 SP371 80 + 35pf Clown 1.30 1.30
B681 SP371 100 +50pf Caravans, big top 1.65 1.65

Surtax for natl. youth welfare organizations.

Mounted Courier of Thurn and Taxis, 18th Cent. — SP372

History of mail carrying: No. B683, Hamburg postal service messenger, 1808. No. B684, Bavarian mail coach, c. 1900.

1989, Oct. 12 **Litho.**

B682 SP372 60 + 30pf multi 98 98
B683 SP372 80 + 35pf multi 1.25 1.25
B684 SP372 100 + 50pf multi 1.65 1.65

Surtax for the benefit of Free Welfare Work.

Christmas
SP373

Wood carvings by Veit Stoss in St. Lawrence's Church, Nuremburg, 1517-18.

1989, Nov. 16 **Litho.**

B685 SP373 60 + 30pf Angel 92 92
B686 SP373 100 +50pf Adoration of the Kings 1.55 1.55

Surtax for benefit of the Federal Working Assoc. of Free Welfare Work.

Popular Sports
SP374

1990, Feb. 15 **Litho.**

B687 SP374 100 + 50pf Handball 1.80 1.80
B688 SP374 140 + 60pf Physical fitness 2.40 2.40

Surtax for the Natl. Sports Promotion Foundation.

Max and Moritz, by Wilhelm Busch, 125th Anniv.
SP375

1990, Apr. 19 **Litho.**

B689 SP375 60 + 30pf Widow Bolte 1.05 1.05
B690 SP375 70 + 30pf Max 1.20 1.20
B691 SP375 80 + 35pf Max and Moritz 1.35 1.35
B692 SP375 100 + 50pf Max and Moritz, diff. 1.75 1.75

Surcharge for the German Youth Stamp Foundation.

Dusseldorf '90 — SP376

Illustration reduced.

1990, June 21 **Litho.**

B693 Sheet of 6 10.80 10.80
a. SP376 100pf + 50pf multi 1.80 1.80

Surtax for the Foundation for Promotion of Philately and Postal History. 10th Intl. Philatelic Exhibition of Youth and 11th Natl. Philatelic Exhibition of Youth.

Post and Telecommunications — SP377

Designs: 60pf+30pf, Postal vehicle, 1900. 80pf+35pf, Telephone exchange, 1890. 100pf+50pf, Post office, 1900.

1990, Sept. 27 **Litho.** ***Perf. 13½x14***

B694 SP377 60pf + 30pf multi 1.05 1.05
B695 SP377 80pf + 35pf multi 1.35 1.35
B696 SP377 100pf + 50pf multi 1.75 1.75

Surtax for welfare organizations.

Christmas
SP378

1990, Nov. 6 **Litho.** ***Perf. 14***

B697 SP378 50pf + 20pf shown 85 85
B698 SP378 60pf + 30pf Smoking manikin 1.05 1.05
B699 SP378 70pf + 30pf Nutcracker 1.20 1.20
B700 SP378 100pf + 50pf Angel, diff. 1.75 1.75

Surtax for welfare organizations.

Sports — SP379

1991, Feb. 14 **Litho.** ***Perf. 14***

B701 SP379 70 +30pf Weight lifting 1.25 1.25
B702 SP379 100 +50pf Cycling 1.85 1.85
B703 SP379 140 +60pf Basketball 2.50 2.50
B704 SP379 170 +80pf Wrestling 3.10 3.10

Surtax for the Foundation for the Promotion of Sports.

Endangered Butterflies
SP380

No. B705, Alpen gelbling, alpine sulphur. No. B706, Grosser eisvogel, Viceroy. No. B707, Grosser schillerfalter, purple emperor. No. B708, Blauschillernder beuerfalter, bluish copper. No. B709, Schwalben-schwanz, swallowtail. No. B710, Alpen apollo, alpine apollo. No. B711, Hochmoor gelbling, moor sulphur. No. B712, Grosser feuerfalter, large copper.

1991, Apr. 9 **Litho.** ***Perf. 13½***

B705 SP380 30 +15pf multi 50 50
B706 SP380 50 +25pf multi 90 90
B707 SP380 60 +30pf multi 1.05 1.05
B708 SP380 70 +30pf multi 1.15 1.15
B709 SP380 80 +35pf multi 1.35 1.35
B710 SP380 90 +45pf multi 1.55 1.55
B711 SP380 100 +50pf multi 1.70 1.70
B712 SP380 140 +60pf multi 2.30 2.30
Nos. B705-B712 (8) 10.50 10.50

Surtax for German Youth Stamp Foundation.
See Nos. B728-B732.

Souvenir Sheet

Otto Lilienthal's First Glider Flight, Cent. — SP381

1991, July 9 Litho. *Perf. 14*
B713 SP381 100pf +50pf multi 1.70 1.70

Surtax benefited Foundation of Philately and Postal History.

Post Offices — SP382

Designs: 30pf+15pf, Bethel. 60pf+30pf, Budingen postal station. 70pf+30pf, Stralsund. 80pf+35pf, Lauscha. 100pf+50pf, Bonn. 140pf+60pf, Weilburg.

1991, Oct. 10 Litho. *Perf. 14*
B714 SP382 30pf +15pf multi 55 28
B715 SP382 60pf +30pf multi 1.10 55
B716 SP382 70pf +30pf multi 1.20 60
B717 SP382 80pf +35pf multi 1.40 70
B718 SP382 100pf +50pf multi 1.80 90
B719 SP382 140pf +60pf multi 2.40 1.20
Nos. B714-B719 (6) 8.45 4.23

Christmas SP383

Paintings by Martin Schongauer (c. 1450-1491): 60pf+30pf, Angel of the Annunciation. 70pf+30pf, The Annunciation. 80pf+35pf, Angel. 100pf+50pf, Nativity.

1991, Nov. 5 Litho. *Perf. 14*
B720 SP383 60pf +30pf multi 1.10 1.10
B721 SP383 70pf +30pf multi 1.20 1.20
B722 SP383 80pf +35pf multi 1.40 1.40
B723 SP383 100pf +50pf multi 1.80 1.80

Surtax for Federal Working Association of Free Welfare Work.

Olympic Sports — SP384

1992, Feb. 6 Litho. *Perf. 14*
B724 SP384 60pf +30pf Women's fencing 1.05 1.05
B725 SP384 80pf +40pf Rowing coxed eights 1.45 1.45
B726 SP384 100pf +50pf Dressage 1.80 1.80
B727 SP384 170pf +80pf Men's slalom skiing 3.00 3.00

Endangered Butterfly Type of 1991

Designs: 60pf+30pf, Purpurbar. 70pf+30pf, Labkraut schwarmer. 80pf+40pf, Silbermonch. 100pf+50pf, Schwarzer bar. 170pf+80pf, Rauschbeeren-fleckenspanner.

1992, Apr. 9 Litho. *Perf. 13½*
B728 SP380 60pf +30pf multi 1.05 1.05
B729 SP380 70pf +30pf multi 1.20 1.20
B730 SP380 80pf +40pf multi 1.45 1.45
B731 SP380 100pf +50pf multi 1.80 1.80
B732 SP380 170pf +80pf multi 3.00 3.00
Nos. B728-B732 (5) 8.50 8.50

Surtax for German Youth Stamp Foundation.

Preservation of Tropical Rain Forests — SP385

1992, June 11 Litho. *Perf. 13*
B733 SP385 100pf +50pf multi 1.80 1.80

Antique Clocks A386

Antique clocks: 60pf+30pf, Turret, c. 1400. 70pf+30pf, Astronomical geographical mantelpiece, 1738. 80pf+40pf, Fluted, c. 1790. 100pf+50pf, Figurine, c. 1580. 170pf+80pf, Table, c. 1550.

1992, Oct. 15 Litho. *Perf. 14*
B734 SP386 60pf +30pf multi 1.10 1.10
B735 SP386 70pf +30pf multi 1.25 1.25
B736 SP386 80pf +40pf multi 1.50 1.50
B737 SP386 100pf +50pf multi 1.85 1.85
B738 SP386 170pf +80pf multi 3.00 3.00
Nos. B734-B738 (5) 8.70 8.70

Surtax for welfare organizations.

Christmas SP387

Carvings from Church of St. Anne, Annaberg-Buchholz, by Franz Maidburg: 60pf + 30pf, Adoration of the Magi. 100pf + 50pf, The Nativity.

1992, Nov. 5
B739 SP387 60pf +30pf multi 1.15 1.15
B740 SP387 100pf +50pf multi 1.90 1.90

Surtax for benefit of free welfare work.

Sports — SP388

Designs: 60pf+30pf, Olympic ski jump, Garmisch-Partenkirchen. 80pf+40pf, Olympic Park, Munich. 100pf+50pf, Olympic Stadium, Berlin. 170pf+80pf, Olympic harbor, Kiel.

1993, Feb. 11 Litho. *Perf. 13½*
B741 SP388 60pf +30pf multi 1.05 1.05
B742 SP388 80pf +40pf multi 1.40 1.40
B743 SP388 100pf +50pf multi 1.75 1.75
B744 SP388 170pf +80pf multi 2.95 2.95

Surtax for Natl. Sports Promotion Foundation.

Beetles — SP389

Designs: No. B745, Alpenbock (Alpine sawyer). No. B746, Rosenkafer (rose chafer). No. B747, Hirschkafer (stag beetle). No. B748, Sandlaufkafer (tiger beetle). 200pf + 50pf, Maikafer (cockchafer).

1993, Apr. 15 Litho. *Perf. 14*
B745 SP389 80pf +40pf multi 1.45 1.45
B746 SP389 80pf +40pf multi 1.45 1.45
B747 SP389 100pf +50pf multi 1.85 1.85
B748 SP389 100pf +50pf multi 1.85 1.85
B749 SP389 200pf +50pf multi 3.00 3.00
Nos. B745-B749 (5) 9.60 9.60

Surtax for German Youth Stamp Foundation.

Stamp Day — SP390

1993, Sept. 16 Litho. *Perf. 13½x14*
B750 SP390 100pf +50pf multi 1.75 1.75

Surtax for the Foundation for Promotion of Philately and Postal History.

Traditional Costumes SP391

Costumes from: No. B751, Rugen, Mecklenburg, Western Pomerania. No. B752, Fohr, Schleswig-Holstein. No. B753, Schwalm, Hesse. No. B754, Oberndorf, Bavaria. 200pf + 40pf, Ernstroda, Thuringia.

1993, Oct. 14 *Perf. 14*
B751 SP391 80pf +40pf multi 1.40 1.40
B752 SP391 80pf +40pf multi 1.40 1.40
B753 SP391 100pf +50pf multi 1.75 1.75
B754 SP391 100pf +50pf multi 1.75 1.75
B755 SP391 200pf +40pf multi 2.75 2.75
Nos. B751-B755 (5) 9.05 9.05

Surtax for welfare organizations.

Christmas SP392

Wings of high altar in choir of Blaubeuren Monastery: 80pf+40pf, Adoraration of Magi. 100pf+50pf, Nativity.

1993, Nov. 10 Litho. *Perf. 14*
B756 SP392 80pf +40pf multi 1.40 1.40
B757 SP392 100pf +50pf multi 1.75 1.75

Surtax for welfare organizations.

Sports — SP393

Designs: 80pf+40pf, Figure skating. No. B759, Olympic Flame. No. B760, Soccer ball, World Cup Trophy. 200pf+80pf, Skiier.

1994, Feb. 10 Litho. *Perf. 14x13½*
B758 SP393 80pf +40pf multi 1.25 1.25
B759 SP393 100pf +50pf multi 1.60 1.60
B760 SP393 100pf +50pf multi 1.60 1.60
B761 SP393 200pf +80pf multi 3.00 3.00

1994 Winter Olympics, Lillehammer (#B758). Intl. Olympic Committee, Cent. (#B759). 1994 World Cup Soccer Championships, US (#B760). 1994 Paralympics, Lillehammer (#B761).

AIR POST STAMPS

Issues of the Republic

Post Horn with Wings — AP1

Biplane — AP2

Perf. 15x14½

1919, Nov. 10 Typo. Unwmk.
C1 AP1 10pf orange 15 *1.75*
C2 AP2 40pf dark green 15 *1.75*
a. Imperf. 675.00
Set value 20
Set, never hinged 75

No. C2a is ungummed.

Carrier Pigeon — AP3

German Eagle — AP4

1922-23 Wmk. 126 *Perf. 14, 14½*
Size: 19x23mm
C3 AP3 25(pf) chocolate 30 *10.00*
C4 AP3 40(pf) orange 30 *14.00*
C5 AP3 50(pf) violet 18 *5.00*
C6 AP3 60(pf) carmine 40 *8.25*
C7 AP3 80(pf) blue grn 40 *10.00*

Perf. 13x13½
Size: 22x28mm
C8 AP3 1m dk grn & pale grn 15 *1.65*
C9 AP3 2m lake & gray 15 *1.65*
C10 AP3 3m dk blue & gray 15 *1.65*
C11 AP3 5m red org & yel 15 *1.65*
C12 AP3 10m vio & rose ('23) 15 *5.25*
C13 AP3 25m brn & yel ('23) 15 *4.00*
C14 AP3 100m ol grn & rose ('23) 15 *4.00*
Nos. C3-C14 (12) 2.63
Set, never hinged 5.75

1923
C15 AP3 5m vermilion 15 *24.00*
C16 AP3 10m violet 15 *7.25*
C17 AP3 25m dark brown 15 *6.00*
C18 AP3 100m olive grn 15 *5.00*

C19 AP3 200m deep blue 15 25.00
a. Imperf. 72.50
Set value 56
Set, never hinged 1.75

Issued: #C15-C18, June 1. #C19, July 25.
Note following #160 applies to #C1-C19.

1924, Jan. 11 *Perf. 14*
Size: 19x23mm

C20 AP3	5(pf)	yellow grn	1.25	1.10
C21 AP3	10(pf)	carmine	1.25	1.90
C22 AP3	20(pf)	violet blue	3.50	5.25
C23 AP3	50(pf)	orange	12.50	14.00
C24 AP3	100(pf)	dull violet	32.50	42.50
C25 AP3	200(pf)	grnsh blue	55.00	67.50
C26 AP3	300(pf)	gray	87.50	110.00
a.		Imperf.	1,900.	
		Nos. C20-C26 (7)	193.50	242.25
		Set, never hinged	1,000.	

1926-27

C27 AP4	5pf	green	70	45
C28 AP4	10pf	rose red	70	45
b.		Tête bêche pair	120.00	140.00
d.		Bklt. pane 10 (6 No. C28 + 4 No. C29)	110.00	
C29 AP4	15pf	lilac rose ('27)	1.50	95
a.		Double impression	1,250.	
C30 AP4	20pf	dull blue	1.50	95
a.		Tête bêche pair	120.00	140.00
b.		Bklt. pane 4 (4 No. C30 + 6 labels)	110.00	
c.		Bklt. pane 5 (5 No. C30 + 5 labels)	300.00	
C31 AP4	50pf	brown org	21.00	3.50
C32 AP4	1m	black & salmon	16.00	4.75
C33 AP4	2m	black & blue	16.00	17.50
C34 AP4	3m	black & ol grn	55.00	55.00
		Nos. C27-C34 (8)	112.40	83.55
		Set, never hinged	850.00	

"Graf Zeppelin" Crossing Ocean — AP5

1928-31 **Photo.**

C35 AP5	1m	carmine ('31)	22.50	25.00
C36 AP5	2m	ultra	35.00	35.00
C37 AP5	4m	black brown	22.50	25.00
		Set, never hinged	325.00	

Issued: 2m, 4m, Sept. 20. 1m, May 8.
For overprints see Nos. C40-C45.

AP6

1930, Apr. 19 **Wmk. 126**

C38 AP6	2m	ultra	165.00	225.00
C39 AP6	4m	black brown	225.00	225.00
		Set, never hinged	1,600.	

First flight of Graf Zeppelin to South America. Nos. C38-C39 exist with watermark vertical or horizontal.
Counterfeits exist of Nos. C38-C45.

Nos. C35-C37 Overprinted in Brown
POLAR-
FAHRT
1931

1931, July 15

C40 AP5	1m	carmine	87.50	60.00
C41 AP5	2m	ultra	140.00	150.00
C42 AP5	4m	black brown	300.00	450.00
		Set, never hinged	2,400.	

Polar flight of Graf Zeppelin.

Nos. C35-C37 Overprinted
Chicagofahrt
Weltausstellung
1933

1933, Sept. 25

C43 AP5	1m	carmine	350.00	225.00
C44 AP5	2m	ultra	32.50	115.00
C45 AP5	4m	black brown	32.50	115.00
		Set, never hinged	2,100.	

Graf Zeppelin flight to Century of Progress International Exhibition, Chicago.

Swastika Sun, Globe and Eagle — AP7

Otto Lilienthal — AP8

Design: 3m, Count Ferdinand von Zeppelin.

Perf. 14, 13½x13
1934, Jan. 21 **Typo.** **Wmk. 237**

C46 AP7	5(pf)	brt green	35	24
C47 AP7	10(pf)	brt carmine	35	35
C48 AP7	15(pf)	ultra	35	35
C49 AP7	20(pf)	dull blue	70	65
C50 AP7	25(pf)	brown	70	65
C51 AP7	40(pf)	red violet	70	45
C52 AP7	50(pf)	dk green	2.25	45
C53 AP7	80(pf)	orange yel	1.65	1.90
C54 AP7	100(pf)	black	2.25	1.40
C55 AP8	2m	green & blk	12.50	12.00
C56 AP8	3m	blue & blk	40.00	25.00
		Nos. C46-C56 (11)	61.80	43.44
		Set, never hinged	325.00	

"Hindenburg" — AP10

Perf. 14, 14½x14
1936, Mar. 16 **Engr.**

C57 AP10	50pf	dark blue	4.50	40
C58 AP10	75pf	dull green	5.25	40
		Set, never hinged	16.00	

Count Zeppelin — AP11

Airship Gondola — AP12

1938, July 5 **Unwmk.** *Perf. 13½*

C59 AP11	25pf	dull blue	2.50	55
C60 AP12	50pf	green	3.00	35
		Set, never hinged	25.00	

Count Ferdinand von Zeppelin (1838-1917), airship inventor and builder.

Catalogue values for unused stamps in this section, from this point to the end of the section, are for Never Hinged items.

Federal Republic

Lufthansa Emblem — AP13

Perf. 13½x13
1955, Mar. 31 **Litho.** **Wmk. 295**

C61 AP13	5pf	lilac rose & blk	60	38
C62 AP13	10pf	green & blk	85	60
C63 AP13	15pf	blue & blk	5.00	3.75
C64 AP13	20pf	red & blk	17.00	5.50

Re-opening of German air service, Apr. 1.

MILITARY AIR POST STAMP

Junkers 52 Transport — MAP1

1942 **Unwmk.** **Typo.** *Perf. 13½*

MC1 MAP1	ultramarine	15	25
	Never hinged	25	
a.	Rouletted	15	50
a.	Never hinged	40	

MILITARY PARCEL POST STAMPS

Nazi Emblem — MPP1

1942 **Unwmk.** **Typo.** *Perf. 13½*
Size: 28x23mm

MQ1 MPP1	red brown	15	30
	Never hinged	25	
a.	Rouletted	15	50
a.	Never hinged	30	

1944 **Size: 22½x18mm** *Perf. 14*

MQ2 MPP1	bright green	75	40.00
	Never hinged	1.50	

See note "Postally Used vs. CTO" after #160.

No. 520 Overprinted in Black
FELDPOST
2kg

1944 **Engr.**

MQ3 A115	on 40pf brt red vio	90	60.00
	Never hinged	1.50	

See note after No. O13.

OFFICIAL STAMPS

Issues of the Republic

In 1920 the Official Stamps of Bavaria and Wurttemberg then current were overprinted "Deutsches Reich" and made available for official use in all parts of Germany. They were, however, used almost exclusively in the two states where they originated and we have listed them among the issues of those states.

O1

O2

O3

O4

O5

O6

O7

O8

O9

O10

O11

O12

1920-21 **Typo.** **Wmk. 125** *Perf. 14*

O1	O1	5pf	deep green	80	3.25
O2	O2	10pf	car rose	15	15
O3	O2	10pf	orange ('21)	50	180.00
O4	O3	15pf	violet brn	15	15
a.			Imperf. ('21)		65.00
O5	O4	20pf	deep ultra	15	15
O6	O5	30pf	org, *buff*	15	15
O7	O6	40pf	carmine	15	15
O8	O7	50pf	violet, *buff*	15	15
O9	O8	60pf	red brown ('21)	15	25
O10	O9	1m	red, *buff*	15	15
O11	O10	1.25m	dk bl, *yel*	15	20
O12	O11	2m	dark blue	4.25	85
O13	O12	5m	brown, *yel*	15	15
			Nos. O1-O13 (13)	7.05	
			Set, never hinged	25.00	

The value of No. O4a is for a copy postmarked at Bautzen.
See No. O15. For surcharges see Nos. O29-O33, O35-O36, O38.

Postally Used vs. CTO
Values quoted for canceled copies of Nos. O1-O46) are for postally used stamps. See note after No. 160.

O13

O14

O15

Wmk. 126, 125 (#O16-O17)
1922-23

O14	O13	75pf	dark blue	15	2.00
O15	O11	2m	dark blue	15	15
a.			Imperf.	125.00	
O16	O14	3m	brown, *rose*	15	15
O17	O15	10m	dk grn, *rose*	15	15
O18	O15	10m	dk grn, *rose*	15	6.50
O19	O15	20m	dk bl, *rose*	15	15
O20	O15	50m	vio, *rose*	15	15
O21	O15	100m	rose red, *rose*	15	15
			Set value	68	
			Set, never hinged	2.75	

Issue date: #O18-O21, 1923. Nos. O20-O21 exist imperf.
For surcharges see Nos. O34, O37, O39.

Regular Issue of 1923 Overprinted

a 

1923

O22 A34 20m red lilac 15 5.00
O23 A34 30m olive grn 15 18.00
O24 A29 40m green 15 2.25
O25 A35 200m car rose 15 32
O26 A35 300m green 15 32
O27 A35 400m dk brn 15 32
O28 A35 500m red orange 15 32
Set value 50
Set, never hinged 2.00

Official Stamps of 1920-23 Surcharged with New Values

Abbreviations:
Th=(Tausend) Thousand
Mil=(Million) Million
Mlrd=(Milliarde) Billion

1923 Wmk. 125

O29 O12 5th m on 5m 15 1.65
a. Inverted surcharge 52.50
O30 O5 20th m on 30pf 15 1.25
a. Inverted surcharge 62.50
b. Imperf. 62.50
O31 O3 100th m on 15pf 15 1.65
a. Imperf. 62.50
b. Inverted surcharge 52.50
O32 O2 250th m on 10pf car rose 15 1.25
a. Double surcharge 52.50
O33 O5 800th m on 30pf 55 150.00

Official Stamps and Types of 1920-23 Surcharged with New Values
Wmk. 126

O34 O15 75th m on 50m 15 1.65
a. Inverted surcharge 52.50
O35 O3 400th m on 15pf brn 15 20.00
O36 O5 800th m on 30pf org, *buff* 15 1.65
O37 O13 1 mil m on 75pf 15 20.00
O38 O2 2 mil m on 10pf car rose 15 1.65
a. Imperf. 70.00
O39 O15 5 mil m on 100m 15 3.25
Set value 1.45
Set, never hinged 2.75

The 10, 15 and 30 pfennig are not known with this watermark and without surcharge.

Nos. 290-291, 295-299 Overprinted Type "a"

1923

O40 A39 100 mil m 15 100.00
O41 A39 200 mil m 15 85.00
O42 A39a 2 mlrd m 15 72.50
O43 A39a 5 mlrd m 15 57.50
O44 A39a 10 mlrd m 3.00 85.00
O45 A39a 20 mlrd m 2.00 100.00
O46 A39a 50 mlrd m 2.00 150.00
Nos. O40-O46 (7) 7.60
Set, never hinged 28.00

Same Overprint on Nos, 323-328, Values in Rentenpfennig

1923

O47 A40 3pf brown 22 15
O48 A40 5pf dk green 22 15
a. Inverted overprint 125.00 110.00
O49 A40 10pf carmine 38 15
a. Inverted overprint 100.00 110.00
b. Imperf. 52.50
O50 A40 20pf dp ultra 75 15
O51 A40 50pf orange 75 48
O52 A40 100pf brown vio 3.50 4.50
Nos. O47-O52 (6) 5.82 5.58
Set, never hinged 22.50

Same Overprint On Issues of 1924

1924

O53 A41 3pf lt brown 55 18
a. Inverted overprint 60.00 160.00
O54 A41 5pf lt green 55 15
a. Imperf. 62.50
b. Inverted overprint 110.00
O55 A41 10pf vermilion 55 15
O56 A41 20pf blue 55 15
O57 A41 30pf rose lilac 1.10 18
O58 A41 40pf olive green 1.10 18
O59 A41 50pf orange 5.00 1.25
O60 A47 60pf red brown 2.25 2.00
O61 A47 80pf slate 12.00 24.00
Nos. O53-O61 (9) 23.65 28.24
Set, never hinged 50.00

O16

Swastika — O17

1927-33 *Perf. 14*

O62 O16 3pf bister 32 15
O63 O16 4pf lt bl ('31) 15 15
O64 O16 4pf blue ('33) 1.25 2.00
O65 O16 5pf green 15 15
O66 O16 6pf pale ol grn ('32) 15 15
O67 O16 8pf dk grn 15 15
O68 O16 10pf carmine 5.00 3.00
O69 O16 10pf ver ('29) 8.50 9.25
O70 O16 10pf red vio ('30) 25 15
a. Imperf. 100.00
O71 O16 10pf choc ('33) 1.10 1.65
O72 O16 12pf org ('32) 20 15
O73 O16 15pf vermilion 1.00 20
O74 O16 15pf car ('29) 32 15
O75 O16 20pf Prus grn 2.00 65
O76 O16 20pf gray ('30) 50 32
O77 O16 30pf olive grn 55 15
O78 O16 40pf violet 55 20
O79 O16 60pf red brn ('28) 85 40
Nos. O62-O79 (18) 22.99 19.02
Set, never hinged 120.00

1934, Jan. 18 Wmk. 237

O80 O17 3pf bister 15 15
O81 O17 4pf dull blue 15 15
O82 O17 5pf brt green 15 15
O83 O17 6pf dk green 15 15
a. Imperf. 90.00
O84 O17 8pf vermilion 40 15
O85 O17 10pf chocolate 32 15
O86 O17 12pf brt carmine 15 15
a. Unwmkd. 1.50 2.00
O87 O17 15pf claret 1.00 1.40
O88 O17 20pf light blue 20 24
O89 O17 30pf olive grn 32 24
O90 O17 40pf red violet 32 24
O91 O17 50pf orange yel 50 28
Nos. O80-O91 (12) 4.21
Set value 3.00
Set, never hinged 8.00

O83 exists imperf.

1942 Unwmk. *Perf. 14*

O92 O17 3pf bister brn 15 15
O93 O17 4pf dull blue 15 15
O94 O17 5pf deep olive 15 15
O95 O17 6pf deep violet 15 15
O96 O17 8pf vermilion 15 32
O97 O17 10pf chocolate 15 25
O98 O17 12pf rose car 22 45
a. Wmk. 237 1.10 2.75
O99 O17 15pf brown car 1.65 2.75
O100 O17 20pf light blue 15 52
O101 O17 30pf olive grn 15 52
O102 O17 40pf red violet 15 52
O103 O17 50pf dk green 1.10 2.75
Nos. O92-O103 (12) 4.32 8.68
Set, never hinged 9.00

LOCAL OFFICIAL STAMPS

For Use in Prussia

("Nr. 21" refers to the district of Prussia) — LO1

1903 Unwmk. Typo. *Perf. 14, 14½*

OL1 LO1 2pf slate 90 3.50
OL2 LO1 3pf bister brn 90 3.50
OL3 LO1 5pf green 22 22
OL4 LO1 10pf carmine 22 15
OL5 LO1 20pf ultra 22 22
OL6 LO1 25pf org & blk, *yel* 22 22
OL7 LO1 40pf lake & blk 22 1.00
OL8 LO1 50pf pur & blk, *sal* 32 1.00
Nos. OL1-OL8 (8) 3.22 9.81
Set, never hinged 11.00

LO2

LO3

LO4

LO5

LO6

LO7

LO8

1920 Typo. Wmk. 125 *Perf. 14*

OL9 LO2 5pf green 22 1.50
OL10 LO3 10pf carmine 80 75
OL11 LO4 15pf vio brn 18 35
OL12 LO5 20pf dp ultra 18 35
OL13 LO6 30pf org, *buff* 16 28
OL14 LO7 50pf brn lil, *buff* 30 35
OL15 LO8 1m red, *buff* 6.00 2.25
Nos. OL9-OL15 (7) 7.84 5.83
Set, never hinged 35.00

For Use in Baden

LO9

1905 Unwmk. Typo. *Perf. 14, 14½*

OL16 LO9 2pf gray blue 37.50 32.50
OL17 LO9 3pf brown 3.50 3.00
OL18 LO9 5pf green 1.75 2.25
OL19 LO9 10pf rose 38 32
OL20 LO9 20pf blue 1.00 1.00
OL21 LO9 25pf org & blk, *yel* 22.50 22.50
Nos. OL16-OL21 (6) 66.63 61.57
Set, never hinged 750.00

NEWSPAPER STAMPS

Newsboy and Globe — N1

Wmk. Swastikas (237)

1939, Nov. 1 Photo. *Perf. 14*

P1 N1 5pf green 30 50
P2 N1 10pf red brown 30 50
Set, never hinged 1.25

FRANCHISE STAMPS

For use by the National Socialist German Workers' Party

Party Emblem — F1

1938 Typo. Wmk. 237 *Perf. 14*

S1 F1 1pf black 55 75
S2 F1 3pf bister 55 52
S3 F1 4pf dull blue 90 52
S4 F1 5pf brt green 55 52
S5 F1 6pf dk green 55 52
S6 F1 8pf vermilion 2.75 60
S7 F1 12pf brt car 3.50 52
S8 F1 16pf gray 90 4.00
S9 F1 24pf citron 1.65 2.50
S10 F1 30pf olive grn 90 2.00
S11 F1 40pf red violet 90 3.25
Nos. S1-S11 (11) 13.70 15.70
Set, never hinged 35.00

1942 Unwmk.

S12 F1 1pf gray blk 38 1.00
S13 F1 3pf bister brn 15 24
S14 F1 4pf dk gray blue 15 30
S15 F1 5pf gray green 15 60
S16 F1 6pf violet 15 30
S17 F1 8pf deep orange 15 24
a. Imperf. 100.00
S18 F1 12pf carmine 18 24
S19 F1 16pf blue green 2.00 3.00
S20 F1 24pf yellow brn 25 1.10
S21 F1 30pf dp olive grn 25 1.25
S22 F1 40pf light rose vio 25 1.10
Nos. S12-S22 (11) 4.06 9.33
Set, never hinged 7.50

OCCUPATION STAMPS

100 Centimes = 1 Franc
100 Pfennig = 1 Mark

Issued under Belgian Occupation

Belgian Stamps of 1915-20 Overprinted

ALLEMAGNE
DUITSCHLAND

Perf. 11½, 14, 14½

1919-21 Unwmk.

1N1 A46 1c orange 40 40
1N2 A46 2c chocolate 40 40
1N3 A46 3c gray blk ('21) 60 1.50
1N4 A46 5c green 80 1.00
1N5 A46 10c carmine 2.25 2.00
1N6 A46 15c purple 1.00 1.00
1N7 A46 20c red violet 1.25 1.25
1N8 A46 25c blue 1.25 1.50
1N9 A54 25c dp blue ('21) 5.00 5.00

Overprinted

ALLEMAGNE
DUITSCHLAND

1N10 A47 35c brn org & blk 1.40 1.25
1N11 A48 40c green & blk 1.50 2.00
1N12 A49 50c car rose & blk 8.00 10.00
1N13 A56 65c cl & blk ('21) 4.25 8.50
1N14 A50 1fr violet 24.00 24.00
1N15 A51 2fr slate 42.50 45.00
1N16 A52 5fr deep blue 9.50 12.00
1N17 A53 10fr brown 60.00 80.00
Nos. 1N1-1N17 (17) 164.10 196.80

Belgian Stamps of 1915 Surcharged

EUPEN & MALMÉDY 5 PF.
Nos. 1N18-1N22

EUPEN & MALMÉDY 1 Mk 25
Nos. 1N23-1N24

Black Surcharge

1920

1N18 A46 5pf on 5c green 42 75
1N19 A46 10pf on 10c carmine 50 75
1N20 A46 15pf on 15c purple 75 90
1N21 A46 20pf on 20c red vio 1.00 1.25
1N22 A46 30pf on 25c blue 1.25 1.50

Red Surcharge

1N23 A49 75pf on 50c car rose & blk 17.50 21.00
1N24 A50 1m25pf on 1fr violet 20.00 22.50
Nos. 1N18-1N24 (7) 41.42 48.65

EUPEN ISSUE

Belgian Stamps of 1915-20 Overprinted:

Eupen
Nos. 1N25-1N36

Eupen
Nos. 1N37-1N41

1920-21 *Perf. 11½, 14, 14½*

1N25 A46 1c orange 42 42
1N26 A46 2c chocolate 42 42
1N27 A46 3c gray blk ('21) 60 1.65
1N28 A46 5c green 70 95
1N29 A46 10c carmine 1.10 1.25
1N30 A46 15c purple 1.25 1.40
1N31 A46 20c red violet 1.25 1.65

1N32	A46	25c blue	1.65	1.90
1N33	A54	25c dp blue ('21)	6.75	9.25
1N34	A47	35c brn org & blk	2.00	2.00
1N35	A48	40c green & blk	2.25	2.00
1N36	A49	50c car rose & blk	6.75	7.75
1N37	A56	65c cl & blk ('21)	4.50	9.25
1N38	A50	1fr violet	20.00	19.00
1N39	A51	2fr slate	37.50	32.50
1N40	A52	5fr deep blue	14.00	15.00
1N41	A53	10fr brown	55.00	57.50
		Nos. 1N25-1N41 (17)	156.14	163.89

MALMEDY ISSUE

Belgian Stamps of 1915-20 Overprinted:

Malmédy — Nos. 1N42-1N50

Malmédy — Nos. 1N51-1N53

Malmédy — Nos. 1N54-1N58

1920-21

1N42	A46	1c orange	40	40
1N43	A46	2c chocolate	40	40
1N44	A46	3c gray blk ('21)	60	1.50
1N45	A46	5c green	65	1.00
1N46	A46	10c carmine	1.00	1.25
1N47	A46	15c purple	1.10	1.25
1N48	A46	20c red violet	1.25	1.50
1N49	A46	25c blue	1.50	1.75
1N50	A54	25c dp blue ('21)	6.50	9.25
1N51	A47	35c brn org & blk	2.00	2.00
1N52	A48	40c grn & blk	2.25	2.00
1N53	A49	50c car rose & blk	7.00	6.75
1N54	A56	65c cl & blk ('21)	4.25	8.50
1N55	A50	1fr violet	21.00	18.00
1N56	A51	2fr slate	35.00	30.00
1N57	A52	5fr deep blue	13.00	14.00
1N58	A53	10fr brown	52.50	55.50
		Nos. 1N42-1N58 (17)	150.40	155.05

OCCUPATION POSTAGE DUE STAMPS

Belgian Postage Due Stamps of 1919-20, Overprinted **Eupen**

1920 **Unwmk.** *Perf. 14½*

1NJ1	D3	5c green	1.10	1.50
1NJ2	D3	10c carmine	2.25	2.25
1NJ3	D3	20c gray green	3.75	3.75
1NJ4	D3	30c bright blue	4.50	4.50
1NJ5	D3	50c gray	11.00	16.00
		Nos. 1NJ1-1NJ5 (5)	22.60	28.00

Belgian Postage Due Stamps of 1919-20, Overprinted **Malmédy**

1NJ6	D3	5c green	1.25	1.25
1NJ7	D3	10c carmine	2.25	1.75
a.		Inverted overprint	35.00	
1NJ8	D3	20c gray green	9.25	10.50
1NJ9	D3	30c bright blue	5.75	6.00
1NJ10	D3	50c gray	9.75	10.50
		Nos. 1NJ6-1NJ10 (5)	28.25	30.00

A. M. G. ISSUE

Issued jointly by the Allied Military Government of the US and Great Britain, for civilian use in areas under Allied occupation.

OS1

Type I. Thick paper, white gum.
Type II. Medium paper, yellow gum.
Type III. Medium paper, white gum.

Perf. 11, 11½ and Compound

1945-46 **Litho.** **Unwmk.**

Type III, Brunswick Printing

Size: 19-19½x22-22½mm

3N1	OS1	1pf slate gray	15	20
3N2	OS1	3pf dull lilac	15	15
3N3	OS1	4pf lt gray	15	15
3N4	OS1	5pf emerald	15	15
3N5	OS1	6pf yellow	15	15
3N6	OS1	8pf orange	60	1.75
3N7	OS1	10pf yel brn	15	15
3N8	OS1	12pf rose vio	15	15
3N9	OS1	15pf rose car	15	15
3N10	OS1	16pf dp Prus grn	15	32
3N11	OS1	20pf blue	15	15
3N12	OS1	24pf chocolate	15	42
3N13	OS1	25pf brt ultra	15	1.40

Size: 21½x25mm

3N14	OS1	30pf olive	18	50
3N15	OS1	40pf dp mag	15	15
3N16	OS1	42pf green	15	15
3N17	OS1	50pf slate grn	15	25
3N18	OS1	60pf vio brn	15	35
3N19	OS1	80pf bl blk	15.00	25.00

Size: 25x29½mm

3N20	OS1	1m dk ol grn ('46)	1.75	4.50
		Nos. 3N1-3N20 (20)	19.93	36.19

Most of Nos. 3N1-3N20 exist imperforate and part-perforate.

Type I, Washington Printing

Size: 19-19½x22-22½mm

Perf. 11

3N2a	OS1	3pf lilac	15	15
3N3a	OS1	4pf light gray	15	15
3N4a	OS1	5pf emerald	15	15
3N5a	OS1	6pf yellow	15	15
3N6a	OS1	8pf deep orange	15	15
3N7a	OS1	10pf brown	15	15
3N8a	OS1	12pf rose vio	15	15
3N9a	OS1	15pf cerise	15	15
3N13a	OS1	25pf bright ultra	15	15
		Set value	45	70

Type II, London Printing

Size: 19-19½x22-22½mm

Photo.

Perf. 14, 14½ and Compound

3N2b	OS1	3pf lilac	15	15
3N3b	OS1	4pf light gray	15	15
3N4b	OS1	5pf deep emerald	30	30
3N5b	OS1	6pf orange yellow	15	15
3N6b	OS1	8pf dark orange	30	38
3N8b	OS1	12pf rose violet	15	15
		Set value	80	1.00

ISSUED UNDER FRENCH OCCUPATION

Coats of Arms

Rhine Province — OS3

Palatinate District — OS4

Saarland OS5

Württemberg OS6

Baden OS7

Johann Wolfgang von Goethe OS8

Friedrich von Schiller — OS9

Heinrich Heine — OS10

Perf. 14x13½

1945-46 **Unwmk.** **Typo.**

4N1	OS3	1pf blk, grn & lem	15	15
4N2	OS4	3pf dk red, blk & dl yel	15	15
4N3	OS6	5pf brn, blk & org yel	15	15
4N4	OS7	8pf brn, yel & red	15	15
4N5	OS3	10pf brn, grn & lem	5.00	12.50
4N6	OS4	12pf red, blk & org yel	15	15
4N7	OS5	15pf blk, ultra & red ('46)	15	15
4N8	OS6	20pf red, org yel & blk	15	15
4N9	OS5	24pf blk, dp ultra & red ('46)	15	15
4N10	OS7	30pf blk, org yel & red	15	15

Perf. 13

Engr.

4N11	OS8	1m lilac brn	1.25	3.00
4N12	OS9	2m dp bl ('46)	1.00	4.50
4N13	OS10	5m dl red brn ('46)	1.25	5.00
		Nos. 4N1-4N13 (13)	9.85	
		Set, never hinged	15.00	

Exist imperf. Value for set of 13, $300.

BADEN

Johann Peter Hebel — OS1

Girl of Constance — OS2

Hans Baldung Grien — OS3

Rastatt Castle — OS4

Black Forest Scene OS5

Cathedral of Freiburg — OS6

1947 **Unwmk.** **Photo.** *Perf. 14*

5N1	OS1	2pf gray	15	15
5N2	OS2	3pf brown	15	15
5N3	OS3	10pf slate blue	15	15
5N4	OS1	12pf dk green	15	15
5N5	OS2	15pf purple	15	15
5N6	OS4	16pf olive green	15	40
5N7	OS3	20pf blue	15	15
5N8	OS4	24pf crimson	15	15
5N9	OS2	45pf cerise	15	15
5N10	OS1	60pf deep orange	15	15
5N11	OS3	75pf brt blue	15	25
5N12	OS5	84pf blue green	15	55
5N13	OS6	1m dark brown	15	15
		Set value	75	2.30
		Set, never hinged	1.00	

Festival Headdress OS7

Grand Duchess Stephanie OS8

1948

5N14	OS1	2pf dp orange	15	24
5N15	OS2	6pf violet brn	15	15
5N16	OS7	8dpf blue green	28	85
5N17	OS3	10pf dark brown	16	15
5N18	OS1	12pf crimson	16	15
5N19	OS2	15pf blue	20	32
5N20	OS4	16dpf violet	52	1.50
5N21	OS3	20dpf brown	2.00	85
5N22	OS4	24pf dark green	28	15
5N23	OS7	30pf cerise	65	70
5N24	OS8	50pf brt blue	65	15
5N25	OS1	60dpf gray	2.00	24
5N26	OS5	84dpf rose brn	4.00	3.00
5N27	OS6	1dm brt blue	4.00	3.00
		Nos. 5N14-5N27 (14)	15.20	11.45
		Set, never hinged	27.50	

Without "PF"

1948-49

5N28	OS1	2(pf) dp orange	38	50
5N29	OS4	4(pf) violet	18	30
5N30	OS2	5(pf) blue	48	60
5N31	OS2	6(pf) violet brn	12.50	8.50
5N32	OS7	8(pf) rose brn	55	50
5N33	OS3	10(pf) dark green	55	15
5N37	OS3	20(pf) cerise	90	25
5N38	OS4	40(pf) brown	35.00	47.50
5N39	OS1	80(pf) red	5.75	4.75
5N40	OS5	90(pf) rose brn	35.00	65.00
		Nos. 5N28-5N40 (10)	91.29	128.05
		Set, never hinged	160.00	

Constance Cathedral and Insel Hotel OS9

Type I. Frameline thick and straight. Inscriptions thick. Shading dark. Upper part of "B" narrow.
Type II. Frameline thin and zigzag. Inscriptions fine. Shading light. Upper part of "B" wide.

1949, June 22

5N41	OS9	30pf dark blue (I)	15.00	60.00
		Never hinged	27.50	
a.		Type II	375.00	1,750.

Issued to publicize the International Engineering Congress, Constance, 1949.

Conradin Kreutzer — OS10

1949, Aug. 27

5N42	OS10	10pf dark green	1.40	2.50
		Never hinged	1.75	

Conradin Kreutzer (1780-1849), composer.

Stagecoach OS11

Design: 20pf, Post bus, trailer and plane.

1949, Sept. 17

5N43	OS11	10pf green	2.75	9.00
5N44	OS11	20pf red brown	2.75	9.00
		Set, never hinged	11.00	

Centenary of German postage stamps.

Globe, Olive Branch and Post Horn — OS12

1949, Oct. 4

5N45	OS12	20pf dark red	2.50	11.00
5N46	OS12	30pf deep blue	2.50	5.25
		Set, never hinged	10.00	

75th anniv. of the UPU.

Allied Military Government stamps can be mounted in the Scott Germany album part I.

OCCUPATION SEMI-POSTAL STAMPS

Arms of Baden OSP1

Cornhouse, Freiburg OSP2

Perf. 13½x14

1949, Feb. 25 Photo. Unwmk.

Cross in Red

5NB1	OSP1	10 + 20pf green	15.00	*52.50*
5NB2	OSP1	20 + 40pf lilac	15.00	*52.50*
5NB3	OSP1	30 + 60pf blue	15.00	*52.50*
5NB4	OSP1	40 + 80pf gray	15.00	*52.50*
a.		Sheet of 4, imperf.	90.00	*1,400.*
a.		Never hinged	110.00	
		Set, never hinged	67.50	

The surtax was for the Red Cross.

No. 5NB4a measures 90x101mm. and contains one each of Nos. 5NB1 to 5NB4, with red inscription in upper margin and no gum.

1949, Feb. 24 *Perf. 14*

Designs: 10pf+20pf, Cathedral tower. 20pf+30pf, Trumpeting angel. 30pf+50pf, Fish pool.

5NB5	OSP2	4 + 16pf dk violet	5.00	*25.00*
5NB6	OSP2	10 + 20pf dk green	7.25	*27.50*
5NB7	OSP2	20 + 30pf carmine	8.75	*27.50*
5NB8	OSP2	30 + 50pf blue	14.00	*32.50*
a.		Sheet of 4, #5NB5-5NB8	47.50	*175.00*
a.		Never hinged	72.50	
b.		As "a," imperf.	47.50	*175.00*
b.		Never hinged	72.50	
		Set, never hinged	60.00	

The surtax was for the reconstruction of historical monuments in Freiburg.

Carl Schurz at Rastatt OSP3

Goethe OSP4

1949, Aug. 23

5NB9	OSP3	10 + 5pf green	6.00	*22.50*
5NB10	OSP3	20 + 10pf cerise	6.00	*22.50*
5NB11	OSP3	30 + 15pf blue	6.00	*22.50*
		Set, never hinged	24.00	

Centenary of the surrender of Rastatt.

1949, Aug. 12

Various Portraits.

5NB12	OSP4	10 + 5pf green	5.50	*16.00*
5NB13	OSP4	20 + 10pf cerise	5.50	*16.00*
5NB14	OSP4	30 + 15pf blue	6.75	*32.50*
		Set, never hinged	24.00	

Johann Wolfgang von Goethe (1749-1832).

RHINE PALATINATE

Beethoven OS1

Wilhelm E. F. von Ketteler OS2

Girl Carrying Grapes OS3

Porta Nigra, Trier OS4

Karl Marx — OS5

"Devil's Table", Near Pirmasens — OS6

Street Corner, St. Martin OS7

Cathedral of Worms OS8

Cathedral of Mainz — OS9

Statue of Johann Gutenberg — OS10

Gutenfels and Pfalzgrafenstein Castles on Rhine — OS11

Statue of Charlemagne — OS12

1947-48 Unwmk. Photo. *Perf. 14*

6N1	OS1	2pf gray	15	15
6N2	OS2	3pf dk brown	15	15
6N3	OS3	10pf slate blue	15	15
6N4	OS4	12pf green	15	15
6N5	OS5	15pf purple	15	15
6N6	OS6	16pf lt ol grn	15	15
6N7	OS7	20pf brt blue	15	15
6N8	OS8	24pf crimson	15	15
6N9	OS10	30pf cerise ('48)	15	30
6N10	OS9	45pf cerise	15	15
6N11	OS9	50pf blue ('48)	15	35
6N12	OS1	60pf dp orange	15	15
6N13	OS10	75pf blue	15	15
6N14	OS11	84pf green	15	45
6N15	OS12	1m brown	15	18
		Set value	75	2.10
		Set, never hinged	1.00	

Exist imperf. Value for set, $600.

1948

6N16	OS1	2pf dp orange	15	20
6N17	OS2	6pf violet brn	15	20
6N18	OS4	8dpf blue green	24	1.00
6N19	OS3	10pf dk brown	24	15
6N20	OS4	12pf crim rose	22	15
6N21	OS5	15pf blue	55	50
6N22	OS6	16dpf dk violet	28	85
6N23	OS7	20dpf brown	55	60
6N24	OS8	24pf green	25	15
6N25	OS9	30pf cerise	52	20
6N26	OS10	50pf brt blue	80	20
6N27	OS1	60dpf gray	5.50	22
6N28	OS11	84dpf rose brown	2.75	3.00
6N29	OS12	1dm brt blue	3.00	2.25
		Nos. 6N16-6N29 (14)	15.20	9.67
		Set, never hinged	27.50	

Exist imperf. Value for set, $600.

Types of 1947 Without "PF"

1948-49

6N30	OS1	2(pf) dp orange	18	30
6N31	OS6	4(pf) violet ('49)	28	18
6N32	OS5	5(pf) blue ('49)	48	40
6N33	OS2	6(pf) violet brn	16.00	12.00
6N33A	OS4	8(pf) rose brn ('49)	45.00	*125.00*
6N34	OS3	10(pf) dk green	50	18
a.		Imperf.	175.00	
6N35	OS7	20(pf) cerise	55	18
6N36	OS8	40(pf) brown ('49)	1.40	2.25
6N37	OS4	80(pf) red ('49)	1.75	3.75
6N38	OS11	90(pf) rose brn ('49)	2.75	*11.00*
		Nos. 6N30-6N38 (10)	68.89	*155.24*
		Set, never hinged	125.00	

Type of Baden, 1949

Designs as in Baden.

1949, Sept. 17

6N39	OS11	10pf green	4.50	*18.00*
6N40	OS11	20pf red brown	4.50	*18.00*
		Set, never hinged	18.00	

UPU Type of Baden, 1949

1949, Oct. 4

6N41	OS12	20pf dark red	3.50	*12.00*
6N42	OS12	30pf deep blue	3.50	7.50
		Set, never hinged	11.00	

OCCUPATION SEMI-POSTAL STAMPS

St. Martin — OSP1

Design: 30pf+50pf, St. Christopher.

1948 Unwmk. Photo. *Perf. 14*

6NB1	OSP1	20pf + 30pf dp claret	65	*3.50*
6NB2	OSP1	30pf + 50pf dp blue	65	*3.50*
		Set, never hinged	2.00	

The surtax was to aid victims of an explosion at Ludwigshafen.

Type of Baden, 1949, Showing Arms of Rhine Palatinate

1949, Feb. 25 *Perf. 13½x14*

Cross in Red

6NB3	OSP1	10pf + 20pf green	15.00	*70.00*
6NB4	OSP1	20pf + 40pf lilac	15.00	*70.00*
6NB5	OSP1	30pf + 60pf blue	15.00	*70.00*
6NB6	OSP1	40pf + 80pf gray	15.00	*70.00*
a.		Sheet of 4, #6NB3-6NB6, imperf.	80.00	*1,400.*
a.		Sheet of #6NB3-6NB6, imperf., never hinged	90.00	
		Set, never hinged	75.00	

The surtax was for the Red Cross.

No. 6NB6a measures 90x100mm and has no gum.

Goethe Type of Baden, 1949

Various Portraits.

1949, Aug. 12

6NB7	OSP4	10pf + 5pf green	3.00	*12.50*
6NB8	OSP4	20pf + 10pf cerise	3.00	*12.50*
6NB9	OSP4	30pf + 15pf blue	6.00	*27.50*
		Set, never hinged	15.00	

WURTTEMBERG

Friedrich von Schiller OS1

Castle of Bebenhausen, near Tübingen OS2

Friedrich Hölderlin OS3

Town Gate of Wangen (Allgäu) OS4

Lichtenstein Castle — OS5

Zwiefalten Church — OS6

1947-48 Unwmk. Photo. *Perf. 14*

8N1	OS1	2pf gray ('48)	15	15
8N2	OS3	3pf brown ('48)	15	15
8N3	OS4	10pf slate bl ('48)	15	15
8N4	OS1	12pf dk green	15	15
8N5	OS3	15pf purple ('48)	15	15
8N6	OS2	16pf ol grn ('48)	15	18
8N7	OS4	20pf blue ('48)	15	15
8N8	OS2	24pf crimson	15	15
8N9	OS3	45pf cerise	15	15
8N10	OS1	60pf dp org ('48)	15	35
8N11	OS4	75pf brt blue	15	35
8N12	OS5	84pf blue grn	15	55
8N13	OS6	1m dk brown	15	35
		Set value	75	2.40
		Set, never hinged	1.00	

The 12pf and 60pf exist imperf. Value, each $35.

Waldsee OS7

Ludwig Uhland OS8

1948

8N14	OS1	2pf dp orange	15	75
8N15	OS3	6pf violet brn	15	22
8N16	OS7	8dpf blue grn	48	*1.75*
8N17	OS4	10pf dk brown	15	42
8N18	OS1	12pf crimson	15	22
8N19	OS3	15pf blue	35	35
8N20	OS2	16dpf dk violet	42	*1.75*
8N21	OS4	20dpf brown	1.00	1.10
8N22	OS2	24pf dk green	38	22
8N23	OS7	30pf cerise	60	35
8N24	OS8	50pf dull blue	1.25	35
8N25	OS1	60dpf gray	6.25	35
8N26	OS5	84dpf rose brn	2.50	3.00
8N27	OS6	1dm brt blue	2.50	3.00
		Nos. 8N14-8N27 (14)	16.33	13.83
		Set, never hinged	29.00	

The 2pf, 10pf, 24pf and 30pf exist imperf. Value, each $35.

Without "PF"

1948-49

8N28	OS1	2(pf) dp orange	65	25
8N29	OS2	4(pf) violet	65	25
8N30	OS3	5(pf) blue	1.10	60
8N31	OS3	6(pf) vio brown	3.75	3.00
8N32	OS7	8(pf) rose brown	3.75	90
8N33	OS4	10(pf) dk green	3.75	15
8N34	OS4	20(pf) cerise	3.75	15
8N35	OS2	40(pf) brown	11.00	*27.50*
8N36	OS1	80(pf) red	30.00	27.50
8N37	OS5	90(pf) rose brn	37.50	*75.00*
		Nos. 8N28-8N37 (10)	95.90	*135.30*
		Set, never hinged	190.00	

The 4pf and 6pf exist imperf. Value, respectively $100 and $37.50.

Type of Baden, 1949

Designs as in Baden.

1949, Sept. 17

8N38	OS11	10pf green	4.00	*8.25*
8N39	OS11	20pf red brown	4.00	*11.00*
		Set, never hinged	14.00	

UPU Type of Baden, 1949

1949, Oct. 4

No.	Type	Description	Unused	Used
8N40	OS12	20pf dark red	3.00	*11.00*
8N41	OS12	30pf deep blue	3.00	4.25
		Set, never hinged	10.00	

OCCUPATION SEMI-POSTAL STAMPS

Type of Baden, 1949

Design: Arms of Württemberg.

Perf. 13½x14

1949, Feb. 25 Photo. Unwmk.

Cross in Red

No.	Type	Description	Unused	Used
8NB1	OSP1	10 + 20pf green	22.50	*85.00*
8NB2	OSP1	20 + 40pf lilac	22.50	*85.00*
8NB3	OSP1	30 + 60pf blue	22.50	*85.00*
8NB4	OSP1	40 + 80pf gray	22.50	*85.00*
		Set, never hinged	130.00	
a.		Sheet of 4, imperf.	125.00	*1,250.*
a.		Sheet of 4, imperf., never hinged	140.00	

The surtax was for the Red Cross.

No. 8NB4a measures 90x100mm and contains one each of Nos. 8NB1 to 8NB4, with red inscription in upper margin and no gum.

View of Isny OSP1

Design: 20pf+6pf, Skier and village.

Wmk. 116

1949, Feb. 11 Typo. *Perf. 14*

No.	Type	Description	Unused	Used
8NB5	OSP1	10 + 4pf dull green	2.50	*11.00*
8NB6	OSP1	20 + 6pf red brown	2.50	*11.00*
		Set, never hinged	9.00	

Issued to commemorate the 1948-49 German Ski Championship at Isny im Allgau.

Gustav Werner — OSP2

1949, Sept. 4

No.	Type	Description	Unused	Used
8NB7	OSP2	10 + 5pf blue green	3.00	*11.00*
8NB8	OSP2	20 + 10pf claret	3.00	*11.00*
		Set, never hinged	9.50	

Cent. of the founding of Gustav Werner's "Christianity in Action" and "House of Brotherhood."

Goethe Type of Baden, 1949

Various Portraits.

1949, Aug. 12

No.	Type	Description	Unused	Used
8NB9	OSP4	10 + 5pf green	4.00	*11.50*
8NB10	OSP4	20 + 10pf cerise	5.00	*18.00*
8NB11	OSP4	30 + 15pf blue	6.50	*27.50*
		Set, never hinged	28.00	

BERLIN

Issued for Use in the American, British and French Occupation Sectors of Berlin

Germany Nos. 557-569, 571-573 Overprinted Diagonally in Black

a

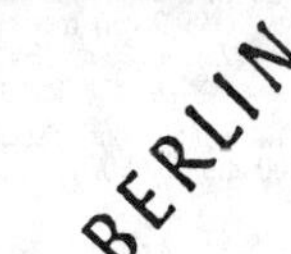

Wmk. 284

1948, Sept. 1 Typo. *Perf. 14*

No.	Type	Description	Unused	Used
9N1	A120	2pf brown blk	90	*1.50*
9N2	A120	6pf purple	60	50
9N3	A121	8pf red	60	50
9N4	A121	10pf yellow grn	38	26
9N5	A122	12pf gray	38	26
9N6	A120	15pf chocolate	3.50	*26.00*
9N7	A123	16pf dk blue grn	65	55
9N8	A121	20pf blue	1.40	*2.50*
9N9	A123	24pf brown org	52	25
9N10	A120	25pf orange yel	9.50	*30.00*
9N11	A122	30pf red	1.50	*3.25*
9N12	A121	40pf red violet	1.10	1.10
9N13	A123	50pf ultra	3.50	*9.00*
9N14	A122	60pf red brown	1.10	15
9N15	A122	80pf dark blue	3.25	*14.00*
9N16	A123	84pf emerald	7.75	*57.50*

Germany Nos. 574-577 Overprinted Diagonally in Black

b

BERLIN

Engr.

No.	Type	Description	Unused	Used
9N17	A124	1m olive	19.00	*82.50*
9N18	A124	2m dk brown vio	27.50	*300.00*
9N19	A124	3m copper red	35.00	*425.00*
9N20	A124	5m dark blue	35.00	*450.00*
		Nos. 9N1-9N20 (20)	153.13	
		Set, never hinged	275.00	

Forged overprints and cancellations are found on Nos. 9N1-9N20.

Stamps of Germany 1947-48 with "a" Overprint in Red

1948-49 Wmk. 284 Typo. *Perf. 14*

No.	Type	Description	Unused	Used
9N21	A120	2pf brn blk ('49)	90	1.40
9N22	A120	6pf purple ('49)	4.75	1.40
9N23	A121	8pf red ('49)	17.50	2.75
9N24	A121	10pf yellow grn	90	42
9N25	A120	15pf chocolate	2.25	1.40
9N26	A121	20pf blue	90	55
9N27	A120	25pf org yel ('49)	42.50	30.00
9N28	A122	30pf red ('49)	27.50	4.50
9N29	A121	40pf red vio ('49)	27.50	7.50
9N30	A123	50pf ultra ('49)	27.50	4.50
9N31	A122	60pf red brown	3.25	42
9N32	A122	80pf dk blue ('49)	47.50	5.75

With "b" Overprint in Red

Engr.

No.	Type	Description	Unused	Used
9N33	A124	1m olive	200.00	275.00
9N34	A124	2m dk brown vio	110.00	110.00
		Nos. 9N21-9N34 (14)	512.95	445.59
		Set, never hinged	1,600.	

Forgeries exist of the overprints on Nos. 9N21-9N34. No. 9N33 exists imperf.

Statue of Heinrich von Stephan
A1 A2

1949, Apr. 9 Litho. *Perf. 14*

No.	Type	Description	Unused	Used
9N35	A1	12pf gray	4.50	3.25
9N36	A1	16pf blue green	11.00	4.75
9N37	A1	24pf orange brn	8.75	28
9N38	A1	50pf brown olive	65.00	10.00
9N39	A1	60pf brown red	67.50	10.00
9N40	A2	1m olive	37.50	47.50
9N41	A2	2m brown violet	45.00	24.00
		Nos. 9N35-9N41 (7)	239.25	99.78
		Set, never hinged	475.00	

75th anniv. of the UPU.

Brandenburg Gate, Berlin — A3

Tempelhof Airport — A4

Designs: 4pf, 8pf, 40pf, Schoeneberg, Rudolf Wilde Square. 5pf, 25pf, 5m, Tegel Castle. 6pf, 50pf, Reichstag Building. 10pf, 30pf, Cloisters, Kleist Park. 15pf, Tempelhof Airport. 20pf, 80pf, 90pf, Polytechnic College, Charlottenburg. 60pf, National Gallery. 2m, Gendarmen Square. 3m, Brandenburg Gate.

1949 Typo. Wmk. 284

Size: 22x18mm

No.	Type	Description	Unused	Used
9N42	A3	1pf black	15	15
a.		Bklt. pane 5 + label	10.00	
b.		Tête bêche	48	60
9N43	A3	4pf yellow brn	20	15
a.		Bklt. pane 5 + label	10.00	
b.		Tête bêche	1.50	1.75
9N44	A3	5pf blue green	20	15
9N45	A3	6pf red violet	35	1.10
9N46	A3	8pf red orange	52	1.10
9N47	A3	10pf yellow grn	42	15
a.		Bklt. pane 5 + label	42.50	
9N48	A4	15pf chocolate	2.75	60
9N49	A3	20pf red	1.90	15
a.		Bklt. pane 5 + label	42.50	
9N50	A3	25pf orange	8.00	60
9N51	A3	30pf violet bl	3.00	60
a.		Imperf.	*850.00*	
9N52	A3	40pf lake	5.50	40
9N53	A3	50pf olive	5.50	40
9N54	A3	60pf red brown	19.00	15
9N55	A3	80pf dark blue	4.50	1.00
9N56	A3	90pf emerald	4.50	1.00

Engr.

Size: 29¼-29¾x24-24½mm

No.	Type	Description	Unused	Used
9N57	A4	1m olive	8.00	60
9N58	A4	2m brown vio	22.50	60
9N59	A4	3m henna brn	80.00	3.75
9N60	A4	5m deep blue	47.50	11.00
		Nos. 9N42-9N60 (19)	214.49	23.65
		Set, never hinged	650.00	

See Nos. 9N101-9N102, 9N108-9N110.

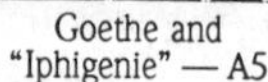

Goethe and "Iphigenie" — A5

Statue of Atlas, New York — A6

Designs (Goethe and scenes from his works): 20pf, "Reineke Fuchs." 30pf, "Faust."

1949, July 29 Litho. *Perf. 14*

No.	Type	Description	Unused	Used
9N61	A5	10pf green	55.00	40.00
9N62	A5	20pf carmine	55.00	50.00
9N63	A5	30pf ultra	10.00	25.00
		Set, never hinged	225.00	

Bicentenary of the birth of Johann Wolfgang von Goethe.

Germany Nos. 550, 565, 572 and 576 Surcharged "BERLIN" and New Value in Dark Green

1949, Aug. 1 Typo.

No.	Type	Description	Unused	Used
9N64	A119	5pf on 45pf	1.50	15
9N65	A123	10pf on 24pf	4.00	20
9N66	A122	20pf on 80pf	20.00	15.00

Engr.

No.	Type	Description	Unused	Used
9N67	A124	1m on 3m	62.50	16.00
		Set, never hinged	190.00	

1950, Oct. 1 Engr. Wmk. 116

No.	Type	Description	Unused	Used
9N68	A6	20pf dk carmine	42.50	35.00
		Never hinged	85.00	

European Recovery Plan.

Albert Lortzing — A7

Freedom Bell, Berlin — A8

1951, Apr. 22

No.	Type	Description	Unused	Used
9N69	A7	20pf red brown	30.00	47.50
		Never hinged	55.00	

Centenary of the death of Albert Lortzing, composer.

1951 *Perf. 14*

No.	Type	Description	Unused	Used
9N70	A8	5pf chocolate	1.25	*1.65*
9N71	A8	10pf deep green	4.25	*7.75*
9N72	A8	20pf rose red	1.50	*3.50*
9N73	A8	30pf blue	16.00	*30.00*
9N74	A8	40pf rose violet	6.75	*17.00*
		Nos. 9N70-9N74 (5)	29.75	59.90
		Set, never hinged	60.00	

Re-engraved

1951-52

No.	Type	Description	Unused	Used
9N75	A8	5pf olive bis ('52)	1.25	85
9N76	A8	10pf yellow grn	3.00	3.50
9N77	A8	20pf brt red	12.00	12.50
9N78	A8	30pf blue ('52)	24.00	26.00
9N79	A8	40pf dp car ('52)	10.00	12.00
		Nos. 9N75-9N79 (5)	50.25	54.85
		Set, never hinged	100.00	

Bell clapper moved from left to right. Imprint "L. Schnell" in lower margin.

No. 9N76 exists imperf. Value $900.

See Nos. 9N94-9N98.

Ludwig van Beethoven — A9

Olympic Symbols — A10

1952, Mar. 26 Engr. Unwmk.

No.	Type	Description	Unused	Used
9N80	A9	30pf blue	22.50	20.00
		Never hinged	27.50	

125th anniversary of the death of Ludwig van Beethoven.

1952, June 20 Litho. Wmk. 116

No.	Type	Description	Unused	Used
9N81	A10	4pf yellow brown	45	80
9N82	A10	10pf green	4.50	8.00
9N83	A10	20pf rose red	8.00	15.00
		Set, never hinged	24.00	

Issued to publicize the pre-Olympic Festival Day, June 20, 1952.

Carl Friedrich Zelter — A11

Arms Breaking Chains — A12

Portraits: 5pf, Otto Lilienthal. 6pf, Walter Rathenau. 8pf, Theodor Fontane. 10pf, Adolph von Menzel. 15pf, Rudolf Virchow. 20pf, Werner von Siemens. 25pf, Karl Friedrich Schinkel. 30pf, Max Planck. 40pf, Wilhelm von Humboldt.

1952-53 Engr. Wmk. 284

No.	Type	Description	Unused	Used
9N84	A11	4pf brown	15	18
9N85	A11	5pf dp blue ('53)	25	38
9N86	A11	6pf choc ('53)	2.00	6.25
9N87	A11	8pf henna brn ('53)	1.10	2.00
9N88	A11	10pf deep green	1.25	52
9N89	A11	15pf purple ('53)	5.00	11.00
9N90	A11	20pf brown red	1.25	60
9N91	A11	25pf dp olive ('53)	19.00	4.50
9N92	A11	30pf brn vio ('53)	6.00	5.50
9N93	A11	40pf black ('53)	10.00	2.50
		Nos. 9N84-9N93 (10)	46.00	33.43
		Set, never hinged	110.00	

Bell Type of 1951-1952

Second Re-engraving

1953 Wmk. 284 *Perf. 14*

No.	Type	Description	Unused	Used
9N94	A8	5pf brown	60	60
9N95	A8	10pf deep green	1.40	1.40
9N96	A8	20pf brt red	3.50	3.00
9N97	A8	30pf blue	6.25	10.00
9N98	A8	40pf rose violet	24.00	25.00
		Nos. 9N94-9N98 (5)	35.75	40.00
		Set, never hinged	62.50	

Bell clapper hangs straight down. Marginal imprint omitted.

For overprint & surcharge see #9N106, 9NB17.

1953, Aug. 17 Typo.

Design: 30pf, Brandenburg Gate.

No.	Type	Description	Unused	Used
9N99	A12	20pf black	1.90	1.00
9N100	A12	30pf dp carmine	10.00	15.00
		Set, never hinged	24.00	

Issued to commemorate the strike of East German workers, June 17, 1953.

Similar to Type of 1949

Designs: 4pf, Exposition halls. 20pf, Olympic Stadium, Berlin.

1953-54 Wmk. 284 *Perf. 14*

9N101 A3 4pf yellow brn ('54)	1.40	1.25
9N102 A3 20pf red	30.00	25
Set, never hinged		60.00

Catalogue values for unused stamps in this section, from this point to the end of the section, are for Never Hinged items.

Allied Council Building — A13

1954, Jan. 25 Litho.

9N103 A13 20pf red 7.00 4.00

Issued to publicize the Four Power Conference, Berlin, 1954.

Prof. Ernst Reuter (1889-1953), Mayor of Berlin (1948-53) — A14

1954, Jan. 18 Engr. Wmk. 284

9N104 A14 20pf chocolate 7.00 1.25

See No. 9N174.

Ottmar Mergenthaler and Linotype — A15

1954, May 11

9N105 A15 10pf dk blue grn 1.75 1.75

Cent. of the birth of Ottmar Mergenthaler.

No. 9N96 Overprinted in Black

Wahl des Bundespräsidenten in Berlin 17. Juli 1954

1954, July 17 *Perf. 13½x14*

9N106 A8 20pf bright red 3.00 3.00

Issued to publicize the West German presidential election held in Berlin July 17, 1954.

Germany in Bondage A16

Richard Strauss — A17

1954, July 20 Typo.

9N107 A16 20pf car & gray 4.00 4.25

10th anniv. of the attempted assassination of Adolf Hitler.

Similar to Type of 1949

Designs: 7pf, Exposition halls. 40pf, Memorial library. 70pf, Hunting lodge, Grunewald.

1954 Wmk. 284 *Perf. 14*

9N108 A3 7pf aqua	6.25	24
9N109 A3 40pf rose lilac	11.00	3.25
9N110 A3 70pf olive green	95.00	17.50

1954, Sept. 18 Engr.

9N111 A17 40pf violet blue 11.50 2.50

5th anniv. of the death of Richard Strauss, composer.

Early Forge — A18

1954, Sept. 25

9N112 A18 20pf reddish brown 7.50 2.00

Centenary of the death of August Borsig, industrial leader.

M. S. Berlin and Arms of Berlin A19

Wilhelm Furtwängler A20

1955, Mar. 12 Wmk. 284

9N113 A19 10pf Prus green	95	28
9N114 A19 25pf violet blue	5.00	2.50

Issued to publicize the resumption of shipping under West German ownership.

Perf. 13½x14

1955, Sept. 17 Unwmk.

9N115 A20 40pf ultra 20.00 13.00

Issued to honor the conductor Wilhelm Furtwängler and to publicize the Berlin Music Festival, September 1955.

Arms of Berlin

A21 A22

1955, Oct. 17 Litho. Wmk. 304

9N116 A21 10pf red, org yel & blk	45	20
9N117 A21 20pf red, org yel & blk	4.00	4.25

Meeting of the German Bundestag in Berlin, Oct. 17-22, 1955.

1956, Mar. 16

9N118 A22 10pf red, ocher & blk	1.10	25
9N119 A22 25pf red, ocher & blk	3.50	2.50

Meeting of the German Bundesrat in Berlin Mar. 16, 1956.

Radio Station, Berlin (A23 has no top inscription. A24 has top inscription.)

A23 A24

Free University A25

Monument of the Great Elector Frederick William A26

Designs: 1pf, 3pf, Brandenburg Gate. 5pf, General Post Office. 8pf, City Hall, Neukölln. 10pf, Kaiser Wilhelm Memorial Church. 15pf, Airlift memorial. 25pf, Lilienthal Monument. 30pf, Pfaueninsel Castle. 40pf, Charlottenburg Castle. 50pf, Reuter power plant. 60pf, Chamber of Commerce and Industry and Stock Exchange. 70pf, Schiller Theater. 3m, Congress Hall.

Typo.; Litho. (3pf, #9N122)

1956-63 Wmk. 304 *Perf. 14*

9N120	A25 1pf gray ('57)	15	15
9N120A	A25 3pf brt pur ('63)	15	15
9N121	A25 5pf rose lilac ('57)	15	15
9N122	A23 7pf blue green	6.00	1.50
9N123	A24 7pf blue green	15	15
9N124	A24 8pf gray	22	35
9N125	A24 8pf red org ('59)	16	15
9N126	A24 10pf emerald	15	15
9N127	A24 15pf chlky blue	16	16
9N128	A25 20pf rose car	15	15
9N129	A24 25pf dull red brn	22	35
	Engr.		
9N130	A24 30pf gray grn ('57)	24	40
9N131	A25 40pf lt ultra ('57)	5.50	4.00
9N132	A24 50pf olive	50	60
9N133	A25 60pf lt brown ('57)	65	75
9N134	A25 70pf violet	21.00	7.50
9N135	A26 1m olive	1.25	1.10
	Size: 29x24½mm		
9N136	A25 3m rose cl ('58)	4.00	4.75
	Nos. 9N120-9N136 (18)	40.80	22.51

No. 9N120 exists on both ordinary and fluorescent paper; No. 9N120A on fluorescent paper only; others on ordinary paper.

Engineers' Society Emblem — A27

Paul Lincke — A28

1956, May 12 Engr. *Perf. 14*

9N140 A27 10pf dark green	1.75	1.00
9N141 A27 20pf dark red	4.25	3.50

Cent. of Soc. of German Civil Engineers.

1956, Sept. 3

9N142 A28 20pf dark red 2.00 2.25

10th anniversary of the death of Paul Lincke, composer.

Radio Station, Berlin-Nikolassee A29

Spandau, 1850 A30

1956, Sept. 15

9N143 A29 25pf brown 6.00 5.75

Issued to publicize the German Industrial Fair, Berlin, Sept. 15-30.

1957, Mar. 7

9N144 A30 20pf gray ol & brn red 55 55

725th anniversary of Spandau.

Hansa Model Town and "B" — A31

Designs: 20pf, View of exposition grounds and "B." 40pf, Auditorium and "B."

1957 Engr.

9N145 A31 7pf violet brown	18	18
9N146 A31 20pf carmine	50	50
9N147 A31 40pf violet blue	85	85

Issued to publicize the International Building Show, Berlin, July 6-Sept. 29, 1957.

Friedrich Karl von Savigny, Law Teacher A32

Uta Statue, Naumburg Cathedral A33

Portraits: 7pf, Theodor Mommsen, historian. 8pf, Heinrich Zille, painter. 10pf, Ernst Reuter, mayor of Berlin. 15pf, Fritz Haber, chemist. 20pf, Friedrich Schleiermacher, theologian. 25pf, Max Reinhardt, theatrical director. 40pf, Alexander von Humboldt, naturalist and geographer. 50pf, Christian Daniel Rauch, sculptor.

1957-59 Wmk. 304 *Perf. 14*

Portraits in Brown

9N148 A32 7pf blue grn ('58)	15	15
9N149 A32 8pf gray ('58)	15	15
9N150 A32 10pf green ('58)	15	15
9N151 A32 15pf dark blue	45	35
9N152 A32 20pf carmine ('58)	15	15
9N153 A32 25pf magenta	58	52
9N154 A32 30pf olive green	90	90
9N155 A32 40pf blue ('59)	26	28
9N156 A32 50pf olive	3.00	2.50
Nos. 9N148-9N156 (9)	5.79	5.15

Issued to honor famous men of Berlin.
See No. 9NB19.

1957, Aug. 6

9N157 A33 25pf brown red 50 50

Issued to publicize the annual meeting of the East German Culture Society in Berlin.

"Unity and Justice and Liberty" A34

Postilion 1897-1925 A35

1957, Oct. 15 **Litho.**

9N158 A34 10pf multicolored	32	40
9N159 A34 20pf multicolored	1.50	1.90

Issued to commemorate the first meeting of the third German Bundesrat, Berlin, Oct. 15.

1957, Oct. 23 **Wmk. 304** ***Perf. 14***

9N160 A35 20pf multicolored	60	50

Issued for Stamp Day and BEPHILA stamp exhibition, Berlin, Oct. 23-27.

World Veterans' Federation Emblem — A36

Christ and the Cosmos — A37

1957, Oct. 28

9N161 A36 20pf bl grn, ol grn & yel	60	50

7th General Assembly of the World Veterans' Federation, Berlin, Oct. 24-Nov. 1.

1958, Aug. 13

9N162 A37 10pf lt bl grn & blk	30	30
9N163 A37 20pf rose lilac & blk	70	70

Issued in honor of the 78th German Catholics Meeting, Berlin, Aug. 13-17.

Prof. Otto Suhr (1894-1957), Mayor of Berlin (1955-57) — A38

1958, Aug. 30 **Engr.** ***Perf. 14***

9N164 A38 20pf rose red	65	75

Pres. Heuss Type of Germany, 1959

1959 **Litho., Engraved (40pf, 70pf)**

9N165 A208 7pf blue green	15	15
9N166 A208 10pf green	28	15
9N167 A208 20pf dk car rose	65	15
9N168 A208 40pf blue	2.00	2.00
9N169 A208 70pf dull purple	6.75	7.00
Nos. 9N165-9N169 (5)	9.83	9.45

Nos. 9N168-9N169 were issued in sheets of 100 and in coils. Every fifth coil stamp has a control number on the back.

Berlin stamps can be mounted in the Scott Germany album part III.

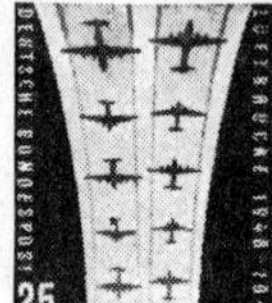
Aerial Bridge to Berlin — A39

Globe and Brandenburg Gate — A40

1959, May 12 **Engr.**

9N170 A39 25pf maroon & blk	25	20

10th anniversary of Berlin Airlift.

1959, June 18 **Litho.** ***Perf. 14***

9N171 A40 20pf lt blue & red	18	20

Issued to publicize the 14th International Municipal Congress, Berlin, June 18-23.

Friedrich von Schiller (1759-1805), Poet — A41

1959, Nov. 10 **Engr.** **Wmk. 304**

9N172 A41 20pf dull red & brn	15	15

Dr. Robert Koch (1843-1910), Bacteriologist — A42

Hans Böckler (1875-1951), Labor Leader — A43

1960, May 27 ***Perf. 14***

9N173 A42 20pf rose lake	15	15

Mayor Type of 1954

Portrait: Dr. Walther Carl Rudolf Schreiber, Mayor of Berlin, 1953-54.

1960, June 30 **Wmk. 304** ***Perf. 14***

9N174 A14 20pf brown car	42	42

1961, Feb. 16 **Litho.** ***Perf. 14***

9N175 A43 20pf dk brick red & blk	15	15

Hans Böckler (1875-1951), labor leader.

Fluorescent Paper

was introduced for all stamps, starting with No. 9N176, and including Nos. 9N120 and 9N120A.

Albrecht Dürer — A44

Louise Schroeder — A45

Portraits: 5pf, Albertus Magnus. 7pf, St. Elizabeth of Thuringia. 8pf, Johann Gutenberg. 15pf, Martin Luther. 20pf, Johann Sebastian Bach. 25pf, Balthasar Neumann. 30pf, Immanuel Kant. 40pf, Gotthold Ephraim Lessing. 50pf, Johann Wolfgang von Goethe. 60pf, Friedrich von Schiller. 70pf, Ludwig van Beethoven. 80pf, Heinrich von Kleist. 1m, Annette von Droste-Hülshoff. 2m, Gerhart Hauptmann.

1961-62 **Typo.** **Wmk. 304**

9N176 A44 5pf olive	15	15
9N177 A44 7pf dk bister	15	15
9N178 A44 8pf lilac	15	15
9N179 A44 10pf olive green	15	15
b. Tête bêche pair	70	65
9N180 A44 15pf blue	15	15
9N181 A44 20pf dark red	15	15
9N182 A44 25pf orange brn	15	15

Engr.

9N183 A44 30pf gray	20	32
9N184 A44 40pf blue	42	52
9N185 A44 50pf red brown	42	52
9N186 A44 60pf dk car rose ('62)	42	52
9N187 A44 70pf green	52	45
9N188 A44 80pf brown	3.25	3.00
9N189 A44 1m violet blue	1.40	1.25
9N190 A44 2m yel grn ('62)	1.75	1.50
Nos. 9N176-9N190 (15)	9.43	9.13

Nos. 9N176-9N182, 9N184 and 9N187 were issued in sheets and in coils. Every fifth coil stamp has a black control number on the back.

1961, June 3 **Engr.** ***Perf. 14***

9N192 A45 20pf dark brown	15	15

Issued to honor Louise Schroeder, acting mayor of Berlin (1947-1948).

Synod Emblem and St. Mary's Church — A46

Berlin Bear with Record, TV Set and Radio Tower — A47

Design: 20pf, Emblem and Kaiser Wilhelm Memorial Church.

1961, July 19 **Litho.** **Wmk. 304**

9N193 A46 10pf green & vio	15	15
9N194 A46 20pf rose claret & vio	16	18
Set value	24	26

10th meeting of German Protestants (Evangelical Synod), Berlin, July 19-23.

1961, Aug. 3 **Engr.**

9N195 A47 20pf brn red & dk brn	15	15

German Radio, Television and Phonograph Exhibition, Berlin, Aug. 25-Sept. 3.

Berlin, 1650 — A48

Views of Old Berlin: 10pf, Spree and Waisenbrücke (Orphans' Bridge). 15pf, Mauer Street, 1780. 20pf, Berlin Palace, 1703. 25pf, Potsdam Square, 1825. 40pf, Bellevue Palace, 1800. 50pf, Fischer Bridge, 1830. 60pf, Halle Gate, 1880. 70pf, Parochial Church, 1780. 80pf, University, 1825. 90pf, Opera House, 1780. 1m, Grunewald Lake, 1790.

1962-63 **Wmk. 304** ***Perf. 14***

9N196 A48 7pf dk gray & gldn brn	15	15
9N197 A48 10pf grn & dk gray	15	15
9N198 A48 15pf bluish gray & dk bl ('63)	15	15
9N199 A48 20pf org brn & sep	15	15
9N200 A48 25pf ol & gray ('63)	16	15
9N201 A48 40pf bluish gray & ultra	28	15
9N202 A48 50pf gray & dk brn ('63)	28	18
9N203 A48 60pf gray & car rose ('63)	32	24
9N204 A48 70pf dk gray & lilac	35	28
9N205 A48 80pf dk gray & dk red ('63)	38	30
9N206 A48 90pf sep & brn org ('63)	38	35
9N207 A48 1m ol gray & dp grn	70	60
Nos. 9N196-9N207 (12)	3.45	
Set value		2.40

Gelber Hund, 1912, and Boeing 707 — A49

Berlin Bear and Radio Tower — A50

1962, Sept. 12 **Litho.**

9N208 A49 60pf brt blue & blk	28	35

50th anniv. of German airmail service.

1963, July 24 **Unwmk.** ***Perf. 14***

9N209 A50 20pf bl, vio bl & gray	15	16

German Radio, Television and Phonograph Exhibition, Berlin, Aug. 30-Sept. 8.

Schöneberg City Hall, John F. Kennedy Place, Berlin — A51

1964, May 30 **Engr.** **Wmk. 304**

9N210 A51 20pf dk brn, *cr*	15	16

700th anniv. of the Schöneberg district of Berlin. The Senate and House of Representatives of West Berlin meet at Schöneberg City Hall.

Lübke Type of Germany, 1964

1964, July 1 **Litho.** **Unwmk.**

9N211 A247 20pf carmine	15	15
9N212 A247 40pf ultra	18	18
Set value	26	26

See Nos. 9N263-9N264.

Capitals Type of Germany

Design: Reichstag Building, Berlin.

1964, Sept. 14 **Litho.** ***Perf. 14***

9N213 A245 20pf blue, blk & grn	15	16

Kennedy Type of Germany

1964, Nov. 21 **Engr.** **Wmk. 304**

9N214 A255 40pf dark blue	16	15

Castle Gate, Ellwangen — A52

Designs (German buildings through 12 centuries): 10pf, Wall pavilion, Zwinger, Dresden. 15pf, Tegel Castle, Berlin. 20pf, Portico, Lorsch. 40pf, Trifels Fortress, Palatinate. 60pf, Treptow Gate, Neubrandenburg. 70pf, Osthofen Gate, Soest. 80pf, Elling Gate, Weissenburg.

1964-65 **Typo.** **Unwmk.**

9N215 A52 10pf brown ('65)	15	15
b. Tête bêche pair	50	50
9N216 A52 15pf dk green ('65)	15	15
9N217 A52 20pf brn red ('65)	15	15

Engr.

9N218 A52 40pf vio bl ('65)	45	40
9N219 A52 50pf olive bis	95	85
9N220 A52 60pf rose red	70	60
9N221 A52 70pf dk green ('65)	1.65	1.40
9N222 A52 80pf chocolate	90	75
Nos. 9N215-9N222 (8)	5.10	4.45

Nos. 9N215-9N218, 9N221 were issued in sheets of 100 and in coils. Every fifth coil stamp has a black control number on the back.

Kaiser Wilhelm Memorial Church
A53

Nordertor, Flensburg
A54

The New Berlin: 15pf, German Opera House, horiz. 20pf, Philharmonic Hall, horiz. 30pf, Jewish Community Center, horiz. 40pf, Regina Martyrum Memorial, horiz. 50pf, Ernst Reuter Square, horiz. 60pf, Europa Center. 70pf, School of Engineering, horiz. 80pf, City Highway. 90pf, Planetarium and observatory, horiz. 1m, Schaeferberg radio tower, Wannsee. 1.10m, University clinic, Steglitz, horiz.

Engraved and Lithographed

1965-66 Unwmk. *Perf. 14*

9N223	A53	10pf multi	15	15
9N224	A53	15pf multi	15	15
9N225	A53	20pf multi	15	15
9N226	A53	30pf multi ('66)	16	15
9N227	A53	40pf multi ('66)	28	20
9N228	A53	50pf multi	30	22
9N229	A53	60pf multi ('66)	30	25
9N230	A53	70pf multi ('66)	38	30
9N231	A53	80pf multi	42	30
9N232	A53	90pf multi ('66)	50	35
9N233	A53	1m multi ('66)	55	45
9N234	A53	1.10m multi ('66)	60	60
		Nos. 9N223-9N234 (12)	3.94	3.27

1966-69 Engr. *Perf. 14*

Designs: 5pf, Berlin Gate, Stettin. 8pf, Castle, Kaub on the Rhine. 10pf, Wall Pavilion, Zwinger, Dresden. 20pf, Portico, Lorsch. 40pf, Trifels Fortress, Palatinate. 50pf, Castle Gate, Ellwangen. 60pf, Treptow Gate, Neubrandenburg. 70pf, Osthofen Gate, Soest. 80pf, Elling Gate, Weissenburg. 90pf, Zschocke Ladies' Home, Königsberg. 1m, Melanchthon House, Wittenberg. 1.10m, Trinity Hospital, Hildesheim. 1.30m, Tegel Castle, Berlin. 2m, Löwenberg Town Hall, interior view.

9N235	A54	5pf olive	15	15
9N236	A54	8pf car rose	15	15
9N237	A54	10pf dk brn ('67)	15	15
9N238	A54	20pf dk grn ('67)	15	15
9N239	A54	30pf yellow grn	16	18
9N240	A54	30pf red ('67)	18	15
9N241	A54	40pf ol bis ('67)	60	60
9N242	A54	50pf blue ('67)	48	48
9N243	A54	60pf dp org ('67)	1.50	1.40
9N244	A54	70pf sl grn ('67)	70	70
9N245	A54	80pf red brn ('67)	1.10	1.10
9N246	A54	90pf black	70	70
9N247	A54	1m dull blue	65	28
9N248	A54	1.10m red brn	1.10	85
9N249	A54	1.30m green ('69)	1.50	1.40
9N250	A54	2m purple	1.50	1.25
		Nos. 9N235-9N250 (16)	10.77	9.69

Brandenburg Gate Type of Germany

1966-70 Typo. *Perf. 14*

9N251	A268	10pf chocolate	15	15
a.		Bklt. pane of 10 (4 #9N251, 2 #9N252, 4 #9N253)	3.00	
b.		Tête bêche pair	60	45
c.		Bklt. pane of 6 (4 #9N251, 2 #9N253) ('70)	2.00	
9N252	A268	20pf dp green	20	15
a.		Bklt. pane of 4 (2 #9N252, 2 #9N253) ('70)	2.00	
9N253	A268	30pf red	20	15
a.		Tête bêche pair	1.25	1.25
9N254	A268	50pf dk blue	85	50
9N255	A268	100pf dk blue ('67)	5.50	2.25
		Nos. 9N251-9N255 (5)	6.90	3.20

Nos. 9N251-9N255 were issued in sheets of 100 and in coils. Every fifth coil stamp has a black control number on the back.

A55

A56

Designs: 10pf, Young Man, by Conrat Meit, 1520. 20pf, The Great Elector Friedrich Wilhelm (1640-88), head from monument by Andreas Schlüter. 30pf, The Evangelist Mark, by Tilman Riemenschneider. 50pf, Head of "Victory" from Brandenburg Gate, by Gottfried Schadow, 1793. 1m, Madonna, by Joseph Anton Feuchtmayer. 1.10m, Jesus and John, wood sculpture, anonymous, c. 1320.

1967 Engr. *Perf. 14*

9N256	A55	10pf sepia & lemon	15	15
9N257	A55	20pf sl grn & bluish gray	15	15
9N258	A55	30pf brown & olive	15	15
9N259	A55	50pf black & gray	22	20
9N260	A55	1m blue & chlky blue	40	38

Size: 22x40mm

9N261	A55	1.10m brown & buff	48	50
		Nos. 9N256-9N261 (6)	1.55	1.53

Issued to publicize Berlin art treasures.

1967, July 19 Litho. and Engr.

Berlin Radio Tower and Television Screens

9N262	A56	30pf multicolored	15	15

25th German Radio, Television and Phonograph Exhibition, Berlin, Aug. 25-Sept. 3.

Lübke Type of Germany, 1964

1967, Oct. 14 Litho.

9N263	A247	30pf carmine	16	20
9N264	A247	50pf ultra	30	45

Old Court Building (Berlin Museum) — A57

Turners' Emblem — A58

1968, Mar. 16 Engr. *Perf. 14*

9N265	A57	30pf black	18	20

500th anniv. of the Berlin Court of Appeal.

1968, Apr. 29 Litho. *Perf. 14*

9N266	A58	20pf gray, blk & red	15	16

Issued to publicize the German Turner Festival, Berlin, May 28-June 3.

Newspaper Vendor by Christian Wilhelm Allers — A59

19th Century Berliners: 5pf, Hack, by Heinrich Zille, horiz. No. 9N269, Horse omnibus, coachman and passengers, 1890, by C. W. Allers. No. 9N270, Cobbler's apprentice, by Franz Kruger. No. 9N271, Cobbler, by Adolph von Menzel. No. 9N272, Blacksmiths, by Paul Meyerheim. No. 9N273, Three Ladies, by Franz Kruger. 50pf, Strollers at Brandenburg Gate, by Christian W. Allers.

1969 Engr. *Perf. 14*

9N267	A59	5pf black	15	15
9N268	A59	10pf dp brown	15	15
9N269	A59	10pf brown	15	15
9N270	A59	20pf dk olive grn	16	15
9N271	A59	20pf green	16	15
9N272	A59	30pf dk red brown	35	32
9N273	A59	30pf red brown	25	25
9N274	A59	50pf ultra	1.50	1.25
		Nos. 9N267-9N274 (8)	2.87	2.57

Souvenir Sheet

Berlin Zoo Animals — A60

Designs: 10pf, Orangutan family. 20pf, White pelicans. 30pf, Gaur and calf. 50pf, Zebra and foal.

Engraved and Lithographed

1969, June 4 *Perf. 14*

9N275	A60	Sheet of 4	1.75	1.75
a.		10pf bister & black	40	40
b.		20pf light green & black	40	40
c.		30pf lilac rose & black	40	40
d.		50pf blue & black	40	40

125th anniversary of the Berlin Zoo. The sheet was sold with a 20pf surtax for the benefit of the Zoo.

Australian Postman — A61

Joseph Joachim — A62

Designs: 20pf, African telephone operator. 30pf, Middle East telecommunications engineer. 50pf, Loading mail on plane.

1969, July 21 Litho. *Perf. 14*

9N276	A61	10pf olive & apple grn	15	15
9N277	A61	20pf dk brn, bis & brn	20	18
9N278	A61	30pf vio blk & bis	30	25
9N279	A61	50pf dk blue & blue	60	55

20th Congress of the Post Office Trade Union Federation, Berlin, July 7-11.

1969, Sept. 12 Photo. *Perf. 14*

Design: 50pf, Alexander von Humboldt, painting by Joseph Stieler.

9N280	A62	30pf multicolored	35	32
9N281	A62	50pf multicolored	55	48

Cent. of the Berlin Music School and honoring its 1st director, Joseph Joachim (1831-1907), violinist, conductor and composer; Alexander von Humboldt (1769-1859), naturalist and explorer.

1970, Jan. 7

Design: 20pf, Theodor Fontane, painting by Hanns Fechner.

9N282	A62	20pf multicolored	20	16

150th anniv. of the birth of Theodor Fontane (1819-1898), poet and writer.
See No. 9N303.

Film Frame — A63

Symbols of Dance, Theater & Art — A64

1970, June 18 Photo. *Perf. 14*

9N283	A63	30pf multicolored	30	25

20th International Film Festival.

President Heinemann Type of Germany Inscribed "Berlin"

1970-73 Engr. *Perf. 14*

9N284	A312	5pf dk gray	15	15
9N285	A312	8pf olive bis	85	90
9N286	A312	10pf brown	15	15
9N286A	A312	15pf olive	15	15
9N287	A312	20pf green	15	15
9N288	A312	25pf dp yel grn	95	1.10
9N289	A312	30pf red brown	1.40	45
9N290	A312	40pf brown org	40	22
9N291	A312	50pf dark blue	45	28
9N292	A312	60pf blue	65	52
9N293	A312	70pf dk brown	60	60
9N294	A312	80pf slate grn	70	60
9N295	A312	90pf magenta	2.25	1.40
9N296	A312	1m olive	85	45
9N296A	A312	110pf olive gray	95	75
9N297	A312	120pf ocher	85	85
9N298	A312	130pf ocher	1.25	90
9N298A	A312	140pf dk blue grn	1.25	90
9N299	A312	150pf purple	1.40	90
9N300	A312	160pf orange	1.25	90
9N300A	A312	170pf orange	1.50	90
9N300B	A312	190pf dp claret	1.65	1.10
9N301	A312	2m dp violet	1.65	90
		Nos. 9N284-9N301 (23)	21.45	15.22

Issue dates: 5pf, 1m, July 23. 10pf, 20pf, Oct. 23. 30pf, 90pf, 2m, Jan. 7, 1971. 8pf, 40pf, 50pf, 70pf, 80pf, Apr. 8, 1971. 60pf, June 25, 1971. 25pf, Aug. 27, 1971. 120pf, 160pf, Mar. 8, 1972. 15pf, 130pf, June 20, 1972. 150pf, July 5, 1972. 170pf, Sept. 11, 1972. 110pf, 140pf, 190pf, Jan. 16, 1973.

1970, Sept. 4 Litho. *Perf. 13½x14*

9N302	A64	30pf gray & multi	28	28

20th Berlin Festival Weeks.

Portrait Type of 1969

Design: 30pf, Leopold von Ranke, by Julius Schrage.

1970, Oct. 23 Photo. *Perf. 13½x14*

9N303	A62	30pf multicolored	32	32

175th anniversary of the birth of Leopold von Ranke (1795-1886), historian.

Imperial Eagle Type of Germany

1971, Jan. 18 Litho. *Perf. 13½x14*

9N304	A317	30pf org, red, gray & blk	25	25

Metropolitan Train, 1932 — A65

Designs: 5pf, Suburban train, 1925. 10pf, Street cars, 1890. 20pf, Horsedrawn trolley. 50pf, Strect car, 1950. 1m, Subway train, 1971.

1971 Litho. *Perf. 14*

9N305	A65	5pf multicolored	15	15
9N306	A65	10pf multicolored	16	16
9N307	A65	20pf multicolored	25	25
9N308	A65	30pf multicolored	42	42
9N309	A65	50pf multicolored	1.25	1.25
9N310	A65	1m multicolored	1.25	1.25
		Nos. 9N305-9N310 (6)	3.48	3.48

Issued: 30pf, 1m, Jan. 18; others, May 3.

Bagpipe Player, by Dürer — A66

1971, May 21 Engr. *Perf. 14*

9N311	A66	10pf black & brown	16	16

500th anniversary of the birth of Albrecht Dürer (1471-1528), painter and engraver.

Score from 2nd Brandenburg Concerto and Bach — A67

1971, July 14 Litho. *Perf. 14*

9N312	A67	30pf buff, brn & slate	40	30

250th anniv. of 1st performance of Johann Sebastian Bach's 2nd Brandenburg Concerto.

A68

A69

1971, July 14 Photo.

Telecommunications tower, Berlin.

9N313 A68 30pf dk blue, blk & car 40 30

Intl. Broadcasting Exhibition, Berlin.

1971, Aug. 27

9N314 A69 25pf multicolored 30 30

Hermann von Helmholtz (1821-94), scientist. See Nos. 9N332-9N333, 9N341.

Souvenir Sheet

Racing Cars — A70

1971, Aug. 27 Litho. *Perf. 14*

9N315 A70 Sheet of 4 1.25 1.25
- *a.* 10pf Opel racer 30 30
- *b.* 25pf Auto Union racer 30 30
- *c.* 30pf Mercedes-Benz SSKL, 1931 30 30
- *d.* 60pf Mercedes and Auto Union cars racing on North embankment 30 30

50th anniversary of Avus Race Track.

Accident Prevention Type of Germany

Designs: 5pf, "Matches cause fires." 10pf, Broken ladder. 20pf, Hand and circular saw. 25pf, "Alcohol and automobile." 30pf, Safety helmets prevent injury. 40pf, Defective plug. 50pf, Nail sticking from board. 60pf, 70pf, Traffic safety (ball rolling before car). 100pf, Hoisted cargo. 150pf, Fenced-in open manhole.

1971-73 Typo. *Perf. 14*

9N316 A328 5pf orange 22 22
9N317 A328 10pf dk brown 22 15
- *a.* Bkt. pane, 2 each #9N317-9N318, 9N320-9N321 ('74) 6.50

9N318 A328 20pf purple 18 15
9N319 A328 25pf green 55 35
9N320 A328 30pf dark red 38 17
9N321 A328 40pf rose cl 30 30
9N322 A328 50pf Prus blue 2.00 55
9N323 A328 60pf violet blue 1.50 85
9N323A A328 70pf green & vio bl 90 60
9N324 A328 100pf olive 1.50 80
9N325 A328 150pf red brown 4.25 1.75
Nos. 9N316-9N325 (11) 12.00 5.89

Issued in sheets of 100 and coils. Every fifth coil stamp has a control number on the back.
Issue dates: 25pf, 60pf, Sept. 10. 5pf, Oct. 29. 10pf, 30pf, Mar. 8, 1972. 40pf, June 20, 1972. 20pf, 100pf, July 5, 1972. 150pf, Sept. 11, 1972. 50pf, Jan. 16, 1973. 70pf, June 5, 1973.

Microscope and Metal Slide — A71

Friedrich Gilly, by Gottfried Schadow — A72

1971, Oct. 26 Photo. *Perf. 14*

9N326 A71 30pf multicolored 25 25

Materials Testing Laboratory centenary.

1972, Feb. 4 Engr. *Perf. 14*

9N327 A72 30pf black & blue 28 28

Friedrich Gilly (1772-1800), sculptor.

Grunewaldsee, by Alexander von Riesen — A73

Paintings of Berlin Lakes: 25pf, Wannsee, by Max Liebermann. 30pf, Schlachtensee, by Walter Leistikow.

1972, Apr. 14 Photo. *Perf. 14*

9N328 A73 10pf blue & multi 15 15
9N329 A73 25pf green & multi 25 25
9N330 A73 30pf black & multi 35 35

A74

A75

1972, May 18

9N331 A74 60pf violet & blk 80 50

E. T. A. Hoffmann (1776-1822), writer and composer. (Portrait by Wilhelm Hensel.)

Portrait Type of 1971

Designs: No. 9N332, Max Liebermann (1847-1935), self-portrait. No. 9N333, Karl August, Duke of Hardenberg (1750-1822), Prussian statesman, by J. H. W. Tischbein.

1972 Photo. *Perf. 14*

9N332 A69 40pf multi 40 40
9N333 A69 40pf multi 40 40

Issue dates: No. 9N332, July 18; No. 9N333, Nov. 10.

1972, Oct. 20 Engr. & Litho.

9N334 A75 20pf Stamp-printing press 18 18

Stamp Day 1972, and for the 5th National Youth Philatelic Exhib., Berlin, Oct. 26-29.

Streetcar, 1907 A76

Designs: No. 9N336, Double-decker bus, 1919. No. 9N337, Double-decker bus, 1925. No. 9N338, Electrobus, 1933. No. 9N339, Double-decker bus, 1970. No. 9N340, Elongated bus, 1973.

1973, Apr. 30 Litho. *Perf. 14*

9N335 A76 20pf gray & multi 35 32
9N336 A76 30pf gray & multi 50 45
9N337 A76 40pf gray & multi 65 55

1973, Sept. 14

9N338 A76 20pf gray & multi 35 32
9N339 A76 30pf gray & multi 50 45
9N340 A76 40pf gray & multi 65 55
Nos. 9N335-9N340 (6) 3.00 2.64

Public transportation in Berlin.

Portrait Type of 1971

Design: 40pf, Ludwig Tieck (1773-1853), poet and writer, by Carl Christian Vogel von Vogelstein.

1973, May 25 Photo. *Perf. 14*

9N341 A69 40pf multicolored 45 45

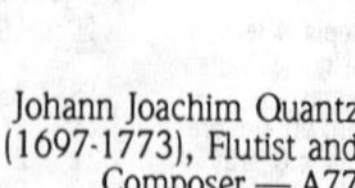

Johann Joachim Quantz (1697-1773), Flutist and Composer — A77

1973, June 12 Engr. *Perf. 14*

9N342 A77 40pf black 45 45

Souvenir Sheet

50 Years of Broadcasting — A78

1973, Aug. 23 Litho. *Perf. 14*

9N343 A78 Sheet of 4 3.50 4.00
- *a.* 20pf Speaker, set, 1926 75 85
- *b.* 30pf Hans Bredow 75 85
- *c.* 40pf Girl, TV, tape recorder 75 85
- *d.* 70pf TV camera 75 85

50 years of German broadcasting. Sold for 1.80m.

Georg W. von Knobelsdorff A79

Gustav R. Kirchhoff A80

1974, Feb. 15 Engr. *Perf. 14*

9N344 A79 20pf chocolate 18 18

275th anniversary of the birth of Georg Wenzelslaus von Knobelsdorff (1699-1753), architect.

1974, Feb. 15 Litho. & Engr.

9N345 A80 30pf gray & dk grn 28 28

Sesquicentennial of the birth of Gustav Robert Kirchhoff (1824-1887), physicist.

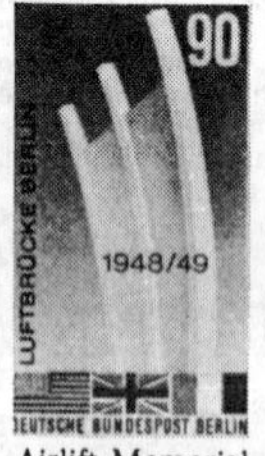

Airlift Memorial, Allied Flags — A81

Adolf Slaby and Waves — A82

1974, Apr. 17 Photo. *Perf. 14*

9N346 A81 90pf multicolored 1.25 85

25th anniversary of the end of the Allied airlift into Berlin.

1974, Apr. 17 Litho. *Perf. 14*

9N347 A82 40pf black & red 40 38

125th anniversary of the birth of Adolf Slaby (1849-1913), radio pioneer.

School Seal Showing Athena and Hermes — A83

1974, July 13 Photo. *Perf. 14*

9N348 A83 50pf multicolored 50 50

400th anniversary of the Gray Brothers' School, a secondary Franciscan school.

Berlin-Tegel Airport A84

Lithographed and Engraved

1974, Oct. 15 *Perf. 14*

9N349 A84 50pf multicolored 50 50

Opening of Berlin-Tegel Airport and Terminal, Nov. 1, 1974.

Venus, by F. E. Meyer, c. 1775 — A85

Gottfried Schadow — A86

Berlin Porcelain: 40pf, "Astronomy," by W. C. Meyer, c. 1772. 50pf, "Justice," by J. G. Müller, c. 1785.

1974, Oct. 29 Litho. *Perf. 14*

9N350 A85 30pf carmine & multi 32 28
9N351 A85 40pf carmine & multi 40 35
9N352 A85 50pf carmine & multi 55 48

1975, Jan. 15 Engr. *Perf. 14*

9N353 A86 50pf maroon 50 50

Johann Gottfried Schadow (1764-1850), sculptor.

S.S. Princess Charlotte A87

Ships: 40pf, S.S. Siegfried. 50pf, S.S. Sperber. 60pf, M.S. Vaterland. 70pf, M.S. Moby Dick.

1975, Feb. 14 Litho. *Perf. 14*

9N354 A87 30pf gray & multi 50 40
9N355 A87 40pf olive & multi 55 45
9N356 A87 50pf ultra & multi 65 48
9N357 A87 60pf red brn & multi 75 60
9N358 A87 70pf dk blue & multi 1.00 80
Nos. 9N354-9N358 (5) 3.45 2.73

Berlin passenger ships

Industry Type of Germany

1975-82 Engr. *Perf. 14*

Type A380

9N359 5pf Symphonie satellite 15 15
9N360 10pf Electric train 15 15
9N361 20pf Old Weger lighthouse 15 15
9N362 30pf Rescue helicopter 22 15
9N363 40pf Space 28 15
9N364 50pf Radar station 35 15
9N365 60pf X-ray machine 55 15
9N366 70pf Shipbuilding 55 24
9N367 80pf Tractor 65 35
9N368 100pf Coal excavator 80 42
9N368A 110pf TV camera 90 38
9N369 120pf Chemical plant 1.00 55
9N369A 130pf Brewery 1.10 45

9N370 140pf Heating plant 1.25 60
9N371 150pf Power shovel 1.50 55
9N372 160pf Blast furnace 1.40 90
9N373 180pf Payloader 1.50 70
9N373A 190pf Shovel dredger 1.50 65
9N374 200pf Oil drill platform 1.50 75
9N375 230pf Frankfurt airport 2.25 70
9N375A 250pf Airport 2.25 90
9N375B 300pf Electric railroad 2.50 1.00
9N376 500pf Radio telescope 4.25 2.50
Nos. 9N359-9N376 (23) 26.75 12.69

Issue dates: 40pf, 50pf, 100pf, May 15. 10pf, 30pf, 70pf, Aug. 14. 80pf, 120pf, 160pf, Oct. 15. 5pf, 140pf, 200pf, Nov. 14. 20pf, 500pf, Feb. 17, 1976. 60pf, Nov. 16, 1978. 230pf, May 17, 1979. 150pf, 180pf, July 12, 1979. 110pf, 130pf, 300pf, June 16, 1982. 190pf, 250pf, July 15, 1982.

Ferdinand Sauerbruch A88

Gymnasts' Emblem A89

Lithographed and Engraved

1975, May 15 ***Perf. 13½x14***
9N379 A88 50pf dull red & dk brn 48 48

Ferdinand Sauerbruch (1875-1951) surgeon, birth centenary.

1975, May 15 **Photo.** ***Perf. 14***
9N380 A89 40pf green, gold & blk 38 38

6th Gymnaestrada, Berlin, July 1-5.

Lovis Corinth (1858-1925), Self-portrait, 1900 — A90

1975, July 15 **Photo.** ***Perf. 14***
9N381 A90 50pf multicolored 48 48

Architecture Type of Germany

Design: Houses, Naunynstrasse, Berlin-Kreuzberg.

1975, July 15 **Litho. & Engr.**
9N382 A381 50pf multicolored 48 48

European Architectural Heritage Year.

Paul Löbe and Reichstag A92

1975, Nov. 14 **Engr.** ***Perf. 14***
9N383 A92 50pf copper red 48 48

Paul Löbe (1875-1967), president of German Parliament 1920-1932, birth centenary.

Grain — A93

1976, Jan. 5 **Photo.** ***Perf. 14***
9N384 A93 70pf green & yellow 60 60

Green Week International Agricultural Exhibition, Berlin, 50th anniversary.

Hockey A94

1976, May 13 **Engr.** ***Perf. 14***
9N385 A94 30pf green 28 28

Women's World Hockey Championships.

Treble Clef — A95

Berlin Fire Brigade Emblem — A96

1976, May 13 **Photo.**
9N386 A95 40pf multicolored 38 38

German Choir Festival.

1976, May 13 **Litho.**
9N387 A96 50pf red & multi 48 48

Berlin Fire Brigade, 125th anniversary.

Sailboat on Havel River — A97

Berlin Views: 40pf, Spandau Castle. 50pf, Tiergarten.

1976, Nov. 16 **Engr.** ***Perf. 14***
9N388 A97 30pf blue & blk 40 30
9N389 A97 40pf brown & blk 50 38
9N390 A97 50pf green & blk 75 55

See Nos. 9N422-9N424.

Castle Type of Germany

1977-79 **Typo.** ***Perf. 14***

Castles: 10pf, Glücksburg. 20pf, 190pf, Pfaueninsel. 25pf, Gemen. 30pf, Ludwigstein. 40pf, Eltz. 50pf, Neuschwanstein. 60pf, Marksburg. 70pf, Mespelbrunn. 90pf, Vischering. 200pf, Bürresheim. 210pf, Schwanenburg. 230pf, Lichtenberg.

9N391 A406 10pf gray blue 15 15
a. Bklt. pane, 4 #9N391, 2 each #9N394, 9N396 2.50
b. Bklt. pane, 4 #9N391, 2 #9N394, 2 #9N440 2.25
c. Bklt. pane, 4 #9N391, 2 #9N440, 2 #9N442 2.25
d. Bklt. pane, 2 each #9N391, 9N394, 9N440-9N441 2.50
9N392 A406 20pf orange 15 15
9N393 A406 25pf crimson 22 15
9N394 A406 30pf olive 25 15
9N395 A406 40pf blue green 45 15
9N396 A406 50pf rose car 55 15
9N397 A406 60pf brown 60 25
9N398 A406 70pf blue 60 35
9N399 A406 90pf dark blue 1.00 45
9N400 A406 190pf red brown 1.75 95
9N401 A406 200pf green 2.00 80
9N402 A406 210pf red brown 2.50 1.00
9N403 A406 230pf dark green 2.75 1.10
Nos. 9N391-9N403 (13) 12.97 5.80

Issued in sheets of 100 and coils. Every fifth coil stamp has a control number on the back.

Issue dates: 60pf, 200pf, Jan. 13. 40pf, 190pf, Feb. 16. 10pf, 20pf, 30pf, Apr. 14. 50pf, 70pf, May 17. 230pf, Nov. 16, 1978. 25pf, 90pf, Jan. 11, 1979. 210pf, Feb. 14, 1979.

See Nos. 9N438-9N445.

Eugenie d'Alton, by Rausch — A98

Eduard Gaertner (1801-77), Painter — A99

1977, Jan. 13 **Photo.** ***Perf. 14***
9N404 A98 50pf violet black 60 48

Christian Daniel Rausch (1777-1857), sculptor, birth bicentenary.

1977, Feb. 16 **Litho. & Engr.**
9N405 A99 40pf lt grn, grn & blk 45 38

Fountain, by Georg Kolbe — A100

"Bear each other's burdens" — A101

1977, Apr. 14 **Photo.** ***Perf. 14***
9N406 A100 30pf dark olive 40 28

Georg Kolbe (1877-1947), sculptor.

1977, May 17 **Litho.** ***Perf. 14***
9N407 A101 40pf green blk & yel 40 38

17th meeting of German Protestants (Evangelical Synod), Berlin.

Patent Office, Berlin-Kreuzberg — A102

1977, July 13 **Litho. & Engr.**
9N408 A102 60pf gray & red 65 50

Centenary of German patent laws.

Telephones, 1905 and 1977 A103

Painting by George Grosz (1893-1959) A104

1977, July 13 **Litho.**
9N409 A103 50pf multicolored 80 50

International Broadcasting Exhibition, Berlin, Aug. 26-Sept. 4, and centenary of telephone in Germany.

1977, July 13
9N410 A104 70pf multicolored 85 65

15th European Art Exhibition, Berlin, Aug. 14-Oct. 16.

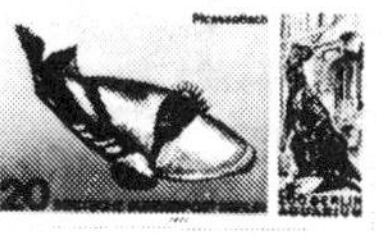

Rhinecanthus Aculeatus A105

Designs: 30pf, Paddlefish. 40pf, Tortoise. 50pf, Rhinoceros iguana. Designs include statue of iguanodon from Aquarium entrance.

1977, Aug. 16 **Photo.** ***Perf. 14***
9N411 A105 20pf multicolored 18 16
9N412 A105 30pf multicolored 40 32
9N413 A105 40pf multicolored 50 40
9N414 A105 50pf multicolored 70 55

25th anniv. of the reopening of Berlin Aquarium.

Walter Kollo (1878-1940), Composer — A106

1978, Jan. 12 **Engr.** ***Perf. 14***
9N415 A106 50pf brn, red & dk brn 65 50

Chamber of Commerce Emblem A107

1978, Apr. 13 **Engr.** ***Perf. 14***
9N416 A107 90pf dk blue & red 90 80

American Chamber of Commerce in Germany, 75th anniversary.

15-Cent Minimum Value
The minimum catalogue value is 15 cents. Separating se-tenant pieces into individual stamps does not increase the value of the stamps since demand for the separated stamps may be small.

Albrecht von Graefe — A108

Friedrich Ludwig Jahn — A109

1978, May 22 Engr. *Perf. 14*
9N417 A108 30pf red brn & blk 35 28

Dr. Albrecht von Graefe (1828-1870) ophthalmologist.

1978, July 13 Engr. *Perf. 14*
9N418 A109 50pf dk carmine 55 50

Friedrich Ludwig Jahn (1778-1852), founder of organized gymnastics.

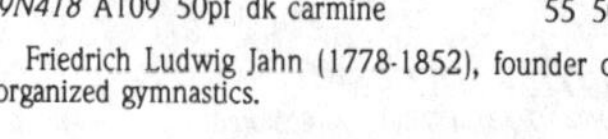

Swimmers A110

1978, Aug. 17 Litho. *Perf. 14*
9N419 A110 40pf multicolored 45 38

3rd World Swimming Championships, Berlin, Aug. 18-28.

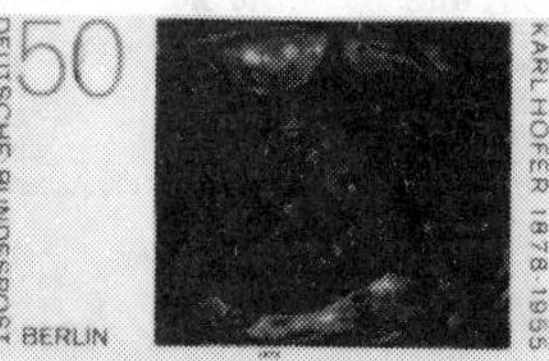

The Boat, by Karl Hofer — A111

1978, Oct. 12 Photo. *Perf. 14*
9N420 A111 50pf multicolored 55 50

Karl Hofer (1878-1955), painter.

National Library A112

1978, Nov. 16 Engr. *Perf. 14*
9N421 A112 90pf red & olive 1.10 80

Opening of new National Library building.

Views Type of 1976

Berlin Views: 40pf, Belvedere, Charlottenburg Castle. 50pf, Shell House on Landwehr Canal. 60pf, Village Church, Alt-Lichtenrade.

1978, Nov. 16
9N422 A97 40pf green & blk 50 40
9N423 A97 50pf lilac & blk 70 45
9N424 A97 60pf brown & blk 1.00 60

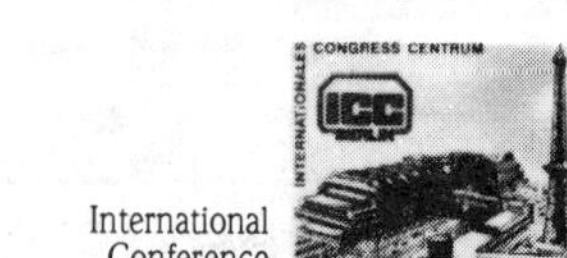

International Conference Center — A113

Photogravure and Engraved

1979, Feb. 14 *Perf. 14*
9N425 A113 60pf multicolored 90 75

Opening of Intl. Conference Center in Berlin.

A114

A115

1979, May 17 Litho. *Perf. 14*
9N426 A114 60pf German eagles 65 55

Cent. of German Natl. Printing Bureau.

1979, July 12 Photo. *Perf. 14*
9N427 A115 60pf TV screen, emblem 60 55

Intl. Broadcasting Exhibition, Berlin.

Target and Arrows A116

1979, July 12
9N428 A116 50pf multicolored 50 50

World Archery Championships, Berlin.

Moses Mendelssohn A117

1979, Aug. 9 Engr. *Perf. 14*
9N429 A117 90pf black 1.00 80

Mendelssohn (1729-86), philosopher.

Gas Lamp — A118

Historic Street Lanterns: 40pf, Carbon arc lamp. 50pf, Hanging gas lamps. 60pf, 5-armed candelabra.

1979, Aug. 9 Litho.
9N430 A118 10pf multicolored 15 15
9N431 A118 40pf multicolored 52 45
9N432 A118 50pf multicolored 70 65
9N433 A118 60pf multicolored 85 80

300 years of street lighting in Berlin.

Orchid A119

1979, Aug. 9
9N434 A119 50pf multicolored 55 50

Botanical Gardens, Berlin, 300th anniv.

Berlin Poster Columns, 125th Anniversary — A120

Lithographed and Engraved

1979, Nov. 14 *Perf. 14*
9N435 A120 50pf multicolored 75 50

Castle Type of Germany

1979-82 Typo. *Perf. 14*
9N438 A406 35pf Lichtenstein 35 15
9N439 A406 40pf Wolfsburg 38 18
9N440 A406 50pf Inzlingen 50 22
9N441 A406 60pf Rheydt 60 15
9N442 A406 80pf Wilhelmsthal 75 35
9N443 A406 120pf Charlottenburg 1.10 52
9N444 A406 280pf Ahrensburg 2.50 1.40
9N445 A406 300pf Herrenhausen 2.75 1.40
Nos. 9N438-9N445 (8) 8.93 4.37

Issue dates: 60pf, Nov. 14. 40pf, 50pf, Feb. 14, 1980. 35pf, 80pf, 300pf, June 16, 1982. 120pf, 280pf, July 15, 1982.

World Map Showing Continental Drift — A121

1980, Feb. 14 Litho. *Perf. 14*
9N451 A121 60pf multicolored 90 75

Alfred Wegener (1880-1930), geophysicist and meteorologist; founded theory of continental drift.

A122 A123

Design: Cardinal Count Preysing (1880-1950).

1980, May 8 Engr. *Perf. 14*
9N452 A122 50pf blk & car rose 60 50

German Catholics Day.

1980, July 10 Litho. *Perf. 14*

Prussian Museum, Berlin, 150th Anniv.: 40pf, Angel, enamel medallion, 12th cent. 60pf, Monks Reading, oak sculpture, by Ernest Barlach (1870-1938).

9N453 A123 40pf multi 40 40
9N454 A123 60pf multi 60 60

Von Steuben Leading Troops — A124

Robert Stolz Conducting — A125

1980, Aug. 14 Litho. *Perf. 14*
9N455 A124 40pf multicolored 50 45

Friedrich Wilhelm von Steuben (1730-94).

1980, Aug. 14
9N456 A125 60pf dk blue & bis 70 60

Robert Stolz (1880-1975), composer.

Lilienthal Memorial — A126

Designs: 50pf, Grosse Neugierde Memorial, 1835. 60pf, Lookout tower, Grunewald Memorial to Kaiser Wilhelm I.

1980, Nov. 13 Engr. *Perf. 14*
9N457 A126 40pf dk green & blk 40 40
9N458 A126 50pf brown & blk 45 45
9N459 A126 60pf dk blue & blk 60 60

Von Gontard and Kleist Park Colonnades, Berlin A127

1981, Jan. 15 Litho. *Perf. 14*
9N460 A127 50pf multicolored 60 50

Karl Philipp von Gontard (1731-91), architect.

Achim von Arnim A128

Adelbert von Chamisso A129

1981, Jan. 15 Engr.
9N461 A128 60pf dark green 55 55

Achim von Arnim (1781-1831), poet.

1981, Jan. 15 Litho.
9N462 A129 60pf brn & gldn brn 55 55

Adelbert von Chamisso (1781-1838), poet.

Berlin-Kreuzberg, Liberation Monument, 1813 — A130

1981, Feb. 12 Engr. *Perf. 14*
9N463 A130 40pf brown 55 45

Karl Friedrich Schinkel (1781-1841), architect, 400th anniversary of birth.

Arts and Science Medal, Awarded 1842-1933
A131

Amor and Psyche, by Reinhold Begas (1831-1911)
A132

1981, July 16 **Litho.** ***Perf. 14***
9N464 A131 40pf multicolored 55 45

"Prussia—an attempt at a balance" exhibition.

1981, July 16 **Photo.**
9N465 A132 50pf multicolored 50 50

Intl. Telecommunications Exhibition — A133

1981, July 16 **Litho.**
9N466 A133 60pf multicolored 80 65

Peter Beuth (1781-1853), Constitutional Law Expert — A134

Nijinsky, by Georg Kolbe, 1914 — A135

Lithographed and Engraved

1981, Nov. 12 ***Perf. 14***
9N467 A134 60pf gold & black 55 55

1981, Nov. 12 **Photo.**

20th Century Sculptures: 60pf, Mother Earth II, by Ernst Barlach, 1920. 90pf, Flora Kneeling, by Richard Scheibe, 1930.

9N468	A135 40pf multicolored	45	40
9N469	A135 60pf multicolored	70	60
9N470	A135 90pf multicolored	1.25	1.10

750th Anniv. of Spandau
A136

Lithographed and Engraved

1982, Feb. 18 ***Perf. 14***
9N471 A136 60pf multicolored 75 60

Berlin Philharmonic Centenary
A137

Salzburg Emigration to Prussia, 250th Anniv.
A138

Lithographed and Embossed

1982, Apr. 15 ***Perf. 14***
9N472 A137 60pf multicolored 75 60

1982, May 5 **Litho.** **Engr.**
9N473 A138 50pf multicolored 50 50

Italian Stone Carriers, by Max Pechstein — A139

Design: 80pf, Two Girls Bathing, by Otto Mueller.

1982, July 15 **Litho.** ***Perf. 14***

9N474	A139 50pf multicolored	75	50
9N475	A139 80pf multicolored	1.10	75

Villa Borsig — A140

1982, Nov. 10 **Engr.** ***Perf. 14***

9N476	A140 50pf shown	60	55
9N477	A140 60pf Sts. Peter and Paul Church	75	70
9N478	A140 80pf Villa von der Heydt	1.00	90

State Theater, Charlottenburg, 1790 — A141

1982, Nov. 10 **Litho. & Engr.**
9N479 A141 80pf multicolored 1.00 85

Carl Gotthard Langhans (1732-1808), architect.

A142

A142a

Various street pumps and fire hydrants, 1900.

1983, Jan. 13 **Litho.** ***Perf. 14***

9N480	A142 50pf multi	65	60
9N481	A142 60pf multi	80	75
9N482	A142 80pf multi	95	90
9N483	A142 120pf multi	1.50	1.40

1983, Feb. 8 **Engr.** ***Perf. 14***
9N484 A142a 80pf dark brown 1.40 1.25

Berlin-Koblenz Telegraph Service sesquicentennial.

A143

A144

Design: Portrait of Barbara Campanini, 1745, by Antoine Pesne (1683-1757).

1983, May 5 **Photo.** ***Perf. 14***
9N485 A143 50pf multicolored 80 65

1983, July 14 **Litho.** ***Perf. 14***
9N486 A144 50pf Silhouette 80 60

Joachim Ringelnatz (1883-1934), painter and writer.

Intl. Radio Exhibition, Sept. 2-11
A145

1983, July 14
9N487 A145 80pf Nipkow's phototelegraphy diagram 1.25 1.00

Ancient Artwork, Berlin Museum — A146

Designs: 30pf, Bust of Queen Cleopatra VII, 69-30 B.C. 50pf, Statue of Egyptian Couple, Giza, 2400 B.C. 60pf, Stone God with Beaded Turban, Mexico, 300 B.C. 80pf, Enamel Plate, 16th century.

1984, Jan. 12 **Litho.** ***Perf. 14***

9N488	A146 30pf multi	42	42
9N489	A146 50pf multi	65	65
9N490	A146 60pf multi	90	85
9N491	A146 80pf multi	1.00	1.00

Electricity Centenary
A147

Conference Emblem
A148

Design: Allegorical figure holding light bulb (symbol of electric power).

1984, May 8 **Litho.** ***Perf. 14***
9N492 A147 50pf black & org 65 50

1984, May 8
9N493 A148 60pf multicolored 90 70

European Ministers of Culture, 4th Conf.

Erich Klausener (1885-1934), Chairman of Catholic Action — A149

1984, May 8 **Engr.** ***Perf. 14x13½***
9N494 A149 80pf dark green 1.00 85

Alfred Brehm (1829-1884), Zoologist — A150

Lithographed and Engraved

1984, Apr. 18 ***Perf. 14***
9N495 A150 80pf Brehm, white stork 1.25 90

A151 A152

1984, Aug. 21 **Engr.** ***Perf. 14***
9N496 A151 50pf brown & blk 80 60

Ernst Ludwig Heim (1747-1834), botanist.

1984, Nov. 8 **Litho.** ***Perf. 14***

Design: Sunflowers, by Karl Schmidt-Rottluff (1884-1976).

9N497 A152 60pf multi 90 70

A153 A154

1985, Feb. 21 **Litho. & Engr.**
9N498 A153 50pf multicolored 90 70

Bettina von Arnim, writer (1785-1859).

1985, Feb. 21 **Engr.**
9N499 A154 80pf blue, blk & red 1.10 85

Wilhelm von Humboldt, statesman (1767-1835).

1985 Berlin Horticultural Show — A155

1985, Apr. 16 **Litho.** ***Perf. 14***
9N500 A155 80pf Symbolic flower 1.00 80

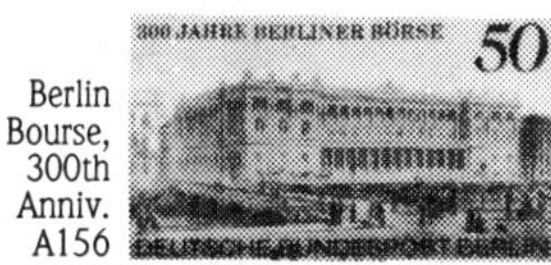

Berlin Bourse, 300th Anniv.
A156

1985, May 7 **Litho. & Engr.**
9N501 A156 50pf multicolored 90 70

Otto Klemperer (1885-1973), Conductor — A157

1985, May 7 **Engr.**
9N502 A157 60pf dp blue violet 1.00 80

Telefunken Camera, 1936
A158

1985, July 16 Litho. *Perf. 14*

9N503 A158 80pf multicolored 1.00 90

German Television, 50th anniv., Intl. Telecommunications Exhibition, Berlin.

9th World Gynecological Congress — A159

Design: Emblem of the Intl. Federation for Gynecology and birth aid.

1985, July 16 Photo. *Perf. 13½x14*

9N504 A159 60pf pale yel, ap grn & dp grn 80 70

Edict of Potsdam, 300th Anniv.
A160

Lithographed and Engraved

1985, Oct. 15 *Perf. 14*

9N505 A160 50pf dk bluish lilac 65 50

Kurt Tucholsky (1890-1935), Novelist, Journalist — A161

1985, Nov. 12 Litho. *Perf. 14*

9N506 A161 80pf multi 1.00 85

Wilhelm Furtwangler (1886-1954), Composer — A162

Score from Sonata in D Sharp.

Lithographed and Engraved

1986, Jan. 16 *Perf. 14*

9N507 A162 80pf multi 1.40 1.10

Ludwig Mies van der Rohe (1886-1969), Architect — A163

1986, Feb. 13

9N508 A163 50pf multi 90 70

New Natl. Gallery, Berlin.

16th European Communities Day — A164

1986, Apr. 10 Litho. *Perf. 14*

9N509 A164 60pf Flags 90 70

Leopold von Ranke (1795-1886), Historian — A165

Gottfried Benn (1886-1956), Writer and Physician — A166

1986, May 5 Litho.

9N510 A165 80pf brn blk & tan 1.25 1.00

Engr.

9N511 A166 80pf brt blue 1.25 1.00

Portals and Gateways — A167

1986, June 20 Litho. & Engr.

9N512 A167 50pf Charlotte Gate 70 80
9N513 A167 60pf Gryphon Gate, Glienicke Castle 85 80
9N514 A167 80pf Elephant Gate, Berlin Zoo 1.25 1.10

King Frederick the Great — A168

Painting: The Flute Concert (detail), by Adolph von Menzel.

1986, Aug. 14 Litho. *Perf. 14*

9N515 A168 80pf multicolored 1.00 80

Famous Women Type of Germany

Designs: 5pf, Emma Ihrer (1857-1911), politician, labor leader. 10pf, Paula Modersohn-Becker (1876-1907), painter. 20pf, Cilly Aussem (1909-63), tennis champion. 40pf, Maria Sibylla Merian. 50pf, Christine Teusch. 60pf, Dorothea Erxleben (1715-62), physician. 80pf, Clara Schumann. 100pf, Therese Giehse (1898-1975), actress. 130pf, Lise Meitner (1878-1968), physicist. 140pf, Cecile Vogt (1875-1962), neurologist. 170pf, Hannah Arendt (1906-75), American political scientist. 180pf, Lotte Lehmann (1888-1976), soprano. 240pf, Mathilde Franziska Anneke, (1817-84), American author. 250pf, Queen Louise of Prussia (1776-1810). 300pf, Fanny Hensel (1805-1847), composer-conductor. 350pf, Hedwig Dransfeld (1871-1925), women's rights activist. 500pf, Alice Salomon (1872-1948), feminist and social activist.

1986-89 Engr. *Perf. 14*

Type A602

9N516 5pf bluish gray & org brn 15 15
9N517 10pf vio & yel brn 15 15
9N518 20pf lake & Prus bl 22 16
9N519 40pf dp bl & dk lil rose 42 38
9N520 50pf gray ol & Prus bl 52 42
9N521 60pf dp vio & grnsh blk 60 55
9N522 80pf dk grn & lt red brn 85 65
9N523 100pf dk red & grnsh blk 1.00 95
9N524 130pf Prus bl & dk vio 1.40 1.40
9N525 140pf blk & dk ol bis 1.65 1.25
9N526 170pf gray grn & dk brn 1.90 1.50
9N527 180pf bl & brn vio 2.00 1.50
9N528 240pf Prus bl & yel brn 2.50 2.25
9N529 250pf dp lil rose & dp bl 2.75 2.25
9N530 300pf dk vio & sage grn 3.25 2.50
9N531 350pf gray grn & lake 3.75 3.25
9N532 500pf slate grn & brt ver 5.50 5.00
Nos. 9N516-9N532 (17) 28.61 24.31

Issue dates: 50pf, 80pf, Nov. 1. 40pf, Sept. 17, 1987. 10pf, Apr. 4, 1988. 20pf, 130pf, May 5, 1988. 60pf, 100pf, 170pf, 240pf, 350pf, Nov. 10, 1988. 500pf, Jan. 12, 1989. 5pf, Feb. 9, 1989. 180pf, 250pf, July 13, 1989. 140pf, 300pf, Aug. 10, 1989.

Berlin 750th Anniv. Type of Germany

Designs: a, Berlin, 1650, engraving by Caspar Merian. b, Charlottenburg Castle, c. 1830. c, AEG Company turbine construction building, by architect Walter Behrens, 1909. d, Philharmonic Concert Hall and Chamber Music Rooms on the Kemperplatz, 1987.

1987, Jan. 15 Litho. *Perf. 14*

9N536 A604 80pf like #1496 1.00 85

Souvenir Sheet

Perf. 14x14½

9N537 Sheet of 4 2.50 2.50
a. A604 40pf multicolored 42 42
b. A604 50pf multicolored 52 52
c. A604 60pf multicolored 65 65
d. A604 80pf multicolored 85 85

No. 9N537 contains four 43x25mm stamps.

A169

A170

1987, Feb. 12 Engr. *Perf. 14*

9N538 A169 50pf sepia & dk red 80 28

Louise Schroeder (1887-1957), politican.

1987, May 5 Litho. & Engr.

Design: Bohemian refugees, bas-relief detail from monument to King Friedrich Wilhelm I of Prussia, 1912.

9N539 A170 50pf sep & pale gray grn 58 30

Settlement of Bohemians at Rixdorf, 250th anniv.

1987 Intl. Architecture Exhibition
A171

1987, May 5 Litho. *Perf. 14x14½*

9N540 A171 80pf lt ultra, sil & blk 90 45

14th Int'l. Botanical Congress — A172

1987, July 16 Litho. *Perf. 14*

9N541 A172 60pf multicolored 75 60

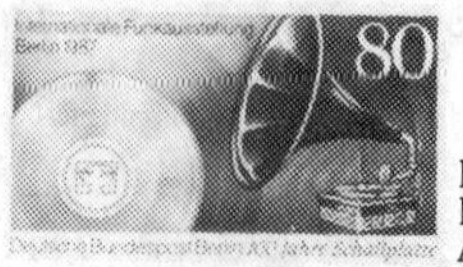

Int'l. Radio Exhibition
A173

1987, Aug. 20

9N542 A173 80pf Gramophone, compact disc 90 75

Historic Sites and Objects Type of Germany

Designs: 5pf, Brunswick Lion. 10pf, Frankfurt Airport. 20pf, No. 9N550, Queen Nefertiti, bust, Egyptian Museum, Berlin. 30pf, Corner tower, Celle Castle, 14th cent. 40pf, Chile House, Hamburg. 50pf, Filigree tracery on spires, Freiburg Cathedral. 60pf, Bavaria Munich, bronze statue above the Theresienwiese, Hall of Fame. No. 9N551, Heligoland. 80pf, Entrance to Zollern II, coal mine, Dortmund. 100pf, Altotting Chapel, Bavaria. 120pf, Schleswig Cathedral. 140pf, Bronze flagon from Reinheim. 300pf, Hambach Castle. 350pf, Externsteine Bridge near Horn-Bad Meinberg.

1987-90 Typo. *Perf. 14*

Type A623

9N543 5pf Prus bl & gray 15 15
9N544 10pf lt chalky bl & slate bl 15 15
9N545 20pf dull blue & tan 22 15
9N546 30pf agua & org brn 35 22
9N547 40pf ultra, dk red brn & org red 45 28
9N548 50pf ultra & yel brn 58 38
9N549 60pf cob & pale gray 68 45
9N550 70pf dull bl & fawn 85 52
9N551 70pf vio bl & henna brn 85 52
9N552 80pf cob & pale gray 90 55
a. Bklt. pane of 8 (4 10pf, 2 50pf, 2 80pf) ('89) 3.45
9N553 100pf brt bluish grn & olive bis 1.10 70
a. Bklt. pane of 8 (2 each 10pf, 60pf, 80pf, 100pf) 5.60
9N554 120pf brn org & lt grnsh bl 1.45 90
9N555 140pf tan & lt grn 1.60 1.00
9N556 300pf dk red brn & tan 3.75 2.25
9N557 350pf brt ultra & ol bis 3.75 2.50
Nos. 9N543-9N557 (15) 16.83 10.72

Issue dates: 30pf, 50pf, 60pf, 80pf, Nov. 6. 10pf, 300pf, Jan. 14, 1988. No. 9N550, 120pf, July 14, 1988. 20pf, 140pf, Jan. 12, 1989. 100pf, 350pf, Feb. 9, 1989. 5pf, Feb. 15, 1990. No. 9N551, June 21, 1990.

European Culture — A175

1988, Jan. 14 Litho. *Perf. 14*

9N568 A175 80pf Berlin Bear 1.00 50

Urania Science Museum, Cent.
A176

1988, Feb. 18

9N569 A176 50pf multicolored 65 50

A177

A178

Design: Thoroughbred Foal, bronze sculpture by Renee Sintenis (1888-1965).

1988, Feb. 18

9N570 A177 60pf multicolored 75 50

1988, May 5 Litho. & Engr.

Design: The Great Elector with Family in Berlin Castle Gardens.

9N571 A178 50pf multicolored 60 45

The Great Elector of Brandenburg (d. 1688), founder of the Hohenzollern Dynasty.

Intl. Monetary Fund and World Bank Congress, Berlin — A179

1988, Aug. 11 **Litho.**
9N572 A179 70pf multicolored 80 60

Berlin-Potsdam Railway, 150th Anniv. — A180

1988, Oct. 13 **Litho.**
9N573 A180 10pf multicolored 15 15

A181

A182

Design: *The Collector,* 1913, by Ernst Barlach (1870-1938).

1988, Oct. 13
9N574 A181 40pf multicolored 45 35

1989, May 5 **Photo.** ***Perf. 14***
9N575 A182 60pf multicolored 68 50

Airlift, 40th anniv.

13th Intl. Congress of the Supreme Audit Office, Berlin A183

1989, May 5 **Litho.**
9N576 A183 80pf multicolored 90 65

Ernst Reuter (1889-1953), Mayor of Berlin — A184

Perf. 14x14½
1989, July 13 **Litho. & Engr.**
9N577 A184 100pf multicolored 1.10 90

Intl. Radio Exhibition, Berlin A185

1989, July 13 **Litho.**
9N578 A185 100pf multicolored 1.10 90

Plans of the Zoological Gardens, Berlin, and Designer Peter Joseph Lenne (1789-1866) — A186

Litho. & Engr.
1989, Aug. 10 ***Perf. 14***
9N579 A186 60pf multicolored 70 50

Carl von Ossietzky (1889-1938), Awarded Nobel Peace Prize of 1935 — A187

1989, Aug. 10 **Photo.**
9N580 A187 100pf multicolored 1.10 80

450th Anniv. of the Reformation — A188

Design: Nikolai Church, Spandau District.

1989, Oct. 12 **Litho.**
9N581 A188 60pf multicolored 75 50

French Gymnasium, 300th Anniv. — A189

Design: School from 1701 to 1873 and frontispiece of *Leges Gymnasie Gallici,* published in 1689.

1989, Oct. 12 **Litho. & Engr.**
9N582 A189 40pf multicolored 55 40

Journalists, 1925, by Hannah Hoch (1889-1978) A190

1989, Oct. 12 **Litho.** ***Perf. 13½***
9N583 A190 100pf multicolored 1.10 75

European Postal Service 500th Anniv. Type

1990, Jan. 12 **Litho. & Engr.** ***Perf. 14***
9N584 A673 100pf *The Young Post Rider* 1.10 90

Public Transportation, 250th Anniv. — A191

1990, Jan. 12 **Litho.**
9N585 A191 60pf multicolored 70 60

Ernst Rudorff (1840-1916), Conservationist — A192

1990, Jan. 12
9N586 A192 60pf multicolored 70 60

People's Free Theater Organization, Cent. — A193

1990, Feb. 15 ***Perf. 13½***
9N587 A193 100pf multicolored 1.10 80

Parliament House, 40th Anniv. A194

1990, Feb. 15 ***Perf. 14x14½***
9N588 A194 100pf multicolored 1.10 90

Bicent. of the Invention of the Barrel Organ — A195

1990, May 3 **Litho.** ***Perf. 14***
9N589 A195 100pf multicolored 1.20 90

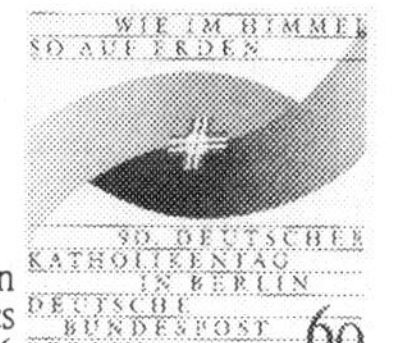
90th German Catholics Day — A196

1990, May 3
9N590 A196 60pf multicolored 70 60

German Pharmaceutical Society, Cent. — A197

1990, Aug. 9 **Litho.** ***Perf. 14***
9N591 A197 100pf multicolored 1.20 1.00

Adolph Diesterweg (1790-1866), Educator — A198

1990, Sept. 27
9N592 A198 60pf multicolored 70 75

Stamps for Berlin were discontinued Oct. 3, 1990, when Germany and the German Democratic Republic merged. The stamps remained valid until Dec. 31, 1991.

OCCUPATION SEMI-POSTAL STAMPS

Offering Plate and Berlin Bear — SP1

Wmk. 284
1949, Dec. 1 **Litho.** ***Perf. 14***

9NB1 SP1	10 + 5pf grn	42.50	*150.00*
9NB2 SP1	20 + 5pf car	42.50	*150.00*
9NB3 SP1	30 + 5pf blue	42.50	*150.00*
	Set, never hinged	275.00	
a.	Souv. sheet of 3, #9NB1-9NB3	475.00	*2,200.*
a.	Souv. sheet, never hinged	700.00	

The surtax was for Berlin victims of currency devaluation.

Harp and Laurel Branch — SP2

"Singing Angels" — SP3

1950, Oct. 29 **Engr.** **Wmk. 116**

9NB4 SP2	10 + 5pf grn	22.50	32.50
9NB5 SP3	30 + 5pf dk sl bl	37.50	*62.50*
	Set, never hinged	120.00	

The surtax was to aid in reestablishing the Berlin Philharmonic Orchestra.

Young Stamp Collectors — SP4

Reconstructed Kaiser Wilhelm Memorial Church — SP5

1951, Oct. 7 ***Perf. 14***

9NB6 SP4	10 + 3pf grn	10.00	*18.00*
9NB7 SP4	20 + 2pf brn red	12.00	*22.50*
	Set, never hinged	47.50	

Stamp Day, Berlin, Oct. 7, 1951.

1953, Aug. 9 Wmk. 284

Design: 20pf+10pf, 30pf+15pf, Ruins of Kaiser Wilhelm Memorial Church.

9NB8 SP5 4 + 1pf choc 15 60
9NB9 SP5 10 + 5pf grn 75 *5.25*
9NB10 SP5 20 + 10pf car 75 *4.75*
9NB11 SP5 30 + 15pf dp bl 8.25 *65.00*
Set, never hinged 20.00

The surtax was to aid in reconstructing the church.

Catalogue values for unused stamps in this section, from this point to the end of the section, are for Never Hinged items.

Prussian Postilion — SP6

Prussian Field Postilion — SP7

1954, Aug. 4 Litho. Wmk. 284
9NB12 SP6 20 + 10pf multi 16.00 *18.00*

National Stamp Exhibition, Berlin, Aug. 4-8.

Perf. 13½x14

1955, Oct. 27 Wmk. 304
9NB13 SP7 25 + 10pf multi 5.50 9.00

The surtax was for the benefit of philately.

St. Otto, Bishop of Bamberg — SP8

Statues: 10pf+5pf, St. Hedwig, Duchess of Silesia. 20pf+10pf, St. Peter.

1955, Nov. 26 Engr. *Perf. 14*
9NB14 SP8 7 + 3pf brown 60 1.25
9NB15 SP8 10 + 5pf gray grn 1.10 1.40
9NB16 SP8 20 + 10pf rose lil 1.25 1.75

25th anniv. of the Bishopric of Berlin.
The surtax was for the reconstruction of destroyed churches throughout the bishopric.

+10
Berlinhilfe
für die
Hochwassergeschädigten

DEUTSCHE BUNDESPOST·BERLIN

Bell Type of 1951 Surcharged

Perf. 13½x14

1956, Aug. 9 Wmk. 284
9NB17 OS8 20pf + 10pf citron 1.75 2.50

The surtax was for help for flood victims.

Postrider of Brandenburg, 1700 — SP9

Ludwig Heck — SP10

Wmk. 304

1956, Oct. 26 Litho. *Perf. 14*
9NB18 SP9 25pf + 10pf multi 1.50 2.00

The surtax was for the benefit of philately.

1957, Sept. 7 Engr. *Perf. 13½x14*
9NB19 SP10 20pf + 10pf red & dk brn 30 35

Dr. Ludwig Heck, zoologist and long-time director of the Berlin Zoo. The surtax was for the Zoo.

Elly Heuss-Knapp and Relaxing Mothers — SP11

Boy at Window — SP12

1957, Nov. 30 *Perf. 14*
9NB20 SP11 20pf + 10pf dk red 1.10 1.25

The surtax was for welfare work among mothers.

1960, Sept. 15 Litho. Wmk. 304

Designs: 10pf+5pf, Girl going to school. 20pf+10pf, Girl with flower and mountains. 40pf+20pf, Girls at seashore.

9NB21 SP12 7pf + 3pf dk brn & brn 15 15
9NB22 SP12 10pf + 5pf ol grn & slate grn 15 15
9NB23 SP12 20pf + 10pf dk car & brn blk 20 16
9NB24 SP12 40pf + 20pf bl & ind 70 90

The surtax was for vacations for the children of Berlin.

Fluorescent Paper was introduced for semipostal stamps, starting with Nos. 9NB25-9NB28.

Fairy Tale Type of 1960

Various Scenes from Sleeping Beauty.

1964, Oct. 6 Unwmk. *Perf. 14*
9NB25 SP285 10pf + 5pf multi 15 16
9NB26 SP285 15pf + 5pf multi 15 15
9NB27 SP285 20pf + 10pf multi 15 15
9NB28 SP285 40pf + 20pf multi 60 90

The surtax was for independent welfare organizations.

Beginning with 9NB25-9NB28 semi-postals are types of Germany inscribed "Berlin" except Nos. 9NB129-9NB131.

Bird Type of 1965

Birds: 10pf+5pf, Woodcock. 15pf+5pf, Ring-necked pheasant. 20pf+10pf, Black grouse. 40pf+20pf, Capercaillie.

1965, Apr. 1 Litho. *Perf. 14*
9NB29 SP289 10pf + 5pf multi 15 15
9NB30 SP289 15pf + 5pf multi 15 20
9NB31 SP289 20pf + 10pf multi 20 25
9NB32 SP289 40pf + 20pf multi 45 70

Issued for the benefit of young people.

Fairy Tale Type of 1965

Various Scenes from Cinderella.

1965, Oct. 6 Litho. *Perf. 14*
9NB33 SP290 10pf + 5pf multi 15 15
9NB34 SP290 15pf + 5pf multi 15 15
9NB35 SP290 20pf + 10pf multi 15 15
9NB36 SP290 40pf + 20pf multi 45 90
Set value 78

The surtax was for independent welfare organizations.

Animal Type of 1966

Designs: 10pf+5pf, Roe deer. 20pf+10pf, Chamois. 30pf+15pf, Fallow deer. 50pf+25pf, Red deer.

1966, Apr. 22 Litho. *Perf. 14*
9NB37 SP291 10pf + 5pf multi 15 15
9NB38 SP291 20pf + 10pf multi 15 15
9NB39 SP291 30pf + 15pf multi 18 18
9NB40 SP291 50pf + 25pf multi 40 75

Issued for the benefit of young people.

Fairy Tale Type of 1965

Various Scenes from The Princess and the Frog.

1966, Oct. 5 Litho. *Perf. 14*
9NB41 SP290 10pf + 5pf multi 15 15
9NB42 SP290 20pf + 10pf multi 15 15
9NB43 SP290 30pf + 15pf multi 20 15
9NB44 SP290 50pf + 25pf multi 42 70
Set value 80

Surtax for independent welfare organizations.

Animal Type of 1966

Designs: 10pf+5pf, Rabbit. 20pf+10pf, Ermine. 30pf+15pf, Hamster. 50pf+25pf, Red fox.

1967, Apr. 4 Unwmk.
9NB45 SP291 10pf + 5pf multi 15 15
9NB46 SP291 20pf + 10pf multi 18 20
9NB47 SP291 30pf + 15pf multi 22 24
9NB48 SP291 50pf + 25pf multi 65 85

Issued for the benefit of young people.

Fairy Tale Type of 1965

Various Scenes from Frau Holle.

1967, Oct. 3 Litho. *Perf. 14*
9NB49 SP290 10pf + 5pf multi 15 18
9NB50 SP290 20pf + 10pf multi 15 15
9NB51 SP290 30pf + 15pf multi 18 16
9NB52 SP290 50pf + 25pf multi 45 95

The surtax was for independent welfare organizations.

Animal Type of 1968

Animals: 10pf+5pf, Wildcat. 20pf+10pf, Otter. 30pf+15pf, Badger. 50pf+25pf, Beaver.

1968, Feb. 2 Photo. *Perf. 14*
9NB53 SP293 10pf + 5pf multi 30 32
9NB54 SP293 20pf + 10pf multi 35 35
9NB55 SP293 30pf + 15pf multi 60 60
9NB56 SP293 50pf + 25pf multi 1.50 1.75

Surtax for benefit of young people.

Doll Type of 1968

Designs: Various 19th century dolls in sitting position.

1968, Oct. 3 Litho. *Perf. 14*
9NB57 SP294 10pf + 5pf multi 15 20
9NB58 SP294 20pf + 10pf multi 15 15
9NB59 SP294 30pf + 15pf multi 18 18
9NB60 SP294 50pf + 25pf multi 55 1.00

The surtax was for independent welfare organizations.

Horse Type of 1969

Horses: 10pf+5pf, Pony. 20pf+10pf, Work horse. 30pf+15pf, Hotblood. 50pf+25pf, Thoroughbred.

1969, Feb. 6 Litho. *Perf. 14*
9NB61 SP295 10pf + 5pf multi 16 16
9NB62 SP295 20pf + 10pf multi 22 22
9NB63 SP295 30pf + 15pf multi 38 38
9NB64 SP295 50pf + 25pf multi 1.25 1.25

Surtax for benefit of young people.

Tin Toy Type of 1969

Tin Toys: 10pf+5pf, Coach. 20pf+10pf, Woman feeding chickens. 30pf+15pf, Woman grocer. 50pf+25pf, Postilion on horseback.

1969, Oct. 2 Litho. *Perf. 13½x14*
9NB65 SP297 10pf + 5pf multi 15 15
9NB66 SP297 20pf + 10pf multi 16 16
9NB67 SP297 30pf + 15pf multi 25 25
9NB68 SP297 50pf + 25pf multi 65 65

The surtax was for independent welfare organizations.

1969, Nov. 13 Litho. *Perf. 13½x14*

Christmas: 10pf+5pf, The Three Kings.

9NB69 SP297 10pf + 5pf multi 35 35

Minnesinger Type of 1970

Minnesingers (and their Ladies): 10pf+5pf, Heinrich von Stretlingen. 20pf+10pf, Meinloh von Sevelingen. 30pf+15pf, Burkhart von Hohenfels. 50pf+25pf, Albrecht von Johansdorf.

1970, Feb. 5 Photo. *Perf. 13½x14*
9NB70 SP298 10pf + 5pf multi 15 15
9NB71 SP298 20pf + 10pf multi 30 30
9NB72 SP298 30pf + 15pf multi 48 48
9NB73 SP298 50pf + 25pf multi 95 95

Surtax for benefit of young people.

Puppet Type of 1970

Puppets: 10pf+5pf, "Kasperl." 20pf+10pf, Polichinelle. 30pf+5pf, Punch. 50pf+25pf, Pulcinella.

1970, Oct. 6 Litho. *Perf. 13½x14*
9NB74 SP300 10pf + 5pf multi 15 15
9NB75 SP300 20pf + 10pf multi 16 16
9NB76 SP300 30pf + 15pf multi 22 22
9NB77 SP300 50pf + 25pf multi 80 80

The surtax was for independent welfare organizations.

1970, Nov. 12

Christmas: 10pf+5pf, Rococo angel, from Ursuline Sisters' Convent, Innsbruck.

9NB78 SP300 10pf + 5pf multi 35 35

Drawings Type of 1971

Children's Drawings: 10pf+5pf, Fly. 20pf+10pf, Fish. 30pf+15pf, Porcupine. 50pf+25pf, Cock. All stamps horizontal.

1971, Feb. 5 Litho. *Perf. 14*
9NB79 SP301 10pf + 5pf multi 16 16
9NB80 SP301 20pf + 10pf multi 35 35
9NB81 SP301 30pf + 15pf multi 45 45
9NB82 SP301 50pf + 25pf multi 95 95

Surtax for the benefit of young people.

Wooden Toy Type of 1971

Wooden Toys: 10pf+5pf, Movable dolls in box. 25pf+10pf, Knight on horseback. 30pf+15pf, Jumping jack. 60pf+30pf, Nurse rocking babies.

1971, Oct. 5
9NB83 SP303 10pf + 5pf multi 15 15
9NB84 SP303 25pf + 10pf multi 18 18
9NB85 SP303 30pf + 15pf multi 28 28
9NB86 SP303 60pf + 30pf multi 70 70

1971, Nov. 11

Christmas: Christmas angel with candles.

9NB87 SP303 10pf + 5pf multi 35 35

Animal Protection Type of 1972

Designs: 10pf+5pf, Boy trying to rob bird's nest. 25pf+10pf, Girl with kittens to be drowned. 30pf+15pf, Watch dog and man with whip. 60pf+30pf, Hedgehog and deer passing before car at night.

1972, Feb. 4
9NB88 SP304 10pf + 5pf multi 15 15
9NB89 SP304 25pf + 10pf multi 28 28
9NB90 SP304 30pf + 15pf multi 45 45
9NB91 SP304 60pf + 30pf multi 1.10 1.10

Surtax for the benefit of young people.

Chess Type of 1972

1972, Oct. 5 Litho. *Perf. 14*
9NB92 SP307 20pf + 10 Knight 22 22
9NB93 SP307 30pf + 15 Rook 32 32
9NB94 SP307 40pf + 20 Queen 40 40
9NB95 SP307 70pf + 35 King 95 95

The surtax was for independent welfare organizations.

Christmas Type of 1972

Design: 20pf+10pf, Holy Family.

1972, Nov. 10 Litho. *Perf. 14*
9NB96 SP308 20pf + 10pf multi 35 35

Bird Type of 1973

Birds of Prey: 20pf+10pf, Goshawk. 30pf+15pf, Peregrine falcon. 40pf+20pf, Sparrow hawk. 70pf+35pf, Golden eagle.

1973, Feb. 6 Photo. *Perf. 14*
9NB97 SP309 20pf + 10pf multi 45 45
9NB98 SP309 30pf + 15pf multi 75 75
9NB99 SP309 40pf + 20pf multi 1.10 1.10
9NB100 SP309 70pf + 35pf multi 1.65 1.65

Surtax was for benefit of young people.

Instrument Type of 1973

Musical Instruments: 20pf+10pf, Hurdygurdy, 17th cent. 30pf+15pf, Drum, 16th cent. 40pf+20pf, Archlute, 18th cent. 70pf+35pf, Organ, 16th cent.

1973, Oct. 5 Litho. *Perf. 14*

9NB101 SP311 20pf + 10pf multi 28 28
9NB102 SP311 30pf + 15pf multi 45 45
9NB103 SP311 40pf + 20pf multi 58 58
9NB104 SP311 70pf + 35pf multi 1.10 1.10

Surtax was for independent welfare organizations.

Star Type of 1973

Christmas: 20pf+10pf, Christmas star.

1973, Nov. 9 Litho. & Engr.

9NB105 SP312 20pf + 10pf multi 40 35

Youth Type of 1974

Designs: 20pf+10pf, Boy photographing. 30pf+15pf, Boy athlete. 40pf+20pf, Girl violinist. 70pf+35pf, Nurse's aid.

1974, Apr. 17 Photo. *Perf. 14*

9NB106 SP313 20pf + 10pf multi 40 40
9NB107 SP313 30pf + 15pf multi 55 55
9NB108 SP313 40pf + 20pf multi 1.00 1.00
9NB109 SP313 70pf + 35pf multi 1.40 1.40

Surtax was for benefit of young people.

Flower Type of 1974

Designs: 30pf+15pf, Spring bouquet. 40pf+20pf, Autumn bouquet. 50pf+25pf, Roses. 70pf+35pf, Winter flowers. All horiz.

1974, Oct. 15 Litho. *Perf. 14*

9NB110 SP314 30pf + 15pf multi 38 38
9NB111 SP314 40pf + 20pf multi 48 48
9NB112 SP314 50pf + 25pf multi 65 65
9NB113 SP314 70pf + 35pf multi 90 90

Surtax was for independent welfare organizations.

1974, Oct. 29

Christmas: Christmas bouquet, horiz.

9NB114 SP314 30pf + 15pf multi 45 45

Locomotive Type of 1975

Steam Locomotives: 30pf+15pf, Dragon. 40pf+20pf, Class 89 (70-75). 50pf+25pf, Class O50. 70pf+35pf, Class O10.

1975, Apr. 15 Litho. *Perf. 14*

9NB115 SP315 30pf + 15pf multi 70 70
9NB116 SP315 40pf + 20pf multi 85 85
9NB117 SP315 50pf + 25pf multi 1.25 1.25
9NB118 SP315 70pf + 35pf multi 2.25 2.25

Surtax was for benefit of young people.

Flower Type of 1975

Alpine Flowers: 30pf+15pf, Yellow gentian. 40pf+20pf, Arnica. 50pf+25pf, Cyclamen. 70pf+35pf, Blue gentian.

1975, Oct. 15 Litho. *Perf. 14*

9NB119 SP316 30pf + 15pf multi 40 40
9NB120 SP316 40pf + 20pf multi 55 55
9NB121 SP316 50pf + 25pf multi 65 65
9NB122 SP316 70pf + 35pf multi 90 90

Surtax was for independent welfare organizations.

1975, Nov. 14

Christmas: 30pf+15pf, Snow heather.

9NB123 SP316 30pf + 15pf multi 50 50

Sports Type of 1976

Designs: 30pf+15pf, Shot put, women's. 40pf+20pf, Hockey. 50pf+25pf, Handball. 70pf+35pf, Swimming.

1976, Apr. 6 Litho. *Perf. 14*

9NB124 SP317 30pf + 15pf multi 45 45
9NB125 SP317 40pf + 20pf multi 60 60
9NB126 SP317 50pf + 25pf multi 75 75
9NB127 SP317 70pf + 35pf multi 1.25 1.25

Youth training for Olympic Games. The surtax was for the benefit of young people.

Iris — SP13

Flowers: 40pf+20pf, Wallflower. 50pf+25pf, Dahlia. 70pf+35pf, Larkspur.

1976, Oct. 14 Litho. *Perf. 14*

9NB128 SP13 30pf + 15pf 35 35
9NB129 SP13 40pf + 20pf 50 50
9NB130 SP13 50pf + 25pf 65 65
9NB131 SP13 70pf + 35pf 1.00 1.00

Surtax was for independent welfare organizations.

Souvenir Sheet
Christmas Type of 1976

Christmas: 30pf+15pf, Annunciation to the Shepherds, stained-glass window, Frauenkirche, Esslingen.

1976, Nov. 16 Litho. & Engr.

9NB132 SP320 30pf + 15pf multi 50 50

Ship Type of 1977

Historic Ships: 30pf+15pf, Bremer Kogge, c. 1380. 40pf+20pf, Helena Sloman, 1850. 50pf+25pf, Passenger ship, Cap Polonio, 1914. 70pf+35pf, Freighter Widar, 1971.

1977, Apr. 14 Litho. *Perf. 14*

9NB133 SP321 30pf + 15pf 45 45
9NB134 SP321 40pf + 20pf 60 60
9NB135 SP321 50pf + 25pf 75 75
9NB136 SP321 70pf + 35pf 1.25 1.25

Surtax was for benefit of young people.

Flower Type of 1977

Meadow Flowers: 30pf+15pf, Daisy. 40pf+20pf, Cowslip. 50pf+25pf, Sainfoin. 70pf+35pf, Forget-me-not.

1977, Oct. 13 Litho. *Perf. 14*

9NB137 SP322 30pf + 15pf 40 40
9NB138 SP322 40pf + 20pf 50 50
9NB139 SP322 50pf + 25pf 65 65
9NB140 SP322 70pf + 35pf 95 95

Surtax was for independent welfare organizations. See Nos. 9NB148-9NB151.

Souvenir Sheet
Christmas Type of 1977

Christmas: 30pf+15pf, Virgin and Child, stained-glass window, Sacristy of St. Gereon Basilica, Cologne.

1977, Nov. 10

9NB141 SP323 30pf + 15pf multi 50 50

Aviation Type of 1978

Designs: 30pf+15pf, Montgolfier balloon, 1783. 40pf+20pf, Lilienthal's glider, 1891. 50pf+25pf, Wright brothers' plane, 1909. 70pf+35pf, Etrich/Rumpler Taube, 1910.

1978, Apr. 13 Litho. *Perf. 14*

9NB142 SP325 30pf + 15pf 40 40
9NB143 SP325 40pf + 20pf 48 48
9NB144 SP325 50pf + 25pf 60 60
9NB145 SP325 70pf + 35pf 90 90

Surtax was for benefit of young people.

Sports Type of 1978

Designs: 50+25pf, Bicycling. 70+35pf, Fencing.

1978, Apr. 13 Litho. *Perf. 14*

9NB146 SP324 50pf + 25pf 70 70
9NB147 SP324 70pf + 35pf 1.10 1.10

Surtax was for German Sports Foundation.

Flower Type of 1977

Woodland Flowers: 30pf+15pf, Solomon's-seal. 40pf+20pf, Wood primrose. 50pf+25pf, Cephalanthera rubra (orchid). 70pf+35pf, Bugle.

1978, Oct. 12 Litho. *Perf. 14*

9NB148 SP322 30pf + 15pf 40 40
9NB149 SP322 40pf + 20pf 48 48
9NB150 SP322 50pf + 25pf 65 65
9NB151 SP322 70pf + 35pf 90 90

Surtax was for independent welfare organizations.

Souvenir Sheet
Christmas Type of 1978

Christmas: 30pf+15pf, Adoration of the Kings, stained glass window, Frauenkirche, Munich.

1978, Nov. 16 Litho. *Perf. 14*

9NB152 SP326 30pf + 15pf multi 60 50

Aviation Type of 1979

Airplanes: 40pf+20pf, Vampyr, 1921. 50pf+25pf, Junkers JU52/3M, 1932. 60pf+30pf, Messerschmitt BF/ME 108, 1934. 90pf+45pf, Douglas DC3, 1935.

1979, Apr. 5 Litho. *Perf. 14*

9NB153 SP327 40pf + 20pf 55 55
9NB154 SP327 50pf + 25pf 75 75
9NB155 SP327 60pf + 30pf 95 95
9NB156 SP327 90pf + 45pf 1.75 1.75

Surtax was for benefit of young people.

Sports Type of 1979

Designs: 60pf+30pf, Runners. 90pf+45pf, Archers.

1979, Apr. 5

9NB157 SP328 60pf + 30pf 90 90
9NB158 SP328 90pf + 45pf 1.40 1.40

Surtax was for German Sports Foundation.

Plant Type of 1979

Woodland Plants: 40pf+20pf, Larch. 50pf+25pf, Hazelnut. 60pf+30pf, Horse chestnut. 90pf+45pf, Blackthorn.

1979, Oct. 11 Litho. *Perf. 14*

9NB159 SP330 40pf + 20pf 55 55
9NB160 SP330 50pf + 25pf 70 70
9NB161 SP330 60pf + 30pf 80 80
9NB162 SP330 90pf + 45pf 1.25 1.25

Surtax was for independent welfare organizations.

Christmas Type of 1979

Christmas: Nativity, medieval manuscript, Cistercian Abby, Altenberg.

1979, Nov. 14 Litho. *Perf. 13½*

9NB163 SP331 40pf + 20pf multi 65 55

Aviation Type of 1979

Designs: 40pf+20pf, Vickers Viscount, 1950. 50pf+25pf, Fokker 27 Friendship, 1955. 60pf+30pf, Sud Aviation Caravelle, 1955. 90pf+45pf, Sikorsky-55, 1949.

1980, Apr. 10 Litho. *Perf. 14*

9NB164 SP327 40 + 20pf multi 70 70
9NB165 SP327 50 + 25pf multi 95 95
9NB166 SP327 60 + 30pf multi 1.00 1.00
9NB167 SP327 90 + 45pf multi 1.75 1.75

Surtax was for benefit of young people.

Sports Type of 1980

Designs: 50pf+25pf, Javelin. 60pf+30pf, Weight lifting. 90pf+45pf, Water polo.

1980, May 8 Photo. *Perf. 14*

9NB168 SP332 50 + 25pf multi 75 75
9NB169 SP332 60 + 30pf multi 1.00 1.00
9NB170 SP332 90 + 45pf multi 1.65 1.65

Surtax was for German Sports Foundation.

Wildflower Type of 1980

Wildflowers: 40pf+20pf, Orlaya. 50pf+25pf, Yellow gagea. 60pf+30pf, Summer pheasant's eye. 90pf+45pf, Small-flowered Venus' looking-glass.

1980, Oct. 9 Litho. *Perf. 14*

9NB171 SP333 40 + 20pf multi 60 60
9NB172 SP333 50 + 25pf multi 75 75
9NB173 SP333 60 + 30pf multi 85 85
9NB174 SP333 90 + 45pf multi 1.50 1.50

Surtax was for independent welfare organizations.

Christmas Type of 1980

Christmas: 40pf+20pf, Annunciation to the Shepherds, from Altomunster manuscript, 12th century.

1980, Nov. 13 Litho. *Perf. 14x13½*

9NB175 SP335 40 + 20pf multi 85 75

Optical Instrument Type of 1981

Designs: 40pf+20pf, Theodolite, 1810. 50pf+25pf, Equatorial telescope, 1820. 60pf +30pf, Microscope, 1790. 90pf+45pf, Sextant, 1830.

1981, Apr. 10 Litho. *Perf. 13½*

9NB176 SP336 40 + 20pf multi 60 60
9NB177 SP336 50 + 25pf multi 80 80
9NB178 SP336 60 + 30pf multi 95 95
9NB179 SP336 90 + 45pf multi 1.65 1.65

Surtax for benefit of young people.

Sports Type of 1981

Designs: 60pf+30pf, Women's gymnastics. 90pf+45pf, Cross-county running.

1981, Apr. 10 *Perf. 14*

9NB180 SP337 60 + 30pf multi 95 90
9NB181 SP337 90 + 45pf multi 1.40 1.40

Surtax for the German Sports Foundation.

Plant Type of 1981

Designs: 40pf+20pf, Common bistort. 50pf+25pf, Pedicularis sceptrum-carolinum. 60pf+30pf, Gladiolus palustris. 90pf+45pf, Iris sibirica.

1981, Oct. 8 Litho.

9NB182 SP338 40 + 20pf multi 60 60
9NB183 SP338 50 + 25pf multi 70 70
9NB184 SP338 60 + 30pf multi 90 90
9NB185 SP338 90 + 45pf multi 1.40 1.40

Surtax was for independent welfare organizations.

Christmas Type of 1981

Christmas: Adoration of the Kings, 19th cent. painting.

1981, Nov. 12 Litho.

9NB186 SP339 40 + 20pf multi 80 65

Antique Car Type of 1982

Designs: 40pf+20pf, Daimler, 1889. 50pf+25pf, Wanderer, 1911. 60pf+30pf, Adler limousine, 1913. 90pf+45pf, DKW-F, 1931.

1982, Apr. 15 Litho.

9NB187 SP340 40 + 20pf multi 70 70
9NB188 SP340 50 + 25pf multi 90 90
9NB189 SP340 60 + 30pf multi 1.10 1.10
9NB190 SP340 90 + 45pf multi 1.65 1.65

Surtax was for benefit of young people.

Sports Type of 1982

Designs: 60pf+30pf, Sprinting. 90pf+45pf, Volleyball.

1982, Apr. 15 Litho.

9NB191 SP341 60 + 30pf multi 1.00 1.00
9NB192 SP341 90 + 45pf multi 1.50 1.50

Surtax was for the German Sports Foundation.

Flower Type of 1982

Designs: 50pf+20pf, Floribunda grandiflora. 60pf+30pf, Tea-rose hybrid, diff. 80pf+40pf, Floribunda, diff. 120pf+60pf, Miniature rose.

1982, Oct. 14 Litho. *Perf. 14*

9NB193 SP342 50 + 20pf multi 75 75
9NB194 SP342 60 + 30pf multi 1.00 1.00
9NB195 SP342 80 + 40pf multi 1.25 1.25
9NB196 SP342 120 + 60pf multi 2.00 2.00

Surtax was for independent welfare organizations.

Christmas Type of 1982

Christmas: Adoration of the Kings, Oak altar, St. Peter's Church, Hamburg, 1380.

1982, Nov. 10

9NB197 SP343 50 + 20pf multi 90 80

Motorcycle Type of 1983

Designs: 50pf+20pf, Hildebrand & Wolfmuller, 1894. 60pf+30pf, Wanderer, 1908. 80pf+40pf, DKW-Lomos, 1922. 120pf+60pf, Mars, 1925.

1983, Apr. 12 Litho. *Perf. 14*

9NB198 SP344 50 + 20pf multi 85 85
9NB199 SP344 60 + 30pf multi 1.10 1.10
9NB200 SP344 80 + 40pf multi 1.40 1.40
9NB201 SP344 120 + 60pf multi 2.25 2.25

Surtax was for benefit of young people.

Sports Type of 1983

Designs: 80pf+40pf, European Latin American Dance Championship. 120pf+60pf, World Hockey Championship.

1983, Apr. 12

9NB202 SP345 80 + 40pf multi 1.40 1.40
9NB203 SP345 120 + 60pf multi 2.00 2.00

Surtax was for German Sports Foundation.

Flower Type of Germany

Designs: 50pf+20pf, Mountain wildflower. 60pf+30pf, Alpine auricula. 80pf+40pf, Little primrose. 120pf+60pf, Einsele's aquilegia.

1983, Oct. 13 Litho. *Perf. 14*

9NB204 SP346 50 + 20pf multi 85 80
9NB205 SP346 60 + 30pf multi 1.10 1.00
9NB206 SP346 80 + 40pf multi 1.40 1.10
9NB207 SP346 120 + 60pf multi 2.25 2.00

Surtax was for welfare organizations.

Christmas Type of Germany

1983, Nov. 10 Litho.

9NB208 SP347 50 + 20pf Nativity 90 80

Surtax was for free welfare work.

Insect Type of 1984

Designs: 50pf+20pf, Trichius fasciatus. 60pf+30pf, Agrumenia carniolioa. 80pf+40pf, Bombus terrestris. 120pf+60pf, Eristalis tenax.

1984, Apr. 12 Litho.

9NB209 SP348 50 + 20pf multi 95 90
9NB210 SP348 60 + 30pf multi 1.25 1.10
9NB211 SP348 80 + 40pf multi 1.65 1.65
9NB212 SP348 120 + 60pf multi 2.50 2.50

Surtax was for German Youth Stamp Foundation.

Olympic Type of 1984

Women's Events: 60pf+30pf, Hurdles. 80pf+40pf, Cycling. 120pf+60pf, Kayak.

1984, Apr. 12

9NB213 SP349 60 + 30pf multi 1.25 1.25
9NB214 SP349 80 + 40pf multi 1.75 1.65
9NB215 SP349 120 + 60pf multi 2.50 2.50

Surtax was for German Sports Foundation.

Orchid Type of 1984

Designs: 50+20pf, Listera cordata. 60pf+30pf, Ophrys insectifera. 80pf+40pf, Epipactis palustris. 120pf+60pf, Ophrys coriophora.

1984, Oct. 18 Litho. *Perf. 14*

9NB216 SP350 50 + 20pf multi 90 80
9NB217 SP350 60 + 30pf multi 1.10 1.00
9NB218 SP350 80 + 40pf multi 1.50 1.40
9NB219 SP350 120 + 60pf multi 2.25 2.25

Surtax was for welfare organizations.

Christmas Type of 1984

1984, Nov. 8 Litho.

9NB220 SP351 50pf + 20pf St. Nicholas 95 80

Surtax was for welfare organizations.

Sport Type of 1985

1985, Feb. 21 Photo.

9NB221 SP352 80 + 40pf Basketball 1.65 1.50
9NB222 SP352 120 + 60pf Table Tennis 2.25 2.00

Surtax was for German Sport Foundation.

Bicycle Type of 1985

Designs: 50pf+20pf, Bussing bicycle, 1868. 60pf+30pf, Child's tricycle, 1885. 80pf+40pf, Jaray bicycle, 1925. 120pf+60pf, Opel racer, 1925.

1985, Apr. 16 Litho.

9NB223 SP353 50 + 20pf multi 85 65
9NB224 SP353 60 + 30pf multi 1.10 85
9NB225 SP353 80 + 40pf multi 1.50 1.10
9NB226 SP353 120 + 60pf multi 2.25 1.65

Surtax was for benefit of young people. Each stamp also shows the International Youth Year emblem.

Prayer Book Type of 1985

1985, Oct. 15 Litho. *Perf. 14*

9NB227 SP355 50 + 20pf multi 85 75
9NB228 SP355 60 + 30pf multi 1.00 95
9NB229 SP355 80 + 40pf multi 1.40 1.25
9NB230 SP355 120 + 60pf multi 2.25 1.90

Surtax for welfare organizations.

Christmas Type of 1985

Woodcut: Worship of the Kings, Epiphany Altar, Frieburg Cathedral, by Hans Baldung Grien (1485-1545).

1985, Nov. 12 Litho. *Perf. 14*

9NB231 SP356 50 + 20pf multi 90 70

Surtax for welfare organizations.

European Sports Championships Type of 1986

1986, Feb. 13 Litho. *Perf. 14*

9NB232 SP357 80 + 40pf Swimming 1.50 1.50
9NB233 SP357 120 + 55pf Show jumping 2.25 2.25

Surtax for the Natl. Sports Promotion Foundation.

Vocational Training Type of 1986

1986, Apr. 10

9NB234 SP358 50 + 25pf Glazier 1.00 95
9NB235 SP358 60 + 30pf Mechanic 1.25 1.10
9NB236 SP358 70 + 35pf Tailor 1.40 1.25
9NB237 SP358 80 + 40pf Carpenter 1.75 1.65

Surtax for German Youth Stamp Foundation.

Glassware Type of 1986

1986, Oct. 16 Litho. *Perf. 13x13½*

9NB238 SP359 50 + 25pf Cantharus, 1st cent. 80 75
9NB239 SP359 60 + 30pf Tumbler, c. 200 95 95
9NB240 SP359 70 + 35pf Jug, 3rd cent. 1.10 1.05
9NB241 SP359 80 + 40pf Diatreta, 4th cent. 1.25 1.20

Surtax for public welfare organizations.

Christmas Type of 1986

Christmas: Adoration of the Magi, Ortenberg Altarpiece, c. 1420.

1986, Nov. 13 Litho. *Perf. 14*

9NB242 SP360 50 + 25pf multi 90 75

Surtax for public welfare organizations.

Sports Championships Type of 1987

1987, Feb. 12 Litho.

9NB243 SP361 80 + 40pf Gymnastics 1.35 1.35
9NB244 SP361 120 + 55pf Judo 1.95 1.95

Surtax for the benefit of the national Sports Promotion Foundation.

Industry Type of 1987

1987, Apr. 9 Litho.

9NB245 SP362 50 + 25pf Cooper 82 82
9NB246 SP362 60 + 30pf Stonemason 1.00 1.00
9NB247 SP362 70 + 35pf Furrier 1.15 1.15
9NB248 SP362 80 + 40pf Painter 1.30 1.30

Surtax for youth organizations.

Gold and Silver Artifacts Type of 1987

1987, Oct. 15

9NB249 SP363 50 + 25pf Bonnet ornament, 5th cent. 85 85
9NB250 SP363 60 + 30pf Athena plate, 1st cent. B.C. 1.00 1.00
9NB251 SP363 70 + 35pf Armilla armlet, c. 1180 1.20 1.20
9NB252 SP363 80 + 40pf Snake bracelet, 300 B.C. 1.35 1.35

Surtax for welfare organizations sponsoring free museum exhibitions.

Christmas Type of 1987

Illustration from Book of Psalms, 13th cent., Bavarian Natl. Museum: Adoration of the Magi.

1987, Nov. 6

9NB253 SP364 50 + 25pf multi 90 75

Surtax for public welfare ogranizations.

Sports Type of 1988

1988, Feb. 18 Litho.

9NB254 SP365 60 + 30pf Trapshooting 1.15 1.15
9NB255 SP365 80 + 40pf Figure skating 1.50 1.50
9NB256 SP365 120 + 55pf Hammer throw 2.20 2.20

Music Type of 1988

Designs: No. 9NB257, Piano terzet. No. 9NB258, Wind quintet. No. 9NB259, Guitar, mandolin, recorder. No. 9NB260, Children's choir.

1988, Apr. 14 Litho. *Perf. 14*

9NB257 SP366 50 +25pf multi 1.05 1.05
9NB258 SP366 60 +30pf multi 1.10 1.10
9NB259 SP366 70 +35pf multi 1.30 1.30
9NB260 SP366 80 +40pf multi 1.50 1.50

Surtax for German Youth Stamp Foundation.

Artifacts Type of 1988

Designs: No. 9NB261, Brooch, c. 1700, Schmuck Jewelry Museum, Pforzheim. No. 9NB262, Lion, 1540, Kunstgewerbe Museum, Berlin. No. 9NB263, Lidded goblet, 1536, Kunstgewerbe Museum. No. 9NB264, Cope clasp, c. 1400, Aachen cathedral.

1988, Oct. 13 Litho.

9NB261 SP367 50 +25pf multi 82 82
9NB262 SP367 60 +30pf multi 95 95
9NB263 SP367 70 +35pf multi 1.15 1.15
9NB264 SP367 80 +40pf multi 1.30 1.30

Surtax for welfare organizations.

Christmas Type of 1988

Illumination from *The Gospel Book of Henry the Lion,* Helmarshausen, 1188, Prussian Cultural Museum, Bavaria: Angels announce the birth of Christ to the shepherds.

1988, Nov. 10 Litho.

9NB265 SP368 50 +25pf multi 82 60

Surtax for public welfare organizations.

Sports Type of 1989

1989, Feb. 9 Litho.

9NB266 SP369 100 +50pf Volleyball 1.75 1.75
9NB267 SP369 140 +60pf Hockey 2.25 2.25

Surtax for the Natl. Sports Promotion Foundation.

Circus Type of 1989

1989, Apr. 20 Litho.

9NB268 SP371 60 +30pf Tamer and tigers 1.00 1.00
9NB269 SP371 70 +30pf Trapeze artists 1.10 1.10
9NB270 SP371 80 +35pf Seals 1.30 1.30
9NB271 SP371 100 +50pf Jugglers 1.65 1.65

Surtax for natl. youth welfare organizations.

Mail Carrying Type of 1989

Designs: No. 9NB272, Messenger, 15th cent. No. 9NB273, Brandenburg mail wagon, c. 1700. No. 9NB274, Prussian postal workers, 19th cent.

1989, Oct. 12 Litho.

9NB272 SP372 60 +30pf multi 1.00 1.00
9NB273 SP372 80 +35pf multi 1.25 1.25
9NB274 SP372 100 +50pf multi 1.65 1.65

Surtax for the benfit of Free Welfare Work.

Christmas Type of 1989

1989, Nov. 16 Litho.

9NB275 SP373 40 +20pf Angel 70 70
9NB276 SP373 60 +30pf Nativity 1.00 1.00

Surtax for the benefit of the Federal Working Assoc. of Free Welfare Work.

Sports Type of 1990

Designs: No. 9NB277, Water polo. No. 9NB278, Wheelchair basketball.

1990, Feb. 15 Litho.

9NB277 SP374 100 +50pf multi 1.75 1.75
9NB278 SP374 140 +60pf multi 2.50 2.50

Surtax for the Natl. Sports Promotion Foundation.

Max and Moritz Type of 1990

1990, Apr. 19 Litho.

9NB279 SP375 60 +30pf Max, Moritz 1.05 1.05
9NB280 SP375 70 +30pf Max, Moritz, diff. 1.20 1.20
9NB281 SP375 80 +35pf Moritz 1.35 1.35
9NB282 SP375 100 +50pf Bug, Uncle 1.75 1.75

Surcharge for the German Youth Stamp Foundation.

Post and Telecommunications Type

Designs: 60pf + 30pf, Railway mail car, 1900. 80pf + 35pf, Telephone installation, 1900. 100pf + 50pf, Mail truck, 1900.

1990, Sept. 27 Litho. *Perf. 13½x14*

9NB283 SP377 60 +30pf multi 1.05 1.05
9NB284 SP377 80 +35pf multi 1.35 1.35
9NB285 SP377 100 +50pf multi 1.75 1.75

Surtax for welfare organizations.

ISSUED UNDER RUSSIAN OCCUPATION

3 Berlin 8

When the mark was revalued in June, 1948, a provisional overprint, consisting of various city and town names and post office or zone numerals, was applied by hand in black, violet or blue at innumerable post offices to their stocks.

For Use in All Provinces in the Russian Zone

Germany Nos. 557 to 573 Overprinted in Black

Sowjetische Besatzungs Zone

1948, July 3 Wmk. 284 *Perf. 14*

10N1 A120 2pf brn blk 15 15
10N2 A120 6pf purple 15 15
10N3 A121 8pf red 15 15
10N4 A121 10pf yel grn 15 15
10N5 A122 12pf gray 15 15
10N6 A120 15pf chocolate 15 15
10N7 A123 16pf dk bl grn 15 15
10N8 A121 20pf blue 15 15
10N9 A123 24pf brn org 15 15
10N10 A120 25pf org yel 15 15
10N11 A122 30pf red 15 18
10N12 A121 40pf red vio 15 18
10N13 A123 50pf ultra 22 28
10N14 A122 60pf red brn 30 30
a. 60pf brown red 19.00 *40.00*
10N15 A122 80pf dk bl 35 40
10N16 A122 84pf emerald 35 40
Set value 2.30 2.30
Set, never hinged 4.00

Same Overprint on Numeral Stamps of Germany, 1946

1948, Sept.

10N17 A119 5pf yel grn 15 15
10N18 A119 30pf olive 22 42
10N19 A119 45pf brt red 15 24
10N20 A119 75pf dp ultra 15 24
10N21 A119 84pf emerald 25 24
Nos. 10N17-10N21 (5) 92 1.29
Set, never hinged 1.50

Nos 10N1-10N21 all exist with inverted overprint, and majority with double overprint.

Same Overprint on Berlin-Brandenburg Nos. 11N1-11N7

1948, Sept. Unwmk. Litho. *Perf. 14*

10N22 OS1 5pf green 15 15
a. Serrate roulette 15 15
10N23 OS1 6pf violet 15 15
10N24 OS1 8pf red 15 15
10N25 OS1 10pf brown 15 15
10N26 OS1 12pf rose 15 35
10N27 OS1 20pf blue 15 20
10N28 OS1 30pf olive 15 30
Set value 85 1.25
Set, never hinged 1.40

The overprint made #10N22-10N28 valid for postage throughout the Russian Zone.

Käthe Kollwitz — OS2

Designs: 60pf, 40pf, Gerhard Hauptmann. 8pf, 50pf, Karl Marx. 10pf, 84pf, August Bebel. 12pf, 30pf, Friedrich Engels. 15pf, 60pf, G. W. F. Hegel. 16pf, 25pf, Rudolf Virchow. 20pf, Käthe Kollwitz. 24pf, 80pf, Ernst Thälmann.

Perf. 13x12½

1948 Typo. Wmk. 292

10N29 OS2	2pf gray		15	15
10N30 OS2	6pf violet		15	15
10N31 OS2	8pf red brn		18	15
10N32 OS2	10pf bl grn		15	15
10N33 OS2	12pf blue		1.90	15
10N34 OS2	15pf brown		25	40
10N35 OS2	16pf turquoise		18	15
10N36 OS2	20pf maroon		18	30
10N37 OS2	24pf carmine		2.25	15
10N38 OS2	25pf olive grn		35	65
10N39 OS2	30pf red		38	50
10N40 OS2	40pf red vio		25	30
10N41 OS2	50pf dk ultra		30	20
10N42 OS2	60pf dl grn		95	20
10N43 OS2	80pf dark blue		55	20
10N44 OS2	84pf brn lake		80	85
Nos. 10N29-10N44 (16)			8.97	4.65
Set, never hinged			17.00	

See German Democratic Republic #122-136.

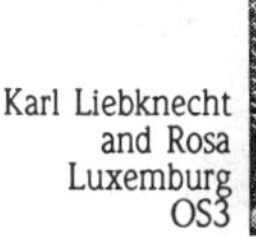

Karl Liebknecht and Rosa Luxemburg OS3

Perf. 13½x13

1949, Jan. 15 Litho. Wmk. 292

10N45 OS3	24pf rose	15	40
Never hinged		20	

30th anniv. of the death of Karl Liebknecht and Rosa Luxemburg, German socialists.

Dove and Laurel — OS4

1949

10N46 OS4	24pf carmine rose	38	95
Never hinged		70	

Overprinted in Black: "3. Deutscher Volkskongress 29.-30. Mai 1949"

1949, May 29

10N47 OS4	24pf carmine rose	30	70
Never hinged		70	

Nos. 10N46 and 10N47 were issued for the 3rd German People's Congress.

For succeeding issues see German Democratic Republic.

RUSSIAN OCCUPATION SEMI-POSTAL STAMPS

Leipzig Fair Issue

Type of German Semi-Postal Stamps of 1947

Designs: 16pf+9pf, First New Year's Fair, 1459. 50pf+25pf, Arrival of clothmakers from abroad, 1469.

Perf. 13½

1948, Aug. 29 Litho. Wmk. 292

10NB1 SP252	16 + 9pf dk vio brn	15	15
10NB2 SP252	50 + 25pf dl vio bl	15	18
Set value		18	
Set, never hinged		45	

The 1948 Leipzig Autumn Fair.

Emblem of Philatelic Institute — OSP1

Goethe — OSP2

1948, Oct. 23 *Perf. 13x13½*

10NB3 OSP1	12 + 3pf red	15	20
Never hinged		16	

Stamp Day, Oct. 26, 1948.

Type of German Semi-Postal Stamps of 1947

Designs: 30pf+15pf, First fair in newly built Town Hall, 1556. 50pf+25pf, Italians at the Fair, 1536.

1949, Mar. 6 Litho. *Perf. 13½*

10NB4 SP252	30 + 15pf red	1.10	1.75
10NB5 SP252	50 + 25pf blue	1.50	2.25
Set, never hinged		5.00	

1949 Leipzig Spring Fair.

1949, July 20 Wmk. 292 *Perf. 13*

Designs: Different Goethe portraits.

10NB6 OSP2	6 + 4pf dl vio	1.00	1.10
10NB7 OSP2	12 + 8pf dl brn	1.00	1.10
10NB8 OSP2	24 + 16pf red brn	90	90
10NB9 OSP2	50 + 25pf dk bl	90	90
10NB10 OSP2	84 + 36pf ol gray	1.50	1.65
Nos. 10NB6-10NB10 (5)		5.30	5.65
Set, never hinged		7.50	

Johann Wolfgang von Goethe, birth bicent.

Souvenir Sheet

Profile of Goethe OSP3

1949, Aug. 22 Engr. *Perf. 14*

10NB11 OSP3	50pf + 4.50m blue	125.00	200.00
Never hinged		175.00	

The sheet measures 106x105mm. The surtax was for the reconstruction of Weimar.

Type of German Semi-Postal Stamps of 1947

Designs: 12pf+8pf, Russian merchants at the Fair, 1650. 24pf+16pf, Young Goethe at the Fair, 1765.

1949, Aug. 30 Litho. *Perf. 13½*

10NB12 SP252	12 + 8pf gray	1.50	2.50
10NB13 SP252	24 + 16pf lake brn	2.25	2.75
Set, never hinged		6.00	

1949 Leipzig Autumn Fair.

BERLIN-BRANDENBURG

Berlin Bear — OS1

1945 Litho. *Perf. 14*

11N1 OS1	5pf shown	15	15
11N2 OS1	6pf Bear holding spade	15	15
11N3 OS1	8pf Bear on shield	15	15
11N4 OS1	10pf Bear holding brick	15	15
11N5 OS1	12pf Bear carrying board	15	15
11N6 OS1	20pf Bear on small shield	15	20
11N7 OS1	30pf Oak sapling, ruins	15	25
Set value		50	1.00

Issue dates: 5pf, 8pf, June 9. 12pf, July 5. Others, July 18.

1945, Dec. 6 ***Serrate Roulette 13½***

11N1a	OS1	5pf	15
11N2a	OS1	6pf	4.00
11N3a	OS1	8pf	3.00
11N4a	OS1	10pf	5.00
11N5a	OS1	12pf	4.00
11N6a	OS1	20pf	4.00
11N7a	OS1	30pf	4.00
Nos. 11N1a-11N7a (7)			24.15

No. 11N1a comes with two different roulettes. The roulette that matches Nos. 11N2a-11N7a is valued at $4. No. 11N5a in the second roulette is rare.

MECKLENBURG-VORPOMMERN

OS1

Plowman — OS2

Design: 12pf, Wheat.

1945-46 Typo. *Perf. 10½*

12N1 OS1	6pf black, *green*		25
12N2 OS1	6pf purple		25
12N3 OS1	6pf purple, *green*		25
12N4 OS2	8pf red, *rose*		25
a.	8pf red lilac, *rose*		35
12N5 OS2	8pf black, *rose*		25
12N6 OS2	8pf red lilac, *green*		25
12N7 OS2	8pf black, *green*		25
12N8 OS2	8pf brown		25
12N9 OS2	12pf black, *rose*		25
12N10 OS2	12pf brown lilac		25
12N11 OS2	12pf red		1.25
12N12 OS2	12pf red, *rose*		25
Nos. 12N1-12N12 (12)			4.00

Many shades.

Issue dates: Nos. 12N1, 12N9, Aug. 28. No. 12N4, Oct. 6. No. 12N5, Oct. 19. No. 12N7, Nov. 2. No. 12N6, Nov. 3. No. 12N10, Nov. 9. No. 12N2, Nov. 16. No. 12N11, Dec. 20. No. 12N8, Jan. 7, 1946. No. 12N3, Jan. 11, 1946. No. 12N12, Jan. 30, 1946.

Buildings — OS3

Designs: 4pf, Deer. 5pf, Fishing boats. 6pf, Harvesting grain. 8pf, Windmill. 10pf, Two-horse plow. 12pf, Bricklayer on scaffolding. 15pf, Tractor plowing field. 20pf, Ship, warehouse. 30pf, Factory. 40pf, Woman spinning.

1946 Typo. *Imperf.*

12N13 OS3	3pf brown	1.25
12N14 OS3	4pf blue	5.00
12N15 OS3	4pf red brown	1.25
12N16 OS3	5pf green	1.25
12N17 OS3	8pf orange	40
12N18 OS3	10pf brown	40

Perf. 10½

12N19 OS3	6pf purple	20
12N20 OS3	6pf blue	3.50
12N21 OS3	12pf red	20
12N22 OS3	15pf brown	30
12N23 OS3	20pf blue	25
12N24 OS3	30pf blue green	25
12N25 OS3	40pf red violet	20
Nos. 12N13-12N25 (13)		14.45

Issue dates: 3pf, No. 12N14, 5pf, 6pf, 8pf, Jan. 17. 10pf, 12pf, 40pf, Jan. 22. 15pf, Jan. 24. 30pf, Jan. 26. 20pf, Jan. 29. No. 12N15, Feb. 25.

Nos. 12N13-12N21 exist on both white and toned paper.

Germany under Russian Occupation stamps can be mounted in the Scott Germany part I and Soviet Republics albums part I.

MECKLENBURG-VORPOMMERN SEMI-POSTAL STAMPS

Rudolf Breitscheid (1874-1944), Politician — OSP1

Designs: 8pf+22pf, Dr. Erich Klausener (1885-1934), theologian. 12pf+28pf, Ernst Thalmann (1886-1944), politician.

1945, Oct. 21 Typo. ***Perf. 10½x11***

12NB1 OSP1	6 +14pf green	3.00
12NB2 OSP1	8 +22pf purple	3.00
12NB3 OSP1	12 +28pf red	3.00

Horsedrawn Plow — OSP2

Child Welfare — OSP3

Designs: 8pf+22pf, Sower. 12pf+28pf, Reaper.

1945

12NB4 OSP2	6 +14pf bl grn	1.75
12NB5 OSP2	6 +14pf grn	1.75
12NB6 OSP2	8 +22pf brn	1.75
12NB7 OSP2	8 +22pf yel brn	1.75
12NB8 OSP2	12 +28pf red	1.75
12NB9 OSP2	12 +28pf org	1.75
Nos. 12NB4-12NB9 (6)		10.50

Issue dates: Nos. 12NB4, 12NB6, 12NB8, Dec. 8, others Dec. 31.

1945, Dec. 31 *Perf. 11*

12NB10 OSP3	6 +14pf Child in hand	50
12NB11 OSP3	8 +22pf Girl in winter	50
12NB12 OSP3	12 +28pf Boy	50

SAXONY PROVINCE

Coat of Arms — OS1

Land Reform — OS2

Perf. 13x12½

1945-46 Typo. Wmk. 48

13N1 OS1	1pf slate	15
a.	Imperf.	30
13N2 OS1	3pf yellow brown	15
a.	Imperf.	30
13N3 OS1	5pf green	15
a.	Imperf.	30
13N4 OS1	6pf purple	15
a.	Imperf.	30
13N5 OS1	8pf orange	15
a.	Imperf.	30
13N6 OS1	10pf brown	15
a.	Imperf.	2.00
13N7 OS1	12pf red	15
a.	Imperf.	30
13N8 OS1	15pf red brown	15
13N9 OS1	20pf blue	15
13N10 OS1	24pf orange brown	15
13N11 OS1	30pf olive green	15
13N12 OS1	40pf lake	15
Set value		1.00

Issue dates: Nos. 13N1-13N12, Dec. 1945. Nos. 13N1a-13N5a, 13N7a, Oct. 10, 1945. No. 13N6a, Jan. 1946.

1945-46 Unwmk. ***Imperf.***

13N13 OS2	6pf green	15

13N14 OS2 12pf red 15

On Thin Transparent Paper

Wmk. 397

Perf. 13x13½

13N15 OS2 6pf green 15
13N16 OS2 12pf red 15
Set value, Nos. 13N13-13N16 30

Issue dates: Nos. 13N13-13N14, Dec. 17, 1945. Others Feb. 21, 1946.

SAXONY PROVINCE SEMI-POSTAL STAMPS

Reconstruction OSP1

Designs: 6+4pf, Housing construction. 12+8pf, Bridge repair. 42+28pf, Locomotives.

1946 Typo. *Perf. 13*

13NB1 OSP1 6pf +4pf green 15
a. Imperf. 15
13NB2 OSP1 12pf +8pf red 15
a. Imperf. 15
13NB3 OSP1 42pf +28pf violet 15
a. Imperf. 15
Set value 18

Issue dates: Perf., Jan. 19. Imperf., Feb. 21.

WEST SAXONY

OS1

Leipzig Fair — OS2

1945 Typo. Wmk. 48 *Perf. 13x12½*

14N1 OS1 3pf brown 15 15
14N2 OS1 4pf slate 15 15
14N3 OS1 5pf green 15 15
a. Imperf. 15
14N4 OS1 6pf violet 15 15
a. Imperf. 15
14N5 OS1 8pf orange 15 15
a. Imperf. 15
14N6 OS1 10pf gray 15 15
14N7 OS1 12pf red 15 15
a. Imperf. 15
14N8 OS1 15pf red brown 15 15
14N9 OS1 20pf blue 25 25
14N10 OS1 30pf olive green 25 35
14N11 OS1 40pf red lilac 25 35
14N12 OS1 60pf maroon 35 45
Set value 1.40 2.00

Issue dates: 3pf, 4pf, 20pf, 30pf, Nov. 9. 5pf, 6pf, 8pf, 12pf, Nov. 12. 10pf, 15pf, 40pf, 60pf, Nov. 15. Imperfs., Sept. 28.

1945, Oct. 18

14N13 OS2 6pf green 15
14N14 OS2 12pf red 15

Leipzig Arms — OS3

Designs: 5pf, 6pf, St. Nicholas Church. 8pf, 12pf, Leipzig Town Hall.

1946, Feb. 12

14N15 OS3 3pf brown 15
a. Unwatermarked 15
14N16 OS3 4pf slate 15
a. Unwatermarked 15
14N17 OS3 5pf green 15
a. Unwatermarked 15
14N18 OS3 6pf violet 15
a. Unwatermarked 15
14N19 OS3 8pf orange 15
a. Unwatermarked 15
14N20 OS3 12pf red 15
a. Unwatermarked 15
Set value 35
Set value, unwatermarked 30

Nos. 14N15a-14N20a issued Mar. 15.

WEST SAXONY SEMI-POSTAL STAMPS

OSP1

Market, Old Town Hall — OSP2

Perf. 13x12½

1946, Jan. 7 Typo. Wmk. 48

14NB1 OSP1 3 +2pf yel brn 15
14NB2 OSP1 4 +3pf slate 15
14NB3 OSP1 5 +3pf green 15
14NB4 OSP1 6 +4pf violet 15
14NB5 OSP1 8 +4pf orange 15
14NB6 OSP1 10 +5pf gray 15
14NB7 OSP1 12 +6pf red 15
14NB8 OSP1 15 +10pf red brn 15
14NB9 OSP1 20 +10pf blue 15
14NB10 OSP1 30 +20pf olive grn 15
14NB11 OSP1 40 +30pf red lilac 15
14NB12 OSP1 60 +40pf lake 15
Set value 1.25

Issue dates: Nos. 14NB1, 14NB4, 14NB7, 14NB11, Jan. 7; others, Jan. 28.

1946, May 8 *Perf. 13*

14NB13 OSP2 6 +14pf violet 15
a. Imperf. 25
b. Unwatermarked 20
14NB14 OSP2 12 +18pf bl gray 15
a. Imperf. 25
b. Unwatermarked 20
14NB15 OSP2 24 +26pf org brn 15
a. Imperf. 25
b. Unwatermarked 25
14NB16 OSP2 84 +66pf green 15
a. Imperf. 25
c. Sheet of 4, #14NB13a-14NB16a 100.00
Set value 30

Issue date: Imperf., May 20.

EAST SAXONY

Type OS1 Inscribed "NOYTA"

1945, June 23 Photo. *Imperf.*

15N1 OS1 12pf red

Withdrawn on day of issue.

OS1

Litho. (3pf, #15N9), Photo.

1945-46

15N2 OS1 3pf sepia 15
15N3 OS1 4pf blue gray 15
a. 4pf gray 15
15N4 OS1 5pf brown 20
15N5 OS1 6pf green 1.00
15N6 OS1 6pf violet 15
15N7 OS1 8pf dark violet 30
15N8 OS1 10pf dark brown 18
15N9 OS1 10pf gray 18
15N10 OS1 12pf red 15
15N11 OS1 15pf lemon 25
15N12 OS1 20pf gray blue 15
a. 20pf blue 15
15N13 OS1 25pf blue 20
15N14 OS1 30pf yellow 15
15N15 OS1 40pf lilac 30

Typo.

Perf. 13x12½

15N16 OS1 3pf brown 15
15N17 OS1 5pf green 15
15N18 OS1 6pf violet 15
15N19 OS1 8pf orange 15
15N20 OS1 12pf vermilion 15

Issue dates: 12pf, June 28. #15N5, June 30. 8pf, #15N8, July 3. 25pf, July 5. 5pf, July 6. 40pf, July 7. 15pf, July 10. #15N12, July 26. #15N9, 15N12a, 15N17-15N20, Nov. 3. #15N3, 30pf, Nov. 5. 3pf, Dec. 5. #15N15, Dec. 21. #15N6, Jan. 22, 1946.

EAST SAXONY SEMI-POSTAL STAMPS

Zwinger, Dresden — OSP1

Design: 12pf+88pf, Rathaus, Dresden.

1946, Feb. 6 Photo. *Perf. 11*

15NB1 OSP1 6pf +44pf green 15
15NB2 OSP1 12pf +88pf red 15

THURINGIA

Fir Trees — OS1

Designs: 6pf, 8pf, Posthorn. 12pf, Schiller. 20pf, 30pf, Goethe.

1945-46 Typo. *Perf. 11*

16N1 OS1 3pf brown 15
16N2 OS1 4pf black 15
16N3 OS1 5pf green 15
a. Souvenir sheet of 3, #16N1-16N3 150.00
16N4 OS1 6pf dark green 15
16N5 OS1 8pf orange 15
16N6 OS1 12pf red 15
16N7 OS1 20pf blue 15
a. Imperf. 15
b. Souv. sheet of 4, #16N2, 16N4, 16N6-16N7, rouletted x imperf. btwn. 500.00
16N8 OS1 30pf gray 30
a. Imperf. 75
Nos. 16N1-16N8 (8) 1.35

#16N3a sold for 2m, #16N7b for 10m.

Issue dates: 6pf, Oct. 1. 12pf, Oct. 19. 5pf, Oct. 20. 8pf, Nov. 3. 20pf, Nov. 24. #16N3a, 16N7b, Dec. 18. 30pf, Dec. 22. 3pf, 4pf, Jan. 4, 1946.

Souvenir Sheet

Rebuilding of German Natl. Theater, Weimar — OS2

Designs: a, 6pf, Schiller. b, 10pf, Goethe. c, 12pf, Liszt. d, 16pf, Wieland. e, 40pf, Natl. Theater.

1946, Mar. 27 Wmk. 48 *Imperf.*

16N9 OS2 Sheet of 5, #a.-e. 10.00
f. Sheet, unwatermarked 25.00

Sold for 7.50 marks.

THURINGIA SEMI-POSTAL STAMPS

Bridge Reconstruction OSP1

Designs: 10pf+60pf, Saalburg Bridge. 12pf+68pf, Camsdorf Bridge, Jena. 16pf+74pf, Goschwitz Bridge. 24pf+76pf, Ilm Bridge, Mellingen.

1946, Mar. 30 Typo. *Imperf.*

16NB1 OSP1 10 +60pf red brown 15
16NB2 OSP1 12 +68pf red 15
16NB3 OSP1 16 +74pf dark green 15
16NB4 OSP1 24 +76pf brown 15
a. Souv. sheet of 4, #16NB1-16NB4 125.00
Set value 30

GERMAN DEMOCRATIC REPUBLIC

LOCATION — Eastern Germany
GOVT. — Republic
AREA — 41,659 sq. mi.
POP. — 16,701,500 (1983)
CAPITAL — Berlin (Soviet sector)

100 Pfennigs = 1 Deutsche Mark (East)
100 Pfennigs = 1 Mark of the Deutsche Notenbank (MDN) (1965)
100 Pfennigs = 1 Mark of the National Bank (M) (1969)
100 Pfennigs = 1 Deutsche Mark (West) (1990)

Catalogue values for all unused stamps in this country are for Never Hinged items.

Watermarks

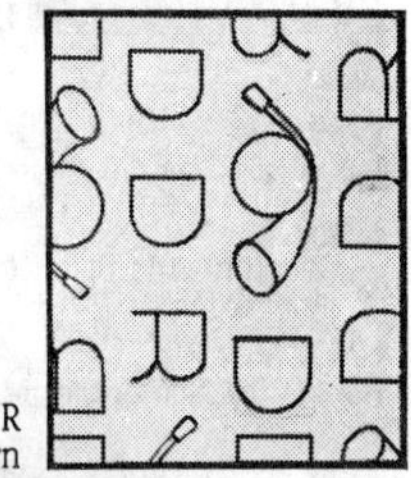

Wmk. 297- DDR and Post Horn

Wmk. 313- Quatrefoil and DDR

Pigeon, Letter and Globe A5

Wmk. Flowers Multiple (292)

1949, Oct. 9 Litho. *Perf. 13½*

48 A5 50pf lt blue & dk blue 7.00 3.25

75th anniv. of the UPU.

Letter Carriers A6

Skier A7

1949, Oct. 27 *Perf. 13*

49 A6 12pf blue 6.00 3.00
50 A6 30pf red 9.00 5.00

"Day of the International Postal Workers' Trade Union," October 27-29, 1949.

1950, Mar. 2 *Perf. 13*

51 A7 12pf shown 5.50 3.00
52 A7 24pf Skater 7.00 4.25

1st German Winter Sport Championship Matches, Schierke, 1950.

Globe and Sun — A8

1950, May 1 Typo.

53 A8 30pf deep carmine 14.00 8.00

60th anniv. of Labor Day.

Pres. Wilhelm Pieck A9 A10

1950-51 Wmk. 292 *Perf. 13x12½*

54 A9 12pf dark blue 12.00 90
55 A9 24pf red brown 27.50 60

Perf. 13x13½

56 A10 1m olive green 25.00 2.25

Litho.

57 A10 2m red brown 12.00 2.25

Engr.

57A A10 5m deep blue ('51) 2.75 20
Nos. 54-57A (5) 79.25 6.20

See Nos. 113-117, 120-121.

Leonhard Euler — A11

Miner — A12

Portraits: 5pf, Alexander von Humboldt. 6pf, Theodor Mommsen. 8pf, Wilhelm von Humboldt. 10pf, H. L. F. von Helmholtz. 12pf, Max Planck. 16pf, Jacob Grimm. 20pf, W. H. Nernst. 24pf, Gottfried von Leibnitz. 50pf, Adolf von Harnack.

Perf. 12½

1950, July 10 Litho. Wmk. 292

58 A11 1pf gray 3.25 1.40
59 A11 5pf dp green 5.00 3.75
60 A11 6pf purple 8.25 4.50
61 A11 8pf orange brn 14.00 8.75
62 A11 10pf dk gray grn 11.00 8.75
63 A11 12pf dk blue 3.25 1.40
64 A11 16pf Prus blue 16.00 11.00
65 A11 20pf violet brn 14.00 8.75
66 A11 24pf red 14.00 2.75
67 A11 50pf dp ultra 20.00 10.50
Nos. 58-67 (10) 108.75 61.55

250th anniv. of the founding of the Academy of Science, Berlin.
See Nos. 352-354.

Canceled to Order

The government stamp agency started about 1950 to sell canceled sets of new issues.

Used values are for CTO's from No. 68 to No. 2831.

1950, Sept. 1 *Perf. 13*

Design: 24pf, Smelting copper.

68 A12 12pf blue 4.00 60
69 A12 24pf dark red 5.00 90

750th anniv. of the opening of the Mannsfeld copper mines.

Symbols of a Democratic Vote — A13

Hand Between Dove and Tank — A14

1950, Sept. 28

70 A13 24pf brown red 10.00 60

Publicizing the election of Oct. 15, 1950.

1950, Dec. 15 Litho. *Perf. 13*

Designs show hand shielding dove from: 8pf, Exploding shell. 12pf, Atomic explosion. 24pf, Cemetery.

71 A14 6pf violet blue 4.00 1.10
72 A14 8pf brown 3.00 55
73 A14 12pf blue 5.00 95
74 A14 24pf red 5.00 45

Issued to publicize the "Fight for Peace."

Tobogganing — A15

Design: 24pf, Ski jump.

1951, Feb. 3 Litho. *Perf. 13*

76 A15 12pf blue 9.00 1.50
77 A15 24pf rose 10.00 2.25

Issued to publicize the second Winter Sports Championship Matches at Oberhof.

A16

1951, Mar. 4 Wmk. 292 *Perf. 13*

78 A16 24pf rose carmine 15.00 3.50
79 A16 50pf violet blue 15.00 3.50

Issued to publicize the 1951 Leipzig Fair.

Pres. Wilhelm Pieck and Pres. Boleslaw Bierut Shaking Hands Across Oder-Neisse Frontier — A17

1951, Apr. 22 *Perf. 13*

80 A17 24pf scarlet 21.00 4.50
81 A17 50pf blue 21.00 4.50

Visit of Pres. Boleslaw Bierut of Poland to the Russian Zone of Germany.

Mao Tse-tung — A18

Redistribution of Chinese Land — A19

1951, June 27 *Perf. 13*

82 A18 12pf dark green *140.00* 7.25
83 A19 24pf deep carmine *200.00* 13.00
84 A18 50pf violet blue *125.00* 5.00

Issued to publicize East Germany's friendship toward Communist China.

Boy Raising Flag A20

5-Year Plan Symbolism A21

Design: 24pf, 50pf, Girls dancing.

1951, Aug. 3

Grayish Paper, Except 30pf

85 A20 12pf choc & org brn 11.00 1.75
86 A20 24pf dk car & yel grn 11.00 1.25
87 A20 30pf dk bl grn & org brn, *cit* 14.00 2.25
88 A20 50pf vio bl & dk car 11.50 1.90

3rd World Youth Festival, Berlin, 1951.

1951, Sept. 2 Typo. Wmk. 292

89 A21 24pf multicolored 4.00 50

East Germany's Five-Year Plan.

Karl Liebknecht A22

Father and Children with Stamp Collection A23

1951, Oct. 7 Litho. *Perf. 13½x13*

90 A22 24pf red & blue gray 4.50 50

80th anniversary of the birth of Karl Liebknecht, socialist.

1951, Oct. 28 *Perf. 13*

91 A23 12pf deep blue 3.50 60

Stamp Day, Oct. 28, 1951.

Stalin and Wilhelm Pieck A24

Design: 12pf, Pavel Bykov and Erich Wirth.

1951

92 A24 12pf deep blue 3.75 90
93 A24 24pf red 4.75 1.10

Month of East German-Soviet friendship.
Issue dates: 12pf, Dec. 15, 24pf, Dec. 1.

Skier A25

Beethoven A26

Design: 24pf, Ski jump.

1952, Jan. 12 Wmk. 292

94 A25 12pf blue green 4.00 70
95 A25 24pf deep blue 4.00 90

Winter Sports Championship Matches, Oberhof, 1952.

1952, Mar. 26 *Perf. 13½*

Design: 12pf, Beethoven full face.

96 A26 12pf bl gray & vio bl 1.50 15
97 A26 24pf gray & red brn 1.50 15

125th anniversary of the death of Ludwig van Beethoven.
See Nos. 100-102.

German Democratic Republic (East Germany) stamps can be mounted in the Scott Germany album part IV.

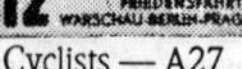
Cyclists — A27

Klement Gottwald — A28

1952, May 5 Photo. *Perf. 13x13½*
98 A27 12pf blue 1.50 15

5th International Bicycle Peace Race, Warsaw-Berlin-Prague.

1952, May 1
99 A28 24pf violet blue 2.25 35

Friendship between German Democratic Republic and Czechoslovakia.

Type of 1952

Portraits: 6pf, G. F. Handel. 8pf, Albert Lortzing. 50pf, C. M. von Weber.

1952, July 5 Litho. Wmk. 297
100 A26 6pf brn buff & choc 1.50 28
101 A26 8pf pink & dp rose pink 2.00 32
102 A26 50pf bl gray & dp bl 3.00 40

Victor Hugo — A29

Portraits: 20pf, Leonardo da Vinci. 24pf, Nicolai Gogol. 35pf, Avicenna.

Wmk. 292
1952, Aug. 11 Photo. *Perf. 13*
103 A29 12pf brown 2.00 50
104 A29 20pf green 2.00 50
105 A29 24pf rose 2.00 50
106 A29 35pf blue 3.00 75

Machine, Globe and Dove — A30

Friedrich Ludwig Jahn — A31

1952, Sept. 7 Wmk. 297 *Perf. 13*
108 A30 24pf red 1.50 15
109 A30 35pf deep blue 1.50 48

Issued to publicize the 1952 Leipzig Fair.

1952, Oct. 15 Litho.
110 A31 12pf blue 1.50 15

Jahn (1778-1852), introduced gymnastics to Germany, and was a politician.

Halle University — A32

Stamp, Flags, Wreath, Dove and Hammer — A33

1952, Oct. 18 Photo.
111 A32 24pf green 1.50 15

450th anniv. of the founding of Halle University, Wittenberg.

1952, Oct. 26
112 A33 24pf red brown 1.50 24

Stamp Day, Oct. 26, 1952.

Pieck Types of 1950
Perf. 13x12½
1952-53 Wmk. 297 Typo.
113 A9 5pf blue green 6.25 38
114 A9 12pf dark blue 19.00 18
115 A9 24pf red brown 19.00 18

Perf. 13x13½
116 A10 1m olive green 27.50 2.75

Litho. *Perf. 13*
117 A10 2m red brown ('53) 27.50 90
Nos. 113-117 (5) 99.25 4.39

Globe, Dove and St. Stephen's Cathedral — A34

Pres. Wilhelm Pieck — A35

1952, Dec. 8 Photo. *Perf. 13*
118 A34 24pf brt carmine 1.50 22
119 A34 35pf deep blue 1.50 28

Issued to publicize the Congress of Nations for Peace, Vienna, Dec. 12-19, 1952.

1953 *Perf. 13x13½*
120 A35 1m olive 12.00 15
a. 1m dark olive ('55) 20.00 15
121 A35 2m red brown 12.00 15
Set value 15

See Nos. 339-340, 532.

Portrait Types of Russian Occupation, 1948

Designs as before.

Perf. 13x12½
1953 Typo. Wmk. 297
122 OS2 2pf gray 1.00 38
123 OS2 6pf purple 1.75 30
124 OS2 8pf red brown 1.00 30
125 OS2 10pf blue grn 2.25 30
126 OS2 15pf brown 7.50 2.50
127 OS2 16pf turquoise 3.25 48
128 OS2 20pf maroon 1.75 30
129 OS2 25pf olive grn 52.50 15.00
130 OS2 30pf red 5.00 1.00
131 OS2 40pf red violet 1.40 48
132 OS2 50pf dk ultra 15.00 4.25
133 OS2 60pf dull green 3.25 45
134 OS2 80pf dark blue 1.75 35
a. Varnish coating 3.50 1.40
135 OS2 80pf crimson 9.50 2.00
136 OS2 84pf brown lake 41.00 12.00
Nos. 122-136 (15) 147.90 40.09

"Industry" and Red Flag — A36

Marx and Engels — A37

Karl Marx Speaking — A38

Karl Marx Medallion — A39

Designs: 12pf, Spasski tower and communist flag. 16pf, Marching workers. 24pf, Portrait of Karl Marx. 35pf, Marx addressing audience. 48pf, Karl Marx and Friedrich Engels. 60pf. Red banner above heads and shoulders of workers.

1953 Photo. *Perf. 13*
137 A36 6pf grnsh gray & red 48 15
138 A37 10pf grnsh gray & dk brn 3.00 15
139 A36 12pf grn, dp plum & dk grn 48 15
140 A37 16pf vio bl & dk car 2.25 38
141 A38 20pf brown & buff 80 20
142 A38 24pf brown & red 2.25 15
143 A36 35pf dp pur & cr 2.25 65
144 A36 48pf dk ol grn & red brn 1.00 20
a. Souvenir sheet of 6 110.00 25.00
145 A37 60pf vio brn & red 3.00 65
146 A39 84pf blue & brown 2.25 48
a. Souvenir sheet of 4 110.00 25.00
Nos. 137-146 (10) 17.76 3.16

No. 144a contains one each of the denominations in types A36 and A38. Perf. and imperf.

No. 146a contains one each of the denominations in types A37 and A39. Perf. and imperf.

Maxim Gorky — A40

Bicycle Racers — A41

1953, Mar. 28
147 A40 35pf brown 25 15

1953, May 2 Wmk. 297 *Perf. 13*

Designs: 35pf, 60pf, Different views of bicycle race.

148 A41 24pf bluish green 1.25 25
149 A41 35pf deep ultra 85 25
150 A41 60pf chocolate 1.25 30

6th International Bicycle Peace Race.

Heinrich von Kleist A42

Coal Miner A43

Designs: 20pf, Evangelical Marienkirche. 24pf, Sailboat on Oder River. 35pf, City Hall, Frankfurt-on-Oder.

1953, July 6 Litho.
151 A42 16pf chocolate 95 22
152 A42 20pf blue green 55 15
153 A42 24pf rose red 95 22
154 A42 35pf violet blue 95 22

700th anniversary of the founding of Frankfurt-on-Oder.

1953 Litho. *Perf. 13x12½*

Designs: 5pf, Woman mariner. 6pf, German and Soviet workers. 8pf, Mother teaching Marxist principles. 10pf, Machinists. 12pf, Worker, peasant and intellectual. 15pf, Teletype operator. 16pf, Steel worker. 20pf, Bad Elster. 24pf, Stalin Boulevard. 25pf, Locomotive building. 30pf, Dancing couple. 35pf, Sports Hall, Berlin. 40pf, Laboratory worker. 48pf, Zwinger Castle, Dresden. 60pf, Launching ship. 80pf, Agricultural workers. 84pf, Dove and East German family.

155 A43 1pf black brown 90 15
156 A43 5pf emerald 1.25 15
157 A43 6pf violet 1.25 15
158 A43 8pf orange brn 1.65 15
159 A43 10pf blue green 1.25 15
160 A43 12pf blue 1.25 15
161 A43 15pf purple 2.50 15
162 A43 16pf dk violet 2.75 15
163 A43 20pf olive 2.75 15
163A A43 24pf carmine 6.75 15
164 A43 25pf dk green 4.00 15
165 A43 30pf dp car 4.00 15
166 A43 35pf violet bl 7.75 15
167 A43 40pf rose red 7.00 15
168 A43 48pf rose red 6.75 15
169 A43 60pf deep blue 6.75 15
170 A43 80pf aqua 9.50 15
171 A43 84pf chocolate 9.50 15
Nos. 155-171 (18) 77.55
Set value 90

See Nos. 187-204, 216-223A, 227-230A, 330-338, 476-482.

Used values of Nos. 155-171 are for cto reprints with printed cancellations. The reprints differ slightly from originals in design and shade.

Power Shovel — A44

Design: 35pf, Road-building machine.

1953, Aug. 29 Photo. *Perf. 13*
172 A44 24pf red brown 1.40 16
173 A44 35pf deep green 2.00 35

The 1953 Leipzig Fair.

G. W. von Knobelsdorff and Berlin State Opera House A45

Design: 35pf, Balthasar Neumann and Wurzburg bishop's palace.

1953, Sept. 16 *Perf. 13x12½*
174 A45 24pf cerise 85 15
175 A45 35pf dk slate blue 1.65 32

200th anniv. of the deaths of G. W. von Knobelsdorff and Balthasar Neumann, architects.

Lucas Cranach — A46

Nurse Applying Bandage — A47

1953, Oct. 16 *Perf. 13x13½*
176 A46 24pf brown 1.90 28

400th anniversary of the death of Lucas Cranach (1472-1553), painter.

Perf. 13½x13
1953, Oct. 23 Wmk. 297
177 A47 24pf brown & red 1.75 15

Issued to honor the Red Cross.

Mail Delivery — A48

Lion and Lioness — A49

1953, Oct. 25 **Photo.**
178 A48 24pf blue gray 1.75 15

Issued to publicize Stamp Day, Oct. 24, 1953.

1953, Nov. 2 ***Perf. 13x13½***
179 A49 24pf olive brown 1.40 15

75th anniversary of Leipzig Zoo.

Thomas Muntzer and Attackers A50

Designs: 16pf, H. F. K. vom Stein. 20pf, Ferdinand von Schill leading cavalry. 24pf, G. L. Blucher and battle scene. 35pf, Students fighting for National Unity. 48pf, Revolution of 1848.

1953, Nov. **Photo.** ***Perf. 13x12½***
180 A50 12pf brown 1.00 15
181 A50 16pf dp brown 1.00 15
182 A50 20pf dk car rose 80 15
183 A50 24pf deep blue 85 15
184 A50 35pf dk green 1.50 28
185 A50 48pf dk brown 1.75 25
Nos. 180-185 (6) 6.90
Set value 88

Issued to honor German patriots.

Franz Schubert — A51

Gotthold E. Lessing — A52

1953, Nov. 13 ***Perf. 13½x13***
186 A51 48pf brt orange brn 3.00 25

125th anniversary of the death of Franz Schubert.

Types of 1953 Redrawn

Designs as before.

1953-54 **Typo.** ***Perf. 13x12½***
187 A43 1pf black brn 55 15
188 A43 5pf emerald 2.50 15
a. Bklt. pane, 3 #188 + 3 #227
b. Bklt. pane, 3 #188 + 3 #228
189 A43 6pf purple 3.75 15
190 A43 8pf orange brn 3.75 15
191 A43 10pf blue grn 6.00 15
192 A43 12pf grnsh blue 3.50 15
193 A43 15pf brt vio ('54) 6.00 15
194 A43 16pf dk purple 2.25 15
195 A43 20pf olive ('54) 7.50 15
196 A43 24pf carmine 6.00 15
197 A43 25pf dk bl grn 2.00 15
198 A43 30pf dp carmine 2.50 15
199 A43 35pf dp vio bl 2.50 15
200 A43 40pf rose red ('54) 7.00 15
201 A43 48pf rose vio 9.25 15
202 A43 60pf blue 9.25 15
203 A43 80pf aqua 3.50 15
204 A43 84pf chocolate 14.00 15
Nos. 187-204 (18) 91.80
Set value 90

Nos. 155-171 were printed from screened halftones, and shading consists of dots. Shading in lines without screen on Nos. 187-204. Designers' and engravers' names added below design on all values except 6, 12, 16 and 35pf. There are many other minor differences.

See note on used values after No. 171.

1954, Jan. 20 **Photo.** ***Perf. 13***
205 A52 20pf dark green 1.75 15

225th anniversary of the birth of G. E. Lessing, dramatist.

Dove Over Conference Table — A53

Joseph V. Stalin — A54

1954, Jan. 25 ***Perf. 12½x13***
206 A53 12pf blue 1.75 15

Four Power Conference, Berlin, 1954.

1954, Mar. 5 **Typo.** ***Perf. 13x12½***
207 A54 20pf gray, dk brn & red org 1.90 15

1st anniv. of the death of Joseph V. Stalin.

Cyclists A55

Design: 24pf, Cyclists passing farm.

1954, Apr. 30 **Photo.**
208 A55 12pf brown 1.10 18
209 A55 24pf dull green 1.40 22

7th International Bicycle Peace Race.

Dancers — A56

Fritz Reuter — A57

Design: 24pf, Boy, two girls and flag.

1954, June 3 ***Perf. 13***
210 A56 12pf emerald 95 15
211 A56 24pf rose brown 95 15

Issued to publicize the 2nd German youth meeting for peace, unity and freedom.

1954, July 12
212 A57 24pf sepia 1.10 16

80th anniversary of the death of Fritz Reuter, writer.

Ernst Thälmann A58

Hall of Commerce, Leipzig Fair A59

1954, Aug. 18 ***Perf. 13½x13***
213 A58 24pf red org & indigo 1.25 15

10th anniv. of the death of Ernst Thälmann (1886-1944), Communist leader.

1954, Sept. 4 ***Perf. 13x13½***
214 A59 24pf dark red 50 15
215 A59 35pf gray blue 60 15
Set value 20

Issued to publicize the 1954 Leipzig Fair.

Redrawn Types of 1953-54 Surcharged with New Value and "X" in Black

1954 **Typo.** ***Perf. 13x12½***
216 A43 5pf on 6pf purple 22 15
217 A43 5pf on 8pf org brn 22 15
218 A43 10pf on 12pf grnsh bl 50 15
219 A43 15pf on 16pf dk pur 22 15
220 A43 20pf on 24pf car 50 15
221 A43 40pf on 48pf rose vio 85 15
222 A43 50pf on 60pf blue 1.25 15
223 A43 70pf on 84pf choc 3.50 15
Nos. 216-223 (8) 7.26
Set value 40

See note on used values after No. 171.

No. 163A Surcharged with New Value and "X" in Black

1955 **Litho.**
223A A43 20pf on 24pf car 32 15

Counterfeit surcharges exist on other values of the lithographed set (Nos. 155-171).

Pres. Wilhelm Pieck and Flags — A60

1954, Oct. 6 **Photo.**
224 A60 20pf brown 55 15
225 A60 35pf greenish blue 1.10 15
Set value 20

5th anniv. of the founding of the German Democratic Republic.

Cologne Cathedral, Leipzig Monument and Unissued Stamp Design — A61

1954, Oct. 23 ***Perf. 13x13½***
226 A61 20pf brt car rose 90 15
a. Souvenir sheet, imperf. 32.00 14.00

Stamp Day. No. 226a has frame and inscription in blue. Size: 60x80mm.

Redrawn Types of 1953-54

Designs: 10pf, Worker, peasant and intellectual. 15pf, Steelworker. 20pf, Stalin Boulevard. 40pf, Zwinger Castle, Dresden. 50pf, Launching ship. 70pf, Dove and East German family.

1955 **Typo.** ***Perf. 13x12½***
227 A43 10pf blue 1.25 15
a. Bklt. pane, 4 #227 + 2 #228
227B A43 15pf violet 1.75 15
228 A43 20pf carmine 1.25 15
229 A43 40pf rose violet 2.00 15
230 A43 50pf deep blue 2.00 15
230A A43 70pf chocolate 5.25 15
Nos. 227-230A (6) 13.50
Set value 20

See note on used values after No. 171.

Soviet Pavilion, Leipzig Spring Fair — A62

Women of Three Nations — A63

Design: 35pf, Chinese pavilion.

Perf. 13x13½
1955, Feb. 21 **Photo.** **Wmk. 297**
231 A62 20pf rose violet 42 15
232 A62 35pf violet blue 1.10 16
Set value 25

Issued to publicize the Leipzig Spring Fair.

1955, Mar. 1 ***Perf. 13x13½***
233 A63 10pf green 75 15
234 A63 20pf red 1.00 15
Set value 15

International Women's Day, 45th year.

Workers' Demonstration — A64

1955, Mar. 15 ***Perf. 13x12½***
235 A64 10pf black & red 90 15

Intl. Trade Union Conference, Apr., 1955.

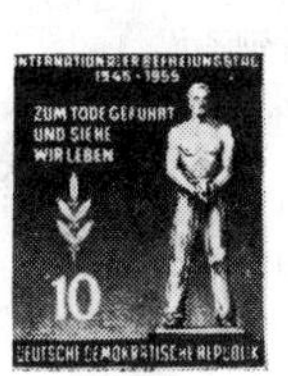

A65

A66

Monument to the Victims of Fascism.

1955, Apr. 9 ***Perf. 13½x13***
236 A65 10pf violet blue 70 15
237 A65 20pf cerise 85 15
a. Souv. sheet of 2, #236-237, imperf. 18.00 6.00
Set value 20

No. 237a sold for 50pf.

1955, Apr. 15 ***Perf. 12½x13***

Russian War Memorial, Berlin.

238 A66 20pf lilac rose 1.25 15

Nos. 236-238 issued for 10th anniv. of liberation, No. 237a for reconstruction of natl. memorial sites.

Cyclists — A67

Friedrich von Schiller — A68

1955 **Wmk. 297** ***Perf. 13½x13***
239 A67 10pf blue green 35 15
240 A67 20pf car rose 85 15
Set value 25

8th International Bicycle Peace Race, Prague-Berlin-Warsaw.

Starting with the 1955 issues, commemorative stamps which are valued in italics were sold on a restricted basis.

1955, Apr. 20

Various Portraits of Schiller.

241 A68 5pf dk gray grn *2.50* *50*
242 A68 10pf brt blue 20 15
243 A68 20pf chocolate 20 15
a. Souv. sheet, #241-243, imperf. *20.00* *6.75*
Set value *65*

150th anniv. of the death of Friedrich von Schiller, poet.

No. 243a sold for 50pf.

Karl Liebknecht A69

Portraits: 10pf, August Bebel. 15pf, Franz Mehring. 20pf, Ernst Thalmann. 25pf, Clara Zetkin. 40pf, Wilhelm Liebknecht. 60pf, Rosa Luxemburg.

1955, June 20 Photo. *Perf. 13x12½*

244 A69	5pf blue green	15	15
245 A69	10pf deep blue	15	15
246 A69	15pf violet	*5.00*	*1.00*
247 A69	20pf red	15	15
248 A69	25pf slate	15	15
249 A69	40pf rose carmine	1.00	15
250 A69	60pf dk brown	24	15
	Nos. 244-250 (7)	*6.84*	
	Set value		*1.50*

Issued to honor German communists.

Optical Goods — A70

Design: 20pf, Pottery and china.

1955, Aug. 29 Photo. *Perf. 13x13½*

253 A70	10pf dark blue	45	15
254 A70	20pf slate green	45	15
	Set value		15

Issued to publicize the 1955 Leipzig Fair.

Farmer Receiving Deed — A71

Harvesters — A72

Design: 10pf, Construction of new farm community.

Perf. 13½x13, 13x13½

1955, Sept. 3

255 A71	5pf dull green	*4.50*	*1.90*
256 A71	10pf ultra	70	15
257 A72	20pf lake	70	15

10th anniv. of the Land-Reform Program.

Man Holding Badge of Peoples' Solidarity — A73

Engels at "First International," 1864 — A74

Perf. 13½x13

1955, Oct. 10 Wmk. 297

258 A73	10pf dark blue	30	15

10th anniv. of the "Peoples' Solidarity."

1955, Nov. 7 *Perf. 13½x13*

Designs: 10pf, Marx and Engels writing the Communist Manifesto. 15pf, Engels as newspaper editor. 20pf, Friedrich Engels. 30pf, Friedrich Engels. 70pf, Engels on the barricades in 1848.

259 A74	5pf Prus blue & olive	25	15
260 A74	10pf dk blue & yel	25	15
261 A74	15pf dk green & ol	25	15
262 A74	20pf brn vio & org	1.75	25
263 A74	30pf org brn & lt bl	*7.75*	*1.50*
264 A74	70pf gray grn & rose car	1.75	25
a.	Souvenir sheet of 6, #259-264	*70.00*	*27.50*
	Nos. 259-264 (6)	*12.00*	*2.45*

Friedrich Engels, 135th birth anniv.

Cathedral at Magdeburg A75

Georgius Agricola A76

German Buildings: 10pf, German State Opera. 15pf, Old City Hall, Leipzig. 20pf, City Hall, Berlin. 30pf, Cathedral at Erfurt. 40pf, Zwinger at Dresden.

1955, Nov. 14

265 A75	5pf black brown	55	15
266 A75	10pf gray green	55	15
267 A75	15pf purple	55	15
268 A75	20pf carmine	55	15
269 A75	30pf dk red brown	*7.00*	*1.90*
270 A75	40pf indigo	80	30
	Nos. 265-270 (6)	*10.00*	*2.80*

For surcharges see Nos. B29-B30.

1955, Nov. 21 Wmk. 297

271 A76	10pf brown	35	15

400th anniv. of the death of Georgius Agricola, mineralogist and scholar.

Portrait of a Young Man, by Dürer — A77

Mozart — A78

Famous Paintings: 10pf, Chocolate Girl, Liotard. 15pf, Portrait of a Boy, Pinturicchio. 20pf, Self-portrait with Saskia, Rembrandt. 40pf, Girl with Letter, Vermeer. 70pf, Sistine Madonna, Raphael.

1955, Dec. 15 *Perf. 13½x13*

272 A77	5pf dk red brown	1.25	15
273 A77	10pf chestnut	1.25	15
274 A77	15pf pale purple	*24.00*	*3.25*
275 A77	20pf brown	1.65	15
276 A77	40pf olive green	1.65	16
277 A77	70pf deep blue	4.25	25
	Nos. 272-277 (6)	*34.05*	*4.11*

Issued to publicize the return of famous art works to the Dresden Art Gallery.
See Nos. 355-360, 439-443.

1956, Jan. 27 Photo.

Designs: 20pf, Portrait facing left.

278 A78	10pf gray green	*9.50*	*1.25*
279 A78	20pf copper brown	2.50	15

200th anniv. of the birth of Wolfgang Amadeus Mozart, composer.

Flag and Schoenefeld Airport, Berlin A79

Lufthansa Plane A80

Designs: 15pf, Plane facing right. 20pf, Plane facing down and left.

1956, Feb. 1 *Perf. 13x12½*

280 A79	5pf multicolored	*9.00*	*1.40*
281 A80	10pf gray green	30	15
282 A80	15pf dull blue	30	15
283 A80	20pf brown red	30	15

Issued to commemorate the opening of passenger service of the German Lufthansa.

Heinrich Heine — A81

Railroad Cranes — A82

Design: 20pf, Heine (different portrait.)

1956, Feb. 17 *Perf. 13½x13*

284 A81	10pf Prus green	*5.25*	*85*
285 A81	20pf dark red	2.50	40

Cent. of the death of Heinrich Heine, poet.

1956, Feb. 26 *Perf. 13x13½*

286 A82	20pf brown red	75	15
287 A82	35pf violet blue	75	15
	Set value		20

Issued to publicize the Leipzig Spring Fair.

Ernst Thälmann — A83

1956, Apr. 16 Litho. *Perf. 13x13½*

288 A83	20pf black olive & red	30	15
a.	Souvenir sheet of 1	*8.00*	*5.25*

Birth of Ernst Thälmann, 70th anniv.
No. 288a was sold at double face value. The proceeds were used for national memorials at former concentration camps.

Wheel, Hand and Olive Branch — A84

City Hall and Old Market — A85

Design: 20pf, Wheel and coats of arms of Warsaw, Berlin, Prague.

Perf. 13½x13

1956, Apr. 30 Wmk. 297

289 A84	10pf lt green	55	15
290 A84	20pf brt carmine	55	15
	Set value		20

9th International Bicycle Peace Race, Warsaw-Berlin-Prague, May 1-15, 1956.

1956, June 1

Designs: 20pf, Hofkirche and Elbe Bridge. 40pf, Technical College.

291 A85	10pf green	18	15
292 A85	20pf carmine rose	18	15
293 A85	40pf brt purple	*2.25*	*75*
	Set value		*80*

750th anniversary of Dresden.

Worker Holding Cogwheel Emblem — A86

Robert Schumann (Music by Schubert) — A87

1956, June 30 *Perf. 13½x13*

294 A86	20pf rose red	45	15

10th anniversary of nationalized industry.

1956, July 20 *Perf. 13x13½*

295 A87	10pf brt green	*1.50*	*40*
296 A87	20pf rose red	40	15
	Set value		*45*

Centenary of the death of Robert Schumann, composer. See Nos. 303-304.

Soccer Players — A88

Thomas Mann — A89

Designs: 10pf, Javelin Thrower. 15pf, Women Hurdlers. 20pf, Gymnast.

1956, July 25 *Perf. 13½x13*

297 A88	5pf green	15	15
298 A88	10pf dk vio blue	15	15
299 A88	15pf red violet	*1.75*	*48*
300 A88	20pf rose red	15	15
	Set value	*2.00*	*60*

Second Sports Festival, Leipzig, Aug. 2-5.

1956, Aug. 13 Wmk. 297

301 A89	20pf bluish black	70	15

1st anniversary of the death of Thomas Mann, novelist.

Jakub Bart Cisinski — A90

Robert Schumann (Music by Schumann) — A91

1956, Aug. 20 Photo.

302 A90	50pf claret	75	15

Birth centenary of Jakub Bart Cisinski, poet.

1956, Oct. 8 *Perf. 13x13½*

303 A91	10pf brt green	*2.50*	*15*
304 A91	20pf rose red	50	15
	Set value	*3.00*	*16*

See Nos. 295, 296.

Lace — A92

Olympic Rings, Laurel and Torch — A93

Design: 20pf, Sailboat.

1956, Sept. 1 Typo. *Perf. 13½x13*

305 A92	10pf green & blk	18	15
306 A92	20pf rose red & blk	22	15
	Set value		15

Leipzig Fair, Sept. 2-9.

1956, Sept. 28 Litho.

Design: 35pf, Classic javelin thrower.

307 A93	20pf brown red	15	15
308 A93	35pf slate blue	18	15
	Set value		15

16th Olympic Games at Melbourne, Nov. 22-Dec. 8, 1956.

Post Runner of 1450 — A94

Greifswald University Seal — A95

1956, Oct. 27

309	A94	20pf	red	40	15

Issued to publicize the Day of the Stamp.

1956, Oct. 17 *Perf. 13x13½*

310	A95	20pf	magenta	45	15

500th anniv. of Greifswald University.

Ernst Abbe — A96

Zeiss Works, Jena — A97

Portrait: 25pf, Carl Zeiss.

Perf. 12½x13, 13x12½

1956, Nov. 9 Photo. Wmk. 297

311	A96	10pf	dark green	15	15
312	A97	20pf	brown red	15	15
313	A96	25pf	bluish black	28	15
			Set value		15

110th anniversary of the Carl Zeiss Optical Works in Jena.

Chinese Girl with Flowers — A98

Designs: 10pf, Negro woman and child. 25pf, European man and dove.

1956, Dec. 10 Litho. *Perf. 13*

314	A98	5pf	ol, *pale lem*	95	30
315	A98	10pf	brown, *pink*	15	15
316	A98	25pf	vio bl, *pale vio bl*	15	15
			Set value	1.10	38

Issued for Human Rights Day.

Elephants A99

1956, Dec. 17 Photo. *Perf. 13x12½*

Design in Gray

317	A99	5pf	shown	15	15
318	A99	10pf	Flamingoes	15	15
319	A99	15pf	White rhinoceros	4.00	75
320	A99	20pf	Mouflon	15	15
321	A99	25pf	Bison	20	15
322	A99	30pf	Polar bear	20	15
			Nos. 317-322 (6)	4.85	
			Set value		90

Issued to publicize the Berlin Zoo.

Freighter A100

Design: 25pf, Electric Locomotive.

1957, Mar. 1 Litho. Wmk. 313

323	A100	20pf	rose red	22	15
324	A100	25pf	bright blue	22	15
			Set value		15

Leipzig Spring Fair.

Silver Thistle A101

Designs: 10pf, Emerald lizard. 20pf, Lady's-slipper.

1957, Apr. 12 Photo. Wmk. 313

325	A101	5pf	chocolate	15	15
326	A101	10pf	dk slate grn	*1.75*	*60*
327	A101	20pf	red brown	15	15
			Set value	*1.90*	*65*

Nature Conservation Week, Apr. 14-20.

Children at Play — A102

Design: 20pf, Friedrich Froebel and Children.

1957, Apr. 18 Litho. *Perf. 13*

328	A102	10pf	dk slate grn & ol	*70*	*32*
329	A102	20pf	black & brown red	30	18

175th anniv. of the birth of Friedrich Froebel, educator.

Redrawn Types of 1953

Designs: 5pf, Woman mariner. 10pf, Worker, peasant and intellectual. 15pf, Steel worker. 20pf, Stalin Boulevard. 25pf, Locomotive building. 30pf, Dancing couple. 40pf, Zwinger Castle, Dresden. 50pf, Launching ship. 70pf, Dove and East German family.

Imprint: "E. Gruner K. Wolf"
No imprint on 10pf, 15pf

Perf. 13x12½, 14 (10pf, 15pf)

1957-58 Typo. Wmk. 313

330	A43	5pf	emerald	15	15
a.			Bklt. pane, 3 #330 + 3 #331		
b.			Bklt. pane, 3 #330 + 3 #333		
c.			Booklet pane of 6	85	
331	A43	10pf	blue ('58)	20	15
a.			Bklt. pane, 4 #331 + 2 #333		
b.			Perf. 13x12½	70	15
332	A43	15pf	violet ('58)	20	15
a.			Perf. 13x12½	25	15
333	A43	20pf	carmine	15	15
a.			Bklt. pane, 5 #333 + 1 #477		
334	A43	25pf	bluish green	25	15
335	A43	30pf	dull red	65	15
336	A43	40pf	rose violet	95	15
337	A43	50pf	bright blue	1.25	15
338	A43	70pf	chocolate	1.40	15

See Nos. 476-482.

Pieck Type of 1953

Photo. *Perf. 13x13½*

339	A35	1m	dk olive grn ('58)	2.25	15
340	A35	2m	red brown ('58)	3.25	15
			Nos. 330-340 (11)	10.70	
			Set value		50

Bicycle Race Route — A103

Perf. 13x13½

1957, Apr. 30 Litho. Wmk. 313

346	A103	5pf	orange	30	15

Issued to publicize the 10th International Bicycle Peace Race, Prague-Berlin-Warsaw.

Steam Shovel A104

Miner — A105

Design: 20pf, Coal conveyor.

Perf. 13x12½, 13½x13 (25pf)

1957, May 3

347	A104	10pf	green	22	15
348	A104	20pf	redsh brown	22	15
349	A105	25pf	blue violet	*1.25*	*28*
			Set value		*40*

Issued in honor of the coal mining industry.

Henri Dunant and Globe A106

Design: 25pf, Henri Dunant facing right and globe.

1957, May 7 Photo. *Perf. 13x12½*

350	A106	10pf	green, red & blk	16	15
351	A106	25pf	brt blue, red & blk	20	15
			Set value		15

Tenth Red Cross world conference.

Portrait Type of 1950, Redrawn

Portraits: 5pf, Joachim Jungius. 10pf, Leonhard Euler. 20pf, Heinrich Hertz.

1957, June 7 Litho.

352	A11	5pf	brown	*75*	*30*
353	A11	10pf	green	15	15
354	A11	20pf	henna brown	15	15
			Set value		*40*

Issued to honor famous German scientists.

Painting Type of 1955.

Famous Paintings: 5pf, Holy Family, Mantegna. 10pf, The Dancer Campani, Carriera. 15pf, Portrait of Morette, Holbein. 20pf, The Tribute Money, Titian. 25pf, Saskia with Red Flower, Rembrandt. 40pf, Young Standard Bearer, Piazetta.

Perf. 13½x13

1957, June 26 Photo. Wmk. 313

355	A77	5pf	dk brown	15	15
356	A77	10pf	lt yellow grn	15	15
357	A77	15pf	brown olive	15	15
358	A77	20pf	rose brown	15	15
359	A77	25pf	deep claret	15	15
360	A77	40pf	dk blue gray	*2.50*	*85*
			Nos. 355-360 (6)	*3.25*	
			Set value		*1.00*

Clara Zetkin — A107

Bertolt Brecht — A108

1957, July 5 *Perf. 13x13½*

361	A107	10pf	dk green & red	40	15

Centenary of the birth of Clara Zetkin, politician and founder of the socialist women's movement.

1957, Aug. 14 *Perf. 13½x13*

362	A108	10pf	dark green	30	15
363	A108	25pf	deep blue	30	15
			Set value		15

Brecht (1898-1956), playwright and poet.

Congress Emblem A109

Fair Emblem A110

1957, Aug. 23 Litho.

364	A109	20pf	brt red & black	35	15

4th International Trade Union Congress, Leipzig, Oct. 4-15.

1957, Aug. 30 Wmk. 313

365	A110	20pf	crimson & ver	18	15
366	A110	25pf	brt blue & lt blue	18	15
			Set value		15

Issued to publicize the 1957 Leipzig Fair.

Savings Book — A111

Postrider, 1563 — A112

1957, Oct. 10 *Perf. 13½x13*

367	A111	10pf	grn & blk, *gray*	*65*	*15*
368	A111	20pf	rose car & blk, *gray*	42	15
			Set value		*25*

Issued to publicize "Savings Weeks."

1957, Oct. 25 Wmk. 313

369	A112	5pf	black, *pale sep*	45	15

Issued for the Day of the Stamp.

Sputnik I — A113

Storming of the Winter Palace — A114

Designs: 20pf, Stratospheric balloon above clouds. 25pf, Ship with plumb line exploring deep sea.

1957-58 *Perf. 12½x13*

370	A113	10pf	blue black	25	15
371	A113	20pf	car rose ('58)	35	15
372	A113	25pf	brt blue ('58)	*1.35*	*35*
			Set value		*45*

IGY. The 10pf also for the launching of the 1st artificial satellite.

1957, Nov. 7 Photo.

373	A114	10pf	yellow grn & red	15	15
374	A114	25pf	brt blue & red	15	15
			Set value		15

40th anniv. of the Russian Revolution.

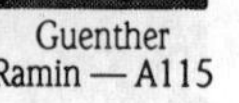

Guenther Ramin — A115

Dove and Globe — A116

Portrait: 20pf, Hermann Abendroth.

Perf. 13½x13

1957, Nov. 22 Litho. Wmk. 313

375 A115 10pf yellow grn & blk 90 26

376 A115 20pf red orange & blk 48 15

Ramin (1898-1956) and Abendroth (1883-1956), musicians, on the 1st anniv. of their death.

1958, Feb. 27 *Perf. 13x13½*

377 A116 20pf rose red 18 15

378 A116 25pf blue 18 15

Set value 15

Issued to publicize the 1958 Leipzig Fair.

Radio Tower, Morse Code and Post Horn A117

Design: 20pf, Radio tower and small post horn.

1958, Mar. 6 *Perf. 13x12½*

379 A117 5pf gray & blk 65 20

380 A117 20pf crim rose & dk red 15 15

Set value 25

Conf. of Postal Ministers of Communist countries, Moscow, Dec. 3-17, 1957.

Sketch by Zille — A118

Symbolizing Quantum Theory — A119

Design: 20pf, Self-portrait of Zille.

1958, Mar. 20 *Perf. 13½x13*

381 A118 10pf green & gray 1.90 20

382 A118 20pf dp car & gray 50 15

Set value 25

Centenary of the birth of Heinrich Zille, artist.

1958, Apr. 23 Litho.

Design: 20pf, Max Planck.

383 A119 10pf gray green 1.25 25

384 A119 20pf magenta 48 15

Set value 30

Centenary of the birth of Max Planck, physicist.

Prize Cow — A120

Charles Darwin — A121

Designs: 10pf, Mowing machine. 20pf, Beet harvester.

Perf. 13x13½

1958, June 4 Wmk. 313

Size: 28x23mm

385 A120 5pf gray & blk 1.65 25

Size: 39x22mm

Perf. 13x12½

386 A120 10pf brt green 15 15

387 A120 20pf rose red 18 15

Set value 30

6th Agricultural Show, Markkleeberg.

1958, June 19 *Perf. 13x13½*

Portrait: 20pf, Carl von Linné.

388 A121 10pf green & black 95 32

389 A121 20pf dk red & black 38 15

Set value 40

Cent. of Darwin's theory of evolution and the bicent. of Linné's botanical system.

Seven Towers of Rostock and Ships — A122

Congress Emblem — A123

Designs: 10pf, Ship at pier. 25pf, Ships in harbor.

1958 *Perf. 13½x13*

390 A122 10pf emerald 15 15

391 A122 20pf red orange 15 15

392 A122 25pf lt blue 1.25 16

Set value 1.40 20

Establishment of Rostock as a seaport.
Issue dates: 20pf, July 5; 10pf and 25pf, Nov. 24.
For overprint see No. 500.

1958, June 25 *Perf. 13x13½*

393 A123 10pf rose red 20 15

5th congress of the Socialist Party of the German Democratic Republic (SED).

Mare and Foal — A124

Designs: 10pf, Trotter. 20pf, Horse race.

1958, July 22 Photo. *Perf. 13x12½*

394 A124 5pf black brown 1.90 22

395 A124 10pf dark olive green 15 15

396 A124 20pf dark red brown 15 15

Set value 26

Issued to publicize the Grand Prize of the DDR, 1958.

Jan Amos Komensky (Comenius) — A125

Design: 20pf, Teacher and pupils, 17th cent.

1958, Aug. 7 Litho. *Perf. 13x13½*

397 A125 10pf brt bl grn & blk 1.40 32

398 A125 20pf org brn & blk 16 15

Set value 40

University Seal A126

Design: 20pf, Schiller University, Jena.

1958, Aug. 19 *Perf. 13x12½*

399 A126 5pf gray & black 1.40 55

400 A126 20pf dark red & gray 16 15

400th anniversary of Friedrich Schiller University in Jena.

Soldier on Obstacle Course — A127

Arms Breaking A-Bomb — A128

Design: 20pf, Spartacist emblem. 25pf, Marching athletes, map and flag.

Perf. 13½x13

1958, Sept. 19 Litho. Wmk. 313

401 A127 10pf emerald & brn 1.25 28

402 A127 20pf brown red & yel 15 15

403 A127 25pf lt blue & red 15 15

Set value 35

Issued to publicize the first Spartacist Sports Meet of Friendly Armies, Leipzig, Sept. 20-28.

1958, Sept. 19 *Perf. 13x13½*

404 A128 20pf rose red 20 15

405 A128 25pf blue 20 15

Set value 15

Issued to publicize the people's fight against atomic death.

Woman and Leipzig Railroad Station A129

Design: 25pf, Woman in Persian lamb coat and old City Hall, Leipzig.

1958, Aug. 29 *Perf. 13x12½*

406 A129 10pf green, brn & blk 15 15

407 A129 25pf blue & black 15 15

Set value 15

Issued to publicize the 1958 Leipzig Fair.

Brandenburg Gate, Berlin — A131

Head from Greek Tomb — A132

Post Wagon, 17th Century A130

Design: 20pf, Mail train and plane.

1958, Oct. 23 Wmk. 313

408 A130 10pf green 1.90 45

409 A130 20pf lake 15 15

Set value 50

Issued for the Day of the Stamp.

1958, Nov. 29 *Perf. 13x13½*

410 A131 20pf rose red 15 15

411 A131 25pf dark blue 2.50 55

Set value 60

Issued to commemorate 10 years of democratic city administration of Berlin.

1958, Dec. 2 *Perf. 13½x13*

Design: 20pf, Giant's head from Pergamum frieze.

412 A132 10pf blue grn & blk 1.25 40

413 A132 20pf dp rose & black 15 15

Set value 45

Return of art treasures from Russia. See #484-486.

Negro and Caucasian Men A133

Design: 25pf, Chinese and Caucasian girls.

1958, Dec. 10 *Perf. 13x12½*

414 A133 10pf brt blue grn & blk 15 15

415 A133 25pf blue & black 1.25 35

Set value 40

10th anniv. of the signing of the Universal Declaration of Human Rights.

Worker and Soldier — A134

Otto Nuschke — A135

1958, Nov. 7 *Perf. 12½x13*

416 A134 20pf blk, ver & dl pur 9.00 3.25

40th anniv. of the Revolution of Nov. 7. (Stamp inscribed Nov. 9.) Withdrawn from sale on day of issue.

Perf. 13½x13

1958, Dec. 27 Wmk. 313

417 A135 20pf red 25 15

First anniversary of the death of Otto Nuschke, vice president of the republic.

Communist Newspaper, "The Red Flag" A136

1958, Dec. 30 *Perf. 13x12½*

418 A136 20pf red 25 15

German Communist Party, 40th anniv.

Rosa Luxemburg Addressing Crowd — A137

Design: 20pf, Karl Liebknecht addressing crowd.

Perf. 13x13½

1959, Jan. 15 Wmk. 313

419 A137 10pf blue green 1.75 52

420 A137 20pf henna brn & blk 32 15

Set value 60

40th anniversary of the death of Rosa Luxemburg and Karl Liebknecht.

Gewandhaus, Leipzig — A138

President Wilhelm Pieck — A139

Design: 25pf, Opening theme of Mendelssohn's A Major symphony.

1959, Feb. 28 Engr. *Perf. 14*

421 A138 10pf green, *grnsh* 15 15
422 A138 25pf blue, *bluish* *1.10* *26*
Set value *30*

150th anniversary of the birth of Felix Mendelssohn-Bartholdy, composer.

1959, Jan. 3 Photo. *Perf. 13½x13*

423 A139 20pf henna brown 30 15

83rd birthday of President Wilhelm Pieck. See No. 511.

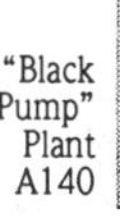

"Black Pump" Plant A140

Design: 25pf, Photographic equipment.

1959, Feb. 28 Litho. *Perf. 13x12½*

424 A140 20pf carmine rose 25 15
425 A140 25pf lt ultra 25 15
Set value 15

1959 Leipzig Spring Fair.

Boy and Girl — A141

Statue of Handel, Halle — A142

1959, Apr. 2 *Perf. 13½x13*

426 A141 10pf blk, *lt grn* *1.25* *32*
427 A141 20pf blk, *salmon* 15 15
Set value *35*

5 years of the Youth Consecration ceremony.

1959, Apr. 27 Wmk. 313

Design: 20pf, Handel by Thomas Hudson, 1749.

428 A142 10pf bluish grn & blk *1.25* *32*
429 A142 20pf rose & blk 15 15
Set value *35*

Bicentenary of the death of George Frederick Handel, composer.

Alexander von Humboldt and Central American View — A143

Post Horn — A144

Design: 20pf, Portrait and Siberian view.

1959, May 6

430 A143 10pf bluish grn *1.25* *32*
431 A143 20pf rose 15 15
Set value *35*

Centenary of the death of Alexander von Humboldt, naturalist and geographer.

1959, May 30 *Perf. 13½x13*

432 A144 20pf scar, yel & blk 15 15
433 A144 25pf lt bl, yel & blk *90* *30*
Set value *35*

Conference of socialist postal ministers.

Gray Heron A145

Designs: 10pf, Bittern. 20pf, Lily of the valley and butterfly. 25pf, Beaver. 40pf, Pussy willows and bee.

1959, June 26 *Perf. 13x12½*

434 A145 5pf lt bl, blk & lil 15 15
435 A145 10pf grnsh bl, dk brn & org 15 15
436 A145 20pf org red, grn & vio 15 15
437 A145 25pf lilac, yel & blk 15 15
438 A145 40pf gray bl, yel & blk *4.25* *75*
Nos. 434-438 (5) *4.85*
Set value *85*

Issued to publicize wildlife protection.

Painting Type of 1955.

Famous Paintings: 5pf, Portrait, Angelica Kauffmann. 10pf, The Lady Lace Maker, Gabriel Metsu. 20pf, Mademoiselle Lavergne, Liotard. 25pf, Old Woman with Brazier, Rubens. 40pf, Young Man in Black Coat, Hals.

1959, June 29 Photo. *Perf. 13½x13*

439 A77 5pf olive 15 15
440 A77 10pf green 15 15
441 A77 20pf dp org 15 15
442 A77 25pf chestnut 15 15
443 A77 40pf dp magenta *4.00* *60*
Nos. 439-443 (5) *4.60*
Set value *72*

Great Cormorant — A146

Youths of Three Races — A147

Birds: 10pf, Black Stork. 15pf, Eagle owl. 20pf, Black grouse. 25pf, Hoopoe. 40pf, Peregrine falcon.

Perf. 13x13½

1959, July 2 Litho. Wmk. 313

Designs in Black

444 A146 5pf yellow 15 15
445 A146 10pf lt green 15 15
446 A146 15pf pale violet *3.50* *60*
447 A146 20pf deep pink 15 15
448 A146 25pf blue 15 15
449 A146 40pf vermilion 15 15
Set value *70*

Protection of native birds.

Perf. 12½x13, 13x12½

1959, July 25

Design: 25pf, Swedish girl kissing African girl, horiz.

450 A147 20pf crimson 20 15
451 A147 25pf bright blue *30* *15*
Set value *15*

7th World Youth Festival, Vienna, July 26-Aug. 14.

Glass Tea Service A148

Design: 25pf, Distilling apparatus, vert.

Perf. 13x12½, 12½x13

1959, Sept. 1

452 A148 10pf bluish brown 20 15
453 A148 25pf bright blue *1.00* *22*
Set value *25*

75 years of Jena glassware.

Lunik 2 Hitting Moon — A149

1959, Sept. 21 *Perf. 13½x13*

454 A149 20pf rose red 50 15

Landing of the Soviet rocket Lunik 2 on the moon, Sept. 13, 1959.

New Buildings, Leipzig, Globe and Fair Emblem A150

1959, Aug. 17 *Perf. 13x12½*

455 A150 20pf gray & rose 25 15

1959 Leipzig Fall Fair.

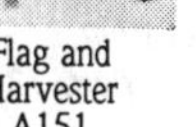

Flag and Harvester A151

Johannes R. Becher A152

Designs (Flag and): 10pf, Fritz Heckert rest home. 15pf, Zwinger, Dresden. 20pf, Steelworker. 25pf, Chemist. 40pf, Central Stadium, Leipzig. 50pf, Woman tractor driver. 60pf, Airplane. 70pf, Merchant ship. 1m, First atomic reactor of the DDR.

1959, Oct. 6 *Perf. 13½x13*

Flag in Black, Red & Orange Yellow Inscription and Design in Black & Red

456 A151 5pf yellow 15 15
457 A151 10pf gray 15 15
458 A151 15pf citron 15 15
459 A151 20pf gray 15 15
460 A151 25pf lt gray olive 15 15
461 A151 40pf citron 15 15
462 A151 50pf salmon 15 15
463 A151 60pf pale bluish grn 15 15
464 A151 70pf pale grnsh yel 20 15
465 A151 1m bis brn 28 15
Nos. 456-465 (10) 1.68
Set value 40

10th anniversary of the German Democratic Republic.

1959, Oct. 28 Litho. *Perf. 13x13½*

466 A152 20pf red & slate 1.00 15

1st anniversary of the death of Johannes R. Becher, writer.

Printed with alternating yellow labels. The label carries in blue a verse from the national anthem and Becher's signature.

Schiller's Home, Weimar A153

Post Rider and Mile Stone, 18th Century A154

Design: 20pf, Friedrich von Schiller.

1959, Nov. 10 Engr. *Perf. 14*

467 A153 10pf dull green, *grnsh* *1.70* *40*
468 A153 20pf lake, *pink* 20 15
Set value *45*

200th anniversary of the birth of Friedrich von Schiller.

1959, Nov. 17 Litho. *Perf. 13½x13*

Design: 20pf, Motorized mailman.

469 A154 10pf green *1.50* *25*
470 A154 20pf dk car rose 15 15
Set value *28*

Issued for the Day of the Stamp.

Red Squirrels A155

1959, Nov. 27 *Perf. 13x12½*

471 A155 5pf shown 15 15
472 A155 10pf Hares 15 15
473 A155 20pf Roe deer 15 15
474 A155 25pf Red deer 15 15
475 A155 40pf Lynx *4.50* *85*
Nos. 471-475 (5) *5.10*
Set value *95*

Redrawn Types of 1953
Without Imprint

1959-60 Wmk. 313 Typo. *Perf. 14*

476 A43 5pf emerald 18 15
477 A43 10pf lt bl grn *(Machinists)* 60 15
a. Perf. 13x12½ 18 15
b. Bklt. pane of 6 #477a 3.00
478 A43 20pf carmine 25 15
a. Se-tenant with DEBRIA label 75 15
479 A43 30pf dull red 15 15
480 A43 40pf rose violet 15 15
481 A43 50pf brt blue 15 15
482 A43 70pf choc ('60) 15 15
Nos. 476-482 (7) 1.63
Set value 35

No. 478a was issued Sept. 3, 1959, to commemorate the 2nd German Stamp Exhibition, Berlin. Sheet contains 60 stamps, 40 labels.

Two other stamps without imprint are Nos. 331-332.

Type of 1958 and

Pergamum Altar of Zeus — A156

Designs: 5pf, Head of an Attic goddess, 580 B.C. 10pf, Head of a princess from Tell el Amarna, 1360 B.C. 20pf, Bronze figure from Toprak-Kale (Armenia), 7th century B.C.

1959, Dec. 29 Litho. *Perf. 13½x13*

484 A132 5pf yellow & black 15 15
485 A132 10pf bluish grn & blk 15 15
486 A132 20pf rose & black 15 15
487 A156 25pf lt blue & blk *1.50* *25*
Set value *34*

Boxing — A157

Designs: 10pf, Sprinters. 20pf, Ski jump. 25pf, Sailboat.

Perf. 13x13½

1960, Jan. 27 Wmk. 313

488 A157 5pf brown & ocher 4.50 *1.10*
489 A157 10pf green & ocher 15 15
490 A157 20pf car & ocher 15 15
491 A157 25pf ultra & ocher 15 15
Set value *1.25*

Issued to publicize the 1960 Winter and Summer Olympic Games.

Technical Fair, North Entrance A158

Design: 25pf, "Ring" Fair building.

1960, Feb. 17 *Perf. 13x12½*

492 A158 20pf red & gray 15 15
493 A158 25pf lt blue & gray 22 15
Set value 15

1960 Leipzig Spring Fair.

Purple Foxglove A159

Lenin A160

Medicinal Plants: 10pf, Camomile. 15pf, Peppermint. 20pf, Poppy. 40pf, Dog rose.

1960, Apr. 7 *Perf. 12½x13*

494 A159 5pf grn, gray & car rose 15 15
495 A159 10pf citron, gray & grn 15 15
496 A159 15pf fawn, gray & grn 15 15
497 A159 20pf grnsh bl, gray & vio 15 15
498 A159 40pf brn, gray, grn & red 4.25 *60*
Nos. 494-498 (5) *4.85*
Set value *68*

1960, Apr. 22 Engr. *Perf. 14*

499 A160 20pf lake 30 15

90th anniversary of the birth of Lenin.

No. 390 Overprinted: "Inbetriebnahme des Hochseehafens 1.Mai 1960"

1960, Apr. 28 Litho. *Perf. 13½x13*

500 A122 10pf emerald 30 15

Inauguration of the seaport Rostock.

Russian Soldier and Liberated Prisoner — A161

1960, May 5 Litho. *Perf. 13x13½*

501 A161 20pf rose red 35 15

15th anniv. of Germany's liberation from fascism.

Model of Vacation Ship — A162

Designs: 25pf, Ship before Leningrad.

Perf. 13½x13

1960, June 23 Wmk. 313

502 A162 5pf slate, cit & blk 15 15
503 A162 25pf blk, yel & ultra *3.25* *1.25*

Launching of the trade union (FDGB) vacation ship, June 25, 1960. See Nos. B58-B59.

Masked Dancer in Porcelain — A163

Lenin Monument, Eisleben — A164

Meissen porcelain: 10pf, Plate with Meissen mark and date. 15pf, Otter. 20pf, Potter. 25pf, Coffee pot.

1960, July 28 *Perf. 12½x13*

504 A163 5pf blue & orange 15 15
505 A163 10pf blue & emerald 15 15
506 A163 15pf blue & purple *3.50* *1.10*
507 A163 20pf blue & orange red 15 15
508 A163 25pf blue & apple grn 15 15
Set value *1.25*

Meissen porcelain works, 250th anniv.

Perf. 13x13½

1960, July 2 Wmk. 313

Design: 20pf, Thälmann monument, gift for Pushkin, USSR.

509 A164 10pf dark green 15 15
510 A164 20pf bright red 25 15
Set value 15

Pieck Type of 1959

1960, Sept. 10 Litho. *Perf. 13½x13*

511 A139 20pf black 40 15
a. Souv. sheet of 1, imperf. 1.50 30

Pres. Wilhelm Pieck (1876-1960).

Modern Postal Trucks A165

Design: 25pf, Railroad mail car, 19th cent.

1960, Oct. 6 *Perf. 13x12½*

512 A165 20pf car rose, blk & yel 15 15
513 A165 25pf blue, gray & blk *1.50* *32*

Issued for the Day of the Stamp, 1960.

New Opera House, Leipzig A166

Design: 25pf, Car, sailboat, tent, campers.

1960, Aug. 29 Wmk. 313

514 A166 20pf rose brn & gray 22 15
515 A166 25pf blue & grysh brn 22 15
Set value 15

1960 Leipzig Fall Fair.

Hans Burkmair Medal, 1518 — A167

Neidhardt von Gneisenau — A168

Design: 25pf, Dancing Peasants by Albrecht Dürer.

1960, Oct. 20 Litho. *Perf. 12½x13*

516 A167 20pf buff, grn & ocher 24 15
517 A167 25pf lt blue & blk *1.50* *35*

400th anniv. of the Dresden Art Gallery.

Perf. 13x12½, 12½x13

1960, Oct. 27

Design: 20pf, Neidhardt von Gneisenau, horiz.

518 A168 20pf dk carmine & blk 15 15
519 A168 25pf ultra *1.40* *40*
Set value *45*

200th anniversary of the birth of Count August Neidhardt von Gneisenau, Prussian Field Marshal.

Rudolf Virchow A169

Humboldt University, Berlin A170

Designs: 10pf, Robert Koch. 25pf, Wilhelm and Alexander von Humboldt medal. 40pf, Wilhelm Griesinger.

1960, Nov. 4 Litho. *Perf. 13x12½*

520 A169 5pf ocher & blk 15 15
521 A169 10pf green & blk 15 15
522 A170 20pf cop red, gray & blk 15 15
523 A170 25pf brt blue & blk 15 15
524 A169 40pf car rose & blk *2.50* *35*
Set value *48*

Nos. 520, 521, 524 for the 250th anniv. of the Charité (hospital), Berlin; Nos. 522-523 the 150th anniv. of Humboldt University, Berlin.

Nos. 520 and 523, and Nos. 521 and 522 are printed se-tenant.

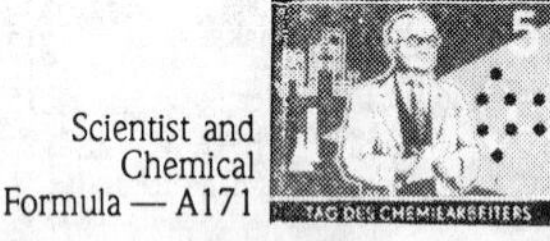

Scientist and Chemical Formula — A171

Designs: 10pf, Chemistry worker (fertilizer). 20pf, Woman worker (automobile). 25pf, Laboratory assistant (synthetic fabrics).

Perf. 13x13½

1960, Nov. 10 Wmk. 313

525 A171 5pf dk red & gray 15 15
526 A171 10pf orange & brt grn 15 15
527 A171 20pf blue & red 15 15
528 A171 25pf yellow & ultra *2.25* *52*
Set value *60*

Day of the Chemistry Worker.

"Young Socialists' Express" — A172

Designs: 20pf, Sassnitz Harbor station and ferry. 25pf, Diesel locomotive and 1835 "Adler."

Perf. 13x13½; 13x12½ (20pf)

1960, Dec. 5

Sizes: 10pf, 25pf, 28x23mm; 20pf, 38½x22mm

529 A172 10pf emerald & blk 15 15
530 A172 20pf red & blk 15 15
531 A172 25pf blue & blk *4.25* *1.50*

125th anniv. of German railroads. No. 530 exists imperf. Value $1.

Pieck Type of 1953 with Dates Added

1961, Jan. 3 Photo. *Perf. 13x13½*

532 A35 20pf henna brn & blk 35 15

Issued on the 85th anniversary of the birth of Pres. Wilhelm Pieck (1876-1960).

380 Kilovolt Switch A173

Lilienstein A174

Design: 25pf, Leipzig Press Center.

1961, Mar. 3 Litho. *Perf. 13½x13*

533 A173 10pf brt grn & dk gray 30 15
534 A173 25pf vio blue & dk gray 40 15
Set value 15

Leipzig Spring Fair of 1961.

1961 Typo. *Perf. 14*

Designs: 5pf, Rudelsburg on Saale. 10pf, Wartburg. No. 538, City Hall, Wernigerode. 25pf, Brocken, Harz Mts., horiz.

535 A174 5pf gray 15 15
536 A174 10pf blue green 15 15
537 A174 20pf red brown 15 15
538 A174 20pf dull red 15 15
539 A174 25pf dark blue 15 15
Set value 50 15

Issue dates: No. 538, 25pf, Mar. 14. 5pf, 10pf, No. 537, June 22.

Trawler — A176

Designs: 20pf, Fishermen. 25pf, S.S. Robert Koch. 40pf, Cannery worker.

1961, Apr. 4 Engr. Wmk. 313

545 A176 10pf gray green 15 15
546 A176 20pf claret 15 15
547 A176 25pf slate 15 15
548 A176 40pf dull violet *2.50* *65*
Set value *75*

Deep-sea fishing industry.

Vostok 1 Leaving Earth A177

Designs: 20pf, Astronaut in capsule. 25pf, Parachute landing of capsule.

1961, Apr. Litho. *Perf. 13x12½*

549 A177 10pf lt blue grn & red 22 15
550 A177 20pf red 30 15
551 A177 25pf lt blue *3.25* *1.50*

1st man in space, Yuri A. Gagarin, Apr. 12, 1961.
Issue dates: 10pf, Apr. 18; others, Apr. 20.

Zebra
A178

Dresden Zoo cent.: 20pf, Black-and-white colobus monkeys.

1961, May 9
552 A178 10pf green & blk 2.50 90
553 A178 20pf lilac rose & blk 52 15

Engels, Marx, Lenin and Crowd — A179

1961, Apr. 20 Litho. *Perf. 13½x13*
554 A179 20pf red 45 15

15th anniversary of Socialist Unity Party of Germany (SED).

Stag Leap — A180

Designs: 20pf, Arabesque. 25pf, Exercise on parallel bars, horiz.

1961, June 3 *Perf. 13½x13, 13x13½*
555 A180 10pf blue green 15 15
556 A180 20pf rose pink 15 15
557 A180 25pf brt blue 4.25 1.25

3rd Europa Cup for Women's Gymnastics.

Salt Miners and Castle Giebichenstein — A181

Design: 20pf, Chemist and "Five Towers" of Halle.

1961, June 22 *Perf. 13x12½*
558 A181 10pf blk, grn & yel 1.40 35
559 A181 20pf blk, dk red & yel 15 15

1000th anniv. of the founding of Halle.

Kayak
Slalom
A182

Designs: 10pf, Canoe. 20pf, Two seater canoe.

1961, July 6 Litho. Wmk. 313
560 A182 5pf gray & Prus bl 2.50 90
561 A182 10pf gray & slate grn 15 15
562 A182 20pf gray & dk car rose 15 15

Canoe Slalom and Rapids World Championships.

Target Line Casting A183

Design: 20pf, River fishing.

1961, July 21
563 A183 10pf green & blue 1.75 75
564 A183 20pf dk red brn & blue 15 15

World Fishing Championships, Dresden.

Tulip — A184

"Alte Waage," Historical Building, Leipzig — A185

1961, Sept. 13 Photo. *Perf. 14*
565 A184 10pf shown 15 15
566 A184 20pf Dahlia 25 15
567 A184 40pf Rose 7.50 3.00

Intl. Horticulture Exhibition, Erfurt.

Perf. 13½x13
1961, Aug. 23 Litho. Wmk. 313

Design: 25pf, Old Exchange Building.

568 A185 10pf citron & bl grn 15 15
569 A185 25pf lt blue & ultra 60 15
Set value 15

Issued to publicize the 1961 Leipzig Fall Fair. See Nos. 595-597.

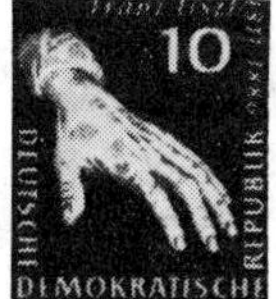

Liszt's Hand, French Sculpture A186

Television Camera and Screen A187

Designs: 5pf, Liszt and Hector Berlioz. 20pf, Franz Liszt, medallion by Ernst Rietschel, 1852. 25pf, Liszt and Frederic Chopin.

1961, Oct.-Nov. Engr. *Perf. 14*
570 A186 5pf gray 15 15
571 A186 10pf blue green 1.65 48
572 A186 20pf dull red 15 15
573 A186 25pf chalky blue 2.75 80

150th anniversary of the birth of Franz Liszt, composer.

1961, Oct. 25 *Perf. 13x13½*

Design: 20pf, Microphone and radio dial.

574 A187 10pf brt green & blk 1.65 35
575 A187 20pf brick red & blk 15 15
Set value 40

Issued for Stamp Day, 1961.

Maj. Gherman Titov and Young Pioneers A188

Designs: 10pf, Titov in Leipzig, vert. 15pf, Titov in spaceship. 20pf, Titov and Walter Ulbricht. 25pf, Spaceship Vostok 2. 40pf, Titov and Ulbricht in Berlin.

1961, Dec. 11 Litho. *Perf. 13½*
576 A188 5pf carmine & vio 15 15
577 A188 10pf olive grn & car 15 15
578 A188 15pf blue & lilac 7.00 2.50
579 A188 20pf blue & car rose 25 15
580 A188 25pf carmine & blue 16 15
581 A188 40pf carmine & dk blue 85 15
Nos. 576-581 (6) 8.56
Set value 2.70

Visit of Russian Maj. Gherman Titov to the German Democratic Republic.

Chairman Walter Ulbricht A189

Red Ants A190

1961-67 Wmk. 313 Typo. *Perf. 14*
Size: 17x21mm
582 A189 5pf slate 15 15
a. Booklet pane of 8
583 A189 10pf brt green 15 15
a. Booklet pane of 8
584 A189 15pf red lilac 15 15
585 A189 20pf dark red 15 15
586 A189 25pf dull bl ('63) 15 15
587 A189 30pf car rose ('63) 15 15
588 A189 40pf brt vio ('63) 20 15
589 A189 50pf ultra ('63) 28 15
589A A189 60pf dp yel grn ('64) 32 15
590 A189 70pf red brn ('63) 48 15
590A A189 80pf brt blue ('67) 60 15

Engr.
Size: 24x28½mm
590B A189 1dm dull grn ('63) 50 15
590C A189 2dm brown ('63) 1.00 15
Nos. 582-590C (13) 4.28
Set value 45

See Nos. 751-752, 1112A-1114A, 1483. Currency abbreviation is "DM" on Nos. 590B-590C, "MDN" on Nos. 751-752, and "M" on Nos. 1113-1114A.

1962, Feb. 16 Photo.
591 A190 5pf shown 3.25 95
592 A190 10pf Weasels 20 15
593 A190 20pf Shrews 20 15
594 A190 40pf Bat 52 16

See Nos. 663-667.

Type of 1961

Buildings: 10pf, "Coffee Tree House." 20pf, Gohlis Castle. 25pf, Romanus House.

1962, Feb. 22 Litho. *Perf. 13x13½*
595 A185 10pf olive grn & brn 30 15
596 A185 20pf orange red & blk 45 15
597 A185 25pf brt blue & brn 75 15
Set value 20

Leipzig Spring Fair of 1962.

Air Defense A191

Designs: 10pf, Motorized infantry. 20pf, Soldier and worker as protectors. 25pf, Sailor and destroyer escort. 40pf, Tank and tankman.

1962, Mar. 1 *Perf. 13x12½*
598 A191 5pf light blue 15 15
599 A191 10pf bright green 15 15
600 A191 20pf red 15 15
601 A191 25pf ultra 18 15
602 A191 40pf brown 1.90 55
Nos. 598-602 (5) 2.53
Set value 65

National People's Army, 6th anniv.

Cyclists and Hradcany, Prague A192

Design: 25pf, Cyclist, East Berlin City Hall and dove.

1962, Apr. 26 Litho. Wmk. 313
603 A192 10pf multicolored 15 15
604 A192 25pf multicolored 1.65 45
Set value 50

15th International Bicycle Peace Race, Berlin-Warsaw-Prague. See No. B89.

Johann Gottlieb Fichte — A193

Design: 10pf, Fichte's birthplace in Rammenau.

1962, May 17 *Perf. 13x13½*
605 A193 10pf brt green & blk 1.25 26
606 A193 20pf vermilion & blk 30 15
Set value 32

Bicentenary of the birth of Johann Gottlieb Fichte, philosopher.

Cross, Crown of Thorns and Rose — A194

George Dimitrov at Reichstag Trial, Leipzig — A195

1962, June 7 *Perf. 12½x13*
607 A194 20pf red & black 20 15
608 A194 25pf brt blue & blk 1.10 30
Set value 36

20th anniversary of the destruction of Lidice in Czechoslovakia by the Nazis.

1962, June 18 Photo. *Perf. 14*

Design: 20pf, Dimitrov as Premier of Bulgaria.

609 A195 5pf blue grn & blk 55 20
610 A195 20pf car rose & blk 15 15
Set value 60 24

George Dimitrov, (1882-1949), communist leader and premier of the Bulgarian Peoples' Republic.

Nos. 609-610 also printed se-tenant, divided by a label inscribed with a Dimitrov quotation.

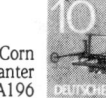

Corn Planter A196

Designs: 20pf, Milking machine. 40pf, Combine harvester.

1962, June 26 Litho. *Perf. 13x12½*
611 A196 10pf multicolored 15 15
612 A196 20pf multicolored 15 15
613 A196 40pf yel, grn & dk red 2.00 70
Set value 80

10th Agricultural Exhibition, Markkleeberg.

Map of Baltic Sea and Emblem — A197

Brandenburg Gate, Berlin — A198

Designs: 20pf, Hotel, Rostock, vert. 25pf, Cargo ship "Frieden" in Rostock harbor.

Perf. 13x13½, 13½x13 (20pf)
1962, July 2 Wmk. 313
614 A197 10pf bluish grn & ultra 15 15
615 A197 20pf dk red & yellow 15 15
616 A197 25pf blue & bister 2.50 65
Set value 75

5th Baltic Sea Week, Rostock, July 7-15.

1962, July 17 *Perf. 13½x13*

Designs: No. 618 Heads of youths of three races. No. 619, Peace dove. No. 620, National Theater, Helsinki.

617 A198	5pf multicolored	*2.50*	*65*
618 A198	5pf multicolored	*2.50*	*65*
619 A198	20pf multicolored	*2.50*	*65*
620 A198	20pf multicolored	*2.50*	*65*
a.	Block of 4, #617-520	*10.00*	*4.00*

8th Youth Festival for Peace and Friendship, Helsinki, July 28-Aug. 6, 1962.

No. 620a forms the festival flower emblem. See Nos. B90-B91.

Free Style Swimming — A199

Municipal Store, Leipzig — A200

Designs: 10pf, Back stroke. 25pf, Butterfly stroke. 40pf, Breast stroke. 70pf, Water polo.

1962, Aug. 7 Litho. *Perf. 13x13½*

Design in Greenish Blue

621 A199	5pf orange	15	15
622 A199	10pf grnsh blue	15	15
623 A199	25pf ultra	15	15
624 A199	40pf brt violet	*1.65*	*1.40*
625 A199	70pf red brown	15	15
	Set value, #621-625, B92	*1.85*	*1.65*

10th European Swimming Championships. Leipzig, Aug. 18-25.

Nos. 621-625 and B92 were also printed in the same sheet, arranged in se-tenant blocks of six.

Engr. & Photo.

1962, Aug. 28 Wmk. 313 *Perf. 14*

Buildings: 20pf, Mädler Passage. 25pf, Leipzig Air Terminal and plane.

626 A200	10pf black & emerald	18	15
627 A200	20pf black & red	35	15
628 A200	25pf black & blue	60	18
	Set value		25

Leipzig Fall Fair of 1962.

"Transportation and Communication" A201

1962, Oct. 3 Litho. *Perf. 13½x13*

629 A201	5pf lt blue & black	25	15

10th anniv. of the Friedrich List Transportation College.

Souvenir Sheet

Pavel R. Popovich, Andrian G. Nikolayev and Space Capsules — A202

1962, Sept. 13 Wmk. 313 *Imperf.*

630 A202	70pf dk blue, lt grn & yel	*2.50*	*70*

1st Russian group space flight of Vostoks III and IV, Aug. 11-13, 1962.

DDR Television Signal — A203

Young Collectors and World Map — A204

1962, Oct. 25 *Perf. 13½x13*

631 A203	20pf green & gray	18	15
632 A204	40pf brt pink & blk	*1.65*	*45*
	Set value		*48*

No. 631 commemorates the 10th anniversary of television in the German Democratic Republic; No. 632 is for Stamp Day.

Gerhart Hauptmann — A205

1962, Nov. 15 *Perf. 13x13½*

633 A205	20pf red & black	30	15

Centenary of the birth of Gerhart Hauptmann, playwright.

Souvenir Sheet

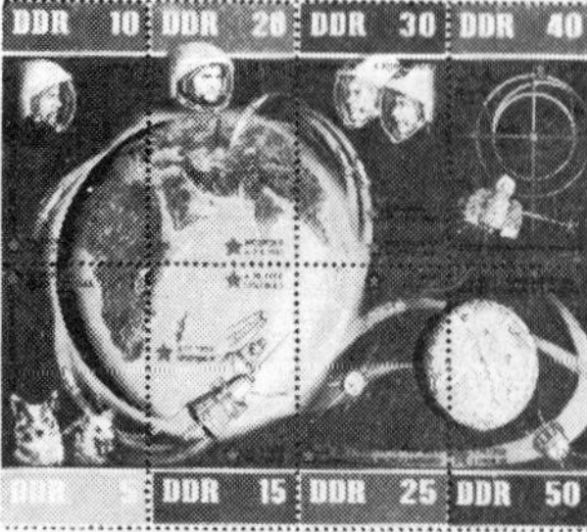

Russian Space Flights and Astronauts — A206

1962, Dec. 28 Litho. *Perf. 12½x13*

634 A206	Sheet of 8	*27.50*	*15.00*
a.	5pf yellow	*1.90*	*1.10*
b.	10pf emerald	*1.90*	*1.10*
c.	15pf magenta	*1.90*	*1.10*
d.	20pf red	*1.90*	*1.10*
e.	25pf greenish blue	*1.90*	*1.10*
f.	30pf red brown	*1.90*	*1.10*
g.	40pf crimson	*1.90*	*1.10*
h.	50pf ultramarine	*1.90*	*1.10*

Issued to show the development of Russian space flights from Sputnik 1 to Vostoks 3 and 4, and to honor the Russian astronauts Gagarin, Titov, Nikolayev and Popovich.

Pierre de Coubertin A207

Congress Emblem, Flag with Marx, Engels and Lenin A208

Design: 25pf, Stadium and Olympic rings.

1963, Jan. 2 *Perf. 13½x13*

635 A207	20pf carmine & gray	32	15
636 A207	25pf blue & bister	*1.95*	*30*
	Set value		*32*

Centenary of the birth of Baron Pierre de Coubertin, organizer of the modern Olympic Games.

1963, Jan. 15 *Perf. 13x13½*

637 A208	10pf yel, org, red & blk	25	15

6th congress of Socialist Unity Party of Germany (SED).

World Map and Exterminator A209

Designs: 25pf, Map, cross and staff of Aesculapius. 50pf, Map, cross, mosquito.

1963, Feb. 6 *Perf. 13x12½*

638 A209	20pf dp org, dk red & blk	15	15
639 A209	25pf multicolored	15	15
640 A209	50pf multicolored	*1.25*	*48*
	Set value		*55*

WHO drive to eradicate malaria.

Silver Fox A210

Design: 25pf, Karakul.

1963, Feb. 14 Photo. *Perf. 14*

641 A210	20pf rose & black	25	15
642 A210	25pf blue & black	*1.25*	*28*
	Set value		*30*

Issued to publicize the International Fur Auctions. Leipzig, Feb. 14-15, Apr. 21-24.

Barthels House, Leipzig — A211

Designs: 20pf, New Leipzig City Hall. 25pf, Belltower Building.

Engr. & Photo.

1963, Feb. 26 Wmk. 313 *Perf. 14*

643 A211	10pf black & citron	20	15
644 A211	20pf black & red org	28	15
645 A211	25pf black & blue	80	28
	Set value		40

1963 Leipzig Spring Fair.

Souvenir Sheet

On March 12, 1963, a souvenir sheet publicizing "Chemistry for Peace and Socialism" was issued. It contains two imperforate stamps, 50pf and 70pf, printed on ungummed synthetic tissue. Size: 105x74mm. Value $1.50.

Richard Wagner and "The Flying Dutchman" A213

Designs (Portrait and Scene from Play): 5pf, Johann Gottfried Seume (1763-1810). 10pf, Friedrich Hebbel (1813-1863). 20pf, Georg Büchner (1813-1837).

1963, Apr. 9 Litho. *Perf. 13x12½*

647 A213	5pf brt citron & blk	15	15
648 A213	10pf brt green & blk	15	15
649 A213	20pf orange & blk	15	15
650 A213	25pf dull blue & blk	*1.65*	*45*
	Set value		*55*

Anniversaries of German dramatists and the 150th anniv. of the birth of Richard Wagner, composer.

First Aid Station A214

Design: 20pf, Ambulance and hospital.

1963, May 14 **Wmk. 313**

651 A214	10pf multicolored	*1.25*	*45*
652 A214	20pf red, blk & gray	15	15
	Set value		*50*

Centenary of International Red Cross.

Eugene Pottier, Writer — A215

Design: 25pf, Pierre-Chretien Degeyter, composer.

1963, June 18 *Perf. 13x13½*

653 A215	20pf vermilion & blk	15	15
654 A215	25pf vio blue & blk	*1.10*	*30*
	Set value		*32*

75th anniv. of the communist song "The International."

Valentina Tereshkova and Vostok 6 — A216

Motorcyclist in "Motocross" at Apolda — A217

Design: No. 656, Valeri Bykovski and Vostok 5.

1963, July 18 Photo. *Perf. 13½*

655 A216 20pf blue, blk & gray bl 1.10 15
656 A216 20pf blue, blk & gray bl 1.10 15
a. Pair, #655-656 2.25 25
Set value 15

Space flights of Valeri Bykovski, June 14-19, and Valentina Tereshkova, 1st woman cosmonaut, June 16-19, 1963.

Engr. & Photo.
1963, July 30 *Perf. 14*

Designs: 20pf, Motorcyclist at Sachsenring, horiz. 25pf, Two motorcyclists at Sachsenring, horiz.

Size: 23x28mm

657 A217 10pf lt grn & dk grn *3.75 1.00*

Size: 48½x21mm

658 A217 20pf rose & dk red 15 15
659 A217 25pf lt blue & dk blue 20 15
Set value *1.10*

Motorcycle World Championships.

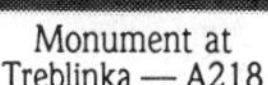

Monument at Treblinka — A218

Globe, Car and Train — A219

Perf. 13x13½
1963, Aug. 20 Litho. Wmk. 313

660 A218 20pf brick red & dk blue 35 15

Erection of a memorial at Treblinka (Poland) concentration camp.

1963, Aug. 27 *Perf. 13½x13*

Design: No. 662, Globe, plane and bus.

661 A219 10pf multicolored 1.25 15
662 A219 10pf multicolored 1.25 15
a. Pair, #661-662 2.50 25
Set value 15

Issued to publicize the 1963 Leipzig Fall Fair.

Fauna Type of 1962

Designs: 10pf, Stag beetle. 20pf, Fire salamander. 30pf, Pond turtle. 50pf, Green toad. 70pf, Hedgehogs.

1963, Sept. 10 Photo. *Perf. 14*

663 A190 10pf emerald, brn & blk 16 15
664 A190 20pf crimson, blk & yel 16 15
665 A190 30pf multicolored 16 15
666 A190 50pf multicolored *3.00 90*
667 A190 70pf claret brn, brn & bis 40 15
Nos. 663-667 (5) *3.88*
Set value *1.10*

Neidhardt von Gneisenau and Gebhard Leberecht von Blücher — A220

Designs: 10pf, Cossacks and home guard, Berlin. 20pf, Ernst Moritz Arndt and Baron Heinrich vom Stein. 25pf, Lützow's volunteers before battle. 40pf, Gerhard von Scharnhorst and Prince Mikhail I. Kutuzov.

1963, Oct. 10 Litho. *Perf. 13½x13*
Center in Tan and Black

668 A220 5pf brt yellow 15 15
669 A220 10pf emerald 15 15
670 A220 20pf dp orange 22 15
671 A220 25pf dp ultra 22 15
672 A220 40pf dark red *1.75 35*
Nos. 668-672 (5) *2.49*
Set value *52*

150th anniversary of War of Liberation.

Valentina Tereshkova and Space Craft — A221

Burning Synagogue and Star of David in Chains — A222

Designs: No. 674, Tereshkova and map of DDR, vert. No. 675, Yuri A. Gagarin and map of DDR, vert. 25pf, Tereshkova in space capsule.

1963 *Perf. 13½x13, 13x13½*
Size: 28x28mm (10pf, 25pf); 28x37mm (20pf)

673 A221 10pf ultra & green 15 15
674 A221 20pf red, blk & ocher 18 15
675 A221 20pf red, grn & ocher 18 15
676 A221 25pf orange & blue *3.00 65*
Set value *70*

Issued to commemorate the visit of astronauts Valentina Tereshkova and Yuri A. Gagarin to the German Democratic Republic.

Perf. 13½x13
1963, Nov. 8 Wmk. 313

677 A222 10pf multicolored 35 15

25th anniversary of the "Crystal Night," the start of the systematic persecution of the Jews in Germany. Inscribed: "Never again Crystal Night."

Letter Sorting Machine A223

Design: 20pf, Mechanized mail loading.

1963, Nov. 25 *Perf. 13x12½*

678 A223 10pf multicolored *1.00 32*
679 A223 20pf multicolored 20 15
Set value *35*

Issued for Stamp Day.

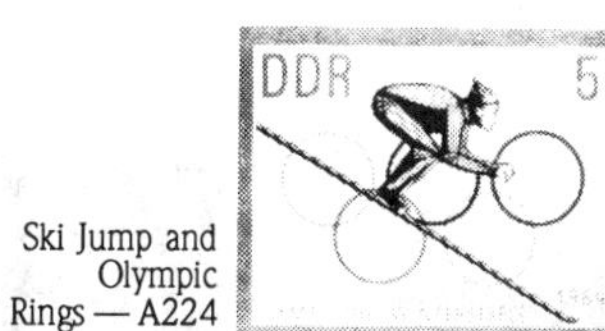

Ski Jump and Olympic Rings — A224

1963, Dec. 16 Litho. *Perf. 13½x13*

680 A224 5pf shown 15 15
681 A224 10pf Start 15 15
682 A224 25pf Landing *1.65 52*
Set value *58*

9th Winter Olympic Games, Innsbruck, Jan. 29-Feb. 9, 1964. See No. B111.

Admiral — A225

Butterflies: 15pf, Alpine Apollo. 20pf, Swallowtail. 25pf, Postilion. 40pf, Great fox.

Wmk. 313
1964, Jan. 15 Photo. *Perf. 14*
Butterflies in Natural Colors

683 A225 10pf citron & blk 15 15
684 A225 15pf pale violet & blk 20 15
685 A225 20pf lt brick red & blk 24 15
686 A225 25pf lt blue & dk brn 28 15
687 A225 40pf lt ultra & blk *3.00 65*
Nos. 683-687 (5) *3.87*
Set value *80*

William Shakespeare A226

Designs: 20pf, Quadriga, Brandenburg Gate, Berlin. 25pf, Keystone, History Museum (Zeughaus), Berlin.

1964, Feb. 6 Litho. *Perf. 13x12½*

688 A226 20pf rose & dk blue 15 15
689 A226 25pf lt blue & mag 15 15
690 A226 40pf lt vio & dk bl grn *1.10 55*
Set value *63*

200th anniv. of the birth of the sculptor Johann Gottfried Schadow (20pf); 300th anniv. of the birth of the sculptor Andreas Schlüter (25pf); 400th anniv. of the birth of William Shakespeare, dramatist (40pf).

Electrical Engineering Exhibit — A227

Design: 20pf, Bräunigkes Court, exhibition hall, 1700.

Perf. 13x13½
1964, Feb. 26 Wmk. 313

691 A227 10pf brt green & blk 5.50 15
692 A227 20pf red & black 6.50 15
Set value 15

Leipzig Spring Fair, Mar. 1-10, 1964.
Nos. 691-692 printed in same sheet with alternating yellow and black label.

Khrushchev and Inventors — A228

Youth Training for Leadership — A229

Design: 40pf, Khrushchev, Tereshkova and Bykovski.

1964, May 15 *Perf. 13x13½*

693 A228 25pf blue 15 15
694 A228 40pf lilac & grnsh blk *2.75 48*
Set value *52*

Issued in honor of Premier Nikita S. Khrushchev of the Soviet Union.

1964, May 13 Litho.

Designs: 20pf, Young athletes. 25pf, Accordion player and girl with flowers.

Center in Black

695 A229 10pf ultra, mag & emer 15 15
696 A229 20pf emerald, ultra & mag 15 15
697 A229 25pf magenta, emer & ultra *85 28*
Set value *1.00 33*

German Youth Meeting, Berlin.

Television Antenna and Puppets — A230

Children's Day: Various characters from children's television programs.

1964, June 1 *Perf. 13x13½*

698 A230 5pf multicolored 15 15
699 A230 10pf multicolored 15 15
700 A230 15pf multicolored 15 15
701 A230 20pf multicolored 15 15
702 A230 40pf multicolored *1.65 65*
Set value *1.95 75*

Woman as Educator and Portrait of Jenny Marx — A231

Designs: 25pf, Women in industry and transistor diagram. 70pf, Women in agriculture.

Perf. 13½x13
1964, June 26 Litho. Wmk. 313

703 A231 20pf crimson, gray & yel 15 15
704 A231 25pf lt blue, gray & red *1.50 42*
705 A231 70pf emerald, gray & yel 18 15
Set value *50*

Congress of Women of the German Democratic Republic, June 25-27.

Bicycling — A232

Diving — A233

Litho. & Engr.
1964, July 15 *Perf. 14*

706 A232 5pf shown 15 15
707 A232 10pf Volleyball 15 15
708 A232 20pf Judo 15 15
709 A232 25pf Woman diver 15 15
710 A232 70pf Equestrian *1.65 70*
Set value, #706-710, B118 *2.20 90*

Litho.
Perf. 13x13½

711 A233 10pf shown 3.00 1.10
712 A233 10pf Volleyball 3.00 1.10
713 A233 10pf Bicycling 3.00 1.10
714 A233 10pf Judo 3.00 1.10
a. Block of 6, #711-714, B119-B120 19.00 9.25

18th Olympic Games, Tokyo, Oct. 10-25, 1964. See Nos. B118-B120. No. 714a printed in 2 horiz. rows: (1st: #711, #B119, #712. 2nd: #713, #B120, #714). The Olympic rings extend over the 6 stamps.

Monument, Leningrad — A234

1964, Aug. 8 Litho. *Perf. 13x13½*

715	A234	25pf	brt blue, blk & yel	45	15

Issued to honor the victims of the siege of Leningrad, Sept. 1941-Jan. 1943.

Bertha von Suttner — A235

Medieval Glazier and Goblet — A236

Designs: 20pf, Frederic Joliot Curie. 50pf, Carl von Ossietzky.

1964, Sept. 1 *Perf. 14*

716	A235	20pf	red & black	15	15
717	A235	25pf	ultra & black	15	15
718	A235	50pf	lilac & black	*1.00*	*42*
			Set value		*50*

Issued to promote World Peace.

1964, Sept. 3 *Perf. 14*

Design: 15pf, Jena glass for chemical industry.

719	A236	10pf	lt ultra & multi	1.10	15
720	A236	15pf	red & multi	1.10	15
			Set value		20

Issued for the Leipzig Fall Fair, 1964. Nos. 719-720 printed as triptychs with label inscribed "800 years Leipzig Fair" between.

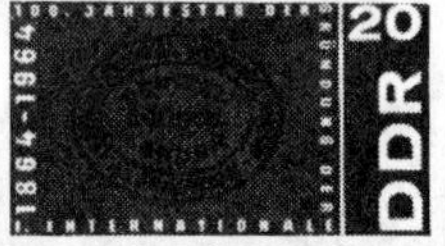

Handstamp of First Socialist International, 1864 — A237

1964, Sept. 16 Photo. Wmk. 313

721	A237	20pf	orange red & blk	15	15
722	A237	25pf	dull blue & blk	*65*	*35*
			Set value		*38*

Centenary of First Socialist International.

Stamp of 1955 (Dürer's Portrait of Young Man) — A238

1964, Sept. 23 Litho. *Perf. 13x13½*

723	A238	50pf	gray & dk red brn	*85*	*45*

Natl. Stamp Exhibition, Berlin, Oct. 3-18. See Nos. B124-B125.

Navigation — A239

Man from Mönchgut, Rügen — A240

Designs: No. 725, Flag and new Berlin buildings. No. 726, Bituminous coal transport and surveyors level. No. 727, Chemist. No. 728, Soldier. No. 729, Farm woman and cows. No. 730, Steel worker. No. 731, Woman scientist and lecture hall. No. 732, Heavy industry. No. 733, Optical industry. No. 734, Consumer goods (woman examining cloth). No. 735, Foreign trade, Leipzig fair emblem. No. 736, Buildings industry. No. 737, Sculptor. No. 738, Woman skier.

Perf. 13½x13

1964, Oct. 6 Litho. Wmk. 313

724	A239	10pf	blue & multi	15	15
725	A239	10pf	blue & multi	15	15
726	A239	10pf	gray & multi	15	15
727	A239	10pf	red & multi	15	15
728	A239	10pf	red & multi	15	15
729	A239	10pf	yel grn & multi	15	15
730	A239	10pf	red & multi	15	15
731	A239	10pf	red & multi	15	15
732	A239	10pf	gray & multi	15	15
733	A239	10pf	gray & multi	15	15
734	A239	10pf	blue & multi	15	15
735	A239	10pf	blue & multi	15	15
736	A239	10pf	yel grn & multi	15	15
737	A239	10pf	yel grn & multi	15	15
738	A239	10pf	blue & multi	15	15
			Set value	1.90	90

German Democratic Republic, 15th anniv.

A souvenir sheet contains 15 imperf. stamps similar to #724-738. Size: 210x287mm. Value, $17.50.

For surcharge see No. B134.

1964, Nov. 25 Photo. *Perf. 14*

Regional Costumes: No. 740, Woman from Mönchgut, Rügen. No. 741, Man from Spreewald. No. 742, Woman from Spreewald. No. 743, Man from Thuringia. No. 744, Woman from Thuringia.

739	A240	5pf	multicolored	*7.50*	*4.25*
740	A240	5pf	multicolored	*7.50*	*4.25*
741	A240	10pf	multicolored	16	15
742	A240	10pf	multicolored	16	15
743	A240	20pf	multicolored	25	15
744	A240	20pf	multicolored	25	15
			Nos. 739-744 (6)	*15.82*	*9.10*

The male and female costume stamps of the same denomination are printed se-tenant in checkerboard arrangement.

See Nos. 859-864.

Souvenir Sheets

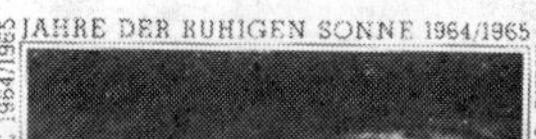

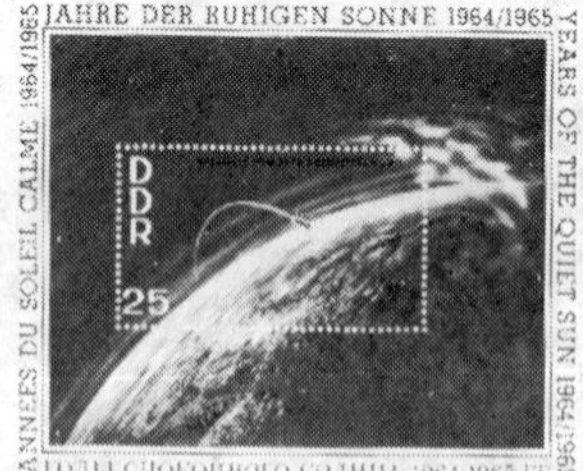

Exploration of Ionosphere — A241

Designs: 40pf, Exploration of sun activities. 70pf, Exploration of radiation belt.

1964, Dec. 29 Litho. *Perf. 13½x13*

745	A241	25pf	vio bl & yel	*6.50*	*1.75*
746	A241	40pf	vio bl, yel & red	*1.50*	*35*
747	A241	70pf	dp grn, vio bl & yel	*1.90*	*42*

Intl. Quiet Sun Year, 1964-65.

Albert Schweitzer as Physician — A242

August Bebel — A243

Designs (Schweitzer): 20pf, As fighter against war and atom bomb. 25pf, At the organ with score of Organ Prelude by Bach.

Wmk. 313

1965, Jan. 14 Photo. *Perf. 14*

748	A242	10pf	emerald, blk & bis	15	15
749	A242	20pf	crimson, blk & bis	20	15
750	A242	25pf	blue, blk & bis	*3.00*	*1.10*
			Set value		*1.20*

90th birthday of Dr. Albert Schweitzer, medical missionary.

Ulbricht Type of 1961-63
Currency in "Mark of the Deutsche Notenbank" (MDN)

1965, Feb. 10 Engr.

Size: 24x28½mm

751	A189	1mdn	dull green	75	15
752	A189	2mdn	brown	75	15
			Set value		15

See note below Nos. 590B-590C.

1965 Photo. *Perf. 14*

Portraits: 10pf, Wilhelm Conrad Roentgen. No. 753A, Adolph von Menzel. 25pf, Wilhelm Külz. 40pf, Erich Weinert. 50pf, Dante Alighieri.

753	A243	10pf	dk brn, yel & emer	15	15
753A	A243	10pf	dk brn, yel & org	15	15
754	A243	20pf	ol brn, red & buff	28	15
754A	A243	25pf	ol brn, yel & bl	28	15
754B	A243	40pf	ol brn, buff & car rose	45	15
755	A243	50pf	dk brn, yel & org	55	15
			Nos. 753-755 (6)	1.86	
			Set value		30

Roentgen (1845-1923), physicist, discoverer of X-rays. Sesquicentennial of the birth of Adolph von Menzel, painter and graphic artist. Bebel, labor leader (1840-1913). 90th anniv. of the birth of Wilhelm Külz, politician. 75th anniv. of the birth of Erich Weinert, poet. Alighieri (1265-1321), Italian poet.

Issue dates: No. 753, Mar. 24; No. 753A, Dec. 8; 20pf, Feb. 22; 25pf, July 5; 40pf, July 28; 50pf, Apr. 15.

A244

A245

Designs: 10pf, Gold Medal, Leipzig Fair. 15pf, Obverse of medal, arms of German Democratic Republic. 25pf, Chemical plant.

1965, Feb. 25 Wmk. 313

756	A244	10pf	lilac rose & gold	20	15
757	A244	15pf	lilac rose & gold	28	15
758	A244	25pf	brt blue, yel & gold	52	15
			Set value		15

1965 Leipzig Spring Fair and 800th anniv. of the Fair.

1965, Mar. 24

Designs: 10pf, Giraffe. 25pf, Common iguana, horiz. 30pf, White-tailed gnu.

759	A245	10pf	green & gray	15	15
760	A245	25pf	dk vio bl & gray	32	15
761	A245	30pf	brown & gray	*2.25*	*42*
			Set value		*50*

10th anniversary of Berlin Zoo.

Col. Pavel Belyayev and Lt. Col. Alexei Leonov — A246

Boxing Glove and Laurel Wreath — A247

Design: 25pf, Lt. Col. Leonov floating in space.

Perf. 13½x13

1965, Apr. 15 Litho. Wmk. 313

762	A246	10pf	red	30	15
763	A246	25pf	dk ultra	*2.25*	*40*
			Set value		*45*

Space flight of Voskhod 2 and the first man walking in space, Lt. Col. Alexel Leonov.

1965, Apr. 27 Photo. *Perf. 14*

764	A247	20pf	blk, red & gold	*80*	*32*

16th European Boxing Championship, Berlin, May, 1965. See No. B126.

Walter Ulbricht and Erich Weinert Distributing "Free Germany" Leaflets on the Eastern Front — A248

Designs: 50pf, Liberation of concentration camps. 60pf, Russian soldiers raising flag on Reichstag, Berlin. 70pf, Political demonstration.

1965, May 5 Photo. *Perf. 14*

Flags in Red, Black & Yellow

765	A248	40pf	blue grn & red	15	15
766	A248	50pf	dull blue & red	15	15
767	A248	60pf	brown & red	*1.75*	*1.25*
768	A248	70pf	vio blue & red	15	15
			Nos. 765-768,B127-B131 (9)	*2.96*	*2.45*

20th anniv. of liberation from fascism.

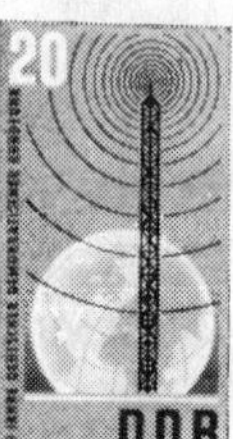

Radio Tower and Globe
A249

ITU Emblem and Frequency Diagram
A250

Design: 40pf, Workers and broadcasting equipment.

1965, May 12 Litho. *Perf. 12½x13*

769	A249	20pf	dk car rose & blk	15	15
770	A249	40pf	vio bl & blk	*70*	*35*
			Set value	*75*	*40*

20th anniv. of the German Democratic broadcasting system.

1965, May 17

Design: 25pf, ITU emblem and telephone diagram.

771 A250 20pf olive, yel & blk 18 15
772 A250 25pf vio, pale vio & blk *1.25 28*
Set value *32*

Cent. of the ITU.

Emblem of Free German Trade Union — A251

Hemispheres with Crowd of Workers A252

1965, June 10 Photo. *Perf. 14*

773 A251 20pf red & gold 15 15
774 A252 25pf gold, blue & blk *65 32*
Set value *70 35*

20th anniv. of the Free German Trade Union (FDGB) and of the World Organization of Trade Unions.

Symbols of Industry — A253

Marx and Lenin — A254

Designs: 20pf, Red Tower. 25pf, City Hall.

1965, June 16

775 A253 10pf gold & emerald 15 15
776 A253 20pf gold & crimson 15 15
777 A253 25pf gold & brt blue *60 35*
Set value *75 45*

800th anniv. of Chemnitz (Karl Marx City).

1965, June 21 Litho. *Perf. 13½x13*

778 A254 20pf red, black & buff 15 15

6th Conference of Postal Ministers of Communist Countries, Peking, June 21-July 15.

"Alte Waage" and New Building, Leipzig — A255

Designs: 25pf, Old City Hall. 40pf, Opera House and General Post Office. 70pf, Hotel "Stadt Leipzig."

Unwmk.

1965, Aug. 25 Photo. *Perf. 14*

781 A255 10pf gold, cl brn & ultra 15 15
a. Souv. sheet of 2, #781, 784 *2.50 90*
782 A255 25pf gold, brn, & ocher 15 15
a. Souv. sheet of 2, #782-783 *1.00 38*
783 A255 40pf gold, brn, ocher & yel grn 15 15
784 A255 70pf gold & ultra *1.40 75*
Set value *1.60 90*

800th anniv. of the City of Leipzig. No. 781a sold for 90pf; No. 782a for 80pf. The souvenir sheets were issued Sept. 4, 1965.

Cameras — A256

Equestrian — A257

Leipzig Fall Fair: 15pf, Electric guitar and organ. 25pf, Microscope.

1965, Sept. 9 *Perf. 14*

785 A256 10pf green, blk & gold 15 15
786 A256 15pf multicolored 15 15
787 A256 25pf multicolored 55 15
Set value 20

Perf. 13½x13

1965, Sept. 15 Litho. Unwmk.

789 A257 10pf shown 15 15
790 A257 10pf Swimmer 15 15
791 A257 10pf Runner *3.00 65*
Set value, #789-791, B135-B136 *80*

Issued to commemorate the International Modern Pentathlon Championships, Leipzig.

Alexei Leonov and Brandenburg Gate — A258

Memorial Monument, Putten — A259

Designs: No. 793, Pavel Belyayev and Berlin City Hall. 25pf, Leonov floating in space and space ship.

Wmk. 313

1965, Nov. 1 Litho. *Perf. 14*

Size: 23½x28½mm

792 A258 20pf blue, sil & red *1.00 42*
793 A258 20pf blue, sil & red *1.00 42*

Size: 51x28½mm

794 A258 25pf blue, sil & red *1.00 42*
a. Strip of 3, #792-794 *3.00 1.50*

Visit of the Russian astronauts to the German Democratic Republic.

1965, Nov. 19 *Perf. 13x13½*

795 A259 25pf brt bl, pale yel & blk 30 15

Issued in memory of the victims of a Nazi attack on Putten, Netherlands, Sept. 30, 1944.

Furnace A260

Designs (after old woodcuts): 15pf, Ore miners. 20pf, Proustite crystals. 25pf, Sulphur crystals.

Perf. 13x12½

1965, Nov. 11 Litho. Unwmk.

796 A260 10pf black & multi 15 15
797 A260 15pf black & multi *65 32*
798 A260 20pf black & multi 15 15
799 A260 25pf black & multi 15 15
Set value *90 40*

Bicentenary of the Mining Academy in Freiberg.

Red Kite A261

Otto Grotewohl A262

Birds: 10pf, Lammergeier. 20pf, Buzzard. 25pf, Kestrel. 40pf, Northern goshawk. 70pf, Golden eagle.

1965, Dec. 8 Photo. *Perf. 14*

Gold Frame

800 A261 5pf orange & blk 15 15
801 A261 10pf emerald, brn & blk 15 15
802 A261 20pf car, red brn & blk 15 15
803 A261 25pf blue, red brn & blk 15 15
804 A261 40pf lilac, blk & dk red 18 15
805 A261 70pf brn, blk & yel *4.25 1.00*
Nos. 800-805 (6) *5.03*
Set value *1.25*

1965, Dec. 14 Photo. Wmk. 313

806 A262 20pf black 25 15

Issued in memory of Otto Grotewohl (1894-1964), prime minister (1949-1964).

Souvenir Sheet

Spartacus Letter, Karl Liebknecht and Rosa Luxemburg — A263

1966, Jan. 3 Unwmk.

807 A263 Sheet of 2 1.10 42
a. 20pf red & black 48 18
b. 50pf red & black 48 18

50th anniv. of the natl. conf. of the Spartacus organization.

Tobogganing, Women's Singles — A264

Tobogganing: 20pf, Men's doubles. 25pf, Men's singles.

Perf. 13½x13

1966, Jan. 25 Litho. Unwmk.

808 A264 10pf citron & dp grn 15 15
809 A264 20pf car rose & dk vio bl 22 15
810 A264 25pf blue & dk blue *1.10 38*
Set value *45*

10th Intl. Tobogganing Championships, Friedrichroda, Feb. 8-13.

Electronic Computer A265

Design: 15pf, Drill and milling machine.

1966, Feb. 24 *Perf. 13x12½*

811 A265 10pf multicolored 15 15
812 A265 15pf multicolored 16 15
Set value 24 15

Leipzig Spring Fair, 1966.

Jan Arnost Smoler and Linden Leaf — A266

Soldier and National Gallery, Berlin — A267

Design: 25pf, House of the Sorbs, Bautzen, Saxony.

1966, Mar. 1 *Perf. 13x13½*

813 A266 20pf brt bl, blk & brt red 15 15
814 A266 25pf brt red, blk & brt bl *60 22*
Set value *25*

Smoler (1816-84), philologist of the Sorbian language. The Sorbs are a small group of slavic people in Saxony.

Wmk. 313

1966, Mar. 1 Photo. *Perf. 14*

Designs (Soldier and): 10pf, Brandenburg Gate. 20pf, Factory. 25pf, Combine.

815 A267 5pf ol gray, blk & yel 15 15
816 A267 10pf ol gray, blk & yel 15 15
817 A267 20pf ol gray, blk & yel 15 15
818 A267 25pf ol gray, blk & yel *90 32*
Set value *1.25 42*

National People's Army, 10th anniversary.

Luna 9 on Moon A268

Medal for Scholarship A269

1966, Mar. 7 Unwmk.

819 A268 20pf multicolored 95 15

Issued to commemorate the first soft landing on the moon by Luna 9, Feb. 3, 1966.

1966, Mar. 7 Litho. *Perf. 13½x13*

820 A269 20pf multicolored 15 15

20th anniv. of the State Youth Organization.

Traffic Signs — A270

Traffic safety: 15pf, Automobile and child with scooter. 25pf, Bicyclist and signaling hand. 50pf, Motorcyclist, ambulance and glass of beer.

1966, Mar. 28 Litho. *Perf. 13*

821 A270 10pf dk & lt bl, red & blk 15 15
822 A270 15pf brt grn, cit & blk 15 15
823 A270 25pf ol bis, brt bl & blk 15 15
824 A270 50pf car, yel, gray & blk *1.10 42*
Set value *55*

Marx, Lenin and Crowd — A271

Designs: 5pf, Party emblem and crowd, vert. 15pf, Marx, Engels and title page of Communist Manifesto, vert. 20pf, Otto Grotewohl and Wilhelm Pieck shaking hands, and Party emblem, vert. 25pf, Chairman Walter Ulbricht receiving flowers.

1966, Mar. 31 **Photo.** ***Perf. 14***

825	A271	5pf multicolored	15	15
826	A271	10pf multicolored	15	15
827	A271	15pf green & blk	15	15
828	A271	20pf dk carmine & blk	18	15
829	A271	25pf multicolored	*1.75*	*70*
		Nos. 825-829 (5)	*2.38*	
		Set value		*90*

20th anniversary of Socialist Unity Party of Germany (SED).

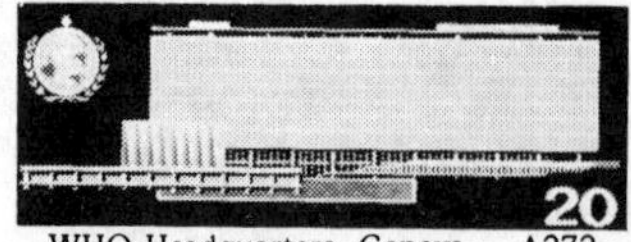

WHO Headquarters, Geneva — A272

Perf. 13x12½

1966, Apr. 26 **Litho.** **Unwmk.**

830	A272	20pf multicolored	45	15

Inauguration of WHO Headquarters, Geneva.

Rügen Island, Königsstuhl A273

National Parks: 10pf, Spree River woodland. 20pf, Saxon Switzerland. 25pf, Dunes at Westdarss. 30pf, Thale in Harz, Devil's Wall. 50pf, Feldberg Lakes, Mecklenburg.

Perf. 13x12½

1966, May 17 **Litho.** **Unwmk.**

831	A273	10pf multicolored	15	15
832	A273	15pf multicolored	15	15
833	A273	20pf multicolored	15	15
834	A273	25pf multicolored	15	15
835	A273	30pf multicolored	15	15
836	A273	50pf multicolored	*1.50*	*65*
		Set value	*1.90*	*80*

Plauen Lace — A274

Various Lace Designs.

1966, May 26 ***Perf. 13x13½***

837	A274	10pf green & lt green	15	15
838	A274	20pf dk blue & lt blue	15	15
839	A274	25pf brown red & ver	15	15
840	A274	50pf dk vio & bluish lil	*1.50*	*90*
		Set value		*98*

Rhododendron A275

Parachutist Landing on Target A276

Flowers: 20pf, Lilies of the Valley. 40pf, Dahlias. 50pf, Cyclamen.

Photo. & Engr.

1966 **Unwmk.** ***Perf. 14x13½***

841	A275	20pf multicolored	15	15
842	A275	25pf multicolored	15	15
843	A275	40pf multicolored	15	15
844	A275	50pf multicolored	*3.75*	*1.10*
		Set value		*1.25*

Intl. Flower Show, Erfurt. Issue dates: 20pf, Aug. 16; others, June 28.

1966, July 12 **Litho.** ***Perf. 12½x13***

Designs: 15pf, Group parachute jump. 20pf, Free fall.

845	A276	10pf blue, blk & ol	15	15
846	A276	15pf multicolored	*70*	*28*
847	A276	20pf sky blue, blk & ol	15	15
		Set value		*35*

Issued to publicize the 8th International Parachute Championships, Leipzig.

Hans Kahle, Song of German Fighters and Medal of Spanish Republic — A277

Design: 15pf, Hans Beimler and street fighting in Madrid.

1966, July 15 **Photo.** ***Perf. 14***

848	A277	5pf multicolored	15	15
849	A277	15pf multicolored	15	15
		Set value, #848-849, B137-B140	*1.60*	*80*

Issued to honor the German fighters in the Spanish Civil War.

Television Set — A278

Design: 15pf, Electric typewriter.

Perf. 13x12½

1966, Aug. 29 **Litho.** **Unwmk.**

850	A278	10pf brt grn, blk & gray	15	15
851	A278	15pf red, blk & gray	22	15
		Set value		15

1966 Leipzig Fall Fair.

Women's Doubles Kayak Race — A279

1966, Aug. 16

852	A279	15pf brt blue & multi	*1.10*	*25*

7th Canoe World Championships, Berlin. See No. B141.

The first value column gives the catalogue value of an unused stamp, the second that of a used stamp.

Oradour sur Glane Memorial and French Flag A280

Emblem of the Committee for Health Education A281

Perf. 13x13½

1966, Sept. 9 **Wmk. 313**

853	A280	25pf ultra, blk & red	25	15

Issued in memory of the victims of the Nazi attack on Oradour, France, June 10, 1944.

1966, Sept. 13 ***Perf. 14***

Designs: 5pf, Symbolic blood donor and recipient, horiz.

854	A281	5pf brt brown & red	15	15
855	A281	40pf brt blue & red	*70*	*50*
		Set value		*55*

Issued to publicize blood donations and health education. See No. B142.

Weight Lifter — A282

Perf. 13½x13

1966, Sept. 22 **Litho.** **Unwmk.**

856	A282	15pf lt brown & blk	*1.50*	*42*

Intl. and European Weight Lifting Championships, Berlin. See No. B143.

Congress Hall A283

Emblem A284

1966, Oct. 10 ***Perf. 13***

857	A283	10pf multicolored	*60*	*15*
858	A284	20pf dk blue & yellow	15	15
		Set value		*15*

6th Congress of the International Organization of Journalists, Berlin.

Costume Type of 1964

Regional Costumes: 5pf, Woman from Altenburg. No. 860, Man from Altenburg. No. 861, Woman from Mecklenburg. 15pf, Man from Mecklenburg. 20pf, Woman from Magdeburg area. 30pf, Man from Magdeburg area.

1966, Oct. 25 **Photo.** ***Perf. 14***

859	A240	5pf multicolored	15	15
860	A240	10pf multicolored	15	15
861	A240	10pf lt green & multi	15	15
862	A240	15pf lt green & multi	15	15
863	A240	20pf yellow & multi	*3.25*	*1.25*
864	A240	30pf yellow & multi	*3.25*	*1.25*
		Nos. 859-864 (6)	*7.10*	
		Set value		*2.65*

The male and female costume designs of the same region are printed se-tenant in checkerboard arrangement.

Megalamphodus Megalopterus — A285

Various Tropical Fish in Natural Colors.

1966, Nov. 8 **Litho.** ***Perf. 13x12½***

865	A285	5pf lt blue & gray	15	15
866	A285	10pf blue & indigo	15	15
867	A285	15pf citron & blk	*2.00*	*80*
868	A285	20pf green & blk	15	15
869	A285	25pf ultra & blk	15	15
870	A285	40pf emerald & blk	22	15
		Nos. 865-870 (6)	*2.82*	
		Set value		*1.00*

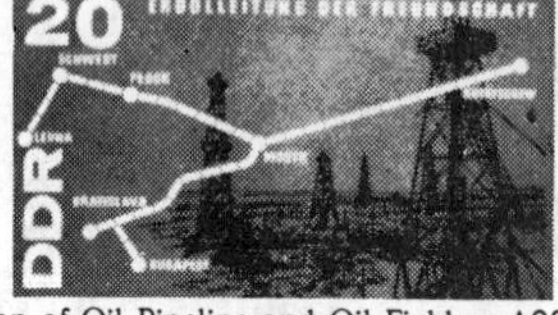

Map of Oil Pipeline and Oil Field — A286

Design: 25pf, Map of oil pipelines and "Walter Ulbricht" Leuna chemical factory.

1966, Nov. 8 ***Perf. 13½x13***

871	A286	20pf red & black	15	15
872	A286	25pf blue & black	*42*	*22*
		Set value		*25*

Chemical industry.

Detail from Ishtar Gate, Babylon, 580 B.C. — A287

Designs from Babylon c. 580 B.C.: 20pf, Mythological animal from Ishtar Gate. 25pf, Lion facing right and ornaments, vert. 50pf, Lion facing left and ornaments, vert.

Perf. 13½x14, 14x13½

1966, Nov. 23 **Photo.**

873	A287	10pf multicolored	15	15
874	A287	20pf multicolored	15	15
875	A287	25pf multicolored	15	15
876	A287	50pf multicolored	*1.00*	*55*
		Set value	*1.20*	*66*

Near East Museum, Berlin.

Wartburg, Thuringia A288

Gentian A289

Design: 25pf, Wartburg, Palace.

1966, Nov. 23 **Litho.** ***Perf. 13x13½***

877	A288	20pf olive	15	15
878	A288	25pf violet brown	*40*	*22*
		Set value	*48*	*26*

900th anniv. (in 1967) of the Wartburg (castle) near Eisenach, Thuringia. See No. B145.

1966, Dec. 8 Litho. *Perf. 12½x13*

Protected Flowers: 20pf, Cephalanthera rubra (orchid). 25pf, Mountain arnica.

Black Background

879	A289	10pf yel, grn & bl	15	15
880	A289	20pf yel, grn & red	15	15
881	A289	25pf red, yel & grn	1.40	45
		Set value		56

Son Leaving Home A290

City Hall, Stralsund A291

Various Scenes from Fairy Tale "The Table, the Ass and the Stick."

1966, Dec. 8 *Perf. 13½x13*

882	A290	5pf multicolored	50	18
883	A290	10pf multicolored	50	18
884	A290	20pf multicolored	50	20
885	A290	25pf multicolored	50	20
886	A290	30pf multicolored	50	18
887	A290	50pf multicolored	50	18
		Nos. 882-887 (6)	3.00	1.12

Nos. 882-887 printed together in sheets of six. See Nos. 968-973, 1063-1068, 1339-1344.

Perf. 14x13½, 13½x14

1967, Jan. 24 Photo.

Buildings: 5pf, Wörlitz Castle, horiz. 15pf, Chorin Convent. 20pf, Ribbeck House, Berlin, horiz. 25pf, Moritzburg, Zeitz. 40pf, Old City Hall, Potsdam.

888	A291	5pf multicolored	15	15
889	A291	10pf multicolored	15	15
890	A291	15pf multicolored	15	15
891	A291	20pf multicolored	15	15
892	A291	25pf multicolored	15	15
893	A291	40pf multicolored	1.40	52
		Set value	1.90	65

See Nos. 1018, 1020, 1071-1076.

Rifle Shooting, Prone — A292

Designs: 20pf, Shooting on skis. 25pf, Relay race with rifles on skis.

1967, Feb. 15 Litho. *Perf. 13x12½*

894	A292	10pf Prus bl gray & brt pink	15	15
895	A292	20pf sl grn, brt bl & grn	15	15
896	A292	25pf ol grn, ol & grnsh bl	75	32
		Set value		40

World Biathlon Championships (skiing and shooting), Altenberg, Feb. 15-19.

Circular Knitting Machine — A293

Mother and Child — A294

Design: 15pf, Zeiss telescope and galaxy.

1967, Mar. 2 *Perf. 13½x13*

897	A293	10pf dull mag & brt grn	15	15
898	A293	15pf ultra & gray	24	15
		Set value		15

Leipzig Spring Fair of 1967.

1967, Mar. 7 *Perf. 13x13½*

Design: 25pf, Working women.

899	A294	20pf rose brn, red & gray	15	15
900	A294	25pf dk bl, brt bl & brn	75	35
		Set value		40

20th anniv. of the Democratic Women's Federation of Germany.

Marx, Engels, Lenin and Electronic Control Center — A295

Designs (Portraits and): 5pf, Farmer driving combine. No. 903, Students and teacher. 15pf, Family. No. 905, Soldier, sailor and aviator. No. 906, Ulbricht among workers. 25pf, Soldier, sailor, aviator and factories. 40pf, Farmers with modern equipment. Nos. 901, 903-905 are vertical.

1967 Photo. *Perf. 14*

901	A295	5pf multicolored	15	15
902	A295	10pf multicolored	15	15
903	A295	10pf multicolored	15	15
904	A295	15pf multicolored	35	25
905	A295	20pf multicolored	15	15
906	A295	20pf multicolored	15	15
907	A295	25pf multicolored	15	15
908	A295	40pf multicolored	75	52
		Set value	1.60	1.00

7th congress of Socialist Unity Party of Germany (SED), Apr. 17.

Nos. 902, 906-908 issued Mar. 22; Nos. 901, 903-905, Apr. 6.

Tahitian Women, by Paul Gauguin — A296

Paintings from Dresden Gallery: 20pf, Young Woman, by Ferdinand Hodler. 25pf, Peter in the Zoo, by H. Hakenbeck. 30pf, Venetian Episode (woman feeding pigeons), by R. Bergander. 50pf, Grandmother and Granddaughter, by J. Scholtz. 70pf, Cairn in the Snow, by Caspar David Friedrich. 20pf, 25pf, 30pf, 50pf are vertical.

1967, Mar. 29

909	A296	20pf multicolored	15	15
910	A296	25pf multicolored	15	15
911	A296	30pf multicolored	15	15
912	A296	40pf multicolored	15	15
913	A296	50pf multicolored	2.00	1.40
914	A296	70pf multicolored	15	15
		Nos. 909-914 (6)	2.75	
		Set value		1.75

Barn Owl — A297

Protected Birds: 10pf, Eurasian crane. 20pf, Peregrine falcon. 25pf, Bullfinches. 30pf, European kingfisher. 40pf, European roller.

1967, Apr. 27 Photo. *Perf. 14*

Birds in Natural Colors

915	A297	5pf gray blue	15	15
916	A297	10pf gray blue	15	15
917	A297	20pf gray blue	16	15
918	A297	25pf gray blue	22	15
919	A297	30pf gray blue	2.75	95
920	A297	40pf gray blue	22	15
		Nos. 915-920 (6)	3.65	
		Set value		1.25

Arms of Warsaw, Berlin and Prague A298

Design: 25pf, Bicyclists and doves.

Perf. 13x12½

1967, May 10 Litho. Wmk. 313

921	A298	10pf org, blk & lil	15	15
922	A298	25pf lt bl & dk car	48	24
		Set value		27

20th Intl. Bicycle Peace Race, Berlin-Warsaw-Prague.

Cat A299

Children's Drawings: 10pf, Snow White and the Seven Dwarfs. 15pf, Fire truck. 20pf, Cock. 25pf, Flowers in vase. 30pf, Children playing ball.

1967, June 1 Unwmk.

923	A299	5pf multicolored	15	15
924	A299	10pf black & multi	15	15
925	A299	15pf dk blue & multi	15	15
926	A299	20pf orange & multi	15	15
927	A299	25pf multicolored	15	15
928	A299	30pf multicolored	90	45
		Nos. 923-928 (6)	1.65	
		Set value		63

Issued for International Children's Day.

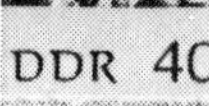

Girl with Straw Hat, by Salomon Bray — A300

Exhibition Emblem and Map of DDR — A301

Paintings: 5pf, Three Horsemen, by Rubens, horiz. 10pf, Girl Gathering Grapes, by Gerard Dou. 20pf, Spring Idyl, by Hans Thoma, horiz. 25pf, Wilhelmine Schroder-Devrient, by Karl Begas. 50pf, The Four Evangelists, by Jacob Jordaens.

1967, June 7 Photo. *Perf. 14*

929	A300	5pf lt & dk blue	15	15
930	A300	10pf lt red brn & red brn	15	15
931	A300	20pf lt & dp yel grn	15	15
932	A300	25pf pale rose & rose lil	15	15
933	A300	40pf pale grn & ol grn	15	15
934	A300	50pf tan & sepia	2.00	95
		Nos. 929-934 (2)	2.75	
		Set value		1.12

Issued to publicize paintings missing from museums since World War II.

Perf. 12½x13

1967, June 14 Litho. Unwmk.

935	A301	20pf dk grn, ocher & red	20	15

15th Agricultural Exhib., Markkleeberg.

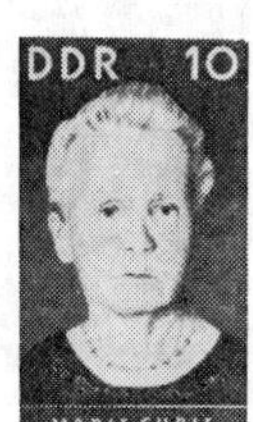

Marie Curie — A302

German Playing Cards — A303

Portraits: 5pf, Georg Herwegh, poet. 20pf, Käthe Kollwitz. 25pf, Johann J. Winckelmann, archaeologist. 40pf, Theodor Storm, writer.

1967 Engr. *Perf. 14*

936	A302	5pf brown	15	15
937	A302	10pf dark blue	15	15
938	A302	20pf dull red	15	15
939	A302	25pf gray	15	15
940	A302	40pf slate green	75	38
		Set value	1.10	52

150th anniv. of the birth of Herwegh, Winckelmann and Storm, and the birth centenaries of Curie and Kollwitz.

1967, July 18 Photo.

Designs: Various German playing cards.

941	A303	5pf red & multi	15	15
942	A303	10pf green & multi	15	15
943	A303	20pf multicolored	22	15
944	A303	25pf multicolored	3.00	1.10
		Set value		1.25

Mare and Foal A304

Horses: 10pf, Stallion. 20pf, Horse race finish. 50pf, Colts, vert.

Perf. 13½x13, 13x13½

1967, Aug. 15 Litho. Unwmk.

945	A304	5pf multicolored	15	15
946	A304	10pf org, blk & dk brn	15	15
947	A304	20pf blue & multi	18	15
948	A304	50pf multicolored	2.50	80
		Set value		95

Thoroughbred Horse Show of Socialist Countries, Hoppegarten, Berlin.

Small Electrical Appliances — A305

Leipzig Fall Fair: 15pf, Woman's fur coat and furrier's trademark.

Perf. 14x13½

1967, Aug. 8 Photo. Unwmk.

949	A305	10pf brt bl, blk & yel	18	15
950	A305	15pf yellow, brn & blk	20	15
		Set value		15

Max Reichpietsch and Warship — A306

Designs: 15pf, Albin Köbis and warship. 20pf, Sailors marching with red flag, and warship.

1967, Sept. 5 Litho. *Perf. 13½x13*
Bluish Paper

951 A306 10pf dk blue, gray & red 15 15
952 A306 15pf dk blue, gray & red *50 22*
953 A306 20pf dk blue, gray & red 15 15
Set value *30*

50th anniv. of the sailors' uprising at Kiel.

Monument at Kragujevac — A307

1967, Sept. 20 *Perf. 13x13½*

954 A307 25pf dk red, yel & blk 30 15

Issued in memory of the victims of the Nazis at Kragujevac, Yugoslavia, Oct. 21, 1941.

Worker and Symbols of Electrification — A308

Designs (Communist Emblem and): 5pf, Worker, and Communist newspaper masthead. 15pf, Russian War Memorial, Berlin-Treptow. 20pf, Russian and German soldiers, and coat of arms. 40pf, Lenin and cruiser Aurora.

1967, Oct. 6 Photo. *Perf. 14x14½*

955 A308 5pf multicolored 15 15
956 A308 10pf multicolored 15 15
957 A308 15pf multicolored 15 15
958 A308 20pf multicolored 15 15
959 A308 40pf multicolored *2.00 1.10*
a. Souvenir sheet of 2 1.00 80
Nos. 955-959 (5) *2.60*
Set value *1.25*

50th anniv. of the Russian October Revolution. No. 959a contains 2 imperf. stamps similar to Nos. 958-959 with simulated perforations. It commemorates the Red October Jubilee Stamp Exhibition, Karl-Marx-Stadt, Oct. 6-15. Sold for 85pf.

Martin Luther, by Lucas Cranach — A309

Young Inventors and Fair Emblem — A310

Designs: 25pf, Luther's House, Wittenberg, horiz. 40pf, Castle Church, Wittenberg.

Engraved and Photogravure
1967, Oct. 17 *Perf. 14*

960 A309 20pf black & rose lilac 15 15
961 A309 25pf black & blue 15 15
962 A309 40pf black & lemon *1.25 52*
Set value *60*

450th anniversary of the Reformation.

1967, Nov. 15 Unwmk. *Perf. 14*

Designs: No. 964, Boy's and girl's heads and emblem of the Free German Youth Organization. 25pf, Young workers receiving awards, and medal.

Size: 23x28½mm

963 A310 20pf multicolored 1.10 45
964 A310 20pf multicolored 1.10 45

Size: 51x28½mm

965 A310 25pf multicolored 1.10 45
a. Strip of 3, #963-965 3.50 1.40

Issued to publicize the 10th Masters of Tomorrow Fair, Leipzig, Nov. 15-26.

Goethe House, Weimar A311

Design: 25pf, Schiller House, Weimar.

1967, Nov. 27 Litho. *Perf. 13x12½*

966 A311 20pf gray, blk & brn 15 15
967 A311 25pf cit, dk grn & brn *75 24*
Set value *28*

Honoring German classical humanism.

Fairy Tale Type of 1966

Various Scenes from King Drosselbart.

1967, Nov. 27 *Perf. 13½x13*

968 A290 5pf multicolored 55 18
969 A290 10pf multicolored 55 18
970 A290 15pf multicolored 55 22
971 A290 20pf multicolored 55 22
972 A290 25pf multicolored 55 18
973 A290 30pf multicolored 55 18
Nos. 968-973 (6) 3.30 1.16

Nos. 968-973 printed together in sheets of 6.

Farmers, Stables and Silos — A312

Perf. 13x12½
1967, Dec. 6 Litho. Unwmk.

974 A312 10pf multicolored 15 15

15th anniversary of the first agricultural co-operatives.

Nutcracker and Figurines A313

Speed Skating A314

Design: 20pf, Candle holders: angel and miner.

1967, Dec. 6 Photo. *Perf. 13½x14*

975 A313 10pf green & multi *65 15*
976 A313 20pf red & multi 30 15
Set value *22*

Issued to publicize local handicrafts of the Erzgebirge in Saxony (Ore Mountains).

Perf. 13½x13
1968, Jan. 17 Litho. Unwmk.

Sport and Olympic Rings: 15pf, Slalom. 20pf, Ice hockey. 25pf, Figure skating, pair. 30pf, Long-distance skiing.

977 A314 5pf blue, dk bl & red 15 15
978 A314 15pf multicolored 15 15
979 A314 20pf grnsh bl, dk bl & red 15 15
980 A314 25pf multicolored 15 15
981 A314 30pf grnsh bl, vio bl & red *1.40 70*
Set value, #977-981, B146 *2.00 90*

10th Winter Olympic Games, Grenoble, France, Feb. 6-18.

Antenna, Cloud Formation and Map of Europe — A315

Designs: 10pf, Actinometer, Sun and Potsdam Meteorological Observatory. 25pf, Weather influence on farming (fields by day and night, produce).

1968, Jan. 24 *Perf. 13½x13*
Size: 23x28mm

982 A315 10pf brt mag, org & blk 1.25 20

Size: 50x28mm

983 A315 20pf multicolored 1.25 20

Size: 23x28mm

984 A315 25pf olive, blk & yel 1.25 20
a. Strip of 3, #982-984 4.00 85

75th anniversary of the Meteorological Observatory in Potsdam.

Venus 4 Interplanetary Station — A316

Design: 25pf, Earth satellites Kosmos 186 and 188 orbiting earth.

1968, Jan. 24 Photo. *Perf. 14*

985 A316 20pf multicolored 15 15
986 A316 25pf multicolored *40 24*
Set value *30*

Russian space explorations.

Fighters of The Underground A317

Designs: 20pf, "The Liberation." 25pf, "The Partisans."

1968, Feb. 21 Photo. *Perf. 14x13½*

987 A317 10pf black & multi 15 15
988 A317 20pf black & multi 15 15
989 A317 25pf black & multi *70 48*
Set value *60*

The designs are from the stained glass window triptych by Walter Womacka in the Sachsenhausen Memorial Museum.

Diesel Locomotive — A318

Design: 15pf, Refrigerator fishing ship.

1968, Feb. 29 *Perf. 14*

990 A318 10pf multicolored 25 15
991 A318 15pf multicolored 45 24
Set value 30

The 1968 Leipzig Spring Fair.

Woman from Hoyerswerda A319

Maxim Gorky and View of Gorky A320

Sorbian Regional Costumes: 20pf, Woman from Schleife. 40pf, Woman from Crostwitz. 50pf, Woman from Spreewald.

1968, Mar. 14

992 A319 10pf citron & multi 15 15
993 A319 20pf fawn & multi 15 15
994 A319 40pf blue grn & multi 15 15
995 A319 50pf green & multi *1.10 65*
Set value *80*

1968, Mar. 14 Engr.

Design: 25pf, Stormy petrel and toppling towers.

996 A320 20pf brown & rose car 15 15
997 A320 25pf brown & rose car *40 24*
Set value *30*

Maxim Gorky (1868-1936), Russian writer.

Ring-necked Pheasants A321

Designs: 15pf, Gray partridges. 20pf, Mallards. 25pf, Graylag geese. 30pf, Wood pigeons. 40pf, Hares.

1968, Mar. 26 Litho. *Perf. 13½x13*

998 A321 10pf gray & multi 15 15
999 A321 15pf gray & multi 15 15
1000 A321 20pf gray & multi 20 15
1001 A321 25pf gray & multi 24 15
1002 A321 30pf gray & multi 30 15
1003 A321 40pf gray & multi *2.50 65*
Nos. 998-1003 (6) *3.54*
Set value *85*

Karl Marx A322

Fritz Heckert A323

Designs: 10pf, Title page of the "Communist Manifesto." 25pf, Title page of "Das Kapital."

1968, Apr. 25 Photo. *Perf. 14*

1004 A322 10pf yel grn & blk 50 18
1005 A322 20pf mag, yel & blk 50 18
1006 A322 25pf lem, blk & red brn 50 18
a. Souvenir sheet of 3 95 80

Karl Marx (1818-83). Nos. 1004-1006 are printed se-tenant. No. 1006a contains 3 imperf. stamps similar to Nos. 1004-1006 with simulated perforations.

1968, Apr. 25

Design: 20pf, Young workers, new apartment buildings and Congress emblem.

1007 A323 10pf multicolored 15 15
1008 A323 20pf multicolored 24 15
Set value 15

7th Congress of the Free German Trade Unions.

"Right to Work" — A324

Designs: 10pf, "Right to Live," tree and globe. 25pf, "Right for Peace," dove and sun.

1968, May 8 Litho. *Perf. 13½x13*

1009 A324 5pf maroon & pink 20 15
1010 A324 10pf brn ol & ol bis 15 15
1011 A324 15pf Prus bl & lt bl *60 24*
Set value *40*

International Human Rights Year.

Angler A325

Designs: No. 1013, Rowing (woman). No. 1014, High jump (woman).

Unwmk.

1968, June 6 Photo. *Perf. 14*

1012 A325 20pf ol grn, sl bl & dk red 15 15
1013 A325 20pf Prus bl, dk bl & ol 15 15
1014 A325 20pf cop red, dp cl & bl *75 28*
Set value *36*

Issued to publicize: World angling championships, Gustrow (No. 1012); European women's rowing championships, Berlin (No. 1013); second European youth athletic competition, Leipzig (No. 1014).

Brandenburg Gate, Torch — A326

Youth Festival Emblem — A327

Design: 25pf, Stadium and torch.

1968, June 20 Litho. *Perf. 13½x13*

1015 A326 10pf multicolored 15 15
1016 A326 25pf multicolored *85 32*
Set value *35*

Issued to publicize the 2nd Children's and Youths' Spartakiad, Berlin.

1968, June 20

1017 A327 25pf multicolored *45 25*

Issued to publicize the 9th Youth Festival for Peace and Friendship, Sofia.
See No. B148.

Type of 1967 and

Moritzburg Castle, Dresden — A328

Buildings: 10pf, City Hall, Wernigerode. 25pf, City Hall, Greifswald. 30pf, Sanssouci Palace, Potsdam.

1968, June 25 Photo. *Perf. 13½x14*

1018 A291 10pf multicolored 15 15
1019 A328 20pf multicolored 15 15
1020 A291 25pf multicolored 15 15
1021 A328 30pf multicolored *70 42*
Set value *52*

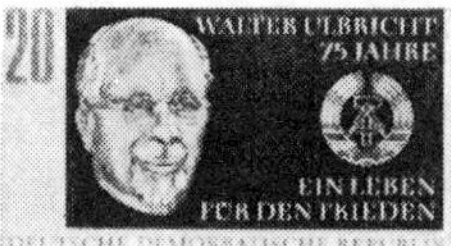

Walter Ulbricht and Arms of Republic A329

Photo. & Engr.

1968, June 27 *Perf. 14*

1022 A329 20pf org, dp car & blk 25 15

75th birthday of Walter Ulbricht, chairman of the Council of State, Communist party secretary and deputy prime minister.

Old Rostock and Arms A330

Design: 25pf, Historic and modern buildings, 1968, and arms of Rostock.

1968, July 9 Photo.

1023 A330 20pf multicolored 15 15
1024 A330 25pf multicolored *55 32*

750th anniv. of Rostock and to publicize the 11th Baltic Sea Week.

Karl Landsteiner, M.D. (1868-1943) — A331

"Trener" Stunt Plane — A332

Portraits: 15pf, Emanuel Lasker (1868-1941), chess champion and writer. 20pf, Hanns Eisler (1898-1962), composer. 25pf, Ignaz Semmelweis, M.D. (1818-1865). 40pf, Max von Pettenkofer (1818-1901), hygienist.

1968, July 17 Engr. *Perf. 14*

1025 A331 10pf gray green 15 15
1026 A331 15pf black 15 15
1027 A331 20pf brown 15 15
1028 A331 25pf gray blue 15 15
1029 A331 40pf rose lake *1.00 52*
Set value *1.35 70*

1968, Aug. 13 Litho. *Perf. 12½x13*

Design: 25pf, Two "Trener" stunt planes in parallel flight.

1030 A332 10pf multicolored 15 15
1031 A332 25pf blue & multi *42 25*
Set value *50 28*

Peasant Woman, by Wilhelm Leibl — A333

Paintings from Dresden Gallery: 10pf, "On the Beach," by Walter Womacka, horiz. 15pf, Mountain Farmers Mowing, by Albin Egger-Lienz, horiz. 40pf, The Artist's daughter, by Venturelli. 50pf, High School Girl, by Michaelis. 70pf, Girl with Guitar, by Castelli.

Perf. 14x13½, 13½x14

1968, Aug. 20 Photo.

1032 A333 10pf multicolored 15 15
1033 A333 15pf multicolored 15 15
1034 A333 20pf multicolored 15 15
1035 A333 40pf multicolored 15 15
1036 A333 50pf multicolored 18 15
1037 A333 70pf multicolored *1.50 1.10*
Set value *1.95 1.50*

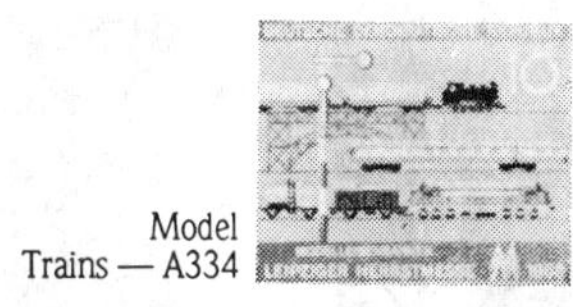

Model Trains — A334

1968, Aug. 29 *Perf. 14x13½*

1038 A334 10pf lt ultra, red & blk 15 15

The 1968 Leipzig Fall Fair.

Spremberg Dam A335

Designs: 10pf, Pöhl Dam, vert. 15pf, Ohra Dam, vert. 20pf, Rappbode Dam.

Perf. 13x12½, 12½x13

1968, Sept. 11 Litho.

1039 A335 5pf multicolored 15 15
1040 A335 10pf multicolored 15 15
1041 A335 15pf multicolored *40 22*
1042 A335 20pf multicolored 15 15
Set value *58 30*

Issued to publicize dams built since 1945.

Runner A336

Designs: 25pf, Woman gymnast, vert. 40pf, Water polo, vert. 70pf, Sculling.

1968, Sept. 18 Photo. *Perf. 14*

1043 A336 5pf multicolored 15 15
1044 A336 25pf multicolored 15 15
1045 A336 40pf multicolored 16 15
1046 A336 70pf blue & multi *1.65 70*
Set value *80*

19th Olympic Games, Mexico City, Oct. 12-27.
See Nos. B149-B150.

Monument, Fort Breendonk, Belgium — A337

Tiger Beetle — A338

1968, Oct. 10 Litho. *Perf. 13x13½*

1047 A337 25pf multicolored 25 15

Issued in memory of the victims of the Nazis at the Fort Breendonk Concentration Camp.

1968, Oct. 16 *Perf. 13½x13*

Insects: 15pf, Ground beetle (Cychrus caraboides). 20pf, Ladybug. 25pf, Ground beetle (Carabus arcensis hrbst.). 30pf, Hister beetle. 40pf, Checkered beetle.

1048 A338 10pf yellow & multi 15 15
1049 A338 15pf bluish lil & blk 15 15
1050 A338 20pf multicolored 15 15
1051 A338 25pf lt lilac & blk *2.25 90*
1052 A338 30pf lt green, blk & red 18 15
1053 A338 40pf pink & black 25 15
Nos. 1048-1053 (6) *3.13*
Set value *1.15*

Lenin and Letter to Spartacists — A339

Designs: 20pf, Workers, soldiers and sailors with masthead and slogans. 25pf, Karl Liebknecht and Rosa Luxemburg.

1968, Oct. 29 Litho. *Perf. 13x12½*

1054 A339 10pf lemon, red & blk 15 15
1055 A339 20pf lemon, red & blk 15 15
1056 A339 25pf lemon, red & blk *38 28*
Set value *52 36*

50th anniv. of the November Revolution in Germany.

Cattleya — A340

Orchids: 10pf, Paphiopedilum albertianum. 15pf, Cattleya fabia. 20pf, Cattleya aclandiae. 40pf, Sobralia macrantha. 50pf, Dendrobium alpha.

1968, Nov. 12 Photo. *Perf. 13*

Flowers in Natural Colors

1057 A340 5pf bluish lilac 15 15
1058 A340 10pf green 15 15
1059 A340 15pf bister 15 15
1060 A340 20pf green 15 15
1061 A340 40pf light brown 22 15
1062 A340 50pf gray *1.90 75*
Set value *1.00*

Fairy Tale Type of 1966

Various Scenes from Puss in Boots.

1968, Nov. 27 Litho. *Perf. 13½x13*

1063 A290 5pf multicolored 60 15
1064 A290 10pf multicolored 60 15
1065 A290 15pf multicolored 60 26
1066 A290 20pf multicolored 60 26
1067 A290 25pf multicolored 60 15
1068 A290 30pf multicolored 60 15
Nos. 1063-1068 (6) 3.60 1.12

#1063-1068 printed together in sheets of 6.

Young Pioneers — A341

Design: 15pf, Five Young Pioneers.

1968, Dec. 3 *Perf. 13x13½*

1069 A341 10pf blue & multi 15 15
1070 A341 15pf multicolored *24 16*
Set value *30 20*

20th anniv. of the founding of the Ernst Thalmann Young Pioneers' organization.

Buildings Type of 1967

Buildings: 5pf, City Hall, Tangermunde. 10pf, German State Opera, Berlin, horiz. 20pf, Wall Pavilion, Dresden. 25pf, Burgher's House, Luckau. 30pf, Rococo Palace, Dornburg, horiz. 40pf, "Stockfish" House, Erfurt.

1969, Jan. 1 Photo. *Perf. 14*

1071 A291 5pf multicolored 15 15
1072 A291 10pf multicolored 15 15
1073 A291 20pf multicolored 15 15
1074 A291 25pf multicolored *95 52*

1075	A291 30pf multicolored	15	15
1076	A291 40pf multicolored	16	15
	Nos. 1071-1076 (6)	*1.71*	
	Set value		*75*

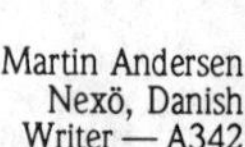

Martin Andersen Nexö, Danish Writer — A342

Portraits: 20pf, Otto Nagel (1894-1967), painter. 25pf, Alexander von Humboldt (1769-1859), naturalist, traveler, statesman. 40pf, Theodor Fontane (1819-1898), writer.

1969, Feb. 5 Engr. *Perf. 14*

1077	A342 10pf grnsh black	15	15
1078	A342 20pf deep brown	15	15
1079	A342 25pf violet blue	*52*	*32*
1080	A342 40pf brown	15	15
	Set value	*80*	*45*

Issued to honor famous men.

Be Attentive and Considerate! A343

Designs: 10pf, Watch ahead! (car, truck and traffic signal). 20pf, Watch railroad crossings! (train and car at crossing). 25pf, If in doubt don't pass! (cars and truck).

1969, Feb. 18 Litho. *Perf. 13x13½*

1081	A343 5pf lt blue & multi	15	15
1082	A343 10pf yellow & multi	15	15
1083	A343 20pf pink & multi	15	15
1084	A343 25pf multicolored	*60*	*25*
	Set value	*75*	*40*

Traffic safety campaign.

Combine A344

Leipzig Spring Fair: 15pf, Planeta-Variant offset printing press.

1969, Feb. 26 Photo. *Perf. 14*

1085	A344 10pf multicolored	15	15
1086	A344 15pf crimson, blk & bl	16	15
	Set value	22	15

Jorinde and Joringel — A345

Various Scenes from Fairy Tale "Jorinde and Joringel."

1969, Mar. 18 Litho. *Perf. 13½x13*

1087	A345 5pf black & multi	38	16
1088	A345 10pf black & multi	38	16
1089	A345 15pf black & multi	38	22
1090	A345 20pf black & multi	38	22
1091	A345 25pf black & multi	38	16
1092	A345 30pf black & multi	38	16
	Nos. 1087-1092 (6)	2.28	1.08

#1087-1092 printed together in sheets of 6. See Nos. 1176-1181.

Spring Snowflake A346

Red Cross, Crescent, Lion and Sun Emblems A347

Protected Plants: 10pf, Adonis. 15pf, Globeflowers. 20pf, Garden Turk's-cap. 25pf, Button snakeroot. 30pf, Dactylorchis latifolia.

1969, Apr. 4 Photo. *Perf. 14*

1093	A346 5pf green & multi	15	15
1094	A346 10pf green & multi	15	15
1095	A346 15pf green & multi	15	15
1096	A346 20pf green & multi	20	15
1097	A346 25pf green & multi	*1.90*	*75*
1098	A346 30pf green & multi	28	15
	Nos. 1093-1098 (6)	*2.83*	
	Set value		*1.00*

1969, Apr. 23 Litho. *Perf. 12½x13*

Design: 15pf, Large Red Cross, Red Crescent and Lion and Sun Emblems.

1099	A347 10pf gray, red & yel	15	15
1100	A347 15pf multicolored	*42*	*16*
	Set value		*20*

50th anniversary of the League of Red Cross Societies.

Conifer Nursery A348

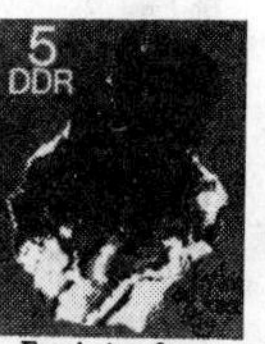

Erythrite from Schneeberg A349

Designs: 10pf, Forests as natural resources (timber and resin). 20pf, Forests as regulators of climate. 25pf, Forests as recreation areas (tents along lake).

1969, Apr. 23

1101	A348 5pf multicolored	15	15
1102	A348 10pf multicolored	15	15
1103	A348 20pf multicolored	15	15
1104	A348 25pf multicolored	*40*	*30*
	Set value	*60*	*40*

Prevention of forest fires.

1969, May 21 Photo. *Perf. 13½x14*

Minerals: 10pf, Fluorite from Halsbrücke. 15pf, Galena from Neudorf. 20pf, Smoky quartz from Lichtenberg. 25pf, Calcite from Niederrabenstein. 50pf, Silver from Freiberg.

1105	A349 5pf tan & multi	15	15
1106	A349 10pf multicolored	15	15
1107	A349 15pf gray & multi	15	15
1108	A349 20pf lemon & multi	15	15
1109	A349 25pf multicolored	*90*	*52*
1110	A349 50pf lt blue & multi	18	15
	Set value	*1.40*	*65*

Women and Symbols of Agriculture, Science and Industry A350

Design: 25pf, Woman's head and symbols.

1969, May 28 Engr. *Perf. 14*

1111	A350 20pf dk red & blue	15	15
1112	A350 25pf blue & dk red	*55*	*22*
	Set value		*28*

2nd Women's Congress of the German Democratic Republic.

Ulbricht Type of 1961-67

1969-71 Wmk. 313 Typo. *Perf. 14*

Size: 17x21mm

1112A	A189 35pf Prus blue ('71)	50	15

Engr. Unwmk.

Size: 24x28½mm

1113	A189 1m dull green	30	22
1114	A189 2m brown	60	45

See note below Nos. 590B-590C.

Coil Stamp

1970, Jan. 20 Typo. Wmk. 313

Size: 17x21mm

1114A	A189 1m olive	55	15

Emblem of DDR Philatelic Society A351

Worker Protecting Children A352

1969, June 4 Photo. Unwmk.

1115	A351 10pf red, gold & ultra	15	15

National Philatelic Exhibition "20 Years DDR," Magdeburg, Oct. 31-Nov. 9.

1969, June 4 Litho. *Perf. 13*

Designs: 25pf, Workers of various races. 20pf+5pf, Berlin buildings: Brandenburg Gate, Council of State, Soviet Cenotaph, Town Hall Tower, Television Tower, Teachers' Building and Hall.

Size: 23x28mm

1116	A352 10pf lemon & multi	1.65	48

Size: 50x28mm

1117	A352 20pf + 5pf multi	1.65	48

Size: 23x28mm

1118	A352 25pf lemon & multi	1.65	48
a.	Strip of 3, #1116-1118	5.00	1.50

Intl. Peace Meeting, Berlin. The surtax on No. 1117 was for the Peace Council of the German Democratic Republic.

Opening Ceremony before Battle of Leipzig Monument A353

Designs: 15pf, Parading athletes and stadium. 25pf, Running, hurdling, javelin and flag waving. 30pf, Presentation of colors before old Leipzig Town Hall.

Photo. & Engr.

1969, June 18 *Perf. 14*

1119	A353 5pf multi & black	15	15
1120	A353 15pf multi & black	15	15
1121	A353 25pf multi & black	*95*	*60*
1122	A353 30pf multi & black	15	15
	Nos. 1119-1122,B152-B153 (6)	*1.70*	
	Set value		*81*

5th German Gymnastic and Sports Festival, Leipzig.

Pierre de Coubertin, by Wieland Forster — A354

Knight — A355

Design: 25pf, Coubertin column, Memorial Grove, Olympia.

1969, June 6 *Perf. 14x13½*

1123	A354 10pf black & lt blue	15	15
1124	A354 25pf black & sal pink	*85*	*26*
	Set value		*30*

75th anniversary of the revival of the Olympic Games.

1969, July 29 Photo. *Perf. 14*

Designs: No. 1126, Bicycle wheel. No. 1127, Volleyball.

1125	A355 20pf red, gold & dk brn	18	15
1126	A355 20pf green, gold & red	18	15
1127	A355 20pf multicolored	18	15
	Set value		35

16th Students' Chess World Championships, Dresden (No. 1125); Indoor Bicycle World Championships, Erfurt (No. 1126); 2nd Volleyball World Cup (No. 1127).

Merchandise — A356

1969, Aug. 27 Litho. *Perf. 12½x13*

1128	A356 10pf multicolored	15	15

Leipzig Fall Fair, Aug. 31-Sept. 7, 1969.

Arms of Republic and View of Rostock A357

Design: 1m, DDR Arms, Town Hall, Marienkirche and Television Tower, Berlin, vert.

1969, Sept. 23 Photo. *Perf. 14*

1129	A357 10pf Rostock	15	15
1130	A357 10pf Neubrandenburg	15	15
1131	A357 10pf Potsdam	15	15
1132	A357 10pf Eisenhüttenstadt	15	15
1133	A357 10pf Hoyerswerda	15	15
1134	A357 10pf Magdeburg	15	15
1135	A357 10pf Halle-Neustadt	15	15
1136	A357 10pf Suhl	15	15
1137	A357 10pf Dresden	15	15
1138	A357 10pf Leipzig	15	15
1139	A357 10pf Karl-Marx-Stadt	15	15
1140	A357 10pf Berlin	15	15
	Set value	96	70

Souvenir Sheet

1141	A357 1m multicolored	1.25	75

#1129-1141, 1142-1145 for 20th anniv. of the German Democratic Republic.
No. 1141 contains one 29x52mm stamp.

Television Tower, Berlin — A358

People and Flags A359

Designs: 20pf, Sphere of Television Tower and TV test picture. No. 1144, Television Tower and TV test picture.

1969, Oct. 6 *Perf. 14*

1142	A358	10pf	multicolored	15	15
1143	A358	20pf	multicolored	20	15
			Set value	35	15

Souvenir Sheets

1144	A358	1m	dk blue & multi	1.40	1.00

Perf. 13x12¹/₂

1145	A359	1m	red & multi	1.10	80

No. 1144 contains one 21¹/₂x60mm stamp.

Cathedral, Otto von Guericke Monument and Hotel International, Magdeburg — A360

1969, Oct. 28 Litho. *Perf. 13x12¹/₂*

1146	A360	20pf	multicolored	15	15

Natl. Postage Stamp Exhibition in honor of the 20th anniv. of the German Democratic Republic, Magdeburg, Oct. 31-Nov. 9. See No. B154.

UFI Emblem — A361

1969, Oct. 28 *Perf. 13x13¹/₂*

1147	A361	10pf	multicolored	15	15
1148	A361	15pf	multicolored	*55*	*15*
			Set value		*18*

36th UFI Congress (Union des Foires Internationales), Leipzig, Oct. 28-30.

Memorial Monument, Copenhagen-Ryvangen A362

Rostock University Seal and Building A363

1969, Oct. 28 *Perf. 13*

1149	A362	25pf	multicolored	25	15

Issued in memory of the victims of the Nazis in Denmark.

1969, Nov. 12 *Perf. 12¹/₂x13*

Design: 15pf, Steam turbine, curve and Rostock University emblem.

1150	A363	10pf	brt blue & multi	15	15
1151	A363	15pf	violet & multi	*32*	*16*
			Set value	*40*	*20*

550th anniversary of Rostock University.

ILO Emblem A364

Mold for Christmas Cookies A365

1969, Nov. 12 *Perf. 13¹/₂x14*

1152	A364	20pf	dp green & silver	15	15
1153	A364	25pf	lil rose & silver	*45*	*26*
			Set value	*50*	*30*

50th anniv. of the ILO.

1969, Nov. 25 Litho. *Perf. 13¹/₂x13*

Design: 50pf, Negro couple, shaped spice cookie.

1154	A365	10pf	dull org, bl & red brn	2.00	60
1155	A365	50pf	lt blue & multi	3.00	90
a.			Pair, #1154-1155	5.00	1.50

Issued to publicize folk art of Lusatia. See No. B155.

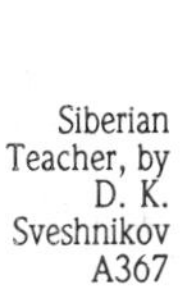

Antonov An-24 A366

Planes: 25pf, Ilyushin Il-18. 30pf, Tupolev Tu-134. 50pf, Mi-8 helicopter.

1969, Dec. 2 *Perf. 13x12¹/₂*

1156	A366	20pf	blue, red & blk	15	15
1157	A366	25pf	vio, red & blk	*1.00*	*80*
1158	A366	30pf	ultra, red & blk	15	15
1159	A366	50pf	olive, red & blk	16	15
			Set value		*1.00*

Siberian Teacher, by D. K. Sveshnikov A367

Russian Paintings from Dresden Gallery of Modern Masters: 10pf, Steelworker, by V. A. Serov. 20pf, Still Life, by E. A. Aslamasjan. 25pf, Hot Day (boats on river), by J. D. Romas. 40pf, Spring is Coming (young woman and snow-covered street), by L. V. Kabatchek. 50pf, Man on River Bank, by V. J. Makovskij.

1969, Dec. 10 Photo. *Perf. 13*

1160	A367	5pf	gray & multi	15	15
1161	A367	10pf	gray & multi	15	15
1162	A367	20pf	gray & multi	15	15
1163	A367	25pf	gray & multi	*1.25*	*75*
1164	A367	40pf	gray & multi	15	15
1165	A367	50pf	gray & multi	16	15
			Set value	*1.75*	*1.00*

Ernst Barlach (1870-1938), Sculptor and Writer — A368

Portraits: 10pf, Johann Gutenberg (1400-68). 15pf, Kurt Tucholsky (1890-1935), writer. 20pf, Ludwig van Beethoven. 25pf, Friedrich Hölderlin (1770-1843), poet. 40pf, Georg Wilhelm Friedrich Hegel (1770-1831), philosopher.

1970, Jan. 20 Engr. *Perf. 14*

1166	A368	5pf	blue violet	15	15
1167	A368	10pf	gray brown	15	15
1168	A368	15pf	violet blue	15	15
1169	A368	20pf	rose lilac	15	15
1170	A368	25pf	blue green	*1.00*	*55*
1171	A368	40pf	rose claret	24	15
			Nos. 1166-1171 (6)	*1.84*	
			Set value		*75*

Rabbit — A369

1970, Feb. 5 Photo. *Perf. 13¹/₂x14*

1172	A369	10pf	shown	15	15
1173	A369	20pf	Red fox	20	15
1174	A369	25pf	Mink	*2.25*	*75*
1175	A369	40pf	Hamster	30	15
			Set value		*85*

Issued to publicize the 525th International Fur Auctions, Leipzig.

Fairy Tale Type of 1969

Various Scenes from Fairy Tale "Little Brother and Sister."

1970, Feb. 17 Litho. *Perf. 13¹/₂x13*

1176	A345	5pf	lilac & multi	50	16
1177	A345	10pf	lilac & multi	50	16
1178	A345	15pf	lilac & multi	50	30
1179	A345	20pf	lilac & multi	50	30
1180	A345	25pf	lilac & multi	50	16
1181	A345	30pf	lilac & multi	50	16
			Nos. 1176-1181 (6)	3.00	1.24

#1176-1181 printed together in sheets of 6.

Telephone Coordinating Station — A370

Design: 15pf, High voltage testing transformer, vert.

Perf. 13x12¹/₂, 12¹/₂x13

1970, Feb. 24

1182	A370	10pf	multicolored	15	15
1183	A370	15pf	multicolored	24	15
			Set value		15

Leipzig Spring Fair, Mar. 1-10, 1970.

Horseman's Tombstone (700 A.D.) A371

Treasures from the Halle Museum: 20pf, Helmet (500 A.D.). 25pf, Bronze basin (1000 B.C.). 40pf, Clay drum (2500 B.C.).

1970, Mar. 3 Photo. *Perf. 13*

1184	A371	10pf	dp grn, gray & dk brn	15	15
1185	A371	20pf	multicolored	15	15
1186	A371	25pf	yellow & multi	*80*	*50*
1187	A371	40pf	multicolored	15	15
			Set value		*65*

Lenin and Clara Zetkin — A372

Designs: 10pf, Lenin, "ISKRA" (newspaper's name), composing frame and printing press. 25pf, Lenin and title page of German edition of "State and Revolution." 40pf, Lenin statue, Eisleben. 70pf, Lenin monument and Lenin Square, Berlin. 1m, Lenin portrait, vert.

Photogravure and Engraved

1970, Apr. 16 *Perf. 14*

1188	A372	10pf	multicolored	15	15
1189	A372	20pf	multicolored	15	15
1190	A372	25pf	multicolored	*1.00*	*65*
1191	A372	40pf	multicolored	15	15
1192	A372	70pf	multicolored	20	15
			Nos. 1188-1192 (5)	*1.65*	
			Set value		*90*

Souvenir Sheet

1193	A372	1m	dk carmine & multi	1.25	1.00

Sea Kale — A373

Red Army Soldier Raising Flag over Berlin Reichstag — A374

Protected Plants: 20pf, European pasqueflower. 25pf, Fringed gentian. 30pf, Galeate orchis. 40pf, Marsh tea. 70pf, Round-leaved wintergreen.

1970, Apr. 28 **Photo.**

1194	A373	10pf	multicolored	15	15
1195	A373	20pf	violet & multi	15	15
1196	A373	25pf	multicolored	*2.25*	*1.10*
1197	A373	30pf	multicolored	15	15
1198	A373	40pf	multicolored	15	15
1199	A373	70pf	multicolored	16	15
			Nos. 1194-1199 (6)	*3.01*	
			Set value		*1.30*

1970, May 5 Litho. *Perf. 13x13¹/₂*

Designs: 20pf, Spasski Tower, Kremlin; State Council Building, Berlin; coats of arms of USSR and German Democratic Republic, and newspaper clipping about friendship treaty with USSR. 25pf, Mutual Economic Aid Building, Moscow, and flags of member countries. 70pf, Memorial monument, Buchenwald, horiz.

1200	A374	10pf	multicolored	15	15
1201	A374	20pf	multicolored	15	15
1202	A374	25pf	multicolored	*55*	*38*

Set value 65 *45*

Souvenir Sheet

1203 A374 70pf multicolored 1.25 65

25th anniv. of liberation from Fascism.

Shortwave Antenna, RBI Emblem and Globe — A375

Grain and Globe — A376

Designs: 15pf, Berlin Radio Station, emblems of Radio Berlin International (RBI), Radio DDR and Radio Germany.

1970, May 13 Litho. ***Perf. 13½x13***

Size: 23x28mm

1204 A375 10pf ap grn, vio bl & bl 90 42

Size: 50x28mm

1205 A375 15pf vio bl, dp rose & ap grn 1.75 80

25th anniv. of the German Democratic Republic broadcasting system.

1970, May 19

Design: 25pf, House of Culture, Dresden, and grain.

1206 A376 20pf vio bl, yel & bl 2.00 85
1207 A376 25pf vio bl, yel & bl 2.00 85
a. Strip of 2, #1206-1207 + label 4.00 2.50

Issued to publicize the 5th World Cereal and Bread Congress, Dresden, May 24-29.

Fritz Heckert Medal A377

Design: 25pf, Globes and "FSM."

1970, June 9 ***Perf. 13x12½***

1208 A377 20pf red, yel & brn 15 15
1209 A377 25pf red, bl & yel *40 26*
Set value *45 30*

25th anniv. of the Free German Trade Union and of the World Organization of Trade Unions.

Traffic Policeman A378

Designs: 10pf, Young Pioneers congratulating police woman. 15pf, Volga police car. 20pf, Railroad policeman with radio-telephone. 25pf, River police in Volga wing-type boat.

1970, June 23 Litho. ***Perf. 13x12½***

1210 A378 5pf ocher & multi 15 15
1211 A378 10pf green & multi 15 15
1212 A378 15pf ultra & multi 15 15
1213 A378 20pf multicolored 15 15
1214 A378 25pf multicolored *65 48*
Set value *80 60*

25th anniversary of the People's Police.

Gods Amon, Shu and Tefnut — A379

Designs from Lion Temple in Musawwarat: 15pf, Head of King Arnekhamani. 20pf, Cow from cattle frieze. 25pf, Head of Prince Arka. 30pf, Head of God Arensnuphis, vert. 40pf, Elephants and prisoners of war. 50pf, Lion God Apedemak.

Perf. 13½x14, 14x13½

1970, June 23 Photo.

1215 A379 10pf multicolored 15 15
1216 A379 15pf multicolored 15 15
1217 A379 20pf multicolored 15 15
1218 A379 25pf multicolored *1.50 90*
1219 A379 30pf multicolored 15 15
1220 A379 40pf multicolored 15 15
1221 A379 50pf multicolored 15 15
Set value *1.95 1.10*

Issued to publicize the archaeological work in the Sudan by the Humboldt University, Berlin.

Arms and Flags of DDR and Poland — A380

1970, July 1 Litho. ***Perf. 13x12½***

1222 A380 20pf multicolored 15 15

20th anniversary of the Görlitz Agreement concerning the Oder-Neisse border.

Culture Association Emblem A381

Athlete on Pommel Horse A382

Design: 25pf, Johannes R. Becher medal.

1970, July 1 Photo. ***Perf. 14***

1223 A381 10pf ultra, sil & brn 4.50 2.00
1224 A381 25pf ultra, gold & brn 4.50 2.00
a. Strip of 2, #1223-1224 + label 9.00 4.50

25th anniv. of the German Kulturbund.

1970, July 1 ***Perf. 14x13½***

1225 A382 10pf blk, yel & brn red 15 15

Issued to publicize the 3rd Children's and Youths' Spartakiad. See No. B156.

Meeting of the American, British and Russian Delegations — A383

Designs: 10pf, Cecilienhof Castle. 20pf, "Potsdam Agreement" in German, English, French and Russian.

1970, July 28 Litho. ***Perf. 13***

Size: 23x28mm

1226 A383 10pf blk, cit & red 38 18
1227 A383 20pf blk, cit & red 38 18

Size: 77x28mm

1228 A383 25pf red & blk 38 18
a. Strip of 3, #1226-1228 1.20 60

25th anniv. of the Potsdam Agreement among the Allies concerning Germany at the end of WWII.

Men's Pocket and Wrist Watches — A384

1970, Aug. 25 Photo. ***Perf. 13½x14***

1229 A384 10pf ultra, blk & gold 20 15

Leipzig Fall Fair, 1970.

Theodor Neubauer and Magnus Poser A385

"Homeland" from Soviet Cenotaph, Berlin-Treptow — A386

Perf. 13x12½, 12½x13

1970, Sept. 2

1230 A385 20pf dk bl, car & pale grn 16 15
1231 A386 25pf dp car, pale bl 28 16
Set value 25

Issued in memory of fighters against "fascism and imperialistic wars."

Competition Map and Compass A387

Design: 25pf, Competition map and runner at 3 different stations.

1970, Sept. 15 Litho. ***Perf. 13x12½***

1232 A387 10pf yellow & multi 15 15
1233 A387 25pf yellow & multi *35 22*
Set value *40 25*

World Orienting Championships.

Mother and Child, by Käthe Kollwitz — A388

Works of Art: 10pf, Forest Worker Scharf's Birthday, by Otto Nagel. 20pf, Portrait of a Girl, by Otto Nagel. 25pf, No More War, (Woman with raised arm) by Käthe Kollwitz. 40pf, Head from Gustrow Memorial, by Ernst Barlach. 50pf, The Flutist, by Ernst Barlach.

Photo.; Litho. (25pf, 30pf)

1970, Sept. 22 ***Perf. 14x13½***

1234 A388 10pf multicolored 15 15
1235 A388 20pf multicolored 15 15
1236 A388 25pf pink & dk brn *1.65 1.00*
1237 A388 30pf sal & blk 15 15
1238 A388 40pf yel & blk 15 15
1239 A388 50pf yel & blk 15 15
Set value *1.90 1.20*

Issued in memory of the artists Otto Nagel, Käthe Kollwitz and Ernst Barlach.

The Little Trumpeter — A389

1970, Oct. 1 Photo.

1240 A389 10pf dp ultra, brn & org 25 15

2nd Natl. Youth Stamp Exhib., Karl-Marx-Stadt, Oct. 4-11. The design shows the memorial in Halle for Fritz Weineck, trumpeter for the Red War Veterans' Organization. See No. B160.

Emblem with Flags of East Block Nations — A390

1970, Oct. 1 Litho. ***Perf. 13x12½***

1241 A390 10pf carmine & multi 15 15
1242 A390 20pf multicolored 24 15
Set value 15

Issued to publicize the Brothers in Arms maneuvers of the East Bloc countries in the territory of the German Democratic Republic.

Musk Ox — A391

Berlin Zoo: 15pf, Shoebill. 20pf, Addax. 25pf, Malayan sun bear.

1970, Oct. 6 Photo. ***Perf. 14***

1243 A391 10pf blue & multi 16 15
1244 A391 15pf green & multi 22 15
1245 A391 20pf org & multi 28 15
1246 A391 25pf multicolored *4.25 65*
Set value *75*

UN Headquarters and Emblem A392

1970, Oct. 20 Photo. ***Perf. 13***

1247 A392 20pf ultra & multi 50 15

25th anniversary of the United Nations.

Friedrich Engels A393 — Epiphyllum A394

Designs: 20pf, Friedrich Engels and Karl Marx. 25pf, Engels and title page of his polemic against Dühring.

Photogravure and Engraved

1970, Nov. 24 *Perf. 14*
1248 A393 10pf ver, gray & blk 15 15
1249 A393 20pf ver, dk grn & blk 15 15
1250 A393 25pf ver, dk car rose & blk *55 32*
Set value *70 42*

Friedrich Engels (1820-1895), socialist, collaborator with Karl Marx.

1970, Dec. 2 Photo. *Perf. 14*

Flowering Cactus Plants: 10pf, Astrophytum myriostigma. 15pf, Echinocereus salm-dyckianus. 20pf, Selenicereus grandiflorus. 25pf, Hamatocactus setispinus. 30pf, Mamillaria boolii.

1251 A394 5pf multicolored 15 15
1252 A394 10pf dk blue & multi 15 15
1253 A394 15pf multicolored 15 15
1254 A394 20pf multicolored 15 15
1255 A394 25pf dk blue & multi *2.00 75*
1256 A394 30pf purple & multi 15 15
Nos. 1251-1256 (6) *2.75*
Set value *90*

Souvenir Sheet

Ludwig van Beethoven — A395

1970, Dec. 10 Engr. *Perf. 14*
1257 A395 1m gray 1.40 90

Bicentenary of the birth of Ludwig van Beethoven (1770-1827), composer.

Dancer's Mask, South Seas — A396

Works from Ethnological Museum, Leipzig: 20pf, Bronze head, Africa. 25pf, Tea pot, Asia. 40pf, Clay figure (jaguar), Mexico.

1971, Jan. 12 Photo. *Perf. 13*
1258 A396 10pf multicolored 15 15
1259 A396 20pf multicolored 15 15
1260 A396 25pf multicolored *75 65*
1261 A396 40pf multicolored 15 15
Set value *1.00 80*

Venus 5, Soft-landing on Moon — A397

Designs: No. 1263, Model of space station. No. 1264, Luna 16 and Luna 10 satellites. No. 1265, Group flight of Sojuz 6, 7 and 8. No. 1266, Proton 1, radiation measuring satellite. No. 1267, Communications satellite Molniya 1. No. 1268, Yuri A. Gagarin, first flight of Vostok 1. No. 1269, Alexei Leonov walking in space, Voskhod 2.

1971, Feb. 11 Litho. *Perf. 13x12½*
1262 A397 20pf dk blue & multi 40 20
1263 A397 20pf dk blue & multi 40 20
1264 A397 20pf dk blue & multi 40 35
1265 A397 20pf dk blue & multi 40 35
1266 A397 20pf dk blue & multi 40 35
1267 A397 20pf dk blue & multi 40 35
1268 A397 20pf dk blue & multi 40 20
1269 A397 20pf dk blue & multi 40 20
Nos. 1262-1269 (8) 3.20 2.20

Soviet space research. Nos. 1262-1269 printed together in sheets of eight.

Johannes R. Becher A398 — Karl Liebknecht A399

Portraits: 10pf, Heinrich Mann. 15pf, John Heartfield. 20pf, Willi Bredel. 25pf, Franz Mehring. 40pf, Rudolf Virchow. 50pf, Johannes Kepler.

1971 Engr. *Perf. 14*
1270 A398 5pf brown 15 15
1271 A398 10pf vio blue 15 15
1272 A398 15pf black 15 15
1273 A398 20pf rose lake 15 15
1274 A398 25pf green *95 48*
1274A A398 40pf pale purple 28 15
1275 A398 50pf dp black 15 15
Set value *1.50 60*

Honoring prominent Germans. See Nos. 1349-1353.

1971, Feb. 23 Photo.

Design: 25pf, Rosa Luxemburg.

1276 A399 20pf gold, mag & blk 28 25
1277 A399 25pf gold, mag & blk 28 25
a. Pair, #1276-1277 56 50

Karl Liebknecht (1871-1919) and Rosa Luxemburg (1871-1919), leaders of Spartacist Movement.

Soldier and Army Emblem — A400

1971, Mar. 1 *Perf. 13½x14*
1278 A400 20pf gray & multi 25 15

15th anniv. of the National People's Army.

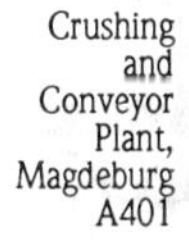

Crushing and Conveyor Plant, Magdeburg A401

Leipzig Spring Fair: 15pf, Dredger for low temperature work.

1971, Mar. 9 Litho. *Perf. 13x12½*
1279 A401 10pf green & multi 15 15
1280 A401 15pf multicolored 18 15
Set value 15

Proclamation of the Commune, Town Hall, Paris — A402

Designs: 20pf, Barricade at Place Blanche, defended by women. 25pf, Illustration by Theophile A. Steinlen for the International. 30pf, Title page for "The Civil War in France," by Karl Marx.

1971, Mar. 9 *Perf. 13*
1281 A402 10pf red, bis & blk 15 15
1282 A402 20pf red, bis & blk 15 15
1283 A402 25pf red, buff & blk *80 55*
1284 A402 30pf red, gray & blk 15 15
Set value *1.00 65*

Centenary of the Paris Commune.

Lunokhod 1 on Moon — A403

1971, Mar. 30 Photo. *Perf. 14*
1285 A403 20pf multicolored 45 15

Luna 17 unmanned, automated moon mission, Nov. 10-17, and the 24th Communist Party Congress of the Soviet Union.

Discobolus — A404

1971, Apr. 6 Litho. *Perf. 13½x13*
1286 A404 20pf dull bl, lt bl & buff 30 15

20th anniversary of the Olympic Committee of German Democratic Republic.

Köpenick Castle — A405 — Clasped Hands — A406

Berlin Buildings: 10pf, St. Mary's Church, vert. 20pf, Old Library. 25pf, Ermeler House, vert. 50pf, New Guard Memorial. 70pf, National Gallery of Art.

Perf. 13½x14, 14x13½

1971, Apr. 6 Photo.
1287 A405 10pf multicolored 15 15
1288 A405 15pf multicolored 15 15
1289 A405 20pf multicolored 15 15
1290 A405 25pf multicolored *2.50 1.10*
1291 A405 50pf multicolored 15 15
1292 A405 70pf multicolored 20 15
Set value *2.90 1.25*

Lithographed and Embossed

1971, Apr. 20 *Perf. 13x13½*
1293 A406 20pf red, blk & gold 25 15

25th anniversary of Socialist Unity Party of Germany (SED).

Dance Costume, Schleife — A407 — Self-Portrait, by Dürer — A408

Sorbian Dance Costumes from: 20pf, Hoyerswerda. 25pf, Cottbus. 40pf, Kamenz.

1971, May 4 Litho. *Perf. 13*
Size: 33x42mm
1294 A407 10pf multicolored 15 15
1295 A407 20pf green & multi 15 15
1296 A407 25pf blue & multi *1.00 80*
1297 A407 40pf multicolored 15 15
Set value *1.20 90*

1971, Nov. 23 *Perf. 13½x13*
Booklet Stamps
Size: 23x28mm
1297A A407 10pf multicolored 20 15
c. Booklet pane of 4 90
d. Booklet pane, 2 #1297A, 2 #1297B 1.75
1297B A407 20pf multicolored 50 32

1971, May 18 *Perf. 12½x13*

Art Works by Dürer: 40pf, Three Peasants. 70pf, Portrait of Philipp Melanchthon.

1298 A408 10pf multicolored 15 15
1299 A408 40pf brown & multi 15 15
1300 A408 70pf gray & multi *1.65 95*
Set value *1.00*

500th anniversary of the birth of Albrecht Dürer (1471-1528), painter and engraver.

Building Industry A409 — Congress Emblem A410

Designs: 10pf, Science and technology. No. 1303, Farming. 25pf, Civilian defense.

1971, June 9 Photo. *Perf. 14*
1301 A409 5pf cream, red & blk 15 15
1302 A409 10pf cream, red & blk 15 15
1303 A409 20pf cream, red, bl & blk 15 15
1304 A410 20pf gold, dp car & red 22 15
1305 A409 25pf cream, red & blk *60 38*
Set value *95 52*

8th Congress of Socialist Unity Party of Germany (SED).

Golden Fleece, 1730 — A411

Treasures from the Green Vault, Dresden: 5pf, Cherry stone with 180 heads carved on it, 1590. 15pf, Tankard, Nuremberg, 1530. 20pf, Moor with drums on horseback, 1720. 25pf, Decorated writing box, 1562. 30pf, St. George pendant, 1570.

1971, June 22 *Perf. 13*
1306 A411 5pf dp car & multi 15 15
1307 A411 10pf green & multi 15 15
1308 A411 15pf violet & multi 15 15

1309 A411 20pf multicolored 15 15
1310 A411 25pf multicolored *1.10* *70*
1311 A411 30pf multicolored 15 15
Set value *1.50* *85*

Prisoners, by Fritz Cremer — A412

Design: 25pf, Brutality in Buchenwald Concentration Camp, by Fritz Cremer.

1971, June 22 Litho. *Perf. 13*
1312 A412 20pf bister & blk 95 42
1313 A412 25pf lt blue & blk 95 42

International Federation of Resistance Fighters (FIR), 20th anniversary. Nos. 1312-1313 printed se-tenant with embossed label with commemorative inscription in between.

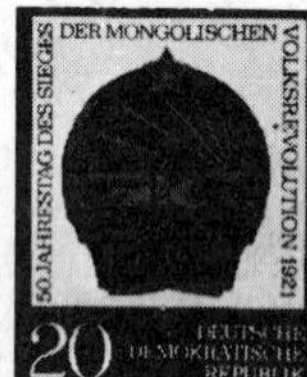

Coat of Arms of Mongolia — A413

1971, July 6 Litho. *Perf. 13*
1314 A413 20pf dk red, yel & blk 25 15

50th anniv. of the Mongolian People's Revolution.

Child's Head, UNICEF Emblem A414

1971, July 13 Photo.
1315 A414 20pf multicolored 25 15

25th anniv. of UNICEF.

Militiaman, Soldier and Brandenburg Gate — A415

Design: 35pf, Brandenburg Gate and new buildings in East Berlin.

1971, Aug. 12
1316 A415 20pf red & multi 75 15
1317 A415 35pf yel & multi 1.25 20
Set value 30

10 years of Berlin Wall.

Passenger Ship Iwan Franko — A416

Ships: 15pf, Freighter, type 17. 20pf, Freighter Rostock, type XD. 25pf, Fish processing ship "Junge Welt." 40pf, Container cargo ship. 50pf, Explorer ship Akademik Kurtschatow.

1971, Aug. 24 Engr.
1318 A416 10pf pale purple 15 15
1319 A416 15pf pale brn & ind 15 15
1320 A416 20pf gray green 15 15
1321 A416 25pf slate *1.65* *1.10*
1322 A416 40pf maroon 15 15
1323 A416 50pf grysh blue 15 15
Set value *2.00* *1.40*

Shipbuilding industry.

Butadiene Plant — A417

Leipzig Fall Fair: 25pf, Refinery.

1971, Sept. 2 Photo. *Perf. 13*
1324 A417 10pf olive, vio & mag 15 15
1325 A417 25pf blue, vio & ol 30 15
Set value 20

Raised Fists, Photo Montage by John Heartfield, 1937 — A418

1971, Sept. 23
1326 A418 35pf grnsh bl, blk & sil 30 15

Intl. Year Against Racial Discrimination.

Karl Marx Monument — A419

1971, Oct. 5 Photo. *Perf. 14x13½*
1327 A419 35pf vio brn, pink & buff 35 15

Unveiling of Karl Marx memorial at Karl-Marx-Stadt (Chemnitz).

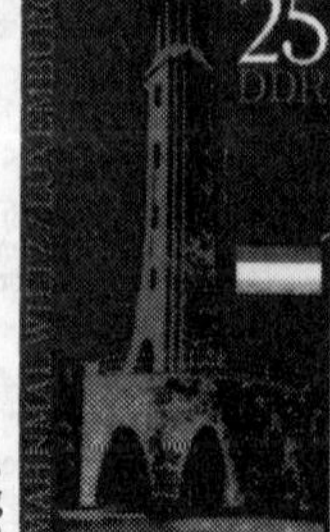

Wiltz Memorial, Flag of Luxembourg A420

1971, Oct. 5
1328 A420 25pf multicolored 20 15

Memorial for Nazi victims, Wiltz, Luxembourg.

Postal Milestones, Saxony, and Zürner's Surveyor Carriage A421

Photo. & Engr.
1971, Oct. 5 *Perf. 14*
1329 A421 25pf blue, olive & lil *50* *30*

Philatelists' Day 1971. See No. B162.

Darbuka, North Africa A422

Geodetic Apparatus A423

Musical Instruments: 15pf, Two morin chuur, Mongolia. 20pf, Violin, Germany. 25pf, Mandolin, Italy. 40pf, Bagpipes, Bohemia. 50pf, Kasso, Sudan.

1971, Oct. 26 Photo. *Perf. 14x13½*
1330 A422 10pf multicolored 15 15
1331 A422 15pf multicolored 15 15
1332 A422 20pf ocher & multi 15 15
1333 A422 25pf blue & multi 15 15
1334 A422 40pf gray & multi 15 15
1335 A422 50pf multicolored *1.50* *1.10*
Set value *1.75* *1.30*

Instruments from the Music Museum in Markneukirchen.

1971, Nov. 9 Photo. *Perf. 13½x14*

Designs: 20pf, Ergaval microscope. 25pf, Planetarium.

Size: 23½x28½mm
1336 A423 10pf blue, blk & red 65 40
1337 A423 20pf blue, blk & red 65 40

Size: 50½x28½mm
1338 A423 25pf blue, vio bl & yel 65 40
a. Strip of 3, #1336-1338 2.00 1.25

125th anniv. of the Carl Zeiss optical works in Jena.

Fairy Tale Type of 1966

Designs: Various Scenes from Fairy Tale "The Bremen Town Musicians."

1971, Nov. 23 Litho. *Perf. 13½x13*
1339 A290 5pf multicolored 42 16
1340 A290 10pf ocher & multi 42 16
1341 A290 15pf gray & multi 42 30
1342 A290 20pf ver & multi 42 30
1343 A290 25pf violet & multi 42 16
1344 A290 30pf yellow & multi 42 16
Nos. 1339-1344 (6) 2.52 1.24

#1339-1344 printed together in sheets of 6.

Olympic Rings and Sledding — A424

Olympic Rings and: 20pf, Long-distance skiing. 25pf, Biathlon. 70pf, Ski jump.

1971, Dec. 7 Photo. *Perf. 13½x14*
1345 A424 5pf green, car & blk 15 15
1346 A424 20pf car rose, vio & blk 15 15
1347 A424 25pf vio, car & blk *1.75* *1.25*
1348 A424 70pf vio bl, vio & blk 20 16
Set value, #1345-1348, B163-B164 *2.10* *1.55*

11th Winter Olympic Games, Sapporo, Japan, Feb. 3-13, 1972.

Portrait Type of 1971

Portraits: 10pf, Johannes Tralow (1882-1968), playwright. 20pf, Leonhard Frank (1882-1961), writer. 25pf, K. A. Kocor (1822-1904), composer. 35pf, Heinrich Schliemann (1822-1890), archaeologist. 50pf, F. Caroline Neuber (1697-1760), actress.

1972, Jan. 25 Engr. *Perf. 14*
1349 A398 10pf green 15 15
1350 A398 20pf rose claret 15 15
1351 A398 25pf dk blue 15 15
1352 A398 35pf brown 15 15
1353 A398 50pf rose violet *1.40* *1.25*
Set value *1.60* *1.40*

Honoring famous personalities.

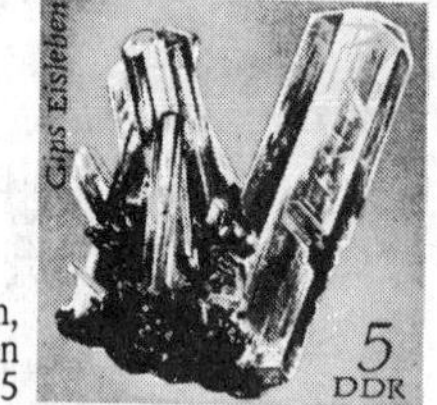

Gypsum, Eisleben A425

Minerals found in East Germany: 10pf, Zinnwaldite, Zinnwald. 20pf, Malachite, Ullersreuth. 25pf, Amethyst, Wiesenbad. 35pf, Halite, Merkers. 50pf, Proustite, Schneeberg.

1972, Feb. 22 Photo. *Perf. 13*
1354 A425 5pf grnsh bl & brn blk 15 15
1355 A425 10pf citron, brn & blk 15 15
1356 A425 20pf multicolored 15 15
1357 A425 25pf multicolored 15 15
1358 A425 35pf lt green, ind & blk 15 15
1359 A425 50pf gray & multi *1.75* *1.10*
Set value *2.00* *1.25*

Russian Pavilion and Fair Emblem A426

Design: 25pf, Flags of East Germany and Russia, and Fair emblem.

1972, Mar. 3 Photo. *Perf. 14*
1360 A426 10pf vio blue & multi 15 15
1361 A426 25pf claret & multi 22 15
Set value 30 16

50 years of Russian participation in the Leipzig Fair.

Miniature Sheets

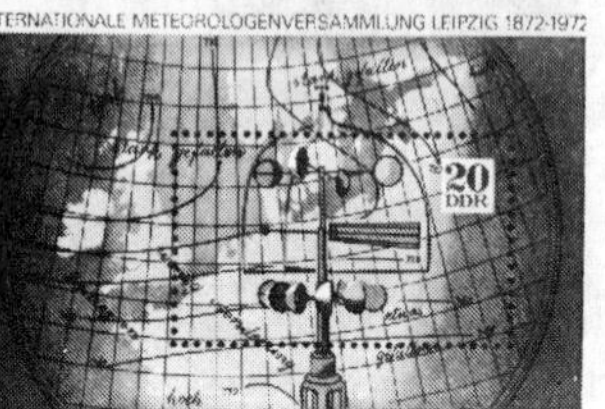

Anemometer, 1896, and Meteorological Chart, 1876 — A427

Designs: 35pf, Dipole and cloud photograph taken by satellite. 70pf, Meteor weather satellite and weather map.

1972, Mar. 23 Litho. *Perf. 13x12½*
1362 A427 20pf multicolored 80 45
1363 A427 35pf multicolored 80 45
1364 A427 70pf green & multi 80 45

Intl. Meteorologists' Cent. Meeting, Leipzig.

World Health Organization Emblem A428

1972, Apr. 4 Photo. *Perf. 13*
1365 A428 35pf lt bl, vio bl & sil 32 15

World Health Day.

Kamov Helicopter A429

Aircraft: 10pf, Agricultural spray plane. 35pf, Ilyushin jet. 1m, Jet and tail with Interflug emblem.

1972, Apr. 25 *Perf. 14*
1366 A429 5pf blue & multi 15 15
1367 A429 10pf multicolored 15 15
1368 A429 35pf blue grn & multi 15 15
1369 A429 1m multicolored *1.90 1.25*
Set value *2.00 1.30*

SPIELE DER XX.OLYMPIADE 1972
Wrestling and Olympic Rings — A430

Sport and Olympic Rings: 20pf, Pole vault. 35pf, Volleyball. 70pf, Women's gymnastics.

1972, May 16 Photo. *Perf. 13½x14*
1370 A430 5pf blue, gold & blk 15 15
1371 A430 20pf mag, gold & blk 15 15
1372 A430 35pf ol bis, gold & blk 15 15
1373 A430 70pf yel grn, gold & blk *1.65 1.50*
Set value, #1370-1373, B166-B167 *1.90 1.80*

20th Olympic Games, Munich, Aug. 26-Sept. 11.

DEUTSCH-SOWJETISCHE FREUNDSCHAFT

10 DDR
FREUNDSCHAFT DES HERZENS UND DER TAT
Flags of USSR and German Democratic Republic — A431

Design: 20pf, Flags, Leonid Brezhnev and Erich Honecker.

1972, May 24 Engr. & Photo.
1374 A431 10pf red, yel & blk 28 15
1375 A431 20pf red, yel & blk 42 15
Set value 24

Society for German-Soviet Friendship, 25th anniversary.

Workers — A432 DDR 10

Design: 35pf, Students.

1972, May 24 Litho. *Perf. 13*
1376 A432 10pf dull yel, org & mag 50 20
1377 A432 35pf dull yel & ultra 50 20
a. Strip of 2, #1376-1377 + label 1.00 50

8th Congress of Free German Trade Unions, Berlin.

Karneol Rose A433

1972, June 13 Photo. *Perf. 13*
Size: 36x36mm
1378 A433 5pf shown 15 15
1379 A433 10pf Berger's Erfurt Rose 15 15
1380 A433 15pf Charme *1.90 1.00*
1381 A433 20pf Izetka Spree-Athens 15 15
1382 A433 25pf Kopenick summer 15 15
1383 A433 35pf Prof. Knoll 15 15
Set value *2.25 1.25*

International Rose Exhibition.

Redrawn

1972, Aug. 22 *Perf. 13½x13*
Booklet Stamps
Size: 23x28mm
1383A A433 10pf multicolored 15 15
d. Booklet pane of 4 55
1383B A433 25pf multicolored 30 18
e. Booklet pane of 4 (2 #1383B, 2 #1383C) 3.00
1383C A433 35pf multicolored 30 18

Young Mother and Child, by Cranach — A434

Paintings by Lucas Cranach: 5pf, Young man. 35pf, Margarete Luther (Martin's mother). 70pf, Reclining nymph, horiz.

1972, July 4 *Perf. 14x13½, 13½x14*
1384 A434 5pf gold & multi 15 15
1385 A434 20pf gold & multi 15 15
1386 A434 35pf gold & multi 15 15
1387 A434 70pf gold & multi *2.25 1.40*

Lucas Cranach (1472-1553), painter.

Compass and Motorcyclist A435

Designs: 10pf, Parachute and light plane. 20pf, Target and military obstacle race. 25pf, Amateur radio transmitter, Morse key and tape. 35pf, Propeller and sailing ship.

1972, Aug. 8 Photo. *Perf. 14*
1388 A435 5pf multicolored 15 15
1389 A435 10pf multicolored 15 15
1390 A435 20pf multicolored 15 15
1391 A435 25pf multicolored *1.00 75*
1392 A435 35pf multicolored 15 15
Set value *1.30 85*

Society for Sport and Technology.

Young Worker Reading, by Jutta Damme — A436

1972, Aug. 22 Photo. *Perf. 13½x14*
1393 A436 50pf multicolored 50 20

International Book Year 1972.

Polylux Writing Projector — A437

George Dimitrov — A438

Design: 25pf, Pentacon-audiovision projector (horiz.).

Perf. 12½x13, 13x12½
1972, Aug. 29 Litho.
1394 A437 10pf crimson & blk 15 15
1395 A437 25pf brt green & blk 28 15
Set value 18

Leipzig Fall Fair, 1972.

1972, Sept. 19 *Perf. 13x13½*
1396 A438 20pf rose red & blk 25 15

George Dimitrov (1882-1949), Bulgarian Communist party leader.

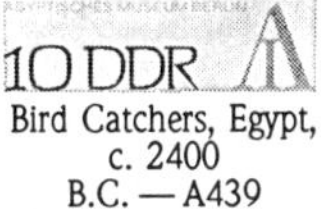

Bird Catchers, Egypt, c. 2400 B.C. — A439

Red Cross Trainees and Red Cross — A440

Design: 20pf, Tapestry with animal design, Anatolia, c. 1400 A.D.

1972, Sept. 19 Photo. *Perf. 14*
1397 A439 10pf multicolored 15 15
1398 A439 20pf multicolored 15 15
Set value 25 15

Interartes Philatelic Exhibition, Berlin, Oct. 4-Nov. 11. See Nos. B168-B169.

1972, Oct. 3 Litho. *Perf. 13*

Designs: 15pf, Red Cross rescue launch in the Baltic. 35pf, Red Cross with world map, ship, plane and vehicles.

Size: 23x28mm
1399 A440 10pf grnsh bl, dk bl & red 40 30
1400 A440 15pf grnsh bl, dk bl & red 40 30

Size: 50x28mm
1401 A440 35pf grnsh bl, dk bl & red 40 30
a. Strip of 3, Nos. 1399-1401 1.25 1.10

Red Cross at work in the DDR.

Arab Celestial Globe, 1279 A441

25 DDR
Anti-Fascists Monument A442

Designs: 10pf, Globe, by Joachim R. Praetorius, 1568. 15pf, Globe clock, by Reinhold and Roll, 1586. 20pf, Globe clock, by J. Bürgi, c. 1590. 25pf, Armillary sphere, by J. Moeller, 1687. 35pf, Heraldic celestial globe, 1690.

1972, Oct. 17 Photo. *Perf. 14x13½*
1402 A441 5pf gray & multi 15 15
1403 A441 10pf gray & multi 15 15
1404 A441 15pf gray & multi *2.50 95*
1405 A441 20pf gray & multi 15 15
1406 A441 25pf gray & multi 15 15
1407 A441 35pf gray & multi 25 15
Nos. 1402-1407 (6) *3.35*
Set value *1.10*

Celestial and terrestrial globes from the National Mathematical and Physics Collection, Dresden.

1972, Oct. 24 Litho. *Perf. 12½x13*
1408 A442 25pf multicolored 30 15

Monument for Polish soldiers and German anti-Fascists, unveiled in Berlin, May 14, 1972.

Young Workers Receiving Technical Education — A443

Design: 25pf, Workers with modern welding machine.

1972, Nov. 2 Photo. *Perf. 13½x14*
1409 A443 10pf blue & multi 25 22
1410 A443 25pf blue & multi 25 22
a. Strip of 2, #1409-1410 + label 55 50

15th Central Fair of Masters of Tomorrow.

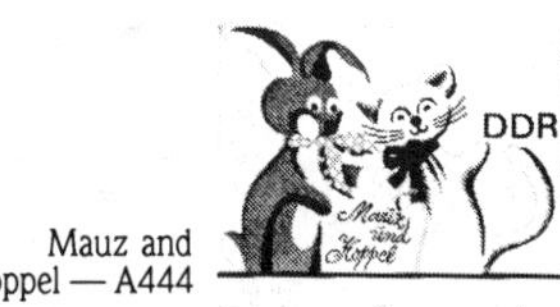

Mauz and Hoppel — A444

Designs: Children's television characters.

1972, Nov. 28 Litho. *Perf. 13½x13*
1411 A444 5pf shown 42 20
1412 A444 10pf Fox and magpie 42 20
1413 A444 15pf Mr. Owl 42 32
1414 A444 20pf Mrs. Hedgehog and Borstel 42 32
1415 A444 25pf Schnuffel and Pieps 42 20
1416 A444 35pf Paul from the Library 42 20
Nos. 1411-1416 (6) 2.52 1.44

#1411-1416 printed together in sheets of 6.

Grandmother, Children, Magic Mirror — A445

Scenes from Hans Christian Andersen's "Snow Queen": 10pf, Kay and Snow Queen. 15pf, Gerda in magic garden. 20pf, Gerda and crows at palace. 25pf, Gerda and reindeer in Lapland. 35pf, Gerda and Kay at Snow Queen's palace.

1972, Nov. 28 ***Perf. 13x13½***

1417	A445	5pf multicolored	45	20
1418	A445	10pf multicolored	45	32
1419	A445	15pf multicolored	45	20
1420	A445	20pf multicolored	45	20
1421	A445	25pf multicolored	45	32
1422	A445	35pf multicolored	45	20
		Nos. 1417-1422 (6)	2.70	1.44

#1417-1422 printed together in sheets of 6.

Souvenir Sheet

Heinrich Heine — A446

1972, Dec. 5 ***Perf. 12½x13***

1423	A446	1m brn ol, blk & red	2.00	1.10

150th anniversary of the birth of Heinrich Heine (1797-1856), poet.

Coat of Arms of USSR A447

Michelangelo da Caravaggio A448

1972, Dec. 5 **Photo.** ***Perf. 13½x14***

1424	A447	20pf red & multi	25	15

50th anniversary of the Soviet Union.

1973 **Litho.** ***Perf. 13½x13***

1425	A448	5pf brown	*1.10*	*80*
1426	A448	10pf dull green	15	15
1427	A448	20pf rose lilac	15	15
1428	A448	25pf blue	15	15
1429	A448	35pf brown red	15	15
1429A	A448	40pf rose claret	35	15
		Set value	*1.75*	*90*

Michelangelo da Caravaggio (1565(?)-1609), Italian painter (5pf). Friedrich Wolf (1888-1953), writer (10pf). Max Reger (1873-1916), composer (20pf). Max Reinhardt (1873-1943), Austrian theatrical director (25pf). Johannes Dieckmann (1893-1969), member and president of People's Chamber (35pf). Hermann Matern (1893-1971), vice-president of DDR (40pf).

Lenin Square, Berlin — A449

Coat of Arms of DDR — A449a

Designs: 5pf, Pelican, Berlin Zoo. 10pf, Neptune Fountain, City Hall Street. 15pf, Fisherman's Island, Berlin. 25pf, World clock, Alexander Square, Berlin. 30pf, Workers' Memorial, Halle. 35pf, Marx monument, Karl-Marx-Stadt. 40pf, Brandenburg Gate, Berlin. 50pf, New Guardhouse, Berlin. 60pf, Zwinger, Dresden. 70pf, Old Town Hall, Office Building, Leipzig. 80pf, Old and new buildings, Rostock-Warnemunde. 1m, Soviet War Memorial, Treptow.

1973-74 **Engr.** ***Perf. 14x13½***
Size: 29x23½mm

1430	A449	5pf blue green	15	15
1431	A449	10pf emerald	15	15
1432	A449	15pf rose lilac	16	15
1433	A449	20pf rose magenta	24	15
1434	A449	25pf grnsh blue	32	15
1435	A449	30pf orange	32	15
1436	A449	35pf grnsh blue	40	15
1437	A449	40pf dull violet	42	15
1438	A449	50pf blue, *bluish*	55	15
1439	A449	60pf lilac ('74)	70	15
1440	A449	70pf redsh brown	85	15
1441	A449	80pf vio blue ('74)	80	15
1442	A449	1m olive	1.10	15
1443	A449a	2m lake	2.25	15
1443A	A449a	3m rose lilac ('74)	3.00	60
		Nos. 1430-1443A (15)	11.41	
		Set value		1.25

See Nos. 1610-1617, 2071-2085.

Lebachia Speciosa (Oldest Conifer) A450

Fossils from Natural History Museum, Berlin: 15pf, Sphenopteris hollandica (carbon fern). 20pf, Pterodactylus kochi (flying reptile). 25pf, Botryopteris (permian fern). 35pf, Archaeopteryx lithographica (primitive reptile-like bird). 70pf, Odontopieura ovata (trilobite).

1973, Feb. 6 **Photo.** ***Perf. 13***

1444	A450	10pf multicolored	15	15
1445	A450	15pf ultra, gray & blk	15	15
1446	A450	20pf yellow & multi	15	15
1447	A450	25pf emerald, blk & brn	15	15
1448	A450	35pf ocher & multi	15	15
1449	A450	70pf ind, blk & yel	*2.00*	*1.75*
		Nos. 1444-1449 (6)	*2.75*	
		Set value		*2.00*

Bobsled Track, Oberhof — A451

1973, Feb. 13 **Litho.** ***Perf. 12½x13***

1450	A451	35pf dk bl, bl & org	35	20

15th Bobsledding Championships, Oberhof.

Combines A452

Leipzig Spring Fair: 25pf, Computerized threshing and silage producing machine.

1973, Mar. 6 **Litho.** ***Perf. 13x12½***

1451	A452	10pf olive & multi	15	15
1452	A452	25pf blue & multi	18	18
		Set value		23

Firecrests — A453

Songbirds: 10pf, White-winged crossbill. 15pf, Waxwing. 20pf, White-spotted and red-spotted bluethroats. 25pf, Goldfinch. 35pf, Golden oriole. 40pf, Gray wagtail. 50pf, Wall creeper.

1973, Mar. 20 **Photo.** ***Perf. 14x13½***

1453	A453	5pf multicolored	15	15
1454	A453	10pf multicolored	15	15
1455	A453	15pf multicolored	15	15
1456	A453	20pf multicolored	15	15
1457	A453	25pf multicolored	15	15
1458	A453	35pf multicolored	15	15
1459	A453	40pf multicolored	15	15
1460	A453	50pf ocher & multi	*3.00*	*2.25*
		Nos. 1453-1460 (8)	4.05	
		Set value		*2.75*

Copernicus and Title Page — A454

1973, Feb. 13 **Litho.** ***Perf. 13½x13***

1461	A454	70pf multicolored	65	32

500th anniversary of the birth of Nicolaus Copernicus (1473-1543), astronomer.

Electric Locomotive — A455

Railroad Cars Manufactured in DDR: 10pf, Refrigerator car. 20pf, Long-distance coach. 25pf, Multiple tank car with pneumatic filling device. 35pf, Two-story coach. 85pf, International coaches.

1973, May 22 **Litho.** ***Perf. 13x12½***

1462	A455	5pf gray & multi	15	15
1463	A455	10pf brt blue & multi	15	15
1464	A455	20pf dk blue & multi	15	15
1465	A455	25pf gray & multi	15	15
1466	A455	35pf multicolored	15	15
1467	A455	85pf green & multi	*2.25*	*1.75*
		Nos. 1462-1467 (6)	*3.00*	
		Set value		*2.00*

King Lear, Staged by Wolfgang Langhoff A456

Great Theatrical Productions: 25pf, Midsummer Marriage, staged by Walter Felsenstein. 35pf, Mother Courage, staged by Bertolt Brecht.

1973, May 29 **Photo.** ***Perf. 13***

1468	A456	10pf maroon, rose & yel	15	15
1469	A456	25pf vio bl, lt bl & rose	15	15
1470	A456	35pf dk gray, bis & bl	*85*	*70*
		Set value	*1.00*	*80*

Goethe and his Home in Weimar — A457

Fireworks, TV Tower, World Clock — A458

Designs (Portraits and Houses): 15pf, Christoph Martin Wieland. 20pf, Friedrich von Schiller. 25pf, Johann Gottfried Herder. 35pf, Lucas Cranach, the Elder. 50pf, Franz Liszt.

1973, June 26 **Litho.** ***Perf. 12½x13***

1471	A457	10pf blue & multi	15	15
1472	A457	15pf multicolored	15	15
1473	A457	20pf multicolored	15	15
1474	A457	25pf multicolored	15	15
1475	A457	35pf green & multi	16	15
1476	A457	50pf multicolored	*2.00*	*90*
		Nos. 1471-1476 (6)	*2.76*	
		Set value		*1.25*

Famous men and their homes in Weimar.

1973

Designs (Festival Emblem and): 15pf, Vietnamese and European men, book and girder. 20pf, Construction workers and valve. 30pf, Negro and European students, dam and retort. 35pf, Emblems of World Federation of Democratic Youth and International Students Union. 50pf, Brandenburg Gate.

1477	A458	5pf vio blue & multi	15	15
a.		Booklet pane of 4	70	
1478	A458	15pf olive & multi	15	15
1479	A458	20pf multicolored	15	15
a.		Booklet pane of 4	75	
1480	A458	30pf blue & multi	*1.25*	*90*
1481	A458	35pf green & multi	15	15
		Set value	*1.50*	*1.00*

Souvenir Sheet

1482	A458	50pf aqua & multi	80	60

10th Festival of Youths and Students, Berlin, July 1973.

Issued: #1477-1481, July 3; #1482, July 26.

Ulbricht Type of 1961-67

1973, Aug. 8 **Engr.** ***Perf. 14***
Size: 24x28½mm

1483	A189	20pf black	25	15

In memory of Walter Ulbricht (1893-1973), chairman of Council of State.

Pylon, Map of Electric Power System — A459

1973, Aug. 14 **Photo.** ***Perf. 14***

1484	A459	35pf mag, org & lt bl	40	20

10th anniversary of the united East European electric power system "Peace."

Sports Equipment A460

Design: 25pf, Sailboat, guitar, electric drill.

1973, Aug. 28 Photo. *Perf. 14*

1485 A460 10pf multicolored 15 15
1486 A460 25pf multicolored 28 15
Set value 20

Leipzig Fall Fair and EXPOVITA exhibition for leisure time equipment.

Militiaman and Emblem A461

Designs: 20pf, Militia guarding border at Brandenburg Gate. 50pf, Representatives of Red Veterans' League, International Brigade in Spain and Workers' Militia in DDR (vert.).

1973, Sept. 11 Litho. *Perf. 13x12½*

1487 A461 10pf multicolored 15 15
1488 A461 20pf tan, red & blk 26 15
Set value 35 20

Souvenir Sheet
Perf. 12½x13

1489 A461 50pf multicolored 75 48

20th anniversary of Workers' Militia of the German Democratic Republic.

Globe and Red Flag Emblem — A462

1973, Sept. 11 Photo. *Perf. 13½x14*

1490 A462 20pf gold & red 25 15

15th anniversary of the review "Problems of Peace and Socialism," published in Prague in 28 languages.

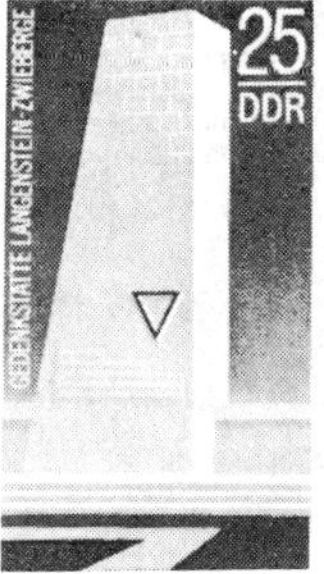

Memorial, Langenstein-Zwieberge — A463

1973, Sept. 18 *Perf. 14x13½*

1491 A463 25pf multicolored 35 15

In memory of the workers who perished in the subterranean munitions works at Langenstein-Zwieberge.

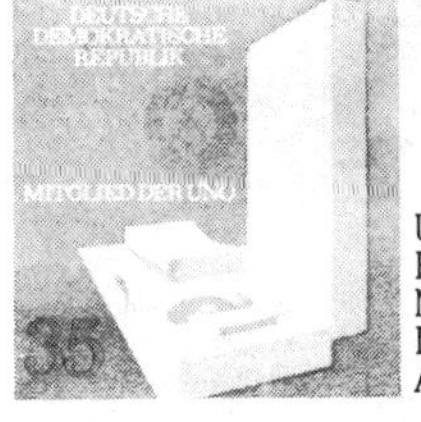

UN Headquarters, NY, UN and DDR Emblems A464

1973, Sept. 21 *Perf. 13*

1492 A464 35pf multicolored 50 15

Admission of the DDR to the UN.

Union Emblem A465

Rocket Launching A466

1973, Oct. 11 Photo. *Perf. 14x13½*

1493 A465 35pf silver & multi 35 15

8th Congress of the World Federation of Trade Unions, Varna, Bulgaria.

1973, Oct. 23 *Perf. 14*

Designs: 20pf, Emblem with map of Russia and hammer and sickle, horiz. 25pf, Oil refinery, Ryazan.

1494 A466 10pf violet bl & multi 15 15
1495 A466 20pf vio bl, red & sil 15 15
1496 A466 25pf multicolored 90 60
Set value 1.00 68

Soviet Science & Technology Days in DDR.

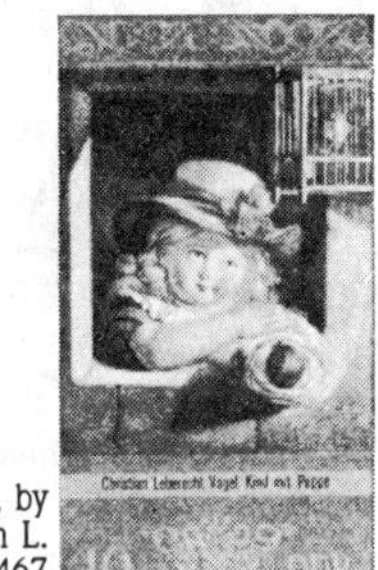
Child with Doll, by Christian L. Vogel — A467

Paintings: 15pf, Madonna with the Rose, by Parmigianino. 20pf, Woman with Plaited Blond Hair, by Rubens. 25pf, Lady in White, by Titian. 35pf, Archimedes, by Domenico Fetti. 70pf, Bouquet with Blue Iris, by Jan D. de Heem.

1973, Nov. 13 Photo. *Perf. 14*

1497 A467 10pf gold & multi 15 15
1498 A467 15pf gold & multi 15 15
1499 A467 20pf gold & multi 15 15
1500 A467 25pf gold & multi 16 15
1501 A467 35pf gold & multi 16 15
1502 A467 70pf gold & multi 2.50 1.75
Set value 2.90 2.10

Human Rights Flame — A468

1973, Nov. 20 *Perf. 13*

1503 A468 35pf dp rose, dk car & sil 40 15

25th anniv. of the Universal Declaration of Human Rights.

Boy Holding Pike — A469

Edwin Hoernle — A470

Designs: Various scenes from Russian Folktale "At the Bidding of the Pike."

1973, Dec. 4 Litho. *Perf. 13x13½*

1504 A469 5pf multicolored 50 30
1505 A469 10pf multicolored 50 48
1506 A469 15pf multicolored 50 30
1507 A469 20pf multicolored 50 30
1508 A469 25pf multicolored 50 48
1509 A469 35pf multicolored 50 30
a. Sheet of 6, #1504-1509 3.00
Nos. 1504-1509 (5) 3.00 2.16

1974 Litho. *Perf. 13½x13*

Portraits: No. 1511, Etkar Andre. No. 1512, Paul Merker. No. 1513, Hermann Duncker. No. 1514, Fritz Heckert. No. 1515, Otto Grotewohl. No. 1516, Wilhelm Florin. No. 1517, Georg Handke. No. 1518, Rudolf Breitscheid. No. 1519, Kurt Bürger. No. 1519A Carl Moltmann.

1510 A470 10pf gray green 15 15
1511 A470 10pf rose violet 15 15
1512 A470 10pf dark blue 15 15
1513 A470 10pf brown 15 15
1514 A470 10pf dull green 15 15
1515 A470 10pf red brown 15 15
1516 A470 10pf vio blue 15 15
1517 A470 10pf olive brown 15 15
1518 A470 10pf slate green 15 15
1519 A470 10pf dull violet 15 15
1519A A470 10pf brown 15 15
Set value 1.30 90

Leaders of German labor movement.
Issued: Nos. 1510-1517, Jan. 8; others July 9.

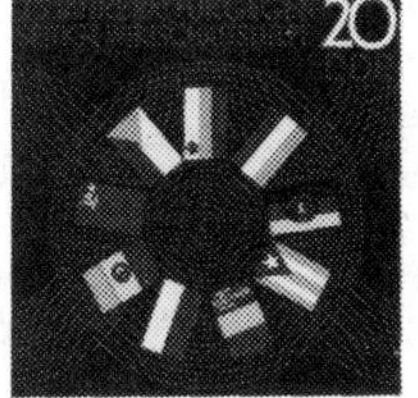

Flags of Comecon Members A471

1974, Jan. 22 Photo. *Perf. 13*

1520 A471 20pf red & multi 20 15

25th anniversary of the Council of Mutual Economic Assistance (Comecon).

Pablo Neruda and Chilean Flag — A472

1974, Jan. 22 *Perf. 14*

1521 A472 20pf multicolored 20 15

Pablo Neruda (Neftali Ricardo Reyes, 1904-1973), Chilean poet.

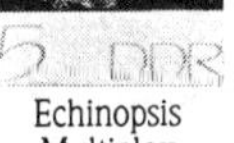
Echinopsis Multiplex A473

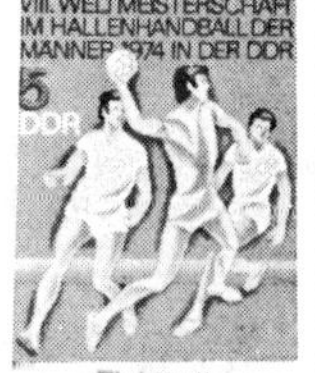

Fieldball A474

Various Flowering Cacti: 10pf, Lobivia haageana. 15pf, Parodia sanguiniflora. 20pf, Gymnocal. monvillei. 25pf, Neoporteria rapifera. 35pf, Notocactus concinnus.

1974, Feb. 12 Photo. *Perf. 14*

1522 A473 5pf multicolored 15 15
1523 A473 10pf tan & multi 15 15
1524 A473 15pf green & multi 2.00 1.40
1525 A473 20pf multicolored 15 15
1526 A473 25pf violet & multi 18 15
1527 A473 35pf multicolored 25 15
Nos. 1522-1527 (6) 2.88
Set value 1.70

1974, Feb. 26 Litho. *Perf. 13*

Design: Various fieldball scenes.

1528 A474 5pf green & multi *35 28*
1529 A474 10pf green & multi *35 28*
1530 A474 35pf green & multi *35 28*
a. Strip of 3, #1528-1530 *1.25 1.00*

8th World Fieldball Championships for Men.

Power Testing Station — A475

Rhodophyllus Sinuatus — A476

Leipzig Spring Fair: 25pf, Robotron EC 2040 data processer, horiz.

1974, Mar. 5 Photo. *Perf. 14*

1531 A475 10pf multicolored 15 15
1532 A475 25pf multicolored 28 15
Set value 20

1974, Mar. 19 Litho. *Perf. 13x13½*

European Poisonous Mushrooms: 10pf, Boletus satanas. 15pf, Amanita pantherina. 20pf, Amanita muscaria. 25pf, Gyromitra esculenta. 30pf, Inocybe patouillardii. 35pf, Amanita phalloides. 40pf, Clitocybe dealbata.

1533 A476 5pf buff & multi 15 15
1534 A476 10pf buff & multi 15 15
1535 A476 15pf buff & multi 15 15
1536 A476 20pf buff & multi 15 15
1537 A476 25pf buff & multi 18 15
1538 A476 30pf buff & multi 22 15
1539 A476 35pf buff & multi 22 15
1540 A476 40pf buff & multi *1.75 1.25*
Nos. 1533-1540 (8) *2.97*
Set value *1.75*

Gustav Robert Kirchhoff — A477

Portraits: 10pf, Immanuel Kant. 20pf, Ehm Welk. 25pf, Johann Gottfried Herder. 35pf, Lion Feuchtwanger.

1974, Mar. 26 Litho. *Perf. 13½x13*

1541 A477 5pf black & gray 15 15
1542 A477 10pf vio bl & dull bl 15 15
1543 A477 20pf maroon & rose 15 15
1544 A477 25pf slate grn & grn 16 15
1545 A477 35pf brn & lt brn *80 52*
Set value *1.20 75*

"Peace" A477a

1974, Apr. 16 *Perf. 13*

1548 A477a 35pf silver & multi 35 15

1st World Peace Congress, 25th anniv.

The lack of a value for a listed item does not necessarily indicate rarity.

Truck Driver and Arms of DDR A477b

1974, Apr. 30 Photo. *Perf. 13*

1549 A477b 10pf shown 15 15
1550 A477b 20pf Students 15 15
1551 A477b 25pf Woman worker 15 15
1552 A477b 35pf Family *95 80*
Set value 90

25th anniv. of the DDR.

Buk Lighthouse, 1878, and Map — A478

Lighthouses, Maps and Nautical Charts: 15pf, Warnemünde, 1898. 20pf, Darsser Ort, 1848. 35pf, Arkona, 1827 and 1902. 40pf, Greifswalder Oie, 1855.

1974, May 7 Litho. *Perf. 14*

1553 A478 10pf multicolored 15 15
1554 A478 15pf multicolored 15 15
1555 A478 20pf multicolored 15 15
1556 A478 35pf multicolored 15 15
1557 A478 40pf multicolored *1.10 90*
Set value 1.50 1.10

Hydrographic Service of German Democratic Republic. See Nos. 1645-1649.

The Ages of Man, by C. D. Friedrich — A479

C. D. Friedrich, Self-portrait — A480

Paintings by Friedrich: 10pf, Two Men Observing Moon. 25pf, The Heath near Dresden. 35pf, View of Elbe Valley.

1974, May 21 Photo. *Perf. 13½*

1558 A479 10pf gold & multi 15 15
1559 A479 20pf gold & multi 15 15
1560 A479 25pf gold & multi *1.50 1.00*
1561 A479 35pf gold & multi 28 15
Set value 1.10

Souvenir Sheet

Engr.

Perf. 14x13½

1562 A480 70pf sepia *1.25 1.25*

200th anniversary of the birth of Caspar David Friedrich (1774-1840), German Romantic painter.

Plauen Lace — A481

Designs: Various Plauen lace patterns.

1974, June 11 Litho. *Perf. 13*

1563 A481 10pf violet, lil & blk 15 15
1564 A481 20pf brown ol & blk 15 15
1565 A481 25pf bl, lt bl & blk *1.10 80*
1566 A481 35pf lil rose, rose & blk 24 15
Set value 1.00

Trotter — A482

Designs: 10pf, Thoroughbred hurdling, vert. 25pf, Haflinger breed horses. 35pf, British thoroughbred race horse.

Perf. 14x13½, 13½x14

1974, Aug. 13 Photo.

1570 A482 10pf olive & multi 15 15
1571 A482 20pf multicolored 20 15
1572 A482 25pf lt blue & multi *1.25 70*
1573 A482 35pf ocher & multi 32 15
Set value 95

International Horse Breeders' of Socialist Countries Congress, Berlin.

Crane Lifting Diesel Locomotive A483

Leipzig Fall Fair: 25pf, Sugar beet harvester, type KS6.

1974, Aug. 27 Litho. *Perf. 13x12½*

1574 A483 10pf multicolored 15 15
1575 A483 25pf orange & multi 28 15
Set value 20

Miniature China and Mirror Exhibits — A484

Designs: Scenes from 18th century Thuringia, Dolls' Village, Arnstadt Castle Museum.

1974, Sept. 10 Photo. *Perf. 14x13½*

1576 A484 5pf shown 15 15
1577 A484 10pf Harlequin barker at Fair 15 15
1578 A484 15pf Wine tasters 15 15
1579 A484 20pf Cooper and apprentice 15 15
1580 A484 25pf Bagpiper *1.50 1.40*
1581 A484 35pf Butcher and beggar, women 22 18
Nos. 1576-1581 (6) 2.32
Set value 1.75

Bound Guerrillas, Ardeatine Caves, Rome — A485

Design: No. 1583, Resistance Fighters, monument near Chateaubriant, France.

1974, Sept. 24 *Perf. 13½x14*

1582 A485 35pf green, blk & red 40 32
1583 A485 35pf blue, blk & red 40 32

International war memorials.

Souvenir Sheet

Family and Flag — A486

1974, Oct. 3 Photo. *Perf. 13*

1584 A486 1m multicolored 1.65 90

25th anniv. of the DDR.

Freighter and Paddle Steamer — A487

"In Praise of Dialectics" — A488

Cent. of the UPU: 20pf, Old steam locomotive and modern Diesel. 25pf, Bi-plane and jet. 35pf, Mail coach and truck.

1974, Oct. 9 *Perf. 14*

1585 A487 10pf green & multi 15 15
1586 A487 20pf multicolored 15 15
1587 A487 25pf blue & multi 18 15
1588 A487 35pf multicolored *1.00 65*
Set value 80

1974, Oct. 24 Litho. *Perf. 13x13½*

Designs: 10pf+5pf, "Praise to the Revolutionaries." 25pf, "Praise to the Party." Designs are from bas-reliefs by Rossdeutscher, Jastram and Wetzel, illustrating poems by Bertholt Brecht.

1589 A488 10pf + 5pf multi *30 22*
1590 A488 20pf multicolored *30 22*
1591 A488 25pf multicolored *30 22*
a. Strip of 3, #1589-1591 *1.00 80*

DDR '74 Natl. Stamp Exhib., Karl-Marx-Stadt.

Souvenir Sheet

Drawings by Young Pioneers — A489

1974, Nov. 26 Litho. *Perf. 14*

1592 A489 Sheet of 4 *1.40 1.10*
a. 20pf Sun shines on everybody *35 28*
b. 20pf My Friend Sascha *35 28*
c. 20pf Carsten, the Best Swimmer *35 28*
d. 20pf Me at the Blackboard *35 28*

Young Pioneers' drawings (7-10 years old).

Man Cutting Tree, and Bird — A490

Meditating Girl, by Wilhelm Lachnit — A491

Designs: Various scenes from Russian folktale "Twittering To and Fro."

1974, Dec. 3 *Perf. 13x13½*

1593 A490 10pf multicolored *60 30*
1594 A490 15pf multicolored *60 45*
1595 A490 20pf multicolored *60 30*
1596 A490 30pf multicolored *60 30*
1597 A490 35pf multicolored *60 45*
1598 A490 40pf multicolored *60 30*
a. Sheet of 6, #1593-1598 *3.60*
Nos. 1593-1598 (6) 3.60 2.10

Perf. 13½x14, 14x13½

1974, Dec. 10

Paintings: 10pf, Still Life, by Ronald Paris, horiz. 20pf, Fisherman's House, Vitte, by Harald Hakenbeck. 35pf, Girl in Red, by Rudolf Bergander, horiz. 70pf, The Artist's Parents, by Willi Sitte.

1599 A491 10pf multicolored 15 15
1600 A491 15pf multicolored 15 15
1601 A491 20pf multicolored 15 15
1602 A491 35pf multicolored 28 15
1603 A491 70pf multicolored *2.25 1.25*
Nos. 1599-1603 (5) 2.98
Set value 1.42

Paintings in Berlin Museums.

Banded Jasper — A492

Minerals from the collection of the Mining Academy in Freiberg: 15pf, Smoky quartz. 20pf, Topaz. 25pf, Amethyst. 35pf, Aquamarine. 70pf, Agate.

1974, Dec. 17 Photo. *Perf. 14*

1604 A492 10pf lt yellow & multi 15 15
1605 A492 15pf lt yellow & multi 15 15
1606 A492 20pf lt yellow & multi 15 15
1607 A492 25pf lt yellow & multi 20 15
1608 A492 35pf lt yellow & multi 25 15
1609 A492 70pf lt yellow & multi *2.00 1.40*
Nos. 1604-1609 (6) 2.90
Set value 1.80

Type of 1973

Coil Stamps

Designs: 5pf, Pelican. 10pf, Neptune Fountain. 20pf, Lenin Square. 25pf, World clock. 50pf, New Guard House. 1m, Soviet War Memorial.

1974-75 Photo. *Perf. 14*

Size: 21x17½mm

1610	A449	5pf blue grn ('74)	15	15
1611	A449	10pf emerald	15	15
1612	A449	20pf rose magenta	32	16
1613	A449	25pf green ('75)	30	15
1615	A449	50pf blue ('74)	70	32
1617	A449	1m olive ('74)	1.50	55
		Nos. 1610-1617 (6)	3.12	1.48

Black control number on back of every fifth stamp.

The 20pf was issued in sheets of 100 in 1975.

Martha Arendsee (1885-1953), Communist Politician — A493

1975, Jan. 14 Litho. *Perf. 13½x13*

1618 A493 10pf dull red 15 15

Souvenir Sheet

Peasants' War, Contemporary Woodcuts — A494

1975, Feb. 11 *Perf. 12½x13*

1619	A494	Sheet of 6 + label	*3.00*	*1.75*
a.		5pf Forced labor	*48*	*24*
b.		10pf Peasant paying tithe	*48*	*24*
c.		20pf Thomas Munzer	*48*	*24*
d.		25pf Armed peasants	*48*	*38*
e.		35pf Peasant, "Liberty" flag	*48*	*38*
f.		50pf Peasant on trial	*48*	*24*

Peasants' War, 450th anniversary.

Black Women — A495

Designs: 20pf, Caucasian women. 25pf, Indian woman and child.

1975, Feb. 25 Litho. *Perf. 13*

1620	A495	10pf red & multi	*26*	*20*
1621	A495	20pf red & multi	*26*	*20*
1622	A495	25pf red & multi	*26*	*20*
a.		Strip of 3, Nos. 1620-1622	*1.00*	*70*

International Women's Year 1975.

Microfilm Pentakta Camera A496

Leipzig Spring Fair: 25pf, Sket cement plant.

1975, Mar. 4 Photo. *Perf. 14*

1623	A496	10pf ultra & multi	15	15
1624	A496	25pf orange & multi	26	15
		Set value		15

Hans Otto (1900-33) Actor — A497

Portraits: 10pf, Thomas Mann (1875-1955), writer. 20pf, Albert Schweitzer (1875-1965), medical missionary. 25pf, Michelangelo (1475-1564), painter and sculptor. 35pf, André Marie Ampère (1775-1836), scientist.

1975, Mar. 18 Litho. *Perf. 13½x13*

1625	A497	5pf dk blue	15	15
1626	A497	10pf dk car rose	15	15
1627	A497	20pf dk green	15	15
1628	A497	25pf sepia	15	15
1629	A497	35pf vio blue	*1.25*	*70*
		Set value	*1.60*	*90*

Famous men, birth anniversaries.

Blue and Yellow Macaws, Magdeburg Zoo — A498

German Zoological Gardens: 10pf, Orangutan family, Dresden. 15pf, Siberian chamois, Halle. 20pf, Rhinoceros, Berlin. 25pf, Dwarf hippopotamus, Erfurt. 30pf, Baltic seal and pup, Rostock. 35pf, Siberian tiger, Leipzig. 50pf, Boehm's zebra, Cottbus. 20pf, 25pf, 30pf, 35pf are horiz.

Perf. 13½x13, 13x13½

1975, Mar. 25

1630	A498	5pf multicolored	15	15
1631	A498	10pf multicolored	15	15
1632	A498	15pf multicolored	15	15
1633	A498	20pf multicolored	15	15
1634	A498	25pf multicolored	16	15
1635	A498	30pf multicolored	18	15
1636	A498	35pf multicolored	26	15
1637	A498	50pf multicolored	*2.00*	*1.00*
		Nos. 1630-1637 (8)	*3.20*	
		Set value		*1.50*

Soldiers, Industry and Agriculture — A499

1975, May 6 Photo. *Perf. 13½x14*

1638 A499 20pf multicolored 40 15

20th anniv. of the signing of the Warsaw Treaty (Bulgaria, Czechoslovakia, DDR, Hungary, Poland, Romania, USSR).

Soviet War Memorial, Berlin-Treptow A500

Ribbons, Youth Organization Emblems of DDR and USSR A501

Designs (Arms of German Democratic Rep. and): 20pf, Buchenwald Memorial (detail). 25pf, Woman reconstruction worker. 35pf, Skyscraper and statue at Orenburg (economic integration). 50pf, Soldier raising Red Flag on Reichstag Building, Berlin.

1975, May 6 *Perf. 14x13½*

1639	A500	10pf red & multi	15	15
1640	A500	20pf red & multi	15	15
1641	A500	25pf red & multi	22	15
1642	A500	35pf red & multi	*95*	*65*
		Set value		*90*

Souvenir Sheet

Imperf

1643 A500 50pf red & multi 65 55

30th anniversary of liberation from fascism.

1975, May 13 *Perf. 14*

1644 A501 10pf multicolored 15 15

Third Friendship Festival of Russian and German Youths, Halle, 1975.

Lighthouse Type of 1974

Lighthouses, Maps and Nautical Charts: 5pf, Timmendorf, 1872. 10pf, Gellen, 1905. 20pf, Sassnitz, 1904. 25pf, Dornbush, 1888. 35pf, Peenemünde, 1954.

1975, May 13 Litho. *Perf. 14*

1645	A478	5pf multicolored	15	15
1646	A478	10pf multicolored	15	15
1647	A478	20pf multicolored	15	15
1648	A478	25pf multicolored	20	15
1649	A478	35pf multicolored	*1.10*	*75*
		Set value	*1.50*	*95*

Hydrographic Service of the DDR.

Wilhelm Liebknecht, August Bebel — A502

Designs: 20pf, Tivoli House and front page of Protocol of Gotha. 25pf, Karl Marx and Friedrich Engels.

1975, May 21 Photo.

1650	A502	10pf buff, brn & red	*32*	*16*
1651	A502	20pf salmon, brn & red	*32*	*16*
1652	A502	25pf buff, brn & red	*32*	*16*
a.		Strip of 3, #1650-1652	*1.00*	*50*

Centenary of the Congress of Gotha, the beginning of German Socialist Workers' Party.

Construction Workers, Union Emblem — A503

1975, June 10 Photo. *Perf. 14*

1653 A503 20pf red & multi 25 15

Free German Association of Trade Unions (FDGB), 30th anniversary.

"Socialist Scientific Cooperation" Mosaic by Walter Womacka — A504

1975, June 10 Litho. *Perf. 13*

1654 A504 20pf multicolored 25 15

Eisenhüttenstadt, first socialist city of DDR, 25th anniversary.

Automatic Clock by Paulus Schuster, 1585 — A505

Clocks, Dresden Museums: 10pf, Astronomical table clock, Augsburg, c. 1560. 15pf, Automatic clock, Hans Schlottheim, c. 1600. 20pf, Table clock, Johann Heinrich Köhler, c. 1720. 25pf, Table clock, Köhler, c. 1700. 35pf, Astronomical clock, Johannes Klein, 1738.

1975, June 24 Photo. *Perf. 14*

1655	A505	5pf multicolored	15	15
1656	A505	10pf ultra & multi	15	15
1657	A505	15pf red & multi	*1.65*	*1.25*
1658	A505	20pf olive & multi	15	15
1659	A505	25pf multicolored	15	15
1660	A505	35pf ocher & multi	22	15
		Nos. 1655-1660 (6)	*2.47*	
		Set value		*1.48*

Dictionary, Compiled by Jacob and Wilhelm Grimm — A506

Designs: 20pf, Karl-Schwarzschild Observatory, Tautenburg near Jena. 25pf, Electron microscope and chemical plant (scientific and practical cooperation). 35pf, Intercosmos 10 satellite.

1975, July 2 Litho. *Perf. 13½x13*

1661	A506	10pf plum, ol & blk	15	15
1662	A506	20pf vio bl & blk	15	15
1663	A506	25pf green, yel & blk	20	15
1664	A506	35pf blue & multi	*1.25*	*85*
		Set value		*1.00*

German Academy of Sciences, 275th anniv.

Torch Bearer — A507

Designs: 20pf, Hurdling. 25pf, Diving. 35pf, Gymnast on bar.

1975, July 15 ***Perf. 13½x13***

1665 A507 10pf sal rose & blk 15 15
1666 A507 20pf yellow & blk 15 15
1667 A507 25pf ultra & blk 18 15
1668 A507 35pf yel grn & blk *1.10* *75*
Set value *90*

5th Children and Youths Spartakiad.

Map of Europe A508

1975, July 30 **Photo.** ***Perf. 13***

1669 A508 20pf multicolored 22 15

European Security and Cooperation Conference, Helsinki, July 30-Aug. 1.

China Aster — A509

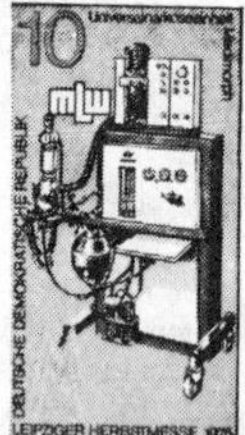

Medimorph Anesthesia Unit — A510

1975, Aug. 19 **Photo.** ***Perf. 13½x14***

1670 A509 5pf shown 15 15
1671 A509 10pf Geranium 15 15
1672 A509 20pf Transvaal daisies 15 15
1673 A509 25pf Carnation 15 15
1674 A509 35pf Chrysanthemum 20 15
1675 A509 70pf Pansies *2.50* *1.25*
Nos. 1670-1675 (6) *3.30*
Set value *1.60*

1975, Aug. 28 ***Perf. 14***

Leipzig Fall Fair: 25pf, Motorcycle, type MZ TS 250, horiz.

1676 A510 10pf multicolored 15 15
1677 A510 25pf yellow & multi 28 15
Set value 20

Children and Child Crossing Guard A511

Designs: 15pf, Traffic policewoman. 20pf, Policeman helping, motorist. 25pf, Motor vehicle inspection. 35pf, Volunteer instructor.

1975, Sept. 9 **Litho.** ***Perf. 13x12½***

1678 A511 10pf multicolored 15 15
1679 A511 15pf green & multi *1.40* *85*
1680 A511 20pf brown & multi 15 15
1681 A511 25pf violet & multi 15 15
1682 A511 35pf multicolored 22 15
Nos. 1678-1682 (5) *2.07*
Set value *1.10*

Traffic police serving and instructing the public.

Soyuz Take-off — A512

Designs: 20pf, Soyuz and Apollo in space. 70pf, Spacecraft after link-up (horiz.; 79x28mm.).

Perf. 14x13½, 13½x14

1975, Sept. 15 **Photo.**

1683 A512 10pf multicolored 15 15
1684 A512 20pf multicolored 15 15
1685 A512 70pf multicolored *1.40* *90*
Set value *1.00*

Apollo Soyuz space test project (Russo-American space cooperation), launching July 15; link-up, July 17.

Weimar, 1630, after Merian — A513

Designs: 20pf, Buchenwald Liberation Monument, vert. 35pf, Composite view of old and new buildings in Weimar.

1975, Sept. 23 **Litho.** ***Perf. 13½x13***

1686 A513 10pf green, gray & blk 15 15
1687 A513 20pf red & multi 15 15
1688 A513 35pf ultra & multi *60* *45*
Set value *75* *55*

Millennium of Weimar.

Monument, Vienna — A514

1975, Oct. 14 **Photo.** ***Perf. 14x13½***

1689 A514 35pf red & multi 30 15

Memorial for the victims of the struggle for a free Austria, 1934-1945.

Louis Braille and Dots — A515 WELT-BRAILLE-JAHR 1975

Designs: 35pf, Hands reading Braille. 50pf, Eyeball and protective glasses.

1975, Oct. 14

1690 A515 20pf gray & multi 15 15
1691 A515 35pf multicolored 25 15
1692 A515 50pf multicolored *1.50* *85*
Set value *1.00*

World Braille Year 1975. Sesquicentennial of the invention of Braille system of writing for the blind, by Louis Braille (1809-1852).

Post Office Bärenfels — A516

1975, Oct. 21 **Photo.** ***Perf. 14***

1693 A516 20pf multicolored 15 15

Philatelists' Day 1975. See No. B177.

Emperor Ordering Clothes — A517

Designs: Scenes from "The Emperor's New Clothes," by Hans Christian Andersen and Andersen portrait.

1975, Nov. 18 **Litho.** ***Perf. 14x13***

1694 A517 20pf ocher & multi *75* *38*
1695 A517 35pf ocher & multi *75* *75*
1696 A517 50pf ocher & multi *75* *38*
a. Sheet of 3, #1694-1696 *2.25* *1.65*

Tobogganing and Olympic Rings — A518

Designs (Olympic Rings and): 20pf, Speed-skating Rink, Berlin. 35pf, Figure-skating Hall, Karl-Marx Stadt. 70pf, Mass skiing at Schmiedefeld. 1m, Innsbruck and surrounding mountains.

1975, Dec. 2 **Photo.** ***Perf. 14***

1697 A518 5pf multicolored 15 15
1698 A518 20pf olive & multi 22 15
1699 A518 35pf multicolored 32 15
1700 A518 70pf multicolored *1.90* *1.00*
Nos. 1697-1700,B178-B179 (6) *2.96* *1.75*

Souvenir Sheet

1701 A518 1m ultra & multi *2.50* *1.10*

12th Winter Olympic Games, Innsbruck, Austria, Feb. 4-15, 1976. No. 1701 contains one stamp (size: 32x27mm).

Wilhelm Pieck A519

Ernst Thälmann (1886-1944) A520

1975, Dec. 30 **Litho.** ***Perf. 13½x13***

1702 A519 10pf lt ultra & blk 15 15

Pres. Pieck (1876-1960), birth cent.

1976, Jan. 13 ***Perf. 13½x13***

Labor Leaders: No. 1704, Georg Schumann (1886-1945). No. 1705, Wilhelm Koenen (1886-1963). No. 1706, John Schehr (1896-1934).

1703 A520 10pf rose & blk 15 15
1704 A520 10pf emerald & blk 15 15
1705 A520 10pf ocher & blk 15 15
1706 A520 10pf violet & blk 15 15
Set value 32 25

See Nos. 1852-1854.

Silbermann Organ, Rötha — A521

Silbermann Organs: 20pf, Freiberg. 35pf, Fraureuth. 50pf, Dresden.

1976, Jan. 27 **Photo.** ***Perf. 14***

1707 A521 10pf green & multi 15 15
1708 A521 20pf red & multi 15 15
1709 A521 35pf multicolored 18 15
1710 A521 50pf brown & multi *1.25* *95*

Organs built by Gottfried Silbermann (1683-1753).

Souvenir Sheet

Richard Sorge — A522

1976, Feb. 3 **Litho.** ***Imperf.***

1711 A522 1m multicolored *2.00* *1.00*

Dr. Richard Sorge (1895-1944), Soviet intelligence agent. No. 1711 contains one stamp with simulated perforations.

Military Flag, Sailor, Soldier, Aviator — A523

Design: 20pf, Military flag, ships, tanks, missile and planes.

1976, Feb. 24 **Litho.** ***Perf. 13½x14***

1712 A523 10pf multicolored 15 15
1713 A523 20pf multicolored 25 15
Set value 15

National People's Army, 20th anniversary.

Telephone A524

Apartment House, Leipzig A525

1976, Mar. 2 ***Perf. 13***

1714 A524 20pf light blue 25 15

Centenary of first telephone call by Alexander Graham Bell, March 10, 1876.

1976, Mar. 9 **Photo.** ***Perf. 14***

Design: 25pf, Ocean super trawler, horiz.

1715 A525 10pf green & multi 15 15
1716 A525 25pf vio blue, blk & grn 35 15
Set value 15

Leipzig Spring Fair.

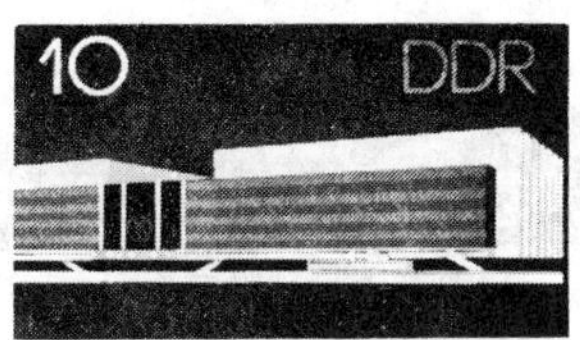

Palace of the Republic — A526

1976, Apr. 22 Photo. *Perf. 14*
1717 A526 10pf vio blue & multi 40 15

Inauguration of Palace of the Republic, Berlin. See No. 1721.

Post Office Radar Station — A527

Marx, Engels, Lenin and Party Flag — A528

1976, Apr. 27 Photo. *Perf. 13½x14*
1718 A527 20pf multicolored 25 15

Intersputnik 1976.

Perf. 14x13½, 13½x14
1976, May 11

Designs: 20pf, New factories and apartment houses, party flag, horiz. 1m, Palace of the Republic.

1719 A528 10pf dp mag, gold & red 18 15
1720 A528 20pf multicolored 35 15
Set value 15

Souvenir Sheet
Perf. 14
1721 A526 1m multicolored *1.50 1.10*

9th Congress of Unity Party (SED).

Peace Bicycle Race and Olympic Rings — A529

Designs: 20pf, Town and sport halls, Suhl. 25pf, Regatta course, Brandenburg. 70pf, 1500-meter race. 1m, Central Stadium, Leipzig.

1976, May 18 Photo. *Perf. 13½x14*
1722 A529 5pf green & multi 15 15
1723 A529 20pf blue & multi 15 15
1724 A529 25pf multicolored 20 15
1725 A529 70pf ultra & multi *2.50 1.40*
Nos. 1722-1725,B180-B181 (6) *3.47*
Set value *1.85*

Souvenir Sheet
Perf. 14
1726 A529 1m multicolored *1.75 1.25*

21st Olympic Games, Montreal, Canada, July 17-Aug. 1. No. 1726 contains one stamp (32x27mm).

Ribbons and Emblem A530

Design: 20pf, Young man and woman, industrial installations.

1976, May 25 *Perf. 14*
1727 A530 10pf blue & multi 15 15
1728 A530 20pf multicolored 25 15
Set value 15

10th Parliamentary Meeting of the Free German Youth Organization.

Himantoglossum Hircinum — A531

Dancer at Rest, by Walter Arnold — A532

Designs: European orchids.

1976, June 15 Litho. *Perf. 12½x13*
1729 A531 10pf *shown* 15 15
1730 A531 20pf *Dactylorhiza incarnata* 15 15
1731 A531 25pf *Anacamptis pyramidalis* 15 15
1732 A531 35pf *Dactylorhiza sambucina* 20 15
1733 A531 40pf *Orchis coriophora* 22 16
1734 A531 50pf *Cypripedium calceolus* *2.00 1.50*
Nos. 1729-1734 (6) *2.87 2.26*

1976, June 22 Photo. *Perf. 14*

Small Sculptures: 10pf, Shetland Pony, by Heinrich Drake, horiz. 25pf, "At the Beach," by Ludwig Engelhardt. 35pf, Hermann Duncker, by Walter Howard. 50pf, "The Conversation," by Gustav Weidanz.

1735 A532 10pf blk & bl grn 15 15
1736 A532 20pf ocher & blk 15 15
1737 A532 25pf ocher & blk 15 15
1738 A532 35pf yel grn & blk 15 15
1739 A532 50pf brick red & blk *2.00 1.00*
Nos. 1735-1739 (5) *2.60*
Set value *1.20*

Marx, Engels, Lenin, Red Flags, Berlin Buildings — A533

1976, June 29 Photo. *Perf. 14*
1740 A533 20pf blue, red & dk red 25 15

European Communist Workers' Congress, Berlin.

Coronation Coach, 1790 A534

Historic Coaches: 20pf, Open carriage, Russia, 1800. 25pf, Court landau, Saxony, 1840. 35pf, State carriage, Saxony, 1860. 40pf, Mail coach, 1850. 50pf, Town carriage, Saxony, 1889.

1976, July 27
1741 A534 10pf multicolored 15 15
1742 A534 20pf multicolored 15 15
1743 A534 25pf multicolored 15 15
1744 A534 35pf multicolored 18 15
1745 A534 40pf multicolored 20 15
1746 A534 50pf multicolored *2.50 1.90*
Nos. 1741-1746 (6) *3.33 2.65*

View of Gera A535

Design: 10pf+5pf, View of Gera, c. 1652.

1976, Aug. 5 Litho. *Perf. 13*
1747 A535 10pf + 5pf multi 22 20
1748 A535 20pf multicolored 22 20
a. Pair, #1747-1748 + label 50 45

4th German Youth Philatelic Exhib., Gera.

Boxer — A536

Dogs: 10pf, Airedale terrier. 20pf, German shepherd. 25pf, Collie. 35pf, Giant schnauzer. 70pf, Great Dane.

1976, Aug. 17 *Perf. 14*
1749 A536 5pf multicolored 15 15
1750 A536 10pf multicolored 15 15
1751 A536 20pf multicolored 15 15
1752 A536 25pf multicolored 15 15
1753 A536 35pf multicolored 25 15
1754 A536 70pf multicolored *2.75 1.25*
Nos. 1749-1754 (6) *3.60*
Set value *1.65*

Oil Distillery A537

Design: 25pf, German Library, Leipzig.

1976, Sept. 1 *Perf. 13x12½*
1755 A537 10pf multicolored 15 15
1756 A537 25pf multicolored 24 15
Set value 22

Leipzig Fall Fair.

Templin Lake Bridge — A538

Designs: 15pf, Overpass, Berlin-Adlergestell. 20pf, Elbe River Bridge, Rosslau. 25pf, Göltzschtal Viaduct. 35pf, Elbe River Bridge, Magdeburg. 50pf, Grosser Dreesch Overpass, Schwerin.

1976, Sept. 21 Photo. *Perf. 14*
1757 A538 10pf multicolored 15 15
1758 A538 15pf multicolored 15 15
1759 A538 20pf multicolored 15 15
1760 A538 25pf multicolored 16 15
1761 A538 35pf multicolored 20 15
1762 A538 50pf multicolored *2.50 1.75*
Nos. 1757-1762 (6) *3.31*
Set value *2.10*

Memorial Monument (detail), Budapest — A539

1976, Oct. 5 Photo. *Perf. 14*
1763 A539 35pf tan & multi 40 15

Memorial to World War II victims.

Brass Jug, c. 1500 — A540

Guppy — A541

Artistic Handicraft Works: 20pf, Faience vase with lid, c. 1710. 25pf, Porcelain centerpiece (woman carrying bowl), c. 1768. 35pf, Porter, gilded silver, c. 1700. 70pf, Art Nouveau glass vase, c. 1900.

1976, Oct. 19
1764 A540 10pf dk car & multi 15 15
1765 A540 20pf ultra & multi 15 15
1766 A540 25pf green & multi 15 15
1767 A540 35pf vio blue & multi 20 15
1768 A540 70pf red brn & multi *2.25 1.75*
Nos. 1764-1768 (5) *2.90*
Set value *2.00*

1976, Nov. 9 Litho. *Perf. 13½x13*

Designs: Various guppies.

1769 A541 10pf multicolored 15 15
1770 A541 15pf multicolored 15 15
1771 A541 20pf multicolored 15 15
1772 A541 25pf multicolored 15 15
1773 A541 35pf multicolored 18 15
1774 A541 70pf multicolored *2.50 1.50*
Nos. 1769-1774 (6) *3.28*
Set value *1.75*

Vessels, c. 3000 B.C. — A542

Designs: 20pf, Cult cart, c. 1300 B.C. 25pf, Roman gold coin, 270-273 A.D. 35pf, Gold pendant, 950 A.D. 70pf, Glass cup, 3rd century A.D.

1976, Nov. 23 Photo. *Perf. 13*
1775 A542 10pf multicolored 15 15
1776 A542 20pf multicolored 15 15
1777 A542 25pf multicolored 16 15
1778 A542 35pf multicolored 22 15
1779 A542 70pf multicolored *2.50 1.40*
Nos. 1775-1779 (5) *3.18*
Set value *1.60*

Archaeological finds in DDR.

"Air," by Rosalba Carriera — A543

Rumpelstiltskin and King — A544

Paintings, Dresden Museum: 15pf, Virgin and Child, by Murillo. 20pf, Woman Viola da Gamba Player, by Bernardo Strozzi. 25pf, Ariadne Forsaken, by Angelica Kauffmann. 35pf, Old Man with Black Cap, by Bartolomeo Nazzari. 70pf, Officer Reading a Letter, by Gerard Terborch.

1976, Dec. 14 Photo. *Perf. 13½x14*

1780 A543 10pf multicolored 15 15
1781 A543 15pf multicolored 15 15
1782 A543 20pf multicolored 15 15
1783 A543 25pf multicolored 15 15
1784 A543 35pf multicolored 22 15
1785 A543 70pf multicolored *2.75 1.75*
Nos. 1780-1785 (6) *3.57*
Set value *2.00*

1976, Dec. 14 Litho. *Perf. 13*

Designs: Scenes from fairy tale "Rumpelstiltskin."

1786 A544 5pf multicolored 45 20
1787 A544 10pf multicolored 45 28
1788 A544 15pf multicolored 45 20
1789 A544 20pf multicolored 45 20
1790 A544 25pf multicolored 45 28
1791 A544 30pf multicolored 45 20
a. Sheet of 6, #1786-1791 2.75
Nos. 1786-1791 (6) 2.70 1.36

Arnold Zweig and Quotation A545

Designs: 20pf, Otto von Guericke and Magdeburg hemispheres. 35pf, Albrecht D. Thaer, wheat, plow and sheep. 40pf, Gustav Hertz and diagram of separation of isotopes.

1977, Feb. 8 Litho. *Perf. 13x12½*

1792 A545 10pf rose & blk 15 15
1793 A545 20pf gray & blk 15 15
1794 A545 35pf lt green & blk 18 15
1795 A545 40pf blue & blk *95 75*
Set value *95*

Honoring Arnold Zweig (1887-1968), novelist; Otto von Guericke (1602-1686), physicist; Albrecht D. Thaer (1752-1828), agronomist and physician; Gustav Hertz (1887-1975), physicist.

Spring near Plaue — A546

Natural Monuments: 20pf, Small Organ, Johnsdorf. 25pf, Ivenacker Oaks, Reuterstadt. 35pf, Stone Rose, Saalburg. 50pf, Rauenscher Stein (boulder), Furstenwalde.

1977, Feb. 24 Litho. *Perf. 12½x13*

1796 A546 10pf multicolored 15 15
1797 A546 20pf multicolored 15 15
1798 A546 25pf multicolored 15 15
1799 A546 35pf multicolored 18 15
1800 A546 50pf multicolored *1.75 1.00*
Nos. 1796-1800 (5) *2.38*
Set value *1.25*

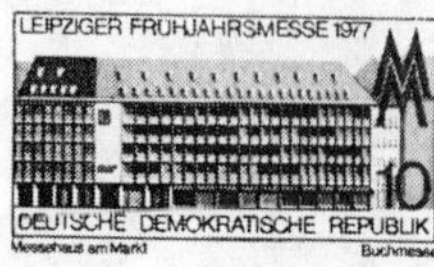

Fair Building, Book Fair — A547

Leipzig Spring Fair: 25pf, Wide aluminum roll casting machine, Nachterstedt factory.

1977, Mar. 8 Photo. *Perf. 14*

1801 A547 10pf multicolored 15 15
1802 A547 25pf multicolored 30 15
Set value 20

Costume Senftenberg A548

Start after Wheel Change A549

Sorbian Costumes from: 20pf, Bautzen. 25pf, Klitten. 35pf, Nochten. 70pf, Muskau.

1977, Mar. 22

1803 A548 10pf multicolored 15 15
1804 A548 20pf multicolored 15 15
1805 A548 25pf multicolored 15 15
1806 A548 35pf multicolored 22 15
1807 A548 70pf multicolored *2.25 1.40*
Nos. 1803-1807 (5) *2.92 2.00*

1977, Apr. 19 Photo. *Perf. 14*

Designs: 20pf, Sprint. 35pf, At finish line.

1808 A549 10pf multicolored *40 24*
1809 A549 20pf multicolored *40 24*
1810 A549 35pf multicolored *40 24*
a. Strip of 3, #1808-1810 *1.25 75*

30th International Peace Bicycling Race.

Carl Friedrich Gauss A550

1977, Apr. 19 Litho. *Perf. 13x12½*

1811 A550 20pf lt ultra & blk 25 15

Carl Friedrich Gauss (1777-1855), mathematician, 200th birth anniversary.

Flags and Handshake A551

1977, May 3 Photo. *Perf. 13*

1812 A551 20pf vio bl & multi 25 15

9th German Trade Union Congress, Berlin.

VKM Channel Converter, Filter and ITU Emblem — A552

1977, May 17 Litho. *Perf. 14*

1813 A552 20pf multicolored 25 15

International Telecommunications Day.

Pistol Shooting A553

Designs: 20pf, Deep-sea diver. 35pf, Radio controlled model boat.

1977, May 17 Photo.

1814 A553 10pf lt green & multi 15 15
1815 A553 20pf lt blue & multi 15 15
1816 A553 35pf salmon & multi *80 52*
Set value *60*

Organization for Physical and Technical Training.

Accordion, c. 1900 — A554

Designs: 20pf, Treble viola da gamba, 1747. 25pf, Oboe, 1785, Clarinet, 1830 and flute, 1817. 35pf, Concert zither, 1891. 70pf, Trumpet, 1860.

1977, June 14

1817 A554 10pf multicolored 15 15
1818 A554 20pf multicolored 15 15
1819 A554 25pf multicolored 15 15
1820 A554 35pf multicolored 16 15
1821 A554 70pf multicolored *2.25 1.90*
Nos. 1817-1821 (5) *2.86*
Set value *2.15*

Vogtland musical instruments from Markneukirchen Museum.

Mercury and Argus, by Rubens — A555

Rubens Paintings in Dresden Gallery: 10pf, Bath of Bathsheba, vert. 20pf, The Drunk Hercules, vert. 25pf, Diana Returning from the Hunt. 35pf, Old Woman with Brazier, vert. 50pf, Leda and the Swan.

1977, June 28 Photo. *Perf. 14*

1822 A555 10pf multicolored 15 15
1823 A555 15pf multicolored 15 15
1824 A555 20pf multicolored 15 15
1825 A555 25pf multicolored 15 15
1826 A555 35pf multicolored 18 15
1827 A555 50pf multicolored *2.25 1.25*
Nos. 1822-1827 (6) *3.03*
Set value *1.45*

Peter Paul Rubens (1577-1640), Flemish painter, 400th birth anniversary.

Souvenir Sheet

Wreath, Flags of USSR and DDR — A556

1977, June 28

1828 A556 50pf multicolored *1.00 70*

Society for German-Soviet Friendship, 30th anniversary.

Tractor with Plow — A557

Designs: 20pf, Fertilizer-spreader. 25pf, Potato digger and loader. 35pf, High-pressure harvester. 50pf, Rotating milking machine.

1977, July 12 Litho. *Perf. 13x12½*

1829 A557 10pf multicolored 15 15
1830 A557 20pf multicolored 15 15
1831 A557 25pf multicolored 15 15
1832 A557 35pf multicolored 18 15
1833 A557 50pf multicolored *2.25 1.40*
Nos. 1829-1833 (5) *2.88*
Set value *1.55*

Motorized modern agriculture.

High Jump A558

Designs: 20pf, Hurdles, girls. 35pf, Dancing. 40pf, Torch bearer and flags.

1977, July 19

1834 A558 5pf red & multi 15 15
1835 A558 20pf lt green & multi 15 15
1836 A558 35pf green & multi 18 15
1837 A558 40pf blue & multi *1.90 1.00*
Nos. 1834-1837,B183-B184 (6) *4.73*
Set value *1.30*

6th Gymnastics and Sports Festival and 6th Children's and Youth Spartacist Games.

"Bread for all" by Wolfram Schubert — A559

Konsument Department Store, Leipzig — A560

Design: 25pf, "When Communists Dream," by Walter Womacka (detail) and Sozphilex emblem.

1977, Aug. 16 Photo. *Perf. 14*

1838 A559 10pf multicolored 20 15
a. Souvenir sheet of 4 1.00 60
1839 A559 25pf multicolored 50 28
a. Souvenir sheet of 4 2.50 1.50

SOZPHILEX '77 Philatelic Exhibition, Berlin, Aug. 19-28. See No. B185.

1977, Aug. 30

Design: 25pf, Glasses and wooden plate.

1840 A560 10pf blue & multi 15 15
1841 A560 25pf multicolored 28 15
Set value 15

Leipzig Fall Fair.

Souvenir Sheet

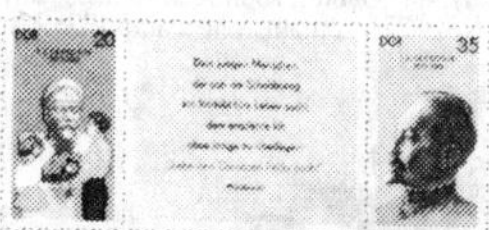

Dzerzhinski and Quotation from Mayakovsky — A561

1977, Sept. 6 Litho. *Perf. 12½x13*

1842 A561 Sheet of 2 *1.40 70*
a. 20pf multicolored *32 22*
b. 35pf multicolored *55 42*

Feliks E. Dzerzhinski (1877-1926), organizer and head of Russian Secret Police (Cheka), birth centenary.

Muldenthal Locomotive, 1861 — A562

Designs: 10pf, Trolley car, Dresden, 1896. 20pf, First successful German plane, 1909. 25pf, 3-wheel car "Phäno-mobile," 1924. 35pf, Passenger steamship on the Elbe, 1837.

1977, Sept. 13 Photo. *Perf. 14*

1843 A562 5pf green & multi 15 15
1844 A562 10pf green & multi 15 15
1845 A562 20pf green & multi 18 15
1846 A562 25pf green & multi 22 15
1847 A562 35pf green & multi *2.25 70*
Nos. 1843-1847 (5) *2.95*
Set value *85*

Transportation Museum, Dresden.

Cruiser "Aurora" A563

Designs: 25pf, Storming of the Winter Palace. 1m, Lenin, vert.

1977, Sept. 20

1848 A563 10pf multicolored *20 15*
1849 A563 25pf multicolored *50 25*

Souvenir Sheet

Perf. 12½x13

1850 A563 1m carmine & blk *2.00 1.10*

60th anniversary of the Russian Revolution.

Mother Russia and Obelisk — A564

1977, Sept. 20 Litho. *Perf. 14*

1851 A564 35pf multicolored 35 15

Soviet soldiers' memorial, Berlin-Schönholz.

Labor Leaders Type of 1976

Portraits: No. 1852, Ernst Meyer (1887-1930). No. 1853, August Fröhlich (1877-1966). No. 1854, Gerhart Eisler (1897-1968).

1977, Oct. 18 Litho. *Perf. 14*

1852 A520 10pf olive & brown 15 15
1853 A520 10pf rose & brown 15 15
1854 A520 10pf lt blue & blk brn 15 15
Set value 30 20

Souvenir Sheet

Heinrich von Kleist, by Peter Friedl, 1801 — A565

1977, Oct. 18

1855 A565 1m multicolored *2.50 1.40*

Heinrich von Kleist (1777-1811), poet and playwright, birth bicentenary.

Rocket A566

Design: 20pf, as 10pf, design reversed.

1977, Nov. 8 Photo. *Perf. 14*

1856 A566 10pf red, blk & sil *20 16*
1857 A566 20pf ultra, blk & gold *20 16*
a. Pair, #1856-1857 + label *52 42*

20th Central Young Craftsmen's Exhibition (Masters of Tomorrow).

Mouflons A567

Children Visiting Firehouse A568

Hunting in East Germany: 15pf, Red deer. 20pf, Retriever with pheasant, hunter. 25pf, Red fox, wild duck. 35pf, Tractor driver saving fawn. 70pf, Wild boars.

1977, Nov. 15

1858 A567 10pf multicolored 15 15
1859 A567 15pf multicolored *2.50 1.40*
1860 A567 20pf multicolored 15 15
1861 A567 25pf multicolored 15 15
1862 A567 35pf multicolored 16 15
1863 A567 70pf multicolored 32 18
Nos. 1858-1863 (6) *3.43*
Set value *1.75*

1977, Nov. 22 Litho. *Perf. 14*

Firemen's Activities: 10pf, Firemen racing with ladders, horiz. 25pf, Fire engines fighting forest and brush fires, horiz. 35pf, Artificial respiration. 50pf, Fireboat alongside freighter, horiz.

1864 A568 10pf multicolored 15 15
1865 A568 20pf multicolored 15 15
1866 A568 25pf multicolored 15 15
1867 A568 35pf multicolored 18 15
1868 A568 50pf multicolored *2.00 1.50*
Nos. 1864-1868 (5) *2.63 2.10*

Knight and King — A569

Designs: Various scenes from fairytale: "Six Men Around the World."

1977, Nov. 22 *Perf. 13x13½*

1869 A569 5pf black & multi 60 28
1870 A569 10pf black & multi 60 42
1871 A569 20pf black & multi 60 28
1872 A569 25pf black & multi 60 28
1873 A569 35pf black & multi 60 42
1874 A569 60pf black & multi 60 28
a. Sheet of 6, #1869-1874 3.60
Nos. 1869-1874 (6) 3.60 1.96

Hips and Dog Rose A570

Medicinal Plants: 15pf, Birch. 20pf, Chamomile. 25pf, Coltsfoot. 35pf, Linden. 50pf, Elder.

1978, Jan. 10 Photo. *Perf. 14*

1875 A570 10pf multicolored 15 15
1876 A570 15pf multicolored 15 15
1877 A570 20pf multicolored 15 15
1878 A570 25pf multicolored 20 15
1879 A570 35pf multicolored 25 15
1880 A570 50pf multicolored *2.75 1.50*
Nos. 1875-1880 (6) *3.65*
Set value *1.85*

Amilcar Cabral A571

Town Hall, Suhl-Heinrichs A572

1978, Jan. 17 Litho. *Perf. 14*

1881 A571 20pf multicolored 25 15

Amilcar Cabral (1924-1973), freedom movement leader from Guinea-Bissau.

1978, Jan. 24 Photo. *Perf. 14*

Half-timbered Buildings, 17th-18th Centuries: 20pf, Farmhouse, Niederoderwitz. 25pf, Farmhouse, Strassen. 35pf, Townhouse, Quedlinburg. 40pf, Townhouse, Eisenach.

1882 A572 10pf multicolored 15 15
1883 A572 20pf multicolored 15 15
1884 A572 25pf multicolored 15 15
1885 A572 35pf multicolored 20 15
1886 A572 40pf multicolored *2.25 1.40*
Nos. 1882-1886 (5) *2.90*
Set value *1.80*

Mail Truck, 1921 A573

Past and Present Mail Transport: 20pf, Mail truck, 1978. 25pf, Railroad mail car, 1896. 35pf, Railroad mail car, 1978.

1978, Feb. 9 Litho. *Perf. 13x12½*

1887 A573 10pf brown & multi 30 18
1888 A573 20pf brown & multi 50 28
1889 A573 25pf brown & multi 70 38
1890 A573 35pf brown & multi 95 52
a. Block of 4, #1887-1890 2.50 1.60

Earring, 11th Century — A574

Royal House, Leipzig — A575

Archaeological Artifacts: 20pf, Earring, 10th century. 25pf, Bronze sheath, 10th century. 35pf, Bronze horse, 12th century. 70pf, Arabian coin, 8th century.

1978, Feb. 21 Photo. *Perf. 14*

1891 A574 10pf multicolored 15 15
1892 A574 20pf multicolored 15 15
1893 A574 25pf multicolored 15 15
1894 A574 35pf multicolored 20 15
1895 A574 70pf multicolored *2.25 1.50*
Nos. 1891-1895 (5) *2.90*
Set value *1.80*

Treasures found on Slavic sites.

1978, Mar. 7

Leipzig Spring Fair: 25pf, Universal measuring instrument by Carl Zeiss.

1896 A575 10pf multicolored 15 15
1897 A575 25pf multicolored 28 15
Set value 20

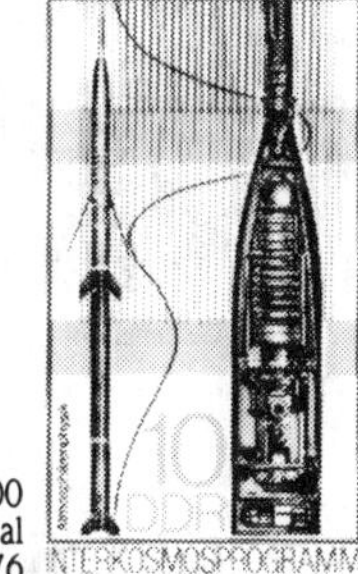

M-100 Meteorological Rocket — A576

Designs: 20pf, Intercosmos I satellite. 35pf, Meteor satellite with spectometric complex. 1m, MFK-6 multi-spectral camera over city.

1978, Mar. 21 Photo. *Perf. 14x13½*

1898 A576 10pf multicolored 15 15
1899 A576 20pf multicolored 15 15
1900 A576 35pf multicolored *90 75*
Set value *85*

Souvenir Sheet

1901 A576 1m multicolored *2.50 1.75*

Achievements in atmospheric and space research.

Samuel Heinicke, Leipzig, c. 1800 A577

Design: 25pf, Deaf child learning sign language.

1978, Apr. 4 Litho. *Perf. 13x12½*

1902 A577 20pf multicolored 15 15
1903 A577 25pf multicolored *52 44*
Set value *50*

National Institute for the Education of the Deaf, established by Samuel Heinicke, 200th anniversary.

Radio Tower, Dequede, TV Truck A578

Saxon Miner, 19th Century A579

Design: 20pf, TV equipment and tower, vert.

Perf. 13½x14, 14x13½

1978, Apr. 25

1904 A578 10pf multicolored 15 15
1905 A578 20pf multicolored *32 26*
Set value *38 30*

World Telecommunications Day.

1978, May 9 *Perf. 12½x13*

Dress Uniforms, 19th Century: 20pf, Foundry worker, Freiberg. 25pf, Mining Academy student. 35pf, Chief Inspector of Mines.

1906 A579	10pf silver & multi		15	15
1907 A579	20pf silver & multi		15	15
1908 A579	25pf silver & multi		15	15
1909 A579	35pf silver & multi		*1.40*	*80*
	Set value			*1.00*

Lion Cub — A580

Young Animals: 20pf, Leopard. 35pf, Tiger. 50pf, Snow leopard.

1978, May 23 **Photo.** *Perf. 14*

1910 A580	10pf multicolored	15	15
1911 A580	20pf multicolored	15	15
1912 A580	35pf multicolored	16	15
1913 A580	50pf multicolored	*1.25*	*95*
	Set value		*1.10*

Centenary of Leipzig Zoo.

Loading Container A581

Ceramic Bull A582

Designs: 20pf, Loading container on flatbed truck. 35pf, Container trains in terminal. 70pf, Loading container on ship.

1978, June 13 **Litho.** *Perf. 12½x13*

1914 A581	10pf multicolored	15	15
1915 A581	20pf multicolored	15	15
1916 A581	35pf multicolored	15	15
1917 A581	70pf multicolored	*2.25*	*1.10*
	Set value		*1.30*

Perf. 14x13½, 13½x14

1978, June 20 **Photo.**

Designs: 10pf, Woman's head, ceramic. 20pf, Gold armband, horiz. 25pf, Animal head, gold ring. 35pf, Seated family from signet ring. 40pf, Necklace, horiz.

1918 A582	5pf multicolored	15	15
1919 A582	10pf multicolored	15	15
1920 A582	20pf multicolored	15	15
1921 A582	25pf multicolored	15	15
1922 A582	35pf multicolored	16	15
1923 A582	40pf multicolored	*2.00*	*1.10*
	Nos. 1918-1923 (6)	*2.76*	
	Set value		*1.50*

African art from 1st and 2nd centuries in Berlin and Leipzig Egyptian museums.

Old and New Buildings, Cottbus A583

Design: 10pf + 5pf, View of Cottbus, 1730.

1978, July 18 **Litho.** *Perf. 13x12½*

1924 A583	10pf + 5pf multi	*30*	*28*
1925 A583	20pf multicolored	*30*	*28*
a.	Strip of 2, #1924-1925 + label	*75*	*70*

5th Youth Philatelic Exhibition, Cottbus.

Justus von Liebig, Wheat and Retort A584

Famous Germans: 10pf, Joseph Dietzgen (1828-1888) and title page. 15pf, Alfred Döblin (1878-1957) and title page. 20pf, Hans Loch (1898-1960) and signature, president of Liberal Democratic Party. 25pf, Dr. Theodor Brugsch (1878-1963), and blood circulation. 35pf, Friedrich Ludwig Jahn (1778-1852) and gymnast. 70pf, Dr. Albrecht von Graefe (1828-1870) and ophthalmological instruments.

1978, July 18

1926 A584	5pf yellow & blk	15	15
1927 A584	10pf gray & blk	15	15
1928 A584	15pf yel grn & blk	15	15
1929 A584	20pf ultra & blk	15	15
1930 A584	25pf salmon & blk	15	15
1931 A584	35pf lt green & blk	16	15
1932 A584	70pf ol & blk	*1.90*	*1.25*
	Nos. 1926-1932 (7)	*2.81*	
	Set value		*1.65*

Festival Emblem and New Buildings, Havana A585

Design: 35pf, Balloons and new buildings, Berlin.

1978, July 25 **Litho.** *Perf. 13x12½*

1933 A585	20pf multicolored	*45*	*40*
1934 A585	35pf multicolored	*45*	*40*
a.	Strip of 2, #1933-1934 + label	*1.00*	*90*

11th World Youth Festival, Havana, July 28-Aug. 5.

Foot Soldier, by Hans Schäufelein A586

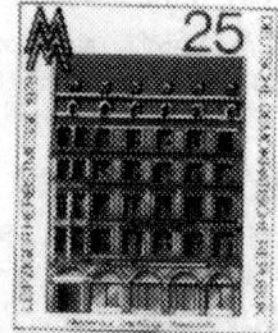

Fair Building "Three Kings," Leipzig A587

Etchings: 20pf, Woman Reading Letter, by Jean Antoine Watteau. 25pf, Seated Boy, by Gabriel Metsu. 30pf, Seated Young Man, by Cornelis Saftleven. 35pf, St. Anthony, by Matthias Grunewald. 50pf, Seated Man, by Abraham van Diepenbeeck.

1978, July 25 *Perf. 13½x14*

1935 A586	10pf lemon & black	60	32
1936 A586	20pf lemon & black	60	52
1937 A586	25pf lemon & black	60	32
1938 A586	30pf lemon & black	60	32
1939 A586	35pf lemon & black	60	52
1940 A586	50pf lemon & black	60	32
a.	Sheet of 6, #1935-1940	3.60	
	Nos. 1935-1940 (6)	3.60	2.32

Etchings from Berlin Museums.

1978, Aug. 29 **Photo.** *Perf. 14*

Leipzig Fall Fair: 10pf, IFA Multicar 25 truck, horiz.

1941 A587	10pf multicolored	15	15
1942 A587	25pf multicolored	28	15

Mauthausen Memorial — A588

1978, Sept. 5 *Perf. 13½x14*

1943 A588	35pf multicolored	40	15

International war memorials.

Soyuz, Intercosmos and German-Soviet Space Flight Emblems — A589

Soyuz, Camera and Space Complex A590

Designs: 10pf, Soyuz and Albert Einstein. 20pf, Sigmund Jähn, 1st German cosmonaut, vert. 35pf, Salyut-Soyuz space station, Otto Lilienthal and his glider. 1m, Cosmonauts Bykovsky and Jähn and space ships.

1978, Sept. **Photo.** *Perf. 14*

1944 A589	20pf multicolored	22	15

Litho.

Perf. 13½x13

1945 A590	5pf multicolored	15	15
1946 A590	10pf multicolored	15	15
1947 A590	20pf multicolored	15	15
1948 A590	35pf multicolored	*95*	*80*
	Set value	*1.35*	*95*

Souvenir Sheet

Perf. 13½x14

1949 A590	1m multicolored	2.50	1.65

1st German cosmonaut on Russian space mission. #1949 contains 1 54x33mm stamp.

Issue dates: #1944, Sept. 4; others, Sept. 21.

Marching Soldiers, Tractor, Factory A591

Design: 35pf, Russian and German Soldiers, Communist war veteran, 1933.

1978, Sept. 19 **Photo.** *Perf. 14*

1950 A591	20pf multicolored	45	35
1951 A591	35pf multicolored	45	35
a.	Strip of 2, #1950-1951 + label	95	75

Workers' military units, 25th anniv.

Seven-person Pyramid — A592

Designs: 10pf, Elephant on tricycle. 20pf, Dressage. 35pf, Polar bear kissing woman trainer.

1978, Sept. 26 **Photo.** *Perf. 14*

1952 A592	5pf black & multi	32	15
1953 A592	10pf black & multi	60	24
1954 A592	20pf black & multi	1.10	45
1955 A592	35pf black & multi	1.90	75
a.	Block of 4, #1952-1955	*4.50*	*1.75*

Circus in German Democratic Republic.

Construction of Gas Pipe Line, Drushba Section — A593

1978, Oct. 3 **Litho.** *Perf. 13x12½*

1956 A593	20pf multicolored	25	15

German youth helping to build gas pipe line from Orenburg to Russian border.

African Behind Barbed Wire — A594

Papilio Hahneli — A595

1978, Oct. 3 **Litho.** *Perf. 12½x13*

1957 A594	20pf multicolored	25	15

Anti-Apartheid Year.

1978, Oct. 24 **Photo.** *Perf. 14*

Designs: 20pf, Agama lehmanni (lizards). 25pf, Agate from Wiederau. 35pf, Paleobatrachus diluvianus. 40pf, Clock, 1720. 50pf, Table telescope, 1750.

1958 A595	10pf multicolored	15	15
1959 A595	20pf multicolored	15	15
1960 A595	25pf multicolored	15	15
1961 A595	35pf multicolored	15	15
1962 A595	40pf multicolored	20	15
1963 A595	50pf multicolored	*2.75*	*1.75*
	Nos. 1958-1963 (6)	*3.55*	
	Set value		*2.00*

Dresden Museum of Natural History, 250th anniversary.

Wheel Lock Gun, 1630 — A596

Hunting Guns: 10pf, Double-barreled gun, 1978. 20pf, Spring-cock gun, 1780. 25pf, Superimposed double-barreled gun, 1978. 35pf, Percussion gun, 1850. 70pf, Three-barreled gun, 1978.

1978, Nov. 21 **Photo.** *Perf. 14*

1964 A596	5pf silver & multi	15	15
1965 A596	10pf silver & multi	22	15
1966 A596	20pf silver & multi	42	25
1967 A596	25pf silver & multi	50	32
1968 A596	35pf silver & multi	65	45
1969 A596	70pf silver & multi	1.65	85
	Nos. 1964-1969 (6)	3.59	2.17

5pf, 20pf, 35pf printed se-tenant in sheets of 9, as are 10pf, 25pf, 70pf.

Rapunzel's Rescuer and Witch — A597

Designs: Scenes from fairy tale "Rapunzel."

1978, Nov. 21 Litho. *Perf. 13*

1970 A597 10pf multicolored 60 32
1971 A597 15pf multicolored 60 52
1972 A597 20pf multicolored 60 32
1973 A597 25pf multicolored 60 32
1974 A597 35pf multicolored 60 52
1975 A597 50pf multicolored 60 32
Nos. 1970-1975 (6) 3.60 2.32

Printed se-tenant in sheets of 6.

Chaffinches A598

Chabo Cock A599

Song Birds: 10pf, Nuthatch. 20pf, Robin. 25pf, Bullfinches. 35pf, Blue tit. 50pf, Red linnets.

1979, Jan. 9 Photo. *Perf. 13½x14*

1976 A598 5pf multicolored 15 15
1977 A598 10pf multicolored 15 15
1978 A598 20pf multicolored 15 15
1979 A598 25pf multicolored 15 15
1980 A598 35pf multicolored 20 15
1981 A598 50pf multicolored *1.90 1.65*
Nos. 1976-1981 (6) *2.70*
Set value *2.00*

1979, Jan. 23 *Perf. 14x13½*

German Cocks: 15pf, Kraienkopp. 20pf, Porcelain-colored bantam. 25pf, Saxonian. 35pf, Phoenix. 50pf, Striped Italian.

1982 A599 10pf multicolored 15 15
1983 A599 15pf multicolored 15 15
1984 A599 20pf multicolored 15 15
1985 A599 25pf multicolored 15 15
1986 A599 35pf multicolored 18 15
1987 A599 50pf multicolored *2.25 1.90*
Nos. 1982-1987 (6) *3.03*
Set value *2.25*

Telephone Operators, 1900 and 1979 — A600

Design: 35pf, Telegraph operators, 1880 and 1979.

1979, Feb. 6 Photo. *Perf. 13½x14*

1988 A600 20pf multicolored 15 15
1989 A600 35pf multicolored *60 52*
Set value *56*

Development of German postal telephone and telegraph service.

Souvenir Sheet

Albert Einstein (1879-1955), Theoretical Physicist A601

1979, Feb. 20 Litho. *Perf. 14*

1990 A601 1m multicolored *2.50 1.75*

Max Klinger House, Leipzig — A602

Leipzig Spring Fair: 25pf, Horizontal drilling and milling machine, horiz.

1979, Mar. 6 Litho. *Perf. 14*

1991 A602 10pf multicolored 15 15
1992 A602 25pf multicolored 28 18
Set value 25

Container Ship, Tug, World Map and IMCO Emblem — A603

1979, Mar. 20 Photo.

1993 A603 20pf multicolored 25 15

World Navigation Day.

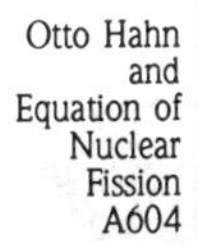

Otto Hahn and Equation of Nuclear Fission A604

Famous Germans: 10pf, Max von Laue (1879-1969) and diagram of sulphide zinc. 20pf, Arthur Scheunert (1879-1957), symbol of nutrition and health. 25pf, Friedrich August Kekulé (1829-1896), and benzene ring. 35pf, George Forster (1754-1794) and Capt. Cook's ship Resolution. 70pf, Gotthold Ephraim Lessing (1729-1781) and title page for Nathan the Wise.

1979, Mar. 20 Litho. *Perf. 13x12½*

1994 A604 5pf pale salmon & blk 15 15
1995 A604 10pf blue gray & blk 15 15
1996 A604 20pf lemon & blk 15 15
1997 A604 25pf lt green & blk 15 15
1998 A604 35pf lt blue & blk 16 15
1999 A604 70pf pink & blk *2.00 1.50*
Nos. 1994-1999 (6) *2.76*
Set value *1.80*

See Nos. 2088-2093.

Miniature Sheet

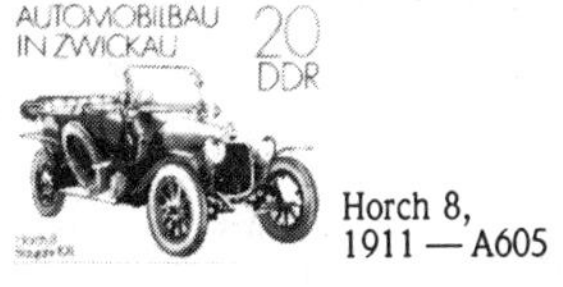

Horch 8, 1911 — A605

Design: 35pf, Trabant 601S de luxe, 1978.

1979, Apr. 3 Litho. *Perf. 14*

2000 Sheet of 2 + label *1.65 1.25*
a. A605 20pf multicolored *55 45*
b. A605 35pf multicolored *90 75*

Sachsenring automobile plant, Zwickau.

Self-Propelled Car — A606

DDR Railroad Cars: 10pf, Self-unloading freight car Us-y. 20pf, Diesel locomotive BR 110. 35pf, Laaes automobile carrier.

1979, Apr. 17 Litho. *Perf. 13*

2001 A606 5pf multicolored 15 15
2002 A606 10pf multicolored 15 15
2003 A606 20pf multicolored 15 15
2004 A606 35pf multicolored *1.25 1.10*
Set value *1.45 1.20*

Durga, 18th Century — A607

Indian Miniatures in Berlin Museums: 35pf, Mahavira, 15th-16th centuries. 50pf, Todi Ragini, 17th century. 70pf, Asavari Ragini, 17th century.

1979, May 8 Photo. *Perf. 14x13½*

2005 A607 20pf multicolored 15 15
2006 A607 35pf multicolored 25 15
2007 A607 50pf multicolored 35 20
2008 A607 70pf multicolored *2.50 1.90*

Youth Gathering A608

Design: 10pf+5pf, Torchlight parade of German youth, Oct. 7, 1949.

1979, May 22 Photo. *Perf. 14*

2009 A608 10pf + 5pf multi *35 28*
2010 A608 20pf multicolored *35 28*
a. Strip of 2, #2009-2010 + label *80 65*

National Youth Festival, Berlin.

Housing Project, Berlin A609

Design: 20pf, Berlin-Marzahn building site and surveyors.

1979, May 22 Litho. *Perf. 13x12½*

2011 A609 10pf multicolored 15 15
2012 A609 20pf multicolored *42 32*
Set value *35*

Berlin Project of Free German Youth.

Children Playing and Reading — A610

Exhibition Emblem — A611

Design: 20pf, Doctor with black and white children.

1979, May 22 Photo. *Perf. 14*

2013 A610 10pf multicolored 15 15
2014 A610 20pf multicolored *60 45*
Set value *65 50*

International Year of the Child.

1979, June 5

2015 A611 10pf multicolored 20 15

Agra '79 Agricultural Exhib., Markkleeberg.

Ferry Boats A612

1979, June 26 Photo. *Perf. 14*

2016 A612 20pf Rostock *60 52*
2017 A612 35pf Rugen *60 52*
a. Strip of 2, #2016-2017 + label *1.40 1.20*

Railroad ferry from Sassnitz, DDR, to Trelleborg, Sweden, 70th anniversary.

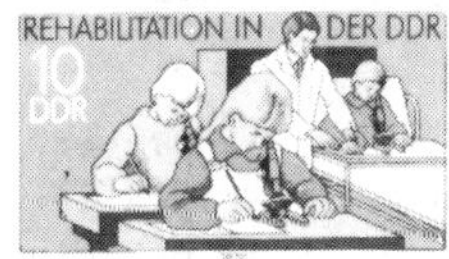

Hospital Classroom A613

Design: 35pf, Handicapped workers.

1979, June 26 Litho. *Perf. 13x12½*

2018 A163 10pf multicolored 15 15
2019 A163 35pf multicolored *60 52*
Set value *66 55*

Rehabilitation in DDR.

Bicyclists A614

Design: 20pf, Roller skating.

1979, July 3

2020 A614 10pf multicolored 15 15
2021 A614 20pf multicolored *50 42*
Set value *56 46*

7th Children's and Youth Spartakiad, Berlin.

Dahlia "Rubens" A615

Dahlias: 20pf, Rosalie. 25pf, Corinna. 35pf, Enzett-Dolli. 50pf, Enzett-Carola. 70pf, Don Lorenzo.

1979, July 17 Photo. *Perf. 13*

2022 A615 10pf multicolored	15	15
2023 A615 20pf multicolored	15	15
2024 A615 25pf multicolored	18	15
2025 A615 35pf multicolored	20	15
2026 A615 50pf multicolored	32	16
2027 A615 70pf multicolored	2.75	*1.90*
Nos. 2022-2027 (6)	*3.75*	*2.66*

Dahlias shown at International Garden Exhibition, Erfurt.

Russian Alphabet Around Congress Emblem A616

1979, Aug. 7 Photo. *Perf. 13*

2028 A616 20pf multicolored 20 15

4th International Congress of Teachers of Russian Language and Literature, Berlin.

Dandelion Fountain, Dresden — A617

Composite of Dresden Buildings — A618

The A618 illustration ias reduced.

1979, Aug. 7 *Perf. 14*

2029 A617 20pf multicolored 15 15

Souvenir Sheet

Litho. *Perf. 13x12½*

2030 A618 1m multicolored *2.50* *1.50*

DDR '79, Natl. Stamp Exhib., Dresden.
See No. B187.

Italian Lira da Gamba, 1592 — A619

Musical Instruments, Leipzig Museum: 25pf, French "serpent," 17th-18th centuries. 40pf, French barrel lyre, 18th century. 85pf, German tenor trumpet, 19th century.

1979, Aug. 21 *Perf. 14*

2031 A619 20pf multicolored	15	15
2032 A619 25pf multicolored	20	15
2033 A619 40pf multicolored	30	15
2034 A619 85pf multicolored	2.75	*2.00*

Galloping — A620

1979, Aug. 21

2035 A620 10pf shown	15	15
2036 A620 25pf Dressage	*90*	*75*

30th International Horse-breeding Congress of Socialist Countries, Berlin.

Memorial Monument, Nordhausen — A621

Teddy Bear — A622

1979, Aug. 28 Photo. *Perf. 14*

2037 A621 35pf dull vio & blk 40 35

Memorial to World War II victims.

1979, Aug. 28

Leipzig Autumn Fair: 25pf, Grosser Blumenberg (building), Leipzig, horiz.

2038 A622 10pf multicolored	15	15
2039 A622 25pf multicolored	*60*	*48*
Set value	*66*	*52*

Philipp Dengel (1888-1948) — A623

Working-Class Movement Leaders: No. 2041, Heinrich Rau (1899-1961). No. 2042, Otto Buchwitz (1879-1964). No. 2043, Bernard Koenen (1889-1964).

1979, Sept. 11 Litho.

2040 A623 10pf multicolored	22	15
2041 A623 10pf multicolored	22	15
2042 A623 10pf multicolored	22	15
2043 A623 10pf multicolored	22	15
Set value		50

See Nos. 2166-2169, 2249-2253, 2314-2318, 2390-2392, 2452-2454.

DDR Arms and Flag, Worker A624

DDR Arms, Flag and: 10pf, Young man and woman. 15pf, Soldiers. 20pf, Workers.

1979, Oct. 2 Photo. *Perf. 13*

2044 A624 5pf multicolored	15	15
2045 A624 10pf multicolored	15	15
2046 A624 15pf multicolored	*50*	*35*
2047 A624 20pf multicolored	15	15
Set value	*70*	*50*

Souvenir Sheet

2048 A624 1m multicolored *1.90* *1.50*

DDR, 30th anniv. No. 2048 contains one stamp (33x55mm).

Altozier Porcelain Coffee Pot — A625

Meissen Porcelain and Hallmark, 18th-20th Centuries: 5pf, Woman applying make-up, 1967. 15pf, "Grosser Ausschnitt" coffee pot, 1974. 20pf, Covered vase. 25pf, Parrot. 35pf, Harlequin drinking. 50pf, Woman selling flowers. 70pf, Sake bottle.

1979, Nov. 6 Photo. *Perf. 14*

2049 A625 5pf multicolored	*15*	*15*
2050 A625 10pf multicolored	*20*	*15*
2051 A625 15pf multicolored	*32*	*24*
2052 A625 20pf multicolored	*42*	*30*
a. Block of 4, #2049-2052	*1.10*	
2053 A625 25pf multicolored	*50*	*35*
2054 A625 35pf multicolored	*70*	*52*
2055 A625 50pf multicolored	*1.00*	*75*
2056 A625 70pf multicolored	*1.50*	*1.10*
a. Block of 4, #2053-2056	*3.75*	
Nos. 2049-2056 (8)	*4.79*	*3.56*

Rag Doll, 1800 — A626

Historic Dolls: 15pf, Ceramic, 1960. 20pf, Wooden, 1780. 35pf, Straw, 1900. 50pf, Jointed, 1800. 70pf, Tumbler, 1820.

1979, Nov. 20 Litho.

2057 A626 10pf multicolored	*65*	*38*
2058 A626 15pf multicolored	*65*	*55*
2059 A626 20pf multicolored	*65*	*38*
2060 A626 35pf multicolored	*65*	*38*
2061 A626 50pf multicolored	*65*	*55*
2062 A626 70pf multicolored	*65*	*38*
a. Sheet of 6, #2057-2062	*4.00*	
Nos. 2057-2062 (6)	*3.90*	*2.62*

Bobsledding, by Gunter Rechn, Olympic Rings — A627

Olympic Rings and: 20pf, Figure Skating, by Johanna Stake, vert. 35pf, Speed Skating, by Axel Wunsch, vert. 1m, Cross-country Skiing, by Lothar Zitzmann.

1980, Jan. 18 Photo. *Perf. 14*

2063 A627 10pf multicolored	15	15
2064 A627 20pf multicolored	15	15
2065 A627 35pf multicolored	*1.40*	*1.10*
Set value		*1.20*

Souvenir Sheet

2066 A627 1m multicolored *2.25* *1.40*

13th Winter Olympic Games, Lake Placid, NY, Feb. 12-24. No. 2066 contains one 29x23½mm stamp. See Nos. 2098-2099, 2119-2121, B189, B190, B192.

"Quiet Music," Grossedlitz — A628

Baroque Gardens: 20pf, Orange grove, Belvedere, Weimar. 50pf, Flower garden, Dornburg Castle. 70pf, Park, Rheinsberg Castle.

1980, Jan. 29

2067 A628 10pf multicolored	15	15
2068 A628 20pf multicolored	15	15
2069 A628 50pf multicolored	28	15
2070 A628 70pf multicolored	*1.90*	*1.50*

Type of 1973

1980-81 Engr. *Perf. 14*

Size: 22x17mm

2071 A449 5pf blue green	15	15
2072 A449 10pf emerald	15	15
2073 A449 15pf rose lilac	15	15
2074 A449 20pf rose mag	15	15
2075 A449 25pf grnsh bl	20	15
2076 A449 30pf org ('81)	28	15
2077 A449 35pf blue	28	15
2078 A449 40pf dull vio	32	15
2079 A449 50pf blue	42	22
2080 A449 60pf lilac ('81)	65	25
2081 A449 70pf redsh brn ('81)	80	35
2082 A449 80pf vio bl ('81)	85	38
2083 A449 1m olive	1.00	45
2084 A449 2m red	1.90	80
2085 A449a 3m rose lil ('81)	3.50	1.25
Nos. 2071-2085 (15)	10.80	4.90

Cable-Laying Vehicle, Dish Antenna — A629

Design: 20pf, Radio tower, television screen.

1980, Feb. 5 Photo.

2086 A629 10pf multicolored	15	15
2087 A629 20pf multicolored	24	15
Set value		15

Famous Germans Type of 1979

Designs: 5pf, Johann Wolfgang Dobereiner (1780-1849), chemist. 10pf, Frederic Joliot-Curie (1900-1958), French physicist. 20pf, Johann Friedrich Naumann (1780-1857), ornithologist. 25pf, Alfred Wegener (1880-1930), geophysicist and meteorologist. 35pf, Carl von Clausewitz (1780-1831), Prussian major general. 70pf, Helene Weigel (1900-1971), actress.

1980, Feb. 26 Litho. *Perf. 13x12½*

2088 A604 5pf pale yel & blk	15	15
2089 A604 10pf multicolored	15	15
2090 A604 20pf lt yel grn & blk	15	15
2091 A604 25pf multicolored	15	15
2092 A604 35pf lt blue & blk	18	15
2093 A604 70pf lt red brn & blk	*1.65*	*1.25*
Nos. 2088-2093 (6)	*2.43*	
Set value		*1.50*

Type ZT-303 Tractor A630

1980 Leipzig Spring Fair: 10pf, Karl Marx University, Leipzig, vert.

1980, Mar. 4 Photo. *Perf. 14*

2094 A630 10pf multicolored	15	15
2095 A630 25pf multicolored	28	18

Werner Eggerath (1900-1977), Labor Leader — A631

1980, Mar. 18 **Litho.**
2096 A631 10pf brick red & blk 15 15

Souvenir Sheet

Cosmonauts, Salyut 6 and Soyuz — A632

1980, Apr. 11 **Litho.** ***Perf. 14***
2097 A632 1m multicolored *2.25 1.50*

Intercosmos cooperative space program.

Olympic Type of 1980

Designs: 10pf, On the Bars, by Erich Wurzer. 50pf, Scull's Crew, by Wilfried Falkenthal.

1980, Apr. 22 **Photo.** ***Perf. 14***
2098 A627 10pf multicolored 15 15
2099 A627 50pf multicolored *90 75*

22nd Summer Olympic Games, Moscow, July 19-Aug. 3. See No. B190.

Flags of Member Countries A633

Bauhaus Cooperative Society Building, 1928, Gropius A634

1980, May 13 **Photo.**
2100 A633 20pf multicolored 30 15

Signing of Warsaw Pact (Bulgaria, Czechoslovakia, DDR, Hungary, Poland, Romania, USSR), 25th anniv.

1980, May 27

Bauhaus Architecture: 10pf, Socialists' Memorial, 1926, by Mies van der Rohe, horiz. 15pf, Monument, 1922, by William Gropius. 20pf, Steel building, 1926, by Muche and Paulick, horiz. 50pf, Trade-Union School, 1928, by Meyer. 70pf, Bauhaus Building, 1926, by Gropius, horiz.

2101 A634 5pf multicolored 15 15
2102 A634 10pf multicolored 15 15
2103 A634 15pf multicolored 15 15
2104 A634 20pf multicolored 15 15
2105 A634 50pf multicolored 30 15
2106 A634 70pf multicolored *2.00 1.40*
Nos. 2101-2106 (6) *2.90*
Set value *1.70*

Rostock View A635

1980, June 10 **Photo.** ***Perf. 14***
2107 A635 10pf shown 15 15
2108 A635 20pf Dancers 25 15
Set value 15

18th Workers' Festival, Rostock, June 27-29.

Dish Antenna, Interflug Airlines A636

1980, June 10 **Litho.** ***Perf. 13x12½***
2109 A636 20pf shown *45 26*
2110 A636 25pf Jet *60 32*
2111 A636 35pf Agricultural plane *80 48*
2112 A636 70pf Aerial photography *1.65 95*
a. Block of 4, #2109-2112 *3.50*

Interflug Airlines. See No. B191

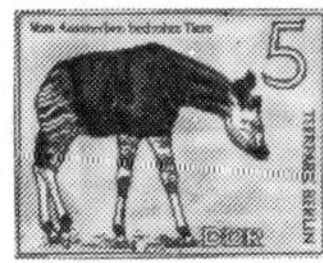

Okapi — A637

1980, June 24 ***Perf. 14***
2113 A637 5pf shown 15 15
2114 A637 10pf Wild cats 15 15
2115 A637 15pf Prairie wolf 15 15
2116 A637 20pf Arabian oryx 15 15
2117 A637 25pf White-eared pheasant 20 15
2118 A637 35pf Musk oxen *1.75 1.25*
Nos. 2113-2118 (6) *2.55*
Set value *1.50*

Olympic Type of 1980

Designs: 10pf, Judo, by Erhard Schmidt. 50pf, Final Spurt, by Siegfried Schreiber. 1m, Spinnaker Yachts, by Karl Raetsch.

1980, July 8 **Photo.** ***Perf. 14***
2119 A627 10pf multicolored 15 15
2120 A627 50pf multicolored *1.10 95*

Souvenir Sheet

2121 A627 1m multicolored *2.25 1.40*

22nd Summer Olympic Games, Moscow, July 19-Aug. 3. No. 2121 contains one stamp (29x24mm). See No. B192.

Old and New Buildings, Suhl A638

Design: 10pf + 5pf, View of Suhl, 1700.

1980, July 22 **Litho.** ***Perf. 13x12½***
2122 A638 10pf + 5pf multi *30 20*
2123 A638 20pf multicolored *30 20*
a. Pair, #2122-2123 + label *75 48*

6th National Youth Philatelic Exhibition, Suhl. Surtax for East German Association of Philatelists.

Huntley Microscope, London, 1740 — A639

Optical Museum, Karl Zeiss Foundation, Jena: 25pf, Magny microscope, Paris, 1751. 35pf, Amici microscope, Modena, 1845. 70pf, Zeiss microscope, Jena, 1873.

1980, Aug. 12 **Photo.** ***Perf. 14***
2124 A639 20pf multicolored 42 32
2125 A639 25pf multicolored 50 40
2126 A639 35pf multicolored 65 52
2127 A639 70pf multicolored 1.50 1.10
a. Block of 4, #2124-2127 3.25 2.60

Maidenek Memorial — A640

1980, Aug. 26
2128 A640 35pf multicolored 35 15

Leipzig 1980 Autumn Fair, Information Center A641

1980, Aug. 26
2129 A641 10pf shown 15 15
2130 A641 25pf Carpet loom 35 18
Set value 25

67th Interparliamentary Conference, Berlin — A642

1980, Sept. 9 **Photo.** ***Perf. 14***
2131 A642 20pf Republic Palace, Berlin 65 15

A643

A644

Designs: Paintings by Frans Hals (1580-1666).

1980, Sept. 23
2132 A643 10pf *Laughing Boy with Flute* 15 15
2133 A643 20pf *Man in Gray Coat* 15 15
2134 A643 25pf *The Mulatto* 16 15
2135 A643 35pf *Man in Black Coat* *1.10 90*

Souvenir Sheet

2136 A643 1m *Self-portrait,* horiz. *1.90 1.40*

1980, Oct. 28 **Litho.** ***Perf. 13x13½***

Edible Mushrooms: 5pf, Leccinum Testaceo Scabrum. 10pf, Boletus erythropus. 15pf, Agaricus campester. 20pf, Xerocomus badius. 35pf, Boletus edulis. 70pf, Cantharellus cibarius.

2137 A644 5pf multicolored 15 15
2138 A644 10pf multicolored 15 15
2139 A644 15pf multicolored 15 15
2140 A644 20pf multicolored 15 15
2141 A644 35pf multicolored 20 15
2142 A644 70pf multicolored *2.00 1.90*
Nos. 2137-2142 (6) *2.80*
Set value *2.25*

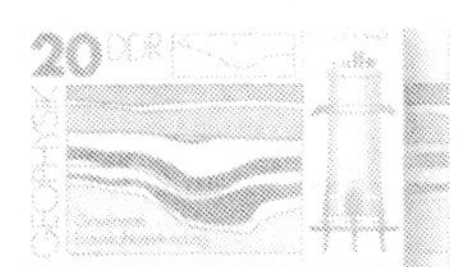

Exploration of Lignite Deposits (Gravimetry) — A645

Geophysical Exploration: 25pf, Bore-hole measuring (water). 35pf, Seismic geology. (mineral oil, natural gas). 50pf, Seismology.

1980, Nov. 11 **Litho.** ***Perf. 13***
2143 A645 20pf multicolored 42 30
2144 A645 25pf multicolored 55 38
2145 A645 35pf multicolored 80 55
2146 A645 50pf multicolored 1.10 75
a. Block of 4, #2143-2146 2.60

Radebeul-Radeburg Railroad Locomotive — A646

1980, Nov. 25 ***Perf. 13x12½***
2147 Strip of 2 + label *1.25 75*
a. A646 20pf shown
b. A646 25pf Passenger car
2148 Strip of 2 + label *1.25 75*
a. A646 20pf Bad Doberan-Osteebad Kuhlungsborn Locomotive
b. A646 35pf Passenger car

Labels show maps of routes and Moritzburg Castle (No. 2147), Bad Doberan Street (No. 2148). See Nos. 2205-2206.

Toy Locomotive, 1850 — A647

1980, Dec. 9 ***Perf. 14***
2149 Sheet of 6 *3.75 2.25*
a. A647 10pf shown *60 32*
b. A647 20pf Airplane, 1914 *60 45*
c. A647 25pf Steam roller, 1920 *60 32*
d. A647 35pf Ship, 1825 *60 32*
e. A647 40pf Car, 1900 *60 45*
f. A647 50pf Balloon, 1920 *60 32*

Souvenir Sheet

Wolfgang Amadeus Mozart, 225th Birth Anniv. — A648

1981, Jan. 13 **Litho.**
2150 A648 1m multicolored *2.00 1.25*

St. John's Apple — A649

Heinrich von Stephan — A650

1981, Jan. 13 **Photo.**
2151 A649 5pf shown 15 15
2152 A649 10pf Snow drop, horiz. 15 15
2153 A649 20pf Bladder bush 15 15
2154 A649 25pf Paulownia tomentose 15 15
2155 A649 35pf German honeysuckle, horiz. 25 15
2156 A649 50pf Genuine spice bush *2.50 1.50*
Nos. 2151-2156 (6) *3.35*
Set value *1.90*

1981, Jan. 20 **Litho.** ***Perf. 13x13½***
2157 A650 10pf lt lemon & blk 15 15

Von Stephan (1831-97), founder of UPU.

Dedication of National Commemorative Plaza, Sachsenhausen — A651

1981, Jan. 27 **Photo.** ***Perf. 14***

2158 A651 10pf shown 15 15
2159 A651 20pf Changing of guard 20 15
Set value 30 15

National People's Forces, 25th anniversary.

Socialist Union Party, 10th Congress — A652

1981, Feb. 10

2160 A652 10pf multicolored 15 15

Postal and Newspaper Apprentice Training — A653

1981, Feb. 10 **Litho.**

2161 A653 5pf shown 15 15
2162 A653 10pf Telephone and telex service 15 15
2163 A653 15pf Radio communications 15 15
2164 A653 20pf School of Engineering, Leipzig 15 15
2165 A653 25pf Communications Academy, Dresden *1.10* 80
Nos. 2161-2165 (5) *1.70*
Set value *1.00*

Working-class Leader Type of 1979

Designs: No. 2166, Erich Baron (1881-1933). No. 2167, Conrad Blenkle (1901-1943). No. 2168, Arthur Ewert (1890-1959). No. 2169, Walter Stoecker (1891-1939).

1981, Feb. 24 **Litho.** ***Perf. 14***

2166 A623 10pf gray grn & blk 15 15
2167 A623 10pf bl vio & blk 15 15
2168 A623 10pf lemon & blk 15 15
2169 A623 10pf lt red brn & blk 15 15
Set value 50 18

Merkur Hotel, Leipzig — A654

Ernst Thälmann, by Willi Sitte — A655

1981 Leipzig Spring Fair: 25pf, Takraf mining conveyor system, horiz.

1981, Mar. 10 **Photo.** ***Perf. 14***

2170 A654 10pf multicolored 15 15
2171 A654 25pf multicolored 35 15
Set value 20

1981, Mar. 24

10th Communist Party Congress (Paintings): 20pf, Worker, by Bernhard Heising. 25pf, Festivities, by Rudolf Bergander. 35pf, Brotherhood in Arms, by Paul Michaelis. 1m, When Communists Dream, by Walter Womacka.

2172 A655 10pf multicolored 15 15
2173 A655 20pf multicolored 15 15
2174 A655 25pf multicolored *1.25* 85
2175 A655 35pf multicolored 18 15
Set value *1.10*

Souvenir Sheet

2176 A655 1m multicolored *2.00 1.50*

Souvenir Sheet

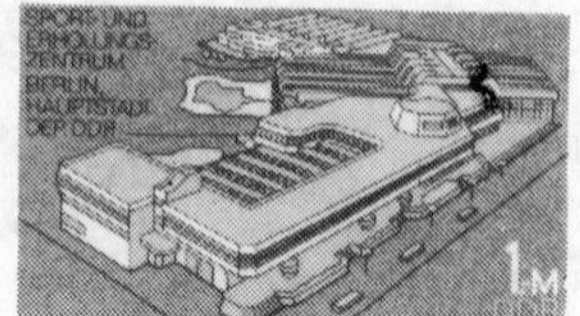

Opening of Sport and Recreation Center, Berlin — A656

1981, Mar. 24 **Litho.**

2177 A656 1m multicolored *2.25 1.40*

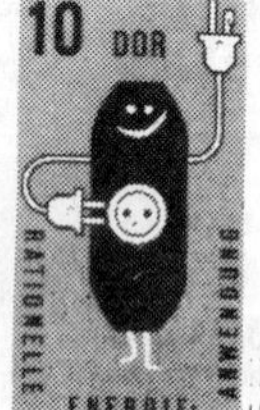

Energy Conservation — A657

1981, Apr. 21 **Litho.** ***Perf. 12½x13***

2178 A657 10pf orange & blk 15 15

Heinrich Barkhausen (1881-1956), Physicist — A658

Famous Men: 20pf, Johannes R. Becher (1891-1958), poet. 25pf, Richard Dedekind (1831-1916), mathematician. 35pf, Georg Philipp Telemann (1681-1767), composer. 50pf, Adelbert V. Chamisso (1781-1838), botanist. 70pf, Wilhelm Raabe (1831-1910), writer.

1981, May 5 ***Perf. 13x12½***

2179 A658 10pf dull bl & blk 15 15
2180 A658 20pf brick red & blk 15 15
2181 A658 25pf dull brn & blk *1.90 1.50*
2182 A658 35pf lt vio & blk 16 15
2183 A658 50pf yel grn & blk 25 15
2184 A658 70pf ol bis & blk 38 20
Nos. 2179-2184 (6) *2.99 2.30*

Free German Youth Members A659

1981, May 19

2185 A659 10pf shown *35 22*
2186 A659 20pf Youths, diff. *35 22*
a. Pair, #2185-2186 + label *75 50*

Free German Youth, 11th Parliament, Berlin.

View and Map of Worlitz Park — A660

1981, June 9 **Litho.** ***Perf. 12½x13***

2187 A660 5pf shown 15 15
2188 A660 10pf Tiefurt 15 15
2189 A660 15pf Marxwalde 15 15
2190 A660 20pf Branitz 18 15
2191 A660 25pf Treptow *1.90 95*
2192 A660 35pf Wiesenburg 24 15
Nos. 2187-2192 (6) *2.77*
Set value *1.25*

Artistic Gymnastics A661

8th Children's and Youth Spartacist Games: No. 2193, children and youths.

1981, June 23 **Photo.** ***Perf. 14***

2193 A661 10pf + 5pf multi *42 32*
2194 A661 20pf multicolored 15 15

Javelin Throwers A662

1981, June 23 **Litho.** ***Perf. 13x12½***

2195 A662 5pf shown 25 16
2196 A662 15pf Men at museum 25 16
a. Pair, #2195-2196 + label 50 35

Intl. Year of the Disabled.

Schinkel's Berlin Playhouse A663

Karl Friedrich Schinkel, (1781-1841), Architect: 25pf, Old Museum, Berlin.

1981, June 23 **Litho. & Engr.**

2197 A663 10pf tan & blk 20 15
2198 A663 25pf tan & blk *1.65 45*
Set value *50*

Sugar Loaf House, Gross Zicker — A664

Frame Houses: 10pf, Zaulsdorf, 19th cent., vert. 25pf, Farmhouse, stable, Weckersdorf, vert. 35pf, Restaurant (former farmhouse), Piligram. 50pf, Eschenbach, vert. 70pf, Farmhouse, Lüdersdorf.

1981, July 7 **Photo.**

2199 A664 10pf multicolored 15 15
2200 A664 20pf multicolored 15 15
2201 A664 25pf multicolored 15 15
2202 A664 35pf multicolored 32 15
2203 A664 50pf multicolored 25 15
2204 A664 70pf multicolored *2.75 1.90*
Nos. 2199-2204 (6) *3.77*
Set value *2.30*

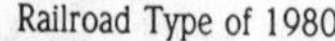

Railroad Type of 1980

1981, July 21 **Litho.** ***Perf. 13x12½***

2205 Strip of 2 + label *50 38*
a. A646 5pf Locomotive, Freital-Kurort-Kipsdorf line
b. A646 15pf Luggage car
2206 Strip of 2 + label *50 38*
a. A646 5pf Locomotive, Putbus-Gohren line
b. A646 20pf Passenger car

Labels show maps of train routes.

Ebers Papyrus (Egyptian Medical Text, 1600 B.C.), Leipzig — A665

Chemical Plant — A666

Literary Treasures in DDR Libraries: 35pf, Maya manuscript, 12th cent., Dresden. 50pf, Petrarch sonnet illustration, 16th century French manuscript, Berlin.

1981, Aug. 18 **Photo.** ***Perf. 14***

2207 A665 20pf multicolored 15 15
2208 A665 35pf multicolored 25 15
2209 A665 50pf multicolored *1.50 1.00*

1981, Aug. 18

Leipzig 1981 Autumn Fair: 25pf, Concert Hall, Leipzig, horiz.

2210 A666 10pf multicolored 15 15
2211 A666 25pf multicolored 30 15
Set value 20

Anti-Fascist Resistance Monument, Sassnitz — A667

Forceps, 18th Cent., Speculum, 17th Cent. — A668

1981, Sept. 8 **Photo.** ***Perf. 14***

2212 A667 35pf multicolored 45 18

1981, Sept. 22

Historic Medical Instruments, Karl Sudhoff Institute, Leipzig: 10pf, Henbana, censer, 16th cent. 20pf, Pelican, dental elevator and extractors, 17th cent. 25pf, Seton forceps, 17th cent. 35pf, Lithotomy knife, 18th cent., hernia scissors, 17th cent. 85pf, Elevators, 17th cent. 10pf, 20pf, 25pf, 35pf horiz.

2213 A668 10pf multicolored 15 15
2214 A668 20pf multicolored 15 15
2215 A668 25pf multicolored 15 15
2216 A668 35pf multicolored 16 15
2217 A668 50pf multicolored *3.00 1.90*
2218 A668 85pf multicolored 42 18
Nos. 2213-2218 (6) *4.03 2.68*

Philatelists' Day A669

1981, Oct. 6 **Photo.** ***Perf. 14***

2219 A669 10pf + 5pf Letter by Engels, 1840 *75 38*
2220 A669 20pf Postcard by Marx, 1878 24 15

River Boat A670

1981, Oct. 20

2221 A670 10pf Tugboat	15	15
2222 A670 20pf Tugboat, diff.	15	15
2223 A670 25pf Diesel paddle liner	18	15
2224 A670 35pf Ice breaker	20	15
2225 A670 50pf Motor freighter	28	15
2226 A670 85pf Bucket dredger	3.00	1.75
Nos. 2221-2226 (6)	3.96	2.50

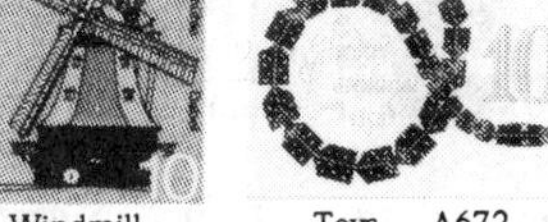

Windmill, Dabel — A671

Toys — A672

1981, Nov. 10 Photo. *Perf. 14*

2227 A671 10pf shown	15	15
2228 A671 20pf Pahrenz	15	15
2229 A671 25pf Dresden-Gohlis	20	15
2230 A671 70pf Ballstadt	1.65	1.25
Set value		1.40

1981, Nov. 24 Litho. *Perf. 13½*

2231 Sheet of 6	4.00	2.75
a. A672 10pf Jointed snake, 1850	65	38
b. A672 20pf Teddy bear, 1910	65	38
c. A672 25pf Fish, 1935	65	55
d. A672 35pf Hobby horse, 1850	65	55
e. A672 40pf Cuckoo, 1800	65	38
f. A672 70pf Frog, 1930	65	38

Meissen Porcelain Teapot, 1715 — A673

1982, Jan. 26 Photo. *Perf. 14*

2232 A673 10pf shown	25	16
2233 A673 20pf Vase, 1715	60	32
2234 A673 25pf Oberon figurine, 1969	75	40
2235 A673 35pf Day and Night vase, 1979	90	50
a. Block of 4, #2232-2235	2.50	

Souvenir Sheet

2236 Sheet of 2	2.00	1.40
a. A673 50pf Portrait	90	65
b. A673 50pf Emblem	90	65

Johann Friedrich Bottger (1682-1719), inventor of Dresden china. No. 2236 contains two 24x29mm stamps.

Post Offices — A674

1982, Feb. 9

2237 A674 20pf Liebenstein	15	15
2238 A674 25pf Berlin	16	15
2239 A674 35pf Erfurt	18	15
2240 A674 50pf Dresden	1.90	1.10

Intl. Fur Auction, Leipzig A675

1982, Feb. 23 Photo. *Perf. 14*

2241 A675 10pf Marmot, vert.	15	15
2242 A675 20pf Polecat	15	15
2243 A675 25pf Mink	16	15
2244 A675 35pf Stone marten	1.25	1.00

Souvenir Sheet

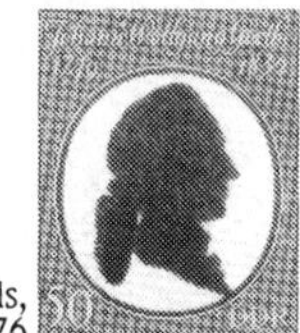

Goethe-Schiller Awards, 1980-1984 — A676

1982, Mar. 9 Litho.

2245 Sheet of 2	2.50	1.40
a. A676 50pf Goethe	1.00	65
b. A676 50pf Schiller	1.00	65

1982 Leipzig Spring Fair — A677

1982, Mar. 9 *Perf. 13x12½*

2246 A677 10pf Entrance	15	15
2247 A677 25pf Exhibit	35	22
Set value		30

Souvenir Sheet

TB Bacillus Centenary — A678

1982, Mar. 23 *Perf. 14*

2248 A678 1m multi	2.50	1.50

Working-class Leader Type of 1979

Designs: No. 2249, Max Fechner (1892-1973). No. 2250, Ottomar Greschke (1882-1957). No. 2251, Helmut Lehmann (1882-1959). No. 2252, Herbert Warnke (1902-1975). No. 2253, Otto Winzer (1902-1975).

1982, Mar. 23 Engr.

2249 A623 10pf dk red brn	15	15
2250 A623 10pf green	15	15
2251 A623 10pf violet	15	15
2252 A623 10pf dull blue	15	15
2253 A623 10pf gray olive	15	15
Set value	50	20

Poisonous Plants — A679

Free Federation of German Trade Unions, 10th Congress — A680

1982, Apr. 6 Litho. *Perf. 14*

2254 A679 10pf Meadow saffron	15	15
2255 A679 15pf Water arum	15	15
2256 A679 20pf Marsh tea	15	15
2257 A679 25pf White bryony	15	15
2258 A679 35pf Common monkshood	18	15
2259 A679 50pf Henbane	1.90	1.50
Nos. 2254-2259 (6)	2.68	
Set value		1.85

1982, Apr. 20 Photo.

Paintings: 10pf, Mother and Child, by Walter Womacka. 20pf, Discussion at the Innovator Collective, by Willi Neubert, horiz. 25pf, Young Couple, by Karl-Heinz Jacob.

2260 A680 10pf multi	15	15
2261 A680 20pf multi	15	15
2262 A680 25pf multi	75	52
Set value		60

A681

A682

1982, Apr. 20

2263 A681 15pf "I"	75	42
2264 A681 35pf Emblem	75	42
a. Pair, #2263-2264 + label	1.50	

Intl. Book Art Exhibition, Leipzig.

Perf. 13½x14, 14x13½

1982, May 18 Photo.

Designs: Protected species. 10pf, 25pf, 35pf vert.

2265 A682 10pf Fish hawk	15	15
2266 A682 20pf Sea eagle	15	15
2267 A682 25pf Tawny eagle	16	15
2268 A682 35pf Eagle owl	1.10	85
Set value		1.00

19th Workers' Festival, Neubrandenburg — A683

1982, June 8 Photo. *Perf. 14*

2269 A683 10pf View of Neubrandenburg	15	15
2270 A683 20pf Traditional costumes	25	16

Souvenir Sheet

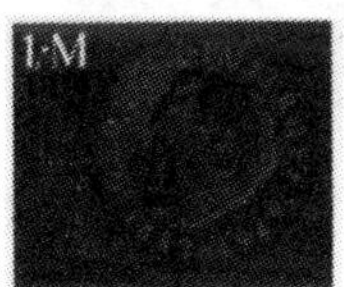

Dimitrov Memorial Medal — A684

1982, June 8

2271 A684 1m multi	2.50	1.40

George Dimitrov (1882-1947), first prime minister of Bulgaria.

Cargo Ship Frieden — A685

1982, June 22

2272 A685 5pf shown	15	15
2273 A685 10pf Fichtelberg	15	15
2274 A685 15pf Brocken	15	15
2275 A685 20pf Weimar	20	15
2276 A685 25pf Vorwarts	25	15
2277 A685 35pf Berlin	1.50	1.00
Nos. 2272-2277 (6)	2.40	
Set value		1.30

Technology — A686

1982, June 22 Litho. *Perf. 13x12½*

2278 A686 20pf multi	25	15

Bird Wedding A687

Sorbian Folklore: 20pf, Zampern masqueraders. 25pf, Easter egg game. 35pf, Painting Easter eggs. 40pf, St. John's Day parade. 50pf, Christmas celebration.

1982, July 6 Litho. *Perf. 13x12½*

2279 Block of 6	4.00	2.75
a. A687 10pf multi	25	18
b. A687 20pf multi	38	28
c. A687 25pf multi	50	35
d. A687 35pf multi	70	55
e. A687 40pf multi	75	60
f. A687 50pf multi	90	75

View of Schwerin A688

7th Youth Stamp Exhibition, Schwerin: 10pf + 5pf, View, 1640.

1982, July 6

2280 A688 10pf + 5pf multi	55	35
2281 A688 20pf multi	55	35
a. Pair, #2280-2281 + label	1.10	

7th Pioneer Meeting, Dresden — A689

1982, July 20 Photo. *Perf. 14x13½*

2282 A689 10pf + 5pf Pioneers, banner	50	45
2283 A689 20pf Bugle, pennant	15	15

Seascape, by Ludolf Backhuysen (1631-1708) — A690

17th Cent. Paintings in Natl. Museum, Schwerin: 10pf, Music Making at Home, by Frans van Mieris (1635-1681), vert. 20pf, The Gate Guard, by Carel Fabritius (1622-1654), vert. 25pf, Farmers Company, by Adriaen Brouwer (1606-1638). 35pf, Breakfast Table with Ham, by Willem Clacsz Heda (1593-1680). 70pf, River Landscape, by Jan van Goyen (1596-1656).

1982, Aug. 10 *Perf. 14*

2284 A690 5pf multi	15	15
2285 A690 10pf multi	15	15
2286 A690 20pf multi	15	15
2287 A690 25pf multi	15	15
2288 A690 35pf multi	18	15
2289 A690 70pf multi	2.00	1.50
Nos. 2284-2289 (6)	2.78	
Set value		1.85

1982 Leipzig Autumn Fair A691

1982, Aug. 24 Litho. *Perf. 13x12½*
2290 A691 10pf Exhibition Hall 15 15
2291 A691 25pf Decorative box, ring 22 15
Set value 25

Karl-Marx-Stadt Buildings and Monument — A692

1982, Aug. 24 Photo. *Perf. 14*
2292 A692 10pf multi 20 15

Org. for the Cooperation of Socialist Countries and Posts and Telecommunications Dept., 13th Conference, Karl-Marx-Stadt, Sept. 6-11. Se-tenant with label showing modes of communication.

Emblem — A693

Auschwitz- Birkenau Intl. Memorial — A694

1982, Sept. 7 Litho. *Perf. 14*
2293 A693 10pf multi 15 15

Intl. Federation of Resistance Fighters, 9th Congress, Berlin.

1982, Sept. 7 Photo.
2294 A694 35pf multi 35 15

Autumn Flowers — A695

1982, Sept. 21
2295 A695 5pf Autumn anemones 15 15
2296 A695 10pf Student flowers 15 15
2297 A695 15pf Hybrid gazanias 15 15
2298 A695 20pf Sunflowers 18 15
2299 A695 25pf Chrysanthemums 22 15
2300 A695 35pf Cosmos bipinnatus *1.75 1.10*
Nos. 2295-2301 (7) *2.75*
Set value *1.40*

Ambulance A696

1982, Oct. 5 Litho. *Perf. 13x12½*
2301 A696 5pf shown 15 15
2302 A696 10pf Street cleaner 15 15
2303 A696 20pf Bus 15 15
2304 A696 25pf Platform truck 18 15
2305 A696 35pf Platform truck, diff. 24 15
2306 A696 85pf Milk truck *2.00 1.65*
Nos. 2301-2306 (6) *2.87*
Set value *2.05*

25th Masters of Tomorrow Central Fair — A697

1982, Oct. 19 *Perf. 14*
2307 A697 20pf multicolored 30 15

Martin Luther (1483-1546) — A698

Toy Carpenter, 1830 — A699

Designs: 10pf, Seal of Eisleben (town of birth and death). 20pf, Portrait, Eisenach, 1521. 35pf, Wittenberg seal, 1500. 85pf, Portrait, after Cranach, 1528.

1982, Nov. 23 Photo. *Perf. 14x13½*
2308 A698 10pf multi 15 15
2309 A698 20pf multi 25 15
a. Miniature sheet of 10 4.00 2.50
2310 A698 35pf multi 35 15
2311 A698 85pf multi *2.50 1.25*
Set value *1.45*

1982, Nov. 23 Litho. *Perf. 14*
2312 Sheet of 6 *4.00 2.50*
a. A699 10pf shown *60 32*
b. A699 20pf Cobbler *60 50*
c. A699 25pf Baker *60 32*
d. A699 35pf Cooper *60 32*
e. A699 40pf Tanner *60 50*
f. A699 70pf Carter *60 32*

Souvenir Sheet

Johannes Brahms (1833-1897), Composer — A700

1983, Jan. 11 Litho. *Perf. 14*
2313 A700 1.15m multi *3.00 1.65*

Working-class Leader Type of 1979

Designs: No. 2314, Franz Dahlem (1892-1981). No. 2315, Karl Maron (1903-1975). No. 2316, Josef Miller (1883-1964). No. 2317, Fred Oelssner (1903-1977). No. 2318, Siegfried Radel (1893-1943).

1983, Jan. 25 Photo.
2314 A623 10pf dark brown 15 15
2315 A623 10pf dark green 15 15
2316 A623 10pf dark olive grn 15 15
2317 A623 10pf deep plum 15 15
2318 A623 10pf dark blue 15 15
Set value 50 20

World Communications Year — A701

1983, Feb. 8 Photo. *Perf. 14*
2319 A701 5pf Telephone receiver, buttons 15 15
2320 A701 10pf Rugen radio 15 15
2321 A701 20pf Surface and air mail 18 15
2322 A701 35pf Optical conductors *1.10 65*
Set value *80*

Otto Nuschke (1883-1957), Statesman — A702

1983, Feb. 8
2323 A702 20pf red brn, bl & blk 25 15

Town Hall, Gera, 1576 — A703

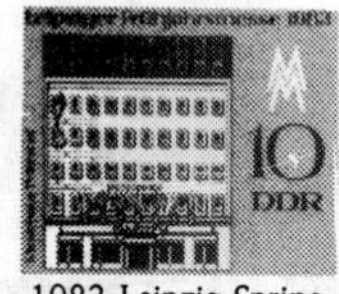

1983 Leipzig Spring Fair — A704

1983, Feb. 22 Photo. *Perf. 14*
2324 A703 10pf Stolberg, 1482, horiz. 15 15
2325 A703 20pf shown 18 15
2326 A703 25pf Possneck, 1486 24 15
2327 A703 35pf Berlin, 1869, horiz. *1.40 90*
Set value *1.10*

1983, Mar. 8
2328 A704 10pf Fair building 16 15
2329 A704 25pf Robotron microcomputer 32 15
Set value 25

Paul Robeson (1898-1976), Singer — A705

1983, Mar. 22 Litho. *Perf. 13x12½*
2330 A705 20pf multicolored 30 15

Souvenir Sheet

Schulze-Boysen/Harnack Resistance Org. — A706

Design: Arvid Harnack (1901-1942), Harro Schulze-Boysen (1909-1942), John Sieg (1903-1942).

1983, Mar. 22
2331 A706 85pf multicolored 1.50 1.10

Karl Marx (1818-1883), and Newspaper Mastheads — A707

Portraits and: 20pf, Lyons silk weavers' revolt, 1831, French-German Yearbook. 35pf, Engels, Communist Manifesto. 50pf, Das Kapital titlepage. 70pf, Program of German Workers' Movement text. 85pf, Engels, Lenin, globe. 1.15m Portrait (24x29mm).

1983, Apr. 11 Photo. *Perf. 13x12½*
2332 A707 10pf multicolored 22 15
2333 A707 20pf multicolored 22 15
2334 A707 35pf multicolored 22 15
2335 A707 50pf multicolored 30 15
2336 A707 70pf multicolored 40 15
2337 A707 85pf multicolored *3.00 1.90*
Nos. 2332-2337 (6) *4.36 2.65*

Souvenir Sheet

Litho. *Perf. 14*
2338 A707 1.15m multi *2.50 1.50*

Works of Art from Berlin State Museums — A708

1983, Apr. 19 Photo. *Perf. 14*
2339 A708 10pf Athena 15 15
2340 A708 20pf Amazon, bronze, 430 BC 24 15
Set value 15

Narrow-Gauge Railroads — A709

1983, May 17 Litho. *Perf. 13x12½*
2341 Pair, Wernigerode-Nordhausen line *1.65 85*
a. A709 15pf Locomotive *75 40*
b. A709 20pf Passenger car *75 40*
2342 Pair, Zittau-Oybin/Johnsdorf line *1.75 85*
a. A709 20pf Locomotive *75 40*
b. A709 50pf Freight car *75 40*

Nos. 2341 and 2342 se-tenant with labels showing maps. See Nos. 2405-2406.

Sand Glasses and Sundials A710

Cacti A711

1983, June 7 Photo. *Perf. 14*
2343 A710 5pf Sand glass, 1674 15 15
2344 A710 10pf Sand glass, 1700 15 15
2345 A710 20pf Sundial, 1611 15 15
a. Sheet of 8 *3.50 2.25*
2346 A710 30pf Sundial, 1750 22 15
2347 A710 50pf Sundial, 1760 30 18
2348 A710 85pf Sundial, 1800 *3.00 1.90*
Nos. 2343-2348 (6) *3.97 2.68*

1983, June 21
2349 A711 5pf Coryphantha elephantidens 15 15
2350 A711 10pf Thelocactus schwarzii 15 15
2351 A711 20pf Leuchtenbergia principis 15 15
2352 A711 25pf Submatucana madisoniorum 15 15
2353 A711 35pf Oroya peruviana 22 16
2354 A711 50pf Copiapoa cinerea *2.25 1.65*
Nos. 2349-2354 (6) *3.07*
Set value *2.00*

Naumberg Cathedral Statues, 15th Cent. — A712

1983, July 5 **Photo.** ***Perf. 13***

2355 A712 20pf Thimo and Wilhelm *50 40*
2356 A712 25pf Gepa and Gerburg *60 50*
2357 A712 35pf Hermann and Reglindis *90 72*
2358 A712 85pf Eckehard and Uta *2.00 1.75*
a. Block of 4, #2355-2358 *4.00*

Technical Training, by Harald Metzkes (b. 1929) A713

SOZPHILEX '83 Junior Stamp Exhibition, Berlin: 10pf+5pf, Glasewaldt and Zinna Defending the Barricade-18th March, 1848, by Theodor Hosemann, vert. Surtax was for exhibition.

1983, July 5 **Litho.** ***Perf. 13x12½***

2359 A713 10pf + 5pf multi *60 45*
2360 A713 20pf multi 15 15

Volleyball — A714

1983, July 19 **Photo.** ***Perf. 14***

2361 A714 10pf + 5pf Passing beach balls *38 28*
2362 A714 20pf shown 15 15

7th Gymnastic and Sports Meeting; 9th Children's and Youth Spartikiade, Leipzig.

Simon Bolivar (1783-1830) A715

1983, July 19

2363 A715 35pf Bolivar, Alexander von Humboldt 50 30

City Arms — A716

1983 Leipzig Autumn Fair — A717

1983, Aug. 9

2364 A716 50pf Berlin *90 50*
2365 A716 50pf Cottbus *90 50*
2366 A716 50pf Dresden *90 50*
2367 A716 50pf Erfurt *90 50*
2368 A716 50pf Frankfurt *90 50*
Nos. 2364-2368 (5) *4.50 2.50*

See Nos. 2398-2402, 2464-2468.

1983, Aug. 30

2369 A717 10pf Central Palace 15 15
2370 A717 25pf Microelectronic pattern 35 25

Leonhard Euler (1707-1783), Mathematician — A718

1983, Sept. 6

2371 A718 20pf multi 35 15

Souvenir Sheet

30th Anniv. of Working-Class Brigade Groups — A719

1983, Sept. 6 **Litho.** ***Perf. 12½x13***

2372 A719 1m multicolored *1.50 1.00*

Governmental Palaces, Potsdam Gardens — A720

1983, Sept. 20 ***Perf. 13x12½***

2373 A720 10pf Sanssouci Palace 15 15
2374 A720 20pf Chinese tea-house 18 15
2375 A720 40pf Charlottenhof Palace 42 22
2376 A720 50pf Royal Stables, Film Museum *2.75 1.50*

Monument, Mamajew-Kurgan Hill — A721

1983, Oct. 4 ***Perf. 14***

2377 A721 35pf Mother Home 50 30

Souvenir Sheet

Martin Luther — A722

1983, Oct. 18 **Litho.** ***Perf. 14***

2378 A722 1m multi *3.00 1.65*

Margin shows title page from Luther Bible, 1541.

Thuringian Glass — A723

1983, Nov. 8 **Photo.** ***Perf. 13½x14***

2379 A723 10pf Cock 15 15
2380 A723 20pf Cup 15 15
2381 A723 25pf Vase 18 15
2382 A723 70pf Ornamental Glass *1.50 1.10*

Souvenir Sheet

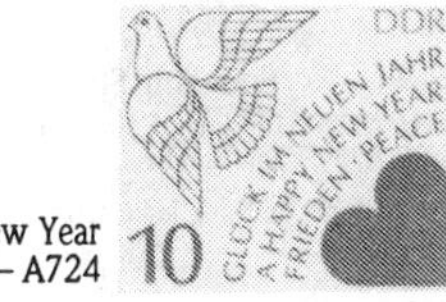

New Year 1984 — A724

1983, Nov. 22 **Litho.** ***Perf. 14***

2383 Sheet of 4 *1.75 1.25*
a. A724 10pf multi *16 15*
b. A724 20pf multi *32 25*
c. A724 25pf multi *48 35*
d. A724 35pf multi *70 55*

Winter Olympics 1984, Sarajevo A725

1983, Nov. 22 **Photo.** ***Perf. 14***

2384 A725 10pf + 5pf 2-man luge 15 15
2385 A725 20pf + 10pf Ski jump 15 15
2386 A725 25pf Skiing 15 15
2387 A725 35pf Biathlon *1.65 1.10*

Souvenir Sheet

2388 A725 85pf Olympic Center *1.90* 1.25

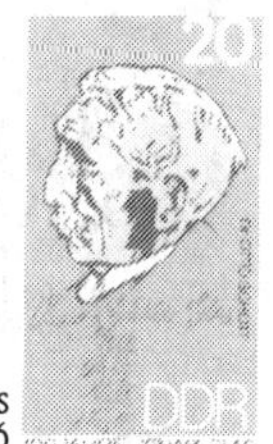

Jena Glass Centenary — A726

1984, Jan. 10 **Litho.** ***Perf. 12½x13***

2389 A726 20pf Otto Schott 35 28

Working-class Leader Type of 1979

Designs: No. 2390, Friedrich Ebert (1894-1979). No. 2391, Fritz Grosse (1904-1957). No. 2392, Albert Norden (1904-1982).

1984, Jan. 24 **Engr.** ***Perf. 14***

2390 A623 10pf black 16 15
2391 A623 10pf dk grn 16 15
2392 A623 10pf dk bl 16 15

Souvenir Sheet

Felix Mendelssohn (1809-1847), Composer — A727

1984, Jan. 24 **Litho.**

2393 A727 85pf multi 1.25 1.00

Margin shows Song Without Words score.

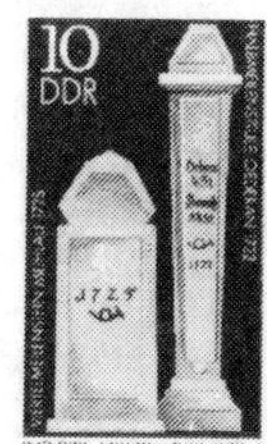

Postal Milestones — A728

Designs: 10pf, Muhlau, 1725; Oederan, 1722. 20pf, Johanngeorgenstadt, 1723; Schonbrunn, 1724. 35pf, Freiberg, 1723. 85pf, Pegau, 1723.

1984, Feb. 7 **Photo.** ***Perf. 14***

2394 A728 10pf multi 15 15
2395 A728 20pf multi 18 16
2396 A728 35pf multi 30 28
2397 A728 85pf multi 70 65

City Arms Type of 1983

1984, Feb. 21

2398 A716 50pf Gera 55 42
2399 A716 50pf Halle 55 42
2400 A716 50pf Karl-Marx-Stadt 55 42
2401 A716 50pf Leipzig 55 42
2402 A716 50pf Magdeburg 55 42
Nos. 2398-2402 (5) 2.75 2.10

1984 Leipzig Spring Fair A729

1984, Mar. 6 ***Perf. 14***

2403 A729 10pf Old Town Hall 15 15
2404 A729 25pf Factory 20 16
Set value 30 23

Railroad Type of 1983

1984, Mar. 20 **Litho.** ***Perf. 13x12½***

2405 Pair, Cranzahl Oberwiesenthal line 1.50 85
a. A709 30pf Locomotive 42 25
b. A709 80pf Passenger car 95 55
2406 Pair, Selke Valley line 1.40 75
a. A709 40pf Locomotive 48 28
b. A709 60pf Passenger car 75 45

Labels show maps of routes.

Stone Door, Rostock A730

Council Building A731

Intl. Society of Monument Preservation 7th General Meeting: 10pf, Town Hall, Rostock. 15pf, Albrecht Castle, Meissen. 85pf, Stable Courtyard, Dresden. 10pf, 15pf, 85pf horiz.

1984, Apr. 24 **Photo.** ***Perf. 14***

2407 A730 10pf multi 15 15
2408 A730 15pf multi 18 15
2409 A730 40pf multi 48 35
2410 A730 85pf multi 95 70

1984, May 8

2411 A731 70pf multi 60 55

Standing Commission of Posts and Telecommunications of Council of Mutual Economic Aid, 25th meeting.

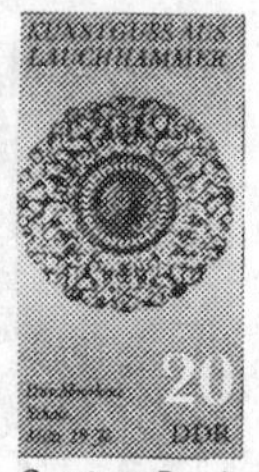

Cast-iron Bowl, 19th Cent. A732

Marionette A733

Cast-Iron, Lauchhammer: 85pf, Ascending Man, by Fritz Cremer, 1967.

1984, May 22

2412 A732 20pf multi 16 15
2413 A732 85pf multi 85 70

1984, June 5

2414 A733 50pf shown 50 40
2415 A733 80pf Puppet 1.10 65

Natl. Youth Festival A734

1984, June 5 Litho. *Perf. 13x12½*

2416 A734 10pf + 5pf Demonstration 22 15
2417 A734 20pf Construction workers 22 15
a. Pair, #2416-2417 + label 45
Set value 24

20th Workers' Festival A735

1984, June 19

2418 A735 10pf View of Gera 15 15
2419 A735 20pf Traditional costumes 30 15
a. Pair, #2418-2419 + label 40
Set value 22

Natl. Stamp Exhib., Halle — A736

Historic Seals, 1442 — A737

1984, July 3 *Perf. 13½x14*

2420 A736 10pf + 5pf Salt carrier 18 15
2421 A736 20pf Wedding couple 22 15
Set value 24

1984, Aug. 7 Litho. *Perf. 14*

2422 A737 5pf Baker, Berlin *35* 15
2423 A737 10pf Wool weaver, Berlin *70* 15
2424 A737 20pf Wool weaver, Cologne *1.25* 15
2425 A737 35pf Shoemaker, Cologne *2.50* 25
a. Block of 4, #2422-2425 *5.00*
Set value 50

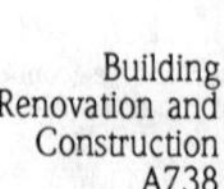

Building Renovation and Construction A738

Ironwork Collective Combine East — A739

Litho., Photo. (#2427, 2429, 25pf)

1984 *Perf. 14x13½*

2426 A738 10pf shown 15 15
2427 A739 10pf shown 15 15
2428 A738 20pf Surface mining 25 16
2429 A739 20pf Armed forces 25 16
2430 A739 25pf Petro-chemical Collective Combine, Schwedt 28 18
Nos. 2426-2430 (5) 1.08
Set value 64

Souvenir Sheets

2431 A738 1m Privy Council Building 1.10 80
2432 A739 1m Family 1.10 80

35th anniv. of DDR. Issue dates: A738, Aug. 21; A739, Sept. 11.

1984 Leipzig Autumn Fair — A740

1984, Aug. 28 Photo. *Perf. 14*

2433 A740 10pf Frege House, Katharine St. 15 15
2434 A740 25pf Crystal bowl, Olbernhau 32 16
Set value 24

Members of the Resistance, Sculpture by Arno Wittig — A741

1984, Sept. 18 Photo. *Perf. 14*

2435 A741 35pf multi 70 22

View of Magdeburg A742

1984, Oct. 4 Litho. *Perf. 13x12½*

2436 A742 10pf + 5pf shown 18 15
2437 A742 20pf Old & modern buildings 22 15
a. Pair, #2436-2437 + label 42
Set value 24

8th Youth Stamp Exhibition, Magdeburg.

35th Anniv. of Republic — A743

1984, Oct. 4 Photo. *Perf. 14*

2438 A743 10pf Construction 15 15
2439 A743 20pf Military 20 15
2440 A743 25pf Heavy industry 25 18
2441 A743 35pf Agriculture 32 22

Souvenir Sheet

2442 A743 1m Arms, dove, vert. 1.10 70

Figurines, Green Vault of Dresden — A744

1984, Oct. 23

2443 A744 10pf Spring 15 15
2444 A744 20pf Summer 22 15
a. Miniature sheet of 8, litho., perf. 12½x13 2.75 1.50
2445 A744 35pf Autumn 40 22
2446 A744 70pf Winter 75 45

Falkenstein Castle — A745

1984, Nov. 6 Litho. *Perf. 14*

2447 A745 10pf shown 15 15
2448 A745 20pf Kriebstein 22 15
2449 A745 35pf Ranis 35 22
2450 A745 80pf Neuenburg 95 60

See Nos. 2504-2507.

Dead Tsar's Daughter and the Seven Warriors A746

Various scenes from the fairytale.

1984, Nov. 27 Litho. *Perf. 13*

2451 Sheet of 6 *15.00* 1.10
a. A746 5pf multi *30* 15
b. A746 10pf multi *50* 15
c. A746 15pf multi *85* 15
d. A746 20pf multi *1.10* 16
e. A746 35pf multi *1.90* 28
f. A746 50pf multi *2.75* 40

Working-class Leader Type of 1979

Designs: No. 2452, Anton Ackermann (1905-1973). No. 2453, Alfred Kurella (1895-1975). No. 2454, Otto Schon (1905-1968).

1985, Jan. 8 Engr. *Perf. 14*

2452 A623 10pf blk brn 15 15
2453 A623 10pf red brn 15 15
2454 A623 10pf gray vio 15 15
Set value 24 22

24th World Luge Championship — A747

1985, Jan. 22 Photo.

2455 A747 10pf Single seat luge 15 15

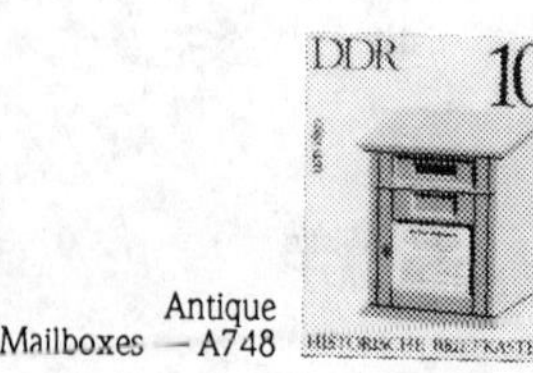

Antique Mailboxes — A748

1985, Feb. 5 Litho. *Perf. 14*

2456 A748 10pf 1850 15 15
2457 A748 20pf 1860 28 16
2458 A748 35pf 1900 45 28
2459 A748 50pf 1920 60 38
a. Block of 4, Nos. 2456-2459 1.50 90

Souvenir Sheet

Dresden Opera House Reopening A749

Litho. & Engr.

1985, Feb. 12 *Perf. 13*

2460 A749 85pf multicolored 1.10 70

1985 Leipzig Spring Fair — A750

Bach, Handel and Schutz Tribute — A751

1985, Mar. 5 Photo. *Perf. 14*

2461 A750 10pf Statue of Bach, Leipzig 15 15
2462 A750 25pf Porcelain pot, Meissen 32 16
Set value 23

Souvenir Sheet

1985, Mar. 19 Litho.

2463 Sheet of 3 1.75 1.00
a. A751 10pf Bach 15 15
b. A751 20pf Handel 22 15
c. A751 85pf Heinrich Schutz (1585-1672) 1.25 75

City Arms Type of 1983

1985, Apr. 9 Photo. *Perf. 14*

2464 A716 50pf Neubrandenburg 60 42
2465 A716 50pf Potsdam 60 42
2466 A716 50pf Rostock 60 42
2467 A716 50pf Schwerin 60 42
2468 A716 50pf Suhl 60 42
Nos. 2464-2468 (5) 3.00 2.10

Seelow Heights Memorial — A752

1985, Apr. 16 Photo. *Perf. 14*

2469 A752 35pf multi 45 28

Egon Erwin Kisch, Journalist (1885-1948) — A753

1985, Apr. 23 Photo. *Perf. 14*

2470 A753 35pf multi 50 28

No. 2470 was printed se-tenant with label showing the house where Kisch was born.

Liberation from Fascism, 40th Anniv. — A754

Designs: 10pf, German and Soviet astronauts. 20pf, Coal miner Adolf Hennecke, symbols of industry and energy. 25pf, farm workers, symbols of socialist agriculture. 50pf, Technicians manufacturing microchips, science and technology.

1985, May 7 Photo. *Perf. 14x13½*

2471 A754 10pf multi 15 15
2472 A754 20pf multi 24 16
2473 A754 25pf multi 28 18
2474 A754 50pf multi 55 38

Souvenir Sheet

Perf. 12½x13

2475 A754 1m Berlin-Treptow Soviet Heroes Monument 1.25 75

Warsaw Treaty, 30th Anniv. — A755

1985, May 14 Litho. *Perf. 13x12½*

2476 A755 20pf Flags of pact nations 45 15

Historical and Modern Buildings A756

12th Youth Parliament, Berlin: 20pf, Ernst Thalmann, flags.

1985, May 21 Litho.

2477 A756 10pf + 5pf multi 15 15
2478 A756 20pf multi 20 15
a. Pair, #2477-2478 + label 35
Set value 23

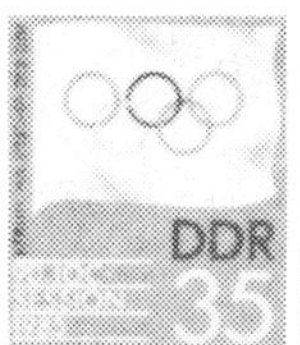

Intl. Olympic Committee 90th Meeting — A757

1985, May 28 Litho. *Perf. 14*

2479 A757 35pf Flag 45 28

No. 2479 was printed se-tenant with label.

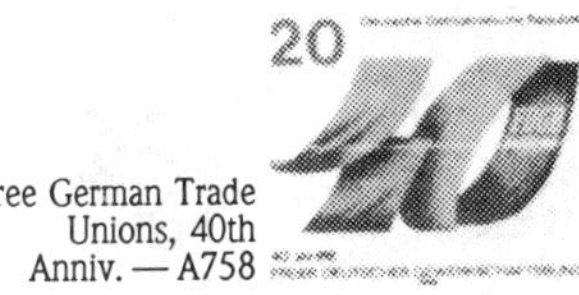

Free German Trade Unions, 40th Anniv. — A758

1985, June 11 Photo.

2480 A758 20pf Red flags 35 22

Wildlife Preservation A759

1985, June 25 Photo.

2481 A759 5pf Harpy eagle, vert. 15 15
2482 A759 10pf Red-necked goose 15 15
2483 A759 20pf Spectacled bear 25 16
2484 A759 50pf Banteng (Javanese) buffalo 60 38
2485 A759 85pf Sunda Straits crocodile 95 65
Nos. 2481-2485 (5) 2.10 1.49

19th Century Steam Engines A760

1985, July 9 Photo.

2486 A760 10pf Bock engine, vert. 15 15
2487 A760 85pf Beam engine 95 60

12th World Youth and Student Festival, Moscow A761

1985, July 23 Litho. *Perf. 13x12½*

2488 A761 20pf + 5pf Students reading 30 15
2489 A761 50pf Student demonstration 70 35
a. Pair, #2488-2489 + label 1.05

2nd World Orienteering and Deep-sea Diving Championship — A762

1985, Aug. 13 Photo. *Perf. 14*

2490 A762 10pf Diver at turning buoy 15 15
2491 A762 70pf Long-distance divers 80 45
Set value 52

Bose House Fair Building, St. Thomas Churchyard — A763

1985, Apr. 27 Photo.

2492 A763 10pf shown 15 15
2493 A763 25pf Bach trumpet 40 18
Set value 25

Leipzig Autumn Fair.

SOZPHILEX '85 — A764

Design: 19th century coach and team, 1878, bas-relief by Hermann Steinemann, in the court of the former Berlin Post Office.

1985, Sept. 10 Litho. *Perf. 13x12½*

2494 A764 5pf multi 15 15
2495 A764 20pf + 5pf multi 40 18
a. Miniature sheet of 8, 4 each 2.00 90
b. Pair, #2494-2495 50
Set value 22

No. 2495b has a continuous design.

Socialist Railway Org. — A765

Designs: 20pf, GS II signal box, track diagram. 25pf, 1838 Saxonia, first German locomotive, designer Johann Andreas Schubert (1808-1870), Model 250 electric locomotive. 50pf, Helicopter lifting cable drum, section electrification. 85pf, Leipzig Central Station.

1985, Sept. 24 Litho. *Perf. 12½x13*

2496 A765 20pf multi 28 18
2497 A765 25pf multi 35 22
2498 A765 50pf multi 70 45
2499 A765 85pf multi 1.10 70

German Railways 150th anniv.

Bridges in East Berlin A766

Photo.; Litho. (#2501a)

1985, Oct. 8 *Perf. 14*

2500 A766 10pf Gertrauden 15 15
2501 A766 20pf Jungfern 24 18
a. Min. sheet of 8, perf. 13x12½ 2.50 1.40
2502 A766 35pf Weidendammer 42 32
2503 A766 70pf Marx-Engels 85 60

Castles Type of 1984

1985, Oct. 15 Litho.

2504 A745 10pf Hohnstein 15 15
2505 A745 20pf Rochsburg 20 15
2506 A745 35pf Schwarzenberg 38 28
2507 A745 80pf Stein 85 65

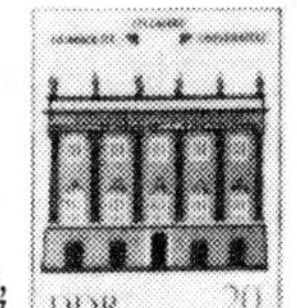

Humboldt University, 175th Anniv. — A767

Anniversaries: 85pf, Charity Hospital, Berlin, 275th anniv.

1985, Oct. 22 *Perf. 14*

2508 A767 20pf Administration bldg. 20 15
2509 A767 85pf Buildings, 1897, 1982 1.25 70

Castle Cacilienhof, UN Emblem A768

1985, Oct. 22 Photo. *Perf. 13*

2510 A768 85pf multi 1.00 70

UN, 40th Anniv.

Circus Art — A769

1985, Nov. 12 *Perf. 14*

2511 A769 10pf Elephant training 20 15
2512 A769 20pf Trapeze artist 85 25
2513 A769 35pf Acrobats on unicycles 1.50 42
2514 A769 50pf Tiger training 2.25 65
a. Block of 4, #2511-2514 5.00

Souvenir Sheet

Brothers Grimm, Fabulists & Philologists A770

Fairy tales compiled by Wilhelm (1786-1859) and Jacob (1785-1863) Grimm.

1985, Nov. 26 Litho. *Perf. 13½x13*

2515 Sheet of 6 2.50 1.65
a. A770 5pf multi 15 15
b. A770 10pf Valiant Tailor 15 15
c. A770 20pf Lucky John 22 16
d. A770 25pf Puss-in-Boots 28 20
e. A770 35pf Seven Ravens 40 28
f. A770 85pf Sweet Porridge 95 70

Monuments to Water Power — A772

Postal Uniforms, c. 1850 — A773

Designs: 10pf, Cast iron hand pump, c. 1900. 35pf, Berlin-Altglienicke water tower, c. 1900. 50pf, Berlin-Friedrichshagen waterworks, 1893. 70pf, Rapphoden Hydro-electric Dam, 1959.

Engr., Photo. & Engr. (35pf)

1986, Jan. 21 *Perf. 14*

2516 A772 10pf dk grn & lake 15 15
2517 A772 35pf buff, blk & dk grn 42 28
2518 A772 50pf dk red brn & lt ol grn 60 38
2519 A772 70pf dk bl & brn 85 52

1986, Feb. 4 Photo. *Perf. 14½x14*

2520 A773 10pf Saxon postillion 18 15
a. Litho., perf. 12½x13 18 15
2521 A773 20pf Prussian postman 32 16
a. Litho., perf. 12½x13 32 16
2522 A773 85pf Prussian P.O. clerk 1.40 70
a. Litho., perf. 12½x13 1.40 70
2523 A773 1m Mecklenburg clerk 1.50 75
a. Litho., perf. 12½x13 1.50 75
b. Block of 4, #2520a-2523a 3.50 1.75

30 JAHRE NATIONALE VOLKSARMEE DDR 20

Natl. People's Army, 30th Anniv. A774

1986, Feb. 18 *Perf. 14*

2524 A774 20pf multi 35 16

No. 2524 printed se-tenant with gold and red inscribed label.

Free German Youth Org., 40th Anniv. — A775

1986, Feb. 18
2525 A775 20pf multi 35 16

Leipzig Spring Fair A776

1986, Mar. 11 Litho. *Perf. 13x12½*
2526 A776 35pf Fair grounds entrance, 1946 40 28
2527 A776 50pf Trawler Atlantik 488 55 42

Manned Space Flight, 25th Anniv. — A777

Designs: 40pf, Yuri Gagarin, Soviet cosomonaut, Vostok rocket, 1961. 50pf, Cosmonauts W. Bykowski, USSR, and S. Jahn, DDR, Vega probe, 1986, Intercosmos emblem. 70pf, Venera probe, Venus, spectrometer. 85pf, MKF-6 multi-spectral reconnaissance camera.

1986, Mar. 25 *Perf. 14*
2528 A777 40pf multi 45 35
2529 A777 50pf multi 60 42
2530 A777 70pf multi 80 60
2531 A777 85pf multi 1.00 70
a. Block of 4, #2528-2531 3.00

Socialist Unity 11th Party Day — A778

Designs: 10pf, Marx, Engels and Lenin. 20pf, Ernst Thalmann. 50pf, Wilhelm Pieck and Otto Grotewohl, Uniting Party Day, 1946. 85pf, Family, motto. 1m, Construction worker, key to economic progress.

1986, Apr. 8 *Perf. 13½x13*
2532 A778 10pf multi 15 15
2533 A778 20pf multi 25 18
2534 A778 50pf multi 60 42
2535 A778 85pf multi 1.00 75

Souvenir Sheet
Perf. 13x14
2536 A778 1m multi 1.25 85

Ernst Thalmann Park Opening, Berlin — A779

1986, Apr. 15 Photo. *Perf. 14*
2537 A779 20pf Memorial statue 30 18

Trams and Streetcars A780

Designs: 10pf, Dresden horse-drawn tram, 1886. 20pf, Leipzig streetcar, 1896. 40pf, Berlin streetcar, 1919. 70pf, Halle streetcar, 1928.

1986, May 20 Photo. *Perf. 14*
2538 A780 10pf multi 15 15
2539 A780 20pf multi 25 16
2540 A780 40pf multi 45 32
2541 A780 70pf multi 80 60

Dresden Zoo, 125th Anniv. — A781

Berlin, 750th Anniv. — A782

1986, May 27 Litho. *Perf. 14*
2542 A781 10pf Orangutan 15 15
2543 A781 20pf Colobus monkey 25 16
2544 A781 50pf Mandrill 65 50
2545 A781 70pf Lemur 95 68

Litho. & Engr., Engr. (70pf, 1m)
1986, June 3 *Perf. 12½x13, 13x12½*
20pf, 50pf are horiz.
2546 A782 10pf City seal, 1253 22 15
2547 A782 20pf Map, 1648 40 16
2548 A782 50pf City arms, 1253 1.00 40
2549 A782 70pf Nicholas Church, 1832 1.50 60

Souvenir Sheet
2550 A782 1m Royal Palace, 1986 1.25 85

21st Workers' Games, Magdeburg A783

Designs: 20pf, Couple in folk dress, house construction. 50pf, Magdeburg Port, River Elbe.

1986, June 17 Litho. *Perf. 13x12½*
2551 A783 20pf multi 20 16
2552 A783 50pf multi 52 40
a. Pair, #2551-2552 + label 75

9th Youth Stamp Exhibition, Berlin A784

1986, July 22 Litho. *Perf. 13x12½*
2553 A784 10pf + 5pf Berlin, c. 1652 20 15
2554 A784 20pf Art, architecture, 1986 25 18
a. Pair, #2553-2554 + label 45

Castles A785

1986, July 29 *Perf. 13x12½*
2555 A785 10pf Schwerin 15 15
a. Miniature sheet of 4 50 35
2556 A785 20pf Gustrow 22 18
a. Miniature sheet of 4 1.25 70
2557 A785 85pf Rheinsberg 95 70
2558 A785 1m Ludwigslust 1.10 90

Intl. Peace Year — A786

1986, Aug. 5 Photo. *Perf. 13*
2559 A786 35pf multi 45 32

Berlin Wall, 25th Anniv. A787

1986, Aug. 5 Litho. *Perf. 14*
2560 A787 20pf Soldiers, Brandenburg Gate 45 18

Souvenir Sheet

Leipzig Autumn Fair — A788

1986, Aug. 19
2561 A788 Sheet of 2 1.40 90
a. 25pf Fair building 70 18
b. 85pf Cloth merchants, 15th cent. 70 70

City Coins — A789

1986, Sept. 2 Photo. *Perf. 13*
2562 A789 10pf Rostock, 1637 15 15
2563 A789 35pf Nordhausen, 1660 40 32
2564 A789 50pf Erfurt, 1633 55 42
2565 A789 85pf Magdeburg, 1638 95 75
2566 A789 1m Stralsund, 1622 1.10 85
Nos. 2562-2566 (5) 3.15 2.49

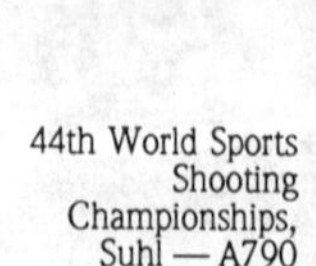

44th World Sports Shooting Championships, Suhl — A790

1986, Sept. 2 *Perf. 14*
2567 A790 20pf Rifle shooting 24 18
2568 A790 70pf Woman firing handgun 80 60
2569 A790 85pf Skeet-shooting 95 70

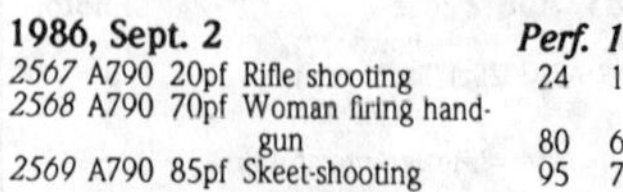

Mukran-Klaipeda Train-Ferry, Inauguration — A795

11th World Trade Unions Congress, Berlin — A791

Border Guards, 40th Anniv. — A792

1986, Sept. 9
2570 A791 70pf multi 75 60

No. 2570 printed se-tenant with label continuing the design.

1986, Sept. 9
2571 A792 20pf multi 30 18

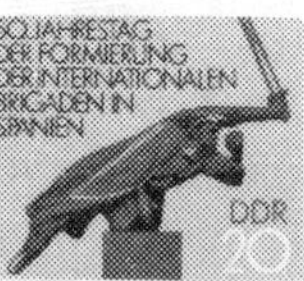

Intl. Brigades in Spain, 50th Anniv. — A793

1986, Sept. 11
2572 A793 20pf Memorial, Friedrichshain 30 18

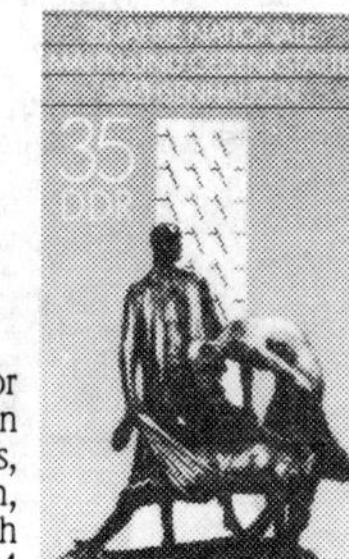

Natl. Memorial for Concentration Camp Victims, Sachsenhausem, 25th Anniv. — A794

1986, Sept. 23
2573 A794 35pf multi 40 32

1986, Sept. 23
2574 A795 50pf Pier, Mukran 60 42
2575 A795 50pf Ferry 60 42
a. Pair, #2574-2575 1.25 1.00

Souvenir Sheet

Carl Maria von Weber (1786-1826), Composer — A796

1986, Nov. 4 Litho. *Perf. 14*
2576 A796 85pf multi 1.00 75

Indira Gandhi (1917-1984), Prime Minister of India — A797

1986, Nov. 18 **Photo.**
2577 A797 10pf multi 25 15

Miniature Sheet

Chandeliers from the Ore Mountains — A798

Wrought iron candle-carrying chandeliers presented to Johann Georgenstadt miners annually by the mine blacksmith.

1986, Nov. 18 **Photo.** ***Perf. 14***
2578 Sheet of 6 2.50 1.90
a. A798 10pf 1778 38 30
b. A798 20pf 1796 38 30
c. A798 25pf 1810 38 30
d. A798 35pf 1821 38 30
e. A798 40pf 1830 38 30
f. A798 85pf 1925 38 30

Statues of Roland, Medieval Hero — A799

1987, Jan. 20 **Photo.** ***Perf. 14½x14***
2579 A799 10pf Stendal, 1525 15 15
2580 A799 20pf Halle, 1719 22 20
2581 A799 35pf Brandenburg, 1474 40 35
2582 A799 50pf Quedlinburg, 1460 55 50

See Nos. 2782-2785.

Historic Post Offices A800

1987, Feb. 3 **Photo.** ***Perf. 14x14½***
2583 A800 10pf Freiberg, 1889 15 15
2584 A800 20pf Perleberg, 1897 24 18
2585 A800 70pf Weimar, 1889 75 60
2586 A800 1.20m Kirschau, 1926 1.40 1.00
a. Block of 4, #2583-2586 2.50 2.00

Nos. 2583-2586 printed in sheets of fifty and se-tenant in sheets of 40.

Berlin, 750th Anniv. A801

Architecture: 20pf, Reconstructed Palais Ephraim, Nikolai Quarter, demolished 1936, reopened 1987, vert. 35pf, Old Marzahn Village, modern housing. 70pf, Marx-Engels Forum, Central Berlin. 85pf, Reconstructed Friedrichstadt Palace Theater, reopened 1984.

Perf. 12½x13, 13x12½
1987, Feb. 17 **Engr.**
2587 A801 20pf vio brn & bluish grn 25 20
2588 A801 35pf sage grn & dk rose brn 45 32
2589 A801 70pf org & dk bl 80 65
2590 A801 85pf dk ol grn & yel grn 1.10 85

See Nos. 2628-2631.

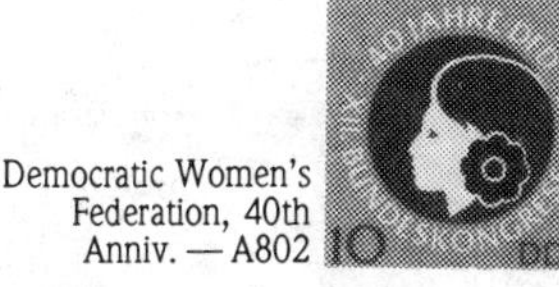

Democratic Women's Federation, 40th Anniv. — A802

1987, Mar. 3 **Litho.** ***Perf. 13½***
2591 A802 10pf sil, dk bl & brt red 18 16

Leipzig Spring Fair A803

1987, Mar. 10 ***Perf. 13x12½***
2592 A803 35pf New Fair Hall No. 20 38 35
2593 A803 50pf Traders at market, c. 1804 55 50

Leaders of the German Workers' Movement — A804

Portraits: No. 2594, Fritz Gabler (1897-1974). No. 2595, Robert Siewert (1887-1973). No. 2596, Walter Vesper (1897-1978). No. 2597, Clara Zetkin (1857-1933).

1987, Mar. 24 **Engr.** ***Perf. 14***
2594 A804 10pf dark gray 15 15
2595 A804 10pf dark green 15 15
2596 A804 10pf black 15 15
2597 A804 10pf vio black 15 15
Set value 40

See Nos. 2721-2724.

K.A. Lingner (1861-1916), Museum — A805

1987, Apr. 7 **Photo.** ***Perf. 14***
2598 A805 85pf multi 90 80

German Hygiene Museum, Dresden, 75th anniv.

Free German Trade Unions 11th Congress A806

1987, Apr. 7 **Litho.** ***Perf. 13x12½***
2599 A806 20pf Construction 22 20
2600 A806 50pf Computer, ship 58 52
a. Pair, #2599-2600 + label 85

German Red Cross 10th Congress A807

1987, Apr. 7 **Photo.** ***Perf. 14***
2601 A807 35pf multi 50 35

Agricultural Cooperative, 35th Anniv. — A808

1987, Apr. 21 **Litho.** ***Perf. 13x12½***
2602 A808 20pf multi 30 22

Famous Men A809

Designs: 10pf, Ludwig Uhland (1787-1862), poet, philologist. 20pf, Arnold Zweig (1887-1968), novelist. 35pf, Gerhart Hauptmann (1862-1946), 1912 Nobel laureate for literature, and scene from The Weavers. 50pf, Gustav Hertz (1887-1975), physicist, and atomic energy transmission diagram.

1987, May 5
2603 A809 10pf multi 15 15
2604 A809 20pf multi 24 22
2605 A809 35pf multi 40 35
2606 A809 50pf multi 58 52

Freshwater Fish A810

1987, May 19 **Litho.** ***Perf. 13x12½***
2607 A810 5pf Abramis brama 15 15
2608 A810 10pf Salmo trutta fario 15 15
2609 A810 20pf Silurus glanis 24 22
2610 A810 35pf Thymallus thymallus 40 35
2611 A810 50pf Barbus barbus 58 52
2612 A810 70pf Esox lucius 80 70
Nos. 2607-2612 (6) 2.32 2.09

Nos. 2608-2609 exist in sheets of 4.

Fire Engines A811

1987, June 16
2613 A811 10pf Hand-operated, 1756 15 15
2614 A811 25pf Steam, 1903 28 25
2615 A811 40pf LF 15, 1919 45 40
2616 A811 70pf LF 16-TS 8, 1971 78 70
a. Block of 4, Nos. 2613-2616 1.65 1.50

Souvenir Sheet

Esperanto Movement, Cent. — A812

1987, July 7 **Litho.** ***Perf. 14***
2617 A812 85pf L.L. Zamenhof, globe 95 85

World Wildlife Fund A813

1987, July 7 **Photo.**
2618 A813 10pf Two otters 15 15
2619 A813 25pf Otter swimming 28 25
2620 A813 35pf Otter 38 35
2621 A813 60pf Close-up of head 68 60

8th Sports Festival and 11th Youth Sports Championships, Leipzig — A814

1987, July 21
2622 A814 5pf Tug-of-war 15 15
2623 A814 10pf Handball 15 15
2624 A814 20pf + 5pf Girls' long jump 28 25
2625 A814 35pf Table tennis 38 35
2626 A814 40pf Bowling 45 40
2627 A814 70pf Running 78 70
Nos. 2622-2627 (6) 2.19 2.00

Berlin Anniversary Type of 1987
Perf. 12½x13, 13x12½
1987, Feb. 17 **Engr.**
2628 A801 10pf like No. 2587 15 15
a. Miniature sheet of 4 48 42
2629 A801 10pf like No. 2588 15 15
a. Miniature sheet of 4 48 42
2630 A801 20pf like No. 2589 24 22
a. Miniature sheet of 4 1.00 90
2631 A801 20pf like No. 2590 24 22
a. Miniature sheet of 4 1.00 90

Assoc. of Sports and Science, 35th Anniv. A815

1987, Aug. 4 **Litho.** ***Perf. 13x12½***
2632 A815 10pf multi 15 15

Stamp Day A816

Designs: 10pf+5pf, Court Post Office, Berlin, 1760. 20pf, Wartenberg Palace, former Prussian General Post Office, 1770.

1987, Aug. 11 **Photo.** ***Perf. 14***
2633 A816 10pf +5pf multi 18 16
2634 A816 20pf multi 24 22
a. Pair, #2633-2634 + label 45

Souvenir Sheet

Leipzig Autumn Fair — A817

Illustration reduced.

1987, Aug. 25 **Litho.** ***Perf. 13½***
2635 A817 Sheet of 2 1.10 1.00
a. 40pf multi 48 42
b. 50pf multi 60 55

Intl. War Victims' Memorial, Budapest — A818

1987, Sept. 8 Photo. *Perf. 14*

2636 A818 35pf Statue of Jozsef Somogyi 50 35

Souvenir Sheet

Thalmann Memorial — A819

Illustration reduced.

1987, Sept. 8 Litho. & Engr. *Perf. 14*

2637 A819 1.35m buff, ver & blk 1.50 1.40

City of Berlin, 750th anniv.

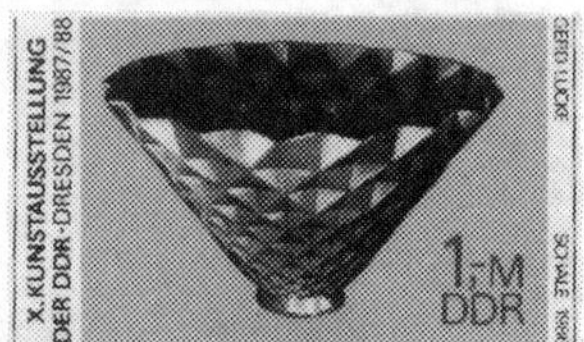

10th Natl. Art Exhibition, Berlin — A820

Designs: 10pf, Weidendamm Bridge, Berlin, 1986, by Arno Mohr. 50pf, They Only Wanted to Learn How to Read and Write, Nicaragua, 1985-86, by Willi Sitte. 70pf, Large Figure of a Man in Mourning, 1983, scupture by Wieland Forster. 1m, Ceramic bowl, 1986, by Gerd Lucke. Nos. 2638-2640, vert.

1987, Sept. 28 Litho.

2638	A820	10pf multi	15	15
2639	A820	50pf multi	55	50
2640	A820	70pf multi	80	70
2641	A820	1m multi	1.15	1.00

Lenin, Flag, Smolny Institute, Cruiser Aurora A821

1987, Oct. 27 Photo. *Perf. 14*

2642	A821	10pf shown	15	15
2643	A821	20pf Spasski Tower	25	20

October Revolution, Russia, 70th anniv.

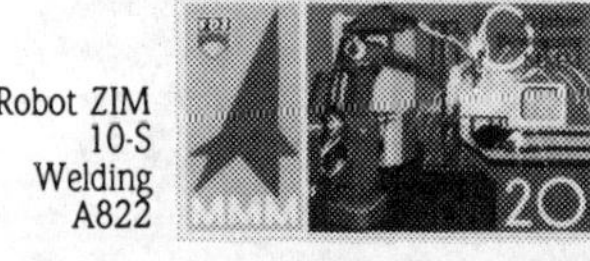

Robot ZIM 10-S Welding A822

1987, Nov. 3 Litho. *Perf. 13x12½*

2644	A822	10pf Personal computer	15	15
2645	A822	20pf shown	25	20

30th MMM Science Fair and 10th Central Industrial Fair for Students and Youth Scientists, Leipzig.

Miniature Sheet

Christmas Candle Carousels from the Ore Mountains — A823

Designs: 10pf, Annaberg, c. 1810. 20pf, Freiberg, c. 1830. 25pf, Neustadtel, c. 1870. 35pf, Schneeberg, c. 1870. 40pf, Lossnitz, c. 1880. 85pf, Seiffen, c. 1910.

1987, Nov. 3 Litho. *Perf. 12½x13*

2646		Sheet of 6	2.50	2.25
a.	A823	10pf multi	15	15
b.	A823	20pf multi	22	20
c.	A823	25pf multi	28	25
d.	A823	35pf multi	40	35
e.	A823	40pf multi	45	40
f.	A823	85pf multi	95	85

1988 Winter Olympics, Calgary — A824

1988, Jan. 19 Photo. *Perf. 14½x14*

2647	A824	5pf Ski jumping	15	15
2648	A824	10pf Speed skating	15	15
2649	A824	20pf +10pf 4-Man bobsled	42	38
2650	A824	35pf Biathlon	48	42

Souvenir Sheet

Perf. 13x12½

2651 A824 1.20m Single and double luge 1.50 1.40

No. 2649 surtaxed for the Olympic Promotion Society.

Postal Buildings, East Berlin A825

1988, Feb. 2 *Perf. 14*

2652	A825	15pf Berlin-Buch post office	22	20
2653	A825	20pf Natl. Postal Museum	28	25
2654	A825	50pf General post office, Berlin-Marzahn	70	65

Souvenir Sheet

Bertolt Brecht (1898-1956), Playwright — A826

1988, Feb. 2 Litho. *Perf. 13x12½*

2655 A826 70pf multi 1.00 90

Flowering Plants — A827

Leipzig Spring Fair — A828

1988, Feb. 16 Photo. *Perf. 14*

2656	A827	10pf Tillandsia macrochlamys	15	15
2657	A827	25pf Tillandsia bulbosa	30	28
2658	A827	40pf Tillandsia kalmbacheri	50	45
2659	A827	70pf Guzmania blassii	85	75

1988, Mar. 8 Litho. *Perf. 12½x13*

Designs: 20pf, Entrance No. 8. 70pf, Faust and Mephistopheles, bronze statue by Matthieu Molitor.

2660	A828	20pf multi	26	22
2661	A828	70pf multi	95	75

Madler Passage (arcade), 75th anniv.

Souvenir Sheet

Joseph von Eichendorff (1788-1857), Poet — A829

1988, Mar. 8 *Perf. 14*

2662 A829 70pf multi 1.40 75

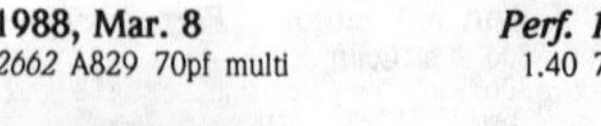

Seals — A830

1988, Mar. 22 Photo. *Perf. 14*

2663	A830	10pf Muhlhausen saddler, 1565	15	15
2664	A830	25pf Dresden butcher, 1564	30	28
2665	A830	35pf Nauen smith, 16th cent.	42	38
2666	A830	50pf Frankfurt-Oder clothier, 16th cent.	60	55
a.		Block of 4, #2663-2666	1.45	1.35

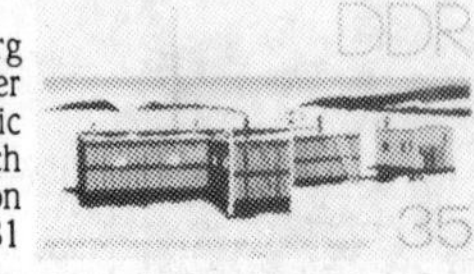

Georg Forster Antarctic Research Station A831

1988, Mar. 22 Litho. *Perf. 13x12½*

2667 A831 35pf multi 42 38

District Capitals A832

1988, Apr. 5 Photo. *Perf. 14*

2668	A832	5pf Wismar	15	15
2669	A832	10pf Anklam	15	15
2670	A832	25pf Ribnitz-Damgarten	30	28
2671	A832	60pf Stralsund	72	65
2672	A832	90pf Bergen	1.10	1.00
2673	A832	1.20m Greifswald	1.45	1.25
		Nos. 2668-2673 (6)	3.87	3.48

Souvenir Sheet

Ulrich von Hutten (1488-1523), Promulgator of the Lutheran Movement — A833

1988, Apr. 5 Litho. *Perf. 12½x13*

2674 A833 70pf multi 1.00 75

USSR-DDR Manned Space Flight, 10th Anniv. — A834

Designs: 5pf, Cosmonauts S. Jahn and Valery Bykowski, Soyuz-29 landing, Sept. 3, 1978. 10pf, MKS-M multi-channel spectrometer. 20pf, MIR space station.

1988, June 21 Litho. *Perf. 14*

2675	A834	5pf multi	15	15
2676	A834	10pf multi	15	15
2677	A834	20pf multi	28	22
		Set value	50	38

See Nos. 2698-2700.

10th Youth Stamp Exhibitions in Erfurt and Karl-Marx-Stadt — A835

Designs: 10pf+5pf, Erfurt. c. 1520. 20+5pf, Chemnitz, c. 1620. 25pf, Historic and modern buildings of Erfurt. 50pf, Historic and modern buildings of Karl-Marx-Stadt.

1988, June 21 **Photo.**

2678 A835 20pf +5pf multi 18 16
2679 A835 20pf +5pf multi 28 25
2680 A835 25pf multi 28 25
a. Pair, #2678, 2680 + label 50
2681 A835 50pf multi 58 52
a. Pair, #2679, 2681 + label 90

Nos. 2678-2679 surtaxed to benefit the Philatelists' League of the DDR Cultural Union.

22nd Workers' Games, Frankfurt-on-Oder — A836

1988, July 7 **Litho.** ***Perf. 13x12½***

2682 20pf multi 24 22
2683 50pf multi, diff. 58 52
a. A836 Pair, #2682-2683 + label 85

Workers' Militia, 35th Anniv. — A837

1988, July 5 **Photo.** ***Perf. 14***

2684 A837 5pf Oath 15 15
2685 A837 10pf Ernst Thalmann tribute 15 15
2686 A837 15pf Roll call 18 16
2687 A837 20pf Weapons exchange 24 22
Set value 60 54

8th Young Pioneers' Congress, Karl-Marx-Stadt — A838

1988, July 19 **Litho.** ***Perf. 13x12½***

2688 A838 10pf shown 15 15
2689 A838 10pf +5pf Youths playing musical instruments 18 16
a. Pair, #2688-2689 + label 35

Surtax financed the congress.

1988 Summer Olympics, Seoul A839

1988, Aug. 9 **Photo.** ***Perf. 14***

2690 A839 5pf Swimming 15 15
2691 A839 10pf Handball 15 15
2692 A839 20pf +10pf Hurdles 32 28
2693 A839 25pf Rowing 28 25
2694 A839 35pf Boxing 38 35
2695 A839 50pf +20pf Cycling 78 70
Nos. 2690-2695 (6) 2.06 1.88

Souvenir Sheet

Litho.

Perf. 13x12½

2696 A839 85pf Relay race 1.25 85

Souvenir Sheet

Leipzig Autumn Fair — A840

1988, Aug. 30 **Litho.** ***Perf. 14***

2697 A840 Sheet of 3 1.50 1.40
a. 5pf Fair, c. 1810 15 15
b. 15pf Battle of Leipzig Memorial 18 16
c. 1m Fair, c. 1820 1.20 1.10

DDR-USSR Manned Space Flight Type

1988, Aug. 30 **Litho.** ***Perf. 14***

2698 A834 10pf like No. 2675 15 15
a. Sheet of 4 50 45
2699 A834 20pf like No. 2676 22 20
a. Sheet of 4 90 80
2700 A834 35pf like No. 2677 38 35
a. Sheet of 4 1.55 1.40

Fascism Resistance Memorial, Como, Italy — A841

1988, Sept. 13 **Photo.**

2701 A841 35pf multi 45 35

Memorial at Buchenwald, 30th Anniv. — A842

1988, Sept. 13 ***Perf. 14***

2702 A842 10pf multi 15 15

Mariner's Soc., Stralsund, 500th Anniv. — A843

Paintings: 5pf, *Adolph Friedrich* at Stralsund, by C. Leplow. 10pf, *Die Gartenlaube* (built in 1872) at Stralsund, by J.F. Kruger. 70pf, Brigantine *Auguste Mathilde* (built in 1830) at Stralsund, by I.C. Grunwaldt. 1.20m, Brig *Hoffnung* at Cologne, by G.A. Luther.

1988, Sept. 20 **Litho.** ***Perf. 13½x13***

2703 A843 5pf multi 15 15
2704 A843 10pf multi 15 15
2705 A843 70pf multi 85 70
2706 A843 1.20m multi 1.40 1.10

Ship Lifts and Bridges A844

1988, Oct. 18 **Photo.** ***Perf. 14x14½***

2707 A844 5pf Magdeburg 15 15
2708 A844 10pf Magdeburg-Rothensee 15 15
2709 A844 35pf Niederfinow 42 38
2710 A844 70pf Altfriesack 82 75
2711 A844 90pf Rugendamm 1.05 95
Nos. 2707-2711 (5) 2.59 2.38

A845

A846

1988, Nov. 8 ***Perf. 14***

2712 A845 35pf Menorah 45 38

1st Nazi Pogrom (Kristallnacht), Nov. 9, 1938.

1988, Nov. 8

Paintings by Max Lingner (1888-1959).

2713 A846 5pf *In the Boat*, 1931 15 15
2714 A846 10pf *Yvonne*, 1939 15 15
2715 A846 20pf *Free, Strong and Happy*, 1944 22 20
2716 A846 85pf *New Harvest*, 1951 1.00 90

Souvenir Sheet

Friedrich Wolf (1888-1953), Playwright — A847

1988, Nov. 22 **Litho.**

2717 A847 1.10m multi 1.40 1.10

WHO, 40th Anniv. — A848

Bone Lace from Erzgebirge — A849

1988, Nov. 22 **Photo.**

2718 A848 85pf multi 1.00 90

Miniature Sheet

Various lace designs.

1988, Nov. 22 **Litho.** ***Perf. 12½x13***

2719 Sheet of 6 3.00 2.75
a. A849 20pf multi 22 20
b. A849 25pf multi 28 25
c. A849 35pf multi 40 35
d. A849 40pf multi 45 40
e. A849 50pf multi 58 52
f. A849 85pf multi 1.00 90

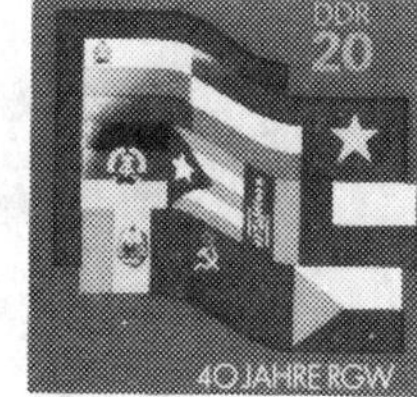

Council for Mutual Economic Aid, 40th Anniv. A850

1989, Jan. 10 **Photo.** ***Perf. 13***

2720 A850 20pf multi 30 20

Labor Leaders Type of 1987

Portraits: No. 2721, Edith Baumann (1909-1973). No. 2722, Otto Meier (1889-1962). No. 2723, Fritz Selbmann (1899-1975). No. 2724, Alfred Oelssner (1879-1962).

1989, Jan. 24 **Engr.** ***Perf. 14***

2721 A804 10pf dark vio brn 15 15
2722 A804 10pf dark grn 15 15
2723 A804 10pf dark blue 15 15
2724 A804 10pf brn blk 15 15
Set value 50 40

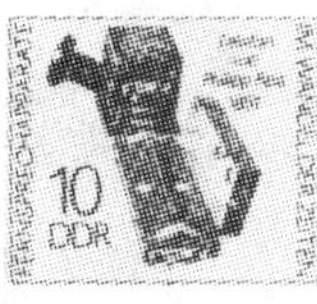

Telephones — A851

Designs: 10pf, Philipp Reis, 1861. 20pf, Siemens & Halske wall model, 1882. 50pf, Wall model OB 03, 1903. 85pf, Table model OB 05, 1905.

1989, Feb. 7 **Litho.**

2725 A851 10pf shown 15 15
2726 A851 20pf multi 22 15
2727 A851 50pf multi 55 30
2728 A851 85pf multi 95 60
a. Block of 4, #2725-2728 1.85 1.10

Famous Men A852

1989, Feb. 28 **Photo.**

2729 A852 10pf Ludwig Renn (1889-1979) 15 15
2730 A852 10pf Carl von Ossietzky (1889-1938) 15 15
2731 A852 10pf Adam Scharrer (1889-1948) 15 15
2732 A852 10pf Rudolf Mauersberger (1889-1971) 15 15
2733 A852 10pf Johann Beckmann (1739-1811) 15 15
Set value 60 55

Leipzig Spring Fair — A853

1989, Mar. 7 **Litho.**

2734 A853 70pf shown 78 70
2735 A853 85pf Buildings, 1690 95 85

Handelshof, 80th anniv. (70pf).

Souvenir Sheet

Thomas Munzer (c. 1468-1525), Religious Reformer — A854

1989, Mar. 21 *Perf. 13x12½*
2736 A854 1.10m multi 1.25 1.10

1st Long-distance German Railway, Leipzig-Dresden, Sesquicentennial A855

Designs: 15pf, Georg Friedrich List (1789-1846), industrialist, economist. 20pf, Dresden Station in Leipzig, 1839. 50pf, Leipzig Station in Dresden, 1839.

1989, Apr. 4 *Perf. 14*
2737 A855 15pf multi 20 16
2738 A855 20pf multi 25 20
2739 A855 50pf multi 65 50

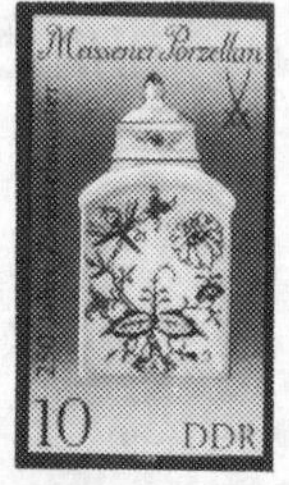

Meissen Onion-pattern Porcelain, 250th Anniv., and Sword Emblem — A856

1989, Apr. 18 Litho. *Perf. 12½x13*
2740 A856 10pf Tea caddy 15 15
2741 A856 20pf Vase 24 20
2742 A856 35pf Breadboard 42 35
2743 A856 70pf Teapot 85 70

Size: 33x56mm

Perf. 14

2744 Block of 4 1.75 1.40
a. A856 10pf like No. 2740 17 15
b. A856 20pf like No. 2741 24 20
c. A856 35pf like No. 2742 42 35
d. A856 70pf like No. 2743 85 70

Intl. Book Fair (IBA), Leipzig — A857

1989, May 2 Photo. *Perf. 14½x14*
2745 A857 20pf "I" 24 20
2746 A857 50pf "B" 60 50
2747 A857 1.35m "A" 1.65 1.40

Student Government — A858

1989, May 9 Litho. *Perf. 13½x12½*
2748 A858 20pf 8th World Youth Festival, Pyongyang 30 20
2749 A858 20pf +5pf Whitsun meeting of Free German Youth 40 25
a. Pair, #2748-2749 + label 70

Princess Luise — A859

Carl Zeiss Foundation, Jena, Cent. — A860

Sculptures by Johann Gottfried Schadow (1764-1850), Prussian Court Sculptor.

1989, May 16 Photo. *Perf. 14½x14*
2750 A859 50pf shown 65 50
2751 A859 85pf Princess Friederike 1.10 80

1989, May 16

Modern medical technology: 50pf, Interference microscope Jenaval. 85pf, Bicoordinate measuring instrument ZKM 01-250C.

2752 A860 50pf multi 65 50
2753 A860 85pf multi 1.10 80
a. Pair, #2752-2753 + label 1.75

Label pictures founder Ernst Abbe (1840-1905).

Jena University Inaugural Address, Bicent. — A861

1989, May 23 Photo. *Perf. 14*
2754 A861 25pf Frontispiece 30 24
2755 A861 85pf Excerpt 1.10 80
a. Pair, #2754-2755 + label 1.40

Label pictures bust of Friedrich Schiller, author of the address.

Souvenir Sheet

Zoologists — A862

1989, June 13 **Litho.**
2756 A862 Sheet of 2 1.75 1.25
a. 50pf Alfred Brehm (1829-1884) 65 45
b. 85pf Christian Brehm (1787-1864) 1.10 80

French Revolution, Bicent. A863

Designs: 5pf, Storming of the Bastille, July 14, 1789. 20pf, Revolutionaries, flag bearer. 90pf, Storming Tuileries Palace, Aug. 10, 1792.

1989, July 4 Photo. *Perf. 13*
2757 A863 5pf multi 15 15
2758 A863 20pf multi 25 18
2759 A863 90pf multi 1.10 80

Intl. Congress of Horse Breeders from Socialist States A864

1989, July 18 Litho. *Perf. 13½*
2760 A864 10pf Haflinger 15 15
2761 A864 20pf English thoroughbred 24 18
2762 A864 70pf Cold blood 85 65
2763 A864 110pf Noble warm blood 1.25 1.00

Natl. Stamp Exhibition, Magdeburg A865

1989, Aug. 8 Litho. *Perf. 13x12½*
2764 A865 20pf Owlglass Fountain 25 20
2765 A865 70pf +5pf Demons Fountain 90 75

No. 2765 surtaxed for the philatelic unit of the Kulturbund.

Souvenir Sheet

Leipzig Autumn Fair — A866

1989, Aug. 22 *Perf. 14*
2766 A866 Sheet of 2 1.50 1.40
a. 50pf Fairground 55 55
b. 85pf Fairground, diff. 92 85

Thomas Munzer (1489-1525), Religious Reformer A867

Various details of the painting *Early Bourgeois Revolution in Germany in 1525,* by W. Tubke.

1989, Aug. 22
2767 A867 5pf Globe 15 15
2768 A867 10pf Fountain 15 15
2769 A867 20pf Battle scene 25 20
a. Souvenir sheet of 4 1.25 80
2770 A867 50pf Ark 65 50
2771 A867 85pf Rainbow, battle 1.10 85
Nos. 2767-2771 (5) 2.30 1.85

Muttergruppe, 1965, Bronze Statue in the Natl. Memorial, Ravensbruck A868

1989, Sept. 5 Photo. *Perf. 14*
2772 A868 35pf multi 45 35

Natl. Memorial, Ravensbruck, 30th anniv.

Flowering Cacti *(Epiphyllum)* A869

1989, Sept. 19 Litho. *Perf. 13*
2773 A869 10m Adriana 15 15
2774 A869 35m Feuerzauber 48 35
2775 A869 50m Franzisko 70 50

DDR, 40th Anniv. — A870

1989, Oct. 3 *Perf. 14*
2776 A870 5pf Education 15 15
2777 A870 10pf Agriculture 15 15
2778 A870 20pf Construction 26 20
2779 A870 25pf Machinist, computer user 32 25
Set value 80 60

Souvenir Sheet

2780 A870 135pf Two workers 1.50 1.40

Jawaharlal Nehru, 1st Prime Minister of Independent India — A871

1989, Nov. 7 Photo. *Perf. 14*
2781 A871 35pf multicolored 40 35

Statues of Roland Type of 1987

1989, Nov. 7 *Perf. 14½x14*
2782 A799 5pf Zerbst, 1445 15 15
2783 A799 10pf Halberstadt, 1433 15 15
2784 A799 20pf Buch-Altmark, 1611 25 20
2785 A799 50pf Perleberg, 1546 65 50
Set value 84

Miniature Sheet

Chandeliers from Erzgebirge — A872

Designs: a, Schneeburg, circa 1860. b, Schwarzenberg, circa 1850. c, Annaberg, circa

1880. d, Seiffen, circa 1900. e, Seiffen, circa 1930. f, Annaberg, circa 1925.

Litho. & Engr.

1989, Nov. 28 *Perf. 14*

2786 Sheet of 6 2.35 2.25
a. A872 10pf multicolored 15 15
b. A872 20pf multicolored 22 20
c. A872 25pf multicolored 28 25
d. A872 35pf multicolored 38 35
e. A872 50pf multicolored 55 50
f. A872 70pf multicolored 78 70

Bees Collecting Nectar — A873

1990, Jan. 9 **Litho.**

2787 A873 5pf Apple blossom 15 15
2788 A873 10pf Blooming heather 15 15
2789 A873 20pf Rape blossom 30 22
2790 A873 50pf Red clover 75 55
Set value 92

The Young Post Rider, an Engraving by Albrecht Durer — A874

1990, Jan. 12 **Litho.** *Perf. 13*

2791 A874 35pf multi 50 38

Postal communications in Europe, 500th anniv.

See Austria No. 1486, Belgium No. 1332, Germany No. 1592 and Berlin No. 9N584.

Labor Leaders — A875

Coats of Arms — A876

Portraits: #2792, Bruno Leuschner (1910-65). #2793, Erich Weinert (1890-1953).

1990, Jan. 16 *Perf. 14*

2792 A875 10pf gray brown 30 15
2793 A875 10pf deep blue 30 15
Set value 22

1990, Feb. 6 **Photo.** *Perf. 14*

Early postal agency insignia: 10pf, Schwarzburg-Rudolstadt and Thurn & Taxis. 20pf, Royal Saxon letter collection. 50pf, Imperial Postal Agency. 1.10pf, Auxiliary post office.

2794 A876 10pf multicolored 15 15
2795 A876 20pf multicolored 30 22
2796 A876 50pf multicolored 75 55
2797 A876 110pf multicolored 1.75 1.10

Size: 32x42mm

Perf. 13½

Litho.

2798 Block of 4 3.00 2.00
a. A876 10pf like No. 2794 15 15
b. A876 20pf like No. 2795 30 22
c. A876 50pf like No. 2796 75 55
d. A876 110pf like No. 2797 1.75 1.10

Posts & Telecommunications Workers' Day.

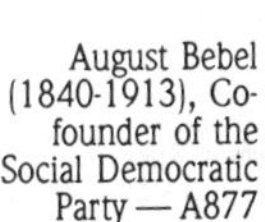

August Bebel (1840-1913), Co-founder of the Social Democratic Party — A877

1990, Feb. 20 **Photo.**

2799 A877 20pf multicolored 45 22

Flying Machine Designed by Leonardo da Vinci — A878

1990, Feb. 20 **Litho.** *Perf. 13½x13*

2800 A878 20pf shown 24 22
2801 A878 35pf +5pf Melchior Bauer 48 42
2802 A878 50pf Albrecht Berblinger 58 52
2803 A878 90pf Otto Lilienthal 1.05 95

LILIENTHAL '91 airmail exhibition. No. 2792 surtaxed for philatelic promotion.

Leipzig Spring Fair Seals — A879

Dying Warriors — A880

1990, Mar. 6 *Perf. 12½x13*

2804 A879 70pf Seal, 1268 85 75
2805 A879 85pf Seal, 1497 1.10 90

City of Leipzig and the Leipzig Spring Fair, 825th annivs.

1990, Mar. 6 **Photo.** *Perf. 13½x14*

Sculptures by Andreas Schluter.

2806 A880 40pf shown 55 42
2807 A880 70pf multi, diff. 95 75

Museum of German History in the Zeughaus of Berlin.

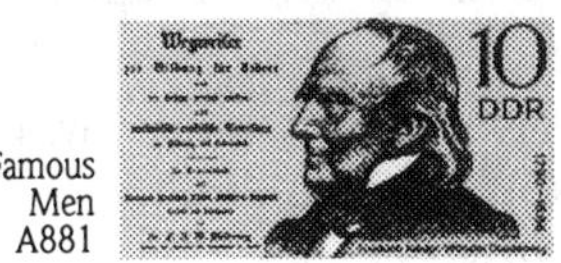

Famous Men A881

Portraits: No. 2808, Friedrich Diesterweg (1790-1866), educator. No. 2809, Kurt Tucholsky (1890-1935), novelist, journalist.

1990, Mar. 20 **Photo.** *Perf. 14*

2808 A881 10pf multicolored 30 15
2809 A881 10pf multicolored 30 15
Set value 20

Labor Day, Cent. — A882

1990, Apr. 3

2810 A882 10pf shown 35 15
2811 A882 20pf Flower, "1890/1990" 60 22

Dicraeosaurus — A883

Perf. 13x12½, 12½x13

1990, Apr. 17 **Litho.**

2812 A883 10pf shown 15 15
2813 A883 25pf Kentrurosaurus 30 28
a. Miniature sheet of 4 1.75 1.10
2814 A883 35pf Dysalotosaurus 42 38
2815 A883 50pf Brachiosaurus 60 55
2816 A883 85pf Brachiosaurus skull 1.10 1.00

Natural History Museum of Berlin, cent. Nos. 2815-2816 vert.

Penny Black, 150th Anniv. — A884

1990, May 8 *Perf. 14*

2817 A884 20pf shown 38 22
2818 A884 35pf +15pf Saxony #1 95 55
2819 A884 110pf No. 48 2.25 1.25

A885

A886

Intl. Telecommunications Union, 125th Anniv.: 10pf, David Edward Hughes (1831-1900), type-printing telegraph, 1855. 20pf, Distribution linkage, Berlin-Kopenick post office. 25pf, TV and microwave tower. 50pf, Molniya news satellite, globe. 70pf, Philipp Reis (1834-1874), physicist, designed sound transmission equipment.

1990, May 15

2820 A885 10pf multicolored 22 15
2821 A885 20pf multicolored 35 22
2822 A885 25pf multicolored 45 28
2823 A885 50pf multicolored 90 55

Souvenir Sheet

2824 A885 70pf multicolored 2.50 80

1990, May 15

2825 A886 35pf multicolored 75 40

Pope John Paul II, 70th birthday.

11th Youth Stamp Exhibition, Halle A887

1990, June 5 *Perf. 13x12½*

2826 A887 10pf +5pf 18th cent. Halle 22 16
2827 A887 20pf 20th cent. Halle 28 22
a. Pair, #2826-2827 + label 50 40

Treasures in the German State Library, Berlin A888

Designs: 20pf, Rules of an order, 1264. 25pf, Rudimentum novitiorum, 1475. 50pf, Chosrou wa Schirin, 18th cent. 110pf, Bookcover of Amalienbibliothek, 18th cent.

1990, June 19

2828 A888 20pf multicolored 32 22
2829 A888 25pf multicolored 42 28
2830 A888 50pf multicolored 85 55
2831 A888 110pf multicolored 1.90 1.25

Castle Albrechtsburg and Cathedral, Meissen — A889

Designs: 30pf, Goethe-Schiller Monument, Weimar. 50pf, Brandenburg Gate, Berlin. 60pf, Kyffhauser Monument. 70pf, Semper Opera, Dresden. 80pf, Castle Sanssouci, Potsdam. 100pf, Wartburg, Eisenach. 200pf, Magdeburg Cathedral. 500pf, Schwerin Castle.

1990, July 2 **Photo.** *Perf. 14*

2832 A889 10pf ultramarine 15 15
2833 A889 30pf olive green 40 18
2834 A889 50pf bluish green 65 30
2835 A889 60pf violet brown 80 36
2836 A889 70pf dark brown 90 42
2837 A889 80pf red brown 1.10 48
2838 A889 100pf dark carmine 1.40 60
2839 A889 200pf dark violet 2.75 1.20
2840 A889 500pf green 6.75 3.00
Nos. 2832-2840 (9) 14.90 6.69

Nos. 2832-2852 have face values based on the Federal Republic's Deutsche mark and were valid for postage in both countries.

Postal System, 500th Anniv. A890

Designs: 30pf, 15th century postman. 50pf, 16th century postrider. 70pf, Post carriages c. 1595, 1750. 100pf, Railway mail carriages 1842, 1900.

1990, Aug. 28 **Litho.** *Perf. 13x13½*

2841 A890 30pf multicolored 52 20
2842 A890 50pf multicolored 90 35
2843 A890 70pf multicolored 1.25 48
2844 A890 100pf multicolored 1.75 70

A891

A892

Designs: 30pf, Louis Lewandowski (1821-94), composer. 50pf+15pf, New Synagogue, Berlin.

1990, Sept. 18 *Perf. 14*

2845 A891 30pf multicolored 55 20
2846 A891 50pf +15pf multi 1.40 45

1990, Oct. 2 **Photo.**

Design: 30pf, shown. 50pf, Schliemann, double pot c. 2600-1900 B.C., horiz.

2847 A892 30pf multicolored 55 20
2848 A892 50pf multicolored 95 35

Heinrich Schliemann (1822-1890), archaeologist.

Intl. Astronautics Federation, 41st Congress, Dresden — A893

1990, Oct. 2

2849 A893 30pf Dresden skyline 42 20
2850 A893 50pf Globe 75 35
2851 A893 70pf Moon 1.00 48
2852 A893 100pf Mars 1.65 70

Stamps of the German Democratic Republic were replaced starting Oct. 3, 1990 by those of the Federal Republic of Germany. #2832-2852 remained valid until Dec. 31, 1991.

SEMI-POSTAL STAMPS

Some se-tenants include a semi-postal stamp. To avoid splitting the se-tenant piece the semi-postal is listed with the regular issue.

Bavaria No. 1 and Magnifier — SP4

Wmk. 292

1949, Oct. 30 Litho. *Perf. 14*

B14 SP4 12pf + 3pf gray blk 6.00 3.00

Stamp Day, 1949. See No. B21a.

Leipzig Fair Issue.
German Type of 1947
Inscribed: "Deutsche Demokratische Republik"

Leipzig Spring Fair: 24pf+12pf, First porcelain at Fair, 1710. 30pf+14pf, First Fair at Municipal Store, 1894.

1950, Mar. 5 *Perf. 13*

B15 SP252 24 + 12pf red vio 7.00 6.25
B16 SP252 30 + 14pf rose car 7.50 6.50

Shepherd Boy with Double Flute — SP5

"Bach Year": 24pf+6pf, Girl with hand organ. 30pf+8pf, Johann Sebastian Bach. 50pf+16pf, Chorus.

1950, June 14 *Perf. 14*

B17 SP5 12pf + 4pf bl grn 3.50 2.50
B18 SP5 24pf + 6pf olive 3.50 2.50
B19 SP5 30pf + 8pf dk red 8.50 6.25
B20 SP5 50pf + 16pf blue 11.50 8.25

Saxony No. 1, Globe and Dove — SP6

1950, July 1 Photo. Wmk. 292

B21 SP6 84 + 41pf brn red 35.00 9.00
a. Souv. sheet of 2, #B14, B21, imperf. *130.00 100.00*

German Stamp Exhib. (DEBRIA) held at Leipzig for the cent. of Saxony's 1st postage stamp.

Canceled to Order
Used values are for CTO's from No. B22 to No. B203.

Clearing Land — SP7

Reconstruction program: 24pf+6pf, Bricklaying. 30pf+10pf, Carpentry. 50pf+10pf, Inspecting plans.

1952, May 1 Litho.

B22 SP7 12pf + 3pf brt vio 70 70
B23 SP7 24pf + 6pf henna brn 75 90
B24 SP7 30pf + 10pf dp grn 75 90
B25 SP7 50pf + 10pf vio bl 1.10 1.50

Dam — SP8

1954, Aug. 16 Unwmk.

B26 SP8 24pf + 6pf green 40 15

The surtax was for flood victims.

Surcharged with New Value and "X"

1955, Feb. 25

B27 SP8 20 +5pf on 24+6pf 50 18

The surtax was for flood victims.

Buchenwald Memorial — SP9

Perf. 13½x13

1956, Sept. 8 Wmk. 297

B28 SP9 20pf + 80pf rose red *1.25 60*

The surtax was for the erection of national memorials at the concentration camps of Buchenwald, Ravensbruck and Sachsenhausen. See No. B43.

Type of 1955 Surcharged "HELFT AGYPTEN +10" (#B29) or "HELFT DEM SOZIALISTISCHEN UNGARN +10" (#B30)

Perf. 13½x13

1956, Dec. 20 Wmk. 313

B29 A75 20pf + 10pf carmine 30 15
B30 A75 20pf + 10pf carmine 30 15
Set value 15

Monument to Ravensbrück SP10

Memorial Park and Lake — SP11

Perf. 13x13½, 13½x13

1957, Apr. 25 Litho.

B31 SP10 5pf + 5pf grn *15 15*
B32 SP11 20pf + 10pf rose red *26 15*
Set value *18*

Intl. Day of Liberation. See Nos. B54, B70.

Ernst Thälmann SP12

Bugler, Flag and Camp SP13

Portraits: 25pf+15pf, Rudolf Breitscheid. 40pf+20pf, Rev. Paul Schneider.

1957, Dec. 3 Photo. *Perf. 13*
Portraits in Gray

B33 SP12 20pf + 10pf dp plum 15 15
B34 SP12 25pf + 15pf dk blue 15 15
B35 SP12 40pf + 20pf violet 30 15
a. Souv. sheet of 3, #B33-B35, imperf. ('58) 35.00 25.00
Set value 25

1958, July 11 Wmk. 313 *Perf. 13*

Portraits: 5pf+5pf, Albert Kuntz. 10pf+5pf, Rudi Arndt. 15pf+10pf, Kurt Adams. 20pf+10pf, Rudolf Renner. 25pf+15pf, Walter Stoecker.

Portraits in Gray

B36 SP12 5pf + 5pf brn blk 15 15
B37 SP12 10pf + 5pf dk sl grn 15 15
B38 SP12 15pf + 10pf dp vio 15 25
B39 SP12 20pf + 10pf dk red brn 15 15
B40 SP12 25pf + 15pf bl blk *65 60*
Set value *1.00 1.00*

Issued to honor the murdered victims of the Nazis at Buchenwald. The surtax was for the erection of national memorials.
See Nos. B49-B53, B55-B57, B60-B64, B71-B75, B79-B81.

1958, Aug. 7 Litho. *Perf. 12½*

Design: 20pf+10pf, Pioneers and flag.

B41 SP13 10pf + 5pf green 28 15
B42 SP13 20pf + 10pf red 28 15
Set value 18

Pioneer organization, 10th anniversary.

Type of 1956 Overprinted in Black "14. September 1958"

Perf. 13½x13

1958, Sept. 15 Unwmk.

B43 SP9 20pf + 20pf rose red *50 15*

Dedication of the memorial at Buchenwald concentration camp, Sept. 14, 1958.

Exercises with Hoops — SP14

Designs: 10pf+5pf, High jump. 20pf+10pf Vaulting. 25pf+10pf, Girl gymnasts. 40pf+20pf, Leipzig stadium and fireworks.

Perf. 13x13½

1959, Aug. 10 Litho. Wmk. 313

B44 SP14 5pf + 5pf org 15 15
B45 SP14 10pf + 5pf grn 15 15
B46 SP14 20pf + 10pf brt car 15 15
B47 SP14 25pf + 10pf brt bl 15 15
B48 SP14 40pf + 20pf red vio *2.00 90*
Nos. B44-B48 (5) *2.60*
Set value *1.10*

3rd German Sports Festival, Leipzig.

Portrait Type of 1957-58

Portraits: 5pf+5pf, Tilde Klose. 10pf+5pf, Kathe Niederkirchner. 15pf+10pf, Charlotte Eisenblatter. 20pf+10pf, Olga Benario-Prestes. 25pf+15pf, Maria Grollmuss.

1959, Sept. 3 Photo. *Perf. 13*
Portraits in Gray

B49 SP12 5pf + 5pf sep 15 15
B50 SP12 10pf + 5pf dp grn 15 15
B51 SP12 15pf + 10pf dp vio 15 15
B52 SP12 20pf + 10pf mag 15 15
B53 SP12 25pf + 15pf dk bl *50 30*
Set value *90 40*

Issued to honor women murdered by the Nazis at Buchenwald.

Ravensbrück Type of 1957 Dated: "12. September 1959"

Perf. 13½x13

1959, Sept. 11 Litho. Wmk. 313

B54 SP11 20pf + 10pf dp car & blk 50 15

Portrait Type of 1957-58

Portraits: 5pf+5pf, Lothar Erdmann. 10pf+5pf, Ernst Schneller. 20pf+10pf, Lambert Horn.

1960, Feb. 25 Photo. *Perf. 13½x13*
Portraits in Gray

B55 SP12 5pf + 5pf ol bis 15 15
B56 SP12 10pf + 5pf dk grn 15 15
B57 SP12 20pf + 10pf dl mag 15 15
Set value 25 15

Issued to honor murdered victims of the Nazis at Sachsenhausen.

Type of Regular Issue, 1960

Designs: 10pf+5pf, Vacation ship under construction, Wismar. 20pf+10pf, Ship before Stubbenkammer and sailboat.

Wmk. 313

1960, June 23 Litho. *Perf. 13*

B58 A162 10pf + 5pf blk, yel & red 18 15
B59 A162 20pf + 10pf blk, red & bl 18 15
Set value 15

Portrait Type of 1957-58

Portraits: 10pf+5pf, Max Lademann. 15pf+5pf, Lorenz Breunig. 20pf+10pf, Mathias Thesen. 25pf+10pf, Gustl Sandtner. 40pf+20pf, Hans Rothbarth.

1960 Wmk. 313 *Perf. 13½x13*
Portraits in Gray

B60 SP12 10pf + 5pf grn 15 15
B61 SP12 15pf + 5pf dp vio *45 42*
B62 SP12 20pf + 10pf maroon 15 15
B63 SP12 25pf + 10pf dk bl 15 15
B64 SP12 40pf + 20pf lt red brn *2.00 85*
Nos. B60-B64 (5) *2.90*
Set value *1.50*

Issued to honor the murdered victims of the Nazis at Sachsenhausen.

Bicyclist — SP15

Design: 25pf+10pf, Bicyclists and spectators.

1960, Aug. 3 *Perf. 13x13½, 13x12½*
Size: 28x23mm

B65 SP15 20pf + 10pf multi 15 15

Size: 38½x21mm

B66 SP15 25pf + 10pf bl, gray & brn *1.25 60*
Set value *65*

Issued to publicize the Bicycling World Championships, Aug. 3-14.

Rook and Congress Emblem — SP16

Designs: 20pf+10pf, Knight. 25pf+10pf, Bishop.

Perf. 14x13½

1960, Sept. 19 Engr. Wmk. 313

B67 SP16 10pf + 5pf blue green 15 15
B68 SP16 20pf + 10pf rose claret 15 15
B69 SP16 25pf + 10pf blue *1.25 52*
Set value *60*

14th Chess Championships, Leipzig.

Type of 1957

Design: Monument and memorial wall of Sachsenhausen National Memorial.

1960, Sept. 8 Litho. *Perf. 13x13½*

B70 SP10 20pf + 10pf dp car 30 15

No. B70 was re-issued Apr. 20, 1961, with gray label adjoining each stamp in sheet, to commemorate the dedication of Sachsenhausen National Memorial.

Type of 1957

Portraits: 5pf+5pf, Werner Kube. 10pf+5pf, Hanno Gunther. 15pf+5pf, Elvira Eisenschneider. 20pf+10pf, Hertha Lindner. 25pf+10pf, Herbert Tschäpe.

1961, Feb. 6 *Perf. 13½x13*
Portraits in Black

B71 SP12	5pf + 5pf brt brn	15	15
B72 SP12	10pf + 5pf bl grn	15	15
B73 SP12	15pf + 5pf brt lilac	*1.50*	*1.10*
B74 SP12	20pf + 10pf dp rose	15	15
B75 SP12	25pf + 10pf brt bl	15	15
	Set value	*1.75*	*1.25*

Surtax for the erection of natl. memorials.

Pioneers Playing Volleyball SP17

Designs: 20pf+10pf, Folk dancing. 25pf+10pf, Building model airplanes.

1961, May 25 *Perf. 13x12½*

B76 SP17	10pf + 5pf multi	15	15
B77 SP17	20pf + 10pf multi	15	15
B78 SP17	25pf + 10pf multi	*2.50*	*85*
	Set value		*90*

Young Pioneers' meeting, Erfurt.

Type of 1957 and

Sophie and Hans Scholl SP18

Portraits: 5pf+5pf, Carlo Schönhaar. 10pf+5pf, Herbert Baum. 20pf+10pf, Liselotte Herrmann. 40pf+20pf, Hilde and Hans Coppi.

Perf. 13½x13, 13x13½
1961, Sept. 7 Litho. Wmk. 313
Portraits in Black

B79 SP12	5pf + 5pf green	15	15
B80 SP12	10pf + 5pf bl grn	15	15
B81 SP12	20pf + 10pf rose car	20	15
B82 SP18	25pf + 10pf blue	30	15
B83 SP18	40pf + 20pf rose brn	*2.25*	*1.25*
	Nos. B79-B83 (5)	*3.05*	
	Set value		*1.50*

Surtax was the support of natl. memorials at Buchenwald, Ravensbrück & Sachsenhausen.

Danielle Casanova of France — SP19

Portraits: 10pf+5pf, Julius Fucik, Czechoslovakia. 20pf+10pf, Johanna Jannetje Schaft, Netherlands. 25pf+10pf, Pawel Finder, Poland. 40pf+20pf, Soya Anatolyevna Kosmodemyanskaya, Russia.

1962, Mar. 22 Engr. *Perf. 13½*

B84 SP19	5pf + 5pf gray	15	15
B85 SP19	10pf + 5pf grn	15	15
B86 SP19	20pf + 10pf maroon	15	15
B87 SP19	25pf + 10pf dp bl	22	15
B88 SP19	40pf + 20pf sepia	*2.00*	*75*
	Set value		*1.00*

Issued in memory of foreign victims of the Nazis.

Type of Regular Issue, 1962

Design: 20pf+10pf, Three cyclists and Warsaw Palace of Culture and Science.

Perf. 13x12½
1962, Apr. 26 Litho. Wmk. 313

B89 A192	20pf + 10pf ver, bl, blk & yel	15	15

Folk Dance — SP20

Design: 15pf+5pf, Youths of three nations parading.

1962, July 17 Wmk. 313 *Perf. 14*

B90 SP20	10pf + 5pf multi	95	20
B91 SP20	15pf + 5pf multi	95	20

Issued to publicize the 8th Youth Festival for Peace and Friendship, Helsinki, July 28-Aug. 6, 1962.

Nos. B90-B91 are printed se-tenant forming the festival emblem.

Type of Regular Issue, 1962

Design: 20pf+10pf, Springboard diving.

1962, Aug. 7 Wmk. 313 *Perf. 13*

B92 A199	20pf + 10pf lil rose & grnsh bl	15	15

René Blieck of Belgium — SP21

Seven Cervi Brothers of Italy — SP22

Portraits: 10pf+5pf, Dr. Alfred Klahr, Austria. 15pf+5pf, José Diaz, Spain. 20pf+10pf, Julius Alpari, Hungary.

1962, Oct. 4 Engr. *Perf. 14*

B93 SP21	5pf + 5pf dk bl gray	15	15
B94 SP21	10pf + 5pf green	15	15
B95 SP21	15pf + 5pf brt vio	15	15
B96 SP21	20pf + 10pf dl red brn	15	15
B97 SP22	70pf + 30pf sepia	*1.40*	*1.10*
	Set value	*1.75*	*1.25*

Issued to commemorate foreign victims of the Nazis.

Walter Bohne, Runner SP23

Gymnasts SP24

Portraits: 10pf+5pf, Werner Seelenbinder, wrestler. 15pf+5pf, Albert Richter, bicyclist. 20pf+10pf, Heinz Steyer, soccer player. 25pf+10pf, Kurt Schlosser, mountaineer.

Engr. & Photo.
1963, May 27 Wmk. 313 *Perf. 14*

B98 SP23	5pf + 5pf yel & blk	15	15
B99 SP23	10pf + 5pf pale yel grn & blk	15	15
B100 SP23	15pf + 5pf rose lil & blk	15	15
B101 SP23	20pf + 10pf pink & blk	16	15
B102 SP23	25pf + 10pf pale bl & blk	*1.75*	*1.50*
	Nos. B98-B102 (5)	*2.36*	
	Set value		*1.70*

Issued to commemorate sportsmen victims of the Nazis. Each stamp printed with alternating label showing sporting events connected with each person honored. The surtax went for the maintenance of national memorials. See Nos. B106-B110.

1963, June 13 Litho. *Perf. 12½x13*

Designs: 20pf+10pf, Women gymnasts. 25pf+10pf, Relay race.

B103 SP24	10pf + 5pf blk, yel grn & lem	15	15
B104 SP24	20pf + 10pf blk, red & vio	15	15
B105 SP24	25pf + 10pf blk, bl, & gray	*2.50*	*1.65*

4th German Gymnastic and Sports Festival, Leipzig. The surtax went to the festival committee.

Type of 1963

Portraits: 5pf+5pf, Hermann Tops, gymnastics instructor. 10pf+5pf, Käte Tucholla, field hockey players. 15pf+5pf, Rudolph Seiffert, long-distance swimmers. 20pf+10pf, Ernst Grube, sportsmen demonstrating for peace. 40pf+20pf, Kurt Biedermann, kayak in rapids.

Engraved and Photogravure
1963, Sept. 24 Wmk. 313 *Perf. 14*

B106 SP23	5pf + 5pf yel & blk	15	15
B107 SP23	10pf + 5pf grn & blk	15	15
B108 SP23	15pf + 5pf lil & blk	15	15
B109 SP23	20pf + 10pf pale pink & blk	15	15
B110 SP23	40pf + 20pf lt bl & blk	*2.25*	*1.65*
	Nos. B106-B110 (5)	*2.85*	*2.25*

See note after No. B102.

Type of Regular Issue, 1963

Design: 20pf+10pf, Ski jumper in mid-air.

Perf. 13½x13
1963, Dec. 16 Litho. Wmk. 313

B111 A224	20pf + 10pf multi	15	15

Surtax for the Natl. Olympic Committee.

Anton Saefkow SP25

Designs: 10pf+5pf, Franz Jacob. 15pf+5pf, Bernhard Bästlein. 20pf+5pf, Harro Schulze-Boysen. 25pf+10pf, Adam Kuckhoff. 40pf+10pf, Mildred and Arvid Harnack. Nos. B112-B114 show group posting anti-Hitler and pacifist posters. Nos. B115-B117 show production of anti-fascist pamphlets.

1964, Mar. 24 Wmk. 313 *Perf. 13*
Size: 41x32mm

B112 SP25	5pf + 5pf	15	15
B113 SP25	10pf + 5pf	15	15
B114 SP25	15pf + 5pf	15	15
B115 SP25	20pf + 5pf	18	15
B116 SP25	25pf + 10pf	24	15

Size: 48½x28mm

B117 SP25	40pf + 10pf	*1.25*	*85*
	Nos. B112-B117 (6)	*2.12*	
	Set value		*1.20*

The surtax was for the support of national memorials for victims of the Nazis.

Olympic Types of Regular Issues

Designs: 40pf+20pf, Two runners. #B119, Equestrian. #B120, Three runners.

Lithographed and Engraved
1964, July 15 Wmk. 313 *Perf. 14*

B118 A232	40pf + 20pf multi	28	15

Litho.
Perf. 13

B119 A233	10pf + 5pf multi	3.00	1.10
B120 A233	10pf + 5pf multi	3.00	1.10

See note after No. 714.

Pioneers Studying — SP26

Designs: 20pf+10pf, Pioneers planting tree. 25pf+10pf, Pioneers playing.

1964, July 29

B121 SP26	10pf + 5pf multi	15	15
B122 SP26	20pf + 10pf multi	28	15
B123 SP26	25pf + 10pf multi	*1.90*	*65*
	Set value		*72*

Fifth Young Pioneers Meeting, Karl-Marx-Stadt.

Stamp Exhibition Type of 1964

Designs: 10pf+5pf, Stamp of 1958 (No. 390). 20pf+10pf, Stamp of 1950 (No. 73).

Perf. 13x13½
1964, Sept. 23 Litho. Wmk. 313

B124 A238	10pf + 5pf org & emer	15	15
B125 A238	20pf + 10pf brt pink & bl	15	15
	Set value	20	15

Boxing Type of Regular Issue

Design: 10pf+5pf, Two boxing gloves and laurel.

Perf. 13½x14
1965, Apr. 27 Photo. Wmk. 313

B126 A247	10pf + 5pf blk, gold, red & blue	15	15

The surtax went to the German Turner and Sport Organization.

Type of Regular Issue, 1965

Designs: 5pf+5pf, George Dimitrov at Leipzig trial and communist newspaper. 10pf+5pf, Anti-fascists clandestinely distributing leaflets. 15pf+5pf, Fighting in Spanish Civil War. 20pf+10pf, Ernst Thalman behind bars and demonstration for his release. 25pf+10pf, Founding of National Committee for Free Germany and signatures.

Wmk. 313
1965, May 5 Photo. *Perf. 14*
Flags in Red, Black and Yellow

B127 A248	5pf + 5pf blk, org & red	15	15
B128 A248	10pf + 5pf grn & red	15	15
B129 A248	15pf + 5pf lil, red & yel	15	15
B130 A248	20pf + 5pf blk & red	15	15
B131 A248	25pf + 10pf ol grn, yel & blk	16	15
	Set value	65	25

The surtax went for the maintenance of national memorials.

Doves, Globe and Finnish Flag — SP27

1965, July 5 Litho. *Perf. 13x13½*

B132 SP27	10pf + 5pf vio bl & emer	15	15
B133 SP27	20pf + 5pf red & vio bl	*55*	*22*
	Set value		*25*

World Peace Congress, Helsinki, July 10-17. The surtax went to the peace council of the DDR.

Hilfe für
VIETNAM

No. 725 Surcharged

+10

Perf. 13½x13
1965, Aug. 23 Wmk. 313

B134 A239	10pf + 10pf multi	25	15

Surtax was for North Viet Nam.

Sports Type of Regular Issue

Sport: No. B135, Fencer. No. B136, Pistol shooter.

Perf. 13½x13

1965, Sept. 15 Litho. Unwmk.

B135 A257 10pf + 5pf vio bl & grnsh bl 18 15
B136 A257 10pf + 5pf dk car rose, gray & blk 18 15
Set value 15

International Modern Pentathlon Championships, Leipzig.

Type of Regular Issue

Designs: 10pf+5pf, Willi Bredel and instruction of International Brigade. 20pf+10pf, Heinrich Rau and parade after battle of Brunete. 25pf+10pf, Hans Marchwitza, international fighters and globe. 40pf+10pf, Artur Becker and battle on the Ebro.

1966, July 15 Photo. *Perf. 14*

B137 A277 10pf + 5pf multi 15 15
B138 A277 20pf + 10pf multi 15 15
B139 A277 25pf + 10pf multi 15 15
B140 A277 40pf + 10pf multi *1.25 65*
Set value 1.50 70

The surtax was for the maintenance of national memorials.

Canoe Type of Regular Issue

Design: 10pf+5pf, Men's single canoe race.

Perf. 13x12½

1966, Aug. 16 Litho. Unwmk.

B141 A279 10pf + 5pf multi 15 15

Red Cross Type of Regular Issue

Design: ICY Red Crescent, Red Cross, and Red Lion and Sun emblems, horiz.

1966, Sept. 13 Wmk. 313 *Perf. 14*

B142 A281 20pf + 10pf vio & red 15 15

International health cooperation. Surtax for German Red Cross.

Sports Type of Regular Issue

Design: 20pf+5pf, Weight lifter.

Perf. 13½x13

1966, Sept. 22 Litho. Unwmk.

B143 A282 20pf + 5pf ultra & blk 15 15

Armed Woman Planting Flower — SP28

1966, Oct. 25 *Perf. 13½x13*

B144 SP28 20pf + 5pf blk & pink 25 15

Surtax was for North Viet Nam.

Wartburg Type of Regular Issue

Design: Wartburg, view from the East.

1966, Nov. 23 *Perf. 13x13½*

B145 A288 10pf + 5pf slate 15 15

See note after No. 878.

Olympic Type of Regular Issue

Design: 10pf+5pf, Tobogganing.

1968, Jan. 17 Litho. *Perf. 13½x13*

B146 A314 10pf + 5pf grnsh bl, vio bl & red 15 15

The surtax was for the Olympic Committee of the German Democratic Republic.

The Scott Catalogue value is a retail price; that is, what you could expect to pay for the stamp in a grade of Fine-Very Fine. The value listed reflects recent actual dealer selling prices.

Armed Mother and Child — SP29

Armed Vietnamese Couple — SP30

1968, May 8 *Perf. 13½x13*

B147 SP29 10pf + 5pf yel & multi 25 15

Surtax was for North Viet Nam.

Festival Type of Regular Issue

1968, June 20 Litho. *Perf. 13½x13*

B148 A327 20pf + 5pf multi 15 15

Olympic Games Type of Regular Issue, 1968

Designs: 10pf+5pf, Pole vault, vert. 20pf+10pf, Soccer, vert.

1968, Sept. 18 Photo. *Perf. 14*

B149 A336 10pf + 5pf multi 15 15
B150 A336 20pf + 10pf multi 15 15
Set value 15 15

The surtax was for the Olympic Committee.

1969, June 4

B151 SP30 10pf + 5pf multi 25 15

Surtax was for North Viet Nam.

Sports Type of Regular Issue, 1969

Designs: 10pf+5pf, Gymnastics. 20pf+5pf, Art Exhibition with sports motifs.

Photo. & Engr.

1969, June 18 *Perf. 14*

B152 A353 10pf + 5pf multi 15 15
B153 A353 20pf + 5pf multi 15 15
Set value 15 15

The surtax was for the German Gymnastic and Sports League.

Otto von Guericke's Vacuum Test with Magdeburg Hemispheres — SP31

1969, Oct. 28 Litho. *Perf. 13x12½*

B154 SP31 40pf + 10pf multi *60 40*

See note after No. 1146.

Folk Art Type of Regular Issue

Design: 20pf+5pf, Decorative plate.

1969, Nov. 25 Litho. *Perf. 13½x13*

B155 A365 20pf + 5pf yel blk & ultra 80 40

Sports Type of Regular Issue

Design: 20pf+5pf, Children hurdling.

1970, July 1 Photo. *Perf. 14x13½*

B156 A382 20pf + 5pf multi 25 15

Pioneer Waving Kerchief, and Pioneer Activities — SP32

Design: 25pf+5pf, Girl Pioneer holding kerchief, and Pioneer activities.

1970, July 28 Litho. *Perf. 13x12½*

B157 SP32 10pf + 5pf multi 50 15
B158 SP32 25pf + 5pf multi 50 15
Set value 20

6th Youth Pioneer Meeting, Cottbus. Printed se-tenant in continuous design.

Ho Chi Minh — SP33

German Democratic Republic No. 460 — SP34

1970, Sept. 2 *Perf. 13x13½*

B159 SP33 20pf + 5pf rose, blk & red 30 15

Surtax was for North Viet Nam.

1970, Oct. 1 Photo. *Perf. 14x13½*

B160 SP34 15pf + 5pf multi 20 15

2nd National Youth Philatelic Exhibition, Karl-Marx-Stadt, Oct. 4-11.

Mother and Child — SP35

Vietnamese Farm Woman — SP36

Photo. & Engr.

1971, Sept. 2 *Perf. 14*

B161 SP35 10pf + 5pf multi 18 15

Surtax was for North Viet Nam.

Type of Regular Issue

Design: 10pf+5pf, Loading and unloading mail at airport.

Photo. & Engr.

1971, Oct. 5 *Perf. 14*

B162 A421 10pf + 5pf multi 15 15

Olympic Games Type of Regular Issue

Olympic Rings and: 10pf+5pf, Figure skating, pairs. 15pf+5pf, Speed skating.

1971, Dec. 7 Photo. *Perf. 13½x14*

B163 A424 10pf + 5pf bl, car & blk 15 15
B164 A424 15pf + 5pf grn, blk & bl 15 15
Set value 15 15

1972, Feb. 22 Litho. *Perf. 13½x13*

B165 SP36 10pf + 5pf multi 20 15

Surtax was for North Viet Nam.

Olympic Games Type of Regular Issue

Sport and Olympic Rings: 10pf+5pf, Diving. 25pf+10pf, Rowing.

1972, May 16 Photo. *Perf. 13½x14*

B166 A430 10pf + 5pf grnsh bl, gold & blk 15 15
B167 A430 25pf + 10pf multi 15 15
Set value 15 15

Interartes Type of Regular Issue

Designs: 15pf+5pf, Spear carrier, Persia, 500 B.C. 35pf+5pf, Grape Sellers, by Max Lingner, 1949, horiz.

1972, Sept. 19 Photo. *Perf. 14*

B168 A439 15pf + 5pf multi *1.25 85*
B169 A439 35pf + 5pf multi 15 15

Flags and World Time Clock SP37

Young Couple, by Günter Glombitza SP38

Design: 25pf+5pf, Youth group with guitar and dove.

1973, Feb. 13 Litho. *Perf. 12½x13*

B170 SP37 10pf + 5pf multi 16 15
B171 SP37 25pf + 5pf multi 35 22
Set value 30

10th World Youth Festival, Berlin.

1973, Oct. 4 Photo. *Perf. 13½x14*

B172 SP38 20pf + 5pf multi 25 15

Philatelists' Day and for the 3rd National Youth Philatelic Exhibition, Halle.

Child, Symbols of Reconstruction SP39

Luis Corvalan, Red Flag SP40

1973, Oct. 11 *Perf. 14x13½*

B173 SP39 10pf + 5pf multi 30 15

Surtax was for North Viet Nam.

1973, Nov. 5 *Perf. 13½x14*

Design: 25pf+5pf, Salvador Allende and Chilean flag.

B174 SP40 10pf + 5pf multi *24 18*
B175 SP40 25pf + 5pf multi *45 35*

Solidarity with the people of Chile.

Raised Fist and Star — SP41

Restored Post Gate, Wurzen, 1734 — SP42

1975, Sept. 23 Litho. *Perf. 13x13½*

B176 SP41 10pf + 5pf multi 25 15

Surtax was for the Solidarity Committee of the German Democratic Republic.

1975, Oct. 21 Photo. *Perf. 14*

B177 SP42 10pf + 5pf multi *32 30*

Philatelists' Day 1975.

Olympic Games Type of 1975

Designs: 10pf+5pf, Luge run, Oberhof. 25pf+5pf, Ski jump, Rennsteig at Oberhof.

1975, Dec. 2 Photo. *Perf. 14*

B178 A518 10pf + 5pf multi 15 15
B179 A518 25pf + 5pf multi 22 15
Set value 20

Olympic Games Type of 1976

Designs: 10pf+5pf, Swimming pool, High School for Physical Education, Leipzig. 35pf+10pf, Rifle range, Suhl.

1976, May 18 Photo. ***Perf. 13½x14***
B180 A529 10pf + 5pf multi 15 15
B181 A529 35pf + 10pf multi 32 15

TV Tower, Berlin, and Perforations
SP43

Hand Holding Torch
SP44

1976, Oct. 19 Litho. ***Perf. 13***
B182 SP43 10pf + 5pf org & bl 16 15

Surtax was for Sozphilex 77, Philatelic Exhibition of Socialist Countries, in connection with 60th anniversary of October Revolution.

Sports Type of 1977

Designs: 10pf+5pf, Young milers. 25pf+5pf, Girls artistic gymnastic performance.

1977, July 19 Litho. ***Perf. 13x12½***
B183 A558 10pf + 5pf multi 15 15
B184 A558 25pf + 5pf multi 15 15
Set value 27 15

Sozphilex Type of 1977
Souvenir Sheet

Design: 50pf+20pf, World Youth Song, by Lothar Zitzmann, horiz.

1977, Aug. 16 Photo. ***Perf. 13***
B185 A559 50pf + 20pf multi *1.25 95*

1977, Oct. 18 Litho. ***Perf. 14***
B186 SP44 10pf + 5pf multi 16 15

Surtax was for East German Solidarity Committee.

Fountain Type of 1979

Design: 10pf+5pf, Goose Boy Fountain.

1979, Aug. 7 Photo. ***Perf. 14***
B187 A617 10pf + 5pf multi *35 35*

Vietnamese Soldier, Mother and Child — SP45

1979, Nov. 6 Litho. ***Perf. 14***
B188 SP45 10pf + 5pf red org & blk 25 15

Surtax was for Vietnam.

Olympic Type of 1980

Design: Ski Jump, sculpture by Gunther Schutz.

1980, Jan. 15 Photo.
B189 A627 25pf + 10pf multi 15 15

1980, Apr. 22 Photo. ***Perf. 14***

Design: 20pf+5pf, Runners at the Finish, by Lothar Zitzmann.

B190 A627 20 + 5pf multi 15 15

Interflug Type of 1980
Souvenir Sheet

1980, June 10 Litho. ***Perf. 13x12½***
B191 A636 1m + 10pf Jet, globe *2.50 1.50*

AEROSOZPHILEX 1980 International Airpost Exhibition, Berlin, Aug. 1-10.

Olympic Type of 1980

Design: Swimmer, by Willi Sitte, vert.

1980, July 8 Photo. ***Perf. 14***
B192 A627 20pf + 10pf multi 25 15

22nd Summer Olympic Games, Moscow, July 19-Aug. 3.

International Solidarity
SP46 SP47

1980, Oct. 14 Photo. ***Perf. 14***
B193 SP46 10pf + 5pf multi 25 15

1981, Oct. 6 Photo. ***Perf. 14***
B194 SP47 10pf + 5pf multi 25 15

SP48 SP49

Palestinian family, Tree of Life.

1982, Sept. 21 Litho. ***Perf. 14***
B195 SP48 10pf + 5pf multi 25 15

Palestinian solidarity.

1983, Nov. 8 Litho. ***Perf. 14x13½***

Literacy, home defense.

B196 SP49 10pf + 5pf multi 25 15

Nicaraguan solidarity.

Solidarity
SP50 SP51

1984, Oct. 23 Photo. ***Perf. 14***
B197 SP50 10pf + 5pf Knot 45 15

1985, May 28 Photo.
B198 SP51 10pf + 5pf Globe, peace dove 25 15

Surtax for the Solidarity Committee.

Technical Assistance to Developing Nations
SP52

1986, Nov. 4 Photo.
B199 SP52 10pf + 5pf multi 25 15

Surtax for the Solidarity Committee.

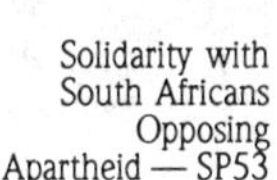

Solidarity with South Africans Opposing Apartheid — SP53

1987, June 16 Litho. ***Perf. 14***
B200 SP53 10pf +5pf multi 25 15

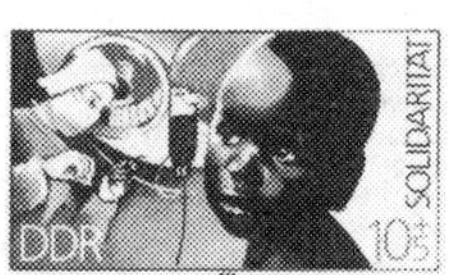

Solidarity
SP54

1988, Oct. 4 Photo. ***Perf. 14***
B201 SP54 10pf +5pf multi 30 15

Surtax for the Solidarity Committee. No. B201 printed se-tenant with label containing a Wilhelm Pieck quote.

UNICEF Emblem and Children of Africa — SP55

1989, Sept. 5 Photo. ***Perf. 14½x14***
B202 SP55 10pf +5pf multi 25 15

Surtax for the Solidarity Committee.

Leipzig Church, Municipal Arms — SP56

1990, Feb. 28 Photo. ***Perf. 13***
B203 SP56 35pf +15pf multicolored 75 55

We are the People.

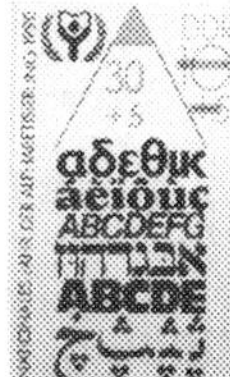
Intl. Literacy Year — SP57

1990, July 24 Photo. ***Perf. 14***
B204 SP57 30pf+5pf on 10pf+5pf 1.50 45

Not issued without surcharge.

AIR POST STAMPS

Canceled to Order
Used values are for CTO's.

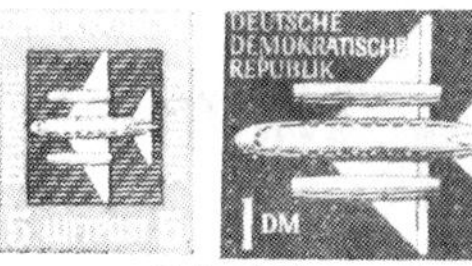

Stylized Plane
AP1 AP2

Perf. 13x12½, 13x13½ (AP2)
1957, Dec. 13 Litho. Wmk. 313
C1 AP1 5pf gray & blk 15 15
C2 AP1 20pf brt car & blk 15 15
C3 AP1 35pf violet & blk 18 15
C4 AP1 50pf maroon & blk 20 15
C5 AP2 1m olive & yel 95 15
C6 AP2 3m choc & yel 2.50 15
C7 AP2 5m dk bl & yel 4.75 15
Nos. C1-C7 (7) 8.88
Set value 50

Plane and Envelope — AP3

1982-87 Photo. ***Perf. 14***
C8 AP3 5pf lt bl & blk 15 15
C9 AP3 15pf brt rose lil & blk 20 15
C10 AP3 20pf ocher & blk 18 15
C11 AP3 25pf ol bis & blk 32 15
C12 AP3 30pf brt grn & blk 30 15
C13 AP3 40pf ol grn & blk 35 18
C14 AP3 1m blue & blk 85 42
C15 AP3 3m brown & blk 3.25 90
C16 AP3 5m dk red & blk 5.50 35
Nos. C8-C16 (9) 11.10 2.60

Issue dates: 30pf, 40pf, 1m, Oct. 26. 5pf, 20pf, Oct. 4, 1983. 3m, Apr. 10, 1984. 5m, Sept. 10, 1985. 15pf, 25pf, Oct. 6, 1987.

OFFICIAL STAMPS

While valid, these Official stamps were not sold to the public unused. After their period of use, some sets were sold abroad by the government stamp sales agency.

Arms of Republic — O1

Perf. 13x12½
1954 Wmk. 297 Litho.
O1 O1 5pf emerald 11.00 15
O2 O1 6pf violet 4.75 15
O3 O1 8pf org brown 11.00 15
O4 O1 10pf lt bl grn 11.00 15
O5 O1 12pf blue 11.00 15
O6 O1 15pf dark violet 11.00 15
O7 O1 16pf dark violet 4.75 15
O8 O1 20pf olive 4.75 15
O9 O1 24pf brown red 4.75 15
O10 O1 25pf sage green 7.50 15
O11 O1 30pf brown red 3.25 15
O12 O1 40pf red 7.50 15
O13 O1 48pf rose lilac 3.75 85
O14 O1 50pf rose lilac 3.75 15
O15 O1 60pf bright blue 3.75 15
O16 O1 70pf brown 3.75 15
O17 O1 84pf brown 3.75 1.50
Nos. O1-O17 (17) 111.00
Set value 3.50

Type of 1954 Redrawn

Arc of compass projects at right except on No. O22.

1954-56 Typo.
O18 O1 5pf emer ('54) 60 15
O19 O1 10pf bl grn 60 15
O20 O1 12pf dk bl ('54) 50 15
O21 O1 15pf dk vio 60 15
O22 O1 20pf ol, arc at left ('55) *4.00* 15
a. Arc of compass projects at right ('56) 175.00 15
O23 O1 25pf dark green 30 15
O24 O1 30pf brown red 80 15
O25 O1 40pf red 50 15
O26 O1 50pf rose lilac 40 15
O27 O1 70pf brown 50 15
Nos. O18-O27 (10) 8.80
Set value 45

Shaded background of emblem consists of vertical lines; on Nos. O1-O17 it consists of dots.

Granite paper was used for a 1956 printing of the 5pf, 10pf, 15pf, 20pf and 40pf. Value for set unused $300, used 30 cents.

See Nos. O37-O43.

O2 O3

1956 Wmk. 297 *Perf. 13x12½*

O28 O2 5pf black 15 15
O29 O2 10pf black 15 15
O30 O2 20pf black 15 15
O31 O2 40pf black 25 15
O32 O2 70pf black 35 15
Set value 82 25

1956 Litho. Wmk. 297

O33 O3 10pf lilac & black 20 18
O34 O3 20pf lilac & black *25.00* 15
O35 O3 40pf lilac & black 20 18
O36 O3 70pf lilac & black 60 55

Nos. O33-O36 exist also with black or violet overprint of 4-digit control number.

See Nos. O44-O45.

No. O34 was reprinted with watermark sideways ("DDR" vertical). Value $2.

Redrawn Type of 1954-56

Perf. 13x12½, 14

1957-60 Typo. Wmk. 313

Granite Paper

O37 O1 5pf emerald 15 15
O38 O1 10pf blue green 15 15
O39 O1 15pf dark vio 15 15
O40 O1 20pf olive 15 15
O41 O1 30pf dark red ('58) 15 15
O42 O1 40pf red 15 15
O42A O1 50pf rose lilac ('60) 40 15
O43 O1 70pf brown ('58) 40 15
Set value 1.20 50

Nos. O37-O43 were all issued in perf. 13x12½. Nos. O37-O40 were also issued perf. 14. Values are the same.

Type of 1956

1957 Litho. *Perf. 13x12½*

O44 O3 10pf lilac & black 25 35
O45 O3 20pf lilac & black 25 55

Nos. O44-O45 have black or violet overprint of four-digit control number.

Stamps similar to type O3 were issued later, with denomination expressed in dashes: one for 10pf, two for 20pf.

GERMAN OFFICES ABROAD

OFFICES IN CHINA

100 Pfennings = 1 Mark
100 Cents = 1 Dollar (1905)

Stamps of Germany, 1889-90, Overprinted in Black at 56 degree Angle

1898 Unwmk. *Perf. 13½x14½*

1 A9 3pf dark brown 4.25 3.50
a. 3pf yellow brown 7.50 7.50
b. 3pf reddish brown 21.00 30.00
2 A9 5pf green 2.25 2.25
3 A10 10pf carmine 6.00 6.00
4 A10 20pf ultramarine 11.50 16.00
5 A10 25pf orange 25.00 27.50
6 A10 50pf red brown 13.00 13.00

Overprinted at 45 degree Angle

1c A9 3pf yellow brown 130.00 *25,000.*
1d A9 3pf reddish brown 165.00
2a A9 5pf green 12.00 12.00
3a A10 10pf carmine 15.00 10.00
4a A10 20pf ultramarine 13.00 10.00
5a A10 25pf orange 52.50 55.00
6a A10 50pf red brown 22.50 18.00

Foochow Issue

Nos. 3 and 3a Handstamp Surcharged

5 pf

16 A10 5pf on 10pf, #3 415.00 525.00
a. On No. 3a 465.00 650.00

For similar 5pf surcharges on 10pf carmine, see Tsingtau Issue, Kiauchau.

Tientsin Issue

German Stamps of 1900 Issue Handstamped

1900

17 A11 3pf brown 525. 525.
18 A11 5pf green 265. 325.
19 A11 10pf carmine 675. 650.
20 A11 20pf ultra 650. 475.
21 A11 30pf org & blk, *sal* *7,750.* *7,750.*
22 A11 50pf pur & blk, *sal* *30,000.* *17,500.*
23 A11 80pf lake & blk, *rose* *4,750.* *4,250.*

This handstamp is known inverted and double on most values.

Excellent faked handstamps are plentiful.

Regular Issue

A3

A4

A5

A6

A7

Overprinted Horizontally in Black

1901 *Perf. 14, 14½*

24 A3 3pf brown 1.75 1.75
a. 3pf light red brown 90.00 110.00
25 A3 5pf green 1.75 1.00
26 A3 10pf carmine 2.75 80
27 A3 20pf ultra 3.25 1.50
28 A3 25pf org & blk, *yel* 11.50 16.00
29 A3 30pf org & blk, *sal* 11.50 13.00
30 A3 40pf lake & blk 11.50 8.75
31 A3 50pf pur & blk, *sal* 11.50 8.75
32 A3 80pf lake & blk, *rose* 14.00 13.00

Overprinted in Black or Red

33 A4 1m car rose 35.00 32.50
34 A5 2m gray blue 30.00 30.00
35 A6 3m blk vio (R) 50.00 65.00
36 A7 5m slate & car, I 275.00 450.00
36A A7 5m slate & car, II 200.00 300.00
Nos. 24-36A (14) 659.50 942.05

Retouched copies of No. 36 sell for ⅔ as much. See note after Germany No. 65A.

Surcharged on German Stamps of 1902 in Black or Red

a

* 1 Dollar *

China

b

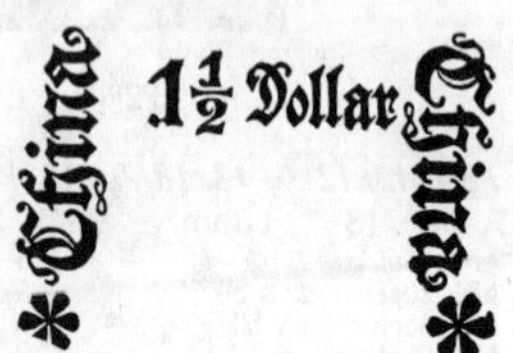

c

1905

37 A16(a) 1c on 3pf 2.50 2.50
38 A16(a) 2c on 5pf 2.50 1.10
39 A16(a) 4c on 10pf 6.00 1.10
40 A16(a) 10c on 20pf 2.50 1.50
41 A16(a) 20c on 40pf 20.00 5.75
42 A16(a) 40c on 80pf 30.00 12.00
43 A17(b) ½d on 1m 12.00 13.00
44 A21(b) 1d on 2m 15.00 14.00
45 A19(c) 1½d on 3m (R) 10.50 *40.00*
46 A20(b) 2½d on 5m 82.50 *225.00*
Nos. 37-46 (10) 183.50 *315.95*

Surcharged on German Stamps of 1905 in Black or Red

1906-13 Wmk. 125

47 A16(a) 1c on 3pf 45 70
48 A16(a) 2c on 5pf 45 70
49 A16(a) 4c on 10pf 45 70
50 A16(a) 10c on 20pf 1.00 *5.25*
51 A16(a) 20c on 40pf 1.40 *2.75*
52 A16(a) 40c on 80pf 1.40 *30.00*
53 A17(b) ½d on 1m 2.75 *27.50*
54 A21(b) 1d on 2m 4.50 *27.50*
55 A19(c) 1½d on 3m (R) 5.25 *75.00*
56 A20(b) 2½d on 5m 22.50 *37.50*
Nos. 47-56 (10) 40.15

Forged cancellations exist.

OFFICES IN MOROCCO

100 Centimos = 1 Peseta

A1

A2

Stamps of Germany Surcharged in Black

1899 Unwmk. *Perf. 13½x14½*

1 A1 3c on 3pf dk brn 3.25 2.00
2 A1 5c on 5pf green 3.25 2.50
3 A2 10c on 10pf car 7.50 7.00
4 A2 25c on 20pf ultra 12.50 12.50
5 A2 30c on 25pf orange 25.00 27.50
6 A2 60c on 50pf red brn 20.00 24.00

Before Nos. 1-6 were issued, the same six basic stamps of Germany's 1889-1900 issue were overprinted "Marocco" diagonally without the currency-changing surcharge line, but were not issued. Value, $1,500.

A3

A4

A5

A6

A7

Black or Red Surcharge

1900 *Perf. 14, 14½*

7 A3 3c on 3pf brn 1.25 1.25
8 A3 5c on 5pf green 1.25 1.00
9 A3 10c on 10pf car 2.00 1.00
10 A3 25c on 20pf ultra 2.75 2.25
11 A3 30c on 25pf org & blk, *yel* 10.00 11.50
12 A3 35c on 30pf org & blk, *sal* 7.25 5.25
13 A3 50c on 40pf lake & blk 7.25 5.25
14 A3 60c on 50pf pur & blk, *sal* 16.00 30.00
15 A3 1p on 80pf lake & blk, *rose* 11.50 11.50
16 A4 1p25c on 1m car rose 30.00 35.00
17 A5 2p50c on 2m gray bl 32.50 40.00
18 A6 3p75c on 3m blk vio (R) 42.50 60.00
19 A7 6p25c on 5m sl & car, type I 230.00 350.00
19A A7 6p25c on 5m sl & car, type II 215.00 215.00
Nos. 7-19A (14) 609.25 769.00

A 1903 printing of Nos. 8, 16-18 and 19A differs in the "M" and "t" of the surcharge. Values are for 1900 printing: Nos. 8, 16-18. 1903 printing: No. 19A.

Retouched copies of No. 19 sell for ⅔ as much. See note after Germany No. 65A.

German Stamps of 1902 Surcharged in Black or Red

Marocco
3 Centimos

a

Marocco 1 Pes. 25 Cts. Marocco

b

Marocco 3 Pes. 75 Cts.

c

1905

20 A16(a) 3c on 3pf 3.25 3.00
21 A16(a) 5c on 5pf 5.25 1.10
22 A16(a) 10c on 10pf 10.50 75
23 A16(a) 25c on 20pf 21.00 3.00
24 A16(a) 30c on 25pf 7.00 4.75
25 A16(a) 35c on 30pf 10.50 5.75
26 A16(a) 50c on 40pf 9.75 9.25
27 A16(a) 60c on 50pf 35.00 25.00
28 A16(a) 1p on 80pf 35.00 22.50
29 A17(b) 1p25c on 1m 45.00 27.50
30 A21(b) 2p50c on 2m 100.00 150.00
31 A19(c) 3p75c on 3m (R) 50.00 50.00
32 A20(b) 6p25c on 5m 140.00 165.00
Nos. 20-32 (13) 472.25 467.60

Surcharged on Germany No. 54

32A A11(a) 5c on 5pf 6.50 *25.00*

German Stamps of 1905 Surcharged

1906-11 Wmk. 125

33 A16(a) 3c on 3pf 9.50 2.25
34 A16(a) 5c on 5pf 9.50 1.10
35 A16(a) 10c on 10pf 9.50 1.10
36 A16(a) 25c on 20pf 16.00 2.25
37 A16(a) 30c on 25pf 18.00 11.00
38 A16(a) 35c on 30pf 18.00 11.00
39 A16(a) 50c on 40pf 35.00 *185.00*
40 A16(a) 60c on 50pf 24.00 16.00
41 A16(a) 1p on 80pf 125.00 225.00
42 A17(b) 1p25c on 1m 60.00 *185.00*
43 A21(b) 2p50c on 2m 60.00 *185.00*
44 A20(b) 6p25c on 5m 125.00 *375.00*
Nos. 33-44 (12) 509.50 *1,199.*

Excellent forgeries exist of No. 41.

Surcharge Spelled "Marokko" in Black or Red

1911

45 A16(a) 3c on 3pf 50 70
46 A16(a) 5c on 5pf 50 90
47 A16(a) 10c on 10pf 50 1.00
48 A16(a) 25c on 20pf 65 1.00
49 A16(a) 30c on 25pf 1.25 *15.00*
50 A16(a) 35c on 30pf 1.25 *8.00*
51 A16(a) 50c on 40pf 1.25 *5.00*
52 A16(a) 60c on 50pf 1.50 *32.50*
53 A16(a) 1p on 80pf 1.75 *26.00*
54 A17(b) 1p25c on 1m 2.00 *60.00*
55 A21(b) 2p50c on 2m 3.50 *52.50*
56 A19(c) 3p75c on 3m (R) 6.00 *125.00*
57 A20(b) 6p25c on 5m 15.00 *200.00*
Nos. 45-57 (13) 35.65

Forged cancellations exist.

OFFICES IN THE TURKISH EMPIRE

> Unused values for Nos. 1-6 are for stamps with original gum. Copies without gum sell for about one-third of the figures quoted.

40 Paras = 1 Piaster

A1

A2

German Stamps of 1880-83 Surcharged in Black or Blue

1884 Unwmk. *Perf. 13½x14½*

No.	Type	Description	Unused	Used
1	A1	10pa on 5pf vio	20.00	18.00
2	A2	20pa on 10pf rose	50.00	18.00
3	A2	1pi on 20pf ultra (Bk)	45.00	2.50
4	A2	1pi on 20pf ultra (Bl)	600.00	45.00
5	A2	1¼pi on 25pf brn	125.00	125.00
6	A2	2½pi on 50pf gray grn	125.00	70.00
a.		2½pi on 50pf deep olive grn	240.00	200.00

There are two types of the surcharge on the 1¼pi and 2½pi stamps, the difference being in the spacing between the figures and the word "PIASTER."

There are re-issues of these stamps which vary only slightly from the originals in overprint measurements.

A3

A4

A5

German Stamps of 1889-1900 Surcharged in Black

1889

No.	Type	Description	Unused	Used
8	A3	10pa on 5pf grn	2.00	60
9	A4	20pa on 10pf car	3.50	1.80
10	A4	1pi on 20pf ultra	4.50	65
11	A5	1¼pi on 25pf org	21.00	14.00
12	A5	2½pi on 50pf choc	35.00	17.00
a.		2½pi on 50pf copper brown	150.00	100.00

A6

A7

A8

A9

A10

A11

1900 *Perf. 14, 14½*

Black or Red Surcharge

No.	Type	Description	Unused	Used
13	A6	10pa on 5pf grn	2.00	2.00
14	A6	20pa on 10pf car	2.50	2.50
15	A6	1pi on 20pf ultra	4.75	1.50
16	A7	1¼pi on 25pf org & blk, *yel*	6.25	3.50
17	A7	1½pi on 30pf org & blk, *sal*	6.25	3.50
18	A6	2pi on 40pf lake & blk	6.25	3.50
19	A7	2½pi on 50pf pur & blk, *sal*	14.00	14.00
20	A6	4pi on 80pf lake & blk, *rose*	14.00	14.00
21	A8	5pi on 1m car rose	35.00	35.00
22	A9	10pi on 2m gray bl	35.00	40.00
23	A10	15pi on 3m blk vio (R)	60.00	80.00
24	A11	25pi on 5m sl & car, type I	250.00	440.00
a.		Double surcharge	*12,500.*	*15,000.*
24B	A11	25pi on 5m sl & car, type II	190.00	325.00
c.		Double surcharge	*11,000.*	*9,000.*
		Nos. 13-24B (13)	626.00	964.50

Retouched copies of No. 24 sell for ⅔ as much. See note after Germany No. 65A.

German Stamps of 1900 Surcharged in Black — 1 PIASTER 1

1903-05

No.	Type	Description	Unused	Used
25	A11	10pa on 5pf green	14.00	10.00
26	A11	20pa on 10pf car	32.50	18.00
27	A11	1pi on 20pf ultra	8.50	3.50

5 PIASTER 5

No.	Type	Description	Unused	Used
28	A12	5pi on 1m car rose	65.00	52.50
29	A13	10pi on 2m bl ('05)	135.00	225.00
30	A15	25pi on 5m sl & car	275.00	*700.00*
a.		Double surcharge	*4,250.*	
		Nos. 25-30 (6)	530.00	*1,009.*

The 1903-05 surcharges may be easily distinguished from those of 1900 by the added bar at the top of the letter "A."

German Stamps of 1902 Surcharged in Black or Red

a — 10 10 Para

b — 5 Piaster 5

1905 Unwmk.

No.	Type	Description	Unused	Used
31	A16(a)	10pa on 5pf	4.50	2.50
32	A16(a)	20pa on 10pf	10.00	3.25
33	A16(a)	1pi on 20pf	11.00	2.50
34	A16(a)	1¼pi on 25pf	11.00	7.00
35	A16(a)	1½pi on 30pf	20.00	18.00
36	A16(a)	2pi on 40pf	32.50	18.00
37	A16(a)	2½pi on 50pf	12.00	*27.50*
38	A16(a)	4pi on 80pf	35.00	16.00
39	A17(b)	5pi on 1m	30.00	27.50
40	A21(b)	10pi on 2m	42.50	47.50
41	A19(b)	15pi on 3m (R)	55.00	47.50
42	A20(b)	25pi on 5m	250.00	325.00
		Nos. 31-42 (12)	513.50	542.25

German Stamps of 1905 Surcharged in Black or Red

1906-12 Wmk. 125

No.	Type	Description	Unused	Used
43	A16(a)	10pa on 5pf	2.00	45
44	A16(a)	20pa on 10pf	2.75	45
45	A16(a)	1pi on 20pf	3.50	50
46	A16(a)	1¼pi on 25pf	16.00	12.50
47	A16(a)	1½pi on 30pf	10.00	5.00
48	A16(a)	2pi on 40pf	4.50	1.25
49	A16(a)	2½pi on 50pf	11.50	8.00
50	A16(a)	4pi on 80pf	10.00	*24.00*
51	A17(b)	5pi on 1m	20.00	30.00
52	A21(b)	10pi on 2m	20.00	*40.00*
53	A19(b)	15pi on 3m (R)	22.50	*450.00*
54	A20(b)	25pi on 5m	27.50	*55.00*
		Nos. 43-54 (12)	150.25	

German Stamps of 1905 Surcharged Diagonally in Black

1908

No.	Type	Description	Unused	Used
55	A16	5c on 5pf	1.25	1.50
56	A16	10c on 10pf	3.00	2.00
57	A16	25c on 20pf	7.25	*27.50*
58	A16	50c on 40pf	32.50	*80.00*
59	A16	100c on 80pf	65.00	90.00
		Nos. 55-59 (5)	109.00	*201.00*

Forged cancellations exist on #37, 53-54, 57-59.

GRAND COMORO

LOCATION — One of the Comoro Islands in the Mozambique Channel between Madagascar and Mozambique.
GOVT. — Former French Colony
AREA — 385 sq. mi. (approx.)
POP. — 50,000 (approx.)
CAPITAL — Moroni

See Comoro Islands

100 Centimes = 1 Franc

Navigation and Commerce — A1

Perf. 14x13½

1897-1907 Typo. Unwmk.

Name of Colony in Blue or Carmine

No.	Type	Description	Unused	Used
1	A1	1c blk, *lil bl*	55	55
2	A1	2c brn, *buff*	60	60
3	A1	4c claret, *lav*	80	80
4	A1	5c grn, *grnsh*	1.50	1.50
5	A1	10c blk, *lavender*	3.50	3.00
6	A1	10c red ('00)	4.50	4.50
7	A1	15c blue, quadrille paper	6.00	4.50
8	A1	15c gray, *lt gray* ('00)	4.50	4.50
9	A1	20c red, *grn*	6.00	5.75
10	A1	25c blk, *rose*	7.00	5.75
11	A1	25c blue ('00)	7.50	4.50
12	A1	30c brn, *bister*	8.00	5.75
13	A1	35c blk, *yel* ('06)	7.50	6.25
14	A1	40c red, *straw*	9.00	5.75
15	A1	45c blk, *gray grn* ('07)	39.00	32.50
16	A1	50c car, *rose*	16.00	8.00
17	A1	50c brn, *bluish* ('00)	18.00	16.00
18	A1	75c dp vio, *org*	25.00	16.00
19	A1	1fr brnz grn, *straw*	15.00	12.00
		Nos. 1-19 (19)	179.95	138.20

Perf. 13½x14 stamps are counterfeits.

Issues of 1897-1907 Surcharged in Black or Carmine

05 — 10

1912

No.	Type	Description	Unused	Used
20	A1	5c on 2c brn, *buff*	45	45
a.		Inverted surcharge	80.00	
21	A1	5c on 4c cl, *lav* (C)	60	60
22	A1	5c on 15c blue (C)	45	45
23	A1	5c on 20c red, *grn*	50	50
24	A1	5c on 25c blk, *rose* (C)	50	50
25	A1	5c on 30c brn, *bis* (C)	60	60
26	A1	10c on 40c red, *straw*	60	60
27	A1	10c on 45c blk, *gray grn* (C)	60	60
28	A1	10c on 50c car, *rose*	65	65
29	A1	10c on 75c dp vio, *org*	65	65
		Nos. 20-29 (10)	5.60	5.60

Two spacings between the surcharged numerals are found on Nos. 20-29.

Nos. 20-29 were available for use in Madagascar and the entire Comoro archipelago.

Stamps of Grand Comoro were superseded by those of Madagascar, and in 1950 by those of Comoro Islands.

GREECE

(Hellas)

LOCATION — Southern part of the Balkan Peninsula in southeastern Europe, bordering on the Ionian, Aegean and Mediterranean Seas
GOVT. — Republic
AREA — 50,949 sq. mi.
POP. — 9,740,417 (1981)
CAPITAL — Athens

In 1923 the reigning king was forced to abdicate and the following year Greece was declared a republic. In 1935, the king was recalled by a "plebiscite" of the people. Greece became a republic in June 1973. The country today includes the Aegean Islands of Chios, Mytilene (Lesbos), Samos, Icaria (Nicaria) and Lemnos, the Ionian Islands (Corfu, etc.) Crete, Macedonia, Western Thrace and part of Eastern Thrace, the Mount Athos District, Epirus and the Dodecanese Islands.

100 Lepta = 1 Drachma

> **Catalogue values for unused stamps in this country are for Never Hinged items, beginning with Scott 601 in the regular postage section, Scott B1 in the semi-postal section, Scott C48 in the airpost section, Scott CB1 in the airpost semi-postal section, Scott RA69 in the postal tax section, and Scott N239 in the occupation and annexation section.**

> Values of early Greek stamps vary according to condition. Quotations for Nos. 1-58 are for fine copies. Very fine to superb specimens sell at much higher prices, and inferior or poor copies sell at reduced prices, depending on the condition of the individual specimen.
> Values for Nos. 1-7 unused are for specimens without gum. Stamps with original gum are worth considerably more.

Watermarks

Wmk. 129- Crown and ET

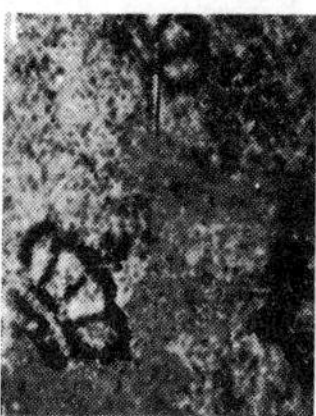
Wmk. 252- Crowns

> Values of early Greek stamps vary according to condition. Quotations for Nos. 1-58 are for fine copies. Very fine to superb specimens sell at much higher prices, and inferior or poor copies sell at reduced prices, depending on the condition of the individual specimen.
> Values for Nos. 1-7 unused are for specimens without gum. Stamps with original gum are worth considerably more.

Hermes (Mercury) — A1

Paris Print, Fine Impression

The enlarged illustrations show the head in various states of the plates. The differences are best seen in the shading lines on the cheek and neck.

1861 Unwmk. Typo. *Imperf.*

Without Figures on Back

1 A1 1 l choc, *cream* 150.00 275.00
a. 1 l red brown, *cream* 165.00 300.00
2 A1 2 l ol bis, *straw* 21.00 35.00
a. 2 l brown buff, *buff* 20.00 32.50
3 A1 5 l yel grn, *grnsh* 150.00 100.00
4 A1 20 l bl, *bluish* 375.00 52.50
a. 20 l deep blue, *bluish* 500.00 160.00
b. On pelure paper *250.00*
5 A1 40 l vio, *bl* 165.00 100.00
6 A1 80 l rose, *pink* 110.00 70.00
a. 80 l carmine, *pink* 110.00 70.00

Large Figures, 8mm high, on Back

7 A1 10 l red org, *bl* 275.00 275.00
a. "01" on back
b. Without "10" on back 475.00
c. "0" of "10" invtd. on back *675.00*
d. "1" of "10" invtd. on back *775.00*

No. 7b was not regularly issued.

Trial impressions of Paris prints exist in many shades, some being close to those of the issued stamps. The gum used was thin and smooth instead of thick, brownish and crackly as on the issued stamps.

See #8-58. For surcharges see #130, 132-133, 137-139, 141-143, 147-149, 153-154, 157-158.

Athens Print, Clear Impression

1861-62

Without Figures on Back

Fine Printing

8 A1 1 l choc, *cr* ('62) 375.00 225.00
a. 1 l dk chocolate, *cream* 675.00 428.00
9 A1 2 l bis brn, *cr* 35.00 47.50
a. 2 l dark brown, *straw*
10 A1 20 l dk bl, *bluish* (coarse print) *10,000.*

No. 10 often shows a quadrille appearance in the background.

With Figures on Back

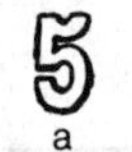

a

b

Fine Printing, #11-14

Coarse Printing, #11a-14a

11 A1 (a) 5 l grn, *grnsh* 175.00 65.00
a. 5 l green, *greenish* 215.00 65.00
b. Double "5" on back *475.00*
12 A1 10 l org, *grnsh* 400.00 67.50
a. 10 l orange, *greenish* 725.00 87.50
13 A1 20 l dk bl, *bluish* *2,500.* 55.00
a. 20 l dull blue, *bluish* *2,750.* 80.00
14 A1 40 l red vio, *bl* *1,500.* 190.00
a. 40 l red violet, *blue* *1,600.* 200.00
15 A1 80 l dl rose, *pink* ('62) 550.00 100.00
a. 80 l carmine, *pink* ('62) 550.00 100.00

The fine stamps can be distinguished by the delicate lines of the numerals on the back as compared with the coarser ones of later printings.

Nos. 15 and 15a have vermilion figures on the back, while those of all later printings are carmine.

Athens Print, Coarse Impression

1862-67

With Figures on Back, Except 1 l and 2 l

16 A1 1 l choc, *cr* 35.00 24.00
a. 1 l red brn, *cr* (poor print) 140.00 70.00
b. 1 l brn, *cr* (poor print) 45.00 22.50
17 A1 2 l brnsh bis, *cr* 7.25 6.50
a. 2 l bister, *cream* 7.25 6.50
18 A1 (b) 5 l grn, *grnsh* 125.00 8.00
a. 5 l yelsh grn, *grnsh* 125.00 8.00
19 A1 10 l yel org, *bluish* 150.00 8.75
a. 10 l org, *blue* (1864) 325.00 10.00
b. "10" on face instead of back (No. 19a) *5,500.*
c. 10 l red org, *bl* (Dec. 1865) *300.00* 10.00
d. "01" on back *500.00*
20 A1 20 l bl, *bluish* 125.00 5.50
a. 20 l lt bl, *bluish* (fine print) 125.00 14.00
b. 20 l dark blue, *bluish* 375.00 14.00
c. 20 l blue, *greenish* *1,000.* 10.00
d. "80" on back *1,300.*
e. Double "20" on back *175.00*
f. Without "20" on back *1,400.*
21 A1 40 l red vio, *bl* 225.00 12.00
a. 40 l brown vio, *blue* 225.00 12.00
b. 40 l lil brown, *lil gray* *1,000.* 14.00
c. Double "40" on back 225.00
22 A1 80 l car, *pale rose* 50.00 10.00
a. 80 l rose, *pale rose* 55.00 10.00
b. "8" on back inverted *1,000.* 175.00
c. "80" on back inverted 225.00
d. "8" only on back 185.00

Faint vertical lines are visible in the background of Nos. 16, 16a and 16b.

Many stamps of this and succeeding issues which are normally imperforate are known rouletted, pin-perforated, percé en scie, etc., all of which are unofficial.

1868-69

Athens Print, From Cleaned Plates

23 A1 1 l redsh brn, *cr* 25.00 22.50
a. 1 l dk redsh brn, *cream* 22.50 27.50
24 A1 2 l gray bis, *cr* 12.00 11.00
25 A1 (b) 5 l grn, *grnsh* *1,100.* 40.00
26 A1 10 l pale org, *bluish* *900.00* 9.00
a. "10" on back inverted *500.00*
27 A1 20 l pale bl, *bluish* *1,000.* 7.00
a. Double "20" on back *200.00*
28 A1 40 l rose vio, *bl* 225.00 17.00
a. "20" on back, corrected to "40" *1,400.* *600.00*
29 A1 80 l rose car, *pale rose* 125.00 72.50

The "0" on the back of No. 29 is printed more heavily than the "8."

1870

Special Athens Printing Made Under Supervision of German Workmen

Good Impression

30 A1 1 l redsh brn, *cr* 60.00 70.00
a. 1 l deep reddish brn, *cream* 80.00 95.00
31 A1 20 l lt bl, *bluish* *1,500.* 13.00
a. 20 l blue, *bluish* *1,600.* 14.00
b. "02" on back 225.00
c. "20" on back inverted 190.00

Nos. 30 and 30a have short lines of shading on cheek. The spandrels of No. 31 are very pale with the lines often broken or missing.

1870-71

Medium to Thin Paper Without Mesh

32 A1 1 l brn, *cream* 57.50 40.00
a. 1 l purple brown, *cream* 47.50 35.00
33 A1 2 l sal bis, *cr* 8.00 8.00
34 A1 (b) 5 l grn, *grnsh* *2,000.* 30.00
35 A1 10 l lt red org, *grnsh* *1,100.* 27.50
a. "01" on back 600.00
36 A1 20 l bl, *bluish* *1,000.* 7.25
a. "02" on back 190.00
b. Double "20" on back 200.00
37 A1 40 l sal, *grnsh* 475.00 40.00
a. 40 l lilac, *greenish*

The stamps of this issue have rather coarse figures on back.

No. 37a is printed in the exact shade of the numerals on the back of No. 37.

1872-75

Thin Transparent Paper Showing Mesh

38 A1 1 l red brn, *yelsh* 32.50 30.00
a. 1 l grayish brown, *straw* 37.50 32.50
39 A1 (b) 5 l grn, *greenish* 425.00 13.00
a. 5 l dark green, *grnsh* 400.00 20.00
b. Double "5" on back 100.00
40 A1 10 l red org, *grnsh* *650.00* 5.00
a. 10 l red orange, *pale lilac* *2,750.* 32.50
b. "10" on back inverted (No. 40) 450.00 60.00
c. Double "10" on back 160.00
d. "0" on back 67.50
41 A1 20 l dk bl, *bluish* 750.00 5.50
a. 20 l blue, *bluish* 700.00 5.50
b. 20 l dark blue, *blue* 800.00 18.00
42 A1 40 l brn, *bl* 18.00 20.00
a. 40 l olive brown, *blue* 18.50 20.00
b. 40 l red violet, *blue* 600.00 18.00
c. 40 l gray violet, *blue* 400.00 16.00
d. Figures on back bister 60.00 16.00

The mesh is not apparent on Nos. 38, 38a.

1875-80

On Cream Paper Unless Otherwise Stated

43 A1 1 l gray brn 17.50 15.00
a. 1 l dark gray brown 17.50 15.00
b. 1 l black brown 22.50 20.00
c. 1 l red brown 22.50 20.00
d. 1 l dark red brown 22.50 20.00
e. 1 l purple brown 30.00 20.00
44 A1 2 l bister 19.00 17.00
45 A1 (b) 5 l dk yel grn 100.00 12.00
a. 5 l pale yellow green 100.00 12.00
46 A1 10 l orange 125.00 6.00
a. 10 l orange, *yellow* 150.00 8.00
c. "00" on back 135.00 65.00
d. "1" on back 150.00 67.50
e. "0" on back 175.00 67.50
f. "01" on back 67.50
g. Double "10" on back 140.00
47 A1 20 l ultra 80.00 4.00
a. 20 l blue 175.00 8.00
b. 20 l dull blue 275.00 10.00
c. "02" on back 135.00
d. "20" on back inverted
e. As "c," inverted
f. Double "20" on back
48 A1 40 l salmon 18.00 30.00

The back figures are found in many varieties, including "1" and "0" inverted in "10."

1876

Without Figures on Back

Paris Print, Clear Impression

49 A1 30 l ol brn, *yelsh* 140.00 25.00
a. 30 l brown, *yellowish* 200.00 47.50
50 A1 60 l grn, *grnsh* 24.00 32.50

Athens Print, Coarse Impression, Yellowish Paper

51 A1 30 l dark brown 32.50 3.00
a. 30 l black brown 35.00 3.50
52 A1 60 l green 260.00 30.00

1880-82 Cream Paper

53 A1 5 l green 6.50 2.25
54 A1 10 l orange 11.00 2.50
a. 10 l yellow 11.00 2.50
b. 10 l red orange *2,250.* 35.00
55 A1 20 l ultra 225.00 65.00
56 A1 20 l rose (aniline ink) ('82) 3.00 1.00
a. 20 l pale rose (aniline ink) ('82) 3.00 1.00
b. 20 l deep carmine 125.00 8.00
57 A1 30 l ultra ('82) 110.00 10.00
a. 30 l slate blue 110.00 10.00
58 A1 40 l lilac 40.00 5.00
a. 40 l violet 40.00 5.00

Stamps of type A1 were not regularly issued with perf. 11½ but were freely used on mail.

Hermes — A2

Lepta denominations have white numeral tablets.

Belgian Print, Clear Impression

1886-88 *Imperf.*

64 A2 1 l brown ('88) 1.25 75
65 A2 2 l bister ('88) 3.00 45.00
66 A2 5 l yel grn ('88) 4.50 1.00
67 A2 10 l yellow ('88) 9.50 1.00
68 A2 20 l car rose ('88) 25.00 1.00
69 A2 25 l blue 95.00 1.00
70 A2 40 l vio ('88) 47.50 17.50
71 A2 50 l gray grn 4.00 1.00
72 A2 1d gray 50.00 1.00

See Nos. 81-116. For surcharges see Nos. 129, 134, 140, 144, 150, 151-152, 155-156.

1891 *Perf. 11½*

81 A2 1 l brown 2.75 1.40
82 A2 2 l bister 10.50 5.00
83 A2 5 l yel grn 13.00 4.50
84 A2 10 l yellow 18.00 4.50
85 A2 20 l car rose 30.00 4.50
86 A2 25 l blue 125.00 22.50
87 A2 40 l violet 95.00 30.00
88 A2 50 l gray grn 12.00 4.50
89 A2 1d gray 125.00 3.00

The Belgian Printings perf. 13½ and most of the values perf. 11½ (Nos. 82-86) were perforated on request of philatelists at the main post office in Athens. While not regularly issued they were freely used for postage.

Athens Print, Poor Impression

Wmk. Greek Words in Some Sheets

1889-95 *Imperf.*

90 A2 1 l blk brn 80 20
a. 1 l brown 80 20
91 A2 2 l pale bister 1.00 65
a. 2 l buff 1.00 65
92 A2 5 l green 2.50 30
a. Double impression
b. 5 l deep green 3.75 30
93 A2 10 l yellow 18.00 25
a. 10 l orange 35.00 25
b. 10 l dull yellow 12.00 25
94 A2 20 l carmine 3.25 15
a. 20 l rose 3.25 15
95 A2 25 l brt bl 40.00 75
a. 25 l indigo 75.00 2.50
b. 25 l ultra 75.00 2.50
c. 25 l dull blue 40.00 2.00
96 A2 25 l red vio ('93) 2.40 25
a. 25 l lilac 2.40 25
97 A2 40 l red vio ('91) 47.50 25.00
98 A2 40 l blue ('93) 6.25 2.00
99 A2 1d gray ('95) 190.00 5.00

Perf. 13½

100 A2 1 l brown 7.50 7.50
101 A2 2 l buff 1.25 1.25
104 A2 20 l carmine 10.00 3.75
a. 20 l rose 10.00 3.75
105 A2 40 l red violet 75.00 30.00

Other denominations of type A2 were not officially issued with perf. 13½.

Perf. 11½

107 A2 1 l brown 1.25 70
a. 1 l black brown 2.75 1.00
108 A2 2 l pale bister 2.00 1.00
a. 2 l buff 2.00 1.00

109 A2 5 l pale grn 3.75 50
a. 5 l deep green 5.75 50
110 A2 10 l yellow 10.00 1.00
a. 10 l dull yellow 19.00 1.00
b. 10 l orange 40.00 1.50
111 A2 20 l carmine 4.50 50
a. 20 l rose 4.50 50
112 A2 25 l dull blue 47.50 3.50
a. 25 l indigo 80.00 5.50
b. 25 l ultra 125.00 7.50
c. 25 l bright blue 47.50 3.75
113 A2 25 l red vio 3.75 50
a. 25 l lilac 3.75 50
114 A2 40 l red vio 60.00 30.00
115 A2 40 l blue 10.00 3.50
116 A2 1d gray 225.00 10.00

Partly-perforated varieties sell for about twice as much as normal copies.

The watermark on Nos. 90-116 consists of three Greek words meaning Paper for Public Service. It is in double-lined capitals, measures 270x35mm, and extends across three panes.

Boxers — A3

Discobolus by Myron — A4

Vase Depicting Pallas Athene (Minerva) — A5

Chariot Driving A6

Stadium and Acropolis A7

Statue of Hermes by Praxiteles — A8

Statue of Victory by Paeonius — A9

Acropolis and Parthenon A10

Perf. 14x13½, 13½x14

1896 Unwmk.

117 A3 1 l ocher 60 30
118 A3 2 l rose 60 30
a. Without engraver's name 10.00 6.00
119 A4 5 l lilac 90 45
120 A4 10 l slate gray 1.25 50
121 A5 20 l red brn 10.00 20
122 A6 25 l red 12.00 45
123 A5 40 l violet 8.00 2.75
124 A6 60 l black 15.00 5.50
125 A7 1d blue 40.00 6.25
126 A8 2d bister 60.00 25.00
a. Horiz. pair, imperf. btwn.
127 A9 5d green 200.00 135.00
128 A10 10d brown 210.00 175.00
Nos. 117-128 (12) 558.35 351.70

1st intl. Olympic Games of the modern era, held at Athens. Counterfeits of Nos. 123-124 and 126-128 exist.

For surcharges see Nos. 159-164.

Preceding Issues Surcharged

ΛΕΠΤΑ
20

1900 Imperf.

129 A2 20 l on 25 l dl bl, #95c 75 50
a. 20 l on 25 l indigo, #95a 47.50 7.50
b. 20 l on 25 l ultra, #95b 67.50 20.00
c. Double surcharge 50.00 30.00
d. Triple surcharge 60.00
e. Inverted surcharge 50.00 30.00
f. "20" above word 50.00 30.00
g. Pair, one without surcharge 100.00
h. "20" without word
130 A1 30 l on 40 l vio, cr, #58a 4.50 4.00
a. 30 l on 40 l lilac, #58 5.25 4.50
b. Broad "0" in "30" 6.00 5.25
c. First letter of word is "A" 50.00 45.00
d. Double surcharge 250.00
132 A1 40 l on 2 l bis, cr, #44 5.25 4.00
a. Broad "0" in "40" 6.00 6.00
b. First letter of word is "A" 50.00 45.00
133 A1 50 l on 40 l sal, cr, #48 6.00 3.75
a. Broad "0" in "50" 5.25 5.25
b. First letter of word is "A" 50.00 45.00
c. "50" without word
d. "50" above word
134 A2 1d on 40 l red vio (No. 97) 10.00 9.25
137 A1 3d on 10 l org, cr, #54 50.00 25.00
a. 3d on 10 l yellow, #54a 50.00 25.00
138 A1 5d on 40 l red vio, bl, #21 90.00 65.00
a. 5d on 40 l red vio, bl, #28 90.00 65.00
b. "20" on back corrected to "40"
139 A1 5d on 40 l red vio, bl, #42b 300.00

Perf. 11½

140 A2 20 l on 25 l dl bl, #112 2.25 1.25
a. 20 l on 25 l indigo, #112a 67.50 17.50
b. 20 l on 25 l ultra, #112b 55.00 20.00
c. Double surcharge 50.00 25.00
d. Triple surcharge 60.00 40.00
e. Inverted surcharge 50.00 25.00
f. "20" above word 75.00
141 A1 30 l on 40 l vio, cr, #58a 6.50 6.00
a. 30 l on 40 l lilac, #58 6.50 6.00
b. Broad "0" in "30" 9.25 9.25
c. First letter of word "A" 50.00 45.00
d. Double surcharge
142 A1 40 l on 2 l bis, cr, #44 6.50 6.00
a. Broad "0" in "40" 9.25 9.25
b. First letter of word "A" 50.00 45.00
143 A1 50 l on 40 l sal, cr, #48 8.00 6.50
a. Broad "0" in "50" 9.25 9.25
b. First letter of word "A" 50.00 45.00
c. "50" without word
144 A2 1d on 40 l red vio, #114 13.00 10.50
147 A1 3d on 10 l org, cr, #54 57.50 20.00
a. 3d on 10 l yel, cream, #54a 57.50 20.00
148 A1 5d on 40 l red vio, bl, #21 80.00 62.50
a. 5d on 40 l red vio, bl, #28 80.00 62.50
149 A1 5d on 40 l red vio, bl, #42 315.00

Perf. 13½

150 A2 2d on 40 l red vio, #105 6.50 6.50

The 1d on 40 l perf. 13½ and the 2d on 40 l, both imperf. and perf. 13½, were not officially issued.

Surcharge Including "A M"

"A M" = "Axia Metalliki" or "Value in Metal (gold)."

1900 Imperf.

151 A2 25 l on 40 l vio, #70 6.00 5.00
152 A2 50 l on 25 l bl, #69 27.50 22.50
153 A1 1d on 40 l brn, bl, #42b 125.00 115.00
154 A1 2d on 5 l grn, cr, #53 15.00 11.50

Perf. 11½

155 A2 25 l on 40 l vio, #87 10.00 10.00
156 A2 50 l on 25 l bl, #86 47.50 40.00
157 A1 1d on 40 l brn, bl, #42b 140.00 125.00
158 A1 2d on 5 l grn, cr, #53 18.00 17.50

Partly-perforated varieties of Nos. 129-158 sell for about two to three times as much as normal copies.

Surcharge Including "A M" on Olympic Issue in Red

1900-01 Perf. 14x13½

159 A7 5 l on 1d blue 11.00 8.00
a. Wrong font "M" with serifs 40.00 37.50
b. Double surcharge 250.00 225.00
160 A5 25 l on 40 l vio 65.00 40.00
161 A8 50 l on 2d bister 45.00 32.50
a. Broad "0" in "50" 50.00 40.00
162 A9 1d on 5d grn ('01) 250.00 150.00
a. Greek "D" instead of "A" as 3rd letter 500.00 450.00
163 A10 2d on 10d brn ('01) 45.00 45.00
a. Greek "D" instead of "A" as 3rd letter 250.00 250.00
Nos. 159-163 (5) 416.00 275.50

Black Surcharge on No. 160

164 A5 50 l on 25 l on 40 l vio (R + Bk) 475.00 450.00
a. Broad "0" in "50" 450.00 525.00

Nos. 151-164 and 179-183, gold currency stamps, were generally used for parcel post and foreign money orders. They were also available for use on letters, but cost about 20 per cent more than the regular stamps of the same denomination.

Counterfeit surcharges exist of #159-164.

Giovanni da Bologna's Hermes
A11 A12

A13

FIVE LEPTA.

Type I- Letters of "ELLAS" not outlined at top and left. Only a few faint horizontal lines between the outer vertical lines at sides.

Type II- Letters of "ELLAS" fully outlined. Heavy horizontal lines between the vertical frame lines.

Perf. 11½, 12½, 13½

1901 Engr. Wmk. 129

165 A11 1 l yel brn 30 15
166 A11 2 l gray 40 15
167 A11 3 l orange 55 15
168 A12 5 l grn, type I 55 15
a. 5 l yellow green, type I 55 15
b. 5 l yellow green, type II 55 15
169 A12 10 l rose 1.65 15
170 A11 20 l red lilac 1.75 15
171 A12 25 l ultra 2.25 15
172 A11 30 l dl vio 10.00 1.75
173 A11 40 l dk brn 18.00 1.75
174 A11 50 l brn lake 16.00 1.75

Perf. 12½, 14 and Compound

175 A13 1d black 45.00 2.75
a. Horiz. pair, imperf. btwn. 300.00
c. Horiz. pair, imperf. vert. 300.00
d. Vert. pair, imperf. horiz. 300.00

Litho.

Perf. 12½

176 A13 2d bronze 6.00 6.00
177 A13 3d silver 6.00 6.00
a. Horiz. pair, imperf. btwn. 450.00
178 A13 5d gold 7.50 7.50
Nos. 165-178 (14) 115.95 28.55

For overprints and surcharges see Nos. RA3-RA13, N16, N109.

Imperf., Pairs

165a A11 1 l 25.00
166a A11 2 l 30.00
167a A11 3 l 30.00
168c A12 5 l 25.00
169a A12 10 l 25.00
170a A11 20 l 30.00
171a A12 25 l 30.00
172a A11 30 l 125.00
173a A11 40 l 130.00
174a A11 50 l 80.00
175b A13 1d 300.00

Hermes — A14

1902, Jan. 1 Engr. Perf. 13½

179 A14 5 l deep orange 2.50 48
a. Imperf., pair 45.00
180 A14 25 l emerald 30.00 1.40
181 A14 50 l ultra 30.00 3.00
a. Imperf., pair 300.00
182 A14 1d rose red 30.00 4.75
183 A14 2d org brn 40.00 32.50
Nos. 179-183 (5) 132.50 42.13

See note after No. 164. In 1913 remainders of Nos. 179-183 were used as postage dues.

Apollo Throwing Discus — A15

Jumper, with Jumping Weights — A16

Victory A17

Atlas and Hercules A18

Struggle of Hercules and Antaeus A19

Wrestlers A20

Daemon of the Games A21

Foot Race A22

Nike, Priest and Athletes in Pre-Games Offering to Zeus — A23

Wmk. Crown and ET (129)

1906, Mar. Engr. Perf. 13½, 14

184 A15 1 l brown 1.90 48
a. Imperf., pair 150.00
185 A15 2 l gray 65 24
a. Imperf., pair 150.00
186 A16 3 l orange 65 24
a. Imperf., pair 180.00
187 A16 5 l green 1.10 20
a. Imperf., pair 60.00
188 A17 10 l rose red 2.50 20
a. Imperf., pair 150.00
189 A18 20 l magenta 5.00 20
a. Imperf., pair 350.00
190 A19 25 l ultra 6.25 40
a. Imperf., pair 350.00
191 A20 30 l dl pur 6.25 4.50
a. Double impression 900.00
192 A21 40 l dk brn 5.00 4.50
193 A18 50 l brn lake 8.25 3.25
194 A22 1d gray blk 52.50 5.25
a. Imperf., pair 800.00
195 A22 2d rose 60.00 14.00
196 A22 3d olive yel 75.00 70.00
197 A23 5d dull blue 75.00 70.00
Nos. 184-197 (14) 300.05 173.46

Greek Special Olympic Games of 1906 at Athens, celebrating the 10th anniv. of the modern Olympic Games.

Surcharged stamps of this issue are revenues.

A24

Iris Holding Caduceus — A25

Hermes Donning Sandals — A26

Hermes Carrying Infant Arcas — A27

Hermes, from Old Cretan Coin — A28

Designs A24 to A28 are from Cretan and Arcadian coins of the 4th Century, B.C.

Serrate Roulette 13½

1911-21		**Engr.**		**Unwmk.**
198	A24	1 l green	30	15
199	A25	2 l car rose	30	15
200	A24	3 l vermilion	20	15
201	A26	5 l green	1.15	15
202	A24	10 l car rose	8.00	15
203	A25	20 l gray lilac	1.75	20
204	A25	25 l ultra	14.00	20
a.		Rouletted in black	90.00	
205	A26	30 l car rose	2.25	70
206	A25	40 l deep blue	6.75	5.00
207	A26	50 l dl vio	14.00	1.50
208	A27	1d ultra	16.00	30
209	A27	2d vermilion	22.50	60
210	A27	3d car rose	25.00	1.00
a.		Size 20¼x25½mm ('21)	75.00	17.50
211	A27	5d ultra	40.00	3.50
a.		Size 20¼x25½mm ('21)	125.00	17.00
212	A27	10d dp bl ('21)	35.00	17.00
a.		Size 20x26½mm ('11)	250.00	175.00
213	A28	25d deep blue	50.00	45.00
		Nos. 198-213 (16)	237.20	75.75

The 1921 reissues of the 3d, 5d and 10d measure 20¼x25½mm instead of 20x26½mm.

See Nos. 214-231. For overprints see Nos. 233-248B, N1, N10-N15, N17-N52A, N110-N148, Thrace 22-30, N26-N75.

Imperf., Pairs

198a	A24	1 l	40.00
200a	A24	3 l	*100.00*
201a	A26	5 l	25.00
202a	A24	10 l	35.00
203a	A25	20 l	80.00
204b	A25	25 l	110.00
206a	A25	40 l	125.00
207a	A26	50 l	150.00
208a	A27	1d	175.00
209a	A27	2d	175.00
210b	A27	3d	175.00
211b	A27	5d	175.00
212b	A27	10d As "a"	*900.00*
213a	A28	25d	*450.00*

Serrate Roulette 10½x13½, 13½

1913-23				**Litho.**
214	A24	1 l green	15	15
a.		Without period after "Ellas"	40.00	40.00
215	A25	2 l rose	15	15
216	A24	3 l vermilion	15	15
217	A26	5 l green	15	15
218	A24	10 l carmine	15	15
219	A25	15 l dl bl ('18)	15	15
220	A25	20 l slate	15	15
221	A25	25 l ultra	2.50	15
a.		25 l blue	15	
c.		Double impression	50.00	
222	A26	30 l rose ('14)	55	15
223	A25	40 l indigo ('14)	1.00	30
224	A26	50 l vio brn ('14)	2.50	15
225	A26	80 l vio brn ('23)	2.50	60
226	A27	1d ultra ('19)	2.75	15
227	A27	2d ver ('19)	6.50	20
228	A27	3d car rose ('20)	7.25	20
229	A27	5d ultra ('22)	11.00	30
230	A27	10d dp bl ('22)	5.50	60
231	A28	25d indigo ('22)	5.50	2.50
		Nos. 214-231 (18)	48.60	6.35

Nos. 221, 223 and 226 were re-issued in 1926, printed in Vienna from new plates. There are slight differences in minor details.

The 10 lepta brown, on thick paper, type A28, is not a postage stamp. It was issued in 1922 to replace coins of this denomination during a shortage of copper.

Imperf., Pairs

214b	A24	1 l	22.50
215a	A25	2 l	30.00
216a	A24	3 l	60.00
217a	A26	5 l	30.00
218a	A24	10 l	30.00
220a	A25	20 l	40.00
221b	A25	25 l	60.00
222a	A26	30 l	65.00
224a	A26	50 l	90.00
225b	A26	80 l	50.00
227a	A27	2d	75.00
228b	A27	3d	90.00
229a	A27	5d	140.00

Raising Greek Flag at Suda Bay, Crete — A29

1913, Dec. 1		**Engr.**		***Perf. 14½***
232	A29	25 l blue & black	4.50	3.50
a.		Imperf., pair	*600.00*	

Union of Crete with Greece. Used only in Crete.

Stamps of 1911-14 Overprinted in Red or Black

Serrate Roulette 13½

1916, Nov. 1				**Litho.**
233	A24	1 l green (R)	15	15
234	A25	2 l rose	20	20
235	A24	3 l vermilion	20	20
236	A26	5 l green (R)	35	15
237	A24	10 l carmine	35	15
238	A25	20 l slate (R)	70	20
239	A25	25 l blue (R)	70	15
a.		25 l ultra	60.00	3.00
240	A26	30 l rose	70	20
a.		Pair, one without overprint		
241	A25	40 l indigo (R)	9.00	2.25
242	A26	50 l vio brn (R)	37.50	2.25

Engr.

243	A24	3 l vermilion	70	70
244	A26	30 l car rose	1.00	1.00
245	A27	1d ultra (R)	32.50	60
a.		Rouletted in black	150.00	
246	A27	2d vermilion	25.00	3.50
247	A27	3d car rose	12.50	3.50
248	A27	5d ultra (R)	47.50	6.75
248B	A27	10d dp bl (R)	15.00	15.00
		Nos. 233-248B (17)	184.05	36.95

Most of Nos. 233-248B exist with overprint double, inverted, etc. Values 2 to 3 times those of normal examples, minimum $3. Excellent counterfeits of the overprint varieties exist.

Issued by the Venizelist Provisional Government

Iris — A32

1917, Feb. 5		**Litho.**		***Perf. 14***
249	A32	1 l dp grn	30	18
250	A32	5 l yel grn	30	25
251	A32	10 l rose	60	25
252	A32	25 l lt bl	95	40
253	A32	50 l gray vio	7.25	1.50
254	A32	1d ultra	1.50	50
255	A32	2d lt red	3.50	1.25
256	A32	3d claret	15.00	5.00
257	A32	5d gray bl	3.00	2.00
258	A32	10d dk bl	57.50	12.00
259	A32	25d slate	80.00	80.00
		Nos. 249-259 (11)	169.90	103.33

The 4d, type A32, was used only as a revenue stamp.

Imperf., Pairs

249a	A32	1 l	6.00
250a	A32	5 l	6.00
251a	A32	10 l	6.00
252a	A32	25 l	12.50
253a	A32	50 l	22.50
254a	A32	1d	25.00
255a	A32	2d	25.00
256a	A32	3d	60.00
257a	A32	5d	65.00
258a	A32	10d	125.00
259a	A32	25d	125.00

Stamps of 1917 Surcharged

ΕΠΑΝΑΣΤΑΣΙΣ
1922
ΛΕΠΤΑ 10

1923				
260	A32	5 l on 10 l rose	15	15
a.		Inverted surcharge	7.00	
261	A32	50 l on 50 l gray vio	15	15
262	A32	1d on 1d ultra	15	15
a.		1d on 1d gray	25	25
263	A32	2d on 2d lt red	25	25
264	A32	3d on 3d claret	1.40	1.40
265	A32	5d on 5d dk bl	1.25	1.25
266	A32	25d on 25d slate	25.00	25.00

Same Surcharge on Occupation of Turkey Stamps, 1913

Perf. 13½

267	O2	5 l on 3 l org	15	15
a.		Inverted surcharge	10.00	
268	O1	10 l on 20 l vio	40	40
a.		Inverted surcharge	20.00	
269	O2	10 l on 25 l pale bl	25	25
270	O1	10 l on 30 l gray grn	25	25
271	O2	10 l on 40 l ind	30	30
272	O1	50 l on 50 l dk bl	25	25
a.		Inverted surcharge	20.00	
273	O1	2d on 2d gray brn	55.00	55.00
274	O2	3d on 3d dl bl	2.75	2.75
a.		Imperf., pair	325.00	
275	O1	5d on 5d gray	3.00	3.00
276	O2	10d on 1d vio brn	6.00	6.00
276A	O2	10d on 10d car	900.00	

Dangerous counterfeits of No. 276A exist.

Same Surcharge on Stamps of Crete

Perf. 14

On Crete #50, 52, 59

276B	A6	5 l on 1 l red brn	35.00	30.00
277	A8	10 l on 10 l red	20	20
277B	A8	10 l on 25 l bl	150.00	

On Crete #66-69, 71

278	A8	10 l on 25 l blue	20	20
279	A6	50 l on 50 l lilac	25	25
279A	A6	50 l on 50 l ultra	3.75	3.75
280	A9	50 l on 1d gray vio	1.75	1.75
280A	A11	50 l on 5d grn & blk	35.00	

On Crete #77-82

281	A15	10 l on 20 l bl grn	120.00	120.00
282	A16	10 l on 25 l ultra	40	40
a.		Double surcharge	20.00	
283	A17	50 l on 50 l yel brn	30	30
284	A18	50 l on 1d rose car & brn	2.50	2.50
a.		Imperf., pair		
285	A19	3d on 3d org & blk	7.50	7.50
286	A20	5d on 5d ol grn & blk	7.50	7.50

On Crete #83-84

287	A21	10 l on 25 l bl & blk	1.10	1.10
a.		Imperf., pair		
287B	A22	50 l on 1d grn & blk	3.00	3.00

On Crete #96

288	A23	10 l on 10 l brn red	20	20
a.		Inverted surcharge	12.00	

On Crete #91

288B	A17	50 l on 50 l yel brn	*1,000.*	

Dangerous counterfeits of the overprint on No. 288B are plentiful. Copies with the surcharge on top of the overprint sell for more.

On Crete #109

289	A19	3d on 3d org & blk	14.00	14.00

On Crete #111, 113-120

290	A6	5 l on 1 l vio brn	15	15
a.		Inverted surcharge	12.00	12.00
291	A13	5 l on 5 l grn	20	20
a.		Inverted surcharge	12.00	
292	A23	10 l on 10 l brn red	20	20
a.		Inverted surcharge	12.00	
293	A15	10 l on 20 l bl grn	25	25
a.		Inverted surcharge	12.00	
294	A16	10 l on 25 l ultra	30	30
a.		Inverted surcharge	12.00	12.00
295	A17	50 l on 50 l yel brn	35	35
296	A18	50 l on 1d rose car & brn	3.00	3.00
a.		Inverted surcharge		
b.		Double surcharge	70.00	
c.		Double surch., one invtd.		
d.		Imperf., pair		
297	A19	3d on 3d org & blk	12.00	12.00
298	A20	5d on 5d ol grn & blk	130.00	130.00

Dangerous counterfeits of No. 298 exist.

Crete #J2-J9

299	D1	5 l on 5 l red	15	15
a.		Inverted surcharge	5.00	5.00
300	D1	5 l on 10 l red	15	15
301	D1	10 l on 20 l red	10.00	10.00
a.		Inverted surcharge		
302	D1	10 l on 40 l red	20	20
303	D1	50 l on 50 l red	20	20
304	D1	50 l on 1d red	50	50
a.		Double surcharge		
305	D1	50 l on 1d on 1d red	6.75	6.75
306	D1	2d on 2d red	75	75

On Crete #J11-J13

307	D1	5 l on 5 l red	3.50	3.50
308	D1	5 l on 10 l red	90	90
a.		"Ellas" inverted	5.00	
309	D1	10 l on 20 l red	32.50	32.50

On Crete #J20-J22, J24-J26

310	D1	5 l on 5 l red	50	50
311	D1	5 l on 10 l red	50	50
a.		Inverted surcharge	10.00	
312	D1	10 l on 20 l red	50	50
313	D1	50 l on 50 l red	1.10	1.10
314	D1	50 l on 1d red	1.40	1.40
315	D1	2d on 2d red	6.00	6.00

These surcharged Postage Due stamps were intended for the payment of ordinary postage.

Nos. 260 to 315 were surcharged in commemoration of the revolution of 1922.

Nos. 59, 91, 109, 111, 113-120, J11-J13, J20-J22, J24-J26 are on stamps previously overprinted by Crete.

Issues of the Republic

Lord Byron — A33

Byron at Missolonghi — A34

1924, Apr. 16		**Engr.**		***Perf. 12***
316	A33	80 l dark blue	50	25
317	A34	2d dk vio & blk	1.00	70
		Set, never hinged	3.25	

Death of Lord Byron (1788-1824) at Missolonghi.

Tomb of Markos Botsaris — A35

Serrate Roulette 13½

1926, Apr. 24				**Litho.**
318	A35	25 l lilac	45	45
		Never hinged	1.00	

Centenary of the defense of Missolonghi against the Turks.

Corinth Canal — A36

Dodecanese Costume — A37

Macedonian Costume — A38

Monastery of Simon Peter on Mt. Athos — A39

White Tower of Salonika — A40

Temple of Hephaestus — A41

The Acropolis — A42

Cruiser "Georgios Averoff" — A43

Academy of Sciences, Athens — A44

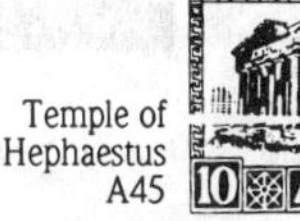

Temple of Hephaestus A45

Acropolis — A46

Perf. 12½x13, 13, 13x12½, 13½, 13½x13

1927, Apr. 1 **Engr.**

321 A36 5 l dark green 15 15
a. Vert. pair, imperf. horiz. 50.00
322 A37 10 l orange red 15 15
a. Horiz. pair, imperf. between 67.50
c. Double impression 20.00
323 A38 20 l violet 15 15
324 A39 25 l slate blue 15 15
a. Imperf., pair 67.50 67.50
b. Vert. pair, imperf. between 67.50
325 A40 40 l slate blue 60 15
326 A36 50 l violet 1.90 15
327 A36 80 l dk bl & blk 95 15
a. Imperf., pair 115.00
328 A41 1d dk bl & bis brn (I) 1.90 15
a. Imperf., pair 175.00
b. Center inverted 5,000.
c. Double impression of center 1,200.
d. Double impression of frame 125.00
329 A42 2d dk green & blk 2.75 18
a. Imperf., pair 150.00
330 A43 3d dp violet & blk 3.75 18
a. Double impression of center 200.00
b. Center inverted 3,500.
331 A44 5d yellow & blk 6.25 55
a. Imperf., pair 375.00
b. Center inverted 1,350.
c. 5d yellow & green 100.00 35.00
332 A45 10d brn car & blk 19.00 1.10
333 A44 15d brt yel grn & blk 19.00 6.75
334 A46 25d green & blk 40.00 6.75
a. Double impression 100.00
Nos. 321-334 (14) 96.70 16.71
Set, never hinged 400.00

See Nos. 364-371 and notes preceding No. 364.
For overprints see Nos. RA55, RA57, RA60, RA66, RA70-RA71.

This series as prepared, included a 1 lepton dark brown, type A37, but that value was never issued. Most copies were burned. Value $250.

Gen. Charles N. Fabvier and Acropolis A47

1927, Aug. 1 *Perf. 12*

335 A47 1d red 95 20
336 A47 3d dark blue 2.25 60
337 A47 6d green 6.75 6.75
Set, never hinged 25.00

Cent. of the liberation of Athens from the Turks in 1826.
For surcharges see Nos. 376-377.

Bay of Navarino and Pylos — A48

Battle of Navarino A49

"Edward" omitted — A50

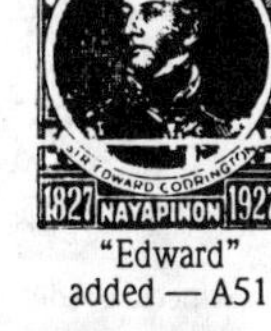
"Edward" added — A51

Admiral de Rigny — A52

Admiral van der Heyden — A53

Designs: #340-341, Sir Edward Codrington.

Perf. 13½x12½, 12½x13½, 13x12½, 12½x13

1927-28 **Litho.**

338 A48 1.50d gray green 1.25 15
a. Imperf., pair 225.00
b. Horiz. pair, imperf. btwn. 225.00
c. Horiz. pair, imperf. vert. 225.00
339 A49 4d dk gray bl ('28) 4.50 35
340 A50 5d dk brn & gray 4.50 2.00
a. 5d blk brn & blk ('28) 10.50 6.00
341 A51 5d dk brn & blk ('28) 18.00 6.50
342 A52 5d vio bl & blk ('28) 13.00 3.00
343 A53 5d lake & blk ('28) 7.25 3.00
Nos. 338-343 (6) 48.50 15.00
Set, never hinged 160.00

Centenary of the naval battle of Navarino.
For surcharges see Nos. 372-375.

Admiral Lascarina Bouboulina A54

Athanasios Diakos A55

Map of Greece in 1830 and 1930 — A56

Sortie from Missolonghi — A58

Patriots Declaring Independence — A57

Portraits: 10 l, Constantine Rhigas Ferreos. 20 l, Gregorios V. 40 l, Prince Alexandros Ypsilantis. No. 345, Bouboulina. No. 355, Diakos. No. 346, Theodoros Kolokotronis. No. 356, Konstantinos Kanaris. No.347, Georgios Karaiskakis. No. 357, Markos Botsaris. 2d, Andreas Miaoulis. 3d, Lazaros Koundouriotis. 5d, Count John Capo d'Istria (Capodistria), statesman and doctor. 10d, Petros Mavromichalis. 15d, Dionysios Solomos. 20d, Adamantios Korais.

Various Frames

1930, Apr. 1 **Engr.** *Perf. 13½, 14*

Imprint of Perkins, Bacon & Co.

344 A55 10 l brown 15 15
345 A54 50 l red 15 15
346 A54 1d car rose 24 15
347 A55 1.50d lt blue 20 15
348 A55 2d orange 30 16
349 A55 5d purple 1.25 1.25
350 A54 10d gray blk 7.00 3.75
351 A54 15d yel grn 7.00 5.50
352 A55 20d blue blk 9.00 7.25

Imprint of Bradbury, Wilkinson & Co.

Perf. 12

353 A55 20 l black 15 15
354 A55 40 l blue grn 15 15
355 A55 50 l brt blue 20 15
356 A55 1d brown org 30 15
357 A55 1.50d dk red 24 15
358 A55 3d dk brown 85 18
359 A56 4d dk blue 1.90 65
360 A57 25d black 9.00 7.00
361 A58 50d red brn 27.50 35.00
Nos. 344-361 (18) 65.58 62.09
Set, never hinged 150.00

Centenary of Greek independence. Some exist imperf.

Arcadi Monastery and Abbot Gabriel (Mt. Ida in Background) A60

1930, Nov. 8 *Perf. 12*

363 A60 8d deep violet 8.00 50
Never hinged 30.00

Issue of 1927 Re-engraved

50 l, Design is clearer, especially "50" and the 10 letters.

Type I 1927

Type II 1931

1d. Type I- Greek letters "L," "A," "D" have sharp pointed tops; numerals "1" are 1½mm wide at the foot, and have a straight slanting serif at top.

1d. Type II- Greek letters "L," "A," "D" have flat tops; numerals "1" are 2mm wide at foot and the serif at top is slightly curved. Perf. 14.

There are many minor differences in the lines of the two designs.

1d. Type III- The "1" in lower left corner has no serif at left of foot. Lines of temple have been deepened, so details stand out more clearly.

2d. On 1927 stamp the Parthenon is indistinct and blurred. On 1933 stamp it is strongly outlined and clear. Between the two pillars at lower right are four blocks of marble. These blocks are clear and distinct on the 1933 stamp but run together on the 1927 issue.

3d. Design is clearer, especially vertical lines of shading in smoke stacks and reflections in the water. Two or more sides perf. 11½.

10d. Background and shading of entire stamp have been lightened. Detail of frame is clearer and more distinct.

15d. Many more lines of shading in sky and foreground. Engraving is sharp and clear, particularly in frame. Two or more sides perf. 11½.

25d. Background has been lightened and foreground reduced until base of larger upright column is removed and fallen column appears nearly submerged.

Sizes in millimeters:
50 l, 1927, 18x24¾. 1933, 18½x24½.
1d, 1927, 24¾x17¾. 1931, 24¾x17¼. 1933, 24½x18¼.
2d, 1927, 24½x17¾. 1933, 24½x18½.

Perf. 11½, 11½x12½, 12½x10, 13, 13x12½, 14

1931-35

364 A36 50 l dk vio ('33) 3.00 50
365 A41 1d dk bl & org brn, type II 6.00 35
366 A41 1d dk bl & org brn, type III ('33) 4.25 22
367 A42 2d dk grn & blk ('33) 2.00 22
368 A43 3d red vio & blk ('34) 2.50 22
a. Imperf., pair
369 A45 10d brn car & blk ('35) 30.00 95
370 A44 15d pale yel grn & blk ('34) 57.50 9.00
a. Imperf., pair
371 A46 25d dk grn & blk ('35) 9.25 6.00
Nos. 364-371 (8) 114.50 17.46
Set, never hinged 365.00

Nos. 336-337, 340-343 Surcharged in Red ΔΡ.1.50

1932 *Perf. 12½x13½, 12½x13*

372 A52 1.50d on 5d 1.75 20
373 A53 1.50d on 5d 1.65 20
a. Double surcharge 60.00
374 A50 2d on 5d 2.00 20
375 A51 2d on 5d 6.25 20

Perf. 12

376 A47 2d on 3d 2.50 20
a. Double surcharge 60.00
377 A47 4d on 6d 3.75 1.00
Nos. 372-377 (6) 17.90 2.00
Set, never hinged 40.00

Adm. Pavlos Koundouriotis and Cruiser "Averoff" — A61

Pallas Athene — A62

Youth of Marathon — A63

1933 *Perf. 13½x13, 13x13½*

378 A61 50d black & ind 27.50 3.00
379 A62 75d blk & vio brn 82.50 120.00
a. Imperf., pair 450.00
380 A63 100d brn & dull grn 275.00 26.00
Set, never hinged 1,000.

For surcharges see Nos. 386-387.

Approach to Athens Stadium A64

Perf. 11½, 11½x10, 13½x11½

1934, Dec. 10

381 A64 8d blue 37.50 50
Never hinged 150.00

Perforations on No. 381 range from 10½ to 13, including compounds.

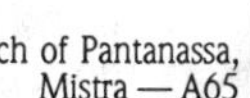

Church of Pantanassa, Mistra — A65

1935, Nov. 1 *Perf. 13x12½*

382 A65 4d brown 10.00 40
Never hinged 27.50
a. Horizontal pair, imperf. between 350.00
b. Imperf., pair 600.00

Issues of the Monarchy

J71, J76, J82, 380, 379 Surcharged in Red or Blue

Nos. 383-385

Nos. 386-387

Serrate Roulette 13½

1935, Nov. 24 **Litho.**

383 D3 50 l on 40 l indigo (R) 20 15
a. Double surcharge 25.00
384 D3 3d on 3d car (Bl) 50 35

Perf. 13

385 D3	3d on 3d rose red (Bl)		2.50	75

Perf. 13x13½

386 A63	5d on 100d (R)	1.50	1.00
387 A62	15d on 75d (Bl)	5.25	4.25
	Set, never hinged	24.00	

King Constantine — A66

Center Engr., Frame Litho.

Perf. 12x13½

1936, Nov. 18 Wmk. 252

389 A66	3d black & brown	50	30
a.	Pair with printer's name in Greek	40.00	
b.	Pair with printer's name in English	40.00	
390 A66	8d black & blue	1.00	1.25
a.	Pair with printer's name in Greek	40.00	
b.	Pair with printer's name in English	40.00	
	Set, never hinged	4.00	

Re-burial of the remains of King Constantine and Queen Sophia.

Two printings exist, the first containing varieties "a" and "b" with gray border; second with black border.

King George II — A67

Pallas Athene — A68

1937, Jan. 24 Engr. *Perf. 12½x12*

391 A67	1d green	15	15
392 A67	3d red brown	18	15
393 A67	8d dp blue	55	35
394 A67	100d car lake	7.25	7.25
	Set, never hinged	20.00	

For surcharges see Nos. 484-487, 498-500, RA86-RA87, N241-N242.

1937, Apr. 17 Unwmk. *Perf. 11½*

395 A68	3d yellow brown	45	35
	Never hinged	1.10	

Centenary of the University of Athens.

Contest with Bull — A69

Lady of Tiryns — A70

Zeus of Dodona — A71

Coin of Amphictyonic League — A72

Diagoras of Rhodes, Victor at Olympics — A73

Venus of Melos — A74

Battle of Salamis — A75

Chariot of Panathenaic Festival — A76

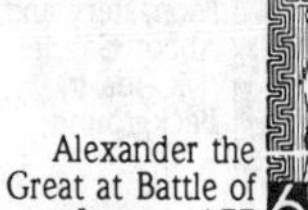

Alexander the Great at Battle of Issos — A77

St. Paul Preaching to Athenians A78

St. Demetrius' Church at Salonika — A79

Leo III Victory over Arabs — A80

Allegorical Figure of Glory — A81

Perf. 13½x12, 12x13½

1937, Nov. 1 Litho. Wmk. 252

396 A69	5 l brn red & bl	15	15
a.	Double impression of frame	60.00	
397 A70	10 l bl & brn red	15	15
a.	Double impression of frame	20.00	
398 A71	20 l black & grn	15	15
399 A72	40 l green & blk	15	15
a.	Green impression doubled	20.00	
400 A73	50 l brown & blk	15	15
401 A74	80 l ind & yel brn	15	15

Engr.

402 A75	2d ultra	15	15
403 A76	5d red	15	15
a.	Printer's name omitted	8.00	8.00
404 A77	6d olive brn	55	40
405 A78	7d dk brown	1.10	45
406 A79	10d red brown	15	15
407 A80	15d green	15	20
408 A81	25d dk blue	15	20
	Set value	2.25	1.90
	Set, never hinged	2.50	

See Nos. 413, 459-466. For overprints and surcharges see Nos. 455-458, 476-477, RA75-RA78, RA83-RA85, N202-N217, N246-N247.

Cerigo, Paxos, Lefkas

Greek stamps with Italian overprints for the islands of Cerigo (Kithyra), Paxos and Lefkas (Santa Maura) are fraudulent.

Royal Wedding Issue

Princess Frederika-Louise and Crown Prince Paul — A82

1938 Wmk. 252 *Perf. 13½x12*

409 A82	1d green	15	15
410 A82	3d orange brn	38	32
411 A82	8d dark blue	1.00	1.00
	Set, never hinged	2.75	

Arms of Greece, Romania, Yugoslavia and Turkey A83

Statue of King Constantine A84

Perf. 12x12½

1938, Feb. 8 Litho. Unwmk.

412 A83	6d blue	4.00	1.40
	Never hinged	12.00	

Balkan Entente.

Tiryns Lady Type of 1937

Corrected Inscription

1938 Wmk. 252 *Perf. 12x13½*

413 A70	10 l blue & brn red	65	65
	Never hinged	1.00	

The first four letters of the third word of the inscription read "TIPY" instead of "TYPI."

Perf. 12x13½

1938, Oct. 8 Engr. Unwmk.

414 A84	1.50d green	55	55
415 A84	30d orange brn	3.00	3.00
	Set, never hinged	4.25	

For overprint see No. N218.

Coats of Arms of Ionian Islands — A85

Fort at Corfu — A86

King George I of Greece and Queen Victoria of England — A87

Perf. 12½x12, 13½x12

1939, May 21 Engr. Unwmk.

416 A85	1d dk blue	85	20
417 A86	4d green	1.65	85
418 A87	20d yellow org	12.50	13.00
419 A87	20d dull blue	12.50	13.00
420 A87	20d car lake	12.50	13.00
	Nos. 416-420 (5)	40.00	40.05
	Set, never hinged	110.00	

75th anniv. of the union of the Ionian Islands with Greece.

Runner with Shield — A88

10th Pan-Balkan Games: 3d, Javelin thrower. 6d, Discus thrower. 8d, Jumper.

Perf. 12x13½

1939, Oct. 1 Litho. Unwmk.

421 A88	50 l slate grn & grn	20	20
422 A88	3d henna brn & dl rose	80	80
423 A88	6d cop brn & dl org	2.00	2.25
424 A88	8d ultra & gray	2.00	2.25
	Set, never hinged	12.00	

Arms of Greece, Romania, Turkey and Yugoslavia — A92

Perf. 13x12½

1940, May 27 Wmk. 252

425 A92	6d blue	3.00	1.00
426 A92	8d blue gray	3.00	1.00
	Set, never hinged	17.50	

Balkan Entente.

Emblem of Youth Organization A93

Boy Member — A94

Designs: 3d, 100d, Emblem of Greek Youth Organization. 10d, Girl member. 15d, Javelin Thrower. 20d, Column of members. 25d, Flag bearers and buglers. 30d, Three youths. 50d, Line formation. 75d, Coat of arms.

Perf. 12½, 13½x12½

1940, Aug. 3 Litho. Wmk. 252

427 A93	3d sil, dp ultra & red	2.25	2.25
428 A94	5d dk bl & blk	6.25	6.00
429 A94	10d red org & blk	7.75	6.50
430 A94	15d dk grn & blk	45.00	45.00
431 A94	20d lake & blk	20.00	17.00
432 A94	25d dk bl & blk	24.00	20.00
433 A94	30d rose vio & blk	26.00	26.00
434 A94	50d lake & blk	26.00	26.00
435 A94	75d dk bl, brn & gold	26.00	27.50
436 A93	100d sil, dp ultra & red	37.50	35.00
	Nos. 427-436,C38-C47 (20)	399.75	380.00
	Set, never hinged	425.00	

4th anniv. of the founding of the Greek Youth Organization. The stamps were good for postal duty Aug. 3-5, 1940, only. They remained on sale until Feb. 3, 1941.

For overprints see Nos. N219-N238.

Windmills on Mykonos A103

Bourtzi Fort — A104

Aspropotamos River — A105

Candia Harbor, Crete — A106

Houses at Hydra — A107

Meteora Monasteries A108

Edessa — A109

Pantokratoros Monastery and Port — A110

Bridge at Konitsa — A111

Ekatontapiliani Church, Paros — A112

Ponticonissi, Corfu (Mouse Island) — A113

Perf. 12½, 13½x12½

1942-44		Litho.	Wmk. 252	
437	A103	2d red brn	15	15
438	A104	5d lt bl grn	15	15
a.		"NAYU . . ."	10.00	10.00
439	A105	10d lt bl	15	15
440	A106	15d red vio	15	15
441	A107	25d org red	15	15
442	A108	50d saph	15	15
443	A109	75d dp rose	15	15
444	A110	100d black	15	15
445	A110	200d ultra	15	15
a.		Imprint omitted	3.00	3.00
446	A111	500d dk olive	15	15
447	A112	1000d org brn	15	15
448	A113	2000d dp bl	15	15
449	A111	5000d rose red	15	15
450	A112	15,000d rose lil	15	15
451	A113	25,000d green	15	15
452	A105	500,000d blue	20	20
453	A103	2,000,000d turq grn	20	20
454	A104	5,000,000d rose brn	20	20
		Set value	1.85	1.85
		Set, never hinged	2.00	

Double impressions exist of 10d, 25d, 50d, 100d, 200d, 1,000d and 2,000d. Value, each $30.

Issue dates: Nos. 439-442, Sept. 1. 200d, Dec. 1. Nos. 446-448, Mar. 15, 1944. Nos. 449-451, July 1, 1944. Nos. 452-454, Sept. 15, 1944.

For surcharges and overprint see Nos. 472C, 473B-475, 478-481, 501-505, B1-B5, B11-B15, RA72-RA74, N239-N240, N243-N245, N248.

Imperf., Pairs

439a	A105	10d	70.00
440a	A106	15d	70.00
441a	A107	25d	70.00
442a	A108	50d	50.00
446a	A111	500d	70.00
447a	A112	1000d	70.00
448a	A113	2000d	70.00
449a	A111	5000d	70.00
450a	A112	15,000d	70.00
451a	A113	25,000d	70.00
452a	A105	500,000d	90.00
454a	A104	5,000,000d	90.00

Nos. 400, 402-404 Surcharged in Blue Black

ΔΡΑΧΜΑΙ ΝΕΑΙ

1944-45			*Perf. 13½x12*	
455	A73	50 l brn & blk	15	15
a.		Double surcharge	12.00	12.00
456	A75	2d ultra	15	15
457	A76	5d red	15	15
a.		Inverted surcharge	20.00	
b.		Double surcharge	20.00	
c.		Printer's name omitted (403a)	10.00	10.00
d.		Pair, one without surcharge	15.00	
458	A77	6d olive brn ('45)	25	25
		Set value	45	45
		Set, never hinged	55	

Glory Type of 1937

Perf. 12½x13½

1945		Litho.	Wmk. 252	
459	A81	1d dull rose vio	15	15
460	A81	3d rose brown	15	15
a.		Imperf., pair	50.00	
461	A81	5d ultra	15	15
a.		Imperf., pair	50.00	
462	A81	10d dull brown	15	15
463	A81	20d dull violet	15	15
464	A81	50d olive black	15	15
465	A81	100d pale blue	2.50	3.25
a.		Imperf., pair	175.00	
466	A81	200d slate	2.00	1.25
		Nos. 459-466 (8)	5.40	5.40
		Set, never hinged	11.00	

Doric Column and Greek Flag — A114

Franklin D. Roosevelt — A115

1945, Oct. 28			Unwmk.	
467	A114	20d orange brown	15	15
468	A114	40d blue	18	18
a.		Double impression	20.00	
		Set, never hinged	40	

Vote of Oct. 28, 1940, refusing Italy's ultimatum. "OXI" means "No."
Exist imperf.

1945, Dec. 21			Unwmk.	
469	A115	30d blk & red brn	15	15
a.		Center double	65.00	65.00
c.		Inverted frame	65.00	
d.		Imperf., pair	70.00	
470	A115	60d blk & sl gray	15	15
a.		Center double	60.00	60.00
b.		60d black & blue gray	10.00	10.00
c.		Imperf., pair	100.00	
d.		Inverted frame	60.00	
471	A115	200d blk & vio brn	15	15
a.		Center double	70.00	70.00
b.		Imperf., pair	125.00	
		Set value	33	33
		Set, never hinged	50	

Death of Pres. Franklin D. Roosevelt.

Nos. C61, C63, 447-451, 453, 398, 401, 454 and 452 Surcharged in Black or Carmine

Perf. 12½, 12x13½, 13½x12½

1946			Wmk. 252	
472	AP35	10d on 10d	15	15
a.		Inverted surcharge	30.00	30.00
b.		Double surcharge	20.00	
472C	A113	10d on 2000d (C)	15	15
473	AP35	20d on 50d (C)	15	15
a.		Inverted surcharge	30.00	
473B	A112	20d on 1000d	20	15
474	A113	50d on 25,000d (C)	20	15
475	A103	100d on 2,000,000d (C)	25	15
476	A71	130d on 20 l (C)	40	15
b.		Double surcharge	25.00	
476A	A71	250d on 20 l (C)	1.00	15
c.		Double surcharge	25.00	
477	A74	300d on 80 l	45	35
a.		Purple brown surcharge	10.00	7.00
b.		Double surcharge	30.00	
478	A104	500d on 5,000,000d	1.75	25
a.		Inverted surcharge	35.00	
b.		Double surcharge	30.00	
479	A105	1000d on 500,000d (C)	5.25	22
a.		Double surcharge	40.00	
480	A111	2000d on 5000d	14.00	2.50
481	A112	5000d on 15,000d	35.00	22.50
a.		Blue surcharge	45.00	45.00
		Nos. 472-481 (13)	58.95	27.02
		Set, never hinged	150.00	

The surcharge exists in various shades on most denominations. A 150d on 20 l is fraudulent.

Eleutherios K. Venizelos A116

Panaghiotis Tsaldaris A117

Perf. 12x13½

1946, Mar. 25		Litho.	Wmk. 252	
482	A116	130d brn ol & buff	15	15
a.		Double impression of brn olive	15.00	
483	A116	300d red brn & pale brn	25	25
a.		Double impression of red brown	15.00	
		Set, never hinged	42	

Venizelos (1864-1936), statesman.

Nos. 391 to 394 Surcharged in Blue Black

1-9-1946

1946, Sept. 28			*Perf. 12½x12*	
484	A67	50d on 1d	15	15
485	A67	250d on 3d	20	15
a.		Date omitted	25.00	
b.		Inverted surcharge	40.00	40.00
486	A67	600d on 8d	75	75
a.		Additional surcharge on back, inverted	30.00	
b.		Carmine surcharge	100.00	
487	A67	3000d on 100d	3.75	85
		Set, never hinged	11.00	

Plebiscite of Sept. 1, 1946, which resulted in the return of King George II to Greece.

Perf. 12½x13½

1946, Nov. 15		Litho.	Unwmk.	
488	A117	250d red brn & buff	55	15
489	A117	600d dp bl & pale bl	1.25	1.10
a.		Double impression	55.00	
		Set, never hinged	4.00	

Naval Convoy — A118

Torpedoing of Cruiser Helle — A119

Women Carrying Ammunition in Pindus Mountains A120

Troops in Albania — A121

Campaign of Greek Troops in Italy — A122

Allegory of Flight — A123

Greek Torpedo Boat Towing Captive Submarine A124

Design: 5000d, Memorial Tomb, El Alamein.

1946-47		Unwmk. Engr.	*Perf. 13*	
490	A118	50d dk bl grn	15	15
491	A119	100d dp ultra	15	15
492	A120	250d yel grn ('46)	15	15
493	A121	500d yel brn	48	15
494	A122	600d dk brown	1.10	22
495	A123	1000d dull lil	1.25	22
496	A124	2000d dp ultra	3.75	3.00
497	A119	5000d dk car	7.75	48
a.		Imperf., pair	400.00	
		Nos. 490-497 (8)	14.78	4.52
		Set, never hinged	40.00	

1947 stamps issued May 1.

King George II Memorial Issue

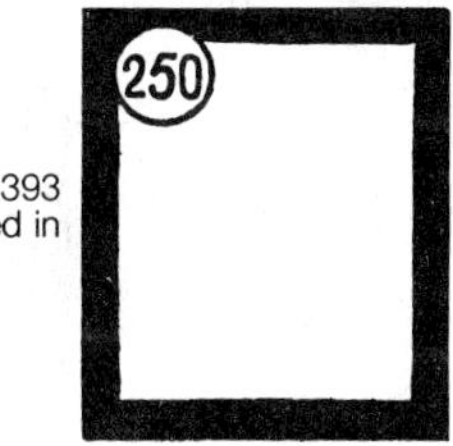

Nos. 391-393 Surcharged in Black

Perf. 12½x12

1947, Apr. 15			Wmk. 252	
498	A67	50d on 1d grn	15	15
a.		Double surcharge	20.00	
499	A67	250d on 3d red brn	28	15
a.		Double surcharge	25.00	
b.		Pair, one without surcharge	12.50	
500	A67	600d on 8d dp bl	80	50
a.		Double surcharge	20.00	
		Set value		62
		Set, never hinged	2.75	

Nos. 446, 438, 442, 439 and 443 Surcharged in Carmine or Black

1947			*Perf. 12½*	
501	A111	20d on 500d	15	15
a.		Double surcharge	25.00	
502	A104	30d on 5d	15	15
503	A108	50d on 50d	15	15
504	A105	100d on 10d	20	15
505	A109	450d on 75d (Bk)	80	1.00
		Set value	1.25	1.10
		Set, never hinged	3.00	

Castellorizo Castle — A126

Dodecanese Vase A127

Dodecanese Costume A128

Monastery where St. John Preached, Patmos — A129

Emanuel Xanthos — A130

Sailing Vessel of 1824 — A131

Revolutionary Stamp of 1912 A132

Statue of Hippocrates A133

Colossus of Rhodes — A134

Perf. 12½x13½, 13½x12½

1947-48 Litho. Wmk. 252

506	A126	20d	ultra	15	15
507	A127	30d	blk brn & buff	15	15
508	A128	50d	chlky bl	15	15
509	A129	100d	blk grn & pale grn	15	15
510	A130	250d	gray grn & pale grn	18	15
511	A132	450d	dp bl ('48)	75	15
512	A131	450d	dp bl & pale bl ('48)	75	15
a.			Imperf., pair	150.00	
513	A132	500d	red	30	15
514	A133	600d	vio brn & pale pink	55	15
515	A134	1000d	brn & cream	85	15
a.			Imperf., pair	150.00	
			Nos. 506-515 (10)	3.98	
			Set value		68
			Set, never hinged	7.50	

Return of the Dodecanese to Greece. See Nos. 520-522, 525-534.

Battle of Crete — A135

1948, Sept. 15 Engr. *Perf. 13x13½*

516	A135	1000d	dark green	1.00	25
			Never hinged	3.50	

Battle of Crete, 7th anniversary.

Abduction of Children A136

Concentration Camp — A137

Protective Mother — A138

Perf. 13½x12½, 12½x13½

1949, Feb. 1 Litho. Wmk. 252

517	A136	450d	dk & lt violet	75	50
518	A137	1000d	dk & lt brown	1.75	25
519	A138	1800d	dk red & cream	2.00	25
			Set, never hinged	10.00	

Types of 1947

1950, Apr. 5 *Perf. 12½x13½*

520	A127	2000d	org brn & sal	8.75	15
a.			Imperf., pair	85.00	
521	A133	5000d	rose vio	21.00	45
522	A134	10,000d	ultra	8.75	30
			Set, never hinged	92.50	

Map of Crete and Flags A139

Perf. 13½x13

1950, Apr. 28 Engr. Wmk. 252

523	A139	1000d	deep blue	1.50	25
			Never hinged	4.00	
a.			Imperf., pair	*425.00*	

Battle of Crete, 9th anniversary.

Youth of Marathon — A140

Engraved and Lithographed

1950, May 21 *Perf. 13x13½*

524	A140	1000d	cream & dp grn	50	20
			Never hinged	1.00	
a.			Without dates	90.00	
b.			"1949" only	80.00	
c.			Dates inverted	80.00	
d.			Dates doubled	80.00	

75th anniv. (in 1949) of the UPU.
Exists imperf., used only.

Types of 1947-48

Perf. 12½x13½, 13½x12½

1950 Litho. Wmk. 252

525	A130	200d	orange	30	15
526	A128	300d	orange	30	15
527	A129	400d	blue	1.65	15
528	A133	700d	lilac rose	1.65	15
529	A133	700d	blue green	1.65	15
a.			Imperf., pair	110.00	
530	A131	800d	pur & pale grn	75	15
531	A132	1300d	carmine	5.00	15
532	A126	1500d	brn org	7.50	15
533	A127	1600d	ultra & bl gray	1.65	15
534	A134	2600d	emer & pale grn	3.50	42
			Nos. 525-534 (10)	23.95	
			Set value		1.35
			Set, never hinged	45.00	

Altar and Sword — A141

St. Paul — A142

St. Paul by El Greco A143

Preaching to Athenians A144

Perf. 13½x12, 12x13½

1951, June 15 Engr. Unwmk.

535	A141	700d	red vio	1.40	35
536	A142	1600d	lt bl	3.00	3.00
537	A143	2600d	dk ol bis	5.25	4.50
538	A144	10,000d	red brn	40.00	30.00
			Set, never hinged	95.00	

1900th anniv. of St. Paul's visit to Athens.

Industrialization A145

Designs: 800d, Fishing. 1300d, Rebuilding. 1600d, Farming. 2600d, Home Industries. 5000d, Electrification and map of Greece.

Perf. 12½x13½

1951, Sept. 20 Wmk. 252

539	A145	700d	red org	2.25	15
540	A145	800d	aqua	3.75	50
541	A145	1300d	grnsh bl	6.75	32
542	A145	1600d	olive grn	11.50	32
543	A145	2600d	vio gray	35.00	50
544	A145	5000d	dp plum	32.50	70
			Nos. 539-544 (6)	91.75	2.49
			Set, never hinged	225.00	

Issued to publicize Greek recovery under the Marshall Plan.

King Paul I — A146

Allegorical Figure and Medal — A147

1952, Dec. 14 Engr. *Perf. 12½x12*

545	A146	200d	dp green	40	15
546	A146	1000d	red	95	15
547	A147	1400d	blue	4.75	1.00
548	A146	10,000d	dk red lil	20.00	8.75
			Set, never hinged	50.00	

50th birthday of King Paul I.

Oranges A148

Tobacco — A149

National Products: 1000d, Olive oil, Pallas Athene. 1300d, Wine. 2000d, Figs. 2600d, Grapes and bread. 5000d, Bacchus holding grapes.

1953, July 1 *Perf. 13½x13, 13x13½*

549	A148	500d	dp car & org	40	16
550	A149	700d	dk brn & org yel	70	16
551	A148	1000d	bl & lt ol grn	85	16
a.			Imperf., pair	100.00	
552	A149	1300d	dp plum & org brn	4.00	16
553	A149	2000d	dk brn & lt grn	6.25	20
554	A149	2600d	vio & ol bis	8.25	1.00
555	A149	5000d	dk brn & yel grn	9.25	35
			Nos. 549-555 (7)	29.70	2.19
			Set, never hinged	60.00	

Pericles A150

Homer A151

Hunting Wild Boar — A152

Shepherd Carrying Calf — A152a

Designs: 200d, Mycenaean oxhead vase. 500d, Zeus of Istiaea. 600d, Head of a youth. 1000d, Alexander the Great. 1200d, Charioteer of Delphi. 2000d, Vase of Dipylon. 4000d, Voyage of Dionysus. 20,000d, Pitcher bearers.

Perf. 13½x13, 12½x12, 13x13½

1954, Jan. 15 Litho.

556	A150	100d	red brn	18	15
557	A150	200d	black	30	15
558	A151	300d	bl vio	80	15
559	A151	500d	green	80	15
560	A151	600d	rose pink	1.00	15
561	A151	1000d	dl bl & blk	1.00	15
562	A150	1200d	ol grn	1.00	15
563	A150	2000d	red brn	2.50	15
564	A152	2400d	grnsh bl	4.00	20
a.			Double impression	125.00	
565	A152a	2500d	dk bl grn	4.00	15
566	A151	4000d	dk car	4.00	24
567	A150	20,000d	rose lilac	42.50	1.50
			Nos. 556-567 (12)	62.08	
			Set value		2.70
			Set, never hinged	140.00	

See Nos. 574-581, 632-638, and 689.

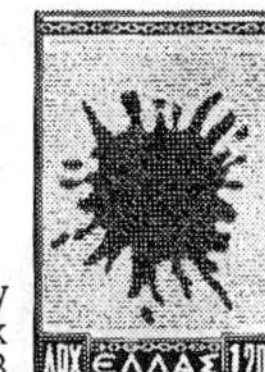

British Parliamentary Debate and Ink Blot — A153

1954, Sept. *Perf. 12½*

Center in Black

568 A153 1.20d cream 1.75 15
569 A153 2d orange 4.50 4.00
570 A153 2d lt bl 4.50 3.50
571 A153 2.40d lilac 4.50 60
572 A153 2.50d pink 4.50 60
573 A153 4d citron 5.75 1.25
Nos. 568-573 (6) 25.50 10.10
Set, never hinged 62.50

Document in English on Nos. 569, 572, 573; in French on Nos. 570, 571 and in Greek on No. 568.
Issued to promote the proposed union between Cyprus and Greece.

Types of 1954

Perf. 13½x13, 12½x12, 13x13½

1955 **Litho.** **Wmk. 252**

Designs: 20 l, Mycenaean oxhead vase. 30 l, Pericles. 50 l, Zeus of Istiaea. 1d, Head of a youth. 2d, Alexander the Great. 3d, Hunting wild boar. 3.50d, Homer. 4d, Voyage of Dionysus.

574 A150 20 l dk grn 55 15
575 A150 30 l yel brn 75 15
576 A151 50 l car lake 1.50 15
577 A151 1d bl grn 1.90 15
578 A151 2d brn & blk 4.75 15
579 A152 3d red org 5.75 15
580 A151 3.50d rose crim 9.25 24
581 A151 4d vio bl 13.00 24
Nos. 574-581 (8) 37.45
Set value 1.15
Set, never hinged 82.50

Samos Coin Picturing Pythagoras A154

Pythagorean Theorem A155

Samos Mapped in Antique Style — A156

1955, Aug. 20 *Perf. 12x13½*

582 A154 2d green 2.25 30
583 A155 3.50d intense blk 6.25 2.75
584 A154 5d plum 13.00 1.10
585 A156 6d blue 6.25 *15.00*
Set, never hinged 62.50

2500th anniv. of the founding of the 1st School of Philosophy by Pythagoras on Samos.

Globe and Rotary Emblem — A157

Perf. 12x13½

1956, May 15 **Litho.** **Wmk. 252**

586 A157 2d ultra 2.25 35
Never hinged 5.50

50th anniv. of Rotary Intl. (in 1955).

King Alexander A158

Crown Prince Constantine — A159

Portraits: 30 l, George I. 50 l, Queen Olga. 70 l, King Otto. 1d, Queen Amalia. 1.50d, King Constantine. 2d, 7.50d, King Paul. 3d, George II. 3.50d, Queen Sophia. 4d, Queen Frederica. 5d, King Paul and Queen Frederica. 10d, King, Queen and Crown Prince.

Perf. 13½x12, 12x13½

1956, May 21 **Engr.**

587 A158 10 l blue vio 16 15
588 A159 20 l dull pur 16 15
589 A159 30 l sepia 16 15
590 A159 50 l red brn 16 15
591 A159 70 l lt ultra 40 15
592 A159 1d grnsh bl 40 15
593 A159 1.50d gray bl 48 15
594 A159 2d black 48 15
595 A159 3d brown 80 15
596 A159 3.50d copper brn 1.90 15
597 A159 4d gray green 1.90 15
598 A158 5d rose car 1.90 15
599 A159 7.50d ultra 4.00 1.25
600 A158 10d dk blue 5.75 70
Nos. 587-600 (14) 18.65
Set value 2.85
Set, never hinged 38.00

See Nos. 604-617.

Catalogue values for unused stamps in this section, from this point to the end of the section, are for Never Hinged items.

Dionysios Solomos and Nicolaos Mantzaros A160

Dionysios Solomos A161

Design: 5d, View on Zante and bust of Solomos.

Perf. 13½x12, 12x13½

1957, Mar. 26 **Litho.** **Wmk. 252**

601 A160 2d red brn & ocher 4.00 18
602 A161 3.50d bl & gray 7.75 3.25
603 A160 5d dk grn & ol bis 8.00 4.75

Centenary of the death of Dionysios Solomos, composer of the Greek national anthem.

Types of 1956

Designs as before.

Perf. 13½x12

1957 **Wmk. 252** **Engr.**

604 A158 10 l rose lake 40 15
605 A159 20 l orange 40 15
606 A159 30 l gray blk 40 15
607 A159 50 l grnsh blk 40 15
608 A159 70 l rose lil 1.00 60
609 A159 1d rose red 85 15
610 A159 1.50d lt ol grn 1.40 15
611 A159 2d carmine 1.40 15
612 A159 3d dk bl 2.00 15
613 A159 3.50d blk vio 5.25 20
a. Imperf., pair
614 A159 4d red brn 5.25 18
615 A158 5d gray blue 5.25 15
616 A159 7.50d yel org 13.00 75
617 A158 10d green 16.00 60
Nos. 604-617 (14) 53.00
Set value 3.00

Oil Tanker — A162

Ships: 1d, Ocean liner. 1.50d, Sailing ship, 1820. 2d, Byzantine vessel. 3.50d, Ship from 6th century B. C. 5d, "Argo."

1958, Jan. 30 **Litho.** *Perf. 13½x12*

618 A162 50 l multi 15 15
619 A162 1d ultra, blk & bis 22 18
620 A162 1.50d blk & car 25 20
a. Double impression of blk 100.00
621 A162 2d vio bl, blk & red brn 35 30
622 A162 3.50d lt bl, blk & red 1.10 1.00
a. Double impression of blk 150.00 120.00
623 A162 5d bl grn, blk & car 7.25 6.00
Nos. 618-623 (6) 9.32 7.83

Issued to honor the Greek merchant marine.

Narcissus — A163

Designs: 30 l, Daphne (laurel) and Apollo. 50 l, Adonis (hibiscus) and Aphrodite. 70 l, Pitys (pine) and Pan. 1d, Crocus. 2d, Iris. 3.50d, Tulips. 5d, Cyclamen.

1958, Sept. 15 **Wmk. 252** *Perf. 13*

Size: 22½x38mm

624 A163 20 l multi 15 15
625 A163 30 l multi 15 15
626 A163 50 l multi 15 15
627 A163 70 l multi 20 15

Perf. 12½x12

Size: 21½x26mm

628 A163 1d multi 35 24

Perf. 12x13½

Size: 22x32mm

629 A163 2d multi 25 16
630 A163 3.50d multi 1.25 90
a. Imperf., pair 250.00
631 A163 5d multi 1.75 1.25
Nos. 624-631 (8) 4.25 3.15

International Congress for the Protection of Nature, held in Athens.

Types of 1954

Designs: 10 l, Pericles. 20 l, Mycenaean oxhead vase. 50 l, Zeus of Istiaea. 70 l, Charioteer of Delphi. 1d, Head of a youth. 1.50d, Pitcher bearers. 2.50d, Alexander the Great.
Two types of 2.50d:
I- 9 dots in upper half of right border.
II- 10 dots.

Perf. 13½x13, 12½x12

1959 **Litho.** **Wmk. 252**

632 A150 10 l emerald 16 16
633 A150 20 l magenta 38 15
634 A151 50 l lt bl grn 1.40 15
635 A150 70 l red org 38 15
636 A151 1d reddish brn 3.50 15
637 A150 1.50d brt bl 6.25 15
638 A151 2.50d mag & blk (II) 10.50 15
a. Type I 55.00 52
Nos. 632-638 (7) 22.57 1.06

Zeus-Eagle Coin A164

Helios-Rose Coin — A165

Ancient Greek Coins: 20 l, Athena & Owl. 50 l, Nymph Arethusa & Chariot. 70 l, Hercules & Zeus. 1.50d, Griffin & Square. 2.50d, Apollo & Lyre. 4.50d, Apollo & Labyrinth. 6d, Aphrodite & Apollo. 8.50d, Ram's Head & Incuse Squares.

1959, Mar. 24 **Wmk. 252** *Perf. 14*

Coins in Various Shades of Gray

639 A164 10 l red brn & blk 50 15
640 A164 20 l dp bl & blk 50 15
641 A164 50 l plum & blk 1.25 15
642 A164 70 l ultra & blk 1.25 15
643 A165 1d dk car rose & blk 2.50 15
644 A164 1.50d ocher & blk 2.50 15
645 A164 2.50d dp mag & blk 3.00 15
646 A165 4.50d Prus grn & blk 4.50 22
647 A165 6d ol grn & blk 5.00 22
648 A165 8.50d dp car & blk 4.50 1.00
Nos. 639-648 (10) 25.50
Set value 1.95

See Nos. 750-758.

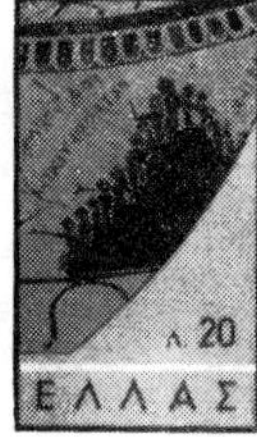

Audience, Vase 580 B. C. — A166

Theater, Delphi A167

Designs: 50 l, Clay tragedy mask, 3rd cent. B.C. 1d, Flute, drum and lyre. 2.50d, Clay statue of an actor, 3rd cent. B.C. 4.50d, Andromeda, vase, 4th cent. B.C. 6d, Actors, bowl 410 B.C.

Perf. 13x13½, 13½x13

1959, June 20 **Litho.** **Wmk. 252**

649 A166 20 l blk, fawn & gray 15 15
650 A166 50 l dk red brn & ol bis 20 15
651 A166 1d grn, brn & ocher 20 15
652 A166 2.50d brn & bl 35 28
653 A167 3.50d red brn, grn & sep 8.75 6.50
654 A167 4.50d blk & fawn 1.25 90
655 A166 6d blk, fawn & gray 1.25 90
Nos. 649-655 (7) 12.15 9.03

Ancient Greek theater.

"Victory" and Soldiers — A168

Perf. 13x13½

1959, Aug. 29 **Wmk. 252**

656 A168 2.50d red brn, ultra & blk 2.50 25

10th anniversary of civil war.

St. Basil — A169

The Good Samaritan — A170

Designs: 20 l, Plane tree of Hippocrates. 50 l, Aesculapius. 2.50d, Achilles and Patroclus. 3d, Globe and Red Cross over people receiving help. 4.50d, Henri Dunant.

Perf. 13½x12, 12x13½

1959, Sept. 21 **Litho.**

No.	Type	Denom. / Color	Unused	Used
657	A170	20 l multi	15	15
658	A169	50 l multi	15	15
659	A169	70 l multi	15	15
660	A169	2.50d multi	15	15
661	A169	3d multi	8.00	6.50
662	A169	4.50d multi	42	35
663	A170	6d multi	52	45
		Nos. 657-663 (7)	9.54	7.90

Cent. of the Red Cross idea. Sizes: Nos. 658-660, 662 24½x32mm, No. 661 32x47mm.

Imre Nagy — A171

Costis Palamas — A172

Perf. 13x13½

1959, Dec. 8 **Wmk. 252**

No.	Type	Denom. / Color	Unused	Used
664	A171	4.50d org brn & dk brn	1.00	1.00
665	A171	6d brt bl, bl & blk	1.00	1.00

3rd anniv. of the crushing of the 1956 Hungarian Revolution, and to honor Premier Imre Nagy, its leader.

1960, Jan. 25 *Perf. 12x13½*

666 A172 2.50d multi 2.75 20

Issued to commemorate the centenary of the birth of Costis Palamas (1859-1943), poet.

Ship Battling Storm A173

Design: 4.50d, Ship in calm sea and rainbow.

Perf. 13½x13

1960, Apr. 7 **Wmk. 252**

No.	Type	Denom. / Color	Unused	Used
667	A173	2.50d multi	35	15
668	A173	4.50d multi	1.00	85

Issued to publicize World Refugee Year, July 1, 1959-June 30, 1960.

Boy Scout on Horseback, St. George and Dragon — A174

Scouts Planting Tree A175

Designs: 30 l, Scout taking oath and boy of ancient Athens. 40 l, Scouts helping in disaster. 70 l, Scouts reading map and tent. 1d, Boy Scout, Sea Scout and Air Scout. 2.50d, Crown Prince Constantine. 6d, Scout flag of Greece and Military Merit medal.

Perf. 13x13½, 13½x13

1960, Apr. 23 **Litho.**

No.	Type	Denom. / Color	Unused	Used
669	A174	20 l multi	15	15
670	A174	30 l multi	15	15
671	A174	40 l multi	15	15
672	A175	50 l multi	18	15
673	A175	70 l multi	18	15
674	A175	1d multi	18	15
675	A174	2.50d multi	40	15
676	A175	6d multi	2.00	1.10
		Nos. 669-676 (8)	3.39	
		Set value		1.65

Greek Boy Scout Organization, 50th anniv.

Greek Holding Sacred Disk Proclaiming Armistice During Games — A176

Lighting Olympic Flame A177

Designs: 70 l, Youth taking oath. 80 l, Boy cutting olive branches for Olympic prizes. 1d, Judges entering stadium. 1.50d, Long jump. 2.50d, Discus thrower. 4.50d, Sprinters. 5d, Javelin thrower. 6d, Crowning the victors. 12.50d, Victor in chariot entering home town.

Perf. 13x13½, 13½x13

1960, Aug. 12 **Wmk. 252**

No.	Type	Denom. / Color	Unused	Used
677	A176	20 l multi	15	15
678	A177	50 l multi	22	15
679	A176	70 l multi	22	15
680	A177	80 l multi	22	15
a.		Imperf., pair	225.00	
681	A177	1d multi	22	15
682	A177	1.50d multi	22	15
683	A176	2.50d multi	50	15
684	A177	4.50d multi	1.00	52
a.		Dbl. impression of black	160.00	160.00
685	A176	5d multi	55	42
686	A177	6d multi	65	52
687	A177	12.50d multi	7.75	5.00
		Nos. 677-687 (11)	11.70	7.51

17th Olympic Games, Rome, Aug. 25-Sept. 11.

Europa Issue, 1960

Common Design Type

Perf. 13½x12

1960, Sept. 19 **Litho.** **Wmk. 252**

Size: 33x23mm

No.	Type	Denom. / Color	Unused	Used
688	CD3	4.50d ultra	3.50	1.65
a.		Double impression	100.00	

Common Design Types pictured in section at front of book.

Shepherd Type of 1954

1960, Sept. 1 **Wmk. 252** *Perf. 13*

689 A152a 3d ultra 2.50 20

Crown Prince Constantine and Yacht A178

1961, Jan. 18 *Perf. 13½x13*

690 A178 2.50d multi 1.50 20

Victory of Crown Prince Constantine and his crew at the 17th Olympic Games, Rome (Gold medal, Yachting, Dragon class).

Castoria A179

Delphi — A180

Landscapes and Ancient Monuments: 20 l, Meteora. 50 l, Hydra harbor. 70 l, Acropolis, Athens. 80 l, Mykonos. 1d, St. Catherine's Church, Salonika. 1.50d, Olympia. 2.50d, Knossos. 3.50d, Rhodes. 4d, Epidauros amphitheater. 4.50d, Temple of Poseidon, Sounion. 5d, Temple of Zeus, Athens. 7.50d, Aslan's mosque, Ioannina. 8d, Mount Athos. 8.50d, Santorini. 12.50d, Marble lions, Delos.

Perf. 13½x12½, 12½x13½

1961, Feb. 15 **Engr.** **Wmk. 252**

No.	Type	Denom. / Color	Unused	Used
691	A179	10 l dk gray bl	20	15
692	A179	20 l dk pur	20	15
693	A179	50 l blue	20	15
694	A179	70 l dk pur	48	15
695	A179	80 l brt ultra	28	15
696	A179	1d red brn	52	15
697	A179	1.50d brt grn	80	15
698	A179	2.50d carmine	5.25	15
699	A179	3.50d purple	1.10	15
700	A179	4d sl grn	1.10	15
701	A179	4.50d dk bl	1.10	15
702	A179	5d claret	2.25	15
703	A180	6d slate grn	2.75	15
704	A179	7.50d black	2.75	24
705	A180	8d dk vio bl	2.75	45
706	A180	8.50d org ver	2.75	45
707	A179	12.50d dk brn	3.25	60
		Nos. 691-707 (17)	27.73	
		Set value		2.50

Issued for tourist publicity.

Lily Vase — A181

Partridge and Fig Pecker A182

Minoan Art: 1d, Fruit dish. 1.50d, Rhyton bearer. 2.50d, Ladies of Knossos Palace. 4.50d, Sarcophagus of Hagia Trias. 6d, Dancer. 10d, Two vessels with spouts.

Perf. 13x13½, 13½x13

1961, June 30 **Litho.**

No.	Type	Denom. / Color	Unused	Used
708	A181	20 l multi	42	35
709	A182	50 l multi	55	35
710	A182	1d multi	85	22
711	A181	1.50d multi	1.25	28
712	A182	2.50d multi	1.50	15
713	A181	4.50d multi	3.50	2.75
714	A182	6d multi	3.75	2.25
715	A182	10d multi	12.00	4.00
		Nos. 708-715 (8)	23.82	10.35

Democritus Nuclear Research Center A183

Democritus A184

1961, July 31 *Perf. 13½x13*

No.	Type	Denom. / Color	Unused	Used
716	A183	2.50d dp lil rose & rose lil	60	15
717	A184	4.50d vio bl & pale vio bl	1.10	95

Inauguration of the Democritus Nuclear Research Center at Aghia Paraskevi.

Europa Issue, 1961

Common Design Type

1961, Sept. 18 *Perf. 13½x12*

Size: 32½x22mm

No.	Type	Denom. / Color	Unused	Used
718	CD4	2.50d ver & pink	15	15
a.		Pink omitted (inscriptions white)	10.00	10.00
719	CD4	4.50d ultra & lt ultra	20	20

Nicephoros Phocas A185

Hermes Head of 1861 A186

1961, Sept. 22 **Wmk. 252**

720 A185 2.50d multi 85 32

1000th anniv. of the liberation of Crete from the Saracens by the Byzantine general (later emperor) Phocas.

1961, Dec. 20 **Litho.** *Perf. 13x13½*

Each denomination shows a different stamp of 1861 issue.

No.	Type	Denom. / Color	Unused	Used
721	A186	20 l brn, red brn & cream	15	15
722	A186	50 l brn, bis & straw	15	15
723	A186	1.50d emer & gray	15	15
724	A186	2.50d red org & ol bis	18	15
725	A186	4.50d dk bl, bl & gray	22	15
726	A186	6d rose lil, pale rose & bl	25	16
727	A186	10d car, rose & cr	1.75	1.10
		Nos. 721-727 (7)	2.85	
		Set value		1.75

Centenary of Greek postage stamps.

Tauropos Dam and Lake — A187

Ptolemais Power Station A188

Designs: 50 l, Ladhon river hydroelectric plant. 1.50d, Louros river dam. 2.50d, Aliverion power plant. 4.50d, Salonika hydroelectric sub-station. 6d, Agra river hydroelectric station, interior.

Perf. 13x13½, 13½x13

1962, Apr. 14 Wmk. 252

728 A187	20 l	multi	15	15
729 A187	50 l	multi	15	15
730 A188	1d	multi	40	15
731 A188	1.50d	multi	40	15
732 A188	2.50d	multi	48	15
733 A188	4.50d	multi	1.90	1.25
734 A188	6d	multi	2.50	1.75
	Nos. 728-734 (7)		5.98	3.75

National electrification project.

Youth with Shield and Helmet from Ancient Vase — A189

Designs: 2.50d, Zappion hall (horiz.). 4.50d, Kneeling soldier from Temple of Aphaea, Aegina. 6d, Standing soldier from stele of Ariston.

Perf. 13½x12, 12x13½

1962, May 3 Litho. Wmk. 252

Sizes: 22x33mm, 33x22mm

735 A189	2.50d	grn, bl, red & brn	38	15
736 A189	3d	brn, buff & red brn	48	20
737 A189	4.50d	bl & gray	60	35

Size: 21x37mm

738 A189	6d	brn red & blk	60	35

Ministerial congress of NATO countries, Athens, May 3-5.

Europa Issue, 1962

Common Design Type

1962, Sept. 17 *Perf. 13½x12*

Size: 33x23mm

739 CD5	2.50d	ver & blk	55	25
740 CD5	4.50d	ultra & blk	1.10	52

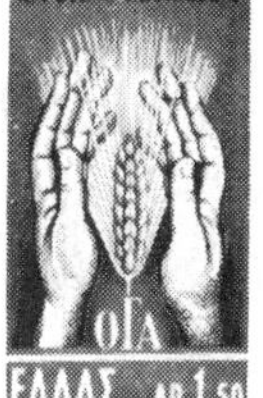
Hands and Grain A190

Demeter A191

1962, Oct. 30 *Perf. 13x13½*

741 A190	1.50d	dp car, blk & brn	38	15
742 A190	2.50d	brt grn, blk & brn	95	25

Agricultural Insurance Program.

Perf. 12x13½

1963, Apr. 25 Wmk. 252

Design: 4.50d, Wheat and globe.

743 A191	2.50d	brn car, gray & blk	35	15
744 A191	4.50d	multi	1.00	65

FAO "Freedom from Hunger" campaign.

George I, Constantine XII, Alexander I, George II and Paul I — A192

Perf. 13½x12½

1963, June 29 Engr.

745 A192	50 l	rose car	22	15
746 A192	1.50d	green	55	15
747 A192	2.50d	redsh brn	70	15
748 A192	4.50d	dk bl	3.25	90
749 A192	6d	violet	2.75	45
	Nos. 745-749 (5)		7.47	
	Set value			1.55

Centenary of the Greek dynasty.

Coin Types of 1959

Ancient Greek Coins: 50 l, Nymph Arethusa & Chariot. 80 l, Hercules & Zeus. 1d, Helios & Rose. 1.50d, Griffin & Square. 3d, Zeus & Eagle. 3.50d, Athena & Owl. 4.50d, Apollo & Labyrinth. 6d, Aphrodite & Apollo. 8.50d, Ram's head & Incuse Squares.

Perf. 13½x13, 13x13½

1963, July 5 Litho. Wmk. 252

Coins in Various Shades of Gray

750 A164	50 l	vio bl	15	15
751 A164	80 l	dp mag	24	15
752 A165	1d	emerald	48	15
753 A164	1.50d	lilac rose	48	15
754 A164	3d	olive	60	15
755 A164	3.50d	vermilion	75	15
756 A165	4.50d	redsh brn	1.10	15
757 A165	6d	bl grn	1.10	15
758 A165	8.50d	brt bl	1.50	50
	Nos. 750-758 (9)		6.40	
	Set value			1.15

"Acropolis at Dawn" by Lord Baden-Powell A193

Jamboree Badge (Boeotian Shield) — A194

Athenian Treasury, Delphi — A195

Designs: 2.50d, Crown Prince Constantine, Chief Scout. 3d, Athanassios Lefkadites (founder of Greek Scouts) and Lord Baden-Powell. 4.50d, Scout bugling with conch shell.

1963, Aug. 1

759 A193	1d	bl, sal & ol	15	15
760 A194	1.50d	dk bl, org brn & brn	15	15
761 A194	2.50d	multi	15	15
762 A193	3d	multi	32	15
763 A194	4.50d	multi	1.50	80
	Nos. 759-763 (5)		2.27	
	Set value			1.15

11th Boy Scout Jamboree, Marathon, July 29-Aug. 16, 1963.

1963, Sept. 16 *Perf. 12x13½*

Designs: 2d, Centenary emblem. 2.50d, Queen Olga, founder of Greek Red Cross. 4.50d, Henri Dunant.

764 A195	1d	multi	15	15
765 A195	2d	multi	15	15
766 A195	2.50d	multi	20	15
767 A195	4.50d	multi	1.25	70
	Set value			96

International Red Cross Centenary.

Europa Issue, 1963

Common Design Type

1963, Sept. 16 *Perf. 13½x12*

Size: 33x23mm

768 CD6	2.50d	green	1.50	50
769 CD6	4.50d	brt magenta	3.00	1.50

Vatopethion Monastery A196

King Paul I (1901-1964) A197

Designs: 80 l, St. Denys' Monastery. 1d, "Protaton" (Founder's) Church, horiz. 2d, Stavronikita Monastery. 2.50d, Jeweled cover of Nicephoros Phocas Gospel. 3.50d, Fresco of St. Athanassios, founder of community. 4.50d, Presentation of Christ, 11th century manuscript. 6d, Great Lavra Church, horiz.

Perf. 13x13½, 13½x13

1963, Dec. 5 Litho. Wmk. 252

770 A196	30 l	multi	15	15
771 A196	80 l	multi	22	15
772 A196	1d	multi	50	15
773 A196	2d	multi	65	15
774 A196	2.50d	multi	65	15
775 A196	3.50d	multi	1.00	40
776 A196	4.50d	multi	1.10	40
777 A196	6d	multi	1.50	52
	Nos. 770-777 (8)		5.77	2.07

Millennium of the founding of the monastic community on Mt. Athos.

1964, May 6 *Perf. 12x13½*

778 A197	30 l	brown	15	15
779 A197	50 l	purple	18	15
780 A197	1d	green	18	15
781 A197	1.50d	orange	30	15
782 A197	2d	blue	35	15
783 A197	2.50d	chocolate	60	15
784 A197	3.50d	red brn	1.10	18
785 A197	4d	ultra	1.10	18
786 A197	4.50d	bluish blk	1.40	25
787 A197	6d	rose pink	2.25	38
	Nos. 778-787 (10)		7.61	
	Set value			1.50

Archangel Michael — A198

Designs: 1d, Bulgaroctonus coin of Emperor Basil II. 1.50d, Two armed saints from ivory triptych by Harbaville, Louvre. 2.50d, Lady, fresco by Panselinos, Protaton Church, Mt. Athos. 4.50d, Angel, mosaic, Daphni Church, Athens.

1964, June 10 *Perf. 12x13½*

788 A198	1d	multi	15	15
789 A198	1.50d	multi	15	15
790 A198	2d	multi	18	15
791 A198	2.50d	multi	28	15
792 A198	4.50d	multi	1.50	1.00
	Nos. 788-792 (5)		2.26	
	Set value			1.20

Byzantine Art and for the Byzantine Art Exhibition, Athens, Apr.-June, 1964.
Exist imperf.

Birth of Aphrodite, Emblem of Kythera — A199

Designs (emblems of islands): 20 l, Trident, Paxos. 1d, Head of Ulysses, Ithaca. 2d, St. George slaying dragon, Lefkas. 2.50d, Zakyntnos, Zante. 4.50d, Cephalus, dog and spear, Cephalonia. 6d, Trireme, Corfu.

Perf. 13½x12

1964, July 20 Litho. Wmk. 252

793 A199	20 l	multi	15	15
794 A199	30 l	multi	15	15
795 A199	1d	multi	15	15
796 A199	2d	multi	16	15
797 A199	2.50d	sl grn & dl grn	20	15
798 A199	4.50d	multi	75	55
799 A199	6d	multi	90	38
	Nos. 793-799 (7)		2.46	
	Set value			1.30

Centenary of the union of the Ionian Islands with Greece.

Child and Sun — A200

1964, Sept. 10 Wmk. 252

800 A200	2.50d	multi	85	25

50th anniv. of the Natl. Institute of Social Welfare for the Protection of Children and Mothers (P.I.K.P.A.).

Europa Issue, 1964

Common Design Type

1964, Sept. 14 Litho. *Perf. 13x13½*

Size: 23x39mm

801 CD7	2.50d	lt grn & dk red	75	18
802 CD7	4.50d	gray & brn	1.10	80

King Constantine II and Queen Anne-Marie A201

Peleus and Atalante Fighting, 6th Cent. B.C. Vase A202

1964, Sept. 18 Engr. *Perf. 13½x14*

803 A201	1.50d	green	15	15
804 A201	2.50d	rose car	15	15
805 A201	4.50d	brt ultra	65	40
	Set value			55

Wedding of King Constantine II and Princess Anne-Marie of Denmark, Sept. 18, 1964.

Perf. 12x13½, 13½x12

1964, Oct. 24 Litho. Wmk. 252

Designs: 1d, Runners on amphora, horiz. 2d, Athlete on vase, horiz. 2.50d, Discus thrower and judge, pitcher. 4.50d, Charioteer, sculpture, horiz. 6d, Boxers, vase, horiz. 10d, Apollo, frieze from Zeus Temple at Olympia.

806 A202	10 l	multi	15	15
807 A202	1d	multi	15	15
808 A202	2d	multi	15	15
809 A202	2.50d	multi	15	15
810 A202	4.50d	multi	32	18
811 A202	6d	multi	32	15
812 A202	10d	multi	90	55
	Nos. 806-812 (7)		2.14	
	Set value			1.15

18th Olympic Games, Tokyo, Oct. 10-25.

Detail from "Christ Stripped of His Garments" by El Greco A203

Aesculapius Theatre, Epidauros A204

Paintings by El Greco: 1d, Concert of the Angels. 1.50d, El Greco's painted signature, horiz. 2.50d, Self-portrait. 4.50d, Storm-lashed Toledo.

Perf. 12x13½, 13½x12

1965, Mar. 6 Litho. Wmk. 252

813	A203	50 l	sepia & multi	15	15
814	A203	1d	gray & multi	15	15
a.			Double impression of black		
815	A203	1.50d	multi	15	15
816	A203	2.50d	slate & multi	15	15
817	A203	4.50d	multi	40	32
			Set value	82	68

350th anniv. of the death of Domenico Theotocopoulos, El Greco (1541-1614).

1965, Apr. 30 Litho. *Perf. 12x13½*

Design: 4.50d, Herod Atticus Theatre, and Acropolis, Athens.

818	A204	1.50d	multi	32	15
819	A204	4.50d	multi	40	25

Epidauros and Athens theatrical festivals.

ITU Emblem, Old and New Telecommunication Equipment — A205

1965, Apr. 30 *Perf. 13½x12*

820	A205	2.50d	multi	30	15

Cent. of the ITU.

Swearing-in Ceremony A206

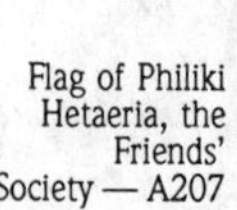

Flag of Philiki Hetaeria, the Friends' Society — A207

Perf. 13½x12

1965, May 31 Litho. Wmk. 252

821	A206	1.50d	multi	20	15
822	A207	4.50d	gray & multi	25	22

150th anniv. of the Friends' Society, a secret organization for the liberation of Greece from Turkey.

Emblem of A.H.E.P.A. A208

1965, June 30

823	A208	6d	lt bl, blk & ol	55	25

Congress of the American Hellenic Educational Progressive Association, Athens.

Eleutherios Venizelos, Therissos, 1905 — A209

Designs: 2d, Venizelos signing Treaty of Sevres, 1920. 2.50d, Venizelos portrait.

1965, June 30 Engr. *Perf. 12½x13*

824	A209	1.50d	green	16	15
825	A209	2d	dk bl	40	25
826	A209	2.50d	brown	48	20

Issued to commemorate the centenary of the birth of Eleutherios Venizelos (1864-1963), statesman and prime minister.

Symbols of Planets — A210

Astronaut in Space — A211

Design: 6d, Two space ships over globe.

Perf. 12½x13½

1965, Sept. 11 Litho. Wmk. 252

827	A210	50 l	multi	15	15
828	A211	2.50d	multi	15	15
829	A211	6d	multi	25	22
			Set value	46	46

Issued to commemorate the 16th Astronautical Congress, Athens, Sept. 12-18.

Victory Medal — A212

Stadium, Phaleron A213

Design: 1d, Games' emblem and "JBA."

Perf. 13½x13, 13x13½

1965, Sept. 11

830	A213	1d	multi	15	15
831	A212	2d	multi	15	15
832	A213	6d	multi	25	22
			Set value	46	40

24th Balkan Games, Sept. 1-10.

Europa Issue, 1965

Common Design Type

1965, Oct. 21 *Perf. 13½x12*

Size: 33x23mm

833	CD8	2.50d	bl gray, blk & dk bl	28	15
834	CD8	4.50d	ol, blk & grn	55	40

Hipparchus and Astrolabe A214

1965, Oct. 21 Litho. Wmk. 252

835	A214	2.50d	bl grn, blk & dk red	22	15

Issued to commemorate the opening of the Evghenides Planetarium, Athens.

St. Andrew's Church, Patras — A215

St. Andrew — A216

1965, Nov. 30 *Perf. 12x13½*

836	A215	1d	multi	15	15
837	A216	5d	multi	18	15
			Set value	27	15

Return of the head of St. Andrew from St. Peter's, Rome to St. Andrew's, Patras. The design of the 5d is from an 11th cent. mosaic at St. Luke's Monastery, Boeotia.

Ants and Anthill — A217

Savings Bank and Book — A218

1965, Nov. 30 Litho. Wmk. 252

838	A217	10 l	grn, blk & bis	15	15
839	A218	2.50d	multi	38	15
			Set value		25

50th anniv. of the Post Office Savings Bank.

Theodore Brysakes — A219

Jean Gabriel Eynard — A220

Banknote of 1867 — A221

Painters: 1d, Nikeforus Lytras. 2.50d, Constantin Volonakes. 4d, Nicolas Gyses. 5d, George Jacobides.

Perf. 13x13½

1966, Feb. 28 Litho. Wmk. 252

840	A219	80 l	multi	15	15
841	A219	1d	multi	15	15
842	A219	2.50d	multi	15	15
843	A219	4d	multi	15	15
844	A219	5d	multi	18	15
			Set value	63	50

Issued to honor Greek painters.

Perf. 12x13½

1966, Mar. 30 Engr. Wmk. 252

Designs: 2.50d, Georgios Stavros. 4d, Bank's first headquarters, etching by Yannis Kefallinos.

845	A220	1.50d	gray grn	15	15
846	A220	2.50d	brown	15	15
847	A221	4d	ultra	15	15
848	A221	6d	black	28	18
			Set value	56	36

National Bank of Greece, 125th anniv.

Symbolic Water Cycle A222

UNESCO Emblem A223

WHO Headquarters, Geneva — A224

Perf. 12x13½, 13½x12

1966, Apr. 18 Litho.

849	A222	1d	multi	15	15
850	A223	3d	multi	15	15
851	A224	5d	multi	28	22
			Set value	48	40

Hydrological Decade (UNESCO), 1965-74, (1d); 20th anniv. of UNESCO (3d); inauguration of the WHO Headquarters, Geneva (5d).

Geannares Michael (Hatzes) A225

Explosion at Arkadi Monastery A226

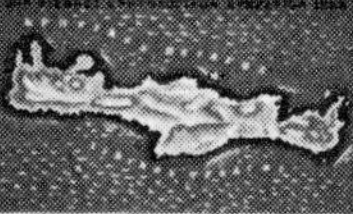

Map of Crete — A227

1966, Apr. 18

852	A225	2d	multi	15	15
853	A226	2.50d	multi	15	15
854	A227	4.50d	multi	28	22
			Set value	48	40

Cent. of the Cretan revolt against the Turks. Geannares Michael (Hatzes), the leader of the revolt, was a member of Cretan government and a writer.

Copper Mask, 4th Century, B.C. — A228

Dionysus on a Thespian Ship-Chariot — A229

Designs: 2.50d, Old Theater of Dionysus, Athens, 6th Century B.C. 4.50d, Dancing Dionysus, from vase by Kleophrades, c. 500 B.C.

Perf. 12x13½, 13½x12

1966, May 26 Litho. Wmk. 252

855	A228	1d	multi	15	15
856	A229	1.50d	multi	15	15
857	A229	2.50d	multi	15	15
858	A228	4.50d	multi	25	22
			Set value	52	50

2500th anniversary of Greek theater.

Boeing 707-320 over New York Buildings and Greek Column
A230

1966, May 26 *Perf. 13x12½*

859 A230 6d blue & dark blue	38	18

Inauguration of transatlantic flights of Olympic Airways.

Tobacco Worker — A231

Design: 5d, Woman sorting tobacco leaves.

Perf. 12½x13½

1966, Sept. 19 Litho. Wmk. 252

860 A231 1d multi	22	15
861 A231 5d multi	42	15
Set value		23

Greek tobacco industry, and 4th Intl. Scientific Tobacco Congress, Athens, Sept. 19-26.

Europa Issue, 1966

Common Design Type

1966, Sept. 19 Litho. Wmk. 252

Size: 23x33mm

862 CD9 1.50d olive	25	15
863 CD9 4.50d lt red brn	52	38

Carved Cases for Knitting Needles — A232

Bridegroom, Embroidery from Epirus
A233

Designs (Popular Art): 50 l, Lyre, Crete. 1d, Massa (stringed instrument). 1.50d, Bas-relief (cross and angels). 2d, Icon (Sts. Constantine and Helena). 2.50d, Virgin (wood carving, Church of St. Nicholas, Galaxeidon). 3d, Embroidery (sailing ship from Skyros). 4d, Embroidery (wedding parade). 4.50d, Carved wooden distaff (Sts. George and Barbara). 5d, Silver and agate necklace and earrings. 20d, Handwoven cloth, Cyprus.

Perf. 12x13½, 13½x12

1966, Nov. 21 Litho. Wmk. 252

864 A232 10 l multi	15	15
865 A233 30 l multi	15	15
866 A232 50 l multi	15	15
867 A232 1d multi	15	15
868 A232 1.50d multi	15	15
869 A232 2d multi	1.10	15
870 A232 2.50d multi	18	15
871 A233 3d multi	20	15
872 A233 4d multi	22	15
873 A232 4.50d multi	30	18
874 A232 5d multi	30	15
875 A233 20d multi	4.00	50
Nos. 864-875 (12)	7.05	
Set value		1.40

King Constantine II, Queen Anne-Marie and Princess Alexia — A234

Designs: 2d, Princess Alexia. 3.50d, Queen Anne-Marie and Princess Alexia.

Perf. 13½x14

1966, Dec. 19 Engr. Wmk. 252

876 A234 2d green	15	15
877 A234 2.50d brown	15	15
878 A234 3.50d ultra	30	20
Set value		35

Issued to honor Princess Alexia, successor to the throne of Greece.

"Night" by John Cossos (1830-73) — A235

Sculptures: 50 l, Penelope by Leonides Drosses (1836-1882). 80 l, Shepherd by George Fytales. 2d, Woman's torso by Constantine Demetriades (1881-1943). 2.50d, "Colocotrones" (equestrian statue) by Lazarus Sochos (1862-1911). 3d, Sleeping Young Lady by John Halepas (1851-1938), horiz. 10d, Woodcutter by George Filippotes (1839-1919), horiz.

Perf. 12x13½, 13½x12

1967, Feb. 28 Litho. Wmk. 252

879 A235 20 l Prus bl, gray & blk	15	15
880 A235 50 l brn, gray & blk	15	15
881 A235 80 l brn red, gray & blk	18	15
882 A235 2d vio bl, gray & blk	15	15
883 A235 2.50d ultra, blk & grn	18	15
884 A235 3d bl, lt bl, gray & blk	18	15
885 A235 10d bl & multi	20	18
Set value	96	62

Issued to honor modern Greek sculptors.

World Map and Olympic Rings
A236

Discus Thrower by C. Demetriades
A237

Designs: 1.50d, Runners on ancient clay vessel. 2.50d, Hurdler and map of Europe and Near East. 6d, Rising sun over Altis ruins at Olympia.

Perf. 13½x12, 12x13½

1967, Apr. 6 Litho. Wmk. 252

886 A236 1d multi	15	15
887 A236 1.50d multi	15	15
888 A236 2.50d multi	15	15
889 A237 5d multi	25	22
890 A236 6d multi	28	20
Set value	82	64

Olympic Games Day, Apr. 6 (1d); Classic Marathon Race, Apr. 6 (1.5d); athletic qualifying rounds for the Cup of Europe, June 24-25 (2.50d); 9th contest for the European Athletic Championships, 1969 (5d); founding of the Intl. Academy at Olympia and the 7th meeting of the Academy, July 29-Aug. 14, 1967 (6d).

Europa Issue, 1967

Common Design Type

Perf. 12x13½

1967, May 2 Litho. Wmk. 252

Size: 23x33½mm

891 CD10 2.50d buff, lt & dk brn	38	15
892 CD10 4.50d grn, lt & dk grn	55	50

Chapel, Skopelos Island — A238

Plaka District, Athens — A239

Intl. Tourist Year: 4.50d, Doric Temple of Epicurean Apollo, by Itkinus, c. 430 B.C.

Perf. 13½x12, 12x13½

1967, June 26 Litho. Wmk. 252

893 A238 2.50d multi	15	15
894 A238 4.50d multi	28	22
a. Double impression of black		
895 A239 6d multi	30	25

Destroyer and Sailor — A240

Training Ship, Merchant Marine Academy — A241

Maritime Week: 2.50d, Merchant Marine Academy, Aspropyrgos, Attica, and rowing crew. 3d, Cruiser Georgios Averoff and Naval School, Poros. 6d, Merchant ship and bearded figurehead.

1967, June 26

896 A240 20 l multi	15	15
897 A241 1d multi	15	15
898 A240 2.50d multi	15	15
899 A240 3d multi	30	20
900 A240 6d multi	30	20
Nos. 896-900 (5)	1.05	
Set value		50

Soldier and Rising Phoenix
A242

Blast Furnaces
A243

Perf. 12x13½

1967, Aug. 30 Litho. Wmk. 252

901 A242 2.50d bl & multi	15	15
902 A242 3d org & multi	15	15
903 A242 4.50d multi	38	38
Set value		56

Revolution of Apr. 21, 1967.

1967, Nov. 29 *Perf. 13x14*

904 A243 4.50d brt bl & dk vio bl	50	35

1st meeting of the UN Industrial Development Organization, Athens, Nov. 29-Dec. 20.

Sailboats
A244

Children's Drawings: 1.50d, Steamship and island. 3.50d, Farmhouse. 6d, Church on hill.

1967, Dec. 20 *Perf. 13½x12½*

905 A244 20 l multi	30	15
906 A244 1.50d grn, dk bl & blk	20	15
907 A244 3.50d multi	32	30
908 A244 6d multi	65	32

Javelin — A245

Apollo, Olympic Academy Seal
A246

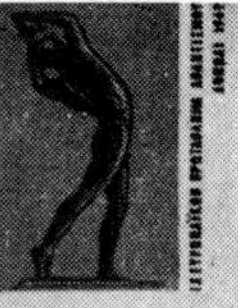

Discus Thrower by Demetriades
A247

Designs: 1d, Jumping. 2.50d, Attic vase showing lighting of Olympic torch. 4d, Olympic rings and map of Europe, horiz. 6d, Long-distance runners, vert.

Perf. 12½

1968, Feb. 28 Wmk. 252 Litho.

909 A245 50 l ultra & bis	15	15
910 A245 1d grn, yel, blk & gray	15	15
911 A246 1.50d blk, bl & buff	15	15
912 A246 2.50d ol grn, blk & org brn	15	15
913 A246 4d gray & multi	42	18
914 A247 4.50d bl, grn, yel & blk	65	42
915 A245 6d brn, red & bl	32	18
Nos. 909-915 (7)	1.99	
Set value		1.00

50 l, 1d, 6d, 27th Balkan Games, Athens, Aug. 29-Sept. 1; 1.50d, Meeting of the Intl. Olympic Academy; 2.50d, Lighting of the Olympic torch for 19th Olympic Games, Mexico City; 4d, Olympic Day, Apr. 6; 4.50d, 9th European Athletic Championships, 1969.

Europa Issue, 1968

Common Design Type

Perf. 13½x12

1968, Mar. 29 Litho. Wmk. 252

Size: 33x23mm

916 CD11 2.50d cop red, bis & blk	52	35
917 CD11 4.50d vio, bis & blk	1.25	75

Set Values

A 15-cent minimum now applies to individual stamps and sets. Where the 15-cent minimum per stamp would increase the value of a set beyond retail, there is a "Set Value" notation giving the retail value of the set.

Emblems of Greek and International Automobile Clubs — A248

1968, Mar. 29 ***Perf. 13x14***

918 A248 5d ultra & org brn 52 35

General Assembly of the International Automobile Federation, Athens, Apr. 8-14.

Athena Defeating Alkyoneus, from Pergamos Altar, 180 B.C. A249

Athena, 2nd Century, B.C. — A250

Winged Victory of Samothrace, c. 190 B.C. — A251

Designs: 50 l, Alexander the Great on horseback, from sarcophagus, c. 310 B.C. 1.50d, Emperors Constantine and Justinian bringing offerings to Virgin Mary, Byzantine mosaic. 2.50d, Emperor Constantine Paleologos, lithograph by D. Tsokos, 1859. 3d, Greece in Missolonghi, by Delacroix. 4.50d, Greek Soldier (evzone), by G. B. Scott.

Perf. 13¹/₂x13, 13x13¹/₂, 13¹/₂x14 (A249)

1968, Apr. 27

919	A249	10 l	gray & multi	15	15
920	A250	20 l	grn & multi	15	15
921	A250	50 l	pur & multi	15	15
922	A249	1.50d	gray & multi	15	15
923	A250	2.50d	multi	15	15
924	A251	3d	multi	15	15
925	A251	4.50d	multi	50	28
926	A251	6d	multi	65	50
			Set value	1.70	1.10

Issued to publicize an exhibition "The Hellenic Fight for Civilization."

Monument to the Unknown Priest and Teacher, Rhodes A252

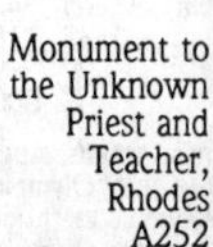

Map & Flag of Greece — A253

Cross and Globe — A254

Perf. 14x13¹/₂, 13¹/₂x14

1968, July 11 **Litho.** **Wmk. 252**

927 A252 2d multi 30 15
928 A253 5d multi 40 40

20th anniv. of the union of the Dodecanese Islands with Greece.

1968, July 11 ***Perf. 13¹/₂x14***

929 A254 6d multi 55 35

19th Biennial Congress of the Greek Orthodox Archdiocese of North and South America.

Antique Lamp (GAPA Emblem) A255

1968, July 11 ***Perf. 14x13¹/₂***

930 A255 6d multi 50 35

Issued to publicize the Regional Congress of the Greek-American Progressive Association, G.A.P.A.

Fragment of Bas-relief, Temple of Aesculapius, Athens — A256

Perf. 13¹/₂x14

1968, Sept. 8 **Litho.** **Wmk. 252**

931 A256 4.50d multi 2.00 90

Issued to publicize the 5th European Cardiology Congress, Athens, Sept. 8-14.

View of Olympia, Site of Ancient Games A257

Pindar and Olympic Ode — A258

Hygeia and WHO Emblem — A259

Design: 2.50d, Panathenaic Stadium, site of 1896 Olympic Games.

Perf. 14x13¹/₂, 13x13¹/₂

1968, Sept. 25 **Litho.** **Wmk. 252**

932 A257 2.50d multi 15 15
933 A257 5d grn & multi 15 15
934 A258 10d bl, yel & brn 1.75 1.00

Issued to publicize the 19th Olympic Games, Mexico City, Oct. 12-27.

On 10d, hyphen is omitted at end of 5th line of ode on 5 of 50 stamps in each sheet.

1968, Nov. 8 ***Perf. 13¹/₂x14***

935 A259 5d gray & multi 55 32

20th anniv. of WHO.

Mediterranean, Breguet 19 and Flight Route, 1928 — A260

Farman, 1912, Plane and F-104G Jet — A261

St. Zeno, The Letter Bearer — A262

Design: 2.50d, Greek air force pilot ramming enemy plane over Langada.

1968, Nov. 8 ***Perf. 14x13¹/₂, 13¹/₂x14***

936 A260 2.50d ultra, blk & yel 15 15
937 A260 3.50d multi 15 15
938 A261 8d multi 1.25 90

Exploits of Royal Hellenic Air Force.

Perf. 13¹/₂x14

1969, Feb. 10 **Litho.** **Wmk. 252**

939 A262 2.50d multi 45 20

Establishment of the feast day of St. Zeno as the day of Greek p.o. personnel.

Hephaestus and Cyclops, Bas-relief A263

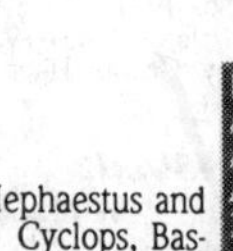

Parade of Harvesters, Minoan Vase — A264

1969, Feb. 10 ***Perf. 13¹/₂x12¹/₂***

940 A263 1.50d multi 35 15
941 A264 10d multi 1.00 65

50th anniv. of the ILO.

Yachts in Vouliagmeni Harbor — A265

Athens Festival, Chorus of Elders — A266

View of Astypalaia A267

Perf. 13¹/₂x12¹/₂, 12¹/₂x13¹/₂

1969, Mar. 3

942 A265 1d multi 15 15
943 A266 5d multi 85 70
944 A267 6d multi 45 15

Issued for tourist publicity.

Attic Shield and Helmet on Greek Coin, 461-450 B.C. — A268

Hoplites and Flutist, from Proto-Corinthian Pitcher, 640-630 B.C. — A269

Perf. 12¹/₂x13¹/₂, 13¹/₂x12¹/₂

1969, Apr. 4 **Litho.** **Wmk. 252**

945 A268 2.50d rose red, blk & sl 35 15
946 A269 4.50d multi 85 65

20th anniv. of NATO.

Europa Issue, 1969

Common Design Type

1969, May 5 ***Perf. 13¹/₂x12¹/₂***

Size: 33x23mm

947 CD12 2.50d multi 65 15
948 CD12 4.50d multi 1.10 90

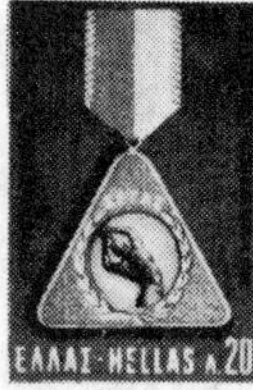

Victory Medal — A270

Pole Vault and Pentathlon (from Panathenaic Amphora) — A271

Designs: 5d, Relay race and runners from amphora, 525 B.C., horiz. 8d, Modern and ancient (Panathenaic amphora, c. 480 B.C.) discus throwers.

Perf. 12¹/₂x13¹/₂, 13¹/₂x12¹/₂

1969, May 5

949	A270	20 l	red & multi	15	15
950	A271	3d	gray & multi	16	15
951	A271	5d	multi	16	15
952	A271	8d	multi	1.40	75
			Set value		1.00

Issued to publicize the 9th European Athletic Championships, Athens, Sept. 16-21.

Greece and the Sea Issue

Oil Tanker — A272

Merchant Vessels and Warships, 1821 A273

Designs: 80 l, Brig and steamship, painting by Ioannis Poulakas, vert. 4.50d, Warships on maneuvers. 6d, Battle of Salamis, 480 B.C., painting by Constantine Volonakis.

Perf. 12½x13½, 13½x12½, 13½x13

1969, June 28 Litho. Wmk. 252

953	A272	80 l	multi	15	15
954	A272	2d	blk, bl & gray	15	15
955	A273	2.50d	dk bl & multi	15	15
956	A272	4.50d	brn, gray & bl	75	35
957	A273	6d	multi	90	45
			Nos. 953-957 (5)	2.10	
			Set value		1.00

Raising Greek Flag — A274

1969, Aug. 31 ***Perf. 13x13½***

958	A274	2.50d	bl & multi	55	20

20th anniv. of the Grammos-Vitsi victory.

Athena Promachos and Map of Greece A275

"National Resistance" A276

Greek Participation in World War II — A277

Perf. 13x13½, 13½x14

1969, Oct. 12 Litho. Wmk. 252

959	A275	4d	multi	15	15
960	A276	5d	multi	60	50
961	A277	6d	multi	45	20

25th anniv. of the liberation of Greece in WW II.
No. 960 exists imperf.

Demetrius Tsames Karatasios, by G. Demetriades A278

Pavlos Melas, by P. Mathiopoulos A279

Designs: 2.50d, Emmanuel Pappas, statue by Nicholas Perantinos. 4.50d, Capetan Kotas.

Perf. 12x13½

1969, Nov. 12 Litho. Wmk. 252

962	A278	1.50d	multi	15	15
963	A278	2.50d	bl & multi	15	15
964	A279	3.50d	gray & multi	22	15
965	A279	4.50d	multi	95	55
			Set value		85

Issued to honor Greek heroes in Macedonia's struggle for liberation.

Angel of the Annunciation, Daphni Church, 11th Century — A280

Dolphins, Delos, 110 B.C. A281

Christ's Descent into Hell, Nea Moni Church, 11th Cent. — A282

Greek Mosaics: 1.50d, The Holy Ghost (dove), Hosios Loukas Monastery, 11th cent. 2d, The Hunter, Pella, 4th cent. B.C. 5d, Bird, St. George's Church, Salonica, 5th cent.

Perf. 12x13½, 13½x12 (1d), 13x13½ (6d)

1970, Jan. 16 Litho. Wmk. 252

966	A280	20 l	multi	15	15
967	A281	1d	multi	15	15
968	A280	1.50d	bl & multi	15	15
969	A280	2d	gray & multi	15	15
970	A280	5d	bis & multi	32	15
971	A282	6d	multi	2.25	1.00
			Nos. 966-971 (6)	3.17	
			Set value		1.25

Hercules and the Cretan Bull — A283

Hercules and the Erymanthian Boar — A284

Labors of Hercules: 30 l, Capture of Cerberus. 1d, Capture of the golden apples of the Hesperides. 1.50d, Lernean Hydra. 2d, Slaying of Geryon. 3d, Centaur Nessus. 4.50d, Fight with the river god Achelos. 5d, Nemean lion. 6d, Stymphalian birds. 20d, Giant Antaeus. Designs of 20 l and 1d are from Temple of Zeus, Olympia; others from various vessels; all from 7th-5th cent. B.C.

Perf. 13½x12, 12x13½

1970, Mar. 16 Litho. Wmk. 252

972	A283	20 l	gray, blk & yel	15	15
973	A283	30 l	ocher & multi	15	15
974	A284	1d	bl gray, blk & bl	15	15
975	A283	1.50d	dk brn, bis & sl grn	15	15
976	A283	2d	ocher & multi	1.65	15
977	A284	2.50d	ocher, dk brn & dl red	32	15
978	A284	3d	multi	1.25	15
979	A283	4.50d	dk bl & multi	70	15
980	A283	5d	multi	90	15
981	A283	6d	multi	90	15
982	A283	20d	blk & multi	4.00	70
			Nos. 972-982 (11)	10.32	
			Set value		1.50

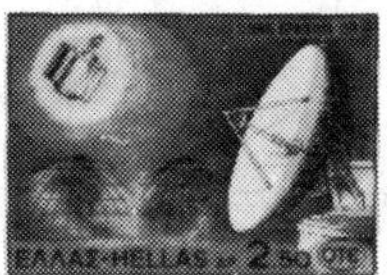
Satellite, Earth Station and Hemispheres A285

1970, Apr. 21 ***Perf. 13½x12***

983	A285	2.50d	bl, gray & yel	70	20
984	A285	4.50d	brn, ol & bl	1.10	85

Opening of the Earth Satellite Telecommunications Station "Thermopylae," Apr. 21, 1970.

Europa Issue, 1970

Common Design Type and

Owl (Post Horns and CEPT) — A287

Perf. 13½x12, 12x13½

1970, Apr. 21

985	CD13	2.50d	rose red & org	55	20
986	A287	3d	brt bl, gray & vio bl	95	38
987	CD13	4.50d	ultra & org	2.00	1.25

St. Demetrius with Cyril and Methodius as Children A288

Emperor Michael III with Sts. Cyril and Methodius A290

St. Cyril A289 — St. Methodius A291

Perf. 13½x14 (50 l); 12x13½ (2d, 10d); 13x13½ (5d)

1970, Apr. 17 Litho. Wmk. 252

988	A288	50 l	multi	20	15
989	A289	2d	multi	65	25
990	A290	5d	multi	65	25
991	A291	10d	multi	1.25	75
a.			Pair, #989, 991	2.00	1.25

Sts. Cyril and Methodius who translated the Bible into Slavonic.

Greek Fir A292

Jankaea Heldreichii A293

Designs: 6d, Rock partridge, horiz. 8d, Wild goat.

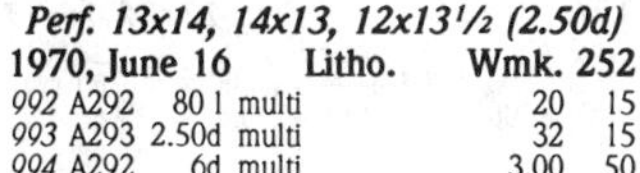

Perf. 13x14, 14x13, 12x13½ (2.50d)

1970, June 16 Litho. Wmk. 252

992	A292	80 l	multi	20	15
993	A293	2.50d	multi	32	15
994	A292	6d	multi	3.00	50
995	A292	8d	multi	5.00	2.50

European Nature Conservation Year, 1970.

Map Showing Link Between AHEPA Members and Greece A294

1970, Aug. 1 ***Perf. 13½x13***

996	A294	6d	blue & multi	1.10	25

48th annual AHEPA (American Hellenic Educational Progressive Assoc.) Cong., Athens, Aug. 1970.

UPU Headquarters, Bern — A295

Education Year Emblem — A296

Mahatma Gandhi — A297

United Nations Emblem — A298

Ludwig van Beethoven — A299

Perf. 13½x12, 13x14, 12x13½

1970, Oct. 7 Litho. Wmk. 252

997	A295	50 l	bis & multi	15	15
998	A296	2.50d	bl & multi	15	15
999	A297	3.50d	multi	95	30
1000	A298	4d	bl & multi	95	25
1001	A299	4.50d	blk & multi	1.65	1.00
			Nos. 997-1001 (5)	3.85	1.85

Inauguration of the UPU Headquarters, Bern (50 l); Intl. Education Year (2.50d); cent. of the birth of Mohandas K. Gandhi (1869-1948), leader in India's struggle for independence (3.50d); 25th anniv. of the UN (4d); Ludwig van Beethoven (1770-1827), composer (4.50d).

The Shepherds (Mosaic) — A300

Christmas (from Mosaic in the Monastery of Hosios Loukas, Boetia, 11th cent.): 4.50d, The Three Kings and Angel. 6d, Nativity, horiz.

1970, Dec. 5 ***Perf. 13x14, 14x13***

No.	Type	Description	Unused	Used
1002	A300	2d bister & multi	28	18
1003	A300	4.50d bister & multi	80	42
1004	A300	6d bister & multi	80	42

"Leonidas"
A301

Priest Sworn in as Fighter, from Commemorative Medal — A302

Eugenius Voulgaris (1716-1806)
A303

Battle of Corinth
A304

Kaltetsi Monastery, Seal of Peloponnesian Senate — A305

Death of Bishop Isaias, Battle of Alamana — A306

Designs: No. 1009, *Pericles*. No. 1010, Sacrifice of Kapsalis. 1.50d, *Terpsichore*. No. 1012, Patriarch Grigorius IV. No. 1013, Suliot women in battle, horiz. No. 1015, *Karteria*. No. 1016, Adamantios Korias, M.D. No. 1017, Memorial column, provincial administrative seal of Epidaurus. 3d, Naval battle, Samos, horiz. 5d, Battle of Athens. 6d, Naval battle, Yeronda. 6.50d, Battle of Maniaki. 9d, Battle of Karpenisi, death of Marcos Botsaris. 10d, Bishop Germanos blessing flag. 15d, *Secret School*. 20d, John Capodistrias' signature and seal.

1971 **Litho.** **Wmk. 252**

No.	Type	Description	Unused	Used
1005	A301	20 l multi	15	15
1006	A302	50 l multi	15	15
1007	A303	50 l multi	15	15
1008	A304	50 l multi	15	15
1009	A301	1d multi	20	15
1010	A304	1d multi	15	15
1011	A301	1.50d multi	20	15
1012	A302	2d multi	20	15
1013	A304	2d multi	20	15
1014	A305	2d multi	20	15
1015	A301	2.50d multi	20	15
1016	A303	2.50d multi	70	35
1017	A305	2.50d multi	20	15
1018	A304	3d multi	42	22
1019	A306	4d multi	32	15
1020	A304	5d multi	65	22
1021	A301	6d multi	65	32
1022	A301	6.50d multi	85	38
1023	A301	9d multi	90	42
1024	A306	10d multi	90	42
1025	A306	15d multi	1.25	60
1026	A305	20d multi	1.50	60
		Nos. 1005-1026 (22)	10.29	
		Set value		4.60

Sesquicentennial of Greece's uprising against the Turks. Emphasize role of Navy (Nos. 1005, 1009, 1011, 1015, 1018, 1021), issued Mar. 15; Church (Nos. 1006, 1012, 1019, 1024), Feb. 8; Instructors (Nos. 1007, 1016, 1025), June 21; Land Forces (Nos. 1008, 1010, 1013, 1020, 1022-1023), Sept. 21; Provincial Administrations (Nos. 1014, 1017, 1026), Oct. 19.

Sizes: 37x24mm: (Nos. 1005, 1009, 1011, 1015); 40x27½mm (No. 1021); 48x33mm (Nos. 1022, 1023).

Perfs.: 14x13 (Nos. 1005, 1009, 1011, 1013, 1015, 1018); 13½x14 (Nos. 1006, 1012); 12x13½ (Nos. 1007, 1016, 1019, 1022-1025); 13x14 (Nos. 1008, 1010, 1020); 13½x13 (Nos. 1014, 1017, 1021, 1026).

Spyridon Louis, Winner of 1896 Marathon Race, Arriving at Stadium
A307

Pierre de Coubertin and Memorial Column — A308

Perf. 13½x13, 13x13½

1971, Apr. 10 **Litho.** **Wmk. 252**

No.	Type	Description	Unused	Used
1027	A307	3d multi	38	28
1028	A308	8d multi	55	52

Olympic Games revival, 75th anniv.

Europa Issue, 1971
Common Design Type

1971, May 18 ***Perf. 13½x12***
Size: 33x22½mm

No.	Type	Description	Unused	Used
1029	CD14	2.50d grn, yel & blk	1.00	32
1030	CD14	5d org, yel & blk	1.25	85

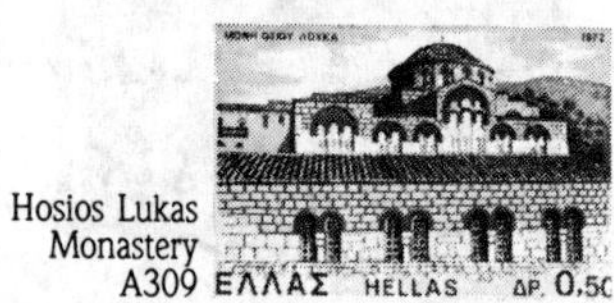

Hosios Lukas Monastery
A309

Monasteries and Churches: 1d, Daphni Church. 2d, St. John the Divine, Patmos. 2.50d, Koumbelidiki Church, Kastoria. 4.50d, Chalkeon Church, Thessalonica. 6.50d, Paregoritissa Church, Arta. 8.50d, St. Paul's Monastery, Mt. Athos.

1972, Jan. 17 ***Perf. 14x13***

No.	Type	Description	Unused	Used
1031	A309	50 l multi	15	15
1032	A309	1d multi	15	15
1033	A309	2d multi	15	15
1034	A309	2.50d multi	15	15
1035	A309	4.50d multi	40	20
1036	A309	6.50d multi	40	15
1037	A309	8.50d multi	1.10	70
		Nos. 1031-1037 (7)	2.50	
		Set value		1.35

Cretan Costume — A310

Designs: Greek regional costumes.

1972, Mar. 1 ***Perf. 12½x13½***

No.	Type	Description	Unused	Used
1038	A310	50 l shown	15	15
1039	A310	1d Woman, Pindus	16	15
1040	A310	2d Man, Missolonghi	18	15
1041	A310	2.50d Woman, Sarakatsan, Attica	25	15
a.		"1972" omitted	3.00	3.00
1042	A310	3d Woman, Island of Nisyros	25	15
1043	A310	4.50d Woman, Megara	50	15
1044	A310	6.50d Woman, Trikeri	70	15
1045	A310	10d Woman, Pylaia, Macedonia	1.40	55
		Nos. 1038-1045 (8)	3.59	
		Set value		1.05

See Nos. 1073-1089, 1121-1135.

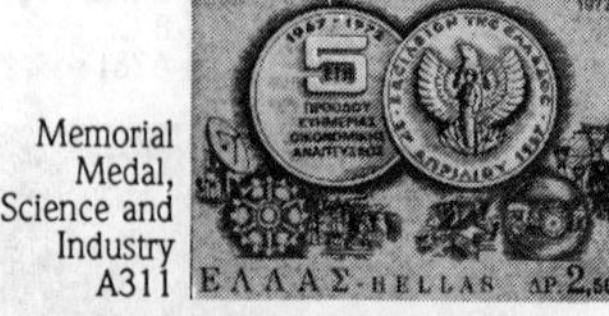

Memorial Medal, Science and Industry
A311

Flag and Map of Greece — A312

Honeycomb, Transportation and Industry — A313

Perf. 13½x13, 13x13½

1972, Apr. 21 **Wmk. 252**

No.	Type	Description	Unused	Used
1046	A311	2.50d blue & multi	15	15
1047	A312	4.50d ocher & multi	25	25
1048	A313	5d multi	38	38

5th anniversary of the revolution.

Europa Issue 1972
Common Design Type

1972, May 2 ***Perf. 12x13½***
Size: 23x33mm

No.	Type	Description	Unused	Used
1049	CD15	3d multi	50	15
1050	CD15	4.50d blue & multi	1.25	1.00

Acropolis and Car — A314

Route of Automobile Rally — A315

1972, May 26 ***Perf. 13½x12***

No.	Type	Description	Unused	Used
1051	A314	4.50d multi	65	50
1052	A315	5d bl & multi	65	50

20th Acropolis Automobile Rally, May 26-29.

Gaia Handing Erecthonius to Athena, Cecrops
A316

Designs: 2d, Uranus, from altar of Zeus at Pergamum. 2.50d, Gods defeating the Giants, Treasury of Siphnos. 5d, Zeus of Dodona.

1972, June 26 **Litho.** ***Perf. 14x13½***

No.	Type	Description	Unused	Used
1053	A316	1.50d yel grn & blk	15	15
1054	A316	2d dk bl & blk	15	15
1055	A316	2.50d org brn & blk	15	15
1056	A316	5d dk brn & blk	40	30
a.		Strip of 4, #1053-1056	80	80
		Set value		54

Greek mythology. No. 1056 issued only se-tenant with Nos. 1053-1055 in sheets of 40 (4x10). Nos. 1053-1055 issued also in sheets of 50 each.

Olympic Rings, Wrestlers
A317

Designs: 50 l, Young athlete, crowning himself, c. 480 B.C., vert. 3.50d, Spartan woman running, Archaic period, vert. 4.50d, Episkyros ball game, 6th century B.C. 10d, Running youths, from Panathenaic amphora.

Perf. 13½x14, 14x13½

1972, July 28 **Litho.** **Wmk. 252**

No.	Type	Description	Unused	Used
1057	A317	50 l mar, blk & gray	15	15
1058	A317	1.50d brn, gray & blk	15	15
1059	A317	3.50d ocher & multi	15	15
1060	A317	4.50d grn, buff & blk	40	25
1061	A317	10d blk & fawn	60	38
		Set value	1.25	80

20th Olympic Games, Munich, Aug. 26-Sept. 11.

Young Stamp Collector — A318

Three Kings and Angels — A319

1972, Nov. 15 ***Perf. 13x14***

No.	Type	Description	Unused	Used
1062	A318	2.50d multi	18	15

Stamp Day.

1972, Nov. 15

No.	Type	Description	Unused	Used
1063	A319	2.50d shown	15	15
1064	A319	4.50d Nativity	15	15
a.		Pair, #1063-1064	30	30

Christmas 1972.

Technical University, 1885, by Luigi Lanza
A320

1973, Mar. 30 ***Perf. 13½x13***

No.	Type	Description	Unused	Used
1065	A320	2.50d multi	18	15

Centenary of the Metsovion National Technical University.

"Spring," Fresco — A321

Breast-form Jug — A322

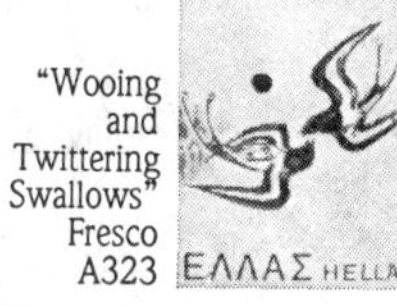

"Wooing and Twittering Swallows" Fresco A323

Designs: 30 l, "Blue Apes" fresco. 1.50d, Jug decorated with birds. 5d, "Wild Goats" fresco. 6.50d, Wrestlers, fresco.

Perf. 13x13½, 13½x13

1973, Mar. 30

1066 A321 10 l multi 15 15
1067 A322 20 l multi 15 15
1068 A323 30 l multi 15 15
1069 A322 1.50d grn & multi 15 15
1070 A323 2.50d multi 15 15
1071 A323 5d multi 25 25
1072 A323 6.50d multi 1.50 1.50
Set value 2.15 2.15

Archaeological treasures from Santorini Island (Thera).

Costume Type of 1972

Designs: Women's costumes except 10 l, 20 l, 50 l, 5d, 15d.

1973, Apr. 18 *Perf. 12½x13½*

1073 A310 10 l Peloponnesus 15 15
1074 A310 20 l Central Greece 15 15
1075 A310 30 l Locris 15 15
1076 A310 50 l Skyros 15 15
1077 A310 1d Spetsai 15 15
1078 A310 1.50d Almyros 15 15
1079 A310 2.50d Macedonia 15 15
1080 A310 3.50d Salamis 18 15
1081 A310 4.50d Epirus 24 15
1082 A310 5d Lefkas 28 15
1083 A310 6.50d Skyros 24 15
1084 A310 8.50d Corinth 35 15
1085 A310 10d Corfu 35 15
1086 A310 15d Epirus 45 15
1087 A310 20d Thessaly 90 18
1088 A310 30d Macedonia 1.10 50
1089 A310 50d Thrace 1.75 65
Nos. 1073-1089 (17) 6.89
Set value 2.80

Europa Issue 1973

Common Design Type

1973, May 2 *Perf. 13½x12½*

Size: 35x22mm

1090 CD16 2.50d dp bl & lt bl 25 15
1091 CD16 3d dp car & dp org 50 30
1092 CD16 4.50d ol grn & yel 75 45

Zeus Battling Typhoeus, from Amphora A324

Designs: 1d, Mount Olympus, after photograph. 2.50d, Zeus battling Giants, from Pergamum Altar. 4.50d, Punishment of Atlas and Prometheus, from vase.

Perf. 14x13½

1973, June 25 **Wmk. 252**

1093 A324 1d gray & blk 15 15
1094 A324 2d multi 15 15
1095 A324 2.50d gray, blk & buff 20 15
1096 A324 4.50d ocher & multi 30 22
a. Strip of 4, #1093-1096 1.25 1.00
Set value 64 48

Greek mythology.

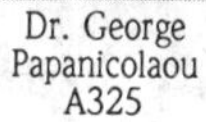

Dr. George Papanicolaou A325

Icon, The Annunciation A326

Perf. 13x13½

1973, Aug. 10 **Litho.** **Wmk. 252**

1097 A325 2.50d multi 30 30
1098 A325 6.50d multi 35 30

Dr. George Papanicolaou (1883-1962), cytologist and cancer researcher.

1973, Aug. 10

1099 A326 2.50d multi 22 15

Miraculous icon of Our Lady of the Annunciation found on Tinos, 1823.

A327

A328

Triptolemus holding wheat on chariot.

Perf. 13x14

1973, Oct. 22 **Litho.** **Wmk. 252**

1100 A327 4.50d buff, dk brn & red 25 22

5th Symposium of the European Conf. of Transport Ministers, Athens, Oct. 22-25.

1973, Nov. 15 **Engr.**

National Benefactors: 1d, Georgios Averoff. 2d, Apostolos Arsakis. 2.50d, Constantine Zappas. 4d, Andrea Sygros. 6.50d, John Varvakis.

1101 A328 1.50d dk red brn 15 15
1102 A328 2d car rose 15 15
1103 A328 2.50d slate green 15 15
1104 A328 4d purple 15 15
1105 A328 6.50d black 15 15
Set value 57 48

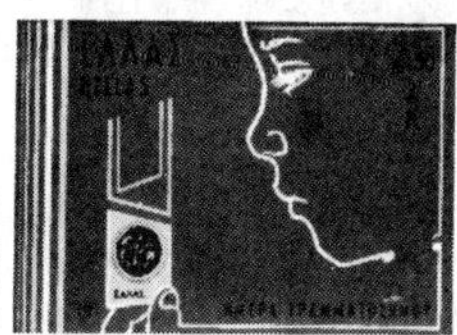

Child Examining Stamp A329

1973, Nov. 15 **Litho.** *Perf. 14x13*

1106 A329 2.50d multi 18 15

Stamp Day.

Lord Byron in Souliot Costume — A330

Byron Taking Oath at Grave of Botsaris — A331

Perf. 13x14

1974, Apr. 4 **Wmk. 252** **Litho.**

1107 A330 2.50d multi 15 15
1108 A331 4.50d multi 15 15
Set value 22 16

George Gordon, Lord Byron (1788-1824), English poet involved in Greek struggle for independence.

Harpist of Keros, c. 2800-2200 B.C. — A332

Europa: 4.50d, Statue of Young Women, c. 510 B.C. 6.50d, Charioteer of Delphi, c. 480-450 B.C.

1974, May 10 *Perf. 13x14*

1109 A332 3d dp bl & multi 16 15
1110 A332 4.50d dl red & multi 20 15
1111 A332 6.50d yel & multi 38 25

Zeus and Hera Enthroned, and Iris — A333

Design from Mycenean Vase and UPU Emblem — A334

Greek mythology (from Vases, 5th Cent. B.C.): 2d, Birth of Athena, horiz. 2.50d, Artemis, Apollo, Leto, horiz. 10d, Hermes, the messenger.

1974, June 24 *Perf. 13x14, 14x13*

1112 A333 1.50d ocher, blk & brn 15 15
1113 A333 2d blk, ocher & brn 15 15
1114 A333 2.50d blk, ocher & brn 15 15
1115 A333 10d blk, ocher & brn 20 15
Set value 54 36

1974, Sept. 14 *Perf. 12½x13½*

UPU cent.: 4.50d, Hermes on the Move, horiz. 6.50d, Woman reading letter.

1116 A334 2d vio & blk 15 15
1117 A334 4.50d vio & blk 15 15
1118 A334 6.50d vio & blk 15 15

Crete No. 80 A335

1974, Nov. 15 **Litho.** *Perf. 13½x13*

1119 A335 2.50d multi 18 15

Stamp Day.

Flight into Egypt — A336

Illustration reduced.

1974, Nov. 15 *Perf. 13½x14*

1120 A336 Strip of 3 38 30
a. 2d ocher & multi 15 15
b. 4.50d ocher & multi 15 15
c. 8.50d ocher & multi 15 15

Christmas 1974. Design is from 11th cent. Codex of Dionysos Monastery on Mount Athos.

Costume Type of 1972

Designs: Women's costumes, except 1.50d.

1974, Dec. 5 *Perf. 12½x13½*

1121 A310 20 l Megara 15 15
1122 A310 30 l Salamis 15 15
1123 A310 50 l Edipsos 15 15
1124 A310 1d Kyme 15 15
1125 A310 1.50d Sterea Hellas 15 15
1126 A310 2d Desfina 15 15
1127 A310 3d Epirus 15 15
1128 A310 3.50d Naousa 15 15
1129 A310 4d Hasia 16 15
1130 A310 4.50d Thasos 16 15
1131 A310 5d Skopelos 18 15
1132 A310 6.50d Epirus 18 15
1133 A310 10d Pelion 20 15
1134 A310 25d Kerkyra 48 18
1135 A310 30d Boeotia 65 30
Set value 2.75 1.60

Secret Vostitsa Assembly, 1821 — A337

Grigorios Dikeos-Papaflessas A338

Aghioi Apostoli Church, Kalamata A339

Perf. 13½x12½, 12½x13½

1975, Mar. 24

1136 A337 4d multi 15 15
1137 A338 7d multi 15 15
1138 A339 11d multi 20 15
Set value 32

Grigorios Dikeos-Papaflessas (1788-1825), priest and leader in Greece's uprising against the Turks, sesquicentennial of death.

Vase with Flowers — A340

Erotokritos and Aretussa — A341

Design: 11d, Girl with Hat. All designs are after paintings by Theophilos Hatzimichael (d. 1934).

Perf. 12½x13½

1975, May 10 **Litho.** **Wmk. 252**

1139 A340 4d multi 20 15
1140 A341 7d multi 32 25
1141 A340 11d multi 50 38

House, Kastoria A342

Greek Houses, 18th Cent.: 40 l, Arnea, Halkidiki. 4d, Veria. 6d, Siatista. 11d, Ambelakia, Thessaly.

1975, June 26 *Perf. 13½x12½*

1142 A342 10 l brt bl & blk 15 15
1143 A342 40 l red org & blk 15 15
1144 A342 4d bister & blk 28 15

1145 A342 6d ultra & multi 20 18
1146 A342 11d org & blk 55 35
Nos. 1142-1146 (5) 1.33
Set value 80

IWY Emblem, Neolithic Goddess — A343

"Looking to the Future" — A344

Design: 8.50d, Confrontation between Antigone and Creon.

Perf. 12½x13½

1975, Sept. 29 Litho. Wmk. 252
1147 A343 1.50d lilac & dk brn 15 15
1148 A343 8.50d bis, blk & brn 18 15
1149 A344 11d bl & blk 20 18
Set value 46 38

International Women's Year 1975.

Papanastasiou and University Buildings A345

First University Building A346

University City Plan — A347

1975, Sept. 29 *Perf. 14x13½*
1150 A345 1.50d tan & sepia 15 15
1151 A346 4d multi 15 15
1152 A347 11d multi 18 15
Set value 42 28

Thessaloniki University, 50th anniversary. Alexandros Papanastasiou (1876-1936), founded University while Prime Minister.

Evangelos Zappas and Zappeion Building A348

National Benefactors: 4d, Georgios Rizaris and Rizarios Ecclesiastical School. 6d, Michael Tositsas and Metsovion Technical University. 11d, Nicolaos Zosimas and Zosimea Academy.

Perf. 14x13

1975, Nov. 15 Litho. Wmk. 252
1153 A348 1d blk & grn 15 15
1154 A348 4d blk & brn 15 15
1155 A348 6d blk & org 15 15
1156 A348 11d blk & brick red 20 20
Set value 52 46

Greece No. 380 — A349

1975, Nov. 15 *Perf. 13x14*
1157 A349 11d dull grn & brn 25 20

Stamp Day 1975.

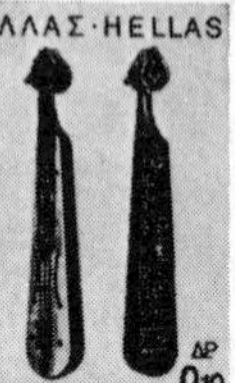

Pontos Lyre — A350

Musicians, Byzantine Mural — A351

Designs: 1d, Cretan lyre. 1.50d, Tambourine. 4d, Guitarist, from amphora, horiz. 6d, Bagpipes. 7d, Lute. 10d, Barrel organ. 11d, Pipes and zournadas. 20d, Musicians and singers praising God, Byzantine mural, horiz. 25d, Drums. 30d, Kanonaki, horiz.

Perf. 12½x13½, 13½x12½

1975, Dec. 15 Litho. Wmk. 252
1158 A350 10 l multi 15 15
1159 A351 20 l multi 15 15
1160 A350 1d ultra & multi 15 15
1161 A350 1.50d multi 15 15
1162 A351 4d multi 15 15
1163 A350 6d multi 16 15
1164 A350 7d multi 20 15
1165 A350 10d multi 30 15
1166 A350 11d red & multi 30 15
1167 A351 20d multi 28 15
1168 A350 25d multi 30 15
1169 A350 30d multi 45 20
Nos. 1158-1169 (12) 2.74
Set value 1.20

Popular musical instruments.

Early Telephone, Globe, Waves — A352

Design: 11d, Globe, waves, telephone 1976.

Perf. 13½x12½

1976, Mar. 23 Litho. Wmk. 252
1170 A352 7d blk & multi 18 15
1171 A352 11d blk & multi 22 15
a. Pair, Nos. 1170-1171 60 60

1st telephone call by Alexander Graham Bell, Mar. 10, 1876.

Sortie of Missolonghi — A353

1976, Mar. 23 *Perf. 13½x13*
1172 A353 4d multi 15 15

Sortie of the garrison of Missolonghi, sesquicentennial.

Florina Jugn — A354

Avramidis Plate — A355

Europa: 11d, Egina pitcher with Greek flags.

Perf. 13x14, 12½x12 (A355)

1976, May 10 Litho. Wmk. 252
1173 A354 7d buff & multi 15 15
1174 A355 8.50d blk & multi 18 15
1175 A354 11d gray & multi 35 24
Set value 46

Lion Attacking Bull — A356

Head of Silenus — A357

Designs: 4.50d, Flying aquatic birds. 7d, Wounded bull. 11d, Cow feeding calf, horiz. Designs from Creto-Mycenaean engraved seals, c. 1400 B.C.

Perf. 13x12½, 13½x14, 14x13½

1976, May 10
1176 A356 2d bis & multi 15 15
1177 A356 4.50d multi 20 15
1178 A356 7d multi 16 15
1179 A357 8.50d pur & multi 16 15
1180 A357 11d brn & multi 20 15
Nos. 1176-1180 (5) 87
Set value 48

Long Jump — A358

Montreal and Athens Stadiums — A359

Designs (Classical and Modern Events): 2d, Basketball. 3.50d, Wrestling. 4d, Swimming. 25d, Lighting Olympic flame and Montreal Olympic Games torch.

Perf. 14x13½, 12½x13½ (A359)

1976, June 25 Litho. Wmk. 252
1181 A358 50 l org & multi 15 15
1182 A358 2d org & multi 15 15
1183 A358 3.50d org & multi 15 15
1184 A358 4d bl & multi 15 15
1185 A359 11d multi 24 15
1186 A358 25d org & multi 50 25
Set value 1.10 68

21st Olympic Games, Montreal, Canada, July 17-Aug. 1.

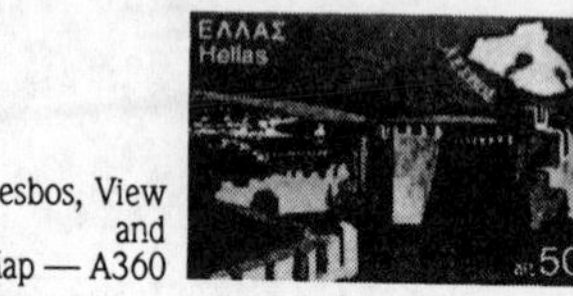

Lesbos, View and Map — A360

Designs (Views and Maps): 30d, Lemnos, vert. 75d, Chios. 100d, Samos.

Perf. 13½x14, 14x13½

1976, July 26 Litho. Wmk. 252
1187 A360 30d blue & multi 70 22
1188 A360 50d blue & multi 1.00 35
1189 A360 75d blue & multi 1.75 40
1190 A360 100d blue & multi 2.00 55

Greek Aegean Islands.

Three Kings Speaking to the Jews — A361

Christmas: 7d, Nativity. Designs from manuscripts in Esfigmenou Monastery, Mount Athos.

1976, Dec. 8 *Perf. 13½x14*
1191 A361 4d yellow & multi 15 15
1192 A361 7d yellow & multi 16 15
Set value 24

Greek Grammar of 1478 A362

1976, Dec. 8 *Perf. 14x13*
1193 A362 4d multi 15 15

500th anniversary of printing of first Greek book by Constantin Lascaris, Milan.

Heinrich Schliemann — A363

Brooch with Figure of Goddess — A364

Designs: 4d, Gold bracelet, horiz. 7d, Gold diadem, horiz. 11d, Gold mask (Agamemnon). Treasures from Mycenaean tombs.

1976, Dec. 8 *Perf. 13x14, 14x13*
1194 A363 2d multi 15 15
1195 A364 4d multi 15 15
1196 A364 5d grn & multi 15 15
1197 A364 7d multi 15 15
1198 A364 11d multi 22 16
Set value 66 50

Cent. of the discovery of the Mycenaean royal shaft graves by Heinrich Schliemann.

Aesculapius with Patients — A365

Patient in Clinic — A366

Designs: 1.50d, Aesculapius curing young man. 2d, Young Hercules with old nurse. 20d, Old man with votive offering of large leg.

Perf. 12½x13½ (A365); 13x12 (A366)

1977, Mar. 15 Litho. Wmk. 252

No.	Type	Value	Color	Unused	Used
1199	A365	50 l	multi	15	15
1200	A366	1d	multi	15	15
1201	A366	1.50d	multi	15	15
1202	A366	2d	multi	15	15
1203	A365	20d	multi	22	18
			Set value	52	42

International Rheumatism Year.

Winged Wheel, Modern Transportation — A367

1977, May 16 Litho. *Perf. 14x13½*

No.	Type	Value	Color	Unused	Used
1204	A367	7d	multi	20	15

European Conference of Ministers of Transport (E.C.M.T.), Athens, June 1-3.

Mani Castle, Vathia A368

Europa: 7d, Santorini, vert. 15d, Windmills on Lasithi plateau.

Perf. 14x13½, 13½x14

1977, May 16 Litho. Wmk. 252

No.	Type	Value	Color	Unused	Used
1205	A368	5d	multi	15	15
1206	A368	7d	multi	15	15
1207	A368	15d	multi	30	22
			Set value		40

Alexandria Lighthouse, from Roman Coin A369

Designs: 1d, Alexander places Homer's works into Achilles' tomb, fresco by Raphael. 1.50d, Alexander descends to the bottom of the sea, Flemish miniature. 3d, Alexander searching for water of life, Hindu plate. 7d, Alexander on horseback, Coptic carpet. 11d, Alexander hearing oracle that his days are numbered, Byzantine manuscript. 30d, Death of Alexander, Persian miniature. All designs include gold coin of Lysimachus with Alexander's head.

1977, July 23 *Perf. 14x13*

No.	Type	Value	Color	Unused	Used
1208	A369	50 l	silver & multi	15	15
1209	A369	1d	silver & multi	15	15
1210	A369	1.50d	silver & multi	15	15
1211	A369	3d	silver & multi	15	15
1212	A369	7d	silver & multi	18	15
1213	A369	11d	silver & multi	18	15
1214	A369	30d	silver & multi	55	32
			Set value	1.20	88

Cultural influence of Alexander the Great (356-323 B.C.), King of Macedonia.

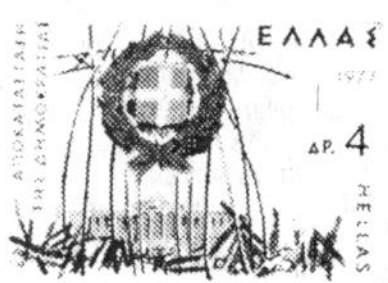

"Greece Rising Again" — A370

People in Front of University A371

Greek Flags, Laurel, University A372

Perf. 13½x12½, 12x12½, 12½x12

1977, July 23 Unwmk.

No.	Type	Value	Color	Unused	Used
1215	A370	4d	multi	15	15
1216	A371	7d	multi	15	15
1217	A372	20d	multi	25	20
			Set value		40

Restoration of Democracy in Greece.

Archbishop Makarios, Map of Cyprus A373

Design: 4d, Archbishop Makarios, vert.

Perf. 13x13½, 13½x13

1977, Sept. 10 Litho. Unwmk.

No.	Type	Value	Color	Unused	Used
1218	A373	4d	sepia & blk	15	15
1219	A373	7d	buff, brn & blk	15	15
			Set value		22

Archbishop Makarios (1913-1977), President of Cyprus.

Old Athens Post Office A374

Neo-Hellenic architecture: 1d, Institution for the Blind, Salonika. 1.50d, Townhall, Syros. 2d, National Bank of Greece, Piraeus. 5d, Byzantine Museum, Athens. 50d, Municipal Theater, Patras.

1977, Sept. 22 *Perf. 13½x13*

No.	Type	Value	Color	Unused	Used
1220	A374	50 l	multi	15	15
1221	A374	1d	multi	15	15
1222	A374	1.50d	multi	15	15
1223	A374	2d	multi	15	15
1224	A374	5d	multi	15	15
1225	A374	50d	multi	60	30
			Set value	1.00	70

Battle of Navarino, Lithograph A375

Adm. Van Heyden, Sir Edward Codrington, Count de Rigny A376

1977, Oct. 20 *Perf. 13½x13*

No.	Type	Value	Color	Unused	Used
1226	A375	4d	brn, buff & blk	15	15
1227	A376	7d	multi	15	15
			Set value	24	21

150th anniversary of Battle of Navarino.

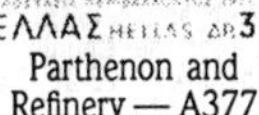

Parthenon and Refinery — A377

Caryatid and Factories — A379

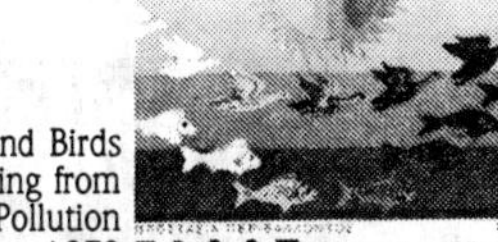

Fish and Birds Suffering from Pollution A378

Design: 7d, Birds and trees in polluted air.

Perf. 13½x14, 14x13½

1977, Oct. 20

No.	Type	Value	Color	Unused	Used
1228	A377	3d	org & blk	15	15
1229	A378	4d	multi	20	15
1230	A378	7d	multi	30	20
1231	A379	30d	blk, gray & slate	42	28

Protection of the environment.

Map of Greece and Ships — A380

Globe and Swallows A381

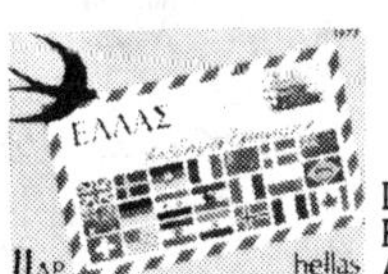

Letter with Flags, Swallow A382

Designs: 5d, Globe with Greek flag. 13d, World map showing dispersion of Greeks abroad.

1977, Dec. 15 *Perf. 13½x12½*

No.	Type	Value	Color	Unused	Used
1232	A380	4d	multi	15	15
1233	A380	5d	multi	15	15
1234	A381	7d	multi	18	15
1235	A382	11d	multi	18	15
1236	A380	13d	multi	22	15
			Nos. 1232-1236 (5)	88	
			Set value		50

Greeks living abroad.

Kalamata Harbor, by Constantine Parthenis — A383

Greek Paintings: 2.50d, Boats, Arsanas, by Spyros Papaloucas, vert. 4d, Santorini, by Constantine Maleas. 7d, The Engagement, by Nicolaus Gyzis. 11d, Woman with Straw Hat, by Nicolaus Lytras, vert. 15d, "Spring" (nude), by Georgio Iacovidis.

Perf. 13½x13, 13x13½

1977, Dec. 15

No.	Type	Value	Color	Unused	Used
1237	A383	1.50d	yel & multi	15	15
1238	A383	2.50d	yel & multi	15	15
1239	A383	4d	yel & multi	15	15
1240	A383	7d	yel & multi	15	15
1241	A383	11d	yel & multi	16	15
1242	A383	15d	yel & multi	30	15
			Set value	88	56

Ebenus Cretica — A384

Greek Flora: 2.50d, Dwarf lily. 3d, Campanula oreadum. 4d, Tiger lily. 7d, Viola delphinantha. 25d, Paeonia rhodia.

1978, Mar. 30 Litho. *Perf. 13x13½*

No.	Type	Value	Color	Unused	Used
1243	A384	1.50d	multi	15	15
1244	A384	2.50d	multi	15	15
1245	A384	3d	multi	15	15
1246	A384	4d	multi	15	15
1247	A384	7d	multi	24	15
1248	A384	25d	multi	24	16
			Set value	86	64

Postrider, Cancellation A385

Designs: 5d, S.S. Maximilianos and Hermes Head. 7d, 19th century mail train and No. 122. 30d, Mailmen on motorcycles and No. 1062.

1978, May 15 *Perf. 13½x12½*

No.	Type	Value	Color	Unused	Used
1249	A385	4d	buff & multi	15	15
1250	A385	5d	buff & multi	18	15
1251	A385	7d	buff & multi	30	15
1252	A385	30d	buff & multi	30	15
a.			Souvenir sheet of 4	1.10	1.10
			Set value		48

150th anniv. of Greek postal service.

No. 1252a issued Sept. 25, contains Nos. 1249-1252 in slightly changed colors. Sold for 60d.

Lighting Olympic Flame, Olympia — A386

Start of 100-meter Race — A387

1978, May 15 *Perf. 13x14*

No.	Type	Value	Color	Unused	Used
1253	A386	7d	multi	20	15
1254	A387	13d	multi	28	20

80th session of International Olympic Committee, Athens, May 10-21.

Europa Issue 1978

St. Sophia, Salonica A388

Lysicrates Monument, Athens — A389

1978, May 15 *Perf. 13x14, 14x13*

1255	A388 4d multi		15	15
1256	A389 7d multi		18	15
	Set value			20

Aristotle, Roman Bust — A390

School of Athens, by Raphael — A391

Map of Chalcidice, Base of Statue from Attalus Arcade — A392

Aristotle the Wise, Byzantine Fresco, St. George's Church, Ioannina — A393

Perf. 13x13¹/₂, 13¹/₂x14 (20d)

1978, July 10 **Litho.**

1257	A390	2d multi	15	15
1258	A391	4d multi	15	15
1259	A392	7d multi	15	15
1260	A393	20d multi	38	25
		Set value	68	48

Aristotle (384-322 B.C.), systematic philosopher.

Rotary Emblem — A394

Surgeons Operating — A395

Ugo Foscolo, View of Zante — A396

Hellenistic Bronze Head — A397

Charioteer's Hand, Delphi — A398

Wright Brothers' Plane, Daedalus and Icarus — A399

1978, Sept. 21 **Litho.** *Perf. 12¹/₂*

1261	A394	1d multi	15	15
1262	A395	1.50d multi	15	15
1263	A396	2.50d multi	15	15
1264	A397	5d multi	15	15
1265	A398	7d multi	15	15
1266	A399	13d multi	16	15
		Set value	68	46

Rotary in Greece, 50th anniv. (1d); 11th Greek Surgery Cong., Salonica (1.50d); Ugo Foscolo (1778-1827), Italian writer (2.50d); European Convention on Human Rights, 25th anniv. (5d); 2nd Conf. of Ministers of Culture of the Council of Europe member countries, Athens, Oct. 23-27 (7d); 75th anniv. of 1st powered flight (13d).

Poor Woman and her 5 Children A400

Scenes from Fairy Tale "The 12 Months": 3d, The poor woman and the 12 months. 4d, The poor woman and the gold coins. 20d, Punishment of the greedy woman.

1978, Nov. 6 **Litho.** *Perf. 13¹/₂x13*

1267	A400	2d multi	15	15
1268	A400	3d multi	15	15
1269	A400	4d multi	15	15
1270	A400	20d multi	28	15
		Set value	56	38

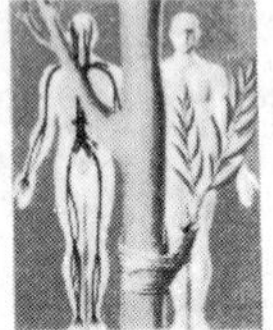

"Transplants" A401

The Miracle of St. Anarghiri A402

1978, Nov. 6 *Perf. 12¹/₂x13¹/₂*

1271	A401	4d multi	15	15
1272	A402	10d multi	20	15
		Set value	30	20

Advancements in organ transplants.

Cruiser — A403

New and Old Greek Naval Ships: 1d, Torpedo boats. 2.50d, Submarine Papanicolis. 4d, Battleship Psara. 5d, Sailing ship "Madonna of Hydra." 7d, Byzantine corvette. 50d, Archaic trireme.

1978, Dec. 15 **Litho.** *Perf. 13¹/₂x12*

1273	A403	50 l multi	15	15
1274	A403	1d multi	15	15
1275	A403	2.50d multi	15	15
1276	A403	4d multi	15	15
1277	A403	5d multi	15	15
1278	A403	7d multi	15	15
1279	A403	50d multi	65	40
		Set value	1.20	88

Cadet Officer, Military School, Nauplia A404

Cadet Officers' School Emblem — A405

Design: 10d, Cadet Officers Military School, Athens, Cadet's uniform, 1978.

Perf. 13¹/₂x12, 12x13¹/₂

1978, Dec. 15

1280	A404	1.50d multi	15	15
1281	A405	2d multi	15	15
1282	A404	10d multi	16	15
		Set value	32	20

Cadet Officers Military School, 150th anniv.

Virgin and Child — A406

Baptism of Christ — A407

Designs from 16th century icon stands in Stavronikita Monastery.

1978, Dec. 15 *Perf. 13x13¹/₂*

1283	A406	4d multi	15	15
1284	A407	7d multi	15	15
		Set value	24	20

Christmas 1978.

Map of Greece A408

1978, Dec. 28 *Perf. 14x13*

1285	A408	7d multi	16	15
1286	A408	11d multi	16	15
1287	A408	13d multi	16	15
		Set value		32

Kitsos Tzavellas A409

Souli Castle A410

Designs: 10d, Fighting Souliots. 20d, Fight of Zalongo.

Perf. 12¹/₂x13¹/₂, 13¹/₂x12¹/₂

1979, Mar. 12 **Litho.**

1288	A409	1.50d buff, blk & brn	15	15
1289	A410	3d multi	15	15
1290	A410	10d multi	20	15
1291	A409	20d buff, blk & brn	32	20
		Set value	72	50

Struggle of the Souliots, 18th century fighters for freedom from Turkey.

Cycladic Figure from Amorgos A411

Mailmen from Crete A412

1979, Apr. 26 **Litho.** *Perf. 12x13¹/₂*

1292	A411	20d multi	40	25

Aegean art.

1979, May 11 *Perf. 13¹/₂x14*

Europa: 7d, Rural mailman on horseback, Crete.

1293	A412	4d multi	15	15
1294	A412	7d multi	22	15
a.		Pair, #1293-1294	30	25
		Set value	30	21

Nicolas Scoufas — A413

Basketball — A415

Locomotives A414

Mene Psarianosi Symeonidis Fossil — A416

Temple of Hephaestus and Byzantine Church — A417

Victory of Paeonius Statue, Flags of Balkan Countries — A418

1979, May 12 *Perf. 13x14, 14x13*

1295	A413	1.50d multi	15	15
1296	A414	2d multi	15	15
1297	A415	3d multi	15	15
1298	A416	4d multi	15	15
1299	A417	10d multi	15	15
1300	A418	20d multi	24	15
		Set value	76	48

Nicolas Scoufas (1779-1818), founder of (patriotic) Friendly Society; Piraeus-Athens-to-the-frontier railroad, 75th anniv.; European Basketball Championship; 7th Intl. Cong. for the Study of the Neocene Period in the Mediterranean; Balkan Tourist Year 1979; 50 years of track and field competitions in Balkan countries.

Wheat with Members' Flags, Greek Coins — A419

European Parliament, Strasbourg A420

Perf. 13x14, 14x13

1979, May 28 **Litho.**

No.	Type	Value	Description	Unused	Used
1301	A419	7d	multi	20	20
1302	A420	30d	multi	30	30

Greece's entry into European Economic Community and Parliament.

Statue of a Girl, IYC Emblem — A421

International Year of the Child: 8d, Girl and pigeons. 20d, Mother and Children, painting by Iacovides.

1979, June 27 **Litho.** *Perf. 13x14*

No.	Type	Value	Description	Unused	Used
1303	A421	5d	multi	20	15
1304	A421	8d	multi	24	15
1305	A421	20d	multi	24	15

Philip II, Bust — A422

Purple Heron — A423

Designs: 8d, Golden wreath. 10d, Copper vessel. 14d, Golden casket, horiz. 18d, Silver ewer. 20d, Golden quiver (detail). 30d, Gold and iron cuirass.

Perf. 13½x14, 14x13½

1979, Sept. 15 **Litho.**

No.	Type	Value	Description	Unused	Used
1306	A422	6d	multi	15	15
1307	A422	8d	multi	15	15
1308	A422	10d	multi	20	15
1309	A422	14d	multi	22	15
1310	A422	18d	multi	30	15
1311	A422	20d	multi	32	18
1312	A422	30d	multi	42	25
			Nos. 1306-1312 (7)	1.76	
			Set value		96

Archaeological finds from Vergina, Macedonia.

1979, Oct. 15

Protected Birds: 8d, Gull. 10d, Falcon, horiz. 14d, Kingfisher, horiz. 20d, Pelican. 25d, White-tailed sea eagle.

No.	Type	Value	Description	Unused	Used
1313	A423	6d	multi	15	15
1314	A423	8d	multi	15	15
1315	A423	10d	multi	22	15
1316	A423	14d	multi	30	20
1317	A423	20d	multi	32	22
1318	A423	25d	multi	32	22
			Nos. 1313-1318 (6)	1.46	1.09

Council of Europe wildlife and natural habitat protection campaign.

Agricultural Bank A424

St. Cosmas — A425

Basil the Great — A426

Balkan Countries, Magnifier — A427

Aristotelis Valaoritis — A428

Golfer A429

Hippocrates A430

Parliament in Session A431

Perf. 14x13½, 13½x14

1979, Nov. 24 **Litho.**

No.	Type	Value	Description	Unused	Used
1319	A424	3d	multi	15	15
1320	A425	4d	multi	15	15
1321	A426	6d	multi	15	15
1322	A427	8d	multi	15	15
1323	A427	10d	multi	18	15
1324	A428	12d	multi	22	15
1325	A429	14d	multi	18	15
1326	A430	18d	multi	18	15
1327	A431	25d	multi	32	18
			Nos. 1319-1327 (9)	1.68	
			Set value		1.00

Agricultural Bank of Greece, 50th anniv.; Cosmas the Aetolian (1714-79), Greek missionary and martyr; Basil the Great (330-379), Archbishop of Caesarea; Balkanfila, Balkan Stamp Exhibition, Athens, Nov. 24-Dec. 2; Aristotelis Valaoritis (1824-79), Greek poet; 27th World Golf Championship, Nov. 8-11; Intl. Hippocratic Foundation of Cos; Greek Parliament, 104th anniv.

Parnassus A432

Tempe Valley A433

Perf. 12½x13½, 13½x12½

1979, Dec. 15 **Litho.**

No.	Type	Value	Description	Unused	Used
1328	A432	50 l	shown	15	15
1329	A433	1d	shown	15	15
1330	A432	2d	Melos	15	15
1331	A432	4d	VikosGorge	15	15
1332	A433	5d	Missolonghi Salt Lake	15	15
1333	A432	6d	Louros Aqueduct	15	15
1334	A432	7d	Samothrace	15	15
1335	A433	8d	Sithonia-Halkidiki	18	15
1336	A433	10d	Samarias Gorge, vert	20	15
1337	A432	12d	Siphnos	22	15
1338	A433	14d	Kyme	25	15
1339	A432	18d	Ios	32	15
1340	A432	20d	Thasos	30	28
1341	A433	30d	Paros	48	18
1342	A432	50d	Cephalonia	55	35
			Set value	3.15	1.80

Byzantine Castle of Thessalonica A434

Designs: 4d, Aegosthena Castle, vert. 8d, Cave of Perama Ioannina, vert. 10d, Cave of Dyros, Mani, vert. 14d, Arta Bridge. 20d, Kalogiros Bridge, Epirus.

Perf. 12½x14, 14x12½

1980, Mar. 15 **Litho.**

No.	Type	Value	Description	Unused	Used
1343	A434	4d	multi	15	15
1344	A434	6d	multi	15	15
1345	A434	8d	multi	20	15
1346	A434	10d	multi	20	15
1347	A434	14d	multi	20	15
1348	A434	20d	multi	22	15
			Nos. 1343-1348 (6)	1.12	
			Set value		72

Gate of Galerius A435

1980, Mar. 15

No.	Type	Value	Description	Unused	Used
1349	A435	8d	multi	18	15

1st Hellenic Congress of Nephrology, Thessalonica, Mar. 20-22.

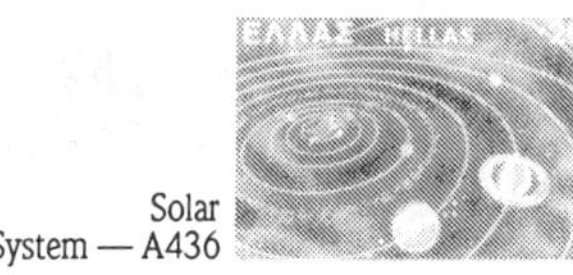

Solar System — A436

Design: 10d, Temple of Hera, Aristarchus' theory and diagram.

1980, May 5 **Litho.** *Perf. 13½x12½*

No.	Type	Value	Description	Unused	Used
1350	A436	10d	multi	22	18
1351	A436	20d	multi	25	20

Aristarchus of Samos, first astronomer to discover heliocentric theory of universe, 2300th birth anniv.; Intl. Scientific Congress on Aristarchus, Samos, June 17-19.

Maria Callas (1923-1977), Opera Singer — A437

Europa: 8d, Georges Seferis (1900-1971), writer and diplomat.

1980, May 5

No.	Type	Value	Description	Unused	Used
1352	A437	8d	multi	18	15
1353	A437	14d	multi	30	22

Energy Conservation Manual — A438

Perf. 13½x12½, 12½x13½

1980, May 5

No.	Type	Value	Description	Unused	Used
1354	A438	8d	shown	20	18
1355	A438	20d	Candle in bulb, vert.	28	24

Firemen — A439

St. Demetrius, Angel, Fresco — A440

Soldiers Marching through Crete — A441

Ancient Vase, Olives — A442

Federation Emblem, Newspaper A443

Constantinos Ikonomos A444

1980, July 14 **Litho.** *Perf. 12½*

No.	Type	Value	Description	Unused	Used
1356	A439	4d	multi	15	15
1357	A440	6d	multi	15	15
1358	A441	8d	multi	18	15
1359	A442	10d	multi	18	15
1360	A443	14d	multi	20	18
1361	A444	20d	multi	24	20
			Nos. 1356-1361 (6)	1.10	
			Set value		72

Fire Brigade, 50th anniv.; St. Demetrius, 1700th birth anniv.; Therissos Revolution, 75th anniv.; 2nd Intl. Olive Oil Year; Intl. Federation of Journalists, 15th Cong., Athens, May 12-16; Constantinos Ikonomos (1780-1857), writer and revolutionary.

Elis Gold Coin, Olympia Stadium, Olympic Rings A445

Olympic Rings and: 14d, Stadium and coin of Delphi 18d, Epidaurus theater, coin of Olympia 20d, Rhodes Stadium, Cos coin. 50d, Panathenean Stadium; 1st Olympic Games medal.

1980, Aug. 11 **Litho.** *Perf. 13½x13*

No.	Type	Value	Description	Unused	Used
1362	A445	8d	multi	18	15
1363	A445	14d	multi	30	15
1364	A445	18d	multi	32	18
1365	A445	20d	multi	35	20
1366	A445	50d	multi	60	40
			Nos. 1362-1366 (5)	1.75	1.08

22nd Summer Olympic Games, Moscow, July 19-Aug. 3.

Asbestos A446

Perf. 13½x12½

1980, Sept. 22 **Litho.**

1367 A446 6d shown 16 15
1368 A446 8d Gypsum, vert. 20 15
1369 A446 10d Copper ore 24 15
1370 A446 14d Barite, vert. 30 15
1371 A446 18d Chromite 30 15
1372 A446 20d Mixed sulphides, vert. 28 15
1373 A446 30d Bauxite, vert. 28 15
Nos. 1367-1373 (7) 1.76 1.05

Tow Truck — A447

Air Force Jet — A448 Airplane and Hangar — A449

Ships in Port A450

Students' Association Headquarters A451

1980, Oct. 31 **Litho.** ***Perf. 12½***

1374 A447 6d multi 20 15
1375 A448 8d multi 25 18
1376 A449 12d multi 25 15
1377 A450 20d multi 25 15
1378 A451 25d multi 25 16
Nos. 1374-1378 (5) 1.20 79

Road Assistance Service of Automobile and Touring Club of Greece, 20th anniv.; Air Force, 50th anniv.; Flyers' Club of Thessaloniki, 50th anniv.; Piraeus Port Organization, 50th anniv.; Association for Macedon ian Studies, 40th anniv.

Madonna and Child, by Theodore Poulakis — A452

Christmas 1980: He is Happy Thanks to You, by Theodore Poulakis. No. 1381a has continuous design.

1980, Dec. 10 ***Perf. 13½***

1379 A452 6d multi 18 15
1380 A452 14d multi 24 18
1381 A452 20d multi 30 22
a. Strip of 3, #1379-1381 75 65

Vegetables for Export — A453

1981, Mar. 16 **Litho.** ***Perf. 12½***

1382 A453 9d shown 28 15
1383 A453 17d Fruits 35 22
1384 A453 20d Cotton 35 22
1385 A453 25d Marble 35 20

Europa Issue 1981

Kira Maria Folk Dance, Alexandria A454

1981, May 4 **Litho.** ***Perf. 14x13***

1386 A454 12d shown 28 20
1387 A454 17d Cretan Sousta (dance) 35 25

Runner, Olympic Stadium, Kalogreza A455

1981, May 4

1388 A455 12d shown 30 24
1389 A455 17d Runners, Europe 30 24

13th European Athletic Championship, Athens, 1982.

Torso Showing Kidneys — A456

Sky Diver and Airplanes — A457

Views of Thessaly and Epirus — A458

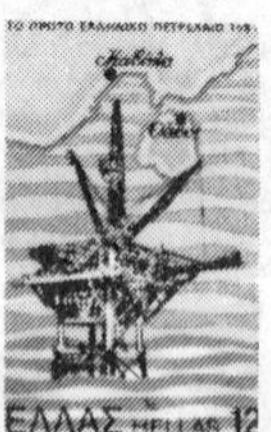

Oil Rig and Map of Thassos Island — A460

Vase with Painted Eyes — A459

Globes and Ancient Coin A461

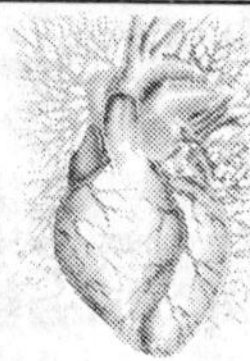
Heart and Vessels — A462

Perf. 13½x14, 14x13½

1981, May 22 **Litho.**

1390 A456 2d multi 15 15
1391 A457 3d multi 15 15
1392 A458 6d multi 20 15
1393 A459 9d multi 30 20
1394 A460 12d multi 32 20
1395 A461 21d multi 32 18
1396 A462 40d multi 40 22
Nos. 1390-1396 (7) 1.84 1.25

8th Intl. Nephrology Conf., Athens, June 7-12; Greek National Air Club, 50th anniv.; Intl. Historical Symposium, Volos, Sept. 27-30; Greek Ophthalmological Society, 50th anniv.; inauguration of oil production at Thassos Island; World Assoc. for Intl. Relations, Athens, 2nd anniv.; 15th Intl. Cardiovascular Surgery Conference, Athens, Sept. 6-10.

Cockles A463

1981, June 30 **Litho.** ***Perf. 14x13½***

1397 A463 4d shown 15 15
1398 A463 5d Parrot fish 15 15
1399 A463 12d Painted comber 30 20
1400 A463 15d Common dentex 35 25
1401 A463 17d Parnassius apollo 42 30
1402 A463 50d Colias hyale 1.50 1.00
Nos. 1397-1402 (6) 2.87 2.05

Bell Tower, Epirus — A464

Altar Gate, St. Paraskevi's Church — A465

Bell Towers and Wood Altar Gates (Iconostases): 9d, Pelion, horiz. 12d, Church of Sts. Constantine and Helen, Epirus. 17d, St. Nicolas Church, Velvendos, horiz. 30d, St. Jacob icon, Church Museum, Alexandroupolis. 40d, St. Nicholas Church, Makrinitsa.

1981, Sept. 30 **Litho.**

1403 A464 4d multi 16 15
1404 A465 6d multi 18 15
1405 A465 9d multi 28 15
1406 A464 12d multi 38 18
1407 A465 17d multi 38 18
1408 A465 30d multi 38 18
1409 A465 40d multi 38 18
Nos. 1403-1409 (7) 2.14 1.17

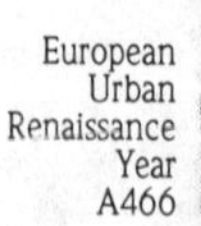

European Urban Renaissance Year A466

St. Simeon, Archbishop of Thessalonica A467

Promotion of Breastfeeding A468

Gina Bachauer, Pianist, 5th Death Anniv. A469

Constantine Broumidis, Artist, Death Centenary A470

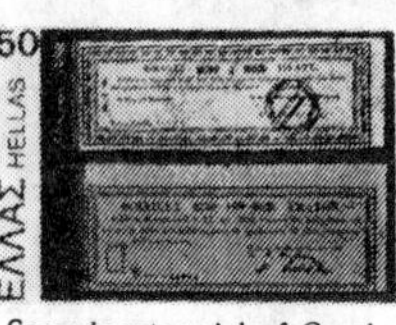

Sesquicentennial of Greek Banknotes — A471

Perf. 14x13½, 13½x14

1981, Nov. 20 **Litho.**

1410 A466 3d multi 18 15
1411 A467 9d multi 24 15
1412 A468 12d multi 30 15
1413 A469 17d multi 45 22
1414 A470 21d multi 50 22
1415 A471 50d multi 52 25
Nos. 1410-1415 (6) 2.19 1.14

Old Parliament Building, Athens — A472

Angelos Sikelianos (1884-1951), Poet A473

Harilaos Tricoupis, Politician, Birth Sesquicentennial A474

Aegean Islands Exhib., Rhodes, Athens — A475

Petralona Cave and Skull — A477

Olympic Airlines, 25th Anniv. — A476

Perf. 13½x12½, 12½x13½

1982, Mar. 15 Litho.

1416 A472 2d multi 15 15
1417 A473 9d multi 30 15
1418 A474 15d multi 42 20
1419 A475 21d multi 55 20
1420 A476 30d multi 55 22
1421 A477 50d multi 60 18
Nos. 1416-1421 (6) 2.57 1.10

Historical and Ethnological Society centennial (2d); 3rd European Anthropology Congress, Halkidiki, Sept. (50d).

Europa 1982 — A478

13th European Athletic Championships, Athens — A479

1982, May 10 Litho. *Perf. 13½x14*

1422 A478 21d Battle of Marathon, 490 BC 55 25
1423 A478 30d 1826 Revolution 75 38

Perf. 14x13½, 13½x14

1982, May 10

1424 A479 21d Pole vaulting, horiz. 32 20
1425 A479 25d Running 40 28
1426 A479 40d Sports, horiz. 75 55

Byzantine Book Illustrations A480

Perf. 13½x12½, 12½x13½

1982, June 26 Litho.

1427 A480 4d Gospel book heading 15 15
1428 A480 6d Illuminated "E," vert. 15 15
1429 A480 12d Illuminated "T," vert. 30 18
1430 A480 15d Gospel reading canon table, vert. 38 24
1431 A480 80d Zoology book heading 1.50 90
Nos. 1427-1431 (5) 2.48 1.62

George Caraiskakis (1782 1827), Liberation Hero — A481

Amnesty Intl. — A482

Designs: 12d, Camp in Piraeus, by von Krazeisen. 50d, Meditating.

1982, Sept. 20 Litho. *Perf. 13x13½*

1432 A481 12d multi 28 16
1433 A481 50d multi 1.00 60

1982, Sept. 20 *Perf. 13x14*

1434 A482 15d Vigil 32 20
1435 A482 75d Prisoners 1.50 75

Natl. Resistance Movement, 1941-44 — A483

Designs: 1d, Demonstration of Mar. 24, 1942. 2d, Sacrifice of Inhabitants of Kalavrita, by S. Vasiliou. 5d, Resistance Fighters in Thrace, by A. Tassos. 9d, The Start of Resistance in Crete, by P. Gravalos. 12d, Partisan Men and Women, by P. Gravalos. 21d, Blowing Up a Bridge, by A. Tassos. 30d, Fighters at a Barricade, by G. Sikeliotis. 50d, The Fight in Northern Greece, by B. Katraki, 5d, 9d, 12d, 21d vert.

1982, Nov. 8 Litho. *Perf. 12½*

1436 A483 1d multi 15 15
1437 A483 2d multi 15 15
1438 A483 5d multi 15 15
1439 A483 9d multi 18 15
1440 A483 12d multi 24 15
1441 A483 21d multi 40 18
a. Souv. sheet, 5d, 9d, 12d, 21d 3.25 3.75
1442 A483 30d multi 60 22
1443 A483 50d multi 90 32
a. Souv. sheet, 1d, 2d, 30d, 50d 2.25 2.25
Nos. 1436-1443 (8) 2.77
Set value 1.10

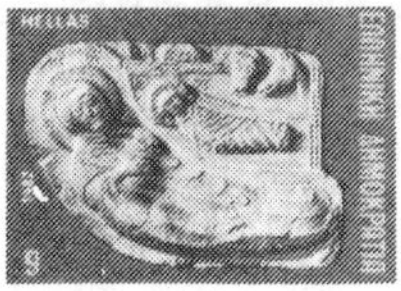

Christmas 1982 — A484

Designs: Various Byzantine Nativity bas-reliefs, Byzantine Museum.

1982, Dec. 6 Litho. *Perf. 13½x12½*

1444 A484 9d multi 20 15
1445 A484 21d multi 35 25
a. Pair, #1444-1445 55 45

25th Anniv. of Intl. Maritime Org. — A485

Ship Figureheads. 15d, 18d, 25d, 40d vert.

Perf. 14x13½, 13½x14

1983, Mar. 14

1446 A485 11d Ares, Tsamados 30 15
1447 A485 15d Ares, Miaoulis 42 18
1448 A485 18d Female figure 45 20
1449 A485 25d Spetses, Bouboulina 55 24
1450 A485 40d Epameinondas, K. Babas 55 24
1451 A485 50d Carteria 1.10 48
Nos. 1446-1451 (6) 3.37 1.49

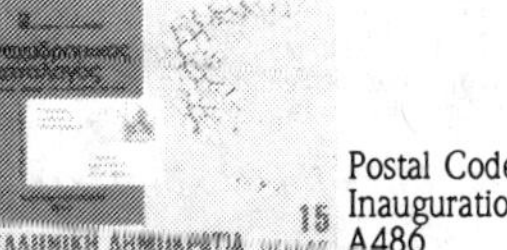

Postal Code Inauguration A486

1983, Mar. 14 Litho. *Perf. 12½*

1452 A486 15d Cover, map 35 22
1453 A486 25d Hermes, post horn, vert. 42 28

Rowing A487

1983, Apr. 28 *Perf. 14x13, 13x14*

1454 A487 15d shown 32 20
1455 A487 18d Water skiing, vert. 40 22
1456 A487 27d Wind surfing, vert. 65 35
1457 A487 50d Skiers on chairlift, vert. 1.10 45
1458 A487 80d Skiing 1.50 75
Nos. 1454-1458 (5) 3.97 1.97

Europa Issue 1983

Acropolis — A488

Archimedes and His Hydrostatic Principle — A489

Perf. 12½x13½, 13x13½

1983, Apr. 28 Litho.

1459 A488 25d multi 85 32
1460 A489 80d multi 2.25 75

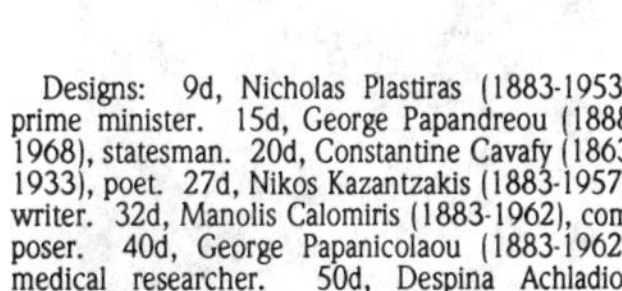

Marinos Antypas (1873-1907), Farmers' Movement Leader — A490

Designs: 9d, Nicholas Plastiras (1883-1953), prime minister. 15d, George Papandreou (1888-1968), statesman. 20d, Constantine Cavafy (1863-1933), poet. 27d, Nikos Kazantzakis (1883-1957), writer. 32d, Manolis Calomiris (1883-1962), composer. 40d, George Papanicolaou (1883-1962), medical researcher. 50d, Despina Achladioti (1890-1982), nationalist.

1983, July 11 Litho. *Perf. 13½x14*

1461 A490 6d multi 15 15
1462 A490 9d multi 18 15
1463 A490 15d multi 25 15
1464 A490 20d multi 38 16
1465 A490 27d multi 48 20
1466 A490 32d multi 75 24
1467 A490 40d multi 80 25
1468 A490 50d multi 95 30
Nos. 1461-1468 (8) 3.94 1.60

A491

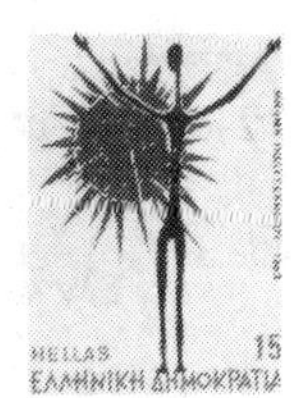

A492

1983, Sept. 26 Litho. *Perf. 13½x13*

1469 A491 50d Portrait bust 1.00 50

1st Intl. Conf. on the Works of Democritus (Philosopher, 460-370 BC), Xanthe, Oct.

1983, Nov. 17 Litho. *Perf. 13*

1470 A492 15d Poster 38 25
1471 A492 30d Flight from school 52 32

Polytechnic School Uprising, 1st anniv.

The Deification of Homer — A493

Homer Inspired Artworks: 3d, The Abduction of Helen by Paris, horiz. 4d, The Wooden Horse, horiz. 5d, Achilles Throwing Dice with Ajax, horiz. 6d, Achilles, vert. 10d, Hector Receiving His Arms from His Parents. 14d, Single-handed Battle Between Ajax and Hector, horiz. 15d, Priam Requesting the Body of Hector, horiz. 20d, The Blinding of Polyphemus, vert. 27d, Ulysses Escaping from Polyphemus' Cave, horiz. 30d, Ulysses Meeting with Nausica. 32d, Ulysses on the Island of the Sirens, horiz. 50d, Ulysses Slaying the Suitors, horiz. 75d, The Heroes of the Iliad, horiz. 100d, Homer.

1983, Dec. 19 Litho. *Perf. 13*

1472 A493 2d multi 15 15
1473 A493 3d multi 15 15
1474 A493 4d multi 15 15
1475 A493 5d multi 15 15
1476 A493 6d multi 15 15
1477 A493 10d multi 16 15
1478 A493 14d multi 20 15
1479 A493 15d multi 24 15
1480 A493 20d multi 32 15
1481 A493 27d multi 40 15
1482 A493 30d multi 48 15
1483 A493 32d multi 52 15
1484 A493 50d multi 75 30
1485 A493 75d multi 1.25 45
1486 A493 100d multi 1.50 85
Nos. 1472-1486 (15) 6.57
Set value 2.60

Horse's Head from Chariot of Seline — A494

Horsemen and Heroes — A495

1984, Mar. 15 Litho. *Perf. 14½x14*

1487 A494 14d shown 22 15
1488 A494 15d Dionysus 24 15
1489 A494 20d Hestia, Dione, Aphrodite 48 15
1490 A494 27d Ilissus 60 25
1491 A494 32d Lapith, centaur 80 30
Nos. 1487-1491 (5) 2.34 1.00

Souvenir Sheet

Perf. 13x13½

1492 Sheet of 4 3.75 3.00
a. A495 15d multi 48 35
b. A495 21d multi 65 55
c. A495 27d multi 85 75
d. A495 32d multi 1.00 85

Marble from the Parthenon. No. 1492 sold for 107d.

Europa (1959-84) A496

1984, Apr. 30 Litho. *Perf. 14x13½*

1493 A496 15d multi 1.00 28
1494 A496 27d multi 1.50 50

Nos. 1493-1494 exist se-tenant.

1984 Summer Olympics — A497

Designs: 14d, Ancient Olympic stadium crypt. 15d, Athletes training. 20d, Broad jump, discus thrower. 32d, Athletes, diff. 80d, Stadium, Demetrius Bikelos, poet, organizer of 1896 Athens games. Nos. 1495-1499 exist se-tenant.

1984, Apr. 30 *Perf. 13½x14*

1495	A497	14d	multi	32	20
1496	A497	15d	multi	35	25
1497	A497	20d	multi	60	35
1498	A497	32d	multi	90	50
1499	A497	80d	multi	2.25	1.10
			Nos. 1495-1499 (5)	4.42	2.40

Also issued in booklets.

Turkish Invasion of Cyprus, 10th Anniv. — A498

1984, July 10 **Litho.** *Perf. 13*

1500	A498	20d	Tank, map, vert.	40	15
1501	A498	32d	Map, barbed wire	70	25

Exist se-tenant. Also issued in booklets.

Greek Railway Centenary A499

Perf. 13x13½, 13½x13

1984, July 20 **Litho.**

1502	A499	15d	Pelion	24	15
1503	A499	20d	Papadia Bridge, vert.	32	15
1504	A499	30d	Piraeus-Peloponnese	70	22
1505	A499	50d	Cogwheel Calavryta, vert.	1.25	35

Sesquicentenary of Athens as Capitol City — A500

Designs: 15d, 4d silver coin, 5th cent. BC, city plan, vert. 100d, Views of ancient and modern Athens.

Perf. 13½x13, 13x13½

1984, Oct. 12 **Litho.**

1506	A500	15d	multi	65	15
1507	A500	100d	multi	1.65	50

10th Anniv. of Democratic Govt. — A501

1984, Oct. 12 **Litho.** *Perf. 13x13½*

1508	A501	95d	"10" on flag	2.00	50

Christmas 1984 — A502

Scenes from 18th cent. icon by Athanasios Tountas.

1984, Dec. 6 **Litho.** *Perf. 13½x13*

1509	A502	14d	Annunciation	25	15
1510	A502	20d	Nativity	35	18
1511	A502	25d	Presentation in the Temple	55	22
1512	A502	32d	Baptism of Christ	1.00	30

Nos. 1509-1512 exist se-tenant. Also issued in booklets.

Runner — A503

Palais des Sports A504

Perf. 13, 13x13½ (#1515)

1985, Mar. 1 **Litho.**

1513	A503	12d	shown	22	15
1514	A503	15d	Shot put	28	15
1515	A504	20d	shown	32	18
1516	A503	25d	Hurdles	55	20
1517	A503	80d	Women's high jump	1.65	75
			Nos. 1513-1517 (5)	3.02	1.43

European Indoor Athletics Championships, Palais des Sports, New Phaleron.

Europa 1985 — A505

CEPT emblem and: 27d, Musical contest between Marsyas and Apollo. 80d, Dimitris Mitropoulos (1896-1960) and Nikos Skalkottas (1904-1949), composers.

1985, Apr. 29 *Perf. 14x14½*

1518	A505	27d	multi	40	30
1519	A505	80d	multi	1.40	1.25

Exist se-tenant. Also issued in booklets.

Melos Catacombs, A.D. 2nd Cent., Trypete — A506

1985, Apr. 29 *Perf. 14½x14*

1520	A506	15d	Niche	22	15
1521	A506	20d	Altar, Central Gallery	55	20
1522	A506	100d	Catacombs	1.75	65

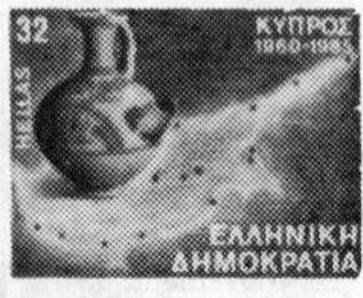

Republic of Cyprus, 25th Anniv. — A507

1985, June 24 *Perf. 13x13½*

1523	A507	32d	Map of Cyprus, urn	70	30

Coin of King Cassander (315 B.C.), Personification of Salonika, Galerius Era Bas-relief A508

Sts. Demetrius and Methodius, Mosaics — A509

Designs: 15d, Emperor sacrificing at Altar, Arch of Galerius, Roman era. 20d, Eastern walls of Salonika, Byzantine era. 32d, Houses in the Upper City. 50d, Liberation of Salonika by the Greek Army, 1912. 80d, German occupation, 1941-44, the Old Mosque. 95d, View of city, Trade Fair grounds, Aristotelian University tower.

Perf. 14½x14 (A508), 14x14½ (A509)

1985, June 24

1524	A508	1d	multi	18	15
1525	A509	5d	multi	45	15
1526	A508	15d	multi	50	15
1527	A508	20d	multi	55	18
1528	A508	32d	multi	60	20
1529	A508	50d	multi	80	22
1530	A508	80d	multi	1.10	38
1531	A509	95d	multi	1.50	45
			Nos. 1524-1531 (8)	5.68	1.88

Salonika City, 2300th anniv. Aristotelian University, Trade Fair, 60th annivs.

Athenian Cultural Heritage A510

Ancient art and architecture: 15d, Democracy Crowning the City, bas-relief from a column, Ancient Agora of Athens, vert. 20d, Mosaic pavement of tritons, nereids, dolphins, etc., Roman baths at Hieratus, Isthmia, A.D. 2nd cent. 32d, Angel, fresco, Grotto of Pentheli, A.D. 13th cent., vert. 80d, Capodistrian University, Athens.

1985, Oct. 7 *Perf. 13½x13, 13x13½*

1532	A510	15d	multi	22	15
1533	A510	20d	multi	28	15
1534	A510	32d	multi	45	25
1535	A510	80d	multi	1.10	65

Intl. Youth Year — A511

UN 40th Anniv. — A512

Design: No. 1540, Girl crowned with flowers, Stadium of Peace and Friendship, Athens.

1985, Oct. 7 *Perf. 14x14½*

1536	A511	15d	Children, olive wreath	28	15
1537	A511	25d	Children, doves	50	15
1538	A512	27d	UN General Assembly, dove	55	18
1539	A512	100d	UN building, emblem	2.00	60

Souvenir Sheet

1985, Nov. 22 *Perf. 14x13 on 3 sides*

1540	A511	100d	multi	1.65	50

No. 1540 contains one 43x47mm stamp.

Pontic Hellenism Cultural Reformation A513

Perf. 14x12½, 12½x14

1985, Dec. 9 **Litho.**

1541	A513	12d	Folk dance	18	15
1542	A513	15d	Our Lady Soumela Monastery	24	15
1543	A513	27d	Folk costumes, vert.	50	16
1544	A513	32d	Trapezus High School	60	20
1545	A513	80d	Sinope Castle	1.50	50
			Nos. 1541-1545 (5)	3.02	1.16

Greek Gods — A514

1986, Feb. 17 **Litho.** *Perf. 13 Horiz.*

1546	A514	5d	Hestia	15	15
1547	A514	18d	Hermes	22	15
1548	A514	27d	Aphrodite	35	20
1549	A514	32d	Ares	38	22
1550	A514	35d	Athena	42	22
1551	A514	40d	Hephaestus	45	25
1552	A514	50d	Artemis	60	25
1553	A514	110d	Apollo	1.25	60
1554	A514	150d	Demeter	1.90	1.00
1555	A514	200d	Poseidon	2.50	1.25
1556	A514	300d	Hera	3.75	2.00
1557	A514	500d	Zeus	6.25	3.25
			Nos. 1546-1557 (12)	18.22	9.54

Each denomination sold in bklts. containing 20 panes of 5 stamps. Also issued perf. 13.

Youth of Antikythera — A515

Soccer Players — A517

Diadoumenos, by Polycleitus A516

Wrestlers, Hellenic Era Statue — A518

Cyclists — A520

Volleyball Players — A519

Commemorative Design for 1st Modern Olympic Games — A521

1986, Mar. 3 *Perf. 12*

1558 A515 18d multi 35 18
1559 A516 27d multi 50 22
1560 A517 32d multi 55 25
1561 A518 35d multi 65 25
1562 A519 40d multi 75 30
1563 A520 50d multi 95 38
1564 A521 110d multi 2.25 90
Nos. 1558-1564 (7) 6.00 2.48

First World Junior Athletic Championships. Pan-European Junior Soccer Championships. Pan-European Free-style and Greco-Roman Wrestling Championships. Men's World Volleyball Championships. Sixth International Round-Europe Cycling Meet. Modern Olympic Games, 90th anniv.

European Traffic Safety Year — A522

1986, Mar. 3 *Perf. 12½x14*

1565 A522 18d Seat belts 30 15
1566 A522 27d Motorcycle 45 18
1567 A522 110d Speed limits 1.75 70

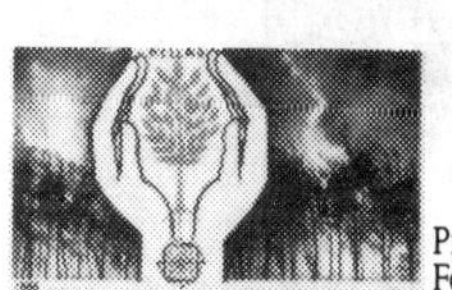

Prevention of Forest Fires A523

1986, Apr. 23 **Litho.** *Perf. 14x13½*

1568 A523 35d shown 75 30
1569 A523 110d Prespa Lakes wetlands 1.75 70
a. Bklt. pane, 2 each 35d, 110d *22.50*
b. Pair, 35d, 110d 2.50 1.50

Europa.

New Postal Services — A524

May Day Strike, Chicago, Cent. — A525

Perf. 13½x14, 14x13½

1986, Apr. 23

1570 A524 18d Intelpost 50 20
1571 A524 110d Express mail, horiz. 1.75 70

1986, Apr. 23 *Perf. 12½*

1572 A525 40d Strikers, monument 65 30

Eleutherios K. Venizelos (1864-1936), Premier A526

Designs: 18d, Venizelos, Ministers taking oath of office, 1917. 110d, Old Hania Harbor, Crete.

1986, June 30 **Litho.** *Perf. 14x12½*

1573 A526 18d multi 30 15
1574 A526 110d multi 1.90 70

6th Intl. Cretological Conference, Crete.

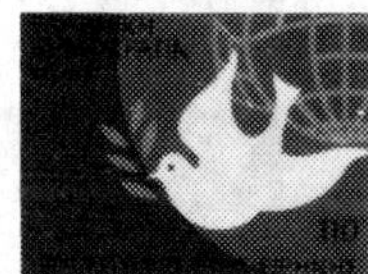
Intl. Peace Year — A527

1986, Oct. 6 **Litho.** *Perf. 12½*

1575 A527 18d Dove, sun, vert. 28 15
1576 A527 35d Flags, dove, vert. 55 22
1577 A527 110d World cage, dove 1.75 70

Christmas — A528

Aesop's Fables — A529

Religious art in the Benaki Museum: 22d, Madonna and Child Enthroned, triptych center panel, 15th cent. 46d, Adoration of the Magi, 15th cent. 130d, Christ Enthroned with St. John the Evangelist, triptych panel.

1986, Dec. 1 **Litho.** *Perf. 13½x14*

1578 A528 22d multi 30 15
1579 A528 46d multi 65 25
1580 A528 130d multi 1.80 70

Size of No. 1579: 27x35mm.

Perf. 12½ Horiz.

1987, Mar. 5 **Litho.**

1581 A529 2d Fox and the Grapes 15 15
1582 A529 5d North Wind and the Sun 15 15
1583 A529 10d Stag and the Lion 15 15
1584 A529 22d Zeus and the Snake 32 15
1585 A529 32d Crow and the Fox 48 20
1586 A529 40d Woodcutter and Hermes 60 24
1587 A529 46d Ass in a Lion's Skin 68 28
1588 A529 130d Tortoise and the Hare 2.00 80
Nos. 1581-1588 (8) 4.53
Set value 1.85

Each denomination sold in booklets containing 20 panes of 5 stamps. Also issued perf. 12½x13.

Europa 1987 — A530

Modern art: 40d, Composition, by Achilleas Apergis. 130d, Delphic Light, by Gerassimos Sklavos.

1987, May 4 **Litho.** *Perf. 12½*

1589 A530 40d multi 68 35
1590 A530 130d multi 2.15 1.10
a. Bklt. pane, 2 each #1589-1590 6.50
b. Pair, 40d, 130d 3.00 2.00

25th European Basketball Championships, Stadium of Peace and Friendship — A531

A532

1987, May 4 *Perf. 13½x14, 12½*

1591 A531 22d Jump shot, stadium, vert. 38 15
1592 A532 25d Emblem, spectators 42 18
1593 A531 130d Two players, vert. 2.15 85

Higher Education Sesquicentenary — A533

Perf. 14x13½, 13½x14

1987, May 4 **Litho.**

1594 A533 3d Students, tapestry 15 15
1595 A533 23d Owl, medallion 40 16
1596 A533 40d Institute, symbols of science 70 28
1597 A533 60d Institute, students 1.00 40

Capodistrias University of Athens (Nos. 1594-1595); The Natl. Metsovio Polytechnic Institute (Nos. 1596-1597). #1596-1597 vert.

Souvenir Sheet

25th European Men's Basketball Championships A534

1987, June 3 **Litho.** *Perf. 13x14*

1598 Sheet of 3 3.00 3.00
a. A534 40d Jump ball 55 55
b. A534 60d Layup 80 80
c. A534 100d Dunk shot 1.40 1.40

Architecture A535

Designs: 2d, Ionic and Corinthian capitals, Archaic Era. 26d, Doric capital, the Parthenon (detail). 40d, Ionic capital and the Erechteum. 60d, Corinthian capital and the Tholos in Epidaurus.

1987, July 1 **Litho.** *Perf. 13½x12½*

1599 A535 2d multi 15 15
1600 A535 26d multi 38 15
1601 A535 40d multi 55 25
1602 A535 60d multi 85 38

Engraving by Yiannis Kephalinos — A536

Panteios School — A537

Perf. 12½x14, 14x12½

1987, Oct. 1 **Litho.**

1603 A536 26d multi 38 15
1604 A537 60d multi 85 38

School of Fine Arts, 150th anniv. (26d), and Panteios School of Political Science, 60th anniv. (60d).

Greek Natl. Team, Winner, 25th European Men's Basketball Championship A538

1987, Oct. 1 *Perf. 13x14*

1605 A538 40d multi 60 25

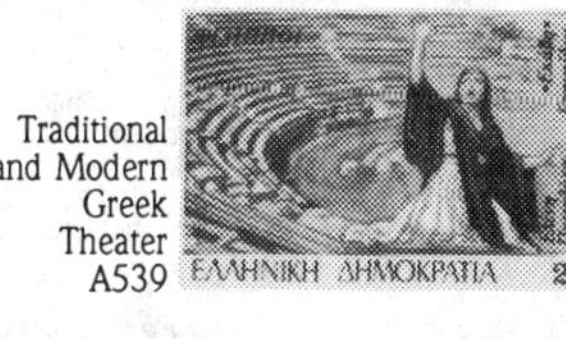

Traditional and Modern Greek Theater A539

Designs: 2d, Eleni Papadaki in Hecuba, by Euripides, and outdoor theater, Philippi. 4d, Christopher Nezer in The Wasps, by Aristophane, and outdoor theater, Dodona. 7d, Emilios Veakis in Oedipus Rex and theater, Delphi. 26d, Marika Cotopouli in The Shepherdess's Love, by Dimitris Koromilas. 40d, Katina Paxinou in Abraham's Sacrifice, by Vitzentzos Cornaros. 50d, Kyveli in Countess Valeraina's Secret, by Gregory Xenopoulos. 60d, Director Carolos Koun, stage setting. 100d, Dimitris Rontiris teaching ancient dance, Greek National Theater.

1987, Dec. 2 **Litho.** *Perf. 14x13½*

1606 A539 2d multi 15 15
1607 A539 4d multi 15 15
1608 A539 7d multi 15 15
1609 A539 26d multi 40 16
1610 A539 40d multi 60 25
1611 A539 50d multi 75 35
1612 A539 60d multi 90 45
1613 A539 100d multi 1.50 75
Nos. 1606-1613 (8) 4.60
Set value 2.10

Christmas — A540

1987, Dec. 2 *Perf. 13x12½*

1614 A540 26d Angel facing right 40 16
1615 A540 26d Angel facing left 40 16
a. Bklt. pane, 5 each #1614-1615 4.00
b. Pair, #1614-1615 80 40

Marine Life — A541

1988, Mar. 2 *Perf. 12½ Vert.*

1616 A541 30d Codonellina 50 20
1617 A541 40d Diaperoecia major 65 28
1618 A541 50d Artemia 82 38
1619 A541 60d Posidonia oceanica 1.00 45
1620 A541 100d Padina pavonica 1.65 80
Nos. 1616-1620 (5) 4.62 2.11

Each denomination sold in bklts. containing 20 panes of 5 stamps. Also issued perf. 14x12½ in sheets of 50.

Europa 1988 — A542

Communication and transport: 60d, Telecommunications satellite, telephone and facsimile machine. 150d, Passenger trains.

1988, May 6 **Litho.** *Perf. 12½*

1621 A542 60d multi *1.75* 75
1622 A542 150d multi *4.25* 1.75
a. Bklt. pane of 4, 2 each #1621-1622, perf. 14 vert. 7.00
b. Pair, 60d, 150d *6.00* 2.75

Single stamps also issued in strips of 5, perf. 14 vert.

1988 Olympics A543

Designs: 4d, Ancient Olympia and Temple of Zeus. 20d, Javelin thrower and and ancient Olympians in open-air gymnasium. 30d, Centenary emblem of the modern Games (cent. in 1996). 60d, Wrestlers, runners and other ancient athletes in training. 170d, Modern torch-bearer.

1988, May 6 *Perf. 14x12*

1623 A543 4d multi 15 15
1624 A543 20d multi 50 25
1625 A543 30d multi 75 35
1626 A543 60d multi 1.50 75
1627 A543 170d multi 4.25 2.25
a. Strip of 5, #1623-1627 7.25
b. Bklt. pane of 5, perf. 12½ vert. 7.25
Nos. 1623-1627 (5) 7.15 3.75

Each denomination also sold in bklts. containing 20 panes of 5 stamps, perf. 12½ vert.
See Korea No. B53.

Waterfalls A544

20th Pan-European Postal Trade Unions Congress A545

Designs: 10d, Catarractis village falls at the foot of the Tzoumerca Mountain Range. 60d, Edessa Waterfalls. 100d, Edessaios River cascades.

1988, July 4 **Litho.** *Perf. 12½x14*

1628 A544 10d multi 20 15
1629 A544 60d multi 1.25 50
1630 A544 100d multi 2.00 95

Each denomination also sold in bklts. containing 20 panes of 5 stamps, perf. 14 vert.

1988, July 4 *Perf. 13x12½*

1631 A545 60d multi 2.00 75

No. 1631 also sold in bklts. containing 20 panes of 5 stamps, perf. 14 vert.

A546

A547

Designs: 30d, Premier Eleutherios Venizelos (1864-1936), natl. flag and map. 70d, Lady liberty, flag and map.

1988, Oct. 7 **Litho.** *Perf. 12½x13*

1632 A546 30d shown 55 22
1633 A546 70d multi 1.40 65

Union of Crete with Greece and liberation of Epirus and Macedonia from Turkish rule, 75th annivs.

Each denomination also sold in bklts. containing 20 panes of 5 stamps, perf. 14 horiz.

1988, Oct. 7 *Perf. 13 Vert. or Horiz.*

Departmental Seats: 2d, Mytilene-Lesbos Harbor, painting by Theophilos. 3d, Alexandroupolis lighthouse. 4d, St. Nicholas bell tower, Kozane. 5d, Labor Center, Hermoupolis. 7d, Sparta Town Hall. 8d, Pegasus of Leukas. 10d, Castle of the Knights, Rhodes. 20d, The Acropolis, Athens. 25d, Kavalla aqueduct. 30d, Statue of Athanasios Diakos and castle, Lamia. 50d, Preveza cathedral bell tower and Venetian clock. 60d, Corfu promenade. 70d, Harbor view of Hagios Nicolaos. 100d, Poligiros public fountains. 200d, Church of the Apostle Paul, Corinth.

1634 A547 2d multi 15 15
1635 A547 3d multi 15 15
1636 A547 4d multi 15 15
1637 A547 5d multi 15 15
1638 A547 7d multi 15 15
1639 A547 8d multi 15 15
1640 A547 10d multi 15 15
1641 A547 20d multi 25 15
a. Bklt. pane, 4 each 3d, 5d, 10d, 20d 2.35
1642 A547 25d multi 35 16
1643 A547 30d multi 40 18
1644 A547 50d multi 60 28
1645 A547 60d multi 75 35
1646 A547 70d multi 90 40
1647 A547 100d multi 1.25 55
1648 A547 200d multi 2.50 1.25
Nos. 1634-1648 (15) 8.05
Set value 3.50

3d-5d, 10d-20d, 30d-50d vert. Nos. 1634-1648 issued in panes of 20, perf. 13 vert. or horiz. and in sheets, perf. 13.

Council of Europe, Rhodes, Dec. 2-3 A548

Christmas A549

Designs: 60d, Map and Castle of the Knights, Rhodes. 100d, Head of Helios, Rhodian 2nd-3rd cent. B.C. coin, and flags.

1988, Dec. 2 **Litho.** *Perf. 12½*

1649 A548 60d multi 1.00 45
1650 A548 100d multi 1.75 75

Nos. 1649-1650 also issued in bklt. panes of 5, perf. 14 horiz.

1988, Dec. 2 *Perf. 12½ on 3 Sides*

Paintings: 30d, *Adoration of the Magi*, by El Greco. 70d, *The Annunciation*, by Costas Parthenis, horiz.

1651 A549 30d multi 45 20
a. Bklt. pane of 10 4.50

Perf. 14

1652 A549 70d multi 1.05 50

No. 1651 issued in booklets. No. 1652 also issued in bklts. containing 20 panes of 5 stamps, perf. 14 vert.

A550

A551

Athens '96 emblem and: 30d, High jumper and ancient Olympia. 60d, Wrestlers and view of Delphi. 70d, Swimmers and The Acropolis, Athens. 170d, Sports complex.

Perf. 13½ Vert.

1989, Mar. 17 **Litho.**

1653 A550 30d multi 48 20
1654 A550 60d multi 95 42
1655 A550 70d multi 1.10 52
1656 A550 170d multi 2.75 1.40
a. Strip of 4, Nos. 1653-1656, perf. 14x13½ 5.50
b. Bklt. pane of 4, #1653-1656 5.50

1989, May 22 **Litho.** *Perf. 12½x14*

Europa: Children's toys.

1657 A551 60d Whistling bird *1.10* 48
1658 A551 170d Butterfly *3.25* 1.75
a. Bklt. pane, 2 each #1657-1658 6.60

Printed se-tenant in sheets of 16. Nos. 1657-1658 also issued separately in booklets containing 20 panes of 5 stamps, perf. 14 vert.

Anniversaries A552

1989, May 22 *Perf. 14x13½*

1659 A552 30d Flags 38 16
1660 A552 50d Flag, La Liberte 65 25
1661 A552 60d Flag, ballot box 75 30
1662 A552 70d Coin, emblem 90 38
1663 A552 200d Flag, "40" 2.50 1.25
Nos. 1659-1663 (5) 5.18 2.34

Six-nation Initiative for Peace and Disarmament, 5th anniv. (30d); French revolution, bicent. (50d); European Parliament Elections in Greece, 10th anniv. (60d); Interparliamentary Union, cent. (70d); and Council of Europe, 40th anniv. (200d).

Nos. 1659-1663 also issued in bklts. containing 20 panes of 5 stamps, perf. 13½ horiz.

A553

BALKANFILA XII, Sept. 30-Oct. 8, Salonica — A554

1989, Sept. 25 **Litho.** *Perf. 14x12½*

1664 A553 60d shown 70 28
1665 A553 70d Eye, magnifying glass 80 35

Souvenir Sheet

Perf. 14x13

1666 A554 200d shown 2.40 2.40

Wildflowers A555

1989, Dec. 8 **Litho.** *Perf. 14x12½*

1667 A555 8d Wild rose 15 15
1668 A555 10d Common myrtle 15 15
1669 A555 20d Field poppy 24 15
1670 A555 30d Anemone 35 15
1671 A555 60d Dandelion, chicory 72 28
1672 A555 70d Mallow 82 35
1673 A555 200d Thistle 2.35 1.10
Nos. 1667-1673 (7) 4.78
Set value 2.00

Ursus arctos — A556

Rare and endangered species.

1990, Mar. 16 **Litho.** *Perf. 14x12½*

1674 A556 40d shown 50 22
1675 A556 70d *Caretta caretta* 90 38
1676 A556 90d *Monachus monachus* 1.15 45
1677 A556 100d *Lynx lynx* 1.25 50

Europa 1990 — A557

Post offices: 70d, Old Central P.O. interior. 210d, Contemporary p.o. exterior.

Perf. 13½x12½

1990, May 11 **Litho.**

1678 A557 70d multicolored 85 35
1679 A557 210d multicolored 2.55 1.00
a. Bklt. pane, 2 each #1678-1679 6.80
b. Pair, #1678-1679 3.40 1.50

Natl. Reconcilation A558

Political Reformers A559

1990, May 11 *Perf. 12½x13½*

1680 A558 40d Flag, handshake 50 20
1681 A558 70d Dove, ribbon 85 35
1682 A558 100d Map, gift of flowers 1.20 48

1990, May 11

1683 A559 40d Gregoris Lambrakis (1912-63) 50 20
1684 A559 40d Pavlos Bakoyiannis (1935-89) 50 20

A560

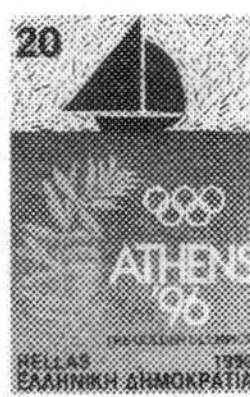

A561

Department Seats: 2d, Karditsa, the commercial-animal fair. 5d, Trikkala fort and clock tower. 8d, Veroia, street with traditional architecture. 10d, Missolonghi, Central Monument of Fallen Heroes in the Exodus. 15d, Chios, view. 20d, Tripolis, street with neoclassical architecture. 25d, Volos, view with town hall, woodcut by A. Tassou. 40d, Kalamata, neoclassical town hall. 50d, Pyrgos, central marketplace. 70d, Ioannina, view of lake and island. 80d, Rethymnon, sculpture at the port. 90d, Argostoli, view before earthquake. 100d, Nauplia, Bourtzi with Palamidi in the background. 200d, Patras, central lighthouse. 250d, Florina, street with neoclassical architecture. Nos. 1685, 1687, 1695, 1698 vert.

Perf. 13½ Horiz. or Vert.

1990, June 20 **Litho.**

1685	A560	2d	multicolored	15	15
1686	A560	5d	multicolored	15	15
1687	A560	8d	multicolored	15	15
1688	A560	10d	multicolored	15	15
1689	A560	15d	multicolored	18	15
1690	A560	20d	multicolored	24	15
1691	A560	25d	multicolored	30	15
1692	A560	40d	multicolored	48	20
1693	A560	50d	multicolored	60	24
1694	A560	70d	multicolored	85	32
1695	A560	80d	multicolored	95	38
1696	A560	90d	multicolored	1.10	45
1697	A560	100d	multicolored	1.20	48
1698	A560	200d	multicolored	2.40	95
1699	A560	250d	multicolored	3.00	1.20
			Nos. 1685-1699 (15)	11.90	5.27

Each denomination sold in booklets containing 20 panes of 5 stamps. Also issued perf. 13x12, 12x13.

See Nos. 1749-1760.

1990, July 13 ***Perf. 12½x13½***

1700	A561	20d	Sailing	24	15
1701	A561	50d	Wrestling	60	24
1702	A561	80d	Sprinting	95	38
1703	A561	100d	Basketball	1.20	48
1704	A561	250d	Soccer	3.00	1.20
a.			Strip of 5, #1700-1704	6.00	
			Nos. 1700-1704 (5)	5.99	2.45

1996 Summer Olympics. Athens, proposed site for centennial Summer Olympic Games. Exists perf. 13½ vert.

Heinrich Schliemann (1822-1890), Archaeologist — A562

1990, Oct. 11 **Litho.** ***Perf. 14x13½***

1705	A562	80d	multicolored	95	38

See Germany No. 1615.

Greco-Italian War, 50th Anniv. — A563

1990, Oct. 11 ***Perf. 12½***

1706	A563	50d	Woman knitting	60	20
1707	A563	80d	Virgin Mary, soldier	95	38
1708	A563	100d	Women volunteers	1.25	42

Souvenir Sheet

Stamp Day — A564

1990, Dec. 14 **Litho.** ***Perf. 14x13***

1709	A564	300d	multicolored	*7.50*	*7.50*

The Muses — A565

Designs: 50d, Calliope, Euterpe, Erato. 80d, Terpsichore, Polyhymnia, Melpomene. 250d, Thalia, Clio, Urania.

1991, Mar. 11 **Litho.** ***Perf. 12½***

1710	A565	50d	multicolored	60	20
1711	A565	80d	multicolored	95	38
1712	A565	250d	multicolored	3.00	1.20

Battle of Crete by Ioannis Anousakis — A566

Design: 300d, Map, flags of participating allied armies.

Perf. 12½x13½

1991, May 20 **Litho.**

1713	A566	60d	multicolored	75	25

Size: 32x24mm

Perf. 12½

1714	A566	300d	multicolored	3.60	1.20

Battle of Crete, 50th anniv.

Europa — A567

Designs: 80d, Icarus pushing modern satellite. 300d, Chariot of the Sun.

1991, May 20 ***Perf. 12½***

1715	A567	80d	multicolored	95	38
1716	A567	300d	multicolored	3.60	1.20
a.			Pair, #1715-1716	4.60	1.60
b.			Bklt. pane, 2 ea. #1715-1716	9.20	3.20

No. 1716a printed in continuous design.

A568

A569

1991, June 25 **Litho.** ***Perf. 13½x14***

1717	A568	10d	Swimming	15	15
1718	A568	60d	Basketball	75	25
1719	A568	90d	Gymnastics	1.10	38
1720	A568	130d	Weight lifting	1.60	52
1721	A568	300d	Hammer throw	3.60	1.20
			Nos. 1717-1721 (5)	7.20	2.50

1991 Mediterranean Games, Athens.

1991, Sept. 20 **Litho.** ***Perf. 13½x14***

1722	A569	100d	multicolored	1.05	35

Athenian Democracy, 2500th anniv.

Souvenir Sheet

Greek Presidency of CEPT — A570

Europe with Zeus metmorphosed into a bull, from Attic vase, c. 500 B.C.

1991, Sept. 20 ***Perf. 14x13***

1723	A570	300d	multicolored	3.10	1.05

A571

A572

Greek Membership in EEC, 10th anniv.: 50d, Pres. Konstantin Karamanlis signing Treaty of Greek entrance into EEC. 80d, Map showing EEC members, Pres. Karamanlis.

1991, Dec. 9 **Litho.** ***Perf. 13x14***

1724	A571	50d	multicolored	55	18
1725	A571	80d	multicolored	90	30

1991, Dec. 9 ***Perf. 12½x13½***

1726	A572	80d	Speed skaters	90	30
1727	A572	300d	Slalom skier	3.30	1.10
a.			Pair, #1726-1727	4.20	1.40

16th Winter Olympics, Albertville.

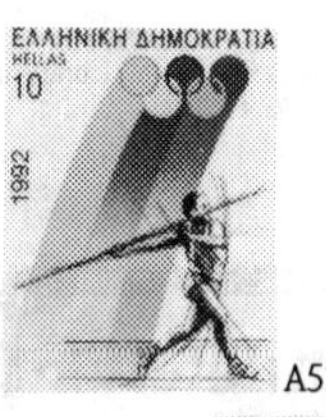

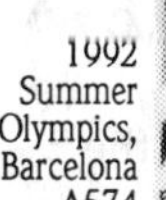

A573

1992 Summer Olympics, Barcelona A574

Perf. 12½, 14x13½ (90d, 340d)

1992, Apr. 3 **Litho.**

1728	A573	10d	Javelin	15	15
1729	A573	60d	Equestrian	62	30
1730	A574	90d	Runner	90	45
1731	A573	120d	Gymnastics	1.25	62
1732	A574	340d	Runners	3.50	1.75
			Nos. 1728-1732 (5)	6.42	3.27

Health — A575

Designs: 60d, Protection against AIDS. 80d, Diseases of digestive system. 90d, Dying flower symbolizing cancer. 120d, Hephaestus at his forge, 6th century BC. 280d, Alexandros S. Onassis Cardiosurgical Center.

1992, May 22 **Litho.** ***Perf. 12½***

1733	A575	60d	multicolored	62	30
1734	A575	80d	multicolored	85	42
1735	A575	90d	multicolored	90	45
1736	A575	120d	multicolored	1.25	62
1737	A575	280d	multicolored	2.90	1.45
			Nos. 1733-1737 (5)	6.52	3.24

No. 1734, 1st United European Gastroenterology Week. No. 1736, European Year of Social Security, Hygiene and Health in the Workplace.

Discovery of America, 500th Anniv. — A576

Europa: 340d, Map of 15th century Chios, Columbus.

1992, May 22 ***Perf. 13½x12½***

1738	A576	90d	shown	90	45
a.			Perf. 12½ vert.	90	45
1739	A576	340d	multicolored	3.50	1.75
a.			Pair, #1738-1739	4.40	2.20
b.			Perf. 12½ vert.	3.50	1.75
c.			Bklt. pane, 2 each #1738a, 1739b	8.80	

Souvenir Sheet

European Conference on Transportion — A577

1992, June 8 ***Perf. 14x13***

1740	A577	300d	multicolored	3.10	3.10

Macedonian Treasures — A578

Designs: 10d, Head of Hercules wearing lion skin, Vergina treasures. 20d, Bust of Aristotle, map of Macedonia, horiz. 60d, Alexander the Great at Battle of Issus, horiz. 80d, Archaeologist Manolis Andronikos, tomb of King Philip II. 90d, Deer hunt mosaic, Pella. 120d, Macedonian tetradrachm. 340d, St. Paul, 4th century church near Philippi.

1992, July 17 **Litho.** ***Perf. 12½***

1741	A578	10d	multicolored	15	15
1742	A578	20d	multicolored	15	15
1743	A578	60d	multicolored	28	15
1744	A578	80d	multicolored	36	18
1745	A578	90d	multicolored	40	20
1746	A578	120d	multicolored	55	28
1747	A578	340d	multicolored	1.55	78
			Nos. 1741-1747 (7)	3.44	1.89

European Unification A579

1992, Oct. 12 Litho. *Perf. 14x13*

1748 A579 90d multicolored 90 45

Departmental Seat Type of 1990

Designs: 10d, Piraeus, the old clock. 20d, Amphissa, view of city with citadel. 30d, Samos (Vathy), the Heraion. 40d, Canea, city in 1800s. 50d, Zakinthos (Zante), view in 1800s. 60d, Karpenision, Velouchi and city. 70d, Kilkis, the cave, vert. 80d, Xanthe, door of Town Hall, vert. 90d, Salonika, Macedonian Struggle Museum. 120d, Komotine, Tsanakleous School. 340d, Drama, spring. 400d, Larissa, Pinios bridge.

1992, Oct. 12 *Perf. 10 Horiz. or Vert.*

1749 A560	10d	multicolored	15	15
1750 A560	20d	multicolored	20	15
1751 A560	30d	multicolored	30	15
1752 A560	40d	multicolored	40	20
1753 A560	50d	multicolored	50	25
1754 A560	60d	multicolored	60	30
1755 A560	70d	multicolored	70	35
1756 A560	80d	multicolored	80	40
1757 A560	90d	multicolored	90	45
1758 A560	120d	multicolored	1.25	65
1759 A560	340d	multicolored	3.50	1.75
1760 A560	400d	multicolored	4.00	2.00
		Nos. 1749-1760 (12)	13.30	6.80

Each denomination sold in booklets containing 20 panes of 5 stamps. Also issued perf. 13 from sheets.

City of Rhodes, 2400th Anniv. — A580

Designs: 60d, Headstone, 4th cent. B.C. 90d, Bathing Aphrodite, 1st cent. B.C. 120d, St. Irene, Church of St. Catherine, 14th cent. 250d, St. Paul's Gate, 15th cent.

1993, Feb. 26 Litho. *Perf. 13x14*

1761 A580	60d	multicolored	55	28
1762 A580	90d	multicolored	82	40
1763 A580	120d	multicolored	1.10	55
1764 A580	250d	multicolored	2.30	1.15

Rememberences of Greek Wars — A581

Designs: 10d, Death of Georgakis Olympios, 1821. 30d, Theodore Kolokotronis in battle, 1821. 60d, Pavlos Melas. 90d, Glory lays wreath over graves of dead from Balkan Wars. 120d, Greek soldiers at Battle of El Alamein, 1942, horiz. 150d, Greek troops in Aegean Islands, 1942, horiz. 200d, Kalavryta Massacre Memorial.

Perf. 13x14, 14x13

1993, May 25 Litho.

1765 A581	10d	multicolored	15	15
1766 A581	30d	multicolored	28	15
1767 A581	60d	multicolored	55	28
1768 A581	90d	multicolored	85	42
1769 A581	120d	multicolored	1.10	55
1770 A581	150d	multicolored	1.35	68
1771 A581	200d	multicolored	1.80	90
		Nos. 1765-1771 (7)	6.08	3.13

The Benefits of Transportation, by K. Parthenis — A582

Europa: 90d, Tree, three people, ships. 350d, Woman and children, town.

1993, May 25 *Perf. 13x14*

1772 A582 90d multicolored		85	42
a.	Perf. 13½ vert.	85	42
1773 A582 350d multicolored		3.20	1.60
a.	Pair, #1772-1773	4.00	2.00
b.	Perf. 13½ vert.	3.20	1.60
c.	Bklt. pane, 2 each #1772a, 1773b	8.10	

Nos. 1772-1773 are a continuous design.

Buildings in Athens A583

Designs: 30d, Concert Hall. 60d, Numismatic Museum (Iliou Melathron). 90d, Natl. Library of Greece. 200d, Opthalmology Hospital.

1993, Oct. 4 Litho. *Perf. 14*

1774 A583	30d	multicolored	25	15
1775 A583	60d	multicolored	50	25
1776 A583	90d	multicolored	75	38
1777 A583	200d	multicolored	1.75	85

Souvenir Sheet

Greek Presidency of the European Community Council of Ministers — A584

1993, Dec. 20 Litho. *Perf. 14*

1778 A584 400d multicolored 3.25 1.65

Chariot of Selene Driven by Hermes — A585

1994, Mar. 7 Litho. *Perf. 13x13½*

1779 A585 200d multicolored 1.65 80

2nd Pan-European Transportation Conference.

Year Sets

Year set values are determined from price lists offering complete sets for each year. Not all dealers offer these sets. Values may be lower or higher than the total value of the individual stamps. Contents of the sets being offered may differ (complete booklets by some, singles from the booklets by others).

1959	#632-665	46.50
1960	#666-689	20.00
1961	#690-727	45.00
1962	#728-742	10.90
1963	#743-777	24.00
1964	#778-812	18.00
1965	#813-839	6.50
1966	#840-878	9.00
1967	#879-908	7.50
1968	#909-938	10.00
1969	#939-965	10.00
1970	#966-1004	25.00
1971	#1005-1030	10.00
1972	#1031-1064	13.00
1973	#1065-1106	11.00
1974	#1107-1135	4.75
1975	#1136-1169	6.00
1976	#1170-1198	7.00
1977	#1199-1242	5.75
1978	#1243-1287	6.50
1979	#1288-1342	9.00
1980	#1343-1381	7.50
1981	#1382-1415	8.50
1982	#1416-1445	16.00
1983	#1446-1486	18.00
1984	#1487-1512	22.50
1985	#1513-1545	18.00
1986	#1546-1580	35.00
1987	#1581-1615	26.00
1988	#1616-1652	54.00
1989	#1653-1673	25.00
1990	#1674-1709	40.00
1991	#1710-1727	36.00
1992	#1728-1760	40.00

SEMI-POSTAL STAMPS

Catalogue values for unused stamps in this section are for Never Hinged items.

Nos. 440-444 Surcharged in Blue

ΒΟΜΒΑΡΔΙΣΜΟΣ
ΠΕΙΡΑΙΩΣ
11-1-1944
ΔΡ. 100.000

1944 Wmk. 252 *Perf. 12½*

B1	A106	100,000d on 15d	90	60
B2	A107	100,000d on 25d	90	60
B3	A108	100,000d on 50d	90	60
B4	A109	100,000d on 75d	90	60
B5	A110	100,000d on 100d	90	60
		Nos. B1-B5,CB1-CB5 (10)	7.75	6.00

The proceeds aided victims of the Piraeus bombing, Jan. 11, 1944. The exceptionally high face value discouraged the use of these stamps.

Nos. 437-441 Surcharged in Blue

1944, July 20

50,000d + 450,000d

B11	A103	on 2d	70	50
B12	A104	on 5d	70	50
B13	A105	on 10d	70	50
B14	A106	on 15d	70	50
a.		Pair, one without surcharge	50.00	
B15	A107	on 25d	70	50
		Nos. B11-B15,CB6-CB10 (10)	7.75	5.00

The surtax aided children's camps.

AIR POST STAMPS

Italy-Greece-Turkey-Rhodes Service

Flying Boat off Phaleron Bay AP1

Flying Boat over Acropolis AP2

Flying Boat over Map of Southern Europe AP3

Flying Boat Seen through Colonnade — AP4

Perf. 11½

1926, Oct. 20 Unwmk. Litho.

C1	AP1	2d multi	40	25
a.		Horiz. pair, imperf. vert.	450.00	
C2	AP2	3d multi	4.50	3.50
C3	AP3	5d multi	40	50
C4	AP4	10d multi	4.50	3.75
		Set, never hinged	32.50	

Graf Zeppelin Issue

Zeppelin over Acropolis — AP5

1933, May 2 *Perf. 13½x12½*

C5	AP5	30d rose red	7.00	7.00
C6	AP5	100d deep blue	35.00	35.00
C7	AP5	120d dark brown	35.00	35.00
		Set, never hinged	210.00	

Propeller and Pilot's Head — AP6

Temple of Apollo, Corinth AP7

Plane over Hermoupolis, Syros — AP8

Allegory of Flight
AP9 AP12

Map of Italy-Greece-Turkey-Rhodes Airmail Route — AP10

Head of Hermes and Airplane — AP11

1933, Oct. 10 **Engr.** *Perf. 12*

C8	AP6	50 l grn & org	16	15
C9	AP7	1d bl & brn org	25	22
C10	AP8	3d dk vio & org brn	38	42
C11	AP9	5d brn org & dk bl	3.75	3.25
C12	AP10	10d dp red & blk	1.25	1.10
C13	AP11	20d blk & grn	3.75	2.50
C14	AP12	50d dp brn & dp bl	37.50	42.50
		Nos. C8-C14 (7)	47.04	50.14
		Set, never hinged	125.00	

By error the 1d stamp is inscribed in the plural "Draxmai" instead of the singular "Draxmh." This stamp exists bisected, used as a 50 lepta denomination.

All values of this set exist imperforate but were not regularly issued.

For General Air Post Service

Airplane over Map of Greece — AP13

Airplane over Map of Icarian Sea — AP14

Airplane over Acropolis AP15

Perf. 13x13½, 13x12½, 13½x13, 12½x13

1933, Nov. 2

C15	AP13	50 l green	16	25
C16	AP13	1d red brn	28	48
C17	AP14	2d lt vio	52	75
C18	AP15	5d ultra	2.75	2.75
a.		Imperf., pair	500.00	500.00
b.		Horiz. pair, imperf. vert.	500.00	
C19	AP14	10d car rose	3.75	4.50
C20	AP13	25d dark blue	27.50	18.00
C21	AP15	50d dark brn	27.50	*37.50*
a.		Imperf., pair	600.00	600.00
		Nos. C15-C21 (7)	62.46	64.23
		Set, never hinged	150.00	

Helios Driving the Sun Chariot AP16

Iris — AP17

Daedalus Preparing Icarus for Flying — AP18

Pallas Athene Holding Pegasus — AP19

Hermes AP20

Zeus Carrying off Ganymede AP21

Triptolemos, King of Eleusis — AP22

Bellerophon and Pegasus — AP23

Phrixos and Helle on the Ram Flying over the Hellespont AP24

Perf. 13x12½, 12½x13

1935, Nov. 10 **Engr.**

Grayish Paper

Size: 34x23½mm, 23½x34mm

C22	AP16	1d dp red	35	35
C23	AP17	2d dl bl	80	50
C24	AP18	5d dk vio	6.25	1.10
C25	AP19	7d bl vio	8.75	2.50
C26	AP20	10d bis brn	2.00	2.00
C27	AP21	25d rose	3.25	*3.25*
C28	AP22	30d dk grn	40	40
C29	AP23	50d violet	2.75	*3.25*
C30	AP24	100d brown	60	*90*
		Nos. C22-C30 (9)	25.15	*14.25*
		Set, never hinged	55.00	

Re-engraved

1937-39

White Paper

Size: 34¼x24mm, 24x34¼mm

C31	AP16	1d red	20	20
C32	AP17	2d gray blue	20	20
C33	AP18	5d violet	20	20
C34	AP19	7d dp ultra	20	20
C35	AP20	10d brn org ('39)	1.75	1.40
		Nos. C31-C35 (5)	2.55	2.20
		Set, never hinged	3.75	

No. C35, Mar. 1, 1939, others Aug. 3, 1937.

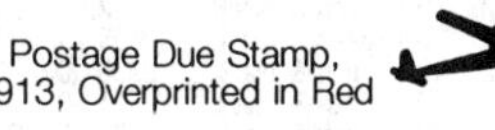
Postage Due Stamp, 1913, Overprinted in Red

Serrate Roulette 13½

1938, Aug. 8 **Litho.** **Unwmk.**

C36	D3	50 l vio brn	15	15
		Never hinged	16	
a.		"O" for "P" in word at foot	27.50	27.50

Same Overprint on No. J79 in Red

1939, June 26 *Perf. 13½x12½*

C37	D3	50 l dark brown	15	15
		Never hinged	16	

Meteora Monasteries, near Trikkala — AP25

Designs: 4d, Simon Peter Monastery. 6d, View of Santorin. 8d, Church of Pantanassa. 16d, Santorin view. 32d, Ponticonissi, Corfu. 45d, Acropolis, Athens. 55d, Erechtheum. 65d, Temple of Nike Apteros. 100d, Temple of the Olympian Zeus, Athens.

Wmk. Crowns (252)

1940, Aug. 3 **Litho.** *Perf. 12½*

C38	AP25	2d red org & blk	2.00	1.75
C39	AP25	4d dk grn & blk	10.00	10.50
C40	AP25	6d lake & blk	10.00	10.50
C41	AP25	8d dk bl & blk	16.00	16.00
C42	AP25	16d rose vio & blk	16.00	16.00
C43	AP25	32d red org & blk	20.00	21.00
C44	AP25	45d dk grn & blk	22.50	21.00
C45	AP25	55d lake & blk	27.50	24.00
C46	AP25	65d dk bl & blk	27.50	24.00
C47	AP25	100d rose vio & blk	27.50	24.00
		Nos. C38-C47 (10)	179.00	168.75
		Set, never hinged	375.00	

4th anniv. of the founding of the Greek Youth Organization. The stamps were good for postal duty on Aug. 3-5, 1940, only. They remained on sale until Feb. 3, 1941.

For overprints see Nos. N229-N238.

Catalogue values for unused stamps in this section, from this point to the end of the section, are for Never Hinged items.

Postage Due Stamps Nos. J81 and J75 Surcharged in Red

1941-42 **Unwmk.** *Perf. 13x12½*

C48	D3	1d on 2d lt red	15	15
a.		Inverted surcharge	20.00	

Serrate Roulette 13½

C49	D3	1d on 2d ver ('42)	15	15
a.		Inverted surcharge	20.00	
b.		Double surcharge	20.00	
		Set value	24	24

Nos. J83, J84, J86, J87 Overprinted in Red

1941-42 *Perf. 13, 12½x13*

C50	D3	5d gray bl ('42)	20	20
a.		Inverted overprint	20.00	
b.		Double overprint	20.00	
c.		Pair, one without ovpt.	20.00	
d.		Surcharge on back	20.00	
e.		On No. J78 ('42)	120.00	*150.00*
C51	D3	10d gray grn	30	30
a.		Inverted overprint	15.00	
b.		Vert. pair, imperf. btwn.	250.00	
C52	D3	25d lt red	75	75
a.		Inverted overprint	30.00	
C53	D3	50d orange	1.40	1.40

Boreas, North Wind — AP35

Winds: 5d, Notus, South. 10d, Apeliotes, East. 20d, Lips, Southwest. 25d, Zephyrus, West. 50d, Kaikias, Northeast.

Perf. 12½

1942, Aug. 15 **Wmk. 252** **Litho.**

C55	AP35	2d emerald	15	15
C56	AP35	5d red org	15	15
a.		Imperf., pair	175.00	
b.		Double impression	50.00	25.00
C57	AP35	10d red brown	15	15
C58	AP35	20d brt blue	15	15
C59	AP35	25d dk red org	15	15
C60	AP35	50d gray blk	1.65	1.65
a.		Double impression	140.00	
		Nos. C55-C60 (6)	2.40	2.40

1943, Sept. 15

Winds: 10d, Apeliotes, East. 25d, Zephyrus, West. 50d, Kaikias, Northeast. 100d, Boreas, North. 200d, Eurus, Southeast. 400d, Skiron, Northwest.

C61	AP35	10d rose red	15	15
C62	AP35	25d Prus grn	15	15
C63	AP35	50d vio bl	15	15
C64	AP35	100d slate blk	15	15
C65	AP35	200d claret	15	15
C66	AP35	400d steel blue	20	20
		Set value	75	75

Double impressions exist of 10d and 400d. Value, each $30.

For surcharges see Nos. 472, 473, CB1-CB10.

Imperf., Pairs

C61a	AP35	10d	85.00
C62a	AP35	25d	75.00
C63a	AP35	50d	75.00
C64a	AP35	100d	80.00
C65a	AP35	200d	120.00
C66a	AP35	400d	90.00

Priest Blessing Troops on Summit of Mt. Grammos
AP36

Torchbearer
AP37

Designs: 1700d, Victory above Mt. Vitsi. 2700d, Battle Scene. 7000d, Victory leading infantry.

1952, Aug. 29 Engr. ***Perf. 12x13½***

C67 AP36 1000d deep blue 85 25
C68 AP36 1700d dp bl grn 3.00 1.10
C69 AP36 2700d brown 8.25 3.75
C70 AP36 7000d olive green 25.00 10.00

Greek army's struggle against communism.

1954, May 15 ***Perf. 13***

Designs: 2400dr, Coin of Amphictyonic League. 4000dr, Pallas Athene.

C71 AP37 1200d dp org 7.50 20
C72 AP37 2400d dk green 30.00 6.25
C73 AP37 4000d dp ultra 67.50 2.50

5th anniv. of the signing of the North Atlantic Treaty.

Piraeus
AP38

Harbors: 15d, Salonika. 20d, Patras. 25d, Hermoupolis (Syra). 30d, Volos. 50d, Cavalla. 100d, Herakleion (Candia).

Perf. 13½x13

1958, July 1 Wmk. 252 Litho.

C74 AP38 10d multi 6.00 18
C75 AP38 15d multi 1.00 32
C76 AP38 20d multi 5.75 25
C77 AP38 25d multi 1.00 50
C78 AP38 30d multi 1.00 32
C79 AP38 50d multi 2.50 32
C80 AP38 100d multi 17.00 2.50
Nos. C74-C80 (7) 34.25 4.39

AIR POST SEMI-POSTAL STAMPS

Catalogue values for unused stamps in this section are for Never Hinged items.

#C61-C65 Surcharged in Blue like #B1-B5

1944, June Wmk. 252 ***Perf. 12½***

CB1 AP35 100,000d on 10d 65 60
CB2 AP35 100,000d on 25d 65 60
CB3 AP35 100,000d on 50d 65 60
a. Inverted overprint 50.00
CB4 AP35 100,000d on 100d 65 60
CB5 AP35 100,000d on 200d 65 60
Nos. CB1-CB5 (5) 3.25 3.00

The exceptionally high face value discouraged the use of these stamps.

The proceeds aided victims of the Piraeus bombing, January 11, 1944.

#C61-C65 Surcharged in Blue like #B11-B15

1944, July

50,000d + 450,000d

CB6 AP35 on 10d 85 50
CB7 AP35 on 25d 85 50
CB8 AP35 on 50d 85 50
CB9 AP35 on 100d 85 50
CB10 AP35 on 200d 85 50
Nos. CB6-CB10 (5) 4.25 2.50

The surtax aided children's camps. Surcharge exists inverted or double. Value, each $55.

POSTAGE DUE STAMPS

D1

D2

Perf. 9, 9½, and 10, 10½ and Compound

1875 Litho. Unwmk.

J1 D1 1 l green & black 2.25 2.00
J2 D1 2 l green & black 2.25 2.00
J3 D1 5 l green & black 2.25 2.00
J4 D1 10 l green & black 8.50 6.00
J5 D1 20 l green & black 45.00 27.50
J6 D1 40 l green & black 10.00 5.75
J7 D1 60 l green & black 20.00 17.50
J8 D1 70 l green & black 11.00 8.50
J9 D1 80 l green & black 11.00 8.50
J10 D1 90 l green & black 11.00 8.50
J11 D1 1d green & black 15.00 8.00
J12 D1 2d green & black 27.50 14.00

Imperforate and part perforated, double and inverted center varieties of Nos. J1-J12 are believed to be printers' waste.

Perf. 12, 13 and 10½x13

J13 D1 1 l green & black 2.25 80
J14 D1 2 l green & black 2.25 2.00
J15 D1 5 l green & black 14.00 8.50
J16 D1 10 l green & black 6.00 5.75
J17 D1 20 l green & black 40.00 22.50
J18 D1 40 l green & black 8.50 2.75
J19 D1 60 l green & black 17.50 14.00
J20 D1 70 l green & black 8.50 7.00
J21 D1 80 l green & black 8.50 6.00
J22 D1 90 l green & black 18.00 14.00
J23 D1 1d green & black 14.00 14.00
J24 D1 2d green & black 27.50 14.00

Redrawn

"Lepton" or "Lepta" in Larger Greek Letters

1876 ***Perf. 9, 9½, and 10, 10½***

J25 D2 1 l green & black 3.00 2.75
J26 D2 2 l dk grn & blk 3.00 2.75
J27 D2 5 l dk grn & blk 375.00 250.00
J28 D2 10 l green & black 2.50 1.75
J29 D2 20 l green & black 5.25 3.25
J30 D2 40 l green & black 25.00 10.50
J31 D2 60 l green & black 11.00 7.25
J32 D2 70 l green & black 27.50 20.00
J33 D2 80 l green & black 22.50 12.50
J34 D2 90 l green & black 35.50 25.00
J35 D2 100 l green & black 27.50 12.50
J36 D2 200 l green & black 22.50 12.50

Perf. 11½ to 13

J37 D2 1 l yel grn & blk 1.75 70
J38 D2 2 l yel grn & blk 1.75 70
J39 D2 5 l yel grn & blk 3.50 90
J40 D2 10 l yel grn & blk 2.00 90
a. Perf. 10-10½x11½-13 3.00
J41 D2 20 l yel grn & blk 2.00 90
J42 D2 40 l yel grn & blk 30.00 16.00
J43 D2 60 l yel grn & blk 9.00 6.25
J47 D2 100 l yel grn & blk 11.00 7.25
J48 D2 200 l yel grn & blk 15.00 7.25

Footnote below #J12 applies also to #J25-J48.

D3

1902 Engr. Wmk. 129 ***Perf. 13½***

J49 D3 1 l chocolate 20 20
J50 D3 2 l gray 20 20
J51 D3 3 l orange 20 20
J52 D3 5 l yel grn 20 20
J53 D3 10 l scarlet 25 20
J54 D3 20 l lilac 30 20
J55 D3 25 l ultra 4.00 1.75
J56 D3 30 l dp vio 30 30
J57 D3 40 l dk brn 35 25
J58 D3 50 l red brn 35 20
J59 D3 1d black 90 60

Litho.

J60 D3 2d bronze 2.25 60
J61 D3 3d silver 2.00 2.00
J62 D3 5d gold 6.00 5.00
Nos. J49-J62 (14) 17.50 11.90

See Nos. J63-J88, J90-J93. For overprints and surcharges see Nos. 383-385, J89, RA56, RA58-RA59, NJ1-NJ31.

Imperf., Pairs

J50a D3 2 l 22.50
J51a D3 3 l 22.50
J52a D3 5 l 22.50
J55a D3 25 l 22.50
J56a D3 30 l 35.00
J58a D3 50 l 35.00
J59a D3 1d 40.00

Serrate Roulette 13½

1913-26 Unwmk.

J63 D3 1 l green 15 15
J64 D3 2 l carmine 15 15
J65 D3 3 l vermilion 15 15
J66 D3 5 l green 15 15
a. Imperf., pair 40.00
b. Double impression 40.00
c. "o" for "p" in lowest word 3.00 3.00
J67 D3 10 l carmine 15 15
J68 D3 20 l slate 20 15
J69 D3 25 l ultra 15 15
J70 D3 30 l carmine 15 15
J71 D3 40 l indigo 20 15
J72 D3 50 l vio brn 30 25
a. "o" for "p" in lowest word 25.00 20.00
J73 D3 80 l lil brn ('24) 40 20
J74 D3 1d blue 2.00 60
a. 1d ultramarine 9.00 3.50
J75 D3 2d vermilion 1.75 35
J76 D3 3d carmine 5.25 3.25
J77 D3 5d ultra 17.50 3.50
J78 D3 5d gray bl ('26) 3.50 90
Nos. J63-J78 (16) 32.15 10.40

In 1922-23 and 1941-42 some postage due stamps were used for ordinary postage.

In 1916 Nos. J52, and J63 to J75 were surcharged for the Mount Athos District (see note after No. N166) but were never issued there. By error some of them were put in use as ordinary postage due stamps in Dec., 1924. In 1932 the balance of them was burned.

Type of 1902 Issue

Perf. 13, 13½x12½, 13½x13

1930 Litho.

J79 D3 50 l dk brn 30 30
J80 D3 1d lt bl 30 30
J81 D3 2d lt red 30 30
J82 D3 3d rose red 35.00 22.50
J83 D3 5d gray blue 30 30
J84 D3 10d gray grn 30 30
J85 D3 15d red brn 30 30
J86 D3 25d light red 65 65
Nos. J79-J86 (8) 37.45 24.95

Type of 1902 Issue

1935 Engr. ***Perf. 12½x13***

J87 D3 50d orange 30 30
J88 D3 100d slate green 30 30

No. J70 Surcharged with New Value in Black

1942

J89 D3 50 (l) on 30 l carmine 90 90

Type of 1902

1943 Wmk. 252 Litho. ***Perf. 12½***

J90 D3 10d red orange 15 15
J91 D3 25d ultramarine 15 15
J92 D3 100d black brown 15 15
J93 D3 200d violet 15 15
Set value 40 40

POSTAL TAX STAMPS

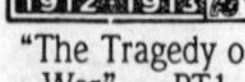

"The Tragedy of War" — PT1

Red Cross, Nurses, Wounded and Bearers — PT1a

Serrate Roulette 13½

1914 Litho. Unwmk.

RA1 PT1 2 l carmine 15 15
a. 2 l red 15 15
b. Imperf., pair 50.00
RA2 PT1 5 l blue 25 20
a. Imperf., pair
Set value 33 28

1915 ***Serrate Roulette 13***

RA2B PT1a (5 l) dk bl & red 10.00 1.50

The tax was for the Red Cross.

Women's Patriotic League Badge — PT1b

1915, Nov. ***Perf. 11½***

RA2C PT1b (5 l) dk bl & car 50 50
d. Horiz. pair, imperf. btwn. 50.00

The tax was for the Greek Women's Patriotic League.

Nos. 165, 167, 170, 172-175 Surcharged in Black or Brown:

Κ. Π. **λεπτοῦ** **1** — a

Κ. Π. **λεπτοῦ** **1** — b

In type "b" the letters, especially those in the first line, are thinner than in type "a," making them appear taller.

Perf. 11½, 12½, 13½ and Compound

1917 Engr. Wmk. 129

RA3 A11(a) 1 l on 1 l 2.00 1.75
a. Double surcharge 5.00
RA4 A11(a) 1 l on 1 l (Br) 20.00 20.00
RA5 A11(a) 1 l on 3 l 30 30
RA6 A11(b) 1 l on 3 l 30 30
a. Triple surcharge 5.00
b. Dbl. surch., one invtd. 5.00
c. "K.M." for "K.Π." 5.00 5.00
RA7 A11(a) 5 l on 1 l 2.00 2.00
a. Double surcharge 5.00
b. Dbl. surch., one invtd. 5.00
c. Inverted surcharge 5.00
RA8 A11(a) 5 l on 20 l 65 65
a. Double surcharge 5.00
b. Dbl. surch., one invtd. 5.00
RA9 A11(b) 5 l on 40 l 65 65
a. Imperf.
RA10 A11(b) 5 l on 50 l 65 65
a. Double surcharge 5.00
b. Dbl. surch., one invtd. 5.00
RA11 A13(b) 5 l on 1d 1.25 1.25
a. Imperf.
b. Inverted surcharge 10.00
RA12 A11(a) 10 l on 30 l 90 90
a. Imperf.
b. Double surcharge 6.00
RA13 A11(a) 10 l on 30 l 90 90
a. Double surcharge 6.00
Nos. RA3-RA13 (11) 29.60 29.35

Same Surcharge On Occupation Stamps of 1912

Serrate Roulette 13½

1917 Litho. Unwmk.

RA14 O2 (b) 5 l on 25 l pale bl 45 45
a. Triple surch., one invtd. 6.00
b. Double surcharge 6.00
RA15 O2 (b) 5 l on 40 l indigo 45 45
a. Double surch., one invtd. 6.00
b. Double surcharge 6.00
RA16 O1 (b) 5 l on 50 l dk bl 45 45
a. Double surcharge 10.00
b. Inverted surcharge 10.00

There are many wrong font, omitted and misplaced letters and punctuation marks and similar varieties in the surcharges on Nos. RA3 to RA16.

Revenue Stamps Surcharged in Brown

"Victory" — R1

Κ. Π. **λεπτοῦ** **1**

1917

RA17 R1 1 l on 10 l blue 60 60
RA18 R1 1 l on 80 l blue 60 60
RA19 R1 5 l on 10 l blue 12.00 8.00
RA20 R1 5 l on 60 l blue 2.50 1.75
a. Perf. vert. through middle 4.25 2.50
RA21 R1 5 l on 80 l blue 1.75 1.75
a. Perf. vert. through middle 7.50 4.00
b. Inverted surcharge
RA22 R1 10 l on 70 l blue 12.50 4.00
a. Perf. vert. through middle 4.25 2.00
RA23 R1 10 l on 90 l blue 4.75 2.00
a. Perf. vert. through middle 12.50 11.00

RA24 R1 20 l on 20 l blue 650.00 475.00
RA25 R1 20 l on 30 l blue 3.50 2.75
RA26 R1 20 l on 40 l blue 9.50 6.75
RA27 R1 20 l on 50 l blue 4.50 3.00
RA28 R1 20 l on 60 l blue 250.00 150.00
RA29 R1 20 l on 80 l blue 32.50 24.00
RA30 R1 20 l on 90 l blue 3.00 1.50
a. Inverted surcharge 45.00
Nos. RA17-RA30 (14) 987.70 681.70

No. RA19 is known only with vertical perforation through the middle.
Counterfeits exist of Nos. RA17-RA43, used.

Surcharged in Brown or Black — Κ. Π. 5 λεπτ. 5

RA31 R1 1 l on 50 l vio (Bk) 95 30
RA32 R1 5 l on 10 l bl (Br) 95 30
a. Inverted surcharge 30.00
b. Left "5" invert. 30.00
RA33 R1 5 l on 10 l vio (Br) 95 30
RA34 R1 10 l on 50 l vio (Br) 1.90 90
RA35 R1 10 l on 50 l vio (Bk) 22.50 7.00
RA36 R1 20 l on 2d bl (Bk) 5.00 3.00
a. Surcharged "20 lept. 30" 30.00 25.00
b. Horiz. pair, imperf. btwn.
Nos. RA31-RA36 (6) 32.25 11.80

The "t," fourth Greek letter of the denomination in the surcharge ("Lept."), is normally omitted on Nos. RA31, RA34-RA36.

Corfu Issue

Surcharged in Black — Κ.Π. 1 ΛΕΠΤΟΝ 1

1917
RA37 R1 1 l on 10 l blue 95 70
RA38 R1 5 l on 50 l blue 32.50 22.50
RA39 R1 10 l on 50 l blue 280.00 200.00
RA40 R1 20 l on 50 l blue 450.00 380.00

Surcharged in Black — Κ.Π. 20 ΛΕΠΤΑ 20

RA41 R1 10 l on 50 l blue 5.50 2.25
RA42 R1 20 l on 50 l blue 13.00 5.25
RA43 R1 30 l on 50 l blue 7.75 6.00

Surcharged in Black — Κ. Π. 5 Λεπτὰ 5

RA44 R1 5 l on 10 l vio & red 5.25 2.00
a. "K" with serifs 7.50 3.50

Counterfeits exist of Nos. RA17-RA44.
Similar stamps with denominations higher than 30 lepta were for revenue use.

Wounded Soldier — PT2

1918 *Serrate Roulette 13½, 11½*
RA45 PT2 5 l bl, yel & red 5.25 2.50

Overprinted — Π.Ι.Π.

RA46 PT2 5 l bl, yel & red 6.00 2.50

The letters are the initials of Greek words equivalent to "Patriotic Relief Institution." The proceeds were given to the Patriotic League, for the aid of disabled soldiers.
Counterfeits exist of Nos. RA45-RA46.

PT3

Surcharge in Red
1922 **Litho.** *Perf. 11½*
Dark Blue & Red
RA46A PT3 5 l on 10 l *250.00* 2.50
RA46B PT3 5 l on 20 l 37.50 19.00
RA46C PT3 5 l on 50 l 190.00 60.00
RA46D PT3 5 l on 1d 3.25 *30.00*

Counterfeit surcharges exist. Copies of Nos. RA46A-RA46C without surcharge, each 50 cents.

Red Cross Help to Soldier and Family
PT3a

St. Demetrius
PT4

1924 *Perf. 11½, 13½ x 12½*
RA47 PT3a 10 l bl, buff & red 30 15
a. Imperf., pair 24.00
b. Horiz. pair, imperf. btwn. 24.00
c. Double impression of cross 24.00

Proceeds were given to the Red Cross.

1934 *Perf. 11½*
RA48 PT4 20 l brown 15 15
a. Horizontal pair, imperf. between 10.00
b. Vertical pair, imperf. between 15.00
c. Imperf., pair 20.00

No. RA48 was obligatory as a tax on all interior mail, including air post, mailed from Salonika.
For surcharge see No. RA69.

"Health"
PT5 PT6

1934, Dec. 28 *Perf. 13, 13x13½*
RA49 PT5 10 l bl grn, org & buff 15 15
a. Vert. pair, imperf. horiz.
RA50 PT5 20 l ultra, org & buff 45 20
RA51 PT5 50 l grn, org & buff 1.25 40

For surcharge see No. RA67.

1935
RA52 PT6 10 l yel grn, org & buff 15 15
RA53 PT6 20 l ultra, org & buff 15 15
RA54 PT6 50 l grn, org & buff 50 35

The use of #RA49-RA54 was obligatory on all mail during 4 weeks each year including Christmas, the New Year and Easter, and on parcel post packages at all times. The benefit of the tubercular clerks and officials of the Post, Telephone and Telegraph Service.
See No. RA64. For surcharge see No. RA68.

No. 364 Overprinted in Red

ΠΡΟΝΟΙΑ

1937, Jan. 20 **Engr.** *Perf. 13x12½*
RA55 A36 50 l violet 1.25 15
a. Inverted overprint 75 15

No. RA55a first appeared as an error, then was issued deliberately in quantity to avoid speculation.

Same Overprint in Blue on No. J67
Litho.
Serrate Roulette 13½
RA56 D3 10 l carmine 15 15
a. Inverted overprint 50.00

No. RA56 with blue overprint double exists only with additional black overprint of Ionian Islands No. NRA1a.

Same Overprint in Green on No. 364
1937 **Engr.** *Perf. 13x12½*
RA57 A36 50 l violet 75 15

Same Overprint, with Surcharge of New Value, on Nos. J66, J68 and 323 in Blue or Black
Serrate Roulette 13½
1938 **Litho.** **Unwmk.**
RA58 D3 50 l on 5 l grn 40 25
a. "o" for "p" in lowest word 25.00 25.00
b. Vert. pair, imperf. horiz. 50.00
RA59 D3 50 l on 20 l slate 90 50

Engr. *Perf. 13x12½*
RA60 A38 50 l on 20 l vio (Bk) 75 15

Surcharge on No. RA60 is 14½x16½mm.

Queens Olga and Sophia — PT7

1939, Feb. 1 **Litho.** *Perf. 13½x12*
RA61 PT7 10 l brt rose, *pale rose* 15 15
RA62 PT7 50 l gray grn, *pale grn* 15 15
RA63 PT7 1d dl bl, *lt bl* 20 20
Set value 40 40

For overprints and surcharges see Nos. RA65, RA79-RA81A, NRA1-NRA3.

"Health" Type of 1935
1939 *Perf. 12½*
RA64 PT6 50 l brn & buff 40 30

No. RA62 Overprinted in Red

ΠΡΟΣΤΑΣΙΑ ΦΥΜΑΤΙΚΩΝ ΤΤΤ

1940 *Perf. 13½x12*
RA65 PT7 50 l gray grn, *pale grn* 25 25
a. Inverted overprint 25.00
b. Pair, one without surcharge 20.00

Proceeds of #RA64-RA65 were used for the benefit of tubercular clerks and officials of the Post, Telephone and Telegraph Service. #RA65 was used in Albania during the Greek occupation, 1940-41 without additional overprint.

No. 321 Surcharged in Carmine — Κ.Π. λεπτῶν 50

1941 **Unwmk.** **Engr.** *Perf. 13½x13*
RA66 A36 50 l on 5 l dk grn 15 15
a. Inverted surcharge 15.00

No. RA49 and Type of 1935 Surcharged with New Value in Black
Perf. 12½x13, 13x13½
Litho.
RA67 PT5 50 l on 10 l 2.00 2.00
RA68 PT6 50 l on 10 l dp bl grn, dl org & buff 15 15
a. Inverted surcharge 20.00
b. Double surcharge 20.00

Catalogue values for unused stamps in this section, from this point to the end of the section, are for Never Hinged items.

No. RA48 Surcharged in Green — ΔΡ. 1

1942 *Perf. 11½*
RA69 PT4 1d on 20 l brn 15 15
a. Pair, one without surcharge 10.00
b. Imperf., pair 15.00
c. Double surcharge 15.00

Nos. 321, 324 Surcharged In Red or Carmine

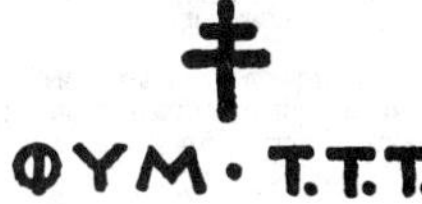

1942-43 **Engr.** *Perf. 13½x13*
RA70 A36 10d on 5 l ('43) 15 15
a. Double surcharge 15.00
RA71 A39 10d on 25 l (C) 15 15
a. Inverted surcharge 15.00
Set value 20 20

No. 444 Overprinted in Red — ΦΥΜ· Τ.Τ.Τ.

1944 **Wmk. 252** **Litho.** *Perf. 12½*
RA72 A110 100d black 15 15
a. Double overprint 9.00
b. Inverted overprint 9.00

No. 443 Surcharged in Blue — ΦΥΜ· Τ.Τ.Τ. ΔΡ. 5000

RA73 A109 5000d on 75d 15 15
a. Double surcharge 20.00

No. 437 Surcharged in Blue — ΥΠΕΡ ΤΩΝ ΦΥΜΑΤΙΚΩΝ Τ.Τ.Τ. ΔΡΧ. 25.000

RA74 A103 25000d on 2d 15 15
a. Double surcharge 15.00
b. Additional surcharge on back 17.50

No. 399 Surcharged in Blue or Carmine — ΥΠΕΡ ΤΩΝ ΦΥΜΑΤΙΚΩΝ Τ.Τ.Τ. ΔΡΑΧΜΗ 1

1945 *Perf. 13½x12*
RA75 A72 1d on 40 l 15 15
a. Double surcharge 10.00
RA76 A72 2d on 40 l (C) 15 15
a. Vert. pair, one without surch. 8.00
b. Surcharged on back 10.00
c. Inverted surcharge 10.00
Set value 20 20

Tax on Nos. RA67, RA68-RA70 to RA76 aided the postal clerks' tuberculosis fund.

Nos. 396 and 399 Surcharged in Carmine — ΠΡΟΝΟΙΑ ΠΡΟΣΩΠΙΚΟΥ Τ.Τ.Τ. ΔΡΑΧΜΑΙ 20

1946
RA77 A72 20d on 40 l 20 20
a. Pair, one without surcharge 15.00
RA78 A69 20d on 5 l 30 20

Same Surcharge in Carmine on Nos. RA62 and RA63
1946-47 **Unwmk.** *Perf. 13½x12*
RA79 PT7 50d on 50 l ('47) 15 15
a. Inverted surcharge 25.00
RA80 PT7 50d on 1d 15 15
a. Violet black surcharge 4.00 1.00
Set value 25 25

The tax on Nos. RA77 to RA80 was for the Postal Clerks' Welfare Fund.

Nos. RA65 and RA62 Surcharged in Carmine

ΔP. ▬ 50

1947

RA81	50d on 50 l (RA65)	35	15
RA81A	50d on 50 l (RA62)	32.50	32.50

The tax was for the postal clerks' tuberculosis fund.

St. Demetrius — PT8

1948 Litho. *Perf. 12x13½*

RA82	PT8 50d yellow brown	20	15

Obligatory on all domestic mail. The tax was for restoration of historical monuments and churches destroyed during World War II.

Nos. 397 and 413 Surcharged in Blue

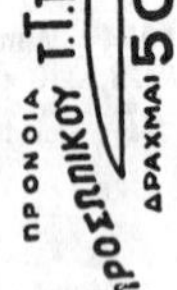

1950 Wmk. 252

RA83	A70 50d on 10 l (#397)	20	15
a.	Stamp with double frame	8.00	
b.	Surcharge reading down	18.00	18.00
RA84	A70 50d on 10 l (#413)	25	15
a.	Surcharge reading down	16.00	16.00
	Set value		20

Tax for the Postal Clerks' Welfare Fund.

No. 396 Surcharged in Carmine

1951 *Perf. 13½x12*

RA85	A69 50d on 5 l	25	15

The tax was for the Postal Employees' Welfare Fund.

No. 392 Surcharged in Black

✝ 50

1951 Wmk. 252 *Perf. 12½x12*

RA86	A67 50d on 3d red brn	15	15
a.	Pair, one without surcharge	15.00	
b.	"50" omitted	18.00	

Tax for the postal clerks' tuberculosis fund.

No. 393 Surcharged in Carmine

ΠΡΟΣΘΕΤΟΝ ΔΡ. 100

1952

RA87	A67 100d on 8d deep blue	15	15

The tax was for the State Welfare Fund.

Greek Occupation and Annexation stamps can be mounted in the Scott Greece album.

Ruins of Church of Phaneromeni, Zante — PT9

Zeus on Macedonian Coin of Philip II — PT10

Design: 500d, Map and scene of destruction, Argostoli.

1953 Wmk. 252 Litho. *Perf. 12½*

RA88	PT9 300d indigo & pale grn	30	15
RA89	PT9 500d dk brn & buff	60	40

The tax was for the reconstruction of Cephalonia, Ithaca, and Zante, Ionian Islands destroyed by earthquake.

1956 *Perf. 13½*

Design: 1d, Aristotle.

RA90	PT10 50 l dk car rose	35	15
a.	Imperf., pair	100.00	
RA91	PT10 1d brt blue	90	60

Tax for archaeological research in Macedonia. The coin on No. RA90 portrays Zeus despite inscription of Philip's name.

POSTAL TAX SEMI-POSTAL STAMPS

Child — PTSP1

Mother and Child — PTSP2

Virgin and Christ Child — PTSP3

Perf. 12x13½

1943 Wmk. 252 Litho.

RAB1	PTSP1	25d + 25d bl grn	15	15
RAB2	PTSP2	100d + 50d rose vio	15	15
RAB3	PTSP3	200d + 100d red brn	15	15
		Set value	30	30

Surtax aided needy children. These stamps were compulsory on domestic mail in Oct. 1943.

OCCUPATION AND ANNEXATION STAMPS

During the Balkan wars, 1912-13, Greece occupied certain of the Aegean Islands and part of Western Turkey. She subsequently acquired these territories and they were known as the New Greece.

Most of the special issues for the Aegean Islands were made by order of the military commanders.

For Use in the Aegean Islands Occupied by Greece

CHIOS

Greece No. 221 Overprinted in Red

Serrate Roulette 13½

1913 Litho. Unwmk.

N1	A25 25 l ultra	65.00	55.00
a.	Inverted overprint	100.00	100.00
b.	Greek "L" instead of "D"	90.00	90.00

ICARIA (NICARIA)

Penelope — I1

1912 Unwmk. Litho. *Perf. 11½*

N2	I1	2 l orange	80	80
N3	I1	5 l bl grn	80	80
N4	I1	10 l rose	80	80
N5	I1	25 l ultra	80	1.25
N6	I1	50 l gray lilac	1.75	2.00
N7	I1	1d dk brn	2.50	*8.25*
N8	I1	2d claret	3.00	*11.00*
N9	I1	5d slate	6.00	*19.00*
		Nos. N2-N9 (8)	16.45	*43.90*

Counterfeits of Nos. N1-N15 are plentiful.

Stamps of Greece, 1911-23, Overprinted Reading Up

ΕΛΛΗΝΙΚΗ ΔΙΟΙΚΗΣΙΣ

1913 Engr.

On Issue of 1911-21

N10	A25	2 l car rose	19.00	19.00
N11	A24	3 l vermilion	19.00	19.00

Litho.

On Issue of 1912-23

N12	A24	1 l green	19.00	19.00
N13	A24	3 l vermilion	19.00	19.00
N14	A26	5 l green	19.00	19.00
N15	A24	10 l carmine	19.00	19.00
		Nos. N10-N15 (6)	114.00	114.00

LEMNOS

Regular Issues of Greece Overprinted in Black

ΛΗΜΝΟΣ

On Issue of 1901

1912 Wmk. 129 Engr. *Perf. 13½*

N16	A11 20 l red lilac	75	75

On Issue of 1911-21

Unwmk.

Serrate Roulette 13½

N17	A24	1 l green	15	15
N18	A25	2 l car rose	15	15
N19	A24	3 l vermilion	15	15
N20	A26	5 l green	30	30
N21	A24	10 l car rose	65	65
N22	A25	20 l gray lilac	35	35
N23	A25	25 l ultra	85	85
N24	A26	30 l car rose	85	85
N25	A25	40 l deep blue	1.50	1.50
N26	A26	50 l dl vio	1.50	1.50
N27	A27	1d ultra	2.00	2.00
N28	A27	2d vermilion	7.00	7.00
N29	A27	3d car rose	10.00	10.00
N30	A27	5d ultra	12.50	12.50
N31	A27	10d deep blue	110.00	110.00
N32	A28	25d deep blue	85.00	85.00

On Issue of 1912-23

Litho.

N33	A24	1 l green	15	15
a.		Without period after "Ellas"	85.00	85.00
N34	A26	5 l green	15	15
N35	A24	10 l carmine	25	25
N36	A25	25 l ultra	1.00	1.00
		Nos. N16-N36 (21)	235.25	235.25

Red Overprint

On Issue of 1911-21

Engr.

N37	A25	2 l car rose	50	50
N38	A24	3 l vermilion	50	50
N39	A25	20 l gray lilac	1.00	1.00
N40	A26	30 l car rose	1.50	1.50
N41	A25	40 l deep blue	1.50	1.50
N42	A26	50 l dl vio	1.50	1.50
N43	A27	1d ultra	1.50	1.50
N44	A27	2d vermilion	9.00	9.00
N45	A27	3d car rose	10.00	10.00
N46	A27	5d ultra	20.00	20.00
N47	A27	10d deep blue	110.00	110.00
N48	A28	25d deep blue	85.00	85.00

On Issue of 1912-23

Litho.

N49	A24	1 l green	50	50
a.		Without period after "Ellas"	85.00	85.00
N50	A26	5 l green	30	30
N51	A24	10 l carmine	1.40	1.40
N52	A25	25 l ultra	80	80
		Nos. N37-N52 (16)	245.00	245.00

The overprint is found inverted or double on many of Nos. N16-N52. There are several varieties in the overprint: Greek "D" for "L," large Greek "S" or "O," and small "O."

No. N49 with Added "Greek Administration" Overprint, as on Nos. N109-N148, in Black

1913

N52A	A24 1 l green	15.00	12.50

Counterfeits of #N16-N52A are plentiful.

MYTILENE (LESBOS)

Turkey Nos. 162, 158 Overprinted in Blue

Ἑλληνικὴ Κατοχὴ Μυτιλήνης

Perf. 12, 13½ and Compound

1912 Typo. Unwmk.

N53	A21	20pa rose	22.50	22.50
N54	A21	10pi dull red	125.00	125.00

On Turkey Nos. P68, 151-155, 137, 157-158 in Black

N55	A21	2pa olive grn	75	75
N56	A21	5pa ocher	1.50	1.50
N57	A21	10pa bl grn	1.50	1.50
N58	A21	20pa rose	75	75
N59	A21	1pi ultra	2.25	2.25
N60	A21	2pi bl blk	15.00	15.00
N61	A19	2½pi dk brn	8.50	8.50
N62	A21	5pi dk vio	19.00	19.00
N63	A21	10pi dl red	110.00	110.00
		Nos. N55-N63 (9)	159.25	159.25

On Turkey Nos. 161-163, 145 in Black

N64	A21	10pa bl grn	4.00	4.00
a.		Double overprint	15.00	
N65	A21	20pa rose	3.00	3.00
N66	A21	1pi ultra	3.00	3.00
N67	A19	2pi bl blk	52.50	52.50

Nos. N55, N58, N65, N59 Surcharged in Blue or Black

N68	A21	25 l on 2pa	4.50	4.50
a.		New value inverted	22.50	
N69	A21	50 l on 20pa	5.75	5.75
b.		New value inverted	22.50	
N70	A21	1d on 20pa (N65) (Bk)	15.00	15.00
a.		New value inverted	45.00	
N71	A21	2d on 1pi (Bk)	20.00	20.00
a.		New value inverted		

Same Overprint on Turkey No. J49

N72	A19 1pi blk, *dp rose*	50.00	50.00

The overprint is found on all values reading up or down with inverted "i" in the first word and inverted "e" in the third word.

No. N72 was only used for postage.

Counterfeits of Nos. N53-N72 are plentiful.

SAMOS

Issues of the Provisional Government

Map of Samos — OS1

1912 Unwmk. Typo. *Imperf.*

No.	Design	Description	Unused	Used
N73	OS1	5 l gray green	20.00	5.50
N74	OS1	10 l red	25.00	6.25
N75	OS1	25 l blue	37.50	9.00
a.		25 l green (error)	*500.00*	*600.00*

Nos. N73-N75 exist in tête bêche pairs. Value per set, $500 unused, $250 used.

Counterfeits exist of Nos. N73 to N75.

Hermes — OS2

1912 Litho. *Perf. 11½*

Without Overprint

No.	Design	Description	Unused	Used
N76	OS2	1 l gray	3.75	85
N77	OS2	5 l lt grn	3.75	85
N78	OS2	10 l rose	47.50	85
b.		Half used as 5 l on cover		15.00
N79	OS2	25 l lt bl	4.25	1.50
N80	OS2	50 l vio brn	12.50	5.50

With Overprint

No.	Design	Description	Unused	Used
N81	OS2	1 l gray	50	50
N82	OS2	5 l bl grn	50	50
N83	OS2	10 l rose	1.00	1.00
b.		Half used as 5 l on cover		20.00
N84	OS2	25 l blue	2.00	1.00
N85	OS2	50 l vio brn	10.50	6.00
N86	OS2	1d orange	10.00	6.00
		Nos. N76-N86 (11)	96.25	24.55

For overprints and surcharge see Nos. N92-N103.

Imperf., Pairs

Without Overprint

No.	Design	Description	Unused	Used
N76a	OS2	1 l	40.00	
N77a	OS2	5 l	40.00	
N78a	OS2	10 l	40.00	
N79a	OS2	25 l	40.00	
N80a	OS2	50 l	40.00	

With Overprint

No.	Design	Description	Unused	Used
N81a	OS2	1 l	80.00	
N82a	OS2	5 l	80.00	
N83a	OS2	10 l	80.00	
N85a	OS2	50 l	60.00	60.00

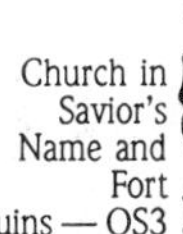

Church in Savior's Name and Fort Ruins — OS3

Manuscript Initials in Red or Black

1913

No.	Design	Description	Unused	Used
N87	OS3	1d brn (R)	14.00	11.50
N88	OS3	2d dp bl (R)	14.00	11.50
N89	OS3	5d gray grn (R)	27.50	22.50
N90	OS3	10d yel grn (R)	100.00	90.00
a.		Black initials	300.00	
N91	OS3	25d red (Bk)	67.50	67.50
a.		Red initials	210.00	
		Nos. N87-N91 (5)	223.00	203.00

Victory of the Greek fleet in 1824 and the union with Greece of Samos in 1912. The manuscript initials are those of Pres. Themistokles Sofulis.

Values the same for copies without initials.

Exist imperf. Counterfeits of Nos. N87-N91 are plentiful.

For overprints see Nos. N104-N108.

Nos. N76 to N80 Overprinted **ΕΛΛΑΣ**

1914

No.	Design	Description	Unused	Used
N92	OS2	1 l gray	4.00	3.00
N93	OS2	5 l lt grn	4.00	3.00
N94	OS2	10 l rose	4.25	3.00
a.		Double overprint	60.00	
N95	OS2	25 l lt bl	12.00	10.50
N96	OS2	50 l vio brn	12.00	5.00
a.		Double overprint	60.00	
		Nos. N92-N96 (5)	36.25	24.50

Charity Issues of Greek Administration

Nos. N81 to N86 Overprinted in Red or Black

1915

No.	Design	Description	Unused	Used
N97	OS2	1 l gray (R)	18.00	18.00
a.		Black overprint	100.00	
b.		Without overprint	60.00	
N98	OS2	5 l bl grn (Bk)	80	80
a.		Red overprint	85.00	
b.		Double overprint	80.00	
N99	OS2	10 l rose (Bk)	90	90
a.		Red overprint	90.00	
b.		Inverted overprint	80.00	
N100	OS2	25 l blue (Bk)	80	80
a.		Red overprint	90.00	
N101	OS2	50 l vio brn (Bk)	1.00	1.00
a.		Red overprint	85.00	
N102	OS2	1d org (R)	2.00	2.00
a.		Inverted overprint	90.00	
b.		Black overprint	100.00	
c.		Double black overprint	90.00	

No. N102 With Additional Surcharge in Black **ΛΕΠΤΟΝ**

No.	Design	Description	Unused	Used
N103	OS2	1 l on 1d org	7.00	7.00
a.		Black surcharge double	90.00	
b.		Black surcharge inverted	100.00	
		Nos. N97-N103 (7)	30.50	30.50

Issue of 1913 Overprinted in Red or Black

1915

No.	Design	Description	Unused	Used
N104	OS3	1d brn (R)	18.00	10.00
N105	OS3	2d dp bl (R)	24.00	14.00
a.		Double overprint		
N106	OS3	5d gray grn (R)	40.00	25.00
N107	OS3	10d yel grn (Bk)	55.00	50.00
a.		Inverted overprint		
N108	OS3	25d red (Bk)	550.00	400.00
		Nos. N104-N108 (5)	687.00	499.00

Nos. N97 to N108 inclusive have an embossed control mark, consisting of a cross encircled by a Greek inscription.

Most copies of Nos. N104-N108 lack the initials.

Counterfeits of Nos. N104-N108 are plentiful.

FOR USE IN PARTS OF TURKEY OCCUPIED BY GREECE (NEW GREECE)

Regular Issues of Greece Overprinted **ΕΛΛΗΝΙΚΗ ΔΙΟΙΚΗΣΙΣ**

Black Overprint Meaning "Greek Administration"

On Issue of 1901

1912 Wmk. 129 Engr. *Perf. 13½*

No.	Design	Description	Unused	Used
N109	A11	20 l red lilac	1.50	50

On Issue of 1911-21

Unwmk.

Serrate Roulette 13½

No.	Design	Description	Unused	Used
N110	A24	1 l green	40	20
N111	A25	2 l car rose	30	20
N112	A24	3 l vermilion	30	20
N113	A26	5 l green	35	20
N114	A24	10 l car rose	55	30
N115	A25	20 l gray lilac	90	30
N116	A25	25 l ultra	1.50	50
N117	A26	30 l car rose	1.50	1.40
N118	A25	40 l deep blue	3.25	1.40
N119	A26	50 l dl vio	3.00	1.40
N120	A27	1d ultra	6.50	1.40
N121	A27	2d vermilion	35.00	20.00
N122	A27	3d car rose	35.00	20.00
N123	A27	5d ultra	11.00	7.00
N124	A27	10d deep blue	275.00	200.00
N125	A28	25d dp bl, ovpt. horiz.	175.00	140.00

On Issue of 1913-23

Litho.

No.	Design	Description	Unused	Used
N126	A24	1 l green	30	18
b.		Without period after "Ellas"	60.00	60.00
N127	A26	5 l green	28	18
N128	A24	10 l carmine	70	24
N129	A25	25 l blue	3.25	1.10
		Nos. N109-N129 (21)	555.58	396.70

Red Overprint

On Issue of 1911-21

Engr.

No.	Design	Description	Unused	Used
N130	A24	1 l green	60	35
N131	A25	2 l car rose	7.00	6.00
N132	A24	3 l vermilion	9.00	6.00
N133	A26	5 l green	90	70
N134	A25	20 l gray lilac	7.00	1.50
N135	A25	25 l ultra	60.00	40.00
N136	A26	30 l car rose	24.00	20.00
N137	A25	40 l deep blue	3.00	2.25
N138	A26	50 l dl vio	4.00	2.75
N139	A27	1d ultra	14.00	5.00
N140	A27	2d vermilion	50.00	40.00
N141	A27	3d car rose	25.00	20.00
N142	A27	5d ultra	315.00	250.00
N143	A27	10d deep blue	25.00	20.00
N144	A28	25d dp bl, ovpt. horiz.	47.50	47.50
a.		Vertical overprint	200.00	200.00

On Issue of 1913-23

Litho.

No.	Design	Description	Unused	Used
N145	A24	1 l green	700	6.00
a.		Without period after "Ellas"	85.00	
N146	A26	5 l green	85	85
N147	A24	10 l carmine	55.00	45.00
N148	A25	25 l blue	2.25	1.75
		Nos. N130-N148 (19)	657.10	515.65

The normal overprint is vertical, reading upward on N109-N124, N126-N143, N145-N148. It is often double or reading downward. There are numerous broken, missing and wrong font letters with a Greek "L" instead of "D" as the first letter of the second word.

Counterfeits exist of Nos. N109-N148.

Cross of Constantine O1

Eagle of Zeus O2

1912 Litho.

No.	Design	Description	Unused	Used
N150	O1	1 l brown	25	20
N151	O2	2 l red	25	20
a.		2 l rose	30	22
N153	O2	3 l orange	30	25
N154	O1	5 l green	60	15
N155	O1	10 l rose red	1.10	15
N156	O1	20 l violet	6.50	1.50
N157	O2	25 l pale blue	1.75	50
N158	O1	30 l gray grn	42.50	1.40
N159	O2	40 l indigo	3.50	1.50
N160	O1	50 l dark blue	2.50	1.00
N161	O2	1d vio brn	4.00	1.75
N162	O1	2d gray brn	40.00	4.00
N163	O2	3d dull blue	125.00	20.00
N164	O1	5d gray	125.00	25.00
N165	O2	10d carmine	135.00	170.00
N166	O1	25d gray blk	135.00	170.00
		Nos. N150-N166 (16)	623.25	397.60

Occupation of Macedonia, Epirus and some of the Aegean Islands.

Sold only in New Greece.

Dangerous forgeries of #N165-N166 exist.

In 1916 some stamps of this issue were overprinted in Greek: "I (era) Koinotis Ag (iou) Orous" for the Mount Athos Monastery District. They were never placed in use and most of them were destroyed.

For surcharges and overprints see Nos. 267-276A, RA14-RA16, Thrace 31-33.

Imperf., Pairs

Without Overprint

No.	Design	Description	Unused	Used
N150a	O1	1 l	175.00	
N151b	O2	2 l	175.00	
N153a	O2	3 l	125.00	
N154a	O1	5 l	70.00	
N155a	O1	10 l	70.00	
N156a	O1	20 l	275.00	
N157a	O2	25 l	275.00	
N158a	O1	30 l	375.00	
N159a	O2	40 l	275.00	
N163a	O2	3d	*900.00*	

CAVALLA

Bulgaria Nos. 89-97 Surcharged in Red

ΕΛΛΗΝΙΚΗ
ΔΙΟΙΚΗΣΙΣ
25 ΛΕΠΤΑ 25

1913 Unwmk. Engr. *Perf. 12*

No.	Design	Description	Unused	Used
N167	A20	5 l on 1s myr grn	*13.50*	*13.50*
N169	A25	10 l on 15s brn bis	*50.00*	*50.00*
N170	A26	10 l on 25s ultra & blk	*15.00*	*15.00*
N171	A21	15 l on 2s car & blk	*25.00*	*25.00*
N172	A22	20 l on 3s lake & blk	*18.00*	*18.00*
N173	A23	25 l on 5s grn & blk	*10.50*	*8.50*
N174	A24	50 l on 10s red & blk	*13.50*	*8.50*
N175	A25	1d on 15s brn bis	*30.00*	*25.00*
N176	A27	1d on 30s bl & blk	*60.00*	*30.00*
N177	A28	1d on 50s ocher & blk	*100.00*	*50.00*

Blue Surcharge

No.	Design	Description	Unused	Used
N178	A24	50 l on 10s red & blk	*13.50*	*9.00*
		Nos. N167-N178 (11)	*349.00*	*252.50*

The counterfeits and reprints of Nos. N167-N178 are difficult to distinguish from originals. Many overprint varieties exist.

Some specialists question the status of Nos. N167-N178.

DEDEAGATCH

(Alexandroupolis)

ΕΛΛΗΝΙΚΗ
ΔΙΟΙΚΗΣΙΣ
ΔΕΔΕΑΓΑΤΣ
ΔΕΚΑ ΛΕΠΤΑ

D1-(10 lepta)

1913 Unwmk. Typeset *Perf. 11½*

Control Mark in Red

No.	Design	Description	Unused	Used
N179	D1	5 l black	35.00	27.50
N180	D1	10 l black	3.00	3.00
N181	D1	25 l black	4.00	4.00
a.		Sheet of 8	100.00	100.00

Nos. N179-N181 issued without gum in sheets of 8, consisting of one 5 l, three 10 l normal, one 10 l inverted, three 25 l and one blank. The sheet yields se-tenant pairs of 5 l & 10 l, 10 l & 25 l; tete beche pairs of 5 l & 10 l, 10 l & 25 l and 10 l & 10 l.

Also issued imperf., value $175 unused, $125 canceled.

The 5 l reads "PENTE LEPTA" in Greek letters; the 10 l is illustrated; the 25 l carries the numeral "25."

Bulgaria Nos. 89-90, 92-93, 95 Surcharged

ΕΛΛΗΝΙΚΗ
ΔΙΟΙΚΗΣΙΣ
ΔΕΔΕΑΓΑΤΣ
10
ΛΕΠΤΑ

Red Surcharge

1913 *Perf. 12*

No.	Design	Description	Unused	Used
N182	A20	5 l on 1s myr grn	72.50	42.50
N183	A26	1d on 25s ultra & blk	72.50	42.50

Blue Surcharge

No.	Design	Description	Unused	Used
N184	A24	10 l on 10s red & blk	27.50	17.00
N185	A23	25 l on 5s grn & blk	32.50	17.00
N187	A21	50 l on 2s car & blk	72.50	42.50
		Nos. N182-N185,N187 (5)	277.50	161.50

The surcharges on Nos. N182 to N187 are printed from a setting of eight, which was used for all, with the necessary changes of value. No. 6 in the setting has a Greek "L" instead of "D" for the third letter of the third word of the surcharge.

The 25 l surcharge also exists on 8 copies of the 25s, Bulgaria No. 95.

ΠΡΟΣΩΡΙΝΟΝ
ΕΛΛΗΝΙΚΗ
ΔΙΟΙΚΗΣΙΣ
ΔΕΔΕΑΓΑΤΣ
1 ΛΕΠΤΟΝ 1
D2

ΠΡΟΣΩΡΙΝΟΝ
ΕΛΛΗΝΙΚΗ
ΔΙΟΙΚΗΣΙΣ
ΔΕΔΕΑΓΑΤΣ
5 ΛΕΠΤΑ 5
D3

1913, Sept. 15 Typeset *Perf. 11½*
Control Mark in Blue

N188 D2 1 l blue 65.00
N189 D2 2 l blue 65.00
N190 D2 3 l blue 65.00
N191 D2 5 l blue 65.00
N192 D2 10 l blue 65.00
N193 D2 25 l blue 65.00
N194 D2 40 l blue 65.00
N195 D2 50 l blue 65.00

Nos. N188 to N195 were issued without gum in sheets of eight containing all values.

1913, Sept. 25 Typeset
Control Mark in Blue

N196 D3 1 l blue, *gray blue* 65.00
N197 D3 5 l blue, *gray blue* 65.00
N198 D3 10 l blue, *gray blue* 65.00
N199 D3 25 l blue, *gray blue* 65.00
N200 D3 30 l blue, *gray blue* 65.00
N201 D3 50 l blue, *gray blue* 65.00

Nos. N196 to N201 were issued without gum in sheets of six containing all values.
Counterfeits of Nos. N182-N201 are plentiful.

FOR USE IN NORTH EPIRUS (ALBANIA)

Greek Stamps of 1937-38 Overprinted in Black ΕΛΛΗΝΙΚΗ ΔΙΟΙΚΗΣΙΣ

Perf. 13½x12, 12x13½
1940 Litho. Wmk. 252

N202 A69 5 l brn red & bl 15 15
a. Inverted overprint 20.00
N203 A70 10 l bl & brn red (No. 413) 15 15
a. Double impression of frame 10.00
N204 A71 20 l blk & grn 15 15
a. Inverted overprint 25.00
N205 A72 40 l grn & blk 15 15
a. Inverted overprint 30.00
N206 A73 50 l brn & blk 18 18
N207 A74 80 l ind & yel brn 18 18
N208 A67 1d green 22 22
a. Inverted overprint 35.00
N209 A75 2d ultra 15 15
N210 A67 3d red brn 15 15
N211 A76 5d red 18 18
N212 A77 6d ol brn 22 22
N213 A78 7d dk brn 38 38
N214 A67 8d deep blue 55 55
N215 A79 10d red brn 55 55
N216 A80 15d green 95 95
N217 A81 25d dark blue 1.10 1.10
a. Inverted overprint 45.00

Engr.
Unwmk.

N218 A84 30d org brn 2.75 2.75
Nos. N202-N218 (17) 8.16 8.16

Same Overprinted in Carmine on National Youth Issue

1941 Litho. *Perf. 12½, 13½x12½*

N219 A93 3d sil, dp ultra & red 1.00 1.00
N220 A94 5d dk bl & blk 1.60 1.60
N221 A94 10d red org & blk 2.00 2.00
N222 A94 15d dk grn & blk 26.00 26.00
N223 A94 20d lake & blk 3.25 3.25
N224 A94 25d dk bl & blk 6.50 6.50
N225 A94 30d rose vio & blk 6.50 6.50
N226 A94 50d lake & blk 6.50 6.50
N227 A94 75d dk bl, brn & gold 6.50 6.50
N228 A93 100d sil, dp ultra & red 6.50 6.50
a. Inverted overprint 175.00
Nos. N219-N228 (10) 66.35 66.35

Same Overprint in Carmine on National Youth Air Post Stamps

N229 AP25 2d red org & blk 65 65
a. Inverted overprint 75.00
N230 AP25 4d dk grn & blk 3.25 3.25
a. Inverted overprint 75.00
N231 AP25 6d lake & blk 3.25 3.25
a. Inverted overprint 75.00
N232 AP25 8d dk bl & blk 3.25 3.25
N233 AP25 16d rose vio & blk 5.00 5.00
N234 AP25 32d red org & blk 5.00 5.00
N235 AP25 45d dk grn & blk 6.50 6.50
N236 AP25 55d lake & blk 6.50 6.50
N237 AP25 65d dk bl & blk 6.50 6.50
N238 AP25 100d rose vio & blk 6.50 6.50
Nos. N229-N238 (10) 46.40 46.40

Some specialists have questioned the status of Nos. N230a and N231a.
For other stamps issued by Greece for use in occupied parts of Epirus and Thrace, see the catalogue listings of those countries.

Catalogue values for unused stamps in this section, from this point to the end of the section, are for Never Hinged items.

FOR USE IN THE DODECANESE ISLANDS

Greece, No. 472C, with Additional Overprint in Carmine or Silver Σ. Δ. Δ.

1947 Wmk. 252 Litho. *Perf. 12½*

N239 A113 10d on 2,000d (C) 30 30
N240 A113 10d on 2,000d (S) 30 30

These stamps sold for 5 lire (100 drachmas) and paid postage for that amount.

King George II Memorial Issue

Greece, Nos. 484 and 485, With Additional Overprint in Black

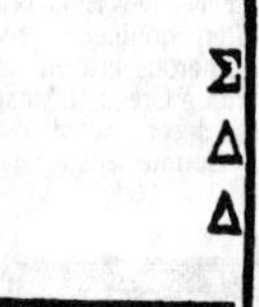

1947 Engr. *Perf. 12½x12*

N241 A67 50d on 1d green 75 75
N242 A67 250d on 3d red brown 75 75

The letters are initials of the Greek words for "Military Administration of the Dodecanese."

Greece, Nos. 501 and 502 Overprinted in Carmine Σ. Δ. Δ.

1947 Wmk. 252 Litho. *Perf. 12½*

N243 A111 20d on 500d dk ol 40 40
N244 A104 30d on 5d lt bl grn 60 60

Greece, Nos. 437, 406, 407 and 445, Surcharged in Black or Carmine

1947 *Perf. 12½, 13½x12*

N245 A103 50d on 2d 70 70

Engr.

N246 A79 250d on 10d 1.40 1.40
N247 A80 400d on 15d (C) 1.75 1.75
a. Inverted surcharge 125.00

Litho.

N248 A110 1000d on 200 (C) 85 85
a. Imprint omitted 70.00

POSTAGE DUE STAMPS

FOR USE IN PARTS OF TURKEY OCCUPIED BY GREECE (NEW GREECE)

Postage Due Stamps of Greece, 1902, Overprinted ΕΛΛΗΝΙΚΗ ΔΙΟΙΚΗΣΙΣ

1912 Wmk. 129 Engr. *Perf. 13½*
Black Overprint

NJ1 D3 1 l chocolate 20 20
NJ2 D3 2 l gray 20 20
NJ3 D3 3 l orange 20 20
NJ4 D3 5 l yel grn 30 30
NJ5 D3 10 l scarlet 30 30
NJ6 D3 20 l lilac 60 60
NJ7 D3 30 l dp vio 2.75 1.75
NJ8 D3 40 l dk brn 2.50 2.50
NJ9 D3 50 l red brn 3.00 3.00
NJ10 D3 1d black 17.50 14.00
NJ11 D3 2d bronze 17.50 11.00
NJ12 D3 3d silver 42.50 27.50
NJ13 D3 5d gold 100.00 85.00
Nos. NJ1-NJ13 (13) 187.55 146.55

Red Overprint

NJ14 D3 1 l chocolate 60 60
NJ15 D3 2 l gray 60 60
NJ16 D3 3 l orange 22.50 22.50
NJ17 D3 5 l yel grn 60 50
NJ18 D3 10 l scar, down 3.00 3.00
NJ19 D3 20 l lilac 60 60
NJ20 D3 30 l dp vio 2.25 2.25
NJ21 D3 40 l dk brn 60 50
NJ22 D3 50 l red brn 60 50
NJ23 D3 1d black 4.00 4.00
NJ24 D3 2d bronze 7.00 6.00
NJ25 D3 3d silver 17.50 17.50
NJ26 D3 5d gold 35.00 35.00
Nos. NJ14-NJ26 (13) 94.85 93.55

The normal position of the overprint is reading upward but it is often reversed. Some of the varieties of lettering which occur on the postage stamps are also found on the postage due stamps. Double overprints exist on some denominations.

FOR USE IN NORTH EPIRUS (ALBANIA)

Postage Due Stamps of Greece, 1930, Surcharged or Overprinted in Black:

ΕΛΛΗΝΙΚΗ
ΔΙΟΙΚΗΣΙΣ
50
ΛΕΠΤΑ
a

ΕΛΛΗΝΙΚΗ
ΔΙΟΙΚΗΣΙΣ
b

Perf. 13, 13x12½
1940 Litho. Unwmk.

NJ27 D3(a) 50 l on 25d lt red 20 30
NJ28 D3(b) 2d light red 25 25
a. Inverted overprint 30.00
NJ29 D3(b) 5d blue gray 25 25
NJ30 D3(b) 10d green 45 45
NJ31 D3(b) 15d red bowrn 60 60
Nos. NJ27-NJ31 (5) 1.75 1.85

POSTAL TAX STAMPS

FOR USE IN NORTH EPIRUS (ALBANIA)

Postal Tax Stamps of Greece, Nos. RA61-RA63, Overprinted Type "b" in Black

1940 Unwmk. Litho. *Perf. 13½x12*

NRA1 PT7 10 l 15 15
NRA2 PT7 50 l 15 15
a. Inverted overprint 35.00
NRA3 PT7 1d 20 20

GREENLAND

LOCATION — North Atlantic Ocean
GOVT. — Danish
AREA — 840,000 sq. mi.
POP. — 52,347 (1984)

In 1953 the colony of Greenland became an integral part of Denmark.

100 Ore = 1 Krone

Catalogue values for unused stamps in this country are for Never Hinged items, beginning with Scott 48 in the regular postage section, Scott B4 in the semi-postal section.

Christian X — A1

Polar Bear — A2

Perf. 13x12½
1938-46 Unwmk. Engr.

1 A1 1o olive black 20 32
2 A1 5o rose lake 1.25 65
3 A1 7o yellow green 1.65 2.75
4 A1 10o purple 85 65
5 A1 15o red 85 65
6 A1 20o red ('46) 85 75
7 A2 30o blue 5.50 7.50
8 A2 40o blue ('46) 16.00 7.50
9 A2 1k light brown 5.75 9.50
Nos. 1-9 (9) 32.90 30.27
Set, never hinged 55.00

Issue dates: Nov. 1, 1938, Aug. 1, 1946.
For surcharges see Nos. 39-40.

Harp Seal — A3

Christian X — A4

Dog Team — A5

Designs: 1k, Polar bear. 2k, Eskimo in kayak. 5k, Eider duck.

1945, Feb. 1 *Perf. 12*

10 A3 1o ol blk & vio 15.00 17.50
11 A3 5o rose lake & ol bister 15.00 17.50
12 A3 7o grn & blk 15.00 17.50
13 A4 10o pur & olive 15.00 17.50
14 A4 15o red & brt ultra 15.00 17.50
15 A5 30o dk bl & red brn 15.00 17.50
16 A5 1k brn & gray blk 15.00 17.50
17 A5 2k sep & dp grn 15.00 17.50
18 A5 5k dk pur & dl brn 15.00 17.50
Nos. 10-18 (9) 135.00 157.50
Set, never hinged 175.00

Nos. 10-18 Overprinted in Carmine or Blue **DANMARK BEFRIET 5 MAJ 1945**

1945

19 A3 1o (C) 21.00 22.50
20 A3 5o (Bl) 21.00 22.50
21 A3 7o (C) 21.00 22.50
22 A4 10o (Bl) 37.50 55.00
a. Overprint in carmine 150.00 225.00
23 A4 15o (C) 35.00 55.00
a. Overprint in blue 75.00 100.00
24 A5 30o (Bl) 35.00 55.00
a. Overprint in carmine 75.00 100.00
25 A5 1k (C) 35.00 55.00
a. Overprint in blue 75.00 100.00
26 A5 2k (C) 35.00 55.00
a. Overprint in blue 75.00 100.00
27 A5 5k (Bl) 35.00 55.00
a. Overprint in carmine 75.00 100.00
Nos. 19-27 (9) 275.50 397.50
Set, never hinged 490.00
Nos. 22a-27a (6) 525.00 725.00
Set, never hinged 700.00

Liberation of Denmark from the Germans. Overprint illustrated as on Nos. 19-21. Larger type and different settings used for Types A4 and A5. Overprint often smudged.
Nos. 19-27 exist with overprint inverted. Value, 1k, $700, others, each $400.

Frederik IX — A6

Polar Ship "Gustav Holm" — A7

1950-60 Unwmk. Engr. *Perf. 13*

28	A6	1o dk olive grn	15	15
29	A6	5o deep car	18	15
30	A6	10o green	28	28
31	A6	15o purple ('60)	55	45
a.		15o dull purple	2.00	1.00
32	A6	25o vermilion	1.10	90
33	A6	30o dk bl ('53)	16.00	1.65
34	A6	30o ver ('59)	48	32
35	A7	50o deep blue	15.00	14.00
36	A7	1k brown	6.50	1.65
37	A7	2k dull red	3.75	1.65
38	A7	5k gray ('58)	1.90	1.40
		Nos. 28-38 (11)	45.89	22.60
		Set, never hinged	65.00	

Issue dates: Nos. 28-30, 31a, 32, 35-37, Aug. 15. No. 33, Dec. 1. No. 38, Aug. 14. No. 34, Oct. 29. No. 31, Oct.

For surcharges see Nos. B1-B2.

Nos. 8 and 9 Surcharged

1956, Mar. 8

39	A2	60o on 40o blue	6.75	1.40
40	A2	60o on 1k lt brn	22.50	6.50
		Set, never hinged	45.00	

Drum Dancer — A8

Designs: 50o, The Boy and the Fox. 60o, The Mother of the Sea. 80o, The Girl and the Eagle. 90o, The Great Northern Diver and the Raven.

1957-69 Engr. *Perf. 13*

41	A8	35o gray olive	1.25	1.00
42	A8	50o brown red	1.25	1.40
43	A8	60o blue	2.75	1.40
44	A8	80o light brn	1.25	1.40
45	A8	90o dark blue	2.75	3.25
		Nos. 41-45 (5)	9.25	8.45
		Set, never hinged	12.00	

Issue dates: 35o, Mar. 16, 1961. 50o, Sept. 22, 1966. 60o, May 2, 1957. 80o, Sept. 18, 1969. 90o, Nov. 23, 1967.

Hans Egede — A9

Knud Rasmussen — A10

1958, Nov. 5

46	A9	30o henna brown	6.00	1.65
		Never hinged	8.50	

200th anniv. of death of Hans Egede, missionary to Eskimos in Greenland.

1960, Nov. 24 *Perf. 13*

47	A10	30o dull red	1.40	1.00
		Never hinged	1.75	

50th anniv. of establishment by Rasmussen of the mission and trading station at Thule (Dundas).

Catalogue values for unused stamps in this section, from this point to the end of the section, are for Never Hinged items.

Northern Lights and Crossed Anchors — A11

Frederick IX — A12

Polar Bear — A13

1963-68 Engr.

48	A11	1o gray	15	15
49	A11	5o rose claret	15	15
50	A11	10o green	42	42
51	A11	12o yellow grn	45	45
52	A11	15o rose vio	60	60
53	A12	20o ultra	4.00	4.00
54	A12	25o lt brn ('64)	40	40
55	A12	30o grn ('68)	28	28
56	A12	35o dl red ('64)	20	20
57	A12	40o gray ('64)	40	40
58	A12	50o grnsh bl ('64)	8.00	7.75
59	A12	50o dk red ('65)	40	28
60	A12	60o rose cl ('68)	42	28
61	A12	80o orange	85	75
62	A13	1k brown	60	28
63	A13	2k dull red	2.50	75
64	A13	5k dark blue	2.50	1.10
65	A13	10k dull sl grn	2.50	1.10
		Nos. 48-65 (18)	24.82	19.34

Issue dates: Nos. 48-52, Mar. 7. Nos. 53, 61, July 25. Nos. 62-65, Sept. 17. Nos. 54, 56-58, Mar. 11. No. 59, Sept. 9. No. 60, Feb. 29. No. 55, Nov. 21.

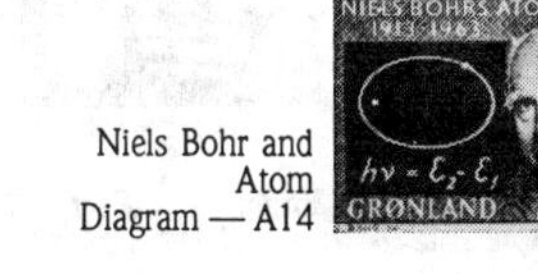

Niels Bohr and Atom Diagram — A14

1963, Nov. 21 Unwmk.

66	A14	35o red brown	45	45
67	A14	60o dark blue	4.00	4.00

50th anniv. of atom theory of Prof. Bohr (1885-1962).

Samuel Kleinschmidt (1814-1886), Philologist — A15

1964, Nov. 26

68	A15	35o brown red	50	50

Princess Margrethe and Prince Henri — A16

1967, June 10

69	A16	50o red	3.75	3.75

Wedding of Crown Princess Margrethe and Prince Henri de Monpezat.

Frederik IX and Map of Greenland — A17

1969, Mar. 11 Engr. *Perf. 13*

70	A17	60o dull red	1.50	1.50

70th birthday of King Frederik IX.

Musk Ox — A18

Liberation Celebration at Jakobshaven — A19

Designs: 1k, Right whale diving off Disko Island. 2k, Narwhal. 5k, Polar bear. 10k, Walruses.

1969-76 Engr. *Perf. 13*

71	A18	1k dark blue	42	35
72	A18	2k gray green	55	42
73	A18	5k blue	1.40	85
74	A18	10k sepia	2.75	1.40
75	A18	25k greenish gray	7.00	2.75
		Nos. 71-75 (5)	12.12	5.77

Issue dates: 1k, Mar. 5, 1970. 2k, Feb. 20, 1975. 5k, Feb. 19, 1976. 10k, Feb. 15, 1973. 25k, Nov. 27, 1969.

1970, May 4

76	A19	60o red brown	2.25	2.25

Hans Egede and Gertrude Rask on the Haabet — A20

1971, May 6 Engr. *Perf. 13*

77	A20	60o brown red	1.65	1.65

250th anniv. of arrival of Hans Egede in Greenland and the beginning of its colonization.

Mail-carrying Kayaks — A21

Designs: 70o, Umiak (women's rowboat). 80o, Catalina seaplane dropping mail by parachute. 90o, Dog sled. 1k, Coaster Kununguak and pilot boat. 1.30k, Schooner Sokongen. 1.50k, Longboat off Greenland coast. 2k, Helicopter over mountains.

1971-77 Engr. *Perf. 13*

78	A21	50o green	25	22
79	A21	70o dl red ('72)	25	25
80	A21	80o black ('76)	45	45
81	A21	90o blue ('72)	35	25
82	A21	1k red ('76)	48	48
83	A21	1.30k dl bl ('75)	60	48
84	A21	1.50k gray grn ('74)	45	45
85	A21	2k blue ('77)	65	65
		Nos. 78-85 (8)	3.48	3.23

Issue dates: No. 78, Nov. 4. No. 81, Feb. 29. No. 79, Sept. 21. No. 84, Feb. 21. No. 83, Apr. 17. Nos. 80, Oct. 11. No. 85, Feb. 24.

Queen Margrethe — A22

1973-79 Engr. *Perf. 13*

86	A22	5o car rose ('78)	15	15
87	A22	10o gray green	15	15
a.		10o emerald	15	15
88	A22	60o sepia	35	24
89	A22	80o sepia ('79)	24	24
90	A22	90o red brn ('74)	60	35
91	A22	1k dk red ('77)	24	24
a.		Bklt. pane, 4 #87a, 6 #91b	2.00	
b.		1k carmine	24	24
92	A22	1.20k dk bl ('74)	60	60
93	A22	1.20k mar ('78)	30	30
94	A22	1.30k dk bl ('77)	40	40
95	A22	1.30k red ('79)	35	35
96	A22	1.60k blue ('79)	60	60
97	A22	1.80k dl grn ('78)	75	75
		Nos. 86-97 (12)	4.73	4.37

#86, 89, 93, 95-97 inscribed "Kalaallit Nunaat."

The background lines on Nos. 87, 91 are sharp and complete. On No. 87a, 91b they are irregular and broken.

Issue dates: Nos. 87-88, Apr. 16. Nos. 90, 92, Oct. 24. Nos. 91, 94, May 26. Nos. 86, 93, 97, Apr. 17. Nos. 89, 95-96, Mar. 29.

Trawler and Kayaks — A23

Falcon and Radar — A24

Design: 2k, Old Trade Buildings, Copenhagen, vert.

1974, May 16 **Engr.** ***Perf. 13***

98 A23 1k lt red brn 60 45
99 A23 2k sepia 70 60

Royal Greenland Trade Dept. Bicentennial.

1975, Sept. 4 **Engr.** ***Perf. 13***

100 A24 90o red 42 42

50th anniversary of Greenland's telecommunications system.

Sirius Sled Patrol A25

1975, Oct. 16 **Engr.** ***Perf. 13***

101 A25 1.20k sepia 42 42

Sirius sled patrol in northeast Greenland, 25th anniversary.

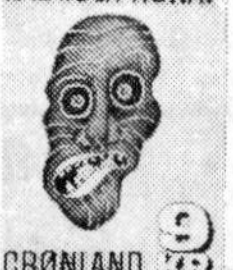

Inuit Cult Mask — A26

Jorgen Bronlund, Jakobshavn, Disko Bay — A27

Designs: 6k, Tupilac, a magical creature, carved whalebone. 7k, Soapstone sculpture. 8k, Eskimo with Family, driftwood sculpture, by Johannes Kreutzmann (1862-1940).

1977-80

102 A26 6k deep rose lilac 1.75 1.75
103 A26 7k gray olive 1.75 1.75
104 A26 8k dark blue 2.00 2.00
105 A26 9k black 3.25 2.75

Issue dates: 6k, Oct. 5, 1978. 7k, Sept. 6, 1979. 8k, Feb. 29, 1980. 9k, Sept. 6, 1977.

The 6k, 7k, 8k are inscribed "Kalaallit Nunaat."

1977, Oct. 20

106 A27 1k red brown 28 25

Jorgen Bronlund, arctic explorer, birth centenary.

Meteorite — A28

1978, Jan. 20 **Engr.** ***Perf. 13***

107 A28 1.20k dull red 40 40

Scientific Research Commission, centenary.

Sun Rising over Mountains — A29

1978, June 5 **Engr.** ***Perf. 13***

108 A29 1.50k dark blue 50 40

25th anniversary of Constitution.

Hans Egede, Settlers, Troops and Drummer A30

1978, Aug. 29 **Engr.** ***Perf. 13***

109 A30 2.50k red brown 75 75

Founding of Godthaab, 250th anniversary.

A31

A32

1979, May 1 **Engr.**

110 A31 1.10k Navigator 42 42

Establishment of home rule, May 1, 1979.

1979, Oct. 18 **Engr.** ***Perf. 13***

Design: Eskimo Boy, aurora borealis, IYC emblem.

111 A32 2k olive green 60 60

International Year of the Child.

The Legend of the Reindeer and the Larva, by Jens Kreutzmann, 1860 — A33

Designs: 2.70k, Harpooning a Walrus, Jakob Danielsen. No. 114, Life in Thule, c. 1900, by Aninaaq. No. 115, Landscape, Ammassalik Fjord, Eastern Greenland, Peter Rosing (1892-1965). 3k, Footrace, woodcut by Aron from Kagec (1822-1869). 3.70k, Polar Bear Killing Seal Hunter, K. Andreassen (1890-1934). 9k, Hares Hunting, Gerhard Kleist (1855-1931).

1980-87 **Engr.** ***Perf. 13***

112 A33 1.60k red 45 45
113 A33 2.70k deep violet 75 75
114 A33 2.80k lake 60 60
115 A33 2.80k lake 40 40
116 A33 3k black 95 95
117 A33 3.70k blue black 95 95
118 A33 9k dark green 2.00 2.00
Nos. 112-118 (7) 6.10 6.10

Issue dates: 1.60k, Mar. 26, 1981. 2.70k, June 24, 1982. No. 114, Sept. 4, 1986. No. 115, Apr. 9, 1987. 3k, Sept. 4, 1980. 3.70k, Feb. 9, 1984, 9k, Sept. 5, 1985.

This is an expanding set. Numbers will change if necessary.

Queen Margrethe, Map of Greenland — A34

1980-89 **Engr.** ***Perf. 13***

120 A34 50o purple ('81) 15 15
121 A34 80o sepia 28 28
122 A34 1.30k red 52 52
123 A34 1.50k royal blue ('82) 45 45
124 A34 1.60k ultra 1.00 1.00
125 A34 1.80k dull red ('82) 38 38
126 A34 2.30k dk grn ('81) 55 55
127 A34 2.50k red ('83) 52 52
128 A34 2.80k copper red ('85) 60 60
129 A34 3k fawn ('88) 70 70
130 A34 3.20k rose ('89) 90 90
a. Bklt. pane of 10 (4 50o, 6 3.20k) 6.00
131 A34 3.80k slate bl ('85) 70 70
132 A34 4.10k bright bl ('88) 95 95
133 A34 4.40k ultra ('89) 1.25 1.25
Nos. 120-133 (14) 8.95 8.95

Issue dates: Nos. 121-122, 124, Apr. 16. Nos. 120, 126, Jan. 29. Nos. 123, 125, May 13. No. 127, Mar. 30. Nos. 128, 131, Feb. 7. Nos. 129, 132, Feb. 4. Nos. 130, 133, Jan. 30.

Rasmus Berthelsen (Teacher, Hymnist), in Training College Library, 1830 — A35

1980, May 29 **Engr.** ***Perf. 13***

134 A35 2k brown, *cream* 65 65

Greenland Public Library Service, 150th anniv.

Ejnar Mikkelsen on board Gustav Holm, 1934 — A36

1980, Oct. 16 **Engr.** ***Perf. 13***

135 A36 4k slate green 1.25 1.25

Ejnar Mikkelsen, inspector of East Greenland, birth centenary.

Pandalus Borealis — A37

Designs: No. 137, Anarhicas minor. No. 138, Reinhardtius Hippoglossoides. No. 139, Mallotus villosus. 25k, Codfish. 50k, Salmo salar.

1981-86 **Engr.** ***Perf. 13***

136 A37 10k multi 2.25 2.25
137 A37 10k dk bl & blk 3.75 3.25
138 A37 10k multi 2.25 2.25
139 A37 10k grnsh blk & blk 2.25 2.25
140 A37 25k multi 5.00 5.00
141 A37 50k multi 10.00 10.00
Nos. 136-141 (6) 25.50 25.00

Issue dates: 25k, May 21. No. 136, Apr. 1, 1982. 50k, Jan. 27, 1983. No. 137, Oct. 11, 1984. No. 138, Oct. 10, 1985. No. 139, Oct. 16, 1986.

This is an expanding set. Numbers will change if necessary.

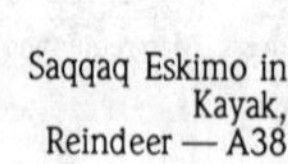

Saqqaq Eskimo in Kayak, Reindeer — A38

Design: 5k, Tunit-Dorset hunters hauling seal.

1981, Oct. 15 **Engr.** ***Perf. 12½***

146 A38 3.50k dark blue 1.05 1.05
147 A38 5k brown 1.50 1.50

Thule District Eskimos Catching Whale, 1000AD — A39

Greenland history: No. 149, Bishop Joen Smyrill's house and staff, 12th cent. No. 150, Wooden dolls, 13th cent. No. 151, Eskimo mummy, sacrificial stones, 14th cent. No. 152, Hans Pothorst, explorer, 15th cent. No. 153, Glass pearls, 16th cent. No. 154, Apostle spoons, 17th cent. No. 155, Key, trading station, 18th cent. No. 156, Trade Ship Hvalfisken, masthead, 19th cent. No. 157, Communications satellite, Earth, 20th cent.

1982, Sept. 30

148 A39 2k brown red 45 45
149 A39 2.70k dark blue 60 60

1983, Sept. 15

150 A39 2.50k red 55 55
151 A39 3.50k brown 80 80
152 A39 4.50k blue 1.00 1.00

1984, Mar. 29

153 A39 2.70k red brown 70 70
154 A39 3.70k dark blue 90 90
155 A39 5.50k brown 1.40 1.40

1985, Mar. 21

156 A39 2.80k violet 55 55
157 A39 6k blue black 1.10 1.10
Nos. 148-157,B10 (11) 8.95 8.95

250th Anniv. of Settlement of New Herrnhut — A40

1983, Nov. 2 **Engr.**

158 A40 2.50k brown 90 90

Henrik Lund, Natl. Anthem Score, Lichtenau Fjord — A41

1984, Sept. 6 **Engr.**

159 A41 5k dark green 1.10 1.10

Henrik Lund (1875-1948), natl. anthem composer, artist, only Greenlander to win Ingenio et Arti medal.

A42

A43

1984, June 6 **Engr.** ***Perf. 13***

160 A42 2.70k dull red 1.10 1.10

Prince Henrik, 50th birthday.

1984, July 25 **Engr.** ***Perf. 13***

161 A43 3.70k Danish grenadier, 1734 80 80

Town of Christianshab, 250th anniv.

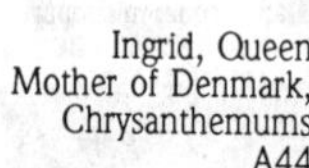

Ingrid, Queen Mother of Denmark, Chrysanthemums A44

1985, May 21 **Litho. & Engr.**

162 A44 2.80k multi 95 95

Arrival in Denmark of Princess Ingrid, 50th anniv. See Denmark No. 775.

Intl. Youth Year — A45

1985, June 27 **Litho.**

163 A45 3.80k Emblem, birds nesting, fiord 1.25 1.25

Greenland Port Post Office, Flags — A46

1986, Mar. 6 **Engr.** ***Perf. 13***
164 A46 2.80k dark red 75 75

Transfer of postal control under Greenland Home Rule, Jan. 1, 1986.

Artifacts — A47

1986-88 **Engr.** ***Perf. 13***
165 A47 2.80k Sewing needles, case 55 55
165A A47 3k Buckets, bowl, scoop 88 88
166 A47 3.80k Ulos 1.10 1.10
167 A47 3.80k Masks 75 75
168 A47 5k Harpoon points 1.45 1.45
169 A47 6.50k Lard lamps 2.00 2.00
172 A47 10k Carved faces 2.90 2.90
Nos. 165-172 (7) 9.63 9.63

Issued: #166, 6.50k, May 22. 2.80k, 3.80k, June 11, 1987. 3k, 5k, 10k, Oct. 27, 1988.
This is an expanding set. Numbers will change if necessary.

Souvenir Sheet

HAFNIA '87 — A48

1987, Jan. 23 **Litho.** ***Perf. 13***
175 A48 Sheet of 3 5.50 5.50
a. 2.80k Gull in flight 1.50 1.50
b. 3.80k Mountain 1.75 1.75
c. 6.50k Gulls in water 2.00 2.00

No. 175 sold for 19.50k.
See No. 199.

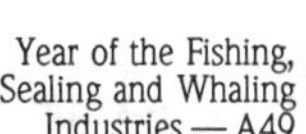

Year of the Fishing, Sealing and Whaling Industries — A49

1987, Apr. 9 **Litho.** ***Perf. 13***
176 A49 3.80k multi 75 75

Lagopus Mutus — A50

Birds of Prey — A51

1987-90 **Litho.** ***Perf. 13***
177 A51 3k Falco rusticolus 95 95
178 A51 3.20k Clangula hyemalis 90 90
179 A51 4k Anser caerulescens 1.15 1.15
180 A51 4.10k Corvus corax 1.30 1.30
181 A51 4.40k Plectrophenax nivalis 1.25 1.25
182 A50 5k shown 1.25 1.25
183 A51 5.50k Haliaeetus albicilla 1.75 1.75
184 A51 5.50k Cepphus grylle 1.55 1.55
185 A51 6.50k Uria lomvia 1.85 1.85
186 A51 7k Gavia immer 2.25 2.25
187 A51 7.50k Stercorarius longicaudus 2.15 2.15
188 A50 10k Nyctea scandiaca 2.50 2.50
Nos. 177-188 (12) 18.85 18.85

Issue dates: 5k, 10k, Sept. 3. 3k, 4.10k, No. 183, 7k, Apr. 14, 1988. 3.20k, 4.40k, No. 184, 6.50k, Mar. 16, 1989. 4k, 7.50k, Jan. 15, 1990.

Plants — A52

1989-92 **Litho.** ***Perf. 13***
189 A52 4k *Campanula gieseckiana* 1.25 1.25
190 A52 4k *Pedicularis hirsuta* 1.25 1.25
191 A52 5k *Eriophorum scheuchzeri* 1.40 1.40
192 A52 5.50k *Ledum groenlandicum* 1.75 1.75
193 A52 6.50k *Cassiope tetragona* 2.00 2.00
194 A52 7.25k *Saxifraga oppositifolia* 2.25 2.25
196 A52 10k *Papaver radicatum*, vert. 2.75 2.75
Nos. 189-196 (7) 12.65 12.65

Issue dates: 5k, 10k, Oct. 12, 1989. No. 189, 5.50k, 6.50k, June 7, 1990; No. 190, 7.25k, Mar. 26, 1992. Nos. 189-190 vert.
This is an expanding set. Numbers will change if necessary.

HAFNIA Type of 1987
Souvenir Sheet

Design: Uummannaq Mountain in winter, horiz.

1987, Oct. 16 **Litho.** ***Perf. 13x12½***
199 A48 2.80k slate blue & lake 1.25 1.25

No. 199 sold for 4k.

Greenland Home Rule, 10th Anniv.
A53 A54

1989, May 1 **Litho.** ***Perf. 13***
200 A53 3.20k Flag, landscape 90 90
201 A54 4.40k Coat of arms 1.25 1.25

Queen Margrethe — A55

1990-94 **Engr.** ***Perf. 13***
214 A55 25o green 15 15
217 A55 1k brown 32 32
a. Bklt. pane of 10, 4 #214, 6 #217 2.25
b. Booklet pane, 4 each #214, 217 1.90
224 A55 4k carmine rose 1.25 1.25
228 A55 6.50k blue 2.00 2.00
229 A55 7k violet 2.25 2.25

Issued: No. 217a, May 3. No. 217b, Sept. 9, 1993. 7k, Feb. 10, 1994. Others, Apr. 5.
This is an expanding set. Numbers will change if necessary.

Frederik Lynge (1889-1957), Politician — A56

Design: 25k, Augo Lynge (1899-1959), politician

1990, Oct. 18 **Engr.** ***Perf. 13x12½***
231 A56 10k rose brn & dk bl 3.25 3.25
232 A56 25k vio & dk bl 8.00 8.00

See Nos. 242-243, 249.

Phoca Hispida — A57

Walrus and Seals.

Litho. & Engr.

1991, Mar. 14 ***Perf. 13***
233 A57 4k shown 1.25 1.25
234 A57 4k Pagophilus groenlandicus 1.25 1.25
235 A57 7.25k Cystophora cristata 2.25 2.25
236 A57 7.25k Odobenus rosmarus 2.25 2.25
237 A57 8.50k Erignatus barbatus 2.65 2.65
238 A57 8.50k Phoca vitulina 2.65 2.65
a. Min. sheet of 8, #233-238 12.30 12.30
Nos. 233-238 (6) 12.30 12.30

Village of Ilulissat, 250th Anniv. — A58

1991, May 15 **Litho.** ***Perf. 13***
239 A58 4k multicolored 1.25 1.25

Tourism — A59

1991, May 15 ***Perf. 12½x13***
240 A59 4k Iceberg 1.25 1.25
241 A59 8.50k Skiers, sled dogs 2.65 2.65

Famous Men Type of 1990

Designs: 10k, Jonathan Petersen (1881-1961), musician. 50k, Hans Lynge (1906-1988), artist and writer. 100k, Lars Moller (1842-1926), newspaper editor.

1991-92 **Engr.** ***Perf. 13x12½***
242 A56 10k black & dk blue 3.10 3.10
243 A56 50k red brn & blue 15.50 15.50
249 A56 100k claret & slate 36.00 18.00

Issued: 10k, 50k, Sept. 5; 100k, Sept. 15, 1992.

Settlement of Paamiut, 250th Anniv. A60

1992, May 14 **Engr.** ***Perf. 13***
252 A60 7.25k dk bl & ol brn 2.25 2.25

Greenland stamps can be mounted in the Scott Scandinavia and Finland album.

Denmark's Queen Margrethe and Prince Henrik, Silver Wedding Anniv. — A61

1992, June 10 **Litho.** ***Perf. 12½x13***
253 A61 4k multicolored 1.25 1.25

A62 A63

1992, Nov. 12 **Litho.** ***Perf. 13***
254 A62 4k Christmas 1.25 1.25

1993, Feb. 4 **Litho.** ***Perf. 13***
255 A63 4k multicolored 1.25 1.25

Intl. Year of Indigenous Peoples.

Crabs — A64

Designs: 4k, Neolithodes grimaldii. 7.25k, Chionoecetes oiliqo. 8.50k, Hyas coarctatus, Hyas araneus.

Litho. & Engr.

1993, Mar. 25 ***Perf. 13***
256 A64 4k multicolored 1.25 1.25
257 A64 7.25k multicolored 2.25 2.25
a. Chionoecetes opilio 2.25 2.25
b. Booklet pane, 4 each #256, 257a 14.00
258 A64 8.50k multicolored 2.65 2.65

Issue date: No. 257b, Sept. 9.

Tourism — A65

1993, May 6 **Litho.** ***Perf. 12½x13***
259 A65 4k Village in winter 1.25 1.25
260 A65 8.50k Ruins, coastline 2.65 2.65

AIDS Research A66

1993, Sept. 9 **Litho.** ***Perf. 13***
261 A66 4k multicolored 1.25 1.25

Native Animals — A67

1993, Oct. 14 Litho. & Engr. *Perf. 13*

262 A67 5k Canis lupus 1.50 1.50
263 A67 8.50k Alopex lagopus 2.75 2.75
264 A67 10k Rangifer tarandus 3.25 3.25

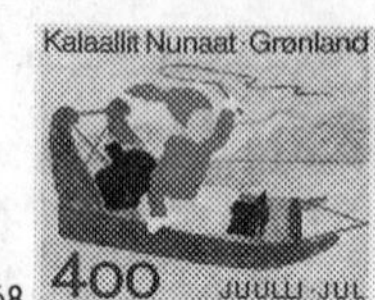

Christmas — A68

1993, Nov. 11 Litho. *Perf. 13*

265 A68 4k multicolored 1.25 1.25

Buksefjord Electrical Project — A69

Litho. & Engr.

1994, Mar. 24 *Perf. 13*

266 A69 4k multicolored 1.25 1.25

Ammassalik, Cent. — A70

1994, Mar. 24

267 A70 7.25k multicolored 2.25 2.25

SEMI-POSTAL STAMPS

No. 35 Surcharged in Red

1958, May 22 Engr. *Perf. 13*

B1 A7 30o + 10o on 50o 3.25 1.75
Never hinged 6.00

The surtax was for the campaign against tuberculosis in Greenland.

No. 32 Surcharged: "Gronlandsfonden 30+10" and Bars

1959, Feb. 23 Unwmk.

B2 A6 30o + 10o on 25o 3.00 3.00
Never hinged 4.00

The surtax was for the benefit of the Greenland Fund.

Two Greenland Boys in Round Tower — SP1

1968, Sept. 12 Engr. *Perf. 13*

B3 SP1 60o + 10o dark red 1.00 2.00
Never hinged 1.25

Surtax for child welfare work in Greenland.

Catalogue values for unused stamps in this section, from this point to the end of the section, are for Never Hinged items.

Hans Egede Explaining Bible to Natives — SP2

1971, July 3 Engr. *Perf. 13*

B4 SP2 60o + 10o red brown 2.50 2.50

See footnote after No. 77.

Frederik IX, "Dannebrog" off Umanak — SP3

1972, Apr. 20

B5 SP3 60o + 10o dull red 1.65 1.65

King Frederik IX (1899-1972). The surtax was for humanitarian and charitable purposes.

Heimaey Town and Volcano — SP4

1973, Oct. 18 Engr. *Perf. 13*

B6 SP4 70o + 20o gray & red 1.65 1.65

The surtax was for the victims of the eruption of Heimaey Volcano.

Arm Pulling, by Hans Egede — SP5

1976, Apr. 8 Engr. *Perf. 12½*

B7 SP5 100o + 20o multi 60 60

Surtax for the Greenland Athletic Union.

Rasmussen and Eskimos — SP6

1979, July Engr. *Perf. 13*

B8 SP6 1.30k + 20o brown red 80 80

Knud Rasmussen (1879-1933), arctic explorer and ethnologist.

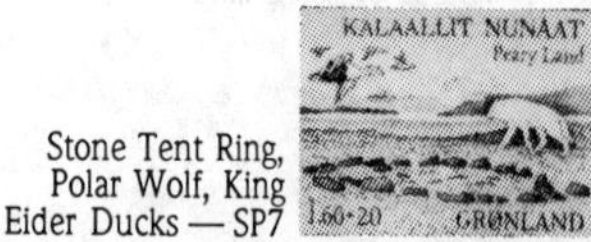

Stone Tent Ring, Polar Wolf, King Eider Ducks — SP7

1981, Sept. 3 Engr. *Perf. 13*

B9 SP7 1.60k + 20o lt red brn 75 75

Surtax was for Peary Land Expeditions.

History Type of 1982

Design: Eric the Red sailing for Greenland.

1982, Aug. 2 Engr. *Perf. 12½*

B10 A39 2k + 40o dk red brn 90 90

Surtax was for Cultural House, Julianehab.

Blind Man — SP8

1983, May 19 Engr.

B11 SP8 2.50k + 40o multi 1.00 1.00

Surtax was for the handicapped.

Greenland Sports Union — SP9

1986, Apr. 17 Litho.

B12 SP9 2.80k + 50o Water game 85 85

Surtax for the Sports Union.

Greenland PO, 50th Anniv. — SP10

1988, Sept. 16 Litho. *Perf. 12½x13*

B13 SP10 300o +50o multi 1.00 1.00

Surtax for the purchase of postal artifacts.

Sled Dog, Common Eider — SP11

1990, Sept. 6 Litho. & Engr. *Perf. 13*

B14 SP11 400o + 50o multi 1.45 1.45

Surtax for the Greenland Environmental Foundation.

SP12

SP13

1991, Sept. 5 Litho. *Perf. 13*

B15 SP12 4k +50o multi 1.40 1.40

Blue Cross of Greenland, 75th Anniv. Surtax benefits Blue Cross of Greenland.

1992, Oct. 8 Litho. *Perf. 13*

B16 SP13 4k +50o multi 1.65 1.65

Cancer research in Greenland.

Red Cross — SP14

Boy Scouts in Greenland, 50th Anniv. SP15

1993, June 17 Litho. *Perf. 13*

B17 SP14 4k +50o red & blue 1.65 1.65
B18 SP15 4k +50o multi 1.65 1.65
a. Souvenir sheet, 2 each #B17-B18 10.00

1994 Winter Olympics, Lillehammer SP16

1994, Feb. 10 Litho. *Perf. 13*

B19 SP16 4k +50o Skiers 1.40 1.40
a. Souvenir sheet of 4 5.75 5.75

Surtax to support Greenlandic athletes.

PARCEL POST STAMPS

Arms of Greenland — PP1

Perf. 11, 11½

1905-37 Unwmk. Typo.

Q1	PP1	1o ol grn ('16)	32.50	30.00
a.		Perf. 12½ ('05)	400.00	450.00
Q2	PP1	2o yellow ('16)	110.00	65.00
Q3	PP1	5o brown ('16)	65.00	57.50
a.		Perf. 12½ ('05)	450.00	525.00
Q4	PP1	10o blue ('37)	25.00	40.00
a.		Perf. 12½ ('05)	425.00	375.00
b.		Perf. 11½ ('16)	32.50	35.00
Q5	PP1	15o violet ('16)	100.00	92.50
Q6	PP1	20o red ('16)	12.00	10.00
a.		Perf. 11 ('37)	26.00	35.00
Q7	PP1	70o violet ('37)	25.00	*55.00*
a.		Perf. 11½ ('30)	110.00	110.00
Q8	PP1	1k yellow ('37)	25.00	*110.00*
a.		Perf. 11½ ('30)	40.00	40.00
Q9	PP1	3k brown ('30)	80.00	100.00

1937 Litho. *Perf. 11*

Q10 PP1 70o pale violet 27.50 *65.00*
Q11 PP1 1k yellow 25.00 55.00

On lithographed stamps, PAKKE-PORTO is slightly larger, hyphen has rounded ends and lines in shield are fine, straight and evenly spaced.

On typographed stamps, hyphen has squared ends and shield lines are coarse, uneven and inclined to be slightly wavy.

Used values are for postally used stamps. Numeral cancels indicate use as postal savings stamps.

Sheets of 25. Certain printings of Nos. Q1-Q2, Q3a, Q4a, and Q5-Q6 were issued without sheet margins. Stamps from the outer rows are straight edged.

The Scott editorial staff regrettably cannot accept requests to identify, authenticate, or appraise stamps and postal markings.

GUADELOUPE

LOCATION — In the West Indies lying between Montserrat and Dominica
GOVT. — Former French colony
AREA — 688 sq. mi.
POP. — 271,262 (1946)
CAPITAL — Basse-Terre

Guadeloupe consists of two large islands, Guadeloupe proper and Grande-Terre, together with five smaller dependencies. Guadeloupe became an integral part of the Republic, acquiring the same status as the departments in metropolitan France, under a law effective Jan. 1, 1947.

100 Centimes = 1 Franc

Catalogue values for unused stamps in this country are for Never Hinged items, beginning with Scott 168 in the regular postage section, Scott B12 in the semi-postal section, Scott C1 in the airpost section, and Scott J38 in the postage due section.

See France Nos. 850, 909, 1280, 1913 for French stamps inscribed "Guadeloupe."

Stamps of French Colonies Surcharged

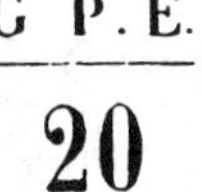

1884 Unwmk. *Imperf.*

1 A8 20c on 30c brn, *bis* 27.50 20.00
a. Large "2" 150.00 110.00
2 A8 25c on 35c blk, *org* 27.50 20.00
a. Large "2" 150.00 110.00
b. Large "5" 65.00 60.00

The 5c on 4c (French Colonies No. 40) was not regularly issued. Value $150.

c

d

1889 *Perf. 14x13½*

Surcharged Type c

3 A9 3c on 20c red, *grn* 1.65 1.65
4 A9 15c on 20c red, *grn* 14.00 14.00
5 A9 25c on 20c red, *grn* 12.50 12.00

Surcharged Type d

6 A9 5c on 1c blk, *lil bl* 6.25 6.25
a. Inverted surcharge 450.00
b. Double surcharge 90.00 90.00
7 A9 10c on 40c red, *straw* 14.00 13.00
a. Double surcharge 160.00 150.00
8 A9 15c on 20c red, *grn* 14.00 11.50
a. Double surcharge 160.00 150.00
9 A9 25c on 30c brn, *bis* 22.50 17.50
a. Double surcharge 160.00 150.00

The word "centimes" in surcharges "b" and "c" varies from 10 to 12½mm.
Issue dates: No. 6, June 25, others, Mar. 22.

5 C.
GPE

1891

10 A9 5c on 10c blk, *lav* 6.75 6.25
11 A9 5c on 1fr brnz grn, *straw* 6.75 6.25

Stamps of French Colonies Overprinted in Black **GUADELOUPE**

1891 *Imperf.*

12 A7 30c brn, *yelsh* 175.00 175.00
13 A7 80c car, *pnksh* 525.00 525.00

Perf. 14x13½

14 A9 1c blk, *lil bl* 70 70
a. Double overprint 12.50 11.00
b. Inverted overprint 60.00 60.00
15 A9 2c brn, *buff* 1.00 65
a. Double overprint 14.00 11.00
16 A9 4c claret, *lav* 2.25 1.75
17 A9 5c grn, *grnsh* 3.00 3.00
a. Double overprint 15.00 11.00
b. Inverted overprint 62.50 62.50
18 A9 10c blk, *lavender* 5.50 5.00
19 A9 15c blue 15.00 2.00
a. Double overprint 42.50 42.50
20 A9 20c red, *grn* 15.00 11.00
a. Double overprint 90.00 80.00
21 A9 25c blk, *rose* 15.00 2.00
a. Double overprint 90.00 85.00
b. Inverted overprint 80.00 80.00
22 A9 30c brn, *bister* 16.00 14.00
a. Double overprint 90.00 90.00
23 A9 35c dp vio, *org* 35.00 27.50
24 A9 40c red, *straw* 20.00 19.00
a. Double overprint 350.00 225.00
25 A9 75c car, *rose* 60.00 57.50
26 A9 1fr brnz grn, *straw* 37.50 35.00

The following errors may be found in all values of Nos. 12-26: "GNADELOUPE," "GUADELOUEP," "GUADELONPE" and "GUADBLOUPE."

Navigation and Commerce — A7

Perf. 14x13½

1892-1901 Typo. Unwmk.

Colony Name in Blue or Carmine

27 A7 1c blk, *lil bl* 62 40
28 A7 2c brn, *buff* 60 40
29 A7 4c claret, *lav* 60 45
30 A7 5c grn, *grnsh* 1.40 40
31 A7 5c yel grn ('01) 1.50 62
32 A7 10c blk, *lavender* 4.00 1.20
33 A7 10c red ('00) 2.50 1.00
a. Imperf. 45.00
34 A7 15c blue, quadrille paper 4.00 40
35 A7 15c gray, *lt gray* ('00) 4.00 62
36 A7 20c red, *grn* 3.25 1.60
37 A7 25c blk, *rose* 3.25 60
38 A7 25c blue ('00) 45.00 45.00
39 A7 30c brn, *bister* 7.50 5.00
40 A7 40c red, *straw* 7.50 4.50
41 A7 50c car, *rose* 14.00 7.00
42 A7 50c brn, *az* ('00) 18.00 11.00
43 A7 75c dp vio, *org* 12.00 8.25
44 A7 1fr brnz grn, *straw* 16.00 14.00
Nos. 27-44 (18) 145.72 102.44

Perf. 13½x14 stamps are counterfeits.
For surcharges see Nos. 45-53, 83-85.

Nos. 39-41, 43-44 Surcharged in Black:

G & D
5
f

G et D
10
g

G & D
1 fr.
h

1903

45 A7 (f) 5c on 30c 1.50 1.50
a. "C" instead of "G" 12.00 12.00
b. Inverted surcharge 15.00 15.00
c. Double surcharge 62.50 62.50
d. Double surch., inverted 65.00
46 A7 (g) 10c on 40c 2.50 2.50
a. "C" instead of "G" 12.00 12.00
b. "1" inverted 20.00 20.00
c. Inverted surcharge 17.50 17.50
47 A7 (f) 15c on 50c 3.50 3.50
a. "C" instead of "G" 15.00 15.00
b. Inverted surcharge 40.00 40.00
c. "15" inverted 150.00 150.00
48 A7 (g) 40c on 1fr 4.00 4.00
a. "C" instead of "G" 16.00 16.00
b. "4" inverted 45.00 45.00
c. Inverted surcharge 45.00 45.00
d. Double surcharge 100.00 100.00
49 A7 (h) 1fr on 75c 16.00 16.00
a. "C" instead of "G" 60.00 60.00
b. "1" inverted 75.00 75.00
c. Value above "G & D" 150.00 150.00
d. Inverted surcharge 45.00 45.00
Nos. 45-49 (5) 27.50 27.50

Letters and figures from several fonts were used for these surcharges, resulting in numerous minor varieties.

Nos. 48-49 With Additional Overprint "1903" in a Frame

1904, Mar.

Red Overprint

50 A7 (g) 40c on 1fr 22.50 22.50
51 A7 (h) 1fr on 75c 27.50 27.50

Blue Overprint

52 A7 (g) 40c on 1fr 16.00 16.00
53 A7 (h) 1fr on 75c 27.50 27.50

The date "1903" may be found in 19 different positions and type faces within the frame. These stamps may also be found with the minor varieties of Nos. 48-49.
The 40c exists with black overprint.

Harbor at Basse-Terre A8

View of La Soufrière — A9

Pointe-à-Pitre, Grand-Terre A10

1905-27 Typo. *Perf. 14x13½*

54 A8 1c blk, *bluish* 15 15
55 A8 2c vio brn, *straw* 15 15
56 A8 4c bis brn, *az* 15 15
57 A8 5c green 45 28
58 A8 5c dp bl ('22) 15 15
59 A8 10c rose 45 15
60 A8 10c green ('22) 15 15
61 A8 10c red, *bluish* ('25) 15 15
62 A8 15c violet 20 15
63 A9 20c red, *grn* 15 15
64 A9 20c bl grn ('25) 15 15
65 A9 25c blue 15 15
66 A9 25c ol grn ('22) 15 15
67 A9 30c black 1.25 90
68 A9 30c rose ('22) 15 15
69 A9 30c brn ol, *lav* ('25) 15 15
70 A9 35c blk, *yel* ('06) 22 15
71 A9 40c red, *straw* 35 35
72 A9 45c ol gray, *lil* ('07) 25 22
73 A9 45c rose ('25) 30 30
74 A9 50c gray grn, *straw* 1.60 90
75 A9 50c dp bl ('22) 38 38
76 A9 50c violet ('25) 15 15
77 A9 65c blue ('27) 30 30
78 A9 75c car, *bl* 42 32
79 A10 1fr blk, *green* 65 65
80 A10 1fr lt bl ('25) 55 55
81 A10 2fr car, *org* 70 65
82 A10 5fr dp bl, *org* 2.50 2.50
Nos. 54-82 (29) 12.52 10.70

Nos. 57 and 59 exist imperf.
For surcharges see Nos. 86-95, 167, B1-B2.

Nos. 29, 39 and 40 Surcharged in Carmine or Black

05 10

1912, Nov.

83 A7 5c on 4c claret, *lav* (C) 35 35
84 A7 5c on 30c brn, *bis* (C) 60 60
85 A7 10c on 40c red, *straw* 80 80

Two spacings between the surcharged numerals are found on Nos. 83 to 85.

Stamps and Types of 1905-27 Surcharged with New Value and Bars

1924-27

86 A10 25c on 5fr dp bl, *org* 30 30
87 A10 65c on 1fr gray grn 60 60
88 A10 85c on 1fr gray grn 60 60
89 A9 90c on 75c dl red 60 60
90 A10 1.05fr on 2fr ver (Bl) 30 30
91 A10 1.25fr on 1fr lt bl (R) 15 15
92 A10 1.50fr on 1fr dk bl 60 60
93 A10 3fr on 5fr org brn 52 52
94 A10 10fr on 5fr vio rose, *org* 4.00 4.00
95 A10 20fr on 5fr rose lil, *pnksh* 4.75 4.75
Nos. 86-95 (10) 12.42 12.42

Years issued: Nos. 87-88, 1925. Nos. 90-91, 1926. Nos. 89, 92-95, 1927.

Sugar Mill — A11

Saints Roadstead A12

Harbor Scene — A13

Perf. 14x13½

1928-40 Unwmk. Typo.

96 A11 1c yel & vio 15 15
97 A11 2c blk & lt red 15 15
98 A11 3c yel & red vio ('40) 15 15
99 A11 4c yel grn & org brn 15 15
100 A11 5c ver & grn 15 15
101 A11 10c bis brn & dp bl 15 15
102 A11 15c brn red & blk 15 15
103 A11 20c lil & ol brn 15 15
104 A12 25c grnsh bl & olvn 15 15
105 A12 30c gray grn & yel grn 15 15
106 A12 35c bl grn ('38) 15 15
107 A12 40c yel & vio 15 15
108 A12 45c vio brn & slate 35 35
109 A12 45c bl grn & dl grn ('40) 30 30
110 A12 50c dl grn & org 15 15
111 A12 55c ultra & car ('38) 35 28
112 A12 60c ultra & car ('40) 15 15
113 A12 65c gray blk & ver 15 15
114 A12 70c gray blk & ver ('40) 15 15
115 A12 75c dl red & bl grn 35 30
116 A12 80c car & brn ('38) 22 22
117 A12 90c dl red & dl rose 80 80
118 A12 90c rose red & bl ('39) 40 40
119 A13 1fr lt rose & lt bl 2.00 1.00
120 A13 1fr rose red & org ('38) 45 45
121 A13 1fr bl gray & blk brn ('40) 20 20
122 A13 1.05fr lt bl & rose 60 60
123 A13 1.10fr lt red & grn 1.20 1.00
124 A13 1.25fr bl gray & blk brn ('33) 15 15
125 A13 1.25fr brt rose & red org ('39) 35 35
126 A13 1.40fr lt bl & lil rose ('40) 22 22
127 A13 1.50fr dl bl & bl 15 15
128 A13 1.60fr lil rose & yel brn ('40) 22 22
129 A13 1.75fr lil rose & yel brn ('33) 1.75 1.00
130 A13 1.75fr vio bl ('38) 2.25 1.60
131 A13 2fr bl grn & dk brn 15 15
132 A13 2.25fr vio bl ('39) 30 30
133 A13 2.50fr pale org & grn ('40) 40 40
134 A13 3fr org brn & sl 20 15
135 A13 5fr dl bl & org 35 28
136 A13 10fr vio & ol brn 42 38
137 A13 20fr grn & mag 50 50
Nos. 96-137 (42) 17.03 14.15

Nos. 96-97 exist imperf.
For surcharges see Nos. 161-166.

Colonial Exposition Issue
Common Design Types

1931, Apr. 13 Engr. *Perf. 12½*

Name of Country in Black

138 CD70 40c dp grn 1.25 1.25
139 CD71 50c violet 1.40 1.40
140 CD72 90c red org 2.50 2.50
141 CD73 1.50fr dull blue 2.00 2.00

Cardinal Richelieu Establishing French Antilles Co., 1635 — A14

Victor Hugues and his Corsairs — A15

1935 *Perf. 13*

142	A14	40c gray brn	4.00	4.00
143	A14	50c dl red	4.00	4.00
144	A14	1.50fr dull blue	4.00	4.00
145	A15	1.75fr lil rose	4.00	4.00
146	A15	5fr dk brn	4.00	4.00
147	A15	10fr bl grn	4.00	4.00
		Nos. 142-147 (6)	24.00	24.00

Tercentenary of the establishment of the French colonies in the West Indies.

Paris International Exposition Issue

Common Design Types

1937 *Perf. 13*

148	CD74	20c dp vio	52	52
149	CD75	30c dk grn	52	52
150	CD76	40c car rose	75	75
151	CD77	50c dk brn & blk	75	75
152	CD78	90c red	75	75
153	CD79	1.50fr ultra	75	75
		Nos. 148-153 (6)	4.04	4.04

Common Design Types pictured in section at front of book.

Colonial Arts Exhibition Issue

Souvenir Sheet

Common Design Type

1937 *Imperf.*

154	CD75	3fr dark blue	2.50	2.50

New York World's Fair Issue

Common Design Type

1939 Engr. *Perf. 12½x12*

155	CD82	1.25fr car lake	45	45
156	CD82	2.25fr ultra	45	45

For surcharges see Nos. 159-160.

La Soufrière View and Marshal Pétain A16

1941 Engr. *Perf. 12½x12*

157	A16	1fr lilac	35	
158	A16	2.50fr blue	35	

Nos. 157-158 were issued by the Vichy government and were not placed on sale in Guadeloupe. This is also true of a 10c stamp, type A11 without "RF," released in 1944.

Nos. 155, 156, 113, 117 and 118 Surcharged with New Values in Black

1943 *Perf. 14x13½, 12½x12*

159	CD82	40c on 1.25fr	35	35
160	CD82	40c on 2.25fr	62	62
161	A12	50c on 65c	42	42
162	A12	1fr on 90c	65	65
163	A12	1fr on 90c	42	42
		Nos. 159-163 (5)	2.46	2.46

Nos. 104, 106, 113 and 90 Surcharged with New Values in Black

1944 *Perf. 14x13½*

164	A12	40c on 35c	35	35
165	A12	50c on 25c	15	15
166	A12	1fr on 65c	42	42
a.		Double surcharge	60.00	
167	A10	4fr on 1.05fr on 2fr	80	80

The surcharge on No. 166 is spelled out.

Catalogue values for unused stamps in this section, from this point to the end of the section, are for Never Hinged items.

Dolphins A17

1945 Unwmk. Photo. *Perf. 11½*

168	A17	10c chlky bl & red org	15	15
169	A17	30c lt yel grn & red	15	15
170	A17	40c lt bl & car	30	22
171	A17	50c red org & yel grn	15	15
172	A17	60c ol bis & lt bl	15	15
173	A17	70c lt gray & yel grn	30	25
174	A17	80c lt bl grn & yel	30	25
175	A17	1fr brn vio & grn	15	15
176	A17	1.20fr brt red vio & yel grn	15	15
177	A17	1.50fr dl brn & car	28	15
178	A17	2fr cer & bl	28	20
179	A17	2.40fr sal & yel grn	62	55
180	A17	3fr gray brn & bl vio	20	20
181	A17	4fr ultra & buff	15	15
182	A17	4.50fr brn org & grn	20	15
183	A17	5fr dk vio & grn	28	22
184	A17	10fr gray grn & red vio	28	22
185	A17	15fr sl gray & org	55	40
186	A17	20fr pale gray & dl org	80	65
		Set value	4.75	3.85

Eboue Issue

Common Design Type

1945 Engr. *Perf. 13*

187	CD91	2fr black	22	22
188	CD91	25fr Prussian green	60	60

Basse-Terre Harbor and Woman — A18

Cutting Sugar Cane — A19

Pineapple Bearer — A20

Guadeloupe Woman — A21

Gathering Coffee — A22

Guadeloupe Woman — A23

1947 Unwmk. Engr. *Perf. 13*

189	A18	10c red brown	15	15
190	A18	30c sepia	15	15
191	A18	50c bl grn	15	15
192	A19	60c blk brn	15	15
193	A19	1fr dp car	25	22
194	A19	1.50fr dk gray bl	60	40
195	A20	2fr bl grn	65	55
196	A20	2.50fr dp car	60	40
197	A20	3fr deep blue	65	55
198	A21	4fr violet	60	45
199	A21	5fr bl grn	60	45
200	A21	6fr red	60	40
201	A22	10fr deep blue	60	40
202	A22	15fr dk vio brn	70	55
203	A22	20fr rose red	80	70
204	A23	25fr blue green	1.40	90
205	A23	40fr red	1.50	1.10
		Nos. 189-205 (17)	10.15	7.67

SEMI-POSTAL STAMPS

Nos. 59 and 62 Surcharged in Red

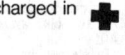

1915-17 Unwmk. *Perf. 14 x 13½*

B1	A8	10c + 5c rose	2.25	1.20
B2	A8	15c + 5c violet	1.50	1.25
a.		Double surcharge	60.00	60.00

Curie Issue

Common Design Type

1938, Oct. 24 *Perf. 13*

B3	CD80	1.75fr + 50c brt ultra	5.25	5.25

French Revolution Issue

Common Design Type

Name and Value Typo. in Black

1939, July 5 Photo. *Perf. 13*

B4	CD83	45c + 25c green	3.25	3.25
B5	CD83	70c + 30c brown	3.75	3.75
B6	CD83	90c + 35c red org	3.75	3.75
B7	CD83	1.25fr + 1fr rose pink	3.75	3.75
B8	CD83	2.25fr + 2fr blue	3.75	3.75
		Nos. B4-B8 (5)	18.25	18.25

Common Design Type and

Colonial Artillery SP1

Colonial Infantry — SP2

1941 Photo. *Perf. 13½*

B9	SP1	1fr + 1fr red	55	
B10	CD86	1.50fr + 3fr maroon	55	
B11	SP2	2.50fr + 1fr blue	55	

Nos. B9-B11 were issued by the Vichy government, and were not placed on sale in Guadeloupe.

Nos. 157-158 were surcharged "OEUVRES COLONIALES" and surtax (including change of denomination of the 2.50fr to 50c). These were issued in 1944 by the Vichy government, and not placed on sale in Guadeloupe.

Catalogue values for unused stamps in this section, from this point to the end of the section, are for Never Hinged items.

Red Cross Issue

Common Design Type

1944 *Perf. 14½x14*

B12	CD90	5fr + 20fr ultra	55	55

The surtax was for the French Red Cross and national relief.

AIR POST STAMPS

Catalogue values for unused stamps in this section are for Never Hinged items.

Common Design Type

1945 Unwmk. Photo. *Perf. 14½x14*

C1	CD87	50fr green	45	45
C2	CD87	100fr deep plum	60	60

Victory Issue

Common Design Type

1946, May 8 Engr. *Perf. 12½*

C3	CD92	8fr redsh brn	60	60

Chad to Rhine Issue

Common Design Types

1946, June 6

C4	CD93	5fr dk slate grn	70	70
C5	CD94	10fr deep blue	70	70
C6	CD95	15fr brt vio	70	70
C7	CD96	20fr brown car	70	70
C8	CD97	25fr black	70	70
C9	CD98	50fr red brown	70	70
		Nos. C4-C9 (6)	4.20	4.20

Gathering Bananas — AP1

Seaplane at Roadstead — AP2

Pointe-a-Pitre Harbor and Guadeloupe Woman — AP3

1947 Unwmk. *Perf. 13*

C10	AP1	50fr dk brn vio	3.50	2.00
C11	AP2	100fr deep blue	4.00	2.50
C12	AP3	200fr red	5.00	3.00

AIR POST SEMI-POSTAL STAMPS

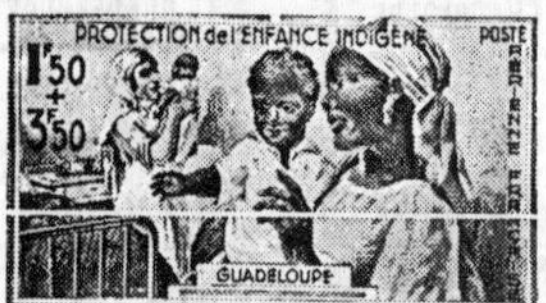

Stamps of the design shown above and stamp of Cameroun type V10 inscribed "Guadeloupe" were issued in 1942 by the Vichy Government, but were not placed on sale in Guadeloupe.

POSTAGE DUE STAMPS

D1 D2 D3

1876 Unwmk. Typeset *Imperf.*

J1	D1	25c black	500.00	400.00
J2	D2	40c black, *blue*		*16,000.*
J3	D3	40c black	600.00	500.00

Twenty varieties of each.

Nos. J1 and J3 have been reprinted on thinner and whiter paper than the originals.

D4 D5

1879

No.	Type	Description	Unused	Used
J4	D4	15c black, *blue*	19.00	14.00
a.		Period after "c" omitted	82.50	82.50
J5	D4	30c black	42.50	27.50
a.		Period after "c" omitted	120.00	110.00

Twenty varieties of each.

1884

No.	Type	Description	Unused	Used
J6	D5	5c black	9.00	9.00
J7	D5	10c black, *blue*	22.50	15.00
J8	D5	15c black, *violet*	42.50	25.00
J9	D5	20c black, *rose*	65.00	45.00
a.		Italic "2" in "20"	450.00	375.00
J10	D5	30c black, *yellow*	60.00	57.50
J11	D5	35c black, *gray*	19.00	16.00
J12	D5	50c black, *green*	9.00	7.50

There are ten varieties of the 35c, and fifteen of each of the other values, also numerous wrong font and missing letters.

Postage Due Stamps of French Colonies Surcharged in Black

1903

No.	Type	Description	Unused	Used
J13	D1	30c on 60c brn, *cr*	140.00	140.00
a.		"3" with flat top	325.00	325.00
b.		Inverted surcharge	400.00	400.00
c.		As "a," inverted	650.00	650.00
J14	D1	30c on 1fr rose, *cr*	160.00	160.00
a.		Inverted surcharge	425.00	425.00
b.		"3" with flat top	425.00	425.00
c.		As "b," inverted	700.00	700.00

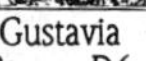

Gustavia Bay — D6

Avenue of Royal Palms — D7

1905-06 Typo. *Perf. 14x13½*

No.	Type	Description	Unused	Used
J15	D6	5c blue	15	15
J16	D6	10c brown	15	15
J17	D6	15c green	25	25
J18	D6	20c black, *yel* ('06)	28	28
J19	D6	30c rose	38	38
J20	D6	50c black	1.40	1.40
J21	D6	60c brn org	60	60
J22	D6	1fr violet	1.50	1.50
		Nos. J15-J22 (8)	4.71	4.71

Type of 1905-06 Issue Surcharged

2
francs
à percevoir

1926-27

No.	Type	Description	Unused	Used
J23	D6	2fr on 1fr gray	70	70
J24	D6	3fr on 1fr ultra ('27)	1.00	1.00

1928, June 18

No.	Type	Description	Unused	Used
J25	D7	2c olive brn & lil	15	15
J26	D7	4c bl & org brn	15	15
J27	D7	5c gray grn & dk brn	15	15
J28	D7	10c dl vio & yel	15	15
J29	D7	15c rose & olive grn	15	15
J30	D7	20c brn org & ol grn	15	15
J31	D7	25c brn red & bl grn	20	20
J32	D7	30c slate & olivine	20	20
J33	D7	50c ol brn & lt red	28	28
J34	D7	60c dp bl & blk	45	45
J35	D7	1fr green & orange	1.40	1.40
J36	D7	2fr bis brn & lt red	1.00	1.00
J37	D7	3fr vio & bl blk	45	45
		Set value	4.35	4.35

Stamps of type D7 without "RF" monogram were issued in 1944 by the Vichy Government, but were not placed on sale in Guadeloupe.

Catalogue values for unused stamps in this section, from this point to the end of the section, are for Never Hinged items.

D8

Perf. 14x13

1947, June 2 Unwmk. Engr.

No.	Type	Description	Unused	Used
J38	D8	10c black	15	15
J39	D8	30c dl bl grn	15	15
J40	D8	50c brt ultra	15	15
J41	D8	1fr dk grn	15	15
J42	D8	2fr dark blue	35	35
J43	D8	3fr blk brn	42	42
J44	D8	4fr lil rose	55	55
J45	D8	5fr purple	62	62
J46	D8	10fr red	80	80
J47	D8	20fr dark violet	1.00	1.00
		Nos. J38-J47 (10)	4.34	4.34

GUATEMALA

LOCATION — Central America, bordering on Atlantic and Pacific Oceans
GOVT. — Republic
AREA — 42,042 sq. mi.
POP. — 6,577,000 (est. 1984)
CAPITAL — Guatemala City

100 Centavos = 8 Reales = 1 Peso
100 Centavos de Quetzal = 1 Quetzal (1927)

Catalogue values for unused stamps in this country are for Never Hinged items, beginning with Scott 316 in the regular postage section, Scott B5 in the semi-postal section, Scott C137 in the air post section, Scott CB5 in the air post semi-postal section and Scott E2 in the special delivery section.

Coat of Arms
A1 A2

Two types of 10c:
Type I - Both zeros in "10" are wide.
Type II - Left zero narrow.

Perf. 14x13½

1871, Mar. 1 Typo. Unwmk.

No.	Type	Description	Unused	Used
1	A1	1c ocher	75	*10.00*
a.		Imperf., pair	5.00	
b.		Printed on both sides, imperf.	75.00	
2	A1	5c lt bister brn	4.00	*7.50*
a.		Imperf., pair	35.00	
b.		Tête bêche pair	150.00	
c.		Tête bêche pair, imperf.	2,600.	
3	A1	10c blue (I)	5.00	*8.00*
a.		Imperf., pair (I)	45.00	
b.		Type II	8.00	10.00
c.		Imperf. pair (II)	60.00	
4	A1	20c rose	4.00	*7.50*
a.		Imperf., pair	45.00	
b.		20c blue (error)	130.00	125.00
c.		As "b," imperf.	*800.00*	

Forgeries exist. Forged cancellations abound. See No. C458.

1873 Litho. *Perf. 12*

No.	Type	Description	Unused	Used
5	A2	4r dull red vio	300.00	75.00
6	A2	1p dull yellow	150.00	100.00

Forgeries exist.

Liberty
A3 A4

A5

A6

1875, Apr. 15 Engr.

No.	Type	Description	Unused	Used
7	A3	¼r black	1.00	*3.50*
8	A4	½r blue green	1.00	*3.00*
9	A5	1r blue	1.00	*3.00*
a.		Half used as ½r on cover		*1,700.*
10	A6	2r dull red	1.00	*3.00*

Nos. 7-10 normally lack gum.
Forgeries and forged cancellations exist.

Indian Woman — A7

Quetzal — A8

Typographed on Tinted Paper

1878, Jan. 10 *Perf. 13*

No.	Type	Description	Unused	Used
11	A7	½r yel grn	75	*3.00*
12	A7	2r car rose	1.25	*4.00*
13	A7	4r violet	1.25	*4.50*
14	A7	1p yellow	2.00	*9.00*
c.		Half used as 4r on cover		*2,200.*

Some sheets of Nos. 11-14 have papermaker's watermark, "LACROIX FRERES," in double-lined capitals appearing on six stamps.

Part perforate pairs of Nos. 11, 12 and 14 exist. Value for each, about $100.

Forgeries of Nos. 11-14 are plentiful. Forged cancellations exist.

For surcharges see Nos. 18, 20.

Imperf., Pairs

No.	Type	Description	Unused
11a	A7	½r yellow green	50.00
12a	A7	2r carmine rose	50.00
13a	A7	4r violet	50.00
14a	A7	1p yellow	50.00

1879 Engr. *Perf. 12*

No.	Type	Description	Unused	Used
15	A8	¼r brown & grn	2.50	2.75
16	A8	1r black & grn	2.50	3.75
a.		Half used as ½r on cover		*1,800.*

For similar types see A11, A72, A103, A121, A146. For surcharges see Nos. 17, 19.

Nos. 11, 12, 15, 16 Surcharged in Black

1
centavo.

1881 *Perf. 12 and 13*

No.	Type	Description	Unused	Used
17	A8	1c on ¼r brn & grn	5.00	6.00
a.		"ecntavo,"	30.00	20.00
b.		Pair, one without surcharge	200.00	
18	A7	5c on ½r yel grn	5.00	7.50
a.		"ecntavos,"	35.00	35.00
b.		"5" omitted	100.00	
c.		Double surcharge	75.00	85.00
19	A8	10c on 1r blk & grn	7.50	7.50
a.		"s" of "centavos" missing	75.00	75.00
b.		"ecntavos"	40.00	45.00
20	A7	20c on 2r car rose	35.00	40.00
a.		Horiz. pair, imperf. between	425.00	

The 5c had three settings.

Surcharge varieties found on Nos. 17-20 include: Period omitted; comma instead of period; "ecntavo." or "ecntavos."; "s" omitted; spaced "centavos."; wider "0" in "20."

Counterfeits of Nos. 17-20 are plentiful.

Quetzal — A11

1881, Nov. 7 Engr. *Perf. 12*

No.	Type	Description	Unused	Used
21	A11	1c black & grn	75	50
22	A11	2c brown & grn	50	50
a.		Center inverted	175.00	150.00
23	A11	5c red & grn	2.25	75
a.		Center inverted	*3,000.*	1,300.
24	A11	10c gray vio & grn	75	50
25	A11	20c yellow & grn	75	1.00
a.		Center inverted	275.00	200.00
		Nos. 21-25 (5)	5.00	3.25

Gen. Justo Rufino Barrios — A12

Black Surcharge

Correos Nacionales
25 c. 25 c.
Guatemala.
25 c. 25 c.
25 centavos.

1886, Mar. 6

No.	Type	Description	Unused	Used
26	A12	25c on 1p ver	50	50
a.		"centovos"	1.00	
b.		"centanos"	1.00	
c.		"255" instead of "25"	150.00	
d.		Inverted "S" in "Nacionales"	20.00	
f.		"cen avos"	20.00	
h.		"Corre cionales"	20.00	
i.		Inverted surcharge	75.00	
27	A12	50c on 1p ver	50	50
a.		"centovos"	1.00	
b.		"centanos"	1.00	
c.		"Carreos"	1.00	
d.		Inverted surcharge	50.00	
e.		Double surcharge	75.00	
f.		Inverted "S" in "Nacionales"	10.00	
g.		"centavo"	20.00	
h.		"cen avos"	20.00	
28	A12	75c on 1p ver	50	50
a.		"centovos"	1.00	
b.		"centanos"	1.00	
c.		"Carreos"	1.00	
d.		"50" for "75" at upper right	1.50	
e.		Inverted "S" in "Nacionales"	10.00	
f.		Double surcharge	75.00	
g.		"ales" inverted	100.00	
29	A12	100c on 1p ver	75	60
a.		"110" at upper left and "á" at lower left, instead of "100"	4.00	
b.		Inverted surcharge	75.00	
c.		"Guatemala" bolder; 23mm instead of 18½mm wide	1.50	
d.		Double surcharge, one diagonal	100.00	
30	A12	150c on 1p ver	50	50
a.		Inverted "G"	5.00	
b.		"Guetemala" and italic "5" in upper 4 numerals	5.00	
d.		Inverted surcharge	90.00	
e.		Pair, one without surcharge	100.00	
f.		Double surcharge	100.00	
		Nos. 26-30 (5)	2.75	2.60

There are many other minor varieties, such as wrong font letters, etc. The surcharge on Nos. 29 and 30 has different letters and ornaments. On No. 29, "Guatemala," normally is 18½mm wide.

Used values of Nos. 26-30 are for canceled to order stamps. Postally used sell for much more.

National Emblem — A13

1886, July 1 Litho. *Perf. 12*

No.	Type	Description	Unused	Used
31	A13	1c dull blue	5.00	2.00
32	A13	2c brown	5.00	3.00
33	A13	5c purple	37.50	75
34	A13	10c red	10.00	75
35	A13	20c emerald	15.00	1.25
36	A13	25c orange	15.00	1.50
37	A13	50c olive grn	10.00	2.00
38	A13	75c car rose	10.00	3.00

39 A13 100c red brown 10.00 3.00
40 A13 150c dark blue 15.00 3.75
41 A13 200c orange yel 17.50 4.75
Nos. 31-41 (11) 150.00 25.75

Used values of Nos. 38-41 are for canceled to order stamps. Postally used sell for more.

See Nos. 43-50, 99-107. For surcharges see Nos. 42, 51-59, 75-85, 97-98, 108-110, 124-130.

No. 32 Surcharged in Black

PROVISIONAL.
1886

UN CENTAVO

Two settings:
I - "1886" (no period).
II - "1886." (period).

1886, Nov. 12

42 A13 1c on 2c brown, I 2.00 2.50
a. Date inverted, I 75.00
b. Date double, I 75.00
c. Date omitted, I 60.00
d. Date double, one invtd., I 100.00
e. Date triple, one inverted, I 100.00
f. Setting II 1.50 1.00
g. Inverted surcharge, II 4.00
h. Double surcharge, II 100.00

Forgeries exist.

Type I Type II

Two types of 5c:
I - Thin "5"
II - Larger, thick "5"

1886-95 Engr. *Perf. 12*

43 A13 1c blue 75 15
44 A13 2c yellow brn 2.25 15
a. Half used as 1c on cover 100.00
45 A13 5c purple (I) 50.00 1.00
46 A13 5c vio (II) ('88) 1.50 15
47 A13 6c lilac ('95) 60 20
48 A13 10c red ('90) 1.50 15
49 A13 20c green ('93) 3.00 75
50 A13 25c red org ('93) 7.50 1.25
Nos. 43-44,46-50 (7) 17.10 2.80

The impression of the engraved stamps is sharper than that of the lithographed. On the engraved stamps the top four lines at left are heavier than those below them. (This is also true of the 1c litho., which is distinguished from the engraved only by a slight color difference and the impression.) The "2" and "5" (I) are more open than the litho. numerals. The "10" of the engraved is wider. The 20c and 25c of the engraved have a vertical line at right end of the "centavos" ribbon.

No. 38 Surcharged in Blue Black

1894

CENTAVOS

"1894" 14½mm wide

1894, Apr. 25

51 A13 10c on 75c car rose 4.50 4.50
a. Double surcharge 75.00
b. Inverted surcharge 100.00

Same on Nos. 38-41 in Blue or Red
"1894" 14mm wide

1894, June 13

52 A13 2c on 100c 7.50 4.25
53 A13 6c on 150c (R) 7.50 3.50
54 A13 10c on 75c 550.00 500.00
55 A13 10c on 200c 7.50 4.25
c. Inverted surcharge 75.00

Nos. 54-55 exist with thick or thin "1" in new value.

Same on Nos. 39-41 in Black or Red
"1894" 12mm wide

1894, July 14

52a A13 2c on 100c red brn (Bk) 4.00 3.50
b. Vert. pair, one without surch. 150.00

53a A13 6c on 150c dk bl (R) 4.50 3.50
55a A13 10c on 200c org yel (Bk) 5.00 3.50
d. Inverted surcharge 100.00
e. Vert. pair, one without surch. 150.00

Nos. 44 and 46 Surcharged in Black, Blue Black, or Red:

1894 — 1 CENTAVO (b) 1895 — 1 CENTAVO (c)
1 CENTAVO — 1895 (d) 1 CENTAVO — 1895 (e)

1894-96

56 A13 (b) 1c on 2c (Bk) 75 30
a. "Centav" 5.00 5.00
b. Double surcharge 75.00
c. As "a," dbl. surcharge 150.00
d. Blue black surcharge 20.00 20.00
e. Dbl. surch., one inverted 150.00
57 A13 (c) 1c on 5c (R) ('95) 50 20
a. Inverted surcharge 3.00 3.00
b. "1894" instead of "1895" 3.50 3.00
c. Double surcharge 50.00
58 A13 (d) 1c on 5c (R) ('95) 75 20
a. Inverted surcharge 50.00 50.00
b. Double surcharge 50.00
59 A13 (e) 1c on 5c (R) ('96) 1.25 40
a. Inverted surcharge 50.00 50.00
b. Double surcharge 50.00

Nos. 56-58 may be found with thick or thin "1" in the new value.

National Arms and President J. M. Reyna Barrios — A21

1897, Jan. 1 Engr. Unwmk.

60 A21 1c blk, *lil gray* 50 50
61 A21 2c blk, *grnsh gray* 50 50
62 A21 6c blk, *brn org* 50 50
63 A21 10c blk, *dl bl* 50 50
64 A21 12c blk, *rose red* 50 50
65 A21 18c blk, *grysh white* 8.00 7.50
66 A21 20c blk, *scarlet* 1.00 1.00
67 A21 25c blk, *bis brn* 1.50 1.00
68 A21 50c blk, *redsh brn* 1.00 1.00
69 A21 75c blk, *gray* 50.00 50.00
70 A21 100c blk, *bl grn* 1.00 1.00
71 A21 150c blk, *dl rose* 100.00 125.00
72 A21 200c blk, *magenta* 1.00 1.00
73 A21 500c blk, *yel grn* 1.00 1.00
Nos. 60-73 (14) 167.00 191.00

Issued for Central American Exposition.

Stamps often sold as Nos. 65, 69 and 71 are copies with telegraph overprint removed.

Used values for Nos. 60-73 are for canceled-to-order copies. Postally used examples are worth more.

The paper of Nos. 64 and 66 was originally colored on one side only, but has "bled through" on some copies.

No. 64 Surcharged in Violet

UN
CENTAVO
1898

1897, Nov.

74 A21 1c on 12c *rose red* 1.00 1.00
a. Inverted surcharge 30.00 30.00
b. Pair, one without surcharge 75.00
c. Dbl. surch., one invtd. 100.00

Stamps of 1886-93 Surcharged in Red

1898 — 1 centavo (f) 1898 — 10 centavos (g)

1898

75 (f) 1c on 5c vio 1.00 1.00
a. Inverted surcharge 75.00
76 (f) 1c on 50c ol grn 1.50 1.25
a. Inverted surcharge 100.00 100.00
77 (f) 6c on 5c vio 4.50 1.50
a. Inverted surcharge 75.00
b. Double surcharge 100.00
78 (f) 6c on 150c dk bl 4.50 3.25
79 (g) 10c on 20c emer 5.00 4.00
a. Double surch., one inverted 125.00 125.00
Nos. 75-79 (5) 16.50 11.00

Black Surcharge

80 (f) 1c on 25c red org 2.00 2.00
81 (f) 1c on 75c car rose 1.50 1.50
a. Double surcharge 100.00
82 (f) 6c on 10c red 10.00 9.00
83 (f) 6c on 20c emer 5.00 4.00
84 (f) 6c on 100c red brn 5.00 4.00
85 (f) 6c on 200c org yel 5.00 4.00
a. Inverted surcharge 50.00 50.00
Nos. 80-85 (6) 28.50 24.50

National Emblem
A24 A25

Revenue Stamp Overprinted or Surcharged in Carmine

Perf. 12, 12x14, 14x12

1898, Oct. 8 Litho.

86 A24 1c dark blue 75 50
a. Inverted overprint 12.50 12.50
87 A24 2c on 1c dk bl 1.00 50
a. Inverted surcharge 12.50 12.50

Counterfeits exist.

See type A26.

Revenue Stamps Surcharged in Carmine

1898 Engr. *Perf. 12½ to 16*

88 A25 1c on 10c bl gray 75 75
a. "ENTAVO" 5.00 5.00
89 A25 2c on 5c pur 1.25 1.00
90 A25 2c on 10c bl gray 6.50 7.00
a. Double surch., car & blk 100.00 75.00
91 A25 2c on 50c dp bl 8.00 9.00
a. Double surch., car & blk 100.00 100.00

Black Surcharge

92 A25 2c on 1c lil rose 3.50 2.00
93 A25 2c on 25c red 7.50 8.00
94 A25 6c on 1p purple 4.00 4.50
95 A25 6c on 5p gray vio 7.50 7.50
96 A25 6c on 10p emer 7.50 7.50
Nos. 92-96 (5) 30.00 29.50

Nos. 88 and 90 are found in shades ranging from Prussian blue to slate blue.

Varieties other than those listed are bogus. Counterfeits exist of No. 92.

Soaking in water causes marked fading.

See type A27.

No. 46 Surcharged in Red

Un I Centavo
1899

1899, Sept. *Perf. 12*

97 A13 1c on 5c violet 40 25
a. Inverted surcharge 7.50 7.50
b. Double surcharge 15.00 15.00
c. Double surcharge, one inverted 15.00 15.00

No. 48 Surcharged in Black

1900
1
CENTAVO

1900, Jan.

98 A13 1c on 10c red 50 50
a. Inverted surcharge 10.00 10.00
b. Double surcharge 75.00 75.00

Quetzal Type of 1886

1900-02 Engr.

99 A13 1c dk grn 60 25
100 A13 2c carmine 60 25
101 A13 5c blue (II) 2.25 1.25
102 A13 6c lt grn 75 25
103 A13 10c bister brn 7.50 1.00
104 A13 20c purple 7.50 7.50
105 A13 20c bis brn ('02) 7.50 7.50
106 A13 25c yellow 7.50 7.50
107 A13 25c bl grn ('02) 7.50 7.50
Nos. 99-107 (9) 41.70 33.00

No. 49 Surcharged in Black

1901
1
CENTAVO

1901, May

108 A13 1c on 20c green 50 50
a. Inverted surcharge 20.00 20.00
b. Double surch., one diagonal 50.00
109 A13 2c on 20c green 1.50 1.50

No. 50 Surcharged in Black

UN
1
CENTAVO
1901

1901, Apr.

110 A13 1c on 25c red org 60 60
a. Inverted surcharge 25.00 25.00
b. Double surcharge 50.00 50.00

A26 A27

Revenue Stamps Surcharged in Carmine or Black

1902, July *Perf. 12, 14x12, 12x14*

111 A26 1c on 1c dk bl 1.00 1.00
a. Double surcharge 20.00
b. Inverted surcharge 20.00
112 A26 2c on 1c dk bl 1.00 1.00
a. Double surcharge 75.00
b. Inverted surcharge 25.00

Perf. 14, 15

113 A27 6c on 25c red (Bk) 2.00 2.50
a. Double surch., one invtd. 75.00 75.00

National Emblem — A28

Statue of Justo Rufino Barrios — A29

"La Reforma" Palace — A30

Temple of Minerva — A31

Lake Amatitlán — A32

Cathedral in Guatemala — A33

Columbus Theater — A34

Artillery Barracks — A35

Monument to Columbus — A36

School for Indians — A37

1902 Engr. *Perf. 12 to 16*

114 A28 1c grn & claret 15 15
 a. Horiz. pair, imperf. vert. 100.00
115 A29 2c lake & blk 15 15
 a. Horiz. or vert. pair, imperf. btwn. 150.00
116 A30 5c bl & blk 20 15
 a. 5c ultra & blk 60 15
 b. Imperf., pair 100.00 100.00
 c. Horiz. pair, imperf. vert. 100.00
117 A31 6c bis & grn 20 15
 a. Horiz. pair, imperf. btwn. 150.00
118 A32 10c org & bl 22 15
 a. Horiz. pair, imperf. vert. 100.00
119 A33 20c rose lil & blk 40 15
 a. Horiz. pair, imperf. vert. 100.00
120 A34 50c red brn & bl 32 15
 a. Vert. pair, imperf. btwn. 350.00
121 A35 75c gray lil & blk 32 15
 a. Horiz. pair, imperf. btwn. 150.00
 b. Horiz. pair, imperf. vert. 100.00
122 A36 1p brn & blk 55 20
 a. Horiz. pair, imperf. btwn. 150.00
123 A37 2p ver & blk 65 40
 Nos. 114-123 (10) 3.16
 Set value 1.55

See Nos. 210, 212-214, 219, 223, 239-241, 243. For overprints and surcharges see Nos. 133, 135-139, 144-157, 168, 170-171, 178, 192-194, 298-299, 301, C19, C27, C123.

1903
Issues of 1886-1900 Surcharged in Black or Carmine **25**
CENTAVOS

1903, Apr. 18 *Perf. 12*

124 A13 25c on 1c dk grn 1.25 50
 a. Inverted surcharge 40.00 40.00
125 A13 25c on 2c car 1.50 50
126 A13 25c on 6c lt grn 2.50 1.75
 a. Inverted surcharge 40.00 40.00
127 A13 25c on 10c bis brn 7.50 7.00
128 A13 25c on 75c rose 10.00 10.00
129 A13 25c on 150c dk bl (C) 9.00 9.00
130 A13 25c on 200c yel 10.00 10.00
 Nos. 124-130 (7) 41.75 38.75

Forgeries and bogus varieties exist.

Declaration of Independence A38

1907, Jan. 1 *Perf. 13½ to 15*

132 A38 12½c ultra & blk 25 15
 a. Horiz. pair, imperf. btwn. 150.00

For surcharge see No. 134.

Nos. 118, 119 and 132 Surcharged in Black or Red
1908
UN 1 UN
CENTAVO

1908, May

133 A32 1c on 10c org & bl 30 25
 a. Double surcharge 25.00
 b. Inverted surcharge 15.00 15.00
 c. Pair, one without surcharge 50.00
134 A38 2c on 12½c ultra & blk (R) 25 25
 a. Horiz. or vert. pair, imperf. btwn. 100.00
 b. Inverted surcharge 15.00 10.00
 c. Double surcharge 30.00
135 A33 6c on 20c rose lil & blk 40 25
 a. Inverted surcharge 20.00 20.00

Similar Surcharge, Dated 1909, in Red or Black on Nos. 121 and 120

1909, Apr.

136 A35 2c on 75c (R) 50 50
137 A34 6c on 50c (R) 50.00 50.00
 a. Double surcharge 100.00 100.00
138 A34 6c on 50c (Bk) 30 30

Counterfeits exist of Nos. 137, 137a.

No. 123 Surcharged in Black
12½
CENTAVOS
1909.

139 A37 12½c on 2p ver & blk 30 30
 a. Inverted surcharge 25.00 25.00
 b. Period omitted after "1909" 12.50 12.50

Counterfeits exist.

Gen. Miguel García Granados, Birth Cent. (in 1909) — A39

1910, Feb. 11 *Perf. 14*

140 A39 6c bis & indigo 50 40
 a. Imperf., pair 50.00

Some sheets used for this issue contained a two-line watermark, "SPECIAL POSTAGE PAPER / LONDON." For surcharge see No. 143.

General Post Office — A40

Pres. Manuel Estrada Cabrera — A41

1911, June *Perf. 12*

141 A40 25c bl & blk 50 15
 a. Center inverted 1,750. 650.00
142 A41 5p red & blk 65 65
 a. Center inverted 25.00 27.50

Nos. 116, 118 and 140 Surcharged in Black or Red:

1911
h
Un Centavo

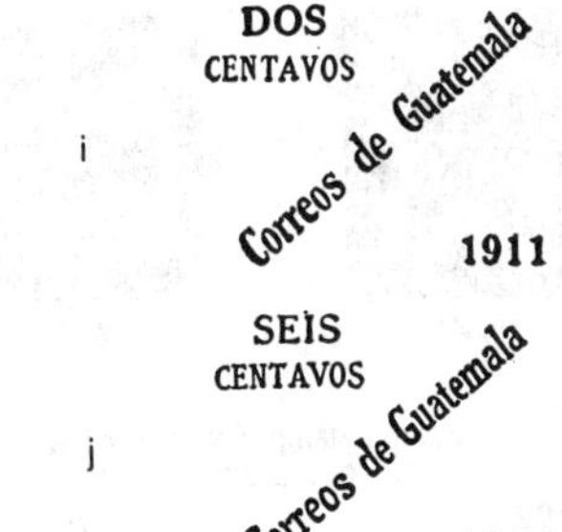
DOS
CENTAVOS
Correos de Guatemala
1911
i

SEIS
CENTAVOS
Correos de Guatemala
1911
j

1911 *Perf. 14*

143 A39 (h) 1c on 6c 20.00 7.50
 a. Double surcharge 75.00
144 A30 (i) 2c on 5c (R) 1.50 75
145 A32 (j) 6c on 10c 1.25 1.25
 a. Double surcharge 50.00

See watermark note after No. 140. Forgeries exist.

Nos. 119-121 Surcharged in Black:

1912
1 UN CENTAVO 1
1912 **1912**
2 CENTAVOS 2
5 5
CINCO CENTAVOS 1912

1912, Sept.

147 A33 1c on 20c 30 30
 a. Inverted surcharge 7.50 7.50
 b. Double surcharge 15.00 15.00
148 A34 2c on 50c 30 30
 a. Inverted surcharge 10.00 10.00
 b. Double surcharge 12.50
 c. Double inverted surcharge 25.00
149 A35 5c on 75c 75 75
 a. "191" for "1912" 7.50 7.50
 b. Double surcharge 15.00 15.00
 c. Inverted surcharge 10.00

Forgeries exist.

Nos. 120, 122 and 123 Surcharged in Blue, Green or Black:

1913
n
UN CENTAVO
1913
o
Seis centavos
1913
p
12½ CENTAVOS

1913, July

151 A34 (n) 1c on 50c (Bl) 25 25
 a. Inverted surcharge 10.00
 b. Double surcharge 17.50
 c. Horiz. pair, imperf. btwn. 100.00

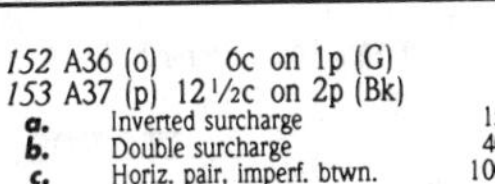
152 A36 (o) 6c on 1p (G) 30 30
153 A37 (p) 12½c on 2p (Bk) 30 30
 a. Inverted surcharge 15.00 15.00
 b. Double surcharge 40.00
 c. Horiz. pair, imperf. btwn. 100.00

Forgeries exist.

Nos. 114 and 115 Surcharged in Black:

DOS
CENTAVOS
q
SEIS
CENTAVOS
r
12½
CENTAVOS
s
VEINTICINCO
CENTAVOS
t

1916-17

154 A28 (q) 2c on 1c ('17) 20 20
155 A28 (r) 6c on 1c 20 20
156 A28 (s) 12½c on 1c 20 20
157 A29 (t) 25c on 2c 20 20

Numerous errors of value and color, inverted and double surcharges and similar varieties are in the market. They were not regularly issued, but were surreptitiously made and sold.
Counterfeit surcharges abound.

"Liberty" and President Estrada Cabrera — A51

Estrada Cabrera and Quetzal — A52

1917, Mar. 15 *Perf. 14, 15*

158 A51 25c dp bl & brn 25 15

Re-election of President Estrada Cabrera.

1918 *Perf. 12*

161 A52 1.50p dark blue 20 15

Radio Station — A54

"Joaquina" Maternity Hospital — A55

"Estrada Cabrera" Vocational School — A56

National Emblem — A57

1919, May 3 *Perf. 14, 15*

162 A54 30c red & blk 2.00 75
163 A55 60c ol grn & blk 75 50
164 A56 90c red brn & blk 75 75
165 A57 3p dp grn & blk 1.50 50

See Nos. 215, 227. For surcharges see Nos. 166-167, 179-185, 188, 195-198, 245-246, C8-C11, C21-C22.

No. 162 Surcharged
1920
2 centavos

Blue Overprint and Black Surcharge

1920, Jan. Unwmk.

166 A54 2c on 30c red & blk 25 25
 a. Inverted surcharge 12.50 12.50
 b. "1920" double 10.00 10.00
 c. "1920" omitted 15.00 15.00
 d. "2 centavos" omitted 20.00
 e. Imperf., pair 100.00
 f. Pair, imperf. btwn. 100.00

Nos. 123 and 163 Surcharged:

2 centavos
u

1920
25
v
Centavos

1920

167 A55 2c on 60c (Bk & R) 25 25
a. Inverted surcharge 10.00 10.00
b. "1920" inverted 7.50 7.50
c. "1920" omitted 10.00 10.00
d. "1920" only 10.00
e. Double surcharge 25.00
168 A37 25c on 2p (Bk) 30 25
a. "35" for "25" 7.50 7.50
b. Large "5" in "25" 7.50 7.50
c. Inverted surcharge 15.00 15.00
d. Double surcharge 25.00

A61

1920

169 A61 25c green 25 15
a. Double overprint 50.00
b. Double overprint, inverted 75.00

See types A65-A66.

No. 119 Surcharged

1921
Doce y medio
cēntavos

1921, Apr.

170 A33 12½c on 20c 25 15
a. Double surcharge 15.00
b. Inverted surcharge 15.00

No. 121 Surcharged

1921
Cincuenta
centavos

1921, Apr.

171 A35 50c on 75c lil & blk 40 30
a. Double surcharge 17.50
b. Inverted surcharge 25.00 25.00

Mayan Stele at Quiriguá — A62

Monument to President Granados — A63

"La Penitenciaria" Bridge — A64

1921, Sept. 1 *Perf. 13½, 14, 15*

172 A62 1.50p bl & org 75 25
173 A63 5p brn & grn 2.50 1.25
174 A64 15p blk & ver 9.00 5.00

See Nos. 216, 228, 229. For surcharges see Nos. 186-187, 189-191, 199-201, 207, 231, 247-251, C1-C5, C12, C23-C24.

A65

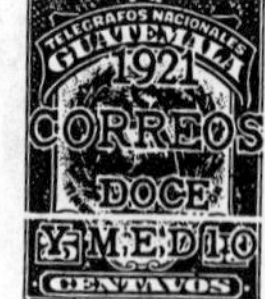
A66

Telegraph Stamps Overprinted or Surcharged in Black or Red

1921 *Perf. 14*

175 A65 25c green 25 20
176 A66 12½c on 25c grn (R) 20 20
177 A66 12½c on 25c grn 15.00 15.00

Nos. 119, 163 and 164 Surcharged in Black or Red:

1922
DOCE Y
MEDIO
CENTAVOS
w

1922
25
CENTAVOS
x

1922, Mar.

178 A33(w) 12½c on 20c 20 20
a. Inverted surcharge 10.00
179 A55(w) 12½c on 60c (R) 50 50
a. Inverted surcharge 25.00
180 A56(w) 12½c on 90c 50 50
a. Inverted surcharge 25.00
181 A55(x) 25c on 60c 1.00 1.00
a. Inverted surcharge 20.00
182 A55(x) 25c on 60c (R) 125.00 125.00
183 A56(x) 25c on 90c 1.00 1.00
a. Inverted surcharge 25.00
184 A56(x) 25c on 90c (R) 4.00 4.00
Nos. 178-181,183-184 (6) 7.20 7.20

Counterfeits exist.

Nos. 165, 173-174 Surcharged in Red or Dark Blue

1922
DOCE
Y MEDIO
CENTAVOS

1922, May

185 A57 12½c on 3p grn & blk (R) 20 15
186 A63 12½c on 5p brn & grn 50 45
187 A64 12½c on 15p blk & ver 50 45

Nos. 165, 173-174 Surcharged in Red or Black

1922
25
CENTAVOS

25 I 25 II 25 III 25 IV

1922

188 A57 25c on 3p (I) (R) 20 20
a. Type II 60 60
b. Type III 60 60
c. Type IV 30 30
d. Inverted surcharge 40.00
e. Horiz. or vert. pair, imperf. between (I) 125.00
189 A63 25c on 5p (I) 1.00 2.00
a. Type II 2.00 3.00
b. Type III 2.00 3.00
c. Type IV 1.00 2.00
190 A64 25c on 15p (I) 1.00 1.50
a. Type II 2.00 3.00
b. Type III 2.00 3.00
c. Type IV 1.00 1.50
191 A64 25c on 15p (I) (R) 22.50 30.00
a. Type II 40.00 45.00
b. Type III 45.00 45.00
c. Type IV 30.00 35.00

Stamps of 1902-21 Surcharged in Dark Blue or Red

1922
25
CENTAVOS

25 V 25 VI 25 VII 25 VIII 25 IX

1922, Aug. **On Nos. 121-123**

192 A35 25c on 75c (V) 35 35
a. Type VI 35 35
b. Type VII 1.75 1.75
c. Type VIII 5.50 4.00
d. Type IX 6.50 6.00
193 A36 25c on 1p (V) 30 30
a. Type VI 30 30
b. Type VII 1.25 1.25
c. Type VIII 2.50 2.50
d. Type IX 4.00 3.50
e. Inverted surcharge 40.00
194 A37 25c on 2p (V) 45 45
a. Type VI 45 45
b. Type VII 1.25 1.25
c. Type VIII 4.00 4.00
d. Type IX 6.50 6.50

On Nos. 162-165

195 A54 25c on 30c (V) 45 45
a. Type VI 45 45
b. Type VII 1.25 1.25
c. Type VIII 5.50 5.50
d. Type IX 6.50 6.50
196 A55 25c on 60c (V) 1.00 1.50
a. Type VI 1.00 1.50
b. Type VII 5.50 7.50
c. Type VIII 8.00 9.00
d. Type IX 10.00 11.00
197 A56 25c on 90c (V) 1.00 1.50
a. Type VI 1.50 2.00
b. Type VII 5.50 6.50
c. Type VIII 8.00 9.00
d. Type IX 10.00 11.00
198 A57 25c on 3p (R) (V) 35 35
a. Type VI 35 35
b. Type VII 1.25 1.00
c. Type VIII 6.00 4.50
d. Type IX 6.50 6.00
e. Invtd. surch. 50.00

On Nos. 172-174

199 A62 25c on 1.50p (V) 30 25
a. Type VI 30 25
b. Type VII 1.25 1.00
c. Type VIII 3.00 3.00
d. Type IX 4.50 4.00
e. Invtd. surch. 40.00
200 A63 25c on 5p (V) 75 90
a. Type VI 80 1.00
b. Type VII 3.00 3.50
c. Type VIII 5.50 6.00
d. Type IX 8.00 8.50
201 A64 25c on 15p (V) 85 90
a. Type VI 1.50 1.50
b. Type VII 5.00 5.50
c. Type VIII 6.50 6.50
d. Type IX 12.00 12.00

Centenary Palace — A69

National Palace at Antigua — A70

1922 *Perf. 14, 14½*

Printed by Waterlow & Sons

202 A69 12½c green 15 15
a. Horiz. or vert. pair, imperf. btwn. 100.00
203 A70 25c brown 15 15
Set value 20

See Nos. 211, 221, 234.

Columbus Theater A71

Quetzal A72

Granados Monument — A73

Litho. by Castillo Bros.

1924, Feb. *Perf. 12*

204 A71 50c rose 50 20
a. Imperf., pair 7.50
b. Horiz. or vert. pair, imperf. btwn. 25.00
205 A72 1p dk grn 75 20
a. Imperf. vertically 15.00
b. Vertical pair, imperf. between 20.00
c. Imperf., pair 7.50
206 A73 5p orange 1.25 50
a. Imperf., pair 7.50
b. Horizontal pair, imperf. between 20.00

For surcharges see Nos. 208-209.

Nos. 172 and 206 Surcharged

1924
—
UN PESO
25 Cents.

1924, July

207 A62 1p on 1.50p bl & org 30 20
208 A73 1.25p on 5p org 50 50
a. "UN PESO 25 Cents." omitted 40.00
b. Horiz. pair, imperf. btwn. 25.00

#208 with two bars over "25 Cents."

1924

209 A73 1p on 5p orange 50 50

Types of 1902-22 Issues

Engr. by Perkins Bacon & Co.

1924, Aug. **Re-engraved** *Perf. 14*

210 A31 6c bister 15 15
211 A70 25c brown 20 15
212 A34 50c red 25 15
213 A36 1p org brn 25 15
214 A37 2p orange 35 25
215 A57 3p dp grn 2.00 50
216 A64 15p black 2.25 75
Nos. 210-216 (7) 5.45 2.10

The designs of the stamps of 1924 differ from those of the 1902-22 issues in many details which are too minute to illustrate. The re-engraved issue may be readily distinguished by the imprint "Perkins Bacon & Co. Ld. Londres."

Pres. Justo Rufino Barrios A74

Lorenzo Montúfar A75

1924, Aug.

217 A74 1.25p ultra 20 15
218 A75 2.50p dk vio 1.00 25

See Nos. 224, 226. For surcharges see Nos. 232, C6, C20.

Aurora Park — A76

National Post Office — A77

National Observatory — A78

Types of 1921-24 Re-engraved and New Designs Dated 1926

Engraved by Waterlow & Sons, Ltd.

1926, July-Aug. *Perf. 12½*

No.	Type	Description		
219	A31	6c ocher	15	15
220	A76	12½c green	15	15
221	A70	25c brown	15	15
222	A77	50c red	15	15
223	A36	1p org brn	20	15
224	A74	1.50p dk blue	20	15
225	A78	2p orange	1.25	1.00
226	A75	2.50p dk vio	1.50	1.25
227	A57	3p dk green	45	20
228	A63	5p brn vio	1.00	40
229	A64	15p black	1.25	60
		Nos. 219-229 (11)	6.45	4.35

These stamps may be distinguished from those of the same designs in preceding issues by the imprint "Waterlow & Sons, Limited, Londres," the date, "1926," and the perforation.

See Nos. 233, 242. For surcharge see No. 230.

Nos. 225-226, 228 Surcharged in Various Colors

1928

½ CENTAVO

DE QUETZAL

1928

No.	Type	Description		
230	A78	½c on 2p (Bl)	60	45
a.		Inverted surcharge	12.50	
231	A63	½c on 5p (Bk)	30	20
a.		Inverted surcharge	10.00	10.00
b.		Double surcharge	50.00	
c.		Blue surcharge	45.00	45.00
d.		Blue and black surcharge	50.00	50.00
232	A75	1c on 2.50p (R)	30	20
b.		Double surcharge		50.00

Barrios
A79

Montúfar
A80

Granados
A81

General Orellana
A82

Coat of Arms of Guatemala City — A83

Engraved by T. De la Rue & Co.

1929, Jan. *Perf. 14*

No.	Type	Description		
233	A78	½c yel grn	75	15
234	A70	1c dk brn	25	15
235	A79	2c dp bl	25	15
236	A80	3c dk vio	20	15
237	A81	4c orange	25	15
238	A82	5c dk car	50	15
239	A31	10c brown	40	15
240	A36	15c ultra	50	15
241	A29	25c brn org	1.00	25
242	A76	30c green	90	40
243	A32	50c pale rose	2.00	75
244	A83	1q black	3.00	50
		Nos. 233-244 (12)	10.00	
		Set value		2.70

Nos. 233, 234 and 239 to 243 differ from the illustrations in many minor details, particularly in the borders.

See No. 300 for bisect of No. 235. For overprints and surcharges see Nos. 297, C13, C17-C18, C25-C26, C28, E1, RA17-RA18.

No. 227 Surcharged in Black or Red

1929, Dec. 28 *Perf. 12½, 13*

No.	Type	Description		
245	A57	3c on 3p dk grn (Bk)	1.25	1.75
a.		Inverted surcharge	15.00	15.00
246	A57	5c on 3p dk grn (R)	1.25	1.75
a.		Inverted surcharge	15.00	15.00

Inauguration of the Eastern Railroad connecting Guatemala and El Salvador.

No. 229 Surcharged in Red

FERROCARRIL DE LOS ALTOS

Inaugurado en 1929

2 CENTAVOS DE QUETZAL

1930, Mar. 30 **Unwmk.**

No.	Type	Description		
247	A64	1c on 15p black	50	50
248	A64	2c on 15p black	50	75
249	A64	3c on 15p black	60	75
250	A64	5c on 15p black	60	75
251	A64	15c on 15p black	60	75
		Nos. 247-251 (5)	2.80	3.50

Opening of Los Altos electric railway.

Hydroelectric Dam — A85

Los Altos Railway — A86

Railroad Station — A87

1930, Mar. 30 **Typo.** *Perf. 12*

No.	Type	Description		
252	A85	2c brn vio & blk	1.00	1.40
a.		Horiz. pair, imperf. btwn.	125.00	
253	A86	3c dp red & blk	1.75	2.00
a.		Vert. pair, imperf. btwn.	125.00	
254	A87	5c buff & dk bl	1.75	2.00

Opening of Los Altos electric railway. Exist imperf.

Mayan Stele at Quiriguá — A91

1932, Apr. 8 **Engr.**

No.	Type	Description		
258	A91	3c carmine rose	1.00	15

See Nos. 302-303.

Flag of the Race, Columbus and Tecum Uman
A92

1933, Aug. 3 **Litho.** *Perf. 12½*

No.	Type	Description		
259	A92	½c dk grn	50	75
260	A92	1c dl brn	1.00	1.25
261	A92	2c dp bl	1.00	1.25
262	A92	3c dl vio	1.00	75
263	A92	5c rose	1.00	1.00
		Nos. 259-263 (5)	4.50	5.00

Day of the Race and 441st anniv. of the sailing of Columbus from Palos, Spain, Aug. 3, 1492, on his 1st voyage to the New World.

The 3c and 5c exist imperf.

Birthplace of Barrios — A93

View of San Lorenzo
A94

Justo Rufino Barrios — A95

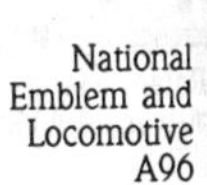

National Emblem and Locomotive
A96

General Post Office — A97

Telegraph Building and Barrios
A98

Military Academy
A99

National Police Headquarters
A100

Jorge Ubico and J. R. Barrios
A101

1935, July 19 **Photo.**

No.	Type	Description		
264	A93	½c yel grn & mag	50	60
265	A94	1c org red & pck bl	50	60
266	A95	2c org & blk	50	70
267	A96	3c car rose & pck bl	1.00	1.00
268	A97	4c pck bl & org red	5.00	6.00
269	A98	5c bl grn & brn	4.00	5.00
270	A99	10c slate grn & rose lake	6.00	7.00
271	A100	15c ol grn & org brn	5.00	6.00
272	A101	25c scar & bl	5.00	6.00
		Nos. 264-272 (9)	27.50	32.90

General Barrios. See Nos. C29-C31.

Lake Atitlán
A102

Quetzal
A103

Legislative Building — A104

1935, Oct. 10

No.	Type	Description		
273	A102	1c brn & crim	25	15
274	A103	3c rose car & pck grn	50	15
275	A103	3c red org & pck grn	50	15
276	A104	4c brt bl & dp rose	35	15
		Set value		40

See No. 277. For surcharges see Nos. B1-B3.

No. 273 perforated diagonally through the center

1935, July *Perf. 12½x12*

No.	Type	Description		
277	A102	(½c) brn & crimson	20	15
a.		Unsevered pair	50	60

Bureau of Printing — A105

Map of Guatemala
A106

1936, Sept. 24 *Perf. 12½*

No.	Type	Description		
278	A105	½c grn & pur	15	15
279	A106	5c bl & dk brn	1.00	15
		Set value		25

For surcharge see No. B4.

Quetzal
A107

Union Park, Quezaltenango
A108

Gen. Jorge Ubico on Horseback
A109

Designs: 1c, Tower of the Reformer. 3c, National Post Office. 4c, Government Building, Retalhuleu. 5c, Legislative Palace entrance. 10c, Custom House. 15c, Aurora Airport Custom House. 25c, National Fair. 50c, Residence of Presidential

Guard. 1.50q, General Ubico, portrait standing, no cap.

1937, May 20

280	A107	½c pck bl & car rose	25	30
281	A107	1c ol gray & red brn	50	30
282	A108	2c vio & car rose	50	35
283	A108	3c brn vio & brt bl	50	20
284	A108	4c yel & dl ol grn	2.00	2.25
285	A107	5c crim & brt vio	1.90	1.75
286	A107	10c mag & brn blk	3.00	3.50
287	A108	15c ultra & cop red	2.50	3.50
288	A108	25c red org & vio	3.00	3.75
289	A108	50c dk grn & org red	4.50	5.50
290	A109	1q mag & blk	22.50	25.00
291	A109	1.50q red brn & blk	22.50	25.00
		Nos. 280-291 (12)	63.65	71.40

Second term of President Ubico.

Mayan Calendar A119

Natl. Flower (White Nun Orchid) A120

Quetzal — A121

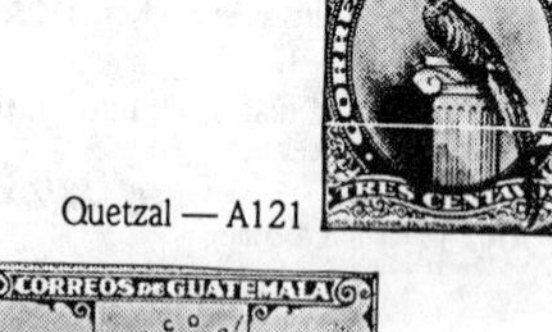

Map of Guatemala A122

1939, Sept. 7 *Perf. 13x12, 12½*

292	A119	½c grn & red brn	25	15
293	A120	2c bl & gray blk	1.50	20
294	A121	3c red org & turq grn	1.00	15
295	A121	3c ol bis & turq grn	1.00	15
296	A122	5c blue & red	1.75	1.75
		Nos. 292-296 (5)	5.50	2.40

For overprints see Nos. 324, C157.

No. 235 Surcharged with New Value in Red

1939, Sept. *Perf. 14*

297 A79 1c on 2c deep blue 20 15

Stamps of 1929 Surcharged in Blue:

y — 1 1 UN CENTAVO

z — 5 5

1940, June

298	A29 (y)	1c on 25c brn org	25	15
299	A32 (z)	5c on 50c pale rose (bar 10x¾mm)	25	15
a.		Bar 12½x2mm	30	15
b.		Bar 12½x1mm	50.00	5.00
		Set value		25

No. 235 perforated diagonally through the center

1941, Aug. 16 *Perf. 14x11½*

300	A79	(1c) deep blue	15	15
a.		Unsevered pair	40	40

No. 241 Surcharged in Black

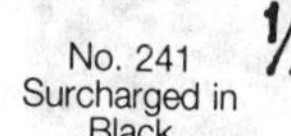

1941, Dec. 24 *Perf. 14*

301 A29 ½c on 25c brn org 15 15

Type of 1932 Inscribed "1942"

1942 Engr. *Perf. 12*

302	A91	3c green	1.00	15
303	A91	3c deep blue	1.00	15
		Set value		20

Issued to publicize the coffee of Guatemala.

Vase of Guastatoya A123

Home for the Aged A124

1942, July 13 **Unwmk.**

304	A123	½c red brn	35	15
305	A124	1c car rose	35	15
		Set value		20

National Printing Works — A125

Rafael Maria Landivar — A126

1943, Jan. 25 Engr. *Perf. 11, 12*

307	A125	2c scarlet	25	15
a.		Vert. pair, imperf. horiz.	35.00	

1943, Aug. *Perf. 11*

308 A126 5c brt ultra 20 15

150th anniv. of the death of Rafael Landivar, poet.

National Palace A127

1944, June 30 *Perf. 11*

309 A127 3c dk bl grn 15 15

Inauguration of the Natl. Palace, Nov. 10, 1943. See Nos. C137A-C139. For overprints see Nos. 311-311A, C133.

Ruins of Zakuleu — A128

1945, Jan. 6

310 A128 ½c blk brn 15 15

Type of 1944 Overprinted in Blue

25 de junio de 1944

PALACIO NACIONAL

1945, Jan. 15

311 A127 3c deep blue 25 15

Overprint Bar 1mm Thick

311A	A127	3c deep blue	75	40
		Set value		45

Allegory of the Revolution A129

Torch A130

1945, Feb. 20

312 A129 3c grysh bl 15 15

Issued to commemorate the Revolution of Oct. 20, 1944. See Nos. C128-C131.

1945, Oct. 20

313 A130 3c deep blue 15 15

1st anniv. of the Revolution of Oct. 20, 1944. See No. C135-C136.

José Milla y Vidaurre — A131

Payo Enriquez de Rivera — A132

1945 *Perf. 11, 12½*

314	A131	1c dp grn	15	15
315	A132	2c dull lilac	15	15
		Set value		15

See Nos. 343-346, 379, C134-C134A, C137, C269, C311-C315.

> **Catalogue values for unused stamps in this section, from this point to the end of the section, are for Never Hinged items.**

José Batres y Montufar A133

UPU Monument Bern, Switzerland A134

1946 **Unwmk.**

316	A133	½c sepia	15	15
317	A133	3c deep blue	15	15
		Set value		15

See Nos. 319, C142.

1946, Aug. 5 Photo. *Perf. 14x13*

318 A134 1c vio & gray brn 25 15

Issued to commemorate the centenary of the first postage stamp. See Nos. C140-C141.

Batres Type of 1946

1947, Nov. 11 Engr. *Perf. 11, 12½*

319 A133 3c dl grn 15 15

Symbolical of Labor A135

Bartolomé de las Casas and Indian A136

1948, May 14 Unwmk. *Perf. 11*

320	A135	1c dp grn	15	15
a.		Perf. 12½	5.00	
321	A135	2c sepia	15	15
a.		Perf. 12½	5.00	
322	A135	3c dp ultra	15	15
a.		Perf. 12½	5.00	
323	A135	5c rose car	15	15
a.		Perf. 12½	5.00	
		Set value		20

Labor Day, May 1, 1948. Other perfs. and compound perfs. exist.

No. 296 Overprinted "1948" in Carmine at Lower Right

1948, May 14 *Perf. 12½*

324 A122 5c bl & red 20 15

1949, Oct. 8 Engr. *Perf. 12½, 13½*

325	A136	½c red	15	15
326	A136	1c blk brn	20	15
327	A136	2c dk bl grn	20	15
a.		2c green, perf. 11, 11½ ('60)	20	15
328	A136	3c rose pink	20	15
a.		3c car perf. 11, 12½, 13½ ('64)	30	15
329	A136	4c ultra	25	15
		Nos. 325-329 (5)	1.00	
		Set value		50

See Nos. 384-386.

Gathering Coffee — A137

Designs: 1c, Poptun Agricultural Colony. 2c, Banana trees. 3c, Sugar cane field. 6c, International Bridge.

1950, Feb. Photo. *Perf. 14*

330	A137	½c vio bl, pink & ol gray	20	15
331	A137	1c red brn, yel & grnsh gray	20	15
332	A137	2c ol grn, pink & bl gray	20	15
333	A137	3c pur, bl & org brn	20	15
334	A137	6c dp org, aqua & vio	35	15
		Nos. 330-334 (5)	1.15	
		Set value		55

See Nos. 347-349.

Badge of Public and Social Assistance Ministry — A138

Nurse — A139

Map Showing Hospitals — A140

1950-51 Litho. *Perf. 12, 12½x12*

335	A138	1c car rose & bl	20	15
336	A139	3c dl grn & rose red	30	15

Perf. 12

337	A140	5c dk bl & choc ('51)	40	20
a.		Souv. sheet, #335-337	2.50	2.50

Issued to publicize the National Hospitals Fund.
No. 337a exists perf. and imperf., same values.
A perforated souvenir sheet is known which is similar to No. 337a, but with the 5c stamp like the

basic stamp of No. C232 (with "BRITISH HONDURAS" inscription).
See #C177-C180a. For overprint see #C232.

Motorcycle Messenger A141

1951, May 22 *Perf. 14x12½*
337B A141 4c bl grn & gray blk 50 20

Issued for regular postage, although inscribed "Expreso." See No. E2.

Souvenir Sheet

A142

Typographed and Engraved

1951, Oct. 22 *Imperf.*
338 A142 Sheet of 2 75 1.00
a. 1c rose carmine 25 25
b. 10c deep ultramarine 25 25

75th anniv. (in 1949) of the UPU.
For overprint see No. 419.

A143

Modern Model Schools A144

1951, Oct. 22 Photo. *Perf. 13½x14*
339 A143 ½c pur & sepia 15 15
340 A144 1c brn car & dl grn 15 15
341 A143 2c grnsh bl & red brn 15 15
342 A144 4c blk brn & rose vio 15 15
Set value 40

Enriquez de Rivera Type of 1945 Re-engraved

1952, June 4 *Perf. 12½*
343 A132 ½c violet 15 15
344 A132 1c rose car 15 15
345 A132 2c green 15 15
346 A132 4c orange 20 15
Set value 50 20

A panel containing the dates "1660-1951" has been added below the portrait.

Produce Type of 1950

Designs: ½c, Sugar cane field. 1c, Banana trees. 2c, Poptun Agricultural Colony.

1953, Feb. 11 Photo. *Perf. 13½*
347 A137 ½c dk brn & dp bl 15 15
348 A137 1c red org & ol grn 15 15
349 A137 2c dk car & gray blk 15 15
Set value 15

Issued to publicize farming.

Rafael Alvarez Ovalle and José Joaquin Palma A145

1953, May 13
350 A145 ½c pur & blk 25 15
351 A145 1c dk grn & org brn 30 15
352 A145 2c org brn & ol grn 30 15
353 A145 3c dk bl & ol brn 30 15
Set value 45

Authors of Guatemala's national anthem.
For overprints see Nos. 374-378.

Quetzal — A146

1954, Sept. 27 Engr. *Perf. 12½, 11*
354 A146 1c dp vio blue 15 15

See Nos. 367-373, 380-382A, 434-444. For overprint see No. 395.

Mario Camposeco A147

Globe and Red Cross A148

Designs: 10c, Carlos Aguirre Matheu. 15c, Goalkeeper.

1955-56 Unwmk. *Perf. 12½*
355 A147 4c violet 1.00 25
356 A147 4c car ('56) 1.00 25
357 A147 4c bl grn ('56) 1.00 25
358 A147 10c bluish grn 3.00 75
359 A147 15c dk bl 3.00 2.00
Nos. 355-359 (5) 9.00 3.50

50 years of Soccer in Guatemala.

1956, May 23 *Perf. 13x12½*

Designs: 3c, Red Cross, Telephone and "5110." 4c, Nurse, patient and Red Cross flag.

360 A148 1c brn & car 25 20
361 A148 3c dk grn & red 25 20
362 A148 4c dk sl grn & red 25 20

Red Cross. See Nos. B5-B7, CB5-CB7. For surcharges see Nos. CB8-CB10.

Dagger-Cross of the Liberation — A149

Designs: 1c, Map showing 2,000 km. (1,243 miles) of new roads. 3c, Oil production.

1956 Engr. *Perf. 12½*
363 A149 ½c violet 15 15
364 A149 1c dk bl grn 15 15

Perf. 11

365 A149 3c sepia 15 15
Set value 35 20

Liberation of 1954-55. Issue dates: ½c, 1c, July 27; 3c, Oct. 31. See Nos. C210-C218.

Quetzal Type of 1954

1957-58 *Perf. 11, 12½*
367 A146 2c violet 15 15
368 A146 3c car rose 15 15
369 A146 3c ultra 15 15
a. 3c dark blue, perf. 11½ ('72) 5.00 5.00
370 A146 4c orange 25 15
371 A146 5c brown 30 15
372 A146 5c org ver ('58) 30 15
373 A146 6c yel grn 30 20
Nos. 367-373 (7) 1.60
Set value 70

No. 368 is only perf. 12½. The 2c, 4c and No. 369 are found in perf. 11 and 12½. Other values are only perf. 11.

No. 350 Overprinted in Blue, Black, Carmine, Red Orange or Green:

1858 1958

CENTENARIO

1958, Nov.-Dec. Photo. *Perf. 13½*
374 A145 ½c pur & blk (Bl) 15 60
375 A145 ½c pur & blk (Bk) 15 60
376 A145 ½c pur & blk (C) 15 60
377 A145 ½c pur & blk (RO) 15 60
378 A145 ½c pur & blk (G) 15 60
Nos. 374-378 (5) 75 3.00

Cent. of the birth of Rafael Alvarez Ovalle, composer of Guatemala's national anthem.

Re-engraved Rivera Type of 1945

1959, Sept. 12 Engr. *Perf. 11, 12½*
379 A132 4c gray blue 15 15

See note after No. 346.

Quetzal Type of 1954

1960-63 Unwmk. *Perf. 11*
380 A146 2c brn ('61) 15 15
381 A146 4c lt vio 15 15
382 A146 5c bl grn 25 15

Perf. 12½

382A A146 5c slate gray ('63) 50 40
Set value 70

Romulus and Remus Statue, Rome A150

1871 Stamp A151

1961 Photo. *Perf. 14*
383 A150 3c blue 15 15

Inauguration of the Plaza Italia.

Las Casas Type of 1949

Perf. 11, 11½, 12½, 13½

1962-64 Engr.
384 A136 ½c blue 15 15
385 A136 1c brt vio ('64) 15 15
386 A136 4c brn ('64) 15 15
Set value 15

1963-66 Unwmk. *Perf. 11*
387 A151 10c carmine 20 15
388 A151 10c slate ('64) 25 15

Perf. 11½

389 A151 10c ol brn ('66) 20 15
390 A151 20c dp pur ('64) 30 25
391 A151 20c dk bl ('65) 30 25
Nos. 387-391 (5) 1.25
Set value 70

For souvenir sheet, see No. C310.

Pedro Bethancourt Comforting Sick Man — A152

1964, Jan. 6 Engr. *Perf. 11*
394 A152 2½c olive bister 15 15

Beatification (1962-63) of Pedro Bethancourt (1626-67). See Nos. C319-C322. For overprints see Nos. C381-C382.

Quetzal Type of 1957-58 Overprinted in Blue

HOMENAJE A LA "I. S. G. C." 1948—1963

1964, Dec. 29 Engr. *Perf. 12½*
395 A146 4c orange 25 15

15th anniv. (in 1963) of the Intl. Soc. of Guatemala Collectors.

Map of Guatemala and British Honduras — A153

Quetzal, Mayan Ball Game Goal — A154

1967, Apr. 28 Litho. *Perf. 14x13½*
396 A153 4c ol, vio bl & dp rose 25 25
397 A153 5c ocher, vio bl & dp org 20 15
398 A153 6c dp org, vio bl & gray 20 15

Issued to state Guatemala's claim to British Honduras.
For overprints see Nos. C411-C413.

Lithographed and Engraved

1968, Oct. 15 *Perf. 11½*
399 A154 1c blk, lt grn & red 15 15
400 A154 5c yel, lt grn & red 20 15
401 A154 8c org, lt grn & red 20 15
402 A154 15c bl, lt grn & red 30 15
403 A154 30c lt vio, lt grn & red 75 1.00
Nos. 399-403 (5) 1.60
Set value 1.30

19th Olympic Games, Mexico City, Oct. 12-27.
The 1c, 5c, 8c, 15c also exist perf 12½, 1c, 8c, perf 13½.
See Nos. 412-415. For overprints see Nos. 408-411, C431-C435.

Child and Poinsettia — A155

1968-70 Typo. *Perf. 13½*
404 A155 2½c grn, dp bis & car 15 15
405 A155 2½c grn, org & car ('70) 40 50
406 A155 5c grn, gray & car 20 15
407 A155 21c grn, lil & car 50 50

Issued to help abandoned children.

Type of 1968 Overprinted in Black or Red

Cincuentenario O. I. T.

1970, Mar. 19 Litho. *Perf. 13½*
408 A154 8c org, lt grn & red 25 50
409 A154 8c org, lt grn & red (R) 25 50

Perf. 12½

410 A154 15c bl, lt grn & red 40 75
411 A154 15c bl, lt grn & red (R) 40 75

50th anniv. of ILO. Gold overprint believed to be a trial color.

Type of 1968

1971 Typo. & Engr. *Perf. 11½*
412 A154 1c gray, yel grn & red 20 15

Typo.

413 A154 5c brt pink, yel grn & red	35	20
414 A154 5c brn, grn & red	35	20
415 A154 5c dk bl, grn & red	35	20

Mayas and CARE Package — A156

1971-72 Typo. *Perf. 13½*

416 A156 1c blk & multi 15 15

Perf. 11½

417 A156 1c vio & multi ('72) 15 15
418 A156 1c brn & multi ('72) 15 15
Set value 30 35

10th anniv. of CARE in Guatemala, a US-Canadian Cooperative for American Relief Everywhere. Exist imperf. See No. C459.

No. 338 (trimmed) Overprinted in Orange with Olympic Rings and: "JUEGOS OLIMPICOS / MUNICH 1972"
Souvenir Sheet

1972, Oct. 23 Typo. & Engr. *Imperf.*

419 A142 Sheet of 2 50 75
a. 1c rose carmine ("Munich") 15 25
b. 10c deep ultra ("1972") 30 50

20th Olympic Games, Munich, Aug. 26-Sept. 11. Commemorative inscriptions on No. 338 at left, top and right have been trimmed off. Size: 61x45mm (approximately). Many varieties exist. Gold overprints probably are proofs.

Pres. Carlos Arana Osorio A157

Designs: 3c, 5c, President Osorio seated, vert. 8c, Pres. Osorio standing, vert.

1973-74 Typo. *Perf. 12½*

420 A157 2c bl & blk 15 15
421 A157 3c org & brn 20 15
422 A157 5c rose car & blk 25 15
423 A157 8c blk & brt grn 30 15
a. Lithographed ('74) 20 15
Set value 45

8th population and 3rd dwellings census, Mar. 26-Apr. 7, 1973.

Francisco Ximenez — A158

Typographed, Lithographed (#426)
1973-77 *Perf. 11½, 13½ (#426)*

424 A158 2c blk & emer 15 15
425 A158 3c dk brn & org 15 15
426 A158 3c blk & yel 25 15
427 A158 6c blk & brt bl 25 20
Set value 40

Brother Francisco Ximenez, discoverer and translator of National Book of Guatemala. No. 427 issued for Intl. Book Year 1972.

Issue dates: 6c, Aug. 2, 1973; 2c, Jan. 14, 1975; No. 425, Mar. 5, 1975; No. 426, Sept. 26, 1977.

Sculpture of Christ, by Pedro de Mendoza, 1643 — A159

Design: 8c, Sculpture by Lanuza Brothers, 18th century.

1977, Apr. 4 Litho. *Perf. 11*

428 A159 6c pur & multi 15 15
429 A159 8c pur & multi 25 15
Nos. 428-429,C614-C619 (8) 2.35 2.15

Holy Week 1977.

INTERFER 77 Emblem — A160

1977, Oct. 31 Litho. *Perf. 11½*

430 A160 7c black & multi 15 15

INTERFER 77, 4th International Fair, Guatemala, Oct. 31-Nov. 13.

Rotary Intl., 75th Anniv. A161

1980, July 31 Litho. *Perf. 11½*

431 A161 4c shown 15 15
432 A161 6c Diamond and Quetzal 15 15
433 A161 10c Paul P. Harris 25 15
Set value 15

Quetzal Type of 1954

1984-86 Engr. *Perf. 12½*

434 A146 1c dp grn 15 15
435 A146 2c deep blue 15 15
436 A146 3c olive green 15 15
437 A146 3c sepia 15 15
438 A146 3c blue 15 15
439 A146 3c red 15 15
440 A146 3c orange 15 15
441 A146 3c vermilion 15 15
442 A146 4c lt red brn 15 15
443 A146 5c magenta 15 15
444 A146 6c deep blue 15 15
Set value 1.10 55

Issue dates: Nos. 436-439, Feb. 20. No. 441, 6c, Apr. 25, 1986. 1c, 4c, 5c, Feb. 16, 1987. 2c, Mar. 25, 1987.

Miguel Angel Asturias Cultural Center — A162

Perf. 12½, 11½ (5c, 9c), 12½x11½ (4c), 13x12½ (6c)

1987-93 Litho.

446 A162 2c bister brown 15 15
447 A162 3c ultra 15 15
448 A162 4c bright pink 15 15
449 A162 5c orange 15 15
450 A162 6c pale green 15 15
451 A162 7c ver 15 15
452 A162 8c brt pink 15 15
453 A162 9c black 15 15
454 A162 10c pale grn 15 15
Set value 1.00 50

Miguel Angel Asturias (1899-1974), 1967 Nobel laureate in literature.

Issue dates: 3c, Nov. 24; 7c, Nov. 17; 8c, Nov. 27; 10c, Dec. 8; 2c, Mar. 2, 1988; 5c, Mar. 23, 1990; 9c, Oct. 1, 1991. 4c, 6c, Mar. 16, 1993.

This is an expanding set. Numbers will change if necessary.

Central American and Caribbean University Games A163

Toucan as a participant in various events.

1990 Litho. *Perf. 12½*

455 A163 15c shown 30 15
456 A163 20c Torch bearer, vert. 40 15
457 A163 25c Volleyball 50 15
458 A163 30c Soccer 60 20
459 A163 45c Karate 90 30
460 A163 1q Baseball 2.00 66
461 A163 2q Basketball 4.00 1.30
462 A163 3q Hurdles 6.00 2.00
Nos. 455-462 (8) 14.70 4.91

Issue dates: 20c, Aug. 22; 30c, 3q, July 10; others, Apr. 25.

SEMI-POSTAL STAMPS

Regular Issues of 1935-36 Surcharged in Blue or Red similar to illustration

EXPOSICION
1937
FILATELICA
+1

1937, Mar. 15 Unwmk. *Perf. 12½*

B1 A102 1c + 1c brn & crim 75 1.00
B2 A103 3c + 1c rose car & pck grn 75 1.00
B3 A103 3c + 1c red org & pck grn 75 1.00
B4 A106 5c + 1c bl & dk brn (R) 75 1.00

1st Phil. Exhib. held in Guatemala, Mar. 15-20.

Catalogue values for unused stamps in this section, from this point to the end of the section, are for Never Hinged items.

Type of Regular Issue, 1956

Designs: 5c+15c, Nurse, Patient and Red Cross Flag. 15c+50c, Red Cross, telephone and "5110." 25c+50c, Globe and Red Cross.

1956, June 19 Engr. *Perf. 13x12½*

B5 A148 5c + 15c ultra & red 90 1.25
a. Imperf. pair 75.00
B6 A148 15c + 50c dk vio & red 2.00 2.50
B7 A148 25c + 50c bluish blk & car 2.00 2.50

The surtax was for the Red Cross.

Jesus and Esquipulas Cathedral — SP1

1957, Oct. 29 *Perf. 13*

B8 SP1 1½c + ½c blk & brn 50 20

The tax was for the Esquipulas highway. See Nos. CB12-CB14.

Type of Air Post Semi-Postal Stamps and

Arms — SP2

Design: 3c+3c, Wounded man, Battle of Solferino.

1960, Apr. 9 Photo. *Perf. 13½x14*
Cross in Rose Red

B9 SP2 1c + 1c red brn & bl 20 30
B10 SPAP2 3c + 3c lil, bl & pink 20 30
B11 SP2 4c + 4c blk & bl 20 30

Cent. (in 1959) of the Red Cross idea. The surtax went to the Red Cross. Exist imperf. See Nos. CB15-CB21.

AIR POST STAMPS

Surcharged in Red on No. 229

SERVICIO
POSTAL AEREO
AÑO DE 1928
Q0.03

1929, May 20 Unwmk. *Perf. 12½*

C1 A64 3c on 15p blk 50 60
C2 A64 5c on 15p blk 30 15
C3 A64 15c on 15p blk 75 20
a. Double surcharge (G & R) 100.00
C4 A64 20c on 15p blk 1.00 1.00
a. Inverted surcharge 100.00
b. Double surcharge 100.00

Surcharged in Red on No. 216

1929, May 20 *Perf. 14*

C5 A64 5c on 15p black 1.50 1.00

Surcharged in Black on No. 218 — A75

SERVICIO
POSTAL
AEREO
AÑO DE 1929
Q0.03

1929, Oct. 9

C6 A75 3c on 2.50p dk vio 1.00 1.00

Airplane and Mt. Agua — AP3

1930, June 4 Litho. *Perf. 12½*

C7 AP3 6c rose red 60 40
a. Double impression 25.00 25.00
b. Imperf., pair 350.00

For overprint see No. C14.

Nos. 227, 229 Surcharged in Black or Red

SERVICIO
AEREO INTERIOR
10 Centavos
DE QUETZAL
1930

1930, Dec. 9 *Perf. 12½*

C8 A57 1c on 3p grn (Bk) 30 30
a. Double surcharge 100.00
C9 A57 2c on 3p grn (Bk) 75 1.00
C10 A57 3c on 3p grn (R) 75 1.00
C11 A57 4c on 3p grn (R) 75 1.00
C12 A64 10c on 15p blk (R) 1.00 1.00
a. Double surcharge 125.00
Nos. C8-C12 (5) 3.55 4.30

No. 237 Overprinted

AEREO EXTERIOR 1931

1931, May 19 *Perf. 14*

C13	A81	4c orange	25	15
a.		Double overprint	40.00	50.00

No. C7 Overprinted

EXTERIOR - 1931

Perf. 12½

C14	AP3	6c rose red	1.00	1.00
a.		On No. C7a	30.00	30.00
b.		Inverted overprint	6.00	7.50

Nos. 240, 242 Overprinted in Red

AEREO INTERNACIONAL 1931

1931, Oct. 21 *Perf. 14*

C15	A36	15c ultra	1.50	20
a.		Double overprint	100.00	100.00
C16	A76	30c green	2.50	85
a.		Double overprint	75.00	75.00

Nos. 235-236 Overprinted in Red or Green

Primer Vuelo Postal BARRIOS-MIAMI 1931

1931, Dec. 5

C17	A79	2c dp bl (R)	2.50	3.00
C18	A80	3c dk vio (G)	2.50	3.00

No. 240 Overprinted in Red

Primer Vuelo Postal BARRIOS-MIAMI 1931

C19	A36	15c ultra	2.50	3.00

Nos. C17-C19 were issued in connection with the 1st postal flight from Barrios to Miami.

No. 224 Surcharged in Red

SERVICIO AEREO INTERIOR 1932 Q0.02

1932-33 *Perf. 12½*

C20	A74	2c on 1.50p dk bl	65	50

Nos. 227, 229 Surcharged in Violet, Red or Blue

SERVICIO AEREO INTERIOR — 1932 Q0.03

C21	A57	3c on 3p grn (V)	75	15
a.		Inverted surcharge	40.00	40.00
b.		Vert. pair, imperf. horiz.	750.00	
C22	A57	3c on 3p grn (R)	75	20
C23	A64	10c on 15p blk (R)	7.50	6.00
b.		First "I" of "Interior" missing	10.00	10.00
C24	A64	15c on 15p blk (Bl)	9.00	8.00
a.		First "I" of "Interior" missing	15.00	15.00
		Nos. C20-C24 (5)	18.65	14.85

Issue dates: No. C22, Jan. 1, 1933; others, Feb. 11, 1932.

No. 237 Overprinted in Green

AEREO INTERIOR 1933

1933, Jan. 1 *Perf. 14*

C25	A81	4c orange	25	15
a.		Double overprint	40.00	40.00

Nos. 235, 238 and 240 Overprinted in Red or Black

AEREO EXTERIOR 1934

1934, Aug. 7

C26	A82	5c dk car (Bk)	1.50	15
C27	A36	15c ultra (R)	1.50	15

Overprinted in Red

AEREO INTERIOR 1934

C28	A79	2c deep blue	50	15

View of Port Barrios — AP7

Designs: 15c, Tomb of Barrios. 30c, Equestrian Statue of Barrios.

1935, July 19 **Photo.** *Perf. 12½*

C29	AP7	10c yel brn & pck grn	2.00	2.00
C30	AP7	15c gray & brn	2.00	2.00
C31	AP7	30c car rose & bl vio	2.00	1.50

Birth cent. of Gen. Justo Rufino Barrios.

Lake Amatitlán AP10

Designs: Nos. C36, C37, C45, C46. Different views of Lake Amatitlan. 3c, Port Barrios. No. C34, C35, Ruins of Port San Felipe. 10c, Port Livingston. No. C39, C40, Port San José. No. C41, C42, View of Atitlan. No. C43, C44, Aurora Airport.

Overprinted with Quetzal in Green

1935-37 **Size: 37x17mm**

C32	AP10	2c org brn	15	15
C33	AP10	3c blue	20	15
C34	AP10	4c black	25	15
C35	AP10	4c ultra ('37)	20	15
C36	AP10	6c yel grn	22	15
C37	AP10	6c blk vio ('37)	4.00	15
C38	AP10	10c claret	50	25
C39	AP10	15c red org	65	40
C40	AP10	15c yel grn ('37)	65	65
C41	AP10	30c olive grn	6.00	6.50
C42	AP10	30c ol bis ('37)	75	50
C43	AP10	50c rose vio	17.50	15.00
C44	AP10	50c Prus bl ('36)	4.00	3.00
C45	AP10	1q scarlet	17.50	20.00
C46	AP10	1q car ('36)	4.50	3.00
		Nos. C32-C46 (15)	57.07	50.20

Issue dates follow No. C69.

For overprints and surcharges see Nos. C70-C79, CB1-CB2.

Central Park, Antigua AP11

Designs: 1c, Guatemala City. 2c, Central Park, Guatemala City. 3c, Monastery. Nos. C50-C51, Mouth of Dulce River. Nos. C52-C53, Plaza Barrios. Nos. C54-C55, Los Proceres Monument. No. C56, Central Park, Antigua. No. C57, Dulce River. Nos. C58-C59, Quezaltenango. Nos. C60-C61, Ruins at Antigua. Nos. C62-C63, Dock at Port Barrios. Nos. C64-C65, Port San Jose. Nos. C66-C67, Aurora Airport. 2.50q, Island off Atlantic Coast. 5q, Atlantic Coast view.

Overprinted with Quetzal in Green

Size: 34x15mm

C47	AP11	1c yel brn	15	15
C48	AP11	2c vermilion	15	15
C49	AP11	3c magenta	50	25
C50	AP11	4c org yel ('36)	1.75	1.50
C51	AP11	4c car lake ('37)	1.00	75
C52	AP11	5c dl bl	20	15
C53	AP11	5c org ('37)	15	15
C54	AP11	10c red brn	50	35
C55	AP11	10c ol grn ('37)	50	30
C56	AP11	15c rose red	25	15
C57	AP11	15c ver ('37)	22	15
C58	AP11	20c ultra	2.50	3.00
C59	AP11	20c dp cl ('37)	50	25
C60	AP11	25c gray blk	3.00	3.50
C61	AP11	25c bl grn ('37)	45	25
a.		Quetzal omitted		*1,100.*
C62	AP11	30c yel grn	1.50	1.50
C63	AP11	30c rose red ('37)	75	15
C64	AP11	50c car rose	7.00	8.00
C65	AP11	50c pur ('36)	6.50	7.50
C66	AP11	1q dk bl	22.50	25.00
C67	AP11	1q dk grn ('36)	7.50	7.50

Size: 46x20mm

C68	AP11	2.50q rose red & ol grn ('36)	5.00	3.00
C69	AP11	5q org & ind ('36)	7.00	4.00
a.		Quetzal omitted	1,500.	1,250.
		Nos. C47-C69 (23)	69.57	67.70

Issue dates of Nos. C32-C69: Nov. 1, 1935; Oct. 1, 1936; Jan. 1, 1937.

Value for No. C61a is for a sound copy.

For overprints and surcharges see Nos. C80-C91, CB3-CB4.

Types of Air Post Stamps, 1935 Overprinted with Airplane in Blue

Designs: 2c, Quezaltenango. 3c, Lake Atitlan. 4c, Progressive Colony, Lake Amatitlan. 6c, Carmen Hill. 10c, Relief map. 15c, National University. 30c, Espana Plaza. 50c, Police Station, Aurora Airport. 75c, Amphitheater, Aurora Airport. 1q, Aurora Airport.

1937, May 18

Center in Brown Black

C70	AP10	2c carmine	15	15
C71	AP10	3c blue	1.00	1.25
C72	AP10	4c citron	15	15
C73	AP10	6c yel grn	35	25
C74	AP10	10c red vio	2.00	2.25
C75	AP10	15c orange	1.50	1.00
C76	AP10	30c ol grn	3.75	3.00
C77	AP10	50c pck bl	5.00	4.25
C78	AP10	75c dk vio	10.00	11.00
C79	AP10	1q dp rose	11.00	12.00
		Nos. C70-C79 (10)	34.90	35.30

Overprinted with Airplane in Black

Designs: 1c, 7th Ave., Guatemala City. 2c, Los Proceres Monument. 3c, National Printing Office. 5c, National Museum. 10c, Central Park. 15c, Escuintla. 20c, Motorcycle Police. 25c, Slaughterhouse, Escuintla. 30c, Exhibition Hall. 50c, Barrios Plaza. 1q, Polytechnic School. 1.50q, Aurora Airport.

Size: 33x15mm

C80	AP11	1c yel brn & brt bl	15	15
C81	AP11	2c crim & dp vio	15	15
C82	AP11	3c red vio & red brn	50	50
C83	AP11	5c pck grn & cop red	4.00	3.00
C84	AP11	10c car & grn	1.25	1.00
C85	AP11	15c rose & dl ol grn	50	25
C86	AP11	20c ultra & blk	3.00	1.75
C87	AP11	25c dk gray & scar	2.50	2.50
C88	AP11	30c grn & dp vio	1.25	1.25
C89	AP11	50c mag & ultra	10.00	12.00

Size: 42x19mm

C90	AP11	1q ol grn & red vio	10.00	12.00
C91	AP11	1.50q scar & ol brn	10.00	12.00
		Nos. C80-C91 (12)	43.30	46.55

Second term of President Ubico.

Souvenir Sheet

AP12

1938, Jan. 10 *Perf. 12½*

C92	AP12	Sheet of 4	1.50	1.50
a.		15c George Washington	30	30
b.		4c Franklin D. Roosevelt	30	30
c.		4c Map of the Americas	30	30
d.		15c Pan American Union Building, Washington, DC	30	30

150th anniv. of US Constitution.

President Arosemena, Panama AP13

Flags of Central American Countries — AP19

Designs: 2c, Pres. Cortés Castro, Costa Rica. 3c, Pres. Somoza, Nicaragua. 4c, Pres. Carias Andino, Honduras. 5c, Pres. Martinez, El Salvador. 10c, Pres. Ubico, Guatemala.

1938, Nov. 20 **Unwmk.**

C93	AP13	1c org & ol brn	15	15
C94	AP13	2c scar, pale pink & sl grn	15	15
C95	AP13	3c grn, buff & ol brn	25	30
C96	AP13	4c dk cl, pale lil & brn	30	35
C97	AP13	5c bis, pale grn & ol brn	50	60
C98	AP13	10c ultra, pale bl & brn	1.00	1.25
		Nos. C93-C98 (6)	2.35	2.80

Souvenir Sheet

C99	AP19	Sheet of 6	1.00	1.00
a.		1c Guatemala	15	15
b.		2c El Salvador	15	15
c.		3c Honduras	15	15
d.		4c Nicaragua	15	15
e.		5c Costa Rica	15	15
f.		10c Panama	15	15

1st Central American Phil. Exhib., Guatemala City, Nov. 20-27.

For overprints see Nos. CO1-CO7.

La Merced Church, Antigua AP20

Designs: 2c, Ruins of Christ School, Antigua. 3c, Aurora Airport. 4c, Drill ground, Guatemala City. 5c, Cavalry barracks. 6c, Palace of Justice. 10c, Customhouse, San José. 15c, Communications Building, Retalhuleu. 30c, Municipal Theater, Quezaltenango. 50c, Customhouse, Retalhuleu. 1q, Departmental Building.

Inscribed "Aéreo Interior" Overprinted with Quetzal in Green

1939, Feb. 14

C100	AP20	1c ol bis & chnt	20	15
C101	AP20	2c rose red & sl grn	20	15
C102	AP20	3c dl bl & bis	25	15
C103	AP20	4c rose pink & yel grn	25	15
C104	AP20	5c brn lake & brt ultra	30	15
C105	AP20	6c org & gray brn	35	15
C106	AP20	10c bis brn & gray blk	50	20
C107	AP20	15c dl vio & blk	75	15
C108	AP20	30c dp bl & dk car	1.10	25
C109	AP20	50c org & brt vio	1.50	40
a.		Quetzal omitted		*1,750.*
C110	AP20	1q yel grn & brt ultra	2.50	1.25
		Nos. C100-C110 (11)	7.90	3.15

See Nos. C111-C122. For overprint and surcharge see No. C124, C132.

1939, Feb. 14

Designs: 1c, Mayan Altar, Aurora Park. 2c, Sanitation Building. 3c, Lake Amatitlan. 4c, Lake Atitlan. 5c, Tamazulapa River bridge. 10c, Los proceres Monument. 15c, Palace of Captains General. 20c, Church on Carmen Hill. 25c, Barrios Park. 30c, Mayan Altar. 50c, Charles III fountain. 1q, View of Antigua.

Inscribed "Aéreo International" or "Aérea Exterior"

Overprinted with Quetzal in Green

C111	AP20	1c ol grn & gldn brn	20	15
C112	AP20	2c lt grn & blk	30	20
C113	AP20	3c ultra & cob bl	20	15
C114	AP20	4c org brn & yel grn	20	15
C115	AP20	5c sage grn & red org	35	15
C116	AP20	10c lake & sl blk	1.75	15

C117 AP20 15c ultra & brt rose 1.75 15
C118 AP20 20c yel grn & ap grn 60 20
C119 AP20 25c dl vio & lt ol grn 60 15
C120 AP20 30c dl rose & blk 80 15
C121 AP20 50c scar & brt yel 1.50 20
C122 AP20 1q org & yel grn 2.50 35
Nos. C111-C122 (12) 10.75
Set value 1.70

No. 240 Overprinted in Carmine

UNION PANAMERICANA
1890 - 1940
CORREO AEREO

1940, Apr. 14 ***Perf. 14***
C123 A36 15c ultra 55 15

Pan American Union, 50th anniversary.

No. C112 Overprinted in Carmine

DICIEMBRE 2
1941

SEGUNDO DIA PAN-
AMERICANO DE LA SALUD

1941, Dec. 2 ***Perf. 12½***
C124 AP20 2c lt grn & blk 40 20

Second Pan American Health Day.

San Carlos University, Antigua AP21

1943, June 25 **Engr.** ***Perf. 11***
C125 AP21 15c dk red brn 40 15
a. Imperf., pair 100.00

Don Pedro de Alvarado AP22

Type I- Diagonal shading lines at inner edges of commemorative tablet.
Type II- Overall shading added to tablet.

1943, Mar. 10 **Unwmk.** ***Perf. 11½***
C126 AP22 15c dp ultra (II) 40 15
a. Type I 15.00 10.00

400th anniv. of the founding of Antigua.

National Police Building AP23

1943, Aug. 3 ***Perf. 11***
C127 AP23 10c dp rose vio 35 15

Allegory of 1944 Revolution — AP24

1945, Apr. 27 **Engr.**
C128 AP24 5c dp rose 25 15
C129 AP24 6c dk bl grn 25 20
a. Imperf., pair 110.00
C130 AP24 10c violet 25 15
C131 AP24 15c aqua 25 20

Revolution of October 20, 1944.

No. C113 Surcharged in Red

1945
FERIA DEL LIBRO
2½ CENTAVOS

1945, July 25 ***Perf. 12½***
C132 AP20 2½c on 3c 1.00 1.25

The 1945 Book Fair.

National Palace AP25

Carmine Overprint

1945, Aug. **Engr.** ***Perf. 11***
C133 AP25 5c rose car 20 15
a. Triple ovpt., one inverted 50.00 25.00
b. Double ovpt., one inverted 65.00

See Nos. C137A-C139.

José Milla y Vidaurre AP26

Torch AP27

AP28

1945
C134 AP26 7½c sepia 75 1.00
C134A AP26 7½c dark blue 40 25

Issued: #C134, Sept. 28; #C134A, Dec. 6.
For overprint see No. C230.

1945, Oct. 19
C135 AP27 5c brt red vio 30 15

Souvenir Sheet

Imperf

C136 AP28 Sheet of 2 1.20 1.20
a. 5c bright red violet 50 50

1st anniv. of the Revolution of Oct. 20, 1944.
See Nos. C147-C150.

Catalogue values for unused stamps in this section, from this point to the end of the section, are for Never Hinged items.

Payo Enriquez de Rivera — AP29

1946, Jan. 22 **Unwmk.** ***Perf. 11***
C137 AP29 5c rose pink 25 15

See Nos. C269, C311-C315.

Palace Type of 1945

1946-47 **Without Overprint**
C137A AP25 5c rose car ('47) 50 15
C138 AP25 10c deep lilac 25 15
a. Imperf., pair 100.00
C139 AP25 15c blue 50 15
a. Imperf., pair 100.00
Set value 35

Sir Rowland Hill — AP30

Globes, Quetzal — AP31

1946, Aug. 5 **Photo.** ***Perf. 14x13***
C140 AP30 5c slate & brn (blk ovpt.) 35 15
a. Without "AEREO" ovpt. 400.00 400.00
C141 AP31 15c car lake, ultra & emer 50 20

Centenary of the first postage stamp.

José Batres y Montufar AP32

Signing the Declaration of Independence AP33

1946, Sept. 16 **Engr.** ***Perf. 11***
C142 AP32 10c Prus grn 25 15
a. Perf. 12½ 10.00 15

1946, Dec. 19 ***Perf. 11***
C143 AP33 5c rose car 15 15
C144 AP33 6c ol brn 20 15
C145 AP33 10c violet 25 15
C146 AP33 20c blue 30 20
Set value 55

125th anniv. of the signing of the Declaration of Independence.

Torch Type of 1945
Dated 1944-1946

1947, Feb. 3 **Engr.**
C147 AP27 1c green 15 15
C148 AP27 2c carmine 15 15
C149 AP27 3c violet 15 15
C150 AP27 5c dp bl 15 15
Set value 40

Inscribed "II Aniversario de la Revolucion." "Aereo" in color on a white background.
2nd anniv. of the Revolution of Oct. 20, 1944.

Franklin D. Roosevelt — AP34

1947, June 6
C151 AP34 5c rose car 20 15
C152 AP34 6c blue 20 15
C153 AP34 10c dp ultra 35 25
C154 AP34 30c gray blk 1.50 1.00
C155 AP34 50c lt vio 2.50 2.50
a. Imperf., pair 125.00
C156 AP34 1q gray grn 4.00 4.00
a. Imperf., pair 125.00
Nos. C151-C156 (6) 8.75 8.05

1948

No. 296 Overprinted in Carmine

AEREO

1948, May 14 ***Perf. 12½***
C157 A122 5c blue & red 15 15

Soccer Game AP35

1948, Aug. 31 **Engr.**

Center in Black

C158 AP35 3c brt car 65 30
C159 AP35 5c bl grn 75 40
C160 AP35 10c dk vio 90 90
C161 AP35 30c dp bl 3.00 3.50
C162 AP35 50c bister 4.00 4.50
Nos. C158-C162 (5) 9.30 9.60

4th Central American and Caribbean Soccer Championship, Mar., 1948.

Seal, University of Guatemala — AP36

1949, Nov. 29 ***Perf. 12½***

Center in Blue

C163 AP36 3c carmine 50 40
C164 AP36 10c green 75 75
C165 AP36 50c yellow 2.75 3.25

1st Latin American Cong. of Universities.

Lake Atitlan AP37

Tecum Uman Monument AP38

Designs: 8c, San Cristobal Church. 13c, Weaver. 35c, Momostenango Cliffs.

1950, Feb. 17 **Photo.** ***Perf. 14***

Multicolored Centers

C166 AP37 3c car rose 35 15
C167 AP38 5c red brn 35 15
C168 AP37 8c dk sl grn 40 15
C169 AP38 13c brown 60 25
C170 AP37 35c purple 2.25 2.75
Nos. C166-C170 (5) 3.95 3.45

See No. C181.

Soccer — AP39

Pole Vault — AP40

Designs: 3c, Foot race. 8c, Tennis. 35c, Diving. 65c, Stadium.

1950, Feb. 25 Engr. *Perf. 12½*

Center in Black

C171	AP39	1c purple	50	20
C172	AP39	3c carmine	60	20
C173	AP40	4c org brn	75	25
C174	AP39	8c red vio	90	30
C175	AP40	35c lt bl	2.00	2.75

Center in Green

C176	AP40	65c dk slate grn	4.25	4.50
		Nos. C171-C176 (6)	9.00	8.20

6th Central American and Caribbean Games.

Nurse and Patient AP41

Designs: 10c, School of Nurses. 50c, Zacapa Hospital. 1q, Roosevelt Hospital.

1950, Sept. 6 Litho. *Perf. 12*

Quetzal in Blue Green

C177	AP41	5c rose vio & car	25	15
a.		Double impression (frame)	25.00	
C178	AP41	10c ol brn & emer	60	35
C179	AP41	50c ver & red vio	2.00	2.50
C180	AP41	1q org yel & sage grn	2.50	2.75
a.		Souv. sheet, #C177-C180	6.50	7.50

National Hospital Fund.

Nos. C177-C180 exist with colors reversed, perf. and imperf. These are proofs.

No. C168 perf. 12½ or 12 diagonally through center

1951, Apr. *Perf. 14*

C181	AP37	(4c) multi	10.00	7.50
a.		Unsevered pair	25.00	15.00

Counterfeits of diagonal perforation exist.

Ceremonial Stone Ax — AP42

National Flag and Emblem — AP43

1953, Feb. 11 Photo. *Perf. 14x13½*

C182	AP42	3c dk bl & ol gray	20	15
C183	AP42	5c dk gray & hn brn	25	15
C184	AP42	10c dk pur & slate	35	25
		Set value		45

1953, Mar. 14 *Perf. 13½*

Multicolored Center

C185	AP43	1c maroon	20	15
C186	AP43	2c slate green	25	15
C187	AP43	4c dark brown	30	15

Issued to mark the passing of the presidency from J. J. Arevalo to Col. Jacobo Arbenz Guzman.

Regional Dance — AP44

Horse Racing — AP45

Designs: 4c, White nun - national flower. 5c, Allegory of the fair. 20c, Zakuleu ruins. 30c, Symbols of Agriculture. 50c, Champion bull. 65c, Bicycle racing. 1q, Quetzal.

1953, Dec. 18 Engr. *Perf. 12½*

C188	AP44	1c dp ultra & car	15	15
C189	AP44	4c org & grn	50	25
C190	AP44	5c emer & choc	30	20
C191	AP45	15c choc & dk pur	1.25	1.00
C192	AP45	20c car & ultra	75	1.00
C193	AP44	30c dp ultra & choc	1.25	1.50
C194	AP45	50c pur & blk	1.50	1.50
C195	AP45	65c lt bl & dk grn	2.50	2.75
C196	AP44	1q dk bl grn & dk red	4.00	4.75
		Nos. C188-C196 (9)	12.20	13.10

National Fair, Oct. 20, 1953.

Indian — AP46

1954, Apr. 21 Unwmk. *Perf. 12½*

C197	AP46	1c carmine	25	15
C198	AP46	2c dp bl	25	15
C199	AP46	4c yel grn	25	15
C200	AP46	5c aqua	50	20
C201	AP46	6c orange	50	20
C202	AP46	10c violet	75	25
C203	AP46	20c blk brn	2.75	3.00
		Nos. C197-C203 (7)	5.25	4.10

Guatemala and ODECA Flags — AP47

Rotary Emblem, Map of Guatemala — AP48

1954, Oct. 13 Photo. *Perf. 14x13½*

C204	AP47	1c multi	15	15
C205	AP47	2c multi	15	15
C206	AP47	4c multi	20	15
		Set value		30

3rd anniv. of the formation of the Organization of Central American States.

1956, Sept. 8 Engr.

C207	AP48	4c bl & dl yel	25	20
C208	AP48	6c lt bl grn & dl yel	25	15
C209	AP48	35c pur & dl yel	1.50	2.00

50th anniv. of Rotary Intl. (in 1955).

Mayan Warrior Holding Dagger Cross of the Liberation — AP49

Designs: 4c, Family looking into the sun. 5c, The dagger of the Liberation destroying communist symbols. 6c, Hands holding cogwheel and map of Guatemala. 20c, Monument to the victims of communism and flag. 30c, Champerico harbor. 65c, Radio tower, Mercury and map of Guatemala. 1q, Flags of the American nations. 5q, Pres. Carlos Castillo Armas.

1956, Oct. 10 Photo. *Perf. 14x13½*

C210	AP49	2c dp grn, red, bl & brn	15	15
C211	AP49	4c dp car & gray blk	15	15
C212	AP49	5c bl & red brn	20	20
C213	AP49	6c dk brn & dp ultra	15	15
C214	AP49	20c vio, brn & bl	1.20	1.50
C215	AP49	30c dp bl & ol	1.50	1.75
C216	AP49	65c chnt brn & grn	2.25	2.75
C217	AP49	1q dk brn & multi	3.25	3.50
C218	AP49	5q multi	13.00	14.00
		Nos. C210-C218 (9)	21.85	24.15

Liberation of 1954-55.

For overprints see Nos. C233, C243, C265-C266, C417.

Red Cross, Map and Quetzal — AP50

Designs: 2c, José Ruiz Augulo and woman with child, vert 3c, Pedro de Bethancourt with sick man. 4c, Rafael Ayau.

Perf. 13½x14, 14x13½

1958, May 13 Unwmk.

C219	AP50	1c multi	22	15
C220	AP50	2c multi	22	15
C221	AP50	3c multi	22	15
C222	AP50	4c multi	22	15

Issued in honor of the Red Cross.

For overprints and surcharges see Nos. C235-C242, C251-C254, C283-C298, C390-C394.

Col. Carlos Castillo Armas AP51

Galleon of 1532 and Freighter "Quezaltenango" AP52

1959, Feb. 27 *Perf. 14x13½*

Center in Dark Blue and Yellow

C223	AP51	1c black	15	15
C224	AP51	2c rose red	15	15
C225	AP51	4c brown	15	15
C226	AP51	6c dk bl grn	15	15
C227	AP51	10c dk pur	25	25
C228	AP51	20c bl grn	75	75
C229	AP51	35c gray	1.20	1.25
		Nos. C223-C229 (7)	2.80	2.85

Pres. Carlos Castillo Armas (1914-1957).

No. C134A Overprinted in Carmine: "HOMENAJE A LAS NACIONES UNIDAS"

1959, Mar. 4 Engr. *Perf. 11*

C230	AP26	7½c dk bl	80	1.00

Issued to honor the United Nations.

1959, May 15 Litho. *Perf. 11*

C231	AP52	6c ultra & rose red	20	15

Issued to honor the formation of the Guatemala-Honduras merchant fleet.

For overprint see No. C467.

Type of 1950 Overprinted in Dark Blue

BELICE ES NUESTRO
AEREO

1959, Oct. 9 *Perf. 12*

C232	A140	5c dk bl & lt brn	50	20
a.		Inverted overprint	200.00	35.00

Issued to state Guatemala's claim to British Honduras. Overprint reads: "Belize is ours." Map includes "BRITISH HONDURAS" and its borderline, and excludes bit extending above "A" of "GUATEMALA" on No. 337.

No. C232 is known without overprint in multiples.

No. C213 Overprinted in Red: "1859 Centenario Primera Exportacion de Cafe 1959"

1959, Oct. 26 Photo. *Perf. 14x13½*

C233	AP49	6c dk brn & dp ultra	50	30

Centenary of coffee export.

Pres. and Mrs. Villeda of Honduras AP53

1959, Nov. 3 Litho. *Perf. 11*

C234	AP53	6c pale brown	15	15

Visit of President Ramon Villeda Morales of Honduras, Oct. 12, 1958.

For overprint see No. C415.

Nos. C219-C222 Overprinted: "AÑO MUNDIAL DE REFUGIADOS" in Green, Violet, Blue or Brown

Perf. 13½x14, 14x13½

1960, Apr. 23 Photo. Unwmk.

C235	AP50	1c multi (G)	60	85
C236	AP50	2c multi (V)	60	85
C237	AP50	3c multi (Bl)	60	85
C238	AP50	4c multi (Br)	60	85

Nos. C219-C222 Overprinted as Above and Surcharged with New Value

C239	AP50	6c on 1c multi	2.25	2.00
C240	AP50	7c on 2c multi	2.25	2.00
C241	AP50	10c on 3c multi	3.75	4.00
C242	AP50	20c on 4c multi	4.00	4.00
		Nos. C235-C242 (8)	14.65	15.40

Nos. C235-C242 issued to publicize World Refugee Year, July 1, 1959-June 30, 1960.

No. C213 Overprinted in Red: "Fundacion de la ciudad Melchor de Mencos, 30-IV-1960"

1960, Apr. 30 *Perf. 14x13½*

C243	AP49	6c dk brn & dp ultra	1.00	1.25

Founding of the city of Melchor de Mencos.

UNESCO and Eiffel Tower, Paris — AP54

1960, Nov. 4 Photo. *Perf. 12½*

C244	AP54	5c dp mag & vio	15	15
C245	AP54	6c ultra & vio brn	15	15
C246	AP54	8c emer & mag	30	15
C247	AP54	20c red brn & dl bl	1.25	1.25

Issued to honor UNESCO.

For overprints see Nos. C258, C267-C268.

Abraham Lincoln — AP55

1960, Oct. 29 Engr. *Perf. 11*

C248	AP55	5c violet blue	20	20
C249	AP55	30c violet	1.00	1.25
C250	AP55	50c gray	5.00	6.00

Issued to commemorate the sesquicentenary of the birth of Abraham Lincoln.

An 8c was also printed, but was not issued and all copies were destroyed.

Nos. C219-C222 Overprinted "Mayo de 1960" in Green, Blue or Brown

Perf. 13½x14, 14x13½

1961, Apr. 20 Photo. Unwmk.

C251 AP50 1c multi (G) 35 25
C252 AP50 2c multi (Bl) 35 25
C253 AP50 3c multi (Bl) 35 25
C254 AP50 4c multi (Br) 35 25

Issued to honor the Red Cross.

Proclamation of Independence AP56

1962 Engr. *Perf. 11*

C255 AP56 4c sepia 20 15
C256 AP56 5c vio bl 25 15
C257 AP56 15c brt vio 75 50

140th anniv. of Independence (in 1961). Issue dates: 4c, 5c, May 23; 15c, Aug. 10.

No. C245 Overprinted in Red: "1962 / EL MUNDO UNIDO / CONTRA LA MALARIA"

1962, Oct. 4 Photo. *Perf. 12½*

C258 AP54 6 ultra & vio brn 80 1.25

WHO drive to eradicate malaria.

Dr. José Luna — AP57

Guatemalan physicians: 4c, Rodolfo Robles. 5c, Narciso Esparragoza y Gallardo. 6c, Juan J. Ortega. 10c, Dario Gonzalez. 20c, José Felipe Flores.

1962, Dec. 12 Photo. *Perf. 14x13½*

C259 AP57 1c ol bis & dl pur 40 15
C260 AP57 4c org yel & gray ol 40 15
C261 AP57 5c pale bl & red brn 40 15
C262 AP57 6c salmon & blk 40 15
C263 AP57 10c pale grn & red brn 60 20
C264 AP57 20c pale pink & bl 70 60
Nos. C259-C264 (6) 2.90
Set value 1.20

No. C213 Overprinted in Red: "PRESIDENTE/ YDIGORAS/ FUENTES/ RECORRE POR TIERRA/ CENTRO AMERICA/ 14 A 20 DIC. 1962"

1962, Dec. Photo. *Perf. 14x13½*

C265 AP49 6c dk brn & dp ultra 1.00 75

Issued to commemorate Pres. Ydigoras' tour of Central America, Dec. 14-20, 1962.

No. C213 Overprinted in Vermilion: "Reunion Presidents: Kennedy, EE. UU. - Ydigoras F., Guat. - Rivera. Salv. -Villeda M., Hond. - Somoza, Nic. - Orlich, C. R. - Chiari, Panama - San Jose, Costa Rica, 18 A 21 de Marzo de 1963"

Perf. 14x13½

1963, Mar. 18 Unwmk.

C266 AP49 6c dk brn & dp ultra 3.50 2.50

Meeting of Pres. John F. Kennedy with the Presidents of the Central American Republics, San Jose, Costa Rica, Mar. 18-21.

Nos. C245-C246 Overprinted "CONMEMORA / CION FIRMA / NUEVA CARTA / ODECA. - 1962" in Magenta or Black

1963, Mar. 14 *Perf. 12½*

C267 AP54 6c ultra & vio brn (M) 25 15
C268 AP54 8c emer & mag 35 15

Issued to commemorate the signing of the new charter of the Organization of Central American States (ODECA).

Enriquez de Rivera Type of 1946

Perf. 11, 11½, 12½

1963, Mar. 26 Engr.

C269 AP29 5c olive bister 15 15

Woman Carrying Fruit Basket — AP58

1963, Mar. 14 Litho. *Perf. 11, 12½*

C270 AP58 1c multi 15 15

Spring Fair, 1960.

Reaper AP59

Ceiba Tree AP60

1963, July 25 Photo. *Perf. 14*

C271 AP59 5c Prus grn 20 20
C272 AP59 10c dk bl 35 20

FAO "Freedom from Hunger" campaign.

1963 Unwmk. *Perf. 12*

C273 AP60 4c brn & grn 25 15

Patzun Palace — AP61

Buildings: 3c, Coban. 4c, Retalhuleu. 5c, San Marcos. 6c, Captains General of Antigua.

1964, Jan. 15 *Perf. 13½x14*

C274 AP61 1c rose red & brn 15 15
C275 AP61 3c rose cl & Prus grn 15 15
C276 AP61 4c vio bl & rose lake 15 15
C277 AP61 5c brn & blue 22 20
C278 AP61 6c grn & slate 22 20
Nos. C274-C278 (5) 89
Set value 70

City Hall, Guatemala City — AP62

Design: 4c, Social Security Institute.

1964, Jan. 15 Photo. *Perf. 12x11½*

C279 AP62 3c brt bl & brn 15 15
C280 AP62 4c brn & brt bl 15 15
Set value 20

See Nos. C281-C282A. For overprints see Nos. C360-C361, C421.

1964-65 Engr. *Perf. 11½*

Designs: 3c, Social Security Institute. 4c, University administration building. No. C282, City Hall, Guatemala City. No. C282A, Engineering School.

Different Frames

C281 AP62 3c dl grn 16 15
C281A AP62 4c gray ('65) 16 15
C282 AP62 7c blue 22 15
C282A AP62 7c ol bis ('65) 20 20

Nos. C219-C222 Overprinted in Green, Blue or Black with Olympic Rings and: "OLIMPIADAS / TOKIO - 1964"

1964 Photo. *Perf. 13½x14, 14x13½*

C283 AP50 1c multi (G) 75 1.00
C284 AP50 2c multi (Bl) 75 1.00
C285 AP50 3c multi (G) 75 1.00
C286 AP50 4c multi (Bk) 75 1.00

Issued to publicize the 18th Olympic Games, Tokyo, Oct. 10-25, 1964.

Nos. C219-C222 Surcharged in Green, Blue or Black with New Value and: "HABILITADA - 1964"

1964

C287 AP50 7c on 1c multi (G) 20 20
C288 AP50 9c on 2c multi (Bl) 25 35
C289 AP50 13c on 3c multi (Bl) 35 45
C290 AP50 21c on 4c multi (Bk) 65 75

Nos. C219-C222 Overprinted "FERIA MUNDIAL / DE NEW YORK" in Green, Blue or Black

1964, June 25

C291 AP50 1c multi (G) 50 75
C292 AP50 2c multi (Bl) 50 75
C293 AP50 3c multi (G) 50 75
C294 AP50 4c multi (Bk) 50 75

New York World's Fair.

Nos. C219-C222 Overprinted in Green, Blue or Black: "VIII VUELTA / CICLISTICA"

1964

C295 AP50 1c multi (G) 65 95
C296 AP50 2c multi (Bl) 65 95
C297 AP50 3c multi (G) 65 95
C298 AP50 4c multi (Bk) 1.25 1.50

Eighth Bicycle Race.

Pres. John F. Kennedy — AP63

Centenary Emblem — AP64

1964 Engr. *Perf. 11½*

C299 AP63 1c violet 60 60
C300 AP63 2c yel grn 60 60
C301 AP63 3c brown 60 60
C302 AP63 7c dp bl 60 60
C303 AP63 50c dk gray 6.00 6.50
Nos. C299-C303 (5) 8.40 8.90

John F. Kennedy (1917-63). Minute letters "TEOK" are in lower right corner of 1c, 2c, 3c and 50c.

Issue dates: 7c, July 10; others, Aug. 21.

Perf. 11x12

1964, Sept. 9 Unwmk. Photo.

C304 AP64 7c ultra, sil & red 40 25
C305 AP64 9c org, sil & red 40 40
C306 AP64 13c pur, sil & red 55 55
C307 AP64 21c brt grn, sil & red 75 1.00
C308 AP64 35c brn, sil & red 1.20 1.40
C309 AP64 1q lem, sil & red 2.50 3.00
Nos. C304-C309 (6) 5.80 6.60

Centenary (in 1963) of the Intl. Red Cross. For overprints see Nos. C323-C327, C395-C400.

Type of Regular Issue 1963

Souvenir Sheet

1964 Engr. *Imperf.*

C310 Sheet of 2 3.50 3.75
a. A151 10c violet blue 1.40 1.50
b. A151 20c carmine 1.40 1.50

15th UPU Congress, Vienna, May-June, 1964.

Enriquez de Rivera Type of 1946

1964, Dec. 18 Engr. *Perf. 11½*

C311 AP29 5c gray 15 15
C312 AP29 5c orange 15 15
C313 AP29 5c lt grn 15 15
C314 AP29 5c lt ultra 15 15
C315 AP29 5c dl vio 15 15
Nos. C311-C315 (5) 75
Set value 50

Bishop Francisco Marroquin — AP65

Guatemalan Boy Scout Emblem — AP66

1965, Jan. 21 Photo. Unwmk.

C316 AP65 4c lil & brn 15 15
C317 AP65 7c gray & sepia 20 15
C318 AP65 9c vio bl & blk 25 15
Set value 35

Issued to honor Bishop Francisco Marroquin.

Bethancourt Type of Regular Issue, 1964

1965, Apr. 20 Engr. *Perf. 11½*

C319 A152 2½c vio bl 15 15
C320 A152 3c orange 15 15
C321 A152 4c purple 15 15
C322 A152 5c yel grn 15 15
Set value 50 40

For overprints see Nos. C381-C382.

Nos. C304-C308 Overprinted in Red: "AYUDENOS / MAYO 1965"

1965, June 18 Photo. *Perf. 11x12*

C323 AP64 7c ultra, sil & red 35 35
C324 AP64 9c org, sil & red 40 40
C325 AP64 13c pur, sil & red 50 50
C326 AP64 21c brt grn, sil & red 65 65
C327 AP64 35c brn, sil & red 1.00 1.10
Nos. C323-C327 (5) 2.90 3.00

1966, Mar. 3 Photo. *Perf. 14x13½*

Designs: 9c, Campfire and Scouts. 10c, Scout emblem and Scout carrying torch and flag. 15c, Scout emblem, flags and Scout giving Scout sign. 20c, Lord Baden-Powell.

C328 AP66 5c multi 50 50
C329 AP66 9c multi 50 50
C330 AP66 10c multi 70 70
C331 AP66 15c multi 80 80
C332 AP66 20c multi 1.00 1.00
Nos. C328-C332 (5) 3.50 3.50

5th Interamerican Regional Training Conf., Guatemala City, Mar. 1-3.

For overprints see Nos. C376-C380.

Central American Independence Issue

Flags of Central American States — AP67

1966, Mar. 9 *Perf. 12½x13½*

C333 AP67 6c multi 20 15

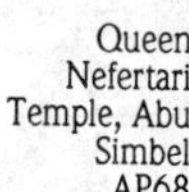

Queen Nefertari Temple, Abu Simbel AP68

1966, Oct. 3 Photo. *Perf. 12*

C334 AP68 21c vio & ocher 55 30

UNESCO world campaign to save historic monuments in Nubia.

Coat of Arms — AP69

1966-70 Engr. *Perf. 13½*

C335 AP69 5c orange 25 15
C336 AP69 5c green 25 15
a. 5c yel grn, perf. 11½ ('69) 25 15

Perf. 11½

C337 AP69 5c bl ('67) 25 15
a. 5c dk bl, perf. 12½ ('69) 25 15

Perf. 12½

C338 AP69 5c gray ('67) 25 15
C339 AP69 5c pur ('67) 25 15
a. 5c bright violet ('69) 25 15

Perf. 11½

C339B AP69 5c dp mag ('70) 25 15
C339C AP69 5c grn, *yel* ('70) 30 15
Nos. C335-C339C (7) 1.80
Set value 80

Issue dates: No. C335, Oct. 31; No. C336, Dec. 15, 1966; No. C337, Feb. 9, 1967; Nos. C338-C339, Apr. 28, 1967; No. C336a, Dec. 3, 1969; No. C339a, Dec. 11, 1969; No. C339B, July 8, 1970; No. C339C, Oct. 16, 1970.

Msgr. Mariano Rossell y Arellano — AP70

1966, Nov. 3 Engr. *Perf. 13½*

C340 AP70 1c dp vio 15 15
C341 AP70 2c green 20 15
C342 AP70 3c brown 20 15
C343 AP70 7c blue 35 15
C344 AP70 50c gray 1.40 1.40
Nos. C340-C344 (5) 2.30 2.00

Issued to honor Msgr. Mariano Rossell y Arellano, apostolic delegate.

Mario Mendez Montenegro AP71

Morning Glory and Map of Guatemala AP72

1966-67 *Perf. 13½*

C345 AP71 2c rose red ('67) 15 15
C346 AP71 3c org ('67) 15 15
C347 AP71 4c rose claret ('67) 20 15
C348 AP71 5c gray 35 20
C349 AP71 5c lt ultra ('67) 35 20
C350 AP71 5c green ('67) 35 20
C351 AP71 5c bluish blk ('67) 35 20
Nos. C345-C351 (7) 1.90 1.25

Mario Mendez Montenegro (1910-65), founder of the Revolutionary Party.

1967, Jan. 12 Photo. *Perf. 12*

Flowers: 8c, Bird of paradise, horiz. 10c, White nun orchid, national flower, horiz. 20c, Nymphs of Amatitlan.

Flowers in Natural Colors

C352 AP72 4c orange 35 25
C353 AP72 8c green 35 15
C354 AP72 10c dk bl 50 50
C355 AP72 20c dk red 1.00 1.00

Pan-American Institute Emblem — AP73

1967, Apr. 13 Photo. *Perf. 13½*

C356 AP73 4c lt brn, lil & blk 20 15
C357 AP73 5c ol, bl & blk 35 15
C358 AP73 7c org yel, bl & blk 50 15

8th Gen. Assembly of the Pan-American Geographical and Historical Institute in 1965.

No. C281 Overprinted

GUATEMALA
CAMPEON
III Norceca Foot-Ball

1967, Apr. 28 Engr. *Perf. 11½*

C360 AP62 3c dull green 50 40

Guatemala's victory in the 3rd Norceca Soccer Games (Caribbean, Central and North American).

No. C281A Overprinted in Red: "REUNION JEFES DE ESTADO / AMERICANO, PUNTA DEL ESTE, / MONTEVIDEO, URUGUAY 1967"

1967, June 28 Engr. *Perf. 11½*

C361 AP62 4c gray 65 65

Meeting of American Presidents, Punta del Este, Apr. 10-12.

Handshake AP74

1967, June 28 Photo. *Perf. 12*

C362 AP74 7c pink, brn & grn 30 15
C363 AP74 21c lt bl, grn & brn 50 50

Issued to publicize "Peace and Progress through Cooperation."
For overprint see No. C416.

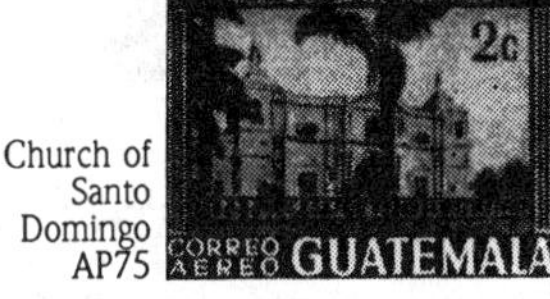

Church of Santo Domingo AP75

Designs: 1c, Yurrita Church, vert. 3c, Church of St. Francis. 4c, Antonio Joséde Irisarri, vert. 5c, Church of the Convent, vert. 7c, Mercy Church, Antigua. 10c, Metropolitan Cathedral.

1967, Aug. *Perf. 11½x12, 12x11½*

C364 AP75 1c grn, lt bl & dk brn 16 15
C365 AP75 2c plum, sal pink & brn 22 15
C366 AP75 3c brt rose, gray & blk 22 15
C367 AP75 4c mar, sl grn & org 22 15
C368 AP75 5c lil, pale grn & dk brn 22 15
C369 AP75 7c ultra, lil rose & blk 35 20
C370 AP75 10c pur, yel & blk 50 22
Nos. C364-C370 (7) 1.89
Set value 95

Abraham Lincoln — AP76

1967 Engr. *Perf. 13½, 11½ (9c)*

C371 AP76 7c gray & dp org 35 20
C372 AP76 9c dk grn & grysh 40 22
C373 AP76 11c brn org & sl 40 30
C374 AP76 15c ultra & vio brn 65 35
C375 AP76 30c mag & grn 1.50 1.50
Nos. C371-C375 (5) 3.30 2.57

Abraham Lincoln (1809-1865).
Issue dates: 7c, 9c, Oct. 9. Others, Dec. 12.
For surcharge see No. C554.

Nos. C328-C332 Overprinted: "VIII Camporee Scout / Centroamericano / Diciembre 1-8/1967"

1967, Dec. 1 Photo. *Perf. 14x13½*

C376 AP66 5c multi 35 35
C377 AP66 9c multi 50 50
C378 AP66 10c multi 65 65
C379 AP66 15c multi 65 65
C380 AP66 20c multi 80 80
Nos. C376-C380 (5) 2.95 2.95

Issued to commemorate the 8th Central American Boy Scout Camporee, Dec. 1-8.

Nos. C320-C321 Overprinted in Four Lines: "Premio Nóbel de Literatura - 10 diciembre 1967 - Miguel Angel Asturias"

1967, Dec. 11 Engr. *Perf. 11½*

C381 A152 3c orange 50 50
C382 A152 4c purple 50 50

Awarding of the Nobel Prize for Literature to Miguel Angel Asturias, Guatemalan writer.

Institute Emblem — AP77

1967, Dec. 12 Engr. *Perf. 11½*

C383 AP77 9c blk & grn 65 65
C384 AP77 25c car & brn 1.40 1.40
C385 AP77 1q ultra & bl 3.50 3.50

25th anniv. of the Inter-American Agriculture Institute.

UNESCO Emblem and Children AP78

1967, Dec. 12

C386 AP78 4c bl grn 20 20
C387 AP78 5c blue 20 20
C388 AP78 7c gray 30 30
C389 AP78 21c brt rose lil 80 80

20th anniv. (in 1966) of UNESCO.

Nos. C219-C221 and C304-C308 Overprinted in Black or Yellow Green: "III REUNION DE / PRESIDENTES / Nov. 15-18, 1967"

Perf. 13½x14, 14x13½, 11x12

1968, Jan. 23 Photo.

C390 AP50 1c multi 65 50
C391 AP50 1c multi (G) 65 75
C392 AP50 2c multi 65 75
C393 AP50 2c multi (G) 65 75
C394 AP50 3c multi 65 75
C395 AP64 3c multi (G) 65 75
C396 AP64 7c multi 65 75
C397 AP64 9c multi 1.00 1.00
C398 AP64 13c multi 1.40 1.00
C399 AP64 21c multi 2.00 1.00
C400 AP64 35c multi 1.60 1.75
Nos. C390-C400 (11) 10.55 9.75

3rd meeting of Central American Presidents, Nov. 15-18, 1967.

Our Lady of the Coro — AP79

Miguel Angel Asturias, Flags of Guatemala and Sweden — AP80

1968-74 Engr. *Perf. 13½, 11½*

C403 AP79 4c ultra 40 15
C404 AP79 7c slate 35 15
C405 AP79 9c green 50 15
C406 AP79 9c lilac ('74) 20 15
C407 AP79 10c brick red 65 20
C408 AP79 10c gray 50 20
C408A AP79 10c vio bl ('74) 35 15
C409 AP79 1q vio brn 3.50 3.00
C410 AP79 1q org yel 3.50 3.00
Nos. C403-C410 (9) 9.95 7.15

Perf. 13½ applies to 4c and Nos. C407, C409-C410; perf. 11½ to 4c, 7c, 9c and Nos. C408, C408A.

Nos. 396-398 Overprinted: "AEREO / XI VUELTA / CICLISTICA / 1967"

1968, Mar. 25 Litho. *Perf. 14x13½*

C411 A153 4c multi 50 50
C412 A153 5c multi 50 50
C413 A153 6c multi 40 40

The 11th Bicycle Race.

1968, June 18 Engr. *Perf. 11½*

C414 AP80 20c ultra 1.00 35

Awarding of the Nobel Prize for Literature to Miguel Angel Asturias.

No. C234 Overprinted in Carmine: "1968. AÑO INTERNACIONAL / DERECHOS HUMANOS. - ONU"

1968, July 18 Litho. *Perf. 11*

C415 AP53 6c pale brown 50 25

International Human Rights Year.

No. C362 Overprinted: "AYUDA A CONSERVAR / LOS BOSQUES. - 1968"

1968, July 18 Photo. *Perf. 12*

C416 AP74 7c pink, brn & grn 35 15

Issued to publicize forest conservation.

No. C213 Overprinted in Brown: "Expedición / Científica / Nahakín / Guatemala-Peru / Ruta de los / Mayas"

1968, Aug. 23 Photo. *Perf. 14x13½*

C417 AP49 6c dk brn & dp ultra 25 15

Nahakin scientific expedition along the route of the Mayas undertaken jointly with Peru.

Views, Quetzal and White Nun Orchid — AP81

1968, Aug. 23 Engr. *Perf. 13½*

C418 AP81 10c dp cl & grn 50 20
C419 AP81 20c dp org & blk 75 50
C420 AP81 50c ultra & car 1.25 1.25

Issued for tourist publicity.

No. C281A Overprinted in Carmine: "CONFEDERACION / DE UNIVERSIDADES / CENTROAMERICANAS / 1948 1968"

1968, Nov. 4 *Perf. 11½*

C421 AP62 4c gray 25 25

20th anniv. of the Federation of Central American Universities.

Presidents Gustavo Diaz Ordaz and Julio Cesar Mendez Montenegro AP82

1968, Dec. 3 **Litho.** ***Perf. 14x13½***

C422	AP82	5c multi	15	15
C423	AP82	10c multi	35	20
C424	AP82	25c multi	80	75

Mutual visits of the Presidents of Mexico and Guatemala.

ITU Emblem, Old and New Communication Equipment — AP83

Engraved and Photogravure

1968-74 ***Perf. 11½, 12½ (21c)***

C425	AP83	7c vio bl	25	15
C426	AP83	15c gray & emer	35	25
C426A	AP83	15c vio brn & org ('74)	50	25
C427	AP83	21c magenta	50	35
C428	AP83	35c rose red & emer	90	50
C429	AP83	75c grn & red	2.00	2.00
C430	AP83	3q brn & red	6.50	6.50
		Nos. C425-C430 (7)	11.00	10.00

Cent. (in 1965) of the ITU.
Nos. C425, C427 are engr. only; on others denominations are photo.. No. C426A is on thin, toned paper.
Dates of issue: No: C426A, Feb. 18, 1974; others Dec. 13, 1968.
For surcharges see Nos. C454, C516.

Nos. 399-403 Overprinted in Red, Black or Gold **AEREO**

Lithographed and Engraved

1969 ***Perf. 11½, 13½ (1c)***

C431	A154	1c blk, lt grn & red (R)	50	50
C432	A154	5c yel, lt grn & red	65	65
C433	A154	8c org, lt grn & red	80	80
C434	A154	15c bl, lt grn & red	1.00	1.00
C435	A154	30c lt vio, lt grn & red (G)	1.40	1.40
		Nos. C431-C435 (5)	4.35	4.35

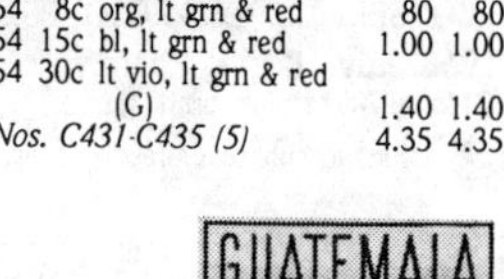

Dante Alighieri — AP84

1969, July 17 **Engr.** ***Perf. 12½***

C436	AP84	7c rose vio & ultra	15	15
C437	AP84	10c dk bl	25	15
C438	AP84	20c green	40	15
C439	AP84	21c gray & brn	70	70
C440	AP84	35c pur & brt grn	1.50	1.50
		Nos. C436-C440 (5)	3.00	2.65

Dante Alighieri (1265-1321), Italian poet.

Map of Latin America AP85

Design: 9c, Seal of University.

1969, Oct. 29 **Typo.** ***Perf. 13***

Size: 44x27mm

C441	AP85	2c brt pink & blk	15	15

Size: 35x27mm

C442	AP85	9c gray & blk	30	20

Souvenir Sheet

Imperf

C443	AP85	Sheet of 2	50	50
a.		2c light blue & black	20	20
b.		9c orange & black	20	20

20th anniv. of the Union of Latin American Universities.

Moon Landing Issue

Moon Landing — AP86

1969-70 **Engr.** ***Perf. 11½***

C444	AP86	50c mar & blk	2.00	2.00
C445	AP86	1q ultra & blk	3.50	3.75

Souvenir Sheet

Imperf

C446	AP86	1q yel grn & ultra	3.75	4.00

See note after US No. C76. No. C446 contains one stamp with simulated perforations.
Issue dates: Nos. C445-C446, Dec. 19, 1969; No. C444, Jan. 6, 1970.

Giant Grebe Family on Lake Atitlan AP87

Designs: 4c, Lake Atitlan. 20c, Grebe chick, eggs atop floating nest, vert.

1970, Mar. 31 **Litho.** ***Perf. 13½***

C447	AP87	4c red & multi	25	15
C448	AP87	9c red & multi	50	30
a.		Souv. sheet of 2, #C447-C448	1.25	1.25
C449	AP87	20c red & multi	75	75

Protection of zambullidor ducks.

Dr. Victor Manuel Calderon — AP88

Hand Holding Bible — AP89

1970 **Litho. & Engr.** ***Perf. 13, 12½***

C450	AP88	1c lt bl & blk	15	15
C451	AP88	2c pale grn & blk	15	15

Perf. 13

C452	AP88	9c yel & blk	30	25
		Set value	50	42

Dr. Victor Manuel Calderon (1889-1969), who described microfilaria, a blood parasite.

1970 **Litho. & Typo.** ***Perf. 13x13½***

C453	AP89	5c red & multi	25	25

Fourth centenary of the Bible in Spanish.

No. C430 Surcharged

VALE Ø0.50

1971, Mar. 11 **Engr.** ***Perf. 11½***

C454	AP83	50c on 3q brn & red	1.75	1.75

Arms of Guatemala, Newspapers — AP90

Official Decree of First Issue — AP91

1971 **Litho.** ***Perf. 11½, 12½***

C455	AP90	2c dk bl & red	15	15
C456	AP90	5c brn & red	16	15
C457	AP90	25c brt bl & red	50	25
		Set value		37

Souvenir Sheet

Lithographed and Engraved

Imperf

C458	AP91	Sheet of 5	1.50	1.50

Cent. of Guatemala's postage stamps.
Nos. C456-C457 have white value tablet.
No. C458 contains a litho. 4c black and engr. reproductions of Nos. 1-4 in colors similar to 1871 issue. Simulated perforations.
In 1974 No. C458 was overprinted "Conmemorativa / al Campeonato Mundial de Foot Ball / Munich 1974" and Munich Games emblem in black. Overprint in gold or other colors was not authorized,
See Nos. C569-C570.

Mayas with CARE Package — AP92

1971 **Typo.** ***Perf. 11½***

C459	AP92	5c multi	30	30
a.		Souv. sheet of 2	1.50	1.50

25th aniversary of CARE, a U.S.-Canadian Cooperative for American Relief Everywhere.
No. C459a contains imperf. stamps similar to Nos. 416 and C459.

J. Rufino Barrios, M. Garcia Granados, Map of Guatemala, Quetzal — AP93

1971, June 30 ***Perf. 11½***

C460	AP93	2c multi, perf 13½	25	15
a.		Value in pink ('72)	15	15
C461	AP93	10c multi	40	20
a.		Value in pink, perf. 12½ ('72)	25	20
C462	AP93	50c multi	1.50	1.50
C463	AP93	1q multi	3.00	3.00

Centenary of the liberal revolution of 1871.

Chavarry Arrué and León Bilak — AP94

Perf. 11½, 11x12½, 12½

1971-72 **Engr.**

C464	AP94	1c grn & blk ('72)	15	15
C465	AP94	2c lt brn & blk ('72)	15	15
C466	AP94	5c org & blk	25	15
		Set value		30

Honoring J. Arnoldo Chavarry Arrué, stamp engraver; León Bilak, philatelist.

No. C231 Overprinted

FERIA INTERNACIONAL "INTERFER—71" 30 Oct. al 21 Nov.

1971, Oct. 25 **Litho.** ***Perf. 11½***

C467	AP52	6c ultra & rose red	25	25

INTERFER 71, Intl. Fair, Guatemala, Oct. 30-Nov. 21.

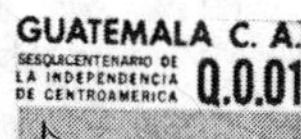

Flag and Map of Guatemala — AP95

UNICEF Emblem and Mayan Figure — AP96

Perf. 13½ (1c), 12½ (3c, 9c), 11 (5c)

1971-75 **Typo.**

C468	AP95	1c blk, bl & lil	15	15
a.		Lithographed ('75)	15	15
C469	AP95	3c brn, brt pink & bl	15	15
C470	AP95	5c brn, org & bl	15	15
a.		Lithographed, perf. 12½ ('74)	15	15
C471	AP95	9c blk, emer & bl	20	15
		Set value	47	20

Sesquicentennial of Central American independence.
Date of issue: #C469-C471, July 10, 1972.

1971-75 **Engr.** ***Perf. 11½***

C472	AP96	1c yel grn	15	15
C472A	AP96	2c purple	15	15
C473	AP96	50c vio brn	1.75	1.75
C474	AP96	1q ultra	3.00	3.00

25th anniv. UNICEF.
Issued: 2c, Feb. 24, 1975; others, Nov. 1971.

Early Boeing Planes — AP97

Design: 10c, Bleriot's plane.

1972 Typo. *Perf. 11½*

C475 AP97 5c lt brn & brt bl 25 15
C476 AP97 10c dark blue 50 15

Military aviation in Guatemala, 50th anniv.

Arches, Antigua — AP98

1972-73 Typo. *Perf. 11½*

Dark Blue and Light Blue

C480 AP98 1c shown 16 15
C481 AP98 1c Cathedral 16 15
C482 AP98 1c Fountain, Central Park 16 15
C483 AP98 1c Capuchin Monastery 16 15
C484 AP98 1c Fountain and Santa Clara 16 15
C485 AP98 1c Portal of San Francisco 16 15
Nos. C480-C485 (6) 96
Set value 60

Black, Lilac Rose, and Silver

C486 AP98 2½c shown 35 15
C487 AP98 2½c Catherdral 35 15
C488 AP98 2½c Fountain and Santa Clara 35 15
C489 AP98 2½c Portal of San Francisco 35 15
C490 AP98 2½c Fountain 35 15
C491 AP98 2½c Capuchin Monastery 35 15
Nos. C486-C491 (6) 2.10 90

Blue, Orange and Black

C492 AP98 5c shown 65 15
C493 AP98 5c Cathedral 65 15
C494 AP98 5c Santa Clara 65 15
C495 AP98 5c Portal of San Francisco 65 15
C496 AP98 5c Fountain 65 15
C497 AP98 5c Capuchin Monastery 65 15
Nos. C492-C497 (6) 3.90 90

Nos. C492-C497 exist perf. 12½, same value.

Perf. 12½

Red, Blue and Black

C498 AP98 1q Fountain 3.50 2.50
C499 AP98 1q Capuchin Monastery 3.50 2.50
C500 AP98 1q shown 3.50 2.50
C501 AP98 1q Cathedral 3.50 2.50
C502 AP98 1q Fountain and Santa Clara 3.50 2.50
C503 AP98 1q Portal of San Francisco 3.50 2.50
Nos. C498-C503 (6) 21.00 15.00
Nos. C480-C503 (24) 27.96

Earthquake ruins of Antigua. 1c printed se-tenant in sheets of 90 (10x9); 2½c, 5c se-tenant in sheets of 30 (5x6); 1q se-tenant in sheets of 6 (3x2).

On Nos. C498-C503 the inks were applied by a thermographic process giving a shiny raised effect.

Issue dates: Nos. C480-C485, Dec. 14, 1972; Nos. C486-C491, Jan. 22, 1973; Nos. C492-C497, Mar. 12, 1973; Nos. C498-C503, Aug. 22, 1973.

Nos. C480-C485 were overprinted "II Feria Internacional" / INTERFER/73 / 31 Octubre - Noviembre 18 / 1973 / GUATEMALA in lilac rose and issued Nov. 3, 1973. Value $3.

The Interfer overprint exists in black on Nos. C480-C485, but these stamps were not decreed or issued.

See Nos. C528-C545, C770-C775F. For overprints see Nos. C517-C523.

Simon Bolivar and Map of Americas — AP99

1973-74 *Perf. 11½*

C504 AP99 3c brt lil rose & blk 15 15
C505 AP99 3c org & dk bl ('74) 15 15
C506 AP99 5c yel & multi 18 15
C507 AP99 5c brt grn & blk 18 15
Set value 25

Indian with CARE Package, World Map — AP100

CARE Package — AP101

1973, June 14 Typo. *Perf. 12½*

C508 AP100 2c blk & multi 20 20
C509 AP101 10c blk & multi 40 40
a. Souvenir sheet of 2 80 90

25th anniversary of CARE (in 1971), a US-sponsored relief organization and 10th anniversary of its work in Guatemala.

No. C509a contains 2 stamps similar to Nos. C508-C509 with simulated perforations.

Guatemala No. 1, Laurel AP102

1973-74 Engr. *Perf. 12½, 11½ (1q)*

C510 AP102 1c yel brn ('74) 20 15
C511 AP102 1q rose claret 2.50 2.50

Centenary (in 1971) of Guatemala postage stamps. See Nos. C574-C576A.

Oak Wreath and Star AP103

1973, Aug. 22 Typo. *Perf. 12½*

C512 AP103 5c brn, yel & bl 15 15

Centenary of Escuela Politecnica, Guatemala's military academy.

See Nos. C552-C553.

Eleanor Roosevelt — AP104

1973, Sept. 11 Engr. *Perf. 12½*

C513 AP104 7c blue 20 15

Eleanor Roosevelt (1884-1962), lecturer, writer, UN delegate.

Boys' School, Chiquimula AP105

1973-74 Typo. *Perf. 12½*

C514 AP105 3c blk & bl 15 15
C515 AP105 5c blk & dp lil rose 15 15
Set value 25 25

Centenary of the Instituto Varones in Chiquimula.

Issued: 5c, Dec. 5, 1973; 3c, June 13, 1974.

No. C430 Surcharged in Red: "Desvalorizadas a Q0.50" and Ornamental Obliteration of Old Denomination

1974 Engr. & Photo. *Perf. 11½*

C516 AP83 50c on 3q brn & red 1.25 1.25

Nos. C480-C485 and C509a Overprinted with UPU Emblem, "UPU / HOMENAJE CENTENARIO / 1874 1974"

1974, June 13 Typo. *Perf. 11½*

C517 AP98 1c dk bl & lt bl 22 30
C518 AP98 1c dk bl & lt bl 22 30
C519 AP98 1c dk bl & lt bl 22 30
C520 AP98 1c dk bl & lt bl 22 30
C521 AP98 1c dk bl & lt bl 22 30
C522 AP98 1c dk bl & lt bl 22 30
Nos. C517-C522 (6) 1.32 1.80

Souvenir Sheet

C523 Sheet of 2 6.50 7.50

Centenary of Universal Postal Union.

No. C523 consists of an overprint on No. C509a, including "UNIVERSAL POSTAL UNION" instead of "UPU."

The overprint on No. C523 in red was not authorized by the Post Office.

Antigua Type of 1972-73

1974, Oct. 8 Typo. *Perf. 11½*

Black and Light Brown

C528 AP98 2c Capuchin Monastery 15 15
C529 AP98 2c Arches 15 15
C530 AP98 2c Cathedral 15 15
C531 AP98 2c Fountain and Santa Clara 15 15
C532 AP98 2c Portal of San Francisco 15 15
C533 AP98 2c Fountain 15 15
Nos. C528-C533 (6) 90
Set value 60

1974, Sept. 24

Black and Yellow

C540 AP98 20c Capuchin Monastery 50 50
C541 AP98 20c Arches 50 50
C542 AP98 20c Cathedral 50 50
C543 AP98 20c Fountain and Santa Clara 50 50
C544 AP98 20c Portal of San Francisco 50 50
C545 AP98 20c Fountain 50 50
Nos. C540-C545 (6) 3.00 3.00

Earthquake ruins of Antigua. Each group of six printed se-tenant in sheets of 30 (5x6).

Nos. C528-C533 were printed in 1975 in black and bister se-tenant in sheets of 24 (4x6) on whiter paper.

Generals Justo Rufino Barrios and M. Garcia Granados AP106

Polytechnic School — AP107

Perf. 12½, 11½ (25c)

1974-75 Typo.

C552 AP106 6c red, gray & bl 15 15
C553 AP107 25c multi 35 25
Set value 30

Centenary (in 1973) of Escuela Politecnica, Guatemala's military academy.

Issued: 6c, Sept. 17, 1974; 25c, Jan. 14, 1975.

No. C373 Surcharged in Black and Green

VALE 10c.

Protección del Ave Nacional el Quetzal

1974, Dec. 3 Engr. *Perf. 13½*

C554 AP76 10c on 11c multi 25 15

Nature protection. The quetzal, Guatemala's national bird.

Costume San Martin Sacatepequez — AP108

Costumes of Women: 2c, Solola. 9c, Coban. 20c, Chichicastenango.

1974-75 Typo. *Perf. 12½*

C556 AP108 2c car & multi 15 15
C557 AP108 2½c bl, car & brn 15 15
C559 AP108 9c bl & multi 30 15
a. Perf. 12½x13½ 30 15
C561 AP108 20c red & multi 50 25
Set value 45

Issue dates: 2½c, Dec. 16, 1974; 20c, Jan. 14, 1975; 2c, 9c, May 19, 1975.

Quetzals and Maya Quekchi Woman Wearing Huipil — AP109

1975, June 25 Litho. *Perf. 13½*

C565 AP109 8c bl & multi 35 15
C566 AP109 20c red & multi 65 15
Set value 25

International Women's Year 1975.

Rotary Emblem AP110

1975-76 Typo. *Perf. 13½*

C567 AP110 10c bl & multi 20 15

Perf. 11½

C568 AP110 15c bl & multi 40 15
Set value 22

Guatemala City Rotary Club, 50th anniversary. Issue dates: 10c, Oct. 1, 1975; 15c, Dec. 21, 1976.

Gaceta Type of 1971 Redrawn

1975-76 Typo. *Perf. 12½*

C569	AP90	5c	brn & red	15	15
C570	AP90	50c	brt rose & brn	1.25	1.25

The white background around numeral and on right of arms has been filled in.

Issued: 5c, Dec. 12, 1975; 50c, Dec. 1, 1976.

IWY Emblem and White Nun Orchid — AP111

1975-76 *Perf. 12½x13½, 11½ (8c)*

C571	AP111	1c	multi	15	15
C572	AP111	8c	yel & multi	25	15
C573	AP111	26c	rose & multi	65	20
			Set value		40

International Women's Year 1975.

Issue dates: 1c, Dec. 19; 8c, Dec. 12; 26c, May 10, 1976.

Stamp Centenary Type of 1973

1975-77 Engr. *Perf. 11½*

C574	AP102	6c	orange	15	15
C575	AP102	6c	green ('76)	15	15
C576	AP102	6c	gray ('77)	15	15
C576A	AP102	6c	vio bl ('77)	15	15
			Set value		40

Centenary (in 1971) of Guatemala's postage stamps.

Issue dates: No. C574, Dec. 31. No. C575, May 10. Others, Aug. 10.

Destroyed Joyabaj Village — AP112

Designs (Guatemala Flag and): 3c, Emergency food distribution. 5c, Jaguar Temple, Tikal. 10c, Destroyed bridge. 15c, Outdoors emergency hospital. 20c, Sugar cane harvest. 25c, Destroyed house. 30c, New building, Tecpan. 50c, Destroyed Cerro del Carmen church. 75c, Cleaning up debris. 1q, Military help. 2q, Lake Atitlan.

1976, June 4 Litho. *Perf. 12½*

C577	AP112	1c	red & multi	15	15
C578	AP112	3c	multi	15	15
C579	AP112	5c	pink & multi	15	15
C580	AP112	10c	red & multi	25	15
C581	AP112	15c	multi	35	15
C582	AP112	20c	pink & multi	45	30
C583	AP112	25c	red & multi	60	35
C584	AP112	30c	multi	75	20
C585	AP112	50c	red & multi	1.25	75
C586	AP112	75c	multi	2.00	1.00
C587	AP112	1q	multi	2.50	1.25
C588	AP112	2q	multi	5.00	3.00
			Nos. C577-C588 (12)	13.60	7.60

Earthquake of Feb. 4, 1976, and gratitude for foreign help. Inscriptions in colored panels vary. 3 imperf. souvenir sheets exist (50c, 1q, 2q). Size: 112x83mm.

Allegory of Independence — AP113

Designs: 2c, Boston Tea Party. 3c, Thomas Jefferson, vert. 4c, 20c, 35c, Allegory of Independence (each different; 4c, 35c, vert.). 5c, Warren's Death at Bunker Hill. 10c, Washington at Valley Forge. 15c, Washington at Monmouth. 25c, The Generals at Yorktown. 30c, Washington Crossing the Delaware. 40c, Declaration of Independence. 45c, Patrick Henry, vert. 50c, Congress Voting Independence. 1q, Washington, vert. 2q, Lincoln, vert. 3q, Franklin, vert. 5q, John F. Kennedy, vert. The historical designs and portraits are after paintings.

1976, July 4 Litho. *Perf. 12½*

Size: 46x27mm, 27x46mm

C592	AP113	1c	multicolored	15	15
C593	AP113	2c	multicolored	15	15
C594	AP113	3c	multicolored	15	15
C595	AP113	4c	multicolored	15	15
C596	AP113	5c	multicolored	15	15
C597	AP113	10c	multicolored	18	15
C598	AP113	15c	multicolored	28	15
C599	AP113	20c	multicolored	35	15
C600	AP113	25c	multicolored	45	16
C601	AP113	30c	multicolored	60	18
C602	AP113	35c	multicolored	65	45
C603	AP113	40c	multicolored	80	55
C604	AP113	45c	multicolored	90	65
C605	AP113	50c	multicolored	1.10	45
C606	AP113	1q	multicolored	2.00	2.00
a.			Souvenir sheet	2.00	2.25
C607	AP113	2q	multicolored	3.75	3.75
a.			Souvenir sheet	4.50	4.75
C608	AP113	3q	multicolored	5.50	5.50
a.			Souvenir sheet	6.00	6.25

Size: 35x55mm

C609	AP113	5q	multicolored	9.00	3.50
a.			Souvenir sheet	11.00	11.50
			Nos. C592-C609 (18)	26.31	18.39

American Bicentennial. Souvenir sheets contain one imperf. stamp each.

1974 Quetzal Coin AP114

Lithographed and Engraved

1976, Dec. 1 *Perf. 11½*

C610	AP114	8c	org, blk & bl	16	15

Perf. 13½

C611	AP114	20c	brt rose, bl & blk	40	15
			Set value		25

50th anniv. of introduction of Quetzal currency.

Engineers at Work AP115

1976, Dec. 21 Engr. *Perf. 11½*

C612	AP115	9c	ultra	16	15
C613	AP115	10c	green	16	15
			Set value		15

School of Engineering, Guatemala City, centenary.

Holy Week Type of 1977

Designs: Sculptures of Christ from various Guatemalan churches. 4c, 7c, 9c, 20c, vert.

1977, Apr. 4 Litho. *Perf. 11*

C614	A159	3c	pur & multi	15	15
C615	A159	4c	pur & multi	15	15
C616	A159	7c	pur & multi	20	15
C617	A159	9c	pur & multi	30	25
C618	A159	20c	pur & multi	50	50
C619	A159	26c	pur & multi	65	65
			Nos. C614-C619 (6)	1.95	1.85

Souvenir Sheet

Roulette 7½

C620	A159	30c	pur & multi	65	1.00

Holy Week 1977.

City Hall and Bank of Guatemala AP116

Designs: 6c, Deed to original site, vert. 8c, Church and farm house, site of first legislative session. 9c, Coat of arms of Pedro Cortes, first archbishop. 22c, Arms of Guatemala City, vert.

Perf. 13½ (6c); 11½ (others)

1977, Aug. 10 Litho.

C621	AP116	6c	multicolored	15	15
C622	AP116	7c	multicolored	16	15
C623	AP116	8c	multicolored	16	15
C624	AP116	9c	multicolored	22	15
a.			Souvenir sheet	25	50
C625	AP116	22c	multicolored	40	25
a.			Souvenir sheet	50	75
			Nos. C621-C625 (5)	1.09	
			Set value		64

Bicentenary of the founding of Nueva Guatemala de la Asuncion (Guatemala City). Nos. C624a-C625a contain one stamp each with simulated perforations.

Arms of Quetzaltenango — AP117

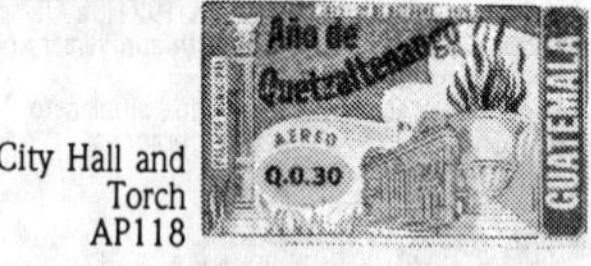

City Hall and Torch AP118

1977, Sept. 11 Litho. *Perf. 11½*

C626	AP117	7c	blk & sil	20	15
C627	AP118	30c	bl & yel	80	20

150th anniversary of the founding of Quetzaltenango.

Mayan Bas-relief AP119

1977, Nov. 7

C628	AP119	10c	brt car & blk	20	15

14th Intl. Cong. of Latin Notaries.

Children Bringing Gifts to Christ Child — AP120

Christmas: 1c, Mother and children, horiz. 4c, Guatemalan children's Nativity scene.

1977, Dec. 16 Litho. *Perf. 11½*

C629	AP120	1c	multicolored	15	15
C630	AP120	2c	multicolored	15	15
C631	AP120	4c	multicolored	15	15
			Set value	30	20

Almolonga Costume, Cancer League Emblem — AP121

Virgin of Sorrows, Antigua — AP122

Regional Costumes after Paintings by Carlos Mérida and Cancer League Emblem: 2c, Nebaj woman. 5c, San Juan Cotzal couple. 6c, Todos Santos couple. 20c, Regidores men. 30c, San Cristobal woman.

Perf. 14 (1c, 5c, No. C636); Perf. 12 (2c, 6c, No. C636a, 30c)

1978, Apr. 3 Litho.

C632	AP121	1c	gold & multi	15	15
C633	AP121	2c	gold & multi	15	15
C634	AP121	5c	gold & multi	15	15
C635	AP121	6c	gold & multi	16	15
C636	AP121	20c	gold & multi	65	50
a.			Souv. sheet of 1	65	75
C637	AP121	30c	gold & multi	65	50
			Nos. C632-C637 (6)	1.91	
			Set value		1.40

Part of proceeds from sale of stamps went to National League to Fight Cancer.

1978 Litho. *Perf. 11½*

Statues from Various Churches: 4c, Virgin of Mercy, Antigua. 5c, Virgin of Anguish, Yurrita. 6c, Virgin of the Rosary, Santo Domingo. 8c, Virgin of Sorrows, Santo Domingo. 9c, Virgin of the Rosary, Quetzaltenango. 10c, Virgin of the Immaculate Conception, Church of St. Francis. 20c, Virgin of the Immaculate Conception, Cathedral Church.

C638	AP122	2c	multicolored	15	15
C639	AP122	4c	multicolored	15	15
C640	AP122	5c	multicolored	15	15
C641	AP122	6c	multicolored	15	15
C642	AP122	8c	multicolored	16	15
C643	AP122	9c	multicolored	20	15
C644	AP122	10c	multicolored	22	15
C645	AP122	20c	multicolored	50	20
			Nos. C638-C645 (8)	1.68	
			Set value		85

Holy Week 1978. A 30c imperf. souvenir sheet shows the Pietà from Calvary Church, Antigua. Size: 71x101mm.

Issued: 6c, 10c, 20c, Sept. 28. Others, May 22.

Soccer Player, Argentina '78 Emblem AP123

Gymnastics AP124

1978, July 3 Litho. *Perf. 12*

C646	AP123	10c	multicolored	20	15

11th World Cup Soccer Championship, Argentina, June 1-25.

1978, Sept. 4 *Perf. 12*

C647	AP124	6c	shown	15	15
C648	AP124	6c	Volleyball	15	15
C649	AP124	6c	Target shooting	15	15
C650	AP124	6c	Weight lifting	15	15
C651	AP124	8c	Track & field	16	15
			Set value	56	30

13th Central American and Caribbean Games, Medellin, Colombia. Nos. C647-C650 printed se-tenant in panes of 50.

Cattleya Pachecoi AP125

Designs: Orchids.

1978, Dec. 7 Litho. *Perf. 12*

C652	AP125	1c	shown	15	15
C653	AP125	1c	Sobralia	15	15
C654	AP125	1c	Cypripedium	15	15
C655	AP125	1c	Oncidium	15	15
C656	AP125	3c	Cattleya bowrigiana	15	15
C657	AP125	3c	Encyclia	15	15
C658	AP125	3c	Epidendrum	15	15
C659	AP125	3c	Barkeria	15	15

C660 AP125	8c Spiranthes	25	25
C661 AP125	20c Lycaste	65	65
	Set value	1.50	1.50

Stamps of same denomination printed se-tenant. Sheets of 60.

Seal of University AP126

Students of Different Departments AP127

Designs: 12c, Student in 17th cent. clothes. 14c, Students, 1978, and molecular model.

1978, Dec. 7

C662 AP126	6c multicolored	15	15
C663 AP127	7c multicolored	15	15
C664 AP126	12c multicolored	20	15
C665 AP126	14c multicolored	25	15
	Set value		40

San Carlos University of Guatemala, tercentenary.

Brown and White Children — AP128

A Helping Hand — AP129

Designs: 7c, Child at play. 14c, Hands sheltering Indian girl.

1978, Dec. 7

C666 AP128	6c multicolored	15	15
C667 AP128	7c multicolored	15	15
C668 AP129	12c multicolored	20	15
C669 AP129	14c multicolored	25	15
	Set value		40

Year of the Children of Guatemala.

Tree Planting and FAO Emblem — AP130

Forest protection: 8c, Burnt forest. 9c, Watershed, river and trees. 10c, Sawmill. 26c, Forests, river and cultivated terraces.

1979, Apr. 16 Litho. *Perf. 13½*

C670 AP130	6c multicolored	15	15
C671 AP130	8c multicolored	15	15
C672 AP130	9c multicolored	15	15
C673 AP130	10c multicolored	15	15
C674 AP130	26c multicolored	35	20
a.	Souv. sheet of 5, #C670-C674	90	1.25
	Set value	80	40

Peten Wild Turkey — AP131

Clay Jar, 50-100 A.D. — AP132

Wildlife conservation: 3c, White-tailed deer, horiz. 5c, King buzzard. 7c, Horned owl. 9c, Young wildcat. 30c, Quetzal.

1979, June 14 Litho. *Perf. 13½*

C675 AP131	1c multicolored	15	15
C676 AP131	3c multicolored	15	15
C677 AP131	5c multicolored	15	15
C678 AP131	7c multicolored	20	15
C679 AP131	9c multicolored	25	15
	Set value	75	35

Souvenir Sheet

C680 AP131	30c multicolored	50	75

1979, Sept. 19 Litho. *Perf. 13*

Archaeological Treasures from Tikal: 3c, Mayan woman, ceramic head, 900 A.D. 4c, Earring, 50-100 A.D. 5c, vase, 700 A.D. 6c, Boy, 200-50 B.C. 7c, Bone carving, 700 A.D. 8c, Striped vase, 700 A.D. 10c, Covered vase on tripod, 450 B.C.

C681 AP132	2c multi	15	15
C682 AP132	3c multi	15	15
C683 AP132	4c multi	15	15
C684 AP132	5c multi	15	15
C685 AP132	6c multi	15	15
C686 AP132	7c multi	15	15
C687 AP132	8c multi	15	15
C688 AP132	10c multi	15	15
	Set value	70	40

Presidential Guard Patches — AP133

Presidential Guard, 30th anniv.: 10c, Guard Headquarters.

1979, Dec. 6 Litho. *Perf. 11½*

C689 AP133	8c multi	15	15
C690 AP133	10c multi	15	15
	Set value	24	15

National Coat of Arms — AP134

Arms of Guatemalan Municipalities.

1979, Dec. 27 Litho. *Perf. 13½*

C691 AP134	8c shown	25	15
C692 AP134	8c Alta Verapaz	25	15
C693 AP134	8c Baja Verapaz	25	15
C694 AP134	8c Chimal Tenango	25	15
C695 AP134	8c Chiquimula	25	15
C696 AP134	8c Escuintla	25	15
C697 AP134	8c Flores	25	15
C698 AP134	8c Guatemala	25	15
C699 AP134	8c Huehuetenango	25	15
C700 AP134	8c Izabal	25	15
C701 AP134	8c Jalapa	25	15
C702 AP134	8c Jutiapa	25	15
C703 AP134	8c Mazatenango	25	15
C704 AP134	8c Progreso	25	15
C705 AP134	8c Quezaltenango	25	15
C706 AP134	8c Quiche	25	15
C707 AP134	8c Retalhuleu	25	15
C708 AP134	8c Sacatepequez	25	15
C709 AP134	8c San Marcos	25	15
C710 AP134	8c Santa Rosa	25	15
C711 AP134	8c Solola	25	15
C712 AP134	8c Totonicapan	25	15
C713 AP134	8c Zacapa	25	15
	Nos. C691-C713 (23)	5.75	3.45

Miniature Sheet

Imperf

C714 AP134	50c 1st & current natl. arms	1.50	50

No. C714 is horizontal.

The Creation of the World — AP135

Designs: Scenes from The Creation, Popul Vuh (Sacred Book of the Ancient Quiches of Guatemala): No. C716, Origin of the Twin Semi-gods. No. C717, Populating the earth. No. C718, Balam Quitze. No. C719, Quiche monarch Cotuha. No. C720, Birth of the Stick Men. No. C721, Princess Xquic's punishment. No. C722, Caha Paluma. No. C723, Cotuha and Iztayul invincible. No. C724, Odyssey of Hun Ahpu and Xbalanque. No. C725, Balam Acab. No. C726, Chief of all Nations. No. C727, Destruction of the Stick Men. No. C728, The Test in Xibalba. No. C729, Chomiha. No. C730, Warrior with captive. No. C731, Creation of the Corn Men. No. C732, Multiplication of the Prodigies. No. C733, Mahucutah. No. C734, Undefeatable king. No. C735, Thanksgiving. No. C736, Deification of Hun Ahpu and Xbalanque. No. C737, Tzununiha. No. C738, Greatness of the Quiches (battle scene).

1981 Litho. *Perf. 12*

C715 AP135	1c multi	15	15
C716 AP135	1c multi	15	15
C717 AP135	2c multi	15	15
C718 AP135	2c multi	15	15
C719 AP135	3c multi	15	15
C720 AP135	4c multi	15	15
C721 AP135	4c multi	15	15
C722 AP135	4c multi	15	15
C723 AP135	4c multi	15	15
C724 AP135	6c multi	15	15
C725 AP135	6c multi	15	15
C726 AP135	6c multi	15	15
C727 AP135	8c multi	20	15
C728 AP135	8c multi	20	15
C729 AP135	8c multi	20	15
C730 AP135	8c multi	20	15
C731 AP135	10c multi	25	15
C732 AP135	10c multi	25	15
C733 AP135	10c multi	25	15
C734 AP135	10c multi	25	15
C735 AP135	22c multi	50	15
C736 AP135	26c multi	60	15
C737 AP135	30c multi	75	25
C738 AP135	50c multi	1.25	30
	Set value	6.00	2.00

Issue dates: Nos. C715, C717, 3c, C727, C731, 22c, Jan. 29. Nos. C716, C718, C721-C722, C724-C725, C728-C729, C732-C733, 26c, 30c, Mar. 16. Other, 1981.

Thomas Edison (Phonograph Centenary) — AP136

Talking Movies, 50th Anniv. — AP137

Telephone Centenary (1976) — AP138

Lindbergh's Atlantic Flight, 50th Anniv. (1977) — AP139

Designs: 12c, Jose Cecilio del Valle, patriot. 25c, Jesus Castillo (1877-1949), composer.

Perf. 11½, 12½ (25c)

1981, June 1 Litho.

C739 AP136	3c multi	15	15
C740 AP137	5c multi	15	15
C741 AP138	6c multi	18	15
C742 AP139	7c multi	20	15
C743 AP139	12c multi	30	15
C744 AP139	25c multi	60	15
	Nos. C739-C744 (6)	1.58	
	Set value		40

First Police Chief Roderico Toledo and Present Chief German Chupina AP140

1981, Sept. 12 Litho. *Perf. 11½*

C745 AP140	2c shown	15	15
C746 AP140	4c Headquarters	15	15
	Set value	20	20

Mayan Rock of the Sun Calendar AP141

1981, Oct. 9

C747 AP141	1c multi	15	15

Gen. Jose Gervasio Artigas of Uruguay — AP142

Liberators of the Americas: 2c, Bernardo O'Higgins (Chile). 4c, Jose de San Martin (Argentina). 10c, Miguel Garcia Granados. 2c, 4c, 10c, 31x47mm.

1982, Apr. 2 Litho. *Perf. 11½*

C748 AP142	2c multi	15	15
C749 AP142	3c multi	15	15

Perf. 12½

C750 AP142	4c multi	15	15
C751 AP142	10c tan & blk	15	15
	Set value	32	20

Occidents Bank Centenary (1981) AP143

Designs: 1c, Justo Rufino Barrios (first pres.), Main Office, Quezaltenango. 2c, Main Office, 3c, Emblem, vert. 4c, Commemorative medals, vert.

1982, July 28 Litho. *Perf. 11½*

No.	Type	Description	Unused	Used
C752	AP143	1c multi	15	15
C753	AP143	2c multi	15	15
C754	AP143	3c multi	15	15
C755	AP143	4c multi	15	15
		Set value	24	20

50th Anniv. of Natl. Mortgage Bank (1980) AP144

Various emblems. 5c vert.

1982, Oct. 18 Litho. *Perf. 11½*

No.	Type	Description	Unused	Used
C756	AP144	1c multi	15	15
C757	AP144	2c multi	15	15
C758	AP144	5c multi	15	15
C759	AP144	10c multi	15	15
		Set value	24	20

AP145

AP146

1983, May 16 Litho. *Perf. 11½*

No.	Type	Description	Unused	Used
C760	AP145	1c Portrait	15	15
C761	AP145	20c Aparition, horiz.	25	15
		Set value	30	15

20th Anniv. of Beatification of Pedro Bethancourt (1626-1667).

1983, July 25 Litho. *Perf. 11½*

No.	Type	Description	Unused	Used
C762	AP146	10c multi	15	15

World Telecommunications and Health Day, May 17, 1981

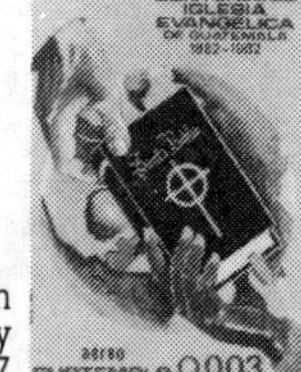

Evangelical Church Centenary (1982) — AP147

1983, Aug. 9

No.	Type	Description	Unused	Used
C763	AP147	3c Hands holding bible	15	15
C764	AP147	5c Church	15	15
		Set value	15	15

Natl. Railroad Centenary AP148

Designs: 10c, First locomotive crossing Puenta de Las Vacas. 25c, General Justo Rufino Barrios, Railroad Yard. 30c, Spanish Diesel, Amatitlan crossing.

1983, Sept. 28 Litho. *Perf. 11½*

No.	Type	Description	Unused	Used
C765	AP148	10c multi	15	15
C766	AP148	25c multi	25	15
C767	AP148	30c multi	40	15
		Set value		18

World Food Day — AP149

1983, Oct. 16 Photo. *Perf. 11½*

No.	Type	Description	Unused	Used
C768	AP149	8c Globe, wheat, vert.	15	15
C769	AP149	1q shown	1.40	1.00

Architecture Type of 1972

1984, Feb. 20 Typo. *Perf. 12½*

Black and Green

No.	Type	Description	Unused	Used
C770	AP98	1c like #C480	15	15
C771	AP98	1c like #C481	15	15
C772	AP98	1c like #C482	15	15
C773	AP98	1c like #C483	15	15
C774	AP98	1c like #C484	15	15
C775	AP98	1c like #C485	15	15
g.		Strip of 6, #C770-C775	30	30

Black, Brown and Orange Brown

No.	Type	Description	Unused	Used
C775A	AP98	5c like #C484	15	15
C775B	AP98	5c like #C485	15	15
C775C	AP98	5c like #C482	15	15
C775D	AP98	5c like #C483	15	15
C775E	AP98	5c like #C480	15	15
C775F	AP98	5c like #C481	15	15
g.		Strip of 6, #C775A-C775F	60	60
		Set value	90	90

Visit of Pope John Paul II, Mar. 8-9, 1983 AP150

1984, Mar. 26 Litho. *Perf. 11½*

No.	Type	Description	Unused	Used
C776	AP150	4c Pope, arms	15	15
C777	AP150	8c Receiving Mayan indian	15	15
		Set value	23	15

Rafael Landivar (1731-93), Poet — AP151

Cardinal Mario Casariego y Acevedo — AP152

1984, Aug. 6 Litho. *Perf. 11½*

No.	Type	Description	Unused	Used
C778	AP151	2c Portrait, vert.	15	15
C779	AP151	4c Tomb	15	15
		Set value	15	15

1984, Aug. 6

No.	Type	Description	Unused	Used
C780	AP152	10c 16th archbishop of Guat. (1909-83)	15	15

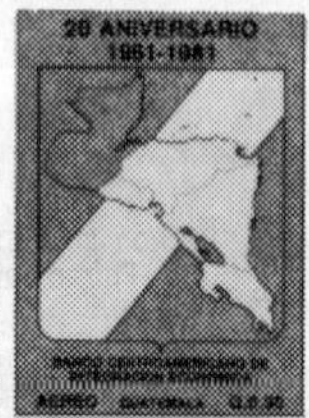

Central American Bank for Economic Integration, 20th Anniv. — AP153

1984, Sept. 10 Litho. *Perf. 11½*

No.	Type	Description	Unused	Used
C781	AP153	30c Bank emblem, map	40	15

Coffee Production, 1870 AP154

Modern Coffee Production AP155

Designs: 1c, Planting coffee. 2c, Harvesting. 3c, Drying beans. 4c, Loading beans on steamer. 5c, Reyna plant grafting method. 10c, Picking beans, coffee cup. 12c, Drying unripened beans, Gardiola Freeze-drying machine. 25c, Cargo transports.

1984, Dec. 19 *Perf. 11½*

No.	Type	Description	Unused	Used
C782	AP154	1c sep & pale brn	15	15
C783	AP154	2c sep & pale org brn	15	15
C784	AP154	3c sep & beige	15	15
C785	AP154	4c sep & pale yel brn	15	15
C786	AP155	5c multi	15	15
C787	AP155	10c multi	15	15
C788	AP155	12c multi	16	15
C789	AP155	25c multi	35	15
		Set value	1.00	50

Natl. coffee production and export. An 86x112mm 25c stamp of Type AP154 and a 105x85mm 30c stamp of Type AP155 exist.

Natl. Scouting Assoc. — AP156

Scouting emblems and: 5c, Beaver scout, Pyramid of Tikal. 6c, Wolf scout, Palace of the Captains-General and Ahua Volcano. 8c, Scout, San Pedro Volcano and Marimba player. 10c, Rover scout and conquest mask dance. 20c, Lord Baden-Powell and Col. Carlos Cipriani, natl. founder.

1985, July 1

No.	Type	Description	Unused	Used
C792	AP156	5c multi	15	15
C793	AP156	6c multi	15	15
C794	AP156	8c multi	15	15
C795	AP156	10c multi	15	15
C796	AP156	20c multi	25	15
		Set value	68	40

Inter-American Family Unity Year — AP157

Central American Aeronautics Admin., 25th Anniv. — AP158

1985, Oct. 16

No.	Type	Description	Unused	Used
C797	AP157	10c multi	15	15

1985, Nov. 11

No.	Type	Description	Unused	Used
C798	AP158	10c multi	15	15

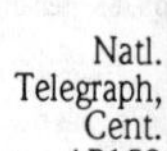

Natl. Telegraph, Cent. AP159

Portraits: Samuel Morse, telegraph inventor, and Justo Rufino Barrios, communications pioneer.

1985, Nov. 20 *Perf. 12*

No.	Type	Description	Unused	Used
C799	AP159	4c brn & blk	15	15

Intl. Olympic Committee, 90th Anniv. AP160

Designs: 8c, Mayan bust of ancient sportsman. 10c, Baron Pierre de Coubertin (1863-1937), father of modern Games, 1st committee president.

1986, Jan. 28 Litho. *Perf. 11½*

No.	Type	Description	Unused	Used
C800	AP160	8c multi	16	15
C801	AP160	10c multi	20	15
		Set value		15

Volunteer Fire Department — AP161

1986, Feb. 6 Litho. *Perf. 11½*

No.	Type	Description	Unused	Used
C802	AP161	6c multi	15	15

Temple of Minerva — AP162

Quetzeltenango Coat of Arms, City Hall — AP163

Perf. 12½, 11½

1986, July 16 Litho.

No.	Type	Description	Unused	Used
C803	AP162	8c multi	16	15
C804	AP163	10c multi	20	15
		Set value		15

Quetzeltenango Independence Fair, cent.

Volunteer Fire Department AP164

1986, Oct. 10 Litho. *Perf. 11½*

No.	Type	Description	Unused	Used
C805	AP164	8c Rescue	16	15
C806	AP164	10c Ruins	20	15
		Set value		15

Assoc. of Telegraphers and Radio-Telegraph Operators, 25th Anniv. — AP165

1986, Oct. 10 *Perf. 12*
C807 AP165 6c multi 15 15

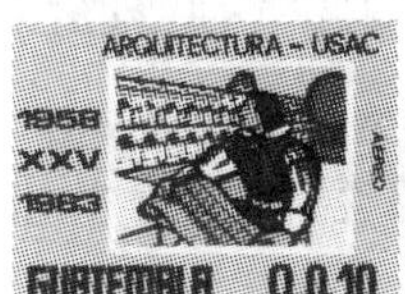

San Carlos University School of Architecture, 25th Anniv. AP166

1987, Feb. 16 **Litho.** *Perf. 11½*
C808 AP166 10c multi 20 15

ICAO, 40th Anniv. (in 1984) AP167

1987, Apr. 2 **Litho.** *Perf. 11½*
C809 AP167 8c Aviateca Airlines jet 16 15
C810 AP167 10c Jet, vert. 20 15
Set value 15

Chixoy Hydroelectric Power Plant — AP168

1987, May 18 **Litho.** *Perf. 11½*
C811 AP168 2c multi 15 15

Nat'l. Electrification Institute inauguration (in 1985).

San Jose de los Infantes College, 200th Anniv. (in 1981) AP169

Designs: 8c, Portrait of Archbishop Cayetano Francos y Monroy, founder, vert. 10c, College crest.

1987, June 10
C812 AP169 8c multi 16 15
C813 AP169 10c multi 20 15
Set value 15

Promotion of Literacy in Latin America and Caribbean AP170

1987, Aug. 20 **Litho.** *Perf. 11½*
C814 AP170 12c apple grn, blk & brt org 25 15

19th Natl. Folklore Carnival of Coban, Alta Verapaz, July 25 — AP171

1987, Oct. 12
C815 AP171 1q Three girls from Tamahu 2.10 70

1987, Dec. 8
C816 AP171 50c Girl weaving 1.00 50

See No. C831.

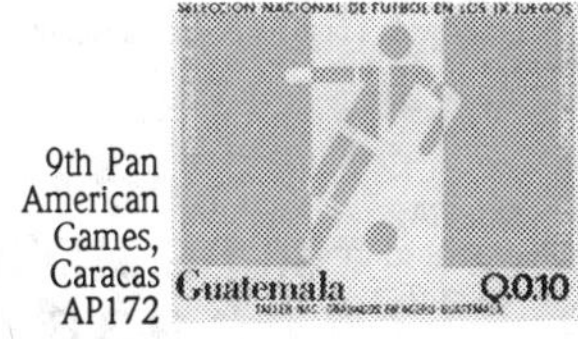

9th Pan American Games, Caracas AP172

1987, Nov. 5 *Perf. 12½*
C817 AP172 10c blk & sky blue 20 15

Writers and Historians AP173

Esquipulas II AP174

Designs: 1c, Flavio Herrera, poet, novelist. 2c, Rosendo Santa Cruz, novelist. 3c, Werner Ovalle Lopez, poet. 4c, Enrique A. Hidalgo, poet, humorist. 5c, Enrique Gomez Carrillo (1873-1927), novelist. 6c, Cesar Branas (1899-1976), journalist. 7c, Clemente Marroquin Rojas, historian. 8c, Rafael Arevalo Martinez (1884-1975), poet. 9c, Jose Milla y Vidaurre (1822-1882), historian. 10c, Miguel Angel Asturias, Nobel laureate for literature.

1987-90 *Perf. 11½*
C818 AP173 1c blk & lil 15 15
C819 AP173 2c blk & dl org 15 15
C820 AP173 3c blk & brt bl 15 15
C821 AP173 4c blk & ver 15 15
C822 AP173 5c blk & org brn 15 15
C823 AP173 6c blk & org 15 15
C824 AP173 7c blk & grn 15 15
C825 AP173 8c blk & brt red 16 15
C826 AP173 9c blk & brt rose lil 18 15
C827 AP173 10c blk & yel 20 15
Set value 1.10 52

Issue dates: 6c, 8c, 9c, Nov. 5. 4c, 5c, Jan. 13, 1988. 7c, Mar. 23, 1990. 1c, 2c, 3c, 10c, Apr. 9, 1990.

1988, Jan. 15 *Perf. 12½*
C828 AP174 10c dark olive grn 20 15
C829 AP174 40c plum 85 30
C830 AP174 60c deep blue vio 1.25 40

2nd Meeting of the Central American Peace Plan. Nos. C828-C829 horiz.

Folklore Festival Type of 1987

1988, Dec. 6 **Litho.** *Imperf.*

Souvenir Sheet

C831 AP171 2q Music ensemble, horiz. 4.00 1.35

St. John Bosco (1815-1888), Educator — AP175

1989, Feb. 1 **Litho.** *Perf. 11½*
C832 AP175 40c gold & blk 80 28

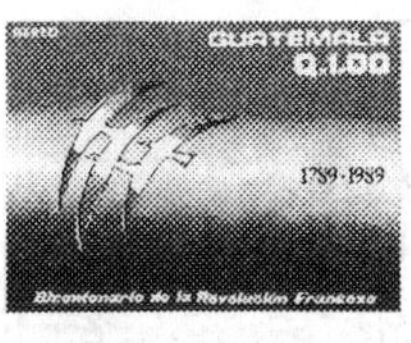

French Revolution, Bicent. AP176

1989, Oct. 18 **Litho.** *Perf. 11½*
C833 AP176 1q dark red, blk & deep blue 2.00 68

America Issue — AP177

UPAE emblem and: 10c, Detail of the *Madrid Codex*. 20c, Temple of the Gran Jaguar of Tikal, Tikal Natl. Park.

1990, Jan. 25 **Litho.** *Perf. 11½*
C834 AP177 10c shown 25 15
C835 AP177 20c brown & multi 52 18
C836 AP177 20c black & multi 52 18

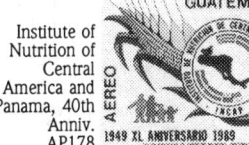

Institute of Nutrition of Central America and Panama, 40th Anniv. AP178

1990, May 18
C837 AP178 20c multicolored 40 15

Red Cross, Red Crescent Societies, 125th Anniv. AP179

1990, June 8
C838 AP179 50c multicolored 1.00 34

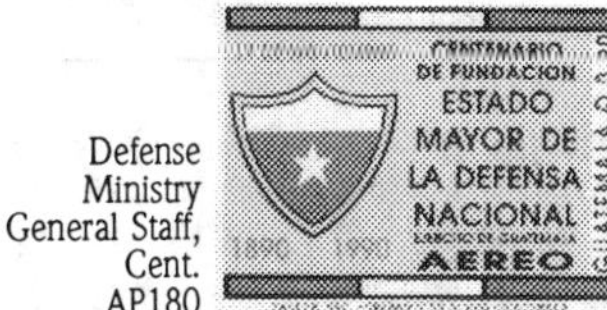

Defense Ministry General Staff, Cent. AP180

1991, May 8 **Litho.** *Perf. 11½*
C839 AP180 20c multicolored 40 15

America AP181

UPAE: 10c, Pacaya Volcano Erupting at Night. 60c, Lake Atitlan.

1991, July 30 **Litho.** *Perf. 11½*
C840 AP181 10c multicolored 20 15
C841 AP181 60c multicolored 1.20 30

America Issue AP182

Designs: 40c, Pinzon brothers, Nina. 60c, Columbus, Santa Maria, vert.

1992, July 27 **Litho.** *Perf. 11½*
C842 AP182 40c green & black 78 20
C843 AP182 60c green & black 1.15 28

AP183 AP184

1992, Oct. 6 **Litho.** *Perf. 12½*
C844 AP183 10c multicolored 15 15

Interamerican Institute for Agricultural Cooperation, 50th anniv.

1992, Dec. 1 **Photo.** *Perf. 11½*
C845 AP184 1q multicolored 2.00 50

World campaign against AIDS.

AIR POST SEMI-POSTAL STAMPS

Air Post Stamps of 1937 Surcharged in Red or Blue

1937

EXPOSICION FILATELICA

+1

1937, Mar. 15 **Unwmk.** *Perf. 12½*
CB1 AP10 4c + 1c ultra (R) 75 85
CB2 AP10 6c + 1c blk vio (R) 75 85
CB3 AP11 10c + 1c ol grn (Bl) 75 85
CB4 AP11 15c + 1c ver (Bl) 75 85

1st Phil. Exhib. held in Guatemala, Mar. 15-20.

Catalogue values for unused stamps in this section, from this point to the end of the section, are for Never Hinged items.

Type of Regular Issue, 1956

Designs: 35c+1q, Red Cross, Ambulance and Volcano. 50c+1q, Red Cross, Hospital and Nurse. 1q+1q, Nurse and Red Cross.

Perf. 13x12½

1956, June 19 **Engr.** **Unwmk.**
CB5 A148 35c + 1q red & ol grn 5.00 5.50
CB6 A148 50c + 1q ultra & red 5.00 5.50
CB7 A148 1q + 1q dk grn & dk red 5.00 5.50

The surtax was for the Red Cross.

Nos. B5-B7 Overprinted **AEREO - 1957**

1957, May 11

CB8	A148 5c + 15c	6.50	7.00
a.	Imperf., pair	225.00	
CB9	A148 15c + 50c	6.50	7.00
a.	Overprint inverted	110.00	
CB10	A148 25c + 50c	6.50	7.00

The surtax was for the Red Cross.

Type of Semi-Postal Stamps, 1957 and

Esquipulas Cathedral SPAP1

Designs: 15c+1q, Cathedral and crucifix. 20c+1q, Christ with crown of thorns and part of globe. 25c+1q, Archbishop Mariano Rossell y Arellano.

Perf. 13½x14½, 13

1957, Oct. 29 Engr. Unwmk.

CB11	SPAP1 10c + 1q choc & emer	6.25	6.75
CB12	SP1 15c + 1q dl grn & sep	6.25	6.75
CB13	SP1 20c + 1q bl gray & brn	6.25	6.75
CB14	SP1 25c + 1q lt vio & car	6.25	6.75

The tax was for the Esquipulas highway.

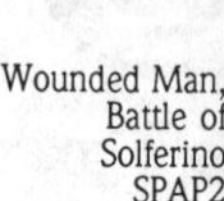

Wounded Man, Battle of Solferino SPAP2

Designs: 6c+6c, 20c+20c, Flood disaster. 10c+10c, 25c+25c, Earth, moon and stars. 15c+15c, 30c+30c, Red Cross headquarters.

1960, Apr. 9 Photo. *Perf. 13½x14*

CB15	SPAP2 5c + 5c multi	2.25	2.50
CB16	SPAP2 6c + 6c multi	2.25	2.50
CB17	SPAP2 10c + 10c multi	2.25	2.50
CB18	SPAP2 15c + 15c multi	2.25	2.50
CB19	SPAP2 20c + 20c multi	2.25	2.50
CB20	SPAP2 25c + 25c multi	2.25	2.50
CB21	SPAP2 30c + 30c multi	2.25	2.50
	Nos. CB15-CB21 (7)	15.75	17.50

Cent. (in 1959) of the Red Cross idea. The surtax went to the Red Cross. Exist imperf.

AIR POST OFFICIAL STAMPS

Nos. C93-C98 Overprinted in Black

OFICIAL

1939, Apr. 29 Unwmk. *Perf. 12½*

CO1	AP13 1c org & ol brn	1.00	1.10
CO2	AP13 2c multi	1.00	1.10
CO3	AP13 3c multi	1.00	1.10
CO4	AP13 4c multi	1.00	1.10
CO5	AP13 5c multi	1.00	1.10
CO6	AP13 10c multi	1.00	1.10
	Nos. CO1-CO6 (6)	6.00	6.60

No. C99 with Same Overprint on each Stamp

1939

CO7	AP19 Sheet of 6	2.50	2.50
a.	1c yel org, blue & blk	30	25
b.	2c lake, org, blue & blk	30	25
c.	3c olive, blue & orange	30	25
d.	4c dk claret, bl, org & blk	30	25
e.	5c grnsh bl, bl, red, org & blk	30	25
f.	10c olive bister, red & org	30	25

SPECIAL DELIVERY STAMPS

No. 237 Overprinted in Red **EXPRESO**

1940, June Unwmk. *Perf. 14*

E1	A81 4c orange	1.25	30

No. E1 paid for express service by motorcycle messenger between Guatemala City and Coban.

Catalogue values for unused stamps in this section, from this point to the end of the section, are for Never Hinged items.

Motorcycle Messenger SD1

Black Surcharge

1948, Sept. 3 Photo. *Perf. 14x12½*

E2	SD1 10c on 4c bl grn & gray blk	1.50	85

No. E2 without surcharge was issued for regular postage, not special delivery. See No. 337B.

OFFICIAL STAMPS

Franqueo Oficial Guatemala. 1902 1 CENTAVO

O1

National Emblem — O2

1902, Dec. 18 Typeset *Perf. 12*

O1	O1 1c green	3.75	1.75
O2	O1 2c carmine	3.75	1.75
O3	O1 5c ultra	4.50	1.50
O4	O1 10c brown violet	5.00	1.50
O5	O1 25c orange	5.25	1.50
a.	Horiz. pair, imperf. between	100.00	
	Nos. O1-O5 (5)	22.25	8.00

Nos. O1-O5 printed on thin paper with sheet watermark "AMERICAN LINEN BOND." Nos. O1-O3 also printed on thick paper with sheet watermark "ROYAL BANK BOND." Values are for copies that do not show the watermark. Counterfeits of Nos. O1-O5 exist.

During the years 1912 to 1926 the Post Office Department perforated the word "OFICIAL" on limited quantities of the following stamps: Nos. 114-123, 132, 141-149, 151-153, 158, 202, 210-229 and RA2. The perforating was done in blocks of four stamps at a time and was of two types.

A rubber handstamp "OFICIAL" was also used during the same period and was applied in violet, red, blue or black to stamps No. 117-118, 121-123, 163-165, 172 and 202-218.

Both perforating and handstamping were done in the post office at Guatemala City and use of the stamps was limited to that city.

1929, Jan. Engr. *Perf. 14*

O6	O2 1c pale grnsh bl	25	25
O7	O2 2c dark brown	25	25
O8	O2 3c green	25	25
O9	O2 4c deep violet	35	35
O10	O2 5c brown car	35	35
O11	O2 10c brown orange	60	60
O12	O2 25c dark blue	1.25	1.00
	Nos. O6-O12 (7)	3.30	3.05

POSTAL TAX STAMPS

National Emblem — PT1

Perf. 13½, 14, 15

1919, May 3 Engr. Unwmk.

RA1	PT1 12½c carmine	16	15

Tax for rebuilding post offices.

G. P. O. and Telegraph Building — PT2

1927, Nov. 10 Typo. *Perf. 14*

RA2	PT2 1c olive green	15	15

Tax to provide a fund for building a post office in Guatemala City.

No. RA2 Overprinted in Green **1871 30 DE JUNIO 1936**

1936, June 30

RA3	PT2 1c olive green	50	40

Liberal revolution, 65th anniversary.

No. RA2 Overprinted in Blue **1821 15 de SEPTIEMBRE 1936**

1936, Sept. 15

RA4	PT2 1c olive green	40	30

115th anniv. of the Independence of Guatemala.

No. RA2 Overprinted in Red Brown **FERIA NACIONAL 1936**

1936, Nov. 15

RA5	PT2 1c olive green	50	40

National Fair.

No. RA2 Overprinted in Red **EXPOSICION FILATELICA 1937**

1937, Mar. 15

RA6	PT2 1c olive green	40	40

No. RA2 Overprinted in Blue **1787-1789 CL ANIVERSARIO DE LA CONSTITUCION EE. UU. 1937-1939**

1938, Jan. 10 *Perf. 14x14½*

RA7	PT2 1c olive green	22	16
a.	"1937-1939" omitted	110.00	

150th anniv. of the US Constitution.

No. RA2 Overprinted in Blue or Red **1938**

1938 *Perf. 14*

RA8	PT2 1c olive green (Bl)	30	20
RA9	PT2 1c olive green (R)	30	15

No. RA2 Overprinted in Violet **Primera Exposicion Filatélica Centroamericana 1938**

1938, Nov. 20

RA10	PT2 1c olive green	30	15

1st Central American Philatelic Exposition.

No. RA2 Overprinted in Green or Black **1939**

1939

RA11	PT2 1c olive green (G)	35	15
RA12	PT2 1c olive green (Bk)	35	15

No. RA2 Overprinted in Violet or Brown **1940**

1940

RA13	PT2 1c olive green (V)	35	15
RA14	PT2 1c olive green (Br)	35	15

No. RA2 Overprinted in Red **Conmemorativo Unión Panamericana 1890-1940**

1940, Apr. 14

RA15	PT2 1c olive green	25	15

Pan American Union, 50th anniversary.

No. RA2 Overprinted in Red **1941**

1941

RA16	PT2 1c olive green	50	15

No. 235 Surcharged in Red **CONSTRUCCION CONSTRUCCION UN CENTAVO**

RA17	A79 1c on 2c deep blue	25	15

No. 235 Surcharged in Carmine **CONSTRUCCION 1942 UN CENTAVO**

1942, Jan.

RA18	A79 1c on 2c deep blue	50	15

Arch of Communications Building PT3 PT4

With Imprint Below Design

1942, June 3 Engr. *Perf. 11, 12x11*

RA19	PT3 1c black brown	5.00	1.00

No imprint; Thin Paper

Perf. 11, 12x11, 11x12, 11x12x11x11

1942, July 18

RA20 PT3 1c black brown 35 15

1943 ***Perf. 11, 12x11, 12***

RA21 PT4 1c orange 25 15

PT5

Perf. 11, 12½ and Compound

1945, Feb. **Unwmk.**

RA22 PT5 1c orange 20 15

1949 ***Perf. 12½***

RA23 PT5 1c deep ultra 30 15

GUINEA

LOCATION — Coast of West Africa, between Guinea-Bissau and Sierra Leone
GOVT. — Republic
AREA — 94,926 sq. mi.
POP. — 5,412,000 (est. 1983)
CAPITAL — Conakry

This former French Overseas Territory of French West Africa proclaimed itself an independent republic on October 2, 1958.

100 Centimes = 1 Franc
100 Caury = 1 Syli (1973)
100 Centimes = 1 CFA Franc (1986)

Catalogue values for all unused stamps in this country are for Never Hinged items.

French West Africa No. 79 Overprinted

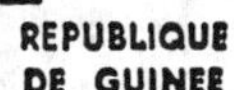

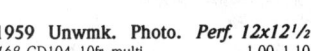

1959 Unwmk. Photo. ***Perf. 12x12½***

168 CD104 10fr multi 1.00 1.10

French West Africa No. 78 Surcharged in Red

45F

REPUBLIQUE DE GUINEE

Engr.

Perf. 13

169 A33 45fr on 20fr multi 1.00 1.10

Common Design Types pictured in section at front of book.

Map, Dove and Pres. Sékou Touré — A12

1959 **Unwmk.** **Engr.** ***Perf. 13***

170 A12 5fr rose car 15 15
171 A12 10fr ultramarine 20 15
172 A12 20fr orange 38 25
173 A12 65fr slate green 1.00 65
174 A12 100fr violet 1.90 1.40
Nos. 170-174 (5) 3.63 2.60

Proclamation of independence, Oct. 2, 1958.

Bananas — A13

Flag Raising, Labé — A15

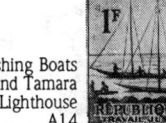

Fishing Boats and Tamara Lighthouse A14

Fruits: 15fr, Grapefruit. 20fr, Lemons. 25fr, Avocados. 50fr, Pineapple.

1959 **Litho.** ***Perf. 11½***

Fruits in Natural Colors

175 A13 10fr red 15 15
176 A13 15fr green & pink 15 15
177 A13 20fr red brn & bl 20 15
178 A13 25fr blue & yel 25 20
179 A13 50fr dark vio bl 42 22
Nos. 175-179 (5) 1.17
Set value 68

For overprints see Nos. 209-213.

1959 **Engr.** ***Perf. 13½***

Designs: 5fr, Coco palms and sailboat, vert. 10fr, Launching fishing pirogue. 15fr, Elephant's head. 20fr, Pres. Sékou Touré and torch, vert. 25fr, Elephant.

180 A14 1fr rose 15 15
181 A14 2fr green 15 15
182 A14 3fr brown 15 15
183 A14 5fr blue 15 15
184 A14 10fr claret 15 15
185 A14 15fr light brn 25 15
186 A14 20fr claret 38 15
187 A14 25fr red brown 40 15
Set value 1.25 60

1959 **Litho.** ***Perf. 12***

188 A15 50fr multicolored 42 20
189 A15 100fr multicolored 90 50

For overprints see Nos. 201-202.

UN Headquarters, New York, and People of Guinea — A16

1959 ***Perf. 12***

190 A16 1fr vio blue & org 15 15
191 A16 2fr red lil & emer 15 15
192 A16 3fr brn & crimson 15 15
193 A16 5fr brn & grnsh bl 15 15
Set value, #190-193, C22-C23 1.40 1.00

Guinea's admission to the UN, first anniv.
For overprints see Nos. 205-208, C27-C28.

Uprooted Oak Emblem — A17

1960 **Photo.** ***Perf. 11½***

Granite Paper

194 A17 25fr multicolored 20 18
195 A17 50fr multicolored 28 20

World Refugee Year, July 1, 1959-June 30, 1960.
For surcharges see Nos. B17-B18.

UPU Monument, Bern — A18

1960 **Granite Paper** **Unwmk.**

196 A18 10fr gray brn & blk 15 15
197 A18 15fr lil & purple 15 15
198 A18 20fr ultra & dk blue 16 15
199 A18 25fr yel grn & sl grn 25 15
200 A18 50fr red org & brown 45 20
Nos. 196-200 (5) 1.16 80

Nos. 199-200 are vertical.
Admission to the UPU, first anniv.

Nos. 188-189 Overprinted in Black, Orange or Carmine: "Jeux Olympiques Rome 1960" and Olympic Rings

1960 **Litho.** ***Perf. 12***

201 A15 50fr multi (Bk) 2.50 2.50
202 A15 100fr multi (O or C) 4.00 4.00
Nos. 201-202,C24-C26 (5) 28.50 26.00

17th Olympic Games, Rome, Aug. 25-Sept. 11.

Map and Flag of Guinea — A19

1960 **Photo.** ***Perf. 11½***

203 A19 25fr multicolored 20 16
204 A19 30fr multicolored 25 20

Second anniversary of independence.

Nos. 190-193 Overprinted

XVÈME ANNIVERSAIRE DES NATIONS UNIES

1961 **Litho.** ***Perf. 12***

205 A16 1fr vio blue & org 15 15
206 A16 2fr red lil & emer 15 15
207 A16 3fr brn & crimson 15 15
208 A16 5fr brn & grnsh bl 15 15

Nos. 175-179 Overprinted in Black or Orange

XVEME ANNIVERSAIRE

DES NATIONS UNIES

Perf. 11½

Fruits in Natural Colors

209 A13 10fr red 15 15
210 A13 15fr grn & pink 16 15
211 A13 20fr red brn & bl 22 20
212 A13 25fr bl & yel (O) 25 22
213 A13 50fr dk vio blue 50 45
Nos. 205-213,C27-C28 (11) 2.98 2.70

15th anniversary of United Nations.

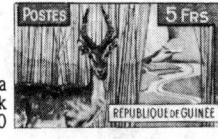

Defassa Waterbuck A20

1961, Sept. 1 **Photo.** ***Perf. 11½***

Multicolored Design; Granite Paper

214 A20 5fr bright grn 15 15
215 A20 10fr emerald 15 15
216 A20 25fr lilac 18 15
217 A20 40fr orange 30 16
218 A20 50fr red orange 40 25
219 A20 75fr ultramarine 65 25
Nos. 214-219 (6) 1.83
Set value 85

For surcharges see Nos. B19-B24.

Exhibition Hall — A21

1961, Oct. 2 ***Perf. 11½***

Flag in Red, Yellow & Green

Granite Paper

220 A21 5fr ultra & red 15 15
221 A21 10fr brown & red 15 15
222 A21 25fr gray grn & red 15 15
Set value 27 27

First Three-Year Plan.

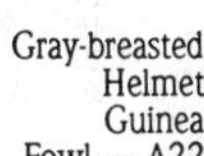

Gray-breasted Helmet Guinea Fowl — A22

1961 **Unwmk.** ***Perf. 13x14***

223 A22 5fr rose lil, sep & bl 15 15
224 A22 10fr dp org, sep & bl 15 15
225 A22 25fr cerise, sep & bl 15 15
226 A22 40fr ocher, sep & bl 25 15
227 A22 50fr lem, sepia & bl 35 16
228 A22 75fr ap grn, sep & bl 70 30
Nos. 223-228 (6) 1.75
Set value 72

For surcharges see Nos. B30-B35.

Patrice Lumumba and Map of Africa — A23

1962, Feb. 13 **Photo.** ***Perf. 11½***

229 A23 10fr multicolored 38 25
230 A23 25fr multicolored 50 25
231 A23 50fr multicolored 30 25

Death anniv. (on Feb. 12, 1961) of Patrice Lumumba, Premier of the Congo Republic.

King Mohammed V of Morocco and Map of Africa — A24

1962, Mar. 15 **Litho.** ***Perf. 13***

232 A24 25fr multicolored 42 16
233 A24 75fr multicolored 90 30

First anniv. of the conference of African heads of state at Casablanca.
For surcharges see Nos. B36-B37.

African Postal Union Issue

Map of Africa and Post Horn — A24a

1962, Apr. 23 Photo. *Perf. 13½x13*

234 A24a 25fr org, blk & grn 50 15
235 A24a 100fr deep brn & org 1.25 25

Establishment of African Postal Union.

Bolon Player — A26

Musical Instruments: 30c, 25fr, 50fr, Bote, vert. 1fr, 10fr, Flute, vert. 1.50fr, 3fr, Koni. 2fr, 20fr, Kora. 40fr, 75fr, Bolon.

Perf. 13½x13, 13x13½

1962, June 15

236 A26 30c bl, dk grn & red 15 15
237 A26 50c sal, brn & brt grn 15 15
238 A26 1fr yel grn, grn & lil 15 15
239 A26 1.50fr yel, red & bl 15 15
240 A26 2fr rose lil, red lil & grn 15 15
241 A26 3fr brn grn, grn & lil 15 15
242 A26 10fr org, brn & bl 15 15
243 A26 20fr ol, dk ol & car 15 15
244 A26 25fr ol, dk ol & lil 20 15
245 A26 40fr bl, grn & red lil 30 20
246 A26 50fr rose, dp rose & Prus bl 40 25
247 A26 75fr dl yel, brn & Prus bl 50 35
Nos. 236-247,C32-C34 (15) 7.35
Set value 4.25

Hippopotamus A27

Designs: 25fr, 75fr, Lion. 30fr, 100fr, Leopard.

1962, Aug. 25 Litho. *Perf. 13x13½*

248 A27 10fr org, grn & brn 15 15
249 A27 25fr emer, blk & brn 25 15
250 A27 30fr yel grn, dk brn & yel 30 15
251 A27 50fr vio bl, dk brn & grn 42 25
252 A27 75fr lil, lt lil & red brn 55 35
253 A27 100fr grnsh bl, dk brn & yel 65 50
Nos. 248-253 (6) 2.32 1.55

See Nos. 340-345

Child at Blackboard A28

Alfa Yaya A29

Designs: 10fr, 20fr, Adult class.

1962, Sept. 19 Photo. *Perf. 13½x13*

254 A28 5fr yel, dk brn & org 15 15
255 A28 10fr org & dk brn 15 15
256 A28 15fr yel grn, dk brn & red 15 15
257 A28 20fr bl & dk brn 15 15
Set value 38 24

Campaign against illiteracy.

> Imperforates
> From late 1962 onward, most Guinea stamps exist imperforate.

1962, Oct. 2 *Perf. 13½*

Portraits: 30fr, King Behanzin. 50fr, King Ba Bemba. 75fr, Almamy Samory. 100fr, Tierno Aliou.

Gold Frame

258 A29 25fr brt bl & sep 22 15
259 A29 30fr yel & sep 35 16
260 A29 50fr brt pink & sep 42 22
261 A29 75fr yel grn & sep 1.00 40
262 A29 100fr org, red & sep 1.20 60
Nos. 258-262 (5) 3.19 1.53

Heroes and martyrs of Africa.

Gray Parrot — A30

Birds: 30c, 3fr, 50fr, Crowned crane (vert). 1fr, 20fr, Abyssinian ground hornbill. 1.50fr, 25fr, White spoonbill. 2fr, 40fr, Bateleur eagle.

1962, Dec. *Perf. 13½x13, 13x13½*

263 A30 30c multicolored 15 15
264 A30 50c multicolored 15 15
265 A30 1fr multicolored 15 15
266 A30 1.50fr multicolored 15 15
267 A30 2fr multicolored 15 15
268 A30 3fr multicolored 15 15
269 A30 10fr multicolored 15 15
270 A30 20fr multicolored 16 15
271 A30 25fr multicolored 20 15
272 A30 40fr multicolored 30 20
273 A30 50fr multicolored 40 25
274 A30 75fr multicolored 50 35
Nos. 263-274,C41-C43 (15) 8.51
Set value 4.40

Wheat Emblem and Globe — A31

1963, Mar. 21 Photo. *Perf. 13x14*

275 A31 5fr red & yellow 15 15
276 A31 10fr emerald & yel 15 15
277 A31 15fr brown & yel 15 15
278 A31 25fr dark ol & yel 20 15
Set value 40 26

FAO "Freedom from Hunger" campaign.

Basketball — A32

Designs: 50c, 4fr, 30fr, Boxing. 1fr, 5fr, Running. 1.50fr, 10fr, Bicycling. 2fr, 20fr, Single sculls.

1963, Mar. 16 Unwmk. *Perf. 14*

279 A32 30c ver, dp cl & grn 15 15
280 A32 50c lil & bl 15 15
281 A32 1fr dl org, sep & grn 15 15
282 A32 1.50fr brown, ultra & mag 15 15
283 A32 2fr aqua, dk bl & mag 15 15
284 A32 3fr ol, dp cl & grn 15 15
285 A32 4fr car rose, pur & bl 15 15
286 A32 5fr brt grn, ol & mag 15 15
287 A32 10fr lil rose, ultra & mag 15 15
288 A32 20fr red org, dk bl & crim 15 15
289 A32 25fr emer, dp cl & dk grn 25 15
290 A32 30fr gray, pur & bl 30 20
Nos. 279-290,C44-C46 (15) 7.20
Set value 3.75

For overprints and surcharges see Nos. 312-314, C58-C60.

A33

Various Butterflies.

1963, May 10 Photo. *Perf. 12*

291 A33 10c dp rose, blk & gray 15 15
292 A33 30c rose, blk & yel 15 15
293 A33 40c yel grn, brn & yel 15 15
294 A33 50c pale vio, blk & grn 15 15
295 A33 1fr yel, blk & emer 15 15
296 A33 1.50fr bluish grn, blk & sep 15 15
297 A33 2fr multi 15 15
298 A33 3fr multi 15 15
299 A33 10fr rose lil, blk & grn 15 15
300 A33 20fr gray, blk & grn 20 15
301 A33 25fr yel grn, blk & gray 30 15
302 A33 40fr multi 40 16
303 A33 50fr ultra, blk & yel 50 20
304 A33 75fr yel, blk & grn 60 35
Nos. 291-304,C47-C49 (17) 9.50
Set value 3.75

Handshake, Map and Dove — A34

1963, May 22 *Perf. 13½x14*

305 A34 5fr bluish grn & dk brn 15 15
306 A34 10fr org yel & dk brn 15 15
307 A34 15fr ol & dk brn 15 15
308 A34 25fr bis brn & dk brn 18 15
Set value 40 28

Conference of African heads of state for African Unity, Addis Ababa.

Globe Encircled by Satellite A35

1963, July 25 Engr. *Perf. 10½*

309 A35 5fr green & car 15 15
310 A35 10fr vio bl & car 15 15
311 A35 15fr yellow & car 15 15
Set value 25 22

Centenary of the International Red Cross. See Nos. C50-C51.

Nos. 279-281 Surcharged in Carmine, Yellow or Orange: "COMMISSION PRÉPARATOIRE AUX JEUX OLYMPIQUES À CONAKRY," New Value and Olympic Rings

1963, Nov. 20 Photo. *Perf. 14*

312 A32 40fr on 30c (C or Y) 1.10 1.00
313 A32 50fr on 50c (C or O) 1.50 1.40
314 A32 75fr on 1fr (C or O) 2.50 2.00
Nos. 312-314,C58-C60 (6) 15.25 12.80

Meeting of the Olympic Games Preparatory Commission at Conakry. The overprint is in a circular line on No. 312, in three lines on each side on Nos. 313-314.

Jewelfish A36

Fish: 40c, 30fr, Golden pheasant. 50c, 40fr, Blue gularis. 1fr, 75fr, Banded Jewelfish. 1.50fr, African lyretail. 2fr, Six-barred epiplatys. 5fr, Jewelfish.

1964, Feb. 15 Litho. *Perf. 14x13½*

315 A36 30c car rose & multi 15 15
316 A36 40c pur & multi 15 15
317 A36 50c car rose & multi 15 15
318 A36 1fr blue & multi 15 15
319 A36 1.50fr blue & multi 15 15
320 A36 2fr pur & multi 15 15
321 A36 5fr blue & multi 15 15
322 A36 30fr grn & multi 20 15
323 A36 40fr pur & multi 50 22
324 A36 75fr multi 65 35
Set value, #315-324, C54-C55 4.35 2.40

John F. Kennedy — A37

1964, Mar. 5 Engr. *Perf. 10½*

Flag in Red and Blue

325 A37 5fr blk & pur 15 15
326 A37 25fr grn & pur 16 15
327 A37 50fr brn & pur 40 25
Set value 42

Issued in sheets of 20 with marginal quotations in English and French. Two sheets for each denomination. See No. C56.

Workers Welding Pipe — A38

Designs: 5fr, Pipe line over mountains, vert. 10fr, Waterworks. 30fr, Transporting pipe. 50fr, Laying pipe.

1964, May 1 Photo. *Perf. 11½*

328 A38 5fr deep mag 15 15
329 A38 10fr bright pur 15 15
330 A38 20fr org red 15 15
331 A38 30fr ultra 15 15
332 A38 50fr yel grn 25 15
Set value 54 35

Completion of the water-supply pipeline to Conakry, Mar. 1964.

Ice Hockey — A39

1964, May 15 *Perf. 13x12½*

333 A39 10fr shown 15 15
334 A39 25fr Ski jump 30 15
335 A39 50fr Slalom 60 35
Set value 55

9th Winter Olympic Games, Innsbruck, Jan. 29-Feb. 9, 1964. See No. C57.

Eleanor Roosevelt Reading to Children A40

1964, June 1 Engr. *Perf. 10½*

336 A40 5fr green 15 15
337 A40 10fr red org 15 15
338 A40 15fr bright bl 15 15
339 A40 25fr car rose 18 15
Nos. 336-339,C61 (5) 1.03
Set value 52

Eleanor Roosevelt, 15th anniv. of the Universal Declaration of Human Rights (in 1963).

Animal Type of 1962

Designs: 5fr, 30fr, Striped hyenas. 40fr, 300fr, Black buffaloes. 75fr, 100fr, Elephants.

1964, Oct. 8 Litho. *Perf. 13x13½*

340 A27 5fr yellow & blk 15 15
341 A27 30fr light bl & blk 18 15
342 A27 40fr lil rose & blk 25 15
343 A27 75fr yel grn & blk 55 22
344 A27 100fr bister & blk 65 38
345 A27 300fr orange & blk 1.90 1.10
Nos. 340-345 (6) 3.68 2.15

Guinea Exhibit, World's Fair — A41

1964, Oct. 26 Engr. *Perf. 10½*

346 A41 30fr vio & emerald 20 15
347 A41 40fr red lil & emer 30 15
348 A41 50fr sepia & emer 40 18
349 A41 75fr rose red & dk bl 60 25

New York World's Fair, 1964-65.
See Nos. 372-375, C62-C63, C69-C70.

Queen Nefertari Crowned by Isis and Hathor — A42

Weight Lifter and Caucasian, Japanese and Negro Children — A43

Designs: 25fr, Ramses II in battle. 50fr, Submerged sphinxes, sailboat, Wadies-Sebua. 100fr, Ramses II holding crook and flail, Abu Simbel. 200fr, Feet and legs of Ramses statues, Abu Simbel.

1964, Nov. 19 Photo. *Perf. 12*

350 A42 10fr dk bl, red brn & cit 15 15
351 A42 25fr blk, dl red & brn 15 15
352 A42 50fr dk brn, bl & vio 22 15
353 A42 100fr dk brn, yel & pur 38 30
354 A42 200fr pur, dl grn & buff 90 55
Nos. 350-354,C64 (6) 3.70 2.40

UNESCO campaign to preserve Nubian monuments.
For overprint see No. 415.

1965, Jan. 18 Photo. *Perf. 13x12½*

Designs: 10fr, Runner carrying torch. 25fr, Pole vaulting and flags. 40fr, Runners. 50fr, Judo. 75fr, Japanese woman, flags and stadium.

355 A43 5fr gold, cl & blk 15 15
356 A43 10fr gold, blk, ver & bl 15 15
357 A43 25fr gold, blk, yel grn & red 15 15
358 A43 40fr gold, blk, brn & yel 20 15
359 A43 50fr gold, blk & grn 35 22
360 A43 75fr gold & multi 60 35
Nos. 355-360,C65 (7) 2.60
Set value 1.25

18th Olympic Games, Tokyo, Oct. 10-25, 1964.
For overprints see Nos. 410-414.

Doudou Mask, Boké — A44

Designs: 40c, 1fr, 15fr, Various Niamou masks, N'Zérékoré region. 60c, "Yoki," woodcarved statuette of a girl, Boke. 80c, Masked woman dancer from Guekedou. 2fr, Masked dancer from Macenta. 20fr, Beater from Tamtam. 60fr, Bird dancer from Macenta. 80fr, Bassari dancer from Koundara. 100fr, Sword dancer from Karana.

1965, Feb. 15 Unwmk. *Perf. 14*

361 A44 20c multicolored 15 15
362 A44 40c multicolored 15 15
363 A44 60c multicolored 15 15
364 A44 80c multicolored 15 15
365 A44 1fr multicolored 15 15
366 A44 2fr multicolored 15 15
367 A44 15fr multicolored 15 15
368 A44 20fr multicolored 20 15
369 A44 60fr multicolored 50 35
370 A44 80fr multicolored 50 38
371 A44 100fr multicolored 70 40
Set value, #361-371, C68 4.50 2.40

World's Fair Type of 1964 Inscribed "1965"

1965, Mar. 24 Engr. *Perf. 10½*

372 A41 30fr grn & orange 15 15
373 A41 40fr car & brt grn 22 15
374 A41 50fr brt grn & vio 35 25
375 A41 75fr brown & vio 50 40

See Nos. C69-C70.

Blacksmith A45

Handicrafts: 20fr, Potter. 60fr, Cloth dyers. 80fr, Basketmaker.

1965, May 1 Photo. *Perf. 14*

376 A45 15fr multicolored 15 15
377 A45 20fr multicolored 15 15
378 A45 60fr multicolored 38 25
379 A45 80fr multicolored 45 35
Nos. 376-379,C71-C72 (6) 3.73 2.05

ITU Emblem, Old and New Communication Equipment — A46

1965, May 17 Unwmk.

380 A46 25fr yel, gray, gold & blk 15 15
381 A46 50fr yel, grn, gold & blk 30 22

ITU centenary. See Nos. C73-C74.

Maj. Virgil I. Grissom A47

Moon from 258mi. A48

Sputnik Over Earth — A49

American Achievements in Space: 10fr, Lt. Com. John W. Young. 25fr, Moon from 115mi. 30fr, Moon from 58mi. 100fr, Grissom and Young in Gemini 2 spaceship.

1965, July 19 Photo. *Perf. 13*

Size: 21x29mm

382 A47 5fr dk red & multi 15 15
383 A47 10fr dk red & multi 15 15
384 A48 15fr gold, bl & dk bl 15 15

Size: 39x28mm

385 A48 25fr gold, bl & dk bl 15 15

Size: 21x29mm

386 A48 30fr gold, bl & dk bl 16 15

Size: 39x28mm

387 A47 100fr multi & dk red 52 40
a. Sheet of 15, #382-387 4.00

Russian Achievements in Space: 5fr, Col. Pavel Belyayev. 10fr, Lt. Col. Alexei Leonov. 15fr, Vostoks 3 & 4 in space. 30fr, Vostoks 5 & 6 over Earth. 100fr, Leonov floating in space.

Size: 21x29mm

388 A47 5fr bl & multi 15 15
389 A47 10fr bl & multi 15 15
390 A49 15fr bl & multi 15 15

Size: 39x28mm

391 A49 25fr bl & multi 15 15

Size: 21x29mm

392 A49 30fr bl & multi 16 15

Size: 39x28mm

393 A47 100fr blk, dk red & gold 52 40
a. Sheet of 15, #388-393 4.00
Set value, #382-393 2.00 1.50

American and Russian achievements in space. Nos. 387a and 393a contain five triptychs each: four rows with 5fr, 100fr and 10fr, and a center row with 15fr, 25fr and 30fr stamps each.

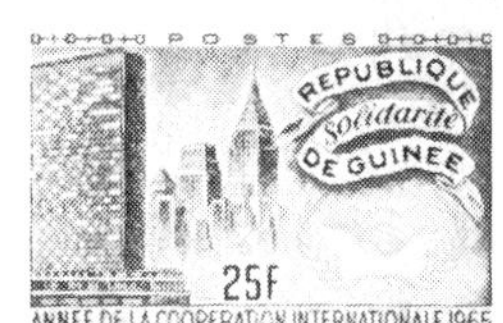
ICY Emblem, UN Headquarters and Skyline, New York — A50

1965, Sept. 8 *Perf. 10½*

394 A50 25fr yel grn & ver 15 15
395 A50 45fr vio & orange 25 18
396 A50 75fr red brn & org 40 25

Intl. Cooperation Year, 1965. See No. C75.

Polytechnic Institute, Conakry — A51

New Projects, Conakry: 30fr, Hotel Camayenne. 40fr, Gbessia Airport. 75fr, Stadium "28 September."

1965, Oct. 2 Photo. *Perf. 13½*

397 A51 25fr multicolored 16 15
398 A51 30fr multicolored 22 15
399 A51 40fr multicolored 42 25
400 A51 75fr multicolored 52 35
Nos. 397-400,C76-C77 (6) 7.07 3.70

Seventh anniversary of independence.

Photographing Far Side of Moon — A52

Designs: 10fr, Trajectories of Ranger VII on flight to moon. 25fr, Relay satellite. 45fr, Vostoks I & II and globe.

1965, Nov. 15 Litho. *Perf. 14x13½*

401 A52 5fr blk, pur & ocher 15 15
402 A52 10fr red brn, lt grn & yel 15 15
403 A52 25fr blk, bl & bis 20 15
404 A52 45fr blk, lt ultra & bis 38 20
Nos. 401-404,C78-C79 (6) 3.13
Set value 1.30

For overprints and surcharges see Nos. 529-530, C112-C112B.

Sword Dance, Karana — A53

Designs: 30c, Dancing girls, Lower Guinea. 50c, Behore musicians of Tiekere playing "Eyoro," horiz. 5fr, Doundouba dance of Kouroussa. 40fr, Bird man's dance of Macenta.

1966, Jan. 5 Photo. *Perf. 13½*

Size: 26x36mm

405 A53 10c multicolored 15 15
406 A53 30c multicolored 15 15

Size: 36x28½mm

407 A53 50c multicolored 15 15

Size: 26x36mm

408 A53 5fr multicolored 15 15
409 A53 40fr multicolored 35 18
Set value, #405-409, C80 1.25 70

Festival of African Art and Culture. See Nos. 436-441.

Engraved Overprint in Red or Orange on Nos. 355-356 and Nos. 358-360

1966, Mar. 14 *Perf. 13x12½*

410 A43 5fr multi (R) 15 15
411 A43 10fr multi (R) 15 15
412 A43 40fr multi (O) 35 25
413 A43 50fr multi (R) 45 35
414 A43 75fr multi (R) 80 58
Nos. 410-414,C81 (6) 2.70 1.86

4th Pan Arab Games, Cairo, Sept. 2-11, 1965. The same overprint was also applied to imperf. sheets of No. 357.

Engraved Red Orange Overprint on No. 352:
"CENTENAIRE DU TIMBRE CAIRE 1966"

1966, Mar. 14 *Perf. 12*

415 A42 50fr dk brn, bl & vio 35 35

First Egyptian postage stamps, cent. See No. C82.

Vonkou Rock, Telimélé — A54

Views: 25fr, Artificial lake, Coyah. 40fr, Kalé waterfalls. 50fr, Forécariah bridge. 75fr, Liana bridge.

1966, Apr. 4 Photo. *Perf. 13½*

416 A54 20fr multicolored 15 15
417 A54 25fr multicolored 15 15
418 A54 40fr multicolored 20 15
419 A54 50fr multicolored 30 15
420 A54 75fr multicolored 42 25
Nos. 416-420,C83 (6) 1.92
Set value 98

See Nos. 475-478, C90-C91. For overprints see Nos. 482-488, C93-C95.

UNESCO Emblem — A55

1966, May 2 Photo. Unwmk.

421 A55 25fr multicolored 20 15

20th anniv. of UNESCO. See Nos. C84-C85.

Woman of Guinea and Morning Glory — A56

Symbolic Water Cycle and UNESCO Emblem — A57

Designs: Women and Flowers of Guinea.

1966, May 30 Photo. *Perf. 13½*

Size: 23x34mm

422 A56 10c multicolored 15 15
423 A56 20c multicolored 15 15
424 A56 30c multicolored 15 15
425 A56 40c multicolored 15 15
426 A56 3fr multicolored 15 15
427 A56 4fr multicolored 15 15
428 A56 10fr multicolored 15 15
429 A56 25fr multicolored 25 15

Size: 28x43mm

430 A56 30fr multicolored 30 15
431 A56 50fr multicolored 40 22
432 A56 80fr multicolored 58 30
Nos. 422-432,C86-C87 (13) 6.68
Set value 2.75

1966, Sept. 26 Engr. *Perf. 10½*

433 A57 5fr bl & dp org 15 15
434 A57 25fr grn & dp org 15 15
435 A57 100fr brt rose lil & dp org 58 35
Set value 75 48

Hydrological Decade (UNESCO), 1965-74.

Dance Type of 1966

Designs: Various folk dances. 25fr, 75fr, horizontal.

1966, Oct. 24 Photo. *Perf. 13½*

Sizes: 26x36mm, 36x28½mm

436 A53 60c multicolored 15 15
437 A53 1fr multicolored 15 15
438 A53 1.50fr multicolored 15 15
439 A53 25fr multicolored 15 15
440 A53 50fr multicolored 35 18
441 A53 75fr multicolored 45 35
Set value 1.10 75

Guinean National Dancers.

Child's Drawing and UNICEF Emblem — A58

Children's Drawings: 2fr, Elephant. 3fr, Girl. 20fr, Village, horiz. 25fr, Boy playing soccer. 40fr, Still life. 50fr, Bird in a tree.

1966, Dec. 12 Photo. *Perf. 13½*

442 A58 2fr multicolored 15 15
443 A58 3fr multicolored 15 15
444 A58 10fr multicolored 15 15
445 A58 20fr multicolored 15 15
446 A58 25fr multicolored 16 15
447 A58 40fr multicolored 25 15
448 A58 50fr multicolored 35 20
Set value 1.10 62

20th anniv. of UNICEF. Printed in sheets of 10 stamps and 2 labels with ornamental borders and inscriptions.

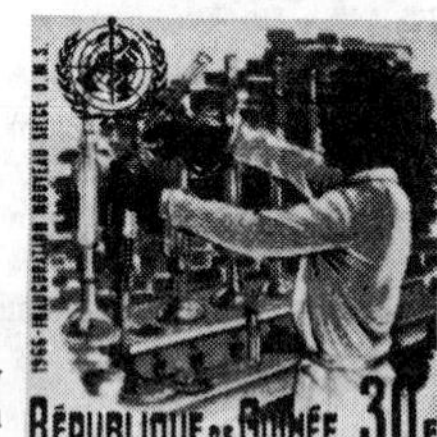

Laboratory Technician A59

Designs (WHO Emblem and): 50fr, Physician examining infant. 75fr, Pre-natal care and instruction. 80fr, WHO Headquarters, Geneva.

1967, Jan. 20 Photo. *Perf. 13½*

449 A59 30fr multicolored 15 15
450 A59 50fr multicolored 25 15
451 A59 75fr multicolored 38 22
452 A59 80fr multicolored 45 35

Inauguration (in 1966) of WHO Headquarters, Geneva.

Niamou Mask, N'Zerekore — A60

Designs: 10c, 1fr, 30fr, Small Banda mask, Kanfarade, Boké region. 1.50fr, 50fr, Like 30c. 50c, 5fr, 75fr, Bearded Niamou mask. 60c, 25fr, 100fr, Horned Yinadjinkele mask, Kankan region.

1967, Mar. 25 Photo. *Perf. 14x13*

453 A60 10c org & multi 15 15
454 A60 30c cit & brn blk 15 15
455 A60 50c dp lil rose, blk & red 15 15
456 A60 60c dp org, blk & bis 15 15
457 A60 1fr yel grn & multi 15 15
458 A60 1.50fr sal pink & brn blk 15 15
459 A60 5fr ap grn, blk & red 15 15
460 A60 25fr red lil, blk & bis 16 15
461 A60 30fr bis & multi 25 15
462 A60 50fr grnsh bl & brn blk 40 15
463 A60 75fr yel, blk & red 60 25
464 A60 100fr lt ultra, blk & bis 90 40
Set value 2.70 1.25

Ball Python A61

Designs: 20c, Pastoria Research Institute. 50c, 75fr, Extraction of snake venom. 1fr, 50fr, Rock python. 2fr, Men holding rock python. 5fr, 30fr, Gaboon viper. 20fr, West African mamba.

1967, May 15 Litho. *Perf. 13½*

Size: 43½x20mm

465 A61 20c multicolored 15 15
466 A61 30c multicolored 15 15
467 A61 50c multicolored 15 15
468 A61 1fr multicolored 15 15
469 A61 2fr multicolored 15 15
470 A61 5fr multicolored 15 15

Size: 56x26mm

471 A61 20fr multicolored 15 15
472 A61 30fr multicolored 35 15
473 A61 50fr multicolored 42 15
474 A61 75fr multicolored 65 20
Nos. 465-474,C88-C89 (12) 6.12
Set value 2.50

Research Institute for Applied Biology of Guinea (Pastoria). For souvenir sheet see No. C88a.

Scenic Type of 1966

Views: 5fr, Loos Island. 30fr, Tinkisso Waterfalls. 70fr, "The Elephant's Trunk" Hotel, Mt. Kakoulima. 80fr, Evening at the shore, Ratoma.

1967, June 20 Photo. *Perf. 13½*

475 A54 5fr multicolored 15 15
476 A54 30fr multicolored 16 15
477 A54 70fr multicolored 42 15
478 A54 80fr multicolored 58 15
Nos. 475-478,C90-C91 (6) 3.31
Set value 1.40

People's Palace, Conakry — A62

Elephant — A63

1967, Sept. 28 Photo. *Perf. 13½*

479 A62 5fr silver & multi 15 15
480 A63 30fr silver & multi 22 16
481 A62 55fr gold & multi 40 20
Set value 66 40

20th anniv. of the Democratic Party of Guinea and the opening of the People's Palace, Conakry. See No. C92.

Nos. 418-420 and 475-478 Overprinted with Lions Emblem and: "AMITIE DES PEUPLES GRACE AU TOURISME 1917-1967"

1967, Nov. 6

482 A54 5fr multicolored 16 15
483 A54 30fr multicolored 38 15
484 A54 40fr multicolored 35 15
485 A54 50fr multicolored 45 20
486 A54 70fr multicolored 55 25
487 A54 75fr multicolored 80 38
488 A54 80fr multicolored 1.00 38
Nos. 482-488,C93-C95 (10) 6.79 3.16

50th anniversary of Lions International.

WHO Office for Africa — A64

1967, Dec. 4 Photo. *Perf. 13½*

489 A64 30fr lt ol grn, bis & dk grn 25 15
490 A64 75fr red org, bis & dk bl 55 25

Inauguration of the WHO Regional Office for Africa in Brazzaville, Congo.

Human Rights Flame — A65

1968, Jan. 15 Photo. *Perf. 13½*

491 A65 30fr ocher, grn & dk car 22 15
492 A65 40fr vio, grn & car 30 15
Set value 22

International Human Rights Year, 1968.

Coyah, Dubréka Region — A66

Homes and People: 30c, 30fr, Kankan Region. 40c, Kankan, East Guinea. 50c, 15fr, Woodlands Region. 60c, Fulahmori, Gaoual Region. 5fr, Cognagui, Kundara Region. 40fr, Fouta Djallon, West Guinea. 100fr, Labé, West Guinea.

1968, Apr. 1 Photo. *Perf. 13½x14*

Size: 36x27mm

493 A66 20c gold & multi 15 15
494 A66 30c gold & multi 15 15
495 A66 40c gold & multi 15 15
496 A66 50c gold & multi 15 15

Perf. 14x13½

Size: 57x36mm

497 A66 60c gold & multi 15 15
498 A66 5fr gold & multi 15 15
499 A66 15fr gold & multi 15 15
500 A66 20fr gold & multi 16 15
501 A66 30fr gold & multi 25 15
502 A66 40fr gold & multi 38 15
503 A66 100fr gold & multi 90 22
Set value, #493-503, C100 4.00 1.60

The Storyteller — A67

African Legends: 15fr, The Little Genie of Mt. Nimba. No. 506, The Legend of the Moons and the Stars. No. 507, Lan, the Child Buffalo, vert. 40fr, Nianablas and the Crocodiles. 50fr, Leuk the Hare Playing the Drum, vert. 75fr, Leuk the Hare Selling his Sister, vert. 80fr, The Hunter and the Antelope-woman. The designs are from paintings by students of the Academy of Fine Arts in Bellevue.

1968 Photo. *Perf. 13½*

504 A67 15fr multicolored 15 15
505 A67 25fr multicolored 15 15
506 A67 30fr multicolored 15 15
507 A67 30fr multicolored 20 15
508 A67 40fr multicolored 30 15
509 A67 50fr multicolored 40 15
a. Souv. sheet of 4 3.75 3.75
510 A67 75fr multicolored 42 25
511 A67 80fr multicolored 65 25
Nos. 504-511,C101-C104 (12) 7.57
Set value 2.50

Issued in sheets of 10 plus 2 labels. No. 509a contains 4 imperf. stamps similar to Nos. 508-509, C101 and C104. "Poste Aerienne" omitted on the 70fr and 300fr of the souvenir sheet.

Issue dates: May 16, Nos. 505-506, 510-511. Sept. 16, Nos. 504, 507-509.

Anubius Baboon A68

African Animals: 10fr, Leopards. 15fr, Hippopotami. 20fr, Nile crocodile. 30fr, Ethiopian wart hog. 50fr, Defassa waterbuck. 75fr, Cape buffaloes.

1968, Nov. 25 Photo. *Perf. 13½*
Size: 44x31mm

512 A68 5fr gold & multi 15 15
513 A68 10fr gold & multi 15 15
514 A68 15fr gold & multi 15 15
a. Souv. sheet of 3, #512-514 30 30
515 A68 20fr gold & multi 22 15
516 A68 30fr gold & multi 30 15
517 A68 50fr gold & multi 40 15
a. Souv. sheet of 3, #515-517 90 90
518 A68 75fr gold & multi 60 25
a. Souv. sheet of 3 3.25 3.25
Nos. 512-518,C105-C106 (9) 4.37
Set value 1.50

No. 518a contains one No. 518 and one each similar to Nos. C105-C106 without "POSTE AERIENNE" inscription. The three souvenir sheets contain 3 stamps and one green and gold label inscribed "FAUNE AFRICAINE."

Senator Robert F. Kennedy — A69

Portraits: 75fr, Rev. Martin Luther King, Jr. 100fr, Pres. John F. Kennedy.

1968, Dec. 16

519 A69 30fr yel & multi 16 15
520 A69 75fr multicolored 50 15
521 A69 100fr multicolored 65 25
Nos. 519-521,C107-C109 (6) 3.96
Set value 1.15

Robert F. Kennedy, John F. Kennedy and Martin Luther King, Jr., martyrs for freedom.

The stamps are printed in sheets of 15 (3x5) containing 10 stamps and five yellow-green and gold center labels. Sheets come either with English or French inscriptions on label.

Sculpture and Runner A70

Sculpture and Soccer — A71

Designs (Sculpture and): 10fr, Boxing. 15fr, Javelin. 30fr, Steeplechase. 50fr, Hammer throw. 75fr, Bicycling.

1969, Feb. 18 Photo. *Perf. 13½*

522 A70 5fr multicolored 15 15
523 A70 10fr multicolored 15 15
524 A70 15fr multicolored 22 15
525 A71 25fr multicolored 25 15
526 A70 30fr multicolored 25 15
527 A70 50fr multicolored 42 15
528 A70 75fr multicolored 55 18
Nos. 522-528,C110-C111A (10) 6.29
Set value 1.85

19th Olympic Games, Mexico City, Oct. 12-27.

No. 404 Surcharged and Overprinted in Red

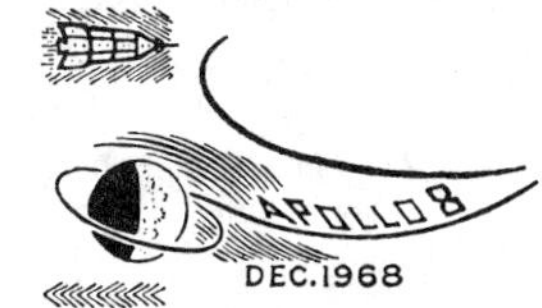

1969, Mar. 17 Litho. *Perf. 14x13½*

529 A52 30fr on 45fr multi 35 35
530 A52 45fr multicolored 35 35
Nos. 529-530,C112-C112B (5) 3.55 2.50

US Apollo 8 mission, the first men in orbit around the moon, Dec. 21-27, 1968.

Nos. 529-530 also exist with surcharge and overprint in black. These sell for about 10% more.

Tarzan — A72

Designs: 30fr, Tarzan sitting in front of Pastoria Research Institute gate. 75fr, Tarzan and his family. 100fr, Tarzan sitting in a tree.

1969, June 6 Photo. *Perf. 13½*

531 A72 25fr orange & multi 16 15
532 A72 30fr bl grn & multi 22 15
533 A72 75fr yel grn & multi 50 18
534 A72 100fr yellow & multi 80 30
Set value 66

Tarzan was a Guinean chimpanzee with superior intelligence and ability.

Campfire A73

Designs: 25fr, Boy Scout and tents. 30fr, Marching Boy Scouts. 40fr, Basketball. 45fr, Senior Scouts, thatched huts and mountain. 50fr, Guinean Boy Scout badge.

1969, July 1

535 A73 5fr gold & multi 15 15
536 A73 25fr gold & multi 16 15
537 A73 30fr gold & multi 20 15
538 A73 40fr gold & multi 30 15
539 A73 45fr gold & multi 35 15
540 A73 50fr gold & multi 40 18
a. Min. sheet of 6, #535-540 2.00 2.00
Nos. 535-540 (6) 1.56
Set value 58

Issued to honor the Boy Scouts of Guinea.

Launching Apollo 11 — A74

Designs: 30fr, Earth showing Africa as seen from moon. 50fr, Separation of lunar landing module and spaceship. 60fr, Astronauts and module on moon. 75fr, Module on moon and earth. 100fr, Module leaving moon. 200fr, Splashdown. "a" stamps are inscribed in French. "b" stamps are inscribed in English.

1969, Aug. 20 Photo. *Perf. 13½*
Size: 34x55mm

541 25fr Pair, #541a, 541b 35 15
542 30fr Pair, #542a, 542b 45 15
543 50fr Pair, #543a, 543b 65 18
544 60fr Pair, #544a, 544b 1.15 30
545 75fr Pair, #545a, 545b 1.30 36

Size: 34x71mm

546 100fr Pair, #546a, 546b 2.10 50

Size: 34x55mm

547 200fr Pair, #547a, 547b 4.25 1.20
Nos. 541-547 (7) 10.25 2.84

Man's 1st landing on the moon, July 20, 1969.

Harvest and ILO Emblem A75

ILO, 50th Anniv.: 25fr, Power lines and blast furnaces. 30fr, Women in broadcasting studio. 200fr, Potters.

1969, Oct. 28 Photo. *Perf. 13½*

548 A75 25fr gold & multi 16 15
549 A75 30fr gold & multi 20 15
550 A75 75fr gold & multi 50 15
551 A75 200fr gold & multi 1.50 50
Set value 75

Mother and Sick Child — A76

Designs: 25fr, Sick child. 40fr, Girl receiving vaccination. 50fr, Boy receiving vaccination. 60fr, Mother receiving vaccination. 200fr, Edward Jenner, M.D.

1970, Jan. 15 Photo. *Perf. 13½*

552 A76 25fr multicolored 15 15
553 A76 30fr multicolored 20 15
554 A76 40fr multicolored 25 15
555 A76 50fr multicolored 40 18
556 A76 60fr multicolored 45 18
557 A76 200fr multicolored 1.50 75
Nos. 552-557 (6) 2.95 1.56

Campaign against smallpox and measles.

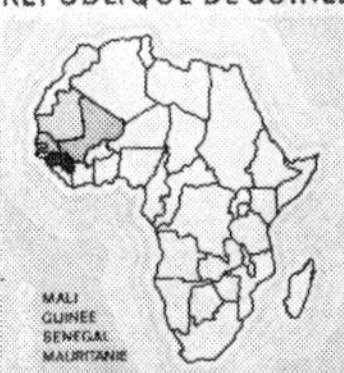

Map of Africa — A77

1970, Feb. 3 Litho. *Perf. 14½x14*

558 A77 30fr lt bl & multi 20 15
559 A77 200fr lt vio & multi 1.40 75

Meeting of statesmen of countries bordering on Senegal River: Mali, Guinea, Senegal and Mauritania.

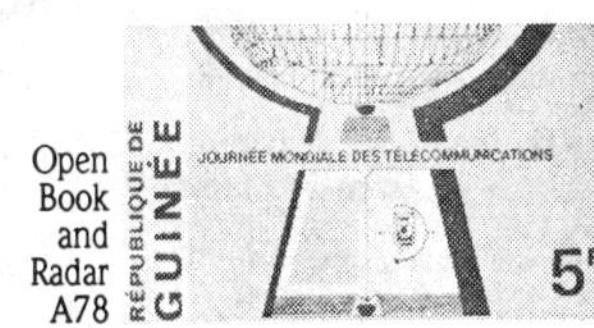
Open Book and Radar A78

1970, July 6 Litho. *Perf. 14*

560 A78 5fr lt bl & blk 15 15
561 A78 10fr rose & blk 15 15
562 A78 50fr yellow & blk 38 15
563 A78 200fr lilac & blk 1.40 75
Set value 90

International Telecommunications Day.

Lenin — A79

Designs: 20fr, Meeting with Lenin, by V. Serov. 30fr, Lenin Addressing Workers, by V. Serov. 40fr, Lenin with Red Guard Soldier and Sailor, by P. V. Vasiliev. 100fr, Lenin Speaking from Balcony, by P. V. Vasiliev. 200fr, Like 5fr.

1970, Nov. 16 Photo. *Perf. 13*

564 A79 5fr gold & multi 15 15
565 A79 20fr gold & multi 16 15
566 A79 30fr gold & multi 22 15
567 A79 40fr gold & multi 38 15
568 A79 100fr gold & multi 80 25
569 A79 200fr gold & multi 1.60 65
Nos. 564-569 (6) 3.31
Set value 1.20

Lenin (1870-1924), Russian communist leader.

Phenecogrammus Interruptus — A80

Designs: Various fish from Guinea.

1971, Apr. 1 Photo. *Perf. 13*

570 A80 5fr gold & multi 15 15
571 A80 10fr gold & multi 15 15
572 A80 15fr gold & multi 15 15
573 A80 20fr gold & multi 15 15
574 A80 25fr gold & multi 20 15
575 A80 30fr gold & multi 25 15
576 A80 40fr gold & multi 25 15
577 A80 45fr gold & multi 30 18
578 A80 50fr gold & multi 35 18
579 A80 75fr gold & multi 60 25

580 A80 100fr gold & multi 70 35
581 A80 200fr gold & multi 1.40 80
Nos. 570-581 (12) 4.65
Set value 2.25

Violet-crested Touraco — A81

Birds: 20fr, European golden oriole. 30fr, Blue-headed coucal. 40fr, Northern shrike. 75fr, Vulturine guinea fowl. 100fr, Southern ground hornbill.

1971, June 18 Photo. *Perf. 13*
Size: 34x34mm

582 A81 5fr gold & multi 15 15
583 A81 20fr gold & multi 15 15
584 A81 30fr gold & multi 16 15
585 A81 40fr gold & multi 30 15
586 A81 75fr gold & multi 70 22
587 A81 100fr gold & multi 90 35
Nos. 582-587,C113-C113B (9) 5.31 2.17

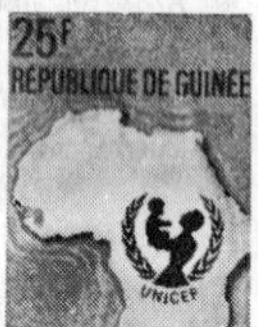

UNICEF Emblem, Map of Africa — A82

1971, Dec. 24 *Perf. 12x12½*
Map in Olive

588 A82 25fr orange & blk 15 15
589 A82 30fr pink & black 16 15
590 A82 50fr gray grn & blk 35 15
591 A82 60fr gray bl & blk 42 15
592 A82 100fr lil rose & blk 70 25
Nos. 588-592 (5) 1.78
Set value 62

UNICEF, 25th anniv.
For overprints see Nos. 625-629.

Imaginary Prehistoric Space Creature — A83

Designs: Various imaginary prehistoric space creatures.

1972, Apr. 1 *Perf. 13½x13*

593 A83 5fr multicolored 15 15
594 A83 20fr multicolored 15 15
595 A83 30fr multicolored 15 15
596 A83 40fr multicolored 25 15
597 A83 100fr multicolored 60 30
598 A83 200fr multicolored 1.10 58
Nos. 593-598 (6) 2.40
Set value 1.15

Black Boy, Men of 4 Races, Emblem — A84

Designs: 20fr, Oriental boy. 30fr, Indian youth. 50fr, Caucasian girl. 100fr, Men of 4 races and Racial Equality emblem.

1972, May 14 *Perf. 13x13½*

599 A84 15fr gold & multi 15 15
600 A84 20fr gold & multi 15 15
601 A84 30fr gold & multi 15 15
602 A84 50fr gold & multi 25 15
603 A84 100fr gold & multi 50 25
Nos. 599-603,C119 (6) 1.80
Set value 92

Intl. Year Against Racial Discrimination, 1971.

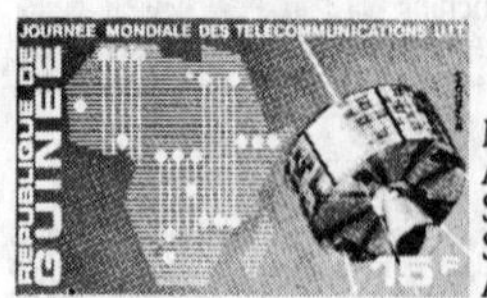

Map of Africa, Syncom Satellite A85

Designs (Map of Africa and Satellites): 30fr, Relay. 75fr, Early Bird. 80fr, Telstar.

1972, May 17 Litho. *Perf. 13*

604 A85 15fr multicolored 15 15
605 A85 30fr red org & multi 15 15
606 A85 75fr grn & multi 38 20
607 A85 80fr multicolored 45 30
Nos. 604-607,C120-C121 (6) 2.63 1.55

4th World Telecommunications Day.

Carrier Pigeon, UPAF Emblem A86

1972, July 10

608 A86 15fr brt bl & multi 15 15
609 A86 30fr multicolored 15 15
610 A86 75fr lil & multi 38 20
611 A86 80fr multicolored 45 30
Nos. 608-611,C122-C123 (6) 2.93 1.70

Book Year Emblem, Reading Child — A87

Designs (Book Year Emblem and): 15fr, Book as sailing ship. 40fr, Young woman with flower and book. 50fr, Book as key. 75fr, Man reading and globe. 200fr, Book and laurel.

1972, Aug. 2 Photo. *Perf. 14x13½*

612 A87 5fr red & multi 15 15
613 A87 15fr multicolored 15 15
614 A87 40fr yel & multi 20 15
615 A87 50fr blue & multi 30 15
616 A87 75fr dk red & multi 50 30
617 A87 200fr org & multi 90 60
Nos. 612-617 (6) 2.20
Set value 1.20

International Book Year 1972.

Javelin, Olympic Emblems, Arms of Guinea — A88

1972, Aug. 26 Photo. *Perf. 13*

618 A88 5fr shown 15 15
619 A88 10fr Pole vault 15 15
620 A88 25fr Hurdles 15 15
621 A88 30fr Hammer throw 15 15
622 A88 40fr Boxing 25 15
623 A88 50fr Vaulting 25 15
624 A88 75fr Running 40 25
Nos. 618-624,C124-C125 (9) 3.25
Set value 1.60

20th Olympic Games, Munich, Aug. 26-Sept. 11.

Nos. 588-592 Overprinted

1972, Sept. 28 Photo. *Perf. 12x12½*
Map in Olive

625 A82 25fr org & blk 15 15
626 A82 30fr pink & blk 15 15
627 A82 50fr gray grn & blk 25 15
628 A82 60fr gray bl & blk 38 15
629 A82 100fr lil rose & blk 45 25
Nos. 625-629 (5) 1.38
Set value 62

UN Conference on Human Environment, Stockholm, June 5-16.

Dimitrov at Leipzig Trial — A89

1972, Sept. 28 *Perf. 13*
Gold, Dark Green & Black

630 A89 5fr shown 15 15
631 A89 25fr In Moabit Prison, 1933 15 15
632 A89 40fr Writing his memoirs 20 15
633 A89 100fr Portrait 55 25
Set value 50

George Dimitrov (1882-1949), Bulgarian Communist party leader and Premier.

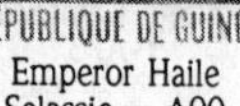

Emperor Haile Selassie — A90

Syntomeida Epilais — A91

Design: 200fr, Emperor facing right.

1972, Oct. 2

634 A90 40fr blk & multi 22 18
635 A90 200fr multicolored 1.10 65

1973, Mar. 5 Photo. *Perf. 14x13½*

Designs: Various insects.

636 A91 5fr shown 15 15
637 A91 15fr Ladybugs 15 15
638 A91 30fr Green locust 15 15
639 A91 40fr Honey bee 20 15
640 A91 50fr Photinus pyralis 25 15
641 A91 200fr Ancyluris formosissima 1.10 70
Nos. 636-641 (6) 2.00
Set value 1.10

Kwame Nkrumah — A92

Designs: Various portraits of Kwame Nkrumah.

1973, May 25 Photo. *Perf. 13½*

642 A92 1.50s lt grn, gold & brn 15 15
643 A92 2.50s lt grn, gold & brn 15 15
644 A92 5s lt grn, gold & brn 25 20
645 A92 10s gold & dark vio 50 35
Set value 68

OAU, 10th anniversary.

Institute for Applied Biology, Kindia A93

Designs (WHO Emblem and): 2.50s, Technicians inoculating egg. 3s, Filling vaccine into ampules. 4s, Sterilization of vaccine. 5s, Assembling of vaccine and vaccination gun. 10s, Inoculation of steer. 20s, Vaccination of woman.

1973, Nov. 16 Photo. *Perf. 13½*
Size: 40x36mm

646 A93 1s gold & multi 15 15
647 A93 2.50s gold & multi 15 15
648 A93 3s gold & multi 20 15
649 A93 4s gold & multi 22 15

Size: 47½x31mm

650 A93 5s gold & multi 35 18
651 A93 10s gold & multi 50 25
652 A93 20s gold & multi 1.20 55
Nos. 646-652 (7) 2.77 1.58

WHO, 25th anniversary.

Copernicus, Heliocentric System, Primeval Landscape — A94

Nicolaus Copernicus A95

Designs (Copernicus and): 2s, Sun rising over volcanic desert, and spacecraft. 4s, Earth, moon and spacecraft. 5s, Moon scape and spacecraft. 10s, Jupiter and spacecraft. 20s, Saturn and heliocentric system.

1973, Dec. 17 Photo. *Perf. 13½*

653 A94 50c gold & multi 15 15
654 A94 2s gold & multi 15 15
655 A94 4s gold & multi 18 15
656 A94 5s gold & multi 30 15
657 A94 10s gold & multi 60 25
658 A94 20s gold & multi 1.20 62
Nos. 653-658 (6) 2.58
Set value 1.20

Souvenir Sheet

659 Sheet of 4 6.50 6.50
a. A95 20s Single stamp 1.40 1.00

Nicolaus Copernicus (1473-1543), Polish astronomer. No. 659 contains center label showing rocket and heliocentric system in gold margin.

Loading Bauxite on Freighter A96

1974, Mar. 1 Litho. *Perf. 13½*

660 A96 4s shown 20 15
661 A96 6s Freight train 30 20
662 A96 10s Mining 50 30

Bauxite mining, Boke.

Clappertonia Ficifolia — A97

1974, May 20 Photo. *Perf. 13*

Size: 25x36mm

663 A97 50c shown 15 15
664 A97 1s Rothmannia longiflora 15 15
665 A97 2s Oncoba spinosa 15 15
666 A97 3s Venidium fastuosum 15 15

Size: 31x42mm

667 A97 4s Bombax costatum 18 15
668 A97 5s Clerodendrum splendens 25 15
669 A97 7.50s Combretuni grandiflorum 38 20
670 A97 10s Mussaendra erythrophylla 55 30

Size: 38x38mm (Diamond)

671 A97 12s Argemone mexicana 65 40
Nos. 663-671,C127-C129 (12) 6.86
Set value 3.50

Drummers, Pigeon, UPAF and UPU Emblems A98

Designs (Carrier Pigeon, African Postal Union and UPU Emblems): 6s, Runner with letter stick. 7.50s, Monorail and mail truck. No. 675, Jet and ocean liner. No. 676, Balloon and dugout canoe. 20s, Satellites over earth.

1974, Oct. 16 Photo. *Perf. 13½x14*

672 A98 5s mag & multi 25 15
673 A98 6s grn & multi 35 20
674 A98 7.50s ver & multi 45 25
675 A98 10s Prus bl & multi 55 45

Souvenir Sheets

Perf. 13½

676 A98 10s ocher & multi 3.50
677 Sheet of 4, multi 4.00
a. A98 20s Single stamp 90 70

Centenary of Universal Postal Union. No. 676 contains one 70x60mm stamp.

Rope Bridge — A99

Designs (Pioneers): 2s, Field observation. 4s, Communication. 5s, Cooking in camp. 7.50s, Salute. 10s, Basketball.

1974, Nov. 22 Photo. *Perf. 14x13½*

678 A99 50c multicolored 15 15
679 A99 2s multicolored 15 15
680 A99 4s multicolored 18 15
681 A99 5s multicolored 25 15
682 A99 7.50s multicolored 38 20
683 A99 10s multicolored 50 30
a. Souv. sheet of 2, #682-683 1.60 1.60
Nos. 678-683 (6) 1.61
Set value 75

National Pioneer Movement.

Souvenir Sheet

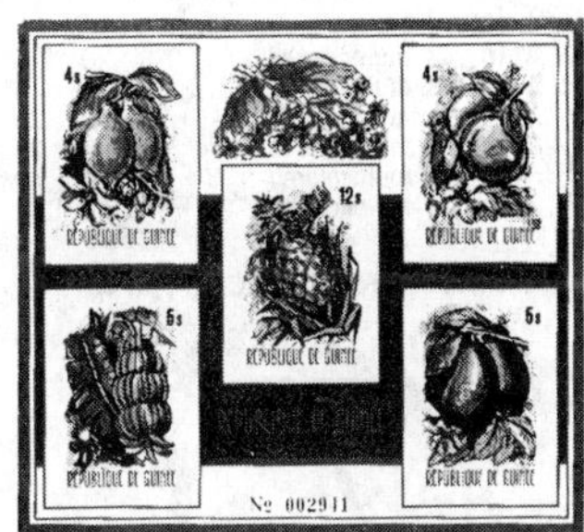

Fruit — A100

1974, Nov. 22 Photo. *Perf. 13x14*

684 A100 Sheet of 5 3.50
a. 4s Limes 25
b. 4s Oranges 25
c. 5s Bananas 35
d. 5s Mangos 35
e. 12s Pineapple 80

Chimpanzee — A101

1975, May 14 Photo. *Perf. 13½*

685 A101 1s shown 15 15
686 A101 2s Impala 15 15
687 A101 3s Wart hog 15 15
688 A101 4s Kobus defassa 18 15
a. Souv. sheet of 4, #685-688 65 65
689 A101 5s Leopard 20 15
690 A101 6s Greater kudu 25 20
691 A101 6.50s Zebra 30 22
692 A101 7.50s Cape buffalo 35 25
a. Souv. sheet of 4, #689-692 1.40 1.40
693 A101 8s Hippopotamus 38 25
694 A101 10s Lion 42 30
695 A101 12s Black rhinoceros 50 35
696 A101 15s Elephant 65 50
a. Souv. sheet of 4, #693-696 2.25 2.25
Nos. 685-696 (12) 3.68 2.82

Sheets exist perf. and imperf.
Stamps in Nos. 692a, 696a are inscribed "Poste Aerienne."

Lions, Pipe Line and ADB Emblem A102

Designs (African Development Bank Emblem, Pipe Line and): 7s, Elephants. 10s, Male lions. 20s, Elephant and calf.

1975, June 16 Photo. *Perf. 13½*

697 A102 5s gold & multi 25 15
698 A102 7s gold & multi 30 16
699 A102 10s gold & multi 45 25
700 A102 20s gold & multi 1.00 60

African Development Bank, 10th anniv.

Women Musicians, IWY Emblem — A103

Designs (IWY Emblem and): 7s, Women banjo and guitar players. 9s, Woman railroad shunter and train. 15s, Woman physician examining infant. 20s, Male and female symbols.

1976, Apr. 12 Photo. *Perf. 13½*

701 A103 5s multicolored 25 15
702 A103 7s multicolored 38 20
703 A103 9s blue & multi 45 30
704 A103 15s multicolored 70 50
a. Souvenir sheet 80 80
705 A103 20s vio bl & multi 1.00 70
a. Souvenir sheet of 4 4.25 4.25
Nos. 701-705 (5) 2.78 1.85

International Women's Year 1975. No. 704a contains one stamp similar to No. 704 with gold frame. No. 705a contains 4 stamps similar to No. 705 with gold frame.

Woman Gymnast A104

Designs (Montreal Olympic Games Emblem and): 4s, Long jump. 5s, Hammer throw. 6s, Discus. 6.50s, Hurdles. 7s, Javelin. 8s, Running. 8.50s, Bicycling. 10s, High jump. 15s, Shot put. 20s, Pole vault. No. 717, Soccer. No. 718, Swimming.

1976, May 17 Photo. *Perf. 13½*

Size: 38x38mm

706 A104 3s multicolored 15 15
707 A104 4s grn & multi 20 15
708 A104 5s yel & multi 25 15
709 A104 6s multicolored 30 20
710 A104 6.50s plum & multi 35 20
711 A104 7s blue & multi 38 22
712 A104 8s ultra & multi 90 25
713 A104 8.50s org & multi 42 25
714 A104 10s multicolored 50 30
715 A104 15s multicolored 70 50
716 A104 20s multicolored 1.00 80
717 A104 25s grn & multi 1.40 80
Nos. 706-717 (12) 6.55 3.97

Souvenir Sheet

718 A104 25s multicolored 2.25 2.25

21st Olympic Games, Montreal, Canada, July 17-Aug. 1. No. 718 contains one 32x32mm stamp. See No. C130.

A. G. Bell, Telephone, 1900 — A105

Designs: 7s, Wall telephone, 1910. 12s, Syncom telecommunications satellite. No. 722, Telstar satellite. No. 723, Telephone switchboard operator, 1914.

1976, Nov. 15 Photo. *Perf. 13*

719 A105 5s multicolored 25 15
720 A105 7s multicolored 38 20
721 A105 12s multicolored 65 40
722 A105 15s multicolored 80 55
a. Souvenir sheet of 4, #719-722 2.25 2.25

Souvenir Sheet

723 A105 15s multicolored 1.00 1.00

Centenary of first telephone call by Alexander Graham Bell, Mar. 10, 1876.

Collybia Fusipes — A106

Mushrooms: 7s, Lycoperdon perlatum. 9s, Boletus edulis. 9.50s, Lactarius deliciosus. 11.50s, Agaricus campestris.

1977, Feb. 6 Photo. *Perf. 13*

Size: 48x26mm

724 A106 5s multicolored 25 15
725 A106 7s multicolored 38 18
726 A106 9s multicolored 45 22
a. Souvenir sheet of 2, #724, 726 1.00 1.00
727 A106 9.50s multicolored 55 30

Size: 48x31mm

728 A106 11.50s multicolored 65 40
Nos. 724-728,C131-C133 (8) 4.33 2.38

Hexaplex Hoplites — A107

Sea Shells: 2s, Perrona lineata. 4s, Marginella pseudofaba. 5s, Tympanotonos radula. 7s, Marginella strigata. 8s, Harpa doris. 10s, Demoulia pinguis. 20s, Bursa scrobiculator. 25s, Marginella adansoni.

1977, Apr. 25 Photo. *Perf. 13*

Size: 50x25mm

729 A107 1s gold & multi 15 15
730 A107 2s gold & multi 15 15
731 A107 4s gold & multi 25 16
732 A107 5s gold & multi 35 20
733 A107 7s gold & multi 45 28
734 A107 8s gold & multi 55 32

Size: 50x30mm

735 A107 10s gold & multi 65 40
736 A107 20s gold & multi 1.40 80
737 A107 25s gold & multi 1.60 1.00
Nos. 729-737 (9) 5.55 3.46

Farmers and Ox Plow A108

Designs: 5s, Pres. Touré addressing rally. 20s, Soldier driving farm tractor. 25s, Pres. Touré addressing UN General Assembly. 30s, 40s, Pres. Sékou Touré, vert.

Perf. 13½x13, 13x13½

1977, May 14

738 A108 5s gold & multi 35 20
739 A108 10s gold & multi 65 40
740 A108 20s gold & multi 1.40 80
741 A108 25s gold & multi 1.60 1.00
a. Souvenir sheet of 4, #738-741 4.25 3.50
742 A108 30s gold & dk brn 2.00 1.20
743 A108 40s gold & sl grn 2.50 1.60
a. Souvenir sheet of 2, #742-743 5.00 4.00
Nos. 738-743 (6) 8.50 5.20

Democratic Party of Guinea, 30th anniv.

Nile Monitor — A109

Reptiles and Snakes: 4s, Frogs. 5s, Lizard (uromastix). 6s, Sand skink. 6.50s, Agama. 7s, Black-lipped spitting cobra. 8.50s, Ball python. 20s, Toads.

1977, Oct. 10 Photo. *Perf. 13½*

Size: 46x20mm

No.	Type	Value	Unused	Used
744	A109	3s multi	20	15
745	A109	4s multi	25	16
746	A109	5s multi	35	20

Size: 46x30mm

No.	Type	Value	Unused	Used
747	A109	6s multi	40	22
748	A109	6.50s multi	42	25
749	A109	7s multi	45	28
750	A109	8.50s multi	55	35
751	A109	20s multi	1.40	80
		Nos. 744-751,C134-C136 (11)	7.27	4.41

Eland — A110

Endangered Animals: 2s, Chimpanzee. 2.50s, Pygmy elephant. 3s, Lion. 4s, Palm squirrel. 5s, Hippopotamus. Each animal shown male, female and young.

1977, Dec. 12 Photo. *Perf. 14x13½*

No.	Type	Value	Unused	Used
752	A110	Strip of 3	22	15
a.-c.		1s any single	15	
753	A110	Strip of 3	42	22
a.-c.		2s any single	15	
754	A110	Strip of 3	50	30
a.-c.		2.50s any single	16	
755	A110	Strip of 3	60	38
a.-c.		3s any single	20	
756	A110	Strip of 3	80	50
a.-c.		4s any single	25	
757	A110	Strip of 3	1.05	60
a.-c.		5s any single	35	
		Nos. 752-757,C137-C142 (12)	15.24	8.85

Lenin Speaking, 1917 A111

Designs: 2.50s, First Lenin debate, Moscow. 7.50s, Lenin and people. 8s, Lenin in first parade on Red Square.

1978, Feb. 27 Photo. *Perf. 14*

No.	Type	Value	Unused	Used
758	A111	2.50s gold & multi	16	15
759	A111	5s gold & multi	35	20
760	A111	7.50s gold & multi	50	30
761	A111	8s gold & multi	55	35
		Nos. 758-761,C143-C144 (6)	4.21	2.60

Russian October Revolution, 60th anniv.

Pres. Giscard d'Estaing at Microphones — A112

Pres. Valery Giscard d'Estaing of France and Pres. Sekou Toure of Guinea: 5s, 10s, In conference. 6.50s, Signing agreement. 7s, Attending official meeting. 8.50s, With their wives. 20s, Drinking a toast.

1979, Sept. 14 Photo. *Perf. 13*

No.	Type	Value	Unused	Used
762	A112	3s lt brn & brn	20	15
763	A112	5s green & brn	35	20
764	A112	6.50s red lil & brn	42	25
765	A112	7s ultra & brn	45	28
766	A112	8.50s dk red & brn	55	35
767	A112	10s vio & brown	65	40
768	A112	20s yel grn & brn	1.40	80
		Nos. 762-768,C145 (8)	5.62	3.43

Visit of Pres. Valery Giscard d'Estaing to Guinea.

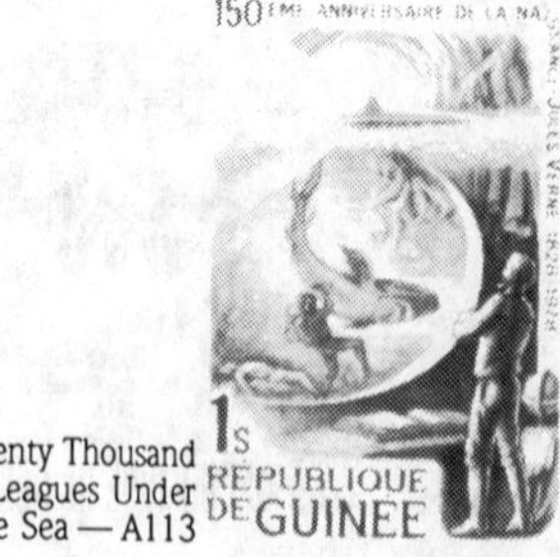

Twenty Thousand Leagues Under the Sea — A113

Jules Verne Stories: 3s, Children of Capt. Grant. 5s, Mysterious Island. 7s, A Captain at Fifteen. 10s, The Borsac Mission.

1979, Nov. 8 Litho. *Perf. 12x12½*

No.	Type	Value	Unused	Used
769	A113	1s multicolored	15	15
770	A113	3s multicolored	20	15
771	A113	5s multicolored	35	20
772	A113	7s multicolored	45	28
773	A113	10s multicolored	65	40
		Nos. 769-773,C146-C147 (7)	4.80	2.98

Jules Verne (1828-1905), French science fiction writer.

"Aerial Steam Carriage," 1842 — A114

Aviation Retrospect: 5s, Wright's Flyer 1 1903. 6.50s, Caudron, 1934. 7s, Spirit of St. Louis, 1927. 8.50s, Bristol Beaufighter, 1940. 10s, Bleriot XI, 1909. No. 780, Concorde. No. 781, Boeing 727, 1963.

1979, Nov. 22 Photo. *Perf. 14*

No.	Type	Value	Unused	Used
774	A114	3s multi	22	15
775	A114	5s multi	40	20
776	A114	6.50s multi	50	30
777	A114	7s multi	55	32
778	A114	8.50s multi	65	38
779	A114	10s multi	80	40
780	A114	20s multi	1.60	80
781	A114	20s multi	1.60	80
		Nos. 774-781 (8)	6.32	3.35

Hafia Soccer Team A115

Designs: 2s, Players and Sekou Touré cup, vert. 5s, Pres. Touré presenting cup. 7s, Pres. Touré and player holding cup, vert. 8s, Sekou Touré cup, vert. 10s, Team captains and referees, vert. 20s, The winning goal.

Perf. 12½x12, 12x12½

1979, Dec. 18 Litho.

No.	Type	Value	Unused	Used
782	A115	1s multicolored	15	15
783	A115	2s multicolored	16	15
784	A115	5s multicolored	40	20
785	A115	7s multicolored	55	28
786	A115	8s multicolored	65	35
787	A115	10s multicolored	80	40
788	A115	20s multicolored	1.60	65
		Nos. 782-788 (7)	4.31	2.18

Hafia Soccer Team, African triple champions, 1977.

Train, IYC Emblem A116

IYC Emblem and: 2s, Children dancing around tree, vert. 4s, "1979" and leaves, vert. 7s, Village. 10s, Boy climbing tree. 25s, Boys of different races, flowers, sun.

Perf. 13x13½, 13½x13

1980, Jan. 14

No.	Type	Value	Unused	Used
789	A116	2s multicolored	20	15
790	A116	4s multicolored	40	16
791	A116	5s multicolored	50	20
792	A116	7s multicolored	65	28
793	A116	10s multicolored	1.00	40
794	A116	25s multicolored	2.50	1.00
		Nos. 789-794 (6)	5.25	2.19

International Year of the Child (1979).

Butterflyfish — A117

1980, Apr. 1 *Perf. 12½x12, 12x12½*

No.	Type	Value	Unused	Used
795	A117	1s shown	15	15
796	A117	2s Porgy	15	15
797	A117	3s Zeus conchifer, vert.	20	15
798	A117	4s Grouper	25	16
799	A117	5s Sea horse, vert.	35	20
800	A117	6s Hatchet fish	40	22
801	A117	7s Pisodonophis semicinctus	45	28
802	A117	8s Flying gurnard, vert.	55	35
803	A117	9s Squirrelfish	60	38
804	A117	10s Psettus sebae, vert.	65	40
805	A117	12s Abudefuf hoeffleri	80	50
806	A117	15s Triggerfish	1.00	60
		Nos. 795-806 (12)	5.55	3.54

Apollo 11 Take-Off — A118

1980, July 20 Photo. *Perf. 14*

No.	Type	Value	Unused	Used
807	A118	1s shown	15	15
808	A118	2s Earth from moon	16	15
809	A118	4s Armstrong leaving module	35	16
810	A118	5s Armstrong on moon	42	20
811	A118	7s Collecting samples	60	28
812	A118	8s Re-entry	65	35
813	A118	12s Recovery	1.00	50
814	A118	20s Crew	1.60	80
		Nos. 807-814 (8)	4.93	2.59

Apollo 11 moon landing, 10th anniv. (1979).

Intl. Palestinian Solidarity Day — A119

1981, Nov. 21 Photo. *Perf. 13½*

No.	Type	Value	Unused	Used
815	A119	8s multicolored	65	35
816	A119	11s multicolored	1.00	42

Soccer A120

1982 Litho. *Perf. 12½x12*

No.	Type	Value	Unused	Used
817	A120	1s shown	15	15
818	A120	2s Basketball	15	15
819	A120	3s Diving	20	15
820	A120	4s Gymnast	25	16
821	A120	5s Boxing	35	20
822	A120	6s Pole vault	40	25
823	A120	7s Running	45	30
824	A120	8s Long jump	55	35
		Nos. 817-824,C148-C152 (13)	7.45	4.81

22nd Summer Olympic Games, Moscow, July 19-Aug. 3, 1980.

5th Anniv. of West African Economic Community A121

1982, May 14 *Perf. 13½*

No.	Type	Value	Unused	Used
825	A121	6s multicolored	50	25
826	A121	7s multicolored	65	35
827	A121	9s multicolored	80	50

Kemal Ataturk Birth Centenary A122

1982, July 19 Photo. *Perf. 13½*

No.	Type	Value	Unused	Used
828	A122	7s multi	45	28
829	A122	10s multi, diff.	65	40
830	A122	25s multi, horiz.	1.60	1.00

See No. C153.

1982 World Cup A123

Designs: Various soccer players.

1982, Aug. 23

No.	Type	Value	Unused	Used
831	A123	6s multicolored	40	25
832	A123	8s multicolored	55	35
833	A123	9s multicolored	60	38
834	A123	10s multicolored	65	40
		Nos. 831-834,C154-C156 (7)	5.85	3.58

Soccer Type of 1982 Nos. 831-834 Overprinted in Green: "CHAMPION ITALIE-11 JUILLET 1982"

1982, Aug. 23 Photo. *Perf. 13½*

835 A123 6s multicolored 40 25
836 A123 8s multicolored 55 35
837 A123 9s multicolored 60 38
838 A123 10s multicolored 65 40
Nos. 835-838,C157-C159 (7) 5.85 3.58

Italy's victory in 1982 World Cup.

23rd Olympic Games, Los Angeles, July 28-Aug. 12, 1984 — A124

1983, July 1 Litho. *Perf. 13½*

839 A124 5s Wrestling 35 20
840 A124 7s Weightlifting 45 28
841 A124 10s Gymnastics 65 40
842 A124 15s Discus 1.00 60
843 A124 20s Kayak 1.40 80
844 A124 25s Equestrian 1.60 1.00
Nos. 839-844 (6) 5.45 3.28

Litho. & Embossed

Size: 39x58mm

844A A124 100s Running

Souvenir Sheets

Litho.

845 A124 30s Running 2.00 1.40

Litho. & Embossed

845A A124 100s Show jumping

Nos. 844A, 845A are airmail. No. 845A contains one 58x39mm stamp.

First Manned Balloon Flight, 200th Anniv. — A125

Designs: 5s, Marquis D'Arlandes, Pilatre de Rozier. 7s, Marie Antoinette Balloon, Rozier. 10s, Dirigible, Dupuy De Lome, horiz. 15s, Dirigible, Major A. Perseval, horiz.

1983, Aug. 1 Litho. *Perf. 13½*

846 A125 5s multicolored 35 20
847 A125 7s multicolored 45 28
848 A125 10s multicolored 65 50
849 A125 15s multicolored 1.00 60
Nos. 846-849,C160-C161 (6) 5.45 3.38

Intl. Year of the Handicapped — A126

1983, Aug. 24 Litho.

850 A126 10s multicolored 80 40
851 A126 20s multicolored 1.60 80

Dr. Robert Koch (1843-1910), TB Bacillus A127

Various phases of research.

1983, Aug. 24 Litho.

852 A127 6s multicolored 40 25
853 A127 10s multicolored 65 40
854 A127 11s multicolored 70 42
855 A127 12s multicolored 80 45
856 A127 15s multicolored 1.10 60
857 A127 20s multicolored 1.40 80
858 A127 25s multicolored 1.60 1.00
Nos. 852-858 (7) 6.65 3.92

Mosque, Conakry A128

1983, Oct. 2 Litho. *Perf. 13½*

859 A128 1s multicolored 15 15
860 A128 2s multicolored 15 15
861 A128 5s multicolored 30 15
862 A128 10s multicolored 60 30
Set value 56

Souvenir Sheet

863 A128 25s multicolored 1.50 70

Natl. independence, 25th anniv. No. 863 airmail.

Mano River Union, 10th Anniv. A129

Designs: 2s, Development program graduates. 7s, Emblem. 8s, Pres. Toure of Guinea, Stevens of Sierra Leone, Doe of Liberia. 10s, 20s, Signing treaty.

1983, Oct. 3

864 A129 2s multicolored 15 15
865 A129 7s multicolored 40 20
866 A129 8s multicolored 50 22
867 A129 10s multicolored 60 30

Souvenir Sheet

868 A129 20s multicolored 1.10 55

No. 868 airmail.

14th Winter Olympics, Sarajevo, Feb. 8-19, 1984 — A130

1983, Dec. 5 Litho. *Perf. 13½*

869 A130 5s Biathlon 35 20
870 A130 7s Bobsledding 45 30
871 A130 10s Downhill skiing 65 40
872 A130 15s Speed skating 1.00 60
873 A130 20s Ski jumping 1.40 80
874 A130 25s Figure skating 1.60 1.00
Nos. 869-874 (6) 5.45 3.30

Litho. & Embossed

Size: 58x39mm

874A A130 100s Downhill skiing

Souvenir Sheets

Litho.

875 A130 30s Hockey 2.00 1.40

Litho. & Embossed

875A A130 100s 4-man bobsled

Nos. 873-875A airmail. No. 875A contains one 58x39mm stamp.

Self-portrait and Virgin with Blue Diadem, by Raphael — A131

Designs: 7s, Self-portrait and Holy Family, by Rubens. 10s, Self-portrait and Portrait of Saskia, by Rembrandt. 15s, Portrait of Goethe and scene from Young Werther. 20s, Scouting Year. 25s, Paul Harris, Rotary emblem. 30s, J.F. Kennedy, Apollo XI. 100s, Paul Harris, 3 other men in Rotary meeting.

1984, Jan 2 Litho. *Perf. 13*

876 A131 5s multicolored 35 20
877 A131 7s multicolored 45 30
878 A131 10s multicolored 65 40
879 A131 15s multicolored 1.00 60
880 A131 20s multicolored 1.40 80
881 A131 25s multicolored 1.60 1.20
Nos. 876-881 (6) 5.45 3.50

Souvenir Sheets

882 A131 30s multicolored 2.00 1.40

Litho. & Embossed

Perf. 13½

882A A131 100s gold & multi

Nos. 880-882A airmail. No. 882A contains one 51x42mm stamp.
For overprints see Nos. C164-C165.

Transportation A132

1984, May 7 Litho. *Perf. 13½*

883 A132 5s Congo River steamer 25 16
884 A132 7s Graf Zeppelin LZ 127 38 20
885 A132 10s Daimler automobile, 1886 55 32
886 A132 15s E. African RR Beyer-Garrat 70 45
887 A132 20s Latecoere 28, 1929 1.10 60
888 A132 25s Sial Marchetti S.M. 73, 1934 1.40 80
Nos. 883-888 (6) 4.38 2.53

Souvenir Sheet

889 A132 30s Series B locomotive 1.60 90

Nos. 887-889 airmail.

Anniversaries and Events — A133

Famous men: 5s, Abraham Lincoln, log cabin, the White House. 7s, Jean-Henri Dunant, Red Cross at Battle of Solferino. 10s, Gottlieb Daimler, 1892 Motor Carriage. 15s, Louis Bleriot, monoplane. 20s, Paul Harris, Rotary Intl. 25s, Auguste Piccard, bathyscaphe Trieste. 30s, Anatoly Karpov, world chess champion, chessboard and knight. 100s, Paul Harris, Rotary Intl. emblem.

1984, Aug. 20 Litho. *Perf. 13½*

890 A133 5s multicolored 30 15
891 A133 7s multicolored 40 20
892 A133 10s multicolored 60 30
893 A133 15s multicolored 90 45
894 A133 20s multicolored 1.10 55
895 A133 25s multicolored 1.50 70
Nos. 890-895 (6) 4.80 2.35

Litho. & Embossed

Size: 60x30mm

895A A133 100s gold & multi
b. Min. sheet of 1, 91x70mm
c. Min. sheet of 1, 121x70mm

Souvenir Sheet

896 A133 30s multicolored 1.90 90

Nos. 894-896 are airmail.
For overprints see Nos. C163, C166.

The Holy Family, by Durer — A134

Painting details: 5s, The Mystic Marriage of St. Catherine and St. Sebastian, by Correggio. 10s, The Veiled Woman, by Raphael. 15s, Portrait of a Young Man, by Durer. 20s, Portrait of Soutine, by Modigliani. 25s, Esterhazy Madonna, by Raphael. 30s, Impannata Madonna, by Raphael.

1984, Aug. 23

897 A134 5s multicolored 25 15
898 A134 7s multicolored 38 22
899 A134 10s multicolored 55 32
900 A134 15s multicolored 70 45
901 A134 20s multicolored 1.10 62
902 A134 25s multicolored 1.40 80
Nos. 897-902 (6) 4.38 2.56

Souvenir Sheet

903 A134 30s multicolored 1.60 90

Nos. 901-903 airmail.

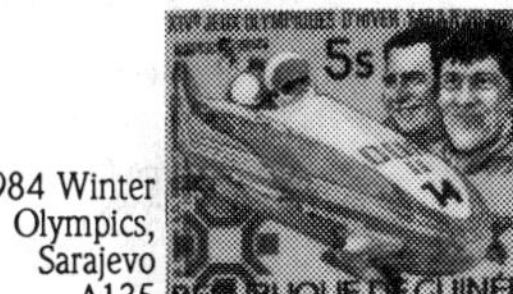

1984 Winter Olympics, Sarajevo A135

Gold medalists: 5s, East German two-man bobsled. 7s, Thomas Wassberg, Sweden, 50-kilometer cross-country. 10s, Gaetan Boucher, Canada, 1000 and 1500-meter speed skating. 15s, Katarina Witt, DDR, singles figure skating. 20s, Bill Johnson, US, men's downhill. 25s, Soviet Union, ice hockey. 30s, Jens Weissflog, DDR, 70-meter ski jump. No. 909A, Phil Mahre, US, slalom skiing. No. 910A, Jayne Torvill & Christopher Dean, Great Britain, ice dancing.

1985, Sept. 23 Litho. *Perf. 13½*

904 A135 5s multicolored 30 15
905 A135 7s multicolored 40 20
906 A135 10s multicolored 60 30
907 A135 15s multicolored 90 45
908 A135 20s multicolored 1.10 55
909 A135 25s multicolored 1.50 70
Nos. 904-909 (6) 4.80 2.35

Litho. & Embossed

Size: 51x36mm

909A A135 100s gold & multi

Souvenir Sheets

Litho.

910 A135 30s multicolored 1.90 90

Litho. & Embossed

910A A135 100s gold & multi

Nos. 908A-910A are airmail. No. 910A contains one 51x36mm stamp.

1984 Los Angeles Summer Olympics — A136

Medalists and various satellites: 5s, T. Ruiz and C. Costie, US, synchronized swimming. 7s, West Germany, team dressage. 10s, US, yachting, flying Dutchman class. 15s, Mark Todd, New Zealand, individual 3-day equestrian event. 20s, Daley Thompson, G.B., decathlon. 25s, US, team jumping. 30s, Carl Lewis, US, long jump, 100 and 200-meter run, 4x100 relay.

1985, Mar. 18 Litho. *Perf. 13½*

911 A136 5s multicolored 20 15
912 A136 7s multicolored 28 16
913 A136 10s multicolored 40 22
914 A136 15s multicolored 60 38
915 A136 20s multicolored 70 45
916 A136 25s multicolored 1.00 60
Nos. 911-917 (7) 4.58 2.76

Souvenir Sheet

917 A136 30s multicolored 1.40 80

Nos. 915-917 airmail.

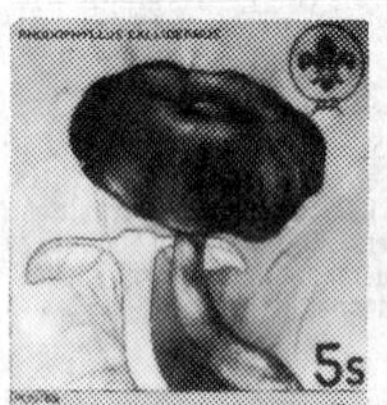

Fungi — A137

1985, Mar. 21 Litho. *Perf. 13½*

918 A137 5s Rhodophyllus callidermus 25 15
919 A137 7s Agaricus niger 38 18
920 A137 10s Thermitomyces globulus 55 25
921 A137 15s Amanita robusta 80 40
922 A137 20s Lepiota subradicans 1.10 55
923 A137 25s Cantharellus rhodophyllus 1.40 65
Nos. 918-923 (6) 4.48 2.18

Souvenir Sheet

924 A137 30s Phlebopus sylvaticus 1.60 80

Nos. 922-924 airmail.
For surcharges see Nos. 962-968.

Scientist Herman J. Oberth, and Two-Stage Rocket — A138

Space achievements: 10s, Lunik 1, USSR, 1959. 15s, Lunik 2 on the Moon, 1959. 20s, Lunik 3 photographing the Moon, 1959. 30s, US astronauts Armstrong, Aldrin, Collins and Apollo 11, 1969. 35s, Sally Ride, 1st American woman in space, 1983. 50s, Recovering a Palapa B satellite, 1984. No. 930A, Guion S. Bluford, 1st black American astronaut. No. 931A, Viking probe on Mars.

1985, May 26 Litho. *Perf. 13½*

925 A138 7s multicolored 28 16
926 A138 10s multicolored 40 22
927 A138 15s multicolored 60 38
928 A138 20s multicolored 70 45
929 A138 30s multicolored 1.40 80
930 A138 35s multicolored 1.50 85
Nos. 925-930 (6) 4.88 2.86

Litho. & Embossed

Size: 51x36mm

930A A138 200s gold & multi

Souvenir Sheet

Litho.

931 A138 50s multicolored 2.00 1.10

Litho. & Embossed

931A A138 200s gold & multi

Nos. 929-931A are airmail. No. 931A contains one 51x36mm stamp.

Maimonides (1135-1204), Jewish Scholar, Cordoba Jewish Quarter — A139

Anniversaries and events: 10s, Christopher Columbus departing from Palos for New World, 1492. 15s, Frederic Auguste Bartholdi (1834-1904), sculptor, architect, and Statue of Liberty, cent. 20s, Queen Mother, 85th birthday. 30s, Ulf Merbold, German physicist, US space shuttle Columbia. 35s, Wedding of Prince Charles and Lady Diana, 1981. 50s, Charles, Diana, Princes Henry and William. 100s, Queen Mother Elizabeth's 85th birthday.

1985, Sept. 23

932 A139 7s multicolored 38 18
933 A139 10s multicolored 55 25
934 A139 15s multicolored 80 40
935 A139 20s multicolored 1.10 55
936 A139 30s multicolored 1.60 80
937 A139 35s multicolored 1.90 90
Nos. 932-937 (6) 6.33 3.08

Litho. & Embossed

Size: 42x51mm

937A A139 100s gold & multi

Souvenir Sheet

Litho.

938 A139 50s multicolored 2.50 1.40

Nos. 936-938 airmail. No. 938 contains one 51x36mm stamp. No. 934 exists in souvenir sheet of one.

Audubon Birth Bicent. — A140

Illustrations of bird species from Birds of America.

1985, Sept. 23 Litho. *Perf. 13½*

939 A140 7s Coccizus erythrophtalmus 40 20
940 A140 10s Conuropsis carolinensis 60 30
941 A140 15s Anhinga anhinga 90 45
942 A140 20s Buteo lineatus 1.10 60
943 A140 30s Otus asio 1.90 90
944 A140 35s Toxostoma rufum 2.00 1.10
Nos. 939-944 (6) 6.90 3.55

Souvenir Sheet

945 A140 50s Zenaidura macroura 3.00 2.25

Nos. 941, 944 vert. Nos. 943-945 are airmail. No. 945 contains one 51x36mm stamp.

1986 World Cup Soccer Championships, Mexico — A141

Famous soccer players: 7s, Bebeto, Brazil. 10s, Rinal Dassaev, USSR. 15s, Phil Neal, Great Britain. 20s, Jean Tigana, France. 30s, Fernando Chalana, Portugal. 35s, Michel Platini, France. 50s, Karl Heinz Rummenigge, West Germany.

1985, Oct. 26

946 A141 7s multicolored 38 18
947 A141 10s multicolored 55 25
948 A141 15s multicolored 80 40
949 A141 20s multicolored 1.10 55
950 A141 30s multicolored 1.60 80
951 A141 35s multicolored 1.90 90
Nos. 946-951 (6) 6.33 3.08

Souvenir Sheet

952 A141 50s multicolored 2.50 1.40

Nos. 950-952 airmail.

Cats and Dogs A142

1985, Oct. 26

953 A142 7s Blue-point Siamese 38 18
954 A142 10s Cocker spaniel 55 25
955 A142 15s Poodles 80 40
956 A142 20s Blue Persian 1.10 55
957 A142 25s European red-and-white tabby 1.40 65
958 A142 30s German shepherd 1.60 80
959 A142 35s Abyssinians 1.90 90
960 A142 40s Boxer 2.25 1.10
Nos. 953-960 (8) 9.98 4.83

Souvenir Sheet

961 A142 50s Pyrenean mountain dog, chartreux cat 2.50 1.40

Nos. 958-961 airmail. No. 961 contains one 51x30mm stamp.

Nos. 918-924 Surcharged with 4 Bars

1985, Nov. 15

962 A137 1s on 5s multi 15 15
963 A137 2s on 7s multi 15 15
964 A137 8s on 10s multi 42 22
965 A137 30s on 15s multi 1.60 80
966 A137 35s on 20s multi 1.90 90
967 A137 40s on 25s multi 2.25 1.10
Nos. 962-967 (6) 6.47 3.32

Souvenir Sheet

968 A137 50s on 30s multi 2.50 1.40

Nos. 966-968 airmail.

Locomotives — A143

Designs: 7s, 8F Class steam, Great Britain. 15s, Bobo 5500 Series III electric, German Fed. Railways. 25s, Pacific A Mazout No. 270, African Railways. 35s, Serie 420 electric train set, Suburban S-Bahn, Germany. 50s, ICE high-speed train, German Fed. Railways.

1985, Dec. 18 Litho. *Perf. 13½*

969 A143 7s multicolored 38 20
970 A143 15s multicolored 80 40
971 A143 25s multicolored 1.40 65
972 A143 35s multicolored 1.90 90

Souvenir Sheet

973 A143 50s multicolored 2.50 1.40

Nos. 972-973 airmail.
For surcharges see Nos. 991-995.

Columbus Discovering America, 1492 — A144

1985, Dec. 18

974 A144 10s Pinta 55 25
975 A144 20s Santa Maria 1.10 55
976 A144 30s Nina 1.60 80
977 A144 40s Santa Maria, sighting land 2.25 1.10

Souvenir Sheet

978 A144 50s Columbus and Nina 2.50 1.40

Nos. 976-979 airmail.

Intl. Youth Year A145

1986, Jan. 21

979 A145 10s Chopin 80 40
980 A145 20s Botticelli 1.60 80
981 A145 25s Picasso 2.00 1.00
982 A145 35s Rossini 2.75 1.40

Souvenir Sheet

983 A145 50s Michelangelo 4.00 2.00

Nos. 981, 983 airmail.
For surcharges see Nos. 996-1000.

Halley's Comet — A146

Sightings: 5fr, Bayeux Tapestry (detail), c. 1092, France. 30fr, Arab, astrolabe, 1400. 40fr, Montezuma II, Aztec deity. 50fr, Edmond Halley, trajectory diagram. 300fr, Halley, Sir Isaac Newton. 500fr, Giotto, Soviet and NASA space probes, comet. 600fr, Hally commemorative medal, Giotto probe.

1986, July 1 Litho. *Perf. 13½*

5fr-500fr Surcharged with New Currency in Silver or Black

984 A146 5fr multi 15 15
985 A146 30fr multi 16 15
986 A146 40fr multi 22 15
987 A146 50fr multi 28 15
988 A146 300fr multi 1.65 82
989 A146 500fr multi 2.75 1.40
Nos. 984-989 (6) 5.21 2.82

Souvenir Sheet

990 A146 600fr multi 3.25 1.65

Nos. 988-990 are airmail. Nos. 984-989 not issued without surcharge.

Nos. 969-973 Surcharged in Black or Black on Silver

1986, Aug. 25 Litho. *Perf. 13½*

991 A143 2fr on 7s multi (B on S) 15 15
992 A143 25fr on 15s multi 15 15
993 A143 50fr on 25s multi 28 15
994 A143 90fr on 35s multi 50 25
Set value 50

Souvenir Sheet

995 A143 500fr on 50s multi 2.75 1.40

Nos. 979-983 Surcharged

1986, Aug. 25

996 A145 5fr on 10s multi 15 15
997 A145 35fr on 20s multi 20 15
998 A145 50fr on 25s multi 28 15
999 A145 90fr on 35s multi 50 25
Set value 52

Souvenir Sheet

1000 A145 500fr on 50s multi 2.75 1.40

Locomotives — A147

Designs: 20fr, Dietrich 640 CV. 100fr, T.13 7906. 300fr, Vapeur 01220. 400fr, ABH Type 3 5020. 600fr, Renault ABH 3 (300 CV).

1986, Nov. 1

1001 A147	20fr multi	15	15
1002 A147	100fr multi	55	28
1003 A147	300fr multi	1.65	82
1004 A147	400fr multi	2.25	1.10

Souvenir Sheet

1005 A147	600fr multi	3.25	1.65

Nos. 1004-1005 are airmail.

Discovery of America, 500th Anniv. (in 1992) — A148

Designs: 40fr, Columbus at Ft. Navidad construction, Santa Maria, 1492. 70fr, Landing at Hispaniola, 2nd voyage, 1494. 200fr, Aboard ship, 3rd voyage, 1498. 500fr, Trading with Indians. 600fr, At court of Ferdinand and Isabella, 1493.

1986, Nov. 1

1006 A148	40fr multi	22	15
1007 A148	70fr multi	40	20
1008 A148	200fr multi	1.10	55
1009 A148	500fr multi	2.75	1.40

Souvenir Sheet

1010 A148	600fr multi	3.25	1.65

Nos. 1009-1010 are airmail.

Anniversaries & Events — A149

Designs: 30fr, Prince Charles and Diana, 5th wedding anniv. 40fr, Alain Prost, San Marino, 1985 Formula 1 Grand Prix world champion. 100fr, Wedding of Prince Andrew and Sarah Ferguson. 300fr, Elvis Presley (1935-1977). 500fr, Michael Jackson (b. 1958). 600fr, M. Dassault (1892-1986), aerospace engineer.

1986, Nov. 12

1011 A149	30fr multi	16	15
1012 A149	40fr multi	22	15
1013 A149	100fr multi	55	28
1014 A149	300fr multi	1.65	82
1015 A149	500fr multi	2.75	1.40
	Nos. 1011-1015 (5)	5.33	2.80

Souvenir Sheet

1016 A149	600fr multi	3.30	1.65

Nos. 1015-1016 are airmail.

1986 World Cup Soccer Championships — A150

Various players and final scores.

1986, Nov. 12

1017 A150	100fr Pfaff	55	28
1018 A150	300fr Platini	1.65	82
1019 A150	400fr Matthaus	2.20	1.10
1020 A150	500fr D. Maradona	2.75	1.40

Souvenir Sheet

1021 A150	600fr Maradona, trophy	3.30	1.65

Nos. 1020-1021 are airmail. No. 1021 contains one 51x42mm stamp.

For surcharge see No. 1182A.

1988 Summer Olympics, Seoul — A151

Pierre de Coubertin (1863-1937), Seoul Stadium, Telecommunications Satellite — A151a

1987, Jan. 17 Litho. *Perf. 13½*

1022 A151	20fr Judo	15	15
1023 A151	30fr High jump	15	15
1024 A151	40fr Team handball	16	15
1025 A151	100fr Women's gymnastics	40	20
1026 A151	300fr Javelin	1.20	60
1027 A151	500fr Equestrian	2.00	1.00
	Nos. 1022-1027 (6)	4.06	2.25

Souvenir Sheet

1028 A151a	600fr multi	2.25	1.20

Dated 1986. Nos. 1026-1028 are airmail.

1988 Winter Olympics, Calgary — A152

1987, Mar. 23 Litho. *Perf. 13½*

1029 A152	50fr on 40fr Biathlon	28	15
1030 A152	100fr Cross-country skiing	55	28
1031 A152	400fr Ski jumping	2.25	2.25
1032 A152	500fr Two-man bobsled	2.75	1.40

Souvenir Sheet

1033 A152	600fr Woman skater, satellite	3.50	1.75

No. 1029 not issued without overprint. Nos. 1031-1033 are airmail.

1988 Winter Olympics, Calgary A153

Telecommunications satellite, athletes and emblem.

1987, May 1

1034 A153	25fr Women's slalom	15	15
1035 A153	50fr Hockey	28	15
1036 A153	100fr Men's figure skating	55	28
1037 A153	150fr Men's downhill skiing	85	42
1038 A153	300fr Speed skating	1.75	90
1039 A153	500fr Four-man bobsled	2.75	1.40
	Nos. 1034-1039 (6)	6.33	3.30

Souvenir Sheet

1040 A153	600fr Ski jumping	3.50	1.75

Nos. 1038-1040 are airmail.

Famous Men — A154

Intl. Cardiology Congresses in Chicago, Washington and New York — A155

Designs: 50fr, Lafayette, military leader during American and French revolutions. 100fr, Ettore Bugatti (1881-1947), Italian automobile manufacturer, 200fr, Garri Kasparov, Russian chess champion. 300fr, George Washington. 400fr, Boris Becker, 1987 Wimbledon tennis champion. 500fr, Sir Winston Churchill.

1987, Nov. 1 Litho. *Perf. 13½*

1041 A154	50fr multi	35	18
1042 A154	100fr multi	70	35
1043 A154	200fr multi	1.40	70
1044 A154	300fr multi	2.05	1.00
1045 A154	400fr multi	2.75	1.40
1046 A154	500fr multi	3.50	1.75
	Nos. 1041-1046 (6)	10.75	5.38

Souvenir Sheet

1047 A155	1500fr multi	10.25	5.00

Nos. 1045-1047 are airmail. Stamp in No. 1047 divided into three sections by simulated perforations.

For surcharge see No. 1182B.

Cave Bear — A156

Prehistoric Animals A157

1987, Nov. 1

1048 A156	50fr Dimetrodon	35	18
1049 A156	100fr Iguanodon	70	35
1050 A156	200fr Tylosaurus	1.40	70
1051 A156	300fr shown	2.05	1.00
1052 A156	400fr Saber-tooth tiger	2.75	1.40
1053 A156	500fr Stegosaurus	3.50	1.75
	Nos. 1048-1053 (6)	10.75	5.38

Souvenir Sheet

1054 A157	600fr Triceratops	4.25	2.10

Nos. 1052-1054 are airmail.

For surcharge see No. 1182C.

1988 Summer Olympics, Seoul — A158

Male and female tennis players in action.

1987, Nov. 28

1055 A158	50fr multi	35	18
1056 A158	100fr multi, diff.	72	35
1057 A158	150fr multi, diff.	1.10	55
1058 A158	200fr multi, diff.	1.45	72
1059 A158	300fr multi, diff.	2.15	1.10
1060 A158	500fr multi, diff.	3.60	1.80
	Nos. 1055-1060 (6)	9.37	4.70

Souvenir Sheet

1061 A158	600fr multi	4.50	2.25

Reintroduction of tennis as an Olympic event. Nos. 1059-1061 are airmail.

1992 Summer Olympics, Barcelona A159

Athletes participating in events, Barcelona highlights: 50fr, Discus, courtyard of St. Croix and St. Paul Hospital. 100fr, High jump, Pablo Casals playing cello. 150fr, Long jump, Labyrinth of Horta. 170fr, Javelin, lizard from Guell Park. 400fr, Gymnastics, Mercy Church. 500fr, Tennis, Picasso Museum. 600fr, Running, tapestry by Miro.

1987, Dec. 28 Litho. *Perf. 13½*

1062 A159	50fr multi	35	18
1063 A159	100fr multi	70	35
1064 A159	150fr multi	1.05	55
1065 A159	170fr multi	1.20	60
1066 A159	400fr multi	2.75	1.40
1067 A159	500fr multi	3.50	1.75
	Nos. 1062-1067 (6)	9.55	4.83

Souvenir Sheet

1068 A159	600fr multi	4.25	2.15

Nos. 1066-1068 are airmail.

For surcharges see Nos. 1182D-1182E.

Wildlife A160

1987, Dec. 28

1069 A160	50fr African wild dog pups	35	18
1070 A160	70fr Adult	42	20
1071 A160	100fr Adults circling gazelle	70	35
1072 A160	170fr Chasing gazelle	1.20	60
1073 A160	400fr Crown cranes	2.75	1.40
1074 A160	500fr Derby elands	3.50	1.75
	Nos. 1069-1074 (6)	8.92	4.48

Souvenir Sheet

1075 A160	600fr Vervet monkeys	4.25	2.15

Nos. 1069-1072 picture World Wildlife Fund emblem; Nos. 1073, 1075, picture Scouting trefoil and No. 1074 pictures Rotary Intl. emblem. Nos. 1073-1075 are airmail.

For surcharges see Nos. 1182F-1182G.

Reconciliation Summit Conference, July 11-12, 1986 — A161

Heads of state and natl. flags: Dr. Samuel Kanyon Doe of Liberia, Colonel Lansana Conte of Guinea and Maj.-Gen. Joseph Saidu Momoh of Sierra Leone.

1987 Litho. *Perf. 13½*

1076 A161 40fr multi 35 18
1077 A161 50fr multi 42 20
1078 A161 75fr multi 65 32
1079 A161 100fr multi 85 42
1080 A161 150fr multi 1.25 62
Nos. 1076-1080 (5) 3.52 1.74

Space Exploration A162

1988, Apr. 16

1081 A162 50fr Galaxie-Grasp 35 16
1082 A162 150fr Energia-Mir 1.05 52
1083 A162 200fr NASA Space Station 1.40 70
1084 A162 300fr Ariane 5-E.S.A. 2.10 1.05
1085 A162 400fr Mars-Rover 2.80 1.40
1086 A162 450fr Venus-Vega 3.25 1.65
Nos. 1081-1086 (6) 10.95 5.48

Souvenir Sheet

1087 A162 500fr Mars-Phobos 3.50 1.75

Nos. 1085-1087 are airmail.

A163 A164

Designs: Boy Scouts watching birds and butterflies.

1988, July 5 Litho. *Perf. 13½*

1088 A163 50fr Spermophaga ruficapilla 32 16
1089 A163 100fr Medon nymphalidae 65 32
1090 A163 150fr Euplecte orix 98 50
1091 A163 300fr Nectarinia pulchella 1.95 1.00
1092 A163 400fr Sophia nymphalidae 2.60 1.30
1093 A163 450fr Rumia nymphalidae 2.90 1.45
Nos. 1088-1093 (6) 9.40 4.73

Souvenir Sheet

1094 A163 750fr Opis nymphalidae, Psittacula krameri 4.85 2.45

Nos. 1092-1094 are airmail. No. 1094 contains one 35x50mm stamp.
For surcharge see No. 1182H.

1988, July 5

Famous People: 200fr, Queen Elizabeth II, Prince Philip and crown jewels. 250fr, Fritz von Opel (1899-1971), German automotive industrialist, and 1928 RAK 2 Opel. 300fr, Wolfgang Amadeus Mozart, composer, and Masonic emblem. 400fr, Steffi Graf, tennis champion. 450fr, Buzz Aldrin and Masonic emblem. 500fr, Paul Harris, Rotary Intl. founder, and organization emblem. 750fr, Thomas Jefferson, horiz.

1095 A164 200fr multi 1.30 65
1096 A164 250fr multi 1.60 80
1097 A164 300fr multi 1.95 1.00
1098 A164 400fr multi 2.60 1.30
1099 A164 450fr multi 2.90 1.45
1100 A164 500fr multi 3.25 1.65
Nos. 1095-1100 (6) 13.60 6.85

Souvenir Sheet

1101 A164 750fr multi 4.85 2.45

40th wedding anniv. of Queen Elizabeth II and Prince Philip (200fr).
Nos. 1099-1101 are airmail. No. 1101 contains one 42x36mm stamp.
For surcharges see Nos. 1182I, 1182Q.

1988 Winter Olympics Gold Medalists A165

Designs: 50fr, Vreni Schneider, Switzerland, women's giant slalom and slalom. 100fr, Frank-Peter Roetsch, East Germany, 10 and 20-kilometer biathlon. 150fr, Matti Nykaenen, Finland, 70 and 90-meter ski jumping. 250fr, Marina Kiehl, West Germany, women's downhill. 400fr, Frank Piccard, France, super giant slalom. 450fr, Katarina Witt, East Germany, women's figure skating. 750fr, Pirmin Zurbriggen, Switzerland, men's downhill. Nos. 1102-1107 vert.

1988, Oct. 2 Litho. *Perf. 13½*

1102 A165 50fr multi 32 16
1103 A165 100fr multi 65 32
1104 A165 150fr multi 98 50
1105 A165 250fr multi 1.60 80
1106 A165 400fr multi 2.60 1.30
1107 A165 450fr multi 2.90 1.45
Nos. 1102-1107 (6) 9.05 4.53

Souvenir Sheet

1108 A165 750fr multi 4.85 2.45

Nos. 1103, 1107-1108 are airmail.
For surcharge see No. 1182J.

African Postal Union, 25th Anniv. A165a

1988 Litho. *Perf. 13½*

1108A A165a 50fr multicolored 35 18
1108B A165a 75fr multicolored 55 28
1108C A165a 100fr multicolored 70 35
1108D A165a 150fr multicolored 1.10 55

World Health Day — A165b

1988 Litho. *Perf. 13½*

1108E A165b 50fr Medical research 40 20
1108F A165b 150fr Immunization 1.15 58
1108G A165b 500fr Dentistry 3.85 1.95

For surcharge see No. 1182K.

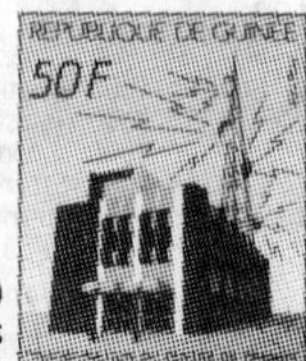

Opening of MT 20 Intl. Communications Center — A165c

1988, Dec. 8 Litho. *Perf. 13½*

1108H A165c 50fr multicolored
1108J A165c 150fr multicolored

A number has been reserved for an additional value in this set.

1992 Summer Olympics, Barcelona — A166

1989, May 3 Litho. *Perf. 13½*

1109 A166 50fr Diving 32 16
1110 A166 100fr Running, vert. 65 32
1111 A166 150fr Shooting 98 50
1112 A166 250fr Tennis, vert. 1.60 80
1113 A166 400fr Soccer 2.60 1.30
1114 A166 500fr Equestrian, vert. 3.25 1.60
Nos. 1109-1114 (6) 9.40 4.68

Souvenir Sheet

1115 A166 750fr Yachting, vert. 4.85 2.45

Nos. 1113-1115 are airmail.
For surcharge see No. 1182M.

French Revolution, Bicent. — A167

Personalities of and scenes from the revolution: 250fr, Jean-Sylvain Bailly (1736-1793) leading proceedings in Tennis Court, June 20, 1789. 300fr, Count Mirabeau (1749-1791) at royal session, June 23, 1789. 400fr, Lafayette (1757-1834), federation anniversary celebration, July 18, 1790. 450fr, Jerome Petion de Villeneuve (1756-1794), king's arrest at Varennes-en-Argonne, June 21, 1791. 750fr, Camille Desmoulins (1760-1794), destruction of the Bastille, July 1789.

1989, July 7 Litho. *Perf. 13½*

1116 A167 250fr multi 1.50 75
1117 A167 300fr multi 1.75 88
1118 A167 400fr multi 2.35 1.20
1119 A167 450fr multi 2.65 1.35

Souvenir Sheet

1120 A167 750fr multi 4.50 2.25

Nos. 1119-1120 airmail.
Nos. 1116-1119 exist in souvenir sheets of 1. Sold for 100fr extra.
For surcharge and overprints see Nos. 1182N, 1216-1220.

Planting A168

1989 Litho. *Perf. 13½*

1121 A168 25fr shown 18 15
1122 A168 50fr Irrigation 35 18
1123 A168 75fr Milking 52 25
1124 A168 100fr Fishing 70 35
1125 A168 150fr Farmers in corn field 1.05 52
1126 A168 300fr Public well 2.10 1.05
Nos. 1121-1126 (6) 4.90 2.50

Natl. Campaign for Self-sufficiency in Food Production and 10th anniv. of the Intl. Fund for Agricultural Development (in 1988). Dated 1988.

African Development Bank, 25th Anniv. — A169

1989, Nov. 4 Litho. *Perf. 13½*

1127 A169 300fr multicolored 2.15 1.10

Mano River Union, 15th Anniv. A170

Design: 300fr, Map of Guinea, Sierra Leone and Liberia, leaders' portraits.

1989, Nov. 4

1128 A170 150fr multicolored 1.10 55
1129 A170 300fr multicolored 2.15 1.10

World Cup Soccer, Italy — A171

Various soccer plays and: 200fr, Spire of San Domenico, Naples. 250fr, Piazza San Carlo, Turin. 300fr, Church of San Cataldo. 450fr, Church of San Francesco, Utine. 750fr, Statue of Dante, Florence and World Cup Soccer Trophy.

1990, Aug. 3 Litho. *Perf. 13½*

1130 A171 200fr multicolored 1.50 75
1131 A171 250fr multicolored 1.90 95
1132 A171 300fr multicolored 2.25 1.15
1133 A171 450fr multicolored 3.40 1.70

Souvenir Sheet

1134 A171 750fr multicolored 5.75 2.85

No. 1133-1134 airmail.

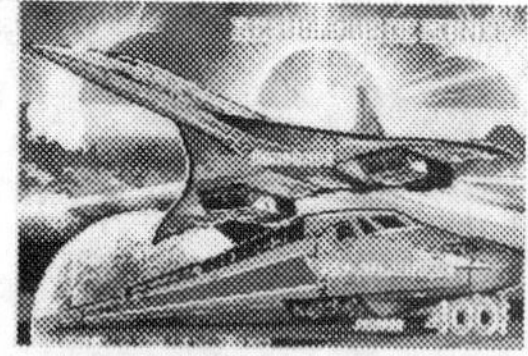

Concorde, TGV Atlantic — A172

1990, Aug. 3

1135 A172 400fr multicolored 3.00 1.50

No. 1135 exists in a souvenir sheet of 1.
For surcharge see No. 1182O.

Pope John Paul II, Pres. Gorbachev — A173

1990, Aug. 3

1136 A173 300fr multicolored 2.30 1.15

Summit Meeting, Dec. 2, 1989. No. 1136 exists in a souvenir sheet of 1.

1992 Winter Olympics, Albertville — A174

1990, Aug. 3

1137 A174 150fr Downhill skiing 1.15 58
1138 A174 250fr Cross country skiing 1.90 1.00
1139 A174 400fr Two-man bobsled 3.00 1.50
1140 A174 500fr Speedskating 3.75 1.90

Souvenir Sheet

1141 A174 750fr Slalom skiing 5.65 2.85

Nos. 1140-1141 airmail. Nos. 1137-1140 exist in souvenir sheets of 1.

For overprints and surcharge see Nos. 1182P, 1225-1230.

Pres. Bush, Pres. Gorbachev — A175

1990 Litho. *Perf. 13½*

1142 A175 200fr multicolored 1.50 75

Summit Meeting Dec. 3, 1989. No. 1142 exists in a souvenir sheet of 1.

De Gaulle's Call for French Resistance, 50th Anniv. — A176

1990

1143 A176 250fr multicolored 1.90 95

No. 1143 exists in a souvenir sheet of 1.

A177

World Cup Soccer Championships, Italy 1990 — A178

Designs: No. 1152, Player, Chateau Saint-Ange.

1991, Apr. 1 Litho. *Perf. 13½*

1144 A177 200fr Rudi Voller 1.50 75
1145 A177 250fr Uwe Bein 1.90 95
1146 A177 300fr Pierre Littbarski 2.30 1.15
1147 A177 400fr Jurgen Klinsmann 3.00 1.50
1148 A177 450fr Lothar Matthaus 3.40 1.70
1149 A177 500fr Andreas Brehme 3.75 1.90
Nos. 1144-1149 (6) 15.85 7.95

Litho. & Embossed

1150 A178 1500fr gold & multi

Souvenir Sheets

Litho.

1151 A177 750fr Brehme, diff. 5.65 2.85

Litho. & Embossed

1152 A178 1500fr gold & multi

Nos. 1148-1152 are airmail. Nos. 1144-1150 exist in souvenir sheets of 1.

Christmas A179

Paintings by Raphael: 50fr, Della Tenda Madonna. 100fr, Cowper Madonna. 150fr, Tempi Madonna. 250fr, Niccolini Madonna. 300fr, Orleans Madonna. 500fr, Solly Madonna. 750fr, Madonna of the Fish.

1991, Apr. 1 Litho.

1153 A179 50fr multi 38 20
1154 A179 100fr multi 75 40
1155 A179 150fr multi 1.15 58
1156 A179 250fr multi 1.90 95
1157 A179 300fr multi 2.30 1.15
1158 A179 500fr multi 3.75 1.90

Souvenir Sheet

1159 A179 750fr multi 5.65 2.85

Nos. 1157-1159 are airmail. Nos. 1153-1158 exist in souvenir sheets of 1.

A180

World War II Battles — A181

Designs: No. 1160, Sinking of the Bismarck, May 27, 1941, Adm. Raeder and Adm. Tovey. No. 1161, Battle of Midway, June 3, 1942, Adm. Yamamoto and Adm. Nimitz. 200fr, Guadalcanal, Oct. 7, 1942, Adm. Kondo and Adm. Halsey. 250fr, Battle of El Alamein, Oct. 23, 1942, Field Marshal Erwin Rommel, Field Marshal Montgomery. 300fr, Battle of the Bulge, Dec. 16, 1944, Gen. Guderian and Gen. Patton. 450fr, Sinking of the Yamato, Apr., 7, 1945, Adm. Kogo and Gen. MacArthur. No. 1166, Review of Free French Forces, July 14, 1940, Gen. Charles De Gaulle. 750fr, Boeing B-17G, Gen. Dwight Eisenhower. No. 1168, De Gaulle's Call for French Resistance, June 18, 1940.

1991, Apr. 8 Litho. *Perf. 13½*

1160 A180 100fr multicolored 75 40
1161 A180 150fr multicolored 1.15 58
1162 A180 200fr multicolored 1.50 75
1163 A180 250fr multicolored 1.90 95
1164 A180 300fr multicolored 2.30 1.15
1165 A180 450fr multicolored 4.90 2.45
a. Sheet of 6, #1160-1165 12.50 6.25
Nos. 1160-1165 (6) 12.50 6.28

Litho. & Embossed

1166 A181 1500fr gold & multi

Souvenir Sheets

Litho.

1167 A180 750fr multicolored 5.65 2.85

Litho. & Embossed

1168 A181 1500fr gold & multi

Nos. 1164-1168 are airmail. No. 1160-1166 exist in souvenir sheets of 1.

Doctors Without Borders A182

1991 Litho. *Perf. 13½*

1169 A182 300fr multicolored 2.40 1.20

Telecom '91 A183

1991

1170 A183 150fr multi, vert. 2.00 1.00
1171 A183 300fr shown 4.00 2.00

6th World Forum and Exposition on Telecommunications, Geneva, Switzerland.

American Entertainers and Films — A184

Designs: 100fr, Nat King Cole Trio. 150fr, Yul Brynner, The Magnificent Seven. 250fr, Judy Garland, The Wizard of Oz. 300fr, Steve McQueen, Papillon. 500fr, Gary Cooper, Sergeant York. 600fr, Bing Crosby, High Society. 750fr, John Wayne, How the West Was Won.

1991, Oct. 2 Litho. *Perf. 13½*

1172 A184 100fr multicolored 75 40
1173 A184 150fr multicolored 1.15 58
1174 A184 250fr multicolored 1.90 95
1175 A184 300fr multicolored 2.30 1.15
1176 A184 500fr multicolored 3.75 1.90
1177 A184 600fr multicolored 8.00 4.00
Nos. 1172-1177 (6) 17.85 8.98

Souvenir Sheet

1178 A184 750fr multicolored 5.65 2.85

Nos. 1176-1178 are airmail. No. 1172-1177 exist in souvenir sheets of 1.

Care Bears Promoting Environmental Protection — A184a

Designs: 50fr, Care Bears circling earth, vert. 100fr, Save water, vert. 200fr, Recycle, vert. 300fr, Control noise, vert. 400fr, Elephant. 500fr, Care Bear emblem, end of rainbow. 600fr, Scout, tent, Lord Baden-Powell.

1991 Litho. *Perf. 13½*

1178A A184a 50fr multicolored 42 22
1178B A184a 100fr multicolored 85 42
1178C A184a 200fr multicolored 1.75 85
1178D A184a 300fr multicolored 2.50 1.25
1178E A184a 400fr multicolored 3.50 1.75

Souvenir Sheets

1178F A184a 500fr multicolored 4.25 2.25
1178G A184a 600fr multicolored 5.00 2.50

Nos. 1178F-1178G each contain one 39x27mm stamp. No. 1178G is airmail.

African Tourism Year A185

1991 Litho. *Perf. 13½*

1179 A185 100fr Dancer, vert. 75 40
1180 A185 150fr Baskets 1.15 58
1181 A185 250fr Drum 1.90 95
1182 A185 300fr Flute player, vert. 2.30 1.15

Stamps of 1986-92 Surcharged in Black or Silver (#1182A-1182B, 1182D, 1182H-1182I, 1182M-1182N, 1182P)

1991 Litho. *Perfs. as Before*

1182A A150 100fr on 400fr #1019 85 42
1182B A154 100fr on 400fr #1045 85 42
1182C A156 100fr on 400fr #1052 85 42
1182D A159 100fr on 170fr #1065 85 42
1182E A159 100fr on 400fr #1066 85 42
1182F A160 100fr on 170fr #1072 85 42
1182G A160 100fr on 400fr #1073 85 42
1182H A163 100fr on 400fr #1092 85 42
1182I A164 100fr on 400fr #1098 85 42
1182J A165 100fr on 400fr #1106 85 42
1182K A165b 100fr on 500fr #1108G 85 42
1182M A166 100fr on 400fr #1113 85 42
1182N A167 100fr on 250fr #1116 85 42
1182O A172 100fr on 400fr #1135 85 42
1182P A174 100fr on 400fr #1139 85 42
1182Q A164 300fr on 450fr #1099 2.50 1.25
1182R AP14 300fr on 450fr #C170 2.50 1.25
Nos. 1182A-1182R (17) 17.75 8.80

Nos. 1182B-1182C, 1182E, 1182G, 1182M, 1182Q-1182R are airmail.

A number has been reserved for an additional surcharge with this set.

Visit by Pope John Paul II — A185a

1992, Feb. 24 Litho. *Perf. 13½*

1182S A185a 150fr multicolored 1.25 60

1994 World Cup Soccer, US — A186

Player, World Cup Trophy and scenes of Atlanta: 100fr, Little Five Points. 300fr, Fulton County Stadium. 400fr, Inman Park. 500fr, High Museum of Art. 1000fr, Intelsat VI, Capitol.

1992, Apr. 27 Litho. *Perf. 13½*

1183 A186 100fr multi 75 40
1184 A186 300fr multi 2.30 1.15
1185 A186 400fr multi 3.00 1.50

1186 A186 500fr multi 3.75 1.90

Souvenir Sheet

1187 A186 1000fr multi 7.50 3.75

Nos. 1186-1187 are airmail. Nos. 1183-1186 exist in souvenir sheets of 1.

1994 World Cup Soccer Championships, US — A186a

Designs: No. 1187A, Player in white shirt. No. 1187B, Player in red.

Litho. & Embossed

1992, Apr. 27 *Perf. 13½*

1187A A186a 1500fr gold & multi

Souvenir Sheet

1187B A186a 1500fr gold & multi

Nos. 1187A-1187B are airmail. No. 1187A exists in souvenir sheet of 1.

Lions Intl., 75th Anniv. — A187

1992, May 22 **Litho.** *Perf. 13½*

1188 A187 150fr blue & multi 1.25 65
1188A A187 400fr lilac rose & multi 3.50 1.75

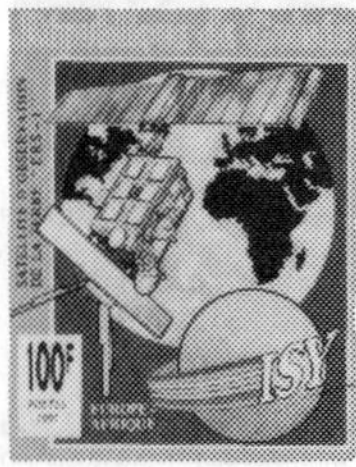

Anniversaries and Events — A188

Designs: 100fr, Satellite ERS-1 in orbit. 150fr, Vase with Fourteen Sunflowers, by Vincent van Gogh. 200fr, Napoleon Bonaparte. 250fr, Henri Dunant, Red Cross workers. 300fr, Brandenburg Gate. 400fr, Pope John Paul II. 450fr, Garry Kasparov, Anatoly Karpov, chess pieces. 500fr, African child, dove, emblems of Rotary and Lions Clubs.

1992, Nov. 10 **Litho.** *Perf. 13½*

1189 A188 100fr multicolored 85 42
1190 A188 150fr multicolored 1.25 65
1191 A188 200fr multicolored 1.70 85
1192 A188 250fr multicolored 2.10 1.05
1193 A188 300fr multicolored 2.50 1.25
1194 A188 400fr multicolored 3.35 1.70
1195 A188 450fr multicolored 3.75 1.90
1196 A188 500fr multicolored 4.15 2.10
Nos. 1189-1196 (8) 19.65 9.92

Intl. Space Year (#1189). Vincent van Gogh, cent. of death (in 1990) (#1190). Napoleon Bonaparte, 170th anniv. of death (in 1991) (#1191). Founding of Red Cross (in 1864) (#1192). Brandenburg Gate, bicent. (#1193). Pope John Paul II's visit to Africa in 1989 (#1194). World Chess Championships (#1195). Lions Intl., 75th anniv. (#1196).

Nos. 1195-1196 are airmail. Nos. 1189-1196 exist in souvenir sheets of one.

Anniversaries and Events — A189

Designs: 200fr, The Devil and Kate, Antonin Dvorak. 300fr, Antonio Vivaldi. 350fr, Graf Zeppelin, flying boat, Count Ferdinand von Zeppelin. 400fr, English Channel Euro-Tunnel Train. 450fr, Konrad Adenauer, Brandenburg Gate. 500fr, Japanese naval ensign, Emperor Hirohito. 750fr, Tunnel Train, diff.

1992, Nov. 10

1197 A189 200fr multicolored 1.70 85
1198 A189 300fr multicolored 2.55 1.25
1199 A189 350fr multicolored 2.90 1.45
1200 A189 400fr multicolored 3.35 1.70
1201 A189 450fr multicolored 3.75 1.90
1202 A189 500fr multicolored 4.15 2.10
Nos. 1197-1202 (6) 18.40 9.25

Souvenir Sheet

1203 A189 750fr multicolored 6.25 3.10

Antonin Dvorak, 90th anniv. of death (in 1994) (#1197). Antonio Vivaldi, 250th anniv. of death (in 1991) (#1198). Count Ferdinand von Zeppelin, 75th anniv. of death (#1199). Opening of English Channel Tunnel (in 1994) (#1200, 1203). Konrad Adenauer, 25th anniv. of death, Brandenburg Gate, bicent. (#1201). Death of Emperor Hirohito (in 1989) (#1202).

Nos. 1201-1203 are airmail. Nos. 1197-1202 exist imperf. and in souvenir sheets of one. No. 1203 exists imperf. and contains one 60x42mm stamp.

Anniversaries and Events — A190

Designs: 50fr, Modern Times, film by Charlie Chaplin. 100fr, Expo '92 Seville, Columbus. 150fr, St. Peter's Square, Rome. 200fr, Marlene Dietrich, roses. 250fr, Michael Schumacher, Benetton Ford B192. 300fr, Mercury rocket, John Glenn. 400fr, Bill Koch, America 3. 450fr, Mark Rypien, quarterback of Washington Redskins. 500fr, Rescue of Intelsat VI by shuttle Endeavour.

1992, Dec. 3

1204 A190 50fr multicolored 42 20
1205 A190 100fr multicolored 85 42
1206 A190 150fr multicolored 1.25 65
1207 A190 200fr multicolored 1.70 85
1208 A190 250fr multicolored 2.10 1.05
1209 A190 300fr multicolored 2.50 1.25
1210 A190 400fr multicolored 3.35 1.70
1211 A190 450fr multicolored 3.70 1.85
1212 A190 500fr multicolored 4.15 2.10
Nos. 1204-1212 (9) 20.02 10.07

Discovery of America, 500th anniv. (#1205). First US orbital space flight, 30th anniv. (#1209). Americas Cup yacht race (#1210). Super Bowl XXVI football game (#1211).

Nos. 1210-1212 are airmail. Nos. 1204-1212 exist in souvenir sheets of one.

Intl. Conference on Nutrition, Rome — A191

1992, Nov. 10 **Litho.** *Perf. 13½*

1213 A191 150fr pink & multi 1.25 65
1214 A191 400fr blue & multi 3.35 1.70
1215 A191 500fr yellow green & multi 4.20 2.10

Nos. 1116-1120 Ovptd. in Silver "BICENTENAIRE / DE L'AN I / DE LA REPUBLIQUE / FRANCAISE"

1992 **Litho.** *Perf. 13½*

1216 A167 250fr multicolored 2.00 1.00
1217 A167 300fr multicolored 2.50 1.25
1218 A167 400fr multicolored 3.25 1.65
1219 A167 450fr multicolored 3.75 1.90

Souvenir Sheet

1220 A167 750fr multicolored 6.25 3.25

Nos. 1219-1220 are airmail. Nos. 1216-1219 exist in souvenir sheets of 1. Sold for 100fr extra.

Nos. 1137-1141 Ovptd. in Gold

1992 **Litho.** *Perf. 13½*

1226 A174 150fr multicolored 1.25 65
1227 A174 250fr multicolored 2.00 1.00
1228 A174 400fr multicolored 3.25 1.65
1229 A174 500fr multicolored 4.00 2.00

Souvenir Sheet

1230 A174 750fr multicolored 6.25 3.00

Overprints read: 150fr, 750fr, "SLALOM GEANT / Alberto Tomba, Italie." 250fr, "SKI NORDIQUE / Vegard Ulvang, Norvege." 400fr, "BOB A DEUX / G. Weder / D Acklin, Suisse." 500fr, "PATINAGE DE VITESSE / Olaf Zinke 1000m., Allemagne."

1994 World Cup Soccer Championships, US — A192

Soccer player, city skyline: 100fr, San Francisco. 300fr, Washington DC. 400fr, Detroit. 500fr, Dallas. 1000fr, New York.

1993 **Litho.** *Perf. 13½*

1233 A192 100fr multicolored 80 40
1234 A192 300fr multicolored 2.50 1.25
1235 A192 400fr multicolored 3.25 1.65
1236 A192 500fr multicolored 4.00 2.00

Souvenir Sheet

1237 A192 1000fr multicolored 8.25 4.25

Nos. 1236-1237 are airmail.

Miniature Sheet

Dinosaurs A193

Designs: No. 1238a, 50fr, Euparkeria. b, 50fr, Plateosaurus. c, 50fr, Anchisaurus. d, 50fr, Ornithosuchus. e, 100fr, Megalosaurus. f, 100fr, Scelidosaurus. g, 100fr, Camptosaurus. h, 100fr, Ceratosaurus. i, 250fr, Ouranosaurus. j, 250fr, Dicraeosaurus. k, 250fr, Tarbosaurus. l, 250fr, Gorgosaurus. m, 250fr, Polacanthus. n, 250fr, Deinonychus. o, 250fr, Corythosaurus. p, 250fr, Spinosaurus.

1000fr, Tyrannosaurus rex.

1993

1238 A193 Sheet of 16, #a.-p. 21.00 10.50

Souvenir Sheet

1239 A193 1000fr multicolored 8.25 4.00

No. 1239 is airmail and contains one 50x60mm stamp.

SEMI-POSTAL STAMPS

Eye Examination SP1

Microscopic Examination — SP2

Designs: 30fr+20fr, Medical laboratory. 40fr+20fr, Insect control. 100fr+100fr, Surgical operation.

Engraved and Lithographed

1960 **Unwmk.** *Perf. 11½*

B12 SP1 20fr + 10fr ultra & car 45 45
B13 SP1 30fr + 20fr brn org & violet 45 45
B14 SP1 40fr + 20fr rose lil & blue 55 55
B15 SP2 50fr + 50fr grn & brn 90 90
B16 SP2 100fr + 100fr lil & grn 1.10 1.10
Nos. B12-B16 (5) 3.45 3.45

Issued for national health propaganda.

For overprints see Nos. B25-B29.

Nos. 194-195 Surcharged "1961" and New Value in Red or Orange

1961, June 6 **Photo.**

B17 A17 25fr + 10fr (R or O) 2.75 2.75
B18 A17 50fr + 20fr (R or O) 2.75 2.75

Nos. B17-B18 exist with orange surcharges transposed: "1961 + 10FRS." on 50fr and "1961 + 20FRS." on 25fr.

Nos. 214-219 Surcharged in Green, Lilac, Orange or Blue: "POUR LA PROTECTION DE NOS ANIMAUX +5 FRS"

Photo., Surcharge Engr.

1961, Dec. 8

Multicolored Design; Granite Paper

B19 A20 5fr + 5fr brt grn (G) 15 15
B20 A20 10fr + 5fr emer (G) 15 15
B21 A20 25fr + 5fr lilac (L) 32 18
B22 A20 40fr + 5fr org (O) 40 22
B23 A20 50fr + 5fr red org (O) 55 35
B24 A20 75fr + 5fr ultra (B) 80 45
Nos. B19-B24 (6) 2.37 1.50

The surtax was for animal protection.

Nos. B12-B16 Overprinted in Red or Orange

1962, Feb. **Engr. & Litho.** *Perf. 11½*

B25 SP1 20fr + 10fr (R or O) 25 25
B26 SP1 30fr + 20fr (R or O) 35 35
B27 SP1 40fr + 20fr (R or O) 38 38
B28 SP2 50fr + 50fr (R or O) 80 80
B29 SP2 100fr + 100fr (R or O) 1.60 1.60
Nos. B25-B29 (5) 3.38 3.38

WHO drive to eradicate malaria.

No. B25 also exists with black overprint.

Nos. 223-228 Surcharged in Red: "POUR LA PROTECTION DE NOS OISEAUX + 5 FRS"

Photo., Surcharge Engr.

1962, May 14 *Perf. 13x14*

B30 A22 5fr + 5fr multi 15 15
B31 A22 10fr + 5fr multi 15 15
B32 A22 25fr + 5fr multi 22 16
B33 A22 40fr + 5fr multi 35 22
B34 A22 50fr + 5fr multi 62 38
B35 A22 75fr + 5fr multi 1.40 70
Nos. B30-B35 (6) 2.89 1.76

The surtax was for bird protection.

Nos. 232-233 Surcharged in Orange or Red and Overprinted: "Aide aux Réfugiés Algeriens"

1962, Nov. 1 **Litho.** *Perf. 13*

B36 A24 25fr + 15fr multi 40 40
B37 A24 75fr + 25fr multi 80 80

Issued to help Algerian refugees.

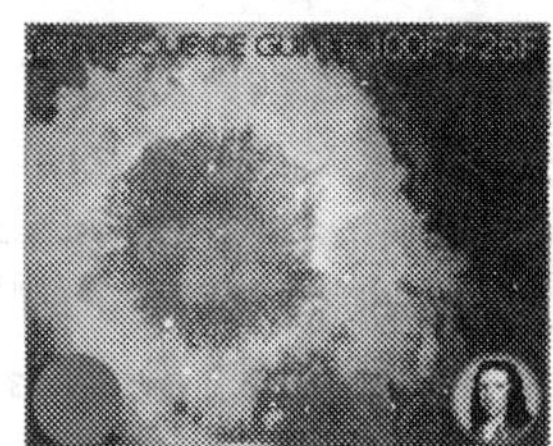

Astronomers and Space Phenomena — SP3

1989, Mar. 7 **Litho.** *Perf. 13½*

B38 SP3 100fr +25fr Helical nebula 82 40
B39 SP3 150fr +25fr Orion nebula 1.15 58
B40 SP3 200fr +25fr Eagle nebula 1.50 75
B41 SP3 250fr +25fr Trifide nebula 1.80 90
B42 SP3 300fr +25fr Eta-carinae nebula 2.10 1.05
B43 SP3 500fr +25fr NGC-2264 nebula 3.40 1.70
Nos. B38-B43 (6) 10.77 5.38

Souvenir Sheet

B44 SP3 750fr +50fr Horse's Head nebula 5.25 2.60

Nos. B42-B44 are airmail.

AIR POST STAMPS

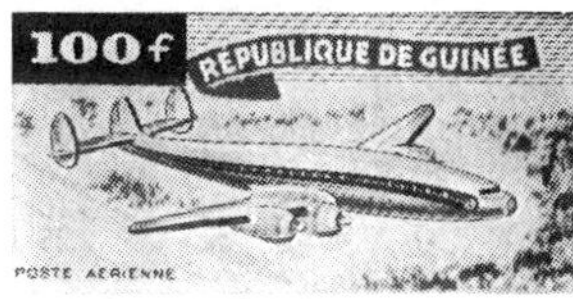

Lockheed Constellation — AP1

Design: 500fr, Plane on ground.

Lithographed and Engraved

1959, July 13 **Unwmk.** *Perf. 11½*

Size: 52½x24mm

C14 AP1 100fr dp car, ultra & emer 1.00 65
C15 AP1 200fr emer, brn & lil 1.40 1.00

Size: 56½x26mm

C16 AP1 500fr multicolored 3.50 2.00

For overprints see Nos. C24-C26, C52-C53.

Doves with Letter and Olive Twig — AP2

1959, Oct. 16 **Engr.** *Perf. 13½*

C17 AP2 40fr blue 20 20
C18 AP2 50fr emerald 38 30
C19 AP2 100fr dk car rose 70 50
C20 AP2 200fr rose red 1.20 1.00
C21 AP2 500fr red orange 3.50 2.50
Nos. C17-C21 (5) 5.98 4.50

For overprints see Nos. C35-C38.

Admission to UN Type of 1959

Engr. & Litho.

1959, Dec. 12 *Perf. 12*

Size: 44x26mm

C22 A16 50fr multicolored 55 40
C23 A16 100fr multicolored 65 50

For overprints see Nos. C27-C28.

Nos. C14-C16 Overprinted in Carmine, Orange or Blue: "Jeux Olympiques Rome 1960" and Olympic Rings

1960 **Litho. & Engr.** *Perf. 11½*

Size: 52½x24mm

C24 AP1 100fr multi (C or O) 2.50 2.00
C25 AP1 200fr multi (Bl) 5.50 3.50

Size: 56½x26mm

C26 AP1 500fr multi (C or O) 14.00 14.00

17th Olympic Games, Rome, Aug. 25-Sept. 11.

Nos. C22-C23 Overprinted

XVÈME
ANNIVERSAIRE
DES NATIONS UNIES

Engr. & Litho.

1961, Oct. 24 *Perf. 12*

C27 A16 50fr multicolored 45 38
C28 A16 100fr multicolored 65 55

United Nations, 15th anniversary.

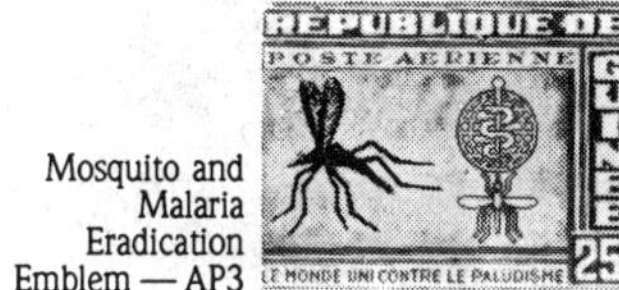

Mosquito and Malaria Eradication Emblem — AP3

1962, Apr. 7 **Engr.** *Perf. 10½*

C29 AP3 25fr orange & blk 25 15
C30 AP3 50fr car rose & blk 38 25
C31 AP3 100fr green & blk 70 45

WHO drive to eradicate malaria.

A souvenir sheet exists containing a 100fr green & sepia stamp, imperf. Sepia coat of arms in margin. Size: 102x76mm.

Musician Type of Regular Issue

Musical Instruments: 100fr, 200fr, Kora. 500fr, Balafon.

1962, June 15 **Photo.** *Perf. 13x13½*

C32 A26 100fr brt pink, dk car & Prus bl 50 40
C33 A26 200fr lt & dk ultra & car rose 1.00 60
C34 A26 500fr dl org, pur & Prus bl 3.25 2.00

Nos. C17-C20 Overprinted in Carmine, Orange or Black: "La Conquête De L'Espace"

Perf. 13½

1962, Nov. 15 **Unwmk.** **Engr.**

C35 AP2 40fr blue (C or O) 40 22
C36 AP2 50fr emer (C or O) 40 22
C37 AP2 100fr dk car rose (B) 65 45
C38 AP2 200fr rose red (B) 1.20 90

The conquest of space. Two types of overprint: Straight lines on 40fr and 50fr in carmine, 100fr (black). Curved lines on 40fr and 50fr in orange, 200fr (black).

Bird Type of Regular Issue

Birds: 100fr, Hornbill. 200fr, White spoonbill. 500fr, Bateleur eagle.

1962, Dec. **Photo.** *Perf. 13x13½*

C41 A30 100fr multicolored 90 40
C42 A30 200fr multicolored 1.50 70
C43 A30 500fr multicolored 3.50 2.00

Sports Type of Regular Issue, 1963

Designs: 100fr, Running. 200fr, Bicycling. 500fr, Single sculls.

1963, Mar. 16 *Perf. 14*

C44 A32 100fr dp rose, sep & grn 65 30
C45 A32 200fr ol bis, ultra & mag 1.50 70
C46 A32 500fr ocher, dk bl & red 3.00 2.00

Butterfly Type of Regular Issue, 1963

Various Butterflies.

1963, May 10 **Unwmk.** *Perf. 12*

C47 A33 100fr cit, dk brn & gray 65 30
C48 A33 200fr sal pink, blk & green 2.00 70
C49 A33 500fr multicolored 3.50 1.60

Red Cross Type of Regular Issue

1963, July 25 **Engr.** *Perf. 10½*

C50 A35 25fr black & car 25 15

Souvenir Sheet

Imperf

C51 A35 100fr green & car 1.50 1.50

Nos. C14-C15 Overprinted:

PREMIER SERVICE DIRECT
CONAKRY-NEW YORK
PAN AMERICAN
30, JUILLET 1963

Lithographed and Engraved

1963, Oct. 28 *Perf. 11½*

C52 AP1 100fr dp car, ultra & emer 1.10 70
C53 AP1 200fr emer, brn & lil 2.50 1.20

1st Pan American air service from Conakry to New York, July 30, 1963.

Fish Type of Regular Issue, 1964

Designs: 100fr, African lyretail. 300fr, Six-barred epiplatys.

1964, Feb. 15 **Litho.** *Perf. 14x13½*

C54 A36 100fr grn & multi 70 40
C55 A36 300fr brn & multi 2.00 1.00

Kennedy Type of Regular Issue, 1964

1964, Mar. 5 **Engr.** *Perf. 10½*

C56 A37 100fr multicolored 80 80

See note after No. 327.

Olympic Type of Regular Issue

Design: 100fr, Women's ice skating.

1964, May 15 **Photo.** *Perf. 13x12½*

C57 A39 100fr gold, brn org & ind 65 42

Nos. C44-C46 Overprinted in Carmine or Orange: "Jeux Olympiques Tokyo 1964" and Olympic Rings

1964, May 15 **Unwmk.** *Perf. 14*

C58 A32 100fr (C or O) 1.65 1.40
C59 A32 200fr (C or O) 2.50 2.00
C60 A32 500fr (C or O) 6.00 5.00

18th Olympic Games, Tokyo, Oct. 10-25.

Mrs. Roosevelt Type of Regular Issue, 1964

1964, June 1 **Engr.** *Perf. 10½*

C61 A40 50fr violet 40 25

Souvenir Sheets

Unisphere, "Rocket Thrower" and Guinea Pavilion AP4

1964, Oct. 26 **Engr.** *Imperf.*

C62 AP4 100fr dk bl & org 00 00
C63 AP4 200fr rose red & emer 1.90 1.90

NY World's Fair, 1964-65. See Nos. C69-C70.

Nubian Monuments Type of Regular Issue, 1964

Design: 300fr, Queen Nefertari, Abu Simbel.

1964, Nov. 19 **Photo.** *Perf. 12*

C64 A42 300fr gold, dl red brn & sal 1.90 1.10

For overprint see No. C82.

Japanese Hostess, Plane and Map of Africa — AP5

1965, Jan. 18 *Perf. 12½x13*

C65 AP5 100fr gold, blk & red lil 1.00 35

18th Olympic Games, Tokyo, Oct. 10-25, 1964. Two multicolored souvenir sheets (200fr vert. and 300fr horiz.) exist, showing different views of Mt. Fuji. Sizes: 86x119mm, 119x86mm.

For overprint see No. C81.

Mask Type of Regular Issue

Design: 300fr, Niamou mask from N'Zérékoré.

1965, Feb. 15 **Photo.** *Perf. 14*

C68 A44 300fr multicolored 2.25 90

World's Fair Type of 1964

Souvenir Sheets

1965, Mar. 24 **Engr.** *Imperf.*

C69 AP4 100fr green & brn 1.00 1.00
C70 AP4 200fr grn & car rose 2.00 2.00

Handicraft Type of Regular Issue

Handicrafts: 100fr, Cabinetmaker. 300fr, Ivory carver.

1965, May 1 **Photo.** *Perf. 14*

C71 A45 100fr multicolored 60 35
C72 A45 300fr multicolored 2.00 80

ITU Type of Regular Issue, 1965

1965, May 17 **Unwmk.**

C73 A46 100fr multicolored 65 30
C74 A46 200fr multicolored 1.60 50

Exist imperf.

ICY Type of Regular Issue, 1965

1965, Sept. 8 **Engr.** *Perf. 10½*

C75 A50 100fr bl & yel org 80 35

West Facade, Polytechnic Institute — AP6

Design: 200fr, North facade.

1965, Oct. 2 **Photo.** *Perf. 13½*

C76 AP6 200fr gold & multi 1.50 80
C77 AP6 500fr gold & multi 4.25 2.00

Seventh anniversary of independence.

For overprints see Nos. C84-C85.

Moon Type of 1965

Designs: 100fr, Ranger VII approaching moon, vert. 200fr, Launching of Ranger VII, Cape Kennedy, vert.

1965, Nov. 15 **Litho.** *Perf. 13½x14*

C78 A52 100fr rose red, yel & dk brown 65 30
C79 A52 200fr multicolored 1.60 60

For overprints and surcharge see Nos. C112-C112B.

Dancer Type of Regular Issue, 1966

Design: 100fr, Kouyate Kandia, national singer, horiz.

1966, Jan. 5 **Photo.** *Perf. 13½*

Size: 36x28½mm

C80 A53 100fr multicolored 70 35

Engraved Overprint on No. C65

1966, Mar. 14 Photo. *Perf. 12½x13*
C81 AP5 100fr gold, blk & red lil 80 38

Fourth Pan Arab Games, Cairo, Sept. 2-11, 1965. The same overprint was applied to two souvenir sheets noted after No. C65 (red ovpt. on 200fr, black ovpt. on 300fr).

Engraved Dark Blue Overprint on No. C64: "CENTENAIRE DU TIMBRE / CAIRE 1966"

1966, Mar. 14 *Perf. 12*
C82 A42 300fr gold, dl red brn & sal 2.00 1.20

Centenary of first Egyptian postage stamp.

Scenic Type of Regular Issue

View: Boulbinet Lighthouse.

1966, Apr. 4 *Perf. 13½*
C83 A54 100fr multicolored 70 35

See Nos. C90-C91. For overprints see Nos. C93-C95.

Nos. C76-C77 Overprinted in Blue or Yellow

1966, May 2 Photo. *Perf. 13½*
C84 AP6 200fr multi (Bl) 1.40 90
C85 AP6 500fr multi (Y) 3.25 2.00

UNESCO, 20th anniv.

Woman-Flower Type of Regular Issue

Designs: Women and flowers of Guinea.

1966, May 30 Photo. *Perf. 13½*
Size: 28x34mm
C86 A56 200fr multicolored 1.60 60
C87 A56 300fr multicolored 2.50 1.10

Snake Type of Regular Issue

Designs: 200fr, Pastoria Research Institute. 300fr, Men holding rock python.

1967, May 15 Litho. *Perf. 13½*
Size: 56x20mm
C88 A61 200fr multicolored 1.40 70
a. Souv. sheet of 3, #471, 474, C88 4.00 3.50
C89 A61 300fr multicolored 2.25 1.10

Scenic Type of Regular Issue

Views: 100fr, House of explorer Olivier de Sanderval. 200fr, Conakry.

1967, June 20 Photo. *Perf. 13½*
C90 A54 100fr multicolored 60 40
C91 A54 200fr multicolored 1.40 70

For overprints see Nos. C94-C95.

Elephant Type of Regular Issue, 1967

1967, Sept. 28 Photo. *Perf. 13½*
C92 A63 200fr gold & multi 1.40 65

Nos. C83 and C90-C91 Overprinted with Lions Emblem and: "AMITIE DES PEUPLES GRACE AU TOURISME 1917-1967"

1967, Nov. 6
C93 A54 100fr multi (#C83) 80 40
C94 A54 100fr multi (#C90) 80 40
C95 A54 200fr multi (#C91) 1.50 70

50th anniversary of Lions International.

Detail from Mural by José Vela Zanetti — AP7

Family, Mural by Per Krohg — AP8

The designs of the 30fr, 50fr and 200fr show mankind's struggle for a lasting peace after the mural in the lobby of the UN Conference Building, NY. The designs of the 100fr and of Nos. C98a-C98b show mankind's hope for the future after a mural in the UN Security Council Chamber.

1967, Nov. 11
C96 AP7 30fr multicolored 22 15
C97 AP7 50fr multicolored 30 15
C98 AP8 100fr multicolored 65 30
a. Souv. sheet of 3, English inscription 1.50 1.50
b. Souv. sheet of 3, French inscription 1.50 1.50
C99 AP7 200fr multi 1.40 45

Nos. C98a and C98b each contain a 100fr stamp similar to No. C98 and two 50fr stamps showing festival scenes. The 50fr stamps have not been issued individually.

People and Dwellings Type of Regular Issue

Design: 300fr, People and village of Les Bassari, Kundara Region.

1968, Apr. 1 Photo. *Perf. 14x13½*
Size: 57x36mm
C100 A66 300fr gold & multi 2.00 80

Legends Type of Regular Issue

Designs: 70fr, The Girl and the Hippopotamus. 100fr, Old Faya's Inheritance, vert. 200fr, Soumangourou Kante Killed by Djegue (woman on horseback). 300fr, Little Gouné, Son of the Lion, vert.

1968 Photo. *Perf. 13½*
C101 A67 70fr multicolored 50 15
C102 A67 100fr multicolored 80 20
C103 A67 200fr multicolored 1.60 38
a. Souv. sheet of 4 4.00 4.00
C104 A67 300fr multicolored 2.25 80

Issued in sheets of 10 plus 2 labels. No. C103a contains 4 imperf. stamps similar to Nos. 510-511 and C102-C103.;
For souvenir sheet see No. 509a.
Issue dates: May 16, Nos. C102-C103. Sept. 16, Nos. C101, C104.

African Animal Type of Regular Issue

1968, Nov. 25 Photo. *Perf. 13½*
Size: 49x35mm
C105 A68 100fr Lions 90 30
C106 A68 200fr Elephant 1.50 60

For souvenir sheet see No. 518a.

Robert F. Kennedy Type of Regular Issue, 1968

Portraits: 50fr, Senator Robert F. Kennedy. 100fr, Rev. Martin Luther King, Jr. 200fr, Pres. John F. Kennedy.

1968, Dec. 16
C107 A69 50fr yel & multi 35 15
C108 A69 100fr multicolored 70 20
C109 A69 200fr multicolored 1.60 45

The stamps are printed in sheets of 15 (3x5) containing 10 stamps and five green and gold center labels. Sheets come either with English or French inscriptions on label.

Olympic Type of Regular Issue

Designs (Sculpture and): 100fr, Gymnast on vaulting horse. 200fr, Gymnast on rings. 300fr, High jump.

1969, Feb. 1 Photo. *Perf. 13½*
C110 A71 100fr multicolored 65 25
C111 A71 200fr multicolored 1.40 40
C111A A71 300fr multicolored 2.25 60

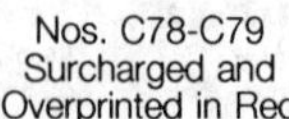
Nos. C78-C79 Surcharged and Overprinted in Red

1969, Mar. 17 Litho. *Perf. 13½x14*
C112 A52 25fr on 200fr multi 35 15
C112A A52 100fr multicolored 90 65
C112B A52 200fr multicolored 1.60 1.00

See note after No. 530.

Nos. C112-C112B also exist with surcharge and overprint in orange (25fr, 200fr) or black (100fr). These sell for a small premium.

Bird Type of Regular Issue

Birds: 50fr, Violet-crested touraco. 100fr, European golden oriole. 200fr, Vulturine guinea fowl.

1971, June 18 Photo. *Perf. 13*
Size: 41x41mm
C113 A81 50fr gold & multi 55 20
C113A A81 100fr gold & multi 80 30
C113B A81 200fr gold & multi 1.60 50

John and Robert Kennedy, Martin Luther King, Jr. — AP9

Embossed on Metallic Foil
1972 *Die Cut Perf. 10½*
C114 AP9 300fr silver

Embossed & Typo.
C114A AP9 1500fr gold, cream & green

Jules Verne, Moon Rocket — AP10

Embossed on Metallic Foil
1972 *Die Cut Perf. 10½*
C115 AP10 300fr silver
C115A AP10 1200fr gold

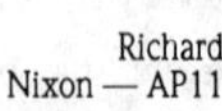
Richard Nixon — AP11

Nixon and Mao — AP12

Nixon's Trip to People's Republic of China: a, Nixon. b, Chinese table tennis player. c, American table tennis player, Capitol dome. d, Mao Tse-tung.

Embossed on Metallic Foil
1972 *Die Cut Perf. 10½*
C116 AP11 90fr Block of 4, #a.-d., silver
C117 AP11 290fr Block of 4, #a.-d., gold

Embossed & Typo.
C118 AP12 1200fr gold & red

Perforations within blocks of 4 are perf. 11.

Racial Equality Year Type of Regular Issue

Design: 100fr, Men of 4 races and racial equality emblem (like No. 603).

1972, May 14 Photo. *Perf. 13x13½*
C119 A84 100fr gold & multi 60 35

Satellite Type of Regular Issue

Designs: 100fr, Map of Africa and Relay. 200fr, Map of Africa and Early Bird.

1972, May 17 Litho. *Perf. 13*
C120 A85 100fr yel & multi 50 25
C121 A85 200fr multicolored 1.00 50

African Postal Union Type of Regular Issue

Designs: 100fr, 200fr, Air mail envelope and UPAF emblem.

1972, July 10
C122 A86 100fr multicolored 60 30
C123 A86 200fr multicolored 1.20 60

Olympic Type of Regular Issue

1972, Aug. 26 Photo. *Perf. 13*
C124 A88 100fr Gymnast on rings 65 30
C125 A88 200fr Bicycling 1.10 60

Souvenir Sheet
C126 A88 300fr Soccer 1.90 1.90

Flower Type of 1974

1974, May 20 Photo. *Perf. 13*
Size: 38x38mm (Diamond)
C127 A97 20s Thunbergia alata 90 45
C128 A97 25s Diascia barberae 1.10 60
C129 A97 50s Kigelia africana 2.25 1.20

Olympic Games Type of 1976
Souvenir Sheet

1976, May 17 Photo. *Perf. 13½*
C130 Sheet of 4 6.50 6.50
a. A104 25s Soccer 1.40 80

No. C130 contains 32x32mm stamps.

Mushroom Type of 1977

Mushrooms: 10s, Morchella esculenta. 12s, Lepiota procera. 15s, Cantharellus cibarius.

1977, Feb. 6 Photo. *Perf. 13*
Size: 48x31mm
C131 A106 10s multicolored 60 30
C132 A106 12s multicolored 65 38
C133 A106 15s multicolored 80 45

Reptile Type of 1977

Reptiles: 10s, Flap-necked chameleon. 15s, Nile crocodiles. 25s, Painted tortoise.

1977, Oct. 10 Photo. *Perf. 13½*
Size: 46x30mm
C134 A109 10s multicolored 65 40
C135 A109 15s multicolored 1.00 60
C136 A109 25s multicolored 1.60 1.00

Animal Type of 1977

Endangered Animals: 5s, Eland. 8s, Pygmy elephant. 9s, Hippopotamus. 10s, Chimpanzee. 12s, Palm squirrel. 13s, Lion. Male, female and young of each animal shown.

1977, Dec. 12 Photo. *Perf. 14x13½*

C137 A110	Strip of 3	1.05	60
a.-c.	5s any single	35	
C138 A110	Strip of 3	1.65	90
a.-c.	8s any single	55	
C139 A110	Strip of 3	1.80	1.10
a.-c.	9s any single	60	
C140 A110	Strip of 3	2.00	1.20
a.-c.	10s any single	65	
C141 A110	Strip of 3	2.40	1.40
a.-c.	12s any single	80	
C142 A110	Strip of 3	2.75	1.50
a.-c.	13s any single	90	
	Nos. C137-C142 (6)	11.65	6.70

Russian Revolution Type, 1978

Designs: 10s, Russian ballet. 30s, Pushkin Monument.

1978, Feb. 27 Photo. *Perf. 14*

C143 A111	10s gold & multi	65	40
C144 A111	30s gold & multi	2.00	1.20

Giscard d'Estaing Type of 1979

Design: Pres. Valery Giscard d'Estaing of France, vert.

1979, Sept. 14 Photo. *Perf. 13*

C145 A112	25s multicolored	1.60	1.00

Jules Verne Type of 1979

Designs: 20s, Five Weeks in a Balloon. 25s, Robur the Conqueror.

1979, Nov. 8 Litho. *Perf. 12x12½*

C146 A113	20s multicolored	1.40	80
C147 A113	25s multicolored	1.60	1.00

Olympic Type of 1982

1982 Litho. *Perf. 12½x12, 12x12½*

C148 A120	9s Fencing	60	38
C149 A120	10s Soccer, vert.	65	40
C150 A120	11s Basketball, vert.	70	42
C151 A120	20s Diving, vert.	1.40	80
C152 A120	25s Boxing, vert.	1.60	1.10

Ataturk Type of 1982

1982, July 19 Photo. *Perf. 13½*

C153 A122	25s like #830	1.60	1.00

World Cup Type of 1982

Designs: Various soccer players.

1982, Aug. 23

C154 A123	10s multicolored	65	40
C155 A123	20s multicolored	1.40	80
C156 A123	25s multicolored	1.60	1.00

Nos. C154-C156 Overprinted in Green "CHAMPION ITALIE - 11 JUILLET 1982"

1982, Aug. 23 Photo. *Perf. 13½*

C157 A123	10s multicolored	65	40
C158 A123	20s multicolored	1.40	80
C159 A123	25s multicolored	1.60	1.00

Balloon Type

Designs: 20s, Graf Zeppelin, Airship (horiz.). 25s, Double Eagle II, L. Newman, B. Abruzzo, M. Anderson. 30s, Le Geant Hot Air Balloon, Nadar; Dirigible, Dumont.

1983, Aug. 1 Litho. *Perf. 13½*

C160 A125	20s multicolored	1.40	80
C161 A125	25s multicolored	1.60	1.00

Souvenir Sheet

C162 A125	30s multicolored	2.00	1.20

Nos. 894, 880-881 and 896 Overprinted

1985, Nov. 5 Litho. *Perf. 13½*

C163 A133	20s "80e Anniversaire / 1905-1985"	1.10	60
C164 A131	20s "Rassemblement / Jambville-1985"	1.10	60
C165 A131	25s "80e Anniversaire / 1905 1985"	1.50	70

Souvenir Sheet

C166 A133	30s "Kasparov / champion / du Monde"	1.90	90

US Space Shuttle Challenger Explosion, Jan. 28, 1986 — AP13

Designs: 100fr, Lift-off, crew names. 170fr, Shuttle design, Christa McAuliffe holding shuttle model. 600fr, Lift-off, vert.

1986, July 1

100fr, 170fr Surcharged in Silver and Black

C167 AP13	100fr multicolored	55	28
C168 AP13	170fr multicolored	95	48

Souvenir Sheet

C169 AP13	600fr multicolored	3.30	1.65

#C167-C168 not issued without surcharge.

Souvenir sheets of one exist containing Nos. C167 and C168.

Robin Yount, Milwaukee Brewers Baseball Player — AP14

1990, Aug. 3 Litho. *Perf. 13½*

C170 AP14	450fr multicolored	3.45	1.75

No. C170 exists in a souvenir sheet of 1. For surcharge see No. 1182R.

Souvenir Sheet

Armstrong, Aldrin, Collins and Apollo 11 Emblem — AP15

1990, Aug. 3 Litho. *Perf. 13½*

C171 AP15	750fr multicolored	5.75	2.85

Galileo Spacecraft — AP16

1990, Aug. 3

C172 AP16	500fr multicolored	3.75	1.90

No. C172 exists as a souvenir sheet of 1.

POSTAGE DUE STAMPS

D5

D6

1959 Unwmk. Litho. *Perf. 11½*

J36 D5	1fr emerald	15	15
J37 D5	2fr lilac rose	15	15
J38 D5	3fr brown	15	15
J39 D5	5fr blue	16	16
J40 D5	10fr orange	60	60
J41 D5	20fr rose lilac	1.10	1.10
	Nos. J36-J41 (6)	2.31	2.31

1960 Engr. *Perf. 13½*

J42 D6	1fr dark carmine	15	15
J43 D6	2fr brown orange	15	15
J44 D6	3fr dark car rose	25	20
J45 D6	5fr bright green	45	40
J46 D6	10fr dark brown	90	65
J47 D6	20fr dull blue	1.90	1.50
	Nos. J42-J47 (6)	3.80	3.05

GUINEA-BISSAU

LOCATION — West coast of Africa between Senegal and Guinea
GOVT. — Republic
AREA — 13,948 sq. mi.
POP. — 844,000 (est. 1984)
CAPITAL — Bissau

Guinea-Bissau, the former Portuguese Guinea, attained independence on September 10, 1974. The state includes the Bissagos Islands.

100 Centavos = 1 Escudo
100 Centavos = 1 Peso

Catalogue values for all unused stamps in this country are for Never Hinged items.

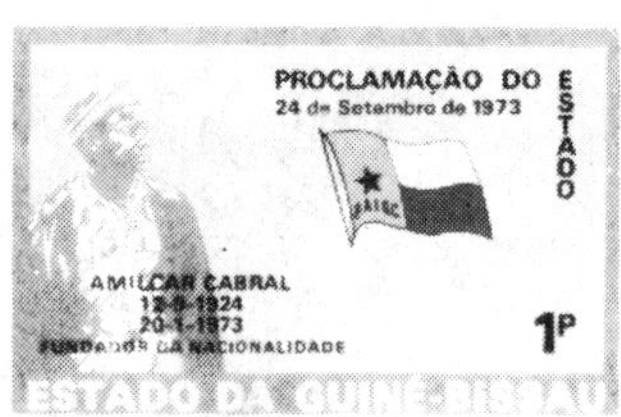

Amilcar Cabral, Map of Africa and Flag — A27

Design: Flag of the PAIGC (African Party of Independence of Guinea-Bissau and Cape Verde) shows location of Guinea-Bissau on map of Africa.

Perf. 11x10½

1974, Sept. 10 Litho. Unwmk.

345 A27	1p brn & multi	50	40
346 A27	2.50p brn & multi	70	60
347 A27	5p brn & multi	*16.00*	*8.00*
348 A27	10p brn & multi	1.90	1.50

First anniv. of Proclamation of Independence, Sept. 24, 1973.

WMO Emblem — A28

Portuguese Guinea No. 344 Overprinted in Black

1975 Litho. *Perf. 13*

349 A28	2c brown & multi	50	50

No. 349 exists with overprint in brown.

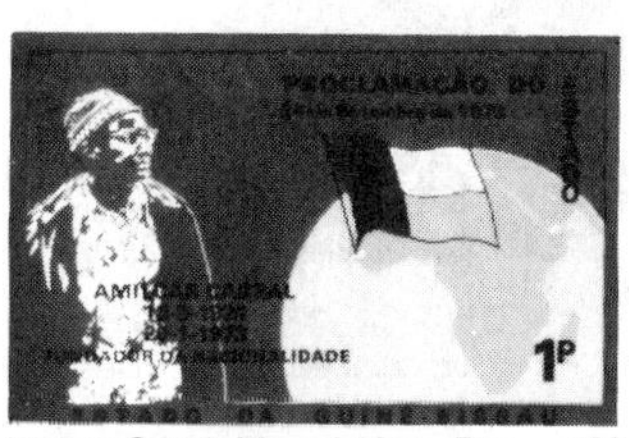

Amilcar Cabral, Map of Africa, Flag — A29

1975 Litho. *Perf. 11*

350 A29	1p brown & multi		
351 A29	2.50p brown & multi		
352 A29	5p brown & multi		
353 A29	10p brown & multi		
	Nos. 350-353 (4)	9.00	6.75

Flag and Arms of Guinea-Bissau and Amilcar Cabral — A30

Designs: (Flag, Arms and): 2e, No. 358, Family. 3e, 5e, Pres. Luiz Cabral. No. 359, like 1e.

1975, Sept. *Perf. 14*

354 A30	1e yel & multi	15	15
355 A30	2e multicolored	15	15
356 A30	3e red & multi	15	15
357 A30	5e yel & multi	20	15
358 A30	10e red & multi	38	25
359 A30	10e brt grn & multi	35	25
	Nos. 354-359 (6)	1.38	
	Set value		80

Amilcar Cabral's 51st birth anniv. (1e, No. 359); African Party of Independence of Guinea-Bissau and Cape Verde, 19th anniv. (2e, No. 358); Proclamation of Independence, 2nd anniv. (3e, 5e).

For surcharges see Nos. 367-367E.

Henry Knox, Cannons of Ticonderoga — A30a

Designs: 10e, Israel Putnam, Battle of Bunker Hill. 15e, Washington crossing the Delaware. 20e, Tadeusz Kosciuszko, Battle of Saratoga. 30e, Von Steuben, winter at Valley Forge. 40e, Lafayette, Washington rallying troops at Monmouth. 50e, Signing the Declaration of Independence.

1976, May 5 Litho. *Perf. 13½*

360	A30a	5e multicolored
360A	A30a	10e multicolored
360B	A30a	15e multicolored
360C	A30a	20e multicolored
360D	A30a	30e multicolored
360E	A30a	40e multicolored

Souvenir Sheet

360F	A30a	50e multicolored

American Revolution, bicentennial. Nos. 360D-360F are airmail. Nos. 360-360E exist in miniature sheets of 1, perf. and imperf. No. 360F contains one 75x45mm stamp and exists imperf.

See Nos. 371-371A.

2P00 PESOS

ESTADO DA GUINÉ-BISSAU

Masked Dancer A30b

1976, May 10 *Perf. 11*

Denomination in Black on Silver Block

361	A30b	2p shown
361A	A30b	3p Dancer, drummer
361B	A30b	5p Dancers on stilts
361C	A30b	10p Dancer with spear, bow
361D	A30b	15p Masked dancer, diff.

361E A30b 20p Dancer with striped cloak

Souvenir Sheet

361F A30b 50p Like No. 361E

Nos. 361C-361F are airmail. Silver block obliterates original denomination. Not issued without surcharge.

Nos. 361-361F Ovptd. in Black

1976, June 8 *Perf. 11*

362 A30b 2p on No. 361
362A A30b 3p on No. 361A
362B A30b 5p on No. 361B
362C A30b 10p on No. 361C
362D A30b 15p on No. 361D
362E A30b 20p on No. 361E

Souvenir Sheet

362F A30b 50p on No. 361F

Nos. 362C-362F are airmail. UPU cent. (in 1974). Nos. 362-362F exist perf. imperf. and Nos. 362-362E in imperf. miniature sheets of 1, all with black or red overprints.

Cabral, Guinean Mother and Children — A31

1976, Aug. **Litho.** *Perf. 13½*

363 A31	3p	multicolored	15	15
364 A31	5p	multicolored	18	15
365 A31	6p	multicolored	22	15
366 A31	10p	multicolored	38	20
		Set value		47

3rd anniv. of assassination of Amilcar Cabral (1924-1973), revolutionary leader.

Nos. 354-359 Surcharged in Black on Silver **1P00 PESOS**

1976, Sept. 12 **Litho.** *Perf. 14*

367 A30 1p on 1e No. 354
367A A30 2p on 2e No. 355
367B A30 3p on 3e No. 356
367C A30 5p on 5e No. 357
367D A30 10p on 10e No. 358
367E A30 10p on 10e No. 359

1876 Bell Telephone and Laying First Trans-Atlantic Cable — A31a

Telephones of: 3p, France, 1890, and first telephone booth, 1893. 5p, Germany, 1903, and automatic telephone, 1898. 10p, England, 1910, and relay station, 1963. 15p, France, 1924, and communications satellite. 20p, Modern telephone, 1970, and Molniya satellite. 50p, Picture phone.

1976, Oct. 18 *Perf. 13½*

368 A31a 2p multicolored
368A A31a 3p multicolored
368B A31a 5p multicolored
368C A31a 10p multicolored
368D A31a 15p multicolored
368E A31a 20p multicolored

Souvenir Sheet

368F A31a 50p multicolored

Nos. 368C-368F are airmail. No. 368F contains one 68x42mm stamp. No. 368F exists imperf. Nos. 368-368E exist in souvenir sheets of one, perf. and imperf.

1976 Winter Olympics, Innsbruck — A31b

1976, Nov. 3 *Perf. 14x13½*

369 A31b 1p Women's figure skating
369A A31b 3p Ice hockey
369B A31b 5p Two-man bobsled
369C A31b 10p Pairs figure skating
369D A31b 20p Cross country skiing
369E A31b 30p Speed skating

Souvenir Sheet

369F A31b 50p Downhill skiing

Nos. 369C-369F are airmail. No. 369F exists imperf. Nos. 369-369E exist in souvenir sheets of one, perf. and imperf.

1976 Summer Olympics, Montreal A31c

1976, Nov. 24 *Perf. 13½*

370 A31c 1p Soccer
370A A31c 3p Pole vault
370B A31c 5p Women's hurdles
370C A31c 10p Discus
370D A31c 20p Sprinting
370E A31c 30p Wrestling

Souvenir Sheet

370F A31c 50p Cycling, horiz.

Nos. 370E-370F are airmail. No. 370F contains one 47x38mm stamp. No. 370F exists imperf. Nos. 370-370E exist in souvenir sheets of one, perf. and imperf.

American Revolution Type of 1976

Designs: 3.50p, Crispus Attucks, Boston Massacre. 5p, Martin Luther King, US Capitol.

1977, Jan. 27 *Perf. 13½*

Denomination in Black on Gold Block

371 A30a 3.50p multicolored
371A A30a 5p multicolored

Gold block obliterates original denomination. Not issued without surcharge. Exist in souvenir sheets of one, perf. and imperf.

Cabral Addressing UN General Assembly A32

Design: 50c, Cabral and guerrilla fighters.

1977, July **Litho.** *Perf. 13½*

372 A32	50c	multicolored	15	15
373 A32	3.50p	multicolored	30	15
		Set value		15

For surcharges see Nos. C12-C13.

Henri Dunant, Nobel Peace Prize, 1901 A32a

Nobel Prize Winners: 5p, Einstein, Physics, 1921. 6p, Irene and Frederic Joliot-Curie, Chemistry, 1935. 30p, Fleming, Medicine, 1945. 35p, Hemingway, Literature, 1954. 40p, J. Tinbergen, Economics, 1969. 50p, Nobel Prize Medal.

1977, July 27

374 A32a 3.50p multicolored
374A A32a 5p multicolored
374B A32a 6p multicolored
374C A32a 30p multicolored
374D A32a 35p multicolored
374E A32a 40p multicolored

Souvenir Sheet

374F A32a 50p multicolored

Nos. 374D-374F are airmail. No. 374F contains one 57x39mm stamp. No. 374F exists imperf. Nos. 374-374E exist in souvenir sheets of one, perf. and imperf.

Postal Runner, Telstar Satellite — A32b

UPU Centenary (in 1974): 5p, Biplane, satellites encircle globe. 6p, Mail truck, satelite control room. 30p, Stagecoach, astronaut canceling letters on Moon. 35p, Steam locomotive, communications satellite. 40p, Space shuttle, Apollo-Soyuz link-up. 50p, Semaphore signalling system, satellite dish.

1977, Sept. 30

375 A32b 3.50p multicolored
375A A32b 5p multicolored
375B A32b 6p multicolored
375C A32b 30p multicolored
375D A32b 35p multicolored
375E A32b 40p multicolored

Souvenir Sheet

375F A32b 50p multicolored

Nos. 375D-375F are airmail. No. 375F exists imperf. Nos. 375-375E exist in souvenir sheets of one, perf. and imperf.

Torch and Party Emblem — A33

1977, Sept. **Litho.** *Perf. 14*

376 A33	3p	yel & multi	15	15
377 A33	15p	sal & multi	60	40
378 A33	50p	lt grn & multi	1.50	1.00

African Party of Independence of Guinea-Bissau and Cape Verde, 20th anniversary.

Queen Elizabeth II, Silver Jubilee — A33a

Designs: 5p, Coronation ceremony. 10p, Yeoman of the Guard, Crown Jewels. 20p, Trumpeter. 25p, Royal Horse Guard. 30p, Royal Family. 50p, Queen Elizabeth II.

1977, Oct. 15

379 A33a 3.50p multicolored
379A A33a 5p multicolored
379B A33a 10p multicolored
379C A33a 20p multicolored
379D A33a 25p multicolored
379E A33a 30p multicolored

Souvenir Sheet

379F A33a 50p multicolored

Nos. 379D-379F are airmail. No. 379F contains one 42x39mm stamp. No. 379F exists imperf. Nos. 379-379E exist in souvenir sheets of one, perf. and imperf.

Massacre of the Innocents by Rubens — A33b

Paintings by Peter Paul Rubens: 5p, Rape of the Daughters of Leukippos. 6p, Lamentation of Christ, horiz. 30p, Francisco IV Gonzaga, Prince of Mantua. 35p, The Four Continents. 40p, Marquise Brigida Spinola Doria. 50p, The Wounding of Christ.

1977, Nov. 15

380 A33b 3.50p multicolored
380A A33b 5p multicolored
380B A33b 6p multicolored
380C A33b 30p multicolored
380D A33b 35p multicolored
380E A33b 40p multicolored

Souvenir Sheet

380F A33b 50p multicolored

Nos. 380D-380F are airmail. Nos. 380-380F exist imperf. Nos. 380-380E exist in souvenir sheets of one, perf. and imperf.

Congress Emblem — A34

1977, Nov. 15 **Litho.** *Perf. 14*

381 A34	3.50p	multicolored	15	15

3rd PAIGC Congress, Bissau, Nov. 15-20.

Santos-Dumont's Airship, 1901 — A34a

Airships: 5p, R-34 crossing the Atlantic, 1919. 10p, Norge over North Pole, 1926. 20p, Graf Zeppelin over Abu Simbel, 1931. 25p, Hindenburg over New York, 1937. 30p, Graf Zeppelin, Concorde, space shuttle. 50p, Ferdinand von Zeppelin, horiz.

1978, Feb. 27

382	A34a	3.50p	multicolored
382A	A34a	5p	multicolored
382B	A34a	10p	multicolored
382C	A34a	20p	multicolored
382D	A34a	25p	multicolored
382E	A34a	30p	multicolored

Souvenir Sheet

382F A34a 50p multicolored

Nos. 382D-382F are airmail. No. 382F exists imperf. Nos. 382-382E exist in souvenir sheets of one, perf. and imperf.

World Cup Soccer Championships, Argentina — A34b

Soccer players and posters from previous World Cup Championships: 3.50p, 1930. 5p, 1938. 10p, 1950. 20p, 1962. 25p, 1970. 30p, 1974. 50p, Argentina '78 emblem.

1978, Mar. 15

383	A34b	3.50p	multicolored
383A	A34b	5p	multicolored
383B	A34b	10p	multicolored
383C	A34b	20p	multicolored
383D	A34b	25p	multicolored
383E	A34b	30p	multicolored

Souvenir Sheet

383F A34b 50p multicolored

Nos. 383D-383F are airmail. Nos. 383-383F exist imperf. Nos. 383-383E exist in miniature sheets of one, perf. and imperf.

For surcharges see Nos. 393-393F.

Endangered Species A34c

1978, Apr. 17

384	A34c	3.50p	Black antelope
384A	A34c	5p	Fennec
384B	A34c	6p	Secretary bird
384C	A34c	30p	Hippopotami
384D	A34c	35p	Cheetahs
384E	A34c	40p	Gorillas

Souvenir Sheet

384F A34c 50p Cercopithecus erythotis

Nos. 384D-384F are airmail. No. 384F contains one 39x42mm stamp. No. 384F exists imperf. Nos. 384-384E exist in souvenir sheets of one, perf. and imperf.

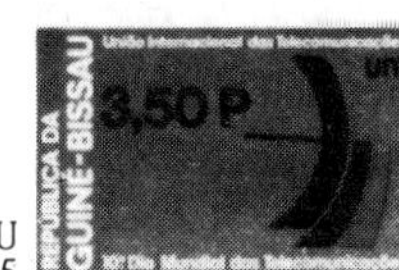

Antenna, ITU Emblem — A35

1978, May 17 Litho. *Perf. 13½*

385	A35	3.50p	silver & multi	15	15
386	A35	10p	gold & multi	42	25

10th World Telecommunications Day.

Boy — A36

Designs: 3p, Infant and grandfather. 5p, Boys. 30p, Girls.

1978 *Perf. 14*

387	A36	50c	yel grn & dk bl	15	15
388	A36	3p	cl & car rose	15	15
389	A36	5p	ocher & brown	20	15
390	A36	30p	car & ocher	1.10	65
			Set value		90

Children's Day.

Queen Elizabeth II, Silver Jubilee A36a

Elizabeth, Imperial State Crown — A36b

Designs: 5p, Queen, Prince Philip in Coronation Coach. 10p, Queen, Prince Philip. 20p, Mounted drummer. 25p, Imperial State Crown, St. Edward's Crown. 30p, Queen holding orb and scepter. 50p, Queen on Throne flanked by Archbishops. No. 391H, Coronation Coach.

1978, June 15

391	A36a	3.50p	multicolored
391A	A36a	5p	multicolored
391B	A36a	10p	multicolored
391C	A36a	20p	multicolored
391D	A36a	25p	multicolored
391E	A36a	30p	multicolored

Litho. & Embossed

391F A36b 100p gold & multi

Souvenir Sheets

391G A36a 50p multicolored

Litho. & Embossed

391H A36b 100p gold & multi

Nos. 391D-391H are airmail. Nos. 391-391E exist in souvenir sheets of one, perf. and imperf. Nos. 391F-391H exist imperf.

History of Aviation — A36c

1978, June 15 Litho. *Perf. 13½*

392	A36c	3.50p	Wright Brothers
392A	A36c	10p	Santos-Dumont
392B	A36c	15p	Bleriot
392C	A36c	20p	Lindbergh, Spirit of St. Louis
392D	A36c	25p	Lunar module
392E	A36c	30p	Space shuttle

Souvenir Sheet

392F A36c 50p Concorde

Nos. 392D-392F are airmail. Nos. 392-392E exist in souvenir sheets of one, perf. and imperf. No. 392F exists imperf.

Nos. 383-383F Ovptd. in Gold

1º ARGENTINA
2º HOLANDA
3º BRASIL

1978, Oct. 2

393	A34b	3.50p	on No. 383
393A	A34b	5p	on No. 383A
393B	A34b	10p	on No. 383B
393C	A34b	20p	on No. 383C
393D	A34b	25p	on No. 383D
393E	A34b	30p	on No. 383E

Souvenir Sheet

393F A34b 50p on No. 383F

Nos. 393D-393F are airmail. Nos. 393-393F exist imperf. Nos. 393-393E exist in miniature sheets of 1 perf. and imperf. No. 393F exists overprinted in silver.

Virgin and Child by Albrecht Durer — A36d

Different Paintings of the Virgin and Child (Virgin only on 30p) by Durer.

1978, Nov. 14

394	A36d	3.50p	multicolored
394A	A36d	5p	multicolored
394B	A36d	6p	multicolored
394C	A36d	30p	multicolored
394D	A36d	35p	multicolored
394E	A36d	40p	multicolored

Souvenir Sheet

394F A36d 50p multicolored

Nos. 394D-394F are airmail. No. 394F contains one 51x56mm stamp. Nos. 394-394E exist in souvenir sheets of one, perf. and imperf. No. 394F exists imperf.

Sir Rowland Hill (1795-1879), Wurttemberg No. 53 — A36e

Hill and: 5p, Belgium #1. 6p, Monaco #10. 30p, Spain 2r stamp of 1851 in blue. 35p, Switzerland #5. 40p, Naples #8. 50p, Portuguese Guinea #13 in brown.

1978, Dec. 15

395	A36e	3.50p	multicolored
395A	A36e	5p	multicolored
395B	A36e	6p	multicolored
395C	A36e	30p	multicolored
395D	A36e	35p	multicolored
395E	A36e	40p	multicolored

Souvenir Sheet

395F A36e 50p multicolored

Nos. 395D-395F are airmail. No. 395F contains one 51x42mm stamp. Nos. 395-395E exist in souvenir sheets of one, perf. and imperf. No. 395F exists imperf.

Intl. Day of the Child A36f

1979, Jan. 15 *Perf. 14*

396	A36f	3.50p	shown
396A	A36f	10p	Children drinking
396B	A36f	15p	Child with book
396C	A36f	20p	Space plane
396D	A36f	25p	Skylab
396E	A36f	30p	Children playing chess

Souvenir Sheet

396F A36f 50p Children watching spaceship

Nos. 396C-396F are airmail. Nos. 396-396E exist in souvenir sheets of one, perf. and imperf. No. 396F exists imperf.

A36g A36h

1979 Litho. *Perf. 13*

397 A36g 4.50p multicolored

Massacre of Pindjiguiti, 20th anniv.

1979 Litho. *Perf. 14*

397A	A36h	50c	shown	16
397B	A36h	4p	People, rainbow, diff.	1.35

World Telecommunications Day.

Family — A37

1979, May Litho. *Perf. 12x11½*

398	A37	50c	multicolored	15	15
399	A37	2p	multicolored	15	15
400	A37	4p	multicolored	20	15
			Set value	35	28

General population census, Apr. 16-30.

Ernst Udet and Fokker D.VII — A38

1980 Litho. *Perf. 13½*

401	A38	3.50p	shown	15	15
401A	A38	5p	Charles Nungesser, Nieuport 17	20	15
401B	A38	6p	von Richthofen, Fokker DR.1	25	20
401C	A38	30p	Francesco Baracca, Spad XIII	1.00	55
			Nos. 401-401C,C14-C14A (6)	4.35	2.35

Lake Placid Emblem, Speed Skating
A39

1980

402 A39 3.50p shown 15 15
402A A39 5p Downhill skiing 20 15
402B A39 6p Luge 25 20
402C A39 30p Cross-country skiing 1.00 55
Nos. 402-402C,C15-C16 (6) 4.35 2.35

13th Winter Olympic Games, Lake Placid, NY, Feb. 12-24.

Shot-put
A40

1980, Aug. Litho. *Perf. 13½*

403 A40 3.50p shown 15 15
403A A40 5p Athlete on rings 20 15
403B A40 6p Running 25 20
403C A40 30p Fencing 1.00 55
Nos. 403-403C,C18-C19 (6) 4.35 2.35

22nd Summer Olympic Games, Moscow, July 19-Aug. 3.

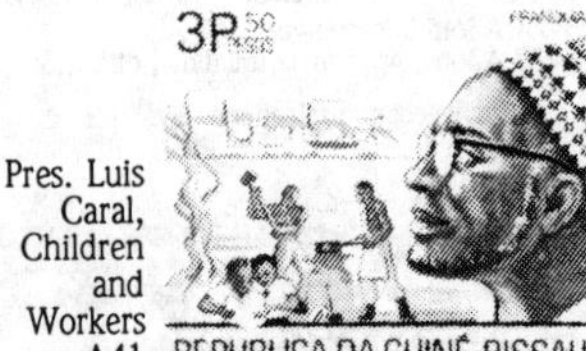

Pres. Luis Caral, Children and Workers
A41

Literacy Campaign: 5p, Pres. Caral holding books.

1980, Aug. Litho. *Perf. 13½*

404 A41 3.50p multicolored 15 15
405 A41 5p multicolored 25 15
Set value 20

See Nos. C21-C22.

Cooperation Among Developing Countries
A42

1980, Aug.

406 A42 3.50p multicolored 15 15
407 A42 6p multicolored 18 15
408 A42 10p multicolored 38 20
Set value 35

Baskets — A43

1980, Aug. Litho. *Perf. 13½*

409 A43 3p Bird, family wood statues, vert. 15 15
410 A43 6p shown 20 15
411 A43 20p Head, doll carvings 70 40
Set value 55

Infant and Toy Train, Locomotive, IYC Emblem — A44

1980

412 A44 6p Classroom, horiz. 25 20
412A A44 10p Boy reading Jules Verne story 38 30
412B A44 25p shown 90 50
412C A44 35p Archer, boy with bow 1.40 70

Souvenir Sheet

412D A44 50p Students in lab 2.00 1.00

International Year of the Child (1979).

Columbia Space Shuttle and Crew — A45

Space Exploration: 3.50p, Galileo, satellites. 5p, Wernher von Braun. 6p, Jules Verne, rocket.

1981, May Litho. *Perf. 13½*

413 A45 3.50p multicolored 20 15
413A A45 5p multicolored 25 15
413B A45 6p multicolored 30 18
413C A45 30p multicolored 1.50 80
Nos. 413-413C,C23-C24 (6) 5.00 2.58

Soccer Players, World Cup, Argentina '78 and Espana '82 Emblems — A46

Soccer scenes and famous players: 3.50p, Platini, France. 5p, Bettega, Italy. 6p, Rensenbrink, Netherlands. 30p, Rivelino, Brazil.

1981, May

414 A46 3.50p multicolored 20 15
414A A46 5p multicolored 25 15
414B A46 6p multicolored 30 18
414C A46 30p multicolored 1.50 60
Nos. 414-414C,C26-C27 (6) 5.00 2.38

Prince Charles and Lady Diana, St. Paul's Cathedral
A47

Royal Wedding (Couple and): 3.50p, Diana leading horse. 5p, Charles crowned Prince of Wales. 6p, Diana with kindergarten children.

1981 Litho. *Perf. 13½*

415 A47 3.50p multicolored 20 15
415A A47 5p multicolored 25 15
415B A47 6p multicolored 30 18
415C A47 30p multicolored 1.50 80
Nos. 415-415C,C29-C30 (6) 6.15 3.53

Woman Before a Mirror, by Picasso (1881-1973)
A48

Picasso Birth Cent.: Various paintings.

1981, Dec. Litho. *Perf. 13½*

416 A48 3.50p multi 20 15
417 A48 5p multi 25 15
418 A48 6p multi 30 18
419 A48 30p multi 1.50 80
Nos. 416-419,C32-C33 (6) 6.15 3.53

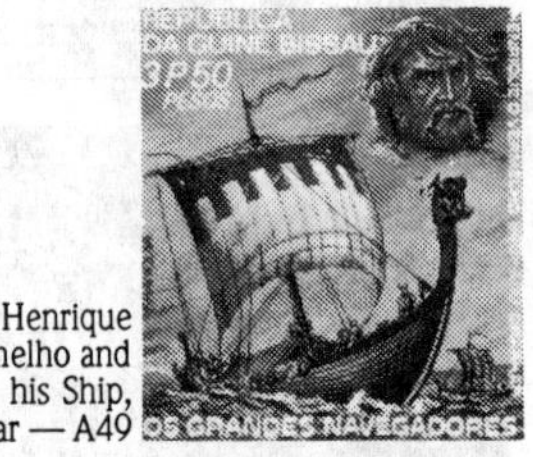

Henrique Vermelho and his Ship, Drakkar — A49

Navigators and their ships: 5p, Vasco de Gama, St. Gabriel. 6p, Ferdinand Magellan, Victoria. 30p, Jacques Cartier, Emerillon.

1981 Litho. *Perf. 13½*

420 A49 3.50p multicolored 20 15
421 A49 5p multicolored 25 15
422 A49 6p multicolored 30 18
423 A49 30p multicolored 1.50 80
Nos. 420-423,C35-C36 (6) 6.15 3.53

Christmas — A50

Designs: Virgin and Child paintings.

1981

424 A50 3.50p Mantegna 20 15
425 A50 5p Bellini 25 15
426 A50 6p Mantegna, diff. 30 18
427 A50 25p Correggio 1.50 80
Nos. 424-427,C38-C39 (6) 6.15 3.53

Scouting Year — A51

1982, June 9 Litho. *Perf. 13½*

428 A51 3.50p Archery 15 15
429 A51 5p First aid training 20 15
430 A51 6p Bugler 25 15
431 A51 30p Cub scouts 1.40 60
Nos. 428-431,C41-C42 (6) 5.40 2.75

1982 World Cup — A52

Various soccer players and cup.

1982, June 13 Litho. *Perf. 13½*

432 A52 3.50p Keegan 15 15
433 A52 5p Rossi 20 15
434 A52 6p Zico 25 15
435 A52 30p Arconada 1.40 60
Nos. 432-435,C44-C45 (6) 5.40 2.75

21st Birthday of Princess Diana — A53

Portraits and scenes of Diana.

1982

436 A53 3.50p multicolored 15 15
437 A53 5p multicolored 20 15
438 A53 6p multicolored 25 15
439 A53 30p multicolored 1.40 60
Nos. 436-439,C47-C48 (6) 5.40 2.75

For overprints see Nos. 450-456.

Manned Flight Bicentenary
A55

Various hot air balloons.

1983, Jan. 15 Litho. *Perf. 11*

442 A55 50c multicolored 15 15
443 A55 2.50p multicolored 15 15
444 A55 3.50p multicolored 18 15
445 A55 5p multicolored 22 15
446 A55 10p multicolored 45 22
447 A55 20p multicolored 1.00 40
448 A55 30p multicolored 1.50 60
Nos. 442-448 (7) 3.65
Set value 1.50

Souvenir Sheet

Perf. 12½

449 A55 50p multicolored 2.50 1.25

No. 449 contains one 47x47mm stamp.

Nos. 436-439, C47-C48, C49A-C49B Overprinted: "21 DE JULHO . GUILHERMO ARTUR FILIPE LUIS PRINCIPE DE GALES"

1982 Litho. *Perf. 13½*

450 A53 3.50p multicolored 15 15
451 A53 5p multicolored 22 15
452 A53 6p multicolored 25 15
453 A53 30p multicolored 1.40 65
454 A53 35p multicolored 1.60 80
455 A53 40p multicolored 1.90 1.00
Nos. 450-455 (6) 5.52 2.90

Souvenir Sheet

456 A53 50p multicolored 2.75 1.20

Litho. & Embossed

456A A53a 200p gold & multi

Souvenir Sheet

456B A53a 200p gold & multi, vert.

Nos. 454-456A are airmail.

African Apes and Monkeys — A56

1983, Mar. 15 Litho. *Perf. 13½*

457 A56	1p	Comopithecus hamadryas	15	15
458 A56	1.50p	Gorilla gorilla	15	15
459 A56	3.50p	Theropithecus gelada	18	15
460 A56	5p	Mandrillus sphinx	25	15
461 A56	8p	Pan trogladytes	42	20
462 A56	20p	Colobus abyssinicus	1.10	50
463 A56	30p	Cercopithecus diana	1.60	70
		Nos. 457-463 (7)	3.85	
		Set value		1.70

Souvenir Sheet

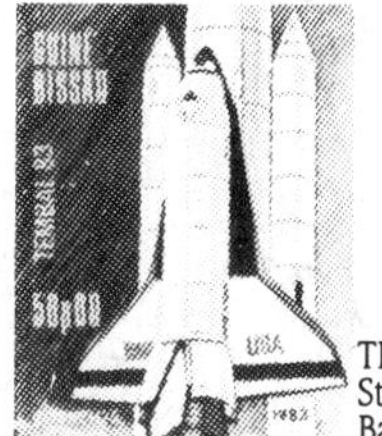

TEMBAL '83, Stamp Exhibition, Basel — A57

1983, May 21

464 A57 50p Space shuttle 2.00 1.25

A58

Designs: Various telecommunications satellites and space shuttles.

1983, May 25 Litho. *Perf. 13½*

465 A58	1p	multicolored	15	15
466 A58	1.50p	multicolored	15	15
467 A58	3.50p	multicolored	18	15
468 A58	5p	multicolored	25	15
469 A58	8p	multicolored	42	20
470 A58	20p	multicolored	1.00	42
471 A58	30p	multicolored	1.50	65
		Nos. 465-471 (7)	3.65	
		Set value		1.55

Souvenir Sheet

472 A58 50p multicolored 2.50 1.25

History of Chess — A59

Early Chess Game — A60

Various chess pieces.

1983, June 13 Litho. *Perf. 12*

473 A59	1p	multicolored	15	15
474 A59	1.50p	multicolored	15	15
475 A59	3.50p	multicolored	15	15
476 A59	5p	multicolored	25	15
477 A59	10p	multicolored	55	25
478 A59	20p	multicolored	1.10	50
479 A59	40p	multicolored	2.25	1.00
		Nos. 473-479 (7)	4.60	
		Set value		2.00

Souvenir Sheet

480 A60 50p brown & blk 2.50 1.25

Raphael, 500th Birth Anniv. — A61

Various paintings.

1983, June 30 Litho. *Perf. 12½*

481 A61	1p	gold & multi	15	15
482 A61	1.50p	gold & multi	15	15
483 A61	3.50p	gold & multi	18	15
484 A61	5p	gold & multi	25	15
485 A61	8p	gold & multi	42	22
486 A61	15p	gold & multi	90	40
487 A61	30p	gold & multi	1.60	65
		Nos. 481-487 (7)	3.65	
		Set value		1.50

Souvenir Sheet

488 A61 50p gold & multi 2.50 1.20

1984 Summer Olympics, Los Angeles — A62

1983, July 20 Litho. *Perf. 12½*

489 A62	1p	Swimming	15	15
490 A62	1.50p	Jumping	15	15
491 A62	3.50p	Fencing	15	15
492 A62	5p	Weightlifting	22	15
493 A62	10p	Running	50	22
494 A62	20p	Equestrian	1.00	50
495 A62	40p	Bicycling	2.00	1.00
		Nos. 489-495 (7)	4.17	
		Set value		2.00

Souvenir Sheet

496 A62 50p Stadium 2.50 1.25

Souvenir Sheet

BRASILIANA '83, Philatelic Exhibition — A63

1983, July 29 Litho. *Perf. 13*

497 A63 50p multicolored 2.50 1.25

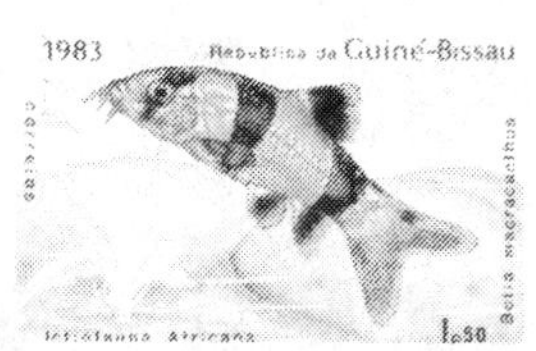

Local Fish A64

Perf. 12x11½, 11½x12

1983, Dec. 8 Litho.

498 A64	1p	Monodactylus sebae, vert.	15	15
499 A64	1.50p	Botia macracanthus	15	15
500 A64	3.50p	Ctenopoma acutirostre	18	15
501 A64	5p	Roloffia bertholdi	25	15
502 A64	8p	Aphyosemion bualanum	42	20
503 A64	10p	Aphyosemion bivittatum	62	30
504 A64	30p	Aphyosemion australe	1.90	90
		Nos. 498-504 (7)	3.67	
		Set value		1.75

1984 Winter Olympics, Sarajevo — A65

1983, Oct. 10 Litho. *Perf. 13*

505 A65	1p	Speed skating	15	15
506 A65	1.50p	Ski jumping	15	15
507 A65	3p	Biathlon	15	15
508 A65	5p	Bobsledding	18	15
509 A65	10p	Hockey	32	18
510 A65	15p	Figure skating	60	30
511 A65	20p	Luge	75	38
		Nos. 505-511 (7)	2.30	
		Set value		1.10

Souvenir Sheet

512 A65 50p Downhill skiing 2.50 1.25

No. 512 contains one 31x40mm stamp.

A66 A67

1983, Nov. 7 *Perf. 12½*

513 A66	4.50p	Emblem	15	15
514 A66	7.50p	Woman, flag	20	15
515 A66	9p	Sewing	25	15
516 A66	12p	Farm workers	32	15
		Set value		42

First anniv. of Women's Federation.

1983, Nov. 12 Litho. *Perf. 13*

Designs: Local flowers.

517 A67	1p	Canna coccinea	15	15
518 A67	1.50p	Bouganville litoralis	15	15
519 A67	3.50p	Euphorbia milii	18	15
520 A67	5p	Delonix regia	25	15
521 A67	8p	Bauhinia variegata	40	20
522 A67	10p	Spathodea campanulata	55	20
523 A67	30p	Hibiscus rosa sinensis	1.50	70
		Nos. 517-523 (7)	3.18	
		Set value		1.40

JAAC Congress, Sept. 8-12 A68

1983, Sept. 1 Litho. *Perf. 13*

524 A68	4p	shown	15	15
524A A68	5p	Emblem	15	15
		Set value		22

World Food Day A69

1983, Oct. 16 Litho. *Perf. 12½x12*

525 A69	1.50p	multicolored	15	15
526 A69	2p	multicolored	15	15
527 A69	4p	multicolored	18	15

Imperf

Size: 61x62mm

528 A69	10p	Hoeing	50	40
		Set value	82	65

1984 Winter Olympics, Sarajevo — A70

1984, Feb. 8 *Perf. 12*

529 A70	50c	Ski jumping	15	15
530 A70	2.50p	Speed skating	15	15
531 A70	3.50p	Hockey	15	15
532 A70	5p	Biathlon	25	15
533 A70	6p	Downhill skiing	35	20
534 A70	20p	Figure skating	1.00	50
535 A70	30p	Bobsledding	1.60	70
		Nos. 529-535 (7)	3.65	
		Set value		1.70

Souvenir Sheet

Perf. 11½

536 A70 50p Skiing 2.50 1.25

No. 536 contains one 32x43mm stamp.

World Communications Year — A71

1983, Aug. 30 Litho. *Perf. 12½*

537 A71	50c	Rowland Hill	15	15
538 A71	2.50p	Samuel Morse	15	15
539 A71	3.50p	H.R. Hertz	18	15
540 A71	5p	Lord Kelvin	25	15
541 A71	10p	Alex. Graham Bell	50	20
542 A71	20p	G. Marconi	1.00	50
543 A71	30p	V. Zworykin	1.40	65
		Nos. 537-543 (7)	3.63	
		Set value		1.70

Souvenir Sheet

544 A71 50p Satellites 2.50 1.25

No. 544 contains one stamp 31x39mm.

Vintage Cars A72

1984, Mar. 20 *Perf. 12*

545 A72	5p	Duesenberg, 1928	15	15
546 A72	8p	MG Midget, 1932	25	15
547 A72	15p	Mercedes, 1928	42	20
548 A72	20p	Bentley, 1928	60	35
549 A72	24p	Alfa Romeo, 1929	70	35

No.	Type	Description	Unused	Used
550	A72	30p Datsun, 1932	80	40
551	A72	35p Lincoln, 1932	1.00	50
		Nos. 545-551 (7)	3.92	2.10

Souvenir Sheet

No.	Type	Description	Unused	Used
552	A72	100p Gottlieb Daimler	2.50	1.50

No. 552 contains one stamp 50x42mm.

Madonna and Child, by Morales — A73

Paintings by Spanish Artists (Espana '84): 6p, Dona Tadea Arias de Enriquez, by Goya. 10p, Santa Cassilda, by Zurbaran. 12p, Saints Andrew and Francis, by El Greco. 15p, Infanta Isabel Clara Eugenia, by Coello. 35p, Queen Maria of Austria, by Velazquez. 40p, Holy Trinity, by El Greco. 100p, Clothed Maja, by Goya.

1984, Apr. 20

No.	Type	Description	Unused	Used
553	A73	3p multicolored	15	15
554	A73	6p multicolored	20	15
555	A73	10p multicolored	30	15
556	A73	12p multicolored	35	20
557	A73	15p multicolored	42	25
558	A73	35p multicolored	1.10	60
559	A73	40p multicolored	1.25	65
		Nos. 553-559 (7)	3.77	2.15

Souvenir Sheet

No.	Type	Description	Unused	Used
560	A73	100p multicolored	3.00	1.50

No. 560 contains one stamp 29x50mm.

Carnivorous Animals — A74

1984, June 28

No.	Type	Description	Unused	Used
561	A74	3p Panthera tigris	15	15
562	A74	6p Panthera leo	20	15
563	A74	10p Neofelis nebulosa	35	15
564	A74	12p Acinonyx jubatus	35	20
565	A74	15p Lynx lynx	42	25
566	A74	35p Panthera pardus	1.10	60
567	A74	40p Uncia uncia	1.25	60
		Nos. 561-567 (7)	3.82	2.10

Intl. Civil Aviation Org., 40th Anniv. A75

1984, Apr. 4 Litho. *Perf. 12½*

No.	Type	Description	Unused	Used
568	A75	8p Caravelle	15	
569	A75	22p DC-6B	40	
570	A75	80p IL-76	1.50	

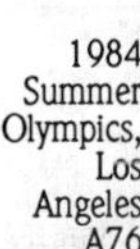

1984 Summer Olympics, Los Angeles A76

1984, May 24 *Perf. 12*

No.	Type	Description	Unused	Used
571	A76	6p Soccer	15	
572	A76	8p Dressage	18	
573	A76	15p Yachting	35	
574	A76	20p Field hockey	45	
575	A76	22p Women's team hand-ball	52	
576	A76	30p Canoeing	70	
577	A76	40p Boxing	90	
		Nos. 571-577 (7)	3.25	

Souvenir Sheet

Perf. 11½

No.	Type	Description	Unused	Used
578	A76	100p Windsurfing	2.25	

World Heritage — A77

Amilcar Cabral, 60th Birth Anniv. — A78

Wood sculptures: 3p, Pearl throne, Cameroun and Central Africa. 6p, Antelope, South Sudan. 10p, Kneeling woman, East Africa. 12p, Mask, West African coast. 15p, Leopard, Guinea coast. 35p, Standing woman, Zaire. 40p, Funerary statues, Southeast Africa and Madagascar.

1984, Aug. 15 *Perf. 12½*

No.	Type	Description	Unused	Used
579	A77	3p multicolored	15	
580	A77	6p multicolored	15	
581	A77	10p multicolored	22	
582	A77	12p multicolored	28	
583	A77	15p multicolored	35	
584	A77	35p multicolored	80	
585	A77	40p multicolored	90	
		Nos. 579-585 (7)	2.85	

1984, Sept. 12 *Perf. 13*

No.	Type	Description	Unused	Used
586	A78	5p Public speaking	15	
587	A78	12p In combat fatigues	20	
588	A78	20p Memorial building, Bafata	35	
589	A78	50p Mausoleum, Bissau	90	

Independence, 11th Anniv. — A79

1984, Sept. 24

No.	Type	Description	Unused	Used
590	A79	3p Mechanic	15	
591	A79	6p Student	15	
592	A79	10p Mason	22	
593	A79	12p Health care, vert.	28	
594	A79	15p Seamstress, vert.	35	
595	A79	35p Telecommunications	80	
596	A79	40p PAIGC building	90	
		Nos. 590-596 (7)	2.85	

Whales A80

1984, Sept. 30 *Perf. 12*

No.	Type	Description	Unused	Used
597	A80	5p Eschrichtius gibbosus	15	
598	A80	8p Balaenoptera musculus	18	
599	A80	15p Tursiops truncatus	35	
600	A80	20p Physeter macrocephalus	45	
601	A80	24p Orcinus orca	55	
602	A80	30p Balaena mysticetus	70	
603	A80	35p Balaenoptera borealis	80	
		Nos. 597-603 (7)	3.18	

The index in each volume of the Scott Catalogue contains many listings that help identify stamps.

Butterflies A81

1984, Oct. 6 *Perf. 12½x13*

No.	Type	Description	Unused	Used
604	A81	3p Hypolimnas dexithea	15	
605	A81	6p Papilio arcturus	15	
606	A81	10p Morpho menelaus terrestris	22	
607	A81	12p Apaturina erminea papuana	28	
608	A81	15p Prepona praeneste	35	
609	A81	35p Ornithoptera paradisea	80	
610	A81	40p Morpho hecuba obidona	90	
		Nos. 604-610 (7)	2.85	

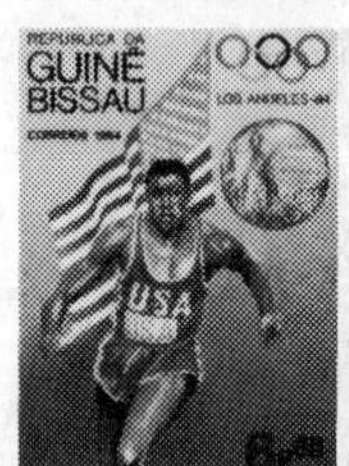

1984 Olympic Winners — A82

National flag, medal and: 6p, Carl Lewis, 4x100 relay, US. 8p, Koji Gushiken, gymnastics, Japan. 15p, Reiner Klimke, equestrian, Federal Republic of Germany. 20p, Tracie Ruiz, synchronized swimming, US. 22p, Mary Lou Retton, gymnastics, US. 30p, Michael Gross, swimming, Federal Republic of Germany. 40p, Edwin Moses, hurdler, US. 100p, Daley Thompson, decathlon, Great Britain.

1984, Nov. 27 *Perf. 13*

No.	Type	Description	Unused	Used
611	A82	6p multicolored	15	
612	A82	8p multicolored	18	
613	A82	15p multicolored	35	
614	A82	20p multicolored	45	
615	A82	22p multicolored	52	
616	A82	30p multicolored	70	
617	A82	40p multicolored	90	
		Nos. 611-617 (7)	3.25	

Souvenir Sheet

No.	Type	Description	Unused	Used
618	A82	100p multicolored	2.25	

No. 618 contains one stamp 32x40mm, perf. 12½.

Locomotives — A83

1984, Dec. 15

No.	Type	Description	Unused	Used
619	A83	5p White Mountain Central No. 4	15	
620	A83	8p Kessler 2-6-OT, 1886	18	
621	A83	15p Langen tram, 1901	35	
622	A83	20p Gurjao No. 6	45	
623	A83	24p Achenseebahn	55	
624	A83	30p Vitznau-Rigi steam locomotive	70	
625	A83	35p Riggenbach rackrail, 1873	80	
		Nos. 619-625 (7)	3.18	

Souvenir Sheet

Perf. 12½

No.	Type	Description	Unused	Used
625A	A83	100p like #621	2.25	

No. 625A contains one stamp 40x32mm.

Native Crafts — A83a

Designs: a, Numbe mask. b, Sono statue. c, Erande statue. d, Kokumba arms. e, Oma mask. f, Koni mask.

1984 Litho. *Perf. 13½*

No.	Type	Description	Unused	Used
626	A83a	7.50p Strip of 6, #a.-f.		

Motorcycle Cent. — A84

1985, Feb. 20 *Perf. 13x12½*

No.	Type	Description	Unused	Used
627	A84	5p Harley-Davidson	15	
628	A84	8p Kawasaki	18	
629	A84	15p Honda	35	
630	A84	20p Yamaha	45	
631	A84	25p Suzuki	55	
632	A84	30p BMW	70	
633	A84	35p Moto Guzzi	80	
		Nos. 627-633 (7)	3.18	

Souvenir Sheet

No.	Type	Description	Unused	Used
634	A84	100p Daimler Motorized Bicycle, 1885, vert.	2.25	

No. 634 contains one stamp 32x40mm, perf. 12½.

Miniature Sheet

Mushrooms — A85

1985, May 15 *Perf. 13*

No.	Type	Description	Unused	Used
635		Sheet of 6	3.10	
a.	A85	7p Clitocybe gibba	16	
b.	A85	9p Morchella elata	22	
c.	A85	12p Lepista nuda	28	
d.	A85	20p Lactarius deliciosus	45	
e.	A85	30p Russula virescens	70	
f.	A85	35p Chroogomphus rutilus	80	

Henri Dunant (1828-1910), Red Cross Founder, Plane — A87

1985, June 12 *Perf. 12½*

No.	Type	Description	Unused	Used
643	A87	20p shown	45	
644	A87	25p Ambulance	52	
645	A87	40p Helicopter	90	
646	A87	80p Speed boat	2.00	

Cats — A88

1985, July 5 *Perf. 13*

647 A88	7p	multicolored	16
648 A88	10p	multicolored	22
649 A88	12p	multicolored	28
650 A88	15p	multicolored	35
651 A88	20p	multicolored	45
652 A88	40p	multicolored	90
653 A88	45p	multicolored	1.20
		Nos. 647-653 (7)	3.56

Souvenir Sheet

654 A88	100p	multicolored	2.25

ARGENTINA '85. No. 654 contains one 40x32mm stamp.

Composers and Musical Instruments A89

Designs: 4p, Vincenzo Bellini (1801-1835), harp, 1820, and descant viol, 16th cent. 5p, Schumann (1810-1856) and Viennese pyramid piano, 1829. 7p, Chopin (1810-1849) and piano-forte, 1817. 12p, Luigi Cherubini (1760-1842) and 18th cent. Baryton violin and Quinton viol. 20p, G. B. Pergolesi (1710-1736) and double-manual harpsichord, 1734. 30p, Handel (1685-1759), valve trumpet, 1825, and timpani drum, 18th cent. 50p, Heinrich Schutz (1585-1672), bass viol and two-stop oboe, 17th cent. 100s, Bach (1685-1750) and St. Thomas Church organ, Leipzig.

1985, Aug. 5 *Perf. 12*

655 A89	4p	multicolored	15
656 A89	5p	multicolored	15
657 A89	7p	multicolored	16
658 A89	12p	multicolored	28
659 A89	20p	multicolored	45
660 A89	30p	multicolored	70
661 A89	50p	multicolored	1.10
		Nos. 655-661 (7)	2.99

Souvenir Sheet

Perf. 11½

662 A89	100p	multicolored	2.25

No. 662 contains one 30x50mm stamp.

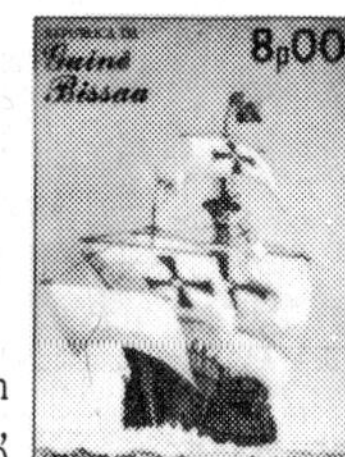

Santa Maria, 15th Cent., Spain — A90

Ships: 15p, Carack, 16th cent., Netherlands. 20p, Mayflower, 17th cent., Great Britain. 30p, St. Louis, 17th cent., France. 35p, Royal Sovereign, 1635, Great Britain. 45p, Soleil Royal, 17th cent., France. 80p, English brig, 18th-19th cent.

1985, Sept. 12 *Perf. 13*

663 A90	8p	multicolored	20
664 A90	15p	multicolored	35
665 A90	20p	multicolored	45
666 A90	30p	multicolored	70
667 A90	35p	multicolored	80
668 A90	45p	multicolored	1.10
669 A90	80p	multicolored	2.00
		Nos. 663-669 (7)	5.60

UN, 40th Anniv. A91

1985, Oct. 17

670 A91	10p	Emblem, doves, vert.	22
671 A91	20p	Emblem, 40	45

Venus and Mars, by Sandro Botticelli (1445-1510) A92

Botticelli paintings (details): 7p, Virgin with Child and St. John. 12p, St. Augustine in the Work Hall. 15p, Awakening of Spring. 20p, Virgin and Child. 40p, Virgin with Child and St. John, diff. 45p, Birth of Venus. 100p, Virgin and Child with Two Angels.

1985, Oct. 25 *Perf. 12½x13*

672 A92	7p	multicolored	16
673 A92	10p	multicolored	22
674 A92	12p	multicolored	28
675 A92	15p	multicolored	35
676 A92	20p	multicolored	45
677 A92	40p	multicolored	90
678 A92	45p	multicolored	1.10

Size: 73x106mm

Imperf

679 A92	100p	multicolored	2.25
		Nos. 672-679 (8)	5.71

ITALIA '85.

Intl. Youth Year A93

1985, Nov. 29 **Litho.** *Perf. 12½*

680 A93	7p	Dance	15
681 A93	13p	Wind surfing	22
682 A93	15p	Rollerskating	25
683 A93	25p	Hang gliding	40
684 A93	40p	Surfing	65
685 A93	50p	Skateboarding	80
686 A93	80p	Parachuting	1.40
		Nos. 680-686 (7)	3.87

Souvenir Sheet

Perf. 13

687 A93	100p	Self-defense	1.60

No. 687 contains one 40x32mm stamp.

Miniature Sheet

Halley's Comet — A94

1986 World Cup Soccer Championships, Mexico — A95

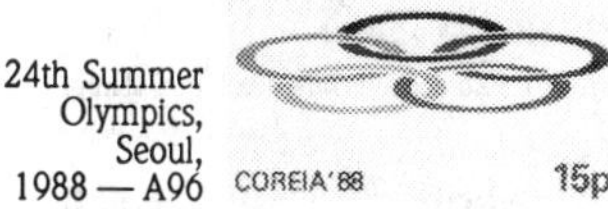

24th Summer Olympics, Seoul, 1988 — A96

Italian Automobile Industry, Cent. — A97

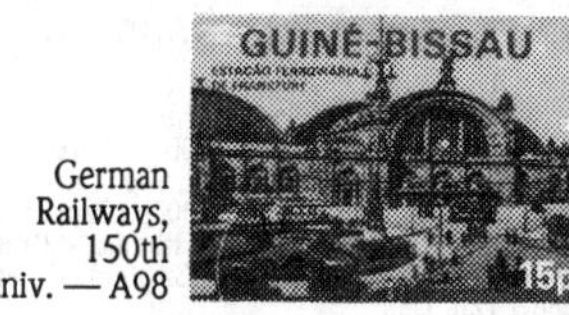

German Railways, 150th Anniv. — A98

Discovery of America, 500th Anniv. (in 1992) — A99

First American Manned Space Flight, 25th Anniv. — A100

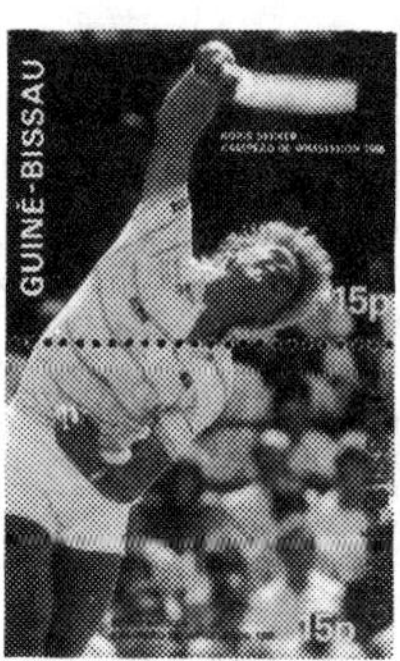

1986 Wimbledon Tennis Championships — A101

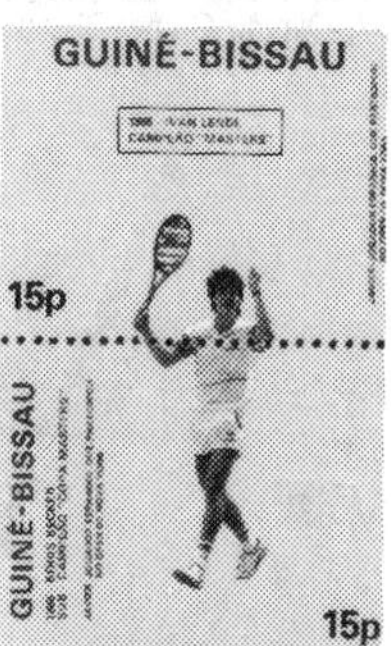

1986 Masters Tennis Championships — A102

Giotto Space Probe A103

Designs: a, Comet tail. b, Comet. c, Trophy. d, Trophy base. e, Five-ring Olympic emblem. f, Alfa Tourer, Italy, c. 1905. g, Railway station, Frankfurt-on Main, c. 1914. h, Barcelona, site of Discovery of America exhibition and 1992 Olympics. i, Space station solar panels and tanks. j, Space station. k, Removing cargo from space shuttle. l, Docking facility, station panels. m, Boris Becker swinging tennis racket. n, Becker, diff. o, Ivan Lendl holding racket. p, Lendl, diff.

1986, Dec. 30 **Litho.** *Perf. 13½*

688	Sheet of 16	*30.00*
a.-p.	A94-A102 15p any single	

Souvenir Sheet

689 A103	100p	multicolored	6.50

Nos. 688a-688b, 688c-688d, 688i-688l, 688m-688n, 688o-688p are se-tenant in continuous designs. Inscription on Nos. 688i-688l incorrect; should read "TRIPULADO MERCURY / 5-5-1961."

Discovery of America, 500th Anniv. (in 1992) — A104

Designs: No. 690, Christopher Columbus aboard caravelle. No. 691, Guadalquivir Port, Seville, c. 1490. No. 692, Pedro Alvars Cabral landing at Bahia, Brazil. No. 693, Bridge over the Guadalquivir River, Seville. No. 694, Port, Lisbon, 15th cent.

1987, Feb. 27

690 A104	50p	multicolored	1.50
691 A104	50p	multicolored	1.50
692 A104	50p	multicolored	1.50
693 A104	50p	multicolored	1.50

Souvenir Sheet

694 A104	150p	multicolored	10.00

No. 694 exists with pink or yellow anniv. emblem pictured in vignette.

Portuguese Guinea Nos. 306-309, 313, 316-317, Ovptd., Guinea-Bissau No. 349 Surcharged

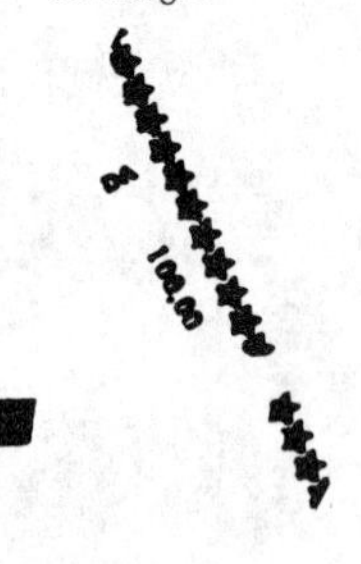

BISSAU

1987, July **Litho.** ***Perf. 13½***

696 A21 100p on 20c #306 *3.00*
697 A21 200p on 35c #307 *6.00*
698 A21 300p on 70c #308 *9.00*
699 A21 400p on 80c #309 *12.00*
700 A21 500p on 3.50e #313 *15.00*
701 A21 1000p on 15e #316 *30.00*
702 A21 2000p on 20e #317 *60.00*

Perf. 13

703 CD61 2500p on 2e #349 *75.00*
Nos. 696-703 (8) *210.00*

Placement of "Bissau," new denomination and obliterating bar varies.

1988 Winter Olympics, Calgary A106

1988, Jan. 15 **Litho.** ***Perf. 13***

704 A106 5p Pairs figure skating 15
705 A106 10p Luge 15
706 A106 50p Skiing 15
707 A106 200p Slalom skiing 36
708 A106 300p Skibobbing 55
709 A106 500p Ski jumping, vert. 90
710 A106 800p Speed skating, vert. 1.45
Nos. 704-710 (7) 3.71

Souvenir Sheet

710A A106 900p Two-man luge 1.60

No. 710A contains one 40x32mm stamp.

Soccer — A107

Various soccer plays.

1988, Apr. 14 **Litho.** ***Perf. 13***

711 A107 5p multi 15
712 A107 10p multi, diff. 15
713 A107 50p multi, diff. 15
714 A107 200p multi, diff. 60
715 A107 300p multi, diff. 88
716 A107 500p multi, diff. 1.50
717 A107 800p multi, diff. 2.35
Nos. 711-717 (7) 5.78

Souvenir Sheet

718 A107 900p multi, diff. 2.65

ESSEN '88 stamp exhibition. No. 718 contains one 32x40mm stamp.

1988 Summer Olympics, Seoul — A108

Perf. 12½x12, 12x12½

1988, Feb. 26 **Litho.**

719 A108 5p Yachting, vert. 15
720 A108 10p Equestrian 15
721 A108 50p High jump 18
722 A108 200p Shooting 72
723 A108 300p Long jump, vert. 1.10
724 A108 500p Tennis, vert. 1.80
725 A108 800p Women's archery, vert. 2.90
Nos. 719-725 (7) 7.00

Souvenir Sheet

Perf. 12½

726 A108 900p Soccer 3.25

No. 726 contains one 40x32mm stamp.

Ancient Ships — A109

Designs: 5p, Egyptian, c. 3300 B.C. 10p, Pharaoh Sahure's ship, c. 2700 B.C. 50p, Queen Hatsepsowe's ship, c. 1500 B.C. 200p, Ramses III's ship, c. 1200 B.C. 300p, Greek trireme, 480 B.C. 500p, Etruscan bireme, 600 B.C. 800p, Venetian galley, 12th cent.

1988 **Litho.** ***Perf. 13x12½***

727 A109 5p multi 15
728 A109 10p multi 15
729 A109 50p multi 18
730 A109 200p multi 72
731 A109 300p multi 1.10
732 A109 500p multi 1.80
733 A109 800p multi 2.90
Nos. 727-733 (7) 7.00

FINLANDIA '88 — A110

Chess champions, board and chessmen.

1988 **Litho.** ***Perf. 12x12½***

734 A110 5p Philidor 15
735 A110 10p Staunton 15
736 A110 50p Anderssen 18
737 A110 200p Morphy 72
738 A110 300p Steinitz 1.10
739 A110 500p Lasker 1.80
740 A110 800p Capablanca 2.90
Nos. 734-740 (7) 7.00

Souvenir Sheet

Perf. 13

741 A110 900p Ruy Lopez 3.25

No. 741 contains one 40x32mm stamp.

Dogs A111

1988 ***Perf. 13x12½***

742 A111 5p Basset hound 15
743 A111 10p Great blue of Gascony 15
744 A111 50p Sabujo of Italy 18
745 A111 200p Yorkshire terrier 72
746 A111 300p Small musterlander 1.10
747 A111 500p Pointer 1.80
748 A111 800p German setter 2.90
Nos. 742-748 (7) 7.00

Souvenir Sheet

Perf. 12½

749 A111 900 German shepherd 3.25

No. 749 contains one 40x32mm stamp.

Intl. Red Cross and Red Crescent Organizations, 125th Annivs. — A112

1988 ***Perf. 13***

750 A112 10p Jean-Henri Dunant 15
751 A112 50p Dr. T. Maunoir 18
752 A112 200p Dr. Louis Appia 72
753 A112 800p Gustave Moynier 2.90

Maps and Fauna — A113

1988 ***Perf. 12½x13, 13x12½***

754 A113 5p *Panthera leo* 15
755 A113 10p *Glaucidium brasilianum* 15
756 A113 50p *Upupa epops* 18
757 A113 200p *Equus burchelli antiquorum* 72
758 A113 300p *Loxodonta africana* 1.10
759 A113 500p *Acryllium vulturinum* 1.80
760 A113 800p *Diceros bicornis* 2.90
Nos. 754-760 (7) 7.00

Nos. 754-755, 758-760 vert. The genus *"Upupa"* is misspelled on the 50p and *"Loxodonta"* is misspelled on the 300p.

Samora Machel (1933-1986), Pres. of Mozambique A114

1988 ***Perf. 13***

761 A114 10p shown 15
762 A114 50p Raising fist 18
763 A114 200p With sentry 75
764 A114 300p Wearing earphones at UN 1.15

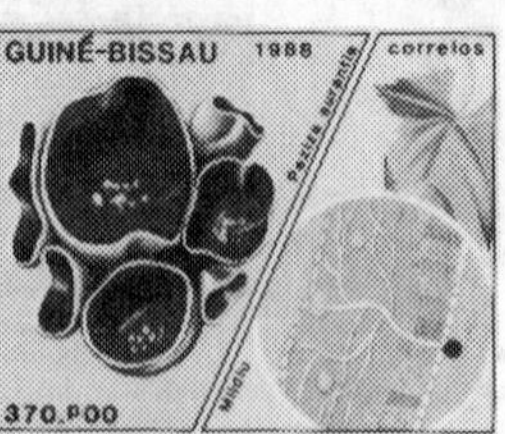

Mushrooms — A115

1988 **Litho.** ***Perf. 13x12½***

765 A115 370p *Peziza aurantia* 1.20
766 A115 470p *Morchella* 1.55
767 A115 600p *Amanita caesarea* 2.00
768 A115 780p *Amanita muscaria* 2.60
769 A115 800p *Amanita phalloides* 2.65
770 A115 900p *Agaricus bisporus* 3.00
771 A115 945p *Cantharellus cibarius* 3.15
Nos. 765-771 (7) 16.15

1992 Winter Olympics, Albertville — A116

1989, Oct. 12 **Litho.** ***Perf. 12½x12***

772 A116 50p Speed skating 15
773 A116 100p Women's figure skating 22
774 A116 200p Ski jumping 45
775 A116 350p Skiing 78
776 A116 500p Skiing, diff. 1.15
777 A116 800p Bobsled 1.80
778 A116 1000p Ice hockey 2.25
Nos. 772-778 (7) 6.80

Souvenir Sheet

Perf. 12½

779 A116 1500p Ice hockey, diff. 3.40

No. 779 contains one 32x40mm stamp.

World Cup Soccer Championships, Italy — A117

Various soccer players.

1989 **Litho.** ***Perf. 12½***

780 A117 50p multicolored 15 15
781 A117 100p multicolored 22 22
782 A117 200p multicolored 45 45
783 A117 350p multicolored 80 80
784 A117 500p multicolored 88 88
785 A117 800p multicolored 1.85 1.85
786 A117 1000p multicolored 2.30 2.30
Nos. 780-786 (7) 6.65 6.65

Souvenir Sheet

Perf. 13

786A A117 1500p multicolored 4.90 4.90

No. 786A contains one 40x32mm stamp.

Lilies (Lilium) — A118

1989 *Perf. 12½*

787 A118 50p Limelight 15 15
788 A118 100p Candidum 22 22
789 A118 200p Pardalinum 45 45
790 A118 350p Auratum 80 80
791 A118 500p Canadense 88 88
792 A118 800p Enchantment 1.85 1.85
793 A118 1000p Black Dragon 2.30 2.30
Nos. 787-793 (7) 6.65 6.65

Souvenir Sheet

794 A118 1500p Lilium pyrenaicum 4.90 4.90

No. 794 contains one 32x40mm stamp.

Trains A119

Various railroad engines.

1989, May 24 Litho. *Perf. 13*

795 A119 50p multicolored 17 17
796 A119 100p multicolored 34 34
797 A119 200p multicolored 68 68
798 A119 350p multicolored 1.25 1.25
799 A119 500p multicolored 1.75 1.75
800 A119 800p multicolored 2.75 2.75

Perf. 12½

Size: 68x27mm

801 A119 1000p multicolored 3.40 3.40
Nos. 795-801 (7) 10.34 10.34

Souvenir Sheet

Perf. 12½

802 A119 1500p multicolored 5.00 5.00

No. 802 contains one 32x40mm stamp.

La Marseillaise by Francois Rude — A120

Paintings: 100p, Armed mob. 200p, Storming the Bastille. 350p, Lafayette, Liberty, vert. 500p, Dancing around the Liberty tree. 800p, Rouget de Lisle singing La Marseillaise by Pils. 1000p, Storming the Bastille, diff. 1500p, Arms of the Republic of France.

Perf. 12½, 12x12½ (350p)

1989, July 5

803 A120 50p shown 17 17
804 A120 100p multicolored 34 34
805 A120 200p multicolored 68 68
806 A120 350p multicolored, 27x44mm 1.25 1.25
807 A120 500p multicolored 1.75 1.75
808 A120 800p multicolored 2.75 2.75
809 A120 1000p multicolored 3.40 3.40
Nos. 803-809 (7) 10.34 10.34

Souvenir Sheet

Perf. 13

810 A120 1500p multicolored 5.00 5.00

Souvenir Sheet

Reinwardtoena Reinwardtsi — A121

1989 Litho. *Perf. 12½*

818 A121 1500p multicolored 4.85 4.85

Pioneers Organization — A122

1989 *Perf. 13*

819 A122 10p Children presenting flag, vert. 15 15
820 A122 50p Children saluting, vert. 21 21
821 A122 200p shown 85 85
822 A122 300p Children playing ball 1.25 1.25

Town of Cacheu, 400th Anniv. A123

1989, Nov. 30

823 A123 10p Monument, vert. 15 15
824 A123 50p shown 21 21
825 A123 200p Old building 85 85
826 A123 300p Church 1.25 1.25

Dated 1988.

A124 A126

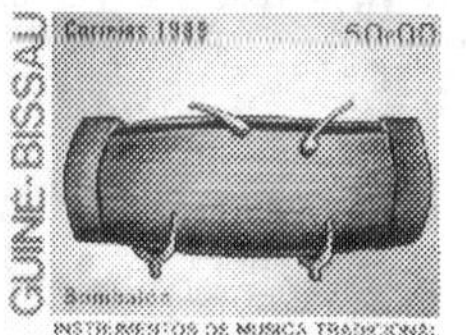

A125

Designs: Prehistoric creatures.

Perf. 13, 12½x12 (100p)

1989, Sept. 15

827 A124 50p Trachodon 15 15
828 A124 100p Edaphosaurus, 68x27mm 24 24
829 A124 200p Mesosaurus 48 48
830 A124 350p Elephas primigenius 80 80
831 A124 500p Tyrannosaurus 1.15 1.15
832 A124 800p Stegosaurus 1.85 1.85
833 A124 1000p Cervus megaceros 2.25 2.25
Nos. 827-833 (7) 6.92 6.92

Nos. 828, 831-833 horiz.

1989, Apr. 10 Litho. *Perf. 13*

Designs: Musical instruments.

834 A125 50p Bombalon 15
835 A125 100p Flauta 30
836 A125 200p Tambor 60
837 A125 350p Dondon 1.05
838 A125 500p Balafon 1.50
839 A125 800p Kora 2.40
840 A125 1000p Nhanhero 3.00
Nos. 834-840 (7) 9.00

1989, July 13 *Perf. 12x12½*

Designs: Indian artifacts.

841 A126 50p Teotihuacan 15 15
842 A126 100p Mochica 24 24
843 A126 200p Jaina 48 48
844 A126 350p Nayarit 80 80
845 A126 500p Inca 1.15 1.15
846 A126 800p Hopewell 1.85 1.85
847 A126 1000p Taina 2.25 2.25
Nos. 841-847 (7) 6.92 6.92

Souvenir Sheet

Perf. 12½

848 A126 1500p Indian statuette 3.50 3.50

Brasiliana '89 Philatelic Exhibition. Nos. 841-847 printed se-tenant with multicolored label showing scenes of colonization. No. 848 contains one 32x40mm stamp.

1992 Summer Olympics, Barcelona A127

1989, June 3 *Perf. 12½x13*

849 A127 50p Hurdles 15 15
850 A127 100p Boxing 16 16
851 A127 200p High jump 32 32
852 A127 350p Sprinters in the blocks 52 52
853 A127 500p Woman sprinter 75 75
854 A127 800p Gymnastics 1.25 1.25
855 A127 1000p Pole vault 1.50 1.50
856 A127 1500p Soccer 2.25 2.25
Nos. 849-856 (8) 6.90 6.90

Wild Animals — A128

1989, Nov. 24 *Perf. 12½*

857 A128 50p Syncerus caffer 15 15
858 A128 100p Equus quagga 16 16
859 A128 200p Diceros bicornis 32 32
860 A128 350p Okapia johnstoni 52 52
861 A128 500p Macaca mulatta 75 75
862 A128 800p Hippopotamus amphibius 1.25 1.25
863 A128 1000p Acinonyx jubatus 1.50 1.50
864 A128 1500p Panthera leo 2.25 2.25
Nos. 857-864 (8) 6.90 6.90

Christmas — A129

Paintings of the Madonna and Child (50p) and the Adoration of the Magi.

1989, Dec. 10 *Perf. 13*

865 A129 50p Fra Filippo Lippi 15 15
866 A129 100p Pieter Brueghel 15 15
867 A129 200p Mostaert 20 20
868 A129 350p Durer 35 35
869 A129 500p Rubens 50 50
870 A129 800p Van der Weyden 80 80
871 A129 1000p Francia, horiz. 1.00 1.00
Nos. 865-871 (7) 3.15 3.15

Womens' Hairstyles — A130

Various hairstyles.

1989, Mar. 8 *Perf. 12½x13*

872 A130 50p multicolored 15 15
873 A130 100p multicolored 16 16
874 A130 200p multicolored 32 32
875 A130 350p multicolored 52 52
876 A130 800p multicolored 1.25 1.25
877 A130 1000p multicolored 1.50 1.50
Nos. 872-877 (6) 3.90 3.90

Vegetables — A131

1989, May 20 *Perf. 12½*

878 A131 50p Capisium annum 15 15
879 A131 100p Solanium 15 15
880 A131 200p Curcumis peco 20 20
881 A131 350p Solanium licopersicum 35 35
882 A131 500p Solanium itiopium 50 50
883 A131 800p Hibiscus esculentus 80 80
884 A131 1000p Oseille de guine 1.00 1.00
Nos. 878-884 (7) 3.15 3.15

Visit of Pope John Paul II — A132

1990, Jan. 27 Litho. *Perf. 13½*

885 A132 500p shown 1.50 1.50
886 A132 1000p multi, diff. 3.00 3.00

Souvenir Sheet

887 A132 1500p multi, diff., vert. 4.50 4.50

Souvenir Sheet

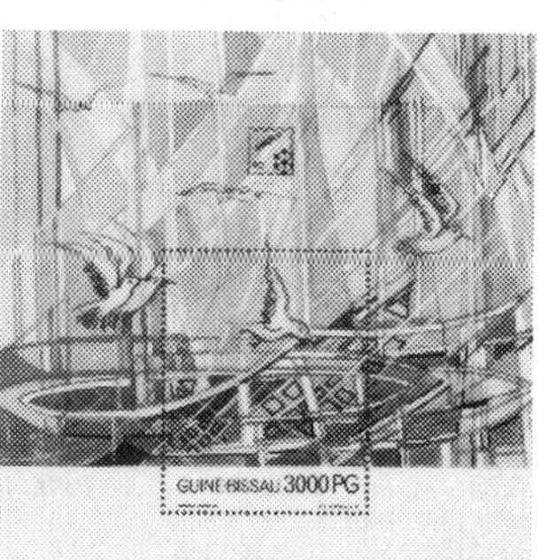

Belgica '90 — A133

1990, June 1 *Perf. 14½*

888 A133 3000p multicolored 4.05 4.05

World Meteorology Day — A134

1990, Oct. 1 Litho. *Perf. 13*

889	A134	1000p	Radar weather map	1.30
890	A134	3000p	Heliograph	3.90

LUBRAPEX '90 — A135

1990, Sept. 21 *Perf. 14*

891	A135	500p	Rooster, hen	65
892	A135	800p	Turkey	1.05
893	A135	1000p	Duck, ducklings	1.30

Souvenir Sheet

Perf. 13½

894	A135	1500p	Rooster, turkey, ducks	2.00

UN Development Program, 40th Anniv. A136

1990 Litho. *Perf. 14*

895	A136	1000p	multicolored	1.35

Fight against AIDS.

Textile Manufacturing A137

No. 896: a, Gossypium hirsutum. b, Processing cotton. c, Spinning thread. d, Picking cotton. e, Moth, silkworms. f, Dyeing thread. g, Weaving. h, Animal design. i, Multi-colored stripes design. j, Stripes, dots design.

1990

896			Sheet of 10	1.50
a.-j.	A137	150p	any single	15
897	A137	400p	like #896a	35
898	A137	500p	like #896g	45
899	A137	600p	like #896h	55

Carnival Masks A138

1990 Litho. *Perf. 14*

900	A138	200p	Mickey Mouse	18
901	A138	300p	Hippopotamus	28
902	A138	600p	Bull	55
903	A138	1200p	Bull, diff.	1.10

Fish — A139

Designs: 300p, Pentanemus quinquarius. 400p, Psettias sabae. 500p, Chaetodipterus goreensis. 600p, Trachinotus goreensis.

1991, Mar. 10 Litho. *Perf. 14*

904	A139	300p	multicolored	25	25
905	A139	400p	multicolored	35	35
906	A139	500p	multicolored	42	42
907	A139	600p	multicolored	50	50

Fire Trucks A140

1991, Aug. 19 Litho. *Perf. 14*

908	A140	200p	shown	15	15
909	A140	500p	Ladder truck	38	38
910	A140	800p	Rescue vehicle	62	62
911	A140	1500p	Ambulance	1.15	1.15

Birds — A141

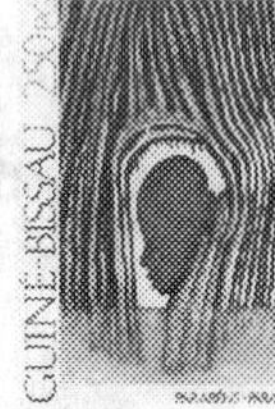
Messages — A142

Designs: 100p, Kaupifalco monogrammicus. 250p, Balearica pavonina. 350p, Bucorvus abyssinicus. 500p, Ephippiorhynchus senegalensis. 1500p, Kaupifalco monogrammicus, diff.

1991, Sept. 10

912	A141	100p	multicolored	15	15
913	A141	250p	multicolored	20	20
914	A141	350p	multicolored	30	30
915	A141	500p	multicolored	38	38

Souvenir Sheet

Perf. 14½

916	A141	1500p	multicolored	1.15	1.15

No. 916 contains one 40x50mm stamp.

1991, Oct. 28 Litho. *Perf. 14*

917	A142	250p	Congratulations	20	20
918	A142	400p	With love	32	32
919	A142	800p	Happiness	65	65
920	A142	1000p	Seasons Greetings	80	80

Fruits — A143

Healthy Hearts — A144

Designs: 500p, Landolfia owariensis. 1500p, Dialium guineensis. 2000p, Adansonia digitata. 3000p, Parkia biglobosa.

1992, Mar. 25 Litho. *Perf. 14*

921	A143	500p	multicolored	28	28
922	A143	1500p	multicolored	75	75
923	A143	2000p	multicolored	1.15	1.15
924	A143	3000p	multicolored	1.70	1.70

1992, Apr. 7

Designs: 1500p, Cigarette butts, healthy heart. 4000p, Heart running over junk food.

925	A144	1500p	multicolored	75	75
926	A144	4000p	multicolored	2.00	2.00

Traditional Costumes — A145

Designs: a, 400p, Fula. b, 600p, Balanta. c, 1000p, Fula, diff. d, 1500p, Manjaco.

1992, Feb. 28 Litho. *Perf. 14*

927	A145		Strip of 4, #a.-d.	1.80	1.80

Canoes A146

Designs: Nos. 928-931, Various types of canoes. No. 932, Alcedo cristata galerita.

1992, May 10

928	A146	750p	multicolored	42	42
929	A146	800p	multicolored	45	45
930	A146	1000p	multicolored	58	58
931	A146	1300p	multicolored	75	75

Souvenir Sheet

Perf. 13½

932	A146	1500p	multicolored	90	90

Trees — A147

Designs: a, 100p, Cassia alata. b, 400p, Perlebia purpurea. c, 1000p, Caesalpina pulcherrima. d, 1500p, Adenanthera pavonina. 3000p, Caesalpina pulcherrima, diff.

1992, May 8 *Perf. 14*

933	A147		Block of 4, #a.-d.	1.75	1.75

Souvenir Sheet

Perf. 13½

934	A147	3000p	multicolored	1.75	1.75

1992 Summer Olympics, Barcelona A148

1992, July 28 Litho. *Perf. 14*

935	A148	600p	Basketball	35	35
936	A148	1000p	Volleyball	60	60
937	A148	1500p	Team handball	90	90
938	A148	2000p	Soccer	1.20	1.20

Trees — A149

Designs: 1000p, Afzelia africana Smith. 1500p, Kaya senegalenses. 2000p, Militia regia. 3000p, Pterocarpus erinaceus.

1992 *Perf. 12*

939	A149	1000p	multicolored	38	38
940	A149	1500p	multicolored	56	56
941	A149	2000p	multicolored	75	75
942	A149	3000p	multicolored	1.15	1.15

Souvenir Sheet

Discovery of America, 500th Anniv. — A150

1992

943	A150	5000p	multicolored	2.00	2.00

Genoa '92.

Procolobus Badius Temminckii — A151

Designs: a, Pair in tree. b, Adult seated in vegetation c, Adult seated in tree fork. d, Female with young.

1992 Litho. *Perf. 12x11½*

944	A151	2000p	Strip of 4, #a.-d.	1.75	1.75

World Wildlife Fund.

Reptiles A152

1993 Litho. *Perf. 14*

945	A152	1500p	Bitis sp.	24	24
946	A152	3000p	Osteolaemus tetraspis	48	48
947	A152	4000p	Varanus nitolicus	65	65
948	A152	5000p	Agama agama	80	80
a.			Souvenir sheet of 4, #945-948	2.20	2.20

Souvenir Sheet

Union of Portuguese Speaking Capitals A153

1993 Litho. *Perf. 13½*
949 A153 6000p Fort 1.00 1.00

Brasiliana '93.

Tourism — A154

Designs: a, 1000p. b, 2000p. c, 4000p. d, 5000p. Illustration reduced.

1993 Litho. *Perf. 14*
950 A154 Block of 4, #a.-d. 2.00 2.00

Traditional Jewelry A155

1993 *Perf. 14½*
951 A155 1500p Bracelet 22 22
952 A155 3000p Mask pendant 45 45
953 A155 4000p Circle pendant 60 60
954 A155 5000p Filigree pendant 75 75

AIR POST STAMPS

Liftoff of Soyuz Spacecraft AP1

Apollo-Soyuz mission: 10p, Launch of Apollo spacecraft. 15p, Leonov, Stafford and meeting in space. 20p, Eclipse of the sun. 30p, Infra-red photo of Earth. 40p, Return to Earth. 50p, Apollo and Soyuz docked, horiz.

1976, Oct. 4 *Perf. 13½*
C10 AP1 5p multicolored
C10A AP1 10p multicolored
C10B AP1 15p multicolored
C10C AP1 20p multicolored
C10D AP1 30p multicolored
C10E AP1 40p multicolored

Souvenir Sheet

C10F AP1 50p multicolored

No. C10F contains one 60x42mm stamp. Nos. C10-C10E exist in souvenir sheets of one, perf. and imperf.

Viking Spacecraft Orbiting Mars — AP2

Design: 35p, Viking gathering Martian soil samples.

1977, Jan. 27
C11 AP2 25p multicolored
C11A AP2 35p multicolored

Nos. 372-373 Surcharged with New Value and "CORREIO AEREO" in Black on Silver Panels

1978 Litho. *Perf. 13½*
C12 A32 15p on 3.50p multi 80 42
C13 A32 30p on 50c multi 1.00 60

History of Aviation Type of 1980

1980 Litho. *Perf. 13½*
C14 A38 35p Willy de Houthulst, Hanriot HD.1 1.25 60
C14A A38 40p Charles Guynemer, Spad S. VII 1.50 70

Souvenir Sheet

C14B A38 50p Comdr. de Rose, Nieuport 2.00 1.00

No. C14B contains one stamp 37x55mm.

Winter Olympics Type of 1980

1980
C15 A39 35p Slalom 1.25 60
C16 A39 40p Figure skating 1.50 70

Souvenir Sheet

C17 A39 50p Ice hockey, horiz. 2.00 1.00

Summer Olympics Type of 1980

1980, Aug. Litho. *Perf. 13½*
C18 A40 35p Somersault 1.25 60
C19 A40 40p Running 1.50 70

Souvenir Sheet

C20 A40 50p Emblem 2.00 1.00

Literacy Type of 1980

1980, Aug. Litho. *Perf. 13½*
C21 A41 15p like #391 60 30
C22 A41 25p like #392 1.00 50

Space Type of 1981

Designs: 35p, Viking 1 and 2. 40p, Apollo-Soyuz craft and crew. 50p, Apollo 11 crew, craft and emblem.

1981, May Litho. *Perf. 13½*
C23 A45 35p multicolored 1.25 60
C24 A45 40p multicolored 1.50 70

Souvenir Sheet

C25 A45 50p multicolored 2.25 1.25

No. C25 contains one stamp 60x42mm.

Soccer Type of 1981

Designs: 35p, Rummenigge, Germany. 40p, Kempes, Argentina. 50p, Juanito, Spain.

1981, May
C26 A46 35p multicolored 1.25 60
C27 A46 40p multicolored 1.50 70

Souvenir Sheet

C28 A46 50p multicolored 2.25 1.25

No. C28 contains one stamp 56x40mm.

Royal Wedding Type of 1981

1981 Litho. *Perf. 13½*
C29 A47 35p Palace 1.90 1.00
C30 A47 40p Prince of Wales arms 2.00 1.25

Souvenir Sheet

C31 A47 50p Couple 2.25 1.25

Picasso Type of 1981

1981, Dec. Litho. *Perf. 13½*
C32 A48 35p multicolored 1.90 1.00
C33 A48 40p multicolored 2.00 1.25

Souvenir Sheet

C34 A48 50p multicolored 2.25 1.25

No. C34 contains one stamp 41x50mm.

Navigator Type of 1981

Designs: 35p, Francis Drake, Golden Hinde. 40p, James Cook, Endeavor. 50p, Columbus, Santa Maria.

1981 Litho. *Perf. 13½*
C35 A49 35p multicolored 1.90 1.00
C36 A49 40p multicolored 2.00 1.25

Souvenir Sheet

C37 A49 50p multicolored 2.25 1.25

Christmas Type of 1981

1981
C38 A50 30p Memling 1.90 1.00
C39 A50 35p Bellini, diff. 2.00 1.25

Souvenir Sheet

C40 A50 50p Fra Angelico 2.25 1.25

No. C40 contains one 35x59mm stamp.

Scout Type of 1982

1982, June 9 Litho. *Perf. 13½*
C41 A51 35p Canoeing 1.50 70
C42 A51 40p Flying model planes 1.90 1.00

Souvenir Sheet

C43 A51 50p Playing chess 2.25 1.25

No. C43 contains one 48x38mm stamp.

Soccer Type of 1982

1982, June 13 Litho. *Perf. 13½*
C44 A52 35p Kempes 1.50 70
C45 A52 40p Kaltz 1.90 1.00

Souvenir Sheet

C46 A52 50p Stadium 2.25 1.25

Diana Type of 1982 and

Princess Diana, 21st Birthday — A53a

1982
C47 A53 35p multicolored 1.50 70
C48 A53 40p multicolored 1.90 1.00

Souvenir Sheet

C49 A53 50p multi, vert. 2.25 1.25

1982, Oct. 1 Litho. & Embossed
C49A A53a 200p gold & multi

Souvenir Sheet

C49B A53a 200p gold & multi, vert.

For overprints see Nos. 456A-456B.

Audubon Birth Bicent. — AP3

1985, Apr. 16 Litho. *Perf. 12*
C50 AP3 5p Brown pelican 15
C51 AP3 10p American white pelican 22
C52 AP3 20p Great blue heron 45
C53 AP3 40p American flamingo 90

HAITI

LOCATION — Western part of Hispaniola
GOVT. — Republic
AREA — 10,700 sq. mi.
POP. — 5,198,000 (est. 1984)
CAPITAL — Port-au-Prince

100 Centimes = 1 Piaster (1906)
100 Centimes = 1 Gourde

Catalogue values for unused stamps in this country are for Never Hinged items, beginning with Scott 370 in the regular postage section, Scott B2 in the semi-postal section, Scott C33 in the air post section, Scott CB10 in the air post semi-postal section, Scott CO6 in the air post official section, Scott CQ1 in the air post parcel post seciton, Scott E1 in the special delivery section, Scott J21 in the postage due section, Scott Q1 in the parcel post section, Scott RA1 in the postal tax section, and Scott RAC1 in the air post postal tax section.

Watermark

Wmk. 131- RH

Liberty Head — A1

1881 Unwmk. Typo. *Imperf.*
1 A1 1c vermilion, *yelsh* 5.25 3.50
2 A1 2c dk violet, *pale lil* 7.00 3.75
3 A1 3c bister, *pale bis* 12.00 4.50
4 A1 5c green, *grnsh* 21.00 7.75
5 A1 7c blue, *grysh* 14.00 2.75
6 A1 20c red brown, *yelsh* 52.50 17.50

Nos. 1-6 were printed from plate I, Nos. 7-13 from plates II and III.

1882 *Perf. 13½*
7 A1 1c ver, *yelsh* 3.50 1.25
c. Horiz. pair, imperf. btwn. 125.00
d. Vert. pair imperf. btwn. 115.00 100.00
8 A1 2c dk vio, *pale lil* 5.25 1.75
a. 2c dark violet 7.00 4.25
b. 2c red violet, *pale lilac* 5.25 2.00
c. Horiz. pair, imperf. vert. 100.00
d. Vert. pair, imperf. horiz. 100.00
e. Horiz. pair, imperf. between 120.00 120.00
9 A1 3c bister, *pale bis* 7.00 2.75
10 A1 5c grn, *grnsh* 4.25 85
a. 5c yellow green, *greenish* 4.25 85
b. 5c deep green, *greenish* 4.25 85
c. Horiz. pair, imperf. vert. 110.00
d. Horiz. or vert. pair, imperf. btwn. 120.00
11 A1 7c blue, *grysh* 6.25 1.40
a. Horiz. pair, imperf. between
12 A1 7c ultra, *grysh* 10.00 2.00
a. Vert. pair, imperf. between
b. Horiz. pair, imperf. vert.
13 A1 20c pale brn, *yelsh* 5.00 1.10
a. 20c red brown, *yellowish* 10.50 2.00
b. Horiz. pair, imperf. vert 90.00
c. Vert. pair, imperf. horiz. 110.00
d. Horiz. or vert. pair, imperf. btwn. 120.00 110.00

Stamps perf. 14, 16 are forgeries which were made to defraud the government and used freely in the mails.

A3

A4

1886-87 *Perf. 13½*

18	A3	1c vermilion, *yelsh*	3.50	1.10
a.		Horiz. pair, imperf. vert.		120.00
b.		Horiz. pair, imperf. between	120.00	120.00
19	A3	2c dk violet, *lilac*	27.50	4.25
20	A4	5c green ('87)	10.50	1.40

Differences between Nos. 18-20 (which were printed from new dies) and the preceding issues are too small to illustrate clearly. These stamps can be identified by the numerals of value, which are larger than the earlier ones and differ slightly in shape. Nos. 18 and 19 show crossed lines of dots on face.

General Louis Etienne Félicité Salomon — A5

1887 **Engr.** *Perf. 14*

21	A5	1c lake	.28	.28
22	A5	2c violet	.70	.52
23	A5	3c blue	.52	.35
24	A5	5c green	3.50	.35

Some experts believe the imperfs. of Nos. 21-24 are plate proofs. Value per pair, $20.

No. 23 Handstamp Surcharged in Red

1890

25	A5	2c on 3c blue	42	35

This surcharge being handstamped is to be found double, inverted, etc. This applies to succeeding surcharged issues.

Coat of Arms — A7

Coat of Arms (Leaves Drooping) — A9

1891 *Perf. 13*

26	A7	1c violet	.35	.25
27	A7	2c blue	.52	.28
28	A7	3c gray lilac	.70	.35
a.		3c slate	.70	.42
29	A7	5c orange	2.50	.28
30	A7	7c red	5.50	2.00
		Nos. 26-30 (5)	9.57	3.16

Nos. 26-30 exist imperf. Value of unused pairs, each $20.

The 2c, 3c and 7c exist imperf. vertically.

No. 28 Surcharged Like No. 25 in Red

1892

31	A7	2c on 3c gray lilac	90	70
a.		2c on 3c slate	90	70

1892-95 **Engr., Litho. (20c)** *Perf. 14*

32	A9	1c lilac	18	15
a.		Imperf., pair		
33	A9	2c deep blue	18	15
34	A9	3c gray	52	35
35	A9	5c orange	1.75	25
36	A9	7c red	25	18
a.		Imperf., pair	4.50	
37	A9	20c brown	1.25	75
		Nos. 32-37 (6)	4.13	1.83

Nos. 32, 33, 35 exist in horiz. pairs, imperf. vert., Nos. 33, 35, in vert. pairs, imperf. horiz.

1896 **Engr.** *Perf. 13½*

38	A9	1c light blue	15	15
39	A9	2c red brown	20	15
40	A9	3c lilac brown	15	15
41	A9	5c slate green	15	15
42	A9	7c dark gray	15	15
43	A9	20c orange	18	18
		Nos. 38-43 (6)	98	
		Set value		75

Nos. 32-37 are 23¼mm high, Nos. 38-43 23½mm to 23½mm. The "C" is closed on Nos. 32-37, open on Nos. 38-43. Other differences exist.

The stamps of the two issues may be readily distinguished by their colors and perfs.

Nos. 38-43 exist imperf. and in horiz. pairs, imperf. vert. The 1c, 3c, 5c, 7c exist in vert. pairs, imperf. horiz. or imperf. between. The 5c, 7c exist in horiz. pairs, imperf. between. Value of unused pairs, $5 and up.

#37, 43 Surcharged Like #25 in Red

1898

44	A9	2c on 20c brown	90	42
45	A9	2c on 20c orange	52	35

No. 45 exists in various part perf. varieties.

Coat of Arms — A11

1898 **Wmk. 131** *Perf. 11*

46	A11	1c ultra	1.00	70
47	A11	2c brown carmine	35	15
48	A11	3c dull violet	85	52
49	A11	5c dark green	35	20
50	A11	7c gray	2.00	1.40
51	A11	20c orange	2.00	1.40
		Nos. 46-51 (6)	6.55	4.37

All values exist imperforate. They are plate proofs.

Pres. T. Augustin Simon Sam — A12

Coat of Arms — A13

1898-99 **Unwmk.** *Perf. 12*

52	A12	1c ultra	15	15
53	A13	1c yel green ('99)	15	15
54	A12	2c deep orange	15	15
55	A13	2c car lake ('99)	15	15
56	A12	3c green	15	15
57	A13	4c red	18	15
58	A12	5c red brown	15	15
59	A13	5c pale blue ('99)	15	15
60	A12	7c gray	15	15
61	A13	8c carmine	18	15
62	A13	10c orange red	18	15
63	A13	15c olive green	52	35
64	A12	20c black	50	35
65	A12	50c rose brown	55	35
66	A12	1g red violet	1.50	1.40
		Nos. 52-66 (15)	4.81	
		Set value		3.50

For overprints see Nos. 67-81, 110-124, 169, 247-248.

Stamps of 1898-99 Handstamped in Black

MAI G^t P^re 1902

1902

67	A12	1c ultra	45	45
68	A13	1c yellow green	35	18
69	A12	2c deep orange	70	70
70	A13	2c carmine lake	35	15
71	A12	3c green	35	35
72	A13	4c red	45	45
73	A12	5c red brown	1.00	1.00
74	A13	5c pale blue	35	35
75	A12	7c gray	70	70
76	A13	8c carmine	70	70
77	A13	10c orange red	70	70
78	A13	15c olive green	3.50	2.50
79	A12	20c black	3.50	2.75
80	A12	50c rose brown	8.75	4.25
81	A12	1g red violet	10.50	8.75
		Nos. 67-81 (15)	32.35	23.98

Many forgeries exist of this overprint.

Centenary of Independence Issues

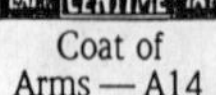

Coat of Arms — A14

Pierre D. Toussaint L'Ouverture — A15

Emperor Jean Jacques Dessalines — A16

Pres. Alexandre Sabes Pétion — A17

1904 **Engr.** *Perf. 13½, 14*

82	A14	1c green	15	15

Center Engr., Frame Litho.

83	A15	2c rose & blk	15	15
84	A15	5c dull blue & blk	15	15
85	A16	7c plum & blk	15	15
86	A16	10c yellow & blk	15	15
87	A17	20c slate & blk	15	15
88	A17	50c olive & blk	15	15
		Nos. 82-88 (7)	1.05	
		Set value		84

Nos. 82 to 88 exist imperforate.

Nos. 83-88 exist with centers inverted. Some are known with head omitted.

Forgeries exist.

Same Handstamped in Blue

1904

89	A14	1c green	25	25
90	A15	2c rose & blk	28	28
91	A15	5c dull blue & blk	28	28
92	A16	7c plum & blk	35	35
93	A16	10c yellow & blk	35	35
94	A17	20c slate & blk	35	35
95	A17	50c olive & blk	35	35
		Nos. 89-95 (7)	2.21	2.21

Two dies were used for the handstamped overprint on Nos. 89-95. Letters and figures are larger on one than on the other. All values exist imperforate.

Pres. Pierre Nord-Alexis — A18

1904 **Engr.** *Perf. 13½, 14*

96	A18	1c green	15	15
97	A18	2c carmine	15	15
98	A18	5c dark blue	15	15
99	A18	10c orange brown	15	15
100	A18	20c orange	15	15
101	A18	50c claret	15	15
a.		Tête bêche pair	35.00	
		Set value	45	45

Used values are for c-t-o's. Postally used examples are worth more.

Nos. 96-101 exist imperforate.

This issue, and the overprints and surcharges, exist in horiz. pairs, imperf. vert., and in vert. pairs, imperf. horiz.

For overprints and surcharges see Nos. 102-109, 150-161, 170-176, 217-218, 235-238, 240-242, 302-303.

Forgeries of Nos. 96, 101, 101a exist.

Stamps of this issue overprinted "T. M." are revenue stamps. The letters are the initials of "Timbre-Mobile."

Reprints or very accurate imitations of this issue exist, including No. 101a.

Some are printed in very bright colors on very white paper and are found both perforated and imperforate. Generally the original stamps are perf. 13¼, the reprints perf 13½.

Same Handstamped in Blue

1904

102	A18	1c green	42	35
103	A18	2c carmine	42	35
104	A18	5c dark blue	42	35
105	A18	10c orange brown	42	35
106	A18	20c orange	42	35
107	A18	50c claret	42	35
		Nos. 102-107 (6)	2.52	2.10

The note after No. 95 applies also to Nos. 102-107. All values exist imperf.

Forgeries exist.

Regular Issue of 1904 Handstamp Surcharged in Black:

1906, Feb. 20

108	A18	1c on 20c orange	18	15
a.		1c on 50c claret	800.00	
109	A18	2c on 50c claret	18	15
		Set value		20

No. 108a is known only with inverted surcharge.

Forgeries exist.

Nos. 52-66 Handstamped in Red

1906

110	A12	1c ultra	90	70
111	A13	1c yellow green	52	52
112	A12	2c deep orange	1.75	1.75
113	A13	2c carmine lake	1.00	1.00
114	A12	3c green	1.00	1.00
115	A13	4c red	4.25	3.50
116	A12	5c red brown	5.25	4.25
117	A13	5c pale blue	70	42
118	A12	7c gray	3.50	3.50
119	A13	8c carmine	70	70
120	A13	10c orange red	1.40	90
121	A13	15c olive green	1.75	1.00
122	A12	20c black	4.25	3.50
123	A12	50c rose brown	4.25	2.75
124	A12	1g red violet	7.00	5.50
		Nos. 110-124 (15)	38.22	30.99

Forgeries of this overprint are plentiful.

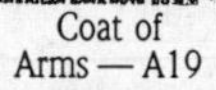

Coat of Arms — A19

President Nord-Alexis — A20

Market at Port-au-Prince A21

Sans Souci Palace A22

Independence Palace at Gonaives
A23

Entrance to Catholic College at Port-au-Prince
A24

Monastery and Church at Port-au-Prince
A25

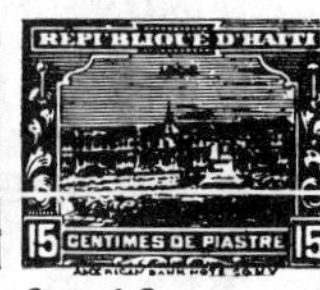

Seat of Government at Port-au-Prince
A26

Presidential Palace at Port-au-Prince — A27

For Foreign Postage (centimes de piastre)

1906-13 *Perf. 12*

125 A19	1c de p green		18	15
126 A20	2c de p ver		35	18
127 A21	3c de p brown		52	18
128 A21	3c de p org yel ('11)		5.00	2.75
129 A22	4c de p car lake		52	28
130 A22	4c de p lt ol grn ('13)		7.00	4.25
131 A20	5c de p dk blue		1.75	18
132 A23	7c de p gray		1.40	70
133 A23	7c de p org red ('13)		21.00	14.00
134 A24	8c de p car rose		1.40	60
135 A24	8c de p ol grn ('13)		12.00	8.50
136 A25	10c de p org red		90	18
137 A25	10c de p red brn ('13)		12.00	8.50
138 A26	15c de p sl grn		1.75	70
139 A26	15c dp p yel ('13)		5.25	2.75
140 A20	20c de p blue grn		1.75	70
141 A19	50c de p red		2.75	2.00
142 A19	50c de p org yel ('13)		6.00	4.25
143 A27	1p claret		5.50	3.50
144 A27	1p red ('13)		6.00	5.00
	Nos. 125-144 (20)		93.02	59.35

All 1906 values exist imperf. These are plate proofs.

For overprints and surcharges see Nos. 177-195, 213-216, 239, 245, 249-260, 263, 265-277, 279-284, 286-301, 304.

Nord-Alexis — A28

Coat of Arms — A29

For Domestic Postage (centimes de gourde)

1906-10

145 A28	1c de g blue	18	15
146 A29	2c de g org yel	35	15
147 A29	2c de g lemon ('10)	52	15
148 A28	3c de g slate	28	15
149 A29	7c de g green	90	35
	Nos. 145-149 (5)	2.23	
	Set value		78

For overprints see Nos. 196-197.

Regular Issue of 1904 Handstamp Surcharged in Red:

1907

150 A18	1c on 5c dk bl	28	20
151 A18	1c on 20c org	20	15
152 A18	2c on 10c org brn	25	18
153 A18	2c on 50c claret	35	20

Black Surcharge

154 A18	1c on 5c dk bl	35	18
155 A18	1c on 10c org brn	25	15
156 A18	2c on 20c org	20	18

Brown Surcharge

157 A18	1c on 5c dk bl	35	35
158 A18	1c on 10c org brn	55	35
159 A18	2c on 20c org	1.75	1.40
160 A18	2c on 50c claret	17.50	16.00

Violet Surcharge

161 A18	1c on 20c org	70.00	

The handstamps are found sideways, diagonal, inverted and double.

Forgeries exist.

President Antoine T. Simon
A30 A31

For Foreign Postage

1910

162 A30	2c de p rose red & blk	52	35
163 A30	5c de p bl & blk	8.75	52
164 A30	20c de p yel grn & blk	7.00	5.50

For Domestic Postage

165 A31	1c de g lake & blk	15	15

For overprint and surcharges see Nos. 198, 262, 278, 285.

A32

A33

Pres. Cincinnatus Leconte — A34

1912

166 A32	1c de g car lake	20	18
167 A33	2c de g dp org	25	18

For Foreign Postage

168 A34	5c de p dp bl	52	18

For overprints see Nos. 199-201.

Stamps of Preceding Issues Handstamped Vertically

GL O.Z.
7 FÉV. 1914

1914

On No. 61

169 A13	8c carmine	8.75	7.00

On Nos. 170-175

170 A18	1c green	25.00	21.00
171 A18	2c carmine	25.00	21.00
172 A18	5c dk bl	45	25
173 A18	10c org brn	45	25
174 A18	20c orange	70	35
175 A18	50c claret	2.00	90

Perforation varieties of Nos. 172-175 exist.

On No. 107

176 A18	50c claret	*10,000.*	*10,000.*

Horizontally on Stamps of 1906-13

177 A19	1c de p grn	35	25
178 A20	2c de p ver	52	25
179 A21	3c de p brn	70	52
180 A21	3c de p org yel	35	25
181 A22	4c de p car lake	70	60
182 A22	4c de p lt ol grn	1.25	65
183 A23	7c de p gray	2.00	2.00
184 A23	7c de p org red	2.75	2.75
185 A24	8c de p car rose	3.50	3.50
186 A24	8c de p ol grn	3.50	3.50
187 A25	10c de p org red	90	52
188 A25	10c de p red brn	1.40	90
189 A26	15c de p sl grn	2.75	2.75
190 A26	15c de p yel	1.25	70
191 A20	20c de p bl grn	2.50	90
192 A19	50c de p red	4.25	4.25
193 A19	50c de p org yel	4.25	4.25
194 A27	1p claret	4.25	4.25
195 A27	1p red	4.25	4.25
196 A29	2c de g lemon	35	18
197 A28	3c de g slate	35	21
	Nos. 177-197 (21)	42.12	37.43

On No. 164

198 A30	20c de p yel grn & blk	2.75	2.75

Vertically on Nos. 166-168

199 A32	1c de g car lake	25	18
200 A33	2c de g dp org	45	35
201 A34	5c de p dp bl	70	20

Two handstamps were used for the overprints on Nos. 169 to 201. They may be distinguished by the short and long foot of the "L" of "GL" and the position of the first "1" in "1914" with regard to the period above it. Both handstamps are found on all these stamps.

Handstamp Surcharged

GL O.Z.
1 CENT DE PIASTRE
7 FÉV. 1914

On Nos. 141 and 143

213 A19	1c de p on 50c de p red	28	20
214 A27	1c de p on 1p claret	45	42

On Nos. 142 and 144

215 A19	1c de p on 50c de p org yel	45	35
216 A27	1c de p on 1p red	52	42

Handstamp Surcharged

On Nos. 100 and 101

217 A18	7c on 20c orange	42	20
218 A18	7c on 50c claret	35	20

The initials on the preceding handstamps are those of Gen. Oreste Zamor; the date is that of his triumphal entry into Port-au-Prince.

Buying Sets
It is often less expensive to purchase complete sets than individual stamps that make up the set. Set values are provided for many such sets.

Pres. Oreste Zamor

Coat of Arms

Pres. Tancrède Auguste

Owing to the theft of a large quantity of this 1914 issue, while in transit from the printers, the stamps were never placed on sale at post offices. A few copies have been canceled through carelessness or favor. Value, set of 10, $4.75.

Preceding Issues Handstamp Surcharged in Carmine or Blue

1

On Nos. 98-101

1915-16

235 A18	1c on 5c dk bl (C)	1.40	1.40
236 A18	1c on 10c org brn	15	15
237 A18	1c on 20c org	42	35
238 A18	1c on 50c claret	15	15

On No. 132

239 A23	1c on 7c de p gray (C)	15	15

On Nos. 106-107

240 A18	1c on 20c org	52	70
241 A18	1c on 50c claret	1.75	52
242 A18	1c on 50c cl (C)	27.50	21.00

Nos. 240-242 are known with two types of the "Post Paye" overprint. No. 237 with red surcharge and any stamps with violet surcharge are unofficial.

No. 143 Handstamp Surcharged in Red

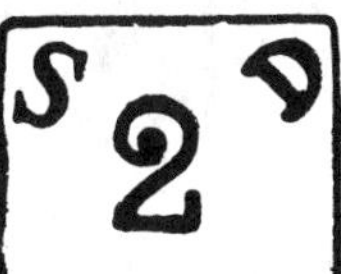

1917-19

245 A27	2c on 1p claret	18	15

Stamps of 1906-14 Handstamp Surcharged in Various Colors

1c, 5c

On Nos. 123-124

247 A12 1c on 50c (R) 17.50 12.50
248 A12 1c on 1g (R) 21.00 16.00

On #127, 129, 134, 136, 138, 140-141

249 A22 1c on 4c de p (Br) 15 15
250 A25 1c on 10c de p (Bl) 15 15
251 A25 1c on 10c de p (Bk) 70 70
252 A20 1c on 20c de p (R) 18 15
253 A20 1c on 20c de p (Bk) 25 15
254 A19 1c on 50c de p (R) 18 15
255 A19 1c on 50c de p (Bk) 25 15
256 A21 2c on 3c de p (R) 28 18
257 A24 2c on 8c de p (R) 18 15
258 A24 2c on 8c de p (Bk) 25 15
259 A26 2c on 15c de p (R) 18 15
260 A20 2c on 20c de p (R) 25 15
Nos. 249-260 (12) 3.00 2.38

On Nos. 164, 128

262 A30 1c on 20c de p (Bk) 3.50 3.50
263 A21 2c on 3c de p (R) 42 28

On #130, 133, 135, 137, 139, 142, 144

265 A22 1c on 4c de p (R) 28 28
266 A23 1c on 7c de p (Br) 42 28
267 A26 1c on 15c de p (R) 42 28
268 A19 1c on 50c de p (Bk) 90 90
269 A27 1c on 1p (Bk) 90 90
270 A24 2c on 8c de p (R) 35 35
271 A25 2c on 10c de p (Br) 35 15
272 A26 2c on 15c de p (R) 45 45
273 A25 5c on 10c de p (Bl) 70 70
274 A25 5c on 10c de p (VBk) 45 45
275 A26 5c on 15c de p (R) 3.50 3.50
Nos. 265-275 (11) 8.72 8.24

"O. Z." Stamps of 1914 Handstamp Surcharged in Red or Brown

276 A26 1c on 15c de p sl grn 18 18
277 A20 1c on 20c de p bl grn 18 18
278 A30 1c on 20c de p yel grn & blk 35 35
279 A27 1c on 1p claret (Br) 22 15
280 A27 1c on 1p claret 1.25 1.25
281 A27 5c on 1p red (Br) 35 35
Nos. 276-281 (6) 2.53 2.46

"O. Z." Stamps of 1914 Handstamp Surcharged in Various Colors as in 1917-19 and

1919-20

282 A22 2c on 4c de p car lake (V) 35 35
283 A24 2c on 8c de p car rose (G) 28 15
284 A24 2c on 8c de p ol grn (R) 18 15
285 A30 2c on 20c de p yel grn & blk (R) 28 15
286 A19 2c on 50c de p red (G) 15 15
288 A19 2c on 50c de p red (R) 45 35
289 A19 2c on 50c de p org yel (R) 25 18
290 A27 2c on 1pi claret (R) 2.00 1.75
291 A27 2c on 1pi red (R) 1.50 1.50
292 A21 3c on 3c de p brn (R) 35 35
293 A23 3c on 7c de p org red (R) 35 18
294 A21 5c on 3c de p brn (R) 42 18
295 A21 5c on 3c de p org yel (R) 1.40 1.40
296 A22 5c on 4c de p car lake (R) 45 45
297 A22 5c on 4c de p ol grn (R) 25 25
298 A23 5c on 7c de p gray (V) 28 28
299 A23 5c on 7c de p org red (V) 35 35
300 A25 5c on 10c de p org red (V) 25 25
301 A26 5c on 15c de p yel (M) 35 35
Nos. 282-301 (19) 9.89 8.77

Nos. 217 and 218 Handstamp Surcharged with New Value

302 A18 5c on 7c on 20c org (M) 35 35
303 A18 5c on 7c on 50c cl (M) 2.75 2.75

No. 187 Handstamp Surcharged

304 A25 5c de p on 10c de p (M) 45 45

Postage Due Stamps of 1906-14 Handstamp Surcharged

On Stamp of 1906

305 D2 5c on 50c ol gray (Bk) 10.50 8.50

On Stamp of 1914

306 D2 5c on 10c vio (Bk) 35 35
307 D2 5c on 50c ol gray (Bk) 45 45
308 D2 5c on 50c ol gray (M) 1.75 1.75

Nos. 299 with red surcharge and 306 and 307 with violet are trial colors or essays.

Allegory of Agriculture — A40 Allegory of Commerce — A41

1920, Apr. **Engr.** ***Perf. 12***

310 A40 3c dp org 18 15
311 A40 5c green 18 15
312 A41 10c vermilion 42 28
313 A41 15c violet 35 25
314 A41 25c dp bl 42 15
Nos. 310-314 (5) 1.55 98

Stamps of this issue overprinted "T. M." are revenue stamps. The letters are the initials of "Timbre-Mobile."

President Louis J. Borno — A42 Christophe's Citadel — A43

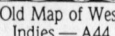

Old Map of West Indies — A44 Borno — A45

National Capitol — A46

1924, Sept. 3

315 A42 5c dp grn 15 15
316 A43 10c carmine 28 15
317 A44 20c vio bl 65 15
318 A45 50c org & blk 65 18
319 A46 1g olive green 1.25 25
Nos. 315-319 (5) 2.98
Set value 73

For surcharge see No. 359.

Coffee Beans and Flowers A47

1928, Feb. 6

320 A47 35c deep green 2.75 35

For surcharge see No. 337.

Pres. Louis Borno — A48

1929, Nov. 4

321 A48 10c car rose 25 15

Signing of the "Frontier" treaty between Haiti and the Dominican Republic.

Presidents Salomon and Vincent — A49

Pres. Sténio Vincent — A50

1931, Oct. 16

322 A49 5c dp grn 90 35
323 A50 10c car rose 90 35

50th anniv. of Haiti's joining the UPU.

President Vincent A52 Aqueduct at Port-au-Prince A53

Fort National — A54 Palace of Sans Souci — A55

Christophe's Chapel at Milot — A56

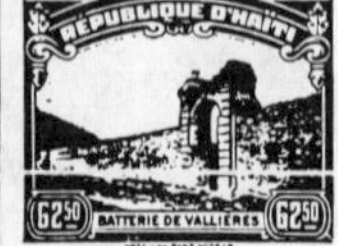

King's Gallery Citadel — A57 Vallières Battery — A58

1933-40

325 A52 3c orange 15 15
326 A52 3c dp ol grn ('39) 15 15
327 A53 5c green 15 15
328 A53 5c ol grn ('40) 42 15
329 A54 10c rose car 35 15
a. 10c vermilion 52 15
330 A54 10c red brn ('40) 35 15
331 A55 25c blue 65 18
332 A56 50c brown 1.75 35
333 A57 1g dk grn 1.75 35
334 A58 2.50g olive bister 2.75 52
Nos. 325-334 (10) 8.47
Set value 1.85

For surcharges see Nos. 357-358, 360.

Alexandre Dumas, His Father and Son — A59

1935, Dec. 29 **Litho.** ***Perf. 11½***

335 A59 10c rose pink & choc 65 25
336 A59 25c bl & chocolate 1.25 28

Issued in honor of the visit of a delegation from France to Haiti. See No. C10.

No. 320 Surcharged in Red

= 25C =

1939, Jan. 24 ***Perf. 12***

337 A47 25c on 35c dp grn 70 28

Statue of Liberty, Map of Haiti and Flags of American Republics — A60

1941, June 30 **Engr.** ***Perf. 12***

338 A60 10c rose car 75 28
339 A60 25c dark blue 65 35

3rd Inter-American Caribbean Conf., held at Port-au-Prince. See Nos. C12-C13.

Patroness of Haiti, Map and Coat of Arms — A61

1942, Dec. 8

Size: 26x36¼mm

340 A61 3c dl vio 30 24
341 A61 5c brt grn 45 24
342 A61 10c rose car 45 24
343 A61 15c orange 60 45
344 A61 20c brown 60 48
345 A61 25c dp bl 1.25 48
346 A61 50c red org 1.75 75
347 A61 2.50g ol blk 6.00 1.50

Size: 32x45mm

348 A61 5g purple 12.00 3.00
Nos. 340-348,C14-C18 (14) 27.80 8.93

Issued in honor of Our Lady of Perpetual Help, patroness of Haiti.
For surcharges see Nos. 355-356.

Adm. Hammerton Killick and Destruction of "La Crête-à-Pierrot" — A62

1943, Sept. 6

349 A62 3c orange 28 15
350 A62 5c turq grn 35 18
351 A62 10c car rose 35 15
352 A62 25c dp bl 42 18
353 A62 50c olive 90 28
354 A62 5g brn blk 4.50 2.50
Nos. 349-354,C22-C23 (8) 8.82 4.94

Nos. 343 and 345 Surcharged with New Value and Bars in Red

1944, July 19

355 A61 10c on 15c org 28 20
356 A61 10c on 25c dp bl 28 20

Nos. 319, 326 and 334 Surcharged with New Values and Bars in Red

1944-45

357 A52 2c on 3c dp ol grn 15 15
358 A52 5c on 3c dp ol grn 20 18
359 A46 10c on 1g ol grn 35 15
a. Surcharged "01.0"
360 A58 20c on 2.50g ol bis 35 28

Nurse and Wounded Soldier on Battlefield — A63

1945, Feb. 20

Cross in Rose

361 A63 3c gray blk 15 15
362 A63 5c dk bl grn 15 15
363 A63 10c red org 18 15
364 A63 20c blk brn 15 15
365 A63 25c dp bl 25 15
366 A63 35c orange 25 18
367 A63 50c car rose 42 20
368 A63 1g ol grn 65 28
369 A63 2.50g pale vio 2.00 35
Nos. 361-369,C25-C32 (17) 12.33 5.06

Issued to honor the Intl. Red Cross.
20c, 1g, 2.50g, Aug. 14. Others, Feb. 20.
For overprints and surcharges see Nos. 456-457, C153-C160.

Catalogue values for unused stamps in this section, from this point to the end of the section, are for Never Hinged items.

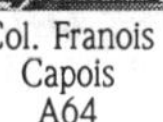

Col. Franois Capois A64

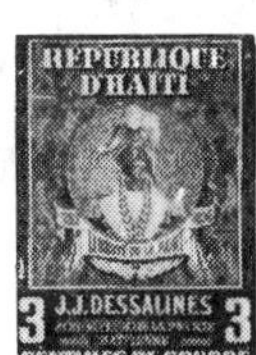

Jean Jacques Dessalines A65

Unwmk.

1946, July 18 Engr. *Perf. 12*

370 A64 3c red org 15 15
371 A64 5c Prus grn 15 15
372 A64 10c red 15 15
373 A64 20c olive black 15 15
374 A64 25c dp bl 15 15
375 A64 35c orange 18 15
376 A64 50c red brown 25 15
377 A64 1g olive brown 35 15
378 A64 2.50g gray 1.00 35
Nos. 370-378,C35-C42 (17) 5.88
Set value 3.15

For surcharges see Nos. 383, 392, C43-C45, C49-C51, C61-C62.

1947-54

379 A65 3c org yel 15 15
380 A65 5c green 15 15
380A A65 5c dp vio ('54) 42 15
381 A65 10c car rose 15 15
382 A65 25c dp bl 18 15
Set value, #379-382, C46 98 34

No. 375 Surcharged with New Value and Rectangular Block in Black

1948

383 A64 10c on 35c orange 18 15

Arms of Port-au-Prince A66

Engraved and Lithographed

1950, Feb. 12 *Perf. 12½*

384 A66 10c multi 20 15

200th anniv. (in 1949) of the founding of Port-au-Prince. See Nos. C47-C48.

Nos. RA10-RA12 and RA16 Surcharged or Overprinted in Black

U P U

1874 1949

■ 0.03 ■

1950, Oct. 4 Unwmk. *Perf. 12*

385 PT2 3c on 5c ol gray 15 15
386 PT2 5c green 25 15
387 PT2 10c on 5c car rose 25 20
388 PT2 20c on 5c blue 35 35
Nos. 385-388,C49-C51 (7) 2.27 2.05

75th anniv. (in 1949) of the UPU.
Exist with inverted or double surcharge and 10c on 5c green.

Cacao — A67

Pres. Paul E. Magloire and Day Nursery, Saline — A68

1951, Sept. 3 Photo. *Perf. 12½*

389 A67 5c dk brn 25 15

See Nos. C52-C54.

1953, May 4 Engr. *Perf. 12*

Design: 10c, Applying asphalt.

390 A68 5c green 15 15
391 A68 10c rose car 15 15
Nos. 390-391,C57-C60 (6) 2.28
Set value 1.40

No. 375 Surcharged in Black

7 AVRIL

1803 - 1953

50

■

1953, Apr. 7

392 A64 50c on 35c orange 35 20

Gen. Pierre Dominique Toussaint L'Ouverture, 1743-1803, liberator.

J. J. Dessalines and Paul E. Magloire — A69

Alexandre Sabes Pétion — A70

Battle of Vertieres — A71

Design: No. 395, Larmartiniere. No. 396, Bois-rond-Tonnerre. No. 397, Toussaint L'Ouverture. No. 399, Capois. No. 401, Marie Jeanne and Lamartiniere leading attack.

1954, Jan. 1 Photo. *Perf. 11½*

Portraits in Black

393 A69 3c blue gray 15 15
394 A70 5c yel grn 18 15
395 A70 5c yel grn 15 15
396 A70 5c yel grn 18 15
397 A70 5c yel grn 15 15
398 A69 10c crimson 15 15
399 A70 15c rose lilac 20 15

Perf. 12½

400 A71 25c dk gray 20 15
401 A71 25c dp org 20 15
Nos. 393-401 (9) 1.56
Set value 78

150th anniv. of Haitian independence.
See Nos. C63-C74, C95-C96.

Mme. Yolette Magloire — A72

1954, Jan. 1 *Perf. 11½*

402 A72 10c orange 15 15
403 A72 10c blue 15 15
Set value 18

See Nos. C75-C80.

Henri Christophe, Paul Magloire and Citadel A73

Tomb and Arms of Henri Christophe — A74

Perf. 13½x13

1954, Dec. 6 Litho. Unwmk.

404 A73 10c carmine 15 15

Perf. 13

405 A74 10c red, blk & car 15 15
Set value 18

Restoration of Christophe's Citadel.
See Nos. C81-C90.

J. J. Dessalines A75

Pres. Magloire and Dessalines Memorial, Gonaives A76

1955-57 Photo. *Perf. 11½*

406 A75 3c ocher & blk 15 15
407 A75 5c pale vio & blk ('56) 15 15
408 A75 10c rose & blk 15 15
a. 10c salmon pink & black ('57) 15 15
409 A75 25c chalky bl & blk ('56) 20 15
a. 25c blue & black ('57) 20 15
Set value, #406-409, C93-C94 63 35

1955, Aug. 1

410 A76 10c deep blue & blk 25 20
411 A76 10c crimson & blk 25 20

21st anniv. of the new Haitian army.
Nos. 410-411 were printed in a single sheet of 20 (5x4). The two upper rows are of No. 410, the two lower No. 411, providing five se-tenant pairs.
See Nos. C97-C98.

Flamingo A77

Mallard A78

1956, Apr. 14 Photo. *Perf. 11½*

Granite Paper

412 A77 10c bl & ultra 18 15
413 A78 25c dk grn & bluish grn 42 18

See Nos. C99-C104.

Immanuel Kant A79

1956, July 19 Granite Paper *Perf. 12*

414 A79 10c brt ultra 15 15

10th anniv. of the 1st Inter-American Philosophical Congress. See Nos. C105-C107a.

Zim Waterfall — A80

J. J. Dessalines and Dessalines Memorial, Gonaives — A81

1957, Dec. 16 Unwmk. *Perf. 11½*
Granite Paper

415 A80 10c org & bl 15 15

See Nos. C108-C111. For surcharge and overprint see Nos. CB49, CO2.

1958, July 1 Photo.

416 A81 5c yel grn & blk 15 15

Bicentenary of birth of J. J. Dessalines.
See Nos. 470-471, C112, C170. For overprints see Nos. 480-482, C183-C184, CO1, O1-O3.

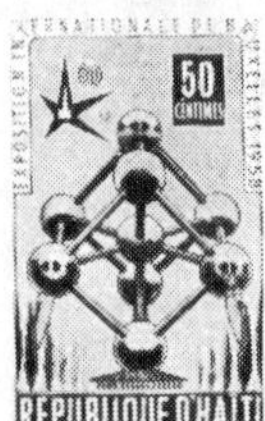

"Atomium" — A82

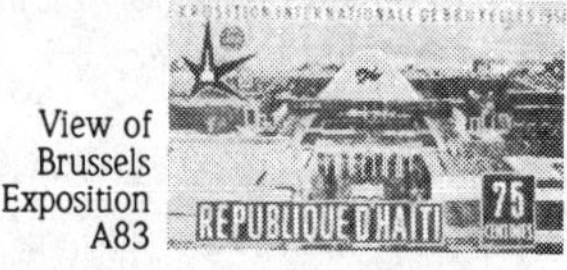

View of Brussels Exposition A83

Perf. 13x13½, 13½x13
1958, July 22 Litho. Unwmk.

417 A82 50c brown 18 15
418 A83 75c brt grn 18 15
419 A82 1g purple 52 18
420 A83 1.50g red org 42 20
Nos. 417-420,C113-C114 (6) 2.85 1.75

Issued for the Universal and International Exposition at Brussels.
For surcharges see Nos. B2-B3, CB9.

Sylvio Cator — A84

U. S. Satellite — A85

1958, Aug. 16 Photo. *Perf. 11½*
Granite Paper

421 A84 5c green 15 15
422 A84 10c brown 15 15
423 A84 20c lilac 15 15
Nos. 421-423,C115-C118 (7) 2.53
Set value 1.15

30th anniversary of the world championship record broad jump of Sylvio Cator.

1958, Oct. 8 *Perf. 14x13½*

Designs: 20c, Emperor penguins. 50c, Modern observatory. 1g, Ocean exploration.

424 A85 10c brt bl & brn red 15 15
425 A85 20c blk & dp org 28 20
426 A85 50c grn & rose brn 42 20
427 A85 1g blk & bl 60 18
Nos. 424-427,C119-C121 (7) 3.98 1.61

Issued for the International Geophysical Year 1957-58. See No. C121a.

President Franois Duvalier — A86

Engraved and Lithographed
1958, Oct. 22 Unwmk. *Perf. 11½*
Commemorative Inscription in Ultramarine

428 A86 10c blk & dp pink 15 15
429 A86 50c blk & lt grn 28 15
430 A86 1g blk & brick red 42 25
431 A86 5g blk & sal 1.75 1.25
Nos. 428-431,C122-C125 (8) 7.15 4.70

1st anniv. of the inauguration of Pres. Dr. Franois Duvalier. See note on souvenir sheets after No. C125.

Regular Issue
Without Commemorative Inscription
1958 Nov. 20

432 A86 5c blk & lt vio bl 15 15
433 A86 10c blk & dp pink 15 15
434 A86 20c blk & yel 15 15
435 A86 50c blk & lt grn 18 15
436 A86 1g blk & brick red 28 15
437 A86 1.50g blk & rose pink 42 28
438 A86 2.50g blk & gray vio 65 42
439 A86 5g blk & sal 1.25 90
Nos. 432-439 (8) 3.23 2.35

For surcharges see Nos. B13, B22-B24.

Map of Haiti — A87

1958, Dec. 5 Photo. *Perf. 11½*
Granite Paper

440 A87 10c rose pink 15 15
441 A87 25c green 15 15
Nos. 440-441,C133-C135 (5) 1.00
Set value 59

Tribute to the UN. See No. C135a. For overprints and surcharges see Nos. 442-443, B4-B5, CB11-CB12.

Nos. 440-441 Overprinted "10th ANNIVERSARY OF THE / UNIVERSAL DECLARATION / OF HUMAN RIGHTS" in English (a), French (b), Spanish (c) or Portuguese (d)

1959, Jan. 28

442 Block of 4 35 35
a.-d. A87 10c any single 15 15
443 Block of 4 90 70
a.-d. A87 25c any single 20 15
Nos. 442-443,C136-C138 (5) 10.65 10.45

10th anniv. of the signing of the Universal Declaration of Human Rights.

Pope Pius XII and Children — A88

Designs: 50c, Pope praying. 2g, Pope on throne.

1959, Feb. 28 Photo. *Perf. 14x13½*

444 A88 10c vio bl & ol 15 15
445 A88 50c grn & dp brn 20 15
446 A88 2g dp claret & dk brn 65 35
Nos. 444-446,C139-C141 (6) 2.15
Set value 1.00

Issued in memory of Pope Pius XII.
For surcharges see Nos. B6-B8.

Abraham Lincoln A89

1959, May 12 Photo. *Perf. 12*

447 A89 50c lt bl & dp claret 25 15

Sesquicentennial of the birth of Abraham Lincoln. Imperf. pairs exist. See Nos. C142-C144a. For surcharges see #B9, CB16-CB18.

Chicago's Skyline and Dessables House A90

Jean Baptiste Dessables and Map of American Midwest, c. 1791 — A91

Design: 50c, Discus thrower and flag of Haiti.

1959, Aug. 27 Unwmk. *Perf. 14*

448 A90 25c blk brn & lt bl 18 15
449 A90 50c multi 42 28
450 A91 75c brown & blue 52 42
Nos. 448-450,C145-C147 (6) 2.89 1.66

Issued to commemorate the 3rd Pan American Games, Chicago, Aug. 27-Sept. 7.
For surcharges see #B10-B12, CB19-CB21.

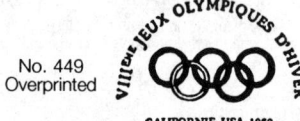

No. 449 Overprinted

VIIIème JEUX OLYMPIQUES D'HIVER
CALIFORNIE USA 1960

1960, Feb. 29

451 A90 50c multi 1.25 1.00

8th Olympic Winter Games, Squaw Valley, Calif., Feb. 18-29, 1960. See Nos. C148-C150.

Uprooted Oak Emblem and Hands — A92

1960, Apr. 7 Litho. *Perf. 12½x13*

452 A92 10c sal & grn 15 15
453 A92 50c vio & mag 18 15
Set value 21

World Refugee Year, July 1, 1959-June 30, 1960. See Nos. 489-490, C151-C152a, C191-C192. For surcharges see Nos. B14-B17, B28-B29, CB24-CB27, CB45-CB46.

No. 406 Surcharged with New Values
1960, Apr. 27 Photo. *Perf. 11½*

454 A75 5c on 3c ocher & blk 15 15
455 A75 10c on 3c ocher & blk 15 15
Set value 21 15

No. 369 Surcharged or Overprinted in Red: "28eme ANNIVERSAIRE"
1960, May 8 Engr. *Perf. 12*
Cross in Rose

456 A63 1g on 2.50g pale vio 65 32
457 A63 2.50g pale vio 90 70

28th anniversary of the Haitian Red Cross. See Nos. C153-C160.

Claudinette Fouchard, Miss Haiti, Sugar Queen — A93

Sugar Queen and: 20c, Sugar harvest. 50c, Beach. 1g, Sugar plantation.

Perf. 11½
1960, May 30 Photo. Unwmk.
Granite Paper

458 A93 10c ol bis & vio 15 15
459 A93 20c red brn & blk 18 15
460 A93 50c brt bl & brn 35 15
461 A93 1g grn & brn 70 20
Nos. 458-461,C161-C162 (6) 2.63
Set value 85

Haitian sugar industry.

Olympic Victors, Athens, 1896, Melbourne Stadium and Olympic Torch — A94

Designs: 20c, Discus thrower and Rome stadium. 50c, Pierre de Coubertin and victors, Melbourne, 1956. 1g, Athens stadium, 1896.

1960, Aug. 18 Photo. *Perf. 12*

462 A94 10c blk & org 15 15
463 A94 20c dk bl & crim 15 15
464 A94 50c grn & ocher 18 15
465 A94 1g dk brn & grnsh bl 28 15
Nos. 462-465,C163-C165 (7) 2.01
Set value 1.00

17th Olympic Games, Rome, Aug. 25-Sept. 11. See No. C165a. For surcharges see Nos. B18-B19, CB28-CB29.

Occide Jeanty and Score from "1804" A95

Designs: 20c, Occide Jeanty and National Capitol.

1960, Oct. 19 *Perf. 14x14½*

466 A95 10c orange & red lilac 15 15
467 A95 20c blue & red lilac 18 15
468 A95 50c green & sepia 42 18
Nos. 466-468,C166-C167 (5) 1.55
Set value 64

Cent. of the birth of Occide Jeanty, composer. Printed in sheets of 12 (3x4) with commemorative inscription and opening bars of "1804," Jeanty's military march, in top margin.

UN Headquarters, NYC — A96

1960, Nov. 25 Engr. *Perf. 10½*

469 A96 1g grn & blk 25 18

15th anniv. of the UN. See Nos. C168-C169a. For surcharges see Nos. B20-B21, CB30-CB31, CB35-CB36.

Dessalines Type of 1958

Perf. 11½

1960, Nov. 5 Unwmk. Photo.

Granite Paper

470 A81 10c red org & blk 15 15
471 A81 25c ultra & blk 18 15
Set value 15

See No. C170.

Alexandre Dumas Père and Musketeer — A97

Designs: 5c, Map of Haiti and birthplace of General Alexandre Dumas, horiz. 50c, Alexandre Dumas, father and son and French and Haitian flags, horiz.

1961, Feb. 10 *Perf. 11½*

Granite Paper

472 A97 5c lt bl & choc 15 15
473 A97 10c rose, blk & sep 15 15
474 A97 50c dk bl & crim 20 15
Nos. 472-474,C177-C179 (6) 1.28
Set value 80

Gen. Dumas (Alexandre Davy de la Pailleterie), born in Jeremie, Haiti, and his son and grandson, French authors.

Privateer in Battle — A98

Tourist publicity: 5c, Map of Tortuga. 10c, Three Pirates. 15c, Pirates. 50c, Pirate with cutlass in rigging.

1961, Apr. 4 Litho. *Perf. 12*

475 A98 5c bl & yel 15 15
476 A98 10c lake & yel 15 15
477 A98 15c ol grn & org 15 15
478 A98 20c choc & org 15 15
479 A98 50c vio bl & org 20 18
Set value, #475-479, C180-C182 1.10 75

For surcharges and overprints see Nos. 484-485, C186-C187.

Nos. 416, 470-471 and 378 Overprinted: "Dr. F. Duvalier / Président / 22 Mai 1961"

1961, May 22 Photo. *Perf. 11½*

480 A81 5c yel grn & blk 15 15
481 A81 10c red org & blk 15 15
482 A81 25c ultra & blk 18 15

Engr.

Perf. 12

483 A64 2.50g gray 70 52
Set value, #480-483, C183-C185 1.55 1.20

Re-election of Pres. Francois Duvalier.

No. 475 Surcharged: "EXPLORATION SPATIALE JOHN GLENN," Capsule and New Value

1962, May 10 Litho.

484 A98 50c on 5c bl & yel 28 20
485 A98 1.50g on 5c bl & yel 1.00 70

US achievement in space exploration and for the 1st orbital flight of a US astronaut, Lt. Col. John H. Glenn, Jr., Feb. 20, 1962. See Nos. C186-C187.

Malaria Eradication Emblem — A99

Design: 10c, Triangle pointing down.

Unwmk.

1962, May 30 Litho. *Perf. 12*

486 A99 5c crimson & dp bl 15 15
487 A99 10c red brn & emer 15 15
488 A99 50c bl & crimson 18 15
Set value, #486-488, C188-C190 88 60

WHO drive to eradicate malaria. Sheets of 12 with marginal inscription. For surcharges see Nos. B25-B27, CB42-CB44.

WRY Type of 1960 Dated "1962"

1962, June 22 *Perf. 12½x13*

489 A92 10c lt bl & org 15 15
490 A92 50c rose lil & ol grn 15 15
Set value 19 19

Issued to publicize the plight of refugees. For souvenir sheet see note after #C191-C192.

Haitian Scout Emblem — A100

Designs: 5c, 50c, Scout giving Scout sign. 10c, Lord and Lady Baden-Powell, horiz.

Perf. 14x14½, 14½x14

1962, Aug. 6 Photo.

491 A100 3c blk, ocher & pur 15 15
492 A100 5c cit, red brn & blk 15 15
493 A100 10c ocher, blk & grn 15 15
494 A100 25c mar, ol & bl 15 15
495 A100 50c vio, grn & red 25 15
Set value, #491-495, C193-C195 1.20 75

22nd anniv. of the Haitian Boy Scouts. For surcharges and overprints see Nos. B31-B34, C196-C199.

Space Needle, Space Capsule and Globe — A101

1962, Nov. 19 Litho. *Perf. 12½*

496 A101 10c red brn & lt bl 15 15
497 A101 20c vio bl & pink 15 15
498 A101 50c emer & yel 20 15
499 A101 1g car & lt grn 35 15
Nos. 496-499,C200-C202 (7) 1.82 1.10

"Century 21" International Exposition, Seattle, Wash., Apr. 21-Oct. 21. For overprints see #503-504, C206-C207.

Plan of Duvalier Ville and Stamp of 1904 — A102

1962, Dec. 10 Photo. *Perf. 14x14½*

500 A102 5c vio, yel & blk 15 15
501 A102 10c car rose, yel & blk 15 15
502 A102 25c bl gray, yel & blk 15 15
Nos. 500-502,C203-C205 (6) 1.52
Set value 1.05

Issued to publicize Duvalier Ville. For surcharge see No. B30.

Nos. 498-499 with Vertical Overprint in Black Similar to

1963, Jan. 23 Litho. *Perf. 12½*

503 A101 50c emer & yel 28 28
a. Claret overprint, horiz. 35 28
504 A101 1g car & lt grn 52 35
a. Claret overprint, horiz. 60 42

"Peaceful Uses of Outer Space." The black vertical overprint has no outside frame lines and no broken shading lines around capsule. Nos. 503a and 504a were issued Feb. 20. See Nos. C206-C207a.

Symbolic Harvest A103

1963, July 12 Photo. *Perf. 13x14*

505 A103 10c org & blk 15 15
506 A103 20c bluish grn & blk 15 15
Set value 17 15

FAO "Freedom from Hunger" campaign. See Nos. C208-C209.

J. J. Dessalines A104

Weight Lifter A105

1963, Oct. 17 *Perf. 14x14½*

507 A104 5c tan & ver 15 15
508 A104 10c yel & blue 15 15
Set value 15 15

See Nos. C214-C215. For overprints see Nos. 509, C216-C217.

No. 508 Overprinted: "FETE DES MERES / 1964"

1964, July 22

509 A104 10c yel & blue 15 15

Issued for Mother's Day, 1964. See Nos. C216-C218.

1964, Nov. 12 Photo. *Perf. 11½*

Granite Paper

Design: 50c, Hurdler.

510 A105 10c lt bl & dk brn 15 15
511 A105 25c sal & dk brn 15 15
512 A105 50c pale rose lil & dk brn 15 15
Set value, #510-512, C223-C226 1.12 78

18th Olympic Games, Tokyo, Oct. 10-25. Printed in sheets of 50 (10x5), with map of Japan in background extending over 27 stamps. For surcharges see #B35-B37, CB51-CB54.

Madonna of Haiti and International Airport, Port-au-Prince — A106

Unisphere, NY World's Fair — A107

1964, Dec. 15 *Perf. 14½x14*

513 A106 10c org yel & blk 15 15
514 A106 25c bl grn & blk 18 15
515 A106 50c brt yel grn & blk 25 15
516 A106 1g ver & blk 35 25
Nos. 513-516,C227-C229 (7) 2.45

Same Overprinted "1965"

1965, Feb. 11

517 A106 10c org, yel & blk 15 15
518 A106 25c bl grn & blk 18 15
519 A106 50c brt yel grn & blk 25 15
520 A106 1g ver & blk 35 25
Nos. 517-520,C230-C232 (7) 2.35
Set value 1.42

1965, Mar. 22 Photo. *Perf. 13½*

Design: 20c, "Rocket Thrower" by Donald De Lue.

521 A107 10c grn, yel ol & dk red 15 15
522 A107 20c plum & org 15 15
523 A107 50c dk brn, dk red, yel & grn 25 15
Nos. 521-523,C233-C235 (6) 2.83 2.38

New York World's Fair, 1964-65.

Merchantmen — A108

1965, May 13 Unwmk. *Perf. 11½*

524 A108 10c blk, lt grn & red 15 15
525 A108 50c blk, lt bl & red 15 15
Set value 19 15

Issued to honor the merchant marine. See Nos. C236-C237.

Market value for a particular scarce stamp may remain relatively low if few collectors want it.

ITU Emblem, Old and New Communication Equipment — A109

1965, Aug. 16 Litho. *Perf. 13½*

526 A109 10c gray & multi 15 15
527 A109 25c multi 15 15
528 A109 50c multi 18 15
Nos. 526-528,C242-C245 (7) 1.98
Set value 1.40

Cent. of the ITU.
For overprints see #537-539, C255-C256.

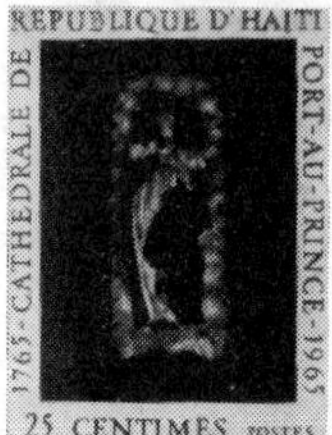

Statue of Our Lady of the Assumption A110

Passionflower A111

Designs: 5c, Cathedral of Port-au-Prince, horiz. 10c, High altar.

Perf. 14x13, 13x14

1965, Nov. 19 Photo.

Size: 39x29mm, 29x39mm

529 A110 5c multi 15 15
530 A110 10c multi 15 15
531 A110 25c multi 15 15
Nos. 529-531,C246-C248 (6) 2.93
Set value 2.15

200th anniv. of the Metropolitan Cathedral of Port-au-Prince.

1965, Dec. 20 Photo. *Perf. 11½*

Granite Paper

Flowers: 5c, 15c, American elder. 10c, Okra.

532 A111 3c dk vio, lt vio bl & grn 15 15
533 A111 5c grn, lt bl & yel 15 15
534 A111 10c multi 15 15
a. "0.10" omitted
535 A111 15c grn, pink & yel 15 15
536 A111 50c dk vio, yel & grn 20 15
Nos. 532-536,C249-C254 (11) 3.49
Set value 2.60

For surcharges see Nos. 566, B38-B40, CB55-CB56.

Nos. 526-528 Overprinted in Red: "20e. Anniversaire / UNESCO"

1965, Aug. 27 Litho. *Perf. 13½*

537 A109 10c gray & multi 15 15
538 A109 25c yel brn & multi 35 35
539 A109 50c pale grn & multi 70 70
Nos. 537-539,C255-C256 (5) 4.20 2.25

20th anniversary of UNESCO.

Amulet — A112

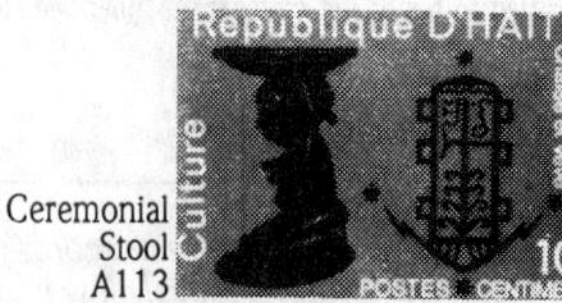

Ceremonial Stool A113

Perf. 14½x14, 14x14½

1966, Mar. 14 Photo. Unwmk.

540 A112 5c grnsh bl, blk & yel 15 15
541 A113 10c multi 15 15
542 A112 50c scar, yel & blk 15 15
Nos. 540-542,C257-C259 (6) 2.07
Set value 1.25

For overprints and surcharges see Nos. 543, 567-570, C260-C261, C280-C281.

No. 541 Overprinted in Red: "Hommage / a Hailé Sélassiéler / 24-25 Avril 1966"

1966, Apr. 24

543 A113 10c multi 18 18

Visit of Emperor Haile Selassie of Ethiopia, Apr. 24-25. See Nos. C260-C262.

Walter M. Shirra, Thomas P. Stafford, Frank A. Borman, James A. Lovell and Gemini VI A114

1966, May 3 *Perf. 13½*

544 A114 5c vio bl, brn & lt bl 15 15
545 A114 10c pur, brn & lt bl 15 15
546 A114 25c grn, brn & lt bl 15 15
547 A114 50c dk red, brn & lt bl 20 15
Set value, #544-547, C263-C265 1.50 1.10

Rendezvous in space of US spacecraft Gemini VI and VII, Dec. 15, 1965.
For overprint see No. 584.

Soccer Ball within Wreath and Pres. Duvalier A115

Design: 10c, 50c, Soccer player within wreath and Duvalier.

Lithographed and Photogravure

1966, June 16 *Perf. 13x13½*

Portrait in Black; Gold Inscription; Green Commemorative Inscription in Two Lines

548 A115 5c pale sal & grn 15 15
549 A115 10c lt ultra & grn 15 15
550 A115 15c lt grn & grn 15 15
551 A115 50c pale lil rose & grn 20 15

Green Commemorative Inscription in 3 Lines; Gold Inscription Omitted

552 A115 5c pale sal & grn 15 15
553 A115 10c lt ultra & grn 15 15
554 A115 15c lt grn & grn 15 15
555 A115 50c pale lil rose & grn 18 15
Set value, #548-555, C266-C269 2.10 1.50

Caribbean Soccer Festival, June 10-22. Nos. 548-551 also for the Natl. Soccer Championships, May 8-22.
For surcharges and overprint see Nos. 578-579, C288, CB57.

"ABC," Boy and Girl — A116

Designs: 10c, Scout symbols. 25c, Television set, book and communications satellite, horiz.

Perf. 14x13½, 13½x14

1966, Oct. 18 Litho. & Engr.

556 A116 5c grn, sal pink & brn 15 15
557 A116 10c red brn, lt brn & blk 15 15
558 A116 25c grn, bl & dk vio 15 15
Set value, #556-558, C270-C272 1.00 95

Issued to publicize education through literacy, Scouting and by audio-visual means.

Dr. Albert Schweitzer, Maps of Alsace and Gabon A117

Designs: 10c, Dr. Schweitzer and pipe organ. 20c, Dr. Schweitzer and Albert Schweitzer Hospital, Deschapelles, Haiti.

Perf. 12½x13

1967, Apr. 20 Photo. Unwmk.

559 A117 5c pale lil & multi 15 15
560 A117 10c buff & multi 15 15
561 A117 20c gray & multi 15 15
Nos. 559-561,C273-C276 (7) 2.13
Set value 1.80

Issued in memory of Dr. Albert Schweitzer (1875-1965), medical missionary to Gabon, theologian and musician.

Watermelon and J. J. Dessalines A118

1967, July 4 Photo. *Perf. 12½*

562 A118 5c shown 15 15
563 A118 10c Cabbage 15 15
564 A118 20c Tangerine 15 15
565 A118 50c Chayote 15 15
Set value, #562-565, C277-C279 1.15 90

No. 532 Surcharged

1967, Aug. 21 Photo. *Perf. 11½*

566 A111 50c on 3c multi 18 15
Nos. 566,B38-B40,CB55-CB56 (6) 1.16 1.10

12th Boy Scout World Jamboree, Farragut State Park, Idaho, Aug. 1-9.

Nos. 540-542 Overprinted and Surcharged

Perf. 14½x14, 14x14½

1967, Aug. 30 Photo.

567 A112 5c grnsh bl, blk & yel 15 15
568 A113 10c multi 15 15
569 A112 50c scar, yel & blk 15 15
570 A112 1g on 5c multi 28 25
Nos. 567-570,C280-C281 (6) 1.95
Set value 1.40

Issued to commemorate EXPO '67 International Exhibition, Montreal, Apr. 28-Oct. 27.

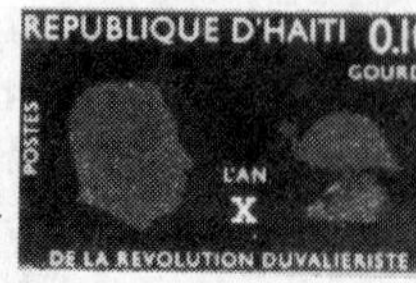

Pres. Duvalier and Brush Turkey A119

1967, Sept. 22 Photo. *Perf. 14x13*

571 A119 5c car rose & gold 15 15
572 A119 10c ultra & gold 15 15
573 A119 25c dk red brn & gold 15 15
574 A119 50c dp red lil & gold 15 15
Set value, #571-574, C282-C284 1.90 1.50

10th anniversary of Duvalier revolution.

Writing Hands — A120

Designs: 10c, Scout emblem and Scouts, vert. 25c, Audio-visual teaching of algebra.

1967, Dec. 11 Litho. *Perf. 11½*

575 A120 5c multi 15 15
576 A120 10c multi 15 15
577 A120 25c dk grn, lt bl & yel 15 15
Set value, #575-577, C285-C287 1.00 85

Issued to publicize the importance of education.
For surcharges see Nos. CB58-CB60.

Nos. 552 and 554 Surcharged

Lithographed and Photogravure

1968, Jan. 18 *Perf. 13x13½*

578 A115 50c on 15c 15 15
579 A115 1g on 5c 25 20

19th Olympic Games, Mexico City, Oct. 12-27. See Nos. C288, CB57.

The 1968 date is missing on 2 stamps in every sheet of 50.

Caiman Woods, by Raoul Dupoux A121

1968, Apr. 22 Photo. *Perf. 12*

Size: 36x26mm

580 A121 5c multi 15 15
581 A121 10c rose red & multi 15 15
582 A121 25c multi 15 15
583 A121 50c dl lil & multi 15 15
Nos. 580-583,C289-C295 (11) 3.98 3.40

Caiman Woods ceremony during the Slaves' Rebellion, Aug. 14, 1791.

No. 547 Overprinted

1968, Apr. 19 Photo. *Perf. 13½*

584 A114 50c dk red, brn & lt bl 70 70

Issued to commemorate the 10th Winter Olympic Games, Grenoble, France, Feb. 6-18, 1968. See Nos. C296-C298.

Monument to the Unknown Maroon — A122

Palm Tree and Provincial Coats of Arms — A123

Madonna, Papal Arms and Arms of Haiti — A124

1968, May 22 *Perf. 11½*

Granite Paper

585	A122	5c	bl & blk	15	15
586	A122	10c	rose brn & blk	15	15
587	A122	20c	vio & blk	15	15
588	A122	25c	lt ultra & blk	15	15
589	A122	50c	brt bl grn & blk	25	15
			Set value, #585-589, C299-C301	1.65	1.10

Unveiling of the monument to the Unknown Maroon, Port-au-Prince.

For surcharges see Nos. C324-C325.

Perf. 13x14, 12½x13½

1968, Aug. 16 **Photo.**

Design: 25c, Cathedral, arms of Pope Paul VI and arms of Haiti.

590	A123	5c	grn & multi	15	15
591	A124	10c	brn & multi	15	15
592	A124	25c	multi	15	15
			Nos. 590-592,C302-C305 (7)	2.00	
			Set value		1.25

Issued to commemorate the consecration of the Bishopric of Haiti, Oct. 28, 1966.

Air Terminal, Port-au-Prince — A125

1968, Sept. 22 **Photo.** *Perf. 11½*

Portrait in Black

593	A125	5c	brn & lt ultra	15	15
594	A125	10c	brn & lt bl	15	15
595	A125	25c	brn & pale lil	15	15
			Set value, #593-595, C306-C308	1.45	1.25

Inauguration of the Francois Duvalier Airport in Port-au-Prince.

Slave Breaking Chains, Map of Haiti, Torch, Conch — A126

1968, Oct. 28 **Litho.** *Perf. 14½x14*

596	A126	5c	brn, lt bl & brt pink	15	15
597	A126	10c	brn, lt ol & brt pink	15	15
598	A126	25c	brn, bis & brt pink	15	15
			Set value, #596-598, C310-C313	1.55	1.30

Slaves' Rebellion, of 1791.

Children Learning to Read — A127

Designs: 10c, Children watching television. 50c, Hands setting volleyball and sports medal.

1968, Nov. 14 *Perf. 11½*

599	A127	5c	multi	15	15
600	A127	10c	multi	15	15
601	A127	50c	multi	15	15
			Set value, #599-601, C314-C316	1.20	90

Issued to publicize education through literacy, audio-visual means and sport.

For surcharges see #B41-B42, CB61-CB62.

Winston Churchill A128

Churchill: 5c, as painter. 10c, as Knight of the Garter. 15c, and soldiers at Normandy. 20c, and early seaplane. 25c, and Queen Elizabeth II. 50c, and Big Ben, London.

1968, Dec. 23 **Photo.** *Perf. 13*

602	A128	3c	gold & multi	15	15
603	A128	5c	gold & multi	15	15
604	A128	10c	gold & multi	15	15
605	A128	15c	gold & multi	15	15
606	A128	20c	gold & multi	15	15
607	A128	25c	gold & multi	15	15
608	A128	50c	gold & multi	18	15
			Set value, #602-608, C319-C322	1.50	1.25

Issued in memory of Sir Winston Spencer Churchill (1874-1965), statesman and World War II leader. Exist imperforate.

For surcharge see No. 828.

1968 Winter Olympics, Grenoble A128a

Designs: 5c, 1.50g, Peggy Fleming, US, figure skating. 10c, Harold Groenningen, Norway, cross-country skiing. 20c, Belousova & Protopopov, USSR, pairs figure skating. 25c, Toini Gustafsson, Sweden, cross country skiing. 50c, Eugenio Monti, Italy, 4-man bobsled. 2g, Erhard Keller, Germany, speed skating. 4g, Jean Claude Killy, France, downhill skiing.

1968 **Litho.** *Perf. 14x13½*

609	A128a	5c	brt bl & multi
609A	A128a	10c	bl grn & multi
609B	A128a	20c	brt rose & multi
609C	A128a	25c	sky bl & multi
609D	A128a	50c	ol bis & multi
609E	A128a	1.50g	vio & multi

Size: 36x65mm

Perf. 12x12½

609F	A128a	2g	emer grn & multi

Souvenir Sheet

609G	A128a	4g	brn & multi

No. 609G contains one 36x65mm stamp. Nos. 609F-609G are airmail. No. 609G exists imperf. with green, brown and blue margin.

No. 589 Surcharged with New Value and Rectangle

1969, Feb. 21 **Photo.** *Perf. 11½*

610	A122	70c	on 50c	32	20

See Nos. C324-C325.

Blue-headed Euphonia A129

Power Lines and Light Bulb A131

Olympic Marathon Winners, 1896-1968 — A130

Birds of Haiti: 10c, Hispaniolan trogon. 20c, Palm chat. 25c, Stripe-headed tanager. 50c, Like 5c.

1969, Feb. 26 *Perf. 13½*

611	A129	5c	lt grn & multi	15	15
612	A129	10c	yel & multi	15	15
613	A129	20c	cream & multi	15	15
614	A129	25c	lt lil & multi	15	15
615	A129	50c	lt gray & multi	25	15
			Nos. 611-615,C326-C329 (9)	2.25	
			Set value		1.50

For overprints see Nos. C344A-C344D.

1969, May 16 *Perf. 12½x12*

Designs: Games location, date, winner, country and time over various stamp designs.

Souvenir sheets do not show location, date, country or time.

Size: 66x35mm (Nos. 616, 616C, 616F, 616O)

616	A130	5c	like Greece #124
616A	A130	10c	like France #124
616B	A130	15c	US #327
616C	A130	20c	like Great Britain #142
616D	A130	20c	Sweden #68
616E	A130	25c	Belgium #B49
616F	A130	25c	like France #198
616G	A130	25c	Netherlands #B30
616H	A130	30c	US #718
616I	A130	50c	Germany #B86
616J	A130	60c	Great Britain #274
616K	A130	75c	like Finland #B110
616L	A130	75c	like Australia #277
616M	A130	90c	Italy #799
616N	A130	1g	like Japan #822
616O	A130	1.25g	like Mexico #C328

Souvenir Sheets

616P	A130	1.50g	US #718, diff.

Imperf

616Q	A130	1.50g	Germany #B86, diff.

Nos. 616H-616O are airmail. Nos. 616P-616Q contain one 66x35mm stamp. A 2g souvenir sheet exists, perf. & imperf.

1969, May 22 **Litho.** *Perf. 13x13½*

617	A131	20c	lilac & blue	15	15

Issued to publicize the Duvalier Hydroelectric Station. See Nos. C338-C340.

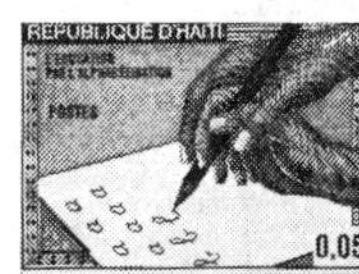

Learning to Write — A132

Designs: 10c, children playing, vert. 50c, Peace poster on educational television, vert.

1969, Aug. 12 **Litho.** *Perf. 13½*

618	A132	5c	multi	15	15
619	A132	10c	multi	15	15
620	A132	50c	multi	15	15
			Set value, #618-620, C342-C344	1.25	82

Issued to publicize national education.

ILO Emblem A133

1969, Sept. 22 *Perf. 14*

621	A133	5c	bl grn & blk	15	15
622	A133	10c	brn & blk	15	15
623	A133	20c	vio bl & blk	15	15
			Set value, #621-623, C345-C347	1.25	75

50th anniv. of the ILO.

Apollo Space Missions — A133a

Designs: 10c, Apollo 7 rendezvous of command module, third stage. 15c, Apollo 7, preparation for re-entry. 20c, Apollo 8, separation of third stage. 25c, Apollo 8, mid-course correction. 70c, Apollo 8, approaching moon. 1g, Apollo 8, orbiting moon, Christmas 1968, vert. 1.25, Apollo 8, leaving moon. 1.50g, Apollo 8, crew, vert. 1.75g, 2g, Apollo 11, first lunar landing.

1969, Oct. 6 *Perf. 12x12½*

624	A133a	10c	brt rose & multi
624A	A133a	15c	vio & multi
624B	A133a	20c	ver & multi
624C	A133a	25c	emer grn & multi
624D	A133a	70c	brt bl & multi
624E	A133a	1g	bl grn & multi
624F	A133a	1.25g	dk bl & multi
624G	A133a	1.50g	dp rose lil & multi

Souvenir Sheets

624H	A133a	1.75g	grn & multi
624I	A133a	2g	sky bl & multi

Nos. 624D-624I are airmail. Nos. 624-624I exist imperf. in different colors.

Papilio Zonaria — A134

Butterflies: 20c, Zerene cesonia cynops. 25c, Papilio machaonides.

1969, Nov. 14 **Photo.** *Perf. 13½*

625	A134	10c	pink & multi	15	15
626	A134	20c	gray & multi	15	15
627	A134	25c	lt bl & multi	15	15
			Nos. 625-627,C348-C350 (6)	1.57	
			Set value		1.10

Martin Luther King, Jr. A135

Perf. 12½x13½

1970, Jan. 12 **Litho.**

628 A135 10c bis, red & blk 15 15
629 A135 20c grnsh bl, red & blk 15 15
630 A135 25c brt rose, red & blk 15 15
Set value, #628-630, C351-C353 1.25 88

Martin Luther King, Jr. (1929-1968), American civil rights leader.

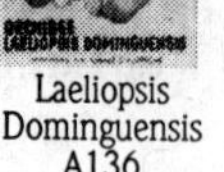

Laeliopsis Dominguensis A136

UPU Monument and Map of Haiti A137

Haitian Orchids: 20c, Oncidium Haitiense. 25c, Oncidium calochilum.

1970, Apr. 3 **Litho.** *Perf. 13x12½*

631 A136 10c yel, lil & blk 15 15
632 A136 20c lt bl grn, yel & brn 20 15
633 A136 25c bl & multi 28 15
Nos. 631-633,C354-C356 (6) 1.85
Set value 1.20

1970, June 23 **Photo.** *Perf. 11½*

Designs: 25c, Propeller and UPU emblem, vert. 50c, Globe and doves.

634 A137 10c blk, brt grn & ol bis 15 15
635 A137 25c blk, brt rose & ol bis 18 15
636 A137 50c blk & bl 35 25
Nos. 634-636,C357-C359 (6) 2.08 1.55

16th Cong. of the UPU, Tokyo, Oct. 1-Nov. 16, 1970.

For overprints see Nos. 640, C360-C362.

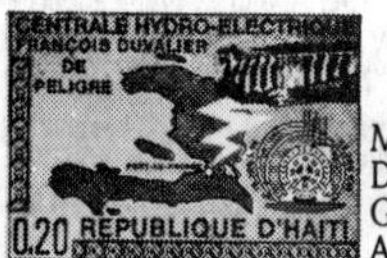

Map of Haiti, Dam and Generator A138

Design: 25c, Map of Haiti, dam and pylon.

1970 **Litho.** *Perf. 14x13½*

637 A138 20c lt grn & multi 15 15
638 A138 25c lt bl & multi 18 15
Set value 17

Issued to publicize the Franois Duvalier Central Hydroelectric Plant.

For surcharges see #B43-B44, RA40-RA41.

Apollo 12 A138a

1970, Sept. *Perf. 13½x14*

639 A138a 5c Lift-off
639A A138a 10c 2nd stage ignition
639B A138a 15c Docking preparations
639C A138a 20c Heading for moon
639D A138a 25c like 639B
639E A138a 25c Lunar exploration
639F A138a 30c Landing on Moon
639G A138a 30c Lift-off from Moon
639H A138a 40c 3rd stage separation
639I A138a 40c Lunar module, crew
639J A138a 50c Lunar orbital activities
639K A138a 50c Leaving Moon orbit
639L A138a 75c In Earth orbit
639M A138a 1g Re-entry
639N A138a 1.25g Landing at sea
639O A138a 1.50g Docking with lunar module

Nos. 639E, 639G, 639I, 639K-639O are airmail. Nos. 639-639O exist imperf. with brighter colors.

For overprints see Nos. 656-656O.

No. 636 Overprinted in Red with UN Emblem and: "XXVe ANNIVERSAIRE / O.N.U."

1970, Dec. 14 **Photo.** *Perf. 11½*

640 A137 50c blk & bl 20 15

UN, 25th anniv. See Nos. C360-C362.

Fort Nativity, Drawing by Columbus — A139

Ascension, by Castera Bazile — A140

1970, Dec. 22

641 A139 3c dk brn & buff 15 15
642 A139 5c dk grn & pale grn 18 15
Set value 23 19

Christmas 1970.

1971, Apr. 29 **Litho.** *Perf. 12x12½*

Paintings: 5c, Man with Turban, by Rembrandt. 20c, Iris in a Vase, by Van Gogh. 50c, Baptism of Christ, by Castera Bazile. No. 647, Young Mother Sewing, by Mary Cassatt. No. 648, The Card Players, by Cezanne.

Size: 20x40mm

643 A140 5c multi 15 15
644 A140 10c multi 15 15

Perf. 13x12½

Size: 25x37mm

645 A140 20c multi 15 15

Perf. 12x12½

Size: 20x40mm

646 A140 50c multi 28 15
Nos. 643-646,C366-C368 (7) 1.78
Set value 1.10

Souvenir Sheets

Imperf

647 A140 3g multi 1.00 1.00
648 A140 3g multi 1.00 1.00

No. 647 contains one stamp, size: 20x40mm, No. 648 contains one stamp, size: 25x37mm.

Soccer Ball — A141

Design: No. 651, 1g, 5g, Jules Rimet cup.

1971, June 14 **Photo.** *Perf. 11½*

649 A141 5c salmon & blk 15 15
650 A141 50c tan & blk 20 15
651 A141 50c rose pink, blk & gold 20 15
652 A141 1g lil, blk & gold 38 28
653 A141 1.50g gray & blk 52 42
654 A141 5g gray, blk & gold 1.75 1.50
Nos. 649-654 (6) 3.20 2.65

Souvenir Sheet

Imperf

655 Sheet of 2 8.50 7.00
a. A141 70c light violet & black
b. A141 1g light green, blue & gold

9th World Soccer Championships for the Jules Rimet Cup, Mexico City, May 30-June 21, 1970. The surface tint of the sheets of 50 (10x5) of Nos. 649-654 includes a map of Brazil covering 26 stamps. Positions 27, 37 and 38 inscribed "Brasilia," "Santos," "Rio de Janeiro" respectively. On soccer ball design the 4 corner stamps are inscribed "Pele."

Nos. 655a and 655b have portions of map of Brazil in background; No. 655a inscribed "Pele" and "Santos," No. 655b "Brasilia."

Nos. 639-639O Ovptd. in Gold

APOLLO XIII RETOUR SUR LA TERRE

1971

656 A138a 5c multicolored
656A A138a 10c multicolored
656B A138a 15c multicolored
656C A138a 20c multicolored
656D A138a 25c multicolored
656E A138a 25c multicolored
656F A138a 30c multicolored
656G A138a 30c multicolored
656H A138a 40c multicolored
656I A138a 40c multicolored
656J A138a 50c multicolored
656K A138a 50c multicolored
656L A138a 75c multicolored
656M A138a 1g multicolored
656N A138a 1.25g multicolored
656O A138a 1.50g multicolored

Nos. 656E, 656G, 656I, 656K-656O are airmail. Exist overprinted in silver.

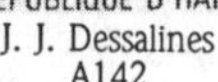

J. J. Dessalines A142

"Sun" and EXPO '70 Emblem A143

1972, Apr. 28 **Photo.** *Perf. 11½*

657 A142 5c grn & blk 15 15
658 A142 10c brt bl & blk 15 15
659 A142 25c org & blk 15 15
Set value, #657-659, C378-C379 1.25 75

See Nos. 697-700, C448-C458, 727, C490-C493, C513-C514. For surcharges see Nos. 692, 705-709, 724-726, C438, C512.

1972, Oct. 27 **Photo.** *Perf. 11½*

660 A143 10c ocher, brn & grn 15 15
661 A143 25c ocher, brn & mar 15 15
Nos. 660-662,C378-C379 (4) 1.38
Set value 1.25

EXPO '70 International Exposition, Osaka, Japan, Mar. 15-Sept. 13, 1970.

Gold Medalists, 1972 Summer Olympics, Munich — A143a

Designs: 5c, L. Linsenhoff, dressage, W. Ruska, judo. 10c, S. Kato, gymnastics, S.Gould, women's swimming. 20c, M. Peters, women's pentathlon, K. Keino, steeplechase. 25c, L. Viren, 5,000, 10,000m races, R. Milburn, 110m hurdles. No. 662D, D. Morelon, cycling, J. Akii-Bua, 400m hurdles. No. 662E, R. Williams, long jump. 75c, G. Mancinelli, equestrian. 1.50g, W. Nordwig, pole vault. 2.50g, K. Wolferman, javelin. 5g, M. Spitz, swimming.

1972, Dec. 29 *Perf. 13½*

662 A143a 5c multicolored
662A A143a 10c multicolored
662B A143a 20c multicolored
662C A143a 25c multicolored
662D A143a 50c multicolored
662E A143a 50c multicolored
662F A143a 75c multicolored
662G A143a 1.50g multicolored
662H A143a 2.50g multicolored
662I A143a 5g multicolored

Nos. 662E-662I are airmail.

Basket Vendors — A144

Designs: 80c, 2.50g, Postal bus.

1973, Jan. **Photo.** *Perf. 11½*

665 A144 50c blk & multi 18 15
666 A144 80c blk & multi 28 16
667 A144 1.50g blk & multi 52 32
668 A144 2.50g blk & multi 1.25 52

20th anniv. of Caribbean Travel Assoc.

Space Exploration

A set of 12 stamps for US-USSR space exploration, the same overprinted for the centenary of the UPU and 3 overprinted in silver for Apollo 17 exist but we have no evidence that they were printed with the approval of the Haitian postal authorities.

Micromelo Undata A145

Designs: Marine life; 50c horizontal.

1973, Sept. 4 **Litho.** *Perf. 14*

669 A145 5c *shown* 15 15
670 A145 10c *Nemaster rubiginosa* 15 15
671 A145 25c *Cyerce cristallina* 15 15
672 A145 50c *Desmophyllum riisei* 15 15
Set value, #669-672, C395-C398 1.65 1.25

For surcharge see No. C439/

Gramma Loreto — A146

1973 *Perf. 13½*

673 A146 10c *shown* 15 15
674 A146 50c *Acanthurus coeruleus* 18 15
Nos. 673-674,C399-C402 (6) 2.55 1.95

For surcharges see Nos. 693, C440.

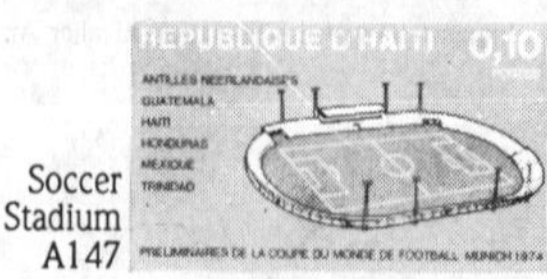

Soccer Stadium A147

Design: 20c, Haiti No. 654.

1973, Nov. 29 *Perf. 14x13*

675 A147 10c bis, blk & emer 15 15
676 A147 20c rose lil, blk & tan 15 15
Nos. 675-676,C407-C410 (6) 3.92 2.98

Caribbean countries preliminary games of the World Soccer Championships, Munich, 1974.

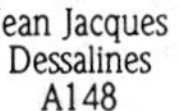

Jean Jacques Dessalines A148

Nicolaus Copernicus A149

1974, Apr. 22 Photo. *Perf. 14*

677 A148 10c lt bl & emer 15 15
678 A148 20c rose & blk 15 15
679 A148 25c yel & vio 15 15
Set value, #677-679, C411-C414 1.30 1.00

For surcharges see Nos. 694, C443.

1974, May 24 Litho. *Perf. 14x13½*

Design: 10c, Symbol of heliocentric system.

680 A149 10c multi 15 15
681 A149 25c brt grn & multi 15 15
Set value, #680-681, C415-C419 1.35 1.00

Copernicus (1473-1543), Polish astronomer.
For overprint and surcharges see Nos. 695, C444, C460-C463.

Pres. Jean-Claude Duvalier — A151

1974 Photo. *Perf. 14x13½*

689 A151 10c grn & gold 15 15
690 A151 20c car rose & gold 15 15
691 A151 50c bl & gold 15 15
Nos. 689-691,C421-C426 (9) 3.42 2.65

For surcharge and overprints see Nos. C445, C487-C489.

Audubon Birds

In 1975 or later various sets of bird paintings by Audubon were produced by government employees without official authorization. They were not sold by the Haiti post office and were not valid for postage. The first set consisted of 23 values and was sold in 1975. A second set containing some of the original stamps and some new stamps appeared unannounced several years later. More sets may have been printed as there are 75 different stamps. These consist of 5 denominations each for the 15 designs.

Nos. 659, 673 and 679-680 Surcharged with New Value and Bar

Perf. 11½, 13½, 14, 14x13½

1976 Photo.; Litho.

692 A142 80c on 25c 35 20
693 A146 80c on 10c 35 20
694 A148 80c on 25c 35 20
695 A149 80c on 10c 35 20

Haiti No. C11 and Bicentennial Emblem — A152

1976, Apr. 22 Photo. *Perf. 11½*
Granite Paper

696 A152 10c multi 15 15
Nos. 696,C434-C437 (5) 2.94 2.28

American Bicentennial.

Dessalines Type of 1972

1977 Photo. *Perf. 11½*

697 A142 10c rose & blk 15 15
698 A142 20c lemon & blk 15 15
699 A142 50c vio & blk 15 15
700 A142 50c tan & blk 15 15
Set value 40 30

Dessalines Type of 1972 Surcharged in Black or Red

1978 Photo. *Perf. 11½*

705 A142 1g on 20c (#698) 28 20
706 A142 1g on 1.75g (#C454) 28 20
707 A142 1.25g on 75c (#C448) 35 26
708 A142 1.25g on 1.50g (#C453) 35 26
709 A142 1.25g on 1.50g (#C453; R) 35 26
Nos. 705-709 (5) 1.61 1.18

Rectangular bar obliterates old denomination on Nos. 705-709 and "Par Avion" on Nos. 706-709.

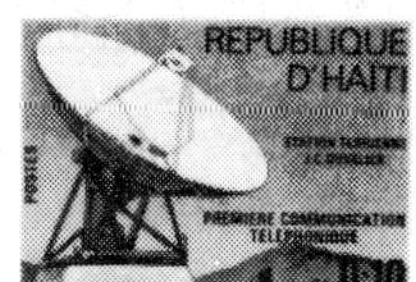

J. C. Duvalier Earth Telecommunications Station — A153

Designs: 20c, Video telephone. 50c, Alexander Graham Bell, vert.

1978, June 19 Litho. *Perf. 13½*

710 A153 10c multi 15 15
711 A153 20c multi 15 15
712 A153 50c multi 15 15
Set value, #710-712, C466-C468 1.42 1.05

Centenary of first telephone call by Alexander Graham Bell, Mar. 10, 1876.

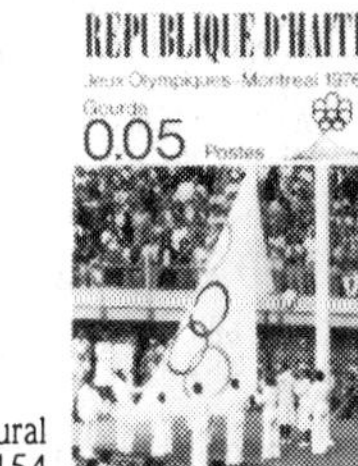

Athletes' Inaugural Parade — A154

1978, Sept. 4 Litho. *Perf. 13½x13*

713 A154 5c shown 15 15
714 A154 25c Bicyclists 15 15
715 A154 50c High jump 15 15
Nos. 713-715,C469-C471 (6) 2.90
Set value 1.72

21st Olympic Games, Montreal, July 17-Aug. 1, 1976.

Mother Nursing Child — A155

Mother Feeding Child — A156

1979, Jan. 15 Photo. *Perf. 14x14½*

716 A155 25c multi 15 15

Inter-American Children's Institute, 50th anniversary. See Nos. C472-C473.

1979, May 11 Photo. *Perf. 11½*

717 A156 25c multi 15 15
718 A156 50c multi 15 15
Nos. 717-718,C474-C476 (5) 1.48 1.18
Set value

30th anniversary of CARE (Cooperative for American Relief Everywhere).

Human Rights Emblem — A157

1979, July 20 Litho. *Perf. 14*

719 A157 25c multi 15 15

30th anniversary of declaration of human rights. See Nos. C477-C479.

Anti-Apartheid Year Emblem, Antenor Firmin, "On the Equality of Human Races" — A158

1979, Nov. 22 Photo. *Perf. 12x11½*

720 A158 50c tan & black 15 15

Anti-Apartheid Year (1978). See Nos. C480-C482.

Children Playing, IYC Emblem A159

1979, Dec. 19 Photo. *Perf. 12*

721 A159 10c multi 15 15
722 A159 25c multi 15 15
723 A159 50c multi 15 15
Nos. 721-723,C483-C486 (7) 3.18 2.43

International Year of the Child.

Nos. C379, C449, C454 Surcharged

TIMBRE POSTE G. 1.00

1980 Photo. *Perf. 11½*
Granite Paper

724 A142 1g on 2.50g lil & blk 28 20
725 A142 1.25g on 80c emer & blk 35 32
726 A142 1.25g on 1.75g rose & blk 35 32

Dessalines Type of 1972

1980, Aug. 27 Photo. *Perf. 11½*
Granite Paper

727 A142 25c org yel & blk 15 15
Nos. 727,C490-C493 (5) 2.73 2.03

Henry Christophe Citadel A160

1980, Dec. 2 Litho. *Perf. 12½x12*

728 A160 5c shown 15 15
729 A160 25c Sans-Souci Palace 15 15
730 A160 50c Vallieres market 15 15
Nos. 728-730,C494-C498 (8) 2.75 2.10

World Tourism Conf., Manila, Sept. 27.
For surcharges see Nos. 738, C511.

Soccer Players, World Cup, Flag of Uruguay (1930 Champion) A161

1980, Dec. 30 Litho. *Perf. 14*

731 A161 10c shown 15 15
732 A161 20c Italy, 1934 15 15
733 A161 25c Italy, 1938 15 15
Nos. 731-733,C499-C506 (11) 4.30
Set value 3.00

World Cup Soccer Championship, 50th anniv.
For surcharges see Nos. 741, 829.

Going to Church, by Gregoire Etienne A162

Paintings: 5c, Woman with Birds and Flowers, by Hector Hyppolite, vert. 20c, Street Market, by Petion Savain. 25c, Market Vendors, by Michele Manuel.

1981, May 12 Photo. *Perf. 11½*

734 A162 5c multi 15 15
735 A162 10c multi 15 15
736 A162 20c multi 15 15
737 A162 25c multi 15 15
Set value, #734-737, C507-C510 2.65 1.95

For surcharges see Nos. 739-740.

Nos. 728, 734-735, 732 Surcharged

Perf. 12½x12, 14, 11½

1981, Dec. 30 Litho., Photo.

738 A160 1.25g on 5c multi 35 28
739 A162 1.25g on 5c multi 35 28
740 A162 1.25g on 10c multi 35 28
741 A161 1.25g on 20c multi 35 28
Nos. 738-741,C511-C512 (6) 2.30 1.85

10th Anniv. of Pres. Duvalier Reforms — A163

1982, June 21 Photo. *Perf. 11½x12*
Granite Paper

742 A163 25c yel grn & blk 15 15
743 A163 50c olive & blk 15 15
744 A163 1g rose & blk 28 20
745 A163 1.25g bl & blk 35 28
746 A163 2g org red & blk 55 42
747 A163 5g org & blk 1.40 1.00
Nos. 742-747 (6) 2.88 2.20

Nos. 742, 744-746 Overprinted in Blue: "1957-1982 / 25 ANS DE REVOLUTION"

1982, Nov. 29 Photo. *Perf. 11½x12*
Granite Paper

748 A163 25c yel grn & blk 15 15
749 A163 1g rose & blk 28 20
750 A163 1.25g blue & blk 35 28
751 A163 2g org red & blk 55 42

25th anniv. of revolution.

Scouting Year A164

Perf. 13½x14, 14x13½

1983, Feb. 26 **Litho.**

752 A164 5c Building campfire 15 15
753 A164 10c Baden-Powell, vert. 15 15
754 A164 25c Boat building 15 15
755 A164 50c like 10c 15 15
756 A164 75c like 25c 20 18
757 A164 1g like 5c 28 20
758 A164 1.25g like 25c 35 28
759 A164 2g like 10c 55 42
Set value 1.65 1.30

Nos. 756-759 airmail.
For surcharge see No. 824.

Patroness of Haiti A165

1983, Mar. 9 **Litho.** *Perf. 14*

760 A165 10c multi 15 15
761 A165 20c multi 15 15
762 A165 25c multi 15 15
763 A165 50c multi 15 15
764 A165 75c multi 20 18
765 A165 1g multi 28 20
766 A165 1.25g multi 35 28
767 A165 1.50g multi 42 35
768 A165 1.75g multi 50 38
769 A165 2g multi 55 42
770 A165 5g multi 1.40 1.00
a. Souvenir sheets 1.40 1.00
Nos. 760-770 (11) 4.30 3.41

Centenary of the Miracle of Our Lady of Perpetual Help. Nos. 764-770 airmail. Sizes of Nos. 770a: 116x90mm; 90x116mm.

UPU Admission, 100th Anniv. A165a

1983, June 10 **Litho.** *Perf. 15x14*

770B A165a 5c shown 15 15
770C A165a 10c L.F. Salomon, J.C. Duvalier 15 15
770D A165a 25c No. 1, UPU emblem 15 15
770E A165a 50c like 5c 15 15
770F A165a 75c like 10c 20 18
770G A165a 1g like 5c 28 20
770H A165a 1.25g like 25c 35 28
770I A165a 2g like 25c 55 42
Set value 1.65 1.30

Nos. 770F-770I airmail.
For surcharge see No. 825.

1982 World Cup — A166

Games and scores. Nos. 776-780 airmail, horiz.

1983, Nov. 22 **Litho.** *Perf. 14*

771 A166 5c Argentina, Belgium 15 15
772 A166 10c Northern Ireland, Yugoslavia 15 15
773 A166 20c England, France 15 15
774 A166 25c Spain, Northern Ireland 15 15
775 A166 50c Italy (champion) 15 15
776 A166 1g Brazil, Scotland 28 20
777 A166 1.25g Northern Ireland, France 35 28
778 A166 1.50g Poland, Cameroun 42 32
779 A166 2g Italy, Germany 55 42
780 A166 2.50g Argentina, Brazil 70 70
Set value 2.65 2.20

For surcharge see No. 826.

Haiti Postage Stamp Centenary — A167

1984, Feb. 28 **Litho.** *Perf. 14½*

781 A167 5c #1 15 15
782 A167 10c #2 15 15
783 A167 25c #3 15 15
784 A167 50c #5 15 15
785 A167 75c Liberty, Salomon 20 16
786 A167 1g Liberty, Salomon 28 20
787 A167 1.25g Liberty, Duvalier 35 28
788 A167 2g Liberty, Duvalier 55 42
Set value 1.65 1.30

Nos. 785-788 airmail.
For surcharge see No. 826A.

World Communications Year — A168

1984, May 30 **Photo.** *Perf. 11½*
Granite Paper

789 A168 25c Broadcasting equipment, horiz. 15 15
790 A168 50c like 25c 15 15
791 A168 1g Drum 28 20
792 A168 1.25g like 1g 35 28
793 A168 2g Globe 55 42
794 A168 2.50g like 2g 70 55
Nos. 789-794 (6) 2.18 1.75

1984 Summer Olympics — A169

1984, July 27
Granite Paper

795 A169 5c Javelin, running, pole vault, horiz. 15 15
796 A169 10c like 5c 15 15
797 A169 25c Hurdles, horiz. 15 15
798 A169 50c like 25c 15 15
799 A169 1g Long jump 28 20
800 A169 1.25g like 1g 35 28
801 A169 2g like 1g 55 42
Set value 1.45 1.15

Souvenir Sheet

802 A169 2.50g like 1g 70 52

No. 802 exists imperf.

Arrival of Europeans in America, 500th Anniv. A170
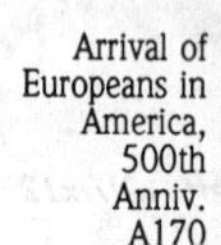

The Unknown Indian, detail or full perspective of statue. Nos. 807-809 are vert. and airmail.

1984, Dec. 5 **Litho.** *Perf. 14*

803 A170 5c multi 15 15
804 A170 10c multi 15 15
805 A170 25c multi 15 15
806 A170 50c multi 15 15
807 A170 1g multi 25 20
808 A170 1.25g multi 30 22
809 A170 2g multi 48 38
a. Souvenir sheet of #806, 809
Set value 1.30 1.00

Simon Bolivar and Alexander Petion A171

Designs: 25c, 1.25g, 7.50g, Portraits reversed. 50c, 4.50g, Bolivar, flags of Grand Colombian Confederation member nations.

1985, Aug. 30 *Perf. 13½x14*

810 A171 5c multi 15 15
811 A171 25c multi 15 15
812 A171 50c multi 15 15
813 A171 1g multi 25 20
814 A171 1.25g multi 30 22
815 A171 2g multi 48 38
816 A171 7.50g multi 1.75 1.40
Nos. 810-816 (7) 3.23 2.65

Souvenir Sheet
Imperf

817 A171 4.50g multi 1.10 80

Nos. 813-817 airmail.

Arrival of Europeans in America, 500th Anniv. — A172

Designs: 10c, 25c, 50c, Henri, cacique of Bahoruco, hero of the Spanish period, 1492-1625. 1g, 1.25g, 2g, Henri in tropical forest.

1986, Apr. 11 **Litho.** *Perf. 14*

818 A172 10c multi 15 15
819 A172 25c multi 15 15
820 A172 50c multi 15 15
821 A172 1g multi 28 20
822 A172 1.25g multi 35 26
823 A172 2g multi 55 42
Set value 1.45 1.10

Nos. 821-823 are airmail. A 3g souvenir sheet exists picturing Henri in tropical forest.

Nos. 770B, 771, 781, 756, C322, C500 Surcharged

1986, Apr. 18

825 A165a 25c on 5c No. 770B 15 15
826 A166 25c on 5c No. 771 15 15
826A A167 25c on 5c No. 781 15 15
827 A164 25c on 75c No. 756 15 15
828 A128 25c on 1.50g No. C322 15 15
829 A161 25c on 75c No. C500 15 15
Set value 36 30

Intl. Youth Year — A173

UNESCO, 40th Anniv. (in 1986) — A174

1986, May 20 **Litho.** *Perf. 14x15*

830 A173 10c Afforestation 15 15
831 A173 25c IYY emblem 15 15
832 A173 50c Girl Guides 15 15
833 A173 1g like 10c 28 20
834 A173 1.25g like 25c 35 26
835 A173 2g like 50c 55 42
Nos. 830-835 (6) 1.63
Set value 1.08

Souvenir Sheet

836 A173 3g multi 3.50 3.50

Nos. 833-836 are airmail.

1987, May 29 **Photo.** *Perf. 11½*
Granite Paper

837 A174 10c multi 15 15
838 A174 25c multi 15 15
839 A174 50c multi 20 15
840 A174 1g multi 40 30
841 A174 1.25g multi 50 38
842 A174 2.50g multi 1.00 75
Nos. 837-842 (6) 2.40 1.88

Souvenir Sheet
Granite Paper

843 A174 2g multi 1.05 1.05

Nos. 840-842 are airmail.

Charlemagne Peralte, Resistance Leader — A175

1988, Oct. 18 **Litho.** *Perf. 14*

844 A175 25c multi 15 15
845 A175 50c multi 22 16
846 A175 1g multi 45 35
847 A175 2g multi 90 68
a. Souvenir sheet of 1 90 90
848 A175 3g multi 1.35 1.00
Nos. 844-848 (5) 3.07 2.34

Nos. 846-848, 847a are airmail.

Slave Rebellion, 200th Anniv. A176

Design: 1g, 2g, 3g, Slaves around fire, vert.

1991, Aug. 22 **Litho.** *Perf. 12x11½*

849 A176 25c brt green & multi 25 15
850 A176 50c pink & multi 50 38

Perf. 11½x12

851 A176 1g blue & multi 1.00 75
852 A176 2g yellow & multi 2.00 1.50
a. Souv. sheet of 2, #850 & 852 2.50 1.90
853 A176 3g buff & multi 3.00 2.25
Nos. 849-853 (5) 6.75 5.03

Nos. 851-853 are airmail.

Discovery of America, 500th Anniv. A177

Designs: 25c, 50c, Ships at anchor, men coming ashore, native. 1g, 2g, 3g, Ships, beached long boats, vert.

1993, July 30 **Litho.** *Perf. 11½*

854 A177 25c green & multi 15 15
855 A177 50c yellow & multi 15 15
856 A177 1g blue & multi 16 15
857 A177 2g pink & multi 32 25
a. Souvenir sheet of 2, #856-857 6.50
858 A177 3g orange yellow & multi 50 38
Set value 1.10 83

Nos. 856-858, 857a are airmail.

SEMI-POSTAL STAMPS

Pierre de Coubertin — SP1

1939, Oct. 3 Unwmk. Engr. ***Perf. 12***
B1 SP1 10c + 10c multi 20.00 20.00

Pierre de Coubertin, organizer of the modern Olympic Games. The surtax was used to build a Sports Stadium at Port-au-Prince.
See Nos. CB1-CB2.

Catalogue values for unused stamps in this section, from this point to the end of the section, are for Never Hinged items.

Nos. 419-420 Surcharged in Deep Carmine

Perf. 13x13½, 13½x13
1958, Aug. 30 Litho. Unwmk.
B2 A82 1g + 50c purple 1.75 1.75
B3 A83 1.50g + 50c red org 1.75 1.75

The surtax was for the Red Cross. Overprint arranged horizontally on No. B3. See No. CB9.

Similar Surcharge in Red on One Line on Nos. 440-441

1959, Apr. 7 Photo. ***Perf. 11½***
Granite Paper
B4 A87 10c + 25c rose pink 18 15
B5 A87 25c + 25c green 25 20

Nos. 444-446 Surcharged Like Nos. B2-B3 in Red
Perf. 14x13½
B6 A88 10c + 50c vio bl & ol 52 35
B7 A88 50c + 50c grn & dp brn 52 42
B8 A88 2g + 50c dp cl & dk brn 70 70
Nos. B4-B8 (5) 2.17 1.82

The surtax from Nos. B4-B8 was for the Red Cross. See Nos. CB10-CB15.

No. 447 Surcharged Diagonally

Nations Unies
ANNEE DES REFUGIES
1959-1960
+ 20
Centimes

Unwmk.
1959, July 23 Photo. ***Perf. 12***
B9 A89 50c + 20c lt bl & dp cl 52 52

Issued for the World Refugee Year, July 1, 1959-June 30, 1960. See Nos. CB16-CB18.

Nos. 448-450 Surcharged in Dark Carmine

POUR LE SPORT
+ 0.75
CENTIMES

1959, Oct. 30 ***Perf. 14***
B10 A90 25c + 75c blk brn & lt bl 50 50
B11 A90 50c + 75c multi 65 52
B12 A91 75c + 75c brn & bl 65 52
Nos. B10-B12,CB19-CB21 (6) 3.75 3.23

The surtax was for Haitian athletes.
On No. B12, surcharge lines are spaced to total depth of 16mm.

No. 436 Surcharged in Red: "Hommage a l'UNICEF +G. 0,50"
Engraved and Lithographed
1960, Feb. 2 ***Perf. 11½***
B13 A86 1g + 50c blk & brick red 65 65

UNICEF. See Nos. CB22-CB23.

Nos. 452-453 Surcharged with Additional Value and Overprinted "ALPHABETISATION" in Red or Black
Perf. 12½x13
1960, July 12 Litho. Unwmk.
B14 A92 10c + 20c sal & grn (R) 18 15
B15 A92 10c + 30c sal & grn 20 18
B16 A92 50c + 20c vio & mag (R) 28 20
B17 A92 50c + 30c vio & mag 42 35
Nos. B14-B17,CB24-CB27 (8) 3.08 2.46

Olympic Games Issue
Nos. 464-465 Surcharged with Additional Value
1960, Sept. 9 Photo. ***Perf. 12***
B18 A94 50c + 25c grn & ocher 25 18
B19 A94 1g + 25c dk brn & grnsh bl 28 20

See Nos. CB28-CB29.

No. 469 Surcharged "UNICEF +25 centimes"
1961, Jan. 14 Engr. ***Perf. 10½***
B20 A96 1g + 25c grn & blk 28 20

UNICEF0. See Nos. CB30-CB31.

No. 469 Surcharged: "OMS SNEM +20 CENTIMES"
1961, Dec. 11
B21 A96 1g + 20c grn & blk 55 52

Haiti's participation in the UN malaria eradication drive. See Nos. CB35-CB36.

Nos. 434, 436 and 438 Surcharged in Black or Red:

(Surcharge arranged to fit shape of stamp.)

1961-62 Engr. & Litho. ***Perf. 11½***
B22 A86 20c + 25c blk & yel 18 15
B23 A86 1g + 50c blk & brick red (R) ('62) 42 35
B24 A86 2.50g + 50c blk & gray vio (R) ('62) 65 52
Nos. B22-B24,CB37-CB41 (8) 3.70 3.27

The surtax was for the benefit of the urban rehabilitation program in Duvalier Ville.

Nos. 486-488 Surcharged: "+25 centimes"
1962, Sept. 13 Litho. ***Perf. 12***
B25 A99 5c + 25c crim & dp bl 15 15
B26 A99 10c + 25c red brn & emer 18 18
B27 A99 50c + 25c bl & crim 20 18
Nos. B25-B27,CB42-CB44 (6) 1.16 1.01

Nos. 489-490 Surcharged in Red: "+0.20"
1962 Unwmk. ***Perf. 12½x13***
B28 A92 10c + 20c bl & org 15 15
B29 A92 50c + 20c rose lil & ol grn 20 15
Set value 24

See Nos. CB45-CB46.

No. 502 Surcharged: "ALPHABETISATION" and "+0,10"
1963, Mar. 15 Photo. ***Perf. 14x14½***
B30 A102 25c + 10c bl gray, yel & blk 15 15

See Nos. CB47-CB48.

Nos. 491-494 Surcharged and Overprinted in Black or Red With Olympic Emblem and: "JEUX OLYMPIQUES / D'HIVER / INNSBRUCK 1964"
Perf. 14x14½, 14½x14
1964, July 27 Unwmk.
B31 A100 50c + 10c on 3c (R) 28 18
B32 A100 50c + 10c on 5c 28 18
B33 A100 50c + 10c on 10c (R) 28 18
B34 A100 50c + 10c on 25c 28 18
Nos. B31-B34,CB49 (5) 1.64 1.14

9th Winter Olympic Games, Innsbruck, Austria, Jan. 20-Feb. 9, 1964. The 10c surtax went for charitable purposes.

Nos. 510-512 Surcharged: "+ 5c." in Black
1965, Mar. 15 Photo. ***Perf. 11½***
Granite Paper
B35 A105 10c + 5c lt bl & dk brn 15 15
B36 A105 25c + 5c sal & dk brn 18 15
B37 A105 50c + 5c pale rose lil & dk brn 25 18
Nos. B35-B37,CB51-CB54 (7) 1.65 1.55

Nos. B35-B37 and CB51-CB54 also exist with this surcharge (without period after "c") in red. They also exist with a similar black surcharge which lacks the period and is in a thinner, lighter type face.

Nos. 533 and 535-536 Surcharged and Overprinted with Haitian Scout Emblem and "12e Jamboree / Mondial 1967" Like Regular Issue
1967, Aug. 21 Photo. ***Perf. 11½***
B38 A111 10c + 10c on 5c multi 15 15
B39 A111 15c + 10c multi 15 15
B40 A111 50c + 10c multi 18 18
Set value 35 35

12th Boy Scout World Jamboree, Farragut State Park, Idaho, Aug. 1-9. The surcharge on No. B38 includes 2 bars through old denomination. See Nos. CB55-CB56.

Nos. 600-601 Surcharged in Red with New Value, Red Cross and: "50ème. Anniversaire / de la Ligue des / Sociétés de la / Croix Rouge"
1969, June 25 Litho. ***Perf. 11½***
B41 A127 10c + 10c multi 15 15
B42 A127 50c + 20c multi 18 18

50th anniv. of the League of Red Cross Societies. See Nos. CB61-CB62.

Nos. 637-638 Surcharged with New Value and: "INAUGURATION / 22-7-71"
1971, Aug. 3 Litho. ***Perf. 14x13½***
B43 A138 20c + 50c multi 25 20
B44 A138 25c + 1.50g multi 65 42

Inauguration of the Franois Duvalier Central Hydroelectric Plant, July 22, 1971.

AIR POST STAMPS

Plane over Port-au-Prince — AP1

1929-30 Unwmk. Engr. ***Perf. 12***
C1 AP1 25c dp grn ('30) 28 25
C2 AP1 50c dp vio 42 18
C3 AP1 75c red brn ('30) 1.35 1.00
C4 AP1 1g dp ultra 1.40 1.25

AP1a

Red Surcharge
1933, July 6
C4A AP1a 60c on 20c blue 35.00 35.00

Issued to commemorate the non-stop flight of Capt. J. Errol Boyd and Robert G. Lyon from New York to Port-au-Prince.

Plane over Christophe's Citadel — AP2

1933-40
C5 AP2 50c org brn 3.50 65
C6 AP2 50c ol grn ('35) 3.25 65
C7 AP2 50c car rose ('37) 2.00 1.25
C8 AP2 50c blk ('38) 1.50 65
C8A AP2 60c choc ('40) 65 15
C9 AP2 1g ultra 1.25 35
Nos. C5-C9 (6) 12.15 3.70

For surcharge see No. C24.

Alexandre Dumas, His Father and Son — AP3

1936, Mar. 1 Litho. ***Perf. 11½***
C10 AP3 60c brt vio & choc 3.25 1.90

Visit of delegation from France to Haiti.

Arms of Haiti and Portrait of George Washington — AP4

1938, Aug. 29 Engr. ***Perf. 12***
C11 AP4 60c deep blue 42 20

150th anniv. of the US Constitution.

Caribbean Conference Type of Regular Issue
1941, June 30
C12 A60 60c olive 2.50 65
C13 A60 1.25g purple 2.25 42

Madonna Type of Regular Issue
1942, Dec. 8 ***Perf. 12***
C14 A61 10c dk olive 28 15
C15 A61 25c brt ultra 42 28
C16 A61 50c turq grn 70 28
C17 A61 60c rose car 1.00 42
C18 A61 1.25g black 2.00 42
Nos. C14-C18 (5) 4.40 1.55

Souvenir Sheets
Perf. 12, Imperf.
C19 A61 Sheet of 2, #C14, C16 3.50 3.50
C20 A61 Sheet of 2, #C15, C17 3.50 3.50
C21 A61 Sheet of 1, #C18 3.50 3.50

Our Lady of Perpetual Help, patroness of Haiti.

Killick Type of Regular Issue
1943, Sept. 6
C22 A62 60c purple 52 25
C23 A62 1.25g black 1.50 1.25

No. C8A Surcharged with New Value and Bars in Red
1944, Nov. 25
C24 AP2 10c on 60c choc 35 25
a. Bars at right vertical 1.75
b. Double surcharge 52.50

Red Cross Type of Regular Issue

1945 **Cross in Rose**

C25 A63	20c yel org	15	15
C26 A63	25c brt ultra	15	15
C27 A63	50c ol blk	18	15
C28 A63	60c dl vio	25	15
C29 A63	1g yellow	1.00	15
C30 A63	1.25g carmine	70	20
C31 A63	1.35g green	70	35
C32 A63	5g black	5.00	2.00
	Nos. C25-C32 (8)	8.13	3.30

Issue dates: 1g, Aug. 14; others, Feb. 20.
For surcharges see Nos. C153-C160.

Catalogue values for unused stamps in this section, from this point to the end of the section, are for Never Hinged items.

Franklin D. Roosevelt — AP11

1946, Feb. 5 **Unwmk.** ***Perf. 12***

C33 AP11	20c black	15	15
C34 AP11	60c black	18	15
	Set value		17

Capois Type of Regular Issue

1946, July 18 **Engr.**

C35 A64	20c car rose	15	15
C36 A64	25c dk grn	15	15
C37 A64	50c orange	15	15
C38 A64	60c purple	18	15
C39 A64	1g gray blk	28	15
C40 A64	1.25g red vio	42	25
C41 A64	1.35g black	52	35
C42 A64	5g rose car	1.50	1.00
	Nos. C35-C42 (8)	3.35	2.35

For surcharges see Nos. C43-C45, C49-C51, C61-C62.

Nos. C37 and C41 Surcharged with New Value and Bar or Block in Red or Black

1947-48

C43 A64	5c on 1.35g (R) ('48)	42	18
C44 A64	30c on 50c	32	20
C45 A64	30c on 1.35g (R)	32	25

Dessalines Type of 1947-54 Regular Issue

1947, Oct. 17 **Engr.**

C46 A65	20c chocolate	18	15

Christopher Columbus and Fleet — AP14

Pres. Dumarsais Estiméand Exposition Buildings — AP15

1950, Feb. 12 ***Perf. 12½***

C47 AP14	30c ultra & gray	70	35
C48 AP15	1g black	70	28

200th anniversary (in 1949) of the founding of Port-au-Prince.

Nos. C36, C39 and C41 Surcharged or Overprinted in Carmine

UPU
1874 1949
30

1950, Oct. 4 ***Perf. 12***

C49 A64	30c on 25c dk grn	20	20
a.	30c on 1g gray black	70.00	
C50 A64	1g gray blk	42	35
a.	"P" of overprint omitted	42.50	42.50
C51 A64	1.50g on 1.35g blk	65	65

75th anniv. (in 1949) of the UPU.

Bananas — AP16

Coffee — AP17

Sisal — AP18

1951, Sept. 3 **Photo.** ***Perf. 12½***

C52 AP16	30c dp org	35	15
C53 AP17	80c dk grn & sal pink	90	42
C54 AP18	5g gray	3.25	2.75

For surcharge see No. C218.

Isabella I — AP19

Cap Haitien Roadstead — AP20

1951, Oct. 12 ***Perf. 13***

C55 AP19	15c brown	18	15
C56 AP19	30c dl bl	32	32

Queen Isabella I of Spain, 500th birth anniv.

1953, May 4 **Engr.** ***Perf. 12***

Designs: 30c, Workers' housing, St. Martin. 1.50g, Restored cathedral. 2.50g, School lunchroom.

C57 AP20	20c dp bl	15	15
C58 AP20	30c red brn	28	15
C59 AP20	1.50g gray blk	55	35
C60 AP20	2.50g violet	1.00	70

Nos. C38 and C41 Surcharged in Black

18 MAI
1803 - 1953
50

1953, May 18

C61 A64	50c on 60c pur	28	15
a.	Double surcharge	*50.00*	*50.00*
C62 A64	50c on 1.35g blk	28	20
a.	Double surcharge	*50.00*	

150th anniv. of the adoption of the natl. flag.

Henri Christophe — AP21

J. J. Dessalines and Paul E. Magloire — AP22

1954, Jan. 1 **Photo.** ***Perf. 11½***

C63 AP21	50c shown	25	18
C64 AP21	50c Toussaint L'Ouverture	25	18
C65 AP21	50c Dessalines	25	18
C66 AP21	50c Petion	25	18
C67 AP21	50c Boisrond-Tonerre	25	18
C68 AP21	1g Petion	50	18
C69 AP21	1.50g Lamartiniere	1.00	65
C70 AP22	7.50g shown	3.25	3.25
	Nos. C63-C70 (8)	6.00	4.98

150th anniv. of Haitian independence.
See Nos. C95-C96.

Marie Jeanne and Lamartinière Leading Attack — AP23

Design: Nos. C73, C74, Battle of Vertieres.

1954, Jan. 1 ***Perf. 12½***

C71 AP23	50c black	18	15
C72 AP23	50c carmine	18	15
C73 AP23	50c ultra	18	15
C74 AP23	50c sal pink	18	15
	Set value		40

150th anniv. of Haitian independence.

Mme. Magloire Type of Regular Issue

1954, Jan. 1 ***Perf. 11½***

C75 A72	20c red org	15	15
C76 A72	50c brown	18	18
C77 A72	1g gray grn	35	28
C78 A72	1.50g crimson	42	35
C79 A72	2.50g bl grn	70	65
C80 A72	5g gray	1.90	1.50
	Nos. C75-C80 (6)	3.70	3.11

Christophe Types of Regular Issue

1954, Dec. 6 **Litho.** ***Perf. 13½x13***

Portraits in Black

C81 A73	50c orange	25	18
C82 A73	1g blue	42	35
C83 A73	1.50g green	65	52
C84 A73	2.50g gray	1.25	70
C85 A73	5g rose car	2.00	1.40

Perf. 13

Flag in Black and Carmine

C86 A74	50c orange	28	18
C87 A74	1g dp bl	42	35
C88 A74	1.50g bl grn	65	52
C89 A74	2.50g gray	1.25	70
C90 A74	5g red org	2.00	1.50
	Nos. C81-C90 (10)	9.17	6.40

Fort Nativity, Drawing by Christopher Columbus — AP27

1954, Dec. 14 **Engr.** ***Perf. 12***

C91 AP27	50c dk rose car	42	20
C92 AP27	50c dk gray	42	20

Dessalines Type of 1955-57 Issue

Perf. 11½

1955, July 14 **Unwmk.** **Photo.**

C93 A75	20c org & blk	15	15
C94 A75	20c yel grn & blk	15	15
	Set value	20	16

For overprint see No. C183a.

Portrait Type of 1954
Dates omitted

Design: J. J. Dessalines.

1955, July 19

Portrait in Black

C95 AP21	50c gray	20	15
C96 AP21	50c blue	20	15
	Set value		20

Dessalines Memorial Type of Regular Issue

1955, Aug. 1

C97 A76	1.50g gray & blk	42	18
C98 A76	1.50g grn & blk	52	20

Types of 1956 Regular Issue and

Car and Coastal View — AP30

Designs: No. C100, 75c, Plane, steamship and Haiti map. 1g, Car and coastal view. 2.50g, Flamingo. 5g, Mallard.

1956, Apr. 14 **Unwmk.** ***Perf. 11½***

Granite Paper

C99 AP30	50c hn brn & lt bl	25	15
C100 AP30	50c blk & gray	20	15
C101 AP30	75c dp grn & bl grn	35	28
C102 AP30	1g ol grn & lt bl	35	20
C103 A77	2.50g dp org & org	2.00	70
C104 A78	5g red & buff	3.50	1.75
	Nos. C99-C104 (6)	6.65	3.23

For overprint see No. C185.

Kant Type of Regular Issue

1956, July 19 **Photo.** ***Perf. 12***

Granite Paper

C105 A79	50c chestnut	18	15
C106 A79	75c dp yel grn	25	18
C107 A79	1.50g dp magenta	90	35
a.	Miniature sheet of 3	2.50	1.90

No. C107a exists both perf. and imperf. Each sheet contains Nos. C105, C106 and a 1.25g gray black of same design.

Waterfall Type of Regular Issue

1957, Dec. 16 ***Perf. 11½***

Granite Paper

C108 A80	50c grn & grnsh bl	15	15
C109 A80	1.50g ol grn & grnsh bl	35	28
C110 A80	2.50g dk bl & brt bl	65	52
C111 A80	5g bluish blk & saph	1.50	1.25

For surcharge and overprint see Nos. CB49, CO2.

Dessalines Type of Regular Issue

1958, July 2

C112 A81	50c org & blk	18	15

For overprints see Nos. C184, CO1.

Brussels Fair Types of Regular Issue, 1958

Perf. 13x13½, 13½x13

1958, July 22 **Litho.** **Unwmk.**

C113 A82	2.50g pale car rose	65	42
C114 A83	5g brt bl	90	65
a.	Souv. sheet of 2, #C113-C114, imperf.	2.50	2.50

For surcharge see No. CB9.

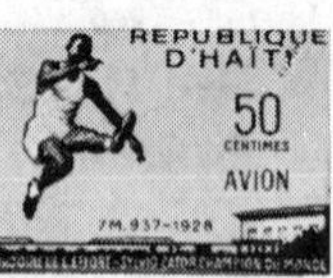

Sylvio Cator — AP33

1958, Aug. 16 **Photo.** ***Perf. 11½***

Granite Paper

C115 AP33	50c green	15	15
C116 AP33	50c blk brn	15	15
C117 AP33	1g org brn	28	18
C118 AP33	5g gray	1.50	70
	Set value		1.00

30th anniversary of the world championship record broad jump of Sylvio Cator.

IGY Type of Regular Issue, 1958

Designs: 50c, US Satellite. 1.50g, Emperor penguins. 2g, Modern observatory.

1958, Oct. 8 *Perf. 14x13½*

C119 A85 50c dp ultra & brn red 28 18
C120 A85 1.50g brn & crim 1.00 35
C121 A85 2g dk bl & crim 1.25 35
a. Souv. sheet of 4, #427, C119-C121, imperf. 3.00 2.50

President Francois Duvalier AP34

Engraved and Lithographed
1958, Oct. 22 Unwmk. *Perf. 11½*
Commemorative Inscription in Ultramarine

C122 AP34 50c blk & rose 65 15
C123 AP34 2.50g blk & ocher 90 35
C124 AP34 5g blk & rose lil 1.25 1.00
C125 AP34 7.50g blk & lt bl grn 1.75 1.40

See note after No. 431.
Souvenir sheets of 3 exist, perf. and imperf., containing one each of Nos. C124-C125 and No. 431. Sheets measure 132x77mm. with marginal inscription in ultramarine. Value, $6.25 each.
For surcharges see Nos. CB37-CB39.

Same Without Commemorative Inscription

1958, Nov. 20

C126 AP34 50c blk & rose 18 15
C127 AP34 1g blk & vio 35 20
C128 AP34 1.50g blk & pale brn 52 28
C129 AP34 2g blk & rose pink 65 28
C130 AP34 2.50g blk & ocher 65 35
C131 AP34 5g blk & rose lil 1.25 90
C132 AP34 7.50g blk & lt bl grn 1.90 1.25
Nos. C126-C132 (7) 5.50 3.41

For surcharges see #CB22-CB23, CB40-CB41.

Type of Regular Issue and

Flags of Haiti and UN — AP35

Perf. 11½
1958, Dec. 5 Unwmk. Photo.
Granite Paper

C133 AP35 50c pink, car & ultra 15 15
C134 A87 75c brt bl 20 15
C135 A87 1g brown 35 18
a. Souv. sheet of 2, #C133, C135, imperf. 2.25 2.25

Issued in tribute to the United Nations.
For surcharges see Nos. CB10-CB12.

Nos. C133-C135 Overprinted: "10th ANNIVERSARY OF THE UNIVERSAL DECLARATION OF HUMAN RIGHTS," in English (a), French (b), Spanish (c) or Portuguese (d)

1959, Jan. 28

C136 Block of 4 1.90 1.90
a.-d. AP35 50c any single 35 35
C137 Block of 4 2.50 2.50
a.-d. A87 75c any single 45 45
C138 Block of 4 5.00 5.00
a.-d. A87 1g any single 1.00 1.00

Pope Pius XII — AP36

Designs: 1.50g, Pope praying. 2.50g, Pope on throne.

1959, Feb. 28 Photo. *Perf. 14x13½*

C139 AP36 50c grn & lil 15 15
C140 AP36 1.50g ol & red brn 35 15
C141 AP36 2.50g pur & dk bl 65 28
Set value 48

Issued in memory of Pope Pius XII.

For surcharges see Nos. CB13-CB15.

Lincoln Type of Regular Issue, 1959

Designs: Various Portraits of Lincoln.

1959, May 12 *Perf. 12*

C142 A89 1g lt grn & chnt 20 15
C143 A89 2g pale lem & sl grn 35 18
C144 A89 2.50g buff & vio bl 42 28
a. Min. sheet of 4, #447, C142-C144, imperf. 2.00 2.00

Imperf. pairs exist.
For surcharges see Nos. CB16-CB18.

Pan American Games Types of Regular Issue

Designs: 50c, Jean Baptiste Dessables and map of American Midwest, c. 1791. 1g, Chicago's skyline and Dessables house. 1.50g, Discus thrower and flag of Haiti.

Unwmk.
1959, Aug. 27 Photo. *Perf. 14*

C145 A91 50c hn brn & aqua 42 18
C146 A90 1g lil & aqua 65 28
C147 A90 1.50g multi 70 35

For surcharges see Nos. CB19-CB21.

Nos. C145-C147 Overprinted

1960, Feb. 29

C148 A91 50c hn brn & aqua 70 70
C149 A90 1g lil & aqua 1.25 1.25
C150 A90 1.50g multi 1.40 1.40

Issued to commemorate the 8th Olympic Winter Games, Squaw Valley, Calif., Feb. 18-29, 1960.

WRY Type of Regular Issue, 1960

1960, Apr. 7 Litho. *Perf. 12½x13*

C151 A92 50c bl & blk 15 15
C152 A92 1g lt grn & mar 28 18
a. Souv. sheet of 4, #452-453, C151-C152, imperf. 3.00 3.00

See Nos. C191-C192. For surcharges see Nos. CB24-CB27, CB45-CB46.

Nos. C31, C28 and 369 Surcharged or Overprinted in Red: "28ème ANNIVERSAIRE"

1960, May 8 Engr. *Perf. 12*
Cross in Rose

C153 A63 20c on 1.35g grn 18 15
C154 A63 50c on 60c dl vio 20 18
C155 A63 50c on 1.35g grn 20 18
C156 A63 50c on 2.50g pale vio 20 18
C157 A63 60c dl vio 25 18
C158 A63 1g on 1.35g grn 28 28
C159 A63 1.35g green 52 42
C160 A63 2g on 1.35g grn 90 70
Nos. C153-C160 (8) 2.73 2.27

28th anniv. of the Haitian Red Cross. Additional overprint "Avion" on No. C156.

Sugar Type of Regular Issue

Designs (Miss Fouchard and): 50c, Harvest. 2.50g, Beach.

Perf. 11½
1960, May 30 Unwmk. Photo.
Granite Paper

C161 A93 50c lil rose & brn 35 15
C162 A93 2.50g ultra & brn 90 35

Olympic Type of Regular Issue

Designs: 50c, Pierre de Coubertin, Melbourne stadium and torch. 1.50g, Discus thrower and Rome stadium. 2.50g, Victors' parade, Athens, 1896, and Melbourne, 1956.

1960, Aug. 18 *Perf. 12*

C163 A94 50c mar & bis 18 15
C164 A94 1.50g rose car & yel grn 42 20
C165 A94 2.50g sl grn & mag 65 28
a. Souv. sheet of 2, #465, C165, imperf. 2.00 2.00

For surcharges see Nos. CB28-CB29.

Jeanty Type of Regular Issue

Designs: 50c, Occide Jeanty and score from "1804." 1.50g, Occide Jeanty and National Capitol.

1960, Oct. 19 *Perf. 14x14½*

C166 A95 50c yel & bl 28 15
C167 A95 1.50g lil rose & sl grn 52 20

Printed in sheets of 12 (3x4) with inscription and opening bars of "1804," Jeanty's military march, in top margin.

UN Type of Regular Issue, 1960

1960, Nov. 25 Engr. *Perf. 10½*

C168 A96 50c red org & blk 15 15
C169 A96 1.50g dk bl & blk 35 25
a. Souv. sheet of 3, #469, C168-C169, imperf. 1.75 1.75
Set value 32

For surcharges see #CB30-CB31, CB35-CB36.

Dessalines Type of Regular Issue

1960, Nov. 5 Photo. *Perf. 11½*
Granite Paper

C170 A81 20c gray & blk 15 15

For overprint see No. C183.

Sud-Caravelle Jet Airliner and Orchid — AP37

Designs: 50c, Boeing 707 jet airliner, facing left, and Kittyhawk. 1g, Sud-Caravelle jet airliner and Orchid. 1.50g, Boeing 707 jet airliner and air post stamp of 1933.

1960, Dec. 17 Photo. Unwmk.
Granite Paper

C171 AP37 20c dp ultra & car 15 15
C172 AP37 50c rose brn & grn 20 15
C173 AP37 50c brt grnsh bl & ol grn 20 15
C174 AP37 50c gray & grn 20 15
C175 AP37 1g gray ol & ver 28 20
C176 AP37 1.50g brt pink & dk bl 52 28
a. Souv. sheet of 3, #C174-C176, imperf. 1.00 70
Nos. C171-C176 (6) 1.55 1.08

Issued for Aviation Week, Dec. 17-23.
#C172-C174 are dated 17 Decembre 1903.
For overprints and surcharges see Nos. CB32-CB34, CO1-CO5.

Dumas Type of Regular Issue.

Designs: 50c, The Three Musketeers and Dumas père, horiz 1g, The Lady of the Camellias and Dumas fils. 1.50g, The Count of Monte Cristo and Dumas père.

1961, Feb. 10 Photo. *Perf. 11½*
Granite Paper

C177 A97 50c brt bl & blk 18 15
C178 A97 1g blk & red 25 18
C179 A97 1.50g brt grn & bl blk 35 25

Type of Regular Issue, 1961

Tourist publicity: 20c, Privateer in Battle. 50c, Pirate with cutlass in rigging. 1g, Map of Tortuga.

1961, Apr. 4 Litho. *Perf. 12*

C180 A98 20c dk bl & yel 15 15
C181 A98 50c brt pur & org 18 15
C182 A98 1g Prus grn & yel 25 18
Set value 34

For overprint and surcharge see #C186-C187.

Nos. C170, C112 and C101 Overprinted: "Dr. F. Duvalier Président 22 Mai 1961"

1961, May 22 Photo. *Perf. 11½*

C183 A81 20c gray & blk 15 15
a. On No. C93
C184 A81 50c org & blk 18 15
C185 AP30 75c dp grn & bl grn 28 25
Set value 45

Re-election of Pres. Francois Duvalier.

No. C182 Overprinted or Surcharged: "EXPLORATION SPATIALE JOHN GLENN" and Capsule

1962, May 10 Litho. *Perf. 12*

C186 A98 1g Prus grn & yel 35 28
C187 A98 2g on 1g Prus grn & yel 90 75

See note after No. 485.

Malaria Type of Regular Issue

Designs: 20c, 1g, Triangle pointing down. 50c, Triangle pointing up.

1962, May 30 Unwmk.

C188 A99 20c lilac & red 15 15
C189 A99 50c emer & rose car 18 15
C190 A99 1g org & dk vio 28 15
a. Souv. sheet of 3 1.40 1.40
Set value 35

Sheets of 12 with marginal inscription.
No. C190a contains stamps similar to Nos. 488 and C189-C190 in changed colors and imperf. Issued July 16.
A similar sheet without the "Contribution . . ." inscription was issued May 30.
For surcharges see Nos. CB42-CB44.

WRY Type of 1960 Dated "1962"

1962, June 22 *Perf. 12½x13*

C191 A92 50c lt bl & red brn 15 15
C192 A92 1g bis & blk 20 20

Plight of refugees. A souvenir sheet exists containing one each of Nos. 489-490 and C191-C192, imperf. Value, $2.
For surcharges see Nos. CB45-CB46.

Boy Scout Type of 1962

Designs: 20c, Scout giving Scout sign. 50c, Haitian Scout emblem. 1.50g, Lord and Lady Baden-Powell, horiz.

Perf. 14x14½, 14½x14
1962, Aug. 6 Photo. Unwmk.

C193 A100 20c multi 15 15
C194 A100 50c multi 20 15
C195 A100 1.50g multi 35 28
Set value 42

A souvenir sheet contains one each of Nos. C194-C195 imperf. Value, 90 cents.
A similar sheet inscribed in gold, "Epreuves De Luxe," was issued Dec. 10. Value $2.

Nos. 495 and C193-C195 Overprinted: "AÉROPORT INTERNATIONAL 1962"

Perf. 14x14½, 14½x14
1962, Oct. 26

C196 A100 20c multi, #C193 15 15
C197 A100 50c multi, #495 15 15
C198 A100 50c multi, #C194 15 15
C199 A100 1.50g multi, #C195 20 15
Set value 40

Proceeds from the sale of Nos. C196-C199 were for the construction of new airport at Port-au-Prince. The overprint on No. C197 has "Poste Aérienne" added.

Seattle Fair Type of 1962

Design: Denomination at left, "Avion" at right.

1962, Nov. 19 Litho. *Perf. 12½*

C200 A101 50c blk & pale lil 20 15
C201 A101 1g org brn & gray 35 15
C202 A101 1.50g red lil & org 42 20
Set value 40

An imperf. sheet of two exists containing one each of Nos. C201-C202 with simulated gray perforations. Size: 133x82mm. Value, $2.50.

Street in Duvalier Ville and Stamp of 1881 AP38

1962, Dec. 10 Photo. *Perf. 14x14½*
Stamp in Dark Brown

C203 AP38 50c orange 20 15
C204 AP38 1g blue 35 28
C205 AP38 1.50g green 52 42

Issued to publicize Duvalier Ville.
For surcharges see Nos. CB47-CB48.

Nos. C201-C202 with Vertical Overprint in Black Similar To

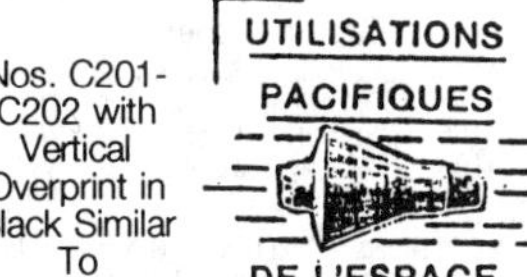

1963, Jan. 23 Litho. *Perf. 12½*
C206 A101 1g org brn & gray 52 45
a. Claret overprint, horiz. 90 60
C207 A101 1.50g red lil & org 70 70
a. Claret overprint, horiz. 1.10 1.10

"Peaceful Uses of Outer Space." The black vertical overprint has no outside frame lines and no broken shading lines around capsule. Nos. C206a and C207a were issued Feb. 20.

Hunger Type of Regular Issue
Perf. 13x14
1963, July 12 Unwmk. Photo.
C208 A103 50c lil rose & blk 15 15
C209 A103 1g lt ol grn & blk 28 15
Set value 22

Dag Hammarskjold and UN Emblem — AP39

Lithographed and Photogravure
1963, Sept. 28 *Perf. 13½x14*
Portrait in Slate
C210 AP39 20c buff & brn 15 15
C211 AP39 50c lt bl & car 20 18
a. Souvenir sheet of 2 1.25 1.25
C212 AP39 1g pink & bl 28 18
C213 AP39 1.50g gray & grn 45 35

Dag Hammarskjold, Sec. Gen. of the UN, 1953-61. Printed in sheets of 25 (5x5) with map of Sweden extending over 9 stamps in second and third vertical rows. No. C211a contains 2 imperf. stamps: 50c blue and carmine and 1.50g ocher and brown with map of southern Sweden in background.
For overprints see Nos. C219-C222, C238-C241, CB50.

Dessalines Type of Regular Issue, 1963
1963, Oct. 17 Photo. *Perf. 14x14½*
C214 A104 50c bl & lil rose 15 15
C215 A104 50c org & grn 15 15
Set value 20

Nos. C214-C215 and C53 Overprinted in Black or Red: "FETE DES MERES / 1964"
1964, July 22 *Perf. 14x14½, 12½*
C216 A104 50c bl & lil rose 20 15
C217 A104 50c org & grn 20 15
C218 AP17 1.50g on 80c dk grn & sal pink (R) 35 20

Issued for Mother's Day, 1964.

Nos. C210-C213 Overprinted in Red

Lithographed and Engraved
1964, Oct. 2 *Perf. 13½x14*
Portrait in Slate
C219 AP39 20c buff & brn 20 15
C220 AP39 50c lt bl & car 20 15
C221 AP39 1g pink & bl 35 28
C222 AP39 1.50g gray & grn 42 35
Nos. C219-C222,CB50 (5) 2.07 1.63

Cent. (in 1963) of the Intl. Red Cross.

Olympic Type of Regular Issue

Designs: No. C223, Weight lifter. Nos. C224-C226, Hurdler.

1964, Nov. 12 Photo. *Perf. 11½*
Granite Paper
C223 A105 50c pale lil & dk brn 15 15
C224 A105 50c pale grn & dk brn 15 15
C225 A105 75c buff & dk brn 20 18
C226 A105 1.50g gray & dk brn 35 18
a. Souv. sheet of 4 90 90

Printed in sheets of 50 (10x5), with map of Japan in background extending over 27 stamps.
No. C226a contains four imperf. stamps similar to Nos. C223-C226 in changed colors and with map of Tokyo area in background.
For surcharges see Nos. CB51-CB54.

Airport Type of Regular Issue, 1964
1964, Dec. 15 *Perf. 14½x14*
C227 A106 50c org & blk 20 15
C228 A106 1.50g brt lil rose & blk 42 20
C229 A106 2.50g lt vio & blk 90 52

Same Overprinted "1965"
1965, Feb. 11 Photo.
C230 A106 50c org & blk 20 15
C231 A106 1.50g brt lil rose & blk 52 25
C232 A106 2.50g lt vio & blk 70 52

World's Fair Type of Regular Issue, 1965

Designs: 50c, 1.50g, "Rocket Thrower" by Donald De Lue. 5g, Unisphere, NY World's Fair.

1965, Mar. 22 Unwmk. *Perf. 13½*
C233 A107 50c dp bl & org 18 15
C234 A107 1.50g gray & org 35 28
C235 A107 5g multi 1.75 1.50

Merchant Marine Type of Regular Issue, 1965
1965, May 13 Photo. *Perf. 11½*
C236 A108 50c blk, lt grnsh bl & red 15 15
C237 A108 1.50g blk, lt vio & red 42 28

O. N. U.

Nos. C210-C213 Overprinted

1945-1965

Lithographed and Photogravure
1965, June 26 *Perf. 13½x14*
Portrait in Slate
C238 AP39 20c buff & brn 15 15
C239 AP39 50c lt bl & car 15 15
C240 AP39 1g pink & bl 25 20
C241 AP39 1.50g gray & grn 20 28
Set value 64

20th anniversary of the United Nations.

ITU Type of Regular Issue
Perf. 13½
1965, Aug. 16 Unwmk. Litho.
C242 A109 50c multi 15 15
C243 A109 1g multi 28 25
C244 A109 1.50g bl & multi 42 35
C245 A109 2g pink & multi 65 50

A souvenir sheet, released in 1966, contains 50c and 2g stamps resembling Nos. C242 and C245, with simulated perforations.
For overprints see Nos. C255-C256.

Cathedral Type of Regular Issue, 1965

Designs: 50c, Cathedral, Port-au-Prince, horiz. 1g, High Altar. 7.50g, Statue of Our Lady of the Assumption.

Perf. 14x13, 13x14
1965, Nov. 19 Photo.
Size: 39x29mm, 29x39mm
C246 A110 50c multi 20 15
C247 A110 1g multi 28 18
Size: 38x52mm
C248 A110 7.50g multi 2.00 1.75

Flower Type of Regular Issue

Flowers: No. C249, 5g, Passionflower. Nos. C250, C252, Okra. Nos. C251, C253, American elder.

1965, Dec. 20 Photo. *Perf. 11½*
Granite Paper
C249 A111 50c dk vio, yel & grn 15 15
C250 A111 50c multi 15 15
C251 A111 50c grn, gray & yel 15 15
C252 A111 1.50g multi 42 35
C253 A111 1.50g grn, tan & yel 42 35
C254 A111 5g dk vio, yel grn & grn 1.40 1.25
Nos. C249-C254 (6) 2.69 2.40

For surcharges see Nos. CB55-CB56.

Nos. C242-C243 Overprinted in Red: "20e. Anniversaire / UNESCO"
1965, Aug. 27 Litho. *Perf. 13½*
C255 A109 50c lt vio & multi 1.00 35
C256 A109 1g citron & multi 2.00 70

20th anniversary of UNESCO.

The souvenir sheet noted below No. C245 was also overprinted "20e. Anniversaire / UNESCO" in red.

Culture Types of Regular Issue and

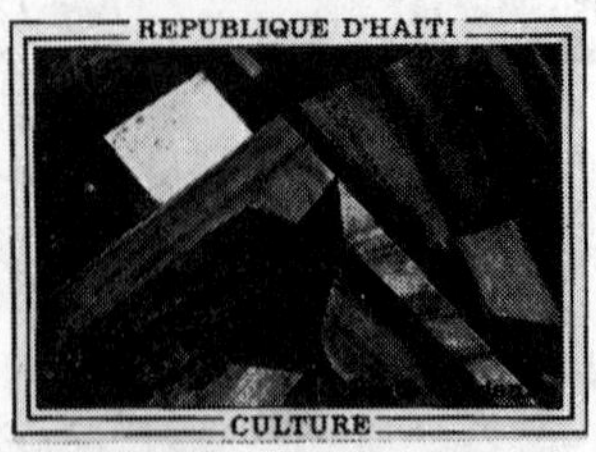

Modern Painting — AP40

Designs: 50c, Ceremonial stool. 1.50g, Amulet.

Perf. 14x14½, 14½x14, 14
1966, Mar. 14 Photo. Unwmk.
C257 A113 50c lil, brn & brnz 20 15
C258 A112 1.50g brt rose lil, yel & blk 52 35
C259 AP40 2.50g multi 90 60

For overprints and surcharge see Nos. C260-C262, C280-C281.

Nos. C257-C259 Overprinted in Black or Red: "Hommage / a Hailé Sélassiéler / 24-25 Avril 1966"
1966, Apr. 24
C260 A112 50c (R) 20 15
C261 A113 1.50g (vert. ovpt.) 52 42
C262 AP40 2.50g (R) 90 70

See note after No. 543.

Walter M. Schirra, Thomas P. Stafford, Frank A. Borman, James A. Lovell and Gemini VI and VII — AP41

1966, May 3 *Perf. 13½*
C263 AP41 50c vio bl, brn & lt bl 20 15
C264 AP41 1g grn, brn & lt bl 35 28
C265 AP41 1.50g car, brn & bl 52 42

See note after No. 547.
For overprints see Nos. C296-C298.

Soccer Type of Regular Issue

Designs: 50c, Pres. Duvalier and soccer ball within wreath. 1.50g, President Duvalier and soccer player within wreath.

Lithographed and Photogravure
1966, June 16 *Perf. 13x13½*
Portrait in Black; Gold Inscription; Green Commemorative Inscription in Two Lines
C266 A115 50c lt ol grn & plum 15 15
C267 A115 1.50g rose & plum 52 42
Green Commemorative Inscription in 3 Lines; Gold Inscription Omitted
C268 A115 50c lt ol grn & plum 15 15
C269 A115 1.50g rose & plum 52 42

Caribbean Soccer Festival, June 10-22. Nos. C266-C267 also for the National Soccer Championships, May 8-22.
For overprint and surcharge see Nos. C288, CB57.

Education Type of Regular Issue

Designs: 50c, "ABC", boy and girl. 1g, Scout symbols. 1.50g, Television set, book and communications satellite, horiz.

Perf. 14x13½, 13½x14
1966, Oct. 18 Litho. and Engraved
C270 A116 50c grn, yel & brn 15 15
C271 A116 1g dk brn, org & blk 28 28
C272 A116 1.50g grn, bl grn & dk bl 42 42

Schweitzer Type of Regular Issue

Designs (Schweitzer and): 50c, 1g, Albert Schweitzer Hospital, Deschapelles, Haiti. 1.50g, Maps of Alsace and Gabon. 2g, Pipe organ.

Perf. 12½x13
1967, Apr. 20 Photo. Unwmk.
C273 A117 50c multi 18 40
C274 A117 1g multi 35 28
C275 A117 1.50g lt bl & multi 50 42
C276 A117 2g multi 65 55

Fruit-Vegetable Type of Regular Issue, 1967
1967, July 4 Photo. *Perf. 12½*
C277 A118 50c Watermelon 15 15
C278 A118 1g Cabbage 28 20
C279 A118 1.50g Tangerine 42 35

No. C258 Overprinted or Surcharged Like EXPO '67 Regular Issue
1967, Aug. 30 Photo. *Perf. 14½x14*
C280 A112 1.50g multi 52 42
C281 A112 2g on 1.50g multi 70 55

Issued to commemorate EXPO '67 International Exhibition, Montreal, Apr. 28-Oct. 27.

Duvalier Type of Regular Issue, 1967
1967, Sept. 22 Photo. *Perf. 14x13*
C282 A119 1g brt grn & gold 35 28
C283 A119 1.50g vio & gold 52 42
C284 A119 2g org & gold 70 55

Education Type of Regular Issue, 1967

Designs: 50c, Writing hands. 1g, Scout emblem and Scouts, vert. 1.50g, Audio-visual teaching of algebra.

1967, Dec. 11 Litho. *Perf. 11½*
C285 A120 50c multi 15 15
C286 A120 1g multi 28 25
C287 A120 1.50g multi 42 35

For surcharges see Nos. CB58-CB60.

No. C269 Overprinted

Lithographed and Photogravure
1968, Jan. 18 *Perf. 13x13½*
C288 A115 1.50g rose & plum 52 42

See note after No. 579.

Caiman Woods Type of Regular Issue
1968, Apr. 22 Photo. *Perf. 12*
Size: 36x26mm
C289 A121 50c multi 15 15
C290 A121 1g multi 28 28
Perf. 12½x13½
Size: 49x36mm
C291 A121 50c multi 15 15
C292 A121 1g multi 28 25
C293 A121 1.50g multi 42 42
C294 A121 2g gray & multi 70 55
C295 A121 5g multi 1.40 1.00
Nos. C289-C295 (7) 3.38 2.80

Xème JEUX OLYMPIQUES D'HIVER–GRENOBLE 1968

Nos. C263-C265 Overprinted

1968, Apr. 19 *Perf. 13½*
C296 AP41 50c multi 52 25
C297 AP41 1g multi 1.00 52
C298 AP41 1.50g multi 1.75 90

See note after No. 584.

Monument Type of Regular Issue
1968, May 22 *Perf. 11½*
Granite Paper
C299 A122 50c ol bis & blk 20 15
C300 A122 1g brt rose & blk 35 25
C301 A122 1.50g org & blk 52 35

For surcharges see Nos. C324-C325.

Types of Regular Bishopric Issue

Designs: 50c, Palm tree and provincial coats of arms. 1g, 2.50g, Madonna, papal arms and arms of Haiti. 1.50g, Cathedral, arms of Pope Paul VI and arms of Haiti.

Perf. 13x14, 12½x13½

1968, Aug. 16 **Photo.**
C302 A123 50c lil & multi 15 15
C303 A124 1g multi 28 25
C304 A124 1.50g multi 42 35
C305 A124 2.50g multi 70 65

Airport Type of Regular Issue

Design: 50c, 1.50g, 2.50g, Front view of air terminal.

1968, Sept. 22 **Photo.** ***Perf. 11½***
Portrait in Black
C306 A125 50c rose lake & pale vio 15 15
C307 A125 1.50g rose lake & bl 42 35
C308 A125 2.50g rose lake & lt grnsh bl 70 65

Pres. Francois Duvalier — AP42

Embossed & Typo. on Gold Foil
1968, Sept. 22 ***Die Cut Perf. 14***
C309 AP42 30g black & red

Freed Slaves' Type of Regular Issue

1968, Oct. 28 **Litho.** ***Perf. 14½x14***
C310 A126 50c brn, lil & brt pink 15 15
C311 A126 1g brn, yel grn & brt pink 28 25
C312 A126 1.50g brn, lt vio bl & brt pink 42 35
C313 A126 2g brn, lt grn & brt pink 55 45

Education Type of Regular Issue, 1968

Designs: 50c, 1.50g, Children watching television. 1g, Hands throwing ball, and sports medal.

1968, Nov. 14 ***Perf. 11½***
C314 A127 50c multi 15 15
C315 A127 1g multi 28 25
C316 A127 1.50g multi 52 35

For surcharges see Nos. CB61-CB62.

Jan Boesman and his Balloon — AP43

Cachet of May 2, 1925 Flight — AP44

1968, Nov. 28 **Litho.** ***Perf. 13½***
C317 AP43 70c lt yel grn & sep 35 28
C318 AP43 1.75g grnsh bl & sep 90 70

Dr. Jan Boesman's balloon flight, Mexico City, Nov. 1968.

Miniature Sheet

1968, Nov. 28 **Litho.** ***Perf. 13½x14***
Black Cachets, Magenta Inscriptions and Rose Lilac Background
C318A Sheet of 12 5.50 7.50
b. AP44 70c 2 Mai 1925 35 45
c. AP44 70c 2 Septembre 1925 35 45
d. AP44 70c 28 Mars 1927 35 45
e. AP44 70c 12 Juillet 1927 35 45
f. AP44 70c 13 Septembre 1927 35 45
g. AP44 70c 6 Fevrier 1928 35 45

Galiffet's 1784 balloon flight and pioneer flights of the 1920's. No. C318A contains 2 each of Nos. C318b-C318g. The background of the sheet shows in white outlines a balloon and the inscription "BALLON GALIFFET 1784." The design of each stamp shows a different airmail cachet, date of a special flight and part of the white background design.

Churchill Type of Regular Issue

Churchill: 50c, and early seaplane. 75c, and soldiers at Normandy. 1g, and Queen Elizabeth II. 1.50g, and Big Ben, London. 3g, and coat of arms, horiz.

1968, Dec. 23 **Photo.** ***Perf. 13***
C319 A128 50c gold & multi 15 15
C320 A128 75c gold & multi 20 18
C321 A128 1g gold & multi 28 25
C322 A128 1.50g gold & multi 42 35

Souvenir Sheet
Perf. 12½x13, Imperf.
C323 A128 3g sil, blk & red 1.00 1.00

Nos. C319-C322 exist imperf.
No. C323 contains one horizontal stamp, size: 38x25½mm.

Nos. C299-C300 Surcharged with New Value and Rectangle

1969, Feb. 21 **Photo.** ***Perf. 11½***
C324 A122 70c on 50c 20 18
C325 A122 1.75g on 1g 52 42

Bird Type of Regular Issue

Birds of Haiti: 50c, Hispaniolan trogon. 1g, Black-cowled oriole. 1.50g, Stripe-headed tanager. 2g, Striated woodpecker.

1969, Feb. 26 ***Perf. 13½***
C326 A129 50c multi 15 15
C327 A129 1g lt bl & multi 28 25
C328 A129 1.50g multi 42 35
C329 A129 2g gray & multi 55 50

For overprints see Nos. C344A-C344D.

Electric Power Type of 1969

1969, May 22 **Litho.** ***Perf. 13x13½***
C338 A131 20c dk bl & lil 15 15
C339 A131 25c grn & rose red 15 15
C340 A131 25c rose red & grn 15 15
Set value 28 23

Education Type of 1969

Designs: 50c, Peace poster on educational television, vert. 1g, Learning to write. 1.50g, Playing children, vert.

1969, Aug. 12 **Litho.** ***Perf. 13½***
C342 A132 50c multi 15 15
C343 A132 1g multi 35 18
C344 A132 1.50g multi 52 35

Nos. C326-C329 Overprinted

1969, Aug. 29 **Photo.** ***Perf. 13½***
C344A A129 50c multi
C344B A129 1g lt bl & multi
C344C A129 1.50g multi
C344D A129 2g gray & multi

ILO Type of Regular Issue

1969, Sept. 22 ***Perf. 14***
C345 A133 25c red & blk 15 15
C346 A133 70c org & blk 25 15
C347 A133 1.75g brt pur & blk 65 42
Set value 62

Butterfly Type of Regular Issue

Butterflies: 50c, Danaus eresimus kaempfferi. 1.50g, Anaea marthesia nemesis. 2g, Prepona antimache.

1969, Nov. 14 **Photo.** ***Perf. 13½***
C348 A134 50c multi 15 15
C349 A134 1.50g multi 42 35
C350 A134 2g yel & multi 55 50

King Type of Regular Issue
Perf. 12½x13½

1970, Jan. 12 **Litho.**
C351 A135 50c emer, red & blk 18 15
C352 A135 1g brick red, red & blk 35 25
C353 A135 1.50g brt bl, red & blk 52 35

Orchid Type of Regular Issue

Haitian Orchids: 50c, Tetramicra elegans. 1.50g, Epidendrum truncatum. 2g, Oncidium desertorum.

1970, Apr. 3 **Litho.** ***Perf. 13x12½***
C354 A136 50c buff, brn & mag 15 15
C355 A136 1.50g multi 42 35
C356 A136 2g lil & multi 65 50

UPU Type of Regular Issue

Designs: 50c, Globe and doves. 1.50g, Propeller and UPU emblem, vert. 2g, UPU Monument and map of Haiti.

1970, June 23 **Photo.** ***Perf. 11½***
C357 A137 50c blk & vio 18 15
C358 A137 1.50g multi 52 35
C359 A137 2g multi 70 50
a. Souvenir sheet of 3, #C357-C359, imperf. 1.50

Nos. C357-C359a Overprinted in Red with UN Emblem and: "XXVe ANNIVERSAIRE / O.N.U."

1970, Dec. 14 **Photo.** ***Perf. 11½***
C360 A137 50c blk & vio 18 15
C361 A137 1.50g multi 52 35
C362 A137 2g multi 70 50
a. Souvenir sheet of 3 1.90

United Nations, 25th anniversary.

Haitian Nativity — AP45

1970, Dec. 22
C363 AP45 1.50g sepia & multi 52 35
C364 AP45 1.50g ultra & multi 52 35
C365 AP45 2g multi 90 50

Christmas 1970.

Painting Type of Regular Issue

Paintings: 50c, Nativity, by Rigaud Benoit. 1g, Head of a Negro, by Rubens. 1.50g, Ascension, by Castera Bazile (like No. 648).

1971, Apr. 29 **Litho.** ***Perf. 12x12½***
Size: 20x40mm
C366 A140 50c multi 18 15
C367 A140 1g multi 35 28
C368 A140 1.50g multi 52 42

Balloon and Haiti No. C2 AP46

Designs: No. C370, as No. C369. No. C373, Haiti No. C2. 1g, 1.50g, Supersonic transport and Haiti No. C2.

1971, Dec. 22 **Photo.** ***Perf. 11½***
C369 AP46 20c bl, red org & blk 15 15
C370 AP46 50c ultra, red org & blk 20 15
C371 AP46 1g org & blk 42 20
C372 AP46 1.50g lil rose & blk 70 32
Set value 66

Souvenir Sheet
Imperf
C373 AP46 50c brt grn & blk 3.50

40th anniv. (in 1969) of air post service in Haiti.
For overprints see #C374-C377, C380-C386.

Nos. C369-C372 Overprinted

INTERPEX 72

1972, Mar. 17 ***Perf. 11½***
C374 AP46 20c multi 15
C375 AP46 50c multi 18
C376 AP46 1g org & blk 35
C377 AP46 1.50g lil rose & blk 52

14th INTERPEX, NYC, Mar. 17-19.

Dessalines Type of Regular Issue

1972, Apr. 28 **Photo.** ***Perf. 11½***
C378 A142 50c yel grn & blk 18 15
C379 A142 2.50g lil & blk 90 52

For surcharge see No. C438.

Nos. C369-C372 Overprinted

HAIPEX 5ème. CONGRES

1972, May 4
C380 AP46 20c multi 15 15
C381 AP46 50c multi 18 15
C382 AP46 1g org & blk 35 20
C383 AP46 1.50g lil rose & blk 52 28
Set value 62

HAIPEX, 5th Congress.

Nos. C370-C372 Overprinted

1972, July
C384 AP46 50c multi 18 15
C385 AP46 1g org & blk 35 20
C386 AP46 1.50g lil rose & blk 52 32

Belgica '72, International Philatelic Exhibition, Brussels, June 24-July 9.

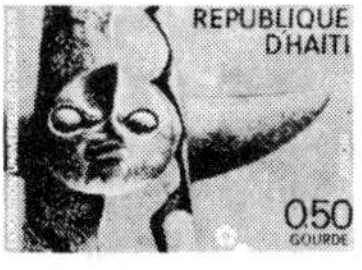

Tower of the Sun, EXPO '70 Emblem — AP47

1972, Oct. 27
C387 AP47 50c bl, plum & dk bl 15 15
C388 AP47 1g bl, plum & red 35 20
C389 AP47 1.50g bl, plum & blk 42 32
C390 AP47 2.50g bl, plum & grn 90 52

EXPO '70 International Exposition, Osaka, Japan, Mar. 15-Sept. 13, 1970.
For surcharge see No. C447.

Souvenir Sheets

1972 Summer Olympics, Munich — AP47a

Designs: 2.50g, Israeli delegation, opening ceremony in Munich Stadium. 5g, Assassinated Israeli athlete David Berger.

1973 ***Perf. 13½***
C390A AP47a 2.50g multi 1.10 75
C390B AP47a 5g multi 2.25 1.50

No. C390B contains one 22½x34mm stamp.

Headquarters and Map of Americas — AP48

1973, Aug. Litho. *Perf. 14½*
C391 AP48 50c dk bl & multi 15 15
C392 AP48 80c multi 22 18
C393 AP48 1.50g vio & multi 42 32
C394 AP48 2g brn & multi 55 42

70th anniversary (in 1972) of the Panamerican Health Organization.

Marine Life Type of Regular Issue

Designs: Marine life; 50c, 1.50g horizontal.

1973, Sept. 4 *Perf. 14*
C395 A145 50c *Platypodia spectabilis* 15 15
C396 A145 85c *Goniaster tessellatus* 25 18
C397 A145 1.50g *Stephanocyathus diadema* 42 32
C398 A145 2g *Phyllangia americana* 55 42

For surcharge see No. C439.

Fish Type of Regular Issue

Designs: Tropical fish.

1973 *Perf. 13½*
C399 A146 50c *Gramma melacara* 15 15
C400 A146 85c *Holacanthus tricolor* 25 18
C401 A146 1.50g *Liopropoma rubre* 42 32
C402 A146 5g *Clepticus parrai* 1.40 1.00

For surcharge see No. C440.

Haitian Flag — AP49

Designs: Nos. C404, C405, Haitian flag and coat of arms. No. C406, Flag and Pres. Jean-Claude Duvalier.

1973, Nov. 18 *Perf. 14½x14*
Size: 35x22½mm
C403 AP49 80c blk & red 22 18
C404 AP49 80c red & blk 22 18

Perf. 14x13½
Size: 42x27mm
C405 AP49 1.85g blk & red 52 32
C406 AP49 1.85g red & blk 52 32

For overprints and surcharges see Nos. C427-C428, C432-C433, C441-C442.

Soccer Type of Regular Issue

Designs: 50c, 80c, Soccer Stadium. 1.75g, 10g, Haiti No. 654.

1973, Nov. 29 *Perf. 14x13*
C407 A147 50c multi 15 15
C408 A147 80c multi 22 18
C409 A147 1.75g multi 50 35
C410 A147 10g multi 2.75 2.00

Dessalines Type of 1974

1974, Apr. 22 Photo. *Perf. 14*
C411 A148 50c brn & grnsh bl 15 15
C412 A148 80c gray & brn 22 18
C413 A148 1g lt grn & mar 28 20
C414 A148 1.75g lil & ol brn 50 35

For surcharge see No. C443.

Copernicus Type of 1974

Designs: No. C415, 80c, 1.50g, 1.75g, Symbol of heliocentric system. No. C416, 1g, 2.50g, Nicolaus Copernicus.

1974, May 24 Litho. *Perf. 14x13½*
C415 A149 50c org & multi 15 15
C416 A149 50c yel & multi 15 15
C417 A149 80c multi 22 18
C418 A149 1g multi 28 20
C419 A149 1.75g brn & multi 50 35

Souvenir Sheet
Imperf
C420 Sheet of 2 1.25
a. A149 1.50g light green & multi 42
b. A149 2.50g deep orange & multi 70

For overprint and surcharges see Nos. C444, C460-C463.

Pres. Duvalier Type of 1974

1974 Photo. *Perf. 14x13½*
C421 A151 50c vio brn & gold 15 15
C422 A151 80c rose red & gold 22 18
C423 A151 1g red lil & gold 28 20
C424 A151 1.50g Prus bl & gold 42 32
C425 A151 1.75g brt vio & gold 50 35
C426 A151 5g ol grn & gold 1.40 1.00
Nos. C421-C426 (6) 2.97 2.20

For surcharge and overprints see Nos. C445, C487-C489.

Nos. C405-C406 Surcharged in Violet Blue

G. 0.80 

1975, July 15 Litho. *Perf. 14x13½*
C427 AP49 80c on 1.85g, #C405
C428 AP49 80c on 1.85g, #C406

Nos. C405-C406 Overprinted in Blue

1874 UPU 1974

100 ANS

1975, July 15 Litho. *Perf. 14x13½*
C432 AP49 1.85g blk & red 52 32
C433 AP49 1.85g red & blk 52 32

Centenary of Universal Postal Union. "100 ANS" in 2 lines on No. C433.

Names of Haitian Participants at Siege of Savannah — AP50

1976, Apr. 22 Photo. *Perf. 11½*
Granite Paper
C434 AP50 50c multi 15 15
C435 AP50 80c multi 22 16
C436 AP50 1.50g multi 42 32
C437 AP50 7.50g multi 2.00 1.50

American Bicentennial.

Stamps of 1972-74 Surcharged with New Value and Bar in Black or Violet Blue

Perf. 11½, 13½, 14x13½, 14
1976 Photogravure; Lithographed
C438 A142 80c on 2.50g, #C379 22 16
C439 A145 80c on 85c, #C396 22 16
C440 A146 80c on 85c, #C400 22 16
C441 AP49 80c on 1.85g, #C405 22 16
C442 AP49 80c on 1.85g, #C406 22 16
C443 A148 80c on 1.75g, #C414 (VB) 22 16
C444 A149 80c on 1.75g, #C419 (VB) 22 16
C445 A151 80c on 1.75g, #C425 22 16
C446 AP50 80c on 1.50g, #C436 22 16
C447 AP47 80c on 1.50g, #C389
Nos. C438-C446 (9) 1.98 1.44

Black surcharge of Nos. C441-C442 differs from the violet blue surcharge of Nos. C427-C428 in type face, arrangement of denomination and bar, and size of bar (10x6mm).

Dessalines Type of 1972

1976-77 Photo. *Perf. 11½*
Granite Paper
C448 A142 75c yel & blk 20 18
C449 A142 80c emer & blk 22 15
C450 A142 1g bl & blk 28 20
C451 A142 1g red brn & blk 28 20
C452 A142 1.25g yel grn & blk 35 26
C453 A142 1.50g bl gray & blk 42 32
C454 A142 1.75g rose & blk 50 38
C455 A142 2g yel & blk 55 42
C457 A142 5g bl grn & blk 1.40 1.00
C458 A142 10g ocher & blk 2.75 2.00
Nos. C448-C458 (10) 6.95 5.11

Issue dates: 75c, 80c, No. C451, 1,75g, 5g, 10g, 1977.

Nos. C415-C416, C418-C419 Overprinted or Surcharged in Black, Dark Blue or Green

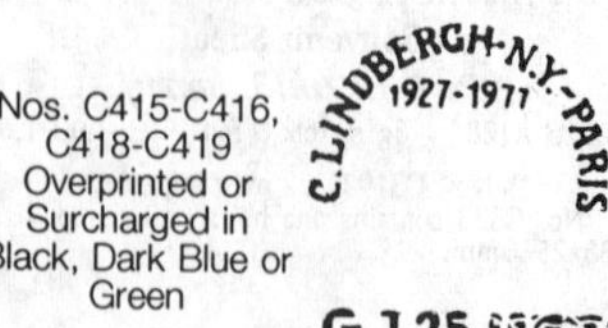

G. 1.25

1977, July 6 Litho. *Perf. 14x13½*
C460 A149 1g (Bk) 28 20
C461 A149 1.25g on 50c (DB) 35 26
C462 A149 1.25g on 50c (G) 35 26
C463 A149 1.25g on 1.75g (Bk) 35 26

Charles A. Lindbergh's solo transatlantic flight from NY to Paris, 50th anniv.

Telephone Type of 1978

Designs: 1g, Telstar over globe. 1.25g, Duvalier Earth Telecommunications Station. 2g, Wall telephone, 1890, vert.

1978, June 19 Litho. *Perf. 13½*
C466 A153 1g multi 28 20
C467 A153 1.25g multi 35 26
C468 A153 2g multi 55 42

Olympic Games Type of 1978

Designs (Montreal Olympic Games' Emblem and): 1.25g, Equestrian. 2.50g, Basketball. 5g, Yachting.

1978, Sept. 4 Litho. *Perf. 13½x13*
C469 A154 1.25g multi 35 26
C470 A154 2.50g multi 70 52
C471 A154 5g multi 1.40 75

Children's Institute Type, 1979

Designs: 1.25g, Mother nursing child. 2g, Nurse giving injection.

1979, Jan. 15 Photo. *Perf. 14x14½*
C472 A155 1.25g multi 35 26
C473 A155 2g multi 55 42

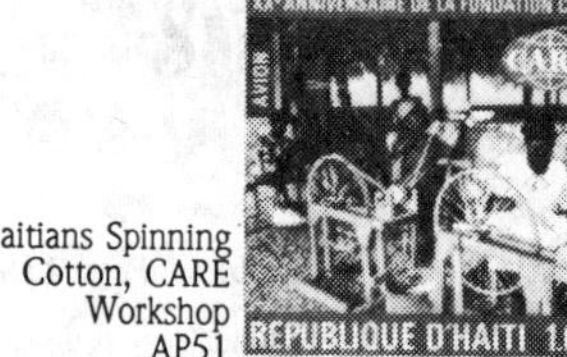

Haitians Spinning Cotton, CARE Workshop AP51

1979, May 11 Photo. *Perf. 11½*
C474 AP51 1g multi 28 20
C475 AP51 1.25g multi 35 26
C476 AP51 2g multi 55 42

30th anniversary of CARE.

Human Rights Type of 1979

1979, July 20 Litho. *Perf. 14*
C477 A157 1g multi 28 20
C478 A157 1.25g multi 35 26
C479 A157 2g multi 55 42

Anti-Apartheid Year Type of 1979

1979, Nov. 22 Photo. *Perf. 12x11½*
C480 A158 1g yel grn & blk 28 20
C481 A158 1.25g bl & blk 35 26
C482 A158 2g gray olive 55 42

IYC Type of 1979

1979, Dec. 19 Photo. *Perf. 12*
C483 A159 1g multi 28 20
C484 A159 1.25g multi 35 26
C485 A159 2.50g multi 70 52
C486 A159 5g multi 1.40 1.00

Nos. C421, C424-C425 Overprinted:

27 JOUR
5
80 FASTE

1980, May 17 Photo. *Perf. 14x13½*
C487 A151 50c multi 15 15
C488 A151 1.50g multi 42 32
C489 A151 1.75g multi 50 38

Wedding of Pres. Duvalier, May 27.

Dessalines Type of 1972

1980, Aug. 27 Photo. *Perf. 11½*
Granite Paper
C490 A142 1g gray vio & blk 28 20
C491 A142 1.25g sal pink & blk 35 26
C492 A142 2g pale grn & blk 55 42
C493 A142 5g lt bl & blk 1.40 1.00

For surcharge see No. C512.

Tourism Type

1980, Dec. 2 Litho. *Perf. 12½x12*
C494 A160 1g like #728 28 20
C495 A160 1.25g like #729 35 25
C496 A160 1.50g Carnival dancers 42 28
C497 A160 2g Vendors 55 42
C498 A160 2.50g like #C497 70 50

For surcharge see No. C511.

Soccer Type of 1980

1980, Dec. 30 Litho. *Perf. 14*
C499 A161 50c Uruguay, 1950 15 15
C500 A161 75c Germany, 1954 20 18
C501 A161 1g Brazil, 1958 28 20
C502 A161 1.25g Brazil, 1962 35 26
C503 A161 1.50g Gt. Britain, 1966 42 32
C504 A161 1.75g Brazil, 1970 50 38
C505 A161 2g Germany, 1974 55 42
C506 A161 5g Argentina, 1978 1.40 1.00

Painting Type of 1981

1981, May 12 Photo. *Perf. 11½*
C507 A162 50c like #734 15 15
C508 A162 1.25g like #735 35 26
C509 A162 2g like #736 55 42
C510 A162 5g like #737 1.40 1.00

Nos. C496, C493 Surcharged

Perf. 12½x12, 11½
1981, Dec. 30 Litho., Photo.
C511 A160 1.25g on 1.50g multi 35 28
C512 A142 2g on 5g multi 55 45

Dessalines Type of 1972

1982, Jan. 25 Photo. *Perf. 11½*
Granite Paper
C513 A142 1.25g lt brn & blk 35 28
C514 A142 2g lilac & blk 55 45

AIR POST SEMI-POSTAL STAMPS

Coubertin Semipostal Type of 1939

1939, Oct. 3 Unwmk. Engr. *Perf. 12*
CB1 SP1 60c + 40c multi 15.00 15.00
CB2 SP1 1.25g + 60c multi 15.00 15.00

Mosquito and National Sanatorium — SPAP2

1949, July 22 Cross in Carmine
CB3 SPAP2 20c + 20c sep 7.00 5.00
CB4 SPAP2 30c + 30c dp grn 7.00 5.00
CB5 SPAP2 45c + 45c lt red brn 7.00 5.00
CB6 SPAP2 80c + 80c pur 7.00 5.00
CB7 SPAP2 1.25g + 1.25g car rose 7.00 5.00
a. Souvenir sheet 24.00 18.00
CB8 SPAP2 1.75g + 1.75g bl 7.00 5.00
a. Souvenir sheet 24.00 18.00
Nos. CB3-CB8 (6) 42.00 30.00

The surtax was used for fighting tuberculosis and malaria.

No. C113 Surcharged in Deep Carmine

+ 50 CENTIMES

1958, Aug. 30 Litho. *Perf. 13x13½*
CB9 A82 2.50g + 50c 2.00 2.00

The surtax was for the Red Cross.

Catalogue values for unused stamps in this section, from this point to the end of the section, are for Never Hinged items.

Similar Surcharge in Red on One Line on Nos. C133-C135

1959, Apr. 7 Photo. *Perf. 11½*
Granite Paper
CB10 AP35 50c + 25c pink, car & ultra 25 18
CB11 A87 75c + 25c brt bl 28 25
CB12 A87 1g + 25c brn 42 35

Nos. C139-C141 Surcharged Like No. CB9 in Red
CB13 AP36 50c + 50c grn & lil 65 65
CB14 AP36 1.50g + 50c ol & red brn 65 65
CB15 AP36 2.50g + 50c pur & dk bl 70 70
Nos. CB10-CB15 (6) 2.95 2.78

Surtax for the Red Cross.

Nos. C142-C144 Surcharged Diagonally

Nations Unies
ANNEE DES REFUGIES
1959-1960
+ 20
Centimes

1959, July 23 Unwmk. *Perf. 12*
CB16 A89 1g + 20c 65 52
CB17 A89 2g + 20c 65 65
CB18 A89 2.50g + 20c 70 70

World Refugee Year, July 1, 1959-June 30, 1960. A similar surcharge of 50c was applied horizontally to stamps in No. C144a. Value $17.50.

C145-C147 Surcharged in Dark Carmine

POUR LE SPORT
+ 0.75
CENTIMES

1959, Oct. 30 Photo. *Perf. 14*
CB19 A91 50c + 75c hn brn & aqua 65 52
CB20 A90 1g + 75c lil & aqua 65 52
CB21 A90 1.50g + 75c multi 65 65

The surtax was for Haitian athletes.
On No. CB19, surcharge lines are spaced to total depth of 16mm.

Nos. C129-C130 Surcharged in Red: "Hommage a l'UNICEF +G. 0,50"

Engraved and Lithographed
1960, Feb. 2 *Perf. 11½*
CB22 AP34 2g + 50c 70 70
CB23 AP34 2.50g + 50c 1.25 1.25

Issued to honor UNICEF.

Nos. C151-C152 Surcharged and Overprinted: "ALPHABETISATION" in Red or Black.

1960, July 12 Litho. *Perf. 12½x13*
CB24 A92 50c + 20c (R) 28 20
CB25 A92 50c + 30c 42 28
CB26 A92 1g + 20c (R) 65 55
CB27 A92 1g + 30c 65 55

Olympic Games Issue
Nos. C163-C164 Surcharged

1960, Sept. 9 Photo. *Perf. 12*
CB28 A94 50c + 25c 18 15
CB29 A94 1.50g + 25c 35 28

Nos. C168-C169 Surcharged: "UNICEF +25 centimes"

1961, Jan. 14 Engr. *Perf. 10½*
CB30 A96 50c + 25c red org & blk 20 15
CB31 A96 1.50g + 25c dk bl & blk 35 25

Issued for the UNICEF.

Nos. C171, C175-C176 Surcharged with Additional Value, Scout Emblem and: "18e Conference Internationale du Scoutisme Mondial Lisbonne Septembre 1961"

1961, Sept. 30 Photo. *Perf. 11½*
CB32 AP37 20c + 25c 18 15
CB33 AP37 1g + 25c 20 18
CB34 AP37 1.50g + 25c 28 28

Issued to commemorate the 18th Boy Scout World Conference, Lisbon, Sept. 19-24, 1961.
The surtax was for the Red Cross. Additional proceeds from the sale of Nos. CB32-CB34 benefited the Port-au-Prince airport project.
The same surcharge was also applied to No. C176a.

Nos. C168-C169 Surcharged: "OMS SNEM +20 CENTIMES"

1961, Dec. 11 Engr. *Perf. 10½*
CB35 A96 50c + 20c 90 90
CB36 A96 1.50g + 20c 1.25 1.25

Issued to publicize Haiti's participation in the UN malaria eradication drive.

Nos. C123, C126-C127 and C131-C132 Surcharged in Black or Red:

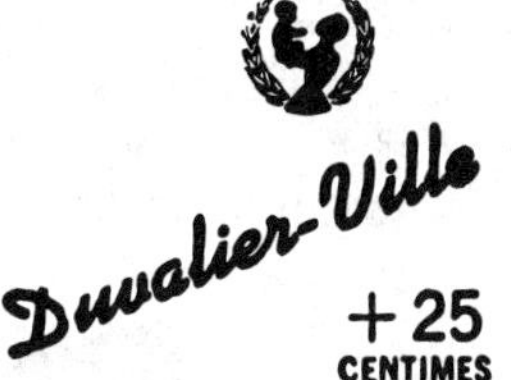

Engraved and Lithographed
1961-62 *Perf. 11½*
CB37 AP34 50c + 25c 15 15
CB38 AP34 1g + 50c 18 15
CB39 AP34 2.50g + 50c (R) ('62) 42 35
CB40 AP34 5g + 50c 70 70
CB41 AP34 7.50g + 50c (R) ('62) 1.00 90
Nos. CB37-CB41 (5) 2.45 2.25

The surtax was for the benefit of the urban rehabilitation program in Duvalier Ville.

Nos. C188-C190 Surcharged: "+25 centimes"

1962, Sept. 13 Litho. *Perf. 12*
CB42 A99 20c + 25c 15 15
CB43 A99 50c + 25c 20 15
CB44 A99 1g + 25c 28 20

Nos. C191-C192 Surcharged in Red: "+0.20"

1962 *Perf. 12½x13*
CB45 A92 50c + 20c 20 15
CB46 A92 1g + 20c 28 20

Nos. C203 and C205 Surcharged: "ALPHABETISATION" and "0, 10"

1963, Mar. 15 Photo. *Perf. 14x14½*
CB47 AP38 50c + 10c 20 15
CB48 AP38 1.50g + 10c 28 28

No. C110 Surcharged in Red with Olympic Emblem and: "JEUX OLYMPIQUES / D'HIVER / INNSBRUCK 1964"

1964, July 27 Photo. *Perf. 11½*
CB49 A80 2.50g + 50c + 10c 52 42

See note after No. B34. The 50c+10c surtax went for charity.

No. C213 Surcharged in Red

Engraved and Photogravure
1964, Oct. 2 *Perf. 13½x14*
CB50 AP39 2.50g + 1.25g on 1.50g 90 70

Issued to commemorate the centenary (in 1963) of the International Red Cross.

Nos. C223-C226 Surcharged: "+ 5c." in Black

1965, Mar. 15 Photo. *Perf. 11½*
CB51 A105 50c + 5c pale lil & dk brn 15 15
CB52 A105 50c + 5c pale grn & dk brn 15 15
CB53 A105 75c + 5c buff & dk brn 25 25
CB54 A105 1.50g + 5c gray & dk brn 52 52

The souvenir sheet No. C226a was surcharged "+25c."
See note following No. B37.

Nos. C251 and C253 Surcharged and Overprinted with Haitian Scout Emblem and "12e Jamboree / Mondial 1967" Like Regular Issue

1967, Aug. 21 Photo. *Perf. 11½*
CB55 A111 50c + 10c multi 15 15
CB56 A111 1.50g + 50c multi 42 35

See note after No. B40.

No. C269 Surcharged Like Regular Issue

Lithographed and Photogravure
1968, Jan. 18 *Perf. 13x13½*
CB57 A115 2.50g + 1.25g on 1.50g 1.00 90

See note after No. 579.

Nos. C285-C287 Surcharged "CULTURE + 10"

1968, July 4 Litho. *Perf. 11½*
CB58 A120 50c + 10c multi 15 15
CB59 A120 1g + 10c multi 28 28
CB60 A120 1.50g + 10c multi 35 35

Nos. C314 and C316 Surcharged in Red with New Value, Red Cross and: "50ème. Anniversaire / de la Ligue des / Sociétés de la / Croix Rouge"

1969, June 25 Litho. *Perf. 11½*
CB61 A127 50c + 20c multi 25 25
CB62 A127 1.50g + 25c multi 65 42

League of Red Cross Societies, 50th anniv.

AIR POST OFFICIAL STAMPS

Nos. C172-C176 and C176a Overprinted: "OFFICIEL"

Perf. 11½
1961, Mar. Unwmk. Photo.
CO1 AP37 50c rose brn & grn 18
CO2 AP37 50c brt grnsh bl & ol grn 18
CO3 AP37 50c gray & grn 18
CO4 AP37 1g gray ol & ver 28
CO5 AP37 1.50g brt pink & dk bl 42
a. Sheet of 3 1.40
Nos. CO1-CO5 (5) 1.24

Nos. CO1-CO5a only available canceled.

Catalogue values for unused stamps in this section, from this point to the end of the section, are for Never Hinged items.

Jean Jacques Dessalines — OA1

1962, Mar. 7 Photo. *Perf. 14x14½*
Size: 20½x38mm
CO6 OA1 50c dk bl & sepia 18 15
CO7 OA1 1g lt bl & maroon 35 26
CO8 OA1 1.50g bister & bl 42 35

Size: 30x40mm
CO9 OA1 5g rose & ol grn 1.25 1.10

Inscription at bottom of #CO9 is in 2 lines.

AIR POST PARCEL POST STAMPS

Catalogue values for unused stamps in this section are for Never Hinged items.

Nos. C112 and C111 Overprinted in Red

COLIS
POSTAUX

Perf. 11½
1960, Nov. 21 Unwmk. Photo.
CQ1 A81 50c orange & black 25 18
CQ2 A80 5g bluish blk & saph 2.00 1.75

Type of Parcel Post Stamps, 1961 Inscribed "Poste Aerienne"

1961, Mar. 24 *Perf. 14*
CQ3 PP1 2.50g yel grn & mar 90 70
CQ4 PP1 5g org & green 1.75 1.40

SPECIAL DELIVERY STAMP

The catalogue value for the unused stamp in this section is for Never Hinged.

Postal Administration Building SD1

Unwmk.
1953, May 4 Engr. *Perf. 12*
E1 SD1 25c vermilion 70 60

POSTAGE DUE STAMPS

D1

D2

1898, May Unwmk. Engr. *Perf. 12*
J1 D1 2c black 25 25
J2 D1 5c red brown 35 35
J3 D1 10c brown orange 52 20
J4 D1 50c slate 1.50 70

For overprints see Nos. J5-J9, J14-J16.

Stamps of 1898 Handstamped

MAI
G^t P^re
1902

1902 Black Overprint
J5 D1 2c black 70 52
J6 D1 5c red brown 70 52
J7 D1 10c brown orange 85 52
J8 D1 50c slate 6.00 3.50

Red Overprint
J9 D1 2c black 85 85
Nos. J5-J9 (5) 9.10 5.91

1906

J10 D2 2c dull red 60 45
J11 D2 5c ultra 1.75 1.75
J12 D2 10c violet 1.75 1.75
J13 D2 50c olive gray 7.50 4.25

For surcharges and overprints see Nos. 305-308, J17-J20.

Preceding Issues Handstamped

Gl O.Z.
7 FÉV. 1914

1914 **On Stamps of 1898**

J14 D1 5c red brown 60 45
J15 D1 10c brown orange 55 55
J16 D1 50c slate 3.75 2.50

On Stamps of 1906

J17 D2 2c dull red 45 30
J18 D2 5c ultra 75 45
J19 D2 10c violet 3.00 2.50
J20 D2 50c olive gray 5.50 3.50

The note after No. 201 applies to Nos. J14-J20 also.

Catalogue values for unused stamps in this section, from this point to the end of the section, are for Never Hinged items.

Unpaid Letter — D3

1951, July **Litho.** ***Perf. 11½***

J21 D3 10c carmine 15 15
J22 D3 20c red brown 15 15
J23 D3 40c green 25 25
J24 D3 50c orange yellow 35 35

PARCEL POST STAMPS

Catalogue values for unused stamps in this section are for Never Hinged items.

Nos. 416, 470-471 and 378 Overprinted in Red

COLIS POSTAUX

Photogravure, Engraved
Perf. 11½, 12

1960, Nov. 21 **Unwmk.**

Q1 A81 5c yel grn & blk 15 15
Q2 A81 10c red org & blk 15 15
Q3 A81 25c ultra & black 15 15
Q4 A64 2.50g gray 1.00 1.00
Set value 1.25 1.25

Coat of Arms — PP1

Unwmk.

1961, Mar. 24 **Photo.** ***Perf. 14***

Q5 PP1 50c bister & purple 35 15
Q6 PP1 1g pink & dark blue 52 28

See Nos. CQ3-CQ4.

POSTAL TAX STAMPS

Catalogue values for unused stamps in this section, are for Never Hinged items.

Haitian Woman, War Invalids and Ruined Buildings PT1

Unwmk.

1944, Aug. 16 **Engr.** ***Perf. 12***

RA1 PT1 5c dull purple 70 28
RA2 PT1 5c dark blue 70 28
RA3 PT1 5c olive green 70 28
RA4 PT1 5c black 70 28

1945, Dec. 17

RA5 PT1 5c dark green 70 28
RA6 PT1 5c sepia 70 28
RA7 PT1 5c red brown 70 28
RA8 PT1 5c rose carmine 70 28

The proceeds from the sale of Nos. RA1 to RA8 were for United Nations Relief.

George Washington, J. J. Dessalines and Simón Bolivar — PT2

1949, Sept. 20

RA9 PT2 5c red brown 20 15
RA10 PT2 5c olive gray 20 15
RA11 PT2 5c blue 20 15
RA12 PT2 5c green 20 15
RA13 PT2 5c violet 20 15
RA14 PT2 5c black 20 15
RA15 PT2 5c orange 20 15
RA16 PT2 5c carmine rose 20 15
Nos. RA9-RA16 (8) 1.60
Set value 96

Bicentenary of Port-au-Prince.
For overprint and surcharges see #385-388.

Helicopter Inspection of Hurricane Damage PT3

Helicopter PT4

1955, Jan. 3 **Photo.** ***Perf. 11½***

RA17 PT3 10c bright green 15 15
RA18 PT3 10c bright blue 15 15
RA19 PT3 10c gray black 15 15
RA20 PT3 10c orange 15 15
RA21 PT3 20c rose carmine 15 15
RA22 PT3 20c deep green 15 15
Set value 60 30

1955, May 3

RA23 PT4 10c black, *gray* 15 15
RA24 PT4 20c violet blue, *blue* 15 15
Set value 24 15

The surface tint of the sheets of 50, (10x5) of #RA23-RA24, RAC1-RAC2 includes a map of Haiti's southern peninsula which extends over the three center rows of stamps.
The tax was for reconstruction.
See Nos. RAC1-RAC2.

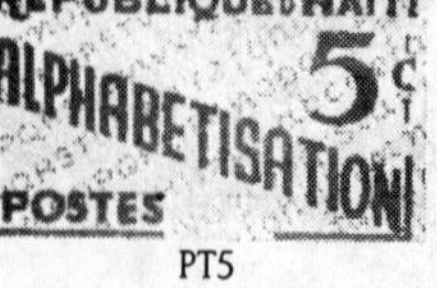
PT5 PT6

1959-60 **Unwmk.** **Photo.** ***Perf. 11½***
Size: 38x22½mm

RA25 PT5 5c green 15 15
RA26 PT5 5c black ('60) 15 15
RA27 PT5 10c red 15 15
Set value 24 16

1960-61
Size: 28x17mm

RA28 PT5 5c green 15 15
RA29 PT5 10c red 15 15
RA30 PT5 10c blue ('61) 15 15
Set value 18 15

1963, Sept. ***Perf. 14½x14***
Size: 13½x21mm

RA31 PT6 10c red orange 15 15
RA32 PT6 10c bright blue 15 15
RA33 PT6 10c olive 15 15
Set value, #RA31-RA33, RAC6-RAC8 33 30

1966-69 **Photo.** ***Perf. 14x14½***
Size: 17x25mm

RA34 PT6 10c bright green 15 15
RA35 PT6 10c violet 15 15
RA36 PT6 10c violet blue 15 15
RA37 PT6 10c brown ('69) 15 15
Set value, #RA34-RA37, RAC9-RAC15 62 55

Nos. RA25-RA37 represent a tax for a literacy campaign.
See Nos. RA42-RA45, RAC20-RAC22.

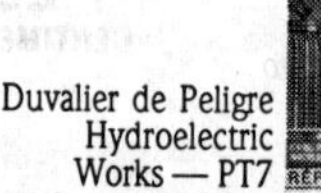
Duvalier de Peligre Hydroelectric Works — PT7

1970-72

RA38 PT7 20c violet & olive 15 15
RA39 PT7 20c ultra & blk ('72) 15 15
Set value 18 15

See Nos. RA46, RAC16-RAC19, RAC23.

Nos. 637-638 Surcharged: "ALPHABETISATION +10"

1971, Dec. 23 **Litho.** ***Perf. 14x13½***

RA40 A138 20c + 10c multi 15 15
a. Inverted surcharge 2.00
RA41 A138 25c + 10c multi 15 15
Set value 18 15

Tax was for the literacy campaign.

"CA" Type of 1963

1972-74 **Photo.** ***Perf. 14x14½***
Size: 17x25mm

RA42 PT6 5c violet blue 15 15
RA43 PT6 5c deep carmine 15 15
RA44 PT6 5c ultra ('74) 15 15
RA45 PT6 5c carmine rose ('74) 15 15
Set value 20 20

Tax was for literacy campaign.

Hydroelectric Type of 1970

1980 **Photo.** ***Perf. 14x14½***

RA46 PT7 25c choc & green 22 15

AIR POST POSTAL TAX STAMPS

Catalogue values for unused stamps in this section, are for Never Hinged items.

Helicopter Type of 1955

1955 **Unwmk.** **Photo.** ***Perf. 11½***

RAC1 PT4 10c red brn, *pale sal* 15 15
RAC2 PT4 20c rose pink, *pink* 15 15
Set value 15

See note after No. RA24.

Type of Postal Tax Stamps, 1960-61

1959
Size: 28x17mm

RAC3 PT5 5c yellow 15 15
RAC4 PT5 10c dull salmon 15 15
RAC5 PT5 10c blue 15 15
Set value 17 15

Type of Postal Tax Stamps, 1963

1963, Sept. ***Perf. 14½x14***
Size: 13½x21mm

RAC6 PT6 10c dark gray 15 15
RAC7 PT6 10c violet 15 15
RAC8 PT6 10c brown 15 15
Set value 15

1966-69 ***Perf. 14x14½***
Size: 17x25mm

RAC9 PT6 10c orange 15 15
RAC10 PT6 10c sky blue 15 15
RAC11 PT6 10c yellow ('69) 15 15
RAC12 PT6 10c carmine ('69) 15 15
RAC13 PT6 10c gray grn ('69) 15 15
RAC14 PT6 10c lilac ('69) 15 15
RAC15 PT6 10c dp claret ('69) 15 15
Set value 40 35

Nos. RAC3-RAC15, RAC20-RAC21 represent a tax for a literacy campaign.

Hydroelectric Type of 1970

1970-74

RAC16 PT7 20c tan & slate 15 15
RAC17 PT7 20c brt bl & dl vio 15 15
RAC18 PT7 25c sal & bluish blk ('74) 18 15
RAC19 PT7 25c yel ol & bluish blk ('74) 18 15
Set value 24

"CA" Type of 1963

1973 **Photo.** ***Perf. 14x14½***
Size: 17x26mm

RAC20 PT6 10c brn & blue 15 15
RAC21 PT6 10c brn & green 15 15
RAC22 PT6 10c brn & orange 15 15
Set value 15

Hydroelectric Power Type of 1970

1980 **Photo.** ***Perf. 14x14½***

RAC23 PT7 25c blue & vio brn 18 15

HATAY

(Formerly Alexandretta)

LOCATION — Northwest of Syria, bordering on Mediterranean Sea.
GOVT. — Former semi-independent republic
AREA — 10,000 sq. mi. (approx.)
POP. — 273,350 (1939)
CAPITAL — Antioch

Alexandretta, a semi-autonomous district of Syria under French mandate, was renamed Hatay in 1938 and transferred to Turkey in 1939.

100 Santims = 1 Kurush
40 Paras = 1 Kurush (1939)

Stamps of Turkey, 1931-38, Surcharged in Black:

HATAY DEVLETİ ■ 75 Sant.
On A77

HATAY DEVLETİ ■ ■ 25 Sant.
On A78

1939 **Unwmk.** ***Perf. 11½x12***

1 A77 10s on 20pa dp org 32 32
a. "Sent" instead of "Sant" 20.00 20.00
2 A78 25s on 1ku dk sl grn 32 32
a. Small "25" 35 35
3 A78 50s on 2ku dk vio 32 32
a. Small "50" 35 35
4 A77 75s on 2½ku green 32 32
5 A78 1ku on 4ku slate 32 32
6 A78 1ku on 5ku rose red 32 32
7 A78 1½ku on 3ku brn org 55 55
8 A78 2½ku on 4ku slate 70 70
9 A78 5ku on 8ku brt blue 2.25 2.25
10 A77 12½ku on 20ku ol grn 3.25 3.25
11 A77 20ku on 25ku Prus bl 3.50 3.50
Nos. 1-11 (11) 12.17 12.17

Map of Hatay — A1

Lions of Antioch A2

Flag of Hatay — A3

Post Office — A4

1939 Unwmk. Typo. Perf. 12

12	A1	10p orange & aqua	24	24
13	A1	30p lt vio & aqua	30	30
14	A1	1½ku olive & aqua	32	32
15	A2	2½ku turq grn	42	42
16	A2	3ku light blue	50	50
17	A2	5ku chocolate	55	55
18	A3	6ku brt blue & car	65	65
19	A3	7½ku dp green & car	55	55
20	A3	12ku violet & car	90	90
21	A3	12½ku dk blue & car	95	95
22	A4	17½ku brown car	2.25	2.25
23	A4	25ku olive brn	3.00	3.00
24	A4	50ku slate blue	6.25	6.25
		Nos. 12-24 (13)	16.88	16.88

Stamps of 1939 Overprinted in Black

T. C.
ilhak tarihi
30-6-1939

1939

25	A1	10p orange & aqua	22	22
a.		Overprint reading up	20.00	
26	A1	30p lt vio & aqua	32	32
27	A1	1½ku ol & aqua	32	32
28	A2	2½ku turq grn	45	45
29	A2	3ku light blue	55	55
30	A2	5ku chocolate	60	60
a.		Overprint inverted	20.00	
31	A3	6ku brt bl & car	60	60
32	A3	7½ku dp grn & car	60	60
33	A3	12ku vio & car	75	75
34	A3	12½ku dk bl & car	90	90
35	A4	17½ku brn car	1.75	1.75
a.		Overprint inverted	20.00	
36	A4	25ku olive brn	3.50	3.50
37	A4	50ku slate blue	7.25	7.25
		Nos. 25-37 (13)	17.81	17.81

The overprint reads "Date of annexation to the Turkish Republic, June 30, 1939."

On Nos. 25-27, the overprint reads down. On Nos. 28-37, it is horizontal.

POSTAGE DUE STAMPS

Postage Due Stamps of Turkey, 1936, Surcharged or Overprinted in Black

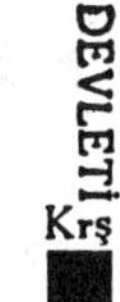

DEVLETİ
Krş

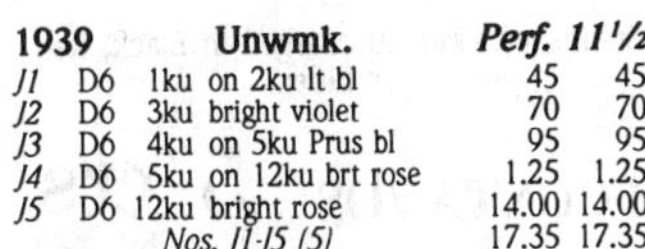

1939 Unwmk. Perf. 11½

J1	D6	1ku on 2ku lt bl	45	45
J2	D6	3ku bright violet	70	70
J3	D6	4ku on 5ku Prus bl	95	95
J4	D6	5ku on 12ku brt rose	1.25	1.25
J5	D6	12ku bright rose	14.00	14.00
		Nos. J1-J5 (5)	17.35	17.35

Castle at Antioch D1

1939 Typo. Perf. 12

J6	D1	1ku red orange	50	50
J7	D1	3ku dk olive brown	70	70
J8	D1	4ku turqoise green	85	85
J9	D1	5ku slate black	1.10	1.10

Nos. J6-J9 Overprinted in Black like Nos. 25-37

1939

J10	D1	1ku red orange	80	80
J11	D1	3ku dk olive brown	95	95
J12	D1	4ku turqoise green	1.00	1.00
J13	D1	5ku slate black	1.25	1.25
a.		Overprint inverted	20.00	

HONDURAS

LOCATION — Central America, between Guatemala on the north and Nicaragua on the south
GOVT. — Republic
AREA — 43,277 sq. mi.
POP. — 4,092,174 (est. 1983)
CAPITAL — Tegucigalpa

8 Reales = 1 Peso
100 Centavos = 1 Peso (1878)
100 Centavos = 1 Lempira (1933)

Catalogue values for unused stamps in this country are for Never Hinged items, beginning with Scott 344 in the regular postage section, Scott C309 in the airpost section, Scott CE3 in the airpost special delivery section, Scott CO110 in the airpost official section, and Scott RA6 in the postal tax section.

Watermark

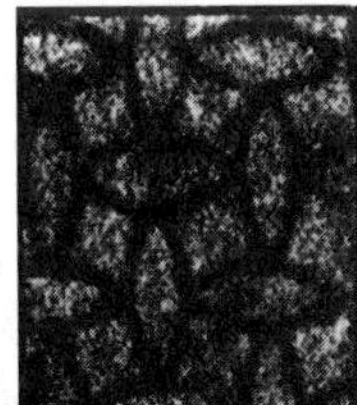
Wmk. 209-Multiple Ovals

Coat of Arms — A1

1865, Dec. Unwmk. Litho. Imperf.

1	A1	2r black, *green*	60
2	A1	2r black, *pink*	60

A2

A3

The actual surcharges are very blurry, distorted and generally unreadable. The above illustrations are only intended to show what the surcharges would look like based on the type face used.

Medio real = ½ real
Un real = 1 real
Dos reales = 2 reales

Comayagua Issue

1877, Apr.

Red Surcharge

3	A2	½r on 2r blk, *grn*	60.00

Blue Surcharge

5	A2	2r on 2r blk, *grn*	95.00
6	A2	2r on 2r blk, *pink*	95.00

Black Surcharge

7	A2	1r on 2r blk, *grn*	75.00
9	A2	2r on 2r blk, *pink*	95.00

Tegucigalpa Issue

1877, June

Black Surcharge

13	A3	1r on 2r blk, *grn*	14.00	16.00
14	A3	1r on 2r blk, *pink*	14.00	
16	A3	2r on 2r blk, *pink*	12.50	

Blue Surcharge

18	A3	½r on 2r blk, *grn*	12.00	
19	A3	½r on 2r blk, *pink*	12.00	
20	A3	1r on 2r blk, *pink*	14.00	
23	A3	2r on 2r blk, *pink*	14.00	16.00

Red Surcharge

24	A3	½r on 2r blk, *grn*	12.00	14.00
25	A3	½r on 2r blk, *pink*	14.00	

Only the stamps valued used were postally used. The others were sold as remainders. #3-25 have been extensively counterfeited.

Regular Issue

President Francisco Morazán — A4

Thin, hard paper, colorless gum
Various Frames

1878, July Engr. Perf. 12
Printed by National Bank Note Co. of N.Y.

30	A4	1c violet	42	42
31	A4	2c brown	42	42
32	A4	½r black	42	42
33	A4	1r green	1.40	1.40
34	A4	2r deep blue	3.00	3.00
35	A4	4r vermilion	2.75	2.50
36	A4	1p orange	3.25	3.25
		Nos. 30-36 (7)	11.66	11.41

Various counterfeit cancellations exist on Nos. 30-36.

Re-Issue
Soft paper, yellowish gum
Various Frames

1889
Printed by American Bank Note Co. of N.Y.

30a	A4	1c deep violet	28
31a	A4	2c red brown	18
32a	A4	½r black	18
33a	A4	1r blue green	22
34a	A4	2r ultramarine	22
35a	A4	4r scarlet vermilion	28
36a	A4	1p orange yellow	35
		Nos. 30a-36a (7)	1.71

Nos. 30a-36a were not for postal use.

Arms of Honduras — A5

1890, Jan. 6

40	A5	1c yellow green	25	28
41	A5	2c red	25	28
42	A5	5c blue	25	28
43	A5	10c orange	32	35
44	A5	20c ocher	32	35
45	A5	25c rose red	32	35
46	A5	30c purple	42	52
47	A5	40c dark blue	42	70
48	A5	50c brown	50	70
49	A5	75c blue green	50	1.75
50	A5	1p carmine	60	2.00
		Nos. 40-50 (11)	4.15	7.56

The tablets and numerals of Nos. 40 to 50 differ for each denomination.

For overprints see Nos. O1-O11.

Used values of Nos. 40-94 are for stamps with genuine cancellations applied while the stamps were valid. Various counterfeit cancellations exist.

President Luis Bográn
A6 A7

1891, July 31

51	A6	1c dark blue	25	28
52	A6	2c yel brown	25	28
53	A6	5c blue green	25	28
54	A6	10c vermilion	25	28
55	A6	20c brown red	25	28
56	A6	25c magenta	35	50
57	A6	30c slate	35	50
58	A6	40c blue green	35	50
59	A6	50c black brown	42	70
60	A6	75c purple	42	1.10
61	A6	1p brown	42	1.40
62	A7	2p brn & black	70	4.25
a.		Head inverted	125.00	
63	A7	5p pur & black	70	5.00
a.		Head inverted	42.50	
64	A7	10p green & blk	70	5.00
a.		Head inverted	42.50	
		Nos. 51-64 (14)	5.66	20.35

#62-64 exist with papermakers watermark.

For overprints see Nos. O12-O22.

Columbus Sighting Honduran Coast — A8

General Trinidad Cabanas — A9

1892, July 31

65	A8	1c slate	35	40
66	A8	2c deep blue	35	40
67	A8	5c yellow grn	35	40
68	A8	10c blue green	35	40
69	A8	20c red	35	40
70	A8	25c orange brn	45	50
71	A8	30c ultramarine	45	52
72	A8	40c orange	45	80
73	A8	50c brown	52	75
74	A8	75c lake	52	1.10
75	A8	1p purple	52	1.25
		Nos. 65-75 (11)	4.66	6.92

Discovery of America by Christopher Columbus, 400th anniv.

1893, Aug.

76	A9	1c green	22	22
77	A9	2c scarlet	22	22
78	A9	5c dark blue	22	22
79	A9	10c orange brn	22	26
80	A9	20c brown red	22	28
81	A9	25c dark blue	28	28
82	A9	30c red orange	40	52
83	A9	40c black	40	70
84	A9	50c olive brn	40	80
85	A9	75c purple	52	1.00
86	A9	1p deep magenta	52	1.10
		Nos. 76-86 (11)	3.62	5.60

Hatay stamps can be mounted in the Scott Turkey album part I.

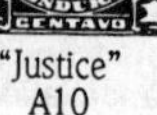
"Justice"
A10

President Celio Arias
A11

1895, Feb. 15

87 A10 1c vermilion 28 28
88 A10 2c deep blue 28 28
89 A10 5c slate 28 42
90 A10 10c brown rose 35 42
91 A10 20c violet 35 45
92 A10 30c deep vio 35 *75*
93 A10 50c olive brn 42 *1.10*
94 A10 1p dark green 50 *1.40*
Nos. 87-94 (8) 2.81 *5.10*

The tablets and numerals of Nos. 76-94 differ for each denomination.

1896, Jan. 1 Litho. *Perf. 11½*

95 A11 1c dark blue 30 35
96 A11 2c yellow brn 30 35
97 A11 5c purple 1.10 28
a. 5c red violet 55 1.10
98 A11 10c vermilion 42 42
99 A11 20c emerald 75 52
a. 20c deep green
100 A11 30c ultramarine 65 70
101 A11 50c rose 90 *1.00*
102 A11 1p black brown 1.25 *1.50*
Nos. 95-102 (8) 5.67 *5.12*

Counterfeits are plentiful. Nos. 95-102 exist imperf. between horiz. or vertically.

Originals of Nos. 95 to 102 are on both thin, semi-transparent paper and opaque paper; reprints are on thicker, opaque paper and usually have a black cancellation "HONDURAS" between horizontal bars.

Railroad Train — A12

1898, Aug. 1

103 A12 1c brown 40 18
104 A12 2c rose 40 18
105 A12 5c dull ultra 75 22
b. 5c red violet (error) 1.00 70
106 A12 6c red violet 60 25
b. 6c dull rose (error)
107 A12 10c dark blue 75 28
108 A12 20c dull orange 1.00 75
109 A12 50c orange red 1.50 1.25
110 A12 1p blue green 3.00 3.00
Nos. 103-110 (8) 8.40 6.11

Excellent counterfeits of Nos. 103-110 exist.
For overprints see Nos. O23-O27.

Laid Paper

103a A12 1c 60 32
104a A12 2c 65 32
105a A12 5c 75 32
106a A12 6c 70 40
107a A12 10c 75 55

General Santos Guardiola
A13

President José Medina
A14

1903, Jan. 1 Engr. *Perf. 12*

111 A13 1c yellow grn 30 18
112 A13 2c car rose 30 25
113 A13 5c blue 30 25
114 A13 6c dk violet 35 25
115 A13 10c brown 35 28
116 A13 20c dull ultra 40 32
117 A13 50c vermilion 1.00 1.00
118 A13 1p orange 1.00 1.00
Nos. 111-118 (8) 4.00 3.53

"PERMITASE" handstamped on stamps of 1896-1903 was applied as a control mark by the isolated Pacific Coast post office of Amapala to prevent use of stolen stamps.

1907, Jan. 1 *Perf. 14*

119 A14 1c dark green 25 25
120 A14 2c scarlet 28 25
120A A14 2c carmine 7.00 4.00
121 A14 5c blue 32 28
122 A14 6c purple 35 28
a. 6c dark violet 70 52
123 A14 10c gray brown 35 35
124 A14 20c ultra 75 75
a. 20c blue violet 100.00 100.00
125 A14 50c deep lake 1.00 1.00
126 A14 1p orange yel 1.25 1.25
Nos. 119-126 (9) 11.55 8.41

All values of the above set exist imperforate, imperforate horizontally and in horizontal pairs, imperforate between.
For surcharges see Nos. 128-130.

1909 Typo. *Perf. 11½*

127 A14 1c green 1.25 1.00
a. Imperf., pair 3.50 3.50
b. Printed on both sides 7.50

The 1909 issue is roughly typographed in imitation of the 1907 design. It exists pin perf. 8, 13, etc.

No. 124 Handstamp Surcharged in Black, Green or Red:

1 5 10

1910, Nov. *Perf. 14*

128 A14 1c on 20c ultra 6.00 5.00
129 A14 5c on 20c ultra (G) 6.00 5.00
130 A14 10c on 20c ultra (R) 6.00 5.00

As is usual with handstamped surcharges inverts and double exist.

Honduran Scene — A15

1911, Jan. Litho. *Perf. 14, 12 (1p)*

131 A15 1c violet 30 15
132 A15 2c green 30 15
a. Perf. 12 1.75 1.00
133 A15 5c carmine 35 15
a. Perf. 12 7.00 3.00
134 A15 6c ultramarine 35 28
135 A15 10c blue 50 35
136 A15 20c yellow 50 42
137 A15 50c brown 1.75 1.50
138 A15 1p olive green 2.00 1.75
Nos. 131-138 (8) 6.05 4.75

For overprints and surcharges see Nos. 139, 141-147, O28-O47.

No. 132a Overprinted in Red

XC
Aniversario de la
Independencia

1911, Sept. 19 *Perf. 12*

139 A15 2c green 15.00 15.00
a. Inverted overprint 20.00 20.00

90th anniversary of Independence.
Counterfeit overprints on perf. 14 stamps exist.

President Manuel Bonilla — A16

1912, Feb. 1 Typo. *Perf. 11½*

140 A16 1c orange red 12.00 12.00

Election of Pres. Manuel Bonilla.

Stamps of 1911 Surcharged in Black, Red or Blue:

2 CENTAVOS
a

5 cts.
b

1913 Litho. *Perf. 14*

141 A15(a) 2c on 1c vio 1.00 65
a. Double surcharge 2.75
b. Inverted surcharge 4.00
c. Double surch., one invtd. 6.00
d. Red surcharge 35.00 35.00
142 A15(b) 2c on 1c vio 6.00 5.00
a. Inverted surcharge 12.50
143 A15(b) 2c on 10c blue 2.50 2.00
a. Double surcharge 5.00 5.00
b. Inverted surcharge
144 A15(b) 2c on 20c yel 6.00 6.00
145 A15(b) 5c on 1c vio 2.00 65
146 A15(b) 5c on 10c bl (Bl) 2.50 1.25
147 A15(b) 6c on 1c vio 2.50 2.00
Nos. 141-147 (7) 22.50 17.55

Counterfeit surcharges exist.

Terencio Sierra — A17

Bonilla — A18

ONE CENTAVO:
Type I - Solid border at sides below numerals.
Type II - Border of light and dark stripes.

1913-14 Typo. *Perf. 11½*

151 A17 1c dark brn, I 20 15
a. 1c brown, type II 35 25
152 A17 2c carmine 25 20
153 A18 5c blue 40 20
154 A18 5c ultra ('14) 40 20
155 A18 6c gray vio 50 25
156 A18 6c purple ('14) 40 25
a. 6c red lilac 60 35
157 A17 10c blue 75 75
158 A17 10c brown ('14) 1.25 50
159 A17 20c brown 1.00 75
160 A18 50c rose 2.00 2.00
161 A18 1p gray green 2.25 2.25
Nos. 151-161 (11) 9.40 7.50

For overprints and surcharges see Nos. 162-173, O48-O57.

Surcharged in Black or Carmine **1 cent.**

1914

162 A17 1c on 2c carmine 75 75
163 A17 5c on 2c carmine 1.25 90
164 A18 5c on 6c gray vio 2.00 2.00
165 A17 10c on 2c carmine 2.00 2.00
166 A18 10c on 6c gray vio 2.00 2.00
a. Double surcharge 10.00
167 A18 10c on 6c gray vio (C) 2.00 2.00
168 A18 10c on 50c rose 6.50 5.00
Nos. 162-168 (7) 16.50 14.65

No. 158 Surcharged with New Value

1915

173 A17 5c on 10c brown 2.50 1.75

Ulua Bridge — A19

Bonilla Theater — A20

1915-16 Typo.

174 A19 1c chocolate 20 15
175 A19 2c carmine 20 15
a. Tête bêche pair 1.00 1.00
176 A20 5c bright blue 25 15
177 A20 6c deep purple 35 18
178 A19 10c dull blue 70 25
179 A19 20c red brown 1.25 1.00
a. Tête bêche pair 4.00 4.00
180 A20 50c red 1.50 1.50
181 A20 1p yellow grn 2.50 2.50
Nos. 174-181 (8) 6.95 5.88

For overprints and surcharges see Nos. 183, 231-232, 237, 239-240, 285, 292, C1-C13, C25, C28, C31, C36, C57, CO21, CO30-CO32, CO42, O58-O65.

Imperf., Pairs

174a A19 1c 2.00 2.00
175b A19 2c 2.00 2.00
176a A20 5c 3.50
178a A19 10c 3.50
179b A19 20c 5.25
180b A20 50c 7.00
181a A20 1p 8.75 8.75

Francisco Bertrand
A21

Statue to Francisco Morazán
A22

1916, Feb. 1

182 A21 1c orange 2.00 2.00

Election of Pres. Francisco Bertrand.
Unauthorized reprints exist.

Official Stamp No. O60 Overprinted **CORRIENTE**

1918

183 A20 5c bright blue 2.00 1.50
a. Inverted overprint 5.00 5.00

1919 Typo.

184 A22 1c brown 15 15
a. Printed on both sides 2.00
b. Imperf., pair 70
185 A22 2c carmine 25 15
186 A22 5c lilac rose 25 15
187 A22 6c bright vio 35 15
188 A22 10c dull blue 75 25
189 A22 15c light blue 75 20
190 A22 15c dark vio 60 20
191 A22 20c orange brn 75 30
a. 20c gray brown 75 30
b. Imperf., pair 2.75
192 A22 50c light brown 1.75 1.25
a. Imperf. pair 6.00
193 A22 1p yellow grn 5.00 3.00
a. Imperf., pair 7.50
b. Printed on both sides 7.50
c. Tête bêche pair 9.00
Nos. 184-193 (10) 10.60 5.80

See note on handstamp following No. 217.
Unauthorized reprints exist.
For overprints and surcharges see Nos. 201-210C, 230, 233, 235-236, 238, 241-243, 287, 289, C58, C61, CO23, CO25, CO33, CO36-CO38, CO39, CO40, O66-O74.

"Dawn of Peace" — A23

1920, Feb. 1

Size: 27x21mm

194 A23 2c rose 2.50 2.50
a. Tête bêche pair 12.50 12.50
b. Imperf., pair 12.50 12.50

Size: 51x40mm

195 A23 2c gold 10.00 10.00
196 A23 2c silver 10.00 10.00
197 A23 2c bronze 10.00 10.00
198 A23 2c red 12.00 12.00
Nos. 194-198 (5) 44.50 44.50

Assumption of power by Gen. Rafael Lopez Gutierrez.
Nos. 195-198 exist imperf.
Unauthorized reprints of #195-198 exist.

Type of 1919, Dated "1920"

1921

201 A22 6c dark violet 5.00 *3.00*
a. Tête bêche pair 15.00
b. Imperf., pair 15.00

Unauthorized reprints exist.

No. 185 Surcharged in Antique Letters

VALE
SEIS CTS.

1922

202 A22 6c on 2c car 40 40
a. "ALE" for "VALE" 2.00 2.00
b. Comma after "CTS" 2.00 2.00
c. Without period after "CTS" 2.00 2.00

d. "CT" for "CTS" 2.00 2.00
e. Double surcharge 4.25
f. Inverted surcharge 4.25

Stamps of 1919 Surcharged in Roman Figures and Antique Letters in Green

$ 0.50
HABILITADO
VALE
CTA. CTS.

1923

203 A22 10c on 1c brown 1.50 1.50
204 A22 50c on 2c car 2.00 2.00
a. Inverted surcharge 10.00 10.00
b. "HABILTADO" 6.00 6.00

Surcharged in Black or Violet Blue

$ 1.00
HABILITADO
VALE
UN PESO

205 A22 1p on 5c lil rose (Bk) 3.50 3.50
a. "PSEO" 20.00 20.00
b. Inverted surcharge 20.00 20.00
206 A22 1p on 5c lil rose (VB) 20.00 20.00
a. "PSEO" 70.00

On Nos. 205-206, "Habilitado Vale" is in Antique letters, "Un Peso" in Roman.

No. 185 Surcharged in Roman Letters in Green

VALE
SEIS CTS

207 A22 6c on 2c carmine 3.50 2.75

Nos. 184-185 Surcharged in Roman Letters in Green

$ 0.50
HABILITADO
VALE
CTA CTS

208 A22 10c on 1c brown 1.75 1.25
a. "DIES" 4.00
b. "DEIZ" 4.00
c. "DEIZ CAS" 4.00
d. "TTS" for "CTS" 4.00
e. "HABILTADO" 4.00
f. "HABILITAD" 4.00
g. "HABILITA" 4.00
h. Inverted surcharge 20.00
209 A22 50c on 2c carmine 3.75 2.75
a. "CAT" for "CTA" 7.50
b. "TCA" for "CTA" 7.50
c. "TTS" for "CTS" 7.50
d. "CAS" for "CTS" 7.50
e. "HABILTADO" 7.50

Surcharge on No. 209 is found in two spacings between value and HABILITADO: 5mm (illustrated) and 1½mm.

No. 186 Surcharged in Antique Letters in Black

$ 1.00
HABILITADO
VALE
UN PESO

210 A22 1p on 5c lil rose 25.00 *25.00*
a. "PFSO" 75.00

In the surcharges on Nos. 202 to 210 there are various wrong font, inverted and omitted letters.

No. 184 Surcharged in Large Antique Letters in Green

$ 0.10
HABILITADO
VALE
DIEZ CTS

210C A22 10c on 1c brown 15.00 15.00
d. "DIFZ" 55.00 55.00

Dionisio de Herrera — A24

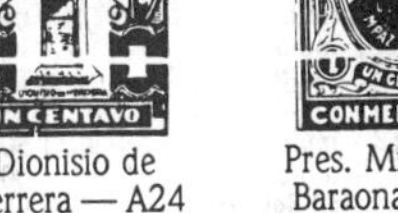
Pres. Miguel Paz Baraona — A25

1924, June **Litho.** ***Perf. 11, 11½***

211 A24 1c olive green 30 15
212 A24 2c deep rose 30 15
213 A24 6c red violet 35 15
214 A24 10c blue 35 15
215 A24 20c yellow brn 70 30
216 A24 50c vermilion 1.50 1.00
217 A24 1p emerald 3.50 2.50
Nos. 211-217 (7) 7.00 4.40

In 1924 a facsimile of the signatures of Santiago Herrera and Francisco Caceres, covering four stamps, was handstamped in violet to prevent the use of stamps that had been stolen during a revolution.

For overprints and surcharges see Nos. 280-281, 290-291, C14-C24, C26-C27, C29-C30, C32-C35, C56, C60, C73-C76, CO1-CO5, CO22, CO24, CO28-CO29, CO34-CO35, CO38A, CO39A, CO41, CO43, O75-O81.

1925, Feb. 1 **Typo.** ***Perf. 11½***

218 A25 1c dull blue 2.00 2.00
a. 1c dark blue 2.00 2.00
219 A25 1c car rose 5.25 5.25
a. 1c brown carmine 5.25 5.25
220 A25 1c olive brn 14.00 14.00
a. 1c orange brown 14.00 14.00
b. 1c dark brown 14.00 14.00
c. 1c black brown 14.00 14.00
221 A25 1c buff 12.00 12.00
222 A25 1c red 52.50 52.50
223 A25 1c green 35.00 35.00
Nos. 218-223 (6) 120.75 120.75

Imperf

225 A25 1c dull blue 5.50 5.50
a. 1c dark blue 5.50 5.50
226 A25 1c car rose 8.75 8.75
a. 1c brown carmine 8.75 8.75
227 A25 1c olive brn 8.75 8.75
a. 1c orange brown 8.75 8.75
b. 1c deep brown 8.75 8.75
c. 1c black brown 8.75 8.75
228 A25 1c buff 8.75 8.75
229 A25 1c red 50.00 50.00
229A A25 1c green 27.50 27.50
Nos. 225-229A (6) 109.25 109.25

Inauguration of President Baraona.
Counterfeits and unauthorized reprints exist.

No. 187 Overprinted in Black and Red

Acuerdo Mayo 3
de 1926
HABILITADO

1926, June ***Perf. 11½***

230 A22 6c bright violet 1.25 1.00

Many varieties of this two-part overprint exist: one or both inverted or double, and various combinations. Value, each $10.

Nos. 177 and 187 Overprinted in Black or Red

1926

1926

231 A20 6c deep pur (Bk) 2.00 2.00
a. Inverted overprint 5.50 5.50
b. Double overprint 5.50 5.50
232 A20 6c deep pur (R) 2.50 2.50
a. Double overprint 5.00 5.00
233 A22 6c lilac (Bk) 60 60
a. 6c violet 75 75
b. Inverted overprint 5.00 5.00
c. Double overprint 5.00 5.00
d. Double ovpt., one inverted 5.00 5.00
e. "192" 7.50 7.50
f. Double ovpt., both inverted 7.50 7.50

Same Overprint on No. 230

235 A22 6c violet 16.00 16.00
a. "1926" inverted 16.00 16.00
b. "Habilitado" triple, one invtd. 16.00 16.00

No. 188 Surcharged in Red or Black

Vale 6 Cts.
1926

236 A22 6c on 10c blue (R) 50 20
c. Double surcharge 2.00 2.00
d. Without bar
e. Inverted surcharge 2.50 2.50
f. "Vale" omitted
g. "6cts" omitted
h. "cts" omitted
k. Black surcharge *50.00 50.00*

Nos. 175 and 185 Overprinted in Green

HABILITADO
1926

237 A19 2c carmine 20 20
a. Tête bêche pair 70 70
b. Double overprint 2.00 1.40
c. "HARILITADO" 2.00 1.40
d. "1926" only 2.75 2.75
e. Double overprint, one inverted 2.75 2.75
f. "1926" omitted 3.50 3.50
g. Triple overprint, two inverted 5.25 5.25
h. Double on face, one on back 5.25 5.25
238 A22 2c carmine 20 20
a. "HARILITADO" 90 90
b. Double overprint 1.40 1.40
c. Inverted overprint 2.00 2.00

No. 177 Overprinted in Red 1926

Large Numerals, 12x5mm

1927

239 A20 6c deep purple 25.00 25.00
a. "1926" over "1927" 35.00 35.00
b. Invtd. ovpt. on face of stamp, normal ovpt. on back 30.00

No. 179 Surcharged

vale 6 cts.
1927

1927

240 A19 6c on 20c brown 75 75
a. Tête bêche pair 2.75 2.75
c. Interted surcharge 2.00 2.00
d. Double surcharge 8.50 8.50

Nos. 8 and 10 in the setting have no period after "cts" and No. 50 has the "t" of "cts" inverted.

Same Surcharge on Nos. 189-191

241 A22 6c on 15c blue 27.50 27.50
a. "c" of "cts" omitted
242 A22 6c on 15c vio 70 70
a. Double surcharge 1.75 1.75
b. Double surch., one invtd. 2.00 2.00
c. "L" of "Vale" omitted
243 A22 6c on 20c yel brn 60 60
a. 6c on 20c deep brown
b. "6" omitted 1.75 1.75
c. "Vale" and "cts" omitted 3.50 3.50

On Nos. 242 and 243 stamps Nos. 12, 16 and 43 in the setting have no period after "cts" and No. 34 often lacks the "s." On No. 243 the "c" of "cts" is missing on stamp No. 38. On No. 241 occur the varieties "ct" or "ts" for "cts." and no period.

Southern Highway — A26

Ruins of Copán — A27

Pine Tree — A28

Presidential Palace — A29

Ponciano Leiva — A30

Pres. M.A. Soto — A31

Lempira — A32

Map of Honduras — A33

President Juan Lindo — A34

Statue of Columbus — A35

1927-29 **Typo.** **Wmk. 209**

244 A26 1c ultramarine 30 15
a. 1c blue 30 18
245 A27 2c carmine 30 15
246 A28 5c dull violet 30 15
247 A28 5c bl gray ('29) 10.00 5.00
248 A29 6c blue black 75 52
a. 6c gray black 75 52
249 A29 6c dark bl ('29) 40 15
a. 6c light blue 40 15
250 A30 10c blue 70 18
251 A31 15c deep blue 1.00 50
252 A32 20c dark blue 1.25 60
253 A33 30c dark brown 1.50 1.00
254 A34 50c light blue 2.50 1.50
255 A35 1p red 5.00 2.50
Nos. 244-255 (12) 24.00 12.40

In 1929 a quantity of imperforate sheets of No. 249 were stolen from the Litografia Nacional. Some of them were perforated by sewing machine and a few copies were passed through the post. To prevent the use of stolen stamps of the 1927-29 issues they were declared invalid and the stock on hand was overprinted "1929 a 1930."

For overprints and surcharges see Nos. 259-278, CO19-CO20B.

Pres. Vicente Mejia Colindres and Vice-Pres. Rafael Diaz Chávez
A36

President Mejia Colindres — A37

1929, Feb. 25

256 A36 1c dk carmine 2.75 2.75
257 A37 2c emerald 2.75 2.75

Installation of Pres. Vicente Mejia Colindres. Printed in sheets of ten.

Nos. 256 and 257 were surreptitiously printed in transposed colors. They were not regularly issued.

Stamps of 1927-29 Overprinted in Various Colors

1929, Oct.

259 A26 1c blue (R) 20 15
a. 1c ultramarine (R) 50 15
b. Double overprint 2.50 1.75
c. As "a", double overprint 2.50 1.75
260 A26 1c blue (Bk) 6.50 6.50
a. 1c ultramarine (Bk)

261 A27 2c car (R Br) 3.50 3.50
a. Double overprint
262 A27 2c car (Bl Gr) 1.00 1.00
a. Double overprint
263 A27 2c car (Bk) 1.00 50
264 A27 2c car (V) 50 25
a. Double overprint
b. Double ovpt., one inverted
265 A27 2c org red (V) 1.50
266 A28 5c dl vio (R) 40 30
a. Double overprint (R+V)
267 A28 5c bl gray (R) 1.00 75
a. Double overprint (R+Bk)
269 A29 6c gray blk (R) 2.50 2.00
a. Double overprint 6.00 6.00
272 A29 6c dk blue (R) 40 15
a. 6c light blue (R) 40 15
b. Double overprint 2.00 2.00
c. Double overprint (R+V)
273 A30 10c blue (R) 40 15
a. Double overprint 2.50 1.75
274 A31 15c dp blue (R) 50 25
a. Double overprint 3.50 2.50
275 A32 20c dark bl (R) 50 35
276 A33 30c dark brn (R) 75 60
a. Double overprint 3.50 2.50
277 A34 50c light bl (R) 1.00 1.00
278 A35 1p red (V) 2.50 2.50
Nos. 259-278 (17) 24.15
Nos. 259-264, 266-278 19.95

Nos. 259-278 exist in numerous shades. There are also various shades of the red and violet overprints. The overprint may be found reading upwards, downwards, inverted, double, triple, tête bêche or combinations.

Status of both 6c stamps with overprint in black is questioned.

A38

1929, Dec. 10
279 A38 1c on 6c lilac rose 70 70
a. "1992" for "1929"
b. "9192" for "1929"
c. Surcharge reading down
d. Dbl. surch., one reading down

Varieties include "1992" reading down and pairs with one surcharge reading down, double or with "1992."

No. 214 Surcharged in Red — **Vale 2 cts. 1930**

Perf. 11, 11½
1930, Mar. 26 **Unwmk.**
280 A24 1c on 10c blue 35 32
a. "1093" for "1930" 1.40
b. "tsc" for "cts" 1.40
281 A24 2c on 10c blue 35 32
a. "tsc" for "cts" 2.00
b. "Vale 2" omitted

Official Stamps of 1929 Overprinted in Red or Violet — **Habilitado para el servicio públi- co. 1930**

1930, Mar. **Wmk. 209** ***Perf. 11½***
282 O1 1c blue (R) 50 50
a. Double overprint 2.00 2.00
284 O1 2c carmine (V) 90 90

Stamps of 1915-26 Overprinted in Blue — **Habilitado julio.—1930**

On No. 174
1930, July 19 **Unwmk.**
285 A19 1c chocolate 28 25
a. Double overprint 1.00 1.00
b. Inverted overprint 1.40 1.40
c. Dbl. ovpt., one inverted 1.40 1.40

On No. 184
287 A22 1c brown 15.00 15.00
a. Double overprint
c. Inverted overprint

On No. 204
289 A22 50c on 2c car 100.00 100.00
b. Inverted surcharge

On Nos. 211 and 212
290 A24 1c olive green 20 18
a. Double overprint 1.75 1.75
b. Inverted overprint 1.75 1.75
d. On No. O75 12.00
291 A24 2c car rose 25 25
a. Double overprint 1.75 1.75
b. Inverted overprint 1.75 1.75

On No. 237
292 A19 2c car (G & Bl) 90.00 90.00

From Title Page of Government Gazette, First Issue — A39

1930, Aug. 11 **Typo.** **Wmk. 209**
295 A39 2c orange 90 90
296 A39 2c ultramarine 90 90
297 A39 2c red 90 90

Publication of the 1st newspaper in Honduras, cent. The stamps were on sale and available for postage on Aug. 11th, 1930, only. Not more than 5 copies of each color could be purchased by an applicant.

Nos. 295-297 exist imperf. and part-perforate. Unauthorized reprints exist.

For surcharges see Nos. CO15-CO18A.

Paz Baraona — A40

Manuel Bonilla — A41

Lake Yojoa — A42

View of Palace at Tegucigalpa — A43

City of Amapala — A44

Mayan Stele at Copán — A45

Christopher Columbus — A46

Discovery of America — A47

Loarque Bridge — A48

1931, Jan. 2 **Unwmk.** **Engr.** ***Perf. 12***
298 A40 1c black brown 20 15
299 A41 2c carmine rose 20 15
300 A42 5c dull violet 30 15
301 A43 6c deep green 30 15
302 A44 10c brown 50 25
303 A45 15c dark blue 50 15
304 A46 20c black 1.00 30
305 A47 50c olive green 2.00 1.00
306 A48 1p slate black 3.50 2.00
Nos. 298-306 (9) 8.50 4.30

Regular Issue of 1931 Overprinted in Black or Various Colors — **T.S.de C.**

1931
307 A40 1c black brown 25 15
308 A41 2c carmine rose 40 15
309 A45 15c dark blue 60 20
310 A46 20c black 1.00 25

Overprinted — **T.S.de C.**

311 A42 5c dull violet 35 18
312 A43 6c deep green 35 15
315 A44 10c brown 50 28
316 A47 50c olive green 4.00 3.50
317 A48 1p slate black 5.00 5.00
Nos. 307-317 (9) 12.45 9.86

The overprint is a control mark. It stands for "Tribunal Superior de Cuentas" (Superior Tribunal of Accounts).

Overprint varieties include: inverted; double; double, one or both inverted; on back; pair, one without overprint; differing colors (6c exists with overprint in orange, yellow and red).

See Nos. C51-C55.

President Carías and Vice-President Williams — A49

1933, Apr. 29
318 A49 2c carmine rose 50 35
319 A49 6c deep green 75 40
320 A49 10c deep blue 1.00 50
321 A49 15c red orange 1.25 75

Inauguration of Pres. Tiburico Carias Andino and Vice-Pres. Abraham Williams, Feb. 1, 1933.

Columbus' Fleet and Flag of the Race A50

Perf. 11½
1933, Aug. 3 **Typo.** **Wmk. 209**
322 A50 2c ultramarine 1.00 65
323 A50 6c yellow 1.00 65
324 A50 10c lemon 1.40 85

Perf. 12
325 A50 15c violet 2.00 1.50
326 A50 50c red 4.00 3.50
327 A50 1 l emerald 7.00 7.00
Nos. 322-327 (6) 16.40 14.15

"Day of the Race," an annual holiday throughout Spanish-American countries. Also for the 441st anniv. of the sailing of Columbus to the New World, Aug. 3, 1492.

Masonic Temple, Tegucigalpa — A51

Designs: 2c, President Carias. 5c, Flag. 6c, Tomás Estrada Palma.

Unwmk.
1935, Jan. 12 **Engr.** ***Perf. 12***
328 A51 1c green 40 15
329 A51 2c carmine 40 18
330 A51 5c dark blue 40 25
331 A51 6c black brown 40 25
a. Vert. pair, imperf. btwn. 20.00 20.00

See Nos. C77-C83.

Gen. Carías Bridge — A55

1937, June 4
332 A55 6c car & ol green 75 35
333 A55 21c grn & violet 1.25 65
334 A55 46c orange & brn 1.75 1.25
335 A55 55c ultra & black 2.50 2.00

Prolongation of the Presidential term to Jan. 19, 1943.

Seal of Honduras — A56

Central District Palace — A57

Designs: 3c, Map of Honduras. 5c, Bridge of Choluteca. 8c, Flag.

1939, Mar. 1 ***Perf. 12½***
336 A56 1c orange yellow 20 15
337 A57 2c red orange 20 15
338 A57 3c carmine 30 15
339 A57 5c orange 30 20
340 A56 8c dark blue 50 20
Nos. 336-340 (5) 1.50 85

Nos. 336-340 exist imperf.
See #C89-C98. For overprints see #342-343.

Nos. 336 and 337 Overprinted in Green — **HABILITADO 1944-45**

1944 ***Perf. 12½***
342 A56 1c orange yellow 30 28
a. Inverted overprint 5.00 5.00
343 A57 2c red orange 1.25 75
a. Inverted overprint 5.00 5.00

Catalogue values for unused stamps in this section, from this point to the end of the section, are for Never Hinged items.

International Peace Movement — A58

1984, Feb. 15 **Litho.** ***Perf. 12***
344 A58 78c multi 65 65
345 A58 85c multi 70 32
346 A58 95c multi 75 35
347 A58 1.50 l multi 1.25 55
348 A58 2 l multi 1.50 70
349 A58 5 l multi 4.00 1.75
Nos. 344-349 (6) 8.85 4.32

Central American Aeronautics Corp., 25th Anniv. — A59

Designs: 2c, Edward Warner Award issued by the Intl. Civil Aviation Organization, vert. 5c, Corp. emblem, flags of Guatemala, Honduras, El Salvador, Costa Rica and Panama. 60c, Transmission tower, plane. 75c, Corp. emblem, vert. 1 l, 1.50 l, Emblem, flags, diff.

1987, Feb. 26 Litho. *Perf. 12*

350 A59 2c multi 15 15
351 A59 5c multi 15 15
352 A59 60c multi 52 25
353 A59 75c multi 65 30
354 A59 1 l multi 90 40
Nos. 350-354 (5) 2.37
Set value 1.00

Souvenir Sheet

355 A59 1.50 l multi 1.40

Housing Institute (INVA), 30th Anniv. — A60

1987, Oct. 9 Litho. *Perf. 13½*

356 A60 5c shown 15 15
357 A60 95c Map, emblem, text 85 40
Set value 45

EXFILHON '88 — A61

1988, Sept. 11 Litho. *Imperf.*

358 A61 3 l dull red brn & brt ultra 3.00 3.00

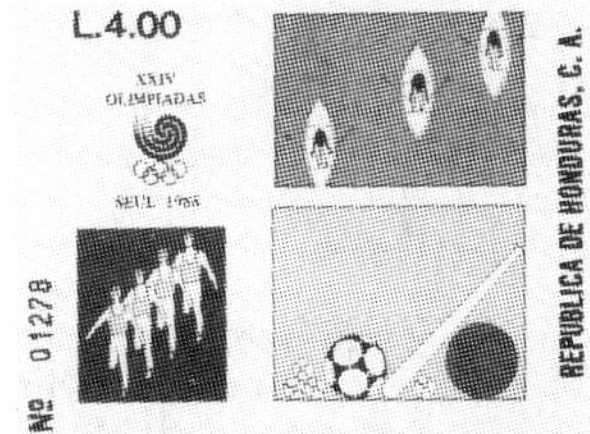

1988 Summer Olympics, Seoul — A62

1988, Sept. 30 Litho. *Imperf.*

359 A62 4 l multi 4.75 4.75

See Nos. C772-C773.

Luis Bogran Technical Institute, Cent. — A63

Design: 85c, Cogwheel, map, flag of Honduras.

1990, Sept. 28 Litho. *Perf. 10½*

360 A63 20c multicolored 15
361 A63 85c multicolored 55

Size: 114x82mm

Imperf

362 A63 2 l like #360 1.25

Nos. 360-361 are airmail.

America Issue — A64

UPAE emblem, land and seascapes showing produce and fish.

1990, Oct. 31 Litho. *Perf. 13½*

363 A64 20c multi, vert. 15
364 A64 1 l multicolored 60

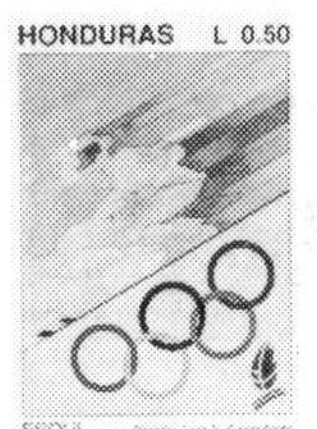

A65

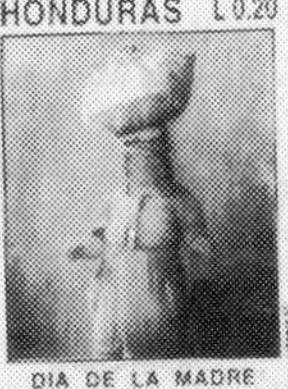

A66

1992

365 A65 50c shown 30
366 A65 3 l Cross-country skiing 1.80

1992 Winter Olympics, Albertville.

1992 Litho. *Perf. 13½*

Mother's Day (Paintings): 20c, Saleswoman, by Manuel Rodriguez. 50c, The Grandmother and Baby, by Rodriguez. 5 l, Saleswomen, by Maury Flores.

367 A66 20c shown 15
368 A66 50c multicolored 30
369 A66 5 l multicolored 3.00

Butterflies A67

Designs: 25c, Melitaeinae chlosyne janais. 85c, Heliconiinae agrilus vanillae. 3 l, Morphinae morpho granadensis. 5 l, Heliconiinae dryadula phalusa.

1992

370 A67 25c multicolored 15
371 A67 85c multicolored 50
372 A67 3 l multicolored 1.75

Size: 108x76mm

Imperf

373 A67 5 l multicolored 3.00

1992 Summer Olympics, Barcelona — A68

1992 Litho. *Perf. 13½*

374 A68 20c Running 15
375 A68 50c Tennis 30
376 A68 85c Soccer 50

AIR POST STAMPS

Regular Issue of 1915-16 Overprinted in Black, Blue or Red

AERO
CORREO

1925 Unwmk. *Perf. 11½*

C1 A20 5c lt blue (Bk) 87.50 87.50
C2 A20 5c lt blue (Bl) 300.00 300.00
a. Inverted overprint *400.00*
b. Vertical overprint *600.00*
c. Double overprint *800.00*
C3 A20 5c lt blue (R) *7,250.*

Value for No. C3 is for copy without gum.

C4 A19 10c dk blue (R) 175.00
a. Inverted overprint 325.00
b. Overprint tête bêche, pair *800.00*
C5 A19 10c dk blue (Bk) *1,100.*
C6 A19 20c red brn (Bk) 175.00 175.00
a. Inverted overprint 250.00
b. Tête bêche pair 400.00
c. Overprint tête bêche, pair *725.00*
d. "AFRO" *1,400.*
e. Double overprint *600.00*
C7 A19 20c red brn (Bl) 175.00 175.00
a. Inverted overprint *500.00*
b. Tête bêche pair *800.00*
c. Vertical overprint 600.00
C8 A20 50c red (Bk) 300.00 300.00
a. Inverted overprint *400.00*
b. Overprint tête bêche, pair *800.00*
C9 A20 1p yel grn (Bk) 600.00 600.00

Surcharged in Black or Blue

AERO
CORREO
25

C10 A19 25c on 1c choc 125.00 125.00
a. Inverted surcharge 600.00
C11 A20 25c on 5c lt bl (Bl) 225.00 225.00
a. Inverted surcharge 550.00
b. Double inverted surcharge *525.00*
C12 A19 25c on 10c dk bl *60,000.*
C13 A19 25c on 20c brn (Bl) 200.00 200.00
a. Inverted surcharge 325.00
b. Tête bêche pair 450.00

Counterfeits of Nos. C1-C13 are plentiful.

Monoplane and Lisandro Garay — AP1

1929, June 5 Engr. *Perf. 12*

C13C AP1 50c carmine 2.00 1.75

No. 216 Surcharged in Blue

Servicio aéreo
Vale 25 centavos oro.—1929.

1929 *Perf. 11, 11½*

C14 A24 25c on 50c ver 5.00 3.50

In the surcharges on Nos. C14 to C40 there are various wrong font and defective letters and numerals, also periods omitted.

Nos. 215-217 Surcharged in Green, Black or Red

Servicio aéreo
Vale 5 cts. oro
1929

1929, Oct.

C15 A24 5c on 20c yel brn (G) 1.40 1.40
a. Double surcharge (R+G) 45.00
C16 A24 10c on 50c ver (Bk) 2.25 1.90
C17 A24 15c on 1p emer (R) 3.50 3.50

Nos. 214 and 216 Surcharged Vertically in Red or Black

Servicio Aéreo Internacional
Vale 5 cts. oro
1929

Servicio Aéreo Internacional.—Vale 20.cts. oro.—1929

1929, Dec. 10

C18 A24(a) 5c on 10c bl (R) 50 50
C19 A24(b) 20c on 50c ver 95 95
a. "1299" for "1929" 190.00
b. "cts. cts." for "cts. oro." 190.00
c. "r" of "Aereo" omitted 2.00
d. Horiz. pair, imperf. btwn. 20.00

Nos. 214, 215 and 180 Surcharged in Various Colors

Servicio Aéreo Internacional
Vale 25 cts. oro
1930

1930, Feb.

C20 A24 5c on 10c (R) 52 52
a. "1930" reading down 3.50
b. "1903" for "1930" 3.50
c. Surcharge reading down 10.00
d. Double surcharge 14.00
e. Dbl. surch., one downward 14.00
C21 A24 5c on 10c (Y) *450.00 450.00*
C22 A24 5c on 20c (Bl) 125.00 125.00
C23 A24 10c on 20c (Bk) 70 70
a. "0" for "10" 3.50
b. Double surcharge 8.75
c. Dbl. surch., one downward 12.00
d. Horiz. pair, imperf. btwn. 70.00
C24 A24 10c on 20c (V) *650.00 650.00*
a. "0" for "10" *1,600.*
C25 A20 25c on 50c (Bk) 95 95
a. "Internaoicnal" 3.50
b. "o" for "oro" 3.50
c. Inverted surcharge 17.50
d. As "a," invtd. surch. *175.00*
e. As "b," invtd. surch. *175.00*

Surcharge on No. C25 is horizontal.

Nos. 214, 215 and 180 Surcharged

Servicio aéreo
Vale 15 centavos oro.—Marzo —1930

1930, Apr. 1

C26 A24 5c on 10c blue 50 50
a. Double surcharge 9.50
b. "Servicioa" 3.50
C27 A24 15c on 20c yel brn 52 52
a. Double surcharge 7.00
C28 A20 20c on 50c red, surch. reading down 95 95
a. Surcharge reading up 7.00

Nos. C22 and C23 Surcharged Vertically in Red

Vale 10
cts. oro

1930

C29 A24 10c on 5c on 20c (Bl+R) 90 90
a. "1930" reading down 9.00 9.00
b. "1903" for "1930" 9.00 9.00
c. Red surch. reading down 14.00
C30 A24 10c on 10c on 20c (Bk+R) 87.50 87.50
a. "0" for "10" 190.00

No. 181 Surcharged as No. C25 and Re-surcharged

Vale 50
cts. oro

C31 A20 50c on 25c on 1p grn 4.25 4.25
a. "Internaoicnal" 7.00
b. "o" for "oro" 7.00
c. 25c surcharge inverted 17.50 17.50
d. 50c surcharge inverted 17.50 17.50
e. As "a" and "c"
f. As "a" and "d"
g. As "b" and "c"
h. As "b" and "d"

No. 215 Surcharged in Dark Blue

Servicio aéreo
Vale 5 centavos oro.
Mayo.

1930, May 22

C32 A24 5c on 20c yel brn 1.00 1.00
a. Double surcharge 5.25 5.25
b. Horiz. pr., imperf. btwn. 60.00 60.00
c. Vertical pair, imperf. between 20.00 20.00

Nos. O78-O80 Surcharged like Nos. C20 to C25 in Various Colors

1930

C33 A24	5c on 10c (R)	350.00	350.00
a.	"1930" reading down	*875.00*	
b.	"1903" for "1930"	*875.00*	
C34 A24	5c on 20c (Bl)	400.00	400.00
C35 A24	25c on 50c (Bk)	175.00	175.00
a.	55c on 50c vermilion	325.00	325.00

No. C35 exists with inverted surcharge.

No. O64 Surcharged like No. C28

C36 A20	20c on 50c red (dbl. surch., reading up)	*350.00*	*350.00*
a.	Dbl. surch., reading down	*350.00*	*350.00*

No. O87 Overprinted

HABILITADO
Servicio Aéreo Internacional
1930

1930, Feb. 21 Wmk. 209 *Perf. 11½*

C37 O1	50c yel, grn & blue	1.25	1.25
a.	"Internacional"	5.25	
b.	"luternacional"	5.25	
c.	Double overprint	5.25	

Nos. O86-O88 Overprinted in Various Colors

HABILITADO
Servicio Aéreo
MAYO 1930

1930, May 23

C38 O1	20c dark blue (R)	1.00	90
a.	Double overprint	8.75	
b.	Triple overprint	12.00	
C39 O1	50c org, grn & bl (Bk)	1.00	90
C40 O1	1p buff (Bl)	1.25	1.25
a.	Double overprint	10.50	

National Palace — AP3

1930, Oct. 1 Unwmk. Engr. *Perf. 12*

C41 AP3	5c yel orange	50	30
C42 AP3	10c carmine	75	60
C43 AP3	15c green	1.00	75
C44 AP3	20c dull violet	1.25	60
C45 AP3	1p light brown	4.00	4.00
	Nos. C41-C45 (5)	7.50	6.25

Same Overprinted in Various Colors

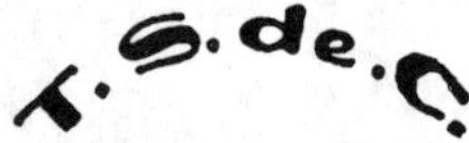

1931 *Perf. 12*

C51 AP3	5c yel orange (R)	2.00	1.50
C52 AP3	10c carmine (Bk)	3.00	2.50
C53 AP3	15c green (Br)	5.00	4.00
C54 AP3	20c dull vio (O)	5.00	4.25
C55 AP3	1p lt brown (G)	10.00	8.75
	Nos. C51-C55 (5)	25.00	21.00

See note after No. 317.

Stamps of Various Issues Surcharged

Servicio aéreo
interior.
Vale 15 cts.
Octubre 1931.

Blue Surcharge

1931, Oct. *Perf. 11½*

On No. 215

C56 A24	15c on 20c yel brn	3.50	2.75
a.	Horiz. pr., imperf. btwn.	42.50	
b.	Green surcharge	20.00	20.00

On No. O64

C57 A20	15c on 50c red	4.25	3.50
a.	Inverted surcharge	10.50	10.50

On No. O72

C58 A22	15c on 20c brn	4.25	4.25
a.	Vert. pair, imperf. between	12.00	

On Nos. C57 and C58 the word "OFICIAL" is canceled by two bars.

Black Surcharge

On No. O88

Wmk. 209

C59 O1	15c on 1p buff	4.25	4.25
a.	Imperf. horizontally, pair	8.75	
b.	"Sevricio"	14.00	14.00

The varieties "Vaie" for "Vale", "aereo" with circumflex accent on the first "e" and "Interior" with initial capital "I" are found on Nos. C56, C58 and C59. No. C57 is known with initial capital in "Interior."

A similar surcharge, in slightly larger letters and with many minor varieties, exists on Nos. 215, O63, O64 and O73. The authenticity of this surcharge is questioned.

Nos. 215, O73, O87-O88 Surcharged in Green, Red or Black

S.—Aéreo
Vl. 15 cts.
XI 1931.

1931, Nov. Unwmk.

C60 A24	15c on 20c (G)	3.50	2.75
a.	Inverted surcharge	6.25	
b.	"XI" omitted	6.25	
c.	"X" for "XI"	6.25	
d.	"PI" for "XI"	6.25	
C61 A22	15c on 50c (R)	3.50	2.75
a.	"XI" omitted	6.75	
b.	"PI" for "XI"	6.75	
c.	Double surcharge	20.00	20.00

On No. C61 the word "OFICIAL" is not barred out.

Wmk. 209

C62 O1	15c on 50c (Bk)	2.75	2.50
a.	"1391" for "1931"	10.50	10.50
b.	Double surcharge	8.75	8.75
C63 O1	15c on 1p (Bk)	2.50	2.25
a.	"1391" for "1931"	12.50	
b.	Surcharged on both sides	7.00	

Nos. O76-O78 Surcharged in Black or Red

Aéreo
interior
VALE
15 Cts.
1932

1932 Unwmk. *Perf. 11, 11½*

C73 A24	15c on 2c	50	50
a.	Double surcharge	5.50	
b.	Inverted surcharge	4.25	
c.	"Ae" of "Aero" omitted	70	
d.	On No. 212 (no "Official")		
C74 A24	15c on 6c	50	50
a.	Double surcharge	3.50	
b.	Horiz. pair, imperf. btwn.	17.50	
c.	"Aer" omitted		
d.	"A" omitted	70	
e.	Inverted surcharge	3.50	
C75 A24	15c on 10c (R)	50	50
a.	Double surcharge	5.50	
b.	Inverted surcharge	3.50	
c.	"r" of "Aereo" omitted	70	

Same Surcharge on No. 214 in Red

C76 A24	15c on 10c dp bl	*87.50*	*87.50*

There are various broken and missing letters in the setting.

A similar surcharge with slightly larger letters exists.

Post Office and National Palace AP4

View of Tegucigalpa AP5

Designs: 15c, Map of Honduras. 20e, Mayo Bridge. 40c, View of Tegucigalpa. 50c, Owl. 1 l, Coat of Arms.

1935, Jan. 10 *Perf. 12*

C77 AP4	8c blue	15	15
C78 AP5	10c gray	25	15
C79 AP5	15c olive gray	40	15
C80 AP5	20c dull green	50	15
C81 AP5	40c brown	70	20
C82 AP4	50c yellow	4.00	1.25
C83 AP4	1 l green	2.50	2.25
	Nos. C77-C83 (7)	8.50	4.30

Flags of US and Honduras — AP11

Engr. & Litho.

1937, Sept. 17 Unwmk.

C84 AP11	46c multicolored	1.00	1.00

US Constitution, 150th anniv..

Comayagua Cathedral AP12

Founding of Comayagua AP13

Alonzo Cáceres and Pres. Carías — AP14

Lintel of Royal Palace — AP15

1937, Dec. 7 Engr.

C85 AP12	2c copper red	15	15
C86 AP13	8c dark blue	35	15
C87 AP14	15c slate black	50	50
C88 AP15	50c dark brown	3.00	2.00

City of Comayagua founding, 400th anniv.

For surcharges see Nos. C144-C146.

Mayan Stele at Copán — AP16

Mayan Temple, Copán — AP17

Designs: 15c, President Carias. 30c, José C. de Valle. 40c, Presidential House. 46c, Lempira. 55c, Church of Our Lady of Suyapa. 66c, J. T. Reyes. 1 l, Hospital at Choluteca. 2 l, Ramón Rosa.

1939, Mar. 1 *Perf. 12½*

C89 AP16	10c orange brn	20	15
C90 AP16	15c grnsh blue	22	15
C91 AP17	21c gray	45	15
C92 AP16	30c dk blue grn	45	15
C93 AP17	40c dull violet	90	15
C94 AP16	46c dk gray brn	90	45
C95 AP16	55c green	1.10	60
a.	Imperf., pair	22.50	
C96 AP16	66c black	1.50	1.10
C97 AP16	1 l olive grn	2.75	90
C98 AP16	2 l henna red	4.00	2.25
	Nos. C89-C98 (10)	12.47	6.05

For surcharges see #C118-C119, C147-C152.

Souvenir Sheets

AP26

Designs: 14c, Francisco Morazan. 16c, George Washington. 30c, J. C. de Valle. 40c, Simon Bolivar.

1940, Apr. 13 Engr. *Perf. 12*

Centers of Stamps Lithographed

C99 AP26	Sheet of 4	2.25	2.25
a.	14c black, yellow, ultra & rose	35	28
b.	16c black, yellow, ultra & rose	42	35
c.	30c black, yellow, ultra & rose	65	55
d.	40c black, yellow, ultra & rose	75	70

Imperf

C100 AP26	Sheet of 4	2.25	2.25
a.	14c black, yellow, ultra & rose	35	28
b.	16c black, yellow, ultra & rose	42	35
c.	30c black, yellow, ultra & rose	65	55
d.	40c black, yellow, ultra & rose	75	70

Pan American Union, 50th anniv.

For overprints see Nos. C153-C154, C187.

Air Post Official Stamps of 1939 Overprinted in Red

Correo Aéreo
Habilitado para
Servicio Publico
Pro-Faro Colon-1940

1940, Oct. 12 *Perf. 12½*

C101 OA2	2c dp bl & green	20	20
C102 OA2	5c dp blue & org	20	20
C103 OA2	8c deep bl & brn	20	20
C104 OA2	15c dp blue & car	40	40
C105 OA2	46c dp bl & ol grn	70	70
C106 OA2	50c dp bl & vio	80	80
C107 OA2	1 l dp bl & red brn	3.50	3.50
C108 OA2	2 l dp bl & red org	7.00	7.50
	Nos. C101-C108 (8)	13.00	13.50

Erection and dedication of the Columbus Memorial Lighthouse.

Air Post Official Stamps of 1939 Overprinted in Black

Habilitada para el
Servicio Público
1941

1941, Aug. 2

C109 OA2	5c deep bl & org	2.50	24
C110 OA2	8c dp blue & brn	5.00	24
a.	Overprint inverted		*225.00*

Nos. CO44, CO47-CO51 Surcharged in Black

Rehabilitada para
el Servicio Público
1941
Vale tres cts.

1941, Oct. 28

C111 OA2	3c on 2c	40	18
C112 OA2	8c on 2c	50	50
C113 OA2	8c on 15c	50	20
C114 OA2	8c on 46c	60	60
C115 OA2	8c on 50c	75	52
C116 OA2	8c on 1 l	1.25	70
C117 OA2	8c on 2 l	2.00	1.50
	Nos. C111-C117 (7)	6.00	4.20

Once in each sheet a large "h" occurs in "ocho" on Nos. C112-C117.

Nos. C90, C94 Surcharged in Red

Correo Aéreo
L 0.08

1942, July 14

C118 AP16	8c on 15c	70	25
a.	"Cerreo"	2.00	2.00
b.	Double surcharge	25.00	25.00
c.	As "a," double surcharge	*175.00*	
C119 AP16	16c on 46c	70	25
a.	"Cerreo"	2.00	2.00

Plaque
AP27

Morazán's Tomb, San Salvador
AP28

Designs: 5c, Battle of La Trinidad. 8c, Morazán's birthplace. 16c, Statue of Morazán. 21c, Church where Morazán was baptized. 1 l, Arms of Central American Federation. 2 l, Gen. Francisco Morazán.

1942, Sept. 15 *Perf. 12*

C120	AP27	2c red orange	15	15
C121	AP27	5c turq green	15	15
C122	AP27	8c sepia	15	15
C123	AP28	14c black	30	30
C124	AP27	16c olive gray	20	20
C125	AP27	21c light blue	85	65
C126	AP27	1 l brt ultra	2.75	2.25
C127	AP28	2 l dl ol brn	7.25	7.25
		Nos. C120-C127 (8)	11.80	11.10

Gen. Francisco Morazan (1799-1842).
For surcharges see Nos. C349-C350.

Coat of Arms — AP35

Cattle — AP36

Bananas — AP37

Pine Tree — AP38

Tobacco Plant — AP39

Orchid
AP40

Coco Palm — AP41

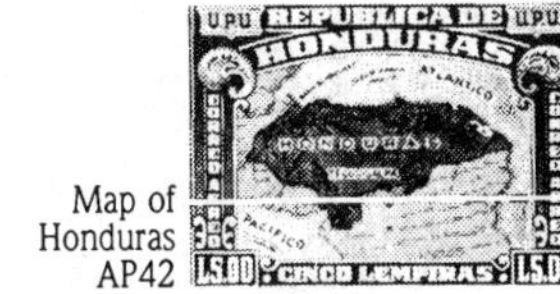

Map of Honduras
AP42

Designs: 2c, Flag. 8c, Rosario. 16c, Sugar cane. 30c, Oranges. 40c, Wheat. 1 l, Corn. 2 l, Map of Americas.

1943, Sept. 14 *Perf. 12½*

C128	AP35	1c light grn	15	15
C129	AP35	2c blue	15	15
C130	AP36	5c green	30	15
C131	AP37	6c dark bl grn	25	15
C132	AP36	8c lilac	30	15
C133	AP38	10c lilac brn	30	15
C134	AP39	15c dp claret	35	15
C135	AP38	16c dark red	35	15
C136	AP40	21c deep blue	75	15
C137	AP39	30c org brown	60	15
C138	AP40	40c red orange	60	15
C139	AP41	55c black	1.00	48
C140	AP41	1 l dark olive	1.50	1.25
C141	AP37	2 l brown red	5.00	3.75
C142	AP42	5 l orange	12.50	12.50
a.		Vert. pair, imperf. btwn.	150.00	
		Nos. C128-C142 (15)	24.10	19.63

Pan-American School of Agriculture
AP50

1944, Oct. 12 *Perf. 12*

C143	AP50	21c dk blue grn	32	16

Inauguration of the Pan-American School of Agriculture, Tegucigalpa.

Air Post Stamps of 1937-39 Surcharged in Red or Green

Correo. Aéreo
HABILITADO
Acd. No 798-1945
L 0.01

1945, Mar. 13 *Perf. 11, 12½*

C144	AP15	1c on 50c dk brn	15	15
C145	AP12	2c on 2c cop red	18	15
C146	AP14	8c on 15c sl blk	22	15
C147	AP16	10c on 10c org brown (G)	35	35
C148	AP16	15c on 15c grnsh blue (G)	22	22
C149	AP17	30c on 21c gray (G)	4.50	2.75
C150	AP17	40c on 40c dull violet (G)	1.75	1.75
C151	AP16	1 l on 46c dk gray brown (G)	1.75	1.25
C152	AP16	2 l on 66c blk (G)	2.50	2.50
		Nos. C144-C152 (9)	11.62	9.27

Souvenir Sheets

Nos. C99 and C100 Overprinted in Red "VICTORIA DE LAS NACIONES UNIDAS, ALEMANIA SE RINDE INCONDICIONALMENTE 8 DE MAYO DE 1945. ACDO. No. 1231 QUE AUTORIZA LA CONTRAMARCA"

1945, Oct. 1 *Perf. 12*

C153	AP26	Sheet of 4	1.90	1.90

Imperf

C154	AP26	Sheet of 4	3.75	3.00

Allied Nations' victory and Germany's unconditional surrender, May 8, 1945.

Seal of Honduras
AP51

Arms of Gracias and Trujillo — AP52

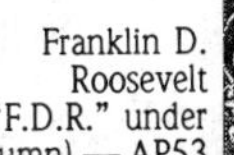

Franklin D. Roosevelt ("F.D.R." under Column) — AP53

Arms of San Miguel de Heredia de Tegucigalpa
AP54

Designs (Coats of Arms): 5c, Comayagua and San Jorge de Olancho. 15c, Province of Honduras and San Juan de Puerto Caballas. 21c, Comayagua and Tencoa. 1 l, Jerez de la Frontera de Choluteca and San Pedro de Zula.

Perf. 12½

1946, Oct. 15 **Unwmk.** **Engr.**

C155	AP51	1c red	15	15
a.		Vert. pair, imperf. between	17.50	
b.		Imperf., pair	70.00	
C156	AP52	2c red orange	15	15
a.		Imperf., pair	70.00	
C157	AP52	5c violet	18	15
C158	AP53	8c brown	70	25
a.		Horiz. pair, imperf. btwn.	70.00	
C159	AP52	15c sepia	35	18
C160	AP52	21c deep blue	35	28
a.		Horiz. pair, imperf. btwn.	15.00	
b.		Imperf., pair	70.00	
C161	AP52	1 l green	1.75	1.25
C162	AP54	2 l dark grn	2.50	2.00
		Nos. C155-C162 (8)	6.13	4.41

No. C158 commemorates the death of Franklin D. Roosevelt and the Allied victory over Japan in World War II.

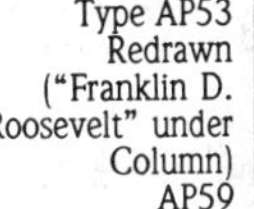

Type AP53 Redrawn ("Franklin D. Roosevelt" under Column)
AP59

1947, Oct. *Perf. 12½*

C163	AP59	8c brown	42	28
a.		Vert. pair, imperf. between	87.50	
b.		Horiz. pair, imperf. btwn.		
c.		Perf. 12x6	*175.00*	

Map, Ancient Monuments and Conference Badge
AP60

1947, Oct. 20 *Perf. 11x12½*

Various Frames

C164	AP60	16c green	35	15
C165	AP60	22c orange yel	30	15
C166	AP60	40c orange	65	25
C167	AP60	1 l deep blue	85	70
C168	AP60	2 l lilac	3.00	2.50
C169	AP60	5 l brown	8.00	6.50
		Nos. C164-C169 (6)	13.15	10.25

1st Intl. Archeological Conference of the Caribbean.
For overprints and surcharges see Nos. C181-C186, C351, C353-C354, C379, C544.

Flag and Arms of Honduras
AP61

Juan Manuel Galvez
AP62

J. M. Galvez, Gen. Tiburcio Carias A. and Julio Lozano
AP63

National Stadium — AP64

Designs: 5c, 15c, Julio Lozano. 9c, Juan Manuel Galvez. 40c, Custom House. 1 l, Recinto Hall. 2 l, Gen. Tiburcio Carias A. 5 l, Galvez and Lozano.

Various Frames

Inscribed: "Conmemorativa de la Sucesion Presidencial para el Periodo de 1949-1955."

1949, Sept. 17 **Engr.** *Perf. 12*

C170	AP61	1c deep blue	15	15
C171	AP62	2c rose car	15	15
C172	AP62	5c deep blue	15	15
C173	AP62	9c sepia	15	15
C174	AP62	15c red brown	25	15
C175	AP63	21c gray black	50	15
C176	AP64	30c olive gray	60	15
C177	AP64	40c slate gray	70	18
C178	AP61	1 l red brown	1.00	35
C179	AP62	2 l violet	2.50	1.50
C180	AP64	5 l rose car	7.00	6.25
		Nos. C170-C180 (11)	13.15	9.33

Presidential succession for the 1949-1955 term.
For overprints and surcharges see Nos. C188-C197, C206-C208, C346, C355, C419-C420, C478, C545.

Nos. C164-C169 Overprinted in Carmine

U. P. U.
75 Aniversario
1874-1949

1951, Feb. 26 *Perf. 11x12½*

C181	AP60	16c green	50	50
a.		Inverted overprint	45.00	45.00
C182	AP60	22c orange yel	75	75
a.		Inverted overprint	45.00	
C183	AP60	40c orange	75	75
C184	AP60	1 l deep blue	2.00	2.00
C185	AP60	2 l lilac	3.00	2.50
a.		Inverted overprint	60.00	
C186	AP60	5 l brown	22.50	18.00
		Nos. C181-C186 (6)	29.50	24.50

Souvenir Sheets

Same Overprint in Carmine on Nos. C99 and C100

Perf. 12

C187	AP26	Sheet of 4	2.75	2.25
a.		Imperf.	*250.00*	*250.00*

UPU, 75th anniv. (in 1949).

Nos. C170 to C179 Overprinted in Carmine

Conmemorativa
Fundación
Banco Central
Administración
Gálvez—Lozano
Julio 1o. de 1950

1951, Feb. 27 *Perf. 12*

C188	AP61	1c deep blue	15	15
C189	AP62	2c rose car	15	15
C190	AP62	5c deep blue	15	15
C191	AP62	9c sepia	15	15
C192	AP62	15c red brown	20	15
C193	AP63	21c gray black	25	20
C194	AP64	30c olive gray	60	30
C195	AP64	40c slate gray	75	50
C196	AP61	1 l red brown	1.75	1.25
C197	AP62	2 l violet	6.00	4.50
		Nos. C188-C197 (10)	10.15	7.50

Founding of Central Bank, July 1, 1950.

Discovery of America AP65

Queen Isabella I — AP66

Designs: 2c, 1 l, Columbus at court. 8c, Surrender of Granada. 30c, Queen Isabella offering her jewels.

Perf. 13½x14, 14x13½

1952, Oct. 11 Engr. Unwmk.

C198	AP65	1c red org & blk	15	15
C199	AP65	2c bl & red brn	15	15
C200	AP65	8c dk grn & dk brown	30	15
C201	AP66	16c dk bl & blk	50	40
C202	AP65	30c pur & dk grn	1.00	60
C203	AP65	1 l dp car & blk	2.50	2.50
C204	AP65	2 l brn & vio	5.00	5.00
C205	AP66	5 l rose lil & ol	8.50	8.50
		Nos. C198-C205 (8)	18.10	17.45

500th birth anniv. of Isabella I of Spain.

For overprints and surcharges see Nos. C209-C221, C377-C378, C404-C406, C489.

No. C175 Surcharged in Carmine

HABILITADO 1953
L 0.05

1953, May 13 *Perf. 12*

C206	AP63	5c on 21c gray blk	15	15
C207	AP63	8c on 21c gray blk	50	15
C208	AP63	16c on 21c gray blk	80	18
		Set value		36

Nos. CO52-CO54 Surcharged "HABILITADO 1953" and New Value in Red

1953, Dec. 8 *Perf. 13½x14, 14x13½*

C209	AP65	10c on 1c	15	15
a.		Inverted surcharge	45.00	45.00
C210	AP65	12c on 1c	15	15
C211	AP65	15c on 2c	20	15
C212	AP65	20c on 2c	30	20
C213	AP65	24c on 2c	30	20
a.		Inverted surcharge	45.00	45.00
C214	AP65	25c on 2c	30	25
C215	AP65	30c on 8c	35	25
C216	AP65	35c on 8c	45	45
C217	AP65	50c on 8c	60	45
C218	AP65	60c on 8c	80	55

Same Overprint on Nos. CO57-CO59

C219	AP65	1 l dk grn & dk brown	2.00	1.75
C220	AP65	2 l bl & red brn	6.00	5.00
C221	AP66	5 l red org & blk	12.00	12.00
a.		Date inverted	150.00	
		Nos. C209-C221 (13)	23.60	21.55

Flags of UN and Honduras AP67

Designs: 2c, UN emblem. 3c, UN building. 5c, Shield. 15c, Juan Manuel Galvez. 30c, UNICEF. 1 l, UNRRA. 2 l, UNESCO. 5 l, FAO.

Engraved; Center of 1c Litho.

1953, Dec. 18 *Perf. 12½*

Frames in Black

C222	AP67	1c ultra & vio bl	15	15
C223	AP67	2c blue	15	15
C224	AP67	3c rose lilac	16	15
C225	AP67	5c green	15	15
C226	AP67	15c red brown	32	22
C227	AP67	30c brown	80	50
C228	AP67	1 l dp carmine	6.25	4.50
C229	AP67	2 l orange	7.00	5.00
C230	AP67	5 l blue green	17.50	15.00
		Nos. C222-C230 (9)	32.48	25.82

Issued to honor the United Nations.

For overprints and surcharges see Nos. C231-C249, C331-C335, C472, C490.

Nos. CO60-CO66 Overprinted in Red

1955, Feb. 23 Unwmk. *Perf. 12½*

Frames in Black

C231	AP67	1c ultra & vio bl	15	15
C232	AP67	2c dp blue grn	15	15
C233	AP67	3c orange	15	15
C234	AP67	5c dp carmine	16	16
C235	AP67	15c dk brown	25	25
C236	AP67	30c purple	75	75
C237	AP67	1 l olive gray	15.00	15.00

Overprint exists inverted on 1c, 3c.

Nos. C231 to C233 Surcharged with New Value in Black

C238	AP67	8c on 1c	15	15
C239	AP67	10c on 2c	15	15
C240	AP67	12c on 3c	18	18
		Nos. C231-C240 (10)	17.09	17.09

50th anniv. of the founding of Rotary International (Nos. C231-C240).

Nos. CO60-CO63, C226-C230 Overprinted

ONU
X ANIVERSARIO
1945 · 1955

1956, July 14 Unwmk. *Perf. 12½*

Frames in Black

C241	AP67	1c ultra & vio bl	15	15
C242	AP67	2c dp bl grn	15	15
C243	AP67	3c orange	18	18
C244	AP67	5c dp car	22	22
C245	AP67	15c red brn	26	26
C246	AP67	30c brown	40	40
C247	AP67	1 l dp car	3.00	2.50
C248	AP67	2 l orange	4.50	4.50
C249	AP67	5 l bl grn	12.00	12.00
		Nos. C241-C249 (9)	20.86	20.36

10th anniv. of UN (in 1955). The red "OFICIAL" overprint was not obliterated.

The "ONU" overprint exists inverted on 1c, 3c, 5c and 1-lempira.

Basilica of Suyapa — AP68

Pres. Julio Lozano Diaz — AP69

Designs: 3c, Southern Highway. 4c, Genoveva Guardiola de Estrada Palma. 5c, Maria Josefa Lastiri de Morazan. 8c, Landscape and cornucopia (5-Year Plan). 10c, National Stadium. 12c, U. S. School. 15c, Central Bank. 20c, Legislative Palace. 25c, Development Bank (projected). 30c, Toncontin Airport. 40c, Juan Ramon Molina Bridge. 50c, Peace Monument. 60c, Treasury Palace. 1 l, Blood bank. 2 l, Communications Building. 5 l, Presidential Palace.

Perf. 13x12½, 12½x13

Engraved; #C255 Litho.

1956, Oct. 3

C250	AP68	1c blk & vio bl	15	15
C251	AP69	2c blk & dk bl	15	15
C252	AP68	3c blk & brown	15	15
C253	AP69	4c blk & lilac	15	15
C254	AP69	5c blk & dk red	15	15
C255	AP68	8c brn & multi	15	15
C256	AP68	10c blk & emer	15	15
C257	AP68	12c blk & green	15	15
C258	AP68	15c dk red & blk	16	15
C259	AP68	20c blk & ultra	16	15
C260	AP69	24c black & lil	22	16
C261	AP68	25c blk & green	25	22
C262	AP68	30c blk & car rose	28	22
C263	AP68	40c blk & red brn	32	25
C264	AP69	50c blk & bl grn	38	32
C265	AP68	60c blk & orange	48	45
C266	AP68	1 l blk & rose vio	1.25	1.00
C267	AP69	2 l black & mag	2.50	2.25
C268	AP69	5 l blk & brn car	5.75	5.00
		Nos. C250-C268 (19)	12.95	11.37

Issued to publicize the Five-Year Plan.

For overprints and surcharges see Nos. C414-C418, C491-C493, C537-C538, C542, C550.

Flag of Honduras — AP70

Designs: 2c, 8c, Monument and mountains. 10c, 15c, 1 l, Lempira. 30c, 2 l, Coat of arms.

1957, Oct. 21 Litho. *Perf. 13*

Frames in Black

C269	AP70	1c buff & ultra	15	15
C270	AP70	2c org, pur & emerald	15	15
C271	AP70	5c pink & ultra	15	15
C272	AP70	8c org, vio & ol	18	15
C273	AP70	10c vio & brown	18	15
C274	AP70	12c lt grn & ultra	25	18
C275	AP70	15c green & brn	32	20
C276	AP70	30c pink & slate	42	25
C277	AP70	1 l blue & brn	1.75	1.50
C278	AP70	2 l lt grn & slate	3.25	3.00
		Nos. C269-C278 (10)	6.80	5.88

First anniv. of the October revolution.

Control marks were handstamped in violet on many current stamps in July and August, 1958, following fire and theft of stamps at Tegucigalpa in April. All post offices were ordered to honor only stamps overprinted with the facsimile signature of their departmental revenue administrator. Honduras has 18 departments.

For surcharge see No. C551.

Flags of Honduras and US — AP71

1958, Oct. 2 Engr. *Perf. 12*

Flags in National Colors

C279	AP71	1c light blue	15	15
C280	AP71	2c red	15	15
C281	AP71	5c green	15	15
C282	AP71	10c brown	15	15
C283	AP71	20c orange	25	18
C284	AP71	30c deep rose	25	22
C285	AP71	50c gray	38	38
C286	AP71	1 l orange yel	1.00	1.00
C287	AP71	2 l gray olive	2.00	2.00
C288	AP71	5 l vio blue	4.00	4.00
		Nos. C279-C288 (10)	8.48	8.38

Honduras Institute of Inter-American Culture. The proceeds were intended for the Binational Center, Tegucigalpa.

For overprints see Nos. C320-C324.

Abraham Lincoln — AP72

Lincoln's Birthplace AP73

Designs: 3c, 50c, Gettysburg Address. 5c, 1 l, Freeing the slaves. 10c, 2 l, Assassination. 12c, 5 l, Memorial, Washington.

1959, Feb. 12 Unwmk. *Perf. 13½*

Flags in National Colors

C289	AP72	1c green	15	15
C290	AP73	2c dark blue	15	15
C291	AP73	3c purple	16	16
C292	AP73	5c dk carmine	16	16
C293	AP73	10c black	24	16
C294	AP73	12c dark brown	24	16
C295	AP72	15c red orange	32	16
C296	AP73	25c dull pur	50	26
C297	AP73	50c ultra	65	50
C298	AP73	1 l red brown	1.40	1.25
C299	AP73	2 l gray olive	2.25	2.00
C300	AP73	5 l ocher	4.75	4.75
a.		Miniature sheet	5.75	5.75
		Nos. C289-C300 (12)	10.97	9.86

Birth sesquicentennial of Abraham Lincoln.

No. C300a contains one each of the 1c, 3c, 10c, 25c, 1 l and 5 l, imperf.

For overprints and surcharges see Nos. C316-C319, C325-C330, C345, C347-C348, C352, C356-C364, C494-C495, C539-C541, C552-C553.

Constitution — AP74

Designs: 2c, 12c, Inauguration of Pres. Villeda Morales, horiz. 3c, 25c, Pres. Ramon Villeda Morales. 5c, 50c, Allegory of Second Republic (Torch and olive branches).

Engr.; Seal Litho. on 1c, 10c

1959, Dec. 21 *Perf. 13½*

C301	AP74	1c red brn, car & ultra	15	15
C302	AP74	2c bister brn	15	15
C303	AP74	3c ultra	15	15
C304	AP74	5c orange	18	15
C305	AP74	10c dull green, car & ultra	22	15
C306	AP74	12c rose red	35	15
C307	AP74	25c dull lilac	85	20
C308	AP74	50c dark blue	1.10	1.10
		Nos. C301-C308 (8)	3.15	
		Set value		1.80

Second Republic of Honduras, 2nd anniv.

For surcharge see No. C543.

Catalogue values for unused stamps in this section, from this point to the end of the section, are for Never Hinged items.

King Alfonso XIII and Map — AP75

Designs: 2c, 1906 award of King Alfonso XIII of Spain. 5c, Arbitration commission delivering its award, 1907. 10c, Intl. Court of Justice. 20c, Verdict of the Court, 1960. 50c, Pres. Morales, Foreign Minister Puerto and map. 1 l, Pres. Davila and Pres. Morales.

1961, Nov. 18 Engr. *Perf. 14½x14*

C309	AP75	1c dark blue	15	15
C310	AP75	2c magenta	15	15
C311	AP75	5c deep green	15	15
C312	AP75	10c brn orange	20	15
C313	AP75	20c vermilion	32	16
C314	AP75	50c brown	95	48
C315	AP75	1 l vio black	1.25	80
		Nos. C309-C315 (7)	3.17	
		Set value		1.70

Judgment of the Intl. Court of Justice at The Hague, Nov. 18, 1960, returning a disputed territory to Honduras from Nicaragua.

Nos. C295-C297 and CO105 Surcharged

L 0.06

1964, Apr. 7 *Perf. 13½*

Flags in National Colors

C316 AP72 6c on 15c red org 22 15
C317 AP73 8c on 25c dl pur 22 15
C318 AP73 10c on 50c ultra 32 16
C319 AP73 20c on 25c black 48 32

The red "OFICIAL" overprint on No. C319 was not obliterated.

See Nos. C345-C355, C419-C421.

Nos. C279-C281, C284 and C287 Overprinted: "FAO / Lucha Contra / el Hambre"

1964, Mar. 23 Unwmk. *Perf. 12*

Flags in National Colors

C320 AP71 1c light blue 16 16
C321 AP71 2c red 16 16
C322 AP71 5c green 20 20
C323 AP71 30c deep rose 1.00 1.00
C324 AP71 2 l gray olive 5.50 5.50
Nos. C320-C324 (5) 7.02 7.02

FAO "Freedom from Hunger Campaign" (1963).

Nos. CO98-CO101, CO104 and CO106 Overprinted in Blue or Black: "IN MEMORIAM / JOHN F. KENNEDY / 22 NOVEMBRE 1963"

1964, May 29 *Perf. 13½*

Flags in National Colors

C325 AP72 1c ocher (Bl) 15 15
C326 AP73 2c gray ol (Bl) 16 16
C327 AP73 3c red brn (Bl) 18 18
C328 AP73 5c ultra (Bk) 32 32
C329 AP72 15c dk brn (Bl) 1.25 1.25
C330 AP73 50c dk car (Bl) 6.25 6.25
Nos. C325-C330 (6) 8.31 8.31

Pres. John F. Kennedy (1917-63). The red "OFICIAL" overprint was not obliterated. The same overprint was applied to the stamps in miniature sheet No. C300a and seal of Honduras and Alliance for Progress emblem added in margin.

Nos. C222-C224, C226 and CO67 Overprinted with Olympic Rings and "1964"

Engr.; Center of 1c Litho.

1964, July 23 *Perf. 12½*

Frames in Black

C331 AP67 1c ultra & vio bl 15 15
C332 AP67 2c blue 18 18
C333 AP67 3c rose lilac 25 25
C334 AP67 15c red brown 48 48
C335 AP67 2 l lilac rose 6.25 6.25
Nos. C331-C335 (5) 7.31 7.31

18th Olympic Games, Tokyo, Oct. 10-25. The red "OFICIAL" overprint on No. C335 was not obliterated.

The same overprint was applied in black to the six stamps in No. CO108a, with additional rings and "1964" in margins of souvenir sheet. Value $50.

View of Copan AP76

Designs: 2c, 12c, Stone marker from Copan. 5c, 1 l, Mayan ball player (stone). 8c, 2 l, Olympic Stadium, Tokyo.

Unwmk.

1964, Nov. 27 Photo. *Perf. 14*

Black Design and Inscription

C336 AP76 1c yellow grn 15 15
C337 AP76 2c pale rose lil 15 15
C338 AP76 5c light ultra 15 15
C339 AP76 8c bluish green 24 24
C340 AP76 10c buff 35 28
C341 AP76 12c lemon 52 35
C342 AP76 1 l light ocher 1.40 1.25
C343 AP76 2 l pale ol grn 3.50 3.50
C344 AP76 3 l rose 4.00 4.00
Nos. C336-C344 (9) 10.46 10.07

18th Olympic Games, Tokyo, Oct. 10-25. Perf. and imperf. souvenir sheets of four exist containing one each of Nos. C338-C339, C341 and C344. Size: 129x110mm.

Nos. C292, C174, CO106, CO104, C124-C125, C165, CO105, C167-C168 and C178 Surcharged **L. 0.12**

1964-65

C345 AP73 4c on 5c dk car, bl & red 15 15
C346 AP62 10c on 15c red brn 18 15
C347 AP73 10c on 50c dk car, bl & red 18 15
C348 AP72 12c on 15c dk brn, bl & red 28 15
C349 AP27 12c on 16c ol gray 28 15
C350 AP27 12c on 21c lt blue 28 15
C351 AP60 12c on 22c org yel 28 15
C352 AP73 12c on 25c blk, bl & red 28 15
C353 AP60 30c on 1 l deep bl 50 22
C354 AP60 40c on 2 l lil ('65) 70 50
C355 AP61 40c on 1 l red brown ('65) 70 28
Nos. C345-C355 (11) 3.81
Set value 1.65

The red "OFICIAL" overprint on Nos. C347-C348 and C352 was not obliterated.

Nos. C289, CO99, C291-C292, C295-C296, CO106 and C299-C300 Overprinted in Black or Green: "Toma de Posesión / General / Oswaldo López A. / Junio 6, 1965"

1965, June 6 Engr. *Perf. 13½*

Flags in National Colors

C356 AP72 1c green 15 15
C357 AP73 2c gray ol (G) 15 15
C358 AP73 3c pur (G) 15 15
C359 AP73 5c dk car (G) 15 15
C360 AP72 15c red orange 25 25
C361 AP73 25c dull pur (G) 40 40
C362 AP73 50c dk car (G) 85 85
C363 AP73 2 l gray ol (G) 3.00 3.00
C364 AP73 5 l ocher (G) 7.50 7.50
Nos. C356-C364 (9) 12.60 12.60

Inauguration of Gen. Oswaldo López Arellano as president. The red "OFICIAL" overprint on Nos. C358 and C362 was not obliterated.

Ambulance and Maltese Cross — AP77

Designs (Maltese Cross and): 5c, Hospital of Knights of Malta. 12c, Patients treated in village. 1 l, Map of Honduras.

1965, Aug. 30 Litho. *Perf. 12x11*

C365 AP77 1c ultra 18 18
C366 AP77 5c dark green 32 32
C367 AP77 12c dark brown 48 48
C368 AP77 1 l brown 1.90 1.90

Knights of Malta; campaign against leprosy.

Father Manuel de Jesus Subirana — AP78

Designs: 1c, Jicaque Indian. 2c, Preaching to the Indians. 10c, Msgr. Juan de Jesus Zepeda. 12c, Pope Pius IX. 20c, Tomb of Father Subirana, Yore. 1 l, Mission church. 2 l, Jicaque mother and child.

Perf. 13½x14

1965, July 27 Litho. Unwmk.

C369 AP78 1c multicolored 15 15
C370 AP78 2c multicolored 15 15
C371 AP78 8c multicolored 15 15
C372 AP78 10c multicolored 15 15
C373 AP78 12c multicolored 18 15
C374 AP78 20c multicolored 35 28
C375 AP78 1 l multicolored 1.75 1.50
C376 AP78 2 l multicolored 3.50 3.00
a. Souv. sheet of 4, #C371, C373, C375-C376 17.50 17.50
Nos. C369-C376 (8) 6.38 5.53

Centenary (in 1964) of the death of Father Manuel de Jesus Subirana (1807-64), Spanish missionary to the Central American Indians.

For overprints and surcharges see Nos. C380-C386, C407-C413, C487-C488, C554.

Nos. C198-C199 and C168 Overprinted: "IN MEMORIAM / Sir Winston Churchill / 1874-1965."

1965, Dec. 20 Engr. *Perf. 13½x14*

C377 AP65 1c red org & blk 35 35
C378 AP65 2c bl & red brn 70 70
C379 AP60 2 l lilac 7.00 7.00

Sir Winston Spencer Churchill (1874-1965), statesman and World War II leader.

Nos. C369-C375 Overprinted

CONMEMORATIVA
Visita S. S.
Pablo VI
a la ONU.
4-X-1965

1966, Mar. 10 Litho. *Perf. 13½x14*

C380 AP78 1c multicolored 15 15
C381 AP78 2c multicolored 15 15
C382 AP78 8c multicolored 25 15
C383 AP78 10c multicolored 25 15
C384 AP78 12c multicolored 28 15
C385 AP78 20c multicolored 35 35
C386 AP78 1 l multicolored 3.25 3.25
Nos. C380-C386 (7) 4.68 4.35

Visit of Pope Paul VI to the UN, New York City, Oct. 4, 1965.

Stamp of 1866, No. 1 — AP79

Tomas Estrada Palma — AP80

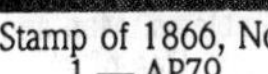

Post Office, Tegucigalpa AP81

Designs: 2c, Air post stamp of 1925, #C1. 5c, Locomotive. 6c, 19th cent. mail transport with mules. 7c, 19th cent. mail room. 8c, Sir Rowland Hill. 9c, Modern mail truck. 10c, Gen. Oswaldo Lopez Arellano. 12c, Postal emblem. 15c, Heinrich von Stephan. 20c, Mail plane. 30c, Flag of Honduras. 40c, Coat of Arms. 1 l, UPU monument, Bern. 2 l, José Maria Medina.

Perf. 14½x14, 14x14½

1966, May 31 Litho. Unwmk.

C387 AP79 1c gold, blk & grnsh gray 15 15
C388 AP79 2c org, blk & lt bl 15 15
C389 AP80 3c brt rose, gold & dp plum 15 15
C390 AP81 4c bl, gold & blk 15 15
C391 AP81 5c pink, gold & blk 52 15
C392 AP81 6c lil, gold & blk 15 15
C393 AP81 7c lt bl grn, gold & black 15 15
C394 AP80 8c lt bl, gold & blk 15 15
C395 AP81 9c lt ultra, gold & black 15 15
C396 AP80 10c cit, gold & blk 15 15
C397 AP79 12c gold, blk, yel & emerald 15 15
C398 AP80 15c brt pink, gold & dp claret 25 25
C399 AP81 20c org, gold & blk 32 32
C400 AP79 30c gold & bl 35 35
C401 AP79 40c multi 52 52
C402 AP79 1 l emer, gold & dk green 1.25 1.00
C403 AP80 2 l gray, gold & black 2.75 2.75
a. Souv. sheet of 6, #C387-C388, C396-C397, C402-C403 3.50 3.50
Nos. C387-C403 (17) 7.46 6.84

Centenary of the first Honduran postage stamp. No. C403a exists perf. and imperf. See No. CE3.

For surcharges see Nos. C473-C474, C479, C486, C496.

Nos. CO53, C201 and C204 Overprinted: "CAMPEONATO DE FOOTBALL Copa Mundial 1966 Inglaterra-Alemania Wembley, Julio 30"

Perf. 13½x14, 14x13½

1966, Nov. 25 Engr.

C404 AP65 2c brown & vio 16 16
C405 AP66 16c dk bl & blk 32 32
C406 AP65 2 l brn & vio 8.50 8.50

Final game between England and Germany in the World Soccer Cup Championship, Wembley, July 30, 1966. The overprint on the 2c and 2 l is in 5 lines, it is in 8 lines on the 16c. There is no hyphen between "Inglaterra" and "Alemania" on the 16c.

Nos. C369-C371 and C373-C376 Overprinted in Red: "CONMEMORATIVA / del XX Aniversario / ONU 1966"

1967, Jan. 31 Litho. *Perf. 13½x14*

C407 AP78 1c multicolored 16 16
C408 AP78 2c multicolored 18 18
C409 AP78 8c multicolored 32 32
C410 AP78 12c multicolore 48 40
C411 AP78 20c multicolore 65 55
C412 AP78 1 l multicolore 1.50 1.50
C413 AP78 2 l multicolore 3.25 3.25
Nos. C407-C413 (7) 6.54 6.36

UN, 20th anniversary.

Nos. C250, C252, C258, C261 and C267 Overprinted in Red: "Siméon Cañas y Villacorta / Libertador de los esclavos / en Centro America / 1767-1967"

1967, Feb. 27 Engr.

C414 AP68 1c blk & vio bl 15 15
C415 AP68 3c blk & brown 25 25
C416 AP68 15c dk red & blk 35 35
C417 AP68 25c blk & grn 70 70
C418 AP69 2 l blk & mag 2.50 2.50
Nos. C414-C418 (5) 3.95 3.95

Birth bicentenary of Father José Siméon Canas y Villacorta, D.D. (1767-1838), emancipator of the Central American slaves. The overprint is in 6 lines on the 2 l, in 4 lines on all others.

Nos. C178-C179 and CE2 Surcharged **L. 0.10**

1967

C419 AP61 10c on 1 l 35 15
C420 AP62 10c on 2 l 35 15
C421 APSD1 10c on 20c 35 15
Set value 30

José Cecilio del Valle, Honduras — AP82

Designs: 12c, Ruben Dario, Nicaragua. 14c, Batres Montufar, Guatemala. 20c, Francisco Antonio Gavidia, El Salvador. 30c, Juan Mora Fernandez, Costa Rica. 40c, Federation Emblem with map of Americas. 50c, Map of Central America.

1967, Aug. 4 Litho. *Perf. 13*

C422 AP82 11c gold, ultra & blk 15 15
C423 AP82 12c lt bl, yel & blk 15 15
C424 AP82 14c sil, grn & blk 15 15
C425 AP82 20c pink, grn & blk 25 25
C426 AP82 30c bluish lil, yel & black 40 35
C427 AP82 40c pur, lt bl & gold 70 70
C428 AP82 50c lem, grn & car rose 70 70
Nos. C422-C428 (7) 2.50 2.45

Founding of the Federation of Central American Journalists.

For surcharges see Nos. C475-C476.

Olympic Rings, Flags of Mexico and Honduras AP83

Olympic Rings and Winners of 1964 Olympics: 2c, Like 1c. 5c, Italian flag and boxers. 10c, French flag and women skiers. 12c, German flag and equestrian team. 50c, British flag and women runners. 1 l, US flag and runners (Bob Hayes).

1968, Mar. 4 Litho. *Perf. 14x13½*

C429	AP83	1c gold & multi	15	15
C430	AP83	2c gold & multi	18	18
C431	AP83	5c gold & multi	25	25
C432	AP83	10c gold & multi	32	25
C433	AP83	12c gold & multi	48	25
C434	AP83	50c gold & multi	1.90	1.10
C435	AP83	1 l gold & multi	6.25	6.25
		Nos. C429-C435 (7)	9.53	8.43

19th Olympic Games, Mexico City, Oct. 12-27. Perf. and imperf. souvenir sheets of 2 exist containing 20c and 40c stamps in design of 1c. Value $4.50 each.

For surcharge see No. C499.

John F. Kennedy, Rocket at Cape Kennedy AP84

ITU Emblem and: 2c, Radar and telephone. 3c, Radar and television set. 5c, Radar and globe showing Central America. 8c, Communications satellite. 10c, 20c, like 1c.

1968, Nov. 28 *Perf. 14x13½*

C436	AP84	1c vio & multi	15	15
C437	AP84	2c sil & multi	20	20
C438	AP84	3c multicolored	25	25
C439	AP84	5c org & multi	30	30
C440	AP84	8c multicolored	35	35
C441	AP84	10c olive & multi	40	40
C442	AP84	20c multicolored	50	50
		Nos. C436-C442 (7)	2.15	2.15

ITU, cent. A 30c in design of 2c, a 1 l in design of 5c and a 1.50 l in design of 1c exist; also two souvenir sheets, one containing 10c, 50c and 75c, the other one 1.50 l.

For overprints see Nos. C446-C453.

Nos. C436, C441-C442 Overprinted: "In Memoriam / Robert F. Kennedy / 1925-1968"

1968, Dec. 23

C446	AP84	1c vio & multi	20	20
C447	AP84	10c olive & multi	30	30
C448	AP84	20c multicolored	50	50

In memory of Robert F. Kennedy. Same overprint was also applied to a 1.50 l and to a souvenir sheet containing one 1.50 l.

Nos. C437-C440 Overprinted in Blue or Red with Olympic Rings and: "Medalias de Oro / Mexico 1968"

1969, Mar. 3

C450	AP84	2c multi (Bl)	20	20
C451	AP84	3c multi (Bl)	30	30
C452	AP84	5c multi (Bl)	40	40
C453	AP84	8c multi (R)	50	50

Gold medal winners in 19th Olympic Games, Mexico City. The same red overprint was also applied to a 30c and a 1 l. The souvenir sheet of 3 noted after No. C442 exists with this overprint in black.

Rocket Blast-off AP85

Designs: 10c, Close-up view of moon. 12c, Spacecraft, horiz. 20c, Astronaut and module on moon, horiz. 24c, Lunar landing module.

Perf. 14½x13½, 13½x14

1969, Oct. 29

C454	AP85	5c multicolored	20	20
C455	AP85	10c multicolored	30	30
C456	AP85	12c multicolored	40	40
C457	AP85	20c multicolored	50	50
C458	AP85	24c multicolored	1.00	1.00
		Nos. C454-C458 (5)	2.40	2.40

Man's first landing on the moon, July 20, 1969. A 30c showing re-entry of capsule, a 1 l in design of 20c and a 1.50 l in design of 24c exist. Two souvenir sheets exist, one containing Nos. C454-C455 and 1.50 l, and the other No. C456, 30c and 1 l.

For the safe return of Apollo 13, overprints were applied in 1970 to Nos. C454-C458, the three unlisted denominations and the two souvenir sheets.

For overprints and surcharges see Nos. C500-C504, C555.

Nos. C224, C393, C395, C422, C424, CE2 and C178 Surcharged with New Value

1970, Feb. 20 Engr.; Litho.

C472	AP67	4c on 3c blk & rose lil	20	15
C473	AP81	5c on 7c multi	25	15
C474	AP81	10c on 9c multi	30	15
C475	AP82	10c on 11c multi	30	15
C476	AP82	12c on 14c multi	35	20
C477	APSD1	12c on 20c blk & red	35	20
C478	AP61	12c on 1 l red brn	35	20
		Nos. C472-C478 (7)	2.10	1.20

No. CE3 Overprinted "HABILITADO"

1970 Litho. *Perf. 14x14½*

C479	AP81	20c bis brn, brn & gold	75	35

Julio Adolfo Sanhueza — AP86

Emblems, Map and Flag of Honduras — AP87

Designs: 8c, Rigoberto Ordoñez Rodriguez. 12c, Forest Fire Brigade emblem (with map of Honduras) and emblems of fire fighters, FAO and Alliance for Progress, horiz. 1 l, Flags of Honduras, UN and US, Arms of Honduras and emblems as on 12c.

Perf. 14½x14, 14x14½

1970, Aug. 15 Litho.

C480	AP86	5c gold, emer & ind	15	15
C481	AP86	8c gold, org brn & indigo	16	15
C482	AP87	12c bl & multi	24	15
C483	AP87	20c yel & multi	40	24
C484	AP87	1 l gray & multi	1.40	1.40
	a.	Souvenir sheet of 5	2.00	2.00
		Nos. C480-C484 (5)	2.35	2.09

Campaign against forest fires and in memory of the men who lost their lives fighting forest fires. No. C484a contains 5 imperf. stamps with simulated perforations and without gum similar to Nos. C480-C484. Sold for 1.45 l.

For surcharges see Nos. C497-C498.

Hotel Honduras Maya — AP88

1970, Oct. 24 Litho. *Perf. 14*

C485	AP88	12c sky bl & blk	30	22

Opening of the Hotel Honduras Maya, Tegucigalpa.

Stamps of 1952-1968 Surcharged

1971 Litho.; Engr.

C486	AP79	4c on 1c (#C387)	15
C487	AP78	5c on 1c (#C369)	15
C488	AP78	8c on 2c (#C370)	25
C489	AP65	10c on 2c (#C199)	35
C490	AP67	10c on 3c (#C224)	35
	a.	Inverted surcharge	
C491	AP68	10c on 3c (#C252)	35
C492	AP68	10c on 3c (#CO71)	35
C493	AP69	10c on 2c (#C251)	35
C494	AP73	10c on 2c (#CO99)	35
C495	AP73	10c on 3c (#CO100)	35
C496	AP80	10c on 3c (#C389)	35
C497	AP87	15c on 12c (#C482)	50
C498	AP87	30c on 12c (#C482)	1.00
C499	AP83	40c on 50c (#C434)	1.25
C500	AP85	40c on 24c (#C458)	1.25
		Nos. C486-C500 (15)	7.35

Red "OFICIAL" overprint was not obliterated on Nos. C492, C494-C495.

No. C491 exists with inverted surcharge.

Nos. C454, C456-C458 Overprinted and Surcharged

Aniversario Gran Logia de Honduras 1922-1972

L 1.00

Perf. 14½x13½, 13½x14½

1972, May 15 Litho.

C501	AP85	5c multi	70	40
C502	AP85	12c multi	1.00	75
C503	AP85	1 l on 20c multi	2.00	1.00
C504	AP85	2 l on 24c multi	4.00	2.00

Masonic Grand Lodge of Honduras, 50th anniv. Overprint varies to fit stamp shape.

Soldier's Bay, Guanaja AP89

Designs: 5c, 7c, 9c, 10c, 2 l, vertical.

1972, May 19 *Perf. 13*

C505	AP89	4c shown	15	15
C506	AP89	5c Taps	15	15
C507	AP89	6c Yojoa Lake	15	15
C508	AP89	7c Banana Carrier, by Roberto Aguilar	15	15
C509	AP89	8c Military parade	15	15
C510	AP89	9c Orchid, national flower	25	15
C511	AP89	10c like 9c	25	15
C512	AP89	12c Soldier with machine gun	20	15
C513	AP89	15c Sunset over beach	30	15
C514	AP89	20c Litter bearers	30	15
C515	AP89	30c Landscape, by Antonio Velasquez	50	25
C516	AP89	40c Ruins of Copan	75	40
	a.	Souv. sheet of 4, #C508, C513, C515-C516	1.40	1.40
C517	AP89	50c Girl from Huacal, by Pablo Zelaya Sierra	60	35
	a.	Souv. sheet of 4, #C506-C507, C514, C517	1.40	1.40
C518	AP89	1 l Trujillo Bay	1.50	1.00
	a.	Souv. sheet of 4, #C505, C509, C512, C518	2.00	1.75
C519	AP89	2 l Orchid, national flower	4.00	3.00
	a.	Souv. sheet of 3, #C510-C511, C519	4.50	3.25
		Nos. C505-C519,CE4 (16)	9.70	6.80

Sesquicentennial of independence (stamps inscribed 1970).

For surcharge see No. CE5.

Sister Maria Rosa and Child — AP90

Designs: 15c, SOS Children's Village emblem, horiz. 30c, Father José Trinidad Reyes. 40c, Kennedy Center, first SOS village in Central America, horiz. 1 l, Boy.

Perf. 13½x13, 13x13½

1972, Nov. 10 Photo.

C520	AP90	10c grn, gold & brn	18	15
C521	AP90	15c grn, gold & brn	25	15
C522	AP90	30c grn, gold & brn	42	15
C523	AP90	40c grn, gold & brn	50	18
C524	AP90	1 l grn, gold & brn	2.00	1.50
		Nos. C520-C524 (5)	3.35	2.13

Children's Villages in Honduras (Intl. SOS movement to save homeless children).

For overprints and surcharges see #C531, C534-C536, C546-C549, C556, C560-C561.

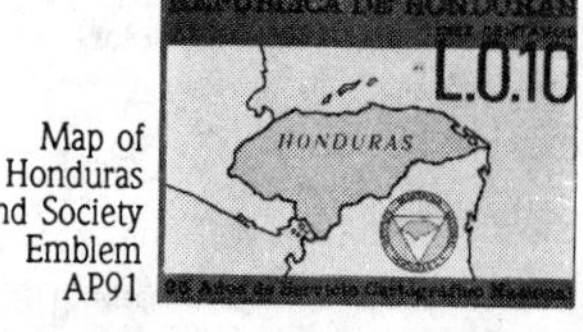

Map of Honduras and Society Emblem AP91

Design: 12c, Map of Honduras, emblems of National Geographic Institute and Interamerican Geodesic Service.

1973, Mar. 27 Litho. *Perf. 13*

C525	AP91	10c multicolored	55	28
C526	AP91	12c multicolored	65	28

25th annivs. of Natl. Cartographic Service (10c) and of joint cartographic work (12c).

For overprints and surcharges see Nos. C532-C533, C557-C558.

Juan Ramón Molina AP92

Designs: 8c, Illustration from Molina's book "Habitante de la Osa." 1 l, Illustration from "Tierras Mares y Cielos." 2 l, "UNESCO."

1973, Apr. 17 Litho. *Perf. 13½*

C527	AP92	8c brn org, blk & red brn	18	15
C528	AP92	20c brt bl & multi	70	25
C529	AP92	1 l green & multi	1.40	1.00
C530	AP92	2 l org & multi	2.75	2.75
	a.	Sheet of 4	5.25	5.25

Molina (1875-1908), poet, and 25th anniv. (in 1971) of UNESCO. No. C530a contains 4 stamps similar to Nos. C527-C530. Exists perf. and imperf.

For surcharge see No. C559.

Nos. C520-C523, C525-C526 Overprinted in Red or Black: "Censos de Población y Vivienda, marzo 1974. 1974, Año Mundial de Población"

Perf. 13½x13, 13x13½, 13

1973, Dec. 28 Photo; Litho.

C531	AP90	10c multi (R)	15	15
C532	AP91	10c multi (B)	15	15
C533	AP91	12c multi (R)	15	15
C534	AP90	15c multi (R)	15	15
C535	AP90	30c multi (R)	28	25
C536	AP90	40c multi (R)	35	35
		Set value	96	90

1974 population and housing census; World Population Year. The overprint is in 7 lines on vertical stamps, in 5 lines on horizontal.

Issues of 1947-59 Surcharged in Red or Black

Perf. 13x12½, 13½, 11x12½, 12

1974, June 28 Engr.

C537	AP68	2c on 1c (#C250) (R)	15	15
C538	AP68	2c on 1c (#CO69)	15	15
C539	AP72	2c on 1c (#C289)	15	15
C540	AP72	2c on 1c (#CO98)	15	15
C541	AP72	3c on 1c (#C289)	15	15
C542	AP68	3c on 1c (#C250) (R)	15	15
C543	AP74	1 l on 50c (#C308)	1.40	1.40

C544 AP60 1 l on 2 l (#C168) 1.40 1.40
C545 AP62 1 l on 2 l (#C179) (R) 1.40 1.40
Nos. C537-C545 (9) 5.10 5.10

Red "OFICIAL" overprint was not obliterated on Nos. C538 and C540.

Nos. C520-C523 Overprinted in Bright Green: "1949-1974 SOS Kinderdorfer International Honduras-Austria"

1974, July 25 **Photo.**
C546 AP90 10c grn, gold & brn 15 15
C547 AP90 15c grn, gold & brn 18 18
C548 AP90 30c grn, gold & brn 25 25
C549 AP90 40c grn, gold & brn 35 35

25th anniversary of Children's Villages in Honduras. Overprint in 6 lines on 10c and 30c, in 4 lines on 15c and 40c.

Stamps of 1956-73 Surcharged

1975, Feb. 24 **Litho.; Engr.**
C550 AP68 16c on 1c (#C250) 20 15
C551 AP70 16c on 1c (#C269) 20 15
C552 AP72 16c on 1c (#C289) 20 15
C553 AP72 16c on 1c (#CO98) 20 15
C554 AP78 16c on 1c (#C369) 30 30
C555 AP85 18c on 12c (#C456) 40 22
C556 AP90 18c on 10c (#C520) 25 18
C557 AP91 18c on 10c (#C525) 25 18
C558 AP91 18c on 12c (#C526) 25 18
C559 AP92 18c on 8c (#C527) 25 18
C560 AP90 50c on 30c (#C522) 75 52
C561 AP90 1 l on 30c (#C522) 1.25 90
Nos. C550-C561,CE5 (13) 5.35 3.86

Denominations not obliterated on Nos. C551, C553-C558, C560-C561; "OFICIAL" overprint not obliterated on No. C553.

Flags of Germany and Austria AP93

Designs (Flags): 2c, Belgium & Denmark. 3c, Spain & France. 4c, Hungary & Russia. 5c, Great Britain & Italy. 10c, Norway & Sweden. 12c, Honduras. 15c, US & Switzerland. 20c, Greece & Portugal. 30c, Romania & Serbia. 1 l, Egypt & Netherlands. 2 l, Luxembourg & Turkey.

1975, June 18 **Litho.** ***Perf. 13***
Gold & Multicolored; Colors Listed are for Shields
C562 AP93 1c lilac 15 15
C563 AP93 2c gold 15 15
C564 AP93 3c rose gray 15 15
C565 AP93 4c light blue 15 15
C566 AP93 5c yellow 15 15
C567 AP93 10c gray 16 16
C568 AP93 12c lilac rose 22 22
C569 AP93 15c bluish green 32 32
C570 AP93 20c bright blue 32 32
C571 AP93 30c pink 48 48
C572 AP93 1 l salmon 1.50 1.50
C573 AP93 2 l yellow green 3.25 3.25
Nos. C562-C573 (12) 7.00 7.00

Souvenir Sheet
C574 AP93 Sheet of 12 *9.50 9.50*

UPU, cent. (in 1974). No. C574 contains 12 stamps similar to Nos. C562-C573 with shields in different colors.

Humuya Youth Center and Mrs. Arellano AP94

Designs (Portrait of First Lady, Gloria de Lopez Arellano, IWY Emblem and): 16c, Jalteva Youth Center. 18c, Mrs. Arellano (diff. portrait) and IWY emblem. 30c, El Carmen de San Pedro Sula Youth Center. 55c, Flag of National Social Welfare Organization, vert. 1 l, La Isla sports and recreational facilities. 2 l, Women's Social Center.

1976, Mar. 5 **Litho.** ***Perf. 13½***
C575 AP94 8c sal & multi 15 15
C576 AP94 16c yel & multi 18 18
C577 AP94 18c pink & multi 18 18
C578 AP94 30c org & multi 35 35
C579 AP94 55c multicolored 52 52
C580 AP94 1 l multicolored 1.10 1.10
C581 AP94 2 l multicolored 2.00 2.00
Nos. C575-C581 (7) 4.48 4.48

International Women's Year (1975).
For surcharges see #C736-C737, C781, C798, C885, C887, C919.

"CARE" and Globe AP95

Designs: 1c, 16c, 30c, 55c, 1 l, Care package and globe, vert. Others like 5c.

1976, May 24 **Litho.** ***Perf. 13½***
C582 AP95 1c blk & lt blue 15 15
C583 AP95 5c rose brn & blk 15 15
C584 AP95 16c black & org 18 18
C585 AP95 18c lemon & blk 22 22
C586 AP95 30c blk & blue 35 35
C587 AP95 50c yel grn & blk 52 52
C588 AP95 55c blk & buff 52 52
C589 AP95 70c brt rose & blk 70 70
C590 AP95 1 l blk & lt grn 1.10 1.10
C591 AP95 2 l ocher & blk 2.00 2.00
Nos. C582-C591 (10) 5.89 5.89

20th anniversary of CARE in Honduras.
For surcharges see Nos. C735, C738, C788, C888, C922.

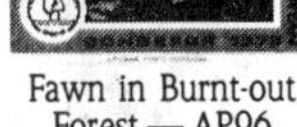

Fawn in Burnt-out Forest — AP96

"Sons of Liberty" — AP97

Forest Protection: 16c, COHDEFOR emblem (Corporacion Hondureña de Desarollo Forestal). 18c, Forest, horiz. 30c, 2 l, Live and burning trees. 50c, like 10c. 70c, Emblem. 1 l, Young forest, horiz.

1976, May 28 **Litho.** ***Perf. 13½***
C592 AP96 10c multicolored 15 15
C593 AP96 16c multicolored 25 15
C594 AP96 18c multicolored 25 15
C595 AP96 30c grn & multi 50 20
C596 AP96 50c multicolored 75 30
C597 AP96 70c brn & multi 1.00 40
C598 AP96 1 l yel & multi 1.60 75
C599 AP96 2 l vio & multi 3.00 3.00
Nos. C592-C599,CE6 (9) 8.10 5.55

For surcharges see Nos. C784, C787, C917.

1976, Aug. 29 **Litho.** ***Perf. 12***

American Bicentennial: 2c, Raising flag of "Liberty and Union." 3c, Bunker Hill flag. 4c, Washington's Cruisers' flag. 5c, 1st Navy Jack. 6c, Flag of Honduras over Presidential Palace, Tegucigalpa. 18c, US flag over Capitol. 55c, Grand Union flag. 2 l, Bennington flag. 3 l, Betsy Ross and her flag.

C601 AP97 1c multicolored 15 15
C602 AP97 2c multicolored 15 15
C603 AP97 3c multicolored 15 15
C604 AP97 4c multicolored 15 15
C605 AP97 5c multicolored 15 15
C606 AP97 6c multicolored 15 15
C607 AP97 18c multicolored 30 35
C608 AP97 55c multicolored 75 70
a. Souv. sheet of 4, #C603, C606-C608 *1.50 1.50*
C609 AP97 2 l multicolored 2.00 1.75
a. Souv. sheet of 3, #C601, C604, C609 *3.25 3.25*
C610 AP97 3 l multicolored 4.50 4.50
a. Souv. sheet of 3, #C602, C605, C610 *4.75 4.75*
Nos. C601-C610 (10) 8.45 8.20

For surcharge see No. C877, C883-C884, C885, C889.

Queen Sophia of Spain — AP98

Designs: 18c, King Juan Carlos. 30c, Queen Sophia and King Juan Carlos. 2 l, Arms of Honduras and Spain, horiz.

1977, Sept. 13 **Litho.** ***Perf. 14***
C611 AP98 16c multicolored 15 15
C612 AP98 18c multicolored 15 15
C613 AP98 30c multicolored 30 22
C614 AP98 2 l multicolored 1.90 1.90

Visit of King and Queen of Spain.
For surcharges see Nos. C890, C918.

Mayan Steles, Exhibition Emblems AP99

Designs: 18c, Giant head. 30c, Statue. 55c, Sun god. 1.50 l, Mayan pelota court.

1978, Apr. 28 **Litho.** ***Perf. 12***
C615 AP99 15c multi 18 18
C616 AP99 18c multi 25 25
C617 AP99 30c multi 35 35
C618 AP99 55c multi 70 70

Imperf
C619 AP99 1.50 l multi 1.75 1.75

Honduras '78 Philatelic Exhibition.
For overprints and surcharge see Nos. C642-C645, C786, C920, C924.

Del Valle's Birthplace AP100

Designs: 14c, La Merced Church, Choluteca, where del Valle was baptized. 15c, Baptismal font, vert. 20c, Del Valle reading independence acts. 25c, Portrait, documents, map of Central America. 40c, Portrait, vert. 1 l, Monument, Central Park, Choluteca, vert. 3 l, Bust, vert.

1978, Apr. 11 **Litho.** ***Perf. 14***
C620 AP100 8c multicolored 15 15
C621 AP100 14c multicolored 15 15
C622 AP100 15c multicolored 15 15
C623 AP100 20c multicolored 20 20
C624 AP100 25c multicolored 26 26
C625 AP100 40c multicolored 38 38
C626 AP100 1 l multicolored 95 95
C627 AP100 3 l multicolored 3.25 3.25
Nos. C620-C627 (8) 5.49 5.49

Bicentenary of the birth of José Cecilio del Valle (1780-1834), Central American patriot and statesman.
For surcharges see Nos. C739, C793, C795, C886A.

Rural Health Center AP101

Designs: 6c, Child at water pump. 10c, Los Laureles Dam, Tegucigalpa. 20c, Rural aqueduct. 40c, Teaching hospital, Tegucigalpa. 2 l, Parents and child. 3 l, National vaccination campaign. 5 l, Panamerican Health Organization Building, Washington, DC.

1978, May 10 **Litho.** ***Perf. 14***
C628 AP101 5c multicolored 15 15
C629 AP101 6c multicolored 15 15
C630 AP101 10c multicolored 15 15
C631 AP101 20c multicolored 22 22
C632 AP101 40c multicolored 45 45
C633 AP101 2 l multicolored 1.90 1.90
C634 AP101 3 l multicolored 3.00 3.00
C635 AP101 5 l multicolored 4.50 4.50
Nos. C628-C635 (8) 10.52 10.52

75th anniv. of Panamerican Health Organization (in 1977).
For surcharge see No. C783.

Luis Landa and his "Botanica" AP102

Designs (Luis Landa and): 16c, Map of Honduras showing St. Ignacio. 18c, Medals received by Landa. 30c, Landa's birthplace in St. Ignacio. 2 l, Brassavola (orchid), national flower. 3 l, Women's Normal School.

1978, Aug. 29 **Photo.** ***Perf. 13x13½***
C636 AP102 14c multicolored 20 16
C637 AP102 16c multicolored 20 16
C638 AP102 18c multicolored 20 16
C639 AP102 30c multicolored 40 20
C640 AP102 2 l multicolored 3.00 1.00
C641 AP102 3 l multicolored 3.50 3.50
Nos. C636-C641 (6) 7.50 5.18

Prof. Luis Landa (1875-1975), botanist.
For surcharges see Nos. C740, C794, C888A, C923.

Nos. C615-C618 Overprinted in Red with Argentina '78 Soccer Cup Emblem and: "Argentina Campeon / Holanda Sub-Campeon / XI Campeonato Mundial / de Football"

1978, Sept. 6 **Litho.** ***Perf. 12***
C642 AP99 15c multicolored 15 15
C643 AP99 18c multicolored 25 18
C644 AP99 30c multicolored 35 28
C645 AP99 55c multicolored 75 52

Argentina's victory in World Cup Soccer Championship. Same overprint was applied to No. C619.
For surcharge see No. C924.

Central University and Coat of Arms — AP103

Designs show for each denomination a 19th century print and a contemporary photograph of same area (except 1.50 l, 5 l): No. C647, University City. 8c, Manuel Bonilla Theater. No. C650, Court House, vert. No. C651, North Boulevard highway intersection, vert. No. C652, Natl. Palace. No. C653, Presidential Palace. 20c, Hospital. 40c, Cathedral. 50c, View of Tegucigalpa. 1.50 l, Aerial view of Tegucigalpa. No. C660, Arms of San Miguel de Tegucigalpa, 18th cent., vert. No. C661, Pres. Marco Aurelio Soto (1846-1908) (painting), vert.

1978, Sept. 29
C646 AP103 6c black & brn 15 15
C647 AP103 6c multicolored 15 15
C648 AP103 8c black & brn 15 15
C649 AP103 8c multicolored 15 15
C650 AP103 10c black & brn 15 15
C651 AP103 10c multicolored 15 15
C652 AP103 16c black & brn 25 16
C653 AP103 16c multicolored 25 16
C654 AP103 20c black & brn 30 16
C655 AP103 20c multicolored 30 16
C656 AP103 40c black & brn 60 45
C657 AP103 40c multicolored 60 45
C658 AP103 50c black & brn 75 48
C659 AP103 50c multicolored 75 48

C660	AP103 5 l black & brn	6.00	6.00
C661	AP103 5 l multicolored	6.00	6.00
	Nos. C646-C661 (16)	16.70	15.40

Souvenir Sheet

C662	AP103 1.50 l multi	2.00	2.00

400th anniv. of the founding of Tegucigalpa.
In the listing the first number is for the 19th cent. design, the second for the 20th cent. design. Stamps of same denomination se-tenant.
For overprints and surcharges see #C724-C725, C740A-C746, C766-C769, C779-C780.

Goalkeeper — AP104

Designs: Various soccer scenes.

1978, Nov. 26 Litho. *Perf. 12*

C663	AP104 15c multi, vert.	16	16
C664	AP104 30c multi	32	32
C665	AP104 55c multi, vert.	50	50
C666	AP104 1 l multi	1.00	1.00
C667	AP104 2 l multi	2.00	2.00
	Nos. C663-C667 (5)	3.98	3.98

7th Youth Soccer Championship, Nov. 26.
For surcharge see No. C797.

UPU Emblem — AP105

Designs: 2c, Postal emblem of Honduras. 25c, Dr. Ramon Rosa, vert. 50c, Pres. Marco Aurelio Soto, vert.

1979, Apr. 1 Litho. *Perf. 12*

C668	AP105 2c multicolored	15	15
C669	AP105 15c multicolored	15	15
C670	AP105 25c multicolored	20	20
C671	AP105 50c multicolored	42	42

Centenary of Honduras joining UPU.

Rotary Emblem and "50" AP106

1979, Apr. 26 Litho. *Perf. 14*

C672	AP106 3c multi	15	15
C673	AP106 5c multi	15	15
C674	AP106 50c multi	42	42
C675	AP106 2 l multi	1.65	1.65

Rotary Intl. of Honduras, 50th anniv.
For surcharge see No. C884A.

Map of Caratasca Lagoon AP107

Designs: 10c, Fort San Fernando de Omoa. 24c, Institute anniversary emblem, vert. 5 l, Map of Santanilla islands.

1979, Sept. 15 Litho. *Perf. 13½*

C676	AP107 5c multi	15	15
C677	AP107 10c multi	15	15
C678	AP107 24c multi	18	18
C679	AP107 5 l multi	3.75	3.75

Panamerican Institute of History and Geography, 50th anniversary.
For surcharge see No. C891.

General Post Office, 1979 — AP108

UPU Membership Centenary: 3 l, Post Office, 19th century.

1980, Feb. 20 Litho. *Perf. 12*

C680	AP108 24c multi	20	20
C681	AP108 3 l multi	2.50	2.50

For surcharge see No. C925.

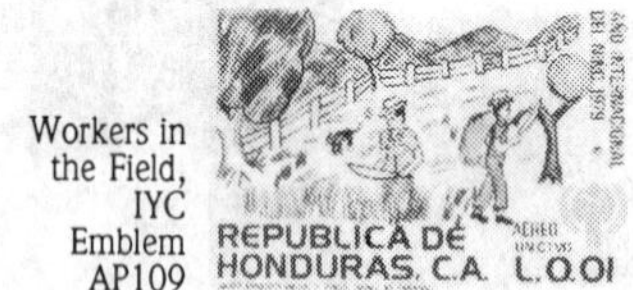

Workers in the Field, IYC Emblem AP109

1980, Dec. 9 Litho. *Perf. 14½*

C682	AP109 1c shown	15	15
C683	AP109 5c Landscape, vert.	15	15
C684	AP109 15c Sitting boy, vert.	15	15
C685	AP109 20c IYC emblem, vert.	20	20
C686	AP109 30c Beach scene	30	30
	Set value	74	74

Souvenir Sheet

C687	AP109 1 l UNICEF and IYC emblems, vert.	1.00	1.00

International Year of the Child (1979).

Maltese Cross, Hill AP110

1980, Dec. 17

C688	AP110 1c shown	15	15
C689	AP110 2c Penny Black	15	15
C690	AP110 5c Honduras type A1	15	15
C691	AP110 10c Honduras type A1	15	15

Size: 47x34mm

C692	AP110 15c Postal emblem	15	15
C693	AP110 20c Flags of Honduras, Gt. Britain	18	18
	Set value	54	54

Souvenir Sheet

C694	AP110 1 l Honduras #C402	85	85

Sir Rowland Hill (1795-1879), originator of penny postage. No. C694 contains one stamp 47x34mm.

Intibucana Mother and Child — AP111

Bernardo O'Higgins, by Jose Gil de Castro — AP112

Inter-American Women's Commission, 50th Anniv.: 2c, Visitacion Padilla, Honduras Section founder. 10c, Maria Trinidad del Cid, Section member. 1 l, Emblem, horiz.

1981, June 15 Litho. *Perf. 14½*

C695	AP111 2c multicolored	15	15
C696	AP111 10c multicolored	15	15
C697	AP111 40c multicolored	32	32
C698	AP111 1 l multicolored	80	80

1981, June 29

Paintings of O'Higgins: 16c, Liberation of Chile, by Cosme San Martin, horiz. 20c, Portrait of Ambrosio O'Higgins (father). 1 l, Abdication of Office, by Antonio Caro, horiz.

C699	AP112 16c multicolored	15	15
C700	AP112 20c multicolored	16	16
C701	AP112 30c multicolored	25	25
C702	AP112 1 l multicolored	85	50

For surcharges see Nos. C785, C888B.

CONCACAF 81 Soccer Cup — AP113

1981, Dec. 30 Litho. *Perf. 14*

C703	AP113 20c Emblem	16	16
C704	AP113 50c Player	42	25
C705	AP113 70c Flags	60	40
C706	AP113 1 l Stadium	85	85

Souvenir Sheet

C707	AP113 1.50 l like #C703	1.25	1.25

For overprint see No. C797.

50th Anniv. of Air Force (1981) AP114

Designs: 3c, Curtiss CT-32 Condor. 15c, North American NA-16. 25c, Chance Vought F4U-5. 65c, Douglas C47. 1 l Cessna A37-B. 2 l, Super Mister SMB-11.

1983, Jan. 14 Litho. *Perf. 12*

C708	AP114 3c multi	15	15
C709	AP114 15c multi	15	15
C710	AP114 25c multi	22	20
C711	AP114 65c multi	55	35
C712	AP114 1 l multi	85	50
C713	AP114 2 l multi	1.75	1.75
	Nos. C708-C713 (6)	3.67	3.10

Souvenir Sheet

C714	AP114 1.55 l Helicopter	1.50	1.50

For surcharge see No. C884B.

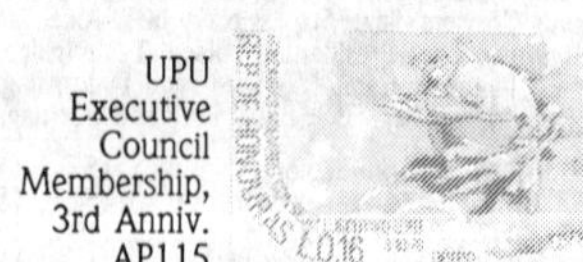

UPU Executive Council Membership, 3rd Anniv. AP115

1983, Jan. 14

C715	AP115 16c UPU monument	15	15
C716	AP115 18c 18th UPU Congress emblem	16	16
C717	AP115 30c Natl. Postal Service emblem	28	28
C718	AP115 55c Rio de Janeiro	45	45
C719	AP115 2 l Dove on globe	1.75	1.75
	Nos. C715-C719 (5)	2.79	2.79

Souvenir Sheet

C720	AP115 1 l like 2 l	90	90

For surcharge see No. C921.

Natl. Library and Archives Centenary (1980) AP116

1983, Feb. 11 Litho. *Perf. 12*

C721	AP116 9c Library	15	15
C722	AP116 1 l Books	80	40

Intl. Year of the Disabled (1979) AP117

1983, Feb. 11

C723	AP117 25c Emblem	22	22

Nos. C656-C657 Overprinted in Red: "CONMEMORATIVA DE LA VISITA / DE SS. JUAN PABLO II / 8 de marzo de 1983"

1983, Mar. 8

C724	AP103 40c multicolored	1.50	1.00
C725	AP103 40c multicolored	1.50	1.00

Visit of Pope John Paul II.

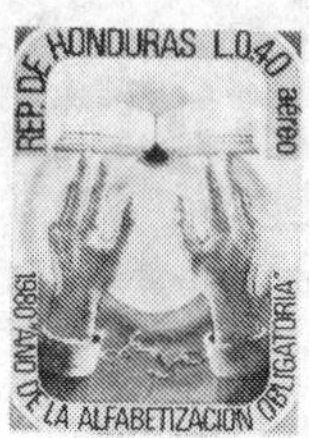

Literacy Campaign (1980) — AP118

World Food Day, Oct. 16, 1981 — AP119

1983, May 18 Litho. *Perf. 12*

C726	AP118 40c Hands, open book	35	35
C727	AP118 1.50 l People holding books	1.40	1.40

1983, May 18

C728	AP119 65c Produce, emblem	60	60

20th Anniv. of Inter-American Development Bank (1980) — AP120

1983, June 17 Litho. *Perf. 12*

C729	AP120 1 l Comayagua River Bridge	85	50
C730	AP120 2 l Luis Bogran Technical Institute of Physics	1.65	1.00

2nd Anniv. of Return to Constitutional Government — AP121

1984, Jan. 27 Litho. *Perf. 12*

C731 AP121 20c Arms, text 18 15
C732 AP121 20c Pres. Suazo Cordova 18 15
a. Pair, #C731-C732 36 30
Set value 20

La Gaceta Newspaper Sesquicentenary (1980) — AP122

1984, May 25 Litho. *Perf. 12*

C733 AP122 10c multicolored 15 15
C734 AP122 20c multicolored 18 15
Set value 27 16

Nos. C582 and C575-C576 Surcharged

1985, June 26 Litho. *Perf. 13½*

C735 AP95 5c on 1c #C582 15 15
C736 AP94 10c on 8c #C575 15 15
C737 AP94 20c on 16c #C576 18 15
C738 AP95 1 l on 1c #C582 90 40
Set value 64

Nos. C621, C636 and C646-C647 Surcharged

Litho., Photo. (No. C740)

1986, Aug. 21 *Perfs. as before*

C739 AP100 50c on 14c #C621 45 25
C740 AP102 60c on 14c #C636 55 30
C740A AP103 85c on 6c #C646 75 40
C740B AP103 85c on 6c #C647 75 40
C741 AP103 95c on 6c #C646 85 45
C742 AP103 95c on 6c #C647 85 45
Nos. C739-C742 (6) 4.20 2.25

Black bar obliterating old values on Nos. C739-C740 also cover "aereo." Nos. C741-C742 se-tenant.

Nos. C656-C657 Ovptd. in Red "EXFILHON '86," "MEXICO '86" and: No. C743 "ARGENTINA CAMPEON" No. C744 "ALEMANIA FEDERAL Sub Campeon" No. C745 "FRANCIA TERCER LUGAR" No. C746 "BELGICA CUARTO LUGAR"

1986, Sept. 12 Litho. *Perf. 12*

C743 AP103 40c No. C656 40 20
C744 AP103 40c No. C657 40 20
C745 AP103 40c No. C657 40 20
C746 AP103 40c No. C656 40 20
a. Block of 4, #C743-C746 1.60

AP123

San Fernando de Omoa Castle — AP124

Designs: 20c, Phulapanzak Falls, vert. 78c, Bahia Isls. beach. 85c, Bahia Isls. cove. 95c, Yojoa Lake, vert. 1 l, Woman painting pottery, vert.

Perf. 13½x14, 14x13½

1986, Nov. 10 Litho.

C747 AP123 20c multi 18 15
C748 AP123 78c multi 70 35
C749 AP123 85c multi 75 35
C750 AP123 95c multi 85 40
C751 AP123 1 l multi 90 45

Size: 84x59mm

Imperf

C752 AP124 1.50 l multi 1.40 1.40
Nos. C747-C752 (6) 4.78 3.10

For overprint see No. C782.

AP125 Flora — AP126

1987, Feb. 2 Litho. *Perf. 13½*

National flag, Pres. Jose Azcona Hoyo.

C753 AP125 20c multicolored 18 15
C754 AP125 85c multicolored 75 30

Democratic government, 1st anniv.

1987, July 8 Litho. *Perf. 13½x14*

C755 AP126 10c Eupatorium cyrillinelsonii 15 15
C756 AP126 20c Salvia ernesti-vargasii 18 15
C757 AP126 95c Robinsonella erasmisosae 85 40
Set value 55

Birds — AP127 AP128

1987, Sept. 10 Litho. *Perf. 13½x14*

C758 AP127 50c Eumomota superciliosa 45 25
C759 AP127 60c Ramphastos sulfuratus 60 30
C760 AP127 85c Amazona autumnalis 75 40

1987, Dec. 10 Litho. *Perf. 13½*

C761 AP128 1 l blk, brt yel & dark red 90 45

Natl. Autonomous University of Honduras, 30th anniv.

AP129 AP130

1987, Dec. 23 Litho. *Perf. 13½*

C762 AP129 20c red & dk ultra 18 15

Natl. Red Cross, 50th anniv.

1988, Jan. 27 Litho. *Perf. 13½*

C763 AP130 95c brt blue & org yel 85 40

17th regional meeting of Lions Intl.

Atlantida Bank, 75th Anniv. AP131

Main offices: 10c, La Ceiba, Atlantida, 1913. 85c, Tegucigalpa, 1988.

1988, Feb. 10

C764 AP131 10c multi 15 15
C765 AP131 85c mutli 75 40
a. Souv. sheet of 2, #358-359, imperf. 90 90
Set value 45

No. C765a sold for 1 l.

L.0.20

Nos. C648-C649 Surcharged

1988, June 9 Litho. *Perf. 12*

C766 AP103 20c on 8c #C648 15 15
C767 AP103 20c on 8c #C649 15 15
Set value 20

L.0.05

Nos. C646-C647 Surcharged

1988, July 8 Litho. *Perf. 12*

C768 AP103 5c on 6c #C646 15 15
C769 AP103 5c on 6c #C647 15 15
Set value 15 15

Postman — AP132

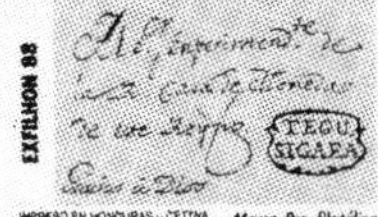

Tegucigalpa Postmark on Stampless Cover, 1789 — AP133

1988, Sept. 11 Litho. *Perf. 13½*

C770 AP132 85c dull red brn 1.05 40
C771 AP133 2 l dull red brn & ver 2.50 1.00

EXFILHON '88.

Summer Olympics Type of 1988

1988, Sept. 30 Litho. *Perf. 13½*

C772 A62 85c Running, vert. 1.05 40
C773 A62 1 l Baseball, soccer, basketball 1.20 50

Discovery of America, 500th Anniv. (in 1992) AP134

Pre-Colombian pottery artifacts: 10c, Footed vase, vert. 25c, Bowl. 30c, Footed bowl. 50c, Pitcher, vert. 1 l, Rectangular footed bowl.

1988 Litho. *Perf. 13½*

C774 AP134 10c multicolored 15 15
C775 AP134 25c multicolored 38 15
C776 AP134 30c multicolored 45 15
C777 AP134 50c multicolored 75 25

Size: 115x83mm

Imperf

C778 AP134 1 l multicolored 1.50

Nos. C652-C653 and C576 Surcharged

1988 Litho. *Perf. 12, 13½*

C779 AP103 10c on 16c #C652 15 15
C780 AP103 10c on 16c #C653 15 15
C781 AP94 50c on 16c #C576 60 40

Issue dates: 10c, Apr. 7, 50c, May 25.

No. C752 Overprinted

"BICENTENARIO DE LA REVOLUCION FRANCESA", 1789-1989

1989, July 14 Litho. *Imperf.*

C782 AP124 1.50 l multi 1.80

French revolution, bicent.

Nos. C629 and C593 Surcharged

L.0.15 I **L. 0.15** II

1989 Litho. *Perf. 14, 13½*

C783 AP101 15c on 6c, I 18
C783A AP101 15c on 6c, II 1.00
C784 AP96 1 l on 16c 1.25

Issue date: 1 l, June 15.

Nos. C699 and C616 Surcharged

1989, Dec. 15 Litho. *Perf. 14½, 12*

C785 AP112 20c on 16c #C699 20
C786 AP99 95c on 18c #C616 75

Issued: #C785, Dec. 15; #C786, Dec. 28.

Nos. C594 and C585 Surcharged with New Denomination and "IV Juegos / Olimpicos / Centroamericanos"

1990, Jan. 12 *Perf. 13½*

C787 AP96 75c on 18c #C594 (S) 98
C788 AP95 85c on 18c #C585 1.10

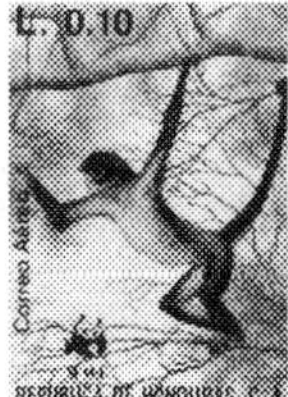

World Wildlife Fund — AP135

Various *Mono ateles.*

1990, Apr. 18 Litho. *Perf. 13½*

C789 AP135 10c shown 35
C790 AP135 10c Adult, young 35
C791 AP135 20c Adult hanging, diff. 70
C792 AP135 20c Adult, young, diff. 70

No. C621 Surcharged

1990, Feb. 8 Litho. *Perf. 14*

C793 AP100 20c on 14c multi 15

Nos. C621 and C636 Surcharged "50 Aniversario / IHCI" / 1939-1989

1990, Mar. 29

C794 AP102 20c on 14c No. 636 15
C795 AP100 1 l on 14c No. 621 45

No. C665 Surcharged

L.1.00

1990, June 14 Litho. *Perf. 12*

C796 AP104 1 l on 55c multi 45

World Cup Soccer Championships, Italy.

No. C707 Ovptd. in Margin "CAMPEONATO MUNDIAL DE FUTBOL Italia '90," and Character Trademark Souvenir Sheet

1990, June 14 *Perf. 14*

C797 AP113 1.50 l multi 70

No. C577 Surcharged in Black

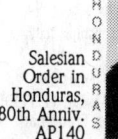

L. 0.20

1990, Feb. 22 Litho. *Perf. 13½*

C798 AP94 20c on 18c multi 15

FAO, 45th Anniv. — AP136

1990, Oct. 16 Litho. *Perf. 13½*

C799 AP136 95c yel, blk, bl, grn 55

17th Interamerican Congress of Industry and Construction — AP137

1990, Nov. 21 Litho. *Perf. 13½*

C800 AP137 20c Map, vert. 15
C801 AP137 1 l Jose Cecilio Del Valle Palace 60

AP138

Christmas — AP139

1990, Nov. 30 Litho. *Perf. 13½*

C802 AP138 20c shown 15
C803 AP138 95c Madonna and Child, vert. 55

Size: 112x82mm

Imperf

C804 AP139 3 l Poinsettia 1.75

Salesian Order in Honduras, 80th Anniv. AP140

1990, Dec. 28 Litho. *Perf. 13½*

C805 AP140 75c St. John Bosco 45
C806 AP140 1 l Natl. Youth Sanctuary 60

Pres. Rafael Leonardo Callejas — AP141

1991, Jan. 31

C807 AP141 30c Taking oath 18
C808 AP141 2 l Portrait 1.20

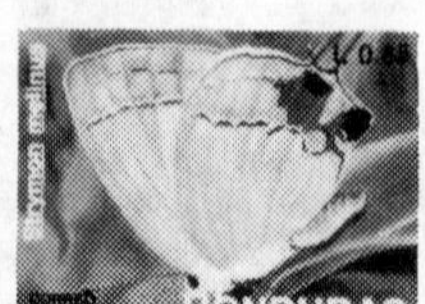

Moths and Butterflies AP142

1991, Feb. 28 Litho. *Perf. 13½*

C809 AP142 85c Strymon melinus 50
C810 AP142 90c Diorina sp. 55
C811 AP142 1.50 l Hyalophora cecropia 90

Size: 114x82mm

Imperf

C812 AP142 5 l Papilio polixenes 3.00

Notary Day — AP143

1991, May 22 Litho. *Perf. 13½*

C813 AP143 50c multicolored 35

Rafael Heliodoro Valle, Birth Cent. — AP144

1991, July 26 Litho. *Perf. 13½*

C815 AP144 2 l pale pink & blk 1.25

Churches AP145

Discovery of America, 500th Anniv. emblem and: 30c, Church of St. Manuel of Colohete, Gracias. 95c, Church of Our Lady of Mercy, Gracias. 1 l, Comayagua Cathedral.

1991, Aug. 30 Litho. *Perf. 13½*

C816 AP145 30c multicolored 18
C817 AP145 95c multicolored 55
C818 AP145 1 l multicolored 60

Latin American Institute, 25th Anniv. AP146

1991, June 20

C819 AP146 1 l multicolored 60

Flowers AP147

1991, Apr. 30

C820 AP147 30c Rhyncholaelia glauca 18
C821 AP147 50c Oncidium splendidum, vert. 30
C822 AP147 95c Laelia anceps, vert. 55
C823 AP147 1.50 l Cattleya skinneri 90

Espamer '91, Buenos Aires AP148

1991, July 1

C824 AP148 2 l multicolored 1.20

Size: 101x82mm

Imperf

C825 AP148 5 l like #C824 3.00

Discovery of America, 500th anniv. (in 1992).

11th Pan American Games, Havana AP149

1991, Aug. 8

C826 AP149 30c Equestrian 18
C827 AP149 85c Judo 50
C828 AP149 95c Men's swimming 55

Size: 114x83mm

Imperf

C829 AP149 5 l Women's swimming 3.00

Pre-Columbian Culture — AP150

UPAEP emblem, artifacts and: 25c, ears of corn. 40c, ear of corn, map. 1.50 l, map.

1991, Sept. 30 Litho. *Perf. 13½*

C830 AP150 25c multicolored 15
C831 AP150 40c multicolored 25
C832 AP150 1.50 l multicolored 90

4th Intl. Congress on Control of Insect Pests — AP151

Designs: 30c, Tactics to control pests. 75c, Integration of science. 1 l, Cooperation between farmers and scientists. 5 l, Pests and biological controls.

1991, Nov. 22

C833 AP151 30c multicolored 18
C834 AP151 75c multicolored 45
C835 AP151 1 l multicolored 60

Size: 115x83mm

Imperf

C836 AP151 5 l multicolored 3.00

America Issue — AP152

1992, Jan. 27 Litho. *Perf. 13½*

C837 AP152 90c Sighting land 55
C838 AP152 1 l Columbus' ships 60
C839 AP152 2 l Ship, map, birds 1.20

Christmas — AP153

1992, Jan. 27

C840 AP153 1 l shown 60
C841 AP153 2 l Poinsettias in rooster vase 1.20

Honduran Savings Insurance Company, 75th Anniv. AP154

1992, Jan. 27

C842 AP154 85c multicolored 50
C843 AP154 1 l Priest saying mass 60

Size: 115x83mm

Imperf

C844 AP154 5 l like #C842 3.00

First mass in New World, 490th anniv. (No. C843). Taking possession of new continent, 490th anniv. (Nos. C842, C844).

Pres. Rafael Leonardo Callejas, 2nd Year in Office AP155

Callejas with: 20c, Italian president Francesco Cossiga. 2 l, Pope John Paul II.

1992, Jan. 27 Litho. *Perf. 13½*

C845 AP155 20c black & purple 15
C846 AP155 2 l black & multi 1.20

Flowers AP156

1992, July 24 Litho. *Perf. 13½*

C847 AP156	20c	Bougainvillea glabra	15
C848 AP156	30c	Canna indica	18
C849 AP156	75c	Epiphyllum	45
C850 AP156	95c	Sobralia macrantha	58

Gen. Francisco Morazan Hydroelectric Complex — AP157

1992, Aug. 17

C851 AP157	85c	Dam face, vert.	50
C852 AP157	4 l	Rear of dam	2.40

AP158

AP159

1992, Aug. 24

C853 AP158	95c	black & multi	58
C854 AP158	95c	multicolored	58

Intl. Conference on Agriculture, 50th anniv.

1992 Litho. *Perf. 13½*

Gen. Francisco Morazan (1792-1842): 5c, Morazan mounted on horseback. 10c, Statue of Morazan. 50c, Watch and sword, horiz. 95c, Portrait of Josefa Lastiri de Morazan. 5 l, Portrait of Morazan in uniform.

C855 AP159	5c	multicolored	15
C856 AP159	10c	multicolored	15
C857 AP159	50c	multicolored	28
C858 AP159	95c	multicolored	52
		Set value	89

Size: 76x108mm

Imperf

C859 AP159	5 l	multicolored	2.75

Children's Day — AP160

Paintings of children: 25c, Musicians. 95c, Boy, dog standing in doorway. 2 l, Flower girl.

1992, Sept. 7

C860 AP160	25c	multicolored	15
C861 AP160	95c	multicolored	52
C862 AP160	2 l	multicolored	1.15

Intl. Conference on Nutrition AP161

1992 Litho. *Perf. 13½*

C863 AP161	1.05 l	multicolored	60

Pan-American Agricultural School, 50th Anniv. — AP162

1992

C864 AP162	20c	Bee keepers	15
C865 AP162	85c	Woman, goats	45
C866 AP162	1 l	Plowing	55
C867 AP162	2 l	Man with tool, vert.	1.10

Exfilhon '92 — AP163

Birds: 1.50 l, F. triquilidos. 2.45 l, Ara macao. 5 l, Quetzal pharomachrus mocinno.

1992

C868 AP163	1.50 l	multicolored	82
C869 AP163	2.45 l	multicolored	1.35

Size: 76x108mm

Imperf

C870 AP163	5 l	multicolored	2.75

Discovery of America, 500th anniv.

America Issue — AP164

Discovery of America, 500th Anniv. — AP165

UPAEP emblem and: 35c, Native settlement. 5 l, Explorers meeting natives in boats.

1992 Litho. *Perf. 13½*

C871 AP164	35c	multicolored	15
C872 AP164	5 l	multicolored	2.75

1992

Details from First Mass, by Roque Zelaya: 95c, Ships off-shore. 1 l, Holding services with natives, horiz. 2 l, Natives, countryside, temples, horiz.

C873 AP165	95c	multicolored	52
C874 AP165	1 l	multicolored	55
C875 AP165	2 l	multicolored	1.10

City of El Progreso, Cent. AP166

1992

C876 AP166	1.55 l	multicolored	85

First Road Conservation Congress of Panama and Central America AP167

1992 *Perf. 13½*

C878 AP167	20c	shown	15
C879 AP167	85c	Bulldozer on highway	45

Pan-American Health Organization, 90th Anniv. — AP168

1992

C880 AP168	3.95 l	multicolored	2.05

Christmas AP169

Paintings by Roque Zelaya: 20c, Crowd watching people climb pole in front of church, vert. 85c, Nativity scene.

1992

C881 AP169	20c	multicolored	15
C882 AP169	85c	multicolored	45

Surcharges on:

L. 0.20
No. C601

L. 0.20
Nos. C606-C607

L 0.50

L. 0.20

Nos. C584, C612, C637

Nos. C672, C678, C708

L 0.50

Nos. C575-C576, C603, C620, C699

1992-93

Perfs. and Printing Methods as Before

C883	AP97	20c on 1c #C601		15
C884	AP97	20c on 3c #C603		16
C884A	AP106	20c on 3c #C672		16
C884B	AP114	20c on 3c #C708		16
C885	AP97	20c on 6c #C606		15
C886	AP94	20c on 8c #C575		16
C886A	AP100	20c on 8c #C620		16
C887	AP94	50c on 16c #C576		40
C888	AP95	50c on 16c #C584		25
C888A	AP102	50c on 16c #C637		25
C888B	AP112	50c on 16c #C699		40
C889	AP97	85c on 18c #C607		45
C890	AP98	85c on 18c #C612		42
C891	AP107	85c on 24c #C678		42
		Nos. C883-C891 (14)		3.69

Size and location of surcharge varies.

Intl. Court of Justice Decision on Border Dispute Between Honduras & El Salvador AP170

Designs: 90c, Pres. of El Salvador and Pres. Callejas of Honduras, vert. 1.05 l, Country flags, map of Honduras and El Salvador.

1993 Litho. *Perf. 13½*

C893 AP170	90c	multicolored	48
C894 AP170	1.05 l	multicolored	55

Third year of Pres. Callejas' term.

Mother's Day — AP171

Endangered Animals — AP172

Paintings of a mother and child, by Sandra Pendrey.

1993 Litho. *Perf. 13½*

C895 AP171	50c	Red blanket	26
C896 AP171	95c	Green blanket	50

1993 *Perf. 13½*

C897 AP172	85c	Manatee, horiz	45
C898 AP172	2.45 l	Puma, horiz.	1.30
C899 AP172	10 l	Jaguar	5.25

Natl. Symbols — AP173

1993 Litho. *Perf. 13½*

C900 AP173	25c	Ara macao	15
C901 AP173	95c	Odocoileus virginianus	45

First Brazilian Postage Stamps, 150th Anniv. AP174

1993 Litho. *Perf. 13½*

C902 AP174	20c	Brazil No. 1	15
C903 AP174	50c	Brazil No. 2	25
C904 AP174	95c	Brazil No. 3	45

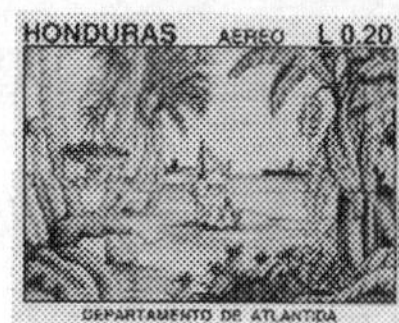

Departments in Honduras AP175

Various scenes, department name: No. C905a, Atlantida. b, Colon. c, Cortes. d, Choluteca. e, El Paraiso. f, Francisco Morazan.
No. C906a, Comayagua. b, Copan. c, Intibuca. d, Islas de la Bahia. e, Lempira. f, Ocotepeque.
No. C907a, La Paz. b, Olancho. c, Santa Barbara. d, Valle. e, Yoro. f, Gracias a Dios.

1993 **Litho.** *Perf. 13½*

C905 AP175 20c Strip of 6, #a.-f. 55
C906 AP175 50c Strip of 6, #a.-f. 1.40
C907 AP175 1.50 l Strip of 6, #a.-f. 4.00

No. C906 is vert.

Endangered Birds — AP176

UN Development Program — AP177

1993 **Litho.** *Perf. 13½*

C908 AP176 20c Spizaetus ornatus 15
C909 AP176 80c Cairina moschata, horiz. 38
C910 AP176 2 l Harpia harpija, horiz. 95

1993

C911 AP177 95c multicolored 45

Christmas — AP178

1993

C912 AP178 20c Church 15
C913 AP178 85c Woman, flowers 42

Nos. C577, C585, C593, C611, C616, C638, C643, C680, C716 Surcharged

L 0.50

1993
Perfs. and Printing Methods as Before

C917 AP96 50c on 16c #C593 25
C918 AP98 50c on 16c #C611 25
C919 AP94 50c on 18c #C577 25
C920 AP99 50c on 18c #C616 25
C921 AP115 50c on 18c #C716 42
C922 AP95 85c on 18c #C585 42
C923 AP102 85c on 18c #C638 42
C924 AP99 85c on 18c #C643 42
C925 AP108 85c on 25c #C680 42
Nos. C917-C925 (9) 3.10

Size and location of surcharge varies. This is an expanding set. Numbers may change.

Fish — AP179

1993 **Litho.** *Perf. 13½*

C931 AP179 20c Pomacanthus arcuatus 15
C932 AP179 85c Holacanthus ciliaris 42
C933 AP179 3 l Chaetodon striatus 1.50

Famous Men — AP180

1993

C934 AP180 25c Ramon Rosa 15
C935 AP180 65c Jesus Aguilar Paz 32
C936 AP180 85c Augusto C. Coello 42

AIR POST SEMI-POSTAL STAMPS

No. C13C Surcharged with Plus Sign and Surtax in Black

Unwmk.

1929, June 5 **Engr.** *Perf. 12*

CB1 AP1 50c + 5c carmine 42 28
CB2 AP1 50c + 10c carmine 52 35
CB3 AP1 50c + 15c carmine 70 52
CB4 AP1 50c + 20c carmine 90 70

AIR POST SPECIAL DELIVERY STAMPS

No. CO52 Surcharged in Red

ENTREGA INMEDIATA 1953 L 0.20

Perf. 13½x14

1953, Dec. 8 **Engr.** **Unwmk.**

CE1 AP65 20c on 1c 2.50 1.00

Transport Plane — APSD1

1956, Oct. 3 *Perf. 13x12½*

CE2 APSD1 20c black & red 75 42

Surcharges on No. CE2 (see Nos. C421, C477) eliminate its special delivery character.

Catalogue values for unused stamps in this section, from this point to the end of the section, are for Never Hinged items.

Stamp Centenary Type of Air Post Issue

Design: 20c, Mailman on motorcycle.

1966, May 31 **Litho.** *Perf. 14x14½*

CE3 AP81 20c bis brn, brn & gold 60 42

Centenary (in 1965) of the first Honduran postage stamp.
The "HABILITADO" overprint on No. CE3 (see No. C479) eliminates its special delivery character.

Independence Type of Air Post Issue

1972, May 19 **Litho.** *Perf. 13*

CE4 AP89 20c Corsair plane 30 30

Same Surcharged

1975

CE5 AP89 60c on 20c 85 60

Forest Protection Type of Air Post

1976, May 28 **Litho.** *Perf. 13½*

CE6 AP96 60c Stag in forest 60 45

AIR POST OFFICIAL STAMPS

Official Stamps Nos. O78 to O81 Overprinted in Red, Green or Black

Servicio aéreo Habilitado VI—1930

1930 *Perf. 11, 11½*

CO1 A24 10c deep blue (R) 1.25 1.25
CO2 A24 20c yel brown 1.25 1.25
a. Vertical pair, imperf. between 14.00
CO3 A24 50c ver (Bk) 1.40 1.40
CO4 A24 1p emerald (R) 1.25 1.25

OA1

Green Surcharge

CO5 OA1 5c on 6c red vio 1.00 1.00
a. "1910" for "1930" 2.75 2.75
b. "1920" for "1930" 2.75 2.75

The overprint exists in other colors and on other denominations but the status of these is questioned.

Official Stamps of 1931 Overprinted

Servicio Aéreo Exterior. Habilitado X. 1931.

1931 **Unwmk.** *Perf. 12*

CO6 O2 1c ultra 35 35
CO7 O2 2c black brn 85 85
CO8 O2 5c olive gray 1.00 1.00
CO9 O2 6c orange red 1.00 1.00
a. Inverted overprint 24.00 24.00
CO10 O2 10c dark green 1.25 1.25
CO11 O2 15c olive brn 2.00 1.75
a. Inverted overprint 20.00 20.00
CO12 O2 20c red brown 2.00 1.75
CO13 O2 50c gray vio 1.40 1.40
CO14 O2 1p dp orange 2.00 1.75
Nos. CO6-CO14 (9) 11.85 11.10

In the setting of the overprint there are numerous errors in the spelling and punctuation, letters omitted and similar varieties.
This set is known with blue overprint. A similar overprint is known in larger type, but its status has not been fully determined.

Postage Stamps of 1918-30 Surcharged Type "a" or Type "b" (#CO22-CO23) in Green, Black, Red and Blue

a **Aéreo Oficial Vale L. 0.70 1933**

b Aéreo oficial Vale L. 0.90 1933

1933 **Wmk. 209, Unwmk.**

CO15 A39 20c on 2c #295 (G) 3.25 3.25
CO16 A39 20c on 2c #296 (G) 3.25 3.25
CO17 A39 20c on 2c #297 (G) 3.25 3.25
CO17A A39 40c on 2c #295 2.00 2.00
CO18 A39 40c on 2c #297 (G) 7.00 7.00
CO18A A39 40c on 2c #297 4.25 4.25
CO19 A28 40c on 5c #246 4.25 4.25
CO19A A28 40c on 5c #247 7.00 7.00
CO20 A28 40c on 5c #266 4.25 4.25
CO20A A28 40c on 5c #267 9.00 9.00
CO20B A28 40c on 5c #267 (R) 14.00 14.00
CO21 A20 70c on 5c #183 3.00 3.00
CO22 A24 70c on 10c #214 (R) 3.25 3.25
CO23 A22 1 l on 20c #191 (Bl) 3.25 3.25
CO24 A24 1 l on 50c #216 (Bl) 14.00 14.00
CO25 A22 1.20 l on 1p #193 (Bl) 1.00 1.00
Nos. CO15-CO25 (16) 86.00 86.00

Official Stamps of 1915-29 Surcharged Type "a" or Type "b" (#CO28-CO29, CO33-CO41, CO43) in Black, Red, Green, Orange, Carmine or Blue

CO26 O1 40c on 5c #O84 (Bk) 95 95
CO27 O1 40c on 5c #O84 (R) 25.00 25.00
CO28 A24 60c on 6c #O77 (Bk) 70 70
CO29 A24 60c on 6c #O77 (G) 25.00 25.00
CO30 A20 70c on 5c #O60 (Bk) 5.25 5.25
CO31 A19 70c on 10c #O62 (R) 9.00 9.00
CO32 A19 70c on 10c #O62 (Bk) 7.75 7.75
CO33 A22 70c on 10c #O70 (R) 4.50 4.00
CO34 A24 70c on 10c #O78 (O) 3.50 3.50
CO35 A24 70c on 10c #O78 (C) 4.50 4.50
CO36 A22 70c on 15c #O71 (R) 87.50 87.50
CO37 A22 90c on 10c #O70 (R) 5.25 5.25
CO38 A22 90c on 15c #O71 (R) 3.75 3.75
CO38A A24 1 l on 2c #O76 1.40 1.40
CO39 A22 1 l on 20c #O72 2.50 2.50
CO39A A24 1 l on 20c #O79 3.75 3.75
CO40 A22 1 l on 50c #O73 1.90 1.90
CO41 A24 1 l on 50c #O80 4.25 4.25
CO42 A20 1.20 l on 1p #O65 9.00 7.00
CO43 A24 1.20 l on 1p #O81 1.50 1.50
Nos. CO26-CO43 (20) 206.95 204.45

Varieties of foregoing surcharges exist.

Merchant Flag and Seal of Honduras — OA2

1939, Feb. 27 **Unwmk.** *Perf. 12½*

CO44 OA2 2c dp bl & grn 15 15
CO45 OA2 5c dp bl & org 15 15
CO46 OA2 8c dp bl & brn 15 15
CO47 OA2 15c dp bl & car 28 20
CO48 OA2 46c dp bl & ol grn 38 28
CO49 OA2 50c dp bl & vio 48 28
CO50 OA2 1 l dp bl & red brown 1.75 1.25
CO51 OA2 2 l dp bl & red orange 3.75 2.25
Nos. CO44-CO51 (8) 7.09 4.71

For overprints and surcharges see Nos. C101-C117.

Types of Air Post Stamps of 1952 Overprinted in Red

OFICIAL

Perf. 13½x14, 14x13½

1952 **Engr.** **Unwmk.**

CO52 AP65 1c rose lil & ol 15 15
CO53 AP65 2c brn & vio 15 15
CO54 AP65 8c dp car & blk 15 15
CO55 AP66 16c pur & dk grn 25 25
CO56 AP65 30c dk bl & blk 52 52
CO57 AP65 1 l dk grn & dk brown 1.75 1.75
CO58 AP65 2 l bl & red brn 3.50 3.50
CO59 AP66 5 l red org & blk 8.50 8.50
Nos. CO52-CO59 (8) 14.97 14.97

Queen Isabella I of Spain, 500th birth anniv.
For surcharge see No. CE1.

No. C222 and Types of Air Post Stamps of 1953 Overprinted in Red

OFICIAL

Engraved; Center of 1c Litho.

1953, Dec. 18 *Perf. 12½*

Frames in Black

CO60 AP67 1c ultra & vio bl 15 15
CO61 AP97 2c dp bl grn 15 15
CO62 AP67 3c orange 15 15
CO63 AP67 5c dp carmine 16 16
CO64 AP67 15c dk brown 20 20
CO65 AP67 30c purple 35 35
CO66 AP67 1 l ol gray 3.25 2.25
CO67 AP67 2 l lilac rose 4.00 3.00
CO68 AP67 5 l ultra 9.25 7.00
Nos. CO60-CO68 (9) 17.66 13.41

Issued to honor the United Nations.

Types of Air Post Stamps Overprinted in Red

OFICIAL

Engraved; 8c Lithographed

1956, Oct. 3 *Perf. 13x12½*

CO69 AP68 1c blk & brn car 15 15
CO70 AP69 2c blk & mag 15 15
CO71 AP68 3c blk & rose vio 15 15
CO72 AP69 4c blk & org 15 15
CO73 AP69 5c blk & bl grn 15 15
CO74 AP68 8c vio & multi 15 15
CO75 AP68 10c blk & red brn 15 15
CO76 AP68 12c blk & car rose 15 15
CO77 AP68 15c car & blk 15 15
CO78 AP68 20c blk & ol brn 15 15
CO79 AP69 24c blk & blue 18 18
CO80 AP68 25c blk & rose vio 18 18
CO81 AP68 30c blk & grn 20 20
CO82 AP68 40c blk & red org 26 26
CO83 AP69 50c blk & brn red 32 32
CO84 AP68 60c blk & rose vio 38 38
CO85 AP68 1 l blk & brn 1.40 1.10
CO86 AP69 2 l blk & dk bl 2.75 2.25
CO87 AP69 5 l blk & vio bl 5.75 5.25
Nos. CO69-CO87 (19) 12.92 11.62

Nos. C269-C278 Overprinted Vertically in Red (Horizontally on Nos. CO89 and CO91) OFICIAL

1957, Oct. 21 Litho. *Perf. 13*

Frames in Black

CO88 AP70 1c buff & aqua 15 15
CO89 AP70 2c org, pur & emer 15 15
CO90 AP70 5c pink & ultra 15 15
a. Inverted overprint
CO91 AP70 8c org, vio & ol 15 15
CO92 AP70 10c vio & brn 15 15
CO93 AP70 12c lt grn & ultra 15 15
CO94 AP70 15c grn & brn 16 15
CO95 AP70 30c pink & sl 55 22
CO96 AP70 1 l bl & brn 1.40 1.00
CO97 AP70 2 l lt grn & sl 2.75 2.25
Nos. CO88-CO97 (10) 5.76 4.52

Types of Lincoln Air Post Stamps 1959 Overprinted in Red OFICIAL

1959 Engr. *Perf. 13½*

Flags in National Colors

CO98 AP72 1c ocher 15 15
CO99 AP73 2c gray olive 15 15
a. Inverted overprint
CO100 AP73 3c red brown 15 15
CO101 AP73 5c ultra 15 15
CO102 AP73 10c dull pur 15 15
a. Overprint omitted
CO103 AP73 12c red org 15 15
CO104 AP72 15c dark brn 15 15
CO105 AP73 25c black 20 15
CO106 AP73 50c dark car 32 25
CO107 AP73 1 l purple 75 65
CO108 AP73 2 l dark bl 1.40 1.10
a. Min. sheet of 6, 2c, 5c, 12c, 15c, 50c, 2 l, imperf. 2.50 2.00
CO109 AP73 5 l green 4.50 3.75
Nos. CO98-CO109 (12) 8.22 6.95

Catalogue values for unused stamps in this section, from this point to the end of the section, are for Never Hinged items.

No. CO55 Overprinted: "IN MEMORIAM / Sir Winston / Churchill / 1874-1965"

1965, Dec. 20 *Perf. 14x13½*

CO110 AP66 16c pur & dk grn 70 70

See note after No. C379.

Nos. C336-C344 Overprinted in Red: OFICIAL

1965 Photo. *Perf. 14*

Black Design and Inscription

CO111 AP76 1c yel grn 15 15
CO112 AP76 2c pale rose lil 15 15
CO113 AP76 5c light ultra 15 15
CO114 AP76 8c bluish grn 15 15
CO115 AP76 10c buff 25 25
CO116 AP76 12c lemon 32 32
CO117 AP76 1 l light ocher 3.50 3.25
CO118 AP76 2 l pale ol grn 7.75 7.00
CO119 AP76 3 l rose 9.50 8.50
Nos. CO111-CO119 (9) 21.92 19.92

OFFICIAL STAMPS

Type of Regular Issue of 1890 Overprinted in Red OFICIAL

1890 Unwmk. *Perf. 12*

O1 A5 1c pale yellow 18
O2 A5 2c pale yellow 18
O3 A5 5c pale yellow 18
O4 A5 10c pale yellow 18
O5 A5 20c pale yellow 18
O6 A5 25c pale yellow 18
O7 A5 30c pale yellow 18
O8 A5 40c pale yellow 18
O9 A5 50c pale yellow 18
O10 A5 75c pale yellow 18
O11 A5 1p pale yellow 18
Nos. O1-O11 (11) 1.98

Type of Regular Issue of 1891 Overprinted in Red

1891

O12 A6 1c yellow 18
O13 A6 2c yellow 18
O14 A6 5c yellow 18
O15 A6 10c yellow 18
O16 A6 20c yellow 18
O17 A6 25c yellow 18
O18 A6 30c yellow 18
O19 A6 40c yellow 18
O20 A6 50c yellow 18
O21 A6 75c yellow 18
O22 A6 1p yellow 18
Nos. O12-O22 (11) 1.98

Nos. O1 to O22 were never placed in use. Cancellations were applied to remainders. They exist with overprint inverted, double, triple and omitted; also, imperf. and part perf.

Regular Issue of 1898 Overprinted OFICIAL

1898-99 *Perf. 11½*

O23 A12 5c dl ultra 20
O24 A12 10c dark bl 20
O25 A12 20c dull org 28
O26 A12 50c org red 35
O27 A12 1p blue grn 60
Nos. O23-O27 (5) 1.63

Counterfeits of basic stamps and of overprint exist.

Regular Issue of 1911 Overprinted OFICIAL

1911-15 *Perf. 12, 14*

Carmine Overprint

O28 A15 1c violet 1.50 60
a. Inverted overprint 2.00
b. Double overprint 2.00
O29 A15 6c ultra 2.50 2.00
a. Inverted overprint 2.50
O30 A15 10c blue 1.50 1.25
a. "OFICAIL" 2.50
b. Double overprint 3.50
O31 A15 20c yellow 10.00 7.50
O32 A15 50c brown 7.00 6.00
O33 A15 1p ol grn 12.00 10.00
Nos. O28-O33 (6) 34.50 27.35

Black Overprint

O34 A15 2c green 1.00 70
a. "CFICIAL" 5.00
O35 A15 5c carmine 1.50 1.00
a. Perf. 12 7.50 5.00
O36 A15 6c ultra 4.50 4.50
O37 A15 10c blue 4.00 4.00
O38 A15 20c yellow 1.75 1.75
O39 A15 50c brown 5.50 4.00
Nos. O34-O39 (6) 18.25 15.95

Counterfeits of overprint of Nos. O28-O39 exist.

With Additional Surcharge 10 cts.

1913-14

O40 A15 1c on 5c car 1.75 1.50
O41 A15 2c on 5c car 2.00 1.50
O42 A15 10c on 1c vio 4.00 3.50
a. "OFICIAL" inverted 7.50
O43 A15 20c on 1c vio 3.00 2.50

On No. O40 the surcharge reads "1 cent." Nos. O40-O43 exist with double surcharge.

No. O43 Surcharged Vertically in Black, Yellow or Maroon OFICIAL 10 cts.

1914

O44 A15 10c on 20c on 1c 7.00 7.00
a. Maroon surcharge 20.00 20.00
O45 A15 10c on 20c on 1c (Y) 35.00 35.00

No. O35 Surcharged 10 c

1915

O46 A15 10c on 5c car 20.00 20.00

No. O39 Surcharged OFICIAL $ 0.20

O47 A15 20c on 50c brn 5.00 5.00

Regular Issues of 1913-14 Overprinted in Red or Black OFICIAL

1915 *Perf. 11½*

O48 A17 1c brn (R) 40 40
a. "OFICAIL" 5.00
O49 A17 2c car (Bk) 40 40
a. "OFICAIL" 5.00
b. Double overprint 4.00
O50 A18 5c ultra (Bk) 40 40
a. "OFIC" 4.00
O51 A18 5c ultra (R) 1.00 1.00
a. "OFIC"
b. "OFICAIL" 5.00
O52 A18 6c pur (Bk) 1.50 1.50
a. 6c red lil (Bk)
O53 A17 10c brn (Bk) 1.25 1.25
O54 A17 20c brn (Bk) 3.00 3.00
O55 A17 20c brn (R) 3.00 3.00
a. Double overprint (R+Bk) 10.00
b. "OFICAIL" 5.00
O56 A18 50c rose (Bk) 6.00 6.00
Nos. O48-O56 (9) 16.95 16.95

The 10c blue has the overprint "OFICIAL" in different type from the other stamps of the series. It is stated that forty copies were overprinted for the Postmaster General but the stamp was never put in use or on sale at the post office.

No. 152 Surcharged OFICIAL. $ 0.01

O57 A17 1c on 2c car 2.00 2.00
a. "0.10" for "0.01" 4.25 4.25
b. "0.20" for "0.01" 4.25 4.25
c. Double surcharge 8.50 8.50
d. As "a," double surcharge 77.50
e. As "b," double surcharge 77.50

Regular Issue of 1915-16 Overprinted in Black or Red. OFICIAL

1915-16

O58 A19 1c choc (Bk) 20 20
O59 A19 2c car (Bk) 20 20
a. Tête bêche pair 1.25 1.25
b. Double overprint 2.00
c. Double overprint, one inverted 2.00
d. "b" and "c" in tête bêche pair
O60 A20 5c brt blue (R) 30 30
a. Inverted overprint 3.00
O61 A20 6c deep pur (R) 40 40
a. Black overprint 3.00
b. Inverted overprint 2.00 2.00
O62 A19 10c dl bl (R) 40 40
O63 A19 20c red brn (Bk) 60 60
a. Tête bêche pair 2.50
O64 A20 50c red (Bk) 1.75 1.75
O65 A20 1p yel grn (C) 3.75 3.75
Nos. O58-O65 (8) 7.60 7.60

The 6c, 10c and 1p exist imperf.

Regular Issue of 1919 Overprinted OFICIAL

1921

O66 A22 1c brown 2.25 2.25
a. Inverted overprint 3.00 3.00
O67 A22 2c carmine 6.50 6.50
a. Inverted overprint 3.00 3.00
O68 A22 5c lilac rose 6.50 6.50
a. Inverted overprint 3.00
O69 A22 6c brt vio 50 50
a. Inverted overprint
O70 A22 10c dull blue 60 60
a. Double overprint
O71 A22 15c light blue 70 70
a. Inverted overprint 2.00
b. Double ovpt., one inverted 4.00
O72 A22 20c brown 1.00 1.00
O73 A22 50c light brown 1.50 1.50
O74 A22 1p yellow green 3.00 3.00
Nos. O66-O74 (9) 22.55 22.55

Regular Issue of 1924 Overprinted

1924 *Perf. 11, 11½*

O75 A24 1c olive brn 15 15
O76 A24 2c deep rose 20 20
O77 A24 6c red vio 30 30
O78 A24 10c deep bl 50 50
O79 A24 20c yel brn 60 60
O80 A24 50c vermilion 1.25 1.25
O81 A24 1p emerald 2.00 2.00
Nos. O75-O81 (7) 5.00 5.00

J. C. del Valle — O1

Designs: 2c, J. R. Molina. 5c, Coffee tree. 10c, J. T. Reyes. 20c, Tegucigalpa Cathedral. 50c, San Lorenzo Creek. 1p, Radio station.

1929 Litho. Wmk. 209 *Perf. 11½*

O82 O1 1c blue 15 15
O83 O1 2c carmine 20 20
a. 2c rose 20 20
O84 O1 5c purple 35 35
O85 O1 10c emerald 50 35
O86 O1 20c dk bl 60 60
O87 O1 50c org, grn & bl 1.00 1.00
O88 O1 1p buff 1.75 1.75
Nos. O82-O88 (7) 4.55 4.40

Nos. O82-O88 exist imperf.

For overprints and surcharges see Nos. 282, 284, C37-C40, C59, C62-C63, CO26-CO27.

View of Tegucigalpa O2

1931 Unwmk. Engr. *Perf. 12*

O89 O2 1c ultra 30 20
O90 O2 2c black brn 30 20
O91 O2 5c olive gray 35 25
O92 O2 6c orange red 40 32
O93 O2 10c dark green 50 35
O94 O2 15c olive brn 65 42
O95 O2 20c red brown 75 50
O96 O2 50c gray vio 1.00 65
O97 O2 1p dp orange 1.75 1.75
Nos. O89-O97 (9) 6.00 4.64

For overprints see #CO6-CO14, O98-O105.

Official Stamps of 1931 Overprinted in Black

HABILITADO 1935-1938

1936-37

O98 O2 1c ultra 25 25
O99 O2 2c black brn 25 25
a. Inverted overprint 10.00
O100 O2 5c olive gray 30 30
O101 O2 6c red orange 40 40
O102 O2 10c dark green 40 40
O103 O2 15c olive brown 50 50
a. Inverted overprint 5.00
O104 O2 20c red brown 1.00 1.00
a. "1938-1935"
O105 O2 50c gray violet 4.00 3.00
Nos. O98-O105 (8) 7.10 6.10

Double overprints exist on 1c and 2c. No. O97 with this overprint is fraudulent.

15-Cent Minimum Value
The minimum value for a single stamp is 15 cents. This value reflects the costs of handling inexpensive stamps.

POSTAL TAX STAMPS

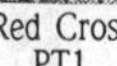

Red Cross
PT1

Francisco Morazán
PT2

Engr.; Cross Litho.

1941 Unwmk. *Perf. 12*

RA1	PT1 1c blue & carmine	25	15

Obligatory on all domestic or foreign mail, the tax to be used by the Honduran Red Cross.

1941 Engr.

RA2	PT2 1c copper brown	40	15

Francisco Morazan, 100th anniv. of death.

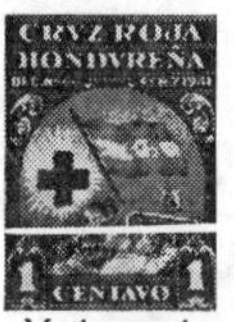

Mother and Child — PT3

Henri Dunant — PT4

1945 Engr.; Cross Litho.

RA3	PT3 1c ol brn, car & bl	25	15

The tax was for the Honduran Red Cross.

Similar to Type of 1945
Large Red Cross

1950

RA4	PT3 1c olive brn & red	25	15

The tax was for the Honduran Red Cross.

1959 *Perf. 13x13½*

RA5	PT4 1c blue & red	25	15

The tax was for the Red Cross.

Henri Dunant — PT5

No. RA7, as PT5, but redrawn; country name panel at bottom, value at right, "El poder . . ." at top.

1964, Dec. 15 Litho. *Perf. 11*

RA6	PT5 1c brt grn & red	25	15
RA7	PT5 1c brown & red	25	15
	Set value		16

The tax was for the Red Cross.

Nurse and Patient — PT6

1969, June Litho. *Perf. 13½*

RA8	PT6 1c light blue & red	25	15

The tax was for the Red Cross.

HORTA

LOCATION — An administrative district of the Azores, consisting of the islands of Pico, Fayal, Flores and Corvo

GOVT. — A district of the Republic of Portugal

AREA — 305 sq. mi.

POP. — 49,000 (approx.)

CAPITAL — Horta

1000 Reis = 1 Milreis

King Carlos
A1 A2

Chalk-surfaced Paper

Perf. 11½, 12½, 13½

1892-93 Typo. Unwmk.

1	A1	5r yellow	1.50	1.00
2	A1	10r reddish violet	1.50	1.25
3	A1	15r chocolate	2.25	1.75
4	A1	20r lavender	2.75	2.00
5	A1	25r dp grn, perf. 11½	4.00	50
a.		Perf. 13½	2.50	2.50
6	A1	50r blue	4.00	2.00
a.		Perf. 13½	10.00	5.25
7	A1	75r carmine	5.25	4.00
8	A1	80r yellow green	9.00	6.00
9	A1	100r brn, *yel* ('93)	6.00	3.50
a.		Perf. 12½	95.00	52.50
10	A1	150r car, *rose* ('93)	30.00	24.00
11	A1	200r dk bl, *bl* ('93)	35.00	22.50
12	A1	300r dark blue ('93)	37.50	27.50
		Nos. 1-12 (12)	138.75	96.00

Bisects of No. 1 were used in Aug. 1894.

The reprints have shiny white gum and clean-cut perforation 13½. The white paper is thinner than that of the originals.

1897-1905 *Perf. 11½*

Name and Value in Black Except 500r

13	A2	2½r gray	45	28
14	A2	5r orange	45	28
15	A2	10r lt green	45	28
16	A2	15r brown	5.25	3.00
17	A2	15r gray grn ('99)	1.00	80
18	A2	20r gray violet	1.10	85
19	A2	25r sea green	2.00	45
20	A2	25r car rose ('99)	90	48
21	A2	50r blue	3.00	70
22	A2	50r ultra ('05)	11.00	8.00
23	A2	65r slate blue ('98)	65	52
24	A2	75r rose	1.90	95
25	A2	75r brn, *yel* ('05)	15.00	10.00
26	A2	80r violet	1.25	1.10
27	A2	100r dk blue, *bl*	1.75	95
28	A2	115r org brn, *pink* ('98)	1.40	1.10
29	A2	130r gray brn, *buff* ('98)	1.40	1.10
30	A2	150r lt brn, *buff*	1.40	1.10
31	A2	180r sl, *pnksh* ('98)	1.50	1.25
32	A2	200r red vio, *pale lil*	4.50	3.75
33	A2	300r dk blue, *rose*	7.50	6.75
34	A2	500r blk & red, *bl*	10.50	8.50
		Nos. 13-34 (22)	74.35	52.19

Stamps of Portugal replaced those of Horta.

HUNGARY

LOCATION — Central Europe

GOVT. — Republic

AREA — 35,911 sq. mi.

POP. — 10,679,000 (est. 1984)

CAPITAL — Budapest

Prior to World War I, Hungary together with Austria comprised the Austro-Hungarian Empire. The Hungarian post became independent on May 1, 1867. During 1850-1871 stamps listed under Austria were also used in Hungary. Copies showing clear Hungarian cancels sell for substantially more.

100 Krajczár (Kreuzer) = 1 Forint 100 Fillér = 1 Korona (1900) 100 Fillér = 1 Pengö (1926) 100 Fillér = 1 Forint (1946)

Catalogue values for unused stamps in this country are for Never Hinged items, beginning with Scott 503 in the regular postage section, Scott B92 in the semi-postal section, Scott C35 in the airpost section, Scott CB1 in the airpost semi-postal section, Scott J130 in the postage due section, and Scott Q9 in the parcel post section.

Watermarks

Wmk. 91- "ZEITUNGS-MARKEN" in Double-lined Capitals across the Sheet

Wmk. 106- Multiple Star

Wmk. 132- kr in Oval

Wmk. 133- Four Double Crosses

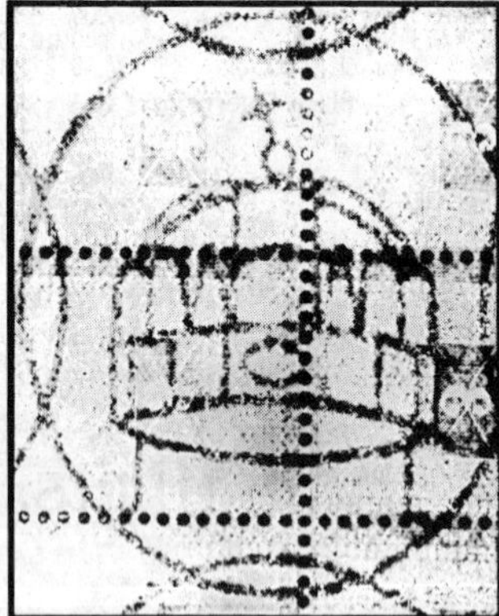

Wmk. 135- Crown in Oval or Circle, Sideways

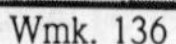

Wmk. 136

Wmk. 136a

Wmk. 137- Double Cross

Wmk. 210- Double Cross on Pyramid

Wmk. 266- Double Barred Cross, Wreath and Crown

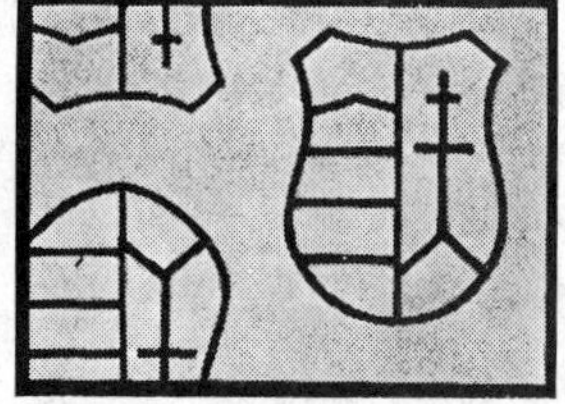

Wmk. 283- Double Barred Cross on Shield, Multiple

Perforations of Nos. 1-12 usually cut into the designs. Well-centered stamps sell at much higher prices.

Issues of the Monarchy

Franz Josef I — A1

1871 Unwmk. Litho. *Perf. 9½*

1	A1	2k orange	160.00	80.00
a.		2k yellow	600.00	150.00
2	A1	3k lt green	425.00	300.00
3	A1	5k rose	150.00	20.00
a.		5k brick red	500.00	45.00
4	A1	10k blue	400.00	95.00
a.		10k pale blue	400.00	100.00
5	A1	15k yellow brn	475.00	125.00
6	A1	25k violet	450.00	125.00
a.		25k bright violet	550.00	200.00

The first printing of No. 1, in dark yellow, was not issued because of spots on the King's face. A few copies were used at Pest in 1873.

1871-72 Engr.

7	A1	2k orange	30.00	8.50
a.		2k yellow	175.00	18.00
b.		Bisect on cover		*425.00*
8	A1	3k green	37.50	20.00
a.		3k blue green	50.00	22.50
9	A1	5k rose	30.00	2.00
a.		5k brick red	100.00	11.00

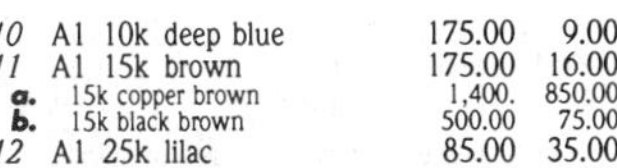
10 A1 10k deep blue 175.00 9.00
11 A1 15k brown 175.00 16.00
a. 15k copper brown 1,400. 850.00
b. 15k black brown 500.00 75.00
12 A1 25k lilac 85.00 35.00

Reprints are perf. 11½ and watermarked "kr" in oval. Value, set $300.

Crown of St. Stephen
A2 A3

Design A3 has an overall burelage of dots.

1874-76 ***Perf. 12½ to 13½***

13 A2 2k rose lilac 22.50 1.50
14 A2 3k yellow green 25.00 1.50
a. 3k blue green 32.50 1.50
15 A2 5k rose 12.50 25
a. 5k dull red 27.50 95
16 A2 10k blue 50.00 1.00
17 A2 20k slate 350.00 7.00

Perf. 11½ and Compound

13a A2 2k rose lilac 57.50 3.00
14b A2 3k yellow green 40.00 5.75
c. 3k blue green 40.00 5.75
d. Perf. 9½ *750.00* *425.00*
15b A2 5k rose 30.00 70
c. 5k dull red 35.00 70
d. Perf. 9½ *290.00* *190.00*
16a A2 10k blue 70.00 2.75
17a A2 20k slate 775.00 40.00

Perf. 11½, 12x11½

1881 **Wmk. 132**

18 A2 2k violet 1.75 25
a. 2k rose lilac 1.75 25
b. 2k slate 8.50 42
19 A2 3k blue green 1.65 15
20 A2 5k rose 10.00 15
21 A2 10k blue 5.00 32
22 A2 20k slate 8.50 65

Perf. 12½ to 13½ and Compound

18c A2 2k violet 85.00 4.00
19a A2 3k blue green 62.50 1.40
20a A2 5k rose 60.00 1.40
21a A2 10k blue 42.50 1.75
22b A2 20k slate 425.00 8.50

1888-98 Typo. ***Perf. 11½, 12x11½***

Numerals in Black

22A A3 1k black, one plate 90 20
c. "1" printed separately 9.50 1.05
23 A3 2k red violet 90 32
a. Perf. 11½ 50.00 3.50
24 A3 3k green 1.40 38
a. Perf. 11½ *27.50* 1.75
25 A3 5k rose 1.65 15
a. Perf. 11½ 27.50 1.40
26 8k orange 4.50 25
a. "8" double *62.50*
27 A3 10k blue 4.00 65
a. Perf. 11½ 125.00 87.50
28 A3 12k brown & green 6.50 25
29 A3 15k claret & blue 6.25 15
30 A3 20k gray 7.00 2.25
a. Perf. 11½ 250.00 160.00
31 A3 24k brn vio & red 14.00 35
32 A3 30k ol grn & brn 14.00 15
33 A3 50k red & org 24.00 60

Numerals in Red

34 A3 1fo gray bl & sil 150.00 1.50
a. Perf. 11½ 165.00 1.75
35 A3 3fo lilac brn & gold 17.50 6.00

Most of Nos. 22A to 103 exist imperforate, but were never so issued.

Perf. 12x11½, 11½

1898-99 **Wmk. 135**

Numerals in Black

35A A3 1k black 75 18
36 A3 2k violet 4.00 18
37 A3 3k green 3.75 18
38 A3 5k rose 2.75 15
39 A3 8k orange 11.00 1.75
40 A3 10k blue 4.00 35
41 A3 12k red brn & grn 57.50 2.00
a. Perf. 11½ 125.00 19.00
42 A3 15k rose & blue 3.50 28
43 A3 20k gray 10.00 1.10
a. Perf. 11½ 140.00 14.50
44 A3 24k vio brn & red 5.00 1.20
a. Perf. 11½ 175.00 45.00
45 A3 30k ol grn & brn 4.50 1.25
a. Perf. 11½ 65.00 19.00
46 A3 50k dull red & org 9.50 4.50
a. Perf. 11½ *225.00* *55.00*
Nos. 35A-46 (12) 116.25 13.12

In the watermark with circles, a four-pointed star and "VI" appear four times in the sheet in the large spaces between the intersecting circles. The paper with the circular watermark is often yellowish and thinner than that with the oval watermark and sell for much higher prices.

See note after No. 35.

"Turul" and Crown of St. Stephen — A4

Franz Josef I Wearing Hungarian Crown — A5

1900-04 **Wmk. 135**

Numerals in Black

47 A4 1f gray 42 35
a. 1f dull lilac 55 35
48 A4 2f olive yel 42 15
49 A4 3f orange 45 22
50 A4 4f violet 45 15
a. Booklet pane of 6 60.00
51 A4 5f emerald 4.25 15
a. Booklet pane of 6 35.00
52 A4 6f claret 50 18
a. 6f violet brown 50 18
53 A4 6f bister ('01) 10.00 70
54 A4 6f olive grn ('04) 3.75 40
55 A4 10f carmine 3.50 15
a. Booklet pane of 6 35.00
56 A4 12f violet ('04) 2.25 35
57 A4 20f brown ('01) 2.75 28
58 A4 25f blue 1.65 28
a. Booklet pane of 6 60.00
59 A4 30f orange brn 25.00 22
60 A4 35f red vio ('01) 10.50 18
a. Booklet pane of 6 70.00
61 A4 50f lake 9.50 90
62 A4 60f green 50.00 42
a. Perf. 11½ 200.00 15.00
63 A5 1k brown red 32.50 55
a. Perf. 11½ 35.00 2.00
64 A5 2k gray blue ('01) 175.00 7.00
a. Perf. 11½ 225.00 45.00
65 A5 3k sea green 25.00 2.50
66 A5 5k vio brown ('01) 30.00 10.00
a. Perf. 11½ 275.00 125.00
Nos. 47-66 (20) 387.89 25.13

The watermark on Nos. 47 to 66 is always the circular form of Wmk. 135 described in the note following No. 46.

Pairs imperf between of Nos. 47-49, 51 were favor prints made for an influential Budapest collector. Value, $45 each.

For overprints and surcharges see Nos. B35-B52, 2N1-2N3, 6N1-6N6, 6NB127N1-7N6, 7NB1, 10N1.

See note after No. 35.

1908-13 **Wmk. 136** ***Perf. 15***

67 A4 1f slate 35 15
68 A4 2f olive yellow 20 15
69 A4 3f orange 30 15
70 A4 5f emerald 15 15
c. Booklet pane of 6
71 A4 6f olive green 25 15
72 A4 10f carmine 15 15
c. Booklet pane of 6
73 A4 12f violet 65 18
74 A4 16f gray green ('13) 38 35
75 A4 20f dark brown 2.50 15
76 A4 25f blue 2.10 15
77 A4 30f orange brown 1.75 15
78 A4 35f red violet 3.50 15
79 A4 50f lake 70 25
80 A4 60f green 2.10 15
81 A5 1k brown red 5.50 15
82 A5 2k gray blue 42.50 55
83 A5 5k violet brown 60.00 7.00
Nos. 67-83 (17) 123.08 10.13

See note after No. 35.

1904-05 **Wmk. 136a** ***Perf. 12x11½***

67a A4 1f slate 95 85
68a A4 2f olive yellow 3.50 18
69a A4 3f orange 52 35
70a A4 5f emerald 1.90 15
71a A4 6f olive green 1.40 20
72a A4 10f carmine 4.00 15
73a A4 12f violet 1.65 1.40
75a A4 20f dark brown 9.50 55
76a A4 25f blue 19.00 42
77a A4 30f orange brown 4.50 22
78a A4 35f red violet 15.00 28
79a A4 50f lake 13.00 2.50
c. 50f magenta 65 90
80a A4 60f green 190.00 90
81a A5 1k brown red 125.00 1.40
82a A5 2k gray blue *350.00* 40.00
c. Perf. 11½ *425.00* 52.50
83a A5 5k violet brown 140.00 50.00

1906 ***Perf. 15***

67b A4 1f slate 1.00 35
68b A4 2f olive yellow 42 15
69b A4 3f orange 90 15
70b A4 5f emerald 42 15
71b A4 6f olive green 1.00 15
72b A4 10f carmine 1.00 15
73b A4 12f violet 1.75 18
75b A4 20f dark brown 3.50 22
76b A4 25f blue 2.50 18
77b A4 30f orange brown 3.25 15
78b A4 35f red violet 19.00 15
79b A4 50f lake 1.90 30
80b A4 60f green 30.00 35
81b A5 1k brown red 30.00 55
82b A5 2k gray blue 105.00 6.50
Nos. 67b-82b (15) 201.64 9.68

1913-16 **Wmk. 137 Vert.** ***Perf. 15***

84 A4 1f slate 25 18
85 A4 2f olive yellow 15 15
86 A4 3f orange 15 15
87 A4 5f emerald 40 15
88 A4 6f olive green 15 15
89 A4 10f carmine 15 15
90 A4 12f violet, *yel* 18 15
91 A4 16f gray green 28 28
92 A4 20f dark brown 22 15
93 A4 25f ultra 22 15
94 A4 30f orange brown 22 15
95 A4 35f red violet 22 15
96 A4 50f lake, *blue* 28 18
a. Cliché of 35f in plate of 50f 165.00 165.00
97 A4 60f green 3.50 1.75
98 A4 60f green, *salmon* 70 15
99 A4 70f red brn, *grn* ('16) 22 15
100 A4 80f dull violet ('16) 22 15
101 A5 1k dull red 1.05 15
102 A5 2k dull blue 3.50 28
103 A5 5k violet brown 10.00 3.50
Nos. 84-103 (20) 22.06
Set value 7.20

See note after No. 35.

For overprints and surcharges see Nos. 2N1-2N3, 6N1-6N6, 6NB127N1-7N6, 7NB1, 10N1.

Wmk. 137 Horiz.

84a A4 1f slate 1.05 1.05
85a A4 2f olive yellow 2.50 1.05
87a A4 5f emerald 70 52
88a A4 6f olive green 90 52
89b A4 10f carmine 1.05 28
90a A4 12f violet, *yellow* 3.25 35
92a A4 20f dark brown 7.75 42
94a A4 30f orange brown 52.50 28
95a A4 35f red violet 175.00 70
96b A4 50f lake, *blue* 15.00 11.50
97a A4 60f green 2.25 2.10
98a A4 60f green, *salmon* 2.00 28
101a A5 1k dull red 22.50 42
102a A5 2k dull blue 125.00 2.10

A5a

1916, July 1 ***Perf. 15***

103A A5a 10f violet brown 50

Although issued as a postal savings stamp, No. 103A was also valid for postage. Used value is for postal usage.

For overprints and surcharges see Nos. 2N59, 5N23, 6N50, 8N13, 10N42.

Queen Zita — A6

Charles IV — A7

1916, Dec. 30

104 A6 10f violet 40 25
105 A7 15f red 40 25

Coronation of King Charles IV and Queen Zita on Dec. 30, 1916.

Harvesting (White Numerals) — A8

1916

106 A8 10f rose 20 15
107 A8 15f violet 20 15
Set value 15

For overprints and surcharges see Nos. B56-B57, 2N4-2N5, 5N1.

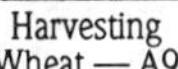
Harvesting Wheat — A9

Parliament Building at Budapest — A10

1916-18 ***Perf. 15***

108 A9 2f brown orange 15 15
109 A9 3f red lilac 15 15
110 A9 4f slate gray ('18) 15 15
111 A9 5f green 15 15
112 A9 6f grnsh blue 15 15
113 A9 10f rose red 35 15
114 A9 15f violet 15 15
115 A9 20f gray brown 15 15
116 A9 25f dull blue 15 15
117 A9 35f brown 15 15
118 A9 40f olive green 15 15

Perf. 14

119 A10 50f red vio & lil 15 15
120 A10 75f brt bl & pale bl 15 15
121 A10 80f grn & pale grn 15 15
122 A10 1k red brn & cl 15 15
123 A10 2k ol brn & bis 15 15
124 A10 3k dk vio & ind 32 15
125 A10 5k dk brn & lt brn 35 15
126 A10 10k vio brn & vio 65 16
Set value 3.00 1.10

See Nos. 335-377, 388-396. For overprints and surcharges see Nos. 153, 167, C1-C5, J76-J99, 1N1-1N21, 1N26-1N30, 1N33, 1N36-1N39, 2N6-2N27, 2N33-2N38, 2N41, 2N43-2N48, 4N1-4N4, 5N2-5N17, 6N7-6N24, 6N29-6N39, 7N7-7N30, 7N38, 7N41-7N42, 8N1-8N4, 9N1-9N2, 9N4, 10N2-10N16, 10N25-10N29, 10N31, 10N33-10N41, Szeged 1-15, 20-24, 27, 30, 32-33.

During 1921-24 various stamps then current were punched with three holes forming a triangle. These were sold at post offices and collectors and dealers who wanted them unpunched would have to purchase them through the philatelic agency at a 10% advance over face value.

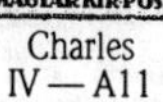

Charles IV — A11

Queen Zita — A12

1918 *Perf. 15*

No.	Type	Description	Unused	Used
127	A11	10f scarlet	15	15
128	A11	15f deep violet	16	15
129	A11	20f dark brown	15	15
130	A11	25f brt blue	15	15
131	A12	40f olive green	15	15
132	A12	50f lilac	15	15
		Set value	50	45

For overprints see Nos. 168-173, 1N32, 1N34-1N35, 2N28-2N32, 2N39-2N40, 2N42, 2N49-2N51, 5N18-5N22, 6N25-6N28, 6N40-6N43, 7N31-7N37, 7N39-7N40, 8N5, 9N3, 10N17-10N21, 10N30, 10N32, Szeged 16-19, 25-26, 28-29, 31.

Issues of the Republic

Hungarian Stamps of 1916-18 Overprinted in Black

1918-19 **Wmk. 137** *Perf. 15, 14*

On Stamps of 1916-18

No.	Type	Description	Unused	Used
153	A9	2f brown orange	15	15
154	A9	3f red lilac	15	15
155	A9	4f slate gray	15	15
156	A9	5f green	15	15
157	A9	6f grnsh blue	15	15
158	A9	10f rose red	15	15
159	A9	20f gray brown	22	22
162	A9	40f olive green	15	15
163	A10	1k red brn & claret	15	15
164	A10	2k ol brn & bis	15	15
165	A10	3k dk violet & ind	20	20
166	A10	5k dk brn & lt brn	75	60
167	A10	10k vio brn & vio	80	80

On Stamps of 1918

No.	Type	Description	Unused	Used
168	A11	10f scarlet	15	15
169	A11	15f deep violet	15	15
170	A11	20f dark brown	15	15
171	A11	25f brt blue	20	20
172	A12	40f olive green	20	20
173	A12	50f lilac	22	22
		Set value	3.30	3.10

Nos. 153-162, 168-173 exist with overprint inverted. Vaue, each $1.

A13

A14

1919-20 *Perf. 15*

No.	Type	Description	Unused	Used
174	A13	2f brown orange	15	15
176	A13	4f slate gray	15	15
177	A13	5f yellow grn	15	15
178	A13	6f grnsh blue	15	15
179	A13	10f red	15	15
180	A13	15f violet	15	15
181	A13	20f dark brown	15	15
182	A13	20f green ('20)	15	15
183	A13	25f dull blue	15	15
184	A13	40f olive green	15	15
185	A13	40f rose red ('20)	15	15
186	A13	45f orange	15	15

Perf. 14

No.	Type	Description	Unused	Used
187	A14	50f brn vio & pale vio	15	15
188	A14	60f brown & bl ('20)	15	15
189	A14	95f dk bl & bl	15	15
190	A14	1k red brn	15	15
191	A14	1k dk bl & dull bl ('20)	15	15
192	A14	1.20k dk grn & grn	15	15
193	A14	1.40k yellow green	15	15
194	A14	2k ol brn & bis	15	15
195	A14	3k dk vio & ind	15	15
196	A14	5k dk brn & brn	15	15
197	A14	10k vio brn & red vio	50	55
		Set value	1.70	1.80

The 3f red lilac, type A13, was never regularly issued without overprint (Nos. 204 and 312). In 1923 a small quantity was sold by the Government at public auction. Value $2.50.

For overprints see Nos. 203-222, 306-330, 1N40, 2N52-2N58, 6N44-6N49, 8N6-8N12, 10N22-10N24, Szeged 34-35.

Issues of the Soviet Republic

Karl Marx — A15

Sándor Petőfi — A16

Ignác Martinovics A17

György Dózsa A18

Friedrich Engels — A19

Wmk. 137 Horiz.

1919, June 14 **Litho.** *Perf. 12½x12*

No.	Type	Description	Unused	Used
198	A15	20f rose & brown	26	40
199	A16	45f brn org & dk grn	26	40
200	A17	60f blue gray & brn	65	90
201	A18	75f claret & vio brn	70	1.10
202	A19	80f olive db & blk brn	65	90
		Nos. 198-202 (5)	2.52	3.70

The 3f red lilac, type A13, was never regularly issued without overprint (Nos. 204 and 312). In 1923 a small quantity was sold by the Government at public auction. Value $2.50. Values are for favor cancels.

Wmk. Vertical

No.	Type	Description	Unused
198a	A15	20f	2.25
199a	A16	45f	4.75
200a	A17	60f	2.25
201a	A18	75f	2.25
202a	A19	80f	27.50
		Nos. 198a-202a (5)	39.00

Nos. 198a-202a were not used postally.

Stamps of 1919 Overprinted in Red

MAGYAR
TANÁCS-
KÖZTÁRSASÁG.

1919, July 21 **Typo.** *Perf. 15*

No.	Type	Description	Unused	Used
203	A13	2f brown orange	15	15
204	A13	3f red lilac	15	15
205	A13	4f slate gray	15	15
206	A13	5f yellow green	15	15
207	A13	6f grnsh blue	15	15
208	A13	10f red	15	15
209	A13	15f violet	15	15
210	A13	20f dark brown	15	15
211	A13	25f dull blue	15	15
212	A13	40f olive green	15	15
213	A13	45f orange	15	15

Overprinted in Red

MAGYAR
TANÁCSKÖZTÁRSASÁG

Perf. 14

No.	Type	Description	Unused	Used
214	A14	50f brn vio & pale vio	15	15
215	A14	95f dk blue & blue	15	15
216	A14	1k red brown	15	15
217	A14	1.20k dk grn & grn	15	15
218	A14	1.40k yellow green	15	15
219	A14	2k ol brn & bister	28	28
220	A14	3k dk vio & ind	28	28
221	A14	5k dk brn & brn	35	35
222	A14	10k vio brn & red vio	60	60
		Set value	2.50	2.50

"Magyar Tanacsköztarsasag" on Nos. 198 to 222 means "Hungarian Soviet Republic."

Issues of the Kingdom

Stamps of 1919 Overprinted in Black

A nemzeti
hadsereg
bevonulása.
1919. XI/16.

1919, Nov. 16

No.	Type	Description	Unused	Used
306	A13	5f green	50	50
307	A13	10f rose red	50	50
308	A13	15f violet	50	50
309	A13	20f gray brown	50	50
310	A13	25f dull blue	50	50
		Nos. 306-310 (5)	2.50	2.50

Issued to commemorate the Romanian evacuation. The overprint reads: "Entry of the National Army-November 16, 1919".

Nos. 203 to 213 Overprinted in Black

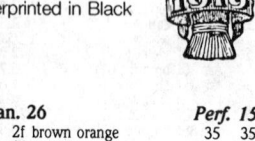

1920, Jan. 26 *Perf. 15*

No.	Type	Description	Unused	Used
311	A13	2f brown orange	35	35
312	A13	3f red lilac	15	15
313	A13	4f slate gray	35	35
314	A13	5f yellow green	15	15
315	A13	6f blue green	15	15
316	A13	10f red	15	15
317	A13	15f violet	15	15
318	A13	20f dark brown	15	15
319	A13	25f dull blue	15	15
320	A13	40f olive green	45	45
321	A13	45f orange	45	45

Nos. 214 to 222 Overprinted in Black

Perf. 14

No.	Type	Description	Unused	Used
322	A14	50f brn vio & pale vio	45	45
323	A14	95f dk bl & bl	45	45
324	A14	1k red brown	45	45
325	A14	1.20k dk grn & grn	1.10	1.10
326	A14	1.40k yellow green	1.10	1.10
327	A14	2k ol brn & bis	1.65	1.65
328	A14	3k dk vio & ind	1.65	1.65
329	A14	5k dk brn & brn	35	35
330	A14	10k vio brn & red vio	2.50	2.50
		Nos. 311-330 (20)	12.35	12.35

Counterfeit overprints exist.

Types of 1916-18 Issue Denomination Tablets Without Inner Frame on Nos. 350 to 363

1920-24 **Wmk. 137** *Perf. 15*

No.	Type	Description	Unused	Used
335	A9	5f brown orange	15	15
336	A9	10f red violet	15	15
337	A9	40f rose red	15	15
338	A9	50f yellow green	15	15
339	A9	50f blue vio ('22)	15	15
340	A9	60f black	15	15
341	A9	1k green ('22)	15	15
342	A9	1½k brown vio ('22)	15	15
343	A9	2k grnsh blue ('22)	15	15
344	A9	2½k dp green ('22)	15	15
345	A9	3k brown org ('22)	15	15
346	A9	4k lt red ('22)	15	15
347	A9	4½k dull violet ('22)	32	15
348	A9	5k deep brown ('22)	15	15
349	A9	6k dark blue ('22)	16	15
350	A9	10k brown ('23)	15	15
351	A9	15k slate ('23)	15	15
352	A9	20k red vio ('23)	15	15
353	A9	25k orange ('23)	15	15
354	A9	40k gray grn ('23)	15	15
355	A9	50k dark blue ('23)	15	15
356	A9	100k claret ('23)	15	15
357	A9	150k dark green ('23)	15	15
358	A9	200k green ('23)	15	15
359	A9	300k rose red ('24)	15	15
360	A9	350k violet ('23)	32	15
361	A9	500k dark gray ('24)	35	15
362	A9	600k olive bis ('24)	35	16
363	A9	800k org yel ('24)	60	20

Perf. 14

No.	Type	Description	Unused	Used
364	A10	2.50k bl & gray bl	15	15
365	A10	3.50k gray	15	15
366	A10	10k brown ('22)	15	15
367	A10	15k dk gray ('22)	15	15
368	A10	20k red vio ('22)	15	15
369	A10	25k orange ('22)	15	15
370	A10	30k claret ('22)	15	15
371	A10	40k gray grn ('22)	15	15
372	A10	50k dp blue ('22)	15	15
373	A10	100k yel brn ('22)	15	15
374	A10	400k turq bl ('23)	48	28
375	A10	500k brt vio ('23)	40	15
376	A10	1000k lilac ('24)	40	15
377	A10	2000k car ('24)	1.40	20
		Set value	7.00	3.00

Nos. 372 to 377 have colored numerals.

Madonna and Child — A23

1921-25 **Typo.** *Perf. 12*

No.	Type	Description	Unused	Used
378	A23	50k dk brn & bl	48	20
379	A23	100k ol bis & yel brn	80	40

Wmk. 133

No.	Type	Description	Unused	Used
380	A23	200k dk bl & ultra	32	18
381	A23	500k vio brn & vio	40	22
382	A23	1000k vio & red vio	40	30
383	A23	2000k grnsh bl & vio	42	45
384	A23	2500k ol brn & buff	52	35
385	A23	3000k brn red & vio	65	35
386	A23	5000k dk grn & yel grn	65	35
a.		Center inverted	*6,000.*	*4,000.*
387	A23	10000k gray vio & pale bl	1.65	1.25
		Nos. 378-387 (10)	6.29	4.05

Issue dates: 50k, 100k, Feb. 27, 1921, 2500k, 10,000k, 1925, others, 1923.

Types of 1916-18 Denomination Tablets Without Inner Frame on Nos. 388-394

1924 **Wmk. 133** *Perf. 15*

No.	Type	Description	Unused	Used
388	A9	100k claret	45	28
389	A9	200k yellow grn	22	15
390	A9	300k rose red	22	15
391	A9	400k deep blue	22	15
392	A9	500k dark gray	22	18
393	A9	600k olive bister	22	22
a.		"800" in upper right corner	140.00	140.00
394	A9	800k org yel	48	35

Perf. 14½x14

No.	Type	Description	Unused	Used
395	A10	1000k lilac	75	18
396	A10	2000k carmine	95	28
		Nos. 388-396 (9)	3.73	1.94

Nos. 395 and 396 have colored numerals.

Maurus Jókai (1825-1904), Novelist — A24

1925, Feb. 1 **Unwmk.** *Perf. 12*

No.	Type	Description	Unused	Used
400	A24	1000k dp grn & blk brn	90	1.65
401	A24	2000k lt brn & blk brn	60	55
402	A24	2500k dk bl & blk brn	90	1.90

Crown of St. Stephen A25

Matthias Cathedral A26

Palace at Budapest — A27

Perf. 14, 15

1926-27 **Wmk. 133** **Litho.**

No.	Type	Description	Unused	Used
403	A25	1f dk gray	20	15
404	A25	2f lt blue	20	15
405	A25	3f orange	20	15
406	A25	4f violet	20	15
407	A25	6f lt green	28	15
408	A25	8f lilac rose	40	15

Typo.

No.	Type	Description	Unused	Used
409	A26	10f deep blue	35	15
410	A26	16f dark violet	35	15
411	A26	20f carmine	35	15
412	A26	25f lt brown	35	18

Perf. 14½x14

No.	Type	Description	Unused	Used
413	A27	32f dp vio & brt vio	1.00	20
414	A27	40f dk blue & blue	1.25	18
		Nos. 403-414 (12)	5.13	
		Set value		1.20

See Nos. 428-436. For surcharges see Nos. 450-456, 466-467.

Madonna and Child — A28

1926-27 Engr. *Perf. 14*

No.	Type	Description	Unused	Used
415	A28	1p violet	14.00	50
416	A28	2p red	7.75	80
417	A28	5p blue ('27)	14.00	2.75

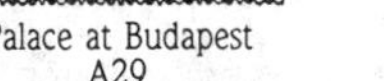

Palace at Budapest A29

St. Stephen A30

1926-27 Typo.

No.	Type	Description	Unused	Used
418	A29	30f blue grn ('27)	1.00	15
419	A29	46f ultra ('27)	1.50	28
420	A29	50f brown blk ('27)	1.00	15
421	A29	70f scarlet	1.50	15

For surcharge see No. 480.

1928-29 Engr. *Perf. 15*

No.	Type	Description	Unused	Used
422	A30	8f yellow grn	42	30
423	A30	8f rose lake ('29)	42	30
424	A30	16f orange red	55	30
425	A30	16f violet ('29)	42	28
426	A30	32f ultra	1.10	1.10
427	A30	32f bister ('29)	1.10	1.10
		Nos. 422-427 (6)	4.01	3.38

890th death anniversary of St. Stephen, the first king of Hungary.

Types of 1926-27 Issue

Perf. 14, 15

1928-30 Typo. Wmk. 210

No.	Type	Description	Unused	Used
428	A25	1f black	24	15
429	A25	2f blue	20	15
430	A25	3f orange	20	15
431	A25	4f violet	20	15
432	A25	6f blue grn	20	15
433	A25	8f lilac rose	24	15
434	A26	10f dp blue ('30)	2.50	15
435	A26	16f violet	50	15
436	A26	20f dull red	38	15
		Nos. 428-436 (9)	4.66	
		Set value		60

On #428-433 the numerals have thicker strokes than on the same values of the 1926-27 issue.

Palace at Budapest — A31

Admiral Nicholas Horthy — A32

Typo A31 resembles A27 but the steamer is nearer the right of the design.

1928-31 *Perf. 14*

No.	Type	Description	Unused	Used
437	A31	30f emerald ('31)	70	20
438	A31	32f red violet	95	32
439	A31	40f deep blue	80	15
440	A31	46f apple green	80	20
441	A31	50f ocher ('31)	80	16
		Nos. 437-441 (5)	4.05	1.03

1930, Mar. 1 Litho. *Perf. 15*

No.	Type	Description	Unused	Used
445	A32	8f myrtle green	1.40	28
446	A32	16f purple	1.40	32
447	A32	20f carmine	3.75	1.05
448	A32	32f olive brown	3.75	3.75
449	A32	40f dull blue	7.00	1.65
		Nos. 445-449 (5)	17.30	7.05

10th anniv. of the election of Adm. Nicholas Horthy as Regent, Mar. 1, 1920.

Stamps of 1926-28 Surcharged

1931, Jan. 1 *Perf. 14, 15*

No.	Type	Description	Unused	Used
450	A25	2f on 3f orange	80	40
451	A25	6f on 8f magenta	80	18
a.		Perf. 14	24.00	24.00
452	A26	10f on 16f violet	65	16

Wmk. 133

No.	Type	Description	Unused	Used
453	A25	2f on 3f orange	3.75	3.00
454	A25	6f on 8f magenta	3.00	3.00
a.		Perf. 14	75.00	75.00
455	A26	10f on 16f dk vio	2.50	1.50
456	A26	20f on 25f lt brn	2.50	1.25
a.		Perf. 14	1.65	1.50
		Nos. 450-456 (7)	14.00	9.49

For surcharges see Nos. 466-467.

St. Elizabeth A33

Ministering to Children A34

Wmk. 210

1932, Apr. 21 Photo. *Perf. 15*

No.	Type	Description	Unused	Used
458	A33	10f ultra	65	30
459	A33	20f scarlet	65	30

Perf. 14

No.	Type	Description	Unused	Used
460	A34	32f deep violet	1.90	2.10
461	A34	40f deep blue	1.50	1.25

700th anniv. of the death of St. Elizabeth of Hungary.

Madonna, Patroness of Hungary — A35

1932, June 1 *Perf. 12*

No.	Type	Description	Unused	Used
462	A35	1p yellow grn	14.00	60
463	A35	2p carmine	14.00	85
464	A35	5p deep blue	57.50	3.50
465	A35	10p olive bister	85.00	37.50

Nos. 451 and 454 Surcharged **2**

1932, June 14 Wmk. 210 *Perf. 15*

No.	Type	Description	Unused	Used
466	A25	2f on 6f on 8f mag	1.50	40

Wmk. 133

No.	Type	Description	Unused	Used
467	A25	2f on 6f on 8f mag	35.00	35.00

Imre Madách — A36

Designs: 2f, Janos Arany. 4f, Dr. Ignaz Semmelweis. 6f, Baron Roland Eotvos. 10f, Count Stephen Szechenyi. 16f, Ferenc Deak. 20f, Franz Liszt. 30f, Louis Kossuth. 32f, Stephen Tisza. 40f, Mihaly Munkacsy. 50f, Alexander Csoma. 70f, Farkas Bolyai.

1932 Wmk. 210 *Perf. 15*

No.	Type	Description	Unused	Used
468	A36	1f slate violet	15	18
469	A36	2f orange	15	15
470	A36	4f ultra	15	15
471	A36	6f yellow grn	15	15
472	A36	10f Prus green	15	15
473	A36	16f dull violet	25	22
474	A36	20f deep rose	15	15
475	A36	30f brown	45	15
476	A36	32f brown vio	70	45
477	A36	40f dull blue	70	15
478	A36	50f deep green	1.10	15
479	A36	70f cerise	1.50	18
		Nos. 468-479 (12)	5.60	
		Set value		1.75
		Set, never hinged	7.50	

Issued in honor of famous Hungarians. See Nos. 509-510.

No. 421 Surcharged

1933, Apr. 15 Wmk. 133 *Perf. 14*

No.	Type	Description	Unused	Used
480	A29	10f on 70f scarlet	40	20
		Never hinged	50	

Leaping Stag and Double Cross — A47

Wmk. 210

1933, July 10 Photo. *Perf. 15*

No.	Type	Description	Unused	Used
481	A47	10f dk green	90	1.00
482	A47	16f violet brn	2.50	2.25
483	A47	20f car lake	1.65	1.25
484	A47	32f yellow	3.75	4.00
485	A47	40f deep blue	3.75	4.00
		Nos. 481-485 (5)	12.55	12.50
		Set, never hinged	16.50	

Boy Scout Jamboree at Gödöllö, Hungary, July 20 - Aug. 20, 1933.

Souvenir Sheet

Franz Liszt A48

1934, May 6 *Perf. 15*

No.	Type	Description	Unused	Used
486	A48	20f lake	50.00	40.00
		Never hinged	75.00	

2nd Hungarian Phil. Exhib., Budapest, and Jubilee of the 1st Hungarian Phil. Soc. Sold for 90f, including entrance fee. Size: 64x76mm.

Francis II Rákóczy (1676-1735), Prince of Transylvania — A49

1935, Apr. 8 *Perf. 12*

No.	Type	Description	Unused	Used
487	A49	10f yellow green	60	52
488	A49	16f brt violet	3.00	2.50
489	A49	20f dark carmine	60	52
490	A49	32f brown lake	5.00	4.50
491	A49	40f blue	5.00	4.00
		Nos. 487-491 (5)	14.20	12.04
		Set, never hinged	18.00	

Cardinal Pázmány — A50

Signing the Charter — A51

1935, Sept. 25

No.	Type	Description	Unused	Used
492	A50	6f dull green	1.10	1.00
493	A51	10f dark green	40	40
494	A50	16f slate violet	1.40	1.25
495	A50	20f magenta	40	40
496	A51	32f deep claret	3.00	1.65
497	A51	40f dark blue	2.75	1.65
		Nos. 492-497 (6)	9.05	6.35
		Set, never hinged	10.00	

Tercentenary of the founding of the University of Budapest by Peter Cardinal Pázmány.

Ancient City and Fortress of Buda — A52

Guardian Angel over Buda — A53

Shield of Buda, Cannon and Massed Flags — A54

First Hungarian Soldier to Enter Buda A55

1936, Sept. 2 *Perf. 11½x12½*

No.	Type	Description	Unused	Used
498	A52	10f dark green	55	32
499	A53	16f deep violet	2.25	2.00
500	A54	20f car lake	55	32
501	A55	32f dark brown	2.50	2.50
502	A52	40f deep blue	2.50	2.50
		Nos. 498-502 (5)	8.35	7.64
		Set, never hinged	12.00	

250th anniv. of the recapture of Budapest from the Turks.

Catalogue values for unused stamps in this section, from this point to the end of the section, are for Never Hinged items.

Budapest International Fair — A56

1937, Feb. 22 *Perf. 12*

No.	Type	Description	Unused	Used
503	A56	2f deep orange	15	18
504	A56	6f yellow green	25	18
505	A56	10f myrtle green	30	18
506	A56	20f deep cerise	50	28
507	A56	32f dark violet	1.00	70
508	A56	40f ultra	1.25	70
		Nos. 503-508 (6)	3.45	2.22

Portrait Type of 1932

Designs: 5f, Ferenc Kolcsey. 25f, Mihaly Vorosmarty.

1937, May 5 *Perf. 15*

No.	Type	Description	Unused	Used
509	A36	5f brown orange	15	15
510	A36	25f olive green	45	20

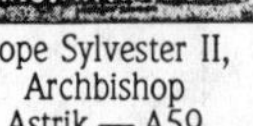
Pope Sylvester II, Archbishop Astrik — A59

Admiral Horthy — A67

Designs: 2f, 16f, Stephen the Church builder. 4f, 20f, St. Stephen enthroned. 5f, 25f, Sts. Gerhardt, Emerich, Stephen. 6f, 30f, St. Stephen offering holy crown to Virgin Mary. 10f, same as 1f. 32f, 50f, Portrait of St. Stephen. 40f, Madonna and Child. 70f, Crown of St. Stephen.

1938, Jan. 1 *Perf. 12*

No.	Type	Value / Color	Unused	Used
511	A59	1f deep violet	18	22
512	A59	2f olive brown	15	15
513	A59	4f brt blue	38	15
514	A59	5f magenta	42	28
515	A59	6f dp yel grn	38	18
516	A59	10f red orange	42	15
517	A59	16f gray violet	75	52
518	A59	20f car lake	55	15
519	A59	25f dark green	1.10	52
520	A59	30f olive bister	1.65	18
521	A59	32f dp claret, *buff*	2.25	1.05
522	A59	40f Prus green	1.65	18
523	A59	50f rose vio, *grnsh*	2.25	32
524	A59	70f ol grn, *bluish*	2.50	42
		Nos. 511-524 (14)	14.63	4.47

900th anniv. of the death of St. Stephen.
For overprints see Nos. 535-536.

1938, Jan. 1 *Perf. 12½x12*

No.	Type	Value / Color	Unused	Used
525	A67	1p peacock green	1.10	15
526	A67	2p brown	1.90	25
527	A67	5p sapphire blue	6.75	1.75

Souvenir Sheet

St. Stephen — A68

1938, May 22 **Wmk. 210** *Perf. 12*

No.	Type	Value / Color	Unused	Used
528	A68	20f carmine lake	13.00	9.50

3rd Hungarian Phil. Exhib., Budapest. Sheet sold only at exhibition with 1p ticket.

College of Debrecen — A69

Three Students — A71

George Marothy — A73

Designs: 10f, 18th century view of College. 20f, 19th century view of College. 40f, Stephen Hatvani.

Perf. 12x12½, 12½x12

1938, Sept. 24 **Wmk. 210**

No.	Type	Value / Color	Unused	Used
529	A69	6f deep green	15	15
530	A69	10f brown	15	15
531	A71	16f brown car	30	18
532	A69	20f crimson	22	15
533	A73	32f slate green	80	45
534	A73	40f brt blue	90	30
		Nos. 529-534 (6)	2.52	1.38

Founding of Debrecen College, 400th anniv.

Types of 1938 Overprinted in Blue or Carmine:

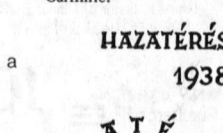

a
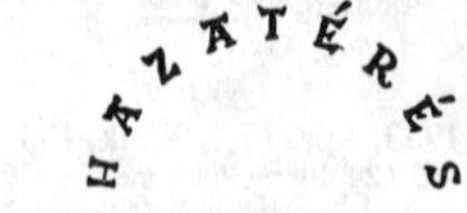

b HAZATÉRÉS 19 38

1938 *Perf. 12*

No.	Type	Value / Color	Unused	Used
535	A59(a)	20f salmon pink (Bl)	70	25
536	A59(b)	70f brn, *grnsh* (C)	80	25

Restoration of the territory ceded by Czechoslovakia.

The 70f exists without overprint. Value, unused, $3500; used, $3000. Forgeries exist.

Crown of St. Stephen A75

St. Stephen A76

Madonna, Patroness of Hungary A77

Coronation Church, Budapest A78

Reformed Church, Debrecen A79

Cathedral, Esztergom A80

Deak Square Evangelical Church, Budapest — A81

Cathedral of Kassa — A82

Wmk. 210

1939, June 1 **Photo.** *Perf. 15*

No.	Type	Value / Color	Unused	Used
537	A75	1f brown car	15	15
538	A75	2f Prus green	15	15
539	A75	4f ocher	15	15
540	A75	5f brown violet	15	15
541	A75	6f yellow green	15	15
542	A75	10f bister brn	15	15
543	A75	16f rose violet	15	15
544	A76	20f rose red	15	15
545	A77	25f blue gray	15	15

Perf. 12

No.	Type	Value / Color	Unused	Used
546	A78	30f red violet	38	15
547	A79	32f brown	35	15
548	A80	40f greenish blue	38	15
549	A81	50f olive	38	15
550	A82	70f henna brown	42	15
		Set value	2.50	85

See #578-596. For overprints see #559-560.

Girl Scout Sign and Olive Branch — A83

Designs: 6f, Scout lily, Hungary's shield, Crown of St. Stephen. 10f, Girls in Scout hat and national headdress. 20f, Dove and Scout emblems.

1939, July 20 **Photo.** *Perf. 12*

No.	Type	Value / Color	Unused	Used
551	A83	2f brown orange	45	42
552	A83	6f green	48	42
553	A83	10f brown	80	42
554	A83	20f lilac rose	1.00	70

Girl Scout Jamboree at Gödöllö.

Admiral Horthy at Szeged, 1919 — A87

Admiral Nicholas Horthy — A88

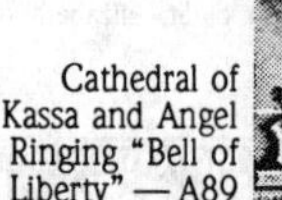

Cathedral of Kassa and Angel Ringing "Bell of Liberty" — A89

1940, Mar. 1

No.	Type	Value / Color	Unused	Used
555	A87	6f green	28	15
556	A88	10f ol blk & ol bis	28	15
557	A89	20f brt rose brown	60	35

20th anniversary of the election of Admiral Horthy as Regent of Hungary.

Crown of St. Stephen — A90

1940, Sept. 5

No.	Type	Value / Color	Unused	Used
558	A90	10f dk green & yellow	18	15

Issued in commemoration of the recovery of northeastern Transylvania from Romania.

Nos. 542, 544 Overprinted in Red or Black DÉL-VISSZATÉR

1941, Apr. 21 *Perf. 15*

No.	Type	Value / Color	Unused	Used
559	A75	10f bister brn (R)	24	15
560	A76	20f rose red (Bk)	24	15
		Set value		24

Return of the Bacska territory from Yugoslavia.

Admiral Nicholas Horthy A92

Wmk. 210

1941, June 18 **Photo.** *Perf. 12*

No.	Type	Value / Color	Unused	Used
570	A92	1p dk green & buff	16	18
571	A92	2p dk brown & buff	35	32
572	A92	5p dk rose vio & buff	1.25	1.40

See Nos. 597-599.

Count Stephen Széchenyi — A93

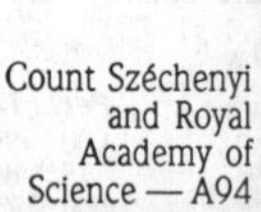

Count Széchenyi and Royal Academy of Science — A94

Representation of the Narrows of Kazán — A95

Chain Bridge, Budapest — A96

Mercury, Train and Boat — A97

1941, Sept. 21

No.	Type	Value / Color	Unused	Used
573	A93	10f dk olive grn	15	15
574	A94	16f olive brown	18	15
575	A95	20f carmine lake	25	16
576	A96	32f red orange	38	25
577	A97	40f royal blue	32	20
		Nos. 573-577 (5)	1.28	91

Count Stephen Szechenyi (1791-1860).

Types of 1939

Perf. 12x12½, 12½x12, 15

1941-43 **Wmk. 266**

No.	Type	Value / Color	Unused	Used
578	A75	1f rose lake ('42)	15	15
579	A75	3f dark brown	15	15
580	A75	5f violet gray ('42)	15	15
581	A75	6f lt green ('42)	15	15
582	A75	8f slate grn	15	15
583	A75	10f olive brn ('42)	15	15
584	A75	12f red orange	15	15
585	A76	20f rose red ('42)	15	15
586	A76	24f brown violet	15	15
587	A78	30f lilac ('42)	15	15
588	A82	30f rose red ('43)	15	15
589	A80	40f blue green ('42)	15	15
590	A79	40f gray black ('43)	15	15
591	A81	50f olive grn ('42)	15	15
592	A80	50f brt blue ('43)	15	15
593	A82	70f copper red ('42)	15	15
594	A81	70f gray green ('43)	15	15
595	A77	80f brown bister	15	15
596	A78	80f bister brn ('43)	18	15
		Set value	1.75	90

Horthy Type of 1941

Perf. 12x12½

1941, Dec. 18 **Wmk. 266**

No.	Type	Value / Color	Unused	Used
597	A92	1p dk green & buff	55	15
598	A92	2p dk brown & buff	20	15
599	A92	5p dk rose vio & buff	48	28
		Set value		50

Stephen Horthy — A98

1942, Oct. 15 *Perf. 12*

No.	Type	Value / Color	Unused	Used
600	A98	20f black	30	20

Death of Stephen Horthy (1904-42), son of Regent Nicholas Horthy, who died in a plane crash.

Arpád — A99

A109

Portraits: 2f, King Ladislaus I. 3f, Miklós Toldi. 4f, János Hunyadi. 5f, Paul Kinizsi. 6f, Count Miklós Zrinyi. 8f, Francis II Rákóczy. 10f, Count Andrew Hadik. 12f, Arthur Görgei. 18f, 24f, Virgin Mary, Patroness of Hungary.

1943-45 *Perf. 15*

601 A99 1f grnsh black 15 15
602 A99 2f red orange 15 15
603 A99 3f ultra 15 15
604 A99 4f brown 15 15
605 A99 5f vermilion 15 15
606 A99 6f slate blue 15 15
607 A99 8f dk ol grn 15 15
608 A99 10f brown 15 15
609 A99 12f dp blue grn 15 15
610 A99 18f dk gray 15 15
611 A109 20f chestnut brn 15 15
612 A99 24f rose violet 15 15
613 A109 30f brt carmine 15 15
614 A109 50f blue 15 15
615 A109 80f yellow brn 15 15
616 A109 1p green 15 15
616A A109 2p brown ('45) 16 15
616B A109 5p dk red violet ('45) 28 28
Set value 1.25 1.25

For overprints and surcharges see Nos. 631-658, 660-661, 664, 666-669, 671-672, 674-677, 679, 680, 682, 685-689, 691-698, 801-803, 805-806, 810-815, F2, Q2-Q3, Q7.

Message to the Shepherds
A110

St. Margaret
A113

Designs: 20f, Nativity. 30f, Adoration of the Magi.

1943, Dec. 1 *Perf. 12x12½*

617 A110 4f dark green 15 18
618 A110 20f dull blue 15 18
619 A110 30f brown orange 15 18

1944, Jan. 19 *Perf. 15*

620 A113 30f deep carmine 15 15

Canonization of St. Margaret of Hungary.
For surcharges see Nos. 662, 673A.

Kossuth with Family
A114

Lajos Kossuth
A117

Honvéd Drummer
A115

Design: 30f, Kossuth orating.

Perf. 12½x12, 12x12½
1944, Mar. 20

621 A114 4f yellow brown 15 15
622 A115 20f dk olive grn 15 15
623 A115 30f henna brown 15 15
624 A117 50f slate blue 15 15
Set value 30 27

Louis (Lajos) Kossuth (1802-94).
For surcharges see Nos. B175-B178.

St. Elizabeth — A118

Portraits: 24f, St. Margaret. 30f, Elizabeth Szilágyi. 50f, Dorothy Kanuizsai. 70f, Susanna Lórántffy. 80f, Ilona Zrinyi.

1944, Aug. 1 *Perf. 15*

625 A118 20f olive 15 15
626 A118 24f rose violet 15 15
627 A118 30f copper red 15 15
628 A118 50f dark blue 15 15
629 A118 70f orange red 15 15
630 A118 80f brown carmine 15 15
Set value 38 44

For overprints and surcharges see Nos. 659, 663, 665, 670, 673, 678, 681, 683-684, 690, 804, 807-809, F1, F3, Q1, Q4-Q6, Q8.

Issues of the Republic

Types of Hungary, 1943 Surcharged in Carmine

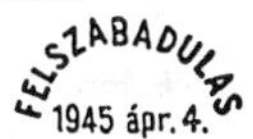

10
fillér

1945, May 1 **Wmk. 266**

Blue Surface-tinted Paper

631 A99 10f on 1f grnsh blk 1.50 1.50
632 A99 20f on 3f ultra 1.50 1.50
633 A99 30f on 4f brown 1.50 1.50
634 A99 40f on 6f slate bl 1.50 1.50
635 A99 50f on 8f dk ol grn 1.50 1.50
636 A99 1p on 10f brown 1.50 1.50
637 A99 150f on 12f dp bl grn 1.50 1.50
638 A99 2p on 18f dk gray 1.50 1.50
639 A109 3p on 20f chnt brn 1.50 1.50
640 A99 5p on 24f rose vio 1.50 1.50
641 A109 6p on 50f blue 1.50 1.50
642 A109 10p on 80f yel brn 1.50 1.50
643 A109 20p on 1p green 1.50 1.50

Yellow Surface-tinted Paper

644 A99 10f on 1f grnsh blk 1.50 1.50
645 A99 20f on 3f ultra 1.50 1.50
646 A99 30f on 4f brown 1.50 1.50
647 A99 40f on 6f slate bl 1.50 1.50
648 A99 50f on 8f dk ol grn 1.50 1.50
649 A99 1p on 10f brown 1.50 1.50
650 A99 150f on 12f dp bl grn 1.50 1.50
651 A99 2p on 18f dk gray 1.50 1.50
652 A109 3p on 20f chnt brn 1.50 1.50
653 A99 5p on 24f rose vio 1.50 1.50
654 A109 6p on 50f blue 1.50 1.50
655 A109 10p on 80f yel brn 1.50 1.50
656 A109 20p on 1p green 1.50 1.50
Nos. 631-656 (26) 39.00 39.00

Hungary's liberation.

Types of Hungary, 1943-45, Surcharged in Carmine or Black

1945
10
fillér

1945

Blue Surface-tinted Paper

657 A99 10f on 4f brn (C) 15 15
658 A99 10f on 10f brn (C) 45 45
659 A118 20f on 20f ol (C) 15 15
660 A99 28f on 5f ver 15 15
661 A109 30f on 30f brt car 15 15
662 A113 30f on 30f dp car 15 15
663 A118 30f on 30f cop red 15 15
664 A99 40f on 10f brown 15 15
665 A118 1p on 70f org red 25 25
666 A109 1p on 80f yel brn (C) 15 15
667 A99 2p on 4f brown 15 15
668 A109 2p on 2p brn (C) 15 15
669 A109 4p on 30f brt car 15 15
670 A118 8p on 20f olive 15 15
671 A99 10p on 2f red org 7.25 7.25
672 A109 10p on 80f yel brn 15 15
673 A118 20p on 30f cop red 15 15

Same Surcharge with Thinner Unshaded Numerals of Value

673A A113 300p on 30f dp car 15 15

Surcharged as Nos. 657-673 Yellow Surface-tinted Paper

674 A99 10f on 12f dp bl grn (C) 15 15
675 A99 20f on 1f grnsh blk (C) 15 15
676 A99 20f on 18f dk gray (C) 15 15
a. Double surcharge

677 A99 40f on 24f rose vio (C) 15 15
678 A118 40f on 24f rose vio (C) 15 15
679 A109 42f on 20f chnt brn (C) 15 15
680 A109 50f on 50f bl (C) 15 15
681 A118 50f on 50f dk bl (C) 15 15
682 A99 60f on 8f dk ol grn (C) 15 15
683 A118 80f on 24f rose vio 20 20
684 A118 80f on 80f brn car (C) 15 15
685 A109 1p on 20f chnt brn 15 15
686 A109 1p on 1p grn (C) 15 15
687 A99 150f on 6f sl bl (C) 90 90
688 A99 1.60p on 12f dp bl grn 15 15
689 A99 3p on 3f ultra (C) 32 32
690 A118 3p on 50f dk bl 15 15
691 A99 5p on 8f dk ol grn 15 15
692 A109 5p on 5p dk red vio (C) 25 25
693 A109 6p on 50f blue 15 15
694 A109 7p on 1p grn 15 15
695 A99 9p on 1f grnsh blk 15 15

Same Surcharge with Thinner, Unshaded Numerals of Value

696 A99 40p on 8f dk ol grn 15 15
697 A99 60p on 18f dk gray 15 15
698 A99 100p on 12f dp bl grn 15 15
Set value, #657-698 11.50 11.50

Various shades and errors of overprint exist on Nos. 657-698.

These surface-tinted stamps exist without surcharge, but were not so issued.

Construction
A124

Designs: 1.60p, Manufacturing. 2p, Railroading. 3p, Building. 5p, Agriculture. 8p, Communications. 10p, Architecture. 20p, Writing.

Wmk. 266
1945, Sept. 11 **Photo.** *Perf. 12*

700 A124 40f gray black 4.50 4.50
701 A124 1.60p olive bis 4.50 4.50
702 A124 2p slate green 4.50 4.50
703 A124 3p dark purple 4.50 4.50
704 A124 5p dark red 4.50 4.50
705 A124 8p brown 4.50 4.50
706 A124 10p deep claret 4.50 4.50
707 A124 20p slate blue 4.50 4.50
Nos. 700-707 (8) 36.00 36.00

World Trade Union Conf., Paris, Sept. 25 to Oct. 10, 1945.

"Reconstruction"
A132

1945-46

708 A132 12p brown olive 24 24
709 A132 20p brt green 15 15
710 A132 24p orange brn 24 24
711 A132 30p gray black 15 15
712 A132 40p olive green 15 15
713 A132 60p red orange 15 15
714 A132 100p orange yel 15 15
715 A132 120p brt ultra 15 15
716 A132 140p brt red 38 38
717 A132 200p olive brn 15 15
718 A132 240p brt blue 15 15
719 A132 300p dk carmine 15 15
720 A132 500p dull green 15 15
721 A132 1000p red violet 15 15
722 A132 3000p brt red ('46) 15 15
Set value 1.80 1.80

Nos. 708 to 721 exist tête bêche. Value: $12.50.

"Liberation"
A133

Postrider
A134

1946, Feb. 12

723 A133 3ez p dark red 15 15
724 A133 15ez p ultra 15 15
Set value 20 20

1946 **Photo.; Values Typo.** *Perf. 15*

725 A134 4ez p brown org 15 15
726 A134 10ez p brt red 15 15
727 A134 15ez p ultra 15 15
728 A134 20ez p dk brown 15 15
729 A134 30ez p red violet 15 15
730 A134 50ez p gray black 15 15
731 A134 80ez p brt ultra 15 15
732 A134 100ez p rose car 15 15
733 A134 160ez p gray green 15 15
734 A134 200ez p yellow grn 15 15
735 A134 500ez p red 15 15
736 A134 640ez p olive bis 15 15
737 A134 800ez p rose violet 15 15
Set value 1.25 1.25

Abbreviations:
Ez (Ezer) = Thousand
Mil (Milpengo) = Million
Mlrd (Milliard) = Billion
Bil (Billio-pengo) = Trillion

Arms of Hungary — A135

1946 **Wmk. 210**

738 A135 1mil p vermilion 15 20
739 A135 2mil p ultra 15 20
740 A135 3mil p brown 15 15
741 A135 4mil p slate gray 15 15
742 A135 5mil p rose violet 15 15
743 A135 10mil p green 15 15
744 A135 20mil p carmine 15 15
745 A135 50mil p olive 15 15

Arms and Post Horn
A136 A137

746 A136 100mil p henna brn 15 15
747 A136 200mil p henna brn 15 15
748 A136 500mil p henna brn 15 15
749 A136 1000mil p henna brn 15 15
750 A136 2000mil p henna brn 15 15
751 A136 3000mil p henna brn 15 15
752 A136 5000mil p henna brn 15 15
753 A136 10,000mil p henna brn 15 15
754 A136 20,000mil p henna brn 15 15
755 A136 30,000mil p henna brn 15 15
756 A136 50,000mil p henna brn 22 28

Denomination in Carmine

757 A137 100mlrd p olive 15 15
758 A137 200mlrd p olive 15 15
759 A137 500mlrd p olive 15 15

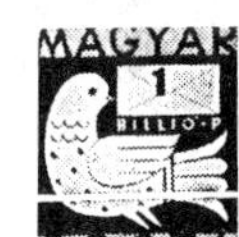

Dove and Letter — A138

Denomination in Carmine

760 A138 1bil p grnsh blk 15 20
761 A138 2bil p grnsh blk 15 20
763 A138 5bil p grnsh blk 15 20
764 A138 10bil p grnsh blk 15 20
765 A138 20bil p grnsh blk 15 20
766 A138 50bil p grnsh blk 15 20
767 A138 100bil p grnsh blk 15 20
768 A138 200bil p grnsh blk 15 20
769 A138 500bil p grnsh blk 15 20
770 A138 1000bil p grnsh blk 15 20
771 A138 10,000bil p grnsh blk 20 20
772 A138 50,000bil p grnsh blk 22 22
773 A138 100,000bil p grnsh blk 22 22
774 A138 500,000bil p grnsh blk 22 22

Denomination in Black

775 A137 5ez ap green 15 15
776 A137 10ez ap green 15 15
777 A137 20ez ap green 15 15
778 A137 50ez ap green 15 15
779 A137 80ez ap green 15 15
780 A137 100ez ap green 15 15
781 A137 200ez ap green 15 15
782 A137 500ez ap green 15 15
783 A137 1mil ap vermilion 15 15
784 A137 5mil ap vermilion 15 15
Set value 5.60 7.00

Denominations are expressed in "ado" or "tax" pengos.

Early Steam Locomotive A139

Designs: 20,000ap, Recent steam locomotive. 30,000ap, Electric locomotive. 40,000ap, Diesel locomotive.

1946, July 15 Wmk. 266 *Perf. 12*

785	A139	10,000ap vio brn	3.00	3.00
786	A139	20,000ap dk blue	3.00	3.00
787	A139	30,000ap dp yel grn	3.00	3.00
788	A139	40,000ap rose car	3.00	3.00

Centenary of Hungarian railways.

Industry A143

Agriculture A144

1946 Wmk. 210 Photo. *Perf. 15*

788A	A143	8f henna brn	15	15
789	A143	10f henna brn	15	15
790	A143	12f henna brn	15	15
791	A143	20f henna brn	15	15
792	A143	30f henna brn	15	15
793	A143	40f henna brn	15	15
794	A143	60f henna brn	16	15
795	A144	1fo dp yel grn	30	15
796	A144	1.40fo dp yel grn	42	15
797	A144	2fo dp yel grn	52	15
798	A144	3fo dp yel grn	4.00	15
799	A144	5fo dp yel grn	1.50	15
800	A144	10fo dp yel grn	3.50	35
		Nos. 788A-800 (13)	11.30	
		Set value		1.10

For surcharges see Nos. Q9-Q11.

Stamps and Types of 1943-45 Overprinted in Carmine or Black to Show Class of Postage for which Valid

"Any." or "Nyomtatv."=Printed Matter.
"Hl" or "Helyi levél"=Local Letter.
"Hlp." or "Helyi lev.-lap"=Local Postcard.
"Tl." or "Távolsági levél"=Domestic Letter.
"Tlp." or "Távolsági lev.-lap"=Domestic Postcard.

a

Nyomtatv
20 gr.
b

1946 Wmk. 266

801	A99(a)	"Any 1." on 1f (#601;C)	15	15
802	A99(a)	"Any 2," on 1f (#601;C)	15	15
803	A99(b)	"Nyomtatv. 20gr" on 60f on 8f (#682;Bk + C)	15	15
804	A118(a)	"Hl. 1" on 50f (#628;C)	15	15
805	A99(a)	"Hl. 2" on 40f on 10f (#664;C + Bk)	15	15
806	A99(b)	"Helyi levél" on 10f brn, *bl* (Bk)	15	15
807	A118(a)	"Hlp.1" on 8p on 20f (#670;C + Bk)	15	15
808	A118(a)	"Hlp.2." on 8p on 20f (#670;C + Bk)	15	15
809	A118(b)	"Helyi lev.-lap" on 20f ol, *bl* (C)	15	15
810	A99(a)	"Tl.1" on 10f (#608;Bk)	15	15
811	A99(a)	"Tl.2." on 10f on 4f (#657;Bk + C)	15	15
812	A99(b)	"Tavolsagi level" on 18f (#610;C)	15	15
813	A99(a)	"Tlp.1." on 4f (#604;Bk)	15	15
814	A99(a)	"Tlp.2." on 4f (#604;Bk)	15	15
815	A99(b)	"Tavolsagi lev.-lap" on 4f (#604;Bk)	15	15
		Set value	90	1.35

Nos. 806 and 809 were not issued without overprint.

György Dózsa — A145

Designs: 10f, Antal Budai-Nagy. 12f, Tamas Esze. 20f, Ignac Martinovics. 30f, Janos Batsanyi. 40f, Lajos Kossuth. 60f, Mihaly Tancsics. 1fo, Alexander Petöfi. 2fo, Andreas Ady. 4fo, Jozsef Attila.

1947, Mar. 15 Photo. Wmk. 210

816	A145	8f rose brown	22	15
817	A145	10f deep ultra	22	15
818	A145	12f deep brown	22	15
819	A145	20f dk yel grn	25	15
820	A145	30f dk ol bis	18	15
821	A145	40f brown car	18	15
822	A145	60f cerise	35	15
823	A145	1fo dp grnsh bl	42	15
824	A145	2fo dk violet	1.10	35
825	A145	4fo grnsh black	1.50	70
		Nos. 816-825 (10)	4.64	
		Set value		1.50

Peace and Agriculture A155

Postal Savings Emblem A156

1947, Sept. 22 *Perf. 12*

826	A155	60f bright red	30	20

Peace treaty.

1947, Oct. 31

Design: 60f, Postal Savings Bank, Budapest.

827	A156	40f rose brown	15	15
828	A156	60f brt rose car	38	15
		Set value		22

Savings Day, Oct. 31, 1947.

Hungarian Flag — A157

1848 Printing Press — A158

Barred Window and Dove — A159

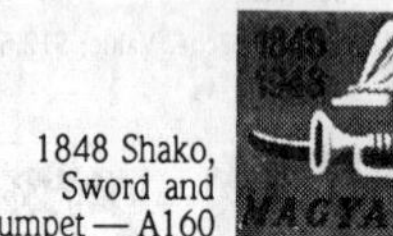

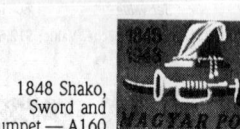

1848 Shako, Sword and Trumpet — A160

"On your feet Hungarian, the Homeland is Calling!" A161

Arms of Hungary A162

Perf. 12½x12, 12x12½

1948 Wmk. 283 Photo.

829	A157	8f dk rose red	24	16
830	A158	10f ultra	24	16
831	A159	12f copper brn	38	24
832	A160	20f deep green	80	15
833	A161	30f olive brown	38	15
834	A157	40f dk vio brn	60	15
835	A161	60f carmine lake	1.00	15
836	A162	1fo brt ultra	1.00	15
837	A162	2fo red brown	1.40	24
838	A162	3fo green	1.65	60
839	A162	4fo scarlet	4.25	80
		Nos. 829-839 (11)	11.94	
		Set value		2.55

Cent. of the beginning of Hungary's war for independence.
#834 is inscribed "Kossuth," #835 "Petofi."

Baron Roland Eötvös — A163

1948, July 27

840	A163	60f deep red	50	25

Centenary of the birth of Roland Eötvös, physicist.

Hungarian Workers — A164

1948, Oct. 17 Wmk. 283 *Perf. 12*

841	A164	30f dk carmine rose	40	30
a.		Sheet of 4	20.00	20.00

The 17th Trade Union Congress, Budapest, October 1948. No. 841a was sold for 2 forint.

Marx Stamp of 1919 and Crowd Carrying Flags — A165

Petöfi Stamp of 1919 and Flags — A166

1949, Mar. 19

Flags in Carmine

842	A165	40f brown	30	25
843	A166	60f olive gray	30	25

1st Hungarian Soviet Republic, 30th anniv.

Workers of the Five Continents and Flag — A167

1949, June 29 *Perf. 12x12½*

Flag in Red

844	A167	30f yellow brown	2.50	2.50
845	A167	40f brown violet	2.50	2.50
846	A167	60f lilac rose	2.50	2.50
847	A167	1fo violet blue	2.50	2.50

2nd Congress of the World Federation of Trade Unions, Milan, 1949.

Sándor Petöfi — A168

Youth of Three Races — A169

Perf. 12½x12

1949, July 31 Engr. Unwmk.

848	A168	40f claret	30	30
849	A168	60f dark red	22	15
850	A168	1fo deep blue	30	16

Cent. of the death of Sándor Petöfi, poet.
See Nos. 867-869.

Perf. 12½x12

1949, Aug. 14 Photo. Wmk. 283

Designs: 30f, Three fists. 40f, Soldier breaking chain. 60f, Soviet youths carrying flags. 1fo, Young workers displaying books.

851	A169	20f dk violet brn	70	70
a.		20f blue green	2.25	2.25
852	A169	30f blue green	80	80
a.		30f violet brown	2.25	2.25
853	A169	40f olive bister	1.00	1.00
a.		40f ultramarine	2.25	2.25
854	A169	60f rose pink	1.00	1.00
855	A169	1fo ultra	1.50	1.50
a.		1fo olive bister	2.75	2.75
b.		Souv. sheet of 5, #851a-855a	25.00	22.50
		Nos. 851-855 (5)	5.00	5.00

World Festival of Youth and Students, Budapest, Aug. 14-28, 1949.

Arms of Hungarian People's Republic — A170

1949 Wmk. 283

Arms in Bister, Carmine Blue and Green

856	A170	20f green	85	48
857	A170	60f carmine	35	20
858	A170	1fo blue	85	55

Adoption of the Hungarian People's Republic constitution. Nos. 856-858 also exist unwatermarked; same values as watermarked.

Imperforates

Nearly all Hungarian stamps from No. 859 on were issued imperforate as well as with perforations. In most cases the imperforate quantities were smaller than the perforated ones. The imperforates were sold at five times face value, and all issued before Feb. 22, 1958, were invalid. Late in 1958, Philatelica Hungarica started selling the imperforates at four to six times face value.

Symbols of the UPU — A171

1949, Nov. 1 *Perf. 12x12½*

859	A171	60f rose red	15	15
a.		Booklet pane of 6	2.50	
860	A171	1fo blue	30	30
a.		Booklet pane of 6	4.00	

75th anniv. of the UPU.

Nos. 859 and 860 exist imperf. and stamps from 859a and 860a in horiz. pairs, imperf. between.
See Nos. C63, C81.

Chain Bridge — A172

1949, Nov. 20 **Wmk. 283**

861 A172 40f blue green	15	15
862 A172 60f red brown	18	18
863 A172 1fo blue	24	24
Nos. 861-863,C64-C65 (5)	2.07	2.07

Cent. of the opening of the Chain Bridge at Budapest to traffic. For souvenir sheet see No. C66.

Joseph V. Stalin — A173

Perf. 12½x12

1949, Dec. 21 **Engr.** **Unwmk.**

864 A173 60f dark red	42	15
865 A173 1fo deep blue	48	32
866 A173 2fo brown	90	65

70th anniv. of the birth of Joseph V. Stalin. See Nos. 1034-1035.

Petőfi Type of 1949

1950, Feb. 5 *Perf. 12½x12*

867 A168 40f brown	15	15
868 A168 60f dark carmine	24	18
869 A168 1fo dark green	65	28

Philatelic Museum, Budapest A174

Perf. 12x12½

1950, Mar. 12 **Photo.** **Wmk. 283**

870 A174 60f gray & brown	2.50	2.25

20th anniv. of the establishment of the Hungarian PO Phil. Museum. See No. C68.

Coal Mining — A175

Designs: 10f, Heavy industry. 12f, Power production. 20f, Textile industry. 30f, "Cultured workers." 40f, Mechanized agriculture. 60f, Village cooperative. 1fo, Train. 1.70fo, "Holiday." 2fo, Defense. 3fo, Shipping. 4fo, Livestock. 5fo, Engineering. 10fo, Sports.

1950 **Wmk. 283**

871 A175 8f gray	45	20
872 A175 10f claret	45	15
873 A175 12f orange ver	70	38
874 A175 20f blue green	28	15
875 A175 30f rose violet	35	15
876 A175 40f sepia	45	15
877 A175 60f red	42	15
878 A175 1fo gray brn, yel & lil	1.90	26
879 A175 1.70fo dk grn & yel	5.50	40
880 A175 2fo vio brn & cr	2.75	20
881 A175 3fo slate & cream	4.50	18
882 A175 4fo blk brn & sal	19.00	4.00
883 A175 5fo rose vio & yel	9.75	1.90
884 A175 10fo dk brn & yel	45.00	11.00
Nos. 871-884 (14)	91.50	19.27

Issued to publicize Hungary's Five Year Plan. See Nos. 945-958.

Citizens Welcoming Liberators A176

1950, Apr. 4 **Unwmk.** *Perf. 12*

885 A176 40f gray black	60	48
886 A176 60f rose brown	40	15
887 A176 1fo deep blue	48	20
888 A176 2fo brown	80	60

Fifth anniversary of Hungary's liberation.

Chess Players A177

Design: 1fo, Iron Workers Union building and chess emblem.

1950, Apr. 9 **Wmk. 106**

889 A177 60f deep magenta	70	42
890 A177 1fo deep blue	1.25	85

Issued to publicize the World Chess Championship Matches, Budapest. See No. C69.

Workers Symbolizing International Proletariat A178

Design: 60f, Blast furnace, tractor, workers holding Maypole.

1950, May 1

891 A178 40f orange brown	35	35
892 A178 60f rose carmine	22	15
893 A178 1fo deep blue	70	42

Issued to publicize Labor Day, May 1, 1950.

Liberty, Cogwheel, Dove and Globes A179

Inscribed: "1950. V. 10.-24."

Design: 60f, Three workers and flag.

1950, May 10 **Photo.** *Perf. 12x12½*

894 A179 40f olive green	16	15
895 A179 60f dark carmine	28	15
Set value		23

Meeting of the World Federation of Trade Unions, Budapest, May 1950.

Doctor Inspecting Baby's Bath A180

Children's Day: 30f, Physical Culture. 40f, Education. 60f, Boys' Camp. 1.70fo, Model plane building.

1950, June 4 **Wmk. 106**

896 A180 20f gray & brown	85	55
897 A180 30f brn & rose lake	42	15
898 A180 40f indigo & dk grn	42	15
899 A180 60f SZABAD	42	15
a. UTANPOTLASUNK..	900.00	850.00
900 A180 1.70fo dp grn & gray	1.65	55
Nos. 896-900 (5)	3.76	1.55

Youths Marching on Globe A181

Working Man and Woman — A182

Designs: 30f, Foundry worker. 60f, Workers on Mt. Gellert. 1.70fo, Worker, peasant and student; flags.

Inscribed: Budapest 1950. VI. 17-18.

Perf. 12x12½, 12½x12

1950, June 17

901 A181 20f dark green	45	40
902 A181 30f deep red org	18	15
903 A182 40f dark brown	18	15
904 A182 60f deep claret	28	15
905 A182 1.70fo dark olive grn	75	32
Nos. 901-905 (5)	1.84	1.17

Issued to publicize the First Congress of the Working Youth, Budapest, June 17-18, 1950.

Peonies — A183

Designs: 40f, Anemones. 60f, Pheasant's-eye. 1fo, Geraniums. 1.70fo, Bluebells.

Engraved and Lithographed

Perf. 12½x12

1950, Aug. 20 **Unwmk.**

906 A183 30f rose brn, rose pink & grn	75	24
907 A183 40f dk green, lil & yel	75	28
908 A183 60f red brn, yel & grn	1.10	45
909 A183 1fo purple, red & grn	2.75	2.00
910 A183 1.70fo dk violet & grn	3.50	2.50
Nos. 906-910 (5)	8.85	5.47

Miner — A184

Designs: 60f, High speed lathe. 1fo, Prefabricated building construction.

Perf. 12x12½

1950, Oct. 7 **Photo.** **Wmk. 106**

911 A184 40f brown	18	18
912 A184 60f carmine rose	20	18
913 A184 1fo brt blue	60	45

Issued to publicize the 2nd National Exhibition of Inventions.

Gen. Josef Bem and Battle at Piski A185

Perf. 12½x12

1950, Dec. 10 **Engr.** **Unwmk.**

914 A185 40f dark brown	80	60
915 A185 60f deep carmine	70	28
916 A185 1fo deep blue	1.00	65

Gen. Josef Bem, death centenary. See No. C80.

Signing Petition — A186

Peace Demonstrator Holding Dove — A187

Design: 1fo, Mother and Children with soldier.

Wmk. 106

1950, Nov. 23 **Photo.** *Perf. 12*

917 A186 40f ultra & red brn	8.75	6.50
918 A187 60f red org & dk grn	2.00	1.50
919 A186 1fo ol grn & dk brn	8.75	5.50

Women Swimmers A188

Designs: 20f, Vaulting. 1fo, Mountain climbing. 1.70fo, Basketball. 2fo, Motorcycling.

1950, Dec. 2 *Perf. 12x12½*

920 A188 10f blue & gray	16	15
921 A188 20f salmon & dk brn	16	15
922 A188 1fo olive & grn	48	45
923 A188 1.70fo ver & brn car	80	55
924 A188 2fo salmon & pur	1.65	1.00
Nos. 920-924,C82-C86 (10)	8.57	6.20

Canceled to Order

The government stamp agency started about 1950 to sell canceled sets of new issues. Values in the second ("used") column are for these canceled-to-order stamps. Postally used copies are worth more.

The practice was to end Apr. 1, 1991.

A189

Worker, Peasant, Soldier and Party Flag — A190

Designs: 60f, Matthias Rakosi and allegory. 1fo, House of Parliament, columns of workers and banner.

Inscribed: "Budapest * 1951 * Februar 24."

Perf. 12½x12, 12x12½

1951, Feb. 24

925 A189 10f yellow green	15	15
926 A190 30f brown	15	15
927 A190 60f carmine rose	22	22
928 A189 1fo blue	60	35

Issued to publicize the 2nd Congress of the Hungarian Workers' Party.

Mare and Foal — A191

Designs: 30f, Sow and shoats. 40f, Ram and ewe. 60f, Cow and calf.

1951, Apr. 5 ***Perf. 12x12½***

929 A191	10f ol bis & rose brn	30	15
930 A191	30f rose brn & ol bis	45	32
931 A191	40f dk green & brn	45	24
932 A191	60f brown org & brn	60	32
	Nos. 929-932,C87-C90 (8)	5.87	3.90

Issued to encourage increased livestock production.

Flags of Russia and Hungary A192

Russian Technician Teaching Hungarians A193

1951, Apr. 4 ***Perf. 12½x12, 12x12½***

933 A192	60f brnsh carmine	18	15
934 A193	1fo dull violet	28	15
	Set value		21

Issued to publicize the "Month of Friendship" between Hungary and Russia, 1951.

Worker Holding Olive Branch and Mallet — A194

Workers Carrying Flags — A195

Design: 1fo, Workers approaching Place of Heroes.

Perf. 12x12½, 12½x12

1951, May 1 Photo. Wmk. 106

935 A194	40f brown	15	15
936 A195	60f scarlet	22	15
937 A194	1fo blue	38	16
	Set value		32

Issued to publicize Labor Day, May 1, 1951.

Leo Frankel — A196

Children of Various Races — A198

Paris Street Fighting, 1871 — A197

1951, May 20

938 A196	60f dark brown	22	18
939 A197	1fo blue & red	28	28

80th anniv. of the Commune of Paris.

1951, June 3 ***Perf. 12½x12***

Designs: 40f, Boy and girl at play. 50f, Street car and Girl Pioneer. 60f, Chemistry students. 1.70fo, Pioneer bugler.

Inscribed: "Nemzetkozi Gyermeknap 1951"

940 A198	30f dark brown	25	15
941 A198	40f green	25	18
942 A198	50f brown red	35	25
943 A198	60f plum	50	35
944 A198	1.70fo blue	95	95
	Nos. 940-944 (5)	2.30	1.88

Issued to publicize the International Day of Children, June 3, 1951.

5-Year-Plan Type of 1950

Designs as before.

1951-52 Wmk. 106 ***Perf. 12x12½***

945 A175	8f gray	40	15
946 A175	10f claret	24	15
947 A175	12f orange ver	24	15
948 A175	20f blue green	24	15
949 A175	30f rose violet	24	15
950 A175	40f sepia	45	15
951 A175	60f red	55	15
952 A175	1fo gray brn, yel & lil	55	15
953 A175	1.70fo dk grn & yel	1.25	18
954 A175	2fo vio brn & cr	1.40	15
955 A175	3fo slate & cream	2.00	25
956 A175	4fo blk brn & sal	2.25	35
957 A175	5fo rose vio & yel ('52)	2.75	60
958 A175	10fo dk brn & yel ('52)	5.75	1.90
	Nos. 945-958 (14)	18.31	
	Set value		4.00

Maxim Gorky — A199

Perf. 12½x12

1951, June 17 Engr. Unwmk.

959 A199	60f copper red	18	15
960 A199	1fo deep blue	32	22
961 A199	2fo rose violet	1.00	75

15th anniversary of the death of Gorky.

Budapest Buildings

Railroad Workshop A200

Building in Lehel Street A201

Suburban Bus Terminal A202

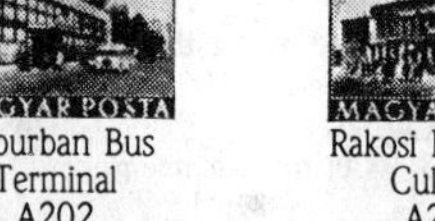

Rakosi House of Culture A203

George Kilian Street School A204

Central Construction Headquarters A205

1951 Wmk. 106 Photo. ***Perf. 15***

962 A200	20f green	20	15
963 A201	30f red orange	20	15
964 A202	40f brown	25	15
965 A203	60f red	32	15
966 A204	1fo blue	65	15
967 A205	3fo deep plum	2.00	15
	Nos. 962-967 (6)	3.62	
	Set value		32

The original size of Nos. 962-967, 22x18mm, was changed to 21x17mm starting in 1958. Values are the same.

See Nos. 1004-1011, 1048-1056C.

Tractor Manufacture A206

Designs: 30f, Fluoroscope examination. 40f, Checking lathework. 60f, Woman tractor operator.

1951, Aug. 20 ***Perf. 12x12½***

968 A206	20f black brown	16	15
969 A206	30f deep blue	16	15
970 A206	40f crimson rose	38	15
971 A206	60f brown	45	16
	Nos. 968-971,C91-C93 (7)	3.15	1.56

Issued to publicize the successful conclusion of the first year under Hungary's 5-year plan.

Soldiers of the People's Army — A207

1951, Sept. 29

972 A207	1fo brown	85	30

Issued to publicize Army Day, Sept. 29, 1951. See No. C94.

Stamp of 1871, Portrait Replaced by Postmark A208

Cornflower A209

Perf. 12½x12

1951, Sept. 12 Engr. Unwmk.

973 A208	60f olive green	2.00	1.75

80th anniv. of Hungary's 1st postage stamp. See Nos. B207-B208, C95, CB13-CB14.

1951, Nov. 4 Engr. & Litho.

974 A209	30f shown	60	20
975 A209	40f Lily of the Valley	75	55
976 A209	60f Tulip	65	20
977 A209	1fo Poppy	1.25	40
978 A209	1.70fo Cowslip	2.50	1.40
	Nos. 974-978 (5)	5.75	2.75

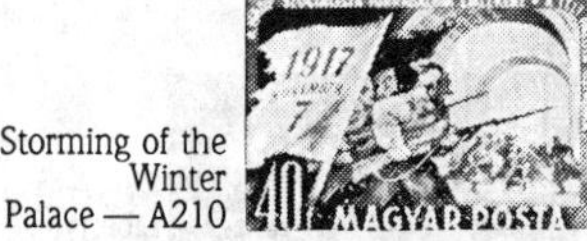

Storming of the Winter Palace — A210

Designs: 60f, Lenin speaking to soldiers. 1fo, Lenin and Stalin.

Perf. 12x12½

1951, Nov. 7 Photo. Wmk. 106

979 A210	40f gray green	40	24
980 A210	60f deep blue	48	16
981 A210	1fo rose lake	85	40

34th anniversary of the Russian Revolution.

Marchers Passing Stalin Monument A211

1951, Dec. 16 Wmk. 106

982 A211	60f henna brown	20	16
983 A211	1fo deep blue	55	32

Joseph V. Stalin, 72nd birthday.

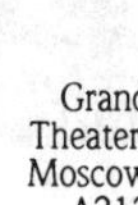

Grand Theater, Moscow A212

Views of Moscow: 1fo, Lenin Mausoleum. 1.60fo, Kremlin.

1952, Feb. 20 ***Perf. 12***

984 A212	60f ol grn & rose brn	28	16
985 A212	1fo lil rose & ol brn	55	28
986 A212	1.60fo red brn & ol	90	55

Hungarian-Soviet Friendship Month.

Rakosi and Farmers A213

Matyas Rakosi — A214

Design: 2fo, Rakosi and Workers.

Perf. 12x12½, 12½x12

1952, Mar. 9 Engr. Unwmk.

987 A213	60f deep plum	25	15
988 A214	1fo dk red brown	35	20
989 A213	2fo dp violet blue	1.10	50

60th anniv. of the birth of Matyas Rakosi, communist leader.

Lajos Kossuth and Speech at Debrecen A215

Designs: 30f, Sándor Petőfi. 50f, Gen. Josef Bem. 60f, Michael Tancsics. 1fo, Gen. János Damjanich. 1.50fo, Gen. Alexander Nagy.

1952, Mar. 15 ***Perf. 12***

990 A215	20f green	15	15
991 A215	30f rose violet	15	15
992 A215	50f grnsh blk	24	24
993 A215	60f brown car	38	16
994 A215	1fo blue	45	28
995 A215	1.50fo redsh brown	52	48
	Nos. 990-995 (6)	1.89	1.46

Heroes of the 1848 revolution.

No. B204 Surcharged in Black with Bars Obliterating Inscription and Surtax

Perf. 12½x12

1952, Apr. 27 Photo. Wmk. 283

996 SP121	60f magenta	37.50	32.50

Budapest Philatelic Exhibition. Counterfeits exist.

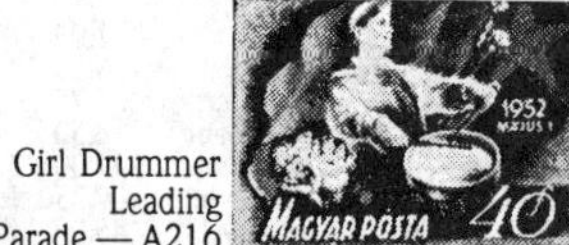

Girl Drummer Leading Parade — A216

Designs: 60f, Workers and soldier. 1fo, Worker, flag-encircled globe and dove.

Perf. 12x12½

1952, May 1 Photo. Wmk. 106

No.	Type	Description	Unused	Used
997	A216	40f dk grn & dull red	30	24
998	A216	60f dk red brn & dull red	30	24
999	A216	1fo sepia & dull red	45	40

Issued to publicize Labor Day, May 1, 1952.

Runner — A217

Designs: 40f, Swimmer. 60f, Fencer. 1fo, Woman gymnast.

1952, May 26 *Perf. 11*

No.	Type	Description	Unused	Used
1000	A217	30f dark red brown	28	15
1001	A217	40f deep green	32	15
1002	A217	60f deep lilac rose	42	25
1003	A217	1fo deep blue	70	50
		Nos. 1000-1003,C107-C108 (6)	3.82	2.65

Issued to publicize Hungary's participation in the Olympic Games, Helsinki, 1952

Building Types of 1951

Buildings: 8f, School, Stalinvarost. 10f, Szekesfehervar Station. 12f, Building, Ujpest. 50f, Metal works, Inotai. 70f, Grain elevator, Hajdunanas. 80f, Tiszalok dam. 4fo, Miners' union headquarters. 5fo, Workers' apartments, Ujpest.

1952 Wmk. 106 *Perf. 15*

No.	Type	Description	Unused	Used
1004	A202	8f green	24	15
1005	A200	10f purple	30	15
1006	A202	12f carmine	24	15
1007	A202	50f gray blue	38	15
1008	A202	70f yellow brn	48	15
1009	A200	80f maroon	85	15
1010	A202	4fo olive grn	1.50	15
1011	A202	5fo gray black	2.75	20
		Nos. 1004-1011 (8)	6.74	
		Set value		60

The original size of Nos. 1004-1011 was 22x18mm. Starting in 1958, this was changed to 21x17mm. Values are the same.

Approaching Train — A218

Railroad Day: 1fo, Railroad Construction.

1952, Aug. 10 *Perf. 12x12½*

No.	Type	Description	Unused	Used
1012	A218	60f red brown	60	18
1013	A218	1fo deep olive grn	65	35

Coal Excavator A219

Miners' Day: 1fo, Coal breaker.

1952, Sept. 7

No.	Type	Description	Unused	Used
1014	A219	60f brown	48	16
1015	A219	1fo dark green	75	24

Lajos Kossuth A220

Janos Hunyadi A221

Design: 60f, Kossuth statue.

1952, Sept. 19 *Perf. 12½x12*

No.	Type	Description	Unused	Used
1016	A220	40f ol brn, *pink*	40	28
1017	A220	60f black brn, *bl*	18	15
1018	A220	1fo purple, *citron*	40	18

150th anniv. of the birth of Lajos Kossuth.

1952, Sept. 28 Engr. Unwmk.

Portraits: 30f, Gyorgy Dozsa. 40f, Miklos Zrinyi. 60f, Ilona Zriuyi. 1fo, Bottyan Vak. 1.50fo, Aurel Stromfeld.

No.	Type	Description	Unused	Used
1019	A221	20f purple	15	15
1020	A221	30f dark green	15	15
1021	A221	40f indigo	15	15
1022	A221	60f dk violet brn	20	15
1023	A221	1fo dk blue grn	48	32
1024	A221	1.50fo dark brown	1.25	90
		Nos. 1019-1024 (6)	2.38	
		Set value		1.38

Army Day, Sept. 28, 1952.

Lenin and Conference at Smolny Palace — A222

Designs: 60f, Stalin and Cavalry Attack. 1fo, Marx, Engels, Lenin and Stalin.

1952, Nov. 7 Wmk. 106

Portraits in Olive Gray

No.	Type	Description	Unused	Used
1025	A222	40f deep claret	65	40
1026	A222	60f gray	35	15
1027	A222	1fo rose red	90	28

Russian Revolution, 35th anniversary.

Peasant Woman Holding Wheat — A223

Peace Meeting A224

Perf. 12½x12, 12x12½

1952, Nov. 22

No.	Type	Description	Unused	Used
1028	A223	60f brn red, *citron*	38	20
1029	A224	1fo brown, *blue*	60	38

Third Hungarian Peace Congress, 1952.

Subway Construction A225

Design: 1fo, Station and map.

1953, Jan. 19 Photo. *Perf. 12x12½*

No.	Type	Description	Unused	Used
1030	A225	60f dk slate green	55	25
1031	A225	1fo brown red	75	45

Completion of the Budapest subway extension.

Tank and Flag — A226

Stalin — A227

Design: 60f, Map of Central Europe and Soldier.

1953, Feb. 18

No.	Type	Description	Unused	Used
1032	A226	40f dark car rose	48	24
1033	A226	60f chocolate	48	15

Battle of Stalingrad, 10th anniversary.

Perf. 12x11½

1953 Engr. Wmk. 106

No.	Type	Description	Unused	Used
1034	A227	60f pur blk	30	15

Souvenir Sheet

No.	Type	Description	Unused	Used
1035	A227	2fo purple black	16.00	16.00

Death of Joseph Stalin (1879-1953).
Issue dates: #1034, Mar. 27, #1035, Mar. 9.

Workers' Rest Home, Galyateto A228

Designs: 40f, Home at Mecsek. 50f, Parad Mineral Baths. 60f, Home at Kekes. 70f, Balatonfured Mineral Baths.

1953, Apr. Photo. *Perf. 12x12½*

No.	Type	Description	Unused	Used
1036	A228	30f fawn	28	15
1037	A228	40f deep blue	28	15
1038	A228	50f dk olive bis	35	15
1039	A228	60f dp yellow grn	38	18
1040	A228	70f scarlet	55	22
		Nos. 1036-1040 (5)	1.84	
		Set value		72

Young Workers with Red Flags — A229

Karl Marx — A230

1953, May 1 *Perf. 12½x12*

No.	Type	Description	Unused	Used
1041	A229	60f brn & red, *yel*	25	15

Issued to publicize Labor Day, May 1, 1953.

1953, May 1 Engr. *Perf. 11½x12*

No.	Type	Description	Unused	Used
1042	A230	1fo black, *pink*	30	15

70th anniv. of the death of Karl Marx. See No. 1898.

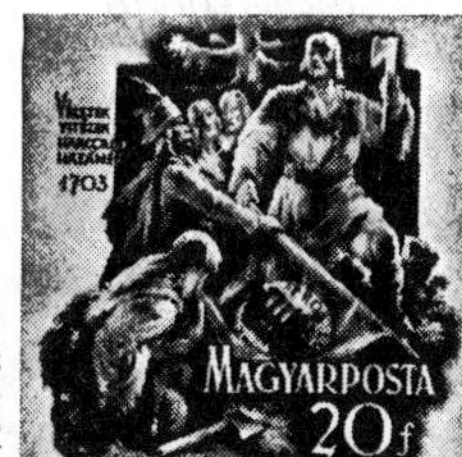

Insurgents in the Forest A231

Designs: 30f, Drummer and fighters. 40f, Battle scene. 60f, Cavalry attack. 1fo, Francis Rákóczy II.

1953, June 14 Photo. *Perf. 11*

No.	Type	Description	Unused	Used
1043	A231	20f dk ol grn & org red, *grnsh*	35	28
1044	A231	30f vio brn & red org	48	40
1045	A231	40f gray bl & red org, *pink*	65	40
1046	A231	60f dk ol brn & org, *yel*	85	75
1047	A231	1fo dk red brn & org red, *yel*	1.10	1.00
		Nos. 1043-1047 (5)	3.43	2.83

250th anniv. of the insurrection of 1703.

Building Types of 1951

Buildings: 8f, Day Nursery, Ozd. 10f, Medical research institute, Szombathely. 12f, Apartments, Komlo. 20f, Department store, Ujpest. 30f, Brick factory, Maly. 40f, Metropolitan hospital. 50f, Sports building, Stalinvaros. 60f, Post office, Csepel. 70f, Blast furnace, Diosgyor. 1.20fo, Agricultural school, Ajkacsinger Valley. 1.70fo, Iron Works School, Csepel. 2fo, Optical works house of culture.

1953 Wmk. 106 *Perf. 15*

No.	Type	Description	Unused	Used
1048	A204	8f olive green	28	15
1049	A204	10f purple	38	15
1050	A205	12f rose carmine	38	15
1051	A204	20f dark green	38	15
1052	A204	30f orange	38	15
1053	A204	40f dark brown	38	15
1054	A205	50f blue violet	60	15
1055	A205	60f rose red	60	15
1056	A204	70f yellow brown	90	15
1056A	A205	1.20fo red	1.40	15
1056B	A204	1.70fo blue	1.25	15
1056C	A204	2fo green	1.40	15
		Nos. 1048-1056C (12)	8.33	
		Set value		75

The original size of Nos. 1048-1056C was 22x18mm. Starting in 1958, this was changed to 21x17mm. Values are the same.

Cycling — A232

1953, Aug. 20 *Perf. 11*

No.	Type	Description	Unused	Used
1057	A232	20f shown	35	24
1058	A232	30f Swimming	15	15
1059	A232	40f Calisthenics	25	15
1060	A232	50f Discus	32	16
1061	A232	60f Wrestling	35	20
		Nos. 1057-1061,C123-C127 (10)	6.22	4.06

Opening of the People's Stadium, Budapest.

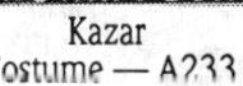

Kazar Costume — A233

Lenin — A234

Provincial Costumes: 30f, Ersekcsanad. 40f, Kalocsa. 60f, Sioagard. 1fo, Sarkoz. 1.70fo, Boldog. 2fo, Orhalom. 2.50fo, Hosszuheteny.

1953, Sept. 12 Engr. *Perf. 12*

No.	Type	Description	Unused	Used
1062	A233	20f blue green	50	28
1063	A233	30f chocolate	50	20
1064	A233	40f ultra	50	28
1065	A233	60f red	65	42
1066	A233	1fo grnsh blue	1.10	85
1067	A233	1.70fo brt green	2.25	1.25
1068	A233	2fo carmine rose	4.00	2.00
1069	A233	2.50fo purple	7.00	4.25
		Nos. 1062-1069 (8)	16.50	9.53

See No. 1189.

1954, Jan. 21 Wmk. 106 *Perf. 12*

Designs: 60f, Lenin and Stalin at meeting. 1fo, Lenin, facing left.

1073	A234	40f dk blue grn	55	55
1074	A234	60f black brown	52	22
1075	A234	1fo dk car rose	85	65

30th anniversary, death of Lenin.

Worker Reading A235

Revolutionary and Red Flag — A236

Design: 1fo, Soldier.

Perf. 12x12½, 12½x12

1954, Mar. 21 Photo.

1076	A235	40f gray blue & red	1.25	65
1077	A236	60f brown & red	1.75	1.50
1078	A235	1fo gray & red	2.50	2.25

35th anniversary of the "First Hungarian Communist Republic."

Blood Test A237

Maypole A238

Designs: 40f, Mother receiving newborn baby. 60f, Medical examination of baby.

1954, Mar. 8 *Perf. 12*

1079	A237	30f brt blue	20	15
1080	A237	40f brown bister	25	15
1081	A237	60f purple	35	15
		Nos. 1079-1081,C146-C148 (6)	2.35	1.60

1954, May 1 *Perf. 12½x12*

Design: 60f, Flag bearer.

1082	A238	40f olive	24	15
1083	A238	60f orange red	28	15
		Set value		24

Issued to publicize Labor Day, May 1, 1954.

Farm Woman with Fruit A239

1954, May 24 *Perf. 12*

1084	A239	60f red orange	25	15

3rd Congress of the Hungarian Workers Party, Budapest, May 24, 1954.

Natl. Museum, Budapest — A240

Peppers — A241

Designs: 60f, Arms of People's Republic. 1fo, Dome of Parliament Building.

1954, Aug. 20 *Perf. 12½x12*

1085	A240	40f brt blue	22	17
1086	A240	60f redsh brown	18	15
1087	A240	1fo dark brown	38	22

Fifth anniversary of the People's Republic Constitution.

1954, Sept. 11 Engr., Fruit Litho.

Fruit: 50f, Tomatoes. 60f, Grapes. 80f, Apricots. 1fo, Apples. 1.20fo, Plums. 1.50fo, Cherries. 2fo, Peaches.

Fruit in Natural Colors

1088	A241	40f gray blue	28	18
1089	A241	50f plum	28	18
1090	A241	60f gray blue	28	18
1091	A241	80f chocolate	38	18
1092	A241	1fo rose violet	40	24
1093	A241	1.20fo dull blue	80	38
1094	A241	1.50fo plum	1.40	1.25
1095	A241	2fo gray blue	1.10	75
		Nos. 1088-1095 (8)	4.92	3.34

National agricultural fair.

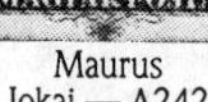

Maurus Jokai — A242

Janos Apacai Csere — A243

1954, Oct. 17 Engr.

1096	A242	60f dk brown olive	42	25
1097	A242	1fo deep claret	85	70

50th anniversary of the death of Maurus Jokai, writer.

No. 1097 in violet blue is from the souvenir sheet, No. C157.

1954, Dec. 5 Photo. *Perf. 12x12½*

Scientists: 10f, Csoma Sandor Korosi. 12f, Anyos Jedlik. 20f, Ignaz Semmelweis. 30f, Janos Irinyi. 40f, Frigyes Koranyi. 50f, Armin Vambery. 60f, Karoly Than. 1fo, Otto Herman. 1.70fo, Tivadar Puskas. 2fo, Endre Hogyes.

1098	A243	8f dk vio brn, *yel*	15	15
1099	A243	10f brn, car, *pink*	20	15
1100	A243	12f gray, *bl*	15	15
1101	A243	20f brn, *yel*	15	15
1102	A243	30f vio bl, *pink*	15	15
1103	A243	40f dk grn, *yel*	15	15
1104	A243	50f red brn, *pale grn*	15	15
1105	A243	60f blue, *pink*	15	15
1106	A243	1fo olive	38	16
1107	A243	1.70fo rose brn, *yel*	60	32
1108	A243	2fo blue green	80	48
		Nos. 1098-1108 (11)	3.03	
		Set value		1.70

Readers in Industrial Library — A244

Industry — A245

Designs: 1fo, Agriculture. 2fo, Liberation monument.

1955, Apr. 4 *Perf. 12½x12, 12x12½*

1109	A244	40f dk car & ol brn	22	16
1110	A245	60f dk green & red	22	16
1111	A245	1fo choc & grn	38	16
1112	A244	2fo blue grn & brn	65	48

10th anniversary of Hungary's liberation.

Date, Flags and Farm — A246

1955, May 1 *Perf. 12x12½*

1113	A246	1fo rose carmine	45	15

Labor Day, May 1, 1955.

Government Printing Plant — A247

1955, May 28 Wmk. 106

1114	A247	60f gray grn & hn brn	25	20

Centenary of the establishment of the government printing plant.

Young Citizens and Hungarian Flag — A248

1955, June 15 *Perf. 12*

1115	A248	1fo red brown	35	15

Issued to publicize the second national congress of the Hungarian Youth Organization.

Truck Farmer — A249

Designs: 10f, Fisherman. 12f, Bricklayer. 20f, Radio assembler. 30f, Woman potter. 40f, Railwayman and train. 50f, Clerk and scales. 60f, Postman emptying mail box. 70f, Cattle and herdsman. 80f, Textile worker. 1fo, Riveter. 1.20fo, Carpenter. 1.40fo, Streetcar conductor. 1.70fo, Herdsman and pigs. 2fo, Welder. 2.60fo, Woman tractor driver. 3fo, Herdsman in national costume and horse. 4fo, Bus driver. 5fo, Lineman. 10fo, Coal miner.

1955 Wmk. 106 *Perf. 12x12½*

1116	A249	8f chestnut	16	15
1117	A249	10f Prus green	16	15
1118	A249	12f red orange	15	15
1119	A249	20f olive green	15	15
1120	A249	30f dark red	42	15
1121	A249	40f brown	15	15
1122	A249	50f violet bl	15	15
1123	A249	60f brown red	35	15
1124	A249	70f olive	35	15
1125	A249	80f purple	45	15
1126	A249	1fo blue	22	15
1127	A249	1.20fo olive bis	22	15
1128	A249	1.40fo deep green	42	15
1129	A249	1.70fo purple	42	15
1130	A249	2fo rose brown	42	15
1131	A249	2.60fo vermilion	50	15
1132	A249	3fo green	90	15
1133	A249	4fo peacock blue	1.10	16
1134	A249	5fo orange brown	1.50	26
1135	A249	10fo violet	2.50	52
		Nos. 1116-1135 (20)	10.69	
		Set value		1.75

For surcharges see Nos. B211-B216.

Postrider Blowing Horn — A250

1955, June 25 *Perf. 12½x12*

1136	A250	1fo rose violet	35	15

Hungarian Postal Museum, 25th anniv.

Exists tete-beche. Value: 2½ times the value of a single.

Mihaly Csokonai Vitez A251

Portraits: 1fo, Mihaly Vorosmarty. 2fo, Attila József.

1955, July 28 *Perf. 12*

1137	A251	60f olive black	40	32
1138	A251	1fo dark blue	70	24
1139	A251	2fo rose brown	90	65

Issued to honor three Hungarian poets.

Bela Bartok — A252

1955, Oct. 9

1140	A252	60f lt brown	1.00	50

10th anniversary of the death of Bela Bartok, composer. See Nos. C168-C169.

Diesel Train A253

Designs: 60f, Bus. 80f, Motorcycle. 1fo, Truck. 1.20fo, Steam locomotive. 1.50fo, Dump truck. 2fo, Freighter.

1955, Dec. 20 *Perf. 14½*

1141	A253	40f grn & vio brn	15	15
1142	A253	60f dp grn & ol	16	15
1143	A253	80f ol grn & brn	25	15
1144	A253	1fo ocher & grn	45	28
1145	A253	1.20fo salmon & blk	65	32
1146	A253	1.50fo grnsh blk & red brn	80	48
1147	A253	2fo aqua & brown	1.10	90
		Nos. 1141-1147 (7)	3.56	2.43

Puli (Sheepdog) — A254

Puli and Steer A255

Hungarian Pointer — A256

Hungarian Dogs: 60f, Pumi (sheepdog). 1fo, Retriever with fowl. 1.20fo, Kuvasz (sheepdog). 1.50fo, Komondor (sheepdog) and cottage. 2fo, Komondor (head).

Perf. 11x13 (A254), 12

1956, Mar. 17 Engr. & Litho.

No.	Type	Description	Unused	Used
1148	A254	40f yellow, blk & red	20	15
1149	A254	50f blue, bis & blk	20	15
1150	A254	60f yel grn, blk & red	20	15
1151	A254	80f bluish grn, ocher & blk	24	15
1152	A254	1fo turq, ocher & blk	32	18
1153	A254	1.20fo salmon, blk & chnt	48	18
1154	A254	1.50fo ultra, blk & buff	90	52
1155	A254	2fo cerise, blk & chnt	1.25	80
		Nos. 1148-1155 (8)	3.79	2.28

Pioneer Emblem — A257

Perf. 12x12½

1956, June 2 Photo. Wmk. 106

No.	Type	Description	Unused	Used
1156	A257	1fo red	25	15
1157	A257	1fo gray	25	15
		Set value		24

Pioneer movement, 10th anniversary.

Janos Hunyadi Statue — A258

Miner — A259

1956, Aug. 12 *Perf. 12*

No.	Type	Description	Unused	Used
1158	A258	1fo brown, *yelsh*	50	35

500th anniv. of the defeat of the Turks at the battle of Pecs under Janos Hunyadi.

Printed in sheets of 50 with alternate vertical rows inverted and center row of perforation omitted, providing 25 tête bêche pairs, of which 5 are imperf. between.

1956, Sept. 2

No.	Type	Description	Unused	Used
1159	A259	1fo dark blue	30	15

Issued in honor of Miners' Day 1956.

Kayak Racer A260

Sports: 30f, Horse jumping hurdle. 40f, Fencing. 60f, Women hurdlers. 1fo, Soccer. 1.50fo, Weight lifting. 2fo, Gymnastics. 3fo, Basketball.

1956, Sept. 25 Wmk. 106 *Perf. 11*

Figures in Brown Olive

No.	Type	Description	Unused	Used
1160	A260	20f lt blue	15	15
1161	A260	30f lt olive grn	15	15
1162	A260	40f deep orange	16	15
1163	A260	60f bluish grn	15	15
1164	A260	1fo vermilion	24	15
1165	A260	1.50fo blue violet	32	22
1166	A260	2fo emerald	45	28
1167	A260	3fo rose lilac	80	60
		Nos. 1160-1167 (8)	2.42	
		Set value		1.55

16th Olympic Games at Melbourne, Nov. 22-Dec. 8, 1956.

Franz Liszt — A261

Portrait: 1fo, Frederic Chopin facing left.

1956, Oct. 7 Photo. *Perf. 12x12½*

No.	Type	Description	Unused	Used
1168	A261	1fo violet blue	90	90
1169	A261	1fo magenta	90	90
a.		Pair, #1168-1169	1.90	1.90

29th Day of the Stamp. Sold only at the Philatelic Exhibition together with entrance ticket for 4fo.

Janos Arany — A262

Arms of Hungary — A263

1957, Sept. 15 Wmk. 106 *Perf. 12*

No.	Type	Description	Unused	Used
1170	A262	2fo bright blue	50	15

75th anniv. of the death of Janos Arany, poet.

1957, Oct. 1

No.	Type	Description	Unused	Used
1171	A263	60f brt red	20	15
1172	A263	1fo dp yellow grn	30	15
		Set value		19

Trade Union Congress Emblem A264

1957, Oct. 4

No.	Type	Description	Unused	Used
1173	A264	1fo dk carmine	25	15

4th Intl. Trade Union Cong., Leipzig, Oct. 4-15.

Dove and Colors of Communist Countries — A265

Design: 1fo, Lenin.

1957, Nov. 7 Litho. *Perf. 12*

No.	Type	Description	Unused	Used
1174	A265	60f gray, blk & multi	24	15
1175	A265	1fo ol bis & indigo	25	16
		Set value		24

Russian Revolution, 40th anniversary.

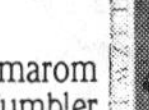

Komarom Tumbler Pigeons — A266

Pigeons: 40f, Two short-beaked Budapest pigeons. 60f, Giant domestic pigeon. 1fo, Three Szeged pigeons. 2fo, Two Hungarian fantails.

Perf. 12x12½

1957-58 Photo. Wmk. 106

No.	Type	Description	Unused	Used
1176	A266	30f yel grn, cl & ocher	20	15
1177	A266	40f ocher & blk	20	15
1178	A266	60f blue & gray	20	15
1179	A266	1fo gray & red brn	45	16
1180	A266	2fo brt pink & gray	1.00	60
		Nos. 1176-1180,C175 (6)	2.80	1.71

Intl. Pigeon Exhibition, Budapest, Dec. 14-16.
Issued: #1176, Jan. 12, 1958; others, Dec. 14, 1957.

Television Station — A267

1958, Feb. 22 Engr. *Perf. 11*

No.	Type	Description	Unused	Used
1181	A267	2fo rose violet	90	65
a.		Perf. 12	2.00	2.00

Souvenir Sheet

No.	Type	Description	Unused	Used
1182	A267	2fo green	22.50	22.50

Issued to publicize the television industry.
No. 1182 sold for 25fo.

Mother and Child A268

Designs: 30f, Old man feeding pigeons. 40f, School boys. 60f, "Working ants and fiddling grasshopper." 1fo, Honeycomb and bee. 2fo, Handing over money.

1958, Mar. 9 Photo. *Perf. 12*

No.	Type	Description	Unused	Used
1183	A268	20f yel grn & ol gray	22	15
1184	A268	30f lt olive & mar	22	15
1185	A268	40f yel bis & brn	22	15
1186	A268	60f rose car & grnsh blk	30	18
1187	A268	1fo ol gray & dk brn	52	35
1188	A268	2fo org & ol gray	1.40	70
		Nos. 1183-1188 (6)	2.88	1.68

Issued to publicize the value of savings and insurance.

Kazar Costume Type of 1953
Souvenir Sheet

1958, Apr. 17 Engr. *Perf. 12*

No.	Type	Description	Unused	Used
1189	A233	10fo magenta	20.00	20.00

Issued for the Universal and International Exposition at Brussels.

Arms of Hungary — A269

1958, May 23 Litho. Wmk. 106

Arms in Original Colors

No.	Type	Description	Unused	Used
1190	A269	60f lt red brn & red	15	15
1191	A269	1fo gray grn & grn	16	15
1192	A269	2fo gray & dk brn	48	20
		Set value		38

1st anniv. of the law amending the constitution.

Youth Holding Book — A270

Post Horn and Town Hall, Prague — A271

1958, June 14 Photo. *Perf. 12½x12*

No.	Type	Description	Unused	Used
1193	A270	1fo brown carmine	45	20

5th Hungarian Youth Festival at Keszthely.
Printed with alternating label, inscribed: V. IFJUSAGI TALALKOZO KESZTHELY 1958.

1958, June 30

No.	Type	Description	Unused	Used
1194	A271	60f green	20	15
a.		Pair, #1194, C184	60	42

Conference of Postal Ministers of Communist Countries at Prague, June 30-July 8.

Dolomite Flax — A272

Hungarian Thistles — A273

Flowers: 30f, Kitaibelia vitifolia. 60f, Crocuses. 1fo, Hellebore. 2fo, Lilies. 2.50fo, Pinks. 3fo, Dog roses.

Perf. 11x13, 12½x12 (A273)

1958, Aug. 12 Photo. Wmk. 106

No.	Type	Description	Unused	Used
1195	A272	20f red vio & yel	1.00	20
1196	A272	30f blue, yel & grn	15	15
1197	A273	40f brown & bis	22	15
1198	A273	60f bl grn & pink	30	15
1199	A273	1fo rose car & yel grn	52	22
1200	A273	2fo green & yellow	95	20
1201	A272	2.50fo vio bl & pink	1.25	42
1202	A272	3fo green & pink	2.00	70
a.		Souvenir sheet of 4, perf. 12	20.00	20.00
		Nos. 1195-1202 (8)	6.39	2.19

No. 1202a and a similar imperf. sheet were issued for the International Philatelic Congress at Brussels, Sept. 15-17, 1958. They contain the triangular 20f, 30f, 2.50fo and 3fo stamps printed in different colors. Sheets measure 111x111mm. and are printed on unwatermarked, linen-finish paper. Background of stamps, marginal inscriptions and ornaments in green. No. 1202a also exists perf. 11; same value.

Paddle, Ball and Olive Branch A274

Designs: 30f, Table tennis player, vert. 40f, Wrestlers, vert. 60f, Wrestlers, horiz. 1fo, Water polo player, vert. 2.50fo, High dive, vert. 3fo, Swimmer.

1958, Aug. 30 Wmk. 106 *Perf. 12*

No.	Type	Description	Unused	Used
1203	A274	20f rose red, *pnksh*	15	15
1204	A274	30f olive, *grnsh*	15	15
1205	A274	40f mag, *yel*	18	15
1206	A274	60f brown, *bluish*	22	15
1207	A274	1fo ultra, *bluish*	38	22
1208	A274	2.50fo dk red, *yel*	75	42
1209	A274	3fo grnsh bl, *grnsh*	1.10	75
		Nos. 1203-1209 (7)	2.93	1.99

Intl. Wrestling and European Swimming and Table Tennis Championships, held at Budapest.

Red Flag — A275

Design: 2fo, Hand holding newspaper.

1958, Nov. 21 *Perf. 12½x12*

1210 A275 1fo brown & red 15 15
1211 A275 2fo dk gray bl & red 28 15
Set value 20

40th anniversary of the founding of the Hungarian Communist Party and newspaper.

Satellite, Sputnik and American Rocket A276

Designs: 10f, Eötvös Torsion Balance and Globe. 20f, Deep sea exploration. 30f, Icebergs, penguins and polar light. 40f, Soviet Antarctic camp and map of Pole. 60f, "Rocket" approaching moon. 1fo, Sun and observatory.

1959, Mar. 14 *Perf. 12x12½*

Size: 32x21mm

1212 A276 10f car rose & sep 30 15
1213 A276 20f brt blue & gray 18 15
1214 A276 30f dk sl grn & bis 28 15

Perf. 12

Size: 35x26mm

1215 A276 40f sl bl & lt bl 18 15

Perf. 15

Size: 58x21mm

1216 A276 60f Prus bl & lem 40 20

Perf. 12

Size: 35x26mm

1217 A276 1fo scarlet & yel 65 32
1218 A276 5fo brn & red brn 1.50 80
Nos. 1212-1218 (7) 3.49 1.92

Intl. Geophysical Year. See No. 1262.

"Revolution" — A277

1959, Mar. 21 *Perf. 12½x12*

1219 A277 20f vio brn & red 20 15
1220 A277 60f blue & red 15 15
1221 A277 1fo brown & red 45 15
Set value 28

40th anniv. of the proclamation of the Hungarian Soviet Republic.

Rose — A278

1959, May 1 **Photo.** *Perf. 11*

1222 A278 60f lilac, dp car & grn 30 15
1223 A278 1fo lt brn, dl red & grn 48 18

Issued for Labor Day, May 1, 1959.

Early Locomotive A279

Designs: 30f, Diesel coach. 40f, Early semaphore, vert. 60f, Csonka automobile. 1fo, Icarus bus. 2fo, First Lake Balaton steamboat. 2.50fo, Stagecoach.

1959, May 26 **Litho.** *Perf. 14½x15*

1224 A279 20f multi 28 15
1225 A279 30f multi 22 16
1226 A279 40f multi 22 16
1227 A279 60f multi 22 16
1228 A279 1fo multi 28 20
1229 A279 2fo multi 55 38
1230 A279 2.50fo multi 85 70
Nos. 1224-1230,C201 (8) 3.87 2.86

Transport Museum, Budapest.

Perf. 10½x11½

1959, May 29 **Wmk. 106**

1231 A279 2.50fo multi 2.00 2.00

Designer's name on No. 1231. Printed in sheets of four with four labels to commemorate the congress of the International Federation for Philately in Hamburg.

Post Horn and World Map — A280

1959, June 1 **Photo.** *Perf. 12*

1232 A280 1fo cerise 40 30

Postal Ministers Conference, Berlin.

Printed in sheets of 25 stamps with 25 alternating gray labels showing East Berlin Opera House.

Great Cormorant — A281

Warrior, 10th Century — A282

Birds: 20f, Little egret and nest. 30f, Purple heron and nest. 40f, Great egret. 60f, White spoonbill. 1fo, Gray heron. 2fo, Squacco heron and nest. 3fo, Glossy ibis.

1959, June 14

1233 A281 10f green & indigo 15 15
1234 A281 20f gray bl & ol grn 22 15
1235 A281 30f org, grnsh blk & vio 15 15
1236 A281 40f dark grn & gray 22 20
1237 A281 60f dp cl & pale rose 35 20
1238 A281 1fo dp bl grn & blk 42 30
1239 A281 2fo dp orange & gray 85 30
1240 A281 3fo bister & brn lake 1.50 95
Nos. 1233-1240 (8) 3.86 2.40

1959, July 11

Designs: 20f, Warrior, 15th century. 30f, Soldier, 18th century. 40f, Soldier, 19th century. 60f, Cavalry man, 19th century. 1fo, Fencer, assault. 1.40fo, Fencer on guard. 3fo, Swordsman saluting.

1241 A282 10f gray & blue 18 15
1242 A282 20f gray & dull yel 20 15
1243 A282 30f gray & gray vio 18 15
1244 A282 40f gray & ver 18 15
1245 A282 60f gray & rose lil 18 18
1246 A282 1fo ind & lt bl grn 35 22
1247 A282 1.40fo orange & blk 75 25
1248 A282 3fo blk & ol grn 1.10 70
Nos. 1241-1248 (8) 3.12 1.95

24th World Fencing Championships, Budapest.

Sailboat, Lake Balaton — A283

Designs: 40f, Vintager and lake, horiz. 60f, Bathers. 1.20fo, Fishermen. 2fo, Summer guests and ship.

1959, July 11 **Photo.** **Wmk. 106**

1249 A283 30f blue, *yel* 15 15
1250 A283 40f carmine rose 15 15
1251 A283 60f dp red brown 15 15
1252 A283 1.20fo violet 35 15
1253 A283 2fo red org, *yel* 70 35
Nos. 1249-1253,C202-C205 (9) 2.57
Set value 1.42

Issued to publicize Lake Balaton and the opening of the Summer University.

Haydn's Monogram A284

Esterhazy Palace A285

Haydn and Schiller Monograms — A286

Design: 1fo, Joseph Haydn and score.

1959, Sept. 20 **Wmk. 106** *Perf. 12*

1254 A284 40f dp claret & yel 20 15
1255 A285 60f Prus bl, gray & yel 80 48
1256 A284 1fo dk vio, lt brn & org 65 40

Designs: 40f, Schiller's monogram. 60f, Pegasus rearing from flames. 1fo, Friedrich von Schiller.

1257 A284 40f olive grn & org 20 15
1258 A285 60f violet bl & lil 40 38
1259 A284 1fo dp cl & org brn 80 40
Nos. 1254-1259 (6) 3.05 1.96

Souvenir Sheet

Imperf

1260 A286 Sheet of 2 8.75 8.75
a. 3fo magenta 2.25 2.25
b. 3fo green 2.25 2.25

150th anniv. of the death of Joseph Haydn, Austrian composer, Nos. 1254-1256; 200th anniv. of the birth of Friedrich von Schiller, German poet and dramatist, Nos. 1257-1259; No. 1260 honors both Haydn and Schiller.

Shepherd — A287

1959, Sept. 25 **Engr.** *Perf. 12*

1261 A287 2fo deep claret 1.65 1.65
a. With ticket 2.00 2.00

Day of the Stamp and Natl. Stamp Exhib. Issued in sheets of 8 with alternating ticket. The 4fo sale price marked on the ticket was the admission fee to the Natl. Stamp Exhib.

Type of 1959 Overprinted in Red

1959, Sept. 24 **Photo.** *Perf. 15*

1262 A276 60f dull blue & lemon 45 25

Landing of Lunik 2 on moon, Sept. 14.

Handing over Letter A288

1959, Oct. 4 **Litho.** *Perf. 12*

1263 A288 60f multicolored 25 15

Intl. Letter Writing Week, Oct. 4-10.

Szamuely and Lenin — A289

Designs: 40pf, Aleksander Pushkin. 60pf, Vladimir V. Mayakovsky. 1fo, Hands holding peace flag.

1959, Nov. 14 **Photo.** **Wmk. 106**

1264 A289 20f dk red & bister 15 15
1265 A289 40f brn & rose lil, *bluish* 15 15
1266 A289 60f dk blue & bis 20 16
1267 A289 1fo bl, car, buff, red & grn 32 28
Set value 60

Soviet Stamp Exhibition, Budapest.

European Swallowtail A290

Worker with Banner A291

Butterflies: 30f, Arctia hebe, horiz. 40f, Lysandra hylas, horiz. 60f, Apatura ilia.

Perf. 11½x12, 12x11½

1959, Nov. 20

Butterflies in Natural Colors

1268 A290 20f blk & yel grn 16 15
1269 A290 30f lt blue & blk 24 15
1270 A290 40f dk gray & org brn 25 16
1271 A290 60f dk gray & dl yel 32 20
Nos. 1268-1271,C206-C208 (7) 5.07 2.55

1959, Nov. 30 *Perf. 14½*

Design: 1fo, Congress flag.

1272 A291 60f brown, grn & red 15 15
1273 A291 1fo brn, red, red & grn 18 15
Set value 15

Issued to commemorate the 7th Congress of the Hungarian Socialist Workers' Party.

Teacher Reading Fairy Tales — A292

Sumeg Castle — A293

Fairy Tales: 30f, Sleeping Beauty. 40f, Matt, the Goose Boy. 60f, The Cricket and the Ant. 1fo, Mashenka and the Three Bears. 2fo, Hansel and Gretel. 2.50fo, Pied Piper. 3fo, Little Red Riding Hood.

1959, Dec. 15 Litho. *Perf. 11½*
Designs in Black

1274 A292	20f gray & multi	15	15
1275 A292	30f brt pink	15	15
1276 A292	40f lt blue grn	18	15
1277 A292	60f lt blue	15	16
1278 A292	1fo yellow	24	24
1279 A292	2fo brt yellow grn	45	24
1280 A292	2.50fo orange	60	38
1281 A292	3fo crimson	90	60
	Nos. 1274-1281 (8)	2.82	2.07

Perf. 14½
1960, Feb. 1 Photo. Wmk. 106

Castles: 20fr, Tata. 30f, Diosgyor. 60f, Saros-Patak. 70f, Nagyvazsony. 1.40fo, Siklos. 1.70fo, Somlo. 3fo, Csesznek, vert. 5fo, Koszeg, vert. 10fo, Sarvar, vert.

Size: 21x17½mm

1282 A293	8f purple	15	15
1283 A293	20f dk yel grn	15	15
1284 A293	30f orange brn	15	15
1285 A293	60f rose red	15	15
1286 A293	70f emerald	18	15

Perf. 12x11½, 11½x12
Size: 28x21mm, 21x28mm

1287 A293	1.40fo ultra	18	15
1288 A293	1.70fo dl vio, "Somlo"	22	15
b.	"Somlyo"	45	15
1289 A293	3fo red brown	38	15
1290 A293	5fo yellow green	75	18
1291 A293	10fo carmine rose	1.65	38
	Nos. 1282-1291 (10)	3.96	
	Set value		1.00

Tinted Paper
Perf. 14½
Size: 21x17½mm

1282a A293	8f pur, *bluish*	15	15
1283a A293	20f dk yel grn, *grnsh*	20	15
1284a A293	30f org brn, *yel*	28	15
1285a A293	60f rose red, *pnksh*	20	15
1286a A293	70f emer, *bluish*	50	15

Perf. 12x11½
Size: 28x21mm

1287a A293	1.40fo ultra, *bluish*	55	28
1288a A293	1.70fo dull vio, *bluish*	70	28
	Nos. 1282a-1288a (7)	2.58	
	Set value		88

See Nos. 1356-1365, 1644-1646.

Halas Lace — A294

Cross-country Skier — A295

Designs: Various Halas lace patterns.

Perf. 11½
1960, Feb. 15 Litho. Wmk. 106
Sizes: 20f, 60f, 1fo, 3fo: 27x37mm
30f, 40f, 1.50fo, 2fo: 37½x43½mm
Inscriptions in Orange

1292 A294	20f brown black	15	15
1293 A294	30f violet	15	15
1294 A294	40f Prus blue	38	15
1295 A294	60f dark brown	20	15
1296 A294	1fo dark green	22	15
1297 A294	1.50fo green	38	18
1298 A294	2fo dark blue	85	22
1299 A294	3fo dk carmine	1.50	55
	Nos. 1292-1299 (8)	3.83	
	Set value		1.32

See Nos. 1570-1577.

Souvenir Sheet

Design as on No. 1299.

1960, Sept. 3
Inscriptions in Orange

1300	Sheet of 4 + 4 labels	6.75	6.75
a.	3fo brown olive	1.25	1.25
b.	3fo bright violet	1.25	1.25
c.	3fo emerald	1.25	1.25
d.	3fo bright blue	1.25	1.25

Fédération Internationale de Philatélie Congress, Warsaw, Sept. 3-11. No. 1300 contains 4 stamps and 4 alternating labels, printed in colors of adjoining stamps.

1960, Feb. 29 Photo. *Perf. 11½x12*

Sports: 40f, Ice hockey player. 60f, Ski jumper. 80f, Woman speed skater. 1fo, Downhill skier. 1.20fo, Woman figure skater.

Inscriptions and Figures in Bister

1301 A295	30f deep blue	15	15
1302 A295	40f brt green	15	15
1303 A295	60f scarlet	15	15
1304 A295	80f purple	22	15
1305 A295	1fo brt grnsh blue	45	22
1306 A295	1.20fo brown red	55	45
	Nos. 1301-1306,B217 (7)	2.92	
	Set value		1.45

8th Olympic Winter Games, Squaw Valley, Calif., Feb. 18-29, 1960.

Clara Zetkin — A296

Portraits: No. 1308, Kato Haman. No. 1309, Lajos Tüköry. No. 1310, Giuseppe Garibaldi. No. 1311, István Türr. No. 1312, Ottó Herman. No. 1313, Ludwig van Beethoven. No. 1314, Ferenc Mora. No. 1315, Istvan Toth Bucsoki. No. 1316, Donat Banki. No. 1317, Abraham G. Pattantyus. No. 1318, Ignaz Semmelweis. No. 1319, Frédéric Joliot-Curie. No. 1320, Ferenc Erkel. No. 1321, Janos Bolyai. No. 1322, Lenin.

1960 Photo. *Perf. 10½*

1307 A296	60f lt red brn	15	15

Engr.

1308 A296	60f pale purple	15	15
1309 A296	60f rose red	15	15
1310 A296	60f violet	15	15
1311 A296	60f blue green	15	15
1312 A296	60f blue	15	15
1313 A296	60f gray brown	15	15
1314 A296	60f salmon pink	15	15
1315 A296	60f gray	15	15
1316 A296	60f rose lilac	15	15
1317 A296	60f green	15	15
1318 A296	60f violet blue	15	15
1319 A296	60f brown	15	15
1320 A296	60f rose brown	15	15
1321 A296	60f grnsh blue	15	15
1322 A296	60f dull red	15	25
	Set value	1.75	1.00

Nos. 1307-1308 commemorate International Women's Day, Mar. 8.

Flower and Quill — A297

Soviet Capt. Ostapenko Statue — A298

Wmk. 106
1960, Apr. 2 Photo. *Perf. 12*

1323 A297	2fo brn, yel & grn	1.25	1.25
a.	With ticket	1.50	1.50

Issued for the stamp show of the National Federation of Hungarian Philatelists. The olive green 4fo ticket pictures the Federation's headquarters and served as entrance ticket to the show. Printed in sheets of 35 stamps and 35 tickets.

Perf. 12½x11½, 11½x12½
1960, Apr. 4

Designs: 60f, Youth holding flag, horiz.

1324 A298	40f dp carmine & brn	15	15
1325 A298	60f red brn, red & grn	16	15
	Set value		16

Hungary's liberation from the Nazis, 15th anniv.

Boxers — A299

Sports: 10f, Rowers. 30f, Archer. 40f, Discus thrower. 50f, Girls playing ball. 60f, Javelin thrower. 1fo, Rider. 1.40fo, Wrestlers. 1.70fo, Swordsmen. 3fo, Hungarian Olympic emblem.

1960, Aug. 21 *Perf. 11½x12*
Designs in Ocher and Black

1326 A299	10f blue	15	15
1327 A299	20f salmon	15	15
1328 A299	30f lt violet	15	15
1329 A299	40f yellow	15	15
1330 A299	50f deep pink	15	15
1331 A299	60f gray	15	15
1332 A299	1fo pale brn vio	24	15
1333 A299	1.40fo lt violet bl	30	15
1334 A299	1.70fo ocher	48	22
1335 A299	3fo multi	1.40	90
	Nos. 1326-1335,B218 (11)	4.27	
	Set value		2.10

17th Olympic Games, Rome, Aug. 25-Sept. 11.

Souvenir Sheet

Romulus and Remus Statue and Olympic Flame A300

1960, Aug. 21

1336 A300	10fo multicolored	10.00	12.00

Winter and Summer Olympic Games, 1960.

Woman of Mezokovesd Writing Letter — A301

Perf. 11½x12
1960, Oct. 15 Photo. Wmk. 106

1337 A301	2fo multicolored	1.40	1.40
a.	With ticket	1.75	1.75

Day of the Stamp and Natl. Stamp Exhib. Issued in sheets of 8 with alternating ticket. The 4fo sale price marked on the ticket was the admission fee to the Natl. Stamp Exhib.

The Turnip, Russian Fairy Tale — A302

Kangaroo — A303

Fairy Tales: 30f, Snow White and the Seven Dwarfs. 40f, The Miller, His Son and the Donkey. 60f, Puss in Boots. 80f, The Fox and the Raven. 1fo, The Maple-Wood Pipe. 1.70fo, The Fox and the Stork. 2fo, Momotaro (Japanese).

1960, Dec. 1 *Perf. 11½x12*

1338 A302	20f multi	15	15
1339 A302	30f multi	15	15
1340 A302	40f multi	15	15
1341 A302	60f multi	15	15
1342 A302	80f multi	18	15
1343 A302	1fo multi	40	15
1344 A302	1.70fo multi	75	40
1345 A302	2fo multi	1.19	70
	Nos. 1338-1345 (8)	3.12	
	Set value		1.40

1961, Feb. 24 *Perf. 11½x12*

Animals: 30f, Bison. 40f, Brown bear. 60f, Elephants. 80f, Tiger with cubs. 1fo, Ibex. 1.40fo, Polar bear. 2fo, Zebra and young. 2.60fo, Bison cow with calf. 3fo, Main entrance to Budapest Zoological Gardens. 30f, 60f, 80f, 1.40fo, 2fo, 2.60fo are horizontal.

1346 A303	20f orange & blk	15	15
1347 A303	30f yel grn & blk brn	15	15
1348 A303	40f org brn & brn	15	15
1349 A303	60f lil rose & gray	15	15
1350 A303	80f gray & yel	15	15
1351 A303	1fo blue grn & brn	15	15
1352 A303	1.40fo grnsh bl, gray & blk	30	18
1353 A303	2fo pink & black	40	24
1354 A303	2.60fo brt vio & brn	60	38
1355 A303	3fo multicolored	1.10	75
	Nos. 1346-1355 (10)	3.30	
	Set value		1.90

Issued for the Budapest Zoo.

Castle Type of 1960

Castles: 10f, Kisvárda. 12f, Szigliget. 40f, Simon Tornya. 50f, Füzér. 80f, Egervár. 1fo, Vitány. 1.20fo, Sirok. 2fo, Boldogkö. 2.60fo, Hollókö. 4fo, Eger.

1961, Mar. 3 Photo. *Perf. 14½*
Size: 21x17½mm

1356 A293	10f orange brn	15	15
1357 A293	12f violet blue	15	15
1358 A293	40f brt green	15	15
1359 A293	50f brown	15	15
1360 A293	80f dull claret	15	15

Perf. 12x11½
Size: 28x21mm

1361 A293	1fo brt blue	15	15
1362 A293	1.20fo rose violet	26	15
1363 A293	2fo olive bister	42	15
1364 A293	2.60fo dull blue	65	15
1365 A293	4fo brt violet	80	20
	Nos. 1356-1365 (10)	3.03	
	Set value		84

Child Chasing Butterfly — A304

Ferenc Rozsa, Journalist — A305

Designs: 40f, Man on operating table. 60f, Ambulance and stretcher. 1fo, Traffic light and scooter. 1.70fo, Syringe. 4fo, Emblem of Health Information Service (torch and serpent).

1961, Mar. 17 Litho. *Perf. 10½*
Cross in Red
Size: 18x18mm

1366 A304	30f org brn & blk	15	15
1367 A304	40f bl grn, bl & sepia	15	15

Size: 25x30mm

1368	A304	60f	multi	15	15
1369	A304	1fo	multi	16	15
1370	A304	1.70fo	multi	52	22
1371	A304	4fo	gray & yel grn	1.25	55
			Nos. 1366-1371 (6)	2.38	
			Set value		1.10

Health Information Service.

Wmk. 106, Unwmk.

1961 Photo. ***Perf. 12***

Portraits: No. 1373, Gyorgy Kilian. No. 1374, Jozsef Rippl-Ronai. No. 1375, Sandor Latinka. No. 1376, Maté Zalka. No. 1377, Jozsef Katona.

1372	A305	1fo	red brown	15	15
1373	A305	1fo	grnsh blue	15	15
1374	A305	1fo	rose brown	15	15
1375	A305	1fo	olive bis	15	15
1376	A305	1fo	olive grn	15	15
1377	A305	1fo	maroon	15	15
			Set value	72	35

Press Day (#1372); the inauguration of the Gyorgy Kilian Sports Movement (#1373); birth cent. of Jozsef Rippl-Ronai, painter (#1374); Sandor Latinka, revolutionary leader, 75th death anniv. (#1375); Mate Zalka, author and revolutionist (#1376); Jozsef Katona, dramatist (#1377).

Nos. 1374, 1375, 1377 are unwmkd. Others in this set have wmk. 106.

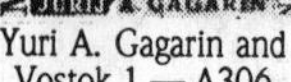

Yuri A. Gagarin and Vostok 1 — A306

Roses — A307

Design: 1fo, Launching Vostok 1.

Perf. 11½x12

1961, Apr. 25 **Wmk. 106**

1381	A306	1fo	dk bl & bis brn	52	52
1382	A306	2fo	dp ultra & bis brn	2.50	2.50

Issued to commemorate the first man in space, Yuri A. Gagarin, Apr. 12, 1961.

1961, Apr. 29 ***Perf. 12½x11½***

Design: 2fo, as 1fo, design reversed.

1383	A307	1fo	grn & dp car	22	15
1384	A307	2fo	grn & dp car	28	15
a.			Pair, #1383-1384	50	30

Issued for May Day, 1961.

"Venus" and Moon A308

Designs: Various Stages of Rocket.

1961, May 24 Wmk. 106 ***Perf. 14½***

1385	A308	40f	grnsh bl, bis & blk	40	22
1386	A308	60f	brt bl, bis & blk	52	22
1387	A308	80f	ultra & blk	1.00	70
1388	A308	2fo	violet & yel	3.00	2.25

Soviet launching of the Venus space probe, Feb. 12, 1961. No. 1388 was also printed in sheets of four, perf. and imperf. Size: 130x76mm.

Warsaw Mermaid, Letter and Sea, Air and Land Transport A309

Mermaid and: 60f, Television screen and antenna. 1fo, Radio.

1961, June 19 Photo. ***Perf. 13½***

1389	A309	40f	red org & blk	15	15
1390	A309	60f	lilac & blk	24	15
1391	A309	1fo	brt blue & blk	38	15
			Set value		27

Conference of Postal Ministers of Communist Countries held at Warsaw.

Flag and Parliament A310

Designs: 1.70fo, Orchid. 2.60fo, Small tortoise-shell butterfly. 3fo, Goldfinch.

1961, June 23 ***Perf. 11***

Background in Silver

1392	A310	1fo	green, red & blk	38	38
1393	A310	1.70fo	red & multi	52	52
1394	A310	2.60fo	purple & multi	85	85
1395	A310	3fo	blue & multi	1.10	1.10

1961, Aug. 19

Background in Gold

1396	A310	1fo	green & blk	38	38
1397	A310	1.70fo	red & multi	48	48
1398	A310	2.60fo	purple & multi	85	85
1399	A310	3fo	blue & multi	1.10	1.10
			Nos. 1392-1399 (8)	5.66	5.66

Issued to publicize the International Stamp Exhibition, Budapest, Sept. 23-Oct. 3, 1961.

Each denomination of Nos. 1392-1399 printed in sheets of four.

In gold background issue the top left inscription is changed on 1fo and 3fo.

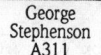

George Stephenson A311

Winged Wheel, Steering Wheel and Road A312

Design: 2fo, Jenö Landler.

Perf. 12½x11½

1961, July 4 Photo. **Wmk. 106**

1400	A311	60f	yellow olive	15	15
1401	A312	1fo	blue & bister	24	15
1402	A311	2fo	yellow brown	42	24

Conference of Transport Ministers of Communist Countries held at Budapest.

Soccer A313

1961, July 8 Unwmk. ***Perf. 14½***

1403	A313	40f	shown	15	15
1404	A313	60f	Wrestlers	15	15
1405	A313	1fo	Gymnast	32	20
			Set value	54	37

50th anniv. of the Steel Workers Sport Club (VASAS). See No. B219.

Galloping Horses — A314

Designs: 40f, Hurdle Jump. 60f, Two trotters. 1fo, Three trotters. 1.70fo, Mares and foals. 2fo, Race horse "Baka." 3fo, Race horse "Kincsem."

1961, July 22

1406	A314	30f	multi	15	15
1407	A314	40f	multi	15	15
1408	A314	60f	multi	15	15
1409	A314	1fo	multi	35	15
1410	A314	1.70fo	multi	60	18
1411	A314	2fo	multi	95	40
1412	A314	3fo	multi	1.50	70
			Nos. 1406-1412 (7)	3.85	1.88

Keyboard, Music and Liszt Silhouette A315

Liszt Monument, Budapest — A316

Designs: 2fo, Academy of Music, Budapest, and bar of music. 10fo, Franz Liszt.

1961, Oct. 2 Unwmk. ***Perf. 12***

1413	A315	60f	gold & blk	18	15
1414	A316	1fo	dark gray	35	20
1415	A315	2fo	dk bl & gray grn	50	40

Souvenir Sheet

1416	A316	10fo	multi	6.00	6.00

150th anniv. of the birth, and the 75th anniv. of the death of Franz Liszt, composer.

Lenin — A317

Monk's Hood — A318

1961, Oct. 22 ***Perf. 11½***

1417	A317	1fo	deep brown	25	15

22nd Congress of the Communist Party of the USSR, Oct. 17-31.

Wmk. 106

1961, Nov. 4 Photo. ***Perf. 12***

1418	A318	20f	shown	15	15
1419	A318	30f	Centaury	15	15
1420	A318	40f	Blue iris	15	15
1421	A318	60f	Thorn apple	15	15
1422	A318	1fo	Purple hollyhock	28	15
1423	A318	1.70fo	Hop	45	20
1424	A318	2fo	Poppy	95	40
1425	A318	3fo	Mullein	1.40	65
			Nos. 1418-1425 (8)	3.68	
			Set value		1.50

Nightingale — A319

Mihaly Karolyi — A320

Birds: 40f, Great titmouse. 60f, Chaffinch, horiz. 1fo, Eurasian jay. 1.20fo, Golden oriole, horiz. 1.50fo, European blackbird, horiz. 2fo, Yellowhammer, 3fo, Lapwing, horiz.

1961, Dec. 18 Unwmk. ***Perf. 12***

1426	A319	30f	multi	15	15
1427	A319	40f	multi	20	15
1428	A319	60f	multi	15	15
1429	A319	1fo	multi	15	15
1430	A319	1.20fo	multi	18	15
1431	A319	1.50fo	multi	48	15
1432	A319	2fo	multi	60	24
1433	A319	3fo	multi	1.25	48
			Nos. 1426-1433 (8)	3.16	
			Set value		1.30

1962, Mar. 18

1434	A320	1fo	black	20	15

Issued in memory of Mihaly Karolyi, (1875-1955), Prime Minister of Hungarian Republic (1918-19).

1962, Mar. 29

Portrait: No. 1435, Ferenc Berkes.

1435	A320	1fo	red brown	16	15

Fifth Congress of the Hungarian Cooperative Movement, and to honor Ferenc Berkes, revolutionary. See Nos. 1457, 1459.

Map of Europe, Train Signals and Emblem — A321

1962, May 2 **Photo.**

1436	A321	1fo	blue green	20	15

14th Intl. Esperanto Cong. of Railway Men.

Xiphophorus Helleri — A322

Tropical Fish: 30f, Macropodus opercularis. 40f, Lebistes reticulatus. 60f, Betta splendens. 80c, Puntius tetrazona. 1fo, Pterophyllum scalare. 1.20fo, Mesogonistius chaetodon. 1.50fo, Aphyosemion australe. 2fo, Hyphessobrycon innesi. 3fo, Symphysodon aequifasciata haraldi.

1962, May 5 ***Perf. 11½x12***

Fish in Natural Colors, Black Inscriptions

1437	A322	20f	blue	15	15
1438	A322	30f	citron	15	15
1439	A322	40f	lt blue	15	15
1440	A322	60f	lt yellow grn	15	15
1441	A322	80f	blue green	28	15
1442	A322	1fo	brt bl grn	16	15
1443	A322	1.20fo	blue green	22	15
1444	A322	1.50fo	grnsh blue	28	15
1445	A322	2fo	green	60	28
1446	A322	3fo	gray grn & yel	90	70
			Nos. 1437-1446 (10)	3.04	
			Set value		1.65

Globe, Soccer Ball and Flags of Colombia and Uruguay — A323

Goalkeeper — A324

Flags of: 40f, USSR and Yugoslavia. 60f, Switzerland and Chile. 1fo, Germany and Italy. 1.70fo, Argentina and Bulgaria. 3fo, Brazil and Mexico.

Unwmk.

1962, May 21 Photo. *Perf. 11*

Flags in National Colors

1447 A323	30f rose & bis	15	15
1448 A323	40f pale grn & bis	15	15
1449 A323	60f pale lil & bis	15	15
1450 A323	1fo blue & bis	38	18
1451 A323	1.70fo ocher & bis	30	24
1452 A323	3fo pink & blue bis	90	45
Nos. 1447-1452,B224,C209A (8)		4.13	
Set value			1.70

Souvenir Sheet

Perf. 12

1453 A324	10fo multicolored	7.00	7.00

World Cup Soccer Championship, Chile, May 30-June 17.

Type of 1961 and

Johann Gutenberg — A325

Portraits: No. 1456, Miklós Misztófalusi Kis, Hungarian printer (1650-1702). No. 1457, Jozsef Pach. No. 1458, András Cházár. No. 1459, Dr. Ferenc Hutyra. No. 1460, Gábor Egressy and National Theater.

1962 Unwmk. Photo. *Perf. 12*

1455 A325	1fo blue black	18	15
1456 A325	1fo red brown	18	15
1457 A320	1fo blue	18	15
1458 A325	1fo violet	18	15
1459 A320	1fo deep blue	18	15
1460 A325	1fo rose red	18	15
Nos. 1455-1460 (6)		1.08	
Set value			42

Cent. of Printers' and Papermakers' Union (Nos. 1455-1456). 75th anniv. of founding, by Jozsef Pech, of Hungarian Hydroelectric Service (No. 1457). András Cházár, founder of Hungarian deaf-mute education (No. 1458). Dr. Ferenc Hutyra, founder of Hungarian veterinary medicine (No. 1459). 125th anniv. of National Theater (No. 1460).

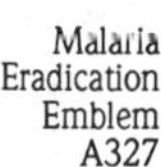

Malaria Eradication Emblem A327

1962, June 25 *Perf. 15*

1461 A327	2.50fo lemon & blk	50	40
a.	2.50fo grn & blk, sheet of 4, perf. 11	5.00	5.00

WHO drive to eradicate malaria. Imperf. sheets with control numbers exist.

Sword-into-Plowshare Statue, United Nations, NY — A328

1962, July 7 *Perf. 12*

1462 A328	1fo brown	15	15

World Congress for Peace and Disarmament, Moscow, July 9-14.

Floribunda Rose A329

Festival Emblem A330

1962 *Perf. 12½x11½*

Various Roses in Natural Colors

1465 A329	20f orange brn	15	15
1466 A329	40f slate grn	15	15
1467 A329	60f violet	15	15
1468 A329	80f rose red	18	15
1469 A329	1fo dark green	24	15
1470 A329	1.20fo orange	28	18
1471 A329	2fo dk blue grn	75	52
1472 A330	3fo multi	1.10	42
Nos. 1465-1472 (8)		3.00	
Set value			1.45

No. 1472 was issued for the 8th World Youth Festival, Helsinki, July 28-Aug. 6.

Weight Lifter — A331

Oil Derrick and Primitive Oil Well — A332

1962, Sept. 16 *Perf. 12*

1473 A331	1fo copper red	30	15

Issued to commemorate the European Weight Lifting Championships.

Perf. 12x11½

1962, Oct. 8 Photo. Unwmk.

1474 A332	1fo green	20	15

25th anniv. of the Hungarian oil industry.

Racing Motorcyclist — A333

Designs: 30f, Stunt racing. 40f, Uphill race. 60f, Cyclist in curve. 1fo, Start. 1.20fo, Speed racing. 1.70fo, Motorcyclist with sidecar. 2fo, Motor scooter. 3fo, Racing car.

1962, Dec. 28 *Perf. 11*

1475 A333	20f multi	15	15
1476 A333	30f multi	15	15
1477 A333	40f multi	15	15
1478 A333	60f multi	15	15
1479 A333	1fo multi	18	15
1480 A333	1.20fo multi	22	15
1481 A333	1.70fo multi	42	15
1482 A333	2fo multi	60	24
1483 A333	3fo multi	1.10	55
Nos. 1475-1483 (9)		3.12	
Set value			1.32

Ice Skater — A334

Designs: 20f-3fo, Various figure skating and ice dancing positions. 20f, 3fo horiz. 10fo, Figure skater and flags of participating nations.

Perf. 12x11½, 11½x12

1963, Feb. 5 Photo. Unwmk.

1484 A334	20f multi	18	15
1485 A334	40f multi	18	15
1486 A334	60f multi	18	15
1487 A334	1fo multi	30	15
1488 A334	1.40fo multi	30	22
1489 A334	2fo multi	42	35
1490 A334	3fo multi	1.00	70
Nos. 1484-1490 (7)		2.56	
Set value			1.55

Souvenir Sheet

Perf. 11½x12

1491 A334	10fo multi	4.75	4.25

European Figure Skating and Ice Dancing Championships, Budapest, Feb. 5-10.

János Batsányi (1763-1845) — A335

Designs: No. 1493, Helicon Monument. No. 1494, Actors before Szeged Cathedral. No. 1495, Leo Weiner, composer. No. 1496, Ferenc Entz, horticulturist. No. 1497, Ivan Markovits, inventor of Hungarian shorthand, 1863. No. 1498, Dr. Frigyes Koranyi. No. 1499, Ferenc Erkel (1810-93), composer. No. 1500, Geza Gardonyi (1863-1922), writer of Hungarian historical novels for youth. No. 1501, Pierre de Coubertin, Frenchman, reviver of Olympic Games. No. 1502, Jozsef Eötvös, author, philosopher, educator. No. 1503, Budapest Industrial Fair emblem. No. 1504, Stagecoach and Arc de Triomphe, Paris. No. 1505, Hungary map and power lines. No. 1506, Roses.

1963 Unwmk. *Perf. 11*

1492 A335	40f dk car rose	15	15
1493 A335	40f blue	15	15
1494 A335	40f violet blue	15	15
1495 A335	40f olive	15	15
1496 A335	40f emerald	15	15
1497 A335	40f dark blue	15	15
1498 A335	60f dull violet	15	15
1499 A335	60f bister brn	15	15
1500 A335	60f gray green	15	15
1501 A335	60f red brown	42	18
1502 A335	60f lilac	15	15
1503 A335	1fo purple	22	15
1504 A335	1fo rose red	25	15
1505 A335	1fo gray	25	15
1506 A335	2fo multi	60	15
Nos. 1492-1506 (15)		3.24	
Set value			1.00

No. 1493, 10th Youth Festival, Keszthely. No. 1494, Outdoor plays, Szeged. No. 1495, Budapest Music Competition. No. 1496, Cent. of professional horticultural training. No. 1498, 50th anniv. of the death of Prof. Koranyi, pioneer in fight against tuberculosis. No. 1499, Erkel Memorial Festival, Gyula. No. 1501, 10th anniv. of the People's Stadium, Budapest. No. 1502, 150th anniv. of birth of Jozsef Eötvös, organizer of modern public education in Hungary. No. 1504, Paris Postal Conf., 1863. No. 1505, Rural electrification. No. 1506, 5th Natl. Rose Show.

Ship and Chain Bridge, Budapest A336

Bus and Parliament A337

Designs: 20f, Trolley. 30f, Sightseeing bus and National Museum. 40f, Bus and trailer. 50f, Railroad tank car. 60f, Trolley bus. 70f, Railroad mail car. 80f, Motorcycle messenger. No. 1516, Mail plane, vert. No. 1517, Television transmitter, Miskolc, vert. 1.40fo, Mobile post office. 1.70fo, Diesel locomotive. 2fo, Mobile radio transmitter and stadium. 2.50fo, Tourist bus. 2.60fo, Passenger train. 3fo, P.O. parcel conveyor. 4fo, Television transmitters, Pecs, vert. 5fo, Hydraulic lift truck and mail car. 6fo, Woman teletypist. 8fo, Map of Budapest and automatic dial phone. 10fo, Girl pioneer and woman letter carrier.

1963-64 Photo. *Perf. 11*

1507 A336	10f brt blue	15	15
1508 A336	20f dp yellow grn	15	15
1509 A336	30f violet	15	15
1510 A336	40f orange	15	15
1511 A336	50f brown	15	15
1512 A336	60f crimson	15	15
1513 A336	70f olive gray	15	15
1514 A336	80f red brn ('64)	28	15

Perf. 12x11½, 11½x12

1515 A337	1fo rose claret	15	15
1516 A337	1.20fo orange brn	1.00	70
1517 A337	1.20fo dp vio ('64)	18	15
1518 A337	1.40fo dp yel grn	24	18
1519 A337	1.70fo maroon	35	15
1520 A337	2fo grnsh blue	40	15
1521 A337	2.50fo lilac	42	15
1522 A337	2.60fo olive	42	15
1523 A337	3fo dk blue ('64)	35	15
1524 A337	4fo blue ('64)	42	15
1525 A337	5fo ol brn ('64)	55	15
1526 A337	6fo dk ol bis ('64)	70	15
1527 A337	8fo red lilac ('64)	1.00	24
1528 A337	10fo emerald ('64)	1.00	50
Nos. 1507-1528 (22)		8.51	
Set value			2.75

Size of 20f, 60f: 20½-21x16¾-17mm.

Minute inscription in lower margin includes year date, number of stamp in set and designer's name (Bokros F. or Legrady S.).

See Nos. 1983-1983B, 2196-2204.

Coil Stamps

1965-67 *Perf. 14*

Size: 21½x16½mm

1508a A336	20f dp yellow green	15	15
1512a A336	60f crimson ('67)	38	15
Set value			20

Black control number on back of every 3th stamp.

Motorboat — A338

Girl, Steamer and Castle — A339

Design: 60f, Sailboat.

1963, July 13 *Perf. 11*

1529 A338	20f sl grn, red & blk	22	15
1530 A339	40f multicolored	22	18
1531 A338	60f bl, blk, brn & org	38	25

Centenary of the summer resort Siofok.

Child with Towel and Toothbrush A340

Karancsság Woman A341

Designs: 40f, Child with medicines. 60f, Girls of 3 races. 1fo, Girl and heart. 1.40fo, Boys of 3 races. 2fo, Medical examination of child. 3fo, Hands shielding plants.

1963, July 27 *Perf. 12x11½*

No.	Type	Value	Color	Unused	Used
1532	A340	30f	multi	15	15
1533	A340	40f	multi	15	15
1534	A340	60f	multi	15	15
1535	A340	1fo	multi	15	15
1536	A340	1.40fo	multi	18	15
1537	A340	2fo	multi	30	28
1538	A340	3fo	multi	75	60
			Nos. 1532-1538 (7)	1.83	
			Set value		1.30

Centenary of the International Red Cross.

1963, Aug. 18 **Engr.** *Perf. 11½*

Provincial Costumes: 30f, Kapuvár man. 40f, Debrecen woman. 60f, Hortobágy man. 1fo, Csököly woman. 1.70fo, Dunántul man. 2fo, Buják woman. 2.50fo, Alföld man. 3fo, Mezökövesd bride.

No.	Type	Value	Color	Unused	Used
1539	A341	20f	claret	15	15
1540	A341	30f	green	15	15
1541	A341	40f	brown	15	15
1542	A341	60f	brt blue	16	15
1543	A341	1fo	brown red	22	15
1544	A341	1.70fo	purple	35	22
1545	A341	2fo	dk blue grn	48	22
1546	A341	2.50fo	dk carmine	60	32
1547	A341	3fo	violet blue	1.10	55
			Nos. 1539-1547 (9)	3.36	
			Set value		1.65

Issued in connection with the Popular Art Exhibition in Budapest.

Slalom and 1964 Olympic Emblem — A342

Sports: 60f, Downhill skiing. 70f, Ski jump. 80f, Rifle shooting on skis. 1fo, Figure skating pair. 2fo, Ice hockey. 2.60fo, Speed ice skating. 10fo, Skier and mountains, vert.

1963-64 **Photo.** *Perf. 12*

1964 Olympic Emblem in Black and Red

No.	Type	Value	Color	Unused	Used
1548	A342	40f	yel grn & bis	15	15
1549	A342	60f	violet & bis	15	15
1550	A342	70f	ultra & bis	15	15
1551	A342	80f	emerald & bis	15	15
1552	A342	1fo	brn org & bis	18	15
1553	A342	2fo	brt blue & bis	45	22
1554	A342	2.60fo	rose lake & bis	70	45
			Nos. 1548-1554,B234 (8)	2.83	
			Set value		1.40

Souvenir Sheet

Perf. 11½x12

No.	Type	Value	Color	Unused	Used
1555	A342	10fo	grnsh bl, red & brn ('64)	5.00	4.75

9th Winter Olympic Games, Innsbruck, Austria, Jan. 29-Feb. 9, 1964.

Four-Leaf Clover — A343

Moon Rocket — A344

Good Luck Symbols: 20f, Calendar and mistletoe, horiz. 30f, Chimneysweep and clover. 60f, Top hat, pig and clover. 1fo, Clown with balloon and clover, horiz. 2fo, Lanterns, mask and clover.

Perf. 12x11½, 11½x12

1963, Dec. 12 **Photo.** **Unwmk.**

Sizes: 28x22mm (20f, 1fo); 22x28mm (40f); 28x39mm (30f, 60f, 2fo)

No.	Type	Value	Color	Unused	Used
1556	A343	20f	multi	15	15
1557	A343	30f	multi	15	15
1558	A343	40f	multi	15	15
1559	A343	60f	multi	15	15
1560	A343	1fo	multi	20	15
1561	A343	2fo	multi	48	22
			Nos. 1556-1561,B235-B236 (8)	2.63	
			Set value		1.25

New Year 1964. The 20f and 40f issued in booklet panes of 10, perf. and imperf.; sold for 2 times and 1½ times face respectively.

1964, Jan. 8 *Perf. 11½x12, 12x11½*

American and Russian Spacecraft: 40f, Venus space probe. 60f, Vostok I, horiz. 1fo, Friendship 7. 1.70fo, Vostok III & IV. 2fo, Telstar 1 & 2, horiz. 2.60fo, Mars I. 3fo, Radar, rockets and satellites, horiz.

No.	Type	Value	Color	Unused	Used
1562	A344	30f	grn, yel & brnz	15	15
1563	A344	40f	pur, bl & sil	15	15
1564	A344	60f	bl, blk, yel, sil & red	15	15
1565	A344	1fo	dk brn, red & sil	18	15
1566	A344	1.70fo	vio bl, blk, tan & red	28	15
1567	A344	2fo	sl grn, yel & sil	50	18
1568	A344	2.60fo	dp bl, yel & brnz	75	35
1569	A344	3fo	dp vio, lt bl & sil	1.00	60
			Nos. 1562-1569 (8)	3.16	
			Set value		1.45

Achievements in space research.

Lace Type of 1960

Various Halas Lace Designs.
Sizes: 20f, 2.60fo: 38x28mm. 30f, 40f, 60f, 1fo, 1.40fo, 2fo: 38x45mm.

Engr. & Litho.

1964, Feb. 28 *Perf. 11½*

No.	Type	Value	Color	Unused	Used
1570	A294	20f	emerald & blk	15	15
1571	A294	30f	dull yel & blk	15	15
1572	A294	40f	deep rose & blk	15	15
1573	A294	60f	olive & blk	16	15
1574	A294	1fo	red org & blk	32	15
1575	A294	1.40fo	blue & blk	45	22
1576	A294	2fo	bluish grn & blk	70	28
1577	A294	2.60fo	lt vio & blk	1.10	60
			Nos. 1570-1577 (8)	3.18	
			Set value		1.45

Special Anniversaries-Events Issue

Imre Madach (1823-64) A345

Shakespeare A346

Karl Marx and Membership Card of International Working Men's Association — A347

Michelangelo — A348

Lajos Kossuth and György Dózsa — A349

Budapest Fair Buildings — A350

Designs: No. 1579, Ervin Szabo. No. 1580, Writer Andras Fay (1786-1864). No. 1581, Aggtelek Cave scene. No. 1582, Excavating bauxite. No. 1584, Equestrian statue, Szekesfehervar. No. 1585, Bowler. No. 1586, Waterfall and forest. No. 1587, Architect Miklos Ybl (1814-91) and Budapest Opera. No. 1590, Armor, saber, sword and foil. No. 1592, Galileo Galilei. No. 1593, Women basketball players. No. 1595, Two runners breaking tape.

Perf. 11½x12, 12x11½, 11

1964 **Photo.** **Unwmk.**

Inscribed: "ÉVFORDULÓK-ESEMÉNYEK"

No.	Type	Value	Color	Unused	Used
1578	A345	60f	brt purple	15	15
1579	A345	60f	olive	15	15
1580	A345	60f	olive grn	15	15
1581	A346	60f	bluish grn	20	15
1582	A346	60f	Prus blue	15	15
1583	A347	60f	rose red	15	15
1584	A348	60f	slate blue	16	15
1585	A345	1fo	car rose	20	15
1586	A346	1fo	dull blue grn	20	15
1587	A348	1fo	orange brn	15	15
1588	A349	1fo	ultra	15	15
1589	A350	1fo	brt green	15	15
1590	A345	2fo	yellow brn	25	15
1591	A346	2fo	magenta	38	15
1592	A346	2fo	red brown	32	15
1593	A346	2fo	brt blue	32	15
1594	A348	2fo	gray brown	38	15
1595	A348	2fo	brown red	32	15
			Nos. 1578-1595 (18)	3.93	
			Set value		1.00

No. 1579, Municipal libraries, 60th anniv., and librarian Szabo (1877-1918). No. 1582, Bauxite mining in Hungary, 30th year. No. 1583, Cent. of 1st Socialist Intl. No. 1584, King Alba Day in Székesfehérvár. No. 1585, 1st European Bowling Championship, Budapest.

No. 1586, Cong. of Natl. Forestry Federation. No. 1588, City of Cegléd, 600th anniv. No. 1589, Opening of 1964 Budapest Intl. Fair. No. 1590, Hungarian Youth Fencing Association, 50th anniv. Nos. 1591-1592, Shakespeare and Galileo, 400th birth anniversaries. No. 1593, 9th European Women's Basketball Championship. No. 1594, Michelangelo's 400th death anniv. No. 1595, 50th anniv. of 1st Hungarian-Swedish athletic meet.

Eleanor Roosevelt — A351

Design, horiz.: a, d, Portrait at right. b, c, Portrait at left.

1964, Apr. 27 *Perf. 12½*

No.	Type	Value	Color	Unused	Used
1596	A351	2fo	gray, black & buff	30	22

Miniature Sheet

Perf. 11

No.	Type	Value	Color	Unused	Used
1597			Sheet of 4	3.75	3.75
a.	A351	2fo	dp cl, brn & blk	75	75
b.	A351	2fo	dk bl, brn & blk	75	75
c.	A351	2fo	grn, brn & blk	75	75
d.	A351	2fo	ol, brn & blk	75	75

Fencing — A352

Sport: 40f, Women's gymnastics. 60f, Soccer. 80f, Equestrian. 1fo, Running. 1.40fo, Weight lifting. 1.70fo, Gymnast on rings. 2fo, Hammer throw and javelin. 2.50fo, Boxing.

1964, June 12 **Photo.** *Perf. 11*

Multicolored Design and Inscription

No.	Type	Value	Color	Unused	Used
1598	A352	30f	lt ver	15	15
1599	A352	40f	blue	15	15
1600	A352	60f	emerald	15	15
1601	A352	80f	tan	15	15
1602	A352	1fo	yellow	15	15
1603	A352	1.40fo	bis brn	15	15
1604	A352	1.70fo	bluish gray	28	15
1605	A352	2fo	gray grn	40	22
1606	A352	2.50fo	vio gray	65	52
			Nos. 1598-1606,B237 (10)	2.98	
			Set value		2.10

Issued to publicize the 18th Olympic Games, Tokyo, Oct. 10-25.

Elberta Peaches — A353

Peaches: 40h, Blossoms (J. H. Hale). 60h, Magyar Kajszi. 1fo, Mandula Kajszi. 1.50fo, Borsi Rozsa. 1.70fo, Blossoms (Alexander). 2fo, Champion. 3fo, Mayflower.

1964, July 24 *Perf. 11½*

No.	Type	Value	Color	Unused	Used
1607	A353	40f	multi	15	15
1608	A353	60f	multi	15	15
1609	A353	1fo	multi	18	15
1610	A353	1.50fo	multi	22	18
1611	A353	1.70fo	multi	28	18
1612	A353	2fo	multi	40	18
1613	A353	2.60fo	multi	48	40
1614	A353	3fo	multi	75	60
			Nos. 1607-1614 (8)	2.61	
			Set value		1.75

National Peach Exhibition, Szeged.

Crossing Street in Safety Zone — A354

Designs: 60f, "Watch out for Children" (child and ball). 1fo, "Look before Crossing" (mother and child).

1964, Sept. 27 *Perf. 11*
1615 A354 20f multicolored 18 15
1616 A354 60f multicolored 18 15
1617 A354 1fo lilac & multi 28 15
Set value 36

Issued to publicize traffic safety.

Souvenir Sheet

Voskhod 1 and Globe — A355

1964, Nov. 6 *Perf. 12x11½*
1618 A355 10fo multicolored 4.00 4.00

Russian space flight of Vladimir M. Komarov, Boris B. Yegorov and Konstantine Feoktistov.

Arpad Bridge — A356

Danube Bridges, Budapest: 30f, Margaret Bridge. 60f, Chain Bridge. 1fo, Elizabeth Bridge. 1.50fo, Freedom Bridge. 2fo, Petőfi Bridge. 2.50fo, Railroad Bridge.

1964, Nov. 21 **Photo.** *Perf. 11x11½*
1619 A356 20f multi 18 15
1620 A356 30f multi 18 15
1621 A356 60f multi 18 15
1622 A356 1fo multi 25 15
1623 A356 1.50fo multi 35 15
1624 A356 2fo multi 60 22
1625 A356 2.50fo multi 1.10 55
Nos. 1619-1625 (7) 2.84
Set value 1.25

Opening of the reconstructed Elizabeth Bridge. See No. C250.

Ring-necked Pheasant and Hunting Rifle — A357

Designs: 30f, Wild boar. 40f, Gray partridges. 60f, Varying hare. 80f, Fallow deer. 1fo, Mouflon. 1.70fo, Red deer. 2fo, Great bustard. 2.50fo, Roebuck and roe deer. 3fo, Emblem of National Federation of Hungarian Hunters (antlers).

1964, Dec. 30 **Photo.** *Perf. 12x11½*
1626 A357 20f multi 15 15
1627 A357 30f multi 15 15
1628 A357 40f multi 15 15
1629 A357 60f multi 15 15
1630 A357 80f multi 15 15
1631 A357 1fo multi 15 15
1632 A357 1.70fo multi 25 15
1633 A357 2fo multi 35 15
1634 A357 2.50fo multi 70 30
1635 A357 3fo multi 1.00 60
Nos. 1626-1635 (10) 3.20
Set value 1.55

Castle Type of 1960

Castles: 3fo, Csesznek, vert. 4fo, Eger. 5fo, Kőszeg, vert.

1964 *Perf. 11½x12, 12x11½*
Size: 21x28mm, 28x21mm
1644 A293 3fo red brown 38 15
1645 A293 4fo brt violet 50 15
1646 A293 5fo yellow grn 65 15
Set value 16

Equestrian, Gold and Bronze Medals — A358

Designs: 30f, Women's gymnastics, silver and bronze medals. 50f, Small-bore rifle, gold and bronze medals. 60f, Water polo, gold medal. 70f, Shot put, bronze medal. 80f, Soccer, gold medal. 1fo, Weight lifting, 1 bronze and 2 silver medals. 1.20fo, Canoeing, silver medal. 1.40fo, Hammer throw, silver medal. 1.50fo, Wrestling, 2 gold medals. 1.70fo, Javelin, 2 silver medals. 3fo, Fencing, 4 gold medals.

1965, Feb. 20 *Perf. 12*
Medals in Gold, Silver or Bronze
1647 A358 20f lt ol grn & dk brn 15 15
1648 A358 30f violet & dk brn 15 15
1649 A358 50f olive & dk brn 15 15
1650 A358 60f lt bl & red brn 15 15
1651 A358 70f lt gray & red brn 15 15
1652 A358 80f yel grn & dk brn 15 15
1653 A358 1fo lil, vio & red brn 15 15
1654 A358 1.20fo lt bl, ultra & red brn 18 18
1655 A358 1.40fo gray & red brn 22 15
1656 A358 1.50fo tan, lt brn & red brn 35 25
1657 A358 1.70fo pink & red brn 70 28
1658 A358 3fo grnsh blue & brn 90 60
Set value 3.00 2.00

Victories by the Hungarian team in the 1964 Olympic Games, Tokyo, Oct. 10-25.

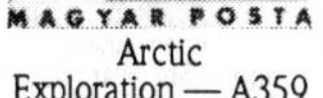

Arctic Exploration — A359

Chrysanthemums — A360

Designs: 30f, Radar tracking rocket, ionosphere research. 60f, Rocket and earth with reflecting layer diagrams, atmospheric research. 80f, Telescope and map of Milky Way, radio astronomy. 1.50fo, Earth, compass rose and needle, earth magnetism. 1.70fo, Weather balloon and lightning, meteorology. 2fo, Aurora borealis and penguins, arctic research. 2.50fo, Satellite, earth and planets, space research. 3fo, IQSY emblem and world map. 10fo, Sun with flares and corona, snow crystals and rain.

Perf. 11½x12
1965, Mar. 25 **Photo.** **Unwmk.**
1659 A359 20f blue, org & blk 15 15
1660 A359 30f gray, blk & emer 15 15
1661 A359 60f lilac, blk & yel 15 15
1662 A359 80f lt grn, yel & blk 15 15
1663 A359 1.50fo lemon, bl & blk 16 15
1664 A359 1.70fo blue, pink & blk 22 15
1665 A359 2fo ultra, sal & blk 25 15
1666 A359 2.50fo org brn, yel & blk 38 22
1667 A359 3fo lt bl, cit & blk 70 50
Nos. 1659-1667 (9) 2.31
Set value 1.25

Souvenir Sheet
1668 A359 10fo ultra, org & blk 3.00 3.00

Intl. Quiet Sun Year, 1964-65.

1965, Apr. 4

Designs: 30f, Peonies. 50f, Carnations. 60f, Roses. 1.40fo, Lilies. 1.70fo, Anemones. 2fo, Gladioli. 2.50fo, Tulips. 3fo, Mixed flower bouquet.

Flowers in Natural Colors
1669 A360 20f gold & gray 15 15
1670 A360 30f gold & gray 15 15
1671 A360 50f gold & gray 15 15
1672 A360 60f gold & gray 15 15
1673 A360 1.40fo gold & gray 15 15
1674 A360 1.70fo gold & gray 18 15
1675 A360 2fo gold & gray 20 15
1676 A360 2.50fo gold & gray 38 16
1677 A360 3fo gold & gray 80 60
Nos. 1669-1677 (9) 2.31
Set value 1.25

20th anniversary of liberation from the Nazis.

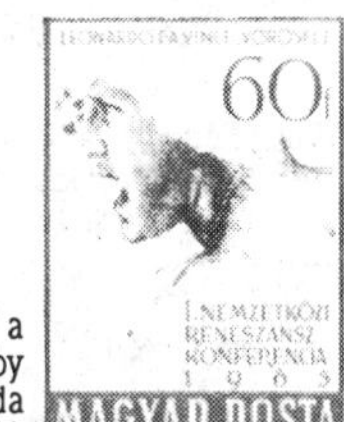

"Head of a Combatant" by Leonardo da Vinci — A361

Perf. 11½x12
1965, May 4 **Photo.** **Unwmk.**
1678 A361 60f bister & org brn 30 15

Issued to publicize the First International Renaissance Conference, Budapest.

Nikolayev, Tereshkova and View of Budapest A362

1965, May 10 *Perf. 11*
1679 A362 1fo dull blue & brn 25 15

Visit of the Russian astronauts Andrian G. Nikolayev and Valentina Tereshkova (Mr. & Mrs. Nikolayev) to Budapest.

ITU Emblem, Old and New Communication Equipment — A363

1965, May 17
1680 A363 60f violet blue 15 15

Cent. of the ITU.

Souvenir Sheet

Austrian WIPA Stamp of 1933 — A363a

1965, June 4 **Photo.** *Perf. 11*
1681 A363a Sheet of 2 + 2 labels 3.75 3.75
a. 2fo gray & deep ultra 1.50 1.50

1965 Vienna Intl. Phil. Exhib. WIPA, June 4-13.

Marx and Lenin, Crowds with Flags — A364

ICY Emblem and Pulley — A365

1965, June 15 *Perf. 11½x12*
1682 A364 60f red, blk & yel 15 15

6th Conference of Ministers of Post of Socialist Countries, Peking, June 21-July 15.

1965, June 25
1683 A365 2fo dark red 20 15
a. Min. sheet of 4, perf. 11 2.75 2.75

Intl. Cooperation Year, 1965. No. 1683a contains rose red, olive, Prussian green and violet stamps.

Musical Clown A366

Dr. Semmelweis A367

Circus Acts: 20f, Equestrians. 40f, Elephant. 50f, Seal balancing ball. 60f, Lions. 1fo, Wildcat jumping through burning hoops. 1.50fo, Black leopards. 2.50fo, Juggler. 3fo, Leopard and dogs. 4fo, Bear on bicycle.

1965, July 26 **Photo.** *Perf. 11½x12*
1684 A366 20f multi 15 15
1685 A366 30f multi 15 15
1686 A366 40f multi 15 15
1687 A366 50f multi 15 15
1688 A366 60f multi 15 15
1689 A366 1fo multi 15 15
1690 A366 1.50fo multi 22 15
1691 A366 2.50fo multi 38 15
1692 A366 3fo multi 60 32
1693 A366 4fo multi 80 48
Nos. 1684-1693 (10) 2.90
Set value 1.50

1965, Aug. 20 **Photo.** **Unwmk.**
1694 A367 60f red brown 15 15

Dr. Ignaz Philipp Semmelweis (1818-1865), discoverer of the cause of puerperal fever and introduced antisepsis into obstetrics.

Runner — A368

Sport: 30f, Swimmer at start. 50f, Woman diver. 60f, Modern dancing. 80f, Tennis. 1.70fo, Fencing. 2fo, Volleyball. 2.50fo, Basketball. 4fo, Water polo. 10fo, People's Stadium, Budapest, horiz.

1965, Aug. 20 *Perf. 11*
Size: 38x38mm
1695 A368 20f multi 15 15
1696 A368 30f blue & red brn 15 15
1697 A368 50f bl grn, blk & red brn 15 15

1698 A368 60f vio, blk & red brn 15 15
1699 A368 80f tan, ol & red brn 18 15
1700 A368 1.70fo multi 30 15
1701 A368 2fo multi 35 18
1702 A368 2.50fo gray, blk & red brn 60 35
1703 A368 4fo bl, red brn & blk 1.00 60
Nos. 1695-1703 (9) 3.03
Set value 1.60

Souvenir Sheet

Perf. 12x11½

1704 A368 10fo bis, red brn & gray 3.25 3.00

Intl. College Championships, "Universiade," Budapest. No. 1704 contains one 38x28mm stamp.

Hemispheres and Warsaw Mermaid A369

1965, Oct. 8 Photo. *Perf. 12x11½*

1705 A369 60f brt blue 20 15

Sixth Congress of the World Federation of Trade Unions, Warsaw.

Phyllocactus Hybridus — A370

Flowers from Botanical Gardens: 30f, Cattleya Warszewiczii (orchid). 60f, Rebutia calliantha. 70f, Paphiopedilum hybridium. 80f, Opuntia cactus. 1fo, Laelia elegans (orchid). 1.50fo, Christmas cactus. 2fo, Bird-of-paradise flower. 2.50fo, Lithops Weberi. 3fo, Victoria water lily.

1965, Oct. 11 *Perf. 11½x12*

1706 A370 20f gray & multi 18 15
1707 A370 30f gray & multi 18 15
1708 A370 60f gray & multi 15 15
1709 A370 70f gray & multi 15 15
1710 A370 80f gray & multi 15 15
1711 A370 1fo gray & multi 18 15
1712 A370 1.50fo gray & multi 24 15
1713 A370 2fo gray & multi 30 18
1714 A370 2.50fo gray & multi 48 30
1715 A370 3fo gray & multi 75 42
Nos. 1706-1715 (10) 2.76
Set value 1.35

"The Black Stallion" — A371

Tales from the Arabian Nights: 30f, Shahriar and Scheherazade. 50f, Sinbad's Fifth Voyage (ship). 60f, Aladdin, or The Wonderful Lamp. 80f, Harun al-Rashid. 1fo, The Flying Carpet. 1.70fo, The Fisherman and the Genie. 2fo, Ali Baba and the Forty Thieves. 3fo, Sinbad's Second Voyage (flying bird).

1965, Dec. 15 Litho. *Perf. 11½*

1716 A371 20f multi 15 15
1717 A371 30f multi 15 15
1718 A371 50f multi 15 15
1719 A371 60f multi 15 15
1720 A371 80f multi 22 15
1721 A371 1fo multi 22 15
1722 A371 1.70fo multi 38 15
1723 A371 2fo multi 50 25
1724 A371 3fo multi 1.10 60
Nos. 1716-1724 (9) 3.02
Set value 1.45

Congress Emblem — A372

Callimorpha Dominula — A373

1965, Dec. 9 Photo. *Perf. 11½x12*

1725 A372 2fo dark blue 30 15

Fifth Congress of the International Federation of Resistance Fighters (FIR), Budapest.

1966, Feb. 1 Photo. *Perf. 11½x12*

Various Butterflies in Natural Colors; Black Inscription

1726 A373 20f lt aqua 16 15
1727 A373 60f pale violet 15 15
1728 A373 70f tan 22 15
1729 A373 80f lt ultra 22 15
1730 A373 1fo gray 15 15
1731 A373 1.50fo emerald 45 15
1732 A373 2fo dull rose 35 15
1733 A373 2.50fo bister 50 30
1734 A373 3fo blue 75 60
Nos. 1726-1734 (9) 2.95
Set value 1.68

Lal Bahadur Shastri A374

Designs: 60f, Bela Kun. 2fo, Istvan Széchenyi and Chain Bridge.

Lithographed; Photogravure (#1736)

1966 *Perf. 11½x12, 12x11½*

1735 A374 60f red & black 15 15
1736 A374 1fo brt violet 22 15
1737 A374 2fo dull yel, buff & sep 30 15
Set value 19

Kun (1886-1939), communist labor leader; Shastri (1904-66), Indian Prime Minister; Count Istvan Széchenyi (1791-1860), statesman.
See Nos. 1764-1765, 1769-1770.

Luna 9 — A375

Crocus — A376

Design: 3fo, Luna 9 sending signals from moon to earth, horiz.

1966, Mar. 12 Photo. *Perf. 12*

1738 A375 2fo violet, blk & yel 45 18
1739 A375 3fo lt ultra, blk & yel 85 60

1st soft landing on the moon by the Russian satellite Luna 9, Feb. 3, 1966.

1966, Mar. 12 *Perf. 11*

Flowers: 30f, Cyclamen. 60f, Ligularia sibirica. 1.40fo, Lilium bulbiferum. 1.50fo, Snake's head. 3fo, Snapdragon and emblem of Hungarian Nature Preservation Society.

Flowers in Natural Colors

1740 A376 20f brown 15 15
1741 A376 30f aqua 15 15
1742 A376 60f rose claret 24 15
1743 A376 1.40fo gray 35 24
1744 A376 1.50fo ultra 50 30
1745 A376 3fo mag & sepia 1.00 52
Nos. 1740-1745 (6) 2.39 1.51

1966, Apr. 16

Designs: 20f, Barn swallows. 30f, Long-tailed tits. 60f, Red crossbill and pine cone. 1.40fo, Middle spotted woodpecker. 1.50fo, Hoopoe feeding young. 3fo, Forest preserve, lapwing and emblem of National Forest Preservation Society.

Birds in Natural Colors

1746 A376 20f brt green 24 15
1747 A376 30f vermilion 15 15
1748 A376 60f brt green 24 17
1749 A376 1.40fo vio blue 30 28
1750 A376 1.50fo blue 90 50
1751 A376 3fo brn, mag & grn 1.10 90
Nos. 1746-1751 (6) 2.93 2.15

Nos. 1740-1751 issued to promote protection of wild flowers and birds.

Locomotive, 1947; Monoplane, 1912; Autobus, 1911; Steamer, 1853, and Budapest Railroad Station, 1846 — A377

Designs: 2fo, Transportation, 1966: electric locomotive V.43; turboprop airliner IL-18; Ikarusz autobus; Diesel passenger ship, and Budapest South Railroad Station.

1966, Apr. 2 Photo. *Perf. 12*

1752 A377 1fo yel, brn & grn 22 15
1753 A377 2fo pale grn, bl & brn 38 22

Issued to commemorate the re-opening of the Transport Museum, Budapest.

Bronze Order of Labor — A378

Decorations: 30f, Silver Order of Labor. 50f, Banner Order, third class. 60f, Gold Order of Labor. 70f, Banner Order, second class. 1fo, Red Banner Order of Labor. 1.20fo, Banner Order, first class. 2fo, Order of Merit. 2.50fo, Hero of Socialist Labor. Sizes: 20f, 30f, 60f, 1fo, 2fo, 2.50fo: 19½x38mm. 50f: 21x29mm. 70f, 25x31mm. 1.20fo: 28x38mm.

1966, Apr. 2 Unwmk. *Perf. 11*

Decorations in Original Colors

1754 A378 20f dp ultra 15 15
1755 A378 30f lt brown 15 15
1756 A378 50f blue green 15 15
1757 A378 60f violet 15 15
1758 A378 70f carmine 15 15
1759 A378 1fo violet bl 15 15
1760 A378 1.20fo brt blue 15 15
1761 A378 2fo olive 28 18
1762 A378 2.50fo dull blue 34 24
Set value 1.30 85

Portrait Type of 1966 and

Dubna Nuclear Research Institute A379

WHO Headquarters, Geneva — A380

Designs: No. 1764, Pioneer girl. No. 1765, Tamás Esze (1666-1708), military hero. No. 1767, Old view of Buda and UNESCO emblem. No. 1768, Horse-drawn fire pump and emblem of Sopron Fire Brigade. No. 1769, Miklos Zrinyi (1508-66), hero of Turkish Wars. No. 1770, Sandor Koranyi (1866-1944), physician and scientist.

1966 Litho. *Perf. 11½x12*

1763 A379 60f blue grn & blk 15 15
1764 A374 60f multicolored 15 15
1765 A374 60f brt bl & blk 15 15
1766 A380 2fo lt ultra & blk 20 15
1767 A380 2fo lt blue & pur 30 15
1768 A380 2fo orange & blk 30 15
1769 A374 2fo ol bis & brn 24 15
1770 A374 2fo multicolored 24 15
Set value 1.50 50

No. 1763, 10th anniv. of the United Institute for Nuclear Research, Dubna, USSR; No. 1764, 20th anniv. of Pioneer Movement; No. 1766, Inauguration of the WHO Headquarters, Geneva; No. 1767, 20th anniv. of UNESCO and 72nd session of Executive Council, Budapest, May 30-31; No. 1768, Cent. of Volunteer Fire Brigade.

Hungarian Soccer Player and Soccer Field — A381

Jules Rimet, Cup and Soccer Ball — A382

Designs (Views of Soccer play): 30f, Montevideo 1930 (Uruguay 4, Argentina 2). 60f, Rome 1934 (Italy 2, Czechoslovakia 1). 1fo, Paris 1938 (Italy 4, Hungary 2). 1.40fo, Rio de Janeiro 1950 (Uruguay 2, Brazil 1). 1.70fo, Bern 1954 (Germany 3, Hungary 2). 2fo, Stockholm 1958 (Brazil 5, Sweden 2). 2.50fo, Santiago 1962 (Brazil 3, Czechoslovakia 1).

Souvenir Sheet

1966, May 16 Photo. *Perf. 11½x12*

1771 A381 10fo multi 3.75 3.50

1966, June 6 *Perf. 12x11½*

1772 A382 20f blue & multi 24 15
1773 A382 30f orange & multi 24 15
1774 A382 60f multi 20 15
1775 A382 1fo multi 20 15
1776 A382 1.40fo multi 15 15
1777 A382 1.70fo multi 20 15
1778 A382 2fo multi 24 18
1779 A382 2.50fo multi 60 50
Nos. 1772-1779,B258 (9) 2.67
Set value 1.75

World Cup Soccer Championship, Wembley, England, July 11-30.

European Red Fox — A383

Hunting Trophies: 60f, Wild boar. 70f, Wildcat. 80f, Roebuck. 1.50fo, Red deer. 2.50fo, Fallow deer. 3fo, Mouflon.

1966, July 4 Photo. *Perf. 11½x12*

Animals in Natural Colors

1780 A383	20f	gray & lt brn	15	15
1781 A383	60f	buff & gray	15	15
1782 A383	70f	lt bl & gray	20	15
1783 A383	80f	pale grn & yel bis	25	15
1784 A383	1.50fo	pale lem & brn	32	16
1785 A383	2.50fo	gray & brn	60	32
1786 A383	3fo	pale pink & gray	95	65
		Nos. 1780-1786 (7)	2.62	
		Set value		1.50

The 80f and 1.50fo were issued with and without alternating labels, which show date and place when trophy was taken; the 2.50fo was issued only with labels, 20f, 60f, 70f and 3fo without labels only.

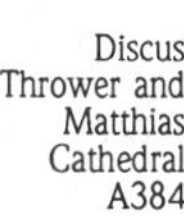

Discus Thrower and Matthias Cathedral A384

Designs: 30f, High jump and Agriculture Museum. 40f, Javelin (women's) and Parliament. 50f, Hammer throw, Mt. Gellert and Liberty Bridge. 60f, Broad jump and view of Buda. 1fo, Shot put and Chain Bridge. 2fo, Pole vault and Stadium. 3fo, Long distance runners and Millenium Monument.

1966, Aug. 30 Photo. *Perf. 12x11½*

1787 A384	20f	grn, brn & org	15	15
1788 A384	30f	multi	28	15
1789 A384	40f	multi	18	15
1790 A384	50f	multi	16	15
1791 A384	60f	multi	16	15
1792 A384	1fo	multi	28	16
1793 A384	2fo	multi	60	25
1794 A384	3fo	multi	1.10	70
		Nos. 1787-1794 (8)	2.91	
		Set value		1.55

8th European Athletic Championships, Budapest, Aug. 30-Sept. 4. See No. C261.

Girl in the Forest by Miklos Barabas A385

Paintings: 1fo, Mrs. Istvan Bitto by Miklos Barabas (1810-98). 1.50fo, Hunyadi's Farewell by Gyula Benczur (1844-1920). 1.70fo, Reading Woman by Gyula Benczur, horiz. 2fo, Woman with Fagots by Mihaly Munkacsi (1844-1900). 2.50fo, Yawning Boy by Mihaly Munkacsi. 3fo, Lady in Violet by Pal Szinyei Merse (1845-1920). 10fo, Picnic in May by Pal Szinyei Merse, horiz.

1966, Dec. 9 *Perf. 12½*

Gold Frame

1795 A385	60f	multi	15	15
1796 A385	1fo	multi	15	15
1797 A385	1.50fo	multi	25	15
1798 A385	1.70fo	multi	55	15
1799 A385	2fo	multi	55	15
1800 A385	2.50fo	multi	75	20
1801 A385	3fo	multi	1.65	1.10
		Nos. 1795-1801 (7)	4.05	2.05

Souvenir Sheet

1802 A385	10fo	multi	8.25	8.25

Issued to honor Hungarian painters. Size of stamp in No. 1802: 56x51mm.

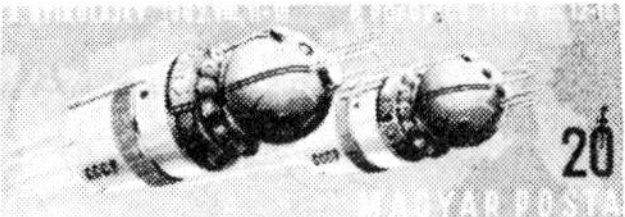

Vostoks 3 and 4 — A386

Space Craft: 60f, Gemini 6 and 7. 80f, Vostoks 5 and 6. 1fo, Gemini 9 and target rocket. 1.50fo, Alexei Leonov walking in space. 2fo, Edward White walking in space. 2.50fo, Voskhod. 3fo, Gemini 11 docking Agena target.

1966, Dec. 29 *Perf. 11*

1803 A386	20f	multi	15	15
1804 A386	60f	multi	15	15
1805 A386	80f	multi	15	15
1806 A386	1fo	multi	18	15
1807 A386	1.50fo	multi	28	18
1808 A386	2fo	multi	40	20
1809 A386	2.50fo	multi	60	35
1810 A386	3fo	multi	1.00	50
		Nos. 1803-1810 (8)	2.91	
		Set value		1.60

American and Russian twin space flights.

Pal Kitaibel and Kitaibelia Vitifolia — A387

Flowers of the Carpathian Basin: 60f, Dentaria glandulosa. 1fo, Edraianthus tenuifolius. 1.50fo, Althaea pallida. 2fo, Centaurea mollis. 2.50fo, Sternbergia colchiciflora. 3fo, Iris Hungarica.

1967, Feb. 7 Photo. *Perf. 11½x12*

Flowers in Natural Colors

1811 A387	20f	rose, blk & gold	15	15
1812 A387	60f	green	15	15
1813 A387	1fo	violet gray	15	15
1814 A387	1.50fo	blue	25	16
1815 A387	2fo	light olive	32	20
1816 A387	2.50fo	gray grn	60	32
1817 A387	3fo	yellow grn	1.10	65
		Nos. 1811-1817 (7)	2.72	
		Set value		1.50

150th anniversary of the death of Pal Kitaibel (1757-1817), botanist, chemist and physician.

Militiaman — A388

1967, Feb. 18 Photo. *Perf. 11½x12*

1818 A388	2fo	blue gray	30	15

Workers' Militia, 10th anniversary.

Mme. Du Barry and Louis XV, by Gyula Benczur (1844-1920) A390

Souvenir Sheet

Painting: 10fo, Milton dictating "Paradise Lost" to his daughters, by Soma Orlai Petrics.

1967, May 6 Photo. *Perf. 12½*

1819 A390	10fo	multi	5.25	5.00

1967, June 22

Paintings: 60f, Franz Liszt by Mihaly Munkacsi (1844-1900). 1fo, Samuel Lanyi, self-portrait, 1840. 1.50fo, Lady in Fur-lined Jacket by Jozsef Borsos (1821-1883). 1.70fo, The Lovers, by Pal Szinyei Merse (1845-1920; horiz.). 2fo, Portrait of Szidonia Deak, 1861, by Alajos Gyorgyi (1821-1863). 2.50fo, National Guardsman, 1848, by Jozsef Borsos.

Gold Frame

1820 A390	60f	multi	15	15
1821 A390	1fo	multi	18	15
1822 A390	1.50fo	multi	22	15
1823 A390	1.70fo	multi	35	15
1824 A390	2fo	multi	42	15
1825 A390	2.50fo	multi	55	22
1826 A390	3fo	multi	90	70
		Nos. 1820-1826 (7)	2.77	
		Set value		1.40

Issued to honor Hungarian painters. No. 1819 commemorates AMPHILEX 67 and the F.I.P. Congress, Amsterdam, May 11-21. No. 1819 contains one 56x50mm stamp.

See #1863-1870, 1900-1907, 1940-1947.

Map of Hungary, Tourist Year Emblem, Plane, Train, Car and Ship A391

1967, May 6 *Perf. 12x11½*

1827 A391	1fo	brt blue & blk	20	15

International Tourist Year, 1967.

S.S. Ferencz Deak, Schönbüchel Castle, Austrian Flag — A392

Designs: 60f, Diesel hydrobus, Bratislava Castle and Czechoslovak flag. 1fo, Diesel ship Hunyadi, Buda Castle and Hungarian flag. 1.50fo, Diesel tug Szekszard, Golubac Fortress and Yugoslav flag. 1.70fo, Towboat Miskolc, Vidin Fortress and Bulgarian flag. 2fo, Cargo ship Tihany, Galati shipyard and Romanian flag. 2.50fo, Hydrofoil Siraly I, Izmail Harbor and Russian flag.

1967, June 1 *Perf. 11½x12*

Flags in National Colors

1828 A392	30f	lt blue grn	38	22
1829 A392	60f	orange brn	38	28
1830 A392	1fo	grnsh blue	75	32
1831 A392	1.50fo	lt green	75	38
1832 A392	1.70fo	blue	1.40	52
1833 A392	2fo	rose lilac	3.00	1.00
1834 A392	2.50fo	lt olive grn	5.25	2.25
		Nos. 1828-1834 (7)	11.91	4.97

25th session of the Danube Commission.

Poodle A393

Collie — A394

Dogs: 1fo, Hungarian pointer. 1.40fo, Fox terriers. 2fo, Pumi, Hungarian sheep dog. 3fo, German shepherd. 4fo, Puli, Hungarian sheep dog.

1967, July 7 Litho. *Perf. 12*

1835 A393	30f	multi	24	15
1836 A394	60f	multi	24	15
1837 A393	1fo	multi	20	15
1838 A394	1.40fo	multi	24	24
1839 A393	2fo	multi	38	18
1840 A394	3fo	multi	60	50
1841 A393	4fo	multi	95	70
		Nos. 1835-1841 (7)	2.85	2.07

Sterlets A395

Fish: 60f, Pike perch. 1fo, Carp. 1.70fo, European catfish. 2fo, Pike. 2.50fo, Rapfin.

1967, Aug. 22 Photo. *Perf. 12x11½*

1842 A395	20f	multi	20	15
1843 A395	60f	bister & multi	15	15
1844 A395	1fo	multi	15	15
1845 A395	1.70fo	multi	15	15
1846 A395	2fo	green & multi	30	15
1847 A395	2.50fo	gray & multi	75	55
		Nos. 1842-1847,B263 (7)	2.60	1.75

14th Cong. of the Intl. Federation of Anglers (C.I.P.S.), Dunaujvaros, Aug. 20-28.

Prince Igor, by Aleksandr Borodin — A396

Opera Scenes: 30f, Freischütz, by Karl Maria von Weber. 40f, The Magic Flute, by Mozart. 60f, Prince Bluebeard's Castle, by Bela Bartok. 80f, Carmen, by Bizet, vert. 1fo, Don Carlos, by Verdi, vert. 1.70fo, Tannhäuser, by Wagner, vert. 3fo. Laszlo Hunyadi, by Ferenc Erkel, vert.

1967, Sept. 26 Photo. *Perf. 12*

1848 A396	20f	multi	20	15
1849 A396	30f	multi	20	15
1850 A396	40f	multi	20	15
1851 A396	60f	multi	20	15
1852 A396	80f	multi	20	15
1853 A396	1fo	multi	25	20
1854 A396	1.70fo	multi	48	32
1855 A396	3fo	multi	1.10	80
		Nos. 1848-1855 (8)	2.83	
		Set value		1.65

Demand, as well as supply, determine a stamp's market value.

Teacher, Students and Stone from Pecs University, 14th Century — A397

1967, Oct. 9 Photo. *Perf. 11½x12*
1856 A397 2fo gold & dp grn 40 15

600th anniv. of higher education in Hungary; University of Pecs was founded in 1367.

Eötvös University, and Symbols of Law and Justice A398

1967, Oct. 12 *Perf. 12x11½*
1857 A398 2fo slate 40 15

300th anniv. of the School of Political Science and Law at the Lorand Eötvös University, Budapest.

Lenin as Teacher, by Sandor Legrady A399

Paintings by Sandor Legrady: 1fo, Lenin. 3fo, Lenin on board the cruiser Aurora.

1967, Oct. 31 *Perf. 12½*

1858 A399 60f gold & multi	15	15
1859 A399 1fo gold & multi	15	15
1860 A399 3fo gold & multi	55	35
Set value		52

50th anniv. of the Russian October Revolution.

Venus 4 Landing on Venus — A400

1967, Nov. 6 *Perf. 12*
1861 A400 5fo gold & multi 1.25 1.10

Landing of the Russian automatic space station Venus 4 on the planet Venus.

Souvenir Sheet

19th Century Mail Coach and Post Horn — A401

Photogravure; Gold Impressed

1967, Nov. 21 *Perf. 12½*
1862 A401 10fo multicolored 3.50 3.50

Hungarian Postal Administration, cent.

Painting Type of 1967

Paintings: 60f, Brother and Sister by Adolf Fenyes (1867-1945). 1fo, Wrestling Boys by Oszkar Glatz (1872-1958). 1.50fo, "October" by Karoly Ferenczy (1862-1917). 1.70fo, Women at the River Bank by Istvan Szönyi (1894-1960), horiz. 2fo, Godfather's Breakfast by Istvan Csok (1865-1961). 2.50fo, "Eviction Notice" by Gyula Derkovits (1894-1934). 3fo, Self-portrait by M. T. Czontvary Kosztka (1853-1919). 10fo, The Apple Pickers by Bela Uitz (1887-).

1967, Dec. 21 Photo. *Perf. 12½*

1863 A390	60f multi	15	15
1864 A390	1fo multi	15	15
1865 A390	1.50fo multi	18	15
1866 A390	1.70fo multi	30	15
1867 A390	2fo multi	38	18
1868 A390	2.50fo multi	50	30
1869 A390	3fo multi	95	60
Nos. 1863-1869 (7)		2.61	1.68

Miniature Sheet

1870 A390 10fo multi 3.00 3.00

Issued to honor Hungarian painters.

Biathlon — A402

Sport (Olympic Rings and): 60f, Figure skating, pair. 1fo, Bobsledding. 1.40fo, Slalom. 1.70fo, Women's figure skating. 2fo, Speed skating. 3fo, Ski jump. 10fo, Ice hockey.

1967, Dec. 30 Photo. *Perf. 12½*

Souvenir Sheet

1871 A402 10fo lilac & multi 3.00 3.00

1968, Jan. 29 *Perf. 11*

1872 A402	30f multi	15	15
1873 A402	60f multi	15	15
1874 A402	1fo multi	15	15
1875 A402	1.40fo rose & multi	16	16
1876 A402	1.70fo multi	20	15
1877 A402	2fo multi	32	16
1878 A402	3fo ol & multi	80	38
Nos. 1872-1878,B264 (8)		2.63	
Set value			1.45

10th Winter Olympic Games, Grenoble, France, Feb. 6-18. No. 1871 contains one 43x43mm stamp.

Kando Statue, Miskolc, Kando Locomotive and Map of Hungary — A403

1968, Mar. 30 Photo. *Perf. 11½x12*
1879 A403 2fo dark blue 35 15

Kalman Kando (1869-1931), engineer, inventor of Kando locomotive.

Domestic Cat — A404

1968, Mar. 30 *Perf. 11*

1880 A404	20f shown	15	15
1881 A404	60f Cream Persian	18	15
1882 A404	1fo Smoky Persian	22	15
1883 A404	1.20fo Domestic kitten	22	15
1884 A404	1.50fo White Persian	32	15
1885 A404	2fo Brown-striped Persian	32	28
1886 A404	2.50fo Siamese	52	32
1887 A404	5fo Blue Persian	1.25	75
Nos. 1880-1887 (8)		3.18	
Set value			1.80

Zoltan Kodaly, by Sandor Légrády A405

1968, Apr. 17 Photo. *Perf. 12½*
1888 A405 5fo gold & multi 1.00 75

Issued in memory of Zoltan Kodaly (1882-1967), composer and musicologist.

White Storks A406

Birds: 50f, Golden orioles. 60f, Imperial eagle. 1fo, Red-footed falcons. 1.20fo, Scops owl. 1.50fo, Great bustard. 2fo, European bee-eaters. 2.50fo, Graylag goose.

1968, Apr. 25

Birds in Natural Colors

1889 A406	20f ver & lt ultra	20	20
1890 A406	50f ver & gray	15	15
1891 A406	60f ver & lt bl	20	15
1892 A406	1fo ver & yel grn	25	15
1893 A406	1.20fo ver & brt grn	25	15
1894 A406	1.50fo ver & lt vio	28	18
1895 A406	2fo ver & pale lil	60	28
1896 A406	2.50fo ver & bl grn	1.25	70
Nos. 1889-1896 (8)		3.18	1.96

International Bird Preservation Congress.

City Hall, Kecskemét A407

Student and Agricultural College A408

1968, Apr. 25 *Perf. 12x11½*
1897 A407 2fo brown orange 30 15

600th anniversary of Kecskemét.

Marx Type of 1953

1968, May 5 Engr. *Perf. 12*
1898 A230 1fo claret 15 15

Karl Marx (1818-1883).

1968, May 24 Photo. *Perf. 12x11½*
1899 A408 2fo dk olive green 30 15

150th anniv. of the founding of the Agricultural College at Mosonmagyaróvár.

Painting Type of 1967

Paintings: 40f, Girl with Pitcher, by Goya (1746-1828). 60f, Head of an Apostle, by El Greco (c. 1541-1614). 1fo, Boy with Apple Basket and Dogs, by Pedro Nunez (1639-1700), horiz. 1.50fo, Mary Magdalene, by El Greco. 2.50fo, The Breakfast, by Velazquez (1599-1660), horiz. 4fo, The Virgin from The Holy Family, by El Greco. 5fo, The Knife Grinder, by Goya. 10fo, Portrait of a Girl, by Palma Vecchio (1480-1528).

1968, May 30 *Perf. 12½*

1900 A390	40f multi	15	15
1901 A390	60f multi	15	15
1902 A390	1fo multi	15	15
1903 A390	1.50fo multi	22	15
1904 A390	2.50fo multi	50	20
1905 A390	4fo multi	70	22
1906 A390	5fo multi	1.00	45
Nos. 1900-1906 (7)		2.87	
Set value			1.18

Souvenir Sheet

1907 A390 10fo multi 3.50 3.50

Issued to publicize art treasures in the Budapest Museum of Fine Arts and to publicize an art exhibition.

Lake Balaton at Badacsony A409

Views on Lake Balaton: 40f like 20f. 60f, Tihanyi Peninsula. 1fo, Sailboats at Almadi. 2fo, Szigliget Bay.

1968-69 Litho. *Perf. 12*

1908 A409	20f multi	15	15
1908A A409	40f multi ('69)	15	15
b.	Bklt. pane, #1909, 1911, 2 each #1908A, 1910	75	
c.	Bklt. pane, #1909-1911, 3 #1908A	75	
d.	Bklt. pane, #1911, 3 #1908A, 2 #1909	75	
1909 A409	60f multi	15	15
1910 A409	1fo multi	20	15
1911 A409	2fo multi	45	22
Set value		92	45

Locomotive, Type 424 — A410

1968, July 14 Photo. *Perf. 12x11½*
1912 A410 2fo gold, lt bl & sl 50 15

Centenary of the Hungarian State Railroad.

Horses Grazing — A411

Designs: 40f, Horses in storm. 60f, Horse race on the steppe. 80f, Horsedrawn sleigh. 1fo, Four-in-hand and rainbow. 1.40fo, Farm wagon drawn by 7 horses. 2fo, One rider driving five horses. 2.50fo, Campfire on the range. 4fo, Coach with 5 horses.

1968, July 25 *Perf. 11*

1913 A411	30f	multi	15	15
1914 A411	40f	multi	15	15
1915 A411	60f	multi	15	17
1916 A411	80f	multi	15	15
1917 A411	1fo	multi	22	15
1918 A411	1.40fo	multi	35	15
1919 A411	2fo	multi	35	16
1920 A411	2.50fo	multi	50	28
1921 A411	4fo	multi	1.10	60
		Nos. 1913-1921 (9)	3.12	
		Set value		1.70

Horse breeding on the Hungarian steppe (Puszta).

Mihály Tompa (1817-68), Poet — A412

1968, July 30 Photo. *Perf. 12x11½*

1922 A412 60f blue black 20 15

Festival Emblem, Bulgarian and Hungarian National Costumes — A413

1968, Aug. 3 Litho. *Perf. 12*

1923 A413 60f multicolored 20 15

Issued to publicize the 9th Youth Festival for Peace and Friendship, Sofia, Bulgaria.

Souvenir Sheet

Runners and Aztec Calendar Stone — A414

1968, Aug. 21 Photo. *Perf. 12½*

1924 A414 10fo multicolored 3.00 3.00

19th Olympic Games, Mexico City, Oct. 12-27.

Scientific Society Emblem A415

Hesperis A416

Perf. 12½x11½

1968, Dec. 10 **Photo.**

1925 A415 2fo brt blue & blk 35 15

Society for the Popularization of Scientific Knowledge.

1968, Oct. 29 *Perf. 11½x12*

Garden Flowers: 60f, Pansy. 80f, Zinnias. 1fo, Morning-glory. 1.40fo, Petunia. 1.50fo, Portulaca. 2fo, Michaelmas daisies. 2.50fo, Dahlia.

Flowers in Natural Colors

1926 A416	20f	gray	16	16
1927 A416	60f	lt green	16	16
1928 A416	80f	bluish lilac	28	16
1929 A416	1fo	buff	28	16
1930 A416	1.40fo	lt grnsh bl	20	16
1931 A416	1.50fo	lt blue	28	20
1932 A416	2fo	pale pink	34	28
1933 A416	2.50fo	lt blue	90	60
		Nos. 1926-1933 (8)	2.60	1.88

Pioneers Saluting Communist Party A417

Children's Paintings: 60f, Four pioneers holding banner saluting Communist Party. 1fo, Pioneer camp.

1968, Nov. 16 Photo. *Perf. 12x11½*

1934 A417	40f buff & multi	22	15
1935 A417	60f buff & multi	22	15
1936 A417	1fo buff & multi	32	22

50th anniv. of the Communist Party of Hungary. The designs are from a competition among elementary school children.

Workers, Monument by Z. Olcsai-Kiss A418

Design: 1fo, "Workers of the World Unite!" poster by N. Por, vert.

Perf. 11½x12, 12x11½

1968, Nov. 24 **Photo.**

1937 A418	1fo gold, red, & blk	15	15
1938 A418	2fo gold & multi	18	15
	Set value	27	16

50th anniv. of the Communist Party of Hungary.

Human Rights Flame — A419

1968, Dec. 10 *Perf. 12½x11½*

1939 A419 1fo dark red brown 25 15

International Human Rights Year.

Painting Type of 1967

Italian Paintings: 40f, Esterhazy Madonna, by Raphael. 60f, The Annunciation, by Bernardo Strozzi. 1fo, Portrait of a Young Man, by Raphael. 1.50fo, The Three Graces, by Battista Naldini. 2.50fo, Portrait of a Man, by Sebastiano del Piombo. 4fo, The Doge Marcantonio Trevisani, by Titian. 5fo, Venus, Cupid and Jealousy, by Angelo Bronzino. 10fo, Bathsheba Bathing, by Sebastiano Ricci, horiz.

1968, Dec. 10 Photo. *Perf. 12½*

1940 A390	40f	multi	15	15
1941 A390	60f	multi	15	15
1942 A390	1fo	multi	15	15
1943 A390	1.50fo	multi	20	15
1944 A390	2.50fo	multi	45	15
1945 A390	4fo	multi	75	30
1946 A390	5fo	multi	1.25	52
		Nos. 1940-1946 (7)	3.10	
		Set value		1.20

Miniature Sheet

Perf. 11

1947 A390 10fo multi 3.00 3.00

Issued to publicize art treasures in the Budapest Museum of Fine Arts. No. 1947 contains one stamp size of stamp: 62x45mm.

1869 and 1969 Emblems of Athenaeum Press — A420

Endre Ady (1877-1919), Lyric Poet — A421

1969, Jan. 27 *Perf. 12½x11½*

1948 A420 2fo gold, gray, lt bl & blk 30 15

Centenary of Athenaeum Press, Budapest.

1969, Jan. 27 *Perf. 11½x12*

1949 A421 1fo multicolored 20 15

Olympic Medal and Women's Javelin — A422

Olympic Medal and: 60f, Canadian singles (canoeing). 1fo, Soccer. 1.20fo, Hammer throw. 2fo, Fencing. 3fo, Greco-Roman Wrestling. 4fo, Kayak single. 5fo, Equestrian. 10fo, Head of Mercury by Praxiteles and Olympic torch.

1969, Mar. 7 Photo. *Perf. 12*

1950 A422	40f	multi	15	15
1951 A422	60f	multi	15	15
1952 A422	1fo	multi	15	15
1953 A422	1.20fo	multi	15	15
1954 A422	2fo	multi	20	15
1955 A422	3fo	multi	35	15
1956 A422	4fo	multi	1.10	20
1957 A422	5fo	multi	1.10	70
		Nos. 1950-1957 (8)	3.35	
		Set value		1.50

Souvenir Sheet

Litho. *Perf. 11½*

1958 A422 10fo multi 3.75 3.75

Victories won by the Hungarian team in the 1968 Olympic Games, Mexico City, Oct. 12-27, 1968. No. 1958 contains one 45x33mm stamp.

1919 Revolutionary Poster — A423

Revolutionary Posters: 60f, Lenin. 1fo, Man breaking chains. 2fo, Industrial worker looking at family and farm. 3fo, Militia recruiter. 10fo, Shouting revolutionist with red banner, horiz.

1969, Mar. 21 Photo. *Perf. 11½x12*

Gold Frame

1960 A423	40f red & black	15	15
1961 A423	60f red & black	15	15
1962 A423	1fo red & black	15	15
1963 A423	2fo black, gray & red	28	15
1964 A423	3fo multicolored	40	20
	Set value	92	42

Souvenir Sheet

Perf. 12½

1965 A423 10fo red, gray & blk 1.50 1.50

50th anniv. of the proclamation of the Hungarian Soviet Republic.

The 60f red lilac with 4-line black printing on back was given away by the Hungarian PO.

No. 1965 contains one 51x38½mm stamp.

Jersey Tiger A424

Designs: Various Butterflies and Moths.

1969, Apr. 15 Litho. *Perf. 12*

1966 A424	40f	shown	15	15
1967 A424	60f	Eyed hawk moth	15	15
1968 A424	80f	Painted lady	15	15
1969 A424	1fo	Tiger moth	15	15
1970 A424	1.20fo	Small fire moth	24	18
1971 A424	2fo	Large blue	38	18
1972 A424	3fo	Belted oak egger	75	45
1973 A424	4fo	Peacock	1.10	70
		Nos. 1966-1973 (8)	3.07	
		Set value		1.85

ILO Emblem A426

1969, May 22 Photo. *Perf. 12x11½*

1974 A426 1fo carmine lake & lake 20 15

50th anniv. of the ILO.

Black Pigs, by Paul Gauguin A427

French Paintings: 60f, These Women, by Toulouse-Lautrec, horiz. 1fo, Venus in the Clouds, by Simon Vouet. 2fo, Lady with Fan, by Edouard Manet, horiz. 3fo, La Petra Camara (dancer), by

Théodore Chassériau. 4fo, The Cowherd, by Constant Troyon, horiz. 5fo, The Wrestlers, by Gustave Courbet. 10fo, Pomona, by Nicolas Fouché.

1969, May 28 Photo. *Perf. 12½*

1975 A427	40f multicolored		15	15
1976 A427	60f multicolored		15	15
1977 A427	1fo multicolored		15	15
1978 A427	2fo multicolored		28	15
1979 A427	3fo multicolored		50	18
1980 A427	4fo multicolored		70	25
1981 A427	5fo multicolored		1.25	52
	Nos. 1975-1981 (7)		3.18	
	Set value			1.25

Miniature Sheet

1982 A427 10fo multicolored 3.50 3.25

Art treasures in the Budapest Museum of Fine Arts. No. 1982 contains one 40x62mm stamp.

Hotel Budapest A428

Budapest Post Office 100 A429

1969, May Photo. *Perf. 11*

1983 A428 1fo brown 15 15

Coil Stamps

1970, Aug. 3 *Perf. 14*

1983B A429 40f gray 24 15
1983a A428 1fo brown 30 15

Yellow control number on back of every 5th stamp.

Arms and Buildings of Vac — A430

Towns of the Danube Bend: 1fo, Szentendre. 1.20fo, Visegrad. 3fo, Esztergom.

1969, June 9 Litho. *Perf. 12*

1984 A430 40f multi		15	15
a. Bklt. pane of 6 (4 #1984, 1 each #1985, 1987)		2.75	
b. Bklt. pane of 6 (1986, 3 #1984, 2 #1985)		2.75	
1985 A430 1fo multi		15	15
1986 A430 1.20fo multi		20	15
1987 A430 3fo multi		35	28
Set value			58

Stamps in booklet panes Nos. 1984a-1984b come in two arrangements.

"PAX" and Men Holding Hands — A431

1969, June 17 Photo. *Perf. 11½x12*

1988 A431 1fo lt bl, dk bl & gold 20 15

20th anniversary of Peace Movement.

The Scholar, by Rembrandt — A432

Fossilized Zelkova Leaves — A433

1969, Sept. 15 *Perf. 11½x12*

1989 A432 1fo sepia 20 15

Issued to publicize the 22nd International Congress of Art Historians, Budapest.

1969, Sept. 21 Photo.

Designs: 60f, Greenockit calcite sphalerite crystals. 1fo, Fossilized fish, clupea hungarica. 1.20fo, Quartz crystals. 2fo, Ammonite. 3fo, Copper. 4fo, Fossilized turtle, placochelys placodonta. 5fo, Cuprite crystals.

1990 A433 40f red, gray & sep		15	15
1991 A433 60f violet, yel & blk		15	15
1992 A433 1fo blue, tan & brn		15	15
1993 A433 1.20fo emer, gray & lil		15	15
1994 A433 2fo olive, tan & brn		16	15
1995 A433 3fo orange, brt & dk grn		32	22
1996 A433 4fo dull blk grn, brn & blk		60	30
1997 A433 5fo multicolored		1.00	48
Nos. 1990-1997 (8)		2.68	
Set value			1.35

Centenary of the Hungarian State Institute of Geology.

Steeplechase — A434

Designs: 60f, Fencing. 1fo, Pistol shooting. 2fo, Swimmers at start. 3fo, Relay race. 5fo, Pentathlon.

1969, Sept. 15 Photo. *Perf. 12x11½*

1998 A434 40f blue & multi		15	15
1999 A434 60f multi		15	15
2000 A434 1fo multi		15	15
2001 A434 2fo violet & multi		34	15
2002 A434 3fo lemon & multi		58	34
2003 A434 5fo bluish grn, gold & dk red		1.25	70
Nos. 1998-2003 (6)		2.62	
Set value			1.42

Hungarian Pentathlon Championships.

First Hungarian Postal Card A435

1969, Oct. 1

2004 A435 60f ver & ocher 15 15

Centenary of the postal card. Hungary and Austria both issued cards in 1869.

Mahatma Gandhi — A436

1969, Oct. 1 *Perf. 11½x12*

2005 A436 5fo green & multi 1.25 70

Mohandas K. Gandhi (1869-1948), leader in India's fight for independence.

World Trade Union Emblem A437

1969, Oct. 17 Photo. *Perf. 12x11½*

2006 A437 2fo fawn & dk blue 30 15

Issued to publicize the 7th Congress of the World Federation of Trade Unions.

Janos Balogh Nagy, Self-portrait — A438

1969, Oct. 17 *Perf. 11½x12*

2007 A438 5fo gold & multi 1.50 80

Janos Balogh Nagy (1874-1919), painter.

St. John the Evangelist, by Anthony Van Dyck A439

Dutch Paintings: 60f, Three Fruit Pickers (by Pieter de Molyn?). 1fo, Boy Lighting Pipe, by Hendrick Terbrughen. 2fo, The Feast, by Jan Steen. 3fo, Woman Reading Letter, by Pieter de Hooch. 4fo, The Fiddler, by Dirk Hals. 5fo, Portrait of Jan Asselyn, by Frans Hals. 10fo, Mucius Scaevola before Porsena, by Rubens and Van Dyck.

1969-70 Photo. *Perf. 12½*

2008 A439 40f multi		15	15
2009 A439 60f multi		15	15
2010 A439 1fo multi		15	15
2011 A439 2fo multi		24	15
2012 A439 3fo multi		45	18
2013 A439 4fo multi		60	40
2014 A439 5fo multi		1.10	70
Nos. 2008-2014 (7)		2.84	
Set value			1.60

Miniature Sheet

2015 A439 10fo multi 3.50 3.50

Treasures in the Museum of Fine Arts, Budapest and the Museum in Eger.

Issue Dates: Nos. 2008-2014, Dec. 2, 1969; No. 2015, Jan. 1970.

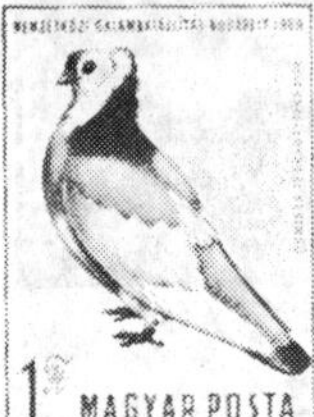

Kiskunfelegyhaza Circling Pigeon — A440

1969, Dec. 12 Photo. *Perf. 11½x12*

2016 A440 1fo multicolored 20 15

Issued to publicize the International Pigeon Show, Budapest, Dec. 1969.

Subway A441

1970, Apr. 3 Photo. *Perf. 12*

2017 A441 1fo blk, lt grn & ultra 20 15

Opening of new Budapest subway.

Souvenir Sheet

Panoramic View of Budapest 1945 and 1970, and Soviet Cenotaph — A442

Illustration reduced.

1970, Apr. 3 *Perf. 12x11½*

2018 A442 Sheet of 2		3.00	3.00
a. 5fo "1945"		1.10	1.10
b. 5fo "1970"		1.10	1.10

25th anniv. of the liberation of Budapest.

Cloud Formation, Satellite, Earth and Receiving Station A443

Lenin Statue, Budapest A444

1970, Apr. 8 Litho. *Perf. 12*

2019 A443 1fo dk bl, yel & blk 20 15

Centenary of the Hungarian Meteorological Service.

1970, Apr. 22 Photo. *Perf. 11*

Design: 2fo, Lenin portrait.

2020 A444 1fo gold & multi		15	15
2021 A444 2fo gold & multi		18	15
Set value		27	15

Lenin (1870-1924), Russian communist leader.

Franz Lehar and "Giuditta" Music — A445

1970, Apr. 30 Photo. *Perf. 12*

2022	A445 2fo multicolored		50	20

Franz Lehar (1870-1948), composer.

Samson and Delilah, by Michele Rocca A446

Paintings: 60f, Joseph Telling Dream, by Giovanni Battista Langetti. 1fo, Clio, by Pierre Mignard. 1.50fo, Venus and Satyr, by Sebastiano Ricci, horiz. 2.50fo, Andromeda, by Francesco Furini. 4fo, Venus, Adonis and Cupid, by Luca Giordano. 5fo, Allegorical Feast, by Corrado Giaquinto. 10fo, Diana and Callisto, by Abraham Janssens, horiz.

1970, June 2 Photo. *Perf. 12½*

2023	A446	40f	gold & multi	15	15
2024	A446	60f	gold & multi	15	15
2025	A446	1fo	gold & multi	24	15
2026	A446	1.50fo	gold & multi	28	15
2027	A446	2.50fo	gold & multi	40	20
2028	A446	4fo	gold & multi	85	40
2029	A446	5fo	gold & multi	1.10	60
			Nos. 2023-2029 (7)	3.17	
			Set value		1.58

Miniature Sheet

Perf. 11

2030	A446	10fo	gold & multi	3.50	3.50

No. 2030 contains one 63x46mm horizontal stamp.

Beethoven Statue, by Janos Pasztor, at Martonvasar A447

1970, June 27 Litho. *Perf. 12*

2031	A447 1fo plum, gray grn & org yel		75	20

Ludwig van Beethoven (1770-1827), composer. The music in the design is from Sonata 37.

Foundryman A448

King Stephen I A449

1970, July 28 Litho. *Perf. 12*

2032	A448 1fo multicolored		25	15

200th anniversary of the first Hungarian steel foundry at Diosgyor, now the Lenin Metallurgical Works.

1970, Aug. 19 Photo. *Perf. 11½x12*

2033	A449 3fo multicolored		1.50	50

Millenary of the birth of Saint Stephen, first King of Hungary.

Women's Four on Lake Tata and Tata Castle A450

1970, Aug. 19 Litho. *Perf. 12*

2034	A450 1fo multicolored		35	15

17th European Women's Rowing Championships, Lake Tata.

Mother Giving Bread to her Children, FAO Emblem A451

1970, Sept. 21 Litho. *Perf. 12*

2035	A451 1fo lt blue & multi		20	15

7th European Regional Cong. of the UNFAO, Budapest, Sept. 21-25.

Boxing and Olympic Rings A452

Designs (Olympic Rings and): 60f, Canoeing. 1fo, Fencing. 1.50fo, Water polo. 2fo, Woman gymnast. 2.50fo, Hammer throwing. 3fo, Wrestling. 5fo, Swimming, butterfly stroke.

1970, Sept. 26 Photo. *Perf. 11*

2036	A452	40f	lt violet & multi	15	15
2037	A452	60f	sky blue & multi	15	15
2038	A452	1fo	orange & multi	15	15
2039	A452	1.50fo	multi	20	15
2040	A452	2fo	multi	35	15
2041	A452	2.50fo	multi	40	18
2042	A452	3fo	multi	60	34
2043	A452	5fo	multi	1.10	55
			Nos. 2036-2043 (8)	3.10	
			Set value		1.45

75th anniv. of the Hungarian Olympic Committee. The 5fo also publicizes the 1972 Olympic Games in Munich.

Flame and Family A453

1970, Sept. 28 Litho. *Perf. 12*

2044	A453 1fo ultra, org & emer		20	15

5th Education Congress, Budapest.

Chalice, by Benedek Suky, 1440 — A454

Hungarian Goldsmiths' Art: 60f, Altar burette, 1500. 1fo, Nadasdy goblet, 16th century. 1.50fo, Coconut goblet, 1600. 2fo, Silver tankard, by Mihaly Toldalaghy, 1623. 2.50fo, Communion cup of Gyorgy Rakoczy I, 1670. 3fo, Tankard, 1690. 4fo, Bell-flower cup, 1710.

1970, Oct. Photo. *Perf. 12*

2045	A454	40f	gold & multi	15	15
2046	A454	60f	gold & multi	15	15
2047	A454	1fo	gold & multi	15	15
2048	A454	1.50fo	gold & multi	15	15
2049	A454	2fo	gold & multi	20	15
2050	A454	2.50fo	gold & multi	24	18
2051	A454	3fo	gold & multi	60	42
2052	A454	4fo	gold & multi	1.00	60
			Nos. 2045-2052 (8)	2.64	
			Set value		1.60

Virgin and Child, by Giampietrino A455

Paintings from Christian Museum, Esztergom: 60f, "Love" (woman with 3 children), by Gregorio Lazzarini. 1fo, Legend of St. Catherine, by Master of Bat. 1.50fo, Adoration of the Shepherds, by Francesco Fontebasso, horiz. 2.50fo, Adoration of the Kings, by Master of Aranyosmarot. 4fo, Temptation of St. Anthony the Hermit, by Jan de Cock. 5fo, St. Sebastian, by Marco Palmezzano. 10fo, Lady with the Unicorn, by Painter of Lombardy.

1970, Dec. 7 Photo. *Perf. 12½*

2053	A455	40f	silver & multi	15	15
2054	A455	60f	silver & multi	15	15
2055	A455	1fo	silver & multi	15	15
2056	A455	1.50fo	silver & multi	18	15
2057	A455	2.50fo	silver & multi	40	20
2058	A455	4fo	silver & multi	75	30
2059	A455	5fo	silver & multi	1.10	70
			Nos. 2053-2059 (7)	2.88	
			Set value		1.55

Souvenir Sheet

2060	A455	10fo	silver & multi	3.50	3.25

No. 2060 contains one 50½x56mm stamp.

Monument to Hungarian Martyrs, by A. Makrisz A456

1970, Dec. 30 Photo. *Perf. 12x11½*

2061	A456 1fo ultra & sepia		15	15

The 25th anniversary of the liberation of the concentration camps at Auschwitz, Mauthausen and Dachau.

Marseillaise, by Francois Rude — A457

Béla Bartók (1881-1945), Composer — A458

1971, Mar. 18 Litho. *Perf. 12*

2062	A457 3fo bister & green		40	20

Centenary of the Paris Commune.

1971

Design: No. 2064, András L. Achim (1871-1911), peasant leader.

2063	A458 1fo gray & dk car		55	18
2064	A458 1fo gray & green		20	15
	Set value			25

Dates of issue: No. 2063, Mar. 25; No. 2064, Apr. 17.

Györ Castle, 1594 A459

1971, Mar. 27

2065	A459 2fo lt blue & multi		40	15

700th anniversary of Györ.

Bison Hunt — A460

Designs: 60f, Wild boar hunt. 80f, Deer hunt. 1fo, Falconry. 1.20fo, Felled stag and dogs. 2fo, Bustards. 3fo, Net fishing. 4fo, Angling.

1971, May Photo. *Perf. 12*

2066	A460	40f	ver & multi	15	15
2067	A460	60f	plum & multi	15	15
2068	A460	80f	multi	15	15
2069	A460	1fo	lilac & multi	16	15
2070	A460	1.20fo	multi	25	22
2071	A460	2fo	multi	45	20
2072	A460	3fo	multi	80	30
2073	A460	4fo	green & multi	1.10	65
			Nos. 2066-2073 (8)	3.21	
			Set value		1.70

World Hunting Exhibition, Budapest, Aug. 27-30. See No. C313.

Souvenir Sheet

Portrait of a Man, by Dürer — A461

1971, May 21 *Perf. 12½*

2074 A461	10fo	gold & multi	3.50	3.25

Albrecht Dürer (1471-1528), German painter and etcher.

Carnation and Pioneers' Emblem A462

1971, June 2 **Photo.** *Perf. 12*

2075 A462	1fo	dark red & multi	20	15

25th anniversary of the Hungarian Pioneers' Organization.

FIR Emblem, Resistance Fighters A463

1971, July 3

2076 A463	1fo	brown & multi	20	15

International Federation of Resistance Fighters (FIR), 20th anniversary.

Walking in Garden, Tokyo School A464

Japanese Prints from Museum of East Asian Art, Budapest: 60f, Geisha in Boat, by Yeishi (1756-1829). 1fo, Woman with Scroll, by Yeishi. 1.50fo, Courtesans, by Kiyonaga (1752-1815). 2fo, Awabi Fisher Women, by Utamaro (1753-1806). 2.50fo, Seated Courtesan, by Harunobu (1725-1770). 3fo, Peasant Woman Carrying Fagots, by Hokusai (1760-1849). 4fo, Women and Girls Walking, by Yeishi.

1971, July 9 *Perf. 12½*

2077 A464	40f	gold & multi	15	15
2078 A464	60f	gold & multi	15	15
2079 A464	1fo	gold & multi	15	15
2080 A464	1.50fo	gold & multi	18	15
2081 A464	2fo	gold & multi	24	15
2082 A464	2.50fo	gold & multi	30	20
2083 A464	3fo	gold & multi	55	24
2084 A464	4fo	gold & multi	1.25	60
		Nos. 2077-2084 (8)	2.97	
		Set value		1.50

Locomotive, Map of Rail System and Danube — A465

1971, July 15 **Litho.** *Perf. 12*

2086 A465	1fo	multi	30	15

125th anniversary of first Hungarian railroad between Pest and Vac.

Griffin Holding Ink Balls A466

1971, Sept. 11 **Photo.** *Perf. 12x11½*

2087 A466	1fo	multicolored	75	60

Centenary of stamp printing in Hungary. Printed se-tenant with 2 labels showing printing presses of 1871 and 1971 and Hungary Nos. P1 and 1171.

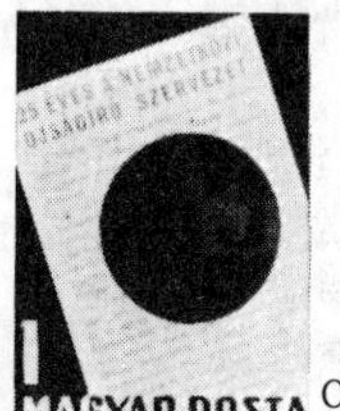

OIJ Emblem and Printed Page — A467

1971, Sept. 21 *Perf. 11½x12*

2088 A467	1fo	dk bl, bl & gold	25	15

25th anniversary of the International Organization of Journalists (OIJ).

Josef Jacob Winterl and Barren Strawberry — A468

Plants: 60f, Bromeliaceae. 80f, Titanopsis calcarea. 1fo, Periwinkle. 1.20fo, Gymnocalycium. 2fo, White water lily. 3fo, Iris arenaria. 5fo, Peony.

1971, Oct. 29 **Litho.** *Perf. 12*

2089 A468	40f	lt vio & multi	15	15
2090 A468	60f	gray & multi	15	15
2091 A468	80f	multi	15	15
2092 A468	1fo	multi	15	15
2093 A468	1.20fo	lilac & multi	18	15
2094 A468	2fo	gray & multi	40	15
2095 A468	3fo	multi	70	35
2096 A468	5fo	multi	1.25	55
		Nos. 2089-2096 (8)	3.13	
		Set value		1.50

Bicentenary of Budapest Botanical Gardens.

Galloping — A469

Equestrian Sports: 60f, Trotting. 80f, Horses fording river. 1fo, Jumping. 1.20fo, Start. 2fo, Polo. 3fo, Steeplechase. 5fo, Dressage.

1971, Nov. 22 **Photo.** *Perf. 12*

2097 A469	40f	blue & multi	15	15
2098 A469	60f	ocher & multi	15	15
2099 A469	80f	olive & multi	15	15
2100 A469	1fo	red & multi	18	15
2101 A469	1.20fo	multi	28	15
2102 A469	2fo	multi	40	18
2103 A469	3fo	violet & multi	60	40
2104 A469	5fo	blue & multi	1.00	70
		Nos. 2097-2104 (8)	2.91	
		Set value		1.75

Beheading of Heathen Chief Koppany A470

Designs: 60f, Samuel Aba pursuing King Peter. 1fo, Basarad's victory over King Charles Robert. 1.50fo, Strife between King Salomon and Prince Geza. 2.50fo, Founding of Obuda Church by King Stephen I and Queen Gisela. 4fo, Reconciliation of King Koloman and his brother Almos. 5fo, Oradea Church built by King Ladislas I. 10fo, Funeral of Prince Emeric and blinding of Vazul.

1971, Dec. 10 **Litho.**

2105 A470	40f	buff & multi	15	15
2106 A470	60f	buff & multi	15	15
2107 A470	1fo	buff & multi	18	15
2108 A470	1.50fo	buff & multi	18	15
2109 A470	2.50fo	buff & multi	30	16
2110 A470	4fo	buff & multi	60	32
2111 A470	5fo	buff & multi	1.10	60
		Nos. 2105-2111 (7)	2.66	
		Set value		1.45

Miniature Sheet

Perf. 11½

2112 A470	10fo	buff & multi	3.25	3.00

History of Hungary, from miniatures from Illuminated Chronicle of King Louis the Great, c. 1370. No. 2112 contains one stamp (size 44½x52mm).

Equality Year Emblem — A471

1971, Dec. 30 **Litho.** *Perf. 12*

2113 A471	1fo	bister & multi	20	15

Intl. Year Against Racial Discrimination.

Ice Hockey and Sapporo '72 Emblem — A472

Sport and Sapporo '72 Emblem: 60f, Men's slalom. 80f, Women's figure skating. 1fo, Ski jump. 1.20fo, Long-distance skiing. 2fo, Men's figure skating. 3fo, Bobsledding. 4fo, Biathlon. 10fo, Buddha.

1971, Dec. 30 *Perf. 12*

2114 A472	40f	black & multi	15	15
2115 A472	60f	black & multi	15	15
2116 A472	80f	black & multi	15	15
2117 A472	1fo	black & multi	15	15
2118 A472	1.20fo	black & multi	24	15
2119 A472	2fo	black & multi	40	20
2120 A472	3fo	black & multi	60	40
2121 A472	4fo	black & multi	1.25	65
		Nos. 2114-2121 (8)	3.09	
		Set value		1.65

Souvenir Sheet

Perf. 11½

2122 A472	10fo	gold & multi	3.50	3.25

11th Winter Olympic Games, Sapporo, Japan, Feb. 3-13, 1972. No. 2122 contains one 86x48mm stamp.

Hungarian Locomotive — A473

Locomotives: 60f, Germany. 80f, Italy. 1fo, Soviet Union. 1.20fo, Japan. 2fo, Great Britain. 4fo, Austria. 5fo, France.

1972, Feb. 23 **Photo.** *Perf. 12x11½*

2123 A473	40f	multi	15	15
2124 A473	60f	ocher & multi	15	15
2125 A473	80f	multi	15	15
2126 A473	1fo	olive & multi	15	15
2127 A473	1.20fo	ultra & multi	40	30
2128 A473	2fo	ver & multi	25	16
2129 A473	4fo	multi	55	30
2130 A473	5fo	multi	1.00	50
		Nos. 2123-2130 (8)	2.80	
		Set value		1.50

Janus Pannonius, by Andrea Mantegna — A474

1972, Mar. 27 **Litho.** *Perf. 12*

2131 A474	1fo	gold & multi	25	15

Janus Pannonius (Johannes Czezmiczei, 1434-1472), humanist and poet.

Mariner 9 — A475

Design: No. 2133, Mars 2 and 3 spacecraft.

1972, Mar. 30 Photo. *Perf. 11½x12*

2132 A475	2fo dk blue & multi	45	45
2133 A475	2fo multi	45	45
a.	Strip #2132-2133 + label	1.35	1.35

Exploration of Mars by Mariner 9 (US), and Mars 2 and 3 (USSR). Issued in sheets containing 4 each of Nos. 2132-2133 and 4 labels inscribed in Hungarian, Russian and English.

13th Century Church Portal — A476

1972, Apr. 11

2134 A476 3fo greenish black 40 15

Centenary of the Society for the Protection of Historic Monuments.

Hungarian Greyhound — A477

Hounds: 60f, Afghan hound (head). 80f, Irish wolfhound. 1.20fo, Borzoi. 2fo, Running greyhound. 4fo, Whippet. 6fo, Afghan hound.

1972, Apr. 14 Litho. *Perf. 12*

2135 A477	40f multi	15	15
2136 A477	60f brown & multi	15	15
2137 A477	80f multi	16	15
2138 A477	1.20fo multi	16	15
2139 A477	2fo multi	35	15
2140 A477	4fo multi	80	24
2141 A477	6fo multi	1.25	90
	Nos. 2135-2141 (7)	3.02	
	Set value		1.55

József Imre, Emil Grósz, László Blaskovics (Ophthalmologists) — A478

Design: 2fo, Allvar Gullstrand, V. P. Filatov, Jules Gonin, ophthalmologists.

1972, Apr. 17

2142 A478	1fo red, brn & blk	45	20
2143 A478	2fo blue, brn & blk	1.10	50

First European Ophthalmologists' Congress, Budapest.

Girl Reading and UNESCO Emblem — A479

Roses — A480

1972, May 27 Photo. *Perf. 11½x12*

2144 A479 1fo multicolored 40 15

International Book Year 1971.

1972, June 1

2145 A480 1fo multicolored 40 15

15th Rose Exhibition, Budapest.

George Dimitrov — A481

1972, June 18 Litho. *Perf. 12*

2146 A481 3fo black & multi 40 15

90th anniversary, birth of George Dimitrov (1882-1949), communist leader.

Souvenir Sheet

St. Martin and the Beggar, Stained-glass Window A482

1972, June 20 *Perf. 10½*

2147 A482 10fo multi 3.50 3.25

Belgica 72, International Philatelic Exhibition, Brussels, June 24-July 9.

Gyorgy Dozsa (1474-1514), Peasant Leader — A483

1972, June 25 Photo. *Perf. 11½x12*

2148 A483 1fo red & multi 20 15

Olympic Rings, Soccer — A484

Designs (Olympic Rings and): 60f, Water polo. 80f, Javelin, women's. 1fo, Kayak, women's. 1.20fo, Boxing. 2fo, Gymnastics, women's. 5fo, Fencing.

1972, July 15 *Perf. 11*

2149 A484	40f multi	15	15
2150 A484	60f multi	15	15
2151 A484	80f multi	15	15
2152 A484	1fo lilac & multi	15	15
2153 A484	1.20fo blue & multi	22	15
2154 A484	2fo multi	50	25
2155 A484	5fo green & multi	1.00	65
	Nos. 2149-2155,B299 (8)	2.87	
	Set value		1.70

20th Olympic Games, Munich, Aug. 26-Sept. 11. See No. C325.

Prince Geza Selecting Site of Székesfehérvár — A485

Designs: 60f, St. Stephen, first King of Hungary. 80f, Knights (country's defense). 1.20fo, King Stephen dictating to scribe (legal organization). 2fo, Sculptor at work (education). 4fo, Merchants before king (foreign relations). 6fo, View of castle and town of Székesfehérvár, 10th century. 10fo, King Andreas II presenting Golden Bull to noblemen.

1972, Aug. 20 Photo. *Perf. 12*

2156 A485	40f slate & multi	15	15
2157 A485	60f multi	20	15
2158 A485	80f lilac & multi	15	15
2159 A485	1.20fo multi	25	15
2160 A485	2fo bister & multi	45	18
2161 A485	4fo blue & multi	75	35
2162 A485	6fo purple & multi	1.10	70
	Nos. 2156-2162 (7)	3.05	
	Set value		1.55

Souvenir Sheet

Perf. 12½

2163 A485 10fo black & multi 3.50 3.25

Millenium of the town of Székesfehérvár and 750th anniversary of the Golden Bull granting rights to lesser nobility. No. 2163 contains one stamp (94x45mm).

Parliament, Budapest — A486

Design: 6fo, Session room of Parliament.

1972, Aug. 20 Litho.

2164 A486	5fo dk blue & multi	60	20
2165 A486	6fo multicolored	95	30

Constitution of 1949.

Eger, 17th Century View, and Bottle of Bull's Blood A487

Design: 2fo, Contemporary view of Tokay and bottle of Tokay Aszu.

1972, Aug. 21 Litho. *Perf. 12*

2166 A487	1fo buff & multi	28	15
2167 A487	2fo green & multi	65	20
	Set value		27

1st World Wine Exhibition, Budapest, Aug. 1972.

Georgikon Emblems, Grain, Potato Flower A488

1972, Sept. 3

2168 A488 1fo multi 20 15

175th anniv. of the founding of the Georgikon at Keszthely, the 1st scientific agricultural academy.

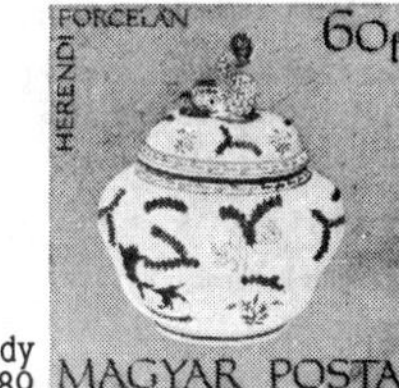

Covered Candy Dish — A489

Herend Porcelain: 40f, Vase with bird. 80f, Vase with flowers and butterflies. 1fo, Plate with Mexican landscape. 1.20fo, Covered dish. 2fo, Teapot, cup and saucer. 4fo, Plate with flowers. 5fo, Baroque vase showing Herend factory.

1972, Sept. 15

Sizes: 23x46mm (40f, 80f, 2fo, 5fo); 33x36mm, others

2169 A489	40f gray & multi	15	15
2170 A489	60f ocher & multi	15	15
2171 A489	80f multi	15	15
2172 A489	1fo multi	15	15
2173 A489	1.20fo green & multi	18	15
2174 A489	2fo multi	35	20
2175 A489	4fo red & multi	70	40
2176 A489	5fo multi	1.10	60
	Nos. 2169-2176 (8)	2.93	
	Set value		1.70

Herend china factory, founded 1839.

UIC Emblem and M-62 Diesel Locomotive — A490

1972, Sept. 19 Photo. *Perf. 11½x12*

2177 A490 1fo dark red 35 15

50th anniversary of International Railroad Union Congress, Budapest, Sept. 19.

"25" and Graph — A491

1972, Sept. *Perf. 11½x12*
2178 A491 1fo yellow & brown 35 15

Planned national economy, 25th anniv.

View of Obuda, 1872 A492

Designs: No. 2180, Budapest, 1972. No. 2181, Buda, 1872. No. 2182, Budapest, 1972. No. 2183, Pest, 1872. No. 2184, Budapest, 1972.

1972, Sept. 26 *Perf. 12x11½*
2179 A492 1fo Prus bl & rose car 16 15
2180 A492 1fo rose car & Prus bl 16 15
a. Pair, #2179-2180 32 20
2181 A492 2fo ocher & olive 28 15
2182 A492 2fo olive & ocher 28 15
a. Pair, #2181-2182 56 35
2183 A492 3fo green & lt brn 42 18
2184 A492 3fo lt brown & grn 42 18
a. Pair, #2183-2184 85 50
Nos. 2179-2184 (6) 1.72
Set value 70

Centenary of unification of Obuda, Buda and Pest into Budapest.

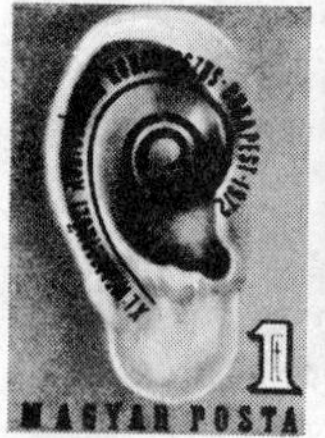

Ear and Congress Emblem — A493

Flora Martos — A494

1972, Oct. 3 *Perf. 11½x12*
2185 A493 1fo brown, yel & blk 20 15

11th Intl. Audiology Cong., Budapest.

1972 **Photo.** *Perf. 11½x12*

Portrait: No. 2187, Miklós Radnóti.

2186 A494 1fo green & multi 15 15
2187 A494 1fo brown & multi 15 15
Set value 15

Flora Martos (1897-1938), Hungarian Labor Party leader, and Miklós Radnóti (1909-1944), poet.

Issued: #2186, Nov. 5; #2187, Nov. 11.

Muses, by Jozsef Rippl-Ronai A495

Stained-glass Windows, 19th-20th Centuries: 60f, 16th century scribe, by Ferenc Sebesteny. 1fo, Flight into Egypt, by Karoly Lotz and Bertalan Székely. 1.50fo, Prince Arpad's Messenger, by Jenö Percz. 2.50fo, Nativity, by Lili Sztehlo. 4fo, Prince Arpad and Leaders, by Karoly Kernstock. 5fo, King Matthias and Jester, by Jenö Haranghy.

1972, Nov. 15 *Perf. 12*
2188 A495 40f multi 15 15
2189 A495 60f multi 15 15
2190 A495 1fo multi 15 15
2191 A495 1.50fo multi 22 15
2192 A495 2.50fo multi 38 16
2193 A495 4fo multi 75 32
2194 A495 5fo multi 1.25 60
Nos. 2188-2194 (7) 3.05
Set value 1.38

Weaver, Cloth and Cogwheel A496

1972, Nov. 27 **Litho.** *Perf. 12*
2195 A496 1fo silver & multi 25 15

Opening of Museum of Textile Techniques, Budapest.

Main Square, Szarvas A497

Church and City Hall, Vac A498

Designs: 1fo, Modern buildings, Salgotarjan. 3fo, Tokay and vineyard. 4fo, Esztergom Cathedral. 7fo, Town Hall, Kaposvar. 20fo, Veszprem.

1972 **Litho.** *Perf. 11*
2196 A497 40f brown & orange 15 15
2197 A497 1fo dk & lt blue 22 15

1973 *Perf. 12x11½*
2198 A498 3fo dk & lt green 60 15
2199 A498 4fo red brn & org 75 15
2200 A498 7fo blue vio & lil 1.40 15
2200A A498 20fo multicolored 3.75 55
Nos. 2196-2200A (6) 6.87
Set value 85

See Nos. 2330-2335.

Coil Stamps
Type of 1963-64

Designs as before

1972, Nov. **Photo.** *Perf. 14*
Size: 21½x17½mm, 17½x21½mm
2201 A336 2fo blue green 38 15
2202 A336 3fo dark blue 55 15
2203 A336 4fo blue, vert. 75 25
2204 A336 6fo bister 1.10 40

Black control number on back of every 5th stamp.

Minute inscription centered in lower margin: "Legrady Sandor".

Arms of Soviet Union — A498a

1972, Dec. 30 **Photo.** *Perf. 11½x12*
2205 A498a 1fo multicolored 15 15

50th anniversary of Soviet Union.

Petöfi Speaking at Pilvax Cafe — A499

Designs: 2fo, Portrait. 3fo, Petöfi on horseback, 1848-49.

1972, Dec. 30 **Engr.** *Perf. 12*
2206 A499 1fo rose carmine 18 15
2207 A499 2fo violet 35 15
2208 A499 3fo Prus green 50 24
Set value 45

Sesquicentennial of the birth of Sandor Petöfi (1823-49), poet and revolutionary.

Postal Zone Map of Hungary and Letter-carrying Crow — A500

1973, Jan. 1 **Litho.** *Perf. 12*
2209 A500 1fo red & black 20 15

Introduction of postal code system.

Imre Madách (1823-64), Poet and Dramatist — A501

1973, Jan. 20 **Photo.** *Perf. 11½x12*
2210 A501 1fo multicolored 20 15

Busho Mask — A502

Designs: Various Busho masks.

1973, Feb. 17 **Litho.** *Perf. 12*
2211 A502 40f tan & multi 15 15
2212 A502 60f dull grn & multi 15 15
2213 A502 80f lilac & multi 15 15
2214 A502 1.20fo multi 20 15
2215 A502 2fo tan & multi 32 16
2216 A502 4fo multi 80 38
2217 A502 6fo lilac & multi 1.25 55
Nos. 2211-2217 (7) 3.02
Set value 1.40

Busho Walk at Mohacs, ancient ceremony to drive out winter.

Nicolaus Copernicus — A503

1973, Feb. 19 **Engr.** *Perf. 12*
2218 A503 3fo bright ultra 75 60

Nicolaus Copernicus (1473-1543), Polish astronomer. Printed with alternating label showing heliocentric system and view of Torun.

Vascular System and WHO Emblem — A504

1973, Apr. 16 **Photo.** *Perf. 12*
2219 A504 1fo sl grn & brn red 25 15

25th anniv. of WHO.

Tank, Rocket, Radar, Plane, Ship and Soldier A505

1973, May 9 **Litho.** *Perf. 12*
2220 A505 3fo blue & multi 40 15

Philatelic Exhibition of Military Stamp Collectors of Warsaw Treaty Member States. No. 2220 was printed with alternating label showing flags of Warsaw Treaty members.

Hungary No. 1396 and IBRA '73 Emblem — A506

1973, May 11 **Litho.** *Perf. 12*
2221 A506 40f shown 15 15
2222 A506 60f No. 1397, POLSKA '73 15 15
2223 A506 80f No. 1398, IBRA '73 15 15
2224 A506 1fo No. 1399, POLSKA 15 15
2225 A506 1.20fo No. B293a, IBRA 16 15
2226 A506 2fo No. B293b, POLSKA 32 16
2227 A506 4fo No. B293c, IBRA 80 38
2228 A506 5fo No. B293d, POLSKA 1.15 50
Nos. 2221-2228 (8) 3.03
Set value 1.40

Publicity for IBRA '73 International Philatelic Exhibition, Munich, May 11-20; and POLSKA '73, Poznan, Aug. 15-Sept. 2. See No. C345.

Typesetting, from "Orbis Pictus," by Comenius — A507

Design: 3fo, Printer and wooden screw press, woodcut from Hungarian translation of Gospels.

1973, June 5 Photo. Perf. 11½x12

2229	A507	1fo black & gold	18	15
2230	A507	3fo black & gold	42	18
		Set value		25

500th anniv. of book printing in Hungary.

Storm over Hortobagy Puszta, by Csontvary — A508

Paintings: 60f, Mary's Well, Nazareth. 1fo, Carriage Ride by Moonlight in Athens, vert. 1.50fo, Pilgrimage to Cedars of Lebanon, vert. 2.50fo, The Lonely Cedar. 4fo, Waterfall at Jajce. 5fo, Ruins of Greek Theater at Taormina. 10fo, Horseback Riders on Shore.

1973, June 18 Perf. 12½

2231	A508	40f	gold & multi	15	15
2232	A508	60f	gold & multi	15	15
2233	A508	1fo	gold & multi	15	15
2234	A508	1.50fo	gold & multi	22	15
2235	A508	2.50fo	gold & multi	48	16
2236	A508	4fo	gold & multi	80	45
2237	A508	5fo	gold & multi	95	70
			Nos. 2231-2237 (7)	2.90	
			Set value		1.60

Souvenir Sheet

2238	A508	10fo gold & multi	3.75	3.25

Paintings by Tividar Kosztka Csontvary (1853-1919). No. 2238 contains one stamp (size: 90x43mm).

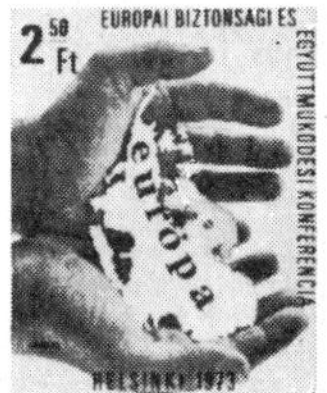

Hands Holding Map of Europe — A509   Flowers — A510

1973, July 3 Photo. Perf. 11½x12

2239	A509	2.50fo blk & gldn brn	3.00	3.00
a.		Souv. sheet of 4 + 2 labels	14.50	14.50

Conference for European Security and Cooperation. Helsinki, July 1973. No. 2239 was printed in souvenir sheet of 4 stamps and 2 blue labels showing conference sites.

1973, Aug. 4

2240	A510	40f	Provence roses	15	15
2241	A510	60f	Cyclamen	15	15
2242	A510	80f	Lungwort	15	15
2243	A510	1.20fo	English daisies	16	15
2244	A510	2fo	Buttercups	32	18
2245	A510	4fo	Violets	80	35
2246	A510	6fo	Poppies	1.25	65
			Nos. 2240-2246 (7)	2.98	
			Set value		1.55

"Let's be Friends in Traffic" — A511

Designs: 60f, "Not even one drink." 1fo, "Light your bicycle."

1973, Aug. 18 Photo. Perf. 12x11½

2247	A511	40f green & orange	15	15
2248	A511	60f purple & orange	15	15
2249	A511	1fo indigo & orange	16	15
		Set value	30	17

To publicize traffic rules.

Adoration of the Kings A512

Paintings: 60f, Angels playing violin and lute. 1fo, Adoration of the Kings. 1.50fo, Annunciation. 2.50fo, Angels playing organ and harp. 4fo, Visitation of Mary. 5fo, Legend of St. Catherine of Alexandria. 10fo, Nativity.

1973, Nov. 3 Photo. Perf. 12½

2250	A512	40f	gold & multi	15	15
2251	A512	60f	gold & multi	15	15
2252	A512	1fo	gold & multi	18	15
2253	A512	1.50fo	gold & multi	25	15
2254	A512	2.50fo	gold & multi	48	22
2255	A512	4fo	gold & multi	70	38
2256	A512	5fo	gold & multi	1.00	65
			Nos. 2250-2256 (7)	2.91	
			Set value		1.55

Souvenir Sheet

Perf. 11

2257	A512	10fo gold & multi	3.50	3.25

Paintings by Hungarian anonymous early masters from the Christian Museum at Esztergom. No. 2257 contains one 49x74mm stamp.

Mihaly Csokonai Vitez — A513   José Marti and Cuban Flag — A514

1973, Nov. 17 Photo. Perf. 11½x12

2258	A513	2fo bister & multi	35	15

Mihaly Csokonai Vitez (1773-1805), poet.

1973, Nov. 30

2259	A514	1fo dk brn, red & bl	15	15

Marti (1853-95), Cuban natl. hero and poet.

Barnabas Pesti (1920-44), Member of Hungarian Underground Communist Party — A515

1973, Nov. 30

2260	A515	1fo blue, brn & buff	15	15

Women's Double Kayak — A516

Designs: 60f, Water polo. 80f, Men's single kayak. 1.20fo, Butterfly stroke. 2fo, Men's fours kayak. 4fo, Men's single canoe. 6fo, Men's double canoe.

1973, Dec. 29 Litho. Perf. 12x11

2261	A516	40f	red & multi	15	15
2262	A516	60f	blue & multi	15	15
2263	A516	80f	multicolored	15	15
2264	A516	1.20fo	green & multi	22	15
2265	A516	2fo	carmine & multi	40	16
2266	A516	4fo	violet & multi	80	38
2267	A516	6fo	multicolored	1.10	60
			Nos. 2261-2267 (7)	2.97	
			Set value		1.40

Hungarian victories in water sports at Tampere and Belgrade.

Souvenir Sheet

Map of Europe — A517

1974, Jan. 15 Photo. Perf. 12x11½

2268		Sheet of 2 + label	10.00	10.00
a.		A517 5fo multicolored	2.25	2.25

European Peace Conference (Arab-Israeli War), Geneva, Jan. 1974.

Lenin A518

1974, Jan. 21 Photo. Perf. 11½x12

2269	A518	2fo gold, dull bl & brn	25	15

50th anniv. of the death of Lenin (1870-1924).

Jozsef Boczor, Imre Békés, Tamás Elek A519

1974, Feb. 21 Perf. 12½

2270	A519	3fo brown & multi	25	15

30th anniversary of the death in France of Hungarian resistance fighters.

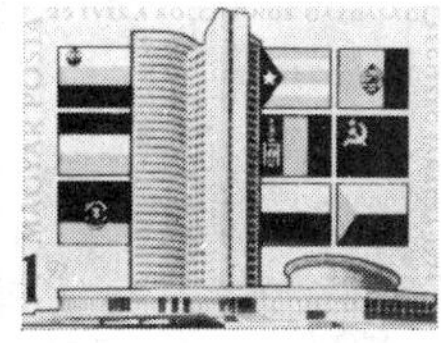

Comecon Building, Moscow and Flags A520

1974, Feb. 26 Photo. Perf. 12x11½

2271	A520	1fo multicolored	25	15

25th anniversary of the Council of Mutual Economic Assistance.

Bank Emblem, Coins and Banknote — A521

1974, Mar. 1 Perf. 11½x12

2272	A521	1fo lt green & multi	25	15

25th anniversary of the State Savings Bank.

Spacecraft on Way to Mars — A522

Designs: 60f, Mars 2 over Mars. 80f, Mariner 4. 1fo, Mars and Mt. Palomar Observatory. 1.20fo, Soft landing of Mars 3. 5fo, Mariner 9 with Mars satellites Phobos and Deimos.

1974, Mar. 11 Photo. Perf. 12½

2273	A522	40f	gold & multi	15	15
2274	A522	60f	silver & multi	15	15
2275	A522	80f	gold & multi	15	15
2276	A522	1fo	silver & multi	22	15
2277	A522	1.20fo	gold & multi	28	15
2278	A522	5fo	silver & multi	95	50
			Nos. 2273-2278,C347 (7)	3.00	
			Set value		1.55

Exploration of Mars. See No. C348.

Salvador Allende (1908-73), Pres. of Chile — A523

1974, Mar. 27 Photo. Perf. 11½x12

2279	A523	1fo black & multi	15	15

Mona Lisa, by Leonardo da Vinci A524

1974, Apr. 19 *Perf. 12½*

2280 A524 4fo gold & multi 7.75 7.50

Exhibition of the Mona Lisa in Asia.
Printed in sheets of 6 stamps and 6 labels with commemorative inscription.

Souvenir Sheet

Issue of 1874 and Flowers — A525

Designs: a, Mallow. b, Aster. c, Daisy. d, Columbine.

1974, May 11 **Litho.** *Perf. 11½*

2281 A525 Sheet of 4 3.50 3.50
a.-d. 2.50fo any single 48 48

Centenary of the first issue inscribed "Magyar Posta" (Hungarian Post).

Carrier Pigeon, World Map, UPU Emblem — A526

1974, May 22 **Litho.** *Perf. 12*

2282 A526	40f	shown	15	15
2283 A526	60f	Mail coach	15	15
2284 A526	80f	Old mail automobile	15	15
2285 A526	1.20fo	Balloon post	20	16
2286 A526	2fo	Mail train	42	25
2287 A526	4fo	Mail bus	90	50
Nos. 2282-2287,C349 (7)			2.13	
Set value				1.20

Centenary of the Universal Postal Union.

Dove of Basel, Switzerland No. 3L1, 1845 — A527

1974, June 7 **Photo.** *Perf. 11½x12*

2288 A527 3fo gold & multi 1.20 1.20

INTERNABA 1974 Philatelic Exhibition, Basel, June 7-16. No. 2288 issued in sheets of 3 stamps and 3 labels showing Internaba 1974 emblem. Size: 104x125mm.

Chess Players, from 13th Century Manuscript A528

Designs: 60f, Chess players, 15th century English woodcut. 80f, Royal chess party, 15th century Italian chess book. 1.20fo, Chess players, 17th century copper engraving by Selenus. 2fo, Farkas Kempelen's chess playing machine, 1769. 4fo, Hungarian Grand Master Geza Maroczy (1870-1951). 6fo, View of Nice and emblem of 1974 Chess Olympiad.

1974, June 6 **Litho.** *Perf. 12*

2289 A528	40f	multi	15	15
2290 A528	60f	multi	15	15
2291 A528	80f	multi	24	15
2292 A528	1.20fo	multi	30	20
2293 A528	2fo	multi	30	18
2294 A528	4fo	multi	75	35
2295 A528	6fo	multi	1.25	70
Nos. 2289-2295 (7)			3.14	1.88

50th anniv. of Intl. Chess Federation and 21st Chess Olympiad, Nice, June 6-30.

Souvenir Sheet

Cogwheel Railroad — A529

Designs: a, Passenger train, 1874. b, Freight train, 1874. c, Electric train, 1929-73. d, Twin motor train, 1973.

1974, June 25 **Litho.** *Perf. 12*

2296 A529 Sheet of 4 3.75 3.75
a.-d. 2.50fo, any single 50 50

Cent. of Budapest's cogwheel railroad.

Congress Emblem (Globe and Parliament) A530

1974, Aug. 18 **Photo.** *Perf. 12*

2297 A530 2fo silver, dk & lt bl 35 15

4th World Congress of Economists, Budapest, Aug. 19-24.

Bathing Woman, by Károly Lotz A531

Paintings of Nudes: 60f, Awakening, by Károly Brocky. 1fo, Venus and Cupid, by Brocky, horiz. 1.50fo, After the Bath, by Lotz. 2.50fo, Resting Woman, by Istvan Csok, horiz. 4fo, After the Bath, by Bertalan Szekely. 5fo, "Devotion," by Erzsebet Korb. 10fo, Lark, by Pál Szinyei Merse.

1974, Aug. *Perf. 12½*

2298 A531	40f	gold & multi	15	15
2299 A531	60f	gold & multi	15	15
2300 A531	1fo	gold & multi	18	15
2301 A531	1.50fo	gold & multi	35	15
2302 A531	2.50fo	gold & multi	45	20
2303 A531	4fo	gold & multi	85	30
2304 A531	5fo	gold & multi	1.00	55
Nos. 2298-2304 (7)			3.13	
Set value				1.40

Souvenir Sheet

Perf. 11

2305 A531 10fo gold & multi 3.75 3.75

No. 2305 contains one stamp (45x70mm).

Mimi, by Béla Czóbel A532

1974, Sept. 4

2306 A532 1fo multicolored 40 20

91st birthday of Béla Czóbel, Hungarian painter.

Intersputnik Tracking Station — A533

High Voltage Line "Peace" and Pipe Line "Friendship" — A534

Perf. 11½x12, 12x11½

1974, Sept. 5 **Litho.**

2307 A533 1fo blue & violet 18 15
2308 A534 3fo multicolored 60 18
Set value 25

Technical assistance and cooperation between Hungary and USSR, 25th anniv.

Pablo Neruda — A535

Sweden No. 1 and Lion from Royal Palace, Stockholm — A536

1974, Sept. 11 **Photo.** *Perf. 11½x12*

2309 A535 1fo multicolored 15 15

Pablo Neruda (Neftali Ricar do Reyes, 1904-1973), Chilean poet.

1974, Sept. 21 *Perf. 12x11½*

2310 A536 3fo ultra, yel grn & gold 1.25 1.25

Stockholmia 74 Intl. Philatelic Exhibition, Stockholm, Sept. 21-29. No. 2310 issued in sheets of 3 stamps and 3 labels showing Stockholmia emblem. White margin inscribed "UPU" multiple in white. Size: 126x104mm.

Tank Battle and Soldier with Anti-tank Grenade — A537

1974, Sept. 28 **Litho.** *Perf. 12*

2311 A537 1fo gold, orange & blk 15 15

Army Day. See Nos. C351-C352.

Segner and Segner Crater on Moon A538

1974, Oct. 5

2312 A538 3fo multicolored 60 25

270th anniversary of the birth of Janos Andras Segner, naturalist. No. 2312 printed se-tenant with label arranged checkerwise in sheet. Label shows Segner wheel.

Rhyparia Purpurata A539

Lepidoptera: 60f, Melanargia galathea. 80f, Parnassius Apollo. 1fo, Celerio euphorbia. 1.20fo, Catocala fraxini. 5fo, Apatura iris. 6fo, Palaeochrysophanus hyppothoe.

1974, Nov. 11 **Photo.** *Perf. 12½*

2313 A539	40f	multicolored	15	15
2314 A539	60f	violet & multi	15	15
2315 A539	80f	multicolored	16	15
2316 A539	1fo	brown & multi	16	15
2317 A539	1.20fo	blue & multi	30	22
2318 A539	5fo	purple & multi	1.00	42
2319 A539	6fo	multicolored	1.25	65
Nos. 2313-2319 (7)			3.17	
Set value				1.60

Motherhood A540

Robert Kreutz A541

1974, Dec. 24 **Litho.** *Perf. 12*

2320 A540 1fo lt blue, blk & yel 25 15

1974, Dec. 24

2321 A541 1fo shown 15 15
2322 A541 1fo István Pataki 15 15
Set value 20 15

30th death anniversary of anti-fascist martyrs Robert Kreutz (1923-1944) and István Pataki (1914-1944).

Puppy — A542

Young Animals: 60f, Siamese kittens, horiz. 80f, Rabbit. 1.20fo, Foal, horiz. 2fo, Lamb. 4fo, Calf, horiz. 6fo, Piglet.

1974, Dec. 30

2323 A542 40f lt blue & multi 15 15
2324 A542 60f multicolored 15 15
2325 A542 80f olive & multi 15 15
2326 A542 1.20fo green & multi 24 15
2327 A542 2fo brown & multi 35 15
2328 A542 4fo orange & multi 75 40
2329 A542 6fo violet & multi 1.25 60
Nos. 2323-2329 (7) 3.04
Set value 1.35

See Nos. 2403-2409.

Building Type of 1972

Designs: 4fo, Szentendre. 5fo, View of Szolnok across Tisza River. 6fo, Skyscraper, Dunáujváros. 10fo, City Hall, Kiskunfélegyháza. 50fo, Church (Turkish Mosque), Hunyadi Statue and TV tower, Pecs.

1974-80 Litho. *Perf. 12x11½*

2330 A498 4fo red brn & pink 80 15
2331 A498 5fo dk blue & ultra 1.00 15
2332 A498 6fo dk brn & org 1.25 15
2333 A498 8fo dk & brt grn 1.65 15
2334 A498 10fo brown & yel 2.00 15
2335 A498 50fo multi 10.00 1.75
Nos. 2331-2335 (5) 15.90 2.35

Issue dates: 8fo, Dec. 7. 10fo, 50fo, Dec. 30. 5fo, Mar. 8, 1975. 6fo, June 10, 1975. 4fo, June 20, 1980.

Hospital, Lambarene — A544

Designs: 60f, Dr. Schweitzer, patient and microscope. 80f, Patient arriving by boat. 1.20fo, Hospital supplies arriving by ship. 2fo, Globe, Red Cross, carrier pigeons. 4fo, Nobel Peace Prize medal. 6fo, Portrait and signature of Dr. Schweitzer, organ pipes and "J. S. Bach."

1975, Jan. 14 Photo. *Perf. 12*

2340 A544 40f gold & multi 15 15
2341 A544 60f gold & multi 15 15
2342 A544 80f gold & multi 15 15
2343 A544 1.20fo gold & multi 24 15
2344 A544 2fo gold & multi 35 18
2345 A544 4fo gold & multi 75 40
2346 A544 6fo lil & multi 1.25 60
Nos. 2340-2346 (7) 3.04
Set value 1.45

Dr. Albert Schweitzer (1875-1965), medical missionary and musician, birth centenary.

Farkas Bolyai — A545

1975, Feb. 7 Litho. *Perf. 11½x12*

2347 A545 1fo gray & red brown 20 15

Bolyai (1775-1856), mathematician.

Mihály Károlyi — A546

1975, Mar. 4 Litho. *Perf. 12*

2348 A546 1fo lt blue & brown 20 15

Birth centenary of Count Mihály Károlyi (1875-1955), prime minister, 1918-1919.

Woman, IWY Emblem A547

1975, Mar. 8 *Perf. 12x11½*

2349 A547 1fo aqua & black 15 15

International Women's Year 1975.

"Let us Build up the Railroads" — A548

Posters: 60f, "Bread starts here." 2fo, "Hungarian Communist Party-a Party of Action." 4fo, "Heavy Industry-secure base of Three-year Plan." 5fo, "Our common interest-a developed socialist society."

1975, Mar. 17 Photo. *Perf. 11*

2350 A548 40f red & multi 15 15
2351 A548 60f red & multi 15 15
2352 A548 2fo red & multi 20 15
2353 A548 4fo red & multi 48 20
2354 A548 5fo red & multi 70 40
Nos. 2350-2354 (5) 1.68
Set value 75

Hungary's liberation from Fascism, 30th anniversary.

Arrow, 1915, Pagoda and Mt. Fuji — A549

Antique Cars: 60f, Swift, 1911, Big Ben and Tower of London. 80f, Model T Ford, 1908, Capitol and Statue of Liberty. 1fo, Mercedes, 1901, Towers of Stuttgart. 1.20fo, Panhard Levassor, 1912, Arc de Triomphe and Eiffel Tower. 5fo, Csonka, 1906, Fishermen's Bastion and Chain Bridge. 6fo, Emblems of Hungarian Automobile Club, Alliance Internationale de Tourisme and Federation Internationale de l'Automobile.

1975, Mar. 27 Litho. *Perf. 12*

2355 A549 40f lt blue & multi 15 15
2356 A549 60f lt green & multi 15 15
2357 A549 80f pink & multi 15 15
2358 A549 1fo lilac & multi 18 15
2359 A549 1.20fo orange & multi 25 15
2360 A549 5fo ultra & multi 90 42
2361 A549 6fo lilac rose & multi 1.40 70
Nos. 2355-2361 (7) 3.18
Set value 1.62

Hungarian Automobile Club, 75th anniv.

The Creation of Adam, by Michelangelo — A550

1975, Apr. 23 Photo. *Perf. 12½*

2362 A550 10fo gold & multi 4.00 3.75

Michelangelo Buonarroti (1475-1564), Italian painter, sculptor and architect.

Academy of Science — A551

Design: 2fo, Dates "1975 1825." 3fo, Count Istvan Szechenyi.

1975, May 5 Litho. *Perf. 12*

2363 A551 1fo green & multi 15 15
2364 A551 2fo green & multi 28 15
2365 A551 3fo green & multi 50 28

Sesquicentennial of Academy of Science, Budapest, founded by Count Istvan Szechenyi.

Emblem of 1980 Olympics and Proposed Moscow Stadium — A553

1975, May 8 Photo. *Perf. 11½x12*

2366 A553 5fo lt blue & multi 1.50 1.25

Socfilex 75 International Philatelic Exhibition, Moscow, May 8-18. No. 2366 issued in sheets of 3 stamps and 3 labels showing Socfilex 75 emblem (War Memorial, Berlin-Treptow). Size: 104x125mm.

France No. 1100 and Venus of Milo — A554

1975, June 3 Photo. *Perf. 11½x12*

2367 A554 5fo lilac & multi 1.50 1.25

ARPHILA 75 International Philatelic Exhibition, Paris, June 6-16. No. 2367 issued in sheets of 3 stamps and 3 labels showing ARPHILA 75 emblem. Size: 104x125mm.

Early Transformer, Kando Locomotive, 1902, Pylon — A555

1975, June 10 Litho. *Perf. 12*

2368 A555 1fo multicolored 30 15

Hungarian Electrotechnical Association, 75th anniversary.

Epée, Saber, Foil and Globe — A556

1975, July 11

2369 A556 1fo multicolored 25 15

32nd World Fencing Championships, Budapest, July 11-20.

Souvenir Sheet

Whale Pavilion, Oceanexpo 75 — A557

1975, July 21 Photo. *Perf. 12½*

2370 A557 10fo gold & multi 3.50 3.50

Oceanexpo 75, International Exhibition, Okinawa, July 20, 1975-Jan. 1976.

Dr. Agoston Zimmermann (1875-1963), Veterinarian A558

1975, Sept. 4 Litho. *Perf. 12*

2371 A558 1fo brown & blue 20 15

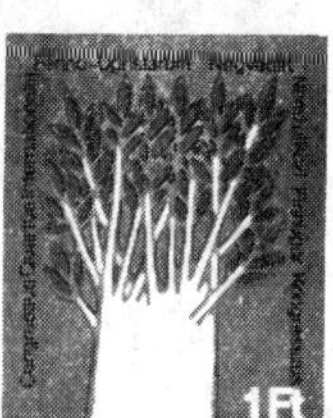

Symbolic of 14 Cognate Languages — A559

1975, Sept. 9

2372 A559 1fo gold & multi 20 15

International Finno-Ugrian Congress.

Voters — A560

Design: No. 2374, Map of Hungary with electoral districts.

1975, Oct. 1

2373	A560	1fo multicolored	15	15
2374	A560	1fo multicolored	15	15
		Set value		15

Hungarian Council System, 25th anniv.

Fish and Waves (Ocean Pollution) — A561

Designs: 60f, Skeleton hand reaching for rose in water glass. 80f, Fish gasping for raindrop. 1fo, Carnation wilting in polluted soil. 1.20fo, Bird dying in polluted air. 5fo, Sick human lung and smokestack. 6fo, "Stop Pollution" (raised hand protecting globe from skeleton hand).

1975, Oct. 16 Litho. *Perf. 11½*

2375	A561	40f multi	15	15
2376	A561	60f multi	15	15
2377	A561	80f multi	15	15
2378	A561	1fo multi	20	15
2379	A561	1.20fo multi	28	18
2380	A561	5fo multi	85	32
2381	A561	6fo multi	1.25	55
		Nos. 2375-2381 (7)	3.03	
		Set value		1.35

Environmental Protection.

Mariska Gárdos (1885-1973) A562

Portraits: No. 2383, Imre Mezö (1905-56). No. 2384, Imre Tarr (1900-37).

1975, Nov. 4 Litho. *Perf. 12*

2382	A562	1fo black & red org	15	15
2383	A562	1fo black & red org	15	15
2384	A562	1fo black & red org	15	15
		Set value	30	15

Famous Hungarians, birth anniversaries.

Treble Clef, Organ and Orchestra — A563

1975, Nov. 14

2385	A563	1fo multicolored	30	15

Franz Liszt Musical Academy, centenary.

Szigetcsep Icon A564

Virgin and Child, 18th Century Icons: 60f, Graboc. 1fo, Esztergom. 1.50fo, Vatoped. 2.50fo, Tottos. 4fo, Gyor. 5fo, Kazan.

1975, Nov. 25 Photo. *Perf. 12½*

2386	A564	40f gold & multi	15	15
2387	A564	60f gold & multi	20	15
2388	A564	1fo gold & multi	16	15
2389	A564	1.50fo gold & multi	25	15
2390	A564	2.50fo gold & multi	40	15
2391	A564	4fo gold & multi	80	35
2392	A564	5fo gold & multi	1.25	90
		Nos. 2386-2392 (7)	3.21	
		Set value		1.70

Members' Flags, Radar, Mother and Child — A565

1975, Dec. 15 Litho. *Perf. 12*

2393	A565	1fo multicolored	20	15

20th anniversary of the signing of the Warsaw Treaty (Bulgaria, Czechoslovakia, German Democratic Rep., Hungary, Poland, Romania, USSR).

Ice Hockey, Winter Olympics' Emblem — A566

Designs (Emblem and): 60f, Slalom. 80f, Ski race. 1.20fo, Ski jump. 2fo, Speed skating. 4fo, Cross-country skiing. 6fo, Bobsled. 10fo, Figure skating, pair.

1975, Dec. 29 Photo. *Perf. 12x11½*

2394	A566	40f silver & multi	15	15
2395	A566	60f silver & multi	15	15
2396	A566	80f silver & multi	15	15
2397	A566	1.20fo silver & multi	24	15
2398	A566	2fo silver & multi	35	18
2399	A566	4fo silver & multi	85	35
2400	A566	6fo silver & multi	1.25	65
		Nos. 2394-2400 (7)	3.14	
		Set value		1.50

Souvenir Sheet

Perf. 12½

2401	A566	10fo silver & multi	3.50	3.50

12th Winter Olympic Games, Innsbruck, Austria, Feb. 4-15, 1976. No. 2401 contains one stamp (59x36mm).

"P," 5-pengö and 500-pengö Notes — A567

1976, Jan. 16 Litho. *Perf. 12*

2402	A567	1fo multicolored	25	15

Hungarian Bank Note Co., 50th anniversary.

Animal Type of 1974

Young Animals: 40f, Wild boars, horiz. 60f, Squirrels. 80f, Lynx, horiz. 1.20fo, Wolves. 2fo, Foxes, horiz. 4fo, Bears. 6fo, Lions, horiz.

1976, Jan. 26

2403	A542	40f multi	15	15
2404	A542	60f blue & multi	15	15
2405	A542	80f multi	15	15
2406	A542	1.20fo multi	24	15
2407	A542	2fo violet & multi	38	18
2408	A542	4fo yellow & multi	85	35
2409	A542	6fo multi	1.25	55
		Nos. 2403-2409 (7)	3.17	
		Set value		1.30

A.G. Bell, Telephone, Molniya I and Radar — A568

1976, Mar. 10 Litho. *Perf. 11½x12*

2410	A568	3fo multicolored	75	75

Centenary of first telephone call by Alexander Graham Bell, Mar. 10, 1876. Issued in sheets of 4.

Battle of Kuruc-Labantz — A569

Paintings: 60f, Meeting of Rakoczi and Tamas Esze, by Endre Veszprem. 1fo, Diet of Onod, by Mor Than. 2fo, Camp of the Kurucs. 3fo, Ilona Zrinyi (Rakoczi's mother), vert. 4fo, Kuruc officers, vert. 5fo, Prince Francis II Rakoczy, by Adam Manyoki, vert. Painters of 40f, 2fo, 3fo, 4fo, are unknown.

1976, Mar. 27 Photo. *Perf. 12½*

2411	A569	40f gold & multi	15	15
2412	A569	60f gold & multi	15	15
2413	A569	1fo gold & multi	28	15
2414	A569	2fo gold & multi	65	18
2415	A569	3fo gold & multi	85	25
2416	A569	4fo gold & multi	1.40	35
2417	A569	5fo gold & multi	1.75	70
		Nos. 2411-2417 (7)	5.23	1.93

Francis II Rakoczy (1676-1735), leader of Hungarian Protestant insurrection, 300th birth anniversary.

Standard Meter, Hungarian Meter Act — A570

Designs: 2fo, Istvan Krusper, his vacuum balance, standard kilogram. 3fo, Interferometer and rocket.

1976, Apr. 5 *Perf. 11½x12*

2418	A570	1fo multicolored	18	15
2419	A570	2fo multicolored	28	18
2420	A570	3fo multicolored	42	28

Centenary of introduction of metric system in Hungary.

US No. 1353 and Independence Hall, Philadelphia — A571

Photogravure and Foil Embossed

1976, May 29 *Perf. 11½x12*

2421	A571	5fo blue & multi	1.40	1.25

Interphil 76 International Philatelic Exhibition, Philadelphia, Pa., May 29-June 6. No. 2421 issued in sheets of 3 stamps and 3 labels showing bells. Size: 115x125mm.

"30" and Various Pioneer Activities A572

1976, June 5 Litho. *Perf. 12*

2422	A572	1fo multicolored	25	15

Hungarian Pioneers, 30th anniversary.

Trucks, Safety Devices, Trade Union Emblem — A573

1976, June *Perf. 12½*

2423	A573	1fo multicolored	15	15

Labor safety.

Intelstat 4, Montreal Olympic Emblem, Canadian Flag — A574

Designs: 60f, Equestrian. 1fo, Butterfly stroke. 2fo, One-man kayak. 3fo, Fencing. 4fo, Javelin. 5fo, Athlete on vaulting horse.

1976, June 29 Photo. *Perf. 11½x12*

2424	A574	40f dk blue & multi	15	15
2425	A574	60f slate grn & multi	15	15
2426	A574	1fo blue & multi	18	15
2427	A574	2fo green & multi	35	15
2428	A574	3fo brown & multi	55	20

2429 A574 4fo bister & multi 75 35
2430 A574 5fo maroon & multi 95 55
Nos. 2424-2430 (7) 3.08
Set value 1.40

21st Olympic Games, Montreal, Canada, July 17-Aug. 1. See No. C365.

Denmark No. 2 and Mermaid, Copenhagen — A575

1976, Aug. 19 Photo. *Perf. 11½x12*
2431 A575 3fo multicolored 1.25 1.25

HAFNIA 76 Intl. Phil. Exhib., Copenhagen, Aug. 20-29. No. 2431 issued in sheets of 3 stamps and 3 labels showing HAFNIA emblem.

Souvenir Sheet

Discovery of Body of Lajos II, by Bertalan Székely — A576

1976, Aug. 27 Photo. *Perf. 12½*
2432 A576 20fo multicolored 3.50 3.50

450th anniversary of the Battle of Mohacs against the Turks.

Flora, by Titian A577

1976, Aug. 27
2433 A577 4fo gold & multi 75 25

Titian (1477-1576), Venetian painter.

Hussar, Herend China — A578

1976, Sept. 28 Litho. *Perf. 12*
2434 A578 4fo multicolored 75 25

Herend China manufacture, sesqui.

Daniel Berzsenyi (1776-1836), Poet — A579

1976, Sept. 28
2435 A579 2fo black, gold & yel 25 15

Pal Gyulai (1826-1909), Poet and Historian — A580

1976, Sept. 28
2436 A580 2fo orange & black 25 15

Tuscany No. 1 and Emblem — A581

1976, Oct. 13 Photo. *Perf. 11½x12*
2437 A581 5fo orange & multi 2.25 2.25

ITALIA 76 International Philatelic Exhibition, Milan, Oct. 14-24. No. 2437 issued in sheets of 3 stamps and 3 labels showing Italia 76 emblem. Size: 106x127mm.

Jozsef Madzsar, M.D. — A582

Labor leaders: No. 2439, Ignac Bogar (1876-1933), secretary of printers' union. No. 2440, Rudolf Golub (1901-44), miner.

1976, Nov. 4 Litho. *Perf. 12*
2438 A582 1fo deep brown & red 15 15
2439 A582 1fo deep brown & red 15 15
2440 A582 1fo deep brown & red 15 15
Set value 15

Science and Culture House, Georgian Dancer, Hungarian and USSR Flags A583

1976, Nov. 4 *Perf. 12½x12*
2441 A583 1fo multicolored 40 15

House of Soviet Science and Culture, Budapest, 2nd anniversary.

Koranyi Sanitarium and Statue — A584

1976, Nov. 11 *Perf. 12*
2442 A584 2fo multicolored 35 15

Koranyi TB Sanitarium, founded by Dr. Frigyes Koranyi, 75th anniversary.

Locomotive, 1875, Enese Station — A585

Designs: 60f, Steam engine No. 17, 1885, Rabatamasi Station. 1fo, Railbus, 1925, Fertoszentmiklos Station. 2fo, Express steam engine, Kapuvar Station. 3fo, Engine and trailer, 1926, Gyor Station. 4fo, Eight-wheel express engine, 1934, and Fertoboz Station. 5fo, Raba-Balaton engine, Sopron Station.

1976, Nov. 26 Litho. *Perf. 12*
2443 A585 40f multicolored 15 15
2444 A585 60f multicolored 15 15
2445 A585 1fo multicolored 18 15
2446 A585 2fo multicolored 35 15
2447 A585 3fo multicolored 48 20
2448 A585 4fo multicolored 75 55
2449 A585 5fo multicolored 1.00 60
Nos. 2443-2449 (7) 3.06
Set value 1.65

Gyor-Sopron Railroad, centenary.

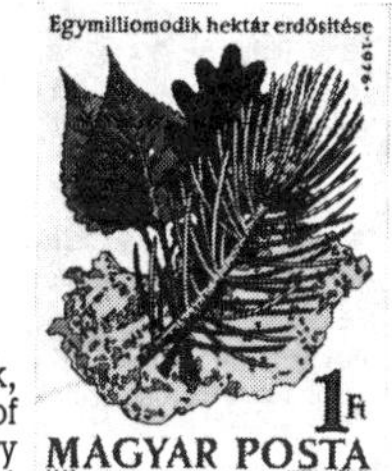

Poplar, Oak, Pine and Map of Hungary A586

1976, Dec. 14
2450 A586 1fo multicolored 25 15

Millionth hectare of reforestation.

Weight Lifting and Wrestling, Silver Medals — A587

Designs: 60f, Kayak, men's single and women's double. 1fo, Horse vaulting. 4fo, Women's fencing. 6fo, Javelin. 20fo, Water polo.

1976, Dec. 14 Photo. *Perf. 11½x12*
2451 A587 40f multicolored 15 15
2452 A587 60f multicolored 15 15
2453 A587 1fo multicolored 18 15
2454 A587 4fo multicolored 85 35
2455 A587 6fo multicolored 1.10 55
Nos. 2451-2455 (5) 2.43
Set value 1.05

Souvenir Sheet

Perf. 12½x11½
2456 A587 20fo multicolored 3.50 3.50

Hungarian medalists in 21st Olympic Games.

Spoonbills A588

Birds: 60f, White storks. 1fo, Purple herons. 2fo, Great bustard. 3fo, Common cranes. 4fo, White wagtails. 5fo, Garganey teals.

1977, Jan. 3 Litho. *Perf. 12*
2457 A588 40f multicolored 18 15
2458 A588 60f multicolored 18 15
2459 A588 1fo multicolored 28 15
2460 A588 2fo multicolored 40 18
2461 A588 3fo multicolored 50 28
2462 A588 4fo multicolored 1.10 40
2463 A588 5fo multicolored 1.40 65
Nos. 2457-2463 (7) 4.04 1.96

Birds from Hortobagy National Park.

1976 World Champion Imre Abonyi Driving Four-in-hand A589

Designs: 60f, Omnibus on Boulevard, 1870. 1fo, One-horse cab at Budapest Railroad Station, 1890. 2fo, Mail coach, Buda to Vienna route. 3fo, Covered wagon of Hajduszoboszlo. 4fo, Hungarian coach, by Jeremias Schemel, 1563. 5fo, Post chaise, from a Lübeck wood panel, 1430.

1977, Jan. 31 Litho. *Perf. 12x11½*
2464 A589 40f multicolored 15 15
2465 A589 60f multicolored 15 15
2466 A589 1fo multicolored 18 15
2467 A589 2fo multicolored 35 18
2468 A589 3fo multicolored 50 20
2469 A589 4fo multicolored 70 48
2470 A589 5fo multicolored 85 60
Nos. 2464-2470 (7) 2.88
Set value 1.65

History of the coach.

Peacock A590

Birds: 60f, Green peacock. 1fo, Congo peacock. 3fo, Argus pheasant. 4fo, Impeyan pheasant. 6fo, Peacock pheasant.

1977, Feb. 22 Litho. *Perf. 12*
2471 A590 40f multicolored 18 15
2472 A590 60f multicolored 18 15
2473 A590 1fo multicolored 20 15
2474 A590 3fo multicolored 50 22
2475 A590 4fo multicolored 80 35
2476 A590 6fo multicolored 1.25 65
Nos. 2471-2476 (6) 3.11
Set value 1.45

Newspaper Front Page, Factories — A591

1977, Mar. 3 Litho. *Perf. 12*
2477 A591 1fo gold, black & ver 15 15

Nepszava newspaper, centenary.

Flowers, by Mihaly Munkacsy A592

Flowers, by Hungarian Painters: 60f, Jakab Bogdany. 1fo, Istvan Csok, horiz. 2fo, Janos Halapy. 3fo, Jozsef Rippl-Ronai, horiz. 4fo, Janos Tornyai. 5fo, Jozsef Koszta.

1977, Mar. 18 Photo. *Perf. 12½*

2478 A592 40f gold & multi 15 15
2479 A592 60f gold & multi 15 15
2480 A592 1fo gold & multi 16 15
2481 A592 2fo gold & multi 32 16
2482 A592 3fo gold & multi 48 20
2483 A592 4fo gold & multi 65 38
2484 A592 5fo gold & multi 95 52
Nos. 2478-2484 (7) 2.86
Set value 1.48

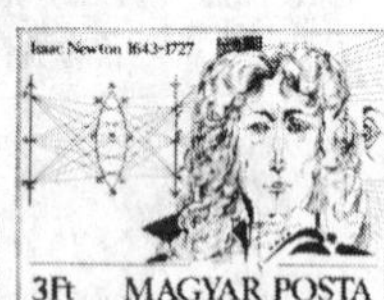

Newton and Double Convex Lens — A593

1977, Mar. 31 Litho. *Perf. 12*

2485 A593 3fo tan & multi 1.00 1.00

Isaac Newton (1643-1727), natural philosopher and mathematician, 250th death anniversary. No. 2485 issued in sheets of 4 stamps and 4 blue and black labels showing illustration from Newton's "Principia Mathematica," and Soviet space rocket.

Janos Vajda (1827-97), Poet — A594

1977, May 2 Litho. *Perf. 12*

2486 A594 1fo green, cream & blk 15 15

Netherlands No. 1 and Tulips — A595

1977, May 23 Photo. *Perf. 11½x12*

2487 A595 3fo multicolored 1.25 1.25

AMPHILEX '77, Intl. Stamp Exhib., Amsterdam, May 26-June 5. Issued in sheets of 3 stamps + 3 labels showing Amphilex poster.

The only foreign revenue stamps listed in this catalogue are those also authorized for prepayment of postage.

Scene from "Wedding at Nagyrede" A596

1977, June 14 Litho. *Perf. 12*

2488 A596 3fo multicolored 50 20

State Folk Ensemble, 25th anniversary.

Souvenir Sheet

Bath of Bathsheba, by Rubens A597

1977, June 14 Photo. *Perf. 11*

2489 A597 20fo multicolored 4.00 4.00

Peter Paul Rubens (1577-1640), Flemish painter.

Medieval View of Sopron, Fidelity Tower, Arms A598

1977, June 25 Litho. *Perf. 12x11½*

2490 A598 1fo multicolored 1.50 1.50

700th anniv. of Sopron. Printed se-tenant with label showing European Architectural Heritage medal awarded Sopron in 1975.

Race Horse Kincsem A599

1977, July 16 Litho. *Perf. 12*

2491 A599 1fo multicolored 1.00 90

Sesquicentennial of horse racing in Hungary. Printed se-tenant with label showing portrait of Count Istvan Szechenyi and vignette from his 1827 book "Rules of Horse Racing in Hungary."

German Democratic Republic No. 370 — A600

1977, Aug. 18 Photo. *Perf. 12x11½*

2492 A600 3fo multicolored 1.25 1.10

SOZPHILEX 77 Philatelic Exhibition, Berlin, Aug. 19-28. No. 2492 issued in sheets of 3 stamps and 3 labels showing SOZPHILEX emblem.

Scythian Iron Bell, 6th Century B.C. — A601

Panel, Crown of Emperor Constantin Monomakhos A602

Designs: No. 2494, Bronze candlestick in shape of winged woman, 12th-13th centuries. No. 2495, Centaur carrying child, copper aquamanile, 12th century. No. 2496, Gold figure of Christ, from 11th century Crucifix. Designs show art treasures from Hungarian National Museum, founded 1802.

1977, Sept. 3 Litho. *Perf. 12*

2493 A601 2fo multicolored 75 75
2494 A601 2fo multicolored 75 75
2495 A601 2fo multicolored 75 75
2496 A601 2fo multicolored 75 75
a. Horiz. strip of 4, #2493-2496 3.00 3.00

Souvenir Sheet

2497 A602 10fo multicolored 3.50 3.00

50th Stamp Day.

Sputnik — A603

Spacecraft: 60f, Skylab. 1fo, Soyuz-Salyut 5. 3fo, Luna 24. 4fo, Mars 3. 6fo, Viking.

1977, Sept. 20

2498 A603 40f multicolored 15 15
2499 A603 60f multicolored 15 15
2500 A603 1fo multicolored 18 15
2501 A603 3fo multicolored 48 24
2502 A603 4fo multicolored 80 38
2503 A603 6fo multicolored 1.25 55
Nos. 2498-2503 (6) 3.01
Set value 1.35

Space explorations, from Sputnik to Viking. See No. C375.

Janos Szanto Kovacs (1852-1908), Agrarian Movement Pioneer — A604

Ervin Szabo (1877-1918), Revolutionary Workers' Movement Pioneer — A605

1977, Nov. 4 Litho. *Perf. 12*

2504 A604 1fo red & black 15 15
2505 A605 1fo red & black 15 15
Set value 16

Monument to Hungarian October Revolutionists, Omsk — A606

1977, Nov. 4

2506 A606 1fo black & red 15 15

60th anniv. of Russian October Revolution.

Hands and Feet Bathed in Thermal Spring — A607

1977, Nov. 1

2507 A607 1fo multicolored 25 15

World Rheumatism Year.

Endre Ady — A608

1977, Nov. 22 Engr. *Perf. 12*

2508 A608 1fo violet blue 35 35

Endre Ady (1877-1919), lyric poet. Issued in sheets of 4.

Lesser Panda — A609

Designs: 60f, Giant panda. 1fo, Asiatic black bear. 4fo, Polar bear. 6fo, Brown bear.

1977, Dec. 16 Litho. *Perf. 11½x12*

2509	A609	40f	yellow & multi	15	15
2510	A609	60f	yellow & multi	15	15
2511	A609	1fo	yellow & multi	35	15
2512	A609	4fo	yellow & multi	95	35
2513	A609	6fo	yellow & multi	1.40	70
			Nos. 2509-2513 (5)	3.00	
			Set value		1.25

Souvenir Sheet

Flags and Ships along Intercontinental Waterway — A610

Flags: a, Austria. b, Bulgaria. c, Czechoslovakia. d, France. e, Luxembourg. f, Yugoslavia. g, Hungary. h, Fed. Rep. of Germany. i, Romania. j, Switzerland. k, USSR.

1977, Dec. 28 Litho. *Perf. 12*

2514	A610	Sheet of 11	15.00	15.00
a.-k.		2fo, any single	1.25	1.25

European Intercontinental Waterway: Danube, Main and Rhine.

Lancer, 17th Century — A611

Hussars: 60f, Kuruts, 1710. 1fo, Baranya, 1762. 2fo, Palatine officer, 1809. 4fo, Sandor, 1848. 6fo, Trumpeter, 5th Honved Regiment, 1900.

1978, Jan. Litho. *Perf. 11½x12*

2515	A611	40f	lilac & multi	15	15
2516	A611	60f	yel grn & multi	15	15
2517	A611	1fo	red & multi	18	15
2518	A611	2fo	dull bl & multi	35	18
2519	A611	4fo	olive bis & multi	75	40
2520	A611	6fo	gray & multi	1.40	60
			Nos. 2515-2520 (6)	2.98	
			Set value		1.40

School of Arts and Crafts A612

1978, Mar. 31 Litho. *Perf. 12*

2521	A612	1fo	multicolored	20	15

School of Arts and Crafts, 200th anniv.

Soccer Players, Flags of West Germany and Poland A613

Designs (Various Soccer Scenes and Flags): No. 2523, Hungary and Argentina. No. 2524, France and Italy. No. 2525, Tunisia and Mexico. No. 2526, Sweden and Brazil. No. 2527, Spain and Austria. No. 2528, Peru and Scotland. No. 2529, Iran and Netherlands. Flags represent first round of contestants. 20fo, Argentina '78 emblem.

1978, May 25 Litho. *Perf. 12*

2522	A613	2fo	multicolored	35	15
2523	A613	2fo	multicolored	35	15
2524	A613	2fo	multicolored	35	15
2525	A613	2fo	multicolored	35	15
2526	A613	2fo	multicolored	35	15
2527	A613	2fo	multicolored	35	15
2528	A613	2fo	multicolored	35	35
2529	A613	2fo	multicolored	1.00	50
			Nos. 2522-2529 (8)	3.45	1.75

Souvenir Sheet

Perf. 11½

2530	A613	20fo	multicolored	3.50	3.50

Argentina '78 11th World Cup Soccer Championships, Argentina, June 2-25.

Vase, Star and Glass Blower's Tube A614

1978, May 20 Litho. *Perf. 12*

2531	A614	1fo	multicolored	20	15

Ajka Glass Works, centenary.

Canada No. 1 and Trillium — A615

1978, June 2

2532	A615	3fo	multicolored	1.00	90

CAPEX '78, Canadian International Philatelic Exhibition, Toronto, Ont., June 9-18. Issued in sheets of 3 stamps and 3 labels showing CAPEX '78 emblem.

Souvenir Sheets

Leif Ericson and his Ship — A616

Explorers and their ships: #2533b, Columbus. c, Vasco da Gama. d, Magellan. #2534a, Drake. b, Hudson. c, Cook. d, Peary.

1978, June 10 Litho. *Perf. 12x11½*

2533		Sheet of 4	4.00	4.00
a.-d.	A616	2fo, any single	75	75
2534		Sheet of 4	4.00	4.00
a.-d.	A616	2fo, any single	75	75

Diesel Train, Pioneer's Kerchief — A617

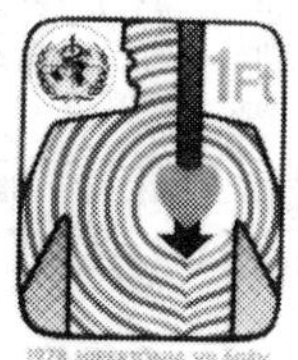

Congress Emblem as Flower — A618

1978, June 10 *Perf. 12*

2535	A617	1fo	multicolored	20	15

30th anniversary of Pioneer Railroad.

1978, June

Design: No. 2537, Congress emblem, "Cuba" and map of Cuba.

2536	A618	1fo	multi	25	15
2537	A618	1fo	multi	25	15
a.			Pair, #2536-2537	50	30

11th World Youth Festival, Havana.

WHO Emblem, Stylized Body and Heart — A619

Clenched Fist, Dove and Olive Branch — A620

1978, Aug. 21 Litho. *Perf. 12*

2538	A619	1fo	multicolored	20	15

Drive against hypertension.

1978, Sept. 1 Litho. *Perf. 12*

2539	A620	1fo	gray, red & black	20	15

Publication of review "Peace and Socialism," 20th anniversary.

Train, Telephone, Space Communication — A621

1978, Sept. 8 Litho. *Perf. 12*

2540	A621	1fo	multicolored	25	15

20th anniv. of Organization for Communication Cooperation of Socialist Countries.

"Toshiba" Automatic Letter Sorting Machine — A622

1978, Sept. 15 Litho. *Perf. 11½x12*

2541	A622	1fo	multicolored	25	20

Introduction of automatic letter sorting. No. 2541 printed with se-tenant label showing bird holding letter.

Eros Offering Grapes, Villa Hercules A623

Roman Mosaics Found in Hungary: No. 2543, Tiger (Villa Hercules, Budapest). No. 2544, Bird eating berries (Balacapuszta). No. 2545, Dolphin (Aquincum). 10fo, Hercules aiming at Centaur fleeing with Deianeira (Villa Hercules).

Photogravure and Engraved

1978, Sept. 16 *Perf. 11½*

2542	A623	2fo	multicolored	1.90	1.90
2543	A623	2fo	multicolored	1.90	1.90
2544	A623	2fo	multicolored	1.90	1.90
2545	A623	2fo	multicolored	1.90	1.90

Souvenir Sheet

2546	A623	10fo	multicolored	12.00	12.00

Stamp Day. No. 2546 contains one stamp (52x35mm).

Count Imre Thököly — A624

1978, Oct. 1 Photo. *Perf. 12½*

2547	A624	1fo	black & yellow	25	15

300th anniv. of Hungary's independence movement, led by Imre Thököly (1657-1705).

Souvenir Sheet

Hungarian Crown Jewels — A625

1978, Oct. 10

2548	A625	20fo	gold & multi	6.00	6.00

Return of Crown Jewels from US, Jan. 6, 1978.

"The Red Coach" A626

1978, Oct. 21 Litho. *Perf. 12*

2549	A626	3fo	red & black	50	15

Gyula Krudy, 1878-1933, novelist.

St. Ladislas I Reliquary, Györ Cathedral — A627

1978, Nov. 15 *Perf. 11½x12½*

2550 A627 1fo multicolored 20 15

Ladislas I (1040-1095), 900th anniversary of accession to throne of Hungary.

Miklos Jurisics Statue, Köszeg A628

1978, Nov. 15 *Perf. 12*

2551 A628 1fo multicolored 20 15

650th anniversary of founding of Köszeg.

Samu Czaban and Gizella Berzeviczy — A629

Photogravure and Engraved

1978, Nov. 24 *Perf. 11½x12*

2552 A629 1fo brown, buff & red 20 15

Samu Czaban (1878-1942) and Gizella Berzeviczy (1878-1954), Communist teachers during Soviet Republic (1918-1919).

Communist Party Emblem — A630

1978, Nov. 24 **Litho.** *Perf. 12*

2553 A630 1fo gray, red & blk 15 15

Hungarian Communist Party, 60th anniv.

Woman Cutting Bread — A631

Ceramics by Margit Kovacs (1902-1976): 2fo, Woman with pitcher. 3fo, Potter.

1978, Nov. 30 **Litho.** *Perf. 11½x12*

2554	A631	1fo multicolored	15	15
2555	A631	2fo multicolored	32	15
2556	A631	3fo multicolored	80	60

Virgin and Child, by Dürer A632

Dürer Paintings: 60f, Adoration of the Kings, horiz. 1fo, Self-portrait, 1500. 2fo, St. George. 3fo, Nativity, horiz. 4fo, St. Eustatius. 5fo, The Four Apostles. 20fo, Dancing Peasant Couple, 1514 (etching).

1979, Jan. 8 **Photo.** *Perf. 12½*

2557	A632	40f gold & multi	15	15
2558	A632	60f gold & multi	15	15
2559	A632	1fo gold & multi	16	15
2560	A632	2fo gold & multi	32	18
2561	A632	3fo gold & multi	40	22
2562	A632	4fo gold & multi	80	35
2563	A632	5fo gold & multi	1.00	90
		Nos. 2557-2563 (7)	2.98	2.10

Souvenir Sheet

Litho.

2564 A632 20fo buff & brown 3.75 3.50

Albrecht Dürer (1471-1528), German painter and engraver.

Human Rights Flame — A633

1979, Feb. 8 **Litho.** *Perf. 11½x12*

2565 A633 1fo dk & lt blue 1.50 1.50

Universal Declaration of Human Rights, 30th anniversary. No. 2565 issued in sheets of 12 stamps (3x4) and 4 labels. Alternating horizontal rows inverted.

Child at Play — A634

IYC Emblem and: No. 2567, Family. No. 2568, 3 children (international friendship).

1979, Feb. 26 *Perf. 12*

2566	A634	1fo multicolored	2.00	75
2567	A634	1fo multicolored	2.00	75
2568	A634	1fo multicolored	6.00	6.50

Soldiers of the Red Army, by Bela Uitz A635

1979, Mar. 21 **Litho.** *Perf. 12*

2569 A635 1fo silver, blk & red 15 15

60th anniv. of Hungarian Soviet Republic.

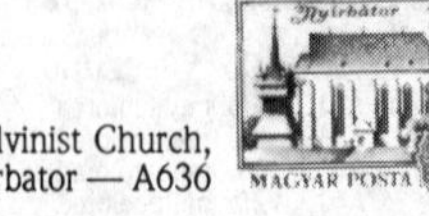

Calvinist Church, Nyirbator — A636

1979, Mar. 28 *Perf. 11*

2570 A636 1fo brown & yellow 15 15

700th anniversary of Nyirbator. See No. 2601.

Chessmen, Gold Cup, Flag A637

1979, Apr. 12 **Litho.** *Perf. 12*

2571 A637 3fo multicolored 50 50

Hungarian victories in 23rd Chess Olympiad, Buenos Aires, 1978.

Alexander Nevski Cathedral, Sofia, Bulgaria No. 1 — A638

1979, May 18 **Litho.** *Perf. 11½x12*

2572 A638 3fo multicolored 75 75

Philaserdica '79 Philatelic Exhibition, Sofia, Bulgaria, May 18-27. No. 2572 issued in sheets of 3 stamps and 3 labels showing Philaserdica emblem and arms of Sofia.

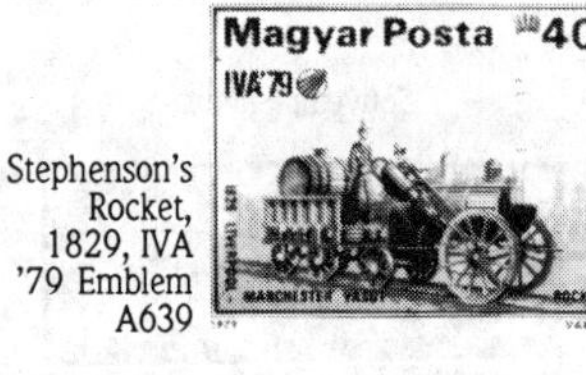

Stephenson's Rocket, 1829, IVA '79 Emblem A639

Railroad Development: 60f, Siemens' first electric locomotive, 1879. 1fo, "Pioneer," Chicago & Northwestern Railroad, 1836. 2fo, Orient Express, 1883. 3fo, Trans-Siberian train, 1898. 4fo, Express train on Tokaido line, 1964. 5fo, Transrapid-O5 train, exhibited 1979. 20fo, Map of European railroad network.

1979, June 8 **Litho.** *Perf. 12x11½*

2573	A639	40f multi	15	15
2574	A639	60f multi	15	15
2575	A639	1fo multi	20	15
2576	A639	2fo multi	35	22
2577	A639	3fo multi	50	35
2578	A639	4fo multi	65	52
2579	A639	5fo multi	1.00	65
		Nos. 2573-2579 (7)	3.00	2.19

Souvenir Sheet

Perf. 12½x11½

2580 A639 20fo multi 4.50 4.50

International Transportation Exhibition (IVA '79), Hamburg. No. 2580 contains one stamp (47x32mm).

Natural Gas Pipeline and Compressor — A640

Designs: 2fo, Lenin power station and dam, Dnieperopetrovsk and pylon. 3fo, Comecon Building, Moscow, and star symbolizing ten member states.

1979, June 26 *Perf. 11½x12*

2581	A640	1fo multi	15	15
2582	A640	2fo multi	28	15
2583	A640	3fo multi	40	20
		Set value		40

30th anniversary of the Council of Mutual Economic Assistance, Comecon.

Zsigmond Moricz (1879-1942), Writer, by Jozsef Ripple-Ronai A641

1979, June 29 *Perf. 12*

2584 A641 1fo multi 20 15

Town Hall, Helsinki, Finnish Flag, Moscow '80 Emblem A642

Designs (Moscow '80 Emblem and): 60f, Colosseum, Rome, Italian flag. 1fo, Asakusa Temple, Tokyo, Japanese flag. 2fo, Mexico City Cathedral, Mexican flag. 3fo, Our Lady's Church, Munich, German flag. 4fo, Skyscrapers, Montreal, Canadian flag. 5fo, Lomonosov University, Misha the bear and Soviet flag.

1979, July 31 *Perf. 12x11½*

2585	A642	40f multi	15	15
2586	A642	60f multi	15	15
2587	A642	1fo multi	18	15
2588	A642	2fo multi	28	20
2589	A642	3fo multi	35	24
2590	A642	4fo multi	48	30
2591	A642	5fo multi	85	55
		Nos. 2585-2591 (7)	2.44	
		Set value		1.50

Pre-Olympic Year.

Boy with Horse and Greyhounds, by Janos Vaszary — A643

Paintings of Horses: 60f, Coach and Five, by Karoly Lotz. 1fo, Boys on Horseback, by Celesztin Pallya. 2fo, Farewell, by Lotz. 3fo, Horse Market, by Pallya. 4fo, Wanderer, by Bela Ivanyi-Grunwald. 5fo, Ready for the Hunt, by Karoly Sterio.

1979, Aug. 11 Photo. *Perf. 12½*

2592 A643 40f multi	15	15
2593 A643 60f multi	15	15
2594 A643 1fo multi	20	15
2595 A643 2fo multi	28	15
2596 A643 3fo multi	50	20
2597 A643 4fo multi	65	35
2598 A643 5fo multi	1.00	50
Nos. 2592-2598 (7)	2.93	
Set value		1.42

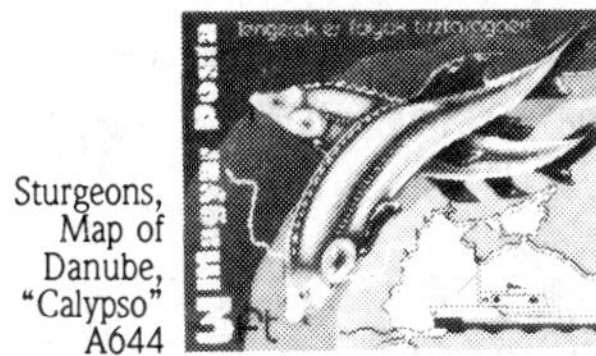

Sturgeons, Map of Danube, "Calypso" A644

1979, Aug. 11

2599 A644 3fo multi	50	15

Environmental protection of rivers and seas.

Pentathlon A645

1979, Aug. 12 Litho. *Perf. 12*

2600 A645 40f multi	50	20

Pentathlon World Championship, Budapest, Aug. 12-18.

Architecture Type of 1979

Design: Vasvar Public Health Center.

1979, Aug. 15 Litho. *Perf. 11*

2601 A636 40f multi	15	15

700th anniversary of Vasvar.

Denarius of Stephen I, 1000-1038, Reverse A646

Hungarian Coins: 2fo, Copper coin of Bela III, 1172-1196. 3fo, Golden groat of King Louis the Great, 1342-1382. 4fo, Golden forint of Matthias I, 1458-1490. 5fo, Silver gulden of Wladislaw II, 1490-1516.

Engraved and Photogravure

1979, Sept. 3 *Perf. 12x11½*

2602 A646 1fo multi	18	20
2603 A646 2fo multi	28	35
2604 A646 3fo multi	35	35
2605 A646 4fo multi	48	35
2606 A646 5fo multi	1.00	85
Nos. 2602-2606 (5)	2.29	2.10

9th International Numismatic Congress, Berne, Switzerland.

Souvenir Sheet

Unofficial Stamp, 1848 — A647

1979, Sept. 15 Litho. *Perf. 12*

2607 A647 10fo dk brown, blk & red	3.00	3.00

Stamp Day.

Souvenir Sheet

Elbel Locomotive A648

Designs: b, Type 424 steam engine. c, "War Locomotive." d, Hydraulic diesel locomotive.

1979, Oct. 19 Litho. *Perf. 12*

2608 Sheet of 4	3.50	3.50
a.-d. A648 5fo, any single	70	70

Gyor-Sopron-Ebenfurt rail service, cent.

Vega-Chess, by Victor Vasarely A649

1979, Oct. 29

2609 A649 1fo multi	15	15

International Savings Day — A650

1979, Oct. 29 Litho. *Perf. 12*

2610 A650 1fo multi	15	15

Otter — A651

Wildlife Protection: 60f, Wild cat. 1fo, Pine marten. 2fo, Eurasian badger. 4fo, Polecat. 6fo, Beech marten.

1979, Nov. 20

2611 A651 40f multi	15	15
2612 A651 60f multi	15	15
2613 A651 1fo multi	18	15
2614 A651 2fo multi	35	20
2615 A651 4fo multi	65	28
2616 A651 6fo multi	1.00	65
Nos. 2611-2616 (6)	2.48	
Set value		1.35

Tom Thumb, IYC Emblem A652

IYC Emblem and Fairy Tale Scenes: 60f, The Ugly Duckling. 1fo, The Fisherman and the Goldfish. 2fo, Cinderella. 3fo, Gulliver's Travels. 4fo, The Little Pigs and the Wolf. 5fo, Janos the Knight. 20fo, The Fairy Ilona.

1979, Dec. 29 Litho. *Perf. 12x11½*

2617 A652 40f multi	15	15
2618 A652 60f multi	15	15
2619 A652 1fo multi	20	15
2620 A652 2fo multi	35	20
2621 A652 3fo multi	50	28
2622 A652 4fo multi	70	40
2623 A652 5fo multi	1.00	70
Nos. 2617-2623 (7)	3.05	2.03

Souvenir Sheet

2624 A652 20fo multi	4.50	4.25

Trichodes Apairius and Yarrow A653

Insects Pollinating Flowers: 60f, Bumblebee and blanketflower. 1fo, Red admiral butterfly and daisy. 20fo, Cetonia aurata and rose. 4fo, Graphosoma lineatum and petroselinum hortense. 6fo, Chlorophorus varius and thistle.

1980, Jan. 25 Litho. *Perf. 12*

2625 A653 40f multi	15	15
2626 A653 60f multi	15	15
2627 A653 1fo multi	15	15
2628 A653 2fo multi	30	18
2629 A653 4fo multi	70	32
2630 A653 6fo multi	95	45
Nos. 2625-2630 (6)	2.40	
Set value		1.15

Hanging Gardens of Semiramis, 6th Century B.C., Map showing Babylon A654

Seven Wonders of the Ancient World (and Map): 60f, Temple of Artemis, Ephesus, 6th century B.C. 1fo, Zeus, by Phidias, Olympia. 2fo, Tomb of Maussolos, Halikarnassos, 3rd century B.C. 3fo, Colossos of Rhodes. 4fo, Pharos Lighthouse, Alexandria, 3rd century B.C. 5fo, Pyramids, 26th-24th centuries B.C.

1980, Feb. 29 Litho. *Perf. 12x11½*

2631 A654 40f multi	15	15
2632 A654 60f multi	15	15
2633 A654 1fo multi	15	15
2634 A654 2fo multi	30	18
2635 A654 3fo multi	42	30
2636 A654 4fo multi	60	38
2637 A654 5fo multi	75	60
Nos. 2631-2637 (7)	2.52	1.91

Tihany Benedictine Abbey and Deed A655

1980, Mar. 19 Litho. *Perf. 12*

2638 A655 1fo multi	15	15

Benedictine Abbey, Tihany, 925th anniversary of deed (oldest document in Hungarian).

Gabor Bethlen, Copperplate Print — A656

1980, Mar. 19

2639 A656 1fo multi	15	15

Gabor Bethlen (1580-1629), Prince of Transylvania (1613-29) and King of Hungary (1620-29).

Easter Casket of Garamszentbenedek, 15th Century (Restoration) — A657

1980, Mar. 19

2640 A657 1fo shown	15	15
2641 A657 2fo Three Marys	30	30
2642 A657 3fo Apostle James	42	42
2643 A657 4fo Thaddeus	60	60
2644 A657 5fo Andrew	85	60
Nos. 2640-2644 (5)	2.32	2.07

Liberation from Fascism, 35th Anniversary A658

1980, Apr. 3 Litho. *Perf. 12*

2645 A658 1fr multi	20	15

Jozsef Attila, Poet and Lyricist — A659

1980, Apr. 11

2646 A659 1fo rose car & olive	20	15

See No. 2675.

Hungary No. 386a — A660

1980, Apr. 28 *Perf. 11½x12*
2647 A660 1fo multi 2.25 1.50

Hungarian Postal Museum, 50th anniv.

Two Pence Blue, Mounted Guardsman, London 1980 Emblem — A661

1980, Apr. 30 *Perf. 11½x12*
2648 A661 3fo multi 1.00 1.00

London 1980 International Stamp Exhibition, May 6-14. No. 2648 issued in sheets of 3 stamps and 3 labels showing London 1980 emblem and arms of city. Size: 104x125mm.

Norway No. B51, Mother with Child, by Gustav Vigeland — A662

1980, June 9 **Litho.** *Perf. 11½x12*
2649 A662 3fo multi 1.00 1.00

NORWEX '80 Stamp Exhibition, Oslo, June 13-22. No. 2649 issued in sheets of 3 stamps and 3 labels showing NORWEX emblem. Size: 108x125mm.

Margit Kaffka (1880-1918), Writer — A663

1980, June 9 *Perf. 12*
2650 A663 1fo blk & pur, *cr* 25 15

Zoltan Schönherz (1905-42), Anti-fascist Martyr A664

1980, July 25 **Litho.**
2652 A664 1fo multi 15 15

Dr. Endre Hogyes and Congress Emblem — A665

Decanter, c. 1850 — A666

1980, July 25
2653 A665 1fo multi 15 15

28th International Congress of Physiological Sciences, Budapest, Dr. Hogyes (1847-1906) first described equilibrium reflex-curve and modified Pasteur's rabies vaccine.

1980, Sept. **Litho.** *Perf. 12*
2654 A666 1fo shown 25 25
2655 A666 2fo Decorated glass 38 38
2656 A666 3fo Stem glass 65 65

Souvenir Sheet

2657 A666 10fo Pecs glass 2.50 2.25

53rd Stamp Day.

Bertalan Por, Self-portrait — A667

Graylag Goose — A668

1980, Nov. 4 **Litho.** *Perf. 12*
2658 A667 1fo Artist (1880-1964) 35 18

1980, Nov. 11 *Perf. 11½x12*
2659 A668 40f shown 15 15
2660 A668 60f Black-crowned night heron 15 15
2661 A668 1fo Shoveler 18 15
2662 A668 2fo Chlidonias leucopterus 38 22
2663 A668 4fo Great crested grebe 75 42
2664 A668 6fo Black-necked stilt 1.25 60
Nos. 2659-2664 (6) 2.86
Set value 1.45

Souvenir Sheet

2665 A668 20fo Great white heron 4.75 4.50

European Nature Protection Year. No. 2665 contains one stamp (37x59mm).

Souvenir Sheet

Dove on Map of Europe — A669

1980, Nov. 11 *Perf. 12½x11½*
2666 A669 20fo multi 4.75 4.50

European Security and Cooperation Conference, Madrid.

Johannes Kepler and Model of his Theory A670

1980, Nov. 21 **Litho.** *Perf. 12*
2667 A670 1fo multi 35 20

Johannes Kepler (1571-1630), German astronomer, 350th anniversary of death. No. 2667 printed se-tenant with label showing rocket and satellites orbiting earth.

Karoly Kisfaludy (1788-1830), Poet and Dramatist A671

1980, Nov. 21
2668 A671 1fo brn red & dull brn 15 15

UN Headquarters, New York — A672

UN membership, 25th anniversary.

Photogravure and Engraved

1980, Dec. 12 *Perf. 11½x12*
2669 A672 40f shown 15 15
2670 A672 60f Geneva headquarters 15 15
2671 A672 1fo Vienna headquarters 15 15
2672 A672 2fo UN & Hungary flags 28 18
2673 A672 4fo UN, Hungary arms 55 35
2674 A672 6fo World map 95 60
Nos. 2669-2674 (6) 2.23
Set value 1.30

Attila Type of 1980

Design: Ferenc Erdei (1910-71), economist and statesman.

1980, Dec. 23 **Litho.** *Perf. 12*
2675 A659 1fo dk green & brown 15 15

Bela Szanto — A674

Count Lajos Batthyany — A675

1981, Jan. 31 **Litho.** *Perf. 12*
2676 A674 1fo multi 15 15

Bela Szanto (1881-1951), labor movement leader.
See Nos. 2698, 2724, 2767.

1981, Feb. 14
2677 A675 1fo multi 15 15

Count Lajos Batthyany (1806-1849), prime minister, later executed.

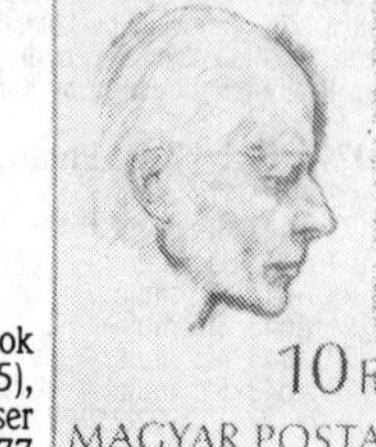

Bela Bartok (1881-1945), Composer A677

Design: b, Cantata Profana illustration.

1981, Mar. 25 **Litho.** *Perf. 12½*
2685 Sheet of 2 2.75 2.75
a.-b. A677 10fo any single 1.25 1.25

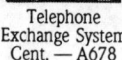

Telephone Exchange System Cent. — A678

Belling Stag — A679

1981, Apr. 29 **Litho.** *Perf. 12*
2686 A678 2fo multi 25 15

1981, Apr. 29
2687 A679 2fo multi 25 15

Flag of the House of Arpad, 11th Cent. — A680

1981, Apr. 29
2688 A680 40f shown 15 15
2689 A680 60f Hunyadi family, 15th cent. 15 15
2690 A680 1fo Gabor Bethlen, 1600 15 15
2691 A680 2fo Ferenc Rakoczi II, 1716 28 15
2692 A680 4fo Honved, 1848 75 28
2693 A680 6fo Troop flag, 1919 1.00 40
Nos. 2688-2693 (6) 2.48
Set value 1.00

Red Cross and Ambulance Vehicles — A681

Map of Europe and J. Henry Dunant (Red Cross Founder) — A682

1981, May 4
2694 A681 2fo multi 25 15

Souvenir Sheet

Perf. 12½x11½

2695 A682 20fo multi 2.75 2.75

Hungarian Red Cross cent. (2fo); 3rd European Red Cross Conf., Budapest, May 4-7 (20fo).

Souvenir Sheet

1933 WIPA Exhibition Seals — A683

1981, May 15 *Perf. 12x12½*
2696 Sheet of 4 2.75 2.75
a.-d. A683 5fo any single 65 65

WIPA 1981 Phil. Exhib., Vienna, May 22-31.

Stephenson and his Nonpareil — A684

1981, June 12 **Litho.** *Perf. 12*
2697 A684 2fo multi 25 15

George Stephenson (1781-1848), British railroad engineer, birth bicentenary.

Famous Hungarians Type

Design: Bela Vago (1881-1939), anti-fascist martyr.

1981, Aug. 7 **Litho.** *Perf. 12*
2698 A685 2fo ocher & brn ol 25 15

Alexander Fleming (1881-1955), Discoverer of Penicillin A686

1981, Aug. 7
2699 A686 2fo multi 25 15

Bridal Chest — A687

Designs: Bridal chests.

1981, Sept. 12 **Litho.** *Perf. 12*
2700 A687 1fo Szentgal, 18th cent. 15 15
2701 A687 2fo Hodmezovasar-hely, 19th cent. 30 18

Souvenir Sheet

2702 A687 10fo Bacs County, 17th cent. 2.00 2.00

54th Stamp Day. No. 2702 contains one stamp (44x25mm).

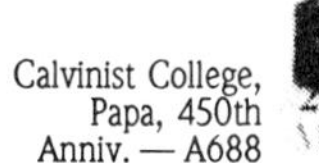

Calvinist College, Papa, 450th Anniv. — A688

1981, Oct. 3 **Litho.** *Perf. 12*
2703 A688 2fo multi 25 15

World Food Day — A689

1981, Oct. 16
2704 A689 2fo multi 25 15

Passenger Ship Rakoczi, 1964, No. 1834 A690

Designs: Sidewheelers and Hungarian stamps.

1981, Nov. 25 *Perf. 12x11½*
2705 A690 1fo Franz I, #1828 16 15
2706 A690 1fo Arpad, #1829 16 15
2707 A690 2fo Szechenyi, #1830 32 16
2708 A690 2fo Grof Szechenyi Istvan, #1831 32 16
2709 A690 4fo Sofia, #1832 65 32
2710 A690 6fo Felszabadulas, #1833 95 48
2711 A690 8fo shown 1.25 65
Nos. 2705-2711 (7) 3.81 2.07

Souvenir Sheet

Perf. 13

2712 A690 20fo Hydrofoil Solyom, #1830 3.50 3.50

European Danube Commission, 125th anniv.

Souvenir Sheet

Slovakian Natl. Costumes — A691

Perf. 12½x11½

1981, Nov. 18 **Litho.**
2713 Sheet of 4 2.25 2.25
a. A691 1fo shown 20 20
b. A691 2fo German 40 40
c. A691 3fo Croatian 60 60
d. A691 4fo Romanian 80 80

Christmas 1981 — A692

Pen Pals, by Norman Rockwell — A693

Sculptures: 1fo, Mary Nursing the Infant Jesus, by Margit Kovacs. 2fo, Madonna of Csurgo.

1981, Dec. 4 *Perf. 12½x11½*
2714 A692 1fo multi 15 15
2715 A692 2fo multi 26 15
Set value 15

1981, Dec. 29 *Perf. 11½x12*

Norman Rockwell Illustrations.

2716 A693 1fo shown 15 15
2717 A693 2fo Courting Under the Clock at Midnight 25 15
2718 A693 2fo Maiden Voyage 25 15
2719 A693 4fo Threading the Needle 52 30
Nos. 2716-2719,C435-C437 (7) 3.47 2.60

Souvenir Sheet

La Toilette, by Pablo Picasso (1881-1973) — A694

1981, Dec. 29 **Litho.** *Perf. 11½*
2720 A694 20fo multicolored 2.75 2.75

25th Anniv. of Worker's Militia — A695

1982, Jan. 26 **Litho.** *Perf. 12*
2721 A695 1fo Shooting practice 18 15
2722 A695 4fo Members, 3 generations 50 35
Set value 43

A696 A698

1982, Feb. 12 **Litho.** *Perf. 12x11½*
2723 A696 2fo multicolored 25 15

10th World Trade Union Cong., Havana, Feb. 10-15.

Famous Hungarians Type

Gyula Alpri (1882-1944), anti-fascist martyr.

1982, Mar. 24 *Perf. 12*
2724 A674 2fo multicolored 25 15

1982, Mar. 24 **Litho.** *Perf. 12*
2725 A698 2fo multicolored 25 15

TB Bacillus centenary.

1982 World Cup — A699

Designs: Hungary in competition with other World Cup teams.

No. 2733a, Barcelona Stadium. b, Madrid Stadium.

1982, Apr. 16 *Perf. 11*
2726 A699 1fo Egypt, 1934 15 15
2727 A699 1fo Italy, 1938 15 15
2728 A699 2fo Germany, 1954 25 16
2729 A699 2fo Mexico, 1958 25 16
2730 A699 4fo England, 1962 50 30
2731 A699 6fo Brazil, 1966 80 45
2732 A699 8fo Argentina, 1978 1.00 60
Nos. 2726-2732 (7) 3.10 1.97

Souvenir Sheet

2733 Sheet of 2 3.00 3.00
a.-b. A699 10fo any single 1.40 1.40

No. 2733 contains 44x44mm stamps.

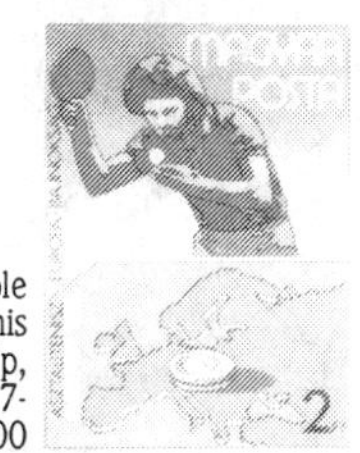

European Table Tennis Championship, Budapest, Apr. 17-25 — A700

1982, Apr. 16 **Litho.** *Perf. 11½x12*
2734 A700 2fo multi 25 15

Roses — A701

25 Years of Space Travel — A702

1982, Apr. 30 *Perf. 12*
2735 A701 1fo Pascali 16 15
2736 A701 1fo Michele Meilland 16 15
2737 A701 2fo Diorama 32 18
2738 A701 2fo Wendy Cussons 32 18
2739 A701 3fo Blue Moon 45 28
2740 A701 3fo Invitation 45 28
2741 A701 4fo Tropicana 65 35
Nos. 2735-2741 (7) 2.51 1.57

Souvenir Sheet

2742 A701 10fo Bouquet 2.50 2.50

No. 2742 contains one stamp (34x59mm, perf. 11).

1982, May 18 **Photo.** *Perf. 11½*
2743 A702 1fo Columbia shuttle, 1981 15 15
2744 A702 1fo Armstrong, Apollo 11, 1969 15 15
2745 A702 2fo A. Leonov, Voskhod 2, 1965 28 18
2746 A702 2fo Yuri Gagarin, Vostok 28 18
2747 A702 4fo Laika, Sputnik 2, 1957 55 35
2748 A702 4fo Sputnik I, 1957 55 35
2749 A702 6fo Space researcher K.E. Ciolkovski 85 50
Nos. 2743-2749 (7) 2.81 1.86

A703

A704

1982, May 7 **Litho.** *Perf. 12*
2750 A703 2fo multi 25 15

George Dimitrov (1882-1947), 1st prime minister of Bulgaria. SOZPHILEX '82 Stamp Exhib., Sofia, Bulgaria, May. No. 2750 se-tenant with label showing Bulgarian 1300th anniv. emblems.

1982, May 27 **Litho.** *Perf. 12x11½*
2751 A704 2fo multi 25 15

Diosgyor paper mill, bicent.

First Rubik's Cube World Championship, Budapest, June 5 — A705

1982, June 4 *Perf. 11½x12*

2752 A705 2fo multi 25 15

Souvenir Sheet

George Washington, by F. Kemmelmeyer — A706

Washington's 250th Birth Anniv.: a, Michael Kovats de Fabricy (1724-1779), Cavalry Commandant, by Sandor Finta.

1982, July 2 **Litho.** *Perf. 11*

2753 Sheet of 2 2.50 2.50
a.-b. A706 5fo any single 75 75

World Hematology Congress, Budapest — A707

Zirc Abbey, 800th Anniv. — A708

1982, July 30 *Perf. 12½x11½*

2754 A707 2fo multi 25 15

1982, Aug. 19 *Perf. 11½x12*

2755 A708 2fo multi 25 15

KNER Printing Office, Gyoma, Centenary — A709

1982, Sept. 23 **Litho.** *Perf. 12x11½*

2756 A709 2fo Emblem 25 15

AGROFILA '82 Intl. Agricultural Stamp Exhibition, Godollo — A710

1982, Sept. 24 *Perf. 11½x12*

2757 A710 5fo Map 1.00 95

Issued in sheets of 3 stamps and 3 labels showing Godollo Agricultural University, emblem. Size: 109x127mm.

Public Transportation Sesquicentennial — A711

1982, Oct. 5 **Litho.** *Perf. 12x11½*

2758 A711 2fo multi 25 15

Vuk and a Bird — A712

Scenes from Vuk the Fox Cub, Cartoon by Attila Dargay.

1982, Nov. 11 *Perf. 12½*

2759	A712 1fo shown		15	15
2760	A712 1fo Dogs		15	15
2761	A712 2fo Rooster		28	18
2762	A712 2fo Owl		28	18
2763	A712 4fo Geese		55	35
2764	A712 6fo Frog		80	60
2765	A712 8fo Master fox		1.10	80
	Nos. 2759-2765 (7)		3.31	2.41

Engineering Education Bicentenary — A713

1982, Oct. 13 *Perf. 12*

2766 A713 2fo Budapest Polytechnical Univ. 25 15

Famous Hungarians Type

Gyorgy Boloni (1882-1959), writer and journalist.

1982, Oct. 29

2767 A674 2fo multi 25 15

October Revolution, 65th Anniv. — A715

Works of Art in Hungarian Chapel, Vatican — A716

1982, Nov. 5 **Litho.** *Perf. 11½x12*

2768 A715 5fo Lenin 75 42

1982, Nov. 30 *Perf. 12x11½*

Designs: No. 2769, St. Stephen, first King of Hungary (1001-1038). No. 2770, Pope Sylvester II making donation to St. Stephen. No. 2771, Pope Callixtus III ordering noon victory bell ringing by St. John of Capistrano, 1456. No. 2772, Pope Paul VI showing Cardinal Lekai location of Hungarian Chapel. No. 2773, Pope John Paul II consecrating chapel, 1980. No. 2774, Madonna and Child. Nos. 2769, 2774 sculptures by Imre Varga; others by Amerigo Tot. Nos. 2770-2773 in continuous design (37x18mm).

2769	A716 2fo multi	38	38
2770	A716 2fo multi	38	38
2771	A716 2fo multi	38	38
2772	A716 2fo multi	38	38
2773	A716 2fo multi	38	38
2774	A716 2fo multi	38	38
a.	Block of 5, #2769-2774	2.50	2.50
	Nos. 2769-2774 (6)	2.28	2.28

Souvenir Sheet

Zoltan Kodaly (1882-1967), Composer — A717

1982, Dec. 16 *Perf. 11½*

2775 A717 20fo multi 2.75 2.75

A718 A719

Perf. 12½x11½

1982, Dec. 16 **Litho.**

2776 A718 2fo multi 25 15

New Year 1983.

1982, Dec. 29 *Perf. 11½x12½*

Design: Johann Wolfgang Goethe (1749-1832), German poet, by Heinrich Kolbe.

Souvenir Sheet

2777 A719 20fo multi 3.00 2.75

10th Anniv. of Postal Code — A720

1983, Jan. 24 *Perf. 11½x12*

2778 A720 2fo multi 25 15

3rd Budapest Spring Festival, Mar. 18-27 A721

1983, Mar. 18 **Litho.** *Perf. 12x11½*

2779 A721 2fo Ship of Peace, by Engre Szasz 25 15

Gyula Juhasz (1883-1937), Poet — A722

1983, Apr. 15 *Perf. 12*

2780 A722 2fo multi 25 15

City of Szentgotthard, 800th Anniv. — A723

1983, May 4 **Litho.** *Perf. 11½*

2781 A723 2fo Monastery, seal, 1489 25 15

Malomto Lake, Tapolca — A724

1983, May 17 *Perf. 11½x12*

2782 A724 5fo multi 80 80

TEMBAL '83 Intl. Topical Stamp Exhibition, Basel, May 21-29. Issued in sheets of 3 stamps and 3 labels.

Souvenir Sheet

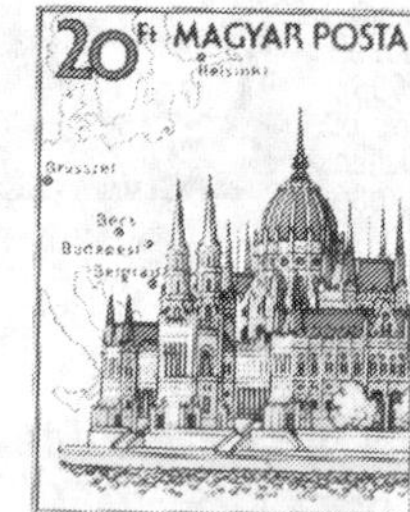

5th Interparliamentary Union Conference on European Cooperation, Budapest, May 30-June 5 — A725

1983, May 30 **Litho.** *Perf. 12½*

2783 A725 20fo Budapest Parliament 3.50 3.50

Jeno Hamburger (1883-1936) A726

1983, May 31 *Perf. 12*

2784 A726 2fo multi 25 15

Lady with Unicorn, by Raphael (1483-1517) A727

Paintings: No. 2786, John of Aragon. No. 2787, Granduca Madonna. No. 2788, Madonna and Child with St. John. 4fo, La Muta. 6fo, La Valeta. 8fo, La Fornarina. 20fo, Esterhazy Madonna.

Perf. 11½x12½

1983, June 29 **Litho.**

2785 A727	1fo multi		15	15
2786 A727	1fo multi		15	15
2787 A727	2fo multi		24	15
2788 A727	2fo multi		24	15
2789 A727	4fo multi		50	28
2790 A727	6fo multi		75	35
2791 A727	8fo multi		85	50
	Nos. 2785-2791 (7)		2.88	1.73

Souvenir Sheet

2792 A727 20fo multi 3.00 3.00

No. 2792 contains one stamp (24x37mm).

Simon Bolivar (1783-1830) — A728

1983, July 22 **Litho.** ***Perf. 12***

2793 A728 2fo multi 25 15

Istvan Vagi (1883-1940), Anti-fascist Martyr — A729

1983, July 22 ***Perf. 11½x12½***

2794 A729 2fo multi 25 15

68th World Esperanto Congress, Budapest, July 30-Aug. 6 — A730

1983, July 29 ***Perf. 12***

2795 A730 2fo multi 25 15

Souvenir Sheet

Martin Luther (1483-1546) — A731

1983, Aug. 12 ***Perf. 12½***

2796 A731 20fo multi 2.75 2.50

A732

A733

Designs: Protected birds of prey and World Wildlife Fund emblem

1983, Aug. 18 ***Perf. 11½x12***

2797 A732	1fo Aquila heliaca	16	15
2798 A732	1fo Aquila pomarina	16	15
2799 A732	2fo Haliaetus albicilla	25	16
2800 A732	2fo Falco vespertinus	25	16
2801 A732	4fo Falco cherrug	50	32
2802 A732	6fo Buteo lagopus	75	40
2803 A732	8fo Buteo buteo	90	85
	Nos. 2797-2803 (7)	2.97	2.19

1983, Aug. 25 ***Perf. 12***

2804 A733 1fo Bee collecting pollen 15 15

29th Intl. Apicultural Congress, Budapest, Aug. 25-31.

Fruit, by Bela Czobel (1883-1976) — A734

1983, Sept. 15 **Litho.** ***Perf. 12x11½***

2805 A734 2fo multi 25 15

A735

A736

World Communications Year: No. 2806, Telecommunications Earth Satellite. No. 2807, Intersputnik Earth Station. 2fo, TMM-81 Telephone Service. 3fo, Intelligent Terminal System. 5fo, OCR Optical Reading Instrument. 8fo, Teletext. 20fo, Molina Communications Satellite.

1983, Oct. 7 **Litho.** ***Perf. 11½x12***

2806 A735	1fo multi	18	15
2807 A735	1fo multi	18	15
2808 A735	2fo multi	28	18
2809 A735	3fo multi	42	25
2810 A735	5fo multi	70	42
2811 A735	8fo multi	1.10	65
	Nos. 2806-2811 (6)	2.86	1.80

Souvenir Sheet

Perf. 12x12½

2812 A735 20fo multi 3.00 3.00

1983, Oct. 10 **Photo.** ***Perf. 12***

2813 A736 2fo multi 25 15

34th Intl. Astronautical Federation Congress.

SOZPHILEX 83, Moscow — A737

1983, Oct. 14 **Litho.** ***Perf. 12***

2814 A737 2fo Kremlin 50 50

Issued in sheets of 3 stamps and 3 labels showing emblem. Size: 101x133mm.

Mihaly Babits (1883-1941), Poet and Translator — A738

1983, Nov. 25

2815 A738 2fo multi 25 15

Souvenir Sheet

European Security and Cooperation Conference, Madrid — A739

Perf. 12½x11½

1983, Nov. 10 **Litho.**

2816 A739 20fo multi 3.75 3.75

1984 Winter Olympics, Sarajevo — A740

Designs: Ice dancers representing the seven phases of a figure cut.

1983, Dec. 22 **Litho.** ***Perf. 12x12½***

2817 A740	1fo Emblem upper right	15	15
2818 A740	1fo Emblem upper left	15	15
2819 A740	2fo Arms extended	28	15
2820 A740	2fo Arms bent	28	15
2821 A740	4fo Man looking down	55	30
2822 A740	4fo Girl looking up	55	30
2823 A740	6fo multi	85	45
a.	Strip of 7, #2817-2823	3.00	2.00
	Nos. 2817-2823 (7)	2.81	1.65
	Set value		

Souvenir Sheet

Perf. 12½

2824 A740 20fo multi 3.00 3.00

No. 2824 contains one 49x39mm stamp.

Christmas — A741

Resorts and Spas — A742

Designs: 1fo, Madonna with Rose, Kassa, 1500. 2fo, Altar piece, Csikmenasag, 1543.

1983, Dec. 13 **Litho.** ***Perf. 11½x12***

2825 A741	1fo multi	15	15
2826 A741	2fo multi	30	15
	Set value		22

1983, Dec. 18

2827 A742	1fo Zanka, Lake Balaton	16	15
2828 A742	2fo Hajduszoboszlo	32	15
2829 A742	5fo Heviz	80	40
	Set value		50

Virgin with Six Saints, by Giovanni Battista Tiepolo — A743

Rest During Flight into Egypt, by Giovanni Domenico Tiepolo — A744

Paintings Stolen and Later Recovered, Museum of Fine Arts, Budapest: b, Esterhazy Madonna, by Raphael. c, Portrait of Giorgione, 16th cent. d, Portrait of a Woman, by Tintoretto. e, Pietro Bempo, by Raphael. f, Portrait of a Man, by Tintoretto.

1984, Feb. 16 ***Perf. 12½x12***

2839	Sheet of 7	3.75	3.75
a.-f.	A743 2fo multi	35	
g.	A744 8fo multi	1.50	

Energy Conservation — A745

1984, Mar. 30 **Litho.** ***Perf. 11½x12***

2840 A745 1fo multi 25 15

Sandor Korosi Csoma (1784-1842), Master of Tibetan Philology — A746

1984, Mar. 30 ***Perf. 11½x12½***

2841 A746 2fo multi 25 18

Stamps with silver inscription and with back inscription "Gift of the Hungarian Post" issued to members of Natl. Fed. of Hungarian Philatelists.

Miniature Sheet

No. 1900 — A747

Designs: b, No. 1346. c, No. 1259.

1984, Apr. 20 **Litho.** ***Perf. 12x11½***

2842	Sheet of 3	2.75	2.75
a.-c.	A747 4fo multi	70	

Espana '84; Ausipex '84; Philatelia '84.

The Scott Catalogue value is a retail price; that is, what you could expect to pay for the stamp in a grade of Fine-Very Fine. The value listed reflects recent actual dealer selling prices.

Post-Roman Archaeological Discoveries — A748

Designs: No. 2843, Round gold disc hair ornaments, Rakamaz. No. 2844, Saber belt plates, Szolnok-Strazsahalom and Galgocz. No. 2845, Silver disc hair ornaments, Sarospatak. No. 2846, Swords. 4fo, Silver and gold bowl, Ketpo. 6fo, Bone walking stick handles, Hajdudorog and Szabadbattyan. 8fo, Ivory saddle bow, Izsak; bit, stirrups, Muszka.

1984, May 15 *Perf. 12*

2843 A748 1fo dk brn & tan 15 15
2844 A748 1fo dk brn & tan 15 15
2845 A748 2fo dk brn & tan 28 15
2846 A748 2fo dk brn & tan 28 15
2847 A748 4fo dk brn & tan 55 22
2848 A748 6fo dk brn & tan 80 32
2849 A748 8fo dk brn & tan 1.10 42
Nos. 2843-2849 (7) 3.31
Set value 1.15

View of Cracow A749

Butterflies A750

Perf. 12½x11½

1984, May 21 **Litho.**

2850 A749 2fo multi 25 15

Permanent Committee of Posts and Telecommunications, 25th Session, Cracow.

1984, June 7 *Perf. 11½x12*

2851 A750 1fo Epiphille dilecta 15 15
2852 A750 1fo Agra sara 15 15
2853 A750 2fo Morpho cypris 26 15
2854 A750 2fo Ancylusis formossissima 26 15
2855 A750 4fo Danaus chrysippus 52 22
2856 A750 6fo Catagramma cynosura 85 35
2857 A750 8fo Ornithoptera paradisea 1.10 48
Nos. 2851-2857 (7) 3.29
Set value 1.30

A751

A752

Design: Archer, by Kisfaludy Strobl (1884-1975).

Perf. 12½x11½

1984, July 26 **Litho.**

2858 A751 2fo multicolored 25 15

1984, July 26

2859 A752 2fo multicolored 25 15

Akos Hevesi (1884-1937), revolutionary. See Nos. 2884-2885, 2910, 2915, 2962.

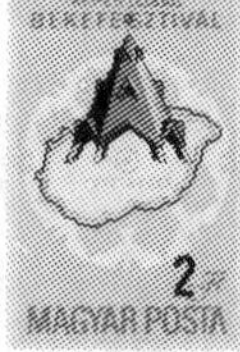
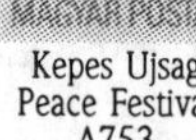

Kepes Ujsag Peace Festival A753

Aerobatic Championship A754

1984, Aug. 3 **Litho.** *Perf. 12½x11½*

2860 A753 2fo Map, building 25 15

1984, Aug. 14

2861 A754 2fo Plane, map 25 15

Horse Team World Championship, Szilvasvarad, Aug. 17-20 — A755

1984, Aug. 17 *Perf. 12*

2862 A755 2fo Horse-drawn wagon 25 15

Budapest Riverside Hotels — A756

1984, Sept.

2863 A756 1fo Atrium Hyatt 18 15
2864 A756 2fo Duna Intercontinental 26 15
2865 A756 4fo Forum 52 26
2866 A756 4fo Thermal Hotel, Margaret Isld. 52 26
2867 A756 5fo Hilton 70 35
2868 A756 8fo Gellert 1.00 52
Nos. 2863-2868 (6) 3.18 1.69

Souvenir Sheet

2869 A756 20fo Hilton, diff. 3.00 3.00

14th Conference of Postal Ministers, Budapest — A757

1984, Sept. 10 *Perf. 12½x11½*

2870 A757 2fo Building, post horn 25 15

57th Stamp Day — A758

1984, Sept. 21 *Perf. 12*

2871 A758 1fo Four-handled vase, Zsolnay 15 15
2872 A758 2fo Platter, vert. 26 15
Set value 20

Souvenir Sheet

2872A A758 10fo #19 on cover 1.75 1.75

No. 2872A contains one stamp (44x27mm, perf. 11).

Edible Mushrooms A759

Photogravure and Engraved

1984, Oct. *Perf. 12x11½*

2873 A759 1fo Boletus edulis 20 15
2874 A759 1fo Marasmius oreades 20 15
2875 A759 2fo Morchella esculenta 30 15
2876 A759 2fo Agaricus campester 30 15
2877 A759 3fo Macrolepiota procera 45 24
2878 A759 3fo Cantharellus cibarius 45 24
2879 A759 4fo Armillariella mellea 65 30
Nos. 2873-2879 (7) 2.55 1.38

Budapest Opera House Centenary A760

1984, Sept. 27 *Perf. 12x11½*

2880 A760 1fo Fresco by Mor Than 15 15
2881 A760 2fo Hallway 26 15
2882 A760 5fo Auditorium 65 30
Set value 48

Souvenir Sheet

2883 A760 20fo Building 2.75 2.75

No. 2883 contains one stamp (49x40mm, perf. 12½).

Famous Hungarians Type of 1984

Designs: No. 2884, Bela Balazs, writer (1884-1949); No. 2885, Kato Haman, labor leader (1884-1936).

1984, Dec. 3 **Litho.** *Perf. 12½x11½*

2884 A752 2fo multi 25 15
2885 A752 2fo multi 25 15
Set value 20

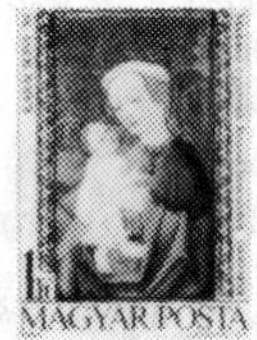

Madonna and Child, Trensceny — A763

Owls — A764

1984, Dec. 17 **Litho.** *Perf. 11½x12*

2886 A763 1fo multi 15 15

Photogravure and Engraved

1984, Dec. 28 *Perf. 12½x11½*

2887 A764 1fo Athene Noctua 16 15
2888 A764 1fo Tyto alba 16 15
2889 A764 2fo Strix aluco 25 15
2890 A764 2fo Asio otus 25 15
2891 A764 4fo Nyctea scadiaca 50 28
2892 A764 6fo Strix uralensis 75 40
2893 A764 8fo Bubo bubo 90 55
Nos. 2887-2893 (7) 2.97
Set value 1.55

Torah Crown, Buda — A765

19th Cent. Art from Jewish Museum, Budapest.

1984, Dec. **Litho.** *Perf. 12*

2894 A765 1fo shown 15 15
2895 A765 1fo Chalice, Moscow 15 15
2896 A765 2fo Torah shield, Vienna 30 15
2897 A765 2fo Chalice, Warsaw 30 15
2898 A765 4fo Container, Augsburg 60 24
2899 A765 6fo Candlestick holder, Warsaw 90 38
2900 A765 8fo Funeral urn, Pest 1.25 48
Nos. 2894-2900 (7) 3.65
Set value 1.40

Souvenir Sheet

Olympics — A766

1985, Jan. 2 **Photo.** *Perf. 12x12½*

2901 A766 20fo Long jump 3.00 3.00

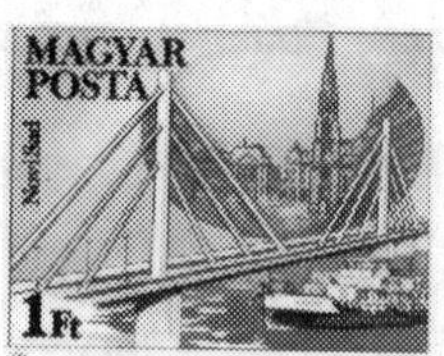

Novi Sad, Yugoslavia A767

Danube Bridges: No. 2903, Baja. No. 2904, Arpad Bridge, Budapest. No. 2905, Bratislava, Czechoslovakia. 4fo, Reichsbrucke, Vienna. 6fo, Linz, Austria. 8fo, Regensburg, Federal Rep. of Germany. 20fo, Elizabeth Bridge, Budapest, and map.

1985, Feb. 12 **Litho.** *Perf. 12x11½*

2902 A767 1fo multi 15 15
2903 A767 1fo multi 15 15
2904 A767 2fo multi 24 15
2905 A767 2fo multi 24 15
2906 A767 4fo multi 52 24
2907 A767 6fo multi 75 38
2908 A767 8fo multi 1.00 48
Nos. 2902-2908 (7) 3.05
Set value 1.40

Souvenir Sheet

Perf. 12½

2909 A767 20fo multi 3.00 3.00

Famous Hungarians Type of 1984

Design: Laszlo Rudas (1885-1950), communist philosopher.

1985, Feb. 21 *Perf. 12½x11½*

2910 A752 2fo gold & brn 25 15

Intl. Women's Day, 75th Anniv. — A769

Perf. 11½x12½

1985, Mar. 5 **Photo.**

2011 A769 2fo gold & multi 25 15

OLYMPHILEX '85, Lausanne — A770

1985, Mar. 14 Litho. *Perf. 11½x12*

2912 A770 4fo No. B81 50 25
2913 A770 5fo No. B82 65 32

Souvenir Sheet

Liberation of Hungary From German Occupation Forces, 40th Anniv. A771

Design: Liberty Bridge, Budapest and silhouette of the Liberation Monument on Gellert Hill illuminated by fireworks.

1985, Mar. 28 *Perf. 12½*

2914 A771 20fo multi 3.25 3.25

Famous Hungarians Type of 1984

Design: Gyorgy Lukacs (1885-1971) communist philosopher, educator.

1985, Apr. 12 *Perf. 12½x11½*

2915 A752 2fo gold & brn 25 15

Totfalusi Bible, 300th Anniv. — A773

1985, Apr. 25 *Perf. 12*

2916 A773 2fo gold & black 25 15

1st Bible printed in Hungarian by Nicolas Totfalusi Kis (1650-1702), publisher, in 1685.

Lorand Eotvos Univ., 350th Anniv. — A774

26th European Boxing Championships, Budapest — A775

Design: Archbishop Peter Pazmany (1570-1637), founder.

1985, May 14

2917 A774 2fo magenta & gray 25 15

No. 2917 printed se-tenant with label picturing obverse and reverse of university commemorative medal.

1985, May 25

2918 A775 2fo multi 25 15

Intl. Youth Year — A776

1985, May 29 *Perf. 11½x12*

2919 A776 1fo Girl's soccer 15 15
2920 A776 2fo Windsurfing 24 15
2921 A776 2fo Aerobic exercise 24 15
2922 A776 4fo Karate 52 24
2923 A776 4fo Go-kart racing 52 24
2924 A776 5fo Hang gliding 70 30
2925 A776 6fo Skateboarding 75 38
Nos. 2919-2925 (7) 3.12
Set value 1.40

Electro-magnetic High-speed Railway — A777

EXPO '85, Tsukuba, Japan: futuristic technology.

1985, May 29 *Perf. 12x11½*

2926 A777 2fo shown 25 15
2927 A777 4fo Fuyo (robot) Theater 50 20
Set value 28

Audubon Birth Bicentenary A778

Audubon illustrations

1985, June 19 *Perf. 12*

2928 A778 2fo Colaptes cafer 28 15
2929 A778 2fo Bombycilla garrulus 28 15
2930 A778 2fo Dryocopus pileatus 28 15
2931 A778 4fo Icterus galbula 58 28
Set value 58

See Nos. C446-C447.

Mezohegyes Stud Farm, Bicent. — A779

Horses: No. 2932, Nonius-36, 1883, a dark chestnut. No. 2933, Furioso-23, 1889, a light chestnut. No. 2934, Gidrian-1, 1935, a blond breed. No. 2935, Ramses-3, 1960, gray sporting horse. No. 2936, Krozus-1, 1970, chestnut sporting horse.

1985, June 28

2932 A779 1fo multi 15 15
2933 A779 2fo multi 28 15
2934 A779 4fo multi 55 22
2935 A779 4fo multi 55 22
2936 A779 6fo multi 85 35
Nos. 2932-2936 (5) 2.38
Set value 94

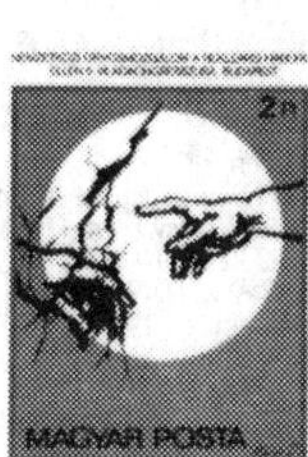

Prevention of Nuclear War — A780

European Music Year — A781

Design: Illustration of a damaged globe and hands, by Imre Varga (b. 1923), 1973 Kossuth prize-winner.

1985, June 28 *Perf. 11½x12*

2937 A780 2fo multi 25 15

Intl. Physician's Movement for the Prevention of Nuclear War, 5th Congress.

1985, July 10 *Perf. 11*

Composers and instruments: 1fo, George Frideric Handel (1685-1759), kettle drum, horn. 2fo, Johann Sebastian Bach (1685-1750), Thomas Church organ. No. 2940, Luigi Cherubini (1760-1842), harp, bass viol, baryton. No. 2941, Frederic Chopin (1810-1849), piano, 1817. 5fo, Gustav Mahler (1860-1911), pardessus de viole, kettle drum, double horn. 6fo, Erkel Ferenc (1810-1893), bass tuba, violin.

2938 A781 1fo multi 15 15
2939 A781 2fo multi 28 15
2940 A781 4fo multi 55 22
2941 A781 4fo multi 55 22
2942 A781 5fo multi 70 28
2943 A781 6fo multi 85 35
Nos. 2938-2943 (6) 3.08 1.37

Souvenir Sheet

12th World Youth Festival, Moscow A782

1985, July 22 *Perf. 12½*

2944 A782 20fo Emblem, Red Square 2.75 2.75

Souvenir Sheet

Helsinki Agreement, 10th Anniv. — A783

1985, Aug. 1 *Perf. 11*

2945 A783 20fo Finlandia Hall, Helsinki 3.25 3.25

World Tourism Day — A784

COMNET '85 — A785

Perf. 12½x11½

1985, Sept. 27 Litho.

2946 A784 2fo Key, globe, heart 25 15

1985, Oct. 1 *Perf. 11½*

2947 A785 4fo Computer terminal 60 30

3rd Computer Sciences Conference, Budapest, Oct. 1-4.

Souvenir Sheet

Danube River, Budapest Bridges — A786

1985, Oct. 15 *Perf. 12*

2948 A786 20fo multi 3.50 3.50

European Security and Cooperation Conference and Cultural Forum, Budapest, Oct. 15-Nov. 25. Exists inscribed "Kuturalis Forum Resztvevoi Tiszteletere" in gold on front and "Gift of the Hungarian Post" on back. Not valid for postage.

EUROPHILEX '85, Oct. 14-31 — A787

16-17th century ceramics: 1fo, Faience water jar and dispenser, 1609. 2fo, Tankard, 1670. 10fo, Hexagonal medicine jar, 1774.

1985, Oct. 18 *Perf. 12½x11½*

2949 A787 1fo multi 15 15
2950 A787 2fo multi 35 15
Set value 16

Souvenir Sheet

2951 A787 10fo multi 1.75 1.75

Italy No. 799, View of Rome — A788

1985, Oct. 21 *Perf. 12x11½*

2952 A788 5fo multi 90 90

Italia '85, Rome, Oct. 25-Nov. 3. Issued in sheets of 3 stamps and 3 labels showing emblem.

UN, 40th Anniv. — A789

1985, Oct. 24 *Perf. 11½x12*

2953 A789 4fo Dove, globe, emblem 50 30

Indigenous Lilies — A790

Photogravure and Engraved

1985, Oct. 28 *Perf. 12x11½*

2954 A790 1fo Lilium bulbiferum 15 15
2955 A790 2fo Lilium martagon 28 15
2956 A790 2fo Erythronium dens-canis 28 15
2957 A790 4fo Fritillaria meleagris 55 22
2958 A790 4fo Lilium tigrinum 55 22
2959 A790 5fo Hemerocallis lilioasphodelus 70 28
2960 A790 6fo Bulbocodium vernum 85 35
Nos. 2954-2960 (7) 3.36
Set value 1.30

Christmas 1985 A791

1985, Nov. 6 Litho. *Perf. 13½x13*

2961 A791 2fo Youths caroling 25 15

Famous Hungarians Type of 1984

Design: Istvan Ries (1885-1950), Minister of Justice (1949), labor movement.

1985, Nov. 11 *Perf. 12½x11½*

2962 A752 2fo gold & ol brn 25 15

Motorcycle Centenary — A793

Photogravure & Engraved

1985, Dec. 28 *Perf. 11½x12*

2963 A793 1fo Fantic Sprinter, 1984 16 15
2964 A793 2fo Suzuki Katana GSX, 1983 25 15
2965 A793 2fo Harley-Davidson Duo-Glide, 1960 25 15
2966 A793 4fo Rudge-Whitworth, 1935 48 20
2967 A793 4fo BMW R47, 1927 48 20
2968 A793 5fo NSU, 1910 65 24
2969 A793 6fo Daimler, 1885 75 28
Nos. 2963-2969 (7) 3.02
Set value 1.15

Bela Kun (1886-1939), Communist Party Founder — A794

Perf. 12½x11½

1986, Feb. 20 Litho.

2970 A794 4fo multi 50 30

Souvenir Sheet

US Shuttle Challenger — A795

1986, Feb. 21 *Perf. 11½*

2971 A795 20fo multi 3.50 3.50

Memorial to the US astronauts who died when the Challenger exploded during takeoff, Jan. 28.

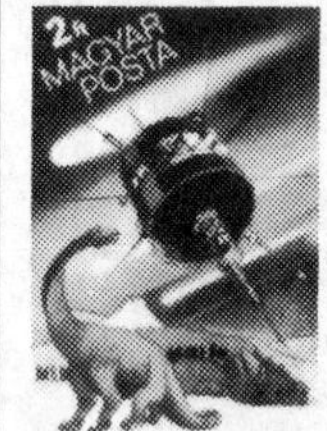

Halley's Comet — A796

Designs: No. 2972, US Ice satellite, dinosaurs. No. 2973, USSR Vega and Bayeaux tapestry detail, 1066, France. No. 2974, Japanese Suisei and German engraving, 1507. No. 2975, European Space Agency Giotto and The Three Magi, tapestry by Giotto. No. 2976, USSR Astron and Apianis constellation, 1531. No. 2977, US space shuttle and Edmond Halley.

Perf. 11½x13½

1986, Feb. 14 Litho.

2972 A796 2fo multi 30 15
2973 A796 2fo multi 30 15
2974 A796 2fo multi 30 15
2975 A796 4fo multi 60 24
2976 A796 4fo multi 60 24
2977 A796 6fo multi 90 38
Nos. 2972-2977 (6) 3.00 1.31

Seeing-eye Dog, Red Cross — A797

Soccer Players in Blue and Red Uniforms — A798

Perf. 12½x11½

1986, Mar. 20 Litho.

2978 A797 4fo multi 60 15

Assistance for the blind.

1986, Apr. 2 *Perf. 11*

Color of Uniforms

2979 A798 2fo shown 35 15
2980 A798 2fo blue & green 35 15
2981 A798 4fo red & black 75 24
2982 A798 4fo yellow & red 75 24
2983 A798 4fo yellow & green 75 24
2984 A798 6fo orange & white 1.00 38
Nos. 2979-2984 (6) 3.95 1.40

Souvenir Sheet

Perf. 12½

2985 A798 20fo Victors 4.00 4.00

1986 World Cup Soccer Championships, Mexico. No. 2979 contains one stamp (size: 41x32mm). Also exists with added inscription "In honor of the winner . . ." and red control number.

Buda Castle Cable Railway Station Reopening — A799

1986, Apr. 30 *Perf. 11½x12*

2986 A799 2fo org, brn & pale yel 40 15

Souvenir Sheet

AMERIPEX '86, Chicago, May 22-June 1 — A800

Designs: a, Yankee doodle rose. b, America rose. c, George Washington, statue by Gyula Bezeredy (1858-1935), Budapest.

1986, Apr. 30 *Perf. 12½x11½*

2987 Sheet of 3 4.00 4.00
a.-b. A800 5fo any single 1.00 1.00
c. A800 10fo multi 2.00 2.00

Size of No. 2987c: 27x74mm.

Hungary Days in Tokyo — A801

1986, May 6 *Perf. 11½x12*

2988 A801 4fo Folk dolls 50 30

Andras Fay (1786-1864), Author, Politician — A802

Lithographed and Engraved

1986, May 29 *Perf. 12*

2989 A802 4fo beige & fawn 50 30

Printed se-tenant with label picturing First Hungarian Savings Bank Union, founded by Fay.

Automobile, Cent. — A803

Designs: No. 2990, 1961 Ferrari Tipo 156, 1985 race car. No. 2991, 1932 Alfa Romeo Tipo B, 1984 race car. No. 2992, 1936 Volkswagen, 1986 Porsche 959. No. 2993, 1902 Renault 14CV, 1985 Renault 5 GT Turbo. No. 2994, 1899 Fiat 3½, 1985 Fiat Ritmo. 6fo, 1886 Daimler, 1986 Mercedes-Benz 230SE.

1986, July 24 Litho. *Perf. 12*

2990 A803 2fo multi 30 15
2991 A803 2fo multi 30 15
2992 A803 2fo multi 30 15
2993 A803 4fo multi 60 24
2994 A803 4fo multi 60 24
2995 A803 6fo multi 90 38
Nos. 2990-2995 (6) 3.00
Set value 1.00

Wasa, 1628, Warship — A804

1986, Aug. 15 Litho. *Perf. 11½x12*

2996 A804 2fo multi 50 50

STOCKHOLMIA '86, Aug. 28-Sept. 7. printed se-tenant with label (size: 27x34mm) picturing exhibition emblem. Printed in sheets of 3.

14th Intl. Cancer Congress, Budapest — A805

Design: Moritz Kaposi (1837-1902), Austrian cancer researcher.

1986, Aug. 21 *Perf. 12½x11½*

2997 A805 4fo multicolored 50 30

Recapture of Buda Castle, by Gyula Benzcur (1844-1920) — A806

1986, Sept. 2 *Perf. 12*

2998 A806 4fo multicolored 50 30

Recapture of Buda from the Turks, 300th anniv.

Tranquility A807

Hope — A808

Stamp Day: Paintings by Endre Szasz.

1986, Sept. 5

2999 A807 2fo shown 30 15
3000 A807 2fo Confidence 30 15
Set value 20

Souvenir Sheet

Perf. 11½

3001 A808 10fo shown 1.75 1.75

5th Intl. Conference on Oriental Carpets, Vienna and Budapest — A809

1986, Sept. 17 Litho. *Perf. 11*

3002 A809 4fo Anatolia crivelli, 15th cent. 60 30

Franz Liszt, Composer A810

1986, Oct. 21 Engr. *Perf. 12*

3003 A810 4fo grayish green 50 30

Intl. Peace Year — A811

1986, Oct. 24 Litho.

3004 A811 4fo multicolored 50 30

No. 3004 printed se-tenant with label.

Souvenir Sheet

Hofburg Palace, Vienna, and Map — A812

1986, Nov. 4 *Perf. 11*

3005 A812 20fo multicolored 2.75 2.75

European Security and Cooperation Conference, Vienna.

Fruits — A813

Photogravure & Engraved

1986, Nov. 25 *Perf. 12x11½*

3006 A813 2fo Sour cherries	28	15
3007 A813 2fo Apricots	28	15
3008 A813 4fo Peaches	55	28
3009 A813 4fo Raspberries	55	28
3010 A813 4fo Apples	55	28
3011 A813 6fo Grapes	85	40
Nos. 3006-3011 (6)	3.06	1.54

Natl. Heroes — A814

Designs: No. 3012, Jozseph Pogany (1886-1939), journalist, martyr. No. 3013, Ferenc Munnich (1886-1967), prime minister, 1958-61.

1986 Litho. *Perf. 12½x11½*

3012 A814 4fo multi 65 32
3013 A814 4fo multi 65 32

Issued: No. 3012, Nov. 6. No. 3013, Nov. 14.

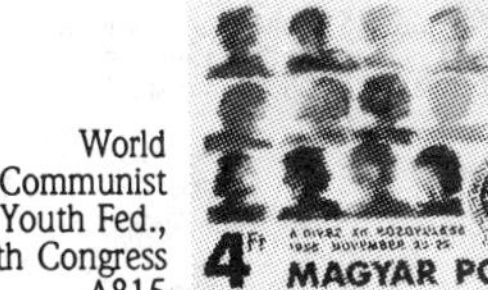

World Communist Youth Fed., 12th Congress A815

1986, Nov. 21 *Perf. 12*

3014 A815 4fo multi 50 30

Castles — A816

Festetics Castle, Keszthely A816a

Designs: 2fo, Forgach, Szecseny. 3fo, Savoya, Rackeve. 4fo, Batthyany, Kormend. 5fo, Szechenyi, Nagycenk. 6fo, Rudnyanszky, Nagyteteny. 7fo, Esterhazy, Papa. 8fo, Szapary, Buk. 10fo, Festetics, Keszthely. 12fo, Dory Castle, Mihalyi. 20fo, Brunswick, Martonvasar. 30fo, De la Motte, Nosvaj. 40fo, L'Huillier-Coborg, Edeleny. 50fo, Teleki-Degenfeld, Szirak. 70fo, Magochy, Pacin. 100fo, Eszterhazy, Fertod.

Perf. 12x11½, 11½x12½ (7fo)

1986-91 Litho.

3015	A816	2fo multi	18	15
3016	A816	3fo multi	24	15
3017	A816	4fo multi	32	20
3018	A816	5fo multi	40	22
3019	A816	6fo multi	48	28
3019A	A816	7fo multi	80	45
3020	A816	8fo multi	60	38
3021	A816	10fo multi	95	55
3021A	A816	12fo multi	1.25	75
3022	A816	20fo multi	2.00	1.10
3023	A816	30fo multi	3.00	1.65
3024	A816	40fo multi	3.75	2.25
3025	A816	50fo multi	5.00	2.75
3026	A816	70fo multi	6.25	4.00
3027	A816	100fo multi	9.50	5.75
		Nos. 3015-3027 (15)	34.72	20.63

Issue dates: 2fo-6fo, 8fo, Nov. 28. 10fo, 20fo, 30fo, 100fo, May 28, 1987. 40fo-60fo, July 30, 1987, 7fo, June 27, 1991. 12fo, Sept. 6, 1991.

For overprint see No. 3320.

1989-92 Litho. & Engr. *Perf. 12*

3028 A816a 10fo multi 1.65 85

Litho.

3029 A816a 15fo multi 1.25 65

Issue dates: 10fo, Feb. 28; 15fo, Mar. 27, 1992.

This is an expanding set. Numbers will change if necessary.

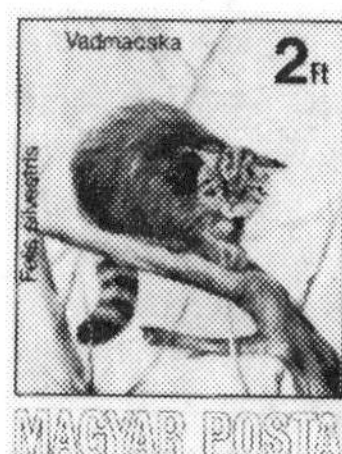

Wildlife Conservation A817

1986, Dec. 15 *Perf. 12*

3035 A817 2fo Felis silvestris	30	15
3036 A817 2fo Lutra lutra	30	15
3037 A817 2fo Mustela erminea	30	15
3038 A817 4fo Sciurus vulgaris	60	30
3039 A817 4fo Erinaceus concolor	60	30
3040 A817 6fo Emys orbicularis	90	45
Nos. 3035-3040 (6)	3.00	1.50

Portraits of Hungarian Kings in the Historical Portrait Gallery — A818

King and reign: No. 3041, St. Steven, 997-1038. No. 3042, Geza I, 1074-1077. No. 3043, St. Ladislas, 1077-1095. No. 3044, Bela III, 1172-1196. No. 3045, Bela IV, 1235-1270.

1986, Dec. 10 *Perf. 11½x12*

3041 A818 2fo multi	30	15
3042 A818 2fo multi	30	15
3043 A818 4fo multi	60	30
3044 A818 4fo multi	60	30
3045 A818 6fo multi	90	45
Nos. 3041-3045 (5)	2.70	1.35

See Nos. 3120-3122.

Fungi — A819

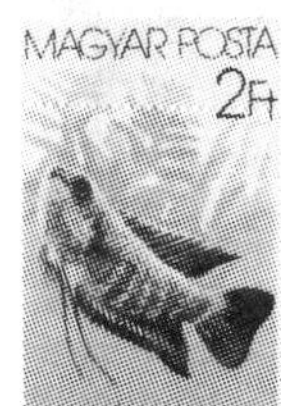

Saltwater Fish — A820

Lithographed and Engraved

1986, Dec. 30 *Perf. 11½*

3046 A819 2fo Amanita phalloides	30	15
3047 A819 2fo Inocybe patouillardi	30	15
3048 A819 2fo Amanita muscaria	30	15
3049 A819 4fo Omphalotus olearius	60	30
3050 A819 4fo Amanita pantherina	60	30
3051 A819 6fo Gyromitra esculenta	90	45
Nos. 3046-3051 (6)	3.00	1.50

1987, Jan. 15 Photo. *Perf. 11½*

3052 A820 2fo Colisa fasciata	30	15
3053 A820 2fo Pseudotropheus zebra	30	15
3054 A820 2fo Iriatherina werneri	30	15
3055 A820 4fo Aphyosemion multicolor	60	30
3056 A820 4fo Papiliochromis ramirezi	60	30
3057 A820 6fo Hyphessobrycon erythrostigma	90	45
Nos. 3052-3057 (6)	3.00	1.50

Seated Woman, 1918, by Bela Uitz (1887-1972), Painter A821

Abstract, 1960, by Lajos Kassak (1887-1967) A822

1987, Mar. 6 Litho. *Perf. 12*

3058 A821 4fo multicolored 50 30

1987, Mar. 20

3059 A822 4fo black & red 50 30

Medical Pioneers — A823

Neolithic and Copper Age Artifacts — A824

Designs: 2fo, Hippocrates (460-377 B.C.), Greek physician. No. 3061, Avicenna or Ibn Sina (A.D. 980-1037), Islamic pharmacist, diagnostician. No. 3062, Ambroise Pare (1510-1590), French surgeon. No. 3063, William Harvey (1578-1657), English physician, anatomist. 6fo, Ignaz Semmelweis (1818-1865), Hungarian obstetrician.

1987, Mar. 31

3060 A823 2fo black & dk red brn	30	15
3061 A823 4fo black & dk grn	60	30
3062 A823 4fo black & steel bl	60	30
3063 A823 4fo black & olive blk	60	30
3064 A823 6fo black & grn blk	90	45
Nos. 3060-3064 (5)	3.00	1.50

1987, Apr. 15 Litho. *Perf. 12*

Designs: 2fo, Urn, Hodmezovasarhely. No. 3066, Altar, Szeged. No. 3067, Deity, Szegvar-Tuzkoves. 5fo, Vase, Center.

3065 A824 2fo pale bl grn & sep	30	15
3066 A824 4fo buff & sepia	60	30
3067 A824 4fo pale org & sep	60	30
3068 A824 5fo pale yel grn & sep	90	45

Souvenir Sheet

Esztergom Cathedral Treasury Reopening — A825

1987, Apr. 28 *Perf. 11*

3069 A825 20fo Calvary of King Matthias 4.00 4.00

No. 3069 margin pictures the Horn Chalice of King Sigismund, Rhineland, 1408 (UL), Crozier of Archbishop Miklos Olah, Hungary, c. 1490 (UR), Monstrance of Imre Eszterhazy, by Gaspar Meichl, Vienna, 1728 (LL), and the Chalice of Matthias, Hungary, c. 1480.

Hungarian First Aid Assoc., Cent. — A826

1987, May 5 ***Perf. 11½x12***

3070 A826 4fo Ambulances, 1887-1987 50 30

Souvenir Sheet

CAPEX '87, Toronto A827

Stamp exhibitions: b, OLYMPHILEX '87, Rome. c, HAFNIA '87, Copenhagen.

1987, May 20 **Litho.** ***Perf. 11***

3071 Sheet of 3 + 3 labels 4.00 3.00
a.-c. A827 5fo any single 1.25 90

Jozsef Marek (1886-1952), Veterinarian — A828

1987, May 25 ***Perf. 12x11½***

3072 A828 4fo multicolored 50 30

Veterinary education, bicent.

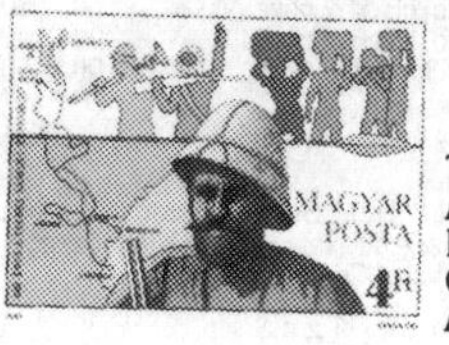
Teleki's African Expedition, Cent. A829

1987, June 10

3073 A829 4fo multicolored 50 30

Samuel Teleki (1845-1916), explorer.

Woodcut by Abraham von Werdt, 18th Cent. — A830

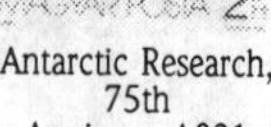
Antarctic Research, 75th Anniv. — A831

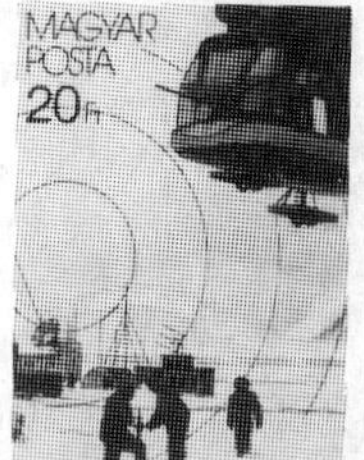
Helicopter Landing, Mirnij Research Station — A832

1987, June 25 Litho. & Engr. ***Perf. 12***

3074 A830 4fo beige & sepia 50 30

Hungarian Printing, Paper and Press Workers' Union, 125th anniv.

1987, June 30 **Litho.**

Map, explorer and scene: No. 3075, James Cook (1728-1779) and ship. No. 3076, Fabian von Bellingshausen (1778-1852) and seals. No. 3077, Ernest H. Shackleton (1874-1922) and penguins. No. 3078, Roald Amundsen (1872-1928) discovering South Pole, dog team. No. 3079, Robert F. Scott (1868-1912) and ship. No. 3080, Richard E. Byrd (1888-1957) and Floyd Bennett monoplane.

3075 A831 2fo multi 30 15
3076 A831 2fo multi 30 15
3077 A831 2fo multi 30 15
3078 A831 4fo multi 60 30
3079 A831 4fo multi 60 30
3080 A831 6fo multi 90 45
Nos. 3075-3080 (6) 3.00 1.50

Souvenir Sheet

Perf. 11½

3081 A832 20fo multi 3.00 3.00

Railway Officers Training Institute, Cent. — A833

Stamp Day, 60th Anniv. — A834

1987, Sept. 4 **Litho.** ***Perf. 11½x12***

3082 A833 4fo blue & black 75 50

Litho. & Engr.

1987, Sept. 18 ***Perf. 12***

Masonry of the medieval Buda Castle: 2fo, Flowers, dolphin. 4fo, Arms of King Matthias. 10fo, Capital inscribed "ONDIDIT/GENEROSVM."

3083 A834 2fo multi 40 25
3084 A834 4fo multi 80 50

Souvenir Sheet

Perf. 11

3085 A834 10fo multi 2.00 2.00

A835

Orchids — A836

A837

1987, Sept. 30 **Litho.** ***Perf. 12***

3086 A835 4fo multi 80 50
a. Se-tenant with label 80 50

No 3086 printed in sheet of 50 and in sheet of 25 plus 25 labels picturing 13th cent. church at Gyongyospata which houses the altar.

1987, Oct. 29 **Litho.** ***Perf. 11***

3087 A836 2fo Cypripedium calceolus 35 25
3088 A836 2fo Orchis purpurea 35 25
3089 A836 4fo Himantoglossum hircinum 70 50
3090 A836 4fo Ophrys scolopax cornuta 70 50
3091 A836 5fo Cephalanthera rubra 85 62
3092 A836 6fo Epipactis atrorubens 1.10 75
Nos. 3087-3092 (6) 4.05 2.87

Miniature Sheet

3093 A837 20fo shown 4.00 4.00

1988 Winter Olympics, Calgary — A838

1987, Nov. 24

3094 A838 2fo Speed skating 35 25
3095 A838 2fo Cross-country skiing 35 25
3096 A838 4fo Biathlon 70 50
3097 A838 4fo Ice hockey 70 50
3098 A838 4fo 4-Man bobsled 70 50
3099 A838 6fo Ski-jumping 1.10 75
Nos. 3094-3099 (6) 3.90 2.75

Souvenir Sheet

3100 A838 20fo Slalom 4.00 4.00

Souvenir Sheet

US-Soviet Summit, Dec. 7-10 — A839

1987, Dec. 7 ***Perf. 12***

3101 A839 20fo Shaking hands 4.00 4.00

Meeting of Gen. Secretary Gorbachev and Pres. Reagan to discuss and sign nuclear arms reduction treaty.

Fairy Tales — A840

Designs: No. 3102, The White Crane, from Japan. No. 3103, The Fox and the Crow, Aesop's Fables. No. 3104, The Tortoise and the Hare, Aesop's Fables. No. 3105, The Ugly Duckling, by Hans Christian Andersen. No. 3106, The Steadfast Tin Soldier, by Andersen.

1987, Dec. 11

3102 A840 2fo multi 40 25
3103 A840 2fo multi 40 25
3104 A840 4fo multi 85 50
3105 A840 4fo multi 85 50
3106 A840 6fo multi 1.25 75
Nos. 3102-3106 (5) 3.75 2.25

Count Ferdinand von Zeppelin (1838-1917), Designer of Dirigibles A841

1988, Jan. 29 **Litho.** ***Perf. 12***

3107 A841 2fo LZ-2, 1905 42 25
3108 A841 4fo LZ-4, 1908 85 50
3109 A841 4fo LZ-10, Schwaben, 1911 85 50
3110 A841 8fo LZ-127, Graf Zeppelin, 1928 1.65 1.00

1988 World Figure Skating Championships, Budapest — A842

Various athletes wearing period costumes.

1988, Feb. 29 **Photo.** ***Perf. 11½***

3111 A842 2fo Male, 20th cent. 35 25
3112 A842 2fo Male, (cap), 19th cent. 35 25
3113 A842 4fo Male (hat), 18th cent. 70 50
3114 A842 4fo Woman, c. 1930 70 50
3115 A842 5fo Woman (contemporary) 85 62
3116 A842 6fo Pair 1.00 75
Nos. 3111-3116 (6) 3.95 2.87

Souvenir Sheet

Perf. 12x11½

3117 A842 20fo Death spiral 4.00 4.00

No. 3117 contains one 37x52mm stamp.

Illes Monus (1888-1944), Party Leader — A843

1988, Mar. 11 **Litho.** ***Perf. 11½x12***

3118 A843 4fo multi 75 50

See Nos. 3152, 3160.

Miniature Sheet

Postmaster's Coat, Hat and Post Horn, 18th Cent. — A844

1988, Mar. 18 Litho. *Perf. 13*

3119 A844 4fo + 4 labels 1.25 1.25

Intl. stamp exhibitions, 1988. No. 3119 contains 4 labels picturing exhibition emblems: JUVALUX '88, Luxembourg, Mar. 29-Apr. 4 (UL), SYDPEX '88, Sydney, Australia, July 30-Aug.7 (UR), FINLANDIA '88, Helsinki, Finland, June 1-12 (LR), and PRAGA '88, Prague, Czechoslovakia, Aug. 26-Sept. 4 (LL).

King Type of 1986

Portraits of Hungarian kings in the Historical Portrait Gallery. King and reign: 2fo, Charles Robert (1308-1342). 4fo, Louis I (1342-1382). 6fo, Sigismund (1387-1437).

1988, Mar. 31 *Perf. 11½x12*

3120 A818 2fo pale grn, sep & red 32 25
3121 A818 4fo pale ultra, sep & red 65 50
3122 A818 6fo pale vio, sep & red 1.00 75

1988 Summer Olympics, Seoul A845

Computer Animation A846

1988, Apr. 20 Litho. *Perf. 13½x13*

3123 A845 2fo Rowing 35 25
3124 A845 4fo Hurdling 70 50
3125 A845 4fo Fencing 70 50
3126 A845 6fo Boxing 1.00 75

Souvenir Sheet

Perf. 12½

3127 A845 20fo Tennis 4.00 4.00

1988, May 12 *Perf. 12*

Design: Graphic from the computer-animated film *Dilemma*, 1972, by graphic artist Janos Kass (b. 1927) and cartoon film director John Halas (b. 1912).

3128 A846 4fo black, pur & ver 75 50

Eurocheck Congress, June 10, Budapest A847

1988, June 10 Litho. *Perf. 12*

3129 A847 4fo multicolored 75 50

Eurocheck as legal tender, 20th anniv.

Sovereign of the Seas — A848

Fight Drug Abuse — A849

1988, June 30

3130 A848 2fo shown 38 25
3131 A848 2fo *Santa Maria* 38 25
3132 A848 2fo *Mayflower* 38 25
3133 A848 4fo *Jylland* 75 50
3134 A848 6fo *St. Jupat* 1.10 75
Nos. 3130-3134 (5) 2.99 2.00

1988, July 7 Litho. *Perf. 12*

3135 A849 4fo multicolored 75 50

Ducks A850

1988, July 29 Litho. *Perf. 13x13½*

3136 A850 2fo Anas crecca 38 25
3137 A850 2fo Bucephala clangula 38 25
3138 A850 4fo Anas penelope 75 50
a. Pane of 10 #3136 + 10 #3138 with gutter btwn. 14.00
3139 A850 4fo Netta rufina 75 50
3140 A850 6fo Anas strepera 1.25 75
Nos. 3136-3140 (5) 3.51 2.25

Souvenir Sheet

Perf. 12½x11½

3141 A850 20fo Anas platyrhynchos 4.00 4.00

No. 3141 contains one 52x37mm stamp.
For surcharges see Nos. 3199-3200.

Antique Toys — A851

Calvinist College, Debrecen, 450th Anniv. — A852

1988, Aug. 12 *Perf. 12*

3142 A851 2fo Train 35 25
3143 A851 2fo See-saw 35 25
3144 A851 4fo +2fo Pecking chickens 1.10 75
3145 A851 5fo String-manipulated soldier 90 62

Surtax for youth philately programs.

1988, Aug. 16 Litho. *Perf. 13½x13*

3146 A852 4fo multi 75 50

58th American Society of Travel Agents World Congress, Oct. 23-29, Budapest A853

1988, Aug. 30 *Perf. 12*

3147 A853 4fo multi 75 50

P.O. Officials Training School, Cent. — A854

1988, Sept. 9 Litho. *Perf. 12*

3148 A854 4fo Badge on collar 75 50

Gabor Baross (1848-1892), Minister of Commerce and Communication — A855

Portrait and: 2fo, Postal Savings Bank, Budapest, emblem and postal savings stamp. 4fo, Telephone and telegraph apparatus, registration label and cancellations. 10fo, East Railway Station, Budapest.

1988, Sept. 16

3149 A855 2fo multi 32 25
3150 A855 4fo multi 65 50

Souvenir Sheet

Perf. 11½

3151 A855 10fo multi 2.00 2.00

No. 3151 contains one 50x29mm stamp.

Famous Hungarians Type of 1988

Design: Gyula Lengyel (1888-1941), political writer.

1988, Oct. 7 *Perf. 11½x12*

3152 A843 4fo multi 75 50

Christmas A857

Nobel Prize Winners A858

Perf. 12½x11½

1988, Nov. 10 Litho.

3153 A857 2fo multi 40 25

Litho. & Engr.

1988, Nov. 30 *Perf. 12*

Designs: No. 3154, Richard Adolf Zsigmondy (1865-1929), Germany, chemistry (1925). No. 3155, Robert Barany (1876-1936), Austria, medicine (1914). No. 3156, Georg von Hevesy (1885-1966), Hungary, chemistry (1943). No. 3157, Albert Szent-Gyorgyi (1893-1986), Hungary-US, medicine (1937). No. 3158, Georg von Bekesy (1899-1972), US, medicine (1961). 6fo, Denis Gabor (1900-1979), Great Britain, physics (1971).

3154 A858 2fo red brown 35 25
3155 A858 2fo green 35 25
3156 A858 2fo deep claret 35 25
3157 A858 4fo rose lake 70 50
3158 A858 4fo steel blue 70 50
3159 A858 6fo sepia 1.00 75
Nos. 3154-3159 (6) 3.45 2.50

Famous Hungarians Type of 1988

Design: Arpad Szakasits (1888-1965), party leader.

1988, Dec. 6 *Perf. 11½x12*

3160 A843 4fo multicolored 75 50

Souvenir Sheet

Medals Won by Hungarian Athletes at the 1988 Seoul Olympic Games — A860

1988, Dec. 19 Litho. *Perf. 12*

3161 A860 20fo multicolored 4.00 4.00

Silver and Cast Iron — A861

1988, Dec. 28 Litho. & Engr.

3162 A861 2fo Teapot, Pest, 1846 38 25
3163 A861 2fo Coffee pot, Buda, 18th cent. 38 25
3164 A861 4fo Sugar bowl, Pest, 1822 75 50
3165 A861 5fo Cast iron plate, Romania, 1850 95 62

Postal Savings Bank Inauguration — A862

1989, Jan. 20 Litho. *Perf. 12x11½*

3166 A862 5fo royal blue, blk & silver 1.00 62

Kalman Wallisch (1889-1934), Labor Leader — A863

1989, Feb. 28 Litho. *Perf. 12*

3167 A863 3fo dk red & brt bl 60 38

See No. 3170.

World Indoor Sports Championships, Budapest, Mar. 3-5 — A864

1989, Mar. 3 *Perf. 13x13½*

3168 A864 3fo multicolored 60 38

Souvenir Sheet

Interparliamentary Union Cent. and 81st Session, Budapest, Mar. 13-18 — A865

Designs: a, Parliament, Big Ben and Tower Bridge, London. b, Parliament and Chain Bridge, Budapest.

1989, Mar. 13 Litho. *Perf. 11*

3169 A865 Sheet of 2	4.00	4.00
a.-b. 10fo any single	2.00	2.00

Exists with red inscriptions and control number.

Famous Hungarians Type of 1989

Design: Janos Gyetvai (1889-1967), journalist, diplomat.

1989, Apr. 7 Litho. *Perf. 12*

3170 A863 3fo dark red & brt grn	60	38

Stud Farm at Babolna, 200th Anniv. — A867

Horses: a, O Bajan. b, Meneskari Csikos. c, Gazal II.

1989, May 18 Litho. *Perf. 12*

3171 Strip of 3	2.00	1.15
a.-c. A867 3fo any single	65	38

ART '89, May 23-27, Budapest A868

1989, May 23 *Perf. 12x11½*

3172 A868 5fo multi	1.00	62

Exhibition for disabled artists.

Flower Arrangements A869

1989, May 31 *Perf. 12*

3173 A869 2fo multi, vert.	38	25
3174 A869 3fo multi, vert.	55	38
3175 A869 3fo shown	55	38
3176 A869 5fo multi, diff.	95	62
3177 A869 10fo multi, vert.	1.90	1.25
Nos. 3173-3177 (5)	4.33	2.88

French Revolution, Bicent. A870

1989, June 1 *Perf. 12*

3178 A870 5fo brt blue, blk & red	1.00	62

Souvenir Sheet

Perf. 11½

3179 A870 20fo like 5fo	4.00	4.00

No. 3179 contains one 50x30mm stamp.

Medieval Church of the Csolts Near Veszto — A871

Photography, 150th Anniv. — A872

1989, June 15 Litho. *Perf. 12*

3180 A871 3fo multi	50	30

1989, June 15

3181 A872 5fo multi	80	50

Old Mills — A873

Designs: 2fo, Water mill, Turistvandi, 18th cent. 3fo, Horse-driven mill, Szarvas, 1836. 5fo, Windmill, Kiskunhalas, 18th cent. 10fo, Water wheel on the Drava River.

1989, June 20

3182 A873 2fo multi	30	20
3183 A873 3fo multi	45	30
3184 A873 5fo multi	75	50
3185 A873 10fo multi	1.50	1.00

Souvenir Sheet

1st Moon Landing, 20th Anniv. — A874

1989, July 12 Litho. *Perf. 12½*

3186 A874 20fo multi	4.50	4.50

Gliders A875

1989, July 20 *Perf. 12*

3187 A875 3fo Futar	45	30
3188 A875 5fo Cimbora	80	60

17th Intl. Old Timers Rally, Budakeszi Airport, and 60th anniv. of glider flying in Hungary.

Reptiles — A876

1989, July 26 *Perf. 11*

3189 A876 2fo *Lacerta agilis*	32	20
3190 A876 3fo *Lacerta viridis*	48	30
3191 A876 5fo *Vipera rakosiensis*	80	50
3192 A876 5fo *Natrix natrix*	80	50
3193 A876 10fo *Emys orbicularis*	1.65	1.00
Nos. 3189-3193 (5)	4.05	2.50

31st Modern Pentathlon World Championships, Aug. 30-Sept. 4, Budapest — A877

1989, July 31 *Perf. 13½x13*

3194 A877 5fo multi	80	50

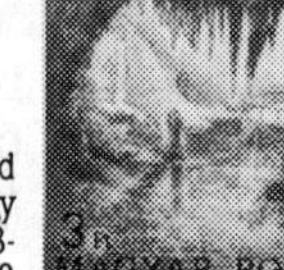

10th World Speleology Congress, Aug. 13-20, Sofia — A878

Caves.

1989, Aug. 14 Litho. *Perf. 11*

3195 A878 3fo Baradla	35	25
3196 A878 5fo Szemlohegy	60	42
3197 A878 10fo Anna	1.10	82
3198 A878 12fo Lake Cave of Tapolca	1.40	1.00

Nos. 3136 and 3138 Surcharged

1989, Aug. 14 *Perf. 13x13½*

3199 A850 3fo on 2fo #3136	45	25
3200 A850 5fo on 4fo #3138	80	42

A879

A880

1989, Aug. 24 *Perf. 12*

3201 A879 5fo multi	80	45

Third World Two-in-Hand Carriage-driving Championships, Balatonfenyves, Aug. 24-27.

1989, Sept. 8 Litho. *Perf. 12*

Nurses: 5fo, Zsuzsanna Kossuth (1820-1854) and emblem. 10fo, Florence Nightingale (1820-1910) and medal awarded in her name by the Red Cross.

3202 A880 5fo multi	70	45
3203 A880 10fo multi	1.25	82

Stamp Day. See No. B341.

Pro-Philatelia 1989 — A881

1989, Oct. 10 Litho. *Imperf.*

3204 A881 50fo #2665, C426, 2742, 3005, B233	7.00	7.00

Dismantling of the Electronic Surveillance System (Iron Curtain) on the Hungary-Austria Border — A882

1989, Oct. 30 *Perf. 11*

3205 A882 5fo multi	75	45

Conquest of Hungary, by Mor Than — A883

1989, Oct. 31

3206 A883 5fo multi	75	45

Arpad, chief who founded the 1st Magyar dynasty of Hungary in 889.

A884 A885

1989, Nov. 10 Litho. *Perf. 11½x12*

3207 A884 3fo Flight to Egypt	45	25

Christmas.

Litho. & Engr.

1989, Nov. 14 *Perf. 12*

3208 A885 3fo buff & rose brn	45	25

Jawaharlal Nehru, 1st prime minister of independent India.

A886 A887

Modern Art (Paintings): 3fo, *Mike,* by Dezso Korniss. 5fo, *Sunrise,* by Lajos Kassak. 10fo, *Grotesque Burial,* by Endre Balint. 12fo, *Memory of Toys,* by Tihamer Gyarmathy.

1989, Dec. 18 Litho. *Perf. 12*

3209	A886	3fo	multicolored	45	30
3210	A886	5fo	multicolored	75	55
3211	A886	10fo	multicolored	1.50	1.05
3212	A886	12fo	multicolored	1.75	1.25

1989, Dec. 29 Engr. *Perf. 12*

Medical Pioneers: #3213, Galen (129-c.199), Greek physician. #3214, Paracelsus (1493-1541), German alchemist. 4fo, Andreas Vesalius (1514-64), Belgian anatomist. 6fo, Rudolf Virchow (1821-1902), German pathologist. 10fo, Ivan Petrovich Pavlov (1849-1936), Russian physiologist.

3213	A887	3fo	olive gray	50	32
3214	A887	3fo	brown	50	32
3215	A887	4fo	black	90	58
3216	A887	6fo	intense black	1.00	65
3217	A887	10fo	brown violet	1.65	1.10
			Nos. 3213-3217 (5)	4.55	2.97

Hungarian Savings Bank, 150th Anniv. — A888

1990, Jan. 11 Litho.

3218	A888	5fo	multicolored	75	45

Singer Sewing Machine, 125th Anniv. A889

Telephone, Budapest Exchange A890

1990, Jan. 15 *Perf. 12*

3219	A889	5fo	brown & sepia	75	45

1990, Jan. 29

Designs: 5fo, Mailbox and main p.o., Budapest, c. 1900.

3220	A890	3fo	shown	38	20
3221	A890	5fo	multicolored	62	30

Coil Stamps

Size: 17x22mm

Perf. 14

Photo.

3222	A890	3fo	shown	38	20
3223	A890	5fo	multi	62	30

Nos. 3220-3221 inscribed "Pj 1989." Nos. 3222-3223 inscribed "1989."

Nos. 3222-3223 do not exist imperf.

A891 A892

Designs: Protected bird species.

1990, Feb. 20 Litho. *Perf. 11½x12*

3224	A891	3fo	*Alcedo atthis*	52	35
3225	A891	3fo	*Pyrrhula pyrrhula*	52	35
3226	A891	3fo	*Dendrocopos syriacus*	52	35
3227	A891	5fo	*Upupa epops*	85	58
3228	A891	5fo	*Merops apiaster*	85	58
3229	A891	10fo	*Coracias garrulus*	1.65	1.10
			Nos. 3224-3229 (6)	4.91	3.31

1990, Mar. 14 Litho. *Perf. 12*

Flowers of the continents (Africa).

3230	A892	3fo	*Leucadendron*	52	35
3231	A892	3fo	*Protea compacta*	52	35
3232	A892	3fo	*Leucadendron spissifolium*	52	35
3233	A892	5fo	*Protea barbigera*	85	58
3234	A892	5fo	*Protea lepidocarpodendron*	85	58
3235	A892	10fo	*Protea cynaroides*	1.65	1.10
			Nos. 3230-3235 (6)	4.91	3.31

Souvenir Sheet

Perf. 12½x12

3236	A892	20fo	Montage of African flowers	5.00	5.00

No. 3236 contains one 27x38mm stamp.

See Nos. 3278-3283, 3371-3375, 3377-3381.

A893

A894

Portraits of Hungarian kings in the Historical Portrait Gallery. King and reign: No. 3237, Janos Hunyadi (c. 1407-1409). No. 3238, Matthias Hunyadi (1443-1490).

1990, Apr. 6 Litho. *Perf. 11½x12*

3237	A893	5fo	multicolored	70	42
3238	A893	5fo	multicolored	70	42
a.			Pair, #3237-3238	1.40	1.00

Souvenir Sheet

Perf. 12½x12

1990, Apr. 17 Litho. & Engr.

3239	A894	20fo	black & buff	5.00	5.00

Penny Black 150th anniv., Stamp World London '90.

Karoli Bible, 400th Anniv. — A895

1990, Apr. 24 Litho.

3240	A895	8fo	Gaspar Karoli	1.00	68

No. 3240 printed se-tenant with label picturing Bible frontispiece.

1990 World Cup Soccer Championships, Italy — A896

Various athletes.

1990, Apr. 27 *Perf. 11½x12*

3241	A896	3fo	Dribble	45	30
3242	A896	5fo	Heading the ball	75	50
3243	A896	5fo	Kick	75	50
3244	A896	8fo	Goal attempt	1.25	82
3245	A896	8fo	Dribble, diff.	1.25	82
3246	A896	10fo	Dribble, diff.	1.50	1.00
			Nos. 3241-3246 (6)	5.95	3.94

Souvenir Sheet

Perf. 12½

3247	A896	20fo	Dribble, diff.	5.00	5.00

No. 3247 contains one 32x42mm stamp.

Kelemen Mikes (1690-1761), Writer — A897

1990, May 31 Litho. *Perf. 13½x13*

3248	A897	8fo	black & gold	1.25	82

Noemi and Beni Ferenczy, Birth Cent. — A898

Designs: 3fo, Painting by Noemi Ferenczy. 5fo, Sculpture by Beni Ferenczy.

1990, June 18 Litho. *Perf. 12*

3249	A898	3fo	multicolored	32	20
3250	A898	5fo	multicolored	55	32

Ferenc Kazinczy (1759-1831), Hungarian Language Reformer — A899

1990, July 18 Litho. *Perf. 12*

3251	A899	8fo	multicolored	75	50

Ferenc Kolcsey (1790-1838), Poet — A900

1990, Aug. 3

3252	A900	8fo	multicolored	75	50

New Coat of Arms A901

1990, Aug. 17 Litho. *Perf. 13½x13*

3253	A901	8fo	multicolored	75	50

Souvenir Sheet

Perf. 11

3254	A901	20fo	multicolored	2.50	1.25

No. 3254 contains one 34x50mm stamp.

Grapes and Wine Producing Areas — A902

Grapes and Growing Area: 3fo, Cabernet franc, Hajos-Vaskut. 5fo, Cabernet sauvignon, Villany-Siklos. No. 3257, Italian Riesling, Badacsony. No. 3258, Kadarka, Szekszard. No. 3259, Leanyka, Eger. 10fo, Furmint, Tokaj-Hegyalja.

1990, Aug. 31 *Perf. 13x13½*

3255	A902	3fo	multicolored	28	20
3256	A902	5fo	multicolored	50	32
3257	A902	8fo	multicolored	75	50
3258	A902	8fo	multicolored	75	50
3259	A902	8fo	multicolored	75	50
3260	A902	10fo	multicolored	95	65
			Nos. 3255-3260 (6)	3.98	2.67

Paintings by Endre Szasz — A903

1990, Oct. 12 Litho *Perf. 12*

3261	A903	8fo	Feast	80	50
3262	A903	12fo	Messsage	1.25	75

Stamp Day. See No. B344.

Prehistoric Animals
A904

1990, Nov. 16 **Litho.** ***Perf. 12***

3263 A904 3fo Tarbosaurus 32 20
3264 A904 5fo Brontosaurus 55 32
3265 A904 5fo Stegosaurus 55 32
3266 A904 5fo Dimorphodon 55 32
3267 A904 8fo Platybelodon 90 50
3268 A904 10fo Mammoth 1.10 65
Nos. 3263-3268 (6) 3.97 2.31

Intl. Literacy Year — A905

1990, Nov. 21 ***Perf. 13x13½***

3269 A905 10fo multicolored 1.00 65

Budapest Stamp Museum, 60th Anniv. — A906

1990, Nov. 23 ***Perf. 12½***

3270 A906 5fo brn red & grn 50 30

Souvenir Sheet

Thurn & Taxis Postal System, 500th Anniv. — A907

Illustration reduced.

1990, Nov. 30 **Litho.** ***Perf. 12½x12***

3271 A907 50fo multicolored *9.00 6.00*

A908 A909

Designs: Antique clocks.

1990, Dec. 14 ***Perf. 12***

3272 A908 3fo Travelling clock, 1576 30 20
3273 A908 5fo Table clock, 1643 50 32
3274 A908 5fo Mantel clock, 1790 50 32
3275 A908 10fo Table clock, 1814 95 65

1990, Dec. 14 ***Perf. 12½x11½***

Christmas: Madonna with Child by Botticelli.

3276 A909 5fo multicolored 52 32

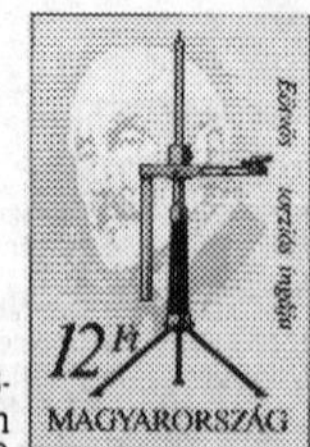

Lorand Eotvos (1848-1919) and Torsion Pendulum — A910

1991, Jan. 31 **Litho.** ***Perf. 11***

3277 A910 12fo multicolored 1.25 75

Flowers of the Continents Type

Flowers of the Americas.

1991, Feb. 28 **Litho.** ***Perf. 12***

3278 A892 5fo Mandevilla splendens 50 32
3279 A892 7fo Lobelia cardinalis 70 45
3280 A892 7fo Cobaea scandens 70 45
3281 A892 12fo Steriphoma paradoxa 1.10 75
3282 A892 15fo Beloperone guttata 1.50 1.00
Nos. 3278-3282 (5) 4.50 2.97

Souvenir Sheet

Perf. 11

3283 A892 20fo Flowers of the Americas 2.00 1.30

No. 3283 contains one 27x44mm stamp.

Post Office, Budapest
A911

Designs: 7fo, Post Office, Pecs.

Perf. 11½x12½

1991, Mar. 22 **Litho.**

3284 A911 5fo multicolored 65 32
3285 A911 7fo multicolored 90 45
a. Pair, #3284-3285 1.55 78

Admission to CEPT.

Europa — A912

1991, Apr. **Litho.** ***Perf. 12½***

3286 A912 12fo Ulysses probe 1.00 75
3287 A912 30fo Cassini-Huygens probe 2.75 1.95

Budapest Zoological and Botanical Gardens, 125th Anniv. — A913

1991, May 15 ***Perf. 13½x13***

3288 A913 7fo Gorilla 70 45
3289 A913 12fo Rhinoceros 1.10 75
3290 A913 12fo Toucan 1.10 75
3291 A913 12fo Polar bear 1.10 75
3292 A913 20fo Orchid 1.90 1.25
Nos. 3288-3292 (5) 5.90 3.95

A914 A915

1991, May 24 **Litho.** ***Perf. 12***

3293 A914 12fo multi 1.25 75

Count Pal Teleki (1879-1941), politician.

1991, June 13 ***Perf. 13x13½***

3294 A915 12fo multicolored 1.25 75

44th World Fencing Championships, Budapest.

Images of the Virgin and Child in Hungarian Shrines — A916

Designs: 7fo, Mariapocs. No. 3296, Mariagyud. No. 3297, Celldomolk. No. 3298, Mariaremete. 20fo, Esztergom.

1991, June 17 ***Perf. 12½***

3295 A916 7fo multicolored 70 45
3296 A916 12fo multicolored 1.10 75
3297 A916 12fo multicolored 1.10 75
3298 A916 12fo multicolored 1.10 75
3299 A916 20fo multicolored 1.90 1.25
Nos. 3295-3299 (5) 5.90 3.95

Compare with design A927.

Souvenir Sheet

Visit of Pope John Paul II, Aug. 16-20, 1991 — A917

1991, July 15 **Litho. & Engr.** ***Perf. 12***

3300 A917 50fo multicolored 6.00 3.25

Karoly Marko (1791-1860), Painter — A918

1991, June 17 ***Perf. 12***

3301 A918 12fo multicolored 1.25 75

Basketball, Cent. — A919

1991, June 27 **Litho.** ***Perf. 12***

3302 A919 10fo multicolored 1.00 62

Otto Lilienthal's First Glider Flight, Cent.
A920

Aircraft of aviation pioneers.

1991, June 27

3303 A920 7fo Otto Lilienthal 65 45
3304 A920 12fo Wright Brothers 1.10 75
3305 A920 20fo Alberto Santos-Dumont 1.90 1.25
3306 A920 30fo Aladar Zselyi 2.75 1.90

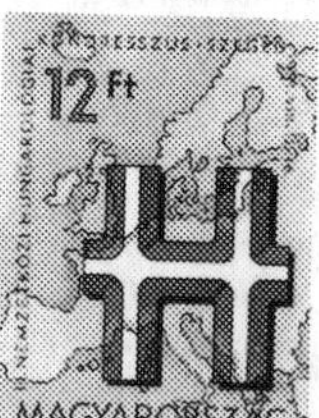

3rd Intl. Hungarian Philological Congress — A921

1991, Aug. 12 **Litho.** ***Perf. 13½x13***

3307 A921 12fo multicolored 1.25 75

A922 A923

1991, Sept. 6 **Engr.** ***Perf. 12***

3308 A922 12fo dark red 75 50

Count Istvan Szechenyi (1791-1860), founder of Academy of Sciences.

1991, Sept. 6 **Litho.**

Designs: Wolfgang Amadeus Mozart (1756-91).

3309 A923 12fo As child 95 50

3310 A923 20fo As adult 1.50 82

Souvenir Sheet

3311 A923 30fo +15fo, in red coat 3.50 1.85

Stamp Day. No. 3311 contains one 30x40mm stamp.

Telecom '91 A924

1991, Sept. 30 Litho. *Perf. 12*
3312 A924 12fo multicolored 90 50

6th World Forum and Exposition on Telecommunications, Geneva, Switzerland.

A925 A926

1991, Oct. 30 Litho. *Perf. 13½x13*
3313 A925 12fo multicolored 90 50

Sovereign Order of the Knights of Malta.

1991, Oct. 30 *Perf. 12*

Early explorers and Discovery of America, 500th anniv. (in 1992): 7fo, Sebastian Cabot, Labrador Peninsula, Nova Scotia. No. 3315, Amerigo Vespucci, South American region. No. 3316, Hernando Cortez, Mexico. 15fo, Ferdinand Magellan, Straits of Magellan. 20fo, Francisco Pizarro, Peru, Andes Mountain region. 30fo, Christopher Columbus and coat of arms.

3314 A926 7fo multicolored 52 30
3315 A926 12fo multicolored 90 50
3316 A926 12fo multicolored 90 50
3317 A926 15fo multicolored 1.10 65
3318 A926 20fo multicolored 1.50 82
Nos. 3314-3318 (5) 4.92 2.77

Souvenir Sheet

3319 A926 30fo multicolored 2.50 1.25

No. 3319 contains one 26x37mm stamp.

No. 3021A Overprinted in Brown

1991, Oct. 22 Litho. *Perf. 12x11½*
3320 A816 12fo on #3021A 1.00 50

Anniversary of Hungarian revolution, 1956.

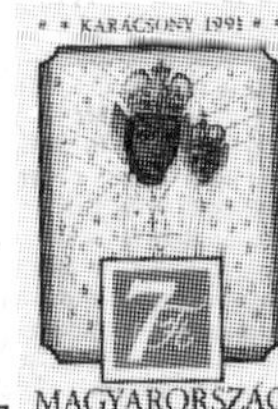

Christmas — A927

Images of the Virgin and Child from: 7fo, Mariapocs. 12fo, Mariaremete.

1991, Nov. 20 *Perf. 13½x13*
3322 A927 7fo multicolored 58 30
3323 A927 12fo multicolored 1.00 50

Nos. 3322-3323 issued in sheets of 20 plus 20 labels.

A928 A929

1991, Nov. 20 *Perf. 12*
3324 A928 12fo multicolored 1.00 50

Fight for human rights.

1991, Dec. 6 *Perf. 13½x13*
3325 A929 7fo Cross-country skiing 58 30
3326 A929 12fo Slalom skiing 1.00 50
3327 A929 15fo Four-man bobsled 1.25 65
3328 A929 20fo Ski jump 1.65 82
3329 A929 30fo Hockey 2.50 1.25
Nos. 3325-3329 (5) 6.98 3.52

Souvenir Sheet

Perf. 12½x11½

3330 A929 30fo Pairs figure skating 2.50 1.25

1992 Winter Olympics, Albertville.

Souvenir Sheet

First Hungarian Postage Stamp, 120th Anniv. — A930

1991, Dec. 20 Litho. *Perf. 12x12½*
3331 A930 50fo No. 6 4.25 2.10

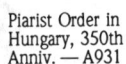

Piarist Order in Hungary, 350th Anniv. — A931

1992, Jan. 22 *Perf. 13½x13*
3332 A931 10fo multicolored 85 42

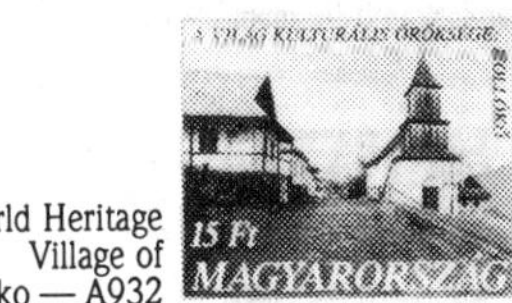

World Heritage Village of Holloko — A932

1992, Jan. 22 *Perf. 12*
3333 A932 15fo multicolored 1.25 65

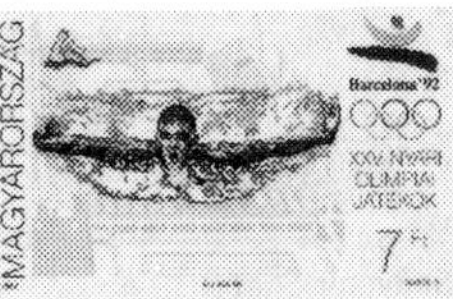

1992 Summer Olympics, Barcelona A933

1992, Feb. 26 Litho. *Perf. 13½x13*
3334 A933 7fo Swimming 58 30
3335 A933 9fo Cycling 75 38
3336 A933 10fo Gymnastics 85 42
3337 A933 15fo Running 1.25 65

Discovery of America, 500th Anniv. — A934

Expo '92, Seville: No. 3338, Map shaped as Indian, Columbus' fleet. No. 3339, Face-shaped map of ocean, sailing ship. No. 3340, Map shaped as European face, ship. No. 3341, Map, square, protractor, compass.

1992, Mar. 27 Litho. *Perf. 12*
3338 A934 10fo multicolored 85 42
3339 A934 10fo multicolored 85 42
3340 A934 15fo multicolored 1.25 65
3341 A934 15fo multicolored 1.25 65

Jozsef Cardinal Mindszenty (1892-1975), Leader of Hungarian Catholic Church — A935

1992, Mar. 27 *Perf. 12½x11½*
3342 A935 15fo red, brn & buff 1.25 65

A936 A937

1992, Mar. 27 *Perf. 13½x13*
3343 A936 15fo multicolored 1.25 65

Jan Amos Komensky (Comenius), writer, 400th birth anniv.

1992, Apr. 14 Litho. *Perf. 13½x13*
3344 A937 15fo Maya Indian sculpture 1.25 65
3345 A937 40fo Indian sculpture, diff. 3.30 1.15

Europa. Discovery of America, 500th anniv..

European Gymnastics Championships, Budapest — A938

1992, May 15 Litho. *Perf. 12*
3346 A938 15fo multicolored 1.25 65

A939 A940

1992, June 26 Litho. *Perf. 13½x13*
3347 A939 15fo multicolored 1.05 52

St. Margaret, 750th Anniv. (in 1991). No. 3347 printed with se-tenant label.

1992, June 26 *Perf. 13x13½*

Protected birds.

3348 A940 9fo Falco cherrug 62 30
3349 A940 10fo Hieraaetus pennatus 70 35
3350 A940 15fo Circaetus gallicus 1.05 52
3351 A940 40fo Milvus milvus 2.75 1.40

Raoul Wallenberg, Swedish Diplomat, 80th Anniv. of Birth — A941

1992, July 30 Litho. *Perf. 12*
3352 A941 15fo gray & red 1.05 52

Theodore von Karman (1881-1963), Physicist and Aeronautical Engineer — A942

Design: 40fo, John von Neumann (1903-1957), mathematician.

1992, Aug. 3 Litho. *Perf. 12x11½*
3353 A942 15fo multicolored 1.05 52
3354 A942 40fo multicolored 2.75 1.40

A943 A945

1992, Aug. 3 *Perf. 13½x13*
3355 A943 15fo multicolored 1.05 52

3rd World Congress of Hungarians.

1992, Oct. 6 Litho. *Perf. 12½x11½*
3360 A945 15fo multicolored 1.05 52

Telecom '92.

Stamp Day — A946

1992, Sept.4 *Perf. 12*

3361 A946 10fo +5fo Coat of arms, vert. 1.05 52
3362 A946 15fo shown 1.05 52
3363 A946 15fo +5fo like #3362, inscribed "65. Bely-egnap" 1.40 70

Souvenir Sheet

3364 A946 50fo +20fo Postilion 5.00 5.00

Eurofilex '92 (#3361, 3363-3364). Nos. 3361, 3363 printed with se-tenant label. No. 3364 contains one 40x30mm stamp.

Famous Men — A947

Postal Uniforms — A948

Designs: 10fo, Stephen Bathory (1533-1586), Prince of Transylvania and King of Poland. 15fo, Stephen Bocskay (1557-1606), Prince of Transylvania. 40fo, Gabriel Bethlen (1580-1629), Prince of Transylvania and King of Hungary.

1992, Oct. 28 **Litho.** *Perf. 12*

3365 A947 10fo multicolored 65 32
3366 A947 15fo multicolored 1.00 50
3367 A947 40fo multicolored 2.60 1.30

1992, Nov. 20 *Perf. 13½x13*

Designs: 10fo, Postrider, 1703-1711. 15fo, Letter carrier, 1874.

3368 A948 10fo multicolored 65 32
3369 A948 15fo multicolored 1.00 50

Christmas A949

Litho. & Engr.

1992, Nov. 20 *Perf. 12*

3370 A949 15fo blue & black 1.00 50

Flowers of the Continents Type of 1990

Flowers of Australia: 9fo, Clianthus formosus. 10fo, Leschenaultia biloba. 15fo, Anigosanthos manglesii. 40fo, Comesperma ericinum. 50fo, Bouquet of flowers.

1992, Nov. 20 **Litho.**

3371 A892 9fo multicolored 60 30
3372 A892 10fo multicolored 65 32
3373 A892 15fo multicolored 1.00 50
3374 A892 40fo multicolored 2.60 1.30

Souvenir Sheet

Perf. 12½

3375 A892 50fo multicolored 3.25 1.65

No. 3375 contains one 32x41mm stamp.

1992 European Chess Championships A950

1992, Oct. 28 *Perf. 11*

3376 A950 15fo multicolored 1.00 50

Flowers of the Continents Type of 1990

Flowers of Asia: No. 3377, Dendrobium densiflorum. No. 3378, Arachnis flos-aeris. No. 3379, Lilium speciosum. No. 3380, Meconopsis aculeata. 50fo, Bouquet of flowers.

1993, Jan. 27 **Litho.** *Perf. 13½x13*

3377 A892 10fo multicolored 60 30
3378 A892 10fo multicolored 60 30
3379 A892 15fo multicolored 90 45
3380 A892 15fo multicolored 90 45

Souvenir Sheet

Perf. 12½

3381 A892 50fo multicolored 3.00 1.50

No. 3381 contains one 32x41mm stamp.

Scythian Archaeological Artifacts A951

1993, Feb. 25 **Litho.** *Perf. 13x13½*

3382 A951 10fo Horse standing 60 30
3383 A951 17fo Horse lying down 95 45

Hungarian Rowing Association, Cent. — A952

1993, Feb. 25 **Litho.** *Perf. 12*

3384 A952 17fo multicolored 95 45

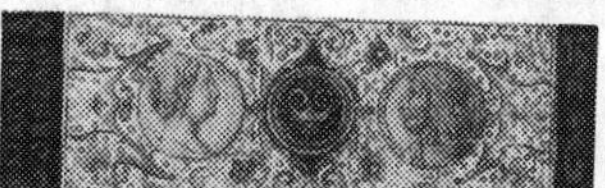

Missale Romanum of Matthias Corvinus (Matyas Hunyadi, King of Hungary) — A953

Design: 40fo, Illuminated page.

1993, Mar. 12 **Litho.** *Perf. 12*

3385 A953 15fo multicolored 75 38

Souvenir Sheet

3386 A953 40fo multicolored 2.10 1.05

Illustration reduced. No. 3386 contains one 60x38mm stamp.

See Belgium Nos. 1474, 1476.

Motocross World Championships A954

1993, May 5 **Litho.** *Perf. 11½x12*

3387 A954 17fo multicolored 95 45

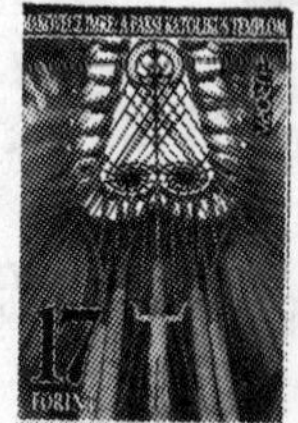

Europa — A955

Buildings designed by Imre Makovecz: 17fo, Roman Catholic Church, Paks. 45fo, Hungarian Pavilion, Expo '92, Seville.

1993, May 5 *Perf. 13x13½*

3388 A955 17fo multicolored 95 45
3389 A955 45fo multicolored 2.50 1.25

Heliocentric Solar System, Copernicus — A956

1993, May 5 *Perf. 12*

3390 A956 17fo multicolored 95 45

Polska '93. No. 3390 issued in sheets of 8 + 4 labels.

Edible Mushrooms — A957

1993, June 18 **Litho.** *Perf. 13½x13*

3391 A957 10fo Ramaria botrytis 60 30
3392 A957 17fo Craterellus cornucopioides 95 45
3393 A957 45fo Amanita caesarea 2.50 1.25

St. Christopher, by Albrecht Durer — A958

1993, June 18 *Perf. 12*

3394 A958 17fo silver, black & buff 95 45

Year of the Elderly.

City of Mohacs, 900th Anniv. — A959

1993, June 18 *Perf. 13½x13*

3395 A959 17fo buff, maroon & red brown 95 45

Hungarian State Railways, 125th Anniv. A960

1993, June 18 *Perf. 13x13½*

3396 A960 17fo lt blue & blue 95 45

Comedians
A961

Butterflies
A962

1993, July 28 Litho. *Perf. 12*

3397	A961	17fo Kalman Latabar	95	45
3398	A961	30fo Charlie Chaplin	1.80	90

1993, July 28 *Perf. 13½x13*

3399	A962	10fo Limenitis populi	60	30
3400	A962	17fo Aricia artaxerxes	95	45
3401	A962	30fo Plebejides pylaon	1.80	90

Souvenir Sheet

Helsinki Conference on European Security and Cooperation, 20th Anniv. — A963

1993, July 28 *Perf. 12*

3402	A963	50fo multicolored	3.00	3.00

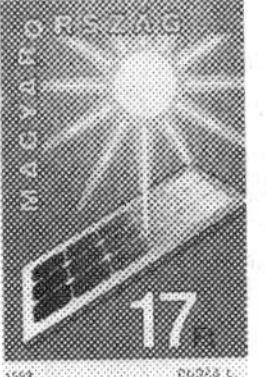
A964

Writers — A965

Perf. 12½x11½
1993, Aug. 23 Litho.

3403	A964	17fo multicolored	35	18

Intl. Solar Energy Society Congress, Budapest. No. 3403 printed se-tenant with label.

1993, Aug. 23 *Perf. 12*

Designs: No. 3404, Laszlo Nemeth (1901-75). No. 3405, Dezso Szabo (1879-1945). No. 3406, Antal Szerb (1901-45).

3404	A965	17fo blue	35	18
3405	A965	17fo blue	35	18
3406	A965	17fo blue	35	18

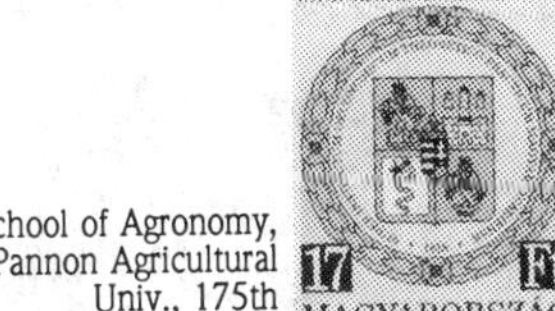
School of Agronomy, Pannon Agricultural Univ., 175th Anniv. — A966

1993, Oct. 22 Litho. *Perf. 12*

3407	A966	17fo multicolored	60	30

Ships — A967

1993, Oct. 27 *Perf. 13x13½*

3408	A967	10fo Steamer with sails	35	18
3409	A967	30fo Battleship	1.00	50
a.		Pair, #3408-3409	1.40	70

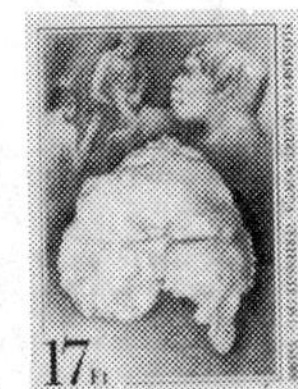
Prehistoric Man — A968

1993, Oct. 27 *Perf. 13½x13*

3410	A968	17fo Skull fragment	60	30
3411	A968	30fo Stone tool	1.00	50

Souvenir Sheet

Roman Roads — A969

1993, Oct. 27 *Perf. 11*

3412	A969	50fo multicolored	1.75	85

Christmas — A970

Altarpiece: 10fo, Virgin and Christ Child, Cathedral of Szekesfehervar, by F. A. Hillebrant.

1993, Nov. 24 *Perf. 13½x13*

3413	A970	10fo multicolored	35	16

Sights of Budapest — A971

Designs: 17fo, Szechenyi Chain Bridge. 30fo, Opera House. 45fo, Matthias Church, vert. Illustration reduced.

Photo. & Engr.
1993, Dec. 16 *Perf. 12*

3414	A971	17fo lt green & dk green	55	28
3415	A971	30fo lt mag & dk mag	1.00	50
3416	A971	45fo lt brown & dk brn	1.50	75

Expo '96.

Josef Antall (1932-93) — A972

1993 Litho. *Perf. 11*

3417	A972	19fo multicolored	65	32
a.		Souvenir sheet	65	32

ICAO, 50th Anniv. A973

1994, Jan. 13 *Perf. 13x13½*

3418	A973	56fo multicolored	1.90	95

1994 Winter Olympics, Lillehammer — A974

1994, Jan. 13 *Perf. 12*

3419	A974	12fo Downhill skiing	40	20
3420	A974	19fo Ice hockey	65	32

SEMI-POSTAL STAMPS

Issues of the Monarchy

"Turul" and St. Stephen's Crown — SP1

Franz Josef I Wearing Hungarian Crown — SP2

Wmk. Double Cross (137)
1913, Nov. 20 Typo. *Perf. 14*

B1	SP1	1f slate	28	28
B2	SP1	2f olive yellow	15	15
B3	SP1	3f orange	15	15
B4	SP1	5f emerald	15	15
B5	SP1	6f olive green	28	22
B6	SP1	10f carmine	15	15
B7	SP1	12f violet, *yellow*	52	42
B8	SP1	16f gray green	22	15
B9	SP1	20f dark brown	1.40	90
B10	SP1	25f ultra	32	15
B11	SP1	30f orange brown	52	22
B12	SP1	35f red violet	32	15
B13	SP1	50f lake, *blue*	2.75	1.25
B14	SP1	60f green, *salmon*	4.00	70
B15	SP2	1k dull red	11.50	5.25
B16	SP2	2k dull blue	35.00	24.00
B17	SP2	5k violet brown	9.25	9.25
		Nos. B1-B17 (17)	66.96	43.54

Nos. B1-B17 were sold at an advance of 2f over face value, as indicated by the label at bottom. The surtax was to aid flood victims.

For overprints see Nos. 5NB1-5NB10, 6NB1-6NB11.

Semi-Postal Stamps of 1913 Surcharged in Red, Green or Brown:

Hadi segély

Özvegyeknek és árváknak két (2) fillér
a

Özvegyeknek és árváknak két (2) fillér
b

1914

B18	SP1(a)	1f slate	24	18
B19	SP1(a)	2f olive yel	22	15
B20	SP1(a)	3f orange	22	15
B21	SP1(a)	5f emerald	15	15
B22	SP1(a)	6f olive green	30	15
B23	SP1(a)	10f carmine (G)	15	15
B24	SP1(a)	12f violet, *yel*	18	15
B25	SP1(a)	16f gray green	15	15
B26	SP1(a)	20f dark brown	22	15
B27	SP1(a)	25f ultra	48	22
B28	SP1(a)	30f orange brn	60	22
B29	SP1(a)	35f red violet	1.65	75
B30	SP1(a)	50f lake, *bl*	1.25	45
B31	SP1(a)	60f green, *sal*	3.75	75
B32	SP2(b)	1k dull red (Br)	32.50	18.00
B33	SP2(b)	2k dull blue	13.50	9.00
B34	SP2(b)	5k violet brn	8.50	6.75
		Nos. B18-B34 (17)	64.06	37.52

Regular Issue of 1913 Surcharged in Red or Green:

Özvegyeknek és árváknak Hadi segély két (2) fillér
c

Hadi segély Özvegyeknek és árváknak két (2) fillér
d

1915, Jan. 1

B35	A4(c)	1f slate	15	15
B36	A4(c)	2f olive yel	15	15
B37	A4(c)	3f orange	15	15
B38	A4(c)	5f emerald	15	15
B39	A4(c)	6f olive grn	15	15
B40	A4(c)	10f carmine (G)	15	15
B41	A4(c)	12f violet, *yel*	15	15
B42	A4(c)	16f gray green	24	24
B43	A4(c)	20f dark brown	28	28

B44 A4(c) 25f ultra 15 15
B45 A4(c) 30f orange brn 15 15
B46 A4(c) 35f red violet 15 15
B47 A4(c) 50f lake, *bl* 18 18
a. On No. 96a
B48 A4(c) 60f green, *sal* 35 28
B49 A5(d) 1k dull red 45 45
B50 A5(d) 2k dull blue 1.50 1.50
B51 A5(d) 5k violet brown 6.25 6.25

Surcharged as Type "c" but in Smaller Letters

B52 A4 60f green, *sal* 1.25 1.00
Nos. B35-B52 (18) 12.00 11.68

Nos. B18-B52 were sold at an advance of 2f over face value. The surtax to aid war widows and orphans.

Soldiers Fighting
SP3 SP4

Eagle with Sword
SP5

Harvesting
SP6

1916-17 *Perf. 15*

B53 SP3 10f + 2f rose red 15 15
B54 SP4 15f + 2f dull violet 15 15
B55 SP5 40f + 2f brn car ('17) 18 18
Set value 38 38

For overprints and surcharge see Nos. B58-B60. 1NB1-1NB3, 2NB1-2NB6, 4NJ1, 5NB11-5NB13, 6NB13-6NB15, 7NB2-7NB3, 9NB1, 10NB1-10NB4, Szeged B1-B4.

1917, Sept. 15

Surcharge in Red

B56 SP6 10f + 1k rose 25 25
B57 SP6 15f + 1k violet 25 25

Nos. B56 and B57 were issued in connection with the War Exhibition of Archduke Josef.

Issues of the Republic

Semi-Postal Stamps of 1916-17 Overprinted in Black

1918

B58 SP3 10f + 2f rose red 15 15
B59 SP4 15f + 2f dull violet 15 15
B60 SP5 40f + 2f brown car 15 15
Set value 30 30

Nos. B58-B60 exist with inverted overprint.

Postally used copies of Nos. B69-B174 sell for more.

Issues of the Kingdom

Released Prisoner Walking Home — SP7

Prisoners of War — SP8

Homecoming of Soldier — SP9

Wmk. 137 Vert. or Horiz.

1920, Mar. 11 *Perf. 12*

B69 SP7 40f + 1k dull red 38 38
B70 SP8 60f + 2k gray brown 30 30
B71 SP9 1k + 5k dk blue 30 30
Set, never hinged 1.75

The surtax was used to help prisoners of war return home from Siberia.

Statue of Petőfi — SP10

Griffin — SP11

Sándor Petőfi — SP12

Petőfi Dying — SP13

Petőfi Addressing People — SP14

1923, Jan. 23 *Perf. 14 (10k, 40k), 12*

B72 SP10 10k slate green 28 28
B73 SP11 15k dull blue 1.25 1.25
B74 SP12 25k gray brown 28 28
B75 SP13 40k brown violet 1.25 1.25
B76 SP14 50k violet brown 1.25 1.25
Nos. B72-B76 (5) 4.31 4.31
Set, never hinged 5.50

Birth centenary of the Hungarian poet Sándor Petőfi. The stamps were on sale at double face value, for a limited time and in restricted quantities, after which the remainders were given to a charitable organization.

Child with Symbols of Peace — SP15

Mother and Infant — SP16

Instruction in Archery — SP17

Wmk. 133

1924, Apr. 8 **Engr.** *Perf. 12*

B77 SP15 300k dark blue 1.40 1.40
a. Perf. 11½ 25.00 25.00
B78 SP16 500k black brown 1.40 1.40
B79 SP17 1000k black green 1.40 1.40
Set, never hinged 5.75

Each stamp has on the back an inscription stating that it was sold at a premium of 100 per cent over the face value.

Parade of Athletes — SP18

Skiing — SP19

Skating — SP20

Diving — SP21

Fencing — SP22

Scouts Camping — SP23

Soccer — SP24

Hurdling — SP25

Perf. 12, 12½ and Compound

1925 **Typo.** **Unwmk.**

B80 SP18 100k bl grn & brn 1.25 1.25
B81 SP19 200k lt brn & myr grn 2.00 2.00
B82 SP20 300k dark blue 2.50 2.50
B83 SP21 400k dp bl & dp grn 3.00 3.00
B84 SP22 500k purple brown 4.00 4.00
B85 SP23 1000k red brown 5.00 5.00
B86 SP24 2000k brown violet 6.00 6.00
B87 SP25 2500k olive brown 7.25 7.25
Nos. B80-B87 (8) 31.00 31.00
Set, never hinged 42.50

These stamps were sold at double face value, plus a premium of 10 per cent on orders sent by mail. They did not serve any postal need and were issued solely to raise funds to aid athletic associations. An inscription regarding the 100 per cent premium is printed on the back of each stamp. Exist imperf.

St. Emerich
SP26

Sts. Stephen and Gisela
SP27

St. Ladislaus
SP28

Sts. Gerhardt and Emerich
SP29

1930, May 15 **Wmk. 210** *Perf. 14*

B88 SP26 8f + 2f deep green 65 52
B89 SP27 16f + 4f brt violet 70 80
B90 SP28 20f + 4f deep rose 2.25 2.75
B91 SP29 32f + 8f ultra 3.25 4.00
Set, never hinged 9.00

900th anniv. of the death of St. Emerich, son of Stephen I, king, saint and martyr.

Catalogue values for unused stamps in this section, from this point to the end of the section, are for Never Hinged items.

St. Ladislaus — SP30

Holy Sacrament — SP31

SP32

1938 May 16 **Photo.** *Perf. 12*

B92 SP30 16f + 16f dull sl bl 2.50 2.50
B93 SP31 20f + 20f dk carmine 2.50 2.50

Souvenir Sheet

B94 SP32 Sheet of 7 17.50 15.00
a. 6f + 6f St. Stephen 1.40 1.10
b. 10f + 10f St. Emerich 1.40 1.10
c. 16f + 16f slate blue (B92) 1.40 1.10
d. 20f + 20f dark carmine (B93) 1.40 1.10
e. 32f + 32f St. Elizabeth 1.40 1.10
f. 40f + 40f St. Maurice 1.40 1.10
g. 50f + 50f St. Margaret 1.40 1.10

Printed in sheets measuring 136½x155mm. Nos. B94c and B94d are slightly smaller than B92 and B93.

Eucharistic Cong. in Budapest, May, 1938.

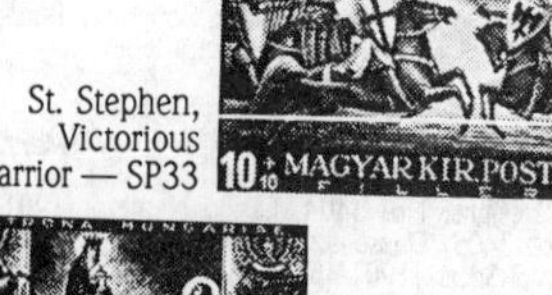

St. Stephen, Victorious Warrior — SP33

St. Stephen, Offering Crown — SP34

SP35

1938, Aug. 12 *Perf. 12*

B95 SP33 10f + 10f violet brn 3.00 2.50
B96 SP34 20f + 20f red orange 3.00 2.50

Souvenir Sheet

B97 SP35 Sheet of 7 17.50 16.00
a. 6f + 6f St. Stephen the Missionary 1.40 1.40
b. 10f + 10f violet brown (B95) 1.40 1.40
c. 16f + 16f Seated Upon Throne 1.40 1.40
d. 20f + 20f red orange (B96) 1.40 1.40
e. 32f + 32f Receives Bishops and Monks 1.40 1.40

f. 40f + 40f St. Gisela, St. Stephen and St. Emerich 1.40 1.40
g. 50f + 50f St. Stephen on Bier 1.40 1.40

Death of St. Stephen, 900th anniversary.
No. B97 is on brownish paper, Nos. B95-B96 on white.

Statue Symbolizing Recovered Territories SP36

Castle of Munkács SP37

Admiral Horthy Entering Komárom — SP38

Cathedral of Kassa — SP39

Girl Offering Flowers to Soldier — SP40

1939, Jan. 16

B98 SP36 6f + 3f myrtle grn 60 35
B99 SP37 10f + 5f olive grn 28 18
B100 SP38 20f + 10f dark red 28 18
B101 SP39 30f + 15f grnsh blue 1.10 60
B102 SP40 40f + 20f dk bl gray 1.10 60
Nos. B98-B102 (5) 3.36 1.91

The surtax was for the aid of "Hungary for Hungarians" patriotic movement.

Memorial Tablets SP41

Gáspár Károlyi, Translator of the Bible into Hungarian SP42

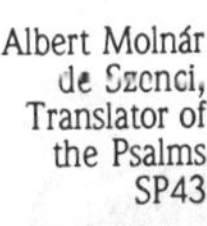
Albert Molnár de Szenci, Translator of the Psalms SP43

Prince Gabriel Bethlen — SP44

Susanna Lórántffy — SP45

Perf. 12x12½, 12½x12

1939 Photo. Wmk. 210

B103 SP41 6f + 3f green 70 55
B104 SP42 10f + 5f claret 70 55
B105 SP43 20f + 10f cop red 80 75
B106 SP44 32f + 16f bister 1.25 1.00
B107 SP45 40f + 20f chlky blue 1.40 1.00
Nos. B103-B107 (5) 4.85 3.85

Souvenir Sheets

Perf. 12

B108 SP44 32f ol & vio brn 14.00 11.50

Imperf

B109 SP44 32f bl grn, cop red & gold 14.00 11.50

National Protestant Day. The surtax was used to erect an Intl. Protestant Institute.
The souvenir sheets sold for 1.32p each.
Issue dates: Nos. B103-B107, Oct. 2. Nos. B108-B109, Oct. 27.

Boy Scout Flying Kite — SP47

Allegory of Flight — SP48

Archangel Gabriel from Millennium Monument, Budapest, and Planes — SP49

1940, Jan. 1 ***Perf. 12½x12***

B110 SP47 6f + 6f yellow grn 24 22
B111 SP48 10f + 10f chocolate 38 35
B112 SP49 20f + 20f copper red 90 80

The surtax was used for the Horthy National Aviation Fund.

SP50

Soldier Protecting Family from Floods — SP51

Souvenir Sheet

Wmk. 210

1940, May 6 Photo. ***Perf. 12***

B113 SP50 20f + 1p dk blue grn 1.75 1.50

1940, May

B114 SP51 10f + 2f gray brown 15 15
B115 SP51 20f + 4f orange red 18 18
B116 SP51 20f + 50f red brown 65 65

The surtax on Nos. B113-B116 was used to aid flood victims.

Hunyadi Coat of Arms — SP52

King Matthias — SP54

Hunyadi Castle — SP53

Equestrian Statue of King Matthias SP55

Corvin Codex — SP56

Equestrian Statue of King Matthias — SP57

1940 ***Perf. 12½x12, 12x12½***

B117 SP52 6f + 3f blue grn 32 28
B118 SP53 10f + 5f gldn brn 26 22
B119 SP54 16f + 8f dk ol bis 32 28
B120 SP55 20f + 10f brick red 45 38
B121 SP56 32f + 16f dk gray 85 70
Nos. B117-B121 (5) 2.20 1.86

Souvenir Sheet

B122 SP57 20f + 1p dk bl grn & pale grn 1.75 1.50

King Matthias (1440-1490) at Kolozsvar, Transylvania. The surtax was used for war relief.
Issued: #B117-B121, July 1. #B122. Nov. 7.

Hungarian Soldier — SP58

Designs: 20f+50f, Virgin Mary and Szekley, symbolizing the return of transylvania. 32f+50f, Szekley Mother Offering Infant Son to the Fatherland.

1940, Dec. 2 Photo. ***Perf. 12½x12***

B123 SP58 10f + 50f dk blue grn 65 50
B124 SP58 20f + 50f brown car 65 50
B125 SP58 32f + 50f yellow brn 95 75

Occupation of Transylvania. The surtax was for the Pro-Transylvania movement.

Symbol for Drama — SP61

Symbol for Sculpture — SP62

Symbols: 16f+16f, Art. 20f+20f, Literature.

Perf. 12x12½, 12½x12

1940, Dec. 15

B126 SP61 6f + 6f dark green 85 70
B127 SP62 10f + 10f olive bis 85 70
B128 SP62 16f + 16f dk violet 85 70
B129 SP61 20f + 20f fawn 85 70

Souvenir Sheet

1941, Jan. 5 ***Imperf.***

B130 Sheet of 4 2.75 2.00
a. SP61 6f + 6f olive brown 55 40
b. SP62 10f + 10f henna brown 55 40
c. SP62 16f + 16f dk blue green 55 40
d. SP61 20f + 20f rose violet 55 40

Surtax on #B126-B130 was used for the Pension and Assistance Institution for Artists.

Winged Head of Pilot — SP66

Designs: 10f+10f, Boy Scout with model plane. 20f+20f, Glider in flight. 32f+32f, Our Lady of Loreto, patroness of Hungarian pilots.

1941, Mar. 24 ***Perf. 12x12½***

B131 SP66 6f + 6f grn olive 45 35
B132 SP66 10f + 10f dp claret 45 35
B133 SP66 20f + 20f org ver 45 35
B134 SP66 32f + 32f turq blue 90 80

The surtax was used to finance civilian and army pilot training through the Horthy National Aviation Fund.

Infantry — SP70

Designs: 12f+18f, Heavy artillery. 20f+30f, Plane and tanks. 40f+60f, Cavalryman and cyclist.

1941, Dec. 1 Photo. Wmk. 266

Inscribed: "Honvedeink Karacsonyara 1941"

B135 SP70 8f + 12f dk green 22 18
B136 SP70 12f + 8f olive grn 22 18
B137 SP70 20f + 30f slate 28 22
B138 SP70 40f + 60f red brown 52 42

The surtax was for the benefit of the Army.

Soldier and Emblem — SP74

1941, Dec. 1

B139 SP74 20f + 40f dark red 1.50 1.25

The surtax was for the soldiers' Christmas.

Aviator and Plane — SP75

Planes and Ghostly Band of Old Chiefs — SP76

Plane and Archer — SP77

Aviators and Plane — SP78

Perf. 12½x12, 12x12½

1942, Mar. 15

B140	SP75	8f + 8f dark green	48	38
B141	SP76	12f + 12f sapphire	48	38
B142	SP77	20f + 20f brown	48	38
B143	SP78	30f + 30f dark red	48	38

The surtax aided the Horthy National Aviation Fund.

Blood Transfusion — SP79

Designs: 8f+32f, Bandaging wounded soldier. 12f+50f, Radio and carrier pigeons. 20f+1p, Widows and orphans.

1942, Sept. 1 *Perf. 12½x12*

B144	SP79	3f + 18f dk ol & red	95	85
B145	SP79	8f + 32f dp brn & red	95	85
B146	SP79	12f + 50f dp cl & red	95	85
B147	SP79	20f + 1p sl bl & red	95	85

The surtax aided the Hungarian Red Cross. Sheets of 10.

Widow of Stephen Horthy — SP83

Red Cross Nurse Aiding Soldier — SP84

Magdalene Horthy Mother of Stephen Horthy — SP85

1942, Dec. 1 *Perf. 13, Imperf.*

B148	SP83	6f + 1p vio bl & red	2.00	1.75
a.		Sheet of 4	15.00	15.00
B149	SP84	8f + 1p dk ol grn & red	2.00	1.75
a.		Sheet of 4	15.00	15.00
B150	SP85	20f + 1p dk red brn & red	2.00	1.75
a.		Sheet of 4	15.00	15.00

The surtax aided the Hungarian Red Cross.

King Ladislaus I
SP86 SP87

1942, Dec. 21 **Wmk. 266** *Perf. 12*

B151	SP86	6f + 6f olive gray	35	35
B152	SP87	8f + 8f green	35	35
B153	SP86	12f + 12f dull violet	35	35
B154	SP87	20f + 20f Prus green	35	35
B155	SP86	24f + 24f brown	35	35
B156	SP87	30f + 30f rose car	35	35
		Nos. B151-B156 (6)	2.10	2.10

900th anniv. of the birth of St. Ladislaus (1040-95), the 700th anniv. of the beginning of the country's reconstruction by King Béla IV (1206-70) and the 600th anniv. of the accession of King Lajos the Great (1326-82).

The surtax aided war invalids and their families.

Archer on Horseback — SP92

Knight with Sword and Shield — SP93

Old Magyar Arms — SP94

Designs: 3f+1f, 4f+1f, Warrior with shield and battle ax. 12f+2f, Knight with lance, 20f+2f, Musketeer. 40f+4f, Hussar. 50f+6f, Artilleryman.

1943

B157	SP92	1f + 1f dk gray	15	15
B158	SP93	3f + 1f dull violet	40	30
B159	SP93	4f + 1f lake	15	15
B160	SP93	8f + 2f green	15	15
B161	SP92	12f + 2f bister brn	15	15
B162	SP93	20f + 2f dp claret	16	15
B163	SP92	40f + 4f gray vio	20	15
B164	SP93	50f + 6f org brn	26	15
B165	SP94	70f + 8f slate blue	26	15
		Nos. B147-B165 (19)	10.93	
		Set value		1.25

The surtax aided war invalids.

Model Glider SP101

Gliders SP102

White-tailed Sea Eagle and Planes SP103

ME-109E Fighter and Gliders SP104

1943, July 17

B166	SP101	8f + 8f green	42	40
B167	SP102	12f + 12f royal blue	42	40
B168	SP103	20f + 20f chestnut	42	40
B169	SP104	30f + 30f rose car	42	40

The surtax aided the Horthy National Aviation Fund.

Stephen Horthy SP105

1943, Aug. 16

B170	SP105	30f + 20f dp rose vio	30	25

The surtax aided the Horthy National Aviation Fund.

Nurse and Soldier — SP106

Designs: 30f+30f, Soldier, nurse, mother and child. 50f+50f, Nurse keeping lamp alight. 70f+70f, Wounded soldier and tree shoot.

1944, Mar. 1

Cross in Red

B171	SP106	20f + 20f brown	20	18
B172	SP106	30f + 30f henna	20	18
B173	SP106	50f + 50f brown vio	20	18
B174	SP106	70f + 70f Prus blue	20	18

The surtax aided the Hungarian Red Cross.

Issues of the Republic

Types of 1944 Surcharged in Red or Black:

a

BÉKE
3P
A NÉPFŐISKOLÁKERT
+9P

b

BÉKE 4P
A NÉP-
FŐISKOLÁKERT
+12P

1945, July 23 **Wmk. 266** *Perf. 12*

B175	A115(a)	3p + 9p on 20f dk ol grn, *yel*	20	20
B176	A114(b)	4p + 12p on 4f yel brn, *bl* (Bk)	20	20
B177	A117(b)	8p + 24p on 50f sl bl, *yel*	20	20
B178	A115(a)	10p + 30p on 30f hn brn, *bl* (Bk)	20	20

The surtax was for the Peoples Universities. "Béke" means "peace".

Imre Sallai and Sandor Fürst — SP110

Designs: 3p+3p, L. Kabok and Illes Monus. 4p+4p, Ferenc Rozsa and Zoltan Schonerz. 6p+6p, Anna Koltai and Mrs. Paul Knurr. 10p+10p, George Sarkozi and Imre Nagy. 15p+15p, Vilmos Tartsay and Jeno Nagy. 20p+20p, Janos Kiss and Andreas Bajcsy-Zsilinszky. 40p+40p, Endre Sagvari and Otto Hoffmann.

1945, Oct. 6 **Photo.**

B179	SP110	2p + 2p yellow brn	1.10	1.10
B180	SP110	3p + 3p deep red	1.10	1.10
B181	SP110	4p + 4p dk purple	1.10	1.10
B182	SP110	6p + 6p dk yel grn	1.10	1.10
B183	SP110	10p + 10p dp car	1.10	1.10
B184	SP110	15p + 15p dk sl grn	1.10	1.10
B185	SP110	20p + 20p dk brown	1.10	1.10
B186	SP110	40p + 40p dp blue	1.10	1.10
		Nos. B179-B186 (8)	8.80	8.80

The surtax was for child welfare.

Andreas Bajcsy-Zsilinszky and Eagle — SP111

1945, May 27

B187	SP111	1p + 1p dk brn vio	25	25

1st anniversary of the death of Andreas Bajcsy-Zsilinszky, hanged by the Nazis for anti-fascist activities.

Lion with Broken Shackles SP112

1946, May 1

B188	SP112	500ez p + 500ez p	95	95
B189	SP112	1mil p + 1mil p	95	95
B190	SP112	1.5mil p + 1.5mil p	95	95
B191	SP112	2mil p + 2mil p	95	95

75th anniv. of Hungary's 1st postage stamp. The surtax was for the benefit of postal employees.

"Agriculture" Holding Wheat — SP113

Physician with Syringe — SP114

1946, Sept. 7 **Photo.**

B192	SP113	30f + 60f dp yel grn	3.50	3.50
B193	SP113	60f + 1.20fo rose brn	3.50	3.50
B194	SP113	1fo + 2fo dp blue	3.50	3.50

1st Agricultural Congress and Exhibition.

Perf. 12½x12

1947, May 16 **Wmk. 210**

Designs: 12f+50f, Physician examining X-ray picture. 20f+50f, Nurse and child. 60f+50f, Prisoner of war starting home.

B195	SP114	8f + 50f ultra	3.00	3.00
B196	SP114	12f + 50f choc	3.00	3.00
B197	SP114	20f + 50f dark green	3.00	3.00
B198	SP114	60f + 50f dark red	85	85

The surtax was for charitable purposes.

Franklin D. Roosevelt and Freedom of Speech Allegory SP115

Pres. F. D. Roosevelt and Allegory: 12f+12f, Freedom of Religion. 20f+20f, Freedom from Want. 30f+30f, Freedom from Fear.

1947, June 11 **Photo.** *Perf. 12x12½*

Portrait in Sepia

B198A	SP115	8f + 8f dark red	2.50	2.50
B198B	SP115	12f + 12f deep green	2.50	2.50

B198C SP115 20f + 20f brown 2.50 2.50
B198D SP115 30f + 30f blue 2.50 2.50
Nos. B198A-B198D,CB1-CB1C (8) 22.00 22.00

Nos. B198A-B198D and CB1-CB1C were also printed in sheets of 4 of each denomination (size: 117x96mm). Value, set of 8, $250.

A souvenir sheet contains one each of Nos. B198A-B198D with border inscriptions and decorations in brown. Size: 161x122mm. Value $80.

Lenin — SP118

XVI Century Mail Coach — SP119

Designs: 60f+60f, Soviet Cenotaph, Budapest. 1fo+1fo, Joseph V. Stalin.

1947, Oct. 29 Photo. Wmk. 283
B199 SP118 40f + 40f ol grn & org brn 4.50 4.50
B200 SP118 60f + 60f red & sl bl 1.00 1.00
B201 SP118 1fo + 1fo vio & brn blk 4.50 4.50

The surtax was for the Hungarian-Soviet Cultural Association.

1947, Dec. 21 ***Perf. 12x12½***
B202 SP119 30f (+ 50f) hn brn 9.50 9.50
Sheet of 4 45.00 45.00

Stamp Day. The surtax paid admission to a philatelic exhibition in any of eight Hungarian towns, where the stamps were sold.

Globe and Carrier Pigeon SP120

Woman Worker SP121

1948, Oct. 17 ***Perf. 12½x12***
B203 SP120 30f (+ 1fo) grnsh bl 3.50 3.50
Sheet of 4 24.00 24.00

5th Natl. Hungarian Stamp Exhib., Budapest. Each stamp sold for 1.30 forint, which included admission to the exhibition.

1949, Mar. 8
B204 SP121 60f + 60f magenta 75 75

Intl. Woman's Day, Mar. 8, 1949. The surtax was for the Democratic Alliance of Hungarian Women.

Aleksander S. Pushkin — SP122

SP123

1949, June 6 Photo.
B205 SP122 1fo + 1fo car lake 7.00 7.00

Souvenir Sheet
Perf. 12½x12, Imperf
B206 SP123 1fo + 1fo red vio & car lake 14.00 14.00

150th anniversary of the birth of Aleksander S. Pushkin. The surtax was for the Hungarian-Russian Culture Society.

Type of Regular Issue of 1951
Perf. 12½x12
1951, Oct. 6 Engr. Unwmk.
B207 A208 1fo + 1fo red 10.00 10.00
B208 A208 2fo + 2fo blue 15.00 15.00

Postwoman Delivering Mail — SP124

1953, Nov. 1 Wmk. 106 ***Perf. 12***
B209 SP124 1fo + 1fo blue grn 1.75 1.75
B210 SP124 2fo + 2fo rose vio 1.75 1.75

Stamp Day, Nov. 1, 1953.

Stamps of 1955 Surcharged in Red or Lake

1957, Jan. 31 Photo. ***Perf. 12x12½***
B211 A249 20f + 20f olive grn 22 20
B212 A249 30f + 30f dk red (L) 22 25
B213 A249 40f + 40f brown 40 25
B214 A249 60f + 60f brn red (L) 60 30
B215 A249 1fo + 1fo blue 85 65
B216 A249 2fo + 2fo rose brn 1.25 1.10
Nos. B211-B216 (6) 3.54 2.75

The surtax was for the Hungarian Red Cross.

Winter Olympic Type of 1960

Design: Olympic Games emblem.

Perf. 11½x12
1960, Feb. 29 Wmk. 106
B217 A295 2fo + 1fo multi 1.25 50

Olympic Type of 1960

Design: 2fo+1fo, Romulus and Remus.

Perf. 11½x12
1960, Aug. 21 Photo. Wmk. 106
B218 A299 2fo + 1fo multi 95 38

Sport Club Type of 1961

Sport: 2fo+1fo, Sailboats.

1961, July 8 Unwmk. ***Perf. 14½***
B219 A313 2fo + 1fo multi 75 48

St. Margaret's Island and Danube SP125

Views of Budapest: No. B221, Fishermen's Bastion. No. B222, Coronation Church and Chain Bridge. No. B223, Mount Gellert.

Unwmk.
1961, Sept. 24 Photo. ***Perf. 12***
B220 SP125 2fo + 1fo multi 70 70
B221 SP125 2fo + 1fo multi 70 70
B222 SP125 2fo + 1fo multi 70 70
B223 SP125 2fo + 1fo multi 70 70
a. Horiz. strip of 4, #B220-B223 3.25 3.25

Stamp Day, 1961, and Budapest Intl. Stamp Exhibition.

No. B223a has a continuous design.

Miniature presentation sheets, perf. and imperf., contain one each of Nos. B220-B223; size: 204x66½mm.

Soccer Type of Regular Issue, 1962

Design: Flags of Spain and Czechoslovakia.

1962, May 21 ***Perf. 11***
Flags in Original Colors
B224 A323 4fo + 1fo lt grn & bis 1.40 32

Austrian Stamp of 1850 with Pesth Postmark — SP126

Stamps: No. B226, #201. No. B227, #C164. No. B228, #C208.

Lithographed and Engraved
1962, Sept. 22 Unwmk. ***Perf. 11***
Design and Inscription in Dark Brown
B225 SP126 2fo + 1fo yellow 55 55
B226 SP126 2fo + 1fo pale pink 55 55
B227 SP126 2fo + 1fo pale blue 55 55
B228 SP126 2fo + 1fo pale yel grn 55 55
a. Horiz. strip of 4, #B225-B228 2.75 2.75
b. Souv. sheet of 4, #B225-B228 5.75 5.75

35th Stamp Day and 10th anniv. of Mabeosz, the Hungarian Phil. Fed.

Emblem, Cup and Soccer Ball — SP127

1962, Nov. 18 Photo. ***Perf. 11½x12***
B229 SP127 2fo + 1fo multi 60 50

Winning of the "Coupe de l'Europe Centrale" by the Steel Workers Sport Club (VASAS) in the Central European Soccer Championships.

Stamp Day — SP128

1963, Oct. 24 ***Perf. 11½x12***
Size: 32x43mm
B230 SP128 2fo + 1fo Hyacinth 50 50
B231 SP128 2fo + 1fo Narcissus 50 50
B232 SP128 2fo + 1fo Chrysanthemum 50 50
B233 SP128 2fo + 1fo Tiger lily 50 50
a. Horiz. strip of 4, #B230-B233 3.00 3.00
b. Min. sheet of 4, #B230-B233 3.75 3.75

#233b contains 25x32mm stamps, perf. 11.

Winter Olympic Type of 1963

Design: 4fo+1fo, Bobsledding.

1963, Nov. 11 ***Perf. 12***
B234 A342 4fo + 1fo grnsh bl & bis 90 38

New Year Type of Regular Issue

Good Luck Symbols: 2.50fo+1.20fo, Horseshoe, mistletoe and clover. 3fo+1.50fo, Pigs, clover and balloon, horiz.

Perf. 12x11½, 11½x12
1963, Dec. 12 Photo. Unwmk.
Sizes: 28x39mm (#B235); 28x22mm (#B206)
B235 A343 2.50fo + 1.20fo multi 55 25
B236 A343 3fo + 1.50fo multi 80 38

The surtax was for the modernization of the Hungarian Postal and Philatelic Museum.

Olympic Type of Regular Issue

Design: 3fo+1fo, Water polo.

1964, June 12 ***Perf. 11***
B237 A352 3fo + 1fo multi 75 90

Exhibition Hall — SP129

1964, July 23 Photo.
B238 SP129 3fo + 1.50fo blk, red org & gray 60 35

Tennis Exhibition, Budapest Sports Museum.

Twirling Woman Gymnast — SP130

1964, Sept. 4 ***Perf. 11½x12***
Size: 27x38mm
B239 SP130 2fo + 1fo Lilac 45 45
B240 SP130 2fo + 1fo Mallards 45 45
B241 SP130 2fo + 1fo Gymnast 45 45
B242 SP130 2fo + 1fo Rocket & globe 45 45
a. Horiz. strip of 4, #B239-B242 2.25 2.25
b. Souv. sheet of 4, #B239-B242 3.75 3.75

37th Stamp Day and Intl. Topical Stamp Exhib., IMEX. No. B242b contains 4 20x28mm stamps, perf. 11.

13th Century Tennis SP131

History of Tennis: 40f+10f, Indoor tennis, 16th century. 60f+10f, Tennis, 18th century. 70f+30f, Tennis court and castle. 80f+40f, Tennis court, Fontainebleau (buildings). 1fo+50f, Tennis, 17th century. 1.50fo+50f, W. C. Wingfield, Wimbledon champion 1877, and Wimbledon Cup. 1.70fo+50f, Davis Cup, 1900. 2fo+1fo, Bela Kehrling (1891-1937), Hungarian champion.

Lithographed and Engraved
1965, June 15 Unwmk. ***Perf. 12***
B243 SP131 30f + 10f mar, *dl org* 15 15
B244 SP131 40f + 10f blk, *pale lil* 15 15
B245 SP131 60f + 10f grn, *ol* 15 15
B246 SP131 70f + 30f lil, *brt grn* 22 15
B247 SP131 80f + 40f dk bl, *lt vio* 22 15
B248 SP131 1fo + 50f grn, *yel* 28 15
B249 SP131 1.50fo + 50f sep, *lt ol grn* 40 28
B250 SP131 1.70fo + 50f ind, *lt bl* 45 28
B251 SP131 2fo + 1fo dk red, *lt grn* 85 42
Nos. B243-B251 (9) 2.87 1.88

Flood Scene SP132

Design: 10fo+5fo, Relief commemorating 1838 flood.

1965, Aug. 14 Photo. *Perf. 12x11½*

B252 SP132 1fo + 50f org brn & bl 30 30

Souvenir Sheet

B253 SP132 10fo + 5fo gldn brn & buff 2.75 2.75

Surtax for aid to 1965 flood victims.

Geranium Stamp of 1950 (No. 909) SP133

Stamp Day: No. B255, #120. No. B256, #1489. No. B257, #1382.

Perf. 12x11½

1965, Oct. 30 Photo. Unwmk.

Stamps in Original Colors

B254 SP133 2fo + 1fo gray & dk bl 65 65
B255 SP133 2fo + 1fo gray & red 65 65
B256 SP133 2fo + 1fo gray & ocher 65 65
B257 SP133 2fo + 1fo gray & vio 65 65
a. Horiz. strip of 4, #B254-B257 3.00 3.00
b. Souv. sheet of 4, #B254-B257 3.75 3.75

#B254b contains 32x23mm stamps, perf. 11.

Soccer Type of Regular Issue

Design: 3fo+1fo, Championship emblem and map of Great Britain showing cities where matches were held.

1966, June 6 Photo. *Perf. 12x11½*

B258 A382 3fo + 1fo multi 60 50

Woman Archer and Danube at Visegrad SP134

Stamp Day: No. B260, Gloria Hungariae grapes and Lake Balaton. No. B261, Red poppies and ruins of Diosgyor Castle. No. B262, Russian space dogs Ugolek and Veterok.

1966, Sept. 16 Photo. *Perf. 12x11½*

B259 SP134 2fo + 50f multi 60 60
B260 SP134 2fo + 50f multi 60 60
B261 SP134 2fo + 50f multi 60 60
B262 SP134 2fo + 50f multi 60 60
a. Horiz. strip of 4, #B259-B262 2.75 2.75
b. Souv. sheet of 4, #B259-B262 3.25 3.25

#B262b contains 4 29x21mm stamps, perf. 11.

Anglers, C.I.P.S. Emblem and View of Danube SP135

1967, Aug. 22 Photo. *Perf. 12x11½*

B263 SP135 3fo + 1fo multi 90 45

See note after No. 1847

Olympic Type of Regular Issue

Design: 4fo+1fo, Indoor stadium and Winter Olympics emblem.

1968, Jan. 29 Photo. *Perf. 11*

B264 A402 4fo + 1fo multi 70 38

Jug, Western Hungary, 1618 — SP136

Hungarian Earthenware: No. B266, Tiszafüred vase, 1847. No. B267, Toby jug, 1848. No. B268, Decorative Baja plate, 1870. No. B269a, Jug, Northern Hungary, 1672. No. B269b, Decorative Mezőcsat plate, 1843. No. B269c, Decorative Moragy plate, 1860. No. B269d, Pitcher, Debrecen, 1793.

1968, Oct. 5 Litho. *Perf. 12*

B265 SP136 1fo + 50f ultra & multi 60 60
B266 SP136 1fo + 50f sky bl & multi 60 60
B267 SP136 1fo + 50f sepia & multi 60 60
B268 SP136 1fo + 50f yel brn & multi 60 60

Miniature Sheet

B269 Sheet of 4 3.25 3.25
a. SP136 2fo + 50f ultra & multi 55 55
b. SP136 2fo + 50f yel brn & multi 55 55
c. SP136 2fo + 50f ol & multi 55 55
d. SP136 2fo + 50f brt rose & multi 55 55

Issued for 41st Stamp Day. No. B269 contains 4 25x36mm stamps. See Nos. B271-B275.

Suspension Bridge, Buda Castle and Arms of Budapest — SP137

Lithographed and Engraved

1969, May 22 *Perf. 12*

B270 SP137 5fo + 2fo sep, pale yel & gray 1.00 1.00

Budapest 71 Philatelic Exposition.

Folk Art Type of 1968

Hungarian Wood Carvings: No. B271, Stirrup cup from Okorag, 1880. No. B272, Jar with flower decorations from Felsötiszavidek, 1898. No. B273, Round jug, Somogyharsagy, 1935. No. B274, Two-legged jug, Alföld, 1740. No. B275a, Carved panel (farm couple), Csorna, 1879. No. B275b, Tankard, Okany, 1914. No. B275c, Round jar with soldiers, Sellye, 1899. No. B275d, Square box with 2 women, Lengyeltoti, 1880.

1969, Sept. 13 Litho. *Perf. 12*

B271 SP136 1fo + 50f rose cl & multi 60 60
B272 SP136 1fo + 50f dp bis & multi 60 60
B273 SP136 1fo + 50f bl & multi 60 60
B274 SP136 1fo + 50f lt bl grn & multi 60 60

Miniature Sheet

B275 Sheet of 4 3.25 3.25
a. SP136 2fo + 50f ultra & multi 60 60
b. SP136 2fo + 50f brn org & multi 60 60
c. SP136 2fo + 50f lt brn & multi 60 60
d. SP136 2fo + 50f bl grn & multi 60 60

Issued for the 42nd Stamp Day. No. B275 contains 4 stamps (size: 25x36mm).

Fishermen's Bastion, Coronation Church and Chain Bridge — SP138

Designs: No. B277, Parliament and Elizabeth Bridge. No. B278, Castle and Margaret Bridge.

1970, Mar. 7 Litho. *Perf. 12*

B276 SP138 2fo + 1fo gldn brn & multi 50 50
B277 SP138 2fo + 1fo bl & multi 50 50
B278 SP138 2fo + 1fo lt vio & multi 50 50

Budapest 71 Philatelic Exhibition, commemorating the centenary of Hungarian postage stamps.

King Matthias I Corvinus — SP139

Initials and Paintings from Bibliotheca Corvina: No. B280, Letter "A." No. B281, Letter "N." No. B282, Letter "O." No. B283a, Ransanus Speaking before King Matthias. No. B283b, Scholar and letter "Q." No. B283c, Portrait of Appianus and letter "C." No. B283d, King David and letter "A."

1970, Aug. 22 Photo. *Perf. 11½x12*

B279 SP139 1fo + 50f multi 45 45
B280 SP139 1fo + 50f multi 45 45
B281 SP139 1fo + 50f multi 45 45
B282 SP139 1fo + 50f multi 45 45

Miniature Sheet

B283 Sheet of 4 3.00 3.00
a.-d. SP139 2fo + 50f, any single 55 55

Issued for the 43rd Stamp Day. No. B283 contains 4 stamps (size: 22½x32mm).

View of Buda, 1470 — SP140

Designs: No. B285, Buda, 1600. B286, Buda and Pest, about 1638. No. B287, Buda and Pest, 1770. No. B288a, Buda, 1777. No. B288b, Buda, 1850. No. B288c, Buda, 1895. No. B288d, Budapest, 1970.

1971, Feb. 26 Litho. *Perf. 12*

B284 SP140 2fo + 1fo blk & yel 60 60
B285 SP140 2fo + 1fo blk & pink 60 60
B286 SP140 2fo + 1fo blk & pale grn 60 60
B287 SP140 2fo + 1fo blk & pale sal 60 60

Souvenir Sheet

Perf. 10½

B288 Sheet of 4 3.00 3.00
a. SP140 2fo + 1fo blk & pale sal 60 60
b. SP140 2fo + 1fo blk & pale grn 60 60
c. SP140 2fo + 1fo blk & lilac 60 60
d. SP140 2fo + 1fo blk & pink 60 60

Budapest 71 Intl. Stamp Exhib. for the cent. of Hungarian postage stamps, Budapest, Sept. 4-12. No. B288 contains 4 stamps, size: 39½x18mm.

Iris and #P1 SP141

Designs: No. B290, Daisy and #199. No. B291, Poppy and #391. No. B292, Rose and #B128. No. B293a, Carnations and #200. No. B292b, Dahlia and #1069. No. B293c, Tulips and #C196. No. B293d, Anenomes and #C251.

1971, Sept. 4 Photo. *Perf. 12x11½*

B289 SP141 2fo + 1fo sil & multi 70 70
B290 SP141 2fo + 1fo sil & multi 70 70
B291 SP141 2fo + 1fo sil & multi 70 70
B292 SP141 2fo + 1fo sil & multi 70 70

Souvenir Sheet

Perf. 11½

B293 Sheet of 4 3.00 3.00
a.-d. SP141 2fo + 1fo, any single 55 55

Cent. of 1st Hungarian postage stamps and in connection with Budapest 71 Intl. Stamp Exhib., Sept. 4-12.

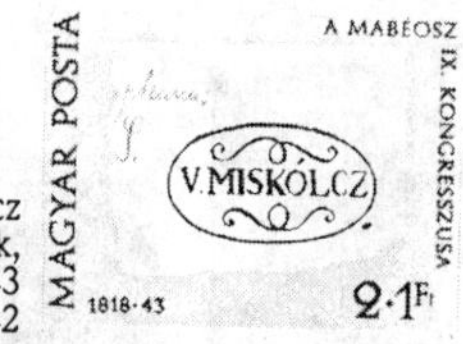

Miskólcz Postmark, 1818-43 SP142

Postmarks: No. B295, Szegedin, 1827-48. No. B296, Esztergom, 1848-51. No. B297, Budapest 1971 Exhibition. No. B298a, Paar family signet, 1593. No. B298b, Courier letter, 1708. No. B298c, First well-known Hungarian postmark "V. TOKAI," 1752. No. B298d, Letter, 1705.

1972, May *Perf. 12x11½*

B294 SP142 2fo + 1fo bl & blk 70 70
B295 SP142 2fo + 1fo yel & blk 70 70
B296 SP142 2fo + 1fo yel grn & blk 70 70
B297 SP142 2fo + 1fo ver & multi 70 70

Souvenir Sheet

B298 Sheet of 4 3.00 3.00
a. SP142 2fo + 1fo yel grn & multi 60 60
b. SP142 2fo + 1fo brn & multi 60 60
c. SP142 2fo + 1fo ultra & multi 60 60
d. SP142 2fo + 1fo red & multi 60 60

9th Congress of National Federation of Hungarian Philatelists (Mabeosz). No. B298 contains 4 stamps (size: 32x23mm).

Olympic Type of Regular Issue

Design: Wrestling and Olympic rings.

1972, July 15 Photo. *Perf. 11*

B299 A484 3fo + 1fo multi 55 40

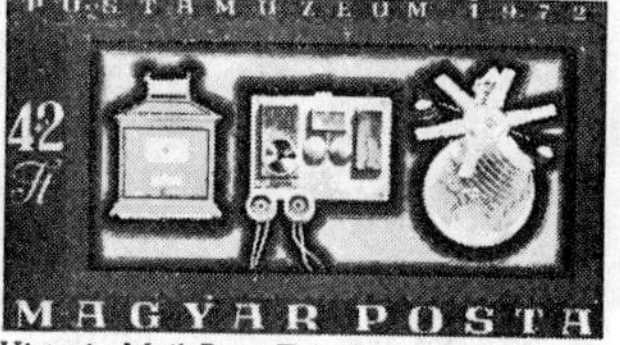

Historic Mail Box, Telephone and Molnya Satellite — SP143

Design: No. B301, Post horn, Tokai postmark, and Nos. 183, 1802, 1809.

1972, Oct. 27 Litho. *Perf. 12*

B300 SP143 4fo + 2fo grn & multi 90 80
B301 SP143 4fo + 2fo bl & multi 90 80

Reopening of the Post and Philatelic Museums, Budapest.

Bird on Silver Disk, 10th Century SP144

Treasures from Hungarian Natl. Museum. No. B303, Ring with serpent's head, 11th cent. No. B304, Lovers, belt buckle, 12th cent. No. B305, Flower, belt buckle, 15th cent. No. B306a, Opal pendant, 16th cent. No. B306b, Jeweled belt buckle, 18th cent. No. B306c, Flower pin, 17th cent. No. B306d, Rosette pendant, 17th cent.

1973, Sept. 22 Litho. *Perf. 12*

B302 SP144 2fo + 50f brn & multi 65 65
B303 SP144 2fo + 50f brt rose lil & multi 65 65
B304 SP144 2fo + 50f dk bl & multi 65 65
B305 SP144 2fo + 50f grn & multi 65 65

Souvenir Sheet

B306	Sheet of 4	2.75	2.75
a.	SP144 2fo + 50f brn & multi	42	42
b.	SP144 2fo + 50f car & multi	42	42
c.	SP144 2fo + 50f ol grn & multi	42	42
d.	SP144 2fo + 50f brt bl & multi	42	42

46th Stamp Day. No. B306 contains 4 stamps (size: 25x35mm).

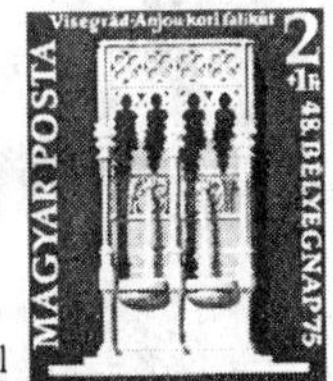

Gothic Wall Fountain — SP145

Visegrad Castle and Bas-reliefs — SP146

Designs: No. B308, Wellhead, Anjou period. No. B309, Twin lion-head wall fountain. B310, Fountain with Hercules riding dolphin. No. B311a, Raven panel. No. B311b, Visegrad Madonna. B311c, Lion panel. No. B311d, Visegrad Castle. Designs show artworks from Visegrad Palace of King Matthias Corvinus I, 15th century. Illustration SP146 is reduced.

1975, Sept. 13 Litho. *Perf. 12*

Multicolored and:

B307	SP145 2fo + 1fo green	2.00	2.00
B308	SP145 2fo + 1fo ver	2.00	2.00
B309	SP145 2fo + 1fo blue	2.00	2.00
B310	SP145 2fo + 1fo lilac	2.00	2.00
a.	Horizontal strip of 4	10.00	10.00

Souvenir Sheet

B311	Sheet of 4	12.00	12.00
a.	SP146 2fo + 1fo 21x32mm	1.65	1.65
b.	SP146 2fo + 1fo 47x32mm	1.65	1.65
c.	SP146 2fo + 1fo 21x32mm	1.65	1.65
d.	SP146 2fo + 1fo 99x32mm	1.65	1.65

European Architectural Heritage Year 1975 and 48th Stamp Day.

Knight — SP147

Gothic Sculptures, Buda Castle — SP148

Designs: Gothic sculptures from Buda Castle.

1976 Photo. *Perf. 12*

B312	SP147 2.50 + 1fo shown	60	60
B313	SP147 2.50 + 1fo Armor-bearer	60	60
B314	SP147 2.50 + 1fo Apostle	60	60
B315	SP147 2.50 + 1fo Bishop	60	60
a.	Horizontal strip of 4, #B312-B315	2.75	2.75

Souvenir Sheet

Designs: a, Man with hat. b, Woman with wimple. c, Man with cloth cap. d, Man with fur hat.

B316	Sheet of 4	3.00	3.00
a.-d.	SP148 2.50 + 1fo any single	55	55

49th Stamp Day.

No. B316 issued in connection with 10th Congress of National Federation of Hungarian Philatelists (Mabeosz).

Issued: #B316, May 22; #B312-B315, Sept. 4.

Young Runners — SP149

1977, Apr. 2 Litho. *Perf. 12*

B317 SP149 3fo + 1.50fo multi 80 80

Sports promotion among young people.

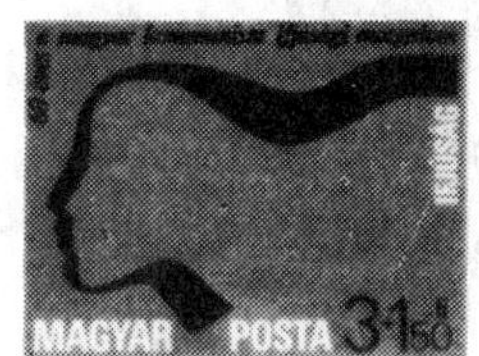

Young Man and Woman, Profiles SP150

1978, Apr. 1 Litho. *Perf. 12*

B318 SP150 3fo + 1.50fo multi 1.00 1.00

Hungarian Communist Youth Movement, 60th anniversary.

"Generations," by Gyula Derkovits — SP151

1978, May 6 Litho. *Perf. 12*

B319 SP151 3fo + 1.50fo multi 1.00 1.00

Szocfilex '78, Szombathely. No. B319 printed in sheets of 3 stamps and 3 labels showing Szocfilex emblem.

Girl Reading Book, by Ferenc Kovacs — SP152

1979, Mar. 31 Litho. *Perf. 12*

B320 SP152 3fo + 1.50fo blk & ultra 50 50

Surtax was for Junior Stamp Exhibition, Bekescsaba.

Watch Symbolizing Environmental Protection SP153

1980, Apr. 3 Litho. *Perf. 12*

B321 SP153 3fo + 1.50fo multi 75 75

Surtax was for Junior Stamp Exhibition, Dunaujvaros.

International Year of the Disabled SP154

Youths and Factory SP155

1981, May 15 Litho. *Perf. 12*

B322 SP154 2fo + 1fo multi 50 50

1981, May 29 *Perf. 12x11½*

B323 SP155 4fo + 2fo multi 80 80

Young Communist League, 10th Congress, Budapest, May 29-31.

European Junior Tennis Cup, July 25-Aug. 1 — SP156

1982, Apr. 2 Litho. *Perf. 12x11½*

B324 SP156 4fo + 2fo multi 80 80

Souvenir Sheet

SP157

Perf. 12½x11½

1982, June 11 Litho.

B325 SP157 20fo + 10fo multi 4.00 4.00

PHILEXFRANCE '82 Stamp Exhibition, Paris, June 11-21.

55th Stamp Day — SP158

Budapest Architecture and Statues: No. B326, Fishermen's Bastion, Janos Hunyadi (1403-1456). No. B327, Parliament, Ferenc Rakoczi the Second (1676-1735).

1982, Sept. 10 Litho. *Perf. 12*

B326	SP158 4fo + 2fo multi	90	90
B327	SP158 4fo + 2fo shown	90	90

Souvenir Sheet

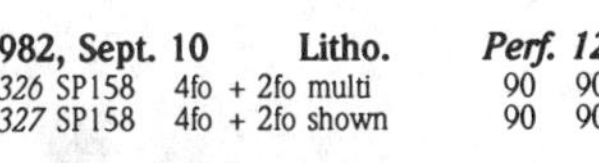

Parliament, Chain Bridge, Buda Castle, Budapest — SP159

Illustration reduced.

1982, Sept. 10 *Perf. 11½*

B328 SP159 20fo + 10fo multi 3.75 3.75

European Security and Cooperation Conference, 10th anniv.

21st Junior Stamp Exhibition, Baja, Mar. 31-Apr. 9 — SP160

1983, Mar. 31 Litho. *Perf. 12x11½*

B329 SP160 4fo + 2fo multi 90 90

Surtax was for show.

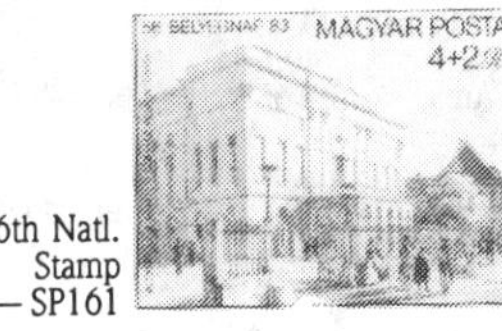

56th Natl. Stamp Day — SP161

Budapest Architecture (19th Cent. Engravings by): Rudolph Alt, H. Luders (No. B331).

1983, Sept. 9 Litho. *Perf. 12*

B330	SP161 4 + 2fo Old Natl. Theater	90	90
B331	SP161 4 + 2fo Municipal Concert Hall	90	90

Souvenir Sheet

Lithographed and Engraved

Perf. 11

B332 SP161 20 + 10fo Holy Trinity Square 4.25 4.00

No. B332 contains one stamp (28x45mm).

Mother and Child — SP162

1984, Apr. 2 Litho. *Perf. 12½x11½*

B333 SP162 4fo + 2fo multi 75 75

Surtax was for children's foundation.

15-Cent Minimum Value

The minimum catalogue value is 15 cents. Separating se-tenant pieces into individual stamps does not increase the value of the stamps since demand for the separated stamps may be small.

Little Red Riding Hood, by the Brothers Grimm — SP163

1985, Apr. 2 Litho. ***Perf. 11½x12***

B334 SP163 4fo + 2fo multi 75 75

Jacob (1785-1863) and Wilhelm (1786-1859) Grimm, fabulists and philologists.

Natl. SOS Children's Village Assoc., 3rd Anniv. SP164

1985, Dec. 10 Litho. ***Perf. 11***

B335 SP164 4fo + 2fo multi 75 75

Surtax for natl. SOS Children's Village.

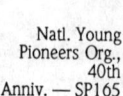

Natl. Young Pioneers Org., 40th Anniv. — SP165

1986, May 30 ***Perf. 11½x12½***

B336 SP165 4fo + 2fo multi 75 60

Souvenir Sheet

Budapest Natl. Theater SP166

Lithographed and Engraved

1986, Oct. 10 ***Perf. 11***

B337 SP166 20fo + 10fo tan, brn & buff 4.00 4.00

Surtax benefited natl. theater construction.

Natl. Communist Youth League, 30th Anniv. — SP167

1987, Mar. 20 ***Perf. 13½x13***

B338 SP167 4fo + 2fo multi 60 60

Souvenir Sheet

SOCFILEX '88, Aug. 12-21, Kecskemet — SP168

1988, Mar. 10 Litho. ***Perf. 11½***

B339 SP168 20fo +10fo multi 4.00 4.00

Surtax for SOCFILEX '88.

Sky High Tree, a Tapestry by Erzsebet Szekeres SP169

1989, Apr. 12 Litho. ***Perf. 12***

B340 SP169 5fo +2fo multi 1.50 1.50

Surtax to promote youth philately.

Souvenir Sheet

Battle of Solferino, by Carlo Bossoli — SP170

1989, Sept. 8 Litho. ***Perf. 10½***

B341 SP170 20fo +10fo multi 5.00 5.00

Stamp Day.

Souvenir Sheet

Martyrs of Arad, Arad, Romania, 1849 — SP171

1989, Oct. 6 ***Perf. 11½x12½***

B342 SP171 20fo +10fo multi 5.00 5.00

Surtax to fund production of another statue.

Teacher's Training High School, Sarospatak Municipal Arms SP172

1990, Mar. 30 Litho. ***Perf. 12x11½***

B343 SP172 8fo +4fo multi 2.00 2.00

28th Youth Stamp Exhibition, Sarospatak, Apr. 6-22.

Souvenir Sheet

Yesterday, by Endre Szasz — SP173

1990, Oct. 12 Litho. ***Perf. 12***

B344 SP173 20fo +10fo multi 3.75 3.75

Stamp Day. Surtax for National Federation of Hungarian Philatelists.

Tapestry, Peter and the Wolf, by Gabriella Hajnal — SP174

1991, Apr. 30 Litho. ***Perf. 12***

B345 SP174 12fo +6fo multi 2.00 1.15

Surtax to promote youth philately.

Children's Drawings SP175

Designs: 9fo + 4fo, Girl holding flower, vert. 10fo + 4fo, Child standing beneath sun. 15fo + 4fo, Boy wearing crown, vert.

1992, May 15 Litho. ***Perf. 12***

B346 SP175 9fo +4fo multi 1.65 1.65
B347 SP175 10fo +4fo multi 1.75 1.75
B348 SP175 15fo +4fo multi 2.40 2.40

Surtax for children's welfare.

Souvenir Sheet

1992 Summer Olympics, Barcelona — SP176

1992, Sept. 4 Litho. ***Perf. 12***

B349 SP176 50fo +20fo multi 5.00 5.00

Textile Art, by Erzsebet Szekeres SP177

1993, Apr. 14 Litho. ***Perf. 12***

B350 SP177 10fo +5fo Outdoor scene 75 75
B351 SP177 17fo +8fo Tree of life 1.25 1.25

Stamp Day SP178

Stamp designers, stamps: 10fo + 5fo, Zoltan Nagy (1916-1987), #1062. 17fo + 5fo, Sandor Legrady (1906-1987), #523. 50fo + 20fo, Ferenc Helbing (1870-1959), #465.

1993, Sept. 10 Litho. ***Perf. 12***

B352 SP178 10fo +5fo multi 32 16
B353 SP178 17fo +5fo multi 48 25

Souvenir Sheet

B354 SP178 50fo +20fo multi 1.50 75

No. B354 contains one 35x27mm stamp.

AIR POST STAMPS

Issues of the Monarchy

Nos. 120, 123 Surcharged in Red or Blue

REPÜLŐ POSTA

4 K 50 f

Wmk. 137

1918, July 4 Typo. ***Perf. 14***

C1 A10 1k 50f on 75f (R) 3.75 4.75
C2 A10 4k 50f on 2k (Bl) 3.00 4.00

Counterfeits exist.

No. 126 Surcharged

LEGI POSTA
12 korona

1920, Nov. 7

C3	A10	3k on 10k (G)	1.25	1.50
C4	A10	8k on 10k (R)	1.25	1.50
C5	A10	12k on 10k (Bl)	1.25	1.50
		Set, never hinged	4.75	

Icarus — AP3

1924-25 *Perf. 14*

C6	AP3	100k red brn & red	52	52
C7	AP3	500k bl grn & yel grn	52	52
C8	AP3	1000k bis brn & brn	52	52
C9	AP3	2000k dk bl & lt bl	52	52

Wmk. 133

C10	AP3	5000k dl vio & brt vio	90	90
C11	AP3	10000k red & dl vio	1.10	1.10
		Nos. C6-C11 (6)	4.08	4.08
		Set, never hinged	4.75	

Issue dates: 100k-2000k, Apr. 11, 1924. Others, Apr. 20, 1925.

For surcharges see Nos. J112-J116.

Mythical "Turul" — AP4

"Turul" Carrying Messenger

AP5 AP6

1927-30 Engr. *Perf. 14*

C12	AP4	4f orange ('30)	28	15
C13	AP4	12f deep green	28	15
C14	AP4	16f red brown	28	18
C15	AP4	20f carmine	28	24
C16	AP4	32f brown vio	1.50	1.00
C17	AP4	40f dp ultra	1.50	24
C18	AP5	50f claret	1.50	75
C19	AP5	72f olive grn	1.50	52
C20	AP5	80f dp violet	1.50	60
C21	AP5	1p emerald ('30)	2.50	60
C22	AP5	2p red ('30)	3.75	2.00
C23	AP5	5p dk blue ('30)	7.50	8.75
		Nos. C12-C23 (12)	22.37	15.18
		Set, never hinged	27.50	

1931, Mar. 27

Overprinted

C24	AP6	1p orange (Bk)	25.00	25.00
C25	AP6	2p dull vio (G)	25.00	25.00
a.		Strip of 7, #2817 2823	3.00	2.00
		Set, never hinged	75.00	

Monoplane over Danube Valley — AP7

Worker Welcoming Plane, Double Cross and Sun Rays — AP8

Spirit of Flight on Plane Wing — AP9

"Flight" Holding Propeller — AP10

Wmk. 210

1933, June 20 Photo. *Perf. 15*

C26	AP7	10f blue green	1.00	35
C27	AP7	16f purple	1.00	55

Perf. 12½x12

C28	AP8	20f carmine	3.25	55
C29	AP8	40f blue	3.25	65
C30	AP9	48f gray black	5.00	1.40
C31	AP9	72f bister brn	6.00	3.50
C32	AP10	1p yellow grn	9.50	2.50
C33	AP10	2p violet brn	25.00	9.00
C34	AP10	5p dk gray	87.50	70.00
		Nos. C26-C34 (9)	141.50	88.50
		Set, never hinged	175.00	

Catalogue values for unused stamps in this section, from this point to the end of the section, are for Never Hinged items.

Fokker F VII over Mail Coach — AP11

Plane over Parliament AP12

Airplane — AP13

1936, May 8 *Perf. 12x12½*

C35	AP11	10f brt green	32	16
C36	AP11	20f crimson	35	20
C37	AP11	36f brown	55	25
C38	AP12	40f brt blue	55	25
C39	AP12	52f red org	1.40	95
C40	AP12	60f brt violet	9.50	95
C41	AP12	80f dk sl grn	1.90	1.10
C42	AP13	1p dk yel grn	2.00	50
C43	AP13	2p brown car	4.25	1.65
C44	AP13	5p dark blue	14.00	9.25
		Nos. C35-C44 (10)	34.82	15.26

Issues of the Republic

Loyalty Tower, Sopron — AP14

Designs: 20f, Cathedral of Esztergom. 50f, Liberty Bridge, Budapest. 70f, Palace Hotel, Lillafüred. 1fo, Vajdahunyad Castle, Budapest. 1.40fo, Visegrád Fortress on the Danube. 3fo, Lake Balaton. 5fo, Parliament Building, Budapest.

Perf. 12½x12

1947, Mar. 5 Photo. Wmk. 210

C45	AP14	10f rose lake	1.00	24
C46	AP14	20f gray green	32	16
C47	AP14	50f copper brn	40	16
C48	AP14	70f olive grn	40	20
C49	AP14	1fo gray blue	75	24
C50	AP14	1.40fo brown	90	40
C51	AP14	3fo green	1.90	24
C52	AP14	5fo rose violet	4.00	1.65
		Nos. C45-C52 (8)	9.67	3.29

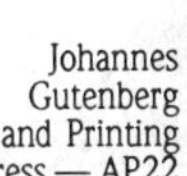

Johannes Gutenberg and Printing Press — AP22

Designs: 2f, Columbus. 4f, Robert Fulton. 5f, George Stephenson. 6f, David Schwarz and Ferdinand von Zeppelin. 8f, Thomas A. Edison. 10f, Louis Bleriot. 12f, Roald Amundsen. 30f, Kalman Kando. 40f, Alexander S. Popov.

Perf. 12x12½

1948, May 15 Wmk. 283

C53	AP22	1f orange red	15	15
C54	AP22	2f dp magenta	15	15
C55	AP22	4f blue	15	15
C56	AP22	5f orange brn	20	20
C57	AP22	6f green	20	20
C58	AP22	8f dp red vio	20	20
C59	AP22	10f brown	25	25
C60	AP22	12f blue grn	30	30
C61	AP22	30f brown rose	85	85
C62	AP22	40f blue violet	1.00	1.00
		Nos. C53-C62 (10)	3.45	3.45

Explorers and inventors.

See Nos. CB3-CB12.

UPU Type

1949, Nov. 1

C63	A171	2fo orange brn	52	52
a.		Booklet pane of 6	7.50	

75th anniv. of the UPU. See No. C81.

Chain Bridge Type and

Symbols of Labor AP25

1949, Nov. 20

C64	A172	1.60fo scarlet	70	70
C65	A172	2fo olive	80	80

Souvenir Sheet

Perf. 12½x12

C66	AP25	50fo carmine lake	140.00	135.00

Cent. of the opening of the Chain Bridge, Budapest.

Postman and Mail Carrying Vehicles AP26

1949, Dec. 11 *Perf. 12*

C67	AP26	50f lilac gray	3.50	3.50
		Sheet of 4	19.00	19.00

Stamp Day, 1949.

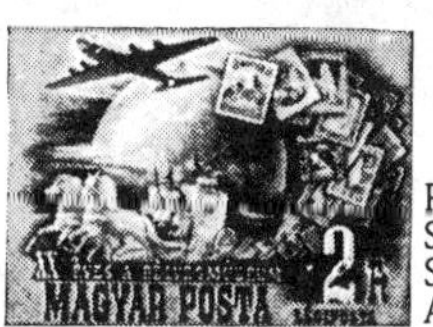

Plane, Globe, Stamps and Stagecoach AP27

1950, Mar. 12 *Perf. 12x12½*

C68	AP27	2fo red brn & yel	2.50	2.50

the 20th anniv. of the establishment of the Hungarian Post Office Philatelic Museum.

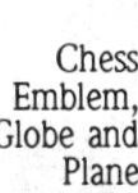

Chess Emblem, Globe and Plane AP28

1950, Apr. 9 Wmk. 106 *Perf. 12*

C69	AP28	1.60fo brown	1.75	1.00

Issued to publicize the World Chess Championship Matches, Budapest.

Globes, Parliament Building and Chain Bridge AP29

1950, May 16 *Perf. 12x12½*

C70	AP29	1fo red brown	40	15

Meeting of the World Federation of Trade Unions, Budapest, May 1950.

Statue of Liberty and View of Budapest — AP30

Designs: 30f, Crane and apartment house. 70f, Steel mill. 1fo, Stalinyec tractor. 1.60fo, Steamship. 2fo, Reaping-threshing machine. 3fo, Passenger train. 5fo, Matyas Rakosi Steel Mill, Csepel. 10fo, Budaörs Airport.

Perf. 12½x12

1950, Oct. 29 Engr. Unwmk.

C71	AP30	20f claret	48	25
C72	AP30	30f blue vio	48	20
C73	AP30	70f violet brn	25	20
C74	AP30	1fo yellow brn	25	20
C75	AP30	1.60fo ultra	48	40
C76	AP30	2fo red org	52	25
C77	AP30	3fo olive blk	75	40
C78	AP30	5fo gray blue	1.50	1.20
C79	AP30	10fo chestnut	4.75	1.75
		Nos. C71-C79 (9)	9.46	4.85

See Nos. C167 and C172.

Bem Type

Souvenir Sheet

1950, Dec. 10 Engr. *Imperf.*

C80	A185	2fo deep plum	20.00	18.00

Stamp Day and Budapest Stamp Exhibition.

UPU Type of 1949

Perf. 12x12½, Imperf.

1950, July 2 Photo. Wmk. 106

C81	A171	3fo dk car & dk brn	20.00	20.00
		Sheet of 4	175.00	175.00

Sports Type

Designs: 30f, Volleyball. 40f, Javelin-throwing. 60f, Sports badge. 70f, Soccer. 3fo, Glider meet.

1950, Dec. 2

C82	A188	30f lilac & magenta	22	20
C83	A188	40f olive & indigo	45	20
C84	A188	60f ol, dk brn & org red	80	40
C85	A188	70f gray & dk brn	1.10	60
C86	A188	3fo buff & dk brn	2.75	2.50
		Nos. C82-C86 (5)	5.32	3.90

Livestock Type

1951, Apr. 5 Photo. *Perf. 12x12½*

C87	A191	20f Mare & foal	22	22
C88	A191	70f Sow & shoats	60	35
C89	A191	1fo Ram & ewe	1.25	90
C90	A191	1.60fo Cow & calf	2.00	1.40

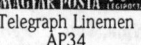

Telegraph Linemen AP34

Tank Column AP35

Designs: 1fo, Workers on vacation. 2fo, Air view of Stalin Bridge.

1951, Aug. 20

C91	AP34	70f henna brown	35	22
C92	AP34	1fo blue green	55	28
C93	AP34	2fo deep plum	1.10	45

Successful conclusion of the 1st year under Hungary's 5-year plan.

1951, Sept. 29 ***Perf. 12½x12***

C94	AP35	60f deep blue	30	20

Army Day, Sept. 29, 1951.

ist Stamp Type
Souvenir Sheet

1951, Oct. 6 Engr. Unwmk.

C95	A208	60f olive green	37.50	37.50

Stamp exhibition to commemorate the 80th anniv. of Hungary's 1st postage stamp.

Twelve hundred copies in rose lilac, perf. and imperf., were presented to exhibitors and members of the arranging committee of the exhibition. Value, each $500.

Avocet — AP37

Hungarian Birds: 30f, White stork. 40f, Golden oriole. 50f, Kentish plover. 60f, Black-winged stilt. 70f, Lesser gray shrike. 80f, Great bustard. 1fo, Redfooted falcon. 1.40fo, European bee-eater. 1.60fo, Glossy ibis. 2.50fo, Great white egret.

Perf. 13x11

1952, Mar. 16 Photo. Wmk. 106

Birds in Natural Colors

C96	AP37	20f emer, *grnsh*	16	15
C97	AP37	30f sage grn, *grysh*	16	15
C98	AP37	40f brown, *cr*	16	15
C99	AP37	50f orange, *cr*	20	15
C100	AP37	60f deep carmine	28	16
C101	AP37	70f red org, *cr*	28	16
C102	AP37	80f olive, *cr*	38	24
C103	AP37	1fo dp blue, *bluish*	55	30
C104	AP37	1.40fo gray, *grysh*	1.25	60
C105	AP37	1.60fo org brn, *cr*	1.40	65
C106	AP37	2.50fo rose vio, *cr*	2.00	90
		Nos. C96-C106 (11)	6.82	3.61

Olympic Games Type

Design: 2fo, Stadium, Budapest.

1952, May 26 ***Perf. 11***

C107	A217	1.70fo dp red orange	1.00	65
C108	A217	2fo olive brown	1.10	95

Issued to publicize Hungary's participation in the Olympic Games, Helsinki, 1952.

Leonardo da Vinci — AP39

1952, June 15 ***Perf. 12½x12***

C109	AP39	1.60fo shown	70	60
C110	AP39	2fo Victor Hugo	80	70

AP40

AP41

1953, Mar. 4 ***Perf. 12x12½***

C111	AP40	20f Red squirrel	42	18
C112	AP41	30f Hedgehog	42	18
C113	AP41	40f Hare	85	18
C114	AP40	50f Beech marten	55	25
C115	AP41	60f Otter	55	25
C116	AP41	70f Red fox	55	38
C117	AP40	80f Fallow deer	75	45
C118	AP41	1fo Roe deer	90	65
C119	AP41	1.50fo Boar	1.25	1.25
C120	AP40	2fo Red deer	1.90	1.40
		Nos. C111-C120 (10)	8.14	5.17

Children at Balaton Lake — AP42

Design: 1.50fo, Workers' Home at Lillafured.

1953, Apr. 19 ***Perf. 12***

C121	AP42	1fo brt grnsh blue	28	30
C122	AP42	1.50fo dp red lilac	65	40

People's Stadium Type

1953, Aug. 20 ***Perf. 11***

C123	A232	80f Water polo	35	16
C124	A232	1fo Boxing	35	20
C125	A232	2fo Soccer	80	40
C126	A232	3fo Track	1.40	1.00
C127	A232	5fo Stadium	1.90	1.40
		Nos. C123-C127 (5)	4.80	3.16

No. C125 Overprinted in Black

1953, Dec. 3

C128	A232	2fo green & brown	12.00	12.00

Hungary's success in the soccer matches at Wembley, England, Nov. 25, 1953. Counterfeits exist.

Janos Bihari and Scene from Verbunkos AP44

Portraits: 40f, Ferenc Erkel. 60f, Franz Liszt. 70f, Mihaly Mosonyi. 80f, Karl Goldmark. 1fo, Bela Bartok. 2fo, Zoltan Kodaly.

1953, Dec. 5 Photo. ***Perf. 12***

Frames and Portraits in Brown

C129	AP44	30f blue gray	15	15
C130	AP44	40f orange	15	15
C131	AP44	60f green	15	15
C132	AP44	70f red	18	16
C133	AP44	80f gray blue	20	24
C134	AP44	1fo olive bis	52	32
C135	AP44	2fo violet	1.00	80
		Nos. C129-C135 (7)	2.35	1.97

Hungarian composers.

Carrot Beetle — AP45

May (or June) Beetle — AP46

Designs: Various beetles. 60f, Bee.

Perf. 12½x12, 12x12½

1954, Feb. 6 Wmk. 106

C136	AP45	30f dp org & dk brn	28	18
C137	AP46	40f grn & dk brn	28	18
C138	AP46	50f rose brn & blk	52	24
C139	AP46	60f vio, dk brn & yel	28	24
C140	AP45	80f grnsh gray, pur & rose	28	24
C141	AP45	1fo ocher & blk	1.00	38
C142	AP46	1.20fo dl grn & dk brn	90	60
C143	AP46	1.50fo ol brn & dk brn	90	80
C144	AP46	2fo hn brn & dk brn	1.40	1.25
C145	AP45	3fo bl grn & dk brn	2.25	2.00
		Nos. C136-C145 (10)	8.09	6.11

Lunchtime at the Nursery AP47

Designs: 1.50fo, Mother taking child from doctor. 2fo, Nurse and children.

1954, Mar. 8 ***Perf. 12***

C146	AP47	1fo olive green	20	15
C147	AP47	1.50fo red brown	45	35
C148	AP47	2fo blue green	90	65

Model Glider Construction — AP48

Boy Flying Model Glider AP49

Designs: 60f, Gliders. 80f, Pilot leaving plane. 1fo, Parachutists. 1.20fo, Biplane. 1.50fo, Plane over Danube. 2fo, Jet planes.

1954, June 25 ***Perf. 11***

C149	AP48	40f brn, ol & dk bl gray	15	15
C150	AP49	50f gray & red brn	15	15
C151	AP48	60f red brn & dk bl gray	15	15
C152	AP49	80f violet & sep	20	15
C153	AP48	1fo brn & dk bl gray	24	16
C154	AP49	1.20fo olive & sep	60	28
C155	AP48	1.50fo cl & dk bl gray	1.00	90
C156	AP49	2fo blue & dk brn	1.25	90
		Nos. C149-C156 (8)	3.74	2.84

Jokai Type
Souvenir Sheet

1954, Oct. 17 Engr. ***Perf. 12½x12***

C157	A242	1fo violet blue	15.00	15.00

Stamp Day. Exists imperforate.

Children on Sled — AP51

Skaters AP52

Designs: 50f, Ski racer. 60f, Ice yacht. 80f, Ice hockey. 1fo, Ski jumper. 1.50fo, Downhill ski racer. 2fo, Man and woman exhibition-skating.

1955 Photo. ***Perf. 12***

C158	AP51	40f multi	58	35
C159	AP52	50f multi	25	18
C160	AP51	60f multi	35	18
C161	AP52	80f multi	42	18
C162	AP51	1fo multi	70	22
C163	AP52	1.20fo multi	95	55
C164	AP51	1.50fo multi	1.65	1.10
C165	AP52	2fo multi	1.65	1.25
		Nos. C158-C165 (8)	6.55	4.01

The 1.20fo and 2fo were issued Jan. 27; others Feb. 26.

Government Printing Plant Type
Souvenir Sheet

1955, May 28 ***Perf. 12x12½***

C166	A247	5fo hn brn & gray grn	14.00	12.50

Cent. of the establishment of the government printing plant.

No. C78 Printed on Aluminum Foil

Perf. 12½x12

1955, Oct. 5 Engr. Unwmk.

C167	AP30	5fo gray blue	7.50	7.50

Intl. Cong. of the Light Metal Industry and for 20 years of aluminum production in Hungary. Imperfs. exist.

Bartok Type

Wmk. 106

1955, Oct. 9 Photo. ***Perf. 12***

C168	A252	1fo gray green	1.25	85
C169	A252	1fo violet brn	2.50	1.75
a.		With ticket	12.50	12.50

10th anniv. of the death of Bela Bartok, composer. No. C169a was issued for the Day of the Stamp, Oct. 16, 1955. The 5fo sales price, marked on the attached ticket, was the admission fee to any one of 14 simultaneous stamp shows.

"Esperanto" AP55

Lazarus Ludwig Zamenhof — AP56

1957, June 8

C170 AP55 60f red brown 25 25
C171 AP56 1fo dark green 30 30

10th anniversary of the death of L. L. Zamenhof, inventor of Esperanto.

Type of 1950

Design: 20fo, Budaörs Airport.

Perf. 12½x12

1957, July 18 Engr. Unwmk.

C172 AP30 20fo dk slate grn 7.00 4.50
Punched 3 holes 6.00 4.00

A few days after issuance, stocks of No. C172 were punched with three holes and used on domestic surface mail.

Courier and Fort Buda AP57

Design: No. C174, Plane over Budapest.

Wmk. 106

1957, Oct. 13 Photo. *Perf. 12*

C173 AP57 1fo ol bis & brn, *buff* 75 75
C174 AP57 1fo ol bis & dp cl, *buff* 75 75
a. Strip of #C173-C174 + label 2.25 2.25

Stamp Day, Oct. 20th. The triptych sold for 6fo.

Type of Regular Pigeon Issue

Design: 3fo, Two carrier pigeons.

1957, Dec. 14 *Perf. 12x12½*

C175 A266 3fo red, grn, gray & blk 75 50

Hungarian Pavilion, Brussels AP58

Designs: 40f, Map, lake and local products. 60f, Parliament. 1fo, Chain Bridge, Budapest. 1.40fo, Arms of Hungary and Belgium. 2fo, Fountain, Brussels, vert. 3fo, City Hall, Brussels vert. 5fo, Exposition emblem.

Perf. 14½x15

1958, Apr. 17 Litho. Wmk. 106

C176 AP58 20f red org & red brn 25 15
C177 AP58 40f lt blue & brn 25 18
C178 AP58 60f crimson & sep 15 15
C179 AP58 1fo bis & red brn 20 15
C180 AP58 1.40fo dull vio & multi 30 22
C181 AP58 2fo gldn brn & dk brn 45 25
C182 AP58 3fo bl grn & sep 1.10 60
C183 AP58 5fo gray ol, blk, red, bl & yel 2.00 1.25
Nos. C176-C183 (8) 4.70 2.95

Universal and Intl. Exposition at Brussels.

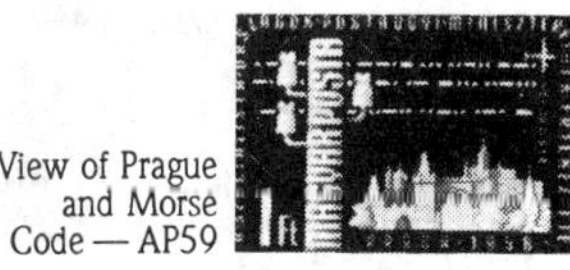

View of Prague and Morse Code — AP59

1958, June 30 Photo. *Perf. 12x12½*

C184 AP59 1fo rose brown 35 20

See No. 1194a for se-tenant pair.

Conference of Postal Ministers of Communist Countries at Prague, June 30-July 8.

Post Horn, Pigeon and Pen — AP60

Design: No. C185, Stamp under magnifying glass.

1958, Oct. 25 Wmk. 106 *Perf. 12*

C185 AP60 1fo dp car & bis 55 55
C186 AP60 1fo yel grn & bis 55 55
a. Strip, #C185-C186 + label 1.50 1.50

Natl. Stamp Exhib., Budapest, Oct. 25-Nov. 2. #C185 inscribed: "XXXI Belyegnap 1958."

1958, Oct. 26

Designs: 60f, as No. C186. 1fo, Ship, plane, locomotive and pen surrounding letter.

C187 AP60 60f dp plum & grysh buff 30 15
C188 AP60 1fo bl & grysh buff 45 20

Issued for Letter Writing Week.

Plane over Heroes' Square Budapest — AP61

Design: 5fo, Plane over Tower of Sopron.

Perf. 12½x12

1958, Nov. 3 Engr. Wmk. 106

C189 AP61 3fo gray, rose vio & red 1.25 60
C190 AP61 5fo gray, dk bl & red 1.50 90

40th anniv. of Hungarian air post stamps.

Same Without Commemorative Inscription

Plane over: 20f, Szeged. 30f, Sarospatak. 70f, Gyor. 1fo, Budapest, Opera House. 1.60fo, Veszprém. 2fo, Budapest, Chain Bridge. 3fo, Sopron. 5fo, Heroes' Square, Budapest. 10fo, Budapest, Academy of Science and Parliament. 20fo, Budapest.

1958, Dec. 31 Engr. Wmk. 106
Yellow Paper and Vermilion Inscriptions

C191 AP61 20f green 15 15
C192 AP61 30f violet 15 15
C193 AP61 70f brown vio 15 15
C194 AP61 1fo blue 15 15
C195 AP61 1.60fo purple 18 15
C196 AP61 2fo Prus green 22 15
C197 AP61 3fo brown 35 15
C198 AP61 5fo olive green 45 20
C199 AP61 10fo dark blue 1.40 35
C200 AP61 20fo brown 2.75 90
Nos. C191-C200 (10) 5.95
Set value 2.05

Transport Type of Regular Issue

Design: 3fo, Early plane.

1959, May Litho. *Perf. 14½x15*

C201 A279 3fo dl lil, blk, yel & brn 1.25 95

Tihany — AP62

Designs: 70f, Ship. 1fo, Heviz and water lily. 1.70fo, Sailboat and fisherman statue.

1959, July 15 Photo. *Perf. 11½x12*

C202 AP62 20f brt green 15 15
C203 AP62 70f brt blue 16 15
C204 AP62 1fo ultra & car rose 24 18
C205 AP62 1.70fo red brn, *yel* 52 30

Issued to publicize Lake Balaton and the opening of the Summer University.

Moth-Butterfly Type of 1959

Butterflies: 1fo, Lycaena virgaureae. 2fo, Acherontia atropos, horiz. 3fo, Red admiral.

Perf. 11½x12, 12x11½

1959, Nov. 20 Wmk. 106
Butterflies in Natural Colors

C206 A290 1fo black & lt bl grn 70 24
C207 A290 2fo black & lilac 1.40 65
C208 A290 3fo dk gray & emer 2.00 1.00

Souvenir Sheet

Rockets in Orbit, Gagarin, Titov & Glenn — AP63

Perf. 11, Imperf.

1962, Mar. 29 Unwmk.

C209 AP63 10fo multi 11.00 10.00

Issued to honor astronauts Yuri A. Gagarin and Gherman Titov of Russia and John H. Glenn, Jr., US.

Soccer Type of 1962

Flags of Hungary and Great Britain.

1962, May 21 Photo. *Perf. 11*
Flags in National Colors

C209A A323 2fo grnsh bis 70 32

Glider and Lilienthal's 1898 Design AP64

Designs: 30f, Icarus and Aero Club emblem. 60f, Light monoplane and 1912 aerobatic plane. 80f, Airship GZ-1 and Montgolfier balloon. 1fo, IL-18 Malev and Wright 1903 plane. 1.40fo, Stunt plane and Nyesterov's 1913 plane. 2fo, Helicopter and Asboth's 1929 helicopter. 3fo, Supersonic bomber and Zhukovski's turbomotor. 4fo, Space rocket and Tsiolkovsky's rocket.

1962, July 19 Unwmk. *Perf. 15*

C210 AP64 30f blue & dull yel 15 15
C211 AP64 40f yel grn & ultra 15 15
C212 AP64 60f ultra & ver 15 15
C213 AP64 80f grnsh bl & sil 15 15
C214 AP64 1fo lilac, sil & bl 18 15
C215 AP64 1.40fo blue & org 18 15
C216 AP64 2fo bluish grn & brn 28 22
C217 AP64 3fo vio, sil & bl 60 28
C218 AP64 4fo grn, sil & blk 1.10 50
Nos. C210-C218 (9) 2.94
Set value 1.45

Issued to show flight development: "From Icarus to the Space Rocket."

Earth, TV Screens and Rockets — AP65

Design: 2fo, Andrian G. Nikolayev, Pavel R. Popovich and rockets.

1962, Sept. 4 *Perf. 12*

C219 AP65 1fo dk bl & org brn 60 35
C220 AP65 2fo dk bl & org brn 70 55

First group space flight of Vostoks 3 and 4, Aug. 11-15, 1962. Printed in alternating horizontal rows.

John H. Glenn, Jr. — AP66

Astronauts: 40f, Yuri A. Gagarin. 60f, Gherman Titov. 1.40fo, Scott Carpenter. 1.70fo, Andrian G. Nikolayev. 2.60fo, Pavel R. Popovich. 3fo, Walter Schirra.

1962, Oct. 27 *Perf. 12x11½*
Portraits in Bister

C221 AP66 40f purple 15 15
C222 AP66 60f dark green 15 15
C223 AP66 1fo dark bl grn 18 15
C224 AP66 1.40fo dark brown 18 15
C225 AP66 1.70fo deep blue 35 24
C226 AP66 2.60fo violet 70 35
C227 AP66 3fo red brown 1.25 60
Nos. C221-C227 (7) 2.96 1.79

Issued to honor the first seven astronauts and in connection with the Astronautical Congress in Paris.

Eagle Owl — AP67

Birds: 40f, Osprey. 60f, Marsh harrier. 80f, Booted eagle. 1fo, African fish eagle. 2fo, Lammergeier. 3fo, Golden eagle. 4fo, Kestrel.

1962, Nov. 18 Litho. *Perf. 11½*
Birds in Natural Colors

C228 AP67 30f yel grn & blk 15 15
C229 AP67 40f org yel & blk 15 15
C230 AP67 60f bister & blk 15 15
C231 AP67 80f lt grn & blk 20 15
C232 AP67 1fo ol bis & blk 24 20
C233 AP67 2fo bluish grn & blk 35 20
C234 AP67 3fo lt vio & blk 75 38
C235 AP67 4fo dp org & blk 1.40 75
Nos. C228-C235 (8) 3.39 2.13

Radio Mast and Albania No. 623 — AP68

Designs (Communication symbols and rocket stamps of various countries): 30f, Bulgaria #C77, vert. 40f, Czechoslovakia #1108. 50f, Communist China #380. 60f, North Korea. 80f, Poland #875. 1fo, Hungary #1386. 1.20fo, Mongolia #189, vert. 1.40fo, DDR #580. 1.70fo, Romania #1200. 2fo, Russia #2456, vert. 2.60fo, North Viet Nam.

Perf. 12x11½, 11½x12

1963, May 9 Photo. Unwmk.
Stamp Reproductions in Original Colors

C236 AP68 20f olive green 15 15
C237 AP68 30f rose lake 15 15
C238 AP68 40f violet 15 15
C239 AP68 50f brt blue 15 15
C240 AP68 60f orange brn 15 15
C241 AP68 80f ultra 15 15
C242 AP68 1fo dull red brn 20 15
C243 AP68 1.20fo aqua 20 15
C244 AP68 1.40fo olive 30 15
C245 AP68 1.70fo brown olive 30 18
C246 AP68 2fo rose lilac 45 24
C247 AP68 2.60fo bluish green 95 48
Nos. C236-C247 (12) 3.30
Set value 1.65

5th Conference of Postal Ministers of Communist Countries, Budapest.

Souvenir Sheet

Globe and Spaceships — AP69

Perf. 11½x12, Imperf.

1963, July 13 **Unwmk.**

C248 AP69 10fo dk & lt blue 8.75 8.75

Space flights of Valeri Bykovski, June 14-19, and Valentina Tereshkova, 1st woman cosmonaut, June 16-19, 1963.

Souvenir Sheet

Mt. Fuji and Stadium — AP70

1964, Sept. 22 Photo. ***Perf. 11½x12***

C249 AP70 10fo multi 5.50 5.00

18th Olympic Games, Tokyo, Oct. 10-24. Exists imperf.

Bridge Type of 1964
Souvenir Sheet

Design: Elizabeth Bridge.

1964, Nov. 21 Photo. ***Perf. 11***

C250 A356 10fo silver & dp grn 3.75 3.50

No. C250 contains one 59x20mm stamp.

Lt. Col. Alexei Leonov in Space — AP71

Design: 2fo, Col. Pavel Belyayev, Lt. Col. Alexei Leonov and Voskhod 2.

1965, Apr. 17 Photo. ***Perf. 11½x12***

C251 AP71 1fo violet & gray 48 15
C252 AP71 2fo rose claret & ocher 1.10 65

Space flight of Voskhod 2 and of Lt. Col. Alexei Leonov, the first man floating in space.

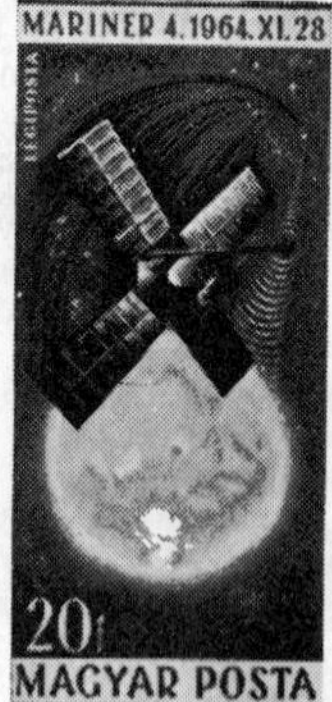

Mariner IV (USA)
AP72

Plane over Helsinki
AP73

New achievements in space research: 30f, San Marco satellite, Italy. 40f, Molniya satellite, USSR. 60f, Moon rocket, 1965, USSR. 1fo, Shapir rocket, France. 2.50fo, Zond III satellite, USSR. 3fo, Syncom III satellite, US. 10fo, Rocket sending off satellites, horiz.

1965, Dec. 31 Photo. ***Perf. 11***

C253 AP72 20f ultra, blk & org yel 15 15
C254 AP72 30f brn, vio & yel 15 15
C255 AP72 40f vio, brn & pink 15 15
C256 AP72 60f lt pur, blk & org yel 16 18
C257 AP72 1fo red lil, blk & buff 32 22
C258 AP72 2.50fo rose cl, blk & gray 80 35
C259 AP72 3fo bl grn, blk & bis 90 70
Nos. C253-C259 (7) 2.63
Set value 1.65

Souvenir Sheet

1965, Dec. 20

C260 AP72 10fo brt bl, yel & dk ol 4.50 4.00

Sport Type of Regular Issue
Souvenir Sheet

Design: 10fo, Women hurdlers and Ferihegy airport.

1966, Sept. 4 Photo. ***Perf. 12x11½***

C261 A384 10fo brt bl, brn & red 4.50 4.50

1966-67 Photo. ***Perf. 12x11½***

Plane over Cities Served by Hungarian Airlines: 50f, Athens. 1fo, Beirut. 1.10fo, Frankfort on the Main. 1.20fo, Cairo. 1.50fo, Copenhagen. 2fo, London. 2.50fo, Moscow. 3fo, Paris. 4fo, Prague. 5fo, Rome. 10fo, Damascus. 20fo, Budapest.

C262 AP73 20f brown org 15 15
C263 AP73 50f brown 15 15
C264 AP73 1fo blue 15 15
C265 AP73 1.10fo black 15 15
C266 AP73 1.20fo orange 15 15
C267 AP73 1.50fo blue grn 15 15
C268 AP73 2fo brt blue 24 15
C269 AP73 2.50fo brt red 20 18
C270 AP73 3fo yel grn 28 18
C271 AP73 4fo brown red 1.00 85
C272 AP73 5fo brt pur 50 24
C273 AP73 10fo violet bl ('67) 1.40 40
C274 AP73 20fo gray ol ('67) 1.25 70
Nos. C262-C274 (13) 5.77
Set value 3.00

See No. C276.

Souvenir Sheet

Icarus Falling — AP73a

1968, May 11 Photo. ***Perf. 11***

C275 AP73a 10fo multicolored 3.50 3.50

In memory of the astronauts Edward H. White, US, Vladimir M. Komarov and Yuri A. Gagarin, USSR.

Type of 1966-67 without "Legiposta" Inscription

Design: 2.60fo, Malev Airlines jet over St. Stephen's Cathedral, Vienna.

1968, July 4 Photo. ***Perf. 12x11½***

C276 AP73 2.60fo violet 50 18

50th anniv. of regular airmail service between Budapest and Vienna.

Women Swimmers and Aztec Calendar Stone — AP74

Aztec Calendar Stone, Olympic Rings and: 60f, Soccer. 80f, Wrestling. 1fo, Canoeing. 1.40fo, Gymnast on rings. 3fo, Fencing. 4fo, Javelin.

1968, Aug. 21 Photo. ***Perf. 12***

C277 AP74 20f brt bl & multi 15 15
C278 AP74 60f green & multi 15 15
C279 AP74 80f car rose & multi 15 15
C280 AP74 1fo grnsh bl & multi 15 15
C281 AP74 1.40fo violet & multi 24 15
C282 AP74 3fo brt lilac & multi 75 35
C283 AP74 4fo green & multi 1.10 60
Nos. C277-C283,CB31 (8) 3.07
Set value 1.70

Issued to publicize the 19th Olympic Games, Mexico City, Oct. 12-27.

Souvenir Sheet

Apollo 8 Trip Around the Moon — AP75

1969, Feb. Photo. ***Perf. 12½***

C284 AP75 10fo multi 3.75 3.75

Man's 1st flight around the moon, Dec. 21-27, 1968.

Soyuz 4 and 5, and Men in Space
AP76

Design: No. C286, Soyuz 4 and 5.

1969, Mar. 21 Photo. ***Perf. 12x11½***

C285 AP76 2fo multi 35 35
C286 AP76 2fo dk bl, lt bl & red 35 35
a. Strip, # C285-C286 + label 85

First team flights of Russian spacecraft Soyuz 4 and 5, Jan. 16, 1969.

Journey to the Moon, by Jules Verne — AP77

Designs: 60f, Tsiolkovski's space station. 1fo, Luna 1. 1.50fo, Ranger 7. 2fo, Luna 9 landing on moon. 2.50fo, Apollo 8 in orbit around moon. 3fo, Soyuz 4 and 5 docking in space. 4fo, Lunar landing module landing on moon. 10fo, Apollo 11 astronauts on moon and lunar landing module.

1969 Photo. ***Perf. 12x11½***

C287 AP77 40f multi 15 15
C288 AP77 60f multi 15 15
C289 AP77 1fo multi 15 15
C290 AP77 1.50fo multi 18 15
C291 AP77 2fo multi 24 15
C292 AP77 2.50fo multi 28 24
C293 AP77 3fo multi 75 24
C294 AP77 4fo multi 1.10 60
Nos. C287-C294 (8) 3.00
Set value 1.50

Souvenir Sheet
Perf. 11

C295 AP77 10fo multi 6.50 6.50

Moon landing issue. See note after Algeria No. 427.

No. C295 contains one 74x49mm stamp. Issued: #C287-C294, Nov. 1; #C295, Aug. 15.

Daimler, 1886 — AP78

Automobiles: 60f, Peugeot, 1894. 1fo, Benz, 1901. 1.50fo, Cudell mail truck, 1902. 2fo, Rolls Royce, 1908. 2.50fo, Model T Ford, 1908. 3fo, Vermorel, 1912. 4fo, Csonka mail car, 1912.

1970, Mar. Photo. ***Perf. 12***

C296 AP78 40f ocher & multi 15 15
C297 AP78 60f multi 15 15
C298 AP78 1fo red & multi 15 15
C299 AP78 1.50fo bl & multi 15 15
C300 AP78 2fo multi 30 22
C301 AP78 2.50fo vio & multi 38 22
C302 AP78 3fo multi 60 42
C303 AP78 4fo multi 1.25 85
Nos. C296-C303 (8) 3.13
Set value 2.00

American Astronauts on Moon
AP79

Design: No. C305, Soyuz 6, 7 and 8 in space.

1970, Mar. 20 Photo. ***Perf. 11***

C304 AP79 3fo blue & multi 75 75
C305 AP79 3fo car rose & multi 75 75

Landing of Apollo 12 on the moon, Nov. 14, 1969, and group flight of Russian spacecraft Soyuz 6, 7 & 8, Oct. 11-13, 1969.

Nos. C304-C305 issued in sheets of 4. Size: 112½x78mm.

"Rain at Foot of Fujiyama," by Hokusai, and Pavilion — AP80

Design: 3fo, Sun Tower, Peace Bell and globe.

1970, Apr. 30 Photo. ***Perf. 12½***

C306 AP80 2fo multi 75 75
C307 AP80 3fo multi 75 75

Issued to publicize EXPO '70 International Exhibition, Osaka, Japan, Mar. 15-Sept. 13.

Miniature Sheets

Phases of Apollo 13 Moon Flight — AP81

Designs of Vignettes of No. C308: Apollo 13 over moon; return to earth; capsule with parachutes; capsule floating, aircraft carrier and helicopter.

Designs of Vignettes of No. C309: Soyuz 9 on way to launching pad; launching of Soyuz 9 capsule in orbit; astronauts Andrian Nikolayev and Vitaly Sevastyanov.

Designs of Vignettes of No. C310: Luna 16 approaching moon; module on moon; landing; nose cone on ground.

Designs of Vignettes of No. C311: Lunokhod 1 on moon; trajectories of Luna 17 around earth and moon.

1970-71 Litho. *Perf. 11½*

C308	AP81	Sheet of 4	3.00	3.00

Photo.

C309	AP81	Sheet of 4	3.00	3.00
C310	AP81	Sheet of 4 ('71)	3.00	3.00
C311	AP81	Sheet of 4 ('71)	3.00	3.00

Nos. C308-C311 were valid for postage only as full sheets. Each contains four 2.50fo vignettes which were not valid singly.

No. C308 for the aborted moon flight and safe return of Apollo 13, American spaceship, Apr. 11-17, 1970. Issued June 10.

No. C309 for the 424-hour flight of Soyuz 9, Russian spaceship, June 1-9. Issued Sept. 4.

No. C310 for Luna 16, the unmanned, automated Russian moon mission, Sept. 12-24, 1970. Issued Jan. 15, 1971.

No. C311 for Luna 17, unmanned, automated Russian moon mission, Nov. 10-17, 1970. Issued Mar. 8, 1971.

Souvenir Sheet

American Astronauts on Moon — AP82

1971, Mar. 31 *Perf. 12½*

C312	AP82	10fo multi	3.75	3.75

Apollo 14 moon landing, Jan. 31-Feb. 9, 1971. See Nos. C315, C326-C328.

Hunting Type of Regular Issue
Souvenir Sheet

Design: 10fo, Red deer group.

1971, Aug. 27 Photo. *Perf. 11*

C313	A460	10fo multi	3.75	3.75

No. C313 contains one 70x45mm stamp.

Astronauts Volkov, Dobrovolsky and Patsayev — AP83

Souvenir Sheet

1971, Oct. 4 Photo. *Perf. 12½*

C314	AP83	10fo multi	2.50	2.50

In memory of the Russian astronauts Vladislav N. Volkov, Lt. Col. Georgi T. Dobrovolsky and Victor I. Patsayev, who died during the Soyuz 11 space mission, June 6-30, 1971.

Apollo 14 Type of 1971
Souvenir Sheet

Design: 10fo, American Lunar Rover on moon.

1972, Jan. 20 Photo. *Perf. 12½*

C315	AP82	10fo multi	3.50	3.50

Apollo 15 moon mission, July 26-Aug. 7, 1971.

Soccer and Hungarian Flag — AP84

Various Scenes from Soccer and Natl. Flags of: 60f, Romania. 80f, DDR. 1fo, Great Britain. 1.20fo, Yugoslavia. 2fo, USSR. 4fo, Italy. 5fo, Belgium.

1972, Apr. 29

C316	AP84	40f gold & multi	15	15
C317	AP84	60f gold & multi	15	15
C318	AP84	80f gold & multi	15	15
C319	AP84	1fo gold & multi	15	15
C320	AP84	1.20fo gold & multi	24	15
C321	AP84	2fo gold & multi	35	18
C322	AP84	4fo gold & multi	85	45
C323	AP84	5fo gold & multi	1.25	75
a.		Sheet of 8, #C316-C323	3.75	3.75
		Nos. C316-C323 (8)	3.29	
		Set value		1.80

European Soccer Championships for the Henri Delaunay Cup.

Nos. C316-C321 were later issued individually in sheets of 20 and in partly changed colors.

Souvenir Sheet

Olympic Rings and Globe — AP85

1972, June 10 Photo. *Perf. 12½*

C324	AP85	10fo multi	8.00	8.00

20th Olympic Games, Munich, Aug. 26-Sept. 11.

Olympic Type of Regular Issue
Souvenir Sheet

Design: Equestrian and Olympic Rings.

1972, July 15 Photo. *Perf. 12½*

C325	A484	10fo multi	3.75	3.75

20th Olympic Games, Munich, Aug. 26-Sept. 11. #C325 contains one 43x43mm stamp.

Apollo 14 Type of 1971
Souvenir Sheets

Design: 10fo, Astronaut in space, Apollo 16 capsule and badge.

1972, Oct. 10 Photo. *Perf. 12½*

C326	AP82	10fo blue & multi	3.75	3.75

Apollo 16 US moon mission, Apr. 15-27, 1972.

1973, Jan. 15

Design: Astronaut exploring moon, vert.

C327	AP82	10fo blue & multi	3.75	3.75

Apollo 17 US moon mission, Dec. 7-19, 1972. No. C327 contains one vertical stamp.

1973, Mar. 12 Photo. *Perf. 12½*

C328	AP82	10fo Venus 8	3.25	3.25

Venus 8 USSR space mission, Mar. 27-July 22, 1972.

Equestrian (Pentathlon), Olympic Rings and Medal — AP86

Designs (Olympic Rings and Medals): 60f, Weight lifting. 1fo, Canoeing. 1.20fo, Swimming, women's. 1.80fo, Boxing. 4fo, Wrestling. 6fo, Fencing. 10fo, Allegorical figure lighting flame, vert.

1973, Mar. 31

C329	AP86	40f multi	15	15
C330	AP86	60f multi	15	15
C331	AP86	1fo blue & multi	15	15
C332	AP86	1.20fo multi	18	15
C333	AP86	1.80fo multi	35	15
C334	AP86	4fo multi	75	40
C335	AP86	6fo multi	1.10	75
		Nos. C329-C335 (7)	2.83	
		Set value		1.60

Souvenir Sheet

Perf. 11

C336	AP86	10fo blue & multi	4.50	4.50

Hungarian medalists at 20th Olympic Games. #C336 contains one 44x71mm stamp.

Wrens — AP87

1973, Apr. 16 Litho. *Perf. 12*

C337	AP87	40f shown	15	15
C338	AP87	60f Rock thrush	15	15
C339	AP87	80f Robins	15	15
C340	AP87	1fo Firecrests	15	15
C341	AP87	1.20fo Linnets	20	15
C342	AP87	2fo Blue titmice	28	20
C343	AP87	4fo White-spotted blue throat	65	30
C344	AP87	5fo Gray wagtails	1.40	85
		Nos. C337-C344 (8)	3.13	
		Set value		1.75

Exhibition Type of Regular Issue
Souvenir Sheet

Design: 10fo, Bavaria No. 1 with mill wheel cancellation; Munich City Hall, TV Tower and Olympic tent.

1973, May 11 Litho. *Perf. 11*

C345	A506	10fo multi	3.50	3.50

No. C345 contains one 83x45mm stamp.

Souvenir Sheet

Skylab over Earth AP88

1973, Oct. 16 Photo. *Perf. 12½*

C346	AP88	10fo dk bl, lt bl & yel	3.25	3.25

First US manned space station.

Space Type of Regular Issue

Designs: 6fo, Mars "canals" and Giovanni V. Schiaparelli. 10fo, Mars 7 spacecraft.

1974, Mar. 11 Photo. *Perf. 12½*

C347	A522	6fo gold & multi	1.10	75

Souvenir Sheet

C348	A522	10fo gold & multi	3.25	3.25

UPU Type of 1974

Designs: a, Mail coach. b, Old mail automobile. c, Jet. d, Apollo 15.

1974, May 22 Litho. *Perf. 12*

C349	A526	6fo UPU emblem and TU-154 jet	1.10	65

Souvenir Sheet

C350		Sheet of 4	3.25	3.25
a.-d.	A526	2.50fo, any single	48	48

No. C350 has bister UPU emblem in center where 4 stamps meet.

Army Day Type of 1974

Designs: 2fo, Ground-to-air missiles, vert. 3fo, Parachutist, helicopter, supersonic jets.

1974, Sept. 28 Litho. *Perf. 12*

C351	A537	2fo gold, emer & blk	24	15
C352	A537	3fo gold, blue & blk	42	18

Carrier Pigeon, Elizabeth Bridge, Mt. Gellert — AP89

1975, Feb. 7 Litho. *Perf. 12*

C353	AP89	3fo multi	1.25	1.25

Carrier Pigeons' Olympics, Budapest, Feb. 7-9. No. C353 printed checkerwise with black and violet coupon showing Pigeon Olympics emblem.

Sputnik 2, Apollo-Soyuz Emblem — AP90

Spacecraft and Apollo-Soyuz Emblem: 60f, Mercury-Atlas 5. 80f, Lunokhod 1 on moon. 1.20fo, Lunar rover, Apollo 15 mission. 2fo, Soyuz take-off, Baikonur. 4fo, Apollo take-off, Cape Kennedy. 6fo, Apollo-Soyuz link-up. 10fo, Apollo, Soyuz, American and Russian flags over earth, horiz.

1975, July 7 Photo. *Perf. 12x11½*

C354	AP90	40f silver & multi	15	15
C355	AP90	60f silver & multi	15	15
C356	AP90	80f silver & multi	16	15
C357	AP90	1.20fo silver & multi	20	15
C358	AP90	2fo silver & multi	25	15
C359	AP90	4fo silver & multi	50	28
C360	AP90	6fo silver & multi	1.25	55
		Nos. C354-C360 (7)	2.66	
		Set value		1.35

Souvenir Sheet

Perf. 12½

C361	AP90	10fo blue & multi	3.50	3.50

Apollo Soyuz space test project (Russo-American cooperation), launching July 15; link-up July 17. No. C361 contains one 59x38mm stamp.

Souvenir Sheet

Map of Europe and Cogwheels — AP91

1975, July 30 Litho. *Perf. 12½*

C362	AP91	10fo multi	7.00	6.50

European Security and Cooperation Conference, Helsinki, July 30-Aug. 1.

Souvenir Sheet

Hungary Nos. 1585, 1382, 2239, 2280, C81 — AP92

1975, Sept. 9 Photo. *Perf. 12½*

C363	AP92	10fo multi	3.50	3.50

30 years of stamps.

A similar souvenir sheet with blue margin, no denomination and no postal validity was released for the 25th anniversary of Filatelica Hungarica.

Souvenir Sheet

Paintings by Károly Lotz and János Halápi AP93

1976, Mar. 19 Photo. *Perf. 12½*

C364	AP93	Sheet of 2	3.25	3.25
a.		5fo Horses in Storm	1.00	1.00
b.		5fo Morning at Tihany	1.00	1.00

Tourist publicity. #C364a and C364b are imperf. between.

Souvenir Sheet

Montreal Olympic Stadium — AP94

1976, June 29 Litho. *Perf. 12½*

C365	AP94	20fo red, gray & blk	4.00	4.00

21st Olympic Games, Montreal, Canada, July 17-Aug. 1.

US Mars Mission AP95

Designs: 60f, Viking in space. 1fo, Viking on moon. 2fo, Venus, rocket take-off. 3fo, Venyera 9 in space. 4fo, Venyera 10, separation in space. 5fo, Venyera on moon. 20fo, Viking 1 landing on Mars, vert.

1976, Nov. 11 Photo. *Perf. 11*

C366	AP95	40f silver & multi	15	15
C367	AP95	60f silver & multi	15	15
C368	AP95	1fo silver & multi	18	15
C369	AP95	2fo silver & multi	24	18
C370	AP95	3fo silver & multi	35	20
C371	AP95	4fo silver & multi	55	28
C372	AP95	5fo silver & multi	1.00	52
		Nos. C366-C372 (7)	2.62	
		Set value		1.40

Souvenir Sheet

Perf. 12½

C373	AP95	20fo black & multi	3.50	3.50

US-USSR space missions. No. C373 contains one stamp (size: 41x64mm).

Hungary No. CB33 — AP96

1977, Apr. Litho. *Perf. 11½x12*

C374	AP96	3fo multi	1.75	1.75

European stamp exhibitions. Issued in sheets of 3 stamps and 3 labels. Labels show exhibition emblems respectively: 125th anniversary of Brunswick stamps, Brunswick, May 5-8; Regiofil XII, Lugano, June 17-19; centenary of San Marino Stamps, Riccione, Aug. 27-29.

Space Type 1977
Souvenir Sheet

Design: 20fo, Viking on Mars.

1977, Sept. 20 Litho. *Perf. 11½*

C375	A603	20fo multi	4.00	4.00

Souvenir Sheet

"EUROPA," Map and Dove — AP97

1977, Oct. 3 *Perf. 12½*

C376	AP97	20fo multi	7.50	7.00

European Security Conference, Belgrade, Oct.-Nov.

TU-154, Malev over Europe — AP98

Planes, Airlines, Maps: 1.20fo, DC-8, Swissair, Southeast Asia. 2fo, IL-62, CSA, North Africa. 2.40fo, A 300B Airbus, Lufthansa, Northwest Europe. 4fo, Boeing 747, Pan Am, North America. 5fo, TU-144, Aeroflot, Northern Europe. 10fo, Concorde, Air France, South America. 20fo, IL-86, Aeroflot, Northeast Asia.

1977, Oct. 26 Litho. *Perf. 11½x12*

Size: 32x21mm

C377	AP98	60f orange & blk	15	15
C378	AP98	1.20fo violet & blk	15	15
C379	AP98	2fo yellow & blk	25	15
C380	AP98	2.40fo bl grn & blk	30	18
C381	AP98	4fo ultra & blk	50	18
C382	AP98	5fo dp rose & blk	60	25
C383	AP98	10fo blue & blk	1.25	42

Perf. 12x11½

Size: 37½x29mm

C384	AP98	20fo green & blk	2.50	90
		Nos. C377-C384 (8)	5.70	2.38

Montgolfier Brothers and Balloon, 1783 — AP99

Designs: 60f, David Schwarz and airship, 1850. 1fo, Alberto Santos-Dumont and airship flying around Eiffel Tower, 1873. 2fo, Konstantin E. Tsiolkovsky, airship and Kremlin, 1857. 3fo, Roald Amundsen, airship Norge, Polar bears and map, 1872. 4fo, Hugo Eckener, Graf Zeppelin over Mt. Fuji, 1930. 5fo, Count Ferdinand von Zeppelin, Graf Zeppelin over Chicago, 1932. 20fo, Graf Zeppelin over Budapest, 1931.

1977, Nov. 1 Photo. *Perf. 12x11½*

C385	AP99	40f gold & multi	15	15
C386	AP99	60f gold & multi	15	15
C387	AP99	1fo gold & multi	15	15
C388	AP99	2fo gold & multi	30	18
C389	AP99	3fo gold & multi	45	28
C390	AP99	4fo gold & multi	60	35
C391	AP99	5fo gold & multi	1.10	60
		Nos. C385-C391 (7)	2.90	
		Set value		1.60

Souvenir Sheet

Perf. 12½

C392	AP99	20fo silver & multi	3.75	3.75

History of airships. No. C392 contains one 60x36mm stamp.

Moon Station — AP100

Science Fiction Paintings by Pal Varga: 60f, Moon settlement. 1fo, Spaceship near Phobos. 2fo, Exploration of asteroids. 3fo, Spaceship in gravitational field of Mars. 4fo, Spaceship and rings of Saturn. 5fo, Spaceship landing on 3rd Jupiter moon.

1978, Mar. 10 Litho. *Perf. 11*

C393	AP100	40f multi	15	15
C394	AP100	60f multi	15	15
C395	AP100	1fo multi	15	15
C396	AP100	2fo multi	30	18
C397	AP100	3fo multi	45	28
C398	AP100	4fo multi	60	35
C399	AP100	5fo multi	85	45
		Nos. C393-C399 (7)	2.65	
		Set value		1.48

Louis Bleriot and La Manche AP101

Designs: 60f, J. Alcock and R. W. Brown, Vickers Vimy, 1919. 1fo, A. C. Read and Navy Curtiss NC-4, 1919. 2fo, H. Köhl, G. Hünefeld, J. Fitzmaurice, Junkers W33, 1928. 3fo, A. Johnson, J. Mollison, Gipsy Moth, 1930. 4fo, G. Endresz, S. Magyar, Lockheed Sirius, 1931. 5fo, W. Gronau, Dornier WAL, 1932. 20fo, Wilbur and Orville Wright and their plane.

1978, May 10 Litho. *Perf. 12*

C400	AP101	40f multi	15	15
C401	AP101	60f multi	15	15
C402	AP101	1fo multi	15	15
C403	AP101	2fo multi	30	18
C404	AP101	3fo multi	45	28
C405	AP101	4fo multi	60	35
C406	AP101	5fo multi	95	50
		Nos. C400-C406 (7)	2.75	
		Set value		1.50

Souvenir Sheet

C407	AP101	20fo multi	3.50	3.50

75th anniv. of 1st powered flight by Wright brothers. #C407 contains one 75x25mm stamp.

Souvenir Sheet

Jules Verne and "Voyage from Earth to Moon" — AP102

1978, Aug. 21 *Perf. 12½x11½*

C408	AP102	20fo multi	3.50	3.50

Jules Verne (1828-1905), French science fiction writer.

Vladimir Remek Postmarking Mail on Board Salyut 6 — AP103

1978, Sept. 1 Photo. *Perf. 11½x12*

C409	AP103	3fo multi	75	75

PRAGA '78 International Philatelic Exhibition, Prague, Sept. 8-17. Issued in sheets of 3 stamps and 3 labels, showing PRAGA '78 emblem and Golden Tower, Prague. FISA emblems in margin.

Ski Jump — AP104

Lake Placid '80 Emblem and: 60f, 20fo, Figure skating, diff. 1fo, Downhill skiing. 2fo, Ice hockey. 4fo, Bobsledding. 6fo, Cross-country skiing.

1979, Dec. 15 Litho. *Perf. 12*

C410	AP104	40f multi	15	15
C411	AP104	60f multi	15	15
C412	AP104	1fo multi	18	15
C413	AP104	2fo multi	35	18
C414	AP104	4fo multi	70	35
C415	AP104	6fo multi	1.10	60
		Nos. C410-C415 (6)	2.63	

Set value 1.32

Souvenir Sheet

C416 AP104 20fo multi 3.00 3.00

13th Winter Olympic Games, Lake Placid, NY, Feb. 12-24, 1980.

Soviet and Hungarian Cosmonauts AP105

1980, May 27 Litho. *Perf. 11½x12*

C417 AP105 5fo multi 75 40

Intercosmos cooperative space program.

Women's Handball, Moscow '80 Emblem, Olympic Rings — AP106

1980, June 16 Photo. *Perf. 11½x12*

C418	AP106	40f shown	15	15
C419	AP106	60f Double kayak	15	15
C420	AP106	1fo Running	15	15
C421	AP106	2fo Gymnast	28	20
C422	AP106	3fo Equestrian	42	28
C423	AP106	4fo Wrestling	60	38
C424	AP106	5fo Water polo	75	60
		Nos. C418-C424 (7)	2.50	1.91

Souvenir Sheet

C425 AP106 20fo Torch bearers 3.25 3.25

22nd Summer Olympic Games, Moscow, July 19-Aug. 3.
See No. C427.

Souvenir Sheet

Cosmonauts Bertalan Farkes and Valery Kubasov, Salyut 6-Soyuz 35 and 36 — AP107

1980, July 12 Litho. *Perf. 12½*

C426 AP107 20fo multi 3.25 3.25

Intercosmos cooperative space program (USSR-Hungary).

Olympic Type of 1900
Souvenir Sheet

1980, Sept. 26 Litho. *Perf. 12½*

C427 AP106 20fo Greek Frieze and gold medal 3.25 3.25

Olympic Champions.

AP108

1981, Mar. 6 Photo. *Perf. 11½*

C427A	AP108	40f Cheetah	15	15
C427B	AP108	60f Lion	15	15
C427C	AP108	1fo Leopard	20	15
C427D	AP108	2fo Rhinoceros	38	20
C427E	AP108	3fo Antelope	60	28
C427F	AP108	4fo African elephant	75	38
C427G	AP108	5fo shown	95	48
		Nos. C427A-C427G (7)	3.18	
		Set value		1.50

Kalman Kittenberger (1881-1958), zoologist and explorer, birth centenary.

Graf Zeppelin over Tokyo, First Worldwide Flight, Aug. 7-Sept. 4, 1929 — AP109

Graf Zeppelin Flights (Zeppelin and): 2fo, Icebreaker Malygin, Polar flight, July 24-31, 1931. 3fo, Nine Arch Bridge, Hortobagy, Hungary, Mar. 28-30, 1931. 4fo, Holsten Tor, Lubeck, Baltic Sea, May 12-15, 1931. 5fo, Tower Bridge, England, Aug. 18-20, 1931. 6fo, Federal Palace, Chicago World's Fair, 50th crossing of Atlantic, Oct. 14-Nov. 2, 1933. 7fo, Lucerne, first flight across Switzerland, Sept. 26, 1929.

Perf. 12½x11½

1981, Mar. 16 Litho.

C428	AP109	1fo multi	15	15
C429	AP109	2fo multi	28	20
C430	AP109	3fo multi	42	28
C431	AP109	4fo multi	60	38
C432	AP109	5fo multi	75	45
C433	AP109	6fo multi	85	60
C434	AP109	7fo multi	95	65
		Nos. C428-C434 (7)	4.00	2.71

LURABA '81, First Aviation and Space Philatelic Exhibition, Lucerne, Switzerland, Mar. 20-29. No. C434 se-tenant with label showing exhibition emblem.

Illustrator Type of 1981

Designs: Illustrations by A. Lesznai.

1981, Dec. 29 Litho. *Perf. 11½x12*

C435	A693	4fo At the End of the Village	60	55
C436	A693	5fo Dance	80	60
C437	A693	6fo Sunday	90	70

Manned Flight Bicentenary AP110

Various hot air balloons.

1983, Apr. 5 Litho. *Perf. 12x11½*

C438	AP110	1fo 1811	16	15
C439	AP110	1fo 1896	16	15
C440	AP110	2fo 1904	28	15
C441	AP110	2fo 1977	28	15
C442	AP110	4fo 1981	55	28
C443	AP110	4fo 1982	55	28
C444	AP110	5fo 1981	75	40
		Nos. C438-C444 (7)	2.73	
		Set value		1.30

Souvenir Sheet

Perf. 12½

C445 AP110 20fo 1983 2.75 2.75

No. C445 contains one 39x49mm stamp.

Audubon Type of 1985

1985, June 19 Litho. *Perf. 12*

C446	A778	4fo Colaptes auratus	60	35
C447	A778	6fo Richmondena cardinalis	85	50

Aircraft — AP111

1988, Aug. 31 Litho. *Perf. 11*

C448	AP111	1fo Lloyd CII	16	15
C449	AP111	2fo Brandenburg CI	30	20
C450	AP111	4fo UFAG CI	55	40
C451	AP111	10fo Gerle 13	1.50	1.00
C452	AP111	12fo WM 13	1.75	1.25
		Nos. C448-C452 (5)	4.26	3.00

AIR POST SEMI-POSTAL STAMPS

Catalogue values for unused stamps in this section are for Never Hinged items.

Roosevelt Type of Semipostal Stamps, 1947

F. D. Roosevelt, Plane and Place: 10f+10f, Casablanca. 20f+20f, Tehran. 50f+50f, Yalta (map). 70f+70f, Hyde Park.

Perf. 12x12½

1947, June 11 Photo. Wmk. 210

Portrait in Sepia

CB1	SP115	10f + 10f red vio	3.00	3.00
CB1A	SP115	20f + 20f brn ol	3.00	3.00
CB1B	SP115	50f + 50f vio	3.00	3.00
CB1C	SP115	70f + 70f blk	3.00	3.00

A souvenir sheet contains one each of Nos. CB1-CB1C with border inscriptions and decorations in brown. Size: 161x122mm. Value $80.
See note below Nos. B198A-B198D.

Souvenir Sheet

Chain Bridge, Budapest — SPAP1

Perf. 12x12½

1948, May 15 Photo. Wmk. 283

CB1D SPAP1 2fo + 18fo brn car 60.00 60.00

Souvenir Sheet

Chain Bridge SPAP2

1948, Oct. 16

CB2 SPAP2 3fo + 18fo dp grnsh bl 55.00 55.00

Type of Air Post Stamps of 1948
Portraits at Right

Writers: 1f, William Shakespeare. 2f, Francois Voltaire. 4f, Johann Wolfgang von Goethe. 5f, Lord Byron. 6f, Victor Hugo. 8f, Edgar Allen Poe. 10f, Sandor Petöfi. 12f, Mark Twain. 30f, Count Leo Tolstoy. 40f, Maxim Gorky.

1948, Oct. 16 Photo.

CB3	AP22	1f dp ultra	15	15
CB4	AP22	2f rose car	15	15
CB5	AP22	4f dp yel grn	15	15
CB6	AP22	5f dp rose lil	15	15
CB7	AP22	6f dp bl	15	15
CB8	AP22	8f ol brn	20	20
CB9	AP22	10f red	28	28
CB10	AP22	12f dp vio	28	28
CB11	AP22	30f org brn	70	70
CB12	AP22	40f sepia	1.00	1.00
		Nos. CB3-CB12 (10)	3.21	3.21

Sold at a 50 per cent increase over face, half of which aided reconstruction of the Chain Bridge and the other half the hospital for postal employees.

Air Post Type of 1951
Souvenir Sheets

Perf. 12½x12

1951, Sept. 12 Engr. Unwmk.

CB13	AP36	1fo + 1fo red	50.00	50.00
CB14	AP36	2fo + 2fo blue	50.00	50.00

Children Inspecting Stamp Album SPAP3

Design: 2fo+2fo, Children at stamp exhibition.

Perf. 12x12½

1952, Oct. 12 Photo. Wmk. 106

CB15	SPAP3	1fo + 1fo blue	2.50	2.50
CB16	SPAP3	2fo + 2fo brn red	2.50	2.50

Stamp week, Oct. 11-19, 1952.

Globe and Mailbox — SPAP4

Designs: 1fo+50f, Mobile post office. 2fo+1fo, Telegraph pole. 3fo+1.50fo, Radio. 5fo+2.50fo, Telephone. 10fo+5fo, Post horn.

1957, June 20 *Perf. 12x12½, 12*

Cross in Red

Size: 32x21mm

CB17	SPAP4	60f + 30f bis brn	52	15
CB18	SPAP4	1fo + 50f lilac	70	35
CB19	SPAP4	2fo + 1fo org ver	95	45
CB20	SPAP4	3fo + 1.50fo blue	1.25	70
CB21	SPAP4	5fo + 2.50fo gray	1.90	1.75

Size: 46x31mm

CB22	SPAP4	10fo + 5fo pale grn	4.00	4.00
		Nos. CB17-CB22 (6)	9.32	7.40

The surtax was for the benefit of hospitals for postal and telegraph employees.

Parachute of Fausztusz Verancsics, 1617 — SPAP5

History of Hungarian Aviation: No. CB24, Balloon of David Schwarz, 1897. No. CB25, Monoplane of Ernö Horvath, 1911. No. CB26, PKZ-2 helicopter, 1918.

Engraved and Lithographed

1967, May 6 *Perf. 10½*

CB23	SPAP5	2fo + 1fo sep & yel	50	50
CB24	SPAP5	2fo + 1fo sep & lt bl	50	50
CB25	SPAP5	2fo + 1fo sep & lt grn	50	50
CB26	SPAP5	2fo + 1fo sep & pink	50	50
a.		Horiz. strip of 4, #CB23-CB26	3.75	3.75
b.		Souv. sheet of 4, #CB23-CB26	3.75	3.75

"AEROFILA 67" International Airmail Exhibition, Budapest, Sept. 3-10.

1967, Sept. 3

Aviation, 1967: No. CB27, Parachutist. No. CB28, Helicopter Mi-1. No. CB29, TU-154 jet. No. CB30, Space station Luna 12.

CB27	SPAP5	2fo + 1fo sl & lt grn	50	50
CB28	SPAP5	2fo + 1fo sl & buff	50	50
CB29	SPAP5	2fo + 1fo sl & yel	50	50

CB30 SPAP5 2fo + 1fo sl & pink 50 50
a. Horiz. strip of 4, #CB27-CB30 2.75 2.75
b. Souv. sheet of 4, #CB27-CB30 3.75 3.75

Issued to commemorate (in connection with AEROFILA 67) the 7th Congress of FISA (Fédération Internationale des Sociétés Aérophilatéliques) and the 40th Stamp Day.

Olympic Games Airmail Type

Design: 2fo+1fo, Equestrian.

1968, Aug. 21 Photo. *Perf. 12*
CB31 AP74 2fo + 1fo multi 38 38

1st Hungarian Airmail Letter, 1918, Plane
SPAP6

Designs: No. CB33, Letter, 1931, and Zeppelin. No. CB34, Balloon post letter, 1967, and balloon. No. CB35, Letter, 1969, and helicopter.
#CB36a, #C1. b, #C7. c, #C305. d, #C312.

1974, Oct. 19 Litho. *Perf. 12*
CB32 SPAP6 2fo + 1fo multi 95 95
CB33 SPAP6 2fo + 1fo multi 95 95
a. Pair, #CB32-CB33 2.00 2.00
CB34 SPAP6 2fo + 1fo multi 95 95
CB35 SPAP6 2fo + 1fo multi 95 95
a. Pair, #CB34-CB35 2.00 2.00

Souvenir Sheet

CB36 Sheet of 4 3.50 3.50
a. SPAP6 2fo+1fo any single 48 48

AEROPHILA, International Airmail Exhibition, Budapest, Oct. 19-27.
No. CB36 contains 4 35x25mm stamps

SPECIAL DELIVERY STAMPS

Issue of the Monarchy

SD1

SD2

1916 Typo. Wmk. 137 *Perf. 15*
E1 SD1 2f gray green & red 15 15

For overprints and surcharges see Nos. 1NE1, 2NE1, 4N5, 5NE1, 6NE1, 7NE1, 8NE1, 10NE1, Szeged E1, J7-J8.

Issue of the Republic

Special Delivery Stamp of 1916 Overprinted

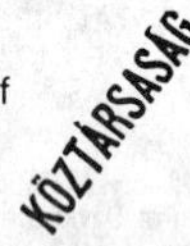

1919
E2 SD1 2f gray green & red 15 15

General Issue

1919
E3 SD2 2f gray green & red 15 15

REGISTRATION STAMPS

Nos. 625, 609 and 626 Overprinted in Carmine

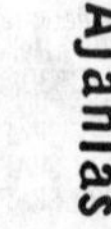

Ajánlás

"Ajl." or "Ajánlás" = Registered Letter.

1946 Wmk. 266 *Perf. 15*
F1 A118(a) "Ajl.1." on 20f 15 15
a. "Ajl.1." 6.00
F2 A99(a) "Ajl.2." on 12f 15 15
F3 A118(b) "Ajánlás" on 24f 15 15
Set value 15 20
Set, never hinged 20

POSTAGE DUE STAMPS

Issues of the Monarchy

D1

Perf. 11½, 11½x12

1903 Typo. Wmk. 135
J1 D1 1f grn & blk 30 25
J2 D1 2f grn & blk 2.00 1.25
J3 D1 5f grn & blk 9.00 5.00
J4 D1 6f grn & blk 6.00 4.50
J5 D1 10f grn & blk 45.00 3.00
J6 D1 12f grn & blk 2.00 2.00
a. Perf. 11½ 110.00 85.00
J7 D1 20f grn & blk 9.00 1.90
a. Perf. 11½ 115.00 32.50
J8 D1 50f grn & blk 12.00 12.00
a. Perf. 11½ 140.00 140.00
J9 D1 100f grn & blk 90 90
Nos. J1-J9 (9) 86.20 30.80

See Nos. J10-J26, J28-J43. For overprints and surcharges see Nos. J27, J44-J50, 1NJ1-1NJ5, 2NJ1-2NJ16, 4NJ2-4NJ3, 5NJ1-5NJ8, 6NJ1-6NJ9, 7NJ1-7NJ4, 9NJ1-9NJ3, 10NJ1-10NJ6, Szeged J1-J6.

1908-09 Wmk. 136 *Perf. 15*
J10 D1 1f green & black 45 45
J11 D1 2f green & black 30 30
J12 D1 5f green & black 2.50 1.10
J13 D1 6f green & black 50 38
J14 D1 10f green & black 1.50 38
J15 D1 12f green & black 50 38
J16 D1 20f green & black 10.00 45
c. Center inverted *4,000.*
J17 D1 50f green & black 95 95
Nos. J10-J17 (8) 16.70 4.39

1905 Wmk. 136a *Perf. 11½x12*
J12a D1 5f green & black 100.00 100.00
J13a D1 6f green & black 10.00 8.00
J14a D1 10f green & black 125.00 7.00
J15a D1 12f green & black 15.00 12.00
J17a D1 50f green & black 9.00 7.00
J18 D1 100f green & black 2.00

1906 *Perf. 15*
J11b D1 2f green & black 2.50 1.90
J12b D1 5f green & black 2.00 1.75
J13b D1 6f green & black 2.00 1.25
J14b D1 10f green & black 15.00 60
J15b D1 12f green & black 60 60
J16b D1 20f green & black 15.00 60
d. Center inverted *3,000.*
J17b D1 50f green & black 1.00 70

1914 Wmk. 137 Horiz. *Perf. 15*
J19 D1 1f green & black 18 18
J20 D1 2f green & black 18 18
J21 D1 5f green & black 40 40
J22 D1 6f green & black 60 60
J23 D1 10f green & black 70 70
J24 D1 12f green & black 35 35
J25 D1 20f green & black 35 35
J26 D1 50f green & black 40 40
Nos. J19-J26 (8) 3.16 3.16

1914 Wmk. 137 Vert.
J20a D1 2f green & black 57.50 57.50
J21a D1 5f green & black 7.50 6.25
J22a D1 6f green & black 16.00 16.00
J25a D1 20f green & black *2,750.* *1,750.*
J26a D1 50f green & black 7.50 7.50

No. J9 Surcharged in Red **20**

1915 Wmk. 135
J27 D1 20f on 100f grn & blk 90 90
a. On No. J18, Wmk. 136a 20.00 20.00

1915-22 Wmk. 137
J28 D1 1f grn & red 15 15
J29 D1 2f grn & red 15 15
J30 D1 5f grn & red 20 15
J31 D1 6f grn & red 15 15
J32 D1 10f grn & red 15 15
J33 D1 12f grn & red 20 15
J34 D1 15f grn & red 18 15
J35 D1 20f grn & red 15 15
J36 D1 30f grn & red 15 15
J37 D1 40f grn & red ('20) 15 15
J38 D1 50f grn & red ('20) 15 15
a. Center inverted 60.00
J39 D1 120f grn & red ('20) 15 15
J40 D1 200f grn & red ('20) 15 15
J41 D1 2k grn & red ('22) 40 40
J42 D1 5k grn & red ('22) 15 15
J43 D1 50k grn & red ('22) 15 15
Set value 2.30 2.00

Issues of the Republic

Postage Due Stamps of 1914-18 Overprinted in Black

1918-19

On Issue of 1914

J44 D1 50f green & black 60 60

On Stamps and Type of 1915-18

J45 D1 2f grn & red 15 15
J46 D1 3f grn & red 15 15
a. "KOZTARSASAG" omitted 200.00
J47 D1 10f grn & red 15 15
J48 D1 20f grn & red 15 15
J49 D1 40f grn & red 15 15
a. Inverted overprint 4.00 4.00
J50 D1 50f grn & red 15 15
a. Center and overprint inverted 10.00 10.00
Set value 1.20 1.20

Issues of the Kingdom

D3

1919-20 Typo.
J65 D3 2f green & black 15 15
a. Inverted center 500.00
J66 D3 3f green & black 15 15
J67 D3 20f green & black 15 15
J68 D3 40f green & black 15 15
J69 D3 50f green & black 15 15
Set value 35 30

Postage Due Stamps of this type have been overprinted "Magyar Tancskztarsasag" but have not been reported as having been issued without the additional overprint "heads of wheat."
For overprints see Nos. J70-J75.

New Overprint in Black over "Magyar Tanacskoztarsasag"

1920
J70 D3 2f green & black 45 45
J71 D3 3f green & black 45 45
J72 D3 10f green & black 1.65 1.65
J73 D3 20f green & black 45 45
J74 D3 40f green & black 45 45
J75 D3 50f green & black 45 45
Nos. J70-J75 (6) 3.90 3.90

Postage Issues Surcharged

PORTÓ
9
KORONA

1921-25

Red Surcharge

J76 A9 100f on 15f vio 15 15
J77 A9 500f on 15f vio 15 15
J78 A9 2½k on 10f red vio 15 15
J79 A9 3k on 15f vio 15 15
J80 A9 6k on 1½k vio 15 15
J81 A9 9k on 40f ol grn 15 15
J82 A9 10k on 2½k grn 15 15
J83 A9 12k on 60f blk brn 15 15
J84 A9 15k on 1½k vio 15 15
J85 A9 20k on 2½k grn 15 15
J86 A9 25k on 1½k vio 15 15
J87 A9 30k on 1½k vio 15 15
J88 A9 40k on 2½k grn 15 15
J89 A9 50k on 1½k vio 15 15
J90 A9 100k on 4½k dl vio 15 15
J91 A9 200k on 4½k dl vio 15 15
J92 A9 300k on 4½k dl vio 15 15
J93 A9 500k on 2k grnsh bl 28 15
J94 A9 500k on 3k org brn 28 28
J95 A9 1000k on 2k grnsh bl 28 15
J96 A9 1000k on 3k org brn 45 18
J97 A9 2000k on 2k grnsh bl 35 15
J98 A9 2000k on 3k org brn 70 35
J99 A9 5000k on 5k brown 90 52
Set value 5.00 2.70

Year of issue: 6k, 15k, 25k, 30k, 50k, 1922. 10k, 20k, 40k, 100k-No. J93, Nos. J95, J97, 1923. 5,000k, 1924. Nos. J94, J96, J98, 1925. Others, 1921.

D6

1926 Wmk. 133 Litho. *Perf. 14, 15*
J100 D6 1f rose red 15 15
J101 D6 2f rose red 15 15
J102 D6 3f rose red 15 15
J103 D6 4f rose red 15 15
J104 D6 5f rose red 38 22
a. Perf. 15 1.10 45
J105 D6 8f rose red 15 15
J106 D6 10f rose red 15 15
J107 D6 16f rose red 22 15
J108 D6 32f rose red 38 15
J109 D6 40f rose red 40 15
J110 D6 50f rose red 42 15
J111 D6 80f rose red 1.10 35
Set value 3.50 1.30

See Nos. J117-J123. For surcharges see Nos. J124-J129.

Nos. C7-C11 Surcharged in Red or Green

1926 Wmk. 137 *Perf. 14*
J112 AP3 1f on 500k (R) 32 22
J113 AP3 2f on 1000k (G) 32 28
J114 AP3 3f on 2000k (R) 32 18

Wmk. 133

J115 AP3 5f on 5000k (G) 65 55
J116 AP3 10f on 10000k (G) 45 35
Nos. J112-J116 (5) 2.06 1.58

Type of 1926 Issue

1928-32 Wmk. 210 *Perf. 14, 15*
J117 D6 2f rose red 15 15
J118 D6 4f rose red ('32) 15 15
J119 D6 8f rose red 15 15
J120 D6 10f rose red 15 15
J121 D6 16f rose red 20 15
J122 D6 20f rose red 32 15
J123 D6 40f rose red 65 15
Nos. J117-J123 (7) 1.77
Set value 50

Postage Due Stamps of 1926 Surcharged in Black

1931-33 Wmk. 133
J124 D6 4f on 5f rose red 28 18
J125 D6 10f on 16f rose red 85 80
J126 D6 10f on 80f rose red ('33) 40 20
J127 D6 12f on 50f rose red ('33) 40 20
J128 D6 20f on 32f rose red 40 28
Nos. J124-J128 (5) 2.33 1.66

Surcharged on No. J121

1931 Wmk. 210 *Perf. 15*
J129 D6 10f on 16f rose red 85 70

Catalogue values for unused stamps in this section, from this point to the end of the section, are for Never Hinged items.

Figure of Value — D7

Coat of Arms and Post Horn — D8

1934 Photo. Wmk. 210

J130 D7 2f ultra 15 15
J131 D7 4f ultra 15 15
J132 D7 6f ultra 15 15
J133 D7 8f ultra 15 15
J134 D7 10f ultra 15 15
J135 D7 12f ultra 18 15
J136 D7 16f ultra 18 15
J137 D7 20f ultra 18 15
J138 D7 40f ultra 55 15
J139 D7 80f ultra 70 28
Nos. J130-J139 (10) 2.54
Set value 85

1941

J140 D8 2f brown red 15 15
J142 D8 4f brown red 15 15
J143 D8 6f brown red 15 15
J144 D8 8f brown red 15 15
J145 D8 10f brown red 15 15
J146 D8 12f brown red 15 15
J147 D8 16f brown red 26 20
J148 D8 20f brown red 40 20
J150 D8 40f brown red 52 25
Nos. J140-J150 (9) 2.08
Set value 90

1941-44 Wmk. 266

J151 D8 2f brown red 15 15
J152 D8 3f brown red 15 15
J153 D8 4f brown red 15 15
J154 D8 6f brown red 15 15
J155 D8 8f brown red 15 15
J156 D8 10f brown red 15 15
J157 D8 12f brown red 15 15
J158 D8 16f brown red 15 15
J159 D8 18f brown red ('44) 22 15
J160 D8 20f brown red 15 15
J161 D8 24f brown red 22 15
J162 D8 30f brown red ('44) 15 15
J163 D8 36f brown red ('44) 15 15
J164 D8 40f brown red 15 15
J165 D8 50f brown red 15 15
J166 D8 60f brown red ('44) 30 15
Set value 2.25 90

For surcharges see Nos. J167-J185.

Issues of the Republic

1945

Types of Hungary Postage Due Stamps, 1941-44, Surcharged in Carmine

10 fillér

1945 Wmk. 266 Photo. *Perf. 15*
Blue Surface-tinted Paper

J167 D8 10f on 2f brn red 15 15
J168 D8 10f on 3f brn red 15 15
J169 D8 20f on 4f brn red 15 15
J170 D8 20f on 6f brn red 6.00 6.00
J171 D8 20f on 8f brn red 15 15
J172 D8 40f on 12f brn red 15 15
J173 D8 40f on 16f brn red 15 15
J174 D8 40f on 18f brn red 15 15
J175 D8 60f on 24f brn red 15 15
J176 D8 80f on 30f brn red 15 15
J177 D8 90f on 36f brn red 15 15
J178 D8 1p on 10f brn red 15 15
J179 D8 1p on 40f brn red 15 15
J180 D8 2p on 20f brn red 15 15
J181 D8 2p on 50f brn red 15 15
J182 D8 2p on 60f brn red 15 15

Surcharged in Black, Thicker Type

J183 D8 10p on 3f brn red 15 15
J184 D8 12p on 8f brn red 15 15
J185 D8 20p on 24f brn red 15 15
Set value 7.25 7.00

D9

1946-50 Wmk. 210 *Perf. 15*
Numerals in Deep Magenta

J186 D9 4f magenta 45 15
J187 D9 10f magenta 1.25 15
J188 D9 20f magenta 45 15
J189 D9 30f magenta 45 15
J190 D9 40f magenta 75 15
J191 D9 50f mag ('50) 2.10 48
J192 D9 60f magenta 1.50 15
J193 D9 1.20fo magenta 2.25 24
J194 D9 2fo magenta 3.50 30
Nos. J186-J194 (9) 12.70
Set value 1.50

1951 Wmk. 106
Numerals in Deep Magenta

J194A D9 4f magenta 15 15
J194B D9 10f magenta 15 15
J194C D9 20f magenta 15 15
j. "fiellr" 3.75
J194D D9 30f magenta 25 15
J194E D9 40f magenta 28 15
J194F D9 50f magenta 1.25 20
J194G D9 60f magenta 45 15
J194H D9 1.20fo magenta 75 15
J194I D9 2fo magenta 1.50 20
Nos. J194A-J194I (9) 4.93
Set value 1.00

Nos. J194A-J194I are found in both large format (about 18x22mm) and small (about 17x21mm).

D10

D11

1951 Unwmk. Typo. *Perf. 14½x15*
Paper with Vertical Lines in Green
Revenue Stamps with Blue Surcharge

J195 D10 8f dark brown 20 20
J196 D10 10f dark brown 20 20
J197 D10 12f dark brown 40 40

1951 Wmk. 106 Photo. *Perf. 14½*

J198 D11 4f brown 15 15
J199 D11 6f brown 15 15
J200 D11 8f brown 16 15
J201 D11 10f brown 15 15
J202 D11 14f brown 32 24
J203 D11 20f brown 15 15
J204 D11 30f brown 15 15
J205 D11 40f brown 15 15
J206 D11 50f brown 24 15
J207 D11 60f brown 28 15
J208 D11 1.20fo brown 28 15
J209 D11 2fo brown 48 32
Set value 2.30 1.15

D12

D13

Photo., Numeral Typo. in Black
1953
Numerals 4½mm High

J210 D12 4f dull green 15 15
J211 D12 6f dull green 15 15
J212 D12 8f dull green 15 15
J213 D12 10f dull green 15 15
J214 D12 12f dull green 15 15
J215 D12 14f dull green 24 16
J216 D12 16f dull green 24 16
J217 D12 20f dull green 15 15
J218 D12 24f dull green 24 16
J219 D12 30f dull green 16 15
J220 D12 36f dull green 24 15
J221 D12 40f dull green 15 15
J222 D12 50f dull green 16 15
J223 D12 60f dull green 20 15
J224 D12 70f dull green 20 15
J225 D12 80f dull green 28 15
J226 D12 1.20fo dull green 40 15
J227 D12 2fo dull green 65 24
a. Small "2" (3mm high) 1.00 60
Nos. J210-J227 (18) 4.06
Set value 1.50

1st Hungarian postage due stamp, 50th anniv.

Photo., Numeral Typo. in Black on Nos. J228-J243
1958 Wmk. 106 *Perf. 14½*
Size: 21x16½mm

J228 D13 4f red 15 15
J229 D13 6f red 15 15
J230 D13 8f red 15 15
J231 D13 10f red 15 15
J232 D13 12f red 15 15
J233 D13 14f red 15 15
J234 D13 16f red 15 15
J235 D13 20f red 15 15
J236 D13 24f red 15 15
J237 D13 30f red 15 15
J238 D13 36f red 15 15
J239 D13 40f red 15 15
J240 D13 50f red 15 15
J241 D13 60f red 18 15
J242 D13 70f red 22 15
J243 D13 80f red 30 15

Perf. 12
Size: 31x21mm

J244 D13 1.20fo dk red brn 45 18
J245 D13 2fo dk red brn 70 28
Set value 2.60 1.25

Photo., Numeral Typo. in Black on Nos. J246-J261
1965-69 Unwmk. *Perf. 11½*
Size: 21x16½mm

J246 D13 4f red 15 15
J247 D13 6f red 15 15
J248 D13 8f red 15 15
J249 D13 10f red 15 15
J250 D13 12f red 15 15
J251 D13 14f red 15 15
J252 D13 16f red 15 15
J253 D13 20f red 15 15
J254 D13 24f red 15 15
J255 D13 30f red 15 15
J256 D13 36f red 15 15
J257 D13 40f red 15 15
J258 D13 50f red 15 15
J259 D13 60f red 15 15
J260 D13 70f red 16 15
J261 D13 80f red 20 15

Perf. 11½x12
Size: 31x21mm

J262 D13 1fo dk red brn ('69) 15 15
J263 D13 1.20fo dk red brn 28 15
J264 D13 2fo dk red brn 40 20
J265 D13 4fo dk red brn ('69) 65 15
Set value 2.60 1.25

Mail Plane and Truck — D14

Postal History — D15

Designs: 20f, Money order canceling machine. 40f, Scales in self-service P.O. 80f, Automat for registering parcels. 1fo, Keypunch operator. 1.20fo, Mail plane and truck. 2fo, Diesel mail train. 3fo, Mailman on motorcycle with sidecar. 4fo, Rural mail delivery. 8fo, Automatic letter sorting machine. 10fo, Postman riding motorcycle.

1973-85 Photo. *Perf. 11*
Size: 21x18mm

J266 D14 20f brn & ver 15 15
J267 D14 40f dl bl & ver 15 15
J268 D14 80f vio & ver 15 15
J269 D14 1fo ol grn & ver 15 15

Perf. 12x11½
Size: 28x22mm

J270 D14 1.20fo grn & ver 18 15
J271 D14 2fo lil & ver 24 15
J272 D14 3fo brt bl & ver 35 15
J273 D14 4fo org brn & ver 45 18
J274 D14 8fo deep mag & dark red 1.50 38
J275 D14 10fo green & dark red 1.75 45
Nos. J266-J275 (10) 5.07
Set value 1.45

Issue dates: 20f-4fo, Dec. 1973. 8fo, 10fo, Dec. 16, 1985.

1987, Dec. 10 Litho. *Perf. 12*

Designs: Excerpt from 18th cent. letter, innovations in letter carrying.

J276 D15 1fo Foot messenger, 16th cent. 25 15
J277 D15 4fo Post rider, 17th cent. 1.00 50
J278 D15 6fo Horse-drawn mail coach, 18th cent. 1.50 75
J279 D15 8fo Railroad mail car, 19th cent. 2.00 1.00
J280 D15 10fo Mail truck, 20th cent. 2.50 1.25
J281 D15 20fo Airplane, 20th cent. 5.00 2.50
Nos. J276-J281 (6) 12.25 6.15

OFFICIAL STAMPS

O1

1921-23 Wmk. 137 Typo. *Perf. 15*

O1 O1 10f brn vio & blk 20 15
O2 O1 20f ol brn & blk 20 15
a. Inverted center 500.00 500.00
O3 O1 60f blk brn & blk 20 15
O4 O1 100f dl rose & blk 20 15
O5 O1 250f bl & blk 20 15
O6 O1 350f gray & blk 24 15
O7 O1 500f lt brn & blk 22 15
O8 O1 1000f lil brn & blk 22 15
O9 O1 5k brn ('23) 15 15
O10 O1 10k choc ('23) 15 15
O11 O1 15k gray blk ('23) 15 15
O12 O1 25k org ('23) 15 15
O13 O1 50k brn & red ('22) 15 15
O14 O1 100k bis & red ('22) 15 15
O15 O1 150k grn & red ('23) 20 15
O16 O1 300k dl red & red ('23) 24 15
O17 O1 350k vio & red ('23) 28 15
O18 O1 500k org & red ('22) 32 15
O19 O1 600k ol bis & red ('23) 80 48
O20 O1 1000k bl & red ('22) 48 16
Nos. O1-O20 (20) 4.90
Set value 2.50

Stamps of 1921 Surcharged in Red

1922

O21 O1 15k on 20f ol brn & blk 15 15
O22 O1 25k on 60f blk brn & blk 15 15
Set value 20 15

Stamps of 1921 Overprinted in Red **KORONA**

1923

O23 O1 350k gray & blk 25 18

With Additional Surcharge of New Value in Red

O24 O1 150k on 100f dl rose & blk 22 15
O25 O1 2000k on 250f bl & blk 60 42

1923-24
Paper with Gray Moiré on Face

O26 O1 500k org & red ('23) 22 15
O27 O1 1000k bl & red ('23) 28 15
O28 O1 3000k vio & red ('24) 60 28
O29 O1 5000k bl & red ('24) 70 48

1924 Wmk. 133

O30 O1 500k orange & red 1.10 55
O31 O1 1000k blue & red 1.10 55

NEWSPAPER STAMPS

Issues of the Monarchy

St. Stephen's Crown and Post Horn
N1 N2

1871-72 Unwmk. Typo. *Imperf.*

P1 N1 (1k) ver red 30.00 12.50
P2 N2 (1k) rose red ('72) 7.00 1.25
a. (1k) vermilion 7.00 1.25
b. Printed on both sides

Reprints of No. P2 are watermarked. Value, $450.

Letter with Crown and Post Horn — N3

N5

1874
P3 N3 1k orange 3.00 35

1881 **Wmk. "kr" in Oval (132)**
P4 N3 1k orange 1.25 15
a. 1k lemon yellow 14.00 2.75
b. Printed on both sides

1898 **Wmk. 135**
P5 N3 1k orange 1.25 20

See watermark note after No. 46.

1900 **Wmk. Crown in Circle (135)**
P6 N5 (2f) red orange 75 15

1905 **Wmk. Crown (136a)**
P7 N5 (2f) red orange 1.00 15
a. Wmk. 136 ('08) 1.00 15

1914-22 **Wmk. Double Cross (137)**
P8 N5 (2f) orange 15 15
a. Wmk. horiz. 4.50 3.75
P9 N5 (10f) deep blue ('20) 15 15
P10 N5 (20f) lilac ('22) 15 15
Set value 27 23

For overprints and surcharges see Nos. 1NJ6-1NJ10, 1NP1, 2NP1, 5NP1, 6NP1, 8NP1, 10NP1, Szeged P1.

NEWSPAPER TAX STAMPS

Issues of the Monarchy

NT1

NT2

NT3

Wmk. 91; Unwmk. from 1871
1868 **Typo.** ***Imperf.***
PR1 NT1 1k blue 5.50 1.50
a. Pair, one sideways
PR2 NT2 2k brown 17.50 15.00
a. 2k red brown 275.00 47.50

1868
PR2B NT3 1k blue *4,750. 4,000.*

No. PR2B was issued for the Military Border District only. All used copies are precanceled (overprinted with newspaper text). A similar 2k was not issued.

1889-90 **Wmk. "kr" in Oval (132)**
PR3 NT1 1k blue 2.00 80
PR4 NT2 2k brown 5.50 4.00

1898 **Wmk. Crown in Oval (135)**
PR5 NT1 1k blue 7.50 5.50

These stamps did not pay postage, but represented a fiscal tax collected by the postal authorities on newspapers.

Nos. PR3 and PR5 have a tall "k" in "kr."

PARCEL POST STAMPS

Nos. 629, 613, 612, 615, 630, 667 and Type of 1943-45 Overprinted in Black or Carmine

Cs. 5-l.
a

Csomag 5 kg.
b

"Cs." or "Csomag"=Parcel

1946 **Wmk. 266** ***Perf. 15***
Q1 A118 "Cs. 5-1." on 70f 15 15
Q2 A109 "Cs. 5-1." on 30f 4.00 4.00
Q3 A99 "Cs. 5-2." on 24f 15 15
Q4 A118 "Cs. 10-1." on 70f 15 15
Q5 A118 "Cs. 10-1." on 80f 4.00 4.00
Q6 A118 "Cs. 10-2." on 80f 15 15
Q7 A99 "Csomag 5kg." on 2p on 4f (C+Bk) 15 15
Q8 A118 "Csomag 10kg." on 30f copper red, *bl* 15 15
Nos. Q1-Q8 (8) 8.90 8.90

No. Q8 was not issued without overprint.

Catalogue values for unused stamps in this section, from this point to the end of the section, are for Never Hinged items.

No. 796 Surcharged with New Value in Red or Black

1954 **Wmk. 210**
Q9 A144 1.70fo on 1.40fo 60 20
Q10 A144 2fo on 1.40fo (Bk) 70 30
Q11 A144 3fo on 1.40fo 85 50

OCCUPATION STAMPS

Issued under French Occupation

ARAD ISSUE

Forged overprints exist.

Stamps of Hungary Overprinted in Red or Blue

Occupation française

On Issue of 1916-18

1919 **Wmk. 137** ***Perf. 15, 14***
1N1 A9 2f brn org (R) 45 45
1N2 A9 3f red lil (R) 25 25
1N3 A9 5f green (R) 65 65
1N4 A9 6f grnsh bl (R) 55 55
a. Inverted overprint 1.00 1.00
1N5 A9 10f rose red 55 55
1N6 A9 15f violet (R) 45 45
a. Double overprint 3.00
1N7 A9 20f gray brn (R) 7.50 7.50
1N8 A9 35f brown (R) 9.00 9.00
1N9 A9 40f ol grn (R) 6.50 6.50
1N10 A10 50f red vio & lil 90 90
1N11 A10 75f brt bl & pale bl 80 80
1N12 A10 80f grn & pale grn 70 70
1N13 A10 1k red brn & cl 1.50 1.50
1N14 A10 2k ol brn & bis 80 80
a. Inverted overprint 3.25
1N15 A10 3k dk vio & ind 2.00 2.00
1N16 A10 5k dk brn & lt brn 2.00 2.00
1N17 A10 10k vio brn & vio 10.00 10.00
Nos. 1N1-1N17 (17) 44.60 44.60

With Additional Surcharge:

45 45 50 50

1N18 A9 (a) 45f on 2f brn org 75 75
1N19 A9 (b) 45f on 2f brn org 1.00 1.00
1N20 A9 (c) 50f on 3f red lil 80 80
1N21 A9 (d) 50f on 3f red lil 80 80

Overprinted On Issue of 1918

1N22 A11 10f scarlet (Bl) 7.50 7.50
1N23 A11 20f dk brn 55 55
1N24 A11 25f brt bl 1.00 1.00
a. Inverted overprint 1.00 1.00
1N25 A12 40f ol grn 1.50 1.50

Ovptd. On Issue of 1918-19, Overprinted "Koztarsasag"

1N26 A9 2f brn org 1.50 1.50
a. Inverted overprint 2.75 2.75
1N27 A9 4f slate gray 1.50 1.50
1N28 A9 5f green 24 24
1N29 A9 6f grnsh bl 2.50 2.50
a. Inverted overprint 4.50 4.50
1N30 A9 10f rose red (Bl) 7.50 7.50
1N31 A9 20f gray brn 1.00 1.00
1N32 A11 25f brt bl 75 75
a. Inverted overprint 4.00 4.00
1N33 A9 40f ol grn 75 75
1N34 A12 40f ol grn 12.50 12.50
a. Inverted overprint 12.50
1N35 A12 50f lilac 60 60
1N36 A10 1k red brn & cl (Bl) 1.10 1.10
1N37 A10 3k dk vio & ind (Bl) 1.75 1.75
Nos. 1N26-1N37 (12) 31.69 31.69

No. 1N36 With Additional Surcharge:

10
e

10
f

1N38 A10 (e) 10k on 1k 2.00 2.00
1N39 A10 (f) 10k on 1k 1.50 1.50

On Issue of 1919
Inscribed "MAGYAR POSTA"

1N40 A13 10f red (Bl) 75 75

SEMI-POSTAL STAMPS

Hungarian Semi-Postal Stamps of 1916-17 Overprinted "Occupation francaise" in Blue or Red

1919 **Wmk. 137** ***Perf. 15***
1NB1 SP3 10f + 2f rose red 8.00 8.00
1NB2 SP4 15f + 2f dl vio (R) 1.00 1.00
1NB3 SP5 40f + 2f brn car 1.00 1.00

SPECIAL DELIVERY STAMP

Hungarian Special Delivery Stamp of 1916 Overprinted "Occupation francaise"

1919 **Wmk. 137** ***Perf. 15***
1NE1 SD1 2f gray green & red 35 35

POSTAGE DUE STAMPS

Hungarian Postage Due Stamps of 1915 Overprinted "Occupation francaise"

1919 **Wmk. 137** ***Perf. 15***
1NJ1 D1 2f green & red 3.50 3.50
1NJ2 D1 10f green & red 1.25 1.25
1NJ3 D1 12f green & red 6.00 6.00
1NJ4 D1 15f green & red 6.00 6.00
1NJ5 D1 20f green & red 3.00 3.00

Hungarian Newspaper Stamp of 1914 Surcharged

Occupation française

12 Porto 12

1NJ6 N5 12f on 2f orange 80 80
1NJ7 N5 15f on 2f orange 80 80
1NJ8 N5 30f on 2f orange 80 80
a. Double surcharge 4.25
1NJ9 N5 50f on 2f orange 4.00 4.00
1NJ10 N5 100f on 2f orange 4.00 4.00
Nos. 1NJ1-1NJ10 (10) 30.15 30.15

NEWSPAPER STAMP

Hungarian Newspaper Stamp of 1914 Overprinted "Occupation francaise"

1919 **Wmk. 137** ***Imperf.***
1NP1 N5 (2f) orange 25 25

ISSUED UNDER ROMANIAN OCCUPATION

FIRST DEBRECEN ISSUE

The first Debrecen overprint was applied to numerous other stamps, also in other colors than are listed. These varieties were not sold to the public but to a favored few.

Excellent forgeries of this overprint are plentiful.

Hungarian Stamps of 1913-19 Overprinted in Blue, Red or Black

1919 **Wmk. 137** ***Perf. 15, 14½x14***

On Stamps of 1913

2N1 A4 2f olive yellow *16.00 16.00*
2N2 A4 3f orange *22.50 22.50*
2N3 A4 6f ol grn (R) 2.50 2.50

On Stamps of 1916

2N4 A8 10f rose 20.00 20.00
2N5 A8 15f vio (Bk) 8.00 8.00

On Stamps of 1916-18

2N6 A9 2f brn org 20 15
2N7 A9 3f red lilac 16 15
2N8 A9 5f grn 80 45
2N9 A9 6f grnsh bl (R) 60 40
2N10 A9 15f vio (Bk) 80 40
2N11 A9 20f gray brn *12.50 12.50*
2N12 A9 25f dl bl (Bk) 80 40
2N13 A9 35f brown 10.00 7.50
2N14 A9 40f ol grn 80 40
2N15 A10 50f red vio & lil 1.50 80
2N16 A10 75f brt bl & pale bl (Bk) 75 35
2N17 A10 80f grn & pale grn (R) 1.00 80
2N18 A10 1k red brn & cl 1.00 80
2N19 A10 2k ol brn & bis (Bk) 80 80
2N20 A10 3k dk vio & ind (R) 2.25 1.50
a. Blue overprint *5.50 5.50*
b. Black overprint *65.00 65.00*
2N21 A10 5k dk brn & lt brn (Bk) 6.50 6.50
2N22 A10 10k vio brn & vio *40.00 40.00*

With New Value Added

2N23 A9 35f on 3f red lil 40 30
2N24 A9 45f on 2f brn org 40 40
2N25 A10 3k on 75f brt bl & pale bl (Bk) 1.25 1.25
2N26 A10 5k on 75f brt bl & pale bl (Bk) 1.25 1.25
2N27 A10 10k on 80f grn & pale grn (R) 1.10 1.10

On Stamps of 1918

2N28 A11 10f scarlet 4.00 4.00
2N29 A11 20f dk brn (R) 4.00 4.00
a. Black overprint 6.00 6.00
b. Blue overprint 6.50 6.50
2N30 A11 25f brt bl (R) 80 80
a. Black overprint 4.00 4.00
2N31 A12 40f olive grn 20 20
2N32 A12 50f lilac 4.00 4.00

On Stamps of 1918-19, Overprinted "Koztarsasag"

2N33 A9 2f brn org 50 25
2N34 A9 3f red lilac 6.50 4.00
2N35 A9 4f sl gray (R) 65 40
2N36 A9 5f grn 20 15
2N37 A9 6f grnsh bl (R) 1.65 80
2N38 A9 10f rose red 2.00 1.10
2N39 A11 10f scarlet 80 40
2N40 A11 15f dp vio (Bk) 2.00 1.65
2N41 A9 20f gray brn 20 18
2N42 A11 20f dk brn (Bk) 3.50 3.50
b. Red overprint 7.00 7.00
2N43 A9 40f olive grn 4.00 4.00
2N44 A10 1k red brn & cl 40 35
2N45 A10 2k ol brn & bis (Bk) 8.00 8.00
2N46 A10 3k dk vio & ind (R) 1.10 1.10
a. Blue overprint 3.50 3.50
b. Black overprint *52.50 52.50*
2N47 A10 5k dk & lt brn (Bk) *50.00 50.00*
2N48 A10 10k vio brn & vio *80.00 80.00*
2N49 A11 25f brt bl (R) 75 65
a. Black overprint 4.00 4.00
2N50 A12 40f olive grn *10.00 10.00*
2N51 A12 50f lilac 1.00 1.00

On Stamps of 1919

2N52 A13 5f green 15 15
2N53 A13 6f grnsh bl (Bk) 1.25 80
2N54 A13 10f red 15 15
2N55 A13 20f dk brn 15 15
2N56 A13 25f dl bl (Bk) 25 16
2N57 A13 45f orange 80 65
2N58 A14 5k dk brn & brn

#2N58 is handstamped. Counterfeits exist.

On No. 103A

2N59 A5a 10f vio brn (R) 3.25 3.25
Nos. 2N1-2N57,2N59 (58) *346.11 333.04*

SEMI-POSTAL STAMPS

Overprinted like Regular Issues in Blue or Black

1919 **Wmk. 137** ***Perf. 15***
2NB1 SP3 10f + 2f rose red 65 65
2NB2 SP4 15f + 2f dl vio (Bk) 1.00 1.00
2NB3 SP5 40f + 2f brn car 80 80

Same Overprint on Hungary Nos. B58-B60 (with "Köztarsasag")

1919

2NB4	SP3	10f + 2f rose red	1.50	1.50
2NB5	SP4	15f + 2f dl vio (Bk)	10.00	9.00
2NB6	SP5	40f + 2f brn car	1.75	1.75

SPECIAL DELIVERY STAMP

Hungarian Special Delivery Stamp of 1916 Overprinted like Regular Issues

1919 Wmk. 137 *Perf. 15*

2NE1	SD1	2f gray grn & red (Bl)	15	15

POSTAGE DUE STAMPS

Hungarian Postage Due Stamps of 1914-19 Overprinted in Black like Regular Issues

1919 Wmk. 137 *Perf. 15*

On Stamp of 1914

2NJ1	D1	50f grn & blk	*26.00*	*26.00*

On Stamps of 1915

2NJ2	D1	1f green & red	8.00	8.00
2NJ3	D1	2f green & red	20	20
2NJ4	D1	5f green & red	*35.00*	*35.00*
2NJ5	D1	6f green & red	*7.50*	*7.50*
2NJ6	D1	10f green & red	50	50
2NJ7	D1	12f green & red	*12.50*	*12.00*
2NJ8	D1	15f green & red	90	90
2NJ9	D1	20f green & red	1.25	1.25
2NJ10	D1	30f green & red	1.25	1.25

On Stamps of 1918-19, Overprinted "Koztarsasag"

2NJ11	D1	2f green & red	2.00	2.00
2NJ12	D1	3f green & red	7.50	7.50
2NJ13	D1	10f green & red	1.25	1.25
2NJ14	D1	20f green & red	1.25	
2NJ15	D1	40f green & red	1.25	1.25
2NJ16	D1	50f green & red	1.25	1.25
		Nos. 2NJ1-2NJ16 (16)	*107.60*	

NEWSPAPER STAMP

Hungarian Newspaper Stamp of 1914 Overprinted like Regular Issues

1919 Wmk. 137 *Imperf.*

2NP1	N5	(2f) orange (Bl)	25	25
a.		Inverted overprint		
b.		Double overprint		

SECOND DEBRECEN ISSUE

Counterfeits exist.

Mythical "Turul" — OS5

Throwing Lariat OS6

Hungarian Peasant OS7

1920 Unwmk. Typo. *Perf. 11½*

3N1	OS5	2f lt brn	60	60
3N2	OS5	3f red brn	60	60
3N3	OS5	4f gray	60	60
3N4	OS5	5f lt grn	60	60
3N5	OS5	6f slate	60	60
3N6	OS5	10f scarlet	60	60
3N7	OS5	15f dk vio	60	60
3N8	OS5	20f dk brn	60	60
3N9	OS6	25f ultra	60	60
3N10	OS6	30f buff	60	60
3N11	OS6	35f claret	60	60
3N12	OS6	40f ol grn	60	60
3N13	OS6	45f salmon	60	60
3N14	OS6	50f pale vio	60	60
3N15	OS6	60f yel grn	60	60
3N16	OS6	75f Prus bl	60	60
3N17	OS7	80f gray grn	60	60
3N18	OS7	1k brn red	80	80
3N19	OS7	2k chocolate	80	80
3N20	OS7	3k brn vio	2.00	2.00
3N21	OS7	5k bis brn	2.00	2.00
3N22	OS7	10k dl vio	2.00	2.00
		Nos. 3N1-3N22 (22)	17.80	17.80

Thick, Glazed Paper

3N23	OS5	2f lt brn	1.25	1.25
3N24	OS5	3f red brn	1.25	1.25
3N25	OS5	4f gray	1.25	1.25
3N26	OS5	5f lt grn	1.25	1.25
3N27	OS5	6f slate	1.25	1.25
3N28	OS5	10f scarlet	1.25	1.25
3N29	OS5	15f dk vio	1.25	1.25
3N30	OS5	20f dk brn	1.25	1.25
3N31	OS7	80f gray grn	1.50	1.50
3N32	OS7	1k brn red	1.50	1.50
3N33	OS7	1.20k orange	10.50	10.50
3N34	OS7	2k chocolate	2.25	2.25
		Nos. 3N23-3N34 (12)	25.75	25.75

SEMI-POSTAL STAMPS

Carrying Wounded SP1

1920 Unwmk. Typo. *Perf. 11½*

3NB1	SP1	20f green	1.00	1.00
3NB2	SP1	50f gray brn	1.00	1.00
3NB3	SP1	1k blue green	1.00	1.00
3NB4	SP1	2k dk grn	1.00	1.00

Colored Paper

3NB5	SP1	20f grn, *bl*	1.00	1.00
3NB6	SP1	50f brn, *rose*	1.00	1.00
3NB7	SP1	1k dk grn, *grn*	1.00	1.00
		Nos. 3NB1-3NB7 (7)	7.00	7.00

POSTAGE DUE STAMPS

D1

1920 Typo. Wmk. 137 *Perf. 15*

3NJ1	D1	5f blue green	40	40
3NJ2	D1	10f blue green	40	40
3NJ3	D1	20f blue green	40	40
3NJ4	D1	30f blue green	40	40
3NJ5	D1	40f blue green	40	40
		Nos. 3NJ1-3NJ5 (5)	2.00	2.00

TEMESVAR ISSUE

Issued under Romanian Occupation

Hungary Nos. 108, 155, 109, 111, E1 Surcharged

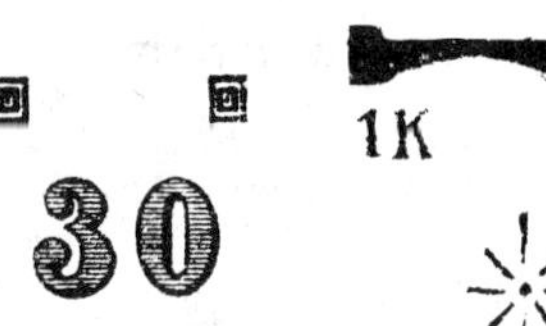

1919 Wmk. 137 *Perf. 15*

4N1	A9	30f on 2f brn org (Bl)	30	30
a.		Red surcharge	65	65
b.		Inverted surcharge (R)		
4N2	A9	1k on 4f sl gray (R)	25	25
4N3	A9	150f on 3f red lil (Bk)	20	20
4N4	A9	150f on 5f grn (Bk)	25	25
4N5	SD1	3k on 2f gray grn & red (Bk)	50	50
a.		Blue surcharge	80	80
		Nos. 4N1-4N5 (5)	1.50	1.50

POSTAGE DUE STAMPS

D1

D2

1919 Wmk. 137 *Perf. 15*

4NJ1	D1	40f on 15f + 2f vio (Bk)	40	40
a.		Red surcharge	70	70
4NJ2	D2	60f on 2f grn & red (Bk)	70	70
a.		Red surcharge	3.50	3.50
4NJ3	D2	60f on 10f grn & red (Bk)	55	55
a.		Red surcharge	3.00	3.00

FIRST TRANSYLVANIA ISSUE

Issued under Romanian Occupation

Both the first and second Transylvania overprints were applied to numerous other stamps and in colors other than listed. These varieties were not sold to the public but to a favored few.

Counterfeits are plentiful.

Issued in Kolozsvar (Cluj)

Hungarian Stamps of 1916-18 Overprinted

1919 Wmk. 137 *Perf. 15, 14*

On Stamp of 1916, White Numerals

5N1	A8	15b violet	60	60

On Stamps of 1916-18

5N2	A9	2b brn org	15	15
5N3	A9	3b red lil	18	18
5N4	A9	5b green	20	20
5N5	A9	6b grnsh bl	20	20
5N6	A9	15b violet	20	20
5N7	A9	25b dl bl	18	18
5N8	A9	35b brown	18	18
5N9	A9	40b ol grn	18	18
5N10	A10	50b red vio & lil	30	30
5N11	A10	75b brt bl & pale bl	18	18
5N12	A10	80b grn & pale grn	18	18
5N13	A10	1 l red brn & cl	18	18
5N14	A10	2 l ol brn & bis	40	40
5N15	A10	3 l dk vio & ind	1.25	1.25
5N16	A10	5 l dk brn & lt brn	1.10	1.10
5N17	A10	10 l vio brn & vio	1.40	1.40

On Stamps of 1918

5N18	A11	10b scarlet	15.00	15.00
5N19	A11	15b dp vio	2.00	2.00
5N20	A11	20b dk brn	15	15
a.		Gold overprint	32.50	32.50
b.		Silver overprint	32.50	32.50
5N21	A11	25b brt bl	40	40
5N22	A12	40b ol grn	25	25

On No. 103A

5N23	A5a	10b vio brn	25	25
		Nos. 5N1-5N23 (23)	25.11	25.11

SEMI-POSTAL STAMPS

Hungarian Semi-Postal Stamps of 1913-17 Overprinted like Regular Issues

On Issue of 1913

1919 Wmk. 137 *Perf. 14*

5NB1	SP1	1 l on 1f slate	16.00	16.00
5NB2	SP1	1 l on 2f ol yel	25.00	25.00
5NB3	SP1	1 l on 3f org	14.00	14.00
5NB4	SP1	1 l on 5f emer	80	80
5NB5	SP1	1 l on 10f car	80	80
5NB6	SP1	1 l on 12f vio,*yel*	5.00	5.00
5NB7	SP1	1 l on 16f gray grn	2.50	2.50
5NB8	SP1	1 l on 25f ultra	20.00	20.00
5NB9	SP1	1 l on 35f red vio	3.00	3.00
5NB10	SP2	1 l on 1k dl red	35.00	35.00

On Issue of 1916-17

Perf. 15

5NB11	SP3	10b + 2b rose red	15	15
5NB12	SP4	15b + 2b dl vio	15	15
5NB13	SP5	40b + 2b brn car	15	15
		Nos. 5NB1-5NB13 (13)	122.55	122.55

SPECIAL DELIVERY STAMP

Hungarian Special Delivery Stamp of 1916 Overprinted like Regular Issues

1919 Wmk. 137 *Perf. 15*

5NE1	SD1	2b gray grn & red	18	18

POSTAGE DUE STAMPS

Hungarian Postage Due Stamps of 1914-18 Overprinted like Regular Issues

On Stamp of 1914

1919 Wmk. 137 *Perf. 15*

5NJ1	D1	50b grn & blk	6.50	6.50

On Stamps of 1915

5NJ2	D1	1b grn & red	*75.00*	*75.00*
5NJ3	D1	2b grn & red	22	22
5NJ4	D1	5b grn & red	14.00	14.00
5NJ5	D1	10b grn & red	80	80
5NJ6	D1	15b grn & red	5.00	5.00
5NJ7	D1	20b grn & red	80	80
5NJ8	D1	30b grn & red	8.50	8.50
		Nos. 5NJ1-5NJ8 (8)	*110.82*	*110.82*

NEWSPAPER STAMP

Hungarian Newspaper Stamp of 1914 Overprinted like Regular Issues

1919 Wmk. 137 *Imperf.*

5NP1	N5	2b orange	1.00	1.00

SECOND TRANSYLVANIA ISSUE

Counterfeits are plentiful.

Issued in Nagyvarad (Oradea)

Hungarian Stamps of 1916-19 Overprinted

1919 Wmk. 137 *Perf. 15, 14*

On Stamps of 1913-16

6N1	A4	2b ol yel	1.10	1.10
6N2	A4	3b orange	2.00	2.00
6N3	A4	6b ol grn	50	50
6N4	A4	16b gray grn	18.50	18.50
6N5	A4	50b lake, *bl*	65	65
6N6	A4	70b red brn & grn	5.00	5.00

On Stamps of 1916-18

6N7	A9	2b brn org	22	22
6N8	A9	3b red lilac	22	22
6N9	A9	5b green	22	22
6N10	A9	6b grnsh bl	80	80
6N11	A9	10b rose red	1.25	1.25
6N12	A9	15b violet	22	22
6N13	A9	20b gray brn	8.00	8.00
6N14	A9	25b dl bl	15	15
6N15	A9	35b brown	22	22
6N16	A9	40b ol grn	15	15
6N17	A10	50b red vio & lil	22	22
6N18	A10	75b brt bl & pale bl	15	15
6N19	A10	80b grn & pale grn	18	18
6N20	A10	1 l red brn & cl	30	30
6N21	A10	2 l ol brn & bis	15	15
6N22	A10	3 l dk vio & ind	2.00	2.00
6N23	A10	5 l dk brn & lt brn	1.25	1.25
6N24	A10	10 l vio brn & vio	80	80

On Stamps of 1918

6N25	A11	10b scarlet	1.40	1.40
6N26	A11	20b dk brn	15	15
6N27	A11	25b brt bl	30	30
6N28	A12	40b ol grn	40	40

On Stamps of 1918-19, Overprinted "Koztarsasag"

6N29	A9	2b brn org	1.75	1.75
6N30	A9	3b red lilac	15	15
6N31	A9	4b slate gray	15	15
6N32	A9	5b green	18	18
6N33	A9	6b grnsh bl	1.00	1.00
6N34	A9	10b rose red	7.50	7.50
6N35	A9	20b gray brn	1.00	1.00
6N36	A9	40b ol grn	25	25
6N37	A10	1 l red brn & cl	18	18
6N38	A10	3 l dk vio & ind	32	32
6N39	A10	5 l dk brn & lt brn	1.40	1.40
6N40	A11	10b scarlet	50.00	50.00
6N41	A11	20b dk brn	1.60	1.60
6N42	A11	25b brt bl	60	60
6N43	A12	50b lilac	18	18

On Stamps of 1919 Inscribed "MAGYAR POSTA"

6N44	A13	5b yel grn	15	15
6N45	A13	10b red	15	15
6N46	A13	20b dk brn	45	45
6N47	A13	25b dl bl	15	15
6N48	A13	40b ol grn	90	90
6N49	A14	5 l dk brn & brn	5.00	5.00

On No. 103A

6N50	A5a	10b vio brn	50	50
		Nos. 6N1-6N50 (50)	120.06	120.06

SEMI-POSTAL STAMPS

Hungarian Semi-Postal Stamps of 1913-17 Overprinted like Regular Issues

On Stamps of 1913

1919 Wmk. 137 *Perf. 14*

6NB1	SP1	1 l on 1f slate	1.00	1.00
6NB2	SP1	1 l on 2f ol yel	5.00	5.00
6NB3	SP1	1 l on 3f orange	1.75	1.75
6NB4	SP1	1 l on 5f emer	60	60
6NB5	SP1	1 l on 6f ol grn	15	15
6NB6	SP1	1 l on 10f car	15	15
6NB7	SP1	1 l on 12f vio, *yel*	40.00	40.00
6NB8	SP1	1 l on 16f gray grn	1.50	1.50
6NB9	SP1	1 l on 20f dk brn	3.75	3.75
6NB10	SP1	1 l on 25f ultra	5.00	5.00
6NB11	SP1	1 l on 35f red vio	5.00	5.00

On Stamp of 1915

Wmk. 135 *Perf. 11½*

6NB12	A4	5b emerald	7.00	7.00

On Stamps of 1916-17

Wmk. 137 *Perf. 15*

6NB13	SP3	10b + 2b rose red	1.25	1.25
6NB14	SP4	15b + 2b dl vio	15	15
6NB15	SP5	40b + 2b brn car	15	15
		Nos. 6NB1-6NB15 (15)	72.45	72.45

SPECIAL DELIVERY STAMP

Hungarian Special Delivery Stamp of 1916 Overprinted like Regular Issues

1919 Wmk. 137 *Perf. 15*

6NE1	SD1	2b gray grn & red	25	25

POSTAGE DUE STAMPS

Hungarian Postage Due Stamps of 1915 Overprinted like Regular Issues

1919 Wmk. 137 *Perf. 15*

6NJ1	D1	1b grn & red	13.00	13.00
6NJ2	D1	2b grn & red	18	18
6NJ3	D1	5b grn & red	25	25
6NJ4	D1	6b grn & red	1.00	1.00
6NJ5	D1	10b grn & red	1.25	1.25
6NJ6	D1	12b grn & red	80	80
6NJ7	D1	15b grn & red	80	80
6NJ8	D1	20b grn & red	15	15
6NJ9	D1	30b grn & red	80	80
		Nos. 6NJ1-6NJ9 (9)	18.23	18.23

NEWSPAPER STAMP

Hungarian Newspaper Stamp of 1914 2 Overprinted like Regular Issues

1919 Wmk. 137 *Imperf.*

6NP1	N5	2b orange	28	28

FIRST BARANYA ISSUE

Issued under Serbian Occupation

Forged overprints abound.

Hungarian Stamps of 1913-18 Overprinted in Black or Red:

1919 Baranya — On A4, A9, A11, A12

1919 Baranya — On A10

1919 Wmk. 137 *Perf. 15*

On Issue of 1913-16

7N1	A4	6f ol grn (R)	65	65
7N2	A4	50f lake, *bl*	15	15
7N3	A4	60f grn, *salmon*	30	30
7N4	A4	70f red brn & grn (R)	1.40	1.40
7N5	A4	70f red brn & grn (Bk)	15	15
7N6	A4	80f dl vio (R)	2.00	2.00

On Issue of 1916-18

7N7	A9	2f brn org (Bk)	2.00	2.00
7N8	A9	2f brn org (R)	20	20
7N9	A9	3f red lil (Bk)	20	20
7N10	A9	3f red lil (R)	20	20
7N11	A9	5f green (Bk)	20	20
7N12	A9	5f green (R)	20	20
7N13	A9	6f grnsh bl (Bk)	20	20
7N14	A9	6f grnsh bl (R)	20	20
7N15	A9	15f violet	20	20
7N16	A9	20f gray brn	15.00	15.00
7N17	A9	25f dl bl	2.00	2.00
7N18	A9	35f brown	4.00	4.00
7N19	A9	40f ol grn	15.00	15.00
7N20	A10	50f red vio & lil	1.75	1.75
7N21	A10	75f brt bl & pale bl	25	25
7N22	A10	80f grn & pale grn	25	25
7N23	A10	1k red brn & cl	25	25
7N24	A10	2k ol brn & bis	25	25
7N25	A10	3k dk vio & ind	25	25
7N26	A10	5k dk brn & lt brn	1.00	1.00
7N27	A10	10k vio brn & vio	4.00	*4.00*

45 45 Baranya 1919

7N28	A9	45f on 2f brn org	15	15
7N29	A9	45f on 5f green	15	15
7N30	A9	45f on 15f vio	15	15

On Issue of 1918

7N31	A11	10f scar (Bk)	15	15
7N32	A11	20f dk brn (Bk)	15	15
7N33	A11	20f dk brn (R)	*22.50*	
7N34	A11	25f dp bl (Bk)	75	75
7N35	A11	25f dp bl (R)	75	75
7N36	A12	40f ol grn (Bk)	5.00	5.00
7N37	A12	40f ol grn (R)	35.00	35.00

On Issue of 1918-19 (Koztarsasag)

7N38	A9	2f brn org (Bk)	4.00	4.00
7N39	A12	40f ol grn (Bk)	*100.00*	*100.00*
7N40	A12	40f ol grn (R)	20.00	20.00

With New Value Added

7N41	A9	45f on 2f brn org (Bk)	25	25
7N42	A9	45f on 2f brn org (R)	25	25

The overprints were set in groups of 25. In each group two stamps have the figures "1" of "1919" with serifs.

No. 7N33 is considered a proof by some specialists.

SEMI-POSTAL STAMPS

Hungarian Semi-Postal Stamps Overprinted Regular Issue First Type

On Stamp of 1915

1919 Wmk. 137 *Perf. 15*

7NB1	A4	50f + 2f lake, *bl*	16.00	16.00

On Stamps of 1916

7NB2	SP3	10f + 2f rose red	15	15
7NB3	SP4	15f + 2f dl vio	15	15

SPECIAL DELIVERY STAMP

SD1

1919 Wmk. 137 *Perf. 15*

7NE1	SD1	105f on 2f gray grn & red	80	80

POSTAGE DUE STAMPS

Overprinted or Surcharged on Hungary Nos. J29, J32, J35 — 1919 Baranya

1919 Wmk. 137 *Perf. 15*

7NJ1	D1	2f grn & red	2.00	2.00
7NJ2	D1	10f grn & red	1.00	1.00
7NJ3	D1	20f grn & red	1.25	1.25

With New Value Added

7NJ4	D1	40f on 2f grn & red	1.50	1.50

SECOND BARANYA ISSUE

Forged overprints exist.

Hungarian Stamps of 1916-19 Surcharged in Black and Red — BARANYA 100

1919 On Stamps of 1916-18

8N1	A9	20f on 2f brn org	1.00	1.00
8N2	A9	50f on 5f green	40	40
8N3	A9	150f on 15f vio	1.00	1.00
8N4	A10	200f on 75f brt bl & pale bl	50	50

On Stamp of 1918-19, Overprinted "Koztarsasag"

8N5	A11	150f on 15f dp vio	25	25

On Stamps of 1919

8N6	A13	20f on 2f brn org	15	15
8N7	A13	30f on 6f grnsh bl	24	30
8N8	A13	50f on 5f yel grn	15	15
8N9	A13	100f on 25f dl bl	15	15
8N10	A13	100f on 40f ol grn	15	15
8N11	A13	100f on 45f orange	35	50
8N12	A13	150f on 20f dk brn	40	60

On No. 103A

8N13	A5a	10f on 10f vio brn	24	35
		Nos. 8N1-8N13 (13)	4.98	5.50

SPECIAL DELIVERY STAMP

Hungarian Special Delivery Stamp of 1916 Surcharged like Regular Issues

1919 Wmk. 137 *Perf. 15*

8NE1	SD1	10f on 2f gray grn & red	40	40

NEWSPAPER STAMP

Hungarian Newspaper Stamp of 1914 Surcharged like Regular Issues

1919 Wmk. 137 *Imperf.*

8NP1	N5	10f on 2f orange	30	30

TEMESVAR ISSUE

Issued under Serbian Occupation

Hungarian Stamps of 1916-18 Surcharged in Black, Blue or Brown:

10 filler — a

50 filler — b

1919

9N1	A9(a)	10f on 2f brn org (Bl)	15	15
a.		Black surcharge	25.00	25.00
9N2	A9(b)	30f on 2f brn org	15	15
a.		Inverted surcharge		
9N3	A11(b)	50f on 20f dk brn (Bl)	15	15
a.		Inverted surcharge		
9N4	A9(b)	1k 50f on 15f vio	25	25
a.		Brown surcharge		
b.		Double surcharge (Bk)		

SEMI-POSTAL STAMP

Hungarian Semi-Postal Stamp of 1916 Surcharged in Blue — 45 fillér

1919 Wmk. 137 *Perf. 15*

9NB1	SP3	45f on 10f + 2f rose red	15	15

POSTAGE DUE STAMPS

Hungarian Postage Due Stamps of 1915 Surcharged — 60 FILLÉR

1919 Wmk. 137 *Perf. 15*

9NJ1	D1	40f on 2f grn & red	80	80
9NJ2	D1	60f on 2f grn & red	80	80
9NJ3	D1	100f on 2f grn & red	80	80

BANAT, BACSKA ISSUE

Issued under Serbian Occupation

Forged overprints exist.

Postal authorities at Temesvar applied these overprints. The stamps were available for postage, but were chiefly used to pay postal employees' salaries.

Hungarian Stamps of 1913-19 Overprinted in Black or Red:

Bánát Bácska 1919. — a

Bánát, Bácska 1919. — b

1919

Type "a" on Stamp of 1913

10N1	A4	50f lake, *blue*	5.00	5.00

Type "a" on Stamps of 1916-18

10N2	A9	2f brn org	15	15
10N3	A9	3f red lilac	15	15
10N4	A9	5f green	15	15
10N5	A9	6f grnsh bl	15	15
10N6	A9	15f violet	15	15
10N7	A9	35f brown	8.50	8.50

Type "b"

10N8	A10	50f red vio & lil (R)	4.25	4.25
10N9	A10	75f brt bl & pale bl	15	15
10N10	A10	80f grn & pale grn	15	15
10N11	A10	1k red brn & cl	15	15
10N12	A10	2k ol brn & bis	15	15
a.		Red overprint	6.00	6.00
10N14	A10	3k dk vio & ind	5.50	5.50
10N15	A10	5k dk brn & lt brn	32	32

10N16 A10 10k vio brn & vio 65 65

Type "a" on Stamps of 1918

10N17 A11 10f scarlet 15 15
10N18 A11 20f dk brn 15 15
10N19 A11 25f brt bl 15 15
10N20 A12 40f ol grn 15 15
10N21 A12 50f lilac 15 15

Type "a" on Stamps of 1919
Inscribed "Magyar Posta"

10N22 A13 10f red *5.50 5.50*
10N23 A13 20f dk brn *2.25 2.25*
10N24 A13 25f dl bl *7.00 7.00*

Type "a" on Stamps of 1918-19
Overprinted "Koztarsasag"

10N25 A9 4f slate gray 15 15
10N26 A9 4f sl gray (R) 5.00 5.00
10N27 A9 5f green 15 15
10N28 A9 6f grnsh bl 15 15
10N29 A9 10f rose red 2.25 2.25
10N30 A11 15f dp vio 1.65 1.65
10N31 A9 20f gray brn 2.75 2.75
10N32 A11 25f brt bl 1.00 1.00
10N33 A9 40f ol grn 15 15
10N34 A9 40f ol grn (R) 5.00 5.00

Type "b"

10N35 A10 1k red brn & cl 15 15
10N36 A10 2k ol brn & bis 2.75 2.75
10N37 A10 3k dk vio & ind 2.75 2.75
10N38 A10 5k dk brn & lt brn 2.75 2.75
10N39 A10 10k vio brn & vio 2.75 2.75

Type "a" on Temesvár Issue

10N40 A9 10f on 2f brn org (Bl & Bk) 40 40
10N41 A9 1k50f on 15f vio 40 40

Bánát Bácska 50 FILLÉR 1919

10N42 A5a 50f on 10f vio brn 85 85
Nos. 10N1-10N42 (41) 72.12 72.12

SEMI-POSTAL STAMPS

Semi-Postal Stamps of 1916-17 Overprinted Type "a" in Black

1919

10NB1 SP3 10f + 2f rose red 15 15
10NB2 SP4 15f + 2f dl vio 15 15
10NB3 SP5 40f + 2f brn car 15 15

Same Overprint on Temesvar Issue

10NB4 SP3 45f on 10f + 2f rose red (Bl & Bk) 40 40

SPECIAL DELIVERY STAMP

Hungary No. E1 Surcharged in Black

1919

10NE1 SD1 30f on 2f gray grn & red 60 60

POSTAGE DUE STAMPS

Postage Due Stamps of 1914-15 Overprinted Type "a" in Black

1919

10NJ1 D1 2f grn & red 38 38
10NJ2 D1 10f grn & red 40 38
10NJ3 D1 15f grn & red 2.50 2.50
10NJ4 D1 20f grn & red 40 40
10NJ5 D1 30f grn & red 1.75 1.75
10NJ6 D1 50f grn & blk 2.50 2.50
Nos. 10NJ1-10NJ6 (6) 7.93 7.91

NEWSPAPER STAMP

Stamp of 1914 Overprinted Type "a" in Black

1919

10NP1 N5 (2f) orange 15 15

SZEGED ISSUE

The "Hungarian National Government, Szeged, 1919," as the overprint reads, was an anti-Bolshevist government which opposed the Soviet Republic then in control at Budapest.

Excellent counterfeits of the overprint exist.

Hungary Stamps of 1916-19 Overprinted in Green, Red and Blue

MAGYAR NEMZETI KORMÁNY Szeged, 1919.

On Stamps of 1916-18

1919 ***Perf. 15, 14***

1 A9 2f brn org (G) 80 80
2 A9 3f red lil (G) 80 80
3 A9 5f green 80 80
4 A9 6f grnsh bl 10.00 10.00
5 A9 15f violet 1.00 1.00
6 A10 50f red vio & lil 6.50 6.50
7 A10 75f brt bl & pale bl 4.00 4.00
8 A10 80f grn & pale grn 6.50 6.50
9 A10 1k red brn & cl (G) 7.50 7.50
10 A10 2k ol brn & bis 7.50 7.50
11 A10 3k dk vio & ind 8.50 8.50
12 A10 5k dk brn & lt brn 22.50 22.50
13 A10 10k vio brn & vio 22.50 22.50

With New Value Added

14 A9 45f on 3f red lil (R & G) 50 50
15 A10 10k on 1k red brn & cl (Bl & G) 6.00 6.00

On Stamps of 1918

16 A11 10f scar (G) 80 80
17 A11 20f dk brn 18 18
18 A11 25f brt bl 5.50 5.50
19 A12 40f ol grn 3.50 3.50

On Stamps of 1918-19
Overprinted "Koztarsasag"

20 A9 3f red lil (G) 12.50 12.50
21 A9 4f slate gray 3.00 3.00
22 A9 5f green 12.50 12.50
23 A9 6f grnsh bl 2.50 2.50
24 A9 10f rose red (G) 2.50 2.50
25 A11 10f scarlet 2.50 2.50
26 A11 15f dp vio 35 35
27 A9 20f gray brn 18.00 18.00
28 A11 20f dk brown 18.00 18.00
29 A11 25f brt blue 6.50 6.50
30 A9 40f oliven 80 80
31 A12 50f lilac 80 80
32 A10 3k dk vio & ind 20.00 20.00

With New Value Added

33 A9 20f on 2f brn org (R & G) 50 50

On Stamps of 1919
Inscribed "Magyar Posta"

34 A13 20f dk brown 35.00 35.00
35 A13 25f dull blue 80 80
Nos. 1-35 (35) 251.63 251.63

SEMI-POSTAL STAMPS

Szeged Overprint on Semi-Postal Stamps of 1916-17 in Green or Red

1919

B1 SP3 10f + 2f rose red (G) 65 65
B2 SP4 15f + 2f dl vio (R) 2.50 2.50
B3 SP5 40f + 2f brn car (G) 6.50 6.50

With Additional Overprint "Koztarsasag"

B4 SP5 40f + 2f brn car (Bk & G) 7.50 7.50

SPECIAL DELIVERY STAMP

Szeged Overprint on Special Delivery Stamp of 1916 in Red

1919

E1 SD1 2f gray grn & red 1.50 1.50

POSTAGE DUE STAMPS

Szeged Overprint on Stamps of 1915-18 in Red

1919

J1 D1 2f green & red 1.25 1.25
J2 D1 6f green & red 4.50 4.50
J3 D1 10f green & red 1.25 1.25
J4 D1 12f green & red 3.00 3.00
J5 D1 20f green & red 3.00 3.00
J6 D1 30f green & red 3.00 3.00

50 Portó 50
MAGYAR NEMZETI KORMÁNY Szeged, 1919

Red Surcharge

J7 SD1 50f on 2f gray grn & red 1.50 1.50
J8 SD1 100f on 2f gray grn & red 1.50 1.50
Nos. J1-J8 (8) 19.00 19.00

NEWSPAPER STAMP

Szeged Overprint on Stamp of 1914 in Green

1919 **Wmk. 137** ***Imperf.***

P1 N5 (2f) orange 40 40

ICELAND

LOCATION — Island in the North Atlantic Ocean, east of Greenland
GOVT. — Republic
AREA — 39,758 sq. mi.
POP. — 238,175 (1983)
CAPITAL — Reykjavik

Iceland became a republic on June 17, 1944. Formerly this country was united with Denmark under the government of King Christian X who, as a ruling sovereign of both countries, was assigned the dual title of king of each. Although the two countries were temporarily united in certain affairs beyond the king's person, both were acknowledged as sovereign states.

96 Skillings = 1 Rigsdaler
100 Aurar (singular "Eyrir") = 1 Krona (1876)

Catalogue values for unused stamps in this country are for Never Hinged items, beginning with Scott 324 in the regular postage section, Scott B14 in the semi-postal section.

Values of early Icelandic stamps vary according to condition. Quotations for Nos. 1-7 are for fine copies. Very fine to superb specimens sell at much higher prices, and inferior or poor copies sell at reduced prices, depending on the condition of the individual specimen.

Watermarks

Wmk. 112- Crown

Wmk. 113- Crown

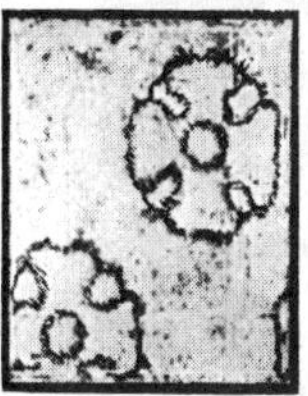
Wmk. 47- Multiple Rosette

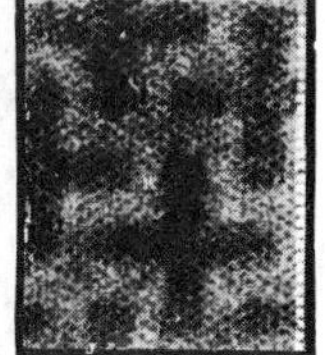
Wmk. 114- Multiple Crosses

A1

Perf. 14x13½

1873 **Typo.** **Wmk. 112**

1 A1 2s ultra 500.00 *1,150.*
a. Imperf. 450.00
2 A1 4s dark carmine 110.00 *575.00*
a. Imperf. 575.00
3 A1 8s brown 175.00 *575.00*
a. Imperf. 225.00
4 A1 16s yellow 825.00 *1,150.*
a. Imperf. 325.00

Perf. 12½

5 A1 3s gray 200.00 *725.00*
a. Imperf. 550.00
6 A1 4s carmine 700.00 *1,200.*
7 A1 16s yellow 67.50 *300.00*

False and favor cancellations are often found on Nos. 1-7. The imperforate varieties lack gum.

A2

Small "3" — A3

Large "3" — A3a

1876

8 A2 5a blue 175.00 *350.00*

Perf. 14x13½

9 A2 5a blue 240.00 *350.00*
10 A2 6a gray 52.50 10.00
11 A2 10a carmine 85.00 3.50
a. Imperf. 350.00 375.00
12 A2 16a brown 62.50 25.00
13 A2 20a dark violet 24.00 *55.00*
14 A2 40a green 62.50 *80.00*

1882-98

15 A3 3a orange 30.00 9.50
16 A2 5a green 25.00 *6.25*
17 A2 20a blue 140.00 18.00
a. 20a ultramarine 275.00 80.00
18 A2 40a red violet 19.00 22.50
a. Perf. 13 ('98) *3,600.*
19 A2 50a bl & car ('92) 45.00 32.50
20 A2 100a brn & vio ('92) 47.50 47.50

See note after No. 68.

1896-1901 ***Perf. 13***

21 A3 3a orange ('97) 45.00 4.00
22 A3a 3a yellow ('01) 2.25 *9.00*
23 A2 4a rose & gray ('99) 10.50 10.00
24 A2 5a green 1.65 1.10
25 A2 6a gray ('97) 7.00 *8.50*
26 A2 10a carmine ('97) 3.00 1.40
27 A2 16a brown 37.50 *45.00*
28 A2 20a dull blue ('98) 14.00 12.00
a. 20a dull ultramarine 200.00 13.00

29 A2 25a yel brown & blue ('00) 13.00 16.00
30 A2 50a bl & car ('98) 225.00 *400.00*

See note after No. 68.
For surcharges see Nos. 31-33A, 45-68.

Black and Red Surcharge

Surcharged **þrír 3**

1897 *Perf. 13*

31 A2 3a on 5a green 300.00 300.00
a. Perf. 14x13½ *2,750.*
b. Inverted surcharge 1,050. 800.00

Surcharged **þrír 3**

32 A2 3a on 5a green 275.00 275.00
a. Inverted surcharge 1,000. 750.00
b. Perf. 14x13½ *8,000.* *1,250.*

Black Surcharge

Surcharged **þrír**

33 A2 3a on 5a green 425.00 375.00

Surcharged **þrír**

33A A2 3a on 5a green 350.00 325.00

Excellent counterfeits are known.

King Christian IX — A4

1902-04 Wmk. 113 *Perf. 13*

34 A4 3a orange 2.75 1.40
35 A4 4a gray & rose 2.25 45
36 A4 5a yel green 11.00 28
37 A4 6a gray brown 8.25 3.50
38 A4 10a car rose 3.75 28
39 A4 16a chocolate 3.75 3.25
40 A4 20a deep blue 1.50 2.25
a. Inscribed "PJONUSTA" 35.00 35.00
41 A4 25a brn & grn 1.50 1.75
42 A4 40a violet 1.75 1.65
43 A4 50a gray & bl blk 3.00 *12.00*
44 A4 1k sl bl & yel brn 4.50 4.25
44A A4 2k olive brn & brt blue ('04) 15.00 *35.00*
44B A4 5k org brn & slate blue ('04) 82.50 *100.00*
Nos. 34-44B (13) 141.50 *166.06*

For surcharge see No. 142.

Stamps of 1882-1901 Overprinted **Í GILDI '02—'03**

1902-03 Wmk. 112 *Perf. 13*

Red Overprint

45 A2 5a green 38 *4.25*
a. Inverted overprint 8.25
b. "I" before Gildi omitted 15.00
c. '03-'03 32.50
d. 02'-'03 32.50
e. Pair, one without overprint 32.50
46 A2 6a gray 28 *3.50*
a. Double overprint 20.00
b. Inverted overprint 16.00
c. '03-'03 90.00
d. 02'-'03 90.00
e. Pair, one with invtd. ovpt. 45.00
f. Pair, one without overprint 25.00
g. As "f", inverted 40.00
47 A2 20a dull blue 38 *4.00*
a. Inverted overprint. 16.00 16.00
b. "I" before Gildi omitted 30.00
c. 02'-'03 82.50
48 A2 25a yel brn & bl 38 *8.25*
a. Inverted overprint 11.00 11.00
b. '03-'03 37.50
c. 02'-'03 37.50
d. Double overprint 55.00

Black Overprint

49 A3 3a orange 75.00 *225.00*
b. Inverted overprint 75.00
c. "I" before Gildi omitted 75.00
d. '03-'03 75.00
e. 02'-'03 75.00 *235.00*
50 A3a 3a yellow 40 *90*
a. Double overprint 35.00
b. Inverted overprint 6.00
c. "I" before Gildi omitted 50.00
d. '02-'03 50.00
51 A2 4a rose & gray 17.00 *27.50*
a. Double overprint 35.00
b. Inverted overprint 19.00 *30.00*
c. Dbl. ovpt., one invtd. 60.00
d. "I" before Gildi omitted 24.00
e. '03-'03 55.00
f. 02'-'03 55.00 60.00
g. Pair, one with invtd. ovpt. 55.00
52 A2 5a green 125.00 *225.00*
a. Inverted overprint 130.00 *225.00*
b. Pair, one without overprint 150.00
c. As "b", inverted 150.00
53 A2 6a gray 250.00 *325.00*
a. Inverted overprint 200.00 250.00
b. Pair, one without overprint 200.00
54 A2 10a carmine 55 *6.00*
a. Inverted overprint 5.50 9.00
b. Pair, one without overprint 24.00
55 A2 16a brown 10.00 *24.00*
a. Inverted overprint 24.00
b. "I" before Gildi omitted 42.50
c. '03-'03 67.50
d. 02'-'03 67.50
56 A2 20a dull blue *4,500.*
a. Inverted overprint *4,750.*
57 A2 25a yel brn & bl *3,750.*
a. Inverted overprint *4,250.*
58 A2 40a red vio 45 *30.00*
a. Inverted overprint 10.00 *30.00*
59 A2 50a bl & car 2.25 *37.50*
a. Double overprint 32.50 40.00
b. 02'-'03 32.50
c. '03-'03 32.50

Perf. 14x13½

Red Overprint

60 A2 5a green 750.00 *1,250.*
a. '03-'03 775.00
b. 02'-'03 750.00
61 A2 6a gray 750.00 1,250.
a. 02'-'03 750.00
62 A2 20a blue *2,600.* *4,500.*

Black Overprint

63 A3 3a orange 400.00 *1,000.*
a. Inverted overprint 475.00
b. 02'-'03 475.00
c. '03-'03 475.00
64 A2 10a carmine *3,500.* *3,750.*
65 A2 16a brown 450.00 *900.00*
a. Inverted overprint 475.00
b. 02'-'03 475.00
d. '03-'03 475.00
65C A2 20a dull blue *3,750.* *4,750.*
66 A2 40a red vio 10.00 *45.00*
a. Inverted overprint 15.00
b. '03-'03 37.50
c. 02'-'03 37.50
67 A2 50a bl & car 14.00 *67.50*
a. Inverted overprint 40.00 *70.00*
b. '03-'03 55.00
c. 02'-'03 55.00
d. As "c," inverted 105.00
68 A2 100a brn & vio 25.00 *32.50*
a. Inverted overprint 32.50 *37.50*
b. 02'-'03 65.00
c. '03-'03 65.00

"I GILDI" means "valid."

In 1904 Nos. 20, 22-30, 45-59 (except 49, 52, 53, 56 and 57) and No. 68 were reprinted for the Postal Union. The reprints are perforated 13 and have watermark type 113. Value $50 each. Without overprint, $100 each.

Kings Christian IX and Frederik VIII — A5

Typo., Center Engr.

1907-08 Wmk. 113 *Perf. 13*

71 A5 1e yel grn & red 70 50
72 A5 3a yel brn & ocher 1.75 50
73 A5 4a gray & red 1.00 50
74 A5 5a green 30.00 30
75 A5 6a gray & gray brn 15.00 1.25
76 A5 10a scarlet 52.50 38
77 A5 15a red & green 3.75 50
78 A5 16a brown 3.75 *12.50*
79 A5 20a blue 4.25 1.40
80 A5 25a bis brn & grn 2.50 *4.00*
81 A5 40a claret & vio 3.25 *5.00*
82 A5 50a gray & vio 3.25 *4.00*
83 A5 1k blue & brn 12.50 *26.00*
84 A5 2k dk brn & dk grn 12.50 *26.00*
85 A5 5k brn & slate 87.50 *165.00*
Nos. 71-85 (15) 234.20 *247.83*

See Nos. 99-107.
For surcharges and overprints see Nos. 130-138, 143, C2, O69.

Jon Sigurdsson — A6

Frederik VIII — A7

1911 Typo. and Embossed

86 A6 1e olive green 1.50 65
87 A6 3a light brown 1.75 *7.00*
88 A6 4a ultramarine 80 *1.00*
89 A6 6a gray 5.50 *10.00*
90 A6 15a violet 14.00 85
91 A6 25a orange 19.00 19.00
Nos. 86-91 (6) 42.55 *38.50*

Sigurdsson (1811-79), statesman and author.
For surcharge see No. 149.

1912, Feb. 17

92 A7 5a green 17.00 6.75
93 A7 10a red 17.00 6.75
94 A7 20a pale blue 25.00 8.50
95 A7 50a claret 7.25 *18.00*
96 A7 1k yellow 12.50 *30.00*
97 A7 2k rose 12.50 *25.00*
98 A7 5k brown 85.00 *110.00*
Nos. 92-98 (7) 176.25 *205.00*

For surcharges and overprints see Nos. 140-141, O50-O51.

Type of 1907-08 and

Christian X — A8

Typo., Center Engr.

1915-18 Wmk. 114 *Perf. 14x14½*

99 A5 1e yel grn & red 4.25 *8.25*
100 A5 3a bister brn 2.00 1.20
101 A5 4a gray & red 2.00 *5.00*
102 A5 5a green 42.50 55
103 A5 6a gray & gray brn 9.00 *65.00*
104 A5 10a scarlet 2.00 55
107 A5 20a blue 105.00 8.25
Nos. 99-107 (7) 166.75 *88.80*

1920-22 Typo.

108 A8 1e yel grn & red 48 50
109 A8 3a bister brn 2.50 *6.25*
110 A8 4a gray & red 2.00 85
111 A8 5a green 1.25 75
112 A8 5a ol green ('22) 2.00 50
113 A8 6a dark gray 7.25 3.50
114 A8 8a dark brown 4.25 85
115 A8 10a red 75 *4.50*
116 A8 10a green ('21) 1.50 65
117 A8 15a violet 18.00 65
118 A8 20a deep blue 1.10 *7.50*
119 A8 20a choc ('22) 30.00 65
120 A8 25a brown & grn 9.25 70
121 A8 25a red ('21) 4.75 *15.00*
122 A8 30a red & green 25.00 1.25
123 A8 40a claret 25.00 1.00
124 A8 40a dk bl ('21) 35.00 5.50
125 A8 50a dk gray & cl 75.00 5.00
126 A8 1k dp bl & dk brn 55.00 70
127 A8 2k ol brn & myr green 90.00 12.50
Revenue cancellation 1.25
128 A8 5k brn & ind 35.00 6.25
Revenue cancellation 1.25
Nos. 108-128 (21) 425.08 *75.05*

Revenue cancellations consisting of "TOLLUR" boxed in frame are found on stamps used to pay the tax on parcel post packages entering Iceland.
See Nos. 176-187, 202.
For surcharges and overprints see Nos. 139, 150, C1, C9-C14, O52, O70-O71.

A9

A10

A11

1921-25 Wmk. 113 *Perf. 13*

130 A9 5a on 16a brown 1.65 *15.00*
131 A11 5a on 16a brown 75 *3.25*
132 A10 20a on 25a brn & green 3.25 2.25
133 A11 20a on 25a bis brn & green 1.65 *2.50*
134 A9 20a on 40a violet 3.25 *7.00*
135 A11 20a on 40a cl & vio 4.50 *7.50*
137 A9 30a on 50a gray & bl blk ('25) 9.00 *12.00*
Revenue cancel 5.00
138 A9 50a on 5k org brn & sl bl ('25) 35.00 15.00
Revenue cancel 4.00
Nos. 130-138 (8) 59.05 *64.50*

No. 111 Surcharged **10 aur.**

1922 Wmk. 114 *Perf. 14x14½*

139 A8 10a on 5a green 2.75 1.25

Nos. 95-96, 44A, 85 Surcharged **Kr. 10**

1924-30 Wmk. 113 *Perf. 13*

140 A7 10k on 50a ('25)	135.00	*225.00*
Revenue cancellation		9.00
141 A7 10k on 1k	200.00	*300.00*
Revenue cancellation		22.50
142 A4 10k on 2k ('29)	40.00	15.00
Revenue cancellation		3.25
143 A5 10k on 5k ('30)	225.00	225.00
Revenue cancellation		3.00

"Tollur" is a revenue cancellation.

Landing the Mail — A12

Designs: 7a, 50a, Landing the mail. 10a, 35a, View of Reykjavik. 20a, Museum building.

Perf. 14x15

1925, Sept. 12 Typo. Wmk. 114

144 A12 7a yel green	25.00	3.00
145 A12 10a dp bl & brn	25.00	25
146 A12 20a vermilion	25.00	25
147 A12 35a deep blue	32.50	5.00
148 A12 50a yel grn & brn	32.50	60
Nos. 144-148 (5)	140.00	9.10

No. 91 Surcharged **2 krónur**

1925 Wmk. 113 *Perf. 13*

149 A6 2k on 25a orange	42.50	*70.00*
Revenue cancellation		6.00

No. 124 Surcharged in Red **EIN KRÓNA**

1926

150 A8 1k on 40a dark blue	72.50	13.00
Revenue cancellation		5.00

Parliament Building — A15

Designs: 5a, Viking ship in storm. 7a, Parliament meeting place, 1690. 10a, Viking funeral. 15a, Vikings naming land. 20a, The dash for Thing. 25a, Gathering wood. 30a, Thingvalla Lake. 35a, Iceland woman in national costume. 40a, Iceland flag. 50a, First Althing, 930 A.D. 1k, Map of Iceland. 2k, Winter-bound home. 5k, Woman spinning. 10k, Viking Sacrifice to Thor.

Perf. 12½x12

1930, Jan. 1 Litho. Unwmk.

152 A15 3a dl vio & gray violet	1.75	*5.00*
153 A15 5a dk bl & sl grn	1.75	*5.00*
154 A15 7a grn & gray grn	1.75	*5.00*
155 A15 10a dk vio & lilac	5.25	*6.00*
156 A15 15a dp ultra & bl gray	1.75	*5.00*
157 A15 20a rose red & sal	23.00	*32.50*
a. Double impression	135.00	
158 A15 25a dk brn & lt brown	4.00	*8.00*
159 A15 30a dk grn & sl grn	4.00	*6.00*
160 A15 35a ultra & bl gray	4.00	*8.50*
161 A15 40a dk ultra, red & slate grn	4.00	*6.00*
162 A15 50a red brn & cinnamon	35.00	*50.00*
163 A15 1k ol grn & gray green	35.00	*50.00*
164 A15 2k turq bl & gray green	42.50	*67.50*
165 A15 5k org & yellow	23.00	*50.00*
166 A15 10k mag & dl rose	23.00	*50.00*
a. Imperf., pair	60.00	
Nos. 152-166 (15)	209.75	354.50

Millenary of the "Althing," the Icelandic Parliament, oldest in the world.
For overprints see Nos. O53-O67.

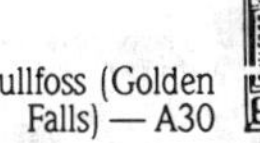
Gullfoss (Golden Falls) — A30

1931-32 Unwmk. Engr. *Perf. 14*

170 A30 5a gray	6.75	48
171 A30 20a red	5.50	18
172 A30 35a ultramarine	10.50	7.50
173 A30 60a red lil ('32)	5.50	75
174 A30 65a red brn ('32)	1.10	55
175 A30 75a grnsh bl ('32)	62.50	19.00
Revenue cancellation		1.90
Nos. 170-175 (6)	91.85	28.46

Issued: 5a-35a, Dec. 15; 60a-75a, May 30.

Type of 1920 Christian X Issue Redrawn

Perf. 14x14½

1931-33 Typo. Wmk. 114

176 A8 1e yel grn & red	60	*65*
177 A8 3a bister brown	3.75	*4.50*
178 A8 4a gray & red	1.00	65
179 A8 6a dark gray	1.00	*3.00*
180 A8 7a yel grn ('33)	40	70
181 A8 10a chocolate	40.00	45
182 A8 25a brn & green	9.00	1.00
183 A8 30a red & green	11.50	2.25
184 A8 40a claret	60.00	6.00
185 A8 1k dk bl & lt brn	25.00	3.50
Revenue cancellation		1.10
186 A8 2k choc & dk grn	77.50	25.00
Revenue cancellation		1.40
187 A8 10k yel grn & blk	175.00	75.00
Revenue cancellation		3.25
Nos. 176-187 (12)	404.75	122.70

On the redrawn stamps the horizontal lines of the portrait and the oval are closer together than on the 1920 stamps and are crossed by many fine vertical lines.
See No. 202.

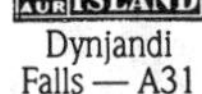
Dynjandi Falls — A31

Mount Hekla — A32

Perf. 12½

1935, June 28 Engr. Unwmk.

193 A31 10a blue	10.00	15
Never hinged	30.00	
194 A32 1k greenish gray	22.50	15
Never hinged	55.00	

Matthias Jochumsson A33

King Christian X A34

1935, Nov. 11

195 A33 3a gray green	38	*1.75*
196 A33 5a gray	8.00	60
197 A33 7a yel green	13.00	75
198 A33 35a blue	38	*75*
Set, never hinged	42.50	

Birth cent. of Matthias Jochumsson, poet.
For surcharges see Nos. 212, 236.

1937, May 14 *Perf. 13x12½*

199 A34 10a green	1.50	*7.00*
200 A34 30a brown	1.50	*3.00*
201 A34 40a claret	1.50	*3.00*
Set, never hinged	9.50	

Reign of Christian X, 25th anniv.

Christian X Type of 1931-33

1937 Unwmk. Typo. *Perf. 11½*

202 A8 1e yel grn & red	50	*50*
Never hinged	85	

Geyser
A35 A36

1938-47 Engr. *Perf. 14*

203 A35 15a dp rose vio	2.75	*6.00*
a. Imperf., pair	*1,000.*	
204 A35 20a rose red	12.50	16
205 A35 35a ultra	48	48
206 A36 40a dk brn ('39)	6.00	*12.00*
207 A36 45a brt ultra ('40)	50	50
208 A36 50a dk slate grn	12.50	50
208A A36 60a brt ultra ('43)	3.75	70
c. Perf. 11½ ('47)	2.00	*2.50*
c. Never hinged	3.00	
208B A36 1k indigo ('45)	1.40	24
d. Perf. 11½ ('47)	2.00	*2.50*
d. Never hinged	3.00	
Nos. 203-208B (8)	39.88	*20.58*
Set, never hinged	90.00	

University of Iceland A37

1938, Dec. 1 *Perf. 13½*

209 A37 25a dark grn	5.00	*7.50*
210 A37 30a brown	5.00	*7.50*
211 A37 40a brt red vio	5.00	*7.50*
Set, never hinged	24.00	

20th anniversary of independence.

No. 198 Surcharged with New Value

1939, Mar. 17 *Perf. 12½*

212 A33 5a on 35a blue	1.00	*1.00*
a. Double surcharge	*160.00*	

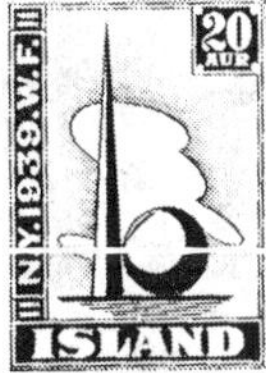
Trylon and Perisphere A38

Leif Ericsson's Ship and Route to America A39

Statue of Thorfinn Karlsefni — A40

1939 Engr. *Perf. 14*

213 A38 20a crimson	2.25	3.25
214 A39 35a bright ultra	3.00	4.25
215 A40 45a bright green	2.75	5.00
216 A40 2k dark gray	32.50	*85.00*
Set, never hinged	67.50	

New York World's Fair.
For overprints see Nos. 232-235.

Codfish — A41

Herring — A42

Flag of Iceland — A43

1939-45 Engr. Perf. 14, 14x13½

217 A41 1e Prussian blue 15 1.40
a. Perf. 14x13½ 1.10 2.00
218 A42 3a dark violet 15 15
a. Perf. 14x13½ 1.00 1.00
219 A41 5a dark brown 15 15
c. Perf. 14x13½ 1.10 50
220 A42 7a dark green 3.00 3.25
221 A42 10a green ('40) 19.00 15
b. Perf. 14 22.50 15
b. Never hinged 50.00
222 A42 10a slate gray ('45) 15 15
223 A42 12a dk grn ('43) 15 15
224 A41 25a brt red ('40) 9.00 15
b. Perf. 14x13½ 22.50 55
b. Never hinged 37.50
225 A41 25a hn brn ('45) 15 15
226 A42 35a carmine ('43) 40 15
227 A41 50a dk bl grn ('43) 35 15

Typo.

228 A43 10a car & ultra 1.40 50
Nos. 217-228 (12) 34.05 6.50
Set, never hinged 55.00

Statue of Thorfinn Karlsefni — A44

1939-45 Engr. Perf. 14

229 A44 2k dark gray 1.60 15
230 A44 5k dk brn ('43) 11.00 20
231 A44 10k brn yel ('45) 10.50 1.40
Set, never hinged 52.50

1947 Perf. 11½

229a A44 2k 4.75 90
230a A44 5k 19.00 1.25
231a A44 10k 14.00 30.00
Set, never hinged 85.00

New York World's Fair Issue of 1939 Overprinted "1940" in Black

1940, May 11 Perf. 14

232 A38 20a crimson 7.75 18.00
233 A39 35a bright ultra 7.75 28.00
234 A40 45a bright green 7.75 18.00
235 A40 2k dark gray 80.00 200.00
Set, never hinged 180.00

No. 195 Surcharged in Red

1941, Mar. 6 Perf. 12½

236 A33 25a on 3a gray green 60 90
Never hinged 95

Statue of Snorri Sturluson — A45

Jon Sigurdsson — A46

1941, Nov. 17 Engr. Perf. 14

237 A45 25a rose red 65 80
238 A45 50a deep ultra 1.65 2.00
239 A45 1k dk olive grn 1.65 2.00
Set, never hinged 6.25

Snorri Sturluson, writer and historian, 700th death anniv.

Republic

1944, June 17 Perf. 14x13½

240 A46 10a gray black 24 60
241 A46 25a dk red brn 32 60
242 A46 50a slate grn 32 60
243 A46 1k blue black 32 60
244 A46 5k henna 6.50 10.50
245 A46 10k golden brn 35.00 67.50
Nos. 240-245 (6) 42.70 80.40
Set, never hinged 80.00

Founding of Republic of Iceland, June 17, 1944.

Eruption of Hekla Volcano
A47 A48

Designs: 35a, 60a, Close view of Hekla.

Unwmk.

1948, Dec. 3 Engr. Perf. 14

246 A47 12a dark vio brn 15 15
247 A48 25a green 60 15
248 A47 35a carmine rose 22 15
249 A47 50a brown 65 15
250 A47 60a bright ultra 2.50 1.65
251 A48 1k orange brown 6.00 15
252 A48 10k violet black 17.50 38
Nos. 246-252 (7) 27.62 2.78
Set, never hinged 62.50

For surcharge see No. 283.

Pack Train and UPU Monument, Bern — A49

UPU, 75th Anniv.: 35a, Reykjavik. 60a, Map. 2k, Thingvellir Road.

1949, Oct. 9

253 A49 25a dark green 20 28
254 A49 35a deep carmine 20 28
255 A49 60a blue 30 70
256 A49 2k orange red 1.00 70
Set, never hinged 2.75

Trawler — A50

Jon Arason — A51

Designs: 20a, 75a, 1k, Tractor plowing. 60a, 5k, Flock of sheep. 5a, 90a, 2k, Vestmannaeyjar harbor.

1950-54 Perf. 13

257 A50 5a dk brn ('54) 15 15
258 A50 10a gray 15 15
259 A50 20a brown 15 15
260 A50 25a car ('54) 15 15
261 A50 60a green 5.50 15.00
262 A50 75a red org ('52) 42 15
263 A50 90a carmine 16 15
264 A50 1k chocolate 2.75 15
265 A50 1.25k red vio ('52) 7.00 15
266 A50 1.50k deep ultra 5.50 15
267 A50 2k purple 10.00 15
268 A50 5k dark grn 17.00 30
Nos. 257-268 (12) 48.93 16.80
Set, never hinged 85.00

For surcharges see Nos. B12-B13.

1950, Nov. 7 Perf. 14

269 A51 1.80k carmine 1.25 1.90
270 A51 3.30k green 50 1.50
Set, never hinged 2.75

Bishop Jon Arason, 400th anniv. of death.

Mail Delivery, 1776 — A52

Design: 3k, Airmail, 1951.

1951, May 13

271 A52 2k deep ultra 1.40 1.10
272 A52 3k dark purple 1.65 1.40
Set, never hinged 4.00

175th anniv. of Iceland's postal service.

Parliament Building — A53

1952, Apr. 1 Perf. 13x12½

273 A53 25k gray black 75.00 14.00
Never hinged 140.00

Sveinn Björnsson A54

Reykjabok A55

1952, Sept. 1 Perf. 13½

274 A54 1.25k deep blue 1.40 15
275 A54 2.20k deep green 35 4.00
276 A54 5k indigo 4.50 70
277 A54 10k brown red 16.00 19.00
Set, never hinged 45.00

Sveinn Björnsson, 1st President of Iceland.

1953, Oct. 1 Perf. 13½x13

Designs: 70a, Lettering manuscript. 1k, Corner of 15th century manuscript, "Stjorn." 1.75k, Reykjabok. 10k, Corner from law manuscript.

278 A55 10a black 15 15
279 A55 70a green 22 18
280 A55 1k carmine 35 15
281 A55 1.75k blue 11.00 75
282 A55 10k orange brn 7.25 35
Nos. 278-282 (5) 18.97 1.58
Set, never hinged 30.00

No. 248 Surcharged With New Value and Bars in Black

1954, Mar. 31 Perf. 14

283 A47 5a on 35a car rose 15 25
a. Bars omitted 35.00
b. Inverted surcharge 92.50

Hannes Hafstein A56

Icelandic Wrestling A57

Portraits: 2.45k, in oval. 5k, fullface.

1954, June 1 Engr. Perf. 13

284 A56 1.25k deep blue 2.50 35
285 A56 2.45k dark green 9.25 17.00
286 A56 5k carmine 9.25 3.00
Set, never hinged 42.50

Appointment of the first native minister to Denmark, 50th anniv.

1955, Aug. 9 Unwmk. Perf. 14

287 A57 75a shown 20 20
288 A57 1.25k Diving 30 30
Set, never hinged 80

See Nos. 300-301.

Skoga Falls — A58

Ellidaar Power Plant — A59

Waterfalls: 60a, Goda. 2kr, Detti. 5kr, Gull. Electric Power Plants: 1.50kr, Sogs. 2.45kr, Andakilsar. 3kr, Laxar.

Perf. 11½, 13½x14 (A59)

1956, Apr. 4 Unwmk.

289 A58 15a vio blue 20 20
290 A59 50a dull green 32 20
291 A59 60a brown 1.65 *3.75*
292 A59 1.50k violet 8.00 25
293 A59 2k sepia 1.20 25
294 A59 2.45k gray black 4.25 4.25
295 A59 3k dark blue 2.25 60
296 A58 5k dark green 6.75 1.50
Nos. 289-296 (8) 24.62 11.00
Set, never hinged 45.00

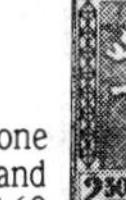
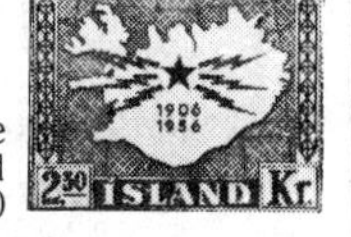

Telegraph-Telephone Emblem and Map — A60

1956, Sept. 29 Engr. *Perf. 13*

297 A60 2.30k ultramarine 25 *60*
Never hinged 35

Telegraph and Telephone service in Iceland, 50th anniv.

Northern Countries Issue

Whooper Swans — A60a

1956, Oct. 30 *Perf. 12½*

298 A60a 1.50k rose red 65 80
299 A60a 1.75k ultra 7.00 *10.00*
Set, never hinged 10.00

To emphasize the bonds among Denmark, Finland, Iceland, Norway and Sweden.

Sports Type of 1955

Designs: 1.50k, Icelandic wrestling. 1.75k, Diving.

1957, Apr. 1 Engr. *Perf. 14*

300 A57 1.50k carmine 50 24
301 A57 1.75k ultramarine 35 24
Set, never hinged 1.10

Type of 1952 Air Post Stamps; Plane Omitted

Glaciers: 2k, Snaefellsjokull. 3k, Eiriksjokull. 10k, Oraefajokull.

1957, May 8 *Perf. 13½x14*

302 AP16 2k green 1.75 15
303 AP16 3k dark blue 1.75 20
304 AP16 10k reddish brn 2.75 32
Set, never hinged 9.00

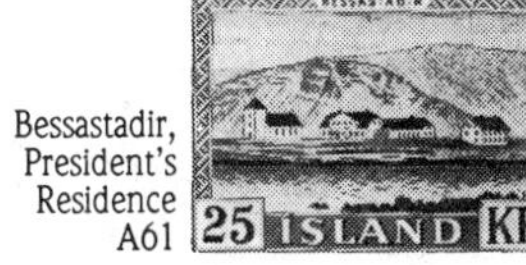

Bessastadir, President's Residence A61

1957, Aug. 1 Engr. Unwmk.

305 A61 25k gray blk 10.50 3.00
Never hinged 17.50

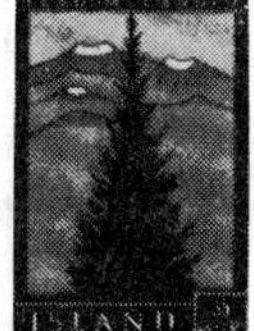
Evergreen and Volcanoes A62

Jonas Hallgrimsson A63

1957, Sept. 4 *Perf. 13½x13*

306 A62 35a shown 15 15
307 A62 70a Birch 15 15
Set value 16 16
Set, never hinged 20

Issued to publicize a reforestation program.

1957, Nov 16

308 A63 5k grn & blk 1.10 45
Never hinged 1.75

150th birth anniv. of Jonas Hallgrimsson, poet.

Willow Herb — A64

Icelandic Pony — A65

1958, July 8 Litho. Unwmk.

309 A64 1k shown 15 15
310 A64 2.50k Wild pansy 35 35
Set, never hinged 55

1958, Sept. 27 Engr.

311 A65 10a gray black 15 15
312 A65 2.25k brown 50 15
Set, never hinged 80

See No. 324.

Flag — A66

Old Icelandic Government Building — A67

Perf. 13½x14

1958, Dec. 1 Litho. Unwmk.

Size: 17½x21mm

313 A66 3.50k brt ultra & red 1.40 65

Size: 23x26½mm

314 A66 50k brt ultra & red 6.25 5.00
Set, never hinged 9.00

40th anniversary of Icelandic flag.

1958, Dec. 9 Photo. *Perf. 11½*

315 A67 2k deep green 45 20
316 A67 4k deep brown 45 35
Set, never hinged 1.10

See Nos. 333-334.

Jon Thorkelsson Teaching — A68

1959, May 5 Engr. *Perf. 13½*

317 A68 2k green 45 45
318 A68 3k dull purple 45 45
Set, never hinged 1.10

Death bicentenary of Jon Thorkelsson, headmaster of Skaholt.

Sockeye Salmon — A69

Eider Ducks — A70

Design: 25k, Gyrfalcon.

1959-60 Engr. *Perf. 14*

319 A69 25a dark blue 15 15
320 A70 90a chestnut & blk 15 15
321 A70 2k olive grn & blk 22 15
322 A69 5k gray green 4.00 65

Litho. *Perf. 11½*

323 A70 25k dl pur, gray & yel 12.00 10.50
Nos. 319-323 (5) 16.52 11.60
Set, never hinged 20.00

Issued: 25k, Mar. 1, 1960; others, Nov. 25.

Catalogue values for unused stamps in this section, from this point to the end of the section, are for Never Hinged items.

Pony Type of 1958

1960, Apr. 7 Engr. *Perf. 13½x13*

324 A65 1k dark carmine 30 15

"The Outlaw" by Einar Jonsson A71

Wild Geranium A72

1960, Apr. 7 *Perf. 14*

325 A71 2.50k reddish brn 20 15
326 A71 4.50k ultramarine 65 75

World Refugee Year, July 1, 1959-June 30, 1960.

Europa Issue, 1960

Common Design Type

1960, Sept. 18 Photo. *Perf. 11½*

Size: 32½x22mm

327 CD3 3k grn & lt grn 85 55
328 CD3 5.50k dk bl & lt bl 65 1.50

1960-62 Photo. *Perf. 11½*

Flowers: 50a, Bellflower. 2.50k, Dandelion. 3.50k, Buttercup.

329 A72 50a gray grn, grn & violet ('62) 15 15
330 A72 1.20k sep, vio & grn 16 16
331 A72 2.50k brn, yel & grn 20 16
332 A72 3.50k dl bl, yel & green ('62) 52 16

See Nos. 363-366, 393-394.

Common Design Types pictured in section at front of book.

Building Type of 1958

1961, Apr. 11 Unwmk. *Perf. 11½*

333 A67 1.50k deep blue 24 15
334 A67 3k dark carmine 24 15

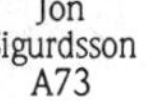

Jon Sigurdsson A73

Reykjavik A74

Typographed and Embossed

1961, June 17 *Perf. 12½x14*

335 A73 50a crimson 15 18
336 A73 3k dark blue 1.10 90
337 A73 5k deep plum 60 55

Jon Sigurdsson (1811-1879), statesman and scholar.

1961, Aug. 18 Photo. *Perf. 11½*

338 A74 2.50k blue & grn 42 25
339 A74 4.50k lilac & vio bl 70 40

Municipal charter of Reykjavik, 175th anniv.

Europa Issue, 1961

Common Design Type

1961, Sept. 18

Size: 32x22½mm

340 CD4 5.50k multicolored 65 80
341 CD4 6k multicolored 65 80

Benedikt Sveinsson A75

University of Iceland A76

Design: 1.40k, Björn M. Olsen.

1961, Oct. 6 Photo. *Perf. 11½*

342 A75 1k red brown 15 20
343 A75 1.40k ultramarine 15 20
344 A76 10k green 1.40 75
a. Souv. sheet of 3, #342-344, imperf. 45 1.00

50th anniv. of the University of Iceland; Benedikt Sveinsson (1827-1899), statesman; and Björn M. Olsen (1850-1919), first rector.

Production Institute — A77

New Buildings: 4k, Fishing Research Institute. 6k, Farm Bureau.

1962, July 6 Unwmk. *Perf. 11½*

345 A77 2.50k ultramarine 35 25
346 A77 4k dull green 45 25
347 A77 6k brown 55 30

Europa Issue, 1962

Common Design Type

1962, Sept. 17 *Perf. 11½*

Size: 32½x22½mm

348 CD5 5.50k yel, lt grn & brn 15 30
349 CD5 6.50k lt grn, grn & brn 40 65

Map Showing Submarine Telephone Cable — A78

1962, Nov. 20

Granite Paper

350 A78 5k multicolored 1.10 55
351 A78 7k grn, lt bl & red 65 45

Inauguration of the submarine telephone cable from Newfoundland, via Greenland and Iceland to Scotland.

Iceland stamps can be mounted in the Scott annually supplemented Scandinavia and Finland album.

Sigurdur Gudmundsson, Self-portrait A79

Herring Boat A80

Design: 5.50k, Knight slaying dragon, Romanesque door from Valthjofsstad Church, ca. 1200 A.D.

1963, Feb. 20 Photo. *Perf. 11½*

352 A79 4k bis brn & choc 48 35
353 A79 5.50k gray ol & brn 48 35

National Museum of Iceland, cent., and its first curator, Sigurdur Gudmundsson.

1963, Mar. 21

354 A80 5k multicolored 90 30
355 A80 7.50k multicolored 25 20

FAO "Freedom from Hunger" campaign.

View of Akureyri — A81

1963, July 2 Unwmk. *Perf. 11½*

356 A81 3k gray green 22 15

Europa Issue, 1963

Common Design Type

1963, Sept. 16

Size: 32½x23mm

357 CD6 6k org brn & yel 45 45
358 CD6 7k blue & yellow 45 45

M.S. Gullfoss A82

1964, Jan. 17 Photo. *Perf. 11½*

359 A82 10k ultra, blk & gray 1.90 1.50
a. Accent on 2nd "E" omitted 25.00 20.00

Iceland Steamship Company, 50th anniv.

Scout Emblem and "Be Prepared" A83

Icelandic Coat of Arms A84

1964, Apr. 24

360 A83 3.50k multicolored 55 20
361 A83 4.50k multicolored 55 30

Issued to honor the Boy Scouts.

1964, June 17 *Perf. 11½*

362 A84 25k multicolored 3.00 2.00

20th anniversary, Republic of Iceland.

Flower Type of 1960-62

Flowers: 50a, Eight-petal dryas. 1k, Crowfoot (Ranunculus glacialis). 1.50k, Buck bean. 2k, Clover (trifolium repens).

1964, July 15

Flowers in Natural Colors

363 A72 50a vio bl & lt vio bl 15 15
364 A72 1k gray & dk gray 15 15
365 A72 1.50k brn & pale brn 15 15
366 A72 2k ol & pale olive 20 15
Set value 52 44

Europa Issue, 1964

Common Design Type

1964, Sept. 14 Photo. *Perf. 11½*

Granite Paper

Size: 22½x33mm

367 CD7 4.50k golden brn, yel & Prus grn 55 50
368 CD7 9k bl, yel & dk brn 60 60

Runner — A85

1964, Oct. 20 Unwmk. *Perf. 11½*

369 A85 10k lt grn & blk 1.10 75

18th Olympic Games, Tokyo, Oct. 10-25.

ITU Emblem A86

1965, May 17 Photo. *Perf. 11½*

370 A86 4.50k green 75 60
371 A86 7.50k bright ultra 15 20

ITU, centenary.

Surtsey Island, April 1964 — A87

Designs: 1.50k, Underwater volcanic eruption, November, 1963, vert. 3.50k, Surtsey, September, 1964.

1965, June 23 Unwmk. *Perf. 11½*

372 A87 1.50k bl, bis & blk 50 50
373 A87 2k multicolored 50 50
374 A87 3.50k bl, blk & red 75 65

Emergence of a new volcanic island off the southern coast of Iceland.

Europa Issue, 1965

Common Design Type

1965, Sept. 27 Photo. *Perf. 11½*

Size: 33x22½mm

375 CD8 5k tan, brn & brt grn 1.10 1.10
376 CD8 8k brt grn, brn & yel green 1.10 1.10

Einar Benediktsson A88

Engr. & Litho.

1965, Nov. 16 *Perf. 14*

377 A88 10k brt blue & brn 3.50 3.00

Einar Benediktsson, poet (1864-1940).

White-tailed Sea Eagle — A89

National Costume — A90

1965-66 Photo. *Perf. 11½*

378 A89 50k multicolored 9.75 7.50
379 A90 100k multicolored 7.75 6.25

Issue dates: No. 378, Apr. 26, 1966; No. 379, Dec. 3, 1965.

West Iceland — A91

Designs: 4k, North Iceland. 5k, East Iceland. 6.50k, South Iceland.

1966, Aug. 4 Photo. *Perf. 11½*

380 A91 2.50k multicolored 38 15
381 A91 4k multicolored 35 15
382 A91 5k multicolored 45 25
383 A91 6.50k multicolored 60 25

Europa Issue, 1966

Common Design Type

1966, Sept. 26 Photo. *Perf. 11½*

Size: 22½x33mm

384 CD9 7k grnsh bl, lt bl & red 1.25 1.25
385 CD9 8k brn, buff & red 1.25 1.25

Literary Society Emblem — A92

1966, Nov. 18 Engr. *Perf. 11½*

386 A92 4k ultramarine 35 32
387 A92 10k vermilion 90 60

Icelandic Literary Society, 150th anniv.

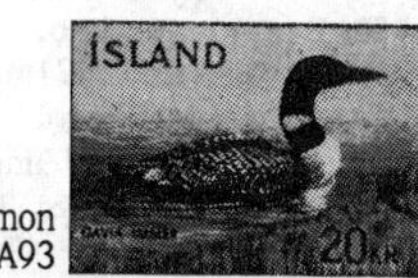

Common Loon — A93

1967, Mar. 16 Photo. *Perf. 11½*

388 A93 20k multicolored 4.25 3.50

Europa Issue, 1967

Common Design Type

1967, May 2 Photo. *Perf. 11½*

Size: 22½x33mm

389 CD10 7k yel, brn & dk bl 1.25 1.25
390 CD10 8k emer, gray & dk bl 1.25 1.25

Old and New Maps of Iceland and North America — A94

1967, June 8 Photo. *Perf. 11½*

391 A94 10k blk, tan & lt bl 35 30

EXPO '67 Intl. Exhibition, Montreal, Apr. 28-Oct. 27, 1967. The old map, drawn about 1590 by Sigurdur Stefansson, is at the Royal Library, Copenhagen.

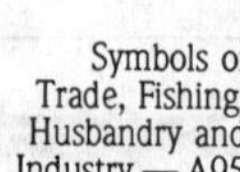

Symbols of Trade, Fishing, Husbandry and Industry — A95

1967, Sept. 14 Photo. *Perf. 11½*

392 A95 5k dk bl, yel & emer 30 25

Icelandic Chamber of Commerce, 50th anniv.

Flower Type of 1960-62

Flowers: 50a, Saxifraga oppositifolia. 2.50k, Orchis maculata.

1968, Jan. 17 Photo. *Perf. 11½*

Flowers in Natural Colors

393 A72 50a green & dk brn 15 15
394 A72 2.50k dk brn, yel & grn 15 15
Set value 23 16

Europa Issue, 1968

Common Design Type

1968, Apr. 29 Photo. *Perf. 11½*

Size: 33½x23mm

395 CD11 9.50k dl yel, car rose & blk 1.00 90
396 CD11 10k brt yel grn, blk & org 1.00 90

Right-hand Driving — A96

1968, May 21 Photo. *Perf. 11½*

397 A96 4k yellow & brn 20 15
398 A96 5k lt reddish brn 20 15

Introduction of right-hand driving in Iceland, May 26, 1968.

Fridrik Fridriksson, by Sigurjón Olafsson — A97

1968, Sept. 5 Photo. *Perf. 11½*

399 A97 10k sky bl & dk gray 45 45

Rev. Fridrik Fridriksson (1868-1961), founder of the YMCA in Reykjavik and writer.

Reading Room, National Library A98

Prime Minister Jon Magnusson (1859-1926) A99

1968, Oct. 30 Photo. *Perf. 11½*

Granite Paper

400 A98 5k yellow & brn 25 15
401 A98 20k lt bl & dp ultra 85 70

Natl. Library, Reykjavik, sesquicentennial.

1968, Dec. 12

Granite Paper

402 A99 4k carmine lake 45 24
403 A99 50k dark brown 3.75 3.50

50th anniversary of independence.

Nordic Cooperation Issue

Five Ancient Ships — A99a

1969, Feb. 28 Engr. *Perf. 12½*

404 A99a 6.50k vermilion 50 50
405 A99a 10k bright blue 50 50

See footnote after Norway No. 524.

Europa Issue, 1969

Common Design Type

1969, Apr. 28 Photo. *Perf. 11½*
Size: 32½x23mm

406 CD12 13k pink & multi 1.65 1.65
407 CD12 14.50k yel & multi 75 75

Flag of Iceland and Rising Sun — A100

1969, June 17 Photo. *Perf. 11½*

408 A100 25k gray, gold, vio bl & red 1.10 70
409 A100 100k lt bl, gold, vio bl & red 5.75 5.25

25th anniversary, Republic of Iceland.

Boeing 727 — A101

Design: 12k, Rolls Royce 400.

1969, Sept. 3 Photo. *Perf. 11½*

410 A101 9.50k dk bl & sky bl 50 50
411 A101 12k dk bl & ultra 50 50

50th anniversary of Icelandic aviation.

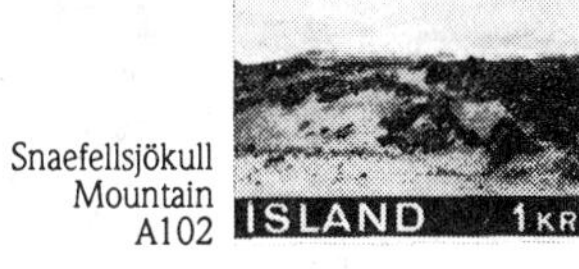

Snaefellsjökull Mountain A102

Views: 4k, Laxfoss. 5k, Hattver, vert. 20k, Fjardargill, vert.

1970, Jan. 6 Photo. *Perf. 11½*

412 A102 1k multicolored 15 15
413 A102 4k multicolored 25 15
414 A102 5k multicolored 25 15
415 A102 20k multicolored 70 32
Set value 62

First Meeting of Icelandic Supreme Court A103

1970, Feb. 16 Photo. *Perf. 11½*

416 A103 6.50k multicolored 25 20

Icelandic Supreme Court, 50th anniv.

Column from "Skarosbók," 1363 (Law Book) — A104

Icelandic Manuscripts: 15k, Preface to "Flateyjarbók" (History of Norwegian Kings), 1387-1394. 30k, Initial from "Flateyjarbók" showing Harald Fairhair cutting fetters of Dofri.

1970, Mar. 20 Photo. *Perf. 11½*

417 A104 5k multicolored 22 22
418 A104 15k multicolored 60 60
419 A104 30k multicolored 1.10 1.10

Europa Issue, 1970

Common Design Type

1970, May 4 Photo. *Perf. 11½*
Size: 32x22mm

420 CD13 9k brn & yellow 85 85
421 CD13 25k brt grn & bis 1.50 1.50

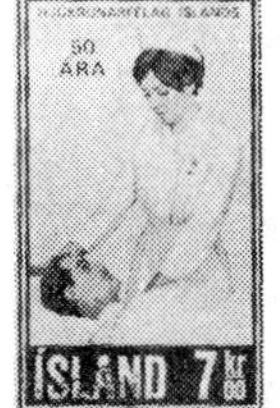

Nurse — A105

Grimur Thomsen — A106

The Rest, by Thorarinn B. Thorlaksson A107

1970, June 19 Photo. *Perf. 11½*

422 A105 7k ultra & lt bl 35 20
423 A106 10k ind & lt grnsh bl 42 30
424 A107 50k gold & multi 2.00 1.25

50th anniv. (in 1969) of the Icelandic Nursing Association (No. 422); 150th birth anniv. of Grimur Thomsen (1820-1896), poet (No. 423); Intl. Arts Festival, Reykjavik, June 1970 (No. 424).

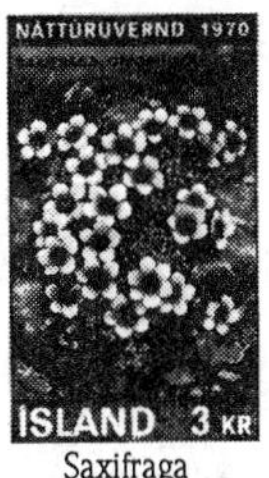

Saxifraga Oppositifolia A108

Lakagigar A109

1970, Aug. 25 Photo. *Perf. 11½*

425 A108 3k multicolored 24 24
426 A109 15k multicolored 75 75

European Nature Conservation Year.

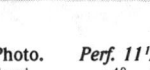

UN Emblem and Map of Iceland — A110

1970, Oct. 23 Photo. *Perf. 11½*

427 A110 12k multicolored 48 48

25th anniversary of United Nations.

"Flight," by Asgrimur Jonsson A111

1971, Mar. 26 Photo. *Perf. 11½*

428 A111 10k multicolored 70 50

Joint northern campaign for the benefit of refugees.

Europa Issue, 1971

Common Design Type

1971, May 3 Photo. *Perf. 11½*
Size: 33x22mm

429 CD14 7k rose cl, yel & blk 1.10 1.10
430 CD14 15k ultra, yel & blk 1.10 1.10

Postal Checking Service Emblem — A112

1971, June 22 Photo. *Perf. 11½*

431 A112 5k vio bl & lt blue 15 15
432 A112 7k dk grn & yel grn 22 20

Introduction of Postal Checking Service, Apr. 30, 1971.

Tryggvi Gunnarsson A113

Haddock Freezing Plant A114

Design: 30k, Patriotic Society emblem.

1971, Aug. 19 Photo. *Perf. 11½*

433 A113 30k lt bl & vio blk 1.25 90
434 A113 100k gray & vio blk 5.50 6.00

Icelandic Patriotic Society, cent.; Tryggvi Gunnarsson (1835-1917), founder and president.

1971, Nov. 18

Fish Industry: 7k, Cod fishing. 20k, Lobster canning plant.

435 A114 5k multicolored 18 15
436 A114 7k multicolored 15 15
437 A114 20k grn & multi 60 50

Herdubreid Mountain A115

1972, Mar. 9 Engr. & Litho. *Perf. 14*

438 A115 250k blue & multi 90 42

Europa Issue 1972

Common Design Type

1972, May 2 Photo. *Perf. 11½*
Size: 22x32mm

439 CD15 9k lt vio & multi 95 60
440 CD15 13k yel grn & multi 1.10 85

"United Municipalities" A116

1972, June 14 Photo. *Perf. 11½*

441 A116 16k multicolored 18 18

Legislation for local government, cent.

Chessboard, World Map, Rook — A117

1972, July 2 Litho. *Perf. 13*

442 A117 15k lt ol & multi 38 30

World Chess Championship, Reykjavik, July-Sept. 1972.

Hothouse Tomatoes A118

Designs: 12k, Steam valve and natural steam. 40k, Hothouse roses.

1972, Aug. 23 Photo. *Perf. 11½*

443 A118 8k Prus bl & multi 15 15
444 A118 12k green & multi 15 15
445 A118 40k dk pur & multi 1.10 75

Hothouse gardening in Iceland, using natural steam and hot springs.

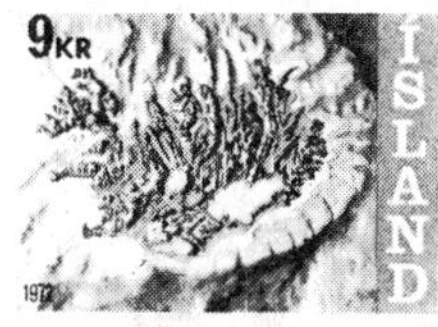

Iceland and the Continental Shelf A119

1972, Sept. 27 Litho. *Perf. 13*

446 A119 9k blue & multi 18 15

To publicize Iceland's offshore fishing rights.

Europa Issue 1973

Common Design Type

1973, Apr. 30 Photo. *Perf. 11½*
Size: 32½x22mm

447 CD16 13k vio & multi 1.25 1.25
448 CD16 25k olive & multi 40 35

Iceland No. 1 and Messenger A120

Designs (First Issue of Iceland and): 15k, No. 5 and pony train. 20k, No. 2 and mailboat "Esja." 40k, No. 3 and mail truck. 80k, No. 4 and Beech-18 mail plane.

Perf. 13x13½

1973, May 23 Litho. & Engr.

449 A120 10k dl bl, blk & ultra 32 32
450 A120 15k grn, blk & gray 15 15
451 A120 20k mar, blk & car 18 18
452 A120 40k vio, blk & brn 18 18
453 A120 80k olive, blk & yel 1.00 65
Nos. 449-453 (5) 1.83 1.48

Centenary of Iceland's first postage stamps.

Nordic Cooperation Issue

Nordic House, Reykjavik A120a

1973, June 26 Engr. *Perf. 12½*
454 A120a 9k multicolored 45 22
455 A120a 10k multicolored 1.40 1.40

A century of postal cooperation among Denmark, Finland, Iceland, Norway and Sweden, and in connection with the Nordic Postal Conference, Reykjavik.

Ásgeir Ásgeirsson, (1894-1972),President of Iceland 1952-1968 — A121

1973, Aug. 1 Engr. *Perf. 13x13½*
456 A121 13k carmine 32 22
457 A121 15k blue 20 15

Islandia 73 Emblem — A122

Design: 20k, Islandia 73 emblem; different arrangement.

1973, Aug. 31 Photo. *Perf. 11½*
458 A122 17k gray & multi 30 30
459 A122 20k brn, ocher & yel 30 25

Islandia 73 Philatelic Exhibition, Reykjavik, Aug. 31-Sept. 9.

Man and WMO Emblem A123

The Settlement, Tapestry by Vigdis Kristjansdottir A124

1973, Nov. 14 Photo. *Perf. 12½*
460 A123 50k sil & multi 75 45

Intl. meteorological cooperation, cent.

1974 Photo. *Perf. 11½*

Designs: 13k, Establishment of Althing, painting by Johannes Johannesson, horiz. 15k, Gudbrandur Thorlakkson, Bishop of Holar 1571-1627. 17k, Age of Sturlungar (Fighting Vikings), drawing by Thorvaldur Skulason. 20k, Stained glass window honoring Hallgrimur Petursson (1614-74), hymn writer. 25k, Illumination from Book of Flatey, 14th century. 30k, Conversion to Christianity (altarpiece, Skalholt), mosaic by Nina Tryggvadottir. 40k, Wood carving (family and plants), 18th century. 60k, Curing the Catch, cement bas-relief. 70k, Age of Writing (Saemundur Riding Seal), sculpture by Asmundur Sveinsson. 100k, Virgin and Child with Angels, embroidered antependium, Stafafell Church, 14th century.

461 A124 10k multicolored 22 15
462 A124 13k multicolored 20 20
463 A124 15k multicolored 20 20
464 A124 17k multicolored 32 22
465 A124 20k multicolored 28 22
466 A124 25k multicolored 15 25
467 A124 30k multicolored 60 45
468 A124 40k multicolored 70 55
469 A124 60k multicolored 85 85
470 A124 70k multicolored 85 85
471 A124 100k multicolored 1.25 70
Nos. 461-471 (11) 5.62 4.64

1100th anniv. of settlement of Iceland.
Issue dates: 10k, 13k, 30k, 70k, Mar. 12; 17k, 25k, 100k, June 11; 15k, 20k, 40k, 60k, July 16.

Horseback Rider, Wood, 17th Century — A125

Europa: 20k, "Through the Sound Barrier," contemporary bronze by Asmundur Sveinsson.

1974, Apr. 29 Photo. *Perf. 11½*
472 A125 13k brn red & multi 15 15
473 A125 20k gray & multi 70 70

Clerk Selling Stamps, UPU Emblem — A126

Design: 20k, Mailman delivering mail.

1974, Oct. 9 Photo. *Perf. 11½*
474 A126 17k ocher & multi 30 28
475 A126 20k olive & multi 30 28

Centenary of Universal Postal Union.

Volcanic Eruption, Heimaey, Jan. 23, 1973 — A127

Design: 25k, Volcanic eruption, night view.

1975, Jan. 23 Photo. *Perf. 11½*
476 A127 20k multicolored 40 40
477 A127 25k multicolored 20 20

Europa Issue 1975

Bird, by Thorvaldur Skulason A128

Sun Queen, by Johannes S. Kjarval — A129

1975, May 12 Photo. *Perf. 11½*
478 A128 18k multicolored 20 20
479 A129 23k gold & multi 55 42

Stephan G. Stephansson — A130

1975, Aug. 1 Engr. *Perf. 13*
480 A130 27k green & brn 55 30

Stephan G. Stephansson (1853-1927), Icelandic poet and settler in North America; centenary of Icelandic emigration to North America.

Petursson, by Hjalti Thorsteinsson A131

Einar Jonsson, Self-portrait A132

Portraits: 23k, Arni Magnusson, by Hjalti Thorsteinsson. 30k, Jon Eiriksson, sculpture by Olafur Olafsson.

1975, Sept. 18 Engr. *Perf. 13*
481 A131 18k slate grn & ind 18 18
482 A131 23k Prussian bl 18 18
483 A131 30k deep magenta 18 18
484 A132 50k indigo 18 18

Famous Icelanders: Hallgrimur Petursson (1614-1674), minister and religious poet; Arni Magnusson (1663-1730), historian, registrar and manuscript collector; Jon Eiriksson (1728-1787), professor of law and cabinet member; Einar Jonsson (1874-1954), sculptor, painter and writer.

Red Cross — A133

1975, Oct. 15 Photo. *Perf. 11½x12*
485 A133 23k multicolored 32 32

Icelandic Red Cross, 50th anniversary.

Abstract Painting, by Nina Tryggvadottir — A134

1975, Oct. 15 Photo. *Perf. 12x12½*
486 A134 100k multicolored 1.25 80

International Women's Year 1975.

Thorvaldsen Statue, by Thorvaldsen A135

Saplings Growing in Bare Landscape A136

1975, Nov. 19 Photo. *Perf. 11½*
487 A135 27k lt vio & multi 70 30

Centenary of Thorvaldsen Society, a charity honoring Bertel Thorvaldsen (1768-1844), sculptor.

1975, Nov. 19 *Perf. 12x11½*
488 A136 35k multicolored 52 40

Reforestation.

Langjökull Glacier, by Asgrimur Jonsson — A137

1976, Mar. 18 Photo. *Perf. 11½*
489 A137 150k gold & multi 1.65 1.00

Asgrimur Jonsson (1876-1958), painter.

Wooden Bowl — A138

Europa: 45k, Spinning wheel, vert.

1976, May 3 Photo. *Perf. 11½*
490 A138 35k ver & multi 70 50
491 A138 45k blue & multi 95 70

No. 9 with First Day Cancel — A139

Decree Establishing Postal Service — A140

1976, Sept. 22 Photo. *Perf. 11½*
Granite Paper
492 A139 30k bis, blk & gray bl 22 22

Centenary of aurar stamps.

1976, Sept. 22 Engr. *Perf. 13*

Design: 45k, Conclusion of Decree with signatures.

493 A140 35k dark brown 40 32
494 A140 45k dark blue 40 32

Iceland's Postal Service, bicentenary.

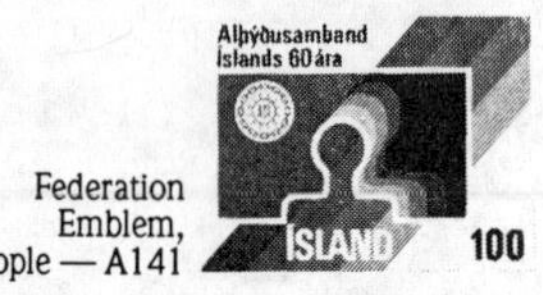

Federation Emblem, People — A141

1976, Dec. 2 Photo. *Perf. 12½*
Granite Paper

495 A141 100k multicolored 1.00 50

Icelandic Federation of Labor, 60th anniv.

Five Water Lilies — A142

Ofaerufoss, Eldgja — A143

Photo. & Engr.

1977, Feb. 2 *Perf. 12½*

496 A142 35k brt grn & multi 85 65
497 A142 45k ultra & multi 85 80

Nordic countries cooperation for protection of the environment and 25th Session of Nordic Council, Helsinki, Feb. 19.

1977, May 2 Photo. *Perf. 12*

Europa: 85k, Kirkjufell Mountain, seen from Grundarfjord.

498 A143 45k multicolored 1.60 90
499 A143 85k multicolored 22 28

Harlequin Duck — A144

1977, June 14 Photo. *Perf. 11½*

500 A144 40k multicolored 22 22

Wetlands conservation, European campaign.

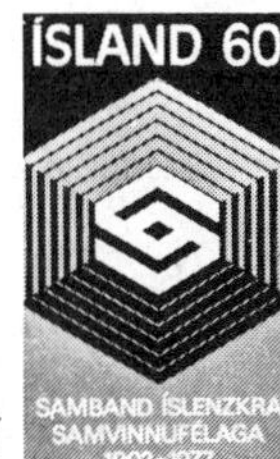

Society Emblem — A145

1977, June 14

501 A145 60k vio bl & ultra 75 42

Federation of Icelandic Cooperative Societies, 75th anniversary.

Hot Springs, Therapeutic Bath, Emblem A146

1977, Nov. 16 Photo. *Perf. 11½*

502 A146 90k multicolored 55 38

World Rheumatism Year.

Stone Marker — A147

1977, Dec. 12 Engr. *Perf. 11½*

503 A147 45k dark blue 85 50

Touring Club of Iceland, 50th anniversary.

Thorvaldur Thoroddsen, (1855-1921), Geologist, Scientist and Writer — A148

Design: 60k, Briet Bjarnhedinsdottir (1856-1940), Founder of Icelandic Women's Association and Reykjavik city councillor.

1977, Dec. 12 Engr. *Perf. 11½*

504 A148 50k brn & sl grn 28 18
505 A148 60k grn & vio brn 55 35

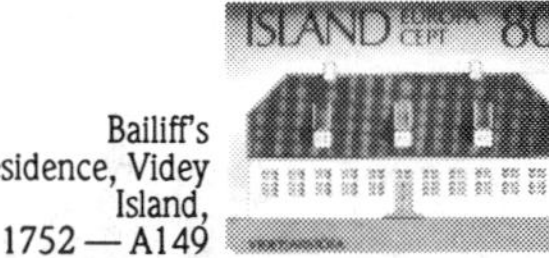

Bailiff's Residence, Videy Island, 1752 — A149

Europa: 120k, Husavik Church, 1906.

1978, May 2 Photo. *Perf. 11½*

506 A149 80k multicolored 48 30
507 A149 120k multi, vert. 70 60

Alexander Johannesson, Junkers Planes — A150

Design: 100k, Fokker Friendship plane over mountains.

1978, June 21 Photo. *Perf. 12½*

508 A150 60k multicolored 35 20
509 A150 100k multicolored 42 28

50th anniv. of domestic flights in Iceland.

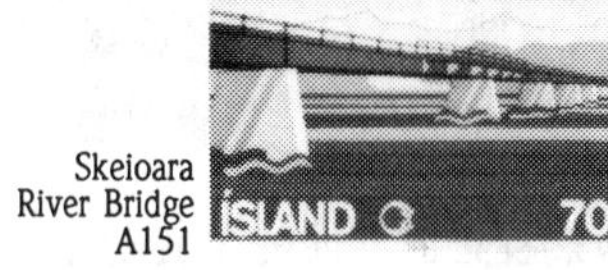

Skeioara River Bridge A151

1978, Aug. 17 Photo. *Perf. 11½*

510 A151 70k multicolored 18 18

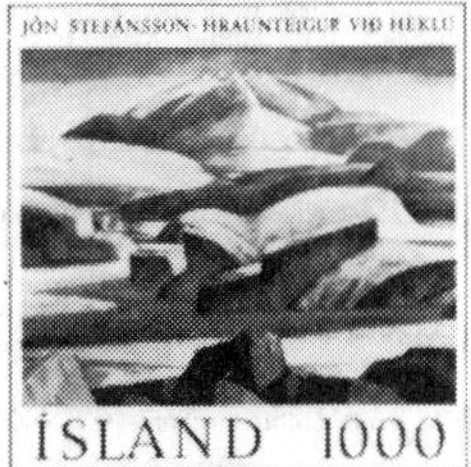

Lava near Mt. Hekla, by Jon Stefansson — A152

1978, Nov. 16 Photo. *Perf. 12*

511 A152 1000k multicolored 4.50 2.25

Jon Stefansson (1881-1962), Icelandic painter.

Ship to Shore Rescue A153

1978, Dec. 1 Engr. *Perf. 13*

512 A153 60k black 18 18

National Life Saving Assoc., 50th anniv.

Halldor Hermannsson (1878-1958), Historian, Librarian — A154

1978, Dec. 1

513 A154 150k indigo 48 32

Lighthouse — A155

Telephone, c. 1900 — A156

1978, Dec. 1 Photo. *Perf. 11½*

514 A155 90k multicolored 48 32

Centenary of Icelandic lighthouses.

1979, Apr. 30 Photo. *Perf. 11½*

Europa: 190k, Post horn and satchel.

515 A156 110k multicolored 55 48
516 A156 190k multicolored 55 55

Jon Sigurdsson and Ingibjorg Einarsdottir A157

1979, Nov. 1 Engr. *Perf. 13x12½*

517 A157 150k black 48 38

Jon Sigurdsson (1811-1879), Icelandic statesman and leader in independence movement.

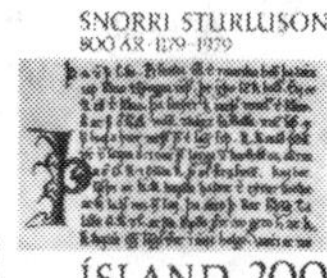

Excerpt from Olafs Saga Helga — A158

1979, Nov. 1 Photo. *Perf. 11½*

518 A158 200k multicolored 48 32

Snorri Sturluson (1178-1241), Icelandic historian and writer.

Children with Flowers ICY Emblem A159

1979, Nov. 12

519 A159 140k multicolored 60 32

International Year of the Child.

A160 A161

Design: Icelandic Arms, before 1904 and 1904-1919.

1979, Nov. 12

520 A160 500k multicolored 1.65 1.10

Home rule, 75th anniversary.

1979 Engr. *Perf. 13*

Designs: 80k, Ingibjorg H. Bjarnason (1867-1941). 100k, Bjarni Porsteinsson (1861-1938), composer. 120k, Petur Gudjohnsen (1812-77), organist. 130k, Sveinbjorn Sveinbjornson (1847-1927), composer. 170k, Torfhildur Holm (1845-1918), poet.

521 A161 80k rose violet 15 15
522 A161 100k black 15 15
523 A161 120k rose carmine 15 15
524 A161 130k sepia 22 22
525 A161 170k carmine rose 40 30
Nos. 521-525 (5) 1.07 97

Issued: 80k, 170k, Aug. 3; others, Dec. 12.

Canis Familiaris — A162

Design: 90k, Alopex lagopus.

1980, Jan. 24

526 A162 10k black 15 15
527 A162 90k sepia 15 15
Set value 21 21

See Nos. 534-536, 543-545, 552, 553, 556-558, 610-612.

Jon Sveinsson Nonni (1857-1944), Writer — A163

Europa: 250k, Gunnar Gunnarsson (1889-1975), writer.

1980, Apr. 28 Photo. *Perf. 11½*
Granite Paper

528 A163 140k dl rose & blk 55 40
529 A163 250k tan & blk 85 65

Mountain Ash Branch and Berries — A164

1980, July 8 Photo. *Perf. 12½*

530 A164 120k multicolored 18 18

Year of the Tree.

Laugardalur Sports Complex, Reykjavik A165

1980, July 8 Engr. *Perf. 13x12½*

531 A165 300k slate green 60 60

1980 Olympic Games.

Carved and Painted Cabinet Door, 18th Cent. — A166

Radio Receiver, 1930 — A168

Nordic Cooperation Issue

Design: 180k, Embroidered cushion, 19th cent.

1980, Sept. 9 Photo. *Perf. 11½*
Granite Paper

532 A166 150k multicolored 70 50
533 A166 180k multicolored 95 60

Animal Type of 1980

1980, Oct. 16 Engr. *Perf. 13*

Designs: 160k, Sebastes marinus. 170k, Fratercula arctica. 190k, Phoca vitulina.

534 A162 160k rose violet 65 32
535 A162 170k black 20 16
536 A162 190k dark brown 20 16

1980, Nov. 20 Photo. *Perf. 12½*
Granite Paper

537 A168 400k multicolored 1.25 1.00

State Broadcasting Service, 50th anniv.

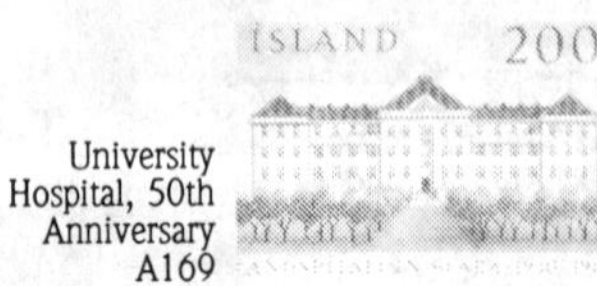

University Hospital, 50th Anniversary A169

1980, Nov. 20 *Perf. 11½*

538 A169 200k multicolored 45 35

A170

A171

Design: 170a, Magnus Stephensen (1762-1833), Chief Justice. 190a, Finnur Magnusson (1781-1847), Privy Archives keeper.

1981, Feb. 24 Engr. *Perf. 13*

539 A170 170a bright ultra 20 20
540 A170 190a olive green 20 20

Europa Issue 1981

1981, May 4 Photo. *Perf. 11½*
Granite Paper

541 A171 180a Luftur the Sorcerer 90 90
542 A171 220a Sea witch 1.00 65

Animal Type of 1980

1981, Aug. 20 Engr. *Perf. 13*

Designs: 50a, Troglodytes troglodytes. 100a, Pluvialis apricaria. 200a, Corvus corax.

543 A162 50a brown 15 15
544 A162 100a blue 15 15
545 A162 200a black 20 15

Intl. Year of the Disabled — A173

Skyggnir Earth Satellite Station, First Anniv. — A174

1981, Sept. 29 Photo. *Perf. 11½*

546 A173 200a multicolored 25 25

1981, Sept. 29 Photo. *Perf. 11½*

547 A174 500a multicolored 1.40 1.00

Hauling the Line, by Gunnlaugur Scheving (1904-1972) A175

1981, Oct. 21 Photo. *Perf. 11½*

548 A175 5000a multi 6.00 5.00

Christian Missionary Work in Iceland Millennium — A176

1981, Nov. 24 Engr. *Perf. 13*

549 A176 200a dark violet 22 22

Christmas — A177

1981, Nov. 24 Photo. *Perf. 12½*
Granite Paper

550 A177 200a Leaf bread 60 52
551 A177 250a Leaf bread, diff. 60 52

Animal Type of 1980

1982, Mar. 23 Engr. *Perf. 13*

Designs: 20a, Buccinum undatum, vert. 600a, Chlamys islandica.

552 A162 20a copper brn 15 15
553 A162 600a vio brown 85 50
Set value 55

Europa Issue 1982

First Norse Settlement, 874 — A179

1982, May 3 Photo. *Perf. 11½*
Granite Paper

554 A179 350a shown 95 75
555 A179 450a Discovery of North America, 1000 95 75

Animal Type of 1980

1982, June 3 Engr. *Perf. 13*

Designs: 300a, Ovis aries, vert. 400a, Bos taurus, vert. 500a, Felis catus, vert.

556 A162 300a brown 95 55
557 A162 400a lake 30 30
558 A162 500a gray 30 30

Kaupfelag Pingeyinga Cooperative Society Centenary A181

1982, June 3

559 A181 1000a black & red 75 75

Man Riding Iceland Pony — A182

1982, July 1 Photo. *Perf. 11½*
Granite Paper

560 A182 700a multicolored 60 60

Centenary of School of Agriculture, Holar — A183

1982, July 1
Granite Paper

561 A183 1500a multi 1.10 1.10

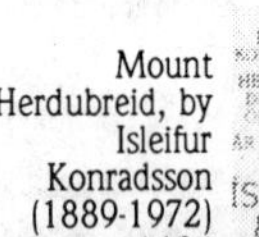

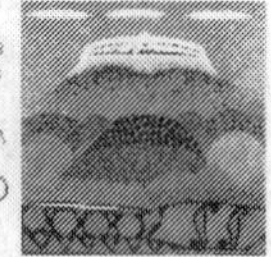

Mount Herdubreid, by Isleifur Konradsson (1889-1972) A184

1982, Sept. 8 Photo. *Perf. 11½*
Granite Paper

562 A184 800a multicolored 85 85

UN World Assembly on Aging, July 26-Aug. 6.

A185

A186

1982, Sept. 8 Engr. *Perf. 13*

563 A185 900a red brown 70 60

Borbjorg Sveinsdottir (1828-1903), midwife and Univ. founder.

Souvenir Sheet

Photo. & Engr.

1982, Oct. 7 *Perf. 13½*

564 Sheet of 2 4.25 4.50
a. A186 400a Reynistaour Monastery seal 2.00 2.25
b. A186 800a Bingeyrar 2.00 2.25

NORDIA '84 Intl. Stamp Exhibition, Reykjavik, July 3-8, 1984. Sold for 18k.
See No. 581.

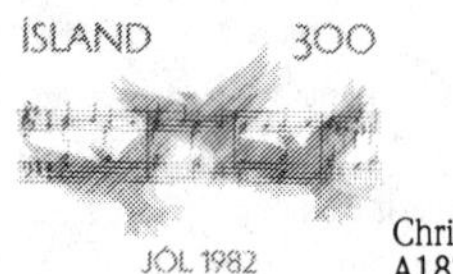

Christmas A187

Score from The Night was Such a Splendid One.

1982, Nov. 16 Photo. *Perf. 11½*
Granite Paper

565 A187 3k Birds 48 48
566 A187 3.50k Bells 60 60

Caltha Palustris — A188

1983, Feb. 10 Photo.
Granite Paper

567 A188 7.50k shown 48 35
568 A188 8k Lychnis alpina 1.00 90
569 A188 10k Potentilla palustris 65 48
570 A188 20k Myosotis scorpioides 2.00 1.75

See #586-587, 593-594, 602-605, 663-664.

Nordic Cooperation A189

1983, Mar. 24
Granite Paper

571 A189 4.50k Mt. Sulur 95 75
572 A189 5k Urridafossar Falls 95 75

Europa Issue, 1983

Thermal Energy Projects — A190

1983, May 5

Granite Paper

573 A190 5k shown 1.25 1.00
574 A190 5.50k multi, diff. 2.00 1.75

Fishing Industry A191

1983, June 8 Engr. *Perf. 13x12½*

575 A191 11k Fishing boats 45 45
576 A191 13k Fishermen 1.40 80

Bicentenary of Skaftareldar Volcanic Eruption A192

1983, June 8 Photo. *Perf. 11½*

Granite Paper

577 A192 15k Volcano, by Finnur Jonsson 1.10 1.10

Skiing — A193

1983, Sept. 8 Photo. *Perf. 11½*

578 A193 12k shown 80 75
579 A193 14k Running 1.25 1.25

World Communications Year — A194

1983, Sept. 8 *Perf. 12½*

580 A194 30k multi 3.00 2.75

NORDIA '84 Type of 1982

Souvenir Sheet

Bishops' Seals: 8k, Magnus Eyjolfsson of Skalholt, 1477-90. 12k, Ogmundur Palsson of Skalhot, 1521-40.

Photo. & Engr.

1983, Oct. 6 *Perf. 13½*

581 Sheet of 2 4.75 5.25
a. A186 8k violet blue & black 2.25 2.50
b. A186 12k pale green & black 2.25 2.50

Sold for 30k.

Christmas A195

Pres. Kristjan Eldjarn (1916-82) A196

1983, Nov. 10 Photo. *Perf. 11½*

Granite Paper

582 A195 6k Virgin and Child 70 55
583 A195 6.50k Angel 70 55

1983, Dec. 6

584 A196 6.50k brn carmine 1.25 1.00
585 A196 7k dark blue 48 32

Flower Type of 1983

1984, Mar. 1 Photo. *Perf. 11½*

Granite Paper

586 A188 6k Rosa pimpinellifolia 80 70
587 A188 25k Potentilla anserium 2.00 1.75

Europa 1959-84 A197

1984, May 3

588 A197 6.50k grnsh bl & blk 1.10 70
589 A197 7.50k rose & black 60 52

A198

A199

Souvenir Sheet

Design: Abraham Ortelius' map of Northern Europe, 1570.

Photo. & Engr.

1984, June 6 *Perf. 14x13½*

590 A198 40k multi 6.25 6.50

NORDIA '84 Intl. Stamp Exhibition, Reykjavik, July 3-8. Sold for 60k.

1984, June 17 Photo. *Perf. 11½*

Granite Paper

591 A199 50k Flags 4.25 3.50

40th Anniv. of Republic.

Good Templars Headquarters, Akureyri A200

1984, July 18 Engr. *Perf. 13*

592 A200 10k green 75 70

Order of the Good Templars, centenary in Iceland, temperance org.

Flower Type of 1983

1984, Sept. 11 Photo. *Perf. 11½*

Granite Paper

593 A188 6.50k Loiseleuria procumbens 45 35
594 A188 7.50k Arctostaphylos uva-ursi 52 35

Christmas A201

Gudbrand's Bible, 400th Anniv. A202

1984, Nov. 29 Photo.

595 A201 600a Madonna and Child 60 36
596 A201 650a Angel, Christmas rose 80 55

1984, Nov. 29 Engr. *Perf. 12½x13*

597 A202 6.50k Text 45 42
598 A202 7.50k Illustration 52 52

First Icelandic Bible.

Confederation of Employers, 50th Anniv. A203

Bjorn Bjarnarson (1853-1918) A204

1984, Nov. 9 Photo. *Perf. 12x12½*

Granite Paper

599 A203 30k Building blocks 2.50 2.50

1984, Nov. 9 Photo. *Perf. 11½*

Granite Paper

600 A204 12k shown 80 65
601 A204 40k New gallery building, horiz. 2.50 2.25

Natl. Gallery centenary.

Flower Type of 1983

1985, Mar. 20 Photo. *Perf. 11½*

Granite Paper

602 A188 8k Rubus saxatilis 70 70
603 A188 9k Veronica fruticans 75 75
604 A188 16k Lathyrus japonicus 1.40 1.40
605 A188 17k Draba alpina 1.50 1.50

Music Year Emblem, Woman Playing the Langspil — A205

Europa: 7.50k, Man playing the Icelandic violin.

1985, May 3 Photo. *Perf. 11½*

Granite Paper

606 A205 6.50k multicolored 60 60
607 A205 7.50k multicolored 60 60

Natl. Horticulture Soc., Cent. — A206

Intl. Youth Year — A207

1985, June 20 Photo. *Perf. 12*

608 A206 20k Sorbus intermedia 1.10 1.00

1985, June 20 Photo. *Perf. 11½*

609 A207 25k Icelandic girl 1.40 1.25

Animal Type of 1980

1985, Sept. 10 Engr. *Perf. 13*

Designs: 700a, Todarodes sagittatus. 800a, Hyas araneus. 900a, Tealia felina.

610 A162 700a brn carmine 40 40
611 A162 800a dk brown 45 45
612 A162 900a carmine 50 50

Hannes Stephensen (1799-1856), Cleric, Politician, Translator A209

Famous men: 30k, Jon Gudmudsson (1807-1875), editor, politician.

1985, Sept. 10 Engr.

613 A209 13k dp magenta 75 75
614 A209 30k deep violet 1.75 1.75

Yearning to Fly, by Johannes S. Kjarval (1885-1972), Reykjavik Natl. Museum A210

1985, Oct. 15 Photo. *Perf. 12x11½*

615 A210 100k multi 5.50 5.00

Abstract Ice Crystal Paintings, by Snorri Sveinn Fridriksson (b. 1934) — A211

1985, Nov. 14 Photo. *Perf. 11½*

616 A211 8k Crucifix 45 45
617 A211 9k Pine Trees 50 50

Christmas.

Birds — A212

1986, Mar. 19 Photo. *Perf. 11½*

Granite Paper

618 A212 6k Motacilla alba 45 45
619 A212 10k Anas acuta 70 70
620 A212 12k Falco columbarius 85 85
621 A212 15k Alca torda 1.00 1.00

See Nos. 642-645, 665-666, 671-672, 686-687, 721, 725.

Europa Issue 1986

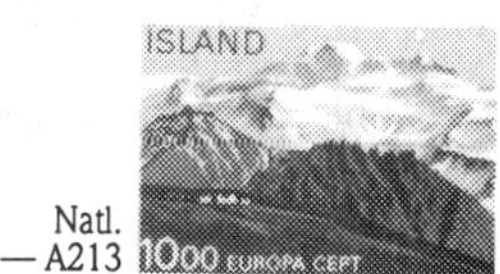

Natl. Parks — A213

1986, May 5

622 A213 10k Skaftafell 1.00 1.00
623 A213 12k Joekulsargljufur 1.40 1.40

Nordic Cooperation Issue — A214

Sister towns.

1986, May 27 *Perf. 11½*

624 A214 10k Stykkisholmur 80 80
625 A214 12k Seydisfjordur 1.00 1.00

Natl. Bank, Cent. A215

1986, July 1 **Engr.** *Perf. 14*

626 A215 13k Headquarters, Reykjavik 70 70
627 A215 250k Banknote reverse, 1928 14.00 12.50

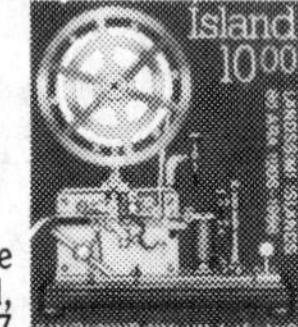

Reykjavik Bicent. A216

1986, Aug. 18 **Engr.** *Perf. 13½x14*

628 A216 10k City seal, 1815 70 70
629 A216 12k View from bank, illustration, 1856 85 85
630 A216 13k Laugardalur hot water brook 90 90
631 A216 40k City Theater 3.00 3.00

Introduction of the Telephone in Iceland, 80th Anniv. — A217

1986, Sept. 29 **Photo.** *Perf. 11½*
Granite Paper

632 A217 10k Morse receiver, 1906 50 50
633 A217 20k Handset, microchip, 1986 1.10 1.10

Souvenir Sheet

Hvita River Crossing, Loa, 1836, by Auguste Mayer — A218

1986, Oct. 9 **Photo. & Engr.** *Perf. 14*

634 A218 20k bluish black 1.90 1.90

Stamp Day. Sold for 30k to benefit philatelic organizations.

Christmas — A219

Paintings by Bjoerg Thorsteinsdottir: 10k, Christmas at Peace. 12k, Christmas Night.

1986, Nov. 13 **Photo.** *Perf. 12*

635 A219 10k multicolored 60 60
636 A219 12k multicolored 75 75

Olafsvik Trading Station, 300th Anniv. A220

1987, Mar. 26 **Engr.** *Perf. 14x13½*

637 A220 50k Merchantman Svanur, 1777 2.40 2.40

Keflavik Intl. Airport Terminal Inauguration A221

1987, Apr. 14 **Photo.** *Perf. 12x11½*

638 A221 100k multi 5.00 5.00

Europa Issue 1987

Stained Glass Windows by Leifur Breidfjoerd, Fossvogur Cemetery Chapel — A222

1987, May 4 **Photo.** *Perf. 12x11½*

639 A222 12k Christ carrying the cross 60 60
640 A222 15k Soldiers, peace dove 75 75

Rasmus Christian Rask (1787-1832), Danish Linguist — A223

1987, June 10 **Engr.** *Perf. 13½*

641 A223 20k black 1.00 1.00

Preservation of the Icelandic language.

Bird Type of 1986

1987, Sept. 16 **Photo.** *Perf. 11½*
Granite Paper

642 A212 13k Asio flammeus 62 62
643 A212 40k Turdus iliacus 1.90 1.90
644 A212 70k Haematopus ostralegus 3.35 3.35
645 A212 90k Anas platyrhynchos 4.25 4.25

Souvenir Sheet

Trading Station of Djupivogur in 1836, by Auguste Mayer — A225

1987, Oct. 9 **Engr.** *Perf. 13½x14*

646 A225 30k black 2.25 2.25

Stamp Day. Sold for 45k to benefit the Stamp and Postal History Fund.

Dental Protection A226

Vulture A227

1987, Oct. 9 **Photo.** *Perf. 11½x12*
Granite Paper

647 A226 12k multi 58 58

Perf. 13 on 3 sides

1987, Oct. 9 **Engr.**

Guardian Spirits of the North, East, South and West.

Booklet Stamps

648 A227 13k shown 62 62
649 A227 13k Dragon 62 62
650 A227 13k Bull 62 62
651 A227 13k Giant 62 62
a. Block of 4, #648-651 2.50 2.50
b. Bklt. pane of 12, 3 #651a 8.50

Legend of Heimskringla, the story of the Norse kings. Haraldur Gormsson, king of Denmark, deterred from invading Iceland after hearing of the guardian spirits.

See Nos. 656-659, 677, 688-695.

Christmas — A228

1987, Oct. 21 **Photo.** *Perf. 11½x12*

652 A228 13k Fir branch 62 62
653 A228 17k Candle flame 80 80

Steinn Steinarr (1908-1958) A229

Poets: 21k, David Stefansson (1895-1964).

1988, Feb. 25 **Photo.** *Perf. 12*

654 A229 16k multi 78 78
655 A229 21k multi 1.00 1.00

Guardian Spirit Type of 1987

Perf. 13 on 3 sides

1988, May 2 **Engr.**

Booklet Stamps

656 A227 16k Vulture 75 75
657 A227 16k Dragon 75 75
658 A227 16k Bull 75 75
659 A227 16k Giant 75 75
a. Block of 4, #656-659 3.00 3.00
b. Bklt. pane of 12, 3 #659a 9.00

Europa Issue, 1988

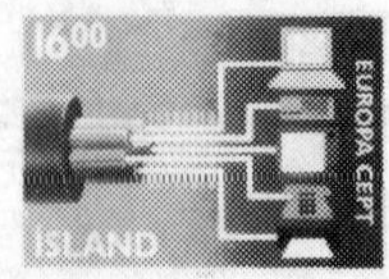

Modern Communication — A230

1988, May 2 **Photo.** *Perf. 12x11½*

660 A230 16k Data transmission system 88 88
661 A230 21k Facsimile machine 1.15 1.15

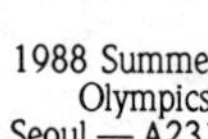

1988 Summer Olympics, Seoul — A231

1988, June 9 **Photo.** *Perf. 12*
Granite Paper

662 A231 18k Handball 95 95

Flower Type of 1983

1988, June 9 *Perf. 11½*
Granite Paper

663 A188 10k Vicia cracca 52 52
664 A188 50k Thymus praecox 2.60 2.60

Bird Type of 1986

1988, Sept. 21 **Photo.** *Perf. 11½*
Granite Paper

665 A212 5k Limosa limosa 22 22
666 A212 30k Clangula hyemalis 1.35 1.35

Souvenir Sheet

Nupsstadur Farm, Fljotshverfi, 1836, by Auguste Mayer — A233

1988, Oct. 9 **Engr.** *Perf. 14*

667 A233 40k black 2.75 2.75

Stamp Day. Sold for 60k to benefit the Stamp and Postal History Fund.

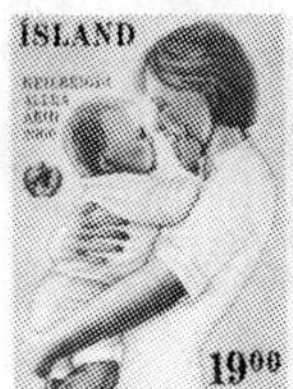

WHO, 40th Anniv. — A234

1988, Nov. 3 **Photo.** *Perf. 11½x12*
Granite Paper

668 A234 19k multicolored 85 85

Christmas A235

1988, Nov. 3 *Perf. 11½*
Granite Paper

669 A235 19k Fisherman at sea 85 85
670 A235 24k Ship, buoy 1.05 1.05

Bird Type of 1986

1989, Feb. 2 **Photo.**

671 A212 19k Phalaropus lobatus 78 78
672 A212 100k Plectrophenax nivalis 4.00 4.00

Women's Folk Costumes — A236

1989, Apr. 20 Photo. *Perf. 11½x12*
Granite Paper

673 A236 21k Peysufot 85 85
674 A236 26k Upphlutur 1.05 1.05

Nordic cooperation.

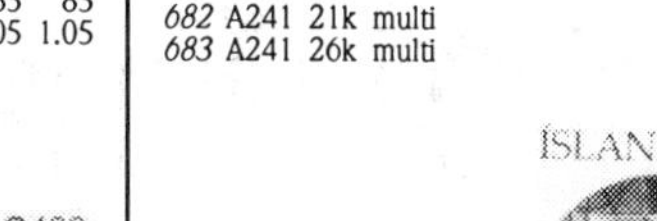
Europa 1989 — A237

Children's games.

1989, May 30 Photo. *Perf. 11½*
Granite Paper

675 A237 21k Sailing toy boats 85 85
676 A237 26k Hoop, stick pony 1.05 1.05

Guardian Spirit Type of 1987

1989, June 27 Engr. *Perf. 13*

677 A227 500k Dragon 16.00 16.00

Landscapes A238

1989, Sept. 20 Photo. *Perf. 11½*
Granite Paper

678 A238 35k Mt. Skeggi, Arnarfjord 1.35 1.35
679 A238 45k Thermal spring, Namaskard 1.70 1.70

See Nos. 713-714, 728, 737.

Agricultural College at Hvanneyri, Cent. A239

1989, Sept. 20 Engr. *Perf. 14*

680 A239 50k multi 1.90 1.90

Souvenir Sheet

NORDIA '91 — A240

Detail of *A Chart and Description of Northern Routes and Wonders to Be Found in the Nordic Countries,* 1539, by Olaus Magnus (1490-1557).

Litho. & Engr.

1989, Oct. 9 *Perf. 12½*

681 A240 Sheet of 3 4.25 4.25
a.-c. 30k any single 1.40 1.40

Stamp Day. Sold for 130k to benefit the exhibition.
See No. 715.

Natural History Soc., Cent. — A241

Flowers or fish and: 21k, Stefan Stefansson (1863-1921), botanist and founder. 26k, Bjarni Saemundsson (1867-1940), chairman.

1989, Nov. 9 Photo. *Perf. 11½*
Granite Paper

682 A241 21k multi 70 70
683 A241 26k multi 85 85

Christmas — A242

Paintings like stained-glass windows by Johannes Johannesson (b. 1921): 21k, Madonna and Child. 26k, Three Wise Men.

1989, Nov. 9
Granite Paper

684 A242 21k multi 70 70
685 A242 26k multi 85 85

Bird Type of 1986

1990, Feb. 15
Granite Paper

686 A212 21k *Anas penelope* 70 70
687 A212 80k *Anser brachyrhynchus* 2.65 2.65

Guardian Spirit Type of 1987
Perf. 13 on 3 Sides

1990, Feb. 15 Engr.

688 A227 5k Vulture 17 17
689 A227 5k Dragon 17 17
690 A227 5k Bull 17 17
691 A227 5k Giant 17 17
a. Block of 4, #688-691 68 68
692 A227 21k Vulture 70 70
693 A227 21k Dragon 70 70
694 A227 21k Bull 70 70
695 A227 21k Giant 70 70
a. Block of 4, #692-695 2.80 2.80
b. Block of 8, #688-695 3.50 3.50
c. Bklt. pane, 2 each #691a, 695a 7.00 7.00
Nos. 688-695 (8) 3.48 3.48

Famous Women — A243

Portraits: No. 696, Gudrun Larusdottir (1880-1938), author and politician, by Halldor Petursson. No. 697, Ragnhildur Petursdottir (1880-1961), educator, by Asgrimur Jonsson.

1990, Mar. 22 Litho. *Perf. 13½x14*

696 A243 21k multicolored 70 70
697 A243 21k multicolored 70 70

Europa 1990 — A244

Old and new post offices in Reykjavik and letter scales.

Perf. 12x11½

1990, May 7 Photo. Granite Paper

698 A244 21k 1915 70 70
699 A244 40k 1989 1.30 1.30

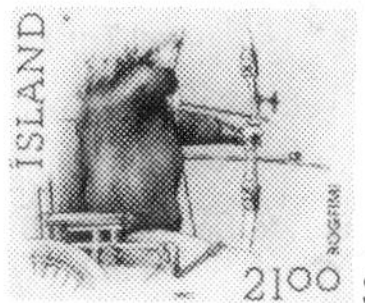
Sports — A245

1990-93 Litho. *Perf. 13x14½*

700 A245 21k Archery 70 70
701 A245 21k Soccer 70 70
706 A245 26k Golf 85 85
707 A245 26k Icelandic wrestling 85 85

Perf. 13½x14½
Photo.

708 A245 30k Volleyball 1.10 1.10
709 A245 30k Skiing 1.10 1.10
710 A245 30k Running 1.00 1.00
711 A245 30k Team handball 1.00 1.00
Nos. 700-711 (8) 7.30 7.30

Issue date: 21k, June 28; 26k, Aug. 14, 1991; 30k, Feb. 20, 1992. Nos. 710-711, Mar. 10, 1993.
This is an expanding set. Numbers will change if necessary.

European Tourism Year — A246

1990, Sept. 6 Litho. *Perf. 13½*

712 A246 30k multicolored 95 95

Landscape Type of 1989

1990, Sept. 6 Photo. *Perf.*

713 A238 25k Hvitserkur 80 80
714 A238 200k Lomagnupur 6.50 6.50

NORDIA '91 Map Type of 1989
Souvenir Sheet

Detail of 1539 Map by Olaus Magnus: a, Dania. b, Gothia. c, Gotlandia.

Litho. & Engr.

1990, Oct. 9 *Perf. 12½*

715 A240 Sheet of 3 6.00 6.00
a.-c. 40k any single 2.00 2.00

Stamp Day. Sold for 170k to benefit the exhibition.

Christmas A247

1990, Nov. 8 *Perf. 13½x13*

716 A247 25k shown 90 90
717 A247 30k Carolers 1.05 1.05

Bird Type of 1986

1991, Feb. 7 Photo. *Perf. 11½*
Granite Paper

721 A212 25k Podiceps auritus 95 95
725 A212 100k Sula bassana 3.75 3.75

This is an expanding set. Numbers will change if necessary.

Landscape Type of 1989

1991, Mar. 7 Photo. *Perf. 11½*
Granite Paper

728 A238 10k Vestrahorn 38 38
737 A238 300k Kverkfjoll 11.25 11.25

This is an expanding set. Numbers will change if necessary.

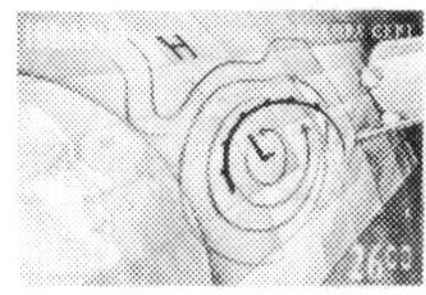
Europa A248

1991, Apr. 29 Litho. *Perf. 14*

738 A248 26k Weather map 90 90
739 A248 47k Solar panels 1.65 1.65

NORDIA '91 Map Type of 1989
Souvenir Sheet

Detail of 1539 Map by Olaus Magnus: a, Iceland's west coast. b, Islandia. c, Mare Glacial.

Litho. & Engr.

1991, May 23 *Perf. 12½*

740 A240 Sheet of 3 7.25 7.25
a.-c. 50k any single 2.42 2.42

Sold for 215k to benefit the exhibition.

Jokulsarlon Lagoon A249

Design: 31k, Strokkur hot spring.

1991, May 23 Litho. *Perf. 15x14*

741 A249 26k multicolored 85 85
742 A249 31k multicolored 1.05 1.05

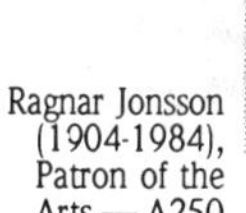
Ragnar Jonsson (1904-1984), Patron of the Arts — A250

Design: 70k, Pall Isolfsson (1893-1974), musician, vert.

1991, Aug. 14 Litho. *Perf. 14*

743 A250 60k multicolored 2.00 2.00
744 A250 70k multicolored 2.30 2.00

Ships A251

Designs: a, Soloven, schooner, 1840. b, Arcturus, steamer with sails, 1858. c, Gullfoss, steamer, 1915. d, Esja II, diesel ship, 1939.

1991, Oct. 9 Litho. *Perf. 14*

745 Block or strip of 4 4.20 4.20
a.-d. A251 30k any single 1.05 1.05
e. A251 Bklt. pane, 2 #745 13.00

No. 745e is distinguished from sheet of 8 by rouletted selvage at left.
Issued in sheet of 8.

College of Navigation, Reykjavik, Cent. — A252

1991, Oct. 9 *Perf. 13½*

746 A252 50k multicolored 1.75 1.75

Christmas — A253

Paintings by Eirikur Smith (b. 1925): 30k, Christmas star. 35k, Star over winter landscape.

1991, Nov. 7 Litho. *Perf. 13½*
747 A253 30k multicolored 1.05 1.05
748 A253 35k multicolored 1.20 1.20

Europa A254

Map and: No. 749, Viking longboat of Leif Erikson. No. 750, Sailing ship of Columbus.

1992, Apr. 6 Litho. *Perf. 13½x14*
749 A254 55k multicolored 1.95 1.95
750 A254 55k multicolored 1.95 1.95

Souvenir Sheet

751 A254 Sheet of 2, #749-750 3.90 3.90

First landing in the Americas by Leif Erikson (#749). Discovery of America by Christopher Columbus, 500th anniv. (#750).

Export Trade and Commerce A255

Designs: 35k, Fishing boat, fish.

1992, June 16 Litho. *Perf. 13½*
752 A255 30k multicolored 1.10 1.10
753 A255 35k multicolored 1.25 1.25

Bridges — A256

1992, Oct. 9 Litho. *Perf. 13½*
754 A256 5k Fnjoska, 1908 18 18
755 A256 250k Olfusa, 1891 9.35 9.35

See Nos. 766-767.

Mail Trucks A257

Designs: No. 756, Mail transport car RE 231, 1933. No. 757, Ford bus, 1946, No. 758, Ford TT, 1920-26. No. 759, Citroen snowmobile, 1929.

1992, Oct. 9 *Perf. 14*
756 A257 30k multicolored 1.15 1.15
757 A257 30k multicolored 1.15 1.15
758 A257 30k multicolored 1.15 1.15
759 A257 30k multicolored 1.15 1.15
a. Block or strip of 4, #756-759 4.60 4.60
b. Booklet pane, 2 each #756-759 13.00

A258 A259

Paintings by Bragi Asgeirsson.

1992, Nov. 9 Litho. *Perf. 13½x13*
760 A258 30k shown 1.10 1.10
761 A258 35k Sun over mountains 1.25 1.25

Christmas.

1992, Dec. 3 Photo. *Perf. 11½*

Falco rusticolus.

Granite Paper

762 A259 5k Adult, two young 18 18
763 A259 10k Adult feeding 36 36
764 A259 20k shown 72 72
765 A259 35k Adult 1.20 1.20

Bridges Type of 1992

1993, Mar. 10 Litho. *Perf. 13½x13*
766 A256 90k Hvita, 1928 3.00 3.00
767 A256 150k Jokulsa a Fjollum, 1947 4.85 4.85

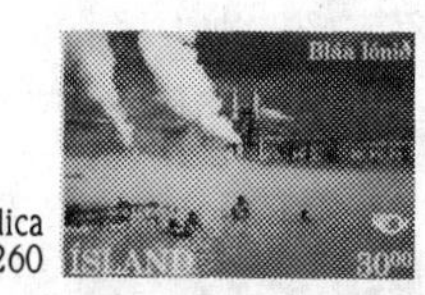
Nordica '93 — A260

Designs: 30k, The Blue Lagoon therapeutic bathing area, hot water plant, Svartsengi. 35k, Perlan hot water storage tanks, restaurant.

1993, Apr. 26 Litho. *Perf. 13½x13*
768 A260 30k multicolored 1.00 1.00
769 A260 35k multicolored 1.15 1.15

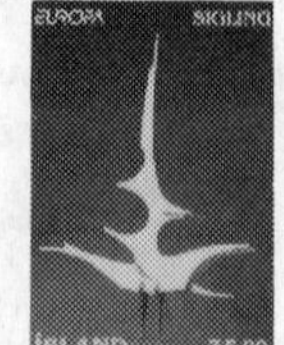
Sculptures — A261

Europa: 35k, Sailing, by Jon Gunnar Arnason. 55k, Hatching of the Jet, by Magnus Tomasson.

1993, Apr. 26 *Perf. 13x13½*
770 A261 35k multicolored 1.15 1.15
771 A261 55k multicolored 1.75 1.75

Souvenir Sheet

Italian Group Flight, 60th Anniv. — A262

1993, Oct. 9 Litho. *Perf. 13½*
772 A262 Sheet of 3, #a.-c. 6.00 6.00
a. 10k #C12 35 35
b. 50k #C13 1.90 1.90
c. 100k #C14 3.75 3.75

No. 772 sold for 200k.

Seaplanes A263

1993, Oct. 9 *Perf. 14*
773 A263 30k Junkers F-13 (D463) 90 90
774 A263 30k Waco YKS-7 (TF-ORN) 90 90
775 A263 30k Grumman G-21A/JRF-5 (RVK) 90 90
776 A263 30k PBY-5 Catalina (TF-ISP) 90 90
a. Block or strip of 4, #773-776 3.75 3.75
b. Booklet pane, 2 each #773-776 12.00

No. 776b is distinguished from sheet of 8 by rouletted selvage at left.
Issued in sheet of 8.

Christmas A264

1993, Nov. 8 Litho. *Perf. 12½*
777 A264 30k Adoration of the Magi 90 90
778 A264 35k Virgin and Child 1.00 1.00

SEMI-POSTAL STAMPS

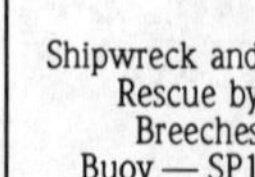

Shipwreck and Rescue by Breeches Buoy — SP1

Children Gathering Rock Plants — SP2

Old Fisherman at Shore — SP3

Unwmk.

1933, Apr. 28 Engr. *Perf. 14*
B1 SP1 10a + 10a red brown 1.10 *3.00*
B2 SP2 20a + 20a org red 1.10 *3.00*
B3 SP1 35a + 25a ultra 1.10 *3.00*
B4 SP3 50a + 25a blue grn 1.10 *3.00*
Set, never hinged 9.50

Receipts from the surtax were devoted to a special fund for use in various charitable works especially those indicated on the stamps: "Slysavarnir" (Rescue work), "Barnahaeli" (Asylum for scrofulous children), "Ellhaeli" (Asylum for the Aged).

Souvenir Sheets

King Christian X — SP4

1937, May 15 Typo.
B5 SP4 Sheet of 3 35.00 *165.00*
a. 15a violet 6.00 *35.00*
b. 25a red 6.00 *35.00*
c. 50a blue 6.00 *35.00*
Never hinged 55.00

Reign of Christian X, 25th anniv. Sheet sold for 2kr.

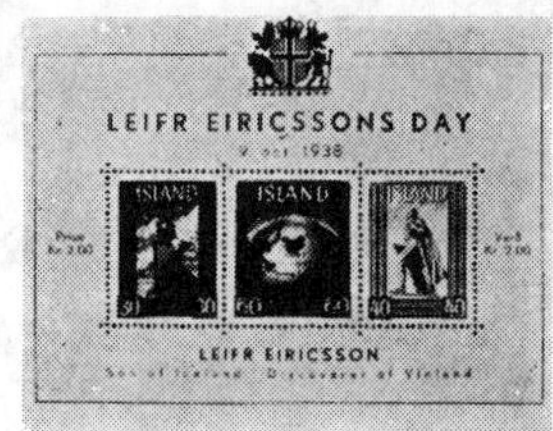
SP5

Designs: 30a, 40a, Ericsson statue, Reykjavik. 60a, Iceland's position on globe.

1938, Oct. 9 Photo. *Perf. 12*
B6 SP5 Sheet of 3 3.50 *27.50*
a. 30a scarlet 75 *6.75*
b. 40a purple 75 *6.75*
c. 60a deep green 75 *6.75*
Never hinged 6.25

Leif Ericsson Day, Oct. 9, 1938.

Ill Child — SP6

Red Cross Nurse and Patient — SP7

Nurse Covering Patient — SP8

Elderly Couple — SP9

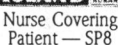

Rescue at Sea — SP10

Unwmk.

1949, June 8 Engr. *Perf. 14*

B7 SP6	10a + 10a olive grn	45	*55*
B8 SP7	35a + 15a carmine	45	*55*
B9 SP8	50a + 25a choc	45	*55*
B10 SP9	60a + 25a brt ultra	45	*55*
B11 SP10	75a + 25a slate gray	45	*55*
	Nos. B7-B11 (5)	2.25	*2.75*
	Set, never hinged	4.00	

The surtax was for charitable purposes.

Nos. 262 and 265 Surcharged in Black

Hollandshjálp
1953
+25

1953, Feb. 12 Unwmk. *Perf. 13*

B12 A50	75a + 25a red org	90	*3.25*
B13 A50	1.25k + 25a red vio	1.40	*3.25*
	Set, never hinged	3.25	

The surtax was for flood relief in the Netherlands.

Catalogue values for unused stamps in this section, from this point to the end of the section, are for Never Hinged items.

St. Thorlacus SP11

Cathedral at Skalholt SP12

Portrait: 1.75k+1.25k, Bishop Jon Thorkelsson Vidalin.

1956, Jan. 23 *Perf. 11½*

B14 SP11	75a + 25a car	32	45
B15 SP12	1.25k + 75a dk brn	32	45
B16 SP11	1.75k + 1.25k black	65	1.25

Bishopric of Skalholt, 900th anniv.
The surtax was for the rebuilding of Skalholt, former cultural center of Iceland.

Ambulance SP13

1963, Nov. 15 Photo. Unwmk.

B17 SP13	3k + 50a multi	22	35
B18 SP13	3.50k + 50a multi	22	35

Centenary of International Red Cross.

Rock Ptarmigan in Summer — SP14

Design: #B20, Rock ptarmigan in winter.

1965, Jan. 27 Photo. *Perf. 12½*
Granite Paper

B19 SP14	3.50k + 50a multi	55	1.25
B20 SP14	4.50k + 50a multi	55	1.25

Ringed Plover's Nest — SP15

Arctic Terns — SP16

Design: 5k+50a, Rock ptarmigan's nest.

1967, Nov. 22 Photo. *Perf. 11½*

B21 SP15	4k + 50a multi	55	1.10
B22 SP15	5k + 50a multi	55	1.10

1972, Nov. 22 Litho. *Perf. 13*

B23 SP16	7k + 1k multi	30	*55*
B24 SP16	9k + 1k multi	38	*55*

AIR POST STAMPS

No. 115 Overprinted

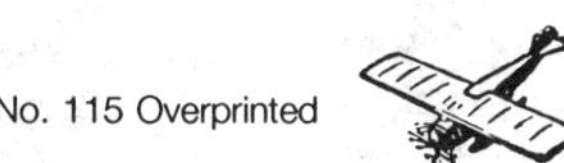

Perf. 14x14½

1928, May 31 Wmk. 114

C1 A8	10a red	90	*7.00*
	Never hinged	1.50	

Same Overprint on No. 82

1929, June 29 Wmk. 113 *Perf. 13*

C2 A5	50a gray & violet	27.50	*42.50*
	Never hinged	70.00	

Gyrfalcon AP1

Perf. 12½x12

1930, Jan. 1 Litho. Unwmk.

C3 AP1	10a dp ultra & gray blue	11.00	*32.50*
a.	Imperf., pair	300.00	
	Never hinged	30.00	

For overprint see No. CO1.

Snaefellsjokull, Extinct Volcano — AP2

Parliament Millenary: 20a, Fishing boat. 35a, Iceland pony. 50a, Gullfoss (Golden Falls). 1k, Ingolfour Arnarson Statue.

Wmk. 47

1930, June 1 Typo. *Perf. 14*

C4 AP2	15a org brn & dl bl	12.00	*30.00*
C5 AP2	20a bis brn & sl bl	12.00	*30.00*
C6 AP2	35a olive grn & brn	27.50	*60.00*
C7 AP2	50a dp grn & dp bl	27.50	*60.00*
C8 AP2	1k olive grn & dk red	27.50	*60.00*
	Nos. C4-C8 (5)	106.50	*240.00*
	Set, never hinged	250.00	

Regular Issue of 1920 Overprinted

Zeppelin
1931

Perf. 14x14½

1931, May 25 Wmk. 114

C9 A8	30a red & green	21.00	*70.00*
C10 A8	1k dp bl & dk brn	10.00	*70.00*
C11 A8	2k ol brn & myr grn	27.50	*70.00*
	Set, never hinged	120.00	

Nos. 185, 128 and 187 Overprinted in Red

1933, June 16

C12 A8	1k dk bl & lt brn	85.00	*425.00*
	Never hinged	165.00	
C13 A8	5k brn & indigo	275.00	*1,100.*
	Never hinged	600.00	
C14 A8	10k yel grn & blk	550.00	*2,000.*
	Never hinged	1,000.	

Excellent counterfeit overprints exist.
Visit of the Italian Flying Armada en route from Rome to Chicago; also for the payment of the charges on postal matter sent from Iceland to the US via the Italian seaplanes.

Plane over Thingvalla Lake — AP7

Designs: 10a, 20a, Plane over Thingvalla Lake. 25a, 50a, Plane and Aurora Borealis. 1k, 2k, Map of Iceland.

Perf. 12½x14

1934, Sept. 1 Engr. Unwmk.

C15 AP7	10a blue	75	*1.00*
C16 AP7	20a emerald	2.50	2.50
a.	Perf. 14	5.00	3.50
C17 AP7	25a dark violet	6.00	*8.00*
a.	Perf. 14	7.00	*8.00*
C18 AP7	50a red vio, perf. 14	2.00	*2.75*
C19 AP7	1k dark brown	11.00	*17.50*
C20 AP7	2k red orange	4.00	*6.00*
	Nos. C15-C20 (6)	26.25	*37.75*
	Set, never hinged	70.00	

Thingvellir, Old Site of the Parliament AP10

Isafjörthur AP11

Eyjafjörthur AP12

Mt. Strandatindur AP13

Mt. Thyrill — AP14

Aerial View of Reykjavik — AP15

1947, Aug. 18 *Perf. 14*

C21 AP10	15a red orange	30	*40*
C22 AP11	30a gray black	30	*40*
C23 AP12	75a brown red	30	*40*
C24 AP13	1k indigo	30	*40*
C25 AP14	2k chocolate	85	*1.00*
C26 AP15	3k dark green	85	*1.00*
	Nos. C21-C26 (6)	2.90	*3.60*
	Set, never hinged	5.00	

Snaefellsjokull AP16

Views: 2.50k, Eiriksjokull. 3.30k, Oraefajokull.

1952, May 2 Unwmk. *Perf. 13½x14*

C27 AP16	1.80k slate blue	5.50	*11.00*
C28 AP16	2.50k green	10.00	1.10
C29 AP16	3.30k deep ultra	4.50	4.25
	Set, never hinged	40.00	

See Nos. 302-304.

Vickers Viscount and Plane of 1919 — AP17

Design: 4.05k, Skymaster and plane of 1919.

1959, Sept. 3 Engr. *Perf. 13½*

C30 AP17	3.50k steel blue	55	55
C31 AP17	4.05k green	45	45
	Set, never hinged	1.20	

40th anniv. of air transportation in Iceland.

AIR POST OFFICIAL STAMPS

No. C3 Overprinted In Red

Þjónustumerki

1930, Jan. 1 Unwmk. *Perf. 12½x12*

CO1 AP1	10a dp ultra & gray blue	20.00	*90.00*
a.	Imperf.		
	Never hinged	37.50	

OFFICIAL STAMPS

O1 O2

O3

Perf. 14x13½

1873 Typo. Wmk. 112

O1 O1	4s green	*4,000.*	*4,000.*
a.	Imperf.	60.00	
O2 O1	8s red lilac	225.00	240.00
a.	Imperf.	225.00	

Perf. 12½

O3 O1	4s green	35.00	*135.00*

The imperforate varieties lack gum.
No. O1 values are for copies with perfs cutting the design on at least one side.

1876-95 *Perf. 14x13½*

O4 O2	3a yellow	12.00	*27.50*
O5 O2	5a brown	3.75	*7.50*
a.	Imperf.	150.00	
O6 O2	10a blue	30.00	7.00
a.	10a ultramarine	165.00	35.00
O7 O2	16a carmine	7.25	*19.00*
O8 O2	20a yellow green	7.00	*12.50*
O9 O2	50a rose lilac ('95)	32.50	*42.50*

1898-1902 *Perf. 13*

O10	O2	3a yellow	6.00	*15.00*
O11	O2	4a gray ('01)	12.00	*17.50*
O12	O2	10a ultra ('02)	25.00	*55.00*

A 5a brown, perf. 13, Wmk. 112, exists. It was not regularly issued.

See note after No. O30.

For overprints see Nos. O20-O30.

1902 Wmk. 113 *Perf. 13*

O13	O3	3a buff & black	1.75	70
O14	O3	4a dp grn & blk	2.50	70
O15	O3	5a org brn & blk	1.25	*1.65*
O16	O3	10a ultra & black	1.25	*1.65*
O17	O3	16a carmine & blk	1.50	*6.00*
O18	O3	20a green & blk	6.50	3.00
O19	O3	50a violet & blk	3.00	*4.00*
		Nos. O13-O19 (7)	17.75	*17.70*

Stamps of 1876-1901 Overprinted in Black **Í GILDI '02—'03**

1902-03 Wmk. 112 *Perf. 13*

O20	O2	3a yellow	70	*1.10*
	a.	"I" before Gildi omitted	15.00	
	b.	Inverted overprint	5.50	6.00
	c.	As "a," invtd.	87.50	
	d.	Pair, one with invtd. ovpt.	40.00	
	e.	'03-'03	65.00	
	f.	02'-'03	65.00	
O21	O2	4a gray	70	*1.10*
	a.	"I" before Gildi omitted	32.00	
	b.	Inverted overprint	14.50	14.00
	e.	'03-'03	100.00	90.00
	f.	02'-'03	100.00	
	g.	Pair, one without ovpt.	32.00	
	h.	Pair, one with invtd. ovpt.	35.00	35.00
	i.	"L" only of "I GILDI" inverted	160.00	
O22	O2	5a brown	52	*1.00*
O23	O2	10a ultramarine	70	*1.25*
	a.	"I" before Gildi omitted	14.00	
	b.	Inverted overprint	8.75	8.75
	c.	'03-'03	60.00	
	d.	02'-'03	60.00	
	e.	"L" only of "I GILDI"	17.50	
	f.	As "e," inverted	24.00	
	g.	"IL" only of "I GILDI"	19.00	
O24	O2	20a yel green	52	*14.00*
		Nos. O20-O24 (5)	3.14	*18.45*

Perf. 14x13½

O25	O2	3a yellow	200.00	*550.00*
	a.	"02'-'03"	240.00	
O26	O2	5a brown	6.00	*60.00*
	a.	Inverted overprint	12.00	*70.00*
	b.	'03-'03	65.00	
	c.	02'-'03	65.00	
	d.	"L" only of "I GILDI" inverted	150.00	
O27	O2	10a blue	225.00	*400.00*
	a.	"I" before Gildi omitted	275.00	
	b.	Inverted overprint	275.00	*500.00*
	c.	'03-'03	275.00	
	d.	02'-'03	275.00	
O28	O2	16a carmine	6.25	*32.50*
	a.	"I" before Gildi omitted	110.00	
	b.	Double overprint	27.50	50.00
	c.	Dbl. ovpt., one inverted	60.00	
	d.	Inverted overprint	30.00	45.00
	e.	'03-'03	110.00	
O29	O2	20a yel green	5.50	*30.00*
	a.	Inverted overprint	45.00	45.00
	b.	'03-'03	87.50	
	c.	02'-'03	87.50	
	d.	"I" before Gildi omitted	80.00	
O30	O2	50a red lilac	5.50	*27.50*
	a.	"I" before Gildi omitted	14.00	
	b.	Inverted overprint	60.00	
		Nos. O25-O30 (6)	448.25	*1,100.*

Nos. O10-O12, O20-O24, O28 and O30 were reprinted in 1904. They have the watermark of 1902 (type 113) and are perf. 13. Value $50 each. Without overprint $100 each.

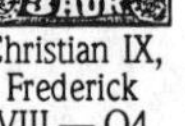

Christian IX, Frederick VIII — O4

Christian X — O5

Engraved Center

1907-08 Wmk. 113 *Perf. 13*

O31	O4	3a yellow & gray	2.00	2.50
O32	O4	4a green & gray	1.25	*3.50*
O33	O4	5a brn org & gray	4.50	1.90
O34	O4	10a deep bl & gray	1.20	*1.50*
O35	O4	15a lt blue & gray	1.50	*2.75*
O36	O4	16a carmine & gray	1.50	*8.00*
O37	O4	20a yel grn & gray	4.50	1.00
O38	O4	50a violet & gray	3.25	2.75
		Nos. O31-O38 (8)	19.70	*23.90*

1918 Wmk. 114 *Perf. 14x14½*

O39	O4	15a lt bl & gray	5.50	*15.00*

1920-30 **Typo.**

O40	O5	3a yellow & gray	1.50	*1.75*
O41	O5	4a dp grn & gray	48	*1.75*
O42	O5	5a orange & gray	50	*60*
O43	O5	10a dk bl & gray	1.00	55
O44	O5	15a lt blue & gray	35	55
O45	O5	20a yel grn & gray	17.50	2.00
O46	O5	50a violet & gray	20.00	85
O47	O5	1k car & gray	19.00	1.25
O48	O5	2k bl & blk ('30)	4.50	5.00
O49	O5	5k brn & blk ('30)	20.00	17.50
		Nos. O40-O49 (10)	84.83	31.80

See No. O68.

Nos. 97 and 98 Overprinted **Þjónusta.**

1922, May Wmk. 113 *Perf. 13*

O50	A7	2k rose, larger letters, no period	17.50	25.00
	a.	As shown	35.00	*27.50*
O51	A7	5k brown	125.00	110.00

No. 115 Surcharged **20 aur. Þjónusta**

1923 Wmk. 114 *Perf. 14x14½*

O52	A8	20a on 10a red	8.50	1.00

Parliament Millenary Issue

#152-166 Overprinted in Red or Blue **Þjónustumerki**

1930, Jan. 1 Unwmk. *Perf. 12½x12*

O53	A15	3a (R)	6.25	*22.50*
O54	A15	5a (R)	6.25	*22.50*
O55	A15	7a (R)	6.25	*22.50*
O56	A15	10a (Bl)	6.25	*22.50*
O57	A15	15a (R)	6.25	*22.50*
O58	A15	20a (Bl)	6.25	*22.50*
O59	A15	25a (Bl)	6.25	*22.50*
O60	A15	30a (R)	6.25	*22.50*
O61	A15	35a (R)	6.25	*22.50*
O62	A15	40a (Bl)	6.25	*22.50*
O63	A15	50a (Bl)	67.50	*110.00*
O64	A15	1k (R)	67.50	*110.00*
O65	A15	2k (R)	67.50	*110.00*
O66	A15	5k (Bl)	67.50	*110.00*
O67	A15	10k (Bl)	67.50	*110.00*
		Nos. O53-O67 (15)	400.00	*775.00*

Type of 1920 Issue Redrawn

1931 Wmk. 114 **Typo.**

O68	O5	20a yel grn & gray	17.50	90

For differences in redrawing see note after No. 187.

No. 82 Overprinted in Black **Þjónusta**

Overprint 15mm long

1936, Dec. 7 Wmk. 113 *Perf. 13*

O69	A5	50a gray & vio	9.00	9.00

Same Overprint on Nos. 180 and 115

Perf. 14x14½

Wmk. 114

O70	A8	7a yellow green	1.40	*22.50*
O71	A8	10a red	1.50	85

IFNI

LOCATION — An enclave in southern Morocco on the Atlantic coast

GOVT. — Former Spanish possession

AREA — 580 sq. mi.

POP. — 51,517 (est. 1964)

CAPITAL — Sidi Ifni

Ifni was ceded to Spain by Morocco in 1860, but the Spanish did not occupy it until 1934. Sidi Ifni was also the administrative capital for Spanish West Africa. Spain turned Ifni back to Morocco June 30, 1969.

100 Centimos = 1 Peseta

Catalogue values for unused stamps in this country are for Never Hinged items, beginning with Scott 51 in the regular postage section, Scott B1 in the semi-postal section, and Scott C47 in the airpost section.

Stamps of Spain, 1936-40, Overprinted in Red or Blue **TERRITORIO DE IFNI**

1941-42 Unwmk. *Imperf.*

1	A159	1c green	4.00	3.75

Perf. 10 to 11

2	A160	2c org brn (Bl)	4.00	3.75
3	A161	5c gray brown	70	35
5	A161	10c dk car (Bl)	2.25	1.25
	a.	Red overprint	12.00	6.00
6	A161	15c light grn	55	35
7	A166	20c bright vio	55	35
8	A166	25c deep claret	55	35
9	A166	30c blue	55	50
10	A166	40c Prus green	85	30
11	A166	50c indigo	4.50	1.00
12	A166	70c blue	4.50	2.75
13	A166	1p gray blk	4.50	28
14	A166	2p dull brown	47.50	12.00
15	A166	4p dl rose (Bl)	185.00	67.50
16	A166	10p light brn	325.00	140.00
		Nos. 1-16 (15)	585.00	234.48

Counterfeit overprints exist.

Nomads — A1

Alcazaba Fortress — A3

Designs: 2c, 20c, 45c, 3p, Marksman.

1943 Litho. *Perf. 12½*

17	A1	1c brn & lil rose	15	15
18	A1	2c yel grn & sl lil	15	15
19	A3	5c magenta & vio	15	15
20	A1	15c sl grn & grn	15	15
21	A1	20c vio & red brn	15	15
22	A1	40c rose vio & vio	18	18
23	A1	45c brn vio & red	20	20
24	A3	75c indigo & bl	20	20
25	A1	1p red & brown	1.25	1.00
26	A1	3p bl vio & sl grn	1.40	1.40
27	A3	10p blk brn & blk	13.00	11.50
		Nos. 17-27 (11)	16.98	15.23

Nos. 17-27 exist imperforate.

See No. E1.

1947, Feb. *Perf. 10*

28	A1	50c Nomad family	6.75	50

Stamps of Spain, 1939-48, Overprinted in Carmine **Territorio de Ifni**

1948, Aug. 2 *Perf. 9½x10½, 11, 13*

29	A161	5c gray brn	1.40	35
30	A194	15c gray grn	2.75	45
31	A167	90c dk grn	8.50	2.50
32	A166	1p gray blk	24	18

Spain Nos. 769 and 770 Overprinted in Violet Blue or Carmine **Territorio de Ifni**

1949, Oct. 9 *Perf. 12½x13*

33	A202	50c red brn (VB)	1.25	70
34	A202	75c vio bl (C)	1.25	70

75th anniv. of the UPU. See No. C40.

Stamps of Spain, 1938-48, Overprinted in Blue or Carmine like Nos. 29-32

Perf. 13, 13½, 12½x13, 9½x10½

1949 Unwmk.

35	A160	2c org brn (Bl)	15	15
37	A161	10c dk car (Bl)	15	15
38	A161	15c dk grn (Il)	15	15
39	A166	25c brn vio	18	15
40	A166	30c blue	18	18
41	A195	40c red brn	18	18
42	A195	45c car rose (Bl)	32	32
43	A166	50c indigo	26	18
44	A195	75c dk vio bl	40	22
47	A167	1.35p purple	3.50	3.25
48	A166	2p dl brn	2.50	1.75
49	A166	4p dl rose (Bl)	9.50	4.50
50	A166	10p lt brn	18.00	16.00
		Nos. 35-50 (13)	35.47	27.18

Catalogue values for unused stamps in this section, from this point to the end of the section, are for Never Hinged items.

Gen. Francisco Franco and Desert Scene — A4

Perf. 12½x13

1951, July 18 Photo. Unwmk.

51	A4	50c dp org	50	15
52	A4	1p chocolate	4.00	1.25
53	A4	5p bl grn	32.50	11.00

Visit of Gen. Francisco Franco, 1950.

View of Granada and Globe — A5

1952, Dec. 10 *Perf. 13x12½*

54	A5	5c red org	15	15
55	A5	35c dk ol grn	15	15
56	A5	60c brown	20	15
		Set value	30	15

400th anniversary of the death of Leo Africanus (c. 1485-c. 1554), Arab traveler and scholar, author of "Descrittione dell' Africa."

Musician A6

Design: 60c, Two musicians.

1953, June 1 *Perf. 12½x13*

57	A6	15c olive gray	15	15
58	A6	60c brown	15	15
		Set value	15	15

Issued to promote child welfare.

See Nos. B13-B14.

Fish and Jellyfish A7

Design: 60c, Fish and seaweed.

1953, Nov. 23

59	A7	15c dark green	15	15
60	A7	60c brown	28	15
		Set value		15

Colonial Stamp Day, Nov. 23, 1953.

See Nos. B15-B16.

Sea Gull — A8

Cactus — A9

Design: 25c, 60c, 2p, 5p, Salsola vermiculata.

Perf. 12½x13, 13x12½

1954, Apr. 22

61	A8	5c red org	15	15
62	A9	10c olive	15	15
63	A9	25c brn car	15	15
64	A8	35c olive gray	15	15
65	A9	40c rose lilac	15	15
66	A9	60c dk brn	15	15
67	A8	1p brown	5.75	60
68	A9	1.25p car rose	15	15
69	A9	2p darp blue	15	15
70	A9	4.50p olive grn	28	28
71	A9	5p olive blk	27.50	4.50
		Nos. 61-71 (11)	34.73	
		Set value		5.75

Mother and Child
A10 A11

1954, June 1 *Perf. 13x12½*

72	A10	15c dk gray grn	15	15
73	A11	60c dk brn	15	15
		Set value	20	15

See Nos. B17-B18.

Lobster — A12

Design: 60c, Hammerhead shark.

1954, Nov. 23 *Perf. 12½x13*

74	A12	15c olive green	15	15
75	A12	60c rose brown	18	15
		Set value	23	15

Issued to publicize Colonial Stamp Day. See Nos. B19-B20.

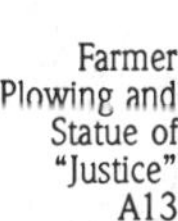

Farmer Plowing and Statue of "Justice" A13

1955, June 1 **Photo.** **Unwmk.**

76	A13	50c gray olive	15	15

See No. B21.

Squirrel A14

1955, Nov. 23

77	A14	70c yellow green	20	15

Issued to publicize Colonial Stamp Day. See Nos. B23-B24.

Senecio Antheuphorbium — A15

Design: 50c, Limoniastrum Ifniensis.

1956, June 1 *Perf. 13x12½*

78	A15	20c bluish green	15	15
79	A15	50c brown	20	15
		Set value	26	15

See Nos. B25-B26.

Arms of Sidi Ifni and Shepherd A16

1956, Nov. 23 *Perf. 12½x13*

80	A16	70c light green	15	15

Issued for Colonial Stamp Day.

Rock Doves — A17

1957, June 1 **Photo.** *Perf. 13x12½*

81	A17	70c yel grn & brn	20	15

See Nos. 86, B29-B30.

Jackal A18

Design: 70c, Jackal's head, vert.

Perf. 12½x13, 13x12½

1957, Nov. 23

82	A18	20c emer & lt grn	15	15
83	A18	70c grn & brn	30	15
		Set value		15

Issued for the Day of the Stamp, 1957. See Nos. 87, B31-B32, B41.

Basketball Players A19

Red-legged Partridges A20

Design: 70c, Cyclists.

1958, June 1 *Perf. 13x12½*

84	A19	20c bluish green	15	15
85	A19	70c olive green	30	15
		Set value		15

See Nos. B36-B37.

Types of 1957 inscribed "Pro-Infancia 1959"

Designs: 20c, Goat. 70c, Ewe and lamb.

1959, June 1 *Perf. 13x12½, 12½x13*

86	A17	20c dull green	15	15
87	A18	70c yellow green	20	15
		Set value		15

Issued to promote child welfare.

1960, June 10 *Perf. 13x12½*

88	A20	35c shown	15	15
89	A20	80c Camels	20	15
		Set value		15

See Nos. B46-B47.

White Stork — A21

Birds: 50c, 1.50p, 5p, European goldfinches. 75c, 2p, 10p, Skylarks, vert.

1960 **Unwmk.** *Perf. 12½x13*

90	A21	25c violet	15	15
91	A21	50c olive blk	15	15
92	A21	75c dull pur	15	15
93	A21	1p org ver	15	15
94	A21	1.50p brt grnsh bl	15	15
95	A21	2p red lilac	15	15
96	A21	3p dark blue	65	15
97	A21	5p red brown	1.25	30
98	A21	10p olive	5.00	1.25
		Nos. 90-98 (9)	7.80	
		Set value		2.00

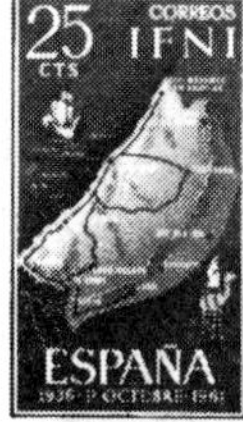
Map of Ifni — A22

General Franco A23

Design: 70c, Government palace.

Perf. 13x12½, 12½x13

1961, Oct. 1 **Photo.**

99	A22	25c gray vio	15	15
100	A23	50c olive brn	15	15
101	A23	70c brt grn	15	15
102	A23	1p red org	15	15
		Set value	33	21

25th anniv. of the nomination of Gen. Francisco Franco as Head of State.

Admiral Jofre Tenoria A24

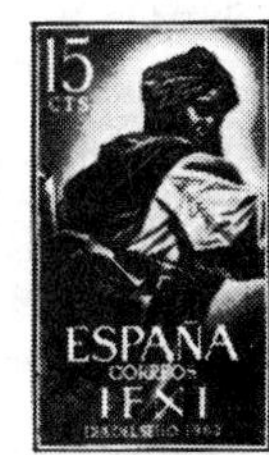
Mailman A25

Design: 50c, Cesareo Fernandez-Duro (1830-1908), writer.

1962, July 10 *Perf. 13x12½*

103	A24	25c dull vio	15	15
104	A24	50c dp bl grn	15	15
105	A24	1p org brn	15	15
		Set value	27	15

1962, Nov. 23 **Unwmk.**

Stamp Day: 35c, Hands, letter and winged wheel.

106	A25	15c dark blue	15	15
107	A25	35c lilac rose	15	15
108	A25	1p rose brown	15	15
		Set value	27	15

Golden Tower, Seville A26

Butterflies A27

1963, Jan. 29 **Photo.**

109	A26	50c green	15	15
110	A26	1p brown orange	15	15
		Set value	20	15

Issued for flood relief in Seville.

1963, July 6 *Perf. 13x12½*

Design: 50c, Butterfly and flower.

111	A27	25c deep blue	15	15
112	A27	50c light green	15	15
113	A27	1p carmine rose	15	15
		Set value	27	16

Issued for child welfare.

Child with Flowers and Arms — A28

1963, July 12 *Perf. 12½x13*

114	A28	50c gray olive	15	15
115	A28	1p reddish brown	15	15
		Set value	20	15

Issued for Barcelona flood relief.

Beetle (Steraspis Speciosa) A29

Mountain Gazelle A30

Stamp Day: 50c, Grasshopper.

1964, Mar. 6 *Perf. 13x12½*

116 A29	25c	violet blue	15	15
117 A29	50c	olive green	15	15
118 A29	1p	red brown	15	15
		Set value	27	18

1964, June 1 **Photo.**

Design: 50c, Head of roebuck.

119 A30	25c	brt vio	15	15
120 A30	50c	slate blk	15	15
121 A30	1p	org red	15	15
		Set value	27	18

Issued for child welfare.

Bicycle Race — A31

Stamp Day: 1p, Motorcycle race.

1964, Nov. 23 *Perf. 12½x13*

122 A31	50c	brown	15	15
123 A31	1p	org ver	15	15
124 A31	1.50p	Prus grn	15	15
		Set value	27	18

Man — A32

Two Boys in School — A33

Cable Cars, Sidi Ifni — A34

Perf. 13x12½, 12½x13

1965, Mar. 1 **Photo.** **Unwmk.**

125 A32	50c	dark green	15	15
126 A33	1p	org ver	15	15
127 A34	1.50p	dark blue	15	15
		Set value	27	18

25 years of peace after the Spanish Civil War.

Eugaster Fernandezi A35

Insect: 1p, Halter halteratus.

1965, June 1 **Photo.** **Unwmk.**

128 A35	50c	purple	15	15
129 A35	1p	rose red	15	15
130 A35	1.50p	violet blue	15	15
		Set value	27	18

Issued for child welfare.

Eagle — A36

Arms of Sidi Ifni — A37

Perf. 13x12½, 12½x13

1965, Nov. 23 **Photo.**

131 A36	50c	dk red brn	15	15
132 A37	1p	org ver	15	15
133 A36	1.50p	grnsh bl	15	15
		Set value	27	18

Issued for Stamp Day 1965.

Jetliner over Sidi Ifni — A38

Syntomis Alicia — A39

Design: 2.50p, Two 1934 biplanes, horiz.

Perf. 13x12½, 12½x13

1966, June 1 **Photo.** **Unwmk.**

134 A38	1p	org brn	15	15
135 A38	1.50p	brt bl	15	15
136 A38	2.50p	dl vio	2.25	1.75

Issued for child welfare.

1966, Nov. 23 **Photo.** *Perf. 13*

Designs: 40c, 4p, Danais chrysippus (butterfly).

137 A39	10c	grn & red	15	15
138 A39	40c	dk brn & gldn brn	15	15
139 A39	1.50p	vio & yel	15	15
140 A39	4p	dk pur & brt bl	25	15
		Set value	42	32

Issued for Stamp Day, 1966.

Coconut Palms — A40

Designs: 40c, 4p, Cactus.

1967, June 1 **Photo.** *Perf. 13*

141 A40	10c	dp grn & brn	15	15
142 A40	40c	Prus grn & ocher	15	15
143 A40	1.50p	bl grn & sepia	15	15
144 A40	4p	sepia & ocher	25	15
		Set value	42	32

Issued for child welfare.

Sidi Ifni Harbor A41

1967, Sept. 28 **Photo.** *Perf. 12½x13*

145 A41	1.50p	grn & red brn	20	15

Modernization of harbor installations.

Needlefish (Skipper) — A42

Fish: 1.50p, John Dory, vert. 3.50p, Gurnard (Trigla lucerna).

1967, Nov. 23 **Photo.** *Perf. 13*

146 A42	1p	bl & grn	15	15
147 A42	1.50p	vio blk & yel	15	15
148 A42	3.50p	brt bl & scar	30	18
		Set value	42	30

Issued for Stamp Day 1967.

Zodiac Issue

Pisces — A43

Signs of the Zodiac: 1.50p, Capricorn. 2.50p, Sagittarius.

1968, Apr. 25 **Photo.** *Perf. 13*

149 A43	1p	brt mag, *lt yel*	15	15
150 A43	1.50p	brn, *pink*	15	15
151 A43	2.50p	dk vio, *yel*	30	15
		Set value	42	27

Issued for child welfare.

Mailing a Letter A44

Designs: 1.50p, Carrier pigeon carrying letter. 2.50p, Stamp under magnifying glass.

1968, Nov. 23 **Photo.** *Perf. 12½x13*

152 A44	1p	org yel & sl grn	15	15
153 A44	1.50p	brt bl & vio blk	15	15
154 A44	2.50p	emer & vio blk	20	15
		Set value	32	27

Issued for Stamp Day.

SEMI-POSTAL STAMPS

Catalogue values for unused stamps in this section are for Never Hinged items.

Gen. Francisco Franco — SP1

Fennec — SP2

Perf. 13x12½

1950, Oct. 19 **Unwmk.**

B1 SP1	50c + 10c	sepia	60	45
B2 SP1	1p + 25c	blue	20.00	6.00
B3 SP1	6.50p + 1.65p	dl grn	7.50	3.25

The surtax was for child welfare.

1951, Nov. 30

B4 SP2	5c + 5c	brown	15	15
B5 SP2	10c + 5c	red org	15	15
B6 SP2	60c + 15c	olive brn	40	15
		Set value	52	22

Colonial Stamp Day, Nov. 23, 1951.

Mother and Child — SP3

Common Shag — SP4

1952, June 1

B7 SP3	5c + 5c	brn	15	15
B8 SP3	50c + 10c	brn blk	15	15
B9 SP3	2p + 30c	dp bl	1.75	65
		Set value		77

The surtax was for child welfare.

1952, Nov. 23

B10 SP4	5c + 5c	brn	20	15
B11 SP4	10c + 5c	brn car	20	15
B12 SP4	60c + 15c	dk grn	35	15
		Set value		36

Colonial Stamp Day, Nov. 23, 1952.

Musician Type of Regular Issue

1953, June 1 *Perf. 12½x13*

B13 A6	5c + 5c	as No. 57	15	15
B14 A6	10c + 5c	as No. 58	15	15
		Set value	16	15

The surtax was for child welfare.

Fish Type of Regular Issue

1953, Nov. 23

B15 A7	5c + 5c	as No. 59	15	15
B16 A7	10c + 5c	as No. 60	15	15
		Set value	24	16

Colonial Stamp Day, Nov. 23, 1953.

Type of Regular Issue

1954, June 1 *Perf. 13x12½*

B17 A10	5c + 5c	org	15	15
B18 A11	10c + 5c	rose vio	15	15
		Set value	24	15

The surtax was for child welfare.

Type of Regular Issue

1954, Nov. 23 *Perf. 12½x13*

B19 A12	5c + 5c	as No. 74	15	15
B20 A12	10c + 5c	as No. 75	15	15
		Set value		15

"Dama de Elche" Protecting Caravan SP5

1955, June 1 **Photo.** **Unwmk.**

B21 A13	10c + 5c	rose lilac	15	15
B22 SP5	25c + 10c	violet	15	15
		Set value		15

The surtax was to help Ifni people.

Squirrel Type of Regular Issue

Design: 15c+5c, Squirrel holding nut.

1955, Nov. 23

B23 A14	5c + 5c	red brown	15	15
B24 A14	15c + 5c	olive bister	15	15
		Set value		15

Type of Regular Issue

1956, June 1 *Perf. 13x12½*

B25 A15	5c + 5c	as No. 78	15	15
B26 A15	15c + 5c	as No. 79	15	15
		Set value		15

The tax was for child welfare.

Dorcas Gazelles and Arms of Spain — SP6

Design: 15c+5c, Arms of Sidi Ifni, boat and woman with drum.

1956, Nov. 23

B27 SP6 5c + 5c dark brown 15 15
B28 SP6 15c + 5c golden brn 15 15
Set value 15 15

Issued for Colonial Stamp Day.

Dove Type of Regular Issue

1957, June 1 Photo. *Perf. 13x12½*

B29 A17 5c + 5c as No. 81 15 15
B30 A17 15c + 5c Stock doves 15 15
Set value 15 15

The surtax was for child welfare.

Type of Regular Issue

Perf. 12½x13, 13x12½

1957, Nov. 23 Photo. Unwmk.

B31 A18 10c + 5c as No. 82 15 15
B32 A18 15c + 5c as No. 83 15 15
Set value 15 15

Swallows and Arms of Valencia and Sidi Ifni — SP7

1958, Mar. 6 *Perf. 12½x13*

B33 SP7 10c + 5c org brn 15 15
B34 SP7 15c + 10c bister 15 15
B35 SP7 50c + 10c brn olive 15 15
Set value 24 18

The surtax was to aid the victims of the Valencia flood, Oct. 1957.

Sport Type of Regular Issue, 1958

1958, June 1 Photo. *Perf. 13x12½*

B36 A19 10c + 5c as No. 84 15 15
B37 A19 15c + 5c as No. 85 15 15
Set value 15 15

The surtax was for child welfare.

Guitarfish — SP8

Sailboats SP9

Stamp Day: 10c+5c, Spotted dogfish.

Perf. 13x12½, 12½x13

1958, Nov. 23

B38 SP9 10c + 5c brn red 15 15
B39 SP8 25c + 10c dull vio 18 15
B40 SP9 50c + 10c olive 25 15
Set value 30

Donkey and Man — SP10

Soccer — SP11

Type of 1957 and SP10

Design: 10c+5c, Ewe and lamb.

Perf. 12½x13, 13x12½

1959, June 1 Photo. Unwmk.

B41 A18 10c + 5c lt red brn 15 15
B42 SP10 15c + 5c golden brn 15 15
Set value 15 15

The surtax was for child welfare.

1959, Nov. 23 *Perf. 13x12½*

Designs: 20c+5c, Soccer players. 50c+20c, Javelin thrower.

B43 SP11 10c + 5c fawn 15 15
B44 SP11 20c + 5c slate green 15 15
B45 SP11 50c + 20c olive gray 25 15
Set value 37 18

Issued for the day of the Stamp, 1959.
See Nos. B52-B54.

Type of Regular Issue, 1960

1960, June 10 *Perf. 13x12½*

B46 A20 10c + 5c as No. 89 15 15
B47 A20 15c + 5c Wild boars 15 15
Set value 15 15

The surtax was for child welfare.

Santa Maria del Mar — SP12

Stamp Day: 20c+5c, 50c+20c, New school building, horiz.

Perf. 13x12½, 12½x13

1960, Dec. 29 Photo.

B48 SP12 10c + 5c org brn 15 15
B49 SP12 20c + 5c dk sl grn 15 15
B50 SP12 30c + 10c red brn 15 15
B51 SP12 50c + 20c sepia 18 15
Set value 36 20

Type of 1959 inscribed: "Pro-Infancia 1961"

Designs: 10c+5c, 80c+20c, Pole vaulting (horiz.). 25c+10c, Soccer player.

Perf. 12½x13, 13x12½

1961, June 21 Unwmk.

B52 SP11 10c + 5c rose brn 15 15
B53 SP11 25c + 10c gray vio 15 15
B54 SP11 80c + 20c dk green 12 15
Set value 28 22

The surtax was for child welfare.

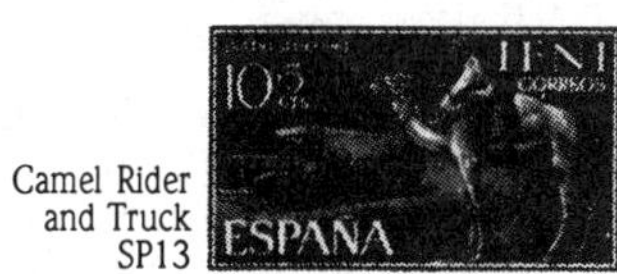

Camel Rider and Truck SP13

Stamp Day: 25c+10c, 1p+10c, Ship in Sidi Ifni harbor.

1961, Nov. 23 *Perf. 12½x13*

B55 SP13 10c + 5c rose brn 15 15
B56 SP13 25c + 10c dk pur 15 15
B57 SP13 30c + 10c dk red brn 15 15
B58 SP13 1p + 10c red org 18 15
Set value 36 24

AIR POST STAMPS

Stamps formerly listed as Nos. C1-C29 were privately overprinted. These include 1936 stamps of Spain overprinted "VIA AEREA" and plane, and 1939 stamps of Spain, type AP30, overprinted "IFNI" or "Territorio de Ifni."

Oasis AP1

The Sanctuary AP2

1943 Unwmk. Litho. *Perf. 12½*

C30 AP2 5c cer & vio brn 18 18
C31 AP1 25c yel grn & ol grn 18 18
C32 AP2 50c ind & turq grn 25 25
C33 AP1 1p pur & grnsh bl 25 25
C34 AP2 1.40p gray grn & bl 25 25
C35 AP1 2p mag & org brn 90 80
C36 AP2 5p brn & pur 1.25 1.25
C37 AP1 6p brt bl & gray grn 15.00 12.50
Nos. C30-C37 (8) 18.26 15.66

Nos. C30-C37 exist imperforate.

Type of Spain, 1939-47, Overprinted in Carmine **IFNI**

1947, Nov. 29

C38 AP30 5c dull yellow 1.75 80
C39 AP30 10c dk bl green 1.75 80

Spain No. C126 Overprinted in Carmine like Nos. 33-34

1949, Oct. 9 *Perf. 12½x13*

C40 A202 4p dk olive grn 1.50 95

75th anniv. of the UPU.

Spain, Nos. C110 and C112 to C116, Overprinted in Blue or Carmine like Nos. 29-32

1949 *Perf. 10*

C41 AP30 25c redsh brn (Bl) 35 15
C42 AP30 50c brown 40 18
C43 AP30 1p chalky blue 40 18
C44 AP30 2p lt gray grn 2.00 50
C45 AP30 4p gray blue 5.75 3.00
C46 AP30 10p brt pur 7.50 6.00
Nos. C41-C46 (6) 16.40 10.01

Catalogue values for unused stamps in this section, from this point to the end of the section, are for Never Hinged items.

Lope Sancho de Valenzuela and Sheik — AP3

Woman Holding Dove — AP4

1950, Nov. 23 Photo. *Perf. 13x12½*

C47 AP3 5p brown black 2.75 70

Stamp Day, Nov. 23, 1950.

1951, Apr. 22 Engr. *Perf. 10*

C48 AP4 5p red 18.00 5.75

Issued to commemorate the 500th anniversary of the birth of Queen Isabella I of Spain.

Ferdinand the Catholic — AP5

Plane and Mountain Gazelle — AP6

Perf. 13x12½

1952, July 18 Photo. Unwmk.

C49 AP5 5p brown 24.00 6.00

500th anniv. of the birth of Ferdinand the Catholic of Spain.

1953, Apr. 1

C50 AP6 60c light grn 15 15
C51 AP6 1.20p brn car 24 15
C52 AP6 1.60p lt brown 28 15
C53 AP6 2p deep blue 2.25 20
C54 AP6 4p grnsh blk 1.25 20
C55 AP6 10p brt red vio 6.50 1.40
Nos. C50-C55 (6) 10.67
Set value 1.95

SPECIAL DELIVERY STAMPS

Type A3 inscribed "URGENTE"

1943 *Perf. 12½*

E1 A3 25c slate green & car 85 70

Spain, No. E20, Overprinted in Blue like Nos. 29-32

1949 Unwmk. *Perf. 10*

E2 SD10 25c carmine 20 15

INDO-CHINA

LOCATION — French possessions on the Cambodian Peninsula in southeastern Asia, bordering on the South China Sea and the Gulf of Siam
GOVT. — Former French Colony and Protectorate
AREA — 280,849 sq. mi.
POP. — 27,030,000 (estimated 1949)
CAPITAL — Hanoi

In 1949, Indo-China was divided into Cambodia, Laos and Viet Nam each issuing its own stamps.

100 Centimes = 1 Franc
100 Cents = 1 Piaster (1918)

Stamps of French Colonies Surcharged in Black or Red:

INDO-CHINE 89 / 5 / R D — a
INDO-CHINE 1889 / 5 / R – D — b

1889 Unwmk. *Perf. 14x13½*
1 A9(a) 5c on 35c dp vio, *org* 3.25 2.50
a. Without date 110.00 90.00
b. Inverted surcharge 160.00 160.00
2 A9(b) 5c on 35c dp vio, *org* (R) 37.50 32.50
a. Date in smaller type 90.00 90.00
b. Inverted surcharge, #2 425.00 425.00
c. Inverted surcharge, #2a 825.00 825.00

Issue dates: No. 1, Jan. 8. No. 2, Jan. 10.
"R" is is the Colonial Governor, P. Richaud, "D" is the Saigon P.M. General P. Demars.

For other overprints on designs A3-A27a see various issues of French Offices in China.

Navigation & Commerce — A3

France — A4

Name of Colony in Blue or Carmine

1892-1900 Typo. *Perf. 14x13½*
3 A3 1c blk, *lil bl* 30 30
4 A3 2c brn, *buff* 45 35
5 A3 4c claret, *lav* 45 35
6 A3 5c grn, *grnsh* 45 25
7 A3 5c yel grn ('00) 35 20
8 A3 10c blk, *lavender* 1.90 35
9 A3 10c red ('00) 80 35
10 A3 15c blue, quadrille paper 11.00 40
11 A3 15c gray ('00) 2.25 35
12 A3 20c red, *grn* 3.00 1.50
13 A3 25c blk, *rose* 4.25 1.10
a. "INDO-CHINE" omitted 3,000. 2,500.
14 A3 25c blue ('00) 5.75 80
15 A3 30c brn, *bis* 7.00 2.00
16 A3 40c red, *straw* 7.00 2.00
17 A3 50c car, *rose* 16.00 5.00
18 A3 50c brn, *az* ('00) 7.00 3.00
19 A3 75c dp vio, *org* 9.00 5.50
a. "INDO-CHINE" inverted 3,000. 2,500.
20 A3 1fr brnz grn, *straw* 16.00 7.50
a. "INDO-CHINE" double 325.00 300.00
21 A3 5fr red lil, *lav* ('96) 50.00 37.50
Nos. 3-21 (19) 142.95 68.80

Perf. 13½x14 stamps are counterfeits.
For surcharges and overprints see Nos. 22-23, Q2-Q4.

Nos. 11 and 14 Surcharged in Black **5**

1903
22 A3 5c on 15c gray 38 30
23 A3 15c on 25c blue 55 30

Issue dates: No. 22, Dec. 4. No. 23, Aug. 8.

1904-06
24 A4 1c olive grn 16 15
25 A4 2c vio brn, *buff* 25 15
26 A4 4c claret, *bluish* 16 15
27 A4 5c deep green 16 15
28 A4 10c carmine 45 15
29 A4 15c org brn, *bl* 30 15
30 A4 20c red, *grn* 80 32
31 A4 25c deep blue 3.75 50
32 A4 30c pale brn 1.65 80
33 A4 35c blk, *yel* ('06) 5.25 60
34 A4 40c blk, *bluish* 1.40 40
35 A4 50c bister brn 2.00 65
36 A4 75c red, *org* 16.00 11.00
37 A4 1fr pale grn 6.00 2.25
38 A4 2fr brn, *org* 16.00 15.00
39 A4 5fr dp vio, *lil* 85.00 70.00
40 A4 10fr org brn, *grn* 80.00 65.00
Nos. 24-40 (17) 219.33 167.42

For surcharges see Nos. 59-64.

Annamite Girl — A5

Cambodian Girl — A6

Cambodian Woman — A7

Annamite Women — A8

Hmong Woman — A9

Laotian Woman — A10

Cambodian Woman — A11

1907 *Perf. 14x13½*
41 A5 1c ol brn & blk 15 15
42 A5 2c yel brn & blk 15 15
43 A5 4c blue & blk 40 35
44 A5 5c grn & blk 16 15
45 A5 10c red & blk 16 15
46 A5 15c vio & blk 55 40
47 A6 20c vio & blk 90 50
48 A6 25c bl & blk 1.90 28
49 A6 30c brn & blk 3.50 2.25
50 A6 35c ol grn & blk 55 35
51 A6 40c yel brn & blk 1.40 65
52 A6 45c org & blk 3.75 2.50
53 A6 50c car & blk 5.00 2.50

Perf. 13½x14
54 A7 75c ver & blk 4.00 3.50
55 A8 1fr car & blk 20.00 6.25
56 A9 2fr grn & blk 5.50 4.50
57 A10 5fr blue & blk 19.00 10.00
58 A11 10fr pur & blk 40.00 35.00
Nos. 41-58 (18) 107.07 69.63

For surcharges see Nos. 65-93, B1-B7.

Stamps of 1904-06 Surcharged in Black or Carmine

05 **10**

1912, Nov. *Perf. 14x13½*
59 A4 5c on 4c cl, *bluish* 2.50 1.60
60 A4 5c on 15c org brn, *bl* (C) 30 30
61 A4 5c on 30c pale brn 30 30
62 A4 10c on 40c blk, *bluish* (C) 30 30
63 A4 10c on 50c bis brn (C) 32 32
64 A4 10c on 75c red, *org* 2.00 1.60
Nos. 59-64 (6) 5.72 4.42

Two spacings between the surcharged numerals are found on Nos. 59 to 64.

Nos. 41-58 Surcharged with New Values in Cents or Piasters in Black, Red or Blue

4 CENTS

1919, Jan.
65 A5 2/5c on 1c 15 15
66 A5 4/5c on 2c 35 25
67 A5 1 3/5c on 4c (R) 60 30
68 A5 2c on 5c 25 15
a. Inverted surcharge 37.50
69 A5 4c on 10c (Bl) 25 15
a. Closed "4" 2.50 50
b. Double surcharge 37.50
70 A5 6c on 15c 70 35
a. Inverted surcharge 42.50
71 A6 8c on 20c 90 65
72 A6 10c on 25c 80 25
73 A6 12c on 30c 2.25 35
74 A6 14c on 35c 45 16
a. Closed "4" 3.50 2.00
75 A6 16c on 40c 2.25 62
76 A6 18c on 45c 2.25 1.10
77 A6 20c on 50c (Bl) 3.25 45
78 A7 30c on 75c (Bl) 3.75 80
79 A8 40c on 1fr (Bl) 6.50 1.10
80 A9 80c on 2fr (R) 7.00 2.00
a. Double surcharge 110.00 80.00
81 A10 2pi on 5fr (R) 37.50 32.50
82 A11 4pi on 10fr (R) 60.00 50.00
Nos. 65-82 (18) 129.20 91.33

Types of 1907 Issue Surcharged with New Values in Black or Red

2 CENTS — Nos. 88-92
12 CENTS — No. 93

1922
88 A5 1c on 5c ocher & blk 35
89 A5 2c on 10c gray grn & blk 80
90 A6 6c on 30c lt red & blk 80
91 A6 10c on 50c lt bl & blk 90
92 A6 11c on 55c vio & blk, *bluish* 80
93 A6 12c on 60c lt bl & blk, *pnksh* (R) 90
Nos. 88-93 (6) 4.55

Nos. 88 to 93 were sold officially in Paris but were never placed in use in the colony.
Nos. 88-93 exist without surcharge but were not regularly issued in that condition. Value, Nos. 88-89, each $100; Nos. 90-91, each $80; Nos. 92-93, each $55.

A12

A13

"CENTS" below Numerals

1922-23 *Perf. 14x13½*
94 A12 1/10c blk & sal ('23) 15 15
a. Double impression of frame
95 A12 1/5c blue & blk 15 15
96 A12 2/5c ol brn & blk 15 15
a. Head and value doubled 100.00 100.00
97 A12 4/5c rose & blk, *lav* 15 15
98 A12 1c yel brn & blk 15 15
99 A12 2c gray grn & blk 25 15
100 A12 3c vio & blk 15 15
101 A12 4c org & blk 15 15
a. Head and value doubled 50.00 50.00
102 A12 5c car & blk 15 15
a. Head and value doubled 110.00 110.00
103 A13 6c dl red & blk 15 15
104 A13 7c grn & blk 15 15
105 A13 8c blk, *lav* 45 38
106 A13 9c ocher & blk, *grnsh* 45 38
107 A13 10c bl & blk 15 15
108 A13 11c vio & blk 15 15
109 A13 12c brn & blk 16 16
a. Head and value double (11c+12c) 190.00 190.00
110 A13 15c org & blk 25 16
111 A13 20c bl & blk, *straw* 35 22
112 A13 40c ver & blk, *bluish* 70 45
113 A13 1pi bl grn & blk, *grnsh* 2.25 2.00
114 A13 2pi vio brn & blk, *pnksh* 3.75 2.50
Nos. 94-114 (21) 10.41 8.20

For overprints see Nos. O17-O32.

Plowing near Tower of Confucius — A14

Bay of Along — A15

Angkor Wat, Cambodia — A16

Carving Wood — A17

That Luang Temple, Laos — A18

Founding of Saigon — A19

1927, Sept. 26
115 A14 1/10c lt olive grn 15 15
116 A14 1/5c yellow 15 15
117 A14 2/5c light blue 15 15
118 A14 4/5c dp brn 20 15
119 A14 1c orange 20 15
120 A14 2c blue grn 45 15
121 A14 3c indigo 20 15
122 A14 4c lil rose 45 32
123 A14 5c dp vio 28 15
a. Booklet pane of 10 11.00
124 A15 6c deep red 80 16
a. Booklet pane of 10 11.00
125 A15 7c lt brn 55 15
126 A15 8c gray green 45 45
127 A15 9c red vio 55 40
128 A15 10c light blue 60 35
129 A15 11c orange 60 45
130 A15 12c myrtle grn 40 16
131 A16 15c dl rose & ol brn 3.25 3.00
132 A16 20c vio & slate 1.40 60
133 A17 25c org brn & lil rose 3.25 2.25
134 A17 30c dp bl & ol gray 1.60 1.25
135 A18 40c ver & lt bl 2.50 80
136 A18 50c lt grn & slate 3.25 1.10
137 A19 1pi dk bl, blk & yel 6.00 3.50
a. Yellow omitted 75.00
138 A19 2pi red, dp bl & org 7.00 5.00
Nos. 115-138 (24) 34.43 21.14

Colonial Exposition Issue
Common Design Types
Surcharged with New Values

1931, Apr. 13 Engr. *Perf. 12½*
Name of Country in Black
140 CD71 4c on 50c violet 90 65
141 CD72 6c on 90c red org 1.10 1.10
142 CD73 10c on 1.50fr dl bl 1.50 90

Junk — A20

Tower at Ruins of Angkor Thom — A21

Planting Rice — A22

Apsaras, Celestial Dancer — A23

1931-41 Photo. *Perf. 13½x13*

No.	Type	Denomination	Color	Unused	Used
143	A20	1/10c	Prus blue	15	15
144	A20	1/5c	lake	15	15
145	A20	2/5c	org red	15	15
146	A20	1/2c	red brn	15	15
147	A20	4/5c	dk vio	15	15
148	A20	1c	blk brn	15	15
149	A20	2c	dk grn	15	15
150	A21	3c	dp brn	15	15
151	A21	3c	dk grn ('34)	2.00	60
152	A21	4c	dk bl	16	15
153	A21	4c	dk grn ('38)	16	15
153A	A21	4c	yel org ('40)	15	15
154	A21	5c	dp vio	15	15
154A	A21	5c	dp grn ('41)	15	15
155	A21	6c	org red	15	15
a.			Bklt. pane 5 + 1 label		
156	A21	7c	blk ('38)	15	15
157	A21	8c	rose lake ('38)	15	15
157A	A21	9c	blk, *yel* ('41)	15	15
158	A22	10c	dark blue	25	15
158A	A22	10c	ultra, *pink* ('41)	15	15
159	A22	15c	dk brn	2.50	42
160	A22	15c	dk bl ('33)	15	15
161	A22	18c	blue ('38)	15	15
162	A22	20c	rose	15	15
163	A22	21c	olive grn	15	15
164	A22	22c	dk grn ('38)	15	15
165	A22	25c	dp vio	1.00	60
165A	A22	25c	dk bl ('41)	15	15
166	A22	30c	org brn ('32)	15	15

Perf. 13½

No.	Type	Denomination	Color	Unused	Used
167	A23	50c	dk brn	15	15
168	A23	60c	dl vio ('32)	15	15
168A	A23	70c	lt bl ('41)	20	20
169	A23	1pi	yel grn	38	25
170	A23	2pi	red	42	25
			Set value	9.00	4.60

Nos. 166, 167, 169 and 170 were issued without the letters "RF" in 1943, by the Vichy Government, but were not placed on sale in the colony.

For surcharge & overprints see #214A, O1-O16.

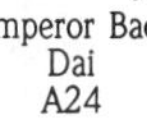

Emperor Bao-Dai A24

King Sisowath Monivong A25

For Use in Annam

1936, Nov. 20 Engr. *Perf. 13*

No.	Type	Denomination	Color	Unused	Used
171	A24	1c	brown	35	35
172	A24	2c	green	35	35
173	A24	4c	violet	45	45
174	A24	5c	red brn	45	45
175	A24	10c	lil rose	62	62
176	A24	15c	ultra	70	70
177	A24	20c	scarlet	90	90
178	A24	30c	plum	1.10	1.10
179	A24	50c	slate grn	1.10	1.10
180	A24	1pi	rose vio	2.00	2.00
181	A24	2pi	black	2.25	2.25
			Nos. 171-181 (11)	10.27	10.27

For Use in Cambodia

No.	Type	Denomination	Color	Unused	Used
182	A25	1c	brown	35	35
183	A25	2c	green	35	35
184	A25	4c	violet	45	45
185	A25	5c	red brn	45	45
186	A25	10c	lil rose	1.10	1.10
187	A25	15c	ultra	1.25	1.25
188	A25	20c	scarlet	90	90
189	A25	30c	plum	90	90
190	A25	50c	slate grn	90	90
191	A25	1pi	rose vio	1.20	1.20
192	A25	2pi	black	2.00	2.00
			Nos. 182-192 (11)	9.85	9.85

Common Design Types pictured in section at front of book.

Paris International Exposition Issue

Common Design Types

1937, Apr. 15

No.	Type	Denomination	Color	Unused	Used
193	CD74	2c	dp vio	45	45
194	CD75	3c	dk grn	45	45
195	CD76	4c	car rose	38	38
196	CD77	6c	dk brn	38	38
197	CD78	9c	red	38	38
198	CD79	15c	ultra	38	38
			Nos. 193-198 (6)	2.42	2.42

Colonial Arts Exhibition Issue

Souvenir Sheet

Common Design Type

1937, Apr. 15 *Imperf.*

No.	Type	Denomination	Color	Unused	Used
199	CD79	30c	dl vio	2.00	2.00

Governor-General Paul Doumer — A26

1938, June 8 Photo. *Perf. 13½x13*

No.	Type	Denomination	Color	Unused	Used
200	A26	5c	rose car	38	25
201	A26	6c	brown	38	25
202	A26	18c	brt bl	38	22

Trans-Indo-Chinese Railway, 35th anniv.

New York World's Fair Issue

Common Design Type

1939, May 10 Engr. *Perf. 12½x12*

No.	Type	Denomination	Color	Unused	Used
203	CD82	13c	car lake	16	16
204	CD82	23c	ultra	28	28

Mot Cot Pagoda, Hanoi — A27

1939, June 12 *Perf. 13*

No.	Type	Denomination	Color	Unused	Used
205	A27	6c	blk brn	35	35
206	A27	9c	vermilion	35	35
207	A27	23c	ultra	25	25
208	A27	39c	rose vio	35	35

Golden Gate International Exposition.

Angkor Wat and Marshal Pétain A27a

1941 Engr. *Perf. 12½x12*

No.	Type	Denomination	Color	Unused	Used
209	A27a	10c	dk car	25	
209A	A27a	25c	blue	25	

Nos. 209-209A were issued by the Vichy government and were not placed on sale in the colony.

For overprints see Nos. 262-263.

Gum

#210-261 issued without gum.

King Norodom Sihanouk of Cambodia A28

Harnessed Elephant on Parade A29

Pin-perf. 12½

1941, Oct. 15 Unwmk. Litho.

No.	Type	Denomination	Color	Unused	Used
210	A28	1c	red org	30	30
211	A28	6c	violet	65	65
212	A28	25c	dp ultra	8.00	8.00

Coronation of Norodom Sihanouk, King of Cambodia, October, 1941.

1942, Mar. 29

No.	Type	Denomination	Color	Unused	Used
213	A29	3c	redsh brn	60	45
214	A29	6c	crimson	60	45

Fête of Nam-Giao in Annam.

No. 165 Surcharged in Black

1942 *Perf. 13*

No.	Type	Denomination	Color	Unused	Used
214A	A22	10c on 25c	dp vio	20	15

View of Saigon Fair — A30

1942, Dec. 20 *Perf. 13½*

No.	Type	Denomination	Color	Unused	Used
215	A30	6c	carmine rose	15	15

Saigon Fair of 1942.

Nam-Phuong, Empress of Annam — A31

Marshal Pétain — A32

1942, Sept. 1 *Pin-perf. 11½*

No.	Type	Denomination	Color	Unused	Used
216	A31	6c	carmine rose	38	15

1942-44 *Perf. 12, 13½*

No.	Type	Denomination	Color	Unused	Used
217	A32	1c	blk brn	15	15
218	A32	3c	olive brn ('43)	15	15
219	A32	6c	rose red	15	15
220	A32	10c	dull grn ('43)	15	15
221	A32	40c	dk blue ('43)	16	16
222	A32	40c	slate bl ('44)	45	45
			Set value	85	85

Bao-Dai, Emperor of Annam A33

Norodom Sihanouk, King of Cambodia A34

1942 *Perf. 13½*

No.	Type	Denomination	Color	Unused	Used
223	A33	1/2c	brown	16	15
224	A33	6c	carmine rose	45	25

Issue dates: 1/2c, Nov. 1. 6c, Sept. 1.

1943 *Perf. 11½*

No.	Type	Denomination	Color	Unused	Used
225	A34	1c	brown	30	25
226	A34	6c	red	25	15

Issue dates: 1c, Mar. 10. 6c, May 10.

Sisavang-Vong, King of Laos — A35

Family, Country and Labor — A36

1943

No.	Type	Denomination	Color	Unused	Used
227	A35	1c	bister brown	15	15
228	A35	6c	carmine rose	16	15
			Set value		22

Issue dates: 1c, Mar. 10. 6c, June 1.

1943, Nov. 5 *Perf. 12*

No.	Type	Denomination	Color	Unused	Used
229	A36	6c	carmine rose	15	15

National revolution, 3rd anniversary.

Admiral Rigault de Genouilly A37

Franois Chasseloup-Laubat A38

Admiral André A. P. Courbet A39

1943 *Perf. 11½, 12, 12x11½*

No.	Type	Denomination	Color	Unused	Used
230	A37	6c	carmine rose	15	15
231	A38	6c	carmine rose	15	15
232	A39	6c	carmine rose	25	15
			Set value		29

Issue dates: Nos. 230, 232, Sept. 1. No. 231, Oct. 5.

A 5c dull brown, type A37, was not regularly issued without the Viet Nam overprint. A 3c light brown, type A39, was prepared but not issued.

Pigneau de Behaine, Bishop of Adran — A40

Alexandre Yersin — A41

1943, June 10 *Perf. 12*

No.	Type	Denomination	Color	Unused	Used
233	A40	20c	dull red	45	45

1943-45 *Perf. 12x11½*

No.	Type	Denomination	Color	Unused	Used
234	A41	6c	carmine rose	50	50
235	A41	15c	vio brn ('44)	15	15
236	A41	1pi	yel grn ('45)	25	25

Issued to honor Dr. Alexandre Yersin (1863-1943), the Swiss bacteriologist who introduced rubber culture into Indo-China.

Issued: 6c, Oct. 5. 15c, Dec. 10. 1pi, Jan. 10.

Lt. M. J. Franois Garnier A42

1943, Sept. ***Perf. 12***

237 A42 1c dull olive bister 40 25

A 15c brown violet was prepared but not issued.

Alexandre de Rhodes A43

1943-45 ***Pin-perf., Perf. 12***

238 A43 15c dk vio brn ('45) 15 15
239 A43 30c org brn 15 15
a. 30c yellow brown, perf. 13½ 15 15

Nos. 239, 239a carry the monogram "EF."
Issue dates: 15c, Mar. 10; 30c, June 15.

Athlete Giving Olympic Salute — A44

1944, July 10 ***Perf. 12***

241 A44 10c dk vio brn & yel 1.25 1.25
242 A44 50c dl red 1.25 1.25

Adm. Pierre de La Grandière A45

1943-45

243 A45 1c dull brn 15 15
244 A45 5c dark brn ('45) 15 15
Set value 17 17

The upper left corner of No. 244 contains the denomination "5c" instead of "EF" monogram.
Issue dates: 1c, Aug. 5c, Jan. 10.

Auguste Pavie — A46

1944 ***Perf. 12***

245 A46 4c org yel 15 15
246 A46 10c dl grn 15 15
Set value 24 24

Issue dates: 4c, Feb. 10. 10c, Jan. 5.
A 20c dark red, type A46, was not regularly issued without the Viet Nam overprint.

Governor-General Pierre Pasquier — A47

1944

247 A47 5c brn vio 28 28
248 A47 10c dl grn 15 15

Issue dates: 5c, Nov. 1. 10c, Sept.

Joost Van Vollenhoven A48

1944, Oct. 10

249 A48 1c olive brown 15 15
250 A48 10c green 28 28

Governor-General J. M. A. de Lanessan — A49

1944

251 A49 1c dl gray brn 15 15
252 A49 15c dl rose vio 30 30

Issue dates: 1c, Dec. 10. 15c, Oct. 16.

Governor-General Paul Doumer — A50

1944

253 A50 2c red vio 15 15
254 A50 4c lt brn 15 15
255 A50 10c yel grn 15 15
Set value 36 36

Issue dates: 2c, May 15. 4c, June 15. 10c, Jan. 5.

Admiral Charner — A51

Doudart de Lagrée — A52

1944

256 A51 10c green 15 15
257 A51 20c brn red 15 15
258 A51 1pi pale yel grn 30 25

Issue dates: 10c, 20c, Aug. 10. 1pi, July.

1944-45

259 A52 1c dl gray brn ('45) 15 15
260 A52 15c dl rose vio 16 16
261 A52 40c brt bl 15 15
Set value 32 32

Issue dates: 1c, Jan. 10. 15c, 40c, Nov.

Nos. 209-209A Overprinted in Black RF

1946 **Unwmk.** ***Perf. 12½x12***

262 A27a 10c dk car 16 16
263 A27a 25c blue 42 42

SEMI-POSTAL STAMPS

No. 45 Surcharged 5 c

1914 **Unwmk.** ***Perf. 14x13½***

B1 A5 10c +5c red & blk 38 25

Nos. 44-46 Surcharged ✚5c

1915-17

B2 A5 5c + 5c grn & blk ('17) 25 25
a. Double surcharge 60.00 60.00
B3 A5 10c + 5c red & blk 70 50
B4 A5 15c + 5c vio & blk ('17) 70 50
a. Triple surcharge 70.00 70.00
b. Quadruple surcharge 65.00 65.00

Nos. B2-B4 Surcharged with New Values in Blue or Black

1918-19

B5 A5 4c on 5c + 5c (Bl) 1.60 1.25
a. Closed "4" 90.00 90.00
B6 A5 6c on 10c + 5c 1.50 1.25
B7 A5 8c on 15c + 5c ('19) 5.50 4.25
a. Double surcharge 80.00 80.00

France Nos. B5-B10 Surcharged INDOCHINE 10 CENTS

1918 (?)

B8 SP5 10c on 15c + 10c 55 55
B9 SP5 16c on 25c + 15c 1.75 1.75
B10 SP6 24c on 35c + 25c 2.75 2.75
a. Double surcharge 250.00
B11 SP7 40c on 50c + 50c 5.00 5.00
B12 SP8 80c on 1fr + 1fr 10.00 10.00
B13 SP8 4pi on 5fr + 5fr 100.00 75.00
Nos. B8-B13 (6) 120.05 95.05

Curie Issue
Common Design Type
Inscription and Date in Upper Margin

1938, Oct. 24 **Engr.** ***Perf. 13***

B14 CD80 18c + 5c brt ultra 4.50 4.50

French Revolution Issue
Common Design Type
Name and Value Typo. in Black

1939, July 5 **Photo.**

B15 CD83 6c + 2c green 3.50 3.50
B16 CD83 7c + 3c brown 3.50 3.50
B17 CD83 9c + 4c red org 3.50 3.50
B18 CD83 13c + 10c rose pink 3.50 3.50
B19 CD83 23c + 20c blue 3.50 3.50
Nos. B15-B19 (5) 17.50 17.50

Common Design Type and

Tonkinese Sharpshooter SP1

Legionary SP2

1941 **Photo.** ***Perf. 13½***

B19A SP1 10c + 10c red 40
B19B CD86 15c + 30c maroon 40
B19C SP2 25c + 10c blue 40

Nos. B19A-B19C were issued by the Vichy government, and were not placed on sale in the colony.
Nos. 209-209A were surcharged "OEUVRES COLONIALES" and surtax (including change of denomination of the 25c to 5c). These were issued in 1944 by the Vichy government and not placed on sale in the colony.

Portal and Flags, City University, Hanoi — SP3

Coat of Arms and Sword — SP4

Perf. 11½

1942, June 1 **Unwmk.** **Litho.**

B20 SP3 6c + 2c car rose 20 20
B21 SP3 15c + 5c brn vio 35 35

No. B20 Surcharged in Black 10c +2c

1944, June 10

B22 SP3 10c + 2c on 6c + 2c 20 20

1942, Aug. 1 ***Perf. 12***

B23 SP4 6c + 2c red & blue 16 16
B24 SP4 15c + 5c vio blk, red & bl 30 30

#B23 Surcharged in Black Like #B22

1944, Mar. 15

B25 SP4 10c + 2c on 6c + 2c 15 15

Aviator Do-Huu-Vi SP5

1943, Aug. 1

B26 SP5 6c + 2c car rose 20 20

#B26 Surcharged in Black Like #B22

1944, Feb. 10

B27 SP5 10c + 2c on 6c + 2c 15 15

Surcharge arranged to fit size of stamp.

Aviator Roland Garros — SP6

1943, Nov. 15

B28 SP6 6c + 2c rose car 15 15

#B28 Surcharged in Black Like #B22

1944, Feb. 10

B29 SP6 10c + 2c on 6c + 2c 15 15

Cathedral of Orléans — SP7

1944, Dec. 20

B30 SP7 15c + 60c brn vio 50 40
B31 SP7 40c + 1.10pi blue 60 58

Type of France, 1945, Surcharged in Black

INDOCHINE
2 P + 2 P

1945 Unwmk. Engr. *Perf. 13*

B32	A152	50c + 50c on 2fr green	25	25
B33	A152	1pi + 1pi on 2fr hn brn	25	25
B34	A152	2pi + 2pi on 2fr Prus grn	40	40

AIR POST STAMPS

Airplane AP1

1933-41 Unwmk. Photo. *Perf. 13½*

C1	AP1	1c ol brn	15	15
C2	AP1	2c dk grn	15	15
C3	AP1	5c yel grn	15	15
C4	AP1	10c red brn	16	15
C5	AP1	11c rose car ('38)	15	15
C6	AP1	15c dp bl	16	15
C6A	AP1	16c brt pink ('41)	15	15
C7	AP1	20c grnsh gray	25	16
C8	AP1	30c org brn	15	15
C9	AP1	36c car rose	80	15
C10	AP1	37c ol grn ('38)	15	15
C10A	AP1	39c dk ol grn ('41)	15	15
C11	AP1	60c dk vio	15	15
C12	AP1	66c olive grn	25	15
C13	AP1	67c brt bl ('38)	45	45
C13A	AP1	69c brt ultra ('41)	25	25
C14	AP1	1pi black	25	15
C15	AP1	2pi yel org	50	15
C16	AP1	5pi purple	80	16
C17	AP1	10pi deep red	1.50	38
		Nos. C1-C17 (20)	6.72	
		Set value		2.60

See Nos. C27-C28.

Issue dates: 11c, 37c, June 8; 67c, Oct. 5; 16c, 39c, 69c, Feb. 5; others, June 1, 1933.

Stamps of type AP1 without "RF" monogram were issued in 1942 and 1943 by the Vichy Government, but were not placed on sale in the colony. On the Vichy stamps, the figure of value has been moved to the lower left corner of the vignette.

Governor-General Paul Doumer — AP2

1938, June 8

C18	AP2	37c red orange	20	15

35th anniv. of the Trans-Indo-Chinese Railway.

Victory Issue
Common Design Type
Perf. 12½

1946, May 8 Unwmk. Engr.

C19	CD92	80c red org	35	25

Chad to Rhine Issue
Common Design Types

1946, June 6

C20	CD93	50c yel grn	30	30
C21	CD94	1pi violet	30	30
C22	CD95	1.50pi carmine	30	30
C23	CD96	2pi vio brn	30	30
C24	CD97	2.50pi dp bl	40	40
C25	CD98	5pi org red	60	60
		Nos. C20-C25 (6)	2.20	2.20

UPU Issue
Common Design Type

1949, July 4 *Perf. 13*

C26	CD99	3pi dp bl, dk vio, grn & red	1.50	1.10

Plane Type of 1933-41

1949, June 13 Photo. *Perf. 13½*

C27	AP1	20pi dk bl grn	4.50	2.00
C28	AP1	30pi brown	5.00	2.00

AIR POST SEMI-POSTAL STAMP

French Revolution Issue
Common Design Type
Unwmk.

1939, July 5 Photo. *Perf. 13*
Name and Value Typo. in Orange

CB1	CD83	39c + 40c brn blk	7.50	7.50

V4

V5

V6

Stamps of the above designs, and of Cameroun type V10 inscribed "Indochine", were issued in 1942 by the Vichy Government, but were not placed on sale in the colony.

POSTAGE DUE STAMPS

French Colonies No. J21 Surcharged

5

1904, June 26 Unwmk. *Imperf.*

J1	D1	5c on 60c brn, *buff*	4.50	3.50

French Colonies Nos. J10-J11 Surcharged in Carmine

1905, July 22

J2	D1	5c on 40c black	11.00	4.00
J3	D1	10c on 60c black	11.00	6.00
J4	D1	30c on 60c black	11.00	6.00

Dragon from Steps of Angkor Wat
D1 D2

1908 Typo. *Perf. 14x13½*

J5	D1	2c black	35	35
J6	D1	4c dp bl	35	35
J7	D1	5c bl grn	35	35
J8	D1	10c carmine	1.10	35
J9	D1	15c violet	1.10	80
J10	D1	20c chocolate	35	35
J11	D1	30c ol grn	35	35
J12	D1	40c claret	3.25	2.75
J13	D1	50c grnsh bl	1.50	45
J14	D1	60c orange	4.00	3.50
J15	D1	1fr gray	7.00	5.50
J16	D1	2fr yel brn	6.00	4.00
J17	D1	5fr red	11.00	7.00
		Nos. J5-J17 (13)	36.70	26.10

Surcharged with New Values in Cents or Piasters

1919

J18	D1	4/5c on 2c blk	65	35
J19	D1	1 3/5c on 4c dp bl	60	40
J20	D1	2c on 5c bl grn	1.10	60
J21	D1	4c on 10c car	65	35
J22	D1	6c on 15c vio	2.25	1.10
J23	D1	8c on 20c choc	2.25	60
J24	D1	12c on 30c ol grn	2.25	65
J25	D1	16c on 40c cl	2.25	60
J26	D1	20c on 50c grnsh bl	4.00	2.25
J27	D1	24c on 60c org	1.00	65
a.		Closed "4"	8.00	6.25
J28	D1	40c on 1fr gray	1.25	65
a.		Closed "4"	9.00	7.00
J29	D1	80c on 20c yel brn	12.00	7.00
J30	D1	2pi on 5fr red	19.00	10.00
a.		Double surcharge	75.00	60.00
b.		Triple surcharge	75.00	55.00
		Nos. J18-J30 (13)	49.25	25.20

"CENTS" below Numerals

1922, Oct.

J31	D2	2/5c black	15	15
J32	D2	4/5c red	15	15
J33	D2	1c buff	16	15
J34	D2	2c gray grn	25	16
J35	D2	3c violet	25	16
J36	D2	4c orange	20	15
a.		"4 CENTS" omitted	250.00	
b.		"4 CENTS" double	25.00	25.00
J37	D2	6c ol grn	35	25
J38	D2	8c blk, *lav*	35	15
J39	D2	10c dp bl	45	15
J40	D2	12c ocher, *grnsh*	50	35
J41	D2	20c dp bl, *straw*	62	25
J42	D2	40c red, *bluish*	62	25
J43	D2	1pi brn vio, *pnksh*	2.00	1.10
		Nos. J31-J43 (13)	6.05	
		Set value		2.90

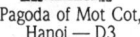

Pagoda of Mot Cot, Hanoi — D3 Dragon of Annam — D4

Perf. 14x13½, 13½x14

1927, Sept. 26

J44	D3	2/5c vio brn & org	15	15
J45	D3	4/5c vio & blk	15	15
J46	D3	1c brn red & sl	35	30
J47	D3	2c grn & brn ol	35	35
J48	D3	3c red brn & bl	35	35
J49	D3	4c ind & brn	35	35
J50	D3	6c dp red & ver	40	40
J51	D3	8c ol brn & vio	40	35
J52	D4	10c dp bl	40	25
J53	D4	12c olive	2.90	1.25
J54	D4	20c rose	1.00	40
J55	D4	40c bl grn	1.25	80
J56	D4	1pi red org	7.00	5.00
		Nos. J44-J56 (13)	15.05	10.10

D5

Value Surcharged in Black or Blue

1931-41 *Perf. 13*

J57	D5	1/5c red, *org* ('38)	15	15
J58	D5	2/5c red, *org*	15	15
J59	D5	4/5c red, *org*	15	15
J60	D5	1c red, *org*	15	15
J61	D5	2c red, *org*	15	15
J62	D5	2.5c red, *org* ('40)	15	15
J63	D5	3c red, *org* ('38)	15	15
J64	D5	4c red, *org*	15	15
J65	D5	5c red, *org* ('38)	15	15
J66	D5	6c red, *org*	15	15
J67	D5	10c red, *org*	15	15
J68	D5	12c red, *org*	15	15
J69	D5	14c red, *org* ('38)	15	15
J70	D5	18c red, *org* ('41)	16	16
J71	D5	20c red, *org*	16	15
J72	D5	50c red, *org*	20	16
J72A	D5	1pi red, *org*	3.50	3.00
J73	D5	1pi red, *org* (Bl)	70	60
		Set value	5.65	5.00

D6 D7

Perf. 12, 13½ and Compound

1943-44 Litho. Unwmk.

J74	D6	1c red, *org*	15	15
J75	D6	2c red, *org*	15	15
J76	D6	3c red, *org*	15	15
J77	D6	4c red, *org*	15	15
J78	D6	6c red, *org*	15	15
J79	D6	10c red, *org*	15	15
J80	D7	12c blue, *pnksh*	15	15
J81	D7	20c blue, *pnksh*	15	15
J82	D7	30c blue, *pnksh*	15	15
		Set value	1.00	1.00

Issue dates: 2c, 3c, July 15, 1943; 6c-30c, Aug. 1943; 1c, 4c, June 10, 1944.

OFFICIAL STAMPS

Regular Issues of 1931-32 Overprinted in Blue or Red

Overprinted SERVICE (vertical)

Perf. 13, 13½

1933, Feb. 27 Unwmk.

O1	A20	1c blk brn (Bl)	30	15
O2	A20	2c dk grn (Bl)	30	16

Overprinted SERVICE

O3	A21	3c dp brn (Bl)	40	28
a.		Inverted overprint	40.00	
O4	A21	4c dk bl (R)	40	30
a.		Inverted overprint	40.00	
O5	A21	5c dp vio (Bl)	65	15
O6	A21	6c org red (Bl)	65	15

Overprinted SERVICE (curved)

O7	A22	10c dk bl (R)	35	25
O8	A22	15c dk brn (Bl)	1.10	60
O9	A22	20c rose (Bl)	80	16
O10	A22	21c ol grn (Bl)	1.10	60
O11	A22	25c dp vio (Bl)	35	16
O12	A22	30c org brn (Bl)	80	35

Overprinted S E R V I C E

O13	A23	50c dk brn (Bl)	5.50	1.25
O14	A23	60c dl vio (Bl)	80	60
O15	A23	1pi yel grn (Bl)	12.00	4.00
O16	A23	2pi red (Bl)	4.25	3.50
		Nos. O1-O16 (16)	29.75	12.66

Type of Regular Issue, 1922-23 Overprinted diagonally in Black or Red "SERVICE"

1934, Oct. 4 *Perf. 14x13*

O17	A13	1c ol grn	30	25
O18	A13	2c brn org	35	28
O19	A13	3c yel grn	30	16
O20	A13	4c cerise	50	50
O21	A13	5c yellow	25	20
O22	A13	6c org red	1.90	1.60
O23	A13	10c gray grn (R)	95	90
O24	A13	15c ultra	75	60
O25	A13	20c gray blk (R)	50	50
O26	A13	21c light vio	3.25	2.75
O27	A13	25c rose lake	3.75	2.25
O28	A13	30c lilac gray	50	40
O29	A13	50c brt vio	2.00	2.75
O30	A13	60c gray	3.75	3.50
O31	A13	1pi blue (R)	9.25	5.50
O32	A13	2pi deep red	14.00	11.00
		Nos. O17-O32 (16)	42.30	33.14

The value tablet has colorless numeral and letters on solid background.

The first value column gives the catalogue value of an unused stamp, the second that of a used stamp.

PARCEL POST STAMPS

French Colonies No. 50 Overprinted — INDO-CHINE TIMBRE COLIS POSTAUX

1891 Unwmk. *Perf. 14x13½*

Q1	A9 10c black, *lavender*	5.00	1.50

The overprint on No. Q1 was also handstamped in shiny ink.

Indo-China No. 8 Overprinted — Colis Postaux

1898

Q2	A3 10c black, *lavender*	6.00	6.25

Nos. 8 and 9 Overprinted — TIMBRE COLIS POSTAUX

1902

Q3	A3 10c black, *lavender*	15.00	9.00
a.	Inverted overprint	40.00	18.00
Q4	A3 10c red	15.00	7.00
a.	Inverted overprint	30.00	18.00
b.	Double overprint	30.00	18.00

INDONESIA

LOCATION — In the East Indies
GOVT. — Republic
AREA — 741,101 sq. mi.
POP. — 158,000,000 (est. 1983)
CAPITAL — Jakarta

Formerly Netherlands Indies, Indonesia achieved independence late in 1949 as the United States of Indonesia and became the Republic of Indonesia August 15, 1950. See Netherlands Indies for earlier issues.

100 Sen = 1 Rupiah

Catalogue values for all unused stamps in this country are for Never Hinged items.

Watermark

Wmk. 228

United States of Indonesia

Mountain, Palms and Flag of Republic — A49

Perf. 12½x12

1950, Jan. 17 Photo. Unwmk.

Size: 20½x26mm

333	A49 15s red	35	15

1950, June *Perf. 11½*

Size: 18x23mm

334	A49 15s red	2.50	40

Netherlands Indies Nos. 307-315 Overprinted in Black — RIS

1950 *Perf. 11½, 12½*

335	A42	1s gray	20	15
336	A42	2s claret	20	15
337	A42	2½s olive brown	25	15
338	A42	3s rose pink	20	15
339	A42	4s green	25	15
340	A42	5s blue	15	15
341	A42	7½s dark green	25	15
342	A42	10s violet	25	15
343	A42	12½s bright red	38	15

Perf. 11½, 1s, 5s. Perf. 12½, 7½s, 12½s. Others, both perfs.

Netherlands Indies Nos. 317-330 Overprinted in Black — R I S

Perf. 11½, 12½

345	A43	20s gray black	2.50	2.25
346	A43	25s ultra	25	15
347	A44	30s bright red	1.40	1.40
348	A44	40s gray green	25	15
349	A44	45s claret	60	20
350	A45	50s orange brown	40	15
351	A45	60s brown	1.90	1.60
352	A45	80s scarlet	1.00	20

Perf. 11½, 20s, 45s, 50s. Others, both perfs.

Overprint 12mm High

Perf. 12½

353	A46	1r purple	60	15
354	A46	2r olive green	90.00	75.00
355	A46	3r red violet	80.00	25.00
356	A46	5r dark brown	25.00	19.00
357	A46	10r gray	45.00	15.00
358	A46	25r orange brown	15.00	6.00
		Nos. 335-358 (23)	266.03	147.60

For overprints see Riau Archipelago #17-22.

Republic of Indonesia

Arms of the Republic A50 — Doves in Flight A51

Perf. 12½x12

1950, Aug. 17 Photo. Unwmk.

359	A50	15s red	25	15
360	A50	25s dull green	65	25
361	A50	1r sepia	4.50	75

5th anniv. of Indonesia's proclamation of independence.

1951, Oct. 24 Engr. *Perf. 12*

362	A51	7½s blue green	1.25	65
363	A51	10s violet	35	15
364	A51	20s red	1.10	40
365	A51	30s carmine rose	1.25	50
366	A51	35s ultra	1.25	50
367	A51	1r sepia	15.00	1.25
		Nos. 362-367 (6)	20.20	3.45

6th anniv. of the UN and the 1st anniv. of the Republic of Indonesia as a member.

A52

Post Office — A53

Mythological Hero — A54

Pres. Sukarno — A55

1951-53 Photo. *Perf. 12½*

368	A52	1s gray	15	15
369	A52	2s plum	15	15
370	A52	2½s brown	2.25	35
371	A52	5s car rose	15	15
372	A52	7½s green	15	15
373	A52	10s blue	15	15
374	A52	15s purple	15	15
375	A52	20s rose red	15	15
376	A52	25s deep green	15	15
377	A53	30s red orange	15	15
378	A53	35s purple	15	15
379	A53	40s dull green	15	15
380	A53	45s deep claret	20	15
381	A53	50s brown	4.00	15
382	A54	60s dark brown	15	15
383	A54	70s gray	15	15
384	A54	75s ultra	15	15
385	A54	80s claret	15	15
386	A54	90s gray green	15	15
		Set value	7.75	1.10

Perf. 12½x12

387	A55	1r purple	15	15
388	A55	1.25r dp orange	15	15
389	A55	1.50r brown	15	15
390	A55	2r green	15	15
391	A55	2.50r rose brown	15	15
392	A55	3r blue	15	15
392A	A55	4r apple green	15	15
393	A55	5r brown	15	15
394	A55	6r rose lilac	15	15
395	A55	10r slate	15	15
396	A55	15r yellow	15	15
397	A55	20r sepia	15	15
398	A55	25r scarlet	15	15
399	A55	40r yellow green	15	15
400	A55	50r violet	15	15
		Set value	75	60

Nos. 368-376, 387, 390, 392, 393, 395, 398 were issued in 1951; Nos. 377-386, 388-389, 391, 392A, 394, 396-397, 399-400 in 1953.

Values are for the later Djakarta printings which have thicker numerals and a darker over-all impression. Earlier printings by Joh. Enschede and Sons, Haarlem, Netherlands, sell for more.

For surcharge see No. B68. For overprints see Riau Archipelago Nos. 1-16, 32-40.

Melati Flowers A56

Crowd Releasing Doves A57

1953, Dec. 22 *Perf. 12½*

401	A56 50s blue green	3.50	25

25th anniv. of the formation of the Indonesian Women's Congress.

1955, Apr. 18 *Perf. 13x12½*

402	A57 15s gray	42	25
403	A57 35s brown	42	25
404	A57 50s deep magenta	1.10	25
405	A57 75s blue green	48	20

Asian-African Conf., Bandung, April 18-24.

Proclamation of Independence A58

Voters A59

1955, Aug. 17 Photo. *Perf. 12½*

406	A58 15s green	30	15
407	A58 35s ultra	30	22
408	A58 50s brown	65	15
409	A58 75s magenta	55	25

Ten years of independence.

1955, Sept. 29 *Perf. 12*

Without gum

410	A59 15s rose violet	42	15
411	A59 35s green	42	20
412	A59 50s carmine rose	1.25	20
413	A59 75s lt ultra	65	25

First free elections in Indonesia.

Mas Soeharto Postmaster General A60

Helmet, Wreath and Monument A61

1955, Sept. 27 *Perf. 12½*

414	A60 15s brown	95	45
415	A60 35s dark carmine	95	45
416	A60 50s ultra	3.75	90
417	A60 75s dull green	2.50	45

Issued to mark 10 years of Indonesia's Postal, Telegraph and Telephone system.

1955, Nov. 10

418	A61 25s bluish green	50	20
419	A61 50s ultra	1.60	40
420	A61 1r dk car rose	5.00	25

Issued in honor of the soldiers killed in the war of liberation from the Netherlands.

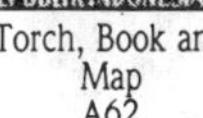

Torch, Book and Map
A62

Lesser Malay Chevrotain
A63

1956, May 26 **Photo.**

421 A62 25s ultra 1.40 16
422 A62 50s carmine rose 4.00 50
423 A62 1r dark green 2.00 50

Issued to publicize the Asia-Africa Student Conference, Bandung, May, 1956.

1956 Unwmk. *Perf. 12½x13½*

Animals: 5s, 10s, Lesser Malay chevrotain. 20s, 25s, Otter. 35s, Malayan pangolin. 50s, Banteng. 75s, Asiatic two-horned rhinoceros.

424 A63 5s deep ultra 15 15
425 A63 10s yellow brown 15 15
426 A63 15s rose violet 15 15
427 A63 20s dull green 15 15
428 A63 25s deep claret 15 15
429 A63 35s brt violet blue 15 15
430 A63 50s brown 15 15
431 A63 75s dark brown 15 15
Set value 40 40

See Nos. 450-456. For overprints see Riau Archipelago Nos. 23-31.

Dancing Girl and Gate — A64

Telegraph Key — A65

1956, Oct. 7 ***Perf. 12½x12***

432 A64 15s slate green 80 25
433 A64 35s brown violet 80 25
434 A64 50s blue black 1.50 40
435 A64 75s deep claret 1.50 15

Founding of the city of Jogjakarta, 200th anniv.

1957, May 10 **Unwmk.**

436 A65 10s lt crimson 1.40 25
437 A65 15s brt blue 32 15
438 A65 25s gray 32 15
439 A65 50s brown red 40 15
440 A65 75s lt blue green 55 15
Nos. 436-440 (5) 2.99
Set value 65

Indonesian telegraph system centenary.

Thrift Symbolism
A66

Douglas DC-3
A67

Design: 15s, 1r, People and hands holding wreath of rice and cotton.

1957, July 12 **Photo.** ***Perf. 12½***

441 A66 10s blue 20 20
442 A66 15s rose carmine 32 20
443 A66 50s green 65 40
444 A66 1r brt violet 85 15

Cooperation Day, July 12.

1958, Apr. 9 ***Perf. 12½x12***

Aircraft: 15s, Helicopter. 30s, Miles Magister. 50s, Two-motor plane of Indonesian Airways. 75s, De Havilland Vampire.

445 A67 10s reddish brown 15 15
446 A67 15s blue 15 15
447 A67 35s orange 15 16
448 A67 50s bright green 16 22
449 A67 75s gray 55 25
Nos. 445-449 (5) 1.16 93

Issued for National Aviation Day, April 9.

Animal Type of 1956

Animals: 30s, Otter. 40s, 45s, Malayan pangolin. 60s, 70s, Banteng. 80s, 90s, Asiatic two-horned rhinoceros.

1958 **Photo.** ***Perf. 12½x13½***

450 A63 30s orange 15 15
451 A63 40s brt yellow grn 15 15
452 A63 45s rose lilac 15 15
453 A63 60s dark blue 15 15
454 A63 70s orange ver 15 15
455 A63 80s red 15 15
456 A63 90s yellow green 15 15
Set value 35 30

Thomas Cup — A68

1958, Aug. 15 ***Perf. 13½x13***

457 A68 25s rose carmine 15 15
458 A68 50s orange 15 15
459 A68 1r brown 15 15
Set value 29 19

Indonesia's victory in the 1958 Thomas Cup World Badminton Championship.

Satellite Circling Globe — A69

1958, Oct. 15 **Litho.** ***Perf. 12½x12***

460 A69 10s dk grn, pink & lt bl 35 15
461 A69 15s vio, gray & pale bluish grn 15 15
462 A69 35s brown, blue & pink 15 15
463 A69 50s bl, redsh brn & gray 15 15
464 A69 75s black, vio & buff 15 15
Set value 75 45

International Geophysical Year, 1957-58.

Bicyclist and Map — A70

1958, Nov. 15 **Photo.** ***Perf. 13½x13***

465 A70 25s bright blue 15 15
466 A70 50s brown carmine 15 15
467 A70 1r gray 15 15
Set value 30

Bicycle Tour of Java, Aug. 15-30.

Man Looking into Light
A71

Wild Boar (Babirusa)
A72

Designs: 15s, Hands and flame. 35s, Woman holding candle. 50s, Family hailing torch. 75s, Torch and "10."

1958, Dec. 10 ***Perf. 12½x12***

468 A71 10s gray brn 15 15
469 A71 15s dull red brn 15 15
470 A71 35s ultra 15 15
471 A71 50s pale brown 15 15
472 A71 75s lt blue grn 15 15
Set value 42 32

10th anniv. of the signing of the Universal Declaration of Human Rights.

1959, June 1 **Photo.** ***Perf. 12***

Animals: 15s, Anoa (smallest buffalo). 20s, Orangutan. 50s, Javan rhinoceros. 75s, Komodo dragon (lizard). 1r, Malayan tapir.

473 A72 10s olive bis & sepia 15 15
474 A72 15s org brn & sepia 15 15
475 A72 20s lt ol grn & sepia 15 15
476 A72 50s bister brn & sepia 15 15
477 A72 75s dp rose & sepia 15 15
478 A72 1r blue grn & blk 15 15
Set value 25 25

Issued to publicize wildlife preservation.

A73

Factories — A74

1959, Aug. 17 **Litho.** ***Perf. 12***

479 A73 20s blue & red 15 15
480 A73 50s rose red & blk 15 15
481 A73 75s brown & red 15 15
482 A73 1.50r lt green & blk 15 15
Set value 27 20

Introduction of the constitution of 1945 embodying "guided democracy."

1959, Oct. 26 **Photo.** ***Perf. 12***

Designs: 20s, 75s, Cogwheel and train. 1.15r, Means of transportation.

483 A74 15s brt green & blk 15 15
484 A74 20s dull org & blk 15 15
485 A74 50s red & black 15 15
486 A74 75s brt grnsh bl & blk 15 15
487 A74 1.15r magenta & blk 15 15
Set value 36 30

11th Colombo Plan Conference, Jakarta.

Mother & Child, WRY Emblem — A75

Tea Plantation — A76

Designs: 15s, 75s, Destroyed town and fleeing family. 20s, 1.15r, World Refugee Year emblem.

1960, Apr. 7 **Unwmk.** ***Perf. 12½x12***

488 A75 10s claret & blk 15 15
489 A75 15s bister & blk 15 15
490 A75 20s org brn & blk 15 15
491 A75 50s green & blk 15 15
492 A75 75s dk blue & blk 15 15
493 A75 1.15r scarlet & blk 15 15
Set value 30 28

Issued to publicize World Refugee Year, July 1, 1959-June 30, 1960.

1960 ***Perf. 12x12½***

Designs: 5s, Oil palms. 10s, Sugar cane and railroad. 15s, Coffee. 20s, Tobacco. 50s, Coconut palms. 75s, Rubber plantation. 1.15r, Rice.

494 A76 5s gray 15 15
495 A76 10s red brown 15 15
496 A76 15s plum 15 15
497 A76 20s ocher 15 15
498 A76 25s brt blue grn 15 15
499 A76 50s deep blue 15 15
500 A76 75s scarlet 15 15
501 A76 1.15r plum 15 15
Set value 35 35

For surcharges see Nos. B132-B134.

Anopheles Mosquito — A77

1960, Nov. 12 **Photo.** ***Perf. 12x12½***

502 A77 25s carmine rose 15 15
503 A77 50s orange brown 15 15
504 A77 75s brt green 15 15
505 A77 3r orange 15 15
Set value 30 20

World Health Day, Nov. 12, 1960, and to promote malaria control.

Pres. Sukarno with Hoe
A78

1961, Feb. 15 ***Perf. 12½x12***

506 A78 75s gray 15 15

Planned National Development.

Dayak Dancer of Borneo
A79

Designs: 10s, Ambonese boat. 15s, Tangkubanperahu crater. 20s, Bull races. 50s, Toradja houses. 75s, Balinese temple. 1r, Lake Toba. 1.50r, Balinese dancer and musicians. 2r, Buffalo hole, view. 3r, Borobudur Temple, Java.

1961 ***Perf. 13½x13***

507 A79 10s rose lilac 15 15
508 A79 15s gray 15 15
509 A79 20s orange 15 15
510 A79 25s orange ver 15 15
511 A79 50s carmine rose 15 15
512 A79 75s red brown 16 20
513 A79 1r brt green 20 25
514 A79 1.50r bister brn 40 25
515 A79 2r grnsh blue 50 35
516 A79 3r gray 60 35
Set of 4 souvenir sheets 4.00 2.25
Nos. 507-516 (10) 2.61
Set value 1.75

Issued for tourist publicity.

The four souvenir sheets among them contain one each of Nos. 507-516 imperf., with two or three stamps to a sheet and English marginal inscriptions: "Visit Indonesia" and "Visit the Orient Year." Size: 139x105mm or 105x139mm.

Sports Hall and Thomas Cup — A80

Perf. 13½x12½

1961, June 1 **Photo.**

517 A80 75s pale violet & blue 15 15
518 A80 1r citron & dk grn 15 15
519 A80 3r salmon pink & dk bl 16 15
Set value 33 26

Issued to commemorate the 1961 Thomas Cup World Badminton Championship.

New Buildings and Workers
A81

1961, July 6 **Unwmk.**

No.	Type	Denom.	Color	Unused	Used
520	A81	75s	violet & grnsh bl	15	15
521	A81	1.50r	emerald & buff	15	15
522	A81	3r	dk red & salmon	15	15
			Set value	20	20

16th anniversary of independence.

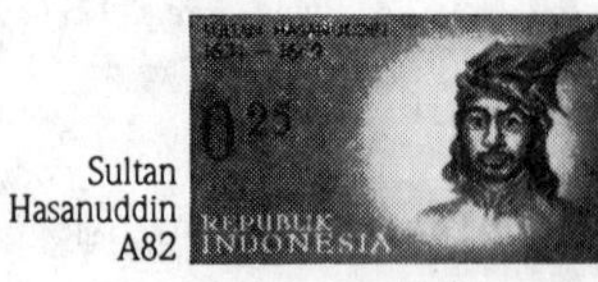

Sultan Hasanuddin A82

Portraits: 20s, Abdul Muis. 30s, Surjopranoto. 40s, Tengku Tjhik Di Tiro. 50s, Teuku Umar. 60s, K. H. Samanhudi. 75s, Captain Pattimura. 1r, Raden Adjeng Kartini. 1.25r, K. H. Achmad Dahlan. 1.50r, Tuanku Imam Bondjol. 2r, Si Singamangaradja XII. 2.50r, Mohammad Husni Thamrin. 3r, Ki Hadjar Dewantoro. 4r, Djenderal Sudirman. 4.50r, Dr. G. S. S. J. Ratulangie. 5r, Pangeran Diponegoro. 6r, Dr. Setyabudi. 7.50r, H. O. S. Tjokroaminoto. 10r, K. H. Agus Salim. 15r, Dr. Soetomo.

Perf. 13½x12½

1961-62 **Unwmk.** **Photo.**

Black Inscriptions; Portraits in Sepia

No.	Type	Denom.	Color	Unused	Used
523	A82	20s	olive	15	15
524	A82	25s	gray olive	15	15
525	A82	30s	brt lilac	15	15
526	A82	40s	brown orange	15	15
527	A82	50s	bluish green	15	15
528	A82	60s	green ('62)	15	15
529	A82	75s	lt red brown	15	15
530	A82	1r	lt blue	15	15
531	A82	1.25r	lt ol grn ('62)	15	15
532	A82	1.50r	emerald	15	15
533	A82	2r	orange red ('62)	15	15
534	A82	2.50r	rose claret	15	15
535	A82	3r	gray blue	15	15
536	A82	4r	olive green	22	15
537	A82	4.50r	red lilac ('62)	15	15
538	A82	5r	brick red	26	18
539	A82	6r	bister ('62)	15	15
540	A82	7.50r	violet bl ('62)	15	15
541	A82	10r	green ('62)	22	15
542	A82	15r	deep orange ('62)	26	15
			Set value	2.40	1.50

Issued to honor national heroes. The 25s, 75s, 1.50r and 5r on Aug. 17, Independence Day; 40s, 50s and 4r on Oct. 5, Army Day; 20s, 30s, 1r, 2.50r and 3r on Nov. 10, Republic Day; 60s, 2r, 7.50r and 15r on Oct. 5, 1962; 1.25r, 4.50r, 6r and 10r on Nov. 10, 1962.

Symbols of Census A83

1961, Sept. 15 *Perf. 13½x12½*

No.	Type	Denom.	Color	Unused	Used
543	A83	75s	rose violet	15	15

First census in Indonesia.

Djataju — A84

Scenes from Ramayana Ballet: 40s, Hanuman. 1r, Dasamuka. 1.50r, Kidang Kentiana. 3r, Dewi Sinta. 5r, Rama.

Perf. 12x12½

1962, Jan. 15 **Unwmk.**

No.	Type	Denom.	Color	Unused	Used
544	A84	30s	ocher & red brn	15	15
545	A84	40s	rose lilac & vio	15	15
546	A84	1r	green & claret	15	15
547	A84	1.50r	sal pink & dk grn	15	15
548	A84	3r	pale grn & dp bl	15	15
549	A84	5r	brn org & dk brn	15	15
			Set value	75	32

Asian Games Emblem — A85

Main Stadium — A86

Designs: 10s, Basketball. 15s, Main Stadium, Jakarta. 20s, Weight lifter. 25s, Hotel Indonesia. 30s, Cloverleaf intersection. 40s, Discus thrower. 50s, Woman diver. 60s, Soccer. 70s, Press House. 75s, Boxers. 1r, Volleyball. 1.25r, 2r, 3r, 5r, Asian Games emblem. 1.50r, Badminton. 1.75r, Wrestlers. 2.50r, Woman rifle shooter. 4.50r, Hockey. 6r, Water polo. 7.50r, Tennis. 10r, Table tennis. 15r, Bicyclist. 20r, Welcome Monument.

1962 **Photo.** *Perf. 12½*

No.	Type	Denom.	Color	Unused	Used
550	A85	10s	green & yel	15	15
551	A86	15s	grnsh blk & bis	15	15
552	A85	20s	red lil & lt grn	15	15
553	A86	25s	car & lt grn	15	15
554	A86	30s	bl grn & yel	15	15
555	A85	40s	ultra & pale bl	15	15
556	A85	50s	choc & gray	15	15
557	A85	60s	lil rose & vio gray	15	15
558	A85	70s	dk brn & rose	15	15
559	A85	75s	choc & org	15	15
560	A85	1r	purple & lt bl	15	15
561	A85	1.25r	dk bl & rose car	15	15
562	A85	1.50r	red org & lil	15	15
563	A85	1.75r	dk car & rose	15	15
564	A85	2r	brn & yel grn	15	15
565	A85	2.50r	dp bl & lt grn	15	15
566	A85	3r	black & dk red	15	15
567	A85	4.50r	dk grn & red	15	15
568	A85	5r	gray grn & lem	15	15
569	A85	6r	brn red & dp yel	16	15
570	A85	7.50r	red brn & sal	16	15
571	A85	10r	dk blue & blue	16	15
572	A85	15r	dl vio & pale vio	20	16
573	A85	20r	dk grn & ol bis	35	25
			Set value	2.50	1.75

4th Asian Games, Jakarta.

Malaria Eradication Emblem — A87

Atom Diagram — A88

1962, Apr. 7 *Perf. 12½x12*

No.	Type	Denom.	Color	Unused	Used
574	A87	40s	dull bl & vio bl	15	15
575	A87	1.50r	yel org & brn	15	15
576	A87	3r	green & indigo	15	15
577	A87	6r	lilac & blk	16	16
			Set value	38	35

WHO drive to eradicate malaria. The 1.50r and 6r have Indonesian inscription on top.

1962, Sept. 24 **Photo.** *Perf. 12x12½*

No.	Type	Denom.	Color	Unused	Used
578	A88	1.50r	dk blue & yel	15	15
579	A88	4.50r	brick red & yel	16	16
580	A88	6r	green & yel	22	16
			Set value	45	39

Development through science.

Pacific Travel Association Emblem — A89

Mechanized Plow — A90

Designs: 1.50r, Prambanan Temple and Mount Merapi. 6r, Balinese Meru (Buildings), Pura Taman Ajun.

1963, Mar. 14 **Unwmk.**

No.	Type	Denom.	Color	Unused	Used
581	A89	1r	grn & indigo	15	15
582	A89	1.50r	olive & indigo	15	15
583	A89	3r	ocher & indigo	15	15
584	A89	6r	dp org & indigo	15	15
			Set value	22	25

Issued to publicize the 12th conference of the Pacific Area Travel Association, Bandung.

Perf. 12½x12, 12x12½

1963, Mar. 21

Design: 1r, 3r, Hand holding rice stalks, vert.

No.	Type	Denom.	Color	Unused	Used
585	A90	1r	blue & yel	15	15
586	A90	1.50r	brt grn & indigo	15	15
587	A90	3r	rose car & org	15	15
588	A90	6r	orange & blk	15	15
			Set value	24	22

FAO "Freedom from Hunger" campaign. English inscription on 3r and 6r.

Long-Armed Lobster — A91

Fish: 1.50r, Little tuna. 3r, River roman. 6r, Chinese pompano.

1963, Apr. 6 *Perf. 12½x12*

No.	Type	Denom.	Color	Unused	Used
589	A91	1r	ver, blk & yel	15	15
590	A91	1.50r	ultra, blk & yel	15	15
591	A91	3r	Prus bl, bis & car	15	15
592	A91	6r	ol grn, blk & ocher	15	15
			Set value	48	22

Pen and Conference Emblem — A92

Designs: 1.50r, Pen, Emblem and map of Africa and Southeast Asia. 3r, Globe, pen and broken chain, vert. 6r, Globe, hand holding pen and broken chain, vert.

Perf. 12½x12, 12x12½

1963, Apr. 24 **Photo.** **Unwmk.**

No.	Type	Denom.	Color	Unused	Used
593	A92	1r	lt bl & dp org	15	15
594	A92	1.50r	pale vio & mar	15	15
595	A92	3r	olive, bl & blk	15	15
596	A92	6r	brick red & blk	15	15
			Set value	22	22

Asian-African Journalists' Conference.

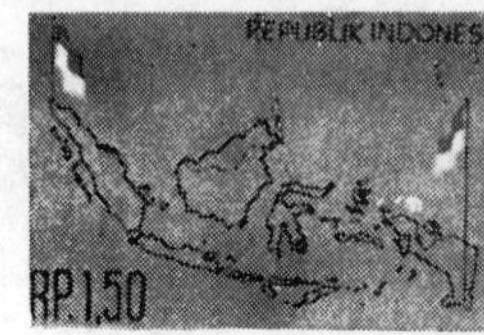

"Indonesia's Flag from Sabang to Merauke" — A93

Designs: 4.50r, Parachutist landing in New Guinea. 6r, Bird of paradise and map of New Guinea.

1963, May 1 *Perf. 12½x12*

No.	Type	Denom.	Color	Unused	Used
597	A93	1.50r	org brn, blk & red	15	15
598	A93	4.50r	multicolored	15	15
599	A93	6r	multicolored	15	15
			Set value	22	17

Issued to mark the acquisition of Netherlands New Guinea (West Irian).

Centenary Emblem — A94

Design: 1.50r, 6r, Red Cross.

1963, May 8 *Perf. 12*

No.	Type	Denom.	Color	Unused	Used
600	A94	1r	brt grn & red	15	15
601	A94	1.50r	lt bl & red	15	15
602	A94	3r	gray & red	15	15
603	A94	6r	yel bis & red	15	15
			Set value	24	22

Centenary of the International Red Cross.

Bank of Indonesia, Djalan A95

Daneswara, God of Prosperity A96

1963, July 5 **Photo.** *Perf. 12*

No.	Type	Denom.	Color	Unused	Used
604	A95	1.75r	lt bl & pur	15	15
605	A96	4r	citron & sl grn	15	15
606	A95	6r	lt green & brn	15	15
607	A96	12r	org & dk red brn	15	15
			Set value	24	22

Issued for National Banking Day.

Standard Bearers A97

Designs: 1.75r, "Pendet" dance. 4r, GANEFO building, Senajan, Jakarta. 6r, Archery. 10r, Badminton. 12r, Javelin. 25r, Sailing. 50r, Torch.

1963, Nov. 10 **Unwmk.** *Perf. 12½*

No.	Type	Denom.	Color	Unused	Used
608	A97	1.25r	gray vio & dk brn	15	15
609	A97	1.75r	org & ol grn	15	15
610	A97	4r	emer & dk brn	15	15
611	A97	6r	rose brn & blk	15	15
612	A97	10r	lt ol grn & dk brn	15	15
613	A97	12r	rose car & grnsh blk	15	15
614	A97	25r	blue & dk blue	15	15
615	A97	50r	red & black	15	15
			Set value	45	45

1st Games of the New Emerging Forces, GANEFO, Jakarta, Nov. 10-22.

Pres. Sukarno — A98

Trailer Truck — A99

1964 Photo. *Perf. 12½x12*

616	A98	6r	brown & dk bl	15	15
617	A98	12r	bister & plum	15	15
618	A98	20r	blue & org	15	15
619	A98	30r	red org & bl	15	15
620	A98	40r	green & brn	15	15
621	A98	50r	red & dp grn	15	15
622	A98	75r	vio & red org	15	15
623	A98	100r	sil & red brn	15	15
624	A98	250r	dk blue & sil	15	15
625	A98	500r	red & gold	15	15
			Set value	45	45

See Nos. B165-B179. For surcharges see Nos. 661, 663-667.

1964 *Perf. 12x12½, 12½x12*

Designs: 1r, Oxcart. 1.75r, Freighter. 2r, Lockheed Electra plane. 2.50r, Buginese sailboat, vert. 4r, Mailman with bicycle. 5r, Dakota plane. 7.50r, Teletype operator. 10r, Diesel train. 15r, Passenger ship. 25r, Convair Coronado Plane. 35r, Telephone switchboard operator.

626	A99	1r	dull claret	15	15
627	A99	1.25r	red brown	15	15
628	A99	1.75r	Prus blue	15	15
629	A99	2r	red orange	15	15
630	A99	2.50r	brt blue	15	15
631	A99	4r	bluish grn	15	15
632	A99	5r	olive bister	15	15
633	A99	7.50r	brt green	15	15
634	A99	10r	orange	15	15
635	A99	15r	dark blue	15	15
636	A99	25r	violet blue	15	15
637	A99	35r	red brown	15	15
			Set value	50	50

For surcharges see Nos. 659-660, 662.

Ramses II — A100

Design: 6r, 18r, Kiosk of Trajan, Philae.

1964, Mar. 8 *Perf. 12½x12*

638	A100	4r	ol bis & ol grn	15	15
639	A100	6r	grnsh bl & ol grn	15	15
640	A100	12r	rose & ol grn	15	15
641	A100	18r	emer & ol grn	15	15
			Set value	22	22

UNESCO world campaign to save historic monuments in Nubia.

Stamps of Netherlands Indies and Indonesia — A101

1964, Apr. 1 *Perf. 12½*

642	A101	10r	gold, dk bl & red org	15	15

Centenary of postage stamps in Indonesia.

Indonesian Pavilion — A102

1964, May 16 *Perf. 12½x12*

643	A102	25r	sil, blk, red & dk bl	15	15
644	A102	50r	gold, Prus bl, red & grn	15	15
			Set value	15	15

New York World's Fair, 1964-65.

Thomas Cup — A103

1964, Aug. 15 *Perf. 12½x13½*

645	A103	25r	brt grn, gold & red	15	15
646	A103	50r	ultra, gold & red	15	15
647	A103	75r	purple, gold & red	20	15
			Set value	40	20

Thomas Cup Badminton World Championship, 1964.

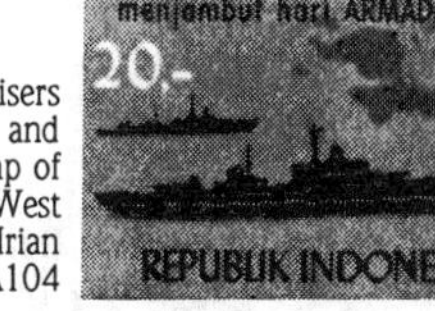

Cruisers and Map of West Irian A104

Designs: 30r, Submarine. 40r, Torpedo boat.

Perf. 12½x12
1964, Oct. 5 Photo. Unwmk.

648	A104	20r	yellow & brn	15	15
649	A104	30r	rose & blk	15	15
650	A104	40r	brt grn & ultra	15	15
			Set value	21	21

Issued to honor the Indonesian Navy.

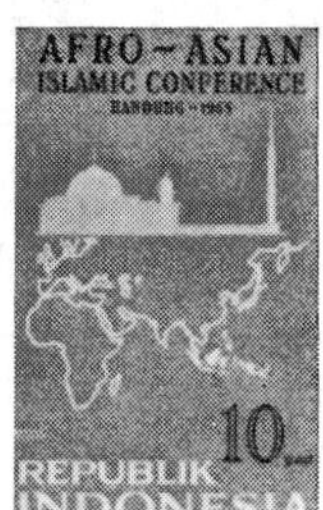

Map of Africa and Asia and Mosque — A105

Design: 15r, 50r, Mosque and clasped hands.

1965, Mar. 6 Photo. *Perf. 12½*

651	A105	10r	lt blue & pur	15	15
652	A105	15r	org & red brn	15	15
653	A105	25r	brt grn & brn	15	15
654	A105	50r	brn red & blk	15	15
			Set value	24	20

Issued to publicize the Afro-Asian Islamic Conference, Bandung, March, 1965.

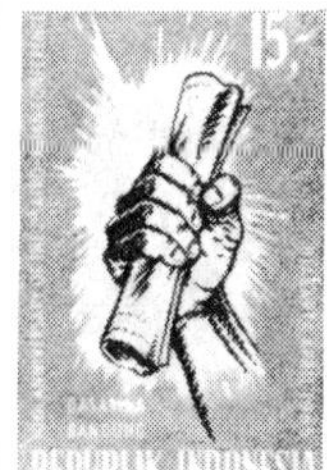

Hand Holding Scroll — A106

Design: 25r, 75r, Conference emblem (globe, cotton and grain).

1965, Apr. 18 Unwmk. *Perf. 12½*

655	A106	15r	silver & dp car	15	15
656	A106	25r	aqua, gold & red	15	15
657	A106	50r	gold & dp ultra	15	15
658	A106	75r	pale vio, gold & red	15	15
			Set value	24	20

10th anniv. of the First Afro-Asian Conf.

Nos. 618-623 and Nos. 634-636 Surcharged in Revalued Currency in Orange or Black

Sen

1965, Dec. *Perf. 12x12½, 12½x12*

659	A99	10s	on 10r (B)	15	15
660	A99	15s	on 15r	15	15
661	A98	20s	on 20r	15	15
662	A99	25s	on 25r (B)	15	15
663	A98	30s	on 30r	15	15
664	A98	40s	on 40r	15	15
665	A98	50s	on 50r	15	15
666	A98	75s	on 75r	15	15
667	A98	100s	on 100r	16	15
			Set value	75	50

The surcharge on Nos. 659-660 and No. 662 is in two lines and larger.

Pres. Sukarno — A107

1966-67 Photo. *Perf. 12½x12*

668	A107	1s	sep & Prus grn	15	15
669	A107	3s	sep & lt ol grn	15	15
670	A107	5s	sep & dp car	15	15
671	A107	8s	sep & Prus grn	15	15
672	A107	10s	sep & vio bl	15	15
673	A107	15s	sep & blk	15	15
674	A107	20s	sep & dp grn	15	15
675	A107	25s	sep & dk red brn	15	15
676	A107	30s	sep & dp bl	15	15
677	A107	40s	sep & red brn	15	15
678	A107	50s	sep & brt vio	15	15
679	A107	80s	sep & org	15	15
680	A107	1r	sep & emer	15	15
681	A107	1.25r	sep & dk gray ol	15	15
682	A107	1.50r	sep & emer	15	15
683	A107	2r	sep & mag	15	15
684	A107	2.50r	sep & gray	15	15
685	A107	5r	sep & ocher	15	15
686	A107	10r	sep & ol grn	15	15
686A	A107	12r	grn & org ('67)	15	15
686B	A107	25r	grn & brt pur ('67)	15	15
			Set value	1.00	50

The 12r is inscribed "1967" instead of "1966."

Dockyard Workers — A108

Gen. Ahmad Yani — A109

Designs: 40s, Lighthouse. 50s, Fishermen. 1r, Maritime emblem (wheel and eagle). 1.50r, Sailboat. 2r, Loading dock. 2.50r, Diver emerging from water. 3r, Liner at pier.

1966 Photo. *Perf. 12x12½*

687	A108	20s	lt ultra & grn	15	15
688	A108	40s	pink & dk bl	15	15
689	A108	50s	green & brn	15	15
690	A108	1r	salmon, bl & yel	15	15
691	A108	1.50r	dull lil & dl grn	15	15
692	A108	2r	gray & dp org	15	15
693	A108	2.50r	rose lil & dk red	15	15
694	A108	3r	brt green & blk	15	15
a.			Souvenir sheet	5.00	3.50
			Set value	50	35

Issued for Maritime Day. Nos. 687-690 issued Sept. 23; Nos. 691-694, Oct. 23.

No. 694a contains one imperf. stamp similar to No. 694.

1966, Nov. 10

Heroes of the Revolution: No. 696, Lt. Gen. R. Suprapto. No. 697, Lt. General Harjono. No. 698, Lt. Gen. S. Parman. No. 699, Maj. Gen. D. I. Pandjaitan. No. 700, Maj. Gen. Sutojo Siswomihardjo. No. 701, Brig. General Katamso. No. 702, Colonel Soegijono. No. 703, Capt. Pierre Andreas Tendean. No. 704, Adj. Insp. Karel Satsuit Tubun.

Deep Blue Frame

695	A109	5r	org brn	15	15
696	A109	5r	brt grn	15	15
697	A109	5r	gray brn	15	15
698	A109	5r	olive	15	15
699	A109	5r	gray	15	15
700	A109	5r	brt purple	15	15
701	A109	5r	red lilac	15	15
702	A109	5r	slate green	15	15
703	A109	5r	dull rose lil	15	15
704	A109	5r	orange	15	15
			Nos. 695-704 (10)	1.50	
			Set value		70

Issued to honor military men killed during the Communist uprising, October, 1965.

Tjlempung, Java — A110

Aviator and MiG-21 — A111

Musical Instruments and Maps: 1r, Sasando, Timor. 1.25r, Foi doa, Flores. 1.50r, Kultjapi, Sumatra. 2r, Arababu, Sangihe and Talaud Islands. 2.50r, Drums, West New Guinea. 3r, Katjapi, Celebes. 4r, Hape, Borneo. 5r, Gangsa, Bali. 6r, Serunai, Sumatra. 8r, Rebab, Java. 10r, Trompet, West New Guinea. 12r, Totobuang, Moluccas. 15r, Drums, Nias. 20r, Kulintang, Celebes. 25r, Keledi, Borneo.

1967 Unwmk. Photo. *Perf. 12½x12*

705	A110	50s	red & gray	15	15
706	A110	1r	brn & dp org	15	15
707	A110	1.25r	mar & ultra	15	15
708	A110	1.50r	grn & lt vio	15	15
709	A110	2r	vio bl & yel bis	15	15
710	A110	2.50r	ol grn & dl red	15	15
711	A110	3r	brt grn & dl cl	15	15
712	A110	4r	vio bl & org	15	15
713	A110	5r	dull red & bl	15	15
714	A110	6r	blk & brt pink	15	15
715	A110	8r	red brn & brt grn	16	15
716	A110	10r	lilac & red	22	15
717	A110	12r	ol grn & lil	25	15
718	A110	15r	vio & lt ol grn	35	15
719	A110	20r	gray & sepia	45	15
720	A110	25r	black & green	60	16
			Set value	2.65	1.00

Issue dates: 1.25r, 10r, 12r, 15r, 20r, 25r, Mar. 1; others Feb. 1.
For surcharges see Nos. J118-J137.

1967, Apr. 9 *Perf. 12½*

Aviation Day: 4r, Traffic control tower and 990A Convair jetliner. 5r, Hercules transport plane.

721	A111	2.50r	multicolored	15	15
722	A111	4r	multicolored	15	15
723	A111	5r	multicolored	15	15
			Set value	22	18

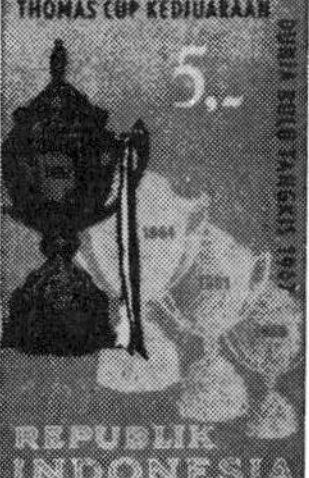

Thomas Cup with Victory Dates — A112

Design: 12r, Thomas Cup and globe.

1967, May 31 ***Perf. 12x12½***

724 A112 5r multicolored 15 15
725 A112 12r multicolored 20 15
Set value 27 15

Issued to commemorate the Thomas Cup Badminton World Championship of 1967.

Balinese Girl in Front of Temple Gate — A113

1967, July 1 **Photo.** ***Perf. 12½***

726 A113 12r multicolored 20 15
a. Souv. sheet of 1, imperf. 1.50 75

Intl. Tourist Year, 1967. See No. 739.

Heroes of the Revolution Monument, Lubang Buaja — A114

Designs: 5r, Full view of monument, horiz. 7.50r, Shrine at monument.

Perf. 12x12½, 12½x12

1967, Aug. 17 **Photo.**

727 A114 2.50r pale grn & dk brn 15 15
728 A114 5r brt rose lil & pale brn 15 15
729 A114 7.50r pink & Prus grn 15 15
Set value 27 18

Issued to publicize the "Heroes of the Revolution" Monument in Lubang Buaja.

Forest Fire, by Raden Saleh A115

Design: 50r, Fight to Death, by Raden Saleh.

1967, Oct. 30 **Photo.** ***Perf. 12½***

730 A115 25r org & gray grn 30 25
a. Souvenir sheet of 1 1.60 1.40
731 A115 50r vio brn & org 65 60

Indonesian painter Raden Saleh (1813-80).

Human Rights Flame — A116

1968, Jan. 1 **Photo.** ***Perf. 12½***

732 A116 5r grn, lt vio bl & red 15 15
733 A116 12r grn, ol bis & red 16 15
Set value 15

International Human Rights Year 1968.

Armed Forces College Emblem — A117

1968, Jan. 29 **Litho.** ***Perf. 12½***

734 A117 10r lt blue, yel & brn 16 15

Integration of the Armed Forces College.

WHO Emblem and "20" — A118

20th anniv. of WHO: 20r, WHO emblem.

1968, Apr. 7 **Photo.** ***Perf. 12½***

735 A118 2r dp yel, pale yel & dk brn 15 15
736 A118 20r emerald & blk 25 15
Set value 32 15

Trains of 1867 and 1967 and Railroad's Emblem — A119

1968, May 15 **Photo.** ***Perf. 12½x12***

737 A119 20r multicolored 25 15
738 A119 30r multicolored 40 16

Indonesian railroad centenary (in 1967).

Tourist Type of 1967

Tourist Publicity: 30r, Butterfly dancer from West Java.

1968, July 1 ***Perf. 12½***

739 A113 30r gray & multi 35 16
a. Souv. sheet of 1 + label 1.60 1.40

Bosscha Observatory and Andromeda Nebula — A120

Design: 30r, Observatory, globe and sky, vert.

1968, Sept. 20 **Photo.** ***Perf. 12½x12***

740 A120 15r ultra & yellow 16 15
741 A120 30r violet & orange 35 15
Set value 17

Bosscha Observatory, 40th anniversary.

Weight Lifting — A121

Designs: 7.50r+7.50r, Sailing, horiz. 12r, Basketball. 30r, Dove, Olympic flame and emblem, horiz.

1968, Oct. 12 ***Perf. 12½***

742 A121 5r ocher, blk & grn 15 15
743 A121 Pair 16 15
a. 7.50r Left half 15 15
b. 7.50r Right half 15 15
c. Souvenir sheet 1.60 1.00
744 A121 12r blue & multi 15 15
745 A121 30r blue grn & multi 25 15
Set value 62 37

19th Olympic Games, Mexico City, Oct. 12-27. No. 743 is perforated vertically in the center, dividing it into two separate stamps, each inscribed "Republic Indonesia" and "7.50r." There is no gutter along the center perforation; and the design is continous over the two stamps.

No. 743c contains one No. 743 with track design surrounding the stamps.

Eugenia Aquea Burm. f. — A122

Fruits: 15r, Papaya. 30r, Durian, vert.

Perf. 12½x12, 12x12½

1968, Dec. 20 **Photo.**

746 A122 7.50r multicolored 15 15
747 A122 15r multicolored 15 15
a. Souvenir sheet of 1 60 50
748 A122 30r multicolored 25 15
a. Souvenir sheet of 1 1.10 1.00
Set value 46 29

Issued for the 11th Social Day.

Globe, ILO and UN Emblems — A123

Designs: 7.50r, 25r, ILO and UN emblems.

1969, Feb. 1 **Photo.** ***Perf. 12½***

749 A123 5r yel grn & scar 15 15
750 A123 7.50r org & dk grn 15 15
751 A123 15r lilac & org 16 15
752 A123 25r bl grn & dull red 22 15
Set value 55 27

50th anniv. of the ILO.

R. Dewi Sartika — A124

Red Crosses — A125

Portraits: No. 754, Tjoet Nja Din. No. 755, Tjoet Nja Meuthia. No. 756, General Gatot Subroto. No. 757, Sutan Sjahrir. No. 758, Dr. F. L. Tobing. Nos. 753-755 show portraits of women.

1969, Mar. 1 **Photo.** ***Perf. 12½x12***

753 A124 15r green & pur 20 15
754 A124 15r red lilac & grn 20 15
755 A124 15r dk blue & ver 20 15
756 A124 15r lilac & dk blue 20 15
757 A124 15r lemon & red 20 15
758 A124 15r pale brn & blue 20 15
Nos. 753-758 (6) 1.20
Set value 30

Heroes of Indonesian independence.

1969, May 5 **Photo.** ***Perf. 12***

Design: 20r, Red Cross surrounded by arms.

759 A125 15r green & dp red 15 15
760 A125 20r org yel & red 20 16
Set value 24

50th anniversary of the League of Red Cross Societies.

"Family Planning Leads to National Development and Prosperity" — A126

Design: 10r, Family, birds and factories.

1969, June 2 **Photo.** ***Perf. 12½***

761 A126 10r blue grn & org 16 15
762 A126 20r gray & magenta 25 15
Set value 21

Planned Parenthood Conference of Southeast Asia and Oceania, Bandung, June 1-7.

Map of Bali and Mask A127

Designs: 15r, Map of Bali and woman carrying basket with offerings on head. 30r, Map of Bali and cremation ceremony.

1969, July 1 **Litho.** ***Perf. 12½x12***

763 A127 12r gray & multi 15 15
764 A127 15r lilac & multi 15 15
765 A127 30r multicolored 22 15
a. Souvenir sheet of 1 1.60 1.00
Set value 17

Issued for tourist publicity.

Agriculture A128

Radar, Djatiluhur Station A129

Designs: 5r, Religious coexistence (roofs of mosques and churches). 10r, Social welfare (house and family). 12r, Import-export (cargo and ship). 15r, Clothing industry (cloth and spindles). 20r, Education (school children). 25r, Research (laboratory). 30r, Health care (people and syringe). 40r, Fishing (fish and net). 50r, Statistics (charts).

1969 **Photo.** ***Perf. 12x12½***

766 A128 5r yel grn & bl 15 15
767 A128 7.50r rose brn & yel 15 15
768 A128 10r slate & red 15 15
769 A128 12r blue & dp org 15 15
770 A128 15r slate grn & org 15 15
771 A128 20r purple & yel 15 15
772 A128 25r orange & blk 15 15
773 A128 30r car rose & gray 16 15
774 A128 40r green & org 20 15
775 A128 50r sepia & org 22 15
Set value 1.15 65

Five-year Development Plan.

See No. 968a.

1969, Sept. 29 *Perf. 12½*

Design: 30r, Communications satellite and earth.

776 A129 15r multicolored 15 15
777 A129 30r multicolored 25 20

Vickers Vimy and Borobudur Temple A130

Design: 100r, Vickers Vimy and map of Indonesia.

1969, Nov. 1 *Perf. 13½x12½*

778 A130 75r dp org & dull pur 40 15
779 A130 100r yellow & green 65 20

50th anniv. of the 1st flight from England to Australia (via Java).

EXPO '70, Indonesian Pavilion — A131

Designs: 15r, Garuda, symbol of Indonesian EXPO '70 committee. 30r, like 5r.

1970, Feb. 15 Photo. *Perf. 12x12½*

780 A131 5r brown, yel & grn 15 15
781 A131 15r dk bl, yel grn & red 20 15
782 A131 30r red, yel & dk bl 35 15
Set value 17

Issued to publicize EXPO '70 International Exposition, Osaka, Japan, Mar. 15-Sept. 13.

Upraised Hands, Bars and Scales of Justice — A132

1970, Mar. 15 Photo. *Perf. 12½*

783 A132 10r red orange & pur 15 15
784 A132 15r brt green & pur 18 15
Set value 15

Rule of law and justice in Indonesia.

UPU Monument, Bern — A133

Timor Dancers — A134

Design: 30r, UPU Headquarters, Bern.

1970, May 20 Photo. *Perf. 12x12½*

785 A133 15r emer & copper red 35 15
786 A133 30r ocher & blue 60 15
Set value 17

Inauguration of the new UPU Headquarters in Bern, Switzerland.

1970, July 1 Photo. *Perf. 12*

787 A134 20r shown 30 15
788 A134 45r Bali dancers 60 18
a. Souvenir sheet of 1 2.00 1.10
Set value 26

Tourist publicity. No. 788a sold for 60r.

Asian Productivity Year — A135

Independence Proclamation Monument — A136

1970, Aug. 1 Photo. *Perf. 12*

789 A135 5r emerald, org & red 25 15
790 A135 30r violet, org & red 70 15
Set value 15

1970, Aug. 17

791 A136 40r lt ultra & magenta *8.00 4.00*

The 25th anniversary of independence.

Post and Telecommunications Emblems — A137

Postal Worker and Telephone Dial — A138

Perf. 12x12½, 12½x12

1970, Sept. 27 **Photo.**

792 A137 10r green, ocher & yel *3.25* 15
793 A138 25r pink, blk & yel *4.25* 22

25th anniversary of the postal service.

UN Emblem A139

Education Year and UNESCO Emblems A140

1970, Oct. 10 Photo. *Perf. 12½*

794 A139 40r pur, red & yel grn *7.50 1.50*

25th anniversary of the United Nations.

1970, Nov. 16 Photo. *Perf. 12½*

Design: 50r, similar to 25r, but without oval background.

795 A140 25r yel, dk red & brn *6.00 1.50*
796 A140 50r lt blue, blk & red *9.00 2.25*

International Education Year.

Batik Worker A141

Designs: 50r, Woman with bamboo musical instrument (angklung), vert. 75r, Menangkabau house and family in traditional costumes.

1971, May 26 Litho. *Perf. 12½*

797 A141 20r multicolored 1.10 15
798 A141 50r multicolored 1.75 15
a. Souvenir sheet of 1 5.50 1.50
799 A141 75r multicolored 2.25 20
Set value 37

"Visit Asian lands." No. 798a sold for 70r.

Fatahillah Park, Djakarta — A142

Designs: 30f, City Hall. 65r, Lenong Theater performance. 80r, Ismail Marzuki Cultural Center.

1971, June 19 Photo. *Perf. 12½*

800 A142 15r yel grn, brn & bl 55 25
801 A142 65r org brn, dk brn & lt grn 2.25 25
802 A142 80r olive, bl & mag 3.25 65

Souvenir Sheet

803 A142 30r bl, yel & lil rose 3.00 1.75

444th anniv. of Djakarta. #803 sold for 60r.

Rama and Sita — A143

Design: 100r, Rama with bow.

1971, Aug. 31

804 A143 30r yellow, grn & blk 50 15
805 A143 100r blue, red & blk 1.75 25

International Ramayana Festival.

Carrier Pigeon and Conference Emblem — A144

1971, Sept. 20

806 A144 50r ocher & dp brown 75 15

5th Asian Regional Postal Conference.

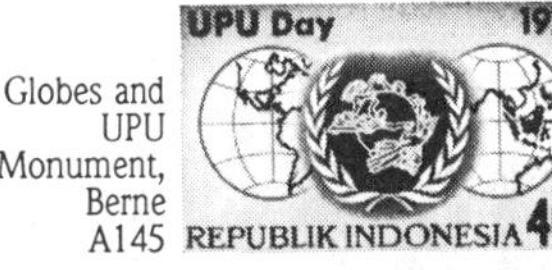

Globes and UPU Monument, Berne A145

1971, Oct. 4 Photo. *Perf. 13½x13*

807 A145 40r blue & dull vio 85 15

Universal Postal Union Day.

Boy Writing, UNICEF Emblem — A146

Design: 40r, Boy with sheaf of rice and UNICEF emblem.

1971, Dec. 11 *Perf. 12½*

808 A146 20r orange & multi 60 15
809 A146 40r blue & multi 70 15
Set value 21

25th anniv. UNICEF.

Lined Tang A147

Fish: 30r, Moorish goddess. 40r, Imperial angelfish.

1971, Dec. 27 Litho. *Perf. 12½*

810 A147 15r lilac & multi 1.10 35
811 A147 30r dull grn & multi 2.50 65
812 A147 40r blue & multi 2.75 1.60

See #834-836, 859-861, 926-928, 959-961.

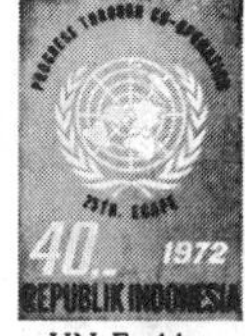

UN Emblem A148

Radio Tower A149

Design: 100r, Road and dam.

1972, Mar. 28 Photo. *Perf. 12½*

813 A148 40r lt grnsh bl & bl 55 15
814 A149 75r dk car, yel & grnsh bl 80 15
815 A148 100r green, yel & blk 1.10 20

UN Economic Commission for Asia and the Far East (ECAFE), 25th anniv.

"Your Heart is your Health" — A150

Woman Weaver, Factories — A151

1972, Apr. 7

816 A150 50r multicolored 70 15

World Health Day.

1972, Apr. 22

817 A151 35r orange, yel & pur 55 15

50th anniv. of the Textile Technology Institute.

Book Readers A152

1972, May 15 *Perf. 13½x12½*

818 A152 75r blue & multi 1.00 20

International Book Year 1972.

Weather Satellite — A153

1972, July 20 Photo. *Perf. 12½*

819 A153 35r shown 55 15
820 A153 50r Astronaut on moon 55 15
821 A153 60r Indonesian rocket Kartika 1 1.10 15
Set value 33

Space achievements.

Hotel Indonesia — A154

1972, Aug. 5
822 A154 50r grn, lt bl & car 80 15

Hotel Indonesia, 10th anniversary.

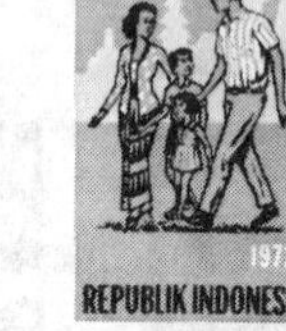

Silat (Self Defense) A155 — Family, Houses of Worship A156

Designs (Olympic Emblems and): 35r, Running. 50r, Diving. 75r, Badminton. 100r, Olympic Stadium.

1972, Aug. 26 **Photo.**
823 A155 20r lt blue & multi 38 15
824 A155 35r multicolored 55 15
825 A155 50r yel grn & multi 70 16
826 A155 75r multicolored 1.10 20
827 A155 100r multicolored 1.25 25
Nos. 823-827 (5) 3.98
Set value 78

20th Olympic Games, Munich, Aug. 26-Sept. 11.

1972, Sept. 27 ***Perf. 12½x13½***

Family planning: 75r, Healthy family. 80r, Working family (national prosperity).

828 A156 30r lemon & multi 35 15
829 A156 75r lilac & multi 80 18
830 A156 80r multicolored 1.10 20

Moluccas Dancer A157 — Thomas Cup, Shuttlecock A158

Designs: 60r, Man, woman and Toradja house, Celebes. 100fr, West Irian house, horiz.

Perf. 12½x13½, 13½x12½
1972, Oct. 28 **Photo.**
831 A157 30r olive pink & brn 55 15
832 A157 60r multicolored 1.00 18
833 A157 100r lt bl, brn & dl yel 1.65 25

Fish Type of 1971

Fish: 30r, Butterflyfish. 50r, Regal angelfish. 100r, Spotted triggerfish.

1972, Dec. 4 **Litho.** ***Perf. 12½***
834 A147 30r blue & multi 95 15
835 A147 50r blue & multi 1.50 15
836 A147 100r blue & multi 3.25 25

1973, Jan. 2 **Litho.** ***Perf. 12½***

Designs (Thomas Cup, Shuttlecock and): 75r, National monument and Istora Sports Hall. 80r, Indonesian flag and badminton player.

837 A158 30r emerald & brt bl 16 15
838 A158 75r dull grn & dk car 70 20
839 A158 80r gold & red 70 20

Thomas Cup Badminton World Championship 1973.

WMO Emblem, Anemometer, Wayang Figure — A159

Perf. 13½x12½
1973, Feb. 15 **Litho.**
840 A159 80r blue, grn & claret 80 20

Cent. of intl. meteorological cooperation.

"Health Begins at Home" — A160

1973, Apr. 7 **Photo.** ***Perf. 12½***
841 A160 80r dk grn, org & ultra 80 20

25th anniv. of WHO.

Ceremonial Mask, Java — A161 — Hand Putting Coin into Bank — A162

1973, June 1 **Photo.** ***Perf. 12½***
842 A161 30r shown 40 15
843 A161 60r Mask, Kalimantan 68 16
844 A161 100r Mask, Bali 1.10 25

Tourist publicity.

1973, July 2 **Photo.** ***Perf. 12½***

Design: 30r, Symbolic coin bank and hand, horiz.

845 A162 25r yellow, lt brn & blk 30 15
846 A162 30r green, yel & gold 42 15
Set value 18

National savings movement.

Chess — A163 — INTERPOL Emblem and Policemen — A164

8th National Sports Week: 60r, Karate. 75r, Hurdling, horiz.

1973, Aug. 4 **Photo.** ***Perf. 12½***
847 A163 30r red, yellow & blk 50 15
848 A163 60r black, ocher & lt grn 65 20
849 A163 75r black, lt bl & rose 1.00 35

1973, Sept. 3

Design: 50r, INTERPOL emblem and guard statue from Sewu Prambanan Temple, vert.

850 A164 30r yellow, grn & blk 35 15
851 A164 50r yellow, brn & blk 50 15
Set value 22

50th anniv. of Intl. Police Organization.

Batik Worker and Parang Rusak Pattern A165

Batik designs: 80r, Man and Pagi Sore pattern. 100r, Man and Merak Ngigel pattern.

1973, Oct. 9 **Photo.** ***Perf. 12½***
852 A165 60r multicolored 80 15
853 A165 80r multicolored 1.00 20
854 A165 100r multicolored 1.25 25

Farmer, Grain, UN and FAO Emblems — A166

1973, Oct. 24 **Photo.** ***Perf. 12½***
855 A166 30r lilac & multi 35 15

World Food Program, 10th anniversary.

Houses of Worship — A167

Family planning: 30r, Classroom. 60r, Family and home.

1973, Nov. 10
856 A167 20r dk bl, lt bl & ver 22 15
857 A167 30r ocher, blk & yel 30 15
858 A167 60r lt grn, yel & blk 62 16
Set value 28

Fish Type of 1971

Fish: 40r, Acanthurus leucosternon. 65r, Chaetodon trifasciatus. 100r, Pomacanthus annularis.

1973, Dec. 10 **Litho.** ***Perf. 12½***
859 A147 40r multicolored 45 15
860 A147 65r multicolored 65 18
861 A147 100r multicolored 1.20 30

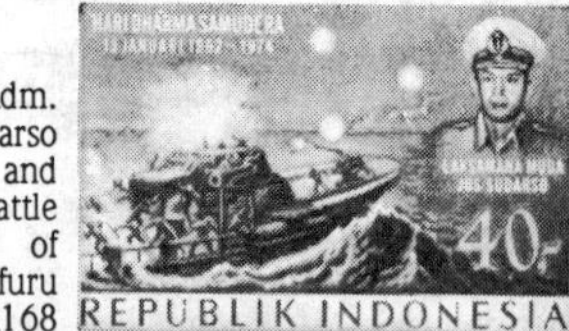

Adm. Sudarso and Battle of Arafuru A168

1974, Jan. 15
862 A168 40r brt blue & multi 50 15

12th Navy Day.

Bengkulu Costume — A169

Designs: Regional Costumes.

1974, Mar. 28 **Litho.** ***Perf. 12½***
863 A169 5r shown
864 A169 7.50r Kalimantan, Timor
865 A169 10r Kalimantan, Tengah
866 A169 15r Jambi
867 A169 20r Sulawesi, Tenggara
868 A169 25r Nusatenggara, Timor
869 A169 27.50r Maluku
870 A169 30r Lampung
871 A169 35r Sumatra, Barat
872 A169 40r Aceh
873 A169 45r Nusatenggara, Barat
874 A169 50r Riouw
875 A169 55r Kalimantan, Barat
876 A169 60r Sulawesi, Utara
877 A169 65r Sulawesi, Tengah
878 A169 70r Sumatra, Selatan
879 A169 75r Java, Barat
880 A169 80r Sumatra, Utara
881 A169 90r Yogyakarta
882 A169 95r Kalimantan, Selatan
883 A169 100r Java, Timor
884 A169 120r Irian, Java
885 A169 130r Java, Tengah
886 A169 135r Sulawesi, Selatan
887 A169 150r Bali
888 A169 160r Djakarta
Nos. 863-888 (26) 30.00 12.50

Baladewa — A170

Designs (Figures from Shadow Plays): 80r, Kresna. 100r, Bima.

1974, June 1 **Photo.** ***Perf. 12½***
889 A170 40r lt violet & multi 70 15
890 A170 80r salmon & multi 1.10 15
891 A170 100r rose 1.40 16
Set value 38

Pres. Suharto A171 — Family and WPY Emblem A172

1974-76 **Photo.** ***Perf. 12½***
Portrait in Dark Brown
901 A171 40r lt green & blk 15 15
903 A171 50r ultra & blk 20 15
906 A171 65r brt pink & blk 28 15
908 A171 75r yellow & blk 38 15
912 A171 100r buff & blk 50 16
913 A171 150r citron & blk 75 25
914 A171 200r green & blue 90 38
915 A171 300r brn org & car 1.40 55
916 A171 400r green & yellow 1.90 75
917 A171 500r lilac & car 2.50 1.00
Nos. 901-917 (10) 8.96 3.69

#914-917 have wavy lines in background.
Issue dates: Nos. 901-913, Aug. 17, 1974. Nos. 914-917, Aug. 17, 1976.

1974, Aug. 19
918 A172 65r ultra, gray & ocher 40 15

World Population Year 1974.

"Welfare" — A173

"Development" A174

"Religion" — A175

1974, Sept. 9

919	A173	25r green & multi	16	15
920	A174	40r yellow grn & multi	35	15
921	A175	65r dk vio brn & multi	50	15
		Set value		27

Family planning.

Mailmen with Bicycles, UPU Emblem — A176

UPU cent.: 40r, Horse-drawn mail cart. 65r, Mailman on horseback. 100r, Sailing ship, 18th century.

1974, Oct. 9

922	A176	20r dk green & multi	15	15
923	A176	40r dull blue & multi	20	15
924	A176	65r black brn & yel	45	20
925	A176	100r maroon & multi	75	16
		Set value		46

Fish Type of 1971

Fish: 40fr, Zebrasoma veliferum. 80r, Euxiphipops navarchus. 100r, Synchiropus splendidus.

1974, Oct. 30 Photo. *Perf. 12½*

926	A147	40r blue & multi	80	15
927	A147	80r blue & multi	1.10	16
928	A147	100r blue & multi	1.25	22

Drill Team Searching for Oil — A177

Designs (Pertamina Emblem and): 75r, Oil refinery. 95r, Pertamina telecommunications and computer center. 100r, Gasoline truck and station. 120r, Plane over storage tanks. 130r, Pipes and tanker. 150r, Petro-chemical storage tanks. 200r, Off-shore drilling platform. 95r, 100r, 120r, 130r, vertical.

1974, Dec. 10 *Perf. 13½*

929	A177	40r black & multi	22	15
930	A177	75r black & multi	42	15
931	A177	95r black & multi	70	18
932	A177	100r black & multi	70	20
933	A177	120r black & multi	90	22
934	A177	130r black & multi	1.00	25
935	A177	150r black & multi	1.20	30
936	A177	200r black & multi	1.60	40
		Nos. 929-936 (8)	6.74	1.85

Pertamina State Oil Enterprise, 17th anniv.

Spittoon, Sumatra — A178

Artistic Metalware: 75r, Condiment dish, Sumatra. 100r, Condiment dish, Kalimantan.

1975, Feb. 24 Photo. *Perf. 12½*

937	A178	50r red & black	45	15
938	A178	75r green & black	60	16
939	A178	100r brt blue & multi	85	20

Blood Donors' Emblem A179

Globe, Standard Meter and Kilogram A180

1975, Apr. 7

940	A179	40r yellow, red & grn	50	15

"Give blood, save lives."

1975, May 20

941	A180	65r blue, red & yel	50	15

Cent. of Intl. Meter Convention, Paris, 1875.

Farmer, Teacher, Mother, Policewoman and Nurse — A181

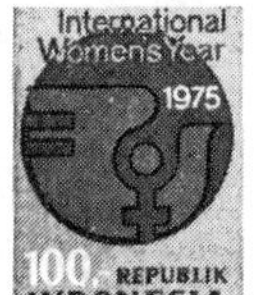

IWY Emblem — A182

1975, June 26 Photo. *Perf. 12½*

942	A181	40r multicolored	25	15
943	A182	100r multicolored	60	20
		Set value		28

International Women's Year 1975.

Dendrobium Pakarena — A183

Stupas and Damaged Temple — A184

Orchids: 70r, Aeridachnis bogor. 85r, Vanda genta.

1975, July 21

944	A183	40r multicolored	60	15
945	A183	70r multicolored	95	15
946	A183	85r multicolored	1.65	22

See Nos. 1010-1012, 1036-1038.

1975, Aug. 10 *Perf. 12½*

Designs (UNESCO Emblem and): 40r, Buddha statues, stupas and damaged wall. 65r, Stupas and damaged wall, horiz. 100r, Buddha statue and stupas, horiz.

947	A184	25r yellow, brn & org	35	15
948	A184	40r black, grn & yel	55	15
949	A184	65r lemon, cl & grn	1.10	16
950	A184	100r bister, brn & sl bl	1.65	20
		Set value		48

UNESCO campaign to save Borobudur Temple, Java.

Banjarmasin Battle — A185

Battle Scenes: 40r, Batua, Sept. 8, 1946. 75r, Margarana, Nov. 20, 1946. 100r, Palembang, Jan. 1, 1947.

1975, Aug. 17

951	A185	25r yellow & blk	16	15
952	A185	40r org ver & red	25	15
953	A185	75r vermilion & blk	55	15
954	A185	100r orange & blk	80	20
		Set value		48

Indonesian independence, 30th anniversary.

"Education" A186

Heroes' Monument, Surabaya A187

Family plannings: 25r, "Religion." 40r, "Prosperity."

1975, Oct. 20 Photo. *Perf. 12½*

955	A186	20r blue, salmon & blk	15	15
956	A186	25r emerald, sal & blk	15	15
957	A186	40r dp org, blue & blk	22	15
		Set value		18

1975, Nov. 10

958	A187	100r maroon & green	55	22

War of independence, 30th anniversary.

Fish Type of 1971

Fish: 40r, Coris angulata. 75r, Chaetodon ephippium. 150r, Platax pinnatus, vert.

1975, Dec. 15 Litho. *Perf. 12½*

959	A147	40r multicolored	70	15
960	A147	75r multicolored	1.40	15
961	A147	150r multicolored	2.75	30

Thomas Cup — A188

Designs: 40r, Uber Cup. 100r, Thomas and Uber Cups.

1976, Jan. 31 Photo. *Perf. 12½*

962	A188	20r blue & multi	15	15
963	A188	40r multicolored	22	15
964	A188	100r green & multi	62	20
		Set value		32

Indonesia, Badminton World Champions.

Refugees on Truck and New Village A189

Designs: 50r, Neglected and restored village streets. 100r, Derelict and rebuilt houses.

1976, Feb. 28 Photo. *Perf. 12½*

965	A189	30r yellow & multi	15	15
966	A189	50r blue & multi	25	15
967	A189	100r ocher & multi	50	20
		Set value		36

World Human Settlements Day.

Telephones, 1876 and 1976 — A190

1976, Mar. 10 Photo. *Perf. 12½*

968	A190	100r yel, org & brn	55	20
a.		Bklt. pane of 8 (4 #968, 4 #775, 2 labels) ('78)	4.25	

Centenary of first telephone call by Alexander Graham Bell, Mar. 10, 1876.

Eye and WHO Emblem — A191

Design: 40r, Blind man, eye and World Health Organization emblem.

1976, Apr. 7 Photo. *Perf. 12½*

969	A191	20r yel, lt grn & blk	15	15
970	A191	40r yel, blue & blk	20	15
		Set value		15

Foresight prevents blindness.

Montreal Stadium A192

1976, May 17

971	A192	100r ultra	50	15

21st Olympic Games, Montreal, Canada, July 17-Aug. 1.

Lake Tondano, Celebes — A193

Tourist publicity: 40r, Lake Kelimutu, Flores. 75r, Lake Maninjau, Sumatra.

1976, June 1

972	A193	35r lt green & blk	28	15
973	A193	40r gray, rose & lt grn	32	15
974	A193	75r blue & sl grn	70	15
a.		Bklt. pane of 8 (7 #974, #998, 2 labels) ('78)	5.00	
		Set value		30

Radar Station — A194

Designs: 50r, Master control radar station. 100r, Apalata satellite.

1976, July 8 Photo. *Perf. 12½*

975	A194	20r multicolored	15	15
976	A194	50r green & blk	28	15
977	A194	100r multicolored	55	20
a.		Bklt. pane of 9 (4 #977, 5 #987, label) ('78)	6.50	
		Set value		35

Inauguration of domestic satellite system.

Arachnis Flos-aeris — A195

Orchids: 40r, Vanda putri serang. 100r, Coelogyne pandurata.

1976, Sept. 7

978	A195	25r multicolored	60	15
979	A195	40r multicolored	90	15
980	A195	100r multicolored	2.50	40
		Set value		60

Tree and Mountain — A196

1976, Oct. 4

981	A196	20r green, blue & brn	15	15

16th National Reforestation Week.

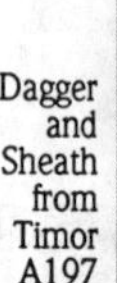

Dagger and Sheath from Timor A197

Historic Daggers and Sheaths: 40r, from Borneo. 100r, from Aceh.

1976, Nov. 1 *Perf. 12½*

982	A197	25r multicolored	32	15
983	A197	40r multicolored	50	20
a.		Souvenir sheet of 1	4.75	4.75
984	A197	100r green & multi	1.10	40
		Set value		65

No. 983a exists imperf.

Open Book A198

Children Reading A199

1976, Dec. 8 **Photo.** *Perf. 12½*

985	A198	20r multicolored	15	15
986	A199	40r multicolored	30	15
		Set value		15

Better books for children.

UNICEF Emblem A200

Ballot Box A201

1976, Dec. 11

987	A200	40r multicolored	25	15

UNICEF, 30th anniv.

1977, Jan. 5 **Photo.** *Perf. 12½*

1977 elections: 75r, Ballot box, grain and factory. 100r, Coat of arms.

988	A201	40r multicolored	30	15
989	A201	75r multicolored	55	16
990	A201	100r multicolored	75	22

Camp and Flags Scout Emblems, — A202

Designs: 30r, Tent, emblems and trees. 40r, Boy and Girl Scout flags and emblems.

1977, Feb. 28

991	A202	25r multicolored	26	15
992	A202	30r multicolored	32	15
993	A202	40r multicolored	35	15
		Set value		20

11th National Scout Jamboree.

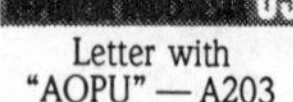
Letter with "AOPU" — A203

Anniversary Emblem, Djakarta Arms — A204

Design: 100r, Stylized bird and letter.

1977, Apr. 1 **Photo.** *Perf. 12½*

994	A203	65r multicolored	35	15
995	A203	100r multicolored	50	20

Asian-Oceanic Postal Union, 15th convention.

1977, May 23 **Photo.** *Perf. 12½*

Designs: Anniversary emblem and arms of Djakarta in different arrangements.

996	A204	20r orange & blue	15	15
997	A204	40r emerald & blue	20	15
998	A204	100r slate & blue	40	22
a.		Souvenir sheet of 1	1.65	1.65
		Set value		35

450th anniversary of Djakarta. No. 998a also issued imperf.

Rose — A205

Various Sports Emblems — A206

1977, May 26 **Photo.** *Perf. 12½*

999	A205	100r shown	75	30
a.		Souvenir sheet	1.75	1.75
1000	A205	100r Envelope	75	30
a.		Souvenir sheet of 4	3.00	3.00

Amphilex 77 Phil. Exhib., Amsterdam, May 26-June 5. Nos. 999-1000 printed se-tenant. No. 999a contains one stamp similar to No. 999 with blue background. No. 1000a contains 2 each of Nos. 999-1000.

Nos. 999a, 1000a exist imperf.

See No. 1013a.

1977, June 22

9th Natl. Sports Week: 50r, 100r, Different sports emblems.

1001	A206	40r silver & multi	38	15
1002	A206	50r silver & multi	55	20
1003	A206	100r gold & multi	1.25	45

Contest Trophy A207

Emblem A208

1977, July 20

1004	A207	40r green & multi	45	15
1005	A208	100r yellow & multi	90	30

10th Natl. Koran Reading Contest, July 20-27.

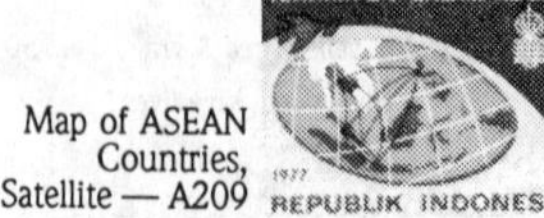

Map of ASEAN Countries, Satellite — A209

Designs: 35r, Map of ASEAN countries. 50r, Flags of founding members: Indonesia, Malaysia, Philippines, Singapore and Thailand; ship, plane and train.

1977, Aug. 8

1006	A209	25r multicolored	25	15
1007	A209	35r multicolored	30	15
1008	A209	50r multicolored	45	20
		Set value		40

Association of South East Asian Nations (ASEAN), 10th anniversary.

Uniform, Jakarta Regiment — A210

1977, Aug. 19

1009	A210	25r green, gold & brn	15	15

Indonesia-Pakistan Economic and Cultural Organization, 1968-1977.

Orchid Type of 1975

Orchids: 25r, Taeniophyllum. 40r, Phalaenopsis violacea. 100r, Dendrobium spectabile.

1977, Oct. 28 **Photo.** *Perf. 12½*

1010	A183	25r orange & multi	60	15
1011	A183	40r blue & multi	1.00	15
1012	A183	100r yel grn & multi	2.50	25
a.		Souvenir sheet of 1	4.00	1.90
		Set value		40

No. 1012a contains one stamp similar to No. 1012 with blue background. No. 1012a exists imperf.

Child and Mosquito — A211

1977, Nov. 7 *Perf. 12½*

1013	A211	40r brt grn, red & blk	22	15
a.		Bklt. pane of 9+label (4 #999, 5 #1013) ('78)		4.75

Natl. Health campaign to eradicate malaria. Issue date: No. 1013a, Sept. 27, 1978.

Proboscis Monkey — A212

Designs: 40r, Indian elephant. 100r, Tiger.

1977, Dec. 22

1014	A212	20r multicolored	25	15
1015	A212	40r multicolored	50	15
1016	A212	100r multicolored	1.90	90
a.		Souvenir sheet of 1	2.25	2.25

Wildlife protection. #1016a exists imperf.

Conference Emblem A213

Mother and Child A214

1978, Mar. 27 **Photo.** *Perf. 12½*

1017	A213	100r lt blue & ultra	65	22

United Nations Conference on Technical Cooperation among Developing Countries.

1978, Apr. 7 **Photo.** *Perf. 12½*

Design: 75r, Mother and child, symbolic design.

1018	A214	40r lt green & blue	25	15
1019	A214	75r orange red & brn	42	16
		Set value		24

Promotion of breast feeding.

Dome of The Rock, Jerusalem — A215

1978, May 15 **Photo.** *Perf. 12½*

1020	A215	100r multicolored	50	20

Palestinian fighters and their families.

Argentina '78 Emblem A216

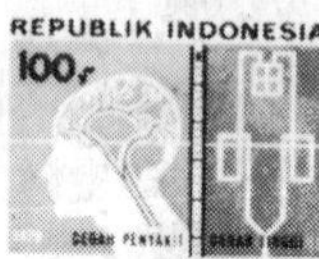

Head and "Blood Circulation" A217

1978, June 1

1021	A216	40r multicolored	22	15
1022	A216	100r multicolored	55	22
		Set value		30

11th World Cup Soccer Championships, Argentina, June 1-25.

1978, June 17 **Photo.** *Perf. 12½*

1023	A217	100r black, blue & red	50	20

World Health Day and drive against hypertension.

Leather Puppets — A218

Art from Wayang Museum, Djakarta: 75r, Wooden puppets. 100r, Actors with puppet masks.

1978, July 22 Litho. *Perf. 12½*

1024 A218 40r multicolored 55 15
1025 A218 75r multicolored 1.25 30
1026 A218 100r multicolored 1.40 40

Congress Emblem A219

IAAY Emblem A220

1978, Aug. 1

1027 A219 100r slate 50 20

27th Congress of World Confederation of Organizations of Teachers (WCOTP), Djakarta, June 26-Aug. 2.

1978, Aug. 16 Photo. *Perf. 12½*

1028 A220 100r orange & dk blue 50 20

International Anti-Apartheid Year.

Congress Emblem A221

Youth Pledge Emblem A222

Design: 100r, People and trees.

1978, Oct. 16 Photo. *Perf. 12½*

1029 A221 40r emerald & blue 22 15
1030 A221 100r emerald & blk 55 20
Set value 28

8th World Forestry Congress, Djakarta.

1978, Oct. 28

1031 A222 40r dk brown & red 16 15
1032 A222 100r salmon, brn & red 40 20
Set value 28

50th anniv. of Youth Pledge. See #1044a.

Wildlife Protection — A223

1978, Nov. 1

1033 A223 40r Porcupine anteater 48 15
1034 A223 75r Deer 95 25
a. Souv. sheet of 5, #1034, 4 #1035 + label 4.00
1035 A223 100r Clouded tiger 1.40 30
a. Souvenir sheet of 1 1.50

Stamps in No. 1034a are in changed colors. Souvenir sheets inscribed for Essen 2nd Intl. Stamp Fair.

Orchid Type of 1975

Orchids: 40r, Phalaenopsis sri rejeki. 75r, Dendrobium macrophilium. 100r, Cymbidium fynlaysonianum.

1978, Dec. 22 Photo. *Perf. 12½*

1036 A183 40r multicolored 50 15
1037 A183 75r multicolored 95 15
1038 A183 100r multicolored 1.40 15
a. Souvenir sheet of 1 3.00 1.00
Set value 20

Douglas DC-3, 1949, over Volcano A224

Designs: 75r, Douglas DC-9 over village. 100r, Douglas DC-10 over temple.

1979, Jan. 26 Photo. *Perf. 12½*

1039 A224 40r multicolored 18 15
1040 A224 75r multicolored 30 15
1041 A224 100r multicolored 48 15
Set value 22

Garuda Indonesian Airways, 30th anniv.

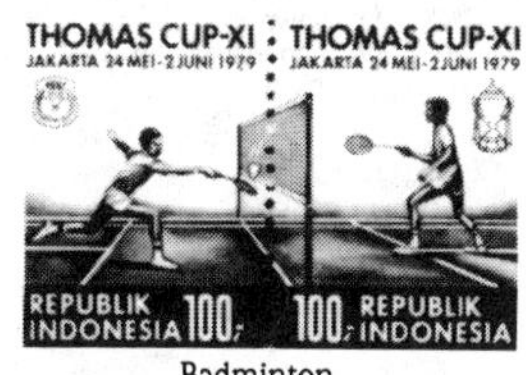

Badminton A225 A226

Design: 40r, Thomas Cup and badminton player.

1979, Feb. 24 Photo. *Perf. 12½*

1042 A225 40r car & blue 15 15
1043 A225 100r car & ocher 40 15
1044 A226 100r car & ocher 50 15
a. Pair, #1043-1044) 90
b. Bklt. pane of 9 + label (3 each #1032, 1043-1044) 4.25
Set value 25

11th Thomas Cup, Djakarta, May 24-June 2.

Paphiopedilum Lowii — A227

Orchids: 100r, Vanda limbata. 125r, Phalaenopsis gigantea.

1979, Mar. 22 Photo. *Perf. 12½*

1045 A227 60r multi 65 18
1046 A227 100r multi 1.00 30
1047 A227 125r multi 1.25 35
a. Souvenir sheet of 1 1.65
b. Souv. sheet of 2 (250r, 300r) 2.50

No. 1047b, issued for Asian Phil. Exhib., Dortmund, West Germany, May 24-27, contains a 250r stamp in design of 60r and 300r stamp in design of 100r. Sold for 650r.

Family and Houses — A228

Third Five-year Plan: 60r, Pylon and fields. 100r, School and clinic. 125r, Factories and trucks. 150r, Motorized mail delivery.

1979-82

1047C A228 12.50r Plane, food ('80) 15 15
1047D A228 17.50r Bridge ('82) 16 15
1048 A228 35r green & olive 16 15
1049 A228 60r blue & olive 22 15
1050 A228 100r blue & dk brn 40 20
1051 A228 125r red brn & ol 55 25
1052 A228 150r carmine & yel 60 32
Nos. 1047C-1052 (7) 2.24
Set value 1.05

See No. 1058a.

R. A. Kartini and Girls' School A229 A230

1979, Apr. 21 Photo. *Perf. 12½*

1053 A229 100r olive & brn 60 30
1054 A230 100r olive & brn 60 30
a. Pair, #1053-1054 1.25 75

Mrs. R. A. Kartini, educator, birth centenary.

Bureau of Education, UNESCO Emblems — A231

1979, May 25 Photo. *Perf. 12½*

1055 A231 150r multicolored 50 22

50th anniversary of the statutes of the International Bureau of Education.

Self Defense — A232

Cooperation Emblem — A233

Designs: 125r, Games' emblem. 150r, Senayan Main Stadium.

1979, June 21 Photo. *Perf. 12½*

1056 A232 60r multicolored 25 15
1057 A232 125r multicolored 45 25
1058 A232 150r multicolored 60 32
a. Bklt. pane of 6+4 labels (#1052, 5 #1058) 5.40

10th South East Asia Games, Djakarta, Sept. 21-30.

Issue date: No. 1058a, Sept. 27.

1979, July 12 Photo. *Perf. 12½*

1059 A233 150r multicolored 50 25

32nd Indonesian Cooperative Day.

A234

TELE COM 79
ITU
A235

Designs: 60r, IYC and natl. IYC emblems. 150r, IYC emblem.

1979, Aug. 4 Photo. *Perf. 12½*

1060 A234 60r emerald & blk 25 15
1061 A234 150r blue & blk 38 25

International Year of the Child.

1979, Sept. 20 Photo. *Perf. 12½*

1062 A235 150r TELECOM 79 50 25

3rd World Telecommunications Exhibition, Geneva, Sept. 20-26.

Fight Drug Abuse — A236

1979, Oct. 17 Photo. *Perf. 12½*

1063 A236 150r deep rose & black 60 32

Dolphin — A237

Wildlife Protection: 125r, Freshwater dolphin. 150r, Leatherback turtle.

1979, Nov. 24 Photo. *Perf. 12½*

1064 A237 60r multi 35 15
1065 A237 125r multi 70 22
1066 A237 150r multi 1.10 25

Souvenir Sheet

1066A A237 200r like #1066 2.00 40

Ship Made of Cloves — A238

Spice Race, Jakarta-Amsterdam (Sailing Ships): 60r, Penisi, vert. 150r, Madurese boat, vert.

1980, Mar. 12 Photo. *Perf. 12½*

1067 A238 60r bright blue 16 15
1068 A238 125r red brown 35 22
1069 A238 150r red lilac 50 25

1980

Souvenir Sheets

1069A A238 300r like #1068 2.50 1.00
1069B A238 500r like #1067 4.50 2.00

Issue dates: 300r, Mar. 12. 500r, May 6. 500r for London 1980 Intl. Stamp Exhib.

Rubber Raft in Rapids A239

Perf. 13½x13, 13x13½

1980, Mar. 21 Photo.

1070 A239 60r shown 16 15
1071 A239 125r Mountain climbing, vert. 35 22
1072 A239 150r Hang gliding, vert. 50 25

Souvenir Sheet

1072A A239 300r like #1070 2.00 65

A240

A241

1980, Apr. 15 *Perf. 12½*
1073 A240 150r multicolored 50 32

Anti-smoking Campaign.

1980, Apr. 21 Photo. *Perf. 12½*
1074 A241 125r Flowers In vase 40 22
1075 A241 150r Bouquet 60 25

2nd Flower Festival, Jakarta, Apr. 19-21. See No. 1080a-1080b.

A242

A243

1980, Apr. 24 *Perf. 13x13½*

Conference building.

1076 A242 150r gold & lil rose 50 25

Souvenir Sheet

1076A A242 300r multicolored 2.00 65

1st Asian-African Conf., 25th anniv.

1980, May 2 *Perf. 12½*

Designs: 60r, Male figure. 125r, Elephant stone. 150r, Taman Bali Stone Sarcophagus, 2000 B.C.

1077 A243 60r multicolored 20 15
1078 A243 125r multicolored 40 22
1079 A243 150r multicolored 55 25

Flower and Sculpture Types of 1980
Souvenir Sheet

1980 Photo. *Perf. 12½*
1080 Sheet of 8 6.00 3.00
a. A241 100r like #1074 42 22
b. A241 100r like #1075 42 22
c. A243 200r like #1077 80 45
d. A243 200r like #1079 80 45

London 1980 Intl. Stamp Exhib., May 6-14. No. 1080 contains 2 stamps of each design (4x2).

Draftsman in Wheelchair A244

Discus Thrower A245

1980, May 18 Photo. *Perf. 12½*
1081 A244 100r multicolored 35 20

Disabled Veterans Corp, 30th anniversary.

1980, May 18
1082 A245 75r dp orange & sep 30 16

Olympics for the Disabled, Arnhem, Netherlands, June 21-July 5.

Pres. Suharto — A246

A246a

A246b

Perf. 13½x12½, 12½

1980-83 **Photo.**
1083 A246 12.50r lt grn & grn 15 15
1084 A246 50r lt grn & bl 16 15
1084A A246 55r red rose & red lil 15 15
1085 A246 75r lem & gldn brn 22 15
1086 A246 100r brt pink & bl 35 20
a. Bklt pane of 8 + 2 labels (6 #1086, 2 #1088, inscribed 1981) 4.00
1087 A246a 110r dull org & dp red lil 15 15
1088 A246 200r dull org & brn 65 40
1088A A246a 250r dull org & brn 1.00 50
1089 A246a 275r lt ap grn & dk grn 38 20
1090 A246 300r rose lil & gold 1.20 60
1091 A246 400r multicolored 1.60 80

Engr. *Perf. 12½x13*
1092 A246b 500r dk red brown 1.60 1.00
Nos. 1083-1092 (12) 7.61 4.45

Issue dates: 12.50r, 50r, 75r, 100r, 200r, June 8. 300r, 400r, June 8, 1981. 250r, Sept. 1982. 500r, Mar. 11, 1983. 55r, July 1983. 110r, 275r, Sept. 27, 1983.

See Nos. 1257-1261, 1266, 1268. For surcharge see No. 1527.

Map of Indonesia, People — A247

1980, July 17 *Perf. 12½*
1093 A247 75r blue & pink 20 16
1094 A247 200r blue & dull yel 60 40

1980 population census.

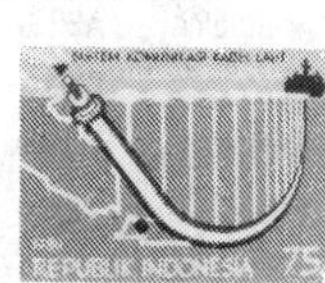

Ship Laying Cable — A248

50s Stamp of 1946 — A249

1980, Aug. 8 Photo. *Perf. 12½*
1095 A248 75r multicolored 20 16
1096 A248 200r multicolored 60 40

Singapore-Indonesia submarine cable opening.

1980, Aug. 17

Designs: 100r, 15s Battle of Surabaya stamp, 1946, horiz. 200r, 15s Independence Fund stamp, 1946.

1097 A249 75r dk brn & dp org 20 16
1098 A249 100r gold & purple 35 22
1099 A249 200r multicolored 60 40

Independence, 35th anniversary.

Asian Oceanic Postal Training School — A250

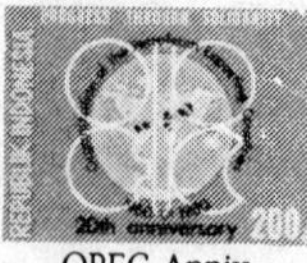

OPEC Anniv. Emblem — A251

1980, Sept. 10 Photo. *Perf. 12½*
1100 A250 200r multicolored 60 40

1980, Sept. 14
1101 A251 200r multicolored 60 40

Organization of Petroleum Exporting Countries, 20th anniversary.

Armed Forces, 35th Anniversary A252

1980, Oct. 5 Photo. *Perf. 13½x13*
1102 A252 75r shown 20 16
1103 A252 200r Service men and emblem 60 40

Vulturine Parrot — A253

One Day Beauty Orchid — A254

Designs: Parrots.

1980, Nov. 25 Photo. *Perf. 13x12½*
1104 A253 75r shown 50 16
1105 A253 100r Yellow-backed lory 90 20
1106 A253 200r Red lory 1.50 40

Souvenir Sheet
Perf. 12½

1106A Sheet of 3 5.25 2.50
b. A253 250r like #1105 90 50
c. A253 350r like #1104 1.40 70
d. A253 400r like #1106 1.50 80

1980, Dec. 10 *Perf. 13x13½*

Designs: Orchids.

1107 A254 75r *shown* 45 16
1108 A254 100r *Dendrobium discolor* 80 20
1109 A254 200r *Dendrobium lasianthera* 1.25 40

Souvenir Sheet

1980 *Perf. 13x13½*
1110 Sheet of 2 4.75 1.40
a. A254 250r like #1109 2.00 50
b. A254 350r like #1108 2.75 80

Heinrich von Stephan (1831-1897), UPU Founder — A255

1981, Jan. 7 *Perf. 13½x12½*
1111 A255 200r brt bl & dk bl 65 40

6th Asian Pacific Scout Jamboree A256

1981 *Perf. 13½x12½, 12½x13½*
1112 A256 75r Emblems 22 16
1113 A256 100r Scouts, vert. 35 20
1114 A256 200r Emblems, diff. 65 40

Souvenir Sheet

1115 A256 150r like #1113 80 35

Issued: #1112-1114, Feb. 22; #1115, Aug. 14.

4th Asian-Oceanian Postal Union Congress A257

Blood Donor Campaign A258

1981, Mar. 18 *Perf. 12½*
1116 A257 200r multicolored 80 40

1981, Apr. 22
1117 A258 75r Girl holding blood drop 22 16
1118 A258 100r Hands holding blood drop 35 20
1119 A258 200r Hands, blood, diff. 65 40

Intl. Family Planning Conference — A259

1981, Apr. 26
1120 A259 200r multicolored 80 40

A261

A260
Natl. Education Day

Traditional Bali Paintings: Nos. 1121-1122, Song of Sritanjung. No. 1123, Birth of the Eagle.

1981, May 2
1121 A260 100r multicolored 35 20
1122 A261 200r multicolored 65 40

Souvenir Sheet

1123 Sheet of 2 4.00 2.00
a. A260 400r multicolored 1.50 75
b. A261 600r multicolored 2.50 1.25

No. 1123 has margin showing WIPA '81 emblem. Sheets exist with marginal inscription "Indonesien grusst WIPA."

A262 A263

1981, May 9

1124 A262 200r multicolored 80 40

ASEAN Building Jakarta, opening.

1981, May 22

1125 A263 200r multicolored 80 40

Uber Cup '81 Badminton Championship, Tokyo.

World Environment Day — A264

Bas-reliefs, Candhi Merut Buddhist Temple, Central Java: 75r, Tree of Life. 200r, Reclining Buddha.

1981, June 5

1126 A264 75r multicolored 22 16
1127 A264 200r multicolored 65 40

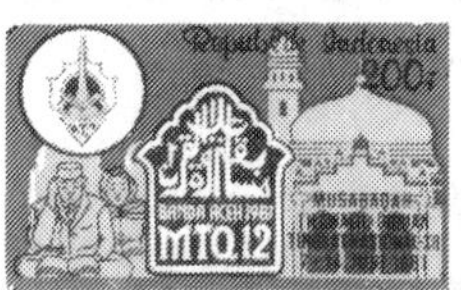

12th Koran Reading Competition, June 7-14 — A265

1981, June 7 *Perf. 13½x12½*

1128 A265 200r multicolored 65 40

Intl. Year of the Disabled — A266

1981, July 31 *Perf. 12½*

1129 A266 75r Blind man 22 16
1130 A266 200r Speech, hearing disabilities 65 40

Soekarno-Hatta Independence Monument, Jakarta — A267

1981, Aug. 17

1131 A267 200r multicolored 65 40

Natl. Sports Week, Sept. 19-30 — A268

World Food Day — A268a

1981, Sept. 19

1132 A268 75r Skydiving 22 16
1133 A268 100r Skin diving, horiz. 35 20
1134 A268 200r Equestrian 65 40

See Nos. 1374-1375 for souvenir sheets containing No. 1134 in different colors.

1981, Oct. 16

1135 A268a 200r multicolored 65 40

Provincial Arms — A269

Natl. Arms A270

1981-83

1136	A269	100r	Aceh	50	30
1137	A269	100r	Bali	50	30
1138	A269	100r	Bengkulu	50	30
1139	A269	100r	Jakarta	50	30
1140	A269	100r	West Irian	50	30
1141	A269	100r	West Java ('82)	50	30
1142	A269	100r	Jambi ('82)	50	30
1143	A269	100r	Central Java ('82)	50	30
1144	A269	100r	East Java ('82)	50	30
1145	A269	100r	South Kalimantan ('82)	50	30
1146	A269	100r	East Kalimantan ('82)	50	30
1147	A269	100r	West Kalimantan ('82)	50	30
1148	A269	100r	Lampung ('82)	50	30
1149	A269	100r	Central Kalimantan ('82)	50	30
1150	A269	100r	Moluccas ('82)	50	30
1151	A269	100r	West Nusa Tenggara ('82)	50	30
1152	A269	100r	East Nusa Tenggara ('82)	50	30
1153	A269	100r	Southeast Celebes ('82)	50	30
1154	A269	100r	Central Celebes ('82)	50	30
1155	A269	100r	West Sumatra ('82)	50	30
1156	A269	100r	North Celebes ('82)	50	30
1157	A269	100r	North Sumatra ('82)	50	30
1158	A269	100r	South Sumatra ('82)	50	30
1159	A269	100r	Riau ('82)	50	30
1160	A269	100r	South Sulawesi ('82)	50	30
1161	A269	100r	Yogyakarta ('82)	50	30
1161A	A269	100r	Timor ('83)	20	15
1162	A270	250r	shown ('82)	1.25	75
			Nos. 1136-1162 (28)	14.45	8.70

Pink-crested Cockatoo — A271

1981, Dec. 10

1163 A271 75r shown 65 16
1164 A271 100r Sulphur-crested cockatoo 90 20
1165 A271 200r King cockatoo 1.65 40

Souvenir Sheet

1166 Sheet of 2 3.50 1.20
a. A271 150r like #1274 85 30
b. A271 350r like #1275 2.50 70

Bumiputra Mutual Life Insurance Co., 70th Anniv. — A272

1982, Feb. 12

1167 A272 75r Family 25 16
1168 A272 100r Family, diff. 35 20
1169 A272 200r Hands holding symbols 65 40

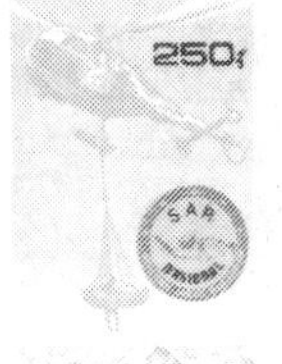

Search and Rescue Institute, 10th Anniv. — A273

General Election — A274

1982, Feb. 28 *Perf. 12½x13½*

1170 A273 250r multicolored 80 50

1982, Mar. 1 *Perf. 12½*

1171 A274 75r Ballot, houses 25 16
1172 A274 100r Farm 35 20
1173 A274 200r Arms 65 40

2nd UN Conference on Exploration and Peaceful Uses of Outer Space, Vienna, Aug. 9-21 — A275

1982, Apr. 19 *Perf. 13x13½*

1174 A275 150r Couple 50 30
1175 A275 150r Emblem 50 30

12th Thomas Badminton Cup, London, May — A276

1982, May 19

1176 A276 250r multicolored 80 50
a. Souvenir sheet of 2 1.60

No. 1176a also exists overprinted "INDONESIE SALUE PHILEXFRANCE" in red or black.

1982 World Cup — A277

1982, June 14

1177 A277 250r multi 80 50
a. Souvenir sheet of 2 2.00
b.-c. Souvenir sheets of 2, each 5.50

No. 1177b overprinted in black; No. 1177c in red.

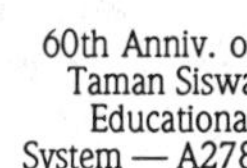

60th Anniv. of Taman Siswa Educational System — A278

1982, July 3

1178 A278 250r multi 80 50

15th Anniv. of Assoc. of South East Asian Nations (ASEAN) — A279

1982, Aug. 8 Photo. *Perf. 12½*

1179 A279 150r Members' flags 50 30

Balinese Starling — A280

Red Birds of Paradise — A281

1982, Oct. 11 Photo. *Perf. 13x13½*

1180 A280 100r shown 35 20
1181 A280 250r King birds of paradise 80 50

Souvenir Sheet

1181A A280 500r Bali dove 3.25 1.00

3rd World Natl. Park Cong., Denpasar Bali.

1982, Dec. 20 *Perf. 12½x13½*

1182 A281 100r Lawe's six-wired parotia 65 20
1183 A281 150r Twelve-wired birds of paradise 95 30
1184 A281 250r shown 1.50 50

Souvenir Sheet

Perf. 12½x13½

1184A Sheet of 2 4.00 1.00
b. A281 200r like 100r 1.50 40
c. A281 300r like 250r 2.25 60

Scouting Year A282

1983, Feb. 22 Photo. *Perf. 13½x13*

1185 A282 250r multi 1.00 50

Restoration of Borobudur Temple — A283

1983, Feb. 23 *Perf. 12½*

1186 A283 100r Scaffolding, crane, vert. 30 15
1187 A283 150r Buddha statue, stupas, vert. 50 20
1188 A283 250r Statue, temple 80 35

Souvenir Sheet

1189 A283 500r Temple 3.50 1.00

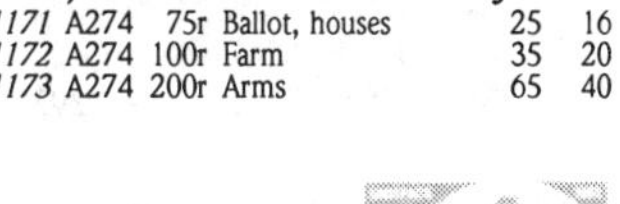

Gas Plant — A284

World Communications Year — A285

1983, May 16 Photo. *Perf. 12½*
1190 A284 275r multi 80 42

7th Intl. Liquefied Natural Gas Conference and Exhibition, Jakarta, May 16-19.

1983, May 17 *Perf. 12½x13½*
1191 A285 75r Dove, ships 30 15
1192 A285 110r Satellite 40 20
1193 A285 175r Dish antenna, jet 60 30
1194 A285 275r Airmail envelope, globe 80 42

See Nos. 1215-1216.

13th Natl. Koran Reading Competition, Padang, May 23-31
A286

1983, May 23 *Perf. 13½x13*
1195 A286 275r multi 80 42

Total Solar Eclipse, June 11
A287

1983, June 11 *Perf. 12½*
1196 A287 110r Map, eclipse 40 20
1197 A287 275r Map 80 42

Souvenir Sheet
1198 A287 500r like 275r 1.50 80

Launch of Palapa B Satellite — A288

Agricultural Census — A289

1983, June 18 *Perf. 12½x13½*
1199 A288 275r multi 80 42

1983, July 1 Photo. *Perf. 12½*
1200 A289 110r Produce 15 15
1201 A289 275r Farmer 30 15
Set value 23

15th Anniv. of Indonesia-Pakistan Economic and Cultural Cooperation Org. — A290

Weavings.

1983, Aug. 19
1202 A290 275r Indonesian, Lombok 30 15
1203 A290 275r Pakistani, Baluchistan 30 15

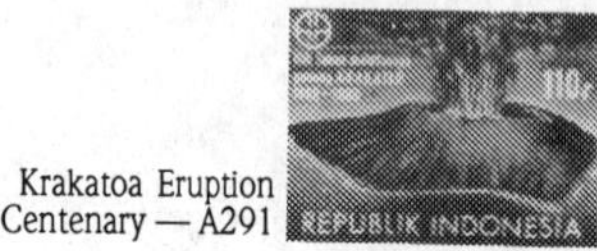

Krakatoa Eruption Centenary — A291

1983, Aug. 26
1204 A291 110r Volcano 15 15
1205 A291 275r Map 30 15
Set value 23

CN-235, Light Air Transport — A292

1983, Sept. 10 Photo. *Perf. 12½*
1206 A292 275r multi 30 15

Tropical Fish
A293

1983, Oct. 17 Photo. *Perf. 12½*
1207 A293 110r Puntius tetrazona 38 15
1208 A293 175r Rasbora einthoveni 55 15
1209 A293 275r Toxotes jaculator 95 20

Canderawasih Birds — A294

1983, Nov. 30 Photo. *Perf. 12½*
1210 A294 110r Diphyllodes respublica 35 15
1211 A294 175r Epimachus fastuosus 50 15
1212 A294 275r Drepanornis albertisi 85 20
1213 A294 500r as #1212 1.50 40
a. Souvenir sheet of 1 3.25 80

Inalienable Rights of the Palestinian People
A295

1983, Dec. 20 *Perf. 13½x13*
1214 A295 275r multi 38 20

WCY Type of 1983
Souvenir Sheets

1983 Photo. *Perf. 12½x13½*
1215 A285 400r like No. 1192 1.25 35
1216 A285 500r like No. 1194 1.90 50

Telecom '83 exhib., Geneva, Oct. 26-Nov. 1 (400r). Philatelic Museum opening, Jakarta (500r). Issue dates: 400r, Oct. 26; 500r, Sept. 29.

Fight Against Polio — A296

4th Five-Year Development Plan — A297

1984, Feb. 17 Photo. *Perf. 12½*
1217 A296 110r Emblem 15 15
1218 A296 275r Stylized person 38 20
Set value 28

1984, Apr. 1 Photo. *Perf. 12½*
1219 A297 55r Fertilizer industry 15 15
1220 A297 75r Aviation 15 15
1221 A297 110r Shipping 15 15
1222 A297 275r Communications 38 20
Set value 70 38

Forestry Resources — A298

1984, May 17 Photo. *Perf. 12½*
1223 A298 75r Forest, paper mill 15 15
1224 A298 110r Seedling 18 15
1225 A298 175r Tree cutting 26 15
1226 A298 275r Logs 45 20
a. Souv. sheet of 2, #1225-1226 1.50 35
Set value 47

17th Annual Meeting of ASEAN Foreign Ministers — A299

1984, July 9 Photo. *Perf. 12½*
1227 A299 275r Flags 38 20

1984 Summer Olympics — A300

Horse Dancers, Central Java — A301

1984, July 28 Photo. *Perf. 12½*
1228 A300 75r Pole vault 15 15
1229 A300 110r Archery 15 15
1230 A300 175r Boxing 22 15
1231 A300 250r Shooting 35 20
1232 A300 275r Weight lifting 38 22
1233 A300 325r Swimming 42 25
Nos. 1228-1233 (6) 1.67
Set value 92

1984, Aug. 17 *Perf. 12½x13½*

Processions.

1234 A301 75r shown 15 15
1235 A301 110r Reyog Ponorogo, East Java 22 15
1236 A301 275r Lion Dance, West Java 55 20
1237 A301 325r Barong of Bali 60 25
Set value 58

Natl. Sports Day — A302

1984, Sept. 9 Photo. *Perf. 13½x13*
1238 A302 110r Thomas Cup victory 15 15
1239 A302 275r Gymnastics 38 20
Set value 28

Postcode System Inauguration
A303

1984, Sept. 27 Photo. *Perf. 12½*
1240 A303 110r multi 15 15
1241 A303 275r multi 38 20
Set value 28

Birds of Irian Jaya — A304

Oath of the Youth — A305

1984, Oct. 15 *Perf. 12½x13½*
1242 A304 75r Chlamydera lauterbachi 30 15
1243 A304 110r Sericulus aureus 45 15
1244 A304 275r Astrapia nigra 1.10 20
1245 A304 325r Lophorhina superba 1.25 25
a. Souv. sheet of 2, #1242, 1245 3.25 3.25
Set value 58

No. 1245a for PHILAKOREA '84.

1984, Oct. 28 *Perf. 12½*
1246 A305 275r Emblem 38 20

ICAO, 40th Anniversary
A306

Perf. 13½x12½
1984, Dec. 7 Photo.
1247 A306 275r Airplane, Emblem 38 20

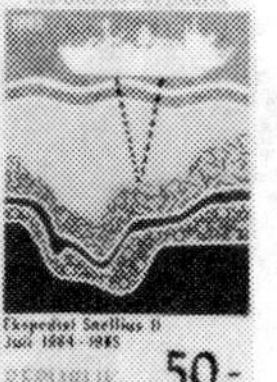

Indonesia Netherlands Marine Exped., 1984-85 — A307

75th Intl. Women's Day — A308

Survey ship Snellius II and: 50r, Marine geological and geophysical exploration. 100r, Mapping ocean currents. 275r, Studying marine flora and fauna.

1985, Feb. 27 Photo. *Perf. 13x13½*

1248	A307	50r	multi	15	15
1249	A307	100r	multi	15	15
1250	A307	275r	multi	40	22
			Set value		35

1985, Mar. 8

1251	A308	100r	Emblem	15	15
1252	A308	275r	Silhouettes, emblem	40	22
			Set value		30

Five Year Plan A309

1985, Apr. 1 *Perf. 13½x13*

1254	A309	75r	Mecca pilgrimage program	15	15
1255	A309	140r	Compulsory education	20	15
1256	A309	350r	Cement industry, Padang works	50	30
			Set value		48

Suharto Type of 1980-83 and

A310

A310a

A310b

A310c

Perf. 13½x12½, 12½ (A310, A310a, A310b, A310c)

1983-90 Photo.

1257	A246	10r	pale grn & dk grn	15	15
1258	A246	25r	pale org & dk cop red	15	15
1259	A246	50r	beige & dark brown	15	15
1260	A246	55r	sal rose & rose	15	15
1261	A246	100r	lt blue green & ultra	15	15
1262	A310	140r	rose & dp brn	20	15
1263	A310c	150r	yellow green & multi	16	15
1264	A310b	200r	pink, bl & red	16	15
1265	A246	300r	lt dull grn, bl grn & gold	40	20
1266	A310c	300r	multicolored	32	16
1267	A310	350r	red & brt lil	50	30
1268	A246	400r	blue grn, int blue & gold	55	25
1268A	A310b	700r	pale grn, rose lil & grn	60	30
1268B	A310c	700r	red & multi	80	40
1269	A310a	1000r	multi	1.40	70
			Nos. 1257-1269 (15)	5.84	
			Set value		1.80

Issue dates: 10r, 25r, Mar. 11. 140r, 350r, Apr. 10, 1985. 50r, 100r, No. 1265, Dec. 24, 1986. 55r, 400r, Dec. 1987. 200r, Dec. 1989. 700r, Mar. 1990. 1000r, Aug. 17, 1988. 150r, Nos. 1266, 1268B, Aug. 17, 1993.

For surcharge see No. 1527.

Asia-Africa Conference, 30th Anniv. — A311

1985, Apr. 24 *Perf. 12½*

1270	A311	350r	Emblem, inscription	50	30

Intl. Youth Year — A312

UN Decade for Women — A313

1985, July 12 *Perf. 12½x13½*

1271	A312	75r	Three youths, globe	15	15
1272	A312	140r	Youths supporting globe	20	15
			Set value		15

1985, July 26

1273	A313	55r	Profiles of women, emblem	15	15
1274	A313	140r	Globe, emblem	20	15
			Set value	28	15

Indonesian Trade Fair — A314

1985, Aug. 1

1275	A314	140r	Hydro-electric plant	20	15
1276	A314	350r	Farmer, industrial plant	50	25

Republic of Indonesia, 40th anniv.

11th Natl. Sports Week, Jakarta, Sept. 9-20 A315

Perf. 13½x12½, 12½x13½

1985, Sept. 9 Photo.

1277	A315	55r	Sky diving	15	15
1278	A315	100r	Combat sports	15	15
1279	A315	140r	High jump	20	15
1280	A315	350r	Wind surfing, vert.	50	25
			Set value		48

Org. of Petroleum Exporting Countries, OPEC, 25th Anniv. — A316

1985, Sept. 14 *Perf. 12½*

1281	A316	140r	multi	20	15

Natl. Oil Industry, Cent. A317

1985, Oct. 8 *Perf. 13½x13*

1282	A317	140r	Oil tankers	20	15
1283	A317	250r	Refinery	35	16
1284	A317	350r	Offshore oil rig	50	25

UN, 40th Anniv. — A318

Design: 140r, Doves, 40, emblem. 300r, Bombs transformed into plants.

1985, Oct. 24 *Perf. 12½*

1285	A318	140r	multicolored	20	15
1286	A318	300r	multicolored	40	20

Wildlife A318a

1985, Dec. 27 Photo. *Perf. 14½x13*

1286A	A318a	75r	Rhinoceros sondaicus	15	15
1286B	A318a	150r	Anoa depressicornis	20	15
1286C	A318a	300r	Varanus komodoensis	40	20
			Set value		35

1986 Industrial Census — A319

1986, Feb. 8 Photo. *Perf. 12½*

1287	A319		Pair	1.10	55
a.			175r Census emblem	55	25
b.			175r Symbols of industry	55	25

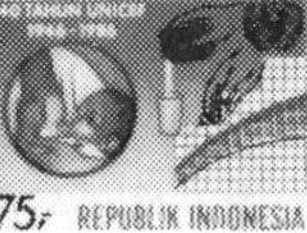

UN Child Survival Campaign — A320

1986, Mar. 15 Photo. *Perf. 12½*

1288	A320	75r	Breastfeeding	15	15
1289	A320	140r	Immunization	25	15
			Set value		20

UNICEF, 40th anniv.

4th 5-year Development Plan — A321

14th Thomas Cup, 13th Uber Cup, Jakarta — A322

1986, Apr. 1 Photo. *Perf. 12½*

1290	A321	140r	Construction	28	15
1291	A321	500r	Agriculture	1.00	50

1986, Apr. 22

1292	A322	55r	Cup, racket	15	15
1293	A322	150r	Cups, horiz.	30	15
			Set value		21

EXPO '86, Vancouver — A323

1986, May 2 *Perf. 12½x14½*

1294	A323	75r	Pinisi junk	15	15
1295	A323	150r	Kentongan, satellite	30	15
1296	A323	300r	Pavilion emblem	60	30

Natl. Scout Jamboree, JAMNAS '86, Cibubur Jakarta East A324

Perf. 13½x12½, 12½x13½

1986, June 21 Photo.

1297	A324	100r	Saluting flag	20	15
1298	A324	140r	Cookout	28	15
1299	A324	210r	Map-reading, vert.	42	20

Air Show '86, Jakarta, June 22-July 1 A325

1986, June 23 *Perf. 13½x12½*

1300	A325	350r	multi	70	35

Folk Dances A326

1986, July 30 Photo. *Perf. 12½*

1301	A326	140r	Legong Kraton	28	15
1302	A326	350r	Barong	70	35
1303	A326	500r	Kecak	1.00	50

19th Congress of Intl. Society of Sugar Cane Technologists, Jakarta — A327

1986, Aug. 5 *Perf. 12½x13½*

1304	A327	150r	Planting	30	15
1305	A327	300r	Sugar	60	30

Values quoted in this catalogue are for stamps graded Fine-Very Fine and with no faults. An illustrated guide to grade is provided beginning on Page 8A.

Sea-Me-We Submarine Cable Inauguration — A328

1986, Sept. 8 *Perf. 12½*

1306 A328 140r shown 28 15
1307 A328 350r Map, diff. 70 35

Southeast Asia, Middle East, Western Europe Submarine Cable.

Intl. Peace Year — A329

1987 General Election — A330

1986, Dec. 17 Photo. *Perf. 12½*

1308 A329 350r shown 70 35
1309 A329 500r Dove circling Earth 1.00 50

1987, Jan. 19

Designs: 75r, Tourism, party emblems, industry. 350r, Emblems, natl. eagle, ballot box.

1310 A330 75r multi 15 15
1311 A330 140r multi 28 15
1312 A330 350r multi 70 35

A331

A332

1987, Mar. 21 Photo. *Perf. 12½*

1313 A331 350r Satellite, horiz. 70 35
1314 A331 500r shown 1.00 50

Launch of Palapa B-2P, Cape Canaveral.

1987, Apr. 1

1315 A332 140r Boy carving figurines, horiz. 28 15
1316 A332 350r shown 70 35

4th 5-Year Development Plan.

Folk Costumes — A333

1987, May 25 *Perf. 13x13½*

1317 A333 140r Kalimantan Timur 28 15
1318 A333 350r Daerah Aceh 70 35
1319 A333 400r Timor Timur 80 40

See Nos. 1358-1363, 1412-1417, 1448-1453, 1464-1469.

14th Southeast Asia Games, Jakarata, Sept. 9-20
A334

Anniv. Emblems
A335

1987, June 10 *Perf. 12½*

1320 A334 140r Weight lifting 28 15
1321 A334 250r Swimming 50 25
1322 A334 350r Running 70 35

1987, June 20

1323 A335 75r multi, horiz. 15 15
1324 A335 100r shown 20 15
Set value 18

City of Jakarta, 460th anniv.; Jakarta Fair, 20th anniv.

Children's Day — A336

ASEAN Headquarters, Jakarta — A337

1987, July 23

1325 A336 100r Education, horiz. 20 15
1326 A336 250r Universal immunization 50 25

1987, Aug. 8

1327 A337 350r multi 70 35

ASEAN, 20th anniv.

Assoc. of Physicians Specializing in Internal Diseases, 30th Anniv. — A338

1987, Aug. 23 **Photo.**

1328 A338 300r Stylized man, caduceus 60 30

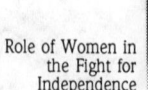

Sand Craters, Mt. Bromo, Timur
A339

1987, Oct. 20 *Perf. 13½x12½*

1329 A339 140r shown 28 15
1330 A339 350r Bratan (Bedugul) Lake, Bali 70 35
1331 A339 500r Sea gardens, Bunaken Is. 1.00 50

Pariwisata (tourism) 1987. See Nos. 1367-1370A, 1408-1410, 1420-1422.

Role of Women in the Fight for Independence
A340

1987, Nov. 10 *Perf. 12½*

1332 A340 75r Veteran 15 15
1333 A340 100r Soldiers, barbed wire (Laskar Wanita) 20 15
Set value 18

Fish — A341

1987, Dec. 30

1334 A341 150r Osphronemus goramy 30 15
1335 A341 200r Cyprinus carpio 40 20
1336 A341 500r Clarias batrachus 1.00 50

Natl. Veteran's League, 31st Anniv. — A342

1988, Jan. 2

1337 A342 250r blue grn & org 50 25

Occupational Health and Safety for Greater Efficiency and Productivity
A343

1988, Jan. 12 *Perf. 13½x12½*

1338 A343 350r Worker using safety equipment 70 35

See No. 1419.

Natl. Craft Council, 8th Anniv. — A344

Crafts: 120r, Carved wood snake and frog. 350r, Cane rocking chair. 500r, Ornate carved bamboo containers and fan.

1988, Mar. 3 Photo. *Perf. 12½*

1339 A344 120r ultra & dark brn 18 15
1340 A344 350r lt blue & dark brn 50 25
1341 A344 500r yel grn & dark brn 70 35

Pelita IV (Five-Year Development Plan) — A345

1988, Apr. 1

1342 A345 140r Oil rig, refinery 20 15
1343 A345 400r Crayfish, trawler 58 30

World Expo '88, Brisbane, Australia
A346

Intl. Red Cross and Red Crescent Organizations, 125th Annivs.
A347

Designs: 200r, Two children, Borobudur Temple in silhouette. 300r, Boy wearing armor and headdress. 350r, Girl, boy and a Tongkonan house, Toraja, South Sulawesi.

1988, Apr. 30 Photo. *Perf. 12½*

1344 A346 200r multi 28 15
1345 A346 300r multi 42 20
1346 A346 350r multi 50 25
a. Souv. sheet of 3, #1344-1346 2.00 2.00

No. 1346a exists imperf.

1988, May 8

1347 A347 350r blk & red 50 25

Orchids — A348

1988, May 17 *Perf. 13x13½*

1348 A348 400r Dendrobium none 58 30
1349 A348 500r Dendrobium abang 70 35

Perf. 13x14½

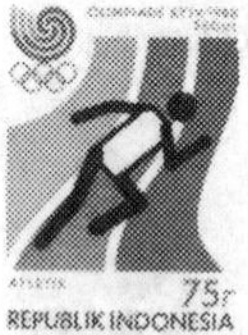
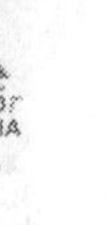

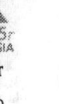

1988 Summer Olympics, Seoul — A349

Intl. Council of Women, Cent. — A350

1988, June 15 Photo. *Perf. 12½*

1350 A349 75r Running 15 15
1351 A349 100r Weight lifting 15 15
1352 A349 200r Archery 28 15
1353 A349 300r Table tennis 42 20
1354 A349 400r Swimming 58 30
a. Souv. sheet of 3 + label, #1351-1352, 1354 2.25 2.25
1355 A349 500r Tennis 70 35
a. Souv. sheet of 3 + label, #1350, 1353, 1355 2.50 2.50
Nos. 1350-1355 (6) 2.28
Set value 1.12

Sheets exist imperf.

1988, June 26

1356 A350 140r brt blue & blk 20 15

7th Natl. Farmers' Week — A351

1988, July 9

1357 A351 350r lake & bister 50 25

Folk Costumes Type of 1987

Traditional wedding attire from: 55r, West Sumatra. 75p, Jambi. 100r, Bengkulu. 120r, Lampung. 200r, Moluccas. 250r, East Nusa.

1988, July 15 *Perf. 12½x14½*

1358 A333 55r multi 15 15

Perf. 12½x13½

1359 A333 75r multi 15 15
1360 A333 100r multi 15 15
1361 A333 120r multi 18 15

Perf. 12½x14½

1362 A333 200r multi 28 15
1363 A333 250r multi 35 18
Nos. 1358-1363 (6) 1.26
Set value 60

A352

A353

1988, Sept. 29 Photo. *Perf. 12½*
1364 A352 500r multi 70 35

13th Congress of the Non-Aligned News Agencies Pool, Jakarta, Sept. 29-Oct. 1.

1988, Oct. 9
1365 A353 140r multi 20 15

Intl. Letter Writing Week.

Transportion and Communications Decade for Asia and the Pacific (1985-1995) A354

1988, Oct. 24
1366 A354 350r blk & lt blue 50 25

Tourism Type of 1987

Architecture: 250r, Al Mashun Mosque, Medan. 300r, Pagaruyung Palace, Batusangkar. 500r, 1000r, Keong Emas Taman Theater, Jakarta.

1988-89 Photo. *Perf. 13½x13*
1367 A339 250r multi 35 18
1368 A339 300r multi 42 20
1369 A339 500r multi 70 35

Souvenir Sheet

Perf. 14½x12½, Imperf

1370 A339 1000r multi 2.25 70

Perf. 14½x13

1370A Sheet of 2 7.25 3.65
b. A339 1500r like No. 1367 2.75 1.35
c. A339 2500r like No. 1368 4.50 2.25

Issue dates: No. 1370A, Nov. 1989; others, Nov. 25, 1988. World Stamp Expo '89, Washington, DC.

Butterflies — A356

Flora — A357

1988, Dec. 20 *Perf. 12½x13½*
1371 A356 400r *Papilio gigon* 65 28
1372 A356 500r *Graphium androcles* 85 35

Souvenir Sheet

Perf. 12½x14½

1373 A356 1000r like 500r 3.00 70

No. 1373 exists imperf.

Equestrian Type of 1981
Souvenir Sheets

1988 *Perf. 12½*
1374 Sheet of 4 2.50 65
a. A268 200r black, dark red & green 60 16
1375 Sheet of 1 + label, dk blue, dk red & dp orange 60 15

FILACEPT '88, The Hague, Oct. 18-23, 1988. Exist imperf., same values.

1989, Jan. 7 Photo. *Perf. 13½x13*
1376 A357 200r *Rafflesia* 30 15
1377 A357 1000r *Amorphophallus titanum* 1.50 70

Souvenir Sheet

Perf. 13½x14½

1378 A357 1000r like No. 1377, value in black 3.75 70

Garuda Indonesia Airlines, 40th Anniv. — A358

1989, Jan. 26 *Perf. 12½*
1379 A358 350r blue grn & brt blue 50 25

World Wildlife Fund — A359

Orangutans, *Pongo pygmaeus.*

1989, Mar. 6 Photo. *Perf. 12½*
1380 A359 75r Adult and young 38 15
1381 A359 100r Adult hanging in tree 48 15
a. Souv. sheet of 2, #1380-1381 3.00
1382 A359 140r Adult, young in tree 70 15
1383 A359 500r Adult's head 2.50 35
a. Souv. sheet of 2, #1382-1383 11.00
Set value 58

Use of Postage Stamps in Indonesia, 125th Anniv. — A360

1989, Apr. 1
1384 A360 1000r grn, rose lilac & deep blue 1.40 70

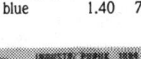

5th Five-year Development Plan — A361

Industries.

1989, Apr. 1
1385 A361 55r Fertilizer 15 15
1386 A361 150r Cilegon Iron and Steel Mill 21 15
1387 A361 350r Petroleum 50 25
Set value 40

See Nos. 1427-1428, 1461-1462, 1488-1489, 1530-1532.

Natl. Education Day — A362

Ki Hadjar Dewantara (b. 1889), founder of Taman Siswa school and: 140r, Graduate. 300r, Pencil, globe and books.

1989, May 2
1388 A362 140r ver, lake & brt rose lil 20 15
1389 A362 300r vio & pale grn 42 20

Terbuka University (140r) and freedom from illiteracy (300r).

Asia-Pacific Telecommunity, 10th Anniv. — A363

Sudirman Cup, Flag — A364

1989, July 1 Photo. *Perf. 12½*
1390 A363 350r grn & vio 50 25

1989, July 3
1391 A364 100r scar, gold & dark red brn 15 15

Sudirman Cup world badminton mixed team championships, Jakarta, May 24-28.

Natl. Children's Day — A365

CIRDAP, 10th Anniv. — A366

1989, July 23
1392 A365 100r Literacy 15 15
1393 A365 250r Physical fitness 35 18
Set value 25

1989, July 29
1394 A366 140r blue & dark red brn 20 15

Center on Integrated Rural Development for Asia and the Pacific.

A367

A368

Paleoanthropological Discoveries in Indonesia: Fossils of *Homo erectus* and *Homo sapiens* men.

1989, Aug. 31
1395 A367 100r Sangiran 17 15 15
1396 A367 150r Perning 1 21 15
1397 A367 200r Sangiran 10 28 15
1398 A367 250r Wajak 1 35 18
1399 A367 300r Sambungmacan 1 42 20
1400 A367 350r Ngandong 7 50 25
Nos. 1395-1400 (6) 1.91 1.08

Nos. 1398-1400 vert.

1989, Sept. 4
1401 A368 350r deep blue & yel grn 50 25

Interparliamentary Union, Cent.

12th Natl. Sports Week — A369

1989, Sept. 18
1402 A369 75r Tae kwando 15 15
1403 A369 100r Tennis 15 15
1404 A369 140r Judo 20 15
1405 A369 350r Volleyball 50 25
1406 A369 500r Boxing 70 35
1407 A369 1000r Archery 1.40 70
Nos. 1402-1407 (6) 3.10
Set value 1.50

Tourism Type of 1987

Structures in Miniature Park: 120r, Taman Burung. 350r, Natl. Philatelic Museum. 500r, Istana Anak-Anak, vert.

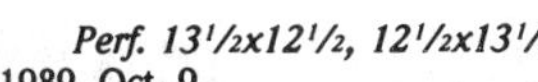
Perf. 13½x12½, 12½x13½

1989, Oct. 9
1408 A339 120r multicolored 17 15
1409 A339 350r multicolored 50 25
1410 A339 500r multicolored 70 35

Film Festival — A370

1989, Nov. 11 Photo. *Perf. 12½*
1411 A370 150r yel bis & blk 15 15

Folk Costumes Type of 1987

Traditional wedding attire from: 50r, North Sumatra. 75r, South Sumatra. 100r, Jakarta. 140r, North Sulawesi. 350r, Mid Sulawesi. 500r, South Sulawesi. 1500r, North Sulawesi.

1989, Dec. 11 *Perf. 13x13½*
1412 A333 50r multicolored 15 15
1413 A333 75r multicolored 15 15
1414 A333 100r multicolored 15 15
1415 A333 140r multicolored 15 15
1416 A333 350r multicolored 35 18
1417 A333 500r multicolored 50 25
Nos. 1412-1417 (6) 1.45 1.03

Souvenir Sheet

Perf. 12½x13½, Imperf.

1418 A333 1500r multicolored 1.50 75

Health and Safety Type of 1988

1990, Jan. 12 *Perf. 13x12½*

Size: 29x21mm

1419 A343 200r Lineman, power lines 20 15

Tourism Type of 1987

Architecture: 200r, Fort Marlborough, Bengkulu. 400r, 1000r, National Museum, Jakarta. 500r, 1500r, Mosque of Baiturrahman, Banda Aceh.

1990, Feb. 1 *Perf. 13½x13*
1420 A339 200r multicolored 20 15
1421 A339 400r multicolored 45 22
1422 A339 500r multicolored 55 28

Souvenir Sheet

1423 Sheet of 2 2.50 1.25
a. A339 1000r multicolored 1.00 50
b. A339 1500r multicolored 1.50 75

Flora A371

1990, Mar. 1
1424 A371 75r Mammilaria fragilis 15 15
1425 A371 1000r Gmelina ellipitca 1.00 50

Souvenir Sheet

1426 A371 1500r like #1425 1.50 75

5th Five-year Development Plan Type of 1989

1990, Apr. 1 *Perf. 12½*
1427 A361 200r Road construction 20 15
1428 A361 1000r Lighthouse, ship 1.00 50

Visit Indonesia Year, 1991 A372

Perf. 13½x12½, 12½x13½

1990, May 1
1429 A372 100r shown 15 15
1430 A372 500r Steps, ruin 50 25

Souvenir Sheet

Perf. 14½x12½

1430A A372 5000r like #1429 5.00 2.50

No. 1430A, Stamp World London '90.

A373

A374

1990, May 18 *Perf. 12½*

1431 A373 1000r gray grn & brn org 1.00 50

Disabled Veterans Corps, 40th anniv.

1990, June 8 *Perf. 12½*

1432 A374 75r shown 15 15
1433 A374 150r multi, diff. 16 15
1434 A374 400r multi, diff. 45 22

Souvenir Sheet

1435 A374 1500r multi 1.50 75

World Cup Soccer Championships, Italy.

Family Planning in Indonesia, 20th Anniv. — A375

1990, June 29

1436 A375 60r brn & red 15 15

Natl. Census — A376

1990, July 1

1437 A376 90r yel grn & dk grn 15 15

Natl. Children's Day — A377

1990, July 23

1438 A377 500r multicolored 55 28

Souvenir Sheet

Traditional Lampung Wedding Costumes — A378

Perf. 12½x14½

1990, June 10 **Photo.**

1439 A378 2000r multicolored 2.00 1.00

Natl. Philatelic Exhibition, Stamp World London '90 and New Zealand '90.

Independence, 45th Anniv. — A379

1990, Aug. 17 *Perf. 12½x13½*

1440 A379 200r Soldier raising flag 35 18
1441 A379 500r Skyscraper, highway 85 42

Souvenir Sheet

1442 A379 1000r like #1442 1.70 85

Indonesia-Pakistan Economic & Cultural Cooperation Organization — A380

Designs: 400r, Woman dancing in traditional costume, vert.

Perf. 13½x12½, 12½x13½

1990, Aug. 19 **Litho.**

1443 A380 75r multicolored 20 15
1444 A380 400r multicolored 1.00 50

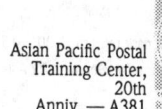

Asian Pacific Postal Training Center, 20th Anniv. — A381

1990, Sept. 10 **Photo.** *Perf. 12½*

1445 A381 500r vio bl, bl & ultra 85 42

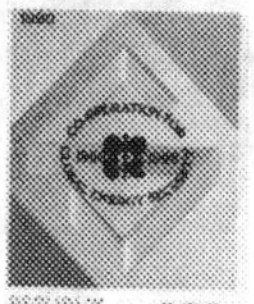

A382

A383

1990, Sept. 14

1446 A382 200r gray, blk & org 36 18

Organization of Petroleum Exporting Countries (OPEC), 30th anniv.

1990, Oct. 24

1447 A383 1000r multicolored 1.70 85

Environmental Protection Laws, 40th anniv.

Folk Costumes Type of 1987

Traditional wedding attire from: 75r, West Java. 100r, Central Java. 150r, Yogyakarta. 200r, East Java. 400r, Bali. 500r, West Nusa Tenggara.

1990, Nov. 1 *Perf. 13x13½*

1448 A333 75r multicolored 15 15
1449 A333 100r multicolored 18 15
1450 A333 150r multicolored 28 15
1451 A333 200r multicolored 36 18
1452 A333 400r multicolored 72 36
1453 A333 500r multicolored 85 42
Nos. 1448-1453 (6) 2.54 1.41

A385

A386

Visit Indonesia Year 1991: Women in traditional costumes.

1991, Jan. 1 **Photo.** *Perf. 12½x13½*

1454 A385 200r multicolored 20 15
1455 A385 500r multicolored 55 28
1456 A385 1000r multicolored 1.00 50

1991, Feb. 4 *Perf. 12½*

1457 A386 200r yel, grn & bl grn 20 15

16th natl. Koran reading competition, Jogjakarta.

Palace of Sultan Ternate, the Moluccas A387

Design: 1000r, 2500r, Bari House, Palembang, South Sumatra.

1991, Mar. 1 *Perf. 13½x12½*

1458 A387 500r multicolored 50 25
1459 A387 1000r multicolored 1.00 50

Souvenir Sheet

1460 A387 2500r multicolored 2.50 1.25

5th Five Year Development Plan Type of 1989

1991, Apr. 1 *Perf. 12½*

1461 A361 75r Steel mill, vert. 15 15
1462 A361 200r Computers 20 15
Set value 28 15

Danger of Smoking — A388

1991, May 31 **Photo.** *Perf. 12½*

1463 A388 90r multicolored 15 15

Folk Costumes Type of 1987

Traditional wedding attire from: 100r, West Kalimantan. 200r, Mid Kalimantan. 300r, South Kalimantan. 400r, Southeast Sulawesi. 500r, Riau. 1000r, Irian Jaya.

1991, June 15 *Perf. 13x13½*

1464 A333 100r multicolored 15 15
1465 A333 200r multicolored 20 15
1466 A333 300r multicolored 30 15
1467 A333 400r multicolored 40 20
1468 A333 500r multicolored 50 25
1469 A333 1000r multicolored 1.00 50
Nos. 1464-1469 (6) 2.55
Set value 1.25

Natl. Scouting Jamboree, Cibubur A389

Monument A390

1991, June 15 *Perf. 12½*

1470 A389 200r multicolored 20 15

1991, July 6

1471 A390 200r multicolored 20 15

Natl. Farmers' Week — A391

Indonesian Chemical Society, 4th Natl. Congress — A392

1991, July 15

1472 A391 500r brt bl, yel & grn 50 25

1991, July 28

1473 A392 400r grn, ver & dull grn 40 20

Chemindo '91.

A393

A394

1991, Aug. 24 **Photo.** *Perf. 12½*

1474 A393 300r blk, red & gray 55 28

5th Junior Men's and 4th Women's Asian Weightlifting Championships.

1991, Aug. 30

1475 A394 500r lilac & sky blue 85 42

World Cup Parachuting Championships.

A395

A396

1991, Sept. 17

1476 A395 200r multicolored 36 18

Indonesian Red Cross, 46th aAnniv.

1991, Oct. 6

1477 A396 300r yellow & blue 55 28

Intl. Amateur Radio Union, 8th regional conf., Bandung.

Istiqlal Festival, Jakarta — A397

1991, Oct. 15
1478 A397 200r gray, blk & ver 35 18

Intl. Conference on the Great Apes — A398

Pongo pygmaeus: 200r, Sitting in tree. 500r, Walking. 1000r, 2500r, Sitting on ground.

1991, Dec. 18 ***Perf. 12½x13½***
1479 A398 200r multicolored 35 18
1480 A398 500r multicolored 85 42
1481 A398 1000r multicolored 1.70 85

Souvenir Sheet

1481A A398 2500r multicolored 2.50 1.25

Intl. Convention on Quality Control Circles, Bali — A399

1991, Oct. 22 ***Perf. 12½***
1482 A399 500r multicolored 85 42

Automation of the Post Office A400

Designs: 200r, Post Office. 500r, Mail sorting equipment.

1992, Jan. 9 Photo. ***Perf. 13½x13***
1483 A400 200r multicolored 24 15
1484 A400 500r multicolored 58 28

National Elections — A401

1992, Feb. 10 ***Perf. 12½***
1485 A401 75r shown 15 15
1486 A401 100r Ballot boxes, globe 15 15
1487 A401 500r Hands dropping ballots in ballot boxes 58 28
Set value 42

5th Five-year Development Plan Type of 1989

1992, Apr. 1 Photo. ***Perf. 12½***
1488 A361 150r Construction worker 18 15
1489 A361 300r Aviation technology 35 18
Set value 27

Visit Asia Year, 1992 A402

1992, Mar. 1 ***Perf. 13½x13***
1490 A402 300r Lembah Baliem, Irian Jaya 35 18
1491 A402 500r Tanah Lot, Bali 58 30
1492 A402 1000r Lombah Anai, Sumatra Barat 1.18 58

Souvenir Sheet

1493 A402 3000r like #1491 3.50 1.75

Birds — A403

1992, July 1 Photo. ***Perf. 12½x13½***
1494 A403 100r Garrulax leucolophus 15 15
1495 A403 200r Dinopium javanense 25 15
1496 A403 400r Buceros rhinoceros 48 24
1497 A403 500r Alisterus amboinensis 60 30
Set value 72

Souvenir Sheet

1498 A403 3000r like #1494 3.50 1.75

Children's Day — A404

Designs: 75r, Street scene. 100r, Children with balloons. 200r, Boating scene. 500r, Girl feeding bird.

1992, July 23 ***Perf. 12½***
1499 A404 75r multicolored 15 15
1500 A404 100r multicolored 15 15
1501 A404 200r multicolored 25 15
1502 A404 500r multicolored 60 30
Set value 53

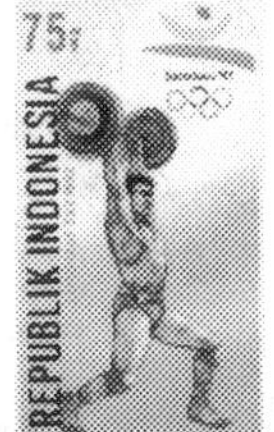

1992 Summer Olympics, Barcelona — A405

Designs: No. 1508a, 2000r, like #1504. b, 3000r, like #1507.

1992, June 1 ***Perf. 12½x13½***
1503 A405 75r Weight lifting 15 15
1504 A405 200r Badminton 24 15
1505 A405 300r Symbols of events 35 18
1506 A405 500r Women's tennis 60 30
1507 A405 1000r Archery 1.20 60
Nos. 1503-1507 (5) 2.54
Set value 1.22

Souvenir Sheet

1508 A405 Sheet of 2, #a.-b. 7.25 3.75

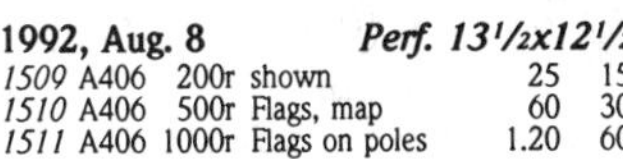

ASEAN, 25th Anniv. A406

1992, Aug. 8 ***Perf. 13½x12½***
1509 A406 200r shown 25 15
1510 A406 500r Flags, map 60 30
1511 A406 1000r Flags on poles 1.20 60

Flowers A407

Designs: 200r, Phalaenopsis ambilis. 500r, Rafflesia arnoldii. 1000r, 2000r, Jasminum sambae.

Perf. 13½x12½

1992, Jan. 20 Photo.
1512 A407 200r multicolored 25 15
1513 A407 500r multicolored 60 30
1514 A407 1000r multicolored 1.20 60

Perf. 13½x13

Souvenir Sheet

1515 A408 2000r multicolored 3.75 1.90

A408 A409

Perf. 12½x13½

1992, Sept. 6 Photo.
1516 A408 200r shown 25 15
1517 A408 500r Flags, emblem 60 30

10th Non-Aligned Summit, Jakarta.

1992, Nov. 29 Photo. ***Perf. 12½***
1518 A409 200r green & blue 25 15

Intl. Planned Parenthood Federation, 40th anniv.

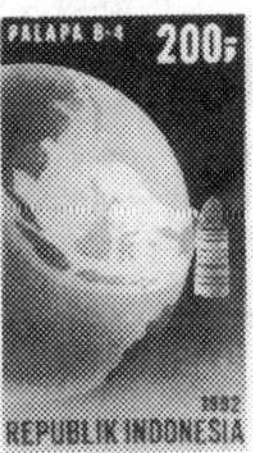

A410 A411

Perf. 12½x13½

1992, Aug. 16 Photo.
1519 A410 200r Globe, satellite 25 15
1520 A410 500r Palapa satellite 60 30
1521 A410 1000r Old, new telephones 1.20 60

Satellite Communications in Indonesia, 16th anniv.

1992 ***Perf. 12½x13½***

Traditional Dances: 200r, 3000r, Tari Ngremo, Timor. 500r, Tari Gending Sriwijaya, Sumatra.

1522 A411 200r multicolored 25 15
1523 A411 500r multicolored 60 30

Souvenir Sheet

1524 A411 3000r like #1518 3.50 1.75

See Nos. 1564-1567.

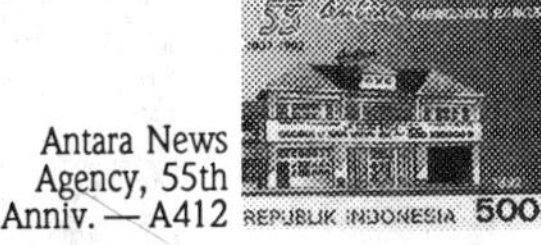

Antara News Agency, 55th Anniv. — A412

1992, Dec. 13 Photo. ***Perf. 12½***
1525 A412 500r blue & black 25 15

Natl. Afforestation Campaign — A413

Perf. 13½x12½

1992, Dec. 24 Photo.
1526 A413 500r multicolored 60 30

No. 1260 Surcharged 50r =

1993, Feb. 1 Photo. ***Perf. 13½x12½***
1527 A246 50r on 55r #1260 15 15

1993 General Session of the People's Consultative Assembly A414

Perf. 13½x12½

1993, Mar. 1 Photo.
1528 A414 300r Building exterior 35 18
1529 A414 700r Building interior 80 40

5th Five Year Development Plan Type of 1989

Designs: 300r, Soldier's silhouettes over city. 700r, Immunizing children. 1000r, Runners.

1993, Apr. 1 ***Perf. 12½***
1530 A361 300r multicolored 35 16
1531 A361 700r multicolored 80 40
1532 A361 1000r multicolored 1.15 58

Ornithoptera Goliath — A415

1993, Apr. 20 Photo. ***Perf. 12½***
1533 A415 1000r multicolored 1.15 58

For overprint see No. 1540.

Surabaja, 700th Anniv. A416

Designs: 300r, Siege of Yamato Hotel. 700r, World Habitat Award, Surabaya skyline. 1000r, Candi Bajang Ratu, natl. monument.

Perf. 13½x12½

1993, May 29 Photo.
1534 A416 300r multicolored 35 16
1535 A416 700r multicolored 78 40
1536 A416 1000r multicolored 1.15 58

For overprints see Nos. 1538-1539, 1541.

Nos. 1533-1536 Ovptd. in Red

and

Indopex '93 — A417

1993 ***Perfs. as Before***
1538 A416 300r on #1534 35 16
1539 A416 700r on #1535 78 40
1540 A415 1000r on #1533 1.15 58
1541 A416 1000r on #1536 1.15 58

Souvenir Sheet
Perf. 13½x12½
1542 A417 3500r multicolored 4.00 2.00

Location of overprint varies. Issued: No. 1540, Apr. 20; others, May 29.

Environmental Protection — A418

Flowers: Nos. 1543a, 1545a, Jasminum sambac. No. 1543b, Phalaenopsis amabilis. No. 1543c, Rafflesia arnoldi.
Wildlife: Nos. 1544a, 1545b, Varanus komodoensis. No. 1544b, Scleropages formasus. No. 1544c, Spizaetus bartelsi.

Perf. 12½x13½
1993, June 5 **Photo.**
1543 A418 300r Triptych, #a.-c. 1.05 52
1544 A418 700r Triptych, #a.-c. 2.40 1.20

Souvenir Sheet
1545 A418 1500r Sheet of 2, #a.-b. 3.50 1.75

1st World Community Development Camp — A419

Designs: 300r, Boy scouts working on road. 700r, Pres. Suharto shaking hands with scout.

Perf. 13½x12½
1993, July 27 **Photo.**
1546 A419 300r multicolored 32 18
1547 A419 700r multicolored 80 40

Papilio Blumei — A420

Armed Forces Day — A421

Perf. 12½x13½
1993, Aug. 24 **Photo.**
1548 A420 700r multicolored 80 40

Souvenir Sheets
1549 A420 3000r multicolored 3.50 1.75
1550 A420 3000r multicolored 3.50 1.75

Inscription at top of No. 1549 is like that on No. 1548. No. 1550 contains a stamp inscribed "1993," a se-tenant label and Bangkok '93 Philatelic Exhibition inscription in sheet margin.

1993, Oct. 5 ***Perf. 12½***
1551 A421 300r Soedirman 35 18
1552 A421 300r Oerip Soemohardjo 35 18
a. Pair, #1551-1552 70 38

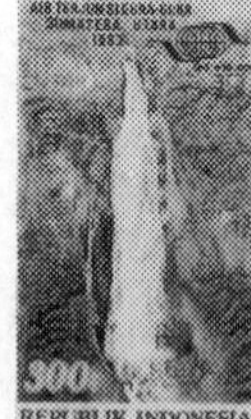

Tourism — A422

13th Natl. Sports Week — A423

Designs: 300r, 3000r, Waterfall. 700r, Cave formations. 1000r, Dormant volcanic crater, horiz.

Perf. 12½x13½, 13½x12½
1993, Oct. 4
1553 A422 300r multicolored 35 18
1554 A422 700r multicolored 80 40
1555 A422 1000r multicolored 1.15 60

Souvenir Sheet
1556 A422 3000r multicolored 3.50 1.75

1993, Sept. 9 ***Perf. 12½x13½***
1557 A423 150r Swimming 16 15
1558 A423 300r Cycling 35 16
1559 A423 700r Mascot 80 40
1560 A423 1000r High jump 1.10 55

Souvenir Sheet
1561 A423 3500r like No. 1560 4.00 2.00

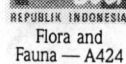

Flora and Fauna — A424

Migratory Farm Workers — A425

Designs: a, Michelia champaca. b, Cananga odorata. c, Copsychus pyrropygus. d, Gracula religiosa robusta.

Perf. 12½x13½
1993, Nov. 5 **Photo.**
1562 A424 300r Block of 4, #a.-d. 1.10 55

1993, Dec. 4 ***Perf. 12½***
1563 A425 700r Field workers 80 40

Traditional Dance Type of 1992

Dance and region: 300r, Gending Sriwijaya, South Sumatra. 700r, Tempayan, West Kalimantan. 1000r, 3500r, Tifa, Irian Jaya.

1993, Dec. 22 ***Perf. 12½x13½***
1564 A411 300r multicolored 32 16
1565 A411 700r multicolored 75 38
1566 A411 1000r multicolored 1.10 55

Souvenir Sheet
1567 A411 3500r multicolored 3.75 1.90

SEMI-POSTAL STAMPS

Symbols of Olympic Games — SP43

Wings and Flame — SP44

Perf. 12½x12
1951, Jan. 2 **Photo.** **Unwmk.**
B58 SP43 5s + 3s gray grn 15 15
B59 SP43 10s + 5s dk vio bl 15 15
B60 SP43 20s + 5s org red 15 15
B61 SP43 30s + 10s dk brn 30 30
B62 SP43 35s + 10s ultra 1.25 1.25
Set value 1.70 1.70

Issued to publicize the Asiatic Olympic Games of 1951 at New Delhi, India.

1951, Oct. 15
B63 SP44 5s + 3s olive green 15 15
B64 SP44 10s + 5s dull blue 15 15
B65 SP44 20s + 5s red 15 15
B66 SP44 30s + 10s brown 15 15
B67 SP44 35s + 10s ultra 15 15
Set value 35 30

Issued to publicize the second National Games, Djakarta, October 21-28, 1951.

19 53
BENTJANA ALAM
+10s

No. 378 Surcharged in Black

1953, May 8 ***Perf. 12½***
B68 A53 35s + 10s purple 15 15

The surcharge reads "Natural Disaster." Surtax was for emergency relief following volcanic eruption and floods.

Merapi Erupting SP45

Young Musicians SP46

1954, Apr. 15 **Litho.** ***Perf. 12½x12***
B69 SP45 15s + 10s bl grn 15 15
B70 SP45 35s + 15s pur 15 15
B71 SP45 50s + 25s red 15 15
B72 SP45 75s + 25s vio bl 18 15
B73 SP45 1r + 25s car 30 22
B74 SP45 2r + 50s blk brn 60 50
B75 SP45 3r + 1r gray grn 7.75 3.75
B76 SP45 5r + 2.50r org brn 11.00 5.50
Nos. B69-B76 (8) 20.28 10.57

The surtax was for victims of the Merapi volcano eruption.

1954, Dec. 22 **Photo.** ***Perf. 12½***

Designs: 15s+10s, Parasol dance. 35s+15s, Girls playing dakon. 50s+15s, Boy on stilts. 75s+25s, Bamboo flute players. 1r+25s, Javanese dancer.

B77 SP46 10s + 10s dk pur 15 15
B78 SP46 15s + 10s dk grn 15 15
B79 SP46 35s + 15s car rose 15 15
B80 SP46 50s + 15s rose brn 15 15
B81 SP46 75s + 25s ultra 15 15
B82 SP46 1r + 25s red org 15 15
Set value 40 40

The surtax was for child welfare.

Scout Emblem SP47

Scout Signaling SP48

Designs: 50s+25s, Campfire. 75s+25s, Scout feeding fawn. 1r+50s, Scout saluting.

1955, June 27 **Unwmk.** ***Perf. 12½***
B83 SP47 15s + 10s bl grn 15 15
B84 SP48 35s + 15s ultra 15 15
B85 SP48 50s + 25s scar 15 15
B86 SP48 75s + 25s brn 15 15
B87 SP48 1r + 50s vio 15 15
Set value 38 30

First National Boy Scout Jamboree.

Blind Weaver — SP49

Red Cross and Heart — SP50

Designs: 35s+15s, Basket weaver. 50s+25s, Boy studying map. 75s+50s, Woman reading Braille.

1956, Jan. 4
B88 SP49 15s + 10s dp grn 15 15
B89 SP49 35s + 15s yel brn 15 15
B90 SP49 50s + 25s rose car 40 25
B91 SP49 75s + 50s ultra 20 18
Set value 70 52

The surtax was for the benefit of the blind.

1956, July 26 **Litho.**

Designs: 35s+15s, 50s+15s, Transfusion bottle. 75s+25s, 1r+25s, Outstretched hands.

Cross in Red
B92 SP50 10s + 10s ultra 15 15
B93 SP50 15s + 10s car 15 15
B94 SP50 35s + 15s lt brn 15 15
B95 SP50 50s + 15s bl grn 15 15
B96 SP50 75s + 25s org 15 15
B97 SP50 1r + 25s brt pur 15 15
Set value 45 45

Surtax for the Indonesian Red Cross.

Invalids Doing Batik Work — SP51

Designs: 15s+10s, Amputee painting. 35s+15s, Lathe operator. 50s+15s, Crippled child learning to walk. 75s+25s, Treating amputee. 1r+25s, Painting with artificial hand.

1957, Mar. 26 **Photo.** ***Perf. 12½***
B98 SP51 10s + 10s dp bl 15 15
B99 SP51 15s + 10s brn 15 15
B100 SP51 35s + 15s red 15 15
B101 SP51 50s + 15s dp vio 15 15
B102 SP51 75s + 25s grn 15 15
B103 SP51 1r + 25s dk car rose 15 15
Set value 45 45

The surtax was for rehabilitation of invalids.

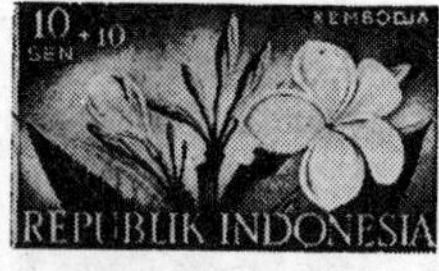

Kembodja Flower SP52

Designs: 15s+10s, Michelia. 35s+15s, Sunflower. 50s+15s, Jasmine. 75s+50s, Orchid.

1957, Dec. 23 ***Perf. 13½x12½***
Flowers in Natural Colors
B104 SP52 10s + 10s bl 35 20
B105 SP52 15s + 10s dp yel grn 30 20
B106 SP52 35s + 15s dk red brn 15 15
B107 SP52 50s + 15s ol & dk brn 15 15
B108 SP52 75s + 60s rose brn 15 15
Nos. B104-B108 (5) 1.10 85

Children SP53

Indonesian Scout Emblem SP54

Design: 15s+10s, 50s+25s, 1r+50s, Girl and boy.

1958, July 1 Photo. *Perf. 12½x12*

B109 SP53 10s + 10s blue 15 15
B110 SP53 15s + 10s rose brown 15 15
B111 SP53 35s + 15s gray green 15 15
B112 SP53 50s + 25s gray olive 16 16
B113 SP53 75s + 50s brn car 20 20
B114 SP53 1r + 50s brown 25 25
Set value 85 85

The surtax was for orphans.

1959, July 17 Photo. Unwmk.

Design: 15s + 10s, 50s + 25s, 1r + 50s, Scout emblem and compass.

Emblem in Red

B115 SP54 10s + 5s bister 15 15
B116 SP54 15s + 10s bluish grn 15 15
B117 SP54 20s + 10s lilac gray 15 15
B118 SP54 50s + 25s olive 15 15
B119 SP54 75s + 35s yel brn 15 15
B120 SP54 1r + 50s dark gray 15 15
Set value 45 45

10th World Scout Jamboree, Makiling National Park near Manila, July 17-26.

Palm-leaf Ribs, Gong and 5 Rings — SP55

Young Couple Holding Sharpened Bamboo Weapon — SP56

Design: 20s+10s, 75s+35s, Bamboo musical instrument and 5-ring emblem.

1960, Feb. 14 *Perf. 12½x12*

B121 SP55 15s + 5s bis & dk brn 15 15
B122 SP55 20s + 10s grn & blk 15 15
B123 SP55 50s + 25s bl & pur 15 15
B124 SP55 75s + 35s ol & dk grn 15 15
B125 SP56 1.15r + 50s car & blk 15 15
Set value 30 26

Issued to commemorate the All-Indonesian Youth Congress, Bandung, Feb. 14-21, 1960.

Social Emblem SP57

Pineapple SP58

Designs: 15s+15s, Rice, lotus and cotton. 20s+20s, Lotus blossom and tree. 50s+25s, Girl and boy. 75s+25s, Watering of plant in man's hand. 3r+50s, Woman nursing infant.

Perf. 12½x12

1960, Dec. 20 Photo. Unwmk.

Inscribed: "Hari Sosial Ke III"

B126 SP57 10s + 10s ocher & blk 15 15
B127 SP57 15s + 15s dp cl & blk 15 15
B128 SP57 20s + 20s bl & blk 15 15
B129 SP57 50s + 25s bis brn & blk 15 15
B130 SP57 75s + 25s emer & blk 15 15
B131 SP57 3r + 50s red & blk 15 15
Set value 45 38

3rd Social Day, Dec. 20.

Type of 1960 Surcharges: "BENTJANA ALAM 1961"

Designs: 15s+10s, Coffee. 20s+15s, Tobacco. 75s+25s, Rubber plantation.

1961, Feb. 17 *Perf. 12x12½*

B132 A76 15s + 10s plum 15 15
B133 A76 20s + 15s ocher 15 15
B134 A76 75s + 25s scarlet 15 15
Set value 18 15

The surtax was for flood relief.

1961, Dec. 20 *Perf. 12½x13½*

4th Social Day: 75s+25s, Mangosteen. 3r+1r, Rambutan.

B135 SP58 20s + 10s bl, yel & red 15 15
B136 SP58 75s + 25s gray, grn & dp claret 15 15
B137 SP58 3r + 1r grn, yel & red 30 15
Set value 47 25

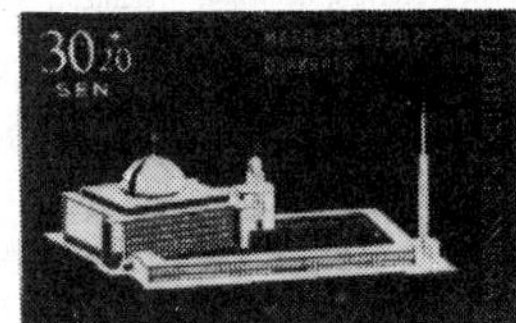

Istiqlal Mosque, Djakarta — SP59

Designs: 40s+20s, 3r+1r, Different view of mosque.

1962, Feb. 22 *Perf. 12½x12*

B138 SP59 30s + 20s Prus grn & yel 15 15
B139 SP59 40s + 20s dk red & yel 15 15
B140 SP59 1.50r + 50s brn & yel 15 15
B141 SP59 3r + 1r grn & yel 16 15
Set value 40 27

Issued for the benefit of the new Istiqlal Mosque.

National Monument, Djakarta — SP60

Design: 1.50r+50s, 6r+1.50r, Aerial view of monument.

1962, May 20 Photo. *Perf. 12x12½*

B142 SP60 1r + 50s org brn & blk 15 15
B143 SP60 1.50r + 50s ol grn & ultra 15 15
B144 SP60 3r + 1r lil rose & dk grn 15 15
B145 SP60 6r + 1.50r vio bl & red 15 15
Set value 27 27

Vanda Tricolor SP61

Orchids: 1.50r+50s, Phalaenopsis amabilis, vert. 3r+1r, Dendrobium phalaenopsis, vert. 6r+1.50r, Paphiopedilum praestans.

Perf. 13½x12½, 12½x13½

1962, Dec. 20 Unwmk.

Orchids in Natural Colors

B146 SP61 1r + 50s ultra & yel 15 15
B147 SP61 1.50r + 50s grnsh bl & ver 15 15
B148 SP61 3r + 1r dp bl & ocher 15 15
B149 SP61 6r + 1.50r org & dl vio 15 15
Set value 28 22

Issued for the 5th Social Day.

West Irian Monument, Djakarta — SP62

1963, Feb. 15 *Perf. 12½x13½*

B150 SP62 1r + 50s rose red & blk 15 15
B151 SP62 1.50r + 50s mag & dk brn 15 15
B152 SP62 3r + 1r bl & dk brn 15 15
B153 SP62 6r + 1.50r grn & brn 15 15
Set value 30 22

The surtax was for the construction of the West Irian Monument in Djakarta.

Erupting Volcano SP63

1963, June 29 Photo. *Perf. 13½x13*

B154 SP63 4r + 2r rose red 15 15
B155 SP63 6r + 3r grnsh bl 15 15
Set value 17 19

The surtax was for victims of national natural disasters.

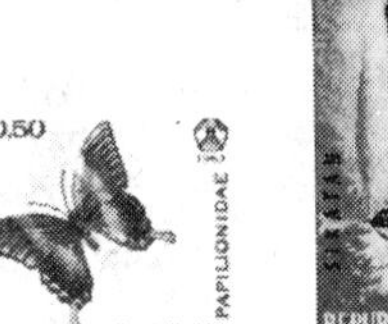

Papilio Blumei, Celebes — SP64

Malaysian Fantails — SP65

Butterflies: 4r+1r, Charaxes Dehaani, Java. 6r+1.50r, Graphium, West Irian. 12r+3r, Troides Amphrysus, Sumatra.

1963, Dec. 20 *Perf. 12x12½*

B156 SP64 1.75r + 50s multi 15 15
B157 SP64 4r + 1r multi 15 15
B158 SP64 6r + 1.50r multi 15 15
B159 SP64 12r + 3r multi 15 15
Set value 25 22

Issued for the 6th Social Day.

Perf. 12½x13½

1965, Jan. 25 Photo. Unwmk.

Birds: 6r+1.50r, Zebra doves. 12r+3r, Black drongos. 20r+5r, Black-naped orioles. 30r+7.50r, Javanese sparrows.

B160 SP65 4r + 1r dl yel, lil & blk 15 15
B161 SP65 6r + 1.50 grn, blk & pink 15 15
B162 SP65 12r + 3r ol & blk 15 15
B163 SP65 20r + 5r gray, yel & red 15 15
B164 SP65 30r + 7.50r car rose, sl bl & blk 15 15
Set value 35 32

Issued for the 7th Social Day.

Type of Regular Issue, 1964, Inscribed Vertically "Conefo"

1965 *Perf. 12½x12*

B165 A98 1r + 1r org red & brn 15 15
B166 A98 1.25r + 1.25r org red & brn 15 15
B167 A98 1.75r + 1.75r org, red & brn blk 15 15
B168 A98 2r + 2r org red & sl grn 15 15
B169 A98 2.50r + 2.50r org red & red brn 15 15
B170 A98 4r + 3.50r org red & dp bl 15 15
B171 A98 6r + 4r org red & emer 15 15
B172 A98 10r + 5r org red & yel grn 15 15
B173 A98 12r + 5.50r org red & org 15 15
B174 A98 15r + 7.50r org red & bl grn 15 15
B175 A98 20r + 10r org red & dk gray 15 15
B176 A98 25r + 10r org red & pur 15 15
B177 A98 40r + 15r ver & plum 15 15
B178 A98 50r + 15r org red & dp vio 15 15
B179 A98 100r + 25r org red & dk ol gray 15 15
Set value 50 50

Conference of New Emerging Forces.

Makara Mask and Magic Rays — SP66

1965, July 17 *Perf. 12*

B180 SP66 20r + 10r red & dk bl 15 15
B181 SP66 30r + 15r bl & dk red 15 15
Set value 15 15

Issued to publicize the fight against cancer.

Family and Produce — SP67

State Principles: 20r+10r, Humanitarianism; clasped hands, globe, flags and chain. 25r+10r, Nationalism; map of Indonesia and tree. 40r+15r, Democracy; conference and bull's head. 50r+15r, Belief in God; houses of worship and star.

1965, Aug. 17 Photo. *Perf. 12½*

B182 SP67 10r + 5r fawn, yel & blk 15 15
B183 SP67 20r + 10r dp yel, red & blk 15 15
B184 SP67 25r + 10r rose red, red, grn & blk 15 15
B185 SP67 40r + 15r bl, red & blk 15 15
B186 SP67 50r + 15r lil, yel & blk 15 15
Set value 25 25

Samudra Beach Hotel and Pres. Sukarno — SP68

Designs: 25r+10r, 80r+20r, Ambarrukmo Palace Hotel and Pres. Sukarno.

1965, Dec. 1 Photo. *Perf. 12½*

B187 SP68 10r + 5r dk bl & lt bl grn 15 15
B188 SP68 25r + 10r vio blk & yel grn 15 15
B189 SP68 40r + 15r dk brn & vio bl 15 15
B190 SP68 80r + 20r dk pur & org 15 15
Set value 24 24

Issued for tourist publicity.

Gloriosa — SP69

Flowers: 40r+15r, Magaguabush. 80r+20r, Balsam. 100r+25r, Crape myrtle.

1965, Dec. 20 Photo. *Perf. 12*

Flowers in Natural Colors

B191 SP69 30r + 10r dp bl 15 15
B192 SP69 40r + 15r dp bl 15 15
B193 SP69 80r + 20r dp bl 15 15
B194 SP69 100r + 25r dp bl 15 15
Set value 27 22

Dated "1966"

Flowers: 10s+5s, Senna. 20s+5s, Crested barleria. 30s+10s, Scarlet ixora. 40s+10s, Rose of China (hibiscus).

1966, Feb. 10

Flowers in Natural Colors

B195 SP69 10s + 5s Prus bl 15 15
B196 SP69 20s + 5s grn 15 15
B197 SP69 30s + 10s grn 15 15
B198 SP69 40s + 10s Prus bl 15 15
Set value 22 22

Nos. B191-B198 issued for the 8th Social Day, Dec. 20, 1965. An imperf. souvenir sheet contains one No. B198. Size: 58x78mm.

Type of 1965 Inscribed: "BENTJANA ALAM / NASIONAL 1966"

Flowers: 15s+5s, Gloriosa. 25s+5s, Magaguabush. 30s+10s, Balsam. 80s+20s, Crape myrtle.

1966, May 2

Flowers in Natural Colors

B199 SP69 15s + 5s blue 15 15
B200 SP69 25s + 5s dk bl 15 15
B201 SP69 30s + 10s dk bl 15 15
B202 SP69 80s + 20s lt bl 15 15
Set value 30 28

The surtax was for victims of national natural disasters.

Reticulated Python — SP70

Reptiles: 3r+50s, Bloodsucker. 4r+75s. Salt-water crocodile. 6r+1r, Hawksbill turtle (incorrectly inscribed *chelonia mydas*, "green turtle").

1966, Dec. 20 Photo. *Perf. 12½x12*

B203 SP70 2r + 25s multi 15 15
B204 SP70 3r + 50s multi 15 15
B205 SP70 4r + 75s multi 15 15
B206 SP70 6r + 1r multi 15 15
Set value 28 28

Flooded Village — SP71

Buddha & Stupa, Borobudur Temple — SP72

Designs: 2.50r+25s, Landslide. 4r+40s, Fire destroying village. 5r+50s, Erupting volcano.

1967, Dec. 20 Photo. *Perf. 12½*

B207 SP71 1.25r + 10s dl vio bl & yel 15 15
B208 SP71 2.50r + 25s dl vio bl & yel 15 15
B209 SP71 4r + 40s dp org & blk 15 15
B210 SP71 5r + 50s dp org & blk 15 15
a. Souv. sheet of 2, #B209-B210 14.00 12.00
Set value 35 35

Surtax for victims of natl. natural disasters.

1968, Mar. 1 Photo. *Perf. 12½*

Designs: No. B211, Musicians. No. B212, Sudhana and Princess Manohara. No. B213, Procession with elephant and horses.

B211 SP72 2.50r + 25s brt grn & gray ol 15 15
B212 SP72 2.50r + 25s brt grn & gray ol 15 15
B213 SP72 2.50r + 25s brt grn & gray ol 15 15
a. Souv. sheet of 3, #B211-B213 11.00 10.00
b. Strip of 3, #B211-B213 30 30
B214 SP72 7.50r + 75s org & gray ol 15 15
Set value 40 40

The surtax was to help save Borobudur Temple in Central Java, c. 800 A.D.

Nos. B211-B213 were printed se-tenant in same sheet. Continuous design shows a frieze from Borobudur.

Scout with Pickax — SP73

Designs: 10r+1r, Bugler. 30r+3r, Scouts singing around campfire, horiz.

1968, June 1 Photo. *Perf. 12½*

Size: 28½x44½mm

B215 SP73 5r + 50 dp org & brn 15 15
B216 SP73 10r + 1r brn & gray ol 20 15

Size: 68x28½mm

B217 SP73 30r + 3r ol gray & grn 45 42

Surtax for Wirakarya Scout Camp.

Woman with Flower SP74

1969, Apr. 21 *Perf. 13½x12½*

B218 SP74 20r + 2r emer, red & yel 40 20

Emancipation of Indonesian women.

Noble Voluta — SP75

Sea shells: 7.50r+50s, Common hairy triton. 10r+1r, Spider conch. 15r+1.50r, Murex ternispina.

1969, Dec. 20 Photo. *Perf. 12½*

B219 SP75 5r + 50s multi 15 15
B220 SP75 7.50r + 50s multi 15 15
B221 SP75 10r + 1r multi 15 15
B222 SP75 15r + 1.50r multi 18 15
Set value 42 34

Issued for the 12th Social Day, Dec. 20.

Chrysocoris Javanus — SP76

Fight Against Cancer — SP77

Insects: 15r+1.50r, Dragonfly. 20r+2r, Carpenter bee.

1970, Dec. 21 Photo. *Perf. 12½*

B223 SP76 7.50r + 50c multi *1.25* 15
B224 SP76 15r + 1.50r multi *3.25* 15
B225 SP76 20r + 2r multi *4.00* 15
Set value 15

The 13th Social Day, Dec. 20.

1983, July 1 Photo. *Perf. 12½*

Patient receiving radiation treatment, Jakarta Hospital.

B226 SP77 55r + 20r multi 15 15
B227 SP77 75r + 25r multi 15 15
Set value 24 15

Children's Day — SP78

Children's Drawings. Surtax was for Children's Palace building fund.

1984, June 17 Photo. *Perf. 13½x13*

B228 SP78 75r + 25r multi 15 15
B229 SP78 110r + 25r multi 18 15
B230 SP78 175r + 25r multi 25 15
B231 SP78 275r + 25r multi 40 20
a. Souv. sheet of 2, #B230-B231 80 40
b. Souv. sheet of 4 + 2 labels 1.60 80
Set value 50

AUSIPEX '84. No. B231b for FILACENTO '84, Netherlands, Sept. 6-9.

SP79

SP80

1987, May 12 Photo. *Perf. 12½*

B232 SP79 350r +25r dark ultra & yel 50 25

Yayasan Cancer Medical Assoc., 10th anniv.

1991, June 1 Photo. *Perf. 12½*

B233 SP80 200r +25r multi 28 15

Natl. Fed. for Welfare of Mentally Handicapped, 24th anniv.

Yayasan Cancer Medical Assoc., 15th Anniv. — SP81

1992, May 12 Photo. *Perf. 12½*

B234 SP81 200r +25r brown & mag 28 15
B235 SP81 500r +50r blue & mag 70 35

SPECIAL DELIVERY STAMPS

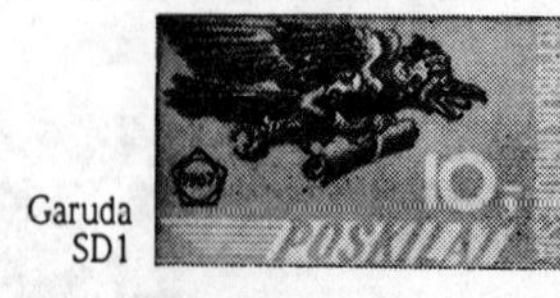

Garuda SD1

Perf. 13½x12½

1967 Unwmk. Photo.

E1 SD1 10r lt ultra & dl pur 16 15
E2 SD1 15r org & dl pur 40 20
Set value 27

Inscribed "1968"

1968

E3 SD1 10r lt ultra & dl pur 15 15
E4 SD1 15r org & dl pur 16 15
E5 SD1 20r yel & dl pur 18 16
E6 SD1 30r brt grn & dl pur 25 25
E7 SD1 40r lil & dl pur 35 35
Nos. E3-E7 (5) 1.09 1.06

Same Inscribed "1969"

1969

E8 SD1 20r yel & dl pur 25 15
E9 SD1 30r brt grn & dl pur 35 20
E10 SD1 40r lil & dl pur 42 25

POSTAGE DUE STAMPS

Netherlands Indies Nos. J57 to J59 Surcharged in Black

BAJAR
2½
sen
PORTO

1950 Wmk. 228 *Perf. 14½x14*

J60 D7 2½s on 50c yellow 38 25
J61 D7 5s on 100c ap grn 75 65
J62 D7 10s on 75c aqua 1.00 75

D8

Perf. 12½

1951-52 Wmk. 228 Litho.

J63 D8 2½s vermilion 15 15
J64 D8 5s vermilion 15 15
J65 D8 10s vermilion 15 15
J66 D8 20s bl ('52) 16 15
J67 D8 25s ol bis ('52) 65 50
J68 D8 50s vermilion 6.50 4.25
J69 D8 1r citron 6.50 3.75
Nos. J63-J69 (7) 14.26 9.10

1953-55 Unwmk.

J70 D8 15s lt mag ('55) 15 15
J71 D8 30s red brn 15 15
J72 D8 40s green 15 15
Set value 38 29

1958-61 *Perf. 13½x12½*

J73 D8 10s orange 15 15
J74 D8 15s org ('59) 15 15
J74A D8 20s org ('61) 15 15
J75 D8 25s org 15 15
J76 D8 30s org ('60) 15 15
J77 D8 50s orange 1.40 38
J78 D8 100s org ('60) 65 15
Set value 2.50 75

1962-65 *Perf. 13½x12½*

J79 D8 50s lt bluish grn 15 15
J80 D8 100s bister 15 15
J81 D8 250s blue 15 15
J82 D8 500s dull yel 15 15
J83 D8 750s pale lilac 15 15
J84 D8 1000s salmon 15 15
J85 D8 50r red ('65) 15 15
J86 D8 100r maroon ('65) 15 15
Set value 45 45

"1966" — D9

1966-67 Unwmk. Photo.

J91 D9 5s dl grn & dl yel 15 15
J92 D9 10s red & lt bl 15 15
J93 D9 20s dk bl & pink 15 15
J94 D9 30s brn & rose 15 15
J95 D9 40s plum & bis 15 15
J96 D9 50s ol grn & pale lil 15 15
J97 D9 100s dk red & yel grn 15 15
J98 D9 200s brt grn & pink ('67) 15 15
J99 D9 500s yel & lt bl ('67) 15 15
J100 D9 1000s rose lil & yel ('67) 22 15
Set value 80 60

Dated "1967"

1967

J101 D9 50s ol grn & pale lil 15 15
J102 D9 100s dk red & yel grn 15 15
J103 D9 200s brt grn & pink 15 15
J104 D9 500s yel & lt bl 15 15
J105 D9 1000s rose lil & yel 25 15

J106	D9	15r org & gray	20	16
J107	D9	25r lil & citron	35	25
		Set value	1.15	80

Similar stamps inscribed "Bajar" or "Bayar", year date and "Sumbangan Ongkos Tjetak" or ". . . Cetak" are revenues.

Dated "1973" or "1974"
Inscribed "BAYAR PORTO"

1973-74

J108	D9	25r lilac & citron	1.00	
J109	D9	65r ol grn & bis ('74)	65	65
J110	D9	125r lil & pale pink ('74)	1.20	1.20

Dated "1975"
Inscribed "BAYAR PORTO"

1975 Photo. *Perf. 13½x12½*

J111	D9	25r lilac & citron	25	25

"1976" — D10

1976

J112	D10	125r lil & pale pur	40	40

Dated "1977"

1977

J113	D10	100r dp vio & pale pink	40	40
J114	D10	200r brt bl & lt lil	80	80
J115	D10	300r choc & lt sal	1.25	1.25
J116	D10	400r brt grn & tan	1.50	1.50
J117	D10	500r red & tan	2.00	2.00
		Nos. J113-J117 (5)	5.95	5.95

See Nos. J138, J139, J142.

Nos. 706, 709, 712-713, 716, 718 Surcharged in Red

BAYAR PORTO

1978 Photo. *Perf. 12½x12*

J118	A110	25r on 1r	15
J119	A110	50r on 2r	20
J120	A110	100r on 4r	60
J121	A110	200r on 5r	1.20
J122	A110	300r on 10r	1.60
J123	A110	400r on 15r	2.25
		Nos. J118-J123 (6)	6.00

Surcharged in Black

J124	A110	25r on 1r	15
J125	A110	50r on 2r	20
J126	A110	100r on 4r	60
J127	A110	200r on 5r	1.20
J128	A110	300r on 10r	1.50
J129	A110	400r on 15r	2.00
		Nos. J124-J129 (6)	5.65

1978

Nos. 710, 717 Surcharged

BAYAR PORTO

1978 Photo. *Perf. 12½x12*

J130	A110	40r on 2.50r	16
J131	A110	40r on 12r	16
J132	A110	65r on 2.50r	25
J133	A110	65r on 12r	25
J134	A110	125r on 2.50r	60
J135	A110	125r on 12r	60
J136	A110	150r on 2.50r	70
J137	A110	150r on 12r	70
		Nos. J130-J137 (8)	3.42

Type of 1976 Dated "1979"

1979 *Perf. 13½x12½*

J138	D10	25r lilac & citron	22	15

Type of 1976 and

D11

Perf. 13½x12½, 13½x13 (#J144-J148, J150-J153), 14½x13 (#J154-J156A)

1980-90 Photo.

Dated "1980"

J139	D10	25r dk lil & beige	15	15
J140	D11	50r multi	20	15
J141	D11	75r rose lake & rose	30	16
J142	D10	125r rose lil & lt pink	30	25

Dated "1981"

J144	D11	25r brt vio & pale yel grn	15	15
J145	D11	50r sl grn & lt vio	20	15
J146	D11	75r rose vio & pink	30	15
J147	D11	125r pur & yel grn	50	25

Dated "1982"

J148	D11	125r dp rose lil & pink	50	25

Dated "1983"

J149	D11	125r dp rose & lil pink	16	15
J150	D11	200r dp vio & lt bl	25	15
J151	D11	300r dk grn & cit	40	20
J152	D11	400r ol grn & brn ol	50	25
J153	D11	500r sepuia & beige	65	32

Dated "1984"

J154	D11	25r brt vio & pale yel grn		
J155	D11	50r sl grn & lt vio		
J156	D11	125r rose lil & lt pink		
J156A	D11	500r sepia & beige		

Dated "1988"

J157	D11	1000r dp vio & gray	36	18
J158	D11	2000r red & dp rose lil	72	36
J159	D11	3000r brn & dl org	1.10	55
J160	D11	5000r grn & bl grn	1.80	90

Dated "1990"

J161	D11	2000r emer & brt yel		
J162	D11	3000r dk bl grn & rose lil		
J163	D11	4000r brn vio & brt yel grn		

RIAU ARCHIPELAGO

(Riouw Archipelago)
100 Sen = 1 Rupiah
(1 rupiah = 1 Malayan dollar)

Indonesia Nos. 371-386 Overprinted in Black

R I A U (vertical) — a

RIAU — b

Overprint "a"

1954 Unwmk. *Perf. 12½*

1	A52	5s car rose	14.00	20.00
2	A52	7½s green	50	50
3	A52	10s blue	12.00	15.00
4	A52	15s purple	50	80
5	A52	20s rose red	65	90
6	A52	25s dp grn	40.00	35.00

Overprint "b"

7	A53	30s red org	40	60
8	A53	35s purple	40	60
9	A53	40s dl grn	40	60
10	A53	45s dp claret	60	80
11	A53	50s brown	100.00	65.00
12	A54	60s dk brn	40	60
13	A54	70s gray	1.00	80
14	A54	75s ultra	1.10	1.40
15	A54	80s claret	80	1.10
16	A54	90s gray grn	80	1.40

Netherlands Indies Nos. 325-330 Overprinted Type "a" in Black
Perf. 12½x12

17	A46	1r purple	6.00	3.00
18	A46	2r ol grn	1.00	3.00
19	A46	3r red vio	1.50	2.25
20	A46	5r dk brn	1.50	2.25
21	A46	10r gray	2.25	3.75
22	A46	25r org brn	2.25	3.75
		Nos. 1-22 (22)	188.05	163.10

Indonesia Nos. 424-428, 450 and 430 Overprinted Type "b" or

RIAU

1957-64 Photo. *Perf. 12½x13½*

23	A63 (b)	5s dp ultra	20	30
24	A63	10s yel brn	3.50	50
25	A63 (b)	10s yel brn	16	22
26	A63 (b)	15s rose vio ('64)	60	1.10
27	A63 (b)	20s dl grn ('60)	16	22
28	A63 (b)	25s dp claret	16	22
29	A63 (b)	30s orange	16	22
30	A63	50s brown	3.50	4.25
31	A63 (b)	50s brown	16	20

The "b" overprint measures 12mm in this set. No. 428 also exists with this overprint.

Sukarno Type of Indonesia Overprinted Type "a"

1960 *Perf. 12½x12*

32	A55	1.25r dp org	15	45
33	A55	1.50r brown	15	45
34	A55	2.50r rose brn	22	65
35	A55	4r apple grn	22	65
36	A55	6r rose lilac	30	90
37	A55	15r yellow	30	90
38	A55	20r sepia	42	1.50
39	A55	40r yel grn	75	2.50
40	A55	50r violet	90	2.50
		Nos. 23-40 (18)	12.01	17.73

INHAMBANE

LOCATION — East Africa
GOVT. — A district of Mozambique, former Portuguese colony
AREA — 21,000 sq. mi. (approx.)
POP. — 248,000 (approx.)
CAPITAL — Inhambane

1000 Reis = 1 Milreis
100 Centavos = 1 Escudo (1913)

Stamps of Mozambique Overprinted

CENTENARIO
DE
S. ANTONIO
—
Inhambane
MDCCCXCV

On 1886 Issue

1895, July 1 Unwmk. *Perf. 12½*

Without Gum

1	A2	5r black	27.50	22.50
2	A2	10r green	25.00	17.50
a.		Perf. 13½	65.00	52.50
3	A2	20r rose	42.50	20.00
4	A2	25r lilac		
5	A2	40r chocolate	42.50	30.00
6	A2	50r blue	42.50	25.00
a.		Perf. 13½	35.00	35.00
7	A2	100r yellow brown		
8	A2	200r gray violet	52.50	47.50
9	A2	300r orange	52.50	47.50

On 1894 Issue
Perf. 11½

10	A3	50r lt blue	35.00	27.50
a.		Perf. 12½	45.00	37.50
11	A3	75r rose	45.00	25.00
12	A3	80r yellow green	37.50	30.00
13	A3	100r brown, *buff*	80.00	52.50
14	A3	150r carmine, *rose*	45.00	40.00

700th anniversary of the birth of St. Anthony of Padua.

The status of Nos. 4 and 7 is questionable. No. 3 is always discolored.

King Carlos — A1

1903, Jan. 1 Typo. *Perf. 11½*

Name and Value in Black except 500r

15	A1	2½r gray	30	28
16	A1	5r orange	30	28
17	A1	10r lt green	60	35
18	A1	15r gray green	85	65
19	A1	20r gray violet	85	55
20	A1	25r carmine	70	55
21	A1	50r brown	1.75	1.25
22	A1	65r dull blue	14.00	9.00
23	A1	75r lilac	2.00	1.40
a.		Imperf.		
24	A1	100r dk blue, *blue*	2.00	1.25
25	A1	115r org brn, *pink*	4.00	4.00
26	A1	130r brown, *straw*	4.25	4.25
27	A1	200r red vio, *pink*	4.25	3.75
28	A1	400r dull bl, *straw*	8.25	6.75
29	A1	500r blk & red, *bl*	12.50	10.00
30	A1	700r gray blk, *straw*	11.00	12.00
		Nos. 15-30 (16)	67.60	56.31

For surcharge & overprints see #31-47, 88-101.

No. 22 Surcharged in Black

50
RÉIS

1905

31	A1	50r on 65r dull blue	2.75	2.00

Nos. 15-21, 23-30 Overprinted in Carmine or Green

1911

32	A1	2½r gray	20	20
33	A1	5r orange	20	20
34	A1	10r lt green	20	20
35	A1	15r gray green	28	28
36	A1	20r gray violet	28	28
37	A1	25r carmine (G)	70	50
38	A1	50r brown	42	42
39	A1	75r lilac	45	42
40	A1	100r dk blue, *bl*	45	42
41	A1	115r org brn, *pink*	85	75
42	A1	130r brown, *straw*	85	75
43	A1	200r red vio, *pink*	90	75
44	A1	400r dull bl, *straw*	1.25	1.00
45	A1	500r blk & red, *bl*	1.50	1.00
46	A1	700r gray blk, *straw*	1.75	1.50
		Nos. 32-46 (15)	10.28	8.67

No. 31 Overprinted in Red

1914

47	A1	50r on 65r dull blue	1.75	1.25
a.		"Republica" inverted		

Vasco da Gama Issue of Various Portuguese Colonies

Common Design Types CD20-CD27 Surcharged

REPUBLICA
INHAMBANE
¼ C.

1913

On Stamps of Macao

48	CD20	¼c on ½a bl grn	1.25	1.25
49	CD21	½c on 1a red	1.25	1.25
50	CD22	1c on 2a red vio	1.25	1.25
a.		Inverted surcharge	20.00	20.00
51	CD23	2½c on 4a yel grn	1.25	1.25
52	CD24	5c on 8a dk bl	1.25	1.25
53	CD25	7½c on 12a vio brn	2.25	2.25
54	CD26	10c on 16a bis brn	1.75	1.75
55	CD27	15c on 24a bis	1.75	1.75
		Nos. 48-55 (8)	12.00	12.00

On Stamps of Portuguese Africa

56	CD20	¼c on 2½r bl grn	1.00	1.00
57	CD21	½c on 5r red	1.00	1.00
58	CD22	1c on 10r red vio	1.00	1.00
59	CD23	2½c on 25r yel grn	1.00	1.00
60	CD24	5c on 50r dk bl	1.00	1.00
61	CD25	7½c on 75r vio brn	2.00	2.00
62	CD26	10c on 100r bis brn	1.50	1.50
63	CD27	15c on 150r bis	1.50	1.50
		Nos. 56-63 (8)	10.00	10.00

On Stamps of Timor

64	CD20	¼c on ½a bl grn	1.25	1.25
a.		Inverted surcharge	20.00	20.00
65	CD21	½c on 1a red	1.25	1.25
66	CD22	1c on 2a red vio	1.25	1.25
67	CD23	2½c on 4a yel grn	1.25	1.25
68	CD24	5c on 8a dk bl	1.25	1.25
69	CD25	7½c on 12a vio brn	2.50	2.50
70	CD26	10c on 16a bis brn	1.75	1.75
71	CD27	15c on 24a bis	1.75	1.75
		Nos. 64-71 (8)	12.25	12.25
		Nos. 48-71 (24)	34.25	34.25

Ceres — A2

1914 Typo. *Perf. 15x14*
Name and Value in Black

72 A2 ¼c olive brown 48 48
73 A2 ½c black 48 48
a. Imperf.
74 A2 1c blue green 48 48
75 A2 1½c lilac brown 48 48
76 A2 2c carmine 48 48
77 A2 2½c lt violet 32 32
78 A2 5c deep blue 80 80
79 A2 7½c yellow brown 1.25 1.25
80 A2 8c slate 1.25 1.25
81 A2 10c orange brown 1.10 1.10
82 A2 15c plum 1.65 1.65
83 A2 20c yellow green 1.65 1.65
84 A2 30c brown, *grn* 2.25 2.25
85 A2 40c brown, *pink* 2.25 2.25
86 A2 50c orange, *sal* 3.25 3.25
87 A2 1e green, *blue* 3.25 3.25
Nos. 72-87 (16) 21.42 21.42

No. 31 Overprinted in Carmine

1915 *Perf. 11½*
88 A1 50c on 65r dull blue 4.75 4.25

Nos. 15-21, 23-30 Overprinted Locally

1917
89 A1 2½r gray 15.00 15.00
90 A1 5r orange 15.00 15.00
91 A1 15r gray green 2.00 2.00
92 A1 20r gray violet 1.50 1.50
93 A1 50r brown 1.75 1.75
94 A1 75r lilac 1.75 1.75
95 A1 100r blue, *blue* 2.00 2.00
96 A1 115r org brn, *pink* 2.00 2.00
97 A1 130r brn, *straw* 2.00 2.00
98 A1 200r red vio, *pink* 2.00 2.00
99 A1 400r dull bl, *straw* 2.50 2.50
100 A1 500r blk & red, *bl* 2.50 2.50
101 A1 700r gray blk, *straw* 11.00 6.00
Nos. 89-101 (13) 61.00 56.00

The stamps of Inhambane have been superseded by those of Mozambique.

ININI

LOCATION — In northeastern South America, adjoining French Guiana
GOVT. — Former territory of French Guiana
AREA — 30,301 sq. mi.
POP. — 5,024 (1946)
CAPITAL — St. Elie

Inini was separated from French Guiana in 1930 and reunited with it in when the colony became an integral part of the Republic, acquiring the same status as the departments of Metropolitan France, under a law effective Jan. 1, 1947.

100 Centimes = 1 Franc

Used values are for canceled-to-order copies.

Stamps of French Guiana, 1929-40, Overprinted in Black, Red or Blue:

TERRITOIRE DE L'ININI
Nos. 1-9

Territoire de l'ININI
Nos. 10-26

Territoire de l'ININI
Nos. 27-40

1932-40 Unwmk. *Perf. 13½x14*
1 A16 1c gray lil & grnsh bl 15 15
2 A16 2c dk red & bl grn 15 15
3 A16 3c gray lil & grnsh bl ('40) 15 15
4 A16 4c ol brn & red vio ('38) 15 15
5 A16 5c Prus bl & red org 15 15
6 A16 10c magenta & brn 15 15
7 A16 15c yel brn & red org 15 15
8 A16 20c dk bl & ol grn 15 15
9 A16 25c dk red & dk brn 22 22

Perf. 14x13½
10 A17 30c dl grn & lt grn 60 60
11 A17 30c grn & brn ('40) 15 15
12 A17 35c Prus grn & ol ('38) 28 28
13 A17 40c red brn & ol gray 15 15
14 A17 45c ol grn & lt grn ('40) 15 15
15 A17 50c dk bl & ol gray 15 15
16 A17 55c vio bl & car ('38) 1.20 1.20
17 A17 60c sal & grn ('40) 15 15
18 A17 65c sal & grn ('38) 40 40
19 A17 70c ind & sl bl ('40) 15 15
20 A17 75c ind & sl bl (Bl) 70 70
21 A17 80c blk & vio bl (R) ('38) 28 28
22 A17 90c dk red & ver 40 40
23 A17 90c red vio & brn ('39) 15 15
24 A17 1fr lt vio & brn 5.00 4.50
25 A17 1fr car & lt red ('38) 28 28
26 A17 1fr blk & vio bl ('40) 15 15
27 A18 1.25fr blk brn & bl grn ('33) 28 28
28 A18 1.25fr rose & lt red ('39) 25 25
29 A18 1.40fr ol brn & red vio ('40) 32 32
30 A18 1.50fr dk bl & lt bl 22 22
31 A18 1.60fr ol brn & bl grn ('40) 32 32
32 A18 1.75fr brn, red & blk brn ('33) 7.50 6.50
33 A18 1.75fr vio bl ('38) 40 40
34 A18 2fr dk grn & rose red 40 40
35 A18 2.25fr vio bl ('39) 35 35
36 A18 2.50fr cop red & brn ('40) 35 35
37 A18 3fr brn red & red vio 40 40
38 A18 5fr dl vio & yel grn 40 40
39 A18 10fr ol gray & dp ultra (R) 40 40
40 A18 20fr ind & ver 60 60
Nos. 1-40 (40) 23.95 22.45

Colonial Arts Exhibition Issue
Souvenir Sheet
Common Design Type

1937 *Imperf.*
41 CD75 3fr red brown 5.00 5.00

New York World's Fair Issue
Common Design Type

1939, May 10 Engr. *Perf. 12½x12*
42 CD82 1.25fr car lake 1.60 1.60
43 CD82 2.25fr ultra 1.60 1.60

French Guiana Nos. 170A-170B Overprinted "ININI" in Green or Red

1941 Engr. *Perf. 12½x12*
44 A21a 1fr deep lilac 40
45 A21a 2.50fr blue (R) 40

Nos. 44-45 were issued by the Vichy government, and were not placed on sale in the territory. This is also true of four stamps of French Guiana types A16-A18 without "RF" and overprinted "TERRITOIRE DE L'ININI," released in 1944.

SEMI-POSTAL STAMPS

Common Design Type
Photo.; Name & Value Typo. in Black
1939, July 5 Unwmk. *Perf. 13*
B1 CD83 45c + 25c green 5.50 5.50
B2 CD83 70c + 30c brown 5.50 5.50
B3 CD83 90c + 35c red org 5.50 5.50
B4 CD83 1.25fr + 1fr rose pink 5.50 5.50
B5 CD83 2.25fr + 2fr blue 5.50 5.50
Nos. B1-B5 (5) 27.50 27.50

Common Design Type and French Guiana Nos. B9 and B11 Overprinted "ININI" in Blue or Red

1941 Photo. *Perf. 13½*
B6 SP1 1fr + 1fr red (B) 80
B7 CD86 1.50fr + 3fr maroon 60
B8 SP2 2.50fr + 1fr blue (R) 65

Nos. B6-B8 and Nos. 44-45 surcharged "OEUVRES COLONIALES" and surtax (including change of denomination of the 2.50fr to 50c) were issued in 1944 by the Vichy government but not placed on sale in Inini.

AIR POST SEMI-POSTAL STAMPS

Stamps of French Guiana type V6 and Cameroun type V10 inscribed "Inini" were issued in 1942 by the Vichy Government, but were not placed on sale in the territory.

POSTAGE DUE STAMPS

Postage Due Stamps of French Guiana, 1929, Overprinted in Black

TERRITOIRE DE L'ININI

1932, Apr. 7 Unwmk. *Perf. 13½x14*
J1 D3 5c indigo & Prus bl 15 15
J2 D3 10c bis brn & Prus grn 15 15
J3 D3 20c grn & rose red 15 15
J4 D3 30c ol brn & rose red 15 15
J5 D3 50c vio & ol brn 45 45
J6 D3 60c brn red & ol brn 45 45

Overprinted in Black or Red

TERRITOIRE DE L'ININI

J7 D4 1fr dp bl & org brn 55 55
J8 D4 2fr brn red & bluish grn 70 70
J9 D4 3fr vio & blk (R) 2.50 2.50
J10 D4 3fr vio & blk 1.00 1.00
Nos. J1-J10 (10) 6.25 6.25

IONIAN ISLANDS

LOCATION — Seven Islands, of which six-Corfu, Paxos, Lefkas (Santa Maura), Cephalonia, Ithaca and Zante-are in the Ionian Sea west of Greece, and a seventh-Cerigo (Kithyra)-is in the Mediterranean south of Greece
GOVT. — Integral part of Kingdom of Greece
AREA — 752 sq. miles
POP. — 231,510 (1938)

These islands were occupied by Italian forces in 1941. The Italians withdrew in 1943 and German forces continued the occupation, using current Greek stamps without overprinting, except for Zante.

For stamps of the Italian occupation of Corfu, see Corfu.

Issued under Italian Occupation

Values of stamps overprinted by letterpress in pairs are for unsevered pairs. Single stamps, unused, sell for one third the price of a pair; used, one half the price of a pair.

Handstamped overprints were also applied to pairs, with "isola" instead of "isole."

Issue for Cephalonia and Ithaca

Stamps of Greece, 1937-38, Overprinted in Pairs Vertically, Reading Down, or Horizontally (H) in Black

ITALIA

Occupazione Militare
Italiana isole
Cefalonia e Itaca

Perf. 12½x12, 13½x12, 12x13½
1941 Wmk. 252, Unwmk.
N1 A69 5 l brn red & bl 2.00 2.00
N2 A70 10 l bl & red brn (#413) (H) 2.00 2.00
a. On No. 397 40.00 45.00
N3 A71 20 l blk & grn (H) 2.00 2.00
a. Overprint inverted 65.00
N4 A72 40 l grn & blk 2.00 2.00
N5 A73 50 l brn & blk 3.00 3.00
N6 A74 80 l ind & yel brn (H) 3.00 3.00
a. Overprint inverted 75.00 80.00
N7 A67 1d green (H) 17.50 10.00
N8 A84 1.50d green (H) 20.00 20.00
a. Overprint inverted 75.00 75.00
N9 A75 2d ultra 2.50 2.00
N10 A76 5d red 4.50 3.75
N11 A77 6d olive brn 5.75 4.50
N12 A78 7d dark brn 5.75 5.75
N13 A67 8d dp bl (H) 21.00 21.00
N14 A79 10d red brn 12.00 9.00
N15 A80 15d green 18.00 18.00
N16 A81 25d dk bl (H) 45.00 30.00
a. Overprint inverted 85.00 77.50
N17 A84 30d org brn (H) 85.00 75.00
a. Overprint inverted 125.00 125.00
Nos. N1-N17 (17) 251.00 213.00

A variety with wrong font "C" in "Cephalonia" is found in several positions in each sheet of all denominations except those overprinted on single stamps. It sells for above three times the price of a normal pair.

Several other minor spelling errors in the overprint occur on several denominations in one of the printings.

Forgeries exist of many of the higher valued stamps and minor varieties of Nos. N1-N17, NC1-NC11 and NRA1-NRA5.

Overprint Reading Up
N1a A69 5 l 4.00 4.00
N4a A72 40 l 2.50 2.50
N5a A73 50 l 5.75 5.75
N9a A75 2d 22.50 15.00
N10a A76 5d 25.00 27.50
N11a A77 6d 5.75 5.75
N12a A78 7d 7.50 7.50
N14a A79 10d 13.00 13.00
N15a A80 15d 22.50 22.50
Nos. N1a-N15a (9) 108.50 103.50

General Issue

Stamps of Italy, 1929, Overprinted in Red or Black

ISOLE JONIE

1941 Wmk. 140 *Perf. 14*
N18 A90 5c ol brn (R) 22 38
N19 A92 10c dk brn (R) 22 38
N20 A91 20c rose red 22 38
N21 A94 25c dp grn 22 38
N22 A95 30c ol brn (R) 22 38
a. "SOLE" for "ISOLE" 25.00
N23 A95 50c purple (R) 22 38
N24 A94 75c rose red 22 38
N25 A94 1.25 l dp bl (R) 22 38
Nos. N18-N25 (8) 1.76 3.04

The stamps overprinted "Isole Jonie" were issued for all the Ionian Islands except Cerigo which used regular postage stamps of Greece.

ISSUED UNDER GERMAN OCCUPATION

Zante Issue

Nos. N21 and N23 with Additional Handstamped Overprint in Black

1943 Wmk. 140 *Perf. 14*
N26 A94 25c deep green 22.50 *45.00*
a. Carmine overprint 40.00 *90.00*
N27 A95 50c purple 22.50 *45.00*
a. Carmine overprint 40.00 *90.00*

No. N19 with this overprint is a proof. Value, black $40; carmine $85.

Nos. N26-N27 were in use 8 days, then were succeeded by stamps of Greece.

Forgeries of Nos. N26-N27, NC13 and their cancellations are plentiful.

Greek stamps with Italian overprints for the islands of Cerigo (Kithyra), Paxos and Lefkas (Santa Maura) are fraudulent.

OCCUPATION AIR POST STAMPS

Issued under Italian Occupation

Issue for Cephalonia and Ithaca

Stamps of Greece Overprinted in Pairs Vertically, Reading Down, or Horizontally (H) in Black Like Nos. N1-N17

Perf. 13x12½, 12½x13

1941 Unwmk.

On Greece Nos. C22, C23, C25 and C27 to C30

Grayish Paper

NC1	AP16	1d dp red	12.00	12.00
NC1A	AP17	2d dl bl	42.50	
NC2	AP19	7d bl vio (H)	72.50	90.00
NC3	AP21	25d rose (H)	80.00	75.00
a.		Overprint inverted	190.00	190.00
NC4	AP22	30d dk grn	50.00	50.00
a.		Overprint reading up	55.00	55.00
b.		Horizontal overprint on single stamp	*125.00*	*125.00*
c.		As "b," inverted	*250.00*	
NC5	AP23	50d vio (H)	*325.00*	325.00
NC6	AP24	100d brown	185.00	175.00
a.		Overprint reading up	200.00	225.00

No. NC1A is known only with overprint reading up.

On Greece Nos. C31-C34

Reengraved; White Paper

NC7	AP16	1d red	5.00	4.50
NC8	AP17	2d gray bl	5.00	4.50
a.		Overprint reading up	5.00	4.50
b.		Horiz. ovpt. on pair	*90.00*	*90.00*
c.		Horizontal overprint on single stamp		
NC9	AP18	5d vio (H)	9.00	7.50
a.		Overprint inverted		
b.		Vert. ovpt. on single stamp, up or down		
NC10	AP19	7d dp ultra (H)	15.00	11.00
a.		Overprint inverted	50.00	50.00

Overprinted Horizontally on No. C36

Rouletted 13½

NC11	D3	50 l vio brn	30.00	30.00
a.		Pair, one without ovpt.	*75.00*	
b.		On No. C36a	*165.00*	

See footnote following No. N17.

General Issue

Italy No. C13 Overprinted in Red Like Nos. N18-N25

1941 Wmk. 140 *Perf. 14*

NC12	AP3	50c olive brn	22	38
a.		"SOLE" for "ISOLE"	18.50	

Used in all the Ionian Islands except Cerigo which used air post stamps of Greece.

No. NC12 with additional overprint "BOLLO" is a revenue stamp.

Issued under German Occupation

ZANTE ISSUE

No. NC12 with Additional Handstamped Overprint in Black Like Nos. N26-N27

1943 Wmk. 140 *Perf. 14*

NC13	AP3	50c olive brown	30.00	*60.00*
a.		"SOLE" for "ISOLE"	*300.00*	
b.		Carmine overprint	135.00	*250.00*

See note after No. N27.

OCCUPATION POSTAGE DUE STAMPS

General Issue

Postage Due Stamps of Italy, 1934, Overprinted in Black Like Nos. N18-N25

1941 Wmk. 140 *Perf. 14*

NJ1	D6	10c blue	22	*75*
NJ2	D6	20c rose red	22	*75*
NJ3	D6	30c red orange	22	*75*
NJ4	D7	1 l red orange	22	*75*

See footnote after No. N25.

OCCUPATION POSTAL TAX STAMPS

Issued under Italian Occupation

Issue for Cephalonia and Ithaca

Greece No. RA56 with Additional Overprint on Horizontal Pair in Black Like Nos. N1-N17

1941 Unwmk. ***Serrate Roulette 13½***

NRA1	D3	10 l car (Bl+Bk)	2.50	2.50
a.		Blue overprint double	27.50	22.50
b.		Inverted overprint	37.50	37.50

Same Overprint Reading Down on Vertical Pairs of Nos. RA61-RA63

Perf. 13½x12

NRA2	PT7	10 l brt rose, *pale rose*	5.00	5.00
a.		Overprint on horiz. pair	40.00	40.00
b.		Horizontal overprint on single stamp	*100.00*	
c.		Overprint reading up	11.00	11.00
NRA3	PT7	50 l gray grn, *pale grn*	1.50	1.40
a.		Overprint reading up	5.00	5.00
b.		Ovpt. on horiz. pair	15.00	15.00
c.		Horizontal overprint on single stamp	*300.00*	
NRA4	PT7	1d dl bl, *lt bl*	12.00	12.00
a.		Overprint reading up	20.00	20.00

Same Overprint Reading Down on Vertical Pair of No. RA65

NRA5	PT7	50 l gray grn, *pale grn*	150.00	
a.		Overprint reading up	200.00	

Nos. NRA5 and NRA5a were not placed in use on any compulsory day.

See footnote following No. N17.

IRAN

(Persia)

LOCATION — Western Asia, bordering on the Persian Gulf and the Gulf of Oman
GOVT. — Islamic republic
AREA — 636,000 sq. mi.
POP. — 43,830,000 (est. 1984)
CAPITAL — Tehran

20 Shahis (or Chahis) = 1 Kran
10 Krans = 1 Toman
100 Centimes = 1 Franc = 1 Kran (1881)
100 Dinars = 1 Rial (1933)
100 Rials = 1 Pahlavi

Catalogue values for unused stamps in this country are for Never Hinged items, beginning with Scott 1054 in the regular postage section, Scott B36 in the semi-postal section, Scott C83 in the airpost section, Scott O72 in the officials section, Scott Q36 in the parcel post section, and Scott RA4 in the postal tax section.

Values of early stamps vary according to condition. Quotations for Nos. 1-20, 33-40 are for fine copies. Very fine to superb specimens sell at much higher prices, and inferior or poor copies sell at reduced prices, depending on the condition of the individual specimen.

Cracked gum on unused stamps does not detract from the value.

Watermarks

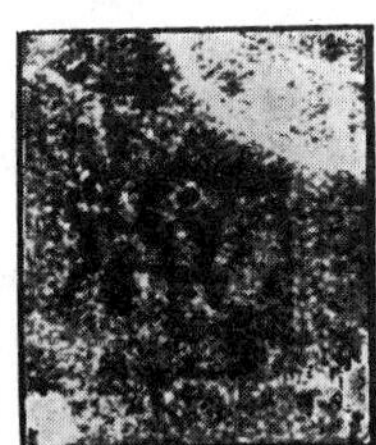

Wmk. 161- Lion

Wmk. 306- Arms of Iran

Wmk. 316- Persian Inscription

Wmk. 349- Persian Inscription and Crown in Circle

Illustration of Wmk. 349 shown sideways. Circles in Wmk. 349 are 95mm apart.

Wmk. 353- Persian Inscription and Coat of Arms in Circle

Wmk. 381- "Islamic Republic of Iran" in Persian (Partial Illustration)

Many issues have handstamped surcharges. As usual with such surcharges there are numerous inverted, double and similar varieties.

Coat of Arms
A1 A2

Design A2 has value numeral below lion.

1868 Unwmk. Typo. ***Imperf.***

1	A1	1s dull violet	65.00
2	A1	2s green	50.00
3	A1	4s greenish blue	50.00
4	A1	8s red	45.00

Values for used copies of Nos. 1-4 are omitted as postmarked copies are not known. Used copies with pen cancellation exist. Many shades exist. Printed in blocks of 4. Forgeries exist.

Printed on Both Sides

1a	A1	1s	650.
2a	A1	2s	700.
3a	A1	4s	1,500.
4a	A1	8s	900.

Vertically Rouletted 10½ on 1 or 2 Sides

1875 Thick Wove Paper

11	A2	1s black	90.00	50.00
a.		Imperf., pair	*400.00*	*400.00*
12	A2	2s blue	82.50	47.50
a.		Tête bêche pair	*10,000.*	
b.		Imperf., pair	*575.00*	*575.00*
13	A2	4s vermilion	110.00	42.50
a.		Imperf., pair	*625.00*	*625.00*
b.		4s bright red, thin paper, imperf.	525.00	
14	A2	8s yellow green	70.00	40.00
a.		Tête bêche pair	*10,000.*	*3,000.*
b.		Imperf., pair	*125.00*	*125.00*

Four varieties of each.

Nos. 11 to 14 also exist pin-perforated and percé en scie.

No. 13b has spacing of 2-3mm; No. 15, 2mm or less. Nos. 11-14 were printed in horizontal strips of 4, with 3-5mm spacing.

See Nos. 15-20, 33-40.

Medium to Thin White or Grayish Paper

1876 ***Imperf.***

15	A2	1s gray black	15.00	15.00
a.		Printed on both sides	500.00	
b.		Laid paper	500.00	
16	A2	2s gray blue	150.00	*250.00*
a.		Printed on both sides	600.00	
17	A2	2s black	450.00	
a.		Tête bêche pair	*3,000.*	
18	A2	4s vermilion	125.00	45.00
a.		Printed on both sides	450.00	325.00
19	A2	1k rose	165.00	50.00
a.		Printed on both sides		475.00
b.		Laid paper	450.00	150.00
c.		1k yellow (error)	*5,000.*	
d.		Tête bêche pair		*12,000.*
20	A2	4k yellow	500.00	70.00
a.		Printed on both sides		*500.00*
b.		Laid paper	600.00	110.00
c.		Tête bêche pair		*9,000.*

Nos. 15-16, 18-20 were printed in blocks of 4, with spacing of 2mm or less, No. 15 also in vertical strip of 4. No. 17 in a vertical strip of 4.

The 2s black and the vertical-strip printing on the 1s are on medium to thick grayish wove paper. Both printings of the 1s are found in black as well as gray black. Forgeries exist.

Official reprints of the 1s and 4s are on thick coarse white paper without gum.

Unofficial Reprints:

1875 and 1876 issues.

The reprints of the 1s and 1k stamps are readily told; the pearls of the circle are heavier, the borders of the circles containing the Persian numeral of value are wider and the figure "1" below the lion is always Roman.

The reprints of the 2s have the outer line of the frame at the left and at the bottom broken and on some specimens entirely missing.

A distinguishing mark by which to tell the 4s and 4k stamps is the frame, the outer line of which is of the same thickness as the inner line, while on the originals the inner line is very thin and the outer line thick; another feature of most of the reprints is a gash in the lower part of the circle below the figure "4."

In the reprints of the 8s stamps the small scroll nearest to the circles with Persian numerals at the bottom of the stamp touches the frame below it; the inner and outer lines of the frame are of equal thickness, while in the originals the outer line is much heavier than the inner one.

All reprints are found canceled to order.

Shah Nasr-ed-Din — A3

Perf. 10½, 11, 12, 13, and Compounds

1876 **Typo.**

27	A3	1s lilac & blk	10.00	4.50
28	A3	2s green & blk	14.00	6.50
29	A3	5s rose & blk	25.00	4.00
30	A3	10s blue & blk	35.00	8.00

Bisects of the 5s (surcharged "2½") and the 10s (surcharged "5 Shahi" or "5 Shahy") exist. Experts variously attribute them to local shortages, a postmaster's inventiveness or fraudulence.

"Imperfs" of the 5s are envelope cutouts.

Forgeries and official reprints exist.

1878 **Typo.** ***Imperf.***

33	A2	1k car rose	150.00	87.50
34	A2	1k red, *yellow*	*1,000.*	70.00
a.		Tête bêche pair		*4,000.*
35	A2	4k ultramarine	140.00	50.00
36	A2	5k gold	*1,000.*	175.00
37	A2	5k violet	250.00	150.00
38	A2	5k red bronze	*2,000.*	350.00
39	A2	5k vio bronze	*2,000.*	475.00
40	A2	1t bronze, *bl*	*15,000.*	*3,000.*

Four varieties of each except for 4k which has 3.

Nos. 33 and 34 are printed from redrawn clichés. They have wide colorless circles around the corner numerals.

Unofficial reprints of the 1 kran and 1 toman are printed from the same die as the reprints of the 1 shahi and 1 kran of the 1876 issue; on these and on the reprints of the 5 krans the outer frame is of irregular thickness. The impression of the reprints of this issue is better than that of the originals.

Nasr-ed-Din
A6

Sun
A7

Perf. 10½, 12, 13, and Compounds

1879

41	A6	1k brown & blk	40.00	3.00
a.		Imperf., pair	*275.00*	
b.		Inverted center		
42	A6	5k blue & blk	50.00	3.00
a.		Imperf., pair	*400.00*	80.00
b.		Inverted center		

1880

43	A6	1s red & black	40.00	3.00
44	A6	2s yellow & blk	50.00	5.00
45	A6	5s green & blk	50.00	2.00
46	A6	10s violet & blk	150.00	15.00

Forgeries and official reprints exist.

The 2, 5 and 10sh of this issue and the 1 and 5kr of the 1879 issue have been reprinted from a new die which resembles the 5 shahi envelope. The aigrette is shorter than on the original stamps and touches the circle above it.

Imperf., Pair

43a	A6	1s	240.00	
44a	A6	2s	400.00	*300.00*
46a	A6	10s		

1881 **Litho.** ***Perf. 12, 13, 12x13***

47	A7	5c dull violet	15.00	5.00
48	A7	10c rose	20.00	5.00
49	A7	25c green	400.00	50.00

1882 **Engr., Border Litho.**

50	A7	5c blue vio & vio	15.00	3.00
51	A7	10c dp pink & rose	15.00	3.00
52	A7	25c deep grn & grn	110.00	10.00

Counterfeits of Nos. 50-52, 53, 53a are plentiful and have been used to create forgeries of Nos. 66, 66a, 70 and 70a. They usually have a strong, complete inner frameline at right. On genuine stamps that line is weak or missing.

A8

Shah Nasr-ed-Din
A9 A10

A11

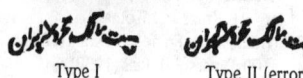

Type I Type II (error)

Type I- Three dots at right end of scroll.
Type II- Two dots at right end of scroll.

1882-84 **Engr.**

53	A8	5s green, type I	10.00	1.50
a.		5s green, type II	20.00	7.50
54	A9	10s buff, org & blk	20.00	3.50
55	A10	50c buff, org & blk	35.00	20.00
56	A10	50c gray & blk ('84)	35.00	10.00
57	A10	1fr blue & black	35.00	6.00
58	A10	5fr rose red & blk	40.00	5.00
59	A11	10fr buff, red & blk	35.00	7.50

Crude forgeries of Nos. 58-59 exist. Halves of the 10s, 50c and 1fr surcharged with Farsi characters in red or black are frauds. The 50c and 1fr surcharged with a large "5" surrounded by rays are also frauds.

No. 59 used is valued for c-t-o.

For overprints and surcharges see #66-72.

A12

A13

1885-86 **Typo.**

60	A12	1c green	10.00	1.00
61	A12	2c rose	10.00	1.00
62	A12	5c dull blue	15.00	50
a.		5c violet blue	90.00	30.00
63	A13	10c brown	7.50	1.00
64	A13	1k slate	7.50	2.00
65	A13	5k dull vio ('86)	60.00	7.00

No. 62a is redrawn.

Nos. 53, 54, 56 and 58 Surcharged in Black:

OFFICIEL 6 — a
OFFICIEL 12 — b
OFFICIEL 18 — c
OFFICIEL 1T — d
OFFICIEL 3 — e
OFFICIEL 8 — f

1885

66	(a)	6c on 5s grn, type I	30.00	4.00
a.		6c on 5s green, type II	55.00	20.00
67	(b)	12c on 50c gray & blk	70.00	15.00
68	(c)	18c on 10s buff, org & black	70.00	15.00
69	(d)	1t on 5fr rose red & black	60.00	15.00

1887

70	(e)	3c on 5s grn, type I	25.00	7.00
a.		3c on 5s green, type II	55.00	20.00
71	(a)	6c on 10s buff, org & black	25.00	7.50
72	(f)	8c on 50c gray & blk	75.00	20.00

The word "OFFICIEL" indicated that the surcharged stamps were officially authorized.

Surcharges on the same basic stamps of values other than those listed are believed to be bogus.

Counterfeits of Nos. 66-72 abound.

A14

A15

1889 **Typo.** ***Perf. 11, 13½, 11x13½***

73	A14	1c pale rose	30	15
74	A14	2c pale blue	30	15
75	A14	5c lilac	30	15
76	A14	7c brown	4.00	40
77	A15	10c black	75	15
78	A15	1k red orange	1.25	15
79	A15	2k rose	7.00	1.50
80	A15	5k green	10.00	2.00
		Nos. 73-80 (8)	23.90	4.65

All values exist imperforate. Canceled to order copies of No. 76 abound.

For surcharges see Nos. 622-625.

A16

A17

1891 ***Perf. 10½, 11½***

81	A16	1c black	1.00	20
82	A16	2c brown	1.00	20
83	A16	5c deep blue	50	15
84	A16	7c gray	45.00	7.00
85	A16	10c rose	1.65	20
86	A16	14c orange	2.00	20
87	A17	1k green	17.50	2.00
88	A17	2k orange	75.00	7.00
89	A17	5k ocher yellow	4.50	4.50
		Nos. 81-89 (9)	148.15	21.45

For surcharges see Nos. 626-629.

A18

Shah Nasr-ed-Din — A19

1894 ***Perf. 12½***

90	A18	1c lilac	50	15
91	A18	2c blue green	50	15
92	A18	5c ultramarine	50	15
93	A18	8c brown	50	15

Perf. 11½x11

94	A19	10c orange	1.00	75
95	A19	16c rose	6.00	10.00
96	A19	1k red & yellow	3.00	75
97	A19	2k brn org & pale bl	3.00	1.00
98	A19	5k violet & silver	4.00	1.50
99	A19	10k red & gold	12.00	10.00
100	A19	50k green & gold	10.00	7.50
		Nos. 90-100 (11)	41.00	32.10

Canceled to order copies sell for one-third of listed values.

Reprints exist. They are hard to distinguish from the originals. Value, set $15.

See Nos. 104-112, 136-144. For overprints see Nos. 120-128, 152-167, 173-181. For surcharges see Nos. 101-103, 168, 206, 211.

Nos. 93, 98 With Violet or Magenta Surcharge

1897 *Perf. 12½, 11½x11*

101 A18	5c on 8c brown (V)		1.50	50
102 A19	1k on 5k vio & sil (V)		2.50	2.00
103 A19	2k on 5k vio & sil (M)		3.50	2.50

Lion Type of 1894 and

Shah Muzaffar-ed-Din — A22

1898 **Typo.** *Perf. 12½*

104 A18	1c gray	45	15
105 A18	2c pale brown	45	15
106 A18	3c dull violet	50	20
107 A18	4c vermilion	50	20
108 A18	5c yellow	35	15
109 A18	8c orange	2.00	1.00
110 A18	10c light blue	2.00	20
111 A18	12c rose	1.00	1.00
112 A18	16c green	3.00	1.00
113 A22	1k ultramarine	4.00	50
114 A22	2k pink	3.00	75
115 A22	3k yellow	2.00	75
116 A22	4k gray	2.00	1.50
117 A22	5k emerald	2.00	3.00
118 A22	10k orange	7.00	7.00
119 A22	50k bright vio	15.00	15.00
	Nos. 104-119 (16)	45.25	32.55

Unauthorized reprints of Nos. 104-119 were made from original clichés. Paper shows a vertical mesh. These abound unused and canceled to order.

See Nos. 145-151. For overprints see Nos. 129-135, 182-188. For surcharges see Nos. 169, 171, 207, 209, 215.

Reprints have been used to make counterfeits of Nos. 120-135, 152-167.

Stamps of 1898 Handstamped in Violet:

1899

120 (a)	1c gray	2.00	2.00
121 (b)	2c pale brown	2.00	2.00
122 (b)	3c dull violet	3.00	2.00
123 (c)	4c vermilion	4.00	4.00
124 (c)	5c yellow	3.00	1.00
125 (d)	8c orange	3.00	1.50
126 (d)	10c light blue	3.00	1.50
127 (d)	12c rose	2.00	1.00
128 (d)	16c green	4.00	2.50
129 (e)	1k ultramarine	4.50	2.00
130 (f)	2k pink	8.00	6.00
131 (f)	3k yellow	12.50	10.00
132 (g)	4k gray	12.50	10.00
133 (g)	5k emerald	12.50	12.50
134 (h)	10k orange	30.00	30.00
135 (h)	50k brt violet	30.00	30.00
	Nos. 120-135 (16)	136.00	118.00

The handstamped control marks on Nos. 120-135 exist sideways, inverted and double. Counterfeits are plentiful.

Types of 1894-98

1899 **Typo.** *Perf. 12½*

136 A18	1c gray, *green*	1.00	15
137 A18	2c brown, *green*	1.00	15
138 A18	3c violet, *green*	1.75	15
139 A18	4c red, *green*	4.00	15
140 A18	5c yellow, *green*	1.00	15
141 A18	8c orange, *green*	5.00	60
142 A18	10c pale blue, *grn*	3.50	15
143 A18	12c lake, *green*	3.50	30
144 A18	16c green, *green*	7.50	60
145 A22	1k red	7.50	50
146 A22	2k deep green	12.50	1.20
147 A22	3k lilac brown	14.00	3.00
148 A22	4k orange red	14.00	3.00
149 A22	5k gray brown	22.50	3.00
150 A22	10k deep blue	60.00	10.00
151 A22	50k brown	45.00	7.00
	Nos. 136-151 (16)	203.75	30.10

Canceled to order copies abound.

Unauthorized reprints of Nos. 136-151 were made from original clichés. Paper is chalky and has white gum. The design can be seen through the back of the reprints.

For surcharges and overprints see Nos. 171, 173-188, 206-207, 209, 211, 215.

Nos. 104-111 Handstamped in Violet

(Struck once on every two stamps.)

1900

152 A18	1c gray	20.00	10.00
153 A18	2c pale brown	20.00	10.00
154 A18	3c dull violet	30.00	10.00
155 A18	4c vermilion	40.00	10.00
156 A18	5c yellow	10.00	5.00
158 A18	10c light blue	75.00	35.00
159 A18	12c rose	30.00	15.00

Pairs of Nos. 152-159 sell for three times the price of singles.

This control mark, in genuine state, was not applied to the 8c orange (Nos. 109, 125).

Same Overprint Handstamped on Nos. 120-127 in Violet

(Struck once on each block of four.)

160 A18	1c gray	40.00	10.00
163 A18	4c vermilion	40.00	25.00
164 A18	5c yellow	20.00	5.00
166 A18	10c light blue	30.00	20.00
167 A18	12c rose	20.00	15.00

Blocks of four of Nos. 160-167 sell for six times the price of singles.

Counterfeits exist of Nos. 152-167.

No. 93 Surcharged in Violet

1900

168 A18	5c on 8c brown	10.00	1.00

No. 145 Surcharged in Violet

1901

169 A22	12c on 1k red	20.00	4.00
a.	Blue surcharge	25.00	6.00

Counterfeits exist.

Some specialists state that No. 169 with black surcharge was made for collectors.

A23

1902 **Violet Surcharge**

171 A23	5k on 50k brown	50.00	50.00
a.	Blue surcharge	55.00	55.00

Counterfeits exist. See No. 207.

Nos. 136-151 Overprinted in Black

1902

173 A18	1c gray, *green*	3.00	2.50
174 A18	2c brown, *green*	3.00	2.50
175 A18	3c violet, *green*	4.00	2.50
176 A18	4c red, *green*	4.00	2.50
177 A18	5c yellow, *green*	3.00	1.50
178 A18	8c orange, *green*	5.00	5.00
179 A18	10c pale blue, *grn*	10.00	3.00
180 A18	12c lake, *green*	10.00	4.00
181 A18	16c green, *green*	10.00	10.00
182 A22	1k red	10.00	6.00
183 A22	2k deep green		
188 A22	50k brown		

Overprinted on No. 168

206 A18	5c on 8c brown	10.00	5.00

Overprinted on Nos. 171 and 171a

207 A23	5k on 50k brown	35.00	25.00
a.	On #171a	40.00	35.00

Overprinted on Nos. 169 and 169a

209 A22	12c on 1k red	10.00	10.00
a.	On #169a	15.00	10.00

Counterfeits of the overprint of Nos. 173-183, 188, 206-207, 209 are plentiful. Practically all examples with overprint sideways, inverted, double and double with one inverted are frauds.

Nos. 142 and 145 Surcharged in Violet

1902

211 A18	5c on 10c pale bl, *grn*	20.00	5.00
215 A22	5c on 1k red	25.00	15.00

Surcharges in different colors were made for collectors.

Initials of Victor Castaigne, Postmaster of Meshed — A24

1902 **Typo.** *Imperf.*

222 A24	1c black	300.00	67.50
b.	Inverted center	*2,750.*	*1,750.*
223 A24	2c black	300.00	90.00
b.	"2" in right upper corner	*2,250.*	*1,750.*
c.	Frame printed on both sides	475.00	
224 A24	3c black	350.00	100.00
225 A24	5c violet	300.00	90.00
a.	"5" in right upper corner		
b.	Frame printed on both sides	*1,650.*	*1,000.*
c.	Inverted center		
226 A24	5c black	250.00	75.00
a.	Persian "5" in lower left corner		
b.	Inverted center		
227 A24	12c dull blue	700.00	300.00
228 A24	1k rose	8,500.	1,000.

The design of No. 228 differs slightly from the illustration.

Pin-perforated

234 A24	12c dull blue		

The post office at Meshed having exhausted its stock of stamps, the postmaster issued the above series provisionally. The center of the design is the seal of the postmaster who also wrote his initials upon the upper part, using violet ink for the 1k and red for the others.

Unauthorized reprints, including pinperforated examples of Nos. 222-226, and forgeries exist.

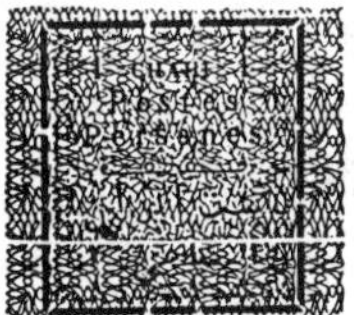

A25

TWO TYPES:

Type I - "CHAHI" or "KRANS" are in capital letters.

Type II - Only "C" of "Chahi" or "K" of "Krans" is a capital.

The 3c and 5c sometimes have a tall narrow figure in the upper left corner. The 5c is also found with the cross at the upper left broken or missing. These varieties are known with many of the overprints that were applied to type A25.

Handstamp Overprinted in Black

1902 **Typeset** *Imperf.*

Type I

235 A25	1c gray & buff	*75.00*
236 A25	2c brown & buff	*75.00*
237 A25	3c green & buff	*75.00*
238 A25	5c red & buff	*75.00*
239 A25	12c ultra & buff	*80.00*
	Nos. 235-239 (5)	*380.00*

Counterfeits abound.

The 3c with violet overprint is believed not to have been regularly issued.

Handstamp Overprinted in Rose

1902 **Type I**

247 A25	1c gray & buff	3.00	50
a.	With Persian numerals "2"	25.00	
248 A25	2c brown & buff	8.00	75
249 A25	3c dp grn & buff	10.00	1.00
250 A25	5c red & buff	3.00	30
251 A25	10c ol yel & buff	8.00	50
252 A25	12c ultra & buff	12.00	1.50
253 A25	1k violet & bl	35.00	3.00
254 A25	2k ol grn & bl	45.00	7.00
256 A25	10k dk bl & bl	125.00	20.00
257 A25	50k red & blue	125.00	75.00

A 5k exists but its' status is doubtful.

Nos. 247-257 and the 12c on brown paper and on blue paper with blue quadrille lines are known without overprint but are not believed to have been regularly issued in this condition.

The 1c to 10k, A25 type I, with violet overprint are believed not to have been regularly issued. Five denominations also exist with overprint in blue, black or green.

Type II

280 A25	1c gray & yellow	20.00	20.00
281 A25	2c brown & yel	40.00	40.00
282 A25	3c dk grn & yel	15.00	
a.	"Persans"	22.50	3.25
283 A25	5c red & yellow	20.00	3.00
284 A25	10c ol yel & yel	20.00	5.00
285 A25	12c blue & yel	20.00	8.00
290 A25	50k org red & bl		

The same overprint in violet was applied to nine denominations of the Type II stamps, but these are believed not to have been regularly issued. The overprint also exists in blue, black and green.

Reprints, counterfeits, counterfeit overprints, with or without cancellations, are plentiful for Nos. 247-257, 280-290.

Five stamps of type A25, type II, in high denominations (10, 20, 25, 50 and 100 tomans), with "Postes 1319" not overprint in blue, were used only on money orders, not for postage. They are usually numbered on the back in red, blue or black.

Handstamp Surcharged in Black

1902

Type I

308	A25	5k on 5k ocher & bl	*50.00*	*25.00*

Counterfeits of No. 308 abound.

This surcharge in rose, violet, blue or green is considered bogus.

This surcharge on 50k orange red and blue, and on 5k ocher and blue, type II, is considered bogus.

Handstamp Overprinted Diagonally in Black

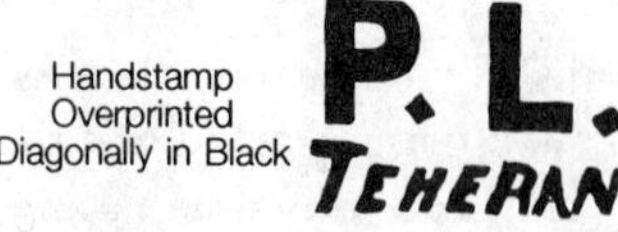

1902

Type I

315	A25	2c brown & buff	30.00	20.00
a.		Rose overprint	30.00	20.00

Type II

316	A25	2c brown & yel	30.00	20.00
a.		Rose overprint	30.00	20.00

"P. L." stands for "Poste Locale."

Counterfeits of Nos. 315-316 exist.

Some specialists believe that Type II stamps were not used officially for this overprint.

Handstamp Overprinted in Black or Rose

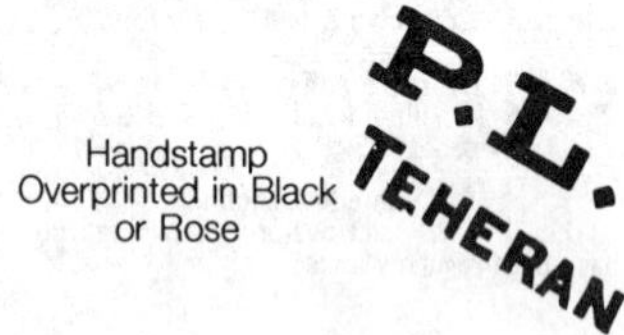

1902 **Type II**

317	A25	2c brn & yellow	20.00	20.00
318	A25	2c brown & yel (R)	20.00	20.00

Counterfeits of Nos. 317-318 exist.

Overprinted in Blue

1903

Type I

321	A25	1k violet & blue	15.00

Type II

336	A25	1c gray & yellow	10.00
337	A25	2c brown & yellow	10.00
338	A25	5c red & yellow	10.00
339	A25	10c olive yel & yel	10.00
340	A25	12c blue & yellow	15.00
		Nos. 321-340 (6)	70.00

The overprint also exists in violet and black, but it is doubtful whether such items were regularly issued.

Forgeries of Nos. 321, 336-340 abound. Genuine unused examples are seldom found.

Arms of Persia
A26

Shah Muzaffar-ed-Din
A27

1903-04 **Typo.** ***Perf. 12½***

351	A26	1c violet	50	15
352	A26	2c gray	50	15
353	A26	3c green	50	15
354	A26	5c rose	50	15
355	A26	10c yellow brn	50	15
356	A26	12c blue	60	15

Engr.

Perf. 11½x11

357	A27	1k violet	1.50	35
358	A27	2k ultramarine	1.50	35
359	A27	5k orange brn	2.50	60
360	A27	10k rose red	3.50	75
361	A27	20k orange ('04)	6.00	3.00
362	A27	30k green ('04)	15.00	5.00
363	A27	50k green	40.00	20.00
		Nos. 351-363 (13)	73.10	30.95

No. 355 exists with blue diagonal surcharge "1 CHAHI"; its status is questioned.

See Nos. 428-433. For surcharges and overprints see #364-420, 446-447, 464-469, O8-O28, P1.

No. 353 Surcharged in Violet or Blue

1903

364	A26	1c on 3c green (V)	10.00	5.00
365	A26	2c on 3c green (Bl)	10.00	8.50

A 2c surcharge on No. 354 exists, but its status is dubious.

No. 360 Surcharged in Blue

366	A27	12c on 10k rose red	10.00	2.00
a.		Black surcharge	15.00	4.00
b.		Violet surcharge	15.00	4.00

No. 363 Surcharged in Blue or Black

1903

368	A27	2t on 50k grn (Bl)	40.00	20.00
a.		Rose surcharge	40.00	25.00
b.		Black surcharge	50.00	30.00
370	A27	3t on 50k grn (Bk)	65.00	20.00
a.		Violet surcharge	40.00	20.00
b.		Rose surcharge	40.00	35.00

No. 363 Surcharged in Blue or Black

1904

372	A27	2t on 50k grn (Bl)	55.00	20.00
375	A27	3t on 50k grn (Bk)	65.00	20.00

The 2t on 50k also exists with surcharge in rose, violet, black and magenta; the 3t on 50k in rose, violet and blue. Values about the same unused; about 50 percent higher used.

No. 352 Overprinted in Violet

1904 ***Perf. 12½***

393	A26	2c gray	10.00	5.00
a.		Black overprint	11.50	5.00
b.		Rose overprint	20.00	5.00

This overprint also exists in blue, violet blue, maroon and gray, but these were not regularly issued.

The 2c overprinted "Controle" in various types is said to be a revenue stamp.

Stamps of 1903 Surcharged in Black:

a

b

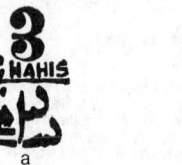

c

1904

400	A26(a)	3c on 5c rose	5.00	25
401	A26(b)	6c on 10c brown	10.00	25
402	A27(c)	9c on 1k violet	10.00	50

Stamps of 1903 Surcharged in Black, Magenta or Violet:

1905-06

404	A26	1c on 3c green ('06)	10.00	3.00
405	A27	1c on 1k violet	10.00	4.00
406	A27	2c on 5k orange brn	20.00	4.00
407	A26	1c on 3c grn (M) ('06)	5.00	1.00
408	A27	1c on 1k violet (M)	10.00	4.00
409	A27	2c on 5k org brn (V)	10.00	4.00
		Nos. 404-409 (6)	65.00	20.00

Nos. 355 and 358 Surcharged in Violet

419	A26	1c on 10c brown	100.00	100.00
420	A27	2c on 2k ultra	125.00	125.00

Forgeries of Nos. 419-420 exist.

A28

Typeset; "Provisoire" Overprint Handstamped in Black

1906 ***Imperf.***

422	A28	1c violet	1.00	25
a.		Irregular pin perf. or perf. 10½	10.00	5.00
423	A28	2c gray	1.00	25
424	A28	3c green	1.00	25
425	A28	6c red	1.00	25
426	A28	10c brown	10.00	1.25
427	A28	13c blue	5.00	65
		Nos. 422-427 (6)	19.00	2.90

Stamps of type A28 have a faint background pattern of tiny squares within squares, an ornamental frame and open rectangles for the value corners.

The 3c and 6c also exist perforated.

Nos. 422-427 are known without overprint but were probably not issued in that condition. Nearly all values are known with overprint inverted and double.

Forgeries are plentiful.

Lion Type of 1903 and

Shah Mohammed Ali
A29 A30

1907-09 **Typo.** ***Perf. 12½***

428	A26	1c vio, *blue*	30	15
429	A26	2c gray, *blue*	30	15
430	A26	3c green, *blue*	30	15
431	A26	6c rose, *blue*	30	15
432	A26	9c org, *blue*	30	15
433	A26	10c brown, *blue*	30	15

Engr.

Perf. 11, 11½

434	A29	13c dark blue	1.00	35
435	A29	1k red	1.00	35
436	A29	26c red brown	1.00	35
437	A29	2k deep grn	1.00	35
438	A29	3k pale blue	1.00	35
439	A29	4k brt yellow	60.00	10.00
440	A29	4k bister	3.00	50
441	A29	5k dark brown	3.00	50
442	A29	10k pink	3.00	1.00
443	A29	20k gray black	4.00	1.50
444	A29	30k dark violet	9.00	5.00
445	A30	50k gold, ver & black ('09)	25.00	10.00
		Nos. 428-445 (18)	113.80	31.15

Frame of No. 445 lithographed. Nos. 434-444 were issued in 1908.

Remainders canceled to order abound.

Nos. 428-429 Overprinted in Black

1909 ***Perf. 12½***

446	A26	1c violet, *blue*	35.00	15.00
447	A26	2c gray, *blue*	35.00	15.00

Counterfeits of Nos. 446-447 exist.

Coat of Arms — A31

1909 **Typo.** ***Perf. 12½x12***

448	A31	1c org & maroon	*75*	25
449	A31	2c vio & maroon	*75*	25
450	A31	3c yel grn & mar	*75*	25
451	A31	6c red & maroon	*75*	25
452	A31	9c gray & maroon	*1.10*	30
453	A31	10c red vio & mar	*1.10*	30
454	A31	13c dk blue & mar	*2.25*	45
455	A31	1k sil, vio & bis brown	*10.00*	60
456	A31	26c dk grn & mar	*5.00*	1.00
457	A31	2k sil, dk grn & bis brown	*20.00*	1.00
458	A31	3k sil, gray & bis brown	*20.00*	2.00
459	A31	4k sil, bl & bis brn	*25.00*	3.00
460	A31	5k gold, brn & bis brown	*22.50*	4.00
461	A31	10k gold, org & bis brown	*30.00*	5.00
462	A31	20k gold, ol grn & bister brn	*37.50*	8.00
463	A31	30k gold, car & bis brown	*57.50*	10.00
		Nos. 448-463 (16)		36.65

The unauthorized "reprints" of Nos. 448-463 abound. Originals have clean, bright colors, centers stand out clearly, and paper is much thinner. Nos. 460-463 originals have gleaming gold margins; reprint margins appear as blackish yellow. Centers of reprints of Nos. 448-454, 456 are brown. **Value for reprints, Nos. 448-463, $10.**

For surcharges & overprints see #541-549, 582-585, 588-594, 597, 601-606, 707-722, C1-C16, O31-O40.

Nos. 428-444, Imperf., Surcharged in Red or Black:

1910 **Blue Paper** ***Imperf.***

464	A26	1c on 1c violet	45.00	32.50
465	A26	1c on 2c gray	45.00	32.50
466	A26	1c on 3c green	45.00	32.50
467	A26	1c on 6c rose (Bk)	45.00	32.50
468	A26	1c on 9c orange	45.00	32.50
469	A26	1c on 10c brown	45.00	32.50

White Paper

470	A29	2c on 13c dp bl	52.50	37.50
471	A29	2c on 26c red brown (Bk)	52.50	37.50
472	A29	2c on 1k red (Bk)	52.50	37.50
473	A29	2c on 2k dp grn	52.50	37.50
474	A29	2c on 3k pale bl	52.50	37.50
475	A29	2c on 4k brt yel	52.50	37.50
476	A29	2c on 4k bister	52.50	37.50
477	A29	2c on 5k dk brn	52.50	37.50
478	A29	2c on 10k pink (Bk)	57.50	37.50
479	A29	2c on 20k gray blk	57.50	37.50
480	A29	2c on 30k dk vio	57.50	37.50
		Nos. 464-480 (17)	862.50	607.50

Nos. 464-480 were prepared for use on newspapers, but nearly the entire printing was sold to stamp dealers. The issue is generally considered speculative. Counterfeit surcharges exist on trimmed stamps

Shah Ahmed — A32

Perf. 11½, 11½x11, 11½x12

1911-13 Engr. center, Typo. frame

No.	Type	Description	Unused	Used
481	A32	1c green & org	50	15
482	A32	2c red & sepia	50	15
483	A32	3c gray brn & grn	50	15
a.		3c bister brown & green	2.00	1.00
484	A32	5c brn & car ('13)	60	75
485	A32	6c gray & car	60	15
486	A32	6c grn & red brown ('13)	75	15
487	A32	9c yel brn & vio	1.00	15
488	A32	10c red & org brn	1.00	15
489	A32	12c grn & ultra ('13)	1.00	15
490	A32	13c violet & ultra	1.00	2.00
491	A32	1k ultra & car	2.00	15
492	A32	24c vio & grn ('13)	1.00	20
493	A32	26c ultra & green	2.00	7.00
494	A32	2k grn & red vio	5.00	50
495	A32	3k violet & blk	3.00	50
496	A32	4k ultramarine & gray ('13)	3.00	17.50
497	A32	5k red & ultra	5.00	1.00
498	A32	10k ol bis & cl	5.00	1.50
499	A32	20k vio brn & bis	5.00	2.00
500	A32	30k red & green	6.00	2.50
		Nos. 481-500 (20)	37.80	

Unauthorized "reprints" of Nos. 481-500 are ubiquitous. Perf. 11½ except 4k which is 11½x12. **Value, set of reprints, $10.**

The reprints include inverted centers for some denominations.

For surcharges and overprints see Nos. 501-540, 586-587, 595, 598, 600, 607-609, 630-634, 646-666.

Stamps of 1911 Overprinted in Black **Officiel**

1912

No.	Type	Description	Unused	Used
501	A32	1c grn & orange	3.00	75
502	A32	2c red & sepia	3.00	75
503	A32	3c gray brn & grn	3.00	75
504	A32	6c gray & carmine	3.00	75
505	A32	9c yel brn & vio	3.00	75
506	A32	10c red & org brn	3.00	75
507	A32	13c vio & ultra	25.00	5.00
508	A32	1k ultra & car	25.00	2.00
509	A32	26c ultra & green	50.00	10.00
510	A32	2k grn & red vio	30.00	1.00
511	A32	3k vio & black	40.00	1.00
512	A32	5k red & ultra	35.00	1.50
513	A32	10k ol bis & claret	65.00	3.50
514	A32	20k vio brn & bis	65.00	5.00
515	A32	30k red & green	65.00	10.00
		Nos. 501-515 (15)	418.00	43.50

The "Officiel" overprint does not signify that the stamps were intended for use on official correspondence but that they were issued by authority. It was applied to the stocks in Tabriz and all post offices in the Tabriz region after a large quantity of stamps had been stolen during the Russian occupation of Tabriz.

The "Officiel" overprint has been counterfeited.

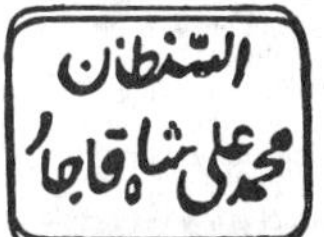

In 1912 this overprint, reading "Sultan Mohammed Ali Shah Kajar," was handstamped on outgoing mail in the Persian Kurdistan region occupied by the forces of the former Shah Mohammed Ali. It was applied after the stamps were on cover and is found on 8 of the Shah Ahmed stamps of 1911 (1c, 2c, 3c, 6c, 9c, 13c, 1k and 26c). Some specialists add the 10c. Forgeries are abundant.

Nos. 490 and 493 Surcharged:

a

b

1914

No.	Type	Description	Unused	Used
535	A32(a)	1c on 13c	10.00	50
536	A32(b)	3c on 26c	15.00	50

In 1914 a set of 19 stamps was prepared as a coronation issue. The 10 lower values each carry a different portrait; the 9 higher values show buildings and scenes. The same set printed with black centers was overprinted in red "SERVICE." The stamps were never placed in use, but were sold to stamp dealers in 1923.

Nos. 484 and 489 Surcharged in Black or Violet:

c

d

1915

No.	Type	Description	Unused	Used
537	A32(c)	1c on 5c	10.00	35
538	A32(c)	2c on 5c (V)	10.00	50
539	A32(c)	2c on 5c	40.00	15.00
540	A32(d)	6c on 12c	15.00	1.00

Nos. 455, 454 Surcharged:

e

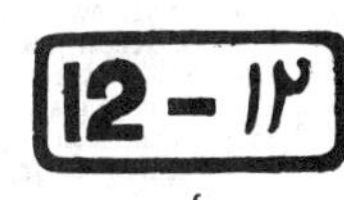
f

1915 *Perf. 12½x12*

No.	Type	Description	Unused	Used
541	A31(e)	5c on 1k multi	15.00	5.00
542	A31(f)	12c on 13c multi	18.00	5.00

Counterfeit surcharges on reprints abound.

Nos. 448-453, 455 Overprinted

1915

No.	Type	Description	Unused	Used
543	A31	1c org & maroon	10.00	2.00
544	A31	2c vio & maroon	10.00	2.00
545	A31	3c grn & maroon	6.00	2.00
546	A31	6c red & maroon	10.00	2.00
547	A31	9c gray & maroon	15.00	3.00
548	A31	10c red vio & mar	20.00	5.00
549	A31	1k sil, vio & bis brn	10.00	3.00
		Nos. 543-549 (7)	81.00	19.00

This overprint ("1333") also exists on the 2k, 10k, 20k and 30k, but they were not issued.

Counterfeit overprints, usually on reprints, abound.

Imperial Crown — A33

King Darius, Farohar overhead — A34

Ruins of Persepolis — A35

Perf. 11, 11½ or Compound

1915 Wmk. 161 Engr., Typo.

No.	Type	Description	Unused	Used
560	A33	1c car & indigo	15	2.00
561	A33	2c bl & carmine	15	2.00
562	A33	3c dark green	15	2.00
a.		Inverted center	110.00	
564	A33	5c red	15	2.50
565	A33	6c olive grn & car	15	2.00
a.		Inverted center	80.00	
566	A33	9c yel brn & vio	15	2.00
567	A33	10c bl grn & yel brn	15	2.00
568	A33	12c ultramarine	15	2.00
569	A34	1k sil, yel brn & gray	65	5.00
570	A33	24c yel brn & dk brn	25	5.00
571	A34	2k silver, bl & rose	65	5.00
572	A34	3k sil, vio & brn	65	5.00
573	A34	5k sil, brn & green	65	7.00
574	A35	1t gold, pur & blk	65	10.00
575	A35	2t gold, grn & brn	1.00	10.00
576	A35	3t gold, cl & red brn	1.00	10.00
577	A35	5t gold, blue & ind	1.00	10.00
		Nos. 560-577 (17)	7.70	

Coronation of Shah Ahmed.

Nos. 560-568, 570 are engraved. Nos. 569, 571-573 are engraved except for silver margins. Nos. 574-577 have centers engraved, frames typographed.

The 3c and 6c with inverted centers are considered genuine errors. Unauthorized reprints exist of these varieties and of other denominations with inverted centers. **Values unused for Nos. 560-577 are for reprints.**

For surcharges and overprints see Nos. 610-616, 635-646, O41-O57, Q19-Q35.

Nos. 455, 461-463 Overprinted

1915 Unwmk. Typo. *Perf. 12½x12*

No.	Type	Description	Unused	Used
582	A31	1k sil, vio & bis brn	10.00	2.50
583	A31	10k multicolored	35.00	10.00
584	A31	20k multicolored	82.50	10.00
585	A31	30k multicolored	40.00	10.00

Counterfeits exist of the overprints on Nos. 582-585 and 588, and of the surcharges on Nos. 586-587.

No. 491 Surcharged **24 Chahis**

1917 *Perf. 11½*

No.	Type	Description	Unused	Used
586	A32	12c on 1k multi	350.00	100.00
587	A32	24c on 1k multi	200.00	125.00

Issued during the Turkish occupation of Kermanshah.

No. 448 Overprinted "1335" in Persian Numerals

1917 *Perf. 12½x12*

No.	Type	Description	Unused	Used
588	A31	1c org & maroon	80.00	40.00

Overprint on No. 588 is similar to date in "k" and "l" surcharges.

Nos. 449, 452-453, 456 Surcharged:

k

l

1917

No.	Type	Description	Unused	Used
589	A31(k)	1c on 2c	10.00	1.00
590	A31(k)	1c on 9c	10.00	1.00
591	A31(k)	1c on 10c	10.00	1.00
592	A31(l)	3c on 9c	10.00	1.00
593	A31(l)	3c on 10c	10.00	1.00
594	A31(l)	3c on 26c	10.00	1.00

Same Surcharge on No. 488

No.	Type	Description	Unused	Used
595	A32(k)	1c on 10c	15.00	50
596	A32(l)	3c on 10c	15.00	50

Nos. 454 & 491 Surcharged Type "e"

No.	Type	Description	Unused	Used
597	A31	5c on 13c	15.00	3.50
598	A32	5c on 1k	15.00	60

Counterfeit surcharges on "canceled" reprints of Nos. 449, 452-454, 456 abound.

No. 489 Surcharged **6Chahis**

No.	Type	Description	Unused	Used
600	A32	6c on 12c grn & ultra	15.00	50

No. 457 Overprinted

1918

No.	Type	Description	Unused	Used
601	A31	2k multi	30.00	5.00

Nos. 459-460 Surcharged:

1918

No.	Type	Description	Unused	Used
602	A31	24c on 4k multi	35.00	7.00
603	A31	10k on 5k multi	35.00	10.00

The surcharges of Nos. 602-603 have been counterfeited.

Nos. 457-463 Overprinted

1918

No.	Type	Description	Unused	Used
603A	A31	2k multicolored	70.00	8.00
604	A31	3k multicolored	30.00	10.00
604A	A31	4k multicolored	40.00	10.00
604B	A31	5k multicolored	80.00	10.00
605	A31	10k multicolored	70.00	8.00
605A	A31	20k multicolored	300.00	80.00
606	A31	30k multicolored	100.00	15.00
		Nos. 603A-606 (7)	690.00	141.00

The overprint has been counterfeited on all values.

Nos. 489, 488 and 491 Surcharged:

m

n

No.	Type	Description	Unused	Used
607	A32(m)	3c on 12c	15.00	1.00
608	A32(n)	6c on 10c	15.00	1.00
609	A32(m)	6c on 1k	15.00	1.00

Nos. 571-577 Overprinted in Black or Red **Novembre ١٣٣٧-1918**

1918 Wmk. 161

No.	Type	Description	Unused	Used
610	A34	2k sil, blue & rose	5.00	5.00
611	A34	3k sil, vio & brn (R)	5.00	5.00
612	A34	5k sil, brn & grn (R)	7.00	7.00
613	A35	1t gold, pur & black (R)	6.00	6.00
614	A35	2t gold, grn & brn	7.00	7.00
615	A35	3t gold, cl & red brn	10.00	10.00
616	A35	5t gold, bl & ind (R)	10.00	10.00
		Nos. 610-616 (7)	50.00	50.00

The overprint commemorates the end of World War I. Counterfeits of this overprint are plentiful.

A36

1919 Unwmk. Typo. *Perf. 11½*

No.	Type	Description	Unused	Used
617	A36	1c yel & black	2.00	20
618	A36	3c green & black	3.00	20
619	A36	5c rose & black	5.00	1.50
620	A36	6c vio & black	10.00	20
621	A36	12c blue & black	15.00	1.25
		Nos. 617-621 (5)	35.00	3.35

Nos. 617-621 exist imperf., in colors other than the originals, with centers inverted and double impressions. Some specialists call them fraudulent, others call them reprints.

Counterfeits having double line over "POSTES" abound.

Nos. 75, 85-86 Surcharged in Various Colors

دو قران
1919
2 Kr.

1919 *Perf. 10½, 11, 11½, 13½*

No.	Type	Description	Unused	Used
622	A14	2k on 5c lilac (Bk)	4.00	2.00
623	A14	3k on 5c lilac (Br)	4.00	2.00
624	A14	4k on 5c lilac (G)	4.00	2.00
625	A14	5k on 5c lilac (V)	4.00	2.00
626	A16	10k on 10c rose (Bl)	6.00	3.00
627	A16	20k on 10c rose (G)	6.00	3.00
628	A16	30k on 10c rose (Br)	6.00	3.00
629	A16	50k on 14c org (V)	6.00	3.00
		Nos. 622-629 (8)	40.00	20.00

Nos. 622-629 exist with inverted and double surcharge. Some specialists consider these fraudulent.

Nos. 486, 489 Handstamp Surcharged

1 KRAN
BENADERS

1921 *Perf. 11½, 11½x11*

No.	Type	Description	Unused	Used
630	A32	10c on 6c	45.00	10.00
631	A32	1k on 12c	45.00	10.00

Counterfeits exist.

No. 489 Surcharged

No.	Type	Description	Unused	Used
632	A32	6c on 12c	80.00	3.00

Nos. 486, 489 Surcharged in Violet:

10 Ch. **1 Kr.**

1921

No.	Type	Description	Unused	Used
633	A32	10c on 6c	45.00	15.00
634	A32	1k on 12c	45.00	15.00

Counterfeits exist.

Coronation Issue of 1915 Overprinted

1921 Wmk. 161 *Perf. 11, 11½*

No.	Type	Description	Unused	Used
635	A33	3c dark grn	5.00	
a.		Center and overprint inverted	40.00	
636	A33	5c red	5.00	
637	A33	6c olive grn & car	5.00	
638	A33	10c bl grn & yel brn	6.00	
639	A33	12c ultramarine	6.00	
640	A34	1k sil, yel brn & gray	8.00	
641	A34	2k sil, blue & rose	7.00	
642	A34	5k sil, brn & green	7.00	
643	A35	2t gold, grn & brn	10.00	
644	A35	3t gold, cl & red brn	7.00	
645	A35	5t gold, bl & ind	7.00	
		Nos. 635-645 (11)	73.00	

Counterfeits of this Feb. 21, 1921, overprint are plentiful. Inverted overprints exist on all values; some specialists consider them fraudulent.

Stamps of 1911-13 Overprinted

1922 Unwmk. *Perf. 11½, 11½x11*

No.	Type	Description	Unused	Used
646	A32	1c grn & orange	3.00	20
a.		Inverted overprint	40.00	
647	A32	2c red & sepia	3.00	20
648	A32	3c brn & green	3.00	20
649	A32	5c brown & car	35.00	15.00
650	A32	6c grn & red brn	3.00	20
651	A32	9c yel brn & vio	3.00	20
652	A32	10c red & org brn	4.00	20
653	A32	12c green & ultra	4.00	30
654	A32	1k ultra & car	15.00	30
655	A32	24c vio & green	10.00	30
656	A32	2k grn & red vio	20.00	30
657	A32	3k vio & black	35.00	35
658	A32	4k ultra & gray	60.00	12.50
659	A32	5k red & ultra	35.00	45
660	A32	10k ol bis & cl	*140.00*	3.00
661	A32	20k vio brn & bis	*140.00*	5.00
662	A32	30k red & green	*140.00*	7.00
		Nos. 646-662 (17)	653.00	45.70

The status of inverted overprints on 5c and 12c is dubious. Unlisted inverts on other denominations are generally considered fraudulent. Counterfeits of this overprint exist.

Nos. 653, 655 Surcharged

1922

No.	Type	Description	Unused	Used
663	A32	3c on 12c	20.00	1.00
664	A32	6c on 24c	35.00	1.50

Nos. 661-662 Surcharged:

ده‌شاهی
1o chahis

یکقران
1 Kran

1923

No.	Type	Description	Unused	Used
665	A32	10c on 20k	25.00	4.00
666	A32	1k on 30k	35.00	10.00

Shah Ahmed — A37

A38

Perf. 11½, 11x11½, 11½x11

1924-25 Engr.

No.	Type	Description	Unused	Used
667	A37	1c orange	1.00	20
668	A37	2c magenta	1.00	20
669	A37	3c orange brown	1.00	20
670	A37	6c black brown	1.00	20
671	A37	9c dark green	2.00	75
672	A37	10c dark violet	2.00	30
673	A37	12c red	2.00	30
674	A37	1k dark blue	2.50	35
675	A37	2k indigo & red	3.00	1.00
a.		Center inverted		*1,500.*
676	A37	3k dk vio & red brown	15.00	1.25
677	A37	5d red & brown	30.00	2.00
678	A37	10k choc & lilac	40.00	10.00
679	A37	20k dk grn & brn	50.00	10.00
680	A37	30k org & blk brn	70.00	10.00
		Nos. 667-680 (14)	220.50	36.75

For overprints see Nos. 703-706.

SIX CHAHIS

P.re. موقتي — Type I

P.re. موقتي — Type II

Surcharge in Black, "1924" etc.

1924 Typo. *Perf. 11*

No.	Type	Description	Unused	Used
681	A38	1c yellow brown	2.00	1.00
682	A38	2c gray	2.00	1.00
683	A38	3c deep rose	2.00	1.00
684	A38	6c orange (I)	4.00	1.50
a.		6c orange (II)	3.00	2.00

The 1c was surcharged "Chahis" by error. Later the "s" was blocked out in black.

Counterfeits having double line over "POSTES" are plentiful.

Similar Surcharge, Dated 1925

1925

No.	Type	Description	Unused	Used
686	A38	2c yellow green	1.50	50
687	A38	3c red	1.50	50
689	A38	6c chalky blue	2.00	50
690	A38	9c light brown	2.00	75
691	A38	10c gray	5.00	1.25
694	A38	1k emerald	10.00	1.25
695	A38	2k lilac	35.00	6.00
		Nos. 686-695 (7)	57.00	10.75

Counterfeits having double line over "POSTES" are plentiful.

A39

Gold Overprint on Treasury Department Stamps

1925

No.	Type	Description	Unused	Used
697	A39	1c red	2.00	1.00
698	A39	2c yellow	2.00	1.50
699	A39	3c yellow green	3.00	2.00
700	A39	5c dark gray	9.00	6.00
701	A39	10c deep orange	3.00	2.00
702	A39	1k ultramarine	8.00	5.00
		Nos. 697-702 (6)	27.00	17.50

Deposition of Shah Ahmed and establishment of provisional government of Riza Khan Pahlavi.

#697-702 have same center (Persian lion in sunburst) with 6 different frames. Overprint reads: "Post / Provisional Government / of Pahlavi / 9th Abanmah / 1304 / 1925."

Nos. 667-670 Overprinted

1926 *Perf. 11½, 11x11½, 11½x11*

No.	Type	Description	Unused	Used
703	A37	1c orange	1.50	50
704	A37	2c magenta	1.50	50
705	A37	3c orange brown	1.50	75
706	A37	6c black brown	32.50	20.00

Overprinted to commemorate the Pahlavi government of 1925. Counterfeits exist.

Nos. 448-463 Overprinted

۱۳۰۵
سلطنت پهلوی
Règne de Pahlavi 1926

1926 *Perf. 11½, 12½x12*

No.	Type	Description	Unused	Used
707	A31	1c org & maroon	75	25
a.		Inverted overprint		
708	A31	2c vio & maroon	75	25
709	A31	3c yel grn & mar	75	25
a.		Inverted overprint	16.00	
710	A31	6c red & maroon	1.00	25
711	A31	9c gray & maroon	1.90	25
712	A31	10c red vio & mar	1.50	35
713	A31	13c dk bl & mar	1.50	35
714	A31	1k multi	2.00	35
715	A31	26c dk grn & mar	3.00	35
716	A31	2k multi	7.00	50
717	A31	3k multi	7.00	50
718	A31	4k sil, bl & bis brn	45.00	5.00
719	A31	5k multi	45.00	5.00
720	A31	10k multi	90.00	7.00
721	A31	20k multi	85.00	7.00
722	A31	30k multi	85.00	7.00
		Nos. 707-722 (16)	377.15	34.65

Overprinted to commemorate the Pahlavi government in 1926.

Nos. 707-722, perf. 11½, are on thick paper, perf. 12½x12 on thin paper.

So far forgeries are perf. 12½x12 only.

Riza Shah Pahlavi
A40 A41

1926-29 Typo. *Perf. 11*

No.	Type	Description	Unused	Used
723	A40	1c yellow green	70	15
724	A40	2c gray violet	70	15
725	A40	3c emerald	1.00	15
727	A40	6c magenta	2.00	15
728	A40	9c rose	6.00	25
729	A40	10c bister brown	10.00	1.50
730	A40	12c deep orange	12.00	35
731	A40	15c pale ultra	15.00	50
733	A41	1k dull bl ('27)	20.00	4.50
734	A41	2k brt vio ('29)	50.00	15.00
		Nos. 723-734 (10)	117.40	22.70

1928 Redrawn

No.	Type	Description	Unused	Used
740	A40	1c yellow green	4.50	20
741	A40	2c gray violet	6.00	20
742	A40	3c emerald	4.50	20
743	A40	6c rose	4.50	20

On the redrawn stamps much of the shading of the face, throat, collar, etc., has been removed. The letters of "Postes Persanes" and those in the circle at upper right are smaller. The redrawn stamps measure 20¼x25¾mm instead of 19¾x25¼mm.

Riza Shah Pahlavi
A42 A43

Perf. 11½, 12, 12½, Compound

1929 Photo.

No.	Type	Description	Unused	Used
744	A42	1c yel grn & cer	1.00	35
745	A42	2c scar & brt blue	1.00	35
746	A42	3c mag & myr grn	1.00	35
747	A42	6c yel brn & ol grn	1.00	35
748	A42	9c Prus bl & ver	2.50	50
749	A42	10c bl grn & choc	2.50	85
750	A42	12c gray blk & pur	4.00	85
751	A42	15c citron & ultra	5.00	85
752	A42	1k dull bl & blk	20.00	1.00
753	A42	24c ol grn & red brn	7.00	1.00

Engr.

Perf. 11½

No.	Type	Description	Unused	Used
754	A42	2k brn org & dk violet	20.00	1.50
755	A42	3k dark grn & dp rose	20.00	2.00
756	A42	5k red brn & dp green	20.00	2.00
757	A42	1t ultra & dp rose	25.00	5.00
758	A42	2t carmine & blk	40.00	15.00

Engr. and Typo.

No.	Type	Description	Unused	Used
759	A43	3t gold & dp vio	40.00	15.00
		Nos. 744-759 (16)	210.00	46.95

For overprints see Nos. 810-817.

Riza Shah Pahlavi — A44

1931-32 Litho. *Perf. 11*

No.	Type	Description	Unused	Used
760	A44	1c ol brn & ultra	1.00	20
761	A44	2c red brn & blk	1.00	20
762	A44	3c lilac rose & ol	1.00	20
763	A44	6c red org & vio	1.00	20
764	A44	9c ultra & red org	10.00	40
765	A44	10c ver & gray	10.00	70
766	A44	11c bl & dull red	17.50	8.00
767	A44	12c turq blue & lil rose	15.00	70
768	A44	16c black & red	17.50	1.75
769	A44	1k car & turq bl	25.00	1.75
770	A44	27c dk gray & dl bl	25.00	1.75
		Nos. 760-770 (11)	124.00	15.85

For overprints see Nos. 818-826.

Riza Shah Pahlavi
A45 A46

1933-34

No.	Type	Description	Unused	Used
771	A45	5d olive brown	1.00	25
772	A45	10d blue	1.00	25
773	A45	15d gray	1.00	25
774	A45	30d emerald	1.00	25
775	A45	45d turq blue	1.50	20
776	A45	50d magenta	1.50	25
777	A45	60d green	3.00	35
778	A45	75d brown	4.00	40
779	A45	90d red	5.00	2.50
780	A46	1r dk rose & blk	5.00	35
781	A46	1.20r gray blk & rose	12.00	1.00
782	A46	1.50 citron & bl	20.00	50
783	A46	2r lt bl & choc	20.00	60
784	A46	3r mag & green	40.00	2.00
785	A46	5r dk brn & red org	75.00	20.00
		Nos. 771-785 (15)	191.00	29.15

For overprints see Nos. 795-809.

"Justice" — A47 "Education" — A49

Ruins of Persepolis A48

Tehran Airport A50

Sanatorium at Sakhtessar A51

Cement Factory, Chah-Abdul-Azim — A52

Gunboat "Palang" A53

Railway Bridge over Karun River A54

Post Office and Customs Building, Tehran A55

1935, Feb. 21 Photo. *Perf. 12½*

No.	Type	Description	Unused	Used
786	A47	5d red brn & grn	25	20
787	A48	10d red org & gray black	25	20
788	A49	15d mag & Prus bl	30	20
789	A50	30d black & green	75	55
790	A51	45d ol grn & red brn	1.25	40
791	A52	75d grn & dark brn	6.00	85
792	A53	90d blue & car rose	10.00	2.50
793	A54	1r red brn & pur	30.00	8.00
794	A55	1½r violet & ultra	15.00	5.00
		Nos. 786-794 (9)	63.80	17.90

Reign of Riza Shah Pahlavi, 10th anniv.

Stamps of 1933-34 Overprinted in Black — POSTES IRANIENNES

1935 *Perf. 11*

No.	Type	Description	Unused	Used
795	A45	5d olive brown	1.00	15
796	A45	10d blue	1.00	15
797	A45	15d gray	1.00	15
798	A45	30d emerald	1.00	15
799	A45	45d turq blue	7.00	5.00
800	A45	50d magenta	2.00	30
801	A45	60d green	2.00	50
802	A45	75d brown	7.50	5.00
803	A45	90d red	20.00	15.00
804	A46	1r dk rose & blk	55.00	50.00
805	A46	1.20r gray black & rose	8.50	2.50
806	A46	1.50r citron & bl	8.50	1.50
807	A46	2r lt bl & choc	12.00	2.50
808	A46	3r mag & green	50.00	3.50
809	A46	5r dk brn & red org	100.00	80.00
		Nos. 795-809 (15)	276.50	166.40

Same Overprint on Stamps of 1929

1935 *Perf. 12, 12x12½*

No.	Type	Description	Unused	Used
810	A42	1c yel green & cer	175.00	
811	A42	2c scar & brt blue	80.00	
812	A42	3c mag & myr grn	45.00	
813	A42	6c yel brn & ol grn	25.00	20.00
814	A42	9c Prus bl & ver	20.00	20.00

Perf. 11½

No.	Type	Description	Unused	Used
815	A42	1t ultra & dp rose	25.00	10.00
816	A42	2t carmine & blk	25.00	6.50
817	A43	3t gold & dp vio	35.00	6.50
		Nos. 810-817 (8)	430.00	

No. 817 is overprinted vertically.
Forged overprints exist.

Same Ovpt. on Stamps of 1931-32

1935 *Perf. 11*

No.	Type	Description	Unused	Used
818	A44	1c ol brn & ultra	165.00	
819	A44	2c red brn & blk	35.00	
820	A44	3c lilac rose & ol	25.00	
821	A44	6c red org & vio	30.00	30.00
822	A44	9c ultra & red org	40.00	40.00
823	A44	11c blue & dull red	5.00	45
824	A44	12c turq bl & lil rose	150.00	
825	A44	16c black & red	7.50	3.00
826	A44	27c dk gray & dull bl	12.00	1.50
		Nos. 818-826 (9)	469.50	

Forged overprints exist.

Riza Shah Pahlavi — A56

1935 Photo. *Perf. 11*

Size: 19x27mm

No.	Type	Description	Unused	Used
827	A56	5d violet	1.00	15
828	A56	10d lilac rose	1.00	15
829	A56	15d turquoise bl	1.00	15
830	A56	30d emerald	1.00	15
831	A56	45d orange	1.50	15
832	A56	50d dull lt brn	2.75	30
833	A56	60d ultramarine	10.00	65
834	A56	75d red orange	10.00	25
835	A56	90d rose	12.50	65

Size: 21½x31mm

No.	Type	Description	Unused	Used
836	A56	1r dull lilac	15.00	50
837	A56	1.50r blue	25.00	2.00
838	A56	2r dk olive grn	20.00	55
839	A56	3r dark brown	25.00	1.00
840	A56	5r slate black	40.00	15.00
		Nos. 827-840 (14)	165.75	21.65

Riza Shah Pahlavi
A57 A58

1936-37 Litho. *Perf. 11*

Size: 20x27mm

No.	Type	Description	Unused	Used
841	A57	5d bright vio	1.00	15
842	A57	10d magenta	1.00	15
843	A57	15d bright ultra	1.00	15
844	A57	30d yellow green	1.00	15
845	A57	45d vermilion	1.25	15
846	A57	50d black brn ('37)	1.25	15
847	A57	60d brown orange	1.50	35
848	A57	75d rose lake	1.50	15
849	A57	90d rose red	3.00	35

Size: 23x31mm

No.	Type	Description	Unused	Used
850	A57	1r turq green	10.00	25
851	A57	1.50r deep blue	10.00	35
852	A57	2r bright blue	20.00	35
853	A57	3r violet brown	30.00	80
854	A57	5r slate green	40.00	1.25
855	A57	10r dark brown & ultra ('37)	55.00	15.00
		Nos. 841-855 (15)	177.50	19.75

1938-39 *Perf. 11*

Size: 20x27mm

No.	Type	Description	Unused	Used
856	A58	5d light violet	1.00	15
857	A58	10d magenta	1.00	15
858	A58	15d violet blue	1.00	15
859	A58	30d bright green	1.00	15
860	A58	45d vermilion	1.00	15
861	A58	50d black brown	1.00	15
862	A58	60d brown orange	1.00	15
863	A58	75d rose lake	1.50	15
864	A58	90d rose red ('39)	4.00	25

Size: 22½x30mm

No.	Type	Description	Unused	Used
865	A58	1r turq green	10.00	20
866	A58	1.50r deep blue	15.00	30
867	A58	2r lt blue ('39)	20.00	30
868	A58	3r violet brown	30.00	45
869	A58	5r gray grn ('39)	35.00	1.00
870	A58	10r dark brown & ultra ('39)	55.00	7.50
		Nos. 856-870 (15)	177.50	11.20

A58a

1939, Mar. 15 *Perf. 13*

No.	Type	Description	Unused	Used
870A	A58a	5d gray blue	60	
870B	A58a	10d brown	60	
870C	A58a	30d green	60	
870D	A58a	60d dark brown	80	
870E	A58a	90d red	1.25	
870F	A58a	1.50r blue	1.50	
870G	A58a	5r lilac	5.50	
870H	A58a	10r carmine	11.00	
		Nos. 870A-870H (8)	21.85	

60th birthday of Riza Shah Pahlavi. Printed in sheets of 4, perf. 13 and imperf. The imperf. sell for 50% more. The 1r violet and 2r orange were not available to the public.

Crown Prince and Princess Fawziya A59

1939, Apr. 25 Photo. *Perf. 11½*

No.	Type	Description	Unused	Used
871	A59	5d red brown	35	20
872	A59	10d bright violet	35	20
873	A59	30d emerald	1.00	35
874	A59	90d red	4.00	60
875	A59	1.50r bright blue	8.00	1.50
		Nos. 871-875 (5)	13.70	2.85

Wedding of Crown Prince Mohammed Riza Pahlavi to Princess Fawziya of Egypt.

Bridge over Karun River — A60

Veresk Bridge, North Iran — A61

Granary, Ahwaz A62

Train and Bridge — A63

Museum, Side View
A64 A67

Ministry of Justice — A65

School Building A66

Mohammed Riza Pahlavi
A68 A69

1942-46 Unwmk. Litho. *Perf. 11*

No.	Type	Description	Unused	Used
876	A60	5d violet	30	15
877	A60	5d red org ('44)	30	15
878	A61	10d magenta	30	15
879	A61	10d pck grn ('44)	30	15
880	A62	20d lt red violet	75	25
881	A62	20d magenta ('44)	75	25
882	A63	25d rose carmine	3.00	50
883	A63	25d violet ('44)	1.50	25
884	A64	35d emerald	80	30
885	A65	50d ultramarine	80	20
886	A65	50d emerald ('44)	80	15
887	A66	70d dull vio brn	60	35
888	A67	75d rose lake	3.00	35
889	A67	75d rose car ('46)	10.00	35
890	A68	1r carmine	2.75	15
891	A68	1r maroon ('45)	8.00	15
892	A68	1.50r red	2.50	15
893	A68	2r light blue	6.50	30
894	A68	2r sage grn ('44)	5.00	30
895	A68	2.50r dark blue	3.50	25
896	A68	3r peacock grn	55.00	75
897	A68	3r brt vio ('44)	17.50	35
898	A68	5r sage green	65.00	7.50
899	A68	5r lt blue ('44)	8.50	50
900	A69	10r brn org & blk	25.00	1.00
901	A69	10r dk org brn & black ('44)	15.00	1.00
902	A69	20r choc & vio	175.00	25.00
903	A69	20r orange & black ('44)	22.50	4.00
904	A69	30r gray blk & emerald	*475.00*	35.00
905	A69	30r emer & black ('44)	17.50	2.50
906	A69	50r dl bl & brn red	50.00	15.00
907	A69	50r brt vio & black ('45)	25.00	5.00
908	A69	100r rose red & blk ('45)	375.00	50.00
909	A69	200r bl & blk ('45)	250.00	40.00
		Nos. 876-909 (34)	1,627.	192.45

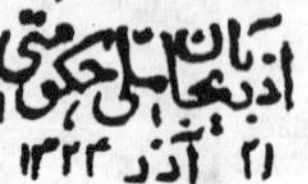

Sixteen denominations of this issue were handstamped at Tabriz in 1945-46 in Persian characters: "Azerbaijan National Government, Dec. 12, 1945." A rebel group did this overprinting while the Russian army held that area.

Flag of Persia A70

Designs: 50d, Docks at Bandar Shapur. 1.50r, Motor convoy. 2.50r, Gorge and railway viaduct. 5r, Map and Mohammed Riza Pahlavi.

Inscribed: "En souvenir des efforts de l'Iran pour la Victoire"

Engr. & Litho.

1949, Apr. 28 *Perf. 12½*

No.	Type	Description	Unused	Used
910	A70	25d multicolored	35	30
		Engr.		
911	A70	50d purple	75	65
912	A70	1.50r carmine rose	1.00	1.25
913	A70	2.50r deep blue	6.00	1.50
914	A70	5r green	10.00	2.50
		Nos. 910-914 (5)	18.10	6.20

Iran's contribution toward the victory of the Allied Nations in World War II.

Bridge over Zaindeh River — A71

National Bank — A72

Former Ministry of P.T.T. — A73

Mohammed Riza Pahlavi — A74

Designs: 5d-20r, Various views and buildings.

1949-50 Unwmk. Litho. *Perf. 10½*

No.	Type	Description	Unused	Used
915	A71	5d rose & dk grn	35	15
916	A71	10d ultra & brown	35	15
917	A71	20d vio & ultra	35	25
918	A71	25d blk brn & dp blue	40	15
919	A71	50d grn & ultra	40	15
920	A71	75d dk brn & red	65	15
921	A72	1r vio & green	1.00	15
922	A72	1.50r dk grn & ver	1.25	15
923	A72	2r dp car & blk brn	1.00	25
924	A72	2.50r chlky bl & bl	1.25	20
925	A72	3r vio bl & red orange	2.50	15
926	A72	5r dp car & vio	3.00	15
927	A73	10r car & blue green ('50)	25.00	45
		a. Inverted center	600.00	
928	A73	20r brown black & red ('50)	150.00	20.00
929	A74	30r choc & deep blue ('50)	45.00	10.00
930	A74	50r red & deep blue ('50)	55.00	10.00
		Nos. 915-930 (16)	287.50	42.50

Globes and Pigeons A75

Symbols of UPU — A76

1950, Mar. 16 Photo.

No.	Type	Description	Unused	Used
931	A75	50d brn carmine	14.00	12.50
932	A76	2.50r deep blue	21.00	17.50

UPU, 75th anniv. (in 1949).

Riza Shah Pahlavi and his Tomb — A77

1950, May 8

No.	Type	Description	Unused	Used
933	A77	50d brown	9.00	6.25
934	A77	2r sepia	21.00	9.00

Re-burial of Riza Shah Pahlavi, May 12, 1950.

Mohammed Riza Pahlavi, 31st Birthday — A78

Various portraits.

1950, Oct. 26 Engr. *Perf. 12½*

Center in Black

No.	Type	Description	Unused	Used
935	A78	25d carmine	2.25	75
936	A78	50d orange	2.25	75
937	A78	75d brown	17.00	6.00
938	A78	1r green	14.00	1.65
939	A78	2.50r deep blue	19.00	1.65
940	A78	5r brown lake	30.00	4.50
		Nos. 935-940 (6)	84.50	15.30

Shah and Queen Soraya A79

A80

1951, Feb. 12 Litho. *Perf. 10½*

No.	Type	Description	Unused	Used
941	A79	5d rose violet	1.10	50
942	A79	25d orange red	1.40	75
943	A79	50d emerald	4.00	2.00
944	A80	1r brown	4.50	2.00
945	A80	1.50r carmine	4.50	2.00
946	A80	2.50r blue	7.00	2.50
		Nos. 941-946 (6)	22.50	9.75

Wedding of Mohammed Riza Pahlavi to Soraya Esfandiari.

Farabi — A81

1951, Feb. 20

No.	Type	Description	Unused	Used
947	A81	50d red	1.90	1.40
948	A81	2.50r blue	9.00	2.50

Death millenary of Farabi, Persian philosopher.

Mohammed Riza Pahlavi
A82 A83

1951-52 Unwmk. Photo. *Perf. 10½*

No.	Type	Description	Unused	Used
950	A82	5d brown orange	25	15
951	A82	10d violet	25	15
952	A82	20d choc ('52)	75	35
953	A82	25d blue ('52)	45	20
954	A82	50d green	65	15
955	A82	75d rose	85	30
956	A83	1r gray green	1.25	15
957	A83	1.50r cerise	1.25	45
958	A83	2r chocolate	2.50	15
959	A83	2.50r deep blue	2.50	25
960	A83	3r red orange	3.50	15
961	A83	5r dark green	12.00	15
962	A83	10r olive ('52)	25.00	50
963	A83	20r org brn ('52)	17.50	3.00
964	A83	30r vio bl ('52)	8.50	2.00
965	A83	50r blk brn ('52)	30.00	4.00
		Nos. 950-965 (16)	107.20	12.10

See Nos. 975-977.

Oil Well and Mosque — A84

Oil Well, Mosque and Monument A85

1953, Feb. 20 Litho.

No.	Type	Description	Unused	Used
966	A84	50d green & yel	1.75	15
967	A85	1r lil rose & yel	2.00	32
968	A84	2.50r blue & yellow	3.00	80
969	A85	5r blk brn & yel	5.75	2.50

Discovery of oil at Qum.

Abadan Oil Refinery A86

Oil Wells — A87

Designs: 1r, Storage tanks. 5r, Pipe lines. 10r, Abadan refinery and wells.

1953, Mar. 20 Photo.

No.	Type	Description	Unused	Used
970	A86	50d blue green	65	45
971	A86	1r rose	1.00	45
972	A87	2.50r bright ultra	2.00	1.10
973	A86	5r red orange	4.25	1.25
974	A86	10r dark violet	6.75	1.90
		Nos. 970-974 (5)	14.65	5.15

Nationalization of oil industry, 2nd anniv.

Shah Types of 1951-52

1953-54 Photo. *Perf. 10½*

No.	Type	Description	Unused	Used
975	A82	50d dark gray grn	15.00	35
976	A83	1r dk blue green	1.50	15
977	A83	1.50r cerise ('54)	1.50	15

The background has been highlighted on the 1r and 1.50r.

Gymnast — A88

Archery A89

Designs: 3r, Climbing Mt. Demavend. 5r, Ancient polo. 10r, Lion hunting.

1953, Oct. 26

978 A88 1r deep green 2.00 1.10
979 A89 2.50fr brt grnsh bl 7.25 3.00
980 A89 3r gray 20.00 3.75
981 A88 5r bister 15.00 7.50
982 A88 10r rose lilac 26.00 7.50
Nos. 978-982 (5) 70.25 22.85

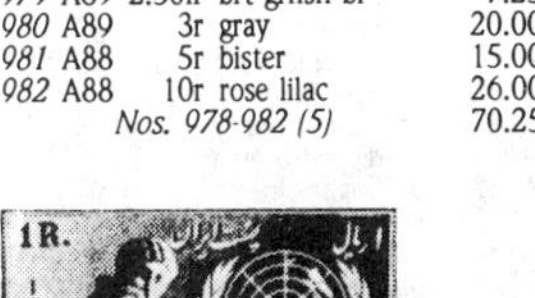
Mother with Children and UN Emblem A90

1953, Oct. 24

983 A90 1r bl grn & dk grn 1.10 20
984 A90 2.50r lt bl & indigo 1.40 50

United Nations Day, Oct. 24.

Herring — A91

Refrigeration Compressor A92

Processing Equipment, National Fisheries — A93

Designs: 2.50r, Sardines. 10r, Sturgeon.

1954, Jan. 31

985 A91 1r multi 3.75 90
986 A91 2.50r multi 20.00 4.50
987 A92 3r vermilion 9.00 4.50
988 A93 5r deep bl grn 13.00 8.00
989 A91 10r multi 20.00 13.00
Nos. 985-989 (5) 65.75 30.90

Nationalization of fishing industry.

Broken Shackles A94

Mother Feeding Baby A95

Designs: 3r, Torch and flag. 5r, Citizen holding flag of Iran.

1954, Aug. 19 **Litho.**

990 A94 2r multicolored 4.50 65
991 A94 3r multicolored 7.50 1.50
992 A94 5r multicolored 10.00 2.75

Return of the royalist government, 1st anniv.

1954, Oct. 24 **Photo.**

993 A95 2r red lil & org 1.75 75
994 A95 3r vio bl & org 1.75 1.25

Issued to honor the United Nations.

Woodsman Felling Tree — A96

Designs: 2.50r, Laborer carrying firewood. 5fr, Worker operating saw. 10r, Wooden galley.

1954, Dec. 11

995 A96 1r brn & grnsh black 13.00 10.00
996 A96 2.50r grnsh blk & bl 18.00 16.50
997 A96 5r lil & dk brn 52.50 21.00
998 A96 10r bl & claret 42.50 35.00

4th World Forestry Congress, Dehra Dun, India, 1954.

Mohammed Riza Pahlavi
A97 A98

1954-55 **Unwmk.**

999 A97 5d yellow brn 30 25
1000 A97 10d violet 30 25
1001 A97 25d scarlet 20 15
1002 A97 50d black brn 20 15
1003 A98 1r blue green 45 15
1004 A98 1.50r cerise 45 25
1005 A98 2r ocher 45 25
1006 A98 2.50r blue 1.00 20
1007 A98 3r olive 1.25 25
1008 A98 5r dk sl grn 5.00 25
1009 A98 10r lilac rose 10.00 1.00
1010 A98 20r indigo 30.00 2.00
1011 A98 30r dp yel grn 110.00 7.50
1012 A98 50r dp orange 30.00 5.00
1013 A98 100r light vio 325.00 40.00
1014 A98 200r yellow 100.00 20.00
Nos. 999-1014 (16) 614.60 77.65

See Nos. 1023-1036.

Regional Costume — A99

Regional Costumes: 1r, 2r, Men's costumes. 2.50r, 3r, 5r, Women's costumes.

Wmk. 306

1955, June 26 **Photo.** ***Perf. 11***

1015 A99 1r bluish gray & black 1.50 90
1016 A99 2r dl rose & blk 3.75 1.75
1017 A99 2.50r buff & black 8.00 2.75
1018 A99 3r rose lil & blk 5.50 3.25
1019 A99 5r gray brn & blk 9.50 6.50
Nos. 1015-1019 (5) 28.25 15.15

Parliament Gate — A100

Designs: 3r, Statue of Liberty, vert. 5r, Old Gate of Parliament.

1955, Aug. 6 ***Perf. 11***

1020 A100 2r red vio & grn 1.65 55
1021 A100 3r dk bl & aqua 5.25 1.65
1022 A100 5r Prus grn & red org 6.50 4.25

50th anniversary of constitution.

Shah Types of 1954-55

1955-56 **Wmk. 306** ***Perf. 11***

1023 A97 5d violet ('56) 50 50
1024 A97 10d carmine ('56) 50 20
1025 A97 25d brown 40 15
1026 A97 50d dk carmine 40 15
1027 A98 1r dark bl grn 50 15
1028 A98 1.50r red brn ('56) 25.00 3.00
1029 A98 2r ol grn ('56) 1.00 25
1030 A98 2.50r blue ('56) 1.50 30
1031 A98 3r bister 3.25 20
1032 A98 5r red lilac 3.00 20
1033 A98 10r brt grnsh bl 5.00 35
1034 A98 20r slate green 17.50 2.00
1035 A98 30r red org ('56) 110.00 14.00
1036 A98 50r red brn ('56) 75.00 16.50
Nos. 1023-1036 (14) 243.55 37.95

UN Emblem and Globes — A101

1955, Oct. 24 ***Perf. 11x12½***

1039 A101 1r dp car & org 1.40 52
1040 A101 2.50r dk bl & grnsh blue 2.25 1.25

UN, 10th anniv.Nations, Oct. 24, 1955.

Wrestlers — A102

1955, Oct. 26 **Wmk. 306** ***Perf. 11***

1041 A102 2.50r multi 3.00 1.75

Victory in intl. wrestling competitions.

Garden, Nemazi Hospital — A103

Soldier — A105

Nemazi Hospital, Shiraz — A104

Designs: 5r, Gate of the Koran. 10r, Hafiz of Shiraz.

1956, Mar. 21 ***Perf. 11x12½***

1042 A103 50d multi 1.65 60
1043 A104 1r multi 3.00 1.00
1044 A105 2.50r multi 8.25 6.00
1045 A104 5r multi 7.25 4.00
1046 A105 10r multi 20.00 6.00
Nos. 1042-1046 (5) 40.15 17.60

Opening of Nemazi Hospital, Shiraz.

Arms of Iran and Olympic Rings — A106

Tomb at Maragheh — A107

1956, May 15 **Wmk. 306**

1047 A106 5r rose lilac 20.00 15.00

National Olympic Committee, 10th anniv.

1956, May 26 **Photo.** ***Perf. 11x12½***

Designs: 2.50r, Astrolabe. 5r, Nasr-ud-Din of Tus.

1048 A107 1r orange 2.50 90
1049 A107 2.50r deep ultra 4.00 90
1050 A107 5r sepia & pur 7.75 1.10

700th death anniv. of Nasr-up-Din of Tus, mathematician.

WHO Emblem — A108

Perf. 11x12½

1956, Sept. 19 **Wmk. 306**

1051 A108 6r cerise 2.25 1.00

6th Regional Congress of the WHO.

Scout Bugler and Camp — A109

Design: 5r, Scout badge and Shah in scout uniform.

1956, Aug. 5 ***Perf. 12½x11***

1052 A109 2.50r ultra & blue 10.50 5.00
1053 A109 5r lil & red lil 14.00 7.50

National Boy Scout Jamboree.

Catalogue values for unused stamps in this section, from this point to the end of the section, are for Never Hinged items.

Former Telegraph Office, Tehran A110

Design: 6r, Telegraph lines and ancient monument.

1956, Oct. 26

1054 A110 2.50r brt bl & grn, *bluish* 8.50 3.50
1055 A110 6r rose car & lil 11.00 5.00

Centenary of Persian telegraph system.

UN Emblem and People of the World — A111

Design: 2.50r, UN Emblem and scales.

1956, Oct. 24

No.	Type	Description	Unused	Used
1056	A111	1r bluish green	1.40	30
1057	A111	2.50r blue & green	2.75	55

United Nations Day, Oct. 24.

Shah and Pres. Iskander Mirza of Pakistan A112

1956, Oct. 31

No.	Type	Description	Unused	Used
1058	A112	1r multicolored	2.00	60

Visit of Pres. General Iskander Mirza of Pakistan to Tehran, Oct. 31-Nov. 10.

Mohammed Riza Pahlavi
A113 A114

Perf. 13½x11

1956-57 Wmk. 306 Photo.

Design A113

No.	Description	Unused	Used
1058A	5d brt car & red	45	1.00
1058B	10d vio bl & dl vio	45	1.00
1059	25d dk brn & brn	65	35
1059A	50d brn & ol brn	70	15
b.	Inverted center		
1060	1r brn & brt grn	70	20
1061	1.50r brt lil & brown	70	20
1062	2r red vio & red	70	20
1063	2.50r ultra & blue	1.00	20
1064	3r brn & dk ol bis	1.00	20
1065	5r ver & mar	1.00	20

Design A114

No.	Description	Unused	Used
1066	6r dk vio & brn lil	4.50	25
1067	10r lt blue & grn	8.50	20
1068	20r green & blue	20.00	3.00
1069	30r rose red & org	25.00	5.00
1070	50r dk grn & ol grn	17.50	4.00
1071	100r lilac & cer	225.00	27.50
1072	200r dp plum & vio bl	100.00	15.00
	Nos. 1058A-1072 (17)	407.85	58.65

Issued: 1.50r, 2r, 3r, 5r, 6r, 1956; others, 1957.
See Nos. 1082-1098.

Lord Baden-Powell A115 — Railroad Tracks A116

Train and Map — A117

1957, Feb. 22 ***Perf. 12½***

No.	Type	Description	Unused	Used
1073	A115	10r dk grn & brn	7.00	4.00

Birth cent. of Robert Baden-Powell, founder of the Boy Scout movement.

1957, May 2 ***Perf. 11x12½, 12½x11***

Design: 10r, Train and mosque.

No.	Type	Description	Unused	Used
1074	A116	2.50r grnsh blk, bl & ocher	7.25	1.00
1075	A117	5r multi	9.50	5.00
1076	A116	10r blk, yel & bl	18.00	9.00

Opening of the Tehran Meshed-Railway.

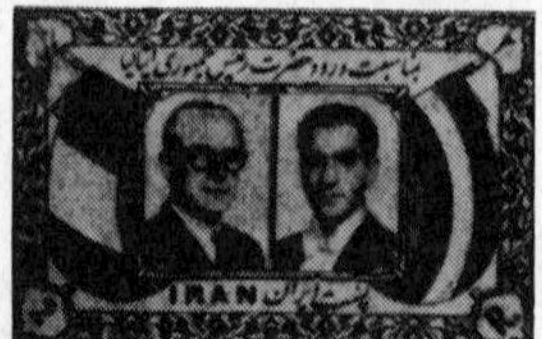

Pres. Giovanni Gronchi of Italy and Shah — A118

Design: 6r, Ruins of Persepolis and Colosseum in Rome and flags.

Wmk. 316

1957, Sept. 7 Photo. ***Perf. 11***

No.	Type	Description	Unused	Used
1077	A118	2r sl bl, grn & red	3.25	1.00
1078	A118	6r sl bl, grn & red	6.75	2.00

Visit of Pres. Giovanni Gronchi of Italy to Iran, Sept. 7.

Queen Soraya and Hospital A119

1957, Sept. 29 Wmk. 316 ***Perf. 11***

No.	Type	Description	Unused	Used
1079	A119	2r lt bl & grn	2.50	45

Sixth Medical Congress, Ramsar.

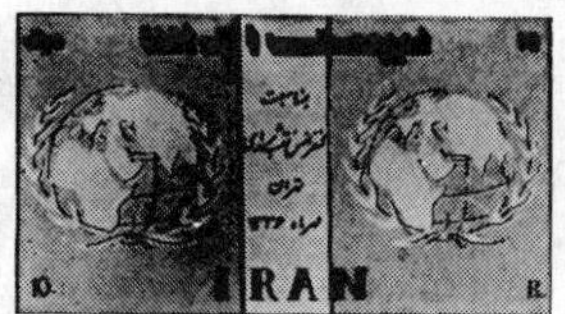

Globes Showing Location of Iran — A120

1957, Oct. 22 Litho. ***Perf. 12½x11***

No.	Type	Description	Unused	Used
1080	A120	10r blk, lt bl, yel & red	7.00	2.00

Intl. Cartographic Conference, Tehran.

Shah and King Faisal II — A121

1957, Oct. 18 Photo.

No.	Type	Description	Unused	Used
1081	A121	2r sl bl, grn & red	2.50	45

Visit of King Faisal of Iraq, Oct. 19.

Shah Types of 1956-57

1957-58 Wmk. 316 ***Perf. 11***

No.	Type	Description	Unused	Used
1082	A114	5d violet & pur	25	2.00
1083	A114	10d claret & rose car	25	2.00
1084	A114	25d rose car & brick red	50	35
1085	A114	50d grn & olive grn	40	15
1086	A114	1r dk grn	40	15
1087	A114	1.50r cl & red lil	50	25
1088	A114	2r bl & grnsh blue	1.65	15
1089	A114	2.50r dk bl & blue	1.65	25
1090	A114	3r rose car & ver	1.65	20
1091	A114	5r vio bl	1.50	15
1092	A113	6r brt bl	1.60	15
1093	A113	10r dp grn	3.00	30
1094	A113	20r grn & olive grn	6.25	45
1095	A113	30r vio bl & dk brn	15.00	4.00
1096	A113	50r dk brn & lt brn	20.00	5.00
1097	A113	100r rose lil & car rose	140.00	25.00
1098	A113	200r vio & yel brn	87.50	20.00
		Nos. 1082-1098 (17)	282.10	60.55

Issued: 1.50r, 2r, 3r, 1957; others, 1958.

Weight Lifter A122 — Modern and Old Houses, Radio Transmitter A123

1957, Nov. 8 ***Perf. 11x14½***

No.	Type	Description	Unused	Used
1099	A122	10r bl, grn & red	2.50	60

Iran's victories in weight lifting.

1958, Feb. 22 Litho.

No.	Type	Description	Unused	Used
1100	A123	10r brn, ocher & bl	4.00	1.50

30th anniversary of radio in Iran.

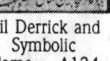

Oil Derrick and Symbolic Flame — A124 — Train on Viaduct — A125

Wmk. 316

1958, Mar. 10 Photo. ***Perf. 11***

No.	Type	Description	Unused	Used
1101	A124	2r gray & multi	3.25	80
1102	A124	10r multicolored	6.00	1.00

Drilling of Iran's 1st oil well, 50th anniv.

1958, Apr. 24 Wmk. 316 ***Perf. 11***

Design: 8r, Train and map.

No.	Type	Description	Unused	Used
1103	A125	6r dull purple	10.00	2.50
1104	A125	8r green	12.00	2.50

Opening of Tehran-Tabriz railway line.

Exposition Emblem A126

1958, Apr. 17 ***Perf. 12½x11***

No.	Type	Description	Unused	Used
1105	A126	2.50r bl & light bl	38	15
1106	A126	6r car & salmon	60	15
		Set value		22

World's Fair, Brussels, Apr. 17-Oct. 19.

Mohammed Riza Pahlavi A127 — UN Emblem and Map of Iran A128

1958-59 Wmk. 316 Photo. ***Perf. 11***

No.	Type	Description	Unused	Used
1107	A127	5d blue violet	50	22
1108	A127	10d lt vermilion	50	22
1109	A127	25d crimson	50	26
1110	A127	50d brt blue	50	22
1111	A127	1r dark green	1.00	15
1113	A127	2r dark brown	8.00	22
1115	A127	3r dk red brown	15.00	18
1117	A127	6r bright blue	4.00	45
1118	A127	8r magenta	5.00	35
1120	A127	14r blue violet	12.00	1.75
1121	A127	20r green	15.00	45
a.		Wmk. 306	20.00	10.00
1122	A127	30r brt car rose	12.00	1.75
1123	A127	50r rose violet	45.00	3.50
1124	A127	100r red orange	20.00	4.50
1125	A127	200r slate green	40.00	8.00
		Nos. 1107-1125 (15)	179.00	22.22

See Nos. 1138-1151, 1173-1179.

1958, Oct. 24

No.	Type	Description	Unused	Used
1126	A128	6r bright blue	1.25	45
1127	A128	10r dk violet & grn	2.25	80

Issued for United Nations Day, Oct. 24.

Globe and Hands — A129

1958, Dec. 10

No.	Type	Description	Unused	Used
1128	A129	6r dk red brn & brn	75	22
1129	A129	8r dk grn & gray grn	1.25	32

Universal Declaration of Human Rights, 10th anniv.

Rudagi — A130 — Wrestlers, Flag and Globe — A131

Flag — A130a

Design: 5r, Rudagi, different pose.

1958, Dec. 24 Photo. Wmk. 306

No.	Type	Description	Unused	Used
1130	A130	2.50r bluish black	6.50	90
1131	A130	5r violet	10.00	1.50
1132	A130	10r dark brown	16.00	2.75

1100th birth anniv. of Rudagi, blind Persian poet.

Perf. 14½x11

1959, May 8 Wmk. 316

No.	Type	Description	Unused	Used
1132A	A130a	1r multicolored	75	38
1132B	A130a	6r multicolored	2.25	50

Centenary of the Red Cross.

1959 Litho. ***Perf. 11x12½***

No.	Type	Description	Unused	Used
1133	A131	6r multicolored	10.00	2.50

World Wrestling Championships, Tehran.

Globe, UN Building and Hand Holding Torch of Freedom A132

1959, Oct. 24 Photo. ***Perf. 11***

No.	Type	Description	Unused	Used
1134	A132	6r gray brn, red & bis	1.50	50

Issued for United Nations Day, Oct. 24.

Shah and Pres. Ayub Khan of Pakistan A133

1959, Nov. 9 Litho. *Perf. 11x16*
1135 A133 6r multicolored 5.00 75

Visit of Pres. Khan to Iran.

ILO Emblem — A134

Uprooted Oak Emblem — A136

Pahlavi Foundation Bridge, Karun River A135

1959, Nov. 12 *Perf. 16*
1136 A134 1r blue 1.10 30
1137 A134 5r brown 1.90 45

ILO, 40th anniversary.

Shah Type of 1958-59

1959-63 Wmk. 316 Photo.			***Perf. 11***	
1138	A127	5d red brown ('60)	35	30
1139	A127	10d Prus green ('60)	35	30
a.		10d Prussian blue ('63)	50	50
1140	A127	25d orange	1.00	20
a.		Perf. 12x11½	10.00	10.00
1141	A127	50d scarlet	1.00	25
1142	A127	1r deep violet	1.00	15
1143	A127	3r olive	3.00	15
1144	A127	8r brown olive	1.50	15
1145	A127	10r olive blk ('60)	1.50	15
1146	A127	14r yel green	1.75	25
1147	A127	20r slate grn ('60)	3.00	35
1148	A127	30r choc ('60)	3.50	65
1149	A127	50r dp blue ('60)	3.50	60
1150	A127	100r green ('60)	110.00	10.00
1151	A127	200r cer ('60)	225.00	15.00
		Nos. 1138-1151 (14)	356.45	28.50

1960, Feb. 29 Litho. *Perf. 16x11*

Design: 5r, Bridge, different view.

1152 A135 1r dk brn & brt bl 1.00 15
1153 A135 5r blue & emerald 2.00 50

Opening of Pahlavi Foundation Bridge at Khorramshahr on the Karun River.

1960, Apr. 7 *Perf. 11*

Design: 6r, Arched frame.

1154 A136 1r brt ultra 50 15
1155 A136 6r gray olive 65 18

World Refugee Year, July 1, 1959-June 30, 1960.

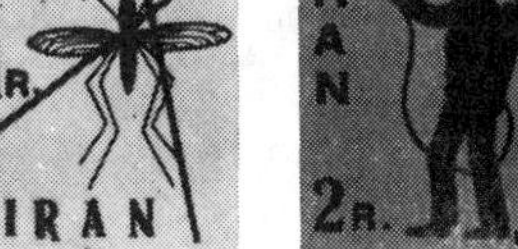

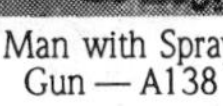

Mosquito — A137

Man with Spray Gun — A138

Design: 3r, Mosquito on water.

1960, Apr. 7 Wmk. 316
1156 A137 1r blk & red, *yel* 1.10 20
1157 A138 2r lt bl, ultra & blk 1.75 30
1158 A137 3r blk & red, *yel grn* 3.75 65

Issued to publicize malaria control.

Polo Player — A139

Design: 6r, Persian archer.

1960, June 9 Litho. Wmk. 316
1159 A139 1r deep claret 75 30
1160 A139 6r dk blue & lt blue 1.90 75

17th Olympic Games, Rome, Aug. 25-Sept. 11.

Shah and King Hussein of Jordan — A140

1960, July 6 *Perf. 11*
1161 A140 6r multicolored 5.00 65

Visit of King Hussein of Jordan to Tehran.

Iranian Scout Emblem in Flower — A141

Tents and Pillars of Persepolis — A142

1960, July 18
1162 A141 1r green 42 22
1163 A142 6r brn, brt bl & buff 65 45

3rd National Boy Scout Jamboree.

Shah and Queen Farah A143

1960, Sept. 9 Litho. *Perf. 11*
1164 A143 1r green 2.25 50
1165 A143 5r blue 4.75 1.00

Marriage of Shah Mohammed Riza Pahlavi and Farah Diba.

UN Emblem and Globe — A144

1960, Oct. 24 Wmk. 316
1166 A144 6r bl, blk & lt brn 50 15

15th anniversary of the United Nations.

Shah and Queen Elizabeth II — A145

1961, Mar. 2 Litho. *Perf. 11*
1167 A145 1r lt red brown 75 15
1168 A145 6r bright ultra 1.65 35

Visit of Queen Elizabeth II to Tehran, Feb. 1961.

Girl Playing Arganoon A146

Safiaddin Amavi A147

1961, Apr. 10 Wmk. 316 *Perf. 11*
1169 A146 1r dk brown & buff 65 15
1170 A147 6r greenish gray 1.40 20

International Congress of Music, Tehran.

Shah Type of 1958-59 Redrawn

1961-62 Litho.			***Perf. 11***	
1173	A127	25d orange	1.10	52
1174	A127	50d scarlet	1.10	42
1175	A127	1r deep violet	2.25	22
1176	A127	2r chocolate	3.75	22
1177	A127	3r olive brown	4.25	52
1178	A127	6r brt blue ('62)	32.50	2.25
1179	A127	8r brown ol ('62)	17.00	2.25
		Nos. 1173-1179 (7)	61.95	6.40

On Nos. 1173-1179 (lithographed), a single white line separates the lower panel from the shah's portrait. On Nos. 1107-1125, 1138-1151 (photogravure), two lines, one in color and one in white, separate panel from portrait. Other minor differences exist.

Shah and Queen Farah Holding Crown Prince — A148

1961, June 2 Litho.
1186 A148 1r bright pink 1.25 75
1187 A148 6r light blue 5.00 2.25

Birth of Crown Prince Riza Cyrus Ali, Oct. 31, 1960.

Swallows and UN Emblem — A149

Planting Tree — A150

1961, Oct. 24 *Perf. 11*
1188 A149 2r blue & car rose 75 15
1189 A149 6r blue & violet 90 28

Issued for United Nations Day, Oct. 24.

1962, Jan. 11
1190 A150 2r ol grn, cit & dk bl 60 16
1191 A150 6r ultra, grn & pale bl 75 32

Tree Planting Day.

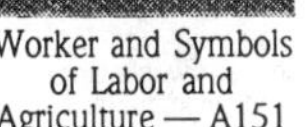

Worker and Symbols of Labor and Agriculture — A151

Map, Family and Cogwheel — A152

1962, Mar. 15 Litho.
1192 A151 2r bl grn, brn & blk 60 15
1193 A151 6r lt ultra, brn & blk 90 28

Issued for Workers' Day.

1962, Mar. 20 *Perf. 11*
1194 A152 2r black, yel & lil 60 15
1195 A152 6r black, bl & ultra 90 28

Social Insurance Week.

Sugar Refinery, Khuzistan A153

1962, Apr. 14 Wmk. 316
1196 A153 2r dk & lt blue & grn 65 15
1197 A153 6r ultra, buff & blue 1.00 30

Opening of sugar refinery in Khuzistan.

Karaj Dam — A154

1962, May 15
1198 A154 2r dk brn & gray grn 1.65 16
1199 A154 6r vio bl & lt blue 1.90 32

Inauguration of Karaj Dam, renamed Amir Kabir Dam.

Sefid Rud Dam A155

1962, May 19 **Litho.**

1200 A155 2r dk grn, lt bl & buff 1.25 25
1201 A155 6r red brn, sl grn & lt blue 1.75 50

Inauguration of Sefid Rud Dam.

"UNESCO" and UN Emblem — A156

1962, June 2 **Wmk. 316** ***Perf. 11***

1202 A156 2r black, emer & red 75 15
1203 A156 6r blue, emer & red 1.50 40

15th anniv. of UNESCO.

Malaria Eradication Emblem and Sprayer — A157

Designs: 2r, Emblem and arrow piercing mosquito, horiz. 10r, Emblem and globe, horiz. Size: 2r and 10r, 40x25mm; 6r, 29½x34½mm.

1962, June 20

1204 A157 2r black & bluish grn 24 15
1205 A157 6r pink & vio blue 95 15
1206 A157 10r lt blue & ultra 2.00 30

WHO drive to eradicate malaria.

Oil Field and UN Emblem — A158

1962, Sept. 1 **Photo.**

1207 A158 6r grnsh blue & brn 1.25 20
1208 A158 14r gray & sepia 2.25 45

2nd Petroleum Symposium of ECAFE (UN Economic Commission for Asia and the Far East).

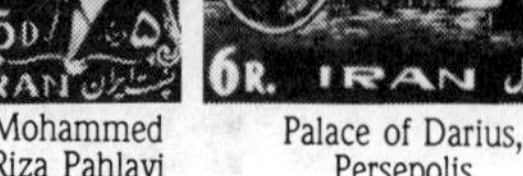

Mohammed Riza Pahlavi A159

Palace of Darius, Persepolis A160

Perf. 11, 10½x11

1962 **Photo.** **Wmk. 316**

1209 A159 5d green 75 25
1210 A159 10d chestnut 75 50
1211 A159 25d dark blue 50 35
1212 A159 50d Prus green 50 15
1213 A159 1r orange 1.50 15
1214 A159 2r violet blue 1.00 15
1215 A159 5r dark brown 2.00 15
1216 A160 6r blue 9.00 2.50
1217 A160 8r yellow grn 4.50 1.00
1218 A160 10r grnsh blue 4.00 15
1219 A160 11r slate green 4.50 65
1220 A160 14r purple 7.00 65
1221 A160 20r red brown 6.00 1.50
1222 A160 50r vermilion 8.00 1.50
Nos. 1209-1222 (14) 50.00 9.65

See Nos. 1331-1344.

Hippocrates and Avicenna A161

1962, Oct. 7 **Litho.**

1226 A161 2r brown, buff & ultra 1.40 25
1227 A161 6r grn, pale grn & ultra 1.65 38

Near and Middle East Medical Congress.

Hands Laying Bricks A162

Design: 6r, Houses and UN emblem, vert.

1962, Oct. 24

1228 A162 6r dk blue & ultra 1.25 20
1229 A162 14r dk blue & emer 1.75 40

Issued for United Nations Day, Oct. 24.

Crown Prince Receiving Flowers A163

1962, Oct. 31

1230 A163 6r blue gray 4.25 65
1231 A163 14r dull green 8.25 1.65

Children's Day, Oct. 31; 2nd birthday of Crown Prince Riza Cyrus Ali.

Map of Iran and Persian Gulf — A164

Hilton Hotel, Tehran — A165

1962, Dec. 12 **Wmk. 316** ***Perf. 11***

1232 A164 6r dk & lt bl, vio bl & rose 1.00 16
1233 A164 14r dk & lt bl, pink & rose 1.50 32

The Persian Gulf Seminar.

1963, Jan. 21 **Photo.**

1234 A165 6r deep blue 2.75 30
1235 A165 14r dark red brown 4.25 45

Opening of the Royal Tehran Hilton Hotel.

Mohammed Riza Shah Dam — A166

1963, Mar. 14 **Litho.**

Center Multicolored

1236 A166 6r violet blue 3.25 30
1237 A166 14r dark brown 5.50 65

Mohammed Riza Shah Dam inauguration.

Worker with Pickax — A167

Stylized Bird over Globe — A168

1963, Mar. 15

1238 A167 2r cream & black 1.10 18
1239 A167 6r lt blue & blk 2.00 32

Issued for Labor Day.

1963, Mar. 21 ***Perf. 11***

Designs: 6r, Stylized globe and "FAO." 14r, Globe in space and wheat emblem.

1240 A168 2r ultra, lt bl & bis 1.50 15
1241 A168 6r lt ultra, ocher & blk 2.25 28
1242 A168 14r slate bl & ocher 3.75 85

FAO "Freedom from Hunger" campaign.

Shah and List of Bills A169

1963, Mar. 21 **Wmk. 316**

1243 A169 6r green & lt blue 3.75 1.10
1244 A169 14r green & dull yel 5.25 1.90

Signing of six socioeconomic bills by Shah, 1st anniv.

Shah and King of Denmark — A170

1963, May 3 **Litho.** ***Perf. 11***

1245 A170 6r indigo & dk ultra 3.00 55
1246 A170 14r dk brn & red brn 4.50 1.00

Visit of King Frederik IX of Denmark.

Flags, Shah Mosque, Isfahan, and Taj Mahal, Agra A171

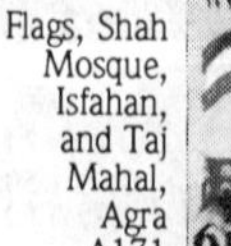

1963, May 19

1247 A171 6r blue, yel grn & red 2.75 65
1248 A171 14r multicolored 4.00 1.25

Visit of Dr. Sarvepalli Radhakrishnan, president of India.

Chahnaz Dam — A172

Cent. Emblem with Red Lion and Sun — A173

1963, June 8 **Wmk. 316** ***Perf. 11***

1249 A172 6r ultra, bl & grn 2.50 38
1250 A172 14r dk grn, bl & buff 2.50 55

Inauguration of Chahnaz Dam.

1963, June 10

1251 A173 6r blue, gray & red 2.50 65
1252 A173 14r buff, gray & red 4.00 90

Centenary of International Red Cross.

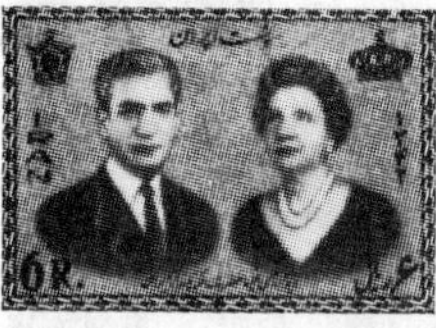

Shah and Queen Juliana A174

Perf. 11x10½

1963, Oct. 3 **Wmk. 349**

1253 A174 6r ultra & blue 3.75 50
1254 A174 14r sl grn & dull grn 5.75 75

Visit of Queen Juliana of the Netherlands.

Literacy Corps Emblem and Soldier Teaching Village Class A175

1963, Oct. 15 **Litho.** ***Perf. 10½***

1255 A175 6r multicolored 3.00 50
1256 A175 14r multicolored 5.00 50

Issued to publicize the Literacy Corps.

Gen. Charles de Gaulle and View of Tehran A176

1963, Oct. 16

1257 A176 6r ultra & blue 4.00 55
1258 A176 14r brn & pale brn 5.25 65

Visit of General de Gaulle of France.

Fertilizer Plant, Oil Company Emblem and Map — A177

Design: 14r, Factory and Iranian Oil Company emblem, horiz.

Perf. 10½x11, 11x10½

1963, Oct. 18 **Wmk. 316**

1259 A177 6r black, yel & red 4.00 50
1260 A177 14r black, bl & yel 5.25 1.50

Opening of Shiraz Chemical Factory.

Pres. Heinrich Lübke of Germany and Mosque in Tehran A178

1963, Oct. 23 Wmk. 349 *Perf. 10½*

1261 A178 6r ultra & dk blue	4.25	65
1262 A178 14r gray & brown	5.00	1.65

Visit of Pres. Lubke of Germany.

UN Emblem and Iranian Flag — A179

1963, Oct. 24

1263 A179 8r multicolored 2.75 50

Issued for United Nations Day.

UN Emblem and Jets — A180

1963, Oct. 24

1264 A180 6r multicolored 2.75 50

Iranian jet fighters with UN Force in the Congo.

Crown Prince Riza — A181

Pres. Brezhnev of USSR — A182

1963, Oct. 31

1265 A181 2r brown	1.75	22
1266 A181 6r blue	4.50	48

Children's Day; Crown Prince Riza's 3rd birthday.

1963, Nov. 16 Wmk. 349 *Perf. 10½*

1267 A182 6r dk brn, yel & bl	2.25	32
1268 A182 11r dk brn, yel & red	5.00	75

Visit of Pres. Leonid I. Brezhnev.

Atatürk's Mausoleum, Ankara — A183

1963, Nov. 28 Litho.

1269 A183 4r shown	2.75	15
1270 A183 5r Kemal Ataturk	2.75	25

25th death anniv. of Kemal Atatürk, president of Turkey.

Scales and Globe — A184

1963, Dec. 10

1271 A184 6r brt yel grn, blk & ultra	2.75	30
1272 A184 14r org brn, blk & buff	3.25	35

Universal Declaration of Human Rights, 15th anniv.

Mother and Child — A185

Map of Iran, Chamber of Industry and Mines Emblem — A186

1963, Dec. 16

1273 A185 2r multicolored	2.25	25
1274 A185 4r multicolored	3.25	50

Issued for Mother's Day.

1963, Dec. 17 Litho.

1275 A186 8r bl grn, buff & dk bl 3.50 40

Chamber of Industry and Mines.

Factories and Hand Holding Bill — A187

Designs: 4r, Factories and bills on scale. 6r, Man on globe carrying torch of education. 8r, Tractor, map and yardstick. 10r, Forest. 12r, Gate of Parliament and heads of man and woman.

1964, Jan. 26 Wmk. 349 *Perf. 10½*

1276 A187 2r multicolored	3.00	75
1277 A187 4r brown & gray	3.00	75
1278 A187 6r multicolored	3.00	75
1279 A187 8r multicolored	3.00	1.00
1280 A187 10r multicolored	5.50	1.25
1281 A187 12r red org & brn	6.50	1.50
Nos. 1276-1281 (6)	24.00	6.00

2nd anniv. of six socioeconomic bills: 2r, Shareholding for factory workers. 4r, Sale of shares in government factories. 6r, Creation of Army of Education. 8r, Land reforms. 10r, Nationalization of forests. 12r, Reforms in parliamentary elections.

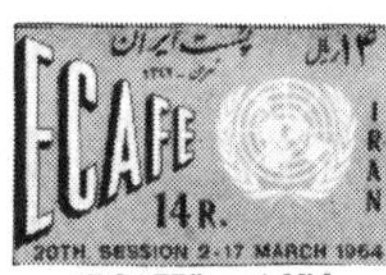
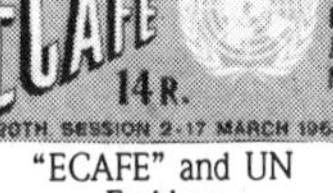
"ECAFE" and UN Emblem A188

Flowering Branch A189

1964, Mar. 2 Wmk. 349

1282 A188 14r brt green & blk 2.25 45

20th session of ECAFE (Economic Commission for Asia and the Far East), Mar. 2-17.

1964, Mar. 5 *Perf. 10½*

1283 A189 50d emerald, blk & org	35	15
1284 A189 1r brt blue, blk & org	35	15
Set value		15

Novrooz, Iranian New Year, Mar. 21.

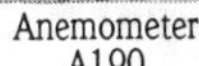
Anemometer A190

Mosque and Arches, Isfahan A191

1964, Mar. 23 Litho.

1285 A190 6r brt blue & vio bl 1.10 25

4th World Meteorological Day.

1964, Apr. 7 *Perf. 10½*

Design: 11r, Griffon and winged bull, Persepolis.

1286 A191 6r lilac, grn & blk	2.00	38
1287 A191 11r orange, brn & blk	2.75	55

Issued for tourist publicity.

Rudaki and Musical Instrument — A192

1964, May 16 Photo. Wmk. 349

1288 A192 6r blue	1.90	32
1289 A192 8r red brown	3.50	45

Opening of an institute for the blind. The inscription translates: "Wisdom is better than eye and sight."

Sculpture, Persepolis A193

Designs: 4r, Achaemenian horse-drawn mail cart, map of Iran, horiz. 6r, Vessel with sculptured animals. 10r, Head of King Shapur, sculpture.

1964, June 5 Wmk. 349 Litho.

1290 A193 2r gray & blue	3.25	1.00
1291 A193 4r vio bl, lt bl & bl	6.50	1.40
1292 A193 6r brown & yellow	6.50	1.40
1293 A193 10r yel & ol grn	8.00	1.40

Opening of the "7000 Years of Persian Art" exhibition in Washington, D.C.

Shah and Emperor Haile Selassie A194

1964, Sept. 14 Wmk. 349 *Perf. 10½*

1294 A194 6r ultra & lt blue 3.00 30

Visit of Emperor Haile Selassie of Ethiopia.

Tooth and Dentists' Assoc. Emblem — A195

"2 I.D.A." — A196

1964, Sept. 14 Litho.

1295 A195 2r blue, red & dk blue	1.00	15
1296 A196 4r ultra, bl & pale brn	1.40	18
Set value		27

Iranian Dentists' Association, 2nd congress.

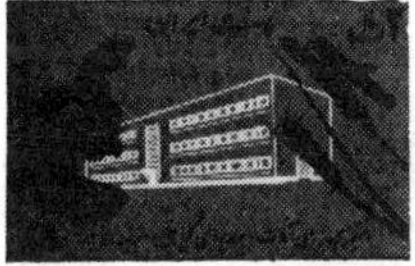
Research Institute, Microscope, Wheat and Locust A197

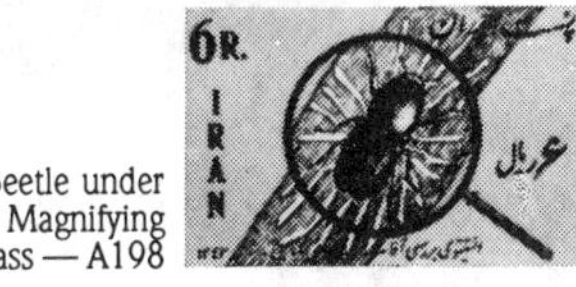
Beetle under Magnifying Glass — A198

1964, Sept. 23 Wmk. 349 *Perf. 10½*

1297 A197 2r red, orange & brn	1.65	22
1298 A198 6r blue, brn & indigo	2.50	40

Fight against plant diseases and damages.

Mithras (Mehr) on Ancient Seal A199

Eleanor Roosevelt (1884-1962) A200

1964, Oct. 8 Litho.

Size: 26x34mm

1299 A199 8r org & brn org 2.00 35

Mehragan celebration. See No. 1406.

1964, Oct. 11

1300 A200 10r vio bl & rose vio 4.00 32

Clasped Hands and UN Emblem — A201

Symbolic Airplane and UN Emblem — A202

1964, Oct. 24 Wmk. 349 *Perf. 10½*

1301 A201 6r ultra, yel, red & blk	1.50	30
1302 A202 14r orange, ultra & red	2.25	50

Issued for United Nations Day.

Persian Gymnast — A203

Polo Player A204

1964, Oct. 26

1303 A203 4r tan, sep & Prus bl 1.25 20
1304 A204 6r red & black 1.75 28

18th Olympic Games, Tokyo, Oct. 10-25.

Crown Prince Riza — A205

1964, Oct. 31 **Litho.**

1305 A205 1r dull green & brn 1.40 30
1306 A205 2r deep rose & ultra 2.75 50
1307 A205 6r ultra & red 4.00 65

Children's Day; Crown Prince Riza's 4th birthday.

UN Emblem, Flame and Smokestack A206

1964, Nov. 16 Wmk. 349 *Perf. 10½*

1308 A206 6r black, lt bl & car 75 15
1309 A206 8r black, emer & car 1.50 20

Petro-Chemical Conference and Gas Seminar, Nov.-Dec. 1964.

Shah and King Baudouin A207

1964, Nov. 17

1310 A207 6r black, org & yel 1.10 16
1311 A207 8r black, org & emer 1.90 28

Visit of King Baudouin of Belgium.

Rhazes — A208

1964, Dec. 27 Wmk. 349 *Perf. 10½*

1312 A208 2r multicolored 1.10 15
1313 A208 6r multicolored 1.90 25

1100th birth anniv. of Rhazes (abu-Bakr Mohammad ibn-Zakariya al-Razi), Persian-born Moslem physician.

Shah and King Olav V A209

1965, Jan. 7 **Litho.**

1314 A209 2r dk brown & lilac 1.10 16
1315 A209 4r brown & green 1.60 25

Visit of King Olav V of Norway.

Map of Iran and Six-pointed Star — A210

1965, Jan. 26 Wmk. 349 *Perf. 10½*

1316 A210 2r black, brt bl & org 1.10 20

3rd anniv. of the Shah's six socioeconomic bills.

Woman and UN Emblem — A211

Green Wheat and Tulip — A212

1965, Mar. 1 Wmk. 349 *Perf. 10½*

1317 A211 6r black & blue 85 15
1318 A211 8r ultra & red 1.25 20

18th session of the UN commission on the status of women.

1965, Mar. 6

1319 A212 50d multicolored 28 15
1320 A212 1r multicolored 28 15
Set value 15

Novrooz, Iranian New Year, Mar. 21.

Pres. Habib Bourguiba and Minarets of Tunis Mosque A213

1965, Mar. 14 Litho. *Perf. 10½*

1321 A213 4r multicolored 90 15

Visit of Pres. Habib Bourguiba of Tunisia.

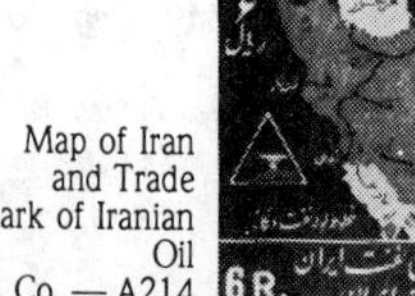

Map of Iran and Trade Mark of Iranian Oil Co. — A214

1965, Mar. 20 **Litho.**

1322 A214 6r multicolored 1.10 18
1323 A214 14r multicolored 1.90 35

Oil industry nationalization, 14th anniv.

ITU Emblem, Old and New Communication Equipment — A215

1965, May 17 Wmk. 349 *Perf. 10½*

1324 A215 14r dp car rose & gray 1.10 18

ITU, centenary.

ICY Emblem A216

1965, June 22 Litho. *Perf. 10½*

1325 A216 10r sl grn & gray bl 2.25 15

International Cooperation Year, 1965.

Iran Airways Emblem A217

1965, July 17 Wmk. 349 *Perf. 10½*

1326 A217 14r multicolored 2.25 30

Tenth anniversary of Iran Airways.

Hands Holding Book — A218

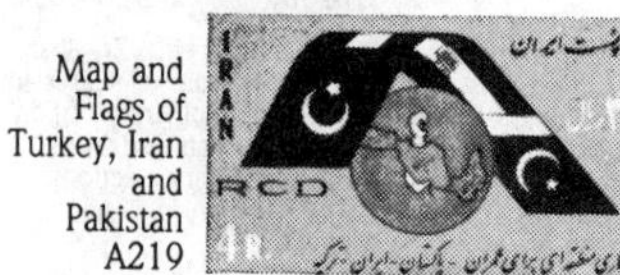

Map and Flags of Turkey, Iran and Pakistan A219

1965, July 21 **Litho.**

1327 A218 2r dk brn, org brn & buff 42 15
1328 A219 4r multicolored 70 20
Set value 30

Signing of the Regional Cooperation for Development Pact by Turkey, Iran and Pakistan, 1st anniv.

Iranian Scout Emblem and Ornament A220

1965, July 23

1329 A220 2r multicolored 70 20
a. Vert. pair, imperf. horiz. 20.00

Middle East Rover Moot (senior Boy Scout assembly).

Majlis Gate A221

1965, Aug. 5 Wmk. 349 *Perf. 10½*

1330 A221 2r lilac rose & brn 40 15

60th anniversary of Iranian constitution.

Types of Regular Issue, 1962

Perf. 10½

1964-65 **Photo.** **Wmk. 349**

1331 A159 5d dk sl grn ('65) 35 30
a. Wmk. 353 35 30
1332 A159 10d chestnut 35 30
1333 A159 25d dk blue ('65) 50 25
1334 A159 50d Prus green 75 15
1335 A159 1r orange 75 15
1336 A159 2r violet blue 50 15
1337 A159 5r dark brown 3.00 50
1338 A160 6r blue ('65) 10.00 1.00
1339 A160 8r yel grn ('65) 3.50 25
1340 A160 10r grnsh bl ('65) 3.00 25
1341 A160 11r sl grn ('65) 10.00 1.50
1342 A160 14r purple ('65) 7.00 1.40
1343 A160 20r red brn ('65) 4.50 1.00
1344 A160 50r org ver ('65) 7.50 2.00
Nos. 1331-1344 (14) 51.70 9.20

Perf. 11x10½

1331b A159 5d Wmk. 353 3.25 1.00
1332a A159 10d 55 50
1333a A159 25d 80 25
1334a A159 50d 3.00 2.00
1335a A159 1r 3.00 2.00
1337a A159 5r 4.00 50

Dental Congress Emblem — A222

1965, Sept. 7 Litho. *Perf. 10½*

1345 A222 6r gray, ultra, & car 60 22

Iranian Dentists' Association, 3rd congress.

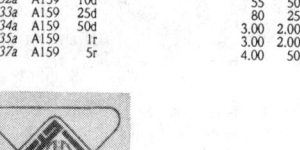

Classroom and Literacy Corps Emblem A223

Alphabets on Globe — A224

Designs: 6r, UNESCO emblem and open book (diamond shape). 8r, UNESCO emblem and inscription, horiz. 14r, Shah Riza Pahlavi and inscription in six languages.

1965, Sept. 8

1346 A223 2r multi 35 20
1347 A224 5r multi 40 25

Size: 30x30mm

1348 A223 6r multi 80 30

Size: 35x23mm

1349 A223 8r dk bl, car emer & buff 80 25

Size: 34x46mm

1350 A223 14r cit, dk bl & brn 2.00 30
Nos. 1346-1350 (5) 4.35 1.30

World Congress Against Illiteracy, Tehran, Sept. 8-19.

Mohammed Riza Pahlavi — A225

1965, Sept. 16 Litho. *Perf. 10½*

1351 A225 1r crim, rose red & gray 90 15
1352 A225 2r dk red, rose red & yel 90 20

Reign of Shah, 25th anniv.

Emblem of Persian Medical Society — A226

1965, Sept. 21 Wmk. 349

1353 A226 5r ultra, dp ultra & gold 50 25

14th Medical Congress, Ramsar.

Pres. Jonas of Austria A227

1965, Sept. 30

1354 A227 6r bl, brt bl & gray 1.50 25

Visit of President Franz Jonas of Austria.

Mithras (Mehr) on Ancient Seal — A228

1965, Oct. 8 Litho. Wmk. 353

1355 A228 4r brt grn, gold, brn & blk 60 16

Mehragan celebration during month of Mehr, Sept. 23-Oct. 22. Persian inscription of watermark vertical on No. 1355.

UN Emblem — A229

1965, Oct. 24 Wmk. 353 *Perf. 10½*

1356 A229 5r bl, grn & rose car 55 15

20th anniversary of the United Nations.

Symbolic Arches — A230

1965, Oct. 26

1357 A230 3r vio bl, blk, yel & red 55 15

Exhibition of Iranian Commodities.

Crown Prince Riza — A231

1965, Oct. 31

1358 A231 2r brown & yellow 1.10 45

Children's Day; Crown Prince Riza's 5th birthday.

Weight Lifters — A232

1965, Nov. 1

1359 A232 10r brt bl, vio & brt pink 60 20

World Weight Lifting Championships, Tehran.

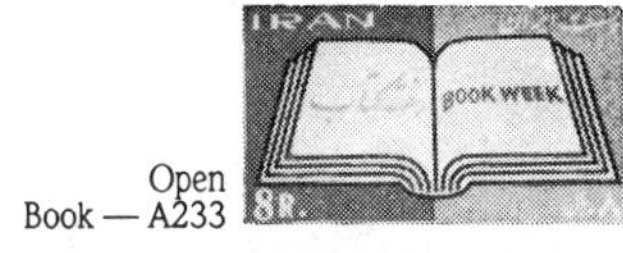

Open Book — A233

1965, Dec. 1 Wmk. 353 *Perf. 10½*

1360 A233 8r bl, brt pink & blk 60 20

Issued for Book Week.

Shah and King Faisal A234

1965, Dec. 8 Litho.

1361 A234 4r olive bis & brn 1.50 35

Visit of King Faisal of Saudi Arabia.

Scales and Olive Branch — A235

1965, Dec. 12

1362 A235 14r multicolored 60 18

Human Rights Day (Dec. 10).

Tractor, "Land Reform" A236

Symbols of Reform Bills: 2r, Trees, nationalization of forests. 3r, Factory and gear wheel, sale of shares in government factories. 4r, Wheels, shareholding for factory workers. 5r, Parliament gate, women's suffrage. 6r, Children before blackboard, Army of Education. 7r, Caduceus, Army of Hygiene. 8r, Scales, creation of rural courts. 9r, Two girders, creation of Army of Progress.

1966, Jan. 26 Wmk. 353 *Perf. 10½*

1363 A236 1r orange & brown 20 15
1364 A236 2r dl grn & green 20 15
1365 A236 3r silver & gray 20 15
1366 A236 4r light & dk vio 30 15
1367 A236 5r rose & brown 40 15
1368 A236 6r olive & brown 60 15
1369 A236 7r bl & vio blue 85 16
1370 A236 8r ultra & dp ultra 1.00 16
1371 A236 9r brn org & dk brn 1.00 20
Nos. 1363-1371 (9) 4.75
Set value 1.15

Parliamentary approval of the Shah's reform plan.

Shah — A237

Ruins of Persepolis — A238

Perf. 10½

1966-71 Wmk. 353 Photo.

1372	A237	5d green	15	15
1373	A237	10d chestnut	20	15
1374	A237	25d dark blue	20	15
1375	A237	50d Prussian green	50	25
a.		50d blue green ('71)	50	30
1376	A237	1r orange	50	15
1377	A237	2r violet	40	15
1377A	A237	4r cl brn ('68)	4.00	1.00
1378	A237	5r dark brn	1.75	25
1379	A238	6r deep blue	60	15
1380	A238	8r yellow grn	60	15
a.		8r dull green ('71)	60	15
1381	A238	10r Prus bl	95	15
1382	A238	11r slate grn	95	15
1383	A238	14r purple	1.25	25
1384	A238	20r brown	9.50	50
1385	A238	50r cop red	3.75	1.50
1386	A238	100r brt blue	12.50	1.75
1387	A238	200r chnt brn	12.50	3.25
		Nos. 1372-1387 (17)	50.30	10.15

Set, except 4r, issued Feb. 22, 1966.

Student Nurse Taking Oath A239

Narcissus A240

1966, Feb. 24 Litho.

1388 A239 5r brt pink & mag 50 15
1389 A239 5r lt bl & brt bl 50 15
Set value 24

Nurses' Day. Nos. 1388-1389 printed in sheets of 50 arranged checkerwise.

1966, Mar. 7

1390 A240 50d ultra, yel & emer 20 15
1391 A240 1r lilac, yel & emer 20 15
Set value 15

Novrooz, Iranian New Year, Mar. 21.

Oil Derricks in Persian Gulf — A241

1966, Mar. 20 *Perf. 10½*

1392 A241 14r blk, brt bl & brt rose lil 1.50 40

Formation of six offshore oil companies.

Radio Tower — A242

Designs: 2r, Radar, horiz. 6r, Emblem and waves. 8r, Compass rose and waves. 10r, Tower and waves.

1966, Apr. 27 Litho. Wmk. 349

1393 A242 2r dark grn 16 15
1394 A242 4r ultra & dp org 20 15
1395 A242 6r gray ol & plum 28 16
1396 A242 8r brt bl & dk bl 35 20
1397 A242 10r brn & bister 52 28
Nos. 1393-1397 (5) 1.51 94

Inauguration of the radio telecommunication system of the Central Treaty Organization of the Middle East (CENTO).

WHO Headquarters, Geneva — A243

1966, May 3 Wmk. 353

1398 A243 10r brt bl, yel & blk 50 18

Opening of the WHO Headquarters, Geneva.

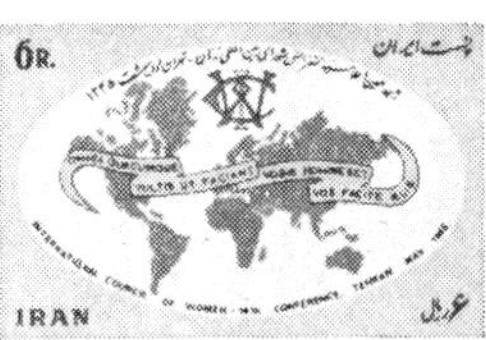

World Map A244

1966, May 14 Litho.

1399 A244 6r bl & multi 38 15
1400 A244 8r multicolored 55 15
Set value 22

Intl. Council of Women, 18th Conf., Tehran, May 1966.

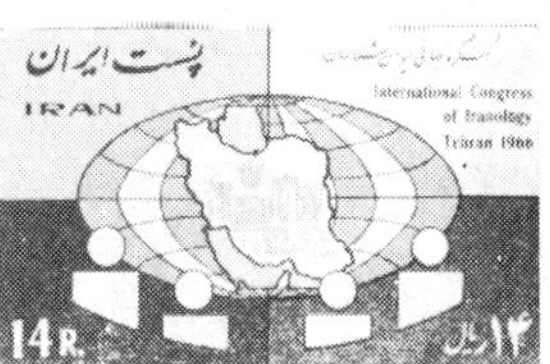

Globe, Map of Iran and Ruins of Persepolis — A245

1966, Sept. 5 Wmk. 353 *Perf. 10½*

1401 A245 14r multicolored 1.00 20

International Iranology Congress, Tehran.

Emblem of Iranian Medical Society — A246

1966, Sept. 21

1402 A246 4r ultra, grnsh bl & bis 30 15

15th Medical Congress, held at Ramsar.

Gate of Parliament, Mt. Demavend and Congress Emblem — A247

Design: 8r, Senate building, Mt. Demavend and emblem.

1966, Oct. 2 Wmk. 353 *Perf. 10½*

1403 A247 6r brick red, ultra & dk grn 25 15
1404 A247 8r lt lil, ultra & dk grn 35 15
Set value 22

55th Interparliamentary Union Conf., Tehran.

Visit of President Cemal Gursel of Turkey — A248

1966, Oct. 2 Litho.

1405 A248 6r vio & dk brn 35 15

Mithras Type of 1964

1966, Oct. 8

Size: 30x40mm

1406 A199 6r olive bis & brn 45 15

Mehragan celebration.

Farmers — A249

1966, Oct. 13

1407 A249 5r olive bis & brn 1.10 50

Establishment of rural courts of justice.

UN Emblem A250

1966, Oct. 24 Wmk. 353 *Perf. 10½*

1408 A250 6r brn org & blk 35 15

21st anniversary of United Nations.

Crown Prince Riza — A251

Symbolic Woman's Face — A252

1966, Oct. 31 Litho.

1409 A251 1r ultramarine 65 15
1410 A251 2r violet 1.00 15
a. Pair, #1409-1410 1.75 30
Set value 24

Children's Day; Crown Prince Riza's 6th birthday.

1966, Nov. 6

1411 A252 5r gold, blk & ultra 30 15

Founding of the Iranian Women's Org.

Film Strip and Song Bird A253

1966, Nov. 6

1412 A253 4r blk, red lil & vio 28 15

First Iranian children's film festival.

"Census Count" — A254

Book Cover — A255

1966, Nov. 11

1413 A254 6r dk brn & gray 28 15

National census.

1966, Nov. 15

1414 A255 8r tan, brn & ultra 35 15

Issued to publicize Book Week.

Riza Shah Pahlavi A256

Design: 2r, Riza Shah Pahlavi without kepi.

1966, Nov. 16 Litho.

1415 A256 1r slate blue 1.25 30
1416 A256 1r brown 1.25 30
1417 A256 2r gray green 1.25 30
1418 A256 2r violet blue 1.25 30

Riza Shah Pahlavi (1877-1944), founder of modern Iran. Stamps of same denomination printed se-tenant.

EROPA Emblem and Map of Persia A257

1966, Dec. 4 Wmk. 353 *Perf. 10½*

1419 A257 8r dk brn & emer 30 15

4th General Assembly of the Org. of Public Administrators, EROPA.

Shah Giving Land Reform Papers to Farmers A258

1967, Jan. 9 Wmk. 353 *Perf. 10½*

1420 A258 6r ol bis, yel & brn 90 15

Approval of land reform laws, 5th anniv.

Shah and 9-Star Crescent A259

Design: 2r, Torch and 9-star crescent.

1967, Jan. 26 Wmk. 353 Litho.

1421 A259 2r multicolored 70 15
1422 A259 6r multicolored 1.25 15
Set value 20

5th anniv. of Shah's reforms, the "White Revolution."

Ancient Sculpture of Bull — A260

Designs: 5r, Sculptured mythical animals. 8r, Pillar from Persepolis.

1967, Feb. 25 Wmk. 353 *Perf. 10½*

1423 A260 3r dk brn & ocher 50 15
1424 A260 5r Prus grn, brn & ocher 50 15
1425 A260 8r vio, blk & sil 1.25 25

Issued to publicize Museum Week.

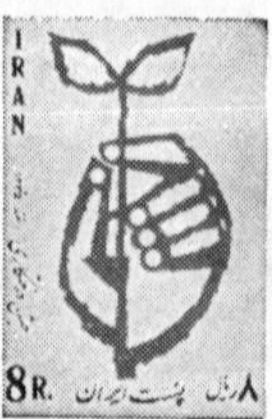

Planting Tree — A261

Goldfish — A262

1967, Mar. 6

1426 A261 8r brn org & grn 30 15

Tree Planting Day.

1967, Mar. 11

Size: 26x20mm

1427 A262 1r shown 25 15

Size: 35x27mm

1428 A262 8r Swallows 70 20
Set value 30

Issued for Novrooz, Iranian New Year.

Microscope, Animals and Emblem — A263

1967, Mar. 11 *Perf. 10½*

1429 A263 5r blk, gray & mag 35 15

Second Iranian Veterinary Congress.

Pres. Arif of Iraq, Mosque A264

1967, Mar. 14 Litho. Wmk. 353

1430 A264 6r brt bl & grn 35 15

Visit of Pres. Abdul Salam Mohammed Arif.

Fireworks A265

1967, Mar. 17

1431 A265 5r vio bl & multi 38 15

Issued for United Nations Stamp Day.

Map of Iran and Oil Company Emblem A266

1967, Mar. 20

1432 A266 6r multicolored 1.00 22

Nationalization of Iranian Oil Industry.

Fencers A267

1967, Mar. 23

1433 A267 5r vio & bister 50 15

Intl. Youth Fencing Championships, Tehran.

Shah and King of Thailand A268

1967, Apr. 23 Wmk. 353 *Perf. 10½*
1434 A268 6r brn org & dk brn 1.10 25

Visit of King Bhumibol Adulyadej.

Old and Young Couples A269

1967, Apr. 24 Litho.
1435 A269 5r ol bis & vio bl 32 15

15th anniversary of Social Insurance.

Skier and Iranian Olympic Emblem — A270

Designs: 6r, Assyrian soldiers, Olympic rings and tablet inscribed "I.O.C." 8r, Wrestlers and Iranian Olympic emblem.

1967, May 5
1436 A270 3r brown & black 25 15
1437 A270 6r multicolored 35 20
1438 A270 8r ultra & brown 65 30

65th Intl. Olympic Congress, Tehran, May 2-11.

Lions International — A271

1967, May 11
Size: 41½x30½mm
1439 A271 3r shown 50 15
Size: 36x42mm
1440 A271 7r Emblem, vert. 75 25

50th anniversary of Lions International.

Visit of Pres. Chivu Stoica of Romania A272

1967, May 13
1441 A272 6r orange & dk bl 30 15

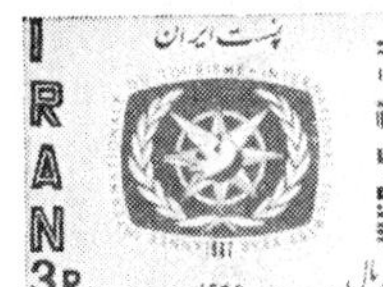

International Tourist Year Emblem A273

1967, June 6 Wmk. 353 *Perf. 10½*
1442 A273 3r brick red & ultra 30 15

Iranian Pavilion and Ornament — A274

1967, June 7 Litho.
1443 A274 4r dk brn, red & gold 16 15
1444 A274 10r red, dk brn & gold 28 15
Set value 23

EXPO '67, Montreal, Apr. 28-Oct. 27.

Stamp of 1870, No. 1 A275

1967, July 23 Wmk. 353 *Perf. 10½*
1445 A275 6r multri 25 15
1446 A275 8r multi 35 15
Set value 24

Centenary of first Persian postage stamp.

World Map and School Children A276

Globe and Oriental Musician A277

1967, Sept. 8 Litho. Wmk. 353
1447 A276 3r ultra & brt & brt bl 15 15
1448 A276 5r brown & yellow 30 20
Set value 30

World campaign against illiteracy.

1967, Sept. 10 *Perf. 10½*
1449 A277 14r brn org & dk brn 75 16

Intl. Conf. on Music Education in Oriental Countries, Sept. 1967.

Child's Hand Holding Adult's — A278

Winged Wild Goat — A279

1967, Sept. 14 Litho. Wmk. 353
1450 A278 8r dk brn & yel 3.25 2.50

Introduction of Children's Villages in Iran. (Modelled after Austrian SOS Villages for homeless children).

1967, Sept. 19
1451 A279 8r dk brn & lemon 60 25

Festival of Arts, Persepolis.

UN Emblem A280

1967, Oct. 17
1452 A280 6r ol bis & vio bl 35 15

Issued for United Nations Day.

Shah and Empress Farah — A281

1967, Oct. 26 Wmk. 353 *Perf. 10½*
Various Frames
1453 A281 2r sil, bl & brn 90 16
1454 A281 10r sil, bl & vio 90 40
1455 A281 14r lt bl, bl, gold & vio 2.25 40

Coronation of Shah Mohammed Riza Pahlavi and Empress Farah, Oct. 26, 1967.
Exist part perf., ungummed.

1967, Oct. 31 Litho.

Design: Crown Prince Riza.

1456 A281 2r silver & violet 90 15
1457 A281 8r sil & red brown 1.25 20
Set value 30

Children's Day; Crown Prince Riza's 7th birthday.

Visit of Pres. Georgi Traikov of Bulgaria — A283

1967, Nov. 20
1458 A283 10r lilac & dk brn 35 15

Persian Boy Scout Emblem A284

1967, Dec. 3 Wmk. 353 *Perf. 10½*
1459 A284 8r olive & red brn 75 15

Cooperation Week of the Iranian Boy Scouts, Dec. 5-12.

Hands Holding Chain Link A285

1967, Dec. 6 Litho.
1460 A285 6r multicolored 32 15

Issued to publicize Cooperation Year.

Visit of Sheik Sabah of Kuwait — A286

1968, Jan. 10 Wmk. 353 *Perf. 10½*
1461 A286 10r lt bl & slate grn 38 20

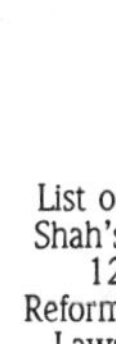

List of Shah's 12 Reform Laws A287

1968, Jan. 27 Litho. Wmk. 353
1462 A287 2r sl grn, brn & sal 38 15
1463 A287 8r vio, dk grn & lt grn 1.25 15
1464 A287 14r brn, pink & lt lil 1.65 20
Set value 40

"White Revolution of King and People."

Almond Blossoms A288

Haji Firooz (New Year Singer) A289

Design: 2r, Tulips.

1968, Mar. 12 Wmk. 353 *Perf. 10½*
1465 A288 1r multi 20 15
1466 A288 2r bluish gray & multi 20 15
1467 A288 2r brt rose lil & multi 20 15
1468 A289 6r multi 80 15
Set value 36

Issued for Novrooz, Iranian New Year.

Oil Worker and Derrick — A290

1968, Mar. 20 **Litho.**
1469 A290 14r grn, blk & org yel 60 15

Oil industry nationalization, 17th anniv.

WHO Emblem — A291

1968, Apr. 7 **Wmk. 353** ***Perf. 10½***
1470 A291 14r brn, bl & org 60 15

WHO, 20th anniversary.

Marlik Chariot, Ancient Sculpture — A292

1968, Apr. 13
1471 A292 8r blue, brn & buff 40 15

Fifth World Congress of Persian Archaeology and Art, Tehran.

Shah and King Hassan II — A293

1968, Apr. 16
1472 A293 6r bright vio & buff 1.10 18

Visit of King Hassan II of Morocco.

Human Rights Flame — A294

Soccer Player — A295

Design: 14r, Frameline inscription reads, "International Conference on Human Rights Tehran 1968"; "Iran" at left.

1968, May 5 **Wmk. 353** ***Perf. 10½***
1473 A294 8r red & dk grn 25 15
1474 A294 14r vio bl & bl 50 15
Set value 24

Intl. Human Rights Year. The 8r commemorates the Iranian Human Rights Committee; the 14r, the Intl. Conference on Human Rights, Tehran, 1968.

1968, May 10 **Litho.**
1475 A295 8r multicolored 25 15
1476 A295 10r multicolored 50 25

Asian Soccer Cup Finals, Tehran.

Tehran Oil Refinery A296

1968, May 21 **Wmk. 353** ***Perf. 10½***
1477 A296 14r brt bl & multi 75 18

Opening of the Tehran Oil Refinery.

Queen Farah as Girl Guide — A297

1968, June 24 **Litho.** ***Perf. 10½***
1478 A297 4r brt rose lil & bl green 1.25 25
1479 A297 6r car & brn 2.00 50

Great Camp of Iranian Girl Guides.

Anopheles Mosquito, Congress Emblem — A298

Winged Figure with Banner, and Globe — A299

1968, Sept. 7 **Wmk. 353** ***Perf. 10½***
1480 A298 6r brt pur & blk 30 15
1481 A298 14r dk grn & mag 45 16

8th Intl. Congress on Tropical Medicine and Malaria, Tehran, Sept. 7-15.

1968, Sept. 8 **Litho.**
1482 A299 6r lt vio, bis & bl 30 15
1483 A299 14r dl yel, sl grn & brn 45 16

World campaign against illiteracy.

Oramental Horse and Flower — A300

1968, Sept. 11
1484 A300 14r sl grn, org & yel grn 65 20

2nd Festival of Arts, Shiraz-Persepolis.

INTERPOL Emblem and Globe — A301

1968, Oct. 6 **Wmk. 353** ***Perf. 10½***
1485 A301 10r dk brn & bl 50 15

37th General Assembly of the Intl. Police Org. (INTERPOL) in Tehran.

Police Emblem on Iran Map in Flag Colors — A302

Peace Dove and UN Emblem — A303

1968, Oct. 7 **Litho.**
1486 A302 14r multicolored 1.00 20

Issued for Police Day.

1968, Oct. 24
1487 A303 14r bl & vio bl 75 20

Issued for United Nations Day.

Empress Farah — A304

Designs: 8r, Shah Mohammed Riza Pahlavi. 10fr, Shah, Empress and Crown Prince.

1968, Oct. 26
1488 A304 6r multi 4.25 1.65
1489 A304 8r multi 4.25 1.65
1490 A304 10r multi 4.25 1.65

Coronation of Shah Riza Pahlavi and Empress Farah, 1st anniv.

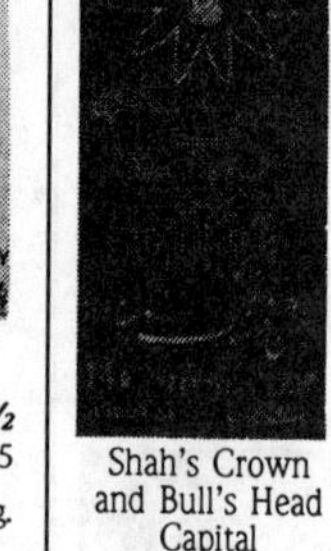
Shah's Crown and Bull's Head Capital A305

UNICEF Emblem and Child's Drawing A306

1968, Oct. 30
1491 A305 14r ultra, gold, sil & red 75 20

Festival of Arts and Culture.

1968, Oct. 31 **Litho.**

Children's Drawings and UNICEF Emblem: 3r, Boat on lake, house and trees, horiz. 5r, Flowers, horiz.

1492 A306 2r dk brn & multi 15 15
1493 A306 3r dk grn & multi 20 15
1494 A306 5r multicolored 30 25

Issued for Children's Day.

Labor Union Emblem A307

Factory and Insurance Company Emblem A308

Designs: 8r, Members of Army of Hygiene, and Insurance Company emblem. 10r, Map of Persia, Insurance Company emblem, car, train, ship and plane.

1968, Nov. 6 **Wmk. 353** ***Perf. 10½***
1495 A307 4r sil & vio bl 16 15
1496 A308 5r multicolored 16 15
1497 A308 8r ultra, gray & yel 25 15
1498 A308 10r multicolored 45 20
Set value 50

Issued to publicize Insurance Day.

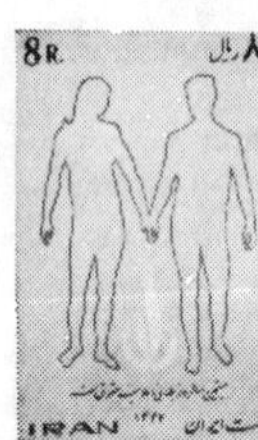

Human Rights Flame, Man and Woman — A309

1968, Dec. 10 **Litho.** ***Perf. 10½***
1499 A309 8r lt bl, vio bl & car 32 15

International Human Rights Year.

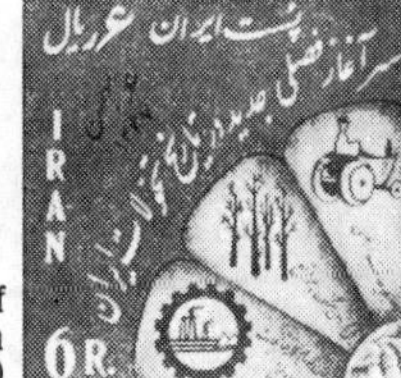

Symbols of Shah's Reform Plan — A310

Design: Each stamp shows symbols of 3 of the Shah's reforms. No. 1503a shows the 12 symbols in a circle with a medallion in the center picturing 3 heads and a torch.

1969, Jan. 26 Wmk. 353 *Perf. 10½*

1500 A310 2r ocher, grn & lil	60	15
1501 A310 4r lil, ocher & grn	60	15
1502 A310 6r lil, ocher & grn	75	25
1503 A310 8r lil, ocher & grn	1.00	25
a. Block of 4, #1500-1503	5.50	2.50

Declaration of the Shah's Reform Plan.

Shah and Crowd A311

1969, Feb. 1 Litho.

1504 A311 6r red, bl & brn 1.50 20

10,000th day of the reign of the Shah.

European Goldfinch A312

Designs: 2r, Ring-necked pheasant. 8r, Roses.

1969, Mar. 6 Wmk. 353 *Perf. 10½*

1505 A312 1r multicolored	15	15
1506 A312 2r multicolored	20	15
1507 A312 8r multicolored	85	20
Set value		36

Issued for Novrooz, Iranian New Year.

"Woman Lawyer" Holding Scales of Justice — A313

Workers, ILO and UN Emblems — A314

1969, Apr. 8 Litho. *Perf. 10½*

1508 A313 6r blk & brt bl 48 15

15th General Assembly of Women Lawyers, Tehran, Apr. 8-14.

1969, Apr. 30 Wmk. 353 *Perf. 10½*

1509 A314 10r bl & vio bl 55 15

ILO, 50th anniversary.

Freestyle Wrestlers and Ariamehr Cup — A315

1969, May 6 Litho.

1510 A315 10r lilac & multi 90 25

Intl. Freestyle Wrestling Championships, 3rd round.

Birds and Flower — A316

1969, June 10 Wmk. 353 *Perf. 10½*

1511 A316 10r vio bl & multi 75 15

Issued to publicize Handicrafts Day.

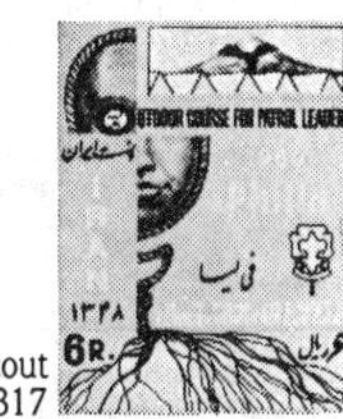

Boy Scout Symbols — A317

1969, July 9 Wmk. 353 *Perf. 10½*

1512 A317 6r lt bl & multi 1.00 15

Philia 1969, an outdoor training course for Boy Scout patrol leaders.

Lady Serving Wine, Safavi Miniature, Iran — A318

Designs: No. 1514, Lady on Balcony, Mogul miniature, Pakistan. No. 1515, Sultan Suleiman Receiving Sheik Abdul Latif, 16th century miniature, Turkey.

1969, July 21 Litho.

1513 A318 25r multi	2.00	50
1514 A318 25r multi	2.00	50
1515 A318 25r multi	2.00	50

Signing of the Regional Cooperation for Development Pact by Turkey, Iran and Pakistan, 5th anniv.

Neil A. Armstrong and Col. Edwin E. Aldrin on Moon — A319

1969, July 26

1516 A319 24r bis, bl & brn 6.00 2.00

See note after Algeria No. 427.

Quotation from Shah's Declaration on Education and Art — A320

1969, Aug. 6 Wmk. 353 *Perf. 10½*

1517 A320 10r car, cr & emer 60 16

Anniv. of educational and art reforms.

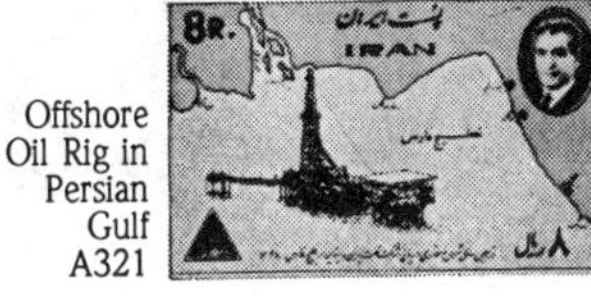

Offshore Oil Rig in Persian Gulf A321

1969, Sept. 1 Litho.

1518 A321 8r multicolored 1.00 16

Marine drillings by the Iran-Italia Oil Co., 10th anniv.

Dancers Forming Flower — A322

Crossed-out Fingerprint, Moon and Rocket — A323

1969, Sept. 6 Wmk. 353 *Perf. 10½*

1519 A322 6r multicolored	28	15
1520 A322 8r multicolored	35	15
Set value		20

3rd Festival of Arts, Shiraz and Persepolis, Aug. 30-Sept. 9.

1969, Sept. 8 Litho.

1521 A323 4r multicolored 30 15

World campaign against illiteracy.

Persepolis, Simulated Stamp with UPU Emblem, and Shah — A324

1969, Sept. 28

1522 A324 10r lt bl & multi	2.25	50
1523 A324 14r multicolored	2.25	50

16th Congress of the UPU, Tokyo.

Fair Emblem A325

Justice A326

Designs: 14r, like 8r, inscribed "ASIA 69." 20r, Fair emblem, world map and "ASIA 69," horiz.

1969, Oct. 5 Wmk. 353 *Perf. 10½*

1524 A325 8r rose & multi	30	15
1525 A325 14r blue & multi	38	18
1526 A325 20r tan & multi	55	25

2nd Asian Trade Fair, Tehran.

1969, Oct. 13 Litho.

1527 A326 8r bl grn & dk brn 60 15

Rural Courts of Justice Day.

UN Emblem A327

Emblem and Column Capital, Persepolis A328

1969, Oct. 24

1528 A327 2r lt bl & dp bl 35 15

25th anniversary of the United Nations.

1969, Oct. 28

1529 A328 2r deep bl & multi 60 15

2nd Festival of Arts and Culture. See Nos. 1577, 1681, 1735.

Child's Drawing and UNICEF Emblem A329

Children's Drawings and UNICEF Emblem: 1r, Boy and birds, vert. 5r, Dinner.

1969, Oct. 31 Wmk. 353 *Perf. 10½*
Size: 28x40mm, 40x28mm

1530 A329 1r lt blue & multi	15	15
1531 A329 2r lt grn & multi	25	15
1532 A329 5r lt lil & multi	55	22

Children's Week. See Nos. 1578-1580.

Globe Emblem A330

1969, Nov. 6

1533 A330 8r dk brn & bl 35 15

Meeting of the Natl. Society of Parents and Educators, Tehran.

Satellite Communications Station — A331

1969, Nov. 19 **Litho.**

1534 A331 6r blk brn & bis 35 15

1st Iranian Satellite Communications Earth Station, Hamadan.

Mahatma Gandhi (1869-1948) — A332

1969, Dec. 29 Wmk. 353 ***Perf.* 10½**

1535 A332 14r gray & dk rose brn 4.25 42

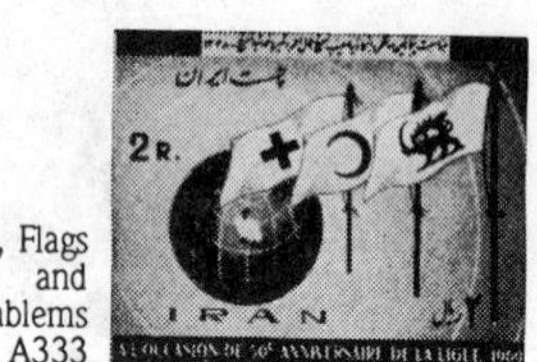

Globe, Flags and Emblems A333

Design: 6r, Globe and Red Cross, Red Lion and Sun, and Red Crescent Emblems.

1969, Dec. 31

1536 A333 2r red & multi 60 15
1537 A333 6r red & multi 90 20
Set value 28

50th anniversary of the League of Red Cross Societies.

Symbols of Reform Laws and Shah A334

1970, Jan. 26 **Litho.** **Wmk. 353**

1538 A334 1r bister & multi 85 15
1539 A334 2r multicolored 85 15

Declaration of the Shah's Reform Plan.

Pansies A335

New Year's Table A336

1970, Mar. 6 Wmk. 353 ***Perf.* 10½**

1540 A335 1r multicolored 22 15
1541 A336 8r multicolored 1.50 30

Issued for the Iranian New Year.

Chemical Plant, Kharg Island, and Iranian Oil Company Emblem — A337

Designs (Iranian Oil Company Emblem and): 2r, Shah's portrait and quotation. 4r, Laying of gas pipe line and tractor. 8r, Tankers at pier of Kharg Island, vert. 10r, Tehran refinery.

1970, Mar. 20 Wmk. 353 ***Perf.* 10½**

1542 A337 2r gray & multi 1.00 20
1543 A337 4r multicolored 1.25 25
1544 A337 6r lt bl & multi 1.40 35
1545 A337 8r multicolored 1.50 45
1546 A337 10r multicolored 1.90 55
Nos. 1542-1546 (5) 7.05 1.80

Nationalization of the oil industry, 20th anniv.

EXPO '70 Emblem — A338

Radar, Satellite and Congress Emblem — A339

1970, Mar. 27 **Litho.**

1547 A338 4r brt rose lil & vio bl 18 15
1548 A338 10r lt bl & pur 42 15
Set value 20

EXPO '70, Osaka, Japan, Mar. 15-Sept. 13.

1970, Apr. 20 Wmk. 353 ***Perf.* 10½**

1549 A339 14r multicolored 75 20

Asia-Australia Telecommunications Congress, Tehran.

UPU Headquarters, Bern — A340

1970, May 10

1550 A340 2r gray, brn & lil rose 50 15
1551 A340 4r lil, brn & lil rose 75 15
Set value 20

Inauguration of the new UPU Headquarters, Bern.

Productivity Year Emblem — A341

1970, May 19 Wmk. 353 ***Perf.* 10½**

1552 A341 8r gray & multi 38 15

Asian Productivity Year, 1970.

Bird Bringing Baby — A342

1970, June 15 **Litho.**

1553 A342 8r brn & dk blue 65 15

Iranian School for Midwives, 50th anniv.

Tomb of Cyrus the Great, Meshed-Morghab in Fars — A343

Designs: 8r, Pillars of Apadana Palace, Persepolis, vert. 10r, Bas-relief from a Mede tomb, Iraq. 14r, Achaemenian officers, bas-relief, Persepolis.

1970, June 21 **Photo.** ***Perf.* 13**

1554 A343 6r gray, red & vio 75 18
1555 A343 8r pale rose, blk & bl grn 1.50 50
1556 A343 10r yel, red & brn 1.90 65
1557 A343 14r bl, blk & red brn 2.25 1.00

2500th anniversary of the founding of the Persian Empire by Cyrus the Great.

See Nos. 1561-1571, 1589-1596, 1605-1612.

Seeyo-Se-Pol Bridge, Isfahan — A344

Designs: No. 1559, Saiful Malook Lake, Pakistan, vert. No. 1560, View of Fethiye, Turkey, vert.

***Perf.* 10½**

1970, July 21 **Litho.** **Wmk. 353**

1558 A344 2r multicolored 75 20
1559 A344 2r multicolored 75 20
1560 A344 2r multicolored 75 20

Signing of the Regional Cooperation for Development Pact by Iran, Turkey and Pakistan, 6th anniv.

Queen Buran, Dirhem Coin A345

Wine Goblet with Lion's Head — A346

Designs: No. 1562, Achaemenian eagle amulet. No. 1563, Mithridates I, dirhem coin. No. 1564, Sassanidae art (arch, coin, jugs). No. 1566, Shapur I, dirhem coin. No. 1567, Achaemenian courier. No. 1568, Winged deer. No. 1569, Ardashir I, dirhem coin. No. 1570, Seal of Darius I (chariot, palms, lion). 14r, Achaemenian tapestry.

1970 Wmk. 353 **Photo.** ***Perf.* 13**

1561 A345 1r gold & multi 1.00 38
1562 A346 2r gold & multi 1.00 38
1563 A345 2r gold & multi 1.25 38
1564 A346 2r lilac & multi 1.25 38
1565 A346 6r lilac & multi 1.25 38
1566 A345 6r lilac & multi 1.75 45
1567 A345 6r lilac & multi 1.75 52
1568 A346 8r lilac & multi 1.75 52
1569 A345 8r lilac & multi 1.75 52
1570 A345 8r lilac & multi 1.75 52
1571 A345 14r lt bl & multi 2.00 1.10
Nos. 1561-1571 (11) 16.50 5.53

2500th anniversary of the founding of the Persian Empire by Cyrus the Great.

Issue dates: 1r, Nos. 1563, 1566, 1569, Aug. 22; Nos. 1562, 1565, 1568, 14r, Aug. 6; others, Sept. 22.

Candle and Globe — A347

Persian Decoration — A348

1970, Sept. 8 **Litho.** ***Perf.* 10½**

1572 A347 1r lt bl & multi 20 15
1573 A347 2r pale sal & multi 25 15
Set value 20

Issued to publicize World Literacy Day.

1970, Sept. 14

1574 A348 6r multi 35 15

Isfahan Intl. Cong. of Architects, Sept. 1970.

Emblem A349

UN Emblem, Dove and Scales A350

1970, Sept. 28 ***Perf.* 10½**

1575 A349 2r lt bl & pur 25 15

Congress of Election Committees of Persian States and Tehran.

1970, Oct. 24 **Litho.** **Wmk. 353**

1576 A350 2r lt bl, mag & dk bl 30 15

Issued for United Nations Day.

Festival Type of 1969

1970, Oct. 28 ***Perf.* 10½**

1577 A328 2r org & multi 40 15

3rd Festival of Arts and Culture.

UNICEF Type of 1969

Children's Drawings and UNICEF Emblem: 50d, Herdsman and goats. 1r, Family picnic. 2r, Mosque.

1970, Oct. 31

Size: 43½x31mm

1578 A329 50d black & multi 15 15
1579 A329 1r black & multi 20 15
1580 A329 2r black & multi 40 15
Set value 30

Issued for Children's Week.

Shah Mohammed Riza Pahlavi A351

1971, Jan. 26 Wmk. 353 *Perf. 10½*
1581 A351 2r lt bl & multi 1.65 35

Publicizing the "White Revolution of King and People" and the 12 reform laws.

Sheldrake — A352

Designs: 2r, Ruddy shelduck. 8r, Flamingo, vert.

1971, Jan. 30 Litho.
1582 A352 1r multicolored 1.00 15
1583 A352 2r multicolored 1.25 20
1584 A352 8r multicolored 1.75 35

Intl. Wetland and Waterfowl Conf., Ramsar.

Riza Shah Pahlavi — A353

1971, Feb. 22 Wmk. 353 *Perf. 10½*
1585 A353 6r multicolored 3.25 45

50th anniversary of the Pahlavi dynasty's accession to power.

Rooster A354

Designs: 2r, Barn swallow and nest. 6r, Hoopoe.

1971, Mar. 6 Photo. *Perf. 13½x13*
1586 A354 1r multicolored 60 15
1587 A354 2r multicolored 1.00 15
1588 A354 6r multicolored 2.75 30

Novrooz, Iranian New Year.

Shapur II Hunting — A355

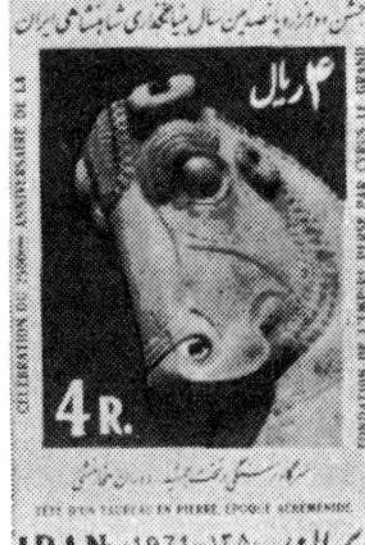

Bull's Head, Persepolis A356

Designs: 1r, Harpist, mosaic. No. 1591, Investiture of Ardashir I, bas-relief. 5r Winged lion ornament. 6r, Persian archer, bas-relief. 8r, Royal audience, bas-relief. 10r, Bronze head of Parthian prince.

1971 Litho. *Perf. 10½*
1589 A356 1r multicolored 1.00 25
1590 A355 2r blk & brn org 1.50 25
1591 A355 2r lil, gldn brn & blk 1.50 25
1592 A356 4r pur & multi 1.50 25
1593 A356 5r multicolored 1.75 50
1594 A356 6r multicolored 1.75 50
1595 A356 8r lt bl & multi 2.25 50
1596 A356 10r dp bis, blk & sl 2.25 65
Nos. 1589-1596 (8) 13.50 3.15

2500th anniversary of the founding of the Persian Empire by Cyrus the Great.
Issued: 4r, 5r, 6r, 8r, May 15; others, June 15.

Prisoners Leaving Jail A357

1971, May 20 Litho. Wmk. 353
1597 A357 6r multicolored 1.50 15
1598 A357 8r multicolored 2.50 15
Set value 24

Rehabilitation of Prisoners Week.

Religious School, Chaharbagh, Ispahan — A358

Designs: No. 1600, Mosque of Selim, Edirne, Turkey. No. 1601, Badshahi Mosque, Lahore, Pakistan, horiz.

1971, July 21 Litho. *Perf. 10½*
1599 A358 2r multicolored 35 15
1600 A358 2r multicolored 35 15
1601 A358 2r multicolored 35 15
Set value 30

7th anniversary of Regional Cooperation among Iran, Pakistan and Turkey.

"Fifth Festival of Arts" — A359

1971, Aug. 26 Litho. & Typo.
1602 A359 2r lt & dk grn, red & gold 70 15

5th Festival of Arts, Shiraz-Persepolis.

"Fight Against Illiteracy" A360

1971, Sept. 8 Litho.
1603 A360 2r grn & multi 50 15

International Literacy Day, Sept. 8.

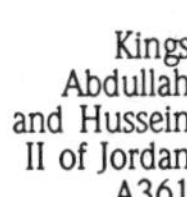

Kings Abdullah and Hussein II of Jordan A361

1971, Sept. 11
1604 A361 2r yel grn, blk & red 40 15

Hashemite Kingdom of Jordan, 50th anniv.

Shahyad Aryamehr Monument — A362

Designs: 1r, Aryamehr steel mill, near Isfahan. 3r, Senate Building, Tehran. 11r, Shah Abbas Kabir Dam, Zayandeh River.

1971, Sept. 22
1605 A362 1r blue & multi 1.00 22
1606 A362 2r multicolored 1.00 36
1607 A362 3r brt pink & multi 1.00 36
1608 A362 11r org & multi 2.25 65

2500th anniversary of the founding of the Persian empire by Cyrus the Great.

Shah Mohammed Riza Pahlavi A363

Designs: 2r, Riza Shah Pahlavi. 5r, Stone tablet with proclamation of Cyrus the Great, horiz. 10r, Crown of present empire (erroneously inscribed *Le Couronne*).

1971, Oct. 12
1609 A363 1r gold & multi 1.65 90
1610 A363 2r gold & multi 1.65 90
1611 A363 5r gold & multi 1.65 90
1612 A363 10r gold & multi 2.75 90

2500th anniversary of the founding of the Persian empire by Cyrus the Great.

Ghatour Railroad Bridge — A364

1971, Oct. 7
1613 A364 2r multicolored 90 25

Iran-Turkey railroad.

Racial Equality Emblem — A365

Mohammed Riza Pahlavi — A366

1971, Oct. 24
1614 A365 2r lt blue & multi 20 15

Intl. Year Against Racial Discrimination.

Perf. 13½x13
1971, Oct. 26 Photo. Wmk. 353
Size: 20½x28mm
1615 A366 5d lilac 15 15
1616 A366 10d henna brown 15 15
1617 A366 50d brt bl grn 20 15
1618 A366 1r dp yel grn 28 15
1619 A366 2r brown 28 15

Size: 27x36½mm
1620 A366 6r slate green 1.10 15
1621 A366 8r violet blue 1.65 1.10
1622 A366 10r red lilac 1.40 30
1623 A366 11r blue green 5.00 1.10
1624 A366 14r brt blue 7.00 50
1625 A366 20r car rose 5.75 65
1626 A366 50r yellow bis 6.75 1.25
Nos. 1615-1626 (12) 29.71 5.80

See Nos. 1650-1661B, 1768-1772.

Child's Drawing and Emblem — A367

Designs: No. 1631, Ruins of Persepolis, vert. No. 1632, Warrior, mosaic, vert.

1971, Oct. 31 Litho. *Perf. 10½*
1630 A367 2r multicolored 25 15
1631 A367 2r multicolored 25 15
1632 A367 2r multicolored 25 15
Set value 30

Children's Week.

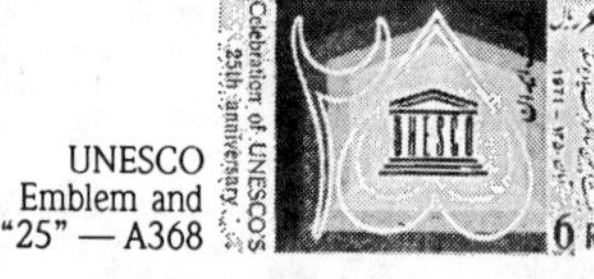
UNESCO Emblem and "25" — A368

1971, Nov. 4
1633 A368 6r ultra & rose claret 40 15

25th anniversary of UNESCO.

Domestic Animals and Emblem A369

1971, Nov. 22
1634 A369 2r gray, blk & car 40 16

4th Iranian Veterinarians' Congress.

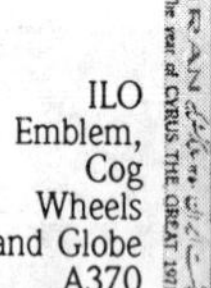

ILO Emblem, Cog Wheels and Globe A370

1971, Dec. 4
1635 A370 2r black, org & bl 35 15

7th ILO Conference for the Asian Region.

UNICEF Emblem, Bird Feeding Young — A371

1971, Dec. 16 ***Perf. 13x13½***
1636 A371 2r lt bl, mag & blk 35 15

25th anniversary of UNICEF.

Mohammed Riza Pahlavi — A372

1972, Jan. 26 Wmk. 353 ***Perf. 10½***
1637 A372 2r lt green & multi 2.50 20
a. 20r Souvenir sheet 7.50 5.25

"White Revolution of King and People" and the 12 reform laws. No. 1637a contains one stamp with simulated perforations.

Pintailed Sandgrouse A373

Designs: No. 1639, Rock ptarmigan. 2r, Yellow-billed waxbill and red-cheeked cordon-bleu.

1972, Mar. 6 Litho. ***Perf. 13x13½***
1638 A373 1r lt green & multi 42 15
1639 A373 1r lt blue & multi 42 15
1640 A373 2r yellow & multi 1.40 24
Set value 42

Iranian New Year.

"Your Heart is your Health" — A374

Film Strip and Winged Antelope — A375

1972, Apr. 4 ***Perf. 10½***
1641 A374 10r lemon & multi 1.75 15

World Health Day; Iranian Society of Cardiology.

1972, Apr. 16 Litho. & Engr.

Design: 8r, Film strips and winged antelope.

1642 A375 6r ultra & gold 80 15
1643 A375 8r yellow & multi 1.50 15
Set value 24

Tehran International Film Festival.

Rose and Bud — A376

1972, May 5 Litho.
1644 A376 1r shown 32 15
1645 A376 2r Yellow roses 60 15
1646 A376 5r Red rose 75 18
Set value 35

See Nos. 1711-1713.

Persian Woman, by Behzad — A377

Paintings: No. 1648, Fisherman, by Cevat Dereli (Turkey). No. 1649, Young Man, by Abdur Rehman Chughtai (Pakistan).

1972, July 21 Wmk. 353
1647 A377 5r gray & multi 1.40 22
1648 A377 5r gray & multi 1.40 22
1649 A377 5r gray & multi 1.40 22

Regional Cooperation for Development Pact among Iran, Turkey and Pakistan, 8th anniv.

Shah Type of 1971

1972-73 Photo. ***Perf. 13½x13***
Bister Frame & Crown
Size: 20½x28mm

1650 A366 5d lilac 15 15
1651 A366 10d henna brown 15 15
1652 A366 50d brt blue grn 18 15
1653 A366 1r dp yellow grn 25 15
a. Brown frame & crown ('73) *55* 15
1654 A366 2r brown 32 15

Size: 27x36½mm

1655 A366 6r slate grn 1.65 20
1656 A366 8r violet blue 1.65 20
1657 A366 10r red lilac 2.00 15
1658 A366 11r blue green 2.75 1.00
1659 A366 14r dull blue 3.50 20
1660 A366 20r car rose 3.75 32
1661 A366 50r grnsh blue 3.75 1.00
1661A A366 100r violet ('73) 5.00 2.00
1661B A366 200r slate ('73) 10.00 3.50
Nos. 1650-1661B (14) 35.10 9.32

Festival Emblem A378

1972, Aug. 31 Litho. ***Perf. 10½***
1662 A378 6r emerald, red & blk 1.10 15
1663 A378 8r brt mag, blk & grn 1.65 25

6th Festival of Arts, Shiraz-Persepolis, Aug. 31-Sept. 8.

Pens and Emblem — A379

"10" and Emblems — A380

1972, Sept. 8
1664 A379 1r lt blue & multi 25 15
1665 A379 2r yellow & multi 38 15
Set value 22

World Literacy Day, Sept. 8.

1972, Sept. 18
1666 A380 1r lilac & multi 25 20
1667 A380 2r dull yel & multi 45 25

10th Congress of Iranian Dentists' Assoc., Sept. 18-22.

Asian Broadcasting Union Emblem — A381

No. 450 on Cover — A382

1972, Oct. 1
1668 A381 6r lt green & multi 75 15
1669 A381 8r gray & multi 1.50 15
Set value 18

9th General Assembly of Asian Broadcasting Union, Tehran, Oct. 1972.

1972, Oct. 9
1670 A382 10r lt blue & multi 2.25 25

International Stamp Day.

Chess and Olympic Rings — A383

Designs (Olympic Rings and): 2r, Hunter. 3r, Archer. 5r, Equestrians. 6r, Polo. 8r, Wrestling.

1972, Oct. 17
1671 A383 1r brown & multi 1.75 75
1672 A383 2r blue & multi 1.75 15
1673 A383 3r lilac & multi 2.25 15
1674 A383 5r bl grn & multi 2.25 22
1675 A383 6r red & multi 2.25 25
1676 A383 8r yel grn & multi 2.25 25
a. Souv. sheet of 6, #1671-1676, imperf. 12.50 3.00
Nos. 1671-1676 (6) 12.50 1.77

20th Olympic Games, Munich, Aug. 26-Sept. 11.

Communications Symbol, UN Emblem — A384

Children and Flowers — A385

1972, Oct. 24
1677 A384 10r multicolored 2.00 15

United Nations Day.

1972, Oct. 31 Litho. Wmk. 353

Children's Drawings and Emblem: No. 1679, Puppet show. 6r, Boys cutting wood, horiz.

1678 A385 2r gray & multi 35 15
1679 A385 2r bister & multi 70 15
1680 A385 6r pink & multi 1.40 15
Set value 26

Children's Week.

Festival Type of 1969

Design: 10r, Crown, emblems and column capital, Persepolis.

1972, Nov. 11
1681 A328 10r dp blue & multi 5.00 28

10th anniv. of White Revolution; Festival of Culture and Art.

Family Planning Emblem A386

1972, Dec. 5
1682 A386 1r blue & multi 15 15
1683 A386 2r brt pink & multi 30 15
Set value 15

To promote family planning.

Iranian Scout Organization, 20th anniv. — A387

1972, Dec. 9
1684 A387 2r multicolored 50 15

Ancient Seal A388

Designs: Various ancient seals.

1973, Jan. 5 *Perf. 10½*

1685	A388	1r blue, red & brn	60	15
1686	A388	1r yellow & multi	60	15
1687	A388	1r pink & multi	60	15
1688	A388	2r lt brick red & multi	60	15
1689	A388	2r dull org & multi	60	15
1690	A388	2r olive & multi	60	15
		Nos. 1685-1690 (6)	3.60	
		Set value		54

Development of writing.

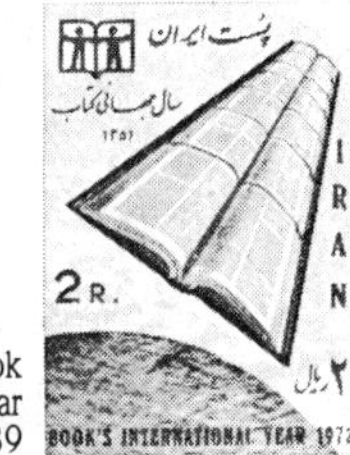

Books and Book Year Emblem — A389

Design: 6r, Illuminated page, 10th century, from Shahnameh, by Firdousi.

1973, Jan. 10

1691	A389	2r black & multi	75	15
1692	A389	6r yellow & multi	1.10	20
		Set value		28

International Book Year.

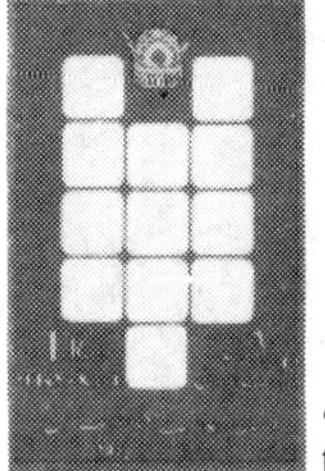

"12 Improvements by the King" — A390

Designs: 2r, 10r, 12 circles symbolizing 12 improvements. 6r, like 1r.

1973, Jan. 26 **Litho.**

Size: 29x43mm

1693	A390	1r gold, ultra, red & yel	25	15
1694	A390	2r sil, plum, ol & yel	25	15

Size: 65x84mm

1695	A390	6r gold, ultra, red & yel	1.75	75
		Set value		86

Souvenir Sheet

Imperf

1696	A390	10r sil, plum, ol & yel	2.75	75

Introduction of the King's socioeconomic reforms, 10th anniv.

Blue Surgeonfish A391

Fish: No. 1698, Gilthead. No. 1699, Banded sergeant major. No. 1700, Porkfish. No. 1701, Black-spot snapper.

1973, Mar. 6 **Wmk. 353** *Perf. 10½*

1697	A391	1r multicolored	65	15
1698	A391	1r multicolored	65	15
1699	A391	2r multicolored	95	18
1700	A391	2r multicolored	95	18
1701	A391	2r multicolored	95	18
		Nos. 1697-1701 (5)	4.15	84

Iranian New Year.

WHO Emblem — A392

1973, Apr. 7 **Litho.** **Wmk. 353**

1702	A392	10r brn, grn & red	1.25	15

25th anniversary of the WHO.

Soccer — A393

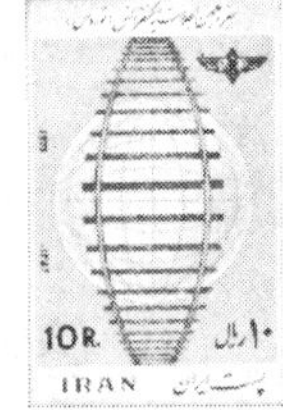

Tracks and Globe — A394

1973, Apr. 13

1703	A393	14r orange & multi	1.40	25

15th Asian Youth Football (soccer) Tournament.

1973, May 10 **Wmk. 353** *Perf. 10½*

1704	A394	10r dk grn, lil & vio bl	1.25	18

13th International Railroad Conference.

Clay Tablet with Aryan Script — A395

Designs: Clay tablets with various scripts.

1973, June 5 *Perf. 10½*

1705	A395	1r shown	50	15
1706	A395	1r Kharoshthi	50	15
1707	A395	1r Achaemenian	50	15
1708	A395	2r Parthian (Mianeh)	90	18
1709	A395	2r Parthian (Arsacide)	90	18
1710	A395	2r Gachtak (Dabireh)	90	15
		Nos. 1705-1710 (6)	4.20	96

Development of writing.

Flower Type of 1972

1973, June 20

1711	A376	1r Orchid	20	15
1712	A376	2r Hyacinth	60	15
1713	A376	6r Columbine	1.25	20
		Set value		32

Statue, Shahdad Kerman, Persia, 4000 B.C. — A396

Designs: No. 1714, Head from mausoleum of King Antiochus I (69-34 B.C.), Turkey. No. 1716, Street, Mohenjo-Daro, Pakistan.

1973, July 21

1714	A396	2r brown & multi	35	16
1715	A396	2r green & multi	35	16
1716	A396	2r blue & multi	35	16
a.		Strip of 3, #1714-1716	1.05	60

Regional Cooperation for Development Pact among Iran, Turkey and Pakistan, 9th anniv.

Shah, Oil Pump, Refinery and Tanker — A397

1973, Aug. 4

1717	A397	5r blue & black	1.40	30

Nationalization of oil industry.

Soldiers and Rising Sun — A398

Gymnasts and Globe — A399

1973, Aug. 19 **Litho.** **Wmk. 353**

1718	A398	2r ultra & multi	32	15

20th anniversary of return of monarchy.

1973, Aug. 23 *Perf. 10½*

1719	A399	2r olive & multi	20	15
1720	A399	2r violet bl & multi	20	15
		Set value		24

7th Intl. Congress of Physical Education and Sports for Girls and Women, Tehran, Aug. 19-25.

Shahyad Monument, Rainbow and WMO Emblem A400

1973, Sept. 4

1721	A400	5r multicolored	75	15

Intl. meteorological cooperation, centenary.

Festival Emblem — A401

Wrestlers — A402

1973, Aug. 31

1722	A401	1r silver & multi	20	15
1723	A401	5r gold & multi	30	15
		Set value		24

7th Festival of Arts, Shiraz-Persepolis.

1973, Sept. 6 **Litho.** **Wmk. 353**

1724	A402	6r lt green & multi	70	20

World Wrestling Championships, Tehran, Sept. 6-14.

"Literacy as Light" — A403

Audio-Visual Equipment — A404

1973, Sept. 8

1725	A403	2r multicolored	20	15

World Literacy Day, Sept. 8.

1973, Sept. 11

1726	A404	10r yellow & multi	65	20

Tehran Intl. Audio-Visual Exhib., Sept. 11-24.

Warrior Taming Winged Bull — A405

1973, Sept. 16

1727	A405	8r blue gray & multi	65	15

Intl. Council of Military Sports, 25th anniv.

abu-al-Rayhan al-Biruni (973-1048), Philosopher and Mathematician — A406

1973, Sept. 16

1728	A406	10r brown & black	1.10	20

Soccer Cup — A407

INTERPOL Emblem — A408

1973, Oct. 2 **Wmk. 353** *Perf. 10½*

1729	A407	2r lilac, blk & buff	35	15

Soccer Games for the Crown Prince's Cup.

1973, Oct. 7

1730	A408	2r multicolored	25	15

50th anniversary of INTERPOL.

Symbolic Arches and Globe A409

1973, Oct. 8

1731	A409	10r orange & multi	55	15

World Federation for Mental Health, 25th anniv.

UPU Emblem, Letter, Post Horn — A410

Honeycomb — A411

1973, Oct. 9

1732	A410	6r blue & orange	50	16

World Post Day, Oct. 9.

1973, Oct. 24

1733	A411	2r lt brown & multi	18	15
1734	A411	2r gray olive & multi	18	15
		Set value		15

UN Volunteer Program, 5th anniv.

Festival Type of 1969

Design: 2r, Crown and column capital, Persepolis.

1973, Oct. 26

1735	A328	2r yellow & multi	40	15

Festival of Culture and Art.

Turkish Bosporus Bridge, Flag — A412

Design: 8r, Kemal Ataturk and Riza Shah Pahlavi.

1973, Oct. 29 Litho. *Perf. 10½*

1736	A412	2r multicolored	75	15
1737	A412	8r multicolored	1.25	25

50th anniversary of the Turkish Republic.

Mother and Child, Emblem — A413

Children's Drawings and Emblem: No. 1739, Wagon, horiz. No. 1740, House and garden with birds.

1973, Oct. 31

1738	A413	2r multicolored	30	15
1739	A413	2r multicolored	30	15
1740	A413	2r multicolored	30	15
		Set value		20

Children's Week.

Cow, Wheat and FAO Emblem A414

1973, Nov. 4

1741	A414	10r multicolored	1.00	20

10th anniversary of World Food Program.

Proclamation of Cyrus the Great; Red Cross, Lion and Crescent Emblems — A415

1973, Nov. 8

1742	A415	6r lt blue & multi	50	18

22nd Intl. Red Cross Conf., Tehran, 1972.

"Film Festival" A416

Globe and Travelers A417

1973, Nov. 26 Wmk. 353 *Perf. 10½*

1743	A416	2r black & multi	20	15

2nd International Tehran Film Festival.

1973, Nov. 26 Litho.

1744	A417	10r orange & multi	50	15

12th annual Congress of Intl. Assoc. of Tour Managers.

Human Rights Flame A418

Score and Emblem A419

1973, Dec. 10

1745	A418	8r lt blue & multi	40	16

Universal Declaration of Human Rights, 25th anniv.

1973, Dec. 21

Design: No. 1747, Score and emblem, diff.

1746	A419	10r yel grn, red & blk	55	15
1747	A419	10r lt bl, ultra & red	55	15
		Set value		24

Dedicated to the art of music.

Forestry, Printing, Education — A420

Designs (Symbols of Reforms): No. 1749, Land reform, sales of shares, women's suffrage. No. 1750, Army of progress, irrigation, women's education. No. 1751, Hygiene, rural courts, housing.

1974, Jan. 26 Litho. *Perf. 10½*

1748	A420	1r lt blue & multi	20	15
1749	A420	1r lt blue & multi	20	15
1750	A420	2r lt blue & multi	25	15
1751	A420	2r lt blue & multi	25	15
a.		Block of 4, #1748-1751	90	75

Imperf

Size: 76½x102mm

1752	A420	20r multicolored	3.25	1.25

"White Revolution of King and People" and 12 reform laws.

Pir Amooz Ketabaty Script A421

Various Scripts: No. 1754, Mo Eghely Ketabaty. No. 1755, Din Dabireh, Avesta script. No. 1756, Pir Amooz, Naskh style. No. 1757, Pir Amooz, decorative style. No. 1758, Decorative and architectural style.

1974, Feb. 14 Wmk. 353 *Perf. 10½*

1753	A421	1r silver, ocher & multi	75	30
1754	A421	1r gold, gray & multi	75	30
1755	A421	1r silver, yel & multi	75	30
1756	A421	2r gold, gray & multi	75	30
1757	A421	2r gold, slate & multi	75	30
1758	A421	2r gold, claret & multi	75	30
		Nos. 1753-1758 (6)	4.50	1.80

Development of writing.

Fowl, Syringe and Emblem A422

1974, Feb. 23

1759	A422	6r red brown & multi	42	15

5th Iranian Veterinary Congress.

Monarch Butterfly — A423

Designs: Various butterflies.

1974, Mar. 6 Litho. *Perf. 10½*

1760	A423	1r rose lilac & multi	80	15
1761	A423	1r brt rose & multi	80	15
1762	A423	2r lt blue & multi	1.00	25
1763	A423	2r green & multi	1.00	25
1764	A423	2r bister & multi	1.00	25
		Nos. 1760-1764 (5)	4.60	1.05

Novrooz, Iranian New Year.

Jalaludin Mevlana (1207-1273), Poet — A424

1974, Mar. 12 *Perf. 13*

1765	A424	2r pale violet & multi	50	15

Shah Type of 1971

1974 Photo. *Perf. 13½x13*

Size: 20½x28mm

1768	A366	50d orange & bl	45	15
1769	A366	1r emerald & bl	50	15
1770	A366	2r red & blue	75	15

Size: 27x36½mm

1771	A366	10r lt green & bl	6.00	15
1772	A366	20r lilac & bl	4.25	20
		Nos. 1768-1772 (5)	11.95	
		Set value		45

Palace of the Forty Columns A425

1974, Apr. 11 Litho. *Perf. 10½*

1773	A425	10r multicolored	50	15

9th Medical Congress of the Near and Middle East, Isfahan.

Onager — A426

Athlete and Games Emblem — A427

1974, Apr. 13

1774	A426	1r shown	40	15
1775	A426	2r Great bustard	50	20
1776	A426	6r Fawn and deer	1.25	35
1777	A426	8r Caucasian black grouse	2.00	40
a.		Strip of 4, #1774-1777	4.25	1.50

Intl. Council for Game and Wildlife Preservation.

1974, Apr. 30

1778	A427	1r shown	42	15
1779	A427	1r Table tennis	42	15
1780	A427	2r Boxing	85	15
1781	A427	2r Hurdles	85	15
1782	A427	6r Weight lifting	1.25	15
1783	A427	8r Basketball	1.75	20
		Nos. 1778-1783 (6)	5.54	
		Set value		64

7th Asian Games, Tehran; first issue.

Pour la Sauvegarde de Venise

Lion of Venice — A428

Design: 8r, Audience with the Doge of Venice (painting).

1974, May 5

1784 A428 6r multicolored 55 15
1785 A428 8r multicolored 1.00 18

Safeguarding Venice.

Links and Grain — A429

1974, May 13 Litho. *Perf. 10½*

1786 A429 2r multicolored 25 15

Cooperation Day.

Military Plane, 1924 A430

1974, June 1

1787 A430 10r shown 2.00 40
1788 A430 10r Jet, 1974 2.00 40

50th anniversary of Iranian Air Force.

Swimmer and Games Emblem — A431 Bicyclists and Games Emblem — A432

1974, July 1 Wmk. 353 *Perf. 10½*

1789 A431 1r shown 65 15
1790 A431 1r Tennis, men's doubles 65 15
1791 A431 2r Wrestling 80 20
1792 A431 2r Hockey 80 20
1793 A431 4r Volleyball 1.25 40
1794 A431 10r Tennis, women's singles 2.50 50
Nos. 1789-1794 (6) 6.65 1.60

7th Asian Games, Tehran; second issue.

1974, Aug. 1

1795 A432 2r shown 90 15
1796 A432 2r Soccer 90 15
1797 A432 2r Fencing 90 15
1798 A432 2r Small-bore rifle shooting 90 15
Set value 48

7th Asian Games, Tehran; third issue.

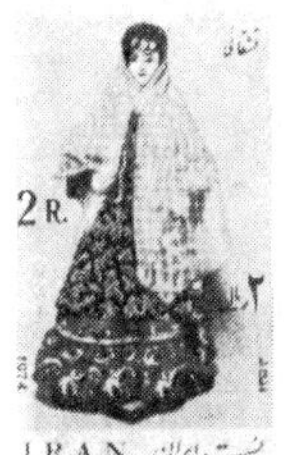

Ghaskai Costume A433

Gold Winged Lion Cup A434

Regional Costumes: No. 1800, Kurdistan, Kermanshah District. No. 1801, Kurdistan, Sanandaj District. No. 1802, Mazandaran. No. 1803, Bakhtiari. No. 1804, Torkaman.

1974, July 6

1799 A433 2r lt ultra & multi 1.40 50
1800 A433 2r buff & multi 1.40 50
1801 A433 2r green & multi 1.40 50
1802 A433 2r lt blue & multi 1.40 50
1803 A433 2r gray & multi 1.40 50
1804 A433 2r dull grn & multi 1.40 50
a. Block of 6, #1799-1804 8.50 4.50
Nos. 1799-1804 (6) 8.40 3.00

1974, July 13

1805 A434 2r dull green & multi 30 15

Iranian Soccer Cup.

Tabriz Rug, Late 16th Century A435

King Carrying Vases, Bas-relief A436

Designs: No. 1807, Anatolian rug, 15th century. No. 1808, Kashan rug, Lahore.

1974, July 21

1806 A435 2r brown & multi 45 15
1807 A435 2r blue & multi 45 15
1808 A435 2r red & multi 45 15
Set value 30
a. Strip of 3, #1806-1808 1.35 45

Regional Cooperation for Development Pact among Iran, Turkey and Pakistan, 10th anniv.

1974, Aug. 15 Litho. *Perf. 10½*

1809 A436 2r black & multi 30 15

8th Iranian Arts Festival, Shiraz-Persepolis.

Aryamehr Stadium, Tehran — A437

Designs: No. 1811, Games' emblem and inscription. No. 1812, Aerial view of games' site.

1974

1810 A437 6r multicolored 1.00 20

Souvenir Sheets

1811 A437 10r multicolored *2.00 1.00*
1812 A437 10r multicolored *2.00 1.00*

7th Asian Games, Tehran; fourth and fifth issues. Nos. 1811-1812 contain one imperf. 51x38mm stamp each.

Issued: #1811-1812, Sept. 1; #1810, Sept. 16.

"Welfare" A438

"Education" A439

1974, Sept. 11

1813 A438 2r orange & multi 22 15
1814 A439 2r blue & multi 22 15
Set value 15

Welfare and free education.

Map of Hasanlu, 1000-800 B.C. — A440

1974, Sept. 24

1815 A440 8r multicolored 42 15

2nd Intl. Congress of Architecture, Shiraz-Persepolis, Sept. 1974.

Achaemenian Mail Cart and UPU Emblem — A441

Design: 14r, UPU emblem and letters.

1974, Oct. 9 Wmk. 353 *Perf. 10½*

1816 A441 6r orange, grn & blk 85 18
1817 A441 14r multicolored 1.25 18

Centenary of Universal Postal Union.

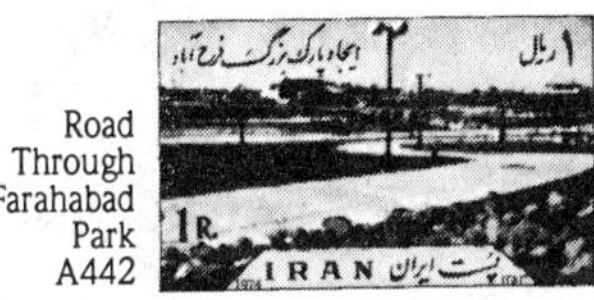

Road Through Farahabad Park A442

1974, Oct. 16

1818 A442 1r shown 15 15
1819 A442 2r Recreation Bldg. 25 15
Set value 15

Inauguration of Farahabad Park, Tehran.

Farahnaz Dam and Mohammed Riza Pahlavi — A443

Designs: 5d, Kharg Island petro-chemical plant. 10d, Ghatour Railroad Bridge. 1r, Tehran oil refinery. 2r, Satellite communication station, Hamadan, and Mt. Alvand. 6r, Aryamehr steel mill, Isfahan. 8r, University of Tabriz. 10r, Shah Abbas Kabir Dam. 14r, Rudagi Music Hall. 20r, Shayad Monument. 50r, Aryamehr Stadium.

1974-75 Photo. *Perf. 13x13½*

Size: 28x21mm

Frame & Shah in Brown

1820 A443 5d slate green 55 15
1821 A443 10d orange 55 15
1822 A443 50d blue green 55 15
1823 A443 1r ultra 55 15
1824 A443 2r deep lilac 55 15

Size: 36x26½mm

Frame & Shah in Dark Blue

1825 A443 6r brown 2.00 35
1826 A443 8r grnsh blue 1.10 45
1827 A443 10r deep lilac 2.25 35
a. Value in Persian omitted 11.00 3.00
1828 A443 14r deep green 9.00 68
1829 A443 20r magenta 3.50 50
1830 A443 50r violet 4.50 1.40
Nos. 1820-1830 (11) 25.10
Set value 3.60

Issued dates: 50d, 1r, 2r, Oct. 16, 1974; 14r, Nov. 1974; others Mar. 6, 1975.

See Nos. 1831-1841. For overprints see Nos. 2008, 2010.

1975-77

Size: 28x21mm

Frame & Shah in Green

1831 A443 5d orange ('77) 50 15
1832 A443 10d rose mag ('77) 50 15
1833 A443 50d lilac 50 15
1834 A443 1r dark blue 30 15
1835 A443 2r brown 35 15

Size: 36x26½mm

Frame & Shah in Brown

1836 A443 6r vio bl ('76) 55 35
1837 A443 8r deep org ('77) 7.50 30
1838 A443 10r dp yel grn ('76) 3.75 20
1839 A443 14r lilac 2.00 20
1840 A443 20r brt green ('76) 3.50 40
1841 A443 50r dp blue ('76) 5.00 90
Nos. 1831-1841 (11) 24.45
Set value 2.70

Festival Emblem, Crown and Column Capital, Persepolis — A444

1974, Oct. 26 Litho. *Perf. 10½*

1842 A444 2r multicolored 30 15

Festival of Culture and Art.

Destroyer "Palang" and Flag A445

1974, Nov. 5

1843 A445 10r multicolored 80 20

Navy Day.

Girl at Spinning Wheel A446

Designs: Children's drawings.

1974, Nov. 7 *Perf. 10½*

1844 A446 2r shown 20 15
1845 A446 2r Scarecrow, vert. 20 15
1846 A446 2r Picnic 20 15
Set value 24

Children's Week.

Winged Ibex — A447

1974, Nov. 25 Litho. Wmk. 353

1847 A447 2r vio, org & blk 20 15

Third Tehran International Film Festival.

WPY Emblem A448

1974, Dec. 1

1848 A448 8r orange & multi 50 20

World Population Year.

Gold Bee A449

Design: 8r, Gold crown, gift of French people to Empress Farah. Bee pin was gift of the Italian people.

1974, Dec. 20

1849 A449 6r multicolored 20 15
1850 A449 8r multicolored 38 15
Set value 20

14th wedding anniv. of Shah and Empress Farah.

Angel with Banner A450

1975, Jan. 7 Litho. *Perf. 10½*

1851 A450 2r org & vio bl 22 15

International Women's Year.

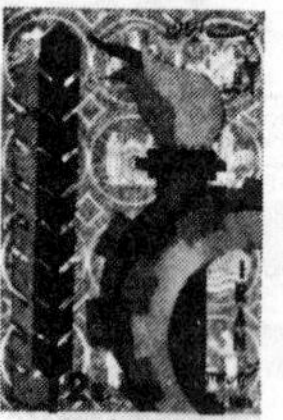

Symbols of Agriculture, Industry and the Arts A451

Tourism Year 75 Emblem A452

1975, Jan. 26 Wmk. 353

1852 A451 2r multicolored 22 15

"White Revolution of King and People."

1975, Feb. 17

1853 A452 6r multicolored 26 15

South Asia Tourism Year.

> *Footnotes near stamp listings often refer to other stamps of the same design.*

"Farabi" in Shape of Musical Instrument or Alembic — A453

Ornament, Rug Pattern — A454

1975, Mar. 1

1854 A453 2r brn red & multi 20 15

Abu-Nasr al-Farabi (870?-950), physician, musician and philosopher, 1100th birth anniversary.

1975, Mar. 6

1855 A454 1r shown 15 15
1856 A454 1r Blossoms and cypress trees 15 15
1857 A454 1r Shah Abbasi flower 15 15
a. Strip of 3, #1855-1857 30 20
Set value 30 15

Novrooz, Iranian New Year. Nos. 1855-1857 printed in sheets of 45 stamps and 15 labels.

Nasser Khosrov, Poet, Birth Millenary — A455

Formula — A456

1975, Mar. 11

1858 A455 2r blk, gold & red 25 15

1975, May 5 Litho. *Perf. 10½*

1859 A456 2r buff & multi 20 15

5th Biennial Symposium of Iranian Biochemical Society.

Charioteer, Bas-relief, Persepolis — A457

Design: 2r, Heads of Persian warriors, bas-relief from Persepolis, vert.

1975, May 5

1860 A457 2r lt brn & multi 1.40 22
1861 A457 10r blue & multi 3.25 40

Rotary International, 70th anniversary.

Signal Fire, Persian Castle A458

Design: 8r, Communications satellite.

1975, May 17

1862 A458 6r multicolored 28 15
1863 A458 8r lil & multi 40 15
Set value 17

7th World Telecommunications Day.

Cooperation Day — A459

1975, May 13

1864 A459 2r multicolored 20 15

Jet, Shayad Monument, Statue of Liberty — A460

1975, May 29 Litho. Wmk. 353

1865 A460 10r org & multi 60 15

Iran Air's 1st flight to New York, May 1975.

Emblem — A461

1975, June 5

1866 A461 6r blue & multi 30 15

World Environment Day.

Dam A462

1975, June 10

1867 A462 10r multicolored 35 15

9th Intl. Congress on Irrigation & Drainage.

Resurgence Party Emblem — A463

Girl Scout Symbols — A464

1975, July 1 Wmk. 353 *Perf. 10½*

1868 A463 2r multicolored 16 15

Organization of Resurgence Party.

1975, July 16

1869 A464 2r multicolored 25 15

2nd Natl Girl Scout Camp, Tehran, July 1976.

Festival of Tus — A465

1975, July 17

1870 A465 2r gray, lil & vio 22 15

Festival of Tus in honor of Firdausi (940-1020), Persian poet born near Tus in Khorasan.

Ceramic Plate, Iran A466

Designs: No. 1872, Camel leather vase, Pakistan, vert. No. 1873, Porcelain vase, Turkey, vert.

1975, July 21

1871 A466 2r bister & multi 20 15
1872 A466 2r bister & multi 20 15
1873 A466 2r bister & multi 20 15
Set value 20

Regional Cooperation for Development Pact among Iran, Pakistan and Turkey.

Majlis Gate A467

1975, Aug. 5 Litho. *Perf. 10½*

1874 A467 10r multi 42 15

Iranian Constitution, 70th anniversary.

Column with Stylized Branches A468

Flags over Globe A469

1975, Aug. 21 Litho. Wmk. 353

1875 A468 8r red & multi 50 15

9th Iranian Arts Festival, Shiraz-Persepolis.

1975, Sept. 8

1876 A469 2r vio bl & multi 20 15

Intl. Literacy Symposium, Persepolis.

Stylized Globe A470

Crown, Column Capital, Persepolis A472

World Map and Envelope — A471

1975, Sept. 13
1877 A470 2r vio & multi 18 15

3rd Tehran International Trade Fair.

1975, Oct. 9 Litho. *Perf. 10½*
1878 A471 14r ultra & multi 60 15

World Post Day, Oct. 9.

1975, Oct. 26 Litho. Wmk. 353
1879 A472 2r ultra & multi 16 15

Festival of Culture and Art. See No. 1954.

Face and Film — A473

1975, Nov. 2
1880 A473 6r multicolored 30 15

Tehran Intl. Festival of Children's Films.

"Mother's Face" — A474

Girl — A475

Design: No. 1882, 2r, "Our House," horiz. All designs after children's drawings.

1975, Nov. 5
1881 A474 2r multicolored 20 15
1882 A475 2r multicolored 20 15
1883 A475 2r multicolored 20 15
Set value 24

Children's Week.

"Film" — A476

1975, Dec. 4 Wmk. 353 *Perf. 10½*
1884 A476 8r multicolored 30 15

4th Tehran International Film Festival.

Symbols of Reforms A477

People A478

1976, Jan. 26 Litho. *Perf. 10½*
1885 A477 2r shown 20 15
1886 A478 2r shown 20 15
1887 A477 2r Five reform symbols 20 15
Set value 24

"White Revolution of King and People."

Motorcycle Policeman — A479

Police Helicopter A480

1976, Feb. 16
1888 A479 2r multicolored 50 15
1889 A480 6r multicolored 85 20

Highway Police Day.

Soccer Cup A481

Candlestick A482

1976, Feb. 24 Litho. Wmk. 353
1890 A481 2r org & multi 22 15

3rd Intl. Youth Soccer Cup, Shiraz and Ahvaz.

1976, Mar. 6

Designs: No. 1892, Incense burner. No. 1893, Rose water container.

1891 A482 1r olive & multi 20 15
1892 A482 1r claret & multi 20 15
1893 A482 1r Prus bl & multi 20 15
a. Strip of 3, #1891-1893 60 30
Set value 20

Novrooz, Iranian New Year.

Telephones, 1876 and 1976 — A483

Eye Within Square — A484

1976, Mar. 10
1894 A483 10r multicolored 42 15

Centenary of first telephone call by Alexander Graham Bell, Mar. 10, 1876.

1976, Apr. 29 Litho. *Perf. 10½*
1895 A484 6r blk & multi 40 15
a. Perf. 12½ 6.00 4.00

World Health Day: "Foresight prevents blindness."

Nurse with Infant A485

Young Man Holding Old Man's Hand — A486

1976, May 10
1896 A485 2r shown 30 15
1897 A485 2r Engineering apprentices 30 15
1898 A486 2r shown 30 15
Set value 30

Royal Org. of Social Services, 30th anniv.

Map of Iran, Men Linking Hands — A487

Waves and Ear Phones — A488

1976, May 13 Wmk. 353
1899 A487 2r yel & multi 30 15

Iranian Cooperatives, 10th anniversary.

1976, May 17
1900 A488 14r gray & multi 55 15

World Telecommunications Day.

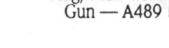

Emblem, Woman with Flag, Man with Gun — A489

1976, June 6
1901 A489 2r bister & multi 30 15

To publicize the power of stability.

Map of Iran, Columns of Persepolis, Nasser Khosrov A490

Riza Shah Pahlavi A491

1976, July 6 Litho. *Perf. 10½*
1902 A490 6r yel & multi 40 16

Tourist publicity.

1976, July 21 Litho. Wmk. 353

Designs: 6r, Mohammed Ali Jinnah. 8r, Kemal Ataturk.

1903 A491 2r gray & multi 30 15
1904 A491 6r gray & multi 60 18
1905 A491 8r gray & multi 60 22

Regional Cooperation for Development Pact among Iran, Turkey and Pakistan, 12th anniversary.

Torch, Montreal and Iranian Olympic Emblems A492

1976, Aug. 1
1906 A492 14r multicolored 75 25

21st Olympic Games, Montreal, Canada, July 17-Aug. 1.

Riza Shah Pahlavi in Coronation Robe — A493

Festival Emblem — A494

Designs: 2r, Shahs Riza and Mohammed Riza Pahlavi, horiz. 14r, 20r, Shah Mohammed Riza Pahlavi in coronation robe and crown.

1976, Aug. 19 Wmk. 353 *Perf. 10½*
1907 A493 2r lilac & multi 65 15
1908 A493 6r blue & multi 1.65 18
1909 A493 14r grn & multi 1.90 30

Souvenir Sheet

1976, Oct. 8 *Imperf.*
1910 A493 20r multi 5.00 2.00

50th anniv. of Pahlavi dynasty; 35th anniv. of reign of Shah Mohammed Riza Pahlavi. No. 1910 contains one stamp 43x62mm.

1976, Aug. 29 Litho. *Perf. 10½*
1911 A494 10r multicolored 50 15

10th Iranian Arts Festival, Shiraz-Persepolis.

Iranian Scout Emblem A495

Cancer Radiation Treatment A496

1976, Oct. 2 Litho. *Perf. 10½*
1912 A495 2r lt bl & multi 25 15

10th Asia Pacific Conference, Tehran 1976.

1976, Oct. 6
1913 A496 2r black & multi 30 15

Fight against cancer.

Target, Police Woman Receiving Decoration A497

1976, Oct. 7
1914 A497 2r lt bl & multi 30 15

Police Day.

UPU Emblem, No. 1907 on Cover A498

1976, Oct. 9
1915 A498 10r multicolored 1.00 16

International Post Day.

Crown Prince Riza with Cup — A499

1976, Oct. 10
1916 A499 6r multicolored 32 15

Natl. Soc. of Village Culture Houses, anniv.

Shahs Riza and Mohammed Riza, Railroad A500

1976, Oct. 15
1917 A500 8r black & multi 2.00 30

Railroad Day.

Emblem & Column Capital, Persepolis A501

Census Emblem A502

1976, Oct. 26
1918 A501 14r blue & multi 50 15

Festival of Culture and Art.

1976, Oct. 30
1919 A502 2r gray & multi 20 15

Natl. Population & Housing Census, 1976.

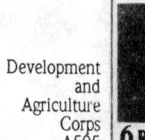

Flowers and Birds — A503

Mohammed Ali Jinnah — A504

Designs: No. 1921, Flowers and bird. No. 1922, Flowers and butterfly. Designs are from covers of children's books.

1976, Oct. 31 *Perf. 10½*
1920 A503 2r multicolored 20 15
1921 A503 2r multicolored 20 15
1922 A503 2r multicolored 20 15
Set value 30

Children's Week.

1976, Dec. 25 Litho. Wmk. 353
1923 A504 10r multicolored 45 15

Jinnah (1876-1948), 1st Governor General of Pakistan.

Development and Agriculture Corps A505

17-Point Reform Law: 5d, Land reform. 10d, Nationalization of forests. 50d, Sale of shares of state-owned industries. 1r, Profit sharing for factory workers. 2r, Woman suffrage. 3r, Education Corps formation. 5r, Health Corps. 8r, Establishment of village courts. 10r, Nationalization of water resources. 12r, Reconstruction program, urban and rural. 14r, Administrative and educational reorganization. 20r, Sale of factory shares. 30r, Commodity pricing. 50r, Free education. 100r, Child care. 200r, Care of the aged (social security).

1977, Jan. 26 Photo. *Perf. 13x13½*
Frame and Shah's Head in Gold

Size: 28x21mm

1924 A505 5d rose & green 15 15
1925 A505 10d lt grn & brn 15 15
1926 A505 50d yel & vio bl 15 15
1927 A505 1r lil & vio bl 15 15
1928 A505 2r org & green 20 15
1929 A505 3r lt bl & red 38 15
1930 A505 5r bl grn & mag 38 15

Size: 37x27mm

1931 A505 6r brn, mar & black 55 15
1932 A505 8r ultra, mar & blk 55 15
1933 A505 10r lt grn, bl & black 1.50 20
1934 A505 12r vio, mar & black 1.10 15
1935 A505 14r org, red & blk 1.65 75
1936 A505 20r gray, ocher & black 3.25 50
1937 A505 30r bl, grn & blk 3.25 65
1938 A505 50r yel, brn & blk 5.50 60
1939 A505 100r multi 4.75 1.25
1940 A505 200r multi 11.00 2.50
Nos. 1924-1940 (17) 34.66
Set value 7.00

"White Revolution of King and People" reform laws.

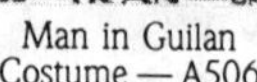

Man in Guilan Costume — A506

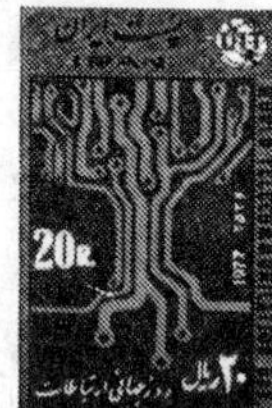

Electronic Tree — A507

Design: 2r, Woman in Guilan costume (Northern Iran).

1977, Mar. 6 Wmk. 353 *Perf. 13*
1941 A506 1r multicolored 15 15
1942 A506 2r multicolored 20 15
Set value 18

Novrooz, Iranian New Year.

1977, May 17 Photo. *Perf. 13*
1943 A507 20r multicolored 65 15

World Telecommunications Day.

Riza Shah Dam A508

1977, May 31 *Perf. 13x13½*
1944 A508 5r multicolored 40 15

Inauguration of Riza Shah Dam.

Olympic Rings — A509

1977, June 23 Litho. *Perf. 10½*
1945 A509 14r multicolored 60 15

Olympic Day.

Terra-cotta Jug, Iran — A510

Designs: No. 1947, Terra-cotta bullock cart, Pakistan. No. 1948, Terra-cotta pot with human face, Turkey.

Perf. 13x13½

1977, July 21 Photo. Wmk. 353
1946 A510 5r violet & multi 28 15
1947 A510 5r emer & multi 28 15
1948 A510 5r green & multi 28 15
Set value 24

Regional Cooperation for Development Pact among Iran, Turkey and Pakistan, 13th anniv.

Flowers with Scout Emblems, Map of Asia — A511

1977, Aug. 5 Litho. *Perf. 13*
1949 A511 10r multicolored 55 16

2nd Asia-Pacific Jamboree, Nishapur.

Map of Eastern Hemisphere with Iran — A512

Tree of Learning, Symbolic Letters — A513

1977, Sept. 20 Photo. Wmk. 353
1950 A512 3r multicolored 20 15

9th Asian Electronics Conference, Tehran.

1977, Oct. 8 Wmk. 353 *Perf. 13*
1951 A513 10r multicolored 32 15

Honoring the teachers.

Globe, Envelope, UPU Emblem A514

1977, Oct. 9 Photo.
1952 A514 14r multicolored 45 15

Iran's admission to the UPU, cent.

Folk Art — A515

1977, Oct. 16
1953 A515 5r multicolored 40 15

Festival of Folk Art.

Festival Type of 1975

Design: 20r, similar to 1975 issue, but with small crown within star.

1977, Oct. 26 *Perf. 10½*
1954 A472 20r bis, grn, car & blk 60 15

Festival of Culture and Art.

Joust — A516

Emblem — A517

Designs: No. 1956, Rapunzel. No. 1957, Little princess with attendants.

1977, Oct. 31 **Photo.**

1955 A516 3r multicolored		20	15
1956 A516 3r multicolored		20	15
1957 A516 3r multicolored		20	15
a. Strip of 3, #1955-1957		60	40
Set value			36

Children's Week.

1977, Nov. 7 **Wmk. 353** ***Perf. 13***

1958 A517 5r multicolored 30 15

First Regional Seminar on the Education and Welfare of the Deaf.

Mohammad Iqbal A518

African Sculpture A519

1977, Nov. 9 **Litho.** ***Perf. 10½***

1959 A518 5r multicolored 45 15

Iqbal (1877-1938), poet and philosopher.

1977, Dec. 14

1960 A519 20r multicolored 3.25 45

African art.

Shah Mosque, Isfahan — A520

Designs: 1r, Ruins, Persepolis. 2r, Khajou Bridge, Isfahan. 5r, Imam Riza Shrine, Meshed. 9r, Warrior frieze, Persepolis. 10r, Djameh Mosque, Isfahan. 20r, King on throne, bas-relief. 25r, Sheik Lotfollah Mosque. 30r, Ruins, Persepolis, diff. view. 50r, Ali Ghapou Palace, Isfahan. 100r, Bas-relief, Tagh Bastan. 200r, Horseman and prisoners, bas-relief, Naqsh Rostam.

1978-79 **Photo.** ***Perf. 13x13½***

"Iran" and Head in Gold

Size: 28x21mm

1961 A520	1r deep brn	30	15
1962 A520	2r emerald	30	15
1963 A520	3r magenta	50	15
1964 A520	5r Prus blue	70	15

Size: 36x27mm

1965 A520	9r sepia ('79)	1.40	55
1966 A520	10r brt bl ('79)	5.50	70
1967 A520	20r rose	1.75	*55*
1968 A520	25r ultra ('79)	25.00	9.75
1969 A520	30r magenta	2.75	55
1970 A520	50r deep yel grn ('79)	4.50	3.50
1971 A520	100r dk bl ('79)	15.00	9.75
1972 A520	200r vio bl ('79)	19.00	19.00
	Nos. 1961-1972 (12)	76.70	44.95

For overprints see Nos. 2009, 2011-2018.

Persian Rug — A521

Designs: Persian rugs.

1978, Feb. 11 **Litho.** ***Perf. 10½***

1973 A521 3r sil & multi	22	15
1974 A521 5r sil & multi	45	15
1975 A521 10r sil & multi	65	30

Opening of Carpet Museum.

Mazanderan Man — A522

Mohammed Riza Pahlavi — A523

Design: 5r, Mazanderan woman.

1978, Mar. 6 ***Perf. 13***

1976 A522 3r yel & multi	22	15
1977 A522 5r lt bl & multi	42	15
Set value		24

Novrooz, Iranian New Year.

1978, Jan. 26

1978 A523 20r multicolored 3.75 1.00

Shah's White Revolution, 15th anniv.

Riza Shah Pahlavi and Crown Prince Inspecting Girls' School A524

Designs (Riza Shah Pahlavi and Crown Prince Mohammed Riza Pahlavi): 5r, Inauguration of Trans-Iranian railroad. 10r, At stairs of Palace, Persepolis. 14r, Shah handing Crown Prince (later Shah) officer's diploma at Tehran Officers' Academy.

1978, Mar. 15

1979 A524 3r multicolored	35	15
1980 A524 5r multicolored	65	20
1981 A524 10r multicolored	1.10	25
1982 A524 14r multicolored	1.50	40

Riza Shah Pahlavi (1877-1944), founder of Pahlavi dynasty.

Communications Satellite over Map of Iran — A525

1978, Apr. 19 **Litho.** ***Perf. 10½***

1983 A525 20r multicolored 1.00 16

ITU, 7th meeting, Tehran; 10th anniv. of Iran's membership.

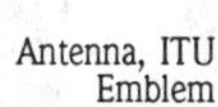

Antenna, ITU Emblem A526

1978, May 17 **Litho.** ***Perf. 10½***

1984 A526 15r multicolored 65 20

10th World Telecommunications Day.

Welfare Legion Emblem — A527

1978, June 13 **Photo.** ***Perf. 13x13½***

1985 A527 10r multicolored 60 15

Universal Welfare Legion, 10th anniversary.

Pink Roses, Iran — A528

Designs: 10r, Yellow rose, Turkey. 15r, Red roses, Pakistan.

Perf. 13½x13

1978, July 21 **Wmk. 353**

1986 A528 5r multicolored	40	15
1987 A528 10r multicolored	65	15
1988 A528 15r multicolored	80	24

Regional Cooperation for Development Pact among Iran, Turkey and Pakistan, 14th anniversary.

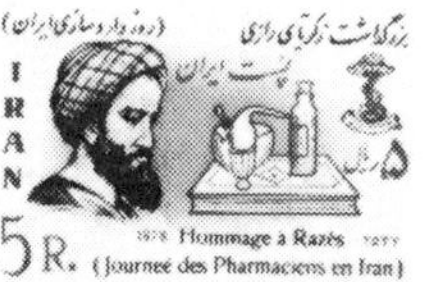
Rhazes, Pharmaceutical Tools — A529

1978, Aug. 26 **Wmk. 353** ***Perf. 13***

1989 A529 5r multicolored 40 15

Pharmacists' Day. Rhazes (850-923), chief physician of Great Hospital in Baghdad.

Girl Scouts, Aryamehr Arch — A530

1978, Sept. 2 ***Perf. 10½***

1990 A530 5r multicolored 35 15

23rd World Girl Scouts Conference, Tehran, Sept. 1978.

Shah Riza Pahlavi A531

Design: 5r, Mohammed Riza Shah Pahlavi.

1978, Sept. 11 **Litho.** ***Perf. 10½***

1991 A531 3r multicolored	1.25	25
1992 A531 5r multicolored	1.50	35

Bank Melli Iran, 50th anniversary.

Girl and Bird — A532

1978, Oct. 31 **Photo.** ***Perf. 13***

1993 A532 3r multicolored 35 20

Children's Week.

Envelope, Map of Iran, UPU Emblem A533

1978, Nov. 22 ***Perf. 13x13½***

1994 A533 14r gold & multi 1.25 18

World Post Day, Oct. 22.

Communications Symbols and Classroom — A534

1978, Nov. 22 ***Perf. 10½***

1995 A534 10r multicolored 1.00 18

Faculty of Communications, 50th anniv.

Human Rights Flame A535

1978, Dec. 17 **Photo.** ***Perf. 13***

1996 A535 20r bl, blk & gold 3.50 26

Universal Declaration of Human Rights, 30th anniv.

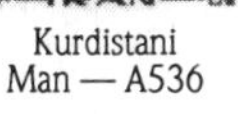
Kurdistani Man — A536

Rose — A537

Design: 5r, Kurdistani woman.

1979, Mar. 17

1997 A536 3r multicolored	90	15
1998 A536 5r multicolored	1.25	15

1979, Mar. 17

1999 A537 2r multicolored 15 15

Novrooz, Iranian New Year.

See No. 2310i.

Islamic Republic

Demonstrators — A538

Islamic revolution: 3r, Demonstrators. 5r, Hands holding rose, gun and torch breaking through newspaper. 20r, Hands breaking prison bars, and dove, vert.

1979, Apr. 20 *Perf. 10½*

2000	A538	3r multicolored	1.50	15
2001	A538	5r multicolored	1.10	15
2002	A538	10r multicolored	1.10	30
2003	A538	20r multicolored	2.50	30

Nos. 1837-1838, 1966, 1970 and Type A520 Overprinted

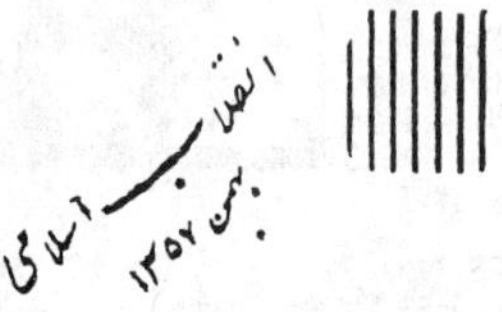

Designs: 15r, Warriors on horseback, bas-relief, Naqsh-Rostam. 19r, Chehel Sotoon Palace, Isfahan.

1979 **Wmk. 353** *Perf. 13x13½*

2008	A443	8r org & brown	*3.00*	1.00
2009	A520	9r gold & dp brn	1.50	1.50
2010	A443	10r gold & dp yel grn	*50.00*	5.00
2011	A520	10r gold & brt bl	1.00	1.00
2012	A520	15r red lilac	1.00	1.00
2013	A520	19r slate green	1.00	1.00
2016	A520	50r gold & dp yel grn	2.00	2.00
2017	A520	100r gold & vio bl	10.00	4.00
2018	A520	200r gold & vio bl	12.50	8.50
		Nos. 2008-2018 (9)	*82.00*	*25.00*

Overprint means Islamic revolution.
Forgeries of No. 2010 exist.

Symbolic Tulip — A539

1979, June 5 **Photo.** *Perf. 13*

2019	A539	5r multicolored	1.50	28

Potters, by Kamalel Molk A540

Paintings: No. 2021, at the Well, by Allah Baksh, Pakistan. No. 2022, Plowing, by Namik Ismail, Turkey.

1979, July 21 **Litho.** *Perf. 10½*

2020	A540	5r multicolored	3.25	15
2021	A540	5r multicolored	2.50	15
2022	A540	5r multicolored	2.50	15

Regional Cooperation for Development Pact among Iran, Turkey and Pakistan, 15th anniv.

"TELECOM 79" — A541

1979, Sept. 20 *Perf. 10½*

2023	A541	20r multicolored	*5.00*	25

3rd World Telecommunications Exhibition, Geneva, Sept. 20-26.

Greeting the Sunrise — A542

Persian Rug Design — A543

Children's Drawings and IYC Emblem: 2r, Tulip over wounded man. 2r, Children with banners.

1979, Sept. 23

2024	A542	2r multicolored	85	20
2025	A542	3r multicolored	85	20
2026	A542	5r multicolored	1.65	20

International Year of the Child.

1979 **Photo.** *Perf. 13½x13*

2027	A543	50d brn & pale sal	15	15
2028	A543	1r dark & lt bl	15	15
2029	A543	2r red & yellow	15	15
2030	A543	3r dk bl & lt lil	15	15
2031	A543	5r sl grn & lt grn	15	15
2032	A543	10r blk & salmon pink ('80)	28	15
2033	A543	20r brn & gray ('80)	55	15
		Size: 27x37½mm		
2034	A543	50r dp violet & gray ('80)	1.40	16
2035	A543	100r blk & slate grn ('80)	5.00	1.40
2036	A543	200r dk bl & cr ('80)	5.50	2.75
		Nos. 2027-2036 (10)	13.48	
		Set value		4.65

Globe in Envelope — A544

1979, Oct. 9 **Litho.** *Perf. 10½*

2041	A544	10r multicolored	*2.00*	25

World Post Day.

Ghyath-al-din Kashani, Astrolabe A545

1979, Dec. 5 **Litho.** *Perf. 10½*

2042	A545	5r ocher & blk	*1.50*	25

Kashani, mathematician, 550th death anniv.

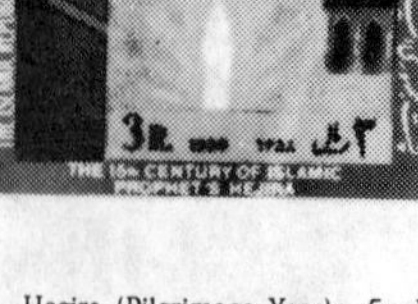

Ka'aba, Flame and Mosque A546

Hegira (Pilgrimage Year): 5r, Koran open over globe, vert. 10r, Salman Farsi (follower of Mohammed), map of Iran.

1980, Jan. 19

2043	A546	3r multicolored	20	15
2044	A546	5r multicolored	25	18
2045	A546	10r multicolored	50	22

Reissued in May-June, 1980, with shiny gum and watermark position changed.

People, Map and Flag of Iran — A547

Dehkhoda, Dictionary Editor, Birth Cent. — A548

Islamic Revolution, 1st Anniversary: 3r, Blood dripping on broken sword. 5r, Window open on sun of Islam, people.

1980, Feb. 11

2046	A547	1r multicolored	18	15
2047	A547	3r multicolored	35	22
2048	A547	5r multicolored	65	30

For similar stamps measuring 24x36mm see Nos. 2310a, 2310b, 2310d.

1980, Feb. 26

2049	A548	10r multicolored	30	15

East Azerbaijani Woman — A549

Mohammed Mossadegh — A550

Novrooz (Iranian New Year): 5r, East Azerbaijani man.

1980, Mar. 5

2050	A549	3r multicolored	15	15
2051	A549	5r multicolored	22	15
		Set value		20

1980, Mar. 19 **Photo.** *Perf. 13x13½*

2052	A550	20r multi	60	16

Oil industry nationalization, 29th anniv.; Mohammed Mossadegh, prime minister who initiated nationalization, birth cent.

Professor Morteza Motahhari, 1st Death Anniversary — A551

1980, May 1 **Litho.** *Perf. 10½*

2053	A551	10r black & red	50	16

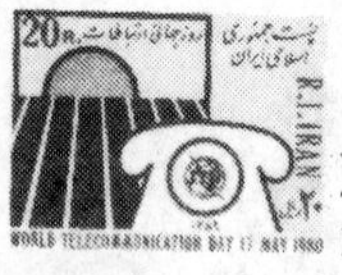

World Telecommunications Day — A552

1980, May 17 **Photo.** *Perf. 13x13½*

2054	A552	20r multicolored	48	15

Interior of Mosque A553

1980, June 11 **Litho.** *Perf. 10½*

2055	A553	50d shown	15	15
2056	A553	1r Demonstration	15	15
2057	A553	3r Avicenna, al-Biruni, Farabi	40	18
2058	A553	5r Hegira emblem	30	15
		Set value		45

Hegira, 1500th anniv.

Ali Sharyati, Educator — A554

1980, June 15 **Photo.** *Perf. 13x13½*

2059	A554	5r multicolored	30	15

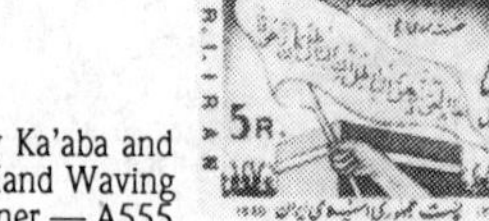

Holy Ka'aba and Hand Waving Banner — A555

1980, June 28

2060	A555	5r multicolored	30	15

Hazrat Mehdi, 12th Imam's birth anniv.

A556

OPEC Emblem — A557

1980, Sept. 10 *Perf. 13½x13*

2061	A556	5r multicolored	30	15

Ayatollah Seyed Mahmood Talegani, death anniv. Compare with design A829.

1980, Sept. 15

2062 A557	5r shown	30	15
2063 A557	10r Men holding OPEC emblem	60	15
	Set value		20

20th anniversary of OPEC.

"Let Us Liberate Jerusalem" A558

Tulip and Fayziyye Mosque, Qum A559

1980, Oct. 9 ***Perf. 13x13½***

2064 A558	5r multicolored	18	15
2065 A558	20r multicolored	75	15
	Set value		20

1981, Feb. 11 ***Perf. 13***

2066 A559	3r shown	15	15
2067 A559	5r Blood spilling on tulip	15	15
2068 A559	20r Tulip, Republic emblem	48	15
	Set value		25

Islamic Revolution, 2nd anniversary.

See Nos. 2310c, 2310e, 2310j, watermark 381 (3r, unserifed "R" in denomination. 5r, bright yellow background; 20r, light blue background behind flower.)

Lorestani Man — A560

Telecommunications Day — A561

Novrooz (Iranian New Year): 10r, Lorestani woman.

1981, Mar. 11

2069 A560	5r multicolored	15	15
2070 A560	10r multicolored	30	15
	Set value		20

Perf. 13½x13

1981, May 17 Photo. Wmk. 353

2071 A561	5r dk grn & org	15	15

Ayatollah Kashani Birth Centenary A562

Adult Education A563

Perf. 13x13½

1981, July 21 Wmk. 381

2072 A562	15r dk grn & dl pur	40	15

Perf. 13x13½, 13½x13 (5r, 10r, 200r)

1981, Aug.

Designs: 50d, Citizens bearing arms. 2r, Irrigation. 3r, Friday prayer service. 5r, Paasdaar emblem and members. 10r, Koran text. 20r, Hejaab (women's veil). 50r, Industrial development. 100r, Religious ceremony, Mecca. 200r, Mosque interior. 5r, 10r, 200r vert.

2073 A563	50d blk & dp bis	15	15
2074 A563	1r dl pur & grn	15	15
2075 A563	2r brn & grnsh bl	15	15

Size: 38x28mm, 28x38mm

2076 A563	3r brt yel grn & black	15	15
2077 A563	5r dk bl & brn org	15	15
2078 A563	10r dk bl & grnsh blue	22	15
2079 A563	20r red & black	45	15
2080 A563	50r lilac & blk	1.10	30
2081 A563	100r org brn & blk	2.25	60
2082 A563	200r blk & bl grn	4.50	1.25
	Nos. 2073-2082 (10)	9.27	
	Set value		2.50

Islamic Iranian Army A564

1981, Sept. 21 Photo. *Perf. 13*

2087 A564	5r multicolored	15	15

World Post Day and 12th UPU Day — A565

Perf. 13x13½

1981, Oct. 9 Wmk. 381

2088 A565	20r black & blue	48	24

Millennium of Nahjul Balaghah (Sacred Book) A566

1981, Oct. 17 *Perf. 13*

2089 A566	25r multicolored	60	16

Martyrs' Memorial — A567

1981, Nov. 9 Photo. *Perf. 13*

2090 A567	3r June 28, 1981 victims	15	15
2091 A567	5r Pres. Rajai, Prime Minister Bahonar	15	15
2092 A567	10r Gen. Chamran	25	15
	Set value		30

Ayatollah M. H. Tabatabaee, Scholar — A568

1981, Dec. 25 Photo. *Perf. 13*

2093 A568	5r multicolored	20	15

Literacy Campaign — A569

Islamic Revolution, 3rd Anniv. — A570

1982, Jan. 20 Photo. *Perf. 13x13½*

2094 A569	5r blue & gold	20	15

1982, Feb. 11 Wmk. 381 *Perf. 13*

2095 A570	5r Map	15	15
2096 A570	10r Tulip	25	15
2097 A570	20r Globe	50	20
a.	Strip of 3, #2095-2097	90	40
	Set value		35

See Nos. 2310f, 2310g, 2310k (5r, orange background, Arabian "5" 6mm above black panel. 10r, dark green background, gray dove with thick black lines around it. 20r, pink background, bright blue globe, faint latitude and longitude lines.)

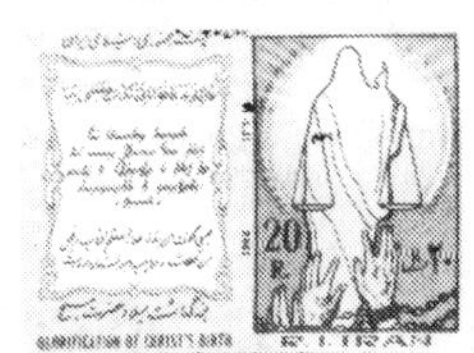

Unity Week — A571

Khuzestan Man — A573

Glorification of Jesus Christ — A572

1982, Feb. 20 Photo. *Perf. 13*

2098 A571	25r multicolored	1.00	20

1982, Mar. 11 Photo. Wmk. 381

2099 A572	20r multicolored	50	20

1982, Mar. 13

2100 A573	3r shown	15	15
2101 A573	5r Khuzestan woman	15	15
a.	Pair, #2100-2101	20	16
	Set value	20	15

Novrooz (New Year).

3rd Anniv. of Islamic Revolution A574

1982, Apr. 1

2102 A574	30r multicolored	90	25

Seyed Mohammad Bagher Sadr — A575

1982, Apr. 8 Photo. *Perf. 13½x13*

2103 A575	50r multicolored	1.00	40

Martyrs of Altar (Ayatollahs Madani and Dastgeyb) — A576

1982, Apr. 21 *Perf. 13*

2104 A576	50r multicolored	1.00	40

Intl. Workers' Solidarity Day — A577

Mab'as Day (Mohammad's Appointment as Prophet) — A579

14th World Telecommunications Day — A578

1982, May 1 Photo. *Perf. 13½x13*

2105 A577	100r multi	2.25	80

1982, May 17 *Perf. 13x13½*

2106 A578	100r multi	2.25	80

1982, May 21 *Perf. 13½x13*

2107 A579	32r multicolored	90	30

1963 Islamic Rising, 19th Anniv. — A580

Lt. Islambuli, Assassin of Anwar Sadat — A581

1982, June 5 Wmk. 381 *Perf. 13*

2108 A580	28r multicolored	60	28

1982, June 17

2109 A581	2r multicolored	20	15

First Death Anniv. of Ayatollah Beheshti — A582

1982, June 28
2110 A582 10r multicolored 40 15
a. Missing dot in Arabic numeral 1.00 1.00

Iran-Iraq War A583

1982, July 7 *Perf. $13x13^1/_2$*
2111 A583 5r multicolored 20 15

Universal Jerusalem Day A584

1982, July 15 *Perf. 13*
2112 A584 1r Dome of the Rock 15 15

Pilgrimage to Mecca — A585

13th World UPU Day — A586

1982, Sept. 28
2113 A585 10r multicolored 30 15

1982, Oct. 9 *Perf. $13^1/_2x13$*
2114 A586 30r multicolored 75 25

4th Anniv. of Islamic Revolution A587

4th Anniv. of Islamic Republic A588

1983, Feb. 11 **Photo.** *Perf. 13*
2115 A587 30r multicolored 75 25

See No. 2310n for stamp with orange or orange red crowd and thick sharp lettering in black panels.

1983, Apr. 1 **Photo.** *Perf. 13*
2116 A588 10r multicolored 30 15

Teachers' Day — A589

World Communications Year — A590

Perf. $13^1/_2x13$

1983, May 1 **Wmk. 381**
2117 A589 5r multicolored 25 15

1983, May 17
2118 A590 20r multicolored 60 15

First Session of Islamic Consultative Assembly A591

1983, May 28 *Perf. 13*
2119 A591 5r multicolored 20 15

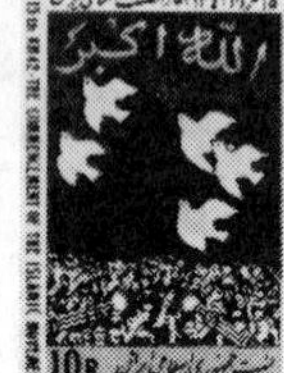

20th Anniv. of Islamic Movement — A592

1983, June 5 **Photo.** *Perf. 13*
2120 A592 10r multicolored 30 15

MiG Bombing Now Rooz Oil Well — A593

1983, June 11 *Perf. $13x13^1/_2$*
2121 A593 5r multicolored 50 15

Ayatollah Mohammad Sadooghi A594

1983, July 2 **Photo.** *Perf. $13^1/_2$*
2122 A594 20r blk & dl red 60 15

Universal Day of Jerusalem A595

Iran-Iraq War, 3rd Anniv. A597

Government Week — A596

1983, July 8
2123 A595 5r Dome of the Rock 20 15

1983, Aug. 30 **Wmk. 381** *Perf. 13*
2124 A596 3r multicolored 15 15

Death of Pres. Rajai and Prime Minister Bahonar, 2nd anniv.

1983, Sept. 28 **Photo.** *Perf. 13*
2125 A597 5r rose red & blk 20 15

Ayatollah Ashrafi Esphahani, Martyr of Altar — A598

Mirza Kuchik Khan — A599

1983, Oct. 15 **Photo.** *Perf. 13*
2126 A598 5r multicolored 15 15

1983-84 **Photo.** *Perf. 13*

Religious and Political Figures: 1r, Sheikh Mohammad Khiabani. 3r, Seyd Majtaba Navab Safavi. 5r, Seyd Jamal-ed-Din Assadabadi. 10r, Seyd Hassan Modaress. 20r, Sheikh Fazel Assad Nouri. 30r, Mirza Mohammed Hossein Naiyni. 50r, Sheikh Mohammad Hossein Kashef. 100r, Seyd Hassan Shirazi. 200r, Mirza Reza Kermani.

2128 A599	1r	black & pink	15	15
2129 A599	2r	org & black	15	15
2130 A599	3r	brt bl & blk	15	15
2131 A599	5r	rose red & blk	15	15
2132 A599	10r	yel grn & blk	30	15
2133 A599	20r	lilac & blk	60	15
2134 A599	30r	gldn brn & blk	90	24
2135 A599	50r	blk & lt bl	1.50	50
2136 A599	100r	blk & org	3.00	1.00
2137 A599	200r	blk & bluish grn	6.00	2.00
		Nos. 2128-2137 (10)	12.90	4.64

Issue dates: 1r, 50r-200r, Feb. 1984. Others, Oct. 23, 1983.

UPU Day — A600

1983, Oct. 9 **Photo.** **Wmk. 381**
2138 A600 10r multi 22 15

Takeover of the US Embassy, 4th Anniv. — A601

1983, Nov. 4 **Photo.** *Perf. 13*
2139 A601 28r multicolored 50 50

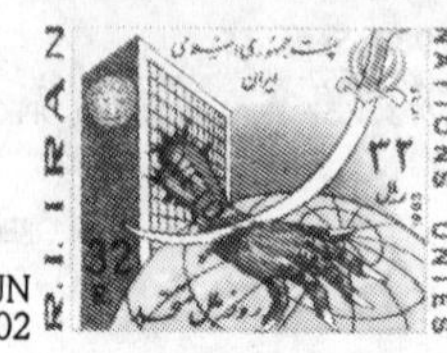

UN Day — A602

1983, Oct. 24 *Perf. $13^1/_2$*
2140 A602 32r multicolored 90 25

Protest of veto by US, Russia, People's Rep. of China, France and Great Britain.

Intl. Medical Seminar, Tehran — A603

1983, Nov. 20
2141 A603 3r Avicenna 20 15

People's Forces Preparation Day — A604

1983, Nov. 26 *Perf. 13*
2142 A604 20r multicolored 60 15

Conference on Crimes of Iraqi Pres. Saddam Hussein A605

1983, Nov. 28 *Perf. $13^1/_2x13$*
2143 A605 5r multicolored 20 15

Mohammad Mofatteh A606

1983, Dec. 18 **Photo.** *Perf. 13*
2144 A606 10r multicolored 30 15

A 5r stamp for the birth anniv. of the prophet Mohammed was withdrawn from sale by the Iranian Post Office because of a spelling error.

5th Anniv. of Islamic Revolution — A608

1984, Feb. 11 **Photo.** *Perf. $13x13^1/_2$*
2146 A608 10r multicolored 75 20

See No. 2310h for stamp with splotchy colors in blue background and denomination, flag colors and darker, thicker black lines around tulips. Background and denominations on No. 2146 have a screened appearance.

Nurses' Day — A609

1984, Feb. 24 *Perf. 13*
2147 A609 20r Attending wounded soldiers 45 20

Invalids' Day A610

Local Flowers A611

1984, Feb. 29
2148 A610 5r Man in wheelchair 15 15

1984, Mar. 10 *Perf. 13½x13*
2149 A611 3r Lotus gebelia 15 15
2150 A611 5r Tulipa chrysantha 15 15
2151 A611 10r Glycyrhiza glabra 22 15
2152 A611 20r Matthiola alyssifolia 45 20
a. Block of 4, #2149-2152 1.00 75
Set value 48

Novrooz (New Year).

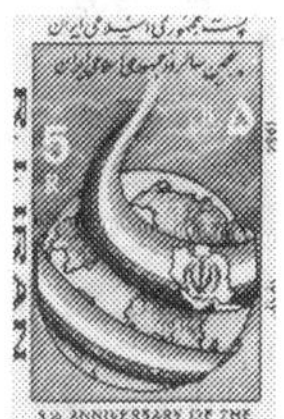

Islamic Republic, 5th Anniv. — A612

Sheik Ragheb Harb, Lebanese Religious Leader — A614

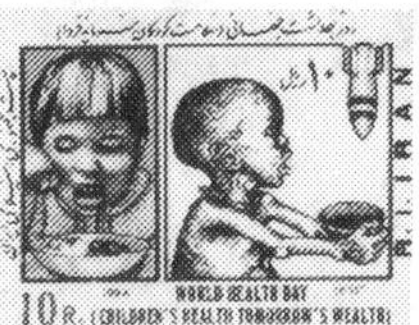

World Health Day — A613

1984, Apr. 1 **Photo.** *Perf. 13*
2153 A612 5r Flag, globe, map 15 15

1984, Apr. 7
2154 A613 10r Children 30 15

1984, Apr. 18
2155 A614 5r multicolored 15 15

World Red Cross Day — A615

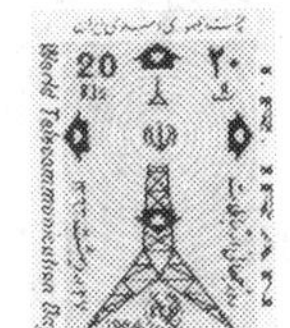

16th World Telecommunications Day — A616

1984, May 8 **Photo.** *Perf. 13½x13*
2156 A615 5r multicolored 15 15

1984, May 17
2157 A616 20r multicolored 45 20

Martyrdom of Seyyed Ghotb — A617

1984, May 28 *Perf. 13*
2158 A617 10r multicolored 30 15

Struggle Against Discrimination — A618

1984, Mar. 21 **Photo.** *Perf. 13*
2159 A618 5r Malcolm X 15 15

Conquest of Mecca Anniv. A619

1984, June 20
2160 A619 5r Holy Ka'aba, idol destruction 15 15

Universal Day of Jerusalem A620

Id Al-fitr Feast A621

1984, June 29
2161 A620 5r Map, Koran 15 15
2162 A621 10r Moon, praying crowd, mosque 25 15
a. Pair, #2161-2162 40 20
Set value 15

Tchogha Zanbil Excavation, Susa — A622

Cultural Heritage Preservation: b, Emamzadeh Hossein Shrine, Kazvin. c, Emam Mosque, Isfahan. d, Ark Fortress, Tabriz. e, Mausoleum of Daniel Nabi, Susa.

1984, Aug. 20 *Perf. 13½*
2163 Strip of 5 75 25
a.-e. A622 5r, any single 15 15

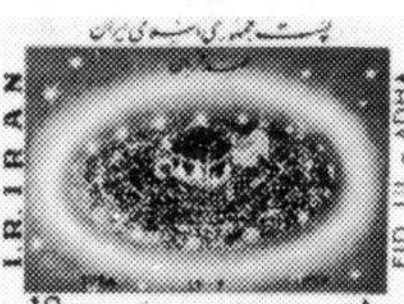

"Eid Ul-Adha" A623

Perf. 13x13½
1984, Sept. 6 **Photo.** **Wmk. 381**
2164 A623 10r Holy Ka'aba 30 15

Feast of Sacrifices (end of pilgrimage to Mecca).

10th Tehran Intl. Trade Fair — A624

Iraq-Iran War, 4th Anniv. — A625

1984, Sept. 11
2165 A624 10r multicolored 30 15

1984, Sept. 22 **Photo.** *Perf. 13x13½*
2166 A625 5r Flower, bullets 15 15

UPU Day — A626

1984, Oct. 9 *Perf. 13½*
2167 A626 20r Dove, UPU emblems 50 20

Haj Seyyed Mostafa Khomeini Memorial A627

1984, Oct. 23
2168 A627 5r multicolored 15 15

Ghazi Tabatabaie Memorial — A628

Mohammed's Birthday, Unity Week — A630

Intl. Saadi Congress A629

1984, Nov. 1 *Perf. 13x13½*
2169 A628 5r Portrait 15 15

1984, Nov. 25 *Perf. 13½*
2170 A629 10r Portrait, mausoleum, emblem 50 15

Saadi (c. 1213-1292), Persian poet.

1984, Dec. 6 **Photo.** *Perf. 13x13½*
2171 A630 5r Koran, mosque 25 15

Islamic Revolution, 6th Anniv. — A631

Arbor Day — A632

1985, Feb. 11 *Perf. 13x13½*
2172 A631 40r multicolored 90 40

See No. 2310o for stamp with bright pink denomination and dove tail.

1985, Mar. 6 *Perf. 13*
2173 A632 3r Sapling, deciduous trees 15 15
2174 A632 5r Maturing trees 15 15
a. Pair, #2173-2174 30 20
Set value 15

Local Flowers — A633

1985, Mar. 9 *Perf. 13½x13*
2175 A633 5r Fritillaria imperialis 15 15
2176 A633 5r Ranunculus ficarioides 15 15
2177 A633 5r Crocus sativus 15 15
2178 A633 5r Primula heterochroma stapf 15 15
a. Block of 4, #2175-2178 50 30
Set value 48 20

Novrooz (New Year).

Women's Day — A634

Republic of Iran, 6th Anniv. — A635

1985, Mar. 13 *Perf. 13x13½*
2179 A634 10r Procession of women 30 15

Birth anniv. of Mohammed's daughter, Fatima.

1985, Apr. 1
2180 A635 20r Tulip, ballot box 45 20

Mab'as Festival A636

1985, Apr. 18
2181 A636 10r Holy Koran 30 15

Religious festival celebrating the recognition of Mohammed as the true prophet.

Day of the Oppressed A637

World Telecommunications Day A638

1985, May 6
2182 A637 5r Koran, flag, globe 15 15

Birthday of the 12th Imam.

1985, May 17 ***Perf. 13½x13***
2183 A638 20r ITU emblem 45 20

Liberation of Khorramshahr, 1st Anniv. — A639

1985, May 24
2184 A639 5r Soldier, bridge 15 15

Fist, Theological Seminary, Qum — A640

Day of Jerusalem — A642

World Handicrafts Day — A641

1985, June 5 ***Perf. 13x13½***
2185 A640 10r multicolored 50 15

1963 Uprising, 22nd Anniv.

1985, June 10 ***Perf. 13½***
2186 A641 20r Plates, flasks 45 20

1985, June 14
2187 A642 5r multicolored 15 15

> ***Set Values***
> *A 15-cent minimum now applies to individual stamps and sets. Where the 15-cent minimum per stamp would increase the value of a set beyond retail, there is a "Set Value" notation giving the retail value of the set.*

Id Al-fitr Feast — A643

Founding of the Islamic Propagation Org. — A644

1985, June 20 ***Perf. 13x13½***
2188 A643 5r multicolored 15 15

1985, June 22
2189 A644 5r tan & emerald 15 15

Ayatollah Sheikh Abdolhossein Amini — A645

1985, July 3 **Photo.** ***Perf. 13***
2190 A645 5r multicolored 25 15

Pilgrimage to Mecca — A646

Goharshad Mosque Uprising, 50th Anniv. — A648

Cultural Heritage Preservation A647

1985, July 20 **Photo.** ***Perf. 13½***
2191 A646 10r multicolored 30 15

1985, Aug. 20

Ceramic plates from Nishabur: a, Swords. b, Farsi script. c, Peacock. d, Four leaves.

2192 Block of 4 60 20
a.-d. A647 5r, any single 15 15

1985, Aug. 21 ***Perf. 13x13½***
2193 A648 10r multicolored 20 15

Week of Government A649

Bleeding Tulips A650

Designs: a, Industry and communications. b, Industry and agriculture. c, Health care, red crescent. d, Education.

1985, Aug. 30 **Photo.** ***Perf. 13x13½***
2194 Block of 4 60 20
a.-d. A649 5r, any single 15 15

1985, Sept. 8
2195 A650 10r multicolored 30 15

17th Shahrivar, Bloody Friday memorial.

OPEC, 25th Anniv. — A651

Design: No. 2196b, OPEC emblem and 25.

1985, Sept. 14 ***Perf. 13½***
2196 Pair 50 15
a.-b. A651 5r, any single 25 15

A652

A653

Designs: a, Dead militiaman. b, Mosque and Ashura in Persian. c, Rockets descending on doves. d, Palm grove, rifle shot exploding rocket.

1985, Sept. 22
2197 Block of 4 60 20
a.-d. A652 5r, any single 15 15

Ashura mourning. Iran-Iraq War, 5th anniv.

1985, Sept. 26 **Photo.** ***Perf. 13x13½***
2198 A653 20r brt bl, lt bl & gold 60 20

Ash-Sharif Ar-Radi, writer, death millennium.

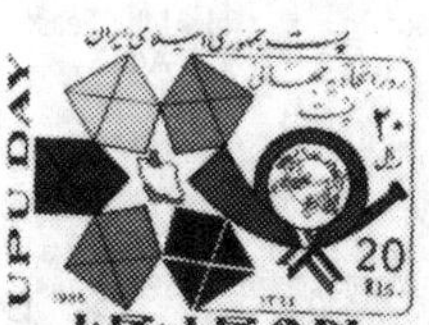
UPU Day — A654

1985, Oct. 9 ***Perf. 13½***
2199 A654 20r multicolored 60 20

World Standards Day — A655

1985, Oct. 14
2200 A655 20r Natl. Standards Office emblem 60 20

Agricultural Training and Development Year — A656

Takeover of US Embassy, 6th Anniv. — A657

1985, Oct. 19 ***Perf. 13x13½***
2201 A656 5r Hand, wheat 15 15

1985, Nov. 4 ***Perf. 13***
2202 A657 40r multicolored 60 40

Moslem Unity Week A658

High Council of the Cultural Revolution A659

1985, Nov. 25 ***Perf. 13x13½***
2203 A658 10r Holy Ka'aba 30 15

Birth of prophet Mohammed, 1015th anniv.

1985, Dec. 10
2204 A659 5r Roses 15 15

Intl. Youth Year — A660

Ezzeddin al-Qassam, 50th Death Anniv. — A661

Designs: a, Education. b, Defense. c, Construction. d, Sports.

1985, Dec. 18 **Photo.** ***Perf. 13x13½***
2205 Block of 4 60 20
a.-d. A660 5r, any single 15 15

1985, Dec. 20 ***Perf. 13½***
2206 A661 20r sil, sep & hn brn 60 20

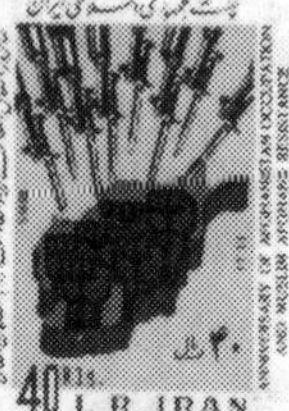
Map, Fists, Bayonets — A662

1985, Dec. 25 **Wmk. 381**
2207 A662 40r multi 1.20 40

Occupation of Afghanistan and Moslem resistance, 6th anniv.

Mirza Taqi Khan Amir Kabir (d. 1851) — A663

1986, Jan. 8 **Litho.** ***Perf. 13***
2208 A663 5r multicolored 80 20

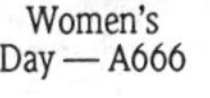

Students Destroying Statue of the Shah, Tulips — A664

Women's Day — A666

Sulayman Khater, 40th Death Anniv. A665

1986, Feb. 11 **Photo.** ***Perf. 13½***
2209 A664 20r multicolored 60 20

Iranian Revolution, 7th anniv.
See No. 2310l for 24x36mm stamp with yellow Arabic script.

1986, Feb. 15 ***Perf. 13***
2210 A665 10r multicolored 30 15

1986, Mar. 3 ***Perf. 13½***
2211 A666 10r multicolored 30 15

Birth anniv. of Mohammed's daughter, Fatima.

Flowers — A667

Designs: a, Papaver orientale. b, Anemone coronaria. c, Papaver bracteatum. d, Anemone biflora.

1986, Mar. 11 **Photo.** ***Perf. 13½***
2212 Block of 4 60 20
a. A667 5r any single 15 15

Novrooz (New Year).

2000th Day of Sacred Defense A668

Intl. Day Against Racial Discrimination A669

1986, Mar. 14 **Photo.** ***Perf. 13x13½***
2213 A668 5r scarlet & grn 15 15

1986, Mar. 21
2214 A669 5r multicolored 15 15

Islamic Republic of Iran, 7th Anniv. A670

1986, Apr. 1 ***Perf. 13***
2215 A670 10r Flag, map 30 15

Mab'as Festival — A671

1986, Apr. 7
2216 A671 40r multicolored 60 20

Army Day A672

Day of the Oppressed A673

1986, Apr. 18 ***Perf. 13½***
2217 A672 5r multicolored 15 15

1986, Apr. 25 ***Perf. 13x13½***
2218 A673 10r blk, gold & dk red 20 15

Helicopter Crash — A674

Teacher's Day — A675

1986, Apr. 25 **Wmk. 381**
2219 A674 40r multicolored 1.40 40

US air landing at Tabass Air Base, 6th anniv.

1986, May 2 **Photo.** ***Perf. 13x13½***
2220 A675 5r multicolored 15 15

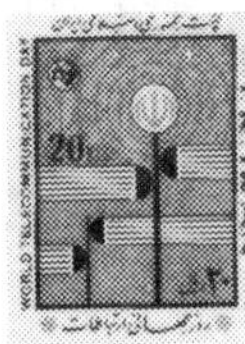

World Telecommunications Day — A676

1986, May 17 ***Perf. 13½x13***
2221 A676 20r blk, sil & ultra 60 20

Universal Day of the Child A677

1986, June 1 ***Perf. 13***
2222 A677 15r Child's war drawing 45 15
2223 A677 15r Hosein Fahmide, Iran-Iraq war hero 45 15
a. Pair, #2222-2223 90 30

1963 Uprising, 23rd Anniv. — A678

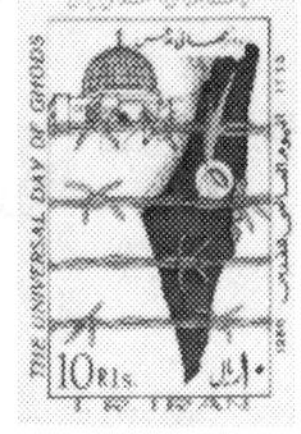

Day of Jerusalem — A679

1986, June 5 ***Perf. 13x13½***
2224 A678 10r Qum Theological Seminary 30 15

1986, June 6
2225 A679 10r multicolored 30 15

Id Al-Fitr Feast A680

1986, June 9 ***Perf. 13***
2226 A680 10r Moslems praying 30 15

World Handicrafts Day — A681

Designs: a, Baluchi cross-hatched rug. b, Craftsman. c, Qalamkar flower rug. d, Copper repousse vase.

1986, June 10 ***Perf. 13½***
2227 Block of 4 1.20 40
a.-d. A681 10r, any single 30 15

Intl. Day for Solidarity with Black So. Africans — A682

Ayatollah Beheshti — A683

1986, June 26
2228 A682 10r multicolored 30 15

1986, June 28 ***Perf. 13x13½***
2229 A683 10r multicolored 30 15

Death of Beheshti and Islamic Party workers, Tehran headquarters bombing, 5th anniv.

Ayatollah Mohammad Taqi Shirazi, Map of Iraq — A684

Shrine of Imam Reza — A685

1986, June 30 **Photo.** **Wmk. 381**
2230 A684 20r multicolored 60 20

Iraqi Moslem uprising against the British.

1986, July 19 ***Perf. 13½***
2231 A685 10r multicolored 30 15

Eid Ul-Adha, Feast of Sacrifice — A686

Eid Ul-Ghadir Feast — A688

Cultural Heritage Preservation A687

1986, Aug. 17 ***Perf. 13x13½***
2232 A686 10r multicolored 30 15

1986, Aug. 20

Designs: No. 2233, Bam Fortress. No. 2234, Kabud (Blue) Mosque, Tabriz. No. 2235, Mausoleum of Sohel Ben Ali at Astenah, Arak. No. 2236, Soltanieh Mosque, Zendjan Province.

2233	A687	5r	Hilltop	25	15
2234	A687	5r	shown	25	15
2235	A687	5r	Intact roof	25	15
2236	A687	5r	Damaged roof	25	15
			Set value		40

1986, Aug. 25

2237 A688 20r multicolored 60 20

Population and Housing Census — A689

Iran-Iraq War, 6th Year — A690

1986, Sept. 9 *Perf. 13½x13*

2238 A689 20r multicolored 40 15

1986, Sept. 22 *Perf. 13*

2239	A690	10r	Battleship Paykan	30	15
2240	A690	10r	Susangerd	30	15
2241	A690	10r	Khorramshahr	30	15
2242	A690	10r	Howeizeh	30	15
2243	A690	10r	Siege of Abadan	30	15
			Nos. 2239-2243 (5)	1.50	
			Set value		50

10th Asian Games, Seoul A691

1986, Oct. 2 Photo. Wmk. 381

2244 A691 15r Wrestling 40 15
2245 A691 15r Rifle shooting 40 15

World Post Day A692

1986, Oct. 9

2246 A692 20r multicolored 50 20

UNESCO, 40th Anniv. — A693

1986, Nov. 4 Photo. *Perf. 13x13½*

2247 A693 45r blk, sky bl & brt rose 1.25 45

Ayatollah Tabatabaie (d. 1981) — A694

1986, Nov. 15 Photo. *Perf. 13½x13*

2248 A694 10r multicolored 30 15

Unity Week — A695

1986, Nov. 20

2249 A695 10r multicolored 30 15

Birth anniv. of Mohammed.

People's Militia — A696

1986, Nov. 26 *Perf. 13*

2250 A696 5r multicolored 15 15

Mobilization of the Oppressed Week.

Afghan Resistance Movement, 7th Anniv. — A697

1986, Dec. 27

2251 A697 40r multicolored 1.20 40

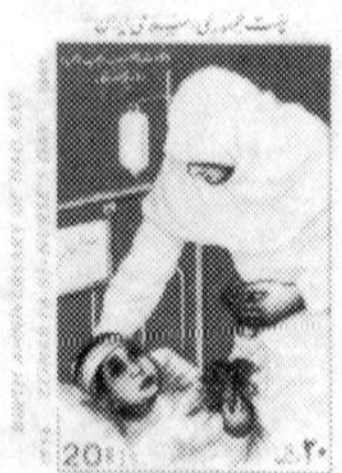

Nurses' Day — A698

1987, Jan. 12 Photo. *Perf. 13*

2252 A698 20r multicolored 60 20

Hazrat Zainab birth anniv.

Fifth Islamic Theology Conference, Tehran — A699

Wmk. 381

1987, Jan. 29 Photo. *Perf. 13*

2253 A699 20r multicolored 60 20

Islamic Revolution, 8th Anniv. A700

1987, Feb. 11

2254 A700 20r multicolored 60 20

See No. 2310m for 24x36mm stamp.

Islamic Revolutionary Committees, 8th Anniv. — A701

1987, Feb. 12

2255 A701 10r brt bl, scar & yel 30 15

Women's Day — A702

1987, Feb. 19

2256 A702 10r multicolored 30 15

Birthday of Fatima, daughter of Mohammed.

Iran Air, 25th Anniv. A703

1987, Feb. 24

2257 A703 30r multicolored 90 30

Ayatollah Mirza Mohammad Hossein Naeini, 50th Death Anniv. — A704

1987, Mar. 6 Photo. *Perf. 13*

2258 A704 10r multicolored 30 15

New Year — A705

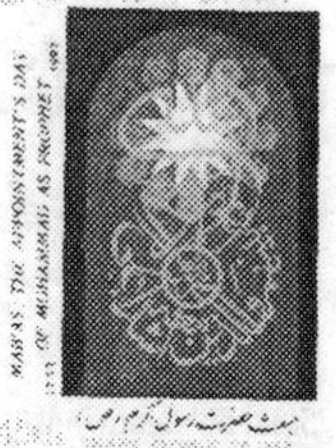

Mab'as Festival — A706

Flowers: a, Iris persica. b, Rosa damascena. c, Iris paradoxa. d, Tulipa clusiana.

1987, Mar. 11 *Perf. 13½x13*

2259 Block of 4 1.00 50
a.-d. A705 5r, any single 25 15

See Nos. 2313, 2361, 2411, 2443.

1987, Mar. 28 *Perf. 13*

2260 A706 45r gold, dk grn & grn 1.35 45

Universal Day of the Oppressed A707

1987, Apr. 14

2261 A707 20r multicolored 60 20

Savior Mahdi's birthday.

Memorial to Lebanese Hizbollah Martyrs — A708

1987, Apr. 5

2262 A708 10r grn, gray & brt car 30 15

Revolutionary Guards Day — A709

1987, Apr. 2
2263 A709 5r multi 15 15

Imam Hossein's birthday.

8th Anniv. of Islamic Republic — A710

1987, Apr. 1
2264 A710 20r multicolored 60 20

World Health Day — A711

Child survival through immunization: 3r, Intravenous. 5r, Oral.

1987, Apr. 7 ***Perf. 13x13½***
2265 A711 3r multicolored 20 15
2266 A711 5r multicolored 30 15
a. Pair, #2265-2266 50 25
Set value 20

Int'l. Labor Day — A712

1987, May 1 Photo. ***Perf. 13***
2267 A712 5r multicolored 15 15

Teachers' Day — A713

1987, May 2 Wmk. 381
2268 A713 5r Ayatollah Mottahari 15 15

A714 A715

1987, May 17 ***Perf. 13½x13***
2269 A714 20r multicolored 60 20

World Telecommunications Day.

1987, May 18 ***Perf. 13***
2270 A715 20r Sassanian silver gilt vase 60 20
2271 A715 20r Bisque pot, Rey, 12th cent. 60 20

Intl. Museum Day.

Universal Day of Jerusalem A716

1963 Uprising, 24th Anniv. A718

World Crafts Day A717

1987, May 22 ***Perf. 13½x13***
2272 A716 20r multicolored 60 20

1987, June 10 ***Perf. 13x13½***

Designs: a, Blown glass tea service. b, Stained glass window. c, Ceramic plate. d, Potter.

2273 Block of 4 60 20
a.-d. A717 5r any single 15 15

1987, June 5 Photo. ***Perf. 13½***
2274 A718 20r multicolored 60 20

Tax Reform Week — A719

1987, July 10 ***Perf. 13***
2275 A719 10r black, sil & gold 30 15

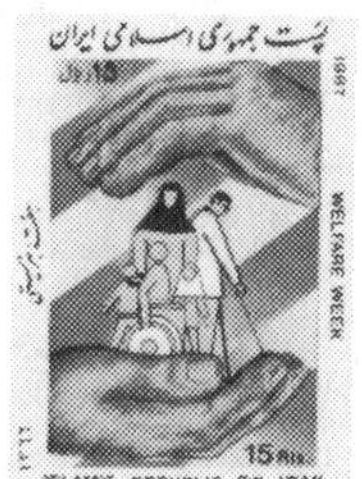
Welfare Week — A720

1987, July 17
2276 A720 15r multicolored 45 15

Eid Ul-adha, Feast of Sacrifice A721

1987, Aug. 6
2277 A721 12r sil, blk & Prus grn 45 15

Eid Ul-Ghadir Festival — A722

Banking Week — A723

1987, Aug. 14
2278 A722 18r black, green & gold 55 18

1987, Aug. 17 ***Perf. 13½x13***
2279 A723 15r red brn, gold & pale grnsh bl 45 15

1st Cultural and Artistic Congress of Iranian Calligraphers A724

1987, Aug. 21 Photo. ***Perf. 13x13½***
2280 A724 20r multicolored 60 20

Memorial to Iranian Pilgrims Killed in Mecca A725

1987, Aug. 26 Wmk. 381 ***Perf. 13***
2281 A725 8r multicolored 30 15

Assoc. of Iranian Dentists, 25th Anniv. — A726

Intl. Peace Day — A727

1987, Aug. 27 Photo. ***Perf. 13½x13***
2282 A726 10r multicolored 30 15

1987, Sept. 1 ***Perf. 13***
2283 A727 20r gold & lt ultra 60 20

Iran-Iraq War, 7th Anniv. — A728

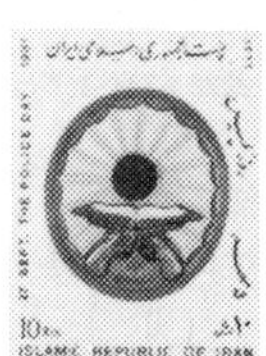
Police Day — A729

1987, Sept. 22 ***Perf. 13½x13***
2284 A728 25r shown 75 25
2285 A728 25r Soldier, battle scene 75 25
a. Pair, #2284-2285

1987, Sept. 28
2286 A729 10r multicolored 30 15

Intl. Social Security Week, Oct. 4-10 — A730

World Post Day — A731

1987, Oct. 4 Wmk. 381
2287 A730 15r blk, gold & brt blue 45 15

1987, Oct. 9 ***Perf. 13x13½***

UPU emblem and: No. 2288, M. Ghandi, minister of the Post and Telecommunications Bureau. No. 2289, Globe, dove.

2288 A731 15r multicolored 45 15
2289 A731 15r multicolored 45 15

Importation Prohibited
Importation of stamps was prohibited effective Oct. 29, 1987.

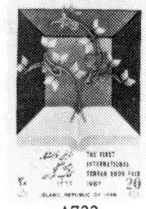

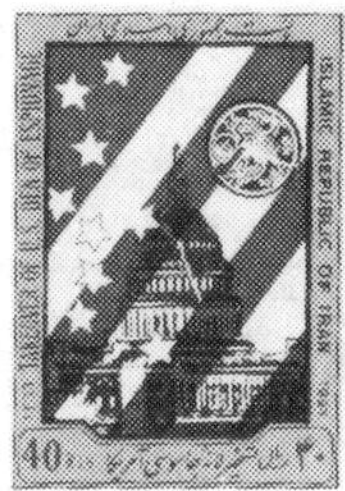
A732 A733

Wmk. 381

1987, Nov. 4 Photo. ***Perf. 13***

2290 A732 40r multicolored

Takeover of US Embassy, 8th anniv.

1987, Nov. 5

2291 A733 20r multicolored

1st Intl. Tehran Book Fair.

Mohammed's Birthday, Unity Week — A734

1987, Nov. 10

2292 A734 25r multicolored

Ayatollah Modarres Martyrdom, 50th Anniv. — A735

1987, Dec. 1

2293 A735 10r brn & bister

Agricultural Training and Extension Week — A736

1987, Dec. 6

2294 A736 10r multicolored

Afghan Resistance, 8th Anniv. — A737

1987, Dec. 27

2295 A737 40r multicolored

Main Mosques — A738

1987-92 ***Perf. 13x13½, 13½x13***

Silver Background

2295A A738 1r Shoushtar
2296 A738 2r Ouroumieh
2296A A738 3r Kerman
2297 A738 5r Kazvin
2298 A738 10r Varamin
a. Unwatermarked ('91)
2299 A738 20r Saveh
a. Unwatermarked ('91)
2300 A738 30r Natanz, vert.
2301 A738 40r Shiraz
a. Unwatermarked ('92)
2302 A738 50r Isfahan, vert.
a. Unwatermarked ('91)
2303 A738 100r Hamadan
a. Unwatermarked ('91)
2304 A738 200r Dezfoul, vert.
a. Unwatermarked ('91)
2305 A738 500r Yazd, vert.
a. Unwatermarked ('91)

Issued: 10r, Dec. 1. 5r, Dec. 30. 500r, Jan. 10, 1988. 20r, Jan. 14, 1988. 2r, Jan. 24, 1988. 50r, Jan. 24, 1989. 100r, Oct. 21, 1989. 200r, Oct. 28, 1989. 30r, 40r, Mar. 17, 1990. 1r, 3r, Mar. 1992.

Qum Uprising, 10th Anniversary — A739

1988, Jan. 9 ***Perf. 13***

2306 A739 20r multicolored

Bombing of Schools by Iraq — A740

1988, Feb. 1 ***Perf. 13x13½***

2307 A740 10r multicolored

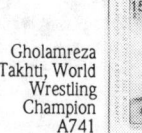

Gholamreza Takhti, World Wrestling Champion A741

1988, Feb. 4 ***Perf. 13½***

2308 A741 15r multicolored

Women's Day — A742

1988, Feb. 9 ***Perf. 13***

2309 A742 20r multicolored

Birth anniv. of Mohammed's daughter, Fatima.

Souvenir Sheet
Types of 1979-88 and

Islamic Revolution, 9th Anniv. — A743

1988, Feb. 11 **Wmk. 381**

2310 Sheet of 16
a. A547 1r like #2046
b. A547 3r like #2047
c. A559 3r like #2066
d. A547 5r like #2048
e. A559 5r like #2067
f. A570 5r like #2095
g. A570 10r like #2096
h. A608 10r like #2146
i. A537 18r like #1999
j. A559 20r like #2068
k. A570 20r like #2097
l. A664 20r like #2209
m. A700 20r like #2254
n. A587 30r like #2115
o. A631 40r like #2172
p. A743 40r shown

Nos. 2310a, 2310b, 2310d, 2310l, 2310m are smaller than the original issues. See original issues for distinguishing features on other stamps.
Exists imperf.

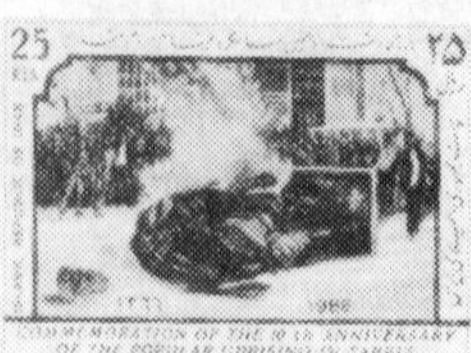

Tabriz Uprising, 10th Anniv. A744

1988, Feb. 18 ***Perf. 13***

2311 A744 25r multicolored

Arbor Day — A745

1988, Mar. 5

2312 A745 15r multicolored

New Year Festival Type of 1987

Flowers: a, Anthemis hyalina. b, Malva silvestria, Viola odorata, Echium amaenum.

1988, Mar. 10 ***Perf. 13½x13***

2313 Block of 4
a.-d. A705 10r any single

Islamic Republic, 9th Anniv. — A746

1988, Apr. 1 ***Perf. 13***

2314 A746 20r multicolored

Universal Day of the Oppressed — A747

1988, Apr. 3

2314A A747 20r multicolored

Savior Mahdi's Birthday.

Cultural Heritage A748

1988, Apr. 18

2315 A748 10r Mosque
2316 A748 10r Courtyard
a. Pair, #2315-2316
2317 A748 10r Minarets, vert.
2318 A748 10r Corridor, vert.
a. Pair, #2317-2318

Chemical Bombardment of Halabja, Iraq — A749

1988, Apr. 26

2319 A749 20r multicolored

A750

A750a

Palestinian Uprising — A750b

1988, May 13

2320 Strip of 5
a. A750 10r multi
b. A750a 10r multi
c. A750b 10r multi
d. A750b 10r multi, diff.
e. A750b 10r Rock in hand, rioters

World Telecommunications Day — A751

1988, May 17 ***Perf. 13x13½***

2321 A751 20r green & blue

Intl. Museum Day — A752

Designs: a, Ceramic vase, 1982. b, Bastan Museum, entranceway. c, Tabriz silk rug, 14th cent. d, Gold ring, 7th cent. B.C.

1988, May 18 *Perf. 13*
2322 Block of 4
a.-d. A752 10r any single

Mining Day — A753

1988, May 22 Photo. Wmk. 381
2323 A753 20r multicolored

Intl. Day of the Child — A754

1988, June 1
2324 A754 10r multicolored

June 5th Uprising, 25th Anniv. — A755

1988, June 5
2325 A755 10r multicolored

World Crafts Day — A756

1988, June 10 *Perf. 13x13½*
2326 A756 10r Straw basket
2327 A756 10r Weaver
a. Pair, #2326-2327
2328 A756 10r Tapestry, vert.
2329 A756 10r Miniature, vert.
a. Pair, #2328-2329

Child Health Campaign — A757

1988, July 6 *Perf. 13*
2330 A757 20r blk, blue & green

Tax Reform Week — A758

1988, July 10
2331 A758 20r multicolored

A759 A760

1988, July 15 *Perf. 13½x13*
2332 A759 20r Allameh Balkhi

1988, July 21 *Perf. 13*
2333 A760 10r Holy Ka'aba, dove, stars
2334 A760 10r shown

Massacre of Muslim Pilgrims at Mecca.

Destruction of Iranian Airliner — A761

1988, Aug. 11
2335 A761 45r multicolored

A762 A763

1988, Aug. 13
2336 A762 20r Seyyed Ali Andarzgou

1988, Sept. 1 *Perf. 13½x13*
2337 A763 20r multicolored

Islamic Banking Week.

Divine Day of 17 Shahrivar, 10th Anniv. — A764

1988, Sept. 8
2338 A764 25r multicolored

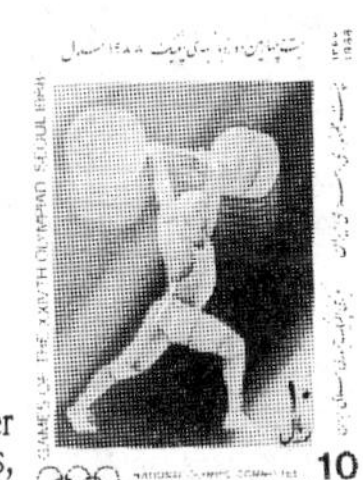

1988 Summer Olympics, Seoul — A765

Designs: a, Weightlifting. b, Pommel horse. c, Judo. d, Soccer. e, Wrestling.

1988, Sept. 10
2339 Strip of 5
a.-e. A765 10r any single

A766 A767

1988, Sept. 17 *Perf. 13½x13*
2340 A766 30r blk, grn & yel

Agricultural census.

1988, Sept. 22 *Perf. 13x13½*
2341 A767 20r multicolored

Iran-Iraq War, 8th anniv.

World Post Day A768

1988, Oct. 9 *Perf. 13*
2342 A768 20r blk, ultra & grn

Parents and Teachers Cooperation Week — A769

1988, Oct. 16
2343 A769 20r multicolored

Mohammed's Birthday, Unity Week — A770

1988, Oct. 29
2344 A770 10r multicolored

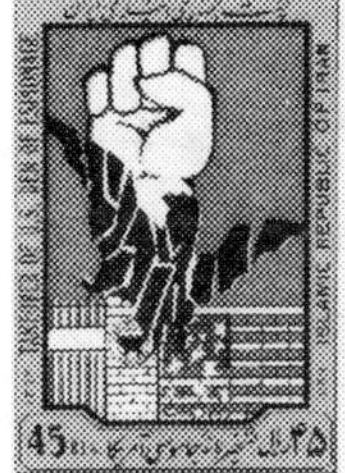

A771 A772

1988, Nov. 4
2345 A771 45r multicolored

Takeover of US embassy, 9th anniv.

1988, Nov. 6 *Perf. 13½x13*
2346 A772 10r multicolored

Insurance Day.

Intl. Congress on the Writings of Hafiz — A773

Illustration reduced.

1988, Nov. 19 *Perf. 13x13½*
2347 A773 20r blue, gold & pink

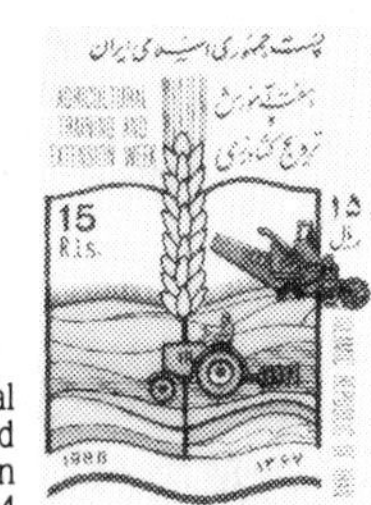

Agricultural Training and Extension Week — A774

1988, Dec. 6 *Perf. 13*
2348 A774 15r multicolored

Scientists, Artists and Writers A775

1988, Dec. 18 *Perf. 13x13½*
2349 A775 10r Parvin E'Tessami
2350 A775 10r Jalal Al-Ahmad
2351 A775 10r Muhammad Mo'in
a. Pair, #2350-2351
2352 A775 10r Qaem Maqam Farahani
2353 A775 10r Kamal Al-Molk
a. Pair, #2352-2353

See Nos. 2398-2402.

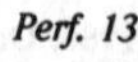

Afghan Resistance, 9th Anniv. — A776

1988, Dec. 27 ***Perf. 13***
2354 A776 40r multicolored

Transportion and Communication Decade — A777

Perf. 13x13½
1989, Jan. 16 **Wmk. 381**
2355 A777 20r Satellite, envelopes, microwave dish
2356 A777 20r Cargo planes
a. Pair, #2355-2356
2357 A777 20r Train, trucks
2358 A777 20r Ships
a. Pair, #2357-2358

Prophethood of Mohammed A778

1989, Mar. 6 ***Perf. 13***
2359 A778 20r multicolored

Mab'as festival.

Arbor Day — A779

1989, Mar. 6
2360 A779 20r multicolored

New Year Festival Type of 1987

Flowers: a, Cephalanthera kurdica. b, Dactylorhiza romana. c, Comperia comperiana. d, Orchis mascula.

1989, Mar. 11 ***Perf. 13½x13***
2361 Block of 4
a.-d. A705 10r any single

A780 A781

1989, Mar. 23
2362 A780 20r shown
2363 A780 30r Meteorological devices, ship
a. Pair, #2362-2363

World Meteorology Day.

1989, Apr. 1 ***Perf. 13***
2364 A781 20r multicolored

Islamic Republic, 10th anniv.

Reconstruction of Abadan Refinery — A782

1989, Apr. 1
2365 A782 20r multicolored

Ayatollah Morteza Motahhari, 10th Death Anniv. — A783

1989, May 2
2366 A783 20r multi

Teachers' Day.

A784 A785

1989, May 5
2367 A784 30r multicolored

Universal Day of Jerusalem.

1989, May 17 ***Perf. 13½x13***
2368 A785 20r multicolored

World Telecommunications Day.

Intl. Museum Day — A786

Gurgan pottery, 6th century.

1989, May 18 ***Perf. 13x13½***
2369 A786 20r Jar
2370 A786 20r Bottle
a. Pair, #2369-2370

Nomads' Day — A787

1989, June 4 ***Perf. 13***
2371 A787 20r multicolored

World Crafts Day — A788

1989, July 5 ***Perf. 13x13½***
2372 A788 20r Engraver
2373 A788 20r Copper vase
a. Pair, #2372-2373
2374 A788 20r Copper plate, vert.
2375 A788 20r Copper wall hanging, vert.
a. Pair, #2374-2375

Ayatollah Khomeini (1900-89) A789

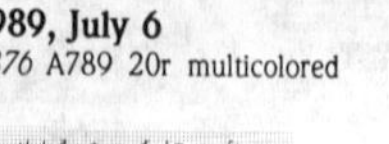

1989, July 6 ***Perf. 13***
2376 A789 20r multicolored

Pasteur and Avicenna — A790

1989, July 7
2377 A790 30r multicolored
2378 A790 50r multicolored
a. Pair, #2377-2378

PHILEXFRANCE.

Asia-Pacific Telecommunity, 10th Anniv. — A791

1989, July 25
2379 A791 30r blk, org brn & bl

Mehdi Araghi, 10th Death Anniv. — A792

1989, Aug. 30
2380 A792 20r brn org & org brn

M.H. Shahryar, Poet A793

1989, Sept. 17
2381 A793 20r multicolored

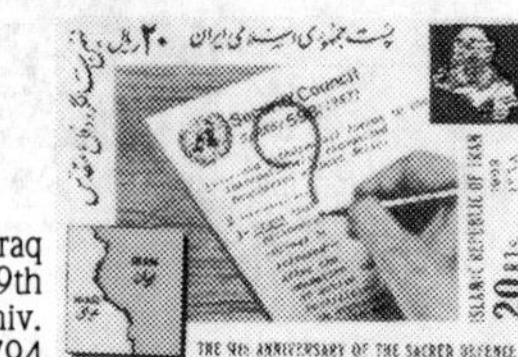

Iran-Iraq War, 9th Anniv. A794

1989, Sept. 22
2382 A794 20r UN Security Council res. 598

Ayatollah Khomeini A795

Designs: 1r, Building courtyard, flower. 2r, Portrait as youth. 3r, Giving speech. 5r, Map, rifles. 10r, Khomeini, others amid flowers. 20r, Khomeini seated before microphone. 30r, Khomeini with child. 40r, Other mullahs. 50r, Khomeini gesturing with hands. 70r, On balcony before crowd. 100r, Slogan. 200r, Empty lectern. 500r, Mausoleum. 1000r, Sun rays.

1989-92 Litho. Unwmk. ***Perf. 13½***
2382A A795 1r green & multi
2382B A795 2r green & multi
2383 A795 3r green & multi
2384 A795 5r brt vio & multi
2385 A795 10r brt bl & multi
2386 A795 20r blue & multi
2387 A795 30r pink & multi
2388 A795 40r red & multi
2389 A795 50r gray & multi
2390 A795 70r brt grn & multi
2391 A795 100r ultra & multi
2392 A795 200r red brn & multi
2393 A795 500r black & multi
2393A A795 1000r multicolored

Issue dates: 1r, Jan. 3, 1991. 3r, Mar. 16, 1990. 5r, Dec. 13. 10r, Oct. 22. 20r, 30r, 50r, Sept. 23,

1990. 40r, Feb. 9, 1990. 100, 200r, Sept. 26. 70r, 500r, June 4, 1991. 2r, 1000r, Mar. 16, 1992.
This is an expanding set. Numbers will change if necessary.

World Post Day A796

Wmk. 381
1989, Oct. 9 Photo. *Perf. 13*
2394 A796 20r multicolored

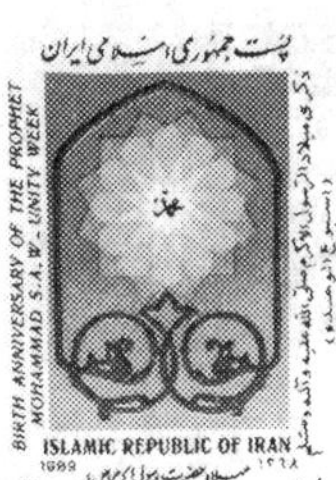

Mohammed's Birthday, Unity Week — A797

1989, Oct. 18
2395 A797 10r multi

Takeover of US Embassy, 10th Anniv. — A798

1989, Nov. 4 *Perf. 13½x13*
2396 A798 40r multicolored

Bassij of the Oppressed (Militia), 10th Anniv. — A799

1989, Nov. 27 *Perf. 13*
2397 A799 10r multicolored

Scientists, Artists and Writers Type of 1988
1989, Dec. 18 *Perf. 13x13½*
2398 A775 10r Mehdi Elahi Ghomshei
2399 A775 10r Dr. Abdulazim Gharib
2400 A775 10r Seyyed Hossein Mirkhani
a. Pair, #2399-2400
2401 A775 10r Ayatollah Seyyed Hossein Boroujerdi
2402 A775 10r Ayatollah Sheikh Abdulkarim Haeri
a. Pair, #2401-2402

Intl. Literacy Year — A800

Perf. 13½
1990, Jan. 1 Photo. Wmk. 381
2403 A800 20r multicolored

Cultural Heritage — A801

Designs: No. 2404, Drinking vessel, 1980. No. 2405, Footed vase, 1979.

1990, Jan. 21 *Perf. 13*
2404 A801 20r blk & deep org
2405 A801 20r blk & yel grn
a. Pair, #2404-2405

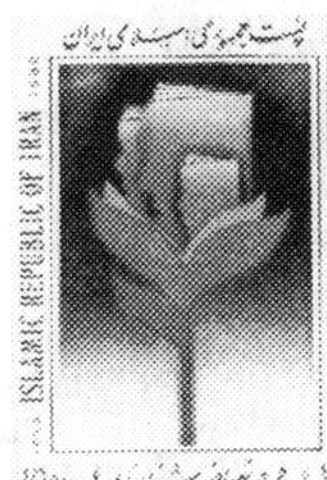

New Identification Card System — A802

1990, Feb. 9
2406 A802 10r multicolored

Islamic Revolution, 11th Anniv. — A803

1990, Feb. 11
2407 A803 50r multicolored

Intl. Koran Recitation Competition A804

1990, Feb. 23
2408 A804 10r blk, bl & grn

A805

A806

1990, Mar. 2 *Perf. 13½x13*
2409 A805 10r multicolored

Invalids of Islamic Revolution.

1990, Mar. 6 *Perf. 13*
2410 A806 20r multicolored

Arbor Day.

New Year Festival Type of 1987

Flowers: a, Coronilla varia. b, Astragalus cornu-caprae. c, Astragalus obtusifolius. d, Astragalus straussii.

1990, Mar. 11 *Perf. 13½x13*
2411 Block of 4
a.-d. A705 10r any single

Islamic Republic, 11th Anniv. — A807

1990, Apr. 1 *Perf. 13*
2412 A807 30r multicolored

World Health Day — A808

1990, Apr. 7
2413 A808 40r multicolored

A809

A810

1990, June 4 Unwmk. *Perf. 11x10½*
2414 A809 50r multicolored

Ayatollah Khomeini, 1st death anniv.

1990, Dec. 15 Litho. *Perf. 10½*
2415 A810 100r multicolored

Jerusalem Day.

A811

A812

1990, Oct. *Perf. 13*
2416 A811 20r Turkoman jewelry
2417 A811 50r Gilded steel bird
a. Pair, #2416-2417

World Crafts Day.

1990, Nov. 17 *Perf. 10½*
2418 A812 20r multicolored

Intl. Day of the Child.

Aid to Earthquake Victims A813

1990, Nov. 19 *Perf. 13x13½*
2419 A813 100r multicolored

Tribute to Former Prisoners of War — A814

1990, Nov. 21 *Perf. 13*
2420 A814 250r multicolored

Ferdowsi Intl. Congress — A815

Illustration reduced.

1990, Dec. 22 Litho. *Imperf.*
Size: 60x75mm
2421 A815 100r Portrait
2422 A815 100r Statue
2423 A815 100r Monument
2424 A815 100r Slogan, diamond cartouche
2425 A815 100r Rectangular slogan
2426 A815 100r Slogan, diff.
2427 A815 200r Two riders embracing
2428 A815 200r Archer, birds
2429 A815 200r Six men
2430 A815 200r White elephant

2431 A815 200r Warrior, genie, horse
2432 A815 200r Hunting scene
2433 A815 200r Riding through fire
2434 A815 200r Four slogan tablets
2435 A815 200r Man with feet shackled
2436 A815 200r Palace scene

Conference on epic poem "Book of Kings" by Ferdowsi.

In 1991 some imperf between blocks of 4 were released.

"Victory Over Iraq" — A816

1991, Feb. 25 *Perf. 13*
2437 A816 100r multicolored

Intl. Museum Day A817

Designs: No. 2438, Gold jug with Kufric inscription, 10th cent. A.D. No. 2439, Silver-inlaid brass basin, 14th cent. A.D.

1991, Feb. 25
2438 A817 50r multicolored
2439 A817 50r multicolored
a. Pair, #2438-2439

A818 A819

1991, Mar. 12 *Perf. 10¹/₂*
2440 A818 50r multicolored

World Telecommunications Day.

1991, Feb. 25 *Perf. 13*
2441 A819 200r org brn & blk

Opening of Postal Museum.

Islamic Revolution, 12th Anniv. — A820

1991, Feb. 11 **Photo.** *Perf. 13*
2442 A820 100r multicolored

New Year Festival Type of 1987

Designs: No. 2443a, Iris spuria. b, Iris lycotis. c, Iris demawendica. d, Iris meda.

1991, Mar. 11 *Perf. 13¹/₂x13*
2443 A705 20r Block of 4, #a.-d.

Saleh Hosseini, 10th Death Anniv. — A821

1991, Mar. 19 *Perf. 13¹/₂x13*
2444 A821 30r red & black

Mab'as Festival A822

1991, Mar. 19 *Perf. 13x13¹/₂*
2445 A822 100r multicolored

Universal Day of the Oppressed A823

1991, Mar. 25 *Perf. 13*
2446 A823 50r multicolored

Savior Mahdi's Birthday.

Revolutionaries, 25th Death Anniv. — A824

1991, Mar. 25
2447 A824 50r maroon & red org

Dated 1990.

Islamic Republic, 12th Anniv. — A825

Unwmk.

1991, Apr. 1 **Photo.** *Perf. 13*
2448 A825 20r blk, slate, grn & red

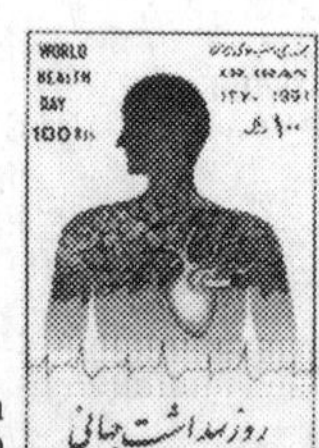

World Health Day — A826

1991, Apr. 7 *Perf. 13¹/₂x13*
2449 A826 100r multicolored

Day of Jerusalem — A827

1991, Apr. 12 *Perf. 13*
2450 A827 100r bl, blk & brn

Women's Day — A828

1991, Apr. 12 **Litho.** *Perf. 10¹/₂*
2451 A828 50r multicolored

Birth anniv. of Mohammed's daughter, Fatima.

Ayatollah Borujerdi, 30th Death Anniv. — A829

Perf. 13¹/₂x13

1991, Apr. 28 **Photo.** **Unwmk.**
2452 A829 200r bl grn & blk

Teachers' Day — A830

Illustration reduced.

1991, May 2 *Perf. 13x13¹/₂*
2453 A830 50r multicolored

Decade for Natural Disaster Reduction — A831

1991, May 11 **Litho.** *Perf. 10¹/₂*
2454 A831 100r multicolored

World Telecommunications Day — A832

Perf. 13¹/₂x13

1991, May 17 **Photo.** **Unwmk.**
2455 A832 100r multicolored

Intl. Museum Day — A833

Flags — A834

Ewers, Kashan, 13th cent.: 20r, With spout. 40r, Baluster.

1991, May 18 *Perf. 13*
2456 A833 20r multicolored
2457 A833 40r multicolored
a. Pair, #2456-2457

1991, May 24 *Perf. 13x13¹/₂*
2458 A834 30r multicolored

Liberation of Khorramshahr, 7th anniv.

A835

Abol-Hassan Ali-ebne-Mosa Rreza, Birth Anniv. — A835a

Views of shrine, Meshed.

1991, May 26 *Perf. 13*

2459 A835 10r Mausoleum
2460 A835a 30r Gravestone
a. Pair, #2459-2460

First Intl. Conf. on Seismology and Earthquake Engineering — A836

1991, May 27 *Perf. 13½x13*

2461 A836 100r multicolored

World Child Day — A837

1991, June 1 Photo. *Perf. 13½*

2462 A837 50r multicolored

Holy Shrine at Karbola, Iraq Destroyed by Invasion — A838

Unwmk.

1991, June 3 Photo. *Perf. 13*

2463 A838 70r multicolored

Ayatollah Khomeini, 2nd Death Anniv. — A839

1991, June 4

2464 A839 100r multicolored

World Handicrafts Day — A840

Designs: No. 2465, Engraved brass wares. No. 2466, Gilded samovar set.

1991, June 10 *Perf. 13½x13*

2465 A840 40r multicolored
2466 A840 40r multicolored
a. Pair #2465-2466

Intl. Congress on Poet Nezami — A841

1991, June 22 *Perf. 13*

2467 A841 50r multicolored

Ali Ibn Abi Talib, 1330th Death Anniv. — A842

1991, July 15 Photo. *Perf. 13*

2468 A842 50r multicolored

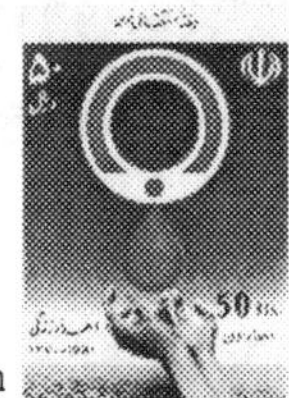

Blood Transfusion Week — A843

Unwmk.

1991, July 29 Photo. *Perf. 13*

2469 A843 50r multicolored

Return of Prisoners of War, First Anniv. — A844

Illustration reduced.

1991, Aug. 27 *Perf. 13x13½*

2470 A844 100r multicolored

Ayatollah Marashi, Death Anniv. — A845

Illustration reduced.

1991, Aug. 29 *Perf. 13½x13*

2471 A845 30r multicolored

Ayatollah-ol-Ozma Seyyed Abdol-Hossein Lary, Revolutionary — A846

Design includes 1909 stamp issued by Lary.

1991, Sept. 9 *Perf. 13x13½*

2472 A846 30r multicolored

Start of Iran-Iraq War, 11th Anniv. — A847

1991, Sept. 22 *Perf. 13½x13*

2473 A847 20r multicolored

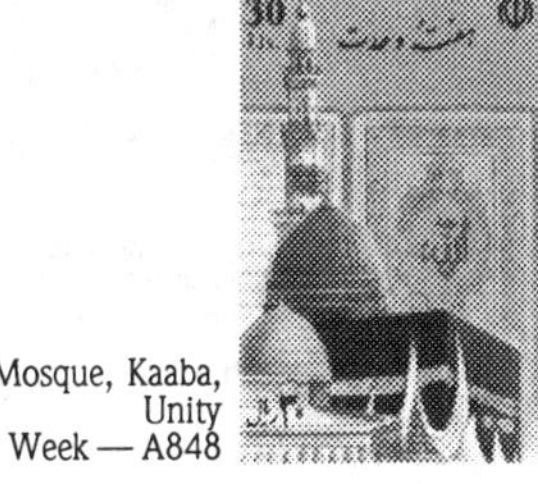

Mosque, Kaaba, Unity Week — A848

1991, Sept. 22 *Perf. 13*

2474 A848 30r multicolored

World Tourism Day — A849

1991, Sept. 27 Photo. *Perf. 13½*

2475 A849 200r multicolored

Dr. Mohammed Gharib — A849a

1991, Sept. 29 Photo. *Perf. 13*

2475A A849a 100r blue & black

World Post Day — A850

Unwmk.

1991, Oct. 9 Photo. *Perf. 13*

2476 A850 70r #2071 on cover

Khaju-ye Kermani Intl. Congress — A851

1991, Oct. 15

2477 A851 30r multicolored

A852 A853

1991, Oct. 16

2478 A852 80r multicolored

World Food Day.

1991, Oct. 19 *Perf. 13½x13*

2479 A853 40r bl vio & gold

Intl. Conference Supporting Palestinians.

Illustrators of Children's Books, 1st Asian Biennial — A854

1991, Oct. 25 *Perf. 13*

2480 A854 100r multicolored

"Children" misspelled.

World Standards Day — A855

1991, Oct. 14 *Perf. 13½*
2481 A855 100r multicolored

1st Seminar on Adolescent and Children's Literature — A856

1991, Nov. 3 *Perf. 13*
2482 A856 20r multicolored

Roshid Intl. Educational Film Festival — A857

1991, Nov. 6
2483 A857 50r multicolored

7th Ministerial Meeting of the Group of 77 — A858

1991, Nov. 16
2484 A858 30r vio & bl grn

Bassij of the Oppressed (Militia), 12th Anniv. — A859

1991, Nov. 25
2485 A859 30r multicolored

Ayatollah Aref Hosseini — A860

1991, Dec. 18 *Perf. 13½*
2486 A860 50r multicolored

Sadek Ghanji A861

1991, Dec. 20
2487 A861 50r multicolored

Agricultural Training and Extension Week — A862

1991, Dec. 22 *Perf. 13*
2488 A862 70r multicolored

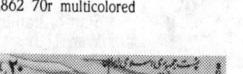

World Telecommunications Day — A863

Designs: No. 2489a, 20r, Telegraph key. b, 20r, Phone lines. c, 20r, Early telephones. d, 40r, Satellite dishes. e, 40r, Telecommunications satellite.

1992, May 17 **Photo.** *Perf. 13*
2489 A863 Strip of 5, #a.-e.

New Year — A863a

1992, Apr. 18 *Perf. 13½x13*
2490 A863a 20r Block of 4, #a.-d.

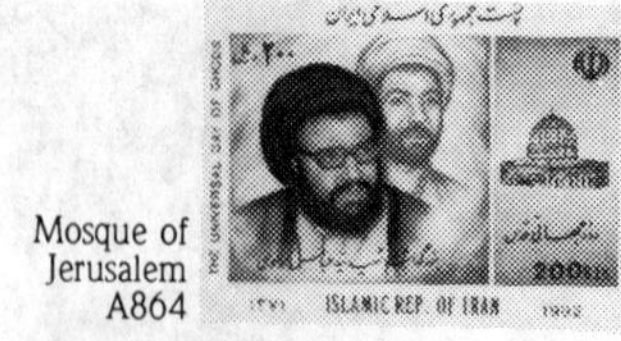

Mosque of Jerusalem A864

1992, Mar. 27 *Perf. 13x13½*
2491 A864 200r multicolored

Day of Jerusalem and honoring A. Mousavi, the Shiva leader of Lebanon.

Reunification of Yemen — A865

1992, May 22 *Perf. 13½x13*
2492 A865 50r multicolored

World Child Day A866

1992, June 1 *Perf. 13x13½*
2493 A866 50r multicolored

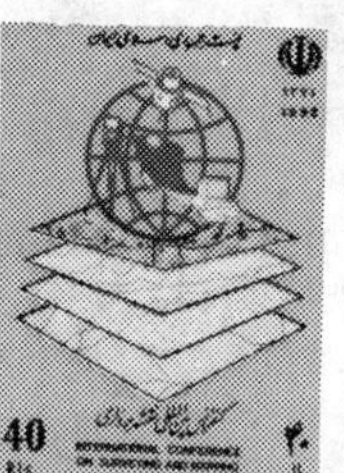

Intl. Conference of Surveying and Mapping — A867

1992, May 25 *Perf. 13*
2494 A867 40r multicolored

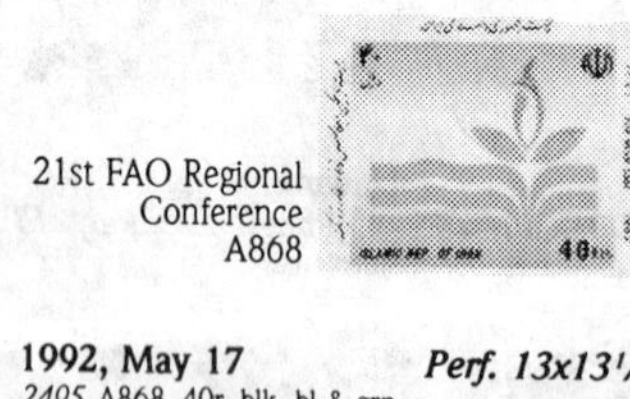

21st FAO Regional Conference A868

1992, May 17 *Perf. 13x13½*
2495 A868 40r blk, bl & grn

South and West Asia Postal Union — A869

Mosques: No. 2496, Imam's Mosque, Isfahan. No. 2497, Lahore Mosque, Pakistan. No. 2498, St. Sophia Mosque, Turkey.

1992, Mar. 27 *Perf. 13½x13*
2496 A869 50r multicolored
2497 A869 50r multicolored
2498 A869 50r multicolored

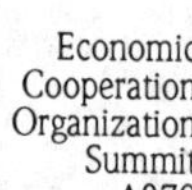

Economic Cooperation Organization Summit A870

Design: 20r, Flags, emblem, vert.

1992 *Perf. 13½x13, 13x13½*
2499 A870 20r multicolored
2500 A870 200r multicolored

Issued: 20r, Apr. 25; 200r, Feb. 17.

Natural Resources — A871

Islamic Republic, 13th Anniv. — A872

1992, Apr. 15 **Litho.** *Perf. 13½x13*
2501 A871 100r multicolored

1992, Apr. 1 *Perf. 13½x13*
2502 A872 50r multicolored

Air Freight Service A873

1992, Apr. 1 *Perf. 13x13½*
2503 A873 60r multicolored

Islamic Revolution, 13th Anniv. — A874

Various scenes of revolution.

Unwmk.

1992, Feb. 11 **Photo.** *Perf. 13*
2504 A874 30r multicolored
2505 A874 50r multicolored
a. Pair, #2504-2505

A875 A876

1992, Mar. 23 **Photo.** *Perf. 13½x13*
2506 A875 100r multicolored

World Meteorological Day.

1992, May 17 *Perf. 13x13½*

Famous Men: No. 2507, Mohammed Bagher Madjlessi. No. 2508, Hadi Sabzevari, wearing turban. No. 2509, Omman Samani, wearing fez. No. 2510, Arabic script, by Ostad Mir Emad.

2507 A876 50r shown
2508 A876 50r brown & multi
2509 A876 50r multicolored
2510 A876 50r multicolored

Intl. Museum Day — A877

Designs: No. 2511, Gray ceramic ware, 1st millennium B.C. No. 2512, Painted ceramic bowl.

1992, May 18
2511 A877 40r multicolored
2512 A877 40r multicolored

Ayatollah Khomeini, 3rd Anniv. of Death — A878

1992, June 4 *Perf. 13*
2513 A878 100r multicolored

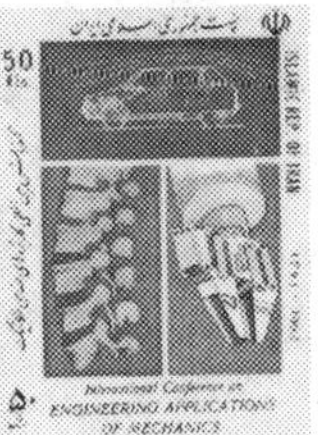

Intl. Conference on Engineering Applications of Mechanics — A879

1992, June 9 *Perf. 13½x13*
2514 A879 50r multicolored

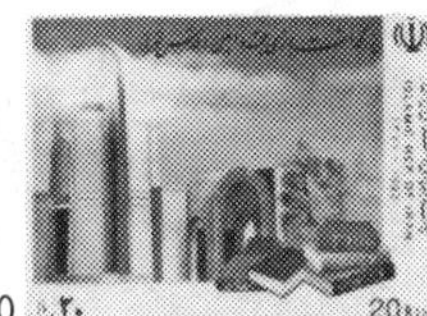

A880

1992, June 13 *Perf. 13x13½*
2515 A880 20r multicolored

Sixth Conference of Nonaligned News Agencies A881

1992, June 15
2516 A881 100r multicolored

A882

A883

1992, June 23 *Perf. 13x13½*
2517 A882 100r green, black & gold

Meeting of Ministers of Industry and Technology.

1992, June 26 *Perf. 13½x13*
2518 A883 100r multicolored

World Anti-narcotics Day.

Holy Ka'aba — A884

Prayer Calligraphy A885

Designs: No. 2520, Ayatollah Khomeini in prayer. No. 2521, Khomeini holding prayer beads. No. 2522, Khomeini unwrapping turban. Nos. 2523-2524, Islamic prayers.

1992 **Photo.** *Perf. 13½x13*
2519 A884 50r multicolored
2520 A884 50r multicolored
2521 A884 50r multicolored
2522 A884 50r multicolored

Perf. 13x13½
2523 A885 50r dk green & lt green
2524 A885 50r dk blue & lt blue

Issue dates: July 27, Aug. 24.

Iran Shipping Line, 25th Anniv. A886

1992, Aug. 24 **Photo.** *Perf. 13x13½*
2525 A886 200r multicolored

A887 A888

1992, Sept. 15 *Perf. 13½x13*
2526 A887 40r multicolored

Mohammad's Birthday, Unity Week.

Perf. 13½x13, 13x13½
1992, Sept. 22

Iranian Defense Forces: 20r, Soldiers on patrol. 40r, Soldier seated at water's edge, horiz.

2527 A888 20r multicolored
2528 A888 40r multicolored

Intl. Congress on the History of Islamic Medicine — A889

1992, Sept. 23 **Litho.** *Perf. 13*
2529 A889 20r Physician, patient
2530 A889 40r Physician's instruments
a. Pair, #2529-2530

Mobarake Steel Plant — A890

1992, Sept. 26 **Photo.** *Perf. 13x13½*
2531 A890 20r Inside plant
2532 A890 70r Outside plant
a. Pair, #2531-2532

No. 2532a has continious design.

Intl. Tourism Day — A891

1992, Sept. 27 *Perf. 13x13½*
2533 A891 20r Mazandaran
2534 A891 20r Isfahan
2535 A891 30r Bushehr (Bushire)
2536 A891 30r Hormozgan

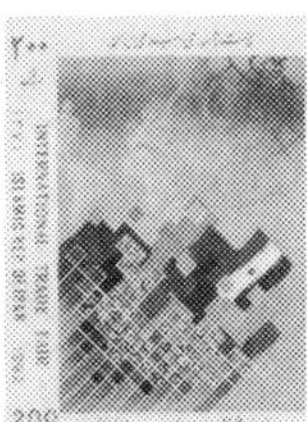

Intl. Trade Fair — A892

1992, Oct. 2 *Perf. 13½x13*
2537 A892 200r multicolored

World Post Day — A893

1992, Oct. 9 *Perf. 13x13½*
2538 A893 30r blue & brown

World Food Day — A894

1992, Oct. 16 *Perf. 13*
2539 A894 100r black, blue & yellow

Intl. Youth Photo Festival — A895

A896

1992, Nov. 1 **Photo.** *Perf. 13½x13*
2540 A895 40r multicolored

1992, Nov. 4 *Perf. 13*

Seizure of US embassy and: No. 2541a, Doves tying up eagle. b, Eagles flying over dead doves. c, Eagles, dove.

2541 A896 100r Strip of 3, #a.-c.

No. 2541 printed in continuous design.

Fighting in Bosnia and Herzegovina A897

Islamic Development Bank A898

1992, Nov. 4 *Perf. 13½x13*
2542 A897 40r multicolored

1992, Nov. 10 **Litho.** *Perf. 13½x13*
2543 A898 20r multicolored

Iran-Azerbaijan Telecommunications — A899

1992, Nov. 21 **Photo.** *Perf. 13x13½*
2544 A899 40r multicolored

Azad University, 10th Anniv. — A900

1992, Nov. 23 *Perf. 13½x13*
2545 A900 200r dark green & emerald

Week of the Basij (Militia) A901

1992, Nov. 26 ***Perf. 13x13½***

2546 A901 40r multicolored

Seyed Mohammed Hosseyn Shahrian, Poet — A902

1992, Dec. 1

2547 A902 80r multicolored

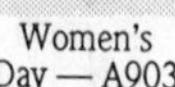

Women's Day — A903

Famous Iranians — A904

1992, Dec. 15

2548 A903 70r multicolored

1992, Dec. 18

Scientists and writers: No. 2551a, Ayatollah Mirza Abolhassan Shar'rani (in turban). b, Prof. Mahmoud Hessabi, U=o formula. c, Mohiyt Tabatabaiy, books on shelves. d, Mehrdad Avesta, calligraphy.

2549 A904 20r Block of 4, #a.-d.

Natl. Iranian Oil Drilling Co. — A905

1992, Dec. 22

2550 A905 100r shown
2551 A905 100r Ocean drilling platform

Promotion of Literacy — A906

1992, Dec. 28 ***Perf. 13½x13***

2552 A906 80r multicolored

Flowers — A907

1993 **Photo.** ***Perf. 13½x13***

2556 A907 20r Narcissus
2560 A907 100r Lily
2561 A907 200r Damascus rose
2562 A907 500r Morning glory
2563 A907 1000r Corn rose

Issue dates: 20r, Jan. 12. 100r, Apr. 21. 200r, Apr. 29. 500r, June 27. 1000r, July 19.

Numbers have been reserved for additional values in this set.

Prophethood of Mohammad A908

1993, Jan. 21 **Photo.** ***Perf. 13x13½***

2567 A908 200r multicolored

Mab'as Festival.

Day of the Disabled — A909

Designs: 40r, Player wearing medal, team memberswith hands raised.

1993, Jan. 27

2568 A909 20r multicolored
2569 A909 40r multicolored
a. Pair, #2568-2569

No. 2569a has continuous design.

Cultural Heritage Preservation A910

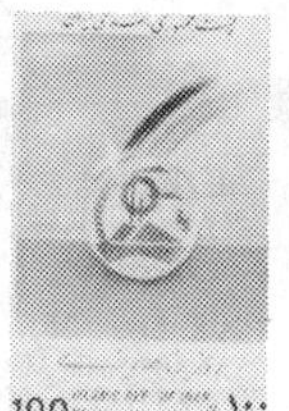

Planning Day A911

1993, Jan. 31 ***Perf. 13½x13***

2570 A910 40r Mosque, exterior
2571 A910 40r Mosque, interior
a. Pair, #2570-2571

1993, Jan. 31 ***Perf. 13***

2572 A911 100r multicolored

Universal Day of the Oppressed A912

1993, Feb. 8 **Litho.** ***Perf. 13***

2573 A912 60r multicolored

Savior Mahdi's Birthday.

Islamic Revolution, 14th Anniv. — A913

Designs: a, Iranian flag. b, Flag, soldiers. c, Soldiers, shellbursts. d, Oil derricks, storage tanks, people harvesting. e, Crowd, car, Ayatollah Khomeini.

1993, Feb. 11 **Photo.** ***Perf. 13x13½***

2574 A913 20r Strip of 5, #a.-e.

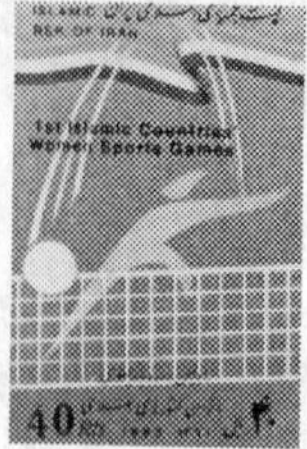

1st Islamic Women's Games — A914

Designs: a, Volleyball. b, Basketball. c, Medal. d, Swimming. e, Running.

1993, Feb. 13 ***Perf. 13***

2575 A914 40r Strip of 5, #a.-e.

Morteza Ansari — A915

1993, Feb. 16 ***Perf. 13½***

2576 A915 40r multicolored

Arbor Day — A916

1993, Mar. 6

2577 A916 70r multicolored

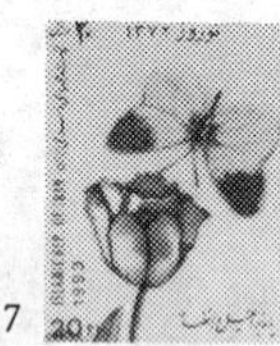

New Year — A917

Designs: a, 20r, Butterfly, tulip. b, 20r, Butterfly, lily. c, 40r, Butterfly, flowers. d, 40r, Butterfly, 3 roses.

1993, Mar. 11 ***Perf. 13½x13***

2578 A917 Block of 4, #a.-d.

World Jerusalem Day — A918

End of Ramadan — A919

1993, Mar. 14 ***Perf. 13½x13***

2579 A918 20r multicolored

1993, Mar. 26 ***Perf. 13½x13***

2580 A919 100r multicolored

Islamic Republic, 14th Anniv. A920

1993, Apr. 1 ***Perf. 13x13½***

2581 A920 40r multicolored

Intl. Congress on the Millennium of Sheik Mofeed — A921

1993, Apr. 17 ***Perf. 13***

2582 A921 80r multicolored

A922

A924

1993, Apr. 21 ***Perf. 13½x13***

2583 A922 100r multicolored

13th Conference of Asian and Pacific Labor Ministers.

1993, May 17 ***Perf. 13½x13***

2585 A924 50r multicolored

Intl. Congress for Advancement of Science and Technology in Islamic World.

A925

A928

1993, May 1

2586 A925 40r multicolored

Intl. Museum Day.

1993, June 1 **Photo.** ***Perf. 13½x13***

2589 A928 50r multicolored

Intl. Child Day.

Ayatollah Khomeini, 4th Death Anniv. — A929

1993, June 4 ***Perf. 13***

2590 A929 20r multicolored

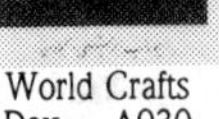

World Crafts Day — A930

World Population Day — A931

1993, June 10 *Perf. 13½x13*
2591 A930 70r multicolored

1993, July 11 *Perf. 13*
2592 A931 30r multicolored

1st Cultural-Athletic Olympiad of Iran University Students — A932

Various sports.

1993, July 22 *Perf. 13x13½*
Background Colors
2593 A932 20r blue
2594 A932 40r henna brown
2595 A932 40r ocher

Intl. Festival of Films for Children and Young Adults, Isfahan A935

1993, Sept. 11 **Photo.** *Perf. 13*
2598 A935 60r multicolored

Illustrators of Children's Books, Intl. Biennial — A939

World of water with fish and: a, Birds. b, Girl. c, Angel with trumpet. d, Trees.

1993, Nov. 5 **Photo.** *Perf. 13½x13*
2602 A939 30r Block of 4, #a.-d.

SEMI-POSTAL STAMPS

Lion and Bull, Persepolis SP1

Persian Soldier, Persepolis SP2

Palace of Darius the Great — SP3

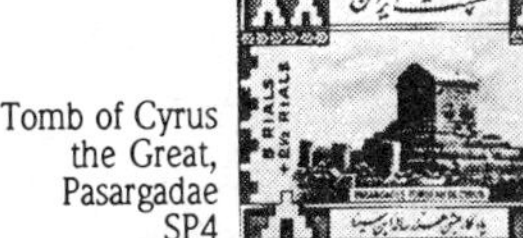

Tomb of Cyrus the Great, Pasargadae SP4

King Darius on his Throne — SP5

Perf. 13x13½, 13½x13
1948, Jan. 30 **Engr.** **Unwmk.**
B1 SP1 50d + 25d emer 1.00 1.00
B2 SP2 1r + 50d red 1.00 1.00
B3 SP3 2½r + 1¼r blue 1.00 1.00
B4 SP4 5r + 2½r pur 1.75 1.75
B5 SP5 10r + 5r vio brn 1.75 1.75
Nos. B1-B5 (5) 6.50 6.50

The surtax was for reconstruction of the tomb of Avicenna (980-1037), Arab physician and philosopher, at Hamadan.

Ardashir II — SP6

Shapur I and Valerian — SP7

Designs: 1r+50d, King Narses, Naqsh-i-Rustam. 5r+2½r, Taq-i-Kisra, Ctesiphon. 10r+5r, Ardashir I and Ahura Mazda.

1949, June 11
B6 SP6 50d + 25d green 80 80
B7 SP6 1r + 50d ver 90 90
B8 SP7 2½r + 1½r blue 90 90
B9 SP7 5r + 2½r magenta 1.40 1.40
B10 SP7 10r + 5r grnsh gray 1.50 1.50
Nos. B6-B10 (5) 5.50 5.50

The surtax was for reconstruction of Avicenna's tomb at Hamadan.

Gunbad-i-Ali SP8

Alaviyan, Hamadan SP9

Seldjukide Coin — SP10

Designs: 1r+½r, Masjid-i-Jami, Isfahan 5r+2½r, Masjid-i-Jami, Ardistan.

1949, Dec. 22
B11 SP8 50d + 25d bl grn 50 50
B12 SP8 1r + ½r dk brn 50 50
B13 SP9 2½r + 1¼r blue 50 50
B14 SP9 5r + 2½r red 1.00 1.00
B15 SP10 10r + 5r olive gray 1.10 1.10
Nos. B11-B15 (5) 3.60 3.60

The surtax was for reconstruction of Avicenna's tomb at Hamadan.

Book, Crescent and Flag — SP11

1950, Oct. 2 **Litho.** *Perf. 11*
B16 SP11 1.50r + 1r multi 22.50 15.00

Economic Conference of the Islamic States.

Tomb of Baba Afzal at Kashan — SP12

Gorgan Vase — SP13

Designs: 2½r+1¼r, Tower of Ghazan. 5r+2½r, Masjid-i Gawhar. 10r+5r, Mihrab of the Mosque at Rezaieh.

Perf. 13x13½, 13½x13
1950, Aug. 23 **Engr.**
B17 SP12 50d + 25d dk grn 50 50
B18 SP13 1r + ½r blue 50 50
B19 SP13 2½r + 1¼r choc 50 50
B20 SP12 5r + 2½r red 1.00 1.00
B21 SP12 10r + 5r gray 1.10 1.10
Nos. B17-B21 (5) 3.60 3.60

The surtax was for reconstruction of Avicenna's tomb at Hamadan.

Mohammed Riza Pahlavi and Map — SP14

Monument to Fallen Liberators of Azerbaijan SP15

Designs: 1r+50d, Marching troops. 1.50r+75d, Running advance with flag. 2.50r+1.25r, Mohammed Riza Pahlavi. 3r+1.50r, Parade of victors.

1950, Dec. 12 **Litho.**
B22 SP14 10d + 5d blk brn 10.00 3.50
B23 SP15 50d + 25d blk brn 8.50 3.50
B24 SP15 1r + 50d brown lake 10.00 4.50
B25 SP14 1.50r + 75d org ver 15.00 9.00
B26 SP14 2.50r + 1.25r blue 17.50 11.00
B27 SP15 3r + 1.50r ultra 19.00 8.50
Nos. B22-B27 (6) 80.00 40.00

Liberation of Azerbaijan Province from communists, 4th anniv.
The surtax was for families of Persian soldiers who died in the struggle.

Koran Gate at Shiraz — SP16

Saadi — SP17

Design: 50d+50d, Tomb of Saadi, Shiraz.

Perf. 11x10½, 10½x11
1952, Apr. 30 **Photo.** **Unwmk.**
B28 SP16 25d + 25d dl bl grn 2.75 1.50
B29 SP16 50d + 50d brn ol 4.00 1.75
B30 SP17 1.50r + 50d vio bl 10.50 6.00

770th birthday of Saadi, Persian poet. The surtax was to help complete Saadi's tomb at Shiraz.
Three stamps of same denominations and colors, with values enclosed in tablets, were prepared but not officially issued.

View of Hamadan SP18

Avicenna SP19

Designs: 2½r+1¼r, Gonbad Qabus (tower of tomb). 5r+2½r, Old tomb of Avicenna. 10r+5r, New tomb.

Perf. 13x13½, 13½x13
1954, Apr. 21 **Engr.** **Unwmk.**
B31 SP18 50d + 25d dp grn 80 80
B32 SP19 1r + ½r vio brn 80 80
B33 SP19 2½r + 1¼r blue 80 80
B34 SP18 5r + 2½r ver 1.25 1.25
B35 SP18 10r + 5r ol gray 2.50 2.50
Nos. B31-B35 (5) 6.15 6.15

The surtax was for reconstruction of Avicenna's tomb at Hamadan.

Catalogue values for unused stamps in this section, from this point to the end of the section, are for Never Hinged items.

Mother with Children and Ruins SP20

Perf. 10½
1963, Feb. 4 **Wmk. 316** **Litho.**
B36 SP20 14r + 6r dk bl grn & lt brn 1.75 50

The surtax was for the benefit of survivors of the Kazvin earthquake.
For overprints see Nos. C86-C88.

AIR POST STAMPS

Type of 1909 Overprinted

POSTE AÉRIENNE

1927 **Unwmk.** **Typo.** *Perf. 11½*
C1 A31 1c org & maroon 35 30
C2 A31 2c vio & maroon 40 30
C3 A31 3c grn & maroon 50 30
C4 A31 6c red & maroon 60 30
C5 A31 9c gray & mar 60 30
C6 A31 10c red vio & mar 70 30
C7 A31 13c dk bl & mar 70 50

C8 A31 1k sil, vio & bis brown 1.25 50
C9 A31 26c dk grn & mar 1.25 70
C10 A31 2k sil, dk grn & bis brown 3.00 1.25
C11 A31 3k sil, gray & bis brown 3.50 2.50
C12 A31 4k sil, bl & bis brown 6.00 3.00
C13 A31 5k gold, brn & bis brown 6.00 4.00
C14 A31 10k gold, org & bis brown 100.00 75.00
C15 A31 20k gold, ol grn & bis brn 100.00 75.00
C16 A31 30k gold, car & bis brown 100.00 75.00
Nos. C1-C16 (16) 324.85 239.25

Counterfeit overprints are plentiful. They are found on Nos. 448-463, perf. 12 1/2x12 instead of 11 1/2.

Nos. C1-C16 exist without overprint. Value, set $600.

AP1

AP2

AP3

AP4

AP5

Airplane, Value and "Poste aérièn" Surcharged on Revenue Stamps

1928 *Perf. 11*
C17 AP1 3k yellow brn 50.00 40.00
C18 AP2 5k dark brown 15.00 10.00
C19 AP3 1t gray vio 12.00 10.00
C20 AP4 2t olive bister 12.00 10.00
C21 AP5 3t deep green 12.00 10.00
Nos. C17-C21 (5) 101.00 80.00

AP6

AP7

"Poste aerienne"

1928-29
C22 AP6 1c emerald 55 50
a. 1c yellow green 25 15
b. Double overprint 16.00
C23 AP6 2c light blue 35 15
C24 AP6 3c bright rose 65 15
C25 AP6 5c olive brn 35 15
a. "5" omitted 400.00 650.00
b. Horiz. pair, imperf. btwn. *200.00*
C26 AP6 10c dark green 35 15
a. "10" omitted 7.00
b. "1" inverted 5.00
C27 AP7 1k dull vio 50 25
a. "1" inverted 5.00
C28 AP7 2k orange 2.00 1.50
Nos. C22-C28 (7) 4.75
Set value 1.75

Counterfeits exist.

Revenue Stamps Similar to Nos. C17 to C21, Overprinted like Nos. C22 to C28: "Poste aerienne"

1929
C29 AP1 3k yellow brn 25.00 7.00
C30 AP2 5k dark brn 9.00 3.00
C31 AP3 10k violet 9.00 5.00
C32 AP4 20k olive grn 22.00 5.00
C33 AP5 30k deep grn 15.00 10.00
Nos. C29-C33 (5) 80.00 30.00

Riza Shah Pahlavi and Eagle AP8

1930, July 6 Photo. ***Perf. 12 1/2x11 1/2***
C34 AP8 1c ol bis & brt bl 30 30
C35 AP8 2c blue & gray blk 30 30
C36 AP8 3c ol grn & dk vio 30 30
C37 AP8 4c dk vio & pck bl 30 30
C38 AP8 5c lt grn & mag 30 30
C39 AP8 6c mag & bl grn 30 30
C40 AP8 8c dk gray & dp violet 30 30
C41 AP8 10c dp ultra & ver 1.00 1.00
C42 AP8 12c slate & org 1.00 1.00
C43 AP8 15c org brn & ol green 2.00 2.00
C44 AP8 1k Prus bl & scar 2.00 2.00

Engr.
C45 AP8 2k black & ultra 2.00 2.00
C46 AP8 3k dk brn & gray green 2.50 2.50
C47 AP8 5k dp red & gray black 3.50 3.50
C48 AP8 1t orange & vio 12.00 5.00
C49 AP8 2t dk grn & red brown 10.00 5.00
C50 AP8 3t brn vio & sl bl 45.00 22.00
Nos. C34-C50 (17) 83.10 48.10

Same Overprinted in Black **Iran**

1935 **Photo.**
C51 AP8 1c ol bis & brt bl 70 60
C52 AP8 2c blue & gray blk 1.50 1.00
C53 AP8 3c ol grn & dk vio 1.90 50
C54 AP8 4c dk vio & pck bl 75 75
C55 AP8 5c lt grn & mag 75 75
C56 AP8 6c mag & bl grn 75 75
C57 AP8 8c dk gray & dp violet 1.25 1.25
C58 AP8 10c dp ultra & ver 1.40 1.50
C59 AP8 12c slate & org 1.75 2.00
C60 AP8 15c org brn & ol green 1.75 2.00
C61 AP8 1k Prus bl & scar 10.00 12.00

Engr.
C62 AP8 2k blk & ultra 5.00 3.00
C63 AP8 3k dk brn & gray green 8.00 4.00
C64 AP8 5k dp red & gray black 3.50 1.10
C65 AP8 1t orange & vio 50.00 30.00
C66 AP8 2t dk grn & red brown 6.00 3.00
C67 AP8 3t brn vio & sl bl 16.00 7.50
Nos. C51-C67 (17) 111.00 71.70

Plane Over Mt. Demavend AP9

Plane above Mosque AP10

Unwmk.
1953, Jan. 21 Photo. ***Perf. 11***
C68 AP9 50d bl green 65 15
C69 AP10 1r car rose 65 15
C70 AP10 2r dark blue 65 15
C71 AP10 3r dark brn 65 15
C72 AP10 5r purple 1.50 15
C73 AP10 10r org ver 2.25 30
C74 AP10 20r vio blue 2.50 50
C75 AP10 30r olive 5.00 1.00
C76 AP10 50r brown 12.00 2.50
C77 AP10 100r black brn 40.00 15.00
C78 AP10 200r dk bl grn 35.00 7.00
Nos. C68-C78 (11) 100.85 27.05

AP11

Golden Dome Mosque and Oil Well — AP12

1953, May 4 Litho. ***Perf. 10 1/2***
Mosque in Deep Yellow
C79 AP11 3r violet 8.00 5.00
C80 AP12 5r chocolate 12.00 5.00
C81 AP11 10r bl green 22.50 12.00
C82 AP12 20r red vio 50.00 30.00

Discovery of oil at Qum.

Catalogue values for unused stamps in this section, from this point to the end of the section, are for Never Hinged items.

Globe and UN Emblem — AP13

Perf. 10 1/2x12 1/2
1957, Oct. 24 Photo. Wmk. 316
C83 AP13 10r brt red lil & rose 2.25 75
C84 AP13 20r dl vio & rose vio 5.00 1.25

United Nations Day, Oct. 24, 1957.

UNESCO Emblem AP14

Perf. 10 1/2
1966, June 20 Wmk. 353 Litho.
C85 AP14 14r multi 95 15

20th anniversary of UNESCO.

No. B36 Surcharged in Maroon, Brown or Red

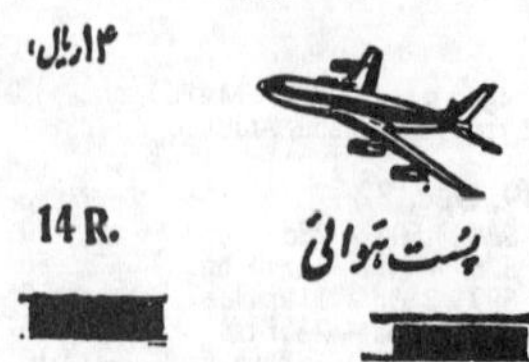

1969, Dec. 4 Wmk. 316 ***Perf. 10 1/2***
C86 SP20 4r on 14r + 6r (M) 2.00 65
C87 SP20 10r on 14r + 6r (B) 2.00 65
C88 SP20 14r on 14r + 6r (R) 2.00 65

1st England-Australia flight, made by Capt. Ross Smith and Lt. Keith Smith, 50th anniv.

IATA Emblem and Persepolis AP15

Perf. 13x13 1/2
1970, Oct. 27 Photo. Wmk. 353
C89 AP15 14r multi 5.00 50

26th meeting of the Intl. Air Transport Assoc. (IATA), Tehran.

"UIT" AP16

1972, May 17 Litho. ***Perf. 10 1/2***
C90 AP16 14r multicolored 2.50 50

4th World Telecommunications Day.

Shah and Jet — AP17

1974, June 1 Photo. ***Perf. 13***
C91 AP17 4r org & black 42 15
C92 AP17 10r blue & black 1.75 15
C93 AP17 12r dull yel & blk 1.75 22
C94 AP17 14r lt green & blk 1.90 25
C95 AP17 20r red lilac & blk 2.50 32
C96 AP17 50r dull bl & blk 6.75 1.40
Nos. C91-C96 (6) 15.07 2.49

Crown Prince at Controls of Light Aircraft — AP18

1974, Oct. 31 Litho. ***Perf. 10 1/2***
C97 AP18 14r gold & multi 1.25 20

Crown Prince Riza's 14th birthday.

Importation Prohibited
Importation of stamps was prohibited effective Oct. 29, 1987.

Islamic Revolution, 10th Anniv. — AP19

1989, Feb. 11 ***Perf. 13x13 1/2***
C98 AP19 40r red vio, blk & gold
C99 AP19 50r bl vio, blk & gold
a. Pair, #C98-C99

Ayatollah Khomeini AP20

1989, July 11 *Perf. 13*
C100 AP20 70r multicolored

OFFICIAL STAMPS

Four bicolored stamps of this design (1s, 2s, 5s, 10s), with centers embossed, exist, but were never issued or used in Iran. They are known imperforate and in many trial colors.

Shah Muzaffar-ed-Din — O1

No. 145 Surcharged in Black

1902 *Perf. 12½*
O5 O1 5c on 1k red 8.50 5.00
O6 O1 10c on 1k red 8.50 5.00
O7 O1 12c on 1k red 8.50 5.00

Nos. 351-363 Overprinted in Black

1903-06
O8 A26 1c violet 60 20
O9 A26 2c gray 60 20
O10 A26 3c green 60 20
O11 A26 5c rose 60 20
O12 A26 10c yel brown 60 20
O13 A26 12c blue 60 20

Perf. 11½x11
O14 A27 1k violet 1.50 50
O15 A27 2k ultra 3.00 50
a. Violet overprint 6.00 5.00
O16 A27 5k org brown 6.00 75
O17 A27 10k rose red 7.50 1.00
a. Violet overprint 12.50
O18 A27 20k orange ('06) 20.00 4.00
O19 A27 30k green ('06) 20.00 4.00
O20 A27 50k green 85.00 45.00
Nos. O8-O20 (13) 146.60 56.95

Overprinted on Nos. 368, 370a
O21 A27 2t on 50k grn (Bl) 60.00 25.00
O22 A27 3t on 50k grn (V) 60.00 25.00

Overprinted on Nos. 372, 375, New Value Surcharged in Blue or Black

1905
O23 A27 2t on 50k grn (Bl) 60.00 25.00
O28 A27 3t on 50k grn (Bk) 60.00 25.00

The 2t on 50k also exists with surcharge in black and magenta; the 3t on 50k in violet and magenta. Values about the same.

Regular Issue of 1909 Overprinted

There is a space between the word "Service" and the Persian characters.

1911 *Perf. 12½x12*
O31 A31 1c org & maroon 6.00 3.00
O32 A31 2c vio & maroon 6.00 3.00
O33 A31 3c yel grn & mar 6.00 3.00
O34 A31 6c red & maroon 6.00 3.00
O35 A31 9c gray & maroon 12.00 5.00
O36 A31 10c multicolored 16.00 5.00
O38 A31 1k multicolored 20.00 10.00
O40 A31 2k multicolored 40.00 20.00
Nos. O31-O40 (8) 112.00 52.00

The 13c, 26c and 3k to 30k denominations were not regularly issued with this overprint.
Dangerous counterfeits exist, usually on reprints.

Regular Issue of 1915 Overprinted

SERVICE

1915 **Wmk. 161** *Perf. 11, 11½*
O41 A33 1c car & indigo 2.00 2.00
O42 A33 2c bl & carmine 2.00 2.00
O43 A33 3c dark green 2.00 2.00
O44 A33 5c red 2.00 2.00
O45 A33 6c ol grn & car 2.00 2.00
O46 A33 9c yel brn & vio 2.00 2.00
O47 A33 10c multicolored 2.00 2.00
O48 A33 12c ultramarine 2.00 2.00
O49 A34 1k multicolored 5.00 5.00
O50 A33 24c multicolored 3.00 3.00
O51 A34 2k sil, bl & rose 5.00 5.00
O52 A34 3k sil, vio & brn 5.00 5.00
O53 A34 5k multicolored 5.00 5.00
O54 A35 1t gold, pur & blk 7.00 7.00
O55 A35 2t gold, grn & brn 7.00 7.00
O56 A35 3t multicolored 9.00 9.00
O57 A35 5t gold, bl & ind 10.00 10.00
Nos. O41-O57 (17) 72.00 72.00

Coronation of Shah Ahmed.
Reprints have dull rather than shiny overprint.
Value, set, $17.50.

Coat of Arms
O2 O3

1941 **Unwmk.** **Litho.** *Perf. 11*
For Internal Postage
O58 O2 5d violet 2.00 20
O59 O2 10d magenta 2.00 20
O60 O2 25d carmine 2.00 20
O61 O2 50d brown black 2.00 20
O62 O2 75d claret 3.50 45

Size: 22½x30mm
O63 O2 1r peacock grn 5.00 45
O64 O2 1½r deep blue 6.00 1.50
O65 O2 2r light blue 8.00 1.00
O66 O2 3r vio brown 15.00 1.50
O67 O2 5r gray green 20.00 2.00
O68 O2 10r dk brn & bl 55.00 5.00
O69 O2 20r chlky bl & brt pink 200.00 20.00
O70 O2 30r vio & brt grn 400.00 45.00
O71 O2 50r turq grn & dk brown 700.00 82.50
Nos. O58-O71 (14) 1,420. 160.20

Catalogue values for unused stamps in this section, from this point to the end of the section, are for Never Hinged items.

Perf. 13½x13
1974, Feb. 25 **Photo.** **Wmk. 353**
Size: 20x28mm
O72 O3 5d vio & lilac 20 25
O73 O3 10d mag & grnsh bl 20 25
O74 O3 50d org & lt green 20 20
O75 O3 1r green & gold 32 20
O76 O3 2r emerald & org 50 20

Perf. 13
Size: 23x37mm
O77 O3 6r slate grn & org 55 20
O78 O3 8r ultra & yellow 70 20
O79 O3 10r dk bl & lilac 3.00 25
O80 O3 11r pur & light bl 1.25 25
O81 O3 14r red & lt ultra 1.25 60
O82 O3 20r vio blue & org 2.50 50
O83 O3 50r dk brn & brt grn 6.50 1.75
Nos. O72-O83 (12) 17.17 4.85

1977-79 **Wmk. 353** *Perf. 13½x13*
Size: 20x28mm
O87 O3 1r black & lt grn 18 15
O88 O3 2r brown & gray 30 15
O89 O3 3r ultra & orange 32 15
O90 O3 5r green & rose 38 15

Perf. 13
Size: 23x37mm
O91 O3 6r dk bl & lt bl ('78) 45 45
O92 O3 8r red & bl grn ('78) 50 50
O93 O3 10r dk grn & yel grn 75 25
O94 O3 11r dk blue & brt yellow ('79) 75 50
O95 O3 14r dl grn & gray 90 50
O96 O3 15r bl & rose lil ('78) 1.00 1.00
O97 O3 20r purple & yel 1.50 40
O98 O3 30r brn & ocher ('78) 2.00 1.25
O99 O3 50r blk & gold ('78) 4.00 1.25
Nos. O87-O99 (13) 13.03 6.70

NEWSPAPER STAMP

No. 429 Overprinted

Imprimés

1909 **Typo.** **Unwmk.** *Perf. 12½*
P1 A26 2c gray, *blue* 15.00 10.00

PARCEL POST STAMPS

Colis Postaux

Colis Postaux

Regular issues of 1907-08 (types A26, A29) with the handstamps above in blue, black or green are of questionable status as issued stamps.

Regular Issue of 1915 Overprinted in Black

COLIS POSTAUX

1915 **Wmk. 161** *Perf. 11, 11½*
Q19 A33 1c car & indigo 2.00 2.00
Q20 A33 2c bl & carmine 2.00 2.00
Q21 A33 3c dark green 2.00 2.00
Q22 A33 5c red 2.00 2.00
Q23 A33 6c ol green & car 2.00 2.00
Q24 A33 9c yel brn & vio 2.00 2.00
Q25 A33 10c bl grn & yel brn 2.00 2.00
Q26 A33 12c ultramarine 2.00 2.00
Q27 A34 1k multicolored 5.00 5.00
Q28 A33 24c multicolored 3.00 3.00
Q29 A34 2k multicolored 5.00 5.00
Q30 A34 3k multicolored 5.00 5.00
Q31 A34 5k multicolored 5.00 5.00
Q32 A35 1t multicolored 7.00 7.00
Q33 A35 2t gold, grn & brn 7.00 7.00
Q34 A35 3t multicolored 9.00 9.00
Q35 A35 5t multicolored 10.00 10.00
Nos. Q19-Q35 (17) 72.00 72.00

Coronation of Shah Ahmed.
Reprints have dull rather than shiny overprint.
Value, set, $16.

Catalogue values for unused stamps in this section, from this point to the end of the section, are for Never Hinged items.

Post Horn — PP1

Black frame and "IRAN" (reversed) are printed on back of Nos. Q36-Q65, to show through when stamp is attached to parcel.

1958 **Wmk. 306** **Typo.** *Perf. 12½*
Q36 PP1 50d olive bis 15 15
Q37 PP1 1r carmine 15 15
Q38 PP1 2r blue 30 15
a. Imperf., pair 32.50
Q39 PP1 3r green 30 15
Q40 PP1 5r purple 70 15
Q41 PP1 10r orange brn 2.75 20
Q42 PP1 20r dp orange 2.75 20
Q43 PP1 30r lilac 3.75 1.40
Q44 PP1 50r dk carmine 4.50 1.75
Q45 PP1 100r yellow 11.00 2.25
Q46 PP1 200r light grn 19.00 4.50
Nos. Q36-Q46 (11) 45.35 11.05

1961-66 **Wmk. 316**
Q51 PP1 5r purple ('66) 1.00 25
Q52 PP1 10r org brn ('62) 3.00 50
Q53 PP1 20r orange 2.75 1.00
Q54 PP1 30r red lil ('63) 4.00 1.50
Q55 PP1 50r dk car ('63) 5.00 2.50
Q56 PP1 100r yellow ('64) 24.00 5.00
Q57 PP1 200r emer ('64) 20.00 10.00
Nos. Q51-Q57 (7) 59.75 20.75

1967-74 **Wmk. 353**
Q58 PP1 2r blue ('74) 15 15
Q59 PP1 5r dk pur ('69) 20 15
Q60 PP1 10r orange brn 40 25
Q61 PP1 20r orange ('69) 2.00 50
Q62 PP1 30r red lilac 1.50 25
Q63 PP1 50r red brn ('68) 2.00 1.25
Q64 PP1 100r yellow 3.50 1.50
Q65 PP1 200r emerald ('69) 6.00 5.00
Nos. Q58-Q65 (8) 15.75 9.05

POSTAL TAX STAMPS

Red Lion and Sun Emblem — PT1

1950 **Unwmk.** **Litho.** *Perf. 11*
RA1 PT1 50d grn & car rose 8.50 40
RA2 PT1 2r vio & lil rose 4.00 40

1955 **Wmk. 306**
RA3 PT1 50d emer & car rose 50.00 5.00

Catalogue values for unused stamps in this section, from this point to the end of the section, are for Never Hinged items.

1957-58 **Wmk. 316**
RA4 PT1 50d emer & rose lil 1.50 30
RA5 PT1 2r vio & car rose ('58) 2.50 1.00

1965 **Wmk. 349** *Perf. 10½*
RA6 PT1 50d emer & car rose 1.50 45
RA7 PT1 2r vio & lil rose 2.00 60

1965-66 **Wmk. 353**
RA8 PT1 50d emer & car rose (I) 1.00 15
a. Type II 3.00 20
RA9 PT1 2r vio & car rose ('66) 3.00 35

No. RA8 was printed in two types: I. Without diagonal line before Persian "50." II. With line.

1976, Sept.-78 **Photo.** *Perf. 13x13½*
RA10 PT1 50d emerald & red 2.50 25
RA11 PT1 2r slate & red ('78) 2.50 25

Nos. RA10-RA11 are redrawn and have vertical watermark.

Nos. RA1-RA11 were obligatory on all mail. 50d stamps were for registered mail, 2r stamps for parcel post. The tax was for hospitals.
The 2.25r and 2.50r of type PT1 were used only on telegrams.

IRAQ

LOCATION — In western Asia, bounded on the north by Syria and Turkey, on the east by Iran, on the south by Saudi Arabia, and on the west by Jordan
GOVT. — Republic
AREA — 167,925 sq. mi.
POP. — 12,029,700 (est. 1982)
CAPITAL — Baghdad

Iraq, formerly Mesopotamia, a province of Turkey, was mandated to Great Britain in 1920. The mandate was terminated in 1932. For earlier issues, see Mesopotamia.

16 Annas = 1 Rupee.
1000 Fils = 1 Dinar (1932)

Catalogue values for unused stamps in this country are for Never Hinged items, beginning with Scott 79 in the regular postage section, Scott C1 in the air post section, Scott CO1 in the air post official section, Scott O90 in the officials section, Scott RA1 in the postal tax section, and Scott RAC1 in the air post postal tax section.

Issues under British Mandate

Sunni Mosque — A1

Gufas on the Tigris — A2

Assyrian Winged Bull — A4

Ctesiphon Arch — A5

Motif of Assyrian Origin — A3

Colors of the Dulaim Camel Corps — A6

Golden Shiah Mosque of Kadhimain — A7

Conventionalized Date Palm or "Tree of Life" — A8

1923-25 Engr. Wmk. 4 ***Perf. 12***

1	A1	½a olive grn	15	15
2	A2	1a brown	25	15
3	A3	1½a car lake	18	15
4	A4	2a brown org	20	15
5	A5	3a dp blue	20	15
6	A6	4a dull vio	25	18
7	A7	6a blue grn	30	15
8	A6	8a olive bis	50	20
9	A8	1r grn & brn	2.50	70
10	A1	2r black	15.00	12.50
11	A1	2r bister ('25)	7.00	1.50
12	A6	5r orange	22.50	12.00
13	A7	10r carmine	50.00	20.00
		Nos. 1-13 (13)	99.03	47.98

For overprints, see Nos. O1-O24, O42, O47, O51-O53.

King Faisal I — A9

1927

14	A9	1r red brown	4.00	1.00

See No. 27. For overprint and surcharges, see Nos. 43, O25, O54.

King Faisal I
A10 A11

1931

15	A10	½a green	15	15
16	A10	1a chestnut	15	15
17	A10	1½a carmine	30	25
18	A10	2a orange	20	15
19	A10	3a light blue	20	15
20	A10	4a pur brown	75	60
21	A10	6a Prus blue	1.00	18
22	A10	8a dark green	2.75	30
23	A11	1r dark brown	3.00	1.25
24	A11	2r yel brown	7.50	1.25
25	A11	5r dp orange	35.00	20.00
26	A11	10r red	70.00	70.00
27	A9	25r violet	750.00	1,000.
		Nos. 15-27 (13)	871.00	1,094.

For overprints, see Nos. O26-O41, O43-O46, O48-O50, O54.

Issues of the Kingdom

Nos. 6, 15-27 Surcharged in "Fils" or "Dinars" in Red, Black or Green:

3 Fils ٣ فلس
a

25Fils ٢٥ فلس
b

100Fils ١٠٠ فلس
c

1 Dinar ١ دينار
d

1932, Apr. 1

28	A10(a)	2f on ½a (R)	15	15
29	A10(a)	3f on ½a	15	15
a.		Double surcharge	250.00	
b.		Inverted surcharge	*250.00*	
30	A10(a)	4f on 1a (G)	15	15
31	A10(a)	5f on 1a	15	15
a.		Double surcharge	250.00	
b.		Inverted Arabic "5"	*50.00*	*60.00*
32	A10(a)	8f on 1½a	25	22
a.		Inverted surcharge	*200.00*	
33	A10(a)	10f on 2a	18	15
34	A10(a)	15f on 3a	35	22
35	A10(a)	20f on 4a	1.25	65
36	A6(b)	25f on 4a	65	65
a.		"Flis" for "Fils"	*550.00*	*650.00*
b.		Inverted Arabic "5"	*550.00*	*650.00*
37	A10(a)	30f on 6a	65	65
38	A10(a)	40f on 8a	1.25	1.25
39	A11(c)	75f on 1r	2.50	1.25
40	A11(c)	100f on 2r	5.00	1.75
41	A11(c)	200f on 5r	12.50	8.00
42	A11(d)	½d on 10r	50.00	32.50
a.		Bar in "½" omitted	*675.00*	*750.00*
43	A9(d)	1d on 25r	110.00	110.00
		Nos. 28-43 (16)	185.18	157.89

King Faisal I
A12 A13

A14

Values in "Fils" and "Dinars"

1932, May 9 Engr.

44	A12	2f ultra	15	15
45	A12	3f green	15	15
46	A12	4f vio brown	15	15
47	A12	5f gray green	15	15
48	A12	8f deep red	15	15
49	A12	10f yellow	15	15
50	A12	15f deep blue	80	15
51	A12	20f orange	50	18
52	A12	25f rose lilac	1.65	15
53	A12	30f olive grn	50	15
54	A12	40f dark vio	2.25	1.00
55	A13	50f deep brown	55	25
56	A13	75f lt ultra	1.65	1.50
57	A13	100f deep green	2.75	35
58	A13	200f dark red	6.75	75
59	A14	½d gray blue	27.50	8.25
60	A14	1d claret	55.00	55.00
		Nos. 44-60 (17)	100.80	68.63

For overprints, see Nos. O55-O71.

A15

A16

King Ghazi — A17

1934-38 Unwmk.

61	A15	1f purple ('38)	15	15
62	A15	2f ultra	15	15
63	A15	3f green	15	15
64	A15	4f pur brown	15	15
65	A15	5f gray green	15	15
66	A15	8f deep red	18	15
67	A15	10f yellow	20	15
68	A15	15f deep blue	20	15
69	A15	20f orange	25	15
70	A15	25f brown vio	50	25
71	A15	30f olive grn	50	15
72	A15	40f dark vio	75	20
73	A16	50f deep brown	80	20
74	A16	75f ultra	1.10	30
75	A16	100f deep green	1.75	35
76	A16	200f dark red	3.75	60
77	A17	½d gray blue	12.50	7.50
78	A17	1d claret	25.00	10.00
		Nos. 61-78 (18)	48.23	20.90

For overprints, see Nos. 226, O72-O89.

Catalogue values for unused stamps in this section, from this point to the end of the section, are for Never Hinged items.

Sitt Zubaidah Mosque — A18

Mausoleum of King Faisal I — A19

Lion of Babylon — A20

Malwiye of Samarra (Spiral Tower) — A21

Oil Wells — A22

Mosque of the Golden Dome, Samarra — A23

Perf. 14, 13½, 12½, 12x13½, 13½x12, 14x13½

1941-42 Engr.

79	A18	1f dark vio ('42)	15	15
80	A18	2f chocolate ('42)	15	15
81	A19	3f brt green ('42)	15	15
82	A19	4f purple ('42)	15	15
83	A19	5f dk car rose ('42)	15	15
84	A20	8f carmine	40	25
85	A20	8f ocher ('42)	15	15
86	A20	10f ocher	8.00	40
87	A20	10f carmine ('42)	15	15
88	A20	15f dull blue	50	20
89	A20	15f black ('42)	15	15
90	A20	20f black	3.00	45
91	A20	20f dull blue ('42)	15	15
92	A21	25f dark violet	20	20
93	A21	30f deep orange	20	20
94	A21	40f brn orange	2.00	30
95	A21	40f chnt ('42)	75	15
96	A21	50f ultra	40	20
97	A21	75f rose vio	60	25
98	A22	100f ol green ('42)	1.00	30
99	A22	200f deep org ('42)	4.00	65
100	A23	½d lt bl, perf. 12x13½ ('42)	7.00	1.00
a.		Perf. 14	6.00	2.50
101	A23	1d grnsh bl ('42)	15.00	6.50
		Nos. 79-101 (23)	44.40	12.40

Nos. 92-95 measure 17¾x21½mm, Nos. 96-97 measure 21x24mm.

For overprints see #O90-O114, O165, RA5.

King Faisal II
A24 A25

Photo.; Frame Litho.

1942 ***Perf. 13 x 13½***

102	A24	1f violet & brown	15	15
103	A24	2f dk blue & brown	15	15
104	A24	3f lt green & brown	15	15
105	A24	4f dull brown & brn	15	15
106	A24	5f sage green & brn	15	15
107	A24	6f red orange & brn	15	15
108	A24	10f dl rose red & lt brn	15	15
109	A24	12f yel green & brown	18	15
		Set value	77	55

For overprints, see Nos. O115-O122.

Perf. 11½x12

1948, Jan. 15 Engr. Unwmk.

Size: 17¾x20½mm

110	A25	1f slate	15	15
111	A25	2f sepia	15	15
112	A25	3f emerald	15	15
113	A25	4f purple	15	15
114	A25	5f rose lake	15	15
115	A25	6f plum	15	15
116	A25	8f ocher	1.50	15
117	A25	10f rose red	15	15
118	A25	12f dark olive	15	15
119	A25	15f black	1.50	15
120	A25	20f blue	15	15
121	A25	25f rose violet	15	15
122	A25	30f red orange	18	15
123	A25	40f orange brn	25	15

Perf. 12x11½

Size: 22x27½mm

124	A25	60f deep blue	75	15
125	A25	75f lilac rose	1.25	25
126	A25	100f olive green	2.00	35
127	A25	200f deep orange	3.00	45
128	A25	½d blue	10.00	2.00
129	A25	1d green	25.00	10.00
		Nos. 110-129 (20)	46.93	15.30

Sheets of 6 exist, perforated and imperforate, containing Nos. 112, 117, 120 and 125-127, with arms and Arabic inscription in blue green in upper and lower margins. Value each, $25.

See Nos. 133-138. For overprints, see Nos. 188-194, O123-O142, O166-O177, O257, O272, O274, O277, O282, RA1-RA4, RA6.

Post Rider and King Ghazi — A26

Designs: 40f, Equestrian statue & Faisal I. 50f, UPU symbols & Faisal II.

1949, Nov. 1 *Perf. 13x13½*

130 A26 20f blue 32 25
131 A26 40f red orange 65 25
132 A26 50f purple 1.25 50

75th anniv. of the UPU.

Type of 1948

1950-51 Unwmk. *Perf. 11½x12*

Size: 17¾x20½mm

133 A25 3f rose lake 3.00 20
134 A25 5f emerald 5.00 28
135 A25 14f dk olive ('50) 55 15
136 A25 16f rose red 2.00 28
137 A25 28f blue 1.00 28

Perf. 12x11½

Size: 22x27½mm

138 A25 50f deep blue ('50) 1.50 35
Nos. 133-138 (6) 13.05 1.54

For overprints, see Nos. 160, O143-O148, O258, O273, O275-O276.

King Faisal II
A27 A28

1953, May 2 Engr. *Perf. 12*

139 A27 3f deep rose car 25 15
140 A27 14f olive 50 15
141 A27 28f blue 1.00 30
b. Souv. sheet of 3, #139-141 60.00 40.00
Set value 50

Coronation of King Faisal II, May 2, 1953.

1954-57 *Perf. 11½x12*

Size: 18x20½mm

141A A28 1f blue ('56) 15 15
142 A28 2f chocolate 15 15
143 A28 3f rose lake 15 15
144 A28 4f violet 15 15
145 A28 5f emerald 15 15
146 A28 6f plum 15 15
147 A28 8f ocher 15 15
148 A28 10f blue 15 15
149 A28 15f black 15 15
149A A28 16f brt rose ('57) 2.25 1.00
150 A28 20f olive 20 15
151 A28 25f rose vio ('55) 35 15
152 A28 30f ver ('55) 50 15
153 A28 40f orange brn 30 15

Size: 22x27½mm

154 A28 50f blue 75 15
155 A28 75f pink 1.25 35
156 A28 100f olive green 1.50 75
157 A28 200f orange 6.00 1.00
Nos. 141A-157 (18) 14.45
Set value 4.00

For overprints, see Nos. 158-159, 195-209, 674, 676, 678, O148A-O161A, O178-O191, O259-O260, O283-O291.

No. 143, 148 and 137 Overprinted in Black

الغاء المعاهدة ٦/٤/٥٥

1955, Apr. 6 *Perf. 11½x12*

158 A28 3f rose lake 15 15
159 A28 10f blue 25 15
160 A25 28f blue 45 30

Abrogation of Anglo-Iraq treaty of 1930.

King Faisal II — A29

1955, Nov. 26 *Perf. 13½x13*

161 A29 3f rose lake 15 15
162 A29 10f light ultra 20 15
163 A29 28f blue 55 45

6th Arab Engineers' Conf., Baghdad, 1955.
For surcharge see No. 227.

Faisal II and Globe — A30

1956, Mar. 3 *Perf. 13x13½*

164 A30 3f rose lake 15 15
165 A30 10f light ultra 25 15
166 A30 28f blue 50 20
Set value 35

Arab Postal Conf., Baghdad, Mar. 3.
For overprint see #173. For surcharge see #251.

Mechanical Loom — A31

Designs: 3f, Dam. 5f, Modern city development. 10f, Pipeline. 40f, Tigris Bridge.

1957, Apr. 8 Photo. *Perf. 11½*

Granite Paper

167 A31 1f Prus bl & org yel 15 15
168 A31 3f multicolored 15 15
169 A31 5f multicolored 15 15
170 A31 10f lt bl, ocher & red 28 15
171 A31 40f lt bl, blk & ocher 60 15
Set value 1.10 45

Development Week, 1957. See #185-187.

Fair Emblem — A32

1957, June 1 Unwmk.

Granite Paper

172 A32 10f brown & buff 25 15

Agricultural and Industrial Exhibition, Baghdad, June 1.

No. 166 Overprinted in Red

اليوبيل الفضي للهلال الاحمر
١٩٥٧

1957, Nov. 14 *Perf. 13x13½*

173 A30 28f blue 1.00 1.00
a. Double overprint 200.00 225.00

Iraqi Red Crescent Soc., 25th anniv.

King Faisal II — A33

Perf. 11½x12

1957-58 Unwmk. Engr.

174 A33 1f blue 15 15
175 A33 2f chocolate 15 15
176 A33 3f dark car ('57) 15 15
177 A33 4f dull violet 15 15
177A A33 5f emerald 1.00 1.50
178 A33 6f plum 15 20
179 A33 8f ocher 35 30
180 A33 10f blue 15 15
Nos. 174-180 (8) 2.25 2.75

Higher denominations exist without Republic overprint. They were probably not regularly issued. See note below No. 225.

For overprints see Nos. 210-225, 675, O162-O164, O192-O199, O292-O294. For types overprinted see #677, 679, O261, O295.

Tanks — A34

King Faisal II — A35

Army Day, Jan. 6: 10f, Marching soldiers. 20f, Artillery and planes.

1958, Jan. 6 *Perf. 13x13½*

181 A34 8f green & black 30 15
182 A34 10f brown & black 40 20
183 A34 20f blue & red brown 50 15
184 A35 30f car & purple 80 30

Type of 1957

Designs: 3f, Sugar beet, bag and refining machinery (vert.). 5f, Farm. 10f, Dervendi Khan dam.

1958, Apr. 26 Photo. *Perf. 11½*

Granite Paper

185 A31 3f gray vio, grn & lt gray 15 15
186 A31 5f multicolored 18 15
187 A31 10f multicolored 35 25

Development Week, 1958.

Republic

Stamps of 1948-51 Overprinted

الجمهورية
العراقية

Perf. 11½x12, 12x11½

1958 Engr. Unwmk.

Size: 17¾x20½mm

188 A25 12f dark olive 20 15
189 A25 14f olive 30 20
190 A25 16f rose red 3.50 2.25
191 A25 28f blue 1.00 45

Size: 22x27½mm

192 A25 60f deep blue 1.25 45
193 A25 ½d blue 10.00 3.25
194 A25 1d green 22.50 11.00
Nos. 188-194 (7) 38.75 17.75

Other denominations of type A25 exist with this overprint, but these were probably not regularly issued.

Same Overprint on Stamps of 1954-57

Size: 18x20½mm

195 A28 1f blue 15 15
196 A28 2f chocolate 15 15
196A A28 4f violet 15 15
196B A28 5f emerald 18 18
197 A28 6f plum 18 15
198 A28 8f ocher 20 20
199 A28 10f blue 24 15
200 A28 15f black 28 15
201 A28 16f bright rose 1.10 35
202 A28 20f olive 40 40
203 A28 25f rose violet 24 18
204 A28 30f vermilion 40 25
205 A28 40f orange brn 48 20

Size: 22½x27½mm

206 A28 50f blue 2.75 2.00
207 A28 75f pink 1.50 1.50
208 A28 100f olive green 2.25 2.00
209 A28 200f orange 7.25 4.00
Nos. 195-209 (17) 17.90 12.16

The lines of this overprint are found transposed on Nos. 195, 196 and 199.

Same Overprint on Stamps and Type of 1957-58

Size: 18x20mm

210 A33 1f blue 15 15
211 A33 2f chocolate 15 15
212 A33 3f dark carmine 18 18
213 A33 4f dull violet 15 15
214 A33 5f emerald 15 15
215 A33 6f plum 15 15
216 A33 8f ocher 15 15
217 A33 10f blue 18 15
218 A33 20f olive 18 15
219 A33 25f rose violet 55 55
220 A33 30f vermilion 70 15
221 A33 40f orange brn 2.25 90

Size: 22x27½mm

222 A33 50f rose violet 1.75 50
223 A33 75f olive 4.50 90
224 A33 100f orange 3.75 90
225 A33 200f blue 6.50 1.40
Nos. 210-225 (16) 21.44 6.68

#218-225 were not issued without overprint.

The lines of this overprint are found transposed on Nos. 210 and 214.
Many errors of overprint exist of #188-226.
For overprint see No. O198.

Same Overprint on No. 78

Perf. 12

226 A17 1d claret 17.50 14.00

No. 163 Surcharged in Red

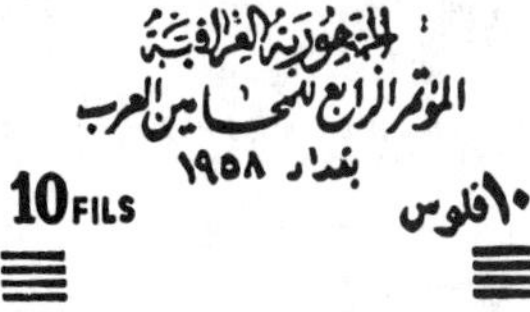

1958, Nov. 26 *Perf. 13x13½*

227 A29 10f on 28f blue 50 25

Arab Lawyers' Conf., Baghdad, Nov. 26.

Soldier and Flag — A36

1959, Jan. 6 Photo. *Perf. 11½*

228 A36 3f bright blue 15 15
229 A36 10f olive green 15 15
230 A36 40f purple 1.00 35
Set value 50

Issued for Army Day, Jan. 6.

Orange Tree — A37

Emblem of Republic — A38

1959, Mar. 21 Unwmk. *Perf. 11½*

231 A37 10f green, dk grn & org 50 15

Issued for Arbor Day.

1959-60 Litho. & Photo. *Perf. 11½*

Granite Paper

Emblem in Gold, Red and Blue; Blue Inscriptions

232 A38 1f gray 15 15
233 A38 2f salmon 15 15
234 A38 3f pale violet 15 15
235 A38 4f bright yel 15 15
236 A38 5f light blue 15 15
237 A38 10f bright pink 15 15
238 A38 15f light green 15 15
239 A38 20f bister brn 15 15
240 A38 30f light gray 20 15
241 A38 40f orange yel 25 15
242 A38 50f yel green 1.75 15
243 A38 75f pale grn ('60) 60 20
244 A38 100f orange ('60) 1.40 30
245 A38 200f lilac ('60) 2.25 60
246 A38 500f bister ('60) 7.25 1.75
247 A38 1d brt grn ('60) 7.25 3.50
Nos. 232-247 (16) 22.15
Set value 7.00

See Nos. 305A-305B. For overprints see Nos. 252, 293-295, O200-O221.

Worker and Buildings — A39

Victorious Fighters A40

Perf. 12½x13, 13x12½

1959, July 14 **Photo.**

248 A39 10f ocher & blue 28 20
249 A40 30f ocher & emerald 80 50

1st anniv. of the Revolution of July 14 (1958), which overthrew the kingdom.

Harvest — A41

1959, July 14 *Perf. 11½*

250 A41 10f lt grn & dk grn 25 15

No. 166 Surcharged in Dark Red

الجمهورية العراقية
يوم الطفل العالمي
١ حزيران ١٩٥٩
10 FILS ١٠ فلوس

1959, June 1 **Engr.** *Perf. 13x13½*

251 A30 10f on 28f blue 40 28

Issued for Children's Day, 1959.

No. 237 Overprinted

اسبوع
الصحة والنظافة

Litho. and Photo.

1959, Oct. 23 *Perf. 11½*

252 A38 10f multicolored 65 35

Health and Sanitation Week.

Abdul Karim Kassem and Army Band — A42

Abdul Karim Kassem and: 16f, Field maneuvers, horiz. 30f, Antiaircraft. 40f, Troops at attention, flag and bugler. 60f, Fighters and flag, horiz.

1960, Jan. 6 **Photo.** *Perf. 11½*

253 A42 10f blue, grn & mar 15 15
254 A42 16f brt blue & red 45 15
255 A42 30f ol grn, yel & brn 45 20
256 A42 40f deep vio & buff 60 25
257 A42 60f dk brown & buff 1.40 40
Nos. 253-257 (5) 3.05 1.15

Issued for Army Day, Jan. 6.

Prime Minister Abdul Karim Kassem — A43

Maroof el Rasafi — A44

1960, Feb. 1 **Engr.** *Perf. 12½*

258 A43 10f lilac 35 15
259 A43 30f emerald 70 18
Set value 24

Issued to honor Prime Minister Kassem on his recovery from an assassination attempt.

1960, May 10 **Photo.** *Perf. 13½x13*

260 A44 10f maroon & blk 65 65
a. Inverted overprint 75.00 60.00

Exists without overprint.

Symbol of the Republic — A45

Unknown Soldier's Tomb and Kassem with Freedom Torch — A46

1960, July 14 *Perf. 11½*

261 A45 6f ol grn, red & gold 15 15
262 A46 10f green, blue & red 15 15
263 A46 16f vio, blue & red 15 15
264 A45 18f ultra, red & gold 18 15
265 A45 30f brown, red & gold 30 20
266 A46 60f dk brn, bl & red 1.00 40
Nos. 261-266 (6) 1.93
Set value 95

2nd anniv. of the July 14, 1958 revolution.

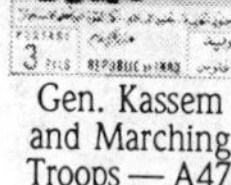

Gen. Kassem and Marching Troops — A47

Gen. Kassem and Arch — A48

1961, Jan. 6 *Perf. 11½*

Granite Paper

267 A47 3f gray ol, emer, yel & gold 15 15
268 A47 6f pur, emer, yel & gold 15 15
269 A47 10f sl, emer, yel & gold 15 15
270 A48 20f bl grn, blk & buff 18 15
271 A48 30f bis brn, blk & buff 35 20
272 A48 40f ultra, black & buff 65 25
Set value 1.30 70

Issued for Army Day, Jan. 6.

Gen. Kassem and Children A49

1961, June 1 **Photo.** **Unwmk.**

Granite Paper

273 A49 3f yellow & brown 15 15
274 A49 6f blue & brown 15 15
275 A49 10f pink & brown 15 15
276 A49 30f yellow & brown 65 20
277 A49 50f lt grn & brown 65 35
Nos. 273-277 (5) 1.75
Set value 70

Issued for World Children's Day.

Gen. Kassem and Flag — A50

Design: 5f, 30f, 40f, Gen. Kassem saluting and flags.

1961, July 14 *Perf. 11½*

Granite Paper

278 A50 1f multicolored 15 15
279 A50 3f multicolored 15 15
280 A50 5f multicolored 15 15
281 A50 6f multicolored 15 15
282 A50 10f multicolored 15 15
283 A50 30f multicolored 42 18
284 A50 40f multicolored 60 22
285 A50 50f multicolored 30 25
286 A50 100f multicolored 4.25 1.65
Nos. 278-286 (9) 6.32
Set value 2.50

3rd anniv. of the July 14, 1958 revolution.

Gen. Kassem and Flag — A51

Gen. Kassem and Symbol of Republic A52

Perf. 11½

1962, Jan. 6 **Unwmk.** **Photo.**

Granite Paper

287 A51 1f multicolored 15 15
288 A51 3f multicolored 15 15
289 A51 6f multicolored 15 15
290 A52 10f blk, lilac & gold 15 15
291 A52 30f black, org & gold 40 18
292 A52 50f blk, pale grn & gold 75 30
Set value 1.35 65

Issued for Army Day, Jan. 6.

Nos. 234, 237 and 240 Overprinted

مؤتمر
العالم الاسلامي
بغداد
١٣٨١هـ-١٩٦٢م

Litho. & Photo.

1962, May 29 *Perf. 11½*

293 A38 3f multicolored 15 15
294 A38 10f multicolored 20 15
295 A38 30f multicolored 80 25
Set value 40

Fifth Islamic Congress.

Hands Across Map of Arabia and North Africa — A53

1962, July 14 **Photo.**

296 A53 1f brn, org, grn & gold 15 15
297 A53 3f brn, yel grn, grn & gold 15 15
298 A53 6f blk, lt brn, grn & gold 15 15
299 A53 10f brn, lil, grn & gold 15 15
300 A53 30f brn, rose, grn & gold 40 20
301 A53 50f brn, gray, grn & gold 75 35
Set value 1.45 75

Revolution of July 14, 1958, 4th anniv.

al-Kindi A54

Emblem of Republic A54a

Designs: 3f, Horsemen with standards and trumpets. 10f, Old map of Baghdad and Tigris. 40f, Gen. Kassem, modern building and flag.

Perf. 14x13½

1962, Dec. 1 **Litho.** **Unwmk.**

302 A54 3f multicolored 15 15
303 A54 6f multicolored 15 15
304 A54 10f multicolored 32 15
305 A54 40f multicolored 90 75
Set value 92

9th century Arab philosopher al-Kindi; millenary of the Round City of Baghdad.

1962, Dec. 20 *Perf. 13½x14*

305A A54a 14f brt green & blk 1.10 25
305B A54a 35f ver & black 1.65 35

Nos. 305A-305B were originally sold affixed to air letter sheets, obliterating the portrait of King Faisal II. They were issued in sheets for general use in 1966.

For overprints, see Nos. RA15-RA16.

Tanks on Parade and Gen. Kassem — A55

Malaria Eradication Emblem — A56

1963, Jan. 6 **Photo.** *Perf. 11½*

306 A55 3f black & yellow 15 15
307 A55 5f brown & plum 15 15
308 A55 6f blk & lt green 15 15
309 A55 10f blk & lt blue 18 15
310 A55 10f black & pink 18 15
311 A55 20f black & ultra 38 15
312 A55 40f blk & rose lilac 55 25
313 A55 50f brn & brt ultra 75 40
Set value 2.15 1.05

Issued for Army Day, Jan. 6.

1962, Dec. 31 *Perf. 14*

Republic Emblem in Red, Blue & Gold

314 A56 3f yel grn, blk & dk grn 15 15
315 A56 10f org, blk & dark blue 20 15
316 A56 40f lilac, black & blue 50 30
Set value 45

WHO drive to eradicate malaria.

Gufas on the Tigris — A57

Shepherd and Sheep — A58

Designs: 2f, 500f, Spiral tower, Samarra. 4f, 15f, Ram's head harp, Ur. 5f, 75f, Map and Republic emblem. 10f, 50f, Lion of Babylon. 20f, 40f, Baghdad University. 30f, 200f, Kadhimain mosque. 100f, 1d, Winged bull, Khorsabad.

Engr.; Engr. and Photo. (bicolored)

1963, Feb. 16 Unwmk. *Perf. 12x11*

317	A57	1f green	15	15
318	A57	2f purple	15	15
319	A57	3f black	15	15
320	A57	4f black & yel	15	15
321	A57	5f lilac & lt grn	15	15
322	A57	10f rose red	15	15
323	A57	15f brn & buff	20	15
324	A57	20f violet blue	20	15
325	A57	30f orange	24	15
326	A57	40f brt green	32	15
327	A57	50f dark brown	3.25	15
328	A57	75f blk & lt grn	1.50	25
329	A57	100f brt lilac	1.50	25
330	A57	200f brown	3.25	75
331	A57	500f blue	5.50	1.75
332	A57	1d deep claret	8.00	3.50
		Nos. 317-332 (16)	24.86	
		Set value		7.00

For overprints, see Nos. RA7-RA12.

1963, Mar. 21 Litho. *Perf. 13½x14*

Designs: 10f, Man holding sheaf. 20f, Date palm grove.

333	A58	3f emerald & gray	15	20
334	A58	10f dp brn & lil rose	15	25
335	A58	20f dk bl & red brn	60	42
a.		Souv. sheet of 3, #333-335	3.00	

FAO "Freeom from Hunger" campaign. No. 335a sold for 50f.

No. 335a was overprinted in 1970 in black to commemorate the UN 25th anniv. Denominations on the 3 stamps were obliterated, leaving "Price 50 Fils" in the margin.

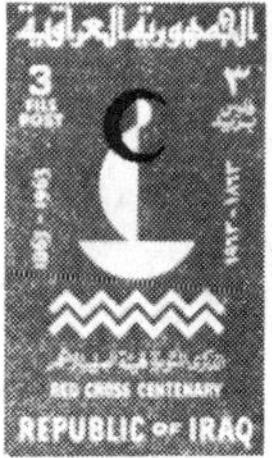

Cent. Emblem — A59

Rifle, Helmet and Flag — A60

Design: 30f, Iraqi Red Crescent Society Headquarters, horiz.

Perf. 11x11½, 11½x11

1963, Dec. 30 Photo.

336	A59	3f violet & red	15	15
337	A59	10f gray & red	15	15
338	A59	30f blue & red	50	20
		Set value		35

Centenary of International Red Cross.

1964, Jan. 6 Unwmk. *Perf. 11½*

Granite Paper

339	A60	3f brn, blue & emer	15	15
340	A60	10f brn, pink & emer	25	15
341	A60	30f brown, yel & emer	50	15
		Set value		35

Issued for Army Day, Jan. 6.

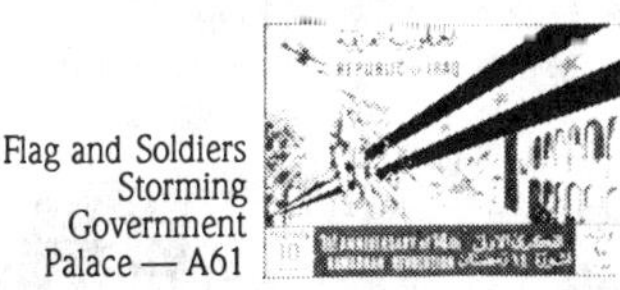
Flag and Soldiers Storming Government Palace — A61

1964, Feb. 8 *Perf. 11½*

Granite Paper

342	A61	10f pur, red, grn & blk	15	15
343	A61	30f red brn, red, grn & blk	40	18
a.		Souv. sheet of 2, imperf	4.25	2.75
b.		Souv. sheet of 2 (4th anniv.) ('67)	4.25	2.75
		Set value		24

Revolution of Ramadan 14, 1st anniv. #343a contains stamps similar to #342-343 in changed colors (10f olive, red, green & black; 30f ultra, red, green & black). Sold for 50f.

No. 343b consists of various block-outs and overprints on No. 343a. It commemorates the 4th anniv. of the Revolution of Ramadan 14. Sold for 70f. Issued Feb. 8, 1967.

Hammurabi and a God from Stele in Louvre A62

Design: 10f, UN emblem and scales.

1964, June 10 Litho. *Perf. 13½*

344	A62	6f lilac & pale grn	15	15
345	A62	10f org & vio blue	20	15
346	A62	30f blue & pale grn	70	25
		Set value		45

15th anniv. (in 1963) of the Universal Declaration of Human Rights.

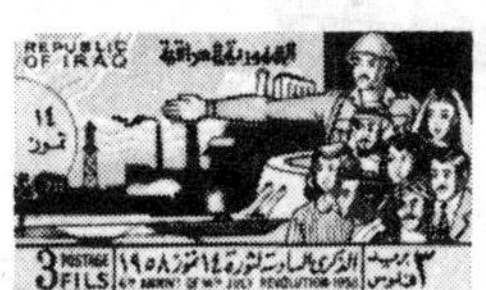

"Industrialization of Iraq" — A63

Soldier Planting New Flag — A64

1964, July 14 *Perf. 11*

347	A63	3f gray, org & black	15	15
348	A64	10f rose red, blk & emer	15	15
349	A64	20f rose red, blk & emer	35	15
350	A63	30f gray, org & black	70	20
		Set value		46

6th anniv. of the July 14, 1958 revolution.

Star and Fighters A65

1964, Nov. 18 Photo. *Perf. 11½*

351	A65	5f sepia & orange	15	15
352	A65	10f lt bl & orange	15	15
353	A65	50f vio & red orange	65	30

Revolution of Nov. 18, 1963, 1st anniv.

Musician with Lute — A66

Perf. 13x13½

1964, Nov. 28 Litho. Unwmk.

354	A66	3f bister & multi	65	45
355	A66	10f dl grn & multi	65	45
356	A66	30f dl rose & multi	90	65

International Arab Music Conference.

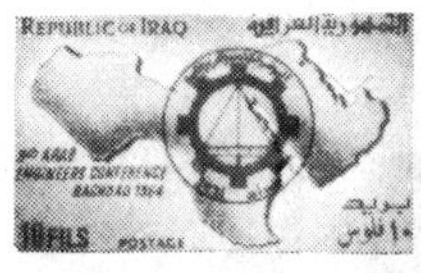
Map of Arab Countries and Emblem A67

1964, Dec. 13 *Perf. 12½x14*

357	A67	10f lt grn & rose lilac	35	15

9th Arab Engineers' Conference, Baghdad.

Arab Postal Union Emblem — A67a

Soldier, Flag and Rising Sun — A68

1964, Dec. 21 Photo. *Perf. 11*

358	A67a	3f sal pink & blue	15	15
359	A67a	10f brt red lil & brn	15	15
360	A67a	30f orange & blue	75	25
		Set value		36

10th anniv. of Permanent Office of Arab Postal Union.

For overprint, see No. 707.

Perf. 14x12½

1965, Jan. 6 Litho. Unwmk.

361	A68	5f dull green & multi	15	15
362	A68	15f henna brn & multi	15	15
363	A68	30f black brn & multi	60	20
		Set value		36

Issued for Army Day, Jan. 6.

An imperf. souvenir sheet carries a revised No. 363 with "30 FILS" omitted, and a portrait of Pres. Abdul Salam Arif. Violet inscriptions including "PRICE 60 FILS."

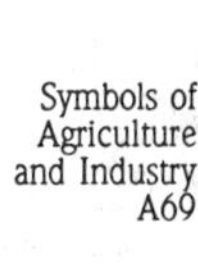

Symbols of Agriculture and Industry A69

1965, Jan. 8 *Perf. 12½x14*

364	A69	10f ultra, brn & blk	25	15

Arab Labor Ministers' Conference.

Tanker A70

1965, Jan. 30 *Perf. 14*

365	A70	10f multicolored	25	15

Inauguration (in 1962) of the deep sea terminal for oil tankers.

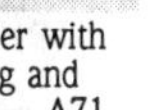
Soldier with Flag and Rifle — A71

Tree Week — A72

1965, Feb. 8 Litho. *Perf. 13½*

366	A71	10f multicolored	25	15

Revolution of Ramadan 14, 2nd anniv.

1965, Mar. 6 Unwmk. *Perf. 13*

367	A72	6f multicolored	15	15
368	A72	20f multicolored	75	15
		Set value		20

Federation Emblem — A73

Dagger in Map of Palestine — A74

1965, Mar. 24 Unwmk. *Perf. 14*

369	A73	3f lt bl, vio bl & gold	15	15
370	A73	10f gray, black & gold	15	15
371	A73	30f rose, car & gold	30	30
		Set value	41	41

Arab Federation of Insurance.

1965, Apr. 9 Litho. *Perf. 14x12½*

372	A74	10f gray & black	15	15
373	A74	20f lt brn & dk blue	25	15
		Set value		18

Deir Yassin massacre, Apr. 9, 1948.

Smallpox Attacking People A75

1965, Apr. 30 Litho. *Perf. 14*

374	A75	3f multicolored	15	15
375	A75	10f multicolored	22	15
376	A75	20f multicolored	65	25

WHO's fight against smallpox. Exist imperf. Value $2.

ITU Emblem, Old and New Telecommunication Equipment — A76

1965, May 17 *Perf. 14, Imperf.*

377	A76	10f multicolored	30	18
378	A76	20f multicolored	75	15
a.		Souv. sheet of 2, #377-378	5.00	5.75

ITU, centenary. No. 378a sold for 40 and exists imperf.

Map of Arab Countries and Banner — A77

1965, May 26 Litho. *Perf. 14x12½*
379 A77 10f multicolored 25 15

Anniversary of the treaty with the UAR.

Library Aflame and Lamp A78

1965, June Photo. *Perf. 11*
380 A78 5f black, grn & red 25 15
381 A78 10f blk, green & red 40 15
Set value 15

Burning of the Library of Algiers, June 2, 1962.

Revolutionist with Torch, Cannon and Flames — A79

1965, June 30 Litho. *Perf. 13*
382 A79 5f multicolored 15 15
383 A79 10f multicolored 20 15
Set value 15

45th anniversary, Revolution of 1920.

Mosque — A80

1965, July 12 Photo. *Perf. 12*
384 A80 10f multicolored 25 15

Prophet Mohammed's birthday. A souvenir sheet contains one imperf. stamp similar to No. 384. Sold for 50f. Value $5

Factories and Grain — A81

Arab Fair Emblem — A82

1965, July 14 Litho. *Perf. 13*
385 A81 10f multicolored 15 15

7th anniv. of the July 14, 1958 Revolution.

1965, Oct. 22 Unwmk. *Perf. 13*
386 A82 10f multicolored 15 15

Second Arab Fair, Baghdad.

Pres. Abdul Salam Mohammed Arif — A83

1965, Nov. 18 Photo. *Perf. 11½*
Granite Paper
387 A83 5f org, buff & dk blue 22 15
388 A83 10f lt ultra, gray & dk brn 30 15
389 A83 50f lil, pale pink & sl blk 1.40 60

Revolution of Nov. 18, 1963, 2nd anniv.

Census Chart and Adding Machine — A84

1965, Nov. 29 Litho. *Perf. 13*
390 A84 3f gray & plum 28 15
391 A84 5f brown red & brn 35 15
392 A84 15f olive bis & dl bl 70 15
Set value 24

Issued to publicize the 1965 census.

Date Palms — A85

Soldiers' Monument — A86

1965, Dec. 27 Litho. *Perf. 13½x14*
393 A85 3f olive bis & multi 16 15
394 A85 10f car rose & multi 32 20
395 A85 15f blue & multi 80 30

2nd FAO Intl. Dates Conference, Baghdad, Dec. 1965.

For surcharges, see Nos. 694, 695.

1966, Jan. 6 Photo. *Perf. 12*
396 A86 2f car rose & multi 15 15
397 A86 5f multicolored 20 15
398 A86 40f yel grn & multi 1.10 75
Set value 85

Issued for Army Day.

Eagle and Flag of Iraq — A87

Perf. 12½
1966, Feb. 8 Photo. Unwmk.
399 A87 5f dl bl & multi 20 15
400 A87 10f orange & multi 40 15
Set value 15

3rd anniv. of the Revolution of Ramadan 14, which overthrew the Kassem government.

Arab League Emblem — A88

Soccer Players — A89

1966, Mar. 22 *Perf. 11x11½*
401 A88 5f org, brn & brt grn 15 15
402 A88 15f ol, rose lil & ultra 40 15

Arab Publicity Week.

1966, Apr. 1 *Perf. 12*

Designs: 5f, Player and goal post. 15f, As 2f. 50f, Legs of player, ball and emblem, horiz.

403 A89 2f multicolored 28 15
404 A89 5f multicolored 15 15
405 A89 15f multicolored 90 45

Miniature Sheet
Imperf
406 A89 50f vio & multi 4.25 10.50

3rd Arab Soccer Cup, Baghdad, Apr. 1-10.

Steam Shovel Within Cogwheel A90

1966, May 1 Litho. *Perf. 13½*
407 A90 15f multicolored 15 15
408 A90 25f red, blk, & sil 25 15
Set value 18

Issued for Labor Day, May 1, 1966.

Queen Nefertari — A91

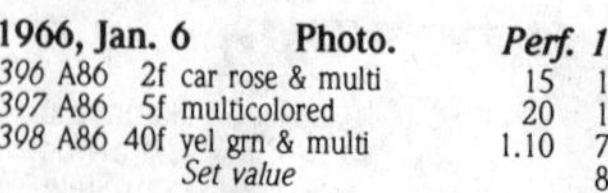

Facade of Abu Simbel A92

Perf. 12½x13, 13½
1966, May 20 Litho.
409 A91 5f olive, yel & blk 15 15
410 A91 15f blue, yel & brn 18 15
411 A92 40f bis brn, red & blk 1.25 1.00

UNESCO world campaign to save historic monuments in Nubia.

President Arif and Flag — A93

1966, July 14 Photo. *Perf. 11½*
412 A93 5f multicolored 15 15
413 A93 15f multicolored 25 15
414 A93 50f multicolored 75 25
Set value 42

8th anniv. of the July 14, 1958 revolution.

A94

1966, July 22 Litho. *Perf. 12*
Multicolored Vignette
415 A94 5f lt olive green 15 15
416 A94 15f lt greenish blue 15 15
417 A94 30f lt yellow green 25 18
Set value 40 30

Mohammed's 1,396th birthday.

Iraqi Museum, Baghdad — A95

Designs: 50f, Golden headdress, Ur. 80f, Carved Sumerian head, vert.

1966, Nov. 9 Litho. *Perf. 14*
418 A95 15f multicolored 22 15
419 A95 50f lt bl, blk, gold & pink 90 50
420 A95 80f crim, blk, bl & gold 2.25 75

Opening of New Iraqi Museum, Baghdad.

UNESCO Emblem — A96

Iraqi Citizens — A97

1966, Dec. *Perf. 13½*
421 A96 5f blue, black & tan 15 15
422 A96 15f brt org brn, blk & gray 15 15
Set value 15 15

20th anniv. of UNESCO.

1966, Nov. 18 *Perf. 13½x13*

423 A97 15f multicolored 40 35
424 A97 25f multicolored 65 85

3rd anniv. of the Revolution of Nov. 18, 1963.

Rocket Launchers and Soldier A98

1967, Jan. 6 **Photo.** *Perf. 11½*

425 A98 15f cit, dk brn & dp bis 20 15
426 A98 20f brt lil, dk brn & dp bis 40 20

Issued for Army Day, Jan. 6.

Oil Derrick, Pipeline, Emblem — A99

Design: 15f, 50f, Refinery and emblem, horiz.

1967, Mar. 6 **Litho.** *Perf. 14*

427 A99 5f ol grn, pale yel & blk 15 15
428 A99 15f multicolored 15 15
429 A99 40f vio, yel & blk 20 16
430 A99 50f multicolored 40 30
Set value 75 58

6th Arab Petroleum Congress, Baghdad, Mar. 1967.

New Year's Emblem and Spider's Web A100

1967, Apr. 11 **Litho.** *Perf. 13½*

431 A100 5f multicolored 15 15
432 A100 15f multicolored 15 15
Set value 15 15

Issued for the Hajeer Year (New Year).

Worker Holding Cogwheel and Map of Arab Countries — A101

1967, May 1 *Perf. 12½x13*

433 A101 10f gray & multi 15 15
434 A101 15f lt ultra & multi 15 15
Set value 16 15

Issued for Labor Day.

A102

1967, June 20 **Litho.** *Perf. 14*

435 A102 5f multicolored 15 15
436 A102 15f blue & multi 25 15
Set value 15

Mohammed's 1,397th birthday.

Flag, Hands with Clubs — A103

1967, July 7 *Perf. 13x13½*

437 A103 5f multicolored 15 15
438 A103 15f multicolored 15 15
Set value 15 15

47th anniversary of Revolution of 1920.

Um Qasr Harbor A104

Designs: 10f, 15f, Freighter loading in Um Qasr harbor.

1967, July 14 **Litho.** *Perf. 14x13½*

439 A104 5f multicolored 15 15
440 A104 10f multicolored 15 15
441 A104 15f multicolored 45 15
442 A104 40f multicolored 1.65 18
Set value 36

9th anniv. of the July 14, 1958 revolution and the inauguration of the port of Um Qasr.

Iraqi Man — A105

President Arif — A106

Iraqi Costumes: 5f, 15f, 25f, Women's costumes. 10f, 20f, 30f, Men's costumes.

1967, Nov. 10 **Litho.** *Perf. 13*

443 A105 2f pale brn & multi 15 15
444 A105 5f ver & multi 15 15
445 A105 10f multicolored 20 15
446 A105 15f ultra & multi 26 15
447 A105 20f lilac & multi 52 18
448 A105 25f lemon & multi 52 20
449 A105 30f fawn & multi 52 26
Nos. 443-449,C19-C21 (10) 6.07
Set value 2.00

For overprints see Nos. 597-599, RA17.

Perf. 11x11½, 11½x11

1967, Nov. 18

Design: 15f, Pres. Arif and map of Iraq, horiz.

450 A106 5f bl, vio blk & yel 15 15
451 A106 15f rose & multi 50 25

4th anniversary of Nov. 18th revolution.

Ziggurat of Ur — A107

Designs: 5f, Gate with Nimrod statues. 10f, Gate, Babylon. 15f, Minaret of Mosul, vert. 25f, Arch and ruins of Ctesiphon.

1967, Dec. 1 **Litho.** *Perf. 13*

452 A107 2f orange & multi 15 15
453 A107 5f lilac & multi 15 15
454 A107 10f orange & multi 15 15
455 A107 15f rose red & multi 28 15
456 A107 25f vio bl & multi 40 15
Nos. 452-456,C22-C26 (10) 32.58 15.87

International Tourist Year.
For overprints, see Nos. 593, 680, RA18.

Iraqi Girl Scout Emblem and Sign — A108

Designs: 5f, Girl Scouts at campfire and Girl Scout emblem. 10f, Boy Scout emblem and Boy Scout sign. 15f, Boy Scouts pitching tent and Boy Scout sign.

1967, Dec. 15

457 A108 2f orange & multi 85 20
458 A108 5f blue & multi 1.00 25
459 A108 10f green & multi 1.10 40
460 A108 15f blue & multi 1.10 50
a. Souv. sheet of 4 5.50 5.50

Issued to honor the Scout movement.
No. 460a contains 4 stamps similar to Nos. 457-460 with simulated perforations. Sold for 50f.
For overprint, see No. RA19.

Soldiers on Maneuvers A109

1968, Jan. 6 **Photo.** *Perf. 11½*

461 A109 5f lt bl, brn & brt grn 15 15
462 A109 15f lt bl, ind & olive 40 15
Set value 15

Issued for Army Day 1968.

White-cheeked Bulbul — A110

Birds: 10f, Hoopoe. 15f, Eurasian jay. 25f, Peregrine falcon. 30f, White stork. 40f, Black partridge. 50f, Marbled teal.

1968, Jan. **Litho.** *Perf. 14*

463 A110 5f org & black 20 15
464 A110 10f blue, blk & brn 25 15
465 A110 15f pink & multi 50 20
466 A110 25f dl org & multi 60 40
467 A110 30f emer, blk & brn 65 20
468 A110 40f rose lil & multi 1.90 20
469 A110 50f multicolored 2.00 45
Nos. 463-469 (7) 6.10 1.75

Fighting Soldiers A111

1968, Feb. 8 *Perf. 11½*

470 A111 15f blk, org & brt bl 1.90 20

Revolution of Ramadan 14, 5th anniv.

Factories, Tractor and Grain A112

1968, May 1 **Litho.** *Perf. 13*

471 A112 15f lt bl & multi 15 15
472 A112 25f multicolored 25 15
Set value 18

Issued for Labor Day.

Soccer — A113

Designs: 5f, 25f, Goalkeeper holding ball, vert.

1968, June 14 *Perf. 13½*

473 A113 2f multicolored 15 15
474 A113 5f multicolored 15 15
475 A113 15f multicolored 22 15
476 A113 25f multicolored 1.50 50
a. Souv. sheet, 70f, imperf. 5.00 8.50
Set value 75

23rd C.I.S.M. (Conseil Internationale du Sports Militaire) Soccer Championships.
No. 476a shows badge of Military Soccer League.

Soldier, Flag, Chain and Rising Sun — A114

1968, July 14 **Photo.** *Perf. 13½x14*

478 A114 15f multicolored 25 15

10th anniv. of the July 14, 1958 revolution.

World Health Organization Emblem — A115

Design: 5f, 10f, Staff of Aesculapius over emblem, vert.

1968, Nov. 29 **Litho.** *Perf. 13½*

479 A115 5f multicolored 15 15
480 A115 10f multicolored 15 15
481 A115 15f blue, red & black 25 15
482 A115 25f yel grn, red & blk 50 15
Set value 30

WHO, 20th anniv. Exist imperf.

Human Rights Flame — A116

Mother and Children — A117

1968, Dec. 22 Litho. *Perf. 13½*

483 A116 10f lt bl, yel & car 15 15
484 A116 25f lt yel grn, yel & car 25 15
a. Souv. sheet, 100f, imperf. 3.00 3.00
Set value 17

International Human Rights Year.

1968, Dec. 31 Litho. *Perf. 13½*

485 A117 15f multi 25 15
486 A117 25f bl & multi 75 15
a. Souv. sheet, 100f, imperf 5.00 3.25
Set value 23

UNICEF. For overprints see Nos. 624-625.

Tanks A118

1969, Jan. 6 Photo.

487 A118 25f vio, car & brn 2.00 1.00

Issued for Army Day, Jan. 6.

Harvester A119

1969, Feb. Photo. *Perf. 13½*

488 A119 15f yel brn & multi 22 15

6th anniv. of the Revolution of Ramadan 14.

Mosque A119a

1969, Mar. 19 Photo. *Perf. 13x13½*

488A A119a 15f multicolored 15 15

Issued for Hajeer (pilgrimage) Year.

Emblem — A120

1969, Apr. 12 Litho. *Perf. 12½x12*

489 A120 10f yel grn & multi 40 15
490 A120 15f orange & multi 60 15

1st conference of the Arab Veterinary Union, Baghdad, Apr. 1969.

Barbus Grypus — A121

Fish: 3f, Barbus puntius sharpeyi. 10f, Pampus argenteus. 100f, Barbus esocinus.

1969, May 9 *Perf. 14*

491 A121 2f multicolored 85 15
492 A121 3f multicolored 85 15
493 A121 10f multicolored 1.00 15
494 A121 100f multicolored 3.25 2.00

Holy Kaaba, Mecca A122

1969, May 28 Photo. *Perf. 12*

495 A122 15f blue & multi 15 15

Mohammed's 1,399th birthday.

ILO Emblem — A123

1969, June 6 Litho. *Perf. 13x12½*

496 A123 5f lt vio, yel & blk 15 15
497 A123 15f grnsh gray, yel & black 20 15
498 A123 50f rose, yel & blk 70 50
a. Souv. sheet, 100f, imperf. 3.00 5.00

ILO, 50th anniv.

Weight Lifting A124

Coat of Arms, Symbols of Industry A125

Design: 5f, 35f, High jump.

1969, June 20 *Perf. 13½x13*

500 A124 3f org yel & multi 15 15
501 A124 5f blue & multi 15 15
502 A124 10f rose pink & multi 20 15
503 A124 35f yellow & multi 70 25
a. Souv. sheet of 4, #500-503, imperf. 6.25 6.25
Set value 1.00 45

19th Olympic Games, Mexico City, Oct. 12-27, 1968. No. 503a sold for 100f.

1969, July 14 Photo. *Perf. 13*

504 A125 10f brn org & multi 20 15
505 A125 15f multicolored 30 15
Set value 15

11th anniv. of the July 14, 1958 revolution.

Street Fighting A126

Pres. Ahmed Hassan al-Bakr A127

Wheat and Fair Emblem A128

Design: 20f, Baghdad International Airport.

1969, July 17 *Perf. 13½*

506 A126 10f yel & multi 28 15
507 A126 15f blue & multi 28 15
508 A126 20f blue & multi 90 25
509 A127 200f gold & multi 9.00 5.00

Coup of July 17, 1968, 1st anniv. #508 also for the inauguration of Baghdad Intl. Airport.

1969, Oct. 1 Photo. *Perf. 13½*

510 A128 10f brt grn, gold & dl red 15 15
511 A128 15f ultra, gold & red 15 15
Set value 20 15

6th International Fair, Baghdad. For overprints see Nos. 567A-567B.

Motor Ship Al-Waleed A129

Designs: 15f, Floating crane Antara. 30f, Pilot ship Al-Rasheed. 35f, Suction dredge Hillah. 50f, Survey ship Al-Fao.

1969, Oct. 8 Litho. *Perf. 12½*

512 A129 15f black & multi 24 18
513 A129 20f black & multi 28 24
514 A129 30f black & multi 48 28
515 A129 35f black & multi 95 55
516 A129 50f black & multi 2.75 1.40
Nos. 512-516 (5) 4.70 2.65

50th anniversary of Basrah Harbor.

Radio Tower and Map of Palestine A130

"Search for Knowledge" A131

1969, Nov. 9 Litho. *Perf. 12½x13*

517 A130 15f multicolored 60 16
518 A130 50f multicolored 1.65 40

10th anniversary of Iraqi News Agency. For overprints see Nos. 698-699.

1969, Nov. 21 Photo. *Perf. 13*

519 A131 15f blue & multi 15 15
520 A131 20f green & multi 20 15
Set value 18

Campaign against illiteracy.

Front Page of First Baghdad Newspaper A132

1969, Dec. 26 Litho. *Perf. 13½*

521 A132 15f yel, org & black 50 30

Centenary of the Iraqi press. For overprint, see No. 552.

Soldier, Map of Iraq and Plane — A133

1970, Jan. 6 Photo. *Perf. 13*

522 A133 15f lt vio & multi 40 15
523 A133 20f yellow & multi 80 30

Issued for Army Day 1970.

Soldier, Farmer and Worker Shoring up Wall in Iraqi Colors — A134

Poppies — A135

1970, Feb. 8 Photo. *Perf. 13*

524 A134 10f multicolored 25 15
525 A134 15f brick red & multi 50 25

7th anniv. of the Revolution of Ramadan 14.

1970, June 12 Litho. *Perf. 13*

Flowers: 3f, Poet's narcissus. 5f, Tulip. 10f, 50f, Carnations. 15f, Rose.

526 A135 2f emer & multi 15 15
527 A135 3f blue & multi 15 15
528 A135 5f multicolored 15 15
529 A135 10f lt grn & multi 15 15
530 A135 15f pale sal & multi 75 15
531 A135 50f lt grn & multi 1.50 75
Nos. 526-531 (6) 2.85
Set value 1.00

The overprinted sets Nos. 532-543 were released before Nos. 526-531.

For overprints see Nos. 621-623, RA20. For surcharge see No. 726.

Nos. 526-531 Overprinted in Ultramarine

عيد نوروز 1970

1970, Mar. 21

532 A135 2f emer & multi 15 15
533 A135 3f lt bl & multi 15 15
534 A135 5f multicolored 15 15
535 A135 10f lt grn & multi 40 15
536 A135 15f pale sal & multi 80 15
537 A135 50f lt grn & multi 3.25 1.50
Nos. 532-537 (6) 4.90
Set value 1.80

Issued for Novrooz (New Year).

Nos. 526-531 Overprinted in Black

مهرجان الربيع الموصل 1970

1970, Apr. 18

538 A135 2f emer & multi 15 15
539 A135 3f lt bl & multi 15 15
540 A135 5f multicolored 15 15
541 A135 10f lt grn & multi 25 15
542 A135 15f pale sal & multi 45 15
543 A135 50f lt grn & multi 2.25 75
Nos. 538-543 (6) 3.40
Set value 1.00

Issued for the Spring Festival, Mosul.

Map of Arab Countries, Slogans A136

Design: 35f, like 15f. 50f, 150f, People, flag, sun and map of Iraq.

1970, Apr. 7 *Perf. 13x12½*

544 A136 15f gold & multi 15 15
545 A136 35f sil & multi 25 20
546 A136 50f red & multi 50 30
a. Souv. sheet, 150f, imperf. 3.00 3.00

23rd anniversary of Al-Baath Party.

Workers and Cogwheel A137

1970, May 1

547 A137 10f silver & multi 20 15
548 A137 15f silver & multi 24 15
549 A137 35f silver & multi 80 40

Issued for Labor Day.

Kaaba, Mecca, and Koran A138

1970, May 17 **Photo.** *Perf. 13*

550 A138 15f brt bl & multi 15 15
551 A138 20f orange & multi 15 15
Set value 18

Mohammed's 1,400th birthday.

No. 521 Overprinted "1970" and Arabic Inscription in Prussian Blue

1970, June 15 **Litho.** *Perf. 13½*

552 A132 15f yel, org & black 20 20

Day of Iraqi press.

Revolutionists and Guns — A139

Designs: 35f, Revolutionist and rising sun.

1970, June 30 **Litho.** *Perf. 13*

553 A139 10f blk & apple grn 15 15
554 A139 15f black & gold 15 15
555 A139 35f blk & red org 50 20
a. Souv. sheet, 100f, imperf. 2.25 2.25
Set value 66 32

50th anniversary, Revolution of 1920.

Broken Chain and New Dawn — A140

1970, July 14 *Perf. 13x13½*

557 A140 15f multicolored 15 15
558 A140 20f multicolored 15 15
Set value 17

12th anniv. of the July 14, 1958 revolution.

Map of Arab Countries and Hands A141

1970, July 17 *Perf. 13*

559 A141 15f gold & multi 15 15
560 A141 25f gold & multi 20 15
Set value 22

2nd anniversary of coup of July 17, 1968.

Pomegranates A142

1970, Aug. 21 *Perf. 14*

561 A142 3f shown 15 15
562 A142 5f Grapefruit 15 15
563 A142 10f Grapes 15 15
564 A142 15f Oranges 45 15
565 A142 35f Dates 90 30
Nos. 561-565 (5) 1.80
Set value 50

The Latin inscriptions on the 5f and 10f have been erroneously transposed.

For overprints, see Nos. 613-615. For surcharge, see No. 725.

Kaaba, Mecca, Moon over Mountain and Spider Web A143

1970, Sept. 4 **Photo.** *Perf. 13*

566 A143 15f multicolored 15 15
567 A143 25f multicolored 20 15
Set value 22

Issued for Hajeer (Pilgrimage) Year.

الدورة السابعة

Nos. 510-511 Overprinted in Red

970 - ٩٧٠

1970, Sept. **Photo.** *Perf. 13½*

567A A128 10f multi 1.10 1.10
567B A128 15f multi 1.65 2.00

7th International Fair, Baghdad.

Intl. Education Year Emblem A144

1970, Nov. 13 **Photo.** *Perf. 13*

568 A144 5f yel green & multi 15 15
569 A144 15f brick red & multi 15 15
Set value 20 15

Flag and Map of Arab League Countries A145

1970 *Perf. 11*

570 A145 15f olive & multi 15 15
571 A145 35f gray & multi 25 20
Set value 27

25th anniversary of the Arab League.

Baghdad Hospital and Emblem A146

1970, Dec. 7 **Litho.** *Perf. 12*

572 A146 15f yellow & multi 15 15
573 A146 40f lt green & multi 50 25
Set value 32

Iraqi Medical Society, 50th anniv.

Sugar Beet — A147

Designs: 15f, Sugar factory, horiz. 30f, like 5f.

Perf. 13x13½, 13½x13

1970, Dec. 25 **Photo.**

574 A147 5f ocher, grn & blk 15 15
575 A147 15f black & multi 15 15
576 A147 30f org ver, grn & blk 18 15
Set value 32 27

Publicity for Mosul sugar factory.

OPEC Emblem A148

1970, Dec. 30 **Litho.** *Perf. 13x13½*

577 A148 10f rose cl, bis & bl 40 20
578 A148 40f emer, bis & blue 1.65 70

OPEC, 10th anniversary.

Soldiers — A149

Soldiers, Maps of Arab Countries and Israel A150

Perf. 13½x14, 11½x12½

1971, Jan. 6

579 A149 15f multicolored 30 15
580 A150 40f red org & multi 1.75 50
a. Souv. sheet of 2, #579-580, imperf. 4.00 6.25

Army Day, 50th anniversary.

No. 580a sold for 100f.

Marchers and Map of Arab Countries A151

1971, Feb. 8 **Litho.** *Perf. 11½x12½*

581 A151 15f yellow & multi 25 15
582 A151 40f pink & multi 75 30

Revolution of Ramadan 14, 8th anniversary.

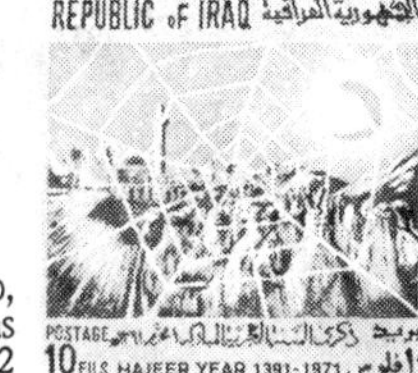

Spider Web, Pilgrims A152

1971, Feb. 26 **Photo.** *Perf. 13*

583 A152 10f pink & multi 15 15
584 A152 15f buff & multi 15 15
Set value 15

Hajeer (New) Year.

President al-Bakr A153

1971, Mar. 11 **Litho.** *Perf. 14*

585 A153 15f orange & multi 50 15
586 A153 100f emer & multi 2.75 85

First anniversary of Mar. 11th Manifesto.

Marshland A154

Tourist Publicity: 10f, Stork flying over Baghdad. 15f, "Summer Resorts." 100f, Return of Sindbad the Sailor.

1971, Mar. 15 *Perf. 13*

587 A154 5f multicolored 24 15
588 A154 10f lt grn & multi 32 15
589 A154 15f pink & multi 70 50
590 A154 100f multicolored 4.75 3.00

Blacksmith Taming Serpent A155

1971, Mar. 21 *Perf. 11½x12*

591 A155 15f multicolored 48 15
592 A155 25f yel & multi 1.00 40

Novrooz Festival.

No. 455 Overprinted

يوم الأنواء
W.M. DAY
1971

1971, Mar. 23 **Litho.** *Perf. 13*

593 A107 15f rose red & multi 3.75 2.50

World Meteorological Day. See No. C39.

Workers, Soldier, Map of Arab Countries A156

1971, Apr. 7

594 A156 15f yel & multi 70 16
595 A156 35f multicolored 1.25 50
596 A156 250f multicolored 10.00 6.25

24th anniv. of the Al Baath Party. No. 596 has circular perforation around vignette set within a white square of paper, perforated on 4 sides. The design of No. 596 is similar to Nos. 594-595, but with denomination within the circle and no inscriptions in margin.

Nos. 443-444, 448 Overprinted

مهرجان الربيع
1971

1971, Apr. 14

597 A105 2f pale brn & multi 45 15
598 A105 5f ver & multi 45 15
599 A105 25f lemon & multi 1.75 1.00

Mosul Festival.

Worker, Farm Woman with Torch A157

1971, May 1 **Litho.** *Perf. 13*

600 A157 15f ocher & multi 15 15
601 A157 40f olive & multi 75 20
Set value 27

Labor Day.

Muslim Praying in Mecca A158

1971, May 7

602 A158 15f yellow & multi 22 15
603 A158 100f pink & multi 2.75 1.00

Mohammed's 1,401st birthday.

People, Fists, Map of Iraq A159

1971, July 14 **Photo.** *Perf. 14*

604 A159 25f green & multi 20 15
605 A159 50f lt bl & multi 40 25

13th anniv. of the July 14, 1958 revolution.

Surveyor, Preacher, Rising Sun — A160

1971, July 17 *Perf. 13*

606 A160 25f multicolored 25 15
607 A160 70f orange & multi 75 45

3rd anniversary of July 17, 1968, coup.

Rafidain Bank Emblem — A161

1971, Sept. 24 **Photo.** *Perf. 13½*

Diameter: 27mm

608 A161 10f multicolored 42 85
609 A161 15f multicolored 85 85
610 A161 25f multicolored 1.65 2.75

Diameter: 32mm

611 A161 65f multicolored 8.50 4.25
612 A161 250f multicolored 21.00 12.50
Nos. 608-612 (5) 32.42 21.20

30th anniversary of Rafidain Bank. Nos. 608-612 have circular perforation around design within a white square of paper, perforated on 4 sides.

Nos. 561, 564-565 Overprinted

التعداد الزراعي العام
١٩٧١/١٠/١٥

1971, Oct. 15 **Litho.** *Perf. 14*

613 A142 3f bl grn & multi 30 15
614 A142 15f red & multi 1.00 50
615 A142 35f orange & multi 2.00 75

Agricultural census, Oct. 15, 1971.

Soccer A162

Designs: 25f, Track and field. 35f, Table tennis. 75f, Gymnastics. 95f, Volleyball and basketball.

1971, Nov. 17 **Litho.** *Perf. 13½*

616 A162 15f green & multi 28 15
617 A162 25f pink & multi 50 30
618 A162 35f lt bl & multi 75 70
619 A162 70f lt grn & multi 3.25 1.00
620 A162 95f yel grn & multi 5.25 2.00
a. Souvenir sheet of 5 11.00 5.50
Nos. 616-620 (5) 10.03 4.15

4th Pan-Arab Schoolboys Sports Games, Baghdad. No. 620a contains 5 stamps similar to Nos. 616-620 with simulated perforations. Sold for 200f.

Nos. 527-528, 530 Overprinted and Surcharged

70 Fils ●●
يوم الطالب
٢٣ تشرين الثاني
٩٦١ - ٩٧١
٧٠ فلسا ●●

1971, Nov. 23 **Litho.** *Perf. 13*

621 A135 15f multicolored 80 25
622 A135 25f on 5f multi 1.50 75
623 A135 70f on 3f multi 5.50 2.00

Students' Day. The 15f has only first 3 lines of Arabic overprint.

Nos. 485-486 Overprinted

25th Anniversary 971

1971, Dec. 11 **Litho.** *Perf. 13½*

624 A117 15f multicolored 2.00 75
625 A117 25f blue & multi 4.75 2.00

25th anniv. of UNICEF.

Children Crossing Street A162a

1971, Dec. 17 **Litho.** *Perf. 13x12½*

625A A162a 15f yel & multi 1.00 50
625B A162a 25f brt rose & multi 2.00 1.00

2nd Traffic Week. For overprints see Nos. 668-669.

Arab Postal Union Emblem A163

1971, Dec. 24 **Photo.** *Perf. 11½*

626 A163 25f emer, yel & brn 30 15
627 A163 70f vio bl, yel & red 1.10 45

25th anniv. of the Conf. of Sofar, Lebanon, establishing Arab Postal Union.

Racial Equality Emblem — A164

1971, Dec. 31 *Perf. 13½x14*

628 A164 25f brt grn & multi 25 15
629 A164 70f orange & multi 65 35

Intl. Year Against Racial Discrimination.

Soldiers with Flag and Torch — A165 Workers — A166

1972, Jan. 6 **Photo.** *Perf. 14x13½*

630 A165 25f blue & multi 70 40
631 A165 70f brt grn & multi 2.75 1.50

Army Day, Jan. 6.

1972, Feb. 8

632 A166 25f brt grn & multi 80 40
633 A166 95f lilac & multi 5.75 1.50

Revolution of Ramadan 14, 9th anniv.

Mosque, Minaret, Crescent and Caravan A167

1972, Feb. 26 **Litho.** *Perf. 12½x13*

634 A167 25f bl grn & multi 25 15
635 A167 35f purple & multi 35 18

Hegira (Pilgrimage) Year.

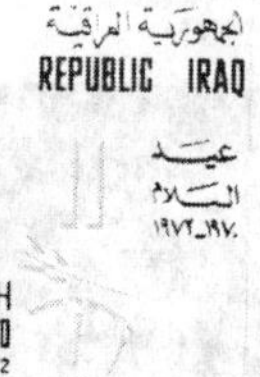

Peace Symbols and "11" — A168

1972, Mar. 11 **Photo.** *Perf. 11x12½*

636 A168 25f lt blue & blk 85 25
637 A168 70f brt lilac & blk 2.50 75

2nd anniversary of Mar. 11 Manifesto.

Mountain Range and Flowers — A169

1972, Mar. 21 *Perf. 11½x11*

638 A169 25f vio blue & multi 90 20
639 A169 70f vio blue & multi 2.75 1.00

Novrooz, New Year Festival.

Party Emblem A170

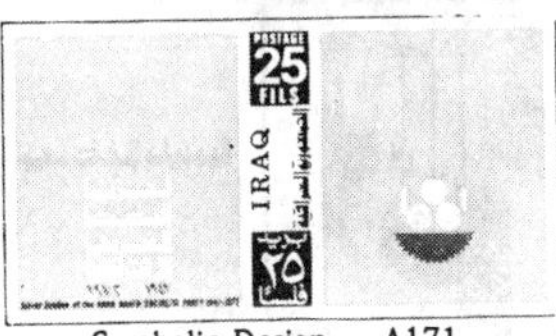

Symbolic Design — A171

Perf. 14 (A170), 13 (A171)

1972 **Litho.**

640	A170 10f brn org & multi	15	15
641	A171 25f bister & multi	24	25
642	A170 35f brn org & multi	40	50
643	A171 70f red & multi	2.50	75

Iraqi Arab Baath Socialist Party, 25th anniv. Issued: 25f, 70f, Mar. 23; 10f, 35f, Apr. 7.

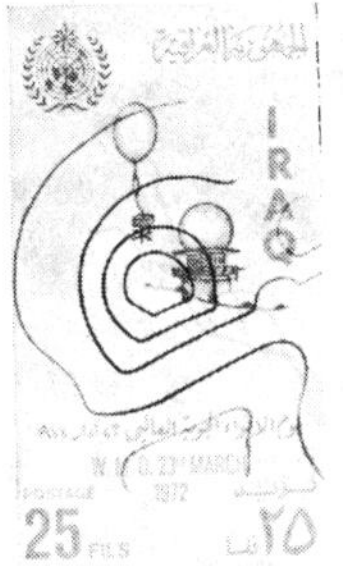

Emblem, Map, Weather Balloons and Chart — A172

Cogwheel and Ship — A173

1972, Mar. 23 **Photo.** *Perf. 14x13½*

644	A172 25f multicolored	65	15
645	A172 35f yel & multi	95	25

12th World Meteorological Day.

1972, Mar. 25 *Perf. 11x11½*

646	A173 25f ocher & multi	25	15
647	A173 35f pink & multi	40	15

Arab Chamber of Commerce.

Derrick and Flame A174

Quill Pens, Map of Arab Countries A175

1972, Apr. 7 *Perf. 13x13½*

648	A174 25f multicolored	50	25
649	A174 35f multicolored	75	30

Opening of North Rumaila (INOC, North Iraq Oil Fields).

1972, Apr. 17 **Photo.** *Perf. 11x11½*

650	A175 25f orange & multi	30	15
651	A175 35f blue & multi	55	18

3rd Congress of Arab Journalists.

Women's Federation Emblem — A176

1972, Apr. 22 **Litho.** *Perf. 13½*

652	A176 25f green & multi	30	15
653	A176 35f lilac & multi	55	18

Iraqi Women's Federation, 4th anniversary.

Hand Holding Globe-shaped Wrench — A177

1972, May 1 **Photo.** *Perf. 11½*

654	A177 25f yel grn & multi	30	15
655	A177 35f orange & multi	55	18

Labor Day.

Kaaba, Mecca, and Crescent — A178

1972, May 26

656	A178 25f green & multi	30	15
657	A178 35f purple & multi	55	18

Mohammed's 1,402nd birthday.

Soldier, Civilian and Guns — A179

1972, July 14 **Photo.** *Perf. 13½x14*

658	A179 35f multicolored	60	25
659	A179 70f lilac & multi	1.90	75

14th anniv. of July 14, 1958, revolution.

Dome of the Rock, Arab Countries' Map, Fists — A180

1972, July 17 *Perf. 13*

660	A180 25f citron & multi	60	15
661	A180 95f blue & multi	1.90	75

4th anniv. of July 17, 1968 coup.

Congress Emblem, Scout Saluting Iraqi Flag — A182

1972, Aug. 12 **Photo.** *Perf. 13½x14*

664	A182 20f multicolored	1.00	55
665	A182 25f lilac & multi	2.00	80

10th Arab Boy Scouts Jamboree and Conference, Mosul, Aug. 10-19.

1972, Aug. 24

Design: Congress emblem and Girl Guide in camp.

666	A182 10f yellow & multi	1.00	45
667	A182 45f multicolored	3.00	90

4th Arab Guides Camp and Conference, Mosul, Aug. 24-30.

No. 625A Overprinted and Surcharged, No. 625B Overprinted with New Date:

1972 ١٩٧٢

●● 70 Fils ٧٠ ●●

1972, Oct. 4 **Photo.** *Perf. 13x12½*

668	A162a 25f brt rose & multi	3.75	1.75
669	A162a 70f on 15f multi	5.00	4.50

Third Traffic Week.

Central Bank of Iraq — A183

1972, Nov. 16 **Photo.** *Perf. 13*

670	A183 25f lt blue & multi	35	30
671	A183 70f lt green & multi	1.00	70

25th anniversary, Central Bank of Iraq.

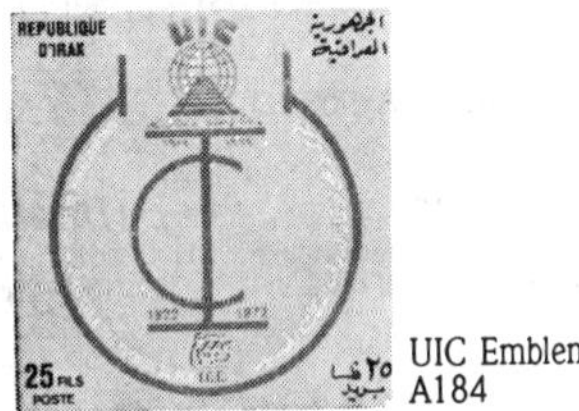

UIC Emblem A184

1972, Dec. 29

672	A184 25f dp rose & multi	65	20
673	A184 45f brt vio & multi	1.40	50

50th anniv., Intl. Railroad Union (UIC).

Nos. 148-149, 151, 180 and Type of 1957-58 Overprinted with 3 Bars

1973, Jan. 29 **Engr.** *Perf. 11½x12*

674	A28 10f blue	40	20
675	A33 10f blue	40	20
676	A28 15f black	80	35
677	A33 15f black	80	35
678	A28 25f rose violet	1.50	50
679	A33 25f rose violet	1.50	50
	Nos. 674-679 (6)	5.40	2.10

The size and position of the bottom bar of overprint differs; the bar can be same size as 2 top bars, short and centered or moved to the right.

No. 455 Overprinted

المؤتمر الدولي
للتاريخ/١٩٧٣

1973, Mar. 25 **Litho.** *Perf. 13*

680	A107 15f rose red & multi	6.00	2.50

Intl. History Cong. See Nos. C52-C53.

Workers and Oil Wells A185

Ram's-head Harp A186

1973, June 1 **Litho.** *Perf. 13*

681	A185 25f yel & multi	1.25	50
682	A185 70f rose & multi	5.50	2.00

1st anniv. of nationalization of oil industry.

1973, June **Litho.** *Perf. 13x12½*

Designs: 25f, 35f, 45f, Minaret, Mosul, 50f, 70f, 95f, Statue of goddess. 10f, 20f, like 5f.

683	A186 5f orange & blk	15	15
684	A186 10f bister & blk	15	15
685	A186 20f brt rose & blk	15	15
686	A186 25f ultra & blk	18	15
687	A186 35f emer & blk	25	18
688	A186 45f blue & black	32	23
689	A186 50f olive & yel	35	25
690	A186 70f violet & yel	50	36
691	A186 95f brown & yel	65	48
	Nos. 683-691 (9)	2.70	
	Set value		1.82

For overprint see No. RA21.

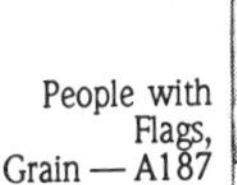

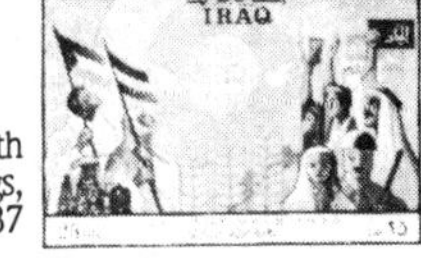

People with Flags, Grain — A187

1973, July 14

692	A187 25f multicolored	20	25
693	A187 35f multicolored	40	30

July Festivals.

Nos. 393 and 395 Surcharged

مهرجان النخيل
وعيد التمور
١٩٧٢
25 Fils ٢٥

1973 **Litho.** *Perf. 13½x14*

694	A85 25f on 3f multi	2.50	1.50
695	A85 70f on 15f multi	6.75	4.00

Festival of Date Trees

INTERPOL Headquarters A188

1973, Sept. 20 **Litho.** *Perf. 12*

696	A188 25f multicolored	30	15
697	A188 70f brt bl & multi	65	35

50th anniv. of Intl. Criminal Police Org.

Nos. 517-518 Overprinted in Silver

I.O.J.
SEPTEMBER
26-29. 1973

1973, Sept. 29 Litho. *Perf. 12½x13*

698 A130 15f multicolored		3.50	1.00
699 A130 50f multicolored		6.00	3.00

Meeting of Intl. Org. of Journalists' Executive Committee, Sept. 26-29.

Flags and Fair Emblem A189

WMO Emblem A190

1973, Oct. 10 Photo. *Perf. 11*

700 A189 10f brt grn & dk brn	15	15
701 A189 20f ocher & multi	32	15
702 A189 65f blue & multi	80	55
Set value		74

10th International Baghdad Fair, Oct. 1-21.

1973, Nov. 15 Litho. *Perf. 12*

703 A190 25f org, blk & green	50	20
704 A190 35f brt rose, blk & grn	70	25

Intl. meteorological cooperation, cent.

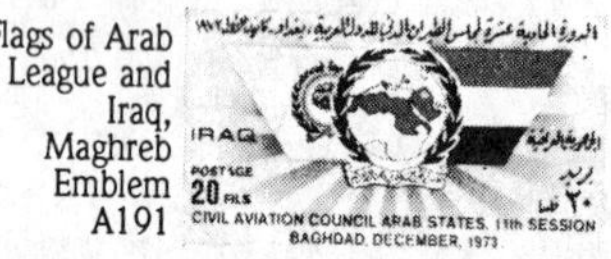

Flags of Arab League and Iraq, Maghreb Emblem A191

1973, Dec. 1 Photo. *Perf. 14*

705 A191 20f dl org & multi	25	15
706 A191 35f blue & multi	35	18

11th session of Civil Aviation Council of Arab States, Baghdad, Dec. 1973.

المجلس التنفيذي

No. 360 Overprinted

بغداد/١٩٧٣

1973, Dec. 12 Photo. *Perf. 11*

707 A67a 30f orange & blue	3.00	2.25

6th Executive Council Meeting of APU.

Human Rights Flame — A192

1973, Dec. 25 *Perf. 11½*

708 A192 25f multicolored	20	15
709 A192 70f ultra & multi	60	35

25th anniversary of Universal Declaration of Human Rights.

Military College Crest and Cadets A193

1974, Jan. 6 *Perf. 12x11½*

710 A193 25f ocher & multi	20	15
711 A193 35f ultra & multi	28	18

50th anniversary of the Military College.

UPU and Arab Postal Union Emblems — A194

1974, May 28 Photo. *Perf. 11½x12*

712 A194 25f gold & multi	45	15
713 A194 35f gold & multi	45	30
714 A194 70f gold & multi	90	75

Centenary of the Universal Postal Union.

Symbols of Ancient Mesopotamia and Oil Industry — A195

1974, June 1 Litho. *Perf. 12½*

715 A195 10f blue & multi	15	15
716 A195 25f ocher & multi	28	25
717 A195 70f rose & multi	1.10	75

Nationalization of the oil industry, 2nd anniv.

Festival — A196

1974, July 17 *Perf. 11½x12*

718 A196 20f lilac & multi	20	15
719 A196 35f dull org & multi	35	18

July Festivals.

National Front Emblem and People A197

1974, July 17 *Perf. 12x11½*

720 A197 25f blue & multi	25	15
721 A197 70f brt grn & multi	65	36

1st anniv. of Progressive National Front.

Cement Plant and Brick Wall — A198

1974, Oct. 19 *Perf. 11½x12*

722 A198 20f gray bl & multi	22	15
723 A198 25f red & multi	28	15
724 A198 70f emerald & multi	90	55

25th anniversary of Iraqi Cement Plant.

Nos. 561 and 527 Surcharged

١٠ فلوس
10 Fils

a

٢٥ فلسا
25 Fils

b

1975, Jan. 9 Litho. *Perf. 13, 14*

725 A142 (a) 10f on 3f multi	2.50	1.50
726 A135 (b) 25f on 3f multi	7.75	5.00

Globe and WPY Emblem — A199

1975, Jan. 30 *Perf. 11½x12*

727 A199 25f dull bl & blk	35	15
728 A199 35f brt pink & ind	75	25
729 A199 70f yel grn & vio	2.00	75

World Population Year 1974.

Festival Symbols — A200

1975, July 17 Litho. *Perf. 12x11½*

730 A200 5f lt brn & multi	15	15
731 A200 10f lt brn & multi	15	15
732 A200 35f lt brn & multi	1.00	75
Set value		90

Festivals, July 1975.

Map of Arab Countries A201

1975, Aug. 5 Photo. *Perf. 13*

733 A201 25f rose & multi	30	15
734 A201 35f multicolored	32	25
735 A201 45f multicolored	52	35

Arab Working Org., 10th anniv.

Symbols of Women, Oil Industry and Agriculture — A202

1975, Aug. 15 *Perf. 14*

736 A202 10f lilac & multi	32	15
737 A202 35f multicolored	65	50
738 A202 70f bl & multi	2.75	1.00
a. Souv. sheet, 100f, imperf.	9.50	11.00

International Women's Year.

Euphrates Dam and Causeway A203

1975, Sept. 5 Litho. *Perf. 12x11½*

739 A203 3f orange & multi	15	15
740 A203 25f purple & multi	38	15
741 A203 70f rose red & multi	2.00	50
Set value		70

Intl. Commission on Irrigation and Drainage, 25th anniv.

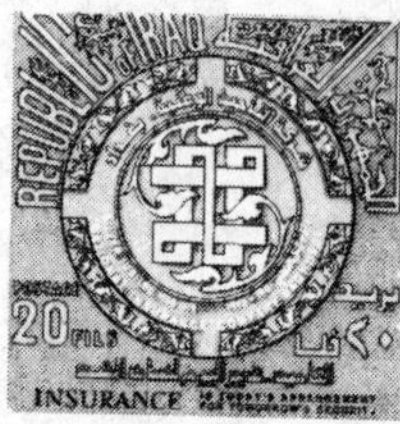

National Insurance Co. Seal — A204

1975, Oct. 11 Photo. *Perf. 13*

742 A204 20f brt bl & multi	55	15
743 A204 25f crim & multi	70	30
a. Souv. sheet, 100f, imperf.	7.00	8.50

Natl. Insurance Co., Baghdad, 25th anniv.

Musician Entertaining King — A205

1975, Nov. 21 *Perf. 14*

744 A205 25f silver & multi	30	15
745 A205 45f gold & multi	55	22

Baghdad Intl. Music Conf., Nov. 1975.

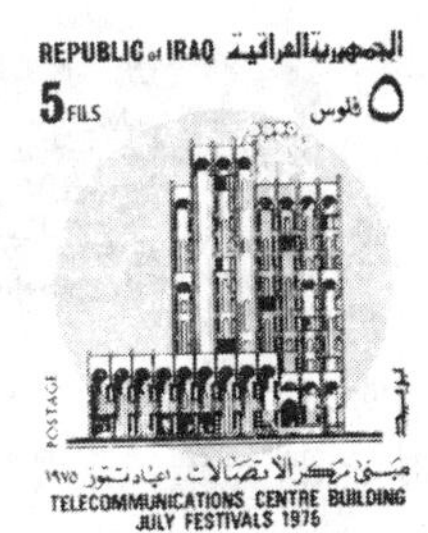

Telecommunications Center — A206

1975, Dec. 22 Litho. *Perf. 12½*

746	A206	5f lil rose & multi	15	15
747	A206	10f blue & multi	18	15
748	A206	60f green & multi	1.10	50
		Set value		65

Inauguration of Telecommunications Center Building during July 1975 Festival.

Diesel Locomotive A207

Conference Emblem and: 30f, Diesel passenger locomotive #511. 35f, 0-3-0 steam tank locomotive with passenger train. 50f, 2-3-0 German steam locomotive, c. 1914.

1975, Dec. 22 Photo. *Perf. 14*

749	A207	25f tan & multi	2.25	38
750	A207	30f tan & multi	3.00	75
751	A207	35f yel grn & multi	4.00	1.50
752	A207	50f yel grn & multi	6.00	4.00

15th Taurus Railway Conference, Baghdad.

A208

A209

Design: Soldier on guard.

1976, Jan. 6 *Perf. 13*

753	A208	5f silver & multi	15	15
754	A208	25f silver & multi	30	15
755	A208	50f gold & multi	90	40
		Set value		58

55th Army Day.

1976, Jan. 8 Photo. *Perf. 13½x13*

Design: Fingerprint crossed out, Arab world.

756	A209	5f violet & multi	15	15
757	A209	15f blue & multi	35	15
758	A209	35f green & multi	1.10	75

Statue of Goddess A210

Iraq Earth Station A211

Designs: 10f, 15f, like 5f. 20f, 25f, 30f, Two female figures forming column. 35f, 50f, 75f, Head of bearded man.

1976, Jan. 1 Litho. *Perf. 13x12½*

759	A210	5f lilac & multi	15	15
760	A210	10f rose & multi	15	15
761	A210	15f yellow & multi	15	15
762	A210	20f bister & multi	16	15
763	A210	25f lt grn & multi	18	15
764	A210	30f blue & multi	20	15
765	A210	35f lil rose & multi	20	18
766	A210	50f citron & multi	32	25
767	A210	75f violet & multi	48	40
		Nos. 759-767 (9)	1.99	
		Set value		1.35

1976, Feb. 8 *Perf. 13x13½*

768	A211	10f silver & multi	25	15
769	A211	25f silver & multi	80	30
770	A211	75f gold & multi	3.25	1.25

Revolution of Ramadan 14, 13th anniv.

Telephones 1876 and 1976 — A212

Map of Maghreb, ICATU Emblem — A213

1976, Mar. 17 Litho. *Perf. 12x12½*

771	A212	35f multicolored	80	30
772	A212	50f multicolored	1.65	50
773	A212	75f multicolored	2.50	75

Centenary of first telephone call by Alexander Graham Bell, Mar. 10, 1876.

1976, Mar. 24 Photo. *Perf. 13½*

774	A213	5f green & multi	15	15
775	A213	10f multicolored	25	15
		Set value	30	20

20th Intl. Conf. of Arab Trade Unions. See #C54.

Map of Iraq, Family, Torch and Wreath — A214

1976, Apr. 1 *Perf. 12½*

776	A214	5f multicolored	15	15
777	A214	15f lilac & multi	24	15
778	A214	35f multicolored	50	25
		Set value		40

Police Day.

Pipeline, Map of Iraq — A215

Pres. A. H. al-Bakr Embracing Vice Pres. Saddam Hussein — A216

1976, June 1 Photo. *Perf. 13*

779	A215	25f multicolored	1.50	75
780	A215	75f multicolored	4.50	2.00

Souvenir Sheet

Imperf

781	A216	150f multicolored	19.00	22.50

4th anniversary of oil nationalization.

"Festival" — A217

1976, July 17 *Perf. 14*

782	A217	15f orange & multi	25	15
783	A217	35f orange & multi	75	50

Festivals, July 1976.

Archbishop Capucci, Map of Palestine A218

1976, Aug. 18 Litho. *Perf. 12*

784	A218	25f multicolored	45	18
785	A218	35f multicolored	70	18
786	A218	75f multicolored	2.25	1.00

Detention of Archbishop Hilarion Capucci in Israel, Aug. 18, 1974.

Common Kingfisher — A219

"15" — A220

Birds: 10f, Turtle dove. 15f, Pin-tailed sandgrouse. 25f, Blue rock thrush. 50f, Purple and gray herons.

1976, Sept. 15 Litho. *Perf. 13½x14*

787	A219	5f multicolored	15	15
788	A219	10f multicolored	16	15
789	A219	15f multicolored	28	15
790	A219	25f multicolored	40	25
791	A219	50f multicolored	1.50	35
		Nos. 787-791 (5)	2.49	1.05

1976, Nov. 23 Photo. *Perf. 13½*

792	A220	30f multicolored	1.00	50
793	A220	70f multicolored	3.00	75

15th anniv. of National Students Union.

Oil Tanker and Emblems — A221

Designs: 15f, like 10f. 25f, 50f, Pier, refinery, pipeline.

1976, Dec. 25 *Perf. 12½x12*

794	A221	10f multicolored	48	15
795	A221	15f multicolored	75	24
796	A221	25f multicolored	2.00	48
797	A221	50f multicolored	2.75	70

1st Iraqi oil tanker (10f, 15f) and Nationalization of Basrah Petroleum Co. Ltd., 1st anniv. (25f, 50f).

Happy Children A222

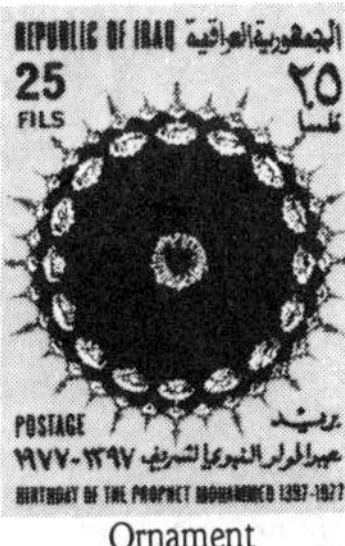

Ornament A223

UNESCO Emblem and: 25f, Children with flowers and butterflies. 75f, Children planting flowers around flagpole.

1976, Dec. 25 *Perf. 12x12½*

798	A222	10f multicolored	18	18
799	A222	25f multicolored	1.75	30
800	A222	75f multicolored	3.00	90

30th anniv. of UNESCO, and Books for Children Campaign.

1977, Mar. 2 Photo. *Perf. 13½*

801	A223	25f gold & multi	48	20
802	A223	35f gold & multi	70	25

Birthday of Mohammed (570-632).

Peace Dove — A224

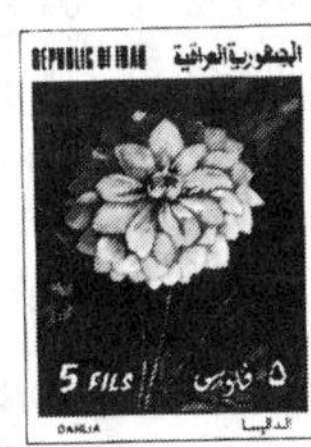

Dahlia — A225

1977, Mar. 11 *Perf. 14x13½*

803	A224	25f lt bl & multi	30	15
804	A224	30f buff & multi	35	15

Peace Day.

1977, Mar. 21 Litho. *Perf. 12½*

Flowers: 10f, Sweet peas. 35f, Chrysanthemums. 50f, Verbena.

805	A225	5f multicolored	20	15
806	A225	10f multicolored	24	15
807	A225	35f multicolored	80	25
808	A225	50f multicolored	1.50	50
		Set value		90

Spring Festivals, Baghdad.

Emblem with Doves A226

Designs: 75f, Emblem with flame. 100f, Dove with olive branch.

1977, Apr. 7 Photo. *Perf. 13*

809	A226	25f yel & multi	60	15
810	A226	75f yel & multi	2.25	40

Souvenir Sheet

Imperf

811	A226	100f multicolored	4.75	6.50

Al Baath Party, 30th anniversary. No. 811 contains one 49x35mm stamp.

APU Emblem, Members' Flags — A227

1977, Apr. 12 Litho. *Perf. 14*

812 A227 25f orange & multi 35 15
813 A227 35f gray & multi 45 18

25th anniversary of Arab Postal Union.

Cogwheel, Globe and "1" — A228

1977, May 1 Litho. *Perf. 14½x14*

814 A228 10f multicolored 15 15
815 A228 30f multicolored 35 15
816 A228 35f multicolored 42 18
Set value 38

Labor Day.

Weight Lifting A229

Designs: 75f, Weight lifter, standing up. 100f, Symbolic weight lifter with Iraqi coat of arms, laurel wreath.

1977, May 8 Photo. *Perf. 14*

817 A229 25f multicolored 60 60
818 A229 75f multicolored 1.25 85

Souvenir Sheet

Imperf

819 A229 100f multicolored 6.50 7.50

8th Asian Weight Lifting Championship, Baghdad, May 1977. No. 819 contains one 42x52mm stamp.

Arabian Garden — A230

Grain and Dove — A231

Arab Tourist Year: 10f, View of town with minarets, horiz. 30f, Landscape with bridge and waterfall. 50f, Hosts welcoming tourists, and drum, horiz.

Perf. 11½x12, 12x11½

1977, June 15 Litho.

820 A230 5f multicolored 15 15
821 A230 10f multicolored 15 15
822 A230 30f multicolored 75 20
823 A230 50f multicolored 2.00 1.25

1977, July 17 Photo. *Perf. 14*

824 A231 25f multicolored 28 15
825 A231 30f multicolored 35 15

Festivals, July 1977.

Map of Arab Countries A232

1977, Sept. 9 Photo. *Perf. 13½x14*

826 A232 30f multicolored 38 25
827 A232 70f multicolored 1.65 50

UN Conference on Desertification, Nairobi, Kenya, Aug. 29-Sept. 9.

Census Emblem A233

Festival Emblem A234

1977, Oct. 17 Litho. *Perf. 14x14½*

828 A233 20f ultra & multi 22 15
829 A233 30f brown & multi 35 15
830 A233 70f gray & multi 70 35

Population Census Day, Oct. 17.

1977, Nov. 1 Photo. *Perf. 14*

831 A234 25f silver & multi 30 15
832 A234 50f gold & multi 60 24

Al Mutanabby Festival, Nov. 1977.

A235

A236

Design: Junblatt, caricatures of Britain, US, Israel.

1977, Nov. 16 Photo. *Perf. 14*

833 A235 20f multicolored 24 15
834 A235 30f multicolored 35 15
835 A235 70f multicolored 80 35

Kemal Junblatt, Druse leader, killed in Lebanese war.

1977, Dec. 12 Photo. *Perf. 14*

836 A236 30f gold & multi 40 15
837 A236 35f silver & multi 50 18

Hegira (Pilgrimage) Year.

Young People and Flags — A237

Coins and Coin Bank — A238

1978, Apr. 7 Photo. *Perf. 11½x11*

838 A237 10f multicolored 15 15
839 A237 15f multicolored 25 15
840 A237 35f multicolored 55 18
Set value 30

Youth Day.

1978, Apr. 15

841 A238 15f multicolored 15 15
842 A238 25f multicolored 30 15
843 A238 35f multicolored 42 18
Set value 38

6th anniversary of postal savings law.

Microwave Transmission and Receiving A239

Emblems and Flags of Participants A240

1978, May 17 Photo. *Perf. 14*

844 A239 25f org & multi 20 15
845 A239 35f lilac & multi 28 18
846 A239 75f emer & multi 60 35

10th World Telecommunications Day and 1st anniversary of commissioning of national microwave network.

Perf. 12½x11½

1978, June 19 Litho.

847 A240 25f multicolored 55 15
848 A240 35f multicolored 85 18

Conference of Postal Ministers of Arabian Gulf Countries, Baghdad (Saudi Arabia, United Arab Emirates, Qatar, Bahrain, Kuwait, Oman, People's Republic of Yemen).

Ancient Coin — A241

Designs: Ancient Iraqi coins. 75f vertical.

Perf. 11½x12½

1978, June 25 Photo.

849 A241 1f citron & multi 15 15
850 A241 2f blue & multi 15 15
851 A241 3f salmon & multi 15 15
852 A241 4f salmon & multi 15 15
853 A241 75f bl grn & multi 2.25 40
Nos. 849-853 (5) 2.85
Set value 60

Festival Emblem — A242

Festival Poster — A243

1978, July 17 *Perf. 13½x13*

854 A242 25f multicolored 20 15
855 A242 35f multicolored 28 18

Souvenir Sheet

Perf. 13x13½

856 A243 100f multicolored 4.25 5.00

Festivals, July 1978.

WHO Emblem, Nurse, Hospital, Sick Child A244

1978, Aug. 18 Photo. *Perf. 14*

857 A244 25f multicolored 24 15
858 A244 35f multicolored 32 18
859 A244 75f multicolored 70 35

Eradication of smallpox.

Maritime Union Emblem A245

1978, Aug. 30 Photo. *Perf. 11½x12*

860 A245 25f multicolored 30 15
861 A245 75f multicolored 90 35

1st World Maritime Day.

Workers A246

1978, Sept. 12 *Perf. 14*

862 A246 10f multicolored 18 15
863 A246 25f multicolored 40 15
864 A246 35f multicolored 70 18
Set value 35

10th anniv. of People's Work Groups.

Fair Emblem with Atom Symbol — A247

Map of Iraq, Ruler and Globe — A248

1978, Oct. 1

865 A247 25f multicolored 24 15
866 A247 35f multicolored 32 18
867 A247 75f multicolored 70 35

15th International Fair, Baghdad, Oct. 1-15.

1978, Oct. 14

868 A248 25f multicolored 24 15
869 A248 35f multicolored 32 18
870 A248 75f multicolored 70 35

World Standards Day.

Altharthar-Euphrates Dam — A249

1978 Photo. *Perf. 11½*

871 A249 5f multicolored 15 15
872 A249 10f multicolored 15 15
873 A249 15f multicolored 15 18
874 A249 25f multicolored 28 15
875 A249 35f multicolored 40 18
876 A249 50f multicolored 60 25
Nos. 871-876 (6) 1.73
Set value 82

Arab Summit Conference A250

Surgeons' Conference Emblem A251

1978, Nov. 2 Photo. *Perf. 14*

890 A250 25f multicolored	22	15
891 A250 35f multicolored	45	25
892 A250 75f multicolored	90	50

9th Arab Summit Conference, Baghdad, Nov. 2-5.

1978, Nov. 8 Litho. *Perf. 12x11½*

893 A251 25f multicolored	25	15
894 A251 75f multicolored	80	35

4th Cong. of the Assoc. of Thoracic & Cardiovascular Surgeons of Asia, Baghdad, Nov. 6-10.

Pilgrims at Mt. Arafat and Holy Ka'aba A252

1978, Nov. 9 Photo. *Perf. 14*

895 A252 25f multicolored	25	15
896 A252 35f multicolored	35	18

Pilgrimage to Mecea.

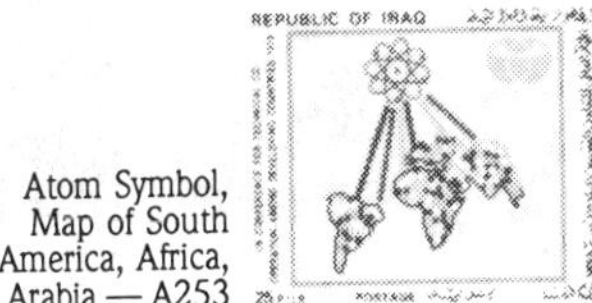
Atom Symbol, Map of South America, Africa, Arabia — A253

1978, Nov. 11 *Perf. 13½*

897 A253 25f multicolored	65	15
898 A253 50f multicolored	55	25
899 A253 75f multicolored	80	35

Technical Cooperation Among Developing Countries Conf., Buenos Aires, Argentina, Sept. 1978.

Hands Holding Emblem — A254

Globe and Flame Emblem — A255

1978, Nov. 30 Litho. *Perf. 13½x13*

900 A254 25f multicolored	30	15
901 A254 50f multicolored	60	25
902 A254 75f multicolored	95	35

Anti-Apartheid Year.

1978, Dec. 20 *Perf. 14*

903 A255 25f multicolored	20	15
904 A255 75f multicolored	60	35

Declaration of Human Rights, 30th anniv.

Candle and Emblem — A256

Book, Pencil and Flame — A257

1979, Jan. 9 Photo. *Perf. 14*

905 A256 10f multicolored	15	15
906 A256 25f multicolored	20	15
907 A256 35f multicolored	28	18
Set value		36

Police Day.

1979, Feb. 15 Photo. *Perf. 14*

908 A257 15f multicolored	25	15
909 A257 25f multicolored	35	15
910 A257 35f multicolored	65	18
Set value		36

Application of Compulsory Education Law, anniversary.

Pupils, School and Teacher — A258

1979, Mar. 1 *Perf. 13*

911 A258 10f multicolored	15	15
912 A258 15f multicolored	20	15
913 A258 50f multicolored	80	25
Set value		38

Teacher's Day.

Pupils, Flag, Pencil — A259

1979, Mar. 10 *Perf. 13½x13*

914 A259 15f multicolored	15	15
915 A259 25f multicolored	25	15
916 A259 35f multicolored	50	18
Set value		38

National Comprehensive Compulsory Literacy Campaign.

Book, World Map, Arab Achievements A260

1979, Mar. 22 *Perf. 13*

917 A260 35f multicolored	28	18
918 A260 75f multicolored	60	38

Achievements of the Arabs.

Girl Playing Flute — A261

1979, Apr. 15 Litho. *Perf. 13½*

919 A261 15f multicolored	22	15
920 A261 25f multicolored	35	15
921 A261 35f multicolored	75	30

Mosul Spring Festival.

Iraqi Flag, Globe, UPU Emblem — A262

1979, Apr. 22 Photo. *Perf. 13x13½*

922 A262 25f multicolored	40	15
923 A262 35f multicolored	45	18
924 A262 75f multicolored	1.00	50

50th anniv. of Iraq's admission to the UPU.

Soccer Tournament Emblem — A263

1979, May 4 Photo. *Perf. 13*

925 A263 10f multicolored	15	15
926 A263 15f multicolored	30	15
927 A263 50f multicolored	1.00	50
Set value		64

5th Arabian Gulf Soccer Championship.

Child With Globe and Candle A264

Design: 100f, IYC emblem, boy and girl reaching for US emblem, vert.

1979, June 1 Photo. *Perf. 13x13½*

928 A264 25f multicolored	38	18
929 A264 75f multicolored	1.25	65

Souvenir Sheet

930 A264 100f multicolored	21.00	17.50

International Year of the Child.
No. 930 contains one stamp 30x42mm.

Leaf and Flower — A265

1979, July 17 Litho. *Perf. 12½*

931 A265 15f multicolored	15	15
932 A265 25f multicolored	20	15
933 A265 35f multicolored	28	18
Set value		38

July festivals.

Students Holding Globe, UNESCO Emblem A266

1979, July 25

934 A266 25f multicolored	40	15
935 A266 40f multicolored	70	25
936 A266 100f multicolored	2.00	50

Intl. Bureau of Education, Geneva, 50th anniv.

S. al Hosari, Philosopher — A267

Designs: No. 938, Mustapha Jawad, historian. No. 939, Jawad Selim, sculptor.

1979, Oct. 15 Litho. *Perf. 12½*

937 A267 25f multicolored	30	15
938 A267 25f multicolored	30	15
939 A267 25f multicolored	30	15
Set value		36

Pilgrimage to Mecca A268

1979, Oct. 25 Litho. *Perf. 12½*

940 A268 25f multicolored	30	15
941 A268 50f multicolored	60	24

Iraqi News Agency, 20th Anniversary A269

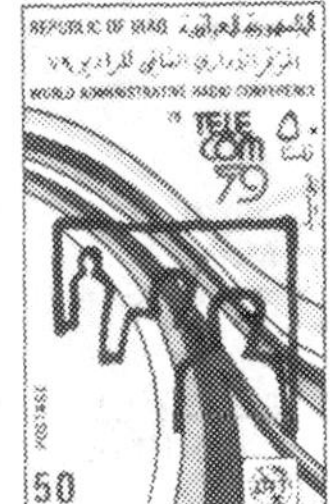
Telecom 79 A270

1979, Nov. 9 Photo. *Perf. 11½*

942 A269 25f multicolored	20	15
943 A269 50f multicolored	40	25
944 A269 75f multicolored	60	35

1979, Nov. 20 Litho. *Perf. 11½*

945 A270 25f multicolored	25	15
946 A270 50f multicolored	50	35
947 A270 75f multicolored	75	50

3rd World Telecommunications Exhibition, Geneva, Sept. 20-26.

International Palestinian Solidarity Day — A271

1979, Nov. 29 Photo. *Perf. 11½x12*

948 A271 25f multicolored	60	15
949 A271 50f multicolored	1.10	35
950 A271 75f multicolored	1.50	50

A272 A273

Designs: 25f, 75f, Ahmad Hassan Al-Bakr. 35f, 100f, Pres. Saddam Hussein.

1979, Dec. 1 Photo. *Perf. 13x13½*

951	A272	25f multicolored	22	15
952	A272	35f multicolored	32	20
953	A272	75f multicolored	65	30
954	A272	100f multicolored	2.75	1.65

1979, Dec. 10 *Perf. 14*

Vanguard Emblem and: 10f, Boy and violin. 15f, Children, map of Iraq. 25f, Youths. 35f, Vanguard emblem alone.

955	A273	10f multicolored	15	15
956	A273	15f multicolored	16	15
957	A273	25f multicolored	25	15
958	A273	35f multicolored	35	18
		Set value		42

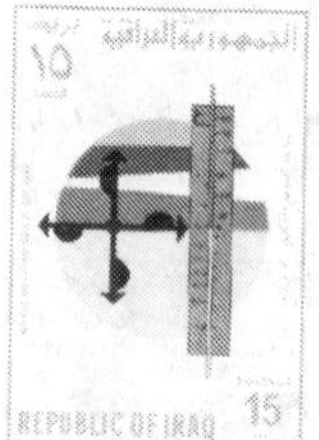

World Meteorological Day — A274

World Health Day — A275

1980, Mar. 23 Photo. *Perf. 14*

959	A274	15f multicolored	16	15
960	A274	25f multicolored	25	15
961	A274	35f multicolored	35	18
		Set value		38

1980, Apr. 7 Photo. *Perf. 14*

962	A275	25f multicolored	24	15
963	A275	35f multicolored	35	18
964	A275	75f multicolored	1.25	38

Festivals Emblem — A276

Pres. Hussein — A277

1980, July 17 Photo. *Perf. 13½x13*

965	A276	25f multicolored	22	15
966	A276	35f multicolored	30	18

Souvenir Sheet

Perf. 13½

967	A277	100f multicolored	3.75	3.75

July Festivals.

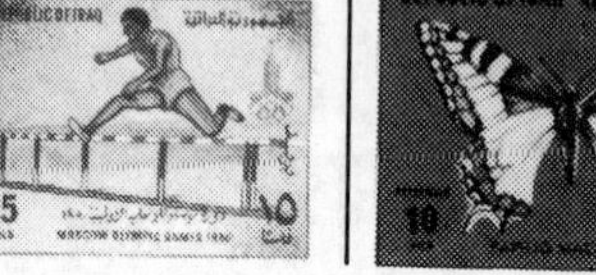

Hurdles, Moscow '80 Emblem — A278

1980, July 30 Photo. *Perf. 14*

968	A278	15f shown	18	15
969	A278	20f Weight lifting, vert.	28	25
970	A278	30f Boxing	55	35
971	A278	35f Soccer, vert.	1.10	55

Souvenir Sheet

972	A278	100f Wrestling	4.75	4.75

22nd Summer Olympic Games, Moscow, July 19-Aug. 3.

Fruits — A279

1980, Aug. 15

973	A279	5f Blackberries	15	15
974	A279	15f Apricots	20	15
975	A279	20f Pears	35	15
976	A279	25f Apples	50	15
977	A279	35f Plums	1.00	25
		Nos. 973-977 (5)	2.20	
		Set value		70

World Tourism Conference, Manila, Sept. 27 — A279a

1980, Aug. 30 Litho. *Perf. 12½*

978	A279a	25f multicolored	28	15
979	A279a	50f multicolored	55	25
980	A279a	100f multicolored	1.10	55

Postal Union Emblem, Posthorn, Map of Arab States — A280

1980, Sept. 8 *Perf. 12*

981	A280	10f multicolored	15	15
982	A280	30f multicolored	35	16
983	A280	35f multicolored	40	18
		Set value		38

Arab Postal Union, 11th Congress, Baghdad.

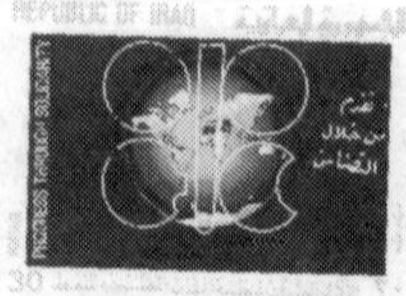

20th Anniversary of OPEC A281

1980, Sept. 30

984	A281	30f multicolored	1.00	25
985	A281	75f multicolored	1.50	50

Papilio Machaon A282

1980, Oct. 20 Photo. *Perf. 13½x14*

987	A282	10f shown	35	15
988	A282	15f Danaus chrysippus	45	20
989	A282	20f Vanessa atalanta	60	25
990	A282	30f Colias croceus	1.00	25

Hegira, 1,500th Anniv. A283

1980, Nov. 9 Litho. *Perf. 11½x12*

991	A283	15f multicolored	18	15
992	A283	25f multicolored	30	15
993	A283	35f multicolored	40	18
		Set value		38

International Palestinian Solidarity Day — A284

1980, Nov. 29

994	A284	25f multicolored	30	15
995	A284	35f multicolored	40	18
996	A284	75f multicolored	80	38

Army Day A285

February Revolution, 18th Anniversary A286

1981, Jan. 6 Photo. *Perf. 14x13½*

997	A285	5f multicolored	15	15
998	A285	30f multicolored	35	16
999	A285	75f multicolored	90	38
		Set value		58

1981, Feb. 8 *Perf. 12*

1000	A286	15f multicolored	18	15
1001	A286	30f multicolored	30	16
1002	A286	35f multicolored	40	18

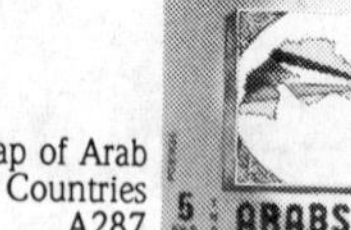

Map of Arab Countries A287

1981, Mar. 22 Litho. *Perf. 12½*

1003	A287	5f multicolored	15	15
1004	A287	25f multicolored	30	15
1005	A287	35f multicolored	40	18
		Set value		34

Battle of Qadisiya — A288

1981, Apr. 7 Photo. *Perf. 13½x13*

1006	A288	30f multicolored	35	16
1007	A288	35f multicolored	40	18
1008	A288	75f multicolored	80	38

Souvenir Sheet

1009	A288	100f multicolored	4.50	5.50

No. 1009 contains one horiz. stamp.

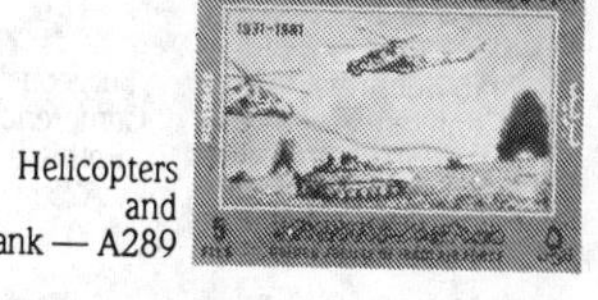

Helicopters and Tank — A289

1981, June 1 Photo.

1010	A289	5f shown	15	15
1011	A289	10f Plane	25	15
1012	A289	15f Rocket	50	15
		Set value		30

Air Force, 50th anniv. See No. C66.

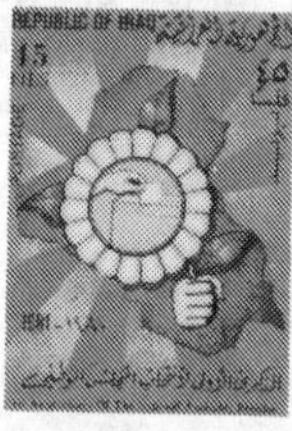

Natl. Assembly Election, First Anniv. — A290

1981, June 20 *Perf. 12½*

1013	A290	30f multicolored	35	16
1014	A290	35f multicolored	40	18
1015	A290	45f multicolored	55	24

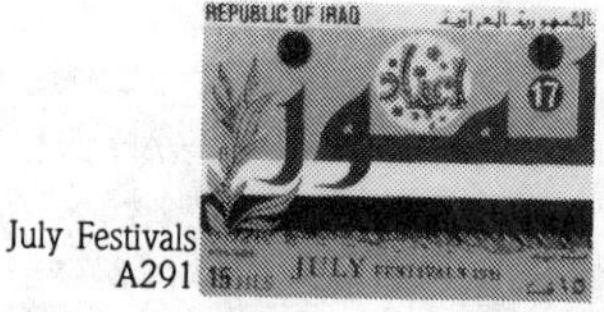

July Festivals A291

1981, July 17 Photo.

1016	A291	15f multicolored	15	15
1017	A291	25f multicolored	30	15
1018	A291	35f multicolored	40	18
		Set value		40

Pottery Maker — A292

Designs: Popular industries.

1981, Aug. 15 *Perf. 14*

1019	A292	5f Straw weaver	15	15
1020	A292	30f Metal worker	35	16
1021	A292	35f shown	40	18
1022	A292	50f Rug maker, horiz.	1.00	28

Islamic Pilgrimage A293

1981, Oct. 7 Photo. *Perf. 12x11½*

1023	A293	25f multicolored	30	15
1024	A293	45f multicolored	55	24
1025	A293	50f multicolored	60	30

World Food Day A294

1981, Oct. 16 Photo. *Perf. 14*

1026	A294	30f multicolored	35	16
1027	A294	45f multicolored	50	24
1028	A294	75f multicolored	80	45

Intl. Year of the Disabled — A295

1981, Nov. 15

1029	A295	30f multicolored	30	16
1030	A295	45f multicolored	50	24
1031	A295	75f multicolored	70	45

5th Anniv. of United Arab Shipping Co. — A296

1981, Dec. 2 *Perf. 13x13½*

1032	A296	50f multicolored	75	30
1033	A296	120f multicolored	2.25	75

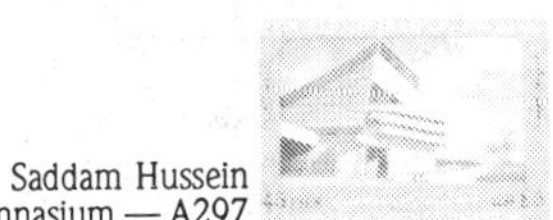

Saddam Hussein Gymnasium — A297

1981, Sept. 26 Litho. *Perf. 12x12½*

1034	A297	45f shown	48	24
1035	A297	50f Palace of Conferences	52	30
1036	A297	120f like #1035	1.25	75
1037	A297	150f like #1034	1.40	90

For surcharges, see Nos. 1097-1099.

35th Anniv. of Al Baath Party — A298

Mosul Spring Festival — A299

1982, Apr. 7 Photo. *Perf. 13½x13*

1038	A298	25f Pres. Hussein, flowers	22	15
1039	A298	30f "7 7 7"	26	16
1040	A298	45f like 25f	40	24
1041	A298	50f like 30f	45	30

Souvenir Sheet

Imperf

1042	A298	150f multicolored	1.75	1.25

1982, Apr. 15 Litho. *Perf. 11½x12*

1043	A299	25f Birds	30	15
1044	A299	30f Girl	35	16
1045	A299	45f like 25f	55	24
1046	A299	50f like 30f	60	30

Intl. Workers' Day — A300

1982, May 1 *Perf. 12½*

1047	A300	25f multicolored	20	15
1048	A300	45f multicolored	36	24
1049	A300	50f multicolored	40	30

14th World Telecommunications Day — A301

1982, May 17 Photo. *Perf. 13x13½*

1050	A301	5f multicolored	15	15
1051	A301	45f multicolored	36	24
1052	A301	100f multicolored	80	60

10th Anniv. of Oil Nationalization A302

1982, June 1 Litho. *Perf. 12½*

1053	A302	5f Oil gusher	15	15
1054	A302	25f like 5f	60	15
1055	A302	45f Statue	1.25	24
1056	A302	50f like 45f	1.40	30
		Set value		72

Martyrs' Day — A303

Women's Day — A304

1981, Dec. 1 Photo. *Perf. 14*

1057	A303	45f multicolored	36	24
1058	A303	50f multicolored	40	30
1059	A303	120f multicolored	1.00	75
		Nos. 1057-1059,O339A-O339C (6)	3.48	2.47

1982, Mar. 4 Litho. *Perf. 12½x13*

1060	A304	25f multicolored	30	15
1061	A304	45f multicolored	55	24
1062	A304	50f multicolored	60	30

A305 A305a

1982, Apr. 12 *Perf. 12½*

1063	A305	25f multicolored	30	15
1064	A305	45f multicolored	55	24
1065	A305	50f multicolored	60	30

Arab Postal Union, 30th anniv.

1982, June 7 Photo. *Perf. 14*

1065A	A305a	30f Nuclear power emblem, lion	50	20
1065B	A305a	45f shown	75	30
1065C	A305a	50f like 30f	90	40
1065D	A305a	120f like 45f	2.00	1.00

First anniv. of attack on nuclear power reactor.

July Festivals — A306

1982, July 17 Photo. *Perf. 14½x14*

1066	A306	25f multicolored	40	15
1067	A306	45f multicolored	55	24
1068	A306	50f multicolored	60	30

Lacerta Viridis A307

1982, Aug. 20 Litho. *Perf. 12½*

1069	A307	25f shown	30	15
1070	A307	30f Vipera aspis	35	16
1071	A307	45f Lacerta virdis, diff.	55	24
1072	A307	50f Natrix tessellata	60	30

7th Non-aligned Countries Conference, Baghdad, Sept. — A308

Designs: No. 1073, Tito. No. 1074, Nehru. No. 1075, Nasser. No. 1076, Kwame Nkrumah. No. 1077, Pres. Hussein.

1982, Sept. 6 Photo. *Perf. 13x13½*

1073	A308	50f multicolored	55	40
1074	A308	50f multicolored	55	40
1075	A308	50f multicolored	55	40
1076	A308	50f multicolored	55	40
1077	A308	100f multicolored	1.10	55
		Nos. 1073-1077 (5)	3.30	2.15

TB Bacillus Centenary A309

1982, Oct. 1 *Perf. 14x14½*

1078	A309	20f multicolored	20	15
1079	A309	50f multicolored	55	30
1080	A309	100f multicolored	1.10	40

1982 World Cup — A310

Designs: Various soccer players. 150f horiz.

1982, July 1 Litho. *Perf. 11½x12*

1081	A310	5f multicolored	15	15
1082	A310	45f multicolored	50	24
1083	A310	50f multicolored	55	30
1084	A310	100f multicolored	1.10	60

Souvenir Sheet

Perf. 12½

1085	A310	150f multicolored	1.75	1.25

13th UPU Day — A311

1982, Oct. 9 *Perf. 12x11½*

1086	A311	5f multicolored	15	15
1087	A311	45f multicolored	40	24
1088	A311	100f multicolored	90	60

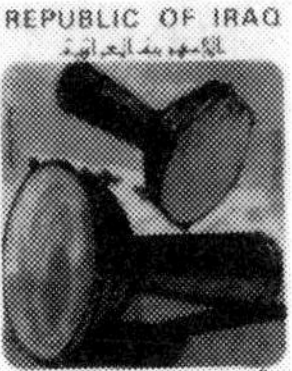

Musical Instruments — A312

1982, Nov. 15 *Perf. 12½x13*

1089	A312	5f Drums	15	15
1090	A312	10f Zither	20	15
1091	A312	35f Stringed instrument	65	35
1092	A312	100f Lute	1.75	85

Birth Anniv. of Mohammed A313

Mecca Mosque views.

1982, Dec. 27 Litho. *Perf. 12x11½*

1093	A313	25f multicolored	20	15
1094	A313	30f multicolored	28	22
1095	A313	45f multicolored	36	24
1096	A313	50f multicolored	40	30

Nos. 1034-1036 Surcharged

1983, May 15 Litho. *Perf. 12x12½*

1097	A297	60f on 50f multi	75	32
1098	A297	70f on 45f multi	90	45
1099	A297	160f on 120f multi	2.00	90

July Festivals A314

1983, July 17 Litho. *Perf. 14½x14*

1100	A314	30f multicolored	35	16
1101	A314	60f multicolored	75	32
1102	A314	70f multicolored	90	45

Local Flowers — A315

1983, June 15 Photo. *Perf. 15x14*

Border Color

1103	A315	10f shown, light blue	15	15
1104	A315	20f Flowers, diff., pale yellow	16	15
1105	A315	30f like 10f, yellow	25	16
1106	A315	40f like 20f, gray	35	25

1107 A315	50f like 10f, pale green	40	30
1108 A315	100f like 20f, pink	80	60
a.	Bklt. pane of 6, #1103-1108	3.00	
	Nos. 1103-1108 (6)	2.11	1.61

Nos. 1103-1108 issued in booklets only.

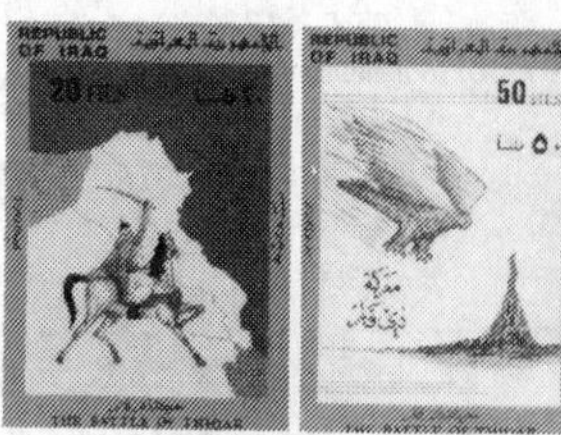

Battle of Thi Qar
A316 A317

1983, Oct. 30 Photo. *Perf. 12½x13*

1109 A316	20f silver & multi	24	15
1110 A317	50f silver & multi	60	30
1111 A316	60f gold & multi	70	32
1112 A317	70f gold & multi	1.10	40

World Communications Year — A318

Design: 25f, 70f show emblem and hexagons.

1983, Oct. 20 Photo. *Perf. 11½x12*

1113 A318	5f brt yel grn & multi	15	15
1114 A318	25f rose lil & multi	30	15
1115 A318	60f brt org yel & multi	70	34
1116 A318	70f brt bl vio & multi	1.10	40

Souvenir Sheet

1117 A318	200f ap grn & multi	3.75	3.75

Baghdad Intl. Fair — A319

Symbolic "9" — A320

1983, Nov. 1 Photo. *Perf. 12½*

1118 A319	60f multicolored	48	32
1119 A319	70f multicolored	56	40
1120 A319	160f multicolored	1.30	90

1983, Nov. 10 Photo. *Perf. 14*

9th Natl. Congress of Arab Baath Socialist Party: 30f, 70f, Symbols of development. 60f, 100f, Torch, eagle, globe, open book.

1121 A320	30f multicolored	24	16
1122 A320	60f multicolored	48	32
1123 A320	70f multicolored	56	40
1124 A320	100f multicolored	80	55

Festival Crowd A321

Various Paintings.

1983, Nov. 20 Litho. *Perf. 12½*

1125 A321	60f shown	48	32
1126 A321	60f Men hauling boat, vert.	48	32
1127 A321	60f Decorations	48	32
1128 A321	70f Village	56	40
1129 A321	70f Crowd	56	40
	Nos. 1125-1129 (5)	2.56	1.76

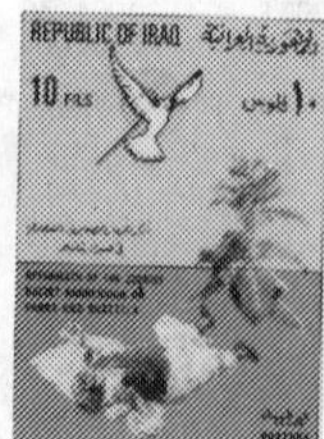

Sabra and Shattela Palestinian Refugee Camp Massacre — A322

Various Victims.

1983, Nov. 29 *Perf. 11½x12*

1130 A322	10f multicolored	15	15
1131 A322	60f multicolored	1.00	32
1132 A322	70f multicolored	1.10	40
1133 A322	160f multicolored	2.00	92

Pres. Hussein, Map — A323

1983 Photo. *Perf. 13½x13*

1134 A323	60f multicolored	60	32
1135 A323	70f multicolored	70	40
1136 A323	250f multicolored	2.50	1.65

Pres. Hussein as head of Al Baath Party, 4th anniv.

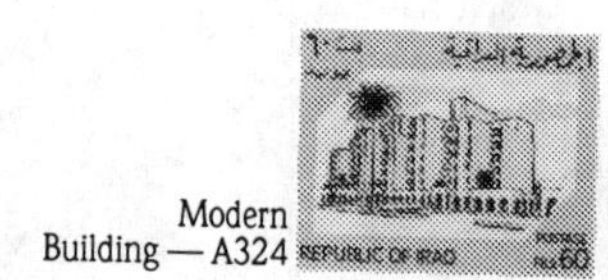

Modern Building — A324

Various buildings.

1983, Dec. 31 Litho. *Perf. 14*

1137 A324	60f multicolored	48	32
1138 A324	70f multicolored	56	40
1139 A324	160f multicolored	1.30	92
1140 A324	200f multicolored	1.60	1.10
	Nos. 1137-1140,O340-O341 (6)	4.98	3.46

Medical Congress Emblem A325

1984, Mar. 10 *Perf. 13x12½*

1141 A325	60f multicolored	60	32
1142 A325	70f multicolored	70	40
1143 A325	200f multicolored	2.00	1.10

25th Intl. Congress of Military Medicine and Pharmacy, Baghdad, Mar. 10-15.

Pres. Hussein's Birthday — A326

Various portraits of Hussein.

1984, Apr. 28 Litho. *Perf. 12½x13*

1144 A326	60f multicolored	48	32
1145 A326	70f multicolored	56	40
1146 A326	160f multicolored	1.30	92
1147 A326	200f multicolored	1.60	1.10

Souvenir Sheet

Imperf

1148 A326	250f multicolored	2.00	1.75

Gold ink on Nos. 1144-1147 and dark green ink in "margin" of No. 1148 was applied by a thermographic process, producing a raised effect. No. 1148 has perf. 12½x13 label picturing Pres. Hussein.

1984 Summer Olympics, Los Angeles A327

1984, Aug. 12 Litho. *Perf. 12x11½*

1149 A327	50f Boxing	32	22
1150 A327	60f Weight lifting	38	25
1151 A327	70f like 50f	45	30
1152 A327	100f like 60f	65	45

Size: 80x60mm

Imperf

1153 A327	200f Soccer	1.40	95
	Nos. 1149-1153 (5)	3.20	2.17

Nos. 1153 contains one 32x41mm perf. 12½ label within the stamp.

A328

A329

Designs: 50f, 70f, Pres. Hussein, flaming horses heads, map. 60f, 100f, Abstract of woman, sapling, rifle. 200f, Shield, heraldic eagle.

1984, Sept. 22 *Perf. 11½x12*

1154 A328	50f multicolored	32	22
1155 A328	60f multicolored	38	25
1156 A328	70f multicolored	45	30
1157 A328	100f multicolored	65	45

Size: 80x60mm

Imperf

1158 A328	200f multicolored	1.40	95
	Nos. 1154-1158 (5)	3.20	2.17

Battle of Qadisiya. No. 1158 contains one 32x41mm perf. 12½ label within the stamp.

1984, Dec. 1 *Perf. 13½*

Martyrs' Day: 50f, 70f, Natl. flag as flame. 60f, 100f, Woman holding rifle, medal.

1159 A329	50f multicolored	32	22
1160 A329	60f multicolored	38	25
1161 A329	70f multicolored	45	30
1162 A329	100f multicolored	65	45

Pres. Hussein's Visit to Al-Mustansiriyah University, 5th Anniv. — A330

1985, Apr. 2 Photo. *Perf. 12x11½*

1163 A330	60f dk bl gray & dk pink	38	25
1164 A330	70f myr grn & dk pink	45	30
1165 A330	250f blk & dk pink	1.75	1.15

Iraqi Air Force, 54th Anniv. — A331

Pres. Hussein, 48th Birthday — A332

Designs: 10f, 160f, Pres. Hussein, fighter planes, pilot's wings. 60f, 70f, 200f, Planes, flag, "54," horiz.

Perf. 13x12½, 13½ (60f, 70f)

1985, Apr. 22 Litho.

1166 A331	10f multicolored	15	15
1167 A331	60f multicolored	38	25
1168 A331	70f multicolored	45	30
1169 A331	160f multicolored	1.05	70

Souvenir Sheet

Perf. 12½

1170 A331	200f multicolored	1.40	95

1985, Apr. 28 *Perf. 13½*

Designs: 30f, 70f, Pres. Hussein, sunflower. 60f, 100f, Pres., candle and flowers. 200f, Flowers and text.

1171 A332	30f multicolored	20	15
1172 A332	60f multicolored	38	25
1173 A332	70f multicolored	45	30
1174 A332	100f multicolored	65	45

Souvenir Sheet

Perf. 13x12½

1175 A332	200f multicolored	1.40	95

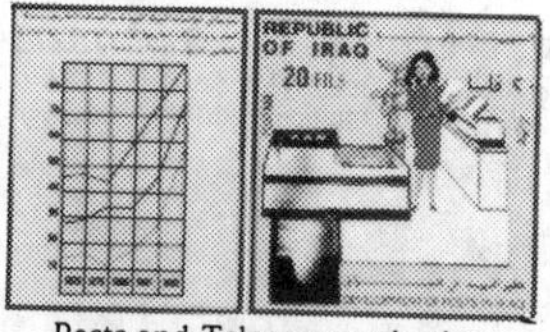

Posts and Telecommunications Development Program — A333

Designs: 20f, 60f, Graph, woman in modern office. 50f, 70f, Satellite dish and graphs.

1985, June 30 *Perf. 12½*

1176 A333	20f multicolored	15	15
1177 A333	50f multicolored	32	22
1178 A333	60f multicolored	38	25
1179 A333	70f multicolored	45	30

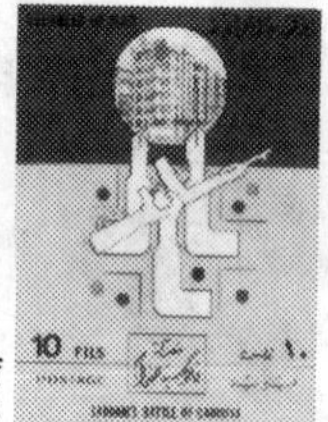

Battle of Qadisiya — A334

Designs: 10f, 60f, Shown. 20f, 70f, Pres. Hussein, Al-Baath Party emblem. 200f, Dove, natl. flag as shield, soldier.

1985, Sept. 4 *Perf. 11½x12*

1180 A334	10f multicolored	15	15
1181 A334	20f multicolored	15	15
1182 A334	60f multicolored	38	25
1183 A334	70f multicolored	45	30

Souvenir Sheet

Perf. 12x12½

1184 A334	200f multicolored	1.40	95

No. 1184 contains one stamp 30x45mm.

Solar Energy Research Center
A335

1985, Sept. 19 *Perf. 13½*

1185 A335 10f multicolored	15	15
1186 A335 50f multicolored	32	22
1187 A335 100f multicolored	65	45

UN Child Survival Campaign
A336

Al Sharif, Poet, Death Millennium
A337

Designs: 10f, 50f, Stop Polio Campaign. 15f, 100f, Girl, infant.

1985, Oct. 10

1188 A336 10f multicolored	15	15
1189 A336 15f multicolored	15	15
1190 A336 50f multicolored	32	22
1191 A336 100f multicolored	65	45
Set value		80

1985, Oct. 20

1192 A337 10f multicolored	15	15
1193 A337 50f multicolored	32	22
1194 A337 100f multicolored	65	45

UN, 40th Anniv.
A338

1985, Oct. 24

1195 A338 10f multicolored	15	15
1196 A338 40f multicolored	28	18
1197 A338 100f multicolored	65	45

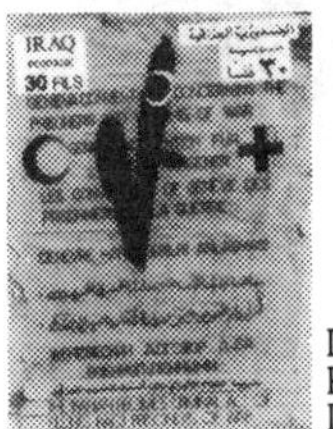
Death of Iraqi Prisoners of War in Iran — A339

Designs: 30f, 100f, Knife, Geneva Convention declaration, red crescent, red cross. 70f, 200f, POWs, gun shell, natl. flag, cherub and dove.

1985, Nov. 10 *Perf. 14*

1198 A339 30f multicolored	20	15
1199 A339 70f multicolored	45	30
1200 A339 100f multicolored	65	45
1201 A339 200f multicolored	1.40	95

Size: 110x80mm

Imperf

1202 A339 250f multicolored	2.75	1.15
Nos. 1198-1202 (5)	5.45	3.00

No. 1202 contains 2 perf. 14 labels similar to 100f and 200f designs within the stamp.

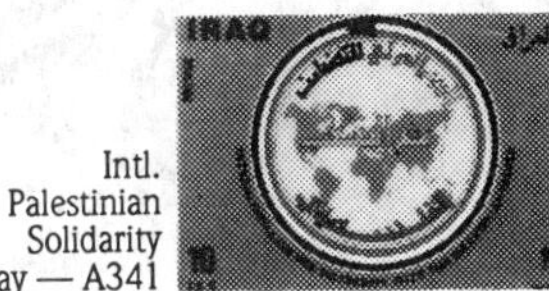
Intl. Palestinian Solidarity Day — A341

1985, Nov. 29 Litho. *Perf. 13½*

1207 A341 10f multicolored	15	15
1208 A341 50f multicolored	50	25
1209 A341 100f multicolored	1.00	50

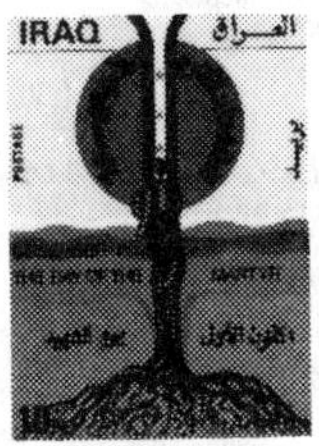
Martyrs' Day — A342

Intl. Youth Year — A343

1985, Dec. 1 *Perf. 11½x12*

1210 A342 10f multicolored	15	15
1211 A342 40f multicolored	28	18
1212 A342 100f multicolored	70	50

1985, Dec. 12 Litho. *Perf. 11½x12*

IYY emblem and: 40f, 100f, Soldier holding flag. 50f, 200f, Youths, flag. 250f, Flag, cogwheel, rifle muzzle, symbols of industry.

1213 A343 40f multicolored	40	18
1214 A343 50f multicolored	45	22
1215 A343 100f multicolored	90	45
1216 A343 200f multicolored	2.00	95

Souvenir Sheet

Perf. 12x12½

1217 A343 250f multicolored	2.50	1.15

No. 1217 contains one stamp 30x45mm. Exists imperf.

Army Day — A344

Pres. Hussein, "6" and: 10f, 50f, Soldier, flowers, vert. 40f, 100f, Flag, cogwheel, rockets. 200f, Al-Baath Party emblem, rifle, waves.

1986, Jan. 6 *Perf. 11½x12, 12x11½*

1218 A344 10f multicolored	15	15
1219 A344 40f multicolored	40	18
1220 A344 50f multicolored	45	22
1221 A344 100f multicolored	90	45

Miniature Sheet

Perf. 12½x11½

1222 A344 200f multicolored	2.00	95

No. 1222 contains one stamp 52x37mm.

Women's Day — A345

Designs: 30f, 100f, Women in traditional and modern occupations, vert. 50f, 150f, Emblem, green flag, battle scene, grapes.

Perf. 11½x12, 12x11½

1986, Mar. 8 Litho.

1223 A345 30f multicolored	22	15
1224 A345 50f multicolored	35	24
1225 A345 100f multicolored	70	48
1226 A345 150f multicolored	1.05	70

Pres. Hussein, 49th Birthday — A346

Designs: 30f, 100f, Children greeting Pres. 50f, 150f, Portrait. 250f, Portrait, flag, flowers.

1986, Apr. 28 Litho. *Perf. 11½x12*

1227 A346 30f multicolored	28	15
1228 A346 50f multicolored	45	22
1229 A346 100f multicolored	90	45
1230 A346 150f multicolored	1.25	65

Size: 80x60mm

Imperf

1231 A346 250f multicolored	2.50	1.15
Nos. 1227-1231 (5)	5.38	2.62

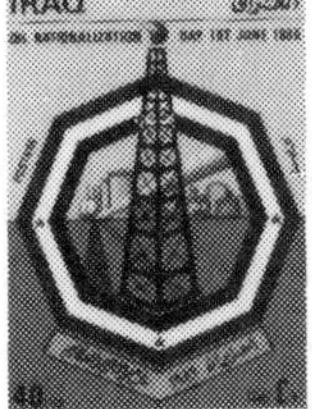
Oil Nationalization Day, June 1 — A347

Labor Day — A348

Designs: 10f, 100f, Symbols of industry, horiz. 40f, 150f, Oil well, pipeline to refinery.

Perf. 12x11½, 11½x12

1986, July 25 Litho.

1232 A347 10f multicolored	15	15
1233 A347 40f multicolored	45	18
1234 A347 100f multicolored	85	45
1235 A347 150f multicolored	1.25	65

1986, July 28 *Perf. 11½x12*

Designs: 10f, 100f, Laborer, cog wheel. 40f, 150f, May Day emblem.

1236 A348 10f multicolored	15	15
1237 A348 40f multicolored	28	18
1238 A348 100f multicolored	65	45
1239 A348 150f multicolored	95	65

Iraqi Air Force, 55th Anniv.
A349

Designs: 30f, 100f, Fighter plane, pilot's wings, natl. flag. 50f, 150f, Fighter planes. 250f, Medal, aircraft in flight.

1986, July 28 *Perf. 12x11½*

1240 A349 30f multicolored	30	15
1241 A349 50f multicolored	42	22
1242 A349 100f multicolored	85	45
1243 A349 150f multicolored	1.25	65

Size: 81x61mm

Imperf

1244 A349 250f multicolored	2.50	1.10
Nos. 1240-1244 (5)	5.32	2.57

No. 1244 also exists perf.

July Festivals — A350

Pres. Hussein and: 20f, 100f, Flag. 30f, 150f, "17." 250f, Inscription, portrait inside medal of honor.

1986, July 29 *Perf. 11½x12*

1245 A350 20f multicolored	15	15
1246 A350 30f multicolored	22	15
1247 A350 100f multicolored	65	45
1248 A350 150f multicolored	95	65

Size: 81x61mm

Imperf

1249 A350 250f multicolored	1.60	1.10
Nos. 1245-1249 (5)	3.57	2.50

1st Qadisiya Battle — A351

Designs: 20f, 70f, Warrior, shield, vert. 60f, 100f, Pres. Hussein, star, battle scene.

Perf. 13x13½, 13½x13

1986, Sept. 4 Litho.

1250 A351 20f multicolored	15	15
1251 A351 60f multicolored	42	28
1252 A351 70f multicolored	50	35
1253 A351 100f multicolored	70	48

Battle between the Arabs and Persian Empire.

Hussein's Battle of Qadisiya — A352

Designs: 30f, 100f, Pres. Hussein, soldiers saluting peace, vert. 40f, 150f, Pres., armed forces. 250f, Pres., soldiers, flags, military scenes.

Perf. 11½x12½, 12½x11½

1986, Sept. 4

1254 A352 30f multicolored	22	15
1255 A352 40f multicolored	28	20
1256 A352 100f multicolored	70	48
1257 A352 150f multicolored	1.05	70

Size: 80x60mm

Imperf

1258 A352 250f multicolored	1.75	1.15
Nos. 1254-1258 (5)	4.00	2.68

Intl. Peace Year — A353

1986, Nov. 15 Litho. *Perf. 11½x12*

1259 A353 50f Dove, flag, G clef	32	24
1260 A353 100f Globe, dove, rifle	65	48
1261 A353 150f like 50f	1.00	70
1262 A353 250f like 100f	1.60	1.10

Size: 80x69mm

Imperf

1263 A353 200f Emblem, flag, map, fist	1.30	1.00
Nos. 1259-1263 (5)	4.87	3.52

Buying Sets
It is often less expensive to purchase complete sets than individual stamps that make up the set. Set values are provided for many such sets.

Pres. Hussein
A354 A355

1986 ***Perf. 12½x12***

1264 A354 30f multicolored 20 15
1265 A355 30f multicolored 20 15
1266 A354 50f multicolored 32 22
1267 A355 50f multicolored 32 22
1268 A354 100f multicolored 65 45
1269 A355 100f multicolored 65 45
1270 A354 150f multicolored 1.00 68
1271 A355 150f multicolored 1.00 68
1272 A354 250f multicolored 1.60 1.05
1273 A354 350f multicolored 2.25 1.50
Nos. 1264-1273 (10) 8.19 5.55

For overprints and surcharge see Nos. 1347-1348, 1455.

Army Day — A356

1987, Jan. 6 Litho. ***Perf. 12x12½***

1274 A356 20f shown 15 15
1275 A356 40f Hussein, armed forces 25 25
1276 A356 90f like 20f 58 58
1277 A356 100f like 40f 65 65

United Arab Shipping Co., 10th Anniv. (in 1986) A357

1987, Apr. 3 Litho. ***Perf. 12½***

1278 A357 50f Cargo ship 32 22
1279 A357 100f Container ship Chaleb Ibn Al Waleeb 65 45
1280 A357 150f like 50f 1.00 68
1281 A357 250f like 100f 1.60 1.05

Size: 102x91mm

Imperf

1282 A357 200f Loading cargo aboard the Waleeb 1.30 1.00

Arab Baath Socialist Party, 40th Anniv. — A358

1987, Apr. 7 Litho. ***Perf. 12x12½***

1283 A358 20f shown 15 15
1284 A358 40f Hussein, "7," map 25 25
1285 A358 90f like 20f 58 58
1286 A358 100f like 40f 65 65

Pres. Hussein's 50th Birthday A359

1987, Apr. 28 ***Perf. 12½x12***

1287 A359 20f shown 15 15
1288 A359 40f Portrait 25 25
1289 A359 90f like 20f 58 58
1290 A359 100f like 40f 65 65

July Festivals — A360

UNICEF, 40th Anniv. — A361

Perf. 12½x12, 12x12½

1987, July 17

1291 A360 20f Hussein, star, flag, horiz. 15 15
1292 A360 40f shown 25 25
1293 A360 90f like 20f, horiz. 58 58
1294 A360 100f like 40f 65 65

1987, Oct. 4 ***Perf. 12x12½, 12½x12***

1295 A361 20f shown 15 15
1296 A361 40f "40," horiz. 25 25
1297 A361 90f like 20f 58 58
1298 A361 100f like 40f, horiz. 65 65

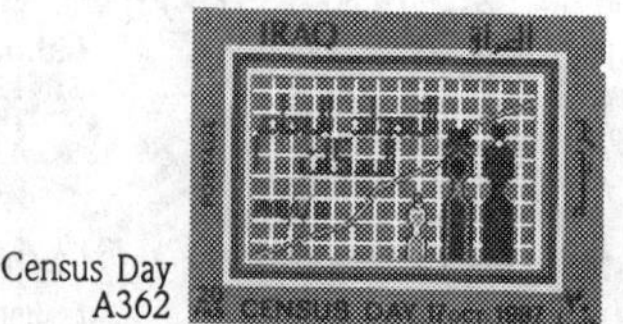

Census Day A362

1987, Nov. 1 ***Perf. 12x11½***

1299 A362 20f shown 15 15
1300 A362 30f Graph, Arabs, diff. 20 20
1301 A362 50f like 30f 35 35
1302 A362 500f like 20f 3.25 3.25

Army Day — A363

Perf. 11½x12, 12x11½

1988, Jan. 6 **Litho.**

1303 A363 20f "6," Hussein, troops, vert. 15 15
1304 A363 30f shown 20 15
1305 A363 50f like 20f, vert. 35 15
1306 A363 150f like 30f 1.00 38
Set value 60

Art Day — A364 A365

1988, Jan. 8 Litho. ***Perf. 11½x12***

1307 A364 20f shown 15 15
1308 A364 30f Hussein, rainbow, gun barrel, music 22 15
1309 A364 50f like 20f 38 15
1310 A364 100f like 30f 75 25

Size: 60x80mm

Imperf

1311 A364 150f Notes, instruments, floral ornament 1.20 80
Nos. 1307-1311 (5) 2.70
Set value 1.30

1988, Feb. 8 ***Perf. 11½x12, 12x11½***

1312 A365 20f "8," troops, Hussein, horiz. 15 15
1313 A365 30f "8," Hussein, eagle 22 15
1314 A365 50f like 20f, horiz. 38 15
1315 A365 150f like 30f 1.20 40
Set value 65

Popular Army, 18th anniv. (20f, 50f); Feb. 8th Revolution, 25th anniv. (30f, 150f).

Al-Baath Arab Socialist Party, 50th Anniv. — A366

President Hussein's 50th Birthday — A367

1988, Apr. 7 ***Perf. 12x12½, 12½x12***

1316 A366 20f Flag, grain, convention, horiz. 15 15
1317 A366 30f shown 22 15
1318 A366 50f like 20f, horiz. 38 15
1319 A366 150f like 30f 1.20 40
Set value 65

1988, Apr. 28 ***Perf. 12x12½***

1320 A367 20f shown 15 15
1321 A367 30f Hussein, 3 hands, flowers 22 15
1322 A367 50f like 20f 38 15
1323 A367 100f like 50f 75 25

Size: 90x99mm

Imperf

1324 A367 150f Sun, Hussein, heart, flowers 1.20 80
Nos. 1320-1324 (5) 2.70
Set value 1.30

World Health Organization, 40th Anniv. — A368

Regional Marine Environment Day, Apr. 4 — A369

1988, June 1 ***Perf. 12½x12, 12x12½***

1325 A368 20f WHO anniv. emblem, horiz. 15 15
1326 A368 40f shown 30 15
1327 A368 90f like 20f, horiz. 68 22
1328 A368 100f like 40f 75 25
Set value 60

Perf. 12x12½, 12½x12

1988, Apr. 24

1329 A369 20f shown 15 15
1330 A369 40f Flag in map, fish, horiz. 30 15
1331 A369 90f like 20f 68 22
1332 A369 100f like 40f, horiz. 75 25
Set value 60

Shuhada School Victims Memorial — A370

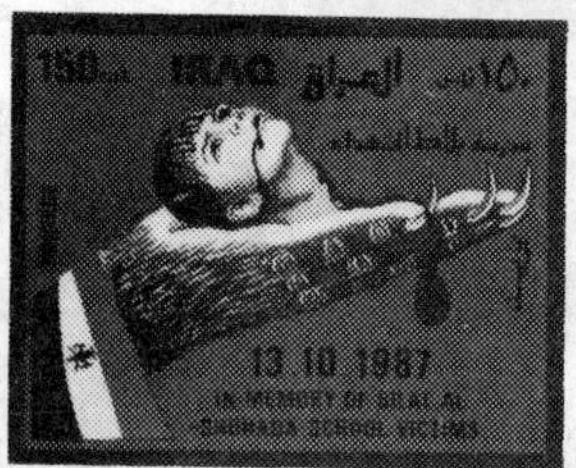

A371

1988, June 1 ***Perf. 11½x12, 12x11½***

1333 A370 20f shown 15 15
1334 A370 40f Girl caught in explosion, horiz. 30 15
1335 A370 90f like 20f 68 22
1336 A370 100f like 40f, horiz. 75 25
Set value 60

Souvenir Sheet

Perf. 12½

1337 A371 150f red, blk & brt grn 1.15 75

Pilgrimage to Mecca — A372

1988, July 24 Litho. ***Perf. 13½***

1338 A372 90f multicolored 70 22
1339 A372 100f multicolored 80 28
1340 A372 150f multicolored 1.20 40

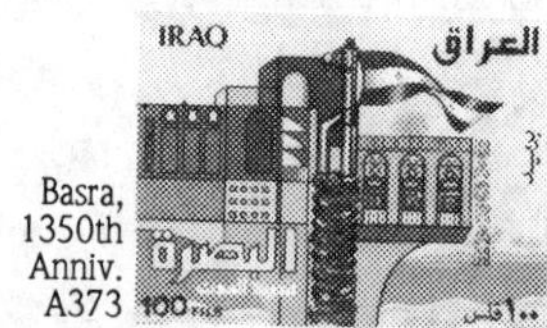

Basra, 1350th Anniv. A373

1988, Oct. 22 ***Perf. 12x11½***

1341 A373 100f multicolored 75 25

Natl. Flag, Grip on Lightning — A374

Pres. Hussein, Natl. Flag — A375

1988, July 17 *Perf. 12x12½*

1342 A374 50f shown 38 15
1343 A374 90f Map, Hussein, desert 68 22
1344 A374 100f like 50f 75 25
1345 A374 150f like 90f 1.15 35

Size: 90x70mm

Imperf

1346 A375 250f shown 1.90 65
Nos. 1342-1346 (5) 4.86 1.62

July Festivals and 9th anniv. of Pres. Hussein's assumption of office.

Nos. 1272-1273 Overprinted

انتصر العراق
١٩٨٨/٨/٨

1988, Aug. 7 **Litho.** *Perf. 12½x12*

1347 A354 250f multicolored 2.90 95
1348 A354 350f multicolored 4.00 1.35

Victory.

Navy Day — A376

1988, Aug. 12 *Perf. 12x12½*

1349 A376 50f shown 58 20
1350 A376 90f Map, boats 1.05 35
1351 A376 100f like 50f 1.15 38
1352 A376 150f like 90f 1.75 58

Size: 91x70mm

Imperf

1353 A376 250f Emblem, Pres. Hussein decorating officers 3.50 1.15
Nos. 1349-1353 (5) 8.03 2.66

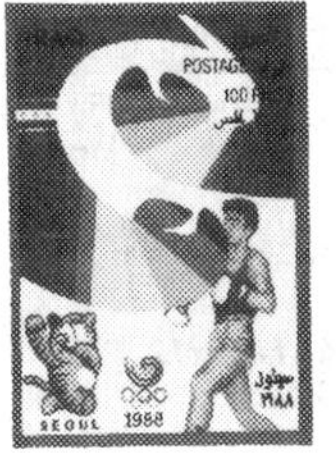

1988 Summer Olympics, Seoul — A377

1988, Sept. 19 *Perf. 12x12½*

1354 A377 100f Boxing, character trademark 1.15 38
1355 A377 150f Flag, emblems 1.75 58

Size: 101x91mm

Imperf

1356 A377 500f Emblem, trademark, Hussein, trophy 7.00 2.35

Liberation of Fao — A378

1988, Sept. 1 *Perf. 12x11½*

1357 A378 100f multicolored 1.15 38
1358 A378 150f multicolored 1.75 58

Size: 60x80mm

Imperf

1359 A378 500f Hussein, text 7.00 2.35

Mosul A379

Baghdad — A380

Ancient cities.

Perf. 12x11½, 11½x12

1988, Oct. 22

1360 A379 50f Fortress 58 20
1361 A380 150f Astrolabe, modern architecture 1.75 58

Al-Hussein Missile — A381

1988, Sept. 10 *Perf. 11½x12*

1362 A381 100f multicolored 80 28
1363 A381 150f multicolored 1.20 40

Size: 80x60mm

Imperf

1364 A381 500f Hussein, map, missile 3.75 1.25

2nd Intl. Festival, Babylon — A382

1988, Sept. 30 *Perf. 11½x12*

1365 A382 100f multicolored 78 25
1366 A382 150f multicolored 1.15 38

Size: 60x80mm

Imperf

1367 A382 500f Medallions 3.75 1.25

Victorious Iraq — A383

1988, Aug. 8 **Litho.** *Perf. 12x11½*

1368 A383 50f multicolored 40 15
1369 A383 100f multicolored 80 28
1370 A383 150f multicolored 1.20 40

Birthday of Mohammed A384

1988, Oct. 23 **Litho.** *Perf. 11½x12*

1371 A384 100f multicolored 75 25
1372 A384 150f multicolored 1.10 38
1373 A384 1d multicolored 7.50 2.50

Martyrs' Day — A385

1988, Dec. 1 **Litho.** *Perf. 13½*

1374 A385 100f multicolored 75 25
1375 A385 150f multicolored 1.10 38
1376 A385 500f multicolored 3.75 1.25

Police Day — A386

1989, Jan. 9 **Litho.** *Perf. 12x11½*

1377 A386 50f multicolored 38 15
1378 A386 100f multicolored 75 25
1379 A386 150f multicolored 1.10 38

Postal Savings Bank — A387

بريد
a

1988 **Litho.** *Perf. 11½x12*

1380 A387 50f shown

Size: 23½x25mm

Perf. 13½x13

1381 A387(a) 100f multi
1382 A387(a) 150f multi

Nos. 1381-1382 without overprint are postal savings stamps.

Arab Cooperation Council A388

1989, Feb. 12 **Litho.** *Perf. 12x11½*

1383 A388 100f shown 78 26
1384 A388 150f Statesmen, diff. 1.15 38

52nd Birthday of Pres. Hussein A392

1989, Apr. 28 **Litho.** *Perf. 12x11½*

1392 A392 100f multicolored 68 22
1393 A392 150f multicolored 1.00 32

Size: 60x81mm

Imperf

1394 A392 250f Hussein, diff. 1.70 58

Fao Liberation, 1st Anniv. A393

1989, Apr. 18 *Perf. 12x11½*

1395 A393 100f multi 68 22
1396 A393 150f multi 1.00 32

Size: 60x81mm

Imperf

1397 A393 250f Calendar 1.70 58

Gen. Adnan Khairalla — A394 Reconstruction of Basra — A395

1989, May 6 **Litho.** *Perf. 13½*

1398 A394 50f gold & multi 48 16
1399 A394 100f copper & multi 95 32
1400 A394 150f silver & multi 1.45 48

Gen. Adnan Khairalla (1940-1989), deputy commander-in-chief of the armed forces and minister of defense.

1989, June 14

1401 A395 100f multi 95 32
1402 A395 150f multi 1.45 48

Reconstruction of Fao — A396 Women — A397

1989, June 25

1403 A396 100f multi 95 32
1404 A396 150f multi 1.45 48

1989, June 25 **Litho.** *Perf. 11½x12*

1405 A397 100f yel & multi 58 20
1406 A397 150f brt pink & multi 88 30
1407 A397 1d brt blue & multi 5.75 2.00
1408 A397 5d white & multi 28.75 9.50

July Festivals — A398

1989, July 17 **Litho.** *Perf. 12x12½*

1409 A398 50f multicolored 40 15
1410 A398 100f multicolored 78 26
1411 A398 150f multicolored 1.20 40

Election of Pres. Hussein, 10th anniv.

Family A399

1989, July 19 *Perf. 13½*

1412	A399	50f multicolored	40	15
1413	A399	100f multicolored	78	26
1414	A399	150f multicolored	1.20	40

A400

Victory Day — A401

1989, Aug. 8 *Perf. 12x12½*

1415	A400	100f multicolored	78	26
1416	A400	150f multicolored	1.20	40

Size: 71x91mm

Imperf

1417	A401	250f multicolored	2.00	68

Interparliamentary Union, Cent. — A402

1989, Sept. 15 *Perf. 12½x12*

1418	A402	25f multicolored	20	15
1419	A402	100f multicolored	78	26
1420	A402	150f multicolored	1.20	40

Ancient Cities A403

1989, Oct. 15 *Perf. 11½x12½*

1421	A403	100f Dhi Qar-ur	78	26
1422	A403	100f Erbil	78	26
1423	A403	100f An Najaf	78	26

5th Session of the Arab Ministers of Transport Council, Baghdad, Oct. 21 — A404

Designs: 100f, Land, air and sea transport, diff. 150f, Modes of transport, flags, vert.

Perf. 12x11½, 11½x12

1989, Oct. 21

1424	A404	50f shown	40	15
1425	A404	100f multicolored	78	26
1426	A404	150f multicolored	1.20	40

Iraqi News Agency, 30th Anniv. A405

1989, Nov. 9 *Perf. 13½*

1427	A405	50f multicolored	40	15
1428	A405	100f multicolored	78	26
1429	A405	150f multicolored	1.20	40

Declaration of Palestinian State, 1st Anniv. — A406

Flowers — A407

1989, Nov. 15 *Perf. 12x12½*

1430	A406	25f shown	20	15
1431	A406	50f Palestinian uprising	40	15
1432	A406	100f like 25f	78	26
1433	A406	150f like 50f	1.20	40

1989, Nov. 20 *Perf. 13½x13*

1434	A407	25f *Viola sp.*	20	15
1435	A407	50f *Antirrhinum majus*	40	15
1436	A407	100f *Hibiscus trionum*	78	26
1437	A407	150f *Mesembryanthemum sparkles*	1.20	40

Miniature Sheet

Perf. 12½x11½

1438	Sheet of 4	4.00	4.00
a.	A407 25f like No. 1434	1.00	1.00
b.	A407 50f like No. 1435	1.00	1.00
c.	A407 100f like No. 1436	1.00	1.00
d.	A407 150f like No. 1437	1.00	1.00

No. 1438 has a continuous design. No. 1438 sold for 500f.

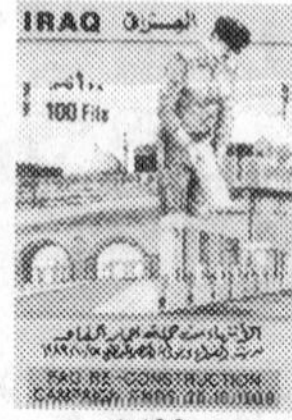

A408

A409

1989, Oct. 25 **Litho.** *Perf. 13½*

1439	A408	100f multicolored	78	26
1440	A408	150f multicolored	1.15	38

Reconstruction of Fao.

1989, Dec. 4 **Litho.** *Perf. 13½*

1441	A409	50f multicolored	38	16
1442	A409	100f multicolored	78	26
1443	A409	150f multicolored	1.15	38

Martyrs' Day.

Iraqi Red Crescent Soc. — A410

1989, Dec. 10 **Litho.** *Perf. 13½*

1444	A410	100f multicolored	38	16
1445	A410	150f multicolored	1.15	38
1446	A410	500f multicolored	3.75	1.25

Arab Cooperation Council, 1st Anniv. — A411

1990, Feb. 16 **Litho.** *Perf. 13x13½*

1447	A411	50f yellow & multi	85	28
1448	A411	100f orange & multi	1.70	55

Size: 80x62mm

Imperf

1449	A411	250f blue & multi	5.00	1.65

Nos. 1435, 1437 Ovptd.

1990, May 28 **Litho.** *Perf. 13½x13*

1450	A407	50f multicolored		
1451	A407	150f multicolored		

Arab League Summit Conf., Baghdad.

End of Iran-Iraq War, 2nd Anniv. — A412

1990, Aug. 30 **Litho.** *Perf. 13½x13*

1452	A412	50f purple & multi		
1453	A412	100f blue & multi		

Imperf

Size: 59x81mm

1454	A412	250f Saddam Hussein, dove		

No. 1269 Surcharged

1992(?) **Litho.** *Perf. 12½x12*

1455	A355	1d on 100f #1269		

No. RA23 Surcharged ١٠٠ فلس

1992 **Photo.** *Perf. 14*

1457	PT3	100f on 5f multi		

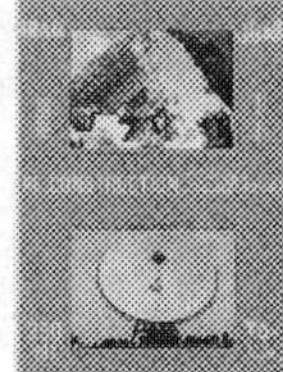

Reconstruction of Iraq — A413

Designs: 250f, Satellite dish. 500f, Bridges. 750f, Power plant, horiz. 1d, Factory.

1993, Sept. **Photo.** *Perf. 14*

1459	A413	250f red & multi		
1460	A413	500f blue & multi		
1461	A413	750f yellow & multi		
1462	A413	1d multicolored		

Stamps of this issue may be poorly centered or have perforations running through the design.

Peace Ship — A414

1993 **Photo.** *Perf. 14*

1463	A414	2d red & multi		
1464	A414	5d green & multi		

AIR POST STAMPS

Catalogue values for unused stamps in this section are for Never Hinged items.

Basra Airport — AP1

Diyala Railway Bridge — AP2

Vickers Viking over: 4f, 20f, Kut Dam. 5f, 35f, Faisal II Bridge.

Perf. 11½, 11½x12

1949, Feb. 1 **Engr.** **Unwmk.**

C1	AP1	3f blue green	15	15
C2	AP1	4f red violet	15	15
C3	AP1	5f red brown	15	15
C4	AP1	10f carmine	15	15
C5	AP1	20f blue	15	15
C6	AP1	35f red orange	25	15
C7	AP2	50f olive	1.50	18
C8	AP2	100f violet	2.00	25
		Nos. C1-C8 (8)	4.50	
		Set value		1.00

Sheets exist, perf. and imperf., containing one each of Nos. C1-C8, with arms and Arabic inscription in blue green in upper and lower margin. Value (2 sheets) $40.

Republic

ICY Emblem AP3

1965, Aug. 13 **Litho.** *Perf. 13½*

C9	AP3	5f brn org & black	42	15
C10	AP3	10f citron & dk brn	60	15
C11	AP3	30f ultra & black	1.65	50

International Cooperation Year.

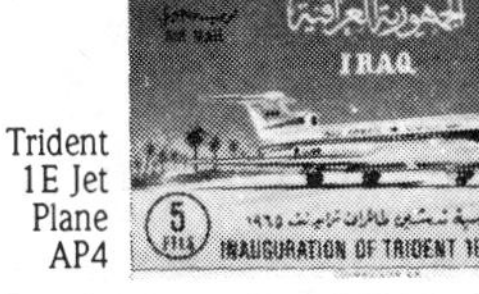

Trident 1E Jet Plane
AP4

1965, Dec. 1 Photo. *Perf. 11½*
Granite Paper

C12	AP4	5f multicolored	15	15
C13	AP4	10f multicolored	20	15
C14	AP4	40f multicolored	2.50	50
		Set value		62

Introduction by Iraqi Airways of Trident 1E jet planes.

Arab International Tourist Union Emblem — AP5

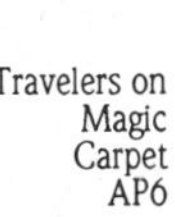

Travelers on Magic Carpet
AP6

1966, Dec. 3 Litho. *Perf. 13½, 14*

C15	AP5	2f multicolored	15	15
C16	AP6	5f yellow & multi	18	15
C17	AP5	15f blue & multi	22	15
C18	AP6	50f multicolored	90	35
		Set value		55

Meeting of the Arab Intl. Tourist Union, Baghdad.
For overprint, see No. RAC1.

Costume Type of Regular Issue

Iraqi Costumes: 40f, Woman's head. 50f, Woman's costume. 80f, Man's costume.

1967, Nov. 10 Litho. *Perf. 13*

C19	A105	40f multicolored	30	15
C20	A105	50f blue & multi	45	24
C21	A105	80f green & multi	3.00	60

International Tourist Year Type of Regular Issue

Designs: 50f, Female statue, Temples of Hatra. 80f, Spiral Tower (Malwiye of Samarra). 100f, Adam's Tree. 200f, Aladdin's Cave. 500f, Golden Shiah Mosque of Kadhimain. 50f, 80f, 100f and 200f are vert.

1967, Dec. 1 Litho.

C22	A107	50f multicolored	60	24
C23	A107	80f multicolored	1.10	40
C24	A107	100f multicolored	2.25	48
C25	A107	200f ver & multi	3.50	2.00
C26	A107	500f brn & multi	24.00	12.00
		Nos. C22-C26 (5)	31.45	15.12

For overprints, see Nos. C39, C52, C53.

Arabian — AP7

Animals: 2f, Striped hyena. 3f, Leopard. 5f, Mountain gazelle. 200f, Arabian stallion.

1969, Sept. 1 Litho. *Perf. 14*

C27	AP7	2f multicolored	15	15
C28	AP7	3f multicolored	15	15
C29	AP7	5f multicolored	15	15
C30	AP7	10f multicolored	25	18
C31	AP7	200f multicolored	6.50	3.50
		Nos. C27-C31 (5)	7.20	4.13

Ross Smith's Vickers Vimy
AP8

1969, Dec. 4 Litho. *Perf. 14*

C32	AP8	15f dk bl & multi	80	35
C33	AP8	35f multicolored	1.65	50
a.		Souv. sheet of 2, #C32-C33, imperf.	7.50	6.00

50th anniv. of the first England to Australia flight of Capt. Ross Smith and Lt. Keith Smith. No. C33a sold for 100f.

View Across Euphrates
AP9

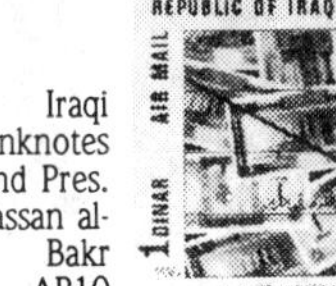

Iraqi Banknotes and Pres. Hassan al-Bakr
AP10

1970, Oct. 30 Litho. *Perf. 13*

C34	AP9	10f brt bl & multi	75	15
C35	AP9	15f multicolored	75	15
C36	AP10	1d multicolored	18.00	7.50

National Development Plan.
For overprints, see Nos. C42-C43.

Telecommunications Emblem — AP11

1970, Dec. 15 Litho. *Perf. 14x13½*

C37	AP11	15f gray & multi	25	15
C38	AP11	25f lt bl & multi	50	35

10th Conf. of Arab Telecommunications Union.

No. C23 Overprinted

يوم الأنواء
W.M. DAY
1971

1971, Apr. 23 *Perf. 13*

C39	A107	80f multicolored	5.50	4.00

World Meteorological Day.

Iraqi Philatelic Society Emblem — AP12

1972, Feb. 25 Litho. *Perf. 13*

C40	AP12	25f multicolored	80	50
C41	AP12	70f pink & multi	2.50	1.50

Iraqi Philatelic Society, 20th anniversary.

Nos. C34-C35 Overprinted

المؤتمر التاسع للاتحاد الوطني
لطلبة العراق
٢٥ شباط – ٢ آذار / ١٩٧٢

1972, Feb. 25

C42	AP9	10f brt bl & multi	1.00	25
C43	AP9	15f multicolored	2.00	1.00

9th Cong. of Natl. Union of Iraqi Students.

Soccer and C.I.S.M. Emblem
AP13

Designs: 20f, 35f, Players, soccer ball, C.I.S.M. emblem. 100f, Winged lion, Olympic and C.I.S.M. emblems.

1972, June 9 Litho. *Perf. 13½*

C46	AP13	10f lt bl & multi	35	15
C47	AP13	20f dp bl & multi	70	15
C48	AP13	25f green & multi	70	20
C49	AP13	35f brt bl & multi	2.75	50
a.		Souv. sheet, 100f, imperf.	8.00	8.00

25th Military Soccer Championships (C.I.S.M.), Baghdad, June 9-19.

Statue of Athlete — AP14

Design: 70f, Mesopotamian archer on horseback, ancient and modern athletes.

1972, Nov. 15 Photo. *Perf. 14x13½*

C50	AP14	25f multicolored	75	50
C51	AP14	70f multicolored	2.25	1.50

Cong. of Asian and World Body Building Championships, Baghdad, Nov. 15-23, 1972.

Nos. C23, C26 Overprinted

المؤتمر الدولي
للتاريخ/١٩٧٣

1973, Mar. 25 Litho. *Perf. 13*

C52	A107	80f multi	11.00	4.50
C53	A107	500f multi	37.50	*52.50*

International History Congress.

ICATU Type of 1976

1976, Mar. 24 Photo. *Perf. 13½*

C54	A213	75f blue & multi	4.00	2.00

Symbolic Eye
AP15

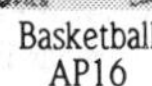

Basketball
AP16

1976, June 20 Photo. *Perf. 14*

C55	AP15	25f ultra & dk brn	20	15
C56	AP15	35f brt grn & dk brn	25	18
C57	AP15	50f orange & multi	40	25

World Health Day: Foresight prevents blindness.

1976, July 30 Litho. *Perf. 12x12½*

Montreal Olympic Games Emblem and: 35f, Volleyball. 50f, Wrestling. 75f, Boxing. 100f, Target shooting, horiz.

C58	AP16	25f yel & multi	50	15
C59	AP16	35f blue & multi	75	25
C60	AP16	50f ver & multi	1.00	50
C61	AP16	75f yel grn & multi	1.50	70

Souvenir Sheet
Imperf

C62	AP16	100f grn & multi	6.00	6.00

21st Olympic Games, Montreal, Canada, July 17-Aug. 1.

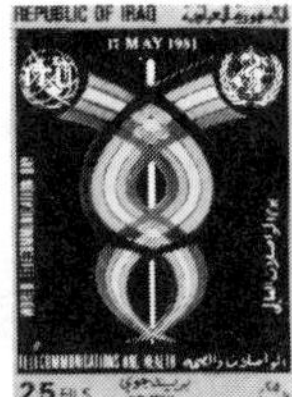

13th World Telecommunications Day — AP17

1981, May 17 Photo. *Perf. 12½*

C63	AP17	25f multicolored	20	15
C64	AP17	50f multicolored	40	25
C65	AP17	75f multicolored	60	38

Air Force Type of 1981

1981, June 1 Photo. *Perf. 14x13½*

C66	A289	120f Planes, vert.	1.00	75

AIR POST OFFICIAL STAMP

Catalogue values for all unused stamps in this section are for Never Hinged items.

Nos. C19-C22 Overprinted

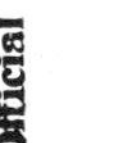

1971 Litho. *Perf. 13*

CO1	A105	40f multicolored	3.25	1.00
CO2	A105	50f multicolored	4.25	1.00
CO3	A105	80f multicolored	4.00	1.00

"Official" Reading Down

CO4	A107	50f multicolored	3.50	2.25

Nos. C27-C28, C30 Overprinted or Surcharged

Official رسمي

25 Fils ٢٥

1971 *Perf. 14*

No.	Type	Description	Unused	Used
CO5	AP7	10f multicolored	55	25
CO6	AP7	15f on 3f multi	80	50
CO7	AP7	25f on 2f multi	1.65	1.00

No bar and surcharge on No. CO5.

OFFICIAL STAMPS

British Mandate

Regular Issue of 1923 Overprinted:

ON STATE SERVICE
k

ON
STATE
SERVICE
l

1923 **Wmk. 4** *Perf. 12*

No.	Type	Description	Unused	Used
O1	A1(k)	½a olive grn	15	15
O2	A2(k)	1a brown	15	15
O3	A3(l)	1½a car lake	35	15
O4	A4(k)	2a brn org	25	15
O5	A5(k)	3a dp blue	35	15
O6	A6(l)	4a dl vio	25	15
O7	A7(k)	6a blue grn	30	25
O8	A6(l)	8a ol bister	35	35
O9	A8(l)	1r grn & brn	5.00	85
O10	A1(k)	2r blk (R)	11.00	1.50
O11	A6(l)	5r orange	32.50	15.00
O12	A7(k)	10r carmine	57.50	40.00
		Nos. O1-O12 (12)	108.15	58.85

Regular Issue of 1923-25 Overprinted:

ON STATE SERVICE
m

ON STATE SERVICE
n

1924-25

No.	Type	Description	Unused	Used
O13	A1(m)	½a olive grn	15	15
O14	A2(m)	1a brown	15	15
O15	A3(n)	1½a car lake	15	15
O16	A4(m)	2a brn org	15	15
O17	A5(m)	3a dp blue	20	15
O18	A6(n)	4a dull vio	30	15
O19	A7(m)	6a blue grn	35	15
O20	A6(n)	8a olive bis	50	15
O21	A8(n)	1r grn & brn	3.00	75
O22	A1(m)	2r bis ('25)	10.00	5.00
O23	A6(n)	5r orange	32.50	20.00
O24	A7(m)	10r brn red	57.50	30.00
		Nos. O13-O24 (12)	104.95	56.95

For overprint, see Nos. O42, O47, O51-O53.

No. 14 Overprinted Type "n"

1927

No.	Type	Description	Unused	Used
O25	A9	1r red brown	3.00	60

Regular Issue of 1931 Overprinted Vertically

ON STATE SERVICE
o

1931

No.	Type	Description	Unused	Used
O26	A10	½a green	15	15
O27	A10	1a chestnut	15	15
O28	A10	1½a carmine	13.00	5.00
O29	A10	2a orange	25	15
O30	A10	3a light blue	30	15
O31	A10	4a purple brn	50	15
O32	A10	6a Prussian bl	16.00	1.25
O33	A10	8a dark green	12.00	1.50

Overprinted Horizontally

ON STATE SERVICE

رسمي

p

No.	Type	Description	Unused	Used
O34	A11	1r dark brown	3.25	1.10
O35	A11	2r yel brown	6.00	6.00
O36	A11	5r deep org	30.00	30.00
O37	A11	10r red	50.00	50.00
		Nos. O26-O37 (12)	131.60	95.60

Overprinted Vertically Reading Up

No.	Type	Description	Unused	Used
O38	A9(p)	25r violet	750.00	800.00

For overprints see Nos. O39-O41, O43-O46, O48-O50, O54.

Kingdom

Nos. O15, O19, O22-O24, O26-O31, O33-O35, O38 Surcharged with New Values in Fils and Dinars, like Nos. 28-43

1932, Apr. 1

No.	Type	Description	Unused	Used
O39	A10	3f on ½a	35	35
O40	A10	4f on 1a (G)	15	15
O41	A10	5f on 1a	18	15
a.		Inverted Arabic "5"	40.00	35.00
O42	A3	8f on 1½a	70	15
O43	A10	10f on 2a	25	15
O44	A10	15f on 3a	40	15
O45	A10	20f on 4a	45	15
O46	A10	25f on 4a	50	25
O47	A7	30f on 6a	60	35
O48	A10	40f on 8a	1.10	35
a.		"Flis" for "Fils"	300.00	450.00
O49	A11	50f on 1r	1.75	80
O50	A11	75f on 1r	3.00	2.75
O51	A1	100f on 2r	6.00	1.00
O52	A6	200f on 5r	12.00	8.00
O53	A7	½d on 10r	35.00	32.50
a.		Bar in "½" omitted	700.00	
O54	A9	1d on 25r	87.50	80.00
		Nos. O39-O54 (16)	149.93	127.25

Regular Issue of 1932 Overprinted Vertically like Nos. O26-O33

1932, May 9

No.	Type	Description	Unused	Used
O55	A12	2f ultramarine	15	15
O56	A12	3f green	15	15
O57	A12	4f vio brown	15	15
O58	A12	5f gray	15	15
O59	A12	8f deep red	15	15
O60	A12	10f yellow	15	15
O61	A12	15f deep blue	1.40	15
O62	A12	20f orange	25	15
O63	A12	25f rose lilac	3.50	40
O64	A12	30f olive grn	75	40
O65	A12	40f dark vio	1.40	40

Overprinted Horizontally Like Nos. O34 to O37

No.	Type	Description	Unused	Used
O66	A13	50f deep brown	1.40	50
O67	A13	75f lt ultra	2.00	25
O68	A13	100f deep green	5.25	50
O69	A13	200f dark red	14.00	2.75

Overprinted Vertically like No. O38

No.	Type	Description	Unused	Used
O70	A14	½d gray blue	14.00	3.50
O71	A14	1d claret	35.00	50.00
		Nos. O55-O71 (17)	79.85	59.90

Regular Issue of 1934-38 Overprinted Type "o" Vertically Reading up in Black

1934-38 **Unwmk.**

No.	Type	Description	Unused	Used
O72	A15	1f purple ('38)	80	15
O73	A15	2f ultramarine	30	15
O74	A15	3f green	15	15
O75	A15	4f purple brn	15	15
O76	A15	5f gray green	15	15
O77	A15	8f deep red	80	15
O78	A15	10f yellow	15	15
O79	A15	15f deep blue	4.00	15
O80	A15	20f orange	25	15
O81	A15	25f brn violet	8.00	1.65
O82	A15	30f olive green	45	18
O83	A15	40f dark violet	1.00	18

Overprinted Type "p"

No.	Type	Description	Unused	Used
O84	A16	50f deep brown	45	20
O85	A16	75f ultramarine	65	52
O86	A16	100f deep green	1.65	45
O87	A16	200f dark red	3.25	65

Overprinted Type "p" Vertically Reading Up

No.	Type	Description	Unused	Used
O88	A17	½d gray blue	12.00	6.25
O89	A17	1d claret	24.00	12.50
		Nos. O72-O89 (18)	58.20	23.93

Catalogue values for unused stamps in this section, from this point to the end of the section, are for Never Hinged items.

Stamps of 1941-42 Overprinted in Black or Red:

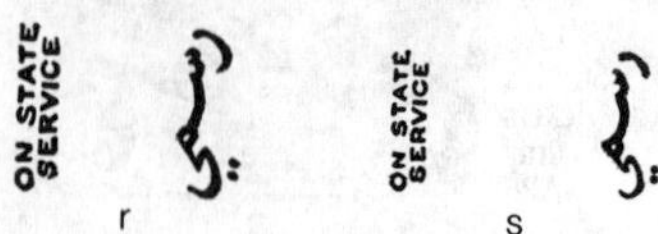

Perf. 11½x13½, 13 to 14 and Compound

1941-42

No.	Type	Description	Unused	Used
O90	A18(r)	1f dk vio ('42)	15	15
O91	A18(r)	2f choc ('42)	15	15
O92	A19(r)	3f brt grn ('42)	15	15
O93	A19(r)	4f pur (R) ('42)	15	15
O94	A19(r)	5f dk car rose ('42)	15	15
O95	A20(s)	8f carmine	50	15
O96	A20(s)	8f ocher ('42)	15	15
O97	A20(s)	10f ocher	2.00	15
O98	A20(s)	10f car ('42)	20	15
O99	A20(s)	15f dull blue	5.50	35
O100	A20(s)	15f blk (R) ('42)	20	15
O101	A20(s)	20f black (R)	1.00	20
O102	A20(s)	20f dl bl ('42)	40	15
O103	A21(s)	25f dark vio	1.50	18
O104	A21(r)	25f dk vio ('42)	30	15
O105	A21(s)	30f dp orange	1.10	15
O106	A21(r)	30f dk org ('42)	25	15
O107	A21(s)	40f brown org	1.10	25
O108	A21(r)	40f chnt ('42)	50	25
O109	A21(r)	50f ultra	1.00	18
O110	A21(r)	75f rose vio	40	30
O111	A22(s)	100f ol grn ('42)	60	40
O112	A22(s)	200f dp org ('42)	1.65	1.65
O113	A23(r)	½d blue ('42)	8.00	5.00
O114	A23(r)	1d grnsh bl ('42)	13.00	10.00
		Nos. O90-O114 (25)	40.10	20.86

The space between the English and Arabic on overprints "r" and "s" varies with the size of the stamps.

For overprints see Nos. O165, RA5.

Stamps of 1942 Overprinted in Black

ON STATE SERVICE

1942 **Unwmk.** *Perf. 13x13½*

No.	Type	Description	Unused	Used
O115	A24	1f violet & brown	15	15
O116	A24	2f dark blue & brn	15	15
O117	A24	3f lt green & brn	15	15
O118	A24	4f dl brown & brn	15	15
O119	A24	5f sage green & brn	15	15
O120	A24	6f red orange & brn	15	15
O121	A24	10f dl rose red & brn	15	15
O122	A24	12f yel green & brn	20	15
		Set value	90	45

Stamps of 1948 Overprinted in Black

ON STATE SERVICE

1948, Jan. 15 *Perf. 11½x12*

Size: 17¾x20½mm

No.	Type	Description	Unused	Used
O123	A25	1f slate	15	15
O124	A25	2f sepia	15	15
O125	A25	3f emerald	15	15
O126	A25	4f purple	15	15
O127	A25	5f rose lake	15	15
O128	A25	6f plum	15	15
O129	A25	8f ocher	15	15
O130	A25	10f rose red	15	15
O131	A25	12f dark olive	15	15
O132	A25	15f black	25	75
O133	A25	20f blue	15	15
O134	A25	25f rose violet	18	15
O135	A25	30f red orange	20	15
O136	A25	40f orange brn	25	15

Perf. 12x11½

Size: 22x27½mm

No.	Type	Description	Unused	Used
O137	A25	60f deep blue	35	25
O138	A25	75f lilac rose	40	40
O139	A25	100f olive grn	55	35
O140	A25	200f dp orange	1.15	1.00
O141	A25	½d blue	5.00	2.75
O142	A25	1d green	10.00	5.50
		Nos. O123-O142 (20)	19.83	12.95

For overprints see Nos. O166-O177, O257, O272, O274, O277, O282, RA1, RA3, RA4.

Same Overprint on Nos. 133-138

1949-51 *Perf. 11½x12*

Size: 17¾x20½mm

No.	Type	Description	Unused	Used
O143	A25	3f rose lake ('51)	80	35
O144	A25	5f emerald ('51)	80	35
O145	A25	14f dk olive ('50)	80	15
O146	A25	16f rose red ('51)	80	35
O147	A25	28f blue ('51)	80	25

Perf. 12x11½

Size: 22x27½mm

No.	Type	Description	Unused	Used
O148	A25	50f deep blue	1.25	50
		Nos. O143-O148 (6)	5.25	1.95

For overprints see Nos. O258, O273, O275, O276.

Same Overprint in Black on Stamps and Type of 1954-57

1955-59 *Perf. 11½x12*

No.	Type	Description	Unused	Used
O148A	A28	1f blue ('56)	15	15
O149	A28	2f chocolate	15	15
O150	A28	3f rose lake	15	15
O151	A28	4f violet	15	15
O152	A28	5f emerald	15	15
O153	A28	6f plum ('56)	15	15
O154	A28	8f ocher ('56)	15	15
O155	A28	10f blue	15	15
O155A	A28	16f brt rose ('57)	12.50	11.00
O156	A28	20f olive	15	15
O157	A28	25f rose violet	80	45
O158	A28	30f vermilion	20	15
O159	A28	40f orange brn	30	20

Size: 22½x27½mm

No.	Type	Description	Unused	Used
O160	A28	50f blue	2.00	30
O161	A28	60f pale purple	7.00	3.00
O161A	A28	100f ol grn ('59)	15.00	3.00
		Nos. O148A-O161A (16)	39.15	19.45

Dates of issue for Nos. O155A and O161A are suppositional.

For overprints see Nos. O178-O191, O259-O260, O283-O291.

Same Ovpt. on Stamps of 1957-58

No.	Type	Description	Unused	Used
O162	A33	1f blue	2.50	60
O162A	A33	2f chocolate	3.00	1.00
O162B	A33	3f dk carmine	3.75	1.50
O162C	A33	4f dull violet	4.50	80
O162D	A33	5f emerald	2.50	80
O163	A33	6f plum	2.50	80
O164	A33	10f blue	2.50	80
		Nos. O162-O164 (7)	21.25	6.30

For overprints see #O192-O199, O292-O293.

Republic

Official Stamps of 1942-51 with Additional Overprint

الجمهورية
العراقية

Perf. 13½x14

1958-59 **Engr.** **Unwmk.**

No.	Type	Description	Unused	Used
O165	A22	200f dp orange	3.25	2.50

Perf. 11½x12, 12x11½

No.	Type	Description	Unused	Used
O166	A25	12f dk olive	60	45
O167	A25	14f olive	60	55
O168	A25	15f black	35	25
O169	A25	16f rose red	1.40	1.40
O170	A25	25f rose vio	2.00	1.25
O171	A25	28f blue	1.00	1.00
O172	A25	40f orange brn	60	60
O173	A25	60f deep blue	1.50	1.40
O174	A25	75f lilac rose	1.25	1.00
O175	A25	200f dp orange	1.50	1.50
O176	A25	½d blue	10.00	3.50
O177	A25	1d green	16.00	7.25
		Nos. O166-O177 (12)	36.80	20.15

Other denominations of types A22 and A25 exist with this overprint, but these were probably not regularly issued.

Same Ovpt. on Nos. O148A-O161A

No.	Type	Description	Unused	Used
O178	A28	1f blue	15	15
O179	A28	2f chocolate	15	15
O180	A28	3f rose lake	15	15
O181	A28	4f violet	15	15
O181A	A28	5f emerald	40	15
O182	A28	6f plum	15	15
O183	A28	8f ocher	30	15
O183A	A28	10f blue	80	25
O184	A28	16f bright rose	3.25	2.00
O185	A28	20f olive	30	15
O186	A28	25f rose violet	30	20
O187	A28	30f vermilion	40	20
O188	A28	40f orange brn	50	25
O189	A28	50f blue	60	40
O190	A28	60f pale purple	75	55
O191	A28	100f olive grn	80	50
		Nos. O178-O191 (16)	9.15	5.55

Same Ovpts. on #O162-O164, 216

No.	Type	Description	Unused	Used
O192	A33	1f blue	15	15
O193	A33	2f chocolate	15	15
O194	A33	3f dark carmine	15	15
O195	A33	4f dull violet	15	15
O196	A33	5f emerald	15	15
O197	A33	6f plum	15	15
O198	A33	8f ocher	15	15
O199	A33	10f blue	15	15
		Set value	92	55

Nos. 232-233, 235-237, 242 Overprinted — On State Service رسمي

Litho. & Photo.

1961, Apr. 1 Unwmk. *Perf.* 11½

O200 A38 1f multi 15 15
O201 A38 2f multi 15 15
O202 A38 4f multi 18 15
O203 A38 5f multi 25 15
O204 A38 10f multi 45 35
O205 A38 50f multi 5.00 2.00
Nos. O200-O205 (6) 6.18 2.95

Nos. 232-247 Overprinted — ON STATE SERVICE رسمي

1961

Emblem in Gold, Red and Blue; Blue Inscriptions

O206 A38 1f gray 15 15
O207 A38 2f salmon 15 15
O208 A38 3f pale violet 15 15
O209 A38 4f bright yel 15 15
O210 A38 5f light blue 15 15
O211 A38 10f bright pink 15 15
O212 A38 15f lt green 15 15
O213 A38 20f bister brn 15 15
O214 A38 30f light gray 25 15
O215 A38 40f orange yel 24 15
O216 A38 50f yel green 30 15
O217 A38 75f pale green 45 25
O218 A38 100f orange 55 40
O219 A38 200f lilac 1.10 55
O220 A38 500f bister 7.50 3.75
O221 A38 1d brt green 15.00 7.50
Nos. O206-O221 (16) 26.59 14.10

Nos. 480-482 Overprinted — Official رسمي

1971 Litho. *Perf.* 13½

O222 A115 10f multicolored 50 1.00
O223 A115 15f blue & multi 5.00 1.00
O224 A115 25f multicolored 5.00 2.00

Overprint lines are spaced 16mm on No. O222, 32½mm on Nos. O223-O224.

Same Overprint on Nos. 453, 455-456

1971 *Perf.* 13

O225 A107 5f lilac & multi 4.75 18
O226 A107 15f rose red & multi 4.75 35
O227 A107 25f vio bl & multi 7.50 1.00

Overprint horizontal on Nos. O225 and O227; vertical, reading down on No. O226. Distance between English and Arabic words: 8mm.

Nos. 446, 448-449 Overprinted

1971 Litho. *Perf.* 13

O228 A105 15f multicolored 1.00 50
O229 A105 15f multicolored 45.00 5.00
O230 A105 25f multicolored 8.00 2.00
O231 A105 30f multicolored 8.00 2.00

No. O229 overprinted "Official" horizontally

Same Overprint on Nos. 483-486

1972 *Perf.* 13½

O232 A116 10f multicolored 1.50 50
O233 A116 25f multicolored 3.00 1.00

1972

O234 A117 15f multicolored 2.00 50
O235 A117 25f multicolored 3.00 1.00

Same Overprint, "Official" Reading Down on Nos. 562-565

1972

O240 A142 5f multicolored 50 25
O241 A142 10f multicolored 2.00 50
O242 A142 15f multicolored 5.00 50
O243 A142 35f multicolored 6.00 1.00

Latin inscription on Nos. O240-O241 obliterated with heavy bar.

No. 487 Overprinted "Official" like No. CO5

1972 Photo. *Perf.* 13½

O244 A118 25f multicolored 20 15

#O134, O148 Ovptd. with 3 Bars

***Perf.* 11½x12, 12x11½**

1973, Jan. 29 Engr.

O257 A25 25f rose violet 6.00 2.00
O258 A25 50f deep blue 6.00 5.00

Same on Nos. O157 and O160

O259 A28 25f rose violet 6.00 6.00
O260 A28 50f blue 6.00 6.00

Type of 1957 Overprinted with 3 Bars and — ON STATE SERVICE رسمي

Size: 22x27½mm

O261 A33 50f rose violet 6.00 6.00

See note after No. 679. No. O261 not issued without overprints.

King Faisal Issues Overprinted

Two sizes of overprint: Arabic 6½mm or 9mm.

1973

O263 A28 15f black (#149) 6.00 6.00
O264 A33 15f black 6.00 1.00
O265 A25 25f rose vio (#121) 8.50 2.00
O266 A28 25f rose vio (#151) 8.50 2.00
O267 A33 25f rose violet 8.50 2.00

Same Overprint on Nos. 674-677

O268 A28 10f blue 1.50 50
O269 A33 10f blue 1.50 50
O270 A28 15f black 6.00 1.00
O271 A33 15f black 6.00 1.00

Official Stamps of 1948-51 Overprinted

Overprint design faces left or right.

1973

O272 A25 12f (#O131) 75 20
O273 A25 14f (#O145) 75 30
O274 A25 15f (#O132) 75 30
O275 A25 16f (#O146) 2.00 50
O276 A25 28f (#O147) 4.00 75
O277 A25 30f (#O135) 4.00 50
O278 A25 40f (#O136) 4.00 90
O279 A25 60f (#O137) 4.00 3.00
O280 A25 100f (#O139) 13.00 5.00
O281 A25 ½d (#O141) 32.50 13.00
O282 A25 1d (#O142) 67.50 67.50
Nos. O272-O282 (11) 133.25 91.95

Same Overprint on Official Stamps of 1955-59

O283 A28 3f (#O150) 20 15
O284 A28 6f (#O153) 20 15
O285 A28 8f (#O154) 20 15
O286 A28 16f (#O155A) *10.00 10.00*
O287 A28 20f (#O156) 1.00 32
O288 A28 30f (#O158) 1.00 50
O289 A28 40f (#O159) 1.00 1.00
O290 A28 60f (#O161) 8.75 2.00
O291 A28 100f (#O161A) *17.50 5.00*

Same Overprint on 1957-58 Issues

O292 A33 3f dk car (#O162B) 20 20
O293 A33 6f plum (#O163) 20 20
O294 A33 8f ocher (#179) 20 20
O295 A33 30f red orange 1.00 1.00

The overprint on Nos. O294-O295 includes the "On State Service" overprint; No. O295 was not issued without overprints. The overprint leaf design faces left or right and varies in size.

Nos. 403, 497, 681 Overprinted — رسمي Official

***Perf.* 12½, 13x12½, 13½**

1974 (?) Photo., Litho.

O296 A89 2f multicolored 1.00
O297 A123 15f multicolored 1.00 50
O298 A185 25f multicolored 3.00 1.00

Size of "Official" on Nos. O297-O298 9mm.

Nos. 683-691 Overprinted — OFFICIAL رسمي

1974 Litho. *Perf.* 13x12½

O299 A186 5f orange & blk 15 15
O300 A186 10f bister & blk 15 15
O301 A186 20f brt rose & blk 35 20
O302 A186 25f ultra & blk 75 75
O303 A186 35f emerald & blk 75 28
O304 A186 45f blue & black 75 35
O305 A186 50f olive & yel 1.00 40
O306 A186 70f violet & yel 1.00 55
O307 A186 95f brown & yel 1.50 75
Nos. O299-O307 (9) 6.40 3.58

Nos. 455 and 467 Overprinted — رسمي Official

1975 Litho. *Perf.* 13, 14

O308 A107 15f multicolored 1.00 35
O311 A110 30f multicolored 4.00 60

Space between Arabic and English lines of overprint is 4mm on No. O308, 13mm on No. O311.

Nos. 491-493 Overprinted or Surcharged like Nos. CO5-CO7

1975 *Perf.* 14

O312 A121 10f multicolored 1.50 70
O312A A121 15f on 3f multi 6.00 1.00
O313 A121 25f on 2f multi 5.00 1.00

Nos. 322-325 Overprinted — رسمي Official

Engr.; Engr. & Photo.

1975 *Perf.* 12x11

O314 A57 10f rose red 8.00 60
O315 A57 15f brown & buff 8.00 75
O316 A57 20f violet blue 8.00 75
O317 A57 30f orange 15.00 80

Arms of Iraq — O1

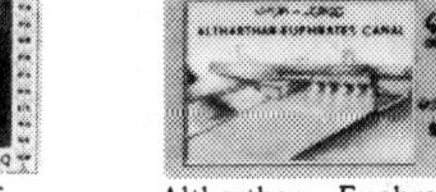

Altharthar - Euphrates Canal — O2

1975 Photo. *Perf.* 14

O318 O1 5f multicolored 15 15
O319 O1 10f blue & multi 15 15
O320 O1 15f yel & multi 24 24
O321 O1 20f ultra & multi 32 32
O322 O1 25f org & multi 40 40
O323 O1 30f rose & multi 50 50
O324 O1 50f multicolored 80 80
O325 O1 100f multicolored 1.65 1.65
Nos. O318-O325 (8) 4.21 4.21

Nos. 787-791 Overprinted "OFFICIAL" in English and Arabic

1976 Litho. *Perf.* 13½x14

O327 A219 5f multicolored 15 15
O328 A219 10f multicolored 15 15
O329 A219 15f multicolored 80 15
O330 A219 25f multicolored 1.00 35
O331 A219 50f multicolored 2.25 75
Nos. O327-O331 (5) 4.35 1.55

1978 Photo. *Perf.* 11½

O332 O2 5f multicolored 15 15
O333 O2 10f multicolored 15 15
O334 O2 15f multicolored 15 15
O335 O2 25f multicolored 40 20
Set value 68 45

Baghdad University Entrance — O3

1981, Oct. 21 Litho. *Perf.* 12x12½

O336 O3 45f multicolored 36 24
O337 O3 50f multicolored 40 30

Nos. O336-O337 Surcharged

1983, May 15 Litho. *Perf.* 12x12½

O338 O3 60f on 45f multi 50 32
O339 O3 70f on 50f multi 60 45

Martyrs Type of 1981

1981 Photo. *Perf.* 14

O339A A303 45f silver border 36 24
O339B A303 50f gold border 40 30
O339C A303 120f metallic bl border 96 64

Building Type of 1983

1982, Dec. 31 Litho. *Perf.* 14

O340 A324 60f multicolored 48 32
O341 A324 70f multicolored 56 40

Martyr Type of 1984

1984, Dec. 1

O342 A329 20f multicolored 15 15
O343 A329 30f multicolored 20 15
O344 A329 50f multicolored 32 22
O345 A329 60f multicolored 38 25

No. RA22 Overprinted — بريد رسمي

1985 (?) Litho. *Perf.* 13x12½

O346 PT2 5f bister, blk & yel 30 30

POSTAL TAX STAMPS

Catalogue values for unused stamps in this section are for Never Hinged items.

Nos. O125 and 115 Surcharged in Carmine or Black — مالية فلسان انقاذ فلسطين

1949 Unwmk. *Perf.* 11½x12

RA1 A25 2f on 3f emer (C) 9.25 5.75
RA2 A25 2f on 6f plum 24.00 3.75

Similar Overprint in Carmine or Black on Nos. O124, O127 and O94 Middle Arabic Line Omitted

***Perf.* 11½x12**

RA3 A25 2f sepia (C) 8.75 1.75
RA4 A25 5f rose lake 25.00 3.75

***Perf.* 12x13½, 14**

RA5 A19 5f dark car rose 6.25 1.90

Larger overprint on #RA5, 20½mm wide.

No. 115 Surcharged in Black — مالية ٥ فلوس انقاذ فلسطين

***Perf.* 11½x12**

RA6 A25 5f on 6f plum 27.50 10.50

The tax on Nos. RA1 to RA6 was to aid the war in Palestine.

Nos. 317, 322-326 Surcharged

دفاع وطني ٥ فلوس

Engr.; Engr. & Photo.

1963 *Perf.* 12x11

RA7 A57 5f on 1f green 60 60
RA8 A57 5f on 10f rose red 60 60
RA9 A57 5f on 15f brn & buff 60 60
RA10 A57 5f on 20f vio blue 60 60
RA11 A57 5f on 30f orange 60 60
RA12 A57 5f on 40f brt green 60 60
Nos. RA7-RA12 (6) 3.60 3.60

Surtax was for the Defense Fund.

PT1

دفــاع
وطــنى
b

1967, Aug. Photo. *Perf. 13½*

RA13 PT1 5f brown 35 15

Surtax was for flood victims.

Same Overprinted "b"

1967, Nov.

RA14 PT1 5f brown 1.00 1.00

Surtax was for Defense Fund.

Nos. 305A-305B with Surcharge Similar to Nos. RA7-RA12

1972 Litho. *Perf. 13½x14*

RA15 A54a 5f on 14f 5.25 3.75
RA16 A54a 5f on 35f 5.25 3.75

Surtax was for the Defense Fund. The 2 disks obliterating old denominations are on one line at the bottom. Size of Arabic inscription: 17x12mm.

No. 452 with Surcharge Similar to Nos. RA7-RA12, and Nos. 443, 457 and 526 Surcharged:

دفاع وطنى
٥ فلوس

1973 Litho. *Perf. 13*

RA17 A105 5f on 2f multi 5.75 40
RA18 A107 5f on 2f multi 5.75 40
RA19 A108 5f on 2f multi 5.75 40
RA20 A135 5f on 2f multi 5.75 40

Surtax was for the Defense Fund. Surcharges on Nos. RA17-RA20 are adjusted to fit shape of stamps and to obliterate old denominations.

No 683 Overprinted

دفاع
وطني

1974 Litho. *Perf. 13x12½*

RA21 A186 5f orange & blk 2.50 2.50

Soldier
PT2

Dome of the Rock, Jerusalem
PT3

1974

RA22 PT2 5f bister, blk & yel 50 30

Surtax of Nos. RA21-RA22 was for the Defense Fund.
For overprint, see No. O346.

1977 Photo. *Perf. 14*

RA23 PT3 5f multicolored 2.00 15

Surtax was for families of Palestinians.
For surcharge see No. 1457.

AIR POST POSTAL TAX STAMPS

Catalogue values for unused stamps in this section are for Never Hinged items.

#C15 Surcharged Like #RA17-RA20

1973 Litho. *Perf. 13½*

RAC1 AP5 5f on 2f multi 5.00 5.00

Surtax was for the Defense Fund.

ISRAEL

LOCATION — Western Asia, bordering on the Mediterranean Sea
GOVT. — Republic
AREA — 8,017 sq. mi.
POP. — 4,150,000 (est. 1984)
CAPITAL — Jerusalem

When the British mandate of Palestine ended in May 1948, the Jewish state of Israel was proclaimed by the Jewish National Council in Palestine.

1000 Mils = 1 Pound
1000 Prutot = 1 Pound (1949)
100 Agorot = 1 Pound (1960)
100 Agorot = 1 Shekel (1980)

Catalogue values for all unused stamps in this country are for Never Hinged items.

Tabs

Stamps of Israel are printed in sheets with tabs (labels) usually attached below the bottom row, sometimes at the sides. Stamps with tab attached are valued by issue or separately through No. 86. From No. 87 onward, stamps with tab attached sell for 10 to 100 per cent higher values than those quoted, except where noted otherwise.

Tabs of the following numbers are in two parts, perforated between: 9, 15, 23-37, 44, 46-47, 50, 55, 62-65, 70-72, 74-77, 86-91, 94-99, 104-118, 123-126, 133-136B, 138-141, 143-151, 160-161, 165-167, 178-179, 182, 187-189, 203, 211-213, 222-223, 228-237, 243-244, 246-250, 256-258, 269-270, 272-273, 275, 294-295, 312, 337-339, 341-344, 346-347, 353-354, C1-C13, C22-C30.

Watermarks

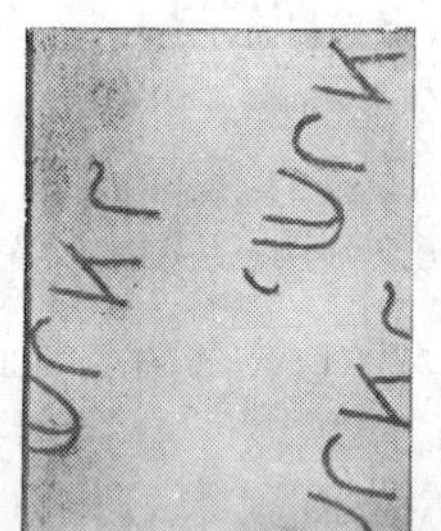
Wmk. 301- ISRAEL in Hebrew

Wmk. 302- Multiple Stag

Ancient Judean Coins
A1 A2

Designs: Nos. 1-6, Various coins.

Perf. 10, 11 and Compound

1948, May 16 Typo. Unwmk.

1	A1	3m orange	40	15
2	A1	5m yellow grn	40	15
3	A1	10m red violet	70	15
4	A1	15m red	1.40	15
5	A1	20m bright ultra	3.50	15
6	A1	50m orange brown	6.50	15
		Nos. 1-6 (6)	12.90	90
		Nos. 1-6 (6) with tabs	250.00	

Size: 34½x22mm

7	A2	250m dark sl grn	50.00	13.00
8	A2	500m red brn, *cr*	170.00	55.00

Size: 36½x24mm

9	A2	1000m blk bl, *pale bl*	225.00	85.00
		Nos. 7-9 (3)	445.00	153.00
		Nos. 7-9 with tabs	*4,500.*	

Nos. 1-9 exist imperf.
See type A6. For overprints see Nos. J1-J5.

Rouletted

1a	A1	3m	90	15
2b	A1	5m	2.75	20
3b	A1	10m	6.25	65
		With tabs	300.00	

Flying Scroll — A3

1948, Sept. 26 Litho. *Perf. 11½*

10	A3	3m brn red & ultra	40	15
11	A3	5m dl grn & ultra	70	22
12	A3	10m dp car & ultra	80	40
13	A3	20m dp ultra & ultra	1.65	65
14	A3	65m brown & red	10.00	3.50
		Nos. 10-14 (5)	13.55	4.92
		With tabs	260.00	

Jewish New Year, 5709.

Flag of Israel — A4

1949, Mar. 31

15	A4	20m bright blue	52	20
		With tab	45.00	

Appointment of the government by the Knesset.

Souvenir Sheet

A5

1949, May 1 *Imperf.*

16	A5	Sheet of 4	100.00	22.50
a.		10m dark carmine rose	25.00	2.75

1st anniv. of Israeli postage stamps.
The sheet was sold at "TABUL," First National Stamp Exhibition, in Tel Aviv, May 1-6, 1949. Tickets, costing 100 mils, covered the entrance fee and one sheet.

Bronze Half-Shekel of 67 A.D. — A6

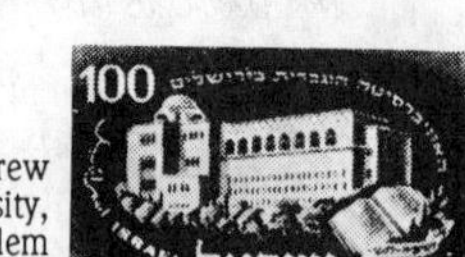
Approach to Jerusalem — A8

Hebrew University, Jerusalem
A7

"The Negev" by Reuven Rubin — A9

1949-50 Unwmk. *Perf. 11½, 14*

17	A6	3p gray black	28	15
18	A6	5p purple	15	15
19	A6	10p green	18	15
20	A6	15p deep rose	25	15
21	A6	30p dark blue	32	15
22	A6	50p brown	1.25	18
23	A7	100p Prus grn ('50)	32	15
		With tab	25.00	
24	A8	250p org brn & gray	1.10	65
		With tab	40.00	
25	A9	500p dp org & brown ('50)	6.25	5.00
		With tab	250.00	
		Nos. 17-25 (9)	10.10	6.73
		Nos. 17-22 with tabs (6)	85.00	
		Tete beche pairs, Nos. 18-21	72.50	72.50

Each of Nos. 17-22 portrays a different coin. For other stamps of coin design, see Nos. 38-43, 56-61, 80-83, and type A1. For overprints see Nos. O1-O4.
25th anniv. of the Hebrew University in Jerusalem (No. 23).

Well at Petah Tikva — A10

1949, Aug. 10 *Perf. 11*

27	A10	40p dk grn & brn	6.50	30
		With tab	80.00	

70th anniv. of Petah Tikva.

Arms and Service Insignia
A11

1949, Sept. 20 *Perf. 11½*

28	A11	5p Air Force	42	20
29	A11	10p Navy	1.10	32
30	A11	35p Army	4.75	2.00
		With tabs	450.00	

Jewish New Year, 5710.

Running Stag — A12

1950, Mar. 26

31	A12	40p purple	75	15
a.		Booklet pane of 4	3.50	

32 A12 80p rose red 75 18
a. Booklet pane of 4 7.00
b. Nos. 31 and 32 tête bêche 45.00 25.00
With tabs 72.50

75th anniv. (in 1949) of the UPU.

Struggle for Free Immigration A13

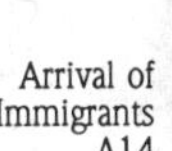

Arrival of Immigrants A14

1950, Apr. 23

33 A13 20p dull brown 2.75 1.25
34 A14 40p dull green 5.25 3.25
With tabs 425.00

Independence Day, Apr. 22, 1950.

Fruit and Star of David — A15

1950, Aug. 31 **Litho.** ***Perf. 14***

35 A15 5p vio blue & org 15 15
36 A15 15p red brn & grn 35 15
Set value 15
With tabs 45.00

Jewish New Year, 5711.

Runner and Track — A16

1950, Oct. 1

37 A16 80p olive & sl blk 1.65 48
With tab 55.00

3rd Maccabiah, Ramat Gan, Sept. 27, 1950.

Coin Type of 1949 Redrawn

Designs: Various coins.

1950

38 A6 3p gray black 15 15
39 A6 5p purple 15 15
a. Tête bêche pair 3.00 3.00
40 A6 10p green 15 15
a. Tête bêche pair 1.25 1.00
41 A6 15p deep rose 15 15
a. Tête bêche pair 2.00 1.75
42 A6 30p dark blue 15 15
a. Tête bêche pair 4.00 4.00
43 A6 50p brown 15 15
Set value 35 30
With tabs 2.75

Inscription at left measures 11mm on Nos. 38-43; 9mm on Nos. 17-22.

Detail from Tablet, "Founding of Tel Aviv" — A17

1951, Mar. 22

44 A17 40p dark brown 28 15
With tab 18.00

40th anniversary of Tel Aviv.

Young Man Holding Outline Map of Israel — A18

1951, Apr. 30 **Litho.**

45 A18 80p red brown 18 15
With tab 4.00

Issued to promote the sale of Independence Bonds.

Metsudat Yesha — A19

Hakastel A20

1951, May 9 **Unwmk.**

46 A19 15p red brown 15 15
47 A20 40p deep blue 50 20
Set value 25
With tabs 45.00

Proclamation of State of Israel, 3rd anniv.

Tractor and Wheat — A21

Tree — A22

Plower and National Fund Stamp of 1902 — A23

1951, June 24 ***Perf. 14***

48 A21 15p red brown 15 15
49 A22 25p Prussian green 15 15
50 A23 80p dull blue 45 15
Set value 62 28
With tabs 100.00

Jewish National Fund, 50th anniversary.

Theodor Zeev Herzl — A24

Carrier Pigeons — A25

1951, Aug. 14

51 A24 80p gray green 16 15
With tab 4.25

23rd Zionist Congress, Jerusalem.

1951, Sept. 16

Designs: 15p, Girl holding dove and fruit. 40p, Scrolls of the law.

52 A25 5p blue 15 15
53 A25 15p cerise 15 15
54 A25 40p rose violet 15 15
Set value 20 18
With tabs 2.50

Jewish New Year, 5712.

Menorah and Emblems of Twelve Tribes — A26

1952, Feb. 27

55 A26 1000p dk blue & gray 15.00 6.25
With tab 250.00

Redrawn Coin Type of 1950

Designs: Various coins.

1952, Mar. 30

56 A6 20p orange 15 15
a. Tête bêche pair 2.50 2.50
57 A6 35p olive green 15 15
58 A6 40p orange brown 15 15
59 A6 45p red violet 15 15
a. Tête bêche pair 4.50 4.50
60 A6 60p carmine 15 15
61 A6 85p aquamarine 15 15
Set value 40 30
With tabs 12.00

Thistle and Yad Mordecai Battlefield A27

Battlefields: 60p, Cornflower and Deganya. 110p, Anemone and Safed.

1952, Apr. 29

62 A27 30p lil rose & vio brn 15 15
63 A27 60p ultra & gray blk 15 15
64 A27 110p crimson & gray 35 24
Set value 56 42
With tabs 22.50

Proclamation of State of Israel, 4th anniv.

Manhattan Skyline and American Zionists' House — A28

1952, May 13

65 A28 220p dark blue & gray 38 20
With tab 14.00

Opening of American Zionists' House, Tel Aviv.

Figs — A29

Unwmk.

1952, Sept. 3 **Litho.** ***Perf. 14***

66 A29 15p shown 15 15
67 A29 40p Lily 15 15
68 A29 110p Dove 20 15
69 A29 220p Nut cluster 30 16
Set value 66 45
With tabs 24.00

Jewish New Year, 5713.

Pres. Chaim Weizmann (1874-1952) and Presidential Standard A30

1952, Dec. 9

70 A30 30p slate 15 15
71 A30 110p black 25 15
Set value 16
With tabs 10.00

Weizmann, president of Israel 1948-52.

Numeral Incorporating Agricultural Scenes A31

1952, Dec. 31

72 A31 110p brown, buff & emer 18 15
With tab 9.00

70th anniversary of B.I.L.U. (Bet Yaakov Lechu Venelcha) immigration.

Five Anemones and State Emblem — A32

1953, Apr. 19
73 A32 110p grnsh bl, bl blk & red 18 15
With tab 4.50

5th anniversary of State of Israel.

Rabbi Moshe ben Maimon (Maimonides) A33

Holy Ark, Jerusalem A34

1953, Aug. 3 Wmk. 301 *Perf. 14x13*
74 A33 110p brown 35 35
With tab 8.00

7th International Congress of History of Science, Jerusalem, Aug. 4-11.

1953, Aug. 11

Holy Arks: 45p, Petah Tikva. 200p, Safed.

75 A34 20p sapphire 15 15
76 A34 45p brown red 15 15
77 A34 200p purple 15 15
Set value 28 18
With tabs 8.50

Jewish New Year, 5714.

Combined Ball-Globe A35

Desert Rose A36

Unwmk.

1953, Sept. 20 Litho. *Perf. 14*
78 A35 110p blue & dark brn 15 15
With tab 4.50

4th Maccabiah, Sept. 20-29, 1953.

1953, Sept. 22
79 A36 200p multicolored 15 15
With tab 4.50

Conquest of the Desert Exhib., Sept. 22-Oct. 14.

Redrawn Type of 1950

Designs: Various coins.

1954, Jan. 5
80 A6 80p olive bister 15 15
81 A6 95p blue green 15 15
82 A6 100p fawn 15 15
83 A6 125p violet blue 15 15
Set value 26 20
With tabs 2.50

Marigold and Ruins at Yehiam — A37

Design: 350p, Narcissus and bridge at Gesher.

1954, May 5 Litho.
84 A37 60p dk bl, mag & ol gray 15 15
85 A37 350p dk brown, grn & yel 15 15
Set value 17 15
With tabs 2.00

Memorial Day and 6th anniversary of proclamation of State of Israel.

Theodor Zeev Herzl (1860-1904), Founder of Zionist Movement A38

1954, July 21 Wmk. 302
86 A38 160p dk bl, dk brn & cr 15 15
With tab 85

Bearers with Grape Cluster A39

1954, Sept. 8 *Perf. 13x14*
87 A39 25p dark brown 15 15

Jewish New Year, 5715.

19th Century Mail Coach and Jerusalem Post Office — A40

Design: 200p, Mail truck and present G.P.O., Jerusalem.

1954, Oct. 13 *Perf. 14*
88 A40 60p blue, blk & yel 15 15
89 A40 200p dk green, blk & red 15 15
Set value 18 15
With tabs 3.25

TABIM, National Stamp Exhibition, Jerusalem, Oct. 13-18.

Baron Edmond de Rothschild (1845-1934) and Grape Cluster — A41

1954, Nov. 23 *Perf. 13x14*
90 A41 300p dark blue green 15 15
With tab 85

Lighted Oil Lamp — A42

1955, Jan. 13 *Perf. 13x14*
91 A42 250p dark blue 15 15
With tab 75

Teachers' Association, 50th anniversary.

Parachutist and Barbed Wire — A43

Lighted Menorah — A44

1955, Mar. 31 Litho. *Perf. 14*
92 A43 120p dk Prus green 15 15
With tab 42

Jewish volunteers from Palestine who served in British army in World War II.

1955, Apr. 26
93 A44 150p dk grn, blk & org 15 15
With tab 32

Proclamation of State of Israel, 7th anniv.

Immigration by Ship — A45

Designs: 10p, Immigration by plane. 25p, Agricultural training. 30p, Gardening. 60p, Vocational training. 750p, Scientific education.

1955, May 10 Unwmk. *Perf. 14*
94 A45 5p brt blue & black 15 15
95 A45 10p red & black 15 15
96 A45 25p deep grn & black 15 15
97 A45 30p orange & black 15 15
98 A45 60p lilac rose & blk 15 15
99 A45 750p olive bis & blk 22 15
With tab 1.75
Set value 45 35

20th anniversary of Israel's Youth Immigration Institution.

Musicians with Tambourine and Cymbals — A46

Mandrake, Reuben — A48

Ambulance A47

Musician with: 60p, Ram's Horn. 120p, Loud Trumpet. 250p, Harp.

1955, Aug. 25 Photo. Wmk. 302
100 A46 25p dark green & org 15 15

Unwmk.

101 A46 60p dk gray & orange 15 15
102 A46 120p dark blue & yel 15 15
103 A46 250p red brn & org 15 15
Set value 36 40

Jewish New Year, 5716.

See Nos. 121-123.

1955, Nov. 1 Wmk. 301 *Perf. 14*
104 A47 160p grn, red & blk 15 15

25th anniversary of Magen David Adom (Israeli Red Cross).

1955-57 Wmk. 302 *Perf. 13x14*

Twelve Tribes: 20p, Gates of Sechem, Simeon. 30p, Ephod, Levi. 40p, Lion, Judah. 50p, Scales, Dan. 60p, Stag, Naphtali. 80p, Tents, Gad. 100p, Tree, Asher. 120p, Sun and stars, Issachar. 180p, Ship, Zebulon. 200p, Sheaf of wheat, Joseph. 250p, Wolf, Benjamin.

105 A48 10p bright green 15 15
106 A48 20p red lilac ('56) 15 15
107 A48 30p bright ultra 15 15
108 A48 40p brown ('56) 15 15
109 A48 50p grnsh bl ('56) 15 15
110 A48 60p lemon 15 15
111 A48 80p deep vio ('56) 15 15
112 A48 100p vermilion 15 15
113 A48 120p olive ('56) 15 15
114 A48 180p lil rose ('56) 15 15
115 A48 200p green ('56) 15 15
116 A48 250p gray ('56) 15 15
Set value 60 50
With tabs 2.00

See Nos. 133-136B.

Albert Einstein (1879-1955) and Equation of his Relativity Theory — A49

1956, Jan. 3 *Perf. 13x14*
117 A49 350p brown 15 15
With tab 60

Technion, Haifa — A50

1956, Jan. 3 Wmk. 302
118 A50 350p lt ol grn & blk 15 15

Israel Institute of Technology, 30th anniv.

"Eight Years of Israel" — A51

Jaffa Oranges — A52

1956, Apr. 12 Litho. *Perf. 14*
119 A51 150p multicolored 15 15

Proclamation of State of Israel, 8th anniv.

1956, May 20 Wmk. 302 *Perf. 14*
120 A52 300p bl grn & orange 15 15

4th Intl. Congress of Mediterranean Citrus Growers.

New Year Type of 1955

Musician with: 30p, Lyre. 50p, Cymbals. 150p, Double oboe, horiz.

1956, Aug. 14 Photo. *Perf. 14x13*
121 A46 30p brown & brt blue 15 15

Perf. 14

122 A46 50p purple & orange 15 15
123 A46 150p dk bl grn & org 15 15
Set value 16 15

Jewish New Year, 5717.

Haganah Insignia A54

Bezalel Museum and Antique Lamp A55

1957, Jan. 1 *Perf. 13x14*

124 A54 20p + 80p brt grn 15 15
125 A54 50p + 150p car rose 15 15
126 A54 50p + 350p ultra 15 15
Set value 18 15

Defense issue. Divided denomination used to show increased postal rate.

1957, Apr. 29 **Litho.** *Perf. 14*

127 A55 400p multicolored 15 15

Bezalel Natl. Museum, Jerusalem, 50th anniv.

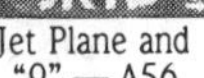
Jet Plane and "9" — A56

Horse and Seal — A57

1957, Apr. 29

128 A56 250p deep bl & blk 15 15

Proclamation of State of Israel, 9th anniv.

1957, Sept. 4 **Wmk. 302** *Perf. 14*

Ancient Seals: 160p, Lion. 300p, Gazelle.

129 A57 50p ocher & blk, *lt bl* 15 15

Perf. 14x13
Photo. **Unwmk.**

130 A57 160p grn & blk, *bis brn* 15 15
131 A57 300p dp car & blk, *pink* 15 15
Set value 15 15

Jewish New Year, 5718.

TABIL
Souvenir Sheet

Bet Alpha Synagogue Mosaic — A58

1957, Sept. 17 **Litho.** *Roulette 13*

132 A58 Sheet of 4 25 20
a. 100p multicolored 15 15
b. 200p multicolored 15 15
c. 300p multicolored 15 15
d. 400p multicolored 15 15

1st Intl. stamp exhibition in Israel, Tel Aviv, Sept. 17-23.

Tribes Type of 1955-57
Perf. 13x14

1957-59 **Unwmk.** **Photo.**

133 A48 10p brt grn ('58) 15 15
133A A48 20p red lilac 15 15
133C A48 40p brown ('59) 75 45
134 A48 50p greenish blue 15 15
135 A48 60p lemon 15 15
136 A48 100p vermilion 18 15
136B A48 120p olive ('58) 20 15
Set value 1.45 85
With tabs 37.50

Hammer Thrower — A59

Menorah and Olive Branch — A61

Ancient Ship — A60

1958, Jan. 20 *Perf. 14x13*

137 A59 500p bister & car 16 15

Maccabiah Games, 25th anniversary.

Wmk. 302
1958, Jan. 27 **Litho.** *Perf. 14*

Ships: 20p, Three-master used for "illegal immigration." 30p, Cargo ship "Shomron." 1000p, Passenger ship "Zion."

Size: 36½x22½mm

138 A60 10p ocher, red & blk 15 15

Photo. *Perf. 13x14*

139 A60 20p brt grn, blk & brn 15 15
140 A60 30p red, blk & grnsh bl 15 15

Size: 56½x22½mm

141 A60 1000p brt bl, blk & grn 15 15
Set value 28 20

Issued to honor Israel's merchant fleet.

Unwmk.
1958, Apr. 21 **Litho.** *Perf. 14*

142 A61 400p gold, blk & grn 15 15

Memorial Day and 10th anniversary of proclamation of State of Israel.

Dancing Youths Forming "10" — A62

1958, July 2

143 A62 200p dk org & dk grn 15 15

First World Conference of Jewish Youth, Jerusalem, July 28-Aug. 1.

Convention Center, Jerusalem A63

1958, July 2

144 A63 400p vio & org, *yellow* 15 15

10th Anniversary of Independence Exhibition, Jerusalem, June 5-Aug. 21.

Wheat — A64

1958, Aug. 27 **Photo.** *Perf. 14x13*

145 A64 50p shown 15 15
146 A64 60p Barley 15 15
147 A64 160p Grapes 15 15
148 A64 300p Figs 15 15
Set value 28 18

Jewish New Year, 5719.

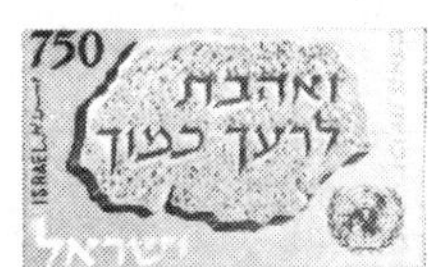
"Love Thy Neighbor . . ." — A65

1958, Dec. 10 **Litho.** *Perf. 14*

149 A65 750p yel, gray & grn 15 15
With tab 90

Universal Declaration of Human Rights, 10th anniversary.

Designing and Printing Stamps — A66

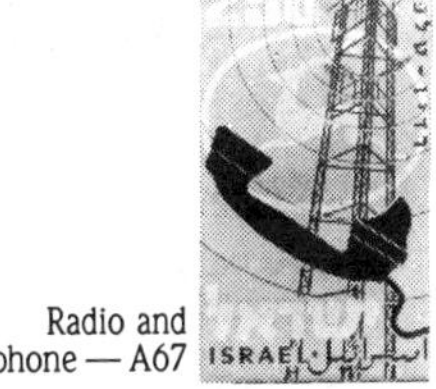
Radio and Telephone — A67

Designs: 120p, Mobile post office. 500p, Teletype.

1959, Feb. 25 **Wmk. 302** *Perf. 14*

150 A66 60p olive, blk & red 15 15
151 A66 120p olive, blk & red 15 15
152 A67 250p olive, blk & red 15 15
153 A67 500p olive, blk & red 15 15
Set value 28 18

Decade of postal activities in Israel.

Shalom Aleichem A68

Cyclamen A69

Portraits: No. 155, Chaim Nachman Bialik. No. 156, Eliezer Ben-Yehuda.

1959 **Unwmk.** **Photo.** *Perf. 14x13*

154 A68 250p yel grn & red brn 15 15
155 A68 250p ocher & ol gray 15 15
Set value 24 20

Litho. *Perf. 14*

156 A68 250p bl & vio bl 15 15
With tab 50

Birth cent. of Aleichem (Solomon Rabinowitz), Yiddish writer (No. 154); 25th death anniv. of Bialik, Hebrew poet (No. 155); birth cent. of Ben-Yehuda, father of modern Hebrew (No. 156).

1959, May 11 **Wmk. 302** *Perf. 14*

Flowers: 60p, Anemone. 300p, Narcissus.

Flowers in Natural Colors

157 A69 60p deep green 15 15
158 A69 120p deep plum 15 15
159 A69 300p blue 15 15
Set value 22 20

Memorial Day and 11th anniversary of proclamation of State of Israel.

Buildings, Tel Aviv — A70

1959, May 4

160 A70 120p multicolored 15 15

50th anniversary of Tel Aviv.

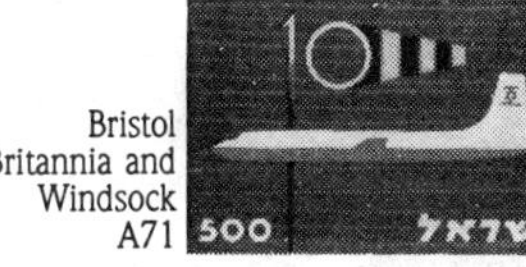
Bristol Britannia and Windsock A71

1959, July 22

161 A71 500p multicolored 16 15
With tab 35

Civil Aviation in Israel, 10th anniversary.

Pomegranates — A72

Perf. 14x13
1959, Sept. 9 **Photo.** **Unwmk.**

162 A72 60p shown 15 15
163 A72 200p Olives 15 15
164 A72 350p Dates 18 15
Set value 32 20
With tabs 2.25

Jewish New Year, 5720.

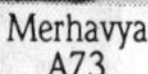
Merhavya
A73

Judean Coin (66-70 A.D.)
A74

Settlements: 120p, Yesud Ha-Maala. 180p, Deganya.

1959, Nov. 25 Photo. *Perf. 13x14*

165 A73 60p citron & dk grn 15 15
166 A73 120p red brn & ocher 15 15
167 A73 180p blue & dk grn 15 15
Set value 28 18
With tabs 2.75

Settlements of Merhavya and Deganya, 50th anniv.; Yesud Ha-Maala, 75th anniv.

1960 Unwmk. *Perf. 13x14*

Denominations in Black

168 A74 1a brn, *pinkish* 15 15
a. On surface colored paper 15 15
As "a," with tab 75
b. Black overprint omitted
169 A74 3a brt red, *pinkish* 15 15
170 A74 5a gray, *pinkish* 15 15
171 A74 6a brt grn, *lt bl* 15 15
171A A74 7a gray, *bluish* 15 15
172 A74 8a mag, *lt blue* 15 15
173 A74 12a grnsh bl, *lt bl* 15 15
a. Black overprint omitted
174 A74 18a orange 15 15
175 A74 25a blue 15 15
176 A74 30a carmine 15 15
177 A74 50a bright lilac 15 15
Set value 55 50
With tabs 1.75

Issue dates: 7a, July 6. Others, Jan. 6.

Operation "Magic Carpet"
A75

Design: 50a, Resettled family in front of house, grapes and figs.

1960, Apr. 7 Unwmk. *Perf. 13x14*

178 A75 25a red brown 15 15
179 A75 50a green 15 15
Set value 16 16
With tabs 40

World Refugee Year, July 1, 1959-June 30, 1960.

Sand Lily — A76

Design: 32a, Evening primrose.

1960, Apr. 27 Litho. *Perf. 14*

180 A76 12a multicolored 15 15
181 A76 32a brn, yel & grn 15 15
Set value 16 15
With tabs 55

Memorial Day; proclamation of State of Israel, 12th anniv. See #204-206, 238-240.

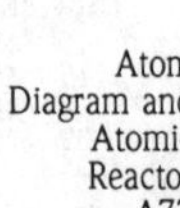
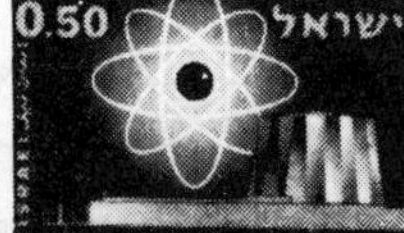

Atom Diagram and Atomic Reactor
A77

1960, July 6 Wmk. 302 *Perf. 14*

182 A77 50a blue, red & blk 15 15
With tab 60

Installation of Israel's first atomic reactor.

Theodor Herzl and Rhine at Basel — A78

King Saul — A79

1960, Aug. 31 Litho. *Perf. 14*

183 A78 25a gray brown 15 15
With tab 40

1960, Aug. 31 Wmk. 302

Designs: 25a, King David. 40a, King Solomon.

Kings in Multicolor

184 A79 7a emerald 15 15

Unwmk.

185 A79 25a brown 15 15
186 A79 40a blue 25 15
Set value 35 20
With tabs 1.25

Jewish New Year, 5721. See Nos. 208-210.

Jewish Postal Courier, Prague, 18th Century
A80

Perf. 13x14

1960, Oct. 9 Photo. Unwmk.

187 A80 25a olive blk, *gray* 22 15
With tab 2.50
a. Souvenir sheet 13.00 6.00

TAVIV Natl. Stamp Exhib., Tel Aviv, Oct. 9-19. No. 187a sold only at Exhibition for 50a.

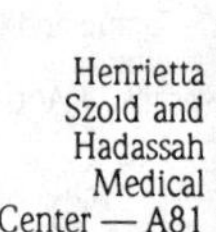

Henrietta Szold and Hadassah Medical Center — A81

1960, Dec. 14 *Perf. 13x14*

188 A81 25a turq bl & vio gray 15 15
With tab 32

Birth cent. of Henrietta Szold, founder of Hadassah, American Jewish women's organization.

Shields of Jerusalem and First Zionist Congress
A82

1960, Dec. 14 Unwmk. *Perf. 14*

189 A82 50a vio bl & turq blue 15 15
With tab 1.10

25th Zionist Congress, Jerusalem, 1960.

Ram — A83

Signs of Zodiac — A84

Signs of the Zodiac: 2a, Bull. 6a, Twins. 7a, Crab. 8a, Lion. 10a, Virgin. 12a, Scales. 18a, Scorpion. 20a, Archer. 25a, Goat. 32a, Water bearer. 50a, Fishes.

1961, Feb. 27 Photo. *Perf. 13x14*

190 A83 1a emerald 15 15
191 A83 2a red 15 15
192 A83 6a ultramarine 15 15
193 A83 7a brown 15 15
194 A83 8a green 15 15
a. Booklet pane of 6 ('65) 42
195 A83 10a orange 15 15
196 A83 12a violet 15 15
a. Booklet pane of 6 ('65) 42
197 A83 18a lilac rose 15 15
198 A83 20a olive 15 15
199 A83 25a red lilac 15 15
200 A83 32a gray 15 15
201 A83 50a greenish blue 15 15

Perf. 14

Litho.

202 A84 £1 dk bl, gold & lt bl 22 15
Set value 1.00 65
With tabs 3.75

Booklet pane sheets (Nos. 194a, 196a) of 36 (9x4) contain 6 panes of 6, with gutters dividing the sheet in four sections. Each sheet yields 4 tete beche pairs and 4 tete beche gutter pairs, or strips. See Nos. 215-217.

Vertical strips of 6 of the 1a, 10a and No. 216 (5a) are from larger sheets from which coils were produced. Regular sheets of 50 are arranged 10x5.

Javelin Thrower and "7" — A85

1961, Apr. 18 Litho. *Perf. 14*

203 A85 25a multicolored 15 15
With tab 42

7th Intl. Congress of the Hapoel Sports Org., Ramat Gan, May 1961.

Flower Type of 1960

Flowers: 7a, Myrtle. 12a, Sea onion. 32a, Oleander.

1961, Apr. 18 Unwmk.

Flowers in Natural Colors

204 A76 7a green 15 15
205 A76 12a rose carmine 15 15
206 A76 32a brt greenish bl 15 15
Set value 30 18
With tabs 1.00

Memorial Day; proclamation of State of Israel, 13th anniv.

Scaffold Around "10" and Sapling — A86

1961, June 14 Photo. *Perf. 14*

207 A86 50a Prussian blue 15 15
With tab 55

Israel bond issue 10th anniv.

Type of 1960

Designs: 7a, Samson. 25a, Judas Maccabaeus. 40a, Bar Cocheba.

1961, Aug. 21 Litho. *Perf. 14*

Multicolored Designs

208 A79 7a red orange 15 15
209 A79 25a gray 15 15
210 A79 40a lilac 20 15
Set value 32 22
With tabs 1.25

Jewish New Year, 5722.

Bet Hamidrash Synagogue, Medzibozh
A87

1961, Aug. 21 Photo. *Perf. 13x14*

211 A87 25a dk brn & yel 15 15
With tab 38

Bicentenary of death of Rabbi Israel Baal-Shem-Tov, founder of Hasidism.

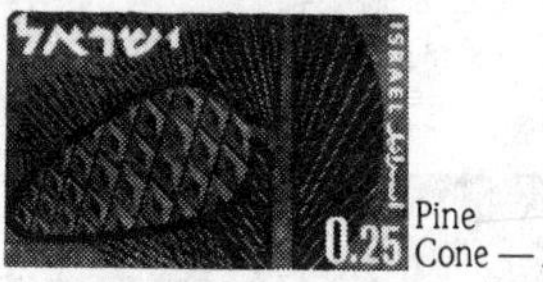

Pine Cone — A88

Design: 30a, Symbolic trees.

1961, Dec. 26 Unwmk. *Perf. 13x14*

212 A88 25a green, yel & blk 15 15
213 A88 30a org, green & ind 15 15
Set value 24 15
With tabs 2.00

Achievements of afforestation program.

Cello, Harp, French Horn and Kettle Drum — A89

1961, Dec. 26 Litho. *Perf. 14*

214 A89 50a multicolored 25 25
With tab 2.00

Israel Philharmonic Orchestra, 25th anniv.

Zodiac Type of 1961 Surcharged with New Value

1962, Mar. 18 Photo. *Perf. 13x14*

215 A83 3a on 1a lt lilac 15 15
a. Without overprint 80.00
216 A83 5a on 7a gray 15 15
217 A83 30a on 32a emerald 15 15
Set value 18 16
a. Without overprint 32.50

See note after No. 202.

Anopheles Maculipennis and Chart Showing Decline of Malaria in Israel — A90

View of Rosh Pinna — A91

1962, Apr. 30 *Perf. 14x13*

218 A90 25a ocher, red & blk 16 15
With tab 48

WHO drive to eradicate malaria.

1962, Apr. 30 **Unwmk.**
219 A91 20a yel, green & brn 18 18
With tab 48

Rosh Pinna agricultural settlement, 80th anniv.

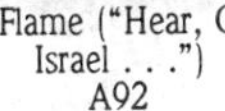
Flame ("Hear, O Israel . . .") A92

Yellow Star of David and Six Candles A93

1962, Apr. 30 **Photo.**
220 A92 12a black, org & red 15 15

Perf. 14

221 A93 55a multicolored 22 15
Set value 30 18
With tabs 1.40

Heroes and Martyrs Day, in memory of the 6,000,000 Jewish victims of Nazi persecution.

Vautour Fighter-Bomber — A94

Design: 30a, Fighter-Bombers in formation.

1962, Apr. 30 ***Perf. 13x14***
222 A94 12a blue 15 15
223 A94 30a olive green 15 15
Set value 18 18
With tabs 1.75

Memorial Day; proclamation of the state of Israel, 14th anniv.

Symbolic Flags — A95

Wolf and Lamb, Isaiah 11:6 — A96

1962, June 5 ***Perf. 14***
224 A95 55a multicolored 18 18
With tab 1.00

Near East Intl. Fair, Tel Aviv, June 5-July 5.

1962, Sept. 5

Designs: 28a, Leopard and kid, Isaiah 11:6. 43a, Child and asp, Isaiah 11:8.

225 A96 8a buff, red & black 15 15
226 A96 28a buff, lilac & black 15 15
227 A96 43a buff, org & black 22 15
Set value 38 22
With tabs 3.00

Jewish New Year, 5723.

Boeing 707 — A97

1962, Nov. 7 ***Perf. 13x14***
228 A97 55a bl, dk bl & rose lil 28 15
With tab 1.10
a. Souvenir sheet 2.50 1.25

El Al Airlines; El Al Philatelic Exhibition, Tel Aviv, Nov. 7-14. Issued in sheets of 15.

No. 228a contains one stamp in greenish blue, dark blue & rose lilac with greenish blue color continuing into margin design (No. 228 has white perforations). Sold for £1 for one day at philatelic counters in Jerusalem, Haifa and Tel Aviv and for one week at the El Al Exhibition.

Cogwheel Symbols of UJA Activities A98

1962, Dec. 26 **Unwmk.** ***Perf. 13x14***
229 A98 20a org red, sil & bl 18 15
With tab 50

25th anniv. of the United Jewish Appeal (United States) and its support of immigration, settlement, agriculture and care of the aged and sick.

Janusz Korczak A99

1962, Dec. 26 **Photo.**
230 A99 30a olive grn & blk 15 15
With tab 45

Dr. Janusz Korczak (Henryk Goldszmit, 1879-1942), physician, teacher and writer, killed in Treblinka concentration camp.

Pennant Coral Fish — A100

Red Sea fish: 6a, Orange butterflyfish. 8a, Lionfish. 12a, Zebra-striped angelfish.

1962, Dec. 26 **Litho.** ***Perf. 14***

Fish in Natural Colors

231 A100 3a green 15 15
232 A100 6a purple 15 15
233 A100 8a brown 15 15
234 A100 12a dark blue 15 15
Set value 28 25
With tabs 60

See Nos. 246-249.

Stockade at Dawn A101

Design: 30a, Completed stockade at night.

1963, Mar. 21 **Unwmk.** ***Perf. 14***
235 A101 12a yel brn, blk & yel 15 15
236 A101 30a dp plum, blk & lt bl 18 15
With tab 1.10
Set value 15

25th anniv. of the "Stockade and Tower" villages.

Hand Offering Food to Bird — A102

1963, Mar. 21 **Photo.** ***Perf. 13x14***
237 A102 55a gray & black 22 15
With tab 1.00
a. Booklet pane of 4 32.50

FAO "Freedom from Hunger" campaign.

Issued in sheets of 15 (5x3) with 5 tabs. The booklet pane sheet of 16 (4x4) is divided into 2 panes of 8 (4x2) by horizontal gutter. The 4 stamps at left in each pane are inverted in relation to the 4 at right, making 4 horizontal tete beche pairs down the center of the sheet.

Flower Type of 1960

Flower: 8a, White lily. 30a, Hollyhock. 37a, Tulips.

1963, Apr. 25 **Litho.** ***Perf. 14***

Flowers in Natural Colors

238 A76 8a slate 15 15
239 A76 30a yellow green 22 15
240 A76 37a sepia 28 15
Set value 35
With tabs 3.25

Memorial Day; proclamation of the State of Israel, 15th anniv.

Typesetter, 19th Century — A103

1963, June 19 **Photo.** ***Perf. 14x13***
241 A103 12a tan & vio brn 65 38
With tab 2.00
a. Sheet of 16 55.00 65.00

Hebrew press in Palestine, cent. Printed in sheets of 16; the background of the sheet shows page of first issue of "Halbanon" newspaper, giving each stamp different background.

"The Sun Beat upon the Head of Jonah" — A104

Hoe Clearing Thistles — A105

Designs: 30a, "There was a mighty tempest in the sea." 55a, "Jonah was in the belly of the fish." 30a, 55a horiz.

1963, Aug. 21 ***Perf. 14x13, 13x14***
242 A104 8a org, lil & blk 15 15
243 A104 30a multicolored 15 15
244 A104 55a multicolored 16 18
Set value 30 32
With tabs 2.75

Jewish New Year, 5724.

1963, Aug. 21 ***Perf. 14***
245 A105 37a multicolored 15 15
With tab 90

80 years of agricultural settlements in Israel; "Year of the Pioneers."

Fish Type of 1962

Red Sea Fish: 2a, Undulate triggerfish. 6a, Radiate turkeyfish. 8a, Bigeye. 12a, Imperial angelfish.

1963, Dec. 16 **Litho.** ***Perf. 14***

Fish in Natural Colors

246 A100 2a violet blue 15 15
247 A100 6a green 15 15
248 A100 8a orange 15 15
249 A100 12a olive green 15 15
Set value 35 25
With tabs 90

S.S. Shalom, Sailing Vessel and Ancient Map of Coast Line — A106

1963, Dec. 16 **Photo.** ***Perf. 13x14***
250 A106 £1 ultra, brt grn & lil 85 45
With tab 9.00

Maiden voyage of S.S. Shalom.

"Old Age and Survivors Insurance" A107

Pres. Izhak Ben-Zvi (1884-1963) A108

Designs (Insurance): 25a, Maternity. 37a, Large family. 50a, Workers' compensation.

1964, Feb. 24 **Litho.** ***Perf. 14***
251 A107 12a multicolored 15 15
252 A107 25a multicolored 15 15
253 A107 37a multicolored 28 20
254 A107 50a multicolored 40 30
Set value 82 65
With tabs 8.75

Natl. Insurance Institute 10th anniv.

1964, Apr. 13 **Photo.** ***Perf. 14x13***
255 A108 12a dark brown 15 15

Terrestrial Spectroscopy A109

Designs: 35a, Macromolecules of the living cell. 70a, Electronic computer.

1964, Apr. 13 ***Perf. 14***
256 A109 8a multicolored 15 15
257 A109 35a multicolored 15 15
258 A109 70a multicolored 22 15
Set value 38 28
With tabs 3.50

Proclamation of the State of Israel, 16th anniv.; Israel's contribution to science.

Basketball Players A110

Serpent of Aesculapius and Menorah A111

Designs: 8a, Runner. 12a, Discus thrower. 50a, Soccer.

1964, June 24 ***Perf. 14x13***
259 A110 8a brt brick red & dk brown 15 15
260 A110 12a rose lil & dk brn 15 15
261 A110 30a bl, car & dk brn 15 15

262 A110 50a yel grn, org red & dk brown 22 18
Set value 45 40
With tabs 90

Israel's participation in the 18th Olympic Games, Tokyo, Oct. 10-25.

1964, Aug. 5 **Unwmk.**
263 A111 £1 ol bis & slate grn 55 28
With tab 95

6th World Congress of the Israel Medical Association, Haifa, Aug. 3-13.

Ancient Glass Vase — A112

Designs: Different glass vessels, 1st to 3rd centuries.

1964, Aug. 5 **Litho.**
264 A112 8a vio, brn & org 15 15
265 A112 35a ol, grn & bl grn 15 15
266 A112 70a brt car rose, blue & violet blue 16 15
Set value 30 18
With tabs 1.15

Jewish New Year, 5725.

Steamer Bringing Immigrants A113

Eleanor Roosevelt (1884-1962) A114

1964, Nov. 2 **Litho.** ***Perf. 14***
267 A113 25a sl bl, bl grn & blk 15 15
With tab 35

30th anniv. of the blockade runners bringing immigrants to Israel.

1964, Nov. 2 **Photo.** ***Perf. 14x13***
268 A114 70a dull purple 18 15
With tab 45

Chess Board, Knight and Emblem of Chess Olympics — A115

1964, Nov. 2 ***Perf. 13x14***
269 A115 12a shown 16 15
270 A115 70a Rook 35 32
Set value 40
With tabs 1.90

16th Chess Olympics, Tel Aviv, Nov. 1964.

"Africa-Israel Friendship" — A116

1964, Nov. 30 **Photo.** ***Perf. 14x13***
271 A116 57a ol, blk, gold & red brown 35 20
With tab 2.75
a. Souvenir sheet 1.75 1.50

TABAI, Natl. Stamp Exhibition, dedicated to African-Israel friendship, Haifa, Nov. 30-Dec. 6. No. 271a contains one imperf. stamp. Sold for £1.

View of Masada from West — A117

Designs: 36a, Northern Palace, lower terrace. £1, View of Northern Palace, vert.

1965, Feb. 3 **Photo.** ***Perf. 13x14***
272 A117 25a dull green 15 15
273 A117 36a bright blue 16 15
274 A117 £1 dark red brn 28 22
Set value 38
With tabs 1.75

Ruins of Masada, the last stronghold in the war against the Romans, 66-73 A.D.

Book Fair Emblem A118

Arms of Ashdod A119

1965, Mar. 24 **Photo.** ***Perf. 13x14***
275 A118 70a gray ol, brt bl & blk 15 15

2nd Intl. Book Fair, Jerusalem, April.

1965-66 ***Perf. 13x14***

Town Emblems: 1a, Lydda (Lod). 2a, Qiryat Shemona. 5a, Petah Tikva. 6a, Nazareth. 8a, Beersheba. 10a Bet Shean. 12a, Tiberias. 20a, Elat. 25a, Acre (Akko). 35a, Dimona. 37a, Zefat. 50a, Rishon Leziyyon. 70a, Jerusalem. £1, Tel Aviv-Jaffa. £3, Haifa.

Size: 17x22½mm

276 A119 1a brown 15 15
277 A119 2a lilac rose 15 15
278 A119 5a gray 15 15
279 A119 6a violet 15 15
280 A119 8a orange 15 15
a. Booklet pane of 6 42
281 A119 10a emerald 15 15
282 A119 12a dark purple 15 15
a. Booklet pane of 6 50
283 A119 15a green 15 15
284 A119 20a rose red 15 15
285 A119 25a ultramarine 15 15
286 A119 35a magenta 15 15
287 A119 37a olive 15 15
288 A119 50a greenish bl 15 15

Perf. 14x13
Size: 22x27mm

289 A119 70a dark brown 20 15
290 A119 £1 dark green 25 15
291 A119 £3 dk carmine rose 52 15
Set value 2.00 1.00
With tabs 10.00

Dates of issue: Nos. 283-286, Mar. 24, 1965. No. 290, Nov. 24, 1965. No. 291, Mar. 14, 1966. Others, Feb. 2, 1966.

The uncut booklet pane sheets of 36 are divided into 4 panes (2 of 6 stamps, 2 of 12) by horizontal and vertical gutters. Half of the stamps in the 2 panes of 12 are inverted, causing 4 horizontal tête bêche pairs and 4 horizontal tête bêche gutter pairs.

Vertical strips of 6 of the 1a, 5a and 10a are from larger sheets, released Jan. 10, 1967, from which coils were produced. Regular sheets of 50 are arranged 10x5.

No. 290 also comes tagged (1975).

See Nos. 334-336, 386-393.

Hands Reaching for Hope, and Star of David — A120

"Irrigation of the Desert" — A121

1965, Apr. 27 **Unwmk.** ***Perf. 14x13***
292 A120 25a gray, black & yel 15 15
With tab 50

Liberation of Nazi concentration camps, 20th anniv.

1965, Apr. 27 **Photo.**
293 A121 37a olive bis & bl 15 15

Memorial Day; proclamation of the state of Israel, 17th anniv.

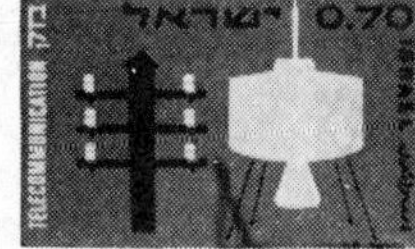

Telegraph Pole and Syncom Satellite A122

1965, July 21 **Unwmk.** ***Perf. 13x14***
294 A122 70a vio, blk & grnsh bl 15 15
With tab 48

ITU, centenary.

Symbol of Cooperation and UN Emblem A123

1965, July 21 **Litho.** ***Perf. 14***
295 A123 36a gray, dp claret, bl, red & bis 15 15
With tab 30

International Cooperation Year.

Dead Sea Extraction Plant A124

"Let There be Light . . ." A125

1965, July 21
296 A124 12a Crane 15 15
297 A124 50a shown 15 15
Set value 20 15
With tabs 1.00

Dead Sea chemical industry.

1965, Sept. 7 **Photo.** ***Perf. 13x14***

Genesis 1, The Creation: 8a, Firmament and Waters. 12a, Dry land and vegetation. 25a, Heavenly lights. 35a, Fish and fowl. 70a, Man.

298 A125 6a dk pur, lil & gold 15 15
299 A125 8a brt grn, dk bl & gold 15 15
300 A125 12a red brn, blk & gold 15 15
301 A125 25a dk pur, pink & gold 15 15
302 A125 35a lt & dk bl & gold 18 15

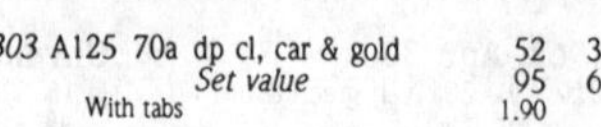
303 A125 70a dp cl, car & gold 52 35
Set value 95 65
With tabs 1.90

Jewish New Year, 5726. Sheets of 20 (10x2).

Charaxes Jasius A126

Flags over Rooftops A127

Butterflies: 6a, Papilio alexanor maccabaeus. 8a, Daphnis nerii. 12a, Zegris eupheme uarda.

1965, Dec. 15 **Litho.** ***Perf. 14***
Butterflies in Natural Colors
304 A126 2a lt olive green 15 15
305 A126 6a lilac 15 15
306 A126 8a ocher 15 15
307 A126 12a blue 15 15
Set value 35 24

1966, Apr. 20 **Litho.** ***Perf. 14***

Designs: 30a, Fireworks over Tel Aviv. 80a, Warships and Super Mirage jets, Haifa.

308 A127 12a multi 15 15
309 A127 30a multi 15 15
310 A127 80a multi 20 15
Set value 35 25

Proclamation of state of Israel, 18th anniv.

Memorial, Upper Galilee — A128

1966, Apr. 20 **Photo.** ***Perf. 14x13***
311 A128 40a olive gray 18 15

Issued for Memorial Day.

Knesset Building, Jerusalem — A129

1966, June 22 **Photo.** ***Perf. 13x14***
312 A129 £1 deep blue 28 15
With tab 60

Inauguration of the Knesset Building (Parliament). Sheets of 12.

Road Sign and Motorcyclist A130

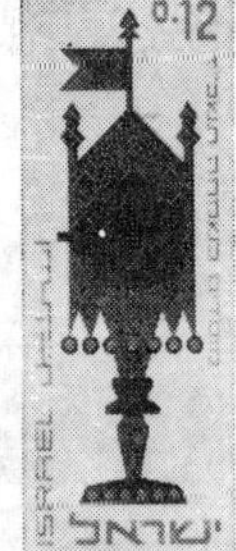

Spice Box A131

Designs (Road Signs and): 5a, Bicyclist. 10a, Pedestrian. 12a, Child playing ball. 15a, Automobile.

1966, June 22 *Perf. 14*

313	A130	2a sl, red brn & lil rose	15	15
314	A130	5a ol bis, sl & lil rose	15	15
315	A130	10a vio, lt bl & lil rose	15	15
316	A130	12a bl, grn & lil rose	15	15
317	A130	15a grn, red & lil rose	15	15
		Set value	28	25

Issued to publicize traffic safety.

1966, Aug. 24 **Photo.** *Perf. 13x14*

Ritual Art Objects: 15a, Candlesticks. 35a, Kiddush cup. 40a, Torah pointer. 80a, Hanging lamp.

318	A131	12a sil, gold, blk & bl	15	15
319	A131	15a sil, gold, blk & lil	15	15
320	A131	35a sil, gold, blk & emer	15	15
321	A131	40a sil, gold, blk & vio bl	15	15
322	A131	80a sil, gold, blk & red	18	18
		Set value	45	45

Jewish New Year, 5727.

Bronze Panther, Avdat, 1st Century, B.C. — A132

Designs: 30a, Stone menorah, Tiberias, 2nd Century. 40a, Phoenician ivory sphinx, 9th century, B.C. 55a, Gold earring (calf's head), Ashdod, 6th-4th centuries B.C. 80a, Miniature gold capital, Persia, 5th century, B.C. £1.15, Gold drinking horn (ram's head), Persia, 5th century, B.C., vert.

1966, Oct. 26 **Litho.** *Perf. 14*

323	A132	15a dp bl & yel brn	15	15
324	A132	30a vio brn & bister	15	15
325	A132	40a sepia & yel bis	15	15
326	A132	55a Prus grn, dp yel & brown	28	16
327	A132	80a lake, dp yel & brown	42	22

Perf. 13x14

328	A132	£1.15 vio, gold & brn	90	55
		Nos. 323-328 (6)	2.05	
		Set value		1.20
		With tabs	6.50	

Israel Museum, Jerusalem. Sheets of 12.

Coach and Mailman of Austrian Levant — A133

Microscope and Cells — A134

Designs: 15a, Turkish mailman and caravan. 40a, Palestinian mailman and locomotive. £1, Israeli mailman and jet liner.

1966, Dec. 14 **Photo.** *Perf. 14*

329	A133	12a ocher & green	15	15
330	A133	15a lt grn, brn & dp car	15	15
331	A133	40a brt rose & dk blue	15	15
332	A133	£1 grnsh bl & brown	22	15
		Set value	48	35
		With tabs	95	

Issued for Stamp Day.

1966, Dec. 14 *Perf. 14x13*

333	A134	15a red & dark sl grn	15	15

Campaign against cancer.

Arms Type of 1965-66

Town Emblems: 40a, Mizpe Ramon. 55a, Ashkelon. 80a, Rosh Pinna.

1967, Feb. 8 **Unwmk.** *Perf. 13x14*

334	A119	40a dark olive	15	15
335	A119	55a dk carmine rose	15	15
336	A119	80a red brown	24	15
		Set value	42	20
		With tabs	2.25	

Port of Acre — A135

Ancient Ports: 40a, Caesarea. 80a, Jaffa.

1967, Mar. 22 **Photo.** *Perf. 13x14*

337	A135	15a dark brown	15	15
338	A135	40a dark blue grn	15	15
339	A135	80a deep blue	25	15
		Set value	45	26
		With tabs	1.25	

Page of Shulhan Aruk and Crowns — A136

1967, Mar. 22 *Perf. 13½x13*

340	A136	40a dk & lt bl, gray & gold	18	15

400th anniv. of the publication (in 1565) of the Shulhan Aruk, a compendium of Jewish religious and civil law, by Joseph Karo (1488-1575).

War of Independence Memorial — A137

1967, May 10 **Unwmk.** *Perf. 13x14*

341	A137	55a lt bl, indigo & sil	18	15
		With tab	42	

Issued for Memorial Day, 1967.

Auster Plane over Convoy on Jerusalem Road A138

Military Aircraft: 30a, Mystère IV jet fighter over Dead Sea area. 80a, Mirage jet fighters over Masada.

1967, May 10 **Photo.**

342	A138	15a lt ol grn & dk bl grn	15	15
343	A138	30a ocher & dark brn	15	15
344	A138	80a grnsh bl & vio bl	20	15
		Set value	35	24
		With tabs	1.10	

Issued for Independence Day, 1967.

Israeli Ships in Straits of Tiran A139

Torah, Scroll of the Law A140

Designs: 15a, Star of David, sword and olive branch, vert. 80a, Wailing (Western) Wall, Jerusalem.

1967, Aug. 16 *Perf. 14x13, 13x14*

345	A139	15a dk red, blk & yel	15	15
346	A139	40a Prussian green	15	15
347	A139	80a deep violet	20	15
		Set value	32	28

Victory of the Israeli forces, June, 1967.

1967, Sept. 13 *Perf. 13x14*

Designs: Various ancient, decorated Scrolls of the Law.

348	A140	12a gold & multi	15	15
349	A140	15a silver & multi	15	15
350	A140	35a gold & multi	15	15
351	A140	40a silver & multi	15	15
352	A140	80a gold & multi	20	16
		Set value	50	40

Jewish New Year, 5728. Sheets of 20 (10x2).

Chaim Weizmann A141

Design: 40a, Lord Balfour.

1967, Nov. 2 **Photo.** *Perf. 13x14*

353	A141	15a dark green	15	15
354	A141	40a brown	15	15
		Set value	17	17

50th anniv. of the Balfour Declaration, which established the right to a Jewish natl. home in Palestine. Issued in sheets of 15.

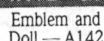

Emblem and Doll — A142

Nubian Ibex — A143

Designs: 30a, Hebrew inscription. 40a, French inscription.

1967, Nov. 2 **Litho.** *Perf. 14*

355	A142	30a yellow & multi	15	15
356	A142	40a brt bl & multi	15	15
357	A142	80a brt grn & multi	16	15
		Set value	30	24

Intl. Tourist Year. Issued in sheets of 15.

1967, Dec. 27 **Litho.** *Perf. 13*

Designs: 18a, Caracal lynx. 60a, Dorcas gazelles.

Animal in Ocher & Brown

358	A143	12a dull purple	15	15
359	A143	18a bright green	15	15
360	A143	60a bright blue	15	15
		Set value	26	20

Flags Forming Soccer Ball — A144

1968, Mar. 11 **Photo.** *Perf. 13*

361	A144	80a ocher & multi	15	15

Pre-Olympic soccer tournament.

Welcoming Immigrants A145

Resistance Fighter A146

Design: 80a, Happy farm family.

1968, Apr. 24 **Litho.** *Perf. 14*

362	A145	15a lt green & multi	15	15
363	A145	80a cream & multi	15	15
		Set value	15	15

Issued for Independence Day, 1968.

1968, Apr. 24 **Photo.** *Perf. 14x13*

364	A146	60a brown olive	15	15

Warsaw Ghetto Uprising, 25th anniv. Design from Warsaw Ghetto Memorial.

Sword and Laurel A147

Rifles and Helmet A148

1968, Apr. 24 **Litho.** *Perf. 14*

365	A147	40a gold & multi	15	15
366	A148	55a black & multi	15	15
		Set value	24	24

Zahal defense army, Independence Day, No. 365; Memorial Day, No. 366.

Candle and Prison Window A149

Prime Minister Moshe Sharett (1894-1965) A150

1968, June 5 Photo. *Perf. 14x13*

367	A149	80a blk, gray & sepia	18	15

Issued to honor those who died for freedom.

1968, June 5 Unwmk.

368	A150	£1 deep brown	18	15

27th Zionist Congress.

Knot Forming Star of David — A151

Dome of the Rock and Absalom's Tomb — A152

1968, Aug. 21 Litho. *Perf. 13*

369	A151	30a multi	15	15

50 years of Jewish Scouting. Sheets of 15.

1968, Aug. 21 Photo. *Perf. 14x13*

Views of Jerusalem: 15a, Church of the Resurrection. 35a, Tower of David and City Wall. 40a, Yemin Moshe District and Mount of Olives. 60a, Israel Museum and "Shrine of the Book."

370	A152	12a gold & multi	15	15
371	A152	15a gold & multi	15	15
372	A152	35a gold & multi	15	15
373	A152	40a gold & multi	15	15
374	A152	60a gold & multi	15	15
		Set value	40	35

Jewish New Year, 5729. Sheets of 15.

Detail from Lions' Gate, Jerusalem (St. Stephen's Gate) — A153

1968, Oct. 8 Unwmk. *Perf. 13x14*

375	A153	£1 brown org	15	15
a.		Souvenir sheet	35	30

TABIRA Natl. Philatelic Exhibition. No. 375a contains one imperf. stamp. Sold only at exhibition for £1.50. No. 375 issued in sheets of 15.

Abraham Mapu A154

Handicapped Boys Playing Basketball A155

1968, Oct. 8 Photo. *Perf. 14x13*

376	A154	30a dark olive grn	15	15

Mapu (1808-1867), novelist and historian.

1968, Nov. 6 Photo. *Perf. 14x13*

377	A155	40a green & yel grn	15	15

17th Stoke-Mandeville Games for the Paralyzed, Nov. 4-13. Sheets of 15.

Port of Elat — A156

Ports of Israel: 60a, Ashdod. £1, Haifa.

1969, Feb. 19 Unwmk. *Perf. 13x14*

378	A156	30a deep magenta	15	15
379	A156	60a brown	16	15
380	A156	£1 dull green	24	15
		Set value	46	34
		With tabs	2.50	

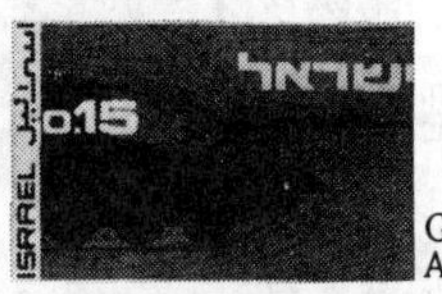

Gun Carrier A157

1969, Apr. 16 Photo. *Perf. 13x14*

381	A157	15a shown	15	15
382	A157	80a Destroyer	15	15
		Set value	22	18

Issued for Independence Day 1969.

Israel's Flag at Half-mast A158

Worker and ILO Emblem A159

1969, Apr. 16

383	A158	55a vio, gold & bl	15	15

Issued for Memorial Day.

1969, Apr. 16

384	A159	80a dark blue grn	15	15

ILO, 50th anniversary.

Hand Holding Torch A160

Arms of Hadera A161

1969, July 9 Photo. *Perf. 14x13*

385	A160	60a gold & multi	15	15
		With tab	60	

Issued to publicize the 8th Maccabiah.

1969-73 *Perf. 13x14*

Town Emblems: 3a, Hertseliya. 5a, Holon. 15a, Bat Yam. 18a, Ramla. 20a, Kefar Sava. 25a, Giv'atayim. 30a, Rehovot. 40a, Netanya. 50a, Bene Beraq. 60a, Nahariyya. 80a, Ramat Gan.

386	A161	2a green	15	15
387	A161	3a deep magenta	15	15
388	A161	5a orange	15	15
389	A161	15a bright rose	15	15
c.		Bklt. pane of 6 (2 #389 + 4 #389A) ('71)	65	
389A	A161	18a ultra ('70)	15	15
d.		Bklt. pane of 6 ('71)	70	
e.		Bklt. pane of 6 (1 #281 + 5 #389A) ('73)	65	
389B	A161	20a brown ('70)	15	15
f.		Bklt. pane of 5 + label ('73)	90	
390	A161	25a dark blue	15	15
390A	A161	30a brt pink ('70)	15	15
391	A161	40a purple	15	15
392	A161	50a greenish bl	18	15
392A	A161	60a olive ('70)	20	15
393	A161	80a dark green	22	15
		Set value	1.20	70
		With tabs	3.75	

Nos. 389c and 389d were also sold in uncut sheets of 36, No. 389e in uncut sheet of 18. See note after No. 291 about similar sheets.

Noah Building the Ark — A162

The Story of the Flood: 15a, Animals boarding the Ark. 35a, The Ark during the flood. 40a, Noah sending out the dove. 60a, Noah and the rainbow.

1969, Aug. 13 Unwmk. *Perf. 14*

394	A162	12a multicolored	15	15
395	A162	15a multicolored	15	15
396	A162	35a multicolored	15	15
397	A162	40a multicolored	15	15
398	A162	60a multicolored	25	15
		Set value	66	50

Jewish New Year, 5730. Sheets of 15.

King David by Marc Chagall — A163

Atom Diagram and Test Tube — A164

1969, Sept. 24 Photo. *Perf. 14*

399	A163	£3 multicolored	80	55
		With tab	1.40	

1969, Nov. 3 *Perf. 14x13*

400	A164	£1.15 vio bl & multi	60	45
		With tab	2.50	

Weizmann Institute of Science, 25th anniv.

Joseph Trumpeldor A165

Dum Palms, Emeq Ha-Arava A166

1970, Jan. 21 Photo. *Perf. 14x13*

401	A165	£1 dark purple	25	15

50th anniv. of the defense of Tel Hay under the leadership of Joseph Trumpeldor.

1970, Jan. 21

Views: 3a, Tahana Waterfall. 5a, Nahal Baraq Canyon, Negev. 6a, Cedars in Judean Hills. 30a, Soreq Cave, Judean Hills.

402	A166	2a olive	15	15
403	A166	3a deep blue	15	15
404	A166	5a orange red	15	15
405	A166	6a slate green	15	15
406	A166	30a brt purple	22	15
		Set value	40	25

Issued to publicize nature reserves.

Magic Carpet Shaped as Airplane A167

Prime Minister Levi Eshkol (1895-1969) A168

1970, Jan. 21 Litho. *Perf. 13*

407	A167	30a multicolored	15	15

20th anniv. of "Operation Magic Carpet" which airlifted the Yemeni Jews to Israel.

1970, Mar. 11 Litho. *Perf. 14*

408	A168	15a bl & multi	15	15

Mania Shochat — A169

Camel and Train — A170

Portrait: 80a, Ze'ev Jabotinsky (1880-1940), writer and Zionist leader.

1970, Mar. 11 Photo. *Perf. 14x13*

409	A169	40a dp plum & buff	16	16
410	A169	80a green & cream	18	18
		With tabs	1.10	

Ha-Shomer (Watchmen defense organization), 60th anniv. (No. 409); defense of Jerusalem, 50th anniv. (No. 410)

1970, Mar. 11 Litho. *Perf. 13*

411	A170	80a orange & multi	38	25
		With tab	1.00	

Opening of Dimona-Oron Railroad.

Scene from "The Dibbuk" — A171

1970, Mar. 11 Photo. *Perf. 14x13*

412 A171 £1 multicolored	22	15
With tab	70	

Habimah Natl. Theater, 50th anniv.

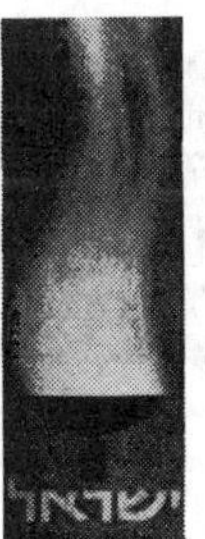
Memorial Flame A172

Orchis Laxiflorus A173

1970, May 6 Photo. *Perf. 13x14*

413 A172 55a vio, pink & blk	18	15

Issued for Memorial Day, 1970.

1970, May 6 Litho. *Perf. 14*

Flowers: 15a, Iris mariae. 80a, Lupinus pilosus.

414 A173 12a pale gray, plum & grn	15	15
415 A173 15a multicolored	15	15
416 A173 80a pale bl & multi	30	30
Set value	46	42
With tabs	1.10	

Issued for Independence Day, 1970.

Charles Netter — A174

420 Class Yachts — A175

Design: 80a, Agricultural College (Mikwe Israel) and garden.

1970, May 6 Photo. *Perf. 14x13*

417 A174 40a lt grn, dk brn & gold	15	15
418 A174 80a gold & multi	22	15
Set value		21
With tabs	1.40	

Centenary of first agricultural college in Israel; its founder, Charles Netter.

1970, July 8 Photo. *Perf. 14x13*

Designs: Various 420 Class yachts.

419 A175 15a grnsh bl, blk & sil	15	15
420 A175 30a ol, red, blk & sil	15	15
421 A175 80a ultra, blk & silver	28	15
Set value	42	22
With tabs	1.10	

World "420" Class Sailing Championships.

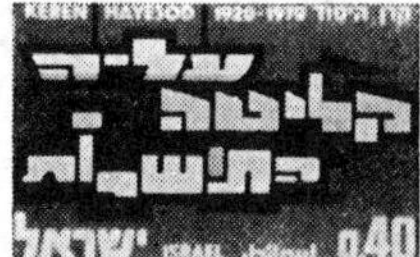
Hebrew Letters Shaped Like Ship and Buildings A176

1970, July 8 *Perf. 13x14*

422 A176 40a gold & multi	15	15

Keren Hayesod, a Zionist Fund to maintain schools and hospitals in Palestine, 50th anniv.

Arava Plane — A177

1970, July 8

423 A177 £1 brt blue, blk & sil	22	15

First Israeli designed and built aircraft.

Bird (Exiles) and Sun (Israel) A178

1970, Sept. 7 Litho. *Perf. 14*

424 A178 80a yel & multi	18	15

"Operation Ezra and Nehemiah," the exodus of Iraqi Jews.

Old Synagogue, Cracow — A179

Historic Synagogues: 15a, Great Synagogue, Tunis. 35a, Portuguese Synagogue, Amsterdam. 40a, Great Synagogue, Moscow. 60a, Shearith Israel Synagogue, New York.

Perf. 14, 13 (15a)

1970, Sept. 7 Photo.

425 A179 12a gold & multi	15	15
426 A179 15a gold & multi	15	15
427 A179 35a gold & multi	15	15
428 A179 40a gold & multi	15	15
429 A179 60a gold & multi	15	15
Set value	42	35

Jewish New Year, 5731.

Tel Aviv Post Office, 1920 — A180

1970, Oct. 18 Photo. *Perf. 14*

430 A180 £1 multicolored	18	15
a. Souvenir sheet	1.25	1.50

TABIT Natl. Stamp Exhibition, Tel Aviv, Oct. 18-29. No. 430a contains an imperf. stamp similar to No. 430. Sold for £1.50.

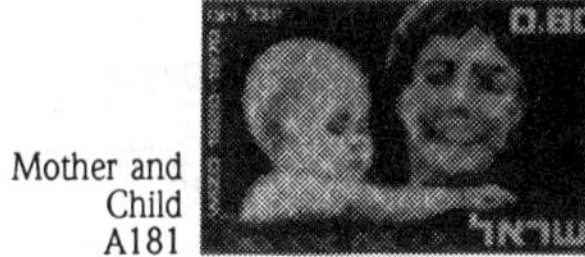
Mother and Child A181

1970, Oct. 18 *Perf. 13x14*

431 A181 80a dp grn, yel & gray	18	15
With tab	48	

WIZO, Women's Intl. Zionist Org., 50th anniv.

Paris Quai, by Camille Pissarro — A182

Paintings from Tel Aviv Museum: 85a, The Jewish Wedding, by Josef Israels. £2, Flowers in a Vase, by Fernand Leger.

1970, Dec. 22 Litho. *Perf. 14*

432 A182 85a black & multi	15	15
433 A182 £1 black & multi	16	15
434 A182 £2 black & multi	52	30
With tabs	2.00	

Hammer and Menorah Emblem — A183

Persian Fallow Deer — A184

1970, Dec. 22

435 A183 35a gold & multi	15	15

General Federation of Labor in Israel (Histadrut), 50th anniversary.

1971, Feb. 16 Litho. *Perf. 13*

Animals of the Bible: 3a, Asiatic wild ass. 5a, White oryx. 78a, Cheetah.

436 A184 2a multicolored	15	15
437 A184 3a multicolored	15	15
438 A184 5a multicolored	15	15
439 A184 78a multicolored	15	15
Set value	25	22

"Samson and Dalila," Israel National Opera — A185

Theater Art in Israel: No. 441, Inn of the Ghosts, Cameri Theater. No. 442, A Psalm of David, Inbal Dance Theater.

1971, Feb. 16 *Perf. 14x13*

440 A185 50a bister & multi	15	15
441 A185 50a lt grn & multi	15	15
442 A185 50a blue & multi	15	15
Set value		30

Basketball A186

Defense Forces Emblem A187

Designs: No. 444, Runner. No. 445, Athlete on rings.

1971, Apr. 13 Litho. *Perf. 14*

443 A186 50a green & multi	15	15
444 A186 50a ocher & multi	15	15
445 A186 50a lt vio & multi	15	15
Set value	36	20

9th Hapoel Games.

1971, Apr. 13 Photo. *Perf. 14x13*

446 A187 78a multicolored	18	15

Memorial Day, 1971, and the war dead.

Jaffa Gate, Jerusalem A188

Gates of Jerusalem: 18c, New Gate. 35c, Damascus Gate. 85c, Herod's Gate.

1971, Apr. 13 *Perf. 14*

Size: 41x41mm

447 A188 15a gold & multi	15	15
448 A188 18a gold & multi	15	15
449 A188 35a gold & multi	25	18
450 A188 85a gold & multi	60	45
a. Souvenir sheet of 4	3.50	3.50

Independence Day, 1971. No. 450a contains 4 stamps similar to Nos. 447-450, but smaller (27x27mm). Sold at the Jerusalem Exhibition for £2.

See Nos. 488-491.

"He Wrote . . . Words of the Covenant" A189

"You shall rejoice in your feast" A190

Designs: 85a, "First Fruits . . ." Exodus 23.19. £1.50, ". . . Feast of Weeks" Exodus 34:22. The quotation on 50a is from Exodus 34:28. The quotations are in English on the tabs.

1971, May 25 Photo. *Perf. 14x13*

451 A189 50a yellow & multi	15	15
452 A189 85a yellow & multi	28	20
453 A189 £1.50 yellow & multi	45	30
With tabs	1.75	

For the Feast of Weeks (Shabuoth).

1971, Aug. 24 Photo. *Perf. 14x13*

Designs: 18a, "You shall dwell in booths for seven days . . ." Leviticus 23:42. 20a, "That I made the people of Israel dwell in booths . . ." Lev.

23:43. 40a, "... when you have gathered in the produce of the land" Lev. 23:39. 65a, "... then I will give you your rains in their season" Lev. 26:4. The quotation on 15a is from Deuteronomy 16:14. The quotations are in English on tabs.

454 A190 15a yellow & multi 15 15
455 A190 18a yellow & multi 15 15
456 A190 20a yellow & multi 15 15
457 A190 40a yellow & multi 15 15
458 A190 65a yellow & multi 15 15
Set value 32 32
With tabs 80

For the Feast of Tabernacles (Sukkoth).

Sun Shining on Fields A191

1971, Aug. 24 ***Perf. 14***

459 A191 40a gold & multi 15 15

1st cooperative settlement in Israel, at Emeq (Valley of Israel), 50th anniv.

Retort and Grain — A192

Negev — A193

1971, Oct. 25 **Litho.** ***Perf. 14***

460 A192 £1 green & multi 18 15

50th anniversary of Volcani Institute of Agricultural Research.

> Tagging
>
> Starting in 1975, vertical luminescent bands were overprinted on various regular and commemorative stamps.
>
> In the 1971-75 regular series, values issued both untagged and tagged are: 20a, 25a, 30a, 35a, 45a, 50a, 65a, £1.10, £1.30, £2 and £3. Also No. 290 was re-issued with tagging in 1975.
>
> Regular issues from 1975 onward, including the £1.70, are tagged unless otherwise noted.
>
> Tagged commemoratives include Nos. 562-563 and all from Nos. 567-569 onward unless otherwise noted.

1971-75 **Photo.** ***Perf. 13x14***

Landscapes: 3a, Judean desert. 5a, Gan Ha-Shelosha. 18a, Kinneret. 20a, Tel Dan. 22a, Fishermen, Yafo. 25a, Arava. 30a, En Avedat. 35a, Brekhat Ram, Golan Heights. 45a, Grazing sheep, Mt. Hermon. 50a, Rosh Pinna. 55a, Beach and park, Netanya. 65a, Plain of Zebulun. 70a, Shore, Engedi. 80a, Beach at Elat. 88a, Boats in Akko harbor. 95a, Hamifratz Hane'elam (lake). £1.10, Aqueduct near Akko. £1.30, Zefat. £1.70, Upper Nazareth. £2, Coral Island. £3, Haifa.

461 A193 3a dp bl ('72) 20 15
462 A193 5a green ('72) 15 15
463 A193 15a dp orange 16 15
464 A193 18a bright mag 65 15
464A A193 20a dk grn ('73) 15 15
465 A193 22a brt bl ('72) 1.00 25
465A A193 25a org red ('74) 15 15
466 A193 30a brt rose ('72) 15 15
466A A193 35a plum ('73) 15 15
467 A193 45a dull vio blue ('73) 15 15
468 A193 50a green 15 15
469 A193 55a olive ('72) 16 15
469A A193 65a black ('73) 16 15
470 A193 70a dp car ('72) 20 15
470A A193 80a dp ultra ('74) 15 15
471 A193 88a greenish bl 1.00 16
472 A193 95a org ver ('73) 80 15
472A A193 £1.10 olive ('73) 16 15
472B A193 £1.30 dp bl ('74) 16 15
472C A193 £1.70 dk brn ('75) 40 15
473 A193 £2 brown ('73) 40 15
474 A193 £3 dp vio ('72) 55 15
Nos. 461-474 (22) 7.20
Set value 1.90
With tabs 14.00

See No. 592.

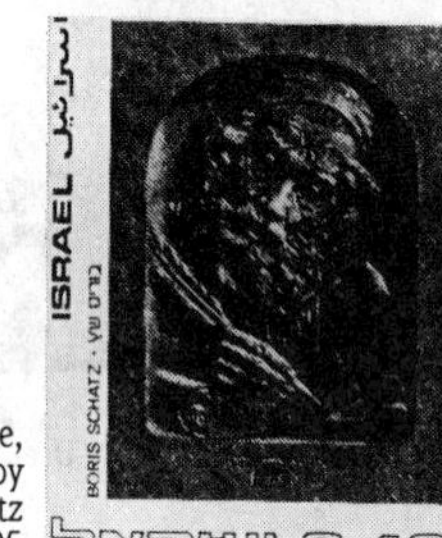

"Get Wisdom" Proverbs 4:7 — A194

Abstract Designs: 18a, Mathematical and scientific formula. 20a, Tools and engineering symbols. 40a, Abbreviations of various college degrees.

1972, Jan. 4 **Litho.** ***Perf. 14***

475 A194 15a brt grn & multi 15 15
476 A194 18a multicolored 15 15
477 A194 20a multicolored 15 15
478 A194 40a red, blk & gold 15 15
Set value 32 25

The Scribe, Sculpture by Boris Schatz A195

Works by Israeli Artists: 55a, Young Girl (Sarah), by Abel Pann. 70a, Zefat (landscape), by Menahem Shemi, horiz. 85a, Old Jerusalem, by Jacob Steinhardt. £1, Resurrection (abstract), by Aharon Kahana.

Perf. 13x14 (40a, 85a), 14

1972, Mar. 7

479 A195 40a black & tan 15 15
480 A195 55a red brn & multi 15 15
481 A195 70a lt grn & multi 16 15
482 A195 85a blk & yellow 32 18
483 A195 £1 blk & multi 35 28
Nos. 479-483 (5) 1.13
Set value 75

Exodus — A196

"Let My People Go" — A197

Passover: 45a, Baking unleavened bread. 95a, Seder.

1972, Mar. 7 **Litho.** ***Perf. 13***

484 A196 18a buff & multi 15 15
485 A196 45a buff & multi 20 15
486 A196 95a buff & multi 32 20
Set value 35
With tabs 1.40

1972, Mar. 7 ***Perf. 14***

487 A197 55a blk, bl & yel grn 45 30
With tab 4.00

No. 487 inscribed in Hebrew, Arabic, Russian and English.

Gate Type of 1971

Gates of Jerusalem: 15a, Lions' Gate. 18a, Golden Gate. 45a, Dung Gate. 55a, Zion Gate.

1972, Apr. 17 **Photo.** ***Perf. 14***

Size: 40x40mm

488 A188 15a gold & multi 15 15
489 A188 18a gold & multi 15 15
490 A188 45a gold & multi 28 25
491 A188 55a gold & multi 35 35
a. Souvenir sheet of 4 3.50 3.50
Set value 75
With tabs 3.00

Independence Day. #491a contains 4 27x27mm stamps similar to #488-491. Sold for £2.

Jethro's Tomb A198

Flowers A199

1972, Apr. 17 **Litho.** ***Perf. 13***

492 A198 55a multicolored 18 15

1972, Apr. 17 ***Perf. 14***

493 A199 55a multicolored 18 15

Memorial Day.

Hebrew Words Emerging from Opened Ghetto — A200

Printed Page — A201

1972, June 6 ***Perf. 13***

494 A200 70a blue & multi 45 35
With tab 2.00

400th anniversary of the death of Rabbi Isaac ben Solomon Ashkenazi Luria ("Ari") (1534-1572), Palestinian cabalist.

1972, June 6 ***Perf. 14x13***

495 A201 95a blk, red & blue 28 15

International Book Year.

Satellite Earth Station, Satellite and Rainbow — A202

1972, June 6 ***Perf. 13***

496 A202 £1 tan & multi 20 15

Opening of satellite earth station in Israel.

17th Cent. Ark, Ancona — A203

Menorah and "25" — A204

Holy Arks from: 45a, Padua, 1729. 70a, Parma, 17th century. 95a, Reggio Emilia, 1756. Arks moved to Israel from Italian synagogues.

1972, Aug. 8 **Photo.** ***Perf. 14x13***

497 A203 15a deep brn & yel 15 15
498 A203 45a dp grn, yel grn & gold 15 15
499 A203 70a brn red, yel & bl 22 15
500 A203 95a magenta & gold 25 20
Set value 62 45
With tabs 1.50

Jewish New Year, 5733.

1972, Aug. 8

501 A204 £1 silver, bl & mag 15 15

25th anniversary of the State of Israel.

Brass Menorah, Morocco, 18th-19th Century A205

Menorahs: 25a, Brass, Poland, 18th century. 70a, Silver, Germany, 17th century.

1972, Nov. 7 **Litho.** ***Perf. 14x13***

502 A205 12a emer, blk & bl grn 15 15
503 A205 25a lil rose, blk & org 15 15
504 A205 70a blue, blk & vio 15 15
Set value 32 25

Hanukkah (Festival of Lights), 1972.

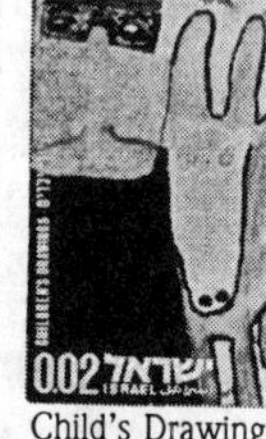

Child's Drawing A206

Pendant A207

Designs: Children's drawings.

1973, Jan. 16 **Litho.** ***Perf. 14***

Sizes: 22½x37mm (2a, 55a); 17x48mm (3a)

505 A206 2a blk & multi 15 15
506 A206 3a multicolored 15 15
507 A206 55a multicolored 15 15
Set value 15 15

Youth Wing of Israel Museum, Jerusalem (2a, 3a) and Youth Workshops, Tel Aviv Museum (55a).

1973, Jan. 16 **Photo.** ***Perf. 14x13***

508 A207 18a silver & multi 15 15

Immigration of North African Jews.

Levi, by Marc Chagall A208

Tribes of Israel: No. 510, Simeon. No. 511, Reuben. No. 512, Issachar. No. 513, Zebulun. No. 514, Judah. No. 515, Dan. No. 516, Gad. No. 517, Asher. No. 518, Naphtali. No. 519, Joseph. No.520, Benjamin.

1973 **Litho.** ***Perf. 14***

509 A208 £1 multicolored 40 40
510 A208 £1 gray grn & multi 40 40
511 A208 £1 olive & multi 40 40
512 A208 £1 gray bl & multi 40 40

513 A208 £1 lemon & multi 40 40
514 A208 £1 gray & multi 40 40
515 A208 £1 bl grn & multi 40 40
516 A208 £1 gray & multi 40 40
517 A208 £1 yel grn & multi 40 40
518 A208 £1 sepia & multi 40 40
519 A208 £1 olive & multi 40 40
520 A208 £1 tan & multi 40 40
Nos. 509-520 (12) 4.80 4.80

Designs from stained glass windows by Marc Chagall, Hadassah-Hebrew University Medical Center Synagogue, Jerusalem.
Issue dates: Nos. 509-514, Mar. 27; Nos. 515-520, Aug. 21.

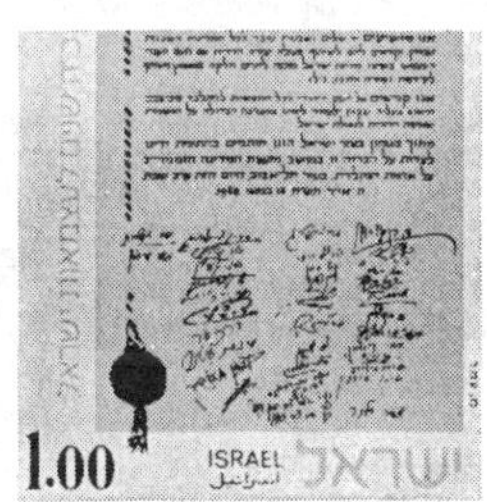

Israel's Declaration of Independence — A209

1973, May 4 Photo. *Perf. 14*
521 A209 £1 ocher & multi 16 15
a. Souvenir sheet 65 75

25 years of Independence. No. 521a sold for £1.50.

Star of David and Runners A210

1973, May 4 Litho.
522 A210 £1.10 multicolored 15 15

9th Maccabiah.

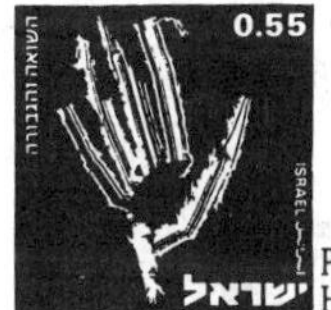

Prison-cloth Hand — A211

1973, May 4 Photo.
523 A211 55a blue black 15 15

Heroes and martyrs of the Holocaust, 1933-1945.

Flame A212

Prophets A213

1973, May 4 Litho.
524 A212 65a multicolored 16 15

Memorial Day.

1973, Aug. 21 Photo. *Perf. 13x14*
525 A213 18a Isaiah 15 15
526 A213 65a Jeremiah 15 15
527 A213 £1.10 Ezekiel 15 15
Set value 32 20

Jewish New Year, 5734.

Torch of Learning, Cogwheel A214

Rescue Boat and Danish Flag A215

1973, Oct. 24 *Perf. 14x13*
528 A214 £1.25 slate & multi 15 15

50th anniversary of the Technion, Israel Institute of Technology.

1973, Oct. 24 *Perf. 13x14*
529 A215 £5 bister, red & blk 55 30

30th anniversary of the rescue by the Danes of the Jews in Denmark.

Spectators at Stamp Show — A216

Design: £1, Spectators, different design.

1973, Dec. 19 Litho. *Perf. 13*
530 A216 20a brown & multi 15 15
531 A216 £1 brown & multi 15 15
Set value 15 15

JERUSALEM '73 Philatelic Exhibition, Mar. 25-Apr. 2, 1974.

Souvenir Sheets

Israel No. 7 — A217

Designs: £2, No. 8. £3, No. 9.

1974, Feb. 19 Photo. *Perf. 14x13*
532 A217 £1 silver & dk slate grn 15 18
533 A217 £2 silver & red brn 22 28
534 A217 £3 silver & blk blue 42 55

Jerusalem '73 Philatelic Exhibition, Mar. 25-Apr. 2, 1974 (postponed from Dec. 1973), 25th anniv. of State of Israel. Each sheet was sold with a 50 per cent surcharge.

Soldier with Prayer Shawl — A218

Quill and Inkwell with Hebrew Letters — A219

1974, Apr. 23 *Perf. 13x14*
535 A218 £1 blk & light bl 15 15

Memorial Day.

1974, Apr. 23 *Perf. 14x13*
536 A219 £2 gold & black 15 15

50th anniversary of Hebrew Writers Assn.

Lady in Blue, by Moshe Kisling A220

Designs: £2, Mother and Child, Sculpture by Chana Orloff. £3, Girl in Blue, by Chaim Soutine.

1974, June 11 Litho. *Perf. 14*
537 A220 £1.25 multicolored 15 15
538 A220 £2 multicolored 18 15
539 A220 £3 multicolored 38 30

Art works from Tel Aviv, En Harod and Jerusalem Museums.

Wrench A221

1974, June 11
540 A221 25a multicolored 15 15

50th anniv. of Working Youth Movement.

Istanbuli Synagogue, Jerusalem — A222

Designs: Interiors of restored synagogues in Jerusalem's Old City.

1974, Aug. 6 Photo. *Perf. 13x14*
541 A222 25a shown 15 15
542 A222 70a Emtzai Synagogue 15 15
543 A222 £1 Rabbi Yohanan Synagogue 15 15
Set value 22 20

Jewish New Year, 5735.

Lady Davis Technical Center "AMAL," Tel Aviv — A223

Designs: 60a, Elias Sourasky Library, Tel Aviv University. £1.45, Mivtahim Rest Home, Zikhron Yaaqov.

1974, Aug. 6 *Perf. 13½x14*
544 A223 25a violet black 15 15
545 A223 60a dark blue 15 15
546 A223 £1.45 maroon 15 15
Set value 28 22

Modern Israeli architecture.

David Ben-Gurion A224

1974, Nov. 5 *Perf. 14*
547 A224 25a brown 15 15
548 A224 £1.30 slate green 15 15
Set value 18 16

David Ben-Gurion (1886-1973), first Prime Minister and Minister of Defense of Israel.

Arrows on Globe — A225

Dove Delivering Letter — A226

1974, Nov. 5 Litho. *Perf. 14*
549 A225 25a black & multi 15 15

Photo.
550 A226 £1.30 gold & multi 15 15
Set value 18 18

Centenary of Universal Postal Union.

Hebrew University, Mount Scopus, Jerusalem — A227

1975, Jan. 14 Litho. *Perf. 13*
551 A227 £2.50 multicolored 18 15

Hebrew University, 50th anniv.

Girl Carrying Plant — A228

Welder — A229

Arbor Day: 35a, Bird singing in tree. £2, Boy carrying potted plant.

1975, Jan. 14 *Perf. 14*

552	A228	1a	multicolored	15	15
553	A228	35a	multicolored	15	15
554	A228	£2	multicolored	15	15
			Set value	18	16

1975, Jan. 14 Photo. *Perf. 14x13*

Designs: 80a, Tractor driver. £1.20, Electrical lineman.

555	A229	30a	multicolored	15	15
556	A229	80a	multicolored	15	15
557	A229	£1.20	ultra & multi	15	15
			Set value	18	18

Occupational safety and publicity for the Institute for Safety and Hygiene.

Hebrew University Synagogue, Jerusalem — A230

Modern Israeli architecture: £1.30, Yad Mordecai Museum. £1.70, Bat Yam City Hall.

Perf. 14, 13½x14 (#559)

1975, Mar. 5 Photo.

558	A230	80a	brown	15	15
559	A230	£1.30	slate green	15	15
560	A230	£1.70	brown olive	18	15
			Set value	38	26

US President Harry S Truman (1884-1972) — A231

1975, Mar. 5 Engr. *Perf. 14*

561	A231	£5	dark brown	35	15

Eternal Flame over Soldier's Grave — A232

Memorial Tablet — A233

1975, Apr. 10 Photo. *Perf. 14x13*

562	A232	£1.45	black & multi	16	15

Memorial Day.

1975, Apr. 10

563	A233	£1.45	black, red & gray	16	15

In memory of soldiers missing in action.

Hurdling A234

1975, Apr. 10 *Perf. 13x14*

564	A234	25a	shown	15	15
565	A234	£1.70	Bicycling	15	15
566	A234	£3	Volleyball	20	16
			Set value	35	30

10th Hapoel Games; 50th anniv. of Hapoel Org.

Hanukkah, by Mortiz D. Oppenheim A235

Paintings: £1.40, The Purim Players, by Jankel Adler, horiz. £4, Yom Kippur, by Maurycy Gottlieb.

1975, June 17 Litho. *Perf. 14*

567	A235	£1	multicolored	15	15
568	A235	£1.40	multicolored	15	15
569	A235	£4	multicolored	32	24
			Set value	48	38

Paintings of religious holidays.

Old Couple A236

1975, June 17 Photo. *Perf. 13x14*

570	A236	£1.85	multicolored	15	15

International Gerontological Association, 10th triennial conference, Jerusalem.

Pres. Zalman Shazar (1889-1974) A237

Pioneer Women's Emblem A238

1975, Aug. 6 Photo. *Perf. 14x13*

571	A237	35a	silver & blk	15	15

1975, Aug. 6 *Perf. 14½*

572	A238	£5	multicolored	30	15

Pioneer Women, 50th anniversary.

Judges of Israel — A239

1975, Aug. 6 *Perf. 13x14*

573	A239	35a	Gideon	15	15
574	A239	£1	Deborah	15	15
575	A239	£1.40	Jephthah	15	15
			Set value	34	26

Jewish New Year, 5736.

Hebrew University, Mt. Scopus — A240

1975, Oct. 14 Photo. *Perf. 14x13*

576	A240	£4	multicolored	30	15

Return of Hadassah to Mt. Scopus, Jerusalem.

Collared Pratincoles — A241

Protected Birds: £1.70, Spur-winged plover. £2, Black-winged stilts.

1975, Oct. 14 Litho. *Perf. 13*

577	A241	£1.10	pink & multi	15	15
578	A241	£1.70	lemon & multi	15	15
579	A241	£2	multicolored	15	15
			Set value	34	26

Butterfly and Factory (Air Pollution) — A242

Designs: 80a, Fish and tanker (water pollution). £1.70, Ear and jet (noise pollution).

1975, Dec. 9 Photo. *Perf. 14*

580	A242	50a	car & multi	15	15
581	A242	80a	green & multi	15	15
582	A242	£1.70	orange & multi	16	15
			Set value	30	22

Environmental protection.

Star of David — A243

1975-80 *Perf. 13x14*

583	A243	75a	vio bl & carmine ('77)	15	15
584	A243	£1.80	violet bl & gray ('79)	15	15
585	A243	£1.85	vio bl & lt brn	24	22
586	A243	£2.45	vio bl & brt green ('76)	30	18
587	A243	£2.70	vio bl & purple ('80)	15	15
588	A243	£4.30	ultra & red ('80)	15	15
589	A243	£5.40	vio bl & ol ('78)	52	18
590	A243	£8	vio bl & bl ('79)	75	24
			Nos. 583-590 (8)	2.41	
			Set value		1.05

Landscape Type of 1971-75

Design: £10, View of Elat and harbor.

1976, Aug. 17 Photo. *Perf. 14x14½*

592	A193	£10	Prussian bl	90	15

No. 592 issued both tagged and untagged.

"In the days of Ahasuerus." — A247

Designs (from Book of Esther): 80a, "He set the royal crown on her head." £1.60, "Thus shall it be done to the man whom the king delights to honor."

1976, Feb. 17 Photo. *Perf. 14*

593	A247	40a	multicolored	15	15
594	A247	80a	multicolored	15	15
595	A247	£1.60	multicolored	15	15
a.			Souv. sheet of 3, #593-595, perf 13x14	45	35
			Set value	32	30

Purim Festival. No. 595a sold for £4.

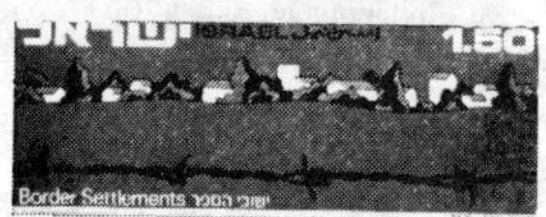

Border Settlement, Barbed Wire — A248

1976, Feb. 17

596	A248	£1.50	olive & multi	15	15

Border settlements, part of Jewish colonization of Holy Land.

Symbolic Key — A249

1976, Feb. 17

597	A249	£1.85	multicolored	15	15

Bezalel Academy of Arts and Design, Jerusalem, 70th anniv.

"200" US Flag — A250

1976, Apr. 25 Photo. *Perf. 13x14*

598	A250	£4	gold & multi	38	22

American Bicentennial.

Dancers of Meron, by Reuven Rubin A251

1976, Apr. 25 Litho. *Perf. 14*

599	A251	£1.30	multicolored	15	15

Lag Ba-Omer festival.

8th Brigade Monument, Ben-Gurion Airport — A252

1976, Apr. 25 Photo. *Perf. 14x13*

600 A252 £1.85 multicolored 24 15

Memorial Day.

Souvenir Sheet

Tourism, Sport and Industry — A253

1976, Apr. 25

601 A253 Sheet of 3 75 50
a. £1 multicolored 15 15
b. £2 multicolored 20 15
c. £4 multicolored 45 28

No. 601 sold for £10.

High Jump A254

1976, June 23 *Perf. 13x14*

602 A254 £1.60 shown 15 15
603 A254 £2.40 Diving 16 16
604 A254 £4.40 Gymnastics 35 30

21st Olympic Games, Montreal, Canada, July 17-Aug. 1.

Tents and Suns — A255

1976, June 23 *Perf. 14*

605 A255 £1.50 green & multi 15 15

Israel Camping Union.

"Truth" A256

Pawn A257

Design: £1.50, "Judgment" (scales). £1.90, "Peace" (dove and olive branch).

1976, Aug. 17 Photo. *Perf. 14x13*
Tagged

606 A256 45a gold & multi 15 15
607 A256 £1.50 gold & multi 15 15
608 A256 £1.90 gold & multi 15 15
Set value 28 25

Festivals 5737.

1976, Oct. 19 Litho. *Perf. 14*

609 A257 £1.30 shown 15 15
610 A257 £1.60 Rook 15 15
Set value 15

22nd Men's and 7th Women's Chess Olympiad, Haifa, Oct. 24-Nov. 11.

Byzantine Building, 6th Century A258

Designs: 70a, City wall, 7th century B.C. £2.40, Robinson's Arch. £2.80, Steps to Gate of Hulda. Both from area leading to 2nd Temple, 1st century B.C. £5, Wall, Omayyad Palace, 8th century A.D.

1976 Litho. *Perf. 14*

611 A258 70a multicolored 15 15
612 A258 £1.30 multicolored 15 15
613 A258 £2.40 multicolored 20 15
614 A258 £2.80 multicolored 35 20
615 A258 £5 multicolored 48 42
Nos. 611-615 (5) 1.33 1.07

Excavations in Old Jerusalem.
Issue dates: Nos. 612-614, Oct. 19; Nos. 611, 615, Dec. 14.

Clearing the Land, 1890 A259

Designs: 10a, Building harbor wall. 60a, Road building, vert. £1.40, Plower and horse-drawn plow. £1.80, Planting trees.

1976, Dec. 14 Photo. *Perf. 13*

616 A259 5a brown & gold 15 15
617 A259 10a purple & gold 15 15
618 A259 60a gold & car 15 15
619 A259 £1.40 gold & blue 15 15
620 A259 £1.80 green & gold 15 15
Set value 40 35

Work of the pioneers.

"Let's Pull up Grandfather's Carrot" — A260

1977, Feb. 15 Litho. *Perf. 14*

621 A260 £2.60 multicolored 25 18

Voluntary service.

Doves, Jew and Arab Shaking Hands A261

Designs: £1.40, Arab and Jew holding hands, and flowers. £2.70, Peace dove, Arab and Jew dancing. Illustrations for the book "My Shalom-My Peace."

1977, Feb. 15

622 A261 50a multicolored 15 15
623 A261 £1.40 multicolored 19 15
624 A261 £2.70 multicolored 32 25
Set value 45

Children's drawings for peace.

"By the Rivers of Babylon . . ." — A262

Drawings by Efraim Moshe Lilien: £1.80, Abraham, vert. £2.10, "May our eyes behold thee when thou returnest to Zion in compassion."

Perf. 14x13, 13x14
1977, Feb. 15 Photo.

625 A262 £1.70 gray, brn & blk 24 18
626 A262 £1.80 yel, blk & brn 25 18
627 A262 £2.10 lt grn & dk grn 30 22

Souvenirs for 5th Zionist Congress, 1902.

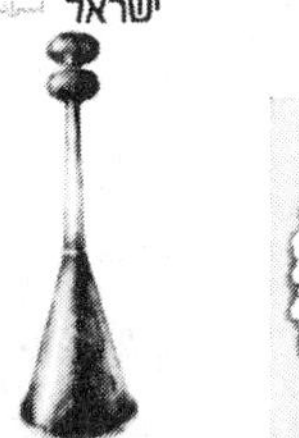

Trumpet A263

Embroidered Sabbath Cloth A264

1977, Apr. 17 Litho. *Perf. 14*

628 A263 £1.50 shown 15 15
629 A263 £2 Lyre 15 15
630 A263 £5 Cymbals 32 24
Set value 42

Ancient musical instruments, Haifa Music Museum and Amli Library.

1977, Apr. 17 *Perf. 13x14*

631 A264 £3 buff & multi 26 15

Importance of Sabbath observation in Jewish life.

Parachutists' Memorial, Bilu-Gedera, Tel Aviv — A265

1977, Apr. 17 *Perf. 13x14*

632 A265 £3.30 gray, blk & grn 38 28

Memorial Day.

10th Maccabiah A266

ZOA Convention Emblem A267

1977, June 23 Photo. *Perf. 14x13*

633 A266 £1 Fencing 16 15
634 A266 £2.50 Shot put 20 15
635 A266 £3.50 Judo 28 20

1977, June 23 *Perf. 14*

636 A267 £4 silver & multi 32 20

Convention of Zionist Organization of America (ZOA), Jerusalem, June 1977.

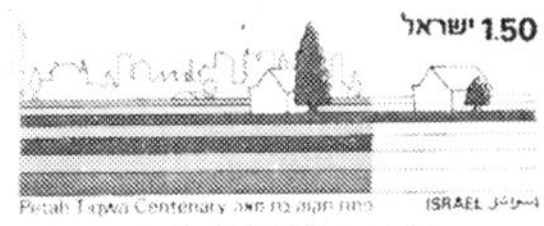

Petah Tikva Centenary — A268

1977, June 23 *Perf. 14x13*

637 A268 £1.50 multicolored 15 15

Matriarchs of the Bible — A269

1977, Aug. 16 Photo. *Perf. 14*

638 A269 70a Sarah 15 15
639 A269 £1.50 Rebekah 15 15
640 A269 £2 Rachel 15 15
641 A269 £3 Leah 20 20
Set value 48 46

Jewish New Year, 5738.

Police — A270

Illuminated Page — A271

1977, Aug. 16 Litho. *Perf. 14*

642 A270 £1 shown 15 15
643 A270 £1 Fronteir Guards 15 15
644 A270 £1 Civil Guard 15 15
Set value 30 20

Israel Police Force, established Mar. 26, 1948.

1977, July 21 Photo. *Perf. 14x13*

645 A271 £4 multicolored 28 15

4th cent. of Hebrew printing at Safad.

15-Cent Minimum Value
The minimum value for a single stamp is 15 cents. This value reflects the costs of handling inexpensive stamps.

Farm Growing from Steel Helmet
A272

Koffler Accelerator
A273

1977, Oct. 18 Litho. *Perf. 14*

646 A272 £3.50 multicolored			28	15

Fighting Pioneer Youth (NAHAL), established 1949.

1977, Oct. 18 Photo. *Perf. 14x13*

647 A273 £8 black & blue			65	42

Inauguration of Koffler accelerator at Weizmann Institute of Science, Rehovot. Untagged.

Caesarea — A274

Scenes: £1, Arava on the Dead Sea. £20, Rosh Pinna.

1977-78 *Perf. 13½x14*

Size: 27x22mm

649 A274	10a	violet blue	15	15
664 A274	£1	olive bister	15	15

Perf. 14½x14

Size: 27½x26½mm

672 A274	£20	org & dk grn ('78)	1.10	15
		Set value		22

The 10a and £20 are untagged.

First Holy Land Locomotive
A276

Locomotives: £1.50, Jezreel Valley train. £2, British Mandate period. £2.50, Israel Railways.

1977, Dec. 13 Photo. *Perf. 13x14*

674 A276	65a	multicolored	15	15
675 A276	£1.50	multicolored	18	15
676 A276	£2	multicolored	28	22
677 A276	£2.50	multicolored	32	28
a.		Souvenir sheet of 4, #674-677	1.40	1.40
		Set value		68

Railways in the Holy Land. #677a sold for £10.

Cypraea Isabella — A277

Designs: Red Sea shells.

1977, Dec. 13 Litho. *Perf. 14*

678 A277	£2	shown	15	15
679 A277	£2	Lioconcha castrensis	15	15
680 A277	£2	Gloripallium pallium	15	15
681 A277	£2	Malea pomum	15	15
		Set value	48	40

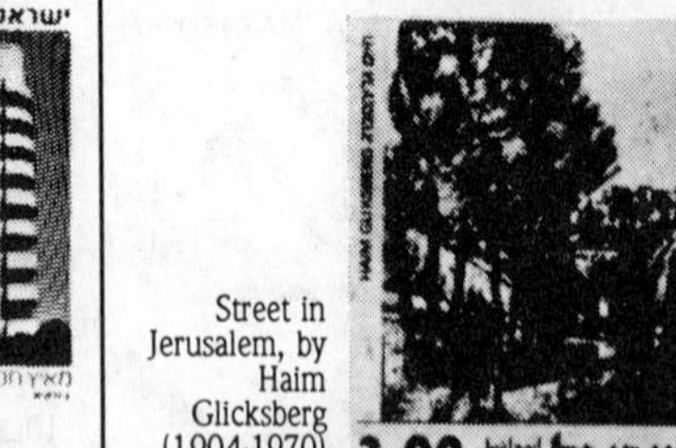

Street in Jerusalem, by Haim Glicksberg (1904-1970)
A278

Paintings: £3.80, Thistles, by Leopold Krakauer (1890-1954). £4.40, An Alley in Zefat, by Mordekhai Levanon (1901-1968).

1978, Feb. 14

682 A278	£3	multicolored	16	15
683 A278	£3.80	multicolored	24	20
684 A278	£4.40	multicolored	28	24

Marriage Contract, Netherlands, 1648 — A279

Marriage Contracts (Ketubah): £3.90, Morocco, 1897. £6, Jerusalem, 1846.

1978, Feb. 14

685 A279	75a	multicolored	15	15
686 A279	£3.90	multicolored	15	16
687 A279	£6	multicolored	25	20
		Set value	45	40

Eliyahu Golomb — A280

Designs: Portraits.

1978, Apr. 23 Photo. *Perf. 14x13*

688 A280	£2	shown	15	15
689 A280	£2	Dr. Moshe Sneh	15	15
690 A280	£2	David Raziel	15	15
691 A280	£2	Yitzhak Sadeh	15	15
692 A280	£2	Abraham Stern	15	15
		Nos. 688-692 (5)	75	75

Heroes of underground movement. Nos. 688-692 issued in sheets of 15.

See Nos. 695-696, 699-700, 705-706, 712-714, 740-742.

Souvenir Sheet

Jerusalem, Mosaic, from Madaba Map — A281

1978, Apr. 23 Litho. *Perf. 14*

693 A281		Sheet of 4	1.75	1.50
a.	£1	multicolored	15	15
b.	£2	multicolored	35	28
c.	£3	multicolored	50	42
d.	£4	multicolored	65	55

Tabir '78 National Stamp Exhibition, Jerusalem, Apr. 23. No. 693 sold for £15.

Flowers
A282

Design: Flowers, after children's paintings on Memorial Wall in Yad-Lebanim Museum, Petah Tikva. Each stamp shows different flowers.

1978, Apr. 23 *Perf. 14*

694	Sheet of 15	1.75	1.25
a.-o.	A282 £1.50 single stamp	15	15

Memorial Day.

Heroes Type

Designs: No. 695, Theodor Herzl. No. 696, Chaim Weizmann.

1978, July 5 Photo. *Perf. 14x13*

695 A280	£2	gray & gray ol	15	15
696 A280	£2	buff & vio bl	15	15
		Set value		15

Herzl, founder of Zionism; Weizmann, 1st President of Israel.

Hatiqwa, 1st Verse
A285

YMCA Building, Jerusalem
A286

1978, July 4 *Perf. 13x14*

697 A285 £8.40 multicolored			48	38

Centenary of Israeli National Anthem, Hatiqwa, by poet Naftali Herz Imber.

1978, July 4 Litho. *Perf. 13*

698 A286 £5.40 multicolored			28	20

Centenary of YMCA in Jerusalem.

Heroes Type

Designs: No. 699, Rabbi Kook (1865-1935). No. 700, Rabbi Ouziel (1880-1963).

1978, Aug. 22 Photo. *Perf. 14x13*

699 A280	£2	pale gray & sl grn	15	15
700 A280	£2	pale gray & dk pur	15	15
		Set value		15

Patriarchs — A288

1978, Aug. 22 *Perf. 14*

701 A288	£1.10	Abraham & Isaac	15	15
702 A288	£5.20	Isaac	28	26
703 A288	£6.60	Jacob	35	32
		Set value		62

Festivals 5739.

Families and Houses
A289

1978, Aug. 22 *Perf. 13x14*

704 A289 £5.10 multicolored			32	20

Social welfare.

Heroes Type

Designs: No. 705, David Ben-Gurion. No. 706, Ze'ev Jabotinsky.

1978, Oct. 31 Photo. *Perf. 14x13*

705 A280	£2	buff & vio brn	16	15
706 A280	£2	gray & indigo	16	15
		Set value		15

30 years of independence. Ben-Gurion, first Prime Minister, and Ze'ev Vladimir Jabotinsky (1880-1940), leader of World Union of Zionist Revisionists.

Star of David and Growing Tree — A291

1978, Oct. 31 Litho. *Perf. 14*

707 A291 £8.40 multicolored			55	38

United Jewish Appeal, established 1939 in US to help Israel.

Old and New Hospital Buildings
A292

1978, Oct. 31

708 A292 £5.40 multicolored			28	22

Opening of new Shaare Zedek Medical Center, Jerusalem.

Silver and Enamel Vase, India — A293

Iris Lortetii — A295

Designs: £3, Elephant with howdah, Persia, 13th century. £4, Mosque lamp, glass and enamel, Syria, 14th century.

1978, Oct. 31

709 A293	£2.40	multicolored	15	15
710 A293	£3	multicolored	20	15
711 A293	£4	multicolored	22	18

Leo Arie Mayer Memorial Museum for Islamic Art, Jerusalem.

Heroes Type

Portraits: No. 712, Menachem Ussishkin (1863-1941). No. 713, Berl Katzenelson (1878-1944). No. 714, Max Nordau (1849-1923).

1978, Dec. 26 Photo. *Perf. 14x13*

712 A280 £2	citron & sl grn	15	15
713 A280 £2	gray & vio blue	15	15
714 A280 £2	buff & black	15	15
	Set value	36	26

30th anniversary of independence.

1978, Dec. 26 Litho. *Perf. 14*

Protected Wild Flowers: £5.40, Iris haynei. £8.40, Iris nazarena.

715 A295 £1.10	multicolored	15	15
716 A295 £5.40	multicolored	32	25
717 A295 £8.40	multicolored	48	35
	Set value		65

Agricultural Mechanization A296

"Hope from Darkness" A297

Symbolic Designs: £2.40, Seawater desalination. £4.30, Electronics. £5, Chemical fertilizers.

1979, Feb. 13 Litho. *Perf. 13*

718 A296 £1.10	multicolored	15	15
719 A296 £2.40	multicolored	20	15
720 A296 £4.30	multicolored	22	20
721 A296 £5	multicolored	25	25
	Set value		62

Technological Achievements.

1979, Feb. 13

722 A297 £5.40	multicolored	38	25

Salute to "the Righteous among Nations," an award to those who helped during Nazi period.

Jewish Brigade Flag — A298

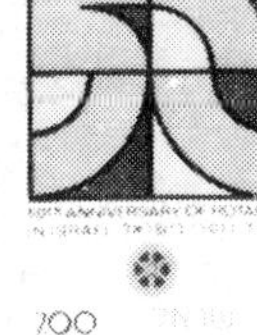

Paper (Prayer for Peace) in Crevice of Western Wall — A299

1979, Feb. 13 Photo. *Perf. 14*

723 A298 £5.10	blue, yel & blk	28	24

Jewish Brigade served with British Armed Forces during WWII.

1979, Mar. 26 Photo. *Perf. 14x13*

724 A299 £10	multicolored	45	24
a.	Souv. sheet of 1, imperf.	50	60

Signing of peace treaty between Israel and Egypt, Mar. 26.

11th Hapoel Games — A300

"50" and Rotary Emblem — A301

1979, Apr. 23 Litho. *Perf. 13*

725 A300 £1.50	Weightlifting	15	15
726 A300 £6	Tennis	32	22
727 A300 £11	Gymnastics	65	42

1979, Apr. 23 Photo. *Perf. 14x13*

728 A301 £7	multicolored	38	25

Rotary Intl. in Israel, 50th anniv.

Navy Memorial, Ashdod A302

1979, Apr. 23

729 A302 £5.10	multicolored	32	32

Memorial Day.

Rabbi Yehoshua ben Hananya A303

Flag Colors as Search Light A304

Craftsmen-Sages: £8.50, Rabbi Meir Baal Ha-Ness, scribe. £13, Rabbi Johanan, sandal maker.

1979, Aug. 14 Photo. *Perf. 14x13*

730 A303 £1.80	multicolored	15	15
731 A303 £8.50	multicolored	22	22
732 A303 £13	multicolored	40	42

Jewish New Year 5740.

1979, Aug. 14

733 A304 £10	multicolored	28	20

Jewish Agency, 50th anniversary.

Hot Springs, Tiberias — A305

Boy Riding Rainbow — A306

Design: £12, Dead Sea health resorts.

1979, Aug. 14 Litho. *Perf. 14*

734 A305 £8	multicolored	20	22
735 A305 £12	multicolored	38	35

1979, Nov. 6 Photo. *Perf. 13x14*

736 A306 £8.50	multicolored	28	28

International Year of the Child.

Jerusalem A307

Sorek Cave A308

Children's Drawings of Jerusalem: £4, People of different nationalities, horiz. £5, Praying at the Western Wall, horiz.

1979 *Perf. 14*

737 A307 £1.80	multicolored	15	15
738 A307 £4	multicolored	15	15
739 A307 £5	multicolored	15	15
	Set value	26	20

Heroes Type

Designs: £7, Arthur Ruppin (1876-1943). £9, Joseph Trumpeldor (1880-1920). £13, Aaron Aaronsohn (1876-1919).

1979, Nov. 6 Photo. *Perf. 14x13*

740 A280 £7	gray & magenta	18	18
741 A280 £9	pale grn & Prus bl	25	25
742 A280 £13	pale yel & dk ol	38	38

1980, Jan. 15 Litho. *Perf. 13x14*

743 A308 £50	multicolored	1.10	52

Star of David in Cogwheel A309

Scolymus Maculatus A310

1980, Jan. 15 *Perf. 14*

744 A309 £13	multicolored	42	40

Organization for Rehabilitation through Training (ORT), centenary.

1980, Jan. 15

Thistles: £5.50, Echinops viscosus. £8.50, Cynara syriaca.

745 A310 50a	multicolored	15	15
746 A310 £5.50	multicolored	15	15
747 A310 £8.50	multicolored	24	20
	Set value	44	36

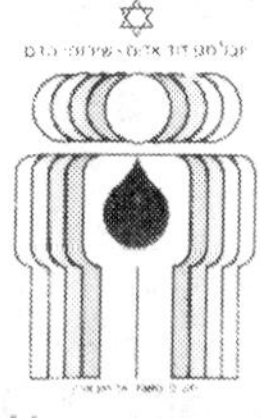

Men and Drop of Blood — A311

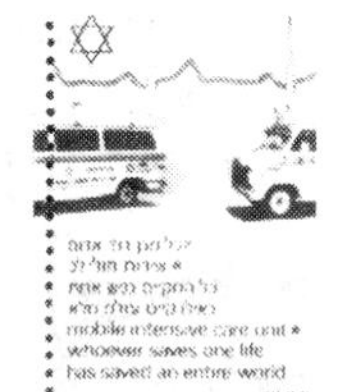

Mobile Intensive Care Unit — A312

1980, Apr. 15 Photo. *Perf. 14x13*

748 A311 £2.70	multicolored	15	15
749 A312 £13	multicolored	32	32
a.	Souv. sheet, 2 each #748-749	1.10	1.10
	Set value	38	36

Magen David Adom (Red Star of David), 50th anniv.

Road of Courage Monument A313

Sabbath Lamp, Netherlands, 18th Century A314

1980, Apr. 15 Litho. *Perf. 14*

750 A313 £12	multicolored	38	38

Memorial Day.

1980, Aug. 5 Photo. *Perf. 13x14*

Sabbath Lamps: £20, Germany, 18th century. £30, Morocco, 19th century.

751 A314 £4.30	multicolored	15	15
752 A314 £20	multicolored	45	45
753 A314 £30	multicolored	65	65

Yizhak Gruenbaum A315

Renewal of Jewish Settlement in Gush Etzion A316

1980, Aug. 5 *Perf. 14x13*

754 A315 £32	sepia	90	85

Yizhak Gruenbaum (1879-1970), first minister of the interior.

1980, Aug. 5

755 A316 £19	multicolored	45	38

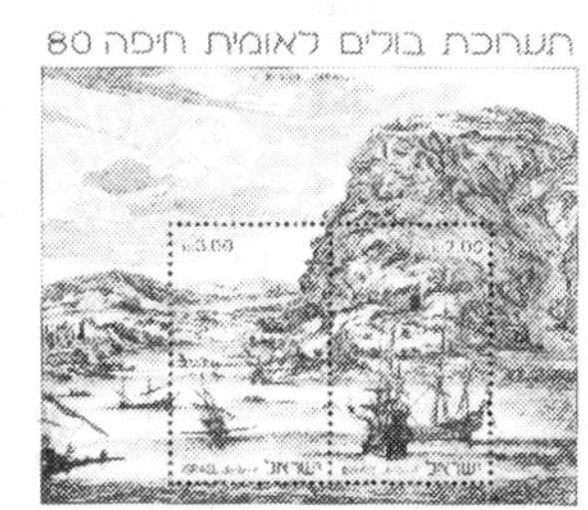

View of Haifa and Mt. Carmel, 17th Century — A317

1980, Sept. 28 Litho. *Perf. 14x13*

756 A317	Sheet of 2	1.75	2.00
a.	2s multicolored	60	70
b.	3s multicolored	90	1.05

Haifa 80 National Stamp Exhibition, Haifa, Sept. 28-Oct. 7.

A318

1980-81 Photo. *Perf. 13x14*

757	A318	5a brt yel grn & green	15	15
758	A318	10a red & brt mag	15	15
759	A318	20a grnsh bl & dk blue	15	15
760	A318	30a lil & dp vio	15	15

761 A318 50a red org & red brown 15 15
762 A318 60a brt yel grn & dk brown 15 15
762A A318 70a Prus bl & black 15 15
763 A318 1s brt mag & dk green 20 15
764 A318 2s dk bl grn & brn red 32 16
765 A318 2.80s brown & grn 40 24
766 A318 3.20s gray & red 45 26
767 A318 4.20s ultra & dk pur 52 32
768 A318 5s green & blk 70 42
769 A318 10s brn org & brn 1.40 70
Nos. 757-769 (14) 5.04
Set value 2.50

Issued: 70a, May 5, 1981; others, Dec. 16, 1980.
See Nos. 784-786, 807-808

Prime Minister Golda Meir (1898-1978) A319

Hand Putting Coin in Light Bulb A321

View of Jerusalem, by Mordechai Ardon — A320

1981, Feb. 10 Photo. *Perf. 14x13*
770 A319 2.60s rose violet 40 40

1981, Feb. 10 Litho. *Perf. 14*

Paintings of Jerusalem by: 50a, Anna Ticho. 1.50s, Joseph Zaritsky, vert.

771 A320 50a multicolored 15 15
772 A320 1.50s multicolored 22 20
773 A320 2.50s multicolored 38 35

1981, Mar. 17 Photo. *Perf. 14*
774 A321 2.60s shown 25 24
775 A321 4.20s Hand squeezing solar energy 40 38

Shmuel Yosef Agnon (1880-1970), Writer — A322

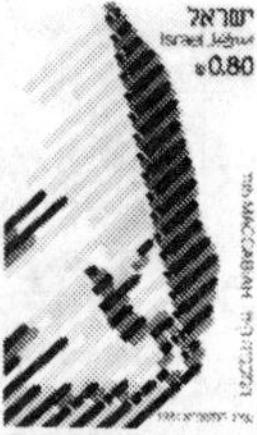

Sailing — A323

Designs: 2.80s, Moses Montefiore (1784-1885), first knighted English Jew. 3.20s, Abba Hillel Silver (1893-1963), statesman.

1981, Mar. 17 *Perf. 14x13, 14 (3.20s)*
776 A322 2s dk blue & blk 25 25
777 A322 2.80s dk bl grn & blk 35 40
778 A322 3.20s deep bis & blk 38 42

1981, May 5 *Perf. 14x13*
779 A323 80a shown 15 15
780 A323 4s Basketball 55 52
781 A323 6s High jump 80 95

11th Maccabiah Games, July 8-16.

Biq'at Hayarden Memorial A324

Jewish Family Heritage A325

1981, May 5 *Perf. 13x14*
782 A324 1s red & black 22 15

1981, May 5 Litho. *Perf. 14*
783 A325 3s multicolored 42 38

Type of 1980

1981, Aug. 25 Photo. *Perf. 13x14*
784 A318 90a dp vio & brn org 15 15
785 A318 3s red & dk blue 45 32
786 A318 4s dk brn vio & dp lil rose 58 35

The Burning Bush — A326

Roses — A327

Festivals 5742 (Book of Exodus): 1s "Let my people go . . ." 3s, Crossing of the Red Sea. 4s, Moses with Tablets.

1981, Aug. 25
787 A326 70a multicolored 15 15
788 A326 1s multicolored 16 15
789 A326 3s multicolored 38 38
790 A326 4s multicolored 45 42

1981, Oct. 22 Litho. *Perf. 14*
791 A327 90a Rosa damascena 16 16
792 A327 3.50s Rosa phoenicia 40 38
793 A327 4.50s Rosa hybrida 50 45

Ha-Shiv'a Interchange, Morasha-Ashod Highway — A328

1981, Oct. 22 Photo. *Perf. 14x13*
794 A328 8s multicolored 95 95

Elat Stone — A329

Wild Strawberry Tree — A330

1981, Dec. 29 Litho. *Perf. 14*
795 A329 2.50s shown 25 25
796 A329 5.50s Star sapphire 55 55
797 A329 7s Emerald 70 70

1981, Dec. 29
798 A330 3s shown 38 38
799 A330 3s Judas tree 38 38
800 A330 3s Balonea oak 38 38
a. Vert. or horiz. strip of 3, #798-800 1.25 1.25

Sheets of 9.

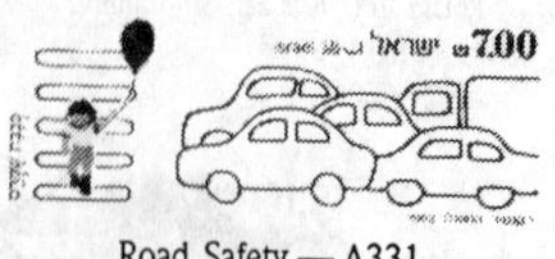

Road Safety — A331

1982, Mar. 2 Photo. *Perf. 14x13*
801 A331 7s multicolored 70 70
a. Souvenir sheet 1.25 1.25

No. 801a sold for 10s.

Joseph Gedalyah Klausner (1874-1958), Historian and Philosopher — A331a

Designs: 7s, Perez Bernstein (1890-1971), writer and editor. 8s, Rabbi Arys Levin (1885-1969).

1982, Mar. 2
802 A331a 7s multi 65 65
803 A331a 8s multi 70 70
804 A331a 9s cream & dk bl 80 80

Type of 1980 and

Produce — A332

1982-83 Photo. *Perf. 13 x 14*
805 A332 40a Prus bl & grn ('83) 15 15
806 A332 80a lt bl & pur ('83) 15 15
807 A318 1.10s ol & red 15 15
808 A318 1.20s bl & red 15 15
809 A332 1.40s ol grn & red 15 15
810 A332 6s red vio & brn org ('83) 26 18
811 A332 7s brn org & ol ('83) 16 15
812 A332 8s brt grn & red brn ('83) 22 15
813 A332 9s ol & brn ('83) 25 18
814 A332 15s ver & brt grn ('83) 40 26
Set value 1.50 1.10

See Nos. 876-879.

Tel Aviv Landscape, by Aryeh Lubin (d. 1980) — A333

Landscapes by: 8s, Sionah Tagger, vert. 15s, Israel Paldi (1892-1979).

1982, Apr. 22 Litho. *Perf. 14*
815 A333 7s multicolored 42 45
816 A333 8s multicolored 48 52
817 A333 15s multicolored 1.00 1.00

Gedudei Nouar Youth Corps A334

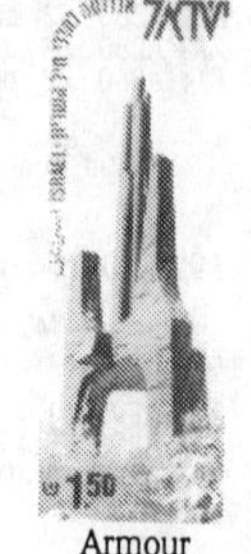

Armour Memorial, En Zetim A335

1982, Apr. 22 Photo. *Perf. 14x13*
818 A334 5s multicolored 42 38

1982, Apr. 22 Litho. *Perf. 14*
819 A335 1.50s multicolored 16 16

Memorial Day.

Joshua Addressing Crowd — A336

Hadassah, 70th Anniv. — A337

Festivals 5743 (Book of Joshua): 5.50s, Crossing River Jordan. 7.50s, Blowing down walls of Jericho. 9.50s, Battle with five kings of Amorites.

1982, Aug. 10 *Perf. 14*
820 A336 1.50s multicolored 15 15
821 A336 5.50s multicolored 32 32
822 A336 7.50s multicolored 45 48
823 A336 9.50s multicolored 55 55

1982, Aug. 10 Litho.
824 A337 12s multicolored 85 70

Rosh Pinna Settlement Centenary A338

1982 Photo. *Perf. 13x14*
825 A338 2.50s shown 20 16
826 A338 3.50s Rishon Leziyyon 24 20
827 A338 6s Zikhron Yaaqov 38 32
828 A338 9s Mazkeret Batya 70 60

Issued: 2.50s, 3.50s, Aug. 10; others, Oct. 5.
See Nos. 849-850.

Olive Branch A339

Emblem of Council for a Beautiful Israel A340

1982, Sept. 12
829 A339 multicolored 15 15
a. Booklet pane of 8 + 8 ('84) 2.75

Sold at various values.

1982, Oct. 5 Litho. *Perf. 14*
830 A340 17s multicolored 95 95
a. Souv. sheet of 1, imperf. 1.50 1.50

No. 830a was for Beer Sheva '82 National Stamp Exhibition. Sold for 25s.

Eliahu Bet Tzuri — A341

Anti-Smoking Campaign — A342

Independence Martyrs: b, Hannah Szenes. c, Shlomo Ben Yosef. d, Yosef Lishanski. e, Naaman Belkind. f, Eliezer Kashani. g, Yechiel Dresner. h, Dov Gruner. i, Mordechai Alkachi. j, Eliahu Hakim. k, Meir Nakar. l, Avshalom Haviv. m, Yaakov Weiss. n, Meir Feinstein. o, Moshe Barazani. p, Eli Cohen. q, Samuel Azaar. r, Moshe Marzouk. s, Shalom Salih. t, Yosef Basri.

1982, Dec. *Perf. 14x13½*
831 Sheet of 20 4.75 4.25
a.-t. A341 3s multicolored 15 16

1983, Feb. 15 Litho. *Perf. 13*
832 A342 7s Candy in ash tray 38 42

Beekeeping A343

1983, Feb. 15 Photo. *Perf. 13x14*
833 A343 30s multi 1.65 1.50

A343a

1983, Feb. 15 Litho. *Perf. 14*
834 A343a 8s Golan 32 30
835 A343a 15s Galil 65 55
836 A343a 20s Yehuda and Shomeron 90 70

Memorial Day (Apr. 17) — A344

1983, Apr. 12 *Perf. 13*
837 A344 3s Division of Steel Memorial, Besor Region 15 15

Independence Day — A345

1983, Apr. 12 *Perf. 14*
838 A345 25s multicolored 1.25 1.00
a. Souvenir sheet, imperf. 2.25 1.90

No. 838a sold for 35s.

12th Hapoel Games — A346

1983, Apr. 12 *Perf. 14x13*
839 A346 6s multicolored 28 25

50th Anniv. of Israel Military Industries — A347

1983, Apr. 12
840 A347 12s multicolored 55 55

Souvenir Sheet

WWII Uprising Leaders — A348

Designs: a, Yosef Glazman (1908-1943), Founder of United Partisans Org. b, Text.1 c, Mordechai Anilewicz (1919-1943), leader of Warsaw Ghetto revolt. No. 841 sold for 45s.

1983, June 7 *Perf. 14*
841 Sheet of 3 2.25 2.25
a. A348 10s multicolored 60 50
b. A348 10s multicolored 60 50
c. A348 10s multicolored 60 50

Raoul Wallenberg (1912-1945), Swedish Diplomat — A349

1983, June 7 *Perf. 14x13*
842 A349 14s multicolored 80 65

The Last Way, by Yosef Kuzkovski — A350

1983, June 7 *Perf. 14*
843 A350 35s multicolored 1.50 1.50

Ohel Moed Synagogue, Tel Aviv — A351

1983, Aug. 23
844 A351 3s shown 15 15
845 A351 12s Yeshurun Society, Jerusalem 38 42
846 A351 16s Ohel Aharon, Haifa 50 50
847 A351 20s Eliyahu Khakascni, Beer Sheva 60 60

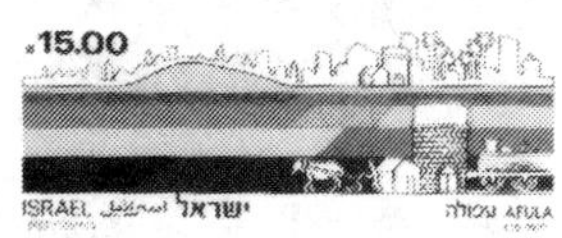
View of Afula, Jezreel Valley — A352

1983, Aug. 23
848 A352 15s multicolored 80 55

Settlement Type of 1982

1983, Aug. 23
849 A338 11s Yesud Ha-Maala 55 42
850 A338 13s Nes Ziyyona 60 48

Souvenir Sheet

Tel Aviv Seashore Promenade — A353

1983, Sept. 25 *Perf. 14x13*
851 Sheet of 2 5.50 4.75
a. A353 30s multicolored 1.50 1.75
b. A353 50s multicolored 2.50 2.75

Tel Aviv '83, 13th Natl. Stamp Show, Sept. Sold for 120s.

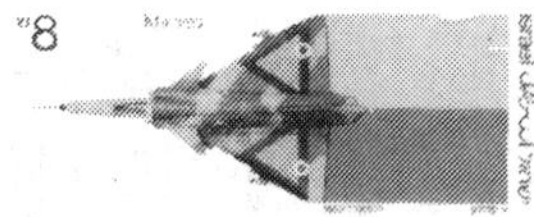
KFIR-C2 Tactical Fighter — A354

1983, Dec. 13 Photo. *Perf. 14*
852 A354 8s shown 15 16
853 A354 18s Reshef class missile boat 35 35
854 A354 30s Merkava-MK1 battle tank 60 60

Rabbi Meir Bar-Ilan (1880-1949), Founder of Mizrachi Movement — A355

1983, Dec. 13 Photo. *Perf. 14x13*
855 A355 9s multicolored 15 15

Jewish Immigration from Germany, 50th Anniv. — A356

1983, Dec. 13 Photo. *Perf. 13x14*
856 A356 14s multicolored 60 35

Michael Halperin (1860-1919), Zionist — A357

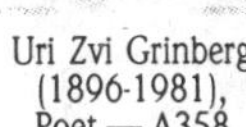
Uri Zvi Grinberg (1896-1981), Poet — A358

Design: 15s, Yigal Allon (1918-1980), military commander, founder of Israel Labor Party.

1984, Mar. 15 Photo. *Perf. 14x13*
857 A357 7s multicolored 15 15

Litho.
Perf. 14
858 A357 15s multicolored 28 25

Perf. 13
859 A358 16s multicolored 30 28

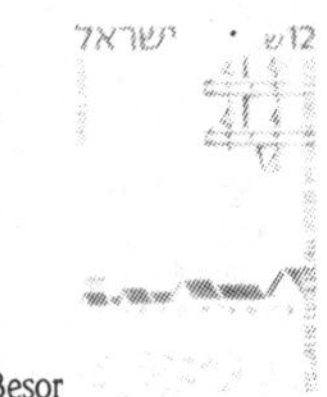
Hevel Ha-Besor Settlement — A359

1984, Mar. 15 *Perf. 14*
860 A359 12s shown 22 15
861 A359 17s Arava 30 24
862 A359 40s Gaza Strip 75 52

Monument of Alexander Zaid, by David Polus — A360

Monuments: No. 864, Tel Hay Defenders (seated lion), by Abraham Melnikov (1892-1960). No. 865, Dov Gruner, by Chana Orloff (1888-1968).

1984, Mar. 15 *Perf. 13x14*
863 A360 15s multicolored 35 26
864 A360 15s multicolored 35 26
865 A360 15s multicolored 35 26

Memorial Day — A361

Natl. Labor Fed., 50th Anniv. — A362

Design: Oliphant House (Druse military memorial), Dalyat Al Karmil.

1984, Apr. 26 Photo. *Perf. 14x13*
866 A361 10s multicolored 15 15

1984, Apr. 26
867 A362 35s multicolored 38 42

Produce Type of 1982-83

1984 Photo. *Perf. 13x14*

876 A332 30s vio brn & red 48 25
877 A332 50s dp bis & rose magenta 80 40
878 A332 100s gray & green 1.65 80
879 A332 500s dp org & bl blk 1.40 90

Leon Pinsker (1821-91), A363

Gen. Charles O. Wingate (1903-44) A364

1984, July 3 *Perf. 14x13*

880 A363 20s Hovevei Zion founder 22 24
881 A364 20s British soldier 22 24

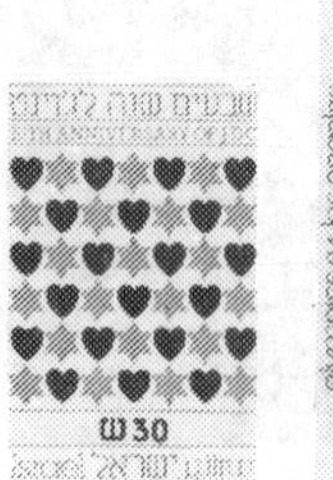

Hearts, Stars — A365

1984 Summer Olympics — A366

1984, July 3

882 A365 30s multicolored 28 28

70th anniv. of American Jewish Joint Distribution Committee (philanthropic org. created during World War I).

1984, July 3 Litho. *Perf. 14*

883 A366 80s Dove 70 70

Souvenir Sheet

Perf. 14x13

884 A366 240s like 80s 4.00 3.25

No. 884 contains one 23x32mm stamp. Sold for 350s.

Biblical Women A367

David Wolffsohn (1856-1914), Jewish Colonial Trust Founder A368

1984, Sept. 4 Photo. *Perf. 13x14*

885 A367 15s Hannah 15 15
886 A367 70s Ruth 38 38
887 A367 100s Huldah 60 60

1984, Sept. 4 *Perf. 14x14½*

888 A368 150s multicolored 1.25 90

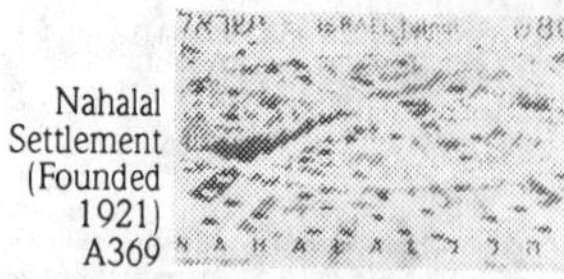

Nahalal Settlement (Founded 1921) A369

1984, Sept. 4 *Perf. 14*

889 A369 80s multicolored 65 48

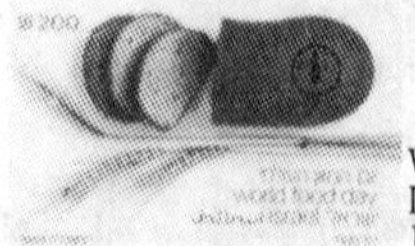

World Food Day, Oct. 16 — A370

1984, Nov. Litho.

891 A370 200s Bread, wheat 70 65

A371

A372

1984, Nov. Photo. *Perf. 14½*

892 A371 400s multicolored 1.65 1.40

Rabbi Isaac Herzog (1888-1959), statesman and scholar.

1984, Nov. Litho. *Perf. 14, 13 (30s)*

Children's Book Illustrations (Authors and their books): 20s, Apartment to Let, by Leah Goldberg (1911-70). 30s, Why is the Zebra Wearing Pajamas, by Omer Hillel (b. 1926) (30x30mm). 50s, Across the Sea, by Haim Nahman Bialik (1873-1934).

893 A372 20s multicolored 15 15
894 A372 30s multicolored 15 15
895 A372 50s multicolored 25 22
Set value 42

Birds of Prey A373

1985, Feb. 5 Litho. *Perf. 14*

896 A373 100s Lappet faced vulture 28 28
897 A373 200s Bonelli's eagle 55 55
898 A373 300s Sooty falcon 80 85
899 A373 500s Griffon vulture 1.40 1.40

Souvenir Sheet

899A Sheet of 4 4.00 3.75
b. A373 100s like #896 32 32
c. A373 200s like #897 65 65
d. A373 300s like #898 1.00 1.00
e. A373 500s like #899 1.50 1.50

No. 899A sold for 1650s.

Aviation in the Holy Land — A374

1985, Apr. 2 Litho. *Perf. 14*

900 A374 50s Bleriot XI, 1913 20 16
901 A374 150s Scipio-Short S-17 Kent, 1931 50 40
902 A374 250s Tiger Moth DH-82, 1934 80 70
903 A374 300s Scion-Short S-16, 1937 85 1.00

Natl. Assoc. of Nurses — A375

1985, Apr. 2 Litho. *Perf. 14*

904 A375 400s multicolored 1.00 95

Golani Brigade Memorial and Museum — A376

1985, Apr. 2 Photo. *Perf. 14x13*

905 A376 50s multicolored 24 20

Zivia (1914-1978) and Yitzhak (1915-1981) Zuckerman, Resistasnce Heroes, Warsaw Ghetto A377

1985, Apr. 2 Photo. *Perf. 13x14*

906 A377 200s multicolored 65 52

Souvenir Sheets

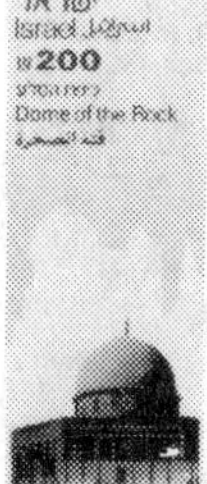

Dome of the Rock A378

16th Cent. Bas-relief, Ottoman Period A379

Adam, Eve and the Serpent (detail) — A380

Designs: No. 907b, The Western Wall. No. 907c, Church of the Holy Sepulchre. No. 908b, Hand, 18th cent. bas-relief, Jewish Quarter. No. 908c, Rosette carving, 12th-13th cent. Crusader capital. No. 909, Frontispiece and detail, Schocken Bible, South Germany, ca. 1290.

1985, May 14 Litho. *Perf. 13x14*

907 Sheet of 3 2.50 2.50
a.-c. A378 200s any single 70 65

Sold for 900s.

Perf. 14x13

908 Sheet of 3 3.75 3.75
a.-c. A379 350s any single 3.25 3.25

Sold for 1500s.

Perf. 14

909 A380 800s multi 3.25 3.25

Sold for 1200s.

The Israeli postal administration authorized the International Philatelic Federation (FIP) to overprint a limited number of these souvenir sheets for sale exclusively at ISRAPHIL '85 to raise funds. The FIP overprints have control numbers and are inscribed "Under the Patronage of the Philatelic Federation" in the sheet margin. The sheets remained valid for postage but were not sold by the post office.

12th Maccabiah Games — A381

1985 Festivals — A382

1985, July 16 Litho. *Perf. 14*

910 A381 400s Basketball 75 75
911 A381 500s Tennis 90 90
912 A381 600s Windsurfing 1.10 1.10

1985, July 16 Litho. *Perf. 14*

Tabernacle utensils: 100sh, Ark of the Covenant. 150sh, Acacia showbread table. 200sh, Menora. 300sh, Incense altar.

913 A382 100s multi 15 15
914 A382 150s multi 30 30
915 A382 200s multi 35 35
916 A382 300s multi 52 52

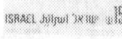

A383

A384

1985, July 16 Litho. *Perf. 14*

917 A383 150s Emblem, badges 48 25

Intl. Youth Year.

1985, Nov. 5 Litho. *Perf. 14*

918 A384 200s multi 80 26

Leon Yehuda Recanati (1890-1945), financier and philanthropist.

Meir Dizengoff (1861-1936), Founder and Mayor of Tel Aviv — A385

1985, Nov. 5

919 A385 500s multi 1.00 65

Gedera Settlement, Cent. A386

1985, Nov. 5 Photo. *Perf. 13x14*

920 A386 600s multi 1.10 80

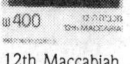

The Kibbutz — A387

1985, Nov. 5 Litho. *Perf. 14*

921 A387 900s multi 1.25 1.10

Theodor Herzl — A388

Capital, Second Temple, Jerusalem — A389

Designs: 1s, Corinthian, A.D. 1st cent. 3s, Ionic, 1st cent. B.C.

1986, Jan. 1 Photo. *Perf. 13x14*

922 A388	1a red & ultra		15	15
923 A388	2a green & ultra		15	15
924 A388	3a brown & ultra		15	15
925 A388	5a blue & ultra		15	15
926 A388	10a org & ultra		15	15
927 A388	20a pink & ultra		24	18
928 A388	30a lemon & ultra		35	26
929 A388	50a pur & ultra		55	42
930 A389	1s multi		1.25	95
931 A389	3s multi		3.25	2.75
	Nos. 922-931 (10)		6.39	5.31

1s and 3s designs with 1000a and 1500a values were not issued.

See Nos. 1014-1020.

Red Sea Coral A390

1986, Mar. 14 Litho. *Perf. 14*

932 A390	30a Balanophyllia	52	52
933 A390	40a Goniopora	70	70
934 A390	50a Dendronephthya	90	90

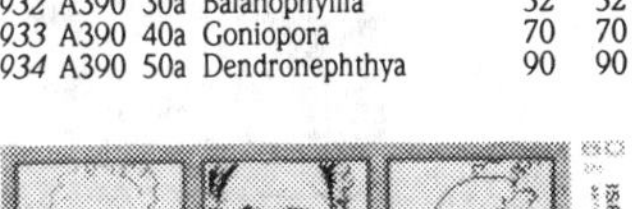
Arthur Rubinstein (1887-1982), Pianist — A391

1986, Mar. 4 Photo. *Perf. 13x14*

935 A391 60a Picasso portraits 90 80

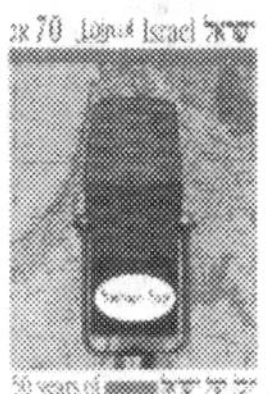
Broadcasting from Jerusalem, 50th Anniv. — A392

1986, Mar. 4 Litho. *Perf. 14*

936 A392 70a Map and microphone, 1936 90 90

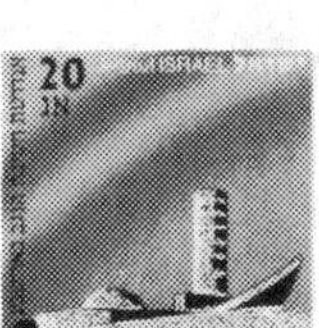
Negev Brigade Memorial, Beer Sheva — A393

Al Jazzar Mosque, Akko — A394

1986, May 4 Litho. *Perf. 13*

937 A393 20a multicolored 30 30

Memorial Day.

1986, May 4 Photo. *Perf. 14x13*

938 A394 30a multicolored 38 38

Id Al-Fitr Feast.

Institutes of Higher Learning in the US — A395

Designs: No. 939, 942a, Hebrew Union College, Jewish Institute of Religion, 1875, Cincinnati. No. 940, 942b, Yeshiva University, 1886, NYC. No. 941, 942c, Jewish Theological Seminary of America, 1886, NYC.

1986, May 4 Litho. *Perf. 14*

939 A395	50a multicolored	60	60
940 A395	50a multicolored	60	60
941 A395	50a multicolored	60	60

Souvenir Sheet

942	Sheet of 3 + label	4.00	4.00
a.-c.	A395 75a any single	1.25	1.25

AMERIPEX '86. Size of Nos. 942a-942c: 36x23mm. No. 942 sold for 3s.

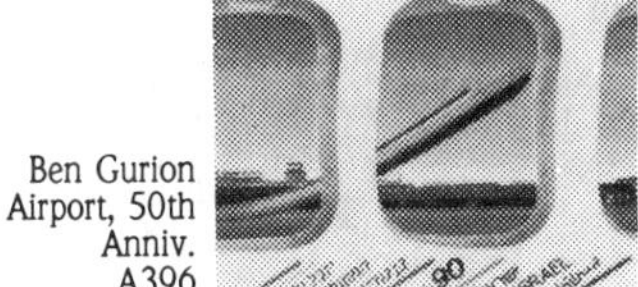
Ben Gurion Airport, 50th Anniv. A396

1986, July 22 *Perf. 14x13*

943 A396 90a Terminal from aircraft 1.25 1.25

"No to Racism" in Graffiti — A397

1986, July 22 *Perf. 14*

944 A397 60a multicolored 90 80

Druze Feast of Prophet Nabi Sabalan A398

1986, July 22 Photo. *Perf. 14*

945 A398 40a Tomb, Hurfeish 52 52

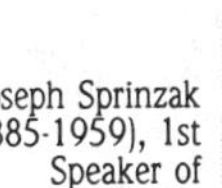
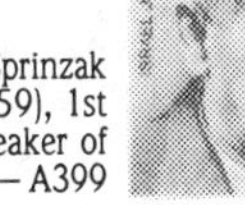
Joseph Sprinzak (1885-1959), 1st Speaker of Knesset — A399

1986, July 22 Litho. *Perf. 13*

946 A399 80a multicolored 1.05 1.05

Worms Illuminated Mahzor, 13th Cent. — A400

1986, Sept. 23 Litho. *Perf. 13x14*

947 A400	20a Gates of Heaven	24	24
948 A400	40a Sheqalim, prayer	48	48
949 A400	90a Rose flower prayer introduction	1.10	1.10

David Ben-Gurion (1886-1973) A401

1986, Oct. 19 Litho. *Perf. 14x13*

950 A401 1s multicolored 1.30 1.30

Souvenir Sheet

Map of the Holyland, by Gerard de Jode, 1578 — A402

1986, Oct. 19 *Perf. 14½*

951 A402 2s multicolored 3.50 3.50

NATANYA '86 Stamp Exhibition; Organized philately in Natanya, 50th anniv. Sold for 3s.

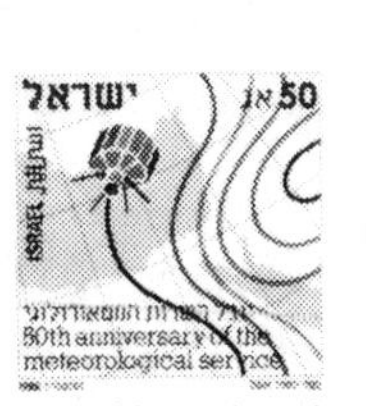
Israel Meteorological Service, 50th Anniv. — A403

Basilica of the Annunciation, Nazareth — A404

1986, Dec. 18 Litho. *Perf. 13*

952 A403 50a multicolored 70 70

1986, Dec. 18 Litho. *Perf. 14*

953 A404 70a multicolored 90 90

Israel Philharmonic Orchestra, 50th Anniv. A405

1986, Dec. 18

954 A405	1.50s Bronislaw Huberman, violinist	2.25	2.00
955 A405	1.50s Arturo Toscanini, conductor	2.25	2.00
a.	Pair, #954-955	4.50	4.00

Owls A406

1987, Feb. 17 Litho. *Perf. 14x13*

956 A406	30a Bubo bubo	55	55
957 A406	40a Otus brucei	70	70
958 A406	50a Tyto alba	90	90
959 A406	80a Strix butleri	1.50	1.50

Souvenir Sheet

960	Sheet of 4	7.00	7.00
a.	A406 30a like #956	1.10	1.10
b.	A406 40a like #957	1.40	1.40
c.	A406 50a like #958	1.75	1.75
d.	A406 80a like #959	2.75	2.75

Sold for 3s.

Ammunition Hill Memorial, Jerusalem A407

1987, Apr. 16 Litho. *Perf. 14*

961 A407 30a multicolored 40 40

Memorial Day.

13th Hapoel Games A408

1987, Apr. 16

962 A408 90a multicolored 1.25 1.25

Souvenir Sheet

HAIFA '87 Stamp Exhibition — A409

1987, Apr. 16 *Perf. 14x13*

963 A409 2.70s No. C8 6.00 6.00

Sold for 4s.

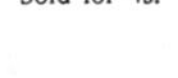

Amateur Radio Operators — A410

1987, June 14 Litho. *Perf. 14*

964 A410 2.50s multi 3.75 3.75

World Dog Show, June 23-27 A411

Clean Environment A412

1987, June 14

965 A411	40a	Saluki	70	70
966 A411	50a	Sloughi	90	90
967 A411	2s	Canaan	4.00	4.00

1987, June 14 ***Perf. 13***

968 A412 40a multicolored 80 80

Rabbi Moshe Avigdor Amiel (1883-1945), Founder of Yeshivas — A413

1987, Sept. 10 Litho. ***Perf. 14***

969 A413 1.40s multi 1.40 1.40

Synagogue Models, Nahum Goldmann Museum, Tel Aviv — A414

Kupat Holim Health Insurance Institute, 75th Anniv. — A415

1987, Sept. 10 ***Perf. 13x14***

970 A414	30a	Altneuschul, Prague, 13th cent.	40	40
971 A414	50a	Aleppo, Syria, 9th cent.	65	65
972 A414	60a	Florence, Italy, 19th cent.	78	78

See Nos. 996-998.

1987, Sept. 10 ***Perf. 14***

973 A415 1.50s multi 1.50 1.50

A416

A417

1987, Nov. 24 Litho. ***Perf. 13***

974 A416 80a multicolored 90 90

Pinhas Rosen (1887-1978), first Minister of Justice.

1987, Nov. 24 ***Perf. 14***

Exploration of the Holy Land, 19th cent.: 30a, Thomas Howard Molyneux (1847) and Christopher Costigan (1835). 50a, William Francis Lynch (1848). 60a, John MacGregor (1868-1869).

975 A417	30a	multi	40	40
976 A417	50a	multi	65	65
977 A417	60a	multi	78	52

Souvenir Sheet

978	Sheet of 3	3.25	3.25
a.	A417 40a like #975	75	75
b.	A417 50a like #976	95	95
c.	A417 80a like #977	1.55	1.55

No. 978 sold for 2.50s.

A418

A419

1988, Jan. 26

979 A418	10a	Computer technology	15	15
980 A418	80a	Genetic engineering	95	95
981 A418	1.40s	Medical engineering	1.65	1.65

Industrialization of Israel, cent.

1988, Jan. 26

982 A419 40a multicolored 52 52

Water conservation.

Australia Bicentennial A420

1988, Jan. 26 ***Perf. 14***

983 A420 1s multi 1.30 1.30

Sunflower — A421

1988, Mar. 9 Photo. ***Perf. 13x14***

984 A421 (30a) dk yel grn & yel 25 25

A422

A423

Design: Anne Frank (1929-45), Amsterdam house where she hid.

1988, Apr. 19 Litho.

985 A422 60a multicolored 55 55

1988, Apr. 19

Design: Modern Jerusalem.

986 A423 1s shown 1.10 1.10

Souvenir Sheet

987 A423 2s detail from 1s 3.25 3.25

Independence 40 Stamp Exhibition, Jerusalem. No. 987 sold for 3s.

Memorial Day — A424

1988, Apr. 19 ***Perf. 14x13***

988 A424 40a multicolored	35	35
a. Souvenir sheet of 1	75	75

Natl. independence, 40th anniv. No. 988a contains one stamp like No. 988 but without copyright inscription LR. Sold for 60a.

Souvenir Sheet

Israel's 40th Anniv. Exhibition, Tel Aviv — A425

Stamps on stamps: a, No. 245. b, No. 297. c, No. 120. d, No. 96. e, Like No. 794. f, No. 252. g, No. 333. h, No. 478.

1988, June 9 Litho. ***Perf. 14***

989	Sheet of 8 + label	3.50	3.50
a.-h.	A425 20a any single	38	38

Sold for 2.40s. Center label pictures Israel 40 emblem.

B'nai B'rith in Jerusalem, Cent. — A426

1988, June 27 ***Perf. 14***

990 A426 70a multicolored 88 88

Nature Reserves in the Negev A427

1988, June 27

991 A427	40a	Ein Zin	42	42
992 A427	60a	She'Zaf	60	60
993 A427	70a	Ramon	75	75

See Nos. 1052-1054, 1154-1156.

Agents Executed During World War II — A428

Portraits: 40a, Havivah Reik (1914-1944). 1.65s, Enzo Hayyim Sereni (1905-1944).

1988, Sept. 1 Litho.

994 A428	40a	multicolored	48	48
995 A428	1.65s	multicolored	1.90	1.90

Synagogue Models Type of 1987

Models in the Nahum Goldmann Museum, Tel Aviv: 35a, Kai-Feng Fu Synagogue, 12th cent., China. 60a, Zabludow Synagogue, 17th cent., Poland. 70a, Touro Synagogue, 1763, Newport, Rhode Island, designed by Peter Harrison.

1988, Sept. 1 ***Perf. 13x14***

996 A414	35a	multicolored	40	40
997 A414	60a	multicolored	70	70
998 A414	70a	multicolored	82	82

A429

A430

1988, Nov. 9 ***Perf. 14***

999 A429 80a multicolored 85 85

Kristallnacht, Nazi pogrom in Germany, 50th anniv.

1988, Nov. 9 ***Perf. 13***

1000 A430 40a multicolored 48 48

Moshe Dayan (1915-1981), Foreign Minister and Minister of Defense.

Jewish Legion, 70th Anniv. A431

1988, Nov. 9 ***Perf. 14***

1001 A431 2s yel brn, sepia & lem 2.35 2.35

Agricultural Achievements A433

Designs: 50a, Avocado (fruit-growing). 60a, Lilium longiflorum (horticulture). 90a, Irrigation.

1988, Dec. 22 ***Perf. 14***

1004 A433	50a	multicolored	58	58
1005 A433	60a	multicolored	70	70
1006 A433	90a	multicolored	1.05	1.05

A434

A435

Design: Natl. tourism and the four seas.

1989, Mar. 12 Litho. ***Perf. 13***

1007 A434	40a	Red Sea	45	30
1008 A434	60a	Dead Sea	65	45
1009 A434	70a	Mediterranean Sea	75	50
1010 A434	1.70s	Sea of Galilee	1.85	1.25

1989, Mar. 12 ***Perf. 14***

1011 A435 1.70s multi 1.85 1.25

Rabbi Judah Leib Maimon (1875-1962), religious scholar.

Rashi, Rabbi Solomon Ben Isaac (b. 1039), Talmudic Commentator A436

1989, Mar. 12

1012 A436 4s buff & black 4.35 2.90

Memorial Day — A437

UNICEF — A438

Design: Fallen Airmen's Memorial at Har Tayassim.

1989, Apr. 30 Litho. *Perf. 14*
1013 A437 50a multi 60 45

Archaeology Type of 1986

Gates of Huldah, Temple Compound, Mt. Moriah: 40a, Rosettes and rhomboids, frieze and columns, facade of the eastern gate, 1st cent. B.C. 60a, Corinthian capital, 6th cent.
70a, Bas-relief from the Palace of Umayade Caliphs, 8th cent. 80a, Corinthian capital from the Church of Ascension on the Mount of Olives, 12-13th cent. 90a, Star of David, limestone relief, northern wall, near the new gate, Suleiman's Wall. 2s, Mamluk relief, 14th century. 10s, Carved frieze from a sepulcher entrance, end of the Second Temple Period.

1988-90 Litho. *Perf. 14*
1014 A389 40a multi 48 48
1015 A389 60a multi 70 70
1016 A389 70a multi 78 58
1017 A389 80a multi 90 68
1018 A389 90a multi 88 65
1019 A389 2s multi 2.00 1.30
1020 A389 10s multi 12.00 8.00
Nos. 1014-1020 (7) 17.74 12.39

Issue dates: 40a, 60a, Dec. 22, 1988. 70a, 80a, June 11, 1989. 10s, Apr. 30, 1989. 90a, Oct. 17, 1989. 2s, June 12, 1990.

1989, Apr. 30 *Perf. 14*
1022 A438 90a multi 1.10 82

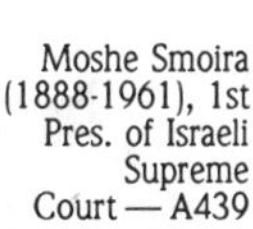

Moshe Smoira (1888-1961), 1st Pres. of Israeli Supreme Court — A439

1989, June 11 Litho. *Perf. 13*
1023 A439 90a deep blue 1.05 78

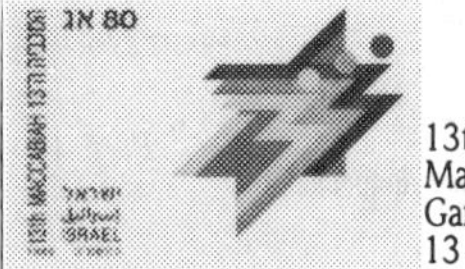
13th Maccabiah Games, July 3-13 — A440

1989, June 11 *Perf. 13x14*
1024 A440 80a multi 90 68

A441 A442

Ducks: a, Garganey. b, Mallard. c, Teal. d, Shelduck.

1989, July 18 Litho. *Perf. 14*
1025 Strip of 4 5.00 5.00
a.-d. A441 80a any single 1.25 85

Souvenir Sheet

1989, Nov. 17
1025E Sheet of 4 4.75 4.75
f. A441 80a like No. 1025d 1.15 1.15
g. A441 80a like No. 1025b 1.15 1.15
h. A441 80a like No. 1025a 1.15 1.15
i. A441 80a like No. 1025c 1.15 1.15

World Stamp Expo '89. No. 1025E contains four 29x33mm stamps. Sold for 5s.

1989, July 18
1026 A442 1s multi 1.00 75

Graphic design industry.

Souvenir Sheet

French Revolution, Bicent. — A443

1989, July 18
1027 A443 3.50s multi 5.00 5.00

Sold for 5s.

Hebrew Language Council, Cent. — A444

Rabbi Yehuda Hai Alkalai (1798-1878), Zionist — A445

1989, Sept. 3 Litho. *Perf. 13x14*
1028 A444 1s multi 95 72

1989, Sept. 3 *Perf. 14*
1029 A445 2.50s multi 2.40 1.80

Mizrah Festival A446

Paper cutouts: 50a, Menorah and lions, by Gadoliahu Neminsky, Holbenisk, Ukraine, 1921. 70a, Menorah and hands, Morocco, 19th-20th cent. 80a, "Misrah," hunting scene and deer, Germany, 1818.

1989, Sept. 3 *Perf. 14x13*
1030 A446 50a multi 48 36
1031 A446 70a multi 68 50
1032 A446 80a multi 78 58

Tevel '89 Youth Stamp Exhibition, Oct. 15-21 A447

1989, Oct. 12 Photo. *Perf. 13x14*
1033 A447 50a multi 48 36

A448

A449

1989, Oct. 17 Litho. *Perf. 14*
1034 A448 1s multi 98 75

1st Israeli Stamp Day.

1989, Nov. 17 Photo. *Perf. 13½x14*
1035 A449 (50a) Good luck 48 35
1036 A449 (50a) With love 48 35
a. Booklet pane of 10 5.15
1037 A449 (50a) See you again 48 35
a. Booklet pane of 10 + 2 labels 5.75
b. Sheet of 20 + 5 labels 11.50

Special occasions. Nos. 1036a, 1037a contain 5 tete-beche pairs, No. 1037b contains 10 tete-beche pairs.
#1037a-1037b had value of 80a when released.
Issued: No. 1036a, Aug. 7, 1990. Nos. 1037a-1037b, June 22, 1993.
See Nos. 1059-1061, 1073-1075.

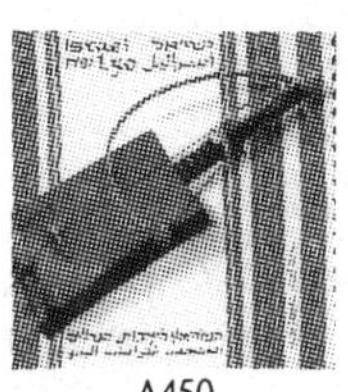
A450

A451

Design: Tapestry and Rebab, a Stringed Instrument, from the Museum of Bedouin Culture.

1990, Feb. 13 Litho. *Perf. 13*
1038 A450 1.50s multicolored 1.45 1.05

1990, Feb. 13 Photo. *Perf. 14x13*

Designs: Circassian folk dancers.

1039 A451 1.50s multicolored 1.45 1.05

The Circassians in Israel.

Rehovot City, Cent. A452

1990, Feb. 13 *Perf. 14*
1040 A452 2s multicolored 1.90 1.40

Souvenir Sheet

Isaiah's Vision of Eternal Peace, by Mordecai Ardon — A453

Series of 3 stained-glass windows, The Hall of Eternal Jewishness and Humanism, Hebrew University Library, Jerusalem: a, "Roads to Jerusalem" (inscription at L). b, Isaiah's prophecy of broken guns beaten into ploughshares (inscription at R).

1990, Apr. 17 Litho. *Perf. 14*
1041 Sheet of 2 4.30 4.30
a.-b. A453 1.50s any single 2.15 2.15

Stamp World London '90. Sold for 4.50s.
Also exists imperf.

Architecture — A454

Design: 75a, School, Deganya Kibbutz, 1930. 1.10s, Dining hall, Kibbutz Tel Yosef by Leopold Krakauer, 1933. 1.20s, Engel House by Ze'ev Rechter, 1933. 1.40s, Home of Dr. Chaim Weizmann, Rehovot by Erich Mendelsohn, 1936. 1.60s, Jewish Agency for Palestine, Jerusalem, by Yohanan Ratner, 1932.

1990-92 Photo. *Perf. 14x13½*
1044 A454 75a black, pale grn & buff 72 55
1046 A454 1.10s blk, yel & grn 1.05 1.05
1047 A454 1.20s blk, bl & yel 1.15 1.15
1049 A454 1.40s blk, lt lil & buff 1.35 1.35
1051 A454 1.60s multicolored 1.15 1.15
Nos. 1044-1051 (5) 5.42 5.25

Issue dates: 75a, Apr. 17. 1.10s, 1.20s, Dec. 12, 1.40s, Apr. 9, 1991. 1.60s, Apr. 26, 1992.
This is an expanding set. Numbers will change if necessary.

Nature Reserves Type of 1988

1990, Apr. 17 Litho. *Perf. 14*
1052 A427 60a Gamla, Yehudiyya 58 45
1053 A427 80a Huleh 78 58
1054 A427 90a Mt. Meron 88 65

Memorial Day — A456

1990, Apr. 17 Photo. *Perf. 13x14*
1055 A456 60a Artillery Corps Memorial 58 45

Intl. Folklore Festival, Haifa
A457 A458

1990, June 12 Litho. *Perf. 14*
1056 A457 1.90s multicolored 2.50 2.50
1057 A458 1.90s multicolored 2.50 2.50
a. Pair, #1056-1057 5.00 5.00

A459 A460

1990, June 12
1058 A459 1.50s multicolored 1.50 1.50

Hagana, 70th anniv.

Special Occasions Type of 1989

1990, June 12 ***Perf. 13½x14***

1059 A449 55a Good luck 52 35
1060 A449 80a See you again 75 50
1061 A449 1s With love 95 62

1990, Sept. 4 Litho. ***Perf. 13x14***

Spice Boxes: 55a, Austro-Hungarian spice box, 19th cent. 80a, Italian, 19th cent. 1s, German, 18th cent.

1062 A460 55a sil, gray & blk 52 52
1063 A460 80a sil, gray & blk 75 75
1064 A460 1s multicolored 95 95
a. Bklt. pane of 6 (3 #1062, 2 #1063, #1064) 4.05 4.05

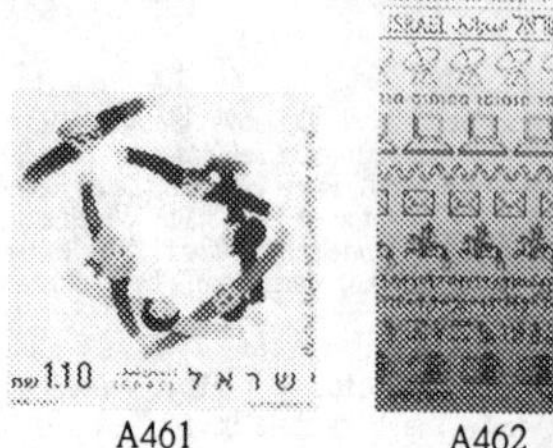

A461 A462

1990, Sept. 4 ***Perf. 13***

1065 A461 1.10s Aliya absorption 1.00 1.00

1990, Sept. 4 ***Perf. 14x13***

1066 A462 1.20s black & grn 1.10 1.10

Electronic mail.

Souvenir Sheet

Beersheba '90 Stamp Exhibition — A463

1990, Sept. 4 ***Perf. 13x14***

1067 A463 3s multicolored 3.50 3.50

Sold for 4s.

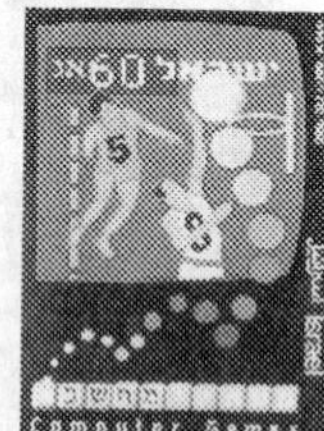

Computer Games — A464

1990, Dec. 12 Litho. ***Perf. 13x14***

1068 A464 60a Basketball 50 50
1069 A464 60a Chess 50 50
1070 A464 60a Auto racing 50 50

A465 A466

1990, Dec. 12 Litho. ***Perf. 13x14***

1071 A465 1.90s multicolored 1.50 1.50

Ze'ev Jabotinsky (1880-1940), Zionist leader.

1990, Dec. 12 ***Perf. 14***

1072 A466 1.20s P.O., Yafo, #5 1.10 1.10

Philately Day.

Special Occasions Type of 1989

1991, Feb. 19 Photo. ***Perf. 13½x14***

1073 A449 (60a) Happy birthday 52 38
1074 A449 (60a) Keep in touch 52 38
1075 A449 (60a) Greetings 52 38

Famous Women A467

Designs: No. 1076, Sarah Aaronsohn (1890-1917), World War I heroine. No. 1077, Rahel Bluwstein (1890-1931), poet. No. 1078, Lea Goldberg (1911-1970), poet.

1991, Feb. 19 ***Perf. 14***

1076 A467 1.30s multicolored 1.10 1.10
1077 A467 1.30s multicolored 1.10 1.10
1078 A467 1.30s multicolored 1.10 1.10

See Nos. 1096-1097, 1102-1103.

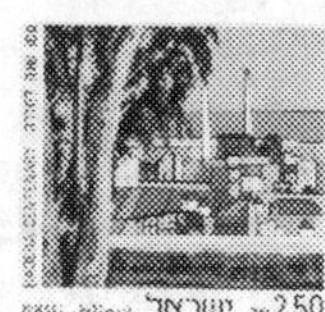

Hadera, Cent. — A468

1991, Feb. 19 ***Perf. 13***

1079 A468 2.50s multicolored 2.45 2.45

Intelligence Services Memorial, G'lilot A469

1991, Apr. 9 Litho. ***Perf. 14***

1080 A469 65a multicolored 60 60

14th Hapoel Games A470

1991, Apr. 9

1081 A470 60a multicolored 58 38
1082 A470 90a multicolored 85 55
1083 A470 1.10s multicolored 1.05 70

Electrification A471

Designs: 70a, First power station, Tel Aviv, 1923. 90a, Yarden Power Station, Naharayim, 1932. 1.20s, Rutenberg Power Station, Ashqelon, 1991.

1991, June 11 Litho. ***Perf. 13***

1084 A471 70a multicolored 70 45
1085 A471 90a multicolored 85 65
1086 A471 1.20s multicolored 1.15 85

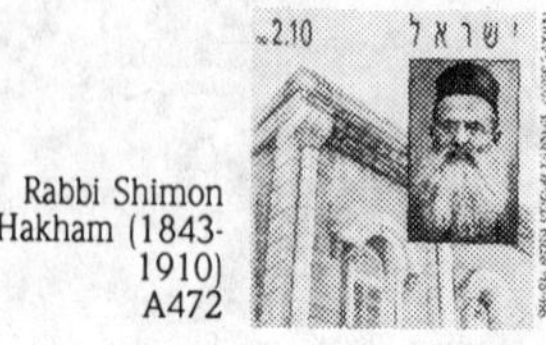

Rabbi Shimon Hakham (1843-1910) A472

1991, June 11

1087 A472 2.10s multicolored 2.00 1.50

Souvenir Sheet

Postal and Philatelic Museum, Tel Aviv — A473

Design: Israel No. 5, Palestine No. 70, and Turkey No. 133.

1991, June 11 ***Perf. 14x13***

1088 A473 3.40s multicolored 4.75 4.75

No. 1088 sold for 5s. Exists imperf.

A474 A475

Jewish Festivals: 65a, Man blowing ram's horn, Rosh Hashanah. 1s, Father blessing children, Yom Kippur. 1.20s, Family seated at harvest table, Sukkot.

1991, Aug. 27 Litho. ***Perf. 14***

1089 A474 65a multicolored 55 55
1090 A474 1s multicolored 85 85
1091 A474 1.20s multicolored 1.00 1.00

1991, Aug. 27

1092 A475 1.50s multicolored 1.25 1.25

Jewish Chronicle, 150th anniv.

Baron Maurice De Hirsch (1831-1896), Founder of Jewish Colonization Assoc. A476

1991, Aug. 27 ***Perf. 14***

1093 A476 1.60s multicolored 1.40 1.40

Souvenir Sheet

Haifa, by Gustav Bauernfeind — A477

1991, Aug. 27 ***Perf. 14x13***

1094 A477 3s multicolored 2.50 2.50

Haifa '91, Israeli-Polish Philatelic Exhibition. Sold for 4s.

A478 A479

1991, Dec. 2 Litho. ***Perf. 13***

1095 A478 70a #2 on piece 60 60

Philately Day.

Famous Women Type of 1991

Designs: 1s, Rahel Yanait Ben-Zvi (1886-1979), politician. 1.10s, Dona Gracia (Nasi, 1510?-1569), philanthropist.

1991, Dec. 2 Litho. ***Perf. 14***

1096 A467 1s multicolored 80 80
1097 A467 1.10s multicolored 85 85

1991, Dec. 2

1098 A479 1.10s multicolored 85 85

1992 Summer Olympics, Barcelona.

Lehi — A480 Etzel — A481

1991, Dec. 2 ***Perf. 14***

1099 A480 1.50s multicolored 1.30 1.30

1991, Dec. 2

1100 A481 1.50s blk & red 1.30 1.30

Wolfgang Amadeus Mozart, Death Bicent. — A482

1991, Dec. 2 ***Perf. 13***

1101 A482 2s multicolored 1.70 1.70
a. Booklet pane of 4 6.80

One pair in No. 1101a is tete beche.

Famous Women Type of 1991

Designs: 80a, Hanna Rovina (1889-1980), actress. 1.30s, Rivka Guber (1902 1981), educator.

1992, Feb. 18 Litho. ***Perf. 14***

1102 A467 80a multicolored 65 65
1103 A467 1.30s multicolored 1.10 1.10

Sea of Galilee — A483

1992, Feb. 18

1104 A483 85a Trees 70 70
1105 A483 85a Sailboat 70 70
1106 A483 85a Fish 70 70
a. Strip of 3, #1104-1106 2.10 2.10

Anemone — A483a

1992, Feb. 18 Photo. *Perf. 13x14*

1107 A483a (75a) multi 65 45

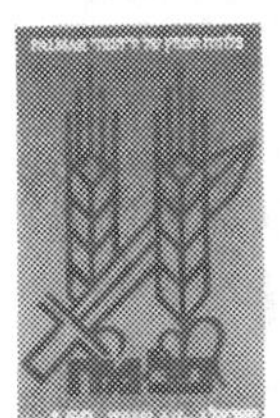
PALMAH, 50th Anniv. A484

The Samaritans A485

1992, Feb. 18 Litho. *Perf. 14*

1108 A484 1.50s multicolored 1.25 1.25

1992, Feb. 18

1109 A485 2.60s multicolored 2.25 2.25

Rabbi Hayyim Joseph David Azulai (1724-1806) A486

Rabbi Joseph Hayyim Ben Elijah (1834-1909) A487

1992, Apr. 26 *Perf. 13*

1110 A486 85a multicolored 75 75

Perf. 14

1111 A487 1.20s multicolored 1.00 1.00

Discovery of America, 500th Anniv. A488

1992, Apr. 26 *Perf. 14*

1112 A488 1.60s multicolored 1.35 1.35

Memorial Day — A488a

1992, Apr. 26 Litho. *Perf. 13*

1113 A488a 85a multicolored 60 60

Souvenir Sheet

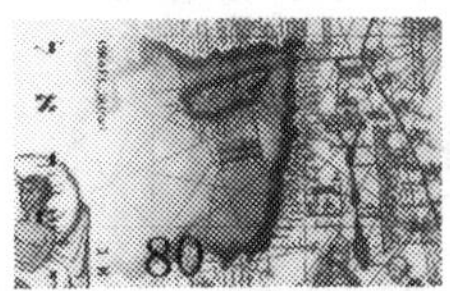
Expulsion of Jews from Spain, 500th Anniv. A489

Designs: No. 1114a, 80a, Map of Palestine. b, 1.10s, Map of Italy, Sicily, Greece and central Mediterranean. c, 1.40s, Map of Spain and Portugal.

1992, Apr. 26 *Perf. 14*

1114 A489 Sheet of 3, #a.-c. 2.75 2.75

Jaffa-Jerusalem Railway, Cent. — A490

Different train and four scenes on each stamp showing railroad equipment and memorabilia.

1992

1115 A490 85a multicolored 70 70
1116 A490 1s multicolored 85 85
1117 A490 1.30s multicolored 1.10 1.10
1118 A490 1.60s multicolored 1.35 1.35
a. Bklt. pane of 4, #1115-1118 4.00

Souvenir Sheet

1118B Sheet of 4 + 4 labels 1.60 1.60
c. A490 50a like #1118 40 40
d. A490 50a like #1117 40 40
e. A490 50a like #1115 40 40
f. A490 50a like #1116 40 40

Nos. 1115 and 1118, 1116 and 1117 are tete beche in No. 1118a. Nos. 1118c and 1118f, 1118d and 1118e are tete beche in No. 1118B.

Issue dates: No. 1118B, Sept. 17; others June 16.

Rabbi Hayyim Benatar (1696-1743) A491

Rabbi Shalom Sharabi (1720-1777) A492

1992, June 16 *Perf. 13*

1119 A491 1.30s multicolored 1.10 1.10
1120 A492 3s multicolored 2.55 2.55

Jewish Natl. & University Library, Jerusalem, Cent. — A493

Designs: 85a, Parables, 1491. 1s, Italian manuscript, 15th cent. 1.20s, Bible translation by Martin Buber.

1992, Sept. 17 Litho. *Perf. 13x14*

1121 A493 85a multicolored 70 70
1122 A493 1s multicolored 85 85
1123 A493 1.20s multicolored 1.00 1.00

Supreme Court A494

1992, Sept. 17 *Perf. 14*

1124 A494 3.60s multicolored 3.00 3.00

Wild Animals A495

Designs: No. 1125, Panthera pardus saxicolor. No. 1126, Elephas maximus. No. 1127, Pan troglodytes. No. 1128, Panthera leo persica.

1992, Sept. 17

1125 A495 50a multicolored 40 40
1126 A495 50a multicolored 40 40
1127 A495 50a multicolored 40 40
1128 A495 50a multicolored 40 40
a. Strip of 4, #1125-1128 1.60 1.60

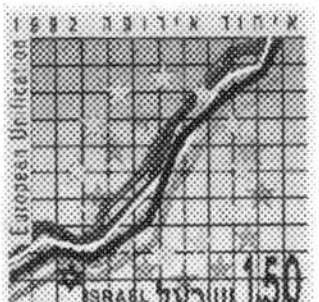
European Unification — A496

1992, Dec. 8 Litho. *Perf. 13*

1129 A496 1.50s multicolored 1.20 1.20

Stamp Day.

First Hebrew Film, 75th Anniv. — A497

Films: 80a, Liberation of the Jews, 1918. 2.70s, Oded, the Vagabond, 1932, first Hebrew feature film. 3.50s, The Promised Land, 1935, first Hebrew talkie.

1992, Dec. 8

1130 A497 80a multicolored 65 65
1131 A497 2.70s multicolored 2.15 2.15
1132 A497 3.50s multicolored 2.80 2.80

Birds — A498

1992-94 Photo. *Perf. 13x14*

1133 A498 10a Wallcreeper 15 15
1134 A498 20a Tristram's grackle 16 16
1135 A498 30a White wagtail 24 24
1137 A498 50a Palestine sunbird 38 25
1141 A498 85a Sinai rosefinch 60 40
1142 A498 90a Swallow 75 75
1143 A498 1.30s Graceful warbler 90 60
1144 A498 1.50s Black-eared wheat-ear 1.10 70
1146 A498 1.70s Common bulbul 1.10 70
Nos. 1133-1146 (9) 5.38 3.95

Issue date: 10a, 20a, 30a, 90a, Dec. 8. 1.30s, 1.70s, Dec. 12, 1993. 50a, 1.50s, Feb. 16, 1993. 85a, Feb. 8, 1994.

This is an expanding set. Numbers may change.

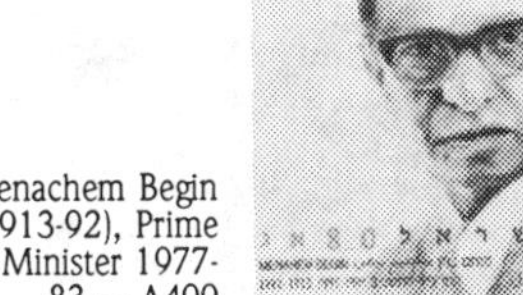
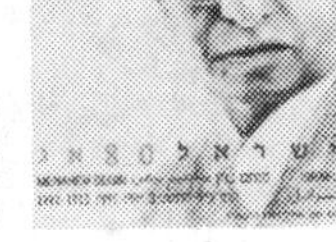
Menachem Begin (1913-92), Prime Minister 1977-83 — A499

1993, Feb. 16 Litho. *Perf. 13*

1153 A499 80a multicolored 60 60

Nature Reserves Type of 1988

1993, Feb. 16 *Perf. 14*

1154 A427 1.20s Hof Dor 90 90
1155 A427 1.50s Nahal Ammud 1.15 1.15
1156 A427 1.70s Nahal Ayun 1.25 1.25

Baha'i World Center, Haifa — A500

1993, Feb. 16 *Perf. 13*

1157 A500 3.50s multicolored 2.60 2.60

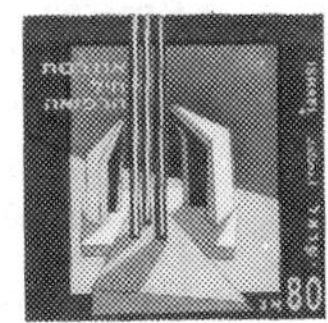
Medical Corps Memorial — A501

1993, Apr. 18 Litho. *Perf. 13*

1158 A501 80a multicolored 60 60

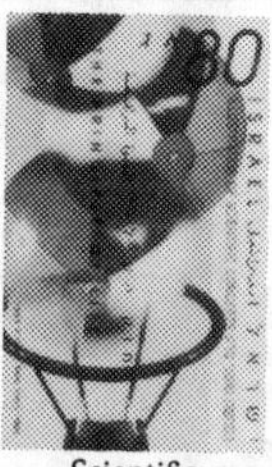

Scientific Concepts — A502

Warsaw Ghetto Uprising, 50th Anniv. — A503

1993, Apr. 18 *Perf. 14*

1159 A502 80a Principle of lift 58 58
1160 A502 80a Waves 58 58
1161 A502 80a Color mixing 58 58
1162 A502 80a Eye's memory 58 58
a. Strip of 4, #1159-1162 2.35 2.35

1993, Apr. 18 *Perf. 14*

1163 A503 1.20s gray, black & yellow 90 90

See Poland No. 3151.

Independence, 45th Anniv. — A504

1993, Apr. 18 *Perf. 14*

1164 A504 3.60s multicolored 2.65 2.65

Guilio Racah (1909-1965), Physicist A505

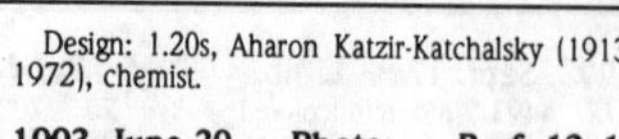

Design: 1.20s, Aharon Katzir-Katchalsky (1913-1972), chemist.

1993, June 29 **Photo.** *Perf. 13x14*

1165 A505 80a magenta, bister & blue 58 58
1166 A505 1.20s magenta, bister & blue 90 90

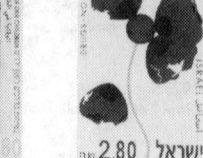

Traffic Safety — A506

Fight Against Drugs — A507

Children's drawings: 80a, Family crossing street. 1.20s, Traffic signs. 1.50s, Traffic director with hand as face.

1993, June 29 **Litho.** *Perf. 14*

1167 A506 80a multicolored 58 58
1168 A506 1.20s multicolored 90 90
1169 A506 1.50s multicolored 1.10 1.10

1993, June 29 *Perf. 14*

1170 A507 2.80s multicolored 2.00 2.00

14th Maccabiah Games A508

1993, June 29 *Perf. 14*

1171 A508 3.60s multicolored 2.60 2.60

Respect for the Elderly — A509

Festivals — A510

1993, Aug. 22 **Litho.** *Perf. 14*

1172 A509 80a multicolored 58 58

1993, Aug. 22 *Perf. 14*

1173 A510 80a Wheat 58 58
1174 A510 1.20s Grapes 85 85
1175 A510 1.50s Olives 1.05 1.05

Environmental Protection — A511

1993, Aug. 22

1176 A511 1.20s multicolored 85 85

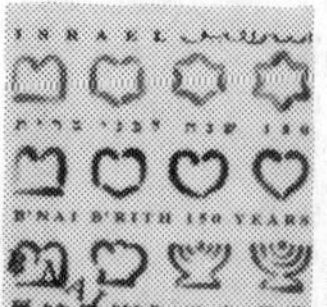

B'nai B'rith, 150th Anniv. — A512

1993, Aug. 22 *Perf. 13*

1177 A512 1.50s multicolored 1.05 1.05

Souvenir Sheet

Telafila '93, Israel-Romania Philatelic Exhibition — A513

Design: 3.60s, Immigrant Ship, by Marcel Janco.

1993, Aug. 21 **Litho.** *Perf. 14x13*

1178 A513 3.60s multicolored 2.50 2.50

Hebrew Magazines for Children, Cent. A514

1993, Dec. 9 **Litho.** *Perf. 14*

1179 A514 1.50s multicolored 1.00 1.00

Philately Day.

Hanukkah A515

Hanukkah lamp with candles lit and: 90a, Oil lamp, Talmudic Period. 1.30s, Hanukkah Lamp, Eretz Israel carved stone, 20th cent. 2s, Lighting the Hanukkah Lamp, Rothschild Miscellany illuminated manuscript, c. 1470.

1993, Dec. 9

1180 A515 90a multicolored 60 60
1181 A515 1.30s multicolored 90 90
1182 A515 2s multicolored 1.40 1.40

This is an expanding set. Numbers have been reserved for additional values.

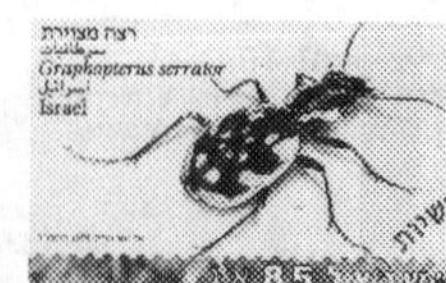

Beetles A516

Designs: No. 1189, Graphopterus serrator. No. 1190, Potosia cuprea. No. 1191, Coccinella septempunctata. No. 1192, Chlorophorus varius.

1994, Feb. 8 **Litho.** *Perf. 14*

1189 A516 85a multicolored 60 40
1190 A516 85a multicolored 60 40
1191 A516 85a multicolored 60 40
1192 A516 85a multicolored 60 40

Health — A517

1994, Feb. 8 *Perf. 13*

1193 A517 85a Exercise 60 40
1194 A517 1.30s Don't smoke 90 60
1195 A517 1.60s Eat sensibly 1.10 75

Mordecai Haffkine (1860-1930), Developer of Cholera Vaccine A518

1994, Feb. 8 *Perf. 14*

1196 A518 3.85s multicolored 2.75 1.75

AIR POST STAMPS

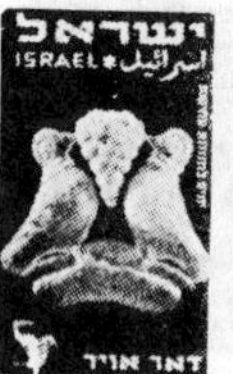

Doves Pecking at Grapes AP1

Marisa Eagle AP2

Designs: 30p, Beth Shearim eagle. 40p, Mosaic bird. 50p, Stylized dove. 250p, Mosaic dove and olive branch.

Perf. 11½

1950, June 25 **Unwmk.** **Litho.**

C1 AP1 5p brt grnsh bl 70 38
C2 AP1 30p gray 22 22
C3 AP1 40p dark green 60 38
C4 AP1 50p henna brown 95 38
C5 AP2 100p rose car 10.00 8.50
C6 AP2 250p dk gray bl 2.75 1.40
Nos. C1-C6 (6) 15.22 11.26
With tabs 250.00

Haifa Bay and City Seal — AP3

Design: 120p, Haifa, Mt. Carmel and city seal.

1952, Apr. 13 *Perf. 14*

Seal in Gray

C7 AP3 100p ultramarine 25 16
C8 AP3 120p purple 32 20
With tabs 18.00

Stamps were available only on purchase of a ticket to the National Stamp Exhibition, Haifa. Price, including ticket, 340p.

Olive Tree — AP4

Tanur Cascade
AP5

Coast at Tel Aviv-Jaffa
AP6

Designs: 70p, En Gev, Sea of Galilee. 100p, Road to Jerusalem. 150p, Lion Rock. 350p, Bay of Elat, Red Sea. 750p, Lake Hule. 3000p, Tomb of Rabbi Meir Baal Haness, Tiberias.

1953-56 Litho.

No.	Type	Value / Color	Unused	Used
C9	AP4	10p olive grn	15	15
C10	AP4	70p violet	15	15
C11	AP4	100p green	15	15
C12	AP4	150p orange brn	15	15
C13	AP4	350p car rose	15	15
C14	AP5	500p dull & dk bl	15	15
C15	AP6	750p brown	15	15
C16	AP6	1000p deep bl grn	1.90	75
		With tab	95.00	
C17	AP6	3000p claret	18	15
		Set value	2.60	1.25
		Nos. C9-C15, C17 with tabs	5.50	

Issue dates: 1000p, Mar. 16, 1953; 10p, 100p, 500p, Mar. 2, 1954; 70p, 150p, 350p, Apr. 6, 1954; 750p, Aug. 21, 1956; 3000p, Nov. 13, 1956.

Old Town, Zefat — AP7

Houbara Bustard — AP9

Port of Elat ('Aqaba) — AP8

Designs: 20a, Ashkelon, Afridar Center. 25a, Acre, tower and boats. 30a, Haifa, view from Mt. Carmel. 35a, Capernaum, ancient synagogue, horiz. 40a, Jethro's tomb, horiz. 50a, Jerusalem, horiz. 65a, Tiberias, tower and lake, horiz. £1, Jaffa, horiz.

1960-61 Photo. Perf. 13x14, 14x13

No.	Type	Value / Color	Unused	Used
C18	AP7	15a light lil & blk	15	15
C19	AP7	20a brt yel grn & blk	15	15
C20	AP7	25a orange & blk ('61)	15	15
C21	AP7	30a grnsh bl & blk ('61)	22	15
C22	AP7	35a yel grn & blk ('61)	24	15
C23	AP7	40a lt vio & blk ('61)	25	15
C24	AP7	50a olive & blk ('61)	20	15
C25	AP7	65a lt ultra & black	24	15
C26	AP7	£1 pink & blk ('61)	50	30
		Set value	1.80	1.00
		With tabs	14.00	

Issue dates: Nos. C18, C19, C25, Feb. 24, 1960. Nos. C20-C22, June 14, 1961. Nos. C23, C24, C26, Oct. 26, 1961.

Wmk. 302

1962, Feb. 21 Litho. Perf. 14

No.	Type	Value / Color	Unused	Used
C27	AP8	£3 multicolored	1.65	1.10
		With tab	11.00	

Perf. 13x14, 14x13

1963 Unwmk. Photo.

Birds: 5a, Sinai rose finch, horiz. 20a, White-breasted kingfisher, horiz. 28a, Mourning wheatear, horiz. 30a, Blue-cheeked bee eater. 40a, Graceful prinia. 45a, Palestine sunbird. 70a, Scops owl. £1, Purple heron. £3, White-tailed Sea eagle.

No.	Type	Value / Color	Unused	Used
C28	AP9	5a dp vio & multi	15	15
C29	AP9	20a red & multi	15	15
C30	AP9	28a emerald & multi	15	15
C31	AP9	30a orange & multi	15	15
C32	AP9	40a multicolored	15	15
C33	AP9	45a yellow & multi	18	18
C34	AP9	55a multicolored	22	22
C35	AP9	70a black & multi	24	24
C36	AP9	£1 multicolored	32	32
C37	AP9	£3 ultra & multi	1.10	1.10
		Nos. C28-C37 (10)	2.81	2.81
		With tabs	6.00	

Issue dates: #C28-C30, Apr. 15. #C31-C33, June 19. #C34-C36, Feb. 13. #C37, Oct. 23.

Diamond and Boeing 707 — AP10

Designs (Boeing 707 and): 10a, Textiles. 30a, Symbolic stamps. 40a, Vase and jewelry. 50a, Chick and egg. 55a, Melon, avocado and strawberries. 60a, Gladioli. 80a, Electronic equipment and chart. £1, Heavy oxygen isotopes (chemical apparatus). £1.50, Women's fashions.

1968 Photo. Perf. 13x14

No.	Type	Value / Color	Unused	Used
C38	AP10	10a ultra & multi	15	15
C39	AP10	30a gray & multi	15	15
C40	AP10	40a multicolored	15	15
C41	AP10	50a multicolored	15	15
C42	AP10	55a multicolored	16	15
C43	AP10	60a sl grn, lt grn & red	18	15
C44	AP10	80a yel, brn & lt bl	22	15
C45	AP10	£1 dark bl & org	28	15
C46	AP10	£1.50 multicolored	35	20
C47	AP10	£3 pur & lt bl	70	38
		Nos. C38-C47 (10)	2.49	
		Set value		1.20
		With tabs	4.75	

Israeli exports. Sheets of 15 (5x3).
Issue dates: Nos. C38-C41, Mar. 11; No. C47, Feb. 7; Nos. C42-C43, C45, Nov. 6; Nos. C44, C46, Dec. 23.

POSTAGE DUE STAMPS

Types of Regular Issue Overprinted in Black דמי דאר

Designs: Various coins, as on postage denominations.

Unwmk.

1948, May 28 Typo. Perf. 11

Yellow Paper

No.	Type	Value / Color	Unused	Used
J1	A1	3m orange	2.00	1.50
J2	A1	5m yellow green	2.75	2.00
J3	A1	10m red violet	8.25	4.75
J4	A1	20m ultramarine	21.00	15.00
J5	A1	50m orange brown	55.00	42.50
		Nos. J1-J5 (5)	89.00	65.75
		With tabs (blank)	1,500.	

The 3m, 20m and 50m are known with overprint omitted.
Nos. J1-J5 exist imperf.

D1

Running Stag — D2

1949, Dec. 18 Litho. Perf. 11½

No.	Type	Value / Color	Unused	Used
J6	D1	2p orange	15	15
J7	D1	5p purple	15	15
J8	D1	10p yellow green	15	15
J9	D1	20p vermilion	22	15
J10	D1	30p violet blue	40	20
J11	D1	50p orange brown	70	28
		Set value	1.45	80
		With tabs (blank)	125.00	

1952, Nov. 30 Unwmk. Perf. 14

No.	Type	Value / Color	Unused	Used
J12	D2	5p orange brown	15	15
J13	D2	10p Prussian blue	15	15
J14	D2	20p magenta	15	15
J15	D2	30p gray black	15	15
J16	D2	40p green	15	15
J17	D2	50p brown	15	15
J18	D2	60p purple	15	15
J19	D2	100p red	15	15
J20	D2	250p blue	15	15
		Set value	50	45
		With tabs (blank)	5.50	

OFFICIAL STAMPS

Redrawn Type of 1950 Overprinted in Black בול שרות

1951, Feb. 1 Unwmk. Perf. 14

No.	Type	Value / Color	Unused	Used
O1	A6	5p bright red violet	15	15
O2	A6	15p vermilion	15	15
O3	A6	30p ultramarine	15	15
O4	A6	40p orange brown	15	15
		Set value	30	20
		With tabs	16.00	

ITALIAN COLONIES

General Issues for all Colonies

100 Centesimi = 1 Lira

Watermark

Wmk. 140

Type of Italy, Dante Alighieri Society Issue, in New Colors and Overprinted in Red or Black

COLONIE ITALIANE

1932, July 11 Wmk. 140 Perf. 14

No.	Type	Value / Color	Unused	Used
1	A126	10c gray blk	25	40
2	A126	15c olive brn	25	40
3	A126	20c slate grn	25	30
4	A126	25c dk grn	25	30
5	A126	30c red brn (Bk)	25	50
6	A126	50c bl blk	25	25
7	A126	75c car rose (Bk)	50	85
8	A126	1.25 l dk bl	50	85
9	A126	1.75 l violet	60	1.10
10	A126	2.75 l org (Bk)	60	1.10
11	A126	5 l + 2 l ol grn	60	1.10
12	A126	10 l + 2.50 l dp bl	60	1.10
		Nos. 1-12,C1-C6 (18)	9.80	16.75

Types of Italy, Garibaldi Issue, in New Colors and Inscribed: "POSTE COLONIALI ITALIANE"

1932, July 1 Photo.

No.	Type	Value / Color	Unused	Used
13	A138	10c green	1.25	2.50
14	A138	20c car rose	1.25	2.50
15	A138	25c green	1.25	2.50
16	A138	30c green	1.25	2.50
17	A138	50c car rose	1.25	2.50
18	A141	75c car rose	1.25	2.50
19	A141	1.25 l deep blue	1.25	2.50
20	A141	1.75 l + 25c dp bl	3.00	7.50
21	A144	2.55 l + 50c ol brn	3.00	7.50
22	A145	5 l + 1 l dp bl	3.00	7.50
		Nos. 13-22,C8-C12 (15)	29.75	67.50

See Nos. CE1-CE2.

Plowing with Oxen — A1

Pack Camel — A2

Lioness — A3

1933, Mar. 27 Wmk. 140

No.	Type	Value / Color	Unused	Used
23	A1	10c ol brn	1.90	3.00
24	A2	20c dl vio	1.90	3.00
25	A3	25c green	1.90	2.00
26	A1	50c purple	1.90	2.00
27	A2	75c carmine	1.90	3.00
28	A3	1.25 l blue	1.90	3.00
29	A1	2.75 l red orange	3.25	6.00
30	A2	5 l + 2 l gray grn	7.00	14.00
31	A3	10 l + 2.50 l org brn	7.00	14.00
		Nos. 23-31,C13-C19 (16)	57.45	101.50

Annexation of Eritrea by Italy, 50th anniv.

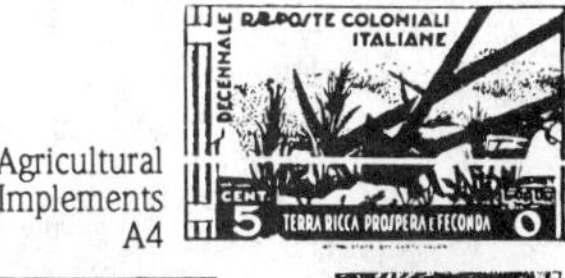
Agricultural Implements A4

Arab and Camel — A5

"Eager with New Life" — A7

Steam Roller — A6

1933 Photo. Perf. 14

No.	Type	Value / Color	Unused	Used
32	A4	5c orange	2.00	2.50
33	A5	25c green	2.00	2.50
34	A6	50c purple	2.00	2.50
35	A4	75c carmine	2.00	3.75
36	A5	1.25 l deep blue	2.00	3.75
37	A6	1.75 l rose red	2.00	4.50
38	A4	2.75 l dark blue	2.00	6.00
39	A5	5 l brnsh blk	3.50	8.75
40	A6	10 l bluish blk	3.50	8.75
41	A7	25 l gray black	5.50	12.00
		Nos. 32-41,C20-C27 (18)	55.25	127.00

10th anniversary of Fascism. Each denomination bears a different inscription.
Issue dates: 25 l, Dec. 26; others, Oct. 5.

Mercury and Fasces — A8

Soccer Kickoff — A10

Scoring a Goal — A9

1934, Apr. 18

No.	Type	Value / Color	Unused	Used
42	A8	20c red orange	50	1.25
43	A8	30c slate green	50	1.25
44	A8	50c indigo	50	1.25
45	A8	1.25 l blue	50	1.25

15th annual Trade Fair, Milan.

1934, June 5

46 A9 10c olive green 8.00 *10.00*
47 A9 50c purple 8.00 7.50
48 A9 1.25 l blue 17.50 *27.50*
49 A10 5 l brown 21.00 *27.50*
50 A10 10 l gray blue 25.00 *27.50*
Nos. 46-50,C29-C35 (12) 160.50 *222.50*

2nd World Soccer Championship.

SEMI-POSTAL STAMPS

Many issues of Italy and Italian Colonies include one or more semi-postal denominations. To avoid splitting sets, these issues are generally listed as regular postage, airmail, etc., unless all values carry a surtax.

AIR POST STAMPS

Italian Air Post Stamps for Dante Alighieri Society Issue in New Colors and Overprinted in Red or Black Like #1-12

1932, July 11 Wmk. 140 *Perf. 14*

C1 AP10 50c gray blk (R) 45 *75*
C2 AP11 1 l indigo (R) 45 *75*
C3 AP11 3 l gray (R) 1.00 *1.75*
C4 AP11 5 l ol brn (R) 1.00 *1.75*
C5 AP10 7.70 l + 2 l car rose 1.00 *1.75*
C6 AP11 10 l + 2.50 l org 1.00 *1.75*
Nos. C1-C6 (6) 4.90 *8.50*

Leonardo da Vinci — AP1

1932, Sept. 7 Photo. *Perf. 14½*

C7 AP1 100 l dp grn & brn 10.00 12.00

Types of Italian Air Post Stamps, Garibaldi Issue, in New Colors and Inscribed: "POSTE AEREA COLONIALE ITALIANA"

1932, July 1

C8 AP13 50c car rose 1.50 *2.50*
C9 AP14 80c green 1.50 *2.50*
C10 AP13 1 l + 25c ol brn 3.00 *7.50*
C11 AP13 2 l + 50c ol brn 3.00 *7.50*
C12 AP14 5 l + 1 l ol brn 3.00 *7.50*
Nos. C8-C12 (5) 12.00 *27.50*

Eagle — AP2

Savoia Marchetti 55 — AP3

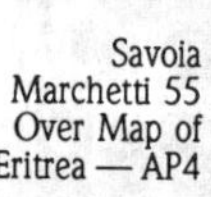

Savoia Marchetti 55 Over Map of Eritrea — AP4

1933 *Perf. 14*

C13 AP2 50c org brn 1.65 *2.50*
C14 AP2 1 l blk vio 1.65 *2.50*
C15 AP3 3 l carmine 2.25 *3.75*
C16 AP3 5 l olive brn 2.25 *3.75*
C17 AP2 7.70 l + 2 l slate 7.00 *13.00*
C18 AP3 10 l + 2.50 l dp bl 7.00 *13.00*
C19 AP4 50 l dk vio 7.00 *13.00*
Nos. C13-C19 (7) 28.80 *51.50*

50th anniv. of Italian Government of Eritrea. Issue dates: 50 l, June 1. Others, Mar. 27.

Macchi-Costoldi Seaplane — AP5

Savoia S73 — AP6

Winding Propeller AP7

"More Efficient Machinery" AP8

1933-34

C20 AP5 50c org brn 2.50 *4.50*
C21 AP6 75c red vio 2.50 *4.50*
C22 AP5 1 l bis brn 2.50 *4.50*
C23 AP6 3 l olive gray 2.50 *9.50*
C24 AP5 10 l dp vio 2.50 *9.50*
C25 AP6 12 l bl grn 2.50 *9.50*
C26 AP7 20 l gray blk 6.00 *15.00*
C27 AP8 50 l blue ('34) 7.75 *15.00*
Nos. C20-C27 (8) 28.75 *72.00*

Tenth anniversary of Fascism. Issue dates: 50l, Dec. 26. Others, Oct. 5.

Natives Hailing Dornier Wal — AP9

1934, Apr. 24

C28 AP9 25 l brown olive 13.00 *37.50*

Issued in honor of Luigi Amadeo, Duke of the Abruzzi (1873-1933).

Airplane over Stadium AP10

Goalkeeper Leaping — AP11

Seaplane and Soccer Ball — AP12

1934, June

C29 AP10 50c yel brn 5.50 *6.25*
C30 AP10 75c dp vio 5.50 *6.25*
C31 AP11 5 l brn blk 14.00 *22.00*
C32 AP11 10 l red org 14.00 *22.00*
C33 AP10 15 l car rose 14.00 *22.00*
C34 AP11 25 l green 14.00 *22.00*
C35 AP12 50 l bl grn 14.00 *22.00*
Nos. C29-C35 (7) 81.00 *122.50*

World Soccer Championship Games, Rome. Issue dates: 50 l, June 21. Others, June 5.

AIR POST SPECIAL DELIVERY STAMPS

Garibaldi Type of Italy
Wmk. 140

1932, Oct. 6 Photo. *Perf. 14*

CE1 APSD1 2.25 l + 1 l dk vio & sl 3.50 *7.50*
CE2 APSD1 4.50 l + 1.50 l dk brn & grn 3.50 *7.50*

ITALIAN E. AFRICA

LOCATION — In eastern Africa, bordering on the Red Sea and Indian Ocean
GOVT. — Former Italian Colony
AREA — 665,977 sq. mi. (estimated)
POP. — 12,100,000 (estimated)
CAPITAL — Asmara

This colony was formed in 1936 and included Ethiopia and the former colonies of Eritrea and Italian Somaliland. For previous issues see listings under these headings.

100 Centesimi = 1 Lira

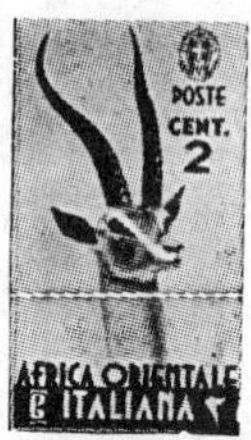

Grant's Gazelle — A1

Eagle and Lion — A2

Victor Emmanuel III — A3

Fascist Legionary — A5

Statue of the Nile — A4

Desert Road — A6

Wmk. 140

1938, Feb. 7 Photo. *Perf. 14*

1 A1 2c red org 35 *45*
2 A2 5c brown 35 35
3 A3 7½c dk vio 65 *75*
4 A4 10c olive brn 35 20
5 A5 15c slate grn 35 42
6 A3 20c crimson 35 20
7 A6 25c green 35 20
8 A1 30c olive brown 45 55
9 A2 35c sapphire 85 *1.25*
10 A3 50c purple 35 20

Engr.

11 A5 75c carmine lake 65 28
12 A6 1 l olive green 55 20
13 A3 1.25 l deep blue 65 24
14 A4 1.75 l orange 6.75 20
15 A2 2 l cerise 75 30
16 A6 2.55 l dark brown 2.75 *4.00*
17 A1 3.70 l purple 17.50 5.50
18 A5 5 l purple 1.90 45
19 A2 10 l henna brown 3.75 1.40
20 A4 20 l dull green 3.75 1.50
Nos. 1-20,C1-C11,CE1-CE2 (33) 70.20 29.89

Augustus Caesar (Octavianus) A7

Goddess Abundantia A8

1938, Apr. 25 Photo. *Perf. 14*

21 A7 5c bister brn 15 35
22 A8 10c copper red 15 35
23 A7 25c deep grn 30 24
24 A8 50c purple 30 24
25 A7 75c crimson 30 *90*
26 A8 1.25 l deep blue 30 *90*
Nos. 21-26,C12-C13 (8) 2.20 *4.68*

Bimillenary of the birth of Augustus Caesar (Octavianus), first Roman emperor.

Native Boat — A9

Native Soldier — A10

Statue Suggesting Italy's Conquest of Ethiopia — A11

1940, May 11 Wmk. 140

27 A9 5c olive brown 15 *28*
28 A10 10c red org 15 *28*
29 A11 25c green 38 *70*
30 A9 50c purple 38 *70*
31 A10 75c rose red 38 *1.10*
32 A11 1.25 l dark blue 38 *1.10*
33 A10 2 l + 75c car 38 *1.65*
Nos. 27-33,C14-C17 (11) 3.38

Issued in connection with the first Triennial Overseas Exposition held at Naples.

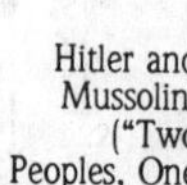

Hitler and Mussolini ("Two Peoples, One War") — A12

1941, June 19

34 A12 5c ocher 15
35 A12 10c chestnut 15
36 A12 20c black 28
37 A12 25c turquoise grn 28
38 A12 50c rose lilac 28
39 A12 75c rose car 28
40 A12 1.25 l brt ultra 28
Nos. 34-40,C18-C19 (9) 15.70

Rome-Berlin Axis.

Four stamps of type AP8, without "Posta Aerea," were prepared in 1941, but not issued. Value, each $1,500.

SEMI-POSTAL STAMPS

Many issues of Italy and Italian Colonies include one or more semi-postal denominations. To avoid splitting sets, these issues are generally listed as regular postage, airmail, etc., unless all values carry a surtax.

AIR POST STAMPS

Plane Flying over Mountains AP1

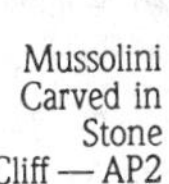

Mussolini Carved in Stone Cliff — AP2

Airplane over Lake Tsana — AP3

Bataleur Eagle — AP4

Eagle Attacking Serpent — AP5

Wmk. Crowns (140)

1938, Feb. 7 — Photo. — *Perf. 14*

C1 AP1	25c slate grn	70	*1.40*
C2 AP2	50c olive brn	15.00	15
C3 AP3	60c red org	70	*1.50*
C4 AP1	75c org brn	1.50	90
C5 AP4	1 l slate blue	18	15

Engr.

C6 AP2	1.50 l violet	42	28
C7 AP3	2 l slate blue	42	42
C8 AP1	3 l car lake	55	60
C9 AP4	5 l red brown	90	60
C10 AP2	10 l vio brn	2.50	1.40
C11 AP1	25 l slate blue	3.25	1.90
	Nos. C1-C11 (11)	26.12	9.30

1938, Apr. 25 — Photo.

C12 AP5	50c bister brown	35	45
C13 AP5	1 l purple	35	*1.25*

Bimillenary of the birth of Augustus Caesar (Octavianus), first Roman emperor.

Tractor — AP6

Plane over City — AP7

1940, May 11

C14 AP6	50c olive gray	24	*1.25*
C15 AP7	1 l purple	24	*1.25*
C16 AP6	2 l + 75c gray blue	35	*1.50*
C17 AP7	5 l + 2.50 l red brn	35	*1.50*

Issued in connection with the first Triennial Overseas Exposition held at Naples.

Hitler and Mussolini ("Two Peoples, One War") AP8

AP9

1941, Apr. 24

C18 AP8	1 l slate blue	12.00
C19 AP9	1 l slate blue	2.00

Issued in commemoration of the Rome-Berlin Axis.

AIR POST SPECIAL DELIVERY STAMPS

Plow and Airplane — APSD1

Wmk. 140

1938, Feb. 7 — Engr. — *Perf. 14*

CE1 APSD1	2 l slate blue	30	*70*
CE2 APSD1	2.50 l dark brown	38	*1.25*

SPECIAL DELIVERY STAMPS

Victor Emmanuel III — SD1

Wmk. 140

1938, Apr. 16 — Engr. — *Perf. 14*

E1 SD1	1.25 l dark green	30	45
E2 SD1	2.50 l dark carmine	38	*2.25*

POSTAGE DUE STAMPS

Italy, Nos. J28 to J40, Overprinted in Black — **A.O.I.**

1941 — Wmk. 140 — *Perf. 14*

J1 D6	5c brown	55
J2 D6	10c blue	55
J3 D6	20c rose red	1.10
J4 D6	25c green	1.10
J5 D6	30c red orange	2.00
J6 D6	40c black brown	2.50
J7 D6	50c violet	2.50
J8 D6	60c slate black	3.75
J9 D7	1 l red orange	20.00
J10 D7	2 l green	20.00
J11 D7	5 l violet	20.00
J12 D7	10 l blue	20.00
J13 D7	20 l carmine rose	20.00
	Nos. J1-J13 (13)	114.05

In 1943 a set of 11 "Segnatasse" stamps, picturing a horse and rider and inscribed "A. O. I.," was prepared but not issued. Value, $4.

ITALIAN STATES

Watermarks

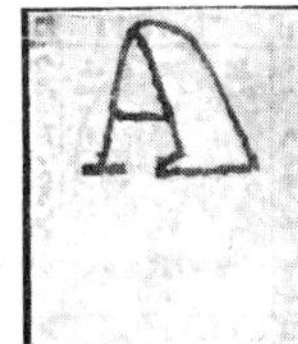
Wmk. 157- Large Letter "A"

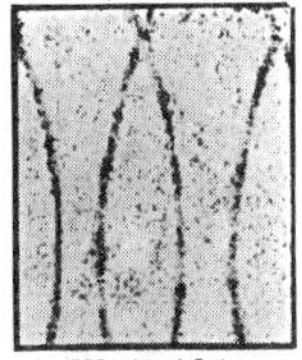
Wmk. 184- Interlaced Wavy Lines

Wmk. 184 has double lined letters diagonally across the sheet readiing: "II R R POSTE TOSCANE."

Wmk. 185- Crowns in the sheet

The watermark consists of twelve crowns, arranged in four rows of three, with horizontal and vertical lines between them. Only parts of the watermark appear on each stamp.
(Reduced illustration.)

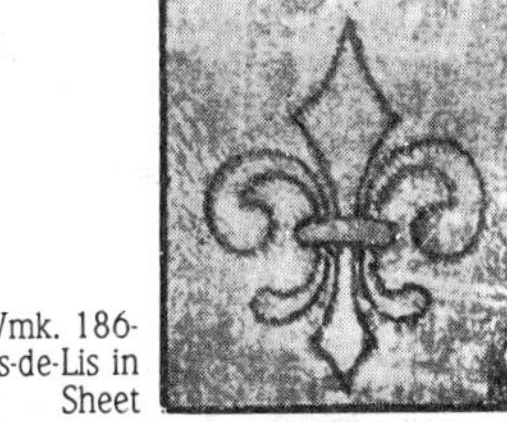
Wmk. 186- Fleurs-de-Lis in Sheet

MODENA

LOCATION — In northern Italy
GOVT. — Former Duchy
AREA — 1,003 sq. mi.
POP. — 448,000 (approx.)
CAPITAL — Modena

In 1852, when the first postage stamps were issued, Modena was under the rule of Duke Francis V of the House of Este-Lorraine. In June, 1859, he was overthrown and the Duchy was annexed to the Kingdom of Sardinia which on March 17, 1861, became the Kingdom of Italy.

100 Centesimi = 1 Lira

> Values of Modena stamps vary according to condition. Quotations are for fine copies, the unused with original gum. Very fine to superb specimens sell at much higher prices, and inferior to poor copies sell at reduced prices, depending on the condition of the individual specimens.

Coat of Arms
A1 A2

1852 — Unwmk. — Typo. — *Imperf.*

Without Period After Figures of Value

1	A1 5c blk, *green*	90.00	6.00
a.	Pair, one with period	180.00	*500.00*
2	A1 10c blk, *rose*	75.00	8.00
a.	"EENT. 10"	*1,800.*	*800.00*
b.	"1" of "10" inverted	*1,800.*	*800.00*
c.	"CNET"	*120.00*	*240.00*
d.	No period after "CENT"	*500.00*	260.00
e.	Pair, #2, 7	225.00	*600.00*
3	A1 15c blk, *yellow*	8.50	8.00
a.	"CETN 15."	*2,250.*	*350.00*
b.	No period after "CENT"	75.00	*180.00*
4	A1 25c blk, *buff*	9.00	6.50
a.	No period after "CENT"	200.00	*400.00*
b.	"ENT.25" omitted	*325.00*	
5	A1 40c blk, *blue*	55.00	35.00
a.	40c black, *pale blue*	*1,500.*	160.00
b.	No period after "CENT"	*600.00*	*400.00*
c.	As "a," no period after "CENT"		*1,300.*
d.	Pair, #5, 8	*140.00*	*700.00*

Unused examples of No. 5a lack gum.

With Period After Figures of Value

6	A1 5c blk, *green*	6.00	12.00
a.	5c black, *olive green*	40.00	20.00
	As "a," without gum	6.00	
b.	"ENT"	*1,400.*	*800.00*
c.	"CNET"	*1,400.*	*1,200.*
d.	As "a," "CNET"	*600.00*	*600.00*
e.	"E" of "CENT" sideways	*2,250.*	*1,600.*
f.	As "a," "CEN1"	*600.00*	*600.00*
g.	As "a," no period after "5"	140.00	*140.00*
h.	Double impression	*300.00*	
i.	As "a," double impression	*260.00*	
7	A1 10c blk, *rose*	20.00	24.00
a.	"CENE"	300.00	*500.00*
b.	"CNET"	150.00	*260.00*
c.	"CE6T"	300.00	*500.00*
d.	"N" of "CENT" sideways	*1,600.*	*1,100.*
e.	Double impression	240.00	*1,200.*
8	A1 40c blk, *blue*	8.00	*45.00*
a.	"CNET"	80.00	*300.00*
b.	"CENE"	160.00	*600.00*
c.	"CE6T"	160.00	*600.00*

d.		"49"	80.00	*300.00*
e.		"4C"	160.00	*600.00*
f.		"CEN.T"	*6,000.*	

Wmk. 157

9	A1	1 l black	10.00	*500.00*
a.		With period after "LIRA"	50.00	*1,400.*

Provisional Government

1859 **Unwmk.**

10	A2	5c green	90.00	*170.00*
a.		5c emerald	110.00	*200.00*
b.		5c dark green	100.00	*180.00*
11	A2	15c brown	40.00	*800.00*
a.		15c gray brown	35.00	
b.		15c black brown	*60.00*	*675.00*
c.		No period after "15"	*200.00*	*1,600.*
d.		Period after "CENT"	*200.00*	*1,600.*
e.		Double impression	*180.00*	
12	A2	20c lilac	10.00	*150.00*
a.		20c violet	60.00	27.50
b.		20c blue violet	130.00	37.50
c.		No period after "20"	12.00	*260.00*
d.		"ECNT"	67.50	*800.00*
e.		"N" inverted	37.50	*400.00*
f.		Double impression		*700.00*
13	A2	40c carmine	10.00	*300.00*
a.		40c brown rose	10.00	*300.00*
b.		No period after "40"	80.00	*1,000.*
c.		Period before "CENT"	80.00	*1,000.*
d.		Inverted "5" before the "C"	*5,500.*	*5,500.*
14	A2	80c buff	14.00	*4,000.*
a.		80c brown orange	16.00	*4,500.*
b.		"CENT 8"	160.00	
c.		"CENT 0"	70.00	
d.		No period after "80"	70.00	
e.		"N" inverted	70.00	

The reprints of the 1859 issue have the word "CENT" and the figures of value in different type from the originals. There is no frame line at the bottom of the small square in the lower right corner.

NEWSPAPER TAX STAMPS

NT1

NT2

B. G. CEN. 9 — Type I

B. G. CEN. 9. — Type II

1853 **Unwmk.** **Typo.** ***Imperf.***

PR1	NT1	9c blk, *violet* (I)	*2,250.*	*650.00*
PR2	NT1	9c blk, *violet* (II)	50.00	12.00
a.		No period after "9"	*180.00*	90.00

All known unused examples of #PR1 lack gum.

1855-57

PR3	A1	9c blk, *violet*	1.50	
a.		No period after "9"	2.50	
PR4	A1	10c blk, *gray vio* ('57)	9.00	*60.00*
a.		"CEN1"	70.00	*775.00*

No. PR3 was never placed in use.

1859

PR5	NT2	10c black	120.00	*480.00*

These stamps did not pay postage, but were a fiscal tax collected by the postal authorities on newspapers arriving from foreign countries.

The stamps of Modena were superseded by those of Sardinia in February, 1860.

PARMA

LOCATION — Comprising the present provinces of Parma and Piacenza in northern Italy.
GOVT. — A former independent Duchy
AREA — 2,750 sq. mi. (1860)
POP. — 500,000 (1860)
CAPITAL — Parma

Parma was annexed to Sardinia in 1860.

100 Centesimi = 1 Lira

Values of Parma stamps vary according to condition. Quotations are for fine copies. Very fine to superb specimens sell at much higher prices, and inferior or poor copies sell at reduced prices, depending on the condition of the individual specimen.
Values for unused are for copies with gum except No. 8 which is known only without gum. Copies of other stamps without gum sell for about a third less.

Crown and Fleur-de-lis
A1 A2

1852 **Unwmk.** **Typo.** ***Imperf.***

1	A1	5c blk, *yellow*	7.50	8.00
2	A1	10c blk, *white*	7.50	8.00
3	A1	15c blk, *pink*	300.00	14.00
a.		Tête bêche pair		*25,000.*
b.		Double impression		*1,000.*
4	A1	25c blk, *violet*	*1,300*	16.00
5	A1	40c blk, *blue*	300.00	75.00
a.		40c black, *pale blue*	*600.00*	80.00

1854-55

6	A1	5c org yel	*600.00*	160.00
a.		5c lemon yellow	*1,600.*	160.00
b.		Double impression		*4,000.*
7	A1	15c red	*800.00*	37.50
8	A1	25c red brn ('55)	*2,600.*	55.00
a.		Double impression		*8,000.*

No. 8 unused is without gum.

1857-59

9	A2	15c red ('59)	26.00	*120.00*
10	A2	25c red brown	30.00	25.00
11	A2	40c bl, wide "0" ('58)	8.00	*110.00*
a.		Narrow "0" in "40"	12.00	*120.00*

Provisional Government

A3

1859

12	A3	5c yel grn	75.00	*2,250.*
a.		5c blue green	160.00	*900.00*
13	A3	10c brown	40.00	*140.00*
a.		10c deep brown	40.00	*140.00*
b.		"1" of "10" inverted	110.00	*1,600.*
c.		Thick "0" in "10"	55.00	*170.00*
14	A3	20c pale blue	30.00	24.00
a.		20c deep blue	45.00	35.00
b.		Thick "0" in "20"	90.00	60.00
15	A3	40c red	67.50	*1,300.*
a.		40c brown red	*1,500.*	*1,300.*
b.		Thick "0" in "40"	85.00	*1,300.*
16	A3	80c org yel	*850.00*	
a.		80c olive yellow	*575.00*	
d.		Thick "0" in "80"	*900.00*	

Nos. 12-16 exist in two other varieties: with spelling "CFNTESIMI" and with small "A" in "STATI." These are valued about 50 per cent more than normal stamps.

See Nos. PR1-PR2.

NEWSPAPER TAX STAMPS

Type of 1859

1853-57 **Unwmk.** **Typo.** ***Imperf.***

PR1	A3	6c blk, *rose* ('57)	10.00	
a.		6c black, *deep rose*	75.00	70.00
PR2	A3	9c black, *blue*	6.50	*5,000.*

These stamps belong to the same class as the Newspaper Tax Stamps of Modena, Austria, etc. No. PR1 was not regularly issued.

Note following No. 16 also applies to Nos. PR1-PR2.

The stamps of Parma were superseded by those of Sardinia in 1860.

ROMAGNA

LOCATION — Comprised the present Italian provinces of Forli, Ravenna, Ferrara and Bologna.
GOVT. — Formerly one of the Roman States
AREA — 5,626 sq. mi.
POP. — 1,341,091 (1853)
CAPITAL — Ravenna

Postage stamps were issued when a provisional government was formed pending the unification of Italy. In 1860 Romagna was annexed to Sardinia and since 1862 the postage stamps of Italy have been used.

100 Bajocchi = 1 Scudo

Values of Romagna stamps vary according to condition. Quotations are for fine copies. Very fine to superb specimens sell at much higher prices, and inferior or poor copies sell at reduced prices, depending on the condition of the individual specimen.

A1

1859 **Unwmk.** **Typo.** ***Imperf.***

1	A1	½b blk, *straw*	7.00	*110.00*
2	A1	1b blk, *drab*	7.00	*50.00*
3	A1	2b blk, *buff*	12.50	*50.00*
4	A1	3b blk, *dk grn*	14.00	*130.00*
5	A1	4b blk, *fawn*	90.00	60.00
6	A1	5b blk, *gray vio*	12.00	*60.00*
7	A1	6b blk, *yel grn*	70.00	*2,600.*
8	A1	8b blk, *rose*	50.00	*425.00*
9	A1	20b blk, *gray grn*	24.00	*800.00*

These stamps have been reprinted several times. The reprints usually resemble the originals in the color of the paper but there are impressions on incorrect colors and also in colors on white paper. They often show broken letters and other injuries. The Y shaped ornaments between the small circles in the corners are broken and blurred and the dots outside the circles are often missing or joined to the circles.

Forged cancellations are plentiful.

The stamps of Romagna were superseded by those of Sardinia in February, 1860.

ROMAN STATES

LOCATION — Comprised most of the central Italian Peninsula, bounded by the former Kingdom of Lombardy-Venetia and Modena on the north, Tuscany on the west, and the Kingdom of Naples on the southeast.
GOVT. — Formerly under the direct government of the See of Rome.
AREA — 16,000 sq. mi.
POP. — 3,124,758 (1853)
CAPITAL — Rome

Upon the formation of the Kingdom of Italy, the area of the Roman States was greatly reduced and in 1870 they disappeared from the political map of Europe. Postage stamps of Italy have been used since that time.

100 Bajocchi = 1 Scudo
100 Centesimi = 1 Lira (1867)

Values of Roman States stamps vary according to condition. Quotations are for fine copies. Very fine to superb specimens sell at much higher prices, and inferior or poor copies sell at reduced prices depending on the condition of the individual specimen.
Values for unused are for copies with original gum.

Papal Arms

A1 A2

A3

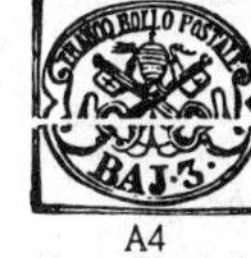

A4

A5

A6

A7 A8

A9

A10

A11

1852 Unwmk. Typo. *Imperf.*

No.	Type	Description	Unused	Used
1	A1	½b blk, *dl vio*	12.00	*24.00*
a.		½b black, *gray blue*	45.00	18.00
b.		½b black, *gray lilac*	30.00	26.00
c.		½b black, *gray*	60.00	18.00
d.		½b black, *reddish violet*	350.00	180.00
e.		½b black, *dark violet*	57.50	60.00
f.		Tête bêche pair		*4,400.*
i.		Double impression		*1,600.*
j.		Impression on both sides		*3,500.*
2	A2	1b blk, *bl grn*	14.00	5.00
a.		1b black, *gray green*	24.00	2.50
c.		Grayish greasy ink	140.00	8.00
d.		Double impression		*1,600.*
e.		Impression on both sides		*3,400.*
3	A3	2b blk, *grnsh white*	1.25	*5.00*
a.		2b black, *yellow green*	26.00	1.60
d.		Grayish greasy ink	180.00	8.00
e.		No period after "BAJ"	60.00	10.00
f.		As "a" and "e"	67.50	6.00
g.		Double impression		*1,200.*
4	A4	3b blk, *brown*	26.00	7.25
a.		3b black, *light brown*	24.00	8.00
b.		3b black, *yellow brown*	40.00	10.00
c.		3b black, *yellow buff*	3.25	*22.50*
g.		Grayish greasy ink		30.00
h.		Impression on both sides		*3,400.*
i.		Double impression		*1,600.*
5	A5	4b blk, *lemon*	26.00	7.00
a.		4b black, *yellow*	26.00	7.00
b.		4b black, *rose brown*	400.00	7.00
c.		4b black, *gray brown*	350.00	7.00
f.		Impression on both sides		*3,400.*
g.		Ribbed paper	30.00	7.00
h.		Grayish greasy ink	*1,000*	40.00
6	A6	5b blk, *rose*	24.00	1.90
a.		5b black, *pale rose*	40.00	2.00
c.		Impression on both sides		*2,600.*
d.		Double impression		*2,000.*
e.		Grayish greasy ink	200.00	12.00
7	A7	6b blk, *grnsh grn*	45.00	6.75
a.		6b black, *gray*	120.00	7.50
b.		6b black, *grayish lilac*	70.00	22.50
c.		Grayish greasy ink	325.00	35.00
d.		Double impression		*1,600.*
8	A8	7b blk, *blue*	80.00	13.00
b.		Double impression		*1,000.*
c.		Grayish greasy ink	360.00	35.00
9	A9	8b black	20.00	6.75
c.		Double impression		
d.		Grayish greasy ink	*450.00*	45.00
10	A10	50b dull blue	*975.00*	400.00
a.		50b deep blue (worn impression)	*1,400.*	575.00
11	A11	1sc rose	*325.00*	*600.00*

Counterfeits exist of Nos. 10-11. Fraudulent cancellations are found on No. 11.

A12 A13

A14

A15

A16

A17

A18

1867 *Imperf.*

Glazed Paper

No.	Type	Description	Unused	Used
12	A12	2c blk, *green*	20.00	*45.00*
a.		No period after "Cent"	24.00	*50.00*
13	A13	3c blk, *gray*	37.50	*1,800.*
a.		3c black, *lilac gray*	240.00	*575.00*
14	A14	5c blk, *lt bl*	16.00	*20.00*
a.		No period after "5"	40.00	*150.00*
15	A15	10c blk, *vermilion*	40.00	9.00
a.		Double impression		*1,600.*
16	A16	20c blk, *cop red* (unglazed)	20.00	8.00
a.		No period after "20"	90.00	45.00
b.		No period after "CENT"	90.00	45.00
17	A17	40c blk, *yellow*	12.00	*40.00*
a.		No period after "40"	12.00	*60.00*
18	A18	80c blk, *lil rose*	12.00	*40.00*
a.		No period after "80"	20.00	*120.00*

Imperforate stamps on unglazed paper, or in colors other than listed, are unfinished remainders of the 1868 issue.

Fraudulent cancellations are found on Nos. 13, 14, 17, 18.

1868 Glazed Paper *Perf. 13*

No.	Type	Description	Unused	Used
19	A12	2c blk, *green*	1.25	*9.00*
a.		No period after "CENT"	1.10	*55.00*
20	A13	3c blk, *gray*	5.00	*750.00*
a.		3c black, *lilac gray*	*550.00*	*3,000.*
21	A14	5c blk, *lt bl*	2.00	*4.00*
a.		No period after "5"	3.00	*9.00*
b.		No period after "Cent"	12.00	*50.00*
c.		5c black, *lt bl* (unglazed, imperf., without gum)	7.50	
22	A15	10c blk, *org ver*	40	*1.75*
a.		10c black, *vermilion*	50.00	2.50
b.		10c black, *ver* (unglazed)	80	
c.		10c black, *ver* (unglazed, imperf., without gum)	15	
23	A16	20c blk, *dp crim*	60	*3.25*
a.		20c black, *magenta*	1.25	*4.00*
b.		20c blk, *mag* (unglazed)	1.25	*4.00*
c.		20c blk, *mag* (imperf., without gum)	15	
d.		20c blk, *cop red* (unglazed)	110.00	3.75
e.		20c blk, *dp crim* (imperf., without gum)	15	
f.		No period after "20" *(copper red)*	*200.00*	14.00
g.		No period after "20" *(mag)*	3.00	*12.00*
h.		No period after "20" *(deep crimson)*	3.00	*12.00*
i.		No period after "CENT" *(copper red)*	*200.00*	14.00
j.		No period after "CENT" *(magenta)*	3.00	*14.00*
k.		No period after "CENT" *(deep crimson)*	3.00	*14.00*
24	A17	40c blk, *grnsh yel*	80	*24.00*
a.		40c black, *yellow*	80	*24.00*
b.		40c black, *orange yellow*	18.00	*140.00*
c.		No period after "40"	2.50	*32.50*
25	A18	80c blk, *rose lilac*	3.00	*50.00*
a.		80c black, *bright rose*	*400.00*	*4,750.*
b.		80c black, *rose* (unglazed)	6.00	
c.		No period after "80" *(rose lilac)*	20.00	

All values except the 3c are known imperforate vertically or horizontally.

Double impressions are known of the 5c. 10c, 20c (all three colors), 40c and 80c.

Fraudulent cancellations are found on Nos. 20, 24 and 25.

The stamps of the 1867 and 1868 issues have been privately reprinted; many of these reprints are well executed and it is difficult to distinguish them from the originals. Most reprints show more or less pronounced defects of the design. On the originals the horizontal lines between stamps are unbroken, while on most of the reprints these lines are broken. Most of the perforated reprints gauge 11½.

Roman States stamps were replaced by those of Italy in 1870.

SARDINIA

LOCATION — An island in the Mediterranean Sea off the west coast of Italy and a large area in northwestern Italy, including the cities of Genoa, Turin and Nice.

GOVT. — A former Kingdom

As a result of war and revolution, most of the former independent Italian States were joined to the Kingdom of Sardinia in 1859 and 1860. On March 17, 1861, the name was changed to the Kingdom of Italy.

100 Centesimi = 1 Lira

Values of Sardinia stamps vary according to condition. Quotations for Nos. 1-9 are for fine copies. Very fine to superb specimens sell at much higher prices, and inferior or poor copies sell at reduced prices, depending on the condition of the individual specimen.

Values for unused are for copies with original gum.

King Victor Emmanuel II

A1 A2

A3

A4

1851 Unwmk. Litho. *Imperf.*

No.	Type	Description	Unused	Used
1	A1	5c gray blk	550.00	550.00
a.		5c black	550.00	550.00
2	A1	20c blue	450.00	35.00
a.		20c deep blue	500.00	45.00
3	A1	40c rose	160.00	*425.00*
a.		40c violet rose	375.00	*500.00*

1853 Embossed

No.	Type	Description	Unused	Used
4	A2	5c blk, *bl grn*	450.00	120.00
a.		Double embossing		*1,000.*
5	A2	20c blk, *dl bl*	300.00	37.50
a.		Double embossing		200.00
6	A2	40c blk, *pale rose*	450.00	80.00
a.		Double embossing		*1,000.*

1854 Lithographed and Embossed

No.	Type	Description	Unused	Used
7	A3	5c yel grn	*3,600.*	140.00
a.		Double embossing		*675.00*
b.		5c green	40.00	
8	A3	20c blue	*900.00*	40.00
a.		Double embossing		*200.00*
b.		20c indigo	20.00	
9	A3	40c rose	*6,000.*	700.00
a.		Double embossing		*2,400.*
b.		40c brown rose	16.00	

Nos. 7b, 8b and 9b, differing in shade from the original stamps, were prepared but not issued.

Typographed Frame in Color, Colorless Embossed Center

1855-63 Unwmk. *Imperf.*

Stamps of this issue vary greatly in color, paper and sharpness of embossing as between the early (1855-59) printings and the later (1860-63) ones. Year dates after each color name indicate whether the stamp falls into the Early or Late printing group.

As a rule, early printings are on smooth thick paper with sharp embossing, while later printings are usually on paper varying from thick to thin and of inferior quality with embossing less distinct and printing blurred. The outer frame shows a distinct design on the early printings, while this design is more or less blurred or even a solid line on the later printings.

No.	Type	Description	Unused	Used
10	A4	5c green ('62-63)	2.00	*2.50*
a.		5c yellow green ('62-63)	2.00	*2.50*
b.		5c olive green ('60-61)	35.00	12.00
c.		5c yellow green ('55-59)	*140.00*	24.00
d.		5c myrtle green ('57)	*800.00*	50.00
e.		5c emerald ('55-57)	*650.00*	55.00
f.		Head inverted		*750.00*
g.		Double head, one inverted		*900.00*
11	A4	10c bis ('63)	80	*1.65*
a.		10c ocher ('62)	60.00	4.00
b.		10c olive bister ('62)	6.00	4.00
c.		10c olive green ('61)	16.00	4.00
d.		10c reddish brown ('61)	70.00	8.00
e.		10c gray brown ('61)	16.00	8.00
f.		10c olive gray ('60-61)	18.00	14.00
g.		10c gray ('60)	24.00	18.00
h.		10c green ('59)	12.00	16.00
i.		10c violet brown ('59)	90.00	40.00

No.	Type	Description	Unused	Used
j.		10c dark brown ('58)	*120.00*	50.00
k.		Head inverted		*800.00*
l.		Double head, one inverted		*675.00*
12	A4	20c indigo ('62)	8.00	1.50
a.		20c blue ('61)	11.00	3.75
b.		20c light blue ('60-61)	14.00	3.75
c.		20c Prussian bl ('59-60)	45.00	5.75
d.		20c indigo ('57-58)	50.00	6.00
e.		20c sky blue ('55-56)	*700.00*	18.00
f.		20c cobalt ('55)	*550.00*	22.50
g.		Head inverted		*300.00*
h.		Double head, one inverted		*450.00*
13	A4	40c red ('63)	1.00	*7.50*
a.		40c rose ('61-62)	6.00	7.00
b.		40c carmine ('60)	40.00	24.00
c.		40c light red ('58-59)	60.00	30.00
d.		40c vermilion ('55-57)	*300.00*	20.00
e.		Head inverted		*1,250.*
f.		Double head, one inverted		*1,000.*
14	A4	80c org yel ('62)	2.00	*25.00*
a.		80c yellow ('60-61)	10.00	*24.00*
b.		80c yellow ocher ('59)	*65.00*	45.00
c.		80c ocher ('58)	20.00	*40.00*
d.		80c brown orange ('58)	35.00	*57.50*
e.		Head inverted		*4,500.*
15	A4	3 l bronze ('61)	50.00	*325.00*

Forgeries of the inverted and double head varieties have been made by applying a faked head embossing to printer's waste without head. These forgeries are plentiful.

Fraudulent cancellations are found on Nos. 13-15.

The 5c, 20c and 40c have been reprinted; the embossing of the reprints is not as sharp as that of the originals, the colors are dull and blurred.

NEWSPAPER STAMPS

N1

Typographed and Embossed

1861 Unwmk. ***Imperf.***

No.	Type	Description	Unused	Used
P1	N1	1c black	20	*1.00*
a.		Numeral "2"	35.00	*300.00*
b.		Figure of value inverted	225.00	*5,500.*
c.		Double impression		*450.00*
P2	N1	2c black	6.75	8.00
a.		Numeral "1"	*1,200.*	*5,500.*
b.		Figure of value inverted	*225.00*	*5,500.*

Forgeries of the varieties of the embossed numerals have been made from printer's waste without numerals.

See Italy No. P1 for 2c buff.

The stamps of Sardinia were superseded in 1862 by those of Italy, which were identical with the 1855 issue of Sardinia, but perforated. Until 1863, imperforate and perforated stamps were issued simultaneously.

TUSCANY

LOCATION — In the north central part of the Apennine Peninsula.
GOVT. — A former Grand Duchy, now a department of Italy.
AREA — 8,890 sq. mi.
POP. — 2,892,000 (approx.)
CAPITAL — Florence

Tuscany was annexed to Sardinia in 1860.

60 Quattrini = 20 Soldi = 12 Crazie = 1 Lira

100 Centesimi = 1 Lira (1860)

Values of Tuscany stamps vary according to condition. They were narrowly spaced. Quotations are for fine copies. Very fine to superb copies with margins all around sell at much higher prices. Inferior specimens with designs partly cut away sell at greatly reduced prices, depending on the individual specimen.

Values for unused stamps are for copies with original gum. Copies without gum sell for about 40 per cent less.

Lion of Tuscany — A1

1851-52 Typo. Wmk. 185 ***Imperf.***

Blue, Grayish Blue or Gray Paper

No.	Type	Description	Unused	Used
1	A1	1q black ('52)	500.00	95.00
2	A1	1s ocher	850.00	190.00
a.		1s orange	1,100.	140.00
b.		1s yellow	1,200.	140.00
3	A1	2s scarlet	*3,250.*	700.00
4	A1	1cr carmine	400.00	6.50
a.		1cr brown carmine	450.00	6.50
5	A1	2cr blue	120.00	8.50
a.		2cr greenish blue	120.00	12.50
6	A1	4cr green	400.00	12.00
a.		4cr bluish green	400.00	12.50
7	A1	6cr blue	400.00	14.00
a.		6cr slate blue	500.00	14.00
b.		6cr indigo	525.00	14.00
8	A1	9cr gray lilac	1,100.	26.00
a.		9cr deep violet	1,100.	26.00
9	A1	60cr red ('52)	*6,000.*	*2,400.*

The first paper was blue, later paper more and more grayish. Stamps on distinctly blue paper sell about 20 percent higher, except Nos. 3 and 9 which were issued on blue paper only. Examples without watermark are proofs.

Reprints of Nos. 3 and 9 have re-engraved value labels, color is too brown and impressions blurred and heavy. Paper same as originals.

1857-59 Wmk. 184

White Paper

No.	Type	Description	Unused	Used
10	A1	1q black	85.00	130.00
11	A1	1s yellow	*2,400.*	450.00
12	A1	1cr carmine	550.00	50.00
13	A1	2cr blue	160.00	12.00
14	A1	4cr blue green	500.00	26.00
15	A1	6cr deep blue	*675.00*	20.00
16	A1	9cr gray lilac ('59)	*180.00*	*500.00*

Provisional Government

Coat of Arms — A2

1860

No.	Type	Description	Unused	Used
17	A2	1c brn lilac	120.00	80.00
a.		1c red lilac	120.00	80.00
b.		1c gray lilac	120.00	80.00
18	A2	5c green	550.00	24.00
a.		5c olive green	550.00	24.00
b.		5c yellow green	550.00	24.00
19	A2	10c gray brn	72.50	5.00
a.		10c deep brown	72.50	5.00
b.		10c purple brown	72.50	5.00
20	A2	20c blue	300.00	14.00
a.		20c deep blue	300.00	14.00
b.		20c gray blue	300.00	14.00
21	A2	40c rose	400.00	26.00
a.		40c carmine	400.00	26.00
22	A2	80c pale red brn	*1,000.*	37.50
a.		80c brown orange	*1,000.*	37.50
23	A2	3 l ocher	*12,000.*	*6,500.*

Dangerous counterfeits exist of #1-PR1c.

NEWSPAPER TAX STAMP

NT1

1854 Unwmk. Typo. ***Imperf.***

Yellowish Pelure Paper

No.	Type	Description	Unused	Used
PR1	NT1	2s black	2.00	
a.		Tête bêche pair	60.00	
b.		as "a," one stamp on back	60.00	
c.		Double impression	40.00	

This stamp represented a fiscal tax on newspapers coming from foreign countries. It was not canceled when used.

The stamps of Tuscany were superseded by those of Sardinia in 1861.

TWO SICILIES

LOCATION — Formerly comprised the island of Sicily and the lower half of the Apennine Peninsula.
GOVT. — A former independent Kingdom
CAPITAL — Naples

The Kingdom was annexed to Sardinia in 1860.

200 Tornesi = 100 Grana = 1 Ducat

Values of Two Sicilies stamps vary according to condition. Quotations for Nos. 1-18 are for fine copies. Very fine to superb specimens sell at much higher prices, and inferior or poor copies sell at reduced prices, depending on the condition of the individual specimen.

Values for unused are for copies with original gum.

Naples

Coat of Arms

A1 A2

A3

A4

A5

A6

A7

1858 Engr. Wmk. 186 ***Imperf.***

No.	Type	Description	Unused	Used
1	A1	½g pale lake	40.00	16.00
a.		½g rose lake	180.00	55.00
b.		½g lake	160.00	75.00
c.		½g carmine lake	160.00	70.00
2	A2	1g pale lake	60.00	6.75
a.		1g rose lake	70.00	8.00
b.		1g brown lake	60.00	8.00
c.		1g carmine lake	60.00	9.00
d.		Printed on both sides		*275.00*
e.		Double impression		60.00
3	A3	2g pale lake	24.00	2.00
a.		2g rose lake	26.00	2.00
b.		2g lake	50.00	5.25
c.		2g carmine lake	60.00	6.00
d.		Impression of 1g on reverse		*500.00*
e.		Double impression	67.50	12.00
f.		Printed on both sides		*500.00*
4	A4	5g rose lake	160.00	10.00
a.		5g brown lake	175.00	14.00
b.		5g carmine lake	290.00	18.00
c.		Double impression	190.00	20.00
d.		Printed on both sides		*2,000.*
5	A5	10g rose lake	300.00	10.00
a.		10g lake	300.00	26.00
b.		10g carmine lake	325.00	26.00
c.		Printed on both sides		*5,000.*
d.		Double impression	600.00	100.00
6	A6	20g rose lake	375.00	30.00
a.		20g lake	375.00	30.00
b.		Double impression	*650.00*	140.00
7	A7	50g rose lake	*3,000.*	750.00
a.		50g lake	*3,250.*	1,500.
b.		Double impression		*4,000.*

As a secret mark, the engraver, G. Masini, placed a minute letter of his name just above the lower outer line of each stamp. There were three plates of the 2g, one plate of the 50g, and two plates of each of the other values.

Nos. 1 to 7, except No. 3, have been reprinted in bright rose and Nos. 1 and 7 in dull brown. The reprints are on thick unwatermarked paper. Value $8 each.

Provisional Government

A8

A9

1860

No.	Type	Description	Unused	Used
8	A8	½t deep blue	*26,000.*	*2,250.*
9	A9	½t blue	*4,500.*	400.00
a.		½t deep blue	*4,500.*	1,000.

100 varieties of each.

No. 8 was made from the plate of No. 1, which was altered by changing the "G" to "T".

No. 9 was made from the same plate after a second alteration erasing the coat of arms and inserting the Cross of Savoy. Dangerous counterfeits exist of Nos. 8-9.

Sicily

Ferdinand II — A10

1859 Unwmk. Engr. ***Imperf.***

No.	Type	Description	Unused	Used
10	A10	½g orange	100.00	*250.00*
a.		½g yellow	*1,500.*	*675.00*
b.		½g olive yellow		*6,000.*
c.		Printed on both sides		*9,000.*
11	A10	1g dk brn	*4,000.*	300.00
a.		1g olive brown (I)	*7,000.*	300.00
12	A10	1g ol grn	32.50	50.00
a.		1g grysh olive grn (II)	60.00	32.50
b.		1g olive brown (II)	160.00	30.00
c.		Double impression	*1,100.*	*1,300.*
13	A10	2g blue	26.00	22.50
a.		2g deep blue	*1,000.*	80.00
b.		Printed on both sides		*6,750.*
14	A10	5g carmine	175.00	140.00
a.		5g deep rose	180.00	130.00
b.		5g brick red	260.00	120.00
15	A10	5g vermilion	65.00	*450.00*
a.		5g orange vermilion	60.00	*500.00*
16	A10	10g dark blue	110.00	70.00
a.		10g indigo	120.00	80.00
17	A10	20g dk gray vio	110.00	130.00
18	A10	50g dk brn red	100.00	*1,250.*

There were three plates each for the 1g and 2g, two each for the ½g and 5g and one plate each for the other values.

Nos. 10a, 10b, 11, 11a, 14, 14a, 14b and 15 are printed from Plate I on which the stamps are 2 to

2½mm apart. On almost all stamps from Plate I, the S and T of POSTA touch.

Nos. 12a, and 15a are from Plate II and No. 12 is from Plate III. On both Plates II and III stamps are spaced 1½mm apart. Most stamps from Plate II have a white line about 1mm long below the beard.

The ½g blue is stated to be a proof of which two copies are known used on cover.

Fraudulent cancellations are known on Nos. 10, 15, 15a and 18.

Neapolitan Provinces

King Victor Emmanuel II — A11

Lithographed, Center Embossed

1861	**Unwmk.**	***Imperf.***	
19	A11 ½t green	1.65	*18.00*
a.	½t yellow green	1.65	*18.00*
b.	½t emerald	500.00	60.00
c.	½t black (error)	*3,500.*	*5,000.*
d.	Head inverted (green)	24.00	
e.	Head inverted (yel grn)		*2,000.*
f.	Printed on both sides		*5,000.*
20	A11 ½g bister	30.00	*35.00*
a.	½g brown	26.00	*35.00*
b.	½g gray brown	500.00	37.50
c.	Head inverted	35.00	
21	A11 1g black	30.00	35.00
a.	Head inverted		*350.00*
22	A11 2g blue	14.00	2.00
a.	2g deep blue	14.00	2.00
b.	Head inverted	*60.00*	*120.00*
c.	2g black (error)		*7,500.*
23	A11 5g car rose	20.00	12.00
a.	5g vermilion	22.50	19.00
b.	5g lilac rose	37.50	24.00
c.	Head inverted	*160.00*	*1,200.*
e.	Printed on both sides		*2,400.*
25	A11 10g orange	12.00	*22.50*
a.	10g ocher	*240.00*	75.00
b.	10g bister	18.00	*37.50*
26	A11 20g yellow	70.00	*160.00*
a.	Head inverted		*3,500.*
27	A11 50g gray	2.00	*1,600.*
a.	50g slate	3.50	*1,600.*
b.	50g slate blue	5.00	*1,700.*

Counterfeits of the inverted head varieties of this issue are plentiful. See note on forgeries after Sardinia No. 15.

Fraudulent cancellations are found on Nos. 19-20, 23-27.

Stamps similar to those of Sardinia 1855-61, type A4 but with inscriptions in larger, clearer lettering, were prepared in 1861 for the Neapolitan Provinces. They were not officially issued although a few are known postally used. Denominations: 5c, 10c, 20c, 40c and 80c.

Stamps of Two Sicilies were replaced by those of Italy in 1862.

ITALY

LOCATION — Southern Europe
GOVT. — Republic
AREA — 119,764 sq. mi.
POP. — 56,929,101 (est. 1983)
CAPITAL — Rome

Formerly a kingdom, Italy became a republic in June 1946

100 Centesimi = 1 Lira

Catalogue values for unused stamps in this country are for Never Hinged items, beginning with Scott 691 in the regular postage section, Scott C129 in the airpost section, Scott D21 in the pneumatic post section, Scott E32 in the special delivery section, Scott EY11 in the authorized delivery section, Scott J83 in the postage due section, Scott Q77 in the parcel post section, Scott QY5 in the parcel post authorized delivery section, Scott 1N1 in the A.M.G. section, Scott 1LN1 in the Venezia Giulia section, 1LNC1 in the occupation air post section, 1LNE1 in the occupation special delivery section, and all of the items in the Italian Social Republic area.

Values of Italy Nos. 17-91, J1-J27, O1-O8 and Q1-Q6 are for specimens in fine condition with original gum. Very fine to superb stamps sell at higher prices. Copies without gum or with perforations cutting into the design sell at much lower prices.

Watermarks

Wmk. 87- Honeycomb

Wmk. 140- Crown

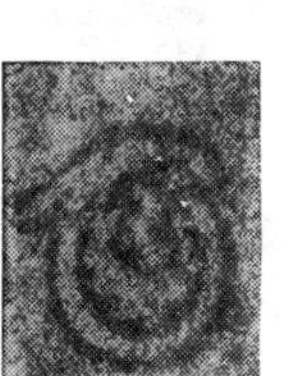

Wmk. 277- Winged Wheel

Wmk. 303- Multiple Stars

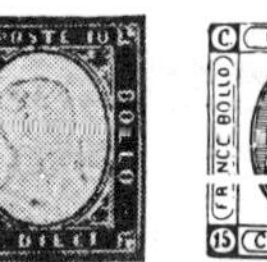

King Victor Emmanuel II
A4 A5

Typographed; Head Embossed

1862	**Unwmk.**	***Perf. 11½x12***	
17	A4 10c bister	*4,000.*	80.00
a.	10c yellow brown	*4,000.*	80.00
b.	10c brown	*7,250.*	120.00
19	A4 20c dark blue	5.50	*9.00*
20	A4 40c red	110.00	60.00
21	A4 80c orange	19.00	*900.00*

The outer frame shows a distinct design on the early printings, while this design is more or less blurred, or even a solid line, on the later printings.

The 20c and 40c exist perf. 11½. These are remainders of Sardinia with forged perforations.

Counterfeit cancellations are often found on No. 21.

Lithographed; Head Embossed

1863		***Imperf.***	
22	A4 15c blue	30.00	17.50
a.	Head inverted		*15,000.*
b.	Double head	45.00	24.00

See note after Sardinia No. 15.

Two types of No. 23:

Type I- First "C" in bottom line nearly closed.
Type II- "C" open. Line broken below "Q."

1863		**Litho.**	
23	A5 15c blue, Type II	1.00	2.00
a.	Type I	300.00	5.50
	Without gum	11.00	

A6

A7

A8

A13

1863-77	**Typo. Wmk. 140**	***Perf. 14***	
24	A6 1c gray green	1.40	40
a.	Imperf., pair		*4,250.*
25	A7 2c org brn ('65)	4.50	38
a.	Imperf., pair	52.50	*135.00*
26	A8 5c slate grn	450.00	40
27	A8 10c buff	450.00	45
a.	10c orange brown	450.00	45
28	A8 10c blue ('77)	850.00	90
29	A8 15c blue	300.00	55
a.	Imperf., pair		*3,600.*
30	A8 30c brown	5.50	1.10
a.	Imperf., pair		*4,250.*
31	A8 40c carmine	725.00	75
a.	40c rose	725.00	75
32	A8 60c lilac	5.50	5.50
33	A13 2 l vermilion	12.50	*30.00*

Nos. 26 to 32 have the head of type A8 but with different corner designs for each value.

Early printings of Nos. 24-27, 29-33 were made in London, later printings in Turin. Values are for Turin printings. London printings of 1c, 2c, 30c, 60c and 2 l sell for more.

For overprints see Italian Offices Abroad Nos. 1-5, 8-11.

No. 29 Surcharged in Brown

1865

Type I - Dots flanking stars in oval, and dot in eight check-mark ornaments in corners.
Type II - Dots in oval, none in corners.
Type III - No dots.

34	A8 20c on 15c bl (I)	135.00	60
a.	Type II	1,500.	3.00
b.	Type III	425.00	38
c.	Inverted surcharge (I)		*18,000.*
d.	Double surcharge (I)		
e.	Double surcharge (III)		*5,750.*

A15

1867-77		**Typo.**	
35	A15 20c blue	135.00	24
36	A15 20c orange ('77)	1,250.	45

For overprints see Italian Offices Abroad #9-10.

Official Stamps Surcharged in Blue

1877

No.	Type	Description	Unused	Used
37	O1	2c on 2c lake	27.50	3.00
38	O1	2c on 5c lake	27.50	4.00
39	O1	2c on 20c lake	165.00	1.25
40	O1	2c on 30c lake	52.50	1.65
41	O1	2c on 1 l lake	120.00	1.40
42	O1	2c on 2 l lake	125.00	2.00
43	O1	2c on 5 l lake	165.00	3.00
44	O1	2c on 10 l lake	95.00	3.75

Inverted Surcharge

No.	Type	Description	Unused	Used
37a	O1	2c on 2c		450.00
38a	O1	2c on 5c		350.00
39a	O1	2c on 20c	*5,500.*	350.00
40a	O1	2c on 30c		275.00
41a	O1	2c on 1 l	*5,500.*	350.00
42a	O1	2c on 2 l	*5,500.*	350.00
43a	O1	2c on 5 l		350.00
44a	O1	2c on 10 l		350.00

King Humbert I — A17

1879 **Typo.** ***Perf. 14***

No.	Type	Description	Unused	Used
45	A17	5c blue green	6.00	30
46	A17	10c claret	65.00	24
47	A17	20c orange	60.00	24
48	A17	25c blue	85.00	55
49	A17	30c brown	52.50	*900.00*
50	A17	50c violet	7.25	2.00
51	A17	2 l vermilion	22.50	*75.00*

Nos. 45 to 51 have the head of type A17 with different corner designs for each value.

For surcharges and overprints see Nos. 64-66, Italian Offices Abroad 12-17.

Arms of Savoy — A24

Humbert I — A25

A26

A27

A28

A29

1889

No.	Type	Description	Unused	Used
52	A24	5c dark green	100.00	75
53	A25	40c brown	4.50	1.00
54	A26	45c gray green	700.00	1.00
55	A27	60c violet	4.50	3.75
56	A28	1 l brown & yel	5.00	1.00
a.		1 l brown & orange	5.00	1.25
57	A29	5 l grn & claret	6.75	*210.00*

Forged cancellations exist on #49, 51, 57.

Parcel Post Stamps of 1884-86 Surcharged in Black

Valevole per le stampe

C.mi = 2

1890

No.	Type	Description	Unused	Used
58	PP1	2c on 10c ol gray	1.10	1.25
a.		Inverted surcharge	45.00	*150.00*
59	PP1	2c on 20c blue	1.40	1.00
60	PP1	2c on 50c claret	9.00	4.50
a.		Inverted surcharge		*4,750.*
61	PP1	2c on 75c blue grn	1.10	75
62	PP1	2c on 1.25 l org	9.50	4.25
a.		Inverted surcharge	*6,000.*	*4,750.*
63	PP1	2c on 1.75 l brn	5.00	*7.50*

Stamps of 1879 Surcharged C.mi 2

1890-91

No.	Type	Description	Unused	Used
64	A17	2c on 5c bl grn ('91)	7.50	12.50
a.		"2" with thin tail	55.00	90.00
65	A17	20c on 30c brown	100.00	1.90
66	A17	20c on 50c violet	105.00	6.00

On Nos. 65-66 the period is omitted in the surcharge.

Arms of Savoy — A33

Humbert I — A34

A35

A36

A37

A38

1891-96 **Typo.**

No.	Type	Description	Unused	Used
67	A33	5c green	100.00	45
68	A34	10c claret ('96)	4.00	28
69	A35	20c orange ('95)	4.00	28
70	A36	25c blue	4.00	40
71	A37	45c ol grn ('95)	4.00	60
72	A38	5 l blue & rose	27.50	*37.50*

Arms of Savoy — A39

A40

A41

1896-97

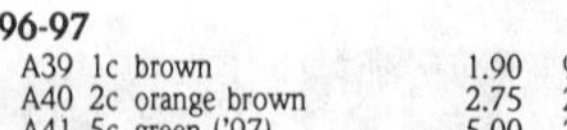

No.	Type	Description	Unused	Used
73	A39	1c brown	1.90	90
74	A40	2c orange brown	2.75	22
75	A41	5c green ('97)	5.00	24

A42

Coat of Arms
A43 A44

Victor Emmanuel III
A45 A46

1901-26

No.	Type	Description	Unused	Used
76	A42	1c brown	15	15
a.		Imperf., pair	225.00	400.00
77	A43	2c org brn	15	15
a.		Double impression	18.00	*67.50*
b.		Imperf., pair	37.50	67.50
78	A44	5c blue grn	15.00	15
a.		Imperf., pair		
79	A45	10c claret	18.00	15
a.		Imperf., pair		*4,500.*
80	A45	20c orange	4.25	15
81	A45	25c dp blue	20.00	15
a.		25c ultra	20.00	15
82	A46	25c grn & pale grn ('26)	24	15
83	A45	40c brown	120.00	1.50
84	A45	45c olive grn	2.25	15
a.		Imperf., pair	90.00	165.00
85	A45	50c violet	120.00	2.50
86	A46	75c dk red & rose ('26)	75	15
87	A46	1 l brown & grn	1.25	15
a.		Imperf., pair	22.50	37.50
88	A46	1.25 l bl & ultra ('26)	1.40	15
89	A46	2 l dk grn & org ('23)	5.50	55
90	A46	2.50 l dk grn & org ('26)	12.50	48
91	A46	5 l blue & rose	7.50	85
		Nos. 76-91 (16)	328.94	7.53

Nos. 83, 85, unused, are valued in fine condition.

The borders of Nos. 79-81, 83-85, 87, 89 and 91 differ slightly for each denomination.

On Nos. 82, 86, 88 and 90, the value is expressed as "Cent. 25," etc.

See No. 87b following No. 174G.

For surcharges and overprints see Nos. 148-149, 152, 158, 174F-174G, B16.

Overprints & Surcharges

See Offices in China, See Offices in Crete, See Offices in Africa, See Offices in Turkish Empire, Albania to Valona, Aegean Islands for types A36-A58 overprinted or surcharged.

No. 80 Surcharged in Black C. 15

1905

No.	Type	Description	Unused	Used
92	A45	15c on 20c org	30.00	28
a.		Double surcharge		*1,200.*

A47

No. 93

No. 111

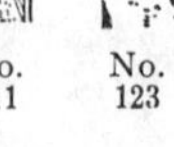
No. 123

1906 **Unwmk.** **Engr.** ***Perf. 12***

No.	Type	Description	Unused	Used
93	A47	15c slate	18.00	24
a.		Imperf. horiz. or vert., pair	67.50	90.00
b.		Booklet pane of 6	210.00	

A48

A49

1906-19 **Wmk. 140** **Typo.** ***Perf. 14***

No.	Type	Description	Unused	Used
94	A48	5c green	15	15
a.		Imperf., pair	17.00	24.00
b.		Printed on both sides	45.00	

95 A48 10c claret	15	15
a. Imperf., pair	17.00	24.00
96 A48 15c slate ('19)	45	15
a. Imperf., pair	55.00	67.50
Set value	60	15

The frame of #95 differs in several details.
See Nos. 96b-96d following No. 174G.
For overprints and surcharge see Nos. 142A-142B, 150, 174A, B5, B9-B10.

1908-27

97 A49 20c brn org ('25)	24	15
98 A49 20c green ('25)	22	15
99 A49 20c lil brn ('26)	45	15
100 A49 25c blue	35	15
a. Imperf., pair	27.50	40.00
b. Printed on both sides	67.50	100.00
101 A49 25c lt grn ('27)	2.25	2.50
102 A49 30c org brn ('22)	70	18
a. Imperf., pair	45.00	67.50
103 A49 30c gray ('25)	45	15
104 A49 40c brown	55	15
a. Imperf., pair	40.00	60.00
105 A49 50c violet	45	15
a. Imperf., pair	32.50	47.50
106 A49 55c dl vio ('20)	1.50	1.50
107 A49 60c car ('17)	45	15
108 A49 60c blue ('23)	2.75	*9.00*
109 A49 60c brn org ('26)	1.40	15
110 A49 85c red brn ('20)	1.65	52
Nos. 97-110 (14)	13.41	*15.05*

The upper panels of Nos. 104 and 105 are in solid color with white letters. A body of water has been added to the background.
See Nos. 100c-105j following No. 174G.
For overprints & surcharges see #142C-142D,147, 151, 153-157, 174B-174E, B7-B8, B12-B15A.

A50

A51

Redrawn

Perf. 13x13½, 13½x14

1909-17 Typo. Unwmk.

111 A50 15c slate black	135.00	40
112 A50 20c brown org ('16)	15.00	75

No. 111 is similar to No. 93, but the design has been redrawn and the stamp is 23mm high instead of 25mm. There is a star at each side of the coat collar, but one is not distinct. See illustrations next to A47.
For overprints see Nos. B6, B11.

Wmk. 140 *Perf. 14*

113 A50 20c brn org ('17)	70	15
a. Imperf., pair	3.75	5.50

Stamps overprinted "Prestito Nazionale, 1917," or later dates, are Thrift or Postal Savings Stamps.

1910, Nov. 1

114 A51 10 l gray grn & red	30.00	4.50

Giuseppe Garibaldi
A52 A53

Perf. 14x13½

1910, Apr. 15 Unwmk.

115 A52 5c green	7.50	7.50
116 A52 15c claret	17.50	12.50

50th anniversary of freedom of Sicily.

1910, Dec. 1

117 A53 5c claret	50.00	27.50
118 A53 15c green	110.00	45.00

50th anniversary of the plebiscite of the southern Italian provinces in 1860.

Symbols of Rome and Turin — A54

Symbol of Valor — A55

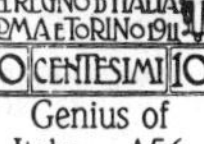

Genius of Italy — A56

Glory of Rome — A57

1911, May 1 Engr. *Perf. 14x13½*

119 A54 2c brown	75	*1.10*
120 A55 5c deep green	3.00	*4.00*
121 A56 10c carmine	4.00	*4.75*
122 A57 15c slate	3.00	*4.75*

50th anniv. of the union of Italian States to form the Kingdom of Italy.
Nos. 115 to 122 were sold at a premium over their face value.
For surcharges see Nos. 126-128.

Victor Emmanuel III — A58

Campanile, Venice — A59

1911, Oct. Re-engraved *Perf. 13½*

123 A58 15c slate	10.00	18
a. Imperf., pair	30.00	55.00
b. Printed on both sides	100.00	150.00
c. Bklt. pane of 6	70.00	

The re-engraved stamp is 24mm high. The stars at each side of the coat collar show plainly and the "C" of "Cent" is nearer the frame than in No. 93. See illustrations next to A47.

For surcharge see No. 129.

1912, Apr. 25 *Perf. 14x13½*

124 A59 5c indigo	70	*1.25*
125 A59 15c dk brn	3.00	*5.75*

Re-erection of the Campanile at Venice.

Nos. 120-121 Surcharged in Black **2** **2**

1913, Mar. 1

126 A55 2c on 5c dp grn	28	55
127 A56 2c on 10c car	38	60

No. 122 Surcharged in Violet **2** **2**

128 A57 2c on 15c slate	28	60

No. 123 Surcharged CENT 20

1916

129 A58 20c on 15c slate	3.00	18
a. Bklt. pane of 6	30.00	
b. Inverted surcharge	47.50	90.00
c. Double surcharge	30.00	55.00

Old Seal of Republic of Trieste A60

Allegory of Dante's Divine Comedy A61

Italy Holding Laurels for Dante — A62

Dante Alighieri — A63

Wmk. 140

1921, June 5 Litho. *Perf. 14*

130 A60 15c blk & rose	55	*5.50*
131 A60 25c bl & rose	55	*5.50*
132 A60 40c brn & rose	55	*5.50*

Reunion of Venezia Giulia with Italy.

1921, Sept. 28 Typo.

133 A61 15c vio brn	45	*3.75*
a. Imperf., pair	14.00	27.50
134 A62 25c gray grn	45	*3.75*
a. Imperf., pair	14.00	27.50
135 A63 40c brown	45	*3.75*
a. Imperf., pair	14.00	27.50

600th anniversary of the death of Dante.
A 15c gray was not issued. Value, $22.50
Nos. 133-135 exist in part perforate pairs.

"Victory" — A64

Perf. 14, 14x13½

1921, Nov. 1 Engr.

136 A64 5c olive green	24	*38*
137 A64 10c red	35	*48*
138 A64 15c slate green	70	*1.50*
139 A64 25c ultra	35	*90*

3rd anniv. of the victory on the Piave.
Nos. 136-137, 139 exist imperf.
For surcharges see Nos. 171-174.

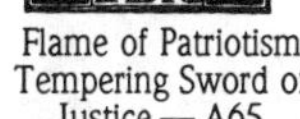

Flame of Patriotism Tempering Sword of Justice — A65

Giuseppe Mazzini — A66

Mazzini's Tomb — A67

1922, Sept. 20 Typo. *Perf. 14*

140 A65 25c maroon	90	*9.00*
141 A66 40c vio brn	1.00	*9.00*
142 A67 80c dk bl	90	*9.00*

Mazzini (1805-1872), patriot and writer.

Nos. 95, 96, 100 and 104 Overprinted in Black

IX CONGRESSO FILATELICO ITALIANO
TRIESTE
1922

1922, June 4 Wmk. 140 *Perf. 14*

142A A48 10c claret	190.00	110.00
142B A48 15c slate	150.00	90.00
142C A49 25c blue	150.00	90.00
142D A49 40c brown	225.00	110.00

9th Italian Philatelic Congress, Trieste. Counterfeits exist.

Christ Preaching The Gospel — A68

Portrait at upper right and badge at lower right differ on each value. Portrait at upper left is of Pope Gregory XV. Others: 20c, St. Theresa. 30c, St. Dominic. 50c, St. Francis of Assisi. 1 l, St. Francis Xavier.

1923, June 11

143 A68 20c ol grn & brn org	75	*15.00*
144 A68 30c claret & brn org	75	*15.00*
145 A68 50c vio & brn org	60	*14.00*
146 A68 1 l bl & brn org	60	*14.00*

300th anniv. of the Propagation of the Faith. Practically the entire issue was delivered to speculators.
Nos. 143-146 exist imperf. and part perf.

Stamps of Previous Issues, Surcharged:

Cent. 7½
a

10 CENTESIMI
b

DIECI
c

Cent. 25
d

Lire 1,75
e

1923-25

147 A49(a) 7½c on 85c	15	35
a. Double surcharge	150.00	*450.00*
148 A42(b) 10c on 1c	15	15
a. Inverted surcharge	3.50	*6.75*
149 A43(b) 10c on 2c	15	15
a. Inverted surcharge	9.00	*18.00*
150 A48(c) 10c on 15c	15	15
151 A49(a) 20c on 25c	15	15
152 A45(d) 25c on 45c	18	*1.50*
153 A49(a) 25c on 60c	70	35
154 A49(a) 30c on 50c	15	15
155 A49(a) 30c on 55c	24	18
156 A49(a) 50c on 40c	15	15
a. Inverted surcharge	45.00	*90.00*
b. Double surcharge	30.00	55.00
157 A49(a) 50c on 55c	14.00	3.25
a. Inverted surcharge	*375.00*	*675.00*
158 A51(e) 1.75 l on 10 l	5.25	5.50
Nos. 147-158 (12)	21.42	12.03

Years of issue: Nos. 148-149, 156-157, 1923; Nos. 147, 152-153, 1924; others, 1925.

Emblem of the New Government
A69

Wreath of Victory, Eagle and Fasces
A70

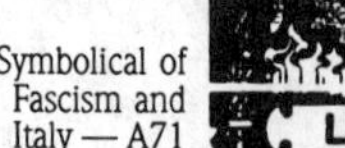

Symbolical of Fascism and Italy — A71

Unwmk.

1923, Oct. 24 Engr. *Perf. 14*

159 A69 10c dark green 80 1.40
a. Imperf., pair 60.00 115.00
160 A69 30c dark violet 90 1.40
161 A69 50c brown carmine 1.25 *2.25*

Wmk. 140 Typo.

162 A70 1 l blue 80 1.40
163 A70 2 l brown 1.25 *2.75*
164 A71 5 l blk & bl 4.00 *11.00*
a. Imperf., pair 75.00
Nos. 159-164 (6) 9.00 *20.20*

Anniv. of the March of the Fascisti on Rome.

Fishing Scene — A72

Designs: 15c, Mt. Resegone. 30c, Fugitives bidding farewell to native mountains. 50c, Part of Lake Como. 1 l, Manzoni's home, Milan. 5 l, Alessandro Manzoni. The first four designs show scenes from Manzoni's work "I Promessi Sposi."

1923, Dec. 29 *Perf. 14*

165 A72 10c brn red & blk 52 *6.00*
166 A72 15c bl grn & blk 52 *6.00*
167 A72 30c blk & slate 52 *6.00*
a. Imperf., pair *1,800.*
168 A72 50c org brn & blk 52 *6.00*
169 A72 1 l blue & blk 9.00 *40.00*
a. Imperf., pair 180.00 *450.00*
170 A72 5 l vio & blk 300.00 *400.00*
a. Imperf., pair 800.00
Nos. 165-170 (6) 311.08 *464.00*

50th anniv. of the death of Alessandro Manzoni.

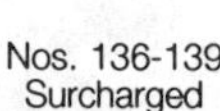
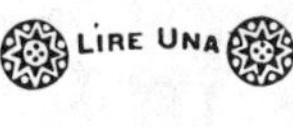
Nos. 136-139 Surcharged

1924, Feb.

171 A64 1 l on 5c ol grn 6.75 *30.00*
172 A64 1 l on 10c red 4.50 *30.00*
173 A64 1 l on 15c slate grn 6.75 *30.00*
174 A64 1 l on 25c ultra 4.50 *30.00*

Surcharge forgeries exist.

Perf. 14x13½

171a A64 1 l on 5c 14.00 *42.50*
172a A64 1 l on 10c 9.00 *42.50*
173a A64 1 l on 15c 14.00 *42.50*
174b A64 1 l on 25c 9.00 *42.50*

Nos. 95, 102, 105, 108, 110, 87 and 89 Overprinted in Black or Red

CROCIERA ITALIANA 1924

1924, Feb. 16

174A A48 10c claret 55 *4.25*
174B A49 30c org brn 55 *4.25*
174C A49 50c violet 55 *4.25*
174D A49 60c bl (R) 5.00 *12.50*
174E A49 85c choc (R) 1.75 *12.50*
174F A46 1 l brn & grn 21.00 *75.00*
174G A46 2 l dk grn & org 14.00 *75.00*
Nos. 174A-174G (7) 43.40 *187.75*

These stamps were sold on an Italian warship which made a cruise to South American ports in 1924.

Overprint forgeries exist of #174D-174G.

Stamps of 1901-22 with Advertising Labels Attached

Perf. 14 all around, Imperf. between

1924-25

No.	Type	Stamp	Label	Unused	Used
96b	A48	15c	+ Bitter Campari	60	2.25
96c	A48	15c	+ Cordial Campari	60	2.25
96d	A48	15c	+ Columbia	5.00	5.50
100c	A49	25c	+ Abrador	20.00	14.00
100d	A49	25c	+ Coen	45.00	6.75
100e	A49	25c	+ Piperno	375.00	80.00
100f	A49	25c	+ Reinach	20.00	9.50
100g	A49	25c	+ Tagliacozzo	160.00	70.00
102a	A49	30c	+ Columbia	5.50	5.50
105b	A49	50c	+ Coen	375.00	9.00
105c	A49	50c	+ Columbia	2.25	70
105d	A49	50c	+ De Montel	45	1.65
105e	A49	50c	+ Piperno	400.00	20.00
105f	A49	50c	+ Reinach	45.00	7.75
105g	A49	50c	+ Siero Casali	2.75	5.50
105h	A49	50c	+ Singer	45	28
105i	A49	50c	+ Tagliacozzo	*600.00*	47.50
105j	A49	50c	+ Tantal	47.50	17.00
87b	A46	1 l	+ Columbia	180.00	95.00
			Nos. 96b-87b (19)	*2,285.*	400.13

No. 113 with Columbia label and No. E3 with Cioccolato Perugina label were prepared but not issued. Values $9, $1.40.

King Victor Emmanuel III — A78

Perf. 11, 13½ (No. 177)

1925-26 Engr. Unwmk.

175 A78 60c brn car 15 15
a. Perf. 13½ 1.50 28
b. Imperf., pair 37.50 55.00
176 A78 1 l dk bl 15 15
a. Perf. 13½ 70 24
b. Imperf., pair 37.50 55.00
177 A78 1.25 l dk bl ('26) 1.35 38
a. Perf. 11 42.50 11.00
b. Imperf., pair 135.00 200.00
Set value 52

25th year of the reign of Victor Emmanuel III.

Nos. 175 to 177 exist with sideways watermark of fragments of letters or a crown, which are normally on the sheet margin.

St. Francis and His Vision
A79

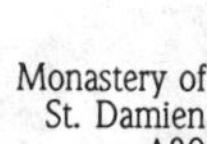

Monastery of St. Damien
A80

Assisi Monastery
A81

St. Francis' Death
A82

St. Francis — A83

1926, Jan. 30 Wmk. 140 *Perf. 14*

178 A79 20c gray grn 15 15
179 A80 40c dk vio 15 15
180 A81 60c red brn 15 15
a. Imperf., pair 110.00 110.00

Unwmk. *Perf. 11*

181 A83 30c slate blk 15 15
a. Perf. 13½ 5.50 1.25
182 A82 1.25 l dark blue 15 18
a. Perf. 13½ 180.00 5.50

Perf. 13½

183 A83 5 l + 2.50 l dk brn 3.50 *37.50*
Nos. 178-183 (6) 4.25 *38.28*

700th anniv. of the death of St. Francis of Assisi.

Alessandro Volta — A84

1927 Wmk. 140 Typo. *Perf. 14*

188 A84 20c dk car 18 15
189 A84 50c grnsh blk 75 15
190 A84 60c chocolate 70 60
191 A84 1.25 l ultra 75 60

Cent. of the death of Alessandro Volta.

The 20c in purple is Cyrenaica No. 25 with overprint omitted. Value, $2,250.

A85

A86

1927-29 Size: 17½x22mm *Perf. 14*

192 A85 50c brn & slate 45 15
a. Imperf., pair 90.00 160.00

Unwmk.

Engr. *Perf. 11*

Size: 19x23mm

193 A85 1.75 l dp brn 1.40 15
a. Perf. 13½ ('29) *6,000.* 400.00
b. Perf. 11x13½ ('29) 600.00
c. Perf. 13½x11 ('29) 600.00
194 A85 1.85 l black 18 18
195 A85 2.55 l brn car 1.40 1.50
196 A85 2.65 l dp vio 1.65 *15.00*
Nos. 192-196 (5) 5.08 *16.98*

1928-29 Wmk. 140 Typo. *Perf. 14*

197 A86 7½c lt brown 45 *1.25*
198 A86 15c brown org ('29) 55 15
199 A86 35c gray blk ('29) 75 *2.75*
200 A86 50c dull violet 90 15

Emmanuel Philibert, Duke of Savoy — A87

Statue of Philibert, Turin — A88

Philibert and Italian Soldier of 1918 — A89

1928 *Perf. 11, 14*

201 A87 20c red brn & ultra 38 40
a. Perf. 13½ 9.00 9.50
202 A87 25c dp red & bl grn 38 40
a. Perf. 13½ 6.75 3.75
203 A87 30c bl grn & red brn 55 45
a. Center inverted *10,000.* *2,500.*
b. Perf. 13½ 2.00 2.00
204 A89 50c org brn & bl 28 15
205 A89 75c dp red 45 18
206 A88 1.25 l bl & blk 65 30
207 A89 1.75 l bl grn 1.10 75
208 A87 5 l vio & bl grn 4.50 *21.00*
209 A89 10 l blk & pink 8.00 *57.50*
210 A88 20 l vio & blk 12.50 *180.00*
Nos. 201-210 (10) 28.79 *261.13*

400th anniv. of the birth of Emmanuel Philibert, Duke of Savoy; 10th anniv. of the victory of 1918; Turin Exhibition.

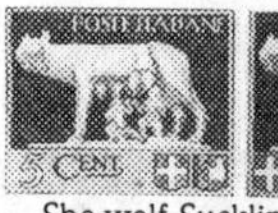
She-wolf Suckling Romulus and Remus
A90 A95a

Julius Caesar — A91

Augustus Caesar — A92

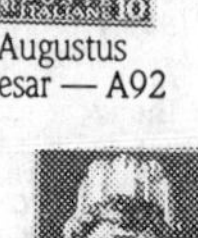
"Italia" — A93

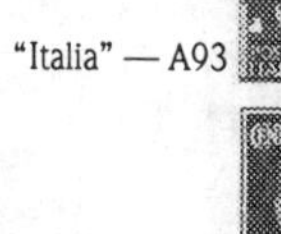
A94 A95

1929-42 Wmk. 140 Photo. *Perf. 14*

213 A90 5c olive brn 15 15
214 A91 7½c deep vio 15 15
215 A92 10c dark brown 15 15
216 A93 15c slate grn 15 15
217 A91 20c rose red 15 15
218 A94 25c dp green 15 15
219 A95 30c olive brn 15 15
a. Imperf., pair 225.00
220 A93 35c dp blue 15 15
221 A95 50c purple 15 15
a. Imperf., pair 75.00 115.00
222 A94 75c rose red 15 15
222A A91 1 l dk pur ('42) 15 15
223 A94 1.25 l dp blue 15 15
224 A92 1.75 l red org 15 15
225 A93 2 l car lake 15 15
226 A95a 2.55 l slate grn 15 15
226A A95a 3.70 l pur ('30) 15 15
227 A95a 5 l rose red 15 15
228 A93 10 l purple 15 24
229 A91 20 l lt green 1.10 *2.25*
230 A92 25 l bluish sl 2.25 *7.75*
231 A94 50 l dp violet 3.50 *14.00*
Set value 8.50

Stamps of the 1929-42 issue overprinted "G.N.R." are 1943 local issues of the Guardia Nazionale Republicana.

See Nos. 427-438, 441-459.

For surcharge and overprints see Nso. 460, M1-M13, 1N10-1N13, 1LN1-1LN1A, 1LN10, Italian Social Republic 1-5A.

Courtyard of Monte Cassino
A96

Monks Laying Cornerstone
A98

St. Benedict of Nursia — A100

Designs: 25c, Fresco, "Death of St. Benedict." 75c+15c, 5 l+1 l, Monte Cassino Abbey.

1929, Aug. 1 Photo. Wmk. 140

232	A96	20c red orange	48	15
233	A96	25c dk green	48	15
234	A98	50c + 10c ol brn	1.40	*3.00*
235	A98	75c + 15c crim	1.50	*4.50*
236	A96	1.25 l + 25c saph	1.75	*5.75*
237	A98	5 l + 1 l dk vio	2.00	*18.00*

Unwmk.

Engr.

238	A100	10 l + 2 l sl grn	3.00	*32.50*
		Nos. 232-238 (7)	10.61	*64.05*

14th cent. of the founding of the Abbey of Monte Cassino by St. Benedict in 529 A.D. The premium on some of the stamps was given to the committee for the celebration of the centenary.

Prince Humbert and Princess Marie José — A101

1930, Jan. 8 Photo. Wmk. 140

239	A101	20c orange red	20	15
240	A101	50c + 10c ol brn	60	90
241	A101	1.25 l + 25c dp bl	85	*3.00*

Marriage of Prince Humbert of Savoy with Princess Marie José of Belgium.

The surtax on Nos. 240 and 241 was for the benefit of the Italian Red Cross Society.

The 20c in green is Cyrenaica No. 35 with overprint omitted. Value, $4,000.

Ferrucci Leading His Army A102

Fabrizio Maramaldo Killing Ferrucci A103

Francesco Ferrucci — A104

1930, July 10

242	A102	20c rose red	15	18
243	A103	25c deep green	15	18
244	A103	50c purple	15	15
245	A103	1.25 l deep blue	35	75
246	A104	5 l + 2 l org red	1.90	*32.50*
		Nos. 242-246 (5)	2.70	*33.76*

4th cent. of the death of Francesco Ferrucci, Tuscan warrior.

See Nos. C20-C22.

Overprints

See Aegean Islands for types A103-A116 Overprinted.

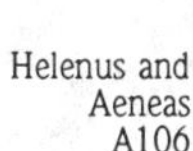

Helenus and Aeneas A106

Designs: 20c, Anchises and Aeneas watch passing of Roman Legions. 25c, Aeneas feasting in shade of Albunea. 30c, Ceres and her children with fruits of Earth. 50c, Harvesters at work. 75c, Woman at loom, children and calf. 1.25 l, Anchises and his sailors in sight of Italy. 5 l+1.50 l, Shepherd piping by fireside. 10 l+2.50 l, Aeneas leading his army.

1930, Oct. 21 Photo. *Perf. 14*

248	A106	15c olive brn	28	20
249	A106	20c orange	28	20
250	A106	25c green	35	18
251	A106	30c dull vio	45	22
252	A106	50c violet	28	15
253	A106	75c rose red	70	55
254	A106	1.25 l blue	90	45

Unwmk. Engr.

255	A106	5 l +1.50 l red brn	21.00	*50.00*
256	A106	10 l +2.50 l gray grn	21.00	*50.00*
		Nos. 248-256 (9)	45.24	*101.95*

Bimillenary of the birth of Virgil. Surtax on Nos. 255-256 was for the National Institute Figli del Littorio.

See Nos. C23-C26.

Arms of Italy (Fascist Emblems Support House of Savoy Arms) — A115

1930, Dec. 16 Photo. Wmk. 140

257	A115	2c deep orange	15	15

St. Anthony being Installed as a Franciscan A116

Olivares Hermitage, Portugal A118

St. Anthony Freeing Prisoners A120

St. Anthony's Death A121

St. Anthony Succoring the Poor — A122

Designs: 25c, St. Anthony preaching to the fishes. 50c, Basilica of St. Anthony, Padua.

Wmk. 140

1931, Mar. 9 Photo. *Perf. 14*

258	A116	20c dull violet	32	18
259	A116	25c gray green	50	18
260	A118	30c brown	65	24
261	A118	50c violet	32	15
262	A120	1.25 l blue	2.00	70

Unwmk. Engr.

263	A121	75c brown red	2.75	1.25
a.		Perf. 12	50.00	57.50
264	A122	5 l + 2.50 l ol grn	13.00	*47.50*
		Nos. 258-264 (7)	19.54	*50.20*

7th centenary of the death of Saint Anthony of Padua.

Tower of Meloria — A123

Training Ship "Amerigo Vespucci" A124

Cruiser "Trento" A125

1931, Nov. 29 Photo. Wmk. 140

265	A123	20c rose red	24	18
266	A124	50c purple	28	15
267	A125	1.25 l dk bl	1.10	55

50th anniv. of the Royal Naval Academy at Leghorn (Livorno) in 1881.

Giovanni Boccaccio A126

Designs: 15c, Niccolo Machiavelli. 20c, Paolo Sarpi. 25c, Count Vittorio Alfieri. 30c, Ugo Foscolo. 50c, Count Giacomo Leopardi. 75c, Giosue Carducci. 1.25 l, Carlo Giuseppe Botta. 1.75 l, Torquato Tasso. 2.75 l, Francesco Petrarca. 5 l+2 l, Ludovico Ariosto. 10 l+2.50 l, Dante Alighieri.

1932, Mar. 14 *Perf. 14*

268	A126	10c olive brn	35	28
269	A126	15c slate green	42	18
270	A126	20c rose red	35	15
271	A126	25c dp green	45	18
272	A126	30c olive brn	65	18
273	A126	50c violet	15	15
274	A126	75c car rose	1.50	1.00
275	A126	1.25 l dp blue	1.00	65
276	A126	1.75 l orange	1.50	1.00
277	A126	2.75 l gray	7.75	*9.00*
278	A126	5 l + 2 l car rose	12.00	*45.00*
279	A126	10 l + 2.50 l ol grn	14.00	*55.00*
		Nos. 268-279 (12)	40.12	*112.77*

Dante Alighieri Society, a natl. literary association founded to promote development of the Italian language and culture. The surtax was added to the Society funds to help in its work.

See Nos. C28-C34.

View of Caprera A138

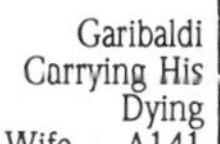

Garibaldi Carrying His Dying Wife — A141

Garibaldi Memorial A144

Giuseppe Garibaldi A145

Designs: 20c, 30c, Garibaldi meeting Victor Emmanuel II. 25c, 50c, Garibaldi at Battle of Calatafimi. 1.25 l, Garibaldi's tomb. 1.75 l+25c, Rock of Quarto.

1932, Apr. 6

280	A138	10c gray blk	40	18
281	A138	20c olive brn	40	18
282	A138	25c dull grn	80	28
283	A138	30c orange	95	28
284	A138	50c violet	45	15
285	A141	75c rose red	2.50	1.00
286	A141	1.25 l dp blue	2.25	70
287	A141	1.75 l + 25c bl gray	9.25	*24.00*
288	A144	2.55 l + 50c red brn	12.00	*30.00*
289	A145	5 l + 1 l cop red	13.00	*35.00*
		Nos. 280-289 (10)	42.00	*91.77*

50th anniv. of the death of Giuseppe Garibaldi, patriot.

See Nos. C35-C39, CE1-CE2.

Plowing with Oxen and Tractor A146

Designs: 10c, Soldier guarding mountain pass. 15c, Marine, battleship and seaplane. 20c, Head of Fascist youth. 25c, Hands of workers and tools. 30c, Flags, Bible and altar. 35c, "New roads for the new Legions." 50c, Mussolini statue, Bologna. 60c, Hands with spades. 75c, Excavating ruins. 1 l, Steamers and galleons. 1.25 l, Italian flag, map and points of compass. 1.75 l, Flag, athlete and stadium. 2.55 l, Mother and child. 2.75 l, Emblems of drama, music, art and sport. 5 l+2.50 l, Roman emperor.

1932, Oct. 27 Photo.

290	A146	5c dk brown	24	15
291	A146	10c dk brown	32	15
292	A146	15c dk gray grn	42	18
293	A146	20c car rose	32	15
294	A146	25c dp green	42	15
295	A146	30c dk brown	48	45
296	A146	35c dk blue	1.40	*1.90*
297	A146	50c purple	24	15
298	A146	60c orange brn	1.50	1.25
299	A146	75c car rose	80	40
300	A146	1 l black vio	1.00	65
301	A146	1.25 l dp blue	75	35
302	A146	1.75 l orange	1.00	35
303	A146	2.55 l dk gray	12.50	*12.00*
304	A146	2.75 l slate grn	12.50	*13.00*
305	A146	5 l + 2.50 l car rose	20.00	*57.50*
		Nos. 290-305 (16)	53.89	*88.78*

10th anniv. of the Fascist government and the March on Rome.

See Nos. C40-C41, E16-E17.

Statue of Athlete A162

Cross in Halo, St. Peter's Dome A163

1933, Aug. 16 *Perf. 14*

306	A162	10c dk brown	15	18
307	A162	20c rose red	15	24
308	A162	50c purple	20	18
309	A162	1.25 l blue	85	1.25

Intl. University Games at Turin, Sept., 1933.

1933, Oct. 23

Designs: 25c, 50c, Angel with cross. 1.25 l, as 20c. 2.55 l, + 2.50 l, Cross with doves.

310	A163	20c rose red	35	18
311	A163	25c green	45	24
312	A163	50c purple	35	15
313	A163	1.25 l dp blue	65	65
314	A163	2.55 l + 2.50 l blk	1.90	*32.50*
		Nos. 310-314 (5)	3.70	*33.72*

Issued at the solicitation of the Order of the Holy Sepulchre of Jerusalem to mark the Holy Year.

See Nos. CB1-CB2.

Anchor of the "Emanuele Filiberto" A166

Antonio Pacinotti A172

Designs: 20c, Anchor. 50c, Gabriele d'Annunzio. 1.25 l, St. Vito's Tower. 1.75 l, Symbolizing Fiume's annexation. 2.55 l+2 l, Victor Emmanuel III arriving aboard "Brindisi." 2.75 l+2.50 l, Galley, gondola and battleship.

1934, Mar. 12

315 A166	10c dk brown		1.90	28
316 A166	20c rose red		18	18
317 A166	50c purple		18	15
318 A166	1.25 l blue		24	*90*
319 A166	1.75 l + 1 l indigo		35	*12.00*
320 A166	2.55 l + 2 l dull vio		35	*16.00*
321 A166	2.75 l + 2.50 l ol grn		35	*18.00*
	Nos. 315-321 (7)		3.55	*47.51*

10th anniversary of annexation of Fiume. See Nos. C56-C61, CE5-CE7.

1934, May 23

322 A172	50c purple	45	15
323 A172	1.25 l sapphire	45	90

75th anniv. of invention of the dynamo by Antonio Pacinotti (1841-1912), scientist.

Guarding the Goal — A173

Players — A175

Soccer Players A174

1934, May 23

324 A173	20c red orange	2.50	1.25
325 A174	25c green	2.50	60
326 A174	50c purple	2.50	18
327 A174	1.25 l blue	8.50	3.25
328 A175	5 l + 2.50 l brn	30.00	*67.50*
	Nos. 324-328 (5)	46.00	*72.78*

2nd World Soccer Championship. See Nos. C62-C65. For overprints see Aegean Islands Nos. 31-35.

Luigi Galvani — A176

1934, Aug. 16

329 A176	30c brown, *buff*	70	24
330 A176	75c carmine, *rose*	70	1.25

Intl. Congress of Electro-Radio-Biology.

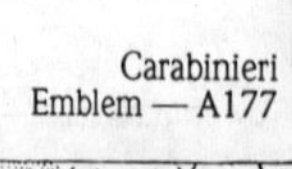

Carabinieri Emblem — A177

Cutting Barbed Wire — A178

Designs: 20c, Sardinian Grenadier and soldier throwing grenade. 25c, Alpine Infantry. 30c, Military courage. 75c, Artillery. 1.25 l, Acclaiming the Service. 1.75 l+1 l, Cavalry. 2.55 l+2 l, Sapping Detail. 2.75 l+2 l, First aid.

1934, Sept. 6 Photo. Wmk. 140

331 A177	10c dk brown	40	28
332 A178	15c olive grn	55	60
333 A178	20c rose red	50	24
334 A177	25c green	65	24
335 A178	30c dk brown	1.10	75
336 A178	50c purple	1.10	18
337 A178	75c car rose	2.25	1.40
338 A178	1.25 l dk blue	2.00	1.00
339 A177	1.75 l + 1 l red org	8.00	*20.00*
340 A178	2.55 l + 2 l dp cl	9.00	*22.50*
341 A178	2.75 l + 2 l vio	10.50	*24.00*
	Nos. 331-341 (11)	36.05	*71.19*

Centenary of Military Medal of Valor. See Nos. C66-C72. For overprints see Aegean Islands Nos. 36-46.

Man Holding Fasces A187

Standard Bearer, Bayonet Attack A188

Design: 30c, Eagle and soldier.

1935, Apr. 23 *Perf. 14*

342 A187	20c rose red	18	18
343 A187	30c dk brown	75	1.10
344 A188	50c purple	15	15

Issued in honor of the University Contests.

Fascist Flight Symbolism A190

Leonardo da Vinci — A191

1935, Oct. 1

345 A190	20c rose red	75	35
346 A190	30c brown	6.00	90
347 A191	50c purple	14.00	24
348 A191	1.25 l dk blue	4.50	1.00

International Aeronautical Salon, Milan.

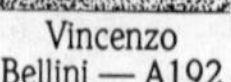

Vincenzo Bellini — A192

Bellini's Villa — A194

Bellini's Piano A193

1935, Oct. 15

349 A192	20c rose red	80	30
350 A192	30c brown	1.25	45
351 A192	50c violet	80	22
352 A192	1.25 l dk blue	2.75	1.40
353 A193	1.75 l + 1 l red org	14.00	*30.00*
354 A194	2.75 l + 2 l ol blk	19.00	*35.00*
	Nos. 349-354 (6)	38.60	*67.37*

Bellini (1801-35), operatic composer. See Nos. C79-C83.

Map of Italian Industries A195

Designs: 20c, 1.25 l, Map of Italian Industries. 30c, 50c, Cogwheel and plow.

1936, Mar. 23

355 A195	20c red	15	15
356 A195	30c brown	18	18
357 A195	50c purple	15	15
358 A195	1.25 l blue	38	40

The 17th Milan Trade Fair.

Flock of Sheep A197

Ajax Defying the Lightning A199

Bust of Horace A200

Designs: 20c, 1.25 l+1 l, Countryside in Spring. 75c, Capitol. 1.75 l+1 l, Pan piping. 2.55 l+1 l, Dying warrior.

Wmk. Crowns (140)

1936, July 1 Photo. *Perf. 14*

359 A197	10c dp green	75	22
360 A197	20c rose red	65	22
361 A199	30c olive brn	75	35
362 A200	50c purple	65	15
363 A197	75c rose red	1.25	70
364 A197	1.25 l + 1 l dk bl	8.50	*15.00*
365 A199	1.75 l + 1 l car rose	10.00	*30.00*
366 A197	2.55 l + 1 l sl blk	17.00	*37.50*
	Nos. 359-366 (8)	39.55	*84.14*

2000th anniv. of the birth of Quintus Horatius Flaccus (Horace), Roman poet. See Nos. C84-C88.

Child Holding Wheat — A204

Child Giving Salute — A205

Child and Fasces A206

"Il Bambino" by della Robbia A207

1937, June 28

367 A204	10c yellow brn	52	24
368 A205	20c car rose	52	24
369 A204	25c green	65	28
370 A206	30c dk brown	1.10	40
371 A205	50c purple	65	18
372 A207	75c rose red	3.00	75
373 A205	1.25 l dk blue	3.75	1.00
374 A206	1.75 l + 75c org	17.00	*30.00*
375 A207	2.75 l + 1.25 l dk bl grn	11.00	*32.50*
376 A205	5 l + 3 l bl gray	11.00	*35.00*
	Nos. 367-376 (10)	49.19	*100.59*

Summer Exhibition for Child Welfare. The surtax on Nos. 374-376 was used to support summer camps for children.

See Nos. C89-C94.

Rostral Column — A208

Designs: 15c, Army Trophies. 20c, Augustus Caesar (Octavianus) offering sacrifice. 25c, Cross and Roman Standards. 30c, Julius Caesar and Julian Star. 50c, Augustus receiving acclaim. 75c, Augustus Caesar. 1.25 l, Symbolizing maritime glory of Rome. 1.75 l+1 l, Sacrificial Altar. 2.55 l+2 l, Capitol.

1937, Sept. 23

377 A208	10c myrtle grn	48	20
378 A208	15c olive grn	48	28
379 A208	20c red	48	22
380 A208	25c green	48	20
381 A208	30c olive bis	75	28
382 A208	50c purple	48	18
383 A208	75c scarlet	95	70
384 A208	1.25 l dk blue	1.25	70
385 A208	1.75 l + 1 l plum	15.00	*22.50*
386 A208	2.55 l + 2 l sl blk	19.00	*24.00*
	Nos. 377-386 (10)	39.35	*49.26*

Bimillenary of the birth of Emperor Augustus Caesar (Octavianus) on the occasion of the exhibition opened in Rome by Mussolini, Sept. 22, 1937.

See Nos. C95-C99. For overprints see Aegean Islands Nos. 47-56.

Gasparo Luigi Pacifico Spontini A218

Antonius Stradivarius A219

Count Giacomo Leopardi A220

Giovanni Battista Pergolesi A221

Giotto di Bondone — A222

1937, Oct. 25

No.	Type	Value	Description	Unused	Used
387	A218	10c	dk brown	15	20
388	A219	20c	rose red	15	20
389	A220	25c	dk green	15	18
390	A221	30c	dk brown	15	28
391	A220	50c	purple	15	18
392	A221	75c	crimson	42	75
393	A222	1.25 l	dp blue	45	90
394	A218	1.75 l	dp orange	45	90
395	A219	2.55 l	+ 2 l gray grn	3.50	*22.50*
396	A222	2.75 l	+ 2 l red brn	3.50	*24.00*
			Nos. 387-396 (10)	9.07	*50.09*

Centennials of Spontini, Stradivarius, Leopardi, Pergolesi and Giotto.

For overprints see Aegean Islands Nos. 57-58.

Guglielmo Marconi — A223

Romulus Plowing — A224

1938, Jan. 24

No.	Type	Value	Description	Unused	Used
397	A223	20c	rose pink	45	15
398	A223	50c	purple	15	15
399	A223	1.25 l	blue	30	60

Guglielmo Marconi (1874-1937), electrical engineer, inventor of wireless telegraphy.

1938, Oct. 28

Designs: 20c, Augustus Caesar (Octavianus). 25c, Dante. 30c, Columbus. 50c, Leonardo da Vinci. 75c, Victor Emmanuel II and Garibaldi. 1.25 l, Tomb of Unknown Soldier, Rome. 1.75 l, Blackshirts' March on Rome, 1922. 2.75 l, Map of Italian East Africa and Iron Crown of Monza. 5 l, Victor Emmanuel III.

No.	Type	Value	Description	Unused	Used
400	A224	10c	brown	24	15
401	A224	20c	car rose	24	15
402	A224	25c	dk green	24	15
403	A224	30c	olive brn	24	18
404	A224	50c	lt violet	24	15
405	A224	75c	rose red	45	28
406	A224	1.25 l	dp blue	60	28
407	A224	1.75 l	vio blk	80	28
408	A224	2.75 l	slate grn	3.75	*7.75*
409	A224	5 l	lt red brn	1.25	*0.25*
			Nos. 400-409 (10)	11.05	*18.62*

Proclamation of the Empire. See #C100-C105.

Wood-burning Engine and Streamlined Electric Engine — A234

1939, Dec. 15 **Photo.** ***Perf. 14***

No.	Type	Value	Description	Unused	Used
410	A234	20c	rose red	15	15
411	A234	50c	brt violet	15	15
412	A234	1.25 l	dp blue	24	60

Centenary of Italian railroads.

Adolf Hitler and Benito Mussolini A235

Hitler and Mussolini A236

1941 **Wmk. 140**

No.	Type	Value	Description	Unused	Used
413	A235	10c	dp brown	15	15
414	A235	20c	red org	15	15
415	A235	25c	dp green	15	15
416	A236	50c	violet	15	15
417	A236	75c	rose red	18	18
418	A236	1.25 l	dp blue	18	28
			Nos. 413-418 (6)	96	1.06

Rome-Berlin Axis.

Stamps of type A236 in the denominations and colors of Nos. 413 to 415 were prepared but not issued. They were sold for charitable purposes in 1948. Value $4 each.

Galileo Teaching Mathematics at Padua — A237

Designs: 25c, Galileo presenting telescope to Doge of Venice. 50c, Galileo Galilei (1564-1642). 1.25 l, Galileo studying at Arcetri.

1942, Sept. 28

No.	Type	Value	Description	Unused	Used
419	A237	10c	dk org & lake	15	18
420	A237	25c	gray grn & grn	15	22
421	A237	50c	brn vio & vio	15	22
a.			Frame missing	*400.00*	
422	A237	1.25 l	Prus bl & ultra	15	45
			Set value	42	
			Set, never hinged	2.25	

Statue of Rossini — A241

Gioacchino Rossini — A242

1942, Nov. 23 **Photo.**

No.	Type	Value	Description	Unused	Used
423	A241	25c	deep green	15	15
424	A241	30c	brown	15	18
425	A242	50c	violet	15	15
426	A242	1 l	blue	15	35
			Set value	36	
			Set, never hinged	1.50	

Gioacchino Antonio Rossini (1792-1868), operatic composer.

"Victory for the Axis" A243

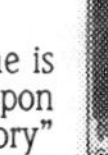

"Discipline is the Weapon of Victory" A244

"Everything and Everyone for Victory" A245

"Arms and Hearts Must Be Stretched Out Towards the Goal" A246

Perf. 14 all around, Imperf. between

1942 **Photo.** **Wmk. 140**

No.	Type	Value	Description	Unused	Used
427	A243	25c	deep green	15	18
428	A244	25c	deep green	15	18
429	A245	25c	deep green	15	18
430	A246	25c	deep green	15	18
431	A243	30c	olive brown	15	*55*
432	A244	30c	olive brown	15	*55*
433	A245	30c	olive brown	15	*55*
434	A246	30c	olive brown	15	*55*
435	A243	50c	purple	15	18
436	A244	50c	purple	15	18
437	A245	50c	purple	15	18
438	A246	50c	purple	15	18
			Set value	80	
			Set, never hinged	5.00	

Issued in honor of the Italian Army.

The left halves of #431-438 are type A95.

For overprints see Italian Socal Republic #6-17.

She-Wolf Suckling Romulus and Remus — A247

Perf. 10½x11½, 11x11½, 11½, 14

1944, Jan. **Litho.** **Wmk. 87**

Without Gum

No.	Type	Value	Description	Unused	Used
439	A247	50c	rose vio & bis rose	28	40

Unwmk.

No.	Type	Value	Description	Unused	Used
440	A247	50c	rose vio & pale rose	15	18

Nos. 439-440 exist imperf., part perf.

Types of 1929

1945, May **Unwmk.** ***Perf. 14***

No.	Type	Value	Description	Unused	Used
441	A93	15c	slate green	15	15
442	A93	35c	deep blue	15	15
443	A91	1 l	deep violet	15	15
			Set value	25	36
			Set, never hinged	90	

Types of 1929 Redrawn

Fasces Removed

Victor Emmanuel III — A248

Julius Caesar — A249

Augustus Caesar — A250

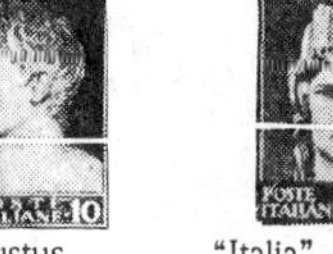

"Italia" — A251

A252

1944-45 **Wmk. 140** **Photo.** ***Perf. 14***

No.	Type	Value	Description	Unused	Used
444	A248	30c	dk brown	15	15
445	A248	50c	purple	18	60
446	A248	60c	slate grn ('45)	15	18
447	A249	1 l	dp blue ('45)	15	15
			Set value	48	
			Set, never hinged	2.25	

1945 **Unwmk.** ***Perf. 14***

No.	Type	Value	Description	Unused	Used
448	A250	10c	dk brown	15	15
448A	A249	20c	rose red	15	15
449	A251	50c	dk violet	15	15
450	A248	60c	slate grn	15	15
451	A251	60c	red org	15	15
452	A249	1 l	dp violet	15	15
452A	A249	1 l	dp vio, redrawn	15	15
452B	A251	2 l	dp car	15	15
452C	A251	10 l	purple	60	1.25
			Set value	1.35	2.00
			Set, never hinged	9.00	

1945 **Wmk. 277**

No.	Type	Value	Description	Unused	Used
453	A249	20c	rose red	15	15
454	A248	60c	slate grn	15	15
455	A249	1 l	dp violet	15	15
456	A251	1.20 l	dk brown	15	15
457	A251	2 l	dk red	15	15
458	A252	5 l	dk red	15	15
459	A251	10 l	purple	70	1.25
			Set value	1.25	1.75
			Set, never hinged	5.00	

Nos. 452A and 457 are redrawings of types A249 and A251. In the redrawn 1 l, the "L" of "LIRE" extends under the "IRE" and the letters of "POSTE ITALIANE" are larger. In the original the "L" extends only under the "I."

In the redrawn 2 l, the "2" is smaller and thinner, and the design is less distinct.

For overprints see Nos. 1LN2-1LN8.

No. 224 Surcharged in Black

1945, Mar. **Wmk. 140**

No.	Type	Value	Description	Unused	Used
460	A92	2.50 l	on 1.75 l red org	15	15
			Never hinged	20	
a.			Six bars at left	70	90

Loggia dei Mercanti, Bologna A253

Basilica of San Lorenzo, Rome A254

Stamps of Italian Social Republic Surcharged in Black

1945, May 2 **Photo.** ***Perf. 14***

No.	Type	Value	Description	Unused	Used
461	A253	1.20 l	on 20c crim	15	15
462	A254	2 l	on 25c green	15	15
a.			2½ mm between "2" and "LIRE"	45	70
			Set value	15	24
			Set, never hinged	30	

Breaking Chain — A255

United Family and Scales — A256

Planting Tree — A257

Tying Tree — A258

Italy stamps can be mounted in the Scott annual Italy supplement.

Torch A259 — "Italia" and Sprouting Oak Stump A260

1945-47 Wmk. 277 Photo. *Perf. 14*

No.	Type	Value	Color	Unused	Used
463	A255	10c	rose brown	15	15
464	A256	20c	dk brown	15	15
464A	A256	25c	brt bl grn ('46)	15	15
465	A257	40c	slate	15	15
465A	A255	50c	dp vio ('46)	15	15
466	A258	60c	dk green	15	15
467	A255	80c	car rose	15	15
468	A257	1 l	dk green	15	15
469	A259	1.20 l	chestnut	15	15
470	A258	2 l	dk cl brn	15	15
471	A259	3 l	red	15	15
471A	A259	4 l	red org ('46)	24	15
472	A256	5 l	deep blue	15	15
472A	A257	6 l	dp vio ('47)	42	15
473	A255	10 l	slate	15	15
473A	A257	15 l	dp bl ('46)	90	15
474	A259	20 l	dk red vio	18	15
475	A260	25 l	dk grn	1.90	15
476	A260	50 l	dk vio brn	75	15
			Set value	5.25	90
			Set, never hinged	40.00	

See Nos. 486-488.
For overprints see Nos. 1LN11-1LN12, 1LN14-1N19, Trieste 1-13, 15-17, 30-32, 58-68, 82-83.

United Family and Scales A261

1946 Engr. *Perf. 14*

No.	Type	Value	Color	Unused	Used
477	A261	100 l	car lake	80.00	1.25
			Never hinged	400.00	
a.			Perf. 14x13½	90.00	1.50

For overprints see Nos. 1LN13, Trieste 14, 69.

Cathedral of St. Andrea, Amalfi — A262

Church of St. Michael, Lucca — A263

"Peace" from Fresco at Siena A264

Signoria Palace, Florence A265

View of Cathedral Domes, Pisa — A266

Republic of Genoa A267

"Venice Crowned by Glory," by Paolo Veronese A268

Oath of Pontida A269

1946, Oct. 30

No.	Type	Value	Color	Unused	Used
478	A262	1 l	brown	15	15
479	A263	2 l	dk blue	15	15
480	A264	3 l	dk bl grn	15	15
481	A265	4 l	dp org	15	15
482	A266	5 l	dp violet	15	15
483	A267	10 l	car rose	15	15
484	A268	15 l	dp ultra	22	28
485	A269	20 l	red brown	15	15
			Set value	65	65
			Set, never hinged	1.40	

Proclamation of the Republic.

Types of 1945

1947-48 Wmk. 277 Photo. *Perf. 14*

No.	Type	Value	Color	Unused	Used
486	A255	8 l	dk green ('48)	25	15
487	A256	10 l	red orange	2.25	15
488	A259	30 l	dk blue ('48)	65.00	15
			Set value		17
			Set, never hinged	300.00	

St. Catherine Giving Mantle to Beggar — A270

Designs: 5 l, St. Catherine carrying cross. 10 l, St. Catherine, arms outstretched. 30 l, St. Catherine and scribe.

1948, Mar. 1 Photo.

No.	Type	Value	Color	Unused	Used
489	A270	3 l	yel grn & gray grn	18	18
490	A270	5 l	vio & bl	28	32
491	A270	10 l	red brn & vio	35	40
492	A270	30 l	bis & gray brn	1.75	2.25
			Nos. 489-492,C127-C128 (6)	29.81	31.90
			Set, never hinged	80.00	

600th anniv. of the birth of St. Catherine of Siena, Patroness of Italy.

"Constitutional Government" — A271

1948, Apr. 12

No.	Type	Value	Color	Unused	Used
493	A271	10 l	rose vio	18	35
494	A271	30 l	blue	85	70
			Set, never hinged	3.75	

Issued to commemorate the proclamation of the constitution of January 1, 1948.

Uprising at Palermo, Jan. 12, 1848 A272

Designs (Revolutionary scenes): 4 l, Rebellion at Padua. 5 l, Proclamation of statute, Turin. 6 l, "Five Days of Milan." 8 l, Daniele Manin proclaming the Republic of Venice. 10 l, Defense of Vicenza. 12 l, Battle of Curtatone. 15 l, Battle of Gioto. 20 l, Insurrection at Bologna. 30 l, "Ten Days of Brescia." 50 l, Garibaldi in Rome fighting. 100 l, Death of Goffredo Mameli.

1948, May 3

No.	Type	Value	Color	Unused	Used
495	A272	3 l	dk brown	15	15
496	A272	4 l	red violet	15	15
497	A272	5 l	dp blue	15	15
498	A272	6 l	dp yel grn	15	35
499	A272	8 l	brown	15	28
500	A272	10 l	orange red	32	15
501	A272	12 l	dk gray grn	55	*1.00*
502	A272	15 l	gray blk	1.50	48
503	A272	20 l	car rose	4.25	3.25
504	A272	30 l	brt ultra	1.90	28
505	A272	50 l	violet	30.00	1.25
506	A272	100 l	blue blk	37.50	9.50
			Nos. 495-506 (12)	76.77	16.99
			Set, never hinged	400.00	

Centenary of the Risorgimento, uprisings of 1848-49 which led to Italian unification.
See No. E26. For overprints see Trieste Nos. 18-29, E5.

Alpine Soldier and Bassano Bridge A273

1948, Oct. 1 Wmk. 277 *Perf. 14*

No.	Type	Value	Color	Unused	Used
507	A273	15 l	dark green	65	75
			Never hinged	2.50	

Re-opening of the Bridge of Bassano, Oct. 3, 1948.
For overprint see Trieste No. 33.

Gaetano Donizetti — A274

1948, Oct. 23 Photo.

No.	Type	Value	Color	Unused	Used
508	A274	15 l	dark brown	65	75
			Never hinged	1.90	

Centenary of the death of Gaetano Donizetti, composer.
For overprint see Trieste No. 34.

Fair Buildings A275

1949, Apr. 12

No.	Type	Value	Color	Unused	Used
509	A275	20 l	dark brown	1.50	1.10
			Never hinged	10.00	

27th Milan Trade Fair, April 1949.
For overprint see Trieste No. 35.

Standard of Doges of Venice — A276

Designs: 15 l, Clock strikers, Lion Tower and Campanile of St. Mark's. 20 l, Lion standard and Venetian galley. 50 l, Lion tower and gulls.

1949, Apr. 12
Buff Background

No.	Type	Value	Color	Unused	Used
510	A276	5 l	red brown	15	15
511	A276	15 l	dk green	1.25	60
512	A276	20 l	dp red brn	1.50	15
513	A276	50 l	dk blue	10.00	60
			Set, never hinged	77.50	

Biennial Art Exhibition of Venice, 50th anniv.
For overprints see Trieste Nos. 36-39.

"Transportation" and Globes — A277

1949, May 2 Wmk. 277 *Perf. 14*

No.	Type	Value	Color	Unused	Used
514	A277	50 l	brt ultra	10.00	2.00
			Never hinged	50.00	

75th anniv. of the UPU.
For overprint see Trieste No. 40.

Workman and Ship — A278

1949, May 30 Photo.

No.	Type	Value	Color	Unused	Used
515	A278	5 l	dk green	1.75	3.00
516	A278	15 l	violet	4.75	*7.25*
517	A278	20 l	brown	27.50	8.25
			Set, never hinged	175.00	

European Recovery Program.
For overprints see Trieste Nos. 42-44.

The Vascello, Rome — A279

1949, May 18

No.	Type	Value	Color	Unused	Used
518	A279	100 l	brown	60.00	35.00
			Never hinged	275.00	

Centenary of Roman Republic.
For overprint see Trieste No. 41.

Giuseppe Mazzini A280

Vittorio Alfieri A281

1949, June 1

No.	Type	Value	Color	Unused	Used
519	A280	20 l	gray	1.90	85
			Never hinged	14.00	

Erection of a monument to Giuseppe Mazzini (1805-72), Italian patriot and revolutionary.
For overprint see Trieste No. 45.

1949, June 4 Photo.

No.	Type	Value	Color	Unused	Used
520	A281	20 l	brown	2.25	85
			Never hinged	9.50	

200th anniv. of the birth of Vittorio Alfieri, tragic dramatist.
For overprint see Trieste No. 46.

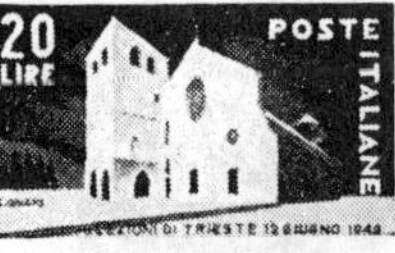

Basilica of St. Just, Trieste A282

1949, June 8

No.	Type	Value	Color	Unused	Used
521	A282	20 l	brown red	4.00	5.50
			Never hinged	13.00	

Trieste election, June 12, 1949.
For overprint see Trieste No. 47.

Staff of Aesculapius, Globe — A283

1949, June 13 Wmk. 277 *Perf. 14*
522 A283 20 l violet 7.00 6.00
Never hinged 42.50

2nd World Health Cong., Rome, 1949.
For overprint see Trieste No. 49.

Lorenzo de Medici A284

Andrea Palladio A285

1949, Aug. 4
523 A284 20 l vio blue 2.00 75
Never hinged 13.00

Birth of Lorenzo de Medici, 500th anniv.
For overprint see Trieste No. 50.

1949, Aug. 4
524 A285 20 l violet 4.00 3.00
Never hinged 17.00

Andrea Palladio (1518-1580), architect.
For overprint see Trieste No. 51.

Tartan and Fair Buildings A286

1949, Aug. 16
525 A286 20 l red 1.25 75
Never hinged 5.00

133th Levant Fair, Bari, September, 1949.
For overprint see Trieste No. 52.

Voltaic Pile — A287

Alessandro Volta — A288

1949, Sept. 14 Engr. *Perf. 14*
526 A287 20 l rose car 1.40 85
a. Perf. 13x14 15.00 2.50
527 A288 50 l deep blue 20.00 6.75
a. Perf. 13x14 150.00 50.00
Set, never hinged 80.00

Invention of the Voltaic Pile, 150th anniv.
For overprints see Trieste Nos. 53-54.

Holy Trinity Bridge — A289

1949, Sept. 19 Photo.
528 A289 20 l deep green 4.00 75
Never hinged 21.00

Issued to publicize plans to reconstruct Holy Trinity Bridge, Florence.
For overprint see Trieste No. 55.

Gaius Valerius Catullus A290

Domenico Cimarosa A291

1949, Sept. 19 Wmk. 277 *Perf. 14*
529 A290 20 l brt blue 3.00 75
Never hinged 16.00

2000th anniversary of the death of Gaius Valerius Catullus, Lyric poet.
For overprint see Trieste No. 57.

1949, Dec. 28
530 A291 20 l violet blk 3.00 75
Never hinged 13.00

Bicentenary of the birth of Domenico Cimarosa, composer.
For overprint see Trieste No. 57.

Milan Fair Scene A292

1950, Apr. 12 Photo.
531 A292 20 l brown 1.10 75
Never hinged 3.50

The 28th Milan Trade Fair.
For overprint see Trieste No. 70.

Flags and Italian Automobile A293

1950, Apr. 29
532 A293 20 l vio gray 2.75 70
Never hinged 12.00

32nd Intl. Auto Show, Turin, May 4-14, 1950.
For overprint see Trieste No. 71.

Pitti Palace, Florence A294

"Perseus" by Cellini — A295

Composite of Italian Cathedrals and Churches — A296

1950, May 22
533 A294 20 l olive grn 1.00 45
534 A295 55 l blue 15.00 2.00
Set, never hinged 75.00

5th General Conf. of UNESCO.
For overprints see Trieste Nos. 72-73.

1950, May 29
535 A296 20 l violet 1.25 28
536 A296 55 l blue 16.00 75
Set, never hinged 82.50

Holy Year, 1950.
For overprints see Trieste Nos. 74-75.

Gaudenzio Ferrari A297

Radio Mast and Tower of Florence A298

1950, July 1 Wmk. 277 *Perf. 14*
537 A297 20 l gray grn 3.00 1.00
Never hinged 17.00

Issued to honor Gaudenzio Ferrari.
For overprint see Trieste No. 76.

1950, July 15 Photo.
538 A298 20 l purple 4.25 4.00
539 A298 55 l blue 75.00 67.50
Set, never hinged 350.00

Intl. Shortwave Radio Conf., Florence, 1950.
For overprints Trieste see Nos. 77-78.

Ludovico A. Muratori A299

Guido d'Arezzo A300

1950, July 22
540 A299 20 l brown 1.40 75
Never hinged 8.25

200th anniv. of the death of Ludovico A. Muratori, writer.
For overprint see Trieste No. 79.

1950, July 29
541 A300 20 l dark green 3.00 75
Never hinged 19.00

900th anniv. of the death of Guido d'Arezzo, music teacher and composer.
For overprint see Trieste No. 80.

Tartan and Fair Buildings A301

1950, Aug. 21
542 A301 20 l chestnut brown 2.50 60
Never hinged 14.00

Levant Fair, Bari, September, 1950.
For overprint see Trieste No. 81.

G. Marzotto and A. Rossi — A302

Tobacco Plant — A303

1950, Sept. 11
543 A302 20 l indigo 30 18
Never hinged 85

Issued to honor the pioneers of the Italian wool industry.
For overprint see Trieste No. 84.

1950, Sept. 11

Designs: 20 l, Mature plant, different background. 55 l, Girl holding tobacco plant.

544 A303 5 l dp claret & grn 48 1.10
545 A303 20 l brown & grn 2.00 20
546 A303 55 l dp ultra & brn 27.50 7.25
Set, never hinged 75.00

Issued to publicize the European Tobacco Conference, Rome, 1950.
For overprints see Trieste Nos. 85-87.

Arms of the Academy of Fine Arts — A304

Augusto Righi — A305

1950, Sept. 16
547 A304 20 l ol brn & red brn 1.90 1.00
Never hinged 4.75

200th anniv. of the founding of the Academy of Fine Arts, Venice.
For overprint see Trieste No. 88.

1950, Sept. 16
548 A305 20 l cream & gray blk 1.40 1.00
Never hinged 3.25

Centenary of the birth of Augusto Righi, physicist.
For overprint see Trieste No. 89.

Blacksmith, Aosta Valley — A306

1851 Stamp of Tuscany — A307

Designs: 1 l, Auto mechanic. 2 l, Mason. 5 l, Potter. 6 l, Lace-making. 10 l, Weaving. 12 l, Sailor steering boat. 15 l, Shipbuilding. 20 l, Fisherman. 25 l, Sorting oranges. 30 l, Woman carrying grapes. 35 l, Olive picking. 40 l, Wine cart. 50 l, Shepherd and flock. 55 l, Plowing. 60 l, Grain cart. 65 l, Girl worker in hemp field. 100 l, Husking corn. 200 l, Woodcutter.

1950, Oct. 20 Wmk. 277 *Perf. 14*
549 A306 50c vio blue 15 15
550 A306 1 l dk bl vio 15 15
551 A306 2 l sepia 15 15
552 A306 5 l dk gray 15 15
553 A306 6 l chocolate 15 15
554 A306 10 l dp green 70 15
555 A306 12 l dp blue grn 20 15
556 A306 15 l dk gray bl 30 15
557 A306 20 l blue vio 1.50 15
558 A306 25 l brn org 80 15
559 A306 30 l magenta 30 15
560 A306 35 l crimson 90 15
561 A306 40 l brown 15 15
562 A306 50 l violet 1.75 15
563 A306 55 l dp blue 30 15
564 A306 60 l red 1.40 15
565 A306 65 l dk grn 22 15

Perf. 13x14, 14x13

Engr.

566 A306 100 l brn org 13.00 15
a. Perf. 13 14.00 15
b. Perf. 14 15.00 15

567 A306 200 l ol brn 3.25 38
a. Perf. 14 3.25 45
Nos. 549-567 (19) 25.52
Set value 1.60
Set, never hinged 115.00

See Nos. 668-673A. For overprints see Trieste Nos. 90-108, 122-124, 178-180.

1951, Mar. 27 Photo. *Perf. 14*

Design: 55 l, Tuscany 6cr.

568 A307 20 l red vio & red 1.00 85
569 A307 55 l ultra & blue 14.00 13.00
Set, never hinged 37.50

Centenary of Tuscany's first stamps.
For overprints see Trieste Nos. 109-110.

Italian Automobile A308

1951, Apr. 2
570 A308 20 l dk green 3.00 1.00
Never hinged 17.00

33rd Intl. Automobile Exhib., Turin, Apr. 4-15, 1951.
For overprint see Trieste No. 111.

Altar of Peace, Medea A309

1951, Apr. 11
571 A309 20 l blue vio 1.90 1.00
Never hinged 11.00

Consecration of the Altar of Peace at Redipuglia Cemetery, Medea.
For overprint see Trieste No. 112.

Helicopter over Leonardo da Vinci Heliport — A310

P. T. T. Building, Milan Fair — A311

1951, Apr. 12 Photo.
572 A310 20 l brown 2.00 70
573 A311 55 l dp blue 18.00 20.00
Set, never hinged 70.00

29th Milan Trade Fair.
For overprints see Trieste Nos. 113-114.

Symbols of the International Gymnastic Festival — A312

Statue of Diana, Spindle and Turin Tower — A313

Wmk. 277
1951, May 18 Photo. *Perf. 14*
Fleur-de-lis in Red

574 A312 5 l dk brown 12.00 *100.00*
575 A312 10 l Prus green 12.00 *100.00*
576 A312 15 l vio blue 12.00 *100.00*
Set, never hinged 75.00

International Gymnastic Festival and Meet, Florence, 1951.
Fake cancellations exist on Nos. 574-576.
For overprints see Trieste Nos. 115-117.

1951, Apr. 26
577 A313 20 l purple 3.75 1.40
Never hinged 27.50

Tenth International Exhibition of Textile Art and Fashion, Turin, May 2-16.
For overprint see Trieste No. 118.

Landing of Columbus A314

1951, May 5
578 A314 20 l Prus green 3.50 1.40
Never hinged 25.00

500th anniversary of birth of Columbus.
For overprint see Trieste No. 119.

Reconstructed Abbey of Montecassino A315

Design: 55 l, Montecassino Ruins.

1951, June 18
579 A315 20 l violet 1.10 70
580 A315 55 l brt blue 14.00 14.00
Set, never hinged 75.00

Issued to commemorate the reconstruction of the Abbey of Montecassino.
For overprints see Trieste Nos. 120-121.

Pietro Vannucci (Il Perugino) A316

Stylized Vase A317

Cartouche of Amenhotep III and Pitcher A318

1951, July 23
581 A316 20 l brn & red brn 1.40 1.50
Never hinged 4.50

500th anniversary (in 1950) of the birth of Pietro Vannucci, painter.
For overprint see Trieste No. 125.

1951, July 23
582 A317 20 l grnsh gray & blk 1.75 1.25
583 A318 55 l vio bl & pale sal 12.50 11.00
Set, never hinged 45.00

Triennial Art Exhibition, Milan, 1951.
For overprints see Trieste Nos. 126-127.

Cyclist — A319

1951, Aug. 23
584 A319 25 l gray blk 1.25 1.40
Never hinged 3.75

World Bicycle Championship Races, Milan, Aug.-Sept. 1951.
For overprint see Trieste No. 128.

Tartan and Globes A320

1951, Sept. 8 Photo.
585 A320 25 l deep blue 1.90 1.10
Never hinged 6.75

15th Levant Fair, Bari, September 1951.
For overprint see Trieste No. 129.

"La Figlia di Jorio" by Michetti A321

1951, Sept. 15 Wmk. 277 *Perf. 14*
586 A321 25 l dk brown 1.50 1.10
Never hinged 6.75

Centenary of the birth of Francesco Paolo Michetti, painter.
For overprint see Trieste No. 130.

Sardinia Stamps of 1851 — A322

1951, Oct. 5
587 A322 10 l shown 1.25 1.90
588 A322 25 l 20c stamp 1.65 1.40
589 A322 60 l 40c stamp 5.75 5.75
Set, never hinged 19.00

Centenary of Sardinia's 1st postage stamp.
For overprints see Trieste Nos. 131-133.

Mercury — A323

Roman Census A324

1951, Oct. 31
590 A323 10 l green 50 85
591 A324 25 l vio gray 1.00 70
Set, never hinged 4.25

3rd Industrial and the 9th General Italian Census.
For overprints see Trieste Nos. 134-135.

Winter Scene A325

Trees A326

1951, Nov. 21
592 A325 10 l ol & dl grn 60 95
593 A326 25 l dull grn 1.50 75
Set, never hinged 7.75

Issued to publicize the Festival of Trees.
For overprints see Trieste Nos. 136-137.

Giuseppe Verdi A327

Designs: Portraits of Verdi, various backgrounds.

1951, Nov. 19 Engr.
594 A327 10 l vio brn & dk grn 48 1.25
595 A327 25 l red brn & dk brn 2.50 85
596 A327 60 l dp grn & ind 5.50 4.25
Set, never hinged 37.50

50th anniversary of the death of Giuseppe Verdi, composer.
For overprints see Trieste Nos. 138-140.

Vincenzo Bellini — A328

Wmk. 277
1952, Jan. 28 Photo. *Perf. 14*
597 A328 25 l gray & gray blk 1.00 55
Never hinged 3.00

150th anniversary of the birth of Vincenzo Bellini, composer.
For overprint see Trieste No. 141.

Palace of Caserta and Statuary A329

1952, Feb. 1
598 A329 25 l dl grn & ol bis 1.00 50
Never hinged 3.75

Issued to honor Luigi Vanvitelli, architect.
For overprint see Trieste No. 142.

Statues of Athlete and River God Tiber — A330

1952, Mar. 22
599 A330 25 l brn & sl blk 32 45
Never hinged 1.10

Issued on the occasion of the first International Exhibition of Sports Stamps.
For overprint see Trieste No. 143.

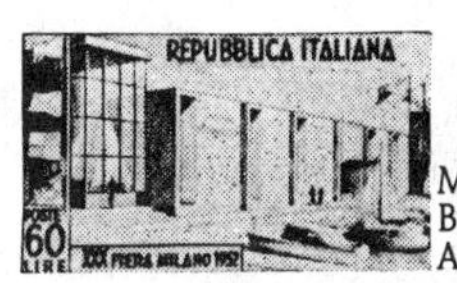

Milan Fair Buildings A331

1952, Apr. 12 **Engr.**

600 A331 60 l ultra 6.00 4.00

Never hinged 17.00

30th Milan Trade Fair.
For overprint see Trieste No. 144.

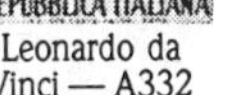

Leonardo da Vinci — A332

Virgin of the Rocks — A332a

1952 **Wmk. 277** **Photo.** ***Perf. 14***

601 A332 25 l deep orange 15 15

Unwmk.

Engr. ***Perf. 13***

601A A332a 60 l ultra 1.25 3.00

Wmk. 277

601B A332 80 l brn car 5.25 15

c. Perf. 14x13 4.25 38

Set, never hinged 30.00

500th anniv. of the birth of Leonardo da Vinci.
For overprints see Trieste Nos. 145, 163-164.

First Stamps and Cathedral Bell Towers of Modena and Parma A333

1952, May 29 ***Perf. 14***

602 A333 25 l blk & red brn 70 35

603 A333 60 l blk & ultra 3.50 3.75

Set, never hinged 10.00

Cent. of the 1st postage stamps of Modena and Parma.
For overprints see Trieste Nos. 146-147.

Globe and Torch — A334

Lion of St. Mark — A335

1952, June 7

604 A334 25 l bright blue 75 40

Never hinged 2.75

Issued to honor the Overseas Fair at Naples and Italian labor throughout the world.
For overprint see Trieste No. 148.

1952, June 14

605 A335 25 l black & yellow 50 40

Never hinged 1.65

26th Biennial Art Exhibition, Venice.
For overprint see Trieste No. 149.

"P" and Basilica of St. Anthony A336

Flag and Basilica of St. Just A337

1952, June 19

606 A336 25 l bl gray, red & dk bl 1.00 40

Never hinged 3.00

30th International Sample Fair of Padua.
For overprint see Trieste No. 150.

1952, June 28

607 A337 25 l dp grn, dk brn & red 65 38

Never hinged 1.90

4th International Sample Fair of Trieste.
For overprint see Trieste No. 151.

Fair Entrance and Tartan A338

1952, Sept. 6 **Wmk. 277** ***Perf. 14***

608 A338 25 l dark green 38 38

Never hinged 1.50

16th Levant Fair, Bari, Sept. 1952.
For overprint see Trieste No. 152.

Girolamo Savonarola A339

Mountain Peak and Climbing Equipment A340

1952, Sept. 20

609 A339 25 l purple 65 40

Never hinged 3.50

500th anniversary of the birth of Girolamo Savonarola.
For overprint see Trieste No. 153.

1952, Oct. 4

610 A340 25 l gray 38 28

Never hinged 80

Issued to publicize the National Exhibition of the Alpine troops, Oct. 4, 1952.
For overprint see Trieste No. 154.

Colosseum and Plane A341

1952, Sept. 29

611 A341 60 l vio bl & dk bl 9.25 5.50

Never hinged 20.00

Issued to publicize the first International Civil Aviation Conference, Rome, Sept. 1952.
For overprint see Trieste No. 155.

Guglielmo Cardinal Massaia and Map — A342

1952, Nov. 21 **Engr.** ***Perf. 13***

612 A342 25 l brn & dk brn 70 40

Never hinged 1.75

Centenary of the establishment of the first Catholic mission in Ethiopia.
For overprint see Trieste No. 156.

Symbols of Army, Navy and Air Force — A343

Sailor, Soldier and Aviator — A344

Design: 60 l, Boat, plane and tank.

1952, Nov. 3 **Photo.** ***Perf. 14***

613 A343 10 l dk green 15 15

614 A344 25 l blk & dk brn 40 15

615 A344 60 l black & blue 1.50 1.50

Set, never hinged 4.00

Armed Forces Day, Nov. 4, 1952.
For overprints see Trieste Nos. 157-159.

Antonio Mancini A345

Vincenzo Gemito A346

1952, Dec. 6

616 A345 25 l dark green 38 35

617 A346 25 l brown 38 28

Set, never hinged 2.00

Birth centenaries of Antonio Mancini, painter, and Vincenzo Gemito, sculptor.
For overprints see Trieste Nos. 160-161.

Martyrs, Jailer and Artist Boldini A347

1952, Dec. 31

618 A347 25 l gray blk & dk blue 1.00 45

Never hinged 1.75

Centenary of the deaths of the five Martyrs of Belfiore.
For overprint see Trieste No. 162.

Antonello da Messina — A349

1953, Feb. 21 **Photo.** ***Perf. 14***

621 A349 25 l car lake 85 38

Never hinged 2.00

Messina Exhibition of the paintings of Antonello and his 15th cent. contemporaries.
For overprint see Trieste No. 165.

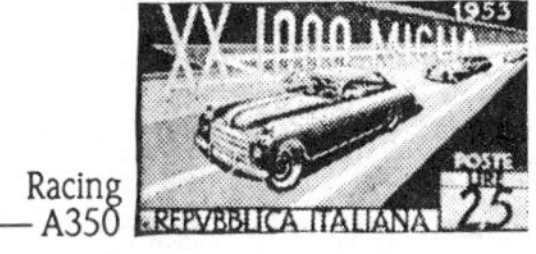

Racing Cars — A350

1953, Apr. 24

622 A350 25 l violet 85 30

Never hinged 1.40

20th 1,000-mile auto race.
For overprint see Trieste No. 166.

Decoration "Knights of Labor" Bee and Honeycomb — A351

Arcangelo Corelli — A352

1953, Apr. 30

623 A351 25 l violet 50 30

Never hinged 1.25

For overprint see Trieste No. 167.

1953, May 30

624 A352 25 l dark brown 38 30

Never hinged 1.25

300th anniv. of the birth of Arcangelo Corelli, composer.
For overprint see Trieste No. 168.

St. Clare of Assisi and Convent of St. Damien — A353

"Italia" after Syracusean Coin — A354

1953, June 27

625 A353 25 l brown & dull red 25 18

Never hinged 80

700th anniv. of the death of St. Clare of Assisi.
For overprint see Trieste No. 169.

1953-54 **Wmk. 277** ***Perf. 14***

Size: 17x21mm

626	A354	5 l gray	15	15
627	A354	10 l org ver	15	15
628	A354	12 l dull green	15	15
628A	A354	13 l brt lil rose ('54)	15	15
629	A354	20 l brown	85	15
630	A354	25 l purple	70	15
631	A354	35 l rose car	26	15
632	A354	60 l blue	2.25	15
633	A354	80 l orange brn	14.00	15
		Nos. 626-633 (9)	18.66	
		Set value		50
		Set, never hinged	85.00	

See Nos. 661-662, 673B-689, 785-788, 998A-998W, 1288-1295. For overprints see Trieste Nos. 170-177.

Mountain Peaks A355

Tyche, Goddess of Fortune A356

1953, July 11

634 A355 25 l blue green 75 18

Never hinged 1.90

Festival of the Mountain.
For overprint see Trieste No. 181.

1953, July 16

635	A356	25 l dark brown	35	15
636	A356	60 l deep blue	1.25	75
		Set, never hinged	5.75	

Issued to publicize the International Exposition of Agriculture, Rome, 1953.

For overprints see Trieste Nos. 182-183.

Continents Joined by Rainbow A357

1953, Aug. 6

637	A357	25 l org & Prus bl	2.75	15
638	A357	60 l lil rose & dk vio bl	6.00	1.40
		Set, never hinged	19.00	

4th anniversary of the signing of the North Atlantic Treaty.

For overprints see Trieste Nos. 184-185.

Luca Signorelli A358

Agostino Bassi A359

1953, Aug. 13

639	A358	25 l dk brn & dull grn	28	20
		Never hinged	70	

Issued to publicize the opening of an exhibition of the works of Luca Signorelli, painter.

For overprint see Trieste No. 186.

1953, Sept. 5

640	A359	25 l dk gray & brown	24	18
		Never hinged	80	

6th International Microbiology Congress, Rome, Sept. 6-12, 1953.

For overprint see Trieste No. 187.

Siena — A360 Rapallo — A361

Views: 20 l, Seaside at Gardone. 25 l, Mountain, Cortina d'Ampezzo. 35 l, Roman ruins, Taormina. 60 l, Rocks and sea, Capri.

1953, Dec. 31 ***Perf. 14***

641	A360	10 l dk brn & red brn	15	15
642	A361	12 l lt blue & gray	15	15
643	A361	20 l brn org & dk brn	15	15
644	A360	25 l dk grn & pale bl	15	15
645	A361	35 l cream & brn	28	18
646	A361	60 l bl grn & ind	48	32
		Set value	1.05	75
		Set, never hinged	7.50	

For overprints see Trieste Nos. 188-193, 204-205.

The values of never-hinged stamps in superb condition are greater than catalogue value.

Lateran Palace, Rome — A362

Television Screen and Aerial — A363

1954, Feb. 11

647	A362	25 l dk brown & choc	24	15
648	A362	60 l blue & ultra	1.00	1.00
		Set, never hinged	4.25	

25th anniv. of the signing of the Lateran Pacts.

For overprints see Trieste Nos. 194-195.

1954, Feb. 25

649	A363	25 l purple	50	15
650	A363	60 l dp blue grn	2.00	1.75
		Set, never hinged	8.50	

Introduction of regular natl. television service.

For overprints see Trieste Nos. 196-197.

"Italia" and Quotation from Constitution A364

194, Mar. 20

651	A364	25 l purple	70	15
		Never hinged	2.00	

Propaganda for the payment of taxes.

For overprint see Trieste No. 198.

Vertical Flight Trophy A365

Eagle Perched on Ruins A366

1954, Apr. 24

652	A365	25 l gray black	50	50
		Never hinged	1.00	

Issued to publicize the experimental transportation of mail by helicopter, April 1954.

For overprint see Trieste No. 199.

1954, June 1

653	A366	25 l gray, org brn & blk	18	18
		Never hinged	50	

10th anniv. of Italy's resistance movement.

For overprint see Trieste No. 200.

Alfredo Catalani, Composer, Birth Centenary — A367

1954, June 19 ***Perf. 14***

654	A367	25 l dk grnsh gray	15	15
		Never hinged	38	

For overprint see Trieste No. 201.

Marco Polo, Lion of St. Mark and Dragon A368

1954, July 8 **Engr.** ***Perf. 14***

655	A368	25 l red brown	24	15

Perf. 13

656	A368	60 l gray green	1.50	1.75
a.		Perf. 13x12	7.50	4.00
		Set, never hinged	4.25	

700th anniv. of the birth of Marco Polo.

For overprints see Trieste Nos. 202-203.

Automobile and Cyclist A369

1954, Sept. 6 **Photo.** ***Perf. 14***

657	A369	25 l dp green & red	18	15
		Never hinged	50	

60th anniv. of the founding of the Italian Touring Club.

For overprint see Trieste No. 206.

St. Michael Overpowering the Devil A370

Pinocchio and Group of Children A371

1954, Oct. 9

658	A370	25 l rose red	28	15
659	A370	60 l blue	85	1.10
		Set, never hinged	2.00	

23rd general assembly of the International Criminal Police, Rome 1954.

For overprints see Trieste Nos. 207-208.

1954, Oct. 26

660	A371	25 l rose red	15	15
		Never hinged	60	

Carlo Lorenzini, creator of Pinocchio.

Italia Type of 1953-54

1954, Dec. 28 **Engr.** ***Perf. 13***

Size: 22½x27½mm

661	A354	100 l brown	26.00	15
662	A354	200 l dp blue	4.75	20
		Set, never hinged	150.00	

Madonna, Perugino A372

Amerigo Vespucci and Map A373

Design: 60 l, Madonna of the Pieta, Michelangelo.

1954, Dec. 31 **Photo.** ***Perf. 14***

663	A372	25 l brown & bister	22	15
664	A372	60 l black & cream	70	1.10
		Set, never hinged	2.00	

Issued to mark the end of the Marian Year.

1954, Dec. 31 **Engr.** ***Perf. 13***

665	A373	25 l dp plum	24	15
a.		Perf. 13x14	2.25	50
666	A373	60 l blue blk	85	1.10
a.		Perf. 13x14	45	1.10
		Set, never hinged	3.75	

500th anniv. of the birth of Amerigo Vespucci, explorer, 1454-1512.

Silvio Pellico (1789-1854), Dramatist — A374

Wmk. 277

1955, Jan. 24 **Photo.** ***Perf. 14***

667	A374	25 l brt blue & vio	28	15
		Never hinged	40	

Italy at Work Type of 1950

1955-57 **Wmk. 303**

668	A306	50c vio bl	15	15
669	A306	1 l dk bl vio	15	15
670	A306	2 l sepia	15	15
671	A306	15 l dk gray bl	22	15
672	A306	30 l magenta	15.00	25
673	A306	50 l violet	9.50	15
673A	A306	65 l dk grn ('57)	5.50	18.00
		Nos. 668-673A (7)	30.67	19.00
		Set, never hinged	140.00	

Italia Type of 1953-54 and

St. George, by Donatello — A374a

1955-58 **Wmk. 303** **Photo.** ***Perf. 14***

Size: 17x21mm

673B	A354	1 l gray ('58)	15	15
674	A354	5 l slate	15	15
675	A354	6 l ocher ('57)	15	15
676	A354	10 l org ver	15	15
677	A354	12 l dull green	15	15
678	A354	13 l brt lil rose	15	15
679	A354	15 l gray vio ('56)	15	15
680	A354	20 l brown	15	15
681	A354	25 l purple	15	15
682	A354	35 l rose car	15	15
683	A354	50 l olive ('58)	22	15
685	A354	60 l blue	15	15
686	A354	80 l brown org	15	15
687	A354	90 l lt red brn ('58)	15	15

Engr. ***Perf. 13½***

Size: 22½x28mm

688	A354	100 l brn ('56)	3.00	15
a.		Perf. 13½x12	3.00	18
b.		Perf. 13½x14	300.00	15.00
689	A354	200 l gray bl ('57)	3.00	15
690	A374a	500 l grn ('57)	75	15
b.		Perf. 14x13½	60	15
690A	A374a	1000 l rose car ('57)	95	15
c.		Perf. 14x13½	1.25	15
		Set value, #673B-690A	8.75	1.00
		Set, never hinged	37.50	

Nos. 690-690A were printed on ordinary and fluorescent paper.

See Nos. 785-788. See Nos. 998A-998W for small-size set.

Catalogue values for unused stamps in this section, from this point to the end of the section, are for Never Hinged items.

"Italia"
A375

Oil Derrick and Old Roman Aqueduct
A376

1955, Mar. 15 **Photo.** ***Perf. 14***
691 A375 25 l rose vio 2.00 15

Issued as propaganda for the payment of taxes.

1955, June 6

Design: 60 l, Marble columns and oil field on globe.

692 A376 25 l olive green 50 15
693 A376 60 l henna brown 1.10 1.25

Issued to publicize the fourth World Petroleum Congress, Rome, June 6-15, 1955.

Antonio Rosmini, Philosopher, Death Centenary
A377

1955, July 1 **Wmk. 303** ***Perf. 14***
694 A377 25 l sepia 75 15

Girolamo Fracastoro and Stadium at Verona
A378

1955, Sept. 1
695 A378 25 l gray blk & brn 70 15

International Medical Congress, Verona, Sept. 1-4.

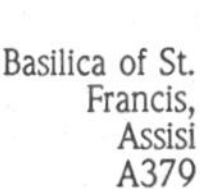

Basilica of St. Francis, Assisi
A379

1955, Oct. 4
696 A379 25 l black & cream 40 15

Issued in honor of St. Francis and to commemorate the 7th centenary (in 1953) of the Basilica in Assisi.

Young Man at Drawing Board — A380

1955, Oct. 15
697 A380 25 l Prus green 40 15

Centenary of technical education in Italy.

Harvester — A381

FAO Headquarters, Rome — A382

1955, Nov. 3
698 A381 25 l rose red & brn 30 15
699 A382 60 l blk & brt pur 1.25 75

50th anniv. of the Intl. Institute of Agriculture and 10th anniv. of the FAO, successor to the Institute.

Giacomo Matteotti
A383

Battista Grassi
A384

1955, Nov. 10
700 A383 25 l rose brown 1.10 15

70th anniversary of the birth of Giacomo Matteotti, Italian socialist leader.

1955, Nov. 19
701 A384 25 l dark green 55 15

30th anniv. of the death of Battista Grassi, zoologist.

"St. Stephen Giving Alms" — A385

"St. Lorenzo Giving Alms"
A386

1955, Nov. 26
702 A385 10 l black & cream 15 18
703 A386 25 l ultra & cream 45 15

Issued to commemorate the 500th anniversary of the death of Fra Angelico, painter.

Giovanni Pascoli
A387

1955, Dec. 31
704 A387 25 l gray black 50 15

Centenary of the birth of Giovanni Pascoli, poet.

Ski Jump "Italia"
A388

Stadiums at Cortina: 12 l, Skiing. 25 l, Ice skating. 60 l, Ice racing, Lake Misurina.

1956, Jan. 26 **Photo.**
705 A388 10 l blue grn & org 15 15
706 A388 12 l yellow & blk 15 20
707 A388 25 l vio blk & org brn 30 15
708 A388 60 l sapphire & org 1.50 1.00

VII Winter Olympic Games at Cortina d'Ampezzo, Jan. 26-Feb. 5, 1956.

Mail Coach and Tunnel Exit — A389

1956, May 19 **Wmk. 303** ***Perf. 14***
709 A389 25 l dk blue grn 1.75 15

50th anniv. of the Simplon Tunnel.

Arms of Republic and Symbols of Industry
A390

1956, June 2
710 A390 10 l gray & slate bl 18 15
711 A390 25 l pink & rose red 30 15
712 A390 60 l lt bl & brt bl 1.90 1.40
713 A390 80 l orange & brn 4.75 15

Tenth anniversary of the Republic.

Amedeo Avogadro
A391

1956, Sept. 8
714 A391 25 l black vio 30 15

Centenary of the death of Amedeo Avogadro, physicist.

Europa Issue

"Rebuilding Europe" — A392

1956, Sept. 15
715 A392 25 l dark green 90 15
716 A392 60 l blue 8.00 32
Set value 38

Issued to symbolize the cooperation among the six countries comprising the Coal and Steel Community.

Globe and Satellites
A393

1956, Sept. 22
717 A393 25 l intense blue 30 15

7th International Astronautical Congress, Rome, Sept. 17-22.

Globe — A394

1956, Dec. 29 **Litho.** **Unwmk.**
718 A394 25 l red & bl grn, *pink* 15 15
719 A394 60 l bl grn & red, *pale bl grn* 48 18
Set value 22

Italy's admission to the United Nations.
The design, viewed through red and green glasses, becomes three-dimensional.

Postal Savings Bank and Notes — A395

1956, Dec. 31 **Photo.** **Wmk. 303**
720 A395 25 l sl bl & dp ultra 20 15

80th anniversary of Postal Savings.

Ovid
A396

Antonio Canova
A397

Paulina Borghese as Venus
A398

1957, June 10 ***Perf. 14***
721 A396 25 l ol grn & blk 18 15

2000th anniversary of the birth of the poet Ovid (Publius Ovidius Naso).

1957, July 15 **Engr.**

Design: 60 l, Sculpture: Hercules and Lichas.

722 A397 25 l brown 15 15
723 A397 60 l gray 24 55
724 A398 80 l vio blue 24 15
Set value 72

Bicentenary of the birth of Antonio Canova, sculptor.

Traffic Light — A399

"United Europe" — A400

Wmk. 303
1957, Aug. 7 **Photo.** ***Perf. 14***
725 A399 25 l green, blk & red 20 15

Campaign for careful driving.

1957, Sept. 16 Litho. *Perf. 14*
Flags in Original Colors

726 A400 25 l light blue 15 15

Perf. 13

727 A400 60 l violet blue 1.40 15
Set value 17

Issued to publicize a united Europe for peace and prosperity.

Giosue Carducci
A401

Filippino Lippi
A402

1957, Oct. 14 Engr. *Perf. 14*

728 A401 25 l brown 20 15

50th anniv. of the death of the poet Giosue Carducci.

1957, Nov. 25 Wmk. 303 *Perf. 14*

729 A402 25 l redsh brown 20 15

500th anniv. of the birth of Filippino Lippi, painter.

2000th Anniv. of the Death of Marcus Tullius Cicero, Roman Statesman and Writer — A403

1957, Nov. 30 Photo.

730 A403 25 l brown red 20 15

St. Domenico Savio and Students of Various Races
A404

1957, Dec. 14

731 A404 15 l brt lil & blk 18 15

Cent. of the death of St. Domenico Savio.

St. Francis of Paola — A405

Giuseppe Garibaldi — A406

1957, Dec. 21 Engr.

732 A405 25 l black 25 15

450th anniv. of the death of St. Francis of Paola, patron saint of seafaring men.

1957, Dec. 14 *Perf. 14x13, 13x14*

Design: 110 l, Garibaldi monument, horiz.

733 A406 15 l slate green 15 15
734 A406 110 l dull purple 38 15
Set value 20

150th anniv. of the birth of Giuseppe Garibaldi.

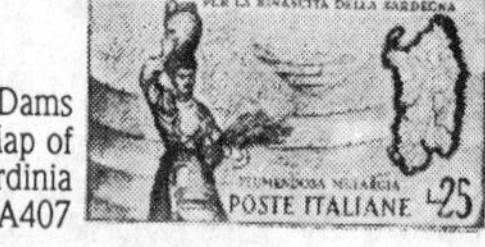

Peasant, Dams and Map of Sardinia
A407

1958, Feb. 1 Engr. *Perf. 14*

738 A407 25 l bluish grn 15 15

Issued to commemorate the completion of the Flumendosa-Mulargia irrigation system.

Immaculate Conception Statue, Rome, and Lourdes Basilica — A408

1958, Apr. 16 Wmk. 303 *Perf. 14*

739 A408 15 l rose claret 15 15
740 A408 60 l blue 15 15
Set value 15

Centenary of the apparition of the Virgin Mary at Lourdes.

Book and Symbols of Labor Industry and Agriculture — A409

Designs: 60 l, "Tree of Freedom," vert. 110 l, Montecitorio Palace.

1958, May 9 Photo. *Perf. 14*

741 A409 25 l bl grn & ocher 15 15
742 A409 60 l blk brn & bl 15 15
743 A409 110 l ol bis & blk brn 35 15
Set value 56 25

10th anniversary of the constitution.

Brussels Fair Emblem
A410

Prologue from Pagliacci
A411

1958, June 12

744 A410 60 l blue & yellow 15 15

Issued for the International and Universal Exposition at Brussels.

1958, July 10

745 A411 25 l dk bl & dk red 15 15

Issued to commemorate the centenary of the birth of Ruggiero Leoncavallo, composer.

Scene from La Bohème
A412

1958, July 10 Engr. Unwmk.

746 A412 25 l dark blue 15 15

Centenary of the birth of Giacomo Puccini, composer.

Giovanni Fattori, Self-portrait
A413

"Ave Maria on the Lake" by Giovanni Segantini
A414

1958, Aug. 7 Wmk. 303 *Perf. 13x14*

747 A413 110 l redsh brown 35 15

50th anniv. of the death of Giovanni Fattori, painter.

1958, Aug. 7 *Perf. 14*

748 A414 110 l slate, *buff* 15 18

Issued to commemorate the centenary of the birth of Giovanni Segantini, painter.

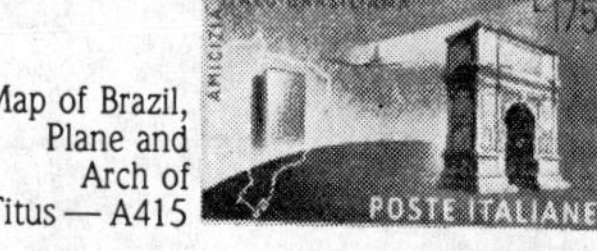

Map of Brazil, Plane and Arch of Titus — A415

1958, Aug. 23 Photo. *Perf. 14*

749 A415 175 l Prus green 60 1.25

Italo-Brazilian friendship on the occasion of Pres. Giovanni Gronchi's visit to Brazil.

Europa Issue, 1958
Common Design Type

1958, Sept. 13
Size: 20½x35½mm

750 CD1 25 l red & blue 15 15
751 CD1 60 l blue & red 15 18
Set value 20

Issued to show the European Postal Union at the service of European integration.

½g Stamp of Naples
A416

Evangelista Torricelli
A417

Design: 60 l, 1g Stamp of Naples.

Perf. 14x13½, 13½

1958, Oct. 4 Engr. Unwmk.

752 A416 25 l brown red 15 15
753 A416 60 l blk & red brn 15 15
Set value 21 17

Centenary of the stamps of Naples.

1958, Oct. 20 Wmk. 303 *Perf. 14*

754 A417 25 l rose claret 40 28

350th anniv. of the birth of Evangelista Torricelli, mathematician and physicist.

"The Triumph of Caesar," Montegna — A418

Persian Style Bas-relief, Sorrento — A419

Designs: 25 l, Coats of Arms of Trieste, Rome and Trento, horiz. 60 l, War memorial bell of Rovereto.

1958, Nov. 3 Engr. *Perf. 14x13½*

755 A418 15 l green 15 15
756 A418 25 l gray 15 15
757 A418 60 l rose claret 18 20
Set value 32 30

40th anniv. of Italy's victory in World War I.

1958, Nov. 27 Photo.

758 A419 25 l sepia, *bluish* 16 15
759 A419 60 l vio bl, *bluish* 45 60
Set value 65

Visit of the Shah of Iran to Italy.

Eleonora Duse — A420

Dancers and Antenna — A421

Unwmk.

1958, Dec. 11 Engr. *Perf. 14*

760 A420 25 l brt ultra 15 15

Issued to commemorate the centenary of the birth of Eleonora Duse, actress.

1958, Dec. 29 Photo. Wmk. 303

Design: 60 l, Piano, dove and antenna.

761 A421 25 l red, bl & blk 15 15
762 A421 60 l ultra & blk 15 15
Set value 20 20

10th anniv. of the Prix Italia (International Radio and Television Competitions).

Stamp of Sicily — A422

Design: 60 l, Stamp of Sicily, 5g.

Perf. 14x13½

1959, Jan. 2 Engr. Unwmk.

763 A422 25 l Prus green 15 15
764 A422 60 l dp orange 15 15
Set value 18 15

Centenary of the stamps of Sicily.

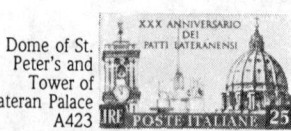

Dome of St. Peter's and Tower of Lateran Palace
A423

Wmk. 303

1959, Feb. 11 **Photo.** ***Perf. 14***

765	A423	25 l ultra	15	15

30th anniversary of the Lateran Pacts.

Common Design Types pictured in section at front of book.

Map of North Atlantic and NATO Emblem A424

1959, Apr. 4

766	A424	25 l dk bl & ocher	15	15
767	A424	60 l dk bl & green	18	22
		Set value	26	28

10th anniv. of NATO.

Arms of Paris and Rome A425

1959, Apr. 9

768	A425	15 l blue & red	15	15
769	A425	25 l blue & red	15	15
		Set value	16	17

Issued to publicize the cultural ties between Rome and Paris.

"A Gentle Peace Has Come" A426

Statue of Lord Byron A427

1959, Apr. 13 **Engr.** **Unwmk.**

770	A426	25 l olive green	15	15

International War Veterans Association convention, Rome.

1959, Apr. 21

771	A427	15 l black	15	15

Unveiling in Rome of a statue of Lord Byron by Bertel Thorvaldson, Danish sculptor.

Camillo Prampolini — A428

1959, Apr. 27 **Unwmk.** ***Perf. 14***

772	A428	15 l car rose	1.65	15

Camillo Prampolini, socialist leader and reformer, birth centenary.

Fountain of Dioscuri and Olympic Rings — A429

Baths of Carcalla A430

Designs: 25 l, Capitoline tower. 60 l, Arch of Constantine. 110 l, Ruins of Basilica of Massentius.

1959, June 23 **Photo.** **Wmk. 303**

Designs in Dark Sepia

773	A429	15 l red orange	15	15
774	A429	25 l blue	15	15
775	A430	35 l bister	15	15
776	A430	60 l rose lilac	22	18
777	A430	110 l yellow	25	15
		Set value	75	48

1960 Olympic Games in Rome.

Victor Emanuel II, Garibaldi, Cavour, Mazzini A431

Battle of San Fermo A432

Designs: 25 l, "After the Battle of Magenta" by Fattori and Red Cross, vert. 60 l, Battle of Palestro. 110 l, "Battle of Magenta" by Induno, vert.

Engr., Cross Photo. on 25 l

1959, June 27 **Unwmk.**

778	A431	15 l gray	15	15
779	A431	25 l brn & red	15	15
780	A432	35 l dk violet	15	15
781	A432	60 l ultra	15	15
782	A432	110 l magenta	15	15
		Set value	32	30

Cent. of the war of independence. No. 779 for the centenary of the Red Cross idea.

Labor Monument, Geneva A433

Stamp of Romagna A434

1959, July 20 ***Perf. 14x13, 14***

783	A433	25 l violet	15	15
784	A433	60 l brown	15	15
		Set value	20	16

40th anniv. of the ILO.

Italia Type of 1953-54

Photo.; Engr. (100 l, 200 l)

1959-66 **Wmk. 303** ***Perf. 14***

Size: 17x21mm

785	A354	30 l bis brn ('60)	38	15
786	A354	40 l lil rose ('60)	1.65	15
786A	A354	70 l Prus grn ('60)	48	15
787	A354	100 l brown	60	15
787A	A354	130 l gray & dl red ('66)	30	15
788	A354	200 l dp blue	60	15
		Nos. 785-788 (6)	4.01	
		Set value		30

1959, Sept. 1 **Photo.**

Design: 60 l, Stamp of Romagna, 20b.

789	A434	25 l pale brn & blk	15	15
790	A434	60 l gray grn & blk	15	15
		Set value	22	17

Centenary of the stamps of Romagna.

Europa Issue, 1959

Common Design Type

1959, Sept. 19

Size: 22x27½mm

791	CD2	25 l olive green	15	15
792	CD2	60 l blue	22	15
		Set value		21

Stamp of 1953 with Facsimile Cancellation A435

Aeneas Fleeing with Father and Son, by Raphael A436

1959, Dec. 20 **Wmk. 303** ***Perf. 14***

793	A435	15 l gray, rose car & blk	15	15

Italy's first Stamp Day, Dec. 20, 1959.

1960, Apr. 7 **Engr.** **Unwmk.**

794	A436	25 l lake	15	15
795	A436	60 l gray violet	15	15
		Set value	25	21

Issued to publicize World Refugee Year, July 1, 1959-June 30, 1960. Design is detail from "The Fire in the Borgo."

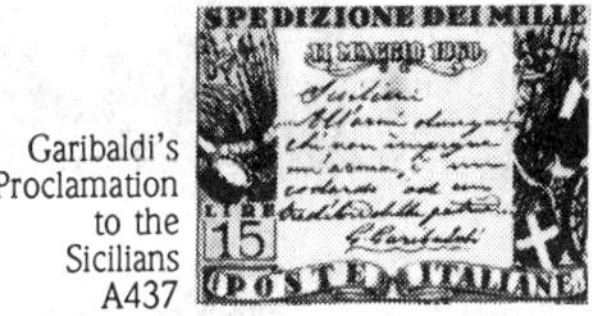

Garibaldi's Proclamation to the Sicilians A437

King Victor Emmanuel and Garibaldi Meeting at Teano — A438

Design: 60 l, Volunteers embarking, Quarto, Genoa.

Wmk. 303

1960, May 5 **Photo.** ***Perf. 14***

796	A437	15 l brown	15	15

Perf. 13x14, 14x13

Engr. **Unwmk.**

797	A438	25 l rose claret	15	15
798	A437	60 l ultramarine	15	15
		Set value	22	20

Cent. of the liberation of Southern Italy (Kingdom of the Two Sicilies) by Garibaldi.

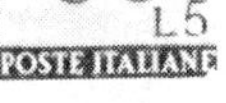

Emblem of 17th Olympic Games — A439

Olympic Stadium A440

Statues: 15 l, Roman Consul on way to the games. 35 l, Myron's Discobolus. 110 l, Seated boxer. 200 l, Apoxyomenos by Lysippus.

Stadia: 25 l, Velodrome. 60 l, Sports palace. 150 l, Small sports palace.

Perf. 14x13½, 13½x14

Photogravure, Engraved

1960 **Wmk. 303, Unwmk.**

799	A439	5 l yellow brn	15	15
800	A440	10 l dp org & dk bl	15	15
801	A439	15 l ultra	15	15
802	A440	25 l lt vio & brn	15	15
803	A439	35 l rose cl	15	15
804	A440	60 l bluish grn & brn	15	15
805	A439	110 l plum	15	15
806	A440	150 l blue & brn	55	55
807	A439	200 l green	22	15
		Set value	1.40	1.00

17th Olympic Games, Rome, Aug. 25-Sept. 11.

The photo. denominations (5, 10, 25, 60, 150-lire) are wmkd.; the engraved (15, 35, 110, 200-lire) are unwmkd.

Bottego Statue, Parma — A441

Michelangelo da Caravaggio — A442

1960 **Unwmk.** **Engr.** ***Perf. 14***

808	A441	30 l brown	15	15

Centenary of the birth of Vittorio Bottego, explorer.

Europa Issue, 1960

Common Design Type

1960 **Photo.** **Wmk. 303**

Size: 37x27mm

809	CD3	30 l dk grn & bis brn	15	15
810	CD3	70 l dk bl & salmon	15	15
		Set value	22	15

1960 **Unwmk.** **Engr.** ***Perf. 13x13½***

811	A442	25 l orange brn	15	15

350th anniv. of the death of Michelangelo da Caravaggio (Merisi), painter.

Mail Coach and Post Horn — A443

1960 **Wmk. 303** **Photo.** ***Perf. 14***

812	A443	15 l blk brn & org brn	15	15

Issued for Stamp Day, Dec. 20.

Slave, by Michelangelo — A444

Designs from Sistine Chapel by Michelangelo: 5 l, 10 l, 115 l, 150 l, Heads of various "slaves." 15 l, Joel. 20 l, Libyan Sybil. 25 l, Isaiah. 30 l, Eritrean Sybil. 40 l, Daniel. 50 l, Delphic Sybil. 55 l, Cumaean Sybil. 70 l, Zachariah. 85 l, Jonah. 90 l, Jeremiah. 100 l, Ezekiel. 200 l, Self-portrait. 500 l, Adam. 1000 l, Eve.

Wmk. 303

1961, Mar. 6 Photo. *Perf. 14*

Size: 17x21mm

813 A444 1 l gray 15 15
814 A444 5 l brown org 15 15
815 A444 10 l red org 15 15
816 A444 15 l brt lil 15 15
817 A444 20 l Prus grn 15 15
818 A444 25 l brown 30 15
819 A444 30 l purple 15 15
820 A444 40 l rose red 15 15
821 A444 50 l olive 42 15
822 A444 55 l red brn 15 15
823 A444 70 l blue 16 15
824 A444 85 l slate grn 18 15
825 A444 90 l lil rose 40 15
826 A444 100 l vio gray 55 15
827 A444 115 l ultra 25 15

Engr.

828 A444 150 l chocolate 55 15
829 A444 200 l dark blue 1.65 15
a. Perf. 13½ 1.65 15

Perf. 13½

Size: 22x27mm

830 A444 500 l blue grn 1.00 15
831 A444 1000 l brown red 1.10 52
Nos. 813-831 (19) 7.76
Set value 1.50

Map Showing Flight from Italy to Argentina
A445

Designs: 185 l, Italy to Uruguay. 205 l, Italy to Peru.

1961, Apr. Photo. *Perf. 14*

832 A445 170 l ultra 4.50 4.50
833 A445 185 l dull green 4.50 4.50
834 A445 205 l violet blk 9.00 9.00
a. 205 l rose lilac 1,500.

Issued to commemorate the visit of President Gronchi to South America, April 1961.

Nos. 832-833 and 834a were issued Apr. 4, to become valid on Apr. 6. The map of Peru on No. 834a was drawn incorrectly and the stamp was therefore withdrawn on Apr. 4. A corrected design in new color (No. 834) was issued Apr. 6. Forgeries of No. 834a exist.

Statue of Pliny, Como Cathedral
A446

Ippolito Nievo (1831-61), Writer
A447

1961, May 27

835 A446 30 l brown 15 15

1900th anniversary of the birth of Pliny the Younger, Roman consul and writer.

1961, June 8 Wmk. 303 *Perf. 14*

836 A447 30 l multi 15 15

St. Paul Aboard Ship — A448

1961, June 28

837 A448 30 l multi 15 15
838 A448 70 l multi 32 40

1,900th anniversary of St. Paul's arrival in Rome. The design is after a miniature from the Bible of Borso D'Este.

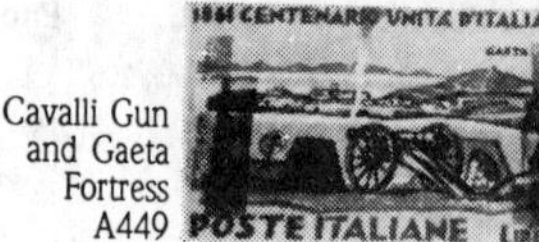

Cavalli Gun and Gaeta Fortress
A449

Cent. of Italian unity: 30 l, Carignano palace, Turin. 40 l, Montecitorio palace, Rome. 70 l, Palazzo Vecchio, Florence. 115 l, Villa Madama, Rome. 300 l, Steel construction, Italia '61 Exhibition, Turin.

1961, Aug. 12 Photo.

839 A449 15 l dk bl & redsh brn 15 15
840 A449 30 l dk bl & red brn 15 15
841 A449 40 l bl & brn 24 24
842 A449 70 l brn & pink 35 15
843 A449 115 l org brn & dk bl 1.25 15
844 A449 300 l brt grn & red 3.75 4.00
Nos. 839-844 (6) 5.89 4.84

Europa Issue, 1961

Common Design Type

1961, Sept. 18 Wmk. 303 *Perf. 14*

Size: 36½x21mm

845 CD4 30 l carmine 15 15
846 CD4 70 l yel grn 15 15
Set value 16 15

Giandomenico Romagnosi — A450

Perf. 13½

1961, Nov. 28 Unwmk. Engr.

847 A450 30 l green 15 15

Bicentenary of the birth of Giandomenico Romagnosi, jurist and philosopher.

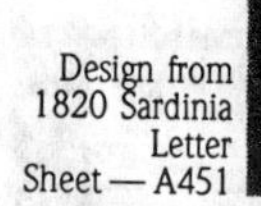

Design from 1820 Sardinia Letter Sheet — A451

Wmk. 303

1961, Dec. 3 Photo. *Perf. 14*

848 A451 15 l lil rose & blk 15 15

Issued for Stamp Day 1961.

Family Scene "I am the Lamp that Glows so Gently . . ."
A452

1962, Apr. 6 Wmk. 303 *Perf. 14*

849 A452 30 l red 15 15
850 A452 70 l blue 24 30

Issued to commemorate the 50th anniversary of the death of Giovanni Pascoli, poet.

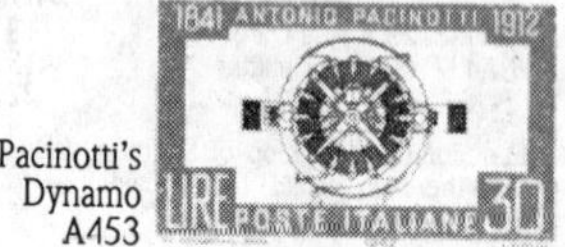

Pacinotti's Dynamo
A453

1962, June 12

851 A453 30 l rose & blk 15 15
852 A453 70 l ultra & blk 24 30

Antonio Pacinotti (1841-1912), physicist and inventor of the ring winding dynamo.

St. Catherine of Siena, by Andrea Vanni — A454

Lion of St. Mark — A455

Design: 70 l, St. Catherine, 15th century woodcut.

1962, June 26 Photo.

853 A454 30 l black 15 15

Engraved and Photogravure

854 A454 70 l red & blk 24 40

500th anniversary of the canonization of St. Catherine of Siena, Patroness of Italy.

1962, Aug. 25 Photo.

Design: 30 l, Stylized camera eye.

855 A455 30 l bl & blk 20 15
856 A455 70 l red org & blk 20 24
Set value 32

Issued to mark the 30th anniversary of the International Film Festival in Venice.

Motorcyclist and Bicyclist
A456

Designs: 70 l, Group of cyclists. 300 l, Bicyclist.

1962, Aug. 30

857 A456 30 l grn & blk 35 15
858 A456 70 l bl & blk 15 15
859 A456 300 l dp org & blk 2.25 2.50

World Bicycle Championship Races.

Europa Issue, 1962

Common Design Type

1962, Sept. 17

Size: 37x21mm

860 CD5 30 l carmine 55 15
861 CD5 70 l blue 55 28

Swiss and Italian Flags, Eugenio and Angela Lina Balzan Medal
A457

1962, Oct. 25 Wmk. 303 *Perf. 14*

862 A457 70 l rose red, grn & brn 30 15

1st distribution of the Balzan Prize by the International Balzan Foundation for Italian-Swiss Cooperation.

Malaria Eradication Emblem
A458

Stamps of 1862 and 1961
A459

1962, Oct. 31 Photo.

863 A458 30 l light violet 15 15
864 A458 70 l light blue 24 30

WHO drive to eradicate malaria.

1962, Dec. 2

865 A459 15 l pur, buff & bis 15 15

Issued for Stamp Day and to commemorate the centenary of Italian postage stamps.

A460

A461

Design: Holy Spirit Descending on Apostles.

1962, Dec. 8

866 A460 30 l org & dk bl grn, *buff* 15 15
867 A460 70 l dk bl grn & org, *buff* 15 18
Set value 25 26

21st Ecumenical Council of the Roman Catholic Church, Vatican II. The design is an illumination from the Codex Syriacus.

1962, Dec. 10 Engr. Unwmk.

Design: Statue of Count Camillo Bensi di Cavour.

868 A461 30 l dk grn 15 15

Centenary of Court of Accounts.

Count Giovanni Pico della Mirandola
A462

Gabriele D'Annunzio
A463

Wmk. 303

1963, Feb. 25 Photo. *Perf. 14*

869 A462 30 l gray blk 15 15

Mirandola (1463-94), Renaissance scholar.

1963, Mar. 12 Engr. Unwmk.

870 A463 30 l dk grn 15 15

Issued to commemorate the centenary of the birth of Gabriele d'Annunzio, author and soldier.

Sower — A464

Design: 70 l, Harvester typing sheaf, sculpture from Maggiore Fountain, Perugia.

1963, Mar. 21 Photo. Wmk. 303

871 A464 30 l rose car & brn 15 15
872 A464 70 l bl & brn 30 30
Set value 38

FAO "Freedom from Hunger" campaign.

Mt. Viso, Alpine Club Emblem, Ax and Rope — A465

Map of Italy and "INA" Initials — A466

1963, Mar. 30 Wmk. 303 *Perf. 14*

873 A465 115 l dk brn & brt bl	15	15

Issued to commemorate the centenary of the founding of the Italian Alpine Club.

1963, Apr. 4

874 A466 30 l grn & blk	15	15

50th anniv. of the Natl. Insurance Institute.

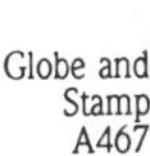

Globe and Stamp A467

1963, May 7 Photo. *Perf. 14*

875 A467 70 l bl & grn	15	15

Cent. of the 1st Intl. Postal Conf., Paris, 1863.

Crosses and Centenary Emblem on Globe — A468

1963, June 8 Wmk. 303 *Perf. 14*

876 A468 30 l dk gray & red	15	15
877 A468 70 l dl bl & red	22	30

Issued to commemorate the centenary of the founding of the International Red Cross.

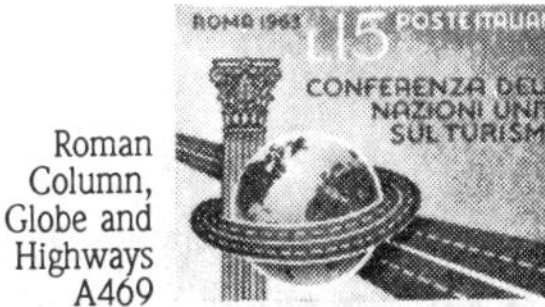
Roman Column, Globe and Highways A469

1963, Aug. 21 Wmk. 303 *Perf. 14*

878 A469 15 l gray ol & dk bl	15	15
879 A469 70 l dl bl & brn	15	24
Set value	22	28

UN Tourist Conf., Rome, Aug. 21-Sept. 5.

Europa Issue, 1963

Common Design Type

1963, Sept. 16

Size: 27½x23mm

880 CD6 30 l rose & brn	15	15
881 CD6 70 l brn & grn	15	15
Set value	22	18

Bay of Naples, Vesuvius and Sailboats — A470

Athlete on Greek Vase — A471

1963, Sept. 21 Wmk. 303 *Perf. 14*

882 A470 15 l bl & org	15	15
883 A471 70 l dk grn & org brn	15	15
Set value	18	17

4th Mediterranean Games, Naples, Sept. 21-29.

Giuseppe Gioachino Belli (1791-1863), Poet A472

Stamps Forming Flower A473

1963, Nov. 14 Wmk. 303 *Perf. 14*

884 A472 30 l red brn	15	15

1963, Dec. 1

885 A473 15 l bl & car	15	15

Issued for Stamp Day.

Pietro Mascagni and Old Costanzi Theater, Rome — A474

Design: No. 886, Giuseppe Verdi and La Scala, Milan.

1963 Photo.

886 A474 30 l gray grn & yel brn	15	15
887 A474 30 l yel brn & gray grn	15	15
Set value	16	15

Verdi (1813-1901), and Mascagni (1863-1945), composers. Dates of issue: No. 886, Oct. 10; No. 887, Dec. 7.

Galileo Galilei A475

Nicodemus by Michelangelo A476

1964, Feb. 15 Wmk. 303 *Perf. 14*

888 A475 30 l org brn	15	15
889 A475 70 l black	15	15
Set value	19	15

Galileo Galilei (1564-1642), astronomer and physicist.

1964, Feb. 18 Photo.

890 A476 30 l brown	15	15

Michelangelo Buonarroti (1475-1564), artist. Head of Nicodemus (self-portrait?) from the Pieta, Florence Cathedral. See No. C137.

Carabinieri A477

Design: 70 l, Charge of Pastrengo, 1848, by De Albertis.

1964, June 5 Wmk. 303 *Perf. 14*

891 A477 30 l vio bl & red	15	15
892 A477 70 l brown	15	15
Set value	16	15

Issued to commemorate the 150th anniversary of the Carabinieri (police corps).

Giambattista Bodoni — A478

Perf. 14x13

1964, July 30 Engr. Unwmk.

893 A478 30 l carmine	15	15
a. Perf. 13	18	15

150th anniversary of the death of Giambattista Bodoni (1740-1813), printer and type designer (Bodoni type).

Europa Issue, 1964

Common Design Type

Wmk. 303

1964, Sept. 14 Photo. *Perf. 14*

Size: 21x37mm

894 CD7 30 l brt rose lil	15	15
895 CD7 70 l bl grn	15	15
Set value	20	15

Walled City — A479

Left Arch of Victor Emmanuel Monument, Rome — A480

1964, Oct. 15 Photo. *Perf. 14*

896 A479 30 l emer & dk brn	15	15
897 A479 70 l bl & dk brn	18	15

Unwmk. Engr.

898 A479 500 l red	90	50
Set value		66

7th Congress of European Towns. The buildings in design are: Big Ben, London; Campodoglio, Rome; Town Hall, Bruges; Römer, Frankfurt; Town Hall, Paris; Belfry, Zurich; Gate, Kampen (Holland).

1964, Nov. 4 Photo. Wmk. 303

899 A480 30 l dk red brn	15	15
900 A480 70 l blue	15	15
Set value	18	16

Issued to commemorate the pilgrimage to Rome of veterans living abroad.

Giovanni da Verrazano and Verrazano-Narrows Bridge, New York Bay — A481

1964, Nov. 21 Wmk. 303 *Perf. 14*

901 A481 30 l blk & brn	15	15

Opening of the Verrazano-Narrows Bridge connecting Staten Island and Brooklyn, NY, and to honor Giovanni da Verrazano (1485-1528), discoverer of New York Bay. See No. C138.

Italian Sports Stamps, 1934-63 — A482

1964, Dec. 6 Photo. *Perf. 14*

902 A482 15 l gldn brn & dk brn	15	15

Issued for Stamp Day.

Italian Soldiers in Concentration Camp — A483

Victims Trapped by Swastika A484

Designs: 15 l, Italian soldier, sailor and airman fighting for the Allies. 70 l, Guerrilla fighters in the mountains. 115 l, Marchers with Italian flag. 130 l, Ruins of city and torn Italian flag.

1965, Apr. 24 Photo. Wmk. 303

903 A483 10 l black	15	15
904 A483 15 l grn & rose car	15	15
905 A484 30 l plum	15	15
906 A483 70 l dp bl	15	15
907 A484 115 l rose car	15	15
908 A484 130 l grn, sep & red	15	15
Set value	40	35

20th anniversary of the Italian resistance movement during World War II.

Antonio Meucci, Guglielmo Marconi and ITU Emblem A485

1965, May 17 *Perf. 14*

909 A485 70 l red & dk grn	15	15

Cent. of the ITU.

Sailboats of Flying Dutchman Class — A486

Designs: 70 l, Sailboats of 5.5-meter class, vert. 500 l, Sailboats, Lightning class.

1965, May 31 Photo. Wmk. 303

910 A486 30 l blk & dl rose	15	15
911 A486 70 l blk & ultra	15	15
912 A486 500 l blk & gray bl	38	32
Set value	55	45

Issued to publicize the World Yachting Championships, Naples and Alassio.

Mont Blanc and Tunnel A487

1965, June 16 Wmk. 303 *Perf. 14*

913 A487 30 l black 15 15

Opening of the Mont Blanc Tunnel connecting Entrayes, Italy, and Le Polerins, France.

Alessandro Tassoni and Scene from "Seccia Rapita" — A488

Unwmk.

1965, Sept. 20 Photo. *Perf. 14*

914 A488 40 l blk & multi 15 15

Tassoni (1565-1635), poet. Design is from 1744 engraving by Bartolomeo Soliani.

Europa Issue, 1965

Common Design Type

1965, Sept. 27 Wmk. 303

Size: 36½x27mm

915 CD8 40 l ocher & ol grn 15 15
916 CD8 90 l ultra & ol grn 15 15
Set value 21 18

Dante, 15th Century Bust A489

House under Construction A490

Designs (from old Manuscripts): 40 l, Dante in Hell. 90 l, Dante in Purgatory led by Angel of Chastity. 130 l, Dante in Paradise interrogated by St. Peter on faith, horiz.

Perf. 13½x14, 14x13½

1965, Oct. 21 Photo. Unwmk.

917 A489 40 l multi 15 15
918 A489 90 l multi 15 15
919 A489 130 l multi 15 15
Set value 28 20

Wmk. 303 *Perf. 14*

920 A489 500 l slate grn 38 32

Dante Alighieri (1265-1321), poet.

1965, Oct. 31 Wmk. 303 *Perf. 14*

921 A490 40 l buff, blk & org brn 15 15

Issued for Savings Day.

Jet Plane, Moon and Airletter Border A491

Design: 40 l, Control tower and plane.

1965, Nov. 3

922 A491 40 l dk Prus bl & red 15 15

Unwmk.

923 A491 90 l red, grn, dp bl & buff 15 15
Set value 15 15

Night air postal network.

Map of Italy with Milan-Rome Highway — A492

Two-Man Bobsled — A493

1965, Dec. 5 Photo. *Perf. 13x14*

924 A492 20 l bl, blk, ocher & gray 15 15

Issued for Stamp Day.

1966, Jan. 24 Wmk. 303 *Perf. 14*

Design: 90 l, Four-man bobsled.

925 A493 40 l dl bl, gray & red 15 15
926 A493 90 l vio & bl 15 15
Set value 15 15

Issued to commemorate the International Bobsled Championships, Cortina d'Ampezzo.

Woman Skater — A494

Benedetto Croce — A495

Winter University Games: 40 l, Skier holding torch, horiz. 500 l, Ice hockey.

1966, Feb. 5 Photo.

927 A494 40 l blk & red 15 15
928 A494 90 l vio & red 15 15
929 A494 500 l brn & red 38 32
Set value 55 45

1966, Feb. 25 Wmk. 303 *Perf. 14*

930 A495 40 l brown 15 15

Benedetto Croce (1866-1952), philosopher, statesman and historian.

Arms of Venice and Other Cities in Venezia A496

1966, Mar. 22 Photo. Unwmk.

932 A496 40 l gray & multi 15 15

Centenary of Venezia's union with Italy.

Battle of Bezzecca — A497

1966, July 21 Wmk. 303 *Perf. 14*

933 A497 90 l ol grn 15 15

Centenary of the unification of Italy and of the Battle of Bezzecca.

Umbrella Pine — A498

Carnations — A499

Designs: 25 l, Apples. 50 l, Florentine iris. 55 l, Cypresses. 90 l, Daisies. 170 l, Olive tree. 180 l, Juniper.

1966-68 Unwmk. *Perf. 13½x14*

934 A498 20 l multi 15 15
934A A498 25 l multi ('67) 15 15
935 A499 40 l multi 15 15
935A A498 50 l multi ('67) 15 15
935B A498 55 l multi ('68) 15 15
936 A499 90 l multi 15 15
937 A498 170 l multi 24 15
937A A498 180 l multi ('68) 24 15
Set value 1.05 45

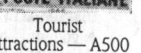

Tourist Attractions — A500

"I" in Flag Colors — A501

1966, May 28 Wmk. 303 *Perf. 14*

938 A500 20 l yel, org & blk 15 15

Issued for tourist publicity and in connection with the National Conference on Tourism, Rome.

Perf. 13½x14

1966, June 2 Photo. Unwmk.

939 A501 40 l multi 15 15
940 A501 90 l multi 15 15
Set value 15 15

20th anniversary of the Republic of Italy.

Singing Angels, by Donatello — A502

Madonna, by Giotto — A503

Perf. 13½x14

1966, Sept. 24 Photo. Unwmk.

941 A502 40 l multi 15 15

Issued to commemorate the centenary of the death of Donatello (1386-1466), sculptor.

Europa Issue, 1966

Common Design Type

1966, Sept. 26 Wmk. 303 *Perf. 14*

Size: 22x38mm

942 CD9 40 l brt pur 15 15
943 CD9 90 l brt bl 15 15
Set value 21 15

Perf. 13½x14

1966, Oct. 20 Photo. Unwmk.

944 A503 40 l multi 15 15

700th anniversary of the birth of Giotto di Bondone (1266?-1337), Florentine painter.

Italian Patriots A504

1966, Nov. 3 Wmk. 303 *Perf. 14*

945 A504 40 l gray & dl grn 15 15

50th anniv. of the execution by Austrians of 4 Italian patriots: Fabio Filzi, Cesare Battisti, Damiano Chiesa and Nazario Sauro.

Postrider — A505

Perf. 14x13½

1966, Dec. 4 Photo. Unwmk.

946 A505 20 l multi 15 15

Issued for Stamp Day.

Globe and Compass Rose — A506

1967, Mar. 20 Photo. Wmk. 303

947 A506 40 l dull blue 15 15

Centenary of Italian Geographical Society.

Arturo Toscanini (1867-1957), Conductor A507

1967, Mar. 25 *Perf. 14*

948 A507 40 l dp vio & cream 15 15

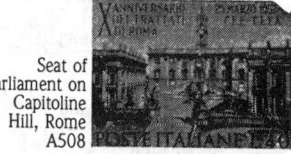

Seat of Parliament on Capitoline Hill, Rome A508

1967, Mar. 25 *Perf. 14*

949 A508 40 l sepia 15 15
950 A508 90 l rose lil & blk 15 15
Set value 23 15

10th anniv. of the Treaty of Rome, establishing the European Common Market.

Europa Issue, 1967
Common Design Type

1967, Apr. 10 Wmk. 303 *Perf. 14*
Size: 22x28mm

951 CD10	40 l plum & pink	15	15
952 CD10	90 l ultra & pale gray	24	15
	Set value	32	15

Alpine Ibex, Grand Paradiso Park — A509

National Parks: 40 l, Brown bear, Abruzzi Apennines, horiz. 90 l, Red deer, Stelvio Pass, Ortler Mountains, horiz. 170 l, Oak and deer, Circeo.

Perf. 13½x14, 14x13½

1967, Apr. 22 Photo.

953 A509	20 l multi	15	15
954 A509	40 l multi	15	15
955 A509	90 l multi	15	15
956 A509	170 l multi	24	15
	Set value	50	32

Claudio Monteverdi and Characters from "Orfeo" A510

1967, May 15 *Perf. 14*

957 A510	40 l bis brn & brn	15	15

Monteverdi (1567-1643), composer.

Bicyclists and Mountains A511

50th Bicycle Tour of Italy: 90 l. Three bicyclists on the road. 500 l, Group of bicyclists.

Perf. 14x13½

1967, May 15 Photo. Unwmk.

958 A511	40 l multi	15	15
959 A511	90 l brt bl & multi	15	15
960 A511	500 l yel grn & multi	70	45
	Set value		58

Luigi Pirandello and Stage — A512

1967, June 28 *Perf. 14x13*

961 A512	40 l blk & multi	15	15

Pirandello (1867-1936), novelist & dramatist.

Stylized Mask — A513

1967, June 30 Wmk. 303 *Perf. 14*

962 A513	20 l grn & blk	15	15
963 A513	40 l car rose & blk	15	15
	Set value	15	15

10th "Festival of Two Worlds," Spoleto.

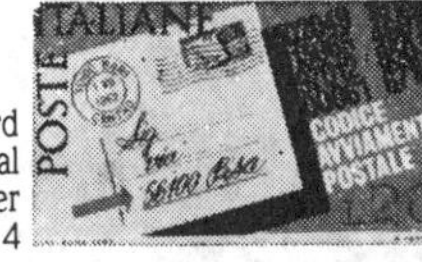

Postal Card with Postal Zone Number A514

Design: 40 l, 50 l, Letter addressed with postal zone number.

Wmk. 303, Unwmkd, (20 l, 40 l)
1967-68

964 A514	20 l multi	15	15
965 A514	25 l multi ('68)	15	15
966 A514	40 l multi	15	15
967 A514	50 l multi ('68)	15	15
	Set value	30	20

Issued to publicize the introduction of postal zone numbers, July 1, 1967.

Pomilio PC-1 Biplane and 1917 Airmail Postmark A515

1967, July 18 Photo. Wmk. 303

968 A515	40 l blk & lt bl	15	15

50th anniv. of the 1st airmail stamp, Italy #C1.

St. Ivo Church, Rome — A516

Umberto Giordano and "Improvisation" from Opera Andrea Chenier — A517

1967, Aug. 2 Unwmk. *Perf. 14*

969 A516	90 l multi	15	15

Francesco Borromini (1599-1667), architect.

1967, Aug. 28 Wmk. 303

970 A517	20 l blk & org brn	15	15

Umberto Giordano (1867-1948), composer.

Oath of Pontida, by Adolfo Cao — A518

ITY Emblem — A519

1967, Sept. 2

971 A518	20 l dk brn	15	15

800th anniv. of the Oath of Pontida, which united the Lombard League against Emperor Frederick I.

Perf. 13½x14

1967, Oct. 23 Photo. Unwmk.

972 A519	20 l blk, cit & brt bl	15	15
973 A519	50 l blk, org & brt bl	15	15
	Set value	15	15

Issued for International Tourist Year, 1967.

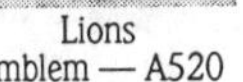

Lions Emblem — A520

Soldier at the Piave — A521

1967, Oct. 30 *Perf. 14x13½*

974 A520	50 l multi	15	15

50th anniversary of Lions International.

1967, Nov. 9 *Perf. 13x14*

975 A521	50 l multi	15	15

50th anniversary of Battle of the Piave.

Enrico Fermi at Los Alamos and Model of 1st Atomic Reactor — A522

"Day and Night" and Pigeon Carrying Italy No. 924 — A523

Wmk. 303
1967, Dec. 2 Photo. *Perf. 14*

976 A522	50 l org brn & blk	15	15

25th anniv. of the 1st atomic chain reaction under Enrico Fermi (1901-54), Chicago, IL.

1967, Dec. 3 Unwmk. *Perf. 13½x14*

977 A523	25 l multi	15	15

Issued for Stamp Day, 1967.

Scouts at Campfire — A524

St. Aloysius Gonzaga, by Pierre Legros — A525

1968, Apr. 23 *Perf. 13x14*

978 A524	50 l multi	15	15

Issued to honor the Boy Scouts.

Europa Issue, 1968
Common Design Type

1968, Apr. 29 Wmk. 303 *Perf. 14x13*
Size: 36½x26mm

979 CD11	50 l blk, rose & sl grn	15	15
980 CD11	90 l blk, bl & brn	15	15
	Set value		18

Perf. 13½x14

1968, May 28 Photo. Wmk. 303

981 A525	25 l red brn & dl vio	15	15

Aloysius Gonzaga (1568-1591), Jesuit priest who ministered to victims of the plague.

Arrigo Boito and Mephistopheles A526

1968, June 10 Unwmk. *Perf. 14*

982 A526	50 l multi	15	15

Boito (1842-1918), composer and librettist.

Francesco Baracca and "Planes," by Giacomo Balla — A527

1968, June 19

983 A527	25 l multi	15	15

Major Francesco Baracca (1888-1918), World War I aviator.

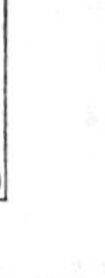

Giambattista Vico — A528

Bicycle Wheel and Velodrome, Rome — A529

Designs: No. 985, Tommaso Campanella. No. 986, Gioacchino Rossini.

Perf. 14x13½

1968 Engr. Wmk. 303

984 A528	50 l ultra	15	15
985 A528	50 l black	15	15
a.	Perf. 13½	90	18
986 A528	50 l car rose	15	15
	Set value	32	18

Vico (1668-1744), philosopher; Campanella (1568-1639), Dominican monk, philosopher, poet and teacher; Rossini (1792-1868), composer.
Issue dates: No. 984, June 24; No. 985, Sept. 5; No. 986, Oct. 25.

Perf. 13x14

1968, Aug. 26 Photo. Unwmk.

Design: 90 l, Bicycle and Sforza Castle, Imola.

987 A529	25 l sl, rose & brn	15	15
988 A529	90 l sl, bl & ver	15	15
	Set value	18	15

Bicycling World Championships: 25 l for the track championships at the Velodrome in Rome; the 90 l, the road championships at Imola.

"The Small St. Mark's Place," by Canaletto — A531

1968, Sept. 30 Unwmk. *Perf. 14*

989 A531	50 l pink & multi	15	15

Canaletto (Antonio Canale, 1697-1768), Venetian painter.

"Mobilization"
A533

Symbolic Designs: 25 l, Trench war. 40 l, The Navy. 50 l, The Air Force. 90 l. The Battle of Vittorio Veneto. 180 l, The Unknown Soldier.

1968, Nov. 2 Photo. Unwmk.

990	A533	20 l	brn & multi	15	15
991	A533	25 l	bl & multi	15	15
992	A533	40 l	multi	15	15
993	A533	50 l	multi	15	15
994	A533	90 l	grn & multi	15	15
995	A533	180 l	bl & multi	15	15
			Set value	62	48

50th anniv. of the Allies' Victory in WW I.

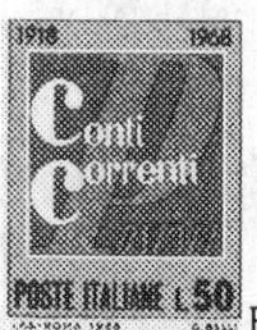

Emblem — A534

1968, Nov. 20 ***Perf. 14x13½***

996	A534	50 l	blk, bl grn & red	15	15

50th anniv. of the Postal Checking Service.

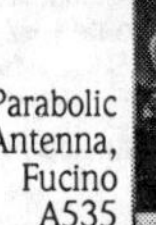

Parabolic Antenna, Fucino
A535

1968, Nov. 25 Photo. ***Perf. 14***

997	A535	50 l	multi	15	15

Issued to publicize the expansion of the space communications center at Fucino.

Development of Postal Service — A536

1968, Dec. 1 Wmk. 303

998	A536	25 l	car & yel	15	15

Issued for the 10th Stamp Day.

Fluorescent Paper was introduced in 1968 for regular and special delivery issues. These stamps are about 1mm. smaller each way than the non-fluorescent ones they replaced, except Nos. 690-690A which remained the same size.

Commemorative or nonregular stamps issued only on fluorescent paper are Nos. 935B, 937A, 965, 967 and from 981 onward unless otherwise noted.

Italia Type of 1953-54
Small Size: 16x19½-20mm
Photo.; Engr. (100, 150, 200-400 l)

1968-76 Wmk. 303 ***Perf. 14***

998A	A354	1 l	dk gray	15	15
998B	A354	5 l	slate	15	15
998C	A354	6 l	ocher	15	15
998D	A354	10 l	org ver	15	15
998E	A354	15 l	gray vio	15	15
998F	A354	20 l	brown	15	15
998G	A354	25 l	purple	15	15
998H	A354	30 l	bis brn	15	15
998I	A354	40 l	lil rose	15	15
998J	A354	50 l	olive	15	15
998K	A354	55 l	vio ('69)	15	15
998L	A354	60 l	blue	15	15
998M	A354	70 l	Prus grn	15	15
998N	A354	80 l	brn org	15	15
998O	A354	90 l	lt red brn	15	15
998P	A354	100 l	redsh brn	15	15
998Q	A354	125 l	ocher & lil ('74)	15	15
998R	A354	130 l	gray & dl red	15	15
998S	A354	150 l	vio ('76)	15	15
998T	A354	180 l	gray & vio brn ('71)	22	15
998U	A354	200 l	slate blue	15	15
998V	A354	300 l	Prus grn ('72)	28	15
998W	A354	400 l	dull red ('76)	28	15
			Set value	2.50	1.25

Memorial Medal — A537

Unwmk.

1969, Apr. 22 Photo. ***Perf. 14***

999	A537	50 l	pink & blk	15	15

Centenary of the State Audit Bureau.

Europa Issue, 1969
Common Design Type

1969, Apr. 28 ***Perf. 14x13***
Size: 35½x25½mm

1000	CD12	50 l	mag & multi	15	15
1001	CD12	90 l	bl & multi	15	15
			Set value		19

Niccolo Machiavelli
A538

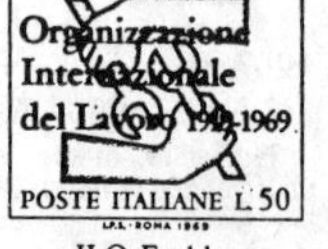

ILO Emblem
A539

1969, May 3 ***Perf. 14x13½***

1002	A538	50 l	blue & multi	15	15

Niccolo Machiavelli (1469-1527), statesman and political philosopher.

Wmk. 303

1969, June 7 Photo. ***Perf. 14***

1003	A539	50 l	grn & blk	15	15
1004	A539	90 l	car & blk	15	15
			Set value	22	15

50th anniv. of the ILO.

Federation Emblem, Tower of Superga Basilica and Matterhorn
A540

1969, June 26 Unwmk. ***Perf. 14***

1005	A540	50 l	gold, bl & car	15	15

50th anniversary of the Federation of Italian Philatelic Societies.

Sondrio-Tirano Stagecoach, 1903 — A541

1969, Dec. 7 Engr. Wmk. 303

1006	A541	25 l	vio bl	15	15

Issued for the 11th Stamp Day.

Downhill Skier — A542

Design: 90 l, Sassolungo and Sella Group, Dolomite Alps.

Perf. 13x14

1970, Feb. 6 Unwmk. Photo.

1007	A542	50 l	bl & multi	15	15
1008	A542	90 l	bl & multi	15	15
			Set value	22	15

World Alpine Ski Championships, Val Gardena, Bolzano Province, Feb. 6-15.

Galatea, by Raphael
A543

Painting: 50 l, Madonna with the Goldfinch (detail), by Raphael, 1483-1520.

1970, Apr. 6 Photo. ***Perf. 14x13***

1009	A543	20 l	multi	15	15
1010	A543	50 l	multi	15	15
			Set value	18	15

Symbol of Flight, Colors of Italy and Japan — A544

1970, May 2 Unwmk. ***Perf. 14***

1011	A544	50 l	multi	15	15
1012	A544	90 l	multi	15	15
			Set value	22	15

50th anniv. of Arturo Ferrarin's flight from Rome to Tokyo, Feb. 14-May 31, 1920.

Europa Issue, 1970
Common Design Type

1970, May 4 Wmk. 303
Size: 36x20mm

1013	CD13	50 l	red & org	15	15
1014	CD13	90 l	bl grn & org	20	15
			Set value		18

Gattamelata, Bust by Donatello — A545

1970, May 30 Engr. ***Perf. 14x13***

1015	A545	50 l	slate grn	15	15

Erasmo de' Narni, called Il Gattamelata (1370-1443), condottiere.

Runner
A546

Unwmk.

1970, Aug. 26 Photo. ***Perf. 14***

1016	A546	20 l	shown	15	15
1017	A546	180 l	Swimmer	18	15
			Set value	27	15

Issued to publicize the 1970 World University Games, Turin, Aug. 26-Sept. 6.

Dr. Maria Montessori and Children
A547

1970, Aug. 31 ***Perf. 14x13***

1018	A547	50 l	multi	15	15

Montessori (1870-1952), educator & physician.

Map of Italy and Quotation of Count Camillo Cavour — A548

1970, Sept. 19 Unwmk. ***Perf. 14***

1019	A548	50 l	multi	15	15

Centenary of the union of the Roman States with Italy.

Loggia of St. Mark's Campanile, Venice
A549

Perf. 14x13½

1970, Sept. 26 Engr. Wmk. 303

1020	A549	50 l	red brown	15	15

Iacopo Tatti "Il Sansovino" (1486-1570), architect.

Garibaldi at Battle of Dijon — A550

1970, Oct. 15 Photo. ***Perf. 14***

1021	A550	20 l	gray & dk bl	15	15
1022	A550	50 l	brt rose lil & dk bl	15	15
			Set value	15	15

Cent. of Garibaldi's participation in the Franco-Prussian War during Battle of Dijon.

Tree and UN Emblem — A551

1970, Oct. 24 Unwmk. ***Perf. 13x14***

1023	A551	25 l	blk, sep & grn	15	15
1024	A551	90 l	blk, brt bl & yel grn	15	15
			Set value	22	15

25th anniversary of the United Nations.

Rotary Emblem A552

1970, Nov. 12 Wmk. 303 *Perf. 14*

1025 A552 25 l bluish vio & org 15 15
1026 A552 90 l bluish vio & org 15 15
Set value 22 15

Rotary International, 65th anniversary.

Telephone Dial and Trunk Lines — A553

1970, Nov. 24

1027 A553 25 l yel grn & dk red 15 15
1028 A553 90 l ultra & dk red 15 15
Set value 22 15

Issued to publicize the completion of the automatic trunk telephone dialing system.

"Man Damaging Nature" — A554

Virgin and Child, by Fra Filippo Lippi — A556

Mail Train — A555

1970, Nov. 28 Wmk. 303 *Perf. 14*

1029 A554 20 l car lake & grn 15 15
1030 A554 25 l dk bl & emer 15 15
Set value 24 18

For European Nature Conservation Year.

1970, Dec. 6 Engr.

1031 A555 25 l black 15 15

For the 12th Stamp Day.

1970, Dec. 12 Photo. Unwmk.

1032 A556 25 l multi 15 15

Christmas 1970. See No. C139.

Saverio Mercadante (1795-1870), Composer A557

1970, Dec. 17 Wmk. 303

1033 A557 25 l vio & gray 15 15

Mercury, by Benvenuto Cellini A558

Bramante's Temple, St. Peter in Montorio A559

1971, Mar. 20 Photo. *Perf. 14*

1034 A558 50 l Prus bl 15 15

400th anniversary of the death of Benvenuto Cellini (1500-1571), sculptor.

Photogravure and Engraved

1971, Apr. 8 *Perf. 13x14*

1035 A559 50 l ocher & blk 15 15

Honoring Bramante (Donato di Angelo di Antonio, 1444-1514), architect.

Adenauer, Schuman, De Gasperi A560

Perf. 14x13½

1971, Apr. 28 Photo. Wmk. 303

1036 A560 50 l blk & lt grnsh bl 15 15
1037 A560 90 l blk & lil rose 15 15
Set value 22 15

20th anniversary of the European Coal and Steel Community.

Europa Issue, 1971

Common Design Type

1971, May 3 *Perf. 14*

1038 CD14 50 l ver & dk red 15 15
1039 CD14 90 l brt rose lil & dk lil 15 15
Set value 18

Giuseppe Mazzini, Italian Flag — A561

Perf. 14x13½

1971, June 12 Unwmk.

1040 A561 50 l multi 15 15
1041 A561 90 l multi 15 15
Set value 17

25th anniversary of the Italian Republic.

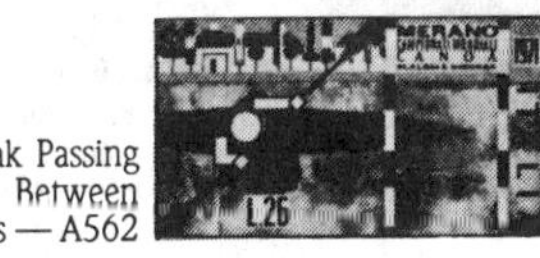
Kayak Passing Between Poles — A562

Design: 90 l, Kayak in free descent.

1971, June 16 Photo. *Perf. 14*

1042 A562 25 l multi 15 15
1043 A562 90 l multi 15 15
Set value 22 15

Canoe Slalom World Championships, Merano.

Skiing, Basketball, Volleyball — A563

Design: 50 l, Gymnastics, cycling, track and swimming.

Perf. 13½x14

1971, June 26 Photo. Unwmk.

1044 A563 20 l emer, ocher & blk 15 15
1045 A563 50 l dl bl, org & blk 15 15
Set value 15 15

Youth Games.

Plane Circling Globe and "A" — A564

Designs: 50 l, Ornamental "A." 150 l, Tail of B747 in shape of "A."

1971, Sept. 16 *Perf. 14x13½*

1046 A564 50 l multi 15 15
1047 A564 90 l multi 15 15
1048 A564 150 l multi 15 15
Set value 30

25th anniversary of the founding of ALITALIA, Italian airlines.

Grazia Deledda (1871-1936), Novelist — A565

Child in Barrel Made of Banknote — A566

Photogravure and Engraved

Perf. 13½x14

1971, Sept. 28 Wmk. 303

1049 A565 50 l blk & salmon 15 15

Perf. 13x14

1971, Oct. 27 Photo. Unwmk.

1050 A566 25 l blk & multi 15 15
1051 A566 50 l multi 15 15
Set value 18 15

Publicity for postal savings bank.

UNICEF Emblem and Children A567

Design: 90 l, Children hailing UNICEF emblem.

1971, Nov. 26 *Perf. 14x13*

1052 A567 25 l pink & multi 15 15
1053 A567 90 l multi 15 15
Set value 22 15

25th anniv. of UNICEF.

Packet Tirrenia and Postal Ensign A568

1971, Dec. 5 Wmk. 303 *Perf. 14*

1054 A568 25 l slate green 15 15

Stamp Day.

Nativity A569

Christmas: 90 l, Adoration of the Kings. Both designs are from miniatures in Evangelistary of Matilda in Nonantola Abbey, 12th-13th centuries.

Perf. 14x13

1971, Dec. 10 Photo. Unwmk.

1055 A569 25 l gray & multi 15 15
1056 A569 90 l gray & multi 15 15
Set value 22 15

Giovanni Verga and Sicilian Cart — A570

1972, Jan. 27

1057 A570 25 l org & multi 15 15
1058 A570 50 l multi 15 15
Set value 15 15

Verga (1840-1922), writer & playwright.

Giuseppe Mazzini (1805-1872), Patriot and Writer — A571

Wmk. 303

1972, Mar. 10 Engr. *Perf. 13*

1059 A571 25 l blk & Prus grn 15 15
1060 A571 90 l black 15 15
1061 A571 150 l blk & rose red 15 15
Set value 32 24

Flags, Milan Fair — A572

Designs: 50 l, 90 l, Different abstract views.

Perf. 14x13½

1972, Apr. 14 Photo. Unwmk.

1062 A572 25 l emer & blk 15 15
1063 A572 50 l dp org & blk 15 15
1064 A572 90 l bl & blk 15 15
Set value 30 22

50th anniversary of the Milan Sample Fair.

Europa Issue 1972

Common Design Type

1972, May 2 *Perf. 13x14*

Size: 26x36mm

1065 CD15 50 l multi 15 15
1066 CD15 90 l multi 15 15
Set value 18

Alpine Soldier and Pack Mule — A573

Designs: 50 l, Mountains, Alpinist's hat, pick and laurel. 90 l, Alpine soldier and mountains.

1972, May 10 *Perf. 14x13*

1067	A573	25 l ol & multi	15	15
1068	A573	50 l bl & multi	15	15
1069	A573	90 l grn & multi	15	15
		Set value	32	20

Centenary of the Alpine Corps.

Brenta Mountains, Society Emblem A574

Designs (Emblem and): 50 l, Mountain climber and Brenta Mountains. 180 l, Sunset over Mt. Crozzon.

Perf. 14x13

1972, Sept. 2 Photo. Unwmk.

1070	A574	25 l multi	15	15
1071	A574	50 l multi	15	15
1072	A574	180 l multi	15	15
		Set value	35	18

Tridentine Alpinist Society centenary.

Conference Emblem, Seating Diagram A575

1972, Sept. 21

1073	A575	50 l multi	15	15
1074	A575	90 l multi	15	15
		Set value	22	15

60th Conference of the Inter-Parliamentary Union, Montecitorio Hall, Rome.

St. Peter Damian, by Giovanni di Paoli, c. 1445 — A576

1972, Sept. 21 **Photo.**

1075	A576	50 l multi	15	15

St. Peter Damian (1007-72), church reformer, cardinal, papal legate.

The Three Graces, by Antonio Canova (1757-1822), Sculptor — A577

1972, Oct. 13 Engr. Wmk. 303

1076	A577	50 l black	15	15

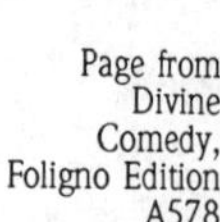

Page from Divine Comedy, Foligno Edition A578

Designs (Illuminated First Pages): 90 l, Mantua edition, vert. 180 l, Jesina edition.

Perf. 14x13½, 13½x14

1972, Nov. 23 Photo. Unwmk.

1077	A578	50 l ocher & multi	15	15
1078	A578	90 l multi	15	15
1079	A578	180 l multi	18	15
		Set value		28

500th anniversary of three illuminated editions of Dante's Divine Comedy.

Angel — A579

Christmas: 25 l, Christ Child in cradle, horiz. 150 l, Angel. All designs from 18th century Neapolitan crèche.

Perf. 13x14, 14x13

1972, Dec. 6 **Photo.**

1080	A579	20 l multi	15	15
1081	A579	25 l multi	15	15
1082	A579	150 l multi	15	15
		Set value	32	24

Passenger and Mail Autobus A580

1972, Dec. 16 Engr. Wmk. 303

1083	A580	25 l magenta	15	15

Stamp Day.

Leòn Battista Alberti — A581

Lorenzo Perosi — A582

1972, Dec. 16 *Perf. 14*

1084	A581	50 l ultra & ocher	15	15

Leòn Battista Alberti (1404-1472), architect, painter, organist and writer.

1972, Dec. 20 Photo. Unwmk.

1085	A582	50 l dk vio brn & org	15	15
1086	A582	90 l blk & yel grn	15	15
		Set value	22	15

Centenary of the birth of Lorenzo Perosi (1872-1956), priest and composer.

Luigi Orione and Boys — A583

Ship Exploring Ocean Floor — A584

1972, Dec. 30

1087	A583	50 l lt bl & dk bl	15	15
1088	A583	90 l ocher & sl grn	15	15
		Set value	22	15

Orione (1872-1940), founder of CARITAS; Catholic Welfare Organization.

1973, Feb. 15 Photo. *Perf. 13x14*

1089	A584	50 l multi	15	15

Cent. of the Naval Hydrographic Institute.

Palace Staircase, Caserta A585

1973, Mar. 1 Engr. *Perf. 14x13½*

1090	A585	25 l gray ol	15	15

Luigi Vanvitelli (1700-1773), architect.

Schiavoni Shore — A586

The Tetrarchs, 4th Century Sculpture — A587

Designs: 50 l, "Triumph of Venice," by Vittore Carpaccio. 90 l, Bronze horses from St. Mark's. 300 l, St. Mark's Square covered by flood.

1973 Photo. *Perf. 14*

1091	A586	20 l ultra & multi	15	15
1092	A587	25 l ultra & multi	15	15
1093	A586	50 l ultra & multi	15	15
1094	A587	90 l ultra & multi	15	15
1095	A586	300 l ultra & multi	38	28
		Set value	72	50

Save Venice campaign. Issue dates: No. 1091, Mar. 5; others Apr. 10.

Verona Fair Emblem — A588

Title Page for Book about Rosa — A589

1973, Mar. 10 *Perf. 13x14*

1096	A588	50 l multi	15	15

75th International Fair, Verona.

1973, Mar. 15 *Perf. 14*

1097	A589	25 l org & blk	15	15

300th anniversary of death of Salvator Rosa (1615-1673), painter and poet.

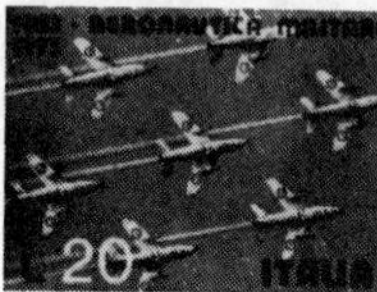

G-91 Jet Fighters A590

Designs: 25 l, Formation of S-55 seaplanes. 50 l, G-91Y fighters. 90 l, Fiat CR-32's flying figure 8. 180 l, Camprini-Caproni jet, 1940.

1973, Mar. 28 *Perf. 14x13½*

1098	A590	20 l multi	15	15
1099	A590	25 l multi	15	15
1100	A590	50 l multi	15	15
1101	A590	90 l multi	15	15
1102	A590	180 l multi	18	15
		Set value, #1098-1102, C140	80	50

50th anniversary of military aviation.

Soccer Field and Ball — A591

Design: 90 l, Soccer players and goal.

1973, May 19 Photo. *Perf. 14x13½*

1103	A591	25 l ol, blk & lt grn	15	15
1104	A591	90 l grn & multi	15	15
		Set value	20	15

75th anniv. of Italian Soccer Federation.

Alessandro Manzoni, by Francisco Hayez — A592

Villa Rotunda, by Andrea Palladio (1508-80), Architect. — A593

1973, May 22 **Engr.**

1105	A592	25 l blk & brn	15	15

Manzoni (1785-1873), novelist and poet.

1973, May 30 Photo. Unwmk.

Perf. 13x14

1106	A593	90 l blk, yel & lem	15	15

Spiral and Cogwheels A594

1973, June 20 *Perf. 14x13*

1107	A594	50 l gold & multi	15	15

50th anniversary of the State Supply Office.

Europa Issue 1973

Common Design Type

1973, June 30 Litho. *Perf. 14*

Size: 36x20mm

1108	CD16	50 l lil, gold & yel	15	15
1109	CD16	90 l lt bl grn, gold & yel	15	15
		Set value	22	18

Catcher and Diamond A595

Design: 90 l, Diamond and batter.

1973, July 21 Photo. ***Perf. 14x13½***

1110	A595	25 l multi	15	15
1111	A595	90 l multi	15	15
		Set value	20	15

International Baseball Cup.

Viareggio by Night — A596

Gaetano Salvemini — A598

Assassination of Giovanni Minzoni A597

1973, Aug. 10 Photo. ***Perf. 13x14***

1112	A596	25 l blk & multi	15	15

Viareggio Carnival.

1973, Aug. 23 ***Perf. 14x13***

1113	A597	50 l multi	15	15

Minzoni (1885-1923), priest & social worker.

1973, Sept. 8 ***Perf. 14x13½***

1114	A598	50 l pink & multi	15	15

Salvemini (1873-1957), historian, anti-Fascist.

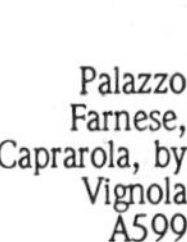

Palazzo Farnese, Caprarola, by Vignola A599

1973, Sept. 21 Engr. ***Perf. 14x13½***

1115	A599	90 l choc & yel	15	15

Giacomo da Vignola (real name, Giacomo Barocchio), 1507-1573, architect.

St. John the Baptist, by Caravaggio A600

Lithographed & Engraved

1973, Sept. 28 ***Perf. 14***

1116	A600	25 l blk & dl yel	15	15

400th anniversary of the birth of Michelangelo da Caravaggio (1573-1610?), painter.

Tower of Pisa — A601

1973, Oct. 8 Photo.

1117	A601	50 l multi	15	15

8th century of Leaning Tower of Pisa.

Sandro Botticelli A602

Trevi Fountain, Rome A603

1973-74 Photo. ***Perf. 14x13½***

1118	A602	50 l shown	15	15
1119	A602	50 l Giambattista Piranesi	15	15
1120	A602	50 l Paolo Veronese	15	15
1121	A602	50 l Andrea del Verrocchio	15	15
1122	A602	50 l Giovanni Battista Tiepolo	15	15
1123	A602	50 l Francesco Borromini	15	15
1124	A602	50 l Rosalba Carriera	15	15
1125	A602	50 l Giovanni Bellini	15	15
1126	A602	50 l Andrea Mantegna	15	15
1127	A602	50 l Raphael	15	15
		Set value	90	45

Famous artists.

Issue dates: Nos. 1118-1122, Nov. 5, 1973. Nos. 1123-1127, May 25, 1974.

Photogravure and Engraved

1973, Nov. 10 ***Perf. 13½x14***

Designs: No. 1129, Immacolatella Fountain, Naples. No. 1130, Pretoria Fountain, Palermo.

1128	A603	25 l blk & multi	15	15
1129	A603	25 l blk & multi	15	15
1130	A603	25 l blk & multi	15	15
		Set value	24	15

See Nos. 1166-1168, 1201-1203, 1251-1253, 1277-1279, 1341-1343, 1379-1381.

Angels, by Agostino di Duccio — A604

Map of Italy, Rotary Emblems — A605

Sculptures by Agostino di Duccio: 25 l, Virgin and Child. 150 l, Angels with flute and trumpet.

1973, Nov. 26

1131	A604	20 l yel grn & blk	15	15
1132	A604	25 l lt bl & blk	15	15
1133	A604	150 l yel & blk	15	15
		Set value	30	18

Christmas 1973.

1973, Nov. 28 Photo.

1134	A605	50 l red, grn & dk bl	15	15

50th anniv. of Rotary International of Italy.

Caravelle A606

Wmk. 303

1973, Dec. 2 Engr. ***Perf. 14***

1135	A606	25 l Prus bl	15	15

15th Stamp Day.

Medal of Valor — A607

Enrico Caruso — A608

Perf. 13½x14

1973, Dec. 10 Photo. Unwmk.

1136	A607	50 l gold & multi	15	15

Gold Medal of Valor, 50th anniversary.

1973, Dec. 15 Engr.

Design: 50 l, Caruso as Duke in Rigoletto.

1137	A608	50 l magenta	15	15

Enrico Caruso (1873-1921), operatic tenor.

Christ Crowning King Roger A609

Luigi Einaudi A610

Norman art in Sicily: 50 l, King William II offering model of church to the Virgin, mosaic from Monreale Cathedral. The design of 20 l, is from a mosaic in Martorana Church, Palermo.

Lithographed and Engraved

1974, Mar. 4 ***Perf. 13½x14***

1138	A609	20 l ind & buff	15	15
1139	A609	50 l red & lt grn	15	15
		Set value	15	15

1974, Mar. 23 Engr. ***Perf. 14x13½***

1140	A610	50 l green	15	15

Luigi Einaudi (1874-1961), Pres. of Italy.

Guglielmo Marconi (1874-1937), Italian Inventor and Physicist A611

Design: 90 l, Marconi and world map.

1974, Apr. 24 Photo. ***Perf. 14x13½***

1141	A611	50 l bl grn & gray	15	15
1142	A611	90 l vio & multi	15	15
		Set value	22	15

David, by Giovanni L. Bernini — A612

Europa: 90 l, David, by Michelangelo.

1974, Apr. 29 Photo. ***Perf. 13½x14***

1143	A612	50 l sal, ultra & gray	15	15
1144	A612	90 l grn, ultra & buff	15	15
		Set value	22	18

Customs Frontier Guards, 1774, 1795, 1817 — A613

Uniforms of Customs Service: 50 l, Lombardy Venetia, 1848, Sardinia, 1815, Tebro Battalion, 1849. 90 l, Customs Guards, 1866, 1880 and Naval Marshal, 1892. 180 l, Helicopter pilot, Naval and Alpine Guards, 1974. All bordered with Italian flag colors.

1974, June 21 Photo. ***Perf. 14***

1145	A613	40 l multi	15	15
1146	A613	50 l multi	15	15
1147	A613	90 l multi	15	15
1148	A613	180 l multi	18	15
		Set value	46	30

Customs Frontier Guards bicentenary.

Sprinter A614

1974, June 28 Photo. ***Perf. 14x13***

1149	A614	40 l shown	15	15
1150	A614	50 l Pole vault	15	15
		Set value	18	15

European Athletic Championships, Rome.

Sharpshooter A615

Design: 50 l, Bersaglieri emblem.

1974, June 27

1151	A615	40 l multi	15	15
1152	A615	50 l grn & multi	15	15
		Set value	18	15

50th anniversary of the Bersaglieri Veterans Association.

View of Portofino — A616

1974, July 10 *Perf. 14*

1153 A616 40 l shown 15 15
1154 A616 40 l View of Gradara 15 15
Set value 18 15

Tourist publicity.

See Nos. 1190-1192, 1221-1223, 1261-1265, 1314-1316, 1357-1360, 1402-1405, 1466-1469, 1520-1523, 1563A-1563D, 1599-1602, 1630-1633, 1708-1711, 1737-1740, 1776-1779, 1803-1806, 1830-1833, 1901-1904.

A617

A618

Petrarch (1304-74), Poet: 50 l, Petrarch at his desk (from medieval manuscript).

Lithographed and Engraved

1974, July 19 *Perf. 13½x14*

1155 A617 40 l ocher & multi 15 15
1156 A617 50 l ocher, yel & bl 15 15
Set value 18 15

1974, July 19

Design: Tommaseo Statue, by Ettore Ximenes, Shibenik.

1157 A618 50 l grn & pink 15 15

Niccolo Tommaseo (1802-1874), writer, Venetian education minister.

A619

A620

1974, Aug. 16 **Photo.**

1158 A619 40 l multi 15 15

Giacomo Puccini (1858-1924), composer.

1974, Sept. 9 **Engr.** *Perf. 14x13½*

1159 A620 50 l King Roland, woodcut 15 15

Lodovico Ariosto (1474-1533), poet. The design is from a contemporary illustration of Ariosto's poem "Orlando Furioso."

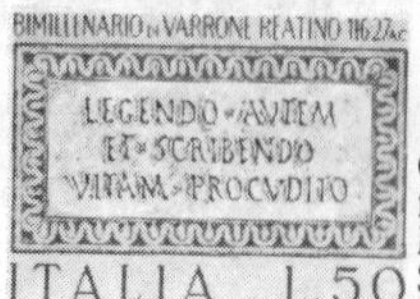

Quotation from Menippean Satire by Varro — A621

1974, Sept. 21

1160 A621 50 l ocher & dk red 15 15

Marcus Terentius Varro (116-27 BC), Roman scholar and writer.

The Scott Catalogue value is a retail price; that is, what you could expect to pay for the stamp in a grade of Fine-Very Fine. The value listed reflects recent actual dealer selling prices.

"October," 15th Century Mural — A622

1974, Sept. 28 **Photo.** *Perf. 14*

1161 A622 50 l multi 15 15

14th International Wine Congress, Trento.

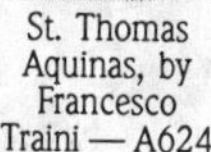

"UPU" and Emblem A623

Design: 90 l, Letters, "UPU" and emblem.

1974, Oct. 19 **Photo.** *Perf. 14*

1162 A623 50 l multi 15 15
1163 A623 90 l multi 15 15
Set value 22 15

Centenary of Universal Postal Union.

St. Thomas Aquinas, by Francesco Traini — A624

Bas-relief from Ara Pacis — A625

1974, Oct. 25 *Perf. 13x14*

1164 A624 50 l multi 15 15

St. Thomas Aquinas (1225-1274), scholastic philosopher, 700th death anniversary.

1974, Oct. 26

1165 A625 50 l multi 15 15

Centenary of the Ordini Forensi (Bar Association).

Fountain Type of 1973

Designs: No. 1166, Oceanus Fountain, Florence. No. 1167, Neptune Fountain, Bologna. No. 1168, Fontana Maggiore, Perugia.

Photogravure and Engraved

1974, Nov. 9 *Perf. 13x14*

1166 A603 40 l blk & multi 15 15
1167 A603 40 l blk & multi 15 15
1168 A603 40 l blk & multi 15 15
Set value 24 15

St. Francis Adoring Christ Child, by Presepe di Greccio A626

Photogravure and Engraved

1974, Nov. 26 *Perf. 14x13½*

1169 A626 40 l multi 15 15

Christmas 1974.

Masked Dancers — A627

1974, Dec. 1 **Photo.** *Perf. 13½x14*

1170 A627 40 l Pulcinella 15 15
1171 A627 50 l shown 15 15
1172 A627 90 l Pantaloon 15 15
Set value 30 18

16th Stamp Day 1974.

God Admonishing Adam, by Jacopo della Quercia A628

Courtyard, Uffizi Gallery, Florence, by Giorgio Vasari — A629

1974, Dec. 20 **Engr.** *Perf. 14*

1173 A628 90 l dk vio bl 15 15

Lithographed and Engraved

1174 A629 90 l multi 15 15
Set value 18

Italian artists: Jacopo della Quercia (1374-c. 1438), sculptor, and Giorgio Vasari (1511-1574), architect, painter and writer.

Angel with Tablet — A630

Angel with Cross — A632

Angels' Bridge, Rome A631

Holy Year 1975: 50 l, Angel holding column. 150 l, Angel holding Crown of Thorns. The angels are statues by Giovanni Bernini on the Angels' Bridge (San Angelo).

1975, Mar. 25 **Photo.** *Perf. 14*

1175 A630 40 l multi 15 15
1176 A630 50 l bl & multi 15 15
1177 A631 90 l bl & multi 15 15
1178 A630 150 l vio & multi 15 15
1179 A632 180 l multi 18 15
Set value 62 40

Pitti Madonna, by Michelangelo A633

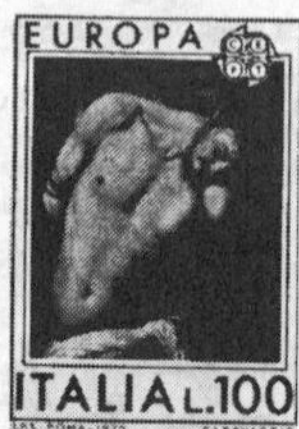

Flagellation of Jesus, by Caravaggio A634

Designs (Works of Michelangelo): 50 l, Niche in Vatican Palace. 90 l, The Flood, detail from Sistine Chapel.

1975, Apr. 18 **Engr.** *Perf. 13½x14*

1180 A633 40 l dl grn 15 15
1181 A633 50 l sepia 15 15
1182 A633 90 l red brn 15 15
Set value 28 18

Michelangelo Buonarroti (1475-1564), sculptor, painter and architect.

1975, Apr. 29 **Photo.** *Perf. 13x14*

Europa: 150 l, Apparition of Angel to Hagar and Ishmael, by Tiepolo (detail).

1183 A634 100 l multi 15 15
1184 A634 150 l multi 15 15
Set value 18

Four Days of Naples, by Marino Mazzacurati A635

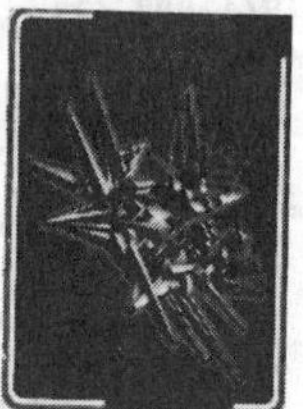
Resistance Fighters of Cuneo, by Umberto Mastroianni A636

Design: 100 l, Martyrs of Ardeatine Caves, by Francesco Coccia.

1975, Apr. 23

1185 A635 70 l multi 15 15
1186 A636 100 l ol & multi 15 15
1187 A636 150 l multi 15 15
Set value 38 26

30th anniversary of victory of the resistance movement.

Globe and IWY Emblem A637

1975, May *Perf. 14x13½*

1188 A637 70 l multi 15 15

International Women's Year 1975.

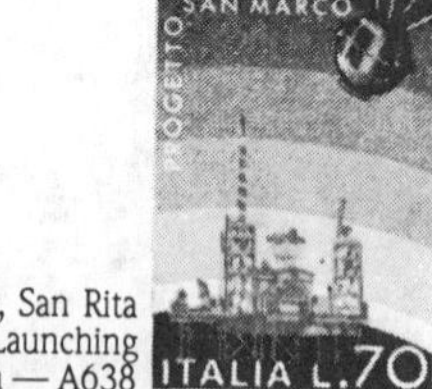

Satellite, San Rita Launching Platform — A638

1975, May 28 *Perf. 13½x14*

1189 A638 70 l multi 15 15

San Marco satellite project.

Tourist Type of 1974

Paintings: No. 1190, View of Isola Bella. No. 1191, Baths of Montecatini. No. 1192, View of Cefalù.

1975, June 16 Photo. *Perf. 14*

1190 A616 150 l grn & multi 18 15
1191 A616 150 l bl grn & multi 18 15
1192 A616 150 l red brn & multi 18 15
Set value 27

Artist and Model, Armando Spadini A640

Painting: No. 1194, Flora, by Guido Reni.

1975, June 20 Engr. *Perf. 14*

1193 A640 90 l blk & multi 15 15
1194 A640 90 l multi 15 15
Set value 18

50th death anniv. of Armando Spadini and 400th birth anniv. of Guido Reni.

Giovanni Pierluigi da Palestrina (1525-94), Composer of Sacred Music — A641

1975, June 27 Engr. *Perf. 13½x14*

1195 A641 100 l magenta & tan 15 15

Emmigrants and Ship — A642

1975, June 30 Photo. *Perf. 14x13½*

1196 A642 70 l multi 15 15

Italian emigration centenary.

Emblem of United Legal Groups A643

Perf. 14x13½

1975, July 25 Photo. Engr.

1197 A643 100 l yel, grn & red 15 15

Centenary of unification of Italian legal organizations.

Locomotive Wheels A644

1975, Sept. 15 Photo. *Perf. 14x13½*

1198 A644 70 l multi 15 15

Intl. Railroad Union, 21st cong., Bologna.

Salvo D'Acquisto, by Vittorio Pisano A645

1975, Sept. 23

1199 A645 100 l multi 15 15

D'Acquisto died in 1943 saving 22 people.

Stylized Syracusean Italia — A646

1975, Sept. 26 Photo. *Perf. 13½x14*

1200 A646 100 l org & multi 15 15

Cent. of unification of the State Archives.

Fountain Type of 1973

Designs: No. 1201, Rosello Fountain, Sassari. No. 1202, Fountain of the 99 Faucets, Aquila. No. 1203, Piazza Fontana, Milan.

Photogravure and Engraved

1975, Oct. 20 *Perf. 13x14*

1201 A603 70 l blk & multi 15 15
1202 A603 70 l blk & multi 15 15
1203 A603 70 l blk & multi 15 15
Set value 36 24

Antonio Vivaldi — A647

1975, Nov. 14 Photo. *Perf. 14x13½*

1204 A647 100 l Alessandro Scarlatti 15 15
1205 A647 100 l shown 15 15
1206 A647 100 l Gaspare Spontini 15 15
1207 A647 100 l F. B. Busoni 15 15
1208 A647 100 l Francesco Cilea 15 15
1209 A647 100 l Franco Alfano 15 15
Nos. 1204-1209 (6) 90
Set value 48

Famous musicians.
See Nos. 1243-1247, 1266-1270.

Annunciation to the Shepherds — A648

"The Magic Orchard" — A649

Christmas: 100 l, Nativity. 150 l, Annunciation to the Kings. Designs from painted wood panels, portal of Alatri Cathedral, 14th century.

Lithographed and Engraved

1975, Nov. 25 *Perf. 13½x14*

1210 A648 70 l grn & multi 15 15
1211 A648 100 l ultra & multi 15 15
1212 A648 150 l brn & multi 15 15
Set value 26

Perf. 14x13½, 13½x14

1975, Dec. 7 Photo.

Designs (Children's Drawings): 70 l, Children on Horseback, horiz. 150 l, Village and procession, horiz.

1213 A649 70 l multi 15 15
1214 A649 100 l multi 15 15
1215 A649 150 l multi 15 15

17th Stamp Day.

Boccaccio, by Andrea del Castagno — A650

State Advocate's Office, Rome — A651

Design: 150 l, Frontispiece for "Fiammetta," 15th century woodcut.

Engraved and Lithographed

1975, Dec. 22 *Perf. 13½x14*

1216 A650 100 l yel grn & blk 15 15
1217 A650 150 l buff & multi 18 15
Set value 18

Giovanni Boccaccio (1313-1375), writer.

1976, Jan. 30 Photo. *Perf. 13½x14*

1218 A651 150 l multi 18 15

State Advocate's Office, centenary.

ITALIA 76 Emblem — A652

Majolica Plate, Deruta — A653

Design: 180 l, Milan Fair pavilion.

1976, Mar. 27 Photo. *Perf. 13½x14*

1219 A652 150 l blk, red & grn 15 15
1220 A652 180 l blk, red, grn & bl 18 15
Set value 22

ITALIA 76 International Philatelic Exhibition, Milan, Oct. 14-24.

Tourist Type of 1974

Tourist publicity: No. 1221, Fenis Castle. No. 1222, View of Ischia. No. 1223, Itria Valley.

1976, May 21 Photo. *Perf. 14*

1221 A616 150 l grn & multi 20 15
1222 A616 150 l plum & multi 20 15
1223 A616 150 l yel & multi 20 15
Set value 27

1976, May 22 *Perf. 13½x14*

Europa: 180 l, Ceramic vase in shape of woman's head, Caltagirone.

1224 A653 150 l multi 15 15
1225 A653 180 l brn & multi 25 15
Set value 18

Italian Flags — A654

Italian Presidents — A655

1976, June 1

1226 A654 100 l multi 15 15
1227 A655 150 l multi 18 15
Set value 18

30th anniversary of Italian Republic.

Fortitude, by Giacomo Serpotta, 1656-1732 A656

Paintings: No. 1229, Woman at Table, by Umberto Boccioni, 1882-1916. No. 1230, The Gunner's Letter, by F. T. Marinetti, 1876-1944.

1976, July 26 Engr. *Perf. 14*

1228 A656 150 l blue 20 15

Lithographed and Engraved

1229 A656 150 l multi 20 15
1230 A656 150 l blk & red 20 15
Set value 27

Italian art.

St. George, by Vittore Carpaccio A657

Design: No. 1231, Dragon, by Vittore Carpaccio, after painting in Church of St. George Schiavoni, Venice.

1976, July 30 Engr. *Perf. 14x13½*

1231 A657 150 l rose lake 20 15
1232 A657 150 l rose lake 20 15
a. Pair, #1231-1232 + label 40 20
Set value 15

Carpaccio (1460-1526), Venetian painter.

Flora, by Titian A658

1976, Sept. 15 Engr. *Perf. 14*

1233 A658 150 l carmine 20 15

Titian (1477-1576), Venetian painter.

St. Francis, 13th Century Fresco — A659

1976, Oct. 2 Engr. *Perf. 14*

1234	A659	150 l brown	20	15

St. Francis of Assisi, 750th death anniv.

Cart, from Trajan's Column A660

Designs: 100 l, Emblem of Kingdom of Sardinia. 150 l, Marble mask, 19th century mail box. 200 l, Hand canceler, 19th century. 400 l, Automatic letter sorting machine.

1976, Oct. 14 Photo. *Perf. 14x13½*

1235	A660	70 l multi	15	15
1236	A660	100 l multi	15	15
1237	A660	150 l multi	18	15
1238	A660	200 l multi	20	15
1239	A660	400 l multi	40	22
		Nos. 1235-1239 (5)	1.08	
		Set value		64

ITALIA 76 International Philatelic Exhibition, Milan, Oct. 14-24.

Girl and Animals — A661

Designs (Children' Drawings): 100 l, Trees, rabbit and flowers. 150 l, Boy healing tree.

1976, Oct. 17 *Perf. 13½x14*

1240	A661	40 l multi	15	15
1241	A661	100 l multi	15	15
1242	A661	150 l multi	15	15
		Set value	38	18

18th Stamp Day and nature protection.

Vivaldi Type of 1975

1976, Nov. 22 Photo. *Perf. 14x13½*

1243	A647	170 l Lorenzo Ghiberti	20	15
1244	A647	170 l Domenico Ghirlandaio	20	15
1245	A647	170 l Sassoferrato	20	15
1246	A647	170 l Carlo Dolci	20	15
1247	A647	170 l Giovanni Piazzetta	20	15
		Nos. 1243-1247 (5)	1.00	
		Set value		25

Famous painters.

The Visit, by Silvestro Lega — A662

1976, Dec. 7 Photo. *Perf. 14x13½*

1248	A662	170 l multi	25	15

Silvestro Lega (1826-1895), painter, sesquicentennial of birth.

Adoration of the Kings, by Bartolo di Fredi — A663

Christmas: 120 l, Nativity, by Taddeo Gaddi.

1976, Dec. 11 *Perf. 13½x14*

1249	A663	70 l multi	15	15
1250	A663	120 l multi	15	15
		Set value		15

Fountain Type of 1973

Designs: No. 1251, Antique Fountain, Gallipoli. No. 1252, Madonna Fountain, Verona. No. 1253, Silvio Cosini Fountain, Palazzo Doria, Genoa.

Lithographed and Engraved

1976, Dec. 21 *Perf. 13½x14*

1251	A603	170 l blk & multi	22	15
1252	A603	170 l blk & multi	22	15
1253	A603	170 l blk & multi	22	15
		Set value		18

Snakes Forming Net — A664

Design: 170 l, Drug addict and poppy.

1977, Feb. 28 Photo. *Perf. 14x13½*

1254	A664	120 l multi	16	15
1255	A664	170 l multi	22	15
		Set value		15

Fight against drug abuse.

Micca Setting Fire — A665

1977, Mar. 5

1256	A665	170 l multi	24	15

Pietro Micca (1677-1706), patriot who set fire to the powder magazine of Turin Citadel, 300th birth anniversary.

Globe with Cross in Center — A666

Design: 120 l, People of the World united as brothers by St. John Bosco.

1977, Mar. 29 Photo. *Perf. 13x13½*

1257	A666	70 l multi	15	15
1258	A666	120 l multi	15	15
		Set value		15

Honoring the Salesian missionaries.

Italian Constitution, Article 53 — A667

1977, Apr. 14 Photo. *Perf. 14*

1259	A667	120 l bis, brn & blk	15	15
1260	A667	170 l lt grn, grn & blk	20	15
		Set value		15

"Pay your taxes."

Tourist Type of 1974

Europa (Europa Emblem and): 170 l, Taormina. 200 l, Castle del Monte.

1977, May 2

1261	A616	170 l multi	20	15
1262	A616	200 l multi	30	15
		Set value		17

Tourist Type of 1974

Paintings: No. 1263, Canossa Castle. No. 1264, Fermo. No. 1265, Castellana Caves.

1977, May 30 Photo. *Perf. 14*

1263	A616	170 l brn & multi	22	15
1264	A616	170 l vio & multi	22	15
1265	A616	170 l gray & multi	22	15
		Set value		15

Vivaldi Type of 1975

1977, June 27 *Perf. 14x13½*

1266	A647	70 l Filippo Brunelleschi	15	15
1267	A647	70 l Pietro Aretino	15	15
1268	A647	70 l Carlo Goldoni	15	15
1269	A647	70 l Luigi Cherubini	15	15
1270	A647	70 l Eduardo Bassini	15	15
		Set value	60	30

Famous artists, writers and scientists.

Justice, by Andrea Delitio A669

Painting: No. 1272, Winter, by Giuseppe Arcimboldi, 1527-c.1593.

Engraved and Lithographed

1977, Sept. 5 *Perf. 14*

1271	A669	170 l multi	25	15
1272	A669	170 l multi	25	15
		Set value		18

Corvette Caracciolo — A670

Italian Ships: No. 1274, Hydrofoil gunboat Sparviero. No. 1275, Paddle steamer Ferdinando Primo. No. 1276, Passenger liner Saturnia.

Photogravure and Engraved

1977, Sept. 23 *Perf. 14x13½*

1273	A670	170 l multi	32	15
1274	A670	170 l multi	32	15
1275	A670	170 l multi	32	15
1276	A670	170 l multi	32	15
a.		Block of 4, #1273-1276 + 2 labels	1.50	
		Set value		32

See #1323-1326, 1382-1385, 1435-1438.

Fountain Type of 1973

Designs: No. 1277, Pacassi Fountain, Gorizia. No. 1278, Fraterna Fountain, Isernia. No. 1279, Palm Fountain, Palmi.

Lithographed and Engraved

1977, Oct. 18 *Perf. 13x14*

1277	A603	120 l blk & multi	15	15
1278	A603	120 l blk & multi	15	15
1279	A603	120 l blk & multi	15	15
		Set value		18

Volleyball — A671

Designs (Children's Drawings): No. 1281, Butterflies and net. No. 1282, Flying kites.

1977, Oct. 23 Photo. *Perf. 13x14*

1280	A671	120 l multi	15	15
1281	A671	120 l multi	15	15
1282	A671	120 l multi	15	15
a.		Block of 3, #1280-1282 + label	50	30
		Set value		24

19th Stamp Day.

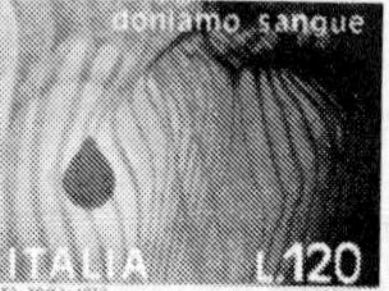

Symbolic Blood Donation A672

Design: 70 l, Blood donation symbolized.

1977, Oct. 26 *Perf. 14x13½*

1283	A672	70 l multi	15	15
1284	A672	120 l multi	15	15
		Set value		15

Blood donors.

Quintino Sella and Italy No. 24 — A673

1977, Oct. 23 *Perf. 13½x14*

1285	A673	170 l ol & blk brn	22	15

Quintino Sella (1827-1884), statesman, engineer, mineralogist, birth sesquicentenary.

Italia Type of 1953-54 and

Italia — A674

1977-87 Wmk. 303 *Perf. 14*

Size: 16x20mm

Photo.

1288	A354	120 l dk bl & emer	18	15

Photo. & Engr.

1292	A354	170 l grn & ocher	35	15

Litho. & Engr.

1295	A354	350 l red, ocher & pur	55	15

Perf. 14x13½

Engr. Unwmk.

1304	A674	1500 l multi	1.50	15
1305	A674	2000 l multi	1.90	15
1306	A674	3000 l multi	3.00	15
1307	A674	4000 l multi	3.75	15
1308	A674	5000 l multi	5.00	38
1308A	A674	10,000 l multi	9.50	1.40
1308B	A674	20,000 l multi	22.50	12.00
		Nos. 1288-1308B (10)	48.23	14.83

Issue dates: Nos. 1288, 1292, 1295, Nov. 22. No. 1308, Dec. 4, 1978. No. 1307, Feb. 12, 1979. No. 1306, Mar. 12, 1979. No. 1305, Apr. 12, 1979. No. 1304, May 14, 1979. No. 1308A, June 27, 1983. No. 1308B, Jan. 5, 1987.

This is an expanding set. Numbers will change if necessary.

Dina Galli — A675

La Scala — A677

Adoration of the Shepherds, by Pietro Testa — A676

Perf. 13½x14

1977, Dec. 2 Photo. Unwmk.
1309 A675 170 l multi 22 15

Dina Galli (1877-1951), actress, birth centenary.

Lithographed and Engraved

1977, Dec. 13 ***Perf. 14***

Christmas: 120 l, Adoration of the Shepherds, by Gian Jacopo Caraglio.

1310 A676 70 l blk & ol 15 15
1311 A676 120 l blk & bl grn 15 15
Set value 15

1978, Mar. 15 Litho. ***Perf. 13½x14***

Design: 200 l, La Scala, auditorium.

1312 A677 170 l multi 22 15
1313 A677 200 l multi 28 15
Set value 17

La Scala Opera House, Milan, bicentenary.

Tourist Type of 1974

Paintings: 70 l, Gubbio. 200 l, Udine. 600 l, Paestum.

1978, Mar. 30 Photo. ***Perf. 14***
1314 A616 70 l multi 15 15
1315 A616 200 l multi 22 15
1316 A616 600 l multi 70 38
Set value 52

Giant Grouper A678

Designs (outline of "Amerigo Vespucci" in background): No. 1318, Leatherback turtle. No. 1319, Mediterranean monk seal. No. 1320, Audouin's gull.

1978, Apr. 3 ***Perf. 14x13***
1317 A678 170 l multi 25 15
1318 A678 170 l multi 25 15
1319 A678 170 l multi 25 15
1320 A678 170 l multi 25 15
a. Strip of 4, #1317-1320 + label 1.25 1.00
Set value 32

Endangered species in Mediterranean.

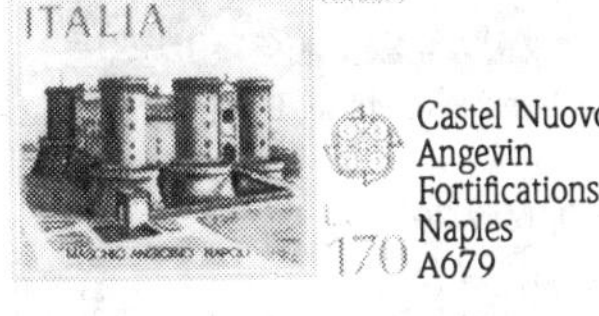

Castel Nuovo, Angevin Fortifications, Naples A679

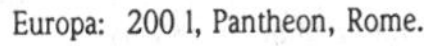
Europa: 200 l, Pantheon, Rome.

1978, Apr. 29 Litho. ***Perf. 14x13½***
1321 A679 170 l multi 20 15
1322 A679 200 l multi 30 15
Set value 15

Ship Type of 1977

Designs: No. 1323, Cruiser Benedetto Brin. No. 1324, Frigate Lupo. No. 1325, Ligurian brigantine Fortuna. No. 1326, Container ship Africa.

1978, May 8 Litho. & Engr.
1323 A670 170 l multi 60 15
1324 A670 170 l multi 60 15
1325 A670 170 l multi 60 15
1326 A670 170 l multi 60 15
a. Block of 4, #1323-1326 + 2 labels 2.50
Set value 36

Matilde Serao — A680

Constitution — A681

Designs: Portraits of famous Italians.

1978, May 10 Engr. ***Perf. 14x13½***
1327 A680 170 l shown 22 15
1328 A680 170 l Vittorino da Feltre 22 15
1329 A680 170 l Victor Emmanuel II 22 15
1330 A680 170 l Pope Pius IX 22 15
1331 A680 170 l Marcello Malpighi 22 15
1332 A680 170 l Antonio Meucci 22 15
a. Block of 6, #1327-1332 1.50
Nos. 1327-1332 (6) 1.32
Set value 48

1978, June 2 Litho. ***Perf. 13½x14***
1333 A681 170 l multi 24 15

30th anniversary of Constitution.

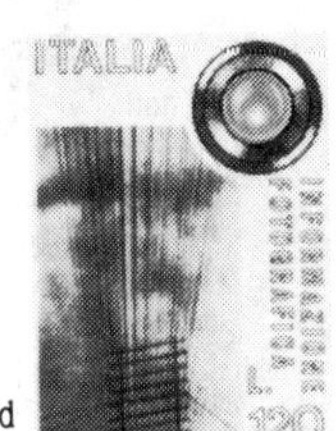

Telegraph Wires and Lens — A682

1978, June 30 Photo.
1334 A682 120 l lt bl & gray 18 15

Photographic information.

The Lovers, by Tranquillo Cremona (1837-1878) A683

Design: 520 l, The Cook (woman with goose), by Bernardo Strozzi (1581-1644).

Engraved and Lithographed

1978, July 12 ***Perf. 14***
1335 A683 170 l multi 1.40 15
1336 A683 520 l multi 4.00 75

Holy Shroud of Turin, by Giovanni Testa, 1578 — A684

1978, Sept. 8 Photo. ***Perf. 14***
1337 A684 220 l yel, red & blk 30 15

400th anniversary of the transfer of the Holy Shroud from Savoy to Turin.

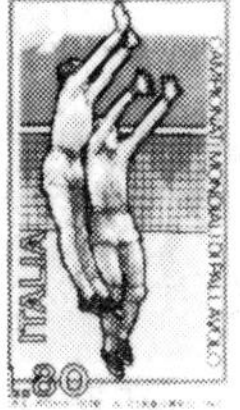

Volleyball A685

Mother and Child, by Masaccio A686

Design: 120 l, Volleyball, diff.

1978, Sept. 20
1338 A685 80 l multi 18 15
1339 A685 120 l multi 30 15
Set value 15

Men's Volleyball World Championship.

1978, Oct. 18 Engr. ***Perf. 13½x14***
1340 A686 170 l indigo 24 15

Masaccio (real name Tommaso Guidi; 1401-1428), painter, 550th death anniversary.

Fountain Type of 1973

Designs: No 1341, Neptune Fountain, Trent. No. 1342, Fortuna Fountain, Fano. No. 1343, Cavallina Fountain, Genzano di Lucania.

1978, Oct. 25 Litho. & Engr.
1341 A603 120 l blk & multi 20 15
1342 A603 120 l blk & multi 20 15
1343 A603 120 l blk & multi 20 15
Set value 18

Virgin and Child, by Giorgione — A687

Adoration of the Kings, by Giorgione — A688

1978, Nov. 8 Engr. ***Perf. 13x14***
1344 A687 80 l dk red 15 15

Photo. ***Perf. 14x13½***
1345 A688 120 l multi 15 15

Christmas 1978.

Flags as Flowers — A689

Designs: No. 1347, European flags. No. 1348, "People hailing Europe."

1978, Nov. 26 Photo. ***Perf. 13x14***
1346 A689 120 l multi 18 15
1347 A689 120 l multi 18 15
1348 A689 120 l multi 18 15
Set value 18

20th Stamp Day on theme "United Europe."

State Printing Office, Stamps A690

Design: 220 l, Printing press and stamps.

1979, Jan. 6 Photo. ***Perf. 14x13½***
1349 A690 170 l multi 18 15
1350 A690 220 l multi 28 15
Set value 17

50th anniversary of first stamps printed by State Printing Office.

St. Francis Washing Lepers, 13th Century Painting A691

1979, Jan. 22
1351 A691 80 l multi 15 15

Leprosy relief.

Bicyclist Carrying Bike — A692

1979, Jan. 27 ***Perf. 13½x14***
1352 A692 170 l multi 18 15
1353 A692 220 l multi 28 15
Set value 17

World Crosscountry Bicycle Championships.

Virgin Mary, by Antonello da Messina A693

Painting: 520 l, Haystack, by Ardengo Soffici (1879-1964).

1979, Feb. 15 Engr. *Perf. 14*

1354 A693 170 l multi 30 15
1355 A693 520 l multi 70 45

A694

A695

Lithographed and Engraved

1979, Mar. 14 *Perf. 13x14*

1356 A694 120 l multi 18 15

Albert Einstein (1879-1955), theoretical physicist and his equation.

Tourist Type of 1974

Paintings: 70 l, Asiago. 90 l, Castelsardo. 170 l, Orvieto. 220 l, Scilla.

1979, Mar. 30 Photo. *Perf. 14*

1357 A616 70 l grn & multi 15 15
1358 A616 90 l car & multi 15 15
1359 A616 170 l ultra & multi 22 15
1360 A616 220 l gray & multi 32 15
Set value 38

1979, Apr. 23 Engr. *Perf. 14x13½*

Famous Italians: No. 1362, Carlo Maderno (1556-1629), architect. No. 1362, Lazzaro Spallanzani (1729-1799), physiologist. No. 1363, Ugo Foscolo (1778-1827), writer. No. 1364 Massimo Bontempelli (1878-1960), journalist. No. 1365, Francesco Severi (1879-1961), mathematician.

1361 A695 170 l multi 24 15
1362 A695 170 l multi 24 15
1363 A695 170 l multi 24 15
1364 A695 170 l multi 24 15
1365 A695 170 l multi 24 15
Nos. 1361-1365 (5) 1.20
Set value 30

Telegraph A696

Europa: 220 l, Carrier pigeons.

1979, Apr. 30 Photo. *Perf. 14*

1366 A696 170 l multi 30 15
1367 A696 220 l multi 40 15
Set value 17

Flags and "E" — A697

1979, May 5 *Perf. 14x13½*

1368 A697 170 l multi 20 15
1369 A697 220 l multi 30 15
Set value 15

European Parliament, first direct elections, June 7-10.

Exhibition Emblem, Dome of Milan A698

1979, June 22 Photo. *Perf. 14*

1370 A698 170 l multi 20 15
1371 A698 220 l multi 30 15
Set value 17

3rd World Machine Tool Exhibition, Milan, Oct. 10-18.

Aeneas and Rotary Emblem — A699

Basket — A700

1979, June 9 *Perf. 13½x14*

1372 A699 220 l multi 30 15

70th World Rotary Cong., Rome, June 1979.

1979, June 13 *Perf. 14*

Design: 120 l, Basketball players.

1373 A700 80 l multi 20 15
1374 A700 120 l multi 30 15
Set value 16

21st European Basketball Championship, June 9-20.

A701 A702

Design: Patient and Physician, 16th cent. woodcut.

1979, June 16 Photo. & Engr.

1375 A701 120 l multi 18 15

Digestive Ailments Study Week.

Lithographed and Engraved

1979, July 9 *Perf. 13x14*

Design: Ottorino Respighi (1879-1936), composer, Roman landscape.

1376 A702 120 l multi 18 15

Woman Making Phone Call — A703

Design: 200 l, Woman with old-fashioned phone.

1979, Sept. 20 Photo. *Perf. 14*

1377 A703 170 l red & gray 20 15
1378 A703 220 l grn & slate 30 15
Set value 21

3rd World Telecommunications Exhibition, Geneva, Sept. 20-26.

Fountain Type of 1973

Designs: No. 1379, Great Fountain, Viterbo. No. 1380, Hot Springs, Acqui Terme. No. 1381, Pomegranate Fountain, Issogne Castle.

Lithographed and Engraved

1979, Sept. 22 *Perf. 13x14*

1379 A603 120 l multi 22 15
1380 A603 120 l multi 22 15
1381 A603 120 l multi 22 15
Set value 18

Ship Type of 1977

Designs: No. 1382, Cruiser Enrico Dandolo. No. 1383, Submarine Carlo Fecia. No. 1384, Freighter Cosmos. No. 1385, Ferry Deledda.

1979, Oct. 12 *Perf. 14x13½*

1382 A670 170 l multi 32 15
1383 A670 170 l multi 32 15
1384 A670 170 l multi 32 15
1385 A670 170 l multi 32 15
a. Block of 4, #1382-1385 + 2 labels 1.50
Set value 36

Penny Black, Rowland Hill — A704

1979, Oct. 25 Photo.

1386 A704 220 l multi 30 15

Sir Rowland Hill (1795-1879), originator of penny postage.

Minstrels and Church A705

1979, Nov. 7 Photo. *Perf. 14x13½*

1387 A705 120 l multi 18 15

Christmas 1979.

Black and White Boys Holding Hands A706

Children's Drawings: 120 l, Children of various races under umbrella map, vert. 150 l, Children and red balloons.

Perf. 14x13½, 13½x14

1979, Nov. 25 Photo.

1388 A706 70 l multi 15 15
1389 A706 120 l multi 15 15
1390 A706 150 l multi 20 15
Set value 18

21st Stamp Day.

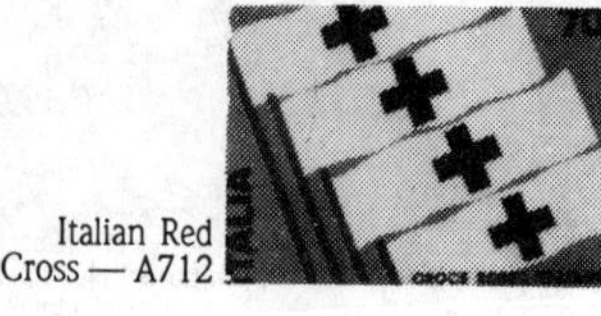

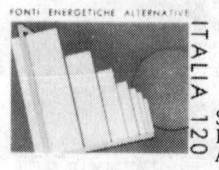

Solar Energy Panels A707

Energy Conservation: 170 l, Sun & pylon.

1980, Feb. 25 Photo. *Perf. 14x13½*

1391 A707 120 l multi 15 15
1392 A707 170 l multi 24 15
Set value 18

A708

A709

1980, Mar. 21 Engr. *Perf. 13½x14*

1393 A708 220 l dark blue 30 15

St. Benedict of Nursia, 1500th birth anniv.

Lithographed and Engraved

1980, Apr. 16 *Perf. 13½x14*

Design: Royal Palace, Naples.

1394 A709 220 l multi 30 15

20th International Philatelic Exhibition, Europa '80, Naples, Apr. 26-May 4.

Antonio Pigafetta, Caravel A710

Europa: 220 l, Antonio Lo Surdo (1880-1949) geophysicist.

1980, Apr. 28 Litho. *Perf. 14x13½*

1395 A710 170 l multi 25 15
1396 A710 220 l multi 35 15
Set value 17

St. Catherine, Reliquary Bust — A711

1980, Apr. 29 Photo.

1397 A711 170 l multi 25 15

St. Catherine of Siena (1347-1380).

Italian Red Cross — A712

1980, May 15 Photo. *Perf. 14x13½*

1398 A712 70 l multi 15 15
1399 A712 80 l multi 15 15
Set value 24 17

Temples of Philae, Egypt — A713

1980, May 20

1400 Pair + label 60 15
a. A713 220 l shown 25 15
b. A713 220 l Temple of Philae, diff. 25 15

Italian civil engineering achievements (Temples of Philae saved from ruin by Italian engineers).

Soccer Player — A714

1980, June 11

1401	A714 80 l multi	20	15

European Soccer Championships, Milan, Turin, Rome, Naples, June 9-22.

Tourist Type of 1974

Paintings: 80 l, Erice. 150 l, Villa Rufolo, Ravello. 200 l, Roseto degli Abruzzi. 670 l, Public Baths, Salsomaggiore Terme.

1980, June 28 ***Perf. 14***

1402	A616 80 l multi	18	15
1403	A616 150 l multi	28	15
1404	A616 200 l multi	35	15
1405	A616 670 l multi	70	40
	Set value		67

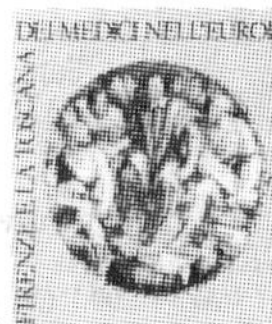

Cosimo I with his Artists, by Giorgio Vasari — A715

1980, July 2 ***Perf. 13½x14***

1406	Pair + label	50	50
a.	A715 170 l shown	20	15
b.	A715 170 l Armillary sphere	20	15

The Medici in Europe of the 16th Century Exhibition, Florence.

Fonte Avellana Monastery Millennium A716

1980, Sept. 3 Engr. ***Perf. 14x13½***

1407	A716 200 l grn & brn	30	15

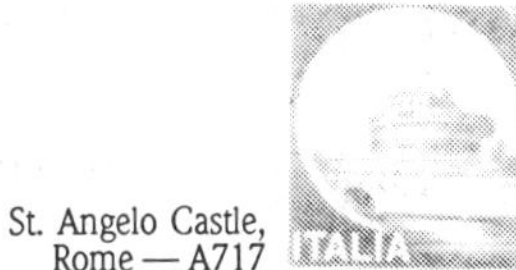

St. Angelo Castle, Rome — A717

Designs: Castles.

Perf. 14x13½

1980, Sept. 22 **Wmk. 303**

Design A717

1408	5 l shown	15	15
1409	10 l Sforzesco, Milan	15	15
1410	20 l Del Monte, Andria	15	15
1411	40 l Ursino, Catania	15	15
1412	50 l Rocca di Calascio	15	15
1413	60 l Norman Tower, St. Mauro Fort	15	15
1414	90 l Isola Capo Rizzuto	18	15
1415	100 l Aragonese, Ischia	18	15
1416	120 l Estense, Ferrara	18	15
1417	150 l Miramare, Trieste	20	15
1418	170 l Ostia, Rome	24	15
1419	180 l Gavone, Savona	24	15
1420	200 l Cerro al Volturno, Isernia	24	15
1421	250 l Rocca di Mondavio	35	15
1422	300 l Svevo, Bari	40	15
1423	350 l Mussomeli, Caltanissetta	45	15
1424	400 l Imperatore-Prato, Florence	52	15
1425	450 l Bosa, Nuoro	60	15
1426	500 l Rovereto, Trento	70	15
1427	600 l Scaligero, Sirmione	75	15
1428	700 l Ivrea, Turin	1.00	15
1429	800 l Rocca Maggiore, Assisi	1.10	15
1430	900 l St. Pierre, Aosta	1.25	15
1431	1000 l Montagnana, Padua	1.25	15
	Nos. 1408-1431 (24)	10.73	
	Set value		1.40

Coil Stamps

Engr. ***Perf. 14 Vert.***

Size: 16x21mm

1432	30 l St. Severna, Rome	15	15
1433	120 l Lombardia, Enna	22	15
a.	Pair, Nos. 1432-1433	40	18
1434	170 l Serralunga d'Alba, Cuneo	30	15
a.	Pair, Nos. 1432, 1434	75	75
	Set value		18

See Nos. 1475-1484, 1657-1666, 1868.

Ship Type of 1977

Designs: No. 1435, Corvette Gabbiano. No. 1436, Torpedo boat Audace. No. 1437, Sailing ship Italia. No. 1438, Floating dock Castoro Sei.

Lithographed and Engraved

1980, Oct. 11 ***Perf. 14x13½***

1435	A670 200 l multi	1.50	15
1436	A670 200 l multi	1.50	15
1437	A670 200 l multi	1.50	15
1438	A670 200 l multi	1.50	15
a.	Block of 4, #1435-1438 + 2 labels		
	Set value		36

Philip Mazzei (1730-1816), Political Writer in United States — A718

1980, Oct. 18 Photo. ***Perf. 13½x14***

1439	A718 320 l multi	45	15

Villa Foscari Malcontenta, Venezia A719

Villas: 150 l, Barbaro Maser, Treviso. 170 l, Godi Valmarana, Vicenza.

Lithographed and Engraved

1980, Oct. 31 ***Perf. 14x13½***

1440	A719 80 l multi	20	15
1441	A719 150 l multi	25	15
1442	A719 170 l multi	30	15
	Set value		25

See Nos. 1493-1495, 1528-1530, 1565-1568, 1606-1609, 1646-1649, 1691-1695.

St. Barbara, by Palma the Elder (1480-1528) A720

Design: No. 1444, Apollo and Daphne, by Gian Lorenzo Bernini (1598-1680).

1980, Nov. 20 ***Perf. 14***

1443	A720 520 l multi	70	42
1444	A720 520 l multi	70	42

Nativity Sculpture by Federico Brandini, 16th Cent. — A721

1980, Nov. 22 **Engr.**

1445	A721 120 l brn org & blk	20	15

Christmas 1980.

View of Verona A722

22nd Stamp Day: Views of Verona drawings by school children.

1980, Nov. 30 Photo. ***Perf. 14x13½***

1446	A722 70 l multi	15	15
1447	A722 120 l multi	20	15
1448	A722 170 l multi	25	15
	Set value		18

Daniele Comboni (1831-1881), Savior of the Africans A723

1981, Mar. 14 **Engr.**

1449	A723 80 l multi	15	15

Alcide de Gasperi (1881-1954), Statesman — A724

International Year of the Disabled — A725

1981, Apr. 3 ***Perf. 13½x14***

1450	A724 200 l olive green	30	15

1981, Apr. 11 **Photo.**

1451	A725 300 l multi	50	15

A726 A727

1981, Apr. 27 Photo. ***Perf. 13½x14***

1452	A726 200 l Roses	30	15
1453	A726 200 l Anemones	30	15
1454	A726 200 l Oleanders	30	15
	Set value		18

See Nos. 1510-1512, 1555-1557.

1981, May 4

Designs: No. 1455, Chess game with human pieces, Marostica. No. 1456, Horse race, Siena.

1455	A727 300 l shown	40	15
1456	A727 300 l	40	15
	Set value		16

Europa.

St. Rita Offering Thorn — A728

Ciro Menotti (1798-1831), Patriot — A729

1981, May 22

1457	A728 600 l multi	80	35

St. Rita of Cascia, 600th birth anniversary.

1981, May 26 Engr. ***Perf. 14x13½***

1458	A729 80 l brn & blk	15	15

G-222 Aeritalia Transport Plane A730

1981, June 1 **Photo.**

1459	A730 200 l shown	30	15
1460	A730 200 l MB-339 Aermacchi jet	30	15
1461	A730 200 l A-109 Agusta helicopter	30	15
1462	A730 200 l P-68 Partenavia transport plane	30	15
a.	Block of 4, #1459-1462 + 2 labels	1.35	
	Set value		36

See Nos. 1505-1508, 1550-1553.

Hydro-geological Research — A731

1981, June 8 ***Perf. 13½x14***

1463	A731 80 l multi	15	15

Sao Simao Dam and Power Station, Brazil — A732

Civil Engineering Works Abroad: No. 1465, High Island Power Station, Hong Kong.

1981, June 26 Engr. ***Perf. 14x13½***

1464	A732 300 l dark blue	50	15
1465	A732 300 l red	50	15
a.	Pair, #1464-1465 + label	1.10	30
	Set value		16

See Nos. 1516-1517, 1538-1539.

Tourist Type of 1974

1981, July 4 Photo. *Perf. 14*

1466 A616 80 l View of Matera 15 15
1467 A616 150 l Lake Garda 32 15
1468 A616 300 l St. Teresa di Gallura beach 48 15
1469 A616 900 l Tarquinia 2.50 45
Set value 68

Naval Academy, Livorno and Navy Emblem A735

Naval Academy of Livorno Centenary: 150 l, View. 200 l, Cadet with sextant, training ship Amerigo Vespucci.

1981, July 24 *Perf. 14x13½*

1472 A735 80 l multi 15 15
1473 A735 150 l multi 20 15
1474 A735 200 l multi 28 15
Set value 22

Castle Type of 1980

Perf. 14x13½

1981-84 Photo. Wmk. 303

1475 A717 30 l Aquila 15 15
1476 A717 70 l Aragonese, Reggio Calabria 15 15
1477 A717 80 l Sabbionara, Avio 16 15

Perf. 13½

1478 A717 550 l Rocca Sinibalda 65 15
1479 A717 1400 l Caldorosco, Vasto 2.00 60
Nos. 1475-1479 (5) 3.11
Set value 85

Issue dates: Nos. 1475-1477, Aug. 20, 1981. Nos. 1478-1479, Feb. 14, 1984.

Coil Stamps

1981-88 Engr. *Perf. 14 Vert.*

Size: 16x21mm

1480 A717 50 l Scilla 15 15
1481 A717 200 l Angionia, Lucera *2.00 2.00*
1482 A717 300 l Norman Castle, Melfi 60 15
1483 A717 400 l Venafro 45 15
1484 A717 450 l Piobbico Pesaro 40 15
a. Pair, #1480, 1484 60 24
Nos. 1480-1484 (5) *3.60 2.60*

Issue dates: Nos. 1481-1482, Sept. 30. No. 1483, June 25, 1983. Nos. 1480, 1484, July 25, 1985. No. 1484a, Mar. 1, 1988.

Palazzo Spada, Rome (Council Seat) A736

1981, Aug. 31 Engr. Unwmk.

1485 A736 200 l multi 30 15

State Council sesquicentennial.

World Cup Races — A737

1981, Sept. 4 Photo. *Perf. 13½x14*

1486 A737 300 l multi 45 15

Harbor View, by Carlo Carra (1881-1966) — A738

Paintings: No. 1488, Castle, by Guiseppe Ugonia (1881-1944).

Lithographed and Engraved

1981, Sept. 7 *Perf. 14*

1487 A738 200 l multi 30 15
1488 A738 200 l multi 30 15

See Nos. 1532-1533, 1638-1639, 1697-1698, 1732.

Riace Bronze, 4th Cent. B.C. — A739

1981, Sept. 9 Photo. *Perf. 13½x14*

1489 A739 200 l shown 30 15
1490 A739 200 l Statue, diff. 30 15
a. Pair, #1489-1490 65 30
Set value 18

Greek statues found in 1972 in sea near Reggio di Calabria.

Virgil, Mosiac, Treviri — A740

1981, Sept. 19 *Perf. 14*

1491 A740 600 l multi 80 42

Virgil's death bimillennium.

Food and Wine, by Gregorio Sciltian A741

1981, Oct. 16 Litho. *Perf. 14*

1492 A741 150 l multi 20 15

World Food Day.

Villa Type of 1980

Lithographed and Engraved

1981, Oct. 17 *Perf. 14x13½*

1493 A719 100 l Villa Campolieto, Ercolano 20 15
1494 A719 200 l Cimbrone, Ravello 40 15
1495 A719 300 l Pignatelli, Naples 55 15
Set value 24

Adoration of the Magi, by Giovanni de Campione d'Italia (Christmas 1981) — A743

1981, Nov. 21 Engr. *Perf. 14*

1496 A743 200 l multi 35 15

Pope John XXIII (1881-1963) A744

Stamp Day A745

1981, Nov. 25 Photo. *Perf. 13½x14*

1497 A744 200 l multi 30 15

Photogravure, Photogravure and Engraved (200 l)

Perf. 14x13½, 13½x14

1981, Nov. 29

1498 A745 120 l Letters, horiz. 25 15
1499 A745 200 l Angel, letter chest 40 15
1500 A745 300 l Letter seal 60 18
Set value 40

A746

A748

Design: St. Francis Receiving the Stigmata, by Pietro Cavaro.

1982, Jan. 6 *Perf. 13½x14*

1501 A746 300 l dk bl & brn 60 15

800th birth anniv. of St. Francis of Assisi.

1982, Feb. 19 Photo. *Perf. 13½x14*

1503 A748 900 l multi 1.40 70

Niccolo Paganini (1782-1840), Composer and Violinist.

Anti-smoking Campaign A749

1982, Mar. 2 Photo. *Perf. 14x13½*

1504 A749 300 l multi 45 15

Aircraft Type of 1981

1982, Mar. 27 Litho. *Perf. 14x13½*

1505 A730 300 l Aeritalia MRCA 45 15
1506 A730 300 l SIAI 260 Turbo 45 15
1507 A730 300 l Piaggio 166-dl3 Turbo 45 15
1508 A730 300 l Nardi NH-500 45 15
a. Block of 4, #1505-1508 + 2 labels 2.00

Sicilian Vespers, 700th Anniv. — A750

1982, Mar. 31 Engr. *Perf. 13½x14*

1509 A750 120 l multi 28 15

Flower Type of 1981

1982, Apr. 10 Photo.

1510 A726 300 l Cyclamens 45 15
1511 A726 300 l Camellias 45 15
1512 A726 300 l Carnations 45 15
Set value 36

Europa 1982 — A751

Photogravure and Engraved

1982, May 3 *Perf. 13½x14*

1513 A751 200 l Coronation of Charlemagne, 799 30 15
1514 A751 450 l Treaty of Rome signatures, 1957 70 15
Set value 24

Engineering Type of 1981

1982, May 29 Photo. *Perf. 14x13½*

1516 A732 450 l Microwaves across Red Sea 70 18
1517 A732 450 l Automatic letter sorting 70 18
a. Pair, #1516-1517 + label 1.50 60

Giuseppe Garibaldi (1807-82) — A753

Game of the Bridge, Pisa — A754

1982, June 2 *Perf. 13½x14*

1518 A753 200 l multi 30 15

1982, June 5

1519 A754 200 l multi 30 15

See Nos. 1562, 1603, 1628-1629, 1655, 1717, 1749, 1775, 1807.

Tourist Type of 1974

1982, June 28 *Perf. 14*

1520 A616 200 l Frasassi Caves 30 15
1521 A616 200 l Paganella Valley 30 15
1522 A616 450 l Temple of Agrigento 70 18
1523 A616 450 l Rodi Garganico Beach 70 18

World Junior Canoeing Championship — A755

1982, Aug. 4 Photo. *Perf. 14*

1524 A755 200 l multi 30 15

Duke Federico da Montefeltro (1422-1482) A756

Photogravure and Engraved

1982, Sept. 10 *Perf. 14x13½*

1525 A756 200 l Urbino Palace, Gubbio Council House 30 15

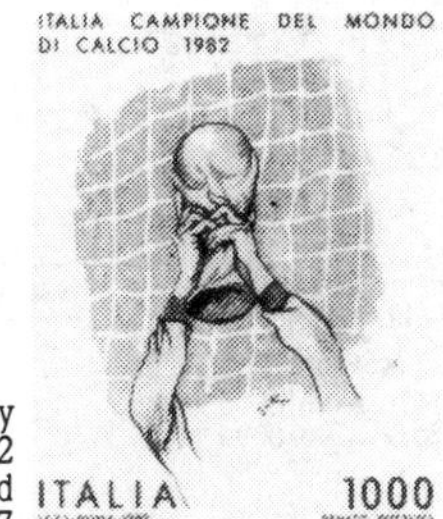
Italy's Victory in 1982 World Cup — A757

1982, Sept. 12 Photo. *Perf. 14*

1526 A757 1000 l World Cup 1.50 75

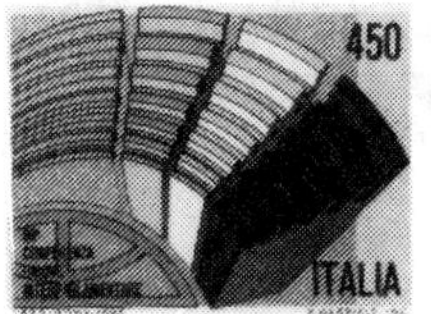
69th Inter-Parliamentary Conference, Rome — A758

1982, Sept. 14 *Perf. 14x13½*

1527 A758 450 l multi 70 15

Villa Type of 1980

Designs: 150 l, Temple of Aesculapius, Villa Borghese, Rome. 250 l, Villa D'Este, Tivoli, Rome. 350 l, Villa Lante, Bagnaia, Viterbo.

Photogravure and Engraved

1982, Oct. 1 *Perf. 14x13½*

1528 A719 150 l multi 25 15
1529 A719 250 l multi 40 15
1530 A719 350 l multi 55 15

Thurn and Taxis Family Postal Service — A759

1982, Oct. 23 Engr. *Perf. 13½x14*

1531 A759 300 l Franz von Taxis (1450-1517) 45 15

Art Type of 1981

Paintings: No. 1532, The Fortune Teller by G.B. Piazzetta (1682-1754). No. 1533, Antonietta Negroni Prati Morosini as a Little Girl by Francesco Hayez (1791-1882).

Lithographed and Engraved

1982, Nov. 3 *Perf. 14*

1532 A738 300 l multi 45 15
1533 A738 300 l multi 45 15

24th Stamp Day — A761

Children's Drawings.

1982, Nov. 28 Photo. *Perf. 14x13½*

1534 A761 150 l multi 25 15
1535 A761 250 l multi 42 15
1536 A761 350 l multi 55 15

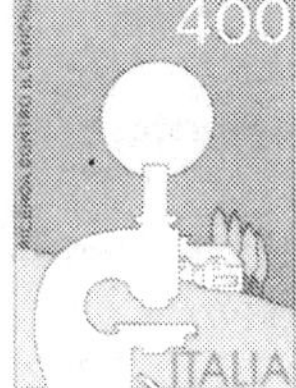
A762

A763

1983, Jan. 14 Photo. *Perf. 13½x14*

1537 A762 400 l multi 45 15

Cancer research.

Engineering Type of 1981

1983, Jan. 20 *Perf. 13½*

1538 A732 400 l Globe, factories 45 15
1539 A732 400 l Automated assembly line 45 15
a. Pair, #1538-1539 1.00 60

1983, Jan. 25 Engr. *Perf. 14x13½*

1540 A763 400 l Emblem 45 15

Crusca Academy, 400th anniv.

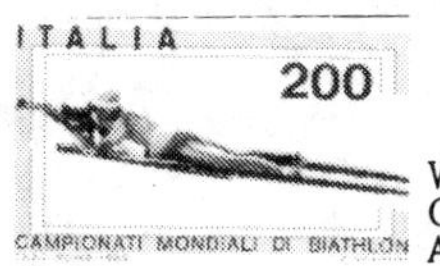
World Biathlon Championship A764

1983, Feb. 5 Photo. *Perf. 14*

1541 A764 200 l multi 22 15

A765

A766

1983, Feb. 28 Engr. *Perf. 14x13½*

1542 A765 300 l dk brn & dk bl 35 15

Gabriele Rossetti (1783-1854), writer.

1983, Mar. 5 Engr. *Perf. 13½x14*

1543 A766 450 l sepia 55 15

Francesco Guicciardini (1483-1540), historian.

Umberto Saba (1883-1957), Poet — A767

1983, Mar. 9 Photo. *Perf. 14x13½*

1544 A767 600 l multi 70 15

Pope Pius XII (1876-1958) — A768

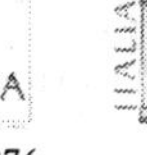
Holy Year — A769

1983, Mar. 21 Engr. *Perf. 13½x14*

1545 A768 1400 l dark blue 1.65 30

1983, Mar. 25 Photo. *Perf. 14*

1546 A769 250 l St. Paul's Basilica 30 15
1547 A769 300 l St. Maria Maggiore Church 35 15
1548 A769 400 l San Giovanni Church 45 15
1549 A769 500 l St. Peter's Church 60 15

Aircraft Type of 1981

1983, Mar. 28 Litho. *Perf. 14x13½*

1550 A730 400 l Caproni C22J glider 45 15
1551 A730 400 l Aeritalia Macchi jet fighter 45 15
1552 A730 400 l SIAI-211 jet trainer 45 15
1553 A730 400 l A-129 Agusta helicopter 45 15
a. Block of 4, #1550-1553 + 2 labels 2.00

Intl. Workers' Day (May 1) — A770

1983, Apr. 29 Engr. *Perf. 14x13½*

1554 A770 1200 l blue 1.75 38

Flower Type of 1981

1983, Apr. 30 Photo. *Perf. 13½x14*

1555 A726 200 l Mimosa 22 15
1556 A726 200 l Rhododendron 22 15
1557 A726 200 l Gladiolus 22 15
Set value 36

Europa 1983 A771

Perf. 14x13½

1983, May 2 Litho. Engr.

1558 A771 400 l Galileo, telescope, 1601 65 15
1559 A771 500 l Archimedes and his screw 85 15

Ernesto T. Moneta (1833-1918), Nobel Peace Prize Winner, 1907 — A772

1983, May 5 Engr. *Perf. 14x13½*

1560 A772 500 l multi 55 15

Monument, Globe, TV Screen A773

20th Natl. Eucharistic Congress A775

1983, May 9 Photo. *Perf. 13½x14*

1561 A773 500 l multi 55 15

3rd Intl. Congress of Jurisdicial Information.

Folk Celebration Type of 1982

Design: No. 1562, La Corsa Dei Ceri Procession, Gubbio.

1983, May 13 *Perf. 13½*

1562 A754 300 l multi 35 15

1983, May 14 *Perf. 14*

1563 A775 300 l multi 35 15

Tourist Type of 1974

1983, July 30 Photo. *Perf. 14*

1563A A616 250 l Alghero 40 20
1563B A616 300 l Bardonecchia 48 24
1563C A616 400 l Riccione 64 32
1563D A616 500 l Taranto 80 40

Girolamo Frescobaldi (1583-1643), Composer — A776

1983, Sept. 14 Engr. *Perf. 13½x14*

1564 A776 400 l brn & grn 50 25

Villa Type of 1980

Designs: 250 l, Fidelia, Spello. 300 l, Imperiale, Pesaro. 400 l, Michetti Convent, Francavilla al Mare. 500 l, Riccia.

Photogravure and Engraved

1983, Oct. 10 *Perf. 14x13½*

1565 A719 250 l multi 30 15
1566 A719 300 l multi 40 20
1567 A719 400 l multi 50 25
1568 A719 500 l multi 60 30

Francesco de Sanctis (1817-1883), Writer A777

1983, Oct. 28 **Photo.**

1569 A777 300 l multi 40 20

Christmas 1983 — A778

25th Stamp Day, World Communications Year — A779

Raphael Paintings: 250 l, Madonna of the Chair. 400 l, Sistine Madonna. 500 l, Madonna of the Candelabra.

1983, Nov. 10 *Perf. 13½x14*

1570 A778 250 l multi 30 15
1571 A778 400 l multi 50 25
1572 A778 500 l multi 60 30

Perf. 14x13½, 13½x14
1983, Nov. 27

Children's Drawings. 200 l, 400 l horiz.

1573 A779 200 l Letters holding hands 25 15
1574 A779 300 l Spaceman 40 20
1575 A779 400 l Flag train, globe 50 25

Road Safety — A780

Perf. 13½x14, 14x13½
1984, Jan. 20 **Photo.**

1576 A780 300 l Bent road sign, vert. 40 20
1577 A780 400 l Accident 55 28

Promenade in Bois de Boulogne, by Giuseppe de Nittis (1846-1884) A781

Design: 400 l, Portrait of Paul Guillaume, 1916, by Amedeo Modigliani (1884-1920).

Lithographed and Engraved
1984, Jan. 25 *Perf. 14*

1578 A781 300 l multi 40 20
1579 A781 400 l multi 50 25

Galaxy-Same Tractor — A782

Italian-made vehicles.

1984, Mar. 10 **Photo.** *Perf. 14x13½*

1580 A782 450 l shown 55 28
1581 A782 450 l Alfa-33 car 55 28
1582 A782 450 l Maserati Biturbo car 55 28
1583 A782 450 l Iveco 190-38 truck 55 28
a. Block of 4, #1580-1583 + 2 labels 2.25 1.50

See Nos. 1620-1623, 1681-1684.

Glass Blower — A783

1984, Apr. 10

1584 A783 300 l Mosaic, furnace 40 20
1585 A783 300 l shown 40 20
a. Pair, #1584-1585 + label 85 45

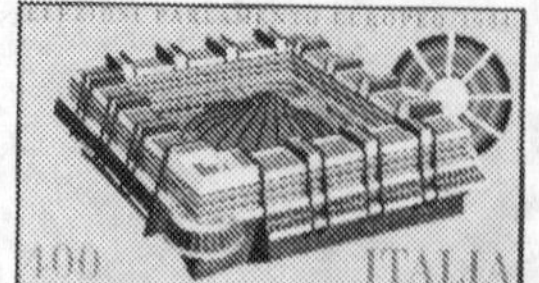

2nd European Parliament Elections — A784

1984, Apr. 16

1586 A784 400 l Parliament Strasbourg 48 24

Forest Preservation A785

1984, Apr. 24 **Photo.** *Perf. 14x13½*

1587 A785 450 l Helicopter fire patrol 55 28
1588 A785 450 l Hedgehog, squirrel, badger 55 28
1589 A785 450 l Riverside waste dump 55 28
1590 A785 450 l Plant life, animals 55 28
a. Block of 4, #1587-1590 2.25 1.50

Italia '85 A786

1984, Apr. 26 *Perf. 14*

1591 A786 450 l Ministry of Posts, Rome 55 28
1592 A786 550 l Via Appia Antiqua, Rome 68 34

Rome Pacts, 40th Anniv. A787

Trade Unionists: Giuseppe di Vittorio, Bruno Buozzi, Achille Grandi.

1984, Apr. 30 *Perf. 14x13½*

1593 A787 450 l multi 55 28

Europa (1959-84) A788

1984, May 5

1594 A788 450 l multi 55 28
1595 A788 550 l multi 68 34

Intl. Telecommunications Symposium, Florence, May — A789

1984, May 7 *Perf. 14*

1596 A789 550 l multi 68 34

Italian Derby Centenary A790

Lithographed and Engraved
1984, May 12 *Perf. 14x13½*

1597 A790 250 l Racing 28 15
1598 A790 400 l Racing, diff. 48 24

Tourist Type of 1974

1984, May 19 **Photo.** *Perf. 14*

1599 A616 350 l Campione d'Italia 45 22
1600 A616 400 l Chianciano Terme baths 48 24
1601 A616 450 l Padula 55 28
1602 A616 550 l Greek ampitheater, Syracuse 68 34

Folk Celebration Type of 1982

Design: La Macchina Di Santa Rosa.

1984, Sept. 3 **Photo.** *Perf. 13½x14*

1603 A754 400 l multi 45 22

Peasant Farming A792

1984, Oct. 1 **Photo.** *Perf. 14x13½*

1604 A792 250 l Grain harvester, thresher 28 15
1605 A792 350 l Cart, hand press 40 20

Villa Type of 1980

Designs: 250 l, Villa Caristo, Stignano. 350 l, Villa Doria Pamphili, Genoa. 400 l, Villa Reale, Stupinigi. 450 l, Villa Mellone, Lecce.

Lithographed and Engraved
1984, Oct. 6 *Perf. 14x13½*

1606 A719 250 l multi 28 15
1607 A719 350 l multi 40 20
1608 A719 400 l multi 45 22
1609 A719 450 l multi 50 25

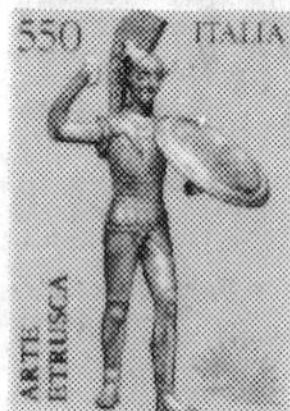

Italia '85 A793

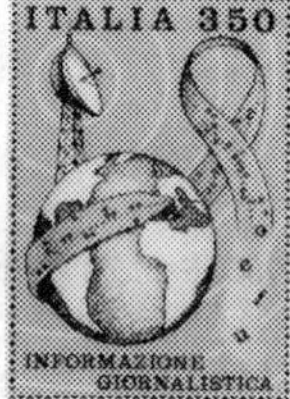

Journalistic Information A794

1984, Nov. 9 *Perf. 13½x14*

1610 A793 550 l Etruscan bronze statue 60 30
1611 A793 550 l Italia '85 emblem 60 30
1612 A793 550 l Etruscan silver mirror 60 30
a. Strip of 3, #1610-1612 2.00 1.50

1985, Jan. 15 **Photo.** *Perf. 13½x14*

1613 A794 350 l Globe, paper tape, microwave dish 40 20

Modern Problems — A795

A796

1985, Jan. 23 **Photo.** *Perf. 13½x14*

1614 A795 250 l Aging 28 15

Photo. and Engr., Photo. (#1616)
1985, Feb. 13 *Perf. 13½x14*

Italia '85. No. 1615, The Hunt, by Raphael (1483-1520). No. 1616, Emblem. No. 1617, Detail from fresco by Baldassare Peruzzi (1481-1536) in Bishop's Palace, Ostia Antica.

1615 A796 600 l multi 60 30
1616 A796 600 l multi 60 30
1617 A796 600 l multi 60 30
a. Strip of 3, #1615-1617 2.00 1.50

Faience Tiles, Plate, Flask and Covered Bowl — A797

Italian ceramics: No. 1619, Tile mural, gladiators in combat.

1985, Mar. 2 **Photo.** *Perf. 14x13½*

1618 A797 600 l multi 60 30
1619 A797 600 l multi 60 30
a. Pair, #1618-1619 + label 1.25 75

Italian Vehicle Type of 1984

1985, Mar. 21

1620 A782 450 l Lancia Thema 45 24
1621 A782 450 l Fiat Abarth 45 24
1622 A782 450 l Fiat Uno 45 24
1623 A782 450 l Lamborghini 45 24
a. Block of 4, #1620-1623 + 2 labels 2.00 1.50

A799

A800

Italia '85: No. 1624, Church of St. Mary of Peace, Rome, by Pietro de Cortona (1596-1669). No. 1625, Exhibition emblem. No. 1626, Church of St. Agnes, Rome, fountain and obelisk.

Photo. and Engr., Photo. (#1625)
1985, Mar. 30 *Perf. 13½x14*

1624 A799 250 l multi 25 15
1625 A799 250 l multi 25 15
1626 A799 250 l multi 25 15
a. Strip of 3, #1624-1626 85 50

1985, Apr. 24 **Litho. and Engr.**

Design: Sixtus V, dome of St. Peter's Basilica, Rome.

1627 A800 1500 l multi 1.75 90

Pope Sixtus V, (1520-1590), 400th anniv. of Papacy

Folk Celebration Type of 1982

Folktales: No. 1628, The March of the Turks, Potenza. No. 1629, San Marino Republican Regatta, Amalfi.

1985, May 29 **Photo.**

1628 A754 250 l multi 28 15
1629 A754 350 l multi 38 20

Tourist Type of 1974

Scenic views: 350 l, Bormio town center. 400 l, Mt. Vesuvius from Castellamare di Stabia. 450 l, Stromboli Volcano from the sea. 600 l, Beach, old town at Termoli.

1985, June 1 *Perf. 14*

1630 A616 350 l multi	38	20
1631 A616 400 l multi	42	22
1632 A616 450 l multi	48	24
1633 A616 600 l multi	65	35

A803

A805

1985, June 5 *Perf. 13½x14*

1634 A803 500 l European beaver	52	28
1635 A803 500 l Primula	52	28
1636 A803 500 l Nebrodi pine	52	28
1637 A803 500 l Italian sandpiper	52	28
a. Block of 4, #1634-1637	2.25	1.50

Nature conservation.

Art Type of 1981

Designs: No. 1638, Madonna bu Il Sassoferrato, G.B. Salvi, 1609-1685. No. 1639, Pride of the Work by Mario Sironi, 1885-1961.

Lithographed and Engraved

1985, June 15 *Perf. 14*

1638 A738 350 l multi	38	20
1639 A738 400 l multi	42	22

1985, June 20 Photo. *Perf. 13½x14*

Europa (tenors and composers): 500 l, Aureliano Pertile (1885-1969) and Giovanni Martinelli (1885-1962). 600 l, Johann Sebastian Bach (1685-1750) and Vincenzo Bellini (1801-1835).

1640 A805 500 l multi	85	30
1641 A805 600 l multi	1.00	35

San Salvatore Abbey, Monte Amiata, 950th Anniv. A806

Lithographed and Engraved

1985, Aug. 1 *Perf. 14x13½*

1642 A806 450 l multi	50	25

World Cycling Championships — A807

1985, Aug. 21 **Photo.**

1643 A807 400 l multi	45	22

7th Intl. Congress for Crime Prevention, Milan, Aug. 26-Sept. 6 — A808

1985, Aug. 26

1644 A808 600 l multi	68	35

Intl. Youth Year — A809

1985, Sept. 3

1645 A809 600 l multi	68	35

Villa Type of 1980

Designs: 300 l, Nitti, Maratea. 400 l, Aldrovandi Mazzacorati, Bologna. 500 l, Santa Maria, Pula. 600 l, De Mersi, Villazzano.

Lithographed and Engraved

1985, Oct. 1 *Perf. 14x13½*

1646 A719 300 l multi	35	18
1647 A719 400 l multi	42	22
1648 A719 500 l multi	58	30
1649 A719 600 l multi	68	35

Natl. and Papal Arms, Treaty Document A810

1985, Oct. 15 **Photo.**

1650 A810 400 l multi	45	22

Ratification of new Concordat with the Vatican.

Souvenir Sheets

Parma #10, View of Parma A812

Switzerland #3L1 A813

Sardinia #1, Great Britain #1 (illustration reduced) — A814

No. 1651b, Two Sicilies #3, Naples. c, Two Sicilies #10, Palermo. d, Modena #3, Modena. e, Roman States #8, Rome. f, Tuscany #5, Florence. g, Sardinia #15, Turin. h, Romagna #7, Bologna. i, Lombardy-Venetia #4, Milan.

No. 1652b, Japan #1. c, US #2. d, Western Australia #1. e, Mauritius #4.

Lithographed and Engraved

1985, Oct. 25 *Perf. 14*

1651 Sheet of 9	3.25	1.75
a.-i. A812 300 l, any single	35	18

Perf. 14x13½

1652 Sheet of 5 + label	3.00	1.50
a.-e. A813 500 l, any single	60	30

Imperf

1653 A814 4000 l multi	4.75	2.50

Italia '85, Rome, Oct. 25-Nov. 3.

Long-distance Skiing A815

1986, Jan. 25 Photo. *Perf. 14x13½*

1654 A815 450 l multi	55	28

Folk Celebration Type of 1982

Design: Procession of St. Agnes, Le Candelore Folk Festival, Catania.

1986, Feb. 3 *Perf. 13½x14*

1655 A754 450 l multi	55	28

Amilcare Ponchielli (1834-1886), Composer A816

Photogravure and Engraved

1986, Mar. 8 *Perf. 14x13½*

1656 A816 2000 l Scene from La Giaconda	2.50	1.25

Castle Type of 1980

Design: 380 l, Vignola, Modena. 650 l, Montecchio Castle, Castiglion Fiorentino. 750 l, Rocca di Urbisaglia.

Perf. 14x13½

1986-90 Photo. Wmk. 303

1657 A717 380 l multi ('87)	60	30
1658 A717 650 l multi	65	32

Engr.

1659 A717 750 l multi ('90)	1.50	75

Issue date: 750 l, Sept. 20.

Coil Stamps

Perf. 14 Vert.

1988-91 Engr. Wmk. 303

Size: 16x21mm

1661 A717 100 l St. Severa	16	15
1662 A717 500 l Norman Castle, Melfi	82	40
1663 A717 600 l Scaligero, Sirmione	1.15	58
1664 A717 650 l Serralunga D'Alba	1.05	52
1665 A717 750 l Venafro	1.25	60
1666 A717 800 l Rocca Maggiore, Assisi	1.50	75
Nos. 1661-1666 (6)	5.93	3.00

Issue dates: 600 l, 800 l, Feb. 20, 1991; others, Mar. 1.

Giovanni Battista Pergolesi (1710-1736), Musician — A817

Perf. 13½x14

1986, Mar. 15 Photo. Unwmk.

1667 A817 2000 l multi	2.50	1.25

The Bay, Acitrezza — A818

1986, Mar. 24 *Perf. 14*

1668 A818 350 l shown	45	22
1669 A818 450 l Piazetta, Capri	58	30
1670 A818 550 l Kursaal, Merano	70	35
1671 A818 650 l Lighthouse, San Benedetto del Tronto	85	42

Europa 1986 — A819

Trees in special shapes: a, Heart (life). b, Star (poetry). c, Butterfly (color). d, Sun (energy).

1986, Apr. 28 Photo. *Perf. 13x14*

1672 Block of 4	3.60	1.80
a.-d. A819 650 l, any single	90	45

25th Intl. Opthalmological Congress, Rome, May 4-10 — A820

1986, May 3 Photo. *Perf. 14*

1673 A820 550 l multi	75	38

Police in Uniform — A821

1986, May 10

1674 A821 550 l multi	75	38
1675 A821 650 l multi	90	45

European Police Conference, Chianciano Terme, May 10-12. Nos. 1674-1675 printed se-tenant with labels picturing male or female police.

Battle of Bezzecca, 120th Anniv. A822

1986, May 31 *Perf. 14x13½*

1676 A822 550 l multi	72	35

Memorial Day for Independence Martyrs — A823

1986, May 31 *Perf. 14*

1677 A823 2000 l multi	2.60	1.30

Bersaglieri Corps of Mountain Troops, 150th Anniv. — A824

1986, June 1 *Perf. 13½x14*

1678 A824 450 l multi 60 30

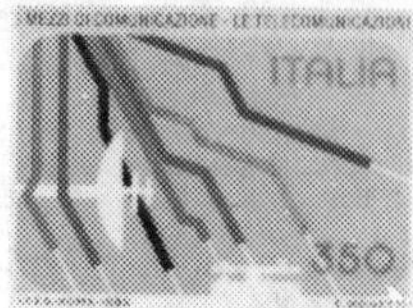

Telecommunications — A825

1986, June 16 *Perf. 14x13½*

1679 A825 350 l multi 48 24

Sacro Monte di Varallo Monastery — A826

1986, June 28 **Engr.** *Perf. 14*

1680 A826 2000 l Prus bl & sage grn 2.70 1.35

Italian Vehicle Type of 1984

1986, July 4 **Photo.** *Perf. 14x13½*

1681 A782 450 l Alfa Romeo AR8 Turbo 62 30
1682 A782 450 l Innocenti 650 SE 62 30
1683 A782 450 l Ferrari Testarossa 62 30
1684 A782 450 l Fiatallis FR 10B 62 30
a. Block of 4, #1681-1684 + 2 labels 2.50

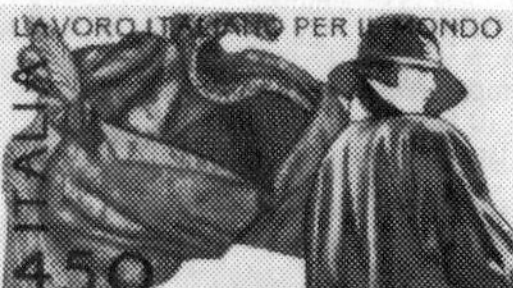

Ladies' Fashions — A827

Breda Heavy Industry — A828

Olivetti Computer Technology — A829

1986, July 14

1685 A827 450 l shown 62 30
1686 A827 450 l Men's fashions 62 30
a. Pair, #1685-1686 + label 1.30 75
1687 A828 650 l shown 90 45
1688 A829 650 l shown 90 45

Alitalia, Italian Airlines, 40th Anniv. A830

1986, Sept. 16 **Photo.** *Perf. 14x13½*

1689 A830 550 l Anniv. emblem 82 40
1690 A830 650 l Jet, runway lights 98 50

Villa Type of 1980

1986, Oct. 1 **Photo. & Engr.**

1691 A719 350 l Necker, Trieste 52 25
1692 A719 350 l Borromeo, Cassano D'Adda 52 25
1693 A719 450 l Palagonia, Bagheria 68 35
1694 A719 550 l Medicea, Poggio a Caiano 82 40
1695 A719 650 l Castello d'Issogne, Issogne 98 50
Nos. 1691-1695 (5) 3.52 1.75

Christmas — A831

Madonna and Child, bronze sculpture by Donatello, Basilica del Santo, Padua.

1986, Oct. 10 **Engr.** *Perf. 14*

1696 A831 450 l brown olive 68 35

Art Type of 1981

Designs: 450 l, Seated Woman Holding a Book, drawing by Andrea del Sarto, Uffizi, Florence, vert. 550 l, Daphne at Pavarola, painting by Felice Casorati, Museum of Modern Art, Turin, vert.

1986, Oct. 11 **Litho. & Engr.**

1697 A738 450 l blk & pale org 68 35
1698 A738 550 l multi 82 40

Memorial, Globe, Plane — A832

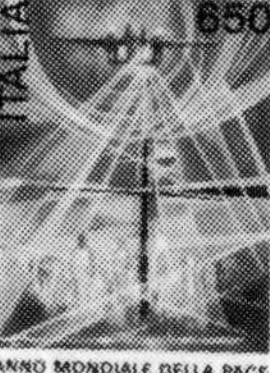

Plane, Cross, Men — A833

1986, Nov. 11 **Photo.** *Perf. 13½x14*

1699 A832 550 l multi 80 40
1700 A833 650 l multi 95 48

Intl. Peace Year, memorial to Italian airmen who died at Kindu, Zaire, while on a peace mission.

Stamp Day — A834

1986, Nov. 29 *Perf. 14x13½*

1701 A834 550 l Die of Sardinia No. 2 85 42

Francesco Matraire, printer of first Sardinian stamps.

A835

Industries — A836

Perf. 14½x13½

1987, Feb. 27 **Photo.**

1702 A835 700 l Marzotto Textile, 1836 1.05 52
1703 A836 700 l Italgas Energy Corp., 1837 1.05 52

See No. 1755-1757.

Environmental Protection — A837

Designs: a, Volturno River. b, Garda Lake. c, Trasimeno Lake. d, Tirso River.

1987, Mar. 6 **Litho.** *Perf. 14x13½*

1704 Block of 4 3.15 1.60
a.-d. A837 500 l, any single 78 40

Antonio Gramsci (1891-1937), Author and Artist — A838

1987, Apr. 27 **Litho.** *Perf. 14x13½*

1705 A838 600 l scar & gray black 95 48

Europa 1987 — A839

Modern architecture: 600 l, Church of Sun Motorway, Florence, designed by Michelucci. 700 l, Railway station, Rome, designed by Nervi.

1987, May 4 **Photo.**

1706 A839 600 l multi 95 48
1707 A839 700 l multi 1.10 55

Tourist Type of 1974

1987, May 9 *Perf. 14*

1708 A616 380 l Verbania Pallanza 60 30
1709 A616 400 l Palmi 65 32
1710 A616 500 l Vasto 80 40
1711 A616 600 l Villacidro 95 48

Naples Soccer Club, Nat'l. Champions — A840

The Absinthe Drinkers, by Degas — A841

1987, May 18 **Litho.** *Perf. 13½x14*

1712 A840 500 l multi 78 40

1987, May 29

1713 A841 380 l multi 60 30

Fight against alcoholism.

St. Alfonso M. de Liguori (1696-1787) and Gulf of Naples A842

1987, Aug. 1 *Perf. 14x13½*

1714 A842 400 l multi 62 30

Events A843

Emblems and natl. landmarks: No. 1715, OLYMPHILEX '87, Intl. Olympic Committee Building, Foro Italico, Rome. No. 1716, World Athletics Championships, Olympic Stadium, Rome.

1987, Aug. 29 **Photo.** *Perf. 14x14½*

1715 A843 700 l multi 1.10 55
1716 A843 700 l multi 1.10 55

Folk Celebration Type of 1982

Design: Quintana Joust, Foligno.

Perf. 13½x14½

1987, Sept. 12 **Photo.**

1717 A754 380 l multi 60 30

Piazzas A844

Designs: 380 l, Piazza del Popolo, Ascoli Piceno. 500 l, Piazza Giuseppe Verdi, Palermo. 600 l, Piazza San Carlo, Turin. 700 l, Piazza dei Signori, Verona.

Perf. 14x13½

1987, Oct. 10 **Litho. & Engr.**

1718 A844 380 l multi 60 30
1719 A844 500 l multi 80 40
1720 A844 600 l multi 95 48
1721 A844 700 l multi 1.10 55

See Nos. 1747-1748, 1765-1766.

Christmas — A845

Paintings by Giotto: 500 l, Adoration in the Manger, Basilica of St. Francis, Assisi. 600 l, The Epiphany, Scrovegni Chapel, Padua.

1987, Oct. 15 Photo. *Perf. 13½x14*
1722 A845 500 l multi 80 40
1723 A845 600 l multi 95 48

Battle of Mentana, 120th Anniv. A846

Perf. 14x13½
1987, Nov. 3 Litho. & Engr.
1724 A846 380 l multi 65 32

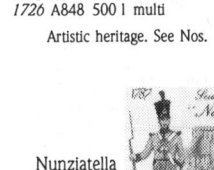

Il Pantocrator (Christ), Mosaic, Monreale Cathedral — A847

Coat of Arms and San Carlo Theater, Naples, from an 18th Cent. Engraving — A848

1987, Nov. 4 *Perf. 14*
1725 A847 500 l multi 85 42
1726 A848 500 l multi 85 42

Artistic heritage. See Nos. 1768-1769.

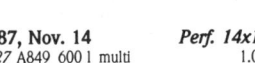

Nunziatella Military School, 200th Anniv. A849

1987, Nov. 14 *Perf. 14x13½*
1727 A849 600 l multi 1.00 50

A850 A851

Stamp Day: Philatelist Marco DeMarchi (d. 1936) holding magnifying glass and stamp album, Milan Cathedral.

1987, Nov. 20 Photo. *Perf. 13½x14*
1728 A850 500 l multi 85 42

Photo. & Engr.
1988, Feb. 6 *Perf. 13½x14*

Design: Homo Aeserniensis (Flint Knapper).

1729 A851 500 l multi 85 42

Remains of Isernia Man, c. 736,000 years-old, discovered near Isernia.

E. Quirino Visconti School, Rome — A852

Perf. 14x13½
Litho. & Engr.
1988, Mar. 1 Unwmk.
1730 A852 500 l multi 82 40

See Nos. 1764, 1824, 1842.

St. John Bosco (1815-1888), Educator — A853

1988, Apr. 2 Photo. *Perf. 13½x14*
1731 A853 500 l multi 82 40

Art Type of 1981

Painting: *Gli Archeologi*, by Giorgio de Chirico (1888-1978).

1988, Apr. 7 Engr. *Perf. 14*
1732 A738 650 l multi, vert. 1.05 52

1st Printed Hebrew Bible, 500th Anniv. A854

Soncino Bible excerpt, 15th cent.

1988, Apr. 22 Photo. *Perf. 14x13½*
1733 A854 550 l multi 90 45

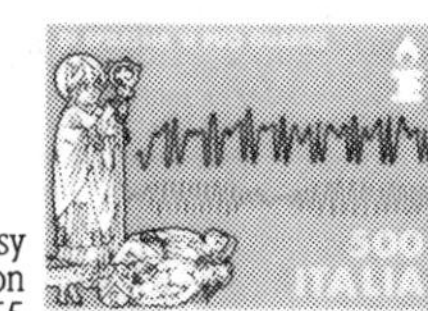
Epilepsy Foundation A855

Design: St. Valentine, electroencephalograph readout, epileptic in seizure and medieval crest.

1988, Apr. 23
1734 A855 500 l multi 82 40

Europa 1988 — A856

Transport and communication: 650 l, ETR 450 locomotive. 750 l, Electronic mail, map of Italy.

1988, May 2
1735 A856 650 l multi 1.05 52
1736 A856 750 l multi 1.25 62

Tourist Type of 1974

Scenic views: 400 l, Castiglione della Pescaia. 500 l, Lignano Sabbiadoro. 650 l, Noto. 750 l, Vieste.

1988, May 7 Photo. *Perf. 14*
1737 A616 400 l multi 62 30
1738 A616 500 l multi 78 40
1739 A616 650 l multi 1.00 50
1740 A616 750 l multi 1.15 58

A858

A860

A859

1988, May 16
1741 A858 500 l Golf 78 40

1988, May 16 Litho. *Perf. 14x13½*
1742 A859 3150 l blk, grn & dark red 4.75 2.40

1990 World Cup Soccer championships.

1988, May 23 *Perf. 13½x14*
1743 A860 650 l multi 1.00 50

1988 Natl. Soccer Championships, Milan.

Bronze Sculpture, Pergola — A861

1988, June 4 Engr. *Perf. 14*
1744 A861 500 l Horse 75 38
1745 A861 650 l Woman 95 48

Bologna University, 900th Anniv. — A862

1988, June 10 Engr. *Perf. 13½x14*
1746 A862 500 l vio 75 38

Piazza Type of 1987

Designs: 400 l, Piazza del Duomo, Pistoia. 550 l, Piazza del Unita d'Italia, Trieste.

Perf. 14x13½
1988, July 2 Litho. & Engr.
1747 A844 400 l multi 60 30
1748 A844 550 l multi 82 40

Folk Celebration Type of 1982

Discesa Dei Candelieri, Sassari: Man wearing period costume, column and bearers.

1988, Aug. 13 Photo. *Perf. 13½x14*
1749 A754 550 l multi 80 40

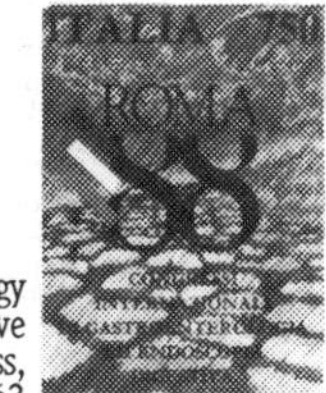
Intl. Gastroenterology and Digestive Endoscopy Congress, Rome — A863

1988, Sept. 5
1750 A863 750 l multi 1.10 55

Surrealistic Films — A864

Italian films amd directors: 500 l, *Ossessione*, 1942, by Luchino Visconti. 650 l, *Ladri di Biciclette*, 1948, by Vittorio DeSica. 2400 l, *Roma Citta Aperta*, 1945, by Roberto Rossellini. 3050 l, *Riso Amaro*, 1949, by Giuseppe DeSantis.

1988, Oct. 13 Litho. *Perf. 14x13½*
1751 A864 500 l multi 80 40
1752 A864 650 l multi 1.05 52
1753 A864 2400 l multi 3.75 1.90
1754 A864 3050 l multi 4.75 2.40

Elsag A865

Aluminia — A866

State Mint and Polygraphic Insitute — A867

Italian Industries.

1988, Oct. 19 **Photo.**

1755 A865 750 l multi 1.30 65
1756 A866 750 l multi 1.30 65

Photo. & Engr.

1757 A867 750 l multi 1.30 65

Christmas: *Nativity,* by Roseto Degli Abruzzi, Church of the Virgin's Assumption — A868

1988, Oct. 29 **Photo.** ***Perf. 13¹/₂x14***

1758 A868 650 l multi 1.05 52

Christmas A869

Photo. & Engr.

1988, Nov. 12 ***Perf. 14x13¹/₂***

1759 A869 500 l dark blue grn & chest brn 78 40

St. Charles Borromeo (1538-1584), Ecclesiastical Reformer A870

1988, Nov. 4 **Litho. & Engr.**

1760 A870 2400 l multi 3.75 1.85

Stamp Day — A871

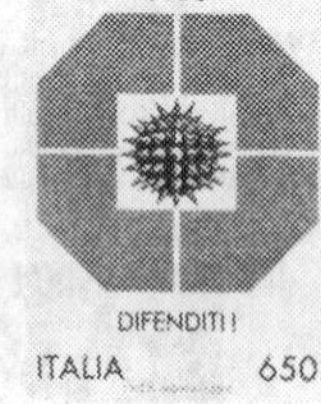

Campaign Against AIDS — A872

Design: Japan No. 69 and stamp designer Edoardo Chiossone.

1988, Dec. 9 **Photo.** ***Perf. 13¹/₂x14***

1761 A871 500 l multi 75 38

1989, Jan. 13

1762 A872 650 l multi 98 50

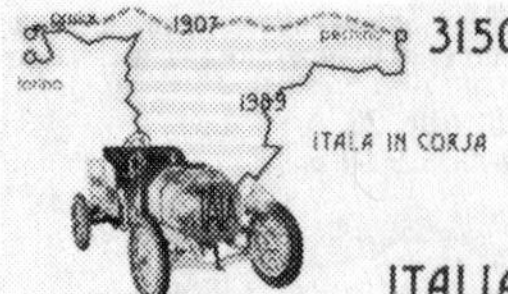

Paris-Peking Rally — A873

1989, Jan. 21 ***Perf. 14¹/₂x13¹/₂***

1763 A873 3150 l Map, Itala race car 4.65 2.30

School Type of 1988

1989 **Photo. & Engr.** ***Perf. 14x13¹/₂***

1764 A852 650 l multi 1.00 50

Piazza Type of 1987

Designs: No. 1765, Piazza Del Duomo, Catanzaro. No. 1766, Piazza Di Spagna, Rome.

Perf. 14x13¹/₂

1989, Apr. 10 **Litho. & Engr.**

1765 A844 400 l multi 60 30
1766 A844 400 l multi 60 30

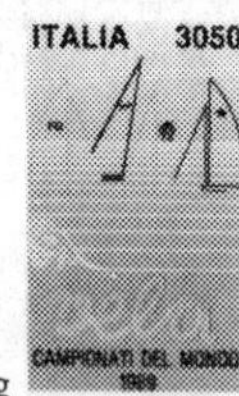

Velo World Yachting Championships — A875

1989, Apr. 8 **Photo.** ***Perf. 14***

1767 A875 3050 l multi 4.60 2.30

Artistic Heritage Type of 1987

Art and architecture: 500 l, King with scepter and orb, Palazzo Della Ragione, Padova, vert. 650 l, Crypt of St. Nicolas, St. Nicolas Basilica, Bari, vert.

1989, Apr. 8 **Litho. & Engr., Engr.**

1768 A847 500 l multi 75 38
1769 A847 650 l indigo 1.00 50

Europa 1989 — A876

European Parliament 3rd Elections — A877

Children's games.

Perf. 14x13¹/₂, 13¹/₂x14

1989, May 8 **Photo.**

1770 A876 500 l Leapfrog, horiz. 72 35
1771 A876 650 l shown 92 45
1772 A876 750 l Sack race, horiz. 1.05 52

1989, June 3 ***Perf. 13¹/₂x14***

1773 A877 500 l multi 72 35

No. 1773 also inscribed in European Currency Units "ECU 0,31."

Pisa University — A878

1989, May 29 **Engr.** ***Perf. 14x13¹/₂***

1774 A878 500 l violet 72 35

Folk Celebration Type of 1982

Design: Priest and Flower Feast street scene.

1989, May 27 **Photo.** ***Perf. 13¹/₂x14***

1775 A754 400 l multi 58 30

Landscape Type of 1974

1989, June 10 **Photo.** ***Perf. 14***

1776 A616 500 l Naxos Gardens 70 35
1777 A616 500 l Spotorno 70 35
1778 A616 500 l Pompei 70 35
1779 A616 500 l Grottammare 70 35

Ministry of Posts, Cent. A879

1989, June 24 ***Perf. 14x13¹/₂***

1780 A879 500 l Posthorn, No. 52 70 35
1781 A879 2400 l Posthorn, Earth 3.25 1.65

INTER Soccer Championships — A880

1989, June 26

1782 A880 650 l multi 90 45

Interparliamentary Union, Cent. — A881

1989, June 28

1783 A881 750 l multi 1.05 52

French Revolution, Bicent. — A882

1989, July 7 **Photo.** ***Perf. 14***

1784 A882 3150 l multi 4.75 2.35

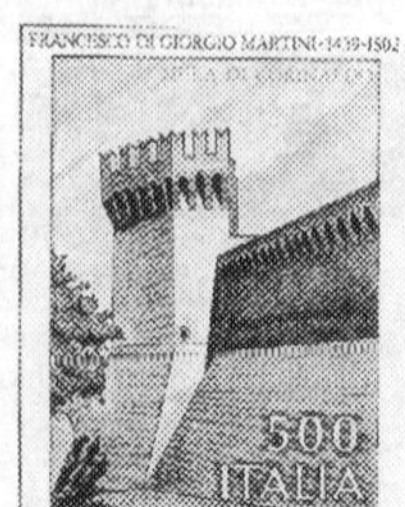

Fortified Walls of Corinaldo, by Francesco di Giorgio Martini (1439-1502) A883

1989, Sept. 2 **Litho. & Engr.** ***Perf. 14***

1785 A883 500 l multi 75 38

Charlie Chaplin (1889-1977) A884

1989, Sept. 23 **Engr.** ***Perf. 14x13¹/₂***

1786 A884 750 l black & sepia 1.10 55

Naples-Portici Railway, 150th Anniv. A885 A886

Illustration reduced.

1989, Oct. 3 **Litho. & Engr.**

1787 A885 550 l multicolored 82 40
1788 A886 550 l multicolored 82 40
a. Pair, #1787-1788 1.75 1.00

Adoration of the Kings, by Correggio A887 A888

1989, Oct. 21 **Photo.** ***Perf. 13¹/₂x14***

1789 A887 500 l multicolored 75 38
1790 A888 500 l multicolored 75 38
a. Pair, #1789-1790 1.65 90

Christmas.

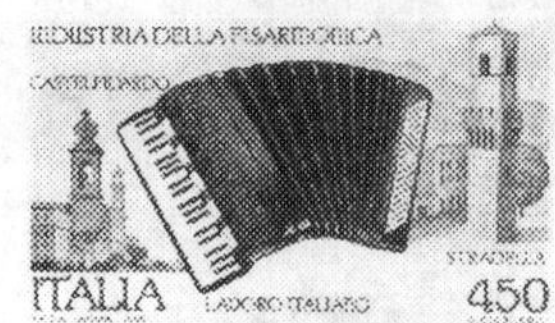

Fidardo Castle, the Stradella, Accordion — A889

Industries.

1989, Oct. 14 **Photo.** ***Perf. 14x13¹/₂***

1791 A889 450 l Music 70 35
1792 A889 450 l Arnoldo World Publishing 70 35

A890 A891

1989, Nov. 24 ***Perf. 13¹/₂x14***

1793 A890 500 l Emilio Diena 78 38

Stamp Day.

1989, Dec. 9 **Engr.** ***Perf. 13¹/₂x14***

1794 A891 450 l multicolored 75 36

1990 World Soccer Championships, Italy.

Columbus's First Voyage, 1474-1484
A892 A893

1990, Feb. 24 **Photo.**

1795 A892 700 l multicolored	1.15	58
1796 A893 700 l multicolored	1.15	58
a. Pair, #1795-1796	2.50	1.50

Souvenir Sheets

1990 World Cup Soccer Championships, Italy — A894

Soccer club emblems and stadiums in Italy.
No. 1797: a, Italy. b, US. c, Olympic Stadium, Rome. d, Municipal Stadium, Florence. e, Austria. f, Czechoslovakia.
No. 1798: a, Argentina. b, Russia. c, St. Paul Stadium, Naples. d, New Stadium, Bari. e, Cameroun. f, Romania.
No. 1799: a, Brazil. b, Costa Rica. c, Alps Stadium, Turin. d, Ferraris Stadium, Genoa. e, Sweden. f, Scotland.
No. 1800: a, UAE. b, West Germany. c, Dall'ara Stadium, Bologna. d, Meazza Stadium, Milan. e, Colombia. f, Yugoslavia.
No. 1801: a, Belgium. b, Uruguay. c, Bentegodi Stadium, Verona. d, Friuli Stadium, Udine. e, South Korea. f, Spain.
No. 1802: a, England. b, Netherlands. c, Sant'elia Stadium, Cagliari. d, La Favorita Stadium, Palermo. e, Ireland. f, Egypt.

1990, Mar. 24 ***Perf. 14x13½***

1797 Sheet of 6	4.50	2.20
a.-f. A894 450 l any single	75	36
1798 Sheet of 6	5.90	2.90
a.-f. A894 600 l any single	98	48
1799 Sheet of 6	6.30	3.15
a.-f. A894 650 l any single	1.05	52
1800 Sheet of 6	6.90	3.50
a.-f. A894 700 l any single	1.15	58
1801 Sheet of 6	7.80	3.90
a.-f. A894 800 l any single	1.30	65
1802 Sheet of 6	11.70	5.90
a.-f. A894 1200 l any single	1.95	98

See No. 1819.

Tourist Type of 1974

1990, Mar. 30 **Photo.** ***Perf. 14***

1803 A616 600 l Sabbioneta	98	50
1804 A616 600 l Montepulciano	98	50
1805 A616 600 l Castellammare del Golfo	98	50
1806 A616 600 l San Felice Circeo	98	50

Folk Celebration Type of 1982

Design: Horse race, Merano.

1990, Apr. 9 ***Perf. 13½x14***

1807 A754 600 l multicolored	98	50

Aurelio Saffi, Death Cent. A895

1990, Apr. 10 ***Perf. 14***

1808 A895 700 l multicolored	1.15	58

Giovanni Giorgi (1871-1950) A896

1990, Apr. 23 ***Perf. 14x13½***

1809 A896 600 l multicolored	1.15	58

Metric System in Italy, 55th. anniv.

A897 A898

1990, Apr. 28 **Photo.** ***Perf. 13½x14***

1810 A897 600 l multicolored	1.15	58

Labor Day, cent.

1990, Apr. 30 ***Perf. 13½x14***

1811 A898 700 l multicolored	1.30	65

Naples Soccer Club, Italian champions.

Europa A899

Post Offices: 700 l, San Silvestro Piazza, Rome. 800 l, Fondaco Tedeschi, Venice.

1990, May 7 ***Perf. 14x13½***

1812 A899 700 l multicolored	1.30	65
1813 A899 800 l multicolored	1.50	75

Giovanni Paisiello (1740-1816), Composer — A900

1990, May 9 ***Perf. 14x13½***

1814 A900 450 l multicolored	82	40

Dante Alighieri (1265-1321), Poet — A901

1990, May 12 ***Perf. 14x13½***

1815 A901 700 l multicolored	1.25	62

Dante Alighieri Soc., cent.

Mosaic (Detail) — A902 Sculpture — A903

Photo. (#1816), Litho. & Engr. (#1817)

1990, May 19 ***Perf. 13½x14***

1816 A902 450 l multicolored	82	40
1817 A903 700 l multicolored	1.25	62

Malatestiana Music Festival, Rimini, 40th Anniv. — A904

1990, June 15 **Photo.** ***Perf. 14***

1818 A904 600 l multicolored	1.15	58

World Cup Soccer Type of 1990 Inscribed "Campione Del Mondo"

1990, July 9 **Litho.** ***Perf. 14x13½***

1819 A894 600 l like No. 1800b	1.15	58

Still Life, by Giorgio Morandi (1890-1964) A905

1990, July 20 **Engr.** ***Perf. 14***

1820 A905 750 l black	1.45	75

Greco-Roman Wrestling, World Championships — A906

1990, Oct. 11 **Litho.** ***Perf. 14x13½***

1821 A906 3200 l multicolored	6.50	3.25

Christmas — A907

Paintings of the Nativity by: 600 l, Emidio Vangelli. 750 l, Pellegrino.

1990, Oct. 26 ***Perf. 14***

1822 A907 600 l multicolored	1.25	65
1823 A907 750 l multicolored	1.60	80

School Type of 1988 and

Italian Schools — A908

Designs: 600 l, Bernardino Telesio gymnasium, Cosenza. 750 l, University of Catania.

Perf. 14x13½

1990, Nov. 5 **Litho. & Engr.**

1824 A852 600 l multicolored	1.25	65

Engr.

1825 A908 750 l multicolored	1.60	80

Self-portrait, Corrado Mezzana (1890-1952) — A909

1990, Nov. 16 **Litho.** ***Perf. 13½x14***

1826 A909 600 l multicolored	1.25	65

Stamp day.

The Nativity — A910 Genoa Flower Show — A911

1991, Jan. 5 **Litho.** ***Perf. 13½x14***

1827 A910 600 l multicolored	1.25	65

1991, Jan. 10 ***Perf. 14***

1828 A911 750 l multicolored	1.60	80

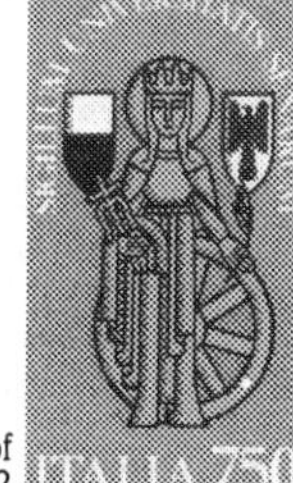

Seal of the Univ. of Siena — A912

1991, Jan. 15 **Photo.** ***Perf. 13½x14***

1829 A912 750 l multicolored	1.60	80

Tourist Type of 1974

1991 **Photo.**

1830 A616 600 l San Remo	1.25	65
1831 A616 600 l Roccaraso	1.25	65
1832 A616 600 l La Maddalena	1.25	65
1833 A616 600 l Calgi	1.25	65

United Europe — A913

Perf. 14x13½

1991, Mar. 12 Photo. Unwmk.

1834 A913 750 l multi 1.45 90

#1834 also carries .48 ECU denomination.

A914

Discovery of America, 500th Anniv. (in 1992) A915

1991, Mar. 22 Litho.

1835 A914 750 l Ships leaving port 1.45 70
1836 A915 750 l Columbus, Queen's court 1.45 70
a. Pair, #1835-1836 2.90 1.50

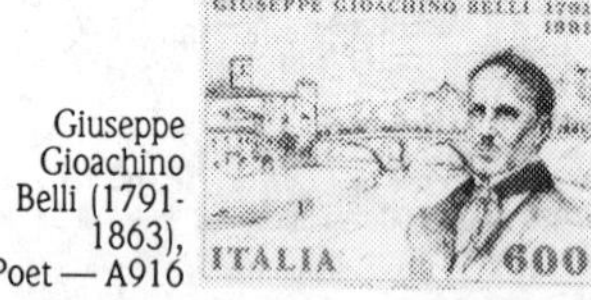

Giuseppe Gioachino Belli (1791-1863), Poet — A916

1991, Apr. 15 Litho. *Perf. 14x13½*

1837 A916 600 l bl & gray blk 1.15 60

Church of St. Gregory, Rome — A917

1991, Apr. 20 Photo. *Perf. 14x13½*

1838 A917 3200 l multicolored 6.00 3.00

Europa A918

1991, Apr. 29 Photo. *Perf. 14x13½*

1839 A918 750 l DRS satellite 1.40 70
1840 A918 800 l Hermes space shuttle 1.50 75

A919

A920

1991, May 2 Engr. *Perf. 13½x14*

1841 A919 600 l brown 1.10 55

Santa Maria Maggiore Church, Lanciano.

Schools Type of 1988

Design: D. A. Azuni school, Sassari.

Perf. 14x13½

1991, May 3 Litho. & Engr.

1842 A852 600 l multicolored 1.10 55

1991, May 27 Photo. *Perf. 13½x14*

1843 A920 3000 l multicolored 5.25 2.60

Team Genoa, Italian soccer champions, 1990-91.

Basketball, Cent. — A921

Children's Rights — A922

1991, June 5

1844 A921 500 l multicolored 90 45

1991, June 14

1845 A922 600 l shown 1.05 52
1846 A922 750 l Man, child with balloon 1.30 65

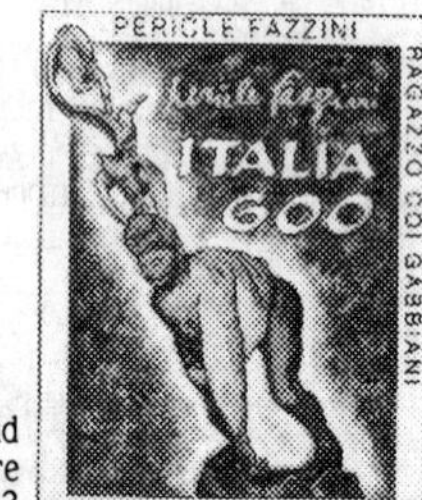

Art and Culture A923

Designs: 600 l, Sculpture by Pericle Fazzini (b. 1913). 3200 l, Exhibition Hall, Turin, designed by Pier Luigi Nervi (1891-1979).

1991, June 21 Litho. & Engr. *Perf. 14*

1847 A923 600 l multicolored 1.05 52
1848 A923 3200 l multicolored 5.60 2.80

Egyptian Museum, Turin — A924

1991, Aug. 31 Litho. *Perf. 13½x14*

1849 A924 750 l grn, yel & gold 1.35 65

Luigi Galvani (1737-1798), Electrophysicist — A925

1991, Sept. 24 *Perf. 14x13½*

1850 A925 750 l multicolored 1.35 65

Radio, cent. (in 1995). See Nos. 1873, 1928.

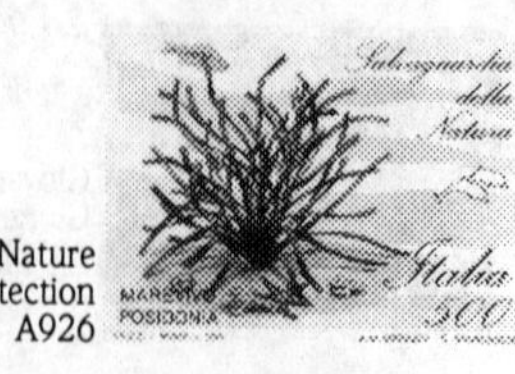

Nature Protection A926

1991, Oct. 10 Photo. *Perf. 14x13½*

1851 A926 500 l Marevivo posidonia 90 45
1852 A926 500 l Falco pellegrino 90 45
1853 A926 500 l Cervo sardo 90 45
1854 A926 500 l Orso marsicano 90 45

World Wildlife Fund.

A927

A928

1991, Oct. 7 *Perf. 13½x14*

1855 A927 800 l multicolored 1.50 75

Wolfgang Amadeus Mozart, death bicent.

1991, Oct. 18

1856 A928 600 l multicolored 1.15 58

Christmas.

Giulio and Alberto Bolaffi, Philatelists — A929

1991, Oct. 25 *Perf. 14*

1857 A929 750 l multicolored 1.45 70

Stamp Day.

Pietro Nenni (1891-1980), Politician — A930

1991, Oct. 30

1858 A930 750 l multicolored 1.45 70

Fountain of Neptune, Florence, by Bartolomeo Ammannati (1511-1592) — A931

1992, Feb. 6 Photo. *Perf. 13½x14*

1859 A931 750 l multicolored 1.40 70

22nd European Indoor Track Championships — A932

1992, Jan. 30 *Perf. 14x13½*

1860 A932 600 l multicolored 1.10 55

University of Ferrara, 600th Anniv. — A933

1992, Mar. 4 Photo. *Perf. 13½x14*

1861 A933 750 l multicolored 1.40 70

Castle Type of 1980

Perf. 14x13½

1992 Photo. Wmk. 303

1868 A717 850 l Arechi, Salerno 1.60 80

Issue date: 850 l, Mar. 7.

This is an expanding set. Numbers will change if necessary.

University of Naples — A934

1992, Mar. 9 Unwmk. *Perf. 14x13½*

1872 A934 750 l multicolored 1.40 70

Radio Cent. Type of 1991

Design: Alessandro Volta (1745-1827), Italian physicist.

1992, Mar. 26

1873 A925 750 l multicolored 1.40 70

Radio, cent. (in 1995).

Genoa '92 Intl. Philatelic Exhibition — A935

1992, Mar. 27 *Perf. 13½x14*

1874 A935 750 l multicolored 1.40 70

Lorenzo de Medici (1449-1492) A936

1992, Apr. 8 *Perf. 14*

1875 A936 750 l bl & org brn 1.40 70

Filippini Institute, 300th Anniv. — A937

1992, May 2 Photo. *Perf. 13½x14*

1876 A937 750 l multicolored 1.40 70

Discovery of America, 500th Anniv. A938

Designs: No. 1877, Columbus seeking Queen Isabella's support. No. 1878, Columbus' fleet. No. 1879, Sighting land. No. 1880, Landing in New World.

1992, Apr. 24 Photo. *Perf. 14x13½*

1877 A938 500 l multicolored 90 45
1878 A938 500 l multicolored 90 45
1879 A938 500 l multicolored 90 45
1880 A938 500 l multicolored 90 45
a. Block of 4, #1877-1880 3.60 1.80

See US Nos. 2620-2623.

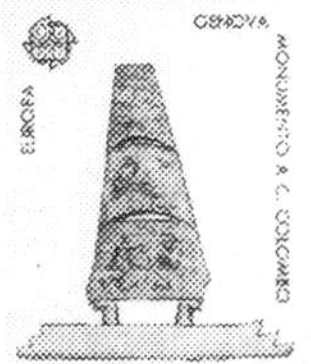

Discovery of America, 500th Anniv. — A939

Designs: 750 l, Monument to Columbus, Genoa. 850 l, Globe, Genoa '92 Exhibition emblem.

1992, May 2 *Perf. 13½x14*

1881 A939 750 l multicolored 1.40 70
1882 A939 850 l multicolored 1.60 80

Europa.

Miniature Sheets

Voyages of Columbus — A940

Designs: No. 1883a, Columbus presenting natives. b, Columbus announcing his discovery. c, Columbus in chains.

No. 1884a, Columbus welcomed at Barcelona. b, Columbus restored to favor. c, Columbus describing his third voyage.

No. 1885a, Columbus in sight of land. b, Fleet of Columbus. c, Queen Isabella pledging her jewels.

No. 1886a, Columbus soliciting aid from Isabella. b, Columbus at La Rabida. c, Recall of Columbus.

No. 1887a, Landing of Columbus. b, Santa Maria. c, Queen Isabella and Columbus. No. 1888, Columbus.

Nos. 1883-1888 are similar in design to US Nos. 230-245.

1992, May 22 Engr. *Perf. 10½*

1883 A940 Sheet of 3 8.10 4.05
a. 50 l olive black 15 15
b. 300 l dark blue green 55 28
c. 4000 l red violet 7.50 3.75
1884 A940 Sheet of 3 7.30 3.65
a. 100 l brown violet 18 15
b. 800 l magenta 1.50 75
c. 3000 l green 5.60 2.80
1885 A940 Sheet of 3 4.90 2.45
a. 200 l dark blue 38 18
b. 900 l ultra 1.70 85
c. 1500 l orange 2.80 1.40
1886 A940 Sheet of 3 3.95 1.95
a. 400 l chocolate 75 35
b. 700 l vermillion 1.30 65
c. 1000 l slate blue 1.90 95
1887 A940 Sheet of 3 5.80 2.90
a. 500 l brown violet 95 45
b. 600 l dark green 1.10 55
c. 2000 l crimson lake 3.75 1.80
1888 A940 5000 l Sheet of 1 9.40 4.70

See US Nos. 2624-2629, Portugal Nos. 1918-1923 and Spain Nos. 2677-2682.

Tour of Italy Bicycle Race A941

1992, May 23 Photo. *Perf. 14x13½*

1889 A941 750 l Ocean 1.50 75
1890 A941 750 l Mountains 1.50 75
a. Pair, #1889-1890 3.00 1.50

No. 1890a printed in continuous design.

Milan, Italian Soccer Champions — A942

1992, May 25 *Perf. 13½x14*

1891 A942 750 l black, red & grn 1.50 75

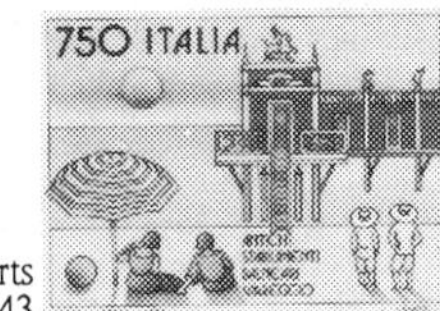

Beach Resorts A943

1992 *Perf. 14x13½*

1892 A943 750 l Viareggio 1.50 75
1893 A943 750 l Rimini 1.50 75

Issue dates: #1892, May 30; #1893, June 13.

Tazio Nuvolari (1892-1953), Race Car Driver A944

1992, June 5 *Perf. 14x13½*

1900 A944 3200 l multicolored 6.25 3.25

Tourism Type of 1974

1992, June 30 *Perf. 14*

1901 A616 600 l Arcevia 1.25 65
1902 A616 600 l Maratea 1.25 65
1903 A616 600 l Braies 1.25 65
1904 A616 600 l Pantelleria 1.25 65

The Shepherds, by Jacopo da Ponte — A945

1992, Sept. 5 Litho. & Engr. *Perf. 14*

1905 A945 750 l multicolored 1.60 80

A946 A947

Discovery of America, 500th Anniv.: 500 l, Columbus' house, Genoa. 600 l, Columbus' fleet. 750 l, Map. 850 l, Columbus pointing to land. 1200 l, Coming ashore.

1992, Sept. 18 Photo. *Perf. 13½x14*

1906 A946 500 l multicolored 1.00 50
1907 A946 600 l multicolored 1.20 60
1908 A946 750 l multicolored 1.50 75
1909 A946 850 l multicolored 1.70 85
1910 A946 1200 l multicolored 2.40 1.20
1911 A946 3200 l multicolored 6.50 3.20
Nos. 1906-1911 (6) 14.30 7.10

Genoa '92.

1992, Sept. 22 *Perf. 14*

1912 A947 750 l multicolored 1.40 70

Self-Adhesive

Perf. 13½

1913 A947 750 l multicolored 1.40 70

Stamp Day.

Lions Intl., 75th Anniv. A948

1992, Sept. 24 *Perf. 14x13½*

1914 A948 3000 l multicolored 5.50 2.75

Single European Market A949

1992, Oct. 5 Photo. *Perf. 14x13½*

1915 A949 600 l multicolored 1.00 50

Intl. Conference on Nutrition, Rome A950

1992, Oct. 16 Photo. *Perf. 14x13½*

1916 A950 500 l multicolored 90 45

15-Cent Minimum Value

The minimum catalogue value is 15 cents. Separating se-tenant pieces into individual stamps does not increase the value of the stamps since demand for the separated stamps may be small.

Christmas A951

1992, Oct. 31

1917 A951 600 l multicolored			1.00	50

Miniature Sheet

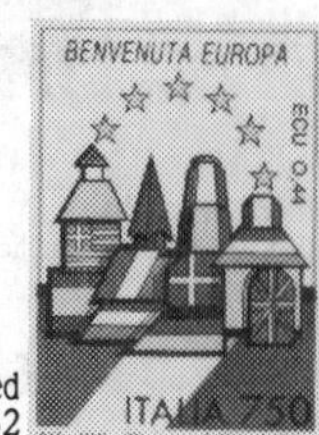

United Europe — A952

Buildings on natl. flags, inscriptions in native language: a, Italy (Benvenuta). b, Belgium (Vienvenue, Welkom). c, Denmark (Velkommen). d, France (Bienvenue L'Europe). e, Germany (Willkommen). f, Greece. g, Ireland (Failte). h, Luxembourg (Bienvenue Europe). i, Netherlands (Welkom). j, Portugal (Bem-Vinda). k, United Kingdom (Welcome). l, Spain (Bienvenida).

1993, Jan. 20 Photo. *Perf. 13½x14*
Sheet of 12

1918 A952 750 l #a.-l.	14.00	14.00

Meeting of Veterans of 1943 Battle of Nikolayev, Ukraine A953

1993, Jan. 23 Litho. *Perf. 14x13½*

1919 A953 600 l multicolored	95	48

Carlo Goldoni (1707-93), Playwright — A954

Paintings depicting scenes from plays: No. 1920, Nude man leaning on picture. No. 1921, Woman seated in front of harlequins.

1993, Feb. 6 Photo. *Perf. 13½x14*

1920 A954 500 l multicolored	80	40
1921 A954 500 l multicolored	80	40

Mosaic from the Piazza Armerina A955

Photo. & Engr.
1993, Feb. 20 *Perf. 14*

1922 A955 750 l multicolored	1.10	55

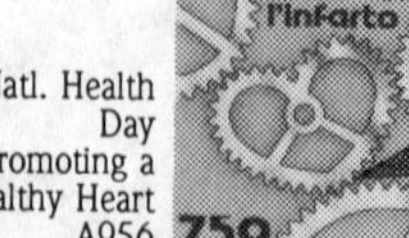

Natl. Health Day Promoting a Healthy Heart A956

1993, Mar. 5 Photo. *Perf. 14x13½*

1923 A956 750 l multicolored	1.10	55

Cats — A957

1993, Mar. 6 *Perf. 14x13½,13½x14*

1924 A957 600 l European	90	45
1925 A957 600 l Maine coon, vert.	90	45
1926 A957 600 l Devon Rex, vert.	90	45
1927 A957 600 l White Persian	90	45

Radio Cent. Type of 1991

Design: 750 l, Temistocle Calzecchi Onesti.

1993, Mar. 26 Litho. *Perf. 14x13½*

1928 A925 750 l multicolored	1.10	55

Radio cent. (in 1995).

City Scene, by Francesco Guardi (1712-1793) A958

1993, Apr. 6 Photo. & Engr. *Perf. 14*

1929 A958 3200 l multicolored	4.65	2.35

Horace (Quintus Horatius Flaccus), Poet and Satirist, 2000th Anniv. of Death — A959

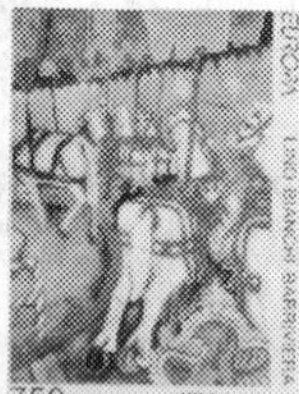

Contemporary Paintings — A960

1993, Apr. 19 Photo. *Perf. 13½x14*

1930 A959 600 l multicolored	90	45

1993, May 3

Europa: 750 l, Carousel Animals, by Lino Bianchi Barriviera. 850 l, Abstract, by Gino Severini.

1931 A960 750 l multicolored	1.15	58
1932 A960 850 l multicolored	1.30	65

Natl. Soccer Champions, Milan — A961

Natl. Academy of St. Luke, 400th Anniv. — A962

1993, May 24

1933 A961 750 l multicolored	1.20	60

1993, May 31 Photo.

1934 A962 750 l multicolored	1.20	60

St. Giuseppe Benedetto Cottolengo (1786-1842) — A963

1993, May Photo. & Engr.

1935 A963 750 l multicolored	1.20	60

Family Fest '93 — A964

1993, June 5 Photo. *Perf. 14x13½*

1936 A964 750 l multicolored	1.20	60

Tourism A965

1993, June 28 Photo. *Perf. 14x13½*

1937 A965 600 l Palmanova	90	45
1938 A965 600 l Senigallia	90	45
1939 A965 600 l Carloforte	90	45
1940 A965 600 l Sorrento	90	45

1993 World Kayaking Championships, Trentino — A966

1993, July 1 *Perf. 13½x14*

1941 A966 750 l multicolored	1.20	60

Regina Margherita Observatory, Cent. — A967

1993, Sept. 4 Photo. *Perf. 14x13½*

1942 A967 500 l multicolored	75	38

Museum Treasures A968

Designs: No. 1943, Concert, by Bartolomeo Manfredi. No. 1944, Ancient map of Foggia. 750 l, Illuminated page with "S," vert. 850 l, The Death of Adonis, by Sebastiano Del Piombo.

Perf. 14x13½, 13½x14

1993, Sept. 15 **Litho.**

1943	A968	600 l multicolored	85	42
1944	A968	600 l multicolored	85	42
1945	A968	750 l multicolored	1.00	50
1946	A968	850 l multicolored	1.25	60

Holy Stairway, Veroli — A969 World War II — A970

1993, Sept. 25 Photo. *Perf. 13½x14*

1947	A969	750 l multicolored	1.10	55

1993, Sept. 25

Events of 1943: No. 1948, Deportation of Jews from Italy, Oct. 16, 1943. No. 1949, Soldiers, helmet (Battle of Naples). No. 1950, Execution of the Cervi Brothers.

1948	A970	750 l multicolored	1.10	55
1949	A970	750 l multicolored	1.10	55
1950	A970	750 l multicolored	1.10	55

Thurn and Taxis Postal History A971

Designs: No. 1951, Coach. No. 1952, Coat of arms. No. 1953, Cart. No. 1954, Post rider on galloping horse. No. 1955, Post rider on walking horse.

1993, Oct. 2 *Perf. 14x13½*

1951	A971	750 l multicolored	1.00	50
1952	A971	750 l multicolored	1.00	50
1953	A971	750 l multicolored	1.00	50
1954	A971	750 l multicolored	1.00	50
1955	A971	750 l multicolored	1.00	50
		Nos. 1951-1955 (5)	5.00	2.50

Perf. 14 Horiz.

1951a	A971	750 l	1.00	50
1952a	A971	750 l	1.00	50
1953a	A971	750 l	1.00	50
1954a	A971	750 l	1.00	50
1955a	A971	750 l	1.00	50
b.		Booklet pane of 5, #1951a-1955a	5.00	

Bank of Italy, Cent. — A972

1993, Oct. 15 *Perf. 14x13½*

1956	A972	750 l Bank exterior	1.10	55
1957	A972	1000 l 1000 Lire note	1.40	70

Christmas — A973

Designs: 600 l, Nativity, by Corchiano. 750 l, Detail of The Annunciation, by Piero Della Francesca.

1993, Oct. 26 Litho. *Perf. 13½x14*

1958	A973	600 l multicolored	85	42
1959	A973	750 l multicolored	1.00	50

Stamp Day — A974

1993, Nov. 12 Photo. *Perf. 14*

1960	A974	600 l blue & red	85	42

First Italian colonial postage stamps, cent.

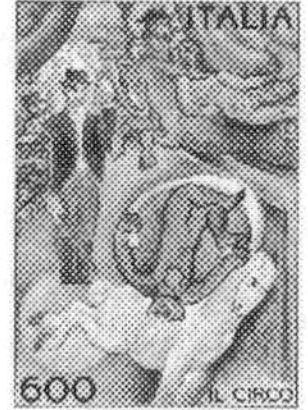

Circus — A975

1994, Jan. 8 Litho. *Perf. 13½x14*

1961	A975	600 l Acrobat, horses	85	42
1962	A975	750 l Clown performing	1.00	50

SEMI-POSTAL STAMPS

Many issues of Italy and Italian Colonies include one or more semi-postal denominations. To avoid splitting sets, these issues are generally listed as regular postage, airmail, etc., unless all values carry a surtax.

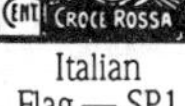

Italian Flag — SP1 Italian Eagle Bearing Arms of Savoy — SP2

1915-16 Typo. Wmk. 140 *Perf. 14*

B1	SP1	10c + 5c rose	1.50	*1.75*
B2	SP2	15c + 5c slate	1.10	*1.75*
B3	SP2	20c + 5c orange	2.00	*5.50*

No. B2 Surcharged **20**

1916

B4	SP2	20c on 15c + 5c	2.50	*6.75*
a.		Double overprint	200.00	
b.		Inverted overprint	200.00	300.00

Regular Issues of 1906-16 Overprinted in Blue or Red **B.L.P.**

1921

B5	A48	10c claret (Bl)	*350.00*	65.00
B6	A50	20c brn org (Bl)	*400.00*	25.00
B7	A49	25c blue (R)	37.50	5.00
B8	A49	40c brn (Bl)	12.00	75
a.		Inverted overprint	12.00	15.00

Regular Issues of 1901-22 Overprinted in Black, Blue, Brown or Red

1922-23

B9	A48	10c cl ('23) (Bk)	25.00	5.00
a.		Blue overprint	30.00	7.50
b.		Brown overprint	30.00	7.50
B10	A48	15c slate (Bl)	90.00	25.00
a.		Red overprint	100.00	30.00
B11	A50	20c brn org (Bk)	90.00	25.00
a.		Blue overprint	200.00	30.00
B12	A49	25c bl ('23) (Bk or Bl)	25.00	7.50
b.		Red overprint	90.00	25.00
B12A	A49	30c org brn (Bk)	37.50	10.00
B13	A49	40c brn (Bl)	40.00	7.50
a.		Black overprint	40.00	8.50
b.		As "a," invtd. ovpt.	30.00	
B14	A49	50c vio ('23) (Bk)	200.00	32.50
a.		Blue overprint		
B15	A49	60c car (Bk)	*850.00*	250.00
B15A	A49	85c choc (Bk)	80.00	22.50
B16	A46	1 l brn & grn ('23) (Bk)	*1,250.*	450.00
a.		Inverted overprint	*600.00*	

The stamps overprinted "B. L. P." were sold by the Government below face value to the National Federation for Assisting War Invalids. Most of them were affixed to special envelopes (Buste Lettere Postali) which bore advertisements. The Federation was permitted to sell these envelopes at a reduction of 5c from the face value of each stamp. The profits for the war invalids were derived from the advertisements.

Values of Nos. B5-B16 unused are for stamps with original gum. Most copies without gum or with part gum sell for about a quarter of values quoted. Uncanceled stamps affixed to the special envelopes usually sell for about half value.

The overprint on Nos. B9-B16 is wider (13½mm) than that on Nos. B5-B8 (11mm). The 1922-23 overprint exists both typo. and litho. on 10c, 15c, 20c and 25c; only litho. on 40c, 50c, 60c and 1 l; and only typo. on 30c and 85c.

Counterfeits of the B.L.P. overprints exist.

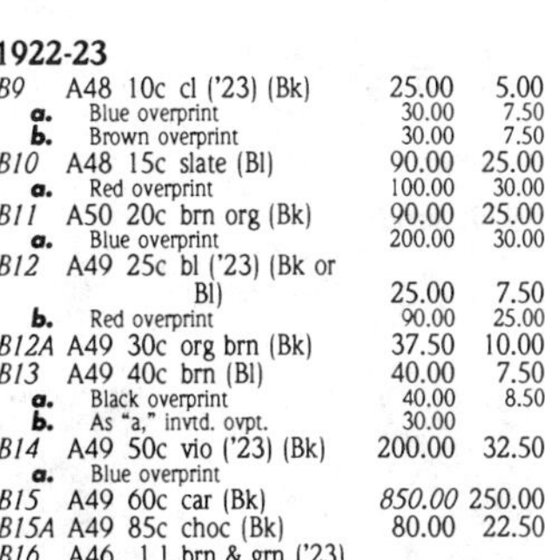

Administering Fascist Oath — SP3

1923, Oct. 29 *Perf. 14x14½*

B17	SP3	30c + 30c brown	9.50	*17.50*
B18	SP3	50c + 50c violet	16.00	*17.50*
B19	SP3	1 l + 1 l gray	9.50	*17.50*

The surtax was given to the Benevolent Fund of the Black Shirts (the Italian National Militia).

Anniv. of the March of the Fascisti on Rome.

St. Maria Maggiore SP4

Pope Opening Holy Door — SP8

Designs: 30c+15c, St. John Lateran. 50c+ 25c, St. Paul's Church. 60c+30c, St. Peter's Basilica. 5 l+2.50 l, Pope closing Holy Door.

1924, Dec. 24 *Perf. 12*

B20	SP4	20c + 10c dk grn & brn	80	*3.75*
B21	SP4	30c + 15c dk brn & brn	80	*3.75*
B22	SP4	50c + 25c vio & brn	80	*3.75*
B23	SP4	60c + 30c dp rose & brn	80	*9.00*
B24	SP8	1 l + 50c dp bl & vio	80	*7.50*
B25	SP8	5 l + 2.50 l org brn & vio	1.00	*19.00*
		Nos. B20-B25 (6)	5.00	*46.75*

The surtax was contributed toward the Holy Year expenses.

Castle of St. Angelo — SP10 Victor Emmanuel II — SP14

Designs: 50c+20c, 60c+30c, Aqueduct of Claudius. 1.25 l+50c, 1.25 l+60c, Capitol, Roman Forum. 5 l+2 l, 5 l+2.50 l, People's Gate.

Unwmk.

1926, Oct. 26 Engr. *Perf. 11*

B26	SP10	40c + 20c dk brn & blk	55	*2.75*
B27	SP10	60c + 30c brn red & ol brn	55	*2.75*
B28	SP10	1.25 l + 60c bl grn & blk	55	*7.75*
B29	SP10	5 l + 2.50 l dk bl & blk	1.00	*24.00*

1928, Mar. 1

B30	SP10	30c + 10c dl vio & blk	2.00	*5.50*
B31	SP10	50c + 20c ol grn & sl	2.00	*3.75*
B32	SP10	1.25 l + 50c dp bl & blk	3.25	*12.50*
B33	SP10	5 l + 2 l brn red & blk	7.50	*35.00*

The tax on Nos. B26 to B33 was devoted to the charitable work of the Voluntary Militia for National Defense.

See Nos. B35-B38.

1929, Jan. 4 Photo. *Perf. 14*

B34	SP14	50c + 10c olive green	75	*1.50*

50th anniv. of the death of King Victor Emmanuel II. The surtax was for veterans.

Type of 1926 Issue

Designs in same order.

1930, July 1 **Engr.**

B35	SP10	30c + 10c dk grn & vio	25	*3.00*
B36	SP10	50c + 10c dk grn & bl grn	25	*1.50*
B37	SP10	1.25 l + 30c ind & grn	35	*6.50*
B38	SP10	5 l + 1.50 l blk brn & ol brn	2.25	*27.50*

The surtax was for the charitable work of the Voluntary Militia for National Defense.

Militiamen at Ceremonial Fire with Quotation from Leonardo da Vinci — SP15 Symbolical of Pride for Militia — SP16

Symbolical of Militia Guarding Immortality of Italy — SP17 Militia Passing Through Arch of Constantine — SP18

1935, July 1 Photo. Wmk. 140

B39	SP15	20c + 10c rose red	2.25	*3.00*
B40	SP16	25c + 15c green	2.25	*3.50*
B41	SP17	50c + 30c purple	2.25	*4.25*
B42	SP18	1.25 l + 75c blue	2.25	*4.50*
		Nos. B39-B42,CB3 (5)	11.25	*21.00*

The surtax was for the Militia.

Roman Battle — SP19

Roman Warriors — SP20

1941, Dec. 13

B43	SP19	20c + 10c rose red	20	55
B44	SP19	30c + 15c brown	20	70
B45	SP20	50c + 25c violet	22	85
B46	SP20	1.25 l + 1 l blue	28	90
		Set, never hinged	4.50	

2,000th anniv. of the birth of Livy (59 B.C.-17 A.D.), Roman historian.

AIR POST STAMPS

Special Delivery Stamp No. E1 Overprinted

ESPERIMENTO POSTA AEREA
MAGGIO 1917
TORINO-ROMA • ROMA-TORINO

1917, May Wmk. 140 *Perf. 14*

C1 SD1 25c rose red 3.00 *5.75*

Type of SD3 Surcharged in Black

IDROVOLANTE

NAPOLI - PALERMO - NAPOLI
25 CENT. 25

1917, June 27

C2 SD3 25c on 40c vio 5.50 *6.00*

Type SD3 was not issued without surcharge.

AP2

1926-28 Typo.

C3	AP2	50c rose red ('28)	1.65	*2.00*
C4	AP2	60c gray	1.25	*1.50*
C5	AP2	80c brn vio & brn ('28)	6.75	*12.50*
C6	AP2	1 l blue	80	*1.50*
C7	AP2	1.20 l brn ('27)	6.75	*20.00*
C8	AP2	1.50 l buff	5.50	5.50
C9	AP2	5 l gray grn	12.50	*15.00*
		Nos. C3-C9 (7)	35.20	*58.00*

Nos. C4 and C6 Surcharged

Cent. 50

1927, Sept. 16

C10	AP2	50c on 60c gray	1.65	*5.75*
a.		Pair, one without surcharge	400.00	
C11	AP2	80c on 1 l blue	6.50	*27.50*

Pegasus AP3

Wings AP4

Spirit of Flight AP5

Arrows AP6

1930-32 Photo. Wmk. 140

C12	AP4	25c dk grn ('32)	15	15
C13	AP3	50c olive brn	15	15
C14	AP5	75c org brn ('32)	15	15
C15	AP4	80c org red	15	30
C16	AP5	1 l purple	15	15
C17	AP6	2 l deep blue	15	18
C18	AP3	5 l dk green	15	30
C19	AP3	10 l dp car	20	60
		Set value		70

The 50c, 1 l and 2 l were reprinted in 1942 with labels similar to those of Nos. 427-438, but were not issued. Value, set of 3, $100.

For overprints see Nos. MC1-MC5. For overprints on type A6 see Nos. C52-C55.

Statue of Ferrucci — AP7

1930, July 10

C20	AP7	50c purple	50	*2.50*
C21	AP7	1 l orange brn	50	*5.00*
C22	AP7	5 l + 2 l brn vio	1.65	*37.50*

400th anniv. of the death of Francesco Ferrucci, Tuscan warrior.

For overprinted types see Aegean Islands Nos. C1-C3.

Jupiter Sending Forth his Eagle — AP8

1930, Oct. 21 Photo. Wmk. 140

C23	AP8	50c lt brown	2.25	*3.00*
C24	AP8	1 l orange	3.00	*4.50*

Engr.
Unwmk.

C25	AP8	7.70 l + 1.30 l vio brn	12.50	*35.00*
C26	AP8	9 l + 2 l indigo	14.00	*35.00*

Bimillenary of the birth of Virgil.

The surtax on Nos. C25 and C26 was for the National Institute Figli del Littorio.

For overprinted types see Aegean Islands Nos. C4-C7.

Trans-Atlantic Squadron — AP9

1930, Dec. 15 Photo. Wmk. 140

C27	AP9	7.70 l Prus bl & gray	125.00	*325.00*
a.		Seven stars instead of six	475.00	*2,000.*

Issued in connection with the flight by Italian aviators from Rome to Rio de Janeiro, Dec., 1930-Jan. 12, 1931.

Leonardo da Vinci's Flying Machine AP10

Leonardo da Vinci — AP11

Leonardo da Vinci — AP12

1932

C28	AP10	50c olive brn	80	*1.50*
C29	AP11	1 l violet	80	*2.00*
C30	AP11	3 l brown red	1.90	*6.50*
C31	AP11	5 l dp green	2.00	*8.00*
C32	AP10	7.70 l + 2 l dk bl	3.00	*27.50*
C33	AP11	10 l + 2.50 l blk brn	3.00	*30.00*
		Nos. C28-C33 (6)	11.50	*75.50*

Engr.
Unwmk.

C34	AP12	100 l brt bl & grnsh blk	21.00	*100.00*
a.		Thin paper	37.50	*150.00*

Dante Alighieri Soc. and especially Leonardo da Vinci, to whom the invention of a flying machine has been attributed. Surtax was for the benefit of the Society.

Inscription on No. C34: "Man with his large wings by beating against the air will be able to dominate it and lift himself above it".

Issued: #C28-C33, Mar. 14; #C34, Aug. 6.

For overprinted types see Aegean Islands Nos. C8-C13.

Garibaldi's Home at Caprera — AP13

Farmhouse where Anita Garibaldi Died — AP14

Designs: 50c, 1 l+25c, Garibaldi's home, Caprera. 2 l+50c, Anita Garibaldi. 5 l+1 l, Giuseppe Garibaldi.

1932, Apr. 6 Photo. Wmk. 140

C35	AP13	50c copper red	65	*1.50*
C36	AP14	80c deep green	1.10	*2.25*
C37	AP13	1 l + 25c red brn	1.75	*7.50*
C38	AP13	2 l + 50c dp bl	3.00	*12.50*
C39	AP14	5 l + 1 l dp grn	3.25	*15.00*
		Nos. C35-C39 (5)	9.75	*38.75*

50th anniv. of the death of Giuseppe Garibaldi, patriot. The surtax was for the benefit of the Garibaldi Volunteers.

For overprinted types see Aegean Islands Nos. C15-C19.

Eagle Sculpture and Airplane AP17

Design: 75c, Italian buildings from the air.

1932, Oct. 27 *Perf. 14*

C40	AP17	50c dark brown	5.75	*2.75*
C41	AP17	75c orange brn	1.25	*6.50*

10th anniversary of the Fascist government and the March on Rome.

Graf Zeppelin Issue

Zeppelin over Pyramid of Caius Cestius AP19

Designs: 5 l, Tomb of Cecilia Metlella. 10 l, Stadium of Mussolini. 12 l, St. Angelo Castle and Bridge. 15 l, Roman Forum. 20 l, Imperial Avenue.

1933, Apr. 24

C42	AP19	3 l black & grn	5.25	*7.50*
C43	AP19	5 l green & brn	3.50	*7.50*
C44	AP19	10 l car & dl bl	3.50	*20.00*
C45	AP19	12 l dk bl & red org	3.50	*25.00*
C46	AP19	15 l dk brn & gray	3.50	*32.50*
C47	AP19	20 l org brn & bl	3.50	*37.50*
a.		Vertical pair, imperf. btwn.	1,850.	
		Nos. C42-C47 (6)	22.75	*130.00*

Balbo's Trans-Atlantic Flight Issue

Italian Flag

King Victor Emmanuel III

Allegory "Flight" — AP25

Design: No. C49, Colosseum at Rome, Chicago skyline. Nos. C48-C49 consist of three parts; Italian flag, Victor Emmanuel III, and scene arranged horizontally.

1933, May 20

C48 AP25 5.25 l + 19.75 l red, grn & ultra	42.50	*325.00*
a. Left stamp without ovpt.	*950.00*	
C49 AP25 5.25 l + 44.75 l grn, red & ultra	42.50	*325.00*

Transatlantic Flight, Rome-Chicago, of 24-seaplane squadron led by Gen. Italo Balbo. Center and right sections paid postage. At left is registered air express label overprinted "APPARECCHIO" and abbreviated pilot's name. Twenty triptychs of each value differ in name overprint.

No. C49 overprinted "VOLO DI RITORNO/ NEW YORK-ROMA" was not issued; flight canceled.

For overprints see Nos. CO1, Aegean Islands C26-C27.

Type of Air Post Stamp of 1930 Surcharged in Black

PRIMO VOLO DIRETTO
ROMA = BUENOS-AYRES
TRIMOTORE "LOMBARDI-MAZZOTTI"
5

1934, Jan. 18

C52 AP6 2 l on 2 l yel	1.25	*19.00*
C53 AP6 3 l on 2 l yel grn	1.25	*22.50*
C54 AP6 5 l on 2 l rose	1.25	*27.50*
C55 AP6 10 l on 2 l vio	1.25	*37.50*

For use on mail carried on a special flight from Rome to Buenos Aires.

View of Fiume Harbor — AP28

Designs: 50c, 1 l+50c, Monument to the Dead. 2 l+1.50 l, Venetian Lions. 3 l+2 l, Julian wall.

1934, Mar. 12

C56 AP28 25c green	18	*55*
C57 AP28 50c brown	18	*38*
C58 AP28 75c org brn	18	*95*
C59 AP28 1 l + 50c dl vio	18	*5.50*
C60 AP28 2 l + 1.50 l dl bl	18	*6.50*
C61 AP28 3 l + 2 l blk brn	18	*7.50*
Nos. C56-C61 (6)	1.08	*21.38*

Annexation of Fiume, 10th anniversary.

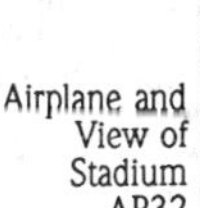

Airplane and View of Stadium AP32

Soccer Player and Plane — AP33

Airplane and Stadium Entrance — AP35

Airplane over Stadium AP34

1934, May 24

C62 AP32 50c car rose	2.50	*3.00*
C63 AP33 75c gray blue	4.00	*4.50*
C64 AP34 5 l + 2.50 l ol grn	11.00	*40.00*
C65 AP35 10 l + 5 l brn blk	15.00	*45.00*

2nd World Soccer Championships.

For overprinted types see Aegean Islands Nos. C28-C31.

Zeppelin under Fire — AP36

Air Force Memorial — AP40

Designs: 25c, 80c, Zeppelin under fire. 50c, 75c, Motorboat patrol. 1 l+50c, Desert infantry. 2 l+1 l, Plane attacking troops.

1934, Apr. 24

C66 AP36 25c dk green	45	*95*
C67 AP36 50c gray	45	*1.25*
C68 AP36 75c dk brown	60	*1.50*
C69 AP36 80c slate blue	90	*2.00*
C70 AP36 1 l + 50c red brn	2.50	*8.00*
C71 AP36 2 l + 1 l brt bl	3.00	*9.00*
C72 AP40 3 l + 2 l brn blk	3.50	*10.50*
Nos. C66-C72 (7)	11.40	*33.20*

Cent. of the institution of the Military Medal of Valor.

For overprinted types see Aegean Islands Nos. C32-C38.

King Victor Emmanuel III — AP41

1934, Nov. 5

C73 AP41 1 l purple	60	*5.50*
C74 AP41 2 l brt blue	60	*6.50*
C75 AP41 4 l red brown	95	*27.50*
C76 AP41 5 l dull green	95	*37.50*
C77 AP41 8 l rose red	5.25	*50.00*
C78 AP41 10 l brown	5.75	*60.00*
Nos. C73-C78 (6)	14.10	*187.00*

65th birthday of King Victor Emmanuel III and the nonstop flight from Rome to Mogadiscio.

For overprint see No. CO2.

Muse Playing Harp AP42

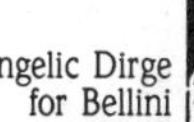

Angelic Dirge for Bellini AP43

Scene from Bellini Opera, La Sonnambula AP44

1935, Sept. 24

C79 AP42 25c dull yellow	60	*1.00*
C80 AP42 50c brown	60	*95*
C81 AP42 60c rose carmine	90	*1.75*
C82 AP43 1 l + 1 l purple	4.25	*30.00*
C83 AP44 5 l + 2 l green	6.50	*37.50*
Nos. C79-C83 (5)	12.85	*71.20*

Vincenzo Bellini, (1801-35), operatic composer.

Seaplane in Flight AP45

Designs: 50c, 1 l+1 l, Monoplane over valley. 60c, Oak and eagle. 5 l+2 l, Ruins of ancient Rome.

1936, July 1

C84 AP45 25c dp green	60	*1.10*
C85 AP45 50c dk brown	75	*1.10*
C86 AP45 60c scarlet	95	*2.00*
C87 AP45 1 l + 1 l vio	4.50	*30.00*
C88 AP45 5 l + 2 l slate bl	6.75	*45.00*
Nos. C84-C88 (5)	13.55	*79.20*

Issued to commemorate the 2000th anniversary of the birth of Quintus Horatius Flaccus (Horace).

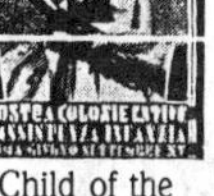
Child of the Balilla AP49

Heads of Children AP50

1937, June 28

C89 AP49 25c dk bl grn	1.25	*2.00*
C90 AP50 50c brown	1.75	*2.00*
C91 AP49 1 l purple	1.25	*3.00*
C92 AP50 2 l + 1 l dk bl	4.75	*27.50*
C93 AP49 3 l + 2 l org	6.50	*32.50*
C94 AP50 5 l + 3 l rose lake	8.25	*37.50*
Nos. C89-C94 (6)	23.75	*104.50*

Issued to commemorate the Summer Exhibition for Child Welfare. The surtax on Nos. C92-C94 was used to support summer camps for poor children.

Prosperous Italy AP51

Designs: 50c, Prolific Italy. 80c, Apollo's steeds. 1 l+1 l, Map and Roman Standard. 5 l+1 l, Augustus Caesar.

1937, Sept. 23

C95 AP51 25c red vio	1.50	*2.00*
C96 AP51 50c olive brn	1.50	*1.50*
C97 AP51 80c org brn	3.00	*3.50*
C98 AP51 1 l + 1 l dk bl	7.00	*19.00*
C99 AP51 5 l + 1 l dl vio	10.50	*30.00*
Nos. C95-C99 (5)	23.50	*56.00*

Bimillenary of the birth of Augustus Caesar (Octavianus) on the occasion of the exhibition opened in Rome by Mussolini on Sept. 22nd, 1937.

For overprinted types see Aegean Islands Nos. C39-C43.

King Victor Emmanuel III — AP56

Designs: 25c, 3 l, King Victor Emmanuel III. 50c, 1 l, Dante Alighieri. 2 l, 5 l, Leonardo da Vinci.

1938, Oct. 28

C100 AP56 25c dull green	70	*70*
C101 AP56 50c dk yel brn	70	*70*
C102 AP56 1 l violet	80	*95*
C103 AP56 2 l royal blue	1.40	*3.75*
C104 AP56 3 l brown car	1.90	*7.50*
C105 AP56 5 l dp green	2.50	*9.00*
Nos. C100-C105 (6)	8.00	*22.60*

Proclamation of the Empire.

Plane and Clasped Hands AP59

Swallows in Flight AP60

1945-47 Wmk. 277 Photo. *Perf. 14*

C106 AP59 1 l slate bl	15	15
C107 AP60 2 l dk blue	15	15
C108 AP59 3.20 l red org	15	15
C109 AP60 5 l dk green	15	15
C110 AP59 10 l car rose	15	15
C111 AP60 25 l dk bl ('46)	4.50	2.75
C112 AP60 25 l brown ('47)	15	15
C113 AP59 50 l dk grn ('46)	6.75	6.00
C114 AP59 50 l violet ('47)	15	15
Nos. C106-C114 (9)	12.30	9.80
Set, never hinged	38.00	

Issue date: Nos. C113-C114, Apr. 21.

See Nos. C130-C131. For surcharges and overprints see Nos. C115, C136, 1LNC1-1LNC7, Trieste C1-C6, C17-C22.

No. C108 Surcharged in Black

1947, July 1

C115 AP59 6 l on 3.20 l	15	15
Never hinged	35	
a. Pair, one without surch.	*975.00*	
b. Inverted surcharge		*5,500.*

Radio on Land — AP61

Plane over Capitol Bell Tower — AP65

Designs: 6 l, 25 l, Radio on land. 10 l, 35 l, Radio at sea. 20 l, 50 l, Radio in the skies.

1947, Sept. 1 Photo. *Perf. 14*

C116 AP61 6 l dp violet	15	15
C117 AP61 10 l dk car rose	15	20
C118 AP61 20 l dp orange	75	20
C119 AP61 25 l aqua	45	20
C120 AP61 35 l brt blue	45	40
C121 AP61 50 l lilac rose	95	1.00
Nos. C116-C121 (6)	2.90	2.15
Set, never hinged	6.00	

50th anniv. of radio.

For overprints see Trieste Nos. C7-C12.

1948

C123 AP65 100 l green 3.00 15
C124 AP65 300 l lilac rose 30 20
C125 AP65 500 l ultra 38 30

Engr.

C126 AP65 1000 l dk brown 1.40 85
a. Vert. pair, imperf. btwn. *250.00 250.00*
b. Perf. 14x13 1.90 1.40
Set, never hinged 7.50

See No. C132-C135. For overprints see Trieste Nos. C13-C16, C23-C26.

St. Catherine Carrying Cross — AP66

Design: 200 l, St. Catherine with outstretched arms.

1948, Mar. 1 Photo.

C127 AP66 100 l bl vio & brn org 20.00 21.00
C128 AP66 200 l dp blue & bis 7.25 7.75
Set, never hinged 67.00

600th anniversary of the birth of St. Catherine of Siena, patroness of Italy.

Catalogue values for unused stamps in this section, from this point to the end of the section, are for Never Hinged items.

Giuseppe Mazzini (1805-1872), Patriot — AP67

1955, Dec. 31 Wmk. 303 *Perf. 14*

C129 AP67 100 l Prus green 1.50 75

Types of 1945-46, 1948

1955-62 Wmk. 303 *Perf. 14*

C130 AP60 5 l green ('62) 15 15
C131 AP59 50 l vio ('57) 15 15
C132 AP65 100 l green 75 15
C133 AP65 300 l lil rose 85 55
C134 AP65 500 l ultra ('56) 1.00 90

Engr.

Perf. 13½

C135 AP65 1000 l maroon ('59) 1.50 1.40
Nos. C130-C135 (6) 4.40 3.30

Fluorescent Paper

See note below No. 998.

No. C132 was issued on both ordinary and fluorescent paper. The design of the fluorescent stamp is smaller.

Airmail stamps issued only on fluorescent paper are Nos. C139-C140.

Type of 1945-46 Surcharged in Ultramarine

1956

L 120

Visita del Presidente della Repubblica negli U.S.A. e nel Canada

1956, Feb. 24

C136 AP59 120 l on 50 l mag 1.50 1.25

Visit of Pres. Giovanni Gronchi to the US and Canada.

Madonna of Bruges, by Michelangelo — AP68

Wmk. 303

1964, Feb. 18 Photo. *Perf. 14*

C137 AP68 185 l black 28 30

400th anniversary of the death of Michelangelo Buonarroti (1475-1564), artist.

Verrazano Type of Regular Issue

1964, Nov. 21 Wmk. 303 *Perf. 14*

C138 A481 130 l blk & dull grn 18 15

See note after No. 901.

Adoration of the Kings, by Gentile da Fabriano — AP69

1970, Dec. 12 Photo. Unwmk.

C139 AP69 150 l multicolored 30 18

Christmas 1970.

Aviation Type of Regular Issue

Design: F-140S Starfighter over Aeronautical Academy, Pozzuoli.

1973, Mar. 28 Photo. *Perf. 14x13½*

C140 A590 150 l multicolored 28 18

AIR POST SEMI-POSTAL STAMPS

Holy Year Issue

Dome of St. Peter's, Dove with Olive Branch, Church of the Holy Sepulcher SPAP1

Wmk. 140

1933, Oct. 23 Photo. *Perf. 14*

CB1 SPAP1 50c + 25c org brn 70 *3.00*
CB2 SPAP1 75c + 50c brn vio 85 *4.50*
Set, never hinged 6.00

Symbolical of Military Air Force — SPAP2

1935, July 1

CB3 SPAP2 50c + 50c brown 2.25 *5.75*
Never hinged 14.00

The surtax was for the Militia.

AIR POST SPECIAL DELIVERY STAMPS

Garibaldi, Anita Garibaldi, Plane APSD1

Wmk. 140

1932, June 2 Photo. *Perf. 14*

CE1 APSD1 2.25 l + 1 l 3.75 *11.50*
CE2 APSD1 4.50 l + 1.50 l 4.00 *12.50*

50th anniversary of the death of Giuseppe Garibaldi.

For overprinted types see Aegean Islands Nos. CE1-CE2.

Airplane and Sunburst APSD2

1933-34

CE3 APSD2 2 l gray blk ('34) 15 *45*
CE4 APSD2 2.25 l gray blk 1.50 *45.00*

For overprint see No. MCE1.

Flag Raising before Fascist Headquarters — APSD3

1934, Mar. 12

CE5 APSD3 2 l + 1.25 l 1.10 *11.50*
CE6 APSD3 2.25 l + 1.25 l 18 *6.50*
CE7 APSD3 4.50 l + 2 l 18 *7.50*
Set, never hinged 3.25

10th anniv. of the annexation of Fiume.

Triumphal Arch in Rome APSD4

1934, Aug. 31

CE8 APSD4 2 l + 1.25 l brown 2.50 *8.75*
CE9 APSD4 4.50 l + 2 l cop red 2.75 *11.00*
Set, never hinged 30.00

Centenary of the institution of the Military Medal of Valor.

For overprinted types see Aegean Islands Nos. CE3-CE4.

AIR POST OFFICIAL STAMPS

Balbo Flight Type of Air Post Stamp of 1933 Overprinted

SERVIZIO DI STATO

1933 Wmk. 140 *Perf. 14*

CO1 AP25 5.25 l + 44.75 l red, grn & red vio 900.00 *6,750.*

Type of Air Post Stamp of 1934 Overprinted in Gold Crown and "SERVIZIO DI STATO"

1934

CO2 AP41 10 l blue blk 275.00 *5,250.*

65th birthday of King Victor Emmanuel III and the non-stop flight from Rome to Mogadiscio.

PNEUMATIC POST STAMPS

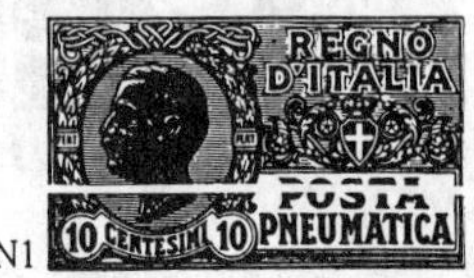

PN1

1913-28 Wmk. 140 Typo. *Perf. 14*

D1 PN1 10c brown 1.00 *5.25*
D2 PN1 15c brn vio ('28) 80 *3.25*
a. 15c dull violet ('21) 2.00 *8.00*
D3 PN1 15c rose red ('28) 2.25 *5.25*
D4 PN1 15c claret ('28) 80 *3.25*
D5 PN1 20c brn vio ('25) 2.75 *10.50*
D6 PN1 30c blue ('23) 2.00 *17.50*
D7 PN1 35c rose red ('27) 4.75 *40.00*
D8 PN1 40c dp red ('26) 5.75 *47.50*
Nos. D1-D8 (8) 20.10 *132.50*

Nos. D1, D2a, D5-D6, D8 Surcharged Like Nos. C10-C11

1924-27

D9 PN1 15c on 10c 1.50 *7.00*
D10 PN1 15c on 20c ('27) 2.75 *7.75*
D11 PN1 20c on 10c ('25) 2.50 *11.00*
D12 PN1 20c on 15c ('25) 1.50 *5.50*
D13 PN1 35c on 40c ('27) 4.75 *37.50*
D14 PN1 40c on 30c ('25) 2.50 *27.50*
Nos. D9-D14 (6) 15.50 *96.25*

Dante Alighieri PN2

Galileo Galilei — PN3

1933, Mar. 29 Photo.

D15 PN2 15c dark violet 15 *50*
D16 PN3 35c rose red 15 *50*
Set value 16

Similar to Types of 1933, Without "REGNO"

1945, Oct. 22 Wmk. 277

D17 PN2 60c dull brown 15 15
D18 PN3 1.40 l dull blue 15 15
Set value 15 16

Minerva — PN6

1947, Nov. 15

D19 PN6 3 l rose lilac 5.00 9.00
D20 PN6 5 l aqua 15 15
Set, never hinged 13.00

Catalogue values for unused stamps in this section, from this point to the end of the section, are for Never Hinged items.

1958-66 Wmk. 303

D21 PN6 10 l rose red 15 15
D22 PN6 20 l sapphire ('66) 20 15
Set value 18

SPECIAL DELIVERY STAMPS

Victor Emmanuel III — SD1

1903-26 Typo. Wmk. 140 *Perf. 14*

E1 SD1 25c rose red 4.75 20
a. Imperf., pair 75.00 150.00
E2 SD1 50c dl red ('20) 75 30
E3 SD1 60c dl red ('22) 75 28
E4 SD1 70c dl red ('25) 15 18
E5 SD1 1.25 l dp bl ('26) 15 15
Nos. E1-E5 (5) 6.55 1.11

For overprint and surcharges see Nos. C1, E11, E13, Offices in Crete, Offices in Africa, Offices in Turkish Empire, .

Victor Emmanuel III — SD2

1908-26

E6 SD2 30c blue & rose 28 80
E7 SD2 2 l bl & red ('25) 38 *14.00*
E8 SD2 2.50 l bl & red ('26) 75 *1.25*

The 1.20 lire blue and red (see No. E12) was prepared in 1922, but not issued. Value $60.

For surcharges and overprints see Nos. E10, E12, Offices in China, Offices in Africa, Offices in Turkish Empire.

SD3

1917, Nov.

E9 SD3 25c on 40c violet 8.25 *18.00*

Type SD3 not issued without surcharge.
For surcharge see No. C2.

No. E6 Surcharged

1921, Oct.

E10 SD2 1.20 l on 30c 38 *4.25*
a. Comma in value omitted 1.65 *18.00*
b. Double surcharge 32.50

No. E2 Surcharged **Cent. 60**

1922, Jan. 9

E11 SD1 60c on 50c dull red 4.50 40
a. Inverted surcharge 27.50 55.00
b. Double surcharge 350.00
c. Imperf., pair 110.00 250.00

Type of 1908 Surcharged

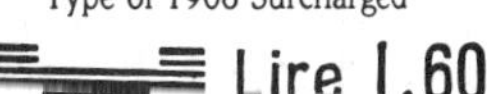

1924, May

E12 SD2 1.60 l on 1.20 l bl & red 38 *15.00*
a. Double surch., one inverted 27.50 *60.00*

No. E3 Surcharged like No. E11

1925, Apr. 11

E13 SD1 70c on 60c dull red 15 40
a. Inverted surcharge 32.50 65.00

Victor Emmanuel III — SD4

1932-33 Photo.

E14 SD4 1.25 l green 15 15
E15 SD4 2.50 l dp org ('33) 15 *1.00*
Set value 22

For overprints see Nos. ME1, Italian Social Republic E1-E2.

Ancient Pillars and Entrenchments — SD5

Design: 2.50 l, Head of Mussolini, trophies of flags, etc.

1932, Oct. 27

E16 SD5 1.25 l dp green 15 *90*
E17 SD5 2.50 l dp orange 1.65 *60.00*

"Italia" SD7

1945, Aug. Wmk. 277 *Perf. 14*

E18 SD7 5 l rose carmine 15 15

Winged Foot — SD8

Rearing Horse and Torch-Bearer SD9

1945-51

E19 SD8 5 l henna brn 15 15
E20 SD9 10 l deep blue 15 15
E21 SD9 15 l dk car rose ('47) 1.75 20
E22 SD8 25 l brt red org ('47) 8.00 20
E23 SD8 30 l dp vio ('46) 2.00 20
E24 SD8 50 l lil rose ('51) 10.00 15
E25 SD9 60 l car rose ('48) 6.25 20
Nos. E19-E25 (7) 28.30 1.25

See No. E32. For overprints see Nos. 1LNE1-1LNE2, Trieste E1-E4, E6-E7.

Type of Regular Issue of 1948
Inscribed: "Espresso"

1948, Sept. 18 Photo. *Perf. 14*

E26 A272 35 l vio *(Naples)* 6.75 6.25

Catalogue values for unused stamps in this section, from this point to the end of the section, are for Never Hinged items.

Type of 1945-51

1955, July 7 Wmk. 303 *Perf. 14*

E32 SD8 50 l lilac rose 4.00 15

Etruscan Winged Horses SD10

1958-76 Photo.

Size: 36 1/2x20 1/4mm

E33 SD10 75 l magenta 20 15

Size: 36x20mm

E34 SD10 150 l dl bl grn ('68) 25 15
a. Size: 36 1/2x20 1/4mm ('66) 1.25 15
E35 SD10 250 l blue ('74) 50 15
E36 SD10 300 l brown ('76) 50 15
Set value 22

Nos. E34-E36 are fluorescent.

AUTHORIZED DELIVERY STAMPS

For the payment of a special tax for the authorized delivery of correspondence privately instead of through the post office.

AD1

Coat of Arms — AD2

1928 Wmk. 140 Typo. *Perf. 14*

EY1 AD1 10c dull blue 38 15
a. Perf. 11 1.75 60

1930 Photo. *Perf. 14*

EY2 AD2 10c dark brown 15 15

For surcharge and overprint see Nos. EY3, Italian Social Republic EY1.

No. EY2 Surcharged in Black

1945

EY3 AD2 40c on 10c dark brown 15 15

Coat of Arms — AD3

"Italia" — AD4

1945-46 Photo. Wmk. 277

EY4 AD3 40c dark brown 15 25
EY5 AD3 1 l dk brown ('46) 40 40

For overprint see Trieste No. EY1.

1947-52

Size: 27 1/2x22 1/2mm

EY6 AD4 1 l brt grnsh bl 15 15
EY7 AD4 8 l brt red ('48) 5.25 15

Size: 20 1/2x16 1/2mm

EY8 AD4 15 l violet ('49) 24.00 20
EY9 AD4 20 l rose vio ('52) 2.00 20
Set, never hinged 150.00

For overprints see Trieste Nos. EY2-EY5.

Catalogue values for unused stamps in this section, from this point to the end of the section, are for Never Hinged items.

Italia Type of 1947

1955-90 Wmk. 303 Photo. *Perf. 14*

Size: 20 1/2x16 1/2mm

EY11 AD4 20 l rose vio 20 20
EY12 AD4 30 l Prus grn ('65) 20 20
EY13 AD4 35 l ocher ('74) 20 20
EY14 AD4 110 l lt ultra ('77) 20 20
EY15 AD4 270 l brt pink ('84) 50 20

Size: 19 1/2x16 1/2mm

EY16 AD4 300 l rose & grn ('87) 60 20
EY17 AD4 370 l tan & brn vio 78 40
Nos. EY11-EY17 (7) 2.68 1.60

Issue date: 370 l, Sept. 24, 1990.

POSTAGE DUE STAMPS

Unused values for Postage Due stamps are for examples with full original gum. Stamps without gum, with part gum or privately gummed sell for much less.

D1

D2

1863 Unwmk. Litho. *Imperf.*

J1 D1 10c yellow 450.00 50.00
a. 10c yellow orange 500.00 50.00
Without gum 30.00

1869 Wmk. 140 Typo. *Perf. 14*

J2 D2 10c buff 750.00 10.00

D3

D4

1870-1925

J3 D3 1c buff & mag 90 1.00
J4 D3 2c buff & mag 5.50 6.00
J5 D3 5c buff & mag 30 15
J6 D3 10c buff & mag ('71) 30 15
b. Imperf., pair *1,100.*
J7 D3 20c buff & mag ('94) 40 15
a. Imperf., pair 37.50 45.00
J8 D3 30c buff & mag 75 22
b. Imperf., pair *3,750.*
J9 D3 40c buff & mag 90 24
J10 D3 50c buff & mag 75 15
b. Imperf., pair *750.00*
J11 D3 60c buff & mag 37.50 45
J12 D3 60c buff & brn ('25) 7.50 1.75
J13 D3 1 l lt bl & brn 1,000. 3.00
J14 D3 1 l bl & mag ('94) 28 18
a. Imperf., pair 37.50 37.50
J15 D3 2 l lt bl & brn 900.00 4.00
J16 D3 2 l bl & mag ('03) 9.00 45
J17 D3 5 l bl & brn ('74) 90.00 3.00
J18 D3 5 l bl & mag ('03) 30.00 1.00
J19 D3 10 l bl & brn ('74) *1,800.* 6.00
J20 D3 10 l bl & mag ('94) 45.00 38

Early printings of 5c, 10c, 30c, 40c, 50c and 60c were in buff and magenta, later ones (1890-94) in stronger shades. The earlier, paler shades and their inverted-numeral varieties sell for considerably more than those of the later shades. Values are for the later shades.

For surcharges and overprints see Nos. J25-J27, Offices in China, Offices in Turkish Empire.

Numeral Inverted

J3a D3 1c 1,300. 600.00
J4a D3 2c *3,500.* 750.00
J5a D3 5c 85 85
J6a D3 10c 1.50 1.50
J7b D3 20c 7.50 9.00
J8a D3 30c 2.00 2.75
J9a D3 40c 125.00 125.00
J10a D3 50c 9.00 9.00
J11a D3 60c 67.50 90.00
J13a D3 1 l *7,500.*
J14b D3 1 l 900.00 450.00
J15a D3 2 l *550.00*
J16a D3 2 l *750.00* *900.00*
J17a D3 5 l 250.00
J19a D3 10 l 140.00

1884-1903

J21 D4 50 l green 15.00 5.50
J22 D4 50 l yellow ('03) 26.00 6.00
J23 D4 100 l claret 16.00 4.25
J24 D4 100 l blue ('03) 17.00 3.00

Nos. J3 & J4 Surcharged in Black

1890-91

J25 D3 10c on 2c 20.00 6.00
J26 D3 20c on 1c 85.00 4.50
a. Inverted surcharge *1,500.*
J27 D3 30c on 2c 275.00 2.50
a. Inverted surcharge *575.00*

Coat of Arms
D6 D7

1934 **Photo.**

No.	Type	Description	Unused	Used
J28	D6	5c brown	15	15
J29	D6	10c blue	15	15
J30	D6	20c rose red	15	15
J31	D6	25c green	15	15
J32	D6	30c red org	15	15
J33	D6	40c blk brn	15	*24*
J34	D6	50c violet	15	15
J35	D6	60c slate blk	22	*50*
J36	D7	1 l red org	15	15
J37	D7	2 l green	15	15
J38	D7	5 l violet	35	15
J39	D7	10 l blue	75	22
J40	D7	20 l car rose	85	50
		Set value	2.60	2.10

For overprints see Italian Social Republic Nos. J1-J13.

D8

D9

1945-46 **Unwmk.** ***Perf. 14***

No.	Type	Description	Unused	Used
J41	D8	5c brn ('46)	15	18
J42	D8	10c blue	15	15
J43	D8	20c rose red ('46)	15	15
J44	D8	25c dk grn	15	15
J45	D8	30c red org	15	15
J46	D8	40c blk brn	15	18
J47	D8	50c violet	15	15
J48	D8	60c black	15	15
J49	D9	1 l red org	28	15
J50	D9	2 l green	15	15
J51	D9	5 l violet	15	15
J52	D9	10 l blue	15	15
J53	D9	20 l car rose	18	15
		Set value	1.20	1.68

Nos. J41 and J43 are printed on grayish paper and have yellow gum.

Wmk. 277

No.	Type	Description	Unused	Used
J54	D8	10c dark blue	15	15
J55	D8	25c dk grn	35	45
J56	D8	30c red org	35	60
J57	D8	40c blk brn	15	15
J58	D8	50c vio ('46)	1.50	45
J59	D8	60c bl blk ('46)	1.75	1.25
J60	D9	1 l red org	15	15
J61	D9	2 l dk grn	15	15
J62	D9	5 l violet	4.00	28
J63	D9	10 l dark blue	5.75	4.00
J64	D9	20 l car rose	8.25	75
		Nos. J54-J64 (11)	22.55	8.38

For overprints see Trieste Nos. J1, J3-J5.

D10

1947-54 **Photo.** ***Perf. 14***

No.	Type	Description	Unused	Used
J65	D10	1 l red orange	15	15
J66	D10	2 l dk green	15	15
J67	D10	3 l carmine	15	45
J68	D10	4 l brown	30	24
J69	D10	5 l violet	48	15
J70	D10	6 l vio blue	1.00	24
J71	D10	8 l rose vio	2.25	60
J72	D10	10 l deep blue	75	15
J73	D10	12 l golden brn	1.40	60
J74	D10	20 l lil rose	24.00	15
J75	D10	25 l dk red ('54)	30.00	45
J76	D10	50 l aqua	19.00	15
J77	D10	100 l org yel ('52)	1.90	15

Engr.

Perf. 13½x14

No.	Type	Description	Unused	Used
J78	D10	500 l dp bl & dk car ('52)	3.50	18
a.		Perf. 11x13	4.50	24
b.		Perf. 13	4.50	18
		Nos. J65-J78 (14)	85.03	
		Set value		3.00

For overprints see Trieste Nos. J2, J6-J29.

Catalogue values for unused stamps in this section, from this point to the end of the section, are for Never Hinged items.

1955-91 **Wmk. 303** **Photo.** ***Perf. 14***

No.	Type	Description	Unused	Used
J83	D10	5 l violet	15	15
J85	D10	8 l rose vio	140.00	140.00
J86	D10	10 l deep blue	15	15
J87	D10	20 l lil rose	15	15
J88	D10	25 l dk red	15	15
J89	D10	30 l gray brn ('61)	15	15
J90	D10	40 l dl brn ('66)	15	15
J91	D10	50 l aqua	15	15
a.		Type II	22	15
J92	D10	100 l org yel ('58)	18	15

Engr.

No.	Type	Description	Unused	Used
J93	D10	500 l dp bl & dk car ('61)	90	18
J94	D10	900 l dp car & gray grn ('84)	80	22
J95	D10	1500 l brown & orange	3.00	1.60
		Set value, #J83, J86-J95	5.45	2.35

Type I imprint on No. J91 reads: "IST POL. STATO OFF. CARET VALORI". Type II imprint reads: "I.P.Z.S. OFF. CARTE VALORI (1993)." No. J91 has lighter background with more distinguishable lettering and design.

No. J92 exists with both Type I & Type II imprints.

No. J93 exists with "I. P. Z. S. ROMA" imprint.

Issue date: 1500 l, Feb. 20, 1991.

MILITARY STAMPS

Regular Stamps, 1929-42, Overprinted **P.M.**

1943 **Wmk. 140** ***Perf. 14***

No.	Type	Description	Unused	Used
M1	A90	5c ol brn	15	24
M2	A92	10c dk brn	15	24
M3	A93	15c slate grn	15	24
M4	A91	20c rose red	15	24
M5	A94	25c dp grn	15	24
M6	A95	30c ol brn	15	24
M7	A95	50c purple	15	15
M8	A91	1 l dk pur	15	*3.00*
M9	A94	1.25 l deep blue	15	*35*
M10	A92	1.75 l red org	15	24
M11	A93	2 l car lake	18	35
M12	A95a	5 l rose red	24	*45*
M13	A93	10 l purple	28	*70*
		Set value	1.75	

Due to a shortage of regular postage stamps during 1944-45, this issue was used for ordinary mail. "P. M." stands for "Posta Militare."

MILITARY AIR POST STAMPS

Air Post Stamps, 1930 Overprinted Like Nos. M1-M13 in Black

1943 **Wmk. 140** ***Perf. 14***

No.	Type	Description	Unused	Used
MC1	AP3	50c ol brn	15	24
MC2	AP5	1 l purple	15	*45*
MC3	AP6	2 l dp bl	15	*1.25*
MC4	AP3	5 l dk grn	18	*3.00*
MC5	AP3	10 l dp car	24	*5.50*
		Set value	70	

MILITARY AIR POST SPECIAL DELIVERY STAMP

#CE3 Overprinted Like #M1-M13

1943 **Wmk. 140** ***Perf. 14***

No.	Type	Description	Unused	Used
MCE1	APSD2	2 l gray black	18	*5.50*

MILITARY SPECIAL DELIVERY STAMP

#E14 Overprinted Like #M1-M13

1943 **Wmk. 140** ***Perf. 14***

No.	Type	Description	Unused	Used
ME1	SD4	1.25 l green	15	*70*

OFFICIAL STAMPS

O1

1875 **Wmk. 140** **Typo.** ***Perf. 14***

No.	Type	Description	Unused	Used
O1	O1	2c lake	70	70
O2	O1	5c lake	70	70
O3	O1	20c lake	18	18
O4	O1	30c lake	18	24
O5	O1	1 l lake	1.50	2.75
O6	O1	2 l lake	10.50	9.00
O7	O1	5 l lake	47.50	42.50
O8	O1	10 l lake	85.00	22.50
		Nos. O1-O8 (8)	146.26	78.57

For surcharges see Nos. 37-44.

Stamps inscribed "Servizio Commissioni" were used in connection with the postal service but not for the payment of postage.

NEWSPAPER STAMP

N1

Typographed, Numeral Embossed

1862 **Unwmk.** ***Imperf.***

No.	Type	Description	Unused	Used
P1	N1	2c buff	15.00	30.00
a.		Numeral double	85.00	*500.00*

Black 1c and 2c stamps of similar type are listed under Sardinia.

PARCEL POST STAMPS

King Humbert I — PP1

1884-86 **Wmk. 140** **Typo.** ***Perf. 14***

Various Frames

No.	Type	Description	Unused	Used
Q1	PP1	10c olive gray	32.50	8.00
Q2	PP1	20c blue	50.00	15.00
Q3	PP1	50c claret	3.00	1.75
Q4	PP1	75c blue grn	3.00	1.75
Q5	PP1	1.25 l orange	5.00	5.50
Q6	PP1	1.75 l brown	6.50	16.00

For surcharges see Nos. 58-63.

Parcel Post stamps from No. Q7 onward were used by affixing them to the waybill so that one half remained on it following the parcel, the other half staying on the receipt given the sender. Most used halves are right halves. Complete stamps were and are obtainable canceled, probably to order.

Both unused and used values are for complete stamps.

PP2

1914-22 **Wmk. 140** ***Perf. 13***

No.	Type	Description	Unused	Used
Q7	PP2	5c brown	15	28
Q8	PP2	10c deep blue	15	28
Q9	PP2	20c black ('17)	15	28
Q10	PP2	25c red	15	28
Q11	PP2	50c orange	15	45
Q12	PP2	1 l violet	20	18
Q13	PP2	2 l green	45	22
Q14	PP2	3 l bister	65	45
Q15	PP2	4 l slate	75	45
Q16	PP2	10 l rose lil ('22)	8.75	1.25
Q17	PP2	12 l red brn ('22)	35.00	75.00
Q18	PP2	15 l ol grn ('22)	35.00	75.00
Q19	PP2	20 l brn vio ('22)	35.00	67.50
		Nos. Q7-Q19 (13)	116.55	221.62

Halves Used

Q7-Q15	15
Q16	18
Q17-Q19	75

Imperfs exist. Value per pair: 20c, 25c, 50c, 2 l, 4 l, 10 l, $50 each; 3 l, $60; 12 l, 15 l, 20 l, $200 each.

No. Q7 Surcharged

60 CENT. 60

No.	Type	Description	Unused	Used
Q20	PP2	30c on 5c brown	25	*2.75*
		Half stamp		15
Q21	PP2	60c on 5c brown	38	*2.75*
		Half stamp		15
Q22	PP2	1.50 l on 5c brown	1.00	*18.00*
		Half stamp		25
a.		Double surcharge	25.00	

No. Q16 Surcharged

LIRE 3 LIRE 3

No.	Type	Description	Unused	Used
Q23	PP2	3 l on 10 l rose lilac	1.00	*10.00*
		Half stamp		20

PP3

1927-39 **Wmk. 140**

No.	Type	Description	Unused	Used
Q24	PP3	5c brn ('38)	15	25
Q25	PP3	10c dp bl ('39)	15	25
Q26	PP3	25c red ('32)	15	25
Q27	PP3	30c ultra	15	45
Q28	PP3	50c org ('32)	15	25
Q29	PP3	60c red	15	45
Q30	PP3	1 l lilac ('31)	15	25
Q31	PP3	1 l brn vio ('36)	12.00	10.00
Q32	PP3	2 l grn ('32)	15	45
Q33	PP3	3 l bister	15	45
a.		Printed on both sides	15.00	
Q34	PP3	4 l gray	15	45
Q35	PP3	10 l rose lil ('34)	20	*1.40*
Q36	PP3	20 l lil brn ('33)	24	*2.75*
		Nos. Q24-Q36 (13)	13.94	17.65

Value of used halves, Nos. Q24-Q36, each 15 cents.

For overprints see Italian Social Republic Nos. Q1-Q12.

Nos. Q24-Q30, Q32-Q36 Overprinted Between Halves in Black

1945 **Wmk. 140** ***Perf. 13***

No.	Type	Description	Unused	Used
Q37	PP3	5c brown	15	45
Q38	PP3	10c dp blue	15	45
Q39	PP3	25c red	15	45
Q40	PP3	30c ultra	2.00	1.90
Q41	PP3	50c orange	15	18
Q42	PP3	60c red	15	18
Q43	PP3	1 l lilac	15	18
Q44	PP3	2 l green	15	18
Q45	PP3	3 l bister	15	28
Q46	PP3	4 l gray	15	22
Q47	PP3	10 l rose lil	1.00	*3.75*
Q48	PP3	20 l lil brn	2.75	*8.00*
		Nos. Q37-Q48 (12)	7.10	*16.22*
		Set, never hinged	11.00	

Halves Used

Q37-Q39, Q41-Q47	15
Q40	18
Q48	15

Type of 1927
With Fasces Removed

1946 **Typo.**

No.	Type	Description	Unused	Used
Q55	PP3	1 l lilac	52	15
Q56	PP3	2 l green	40	15
Q57	PP3	3 l yel org	70	28
Q58	PP3	4 l gray	1.00	18
Q59	PP3	10 l rose lilac	20.00	3.00
Q60	PP3	20 l lilac brn	26.00	9.75
		Nos. Q55-Q60 (6)	48.62	13.51
		Set, never hinged	85.00	

Halves Used

Q55-Q58	15
Q59	25
Q60	30

PP4

PP5

Perf. 13, 13x14, 12½x13

1946-54 Photo. Wmk. 277

Q61 PP4 25c dl vio bl ('48)	15	15
Q62 PP4 50c brn ('47)	15	15
Q63 PP4 1 l golden brn ('47)	15	15
Q64 PP4 2 l lt bl grn ('47)	18	18
Q65 PP4 3 l red org ('47)	15	15
Q66 PP4 4 l gray blk ('47)	90	1.40
Q67 PP4 5 l lil rose ('47)	15	15
a. Perf. 13	15	15
Q68 PP4 10 l violet	1.25	15
a. Perf. 13	1.65	90
Q69 PP4 20 l lil brn	70	24
a. Perf. 13	4.50	45
Q70 PP4 30 l plum ('52)	1.10	1.25
a. Perf. 13	70	90
Q71 PP4 50 l rose red	3.50	55
a. Perf. 13	3.50	70
Q72 PP4 100 l sapphire	11.50	7.00
a. Perf. 13	70.00	11.00
Q73 PP4 200 l grn ('48)	14.00	14.00
a. Perf. 13	18.00	18.00
Q74 PP4 300 l brn car ('48)	300.00	180.00
a. Perf. 13	300.00	180.00
Q75 PP4 500 l brn ('48)	40.00	35.00

Engr.

Perf. 13

Q76 PP5 1000 l ultra ('54)	1,200.	975.00
Nos. Q61-Q76 (16)	1,573.	1,215.
Set, never hinged	5,000.	

Halves Used

Q61-Q69, Q70, Q71, Q72	15
Q69a, Q70a, Q71a	15
Q72a	15
Q73,Q75	18
Q73a	25
Q74	30
Q74a	40
Q76	1.25

For overprints see Trieste Nos. Q1-Q26.

Catalogue values for unused stamps in this section, from this point to the end of the section, are for Never Hinged items.

Perf. 12½x13

1955-59 Wmk. 303 Photo.

Without Imprint

Q77 PP4 25c vio bl	28	38
Q77A PP4 50c brn ('56)	8.00	11.50
Q78 PP4 5 l lil rose ('59)	15	15
Q79 PP4 10 l violet	15	15
Q80 PP4 20 l lil brn	15	15
Q81 PP4 30 l plum ('56)	15	15
Q82 PP4 40 l dl vio ('57)	15	15
Q83 PP4 50 l rose red	15	15
Q84 PP4 100 l sapphire	16	15
Q85 PP4 150 l org brn ('57)	22	22
Q86 PP4 200 l grn ('56)	28	22
Q87 PP4 300 l brn car ('58)	48	38
Q88 PP4 400 l gray blk ('57)	55	45
Q89 PP4 500 l brn ('57)	1.00	60

Engr.

Perf. 13

Q90 PP5 1000 l ultra ('57)	1.25	95
Q91 PP5 2000 l red brn & car ('57)	3.25	1.90
Nos. Q77-Q91 (16)	16.37	17.65

Halves Used

Q77-Q89	15
Q90-Q91	40

1960-66 Photo. *Perf. 12½x13*

Q92 PP4 60 l bright lilac	15	15
Q93 PP4 140 l dull red	22	30
Q94 PP4 280 l yellow	60	45
Q95 PP4 600 l olive bister	70	75
Q96 PP4 700 l blue ('66)	1.10	75
Q97 PP4 800 l dp org ('66)	1.25	95
Nos. Q92-Q97 (6)	4.02	3.35

Halves Used

Q92-Q93	15
Q94	18
Q95	40
Q96-Q97	25

Imprint: "I.P.S.-Off. Carte Valori-Roma"

1973, Mar. Photo. Wmk. 303

Q98 PP4 20 l lilac brown	20	15
Q99 PP4 30 l plum	20	15
Set value		15

PARCEL POST AUTHORIZED DELIVERY STAMPS

For the payment of a special tax for the authorized delivery of parcels privately instead of through the post office.

PAD1

1953 Wmk. 277 Photo. *Perf. 13*

QY1 PAD1 40 l orange red	1.75	2.25
QY2 PAD1 50 l ultra	65.00	72.50
QY3 PAD1 75 l brown	40.00	45.00
QY4 PAD1 110 l lil rose	40.00	50.00
Set, never hinged	260.00	

Halves Used

QY1	30
QY2	60
QY3	1.50
QY4	1.90

For overprints see Trieste Nos. QY1-QY4.

Catalogue values for unused stamps in this section, from this point to the end of the section, are for Never Hinged items.

1956-58 Wmk. 303 *Perf. 12½x13*

QY5 PAD1 40 l orange red	1.65	90
QY6 PAD1 50 l ultra	3.25	2.25
QY7 PAD1 60 l brt vio bl ('58)	9.00	5.25
QY8 PAD1 75 l brown	350.00	150.00
QY9 PAD1 90 l lil ('58)	32	18
QY10 PAD1 110 l lil rose	350.00	125.00
QY11 PAD1 120 l grnsh bl ('58)	32	18
Nos. QY5-QY11 (7)	714.54	283.76

Halves Used

QY5-QY6	15
QY7	90
QY8,QY10	4.00
QY9	30
QY11	22

1960-79

QY12 PAD1 70 l green ('66)	32.50	32.50
QY13 PAD1 80 l brown	40	40
QY14 PAD1 110 l org yel	40	40
QY15 PAD1 140 l black	45	50
QY16 PAD1 150 l car rose ('68)	30	50
QY17 PAD1 180 l red ('66)	38	60
QY18 PAD1 240 l dk bl ('66)	45	70

Perf. 13½

QY19 PAD1 500 l ocher ('76)	1.40	1.40
QY20 PAD1 600 l bl grn ('79)	1.40	1.40
QY21 PAD1 900 l ultra ('81)	1.10	1.40
Nos. QY12-QY21 (10)	38.78	39.80

Halves Used

QY12	4.00
QY13-QY15, QY18, QY21	20
QY16, QY17, QY19	25
QY20	35

PAD2

Perf. 14x13½

1984 Photo. Wmk. 303

QY22 PAD2 3000 l multi	3.75	3.75

OCCUPATION STAMPS

Issued under Austrian Occupation

Emperor Karl of Austria
OS1 OS2

1918 Unwmk. *Perf. 12½*

N1 OS1 2c on 1h grnsh bl	18	40
N2 OS1 3c on 2h red org	18	40
N3 OS1 4c on 3h ol gray	18	40
N4 OS1 6c on 5h ol grn	18	40
N5 OS1 7c on 6h vio	18	40
a. Perf. 12½x11½	14.00	27.50
N6 OS1 11c on 10h org brn	18	40
N7 OS1 13c on 12h blue	18	40
N8 OS1 16c on 15h brt rose	18	40
N9 OS1 22c on 20h red brn	18	40
a. Perf. 11½	6.75	14.00
N10 OS1 27c on 25h ultra	45	40
N11 OS1 32c on 30h slate	24	40
N12 OS1 43c on 40h ol bis	18	40
a. Perf. 11½	6.75	14.00
N13 OS1 53c on 50h dp grn	18	40
N14 OS1 64c on 60h rose	18	40
N15 OS1 85c on 80h dl bl	18	40
N16 OS1 95c on 90h dk vio	18	40
N17 OS1 2 l 11c on 2k rose, *straw*	28	40
N18 OS1 3 l 16c on 3k grn, *bl*	1.00	2.00
N19 OS1 4 l 22c on 4k rose, *grn*	1.00	2.00
Nos. N1-N19 (19)	5.49	10.80

Emperor Karl — OS3

1918

N20 OS3 2c on 1h grnsh bl	2.50
N21 OS3 3c on 2h orange	2.50
N22 OS3 4c on 3h ol gray	2.50
N23 OS3 6c on 5h yel grn	2.50
N24 OS3 11c on 10h dk brn	2.50
N25 OS3 22c on 20h red	2.50
N26 OS3 27c on 25h blue	2.50
N27 OS3 32c on 30h bister	2.50
N28 OS3 48c on 45h dk sl	2.50
N29 OS3 53c on 50h dp grn	2.50
N30 OS3 64c on 60h violet	2.50
N31 OS3 85c on 80h rose	2.50
N32 OS3 95c on 90h brn vio	2.50
N33 OS3 1 l 6c on 90h brn vio	2.50
Nos. N20-N33 (14)	35.00

Nos. N20 to N33 inclusive were never placed in use in the occupied territory. They were, however, on sale at the Post Office in Vienna for a few days before the Armistice.

OCCUPATION SPECIAL DELIVERY STAMPS

Special Handling Stamps of Bosnia Surcharged **3 Centesimi**

1918 Unwmk. *Perf. 12½*

NE1 SH1 3c on 2h ver	5.50	11.00
NE2 SH1 6c on 5h dp grn	5.50	11.00

Nos. NE1-NE2 are on yellowish paper. Reprints on white paper sell for about 70 cents a set.

OCCUPATION POSTAGE DUE STAMPS

Postage Due Stamps of Bosnia Surcharged Like Nos. NE1-NE2

1918 Unwmk. *Perf. 12½*

NJ1 D2 6c on 5h red	1.90	3.75
a. Perf. 11½	5.50	11.00
NJ2 D2 11c on 10h red	1.90	3.75
a. Perf. 11½	5.50	11.00
NJ3 D2 16c on 15h red	90	1.90
NJ4 D2 27c on 25h red	90	1.90
NJ5 D2 32c on 30h red	90	1.90
NJ6 D2 43c on 40h red	90	1.90
NJ7 D2 53c on 50h red	90	1.90
Nos. NJ1-NJ7 (7)	8.30	17.00

OCCUPATION NEWSPAPER STAMPS

Austrian Military Newspaper Stamps Surcharged **3 Centesimi**

1918 Unwmk. *Perf. 12½*

NP1 MN1 3c on 2h blue	15	24
a. Perf. 11½	2.75	5.50
NP2 MN1 7c on 6h org	45	90
NP3 MN1 11c on 10h car	45	90
NP4 MN1 22c on 20h brn	35	70
a. Perf. 11½	15.00	30.00

A.M.G.

Issued jointly by the Allied Military Government of the United States and Great Britain, for civilian use in areas under Allied occupation.

Catalogue values for unused stamps in this section are for Never Hinged items.

OS4

Offset Printing
"Italy Centesimi" (or "Lira") in Black

1943 Unwmk. *Perf. 11*

1N1 OS4 15c pale orange	1.00	80
1N2 OS4 25c pale citron	1.00	80
1N3 OS4 30c light gray	1.00	80
1N4 OS4 50c light violet	1.00	80
1N5 OS4 60c orange yellow	1.00	90
1N6 OS4 1 l lt yel green	1.00	80
1N7 OS4 2 l deep rose	1.00	1.00
1N8 OS4 5 l light blue	1.00	*2.00*
1N9 OS4 10 l buff	1.00	*3.50*
Nos. 1N1-1N9 (9)	9.00	*11.40*

Italy Nos. 217, 220 and 221 Overprinted in Blue, Vermilion, Carmine or Orange **GOVERNO MILITARE ALLEATO**

1943, Dec. 10 Wmk. 140 *Perf. 14*

1N10 A91 20c rose red (Bl)	1.50	3.00
1N11 A93 35c dp blue (C)	15.00	*17.50*
a. 35c deep blue (V)	35.00	*50.00*
1N13 A95 50c purple (C)	75	1.10
a. 50c purple (O)	90	2.00

Nos. 1N1-1N9 were for use in Sicily, Nos. 1N10-1N13 for use in Naples.

VENEZIA GIULIA

Catalogue values for unused stamps in this section are for Never Hinged items.

Stamps of Italy, 1929 to 1945 Overprinted in Black:

On Stamps of 1929

1945-47 Wmk. 140 *Perf. 14*

1LN1 A92 (a) 10c dk brown	28	32
1LN1A A91 (a) 20c rose red ('47)	38	50

On Stamps of 1945

1945 Wmk. 277 *Perf. 14*

1LN2 A249 (a) 20c rose red	30	50
1LN3 A248 (a) 60c sl grn	42	35
1LN4 A249 (a) 1 l dp vio	30	35
1LN5 A251 (a) 2 l dk red	35	35
1LN6 A252 (b) 5 l dk red	65	50
1LN7 A251 (a) 10 l purple	90	1.25
Nos. 1LN2-1LN7 (6)	2.92	3.30

On Stamps of 1945

1945-46 Unwmk.

1LN7A A250(a) 10c dk brn ('46)	30	25
1LN7B A249(a) 20c rose red ('46)	26	50
1LN8 A251(a) 60c red org	26	25

On Air Post Stamp of 1930

1945 Wmk. 140 *Perf. 14*

1LN9 AP3 (a) 50c olive brn	26	50

On Stamp of 1929

1946

1LN10 A91 (a) 20 l lt green	2.25	3.50

On Stamps of 1945

Wmk. 277

1LN11	A260 (a)	25 l dk green	4.25	6.50
1LN12	A260 (a)	50 l dk vio brn	4.75	7.50

Italy No. 477 Overprinted in Black

1LN13	A261	100 l car lake	17.50	25.00

Stamps of Italy, 1945-47 Overprinted Type "a" in Black

1947

1LN14	A259	25c brt bl grn	26	30
1LN15	A258	2 l dk cl brn	60	75
1LN16	A259	3 l red	45	30
1LN17	A259	4 l red org	70	40
1LN18	A257	6 l dp vio	1.75	2.25
1LN19	A259	20 l dk red vio	*26.00*	1.50
		Nos. 1LN14-1LN19 (6)	*29.76*	5.50

Some denominations of the Venezia Giulia A.M.G. issues exist with inverted overprint; several values exist in horizontal and vertical pairs, one stamp without overprint.

OCCUPATION AIR POST STAMPS

Catalogue values for unused stamps in this section are for Never Hinged items.

Italy Nos. C106-C107 and C109-C113 Overprinted Like 1LN13 in Black

1946-47 Wmk. 277 *Perf. 14*

1LNC1	AP59	1 l sl blue ('47)	26	50
1LNC2	AP60	2 l dk blue ('47)	26	50
1LNC3	AP60	5 l dk green ('47)	1.75	*2.50*
1LNC4	AP59	10 l car rose ('47)	1.75	*2.50*
1LNC5	AP60	25 l dk blue	1.75	*2.50*
1LNC6	AP60	25 l brown ('47)	15.00	*20.00*
1LNC7	AP59	50 l dk green	3.25	*5.00*
		Nos. 1LNC1-1LNC7 (7)	24.02	*33.50*

Nos. 1LNC5 and 1LNC7 exist with inverted overprint; No. 1LNC5 with double overprint, one inverted.

OCCUPATION SPECIAL DELIVERY STAMPS

Catalogue values for unused stamps in this section are for Never Hinged items.

Italy Nos. E20 and E23 Overprinted Like 1LN13 in Black

1946 Wmk. 277 *Perf. 14*

1LNE1	SD9	10 l deep blue	3.50	4.50
1LNE2	SD8	30 l deep violet	8.75	12.50

ITALIAN SOCIAL REPUBLIC

On Sept. 15, 1943, Mussolini proclaimed the establishment of a Republican fascist party and a new fascist government. This government's authority covered only the Northern Italy area occupied by the Germans.

Catalogue values for unused stamps in this section are for Never Hinged items.

Italy Nos. 218, 219, 221 to 223 and 231 Overprinted in Black or Red:

a

b

REPUBBLICA
SOCIALE
ITALIANA

c

1944 Wmk. 140 *Perf. 14*

1	A94(a)	25c deep grn	22	15
2	A95(b)	30c ol brn (R)	22	15
3	A95(c)	50c pur (R)	22	15
4	A94(a)	75c rose red	22	15
5	A94(b)	1.25 l dp bl (R)	22	15
5A	A94(b)	50 l dp vio (R)	200.00	*675.00*

Nos. 1 to 5 exist with overprint inverted. No. 1 exists with overprint "b." Counterfeits of No. 5A exist.

Italy Nos. 427 to 438 Overprinted Same in Black or Red

6	A243(a)	25c deep green	35	*55*
7	A244(a)	25c deep green	35	*55*
8	A245(a)	25c deep green	35	*55*
9	A246(a)	25c deep green	35	*55*
10	A243(b)	30c ol brn (R)	42	*75*
11	A244(b)	30c ol brn (R)	42	*75*
12	A245(b)	30c ol brn (R)	42	*75*
13	A246(b)	30c ol brn (R)	42	*75*
14	A243(c)	50c pur (R)	35	*55*
15	A244(c)	50c pur (R)	35	*55*
16	A245(c)	50c pur (R)	35	*55*
17	A246(c)	50c pur (R)	35	*55*
		Nos. 6-17 (12)	4.48	*7.40*

Loggia dei Mercanti, Bologna — A1

Basilica of San Lorenzo, Rome — A2

Drummer Boy — A3

1944 Photo. *Perf. 14*

18	A1	20c crimson	15	15
19	A2	25c green	15	15
20	A3	30c brown	15	15
21	A3	75c dark red	15	15
		Set value	48	20

Church of St. Ciriaco, Ancona — A4

Monte Cassino Abbey — A5

Loggia dei Mercanti, Bologna — A6

Basilica of San Lorenzo, Rome — A7

Statue of "Rome" A8

Basilica of St. Maria delle Grazie, Milan A9

1944 Unwmk.

22	A4	5c brown	15	15
23	A5	10c brown	15	15
24	A6	20c rose red	15	15
25	A7	25c deep green	15	15
26	A3	30c brown	15	15
27	A8	50c purple	18	15
28	A3	75c dark red	15	15
29	A5	1 l purple	15	15
30	A9	1.25 l blue	15	*30*
31	A9	3 l deep green	15	*15.00*
		Set value	1.15	

Bandiera Brothers — A10

1944, Dec. 6

32	A10	25c deep green	15	*22*
33	A10	1 l purple	15	*22*
34	A10	2.50 l rose red	15	*2.75*
		Set value	34	

Cent. of the execution of Attilio (1811-44) and Emilio Bandiera (1819-44), revolutionary patriots who were shot at Cosenza, July 23, 1844, by Neapolitan authorities after an unsuccessful raid.

This set was overprinted in 1945 by the committee of the National Philatelic Convention to publicize that gathering at Venice.

SPECIAL DELIVERY STAMPS

Catalogue values for unused stamps in this section are for Never Hinged items.

Italy Nos. E14 and E15 Overprinted in Red or Black

REPUBBLICA
SOCIALE
ITALIANA

1944 Wmk. 140 *Perf. 14*

E1	SD4	1.25 l green (R)	15	*22*
E2	SD4	2.50 l deep orange	15	*1.25*
		Set value	24	

Cathedral, Palermo SD1

1944 Photo.

E3	SD1	1.25 l green	24	*55*

AUTHORIZED DELIVERY STAMP

Catalogue values for unused stamps in this section are for Never Hinged items.

Italy No. EY2 Overprinted

1944 Wmk. 140 *Perf. 14*

EY1	AD2	10c dark brown	30	15

POSTAGE DUE STAMPS

Catalogue values for unused stamps in this section are for Never Hinged items.

Italy Nos. J28 to J40 Overprinted Like No. EY1

1944 Wmk. 140 *Perf. 14*

J1	D6	5c brown	15	*38*
J2	D6	10c blue	15	*38*
J3	D6	20c rose red	15	*38*
J4	D6	25c green	15	*38*
J5	D6	30c red org	15	*1.10*
J6	D6	40c blk brn	15	*1.50*
J7	D6	50c violet	15	*22*
J8	D6	60c slate blk	1.00	*4.50*
J9	D7	1 l red org	15	*22*
J10	D7	2 l green	1.50	*3.00*
J11	D7	5 l violet	20.00	*25.00*
J12	D7	10 l blue	40.00	*55.00*
J13	D7	20 l car rose	40.00	*55.00*
		Nos. J1-J13 (13)	103.70	*147.06*

PARCEL POST STAMPS

Both unused and used values are for complete stamps.

Catalogue values for unused stamps in this section are for Never Hinged items.

Italian Parcel Post Stamps and Types of 1927-39 Overprinted Like No. EY1

1944 Wmk. 140 *Perf. 13*

Q1	PP3	5c brown	2.25	1.75
Q2	PP3	10c deep blue	2.25	1.75
Q3	PP3	25c carmine	2.25	1.75
Q4	PP3	30c ultra	2.25	1.75
Q5	PP3	50c orange	2.25	1.75
Q6	PP3	60c red	2.25	1.75
Q7	PP3	1 l lilac	2.25	1.75
Q8	PP3	2 l green	165.00	165.00
Q9	PP3	3 l yel grn	4.50	4.75
Q10	PP3	4 l gray	4.50	4.75
Q11	PP3	10 l rose lilac	120.00	120.00
Q12	PP3	20 l lilac brn	285.00	285.00
		Nos. Q1-Q12 (12)	594.75	591.75

No parcel post service existed in 1944. Nos. Q1-Q12 were used undivided, for regular postage.

ITALIAN OFFICES ABROAD

Stamps listed under this heading were issued for use in the Italian Post Offices which, for various reasons, were maintained from time to time in foreign countries.

100 Centesimi = 1 Lira

GENERAL ISSUE

Values of early Italian Offices Abroad vary according to condition. Quotations for Nos. 1-11 are for fine copies. Very fine to superb specimens sell at much higher prices, and inferior or poor copies sell at reduced prices, depending on the condition of the individual specimen.

Italian Stamps with Corner Designs Slightly Altered and Overprinted

1874-78 Wmk. 140 *Perf. 14*

1	A6	1c gray grn	35	*2.75*
a.		Inverted overprint	*5,000.*	
c.		2 dots in lower right corner	5.50	*27.50*
d.		Three dots in upper right corner	67.50	*160.00*
e.		Without overprint	450.00	
2	A7	2c org brn	45	*3.50*
a.		Without overprint	375.00	
3	A8	5c slate grn	45.00	2.75
a.		Lower right corner not altered	*3,000.*	450.00
4	A8	10c buff	135.00	6.75
a.		Upper left corner not altered	*2,750.*	225.00
b.		None of the corners altered	*13,000.*	*13,500.*
c.		Lower corners not altered	*5,000.*	*800.00*
5	A8	10c blue ('78)	27.50	1.90
6	A15	20c blue	125.00	3.50
7	A15	20c org ('78)	350.00	1.50
8	A8	30c brown	52	1.80
a.		None of the corners altered		*5,500.*
b.		Right lower corner not altered		
c.		Double overprint		*3,000.*
9	A8	40c rose	45	*2.00*
10	A8	60c lilac	60	*11.50*
11	A13	2 l vermilion	16.00	*85.00*

1881

12	A17	5c green	1.00	1.65
13	A17	10c claret	60	90
14	A17	20c orange	60	90
a.		Double overprint		*900.00*
15	A17	25c blue	60	1.25
16	A17	50c violet	75	*9.75*
17	A17	2 l vermilion	3.00	

The "Estero" stamps were used in various parts of the world, South America, Africa, Turkey, etc.

Forged cancellations exist on Nos. 1-2, 9-11, 16.

OFFICES IN CHINA

100 Cents = 1 Dollar

PEKING

Italian Stamps of 1901-16 Handstamped — PECHINO 2 CENTS

Wmk. 140, Unwmk.

1917 *Perf. 12, 13½, 14*

1 A48 2c on 5c green 24.00 11.50
c. 4c on 5c green *775.00*
3 A48 4c on 10c claret (No. 95) 47.50 20.00
c. 4c on 10c claret (No. 79)
5 A58 6c on 15c slate 95.00 50.00
b. 8c on 15c slate 500.00 375.00
7 A58 8c on 20c on 15c slate 625.00 275.00
8 A50 8c on 20c brn org (No. 112) *1,000.* 350.00
9 A49 20c on 50c vio *6,000.* *3,750.*
b. 40c on 50c violet *1,400.* *1,400.*
11 A46 40c on 1 l brn & grn *37,500.* *4,250.*

Inverted surcharges are found on Nos. 1, 3, 3c, 5, 7-9; values same. Double surcharge one inverted exist on Nos. 1, 3; value about double.

Excellent forgeries exist of the higher valued stamps of Offices in China.

Italian Stamps of 1901-16 Overprinted — Pechino

1917-18

12 A42 1c brown 1.00 1.65
13 A43 2c orange brown 1.00 1.65
a. Double overprint 57.50
14 A48 5c green 20 35
a. Double overprint 22.50
15 A48 10c claret 20 35
16 A50 20c brn org (No. 112) 8.00 9.00
17 A49 25c blue 25 45
18 A49 50c violet 38 70
19 A46 1 l brown & grn 52 1.00
20 A46 5 l blue & rose 60 2.00
21 A51 10 l gray grn & red 12.00 *14.00*
Nos. 12-21 (10) 24.15 31.15

Italy No. 113, the watermarked 20c brown orange, was also overprinted "Pechino," but not issued. Value $2.50.

Italian Stamps of 1901-16 Surcharged:

1 CENT — 2 dollari

Pechino a — Pechino b

TWO DOLLARS:
Type I - Surcharged "2 dollari" as illustration "b."
Type II - Surcharged "2 DOLLARI."
Type III - Surcharged "2 dollari." "Pechino" measures 11½mm wide, instead of 13mm.

1918-19 *Perf. 14*

22 A42 ½c on 1c brown 8.00 11.50
a. Surcharged "1 cents" 55.00 67.50
23 A43 1c on 2c org brn 20 45
a. Surcharged "1 cents" 27.50 35.00
24 A48 2c on 5c green 20 45
25 A48 4c on 10c claret 20 45
26 A50 8c on 20c brn org (No. 112) 1.00 1.40
27 A49 10c on 25c blue 48 90
28 A49 20c on 50c violet 60 1.25
29 A46 40c on 1 l brn grn 12.00 16.00
30 A46 $2 on 5 l bl & rose (type I) 47.50 60.00
a. Type II *10,000.* *10,000.*
b. Type III *1,500.* *1,150.*

Italy No. 100 Surcharged — 10 CENTS Pechino

1919

32 A49 10c on 25c blue 32 70

PEKING SPECIAL DELIVERY STAMPS

Italian Special Delivery Stamp 1908 Overprinted Like Nos. 12-21

1917 **Wmk. 140** *Perf. 14*

E1 SD2 30c blue & rose 1.00 1.50

No. E1 Surcharged — 12 CENTS

1918

E2 SD2 12c on 30c bl & rose 7.25 16.00

PEKING POSTAGE DUE STAMPS

Italian Postage Due Stamps Overprinted Like Nos. 12-21

1917 **Wmk. 140** *Perf. 14*

J1 D3 10c buff & magenta 45 90
J2 D3 20c buff & magenta 45 90
J3 D3 30c buff & magenta 45 90
J4 D3 40c buff & magenta 60 90

Nos. J1-J4 Surcharged Like No. E2

1918

J5 D3 4c on 10c *11,000.* *8,250.*
J6 D3 8c on 20c 95 1.50
J7 D3 12c on 30c 6.50 10.00
J8 D3 16c on 40c 27.50 37.50

In 1919, the same new values were surcharged on Italy Nos. J6-J9 in a different style: four lines to cancel the denomination, and "-PECHINO- 4 CENTS." These were not issued. Value $1.10 each.

TIENTSIN

Italian Stamps of 1906 Handstamped — TIENTSIN 2 CENTS

Wmk. 140, Unwmk.

1917 *Perf. 12, 13½, 14*

1 A48 2c on 5c green 47.50 35.00
c. 4c on 5c green *1,400.*
2 A48 4c on 10c claret 80.00 57.50
4 A58 6c on 15c slate 190.00 115.00
b. 4c on 15c slate 725.00 375.00

Italian Stamps of 1901-16 Overprinted — Tientsin

1917-18

5 A42 1c brown 1.00 1.65
a. Inverted overprint 37.50 35.00
6 A43 2c orange brn 1.00 1.65
7 A48 5c green 20 35
8 A48 10c claret 20 35
9 A50 20c brn org (#112) 8.75 9.00
10 A49 25c blue 24 45
11 A49 50c violet 38 70
12 A46 1 l brown & grn 55 1.00
13 A46 5 l blue & rose 1.00 2.00
14 A51 10 l gray grn & red 13.00 *14.00*
Nos. 5-14 (10) 26.32 31.15

Italy No. 113, the watermarked 20c brown orange was also overprinted "Tientsin," but not issued. Value $2.50.

Italian Stamps of 1901-16 Surcharged:

1 CENT — 2 Dollari

Tientsin a — Tientsin b

TWO DOLLARS:
Type I - Surcharged "2 Dollari" as illustration "b".
Type II - Surcharged "2 dollari".
Type III - Surcharged "2 Dollari". "Tientsin" measures 10mm wide instead of 13mm.

1918-21 *Perf. 14*

15 A42 ½c on 1c brown 8.00 11.50
a. Inverted surcharge 27.50 35.00
b. Surcharged "1 cents" 55.00 70.00
16 A43 1c on 2c org brn 20 45
a. Surcharged "1 cents" 27.50 35.00
b. Inverted surcharge 37.50 35.00
17 A48 2c on 5c green 20 45
18 A48 4c on 10c claret 20 45
19 A50 8c on 20c brn org (#112) 1.00 1.40
20 A49 10c on 25c blue 48 90
21 A49 20c on 50c violet 60 1.25
22 A46 40c on 1 l brn & grn 12.00 16.00
23 A46 $2 on 5 l bl & rose (type I) 57.50 70.00
a. Type II *1,600.* *1,250.*
b. Type III ('21) *1,500.* *1,050.*
Nos. 15-23 (9) 80.18 102.40

SPECIAL DELIVERY STAMPS

Italian Special Delivery Stamp of 1908 Overprinted — Tientsin

1917 **Wmk. 140** *Perf. 14*

E1 SD2 30c blue & rose 1.00 1.50

No. E1 Surcharged — 12 CENTS

1918

E2 SD2 12c on 30c bl & rose 7.25 16.00

POSTAGE DUE STAMPS

Italian Postage Due Stamps Overprinted — Tientsin

1917 **Wmk. 140** *Perf. 14*

J1 D3 10c buff & magenta 45 90
a. Double overprint 27.50
J2 D3 20c buff & magenta 45 90
J3 D3 30c buff & magenta 45 90
a. Double overprint 27.50
J4 D3 40c buff & magenta 45 90

Nos. J1-J4 Surcharged — 8 CENTS

1918

J5 D3 4c on 10c *325.00* *500.00*
J6 D3 8c on 20c 95 1.50
J7 D3 12c on 30c 6.50 9.75
J8 D3 16c on 40c 27.50 37.50

In 1919, the same new values were surcharged on Italy Nos. J6-J9 in a different style: four lines to cancel the denomination, and "-TIENTSIN- 4 CENTS." These were not issued. Value $1.10 each.

OFFICES IN CRETE

40 Paras = 1 Piaster
100 Centesimi = 1 Lira (1906)

Italy Nos. 70 and 81 Surcharged in Red or Black

LA CANEA

1 PIASTRA 1 a — 1 PIASTRA 1 b

1900-01 **Wmk. 140** *Perf. 14*

1 A36(a) 1pi on 25c blue 1.25 3.50
2 A45(b) 1pi on 25c dp bl (Bk) ('01) 1.25 1.50

Italian Stamps Overprinted — LA CANEA

1906

On Nos. 76-79, 92, 81, 83-85, 87, 91

3 A42 1c brown 15 28
a. Pair, one without ovpt. 75.00
4 A43 2c org brn 15 28
a. Imperf., pair 180.00
b. Double overprint 45.00
5 A44 5c bl grn 18 38
6 A45 10c claret 30.00 22.50
7 A45 15c on 20c org 24 45
8 A45 25c blue 1.25 1.25
9 A45 40c brown 70 1.25
10 A45 45c ol grn 70 1.25
11 A45 50c violet 75 1.40
12 A46 1 l brn & grn 4.50 5.50
13 A46 5 l bl & rose 18.00 30.00
Nos. 3-13 (11) 56.62 64.54

On Nos. 94-95, 100, 104-105

1907-10

14 A48 5c green 15 28
a. Inverted overprint 57.50
15 A48 10c claret 15 28
16 A49 25c blue 35 70
17 A49 40c brown 2.25 4.50
18 A49 50c violet 35 70
Nos. 14-18 (5) 3.25 6.46

On No. 111 in Violet

1912 **Unwmk.** *Perf. 13x13½*

19 A50 15c slate black 24 45

SPECIAL DELIVERY STAMP

Special Delivery Stamp of Italy Overprinted — LA CANEA

1906 **Wmk. 140** *Perf. 14*

E1 SD1 25c rose red 70 1.40

OFFICES IN AFRICA

40 Paras = 1 Piaster
100 Centesimi = 1 Lira (1910)

BENGASI

Italy No. 81 Surcharged in Black — BENGASI 1 PIASTRA 1

1901 **Wmk. 140** *Perf. 14*

1 A45 1pi on 25c dp bl 8.00 *18.00*

Same Surcharge on Italy No. 100

1911

2 A49 1pi on 25c blue 9.50 *18.00*

TRIPOLI

Italian Stamps of 1901-09 Overprinted in Black or Violet — Tripoli di Barberia

1909 **Wmk. 140**

2 A42 1c brown 45 *70*
a. Inverted overprint 27.50
3 A43 2c orange brn 24 *45*
4 A48 5c green 8.00 2.25
a. Double overprint 55.00
5 A48 10c claret 28 *55*
a. Double overprint 27.50 35.00
6 A49 25c blue 35 *70*
7 A49 40c brown 70 *1.40*
8 A49 50c violet 75 *1.50*

Perf. 13½x14

Unwmk.

9 A50 15c slate blk (V) 45 *90*
Nos. 2-9 (9) 20.72 *26.45*

Italian Stamps of 1901 Overprinted **TRIPOLI DI BARBERIA**

1909 Wmk. 140 *Perf. 14*
10 A46 1 l brown & grn 24.00 16.00
11 A46 5 l blue & rose 10.00 32.50

Same Overprint on Italy Nos. 76-77

1915
12 A42 1c brown 45
13 A43 2c orange brown 35

Nos. 12-13 were prepared but not issued.

SPECIAL DELIVERY STAMPS

Italy Nos. E1, E6 Overprinted Like Nos. 10-11

1909 Wmk. 140 *Perf. 14*
E1 SD1 25c rose red 70 *1.40*
E2 SD2 30c blue & rose 2.50 *2.75*

Tripoli was ceded by Turkey to Italy in Oct., 1912, and became known as the Colony of Libia. Later issues will be found under Libya.

OFFICES IN TURKISH EMPIRE

40 Paras = 1 Piaster

Various powers maintained post offices in the Turkish Empire before World War I by authority of treaties which ended with the signing of the Treaty of Lausanne in 1923. The foreign post offices were closed Oct. 27, 1923.

GENERAL ISSUE

Italian Stamps of 1906-08 Surcharged **10 Parà 10**

Printed at Turin

1908 Wmk. 140
1 A48 10pa on 5c green 15 35
2 A48 20pa on 10c claret 15 35
3 A49 40pa on 25c blue 30 38
4 A49 80pa on 50c violet 38 55

See Janina Nos. 1-4.

Surcharged in Violet **30 Parà 30**

Unwmk.

5 A47 30pa on 15c slate 24 35
Nos. 1-5 (5) 1.22 1.98

Nos. 1, 2, 3 and 5 were first issued in Janina, Albania, and subsequently for general use. They can only be distinguished by the cancellations.

Italian Stamps of 1901-08 Surcharged:

10 PARA Nos. 6-8 — **1 PIASTRA** No. 9 — **2 PIASTRE** Nos. 10-12

Printed at Constantinople

1908 First Printing
6 A48 10pa on 5c green 35.00 30.00
7 A48 20pa on 10c claret 35.00 30.00
8 A47 30pa on 15c slate 125.00 90.00
9 A49 1pi on 25c blue 125.00 105.00
a. "PIASTRE" 140.00 115.00
10 A49 2pi on 50c violet 375.00 225.00
11 A46 4pi on 1 l brn & grn *1,350. 850.00*
12 A46 20pi on 5 l bl & rose *4,250. 2,900.*

On Nos. 8, 9 and 10 the surcharge is at the top of the stamp. No. 11 has the "4" closed at the top. No. 12 has the "20" wide.

Second Printing

Surcharged:

10 PARA Nos. 13-15 — **1 PIASTRA** No. 16 — **2 PIASTRE** Nos. 17-19

13 A48 10pa on 5c green 45 70
14 A48 20pa on 10c claret 45 70
15 A47 30pa on 15c slate 2.25 2.75
a. Double surcharge 14.00 14.00
16 A49 1pi on 25c blue 60 75
a. "PIPSTRA" 14.00 14.00
b. "1" omitted 14.00 14.00
17 A49 2pi on 50c violet 8.00 9.00
a. Surcharged "20 PIASTRE" 135.00 135.00
b. "20" with "0" scratched out 57.50 57.50
c. "2" 5mm from "PIASTRE" 27.50 27.50
18 A46 4pi on 1 l brn & grn 180.00 160.00
19 A46 20pi on 5 l bl & rose 750.00 550.00
Nos. 13-19 (7) 941.75 723.90

On No. 18 the "4" is open at the top.

Third Printing

Surcharged in Red **30 PARA**

20 A47 30pa on 15c slate 35 60
a. Double surcharge 27.50 27.50

Fourth Printing

Surcharged:

4 4 PIASTRE — **20 20 PIASTRE**

20B A46 4pi on 1 l brn & grn 9.50 9.00
c. Inverted "S" 18.00 18.00
20D A46 20pi on 5 l bl & rose 32.50 42.50
i. Inverted "S" 120.00 120.00

Fifth Printing

Surcharged

4 4 PIASTRE — **20 20 PIASTRE**

20E A46 4pi on 1 l brn & grn 9.50 8.00
f. Surch. "20 PIASTRE" 275.00
20G A46 20pi on 5 l bl & rose 9.50 8.00
h. Double surcharge 225.00 275.00

Italian Stamps of 1906-19 Surcharged **2 PIASTRE**

1921
21 A48 1pi on 5c green 37.50 80.00
22 A48 2pi on 15c slate 45 60
23 A50 4pi on 20c brn org (No. 113) 3.75 5.50
24 A49 5pi on 25c blue 3.75 5.50
a. Double surcharge 45.00
25 A49 10pi on 60c carmine 24 35
Nos. 21-25 (5) 45.69 91.95

On No. 25 the "10" is placed above "PIASTRE."

Italian Stamps of 1901-19 Surcharged

PARA 30 n — **PIASTRE 1 PARA 20** o

1922
26 A42(n) 10pa on 1c brown 24 45
27 A43(n) 20pa on 2c org brn 24 45
28 A48(n) 30pa on 5c green 35 60
29 A48(o) 1pi20pa on 15c slate 35 60
30 A50(n) 3pi on 20c brn org (#113) 1.35 2.25
31 A49(o) 3pi30pa on 25c blue 35 60
32 A49(o) 7pi20pa on 60c carmine 45 70
33 A46(n) 15pi on 1 l brn & grn 2.25 3.75
Nos. 26-33 (8) 5.58 9.40

Italy No. 100 Surcharged **Piastre 3,75**

34 A49 3.75pi on 25c blue 28 28

Italian Stamps of 1901-20 Surcharged:

30 PARÀ q — **PIASTRE 3,75** r

1922
35 A48 30pa on 5c green 90 1.50
36 A49 1.50pi on 25c blue 35 90
37 A49 3.75pi on 40c brown 35 1.00
38 A49 4.50pi on 50c violet 70 1.25
39 A49 7.50pi on 60c carmine 70 1.25
40 A49 15pi on 85c red brn 1.35 2.50
41 A46 18.75pi on 1 l brn & grn 90 2.00

On No. 40 the numerals of the surcharge are above "PIASTRE."

Surcharged **45 PIASTRE**

42 A46 45pi on 5 l bl & rose 50.00 60.00
43 A51 90pi on 10 l gray grn & red 55.00 90.00

Italian Stamps of 1901-17 Surcharged Type "q" or: **1,50 PIASTRE**

44 A43 30pa on 2c org brn 18 60
45 A50 1.50pi on 20c brn org (#113) 24 60
Nos. 35-45 (11) 110.67 161.60

Italian Stamps of 1901-20 Surcharged in Black or Red **1½ PIASTRE**

46 A48 30pa on 5c green 15 24
47 A48 1½pi on 10c claret 18 38
48 A49 3pi on 25c blue 1.25 75
49 A49 3¾pi on 40c brown 24 35
50 A49 4½pi on 50c violet 5.50 5.50
51 A49 7½pi on 85c red brn 90 1.90
a. "PIASIRE" 9.00 14.00
52 A46 7½pi on 1 l brn & grn (R) 1.25 2.00
a. Double surcharge 27.50 27.50
b. "PIASIRE" 11.00 17.00
53 A46 15pi on 1 l brn & grn 15.00 18.00
54 A46 45pi on 5 l blue & rose 9.00 14.00
55 A51 90pi on 10 l gray grn & red 8.00 14.00
Nos. 46-55 (10) 41.47 57.12

Italian Stamps of 1901-20 Surcharged Type "o" or:

4 PIASTRE 20 PARA No. 58 — **15 PIASTRE** No. 59 — **45 PIASTRE** Nos. 61-62

1923
56 A49 1pi20pa on 25c blue 1.90
57 A49 3pi30pa on 40c brown 1.90
58 A49 4pi20pa on 50c violet 1.90
58A A49 7pi20pa on 60c car 6.75
59 A49 15pi on 85c red brn 1.90
60 A46 18pi30pa on 1 l brn & grn 1.90
61 A46 45pi on 5 l bl & rose 4.50
62 A51 90pi on 10 l gray grn & red 2.25
Nos. 56-62 (8) 23.00

Nos. 56-62 were not issued.

SPECIAL DELIVERY STAMPS

Italian Special Delivery Stamps Surcharged

Surcharged **LEVANTE 1 PIASTRA 1**

1908 Wmk. 140 *Perf. 14*
E1 SD1 1pi on 25c rose red 20 35

Surcharged **LEVANTE 60 Parà 60**

1910
E2 SD2 60pa on 30c blue & rose 38 75

Surcharged **15 PIASTRE**

1922
E3 SD2 15pi on 1.20 l on 30c bl & rose 2.75 *6.75*

On No. E3, lines obliterate the first two denominations.

Surcharged **15 PIASTRE**

E4 SD2 15pi on 30c bl & rose 47.50 *90.00*

Surcharged **15 PIASTRE**

1924
E5 SD2 15pi on 1.20 l blue & red 1.90

No. E5 was not regularly issued.

ALBANIA

Stamps of Italy Surcharged in Black **ALBANIA 10 Parà 10**

1902 Wmk. 140 *Perf. 14*
1 A44 10pa on 5c green 35 38
2 A45 35pa on 20c orange 75 1.00
3 A45 40pa on 25c blue 1.25 90

1907
4 A48 10pa on 5c green 12.50 *27.50*
5 A48 20pa on 10c claret 1.25 2.25
6 A45 80pa on 50c violet 1.50 3.25

CONSTANTINOPLE

Stamps of Italy Surcharged in Black or Violet **Costantinopoli 10 Parà 10**

Wmk. 140, Unwmk. (#3)

1909-11 *Perf. 14, 12*
1 A48 10pa on 5c green 15 24
2 A48 20pa on 10c claret 15 24
3 A47 30pa on 15c slate (V) 15 24
4 A49 1pi on 25c blue 15 24
a. Double surcharge 27.50 35.00
5 A49 2pi on 50c violet 18 35

Surcharged **COSTANTINOPOLI 4 PIASTRE 4**

6 A46 4pi on 1 l brn & grn 28 45
7 A46 20pi on 5 l bl & rose 4.75 1.90
8 A51 40pi on 10 l gray grn & red 1.00 2.25
Nos. 1-8 (8) 6.81 5.91

Italian Stamps of 1901-19 Surcharged:

COSTANTINOPOLI PIASTRE 1 PARA 20 Nos. 10, 12-13 — **COSTANTINOPOLI PIASTRE 3** Nos. 9, 11

1922
9 A48 20pa on 5c green 1.90 3.75
10 A48 1pi20pa on 15c slate 24 35
11 A49 3pi on 30c org brn 24 60
12 A49 3pi30pa on 40c brown 24 45
13 A46 7pi20pa on 1 l brn & grn 24 45
Nos. 9-13 (5) 2.86 5.60

Italian Stamps of 1901-20 Surcharged **COSTANTINOPOLI PIASTRE 1 PARÀ 20**

1923
14 A48 30pa on 5c green 30 50
15 A49 1pi20pa on 25c blue 30 50
16 A49 3pi30pa on 40c brown 30 50
17 A49 4pi20pa on 50c violet 30 50

18 A49 7pi20pa on 60c car 30 50
19 A49 15pi on 85c red brn 30 50
20 A46 18pi30pa on 1 l brn & grn 45 75
21 A46 45pi on 5 l bl & rose 60 1.00
22 A51 90pi on 10 l gray grn & red 60 1.25
Nos. 14-22 (9) 3.45 6.00

CONSTANTINOPLE SPECIAL DELIVERY STAMP

Unissued Italian Special Delivery Stamp of 1922 Surcharged in Black

COSTANTINOPOLI
15
PIASTRE

1923 Wmk. 140 *Perf. 14*
E1 SD2 15pi on 1.20 l bl & red 75 2.25

CONSTANTINOPLE POSTAGE DUE STAMPS

Italian Postage Due Stamps of 1870-1903 Overprinted

Costantinopoli

1922 Wmk. 140 *Perf. 14*
J1 D3 10c buff & mag 60 1.25
J2 D3 30c buff & mag 75 1.25
J3 D3 60c buff & mag 75 1.25
J4 D3 1 l blue & mag 60 1.25
J5 D3 2 l blue & mag 275.00 425.00
J6 D3 5 l blue & mag 70.00 90.00
Nos. J1-J6 (6) 347.70 520.00

A circular control mark, having the appearance of a cancellation, was applied to each block of four of these stamps.

DURAZZO

Stamps of Italy Surcharged in Black or Violet

Durazzo
10 Parà 10

Wmk. 140, Unwmk. (#3)
1909-11 *Perf. 14, 12*
1 A48 10pa on 5c green 15 35
2 A48 20pa on 10c claret 15 35
3 A47 30pa on 15c slate (V) 1.40 1.40
4 A49 1pi on 25c blue 15 35
5 A49 2pi on 50c violet 18 45

Surcharged

DURAZZO
4 PIASTRE 4

6 A46 4pi on 1 l brn & grn 30 70
7 A46 20pi on 5 l bl & rose 27.50 18.00
8 A51 40pi on 10 l gray grn & red 3.75 *12.50*
Nos. 1-8 (8) 33.58 34.10

No. 3 Surcharged

CENT 20

1916 Unwmk. *Perf. 12*
9 A47 20c on 30pa on 15c sl 60 *3.50*

JANINA

Stamps of Italy Surcharged

10 Parà 10

1902-07 Wmk. 140 *Perf. 14*
1 A44 10pa on 5c green 1.25 60
2 A45 35pa on 20c orange 60 75
3 A45 40pa on 25c blue 3.50 1.40
4 A45 80pa on 50c vio ('07) 5.25 8.50

Surcharged in Black or Violet

Janina
10 Parà 10

Wmk. 140, Unwmk. (#7)
1909-11 *Perf. 14, 12*
5 A48 10pa on 5c green 15 35
6 A48 20pa on 10c claret 15 35
7 A47 30pa on 15c slate (V) 15 45
8 A49 1pi on 25c blue 15 45
9 A49 2pi on 50c violet 15 60

Surcharged

JANINA
4 PIASTRE 4

10 A46 4pi on 1 l brn & grn 18 70
11 A46 20pi on 5 l bl & rose 35.00 32.50
12 A51 40pi on 10 l gray grn & red 3.75 11.50
Nos. 5-12 (8) 39.68 46.90

JERUSALEM

Stamps of Italy Surcharged in Black or Violet

Gerusalemme
10 Parà 10

Wmk. 140, Unwmk. (#3)
1909-11 *Perf. 14, 12*
1 A48 10pa on 5c green 32 *1.25*
2 A48 20pa on 10c claret 32 *1.25*
3 A47 30pa on 15c slate (V) 32 *1.25*
4 A49 1pi on 25c blue 32 *1.25*
5 A49 2pi on 50c violet 95 *2.25*

Surcharged

GERUSALEMME
4 PIASTRE 4

6 A46 4pi on 1 l brn & grn 1.65 *4.50*
7 A46 20pi on 5 l bl & rose 60.00 *75.00*
8 A51 40pi on 10 l gray grn & red 9.00 *35.00*
Nos. 1-8 (8) 72.88

Forged cancellations exist on Nos. 1-8.

SALONIKA

Stamps of Italy Surcharged in Black or Violet

Salonicco
10 Parà 10

Wmk. 140, Unwmk. (#3)
1909-11 *Perf. 14, 12*
1 A48 10pa on 5c green 15 35
2 A48 20pa on 10c claret 15 35
3 A47 30pa on 15c slate (V) 15 35
4 A49 1pi on 25c blue 15 35
5 A49 2pi on 50c violet 22 70

Surcharged

SALONICCO
4 PIASTRE 4

6 A46 4pi on 1 l brn & grn 24 75
7 A46 20pi on 5 l bl & rose 60.00 60.00
8 A51 40pi on 10 l gray grn & red 4.50 14.00
Nos. 1-8 (8) 65.56 76.85

SCUTARI

Stamps of Italy Surcharged in Black or Violet

Scutari
di Albania
10 Parà 10

Wmk. 140, Unwmk. (#3)
1909-11 *Perf. 14, 12*
1 A48 10pa on 5c green 15 35
2 A48 20pa on 10c claret 15 35
3 A47 30pa on 15c slate (V) 2.25 1.50
4 A49 1pi on 25c blue 15 45
5 A49 2pi on 50c violet 15 60

Surcharged

SCUTARI
DI ALBANIA
4 PIASTRE 4

6 A46 4pi on 1 l brn & grn 28 75
7 A46 20pi on 5 l bl & rose 1.25 3.50
8 A51 40pi on 10 l gray grn & red 11.00 22.50
Nos. 1-8 (8) 15.38 30.00

Surcharged like Nos. 1-5

1915
9 A43 4pa on 2c orange brn 24 45

No. 3 Surcharged

CENT 20

1916 Unwmk. *Perf. 12*
10 A47 20c on 30pa on 15c sl 90 3.50

SMYRNA

Stamps of Italy Surcharged in Black or Violet

Smirne
10 Parà 10

Wmk. 140, Unwmk. (#3)
1909-11 *Perf. 14, 12*
1 A48 10pa on 5c green 15 35
2 A48 20pa on 10c claret 15 35
3 A47 30pa on 15c slate (V) 15 35
4 A49 1pi on 25c blue 15 45
5 A49 2pi on 50c violet 15 45

Surcharged

SMIRNE
4 PIASTRE 4

6 A46 4pi on 1 l brn & grn 22 60
7 A46 20pi on 5 l bl & rose 14.00 6.75
8 A51 40pi on 10 l gray grn & red 6.50 14.00
Nos. 1-8 (8) 21.47 23.30

Italian Stamps of 1901-22 Surcharged:

SMIRNE
PIASTRE 1
PARÀ 20
Nos. 10, 12-13

SMIRNE
PIASTRE 3
Nos. 9, 11

1922
9 A48 20pa on 5c green 4.75
10 A48 1pi20pa on 15c slate 15
11 A49 3pi on 30c org brn 15
12 A49 3pi30pa on 40c brown 15
13 A46 7pi20pa on 1 l brn & grn 15
Nos. 9-13 (5) 5.35

Nos. 9-13 were not issued.

VALONA

Stamps of Italy Surcharged in Black or Violet

Valona
10 Parà 10

Wmk. 140, Unwmk. (#3)
1909-11 *Perf. 14, 12*
1 A48 10pa on 5c green 15 35
2 A48 20pa on 10c claret 15 35
3 A47 30pa on 15c slate (V) 2.25 1.50
4 A49 1pi on 25c blue 15 45
5 A49 2pi on 50c violet 15 60

Surcharged

VALONA
4 PIASTRE 4

6 A46 4pi on 1 l brn & grn 28 75
7 A46 20pi on 5 l bl & rose 9.50 *5.00*
8 A51 40pi on 10 l gray grn & red 14.00 27.50
Nos. 1-8 (8) 26.63 36.50

Italy No. 123 Surcharged in Violet or Red Violet

VALONA
30 PARA 30

1916
9 A58 30pa on 15c slate (V) 45 1.40
a. Red violet surcharge 70 3.50

No. 9 Surcharged

CENT 20

10 A58 20c on 30pa on 15c sl 24 1.90

AEGEAN ISLANDS

(Dodecanese)

A group of islands in the Aegean Sea off the coast of Turkey. They were occupied by Italy during the Tripoli War and were ceded to Italy by Turkey in 1924 by the Treaty of Lausanne. Stamps of Italy overprinted with the name of the island were in use at the post offices maintained in the various islands.

Rhodes, on the island of the same name, was capital of the entire group.

100 Centesimi = 1 Lira

GENERAL ISSUE

Italian Stamps of 1907-08 Overprinted

EGEO

1912 Wmk. 140 *Perf. 14*
1 A49 25c blue 4.25 5.50
a. Inverted overprint 35.00 57.50
2 A49 50c violet 4.25 5.50
a. Inverted overprint 35.00 57.50

Virgil Issue

Types of Italian Stamps of 1930 Overprinted in Red or Blue

ISOLE ITALIANE DELL'EGEO

1930 Photo. Wmk. 140 *Perf. 14*
3 A106 15c vio blk 24 *1.40*
4 A106 20c org brn 24 *1.40*
5 A106 25c dk green 24 *1.40*
6 A106 30c lt brown 24 *1.40*
7 A106 50c dull vio 24 *1.40*
8 A106 75c rose red 24 *1.40*
9 A106 1.25 l gray bl 24 *1.40*

Engr.
Unwmk.
10 A106 5 l + 1.50 l dk vio 1.00 *3.50*
11 A106 10 l + 2.50 l dk brn 1.00 *3.50*
Nos. 3-11,C4-C7 (13) 7.48

St. Anthony of Padua Issue

Types of Italian Stamps of 1931 Overprinted in Blue or Red

ISOLE ITALIANE
DELL'EGEO

1932 Photo. Wmk. 140 *Perf. 14*
12 A116 20c black brn 5.25 5.50
13 A116 25c dull grn 5.25 3.50
14 A118 30c brown org 5.25 5.50
15 A118 50c dull vio 5.25 3.50
16 A120 1.25 l gray bl 5.25 5.50

Engr.
Unwmk.
17 A121 75c lt red 5.25 5.50
18 A122 5 l + 2.50 l dp org 5.25 *18.00*
Nos. 12-18 (7) 36.75 47.00

Dante Alighieri Society Issue

Types of Italian Stamps of 1932 Overprinted

ISOLE
DELL'

ITALIANE
EGEO

1932 Photo. Wmk. 140
19 A126 10c grnsh gray 38 60
20 A126 15c black vio 38 60
21 A126 20c brown org 38 60
22 A126 25c dp green 38 35
23 A126 30c dp org 38 60
24 A126 50c dull vio 38 35
25 A126 75c rose red 38 60
26 A126 1.25 l blue 38 60
27 A126 1.75 l ol brn 50 90
28 A126 2.75 l car rose 50 90
29 A126 5 l + 2 l dp vio 75 1.50
30 A126 10 l + 2.50 l dk brn 75 1.50
Nos. 19-30 (12) 5.54 9.10

See Nos. C8-C14.

Soccer Issue

Types of Italy, "Soccer" Issue, Overprinted in Black or Red

ISOLE ITALIANE DELL'EGEO

1934

31 A173 20c brn rose (Bk) 10.00 *9.00*
32 A174 25c green (R) 10.00 *9.00*
33 A174 50c violet (R) 42.50 6.75
34 A174 1.25 l gray bl (R) 10.00 *16.00*
35 A175 5 l +2.50 l bl (R) 10.00 *50.00*
Nos. 31-35 (5) 82.50 *90.75*

See Nos. C28-C31.

Same Overprint on Types of Medal of Valor Issue of Italy, in Red or Black

1935

36 A177 10c sl gray (R) 12.50 *22.50*
37 A178 15c brn (Bk) 12.50 *22.50*
38 A178 20c red org (Bk) 12.50 *22.50*
39 A177 25c dp grn (R) 12.50 *22.50*
40 A178 30c lake (Bk) 12.50 *22.50*
41 A178 50c ol grn (Bk) 12.50 *22.50*
42 A178 75c rose red (Bk) 12.50 *22.50*
43 A178 1.25 l dp bl (R) 12.50 *22.50*
44 A177 1.75 l + 1 l pur (R) 10.00 *22.50*
45 A178 2.55 l + 2 l dk car (Bk) 10.00 *22.50*
46 A178 2.75 l + 2 l org brn (Bk) 10.00 *22.50*
Nos. 36-46 (11) 130.00 *247.50*

See Nos. C32-C38, CE3-CE4.

Types of Italy, 1937, Overprinted in Blue or Red

ISOLE
ITALIANE
DELL'EGEO

1938 Wmk. 140 *Perf. 14*

47 A208 10c dk brn (Bl) 85 80
48 A208 15c pur (R) 85 80
49 A208 20c yel bis (Bl) 85 80
50 A208 25c myr grn (R) 85 80
51 A208 30c dp cl (Bl) 85 80
52 A208 50c sl grn (R) 85 80
53 A208 75c rose red (Bl) 85 85
54 A208 1.25 l dk bl (R) 85 85
55 A208 1.75 l + 1 l dp org (Bl) 1.10 1.25
56 A208 2.55 l + 2 l ol brn (R) 1.10 1.25
Nos. 47-56 (10) 9.00 9.00

Bimillenary of birth of Augustus Caesar (Octavianus), first Roman emperor.
See Nos. C39-C43.

Same Overprint of Type of Italy, 1937, in Red

1938

57 A222 1.25 l deep blue 60 70
58 A222 2.75 l + 2 l brown 75 *2.75*

600th anniversary of the death of Giotto di Bondone, Italian painter.

Statue of Roman Wolf — A1

Arms of Rhodes — A2

Dante's House, Rhodes — A3

1940 Photo.

59 A1 5c lt brown 15 15
60 A2 10c pale org 15 15
61 A3 25c blue grn 40 40
62 A1 50c rose vio 40 40
63 A2 75c dull ver 40 40
64 A3 1.25 l dull blue 40 40
65 A2 2 l + 75c rose 40 40
Nos. 59-65,C44-C47 (11) 4.70 4.70

Triennial Overseas Exposition, Naples.

AIR POST STAMPS

Ferrucci Issue

Types of Italian Air Post Stamps of 1930 Overprinted in Blue or Red Like Nos. 12-18

1930 Wmk. 140 *Perf. 14*

C1 AP7 50c brn vio (Bl) 3.00 *4.50*
C2 AP7 1 l dk bl (R) 3.00 *4.50*
C3 AP7 5 l + 2 l dp car (Bl) 6.00 *11.50*

Nos. C1 to C3 were sold at Rhodes only.

Virgil Issue

Types of Italian Air Post Stamps of 1930 Overprinted in Red or Blue Like Nos. 3-11

Photo.

C4 AP8 50c dp grn (R) 90 *2.25*
C5 AP8 1 l rose red (Bl) 90 *2.25*

Engr.
Unwmk.

C6 AP8 7.70 l + 1.30 l dk brn (R) 1.00 *4.50*
C7 AP8 9 l + 2 l gray (R) 1.00 *4.50*

Dante Alighieri Society Issue

Types of Italian Air Post Stamps of 1932 Overprinted Like Nos. 19-30

1932 Wmk. 140

C8 AP10 50c car rose 70 90
C9 AP11 1 l dp grn 45 90
C10 AP11 3 l dl vio 45 90
C11 AP11 5 l dp org 45 90
C12 AP10 7.70 l + 2 l ol brn 75 1.65
C13 AP11 10 l + 2.50 l dk bl 75 1.65
Nos. C8-C13 (6) 3.55 6.90

Leonardo da Vinci — AP12

1932 Photo. *Perf. 14½*

C14 AP12 100 l dp bl & grnsh gray 7.25 *14.00*

Garibaldi Types of Italian Air Post Stamps of 1932 Overprinted in Red or Blue Like Nos. 12-18

1932

C15 AP13 50c deep green 10.50 *20.00*
C16 AP14 80c copper red 10.50 *20.00*
C17 AP13 1 l + 25c dl bl 10.50 *20.00*
C18 AP13 2 l + 50c red brn 10.50 *20.00*
C19 AP14 5 l + 1 l bluish sl 10.50 *20.00*
Nos. C15-C19 (5) 52.50 *100.00*

See Nos. CE1-CE2.

Graf Zeppelin over Rhodes AP17

1933 *Perf. 14*

C20 AP17 3 l olive brn 22.50 *50.00*
C21 AP17 5 l dp vio 14.00 *50.00*
C22 AP17 10 l dk green 14.00 *100.00*
C23 AP17 12 l dk blue 14.00 *100.00*
C24 AP17 15 l car rose 14.00 *100.00*
C25 AP17 20 l gray blk 14.00 *100.00*
Nos. C20-C25 (6) 92.50 *500.00*

Balbo Flight Issue

Types of Italian Air Post Stamps of 1933 Overprinted

ISOLE ITALIANE DELL EGEO

1933 Wmk. 140 *Perf. 14*

C26 AP25 5.25 l + 19.75 l grn, red & bl gray 17.00 35.00
C27 AP25 5.25 l + 44.75 l red, grn & bl gray 17.00 35.00

Soccer Issue

Types of Italian Air Post Stamps of 1934 Overprinted in Black or Red Like Nos. 31-35

1934

C28 AP32 50c brown (R) 3.00 *6.00*
C29 AP33 75c rose red) 3.00 *6.00*
C30 AP34 5 l + 2.50 l red org 6.25 *10.00*
C31 AP35 10 l + 5 l grn (R) 6.25 *10.00*

Types of Medal of Valor Issue of Italy Overprinted in Red or Black Like Nos. 31-35

1935

C32 AP36 25c dp grn 17.00 *30.00*
C33 AP36 50c blk brn (R) 17.00 *30.00*
C34 AP36 75c rose 17.00 *30.00*
C35 AP36 80c dk brn 17.00 *30.00*
C36 AP36 1 l + 50c ol grn 12.00 *30.00*
C37 AP36 2 l + 1 l dp bl (R) 12.00 *30.00*
C38 AP40 3 l + 2 l vio (R) 12.00 *30.00*
Nos. C32-C38 (7) 104.00 *210.00*

Types of Italy Air Post Stamps, 1937, Overprinted in Blue or Red Like Nos. 47-56

1938 Wmk. 140 *Perf. 14*

C39 AP51 25c dl gray vio (R) 1.75 1.25
C40 AP51 50c grn (R) 1.75 1.25
C41 AP51 80c brt bl (R) 1.75 1.25
C42 AP51 1 l + 1 l rose lake 2.00 1.90
C43 AP51 5 l + 1 l rose red 2.00 2.75
Nos. C39-C43 (5) 9.25 8.40

Bimillenary of the birth of Augustus Caesar (Octavianus).

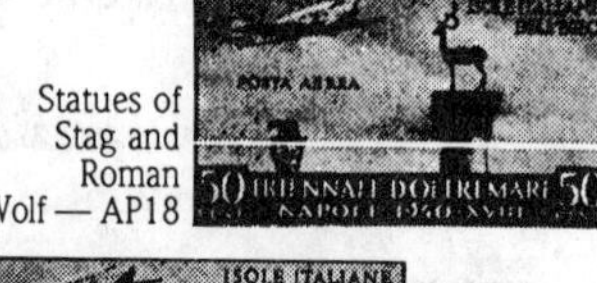

Statues of Stag and Roman Wolf — AP18

Plane over Government Palace, Rhodes AP19

1940 Photo.

C44 AP18 50c olive blk 60 60
C45 AP19 1 l dk vio 60 60
C46 AP18 2 l + 75c dk bl 60 60
C47 AP19 5 l + 2.50 l cop brn 60 60

Triennial Overseas Exposition, Naples.

AIR POST SPECIAL DELIVERY STAMPS

Type of Italian Garibaldi Air Post Special Delivery Stamps Overprinted in Blue or Ocher Like Nos. 12-18

1932 Wmk. 140 *Perf. 14*

CE1 APSD1 2.25 l + 1 l bl & rose (Bl) 17.00 *20.00*
CE2 APSD1 4.50 l + 1.50 l ocher & gray (O) 17.00 *20.00*

Type of Medal of Valor Issue of Italy, Overprinted in Black Like Nos. 31-35

1935

CE3 APSD4 2 l + 1.25 l dp bl 15.00 *30.00*
CE4 APSD4 4.50 l + 2 l grn 15.00 *30.00*

ISSUES FOR THE INDIVIDUAL ISLANDS

Italian Stamps of 1901-20 Overprinted with Names of Various Islands as

Caso
a

CASO
b

CASO
c

The 1912-22 issues of each island have type "a" overprint in black on all values except 15c (type A58) and 20c on 15c, which have type "b" overprint in violet.

The 1930-32 Ferruci and Garibaldi issues are types of the Italian issues overprinted type "c."

CALCHI

Overprinted "Karki" in Black or Violet

1912-22 Wmk. 140 *Perf. 13½, 14*

1 A43 2c orange brn 90 1.40
a. Double overprint 57.50
2 A48 5c green 15 *1.40*
a. Double overprint 42.50
3 A48 10c claret 15 *1.40*
4 A48 15c slate ('22) 90 *10.00*
a. Double overprint 57.50
5 A50 20c brn org ('21) 70 *10.00*
6 A49 25c blue 15 *1.40*
7 A49 40c brown 15 *1.40*
8 A49 50c violet 15 *1.40*

Unwmk.

9 A58 15c slate (V) 5.75 1.40
10 A50 20c brn org ('17) 15.00 *24.00*
Nos. 1-10 (10) 24.00 *53.80*

No. 9 Surcharged ≡ CENT 20 ≡

1916 *Perf. 13½*

11 A58 20c on 15c slate 35 5.00

Ferrucci Issue

Overprinted in Red or Blue

1930 Wmk. 140 *Perf. 14*

12 A102 20c vio (R) 24 *60*
13 A103 25c dk grn (R) 24 *60*
14 A103 50c blk (R) 24 *60*
15 A103 1.25 l dp bl (R) 24 *60*
16 A104 5 l + 2 l dp car (Bl) 1.25 *1.90*
Nos. 12-16 (5) 2.21 *4.30*

Garibaldi Issue

Overprinted "CARCHI" in Red or Blue

1932

17 A138 10c brown 1.50 *3.50*
18 A138 20c red brn (Bl) 1.50 *3.50*
19 A138 25c dp grn 1.50 *3.50*
20 A138 30c bluish sl 1.50 *3.50*
21 A138 50c red vio (Bl) 1.50 *3.50*
22 A141 75c cop red (Bl) 1.50 *3.50*
23 A141 1.25 l dl bl 1.50 *3.50*
24 A141 1.75 l + 25c brn 1.50 *3.50*
25 A144 2.55 l + 50c org (Bl) 1.50 *3.50*
26 A145 5 l + 1 l dl vio 1.50 *3.50*
Nos. 17-26 (10) 15.00 *35.00*

CALINO

Overprinted "Calimno" in Black or Violet

1912-21 Wmk. 140 *Perf. 13½, 14*

1 A43 2c orange brn 1.25 1.40
2 A48 5c green 35 *1.40*
3 A48 10c claret 15 *1.40*
4 A48 15c slate ('21) 1.00 *10.00*
5 A50 20c brn org ('21) 1.00 *10.00*
6 A49 25c blue 90 *1.40*
7 A49 40c brown 15 *1.40*
8 A49 50c violet 15 *1.40*

Unwmk.

9 A58 15c slate (V) 8.25 1.40
10 A50 20c brn org ('17) 19.00 *24.00*
Nos. 1-10 (10) 32.20 *53.80*

No. 9 Surcharged Like Calchi No. 11

1916 *Perf. 13½*

11 A58 20c on 15c slate 4.75 *5.00*

Ferrucci Issue

Overprinted in Red or Blue

1930 Wmk. 140 *Perf. 14*

12 A102 20c violet (R) 35 *60*
13 A103 25c dk green (R) 35 *60*
14 A102 50c black (R) 35 *60*
15 A102 1.25 l dp bl (R) 35 *60*
16 A104 5 l + 2 l dp car (Bl) 1.90 *1.90*
Nos. 12-16 (5) 3.30 *4.30*

Garibaldi Issue

Overprinted in Red or Blue

1932

17 A138 10c brown 2.25 *3.50*
18 A138 20c red brn (Bl) 2.25 *3.50*
19 A138 25c dp grn 2.25 *3.50*
20 A138 30c bluish sl 2.25 *3.50*
21 A138 50c red vio (Bl) 2.25 *3.50*
22 A141 75c cop red (Bl) 2.25 *3.50*
23 A141 1.25 l dull blue 2.25 *3.50*
24 A141 1.75 l + 25c brn 2.25 *3.50*
25 A144 2.55 l + 50c org (Bl) 2.25 *3.50*
26 A145 5 l + 1 l dl vio 2.25 *3.50*
Nos. 17-26 (10) 22.50 *35.00*

CASO

Overprinted "Caso" in Black or Violet

1912-21 Wmk. 140 *Perf. 13½, 14*

1	A43	2c orange brn	1.25	1.40
2	A48	5c green	15	*1.40*
3	A48	10c claret	15	*1.40*
4	A48	15c slate ('21)	1.00	*10.00*
5	A50	20c brn org ('20)	90	*10.00*
6	A49	25c blue	15	*1.40*
7	A49	40c brown	15	*1.40*
8	A49	50c violet	15	*1.40*

Unwmk.

9	A58	15c slate (V)	8.25	*1.40*
10	A50	20c brn org ('17)	19.00	*24.00*
		Nos. 1-10 (10)	31.15	*53.80*

No. 9 Surcharged Like Calchi No. 11

1916 *Perf. 13½*

11	A58	20c on 15c slate	35	*5.00*

Ferrucci Issue

Overprinted in Red or Blue

1930 Wmk. 140 *Perf. 14*

12	A102	20c vio (R)	35	*60*
13	A103	25c dk grn (R)	35	*60*
14	A103	50c blk (R)	35	*60*
15	A103	1.25 l dp bl (R)	35	*60*
16	A104	5 l + 2 l dp car (Bl)	1.90	*1.90*
		Nos. 12-16 (5)	3.30	*4.30*

Garibaldi Issue

Overprinted in Red or Blue

1932

17	A138	10c brown	2.25	*3.50*
18	A138	20c red brn (Bl)	2.25	*3.50*
19	A138	25c dp grn	2.25	*3.50*
20	A138	30c bluish sl	2.25	*3.50*
21	A138	50c red vio (Bl)	2.25	*3.50*
22	A141	75c cop red (Bl)	2.25	*3.50*
23	A141	1.25 l dl bl	2.25	*3.50*
24	A141	1.75 l + 25c brn	2.25	*3.50*
25	A144	2.55 l + 50c org (Bl)	2.25	*3.50*
26	A145	5 l + 1 l dl vio	2.25	*3.50*
		Nos. 17-26 (10)	22.50	*35.00*

COO

(Cos, Kos)

Overprinted "Cos" in Black or Violet

1912-22 Wmk. 140 *Perf. 13½, 14*

1	A43	2c orange brn	1.20	1.40
2	A48	5c green	7.25	1.40
3	A48	10c claret	15	*1.40*
4	A48	15c slate ('22)	95	*10.00*
5	A50	20c brn org ('21)	1.20	*10.00*
6	A49	25c blue	5.50	1.40
7	A49	40c brown	15	*1.40*
8	A49	50c violet	15	*1.40*

Unwmk.

9	A58	15c slate (V)	7.25	1.40
10	A50	20c brn org ('17)	10.00	*24.00*
		Nos. 1-10 (10)	33.80	*53.80*

No. 9 Surcharged Like Calchi No. 11

1916 *Perf. 13½*

11	A58	20c on 15c slate	4.25	*5.00*

Ferrucci Issue

Overprinted in Red or Blue

1930 Wmk. 140 *Perf. 14*

12	A102	20c vio (R)	35	*60*
13	A103	25c dk grn (R)	35	*60*
14	A103	50c blk (R)	35	*60*
15	A103	1.25 l dp bl (R)	35	*60*
16	A104	5 l + 2 l dp car (Bl)	1.65	*1.90*
		Nos. 12-16 (5)	3.05	*4.30*

Garibaldi Issue

Overprinted in Red or Blue

1932

17	A138	10c brown	2.00	*3.50*
18	A138	20c red brn (Bl)	2.00	*3.50*
19	A138	25c dp grn	2.00	*3.50*
20	A138	30c bluish sl	2.00	*3.50*
21	A138	50c red vio (Bl)	2.00	*3.50*
22	A141	75c cop red (Bl)	2.00	*3.50*
23	A141	1.25 l dl bl	2.00	*3.50*
24	A141	1.75 l + 25c brn	2.00	*3.50*
25	A144	2.55 l + 50c org (Bl)	2.00	*3.50*
26	A145	5 l + 1 l dl vio	2.00	*3.50*
		Nos. 17-26 (10)	20.00	*35.00*

LERO

Overprinted "Leros" in Black or Violet

1912-22 Wmk. 140 *Perf. 13½, 14*

1	A43	2c orange brn	1.00	1.40
2	A48	5c green	30	*1.40*
3	A48	10c claret	15	*1.40*
4	A48	15c slate ('22)	75	*10.00*
5	A50	20c brn org ('21)	19.00	10.00
6	A49	25c blue	8.00	1.40
7	A49	40c brown	15	*1.40*
8	A49	50c violet	15	*1.40*

Unwmk.

9	A58	15c slate (V)	6.50	1.40
10	A50	20c brn org ('17)	8.00	*24.00*
		Nos. 1-10 (10)	44.00	*53.80*

No. 9 Surcharged Like Calchi No. 11

1916 *Perf. 13½*

11	A58	20c on 15c slate	3.50	*5.00*

Ferrucci Issue

Overprinted in Red or Blue

1930 *Perf. 14*

12	A102	20c violet (R)	25	*60*
13	A103	25c dk green (R)	25	*60*
14	A103	50c black (R)	25	*60*
15	A103	1.25 l dp bl (R)	25	*60*
16	A104	5 l + 2 l dp car (Bl)	1.40	*1.90*
		Nos. 12-16 (5)	2.40	*4.30*

Garibaldi Issue

Overprinted in Red or Blue

1932

17	A138	10c brown	1.65	*3.50*
18	A138	20c red brn (Bl)	1.65	*3.50*
19	A138	25c dp grn	1.65	*3.50*
20	A138	30c bluish sl	1.65	*3.50*
21	A138	50c red vio (Bl)	1.65	*3.50*
22	A141	75c cop red (Bl)	1.65	*3.50*
23	A141	1.25 l dl bl	1.65	*3.50*
24	A141	1.75 l + 25c brn	1.65	*3.50*
25	A144	2.55 l + 50c org (Bl)	1.65	*3.50*
26	A145	5 l + 1 l dl vio	1.65	*3.50*
		Nos. 17-26 (10)	16.50	*35.00*

LISSO

Overprinted "Lipso" in Black or Violet

1912-22 Wmk. 140 *Perf. 13½, 14*

1	A43	2c orange brn	1.25	1.40
2	A48	5c green	15	*1.40*
3	A48	10c claret	15	*1.40*
4	A48	15c slate ('22)	1.00	*10.00*
5	A50	20c brn org ('21)	1.00	*10.00*
6	A49	25c blue	15	*1.40*
7	A49	40c brown	15	*1.40*
8	A49	50c violet	15	*1.40*

Unwmk.

9	A58	15c slate (V)	8.25	1.40
10	A50	20c brn org ('17)	11.00	*24.00*
		Nos. 1-10 (10)	23.25	*53.80*

No. 9 Surcharged Like Calchi No. 11

1916 *Perf. 13½*

11	A58	20c on 15c slate	35	*5.00*

Ferrucci Issue

Overprinted in Red or Blue

1930 Wmk. 140 *Perf. 14*

12	A102	20c vio (R)	35	*60*
13	A103	25c dk grn (R)	35	*60*
14	A103	50c blk (R)	35	*60*
15	A103	1.25 l dp bl (R)	35	*60*
16	A104	5 l + 2 l dp car (Bl)	1.90	*1.90*
		Nos. 12-16 (5)	3.30	*4.30*

Garibaldi Issue

Overprinted "LIPSO" in Red or Blue

1932

17	A138	10c brown	2.75	*3.50*
18	A138	20c red brn (bl)	2.75	*3.50*
19	A138	25c dp grn	2.75	*3.50*
20	A138	30c bluish sl	2.75	*3.50*
21	A138	50c red vio (Bl)	2.75	*3.50*
22	A141	75c cop red (Bl)	2.75	*3.50*
23	A141	1.25 l dl bl	2.75	*3.50*
24	A141	1.75 l + 25c brn	2.75	*3.50*
25	A144	2.55 l + 50c org (Bl)	2.75	*3.50*
26	A145	5 l + 1 l dl vio	2.75	*3.50*
		Nos. 17-26 (10)	27.50	*35.00*

NISIRO

Overprinted "Nisiros" in Black or Violet

1912-22 Wmk. 140 *Perf. 13½, 14*

1	A43	2c orange brn	1.10	1.40
2	A48	5c green	15	*1.40*
3	A48	10c claret	15	*1.40*
4	A48	15c slate ('22)	3.25	*10.00*
5	A50	20c brn org ('21)	17.50	10.00
6	A49	25c blue	15	*1.40*
7	A49	40c brown	15	*1.40*
8	A49	50c violet	15	*1.40*

Unwmk.

9	A58	15c slate (V)	6.50	1.40
10	A50	20c brn org ('17)	15.00	*24.00*
		Nos. 1-10 (10)	44.10	*53.80*

No. 9 Surcharged Like Calchi No. 11

1916 *Perf. 13½*

11	A58	20c on 15c slate	30	*5.00*

Ferrucci Issue

Overprinted in Red or Blue

1930 Wmk. 140 *Perf. 14*

12	A102	20c vio (R)	30	*60*
13	A103	25c dp grn (R)	30	*60*
14	A103	50c blk (R)	30	*60*
15	A103	1.25 l dp bl (R)	30	*60*
16	A104	5 l + 2 l dp car (Bl)	1.50	*1.90*
		Nos. 12-16 (5)	2.70	*4.30*

Garibaldi Issue

Overprinted in Red or Blue

1932

17	A138	10c brown	1.75	*3.50*
18	A138	20c red brn (Bl)	1.75	*3.50*
19	A138	25c dp grn	1.75	*3.50*
20	A138	30c bluish slate	1.75	*3.50*
21	A138	50c red vio (Bl)	1.75	*3.50*
22	A141	75c cop red (Bl)	1.75	*3.50*
23	A141	1.25 l dull blue	1.75	*3.50*
24	A141	1.75 l + 25c brn	1.75	*3.50*
25	A144	2.55 l + 50c org (Bl)	1.75	*3.50*
26	A145	5 l + 1 l dl vio	1.75	*3.50*
		Nos. 17-26 (10)	17.50	*35.00*

PATMO

Overprinted "Patmos" in Black or Violet

1912-22 Wmk. 140 *Perf. 13½, 14*

1	A43	2c orange brn	1.10	1.40
2	A48	5c green	15	*1.40*
3	A48	10c claret	15	*1.40*
4	A48	15c slate ('22)	85	*10.00*
5	A50	20c brn org ('21)	24.00	10.00
6	A49	25c blue	15	*1.40*
7	A49	40c brown	15	*1.40*
8	A49	50c violet	15	*1.40*

Unwmk.

9	A58	15c slate (V)	8.75	1.40
10	A50	20c brn org ('17)	8.75	*24.00*
		Nos. 1-10 (10)	44.20	*53.80*

No. 9 Surcharged Like Calchi No. 11

1916 *Perf. 13½*

11	A58	20c on 15c slate	3.25	*5.00*

Ferrucci Issue

Overprinted in Red or Blue

1930 Wmk. 140 *Perf. 14*

12	A102	20c vio (R)	30	*60*
13	A103	25c dk grn (R)	30	*60*
14	A103	50c blk (R)	30	*60*
15	A103	1.25 l dp bl (R)	30	*60*
16	A104	5 l + 2 l dp car (Bl)	1.50	*1.90*
		Nos. 12-16 (5)	2.70	*4.30*

Garibaldi Issue

Overprinted in Red or Blue

1932

17	A138	10c brown	1.75	*3.50*
18	A138	20c red brn (Bl)	1.75	*3.50*
19	A138	25c dp grn	1.75	*3.50*
20	A138	30c bluish slate	1.75	*3.50*
21	A138	50c red vio (Bl)	1.75	*3.50*
22	A141	75c cop red (Bl)	1.75	*3.50*
23	A141	1.25 l dl bl	1.75	*3.50*
24	A141	1.75 l + 25c brn	1.75	*3.50*
25	A144	2.55 l + 50c org (Bl)	1.75	*3.50*
26	A145	5 l + 1 l dl vio	1.75	*3.50*
		Nos. 17-26 (10)	17.50	*35.00*

PISCOPI

Overprinted "Piscopi" in Black or Violet

1912-21 Wmk. 140 *Perf. 13½, 14*

1	A43	2c orange brn	1.20	1.40
2	A48	5c green	15	*1.40*
3	A48	10c claret	15	*1.40*
4	A48	15c slate ('21)	2.00	*10.00*
5	A50	20c brn org ('21)	10.00	10.00
6	A49	25c blue	15	*1.40*
7	A49	40c brown	15	*1.40*
8	A49	50c violet	15	*1.40*

Unwmk.

9	A58	15c slate (V)	7.50	1.40
10	A50	20c brn org ('17)	10.00	*24.00*
		Nos. 1-10 (10)	31.45	*53.80*

No. 9 Surcharged Like Calchi No. 11

1916 *Perf. 13½*

11	A58	20c on 15c slate	32	*5.00*

Ferrucci Issue

Overprinted in Red or Blue

1930 Wmk. 140 *Perf. 14*

12	A102	20c vio (R)	32	*60*
13	A103	25c dk grn (R)	32	*60*
14	A103	50c blk (R)	32	*60*
15	A103	1.25 l dp bl (R)	32	*60*
16	A104	5 l + 2 l dp car (Bl)	1.65	*1.90*
		Nos. 12-16 (5)	2.93	*4.30*

Garibaldi Issue

Overprinted in Red or Blue

1932

17	A138	10c brown	2.00	*3.50*
18	A138	20c red brn (Bl)	2.00	*3.50*
19	A138	25c dp grn	2.00	*3.50*
20	A138	30c bluish sl	2.00	*3.50*
21	A138	50c red vio (Bl)	2.00	*3.50*
22	A141	75c cop red (Bl)	2.00	*3.50*
23	A141	1.25 l dl bl	2.00	*3.50*
24	A141	1.75 l + 25c brn	2.00	*3.50*
25	A144	2.55 l + 50c org (Bl)	2.00	*3.50*
26	A145	5 l + 1 l dl vio	2.00	*3.50*
		Nos. 17-26 (10)	20.00	*35.00*

RHODES

(Rodi)

Overprinted "Rodi" in Black or Violet

1912-24 Wmk. 140 *Perf. 13½, 14*

1	A43	2c org brn	15	*90*
2	A48	5c green	15	*60*
a.		Double overprint	57.50	
3	A48	10c claret	15	*60*
4	A48	15c slate ('21)	20.00	11.50
5	A45	20c org ('16)	15	*1.00*
6	A50	20c brn org ('19)	24	45
a.		Double overprint	11.50	
7	A49	25c blue	15	*75*
8	A49	40c brown	15	*90*
9	A49	50c violet	15	*90*
10	A49	85c red brn ('22)	4.25	*14.00*
11	A46	1 l brn & grn ('24)	24	

No. 11 was not regularly issued.

Unwmk.

12	A58	15c slate (V)	6.75	90
13	A50	20c brn org ('17)	30.00	24.00
		Nos. 1-13 (13)	62.53	

No. 12 Surcharged Like Calchi No. 11

1916 *Perf. 13½*

14	A58	20c on 15c slate	20.00	32.50

Windmill, Rhodes — A1

Medieval Galley — A2

Christian Knight — A3

Crusader Kneeling in Prayer — A4

Crusader's Tomb — A5

No Imprint

1929 Unwmk. Litho. *Perf. 11*

15	A1	5c magenta	1.00	18
16	A2	10c olive brn	1.00	18
17	A3	20c rose red	1.00	18
18	A3	25c green	1.00	15

19	A4	30c dk blue	1.00	30
20	A5	50c dk brown	1.50	15
21	A5	1.25 l dk blue	1.00	28
22	A4	5 l magenta	6.25	9.00
23	A4	10 l olive brn	12.50	*22.50*
		Nos. 15-23 (9)	26.25	*32.92*

Visit of the King and Queen of Italy to the Aegean Islands. The stamps are inscribed "Rodi" but were available for use in all the Aegean Islands.

Nos. 15-23 and C1-C4 were used in eastern Crete in 1941-42 with Greek postmarks.

See Nos. 55-63.

Ferrucci Issue

Overprinted in Red or Blue

1930 Wmk. 140 *Perf. 14*

24	A102	20c violet (R)	24	*60*
25	A103	25c dk green (R)	24	*60*
26	A103	50c black (R)	24	*60*
27	A103	1.25 l dp blue (R)	24	*60*
28	A104	5 l + 2 l dp car (Bl)	1.25	*1.90*
		Nos. 24-28 (5)	2.21	*4.30*

Hydrological Congress Issue

Rhodes Issue of 1929 Overprinted

XXI Congresso Idrologico

1930 Unwmk. *Perf. 11*

29	A1	5c magenta	70	1.90
30	A2	10c ol brn	70	1.40
31	A3	20c rose red	1.25	1.40
32	A3	25c green	1.40	1.40
33	A4	30c dk bl	70	1.90
34	A5	50c dk brn	110.00	13.00
35	A5	1.25 l dk bl	85.00	17.00
36	A4	5 l magenta	17.00	27.50
37	A4	10 l ol grn	17.00	27.50
		Nos. 29-37 (9)	233.75	93.00

Rhodes Issue of 1929 Overprinted in Blue or Red

1931 CONGRESSO EUCARISTICO ITALIANO

1931

38	A1	5c mag (Bl)	30	1.40
39	A2	10c ol brn (R)	30	1.40
40	A3	20c rose red (Bl)	30	1.40
41	A3	25c green (R)	30	1.40
42	A4	30c dk blue (R)	30	1.40
43	A5	50c dk brown (R)	21.00	11.00
44	A5	1.25 l dk bl (R)	15.00	15.00
		Nos. 38-44 (7)	37.50	33.00

Italian Eucharistic Congress, 1931.

Garibaldi Issue

Overprinted in Red or Blue

1932 Wmk. 140 *Perf. 14*

45	A138	10c brown	1.75	*3.50*
46	A138	20c red brn (Bl)	1.75	*3.50*
47	A138	25c dp grn	1.75	*3.50*
48	A138	30c bluish sl	1.75	*3.50*
49	A138	50c red vio (Bl)	1.75	*3.50*
50	A141	75c cop red (Bl)	1.75	*3.50*
51	A141	1.25 l dl bl	1.75	*3.50*
52	A141	1.75 l + 25c brn	1.75	*3.50*
53	A144	2.55 l + 50c org (Bl)	1.75	*3.50*
54	A145	5 l + 1 l dl vio	1.75	*3.50*
		Nos. 45-54 (10)	17.50	*35.00*

Types of Rhodes Issue of 1929

Imprint: "Officina Carte-Valori Roma"

1932

55	A1	5c rose lake	15	15
56	A2	10c dk brn	15	15
57	A3	20c red	15	15
58	A3	25c dl grn	15	15
59	A4	30c dl bl	15	15
60	A5	50c blk brn	15	15
61	A5	1.25 l dp bl	15	15
62	A4	5 l rose lake	15	15
63	A4	10 l ol brn	15	15
		Set value	55	75

Aerial View of Rhodes — A6

Map of Rhodes — A7

Deer and Palm — A8

1932 Wmk. 140 Litho. *Perf. 11*

Shield in Red

64	A6	5c blk & grn	90	1.40
65	A6	10c blk & vio bl	90	1.40
66	A6	20c blk & dl yel	90	1.40
67	A6	25c lil & blk	90	1.40
68	A6	30c blk & pink	90	1.40

Shield and Map Dots in Red

69	A7	50c blk & gray	90	1.40
70	A7	1.25 l red brn & gray	90	1.40
71	A7	5 l dk bl & gray	5.50	9.00
72	A7	10 l dk grn & gray	12.50	18.00
73	A7	25 l choc & gray	350.00	*525.00*
		Nos. 64-73 (10)	374.30	*561.80*

20th anniv. of the Italian occupation and 10th anniv. of Fascist rule.

1935, Apr. Photo. Wmk. 140

74	A8	5c orange	1.65	*5.50*
75	A8	10c brown	1.65	*5.50*
76	A8	20c car rose	1.65	*5.50*
77	A8	25c green	1.65	*5.50*
78	A8	30c purple	1.65	*5.50*
79	A8	50c red brn	1.65	*5.50*
80	A8	1.25l blue	1.65	*5.50*
81	A8	5 l yellow	37.50	*80.00*
		Nos. 74-81 (8)	49.05	*118.50*

Holy Year.

WEIHNACHTEN 1944 WEIHNACHTEN 1944

The above overprints on No. 55 are stated to have been prepared locally for use on German military correspondence, but banned by postal authorities in Berlin.

RHODES SEMI-POSTAL STAMPS

Rhodes Nos. 55 to 62 Surcharged in Black or Red

CENT. 5 PRO ASSISTENZA EGEO

1943 Wmk. 140 *Perf. 14*

B1	A1	5c + 5c rose lake	30	28
B2	A2	10c + 10c dk brn	30	28
B3	A3	20c + 20c red	30	28
B4	A3	25c + 25c dl grn	30	28
B5	A4	30c + 30c dl bl (R)	42	35
B6	A5	50c + 50c blk brn	55	45
B7	A5	1.25 l + 1.25 l dp bl (R)	75	60
B8	A4	5 l + 5 l rose lake	27.50	22.50
		Nos. B1-B8 (8)	30.42	25.02

The surtax was for general relief.

Rhodes Nos. 55 to 58, 60 and 61 Surcharged in Black or Red

1944

B9	A1	5c + 3 l rose lake	48	*90*
B10	A2	10c + 3 l dk brn (R)	48	*90*
B11	A3	20c + 3 l red	48	*90*
B12	A3	25c + 3 l dl grn (R)	48	*90*
B13	A5	50c + 3 l blk brn (R)	48	*90*
B14	A5	1.25 l + 5 l dp bl (R)	7.50	9.00
		Nos. B9-B14 (6)	9.90	13.50

The surtax was for war victims.

Rhodes Nos. 62 and 63 Surcharged in Red

+ 10 FEBBRAIO 1945

1945

B17	A4	5 l + 10 l rose lake	3.00	4.50
B18	A4	10 l + 10 l ol brn	3.00	4.50

The surtax was for the Red Cross.

RHODES AIR POST STAMPS

Symbolical of Flight — AP18

1934 Typo. Wmk. 140 *Perf. 14*

C1	AP18	50c black & yellow	15	15
C2	AP18	80c black & mag	35	*1.25*
C3	AP18	1 l black & green	15	15
C4	AP18	5 l black & red vio	35	*2.00*

RHODES AIR POST SEMI-POSTAL STAMPS

Rhodes Nos. C1 to C4 Surcharged in Silver

PRO SINISTRATI DI GUERRA £ 2

1944 Wmk. 140 *Perf. 14*

CB1	AP18	50c + 2 l	2.50	2.00
CB2	AP18	80c + 2 l	3.00	2.75
CB3	AP18	1 l + 2 l	3.75	3.50
CB4	AP18	5 l + 2 l	19.00	20.00

The surtax was for war victims.

RHODES SPECIAL DELIVERY STAMPS

Stag — SD1

1936 Photo. Wmk. 140 *Perf. 14*

E1	SD1	1.25 l green	24	24
E2	SD1	2.50 l vermilion	35	35

Nos. 58 and 57 Surcharged in Black

LIRE 1,25 ESPRESSO

1943

E3	A3	1.25 l on 25c dl grn	15	*45*
E4	A3	2.50 l on 20c red	15	*45*
		Set value	16	

RHODES SEMI-POSTAL SPECIAL DELIVERY STAMPS

Rhodes Nos. E1 and E2 Surcharged in Red or Black

L.RE 1,25 PRO ASSISTENZA EGEO

1943 Wmk. 140 *Perf. 14*

EB1	SD1	1.25 l + 1.25 l (R)	8.50	6.75
EB2	SD1	2.50 l + 2.50 l	11.00	9.00

The surtax was for general relief.

RHODES POSTAGE DUE STAMPS

Maltese Cross PD1

Immortelle PD2

1934 Photo. Wmk. 140 *Perf. 13*

J1	PD1	5c vermilion	15	15
J2	PD1	10c carmine	15	15
J3	PD1	20c dk grn	15	15
J4	PD1	30c purple	15	15
J5	PD1	40c dk bl	15	15
J6	PD2	50c vermilion	15	15
J7	PD2	60c carmine	15	15
J8	PD2	1 l dk grn	15	15
J9	PD2	2 l purple	15	15
		Set value	80	

RHODES PARCEL POST STAMPS

Both unused and used values are for complete stamps.

PP1

PP2

1934 Photo. Wmk. 140 *Perf. 13*

Q1	PP1	5c vermilion	24	18
Q2	PP1	10c carmine	24	18
Q3	PP1	20c dk grn	24	18
Q4	PP1	25c purple	24	18
Q5	PP1	50c dk bl	24	18
Q6	PP1	60c black	24	18
Q7	PP2	1 l vermilion	24	18
Q8	PP2	2 l carmine	24	18
Q9	PP2	3 l dk grn	24	18
Q10	PP2	4 l purple	24	18
Q11	PP2	10 l dk bl	24	18
		Nos. Q1-Q11 (11)	2.64	1.98

Value of used halves, Nos. Q1-Q11, each 15 cents.

See note preceding No. Q7 of Italy.

SCARPANTO

Overprinted "Scarpanto" in Black or Violet

1912-22 Wmk. 140 *Perf. 13½, 14*

1	A43	2c org brn	1.10	1.40
2	A48	5c green	15	*1.40*
3	A48	10c claret	15	*1.40*
4	A48	15c slate ('22)	2.25	*10.00*
5	A50	20c brn org ('21)	8.75	10.00
6	A49	25c blue	85	*1.40*
7	A49	40c brown	15	*1.40*
8	A49	50c violet	15	*1.40*

Unwmk.

9	A58	15c slate (V)	6.50	1.40
10	A50	20c brn org ('17)	21.00	24.00
		Nos. 1-10 (10)	41.05	53.80

No 9 Surcharged Like Calchi No. 11

1916 *Perf. 13½*

11	A58	20c on 15c slate	30	*5.00*

Ferrucci Issue

Overprinted in Red or Blue

1930 Wmk. 140 *Perf. 14*

12	A102	20c vio (R)	30	*60*
13	A103	25c dk grn (R)	30	*60*
14	A103	50c blk (R)	30	*60*
15	A103	1.25 l dp bl (R)	30	*60*
16	A104	5 l + 2 l dp car (Bl)	1.50	*1.90*
		Nos. 12-16 (5)	2.70	*4.30*

Garibaldi Issue
Overprinted in Red or Blue

1932
17 A138 10c brown 1.75 3.50
18 A138 20c red brn (Bl) 1.75 3.50
19 A138 25c dp grn 1.75 3.50
20 A138 30c bluish sl 1.75 3.50
21 A138 50c red vio (Bl) 1.75 3.50
22 A141 75c cop red (Bl) 1.75 3.50
23 A141 1.25 l dl bl 1.75 3.50
24 A141 1.75 l + 25c brn 1.75 3.50
25 A144 2.55 l + 50c org (Bl) 1.75 3.50
26 A145 5 l + 1 l dl vio 1.75 3.50
Nos. 17-26 (10) 17.50 35.00

SIMI

Overprinted "Simi" in Black or Violet

1912-21 Wmk. 140 *Perf. 13½, 14*
1 A43 2c org brn 1.10 1.40
2 A48 5c green 3.00 1.40
3 A48 10c claret 15 1.40
4 A48 15c slate ('21) 24.00 10.00
5 A50 20c brn org ('21) 8.75 10.00
6 A49 25c blue 32 1.40
7 A49 40c brown 15 1.40
8 A49 50c violet 15 1.40

Unwmk.
9 A58 15c slate (V) 7.25 1.40
10 A50 20c brn org ('17) 15.00 24.00
Nos. 1-10 (10) 59.87 53.80

No. 9 Surcharged Like Calchi No. 11

1916 *Perf. 13½*
11 A58 20c on 15c slate 4.00 5.00

Ferrucci Issue
Overprinted in Red or Blue

1930 Wmk. 140 *Perf. 14*
12 A102 20c vio (R) 30 60
13 A103 25c dk grn (R) 30 60
14 A103 50c blk (R) 30 60
15 A103 1.25 l dp bl (R) 30 60
16 A104 5 l + 2 l dp car (Bl) 1.50 1.90
Nos. 12-16 (5) 2.70 4.30

Garibaldi Issue
Overprinted in Red or Blue

1932
17 A138 10c brown 1.75 3.50
18 A138 20c red brn (Bl) 1.75 3.50
19 A138 25c dp grn 1.75 3.50
20 A138 30c bluish sl 1.75 3.50
21 A138 50c red vio (Bl) 1.75 3.50
22 A141 75c cop red (Bl) 1.75 3.50
23 A141 1.25 l dl bl 1.75 3.50
24 A141 1.75 l + 25c brn 1.75 3.50
25 A144 2.55 l + 50c org (Bl) 1.75 3.50
26 A145 5 l + 1 l dl vio 1.75 3.50
Nos. 17-26 (10) 17.50 35.00

STAMPALIA

Overprinted "Stampalia" in Black or Violet

1912-21 Wmk. 140 *Perf. 13½, 14*
1 A43 2c org brn 1.10 1.40
2 A48 5c green 15 1.40
3 A48 10c claret 15 1.40
4 A48 15c slate ('21) 1.75 10.00
5 A50 20c brn org ('21) 6.50 10.00
6 A49 25c blue 15 1.40
7 A49 40c brown 15 1.40
8 A49 50c violet 15 1.40

Unwmk.
9 A58 15c slate (V) 7.00 1.40
10 A50 20c brn org ('17) 21.00 24.00
Nos. 1-10 (10) 38.10 53.80

No. 9 Surcharged Like Calchi No. 11

1916 *Perf. 13½*
11 A58 20c on 15c slate 30 5.00

Ferrucci Issue
Overprinted in Red or Blue

1930 Wmk. 140 *Perf. 14*
12 A102 20c vio (R) 30 60
13 A103 25c dk grn (R) 30 60
14 A103 50c blk (R) 30 60
15 A103 1.25 l dp bl (R) 30 60
16 A104 5 l + 2 l dp car (Bl) 1.50 1.90
Nos. 12-16 (5) 2.70 4.30

Garibaldi Issue
Overprinted in Red or Blue

1932
17 A138 10c brown 1.75 3.50
18 A138 20c red brn (Bl) 1.75 3.50
19 A138 25c dp grn 1.75 3.50
20 A138 30c bluish sl 1.75 3.50
21 A138 50c red vio (Bl) 1.75 3.50
22 A141 75c cop red (Bl) 1.75 3.50
23 A141 1.25 l dull blue 1.75 3.50
24 A141 1.75 l + 25c brn 1.75 3.50
25 A144 2.55 l + 50c org (Bl) 1.75 3.50
26 A145 5 l + 1 l dl vio 1.75 3.50
Nos. 17-26 (10) 17.50 35.00

TRIESTE

A free territory (1947-1954) on the Adriatic Sea between Italy and Yugoslavia. In 1954 the territory was divided, Italy acquiring the northern section and seaport, Yugoslavia the southern section (Zone B).

Catalogue values for all unused stamps in this country are for Never Hinged items.

ZONE A

Issued jointly by the Allied Military Government of the United States and Great Britain

Stamps of Italy 1945-47 Overprinted:

A.M.G. F.T.T. — a
A.M.G. F.T.T. — b
A.M.G. F.T.T. — c

1947, Oct. 1 Wmk. 277 *Perf. 14*
1 A259(a) 25c brt bl grn 15 28
2 A255(a) 50c dp vio 15 28
3 A257(a) 1 l dk grn 15 15
4 A258(a) 2 l dk cl brn 15 15
5 A259(a) 3 l red 15 15
6 A259(a) 4 l red org 15 15
7 A256(a) 5 l deep blue 24 15
8 A257(a) 6 l dp vio 30 15
9 A255(a) 10 l slate 30 15
10 A257(a) 15 l deep blue 55 15
11 A259(a) 20 l dk red vio 30 15
12 A260(b) 25 l dk grn 2.25 1.90
13 A260(b) 50 l dk vio brn 3.50 1.40

Perf. 14x13½
14 A261(c) 100 l car lake 14.00 5.75
Nos. 1-14 (14) 22.34 10.96

The letters "F. T. T." are the initials of "Free Territory of Trieste."

Italy Nos. 486-488 Ovptd. Type "a"

1948, Mar. 1 *Perf. 14*
15 A255 8 l dk green 2.25 2.75
16 A256 10 l red org 6.75 15
17 A259 30 l dk blue 80.00 2.25

Italy Nos. 495 to 506 Overprinted

A.M.G.-F.T.T. — d

1948, July 1
18 A272 3 l dk brn 24 15
19 A272 4 l red vio 15 15
20 A272 5 l deep blue 18 15
21 A272 6 l dp yel grn 35 25
22 A272 8 l brown 24 20
23 A272 10 l org red 35 15
24 A272 12 l dk gray grn 45 1.10
25 A272 15 l gray blk 7.75 7.00
26 A272 20 l car rose 12.00 7.00
27 A272 30 l brt ultra 75 1.10
28 A272 50 l violet 6.00 11.00
29 A272 100 l bl blk 30.00 47.50
Nos. 18-29 (12) 58.46 75.75

Italy, Nos. 486 to 488, Overprinted in Carmine

1948, Sept. 8
30 A255 8 l dk green 30 24
31 A256 10 l red org 30 24
32 A259 30 l dk blue 1.65 2.25
Nos. 30-32,C17-C19 (6) 4.00 4.88

The overprint is embossed.

Italy, No. 507, Overprinted Type "d" in Carmine

1948, Oct. 15
33 A273 15 l dk green 1.25 1.10

Italy, No. 508, Overprinted in Green

A.M.G. F.T.T. — e

1948, Nov. 15
34 A274 15 l dk brown 3.00 1.10

Italy, No. 509, Overprinted Type "d" in Red

1949, May 2 Wmk. 277 *Perf. 14*
35 A275 20 l dk brown 6.50 1.90

Italy, Nos. 510 to 513, Overprinted

A.M.G. F.T.T. — f

1949, May 2 Buff Background
36 A276 5 l red brown 45 85
37 A276 15 l dk green 11.00 12.50
38 A276 20 l dp red brn 4.00 1.25
39 A276 50 l dk blue 17.50 12.00

Italy, No. 514, Overprinted Type "d" in Red

1949, May 2
40 A277 50 l brt ultra 4.00 5.00

Italy, No. 518, Overprinted Type "d" in Red

1949, May 30
41 A279 100 l brown 57.50 87.50

Italy, Nos. 515-517, Ovptd. Type "f"

1949, June 15
42 A278 5 l dk green 7.00 8.75
43 A278 15 l violet 8.00 12.50
44 A278 20 l brown 12.50 16.00

Italy, Nos. 519 and 520, Overprinted Type "e" in Carmine

1949, July 16
45 A280 20 l gray 8.75 2.75
46 A281 20 l brown 7.25 2.75

Italy, No. 521 Overprinted in Green

AMG-FTT — g

1949, June 8
47 A282 20 l brown red 3.50 2.00

Italy, No. 522, Overprinted Type "f" in Carmine

1949, July 8
49 A283 20 l violet 17.50 5.00

Italy, No. 523 Overprinted Type "e", without Periods, in Black

1949, Aug. 27
50 A284 20 l violet blue 7.75 3.25

Italy, No. 524 Ovptd. Type "f"

1949, Aug. 27
51 A285 20 l violet 17.50 13.00

Italy, No. 525, Overprinted Type "d" in Green

1949, Sept. 10
52 A286 20 l red 6.25 3.75

Italy Nos. 526 and 527 Overprinted

AMG-FTT — h

Wmk. 277
1949, Nov. 7 Photo. *Perf. 14*
53 A287 20 l rose car 3.00 2.50
54 A288 50 l deep blue 9.00 7.50

Same Overprint on No. 528

1949, Nov. 7
55 A289 20 l dp grn 3.25 2.75

Same Overprint on No. 529

1949, Nov. 7
56 A290 20 l brt blue 3.25 2.75

Same Overprint in Red on No. 530

1949, Dec. 28
57 A291 20 l violet blk 3.25 2.00

Same Overprint in Black on Italian Stamps of 1945-48

1949-50 Photo.
58 A257 1 l dk green 18 15
59 A258 2 l dk cl brn 18 15
60 A259 3 l red 18 15
61 A256 5 l deep blue 22 15
62 A257 6 l dp violet 18 15
63 A255 8 l dk green 6.50 9.00
64 A256 10 l red org 30 15
65 A257 15 l deep blue 1.25 35
66 A259 20 l dk red vio 48 15
67 A260 25 l dk grn ('50) 13.00 1.90
68 A260 50 l dk vio brn ('50) 25.00 90

Engr.
69 A261 100 l car lake 50.00 6.00
Nos. 58-69 (12) 97.47 19.20

Issue dates: 3 l, 20 l, Oct. 21. 5 l, Nov. 5. 10 l, Nov. 7. 100 l, Nov. 23. 15 l, Nov. 28. 1 l, 2 l, 6 l, 8 l, Dec. 28. 50 l, Jan. 19. 25 l, Feb. 25.

Italy, No. 531, Overprinted Type "g" in Carmine

1950, Apr. 12
70 A292 20 l brown 2.50 1.50

Same Overprint in Carmine on Italy, No. 532

1950, Apr. 29
71 A293 20 l vio gray 1.75 1.65

Same Overprint in Carmine on Italy, Nos. 533 and 534

1950, May 22
72 A294 20 l olive green 2.00 1.65
73 A295 55 l blue 7.50 12.00

Italy, Nos. 535 and 536, Overprinted Type "h" in Black

1950, May 29
74 A296 20 l violet 2.25 1.65
75 A296 55 l blue 8.00 12.00

Italy, No. 537, Overprinted Type "g" in Carmine

1950, July 10
76 A297 20 l gray grn 2.75 2.00

Same Overprint in Carmine on Italy, Nos. 538-539

1950, July 15
77 A298 20 l purple 5.75 5.00
78 A298 55 l blue 18.00 25.00

Italy, No. 540, Overprinted Type "h"

1950, July 22
79 A299 20 l brown 2.75 2.00

Italy, No. 541 Overprinted in Carmine

AMG FTT — i

1950, July 29
80 A300 20 l dk grn 2.75 2.00

Italy, No. 542, Overprinted Type "g"

1950, Aug. 21
81 A301 20 l chnt brn 2.50 2.00

Italy, Nos. 473A and 474, Overprinted

1950, Aug. 27
82 A257 15 l deep blue 1.75 1.65
83 A259 20 l dk red vio 1.75 60

Trieste Fair.

Italy, No. 543, Overprinted Type "i" in Carmine

1950, Sept. 11
84 A302 20 l indigo 1.25 1.10

Italy Nos. 544-546, Ovptd. Type "h"

1950, Sept. 16 Wmk. 277 *Perf. 14*
85 A303 5 l dp cl & grn 80 *2.25*
86 A303 20 l brn & grn 3.50 2.25
87 A303 55 l dp ultra & brn 24.00 *27.50*

Same, in Black, on Italy No. 547

1950, Sept. 16
88 A304 20 l ol brn & red brn 2.50 1.65

Same, in Black, on Italy No. 548

1950, Sept. 16
89 A305 20 l cr & gray blk 2.25 1.65

Italy, Nos. 549 to 565, Overprinted Type "g" in Black

1950, Oct. 20
90 A306 50c vio bl 15 15
91 A306 1 l dk bl vio 15 15
92 A306 2 l sepia 15 15
93 A306 5 l dk gray 15 15
94 A306 6 l chocolate 25 15
95 A306 10 l dp grn 25 15
96 A306 12 l dp bl grn 35 *1.00*
97 A306 15 l dk gray bl 1.00 15
98 A306 20 l bl vio 1.00 15
99 A306 25 l brn org 2.00 15
100 A306 30 l magenta 75 60
101 A306 35 l crimson 2.00 1.50
102 A306 40 l brown 1.25 80
103 A306 50 l violet 25 32
104 A306 55 l deep blue 25 *60*
105 A306 60 l red 6.75 3.75
106 A306 65 l dk green 25 *55*

Italy Nos. 566 and 567 Overprinted

k AMG-FTT

Perf. 14, 14x13½
Engr.
107 A306 100 l brown org 2.50 45
108 A306 200 l olive brn 2.50 *5.50*
Nos. 90-108 (19) 21.95 *16.42*

Italy Nos. 568 and 569 Overprinted Type "k" in Black

1951, Mar. 27 Photo. *Perf. 14*
109 A307 20 l red vio & red 2.00 2.50
110 A307 55 l ultra & bl 30.00 37.50

Italy No. 570 Overprinted Type "g"

1951, Apr. 2
111 A308 20 l dk grn 1.75 2.00

Same, on Italy No. 571

1951, Apr. 11
112 A309 20 l bl vio 1.65 *2.00*

Italy Nos. 572 and 573 Overprinted

1951, Apr. 12
113 A310(h) 20 l brown 1.65 *2.75*
114 A311(g) 55 l deep blue 3.25 *4.75*

Italy Nos. 574 to 576 Overprinted Type "h" in Black

1951, May 18 Fleur-de-Lis in Red
115 A312 5 l dk brown 5.75 *11.00*
116 A312 10 l Prus grn 5.75 *11.00*
117 A312 15 l vio bl 5.75 *11.00*

Italy No. 577 Overprinted

m AMG-FTT

1951, Apr. 26
118 A313 20 l purple 1.65 2.00

Italy No. 578 Overprinted Type "h"

1951, May 5
119 A314 20 l Prus green 2.75 3.25

Italy Nos. 579-580 Ovptd. Type "g"

1951, June 18
120 A315 20 l violet 60 *1.25*
121 A315 55 l brt blue 1.90 *3.50*

Nos. 94, 98 and 104 Overprinted

FIERA di TRIESTE 1951

1951, June 24
122 A306 6 l chocolate 42 *75*
123 A306 20 l blue violet 55 60
124 A306 55 l deep blue 70 *1.20*

Issued to publicize the Trieste Fair, 1951.

Italy No. 581 Overprinted

n AMG FTT

1951, July 23
125 A316 20 l brn & red brn 1.00 1.10

Italy Nos. 582 and 583 Overprinted Types "n" and "h" in Red

1951, July 23
126 A317(n) 20 l grnsh gray & blk 1.10 1.25
127 A318(h) 55 l vio bl & pale sal 2.50 *3.75*

Italy No. 584 Overprinted Type "g" in Carmine

1951, Aug. 23
128 A319 25 l gray blk 1.00 1.10

Overprint "g" on Italy No. 585

1951, Sept. 8
129 A320 25 l deep blue 1.00 1.10

Italy No. 586 Overprinted Type "h" in Red

1951, Sept. 15
130 A321 25 l dk brn 1.00 1.10

Italy Nos. 587-589 Overprinted in Blue

o AMG FTT

1951, Oct. 11
131 A322 10 l dk brn & gray 40 *75*
132 A322 25 l rose red & bl grn 75 75
133 A322 60 l vio bl & red org 1.10 1.50

Italy Nos. 590-591 Overprinted

p AMG FTT

1951, Oct. 31 Photo.
Overprint Spaced to Fit Design
134 A323 10 l green 75 90
135 A324 25 l vio gray 75 90

Italy Nos. 592-593 Ovptd. Type "k"

1951, Nov. 21
136 A325 10 l ol & dull grn 80 1.25
137 A326 25 l dull green 1.00 80

Italy Nos. 594-596 Overprinted Types "k" or "p" in Black

1951, Nov. 23
Overprint "p" Spaced to Fit Design
138 A327(p) 10 l vio brn & dk grn 52 *90*
139 A327(k) 25 l red brn & dk brn 90 90
140 A327(p) 60 l dp grn & ind 1.40 1.90

Italy No. 597 Overprinted Type "p"

1952, Jan. 28 Wmk. 277 *Perf. 14*
Overprint Spaced to Fit Design
141 A328 25 l gray & gray blk 1.00 70

Italy No. 598 Overprinted Type "k"

1952, Feb. 2
142 A329 25 l dl grn & ol bis 1.00 70

Same on Italy No. 599

1952, Mar. 26
143 A330 25 l brn & sl blk 85 70

Same on Italy No. 600

1952, Apr. 12
144 A331 60 l ultra 2.50 *3.25*

Same on Italy No. 601

1952, Apr. 16
145 A332 25 l dp orange 75 15

Stamps of Italy Overprinted "AMG FTT" in Various Sizes and Arrangements
On Nos. 602-603

1952, June 14 Wmk. 277 *Perf. 14*
146 A333 25 l blk & red brn 65 60
147 A333 60 l blk & ultra 1.10 *1.75*

On No. 604

1952, June 7
148 A334 25 l bright blue 90 70

On No. 605

1952, June 14
149 A335 25 l black & yellow 90 70

On No. 606

1952, June 19
150 A336 25 l bl gray, red & dk bl (R) 90 70

On No. 607

1952, June 28
151 A337 25 l dp grn, dk brn & red 90 70

On No. 608

1952, Sept. 6
152 A338 25 l dark green 90 70

On No. 609 in Bronze

1952, Sept. 20
153 A339 25 l purple 90 70

On No. 610

1952, Oct. 4
154 A340 25 l gray 90 70

On No. 611

1952, Oct. 1
155 A341 60 l vio bl & dk bl 2.25 *3.25*

On No. 612

1952, Nov. 21 *Perf. 13*
156 A342 25 l brn & dk brn 90 70

On Nos. 613-615

1952, Nov. 3 *Perf. 14*
157 A343 10 l dk green 20 35
158 A344 25 l blk & dk brn 80 30
159 A344 60 l blk & blue 80 *1.50*

On Nos. 616-617

1952, Dec. 6
160 A345 25 l dk green 90 70
161 A346 25 l brown 90 70

On No. 618

1953, Jan. 5
162 A347 25 l gray blk & dk bl (Bl) 90 70

On Nos. 601A-601B

1952, Dec. 31
163 A332a 60 l ultra (G) 75 *1.25*
164 A332 80 l brown car 1.65 50

On No. 621

1953, Feb. 21
165 A349 25 l car lake 90 70

On No. 622

1953, Apr. 24
166 A350 25 l violet 90 70

On No. 623

1953, Apr. 30
167 A351 25 l violet 90 70

On No. 624

1953, May 30
168 A352 25 l dark brown 90 70

On No. 625

1953, June 27
169 A353 25 l brn & dull red 90 70

On Nos. 626-633

1953-54
170 A354 5 l gray 15 15
171 A354 10 l org ver 25 15
172 A354 12 l dull grn 25 18
172A A354 13 l brt lil rose ('54) 25 18
173 A354 20 l brown 25 15
174 A354 25 l purple 25 15
175 A354 35 l rose car 50 *90*
176 A354 60 l blue 60 *1.25*
177 A354 80 l org brn 65 *1.40*
Nos. 170-177 (9) 3.15 *4.51*

Issue dates: 13 l, Feb. 1. Others, June 16.

Italy, Nos. 554, 558 and 564 Overprinted in Red or Green

FIERA DI TRIESTE AMG FTT 1953

1953, June 27
178 A306 10 l dp green (R) 40 *65*
179 A306 25 l brown org 50 40
180 A306 60 l red 60 1.00

5th International Sample Fair of Trieste.

On No. 634

1953, July 11
181 A355 25 l blue green 95 70

On Nos. 635-636

1953, July 16
182 A356 25 l dark brown 45 50
183 A356 60 l deep blue 70 1.00

On Nos. 637-638

1953, Aug. 6
184 A357 25 l org & Prus bl 1.00 70
185 A357 60 l lil rose & dk vio bl 3.00 3.25

On No. 639

1953, Aug. 13
186 A358 25 l dk brn & dl grn 90 70

On No. 640

1953, Sept. 5
187 A359 25 l dk gray & brn 90 70

On Nos. 641-646

1954, Jan. 26
188 A360 10 l dk brn & red brn 25 32
189 A361 12 l lt bl & gray 30 50
190 A361 20 l brn org & dk brn 40 35
191 A360 25 l dk grn & pale bl 40 18
192 A361 35 l cream & brn 40 *80*
193 A361 60 l bl grn & ind 55 *1.00*
Nos. 188-193 (6) 2.30 *3.15*

On Nos. 647-648

1954, Feb. 11
194 A362 25 l dk brn & choc 45 52
195 A362 60 l bl & ultra 65 1.00

On Nos. 649-650

1954, Feb. 25
196 A363 25 l purple 42 35
197 A363 60 l dp bl grn 95 *1.50*

On No. 651

1954, Mar. 20
198 A364 25 l purple 90 48

On No. 652

1954, Apr. 24
199 A365 25 l gray blk 90 70

On No. 653

1954, June 1
200 A366 25 l gray, org brn & blk 90 70

On No. 654

1954, June 19
201 A367 25 l dk grnsh gray 90 70

On Nos. 655-656

1954, July 8
202 A368 25 l red brown 42 55
203 A368 60 l gray green 95 1.25

Nos. 644, 646 With Additional Overprint

FIERA DI TRIESTE 1954

1954, June 17
204 A360 25 l dk grn & pale bl 45 52
205 A361 60 l bl grn & ind 65 1.00

International Sample Fair of Trieste.

On No. 657

1954, Sept. 6
206 A369 25 l dp grn & red 90 70

On Nos. 658-659

1954, Oct. 30

207 A370 25 l rose red 32 42
208 A370 60 l blue 55 65

OCCUPATION AIR POST STAMPS

Air Post Stamps of Italy, 1945-47, Overprinted Type "c" in Black

1947, Oct. 1 Wmk. 277 *Perf. 14*

C1 AP59 1 l slate bl 20 30
C2 AP60 2 l dk blue 25 30
C3 AP60 5 l dk green 1.00 *1.50*
C4 AP59 10 l car rose 1.00 *1.50*
C5 AP60 25 l brown 1.25 *2.00*
C6 AP59 50 l violet 5.75 2.25
Nos. C1-C6 (6) 9.45 *7.85*

Italy, Nos. C116 to C121, Overprinted Type "b" in Black

1947, Nov. 19

C7 AP61 6 l dp violet 60 *1.00*
C8 AP61 10 l dk car rose 60 *1.00*
C9 AP61 20 l dp org 3.50 2.75
C10 AP61 25 l aqua 60 *1.65*
C11 AP61 35 l brt blue 60 *1.65*
C12 AP61 50 l lilac rose 3.50 1.65
Nos. C7-C12 (6) 9.40 *9.70*

Italy, Nos. C123 to C126, Overprinted Type "f" in Black

1948

C13 AP65 100 l green 27.50 2.75
C14 AP65 300 l lil rose 15.00 *15.00*
C15 AP65 500 l ultra 20.00 *20.00*
C16 AP65 1000 l dk brown 150.00 *190.00*

Issue date: Nos. C13-C15, Mar. 1.

Italy, No. C110, C113 and C114, Overprinted in Black

(Reduced Illustration) 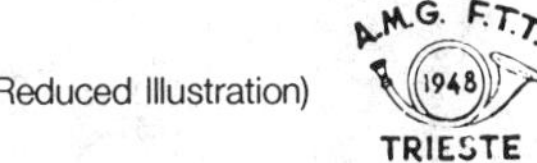

1948, Sept. 8

C17 AP59 10 l carmine rose 35 35
C18 AP60 25 l brown 70 *90*
C19 AP59 50 l violet 70 *90*

The overprint is embossed.

Italy Air Post Stamps of 1945-48 Overprinted Type "h" in Black

1949-52

C20 AP59 10 l car rose 30 15
C21 AP60 25 l brown ('50) 30 30
C22 AP59 50 l violet 30 32
C23 AP65 100 l green 55 30
C24 AP65 300 l lil rose ('50) 7.25 *9.00*
C25 AP65 500 l ultra ('50) 6.75 *12.00*
C26 AP65 1000 l dk brn ('52) 20.00 *22.50*
Nos. C20-C26 (7) 35.45 *44.57*

No. C26 is found in two perforations: 14 and 14x13.

Issue dates: 100 l, Nov. 7. 50 l, Dec. 5. 10 l, Dec. 28. 25 l, Jan. 23. 300 l, 500 l, Nov. 25. 1000 l, Feb. 18.

OCCUPATION SPECIAL DELIVERY STAMPS

Special Delivery Stamps of Italy 1946-48 Overprinted Type "c"

1947-48 Wmk. 277 *Perf. 14*

E1 SD9 15 l dk car rose 28 30
E2 SD8 25 l brt red org ('48) 10.50 5.50
E3 SD8 30 l dp vio 65 *90*
E4 SD9 60 l car rose ('48) 10.50 *10.00*

Issue dates: Oct. 1, 1947. Mar. 1, 1948.

Italy No. E26, Overprinted Type "d"

1948, Sept. 24

E5 A272 35 l violet 5.00 *3.50*

Italy No. E25, Overprinted Type "h"

1950, Sept. 27

E6 SD9 60 l car rose 1.75 1.40

Italy No. E32 Overprinted Type "k"

1952, Feb. 4

E7 SD8 50 l lilac rose 1.65 1.40

OCCUPATION AUTHORIZED DELIVERY STAMPS

Authorized Delivery Stamp of Italy, 1946 Overprinted Type "a" in Black

1947, Oct. 1 Wmk. 277 *Perf. 14*

EY1 AD3 1 l dark brown 24 15

Italy, No. EY7 Overprinted in Black **A.M.G. F.T.T.**

1947, Oct. 29

EY2 AD4 8 l bright red 2.50 65

Italy, No. EY8, Overprinted Type "a" in Black

1949, July 30

EY3 AD4 15 l violet 10.00 1.90

Same, Overprinted Type "h" in Black

1949, Nov. 7

EY4 AD4 15 l violet 90 15

Italy No. EY9 Overprinted Type "h" in Black

1952, Feb. 4

EY5 AD4 20 l rose violet 1.40 15

OCCUPATION POSTAGE DUE STAMPS

Postage Due Stamps of Italy, 1945-47, Overprinted Type "a"

1947, Oct. 1 Wmk. 277 *Perf. 14*

J1 D9 1 l red orange 25 28
J2 D10 2 l dk green 30 15
J3 D9 5 l violet 1.90 28
J4 D9 10 l dk blue 2.25 90
J5 D9 20 l car rose 9.75 90
J6 D10 50 l aqua 1.75 15
Nos. J1-J6 (6) 16.20 2.66

Same Overprint on Postage Due Stamps of Italy, 1947

1949

J7 D10 1 l red orange 40 25
J8 D10 3 l carmine 1.10 *1.25*
J9 D10 4 l brown 7.00 *7.00*
J10 D10 5 l violet 37.50 *7.00*
J11 D10 6 l vio blue 15.00 *14.00*
J12 D10 8 l rose vio 21.00 *22.50*
J13 D10 10 l deep blue 47.50 2.75
J14 D10 12 l golden brn 16.00 *14.00*
J15 D10 20 l lilac rose 12.00 80
Nos. J7-J15 (9) 157.50 *69.55*

Issue dates: 3 l, 4 l, 6 l, 8 l, 12 l, Jan. 24. Others, Apr. 15.

Postage Due Stamps of Italy, 1947-54, Overprinted Type "h"

1949-54

J16 D10 1 l red orange 18 15
J17 D10 2 l dk green 18 15
J18 D10 3 l car ('54) 30 70
J20 D10 5 l violet 38 20
J21 D10 6 l vio bl ('50) 30 15
J22 D10 8 l rose vio ('50) 30 15
J23 D10 10 l deep blue 38 15
J24 D10 12 l gldn brn ('50) 90 70
J25 D10 20 l lilac rose 1.50 48
J26 D10 25 l dk red ('54) 3.75 6.50
J27 D10 50 l aqua ('50) 2.50 15
J28 D10 100 l org yel ('52) 4.25 48
J29 D10 500 l dp bl & dk car ('52) 25.00 12.00
Nos. J16-J29 (13) 39.92 21.96

Issue dates: 5 l, 10 l, Nov. 7. 1 l, Nov. 22. 2 l, 20 l, Dec. 28. 6 l, 8 l, 12 l, May 16. 50 l, Nov. 25. 100 l, Nov. 11. 500 l, June 19. 3 l, Jan. 24. 25 l, Feb. 1.

OCCUPATION PARCEL POST STAMPS

See note preceding Italy No. Q7.

Parcel Post Stamps of Italy, 1946-48, Overprinted:

A.M.G. F.T.T.   **A.M.G. F.T.T.**

1947-48 Wmk. 277 *Perf. 13½*

Q1 PP4 1 l golden brn 24 *38*
Q2 PP4 2 l lt bl grn 35 *48*
Q3 PP4 3 l red org 40 *60*
Q4 PP4 4 l gray blk 50 *75*
Q5 PP4 5 l lil rose ('48) 1.40 *2.00*
Q6 PP4 10 l violet 2.75 *4.00*
Q7 PP4 20 l lilac brn 4.00 *6.00*
Q8 PP4 50 l rose red 6.50 *9.00*
Q9 PP4 100 l sapphire 8.00 *12.00*
Q10 PP4 200 l grn ('48) 325.00 *450.00*
Q11 PP4 300 l brn car ('48) 160.00 *225.00*
Q12 PP4 500 l brn ('48) 95.00 *140.00*
Nos. Q1-Q12 (12) 604.14 *850.21*

Halves Used

Q1-Q4 15
Q5 15
Q6-Q7 15
Q8 15
Q9 22
Q10 5.75
Q11 4.50
Q12 1.90

Issue dates: Nos. Q1-Q4, Q6-Q9, Oct. 1. Others, Mar. 1.

Parcel Post Stamps of Italy, 1946-54, Overprinted:

AMG-FTT   **AMG-FTT**

1949-54

Q13 PP4 1 l gldn brn ('50) 1.10 *1.25*
Q14 PP4 2 l lt bl grn ('51) 25 *28*
Q15 PP4 3 l red org ('51) 25 *28*
Q16 PP4 4 l gray blk ('51) 32 30
Q17 PP4 5 l lilac rose 35 *40*
Q18 PP4 10 l violet 45 28
Q19 PP4 20 l lil brn 48 28
Q20 PP4 30 l plum ('52) 65 *70*
Q21 PP4 50 l rose red ('50) 80 28
Q22 PP4 100 l saph ('50) 2.50 *3.00*
Q23 PP4 200 l green 22.50 *32.50*
Q24 PP4 300 l brn car ('50) 67.50 *85.00*
Q25 PP4 500 l brn ('51) 42.50 *50.00*

Perf. 13x13½

Q26 PP5 1000 l ultra ('54) 110.00 *150.00*
Nos. Q13-Q26 (14) 249.65 *324.55*

Halves Used

Q13-Q18, Q20 15
Q19, Q22 15
Q21 15
Q23 15
Q24 60
Q25 70
Q26 1.40

Pairs of Q18 exist with 5mm between overprints instead of 11mm. Value $800.

Issue dates: 20 l, 200 l, Nov. 22. 5 l, 10 l, Nov. 28. 300 l, Jan. 19. 50 l, Mar. 10. 1 l, Oct. 7. 100 l, Nov. 9. 500 l, Nov. 25. 2 l, 3 l, 4 l, Aug. 1. 30 l, Mar. 6. 1000 l, Aug. 12.

PARCEL POST AUTHORIZED DELIVERY STAMPS

For the payment of a special tax for the authorized delivery of parcels privately instead of through the post office. Both unused and used values are for complete stamps.

Parcel Post Authorized Delivery Stamps of Italy 1953 Overprinted in Black like Nos. Q13-Q26

1953, July 8 Wmk. 277

QY1 PAD1 40 l org red 2.50 *1.00*
QY2 PAD1 50 l ultra 2.50 *1.00*
QY3 PAD1 75 l brown 2.50 *1.00*
QY4 PAD1 110 l lilac rose 2.50 *1.00*

Halves Used

QY1 15
QY2 20
QY3-QY4 35

IVORY COAST

LOCATION — West coast of Africa, bordering on Gulf of Guinea

GOVT. — Republic

AREA — 127,520 sq. mi.

POP. — 13,107,000 (est. 1991)

CAPITAL — Yamoussoukro

The former French colony of Ivory Coast became part of French West Africa and used its stamps, starting in 1945. On December 4, 1958, Ivory Coast became a republic, with full independence on August 7, 1960.

100 Centimes = 1 Franc

Catalogue values for unused stamps in this country are for Never Hinged items, beginning with Scott 167 in the regular postage section, Scott B15 in the semi-postal section, Scott C14 in the airpost section, Scott J19 in the postage due section, Scott M1 in the military section, and Scott O1 in the official section.

Navigation and Commerce — A1

Perf. 14x13½

1892-1900 Typo. Unwmk.

Name of Colony in Blue or Carmine

1 A1 1c black, *lil bl* 60 60
2 A1 2c brown, *buff* 85 85
3 A1 4c claret, *lav* 1.50 1.25
4 A1 5c green, *grnsh* 4.50 2.75
5 A1 10c blk, *lavender* 5.25 3.75
6 A1 10c red ('00) 47.50 42.50
7 A1 15c blue, quadrille paper 7.00 4.25
8 A1 15c gray ('00) 3.75 1.25
9 A1 20c red, *green* 7.00 6.00
10 A1 25c black, *rose* 7.00 1.25
11 A1 25c bl ('00) 13.00 8.50
12 A1 30c brn, *bister* 10.50 8.50
13 A1 40c red, *straw* 8.00 7.00
14 A1 50c car, *rose* 37.50 24.00
15 A1 50c brn, *azure* ('00) 7.50 4.75
16 A1 75c deep vio, *org* 15.00 8.50
17 A1 1fr brnz grn, *straw* 17.50 15.00
Nos. 1-17 (17) 193.95 140.70

Perf. 13½x14 stamps are counterfeits.

For surcharges see Nos. 18-20, 37-41.

Nos. 12, 16-17 Surcharged in Black **0,05**

1904

18 A1 0,05c on 30c brn, *bis* 32.50 32.50
19 A1 0,10c on 75c vio, *org* 6.25 6.25
20 A1 0,15c on 1fr brnz grn, *straw* 6.50 6.50

Gen. Louis Faidherbe — A2

Oil Palm — A3

Dr. N. Eugène Ballay — A4

1906-07

Name of Colony in Red or Blue

21 A2 1c slate 60 60
22 A2 2c chocolate 60 60
23 A2 4c choc, *gray bl* 75 75
a. Name double 75.00 75.00
24 A2 5c green 75 75
25 A2 10c carmine (B) 2.50 1.90
26 A3 20c black, *azure* 3.25 2.75
27 A3 25c bl, *pinkish* 2.50 1.90
28 A3 30c choc, *pnksh* 5.25 2.75
30 A3 35c black, *yel* 5.25 1.75
31 A3 45c choc, *grnsh* 6.00 4.50
32 A3 50c deep violet 6.00 4.50
33 A3 75c blue, *org* 6.75 4.50
34 A4 1fr black, *azure* 15.00 11.50

35 A4 2fr blue, *pink* 22.50 15.00
36 A4 5fr car, *straw* (B) 37.50 32.50
Nos. 21-36 (15) 115.20 86.25

Stamps of 1892-1900 Surcharged in Carmine or Black

05 **10**

1912

37 A1 5c on 15c gray (C) 32 32
38 A1 5c on 30c brn, *bis* (C) 60 60
39 A1 10c on 40c red, *straw* 60 60
a. Pair, one without surcharge 62.50
40 A1 10c on 50c brn, *az* (C) 70 70
41 A1 10c on 75c dp vio, *org* 4.00 4.00
Nos. 37-41 (5) 6.22 6.22

Two spacings between the surcharged numerals are found on Nos. 37 to 41.

River Scene — A5

1913-35

42 A5 1c vio brn & vio 15 15
43 A5 2c brown & blk 15 15
44 A5 4c vio & vio brn 15 15
45 A5 5c yel grn & bl grn 15 15
46 A5 5c choc & ol brn ('22) 15 15
47 A5 10c red org & rose 35 30
48 A5 10c yel grn & bl grn ('22) 15 15
49 A5 10c car rose, *bluish* ('26) 15 15
50 A5 15c org & rose ('17) 32 15
51 A5 20c black & gray 25 15
52 A5 25c ultra & bl 2.75 1.90
53 A5 25c blk & vio ('22) 15 15
54 A5 30c choc & brn 60 40
55 A5 30c red org & rose ('22) 60 60
56 A5 30c lt bl & rose red ('26) 15 15
57 A5 30c dl grn & grn ('27) 15 15
58 A5 35c vio & org 25 15
59 A5 40c gray & bl grn 60 32
60 A5 45c red org & choc 25 18
61 A5 45c dp rose & mar ('34) 2.50 2.25
62 A5 50c black & vio 1.40 1.25
63 A5 50c ultra & bl ('22) 25 25
64 A5 50c ol grn & bl ('25) 15 15
65 A5 60c vio, *pnksh* ('25) 15 15
66 A5 65c car rose & ol grn ('26) 60 60
67 A5 75c brn & rose 25 22
68 A5 75c ind & ultra ('34) 1.25 1.10
69 A5 85c red vio & blk ('26) 60 60
70 A5 90c brn red & rose ('30) 5.00 5.00
71 A5 1fr org & black 55 50
72 A5 1.10fr dl grn & dk brn ('28) 2.50 2.50
73 A5 1.50fr lt bl & dp bl ('30) 3.25 2.50
74 A5 1.75fr lt ultra & mag ('35) 4.50 2.75
75 A5 2fr brn & blue 1.50 75
76 A5 3fr red vio ('30) 3.25 2.75
77 A5 5fr dk bl & choc 3.25 1.90
Nos. 42-77 (36) 38.42 30.87

Nos. 45, 47, 50 and 58 exist on both ordinary and chalky paper.

For surcharges see Nos. 78-91, B1.

Stamps and Type of 1913-34 Surcharged

60 **60**

1922-34

78 A5 50c on 45c dp rose & maroon ('34) 1.40 75
79 A5 50c on 75c indigo & ultra ('34) 75 75
80 A5 50c on 90c brn red & rose ('34) 75 75
81 A5 60c on 75c vio, *pnksh* 16 16
82 A5 65c on 15c orange & rose ('25) 50 50
83 A5 85c on 75c brown & rose ('25) 50 50
Nos. 78-83 (6) 4.06 3.41

Stamps and Type of 1913 Surcharged with New Value and Bars

1924-27

84 A5 25c on 2fr (R) 40 35
85 A5 25c on 5fr 40 35
86 A5 90c on 75c brn red & cer ('27) 50 40
87 A5 1.25fr on 1fr dk bl & ultra (R) ('26) 30 22
88 A5 1.50fr on 1fr lt bl & dk blue ('27) 60 50
89 A5 3fr on 5fr brn red & bl grn ('27) 1.25 1.25
90 A5 10fr on 5fr dl red & rose lil ('27) 6.75 6.25
91 A5 20fr on 5fr bl grn & ver ('27) 7.50 7.25
Nos. 84-91 (8) 17.70 16.57

Colonial Exposition Issue

Common Design Types

Name of Country in Black

1931 **Engr.** ***Perf. 12½***

92 CD70 40c deep green 1.25 1.25
93 CD71 50c violet 2.50 2.50
94 CD72 90c red orange 1.10 1.10
95 CD73 1.50fr dull blue 2.50 2.50

Côte d'Ivoire

Stamps of Upper Volta 1928, Overprinted

1933 ***Perf. 13½x14***

96 A5 2c brown & lilac 15 15
97 A5 4c blk & yellow 15 15
98 A5 5c ind & gray bl 22 18
99 A5 10c indigo & pink 25 22
100 A5 15c brown & blue 30 25
101 A5 20c brown & green 30 30
102 A6 25c brn & yellow 75 60
103 A6 30c dp grn & brn 90 75
104 A6 45c brown & blue 3.75 3.00
105 A6 65c indigo & bl 1.25 90
106 A6 75c black & lilac 1.50 1.10
107 A6 90c brn red & lil 1.25 1.10

Common Design Types pictured in section at front of book.

Overprinted

Côte d'Ivoire

108 A7 1fr brown & green 1.25 1.10
109 A7 1.50fr ultra & grysh 1.25 1.10

Surcharged **Côte d'Ivoire 1F.25**

110 A6 1.25fr on 40c blk & pink 1.10 75
111 A6 1.75fr on 50c blk & green 1.25 80
Nos. 96-111 (16) 15.62 12.45

Baoulé Woman — A6

Rapids on Comoe River — A9

Mosque at Bobo-Dioulasso — A7

Coastal Scene — A8

1936-44 ***Perf. 13***

112 A6 1c carmine rose 15 15
113 A6 2c ultramarine 15 15
114 A6 3c dp grn ('40) 15 15
115 A6 4c chocolate 15 15
116 A6 5c violet 15 15
117 A6 10c Prussian bl 15 15
118 A6 15c copper red 15 15
119 A7 20c ultramarine 15 15
120 A7 25c copper red 15 15
121 A7 30c blue green 15 15
122 A7 30c brown ('40) 15 15
123 A6 35c dp grn ('38) 15 15
124 A7 40c carmine rose 15 15
125 A7 45c brown 25 22
126 A7 45c blue grn ('40) 15 15
127 A7 50c plum 15 15
128 A7 55c dark vio ('38) 15 15
129 A8 60c car rose ('40) 15 15
130 A8 65c red brown 15 15
131 A8 70c red brn ('40) 22 22
132 A8 75c dark violet 25 15
133 A8 80c blk brn ('38) 30 30
134 A8 90c carmine rose 3.75 2.25
135 A8 90c dk grn ('39) 22 22
136 A8 1fr dark green 1.25 60
137 A8 1fr car rose ('38) 22 15
138 A8 1fr dk vio ('40) 15 15
139 A8 1.25fr copper red 22 15
140 A8 1.40fr ultra ('40) 15 15
141 A8 1.50fr ultramarine 15 15
141A A8 1.50fr grnsh blk ('44) 16 16
142 A8 1.60fr blk brn ('40) 35 35
143 A9 1.75fr carmine rose 16 15
144 A9 1.75fr dull bl ('38) 25 22
145 A9 2fr ultramarine 25 15
146 A9 2.25fr dark bl ('39) 35 35
147 A9 2.50fr rose red ('40) 40 40
148 A9 3fr green 35 22
149 A9 5fr chocolate 40 35
150 A9 10fr violet 52 45
151 A9 20fr copper red 1.25 90
Set value 12.50 9.25

Stamps of types A7-A9 without "RF" were issued in 1944, but were not placed on sale in the colony.

For surcharges see Nos. B8-B11.

Paris International Exposition Issue

Common Design Types

1937 ***Perf. 13***

152 CD74 20c deep vio 45 45
153 CD75 30c dark grn 45 45
154 CD76 40c car rose 60 60
155 CD77 50c dk brn & bl 45 45
156 CD78 90c red 45 45
157 CD79 1.50fr ultra 60 60
Nos. 152-157 (6) 3.00 3.00

Colonial Arts Exhibition Issue

Souvenir Sheet

Common Design Type

1937 ***Imperf.***

158 CD76 3fr sepia 2.00 2.00

Louis Gustave Binger — A10

1937 ***Perf. 13***

159 A10 65c red brown 15 15

Death of Governor General Binger; 50th anniv. of his exploration of the Niger.

Caillie Issue

Common Design Type

1939 **Engr.** ***Perf. 12½x12***

160 CD81 90c org brn & org 32 32
161 CD81 2fr bright violet 50 50
162 CD81 2.25fr ultra & dk bl 50 50

New York World's Fair Issue

Common Design Type

1939

163 CD82 1.25fr carmine lake 65 65
164 CD82 2.25fr ultramarine 65 65

Ebrié Lagoon and Marshal Pétain A11

1941

165 A11 1fr green 40
166 A11 2.50fr deep blue 40

It is doubtful whether Nos. 165-166 were placed in use.

For other stamps inscribed Cote d'Ivoire and Afrique Occidental Francaise see French West Africa Nos. 58, 72, 77.

Catalogue values for unused stamps in this section, from this point to the end of the section, are for Never Hinged items.

Republic

Elephant A12

President Felix Houphouet-Boigny A13

1959, Oct. 1 **Engr.** ***Perf. 13***

167 A12 10fr black & emerald 16 15
168 A12 25fr vio brn & olive 32 20
169 A12 30fr ol blk & grnsh bl 35 25

Imperforates

Most Ivory Coast stamps from 1959 onward exist imperforate in issued and trial colors, and also in small presentation sheets in issued colors.

1959, Dec. 4 **Unwmk.**

170 A13 25fr violet brown 30 20

Proclamation of the Republic, 1st anniv.

Bété Mask — A14

Designs: Masks of 5 tribes: Bété, Gueré, Baoulé, Senufo and Guro. #174-176 horiz.

1960 ***Perf. 13***

171 A14 50c pale brn & vio brn 15 15
172 A14 1fr violet & mag 15 15
173 A14 2fr ultra & bl grn 15 15
174 A14 4fr dk grn & org 15 15
175 A14 5fr ver & brown 15 15
176 A14 6fr dark brn & vio 15 15
177 A14 45fr dk grn & brn vio 60 22
178 A14 50fr dk brn & grnsh bl 65 25
179 A14 85fr car & slate grn 1.10 60
Set value 2.70 1.35

C.C.T.A. Issue
Common Design Type

1960, May 16 Engr. *Perf. 13*
180 CD106 25fr grnsh bl & vio 40 38

Emblem of the Entente — A14a

Blood Lilies — A16

Young Couple with Olive Branch and Globe — A15

1960, May 29 Photo. *Perf. 13x13½*
181 A14a 25fr multicolored 42 42

1st anniv. of the Entente (Dahomey, Ivory Coast, Niger and Upper Volta).

1961, Aug. 7 Engr. *Perf. 13*
182 A15 25fr emer, bis & blk 30 20

First anniversary of Independence.

1961-62

Designs: Various Local Plants & Orchids.

183 A16 5fr dk grn, red & orange ('62) 15 15
184 A16 10fr ultra, claret & yel 15 15
185 A16 15fr org, rose lil & green ('62) 20 15
186 A16 20fr brn, dk red & yel 25 16
187 A16 25fr grn, red brn & yel 38 20
188 A16 30fr blk, car & green 40 25
189 A16 70fr green, ver & yel 90 40
190 A16 85fr brn, lil, yel & grn 1.20 75
Nos. 183-190 (8) 3.63 2.21

Early Letter Carrier and Modern Mailman — A17

1961, Oct. 14 Unwmk. *Perf. 13*
191 A17 25fr choc, emer & bl 35 25

Issued for Stamp Day.

Ayamé Dam — A18

1961, Nov. 18 Engr.
192 A18 25fr grnsh bl, blk & grn 30 18

Swimming Race — A19

1961, Dec. 23 Unwmk. *Perf. 13*
193 A19 5fr shown 15 15
194 A19 20fr Basketball 20 15
195 A19 25fr Soccer 25 15
Set value 50 35

Abidjan Games, Dec. 24-31. See No. C17.

Palms — A20

1962, Feb. 5 Photo. *Perf. 12x12½*
196 A20 25fr brn, blue & org 30 18

Commission for Technical Co-operation in Africa South of the Sahara, 17th session, Abidjan, Feb. 5-16.

Fort Assinie and Assinie River — A21

1962, May 26 Engr. *Perf. 13*
197 A21 85fr Prus grn, grn & dl red brn 1.00 55

Centenary of the Ivory Coast post.

African and Malagasy Union Issue
Common Design Type

1962, Sept. 8 Photo. *Perf. 12½x12*
198 CD110 30fr multicolored 75 55

African and Malagasy Union, 1st anniv.

Fair Emblem, Cotton and Spindles — A22

1963, Jan. 26 Engr. *Perf. 13*
199 A22 50fr grn, brn org & sepia 45 25

Bouake Fair, Jan. 26-Feb. 4.

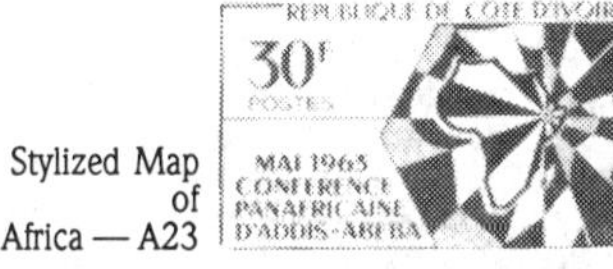

Stylized Map of Africa — A23

1963, May 25 Photo. *Perf. 12½x12*
200 A23 30fr ultra & emerald 40 40

Conference of African heads of state for African unity, Addis Ababa.

Hartebeest A24

UNESCO Emblem, Scales and Globe A25

Designs: 1fr, Yellow-backed duiker, horiz. 2fr, Potto. 4fr, Beecroft's hyrax, horiz. 5fr, Water chevrotain. 15fr, Forest hog, horiz. 20fr, Wart hog, horiz. 25fr, Bongo (antelope). 45fr, Cape hunting dogs, or hyenas, horiz. 50fr, Black-and-white colobus (monkey).

1963-64 Engr. *Perf. 13*
201 A24 1fr choc, grn & yellow ('64) 15 15
202 A24 2fr blk, dk bl, gray ol & brown ('64) 15 15
203 A24 4fr red brn, dk bl, brn & black ('64) 15 15
204 A24 5fr sl grn, brn & citron ('64) 15 15
205 A24 10fr ol grn & ocher 16 15
206 A24 15fr red brn, grn & black ('64) 25 15
207 A24 20fr red org grn & blk 40 16
208 A24 25fr red brn & green 42 16
209 A24 45fr choc, bl grn & yel green 75 42
210 A24 50fr red brn, grn & blk 80 40
a. Min. sheet of 4, #205, 207, 209-210 1.75 1.75
Nos. 201-210 (10) 3.38
Set value 1.55

See Nos. 218-220.

1963, Dec. 10 Unwmk.
211 A25 85fr dk bl, blk & org 80 50

Universal Declaration of Human Rights, 15th anniv.

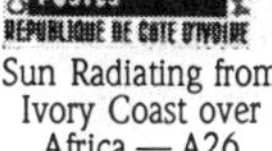

Sun Radiating from Ivory Coast over Africa — A26

Weather Station and Balloon — A27

1964, Mar. 17 Photo. *Perf. 12x12½*
212 A26 30fr grn, dl vio & red 35 20

Inter-African Conference of Natl. Education Ministers.

1964, Mar. 23 *Perf. 13x12½*
213 A27 25fr multicolored 30 22

World Meteorological Day, Mar. 23.

Physician Vaccinating Child — A28

1964, May 8 Engr. *Perf. 13*
214 A28 50fr dk brn, bl & red 55 35

Issued to honor the National Red Cross.

Wrestlers, Globe and Torch — A29

1964, June 27 Unwmk. *Perf. 13*
215 A29 35fr Globe, torch, athletes, vert. 45 35
216 A29 65fr shown 80 65

18th Olympic Games, Tokyo, Oct. 10-25.

Europafrica Issue, 1964
Common Design Type

Design: 30fr, White man and black man beneath tree of industrial symbols.

1964, July 20 Photo. *Perf. 12x13*
217 CD116 30fr multicolored 30 20

Animal Type of 1963-64

Designs: 5fr, Manatee, horiz. 10fr, Pygmy hippopotamus, horiz. 15fr, Royal antelope.

1964, Oct. 17 Engr. *Perf. 13*
218 A24 5fr yel grn, sl grn & brn 15 15
219 A24 10fr sep, Prus grn & dp cl 20 15
220 A24 15fr lil rose, grn & org brn 35 20
Set value 35

Co-operation Issue
Common Design Type

1964, Nov. 7 Unwmk. *Perf. 13*
221 CD119 25fr grn, dk brn & red 30 22

Korhogo Mail Carriers with Guard, 1914 — A30

1964, Nov. 28 Engr.
222 A30 85fr blk, brn, bl & brn red 80 60

Issued for Stamp Day.

Potter — A31

Artisans: 10fr, Wood carvers. 20fr, Ivory carver. 25fr, Weaver.

1965, Mar. 27 Engr. *Perf. 13*
223 A31 5fr mag, green & blk 15 15
224 A31 10fr red lil, grn & blk 15 15
225 A31 20fr bis, dp bl & dk brn 20 15
226 A31 25fr brn, olive & car 25 16
Set value 64 38

Unloading Mail, 1900 — A32

1965, Apr. 24 Unwmk. *Perf. 13*
227 A32 30fr multicolored 35 22

Issued for Stamp Day.

Values quoted in this catalogue are for stamps graded Fine-Very Fine and with no faults. An illustrated guide to grade is provided beginning on Page 8A.

ITU Emblem, Old and New Telecommunication Equipment — A32a

1965, May 17

228 A32a 85fr mar, brt grn & dk bl	90	60

ITU, centenary.

Abidjan Railroad Station — A33

1965, June 12 **Engr.** ***Perf. 13***

229 A33 30fr mag, bl & brn ol	35	22

Pres. Felix Houphouet-Boigny and Map of Ivory Coast — A34

1965, Aug. 7 **Photo.** ***Perf. 12½x13***

230 A34 30fr multicolored	35	22

Fifth anniversary of Independence.

Hammerhead Stork — A35

Baoulé Mother and Child, Carved in Wood — A37

Mail Train, 1906 — A36

Birds: 1fr, Bruce's green pigeon, horiz. 2fr, Spur-winged goose, horiz. 5fr, Stone partridge. 15fr, White-breasted guinea fowl. 30fr, Namaqua dove, horiz. 50fr, Lizard buzzard, horiz. 75fr, Yellow-billed stork. 90fr, Forest (or Latham's) francolin.

1965-66 **Engr.** ***Perf. 13***

231 A35 1fr yel grn, pur & yellow ('66)	15	15
232 A35 2fr slate grn, blk & red ('66)	15	15
233 A35 5fr dk ol, dk brn & brn red ('66)	15	15
234 A35 10fr red lil, blk & red brown	15	15
235 A35 15fr sl grn, gray & ver	20	15
236 A35 30fr sl grn, mar & red brown	40	20
237 A35 50fr brn, blk & chky bl	60	35
238 A35 75fr org, mar & sl grn	80	40
239 A35 90fr emerald, blk & brown ('66)	1.25	65
Nos. 231-239 (9)	3.85	2.35

1966, Mar. 26 **Engr.** ***Perf. 13***

240 A36 30fr grn, blk & mar	38	22

Issued for Stamp Day.

1966, Apr. 9 **Unwmk.**

Designs: 10fr, Unguent vessel, Wamougo mask lid. 20fr, Atié carved drums. 30fr, Bété female ancestral figure.

241 A37 5fr blk & emerald	15	15
242 A37 10fr purple & blk	16	15
243 A37 20fr orange & blk	35	22
244 A37 30fr red & black	45	25
Set value		66

Intl. Negro Arts Festival, Dakar, Senegal, Apr. 1-24.

Hotel Ivoire — A38

1966, Apr. 30 **Engr.** ***Perf. 13***

245 A38 15fr bl, grn, red & ol	20	15

Farm Tractor A39

1966, Aug. 7 **Photo.** ***Perf. 12½x12***

246 A39 30fr multicolored	30	22

6th anniversary of independence.

Uniformed Teacher and Villagers A40

1966, Sept. 1 **Engr.** ***Perf. 13***

247 A40 30fr dk red, ind & dk brn	30	22

National School of Administration.

Veterinarian Treating Cattle — A41

1966, Oct. 22 **Engr.** ***Perf. 13***

248 A41 30fr ol, bl & dp brn	35	25

Campaign against cattle plague.

Man, Waves, UNESCO Emblem — A42

Delivery of Gift Parcels — A43

1966, Nov. 14 **Engr.** ***Perf. 13***

249 A42 30fr dp bl & vio brn	35	25

UNESCO, 20th anniv.

1966, Dec. 11 **Engr.** ***Perf. 13***

250 A43 30fr dk bl, brn & blk	35	25

UNICEF, 20th anniv.

Bouaké Hospital and Red Cross — A44

1966, Dec. 20

251 A44 30fr red brn, red & lil	35	25

Sikorsky S-43 Seaplane and Boats — A45

1967, Mar. 25 **Engr.** ***Perf. 13***

252 A45 30fr ind, bl grn & brn	40	25

Stamp Day; 30th anniv. of the Sikorsky S-43 flying boat route.

Pineapple Harvest A46

1967 **Engr.** ***Perf. 13***

253 A46 20fr shown	20	15
254 A46 30fr Cabbage tree	30	15
255 A46 100fr Bananas	1.10	60

Issue dates: 30fr, June 24; others, Mar. 25.

Genie, Protector of Assamlangangan — A47

1967, July 31 **Engr.** ***Perf. 13***

256 A47 30fr grn, blk & mar	30	15

Intl. PEN Club (writers' organization), 25th Congress, Abidjan, July 31-Aug. 5.

Old and New Houses A48

1967, Aug. 7 **Photo.** ***Perf. 12½x12***

257 A48 30fr multicolored	30	16

7th anniversary of independence.

Lions Emblem and Elephant's Head — A49

1967, Sept. 2 **Photo.** ***Perf. 12½x13***

258 A49 30fr lt bl & multi	40	30

50th anniversary of Lions International.

Monetary Union Issue
Common Design Type

1967, Nov. 4 **Engr.** ***Perf. 13***

259 CD125 30fr car, sl grn & blk	25	20

Allegory of French Recognition of Ivory Coast — A50

Tabou Radio Station — A51

1967, Nov. 17 **Photo.** ***Perf. 13x12½***

260 A50 90fr multicolored	80	50

Days of Recognition, 20th anniv. See No. 298.

1968, Mar. 9 **Engr.** ***Perf. 13***

261 A51 30fr dk grn, brn & brt grn	35	20

Issued for Stamp Day.

Cotton Mill — A52

Designs: 5fr, Palm oil extraction plant. 15fr, Abidjan oil refinery. 20fr, Unloading raw cotton and spinning machine, vert. 30fr, Flour mill. 50fr, Cacao butter extractor. 70fr, Instant coffee factory, vert. 90fr, Saw mill and timber.

1968 **Engr.** ***Perf. 13***

262 A52 5fr ver, sl grn & blk	15	15
263 A52 10fr dk grn, gray & olive bister	15	15
264 A52 15fr ver, lt ultra & blk	20	15
265 A52 20fr Prus blue & choc	20	15
266 A52 30fr dk grn, brt bl & brown	35	16
267 A52 50fr red, brt grn & blk	45	22
268 A52 70fr dk brn, bl & brn	65	40
269 A52 90fr dp bl, blk & brn	90	42
Nos. 262-269 (8)	3.05	
Set value		1.50

Issue dates: 5fr, 15fr, June 8. 10fr, 20fr, 90fr, Mar. 23. Others, Oct. 5.

Canoe Race — A53

1968, Apr. 6 Engr. *Perf. 13*
270 A53 30fr shown 35 20
271 A53 100fr Runners 1.00 60

19th Olympic Games, Mexico City, Oct. 12-27.

Queen Pokou Sacrificing her Son — A54

1968, Aug. 7 Photo. *Perf. 12½x12*
272 A54 30fr multicolored 30 16

8th anniversary of independence.

Vaccination, WHO Emblem and Elephant's Head — A55

1968, Sept. 28 Engr. *Perf. 13*
273 A55 30fr choc, brt bl & mar 35 20

WHO, 20th anniversary.

Antelope in Forest — A56

1968, Oct. 26 Engr. *Perf. 13*
274 A56 30fr ultra, brn & olive 40 20

Protection of fauna and flora.

Abidjan Anthropological Museum and Carved Screen — A57

1968, Nov. 2
275 A57 30fr vio bl, ol & rose mag 30 16

Human Rights Flame and Statues of "Justitia" A58

1968, Nov. 9 Engr. *Perf. 13*
276 A58 30fr sl, org & dk brn 35 20

International Human Rights Year.

"Ville de Maranhao" at Grand Bassam A59

1969, Mar. 8 Engr. *Perf. 13*
277 A59 30fr brn, brt bl & grn 38 20

Issued for Stamp Day.

Opening of Hotel Ivoire, Abidjan — A60

1969, Mar. 29
278 A60 30fr ver, bl & grn 30 16

Carved Figure — A61

Mountains and Radio Tower, Man — A62

1969, July 5 Engr. *Perf. 13*
279 A61 30fr red lil, blk & red org 30 16

Ivory Coast art exhibition, Fine Arts Museum, Vevey, Switzerland, July 12-Sept. 22.

1969, Aug. 7 Engr. *Perf. 13*
280 A62 30fr dl brn, sl & grn 35 20

9th anniversary of independence.

Development Bank Issue
Common Design Type

Design: Development Bank emblem and Ivory Coast coat of arms.

1969, Sept. 6
281 CD130 30fr ocher, grn & mar 30 16

Arms of Bouake A63

Sport Fishing and SKAL Emblem A64

Coats of Arms: 15fr, Abidjan. 30fr, Ivory Coast.

1969 Photo. *Perf. 13*
282 A63 10fr multicolored 15 15
283 A63 15fr multicolored 15 15
284 A63 30fr multicolored 22 15
Set value 18

Issue dates: 10fr, Oct. 25; 15fr, Dec. 27; 30fr, Dec. 20.
See Nos. 335-336, designs A113, A297.

1969, Nov. 22 Engr. *Perf. 13*
285 A64 30fr shown 35 20
286 A64 100fr Vacation village, SKAL emblem 1.00 50

1st Intl. Congress in Africa of the SKAL Tourist Assoc., Abidjan, Nov. 23-28.

ASECNA Issue
Common Design Type

1969, Dec. 13 Engr. *Perf. 13*
287 CD132 30fr vermilion 30 16

University Center, Abidjan — A65

1970, Feb. 26 Engr. *Perf. 13*
288 A65 30fr indigo & yel grn 25 15

Higher education in Ivory Coast, 10th anniv.

Gabriel Dadié and Telegraph Operator A66

1970, Mar. 7 Engr. *Perf. 13*
289 A66 30fr dk red, sl grn & blk 25 15

Stamp Day; Gabriel Dadié (1891-1953) 1st native-born postal administrator.

University of Abidjan — A67

1970, Mar. 21 Photo.
290 A67 30fr Prus bl, dk pur & dk yel grn 25 15

3rd General Assembly of the Assoc. of French-language Universities (A.U.P.E.L.F.).

Safety Match Production — A68

1970, May 9 Engr. *Perf. 13*
291 A68 5fr shown 15 15
292 A68 20fr Textile industry 16 15
293 A68 50fr Shipbuilding 40 20
Set value 60 30

Radar, Classroom with Television — A69

1970, May 17
294 A69 40fr red, grn & gray ol 40 35

Issued for World Telecommunications Day.

UPU Headquarters Issue
Common Design Type

1970, May 20
295 CD133 30fr lil, brt grn & ol 35 16

UN Emblem, Lion, Antelopes and Plane — A70

1970, June 27 Engr. *Perf. 13*
296 A70 30fr dk red brn, ultra & dk green 38 25

25th anniversary of the United Nations.

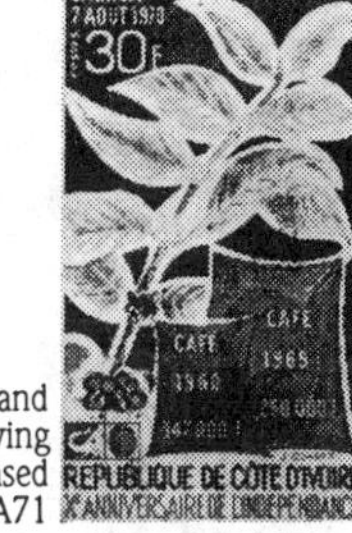

Coffee Branch and Bags Showing Increased Production — A71

1970, Aug. 7 Engr. *Perf. 13*
297 A71 30fr org, bluish grn & gray 25 15

Tenth anniversary of independence.

Type of 1967

1970, Oct. 29 Photo. *Perf. 12x12½*
298 A50 40fr multicolored 38 20

Ivory Coast Democratic Party, 5th Congress.

Power Plant at Uridi — A73

1970, Nov. 21 Engr. *Perf. 13*
299 A73 40fr multicolored 38 16

Independence, 10th Anniv. — A73a

Designs: Nos. 299A, 299D, Pres. Houphouet-Boigny, Gen. Charles DeGaulle. Nos. 299B, 299F, Pres. Houphouet-Boigny, elephants. Nos. 299C, 299E, Coat of arms.

1970, Nov. 27 Embossed *Perf. 10½*
Die Cut

299A A73a 300fr Silver
299B A73a 300fr Silver
299C A73a 300fr Silver
g. Pair, #299B-299C
299D A73a 1000fr Gold
299E A73a 1000fr Gold

Litho. & Embossed

299F A73a 1200fr Gold & multi
h. Pair, #299E-299F

Nos. 299B, 299F are airmail.

Postal Service Autobus, 1925 — A74

1971, Mar. 6 **Engr.** *Perf. 13*
300 A74 40fr dp grn, dk brn & gldn brn 35 16

Stamp Day.

Marginella Desjardini A75

Marine Life: 1fr, Aporrhaispes gallinae. 5fr, Neptunus validus. 10fr, Hermodice carunculata, vert. No. 305, Natica fanel, vert. No. 306, Goniaster cuspidatus, vert. No. 307, Xenorhora digitata. 25fr, Conus prometheus. 35fr, Polycheles typhlops, vert. No. 310, Conus genuanus. No. 311, Chlamys flabellum. 45fr, Strombus bubonius. 50fr, Enoplometopus callistus, vert. 65fr, Cypraea stercoraria.

1971-72 **Engr.** *Perf. 13*

301 A75	1fr	olive & multi	15	15
302 A75	5fr	red & multi	15	15
303 A75	10fr	emer & multi	15	15
304 A75	15fr	brt bl & multi	16	15
305 A75	15fr	dp car & multi ('72)	16	15
306 A75	20fr	ocher & car	20	15
307 A75	20fr	ver & multi ('72)	22	15
308 A75	25fr	dk car, rose brn & black ('72)	22	15
309 A75	35fr	yel & multi	30	16
310 A75	40fr	emer & multi	45	25
311 A75	40fr	brown & multi	38	20
312 A75	45fr	multi ('72)	40	25
313 A75	50fr	green & multi	60	38
314 A75	65fr	bl, rose brn & sl grn ('72)	60	40
		Nos. 301-314 (14)	4.14	
		Set value		2.30

Issue dates: Nos. 304, 306, 310, Apr. 24, 1971; 5fr, 35fr, 50fr, June 5, 1971; 1fr, 10fr, No. 311, Oct. 23, 1971; 25fr, 65fr, Jan. 29, 1972; Nos. 305, 307, 45fr, June 3, 1972.

Submarine Cable Station, 1891 — A76

1971, May 17
315 A76 100fr bl, ocher & olive 75 45

3rd World Telecommunications Day.

Apprentice and Lathe — A77

1971, June 19 **Engr.** *Perf. 13*
316 A77 35fr grn, slate & org brn 30 16

Technical instruction and professional training.

Map of Africa and Telecommunications System — A78

1971, June 26 *Perf. 13x12½*
317 A78 45fr magenta & multi 38 20

Pan-African Telecommunications system.

Bondoukou Market — A79

1971, Aug. 7 **Engr.** *Perf. 13*
Size: 48x27mm
318 A79 35fr ultra, brn & slate 30 16

11th anniv. of independence. See No. C46.

White, Black and Yellow Girls — A80

1971, Oct. 10 **Photo.** *Perf. 13*
319 A80 40fr shown 35 16
320 A80 45fr Boys around globe 38 20

Intl. Year Against Racial Discrimination.

Gaming Table and Lottery Tickets A81

1971, Nov. 13 *Perf. 12½*
321 A81 35fr green & multi 25 16

National lottery.

Electric Power Installations — A82

1971, Dec. 18 *Perf. 13*
322 A82 35fr red brn & multi 35 16

Cogwheel and Workers A83

1972, Mar. 18 **Engr.** *Perf. 13*
323 A83 35fr org, bl & dk brn 25 15

Technical Cooperation Week.

"Your Heart is Your Health" — A84

Girls Reading, Book Year Emblem — A85

1972, Apr. 7 **Photo.** *Perf. 12½x13*
324 A84 40fr blue, olive & red 35 20

World Health Day.

Perf. 12½x13, 13x12½
1972, Apr. 22 **Engr.**
325 A85 35fr Boys reading, horiz. 25 15
326 A85 40fr shown 35 20

International Book Year.

Postal Sorting Center, Abidjan A86

1972, May 13 *Perf. 13*
327 A86 40fr dk grn, rose lil & bis 35 15

Stamp Day.

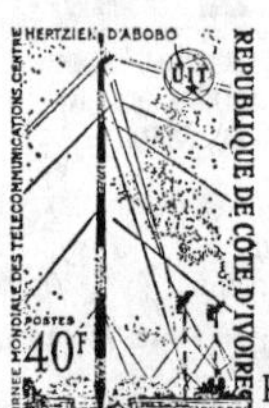

Radio Tower, Abobo, and ITU Emblem — A87

1972, May 17 **Engr.** *Perf. 13*
328 A87 40fr blue, red & grn 35 16

4th World Telecommunications Day.

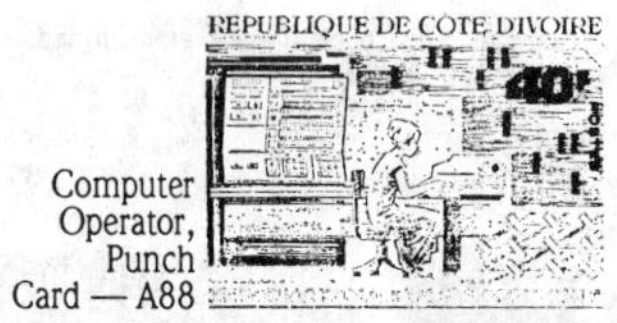

Computer Operator, Punch Card — A88

1972, June 24
329 A88 40fr brt grn, bl & red 35 16

Development of computerized information.

View of Odienné — A89

1972, Aug. 7 **Engr.** *Perf. 13*
330 A89 35fr bl, grn & brn 25 16

12th anniversary of independence.

West African Monetary Union Issue
Common Design Type

1972, Nov. 2 **Engr.** *Perf. 13*
331 CD136 40fr brn, gray & red lil 30 15

Diamond and Diamond Mine — A90

1972, Nov. 4
332 A90 40fr Prus bl, sl & org brn 35 16

Pasteur Institute, Louis Pasteur — A91

1972, Nov. 21
333 A91 35fr vio bl, grn & brn 30 20

Pasteur (1822-1895), chemist and bacteriologist.

Children at Village Pump — A92

1972, Dec. 9 **Engr.** *Perf. 13*
334 A92 35fr dk red, grn & blk 25 15

Water campaign. See No. 360.

Arms Type of 1969

1973 **Photo.** *Perf. 12*
335 A63 5fr Daloa 15 15
336 A63 10fr Gagnoa 15 15
Set value 15 15

Nos. 335-336 are 16½-17x22mm and have "DELRIEU" below design at right. Nos. 282-284 are 17x23mm and have no name at lower right.

Dr. Armauer G. Hansen — A93

1973, Feb. 3 **Engr.** *Perf. 13*
342 A93 35fr lil, dp bl & brn 30 16

Centenary of the discovery of the Hansen bacillus, the cause of leprosy.

Lake Village Bletankoro — A94

1973, Mar. 10 **Engr.** *Perf. 13*
343 A94 200fr choc, bl & grn 1.50 80

Balistes Capriscus A95

Fish: 20fr, Pseudupeneus prayensis. 25fr, Cephalopholis taeniops. 35fr, Priacanthus arenatus. 50fr, Xyrichthys novacula.

1973-74 Engr. *Perf. 13*

344 A95 15fr ind & slate grn 15 15
345 A95 20fr lilac & multi 18 15
346 A95 25fr sl grn & rose ('74) 15 15
347 A95 35fr rose red & sl grn 30 16
348 A95 50fr blk, ultra & rose red 42 30
Nos. 344-348 (5) 1.20
Set value 70

Issue dates: 50fr, Mar. 24; 15fr, 20fr, July 7; 35fr, Dec. 1. 25fr, Mar. 2, 1974.

Children A96

1973, Apr. 7 Engr. *Perf. 13*

354 A96 40fr grn, blk & dl red 35 16

Establishment of first children's village in Africa (SOS villages for homeless children).

Parliament, Abidjan — A97

1973, Apr. 24 Photo. *Perf. 13x12½*

355 A97 100fr multicolored 70 40

112th session of the Inter-parliamentary Council.

Teacher and PAC Store — A98

1973, May 12 Photo. *Perf. 13x12½*

356 A98 40fr multicolored 25 15

Commercial Action Program (PAC).

Mother, Typist, Dress Form and Pot — A99

1973, May 26

357 A99 35fr multicolored 22 15

Technical instruction for women.

Farmers, African Scout Emblem A100

1973, July 16 Photo. *Perf. 13x12½*

358 A100 40fr multicolored 25 16

24th Boy Scout World Conference, Nairobi, Kenya, July 16-21.

Party Headquarters, Yamoussokro — A101

1973, Aug. 7 Photo. *Perf. 13*

359 A101 35fr multicolored 22 15

Children at Dry Pump — A102

1973, Aug. 16 Engr.

360 A102 40fr multicolored 25 15

African solidarity in drought emergency.

African Postal Union Issue
Common Design Type

1973, Sept. 12 Engr. *Perf. 13*

361 CD137 100fr pur, blk & red 65 40

Decorated Arrow Heads, Abidjan Museum — A103

1973, Sept. 15 Photo. *Perf. 12½x13*

362 A103 5fr blk, brn red & brn 15 15

Ivory Coast No. 1 A104

1973, Oct. 9 Engr. *Perf. 13*

363 A104 40fr emer, blk & org 30 20

Stamp Day.

Highway Intersection A105

1973, Oct. 13

364 A105 35fr bl, blk & grn 22 15

Indenie-Abidjan intersection.

Map of Africa, Federation Emblem A106

Elephant Emblem A107

1973, Oct. 26 Photo. *Perf. 13*

365 A106 40fr ultra, red brn & vio bl 22 15

Intl. Social Security Federation, 18th General Assembly, Abidjan, Oct. 26-Nov. 3.

1973, Nov. 19

366 A107 40fr blk & bister 22 15

7th World Congress of the Universal Federation of World Travel Agents' Associations, Abidjan.

Kong Mosque — A108

1974, Mar. 9

367 A108 35fr bl, grn & brn 20 15

People and Sun — A109

1974, Apr. 20 Photo. *Perf. 13*

368 A109 35fr multicolored 20 15

Permanent Mission to UN.

Grand Lahou Post Office — A110

1974, May 17 Engr. *Perf. 13*

369 A110 35fr multicolored 20 15

Stamp Day.

Map and Flags of Members A110a

1974, May 29 Photo. *Perf. 13x12½*

370 A110a 40fr blue & multi 22 15

15th anniversary of the Council of Accord.

Pres. Houphouet-Boigny A111 A112

1974-76 Engr. *Perf. 13*

371 A111 25fr grn, org & brn 15 15
a. Booklet pane of 10 1.60
b. Booklet pane of 20 3.50
373 A112 35fr org, grn & brn 20 15
a. Booklet pane of 10 2.25
b. Booklet pane of 20 4.50
374 A112 40fr grn, org & brn 22 15
a. Booklet pane of 10 2.50
375 A112 60fr bl, car & brn ('76) 35 15
376 A112 65fr car, bl & brn ('76) 35 15
Nos. 371-376 (5) 1.27
Set value 36

See Nos. 783-792.

Arms of Ivory Coast A113

WPY Emblem A114

1974, June 29 Photo. *Perf. 12*

377 A113 30fr emer, brn & gold
378 A113 35fr brn, emer & gold 20 15
a. Booklet pane of 10 2.25
b. Booklet pane of 20 4.50
379 A113 40fr vio, bl, emer & gold 20 15
a. Booklet pane of 10 2.50
b. Booklet pane of 20 5.50

1976, Jan.
Inscribed: "COTE D'IVOIRE"

380 A113 60fr car, gold & emer 30 16
381 A113 65fr grn, gold & emer 35 20
382 A113 70fr bl, gold & emer 38 22
Nos. 378-382 (5) 1.43
Set value 72

See design A297.

1974, Aug. 19 Engr. *Perf. 13*

383 A114 40fr emer & bl 22 15

World Population Year.

Cotton Harvest — A115

1974, Sept. 21 Litho. *Perf. 12½x13*

384 A115 50fr multicolored 25 15

UPU Centenary A116

1974, Oct. 9 Engr. *Perf. 13*

385 A116 40fr multicolored 22 15

See Nos. C59-C60.

Plowing Farmer, Service Emblem A117

1974, Dec. 7 **Photo.** ***Perf. 13***
386 A117 35fr multicolored 20 15

14th anniversary of independence.

National Library, First Anniv. — A118

1975, Jan. 9 **Photo.** ***Perf. 13***
387 A118 40fr multicolored 22 15

Raoul Follereau and Blind Students — A119

1975, Jan. 26 **Engr.** ***Perf. 13***
388 A119 35fr multicolored 20 15

Follereau, educator of the blind and lepers.

Congress Emblem A120

Coffee Cultivation A121

1975, Mar. 4 **Photo.** ***Perf. 12½x13***
389 A120 40fr blk & emerald 22 15

52nd Congress of the Intl. Assoc. of Seed Crushers, Abidjan, Mar. 2-7.

1975, Mar. 15 ***Perf. 13½x13***
390 A121 5fr Flowering branch 15 15
391 A121 10fr Branch with beans 15 15
Set value 15 15

Sassandra Wharf — A122

1975, Apr. 19 **Engr.** ***Perf. 13***
392 A122 100fr multicolored 50 35

Letter Sorting A123

1975, Apr. 26 **Photo.** ***Perf. 13***
393 A123 40fr multicolored 22 16

Stamp Day.

Cotton Flower — A124

Cotton Bolls — A125

1975, May 3 **Photo.** ***Perf. 13***
394 A124 5fr multicolored 15 15
395 A125 10fr multicolored 15 15
Set value 15 15

Cotton cultivation.

Marie Kore, Women's Year Emblem — A126

1975, May 19 **Engr.** ***Perf. 13***
396 A126 45fr lt bl, yel grn & brn 25 20

International Women's Year.

Fort Dabou — A127

1975, June 7 **Engr.** ***Perf. 13***
397 A127 50fr multicolored 25 20

Abidjan Harbor — A128

Designs: 40fr, Grand Bassam wharf, 1906, vert. 100fr, Planned harbor expansion on Locodjro.

1975, July 1 **Photo.** ***Perf. 13***
398 A128 35fr multicolored 20 15

Miniature Sheet

399 Sheet of 3 1.10 1.10
a. A128 40fr multicolored 20 20
b. A128 100fr multicolored 50 50

25th anniversary of Abidjan Harbor. No. 399 contains Nos. 398, 399a, 399b.

Cacao Pods on Tree — A129

1975, Aug. 2
400 A129 35fr multicolored 20 15

Farm Workers A130

1975, Oct. 4 **Photo.** ***Perf. 13x12½***
401 A130 50fr multicolored 25 16

Natl. Org. for Rural Development.

Railroad Bridge, N'zi River A131

1975, Dec. 7 **Photo.** ***Perf. 13***
402 A131 60fr multicolored 35 20

15th anniversary of independence.

Baoulé Mother and Child, Carved in Wood — A132

1976, Jan. 24 **Litho.** ***Perf. 13***
403 A132 65fr black & multi 38 22

Baoulé Mask — A133

1976, Feb. 7 **Photo.** ***Perf. 12½***
404 A133 20fr shown 15 15
405 A133 150fr Chief Abron's chair 80 50

Senufo Statuette — A134

Telephones 1876 and 1976 — A135

1976, Feb. 21 ***Perf. 13x13½***
406 A134 25fr ocher & multi 15 15

1976, Mar. 10 **Litho.** ***Perf. 12***
407 A135 70fr multicolored 38 25

Centenary of first telephone call by Alexander Graham Bell, Mar. 10, 1876.

Ivory Coast Map, Pigeon, Carving A136

1976, Apr. 10 **Photo.** ***Perf. 12½***
408 A136 65fr multicolored 35 25

20th Stamp Day.

Smiling Trees and Cat — A137

Children with Books — A138

1976, June 5 **Litho.** ***Perf. 12½***
409 A137 65fr multicolored 35 20

Nature protection.

1976, July 3 **Photo.** ***Perf. 12½x13***
410 A138 65fr multicolored 35 22

Runner, Maple Leaf, Olympic Rings — A139

1976, July 17 **Litho.** ***Perf. 12***
411 A139 60fr Javelin, vert. 35 22
412 A139 65fr shown 35 25

21st Olympic Games, Montreal, Canada, July 17-Aug. 1.

Mohammad Ali Jinnah — A139a

1976, Aug. 14 **Litho.** ***Perf. 13***

412A	A139a	50fr	multicolored		

1st Governor-General of Pakistan.

Cashew A140

1976, Sept. 18 ***Perf. 12½***

413	A140	65fr	blue & multi	35	20

Highway and Conference Emblem — A141

1976, Oct. 25 **Litho.** ***Perf. 12½x12***

414	A141	60fr	multicolored	35	22

3rd African Highway Conference, Abidjan, July 25-30.

Pres. Houphouet-Boigny — A142

1976-77 **Photo.** ***Perf. 13½x12½***

415	A142	35fr	brn, red lil & blk ('77)		
416	A142	40fr	brt grn, ocher & brn blk	20	15
a.			Bklt. pane of 12 (8#416, 4#417)	7.50	
417	A142	45fr	ocher, brt grn & brn blk	22	15
418	A142	60fr	brn, mag & brn blk	35	15
419	A142	65fr	grn, org & brn blk	35	15
			Set value, #416-419		26

The 40fr and 45fr issued in booklet and coil; 35fr, 60fr and 65fr in coil only.

Stamps from booklets are imperf. on one side or two adjoining sides. Coils have control number on back of every 10th stamp.

John Paul Jones, American Marine and Ship — A143

American Bicentennial: 125fr, Count de Rochambeau and grenadier of Touraine Regiment. 150fr, Admiral Count Jean Baptiste d'Estaing and French marine. 175fr, Lafayette and grenadier of Soissons Regiment. 200fr, Jefferson, American soldier, Declaration of Independence. 500fr, Washington, US flag, Continental officer.

1976, Nov. 27 **Litho.** ***Perf. 11***

421	A143	100fr	multicolored	60	28
422	A143	125fr	multicolored	80	35
423	A143	150fr	multicolored	1.00	40
424	A143	175fr	multicolored	1.10	42
425	A143	200fr	multicolored	1.25	50
			Nos. 421-425 (5)	4.75	1.95

Souvenir Sheet

426	A143	500fr	multicolored	3.00	1.40

"Development and Solidarity" — A144

1976, Dec. 7 **Photo.** ***Perf. 13***

427	A144	60fr	multicolored	35	20

16th anniversary of independence.

Benin Head, Ivory Coast Arms — A145

1977, Jan. 15 **Photo.** ***Perf. 13***

428	A145	65fr	gold, dk brn & grn	35	20

2nd World Black and African Festival, Lagos, Nigeria, Jan. 15-Feb. 12.

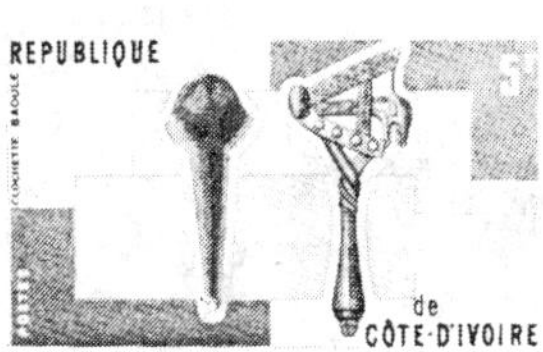

Musical Instruments — A146

1977, Mar. 5 **Engr.** ***Perf. 13***

429	A146	5fr	Baoule bells	15	15
430	A146	10fr	Senufo balafon	15	15
431	A146	20fr	Dida drum	15	15
			Set value	24	16

Air Afrique Plane Unloading Mail — A147

1977, Apr. 9 **Litho.** ***Perf. 13***

432	A147	60fr	multicolored	35	22

Stamp Day.

Sassenage Castle, Grenoble — A148

1977, May 21 **Litho.** ***Perf. 12½***

433	A148	100fr	multicolored	50	35

Intl. French Language Council, 10th anniv.

Orville and Wilbur Wright, "Wright Flyer," 1903 — A149

History of Aviation: 75fr, Louis Bleriot crossing English Channel, 1909. 100fr, Ross Smith and Vickers-Vimy (flew England-Australia, 1919). 200fr, Charles A. Lindbergh and "Spirit of St. Louis" (flew New York-Paris, 1927). 300fr, Supersonic jet Concorde, 1976. 500fr, Lindbergh in flying suit and "Spirit of St. Louis."

1977, June 27 **Litho.** ***Perf. 14***

434	A149	60fr	multi	40	16
435	A149	75fr	multi	50	20
436	A149	100fr	multi	65	20
437	A149	200fr	multi	1.25	40
438	A149	300fr	multi	2.00	60
			Nos. 434-438 (5)	4.80	1.56

Souvenir Sheet

439	A149	500fr	multi	3.25	1.40

Santos Dumont's "Ville de Paris," 1907 — A150

Designs: 65fr, LZ 1 at takeoff. 150fr, "Schwaben" LZ 10 over Germany. 200fr, "Bodensee" LZ 120, 1919. 300fr, LZ 127 over Sphinx and pyramids.

1977, Sept. 3 **Litho.** ***Perf. 11***

440	A150	60fr	multi	38	16
441	A150	65fr	multi	40	16
442	A150	150fr	multi	90	38
443	A150	200fr	multi	1.20	50
444	A150	300fr	multi	1.75	75
			Nos. 440-444 (5)	4.63	1.95

History of the Zeppelin. Exist imperf.
See No. C63.

Congress Emblem — A151

1977, Sept. 12 **Photo.** ***Perf. 12½***

445	A151	60fr	lt & dk grn	35	22

17th Intl. Congress of Administrative Sciences in Africa, Abidjan, Sept. 12-16.

Yamoussoukro, First Ivory Coast Container Ship — A152

1977, Nov. 12 **Photo.** ***Perf. 13½x14***

446	A152	65fr	multicolored	35	22

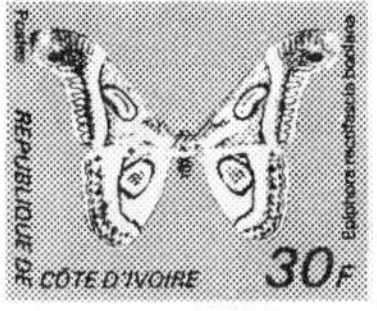

Butterflies A152a

Designs: 30fr, Epiphora rectifascia boolana. 60fr, Charaxes jasius epijasius. 65fr, Imbrasia arata. 100fr, Palla decius.

1977, Nov. **Photo.** ***Perf. 14x13***

446A	A152a	30fr	multicolored		
446B	A152a	60fr	multicolored		
446C	A152a	65fr	multicolored		
446D	A152a	100fr	multicolored		

A153 Flowers — A153a

Design: Hand Holding Produce, Generators, Factories.

1977, Dec. 7 **Photo.** ***Perf. 13½***

447	A153	60fr	multicolored	35	22

17th anniversary of independence.

1977 **Photo.** ***Perf. 13x14***

447A	A153a	5fr	Strophanthus hispidus		
447B	A153a	20fr	Anthurium cultorum		
447C	A153a	60fr	Arachnis flos-aeris		
447D	A153a	65fr	Renanthera storiei		

Presidents Giscard d'Estaing and Houphouet-Boigny — A154

1978, Jan. 11 ***Perf. 13***

448	A154	60fr	multicolored	35	22
449	A154	65fr	multicolored	35	22
450	A154	100fr	multicolored	50	38
a.			Souvenir sheet, 500fr	3.25	1.40

Visit of Pres. Valery Giscard d'Estaing. No. 450a contains one stamp.

St. George and the Dragon, by Rubens — A155

Paintings by Peter Paul Rubens (1577-1640): 150fr, Child's head. 250fr, Annunciation. 300fr, The Birth of Louis XIII. 500fr, Virgin and Child.

1978, Mar. 4 Litho. *Perf. 13½*

451 A155 65fr gold & multi 40 20
452 A155 150fr gold & multi 90 38
453 A155 250fr gold & multi 1.60 55
454 A155 300fr gold & multi 1.90 70

Souvenir Sheet

455 A155 500fr gold & multi 3.25 1.40

Royal Guards — A156

1978, Apr. 1 Litho. *Perf. 12½*

456 A156 60fr shown 30 16
457 A156 65fr Cosmological figures 35 20

Rural Postal Center — A157

1978, Apr. 8

458 A157 60fr multicolored 30 16

Stamp Day.

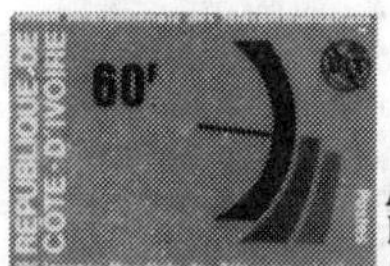

Antenna, ITU Emblem A158

1978, May 17 *Perf. 13*

459 A158 60fr multicolored 30 16

10th World Telecommunications Day.

Svante August Arrhenius, Electrolytic Apparatus — A159

Nobel Prize Winners: 75fr, Jules Bordet, child, mountains, eagle and Petri dish. 100fr, André Gide, and St. Peter's, Rome. 200fr, John Steinbeck and horse farm. 300fr, Children with flowers and UNICEF emblem. 500fr, Max Planck, rockets and earth.

1978, May 27 Litho. *Perf. 13½*

460 A159 60fr multi 38 16
461 A159 75fr multi 45 22
462 A159 100fr multi 60 30
463 A159 200fr multi 1.40 60
464 A159 300fr multi 1.90 90
Nos. 460-464 (5) 4.73 2.18

Souvenir Sheet

465 A159 500fr multi 3.25 1.40

Soccer Ball, Player and Argentina '78 Emblem — A160

Soccer Ball, Argentina '78 Emblem and: 65fr, Player, vert. 100fr, Player, diff. 150fr, Goalkeeper. 300fr, Ball as sun, and player, vert. 500fr, Ball as globe with Argentina on map of South America.

1978, June 17

466 A160 60fr multi 40 16
467 A160 65fr multi 42 20
468 A160 100fr multi 60 30
469 A160 150fr multi 90 42
470 A160 300fr multi 1.90 90
Nos. 466-470 (5) 4.22 1.98

Souvenir Sheet

471 A160 500fr multi 2.50 1.40

11th World Cup Soccer Championship, Argentina, June 1-25.

Miniodes Discolor A161

Butterflies: 65fr, Charaxes lactetinctus. 100fr, Papilio zalmoxis. 200fr, Papilio antimachus.

1978, July 8 Photo. *Perf. 14x13*

472 A161 60fr multicolored 30 16
473 A161 65fr multicolored 35 20
474 A161 100fr multicolored 50 30
475 A161 200fr multicolored 1.00 60

Cricket A162

Insects: 20fr, 60fr, Various hemiptera. 65fr, Goliath beetle.

1978, Aug. 26 Litho. *Perf. 12½*

476 A162 10fr multicolored 15 15
477 A162 20fr multicolored 15 15
478 A162 60fr multicolored 30 16
479 A162 65fr multicolored 35 35
Set value 80 62

Stylized Figures Emerging from TV Screen A163

Design: 65fr, Passengers on train made up of TV sets.

1978, Sept. 18 *Perf. 13*

480 A163 60fr multicolored 30 16
481 A163 65fr multicolored 35 22

Educational television programs.

Map of Ivory Coast, Mobile Drill Platform Ship — A164

Map of Ivory Coast, Ram at Discovery Site and: 65fr, Gold goblets. 500fr, Pres. Houphouet-Boigny holding gold goblets.

1978, Oct. 18 Litho. *Perf. 12½x12*

482 A164 60fr multicolored 30 16
483 A164 65fr multicolored 35 22

Souvenir Sheet

484 A164 500fr multicolored 2.50 1.40

Announcement of oil discovery off the coast of Ivory Coast, 1st anniv.

National Assembly, Paris, UPU Emblem A165

1978, Dec. 2 Litho. *Perf. 13½*

485 A165 200fr multicolored 1.25 60

Congress of Paris, centenary.

Drummer — A166

Poster — A167

1978, Dec. 7 Photo. *Perf. 12½x13*

486 A166 60fr multicolored 30 16

18th anniversary of independence.

1978, Dec. 12

Design: 65fr, Arrows made of flags, and television screen.

487 A167 60fr multicolored 30 16
488 A167 65fr multicolored 35 22

Technical cooperation among developing countries with the help of educational television.

Plowing A168

1979, Jan. 27 Photo. *Perf. 13*

489 A168 100fr multicolored 50 30

King Hassan II, Pres. Houphouet-Boigny, Flags and Map of Morocco and Ivory Coast — A169

1979, Jan. 27 Photo. *Perf. 13*

490 A169 60fr multicolored *10.00*
491 A169 65fr multicolored *10.00*
492 A169 500fr multicolored *10.00*

Visit of King Hassan of Morocco to Ivory Coast. The visit never took place and the stamps were not issued. To recover the printing costs the stamps were sold in Paris for one day.

Horus — A170

1979, Feb. 17 Litho. *Perf. 12½*

493 A170 200fr multi 1.00 60
494 A170 500fr Vulture with ankh, cartouches 2.50 1.50

UNESCO drive to save Temples of Philae.

Flowers — A171

1979, Feb. 24

495 A171 30fr Locranthus 15 15
496 A171 60fr Vanda Josephine 30 20
497 A171 65fr Renanthera storiei 35 22

Wildlife Protection A172

1979, Mar. 24 Photo. *Perf. 13x13½*

498 A172 50fr Hippopotamus 35 25

Globe and Emblem A173

Child Riding Dove A174

1979, Apr. 1 Litho. *Perf. 12x12½*

499 A173 60fr multicolored 40 32
500 A174 65fr multicolored 42 35
501 A173 100fr multicolored 65 55
502 A174 500fr multicolored 3.50 2.50

International Year of the Child.

Rural Mail Delivery — A175

1979, Apr. 7 *Perf. 12½*

503 A175 60fr multicolored 40 32

Stamp Day.

Korhogo Cathedral — A176

1979, Apr. 9 *Perf. 13*

504 A176 60fr multicolored 40 32

Arrival of Catholic missionaries, 75th anniv.

Crying Child — A177

1979, May 17 Litho. *Perf. 12½*

505 A177 65fr multicolored 42 35

10th anniv. of SOS Village (for homeless children).

Euphaedra Xypete A178

Butterflies: 65fr, Pseudacraea bois duvali. 70fr, Auchenisa schausi.

1979, May 26 *Perf. 13x13½*

506 A178 60fr multicolored 40 25
507 A178 65fr multicolored 42 25
508 A178 70fr multicolored 45 28

Endangered Animals A179

1979, June 2

509 A179 5fr Antelopes 15 15
510 A179 20fr Duikerbok 15 15
511 A179 60fr Aardvark 40 25
Set value 58 38

UPU Emblem, Radar, Truck and Ship — A180

Design: No. 513, Ancestral figure and antelope, vert.

1979, June 8 Engr. *Perf. 13*

512 A180 70fr multi 45 28

Photo.

513 A180 70fr multi 45 28

Philexafrique II, Libreville, Gabon, June 8-17. Nos. 512, 513 each printed in sheets of 10 with 5 labels showing exhibition emblem.

Rowland Hill, Steam Locomotive, Great Britain No. 75 — A181

Rowland Hill, Locomotives and: 75fr, Ivory Coast #125. 100fr, Hawaii #4. 150fr, Japan #30, syll. 3. 300fr, France #2. 500fr, Ivory Coast #123.

1979, July 7 Litho. *Perf. 13½*

514 A181 60fr multi 40 25
515 A181 75fr multi 50 30
516 A181 100fr multi 65 40
517 A181 150fr multi 1.00 60
518 A181 300fr multi 2.00 1.20
Nos. 514-518 (5) 4.55 2.75

Souvenir Sheet

519 A181 500fr multi 3.50

Sir Rowland Hill (1795-1879), originator of penny postage.

Insects — A181a A181b

1979 Photo. *Perf. 14x13, 13x14*

519A A181a 30fr Wasp, horiz.
519B A181a 60fr Praying mantis
519C A181a 65fr Cricket, horiz.

1979 Photo. *Perf. 13x14*

Musical instruments.

519D A181b 100fr Harp
519E A181b 150fr Whistles

"TELECOM 79" — A182

Culture Day — A183

1979, Sept. 20 Litho. *Perf. 13x12½*

520 A182 60fr multicolored 40 25

3rd World Telecommunications Exhibition, Geneva, Sept. 20-26.

1979, Oct. 13 *Perf. 12½*

521 A183 65fr multicolored 42 25

Fish — A183a

1979 Photo. *Perf. 14x13*

521A A183a 60fr Pterois volitans
521B A183a 65fr Coelacanth

Boxing A184

1979, Oct. 27 Litho. *Perf. 14x13½*

522 A184 60fr shown 40 25
523 A184 65fr Running 42 25
524 A184 100fr Soccer 65 40
525 A184 150fr Bicycling 1.00 65
526 A184 300fr Wrestling 2.00 1.40
Nos. 530-534 (5) 4.55 3.02

Souvenir Sheet

527 A184 500fr Gymnastics 3.50 2.00

Pre-Olympic Year.

Wildlife Fund Emblem and Jentink's Duiker — A185

Wildlife Protection: 60fr, Colobus Monkey. 75fr, Manatees. 100fr, Epixerus ebii. 150fr, Hippopotamus. 300fr, Chimpanzee.

1979, Nov. 3 Litho. *Perf. 14½*

528 A185 40fr multi 25 16
529 A185 60fr multi 40 22
530 A185 75fr multi 50 35
531 A185 100fr multi 65 40
532 A185 150fr multi 1.00 65
533 A185 300fr multi 2.00 1.40
Nos. 528-533 (6) 4.80 3.18

Raoul Follerau Institute, Adzope — A186

1979, Dec. 6 Litho. *Perf. 12½*

534 A186 60fr multi 40 22

Independence, 19th Anniversary — A187

1979, Dec. 7 Litho. *Perf. 14x13½*

535 A187 60fr multicolored 40 22

Fireball A188

Local Flora: 5fr, Clerodendron thomsonae, vert. 50fr, Costus incanusiamus, vert. 60fr, Ficus elastica abidjan, vert.

1980 Litho. *Perf. 12½*

536 A188 5fr multicolored 15 15
537 A188 10fr multicolored 15 15
538 A188 50fr multicolored 35 20
539 A188 60fr multicolored 40 22
Set value 86 50

Issued: 5fr, 10fr, Jan. 26; 50fr, 60fr, Feb. 16.

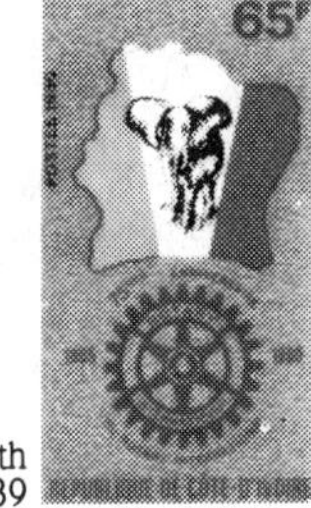

Rotary Intl., 75th Anniv. — A189

1980, Feb. 23 Photo. *Perf. 13½*

540 A189 65fr multicolored 42 30

International Archives Day A190

1980, Feb. 26 Litho.

541 A190 65fr multicolored 42 30

Astronaut Shaking Hands with Boy — A191

Path of Apollo 11 — A192

1980, July 6 **Photo.**
542 A191 60fr multicolored 40 25
543 A192 65fr multicolored 42 30
544 A191 70fr multicolored 45 35
545 A192 150fr multicolored 1.00 65

Apollo 11 moon landing, 10th anniv. (1979).

Jet and Map of Africa — A193

1980, Mar. 22 ***Perf. 12½***
546 A193 60fr multicolored 40 22

ASECNA (Air Safety Board), 20th anniv.

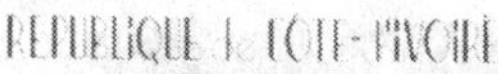
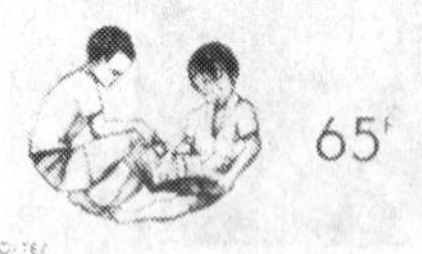

Boys and Stamp Album, Globe — A194

1980, Apr. 12 **Litho.** ***Perf. 12½***
547 A194 65fr bl grn & red brn 42 25

Stamp Day; Youth philately.

Missionary and Church, Aboisso A195

1980, Apr. 26 **Photo.** ***Perf. 13x13½***
548 A195 60fr multicolored 40 22

Settlement of the Holy Fathers at Aboisso, 75th anniversary.

Fight Against Cigarette Smoking A196

1980, May 3 ***Perf. 12½***
549 A196 60fr multicolored 40 22

Foreign postal stationery (stamped envelopes, postal cards and air letter sheets) is beyond the scope of this catalogue.

Pope John Paul II, Pres. Houphouet-Boigny — A197

1980, May 10 **Photo.** ***Perf. 13***
550 A197 65fr multicolored 42 30

Visit of Pope John Paul II to Ivory Coast.

Le Belier Locomotive A198

1980, May 17 **Litho.** ***Perf. 13***
551 A198 60fr shown 40 22
552 A198 65fr Abidjan Railroad Station, 1904 42 30
553 A198 100fr Passenger car, 1908 65 40
554 A198 150fr Steam locomotive, 1940 1.00 60

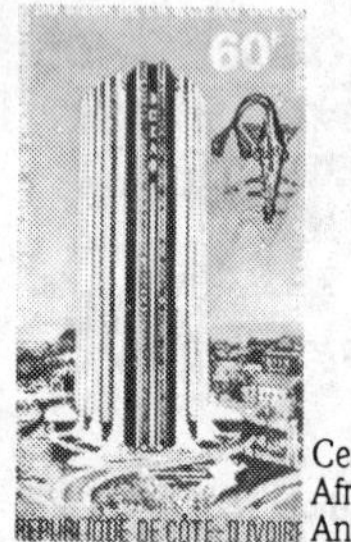

Central Bank of West African States, 1st Anniversary — A199

1980, May 26 **Litho.** ***Perf. 12x12½***
555 A199 60fr multicolored 40 22

Lujtanus Sebae — A200

1980, Apr. 19 **Photo.** ***Perf. 14***
556 A200 60fr shown 40 22
557 A200 65fr Monodactylus sebae, vert. 42 30
558 A200 100fr Colisa fasciata 65 42

Snake A201

1980, July 12 **Litho.** ***Perf. 12½***
559 A201 60fr shown 40 22
560 A201 150fr Toad 1.00 55

Tourists in Village, by K. Ehouman Pierre — A202

Conference Emblem — A203

1980, Aug. 9
561 A202 60fr multicolored 40 22
562 A203 65fr multicolored 42 25

National Tourist Office, Abidjan; World Tourism Conference, Manila.

Forticula Auricularia A204

Perf. 14x13, 13x14
1980, Sept. 6 **Photo.**
563 A204 60fr shown 40 22
564 A204 65fr Praying mantis, vert. 42 25

Perf. 13½x13, 13x13½
1980, Oct. 11 **Photo.**

Designs: 60fr, 200fr, Various grasshoppers.

565 A204 60fr multi, vert. 40 22
566 A204 200fr multi 1.40 70

Hands Free from Chain, Map of Ivory Coast, Pres. Houphouet-Boigny — A205

Pres. Houphouet-Boigny, Symbols of Development — A206

Perf. 12½x13, 14x14½ (A206)
1980, Oct. 18
567 A205 60fr shown 40 22
578 A206 65fr shown 42 25
569 A205 70fr Map, colors, document 45 25
570 A205 150fr like #567 1.00 55
571 A206 300fr like #568 2.00 1.10
Nos. 567-571 (5) 4.27 2.37

Pres. Houphouet-Boigny, 75th birthday.

7th PDCI and RDA Congress A207

1980, Oct. 25 ***Perf. 12½***
572 A207 60fr multicolored 40 22
573 A207 65fr multicolored 42 25

River Cruise Boat Sotra — A208

1980, Dec. 6 **Litho.** ***Perf. 13x13½***
574 A208 60fr multicolored 40 22

View of Abidjan — A209

1980, Dec. 7 ***Perf. 13x12½***
575 A209 60fr multicolored 40 22

20th anniversary of independence.

Universities Association Emblem A210

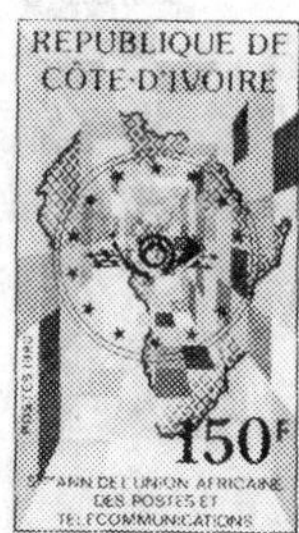

African Postal Union, 5th Anniversary A211

1980, Dec. 16 ***Perf. 12½***
576 A210 60fr multicolored 40 22

African Universities Assoc., 5th General Conference.

1980, Dec. 24 **Photo.** ***Perf. 13½***
577 A211 150fr multi 1.00 55

Herichtys Cyanoguttatum — A212

1981, Mar. 14 **Litho.** ***Perf. 12½***
578 A212 60fr shown 40 22
579 A212 65fr Labeo bicolor 42 25
580 A212 200fr Tetraodon fluviatilis 1.40 1.80

Birds — A212a

1980, Dec. 30 **Photo.** ***Perf. 14½x14***
580A A212a 60fr Spreo superbus
580B A212a 65fr Tockus camurus
580C A212a 65fr Balearica pavonina
580D A212a 100fr Ephippiorhynchus

Post Office, Grand Lahou A213

25th Anniv. of Ivory Coast Philatelic Club — A214

1981, May 2 Litho. *Perf. 12½*

581 A213	60fr multicolored		40	22
582 A214	65fr multicolored		42	25

Stamp Day.

13th World Telecommunications Day — A215

1981, May 17

583 A215	30fr multicolored	20	15
584 A215	60fr multicolored	40	22

Viking Satellite Landing, 1976 — A216

Space Conquest: Columbia space shuttle.

1981, June 13 Litho. *Perf. 13½*

585 A216	60fr multi	40	22
586 A216	75fr multi	50	30
587 A216	125fr multi	80	50
588 A216	300fr multi	2.00	1.10

Souvenir Sheet

589 A216	500fr multi	3.50	1.50

Local Flowers — A217

Elephant on Flag and Map — A219

Prince Charles and Lady Diana, Coach — A218

1981, July 4 Photo. *Perf. 14½x14*

590 A217	50fr Amorphophallus	35	20
591 A217	60fr Sugar Cane	40	22
592 A217	100fr Heliconia ivoirea	65	38

1981, Aug. 8 Litho. *Perf. 12½*

Royal Wedding: Couple and coaches.

593 A218	80fr multi	55	30
594 A218	100fr multi	65	38
595 A218	125fr multi	80	42

Souvenir Sheet

596 A218	500fr multi	3.50	1.50

For overprints see Nos. 642-645.

1981, Sept. Litho. *Perf. 12½*

597 A219	80fr multicolored	55	30
598 A219	100fr multicolored	65	38
599 A219	125fr multicolored	80	42

See Nos. 662-666, 833.

Soccer Players A220

Designs: Soccer players. 70fr, 80fr, 500fr, horiz.

1981, Sept. 19 *Perf. 14*

600 A220	70fr multi	45	25
601 A220	80fr multi	55	30
602 A220	100fr multi	65	38
603 A220	150fr multi	1.00	60
604 A220	350fr multi	2.25	1.40
	Nos. 600-604 (5)	4.90	2.93

Souvenir Sheet

605 A220	500fr multi	3.50	1.50

ESPANA '82 World Cup Soccer Championship. For overprints see Nos. 651-656.

West African Rice Development Assoc., 10th Anniv. A221

1981, Oct. 3 *Perf. 12½*

606 A221	80fr multicolored	55	30

World Food Day — A222

1981, Oct. 18

607 A222	100fr multicolored	65	38

Post Day A223

1981, Oct. 9 Litho. *Perf. 12½*

608 A223	70fr multicolored	45	25
609 A223	80fr multicolored	55	30
610 A223	100fr multicolored	65	38

75th Anniv. of Grand Prix — A224

Designs: Winners and their cars.

1981, Nov. 21 *Perf. 14*

611 A224	15fr Felice Nazarro, 1907	15	15
612 A224	40fr Jim Clark, 1962	25	15
613 A224	80fr Fiat, 1907	55	30
614 A224	100fr Auto Union, 1936	65	38
615 A224	125fr Ferrari, 1961	80	42
	Nos. 611-615 (5)	2.40	1.40

Souvenir Sheet

616 A224	500fr 1933 car	3.50	1.90

21st Anniv. of Independence — A225

1981, Dec. 7 *Perf. 13x12½*

617 A225	50fr multicolored	35	20
618 A225	80fr multicolored	55	30

Traditional Hairstyle — A226

Rotary Emblem on Map of — A228

Stamp Day Africa — A227

Designs: Various hairstyles.

1981, Dec. 19 Photo. *Perf. 14½x14*

619 A226	80fr multicolored	55	30
620 A226	100fr multicolored	65	40
621 A226	125fr multicolored	80	50

1982, Apr. 3 Litho. *Perf. 12½x12*

622 A227	100fr Bingerville P.O., 1902	65	40

1982, Apr. 13 *Perf. 12½*

623 A228	100fr ultra & gold	65	40

Pres. Houphouet-Boigny's Rotary Goodwill Conference, Abidjan, Apr. 13-15.

250th Birth Anniv. of George Washington A229

Anniversaries: 100fr, Auguste Piccard (1884-1962), Swiss physicist. 350fr, Goethe (1749-1832). 450fr, 500fr, Princess Diana, 21st birthday (portraits).

1982, May 15 Litho. *Perf. 13*

624 A229	80fr multi	55	30
625 A229	100fr multi	65	40
626 A229	350fr multi	2.25	1.25
627 A229	450fr multi	3.00	1.90

Souvenir Sheet

628 A229	500fr multi	3.50	2.00

Visit of French Pres. Mitterand, May 21-24 — A230

1982, May 21 Photo. *Perf. 13½*

629 A230	100fr multicolored	65	40

14th World Telecommunications Day — A231

1982, May 29 Litho. *Perf. 13*

630 A231	80fr multicolored	55	30

Scouting Year — A232

Designs: Scouts sailing. 80fr, 150fr, 350fr, 500fr vert.

1982, May 29 *Perf. 12½*

631 A232	80fr multi	55	30
632 A232	100fr multi	65	40
633 A232	150fr multi	1.00	60
634 A232	350fr multi	2.25	1.25

Souvenir Sheet

635 A232	500fr multi	3.50	2.00

TB Bacillus Centenary A233

1982, June 5 Photo. *Perf. 13x13½*

636 A233	30fr brown & multi	20	15
637 A233	80fr lt grn & multi	55	30

UN Conference on Human Environment, 10th Anniv. — A234

League of Ivory Coast Secretaries, First Congress — A235

1982, July Photo. *Perf. 13½x13*
638 A234 40fr multicolored 25 15
639 A234 80fr multicolored 55 30

1982, Aug. 9 Litho. *Perf. 12½x13*
640 A235 80fr tan & multi 55 30
641 A235 100fr silver & multi 65 40

593-596 Overprinted in Blue: "NAISSANCE / ROYALE 1982"

1982, Aug. 21 *Perf. 12½*
642 A218 80fr multi 55 30
643 A218 100fr multi 65 40
644 A218 125fr multi 80 50

Souvenir Sheet

645 A218 500fr multi 3.50 2.00

Birth of Prince William of Wales, June 21.

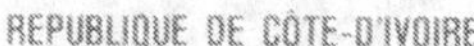

La Colombe de l'Avenir, 1962, by Pablo Picasso (1881-1973) — A236

Picasso Paintings: 80fr, Child with Dove, 1901. 100fr, Self-portrait, 1901. 185fr, Les Demoiselles d'Avignon, 1907. 350fr, The Dream, 1932. Nos. 646-649 vert.

1982, Sept. 4 Litho. *Perf. 13*
646 A236 80fr multi 55 30
647 A236 100fr multi 65 40
648 A236 185fr multi 1.25 70
649 A236 350fr multi 2.25 1.40
650 A236 500fr multi 3.50 2.00
Nos. 646-650 (5) 8.20 4.80

Nos. 600-605 Overprinted with World Cup Winners 1966-1982 in Black on Silver

1982, Oct. 9 Litho. *Perf. 14*
651 A220 70fr multi 45 25
652 A220 80fr multi 55 30
653 A220 100fr multi 65 38
654 A220 150fr multi 75 45
655 A220 350fr multi 2.25 1.40
Nos. 651-655 (5) 4.65 2.78

Souvenir Sheet

656 A220 500fr multi 2.75 1.50

Italy's victory in 1982 World Cup.

13th World UPU Day A237

Designs: 80fr, P.O. counter. 100fr, Postel-2001 building, Abidjan, vert. 350fr, Postal workers. 500fr, Postel-2001 interior.

1982, Oct. 23 *Perf. 12½*
657 A237 80fr multi 55 30
658 A237 100fr multi 65 38
659 A237 350fr multi 2.25 1.40

Size: 48x37mm
Perf. 13

660 A237 500fr multi 3.50 1.50

22nd Anniv. of Independence — A238

1982, Dec. 7 *Perf. 13*
661 A238 100fr multicolored 65 38

Elephant Type of 1981

1982-84
662 A219 5fr multicolored 15 15
662A A219 10fr multi ('84) 15 15
662B A219 20fr multicolored 15 15
663 A219 25fr multicolored 16 15
664 A219 30fr multicolored 20 15
665 A219 40fr multicolored 25 15
666 A219 50fr multicolored 35 20
Set value 1.10 70

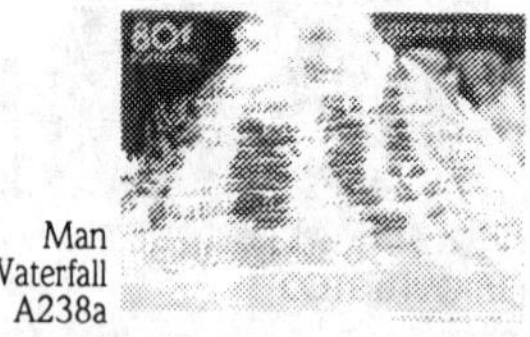
Man Waterfall A238a

1982 Photo. *Perf. 15x14*
666A A238a 80fr shown 55 30
666B A238a 80fr Boisee Savanna 55 30
666C A238a 500fr like #666A 3.50 1.90

Issue dates: No. 666B, Dec. 18; others, Nov. 27.

20th Anniv. of West African Monetary Union A239

1982, Dec. 21 Litho. *Perf. 12½*
667 A239 100fr Emblem 65 38

Abouissa Children's Village — A240

1983, Mar. 5 Photo. *Perf. 13½x13*
668 A240 125fr multicolored 80 42

Anteater A241

1983, Mar. 12 Litho. *Perf. 12½x13*
669 A241 35fr Pangolin, vert. 22 15
670 A241 90fr shown 60 35
671 A241 100fr Colobus monkey, vert. 65 38
672 A241 125fr Buffalo 80 42

Stamp Day A242

1983, Mar. 19 Litho. *Perf. 12½*
673 A242 100fr Grand Bassam P.O., 1903 65 38

Easter 1983 — A243

Paintings by Rubens (1577-1640). 100fr, 400fr, 500fr vert.

1983, Apr. 9 *Perf. 13*
674 A243 100fr Descent from the Cross 65 38
675 A243 125fr Resurrection 80 42
676 A243 350fr Crucifixion 2.25 1.40
677 A243 400fr Piercing of the Sword 2.50 1.50
678 A243 500fr Descent, diff. 3.50 1.90
Nos. 674-678 (5) 9.70 5.60

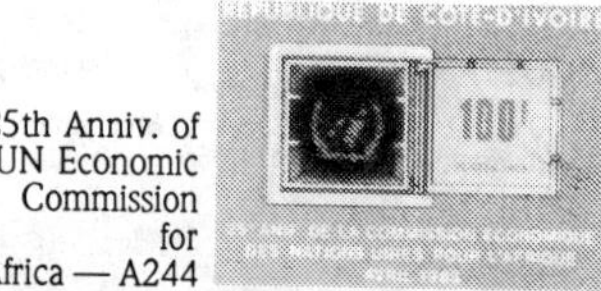
25th Anniv. of UN Economic Commission for Africa — A244

1983, Apr. 29 Litho. *Perf. 13x12½*
679 A244 100fr multicolored 65 38

Gray Parakeet A245

1983, June 11
680 A245 100fr Fish eagle, vert. 65 38
681 A245 125fr shown 80 42
682 A245 150fr Touracoes 1.00 50

World Communications Year — A245a

1983, July 16 *Perf. 12½x13*
682A A245a 100fr shown
682B A245a 125fr diff.

Traditional Dances — A246

1983, Sept. 3 Litho. *Perf. 12½*
683 A246 50fr Flali, Gouro 35 20
684 A246 100fr Masked dancer, Guere 65 38
685 A246 125fr Stilt dancer, Yacouba 80 45

20th Anniv. of the Ivory Hotel, Abidjan — A249

1983, Sept. 7 *Perf. 13*
693 A249 100fr multicolored 65 38

Ecology in Action — A250

1983, Oct. 24 Litho.
694 A250 25fr Forest after fire 15 15
695 A250 100fr Animals fleeing 32 20
696 A250 125fr Animals grazing 40 22
Set value 47

Raphael (1483-1520), 500th Birth Anniv. — A252

Paintings: 100fr, Christ and St. Peter. 125fr, Study for St. Joseph, vert. 350fr, Virgin of the House of Orleans, vert. 500fr, Virgin with the Blue Diadem, vert.

1983, Nov. 5 Litho. *Perf. 13*
698 A252 100fr multi 32 20
699 A252 125fr multi 40 22
700 A252 350fr multi 1.10 62
701 A252 500fr multi 1.60 1.00

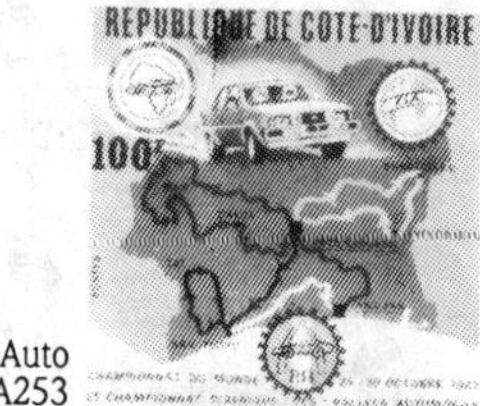
Auto Race — A253

1983, Oct. 24 Litho. *Perf. 12½*
702 A253 100fr Car, map 32 20

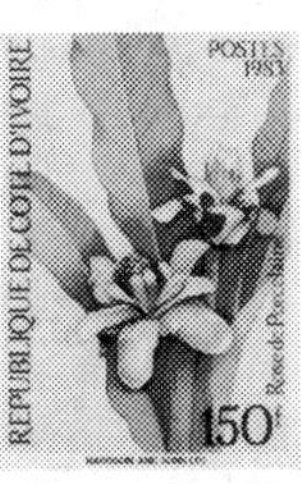

Flowers — A254

1983, Nov. 26 Photo. *Perf. 14x15*
703 A254 100fr Fleurs d'Ananas
704 A254 125fr Heliconia Rostrata
705 A254 150fr Rose de Porcelaine

23rd Anniv. of Independence A255

1983, Dec. 7
706 A255 100fr multicolored 32 20

First Audio-visual Forum, Abidjan A256

1984, Jan. 25 Litho. *Perf. 13x12½*
707 A256 100fr Screen, arrow 30 16

14th African Soccer Cup — A257

1984, Mar. 4 Photo. *Perf. 12½*
708 A257 100fr Emblem 30 16
709 A257 200fr Maps shaking hands 60 35

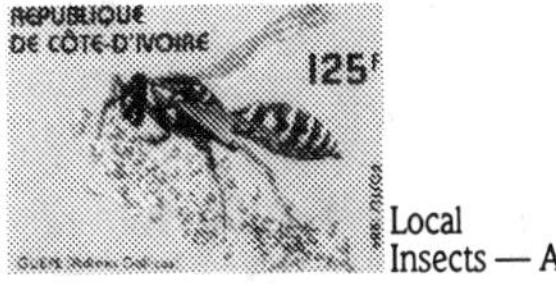

Local Insects — A258

1984, Mar. 24 Litho. *Perf. 13*
710 A258 100fr Argiope, vert. 30 16
711 A258 125fr Polistes gallicus 38 20

Stamp Day A259

1984, Apr. 7 Litho. *Perf. 12½*
712 A259 100fr Abidjan P.O., 1934 32 20

Lions Emblem A260

1984, Apr. 27 *Perf. 13½x13*
713 A260 100fr multicolored 32 20
714 A260 125fr multicolored 40 22

3rd Convention of Multi-district 403, Abidjan, Apr. 27-29.

16th World Telecommunications Day — A261

1984, May 17 *Perf. 12½*
715 A261 100fr multi 32 20

Council of Unity, 25th Anniv. — A262

1984, May 29
716 A262 100fr multicolored 32 20
717 A262 125fr multicolored 40 22

First Governmental Palace, Grand-Bassam — A263

1984, July 14 Litho. *Perf. 12½*
718 A263 100fr shown 32 16
719 A263 125fr Palace of Justice, Grand-Bassam 38 20

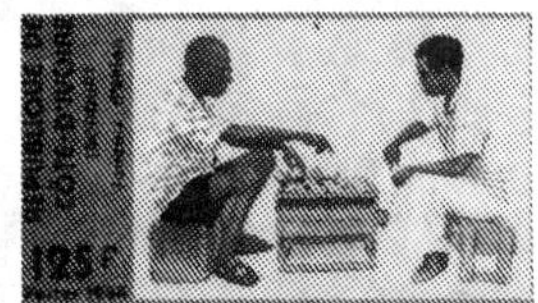

Men Playing Eklan — A264

1984, Aug. 11 *Perf. 13*
720 A264 100fr Board 30 16
721 A264 125fr shown 38 20

Locomotive "Gazelle" — A265

1984 *Perf. 12½*
722 A265 100fr shown 30 16
723 A265 100fr Cargo ship 30 16
724 A265 125fr Superpacific 38 20
725 A265 125fr Cargo ship, diff. 38 20
726 A265 350fr Pacific type 10 1.10 62
727 A265 350fr Ocean liner 1.10 62
728 A265 500fr Mallet class GT2 1.50 90
729 A265 500fr Ocean liner, diff. 1.50 90
Nos. 722-729 (8) 6.56 3.76

Issue dates: trains, Aug. 25; ships, Sept. 1.

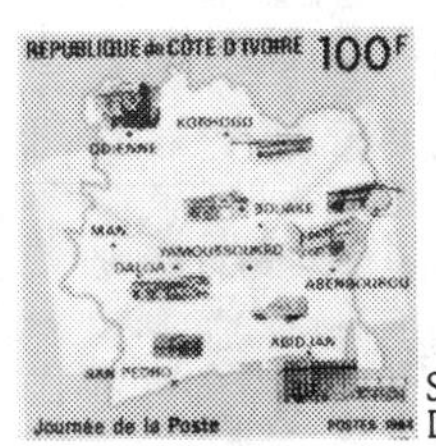

Stamp Day — A266

1984, Oct. 20 Litho. *Perf. 12½*
730 A266 100fr Map, post offices 25 16

10th Anniv., West African Union A267

1984, Oct. 27 Litho. *Perf. 13½*
731 A267 100fr Map, member nations 25 16

Wildlife — A267a

1984, Nov. 3 Photo. *Perf. 14½x15*
731A A267a 100fr Tragelaphus scriptus
731B A267a 150fr Felis serval

Tourism A267b

1984, Nov. 10 Photo. *Perf. 15x14½*
731C A267b 50fr Le Club Valtur
731D A267b 100fr Grand Lahou

Flowers — A267c

1984, Nov. 17 Photo. *Perf. 14½x15*
731E A267c 100fr Allamanda carthartica
731F A267c 125fr Baobob

90th Anniv., Ivory Coast Postage Stamps A268

1984, Nov. 23 Litho. *Perf. 12½*
732 A268 125fr Book cover 35 20

24th Anniv. of Independence A269

1984, Dec. 7 Litho. *Perf. 12½*
733 A269 100fr Citizens, outline map 25 16

Rotary Intl. Conf. — A270

Traditional Costumes — A271

1985, Jan. 16 Litho. *Perf. 12½x13*
734 A270 100fr multicolored 25 16
735 A270 125fr multicolored 35 20

1985, Feb. 16 Litho. *Perf. 13½*
736 A271 90fr Dan le Babou 22 15
737 A271 100fr Post-natal gown 25 15

Birds — A271a

1985, Mar. Photo. *Perf. 14½x15*
737A A271a 25fr Marabout
737B A271a 100fr Jacanda
737C A271a 350fr Ibis

Stamp Day — A272

1985, Apr. 13 Litho. *Perf. 12½*
738 A272 100fr Riverboat Adjame 25 15

18th District of Zonta Intl., 7th Conference, Abidjan, Apr. 25-27
A273

1985, Apr. 25 Litho. *Perf. 13½*
739 A273 125fr Zonta Intl. emblem 35 16

Bondoukou
A273a

1985 Litho. *Perf. 14½x13½*
739A A273a 100fr Marche de Bondoukou
739B A273a 125fr Mosque, Samatiguila
739C A273a 200fr shown

PHILEXAFRICA '85, Lome — A274

1985, May 15 *Perf. 13*
740 A274 200fr Factory, jet, van 55 25
741 A274 200fr Youth sports, farming 55 25

Nos. 740-741 printed se-tenant with center label picturing map of Africa or the UAPT emblem.

African Development Bank, 20th Anniv. — A275

1985, June 18
742 A275 100fr Senegal chemical industry 25 15
743 A275 125fr Gambian tree nursery 35 16

Intl. Youth Year
A276

1985, July 20 *Perf. 12½*
744 A276 125fr Map, profiles, dove 38 20

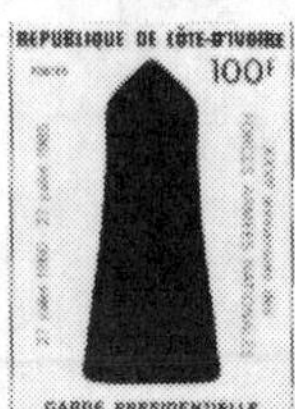

Natl. Armed Forces, 25th Anniv. — A277

Emblems: No. 745, Presidential Guard. No. 746, F.A.N.C.I. 125fr, Air Transport & Liaison Group, G.A.T.L. 200fr, National Marines. 350fr, National Gendarmerie.

1985, July 27 *Perf. 12½x13*
745 A277 100fr dp rose lil & gold 30 15
746 A277 100fr dark bl & gold 30 15
747 A277 125fr blk brn & gold 38 20
748 A277 200fr blk brn & gold 60 30
749 A277 350fr brt ultra & sil 1.00 50
Nos. 745-749 (5) 2.58 1.30

1986 World Cup Soccer Preliminaries, Mexico — A279

1985, Aug. *Perf. 13*
751 A279 100fr Heading the ball 30 15
752 A279 150fr Tackle 42 20
753 A279 200fr Dribbling 60 30
754 A279 350fr Passing 1.00 50

Souvenir Sheet

755 A279 500fr Power shot 1.40 65

Ivory Coast - Sovereign Military Order of Malta Postal Convention, Dec. 19, 1984 — A280

1985, Aug. 31 *Perf. 13x12½*
756 A280 125fr Natl. arms 38 20
757 A280 350fr S.M.O.M. arms 1.00 50

Visit of Pope John Paul II
A281

1985, Sept. 24 *Perf. 13*
Overprint in Black
758 A281 100fr Portrait, St. Paul's Cathedral, Abidjan 30 15

The overprint, "Consecration de la Cathedrale Saint Paul d'Abidjan," was added to explain the reason for the visit of the Pope. Copies without overprint exist but were not issued.

UN Child Survival Campaign
A282

1985, Oct. 5 Litho. *Perf. 13½x14*
759 A282 100fr Breast-feeding 35 16
760 A282 100fr Oral rehydration therapy 35 16
761 A282 100fr Mother and child 35 16
762 A282 100fr Vaccination 35 16

UN 40th Anniv. — A283

1985, Oct. 31 *Perf. 13*
763 A283 100fr multicolored 35 16

Admission to UN, 25th anniv.

World Wildlife Fund — A284

Striped antelopes.

1985, Nov. 30
764 A284 50fr multicolored 16 15
765 A284 60fr multicolored 20 15
766 A284 75fr multicolored 25 15
767 A284 100fr multicolored 35 16
Set value 46

City Skyline — A285

1985, Nov. 21 Litho. *Perf. 13*
768 A285 125fr multicolored 42 20

Expo '85 national industrial exhibition.

Return to the Land Campaign
A286

Handicrafts
A287

1985, Dec. 7 *Perf. 12½*
769 A286 125fr multicolored 42 20

Natl. independence, 25th anniv.

Flowers — A286a

1985, Dec. 28 Litho. *Perf. 14x15*
769A A286a 100fr L'Amorphophallus staudtii
769B A286a 125fr Crinum sccillifolium
769C A286a 200fr Triphyophyllum peltatum

1986, Jan. *Perf. 13½*
770 A287 125fr Spinning thread 65 32
771 A287 155fr Painting 80 40

Flora — A288

Cooking Utensils, Natl. Museum, Abidjan — A289

1986, Feb. 22 Litho. *Perf. 13½*
772 A288 40fr Omphalocarpum elatum 22 15
773 A288 50fr Momordica charantia 28 15
774 A288 125fr Millettia takou 68 35
775 A288 200fr Costus afer 1.10 55

1986, Mar. 6 *Perf. 13x12½, 12½x13*
776 A289 20fr We bowl 15 15
777 A289 30fr Baoule bowl 18 15
778 A289 90fr Baoule platter 50 25
779 A289 125fr Dan scoop 68 35
780 A289 440fr Baoule lidded pot 2.50 1.25
Nos. 776-780 (5) 4.01 2.15

Nos. 776-778 horiz.

Natl. Pedagogic and Vocational School, 10th Anniv. — A290

1986, Mar. 20 *Perf. 13½*
781 A290 125fr multicolored 68 35

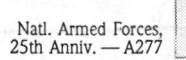

Cable Ship Stephan, 1910 — A291

1986, Apr. 12 Litho. *Perf. 12½*
782 A291 125fr multicolored 68 35

Stamp Day.

Houphouet-Boigny Type of 1974-76

1986, Apr. Engr. *Perf. 13*
783 A112 5fr dk red, dp rose lil & brn 15 15
784 A112 10fr gray grn, brt bl & brn 15 15
785 A112 20fr brt ver, blk brn & brn 15 15
786 A112 25fr bl, dp rose lil & brn 15 15
787 A112 30fr brt ver, blk brn & brn 16 15
789 A112 50fr lake, dk vio & brn 28 15
790 A112 90fr dk brn vio, rose lake & brn 50 25
791 A112 125fr brt lil rose, brt ver & brn 68 35
792 A112 155fr dk brn vio, Prus bl & brn 85 42
Nos. 783-792 (9) 3.07
Set value 1.45

The 1986 printing of the 40fr is in slightly darker colors.

Natl. Youth and Sports Institute, 25th Anniv. — A293

1986, May 9 **Litho.** ***Perf. 12½***
793 A293 125fr brt org & dk yel grn 68 35

Fish
A294

Designs: 5fr, Polypterus endlicheri. 125fr, Synodontis punctifer. 150fr, Protopterus annectens. 155fr, Synodontis koensis. 440fr, Malapterurus electricus.

1986, July 5 **Litho.** ***Perf. 14½x13½***
794 A294 5fr multi 15 15
795 A294 125fr multi 75 38
796 A294 150fr multi 90 45
797 A294 155fr multi 95 48
798 A294 440fr multi 2.75 2.00
Nos. 794-798 (5) 5.50 3.46

Enthronement of a Chief, Agni District — A295

1986, July 19 ***Perf. 13½x14½***
799 A295 50fr Drummer, vert. 28 15
800 A295 350fr Chief in litter 2.00 1.00
801 A295 440fr Royal entourage 2.75 2.00

Rural Houses
A296

1986, Aug. 2 **Litho.** ***Perf. 14x15***
802 A296 125fr Baoule aoulo 75 38
803 A296 155fr Upper Antiam eva 95 48
804 A296 350fr Lobi soukala 2.00 1.00

Coat of Arms
A297

Coastal Landscapes
A298

1986-87 **Engr.** ***Perf. 13***
807 A297 50fr bright org 28 15
810 A297 125fr dark green 75 38
813 A297 155fr crimson 95 48
815 A297 195fr blue ('87) 1.10 55

Issue dates: 50fr, 125fr, 155fr, Aug. 23.
This is an expanding set. Numbers will change if necessary.

Perf. 14x15, 15x14
1986, Aug. 30 **Litho.**
820 A298 125fr Grand Bereby 75 38
821 A298 155fr Sableux Boubele, horiz. 95 48

Oceanographic Research Center — A299

Perf. 14½x13½
1986, Sept. 13 **Litho.**
822 A299 125fr Fishing grounds 68 35
823 A299 155fr Net fishing 85 42

Intl. Peace Year — A300

1986, Oct. 16 **Litho.** ***Perf. 14x13½***
824 A300 155fr multicolored 85 42

Research and Development
A301

1986, Nov. 15 ***Perf. 13½x14***
825 A301 125fr Bull 68 35
826 A301 155fr Wheat 85 42

Natl. Independence, 26th Anniv. — A302

1986, Dec. 6 **Litho.** ***Perf. 13½x14***
827 A302 155fr multicolored 85 42

Rural Housing
A303

1987, Mar. 14 **Litho.** ***Perf. 13½x14***
828 A303 190fr Guesseple Dan 1.05 52
829 A303 550fr M'Bagui Senoufo 3.00 1.50

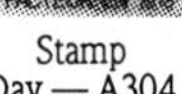

Stamp Day — A304

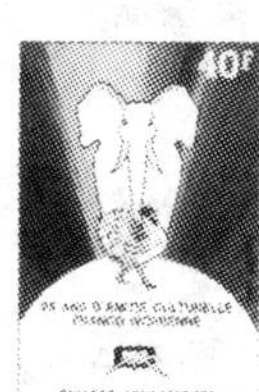

Jean Mermoz College, 25th Anniv. — A305

1987, Apr. 4 ***Perf. 13x13½***
830 A304 155fr Mailman, 1918 85 42

1987, Apr. 9 ***Perf. 13***
831 A305 40fr Cock, elephant 22 15
832 A305 155fr Dove, children 85 42

Elephant Type of 1981

1987, Apr. 9
833 A219 35fr multicolored 20 15

This is an expanding set. Numbers will change if necessary.

Fouilles, by Krah N'Guessan — A306

Paintings by local artists: 500fr, Cortege Ceremonial, by Santoni Gerard.

1987, Aug. 14 **Litho.** ***Perf. 14½x15***
841 A306 195fr multi 1.35 68
842 A306 500fr multi 3.50 1.75

World Post Day, Express Mail Service
A307

1987, Oct. 9 ***Perf. 13½***
843 A307 155fr multi 1.05 52
844 A307 195fr multi 1.30 65

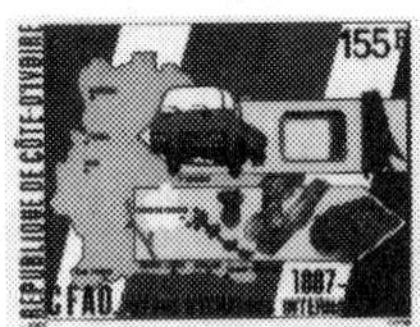

Intl. Trade Cent.
A308

1987, Oct. 24
845 A300 155fr multi 1.05 52

A309 A310

1987, Dec. 5 **Litho.** ***Perf. 14x13½***
846 A309 155fr multicolored 1.05 52

Natl. Independence, 27th anniv.

1988, Feb. 20 **Litho.** ***Perf. 14x13½***
847 A310 155fr multicolored 1.10 55

Lions Club for child survival.

The Modest Canary, by Monne Bou
A311

Paintings by local artists: 20fr, The Couple, by K.J. Houra, vert. 150fr, The Eternal Dance, by Bou, vert. 155fr, La Termitiere, by Mathilde Moro, vert. 195fr, The Sun of Independence, by Michel Kodjo, vert.

Perf. 12½x13, 13x12½
1988, Jan. 30
848 A311 20fr multi 15 15
849 A311 30fr shown 20 15
850 A311 150fr multi 1.05 52
851 A311 155fr multi 1.10 55
852 A311 195fr multi 1.35 68
Nos. 848-852 (5) 3.85 2.05

Stamp Day — A312

1988, Apr. 4 **Litho.** ***Perf. 13***
853 A312 155fr Bereby P.O., c. 1900 1.05 52

15th French-Language Nations Cardiology Congress, Abidjan, Apr. 18-20 — A313

1988, Apr. 18 **Litho.** ***Perf. 15x14***
854 A313 195fr blk & dark red 1.30 65

Intl. Fund for Agricultural Development (IFAD), 10th Anniv. — A314

1988, May 21 **Litho.** ***Perf. 12x13***
855 A314 195fr multicolored 1.35 68

1st Intl. Day for the Campaign Against Drug Abuse and Drug Trafficking A315

1988, Aug. 27 Litho. *Perf. 13½*
856 A315 155fr multi 1.05 52

Stone Heads — A316

Natl. Independence 28th Anniv. — A318

World Post Day — A317

Various stone heads from the Niangoran-Bouah Archaeological Collection.

Perf. 13x14½
1988, July 9 Litho. & Engr.
857 A316 5fr beige & sep 15 15
858 A316 10fr buff & sep 15 15
859 A316 30fr pale grn & sep 20 15
860 A316 155fr pale yel & sep 1.05 52
861 A316 195fr pale yel grn & sep 1.20 60
Nos. 857-861 (5) 2.75
Set value 1.30

1988, Oct. 15 Litho. *Perf. 14*
862 A317 155fr multi 1.00 50

1988, Dec. 6 *Perf. 11½x12*

Year of the Forest: 40fr, Healthy trees. No. 864, Stop forest fires. No. 865, Planting trees.

863 A318 40fr multi 25 15
864 A318 155fr multi 1.00 50
865 A318 155fr multi 1.00 50

History of Money — A319

Perf. 12x11½
1989, Feb. 25 Litho. Granite Paper
866 A319 50fr shown 32 16
867 A319 195fr Senegal bank notes, 1854, 1901 1.25 62

See Nos. 885-886, 896-898, 915. For surcharges see Nos. 904-905.

"Valeur d'echange 0fr.25" on 25c Type A5, 1920 — A320

1989, Apr. *Perf. 12½*
868 A320 155fr multi 1.00 50

Stamp Day.

Jewelry from the National Museum Collection A321

1989, Mar. 25 Litho. *Perf. 14*
869 A321 90fr Voltaic bracelets 55 28
870 A321 155fr Anklets 95 48

Sculptures by Christian Lattier A322

Perf. 11½x12, 12x11½
1989, May 13 Granite Paper
871 A322 40fr *The Old Man and the Infant*, vert. 25 15
872 A322 155fr *The Saxophone Player*, vert. 95 48
873 A322 550fr *The Panther* 3.25 1.65

For surcharge see No. 903.

Council for Rural Development, 30th Anniv. — A323

1989, May 29 *Perf. 15x14*
874 A323 75fr Flags, well, tractor, field 45 22

See Togo No. 1526.

Intl. Peace Congress — A324

1989, June Litho. *Perf. 13*
875 A324 195fr multi 1.15 58

Rural Habitat A325

1989, June 10 Litho. *Perf. 14*
876 A325 155fr Hut, Sirikukube Dida 1.00 50

For surcharge see No. 902.

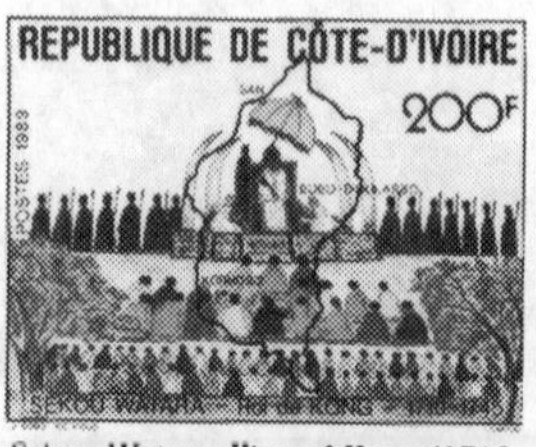
Sekou Watara, King of Kong (1710-1745) — A326

Designs: No. 878, Bastille, Declaration of Human Rights and Citizenship.

1989, July 7 Litho. *Perf. 13*
877 A326 200fr shown 1.20 60
878 A326 200fr multi 1.20 60

PHILEXFRANCE '89, French revolution bicent. Nos. 877-878 printed se-tenant with center label picturing exhibition emblem.

Endangered Species A327

Perf. 12x11½
1989, Sept. 16 Granite Paper
879 A327 25fr *Varanus niloticus* 16 15
880 A327 100fr *Crocodylus niloticus* 65 32

World Post Day — A328

1989, Oct. 9 Litho. *Perf. 12½x13*
881 A328 195fr multi 1.30 65

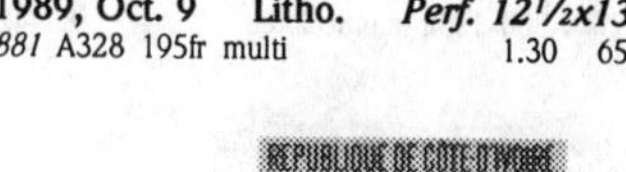

CAPTEAO, 30th Anniv. A329

1989, Oct. 28 Litho. *Perf. 12½*
882 A329 155fr multicolored 1.10 55

Conference of Postal and Telecommunication Administrations of West African Nations.

A330 A331

1989, Dec. 7 *Perf. 13*
883 A330 155fr multicolored 1.10 55

Natl. independence, 29th anniv.

1990, Jan. 18 Litho. *Perf. 13*
884 A331 155fr multicolored 1.10 55

Pan-African Union, 10th anniv.

History of Money Type of 1989
1990, Mar. 17 Litho. *Perf. 12x11½*
Granite Paper
885 A319 155fr 1923 25fr note 1.25 62
886 A319 195fr 1, 2, 5fr notes 1.50 75

Stamp Day — A332

1990, Apr. 21 Litho. *Perf. 13x12½*
887 A332 155fr Packet Africa 1.25 62

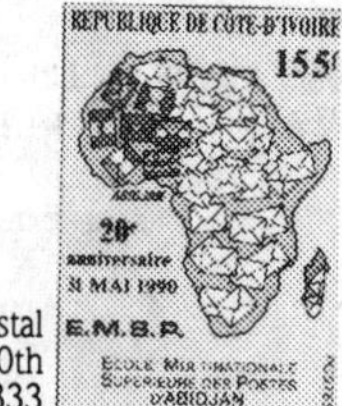
Multinational Postal School, 20th Anniv. — A333

1990, May 31 *Perf. 12½*
888 A333 155fr multicolored 1.25 62

Rural Village A334

1990, June 30 *Perf. 14*
889 A334 155fr multicolored 1.25 62

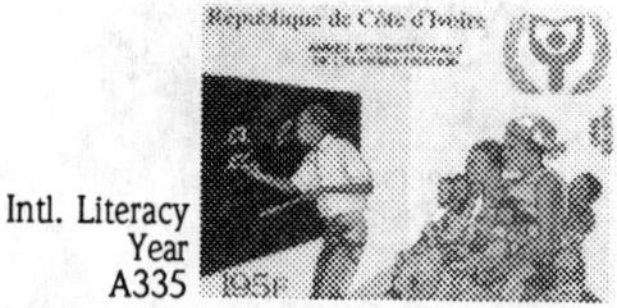
Intl. Literacy Year A335

1990, July 28 *Perf. 15x14*
890 A335 195fr multicolored 1.50 75

Dedication of Basilica of Notre Dame of Peace, Yamoussoukro A336

1990, Sept. 8 *Perf. 14½x13½*
891 A336 155fr shown 1.25 62
892 A336 195fr Basilica, diff. 1.50 75

Visit of Pope John Paul II — A337

1990, Sept. 9 *Perf. 13*
893 A337 500fr multicolored 4.00 2.00

World Post Day — A338

1990, Oct. 9 Litho. *Perf. 14x15*

894 A338 195fr multicolored 1.75 88

Independence, 30th Anniv. — A339

1990, Dec. 6 Litho. *Perf. 13½x14½*

895 A339 155fr multicolored 1.35 70

History of Money Type of 1989

1991, Mar. 1 Litho. *Perf. 11½*

Granite Paper

896 A319 40fr French West Africa 1942 5fr, 100fr notes 30 15
897 A319 155fr like #896 1.10 55
898 A319 195fr French West Africa & Togo 50fr, 500fr notes 1.40 70

For surcharges see Nos. 904-905.

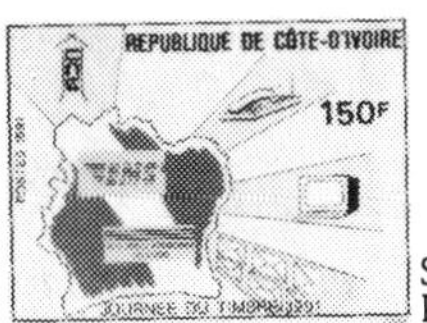

Stamp Day — A340

1991, May 18 Litho. *Perf. 13½*

899 A340 150fr multicolored 1.10 55

Miniature Sheets

French Open Tennis Championships, Cent. — A341

Tennis Players: No. 900a, Henri Cochet. b, Rene Lacoste. c, Jean Borotra. d, Don Budge. e, Marcel Bernard. f, Ken Rosewall. g, Rod Laver. h, Bjorn Borg. i, Yannick Noah.

No. 901a, Suzanne Lenglen. b, Helen Wills Moody. c, Simone Mathieu. d, Maureen Connolly. e, Francoise Durr. f, Margaret Court. g, Chris Evert. h, Martina Navratilova. i, Steffi Graf.

1991, May 24 Litho. *Perf. 13½*

900 A341 200fr Sheet of 9, #a.-i. 13.50 6.75
901 A341 200fr Sheet of 9, #a.-i. 13.50 6.75

Nos. 872, 876, 897-898 Surcharged

150F

1991, July 15 Litho. *Perfs. as Before*

902 A325 150fr on 155fr #876 1.10 55

Granite Paper

903 A322 150fr on 155fr #872 1.10 55
904 A319 150fr on 155fr #897 1.10 55
905 A319 200fr on 195fr #898 1.50 75

Location of obliterator and surcharge varies.

Packet Boats — A342

1991, June 28 Litho. *Perf. 12x11½*

Granite Paper

906 A342 50fr Europe 40 20
907 A342 550fr Asia 4.30 2.15

World Post Day — A343

1991, Oct. 9 *Perf. 13*

908 A343 50fr shown 40 20
909 A343 100fr SIPE, globe 80 40

Tribal Drums — A344

1991 Litho. *Perf. 14x15*

910 A344 5fr We 15 15
911 A344 25fr Krou, Soubre region 20 15
912 A344 150fr Sinematiali 1.20 60
913 A344 200fr Akye, Alepe region 1.60 80

Independence, 31st Anniv. — A345

1991, Dec. 7 Litho. *Perf. 13½x14½*

914 A345 150fr multicolored 1.25 65

History of Money Type of 1989

1991, Dec. 8 *Perf. 12x11½*

Granite Paper

915 A319 100fr like #898 88 45

Flowers A346

Various flowers.

1991, Dec. 20 Engr. *Perf. 13*

916 A346 150fr grn, blk & mag, vert. 1.25 65
917 A346 200fr grn, olive & rose car 1.65 85

African Soccer Championships — A347

Designs: 150fr, Elephants holding trophy, map, soccer ball, vert.

1992, Apr. 22 Litho. *Perf. 13*

918 A347 20fr multicolored 16 15
919 A347 150fr multicolored 1.25 65

Animals A348

1992, May 5 Engr. *Perf. 13x12½*

920 A348 5fr Viverra civetta 15 15
921 A348 40fr Nandinia binotata 35 18
922 A348 150fr Tragelaphus eurycer-os 1.30 65
923 A348 500fr Panthera pardus 4.35 2.20

World Post Day — A349

1992, Oct. 7 Litho. *Perf. 13*

924 A349 150fr black & blue 1.30 65

First Ivory Coast Postage Stamp, Cent. — A350

Designs: a, #3, #197. b, #182, #909 with mail trucks, post office boxes.

1992, Oct. 7

925 A350 150fr Pair, #a.-b. + label 2.60 1.30

Funeral Monuments A351

Various grave site monuments.

1992, Dec. 30 Engr. *Perf. 13*

926 A351 5fr multicolored 15 15
927 A351 50fr multicolored 40 20
928 A351 150fr multicolored 1.20 60
929 A351 400fr multicolored 3.15 1.60

Stamp Day — A352

Designs showing children interested in philately: No. 930, Girl, stamp collection, #169. No. 931, Girl, #431, #446B, #186, and #920. 150fr, Boy sitting under tree, stamp exhibition.

1993, Apr. 17 Litho. *Perf. 13½*

930 A352 50fr multicolored 40 20
931 A352 50fr multicolored 40 20
932 A352 150fr multicolored 1.20 60

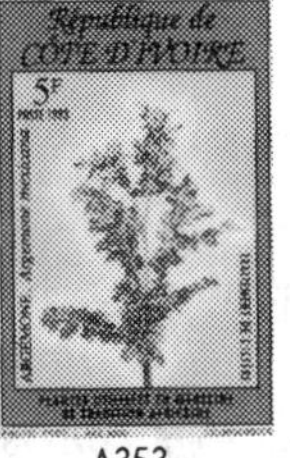

A353 A354

Medicinal plants.

1993, May 14 Litho. *Perf. 11½x12*

Granite Paper

933 A353 5fr Argemone mexicana 15 15
934 A353 20fr Hibiscus esculentus 16 15
935 A353 200fr Cassia alata 1.60 80

1993, Aug. 27 Photo. *Perf. 12x11½*

Orchids: 10fr, Calyptrochilum emarginatum. 50fr, Plectrelminthus caudathus. 150fr, Eulophia guineensis.

Granite Paper

936 A354 10fr multicolored 15 15
937 A354 50fr multicolored 40 20
938 A354 150fr multicolored 1.25 65

Ivory Coast Colony, Cent. — A355

Designs: 25fr, Organization charter. 100fr, Colonial Governor Louis Gustave Binger, and Pres. F. Houphouet-Boigny. 500fr, Natives selecting goods for trade.

1993, Sept. 17 *Perf. 13x12½*

939 A355 25fr green & black 15 15
940 A355 100fr blue & black 80 40
941 A355 500fr brown & black 4.00 2.00

Elimination Round of 1994 World Cup Soccer Championships, US — A356

Designs: 150fr, Cartoon soccer players. 200fr, Three players. 300fr, Two players. 400fr, Cartoon players, diff.

1993, Sept. 24 Litho. *Perf. 14x15*

942 A356 150fr multicolored 1.10 55
943 A356 200fr multicolored 1.50 75
944 A356 300fr multicolored 2.25 1.10
945 A356 400fr multicolored 3.00 1.50

World Post Day — A357

Designs: 30fr, Map of Ivory Coast. 200fr, Post office, Bouake.

1993, Oct. 9 *Perf. 13x13½*

946 A357 30fr multicolored 22 15
947 A357 200fr multicolored 1.50 75

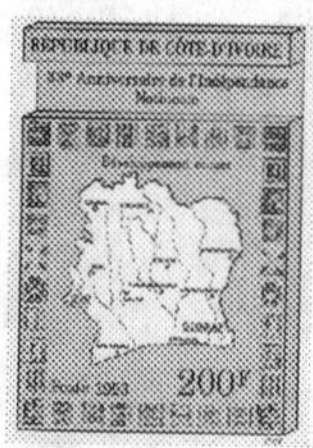

Independence, 33rd Anniv. — A359

1993, Dec. 7 Litho. *Perf. 13½x13*

950 A359 200fr multicolored 1.50 75

SEMI-POSTAL STAMPS

No. 47 Surcharged in Red ✚5c

1915 Unwmk. *Perf. 14x13½*

B1 A5 10c + 5c 35 35
a. Double surcharge 27.50 27.50

Issued on ordinary and chalky paper.

Curie Issue
Common Design Type

1938 *Perf. 13*

B2 CD80 1.75fr + 50c brt ultra 3.75 3.75

French Revolution Issue
Common Design Type

1939 Photo.
Name and Value Typo. in Black

B3	CD83	45c + 25c grn	3.00	3.00
B4	CD83	70c + 30c brn	3.00	3.00
B5	CD83	90c + 35c red org	3.00	3.00
B6	CD83	1.25fr + 1fr rose pink	3.00	3.00
B7	CD83	2.25fr + 2fr blue	3.00	3.00
		Nos. B3-B7 (5)	15.00	15.00

Stamps of 1936-38 Surcharged in Red or Black SECOURS + 1 fr. NATIONAL

1941

B8	A7	50c + 1fr plum (Bk)	65	65
B9	A8	80c + 2fr blk brn (R)	5.00	5.00
B10	A8	1.50fr + 2fr ultra (R)	5.00	5.00
B11	A9	2fr + 3fr ultra (Bk)	5.00	5.00

Common Design Type and

Native Engineer SP1

Senegalese Light Artillery SP2

1941 Photo. *Perf. 13½*

B12 SP1 1fr + 1fr red 45
B13 CD86 1.50fr + 3fr claret 45
B14 SP2 2.50fr + 1fr blue 45

It is doubtful whether Nos. B12-B14 were placed in use. They were issued by the Vichy government.

Nos. 165-166 were surcharged "OEUVRES COLONIALES" and surtax (including change of denomination of the 2.50fr to 50c). These were issued in 1944 by the Vichy government and not placed on sale in the colony.

Catalogue values for unused stamps in this section, from this point to the end of the section, are for Never Hinged items.

Republic
Anti-Malaria Issue
Common Design Type

1962, Apr. 7 Engr. *Perf. 12½x12*

B15 CD108 25fr + 5fr ol grn 65 65

Freedom from Hunger Issue
Common Design Type

1963, Mar. 21 *Perf. 13*

B16 CD112 25fr + 5fr red lil, dk vio & brn 80 80

Red Cross - Red Crescent Soc., Child Survival Campaign — SP3

1987, May 8 Litho. *Perf. 13½*

B17 SP3 195fr +5fr multi 1.15 1.15

No. B17 surcharged "+5fr" in red. Not issued without surcharge. Surtax for the Red Cross - Red Crescent Soc.

Organization of African Unity, 25th Anniv. — SP4

1988, Nov. 19 Litho. *Perf. 12½x13*

B18 SP4 195fr +5fr multi 1.40 1.40

Marie Therese Houphouet-Boigny and N'Daya Intl. Emblem — SP5

1988, Dec. 9 Litho. *Perf. 13*

B19 SP5 195fr +5fr multi 1.35 1.35

N'Daya Intl., 1st anniv.

AIR POST STAMPS

Common Design Type

1940 Unwmk. Engr. *Perf. 12½x12*

C1	CD85	1.90fr ultramarine	16	16
C2	CD85	2.90fr dark red	16	16
C3	CD85	4.50fr dk gray grn	22	22
C4	CD85	4.90fr yel bister	28	28
C5	CD85	6.90fr deep orange	65	65
		Nos. C1-C5 (5)	1.47	1.47

Common Design Types

1942

C6	CD88	50c car & blue	15	
C7	CD88	1fr brn & black	25	
C8	CD88	2fr dk grn & red brn	28	
C9	CD88	3fr dk blue & scar	32	
C10	CD88	5fr vio & dk red	35	

Frame Engraved, Center Typographed

C11	CD89	10fr multicolored	42	
C12	CD89	20fr multicolored	50	
C13	CD89	50fr multicolored	60	90
		Nos. C6-C13 (8)	2.87	

There is doubt whether Nos. C6-C12 were officially placed in use.

Catalogue values for unused stamps in this section, from this point to the end of the section, are for Never Hinged items.

Republic

Lapalud Place and Post Office, Abidjan — AP1

Designs: 200fr, Houphouet-Boigny Bridge. 500fr, Ayamé dam.

1959, Oct. 1 Engr. *Perf. 13*

C14	AP1	100fr multicolored	1.10	38
C15	AP1	200fr multicolored	1.50	1.10
C16	AP1	500fr multicolored	5.25	2.25

Sports Type of 1961

1961, Dec. 23

C17 A19 100fr High jump 90 65

Air Afrique Issue
Common Design Type

1962, Feb. 17 Unwmk. *Perf. 13*

C18 CD107 50fr Prus bl, choc & org brn 65 50

Village in Man Region — AP2

1962, June 23 Engr. *Perf. 13*

C19 AP2 200fr Street in Odienne, vert. 2.25 90
C20 AP2 500fr shown 4.50 2.00

UN Headquarters, New York — AP3

1962, Sept. 20 *Perf. 13*

C21 AP3 100fr multi 1.10 70

Admission to the UN, 2nd anniv.

Sassandra Bay — AP4

1963 Unwmk. *Perf. 13*

C22	AP4	50fr Moossou bridge	50	25
C23	AP4	100fr shown	1.10	65
C24	AP4	200fr Comoe River	2.00	1.00

African Postal Union Issue
Common Design Type

1963, Sept. 8 Photo. *Perf. 12½*

C25 CD114 85fr org brn, ocher & red 90 75

1963 Air Afrique Issue
Common Design Type

1963, Nov. 19 Unwmk. *Perf. 13x12*

C26 CD115 25fr crim, gray, blk & grn 35 25

Ramses II and Queen Nefertari — AP5

President John F. Kennedy (1917-63) — AP7

Arms of Republic — AP6

1964, Mar. 7 Engr. *Perf. 13*

C27 AP5 60fr car, blk & red brn 80 65

UNESCO campaign to save historic monuments in Nubia.

1964, June 13 Photo.

C28 AP6 200fr ultra, yel grn & gold 1.75 75

1964, Nov. 14 Unwmk. *Perf. 12½*

C29 AP7 100fr gray, cl brn & blk 1.20 80
a. Souvenir sheet of 4 4.00 4.00

Liana Bridge, Lieupleu — AP8

1965, Dec. 4 Engr. *Perf. 13*

C30 AP8 100fr ol grn, dk grn & dk red brn 1.00 65

Street in Kong AP9

1966, Mar. 5 Engr. *Perf. 13*

C31 AP9 300fr brt bl, bis brn & vio brn 3.25 1.60

Air Afrique Issue, 1966
Common Design Type

1966, Aug. 20 Photo. *Perf. 13*

C32 CD123 30fr dk grn, blk & gray 35 20

Air Afrique Headquarters AP10

1967, Feb. 4 Engr. *Perf. 13*
C33 AP10 500fr emer, ind & ocher 5.00 2.00

Opening of Air Afrique headquarters in Abidjan.

African Postal Union Issue, 1967
Common Design Type

1967, Sept. 9 Engr. *Perf. 13*
C34 CD124 100fr blk, vio & car lake 1.10 65

Senufo Village — AP11

1968 Engr. *Perf. 13*
C35 AP11 100fr shown 1.10 70
C36 AP11 500fr Tiegba village 4.50 2.00

Issue dates: 100fr, Feb. 17; 500fr, Apr. 27.

PHILEXAFRIQUE Issue

Street in Grand Bassam, by Achalme — AP12

1969, Jan. 11 Photo. *Perf. 12x12½*
C37 AP12 100fr grn & multi 1.10 1.10

PHILEXAFRIQUE Phil. Exhib., Abidjan, Feb. 14-23. Printed with alternating green label.

2nd PHILEXAFRIQUE Issue
Common Design Type

Designs: 50fr, Ivory Coast No. 130 and view of San Pedro. 100fr, Ivory Coast No. 149 and man wearing chief's garments, vert. 200fr, Ivory Coast No. 77 and Exhibition Hall, Abidjan.

1969, Feb. 14 Engr. *Perf. 13*
C38 CD128 50fr grn, brn red & deep bl 50 50
C39 CD128 100fr brn, org & dp blue 1.00 1.00
C40 CD128 200fr brn, gray & dp blue 1.75 1.75
a. Min. sheet of 3, #C38-C40 3.50 3.50

Opening of PHILEXAFRIQUE.

Man Waterfall — AP13

Mount Niangbo — AP14

1970 Engr. *Perf. 13*
C41 AP13 100fr ocher, sl grn & vio bl 75 45
C42 AP14 200fr hn brn, grn & lt ol 1.75 75

Issue dates: 100fr, Jan. 6; 200fr, July 18.

San Pedro Harbor — AP15

1971, Mar. 21 Engr. *Perf. 13*
C43 AP15 100fr sl grn, red brn & brt bl 80 45

Treichville Swimming Pool — AP16

1971, May 29 Photo. *Perf. 12½*
C44 AP16 100fr multicolored 80 50

Aerial View of Coast Line AP17

1971, July 3 Engr. *Perf. 13*
C45 AP17 500fr multi 4.25 2.00

Tourist publicity for the African Riviera.

Bondoukou Market Type of Regular Issue

Design: 200fr, Similar to No. 318, but without people at left and in center.

Embossed on Gold Paper

1971, Aug. 7 *Perf. 12½*
Size: 36x26mm
C46 A79 200fr gold, ultra & blk 1.90 1.50

African Postal Union Issue, 1971
Common Design Type

Design: 100fr, Ivory Coast coat of arms and UAMPT building, Brazzaville, Congo.

1971, Nov. 13 Photo. *Perf. 13x13½*
C47 CD135 100fr bl & multi 80 45

Lion of St. Mark AP18

1972, Feb. 5 Photo. *Perf. 12½*
C48 AP18 100fr shown 1.00 65
C49 AP18 200fr Waves, St. Mark's Basilica, Venice 2.25 1.50

UNESCO campaign to save Venice.

Kawara Mosque — AP19

1972, Apr. 29 Engr. *Perf. 13*
C50 AP19 500fr bl, brn & ocher 4.00 1.90

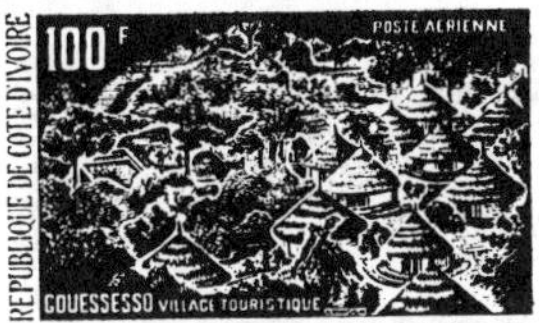

View of Gouessesso — AP20

1972 Engr. *Perf. 13*
C51 AP20 100fr shown 80 45
C52 AP20 200fr Jacqueville Lake 2.00 80
C53 AP20 500fr Kossou Dam 4.00 2.00

Issue dates: 100fr, June 10; 200fr, Oct. 28; 500fr, Nov. 17.

Akakro Radar Earth Station — AP21

1972, Nov. 27 Engr. *Perf. 13*
C54 AP21 200fr brt bl, sl grn & choc 1.75 90

The Judgment of Solomon, by Nandjui Legue — AP22

1973, Aug. 26 Photo. *Perf. 13*
C55 AP22 500fr multi 3.75 2.00

6th World Peace Conference for Justice.

Sassandra River Bridge — AP23

1974, May 4 Engr. *Perf. 13*
C56 AP23 100fr blk & yel grn 55 30
C57 AP23 500fr sl grn & brn 2.50 1.50

Vridi Soap Factory, Abidjan AP24

1974, July 6 Photo. *Perf. 13*
C58 AP24 200fr multi 1.10 65

UPU Emblem, Ivory Coast Flag, Post Runner and Jet — AP25

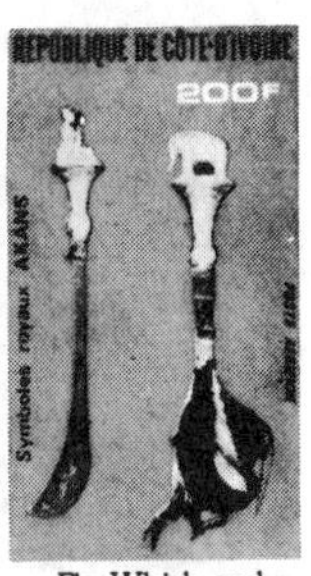

Fly Whisk and Panga Knife, Symbols of Akans Royal Family — AP26

1974, Oct. 9 Photo. *Perf. 13*
C59 AP25 200fr multi 1.10 90
C60 AP25 300fr multi 1.75 1.25

Centenary of Universal Postal Union.

1976, Apr. 3 Photo. *Perf. 12½x13*
C61 AP26 200fr brt bl & multi 1.10 65

Tingrela Mosque — AP27

1977, May 7 Engr. *Perf. 13*
C62 AP27 500fr multi 2.50 1.50

Zeppelin Type of 1977
Souvenir Sheet

Design: "Graf Zeppelin" LZ 127 over New York.

1977, Sept. 3 Litho. *Perf. 11*
C63 A150 500fr multi 3.25 1.40

Exists imperf.

Philexafrique II - Essen Issue
Common Design Types

Designs: No. C64, Elephant and Ivory Coast No. 239. No. C65, Pheasant and Bavaria No. 1.

1978, Nov. 1 Litho. *Perf. 13x12½*
C64 CD138 100fr multi 50 30
C65 CD139 100fr multi 50 30
a. Pair, #C64-C65 + label 1.00 75

Gymnast, Olympic Rings AP28

Designs: Various gymnasts. 75fr, 150fr, 350fr, vert.

1980, July 24 Litho. *Perf. 14½*
C66 AP28 75fr multi 50 30
C67 AP28 150fr multi 1.00 60
C68 AP28 250fr multi 1.60 1.00
C69 AP28 350fr multi 2.25 1.25

Souvenir Sheet

C70 AP28 500fr multi 3.50 2.00

22nd Summer Olympic Games, Moscow, July 19-Aug. 3.

The lack of a value for a listed item does not necessarily indicate rarity.

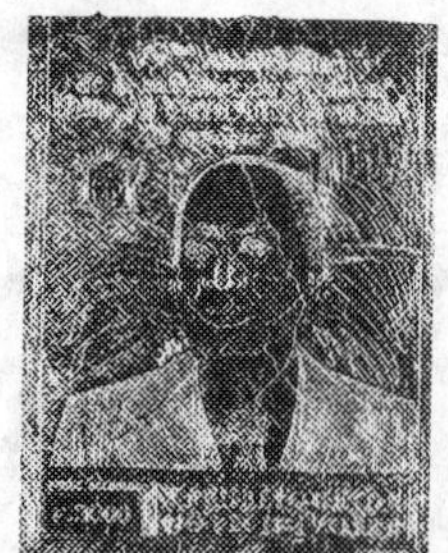

President Houphouet-Boigny, 75th Birthday — AP28a

Embossed Die Cut

1980, Oct. 18 *Perf. 10½*

C70A AP28a 2000fr Silver
C70B AP28a 3000fr Gold

Manned Flight Bicentenary — AP29

Various balloons. 100fr, 125fr, 350fr vert.

1983, Apr. 2 **Litho.** *Perf. 13*

C71	AP29 100fr	Montgolfier, 1783	65	38
C72	AP29 125fr	Hydrogen, 1783	80	42
C73	AP29 150fr	Mail transport, 1870	1.00	55
C74	AP29 350fr	Double Eagle II, 1978	2.25	1.40
C75	AP29 500fr	Dirigible	3.50	1.75
		Nos. C71-C75 (5)	8.20	4.50

Pre-Olympic Year — AP30

Various swimming events.

1983, July 9 **Litho.** *Perf. 14*

C76	AP30 100fr	Crawl	25	16
C77	AP30 125fr	Diving	35	20
C78	AP30 350fr	Backstroke	90	55
C79	AP30 400fr	Butterfly	1.10	62

Souvenir Sheet

C80 AP30 500fr Water polo 1.40 80

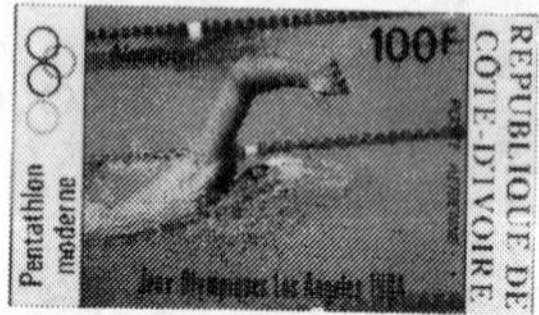

1984 Summer Olympics — AP31

Pentathlon.

1984, Mar. *Perf. 12½*

C81	AP31 100fr	Swimming	30	16
C82	AP31 125fr	Running	40	22
C83	AP31 185fr	Shooting	55	35
C84	AP31 350fr	Fencing	1.10	70

Souvenir Sheet

C85 AP31 500fr Equestrian 1.50 70

Los Angeles Olympics Winners AP32

1984, Dec. 15 **Litho.** *Perf. 13*

C86	AP32 100fr	Tiacoh, silver	25	16
C87	AP32 150fr	Lewis, gold	40	22
C88	AP32 200fr	Babers, gold	65	35
C89	AP32 500fr	Cruz, gold	1.40	80

Christmas AP33

Paintings: 100fr, Virgin and Child, by Correggio. 200fr, Holy Family with Angels, by Andrea del Sarto. 400fr, Virgin and Child, by Bellini.

1985, Jan. 12 *Perf. 13*

C90	AP33 100fr	multi	25	16
C91	AP33 200fr	multi	60	35
C92	AP33 400fr	multi	1.10	65

Nos. C91-C92 have incorrect frame inscriptions.

Audubon Birth Bicentenary — AP34

Birds: 100fr, Mergus serrator. 150fr, Pelecanus erythrorhynchos. 200fr, Mycteria americana. 350fr, Melanitta deglandi.

1985, June 8 **Litho.** *Perf. 13*

C93	AP34 100fr	multi	25	15
C94	AP34 150fr	multi, vert.	40	20
C95	AP34 200fr	multi, vert.	55	25
C96	AP34 350fr	multi	90	45

PHILEXAFRICA '85, Lome, Togo — AP35

1985, Nov. 16 **Litho.** *Perf. 13*

C97	AP35 250fr	shown	65	35
C98	AP35 250fr	Soccer, boys and deer	65	35
a.		Pair, #C97-C98 + label	1.30	1.00

Edmond Halley, Computer Drawing of Comet — AP36

Return of Halley's Comet: 155fr, Sir William Herschel, Uranus. 190fr, Space probe, comet. 350fr, MS T-5 probe, comet. 440fr, Skylab, Kohoutek comet.

1986, Jan. **Litho.** *Perf. 13*

C99	AP36 125fr	shown	50	25
C100	AP36 155fr	multi	62	30
C101	AP36 190fr	multi	75	38
C102	AP36 350fr	multi	1.40	70
C103	AP36 440fr	multi	1.75	85
		Nos. C99-C103 (5)	5.02	2.48

1986 World Cup Soccer Championships, Mexico — AP37

Various soccer plays.

1986, Apr. 26 **Litho.** *Perf. 13*

C104	AP37 90fr	multi	50	25
C105	AP37 125fr	multi	68	35
C106	AP37 155fr	multi	85	42
C107	AP37 440fr	multi	2.40	1.20
C108	AP37 500fr	multi	2.75	1.40
		Nos. C104-C108 (5)	7.18	3.62

Souvenir Sheet

Perf. 13½x13

C109 AP37 600fr multi 3.25 1.75

AP38

1988 Summer Olympics, Seoul — AP39

Sailing sports.

1987, May 23 **Litho.** *Perf. 12½*

C110	AP38 155fr	Soling Class	85	42
C111	AP38 195fr	Windsurfing	1.10	55
C112	AP38 250fr	470 Class	1.40	70
C113	AP38 550fr	Windsurfing, diff.	3.00	1.50

Souvenir Sheet

C114 AP39 650fr 470 Class, diff. 3.75 2.00

1988 Summer Olympics, Seoul — AP40

1988, June 18 **Litho.** *Perf. 13*

C115	AP40 100fr	Gymnastic rings	65	32
C116	AP40 155fr	Women's handball	1.00	50
C117	AP40 195fr	Boxing	1.25	62
C118	AP40 500fr	Parallel bars	3.25	1.65

Souvenir Sheet

C119 AP40 500fr Horizontal bar 3.25 1.65

1990 World Cup Soccer Championships, Italy — AP41

Italian monuments and various athletes.

1989, Nov. 25 **Litho.** *Perf. 13*

C120	AP41 195fr	Milan Cathedral	1.40	70
C121	AP41 300fr	Columbus Monument, Genoa	2.10	1.05
C122	AP41 450fr	Turin	3.20	1.60
C123	AP41 550fr	Bologna	3.85	3.85

World Cup Soccer Championships, Italy — AP42

Various plays.

1990, May 31 **Litho.** *Perf. 13*

C124	AP42 155fr	multicolored	1.25	62
C125	AP42 195fr	multicolored	1.50	75
C126	AP42 500fr	multicolored	3.75	1.90
C127	AP42 600fr	multicolored	4.75	2.40

AIR POST SEMI-POSTAL STAMPS

Stamps of Dahomey types V1, V2, V3 and V4 inscribed "Côte d'Ivoire" were issued in 1942 by the Vichy Government, but were not placed on sale in the colony.

POSTAGE DUE STAMPS

Natives — D1

D2

Perf. 14x13½

1906-07 **Unwmk.** **Typo.**

J1	D1 5c	grn, *greenish*	1.25	1.25
J2	D1 10c	red brown	1.40	1.40
J3	D1 15c	dark blue	2.25	2.25
J4	D1 20c	blk, *yellow*	3.25	3.25
J5	D1 30c	red, *straw*	3.25	3.25
J6	D1 50c	violet	2.50	2.50

J7 D1 60c black, *buff* 12.50 12.50
J8 D1 1fr blk, *pinkish* 15.00 15.00
Nos. J1-J8 (8) 41.40 41.40

1914

J9 D2 5c green 15 15
J10 D2 10c rose 15 15
J11 D2 15c gray 15 15
J12 D2 20c brown 15 15
J13 D2 30c blue 25 25
J14 D2 50c black 40 40
J15 D2 60c orange 50 50
J16 D2 1fr violet 60 60
Set value 2.00 2.00

Type of 1914 Issue Surcharged **2F.**

1927

J17 D2 2fr on 1fr lilac rose 60 60
J18 D2 3fr on 1fr org brown 60 60

> Catalogue values for unused stamps in this section, from this point to the end of the section, are for Never Hinged items.

Republic

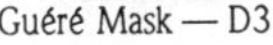
Guéré Mask — D3

Mask — D4

1960 **Engr.** ***Perf. 14x13***
Denomination Typographed in Black

J19 D3 1fr purple 15 15
J20 D3 2fr bright green 15 15
J21 D3 5fr orange yellow 25 25
J22 D3 10fr ultramarine 50 50
J23 D3 20fr lilac rose 80 80
Nos. J19-J23 (5) 1.85 1.85

1962, Nov. 3 **Typo.** ***Perf. 13½x14***

Designs: Various masks and heads, Bingerville school of art.

J24 D4 1fr org & brt blue 15 15
J25 D4 2fr black & red 15 15
J26 D4 5fr red & dark grn 15 15
J27 D4 10fr green & lilac 45 45
J28 D4 20fr dark pur & blk 80 80
Nos. J24-J28 (5) 1.70 1.70

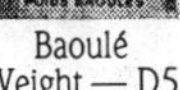
Baoulé Weight — D5

Gold Weight — D6

Designs: Various Baoulé weights.

1968, May 18 **Photo.** ***Perf. 13***

J29 D5 5fr cit, brn & bl grn 15 15
J30 D5 10fr lt bl, brn & bl grn 15 15
J31 D5 15fr sal, brn & bl grn 40 40
J32 D5 20fr gray, car & bl grn 60 60
J33 D5 30fr bis, brn & bl grn 70 70
Nos. J29-J33 (5) 2.00 2.00

1972, May 27 **Engr.**

Designs: Various gold weights.

J34 D6 20fr vio bl & org red 42 42
J35 D6 40fr ver & ocher 65 65
J36 D6 50fr orange & choc 90 90
J37 D6 100fr sl grn & ocher 2.00 2.00

MILITARY STAMP

> The catalogue value for the unused stamp in this section is for Never Hinged.

Coat of Arms — M1

Perf. 13x14

1967, Jan. 1 **Unwmk.** **Typo.**

M1 M1 multi 1.60 1.60

OFFICIAL STAMPS

> Catalogue values for unused stamps in this section are for Never Hinged items.

Ivory Coast Coat of Arms O1

1974, Jan. 1 **Photo.** ***Perf. 12***

O1 O1 (35fr) green & multi 42 22
O2 O1 (75fr) orange & multi 65 35
O3 O1 (100fr) lil rose & multi 90 60
O4 O1 (250fr) violet & multi 2.50 1.20

PARCEL POST STAMPS

Postage Due Stamps of French Colonies Overprinted

Overprinted in Black

Côte d'Ivoire
COLIS
Postaux

1903 **Unwmk.** ***Imperf.***

Q1 D1 50c lilac 17.50 17.50
Q2 D1 1fr rose, *buff* 17.50 17.50

Overprinted in Black

Colis
Postaux

Q3 D1 50c lilac *2,000.* *2,000.*
Q4 D1 1fr rose, *buff* *2,000.* *2,000.*

> **Accents on "C" of "COTE"**
> Nos. Q7-Q8, Q11-Q12, Q15, Q17-Q18, Q21-Q22, Q24-Q25 exist with or without accent.

Overprinted

Côte d'Ivoire
Colis Postaux

Red Overprint

Q5 D1 50c lilac 50.00 50.00
a. Inverted overprint 175.00 175.00

Blue Black Overprint

Q6 D1 1fr rose, *buff* 30.00 30.00
a. Inverted overprint 175.00 175.00

Surcharged in Black

Cote d Ivoire
50c
Colis Postaux

Cote d'Ivoire XX 1FR Colis Postaux — a
Cote d'Ivoire 1FR Colis Postaux — b
Cote d'Ivoire fr 1 fr Colis Postaux — c
Cote d'Ivoire fr 1 fr Colis Postaux — d
Cote d'Ivoire fr 1 fr Colis Postaux — e
Cote d'Ivoire fr 1 fr Colis Postaux — f
Côte d'Ivoire UN FR Colis Postaux — g
Côte d'Ivoire UN FR Colis Postaux — h

1903

Q7 D1 50c on 15c pale grn 5.00 5.00
a. Inverted surcharge 75.00 75.00
Q8 D1 50c on 60c brn, *buff* 17.50 15.00
a. Inverted surcharge 75.00 75.00

Q9 (a) 1fr on 5c blue *2,000.* *2,000.*
Q10 (b) 1fr on 5c blue *2,000.* *1,400.*
Q11 (c) 1fr on 5c blue 6.00 5.25
a. Inverted surcharge 125.00 125.00
Q12 (d) 1fr on 5c blue 8.75 8.00
Q13 (e) 1fr on 5c blue *2,250.* *2,250.*
Q14 (f) 1fr on 5c blue *5,500.* *5,500.*
Q15 (g) 1fr on 5c blue 50.00 50.00
Q16 (h) 1fr on 5c blue *1,800.* *1,800.*
Q17 (c) 1fr on 10c gray brn 8.50 6.00
a. Inverted surcharge 100.00 100.00
Q18 (d) 1fr on 10c gray brn 9.00 9.00
a. Inverted surcharge 100.00 100.00
Q19 (g) 1fr on 10c gray brn *1,500.* *1,500.*
Q20 (h) 1fr on 10c gray brn *22,500.*

Some authorities regard Nos. Q9 and Q10 as essays. A sub-type of type "a" has smaller, bold "XX" without serifs.

Surcharged in Black:

Côte d'Ivoire fr 4 fr Colis Postaux — i
Cote d Ivoire fr 4 fr Colis Postaux — k
Côte d'Ivoire fr 4 fr Colis Postaux — l

Q21 (i) 4fr on 60c brn, *buff* 60.00 42.50
a. Double surcharge *110.00*
Q22 (k) 4fr on 60c brn, *buff* 160.00 125.00
Q23 (l) 4fr on 60c brn, *buff* 525.00 425.00

Surcharged in Black

Colis Postaux
★ 4 Francs ★
Côte d'Ivoire

Q24 D1 4fr on 15c green 60.00 42.50
a. One large star 275.00 175.00
b. Two large stars 90.00 75.00
Q25 D1 4fr on 30c rose 60.00 42.50
a. One large star 275.00 175.00
b. Two large stars 90.00 75.00

Overprinted in Black

C. P.
Cote d'Ivoire

1904

Q26 D1 50c lilac 15.00 15.00
a. Inverted overprint
Q27 D1 1fr rose, *buff* 15.00 15.00
a. Inverted overprint

Overprinted in Black

Cote d'Ivoire
C. P.

Q28 D1 50c lilac 15.00 15.00
a. Inverted overprint 70.00 70.00
Q29 D1 1fr rose, *buff* 16.00 16.00
a. Inverted overprint 70.00 70.00

Surcharged in Black

Colis Postaux
4 Francs
Cote d'Ivoire

Q30 D1 4fr on 5c blue 100.00 100.00
Q31 D1 8fr on 15c green 150.00 150.00

Overprinted in Black

Cote d'Ivoire
C.
P.

1905

Q32 D1 50c lilac 17.50 17.50
Q33 D1 1fr rose, *buff* 17.50 17.50

Surcharged in Black

Cote d'Ivoire
2 Francs
C. P.

Q34 D1 2fr on 1fr rose, *buff* 110.00 110.00
Q35 D1 4fr on 1fr rose, *buff* 125.00 125.00
a. Italic "4" 750.00 750.00
Q36 D1 8fr on 1fr rose, *buff* 275.00 275.00

1995 Vol. 3 Number Changes

Number in 1994 Catalogue	Number in 1995 Catalogue
Denmark	
892a	deleted
Egypt	
98a	deleted
O112	O103
O103-O105	O104-O106
O109	O107
O106-O107	O108-O109
O113	O110
O110	O111
O108	O112
O111	O113
Estonia	
217-218A	216-218
Finland - Aland	
40-41B	35-38
42-42C	39-42
43A, 43AA, 43B	44-46
44	47
46-46A	48-49
47-48	50-51
51	52
54	53
56	54
France	
2182A-2184	2183-2185
2184A-2186	2186-2188
2188-2189	2189-2190
2192A-2194	2193-2195
2200-2200A	2198-2199
2201-2202	2200-2201
2204, 2204a	2202, 2202a
2204B, 2204c, 2204f	2203, 2203a, 2203b
2204D, 2204e	2204, 2204a
Gabon	
609AA	609A
609A	609B
Germany	
1521AA	1522
1521A	1523
1522-1524A	1524-1527
1525-1529	1528-1532
1532	1533
1537-1540C	1535-1540A
German Democratic Republic	
331	331b
331b	331
332	332a
332a	332
Greece	
103	deleted
164a	deleted
Guatemala	
79b, 82a	deleted
Honduras	
C877	C883
C883AA, C883A-C883B	C884-C884B
C884-C884B	C885-C886A
C884C	C887
C885-C886A	C888-C888B
C888	C889
C887	C890
C889	C891
Indonesia	
1044a	1044b
1266-1266A	1265-1266
Iran	
280a, 283a	deleted
1375	1375a
1375a	1375
Italy	
1660, 1662	deleted
1663-1663A	1662-1663

Numerical Index of Vol. 3 Watermark Illustrations

Watermark	Country
47	Iceland
48	Germany
87	Italy
91	Hungary Montenegro
92-95	Bavaria 95v-95h
102	Brunswick
106	Hungary
108-110	Danzig
111-114	Danish West Indies
112-114	Iceland
115-116	Dominican Republic
116	Germany Wurttemberg Liberia
117	Ecuador
118-120	Egypt
121	Finland
122-124	French Congo
125-127	Germany
128	Hamburg
129	Greece
130	Hanover
131	Haiti
132-133	Hungary
135-137	Hungary
140	Italian Colonies Italy
161	Iran
195	Egypt
184-185	Tuscany
186	Two Sicilies
192	Wurttemberg Germany
195	Egypt
207	Estonia Lithuania Nicaragua
208	Finland
209	Honduras
210	Hungary
223	Germany
228	Indonesia Netherlands Indies
233	Ecuador
237	Danzig
237	Germany
241	Germany
252	Greece
266	Hungary
273	Finland
277	Italy
282	Ethiopia
283	Hungary
284-286	Germany
292	Germany (Russian Zone)
295	Germany
297	German Dem. Rep.
301-302	Israel
303	Italy
304	Germany
306	Iran
315	Egypt
318	Egypt
316	Iran
328	Egypt
340	Ecuador
342	Egypt
349	Iran
353	Iran
363	Finland
367	Ecuador

END OF LISTING

Notes

Notes

Notes

Index and Identifier

All pages numbers are those of this Volume 3.

Illustrated Identifier

This section pictures stamps or parts of stamp designs that will help identify postage stamps that do not have English words on them.

Many of the symbols that identify stamps of countries are shown here as well as typical examples of their stamps.

See the Index and Identifier on page 956-961 for stamps with inscriptions such as "sen," "posta," "Baja Porto," "Helvetia," "K.S.A.", etc.

Linn's Stamp Identifier is now available. The 144 pages include more 2,000 inscriptions and over 500 large stamp illustrations. Available from Linn's Stamp News, P.O. Box 29, Sidney, OH 45365.

HEADS, PICTURES AND NUMERALS

GREAT BRITAIN

Great Britain stamps never show the country name, but, except for postage dues, show a picture of the reigning monarch.

Queen Victoria King Edward VII

King George V King Edward VIII

King George VI

Queen Elizabeth

Silhouette (sometimes facing right, generally at the top of stamp)

VICTORIA

Queen Victoria

INDIA

Other stamps of India show this portrait of Queen Victoria and the words "Service" and "Annas."

AUSTRIA

YUGOSLAVIA

(Also BOSNIA & HERZEGOVINA if imperf.)

BOSNIA & HERZEGOVINA

Denominations also appear in top corners instead of bottom corners.

HUNGARY

BRAZIL

AUSTRALIA

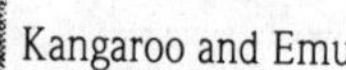

Kangaroo and Emu

NEW ZEALAND

GERMANY - MECKLENBURG-VORPOMMERN

ORIENTAL INSCRIPTIONS

CHINA

Most stamps of Republic of China show this series of characters.

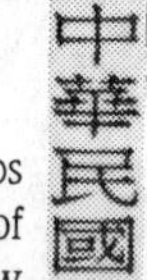

Sun

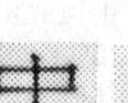

Any stamp with this one character is from China (Imperial, Republic or People's Republic).

Stamps with the China character and this character are from People's Republic of China.

Calligraphic form of People's Republic of China

Chinese stamps without China character

REPUBLIC OF CHINA

PEOPLE'S REPUBLIC OF CHINA

MANCHUKUO

政郵國 政郵國

The first 3 characters are common to many Manchukuo stamps.

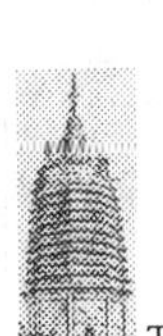
Temple

Emperor Pu-Yi

The last 3 characters are common to other Manchukuo stamps

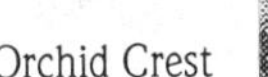
Orchid Crest

Manchukuo stamp without these elements

JAPAN

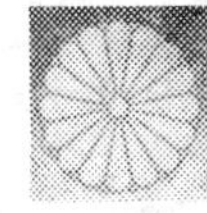
Chrysanthemum Crest

Country Name

RYUKYU ISLANDS

琉球郵便

Country Name

PHILIPPINES (JAPANESE OCCUPATION)

比島郵便

Country Name

MALAYA (JAPANESE OCCUPATION)

Indicates Japanese Occupation

マライ Country Name

BURMA (JAPANESE OCCUPATION)

大日本帝國郵便

Indicates Japanese Occupation

シヤン Country Name

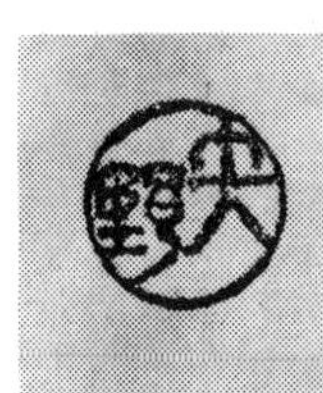

KOREA

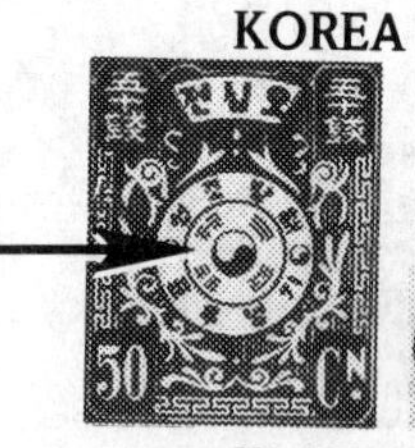

Yin Yang

Indicates Republic of Korea (South Korea)

These two characters, in any order, are common to stamps from the Republic of Korea (South Korea) or the unlisted stamps of the People's Democratic Republic of Korea (North Korea)

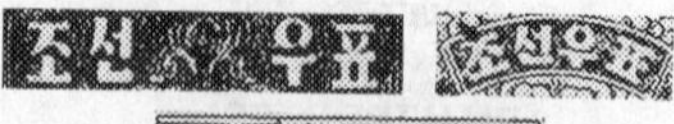

This series of four characters can be found on the stamps of both Koreas.

THAILAND

Country Name

King Prajadhipok and Chao P'ya Chakri

CENTRAL AND EASTERN ASIAN INSCRIPTIONS

INDIA - FEUDATORY STATES

BHOR

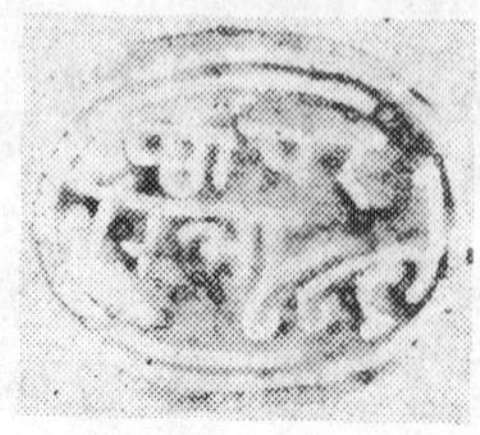

ALWAR

BUNDI

FARIDKOT

HYDERABAD

Similar stamps with different central design are inscribed "Postage" or "Post & Receipt."

INDORE

JAMMU & KASHMIR

JHALAWAR

NOWANUGGUR

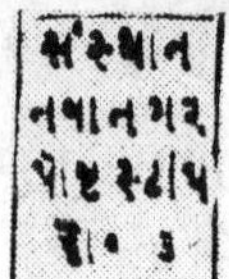

RAJPEEPLA

SORUTH

BANGLADESH

NEPAL

Other similar stamps have more characters.

TANNU TUVA

ISRAEL

GEORGIA

ARMENIA

The four characters are found somewhere on pictorial stamps.

ARABIC INSCRIPTIONS

AFGHANISTAN

BAHRAIN

EGYPT

IRAN

Note Crown

"Iran" is printed on back, shows through paper.

Lion with Sword

JORDAN

LEBANON

LIBYA

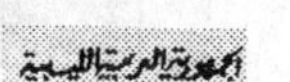
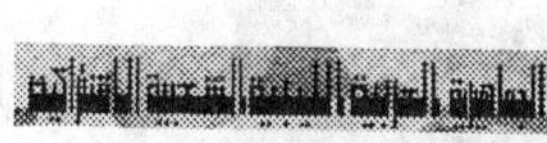

Country Name in various styles

Other Libya stamps show Eagle and Shield (head facing either direction) or Red, White and Black Shield (with or without eagle in center).

SAUDI ARABIA

Note Palm Tree and Swords

SYRIA

THRACE

PAKISTAN - BAHAWALPUR

Country Name in top panel, note star and crescent

TURKEY

Tughra (similar tughras can be found on stamps of Afghanistan and Saudi Arabia)

Plane, Star and Crescent

TURKEY IN ASIA

YEMEN

GREEK INSCRIPTIONS

GREECE

Country Name in various styles (Some Crete stamps overprinted with the Greece country name are listed in Crete.)

ΔΡΑΧΜΗ Drachma | ΔΡΑΧΜΑΙ Drachmas | ΛΕΠΤΟΝ Lepton

ΕΛΛ

Abbreviated Country Name

Other forms of Country Name

No country name

CRETE

Crete stamps with a surcharge that have the year "1922" are listed under Greece.

EPIRUS

IONIAN ISLANDS

CYRILLIC INSCRIPTIONS

RUSSIA

Postage in various styles

Abbreviation for Kopeck

Abbreviation for Ruble

Russia

Abbreviation for Russian Soviet Federated Socialist Republic

Abbreviation for Union of Soviet Socialist Republics

RUSSIA - ARMY OF THE NORTH

"OKCA"

RUSSIA - WENDEN

RUSSIAN OFFICES IN THE TURKISH EMPIRE

These letters appear on other stamps of the Russian offices.

These letters appear on other stamps of the Russian offices. The unoverprinted version of this stamp and a similar stamp were overprinted by various countries (see below).

ARMENIA

FAR EASTERN REPUBLIC

SOUTH RUSSIA

Country Name

FINLAND

Circles and Dots on stamps similar to Imperial Russia issues

BATUM

TRANSCAUCASIAN FEDERATED REPUBLICS

Abbreviation for Country Name

KAZAKHSTAN

KYRGYZSTAN

UKRAINE

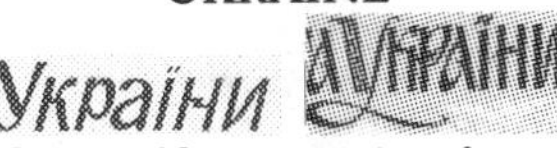

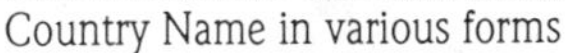

Country Name in various forms

The trident appears on many stamps, usually as an overprint.

Abbreviation for Ukrainian Soviet Socialist Republic

WESTERN UKRAINE

Abbreviation for Country Name

AZERBAIJAN

ACCP

Azerbaijan Soviet Socialist Republic

MONTENEGRO

ЦРНА ГОРА

Country Name in various forms

SERBIA

YUGOSLAVIA

Showing country name

No Country Name

BULGARIA

Country Name in various forms and styles

MONGOLIA

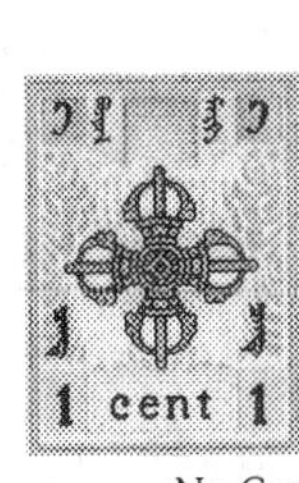

No Country Name

ROMANIA

SCOTT Auction House DIRECTORY

AUSTRALIA

STANLEY GIBBONS AUSTRALIA
343 Little Collins Street
Melbourne, Victoria
Australia 3000
FAX +613-600-0501

CANADA

MONTREAL STAMPS & COINS INC.
1878 Ste. Catherine Est.
Montreal, Quebec H2K 2H5
Canada
514-527-1526

HONG KONG

JOHN BULL STAMPS LTD.
G.P.O. Box 10-009
G.P.O. Hong Kong
+852-890-5767

TREASURE-HUNTERS LTD.
9/F, 280 Lockhart Road
Hong Kong
+852-507-3773

INDIA

STAMP ENTERPRISES
4 CHANDNI CHOWK STREET
CALCUTTA 700072
INDIA
FAX +33 262-336

NEW ZEALAND

ABBEY STAMP AUCTIONS
Box 217
Whangaparaoa
New Zealand
+64-9-424-5542

SWEDEN

POSTILJONEN AB
Box 4118
S-20312 Malmo
Sweden
FAX +46-407-2299

SWITZERLAND

CORINPHILA AUCTIONS LTD.
Bellerivestrasse 34
CH-8034
Zurich, Switzerland
+41-1-383-1060

UNITED STATES

B TRADING CO.
114 Quail Street
Albany, NY 12206
518-465-3497

TED CONWAY
P.O. Box 1950
Hallandale, FL 33008-1950
305-923-3744

DOWNEAST STAMPS
52 Fern Street
Bangor, ME 04401-5599
800-891-3826

CHARLES G. FIRBY AUCTIONS
6695 Highland Rd. #106
Waterford, MI 48327
810-887-3091

HERB LATUCHIE AUCTIONS
P.O. Box 67099
Cuyahoga Falls, OH 44222
216-928-2844

ROBERT E. LIPPERT CO.
23800 Greater Mack Ave.
St. Clair Shores, MI 48080
810-776-8990

LOWELL NEWMAN & CO.
1500 Harbor Blvd.
Weehawken, NJ 07087
201-223-0100

RASDALE STAMP CO.
36 So. State St.
Chicago, IL 60603
312-263-7334

STAMP CENTER/DUTCH COUNTRY AUCTION
4115 Concord Pike
Wilmington, DE 19803
302-478-8740

International DIRECTORY

United States
Scott Authorized
DEALER DIRECTORY

Listings are arranged by zip codes within each state

ARIZONA

NIT WIT STAMPS & SPORTS CARDS
1226 E. Florence Blvd.
Casa Grande, AZ **85222**
602-836-4785

B.J.'S STAMPS - BARBARA J. JOHNSON
6342 W. Bell Rd.
Glendale, AZ **85308**
602-878-2080

AMERICAN PHILATELIC BROKERAGES
7225 N. Oracle Rd.
Suite #102
Tucson, AZ **85704**
602-297-3456

ARKANSAS

THE COIN AND STAMP SHOP
1 Donaghey Building
Little Rock, AR **72201**
501-375-2113

CALIFORNIA

HARRY LEWIS WEISS
P.O. Box 3396
Beverly Hills, CA **90212**
310-276-7252

BROSIUS STAMP AND COIN
2105 Main St.
Santa Monica, CA **90405**
310-396-7480

SAN RAFAEL PHILATELICS
122 Patrician Way
Pasadena, CA **91105**
818-449-7499

BICK INTERNATIONAL
P.O. Box 854
Van Nuys, CA **91408**
818-997-6496

SCOTT WESTERN DISTRIBUTING
5670 Schaefer Ave. No. L
Chino, CA **91710**
909-590-5030
See our Display Advertisement on Page 975

GLOBAL STAMPS
109 W. Center Street
Pomona, CA **91768**
909-629-5501

STAMPS FROM SYLVIA
P.O. Box 226
Redlands, CA **92373**
909-845-7201

FRED COOPS & COMPANY
115 Carousel Mall
San Bernadino, CA **92401**
909-885-2507

COAST PHILATELICS
1113-D Baker St.
Costa Mesa, CA **92626**
714-545-1791

SCOTT-EDELMAN SUPPLY CO.
1111 E. Truslow Ave.
Fullerton, CA **92631**
714-680-6188

ALISO HILLS STAMP & COIN
25381 I Alicia Pkwy.
Laguna Hills, CA **92653**
714-855-0344

FISCHER-WOLK PHILATELICS
24771 "G" Alicia Parkway
Laguna Hills, CA **92653**
714-837-2932

LAGUNA HILLS STAMP CO.
24310 Moulton Pkwy.
Suite M
Laguna Hills, CA **92653**
714-581-5750

BREWART COINS, STAMPS & BASEBALL CARDS
403 W. Katella Ave.
Anaheim, CA **92802**
714-533-0400

JOSEPH I. CALDWELL STAMPS
6659 Arozena Lane
Carpinteria, CA **93013**
805-684-4065

CALIFORNIA COIN & STAMP
243 D Granada Dr.
San Luis Obispo, CA **93401-7337**
805-541-8775

L. & M. STAMP CO.
1738 10th St.
Los Osos, CA **93402**
805-528-6420

ASHTREE STAMP & COIN
2410 N. Blackstone
Fresno, CA **93703**
209-227-7167

PHILATELIC GEMS
320 W. Shaw
Fresno, CA **93704**
209-224-5292

MR. Z'S STAMP SHOP
1231 Burlingame Avenue
Burlingame, CA **94010**
415-344-3401

THE STAMP GALLERY
1515 Locust St.
Walnut Creek, CA **94596**
510-944-9111

STANLEY M. PILLER
3351 Grand Ave.
Oakland, CA **94610**
510-465-8290

ASIA PHILATELICS/OWL STUDIO
P.O. Box 1607
San Jose, CA **95109**
408-238-0893

FTACEK STAMP CO.
P.O. Box 1023
Manteca, CA **95336**
209-823-7018

GILES A. GIBSON
P.O. Drawer B
Rio Nido, CA **95471**
707-869-0362

SACRAMENTO STAMP MART/JOHN VAN ALSTYNE
1487 Tribute Road
Suite J
Sacramento, CA **95815**
916-565-0600

CLASSIC STAMPS & COVERS
3021 Arden Way
Sacramento, CA **95825**
916-972-8235

COLORADO

AURORA STAMPS AND COINS
9818 E. Colfax Ave.
Aurora, CO **80010**
303-364-3223

SHOWCASE STAMPS
3865 Wadsworth Blvd.
Wheat Ridge, CO **80033**
303-425-9252

ARAPAHOE COIN & STAMP
1216 W. Littleton Blvd.
Littleton, CO **80120**
303-797-0466

MAX HICKOX
Box 21081
Denver, CO **80221**
303-425-6281

ACKLEY'S ROCKS & STAMPS
3230 N. Stone Ave.
Colorado Springs, CO **80907**
719-633-1153

CONNECTICUT

MILLER'S STAMP SHOP
41 New London Tpke.
Uncasville, CT **06382**
203-848-0468

J & B STAMPS & COLLECTIBLES
41 Colony Street
Meriden, CT **06451**
203-235-7634

THE KEEPING ROOM
P.O. Box 257
Trumbull, CT **06611-0257**
203-372-8436

COLLECTOR'S MARKET
7 West State Drive
E. Litchfield, CT **06759**
203-482-4840

DISTRICT OF COLUMBIA

WOODWARD & LOTHROP STAMP DEPT.
11th & G St. NW
Washington, DC **20013**
202-879-8028

FLORIDA

ARLINGTON STAMP & COIN CO.
1350 University Blvd., North
Jacksonville, FL **32211-5226**
904-743-1776

TOM'S STAMPS
2810 Sharer Rd.
Tallahassee, FL **32312**
800-252-7117

INTERNATIONAL LIAISON
P.O. Box 825
Milton, FL **32572**
904-623-6050

PHILAETELICS
S.R. 19 & Old 441
Tavares, FL **32778**
904-343-2761

WINTER PARK STAMP SHOP
199 E. Welbourne Avenue, Suite 201
Winter Park, FL **32789**
407-628-1120

BEACH STAMP & COIN
971 E. Eau Gallie Blvd.
and Highway A1A
Suite G
Melbourne Beach, FL **32937**
407-777-1666

JERRY SIEGEL/STAMPS FOR COLLECTORS
1920 E. Hallandale Beach Blvd.
Suite 507
Hallandale, FL **33009**
305-457-0422

RICARDO DEL CAMPO
7379 Coral Way
Miami, FL **33155-1402**
305-262-2919

JACK'S COINS & STAMPS
801 Northlake Blvd.
North Palm Beach, FL **33408**
407-844-7710

A-Z SERVICES
3923 Lake Worth Rd., Suite 111
Lake Worth, FL **33461**
407-439-7060

HUGO'S STAMP EMPORIUM
P.O. Box 5527
Lake Worth, FL **33466**
407-966-7517

HAUSER'S COIN & STAMP
3425 S. Florida Ave.
Lakeland, FL **33803**
813-647-2052

NEW ENGLAND STAMP
4987 Tamiami Trail East
Village Falls Professional Center
Naples, FL **33962**
813-732-8000

HERB'S COINS, STAMPS AND BASEBALL CARDS
21340 Gertrude Ave.
Port Charlotte, FL **33952**
813-629-5777

MOLNAR'S STAMP & COIN
1553 Main St.
Sarasota, FL **34236**
800-516-4850

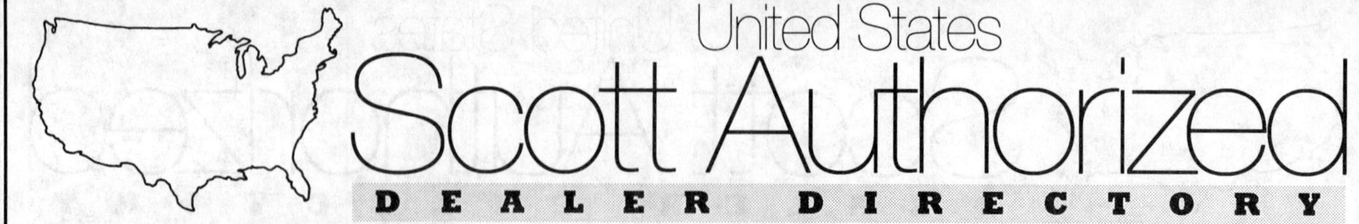

FLORIDA CONT.

JOSEPH BANFI
Cove Center 5965 SE Federal Hwy.
Stuart, FL **34997**
407-283-2128

GEORGIA

COL. LARRY R. DAVIDSON
P.O. Box 965097
Marietta, GA **30066-0002**
404-427-7553

STAMPS UNLIMITED OF GEORGIA
133 Carnegie Way
Room 250
Atlanta, GA **30303**
404-688-9161

PHILATELIC DISTRIBUTORS, INC.
4222 Pleasantdale Rd.
Atlanta, GA **30340**
404-446-5225

NORTHLAKE STAMP AND COIN
1153 Northlake Mall
Atlanta, GA **30345**
800-752-8162

HAWAII

H & P SALES
P.O. Box 10020
Honolulu, HI **96816-0020**
808-955-4004

IDAHO

LEDO SUPPLY CO.
P.O. Box 1749
Sandpoint, ID **83864**
800-257-8331

ILLINOIS

DOUBLE J. STAMPS
P.O. Box 1127
Arlington Heights, IL **60006**
708-843-8700

H.C. STAMP & COIN CO.
10 Crystal Lake Plaza
Crystal Lake, IL **60014**
815-459-3940

JAMES E. LEE
P.O. Drawer 250
Wheeling, IL **60090**
708-215-1231

ROBERT'S STAMP EXCHANGE
P.O. Box 362
Carpentersville, IL **60110**
708-695-6568

AM-NAT/AUSARIUS
221 W. Main St.
St. Charles, IL **60174**
708-584-3112

VERUS DISCOUNT SUPPLY CO.
P.O. Box 187
West Chicago, IL **60186**
708-896-8938

MITCH'S STAMPS & COINS
6333 W. Cermak Rd.
Berwyn, IL **60402**
708-795-7114

ROSEMOOR STAMP & COIN CO.
2021 Ridge Road
Homewood, IL **60430**
708-799-0880

DON CLARK'S STAMPS
937 1/2 Galena Blvd.
Aurora, IL **60506**
708-896-4606

MARSHALL FIELD'S STAMP DEPT.
111 N. State St.
Chicago, IL **60602**
312-781-4237

LIBERTY STAMP SHOP INC.
140 S. Dearborn Street
Chicago, IL **60603**
312-332-4464

RICHARD E. DREWS/STAMP KING
7139 W. Higgins
Chicago, IL **60656**
312-775-2100

INDIANA

VILLAGE STAMP AND COIN
40 E. Cedar
Zionsville, IN **46077**
317-873-6762

THE STAMP SHOP
614 Massachusetts Ave.
Indianapolis, IN **46204**
317-631-0631

CALUMET STAMPS
P.O. Box 83
Griffith, IN **46319**
219-924-4836

IOWA

TRAVEL GENIE MAPS-BOOKS-GIFTS
620 W. Lincolnway
Ames, IA **50010**
515-232-1070

STAMPS "N" STUFF
2700 University
Suite 214
West Des Moines, IA **50266**
515-224-1737

J & K STAMPS & SUPPLIES
1720 Jefferson St.
Waterloo, IA **50702**
319-234-7949

THE HOBBY CORNER
1700 First Ave.
Eastdale Plaza
Iowa City, IA **52240**
319-338-1788

KENTUCKY

TREASURE ISLAND COINS & STAMPS
1433 Bardstown Road
Louisville, KY **40204**
502-454-0334

COLLECTORS STAMPS LTD.
4012 Dupont Circle, #313
Louisville, KY **40207**
502-897-9045

LOUISIANA

J.M. FUSSELL
P.O. Box 24015
New Orleans, LA **70184**
504-486-8213

MAINE

M.A. STORCK CO.
652 Congress St.
Portland, ME **04104**
207-774-7271

JOHN B. HEAD
P.O. Drawer 7
Bethel, ME **04217**
207-824-2462

CTC STAMPS
426 Pleasant Street
Lewiston, ME **04240**
207-784-7892

THE STAMP ACT
Rt. 1 P.O. Box 93
East Orland, ME **04431**
800-743-7832

D & G STAMP & COIN
15 Water St.
Caribou, ME **04736**
207-498-2106

MARYLAND

BULLDOG STAMP CO.
4641 Montgomery Ave.
Bethesda, MD **20814**
301-654-1138

UNIVERSAL STAMPS
1331-F Rockville Pike
Rockville, MD **20852**
301-340-1640

BALTIMORE COIN & STAMP EXCHANGE INC.
10194 Baltimore National Pike
Unit 104
Ellicott City, MD **21042**
410-418-8282

STAMP & COIN WORLD
511-A Delaware Avenue
Towson, MD **21286**
410-828-4465

LPH STAMPS
P.O. Box 356
Hagerstown, MD **21741-0356**
301-714-1423

MASSACHUSETTS

BAY STATE COIN CO.
P.O. Box 6349
Holyoke, MA **01041**
413-538-7342

SUBURBAN STAMP INC.
176 Worthington St.
Springfield, MA **01103**
413-785-5348

J & N FORTIER
484 Main St.
Worcester, MA **01608**
508-757-3657

LINCOLN STAMP & COIN SHOP
50 Franklin Street
Worcester, MA **01608**
508-755-7924

WESTSIDE STAMP & COIN CO. INC.
632 B Washington St.
Canton, MA **02021-0562**
617-828-9464

FREDERICK L. HALL
P.O. Box 236
Marshfield Hills, MA **02051**
617-834-7456

KAPPY'S COINS & STAMPS
534 Washington St.
Norwood, MA **02062**
617-762-5552

BATTLE GREEN STAMP COMPANY
4 Muzzey Street
Lexington, MA **02173**
617-862-2330

FALMOUTH STAMP & COIN
11 Town Hall Square
Falmouth, MA **02540**
508-548-7075

MICHIGAN

BIRMINGHAM COIN AND JEWELRY
1287 S. Woodward
Birmingham, MI **48009**
810-642-1234

MEL COON STAMPS
3833 Twelve Mile
Berkley, MI **48072**
810-398-6085

HUDSON'S - DEPT. 706
Northland Mall
21500 Northwestern Hwy.
Southfield, MI **48075**
810-569-1690

BUTLER PHILATELICS
P.O. Box 2821
Ann Arbor, MI **48106-2821**
313-994-0890

THE MOUSE AND SUCH
696 N. Mill Street
Plymouth, MI **48170**
313-454-1515

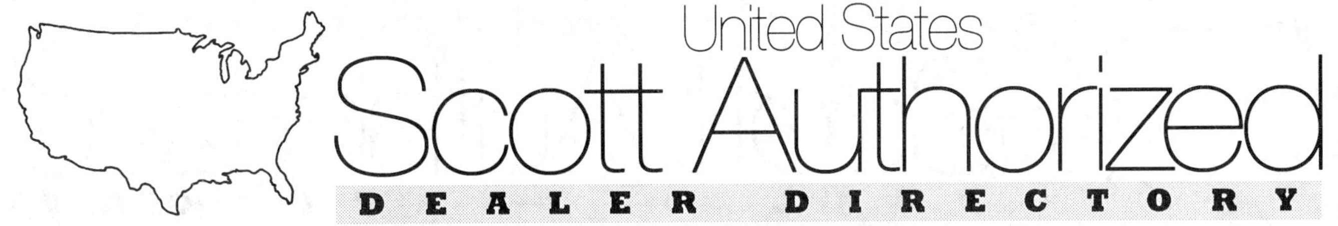

MICHIGAN CONT.

MODERN STAMPS, INC.
25900 Greenfield Rd. #136
Oak Park, MI **48237**
810-968-3505

PHILATELIC APPRAISAL COMPANY
9882 Sonora Street
Freeland, MI **48623**
517-781-2766

PARCHMENT STAMP CO.
2324 Olmstead
Kalamazoo, MI **49001**
616-344-3232

MINNESOTA

BEL-AIRE/MICHAEL E. ALDRICH
2575 N. Fairview Ave.
Suite 200
St. Paul, MN **55113**
612-633-6610

GOPHER SUPPLY CO.
2489 Rice St.
Suite 232
Roseville, MN **55113**
612-486-8007

CROSSROADS STAMP SHOP
2211 West 54th Street
Minneapolis, MN **55419-1515**
612-928-0119

LIBERTY STAMP & COIN SUPPLY
10740 Lyndale Avenue South
Suite 17W
Bloomington, MN **55420**
612-888-4566

RFW STAMPS & SUPPLIES
765 Windemere Drive
Plymouth, MN **55441**
612-545-6655

JW STAMP COMPANY
5300 250th Street
Saint Cloud, MN **56301**
612-252-2996

MISSOURI

THE STAMP CORNER
8133 Delmar Blvd.
St. Louis, MO **63130**
314-721-1083

REGENCY STAMPS, LTD.
Le Chateau Village #106
10411 Clayton Road
St. Louis, MO **63131**
800-782-0066

SOUTHWEST STAMP SUPPLIES
4225 East 25th
Joplin, MO **64804**
800-955-3181

KNIGHT'S COINS & STAMPS
323 South Ave.
Springfield, MO **65806**
417-862-3018

NEBRASKA

TUVA ENTERPRISES
209 So. 72nd Street
Omaha, NE **68114**
402-397-9937

NEW HAMPSHIRE

PINE TREE STAMPS
427-3 Amherst St.
Suite 419
Nashua, NH **03063**
508-454-7365

NEW JERSEY

SCRIVENER'S COLLECTIBLES
178 Maplewood Avenue
Maplewood, NJ **07040**
201-762-5650

BERGEN STAMPS & COLLECTABLES
717 American Legion Dr.
Teaneck, NJ **07666**
201-836-8987

COLONIAL COINS & STAMPS
1865 Rt. #35
Wall Township, NJ **07719**
908-449-4549

BEACHCOMBER COLLECTIBLES
Shore Mall
Pleasantville, NJ **08232**
609-645-1031

TRENTON STAMP & COIN CO.
1804 Rt. 33
Hamilton Square, NJ **08690**
800-446-8664

A.D.A. STAMP CO. INC.
910 Boyd Street
Toms River, NJ **08753**
908-240-1131

CHARLES STAMP SHOP
47 Old Post Road
Edison, NJ **08817**
908-985-1071

AALL STAMPS
38 N. Main Street
Milltown, NJ **08850**
908-247-1093

NEW MEXICO

THE CLASSIC COLLECTOR
7102 Menaul Blvd. NE
Albuquerque, NM **87110**
505-884-9516

NEW YORK

S.R.L. STAMPS
P.O. Box 404
New York, NY **10014**
212-989-6192

SUBWAY STAMP SHOP
111 Nassau Street
New York, NY **10038**
800-221-9960

DART STAMP & COIN SHOP
330 Route 211 East
Middletown, NY **10940**
914-343-2716

BROOKLYN GALLERY COIN & STAMP
8725 4th Ave.
Brooklyn, NY **11209**
718-745-5701

B.B.C. STAMP & COIN INC.
P.O. Box 2141
Setauket, NY **11733-0715**
516-751-5662

FARMINGDALE STAMPS & COINS
356 Conklin Street
Farmingdale, NY **11735**
516-420-8459

MILLER'S MINT LTD.
313 E. Main St.
Patchogue, NY **11772**
516-475-5353

COLONIAL STAMP & COIN STORE
91 Boices Lane
Kingston, NY **12401**
914-336-5390

SUBURBAN STAMPS, COINS AND COLLECTIBLES
120 Kreischer Road
North Syracuse, NY **13212**
315-452-0593

BIG "E" COINS & STAMPS
RD #2 Box 158
Munnsville, NY **13409**
315-495-6235

VILLAGE STAMPS
22 Oriskany Blvd.
Yorkville Plaza
Yorkville, NY **13495**
315-736-1007

GLOBAL STAMP & COIN
460 Ridge Street
Lewiston, NY **14092**
800-368-4328

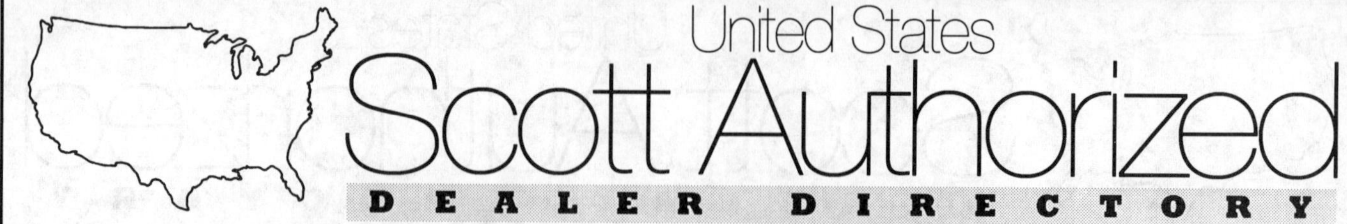

NEW YORK CONT.

LINCOLN COIN & STAMP
33 West Tupper Street
Buffalo, NY **14202**
716-856-1884

JAMESTOWN STAMP CO. INC.
341-343 East Third St.
Jamestown, NY **14701-0019**
716-488-0763

NORTH CAROLINA

NORTH DAKOTA

TREASURE ISLAND COINS INC.
West Acres Shopping Center
Fargo, ND **58103**
701-282-4747

OHIO

NEWARK STAMP COMPANY
49 North Fourth Street
Newark, OH **43055**
614-349-7900

CROWN & EAGLE
5303 N. High Street
Columbus, OH **43214**
614-436-2042

LAZARUS STAMP DEPT.
141 S. High St.
5th Floor
Columbus, OH **43215**
614-463-3214

LINK STAMP CO.
3461 E. Livingston Ave.
Columbus, OH **43227**
614-237-4125

CHAMPAGNE'S GREAT LAKES STAMP CO.
3237 W. Sylvania Ave.
Toledo, OH **43613**
419-475-2991

FEDERAL COIN AND STAMP EXCHANGE, INC.
39 The Arcade
Cleveland, OH **44114**
216-861-1160

JLF STAMP STORE
3041 East Waterloo Road
Akron, OH **44312**
216-628-8343

PILLOLI STAMP CO.
7229 Market St.
Youngstown, OH **44512**
216-758-3859

HILLTOP STAMP SERVICE
P.O. Box 626
Wooster, OH **44691**
216-262-5378

FOUNTAIN SQUARE STAMP & COIN INC.
27 Fountain Square Plaza
Cincinnati, OH **45202**
513-621-6696

SIGNIFICANT BOOKS AND STAMPS
3053 Madison Road
Cincinnati, OH **45209**
513-321-7567

RANDY SCHOLL STAMP COMPANY
Southampton Square
7460 Jager Court
Cincinnati, OH **45230**
513-624-6800

OKLAHOMA

MID-AMERICA STAMPS
P.O. Box 720111
Oklahoma City, OK **73172**
405-942-2122

GARY'S STAMP SHOPPE
120 E. Broadway
Enid, OK **73701**
405-233-0007

OREGON

UNIQUE ESTATE APPRAISALS
1937 NE Broadway
Portland, OR **97232**
503-287-4200

AL SOTH
P.O. Box 22081
Milwaukie, OR **97269**
503-794-0956

AL'S STAMP & COIN
2132 West 6th
Eugene, OR **97402**
503-343-0091

D'S TOYS & HOBBIES
3312 N. Highway 97
Bend, OR **97701**
503-389-1330

PENNSYLVANIA

LIMITED EDITION STAMP AND COIN
510 Tevebaugh Rd.
Freedom, PA **15042**
412-869-9369

KAUFMANN'S STAMP DEPT.
400 Fifth Ave.
Pittsburgh, PA **15219**
412-232-2598

RICHARD FRIEDBERG STAMPS
310 Chestnut St.
Masonic Building
Meadville, PA **16335**
814-724-5824

JAMES REEVES
P.O. Box 219B
Huntingdon, PA **16652**
814-643-5497

LIMOGES STAMP SHOP
123 S. Fraser St.
State College, PA **16801**
800-2-STAMPS

LARRY LEE STAMPS
322 S. Front Street
Wormleysburg, PA **17043**
717-763-7605

DALE ENTERPRISES INC.
P.O. Box 539-C
Emmaus, PA **18049**
610-433-3303

AARON'S COIN CENTER
P.O. Box 1729
Media, PA **19063**
215-565-5449

PHILLY STAMP & COIN CO., INC.
1804 Chestnut St.
Philadelphia, PA **19103**
215-563-7341

STRATACON GAMES & STAMPS COMPANY
1834 Tomlinson Road
Philadelphia, PA **19116-3850**
215-673-2999

TRENTON STAMP & COIN CO.
1804 Rt. 33
Trenton, NJ **08690**
800-446-8664

RHODE ISLAND

PODRAT COIN EXCHANGE INC.
769 Hope Street
Providence, RI **02906**
401-861-7640

SOUTH CAROLINA

THE STAMP OUTLET
Oakbrook Center #9
Summerville, SC **29484**
803-873-4655

BOB BECK
Box 3209 Harbourtown Station
Hilton Head Island, SC **29928**
803-671-3241

TENNESSEE

AMERICAN COIN & STAMP EXCHANGE
330 So. Gallatin Road
Madison, TN **37115**
615-865-8791

THE STAMP DEN
3393 Park Avenue
Memphis, TN **38111**
901-323-2580

HERRON HILL, INC.
5007 Black Rd.
Suite 140
Memphis, TN **38117-4505**
901-683-9644

TEXAS

WARREN A. WASSON
1002 N. Central, Suite 501
Richardson, TX **75080**
800-759-9109
See our Display Advertisement on Page 959

PARK CITIES STAMPS
6440 N. Central Expressway
Suite 409
Dallas, TX **75206**
214-361-4322

METROPLEX STAMP CO.
11811 Preston Rd. at Forest Lane
Dallas, TX **75230**
214-490-1330

ARTEX STAMPS FOR COLLECTORS
3216 W. Park Row
Suite M
Arlington, TX **76013**
817-265-8645

MONEY INVESTMENTS
2352 F.M. 1960 West
Houston, TX **77068**
713-580-1800

SAM HOUSTON PHILATELICS
13310 Westheimer #150
Houston, TX **77077**
713-493-6386

ALAMO HEIGHTS STAMP SHOP
1201 Austin Hwy
Suite 128
San Antonio, TX **78209**
210-826-4328

GLASCOCK DEALER WHOLESALE
P.O. Box 18888
San Antonio, TX **78218**
210-655-2498

HUNT & CO.
26 Doors Shopping Center
1206 West 38th St.
Austin, TX **78705**
512-458-5687

AUSTIN STAMP & COIN
13107 F M 969
Austin, TX **78724**
512-276-7793

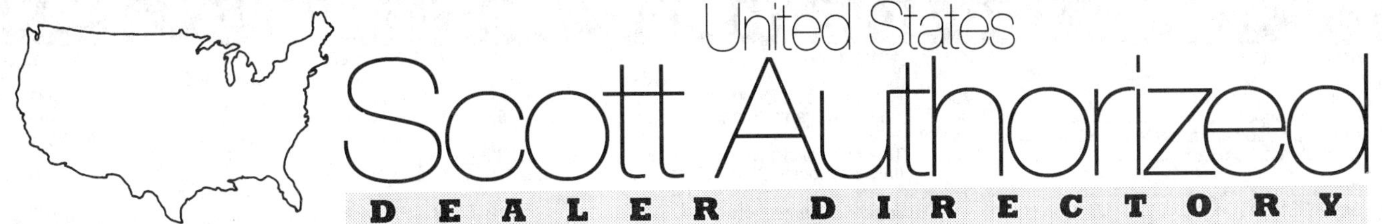

UTAH

HIGHLAND STAMP SHOP
4835 S. Highland Dr. #1346
Salt Lake City, UT **84117**
801-272-1141

J P PHILATELICS
P.O. Box 21548
Salt Lake City, UT **84121-0548**
801-943-5824

VIRGINIA

PRINCE WILLIAM STAMP & COIN CO.
14011 H St. Germain Dr.
Centreville, VA **22020**
703-830-4669

KENNEDY'S STAMPS & COINS
7059 Brookfield Plaza
Springfield, VA **22150**
703-569-7300

LATHEROW & CO. INC.
5054 Lee Highway
Arlington, VA **22207**
703-538-2727

CANDL COINS AND STAMPS
2728 North Mall Drive
Virginia Beach, VA **23452**
804-431-2849

BEACH PHILATELICS
P.O. Box 150
Virginia Beach, VA **23458-0150**
804-425-8566

CANDL COINS AND STAMPS
373 Independence Blvd.
Virginia Beach, VA **23462**
804-499-5156

WASHINGTON

THE STAMP GALLERY
10335 Main Street
Bellevue, WA **98004**
206-455-3781

ED'S STAMPS
14100 NE 20th Street
Bellevue, WA **98007**
206-747-2443

RENTON COINS & STAMPS
225 Wells Avenue South
Renton, WA **98055**
206-226-3890

THE STAMP & COIN PLACE
1310 Commercial
Bellingham, WA **98225**
206-676-8720

PEOPLE'S STAMP SERVICE
4132 F. St.
West Bremerton, WA **98312**
206-377-1210

HIDDEN TREASURES INC.
3276 NW Plaza Road
Suite 111
Silverdale, WA **98383**
206-692-1999

TACOMA MALL BLVD. COIN & STAMP
5225 Tacoma Mall Blvd. E-101
Tacoma, WA **98409**
206-472-9632

MICHAEL JAFFE STAMPS INC.
P.O. Box 61484
Vancouver, WA **98666**
800-782-6770

APX
P.O. Box 952
Yakima, WA **98907**
509-452-9517

HALL'S STAMPS ITEX
2818 East 29th Ave.
Spokane, WA **99223**
800-742-9167

LOWRY'S STAMPS
308 Abbot
Richland, WA **99352**
509-946-7771

WEST VIRGINIA

DAVID HILL LIMITED
6433 U.S. Rt. 60 East
Barboursville, WV **25504**
304-736-4383

ALEX LUBMAN
289 Franklin St.
Morgantown, WV **26505**
304-291-5937

WISCONSIN

MAIN EXCHANGE
496 W. Main Street
Waukesha, WI **53186**
414-542-4266

MILWAUKEE LINCOLN LINDY MINT STAMP CO.
7040 W. Greenfield Ave.
West Allis, WI **53214**
414-774-3133

HERITAGE STAMPS
11400 W. Bluemound Rd.
Milwaukee, WI **53226**
800-231-6080

UNIVERSITY COIN, STAMP & JEWELRY
6801 University Ave.
Middleton, WI **53562**
608-831-1277

JIM LUKES' STAMP & COIN
815 Jay Street
Manitowoc, WI **54221**
414-682-2324

GREEN BAY STAMP SHOP
1134 W. Mason St.
Green Bay, WI **54304**
414-499-6886

PLEASE SUPPORT YOUR FAVORITE AUTHORIZED SCOTT DEALER!

INDEX TO ADVERTISERS - 1995 VOLUME 3

SCOTT CATALOGUE PHILATELIC MARKETPLACE

1995 VOLUME 3

This "Yellow Pages" section of your Scott Catalogue contains advertisements to help you find what you need, when you need it...conveniently!

AUCTIONS

Schiff Auctions

Buyers, Auctioneers & Appraisers of U.S. & Worldwide Stamps & Covers

We have been catering to the individual buyer and seller since 1947. Let us put our expertise to work for you when selling your stamps, covers or your collection. Whether consigning to public auction or selling outright, call us first. Contact us before sending stamps.
Be sure to include your address and telephone number.

CATALOG SUBSCRIPTIONS	N. AMERICA	OVERSEAS
1 Year with Realizations	$10.00	$18.00
1 Year Catalog Only	$7.50	$15.00
1 Catalog with Realizations	$1.50	$2.50
1 Catalog Only	$1.00	$1.50

JACQUES C. SCHIFF, JR., INC.

195 Main St., Ridgefield Park, NJ 07660 USA
Telephone 201-641-5566 from NYC 662-2777
FAX 201-641-5705

OFFICIAL AUCTIONEERS:
AMERIPEX 1986.
WORLD STAMP EXPO 1989.
WORLD COLUMBIAN STAMP EXPO 1992.
YEARLY: COMPEX-CHICAGO.

PTS

QUALIFIED AUCTIONEER

COLLECTIONS

1993 RUSSIA

Complete Mint, 79 Values plus 3 Souv. Sheets and 13 Min. Sheets.
FOR ONLY $38.00

1993 SOUTH KOREA	1992 RUSSIA	1993 CROATIA
Mint (48 values + 9 S/S) **$25.50**	Mint (77vals.+3 S/S &13 M/S) **$35.00**	Mint (49 values + 5 S/S) **$45.00**
1993 P.R. CHINA	**1993 BULGARIA**	**1993 YUGOSLAVIA**
Mint (47 values + 3 S/S) **$15.25**	Mint (55 values + 2 S/S) **$18.50**	Mint (54 values + 1 S/S) **$41.50**

• 5% DISCOUNT ON ORDERS OVER $100 •
VISA & MC ACCEPTED over $50. NY RESIDENTS: Please add NY Sales Tax.

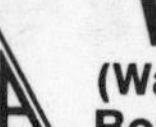

WALLACE STAMPS
(Wallace Haberman) Ph. 516-883-5578
Box 82, Port Washington, NY 11050

FRANK P. GEIGER

PHILATELISTS

212 COUNTRIES

YEAR SETS, MINT STAMPS, S/S, BOOKLETS

We maintain an excellent stock of Never Hinged and Hinged complete sets and singles, booklets, coils varieties and rarities from over 212 countries of the world including up-to-the-minute Year Sets! All the "New Republics of Europe and Asia" are available including many Scott unlisted Locals and Propaganda Issues.

Our Price Lists are available for $1 (deductible from an order). Please indicate your areas of interest as we have separate lists for individual countries of Western Europe, Eastern Europe, Asia including North Vietnam, W.W.F., British Commonwealth, United States, United Nations, "New Republics," Europe-CEPT, Hungarian Imperfs, Belgium Imperfs, Proofs and DeLuxe Sheets. Our Year Set Catalog offers 22 pages of Worldwide NH Year Sets 1930-1994.

RUSSIA 1993 NH COMPLETE

SPECIAL OFFER (with Miniature Sheets) JUST $36.50!!

BEST PRICES on ACCURATE YEAR SETS!

OVER 26 YEARS OF PROFESSIONAL EXPERIENCE

ASDA Since 1969

242 W. SADDLE RIVER ROAD, #2, UPPER SADDLE RIVER, NJ 07458

Since 1971

BUYING & SELLING

WE CARE ABOUT YOU AND YOUR COLLECTION

In addition to our large country packet list, we also offer new issues of the following on approval:

Austria	Croatia	India	Lithuania	Sri Lanka
Azerbaijan	Czec Rep.	Israel	Macau	Tadzhikistan
Belarus	Ethiopia	Japan	Macedonia	Taiwan
Belgium	Estonia	Kazakhstan	Moldova	Tajikistan
Bhutan	Ghana	Khirgistan	Nigeria	Turkey
Brazil	Greenland	Korea S.	Singapore	Turkmenistan
Chile	Hong Kong	Latvia	Slovakia	Ukraine
China P.R.	Iceland	Liechtenstein	Slovenia	Uzbekistan

SEND FOR OUR FREE PRICE LIST AND SPECIAL OFFERS

MODLOW-ARVAI STAMPS

ASDA Est. 1914

RR1, Box 138-G, Mount Vision, NY 13810
Phone 607-293-7975

IFSDA

DUCK STAMPS

Your Source For Federal, State and International Duck Stamps!

CALL, WRITE OR FAX
For Information Regarding New Issues and Rare Offerings

1-800-382-5562
FAX 217-728-8480

DUCK STAMP FULFILLMENT CENTER
1015 W. Jackson, Sullivan, IL 61951

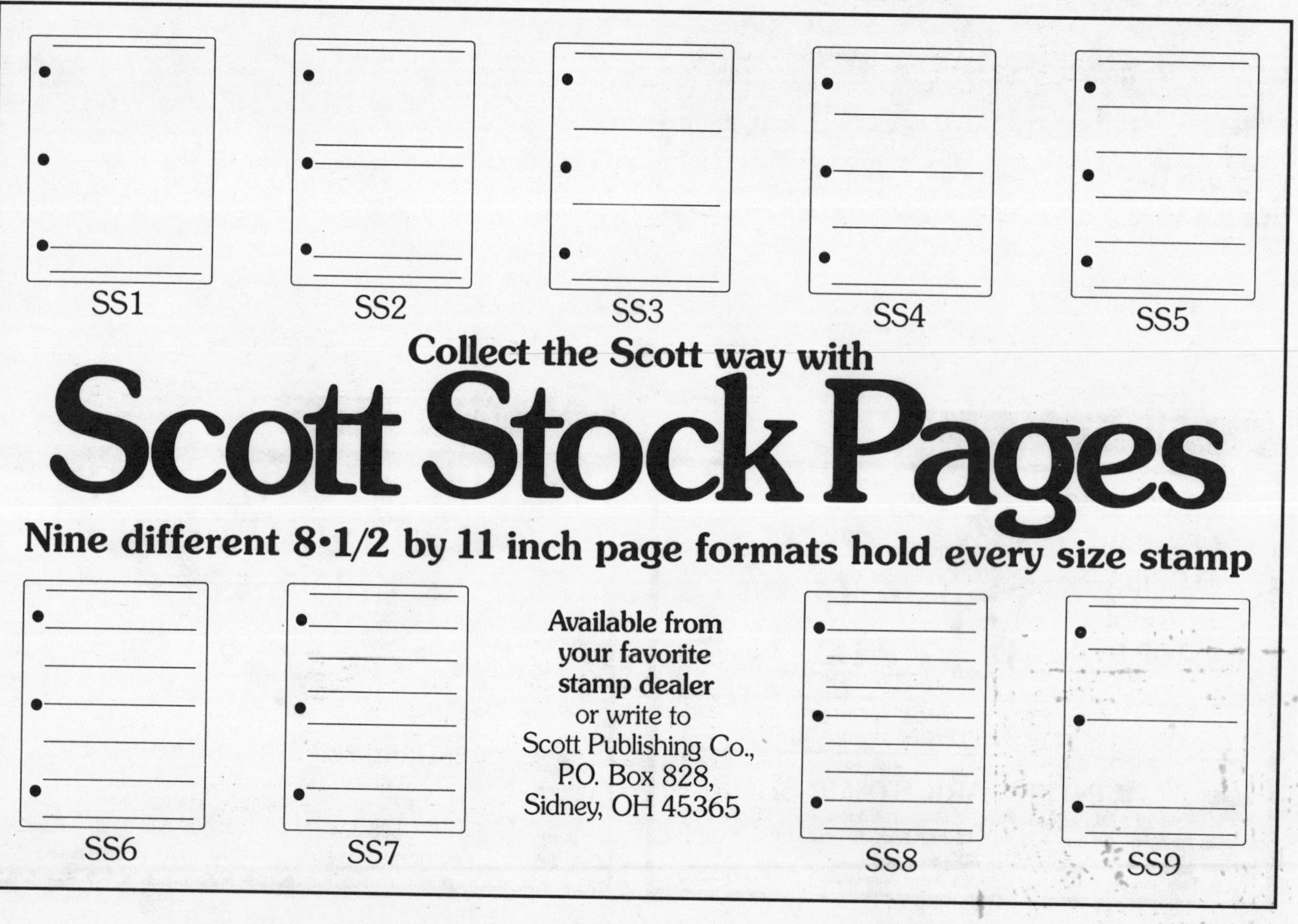
SS1
SS2
SS3
SS4
SS5
Collect the Scott way with
Scott Stock Pages
Nine different 8•1/2 by 11 inch page formats hold every size stamp
Available from
your favorite
stamp dealer
or write to
Scott Publishing Co.,
P.O. Box 828,
Sidney, OH 45365
SS6
SS7
SS8
SS9